Who'sWho in Medicine and Healthcare®

Who's Who in Medicine and Healthcare®

2011~2012

8th Edition

Published by Marquis Who's Who LLC.

Copyright ©2011 by Marquis Who's Who LLC. All rights reserved.

No part of this publication may be reproduced, stored in a retrieval system, or transmitted in any form or by any means—including, but not limited to, electronic, mechanical, photocopying, recording, or otherwise—or used for any commercial purpose whatsoever without the prior written permission of the publisher and, if publisher deems necessary, execution of a formal license agreement with publisher.

For information, contact: Marquis Who's Who, 300 Connell Drive, Suite 2000
Berkeley Heights, New Jersey 07922
1-800-473-7020; www.marquiswhoswho.com

WHO'S WHO IN MEDICINE AND HEALTHCARE is a registered trademark of Marquis Who's Who LLC.

International Standard Book Number: 978-0-8379-0017-9
International Standard Serial Number: 0000-1708

MARQUIS
Who'sWho®   300 Connell Drive, Suite 2000
Berkeley Heights, NJ 07922 U.S.A.
www.marquiswhoswho.com

Who'sWho in Medicine and Healthcare®
Marquis Who's Who

Published by Marquis Who's Who LLC.

For information, contact: Marquis Who's Who, 300 Connell Drive, Suite 2000
Berkeley Heights, New Jersey 07922
1-800-473-7020; www.marquiswhoswho.com

WHO'S WHO IN MEDICINE AND HEALTHCARE® is a registered trademark of Marquis Who's Who LLC.

International Standard Book Number   978-0-8379-0017-9
International Standard Serial Number   0000-1708

Manufactured in the United States of America.

Table of Contents

Preface

Marquis Who's Who is proud to present the 2011-2012 edition of *Who's Who in Medicine and Healthcare*. The 8th edition covers over 27,000 biographical profiles of key individuals specializing in hundreds of fields in medicine and healthcare.

Thanks in great part to the work of those profiled in this volume, there have been dramatic advances in virtually every field of medicine, healthcare, and well-being. Those profiled in the pages that follow have:

- Allowed us to gain a better understanding of the causes and prevention of many diseases

- Developed advanced drugs and aggressive treatments that not only prolong life, but improve the quality of life

- Invented new surgical and diagnostic technologies that can be utilized to treat and cure certain medical conditions

- Provided us with a better understanding of the preventive and therapeutic effects of nutrition, fitness, and mental well-being overall

On the pages of this book, you will find the profiles of leading educators, medical professionals, physicians/specialists, administrators, researchers, clinicians, and industry leaders from around the country and around the globe. Some have gained fame as Nobel Prize winners; others have quietly made significant contributions in the relative anonymity of laboratories, hospitals, and research centers.

Each profile provides you with critical biographical information, including educational background, family history, work history, civic activity, memberships, honors and awards. In many cases hobbies and special interests are also listed.

Factors such as position, professional and personal noteworthy accomplishments and breakthroughs, media/publications and prominence in a field are all taken into account in making selections for the book. Final decisions concerning inclusion or exclusion are made following extensive discussion, evaluation, and deliberation.

Biographical information is gathered in a variety of manners. In most cases, we invite our biographees to submit their biographical details. In many cases, though, the information is collected independently by our research and editorial staffs, which use a wide assortment of tools to gather complete, accurate, and up-to-date information. Biographies marked with an asterisk (*) have been specifically researched by Marquis Who's Who.

While the Marquis Who's Who editors exercise the utmost care in preparing each biographical sketch for publication, in a publication involving so many profiles, occasional errors may appear. Users of this publication are urged to notify the publisher of any issues so that adjustments can be made.

All of the profiles featured in *Who's Who in Medicine and Healthcare* are available on www.marquiswhoswho.com through a subscription. At the present time, subscribers to *Marquis Biographies Online* have access to all of the names included in all of the Marquis Who's Who publications, as well as many new biographies that will appear in upcoming publications.

We sincerely hope that this volume will be an indispensable reference tool for you. We are always looking for ways to better serve you and welcome your ideas for improvements. In addition, we continue to welcome your Marquis Who's Who nominations. *Who's Who in Medicine and Healthcare* and all Marquis Who's Who publications pay tribute to those individuals who make significant contributions to our society. It is our honor and privilege to present their profiles to you.

Key to Information

[1] **COOKE, NANCY ELIZABETH,** [2] healthcare company executive; [3] b. Troy, NY, February 18, 1955; [4] d. Joseph and Carolyn (James) C.; [5] m. Joel Kevin Sullivan, Aug. 27, 1988; [6] children: Calvin Thomas, Katelyn Alyssa. [7] BS cum laude, SUNY Albany, 1977. [8] Cert. CPA. [9] Corp. accts. mgr., Tri-State Med. Ptnrs., NYC, 1977-83; exec. dir., 1983-88; v.p. 1988-92; exec. v.p. HealthSystems Corp., Syracuse, NY, 1992—. [10] Vis. lectr., Onondaga CC, 1992-93; cons. on healthcare and bus. edn., 1992—. [11] Contbr. articles to trade mags. [12] Chmn. planning com., Greater Onondaga Task Force on AIDS, 1992-1993; bd. of trustees, Lake Dist. Shelter for Women, 1993—, United Way 1997—. [13] With USNG, 1977-82. [14] Recipient Cmty. Svc. award, Syracuse, 1995. [15] Mem. Assn. of Healthcare Profls., Health Care Execs. Forum, Soroptimist Internat. [16] Democrat. [17] Episcopalian. [18] Home: 44 Pleasant St Syracuse NY 13244 [19] Office: HealthSystems Corp 100 Corporate Circle Syracuse NY 13240*

KEY

[1]	Name
[2]	Occupation
[3]	Vital statistics
[4]	Parents
[5]	Marriage
[6]	Children
[7]	Education
[8]	Professional certifications
[9]	Career
[10]	Career-related activities
[11]	Writings and creative works
[12]	Civic and political activities
[13]	Military
[14]	Awards and fellowships
[15]	Professional and association memberships, clubs and lodges
[16]	Political affiliation
[17]	Religion
[18]	Home address
[19]	Office address
[*]	Researched by Marquis Who's Who

Table of Abbreviations

The following abbreviations and symbols are frequently used in this book.

A

A Associate (used with academic degrees)
AA Associate in Arts
AAAL American Academy of Arts and Letters
AAAS American Association for the Advancement of Science
AACD American Association for Counseling and Development
AACN American Association of Critical Care Nurses
AAHA American Academy of Health Administrators
AAHP American Association of Hospital Planners
AAHPERD American Alliance for Health, Physical Education, Recreation, and Dance
AAS Associate of Applied Science
AASL American Association of School Librarians
AASPA American Association of School Personnel Administrators
AAU Amateur Athletic Union
AAUP American Association of University Professors
AAUW American Association of University Women
AB Arts, Bachelor of
AB Alberta
ABA American Bar Association
AC Air Corps
acad. academy
acct. accountant
acctg. accounting
ACDA Arms Control and Disarmament Agency
ACHA American College of Hospital Administrators
ACLS Advanced Cardiac Life Support
ACLU American Civil Liberties Union
ACOG American College of Ob-Gyn
ACP American College of Physicians
ACS American College of Surgeons
ADA American Dental Association
adj. adjunct, adjutant
adm. admiral
adminstr. administrator
adminstrn. administration
adminstrv. administrative
ADN Associate's Degree in Nursing
ADP Automatic Data Processing
adv. advocate, advisory
advt. advertising
AE Agricultural Engineer
AEC Atomic Energy Commission
aero. aeronautical, aeronautic
aerodyn. aerodynamic
AFB Air Force Base

AFTRA American Federation of Television and Radio Artists
agr. agriculture
agrl. agricultural
agt. agent
AGVA American Guild of Variety Artists
agy. agency
A&I Agricultural and Industrial
AIA American Institute of Architects
AIAA American Institute of Aeronautics and Astronautics
AIChE American Institute of Chemical Engineers
AICPA American Institute of Certified Public Accountants
AID Agency for International Development
AIDS Acquired Immune Deficiency Syndrome
AIEE American Institute of Electrical Engineers
AIME American Institute of Mining, Metallurgy, and Petroleum Engineers
AK Alaska
AL Alabama
ALA American Library Association
Ala. Alabama
alt. alternate
Alta. Alberta
A&M Agricultural and Mechanical
AM Arts, Master of
Am. American, America
AMA American Medical Association
amb. ambassador
AME African Methodist Episcopal
Amtrak National Railroad Passenger Corporation
AMVETS American Veterans
ANA American Nurses Association
anat. anatomical
ANCC American Nurses Credentialing Center
ann. annual
anthrop. anthropological
AP Associated Press
APA American Psychological Association
APHA American Public Health Association
APO Army Post Office
apptd. appointed
Apr. April
apt. apartment
AR Arkansas
ARC American Red Cross
arch. architect
archeol. archeological
archtl. architectural
Ariz. Arizona
Ark. Arkansas
ArtsD Arts, Doctor of

arty. artillery
AS Associate in Science, American Samoa
ASCAP American Society of Composers, Authors and Publishers
ASCD Association for Supervision and Curriculum Development
ASCE American Society of Civil Engineers
ASME American Society of Mechanical Engineers
ASPA American Society for Public Administration
ASPCA American Society for the Prevention of Cruelty to Animals
assn. association
assoc. associate
asst. assistant
ASTD American Society for Training and Development
ASTM American Society for Testing and Materials
astron. astronomical
astrophys. astrophysical
ATLA Association of Trial Lawyers of America
ATSC Air Technical Service Command
atty. attorney
Aug. August
aux. auxiliary
Ave. Avenue
AVMA American Veterinary Medical Association
AZ Arizona

B

B Bachelor
b. born
BA Bachelor of Arts
BAgr Bachelor of Agriculture
Balt. Baltimore
Bapt. Baptist
BArch Bachelor of Architecture
BAS Bachelor of Agricultural Science
BBA Bachelor of Business Administration
BBB Better Business Bureau
BC British Columbia
BCE Bachelor of Civil Engineering
BChir Bachelor of Surgery
BCL Bachelor of Civil Law
BCS Bachelor of Commercial Science
BD Bachelor of Divinity
bd. board
BE Bachelor of Education

BEE Bachelor of Electrical Engineering
BFA Bachelor of Fine Arts
bibl. biblical
bibliog. bibliographical
biog. biographical
biol. biological
BJ Bachelor of Journalism
Bklyn. Brooklyn
BL Bachelor of Letters
bldg. building
BLS Bachelor of Library Science
Blvd. Boulevard
BMI Broadcast Music, Inc.
bn. battalion
bot. botanical
BPE Bachelor of Physical Education
BPhil Bachelor of Philosophy
br. branch
BRE Bachelor of Religious Education
brig. gen. brigadier general
Brit. British
Bros. Brothers
BS Bachelor of Science
BSA Bachelor of Agricultural Science
BSBA Bachelor of Science in Business Administration
BSChemE Bachelor of Science in Chemical Engineering
BSD Bachelor of Didactic Science
BSEE Bachelor of Science in Electrical Engineering
BSN Bachelor of Science in Nursing
BST Bachelor of Sacred Theology
BTh Bachelor of Theology
bull. bulletin
bur. bureau
bus. business
BWI British West Indies

C

CA California
CAD-CAM Computer Aided Design–Computer Aided Model
Calif. California
Can. Canada, Canadian
CAP Civil Air Patrol
capt. captain
cardiol. cardiological
cardiovasc. cardiovascular
Cath. Catholic
cav. cavalry
CBI China, Burma, India Theatre of Operations
CC Community College
CCC Commodity Credit Corporation
CCNY City College of New York
CCRN Critical Care Registered Nurse
CCU Cardiac Care Unit
CD Civil Defense

CE Corps of Engineers, Civil Engineer
CEN Certified Emergency Nurse
CENTO Central Treaty Organization
CEO chief executive officer
CERN European Organization of Nuclear Research
cert. certificate, certification, certified
CETA Comprehensive Employment Training Act
CFA Chartered Financial Analyst
CFL Canadian Football League
CFO chief financial officer
CFP Certified Financial Planner
ch. church
ChD Doctor of Chemistry
chem. chemical
ChemE Chemical Engineer
ChFC Chartered Financial Consultant
Chgo. Chicago
chirurg., der surgeon
chmn. chairman
chpt. chapter
CIA Central Intelligence Agency
Cin. Cincinnati
cir. circle, circuit
CLE Continuing Legal Education
Cleve. Cleveland
climatol. climatological
clin. clinical
clk. clerk
CLU Chartered Life Underwriter
CM Master in Surgery
CM Northern Mariana Islands
cmty. community
CO Colorado
Co. Company
COF Catholic Order of Foresters
C. of C. Chamber of Commerce
col. colonel
coll. college
Colo. Colorado
com. committee
comd. commanded
comdg. commanding
comdr. commander
comdt. commandant
comm. communications
commd. commissioned
comml. commercial
commn. commission
commr. commissioner
compt. comptroller
condr. conductor
conf. Conference
Congl. Congregational, Congressional
Conglist. Congregationalist
Conn. Connecticut
cons. consultant, consulting
consol. consolidated
constl. constitutional
constn. constitution
constrn. construction

contbd. contributed
contbg. contributing
contbn. contribution
contbr. contributor
contr. controller
Conv. Convention
COO chief operating officer
coop. cooperative
coord. coordinator
corp. corporation, corporate
corr. correspondent, corresponding, correspondence
coun. council
CPA Certified Public Accountant
CPCU Chartered Property and Casualty Underwriter
CPH Certificate of Public Health
cpl. corporal
CPR Cardio-Pulmonary Resuscitation
CS Christian Science
CSB Bachelor of Christian Science
CT Connecticut
ct. court
ctr. center
ctrl. central

D

D Doctor
d. daughter of
DAgr Doctor of Agriculture
DAR Daughters of the American Revolution
dau. daughter
DAV Disabled American Veterans
DC District of Columbia
DCL Doctor of Civil Law
DCS Doctor of Commercial Science
DD Doctor of Divinity
DDS Doctor of Dental Surgery
DE Delaware
Dec. December
dec. deceased
def. defense
Del. Delaware
del. delegate, delegation
Dem. Democrat, Democratic
DEng Doctor of Engineering
denom. denomination, denominational
dep. deputy
dept. department
dermatol. dermatological
desc. descendant
devel. development, developmental
DFA Doctor of Fine Arts
DHL Doctor of Hebrew Literature
dir. director
dist. district
distbg. distributing
distbn. distribution
distbr. distributor
disting. distinguished

div. division, divinity, divorce
divsn. division
DLitt Doctor of Literature
DMD Doctor of Dental Medicine
DMS Doctor of Medical Science
DO Doctor of Osteopathy
docs. documents
DON Director of Nursing
DPH Diploma in Public Health
DPhil, Doctor of Philosophy
DR Daughters of the Revolution
Dr. Drive, Doctor
DRE Doctor of Religious Education
DrPH Doctor of Public Health
DSc Doctor of Science
DSChemE Doctor of Science in Chemical
    Engineering
DSM Distinguished Service Medal
DST Doctor of Sacred Theology
DTM Doctor of Tropical Medicine
DVM Doctor of Veterinary
    Medicine
DVS Doctor of Veterinary Surgery

E

E East
ea. eastern
Eccles. Ecclesiastical
ecol. ecological
econ. economic
ECOSOC UN Economic and Social Council
ED Doctor of Engineering
ed. educated
EdB Bachelor of Education
EdD Doctor of Education
edit. edition
editl. editorial
EdM Master of Education
edn. education
ednl. educational
EDP Electronic Data Processing
EdS Specialist in Education
EE Electrical Engineer
EEC European Economic Community
EEG Electroencephalogram
EEO Equal Employment Opportunity
EEOC Equal Employment Opportunity
    Commission
EKG electrocardiogram
elec. electrical
electrochem. electrochemical
electrophys. electrophysical
elem. elementary
EM Engineer of Mines
EMT Emergency Medical Technician
ency. encyclopedia
Eng. England
engr. engineer
engring. engineering
entomol. entomological
environ. environmental

EPA Environmental Protection Agency
epidemiol. epidemiological
Episc. Episcopalian
ERA Equal Rights Amendment
ERDA Energy Research and Development
    Administration
ESEA Elementary and Secondary Education
    Act
ESL English as Second Language
ESSA Environmental Science Services
    Administration
ethnol. ethnological
ETO European Theatre of Operations
EU European Union
Evang. Evangelical
exam. examination, examining
Exch. Exchange
exec. executive
exhbn. exhibition
expdn. expedition
expn. exposition
expt. experiment
exptl. experimental
Expy. Expressway
Ext. Extension

F

FAA Federal Aviation Administration
FAO UN Food and Agriculture Organization
FBA Federal Bar Association
FBI Federal Bureau of Investigation
FCA Farm Credit Administration
FCC Federal Communications Commission
FCDA Federal Civil Defense Administration
FDA Food and Drug Administration
FDIA Federal Deposit Insurance
    Administration
FDIC Federal Deposit Insurance
    Corporation
FEA Federal Energy Administration
Feb. February
fed. federal
fedn. federation
FERC Federal Energy Regulatory
    Commission
fgn. foreign
FHA Federal Housing Administration
fin. financial, finance
FL Florida
Fl. Floor
Fla. Florida
FMC Federal Maritime Commission
FNP Family Nurse Practitioner
FOA Foreign Operations Administration
found. foundation
FPC Federal Power Commission
FPO Fleet Post Office
frat. fraternity
FRS Federal Reserve System
FSA Federal Security Agency
Ft. Fort

FTC Federal Trade Commission
Fwy. Freeway

G

GA, Ga. Georgia
GAO General Accounting Office
gastroent. gastroenterological
GATT General Agreement on Tariffs and
    Trade
GE General Electric Company
gen. general
geneal. genealogical
geog. geographic, geographical
geol. geological
geophys. geophysical
geriat. geriatrics
gerontol. gerontological
GHQ General Headquarters
gov. governor
govt. government
govtl. governmental
GPO Government Printing Office
grad. graduate, graduated
GSA General Services Administration
Gt. Great
GU Guam
gynecol. gynecological

H

hdqs. headquarters
HEW Department of Health, Education
    and Welfare
HHD Doctor of Humanities
HHFA Housing and Home Finance
    Agency
HHS Department of Health and Human
    Services
HI Hawaii
hist. historical, historic
HM Master of Humanities
homeo. homeopathic
hon. honorary, honorable
House of Dels. House of Delegates
House of Reps. House of Representatives
hort. horticultural
hosp. hospital
HS High School
HUD Department of Housing and Urban
    Development
Hwy. Highway
hydrog. hydrographic

I

IA Iowa
IAEA International Atomic Energy
    Agency
IBRD International Bank for
    Reconstruction and Development
ICA International Cooperation

Administration
ICC Interstate Commerce Commission
ICCE International Council for Computers in Education
ICU Intensive Care Unit
ID Idaho
IEEE Institute of Electrical and Electronics Engineers
IFC International Finance Corporation
IL, Ill. Illinois
illus. illustrated
ILO International Labor Organization
IMF International Monetary Fund
IN Indiana
Inc. Incorporated
Ind. Indiana
ind. independent
Indpls. Indianapolis
indsl. industrial
inf. infantry
info. information
ins. insurance
insp. inspector
inst. institute
instl. institutional
instn. institution
instr. instructor
instrn. instruction
instrnl. instructional
internat. international
intro. introduction
IRE Institute of Radio Engineers
IRS Internal Revenue Service

J

JAG Judge Advocate General
JAGC Judge Advocate General Corps
Jan. January
Jaycees Junior Chamber of Commerce
JB Jurum Baccalaureus
JCB Juris Canoni Baccalaureus
JCD Juris Canonici Doctor, Juris Civilis Doctor
JCL Juris Canonici Licentiatus
JD Juris Doctor
jg. junior grade
jour. journal
jr. junior
JSD Juris Scientiae Doctor
JUD Juris Utriusque Doctor
jud. judicial

K

Kans. Kansas
KC Knights of Columbus
KS Kansas
KY, Ky. Kentucky

L

LA, La. Louisiana
LA Los Angeles

lab. laboratory
L.Am. Latin America
lang. language
laryngol. laryngological
LB Labrador
LDS Latter Day Saints
lectr. lecturer
legis. legislation, legislative
LHD Doctor of Humane Letters
LI Long Island
libr. librarian, library
lic. licensed, license
lit. literature
litig. litigation
LittB Bachelor of Letters
LittD Doctor of Letters
LLB Bachelor of Laws
LLD Doctor of Laws
LLM Master of Laws
Ln. Lane
LPGA Ladies Professional Golf Association
LPN Licensed Practical Nurse
lt. lieutenant
Ltd. Limited
Luth. Lutheran
LWV League of Women Voters

M

M Master
m. married
MA Master of Arts
MA Massachusetts
MADD Mothers Against Drunk Driving
mag. magazine
MAgr Master of Agriculture
maj. major
Man. Manitoba
Mar. March
MArch Master in Architecture
Mass. Massachusetts
math. mathematics, mathematical
MB Bachelor of Medicine, Manitoba
MBA Master of Business Administration
MC Medical Corps
MCE Master of Civil Engineering
mcht. merchant
mcpl. municipal
MCS Master of Commercial Science
MD Doctor of Medicine
MD, Md. Maryland
MDiv Master of Divinity
MDip Master in Diplomacy
mdse. merchandise
MDV Doctor of Veterinary Medicine
ME Mechanical Engineer
ME Maine
M.E.Ch. Methodist Episcopal Church
mech. mechanical
MEd. Master of Education

med. medical
MEE Master of Electrical Engineering
mem. member
meml. memorial
merc. mercantile
met. metropolitan
metall. metallurgical
MetE Metallurgical Engineer
meteorol. meteorological
Meth. Methodist
Mex. Mexico
MF Master of Forestry
MFA Master of Fine Arts
mfg. manufacturing
mfr. manufacturer
mgmt. management
mgr. manager
MHA Master of Hospital Administration
MI Military Intelligence, Michigan
Mich. Michigan
micros. microscopic
mid. middle
mil. military
Milw. Milwaukee
Min. Minister
mineral. mineralogical
Minn. Minnesota
MIS Management Information Systems
Miss. Mississippi
MIT Massachusetts Institute of Technology
mktg. marketing
ML Master of Laws
MLA Modern Language Association
MLitt Master of Literature, Master of Letters
MLS Master of Library Science
MME Master of Mechanical Engineering
MN Minnesota
mng. managing
MO, Mo. Missouri
moblzn. mobilization
Mont. Montana
MP Member of Parliament
MPA Master of Public Administration
MPE Master of Physical Education
MPH Master of Public Health
MPhil Master of Philosophy
MPL Master of Patent Law
Mpls. Minneapolis
MRE Master of Religious Education
MRI Magnetic Resonance Imaging
MS Master of Science
MS, Ms. Mississippi
MSc Master of Science
MSChemE Master of Science in Chemical Engineering
MSEE Master of Science in Electrical Engineering
MSF Master of Science of Forestry

MSN Master of Science in Nursing
MST Master of Sacred Theology
MSW Master of Social Work
MT Montana
Mt. Mount
mus. museum, musical
MusB Bachelor of Music
MusD Doctor of Music
MusM Master of Music
mut. mutual
MVP Most Valuable Player
mycol. mycological

N

N. North
NAACOG Nurses Association of the American College of Obstetricians and Gynecologists
NAACP National Association for the Advancement of Colored People
NACA National Advisory Committee for Aeronautics
NACDL National Association of Criminal Defense Lawyers
NACU National Association of Colleges and Universities
NAD National Academy of Design
NAE National Academy of Engineering, National Association of Educators
NAESP National Association of Elementary School Principals
NAFE National Association of Female Executives
N.Am. North America
NAM National Association of Manufacturers
NAMH National Association for Mental Health
NAPA National Association of Performing Artists
NARAS National Academy of Recording Arts and Sciences
NAREB National Association of Real Estate Boards
NARS National Archives and Record Service
NAS National Academy of Sciences
NASA National Aeronautics and Space Administration
NASP National Association of School Psychologists
NASW National Association of Social Workers
nat. national
NATAS National Academy of Television Arts and Sciences
NATO North Atlantic Treaty Organization

NBA National Basketball Association
NC North Carolina
NCAA National College Athletic Association
NCCJ National Conference of Christians and Jews
ND North Dakota
NDEA National Defense Education Act
NE Nebraska
NE Northeast
NEA National Education Association
Nebr. Nebraska
NEH National Endowment for Humanities
neurol. neurological
Nev. Nevada
NF Newfoundland
NFL National Football League
Nfld. Newfoundland
NG National Guard
NH New Hampshire
NHL National Hockey League
NIH National Institutes of Health
NIMH National Institute of Mental Health
NJ New Jersey
NLRB National Labor Relations Board
NM, N.Mex. New Mexico
No. Northern
NOAA National Oceanographic and Atmospheric Administration
NORAD North America Air Defense
Nov. November
NOW National Organization for Women
nr. near
NRA National Rifle Association
NRC National Research Council
NS Nova Scotia
NSC National Security Council
NSF National Science Foundation
NSTA National Science Teachers Association
NSW New South Wales
nuc. nuclear
numis. numismatic
NV Nevada
NW Northwest
NWT Northwest Territories
NY New York
NYC New York City
NYU New York University
NZ New Zealand

O

ob-gyn obstetrics-gynecology
obs. observatory
obstet. obstetrical
occupl. occupational
oceanog. oceanographic
Oct. October
OD Doctor of Optometry
OECD Organization for Economic Cooperation and Development
OEEC Organization of European Economic Cooperation
OEO Office of Economic Opportunity
ofcl. official
OH Ohio
OK, Okla. Oklahoma
ON, Ont. Ontario
oper. operating
ophthal. ophthalmological
ops. operations
OR Oregon
orch. orchestra
Oreg. Oregon
orgn. organization
orgnl. organizational
ornithol. ornithological
orthop. orthopedic
OSHA Occupational Safety and Health Administration
OSRD Office of Scientific Research and Development
OSS Office of Strategic Services
osteo. osteopathic
otol. otological
otolaryn. otolaryngological

P

PA, Pa. Pennsylvania
paleontol. paleontological
path. pathological
pediat. pediatrics
PEI Prince Edward Island
PEN Poets, Playwrights, Editors, Essayists and Novelists
penol. penological
pers. personnel
PGA Professional Golfers' Association of America
PHA Public Housing Administration
pharm. pharmaceutical
PharmD Doctor of Pharmacy
PharmM Master of Pharmacy
PhB Bachelor of Philosophy
PhD Doctor of Philosophy
PhDChemE Doctor of Science in Chemical Engineering
PhM Master of Philosophy
Phila. Philadelphia
philharm. philharmonic
philol. philological
philos. philosophical
photog. photographic
phys. physical
physiol. physiological
Pitts. Pittsburgh
Pk. Park
Pky. Parkway
Pl. Place
Plz. Plaza
PO Post Office

polit. political
poly. polytechnic, polytechnical
PQ Province of Quebec
PR Puerto Rico
prep. preparatory
pres. president
Presbyn. Presbyterian
presdl. presidential
prin. principal
procs. proceedings
prod. produced
prodn. production
prodr. producer
prof. professor
profl. professional
prog. progressive
propr. proprietor
pros. prosecuting
pro tem. pro tempore
psychiat. psychiatric
psychol. psychological
PTA Parent-Teachers Association
ptnr. partner
PTO Pacific Theatre of Operations, Parent Teacher Organization
pub. publisher, publishing, published, public
publ. publication
pvt. private

Q

quar. quarterly
qm. quartermaster
Que. Quebec

R

radiol. radiological
RAF Royal Air Force
RCA Radio Corporation of America
RCAF Royal Canadian Air Force
Rd. Road
R&D Research & Development
REA Rural Electrification Administration
rec. recording
ref. reformed
regt. regiment
regtl. regimental
rehab. rehabilitation
rels. relations
Rep. Republican
rep. representative
Res. Reserve
ret. retired
Rev. Reverend
rev. review, revised
RFC Reconstruction Finance Corporation
RI Rhode Island
Rlwy. Railway
Rm. Room
RN Registered Nurse
roentgenol. roentgenological

ROTC Reserve Officers Training Corps
RR rural route, railroad
rsch. research
rschr. researcher
Rt. Route

S

S. South
s. son
SAC Strategic Air Command
SAG Screen Actors Guild
S.Am. South America
san. sanitary
SAR Sons of the American Revolution
Sask. Saskatchewan
savs. savings
SB Bachelor of Science
SBA Small Business Administration
SC South Carolina
ScB Bachelor of Science
SCD Doctor of Commercial Science
ScD Doctor of Science
sch. school
sci. science, scientific
SCV Sons of Confederate Veterans
SD South Dakota
SE Southeast
SEC Securities and Exchange Commission
sec. secretary
sect. section
seismol. seismological
sem. seminary
Sept. September
s.g. senior grade
sgt. sergeant
SI Staten Island
SJ Society of Jesus
SJD Scientiae Juridicae Doctor
SK Saskatchewan
SM Master of Science
SNP Society of Nursing Professionals
So. Southern
soc. society
sociol. sociological
spkr. speaker
spl. special
splty. specialty
Sq. Square
SR Sons of the Revolution
sr. senior
SS Steamship
St. Saint, Street
sta. station
stats. statistics
statis. statistical
STB Bachelor of Sacred Theology
stblzn. stabilization
STD Doctor of Sacred Theology
std. standard
Ste. Suite
subs. subsidiary

SUNY State University of New York
supr. supervisor
supt. superintendent
surg. surgical
svc. service
SW Southwest
sys. system

T

Tb. tuberculosis
tchg. teaching
tchr. teacher
tech. technical, technology
technol. technological
tel. telephone
telecom. telecommunications
temp. temporary
Tenn. Tennessee
TESOL Teachers of English to Speakers of Other Languages
Tex. Texas
ThD Doctor of Theology
theol. theological
ThM Master of Theology
TN Tennessee
tng. training
topog. topographical
trans. transaction, transferred
transl. translation, translated
transp. transportation
treas. treasurer
TV television
twp. township
TX Texas
typog. typographical

U

U. University
UAW United Auto Workers
UCLA University of California at Los Angeles
UK United Kingdom
UN United Nations
UNESCO United Nations Educational, Scientific and Cultural Organization
UNICEF United Nations International Children's Emergency Fund
univ. university
UNRRA United Nations Relief and Rehabilitation Administration
UPI United Press International
urol. urological
US, USA United States of America
USAAF United States Army Air Force
USAF United States Air Force
USAFR United States Air Force Reserve
USAR United States Army Reserve
USCG United States Coast Guard
USCGR United States Coast Guard Reserve
USES United States Employment Service

USIA United States Information Agency
USMC United States Marine Corps
USMCR United States Marine Corps Reserve
USN United States Navy
USNG United States National Guard
USNR United States Naval Reserve
USO United Service Organizations
USPHS United States Public Health Service
USS United States Ship
USSR Union of the Soviet Socialist Republics
USTA United States Tennis Association
UT Utah

V

VA Veterans Administration
VA, Va. Virginia
vet. veteran, veterinary
VFW Veterans of Foreign Wars
VI Virgin Islands

vis. visiting
VISTA Volunteers in Service to America
vocat. vocational
vol. volunteer, volume
v.p. vice president
vs. versus
VT, Vt. Vermont

W

W West
WA, Wash. Washington (state)
WAC Women's Army Corps
WAVES Women's Reserve, US Naval Reserve
WCTU Women's Christian Temperance Union
we. western
WHO World Health Organization
WI Wisconsin, West Indies

Wis. Wisconsin
WV, W.Va. West Virginia
WY, Wyo. Wyoming

X, Y, Z

YK Yukon Territory
YMCA Young Men's Christian Association
YMHA Young Men's Hebrew Association
YM & YWHA Young Men's and Young Women's Hebrew Association
yr. year
YT Yukon Territory
YWCA Young Women's Christian Association
zool. zoological

Alphabetical Practices

Names are arranged alphabetically according to the surnames, and under identical surnames according to the first given name. If both surname and first given name are identical, names are arranged alphabetically according to the second given name.

Surnames beginning with De, Des, Du, however capitalized or spaced, are recorded with the prefix preceding the surname and arranged alphabetically under the letter D.

Surnames beginning with Mac and Mc are arranged alphabetically under M.

Surnames beginning with Saint or St. appear after names that begin Sains, and are arranged according to the second part of the name, e.g., St. Clair before Saint Dennis.

Surnames beginning with Van, Von, or von are arranged alphabetically under the letter V.

Compound surnames are arranged according to the first member of the compound.

Many hyphenated Arabic names begin Al-, El-, or al-. These names are alphabetized according to each biographee's designation of last name. Thus Al-Bahar, Neta may be listed either under Al- or under Bahar, depending on the preference of the listee.

Also, Arabic names have a variety of possible spellings when transposed to English. Spelling of these names is always based on the practice of the biographee. Some biographees use a Western form of word order, while others prefer the Arabic word sequence.

Similarly, Asian names may have no comma between family and given names, but some biographees have chosen to add the comma. In each case, punctuation follows the preference of the biographee.

Parentheses used in connection with a name indicate which part of the full name is usually omitted in common usage. Hence, Chambers, E(lizabeth) Anne indicates that the first name, Elizabeth, is generally recorded as an initial. In such a case, the parentheses are ignored in alphabetizing and the name would be arranged as Chambers, Elizabeth Anne.

However, if the entire first name appears in parentheses, for example, Chambers, (Elizabeth) Anne, the first name is not commonly used, and the alphabetizing is therefore arranged as though the name were Chambers, Anne.

If the entire middle name is in parentheses, it is still used in alphabetical sorting. Hence, Belamy, Katherine (Lucille) would sort as Belamy, Katherine Lucille. The same occurs if the entire last name is in parentheses, e.g., (Brandenberg), Howard Keith would sort as Brandenberg, Howard Keith.

For visual clarification:

Smith, H(enry) George: Sorts as Smith, Henry George
Smith, (Henry) George: Sorts as Smith, George
Smith, Henry (George): Sorts as Smith, Henry George
(Smith), Henry George: Sorts as Smith, Henry George

AAMOTH, GORDON M., medical association administrator; b. Apr. 12, 1940; MD, Northwestern U., 1966. Intern U. Calif., San Francisco, 1966—67, fellow, 1968—69, residency, 1969—73; clinical prof. of orthopaedic surgery U. Minn.; dir. private rotation in dept. orthopaedic surgery Abbott Northwestern Hosp., pres., med. staf; faculty mem. Hennepin County Gen. Hosp., Mpls.; pres., CEO Robin Found., Mpls. Spkr. in field; vis. prof. for several universities. Assoc. editor Clinical Orthopaedics and Related Research, consulting reviewer Journal of Bone and Joint Surgery. Recipient Charles Bowles-Bowles Rogers award, Hennepin County Med. Soc., 2004. Mem.: Am. Bd. Med. Specialties, Am. Orthopaedic Assn., Assn. Bone and Joint Surgeons, Am. Acad. Orthopaedic Surgeons (mem-at-large bd. dirs. 2005—), Am. Bd. of Orthopaedic Surgery (past pres., bd. dir.). Office: U Minn Depart of Orthopaedic Surgery 2512 S 7th St R200 Minneapolis MN 55454 Office Phone: 612-273-9400. E-mail: gaamoth@msn.com.

AARAS, ARNE, physician, ergonomist; b. Holla, Norway, Mar. 7, 1937; s. Halvor and Kristine Anette (Romnes) A.; m. Astrid Dorthea Bakas, Mar. 7, 1959, children: Halvor, Marianne, Kristine Irene. MD, U. Oslo, 1964, PhD, 1987. Occupl. physician Ctr. for Occupl. Medicine, Sweden; coord. occupl. medicine Std. Telefon og Kabelfabrikk A/S; prof. Dept. Optometry and Visual Sci. Buskerud Univ. Coll. Contbr. articles to profl. jours. including Ergonomics, Applied Ergonomics, among others, also about 100 sci. papers. Recipient award Nordic Ergonomic Soc., 1995, Disting. Internat. Colleague award Human Factors and Ergonomics Soc., 1999. Fellow Internat. Ergonomus Assn.; mem. Norwegian Employer Fedn. Avocations: sports, physical activities, astronomy. Home: Finstadkroken 12 1475 Finstadjordet Norway Office: Alcatel STK A/S Med Dept PO Box 60 Okern 0508 Oslo Norway Office Phone: 4799468166. Personal E-mail: arne.aaras@hibu.no. Business E-Mail: arne.aaras@alcatel.no.

AARIMAA, TUULA MARJATTA, retired pediatrician; b. Vaasa, Mar. 2, 1941; MD, Turku U., 1967, PhD in Child neurology, 1988. Specialist neurology Turku U. Ctrl. Hosp., 1988—2004, cons. pediat., 1978—88, acting prof. Turku U., 2002—04. Recipient Diagnostic Eye award, Turku U. Ctrl. Hosp.; grant, The State of Finland. Mem.: SLNY, SLL. Avocation: gardening. Home: Kanervak11 Raisio 21260 Finland Personal E-mail: tuuaar@utu.fi.

AARNE-GROSSMAN, VALERIE G., nurse; b. NY, May 20, 1959; BSN magna cum laude, SUNY, Brockport, 1999; student, SUNY, 2008—. RN Crouse Irvins Meml. Hosp., 1981; cert. emergency nurse, critical care registered nurse. Staff nurse Arnot-Ogden Meml. Hosp, Elmira, NY, 1981—82; grad. nurse cardiopulmonary intensive care unit Upstate Med. Ctr, Syracuse, NY, 1981, staff nurse: emergency dept., 1983—94, clin. mgr. emergency, 1989—91; nurse mgr. urgent care ctr. Syracuse Cmty. Health Ctr., 1991—94; staff nurse: emergency dept. (pediatric and adult) U. Rochester Strong Meml. Hosp., NY, 1994—95, staff nurse: cmty. pediatric telephone triage, 1996—2000, staff nurse: imaging scis. (radiology), 2008—; head nurse emergency dept. Myers Cmty. Hosp., 1995—96, nursing dir. for acute svcs, 1995—2002, Newark-Wayne Cmty. Hosp.; staff nurse Rochester Gen. Hosp. Pediatric Ambulatory Care Ctr., 1997—99, Sr. Nurse Counselor Call Ctr., 2004—08, Cmty. Pediatric Telephone Triage, 2004—08, Diagnostic Imaging (Radiology), 2006—08. Nat. facilitator telephone triage special interest group volunteer Emergency Nurses Assn., 1997—99, clin. expert triage, 2002—04, vol., 2008—; cons. Am. Healthcare Inst., Silver Springs, Md., 1999, Triage First, Inc., 1999—; nurse cons. FONEMED North America Inc., St. John's, New Foundland, Canada, 2000; expert witness (plaintiff): telephone triage case Parson, Behle, & Latimer, Salt Lake City, 2007; vol. NY State Dept.Health, 2008—; editl. bd. mem. Emergency Dept. Compliance Manual, 2010, Jour.Radiology Nursing, 2011—; reviewer in fileds; bd. dirs. Jour. Radiology, 2011—, ARIN PAD Liaison, 2011—; nurse mgr. radiology URMC Highland Hosp., 2011—. Contbr. articles to jours.; co-author (with Julie K Briggs): Emergency Nursing: 5 Tier Triage Protocols, 2010; author: Quick Reference to Triage, 2003; contbr. chapters to books. Staff nurse emergency dept St. Mary's Hosp., Rochester, NY, 1995; camp nurse Jewish Cmty. Ctr., Rochester, NY, 1995; chair Certification Exam Content Team, 1999—2003; bd.dirs. Nat. Cert. Corp., Chgo., 2002—03; health svc. administr. Monroe County Jail Sys., 2004; caring clown vol. Rochester Gen. Hosp. Therapeutic Humor Program, 2006; vol. Monroe County Med. Res. Corps, 2008—09; rsch. subjects review bd. U. Rochester Med. Ctr, 2010—. Recipient Disting. Svc. award, 1999. Mem.: Emergency Nurses Assn., Crouse-Irving Memorial Hosp. Alumni Assn., Assn. for Radiologic & Imaging Nursing, Am. Inst. Biol. Scis., Upsilon Upsilon, Sigma Theta Tau Internat., Alpha Chi. Personal E-mail: valerie210@aol.com.

AARON, HENRY JACOB J., economics professor; b. Chgo., June 16, 1936; s. David and Betty (Cooper) A.; m. Ruth Kotell, May 5, 1963; children: Jeffrey, Melissa. AB, UCLA, 1958; MA, Harvard U., 1960, PhD, 1963. Assoc. prof. econs. U. Md., 1967-75, prof., 1975-77, 79-89; sr. fellow Brookings Instn., 1968-78, 96—, 1996—, dir. econ. studies, 1990-96; asst. sec. planning and evaluation HEW, Washington, 1977-78. Sr. staff economist Pres.'s Coun. Econ. Advisers, 1966-67; mem. Gov. Md. Coun. Econ. Advisers, 1968-75; vis. prof. econs. Harvard U., 1974; mem. bd. dirs. Abt Assocs., 1979—, Ctr. on Budget and Policy Priorities, 1994—; chmn. Adv. Coun. on Social Security, 1978-79; trustee Tchrs. Ins. and Annuity Assn., 1984-87; trustee Georgetown U., 1995-97, bd. dirs.; mem. vis. com. dept. econs. Harvard U., 1985-89; mem. Inst. Medicine, 1986—, mem. com. on econ. future of baseball, 1990-92; rsch. adv. coun. Joint Ctr. Polit. Studies, 1984-89; v.p. Nat. Acad. Social Ins., 1986-96, chmn. bd. dirs., 1998—; rsch. adv. bd. Com. Econ. Devel., 1988-92; mem. adv. com. Stanford Inst. Econ. Policy Rsch. Stanford U., 1991—; mem. vis. com. Harvard Med. and Dental Schs., 2006-. Author: Who Pays the Property Tax?, 1974, Politics and the Professors, 1978, Serious and Unstable Condition: Financing America's Health Care; co-author: The Peculiar Problem of Taxing Life Insurance Companies, 1983, The Economic Effects of Social Security, 1984, The Painful Prescription: Rationing Hospital Care, 1984, Assessing Tax Reform, 1985, Can America Afford To Grow Old?, 1988, (with Robert Reischauer) Countdown to Reform: The Great Social Security Debate; editor: Setting National Priorities: Policies for the Nineties, 1990, Serious and Unstable Condition: Financing America's Health Care, 1991; co-editor: Setting Domestic Priorities: What Can Government Do?, 1992, Values and Public Policy, 1994. Economic Effects of Fundamental Tax Reform (edited with William Gale), 1996, (with Robert D. Reischauer) Countdown to Reform: The Great Social Security Debate, 1998, Jour. Econ. Perspectives, Jour. Pub. Econs., Jour. Health Econs.; contbr. articles to profl. jours. Mem. adv. com. Ctr. Econ. Policy Rsch., Stanford U. Ctr. for Advanced Study in the Behavioral Scis. fellow, 1996-97, Guggenheim fellow, 1996-97. Mem. Am. Econ. Assn. (exec. com. 1978-81, v.p. 1991), Am. Acad. Arts and Scis., Assn. Pub. Policy and Mgmt. (pres. 1998-99). Home: Apt #41 2101 Connecticut Ave NW Washington DC 20008 Office: 1775 Massachusetts Ave NW Washington DC 20036-2103 Office Phone: 202-797-6128. Business E-Mail: haaron@brookings.edu.

AARONSON, GARY, pulmonologist; BS in Biology, Ursinus Coll.; MD, Philadelphia U. Fellow Hahnemann Univ. Hosp.; dir. pulmonary medicine divsn. Aria Health, 1988—. Named one of the Top Docs, Phila. Mag., 2011. Fellow: Am. Coll. of Chest Physicians. Office: Aria Health - Torresdale Knights & Red Lion Roads Ste 250 Philadelphia PA 19114 Office Phone: 215-612-8500.

AARONSON, KEITH DAVID, cardiologist, educator; b. Queens, NY, Jan. 1, 1959; MS in Clin. Rsch. Design & Statis. Analysis, U. Mich., 1980; MD, Baylor Coll. Medicine, 1984. Asst. prof. internal medicine Columbia U. Coll. Physicians and Surgeons, 1993—96; prof. internal medicine, divsn. cardiovasc. medicine U. Mich. Med. Sch., 1996—. Exec. com. clin. affairs U. Mich. Health Sys., 2011—. Grant, Nat. Heart Lung and Blood Inst. Mem.: Am. Heart Assn., Heart Failure Soc. Am., Internat. Soc. Heart and Lung Transplantation. Avocation: running. Office: University Mich Med Ctr Ann Arbor MI 48109-5853 Business E-Mail: keith@umich.edu.

A BA-BAI-KE-RE, MA-MU-TI-JIANG, surgeon; b. XinJiang, China, Feb. 6, 1976; M, XinJiang Med. U., 2004, D, 2011. Surgeon First Affiliated Hosp. XinJiang Med. U., 2004—, adj. dir. anorectal dept., 2009—. Avocation: football. Office: Liyushan Rd 1 Urumqi XinJiang 830011 China Office Fax: 0991-4366229. Business E-Mail: mamutjan206@sina.com.

ABAD, LUIS EMILIO, research scientist; b. Córdoba, Argentina, Oct. 31, 1969; PhD, Cordoba Nat. U., 1995; MBA, PhD, Bircham Internat. U., D honoris causa, 2008. Rschr. Zaldivar Inst., 2010—. Home: Adolfo Calle 77 Dorrego Guaymallén Mendoza 5519 Argentina Personal E-mail: prof.abad@hotmail.com.

ABADIR, PETER M., physician, educator; b. Tanta, Egypt, Jan. 26, 1973; s. Magdy Aziz Abadir and Fiby Georgy AsaadGergess; m. Magdoline M Gabrawy, July 23, 2001; children: Michael Peter, Luke Peter. MD, U. Alfateh, Tripoli, Libya, 1997. Diplomate Am. Bd. of family Medicine, Kans., 2007. NIH post doctoral rsch. fellow endocrine divsn. U. Va., Charlottesville, 2001—04; resident in medicine dept. family medicine U. Ky., Lexington, 2004—06, chief clin. resident, 2006—07; geriat. post doctoral clin. fellow geriat. divsn. Johns Hopkins U., Balt., 2007—09; asst. prof. Geriatrics Medicine Johns Hopkins U., 2009—. Med. resident rep. North Am. Primary care Rsch. Group, Kansas City, 2006—07. Recipient Pharmacia New Investigator award, Am. Heart Assn., 2002, Aventis New Investigator award, 2003, Merck New Investigator award, 2004, Chief Resident of Yr. award, U. Ky., 2007, Residency Intern of Yr. award, 2005, Resident Merit award, 2007, Recognition award, N.Am. Primary Care Rsch. Group, 2007, Hot Topics in Endocrinology award, Endocrine Soc., 2003, Cmty. Outreach award, Am. Acad. Family Physicians, 2006, Excellence in Grad. Med. edn. award, 2006, Scholarship award for Residents, 2007; named to Hon. Order of Ky. Colonels., Commonwealth of Ky., 2007; Tng. grant, NIH, 2002. Mem.: Am. Geriat. Soc. Conservative. Achievements include patents for use of novel receptor in the treatment of hypertension. Avocations: chess, swimming, travel, reading. Office: Johns Hopkins U/ Geriat Divsn 5505 Hopkins Baview Circle Ter level Baltimore MD 21224 Personal E-mail: magdolinep@msn.com. Business E-Mail: pabadir1@jhmi.edu.

ABATE, VINCENZO, surgeon; b. Sept. 20, 1934; Degree in Medicine and Surgery, U. Naples, Italy, Columbia U., NYC, 1955; ACOG, NY Poly. Med. Sch. and Hosp., 1959; DOG, Cleve., 1964. Bar: Law Sch. U. Naples 1993; specialist in ob-gyn. U. Pisa, 1993. Physician U. Naples, 1948—54; resident NY Poly. Med. Sch. and Hosp., 1954—59; chief resident St. Joseph's Hosp., Paterson, NJ, 1959—60; with Am. Bd. Specialization Ob-Gyn., 1964; habilitation head surgeon Rome, 1972; internship NY M.C. Hosp., NY, 1955—56. Chmn. Abate Fertility Ctr. Biol. Reproduction, Naples, Italy; instr., ob-gyn. NY Polyclinic Hosp. and Med. Sch.; cons., ob-gyn. US Naval Hosps. Europe; tchr. established staff Montefiore Morrisania Hosp. Assn., A. Enstein U. Bronx, NYC; mem. editl. staff Internat. Jour. Fertility, Internat. Coll. Surgeons, Internat. Found. Rsch. in Reproduction. Author: (poetry) Onde e frammenti2, 1993; Numerous original works in the fields of cytology, endocrinology, fertility and medicine. Recipient Sci. Achievement award, Gallo Meml. Found. Naples, Rotary Internat. San Severo, Robert Shroeder award, Kiel, 1984, Richard Albert Louis Werth award, 1985, Gustav Adolf Micaelis award, 1986, award, Indian Fertility Soc., 1st prize, Am. Fertility Soc., Toronto Film Festival, 1986, Knight of Order of North Star, Sweden, 1988, Sebetia Ter Medicine and Surgery, 1995. Mem.: Numerous Internat. Socs., Colls. and Assns., Dr. Sibhou Mukherjee Meml. Reproductive Rsch. Ctr. (VCalcutta, India). Achievements include first to have introduced and published intratubal insemination, first in Italy 1983 to have attained birtsh from in-vitro fertilization and egg recovery through vaginal fornices. Avocations: sailing, swimming, jogging, gymnastics. Address: 289 Berdan Ave Wayne NJ 07470 Office: Via Francesco Petrarca 203 80122 Naples NA Italy Office Fax: 081 575 2833. Business E-Mail: doctorvincenzo.abate@aucevizag.ac.

ABAZA, MONA M., otolaryngologist, educator; MD, The Med. Coll. of Pa., Phila., 1991; MS in Higher Edn, Drexel U., Phila., Pa., 2010. Diplomate Am. Bd. Otolaryngology, 1999. Intern gen. surgery Univ. of Medicine and Dentistry of NJ Sch. of Medicine, Newark, 1991—92; fellow intramural rsch. tng. Nat. Inst. of Deafness and Other Communication Disorders, 1992—94, Nat. Insts. of Health, Bethesda, Md., 1992—94; resident otolaryngology-head and neck surgery The Univ. of Tex. Health Sciences Ctr., San Antonio; fellow laryngology profl. voice care Grad. Hosp., 1998—99, Thomas Jefferson Univ. Sch. of Medicine, 1998—99, Am. Inst. for Voice and Ear Rsch., Phila., 1998—99; hosp. affiliations include Univ. of Colo. Hosp., The Children's Hosp., Denver Veteran's Adminstrn. Med. Ctr., Denver Health; assoc. prof., residency program dir. dept. of otolaryngology Univ. of Colo. Anschutz Med. Campus. Chair Women's Com.; mem. CORE Otolaryngology Edn. Com., Neurolaryngology Subcommittee, Laryngology and Bronchoesophagology Edn. Com., Home-study Course Com.; mem., cons. Women in Otolaryngology Com.; mem. voice Com. (Sch. of Medicine Ednl. Oversight) Univ. of Colo. Denver Sch. of Medicine, Aurora, Colo., mem. admissions com., exec. comm. mem. dept. of otolaryngology, resident com. mem. dept. of otolaryngology, mem. grad. med. edn. com., curriculum com., Denver; stipend sub-com. mem.; internal reviewer pediatric surgery, neurology, invasive radiology, urology; internat. subcommittee mem. Co-author: (publs.) Unusual Presentations of Pharyngitis, 1999, Laryngeal Manifestations of Postpoliomyelitis Syndrome, 2001, Cough, Paradoxical Vocal Fold Motion and Disordered Breathing, Objective Measurement of Vocal Fatigue in Classically Trained Singers: A Pilot Study of Vocal Dosimetry Data, 2006, Effects of medications on the voice, 2007. Sci. adv. bd. mem., editl. bd. mem. The Voice Found. Fellow: Internat. Assn. of Phonosurgeons, Am. Bronchoesophagology Assn.; mem.: Soc. of Univ. Otolaryngologists, Am. Assn. of Med. Colleges, Am. Acad. of Otolaryngology-Head and Neck Surgery, Univ. of Colo. Sch. of Medicine: Acad. of Med. Educators. Office: University of Colorado Hospital Department of Otolaryngology- Ear Nose and Throat 1635 Aurora Court 6th Fl Aurora CO 80045 Office Phone: 720-848-2820. E-mail: Mona.Abaza@ucdenver.edu.

ABBAS, ABUL K., pathologist, educator; MBBS, All-India Inst. Med. Sci. Resident pathology Peter Bent Brigham Hosp., Boston; fellow pathology Harvard Med. Sch., Boston, from instr. to prof., prof., head immunology rsch. divsn.; prof. and chmn. Dept. of Pathology U. Calif., San Francisco, 1999—. Vis. sci. Divsn. Immunology Nat. Inst. Med. Rsch., London. Editor: Immunity, 1993—96; assoc. editor: The Jour. of Immunology, 1981—85, section editor:, 1987—91, assoc. editor: The Am. Jour. of Pathology, 1992—96, Immunity, 2002—; contbr. over 150 articles to profl. jours. Recipient Warner-Lambert/Parke-Davis award, Am. Soc. Investigative Pathology, 1987. Mem.: Am. Acad. Arts & Sciences. Office: Univ Calif Box 0511 M M590B Dept Pathology San Francisco CA 94143-0511

ABBAS, HEBAT-ALLAH SAYED, chemistry professor; b. Cairo, Mar. 24, 1976; BSc in Chemistry, Azhar U., 1998, PhD in Chemistry, 2004. Asst. prof. Nat. Rsch. Ctr., 2011—. Mem.: Soc. Heterocyclic Compounds, Egyptian Chem. Soc. Office: El-Tahrrir St 12622 Dokki Cairo 11381 Egypt E-mail: hebanrc@yahoo.com.

ABBAS, ISMAIL, science educator, researcher; b. Syria, Aug. 22, 1970; Degree in Informatics, U. Sci. and Tech. Beijing, 1994; MS, PhD, U. Politecnica Catalunya, 2004. Scientist rschr. U. Politecnica Catalunya, 1997—, assoc. prof.-PDI, 2006—. Avocations: football, volleyball. Office: University Politecnica Catalunya Barcelona Catalunya 08013 Spain

ABBASI, ARJANG, physician; DO, UMDNJ-SOM, 2001; degree in Phys. Medicine & Rehab. Residency, UMDNJ-Kessler Inst. Rehab., 2005. Interventional spine and sports medicine fellow Beth Israel Med. Ctr., NY, 2005—06; with interventional pain mgmt. and sports medicine Li Spine Specialists PC, 2006—. Fellow: Am. Assn. Phys. Medicine & Rehab. Office: 763 Larkfield Rd Commack NY 11725

ABBATE, ANTONIO, cardiologist; b. Formia, Latina, Italy, Nov. 5, 1976; s. Gerardo Abbate and Amalia Ferraro; m. Vera Di Trocchio, May 15, 2004. MD, U. Campus Bio-Medico, 2000. Lic. Italy, 2001. Cardiology fellow Cath. U. of Sacred Heart, Rome, 2000—04; internal medicine Va. Commonwealth U. Med. Coll., Richmond, 2004—07, asst. prof. medicine, 2007—. Contbr. articles to profl. jours. Finalist Young Investigator award, Am. Coll. Cardiology, 2003, Transcatheter Cardiovascular Therapeutics, 2004, Italian Soc. Cardiology, 2002, 2003, 2004. Office: Va Commonwealth Univ Med Coll Virginia Campus Richmond VA Home: 12409 Amerishire LN Glen Allen VA 23059-6924 Personal E-mail: abbatea@yahoo.com.

ABBITT, PATRICIA L., diagnostic radiologist, educator; MD, Tufts U., 1981. Diplomate Am. Bd. Radiology-diagnostic radiology, 1986. Resident diagnostic radiology Univ. Va. Med. Ctr., Charlottesville, 1983—86, fellow breast imaging, 1986—87; prof. radiology Coll. of Medicine Univ. of Fla.; hosp. affiliation includes Shands at the Univ. of Fla. Named one of the Top Doctor, US News, 2011. Office: Shands Healthcare Department of Radiology 1600 SW Archer Rd Gainesville FL 32610 Office Phone: 352-265-0291.

ABBOTT, ALLAN V., family medicine physician, educator; MD, Ind. U., 1969. Diplomate Am. Bd. Internal Medicine, 1993, Am. Bd. Family Medicine, 1996, Am. Bd. Family Medicine-sports medicine. Intern LAC+USC Med. Ctr., 1969—70; resident family medicine San Bernardino County Med. Ctr., 1975—77; fellow family practice Am. Acad. of Family Practice, 1982; clin. affiliation include/s USC Healthcare Consultation Ctr., USC Med. Group, USC Univ. Hosp.; prof. clin. family medicine Keck Sch. of Medicine of USC. Author:

(book) Human-Powered Vehicles, 1995. Recipient Preceptor of the Year award, Outstanding Speaker award, USC Sch. of Medicine, 1989—2007; named one of Best Doctors of America, 2003—. Fellow: Am. Acad. of Family Physicians; mem.: Soc. of Tchrs. of Family Medicine, Am. Med. Soc. of Sports Medicine, Am. Coll. of Sports Medicine. Office: University of Southern California Keck School of Medicine 1510 San Pablo St HCC-104 Los Angeles CA 90033 Office Phone: 323-442-1703. Office Fax: 323-442-3070. E-mail: allana@usc.edu.

ABBOTT, ANN AUGUSTINE, social worker, educator; b. Green Bay, Wis., July 6, 1943; d. Walter A. and Ethel D. Augustine. BS in Psychology, St. Norbert Coll., W. DePere, Wis., 1965; MSS in Social Work, Bryn Mawr Coll., 1969, PhD (NIMH fellow), 1977, postgrad. in higher edn. adminstrn., 1978. Acad. tutor, counselor Devereux Schs., Devon, Pa., 1965-67; psychol. clin. coord. Pa. State U., University Park, 1969-71; social worker Tidewater Mental Health Clinic, Williamsburg, Va., 1971-72; adj. prof. Pa. State U., King of Prussia, 1973-75; vis. lectr. C.C. of Phila., 1975-76; asst. prof. dir. social work, cmty. psychology Widener U., Chester, Pa., 1976-81, project dir. Univ. Yr. for Action, 1976-81, project cons. Adult Competency Tng. Grant, 1976-81, Rutgers U., Camden, 1981—2001, assoc. prof., 1987—2001, assoc. dean, 1993—2001; prof., MSW program dir. grad. social work dept. West Chester U., Pa., 2001—. Faculty fellow NIAAA/NIDA/OSAP, 1990-93. Tennis coach Nat. Jr. Tennis League, Phila., 1974-76; budget rev. bd. United Way, vice-chair allocations com., 1979-86; trustee Ins. Trust, 1995-98, chair, 1996-98. Vocation Rehab. Tng. grantee, 1964. Fellow Am. Orthopsychiat. Assn., Coll. Physicians of Phila.; mem. NASW (nat. bd. mem. region IV 1988-91, del. assembly rep. 1979-89, pres. Pa. state chpt. 1987-89, nat. pres.-elect 1992-93, nat. pres. 1993-95), Coun. on Social Work Edn. (commn. on accreditation 1997-2000), Am. Group Psychotherapy Assn., Internat. Fed. Social Workers (v.p. for N.Am. 1994-96), Eastern Evaluation Rsch. Soc. (bd. mem. 2002-). Home: PO Box 637 Villanova PA 19085-0637 Office: Grad Social Work Dept West Chester U Reynolds Hall West Chester PA 19383 Office Phone: 610-738-0351. Business E-Mail: aabbott@wcupa.edu.

ABBOTT, GEOFFREY WINSTON, physiologist; b. Bradford-On-Avon, Wiltshire, Eng., June 14, 1970; arrived in US, 1997, permanent resident; s. Ronald and Helen Mary (Black) Abbott. BSc in Zoology (hon.), Durham U., Eng., 1991; MSc in Molecular Pathology, Toxicology, U. Leicester, Eng., 1993; PhD in Biochemistry, U. London, 1997. Wellcome trust prize travelling postdoctoral rsch. fellow Yale U. Sch. Medicine, New Haven, 1997—99, assoc., 1999—2001; asst. prof. dept. medicine Cornell U. Weill Med. Coll., NYC, 2001—, asst. prof. dept. pharmacology, 2001—07, assoc. prof. dept. medicine, 2001—07, assoc. prof. dept. pharmacology, 2001—07. Mem. editl. adv. bd. Jour. Pharmacology and Exptl. Therapeutics, 2004—, Current Pharm. Design, 2007—; mem. editl. bd. Jour. Cardiovascular Pharmacology and Therapeutics, 2006—; dir. grad. program pharmacology Weill Cornell Med. Coll., 2007—. Contbr. chapters to books, articles to profl. jours. Recipient Cornell U. Weill Med. Coll. Investigator award, Michael Wolk Found., 2002; grantee, Am. Heart Assn., 2002—, NIH, 2004—. Mem.: Am. Heart Assn., Biophysical Soc. Achievements include patents for MinK-related genes, formation of potassium channels and association with cardiac arrhythmia; novel small molecule modulators of ion channels; first to use RNA interference technique in Xenopus oocytes; co-discoverer of the KCNE gene family of potassium channel beta subunits; co-discoverer of the first example of a molecular genetic basis for acquired cardiac arrhythmia; co-discoverer of novel roles for potassium channel ancillary subunits in mammalian brain; co-discoverer of the molecular basis for bradycardia in patients under propofol general anesthesia; co-discoverer of genetic evidence of requirement for KCNE2 in gastric acid secretion and cardiac repolarization. Office: Cornell University Weill Med College Starr 463 520 East 70th Street New York NY 10021 Office Fax: 212-746-7984. Personal E-mail: gwa2001@med.cornell.edu.

ABBOTT, IRA RICHMOND, III, (RICK ABBOTT), pediatric neurosurgeon, educator; b. Schnectady, NY, Aug. 31, 1950; s. Ira Richmond and Anne Elizabeth Abbott; m. Elaine L. Luckadoo, June 5, 1975; children: Richmond, John. BA, Colo. Coll., Colorado Springs, 1972; MD, Baylor Col. Med., Houston, 1980. Diplomate Am. Bd. Neurol. Surgery, 1991, Am. Bd. Pediatric Neurol. Surgery, 1996. Intern Baylor Affiliated Hosps., 1980—81; resident neurosurgery Baylor Hosps., 1981—86; fellow pediat. neurosurgery NYU Med. Ctr., 1986—87; asst. prof. dept. neurosurgery NYU, NYC, 1989—94, assoc. prof., 1994—96, Albert Einstein Coll. Medicine, Bronx, NY, 1996—2006, prof. clin. neurosurgery, 2006—, prof. clin. pediats., 2010; physician Montefiore Med. Ctr., NY, 2007—. Chmn. credential com. Am. Bd. Pediat. Neurol. Surgery, 2004—10. Contbr. more than 50 articles to profl. jours., 15 chpts. to books. Sgt. USAF, 1973—76. Fellow: Am. Acad. Pediats.; mem.: Congress of Neurol. Surgeons, Am. Assn. Neurol. Surgeons (chmn. joint sect. pediat. neurosurgery congress neurol. surgeons 2005—07), Am. Soc. Pediat. Neurosurgery (pres.-elect 2010), Internat. Soc. Pediat. Neurosurgery (pres. 2007—08). Avocations: sailing, skiing, activities with children. Home: 30 Standish Dr Scarsdale NY 10583 Office: Dept Neurosurgery Montefiore Med Ctr 110 E 210th Bronx NY 10457 Office Phone: 718-920-8512. Business E-Mail: rickabbott@montefiore.org.

ABBOTT, REGINA A., neuroscience consultant, business owner; d. Frank A. and Ann (Drelick) A. Student, Pierce Bus. Sch., Boston, 1967-70, Seizure Unit Children's Hosp. Med. Ctr. Sch. EEG Tech., 1970-71. Registered electroneurodiagnostic technologist Advanced Fuller Sch. Massage Therapy, 2001, nat. cert. massage therapist Nat. Cert. Bd. Therapeutic Massage and Bodywork. Tech. dir. electrodiagnostic labs. Salem Hosp., 1972-76; lab. dir. clin. neurophysiology Tufts U. New Eng. Med. Ctr., Boston, 1976-78; clin. instr. EEG program Laboure Coll., Boston, 1977-81; adminstrv. dir. dept. Neurology Mt. Auburn Hosp., Cambridge, Mass., 1978-81; tech. dir. clin. neurophysiology Drs. Diagnostic Service, Virginia Beach, Va.; tech. dir. neurodiagnostic ctr. Portsmouth Psychiatric Ctr., 1981-87; founder, pres., owner Commonwealth Neurodiagnostic Services, Inc., 1986—, Hands on HealthCare, 2001—, Hands On-Site, LLC, 2004—. Co-dir. continuing edn. program EEG Tech., Boston, 1977-78; mem. adv. com. sch. neurodiagnostic tech. Laboure Coll., 1977-81, Sch. EEG Tech. Children's Hosp. Med. Ctr., Boston, 1980-81; assoc. examiner Am. Bd. Registration of Electroencephalographic Technologists, 1977-83; mem. guest faculty Oxford Medilog Co.; cons. Nihon Kohden Am., 1981-83, Teca Corp., Pleasantville, N.Y., 1981-87, educator; clin. evaluator Calif. Coll. for Health Scis., 1995—; mem. adv. bd. Centura Coll. Massage Therapy Program, Virginia Beach, 2006. Contbr. articles to profl. jours. EIL scholar, Poland/USSR, 1970 Mem.: NAFE, Am. Soc. Electroneurodiagnostic Technologists, Am. Massage Therapy Assn. Avocations: running, art collecting, photography, reading, investing.

ABBOTT, RICHARD LEE, ophthalmologist, educator; s. Joseph C. and Anne Abbott; m. Cecilia V. BrundelRe, June 19, 1971; children: Galen Alexander, Alison Abbott Chassin, Lauren Abbott Maucere. BS, Tufts U., Medford, Mass., 1967; MD, George Washington U., Washington, 1971. Diplomate Am. Bd. of Ophthalmology, 1978. Dir. corneal diseases Calif. Pacific Med. Ctr., San Francisco, 1985—95; prof., dir. cornea svc. U. Calif. San Francisco, 1995—2003, Thomas W. Boyden endowed chair, 2003—. Bd. dirs. Internat. Coun. Ophthalmology, San Francisco, That Man May See, Ophthalmic Found., 1998—2009, Tissue Banks Internat., 2001—08; bd. dirs., chair of underwriting Ophthalmic Mut. Ins. Co., San Francisco, mem. FDA ophthalmic devices panel, 1994—2001, bd. chmn., 2009—11. Author: (medical text book) Surgical Intervention in Corneal and External Diseases. Rsch. assoc. Francis I. Proctor Found.; pres. Pan Am. Assn. Ophthalmology Found., 2003—06; trustee Heed Soc. Fellows, 2001—; adv. capacity for ednl. activities Project ORBIS, NYC, 2003—. Capt. US Indian Pub. Health Svc., 1972—74, Gallup, N.Mex. Grantee Rsch. grantee, Fight for Sight, Inc, 1977—78; fellow Heed Ophthalmic fellow, Heed Found., 1977—78. Fellow: Am. Acad. Ophthalmology (licentiate; sec. 1995—, bd. trustees 1996—2001, sec. quality care 2002—08, sec., knowledge base devel. 2002—08, bd. trustees 2009—, pres. 2011—); mem.: Pan Am. Assn. Ophthalmology (pres. 2007—09), Acad. Ophthalmologica Internat. (life), Am. Ophthal. Soc. (life). Independent. Avocations: travel, photography, tennis, hiking. Office: Univ California 10 Koret Way K301 San Francisco CA 94143 Office Fax: 415-502-7418. Business E-Mail: richard.abbott@ucsf.edu. *

ABBOTT-JOHNSON, WINSOME JOY, dietician, nutritionist, researcher; b. Geraldton, Australia, Sept. 17, 1947; d. Robert Harold Abbott and Beryl Lucille Rampton; m. Warren Godfrey Johnson, Apr. 10, 2001 (dec.); children from previous marriage: Lynlee Rampton, Robert McHarg. BSc, London U., 1969; diploma in nutrition and dietetics, Sydney U., Australia, 1971; M in Applied Sci., Queensland U. Tech., Brisbane, Australia, 1995; PhD, U. Queensland, 2008. Dietitian Sydney Adventist Hosp., 1971—72; dietitian nutritionist Princess Alexandra Hosp., Brisbane, Queensland, Australia, 1979—90, sr. dietitian nutritionist, 1990—98, sr. advanced level dietitian nutritionist, 1998—; pvt. practice Brisbane, 1998—. Part time lectr. Queensland U. Tech., Brisbane, 1988—2002; mem. dietitian's job redesign working party Queensland Health, Brisbane, 1992; staff dietitian team leader Princess Alexandra Hosp., Brisbane, 1999, 2006. Contbr. articles, conf. proceedings and abstracts to profl. jours. Chair Adventist Health Assn., Brisbane, 1994—95. Recipient 1st and 2d Mead-Johnson profl. devel. awards, Australian Soc. Parenteral and Enteral Nutrition, 1986, 1987, Joint award-Bob McMahon Sci. prize, 1990, Joint award-David Russell clin. prize, 1994; grantee, Princess Alexandra Hosp., 1990, 1994, 1997, 2002, 2007; scholar, U. Queensland, 2005, 2006, 2007. Mem.: Assn. for Rsch. in Vision and Opthalmology, Transplantation Soc. Australia and New Zealand, Dietitians Assn. Australia. Avocations: music, reading, bushwalking. Home: 29 Brooke St 4132 Crestmead QLD Australia Office Phone: 617-3240-2111. Personal E-mail: winsome@universal.net.au.

ABBOUDI, JACK, orthopaedic hand surgeon, educator; Attended, U. Medicine and Dentistry of NJ-Sch. Health Related Prof, Newark, NJ. Diplomate Am. Bd. Orthopaedic Surgery, 2002, Am. Bd. Orthopaedic Surgery-hand surgery, 2003. Intern Thomas Jefferson Univ. Hosp., resident; clin. instr. orthop. surgery dept. Jefferson Med. Coll.; hosp. affiliations include Lankenau Med. Ctr., 2000, Paoli hosp., 2002; attending surgeon Bryn Mawr Hosp., attending physician. Contbr. chapters to books Pedicle screw fixation for thoracolumbar trauma, (Chpt. 11)Thoracolumbar Transpedicular Instrumentation; co-author: (clin. studies) Supination lag for the diagnosis of posterior tibial tendon dysfunction, 1998, "Supination lag for the diagnosis of posterior tibial tendon dysfunction", Jefferson Orthop. Jour., 1998, "Forearm abscess presenting as a malignant fibrous histiocytoma five years following wrist external fixation", Jefferson Orthop. Jour., 1998. Named one of the Top Doctors, Phila. Mag., 2011. Mem.: Pa. Med. Soc., Honor Med. Soc., Am. Soc. Surgery of the Hand, Am. Acad. Orthop. Surgeons. Office: Bryn Mawr Hospital Health Center Ste 340 3855 W Chester Pike Medical Dr Sq Newtown Square PA 19073 Office Phone: 610-527-9000. Office Fax: 610-707-4025.

ABBRECHT, PETER HERMAN, medical educator; b. Toledo, Nov. 27, 1930; s. Hermann Richard and Paula Katherine (Schwenk) Abbrecht; m. Anne Patterson Lampman, Feb. 16, 1957 (div. 1996); children: Elaine, Brian; m. Dianna S. Miller, Dec. 11, 2000. BS, Purdue U., Lafayette, Ind., 1952; MS, U. Mich., Ann Arbor, 1953, PhD in Chem. Engring, 1957, MD, 1962. Diplomate: Am. Bd. Internal Medicine, Am. Bd. Pulmonary Disease. Sr. chem. engr. Minn. Mining & Mfg. Co., Detroit, 1956-58; mem. spl. faculty Wayne U., Detroit, 1956—58; intern UCLA Hosp., 1962-63; mem. faculty U. Mich. Med. Sch., Ann Arbor, 1963-80, prof. physiology, 1972-80; resident in internal medicine U. Mich. Hosp., Ann Arbor, 1971-72, fellow in pulmonary disease, 1974-75; chmn. bioengring. program U. Mich. Med. Sch., Ann Arbor, 1972-77, prof. medicine, 1976-80; prof. medicine and physiology Uniformed Svcs. U. Health Scis., Bethesda, Md., 1980—2000, chmn. dept. physiology, 1987-97, prof. emeritus, 2000—; cons. physician Walter Reed Army Med. Ctr., Washington, 1980—2000; med. expert U.S. Dept. HHS, Office of Rsch. Integrity, Rockville, Md., 2000—; cons. expert witness, medicine, malpractice and injury biomechanics, 1985—. Guest scientist Naval Med. Rsch. Inst., 1980-82; vis. prof. bioengring. U. Calif., San Diego, 1973; prof. physiology Ross U., Dominica, Wis., 1997—2006, interim chmn. physiology, 2003; dir. physiology and biomed. engring. program NIGMS, NIH, 1977-78; cons. VA, NASA, Air Force Office Sci. Rsch., NSF; mem., nat. rsch. resources adv. coun. DRR, 1975-78; mem. biomed. rsch. tech. com. NIH, 1986-90, chmn., 1989-90; mem. U.S. Nat. Com. on Biomechanics, 1994-96. Editor in chief Internat. Jour. Biomed. Engring, 1972-74; editor: Annals Biomed. Engring., 1978-84; mem. editorial bd. Jour. Biomechanics; contbr. over 100 articles to profl. jours. Recipient outstanding research award Mich. Heart Assn., 1960; research career devel. award NIH, 1969-73 Fellow ACP, Am. Coll. Chest Physicians, Biomed. Engring. Soc. (hon.; dir. 1970-72); mem. AAAS, Am. Physiol. Soc., Am. Thoracic Soc. Home: 1352 Steamboat Run Rd Shepherdstown WV 25443-4005 Business E-Mail: peter.abbrecht@hhs.gov.

ABCARIAN, HERAND, surgeon, educator; b. Ahvaz, Iran, Jan. 23, 1941; arrived in U.S., 1966; s. Joseph and Stella (Banki) A.; m. Karen Jane Berger, May 10, 1969; children: Gregory, Ariane, Margot. MD, Teheran U., 1965. Intern Cook County Hosp., Chgo., 1966—67, resident in gen. surgery, 1967—71, resident in colon and rectal surgery, 1971—72, chmn. colon and rectal surgery, 1972—93; head dept. surgery, Turi Josefson prof. U. Ill. Coll. Med., Chgo., 1989—; exec. dir./sec. treas. Am. Bd. Colon & Rectal Surgery, Taylor, Mich., 1986—2006. Assoc. editor: Diseases of Colon and Rectum, 1981—95. Fellow ACS (various coms. and offices), Am. Soc. Colon and Rectal Surgeons (sec. 1985-87, pres. 1988-89), Can. Soc. Colon and Rectal Surgeons (hon.); mem. Am. Surg. Assn., Soc. Am. Gastroendoscopic Surgeons (founder), Sydney Soc. Colon and Rectal Surgeons (hon.), Assn. Coloproctology of Gt. Britain (hon. fellow). Republican. Roman Catholic. Avocations: visual arts, music, philately. Office: U Ill 840 S Wood St 518 Chicago IL 60612-7317 Address: Am Bd Colon & Rectal Surgery 20600 Eureka Rd Ste 713 Taylor MI 48180-5376 Home Phone: 708-366-5065; Office Phone: 312-996-2061. Business E-Mail: abcarian@uic.edu.

ABDALIAN, SUE ELLEN (SUSAN ABDALIAN), internist, educator; MD, Tulane U., New Orleans, 1979. Diplomate Am. Bd. Internal Medicine, 1983, Am. Bd. Internal Medicine-adolescent medicine, 1994. Resident internal medicine Mayo Clinic, Rochester, 1980—82; fellow Univ. Minn. Hosp., Mpls., 1985—87; prof. medicine Tulane Univ.; physician Tulane Med. Ctr. Office: Tulane Medical Center 1415 Tulane Ave New Orleans LA 70112 Office Phone: 504-988-8000.

ABD EL BAGI, MOHAMED ELMUTASIM, radiologist, consultant; b. Elobeid, Kordofan, Sudan, June 15, 1948; s. Abd El Bagi Mohamed and Omalhassan Alsayed Abd El Bagi; m. Badria Abdelraheem Elfaki, Aug. 24, 1984; children: Issra Mohamed, Ahmed Mohamed, Ali Mohamed, Omar Mohamed, Ameen Mohamed. MB-BCh, Cairo U., 1972. Cert. DMRD Conjoint Bd. Royal Coll., London, 1980. Sr. lectr. U. Khartoum, Sudan, 1983—88; act. head radiology dept. King Fahd Mil. Med. Complex, Dhahran, Eastern, Saudi Arabia, 1988—91; sr. cons. radiologist Mil. Hosp., Riyadh, 1994—; head radiology dept. Soc. Ins. Hosp., Riyadh, 2001—04. Mem. internat. rels. com. European Congress Radiology, Vienna, 1996—2004. Contbr. scientific papers, chapters to books. Fellow: RCS (Ireland) (faculty radiologists), Royal Coll. Radiologists (London); mem.: European Soc. Radiologists (Vienna). Office: Mil Hosp King Abdulaziz 11159 Riyadh Saudi Arabia Office Phone: 0096614777714. Office Fax: 009661 4767348; Home Fax: 0096614503502. Personal E-mail: drm_bagi@hotmail.com.

ABDEL DAYEM, HUSSEIN MAHMOUD, retired nuclear medicine physician, radiology educator; b. Cairo, Apr. 5, 1934; s. Mahamaud and Shafika (El Sayed) A.D.; m. Ayda M. El-Shirbiny, Sept. 19, 1968; children: Amani, Essmaeel. MB, BChir, Cairo U., 1959, MD in Radiology, 1967. Diplomate Am. Bd. Nuclear Medicine, Am. Bd. Radio Therapy. Instr. radiology Faculty of Medicine Cairo U., Egypt, 1967-70; resident, fellow Roswell Park Cancer Inst., Buffalo, 1970-72; dir. nuc. medicine Erie County Med. Ctr., Buffalo, 1972-81; assoc. prof. radiology SUNY, Buffalo, 1972-81; prof., chmn. dept. nuc. medicine Kuwait U., 1981-90; adj. mem. Meml. Sloan Kettering Cancer Ctr., NYC, 1990-92; dir. nuc. medicine St. Vincent's Hosp., NYC, 1992—2010; prof. radiology N.Y. Med. Coll., NYC, 1992—2010. Sr. registrar Cancer Ctr. Kuwait, 1969-70; vis. prof. Med. Coll. Wis., 1990. Contbr. articles to profl. jours. and chpts. to books; mem. editl. bd. European Jour. Nuc. Medicine. Fellow: N.Y. Acad. Medicine (pres. nuc. medicine sect. 2001—03), Am. Coll. Nuc. Medicine (pres. 2006), Am. Coll. Nuc. Physicians; mem.: Radiol. Soc. N.Am. (bd. trustees), Soc. Nuc. Medicine (pres. Asia and Oceana fedn. 1988—92, vice chmn. sci. program 1994, pres. N.E. chpt. 2001—03, 1st prize nuc. medicine rsch. 1984, 3rd prize 1986, Berson Yalow award 2004). Muslim. Achievements include research in nuc. medicine.

ABDEL-FATTAH, YASSER REFAAT, microbiologist, educator; b. Alexandria, Egypt, Feb. 6, 1967; s. Refaat Mohamed Abdel-Fattah and Dawlat El-Masry; m. Mona El-Saiy; children: Nour Yasser, Nada Yasser. PhD, Alexandria U., 1997. Rsch. asst. Nat. Rsch. Ctr., Cairo, 1989—93; asst. prof. Mubarak City Sci. Rsch. Tech. Applications Genetic Engring. and Biotechnology Rsch. Inst., Alexandria, Egypt, 1997—2003, assoc. prof., 2003—. Head in dep. of dept. bio process devel. dept. Genetic Engring. and Biotech. Rsch. Inst., Alexandria, Egypt, 2005—; mgr. patent office Mubarak City for Sci. Rsch. and Tech. Applications, Alexandria, Egypt, 2005. Recipient Best Sci. Achievement of Year award, Mubarak City for Sci. Rsch. and Tech. Applications, 2002. Mem.: Horse Hon. Club (life). Achievements include patents for diagnostic kit for isolation of genomic DNA from blood and body fluids; patents pending for diagnostic kit for bacterial plasmid isolation; method for preparation of DNA ladder and optimization of its yield by application of numerical modeling. Personal E-mail: yasser1967@yahoo.com.

ABD EL-GHAFFAR, HASAN AHMED, hematologist, educator; b. Dekrnes, Egypt, Aug. 18, 1952; s. Ahmed Abd El-Ghaffar Awad and El-Taowely; m. Hanan El-Soutouhy Gawish; children: Mohamed Hasan Abd El-Ghaffar, Hagar Hasan Abd El-Ghaffar. MD, Mansoura Faculty Medicine, PhD, 1987. Prof. HS Ali Mobark, Dekerns, 1967—70; resident hematology Mansoura Faculty Medicine, 1979—81, asst. lectr. hematology, 1981—84, lectr. hematology, 1987—90; asst. prof. hematology Mansoura Facultyof Medicine, 1993—97, prof. hematology, 1997—2003; prof. hematology and dir. Faculty Medicine, Mansoura Oncology Lab. Ctr., 2003—08, med. dir., Molecular Hematology and Stem Cell Lab. Guest worker Immunology Sect. FDA, NIH, Bethesda, Md., 1984—86; vis. scientist hematology and oncology dept. Giessen U. Hosp., Germany, 1991—93; dir. Molecular Hematology Lab., Egypt; coord. Stem Cell Project, Egypt; regional supr. Egyptian Bd. Clin. Pathology; cons. hematology Mansoura Ins. Hosp. With Med. svc. Egyptian Mil. Achievements include establishment of molecular hematology lab for international integration and research; establishment of stem cell laboratory for stem cell research. Office: Mansoura Faculty Med El-Gomhorya St Mansoura 35516 Egypt Home: 72, El-Mashaya 35516 Mansoura Egypt Office Phone: 002 50 223 0552. Office Fax: 2 050 226 756 3; Home Fax: 2 050 225 720 2. Personal E-mail: haabd-elghaffar@mans.edu.eg.

ABDELHADY, AMR MOHAMAD, orthopedist; b. Egypt, Dec. 20, 1966; MBBCh, Ain Shams U., 1989, MD, 2001. Asst. prof. Ain Shams U., 2006—11, prof. dept. orthop., 2011. Avocations: reading, tennis, soccer. Office: 69 Elmerghani St Helioplois dist Cairo Egypt Office Fax: 22914069. Personal E-mail: amelhady1@yahoo.com.

ABDELHALIM, MOHAMED ANWAR K., physics professor; b. Cairo, Aug. 23, 1954; MSc, Ain Shams U., 1987; PhD, Tsukaba U., Japan, 1994. Demonstrator faculty engring., tech. Helwan U., Egypt, 1983—87, asst. prof. faculty sci. dept. physics, 1994—2004; rschr. med. sci. U. Tsukuba, Japan Inst. Basic med. Scis., 1988—90; asst. prof. dept. physics and astronomy King Saud U., Coll. Sci., Dept. Physics and Astronomy, Saudi Arabia, 2004—08, assoc. prof., 2009—11, prof., 2011—. Recipient Editor's Recognition award, European Jour. Radiology, 2005; fellow scholarship, Japanese Govt. Master: Ain Shams U.-Coll. Sci. Avocations: reading, sports. Home: King Saud University Coll Sci Riyadh 2455 Saudi Arabia Personal E-mail: abdelhalimmak@yahoo.com.

ABD ELHAMID, EHAB SA'EED, medical educator; b. Cairo, July 25, 1967; BDS, Cairo U., 1990; PhD, Ain Shams U., 2000. Prof., oral pathology Ain Shams U., 2011—. Recipient Excellence Rsch. award, Ain Shams U. Office: Alwehda Alafriquia Orgn Faculty Abassia Cairo 002 Egypt Office Fax: 002-22639088. Personal E-mail: ihabema2033@yahoo.com.

ABDELLAH, FAYE GLENN, retired public health service officer; d. H. B. and Margaret (Glenn) Abdellah. BS in Tchg., Columbia U., 1945; MA in Tchg., Rutgers U., NJ, 1947, EdD, 1955; LLD (hon.), Case Western Res. U., 1967, Rutgers U., 1973; DSc in Nursing (hon.), U. Akron, 1978; DSc (hon.), Cath. U. Am., 1981; DSc in Public Svc. (hon.), Monmouth Coll., 1982; DSc (hon.), Ea. Mich U., 1987, U. Bridgeport, 1987, Georgetown U., 1989; D in Pub. Svc. (hon.), Am. U., 1987; LHD (hon.), Georgetown U., 1989, U. SC, 1991, D in Pub. Svc., 1991; D, Norwich U., Vt., 1996; D in Mil. Nursing (hon.), USUHS, 2002. RN NY, DC. Commd. officer USPHS, Rockville, Md., 1949, advanced through grades to rear adm., 1970, dep., Surgeon Gen., chief nurse officer, 1970—87, dep. Surgeon Gen., 1981—89, chief nursing edn. br., divsn. nursing, 1949—59, Surgeon Gen., 1989; chief rsch. grants br. Bur. Health Manpower Edn., NIH, HEW, Rockville, 1959—69; dir. Office Rsch. Tng. Nat. Ctr. for Health Svcs. R & D, Health Svcs. Mental Health Adminstrn., Rockville, 1969; acting dep. dir. Nat. Ctr. Health Svcs. R & D, Rockville, 1971, Bur. Health Svcs. Rsch. and Evaluation, Health Resources Adminstrn., Rockville, 1973; dir. Office Long-Term Care, Office Asst. Sec. for Health, HEW, Rockville, 1973—80; exec. dir. Grad. Sch. Nursing Uniformed Svcs. U. Health Scis., Bethesda, Md., 1993—, founding dean, prof. emeritus, 2001—. Prof. nursing, Emily Myrtle Smith chair U. SC, Columbia, 1990—91; dean, prof. Grad. Sch. Nursing, Uniformed Svcs. U. Health Scis., 1993—2002, founding dean, prof. emeritus, 1993—2002, mem. US Dels. Exchange Missions to USSR, Yugoslavia and France; coord. nursing US-Argentina Cooperation Health and Med. Rsch. Project. Author: Effect of Nurse Staffing on Satisfactions with Nursing Care, 1959, Patient Centered Approaches to Nursing, 1960, Better Patient Care Through Nursing Research, 1965, Better Patient Care Through Nursing Research, 2nd edit., 1979, Better Patient Care Through Nursing Research, 3rd edit., 1986, Intensive Care, Concepts and Practices for Clinical Nurse Specialists, 1969, New Directions in Patient Centered Nursing, 1972, Preparing Nursing Research for the 21st Century, 1994; contbr. several articles to profl. pubs.:. Recipient Mary Adelaide Nutting award, 1983, Outstanding Leadership award, U. Pa., 1987, 1999, Disting. Svc. award, 1973—89, Surgeon Gen.'s medal and medallion, 1989, Achievement award in aging, Allied-Signal, 1989, Gustav O. Lienhard award, Inst. Medicine NAS, 1992, Breaking Ground in Women's Health award, 2001, G.W. "Sonny" Montgomery award, Dept. Vets. Affairs, 2002, Centennial award for Achievements in Nursing, Ohio State U., 1970; named to TC Nursing Hall of Fame, Columbia U., 1999, Nat. Women's Hall of Fame, 2000. Fellow: Am. Acad. Nursing (charter, past v.p., pres., Living Legend award); mem.: AAAS, ANA (hon.), APA, Assn. Mil. Surgeons US, Douglas Soc., Phi Lambda Theta, Sigma Theta Tau (Disting. Rsch. Fellow award 1989, Nells Watt Lifetime Achievement Nursing award 2005, Life Time award 2006). Achievements include establishing the first military school of nursing at Uniformed Services University of Health Sciences and served as the school's first dean 1993; receiving congressional tributes for United States Senator Daniel K. Inouye in 2000 and 2002; first nurse officer to receive the rank of two-star rear admiral; first nurse and first woman to serve as a Deputy Surgeon General.

ABDELMAKSOUD, ALAA ELDIN AHMED, urologist, consultant; b. Cairo, May 12, 1970; s. Ahmed Abdelmaksoud and Samia Mohamed Kilany; m. Marwa Mohamed Saleh; 1 child, Yara Alaa. MD, Ain Shams U., Cairo, PhD, 2004. Urology resident Ain Shams U. Hosp., Cairo, 1995—96, lectr. in urology, 2000—. Clin. fellow Elizabethinen Hosp., Linz, Austria, 2002—03. Contbr. articles to profl. jours. Helping orphaned children, Cairo, 1994—2005. Travelling scholar, Internat. Urol. Soc., 2003. Mem.: European Urologic Assn. (life). Achievements include research in urologic laparoscopy. Home: POBox 9535 SOS Cairo Nasr City 11787 Egypt

ABDEL-RAHEEM, IHAB TALAT AHMED, medical researcher; b. Tanta, Egypt, Jan. 24, 1971; Degree, Sch. Medicine, Hiroshima U., Japan, 2005, Sch. Pharmacy, 2011. Rsch. scientist dept. pharmacology and toxicology, faculty pharmacy Al-Azhar U., 1996—. Office: Faysal-Al-Azhar University Assiut Egypt E-mail: ihabpharma@yahoo.com.

ABDELRAHMAN, ABDELRAHMAN MOHAMED, thoracic surgeon, educator; b. Cairo, Mar. 20, 1965; MBBCh, Kasr Eleini Sch. Medicine, 1990; PhD in Surg. Oncology, Nat. Cancer Inst., 2000. Assoc. prof. Nat. Cancer Inst., 2006—. Cons. thoracic surg. oncology Aswan Cancer Inst., 2003—. Named one of Best Dr. of Yr., Egyptian Med. Syndicate, 2003. Mem.: Internat. Union Against Cancer, Soc. Thoracic Surgeon. Avocation: tennis. Office: 127 Mohamed Farid St Cairo 11122 Egypt Personal E-mail: rahmannci@yahoo.com.

ABDEL-RAHMAN, EMAAD M., nephrologist, educator; b. Oct. 20, 1959; MD, Ain Shams U., Cairo, 1982; PhD, Cairo U., 1994. Med. dir., hemodialyis unit U. Va., 1996, nephrology cons., 1996, asst. prof., internal medicine, nephrology, 1996—2003, assoc. prof., 2003—, head, sect., geriatric nephrology, 2001. Recipient Clin. Excellence award, U. Va. Fellow: Am. Soc. Nephrology; mem.: Renal Physician Assn., Nat. Kidney Found. (Va.) (grant). Avocations: chess, soccer, reading. Office: PO Box 800133 Divsn Nephrology Charlottesville VA 22908-0133 Office Fax: 434-924-5848. Business E-Mail: ea6n@virginia.edu.

ABDELRAHMAN, TAREK FTOHY, surgeon, educator; b. Sohag, Egypt, Sept. 21, 1978; MB, Sohag Faculty Medicine, 2001, PhD in Surgery, 2011. Resident gen. surgery Sohag U. Hosp., Egypt, 2002—05, asst. lectr. maxillofacial & head and neck surgery, 2006—08, lectr. surgery, 2011—; clin. and rsch. fellow, dept. maxillofacial & head and neck surgery Kyoto U. Hosp., Japan, 2008—10. Cons. maxillofacial & head and neck surgery dept. Sohag Faculty Medicine, 2010—. Named one of Best Rschr., Kyoto U. Global Ctr. Excellence. Mem.: Egyptian Soc. Surgeons, Egyptian Soc. Craniomaxillofacial Surgeons, Japanese Soc. Promotion Sci., Am. Thyroid Asssn. Avocations: travel, football. Office: Sohag University Hosp Naser City Sohag 12089 Egypt Personal E-mail: tarekftohy2@gmail.com.

ABDEL RAZEK, AHMED KHALEK, radiologist, educator; b. Mansoura, Egypt, Sept. 9, 1961; s. Abdel Khalek Abdel Razek Mohamed and Amal Hasan Eldeab; m. Dalia Ramadan Mahfouz, Dec. 6, 1991; children: Mohamed Ahmed, Amro Ahmed. MD, Mansoura U., Egypt, 1994. Assoc. prof. diagnostic radiology Mansoura U., 1989—2003, prof. diagnositc radiology, 2003—. Cons. Mansoura U., 1994—. Reviewer Egyptain Jour. Radiology, 2003. Solider med. corp, 1987—88, Egypt. Scholar, Thomas Jerffeson U. Hosp., 1991. Mem.: Radiologic Soc. N.Am. (corr.). Achievements include research in reseach in recent advance in diffusion and perfusion magnetic resonance imaging. Home: 62 ElNokrasi St Meet Hadr Mansoura Egypt Office: Mansoura Univ Hosp Elgohmeryia St Mansoura Egypt Business E-Mail: arazek@mans.eun.eg.

ABDELWAHAB, SHERIF AHMED, oncologist, educator; b. Giza, Egypt, Apr. 14, 1969; MBBCh, Ain Shams Faculty Medicine, 1992, MD, 2002. Prof. Ain Shams U., 2008—. Fellowship, Academic Med. Ctr., U. Amsterdam. Office: 17 Emtedad Abbas Akkad St Nasr City Cairo 11371 Egypt E-mail: sherifok69@hotmail.com.

ABDELWHAB, SAEED, medical educator; b. Egypt, Dec. 29, 1966; MD, PhD, Ain Shams U., 1998. Prof., internal medicine and nephrology Faculty Medicine Ain Shams U., 2010—. Office: Faculty Medicine Ain Shams University Cairo 2322 Egypt Business E-Mail: drsas@gmx.com.

ABDOOL KARIM, SALIM SAFURDEEN, epidemiologist; b. Durban, South Africa, July 29, 1960; s. Safurdeen Hassanally and Zubada Bibi (Safeda) Abdool K.; m. Quarraisha Khan, Apr. 18, 1989; children: Safura, Aisha. MBChB, U. Natal, Durban, 1978-83, MMEd, 1992; PhD, U. Natel, Durban, 1999; MS, Columbia U., 1988. Registered specialistin cmty. medicine. Post-intern scholar Med. Rsch. Coun., Durban, 1985; registrar in virology U. Natal, 1986-87, registrar in cmty. health, 1989-91; sr. epidemiologist Med. Rsch. Coun., Durban, 1992, dir. Ctr. for Epidemiol. Rsch., 1993—. Tech. advisor Min. of Health, South Africa, 1994; vis. prof. Columbia U., N.Y.C., 1994; mem. 3 expert coms. Dept. Health, South Africa, 1993-; prin. investigator, Columbia U. South Arfrican AIDS Tng. Program; chair, Nat. Adv. Group of Immunisation, South Africa, 1997-; mem. HIV/AIDS and STD adv. group, Dept. Health, South Africa, 1995-97. Co-editor: Epidemiology Manual, 1995; editor So. African Jour. Pub. Health, 1995; mem. editl. bd. Southern African Journal HIV Medicine and Sexuallly Transmitted Diseases; corresponding editor, International Journal of Infectious Diseases; assoc. editor, AIDS Clinical Care. Chair Nat. Emergency Svcs. Group, South Africa, 1986-87; mem. Phoenix Child Welfare Soc., South Africa, 1982-86; trustee Mahatma Ghandi Settlement, Phoenix, 1981-86; exec. mem. Com. for Health in So. Africa, N.Y.C., 1988. Rockefeller Fellowship, 1987. Fellow Coll. Medicine South Africa; mem. Nat. Med. and Dental Assn. (asst. gen. sec. 1986), Internat. Epidemiol. Assn., Epidemiol. Soc. So. Africa (exec. com. 1989), Acad. Sci. South Africa, Internat. Soc. Infectious Disease, Soc. Epidemiol. Rsch., Internat. AIDS Soc. Avocations: squash, chess, gardening. Office: 722 W 168th St R1605 New York NY 10032 E-mail: ssa16@columbia.edu.

ABDOU, NABIH I., physician, educator; b. Cairo, Oct. 11, 1934; came to U.S., 1962, naturalized, 1972; m. Nancy L. Layle, Aug. 26, 1939; children— Mark L., Marie L. MD, Cairo U., 1958; MSc, U. Pa., 1965; PhD, McGill U., 1969. Intern then resident Cairo Univ. Hosp., 1959-62; resident, fellow in allergy and immunology Hosp. U. Pa., 1963-65, Mayo Clinic, 1965-67, Royal Victoria Hosp., Montreal, Que., Can., 1967-69; asst., assoc. prof. U. Pa., 1969-75; assoc. prof. medicine U. Kans. Med. Ctr., Kansas City, 1975-78, prof. medicine, 1978-89; pvt. practice Ctr. for Rheumatic Disease and Ctr. for Allergy Immunology, Kansas City, 1989—2011. Clin. prof. medicine U. Mo., 1989—2011. Contbr. 154 articles to profl. jours. Founder, vol., Kans. City chpt. Lupus Found., Vasculitis Found., Immune Deficiency Sjorgren Found. Fulbright scholar, 1962-65 Fellow ACP, Am. Acad. Allergy, Asthma & Immunology, Am. Coll. Rheumatology; mem. Am. Assn. Immunologists, Clin. Immunology Soc., Kans. City Allergy and Rheumatology Soc. Home: PO Box 8671 Prairie Village KS 66208 E-mail: niabdou@centerforrheumatic.com.

ABDUELKAREM, ABDUELMULA RAJAB, pharmacist, professor; b. Tripoli, Libya, Apr. 13, 1961; s. Rajab Mohamed Abduelkarem and Salima Mohamed Sulabi; m. Seham H Buik, Dec. 29, 1967; children: Jana Abduelmula children: Amira Abduelmula, Mohammed Abduelmula, Norlhoda Abduelmula, Dania Abduelmula. MPhil, Welsh Sch. Pharmacy, Cardiff, Wales; PhD, Sunderland Sch. Pharmacy, Eng. Chmn. clin. pharmacy and pharmacy practice dept. Ajman U. Sci. and Tech., United Arab Emirates, 1999—, acting dean for pharmacy tng. programs, 1999—2004, chmn., ctrl. rsch. and postgrad. com., 1999—, chmn., ctrl. tng. com. Drug info. dept. cons. Nat. Co. for Pharm. Industries, Tripoli, Libya, 1996—99. Contbr. articles to numerous profl. jours., scientific papers to more than 35 nat. & internat. confs. Recipient trophy, Rsch., Info. and Tng. Coun., 2003—04, 2005—06, 1st Pl., Thalassemias Nat. Competition, UAE, 2008. Mem.: Libyan Soc. Pharm. Sci. Muslim. Avocations: travel, reading, recreational sports. Home: Sug Elgoma Tripoli Libya Office: Ajman Univ Sci and Tech Al-Jaraf Ajman United Arab Emirates Home Phone: 218927320082; Office Phone: 9717056242. Personal E-mail: karem1961@hotmail.com.

ABDUL HAMID, HAMZAINI, radiologist; b. Malaysia, Aug. 10, 1969; MBBCh, Royal Coll. Surgeons, Ireland, 1995; MMed in Radiology, U. Kebangsaan Malaysia, 2004. Physician U. Kebangsaan Malaysia, 2002—. Cons. U Kebangsaan Malaysia Med. Ctr., 2006—. Recipient Employee Excellence award, U. Kebangsaan Malaysia, Gold medal, Internat. Innovation and Invention Tech. Exhbn., 2008, Sanofi-Aventis Prostate Rsch. award, 2008. Mem.: Asian Oceanic Soc. Pediatric Radiology. Avocation: travel. Office: Jalan Yaakob Latiff Bandar Tun Razak Twp Kuala Lumpur 56000 Malaysia Personal E-mail: drzanid@yahoo.com.

ABDUL JAMEEL, ABDUL KAREEM, chemistry professor; b. Labbaikudikadu, India, July 2, 1953; MSc, Madras U., 1976; PhD, Bharathidasan U., 1990. Assoc. prof., head, dean, scis. Jamal Mohamed Coll., Tiruchirappalli, 1976—, tchr., curriculum devel. & adminstrn., 1990—2011. Recipient Best Educationist award, Jamal Mohamed Coll. Fellow: Indian Assn. Nuc. and Allied Scientists (Mumbai), Indian Chem. Soc. (Kolkata). Avocations: reading, writing, travel. Home: 13 C Valluvar St Subramaniapuram Tiruchirappalli Tamil Nadu 620020 India Personal E-mail: jameelchem2001@yahoo.com.

ABDULLA, MOHAMED, physician, educator; b. Alwaye, Kerala, India, Dec. 8, 1937; s. Mohamed Moulavi and Nacheema Mohamed; m. Nasemma Abdulla, Jan. 16, 1976; children: Nadia, Sabina. BSc, U. Punjab, Lahore, Pakistan, 1958; MB, U. Lund, Sweden, 1974, MD, 1978, PhD, 1985. Cert. specialist in clin. chemistry. Sales officer Packages Ltd., Lahore, 1960-62; lab. technician Tottenham County Sch., London, 1962-64; engr. PLM, Malmö, Sweden, 1964-67; rschr. McMaster U., Hamilton, Ont., Canada, 1967-69; rsch. assoc. Swedish Med. Bd., Dalby, 1970-76; physician, rschr. U. Hosp., Lund, 1976-88; prof., chmn. Baqai Med. Coll., Karachi, Pakistan, 1988-90; prof. Hamdard U., New Delhi, 1990—; dir. Primary Care Med. Ctr., Punjab Med. Ctr., Lahore. Vis. prof. Kuwait U., 1993-96; UN expert to Portugal, 1993-95; organizer internat. sci. meetings, Sweden, Denmark, Norway, U.S.A., Japan, Portugal, Turkey, India and Pakistan; sci. advisor to several pharm. cos. worldwide; cons. WHO, UNESCO, IAEA; mem. UN team to Chernobyl, 1990; resident amb. Trace Element Inst. for UNESCO, Lyon, France; pres., amb. Unesco Inst., 1997. Editor: Nutrition and Old Age, 1979, other books, 1975-90; contbr. over 200 articles to profl. jours. Founder, v.p. UNESCO Inst., Lyon, France; pres. Global Coun. Nutrition, Environment & Health, 2009 . Fellow: Swedish Med. Soc.; mem.: Pronutria Internat. (dir.), Internat. Union Elementologists (v.p. 1984—), Internat. Coll. Nutrition, Internat. Soc. Trace Elements Rsch. in Humans (sec. 1985—88, v.p. 2002—). Avocations: cricket, golf, fishing, music, writing. Home: Harjagersvägen 9 S 232 54 Akarp Sweden Office: Hâlsokâllan VC Torgvâgen 7 Kyrkhult SE 290 60 Sweden Office Phone: 46 454 733324. Personal E-mail: abdulla39@hotmail.com.

ABDULLA, MOHAMMED H., medical researcher; b. Baghdad, Iraq, Apr. 6, 1978; BSc in Pharmacy, U. Baghdad, 2009; MSc in Pharmacology and Physiology, Sch. Pharm. Scis., 2009. Tchg. fellow Coll. Pharmacy U. Baghdad, 2002—07; rsch. fellow U. Sains Malaysia, 2007—. Recipient Vice Chancellor's award, U. Sains Malaysia, 2010, Sanggar Sanjung award, 2010. Home: 3A-27-04 N Pk Condominium Batu Uban Penang 11700 Malaysia Personal E-mail: mdapharm78@yahoo.co.uk.

ABDULLAEV, YALCHIN, neuroscientist, educator; b. Baku, Azerbaijan, Aug. 19, 1960; s. Gyulguseyn and Almas Abdullaev; m. Naida Velieva, Nov. 24, 1987 (div. June 20, 2003); 1 child, Mikail; m. Amy Nuetzman, July 30, 2010. MS, Azerbaijan State U., Baku, 1982; PhD, Inst. Exptl. Medicine, St. Petersburg, Russia, 1987; MD, St. Petersburg Med. Acad., 1994. Rsch. asst. Inst. Physiology, Azerbaijan Acad. Scis., Baku, 1982-84; grad. stud. Inst. Exptl. Medicine, St. Petersburg, 1984-87, jr. rsch. scientist, 1987-89, sr. rsch. scientist, 1989-90, Brain Ctr., St. Petersburg, 1990-94; asst. prof. U. Oreg., Eugene, 1994-96, U. Louisville, 1996—2005; rsch. scientist U. Oreg., 2005—; instr. Pioneer Pacific Coll., Springfield, Oreg. Mem. grad. faculty U. Louisville, 1996—2005; rsch. dir. Cognitive Neurosci. Lab., 1996—2005. Mem. editl. bd.: Internat. Jour. Psychophysiology, 1992—96; mem. editl. bd. The Sci. World, 2002—, Med. Sci. Monitor, 2003—; contbr. more than 70 rsch. articles to profl. jours. Mem.: Internat. Orgn. Psychophysiology, Internat. Orgn. Human Brain Mapping, Soc. Neurosci., Am. Psychol. Soc. Avocations: swimming, running, Judo, reading. Personal E-mail: yabdullaev@yahoo.com.

ABDULLAH, NURUL ASMA, immunologist, educator; b. Kota Bharu, Kelantan, Mar. 7, 1981; BS in Health Scis. with honors, Sch. Health Scis., 2003, PhD, 2008. Postdoc. rsch. officer U. Sains Malaysia, 2008—09, lectr., rschr., 2009—, lead auditor, 2010. Tech. assessor Animal Ethics Com., 2009; head cluster Immunology Cluster Rsch., 2010; grant tech. assessor Biomed. & Health Rsch. Platform, 2010. Recipient Global Health Travel award, Bill and Melinda Gates Found.; Nat. Sci. fellowship, Ministry Sci. and Innovation Malaysia, Vis. Rsch. fellow, Med. Rsch. Coun., Travel grant, European Fedn. Immunology Soc. Mem.: Internat. Assn. Dental Rsch. (Malaysia sect.), Malaysia Soc. Parasitology and Tropical Medicine, Internat. Soc. Infectious Diseases. Avocations: travel, Web surfing, cooking. Office: Universiti Sains Malaysia Health Campus Kubang Kerian Kelantan 16150 Malaysia Office Fax: 6097642026. Business E-Mail: nurulasma@kk.usm.my.

ABDUL MUTALIB, HALIZA, optometrist, educator; b. Perak, Malaysia, July 11, 1970; B, U. Kebangsaan Malaysia, 1993; MSc, UMIST, Manchester, PhD, 2000. Assoc. prof. U. Kebangsaan Malaysia, 2000—. Head dept. optometry, 1996. Recipient Best Rsch. award, VDC Peter Abel, Germany, 2000. Mem.: Malaysian Optical Coun. JTC. Avocations: music, reading. Office: Dept Optometry FAHS Jalan Raj Kuala Lumpur 50300 Malaysia Office Fax: 603-26910488. Business E-Mail: haliza@medic.ukm.my.

ABDUL RAZACK, HABEEB IBRAHIM, medical researcher, medical writer and editor; b. Kayalpatnam, India, May 19, 1983; B in Pharmacy, Tamil Nadu Dr MGR Med. U., 2006; MSc in Clin. Rsch. & Regulatory Affairs, Sikkum Manipal U., 2011. Clin. rsch. assoc. Quest Life Sci. Pvt Ltd., 2005—06; exec. clin. rsch. assoc. Nicholas Piramal India Ltd., 2006—07; jr. rsch. assoc. GVK Biosci. Pvt Ltd., 2007—10; sr. process expert, med. writing Accenture Svcs. Ltd., 2010—. Mem., advisor Elsevier's Innovation Explorers, 2008—; adv. bd. mem. Clin. Trial Magnifier, 2009—; jr. officer Conf. Students Bd., 2009—10; editl. mgr. Pharma Scientist Jour., 2011—. Recipient Bio Value Star award, GVK Bioscis. Pvt. Ltd., 2008; Travel grant, Geneva Health Forum, Switzerland, 2008, 2010, SICOBAIR, Tehran, Iran,

2009. Mem.: InPharm Assn., Indian Pharm. Assn. Avocation: writing. Home: 141/57 Appa Palli St Kayalpatnam Thoothukkudi Tamil Nadu 628204 India Personal E-mail: habeebibrahim_ar@yahoo.co.in.

ABE, HARUHIKO, cardiologist, educator; b. Oomuta, Fukuoka, Japan, Mar. 20, 1959; children: Miyuki, Yujiro. MD, Univ. Occup & Environ. Health, Kitakyushu, Japan, 1985. Rsch. fellow Case We. Res. U., Cleve.; clin. fellow Good Samaritan Hosp., LA; resident in internal medicine U. Occupl. & Environ. Health, Kitakyushu, Japan, 1985—87, clin. fellow cardiology, 1987—91, rsch. assoc., 1991—97, asst. prof. medicine, 1997—. Contbr. articles to profl. jours., chapters to books. Rsch. grantee, Ministry of Japan, 1995—. Fellow: Am. Coll. Cardiology (licentiate). Office: Univ Occupl & Environ Health 2d Dept Internal Medicine 1-1 Iseigaoka Yahatanishi-ku Kitakyushu 807-8555 Japan Office Fax: 81-93-691-6913. Personal E-mail: haru-abe@med.uoeh-u.ac.jp.

ABE, HARUKI, ophthalmologist, educator; b. Kashiwazaki, Niigata, Japan, Mar. 24, 1947; MD, Niigata U., 1971, PhD, 1980. Prof., dir. Divsn. Ophthalmology and Visual Sci., Grad. Sch. Med. and Dental Scis., Niigata U., 1993—. Vis. scientist Ax-lanck Inst. Germany, 1976—78; vis. prof. Harvin Med. U. China, 2008—11. Mem.: Am. Acad. Ophthalmology, Internat. Glaucoma Soc. Avocations: tennis, swimming. Office: 1-757 Asahi-achi Chuouku Niigata 951-8510 Japan Office Fax: 81-25-227-0785. Business E-Mail: abechan@med.niigata-u.ac.jp.

ABE, KEIKO, science educator; b. Japan, Mar. 8, 1947; M, Ochanomizu U., 1970; PhD, U. Tokyo, 1983. Prof. Grad. Sch. Agrl. & Life Scis., U. Tokyo, 1996—; prof. emeritus U. Tokyo, 2010—. Project leader Kanagawa Acad. Sci. & Tech., 2008—. Recipient medal with Purple Ribbon, Cabinet Office, Govt. of Japan, Highest prize, Japanese Assn. Study Taste & Smell, IFF award, AChems, Ando Momofuku Prize, ANDO Found. Mem.: Japan Soc. Biochemistry, Japan Soc. Nutrition & Food Sci., Agrl. Chem. Soc. Japan, Internat. Soc. Olfaction & Taste, Am. Chem. Soc. Office: 301-1 Food Sci Bldg 1-1-1 Yayoi Bunkyo-ku Tokyo 113-8657 Japan Office Fax: 81-3-5841-8006. Business E-Mail: aka7308@mail.ecc.u-tokyo.ac.jp.

ABE, MOTOHARU, research scientist; b. Fukuoka, Jan. 1, 1972; MSc, Yamaguchi U., 1997; DSc, Kumamoto U., 2007. Sr. rsch. scientist Chemo-Sero-Therapeutic Rsch. Inst., 1997. Office: Kyokush-iKawabe Kikuchi Kumamoto 8691298 Japan E-mail: abe-mo@kaketsuken.or.jp.

ABE, TOMONOBU, surgeon; b. Nagoya, Japan, Oct. 18, 1966; MD, Nagoya U. Sch. Medicine, 1992, PhD. Staff surgeon, head, adult cardiac surgery divsn. Dept. Cardiovasc. Surgery Chukyo Hosp., 2009—. Mem.: Japanese Assn. Thoracic Surgery. Office: 1-1-10 Sanjyo Minami-ku Nagoya Aichi 4650092 Japan Office Fax: 81-52-692-5220. Business E-Mail: tomonobu_abe@chukyo-hosp.jp.

ABE, YUKI, pediatrician; b. Niigata, Niigata, Japan, July 18, 1970; s. Yuichi and Chiyoko Abe; m. Masako Tamaki; children: Meiko, Takumi, Saeko. MD in Pediat., Niigata U. Grad. Sch. Med. and Dental Scis., 1995, PhD in Homeostatic Regulation and Devel., 2009. Specialist Japan Pediat. Soc., 2002, diplomate pediat. advanced life support instr. Am. Heart Assn., 2007. Resident Niigata City Gen. Hosp., 1995—97, staff, dept. pediat, 1998—2002, chief physician, dept. pediat, 2003—09, vice mgr. dept. pediat, 2010—. Contbr. articles to sci. rsch. jours. Fellow: Japan Pediat. Soc.; mem.: Japan Diabetes Soc., Japan Soc. Study Obesity, Japanese Soc. Emergency Pediat., Japanese Soc. Pediat. Allergy and Clin. Immunology, Japanese Soc. Diabetes and Pregnancy, Japanese Soc. Pediat. Pulmonology, Japanese Soc. Pediat Intensive and Critical Care, Japan Endocrine Soc., Japanese Soc. Hypertension, Japanese Soc. Pediat. Endocrinology. Office: Niigata City Gen Hosp 463-7 Shumoku Chuo-ku Niigata 950-1197 Japan Office Fax: 81-25-281-5187. Business E-Mail: y-abe@hosp.niigata.niigata.jp.

ABECK, DIETRICH, dermatologist, educator; b. Essen, Germany, Aug. 8, 1959; s. Wilhelm and Barbara (Wendt) A.; m. Kathrin Gerda Bergerhof, Oct. 19, 1990; children: Ina-Marie, Finn. MD, Ludwig-Maximilian U., Munich, 1985; cert. in dermatology, U. Hosp. Hamburg, Germany, 1991, cert. in allergy, 1993, cert. in tchr., 1994. Scholar German Rsch. Found., Med. Rsch. Ctr., Harrow, Eng., 1985-87; houseman dept. dermatology Ludwig-Maximilian U., Munich, 1987-91, U. Hosp. Hamburg-Eppendorf, 1991-93, asst. prof. dept. dermatology, 1993-95; asst. prof. in-charge dept. dermatology Tech. U., Munich, 1995—2003, univ. prof., 2003—. Mem. Deutsche Dermatologische Geselschaft, Arbeits Gemeinschaft Dermatologische Intektiologie, NCPD, DGAI. Roman Catholic. Avocations: tennis, squash. Office: Renatastr 72 Munich Germany 80639 Office Phone: 0049-89-50-7000. Business E-Mail: professorabeck@mytum.de.

ABEL, EDWIN GEORGE, III, (TED ABEL), biologist, educator, researcher; b. Winston-Salem, NC, Nov. 10, 1963; s. Edwin G. and Anne G. Abel; m. Noreen M. O'Connor, July 24, 1993; 1 child, Seamus C. Abel. BA in Chemistry, Swarthmore Coll., 1985; MPhil in Biochemistry, U. Cambridge, Christ's Coll., 1987; PhD in Biochemistry and Molecular Biology, Harvard U., 1993. Rsch. fellow, Ctr. for Neurobiology and Behavior Coll. Physicians and Surgeons, Columbia U., NYC, 1993—97; asst. prof. to prof., dept. biology U. Pa., Phila., 1998—, dir., biol. basis of behavior program. Mem. adv. grant panels NSF, 1998—2003, NIH. Mem. editl. bd. Hippocampus, Malden, Mass.; assoc. editor Behavioral Neuroscience, Washington; contbr. articles to profl. jours. Mem. sci. review coun., bd. dirs. Cure Autism Now; mem. sci. adv. com. Autism Speaks. Named Biological Basis of Behavior Soc. Prof. of Yr., U. Pa., 2001, 2005; recipient Young Investigator award, Mental Retardation and Develop. Disabilities Rsch. Ctr., Children's Hosp. Phila., 1999, Daniel X. Freedman award for outstanding rsch. by a young investigator, Nat. Alliance for Rsch. on Schizophrenia and Depression, 2000, Dean's award, U. Pa. Sch. Arts and Scis., 2006; fellow NSF, 1987-90, Damon Runyon-Walter Winchell Cancer Rsch. Fund, 1993-96, David and Lucile Packard Found. fellow in sci. and engring., 2000-06; Marshall scholar British Govt., 1985-87; scholar John Merck Scholars award, 1998-2002. Mem.: Am. Coll. Neuropsychopharmacology, Sigma Xi, Phi Beta Kappa. Democrat. Episcopalian. Office: U Pa Dept Biology 204G Carolyn Lynch Laboratory Philadelphia PA 19104 Office Phone: 215-898-3100. Office Fax: 215-898-8780. E-mail: abele@sas.upenn.edu.

ABEL, ELIZABETH ANN, dermatologist; b. Hartford, Conn., Mar. 16, 1940; d. Frederick A. and Rose (Borovicka) Abel; m. Barton Lane; children: Barton F. Lane, Geoffrey Lane, Suzanne Lane Franklin. Student, Colby-Sawyer Coll., 1957-60; BS, Wash. Hosp. Ctr. Sch. Med. Tech., 1961, U. Md., 1965, MD cum laude, 1967; PhD. Diplomate Am. Bd. Dermatology. Intern San Francisco Gen. Hosp., 1967-68; resident in medicine, fellow in oncology U. Calif. Med. Ctr., San Francisco, 1968-69; resident in dermatology NYU Med. Ctr., 1969-72, chief resident, 1971-72, USPHS research trainee in immunology, 1972-73; dep. chief dept. dermatology USPHS Hosp., SI, NY, 1973-74; instr. clin. dermatology Columbia U. Coll. Physicians and Surgeons, NYC, 1974-75, Stanford (Calif.) U. Sch. Medicine, 1975-77, adj. clin. asst. prof. dermatology, 1977-82, asst. prof. dermatology, 1982-90, clin. assoc. prof., 1990-96, clin. prof., 1996—. Asst. editor Jour. Am. Acad. Dermatology, 1993-98; mem. med. adv. bd. The Nat. Psoriasis Found., 1993-95. Contbr. articles to profl. sci. jours. Mellon Found. fellow, 1983, 87. Fellow Am. Acad. Dermatology; mem. N.Am. Clin. Dermatologic Soc., San Francisco Dermatologic Soc., Pacific Dermatologic Soc.(pres., 2010-11), Pacific Dermatologic Assn., Women's Dermatologic Soc., Noah Worcester Dermatologic Soc., Alpha Omega Alpha. Avocations: piano, golf, travel, reading. Office: California Skin Institute 525 South Dr, Ste 115 Mountain View CA 94040 Office Phone: 650-969-5600. Personal E-mail: eaabelmd@aol.com.

ABELES, NORMAN, psychologist, educator; came to U.S., 1939, naturalized, 1944; s. Felix and Bertha (Gronich) A.; m. Jeanette Bueller, Apr. 14, 1957; children: Linda, Mark. BA, NYU, 1949; MA, U. Tex., 1952, PhD, 1958. Diplomate: Am. Bd. Profl. Psychology (Midwest regional bd. 1972-78, chmn. regional bd. 1975-77; nat. trustee 1975-77). Fellow in counseling U. Tex., Austin, 1956-57; instr. Mich. State U., East Lansing, 1957-59, asst. prof., 1959-64, asso. prof., 1964-67, prof. psychology, 1968—2008, prof. emeritus, 2008, dir. psychol. clinic, 1978—2004, co-dir. clin. tng., 1981-96, asst. dir. counseling center, 1965-71. U.S. State Dept. ednl. exch. prof. U. Utrecht, Netherlands, 1969, vis. prof., 1975; cons. Peace Corps, 1965-69; vocat. cons. Social Security Office of Hearings and Appeals, 1962—; med. advisor Social Security Office of Hearings and Appeals, 1986—; mem. Mich. Commn. Cert. of Psychologists, 1962-77, chmn., 1966-68; mem. coun. Nat. Register Health Svc. Providers in Psychology, 1974—, vice chmn., 1975-80, bd. dirs. 2005—2010; del. White House Conf. on Aging, 1995, 2005; mem. geriatric and gerontology adv. com. to Sec. of VA, 2002—. Editor: Acad. Psychology bull., 1978-82; cons. editor Am. Jour. Alzheimers Disease and other Dementias, Jour. Personality Assessment, 1988-2005, Clin. Psychology: Sci. and Practice, 1994-2004, Clin. Psychology Rev., 1995-98, Profl. Psychology: Rsch. and Practice, 1979-81, 89—, editor, 1983-88; contbr. articles to profl. jours. Served with U.S. Army, 1954-56. Fulbright-Hays grantee, 1969; recipient Disting. Psychologist award Mich. Soc. Clin. Psychologists, 1984; Disting. Practitioner, Nat. Acad. Practice, 1982; Sr. Contbr. award, APA Disting. Ctr., 2010, Arthur Furst Ethics Lectureship medal Pacific Grad. Sch. Psychology, 1996; Dept. Vets. Affairs Spl. Contbns. award, Battle Creek Mich., 1997, APA Presdl. Citation award, 2008, Carl Heiselt award, 2010 Fellow APA (coun. reps. 1972-75, 77-79, 89-91, 93-95, 99-2001, 06-07, 08—10, policy and planning bd. 1975-79, chmn. 1976, rec. sec. 1980-86, chmn. edn. and tng. bd. 1988, bd. ednl. affairs 1999-2001, com. on internat. rels. in psychology 2002-04, pres. divsn. psychotherapy and divsn. clin. psychology 1990, publs. and comm. bd. 1990-96, 2008—, chmn. 1995, pres.-elect 1996, pres. 1997, bd. dirs. divsn. psychotherapy 2000-2005, 2007-, pres. divsn. 7 geropsychology/internat. psychology 2005, pres. sect. IX assessment divsn. clin. psychology 2004, ethics com. 2005-07, bd. dirs., 2008—presdl. award, 2008), Am. Psychol. Found. (sec. 2002-07), Coun. Sci. Socs. Pres.; mem. Midwestern Psychol. Assn., Mich. Psychol. Assn. (legis. chmn. 1964-72, pres. 1971-72, Disting. Psychologist 1974), Internat. Union Psychol. Scis. (U.S. com. 1999-2005), Sigma Xi. Home: 953 Rosewood Ave East Lansing MI 48823-3126 Home Phone: 517-337-0853. Business E-Mail: abeles@msu.edu.

ABELIN, THEODOR, retired medical educator, epidemiologist; b. Berne, Switzerland, Aug. 19, 1935; MD, U. Berne, 1960; MPH, Harvard U., 1963. Rsch. fellow Swiss Fed. Inst. Tech., Zurich, 1961—62, Harvard U., Boston, 1963—64, 1964—65, asst. prof., 1965—70, assoc. prof. epidemiology and behavioral sci., 1970—71; prof. U. Berne Med. Sch., Switzerland, 1971—2000, head dept. social and preventive medicine, 1971—2000, prof. emeritus, 2000—. Assoc. registrar Mass. Tumor Registry, Boston, 1964—67, sr. cons., 1967—71. Chief editor Sozial und Praventivmedizin, 1972—80; author, editor: Measurement in Health Promotion and Protection, 1987; contbr. articles to profl. jours. Mem. World Health Org., 1977—97; chair Swiss Assn. for Tobacco Prevention, 1973—92; coun. mem. for Europe Internat. Epidemiological Assn., 1987—90; co-pres. World Fed. Pub. Health Assn., 2003—04; vice chair Swiss Fed. Commn. Tobacco Prevention, 1999—2007; pres. World Fed. Pub. Health Assn., 2001—03. Recipient Andrija Stampar medal, Assn. Schs. Pub. Health in the European Region, 2004. E-mail: th.abelin@bluewin.ch.

ABELL, THOMAS LYMAN, physician; b. Vermillion, SD, Mar. 9, 1948; married; 2 children. BA, Yale U., 1971; BSM, U. S.D., 1975, MD, 1977. Diplomate Am. Bd. Family Practice, Am. Bd. Internal Medicine, sub. bd. gastroenterology. Intern So. Ill. U. Affiliated Hosps., Springfield, 1977-78; resident in family medicine Ohio State U. Hosp., Columbus, 1978-80, instr., 1978-80; preceptor in family medicine Mayor Med. Sch., U. Minn., Rochester, Minn., 1981-84; instr. family medicine Mayor Med. Sch., Rochester, Minn., 1985-86; internal medicine coord. U. Tenn. HealthPlex Family Medicine Residency/Bapt. Hosp., Memphis, 1986-87; asst. prof. dept. medicine U. Tenn., Memphis, 1988—, asst. prof. dept. family medicine, 1989—, asst. prof. dept. pharmacology, 1991—, assoc. prof. dept. medicine, 1992—. Vis. scientist in gastroenterology dept. medicine Mayor Clinic, Rochester, 1982-86; staff Olmsted Cmty. Hosp., Rochester, 1980-86, Rochester Health Care Ctr., 1980-86, U. Tenn. Med. Ctr. (Bowld Hosp.), 1988—, Regional Med. Ctr., VA Med. Ctr., 1988—, Bapt. Meml. Hosp., 1988—, LeBonheur Children's Hosp., Memphis, 1988—; mem. behavioral medicine study sect. NIH, 1989-90; med. staff U. Tenn. Med. Group, Memphis, 1988—; mem. clin. rsch. ctr. renewal com., 1992, staff, assoc. prof. UAMS Hosp., Little Pk.2000-07, staff, prof. UMMC, 2001-, chief, 2007-, UA Hosp. Jackson Mich., 2005-, Meth. Rep. Hosp., 2003-. Cons. editor Behavioral Medicine Abstracts, 1983-86; abstract reviewer Soc. Behavioral Medicine Ann. Meeting, 1985, Soc. Tchrs. Family Medicine Ann. Meeting, 1986; reviewer Diabetes Care, 1985-86, Gastroenterology, 1988—, Am. Jour. Gastroenterology, 1988—, Dig Dis Sci, 1988—, Am. Jour. Physiology, 1988—; book reviewer Psychosomatics, 1986; contbr. numerous articles to profl. jours. Grantee Olmsted Med. Group, 1982-83, Mayo Found., 1984-85, Janssen Pharmeceutica, 1985—, Ross Labs., 1988, CRC, 1989-91, NIH, 1992, Glaxo Pharms., 1993, TAP Pharms., 1993-96, Medtronics Inc., 1993—, Pfizer Inc., 1997-98, NI & CRC, 2006. Mem. ACP, AMA, Tenn. Acad. Family Practice, Am. Acad. Family Practice, Med. Assn. Soc. of Psychophysiologic Rsch., Soc. for Behavioral Medicine, Am. Gastroenterol. Assn., Am. Fedn. for Clin. Rsch., Janssen Rsch. Coun., Am. Soc. Internal Medicine, Am. Motility Soc., Gastroenterology Rsch. Group(cons. med. trainee 2001-, investigator, med. trainee 2001-06), ASOE. Office: UMMC 2500 N State St Jackson MS 39216 Office Phone: 601-984-4540. Office Fax: 601-984-4548. Personal E-mail: gidivisim@hotmail.com. Business E-Mail: tabell@umc.edu.

ABELMANN, WALTER H., internist, educator; b. Frankfurt, Germany, May 16, 1921; s. Arthur and Else (Weill) A.; m. Rena J. White, June 8, 1958; children: Karen, Nancy, Ruth, Arthur, Charles. AB magna cum laude, Harvard Coll., 1943; MD, U. Rochester, 1946. Diplomate Am. Bd. Internal Medicine. Prof. medicine Harvard Med. Sch., Boston, 1972-91, prof. medicine emeritus, 1991—; prof. medicine Harvard-MIT Div. Health Sci. & Tech., Cambridge, 1974—; chief cardiology Beth Israel Hosp., Boston, 1974-78, physician, 1974-88, dir. cardiovascular rsch., 1978-88, sr. physician, 1989—90; interim co-dir. Harvard-MIT Div. Health Sci. & Tech., Cambridge, 1990-92. Contbr. over 350 articles to profl. jours. Recipient Paul Dudley White award, Am. Heart Assn., 1979. Fellow ACP, AAAS, Am. Coll. Cardiology; mem. New Eng. Cardiovascular Soc. (pres. 1965-66), Assn. Am. Physicians, Am. Soc. Clin. Investigation, Am. Univ. Cardiologists. Home: 975 Memorial Dr Apt 406 Cambridge MA 02138-5803 Office: MIT E25-519 77 Massachusetts Ave Cambridge MA 02139 *

ABELS, CHRISTOPH, dermatologist, educator; b. Cologne, Germany, June 21, 1965; married. MD, Med. Sch. U., Munich; PhD, U. Munich, 1997. Cert. allergology, dermatologist Bavaria, 2001. Assoc. prof., dermatology U. Regensburg, 2004—10, prof., dermatology Germany, 2010—; med. dir. Dr. Wolff, Bielefeld, Germany, 2005—. Office: Dr Wolff Sudbrackstrasse 56 Bielefeld D-33611 Germany Office Phone: 495218808451. Business E-Mail: christoph.abels@wolff-arzneimittel.de.

ABENAVOLI, LUDOVICO, physician, researcher; b. Catanzaro, Italy, Oct. 19, 1976; s. Saverio Abenavoli and Maria Teresa Samà. Degree, U. Cattolica, Sacro Cuore, Italy, 2002. Resident U. Sacre Heart, Rome, 2002—07; rschr. U. Magna Graecia, Catanzaro, Italy, 2008—, asst. prof. gastroenterology. Recipient Young Investigator award, Italian Soc. Internal Medicine, 2007. Mem.: Italian Assn. Study Liver, Italian Soc. Gastroenterology, Italian Soc. Internal Medicine. Achievements include research in role of elastography assessment to evaluate liver fibrosis, celiac disease & exteintestinal manifestations, non alcoholic stestohepetities. Office: Univ Magna Graecia Dept Exptl & Clin Medicine Viale Europa 88100 Catanzaro CZ Italy Business E-Mail: l.abenavoli@unicz.it.

ABENDSTEIN, HELMUT, otolaryngologist; b. Munich, May 12, 1955; B, Ludwigs Maximilians U., Munich, 1979, MD, 1986. Sr. cons. ENT dept. St. Olavs U. Hosp., Trondheim, Norway, 1996—. Rsch. scientist, asst. prof. Norwegian U. Sci. and Tech., 1997—2011. Mem.: Norwegian Med. Assn. Avocations: literature, history, music. Office: Olav Kyrres Gate 17 Trondheim South Troendelag 7048 Norway Business E-Mail: helmut.abendstein@stolav.no.

ABERMAN, HAROLD MARK, veterinarian; b. Chgo., Aug. 5, 1956; s. Howard Oscar and Goldie Esther Aberman. BS, Purdue U., 1979, MSE, 1987, BSE, 1986, DVM, 1983. NIH postdoctoral fellow Purdue U., West Lafayette, 1983-87; dir. sci. and biol. affairs Howmedica div. Pfizer, Rutherford, 1987-99; pres. Applied Biol. Concepts, Los Alamitos, Calif., 1996—; dir. devel. Orthop. Rsch. Inst., Long Beach, Calif., 1999-2001, med. device cons., 2001—; dir. sci. affairs, global sci. program dir. Synthes, West Chester, Pa., 2003—. Adj. prof. N.C. State U., Raleigh, 1988—, Miss. State U., Starkville, Miss., 1990—, Purdue U., 1991—. Contbr. articles to profl. jours. Mem. ASME, AVMA, ASTM, Ortho. Rsch. Soc., Soc. Biomechanics, Soc. Biomaterial, Soc. Biomaterials, ICRS. Jewish. Office: Applied Biol Concepts 12581 Silver Fox Rd Los Alamitos CA 90720-5234 also: 1301 Goshen Pky West Chester PA 19380 Office Phone: 949-500-5211. Personal E-mail: haroldabc@aol.com.

ABERNATHY, GEORGE THOMAS, cardiologist, consultant; b. Atlanta, Oct. 31, 1943; s. Ira Raulston and Stella Eulalia Abernathy. BA, Emory Coll. Arts and Scis., Atlanta, 1964; MD, Emory U. Sch. Medicine, Atlanta, 1968. Diplomate internal medicine and cardiovasc. diseases Am. Bd. Internal Medicine, 1973, Am. Bd. Cardiovasc. Disease, 1985. Intern Emory U. Sch. Medicine, Atlanta, 1968—69; resident U. Minn., Mpls., 1971—73; cardiology fellow Emory U. Sch. Medicine, Atlanta, 1973—75; pvt. practice cardiologist Ft. Lauderdale, Fla., 1975—78, Tampa, Fla., 1986—91, Ruskin, Fla., 1991—96, Venice, Fla., 1996—; with Wilford Hall USAF Med. Ctr., Lackland AFB, San Antonio, 1984—86. Col. med. USAF, 1978—86, US, Germany. Fellow: Am. Heart Assn., Am. Coll. Cardiology; mem.: Am. Soc. Nuc. Cardiology, Am. soc. Echocardiography, Alpha Omega Alpha Honor Med. Soc. Avocations: boating, fishing, scuba diving, horse breeding. Office: Heart Inst Venice 1370 E Venice Ave Ste102 Venice FL 34285 Office Phone: 941-412-0026.

ABERNATHY, SHIELDS B., allergist, immunologist, internist; b. Bronxville, NY, Mar. 14, 1951; m. Leslie Abernathy; children: Amelia, Camille, Lant. BA, Ohio Wesleyan U., 1973; MS, Harvard U., 1975; MD, Med. Coll. Pa., 1979. Diplomate Am. Bd. Internal Medicine, Am. Bd. Allergy and Immunology, eligible Am. Preventive Medicine, Nat. Bd. Med. Examiners; Qualified Med. Examiner Calif.; Fed. Aviation Med. Examiner; ACLS Am. Heart Assn. Intern in internal medicine L.A. County/U. So. Calif. Med. Ctr., LA, 1979-80; resident in internal medicine Hosp. of Good Samaritan, LA, 1980-81; resident UCLA Wadsworth VA Med. Ctr., 1981-82, fellow allergy and immunology, 1982-84. Med. philanthropic facilitator, Philippines, 2000, India, 2001, Indochina, 2001, Amazon, 2002, Africa, 2004, Honduras, 2008, Kingdom of Bhutan, 2011, extern med. student proctor; rschr. in field. Fellow Am. Coll. Allergy and Immunology, Am. Acad. Allergy and Immunology; mem. Am. Med. Health Assn., Am. Pub. Health Assn. (internat. health sect.). Office: 1050 Las Tablas Rd Ste 3 Templeton CA 93465-9792 Office Phone: 805-434-1000. E-mail: sabernats@sbcglobal.net.

ABEYWARDENA, MAHINDA YAPA, cardiovascular scientist, educator; b. Matara, Sri Lanka, Sept. 12, 1953; BSc in Biol. Scis. (hon.), U. Wolverhampton, 1977; PhD in Pharmacology, U. Alberta, 1981. Prin. rsch. scientist CSIRO Food & Nutritional Scis., 1981—. Affiliate staff mem. U. Adelaide, 1990—; vis. prof. Chulalongkorn U., 1998—, U. Putra Malaysia, 1998—2009; editl. panel mem. Nutrition, 2000—, Recent Patents Cardiovasc. Drugs, 2005—. Recipient Rsch. Achievement medal, Commonwealth Sci. Indsl. Rsch. Orgn.; Rsch. grant, Nat. Heart Found. and Similar Agys. & Pharma Food Industry. Fellow: Malaysian Oil Scientists & Technologists Assn.; mem.: Internat. Soc. for Study of Fatty Acids and Lipids, Australian Atherosclerosis Soc., Nutrition Soc. Australia, Am. Oil Chemists Soc. Avocations: cricket, gardening, cooking. Office: CSIRO-FNS Kintore Ave Adelaide SA 5000 Australia Office Fax: 61-8-8303-8899. Business E-Mail: mahinda.abeywardena@csiro.au.

ABI ABBOUD, ANTOINE, plastic surgeon; MD, St. Joseph U., Beirut, Lebanon. Fellow cosmetic and plastic surgery Univ. of Montreal, Canada; aesthetic surgeon Lyon, France, Montreal, Canada, Beirut; head plastic and aesthetic surgery dept. Mt. Lebanon Hosp., 2004—; cons. plastic and aesthetic surgery Kingdom of Saudi Arabia, 2010—; plastic surgeon Beirut Beauty Clinic, Zalka, Lebanon. Mem.: European Soc. of Plastic Reconstructive and Aesthetic Surgery, Internat. Confederation for Plastic, Reconstructive and Aesthetic Surgery (IPRAS), Lebanese Soc. of Plastic Surgery. Office: Beirut Beauty Clinic 4th Fl Warde Bldg Zalka Hwy Lebanon Office Phone: 9611894895. *

ABID, AMR, pharmacologist; b. Constantine, Algeria, May 3, 1964; s. Khoutir Abid and Cherifa Bouafia; m. Allison Ruth Sharp, Sept. 13, 1973. BSc in Molecular and Cellular Biology, U. Constantine, Algeria, 1989; MSc in Pharmacology, Faculty of Pharmacy, Nancy, France, 1991, PhD in Pharmacology, 1994. Rsch. scientist Faculty of Medicine, Vandoeuvre Les Nancy, France, 1995—2000; European bus. mgr. Invitrogen, Paisley, England, 2000—. Contbr. articles to profl. jours. Achievements include patents pending for Oligonucletitide anti-Tumor Necrosis Factor. Office: Invitrogen 3 Fountain Dr Inchinnan Bus Pk Paisley PA4 9RF Scotland Office Phone: 00 44 773 030 3877. Personal E-mail: abidamr@yahoo.fr. Business E-Mail: amr.abid@invitrogen.com, amr.abid@lifetech.com.

ABIGAIL, WENDY FAY, nursing educator; b. Victoria, Aug. 28, 1959; BSN with honors, Flinders U., Adelaide, Australia, 2007, PhD, 2011. ACSC family adv. unit coord. Noarlunga Health Svcs., Adelaide, 1991—2011; lectr. Flinders U., 2011—. Chair Australian Women's Health Assn., SA, 2007—11. Contbr. articles to profl. jours. Recipient Deane Southgate award, Noarlunga Health Svcs., 2006; scholarship, Australian Govt., 2007—10. Mem.: Women's Svcs. Network SA, Australian Women's & Gender Studies Assn., ShineSA, Abortion Providers Exec., Nat. Coun. Women Australia, SA. Office: Flinders University SONM PO Box 2100 Adelaide South Australia 5001 Australia Office Phone: 61 882015433. Business E-Mail: wendy.abigail@flinders.edu.au.

ABIKO, HIRONOBU, research scientist; b. Kawasaki, Kanagawa, Japan, Feb. 15, 1973; BE, U. Tokyo, 1996, PhD in Engring., 2001. Staff rsch. Nat. Inst. Indsl. Health, 2001—06, Nat. Inst. Occupl. Safety and Health, Japan, 2006—09, sr. rschr., 2009—. Tchg. asst., dept. applied chemistry, rsch. asst. U. Tokyo, 1998—2000. Fellow: Eco-carbon Workshop (Japan); mem.: Japan Soc. Occupl. Health, Materials Sci. Soc. Japan, Chem. Soc. Japan, Carbon Soc. Japan. Office: 6-21-1 Nagao Tama ward Kawasaki Kanagawa 214-8585 Japan Office Fax: 81-44-865-6124. Business E-Mail: abiko@h.jniosh.go.jp.

ABIKOFF, HOWARD, psychologist; b. Bklyn., Jan. 3, 1945; BA, Bklyn. Coll., CUNY, 1965; PhD, Adelphi U., 1976. Dir. Inst. Attention Deficit Hyperactivity and Behavior Disorders NYU Child Study Ctr., NYU Sch. Medicine, 1996—2011, dir. rsch., 1996—2003, Pevaroff Cohn prof. child and adolescent psychiatry, 1996—. Dir. rsch. divsn. child and adolescent psychiatry LI Jewish Med. Ctr., 1986—96; rsch. scientist Nathan Kline Inst. Psychiat. Rsch., 1996—99. Named to Hall of Fame, Children and Adults with Attention-Deficit/Hyperactivity Disorder, 2004; grant, NIMH. Mem.: APA, Internat. Soc. Rsch. in Child and Adolescent Psychopathology, Am. Psychopath. Assn. Avocations: tennis, theater. Office: NYU Child Study Ctr 215 Lexington Av New York NY 10016 Business E-Mail: howard.abikoff@nyumc.org.

ABIMANNAN, SATHEESH, engineering educator; b. June 4, 1976; BSc, Sch. Sci. and Humanities, 1996; MCA, ME, Sch. Computing Scis. and Engring., PhD, 1999. Asst. prof. Periyar Maniammai U., 1999—, dept. head, 2010. Mem.: IEEE, Indian Soc. Tech. Edn. (New Delhi) (Young Tchr. award 2010), CSI. Avocations: singing, reading. Home: 6 Second St Sundaram Nagar MC Thanjavur Tamil Nadu 613 004 India Personal E-mail: vbsatheesh@yahoo.com.

ABINA, JELENA, medical researcher; b. Murom, Vladimir, Russia, Dec. 15, 1958; d. Aleksey Lashmanov and Zoya Lashmanova; 1 child, Pavel Abin. MS, Gorky Med. U., Nizhni Novgorod, Russia, 1983. Resident Gorky Regional Hosp., Nizhni Novgorod, 1983—84; rschr. Estonian Inst. Cardiology, Tallinn, Harju, Estonia, 1984—2006, prin. investigator, 1987—2005; epidemiologist, CVD Sci. Ctr. Preventive Cardiology, Moscow, 1985; specialist rschr. Technomedicum TUT, Tallinn, 2007—, prin. investigator, WHO, 2007—. Contbr. articles to profl. jours. Mem.: Estonian Soc. Hypertension, Estonian Soc. Cardiology, European Soc. Cardiology. Avocations: reading, movies, travel, swimming, gardening.

ÅBLAD, BENGT HJALMAR, pharmacologist; b. Falköping, Sweden, Feb. 3, 1932; MD, Gothenburg U., 1961, PhD in Pharmacology, 1963. Adj. prof. applied pharmacology Gothenburg U., 1973—2011, asst. prof., dept. pharmacology, 1965—2011; pharmacologist Drug Co. Hässle (later Astra-Hässle and AstraZeneca), 1963—2011. Vis. scientist Important Drug Companies, Physiol. and Pharmacological U., 1963. Contbr. articles to profl. jours. Co-recipient prize, Bd. Tech. Devel. Home: Sundshagsgatan 22 Gothenburg Västra Götaland 41476 Sweden Personal E-mail: bengtablad@hotmail.com.

ABLIN, RICHARD JOEL, immunologist, educator; b. Chgo., May 15, 1940; s. Robert Benjamin and Minnie Edith (Gordon) A.; m. Linda Lee Lutwack; 1 son, Michael David. AB, Lake Forest Coll., Ill., 1962, DSc (hon.), 2005; PhD in Microbiology, SUNY, Buffalo, 1967. Diplomate Am. Bd. Clin. Immunology and Allergy; cert. specialist in pub. health and med. lab. microbiology Nat. Registry Microbiologists of Am. Acad. Microbiology, Am. Soc. Clin. Pathology Bd. Registry. Grad. asst. dept. biology SUNY-Buffalo, 1963-65, rsch. asst., 1963, rsch. fellow, 1965-66; USPHS postdoctoral fellow dept. microbiology Sch. Medicine, lectr., lab instr., 1966-68; instr., rsch. asst. Rosary Hill Coll., 1965-66; rsch. cons. program med. edn. AID, Paraguay, 1968; dir. divsn. immunology Millard Fillmore Hosp. Rsch. Inst., Buffalo, 1968-70; head sect. immunology, renal unit Meml. Hosp. Springfield, 1970-73; dir. sect. immunobiology div. urology dept. surgery Cook County Hosp. and Hektoen Inst. Med. Rsch., Chgo., 1973-75, sr. sci. officer divsn. immunology, 1976-83; sr. mem. sci. staff, clin. immunologist Cook County Hosp., 1973-75; asst. prof. medicine So. Ill. U., 1971-73; assoc. prof. microbiology Univ. Health Sci. (Chgo. Med. Sch.), 1973-74; pres., dir. Robert Benjamin Ablin Found. for Cancer Rsch., Evergreen Park, Ill., 1979—; rsch. assoc. prof. urology, dir. immunology unit dept. urology SUNY, Stony Brook, 1983—89, mem. U. Senate, 1986—89, 1989—92, mem. U. Gov. Coms., 1984—92; acad. del. United U. Professions, 1986—88, 1988—90; dir. sci. investigation Tetragenex Pharms., Inc., Park Ridge, NJ, 1991—2003, consulting scientist, 2003—08. Vis. rsch. prof. Coll. Medicine U. Ariz., Tucson, 2001-04; rsch. prof., interim dir., 2006-08; asst. dir., 2008-10; grad. edn. program, dept. immunobiology, rsch. prof. dept. pathology Ariz. Coll. Medicine, Ariz. Cancer Ctr. and BIO5 Inst., Tucson, 2005—, Clin. Medicine Insights: Pathology, 2011-; organizer, presenter, instr., participant numerous nat. and internat. profl. meetings, symposia, seminars; mem. editl. bd. Translational Medicine Current Rsch., 2011-, Brit. Med. Jour. Open, 2011-, Clin. Medicine Insights: Pathology, 2011-. Editor: Allergologia et Immunopathologia, 1980—84; co-editor: Cancer Metastasis-Biology and Treatment, 2000—; contbg. editor: Allergologia et Immunopathologia, 1974—84, Seminars in Immunopathology and Oncology, Ill. Med. Jour., 1975—88, Cancer Watch, 2001—; adv. editor: Jour. Cancer, 1976—89, Jour. Translational Medicine, 2006—, Current Cancer Therapy Reviews, 2008—, assoc. editor: Low Temperature Medicine, 1975—, Jour. Investigational Allergology and Clin. Immunology (formerly Allergologia et Immunopathologia), 1985—95, Jour. Exptl. Therapeutics and Oncology, 2003—, Cancer Science, 2007—, mem. editl. adv. bd.: Med. Sci. Rsch., 1984—2000, Cancer Epidemiology (formerly Cancer Detection and Prevention), 2006—; mem. editl. bd. Medikon, 1974—80, Immunology and Allergy Practice, 1979—95, Tumor Diagnostik and Therapie, 1980—98, Am. Jour. Reproductive Immunology and Microbiology, 1980—91, Cellular and Molecular Biology, 1985—87, Chemistry Today, 1991—97, Early Pregnancy: Biology and Medicine, 1995—, Internat. Jour. Oncology, 1996—2008, Advances in Therapy, 1999—, Prostate Jour., 1999—2001, Bratislava Med. Jour., 1999—, Exptl. Biology and Medicine, 2000—06, UroOncology, 2000—08, Annals Clin. and Lab.Sci., 2000—, Clin. and Applied Immunology Revs., 2001—07, Clin. and Vaccine Immunology (formerly Clin. and Diagnostic Lab. Immunology), 2002—07, Expert Rev. Anticancer Therapy, 2002—, Cancer Therapy, 2003—, Internat. Jour. Cancer Prevention, 2003—, Current Opinion in Oncology, 2005—, Biomarkers in Medicine, 2008—, Cancer Cell Internat., 2008—, Jour. Exptl. and Clin. Cancer Rsch., 2008—, Current Oncology, 1998—, dep. editor, 2007—09, Immunotherapy, 2009—, Current Signal Transduction Therapy, 2010—; contbr. chapters to books, articles to profl. jours. Chief Sangamo Nation Y-Indian Guides, Springfield, 1972-73; mgr. Skokie Indians' Boys' Baseball, Ill., 1973-74, 77, 80, 81, bd. dirs., 1979-83, exec. v.p., 1981-82; mgr. Little League Three Villages, Setauket, NY, 1986; cubmaster NW Suburban coun. Boy Scouts Am., 1974-78, asst. scoutmaster, 1975-77; mem. exploring divsn. Suffolk County coun. Boy Scouts Am., 1985-88; pres., dir. Spirit of Chgo. Hockey Club Found., Evergreen Park, Ill., 1982—. Recipient Nat. Pres. Leader's Dist. Boy Scouts Am., 1975, 1st award for sci. excellence The Haakon Radge Found. Advanced Cancer Studies, 2007, Theresa Funds Educator Excellence award in critical rsch., 2009, Disting. Alumni award, U. Buffalo, 2010; named Cubmaster of Yr. Boy Scouts Am., 1977, Gold award Magister in Cryosurgery, Internat. Soc. Cryosurgery, 2007, Theresa Funds Educator Excellence award, 2009. Fellow: Assn. Clin. Scientists, Am. Coll. Cryosurgery (adv. bd. 1977—78, v.p. 1977—79, parliamentarian 1977—79, adv. bd. 1980—81, 1984—99), Am. Coll. Allergy and Immunology (bd. registry), Indian Cryogenics Coun. (hon.); mem.: AAAS, Am. Soc. Cell Biology, Am. Soc. Cell Biology, Anticancer Therapeutics and Oncology Soc., Am. Soc. Clin. Pathology, Metastasis Rsch. Soc., Am. Assn. Cancer Rsch., Am. Assn. Immunologists, Am. Soc. Microbiology, Assn. Med. Lab Immunologists, Brit. Assn. Surg. Oncology, Buffalo Collegium Immunology, Internat. Soc. Immunology Reprodn., N.Y. Acad. Scis., Soc. Exptl. Biology and Medicine, Soc. Leukocyte Biology, Internat. Soc. Protozoologists, Soc. Study Reprodn., Japan Soc. Low Temperature Medicine (hon.), Internat. Soc. Cryosurgery (hon.; pres. 1977—80, bd. dirs. 1980—, hon. life pres.), Transplantation Soc., Cryoimmunotherapeutic Study Group (chmn.), Witebsky Ctr. Microbial Pathogenesis and Immunology, Sigma Xi, Phi Beta Kappa. Achievements include identification of prostate specific antigen, used as tumor marker in prostate cancer, and of human thymic specific antigen providing means for differentiation of thymic lymphocytes from other lymphoid cells and the development of antithymocyte globulin (selectively immunosuppressive for thymocytes) used in renal allograft (transplant) recipients; development of concept of cryoimmunotherapy for treatment of cancer. Office: Univ Ariz Coll Medicine Health Scis Ctr Dept Pathology 1501 N Campbell Ave PO Box 245043 Tucson AZ 85724-5043 Office Phone: 520-626-6283. Business E-Mail: ablinrj@email.arizona.edu, ablinrj@ix.netcom.com.

ABLON, GLYNIS, dermatologist, educator; b. Calif., July 14, 1966; MD, GWU, 1992. Dir., owner Ablon Skin Inst. and Rsch. Ctr., 2001—. Asst. clin. prof. UCLA, 1998—. Contbr. chapters to books, articles to profl. jours. Recipient Rosenberg Dermatology award, GWU. Fellow: Am. Soc. Derm Surgery, Am. Soc. Laser Medicine and Surgery, Am. Acad. Dermatology. Avocation: boxing. Office: 1600 Rosecrans Ave 6A #12 Manhattan Beach CA 90266 Office Fax: 310-727-3377. Business E-Mail: grablon@verizon.net.

ABLOW, KEITH RUSSELL, psychiatrist, writer; b. Marblehead, Mass., Nov. 23, 1961; s. Allan Murray and Jeanette Norma (Mezansky) Ablow. BS, Brown U., Providence, 1983; MD, Johns Hopkins U. Sch. Medicine, Balt., 1987. Diplomate American Bd. Psychiatry & Neurology, American Acad. Experts in Traumatic Stress, cert. in forensic and gen. adult psychiatry. Reporter Newsweek, NYC, 1984; columnist Balt. Evening Sun, Boston Herald, 1985-89; intern in psychiatry Tufts New Eng. Med. Ctr., Boston, 1987-88, resident, 1988-91; cons. psychiatrist WCVB TV, Boston, 1992—; med. dir. Tri-City Mental Health Centers, 1992-94; assoc. med. dir. Heritage Health Systems, 1993-94; corr. Med. News Network, 1993—; med. dir. FHC New Eng., 1994-96; outpatient psychiatrist Boston Regional Med. Ctr., 1996—; pvt. practice Newburyport, Mass., 1996—. Med. editor, prodr. Lifetime Med. TV, NYC, LA, 1985—89; contbg. editor Good Housekeeping Mag., Men's Fitness; on-air psychiatry contbr. Fox News Channel. Author: (nonfiction) Medical School: Getting In, Staying In, Staying Human, 1987, How to Cope with Depression, 1989, To Wrestle With Demons: A Psychiatrist Struggles to Understand His Patients and Himself, 1992, Anatomy of a Psychiatric Illness: Healing the Mind and Brain, 1993, The Strange Case of Dr. Kappler: The Doctor Who Became a Killer, 1994, Without Mercy: The Shocking True Story of a Doctor Who Murdered, 1996, Inside the Mind of Scott Peterson, 2005, Living the Truth: Transform Your Life Through the Power of Insight and Honesty, 2007, (novels) Denial, 1998, Projection, 1999, Compulsion, 2002, Psychopath, 2003, Murder Suicide, 2004, The Architect, 2005; co-author: (with Glenn Beck) The 7: Seven Wonders That Will Change Your Life, 2011; exec. prodr., host The Dr. Keith Ablow Show, 2006—07, appearances include Oprah Winfrey Show, Today Show, Howard Stern Show, Good Morning America, Catherine Crier Live, O'Reilly Factor, Larry King Live, others. Recipient Optimate award, American Soc. Profl. Italians, 1990. Mem.: AMA (Jerry L. Pettis award 1987), AAAS, American Med. Writers Assn. (Will Solimene award 1991), American Psychiat. Assn. Democrat. Avocation: writing fiction. Office: Keith Ablow MD 36 Water St Newburyport MA 01950 *

ABO, TORU, immunologist, researcher; b. Aomori, Japan, Oct. 9, 1947; MD, Tohoku U., 1972, PhD, 1977. Rsch. scientist, dept. immunology Niigata U. Sch. Medicine, 1991—. Mem.: Am. Assn. Immunologist. Office: 1-757 Asahimachi Dori Chuo-ku Niigata 951-8510 Japan Office Fax: 81-25-227-0766. Business E-Mail: immunol2@med.niigata-u.ac.jp.

ABO EL-ENEN, MOHAMED, urologist, educator; b. El Mahalah Elkobra, Gharbia, Egypt, July 1, 1964; s. Abo El-enen and Amal Sheta; m. Mahi Abd Elsatar, Nov. 10, 1993; children: Haneen, Ahmed, Habiba. M in Urology, Tanta U., Egypt, 1993, MD in Urology, 2004. Med. doctorate urology Faculty Medicine-Tanta U., 2004. House officer Tanta U. Hosp., 1989—90, resident urology, 1990—93; asst. lectr. urology Faculty Medicine-Tanta U., 1994—2004, lectr. & cons. urology, 2004—; cons. urology Pvt. Med. Ins. Hosp. Group, Royal Makkah, Saudi Arabia, 2005—; assoc. prof. urology, faculty medicine Tanta U., 2011—. Master: Regency. Avocations: football, reading, politics. Home: Elzokpi Elgomhorea St Elmahalah Elkobra Gharbia 012345678 Egypt Office: Tanta University Hosp Elbahr St-Faculty medicine Tanta Gharbia Egypt Personal E-mail: m.aboelenen@yahoo.com.

ABOLFOTOUH, MOSTAFA ABDELFATTAH, public and family health educator, researcher; b. Alexandria, Egypt, Dec. 18, 1953; s. Abdelfattah Abolfotouh Ali and Neama Ibrahim Khamis; m. Siham Hussein Shukry, Mar. 22, 1985; children: Sameh, Sherif. MBChB, Faculty of Medicine, Alexandria, 1978; MPH, High Inst. of Pub. Health, Alexandria, 1983; DCH, Glasgow U., 1986; DrPH, High Inst. of Pub. Health, Alexandria, 1987. Rural health physician MOH, Behaira Governorate, Egypt, 1979-80; demonstrator of family health High Inst. of Pub. Health, Alexandria U., 1980-83, lectr. of family health, 1983-85, asst. prof., 1986-90, Abha Coll. of Medicine, 1990-95, assoc. prof., 1995-99; prof. family health Alexandria U., 1998—; prof. family and cmty. medicine Abha Coll. Medicine King Saud U., 1999-2000. Rsch. counsellor Am. Sch. Health Assn., 1992—; cons. Modern Medicine, France, 1992—. Author: (book) Principles of Public Health and Social Medicine (Arabic), 1990; editl. bd.: Alexandria Jour. of Paediatrics, 1988-89; contbr. more than 90 articles to profl. jours. Fellow Am. Sch. Health Assn.; mem. N.Y. Acad. of Sci., AAAS, Internat. Edn. Assn., Am. Sch. Health Assn. (life). Avocations: travel, listening to music. Office: Alexandria U High Inst Pub Health 165 Al-Horreya Ave Alexandria Egypt E-mail: mabolfotouh@yahoo.com.

ABOU-CHEBL, ALEX, medical educator; b. Aug. 21, 1969; BS, U. Mich., 1991; MD, Case Western Res. U., 1995. Faculty Cleve. Clinic, 2002—07; assoc. prof. U. Louisville, 2007—. Office: University Louisville Dept Neurology Louisville KY 40202 Business E-Mail: a0abou03@louisville.edu.

ABOUDIAB, TAAN, pediatrician; arrived in France, 1982, naturalized, 1991; s. Farid and Bahija Aboudiab; m. Christine Flandrin, July 12, 1997; children: Rémi, Maxime, Alexandre. MD, U. Libre Bruxelles, Brussels, 1982. Pediatrician U. Jules Verne, Amiens, Picardie, France, 1982—86; resident St. Quentin Regional Hosp., 1982—86, asst. dept. neonatology and blood transfusion lab., 1986—93, part-time practitioner dept. neonatology, 1993. Contbr. articles to profl. jours. Mem.: French Assn. Ambulatory Pediatricians, French Pediatricians Assn. Achievements include invention of dietetic milk and soy substitute. Office: Hosp Ctr Saint Quentin 1 Ave Michel de L'Hôpital Saint Quentin 02321 France E-mail: t.aboudiab@ch-stquentin.fr.

ABOU-EISHA, AHMED MOHAMED, biology professor; b. Cairo, July 17, 1963; BSc, Cairo U., 1985, PhD in Biochemistry, 2000. Assoc. prof., cell biology dept. Nat. Rsch. Ctr., Egypt, 2008—. Avocation: sports. Office: El Buhouth St Dokki Cairo Giza 12311 Egypt Office Fax: (202)33370391.

ABOU-KHALIL, BASSEL WILLIAM, neurologist, epileptologist; s. William and Wafa Abou-Khalil; m. Rima Khallouf, Aug. 6, 1988; children: May Wafa, Lena Noor. BS, Am. U. Beirut, Lebanon, 1974, MD, 1978. Cert. Am. bd. Clin. Neurophysiol. Inc., 1986, in neurology Am. Bd. Psychiatry and Neurology, 1986, in clin. neurophysiol. Am. Bd. Psychiatry and Neurology, 1992. Epilepsy monitoring unit dir. Vanderbilt U., Nashville, 1988—, epilepsy program dir., 1988—, asst. prof. neurology, 1988—95, assoc. prof. neurology, 1995—2001, prof. neurology, 2001—, clin. neurophysiol. and epilepsy tng. program dir., 1990—. Fellow: Am. Clin. Neurophysiol. Soc., Am. Acad. Neurology; mem.: So. Clin. Neurol. Soc., So. Epilepsy and EEG Soc. (pres. 2000—01), Am. Clin. Neurophysiol. Soc., Am. Epilepsy Soc., Am. Neurol. Assn.

ABOULAFIA, ELIE DAVID, vascular surgeon; b. Jerusalem, June 16, 1928; arrived in US, 1953, naturalized, 1958; s. David and Mathilda (Yeshaya) Aboulafia. BSc in Medicine, U. Geneva, 1949, MD, 1953; MSc in Surgery, Tufts U., 1960. Diplomate Am. Bd. Surgery, Am. Bd. Gen. Vascular Surgery. Intern Michael Reese Hosp., Chgo., 1953-54; resident in surgery NYU-Bellevue Med. Ctr., NYC, 1954-56; surg. rsch. fellow Tufts-New Eng. Med. Ctr., Boston, 1958-59, chief surg. resident, 1959-61; dir. surg. rsch. Sinai Hosp.,

Detroit, 1961-63; head sect. vascular surgery Botsford Gen. Hosp., Farmington Hills, Mich., 1963-95; dir. surg. edn. Highland Park (Mich.) Gen. Hosp., Detroit, 1969-73; dir. vascular med. svcs. DMC/Sinai-Grace Hosp., Detroit, 1995—2006. Clin. prof. surgery Mich. State U., East Lansing, 1977—; clin. prof. medicine Wayne State U., Detroit, 1998—. Mem. editl. bd. Internat. Jour. Surgery, 1972—95, Itnernat. Jour. Angiology, 1992—; contbr. articles to profl. jours. Trustee Jewish Mus. Greece, Athens, 1991—. Lt. comdr. USNR, 1956—58. Fellow: Mich. Vascular Surg. Soc., Midwest Vasular Surg. Soc., Soc. Vascular Surgery, Internat. Coll. Surgeons (pres. 1991, Disting. Svc. award 1992, emeritus fellow 1995), Internat. Soc. Vascular Surgery, Soc. Clin. Vascular Surgery; mem.: Maimonides Med. Soc. (pres. 1966—68), Southeastern Mich. Surg. Soc. (pres. 1984—85), Mich. State Med. Soc. (Spl. Recognition Leadership award 1991, 2005), Internat. Coll. Angiology (vice chair sci. coun. 1994—, sec. 2002, pres. 2003), US/Internat. Coll. Surgeons (pres. 1991), Sigma Xi. Home Phone: 248-851-2997. Personal E-mail: vascelie@gmail.com.

ABOUL NASR, GAMAL MOHAMED, cardiologist, educator; b. Cairo, Mar. 3, 1955; s. Mohamed Ibrahim Aboul Nasr and Houria Ramadan Hasan; m. Raghda Moustafa Kharsa, Mar. 13, 1989; children: Hana Gamal, Hala Gamal. MBChB, Cairo U., 1979, M in Cardiovasc. Medicine, 1984, D in Cardiovasc. Medicine, 1991. Resident in cardiology Cairo U. Hosp., 1981—84; sr. registerar Nat. Heart Inst., Cairo, 1985—91, assoc. cons., 1998—2003, cons., prof. cardiology, 2003—, vice dean, tchr., trainer cardiovasc. medicine, 2004. Dir. med. emergency unit Nat. Heart Inst., Cairo, 1992—97, dir. rsch. and tng. com., 2000—, assoc. dir. Egyptian cardiology fellwoship program, 2001—. Assoc. editor: Egyptian Heart Jour., 1997—. Mem. Rodat Abou-Ghalib, Giza, Egypt, 2001. Grantee, Nat. Heart Inst., 1992—98. Mem.: Nahdet Misr Med. Assn., Am. Coun. High Blood Pressure Rsch., Arab Soc. Interventional Cardiology, European Soc. Cardiology, Am. Coll. Cardiology, Egyptian Soc. Cardiology. Muslim. Achievements include first to Establishment of a comprehensive training program for youger colleagues in coronary angiography & intervention at the National heart Institute as well as at Benha University (45 km from Cairo city). Avocations: music, reading, cars, computers. Home: 7 Aboul Mahassen El-Shazly square Egypt Cairo 000 Egypt Office: National Heart Inst 9 Midan Ebn-Elnafees Giza Egypt Home Fax: 002/0122165548. Personal E-mail: gnasr@soficom.com.eg.

ABRAHAM, EDWARD, dean, medical educator; b. Chgo., Apr. 17, 1952; s. Willard and Dale Abraham; m. Norma-May Isakow, Nov. 22, 1989; children: Claire, Erin. BA, Stanford U., 1974, MD, 1978. Diplomate Am. Bd. Internal Medicine, Critical Care. Asst. prof. UCLA Sch. Medicine, LA, 1981—87, assoc. prof., 1987—93, U. Colo. Health Sciences Ctr., Denver, 1993—95, prof. medicine, 1995—2000, Roger Sherman Mitchell prof. pulmonary and critical care medicine, 2000—06, head divsn. pulmonary scis. and critical care medicine, 2000—06, vice chair dept. medicine, 2002—06; prof., chair dept. medicine U. Ala., Birmingham, 2006—11, Spencer chair in med. sci. leadership, 2006—11; dean Wake Forest U. Sch. Medicine, Winston-Salem, NC, 2011—. Editor: Textbook of Critical Care Medicine; editor: Am. Jour. Respiratory Critical Care Medicine, 2004-09; sect. editor assoc. editor Jour. Immunology, 2007-; contbr. articles to profl. jours.; chpts. to books. Area program com. Am. Friends Svc. Com., Denver, 2004—06. Recipient Pres.'s citation, Soc. Critical Care Medicine, 1999, 2002, 2004, Young Investigator award, Soc. of Critical Care Medicine, 1985, Winthrop Breon Young Scholar award, 1986; named Best Doctors in America, 2001—. Fellow Am. Coll. Critical Care Medicine; mem. Soc. Critical Care Medicine (Young Investigator award 1985), Am. Thoracic Soc., Shock Soc., Am. Soc. Clin. Investigation, Assn. Am. Physicians. Avocations: jogging, gardening. Office: Wake Forest Bapt Med Ctr Medical Center Blvd Winston Salem NC 27157 *

ABRAHAM, JOHN A., orthopaedic surgeon; Attended, Yale U., New Haven, Conn., 2000. Diplomate Am. Bd. Orthopaedic Surgery. Intern Mass. Gen. Hosp., Boston, resident, fellow; hosp. affiliations include Methodist Hosp., Thomas Jefferson Univ. Hosp. Named one of the Top Doctors, Phila. Mag., 2011. Office: Thomas Jefferson University Hospital 925 Chesnut St 5th Fl Philadelphia PA 19107 Office Phone: 800-321-9999. Office Fax: 215-503-0580.

ABRAHAMSEN, PÅL, psychiatrist, consultant; b. Oslo, Oct. 30, 1943; s. Odd H. and Jenny B. (Ruud) A.; (div. 1990); children: Øystein, Geir, Bjarne, Line. MD, U. Bergen, Norway, 1968, degree in sociology, 1969. Resident, rsch. fellow U. Bergen, 1969-70, 1971-72, 1973-76; advanced resident Beth Israel Hosp., Boston, 1972-73; med. officer Gaustad Hosp., Ullevål Hosp., Oslo, 1976-83; med. supt. Oslo Hosp., 1983-90; med. cons. Ostensjo Family Guidance Clin., Oslo, 1990—2002; pvt. practice Oslo, 1990—; med. supt. DPS, Hadeland, Gran, Norway, 1997-2001; intern Hosp. & Dist., 1969-70. Assoc. prof. U. Oslo Inst. Behavioral Scis. in Medicine, 1976-80; police psychiatrist, Oslo, 1979-93; forensic psychiatrist, cons., 1979—; med. cons. Child Guidance Clinic, Karasjok, 2002-08, Finnmarksklinikken, 2004- Author: People in Dispair, 1982, Always New Possibilities, 2001, The World of Psychosis, 2004, others; contbr. articles to profl. pubs. Capt. Norwegian Army, 1974-75. Fellow Harvard U., 1972-73; Fulbright grantee Fulbright Assn. Norway, 1972. Mem. Norwegian Med. Assn., Norwegian Psychiatric Assn., Norwegian Assn. Family Therapy (gen. sec. 1983—, editor Metaforum), Norwegian Assn. Non-fiction Authors. Home and Office: Seilduksinst AS Markveien 23 N-0554 Oslo Norway Home Phone: 47 22 35 22 20; Office Phone: 47 22 71 75 05, 47 95 22 26 04. Personal E-mail: seilduk@online.no. Business E-Mail: paabraha@online.no.

ABRAHAMSON, DALE RAYMOND, cell biology educator, researcher; b. Washington, June 18, 1949; s. Sherman R. and Katherine (Seglem) A.; m. Susan K. Spell, Aug. 14, 1971; 1 child, Katherine L. BA, U. Va., 1971, George Mason U., 1976; PhD, U. Va., 1981. Postdoctoral fellow Harvard Med. Sch., Boston, 1980-83; asst. prof. U. Ala., Birmingham, 1983-87, assoc. prof., 1987-92, prof., 1992—. Contbr. articles to profl. Rsch. grantee NIH, 1985—. Mem. Am. Assn. Anatomists, Am. soc. for Cell Biology, Am. Soc. Nephrology, Am. Heart Assn. (rsch. grantee 1986—). Avocations: gardening, tennis. Office: U Ala Uab # 302 Birmingham AL 35294-0001

ABRAHM, JANET LEE, hematologist, oncologist, educator, palliative care specialist; b. San Francisco, Mar. 14, 1949; d. Paul Milton and Helen Lesser Abrahm; m. David Rytman Slavitt, Apr. 16, 1978. Student, U. Calif., Berkeley, 1969; BA, U. Calif., San Francisco, 1970, MD, 1973. Diplomate in internal medicine, hematology and oncology and Hospice and Palliative Medicine Am. Bd. Internal Medicine; diplomate Am. Bd. Hospice and Palliative Medicine. Intern and resident medicine Mass. Gen. Hosp., Boston, 1973-75, hematology fellow, 1975-76; chief resident medicine Moffitt Hosp. U. Calif., San Francisco, 1976-77; hematology/oncology fellow Hosp. U. Pa., Phila., 1977-80; postdoctoral fellow medicine U. Pa., Phila., 1977-78, postdoctoral trainee medicine, 1977-80, asst. prof. medicine, 1980-86, Hosp. U. Pa. and VA Med. Ctr., Phila., 1986-89, assoc. prof. medicine, 1989-2000; attending physician Hosp. U. Pa., Phila., 1980-93; from staff physician to assoc. chief of staff, primary care and consultation medicine Phila. VA Med. Ctr., 1982—97, faculty scholar Project Death in Am., 1997—2000, Harvard Bus. Sch., BWH Leadership Course, 2008—09; med. dir. Wissahickon Hospice UPHS, 1998-2000; assoc. prof. medicine Harvard Med. Sch., 2001—; attending physician Dana-Farber Cancer Inst., Brigham and Women's Hosp., Boston, 2001—; dir., palliative fellowship Dana-Farber Cancer Inst., Boston, 2001—07, divsn. chief, adult palliative care, 2008—. Prin. investigator Palliative Care Fellowship Grant, 1996-2001, 03-; mem. concensus panel on End-of-Life Care, ACP, 1997-2000; chmn. adv. com. Cancer Care VA Dist. 4, 1987-90; sec. subsplty. bd. hematology Am. Bd. Internal Medicine, 1987-92, sec. SEP subcom. hematology, 1993-95; mem. test writing com. hospice and palliative medicine exam., Am. Bd. Internal Medicine, 2007-. Author: Pain Management and Antiemetic Therapy in Hematologic Disorders in Hematology: Basic Principles and Practice, 1994, 2005, 2009, A Physician's Guide to Pain and Symptom Management in Cancer Patients, 2000, 2d edit., 2005, Japanese edit., 2009, Caring For Patients at the End of Life Clinical Oncology, 2004, 2008—10, Specialized Care of the Terminally Ill, In Cancer, Principles & Practices of Oncology, 2005, 2008, Sect. edit.; reviewer New Eng. Jour. Medicine, JAMA, Annals Internal Medicine; mem. editl. bd.: Jour. Palliative Medicine, 2004—08, Cancer, 2007—; contbr. numerous articles to profl. jours. Fellow: ACP, Am. Acad. Hospice and Palliative Medicine (bd. dirs. 2002—07, sec. 2007—09); mem.: Am. Pain Soc., Am. Soc. Clin. Oncology, Am. Soc. Clin. Hypnosis, Am. Soc. Hematology, Alpha Omega Alpha, Phi Beta Kappa. Home: 35 West St #5 Cambridge MA 02139 Office: Dana Farber Cancer Inst 44 Binney St Boston MA 02115 Office Phone: 617-632-6464. Business E-Mail: jabrahm@partners.org.

ABRAM, ZOLTAN SAMOIL, medicine educator; b. Seini, Maramures, Romania, Dec. 9, 1963; s. Samoil Abram and Lydia (Idem) Sarkozi; m. Noemi Bako, Apr. 1, 1989; children: Peter, Endre, Noemi, Erzsebet, Julia. Degree in Medicine, U. Medicine and Pharmacy, Targu Mures, Romania, 1989; degree in Journalism, Balint Gyorgy Journalist Sch., Budapest, Hungary, 1991. Physician City Hosp., Targu Mures, 1990-91; asst. lectr. U. Medicine and Pharmacy, 1991-96, lectr., 1997—, reader, 2001—06, prof., 2006—. Author: Hungarians Around the World, 1995, The Muddy Nyarad, 1996, In Memorial of Communitas, 1996, Environmental Protection, 1997, Szentegyhaza, 1998, Dietetics, 1999, Lifestyle-Health, 2000, Nutrition and Alimentation, 2001, The Pollution of Mures River, 2002, Community Health, 2006, Public Health Guide, 2010; contbr. articles to profl. jours. and newspapers. Bd. dirs. Hungarian Youth Assn., 1990-92, 2006—; dir. bd. dirs. Peter Charity Ctr.; co-pres. Hungarian Folk H.S. Soc., 1992—; co-pres. Rhododendron Ecol. Assn., 1993—; pres. Diakonia Christian Found., 2005—. Recipient Pro Hygiene award Fodor József Nat. Inst., 1999. Mem. Romanian Hygiene and Pub. Health Soc. (sec. 1992—), Transilvanian Med. Soc. (sec. 1992—), N.Y. Acad. Scis., Preventio Health Promotion Assn. (pres. 1998). Mem. UDMR. Avocations: photography, literature. Home: Borsos Tamás 25 540065 Targu Mures Romania Office: U Medicine & Pharmacy Gh Marinescu 38 540138 Targu Mures Romania Office Phone: 00-40-265-215551. E-mail: abramzoltan@yahoo.com.

ABRAMOWICZ, JACQUES SYLVAIN, obstetrician, perinatologist; b. Paris, Dec. 5, 1948; s. Theodore Dov and Sara Ethel (Cukiernik) A.; m. Annie Sternelicht, Aug. 1, 1972; children: Shelly, Ory. MD, Sackler Sch. Medicine, Tel-Aviv, 1975. Diplomate Israel Bd. Ob-Gyn., Am. Bd. Ob-Gyn. Rotating intern Tel-Aviv Mcpl. Med. Ctr., 1973—74; resident dept. ob-gyn. Sapir Med. Ctr., Kfar-Saba, Israel, 1978—85; rsch. registrar ultrasound dept. ob-gyn. King's Coll. Hosp., London, 1981; resident dept. gen. surgery Sapir Med. Ctr., 1982—83, resident dept. urology, 1983; cons. Timsit Inst. Reproductive Medicine, Tel-Aviv, 1986—87; dir. clin. rsch. Div. Maternal-Fetal Medicine, Ea. Va. Med. Sch., Norfolk, 1987—89; assoc. researcher Jones Inst. Reproductive Medicine, Norfolk, 1989; dir. perinatal ultrasound, asst. prof. dept. ob-gyn. U. Rochester Med. Ctr., 1990—93, assoc. prof., 1993—99, prof., 1999—2000, assoc. prof. radiology, 1995—99, prof. radiology, 1999—2000; prof. dept. ob-gyn. and dept. radiology U. Chgo., 2000—04; prof. dept. ob-gyn. Rush Univ., Chgo., 2004—. Co-dir. Rush Fetal and Neonatal Medicine Ctr. Co-editor: Handbook of Ultrasound in Obstetrics and Gynecology, 1997, Imaging in Infertility and Reproductive Endocrinology, 1994; contbr. articles to profl. jours. including Am. Jour. Ob-Gyn., Obstet. Gynecology, Jour. Ultrasound Medicine, Prenatal Diagnosis, Am. Jour. Perinatology, Fetal Therapy, Jour. Perinatal Medicine, Jour. Clin. Ultrasound, Ultrasound Med. Biology, also chpts. to books; referee various jours. Maj. Israel Def. Forces, 1974—78. Fellow: AGOS, ACOG (Ill. section vice-chair 2008—11, chair 2011), Am. Inst. Ultrasound in Medicine (sr.; internat. rels. com. 1988—91, stds. com. 1991—93, mfrs. commendation panel 1991—93, chair mfrs. commendation panel 1993—94, chair epidemiology subcom. 1999—2008, chair bioeffects com. 2005—08); mem.: Internat. Soc. Ultrasound in Ob-Gyn. (chair bioeffects and safety com. 2001—09). Jewish. Achievements include research in prenatal diagnosis and therapy; ultrasound; Doppler velocimetry; ultrasound contrast media; placental perfusion; bioeffects of ultrasound; ovarian cancer. Office: Rush Univ 1653 W Congress Pkwy Chicago IL 60612-3833 Office Phone: 312-942-9428. Business E-Mail: jacques_abramowicz@rush.edu.

ABRAMS, ARTHUR JAY, retired physician; b. Camden, NJ, Apr. 9, 1938; s. Morris and Sophia Sarah (Kates) A.; m. Marianne Ritto Abrams, June 8, 1963; children: Suzanne Beth, Cheryl Lyn, Robert Dwight. BA, Rutgers U., Camden, NJ, 1959; MD, Hahnemann U., 1963. Diplomate Am. Bd. Dermatology. Intern Madigan Army Med. Ctr., Tacoma, 1963-64; resident, chief resident Letterman Army Med. Ctr., San Francisco, 1964-67; dermatologist, Far East cons. 249th Gen. Hosp. U.S. Army, Tokyo, 1967-69; asst. chief dermatologist Tripler Army Med. Ctr., Honolulu, 1969-70; staff dermatologist El Camino Hosp., Mountain View, Calif., 1970—2005; clin. prof. dermatology Stanford U. Med. Ctr., 1979—; dermatology cons. San Jose State U., Calif., 1994—; maj. U.S. Army, 1963-70. Mem. AMA, Calif. Med. Assn., Pacific Dermatol. Assn., San Francisco Dermatol. Soc. Avocations: volleyball, walking.

ABRAMS, DAVID B., nonprofit organization director, former federal agency administrator; BSc in Computer Sci. and Psychology, U. Witwatersrand, Johannesburg, South Africa; MS in Clin. Psychology, Rutgers U., NJ, PhD. Prof. psychiatry/human behavior Brown U. Med. Sch., Providence, 1978—2005, also prof. cmty. health; founding dir. Ctr.'s for Behavioral & Preventive Medicine Miriam Hosp., Providence; co-dir. Transdisciplinary Rsch. Butler Hosp., Providence; dir. Office Behavioral & Social Scis. Rsch., NIH, Bethesda, Md., 2005—08; exec. dir. Steven A. Schroeder Nat. Inst. Tobacco Rsch. & Policy Studies, Am. Legacy Found., Washington, 2008—. Co-dir. Robert Wood Johnson Found. Transdisciplinary Tobacco Etiology Rsch. Network, 1999—2004; mem. sci. adv. bd. Nat. Cancer Inst., 1999—2005. Author: The Tobacco Dependence Treatment Handbook: A Guide to Best Practices, 2003 (Am. Jour. Nursing Book of Yr., 2004); contbr. articles to profl. jours., chapters to books. Fellow: Am. Psychol. Assn., Soc. Behavioral Medicine (pres. 2002, Disting. Scientist award). Office: Am Legacy Found 1724 Massachusetts Ave NW Washington DC 20036 Office Phone: 202-454-5936, 202-454-5555. Office Fax: 301-402-1150. Business E-Mail: dabrams@americanlegacy.org.

ABRAMS, DONALD IRA, medical educator; b. NYC, June 1, 1950; AB, Brown U., 1972; MD, Stanford U. Sch. Medicine, 1977. Prof. clin. medicine U. Calif., San Francisco, 1983—. Chief, hematology-oncology San Francisco Gen. Hosp., 2003. Office: Ward 84 995 Potrero Ave San Francisco CA 94110 Office Fax: 415-502-2991. Business E-Mail: dabrams@hemeonc.ucsf.edu.

ABRAMS, FREDRICK RALPH, physician, clinical ethicist; b. NYC, June 18, 1928; s. David and Jane R. (Rein) A.; m. Alice Marilyn Engelhard, Nov. 25, 1949; children: Reid, Glenn, Hal. BA, Cornell U., 1950, MD, 1954. Diplomate Am. Bd. Ob-Gyn. Intern Letterman Army Hosp., San Francisco, 1954-55; pvt. practice gynecology Denver, 1962-96; ret.; resident Fitzsimons Army Hosp., Denver, 1956-59; prof. U. Colo. Grad. Sch. Pub. Affairs, Denver, 1987—; dir. biomed. ethics Ctr. for Health Ethics and Policy, U. Colo., 1987-92; commr. Govs. Commn. on Life and the Law, State of Colo., 1991—. Vis. prof. Iliff Sch. Theology; founder Ctr. for Applied Biomed. Ethics Rose Med. Ctr., Denver, 1982-87; assoc. med. dir. Colo. Found. for Med. Care, 1992—; Lectr. for pub. edn. in med. ethics; mem. Nat. Adv. Bd. on Ethics in Reproduction, 1995—; sr. rsch. assoc. Denver U. Ctr. Health Policy and Contemporary Affairs, with U. Colo. Med. Ctr. Bioethics & Humanities. Contbr. chpts. to book and articles to profl. jours.; author Doctors On Theedge:Will Your Doctor Break The Rules For You, 2006 Maj. U.S. Army, 1955-62, bd. mem. Acad. Lifelong Learning, WFE Quality Inst.-HospiceMetro Denver, adv. bd. Safe Quality Insulate Palliative Care Grantee Robert Wood Johnson, 1988-89, Colo. Trust, 1987-90, Rose Found., 1982-87, Issac Hays, MD and John Bell, MD award for Leadership in Med. Ethics and Professionalism, AMA, 2006. Mem. Internat. Soc. for Advancement of Humanistic Studies in Gynecology (past pres.), Denver Med. Soc. (past v.p.), Colo. Med. Soc., Am. Coll. Ob-Gyn. (past chmn. ethics com.). Avocations: sculpture, jewelry, fly fishing, poetry, gardening. Office Phone: 303-781-7730. Personal E-mail: frabrams@aol.com.

ABRAMS, GERALD DAVID, pathologist, educator; b. Detroit, Apr. 27, 1932; s. Arthur and Esther (Kushner) A.; m. Gloria Sandra Turner, June 6, 1954; children— Kathryn, Nancy AB, Wayne U., 1951; MD, U. Mich., 1955. Diplomate Am. Bd. Pathology. House officer pathology U. Mich., Ann Arbor, 1955-59, instr. pathology, 1959-60, asst. prof. pathology, 1963-66, assoc. prof. Ann Arbor, Mich., 1966-69, prof., 1969—2002, prof. emeritus, 2002—, dir. anatomic pathology, 1985-89; asst. chief dept. exptl. pathology Walter Reed Army Inst. Rsch., 1961-62. Cons. physician Ann Arbor VA Hosp., 1970—2002. Served to capt. M.C., US Army, 1961-62 Markle scholar John and Mary Markle Found., 1963-68; recipient Elizabeth Crosby Teaching award U. Mich., 1969, 87, 96, Kaiser-Permanente Teaching award U. Mich., 1978, Lifetime Achievement award in Med. Edn., 2002, Disting. Svc. award U. Mich. Med. Ctr. Alumni Soc., 2005. Mem. AAAS, US-Can. Acad. Pathology, Mich. Soc. Pathologists Office: U Mich Dept Pathology Ann Arbor MI 48109 Office Phone: 734-936-6770. Business E-Mail: gabrams@umich.edu.

ABRAMS, HERBERT LEROY, radiologist, educator; b. NYC, Aug. 16, 1920; s. Morris and Freda (Sugarman) Abrams; m. Marilyn Spitz, Mar. 23, 1943; children: Nancy, John. BA, Cornell U., 1941; MD, Downstate Med. Ctr., NYC, 1946. Diplomate Am. Bd. Radiology. Intern L.I. Coll. Hosp., 1946—47; resident in internal medicine Montefiore Hosp., Bronx, NY, 1947—48; resident in radiology Stanford (Calif.) U. Hosp., 1948—51; practice medicine specializing in radiology Stanford U., Calif., 1951—67, mem. faculty Sch. Medicine, 1951—67, dir. divsn. diagnostic roentgenology Sch. Medicine, 1961—67, prof. radiology Sch. Medicine, 1962—67; Philip H. Cook prof. radiology Harvard U., 1967—85, now prof. emeritus, chmn. dept. radiology, 1967—80; prof. radiology Stanford U. Sch. Medicine, 1985—90, prof. emeritus, 1990—; clin. prof. U. Calif. Sch. Medicine, San Francisco, 1986—. Radiologist-in-chief Peter Bent Brigham Hosp., Boston, 1967—80; chmn. dept. radiology Brigham and Women's Hosp., Boston, 1981—85; radiologist-in-chief Sidney Farber Cancer Inst., Boston, 1974—85; R.H. Nimmo vis. prof. U. Adelaide, Australia; mem.-in-residence Ctr. for Internat. Security and Cooperation, Stanford U., 1985—; mem. radiation study sect. NIH, 1962—66; cons. to hosps., profl. socs. Author (with others): Angiocardiography in Congenital Heart Disease, 1956, Congenital Heart Disease, 1965, Coronary Arteriography: A Practical Approach, 1983, Brigham Guide to Diagnostic Imaging, 1986, Assessment of Diagnostic Technology in Health Care; editor: Abrams' Angiography, 3d edit., 1983; author: The President Has Been Shot: Confusion, Disability and the 25th Amendment, 1992, 1994, The History of Cardiac Radiology, 1996; mem. editl. bd.: Investigative Radiology, editor-in-chief, founder: Cardiovasc. and Interventional Radiology, 1978—88, Postgrad. Radiology, 1983—99. Named David M. Gould Meml. lectr., Johns Hopkins, 1964, William R. Whitman Meml. lectr., 1968, Leo G. Rigler lectr., Tel Aviv U., 1969, Holmes lectr., New Eng. Roentgen Ray Soc., Boston, 1970, Ross Golden lectr., N.Y. Roentgen Ray Soc., N.Y.C., 1971, Stauffer Meml. lectr., Phila. Roentgen Ray Soc., 1971, J.M.T. Finney Fund lectr., Md. Radiol. Soc., Ocean City, 1972, Aubrey Hampton lectr., Mass. Gen. Hosp., Boston, 1974, Kirklin-Weber lectr., Mayo Clinic, 1974, Crookshank lectr., Royal Coll. Radiology, 1980, Alpha Omega Alpha lectr., vis. prof., U. Calif. Med.

Sch., San Francisco, 1961—65, W.H. Herbert lectr., U. Calif., Caldwell lectr., Am. Roentgen Ray Soc., 1982, Percy lectr., McMaster Med. Sch., 1983, Charles Dotter lectr., Soc. Cardiovasc. and Interventional Radiology, 1988, Philip Hodes lectr., Jefferson Med. Coll., 1988, David Gould Meml. lectr., Johns Hopkins U., 1991, Hymer Friedell lectr., Western Res. Sch. Medicine, 1993, Felix Fheischner Meml. lectr., Harvard Med. Sch., 1997, Charles Dotter Meml. lectr., Am. Heart Assn., 1998; fellow, Nat. Cancer Inst., 1950, Spl. Rsch. fellow, Nat. Heart Inst., 1960, 1973—74, Henry J. Kaiser sr. fellow, Ctr. for Advanced Study in Behavioral Sci., 1980—81. Fellow: Am. Coll. Cardiology, Am. Coll. Radiology, Royal Coll. Radiology (Gt. Britain) (hon.), Royal Coll. Surgery (Ireland) (hon.); mem.: NIH (working group on disability of U.S. pres. 1995—98, internat. blue ribbon panel radiation effects rsch. found. Hiroshima 1996, chmn. consensus panel on MRI), NAS (com. biol. effects of low-level ionizing radiation BEIR VII 1999—2005), Nat. Coun. Health Tech. Assessment, Soc. Chmn. Acad. Radiology Depts. (pres. 1970—71), Soc. Cardiovasc. Radiology (Gold medal 2000), Internat. Physicians for Prevention of Nuc. War (founding v.p., participant Nobel Peace prize 1985), N.Am. Soc. Cardiac Radiology (pres. 1979—80), Radiol. Soc. N.Am. (Gold medal 1995), Am. Soc. Nephrology, Am. Heart Assn., Inst. Medicine, Assn. Univ. Radiologists (Gold medal 1984), Alpha Omega Alpha, Phi Beta Kappa. Achievements include naming of Abrams conference room in radiology and Women's Hospital; development of Herbert L. Abrams annual lectures of Harvard Medical School. Office: Stanford U Sch Medicine 300 Pasteur Dr Stanford CA 94305-5105 Home: 620 Sand Hill Rd Apt 109G Palo Alto CA 94304 Business E-Mail: hlabrams@stanford.edu.

ABRAMSON, HANLEY NORMAN, pharmacy educator; b. Detroit, June 10, 1940; s. Frederick Jacob and Lillian (Kampner) A.; m. Young Hee Kim, Aug. 4, 1967; children: Nathaniel, Deborah, Stephen. BS in Pharmacy, Wayne State U., 1962; MS in Pharm. Chemistry, U. Mich., 1963, PhD in Pharm. Chemistry, 1966. Registered pharmacist. Rsch. assoc. The Hebrew U., Jerusalem, 1966-67; asst. prof. Wayne State U., Detroit, 1967-73, assoc. prof., 1973-78, prof., 1978—, chmn. dept. pharm. sci., 1986-95, interim dean Eugene Applebaum Coll. of Pharmacy and Health Scis., 1987—88, assoc. provost, 1991-95, assoc. dean, 1996-99, dep. dean pharmacy, 2000—02. Author numerous published articles in field of medicinal chemistry. Bd. trustees 1st Bapt. Ch. of Oak Park, Mich., 1974-78; deacon Bloomfield Hills (Mich.) Bapt. Ch., 1986-89; dir. Met. Detroit Alliance for Minority Participation, 1994-2000. Recipient rsch. grants Mich. Heart Assn., Detroit, 1967-76, Nat. Cancer Inst., Bethesda, Md., 1982-91. Mem. AAAS, Am. Chem. Soc., Am. Pharm. Assn., Am. Assn. Colls. Pharmacy. Baptist. Avocations: astronomy, coin collecting/numismatics, baseball, music. Home: 5530 Hammersmith Dr West Bloomfield MI 48322-1452 Office: Wayne State U 3607 Applebaum Bldg Detroit MI 48201 Home Phone: 248-661-0419; Office Phone: 313-577-1711. Business E-Mail: ac2531@wayne.edu.

ABRASHKIN ROTARU, LAILA, medical technician; b. Santiago, Chile, Feb. 5, 1952; arrived in Israel, 1970, naturalized, 2005; married; 4 children. AA, U. Chile, Santiago, 1970; BSc in Med. Lab. Scis., Hadassah Coll., Jerusalem, 1973; diploma in Molecular Pharmacology, Hadassah Med. Sch., Jerusalem, 1980; diploma in Stats., Hebrew U., Jerusalem, 1981; diploma in Electron Microscopy, Hebrew U., 1986, diploma in Advances Studies in Biology, 1994; diploma, Tchg. Ctr. Clalit Medical Svcs., Tel-Aviv, 2001; diploma in Mediation, Gevim Mediation Ctr., Jerusalem, 2006; AA in Mgmt. and Mktg., E-learning Liverpool U., 2001. Cert. med. technologist Pediat. Rsch. Lab., Hadassah Hosp. Ein Kerem, Jerusalem, 1973. Sec. Latin Am. Sect., Keren Hayesod Found. Fund, 1995; adminstrv. sec. Overseas Mktg. Divsn., Satec Hi-Tech Plant, 1995—96; adminstrv. sec., dept. physiology Sch. Medicine, Hebrew U., 1997—98; sec. head delivery unit, maternal & fatal unit Hadassah Hosp., 1998—99; adminstrv. office mgr. Novamed, 1999; clin. adminstr., health svcs., 1999—2005, med. technologist Ctrl. Lab. HMO, Jerusalem, 2005—. Mem. Movement Quality Govt. Israel. Mem.: Israeli Found. Osteoporosis & Bone Diseases. Jewish. Avocations: stamp collecting/philately, astrology, ancient civilitations. Home: HA-Mehanehet St 7/2 Jerusalem Gilo 93844 Israel Home Phone: 0972545577010. Personal E-mail: s05a02@gmail.com, s05a02@hotmail.com.

ABREU, DANIELA CRISTINA CARVALHO DE, medical educator; b. Campinas, São Paulo, Brazil, Sept. 3, 1977; d. Marinho Leite de and Lúcia Shizue Leite de Carvalho; m. Fernando Mangili Abreu, Jan. 26, 2007. MSc, U. São Paulo, São Carlos, 2001; ScD, State U. Campinas, São Paulo, 2005; PhD, U. Campinas, São Paulo, 2006. Cert. in phys. therapy Fed. U. São Carlos, 1999. Prof. Unipinhal, Espírito Santo do Pinhal, São Paulo, Brazil, 2002—05; vol. rschr. State U. of Campinas, Campinas, São Paulo, Brazil, 2005—06; prof. U. of São Paulo, Ribeirão Preto, São Paulo, Brazil, 2007—. Contbr. articles to sci. jours. Phys. therapist Assn. parents and friends exceptionals, Espírito Santo do Pinhal, São Paulo, 2004—05. Rsch. grant, FAPESP, State São Paulo Found. Rsch., 2008. Office: Univ São Paulo Avenida Bandeirantes 3900 Ribeirão Preto São Paulo Brazil Office Fax: +55 16 3602-4413. E-mail: dabreu@fmrp.usp.br.

ABREU, GLAUCIA RODRIGUES, nursing educator; b. Espirito Santo, Brazil, Apr. 5, 1964; PhD, U. Sao Paulo, 1996. RN Fed. U. Espirito Santo, 1987. Prof. Fed. U. Espirito Santo, 1994, bd. dirs., 2010. Young Investigator grant, CNPq. Mem.: Brazilian Soc. Physiology. Home: Rua Jose Teixeira 228 Apt 1401 Vitoria Espírito Santo 29043-900 Brazil Home Fax: 55-27-33357330. Business E-Mail: grabreu@npd.ufes.br.

ABREU, MARCELO EMIR REQUIA, dentist; b. Santa Maria, Brazil, May 20, 1978; MS, Pontifical U. Cath. Rio Grande do Sul, 2007; grad. in Medicine, 2007. Dentist Pontifical U. Cath. Rio Grande do Sul, 2003. Dentist, pvt. practice, facial trauma, bone reconstruction, orthognathic surgery and dental implants, 2003—; maxillofacial surgeon, 2005—. Adj. prof. Brazilian Assn. Dentistry, 2010; cons. Guidepoint Global Advisors, 2010. Avocation: travel. Office: Ave Princesa Isabel 729/301 Porto Alegre Rio Grande do Sul 90620-001 Brazil Business E-Mail: marceloemir@uol.com.br.

ABREU, MARIA T., gastroenterologist, educator; MD, U. Miami Sch. of Medicine, 1986. Diplomate Am. Bd. Internal Medicine-gastroenterology, 2005, Am. Bd. of Med. Examiners, Am. Bd. of Gastroenterology. Resident Brigham and Women's Hosp., Boston, 1990—92; fellow gastroenterology UCLA, 1992—95; postdoc. rsch. fellow Cedars-Sinai Med. Ctr., LA, 1993—96; dir. inflammatory bowel disease Mt. Sinai Sch. of Medicine, assoc. prof. medicine gastroenterology divsn.; chief gastroenterology divsn. Univ. of Miami Sch. of Medicine, prof. medicine, prof. microbiology and immunology. Author: (articles) Practical techniques for detection of Toll-like receptor-4 in the human intestine, 2009, A novel Toll-like receptor 4 antagonist antibody ameliorates inflammation but impairs mucosal healing in murine colitis, 2009, Innate Immune Signaling by Toll-like receptors-4 (TLR4) shapes the inflammatory microenvironment of colitis-associated tumors, 2009, and several others. Fellow: ACP; mem.: NIH Gastrointestinal Mucosal Pathobiology, Am. Gastroent. Assn. (com.), Am. Coll. of Gastroenterology (com.), Am. Soc. of Clin. Investigators. Office: University of Miami School of Medicine Rm 534 Gautier Medical Research Bldg 1011 N W 15th St Miami FL 33136 Office Phone: 305-243-8644.

ABREU, MURILO CESAR MEDEIROS, plastic surgeon; b. Fortaleza, Ceará, Brazil, Sept. 5, 1959; s. Murilo Washington and Francinetti Medeiros Abreu; m. Tania Caldas Abreu, Sept. 10, 1988; children: Jessica Medeiros, Murilo Arthur. Diploma, U. Fed. Do Ceara, 1984. Master: Pontifícia U. Cath. Rio De Janeiro; fellow: ACS; mem.: Coll. Brasileiro Cirurgioes, Soc. Brasileira Plastic Surgery. Home: Rua Cinco de Julho 108/602 Rio de Janeiro 22051030 Brazil Office: Rua Figueredo de Magalhães 286/1004 Rio de Janeiro 22051-030 Brazil Personal E-mail: m.abreu@terra.com.br.

ABU, EMMANUEL OGBOLE, pathologist, researcher; b. Kaduna, Nigeria, Dec. 19, 1964; s. Abu Ochenehi and Ede Ogbole. MBBS, U. of Ibadan, Nigeria, 1987; MS in Clin. BioChemistry, U. of Surrey, Eng., 1993; PhD, U. of Cambridge, Eng., 1997, St. John's Coll., Cambridge, Eng., 1998; cert. in Forensic Medicine, U. of Glasgow, Scotland, 2003. Cert. Royal Coll. of Pathologists, Eng., 2000. Resident physician in chem. pathology U. of Ilorin (Nigeria) Tchg. Hosp., 1992—94; sr. ho. officer in metabolic medicine Royal Postgraduate Med. Sch., Hammersmith Hosp., London, 1997—98; cons., chem. pathol. Southampton Gen. Hosp., England, 2002—. Specialist registrar in clin. chemistry Royal Liverpool (Nigeria) U. Tchg. Hosp., 1998—2001. Recipient Chancellors award, Eng. Chancellors, 1994—97; fellow, Cambridge Commonwealth Trusts, U. of Cambridge, U. of Southampton Tchg. Hosp., 2003—; scholar, Overseas Devel. Ministry, Eng., 1992—93; Scholarship, Cambridge Commonwealth Trusts, U. of Cambridge, 1994—97, Blue Circles PLC, 1994—97. Fellow: Cambride Commonwealth Trusts, U. of Cambridge (life); mem.: Royal Coll. of Pathologists (life), Assn. of Clin. Biochemists (life). Achievements include research in First to show the presence of the above receptors in human bone in situ. Home: 18 Woodview Close Hampshire Southampton SO16 3PZ England Office: Dept Chemical Pathology Tremona Rd Hampshire Southampton SO16 6YD England Office Fax: 02380796339. Personal E-mail: emmanuel.abu@suht.swest.nhs.uk.

ABU-ARAB, MAHMOUD, psychologist; b. Majd El-Korum, Acre, Israel, Sept. 3, 1953; arrived in Australia, 1988; parents Mohammad and Zena (Askari) Abu-Arab; m. Zlatica Minichova, Mar. 21, 1981 (div. Apr. 1993); children: Maria, Silvia; m. Mariola Zuk, Jan. 27, 1999; 1 child, Adam. MA, Comenius U., Bratislava, Slovakia, 1981, PhD, 1985. Psychologist Bratislava City Coun., 1982-83, Psychiat. Hosp., Pezenok, Slovakia, 1984; lectr. Ibrahimieh Coll., Jerusalem, 1985-88; dir. Palestinian Counseling Ctr., Jerusalem, 1986-88; rsch. officer Arab Studies Soc., Jerusalem, 1987-88; counsellor Granville Tafe Coll., Sydney, NSW, 1988—2003. Head dept. psychology Al-Amal Hosp., Jeddah, Saudi Arabia, 1993-94; pvt. practice, 1994—; spkr., presenter in field. Author standardization Psychol. Screening Inventory on Slovak Population, 1984, Psychol. Test on Palestinian Population, 1988; contbr. articles to profl. jours. Justice of the peace Min. for Justice, NSW, 1992; rep. Palestinian Charity Instns. Week of Peace Conf., Tokyo, 1987, Drug Abuse Prevention Conf., 1988. Mem.: Australian Pain Soc., Coll. Health Psychologists, Coll. Counseling Psychologists, Coll. Independently Practising Psychologists, Coll. Clin. Psychologists, Australian Psychol. Soc. Avocations: bushwalking, skiing, travel, reading. Home: PO Box 391 Granville Sydney NSW 2142 Australia

ABU DAGGA, ZIYAD MAHMOUD, dermatologist; b. Bany suhaila, Gaza Strip, Palestinian Authority, Feb. 14, 1966; s. Mahmoud Mansour and Hamda Mustafa Abu Dagga; life ptnr. Donia Issa Samour, Aug. 17, 1997; children: Nardeen Ziyad, Talla Ziyad, Lana Ziyad, Qusai Ziyad, Layan Abu Dagga. MBBS, Chittagong Med. Coll., Bangladesh, 1994; MSc in Clin. Dermatology, Kings Coll. London, 2001. Cert. dermatologist Ministry of Health, Abu Dhabi, 2001. Physician UN Relief and Welfare Agy., Rafah, Gaza Strip, Palestine, 1996—96, Alkarama Hosp., Abassan, 1996—2000, dermatologist, 2001—; acne specialist, 2001. Com. mem. dermatologist Ministry of Health, Gaza, 2004—. Dermatologist Benevolence Soc., Bany Sohaila, Gaza Strip, 2001, physician Bany Suhaila, Khanyounis, Gaza, Rafa, 1996—2000. Fellow: Am. Acad. Dermatology Assn., Am. Acad. Dermatology; mem.: Internat. Soc. Dermatology (Maria M. Duran fellow 2005). Independent. Muslim. Avocations: tennis, travel, tv, new treatment invention. Home: 36 Abu Samra St Gaza Strip Bany suhaila Palestine Home Fax: 0097282064644. Personal E-mail: ziyadpal@hotmail.com.

ABUHAMAD, ALFRED Z., obstetrician, gynecologist, educator; b. Lebanon, May 2, 1961; arrived in U.S., 1985; m. May R. Habib; children: Sami Michael, Nicole Catherine. BS, Am. U. Beirut, Lebanon, 1981, MD, 1985. Adminstrv. chief resident dept. ob-gyn. U. Miami, 1988—89; dir. ultrasonography Ea. Va. Med. Sch., Norfolk, 1992—, dir. divsn. maternal/fetal medicine, 1992—, prof. ob-gyn., 2002—, prof. radiology, Mason C. Andrews prof., chmn. dept. ob-gyn., 2004—, assoc. dean clin. affairs, 2005—; med. dir. maternal transport team Sentan Health Svcs., Norfolk, 1996—. Mem. editl. bd. Am. Jour. Perinatology, 2006—; mem. nuchal trnaslucency nat. oversight com., nat. coord. Maternal-Fetal Found., 2005—; mem. editl. adv. bd. Current Med. Imaging Rev., 2005—; mem. editl. bd. Jour. Ultrasound in Medicine, 2000—. Mem. Physicians for Peace, 1997; bd. dirs. Jones Inst. Found., Norfolk, 2004—. Recipient 1st prize for sci. paper presentation, William A. Little Soc. Ob-Gyn., 1986, 1988, 1991, Outstanding Resident award, U. Miami, 6th ann. John Ford award, 1989, Nathan Kase award, Yale U. Sch. Medicine, 1992, Resident Edn. award, Berlex Found., 1987; named to Best Drs. Am., 1998, 2005—06, Hampton Rds. Top Drs., 2003. Fellow: ACOG; mem.: Soc. Maternal-Fetal Medicine, Internat. Soc. Ultrasound in Ob-Gyn. (assoc. editor jour. 2002—, bd. dirs. 2003—), Internat. Perinatal Doppler Soc., Assn. Profs. Gynecology and Obstetrics, Chilean Soc. Ultrasound in Medicine and Biology (hon.), Am. Inst. Ultrasound in Medicine (sr.; chmn. patient edn. and resource com. 2000—04, chmn. nat. accreditation coun. 2002—08, mem. nominating com. 2003—, bd. govs. 2004—, chmn. ann. convention com. 2005—08, mem. fin. and exec. com. 2008—, pres. 2011—, Presdl. Recognition award 2004). Office: Eastern Va Med Sch Hofheimer Hall 825 Fairfax Ave Ste 310 Norfolk VA 23507 Office Phone: 757-446-7900. Office Fax: 757-624-2254. *

ABU HASHIM, HATEM, obstetrician, educator; b. El-Sinbellawin, Dakahlia Governorate, Egypt, May 1, 1968; MBBCh, Mansoura U. Egypt, 1991, MD, 2001. Resident ob-gyn. Mansoura U. Hosps., Egypt, 1993—97, asst. lectr. & registrar, ob-gyn., 1997—2002, lectr. & sr. registrar, ob-gyn., 2002—07, assoc. prof., ob-gyn., 2007—, cons., ob-gyn., 2007. Mem.: Egyptian Med. Assn., Egyptian Fertility Sterility Soc., Royal Coll. Obstetricians & Gynaecologists. Office: Bank Misr St Mansoura Dakahlia Governorate 35511 Egypt Personal E-mail: hatem_ah@hotmail.com.

ABUJUDEH, HANI H., radiologist; b. Jerusalem, May 1, 1971; MD, UMDNJ, 1995; MBA, Columbia, 2004. Resident St. Vincent's Hosp. & Med. Ctr., NYC, Univ. Hosp.; fellow NY Presbyn. Hosp. Weill Cornel; radiologist Mass. Gen. Hosp., Boston, 2004—, assoc. prof. radiology. Office: Radiological Associates 55 Fruit St Boston MA 02114-2696 Office Phone: 617-726-2696. Office Fax: 617-726-3634. Business E-Mail: habujudeh@partners.org.

ABULARRAGE, JOSEPH J., pediatrician, educator; B, Fordham U., 1971; med. degree, NYU, 1975; M in Pub. Health, Columbia U., 1975, MPhil, 1981. Lic. NY, 1976, diplomate Am. Bd. Pediatrics, 1981. Asst. pediatrician coll. physicians and surgeons Columbia Univ., 1978—81; intern NYU Bellevue Hosp. Med. Ctr., resident in pediat., 1979; tchg. asst. sch. medicine NYU, 1977—78, clin. asst. prof. pediat. sch. medicine, 1979—85, clin. assoc. prof. pediat. sch. medicine, 1985—90, clin. prof. pediat. sch. medicine, 1990—; program dir. pediatric epidemiology NYU Hosp., 1980—83, asst. attending pediatrician, 1980—; epidemiologist hydrocephalus clinic NYU Med. Ctr., 1981—83; clin. assoc. prof. pediat. Weil Med. Coll Cornell Univ., 1996—2000, clin. prof. pediat., 2000—; assoc. pediatrician Babies Hosp. Presbyn. Med. Ctr., 1971—81; chief and dir. pediat. NY Infirmary/Beekman Downtown Hosp., 1983—92, attending physician, 1983—; chmn. pediat. dept. NY Hosp. Med. Ctr. of Queens, 1992—. Mem.: NY Acad. Medicine, APHA, AMA, Queens Pediatric Soc. (exec. bd. 1993—). Office: New York Hospital Queens 56-45 Main St Flushing NY 11355 Office Phone: 718-670-1033.

ABULEZZ, TAREK ABDELHAMEED, plastic surgeon, educator; m. Elham Omar; children: Abdallah Tarek, Ahmed Tarek. MD, South Valley U., Sohag, Egypt. Cert. Egyptian Med. Syndicate, 1993. Postdoc. rsch. fellow UT Southwestern Med. Ctr., Dallas, 2001—03; lectr., plastic surgery Sohag U., 2004—. Cons., plastic surgery, Sohag, 2005—. Mem.: Mediterranean Coun. Burns and Fire Disasters, Internat. Soc. Burn Injuries, Egyptian Soc. Plastic and Reconstructive Surgery (Best Rsch. award 2006). Achievements include research in modified technique for closing recurrent midline abdominal wall dehiscence. Office: Faculty Medicine Sohag Univ University St Sohag 82524 Egypt Office Phone: 0020103674340. Office Fax: 0020934602963. E-mail: t_abulezz@yahoo.com.

ABUL-HAJ, SULEIMAN KAHIL, pathologist; b. Palestine, Apr. 20, 1925; came to U.S., 1946, naturalized, 1955; s. Sheik Khalil and S. Butelna (Oda) Abul-H.; m. Elizabeth Abood, Feb. 11, 1948; children: Charles, Alan, Cary. BS, U. Calif., Berkeley, 1949; MS, U. Calif., San Francisco, 1951, MD, 1955. Intern Cook County Hosp., Chgo., 1955-56; resident U. Calif. Hosp., San Francisco, 1949, Brooke Gen Hosp., 1957-59; chief clin. and anatomic pathology Walter Reed Army Hosp., Washington, 1959-62; assoc. prof. U. So. Calif. Sch. Medicine, LA, 1963-96; sr. surg. pathologist Los Angeles County Gen. Hosp., 1963; dir. dept. pathology Cmty. Meml. Hosp., Ventura, Calif., 1964-80, Gen. Hosp. Ventura County, 1966-74; dir. Pathology Svc. Med. Group, 1970—. Cons. Calif. Tumor Tissue Registry, 1962-96, Camarillo State Hosp., 1964-70, Tripler Gen. Hosp., Hawaii, 1963-67, Armed Forces Inst. Pathology, 1960-69. Contbr. articles to profl. jours. Bd. dirs. Tri-Counties Blood Bank, Am. Cancer Soc. Maj., M.C., US Army, 1956-65; adv. bd. mem. Salvation Army, attending staff physician, surgeon, Free Med. Clinic. Recipient Calif. Honor Soc. award U. Calif., Berkely, 1949, award Borden Co., 1955, Achievement cert. Surgeon Gen. Army, 1962, Internat. medal of Honor, Am. medal of Honor, Internat. Living Legends Leading Scientists of the World, commendation, US Army 2008. Fellow Coll. Am. Pathologists; mem. AMA, Internat. Coll. Surgeons, World Affairs Coun., World Peace and Diplomacy Forum. Achievements include research in cancer, cardiovascular disease, endocrine, renal, and skin diseases. Home and Office: 105 Encinal Way Ventura CA 93001-3317 Home Phone: 805-643-5236; Office Phone: 805-648-1232.

ABU-MOUSTAFA, ADEL H., medical educator, dean; b. Cairo, Nov. 18, 1939; came to U.S., 1962; s. Abdulhamid and Zanab (Ayad) Abu-moustafa; m. Magda Ismail Kabbany, Oct. 10, 1962; children: Heidi, Sally, Sherief. BSc, Cairo U., 1960; MA, Harvard U., 1964; PhD, Boston U., 1969. Instr. Boston Coll., Chestnut Hill, Mass., 1964-67; from asst. prof. to assoc. prof. Salem (Mass.) State Coll., 1967-70, prof., 1970-72, dean undergrad studies, 1972-74, acting acad. dean, 1974-76, dean acad. svcs., 1976-79, exec. v.p., 1979-83; adminstrv. counselor King Faisal U., Saudi Arabia, 1983-86; dir. svcs. to higher edn. Acad. for Ednl. Devel., Washington, 1983-87; dir. assoc. dean internat. health affairs Tufts U. Sch. Medicine, Boston, 1987—, dean internat. health affairs, 1997—. Team leader consortium of U.S. Univs. and U.S. Dept. Treasury, U.S. Saudi Commn. on Econ. Cooperation to assist King Faisal U., Saudi Arabia, 1983-87. Contbr. articles to profl. jours. Mem. exec. com. Fletcher Sch. Law and Diplomacy, 1987—. Mem. Arab Am. Physicians. Muslim. Avocation: politics. Office: Tufts U Sch Medicine 136 Harrison Ave Boston MA 02111-1817 Office Phone: 617-636-0355. Business E-Mail: adel.abu-moustafa@tufts.edu.

ABU-RUSTUM, NADEEM R., gynecologic oncologist, educator; Diplomate Am. Bd. Ob-Gyn., 2009. Faculty McGill Univ.; dir. minimally invasive surgery gynecology svc. Meml. Sloan-Kettering Cancer Ctr., dir. resident, dir. med. student edn., fellow gynecologic oncology; resident ob-gyn. Greater Baltimore Med. Ctr.; prof. ob-gyn. Weill Med. Coll. Cornell Univ. Chair surgical quality assessment com. Meml. Sloan-Kettering Cancer Ctr.; mem. cervical cancer screening panel Nat. Comprehensive Cancer Network, mem. endometrial cancer and uterine sarcoma panel, mem. cervical cancer panel; mem.

Gynecologic Oncology Group Cervix Com. Mem.: Am. Coll. Surgeons Com. Emerging Surg. Tech. and Edn. Office: Memorial Sloan-Kettering Cancer Center 1275 York Avenue New York NY 10065 Office Phone: 212-639-2000.

ACHARYA, AMIT, dentist; s. Lakshminarayana and Savithri Acharya; m. Rohini Hebbar, Aug. 29, 2004. B in Dental Surgery, Govt. Dental Coll., Bangalore, India, 1999; M in Computer Sci., Western Ky. U., Bowling Green, 2004; PhD in Biomedical Informatics, U. Medicine & Dentistry NJ, Newark, 2010. Dentist Chitra Dental Clinic, Bangalore, 1998—99; hon. surgeon Sanjay Gandhi Trauma Ctr., Bowring & Lady Curzon Hosp., Victoria Hosp. & KC Gen. Hosp., Bangalore, 1998—99; dental surgeon Poly Vignesh Clinic, Bangalore, 1999—2000; grad. asst. U. Medicine & Dentistry NJ, 2005—06; vis. scholar U. Pitts., 2006—09; dental informatics scientist Marshfield Clinic Rsch. Found., Wis., 2009—. Rev.: Jour. Am. Dental Edn. Assn., 2008; contbr. articles to jours. Mem.: IEEE, ADA, Am. Dental Association's Standards Com. Dental Informatics, Am. Med. Informatics Assn., Internat. Assn. Dental Rsch., Am. Assn. Dental Rsch., Am. Dental Edn. Assn. (rev. 2010 ann. session 2009). Hindu. Achievements include research in electronic dental record information model appropriate for general dentistry; dental data element list. Avocations: cooking, travel, music, winemaking, history. Office: Marshfield Clinic Rsch Found 1000 N Oak Ave Marshfield WI 54449

ACHARYA, SOURYA, physician, educator; b. Cuttack, Mar. 20, 1974; MBBS, 1998; DNB, JN Med. Coll., 2003. Assoc. prof. medicine, cons. physician JN Med. Coll., 2007—. Avocations: running, music. Office: Sawangi Meghe Wardha Maharashtra 442004 India E-mail: sacharya_1@hotmail.com.

ACHOLONU, WILFRED W., JR., clinical pharmacy specialist, educator; b. Owerri, Imo, Nigeria, July 18, 1953; arrived in U.S., 1974; s. Wilfred W. and Esther Rose Acholonu; m. Ezioma G. Onwuchekwa, May 25, 1991; children: Ikenna Colin, Ezioge Celest. BS in Pharmacy, Oreg. State U., 1980, MS in Pharmacology and Toxicology, 1984; PharmD, U. Fla., 1994. Cert. Bd. Pharm. Spltys. Resident hosp. pharm. VA Med. Ctr., Portland, Oreg., 1983—84; staff pharmacist Olin E. Teague VA Med. Ctr., Temple, Tex., 1984—89, VA Med. Ctr., Gainesville, Fla., 1989—94; assoc. clin. prof. pharmacy practice U. Fla., Gainesville, 1996—; clin. pharmacy specialist VA Med. Ctr., Gainesville, 1994—. Mem. PET com. VA Med. Ctr., Gainesville. Contbr. articles to profl. jours. Mem.: Am. Soc. Health Sys. Pharmacists, Am. Coll. Clin. Pharmacy, Coll. Psychiatric and Neurologic Pharmacists. Avocations: tennis, racquetball, basketball. Office: North Fla/South Ga VHS 1601 SW Archer Rd Gainesville FL 32608 Office Phone: 352-376-1611 ext. 6459. E-mail: wilfred.acholonu@med.va.gov.

ACHORD, JAMES LEE, retired gastroenterologist; b. Dayton, Ohio, Sept. 24, 1931; s. Lonnie M. and Ethel E. (Collins) A.; m. Patsy Jane Moore, Dec. 18, 1954; children: J. Michael, Ann Elizabeth, Andrew P. DMD, Emory U., 1952, MD, 1956. Intern Emory Hosp., 1956-57; resident Emory U., Atlanta, 1959-62, instr., assoc. prof., 1962-71; med. dir. Med. Ctr. Cen. Ga., Macon, 1971-75; assoc. dean, prof. East Tenn. State Sch. Medicine, Johnson City, 1975-76; prof., dir. div. digestive diseases U. Miss. Med. Ctr., Jackson, 1976-98, prof. emeritus, 1998. Editor book revs. Am. Jour. Gastroenterology, 1985-91, Dig. Dis. Sci., 1994-96; mem. editl. bd. Am. Jour. Clin. Gastroenterology, 1999—08; contbr. numerous articles and editls. to profl. jours. and chpts. to books. Capt. U.S. Army, 1957-59. Master ACP (gov. Miss. chpt. 1993-97), Am. Coll. Gastroenterology (pres. 1983-84), Am. Soc. Gastroenterologic Endoscopy; mem. Am. Assn. Study Liver Disease, Am. Gastroent. Assn.

ACHOUI, MUSTAPHA MOULOUD, psychologist, educator; b. Akfadou, Bejaia, Algeria, Feb. 28, 1952; s. Mouloud Omar Achoui and Mahrez Arezki Yakout; m. Alghaia Shabane Mahrez; children: Toufik, Farouk, Sarah, Mouna. BS, Algiers U., 1977; MS, Rensselaer Poly. Inst., 1980, PhD, 1983. Prof. Algiers U., Algeria, 1990—95, Internat. Islamic U., Malaysia, 1995—2000, King Fahd U. Petroleum and Minerals, Daharan, Saudi Arabia, 2000—. Dir. Nat. Inst. of Strategic Studies, Algeria, 1987—92; dean Internat. Islamic U., Malaysia, 1997—98, dep. dean acad. affairs, Malaysia, 1998—2000. Author: Al-Balkhi: A Pioneer Psychologist, 2000. V.p. Nat. Found. of Health & Rsch., Algeria, 1993—96. Fellow: APA; mem.: Internat. Assn. for Cross Cultural Psychology. Avocation: swimming. Home: 16 Youcef Lamine Bologhine Algeria Mailing: King Fahd Univ Petroleum and Minerals PO Box 2018 31942 Dhahran Saudi Arabia Office Phone: 9663 8604780. Personal E-mail: mustafait@hotmail.com.

ACHUFF, STEPHEN CHARLES, cardiologist; b. St. Louis, Mar. 12, 1943; m. Cary Williams Lipscomb, Dec. 27, 1970; children: Catherine Elise, Jeanne Ann, Charles Walter. BA in Religion, Philosophy, Wesleyan U., 1964; MD, U. Mo., 1969. Diplomate Am. Bd. Internal Medicine, Am. Bd. Cardiovasc., Am. Bd. Med. Examiners. Intern, jr. asst. resident John Hopkins Hosp., 1969-71, fellow medicine, 1971-73, chief resident medicine, 1973-74, asst. dir. Adult Cardia Catheterization Lab., 1975-77, cardiologist Lipid Rsch. Clinic, 1975-84, dir. Adult Cardiology Clin. Program, 1980—2000; instr. medicine John Hopkins U., 1973-74, from asst. prof. to assoc. prof., 1975-90, prof. medicine, 1990—. Rsch. fellow Am. Heart Assn., 1971-73; rsch. fellow, hon. sr. registrar dept. cardiology Royal Infirmary Edinburgh, Scotland, 1974-75; mem. adv. bd. John Hopkins U., 1979-80, Pinnaclecare; vis. prof. Guy's Hosp., London, 1990. Mem. editl. bd. Audiovisual Programs Continuing Edn., John Hopkins U., 1976-92; contbr. articles to profl. jours. Recipient Oustanding Grad. award Mo. State Med. Assn., 1969, Pfizer award U. Mo., 1968; USPHS fellow U. Mo., 1966-67. Fellow Am. Coll. Cardiology, Am. Heart Assn. (mem. coun. clin. cardiology 1979, v.p., bd. dirs. 1979-80); mem. Internat. Soc. Heart Tranplantation, Alpha Omega Alpha. Office: Cardiology Johns Hopkins Hosp 600 N Wolfe St Baltimore MD 21287 Office Phone: 410-955-7670. Business E-Mail: sachuff@jhmi.edu.

ACKER, LOREN CALVIN, medical products executive; b. Lamar, Colo., Mar. 3, 1934; s. John C. and Ada M. (Ecton) Acker; m. Judy N. Willms, Sept. 17, 1955 (dec. Oct. 1968); children: Cheryl Acker Hoge, Keith B., Karen Acker Kime; m. Darla S. Copeland, July 24, 1976. BSME, Fresno State Coll., 1956; cert. in bus. and mgmt., U. Calif., Berkeley, 1961; MBA, U. Santa Clara, 1966. Flight test NASA, Edwards, Calif., 1954-56; engring. mgr. Westinghouse, Sunnyvale, Calif., 1956—68; engring. mgr., assoc. dir. Kitt Peak Nat. Obs., Assn. U. Rsch. in Astronomy, Tucson, 1968—73; founder, bd. dirs. led Engr. & Rsch. Assocs., Inc. (Vante), Tucson, 1973—. Co founder Winged Foot Assocs., Tucson, 1974—; founder ERA LLC, Tucson, 1999, WoofSpa and Resort, NYC, 2003, Electrophysiology LLC, Tucson, 2000, NYPA Inc., Tucson, 1986; co-founder Acker Mgmt. Group LLC, Tucson, 2006, Mankinddog LLC, Tubac, 2008—, Karma Day Spa, Tubac, 2009. Chmn. pk. and recreation City of Cupertino, Calif., 1968; co founder, mem. So. Ariz. Leadership Coun., 1997—; bd. dirs. Sonoran Sea Aquarium, 1999—; chmn. bioindustry Greater Tucson Econ. Coun., 1994—99; mem. master engring. Ariz. U./Indsl. Partnership, 2000—06; mem. agrl. and biosystem coun. U. Ariz., 1999—. Entrepreneurial fellow, U. Ariz., 1999. Mem.: Internat. Soc. Cellular Therapy, Am. Soc. Apherises, Am. Assn. Blood Banks, Audubon Soc., Nature Conservancy, Sierra Club. Republican. Achievements include patents in field. Avocations: skiing, tennis. Home: 4831 E Winged Foot Pl Tucson AZ 85718-1727 Office: 100 N Tucson Blvd Tucson AZ 85716-4740

ACKER, MICHAEL A., thoracic surgeon, educator; b. Phila., May 15, 1956; BS, Brown U., Providence, 1978, MD, 1981. Diplomate Am. Bd. Thoracic Surgery, Am. Bd. Surgery. Intern surgery U. Pa. Hosp., Phila., 1981—82, resident cardiothoracic surgery, 1982—88; asst. instr. surgery U. Pa. Sch. Medicine, 1982—87, asst. prof. surgery, 1993—97, assoc. prof. surgery, 1997—2004, prof. surgery, 2004—, William Maul Measey prof. surgery, 2006—; resident cardiac surgery Johns Hopkins Hosp., Balt., 1988—91; asst. prof. surgery John Hopkins U. Sch. Medicine, 1991—93. Attending cardiac surgeon Johns Hopkins Hosp., 1991—93, Sinai Hosp., Balt., 1991—93; attending cardiothoracic surgeon Vet.'s Adminstrn. Hosp., Phila., 1994—99, Presbyn. Med. Ctr., Phila., 1996—, Pa. Hosp., 1997—, U. Pa. Med. Ctr., 1993—, surg. dir. cardiac transplant/mech. assist prog., 1994—, chief divsn. cardiothoracic surgery, 2003—. Contbr. articles to profl. jours. Fellow: ACS, Am. Call. Cardiology, Am. Coll. Chest Physicians; mem.: Am. Soc. Artificial Internal Organs, Soc. Critical Care Medicine, Am. Cardiomyoplasty Group, Assn. Academic Surgery, Soc. Thoracic Surgeons, Internat. Soc. Heart/Lung Transplantation, Am. Soc. Transplant Surgeons, Internat. Soc. Surgery, Soc. Univ. Surgeons, Heart Failure Soc. America, Am. Assn. Thoracic Surgery, Pa. Acad. Surgery, Greater Del. Valley Soc. Transplant Surgeons, Pa. Assn. Thoracic Surgery. Office: Hosp U Pa 3400 Spruce St 6 Silverstein Pavilion Philadelphia PA 19104 also: Penn Presbyn Med Ctr Dept Surgery 39th & Market St 101 Med Arts Bldg Philadelphia PA 19104 Office Phone: 215-349-8305, 215-662-9595. Office Fax: 215-349-5798, 215-243-3243. Business E-Mail: michael.acker@uphs.upenn.edu.

ACKER, ROBERT FLINT, retired microbiologist; b. Chgo., Aug. 24, 1920; s. Robert Booth and Mary (Flint) A.; m. Phyllis Catharine Fry, Jan. 2, 1948 (dec. Apr. 2005); children: Catharine Elizabeth, Barbara Fenner, Robert Macdonald, James Christopher; m. Helen Crawford Stephens, Apr. 8, 2006. BA, Ind. U., 1942, MA, 1948; PhD, Rutgers U., 1953. Asst. prof. Iowa State U., Ames, 1954-59; asst. chief cancer chemotherapy dept., chief quality control dept. Microbiol. Assocs., Inc., Bethesda, Md., 1959-61, chief dept. cell and media prodn., 1961-62; dir. microbiology program Office of Naval Research, Dept. Navy, Washington, 1962-69; dir. office of rsch. coord., asst. dean faculties for research, prof. biol. scis. Northwestern U., Evanston, Ill., 1969-74; exec. dir. Am. Soc. Microbiology, Washington, 1974-81, Nat. Found. Infectious Diseases, Bethesda, Md., 1981-86; pres. Bionox Corp., Tucson, 1985-92. Mem. bacteriology and mycology study sect. NIH, 1964. Author: (with R.R. Jennings) The Protistan Kingdom, 1970; editor: Proc. 24th Internat. Congress on Marine Corrosion and Fouling, 1972; editorial bd.: Applied Microbiology, 1962-73. V.p., bd. dirs. Iona House Sr. Svc. Ctr., Washington, 1978-79, pres., 1979-81; trustee Massanetta Conf. Ctr., 1983-86; bd. dirs. Am. Type Culture Collection, 1983-89; pres. Sunrise Mountain Ridge Homeowners Assn., 1994-95; bd. elders Potomac United Presbyn. Ch., Md., 1967-69, Winnetka (Ill.) Presbyn. Ch., 1972-74, Nat. Presbyn. Ch., Washington, 1983-86, St. Andrew's Presbyn. Ch., Tucson, 1989-91, 1998-2000. Eli Lilly & Co. postdoctoral fellow, 1953—54. Fellow Am. Acad. Microbiology, Soc. for Indsl. Microbiology (pres. 1986-87, Charles Porter award 2001); mem. Am. Soc. for Microbiology, Am. Inst. Biol. Sci. (coun. 1983-91), Cosmos Club, Sigma Chi (award 2011).

ACKERMAN, JACOB LEWIS, ophthalmologist; b. Berlin, July 22, 1947; s. Joseph and Pearl (Ziment) A.; m. Elaine Marsha Horowitz, Aug. 10, 1969 (dec. Mar. 2002); children: Rita, Karen, Steven, Julie; m. Judith Fay Rosenfeld, Oct. 6, 2002. MD, Albert Einstein Coll. Medicine, 1971. Assoc. dir. Brook Plaza Ophthalmology, Bklyn., 1975—, Brook Plaza Ambulatory Surgery Ctr., Bklyn., 1989—; asst. prof. of ophthalmology SUNY Health Sci. Ctr., Down State Med. Ctr., 1981—. Exec. bd. dirs. Met. Ophthalmic Ambulatory Surg. Ctr. Assn., Bronx. Contbr. articles to profl. jours. Sec. Young Israel of Lawrence-Cedarhurst, 1993. Avocations: tennis, writing, talmud, art, torah. Office: Brook Plaza Ophthalmology Assocs 1901 Utica Ave Brooklyn NY 11234-3213 Home: 138-15 Union Turnpike Flushing NY 11367-3250 Office Phone: 718-968-8700. Personal E-mail: jfjamd2000@yahoo.com.

ACKERMAN, SIGURD HOWARD, psychiatrist; b. Millville, NJ, Feb. 25, 1940; s. William H. and Ethel (Kessler) A.; m. Cecelia M. McCarton, Apr. 25, 1983; children: Elizabeth, Rebecca, McCarton. BA, Harvard U., 1962; MD, Tufts U., 1966. Intern Kings County Hosp., Bklyn., 1966-67, resident in medicine, 1967-68; resident in psychiatry Montefiore Med. Ctr., Bronx, NY, 1970-73; dir. psychiatry St. Luke's Roosevelt Hosp. Ctr., NYC, 1989—98, med. dir., exec. v.p., 1991-93; prof. clin. psychiatry Columbia U. Coll. Physicians and Surgeons, NYC, 1989—, assoc. dean, 1991-93; pres., CEO St. Luke's-Roosevelt Med. Ctr., NYC, 1998—2001; pres., med. dir. Silver Hill Hosp., Inc., New Canaan, Conn., 2003—. Rsch. Scientist Devel. award level I and II, NIMH, 1976-84. Home: 97 Sagamore Rd Stamford CT 06902-8007 Office: Silver Hill Hosp 208 Valley Rd New Canaan CT 06840 Office Phone: 203-801-2215.

ACKLAND, DAVID C., research scientist; b. Melbourne, Australia, Dec. 28, 1979; BE, U. Melbourne, 2003, PhD, 2008. Rsch. fellow, dept. mech. engring. U. Melbourne, 2009—. Office: University Melbourne Bldg 170 Parkville Victoria 3103 Australia Business E-Mail: dackland@unimelb.edu.au.

ACKLER, SCOTT L., pharmacologist; b. Phila., Mar. 25, 1970; BS, U. Scis., 1992; PhD, Georgetown U., 2003. Rsch. assoc. Glaxo Inc., 1993—94, Nobex Corp., 1994—97; assoc. rsch. scientist Bayer Pharm., 1997—98; sr. scientist II Abbott Labs., 2003—. Mem.: Am. Assn. Cancer Rschrs. Office: 100 Abbott Park Rd Bldg AP9 Rm 2185 Abbott Park IL 60064 Business E-Mail: scott.ackler@abbott.com.

ACOSTA, JULIO BERNARD, retired obstetrician, retired gynecologist; b. Yurimaguas, Loreto, Peru, July 29, 1927; came to U.S., 1955, naturalized, 1960; s. Miguel and Flor Maria (Solis) A.; m. Mary Jane Aedinvice, Aug. 30, 1974; children: Raul, Luis-Miguel, Patricia, Silvia, Douglas, Jill. MD, St. Marcos U., Peru, 1955. Diplomate Am. Bd. Obstetrics and Gynecology. Intern St. Alexis Hosp., Cleve., 1955-56, resident, 1956-57, St. Ann Hosp., Cleve., 1957-59; pvt. practice medicine specializing in obstetrics and gynecology Livonia, Mich., 1964-86; retired, 1986; pvt. practice, 1986—2000. Chief staff Plymouth Gen. Hosp., Detroit, 1970-73, chief gynecologic sect., 1974-83, med. dir.; active staff St. Mary Hosp., Livonia, 1964-86, Grace-Harper Hosp., Detroit, 1973-86; clin. instr. Wayne State U. Sch. Medicine, 1983-87; sr. physician Kaiser Permanente Med. Ctr., Walnut Creek, Calif., 1986-2000; clin. faculty U. Calif., San Francisco, 1988-2000. Contbr. articles to profl. jours. Capt. M.C., USAR, 1959-62. Capt. USAR, 1959, with US Army Hosp., Aberdeen Proving Ground, Md. Fellow ACOG (life), Am. Fertility Soc., Am. Soc. Colposcopy and Cervical Pathology, Am. Soc. Abdominal Surgeons; mem. Peruvian-Am. Med. Soc. Democrat. Unitarian Universalist. *

ACOSTA, RODRIGO, physician; Studied, U. Tex. Southwestern. Diplomate Am. Bd. Family Practice, cert. geriatric medicine. Resident family medicine St. Joseph's Hosp.; physician Stamford Hosp. Office: Stamford Hospital 32 Strawberry Hill Crt St 41096 Stamford CT 06902 Office Phone: 203-977-2566. Office Fax: 203-977-2568.

ACWORTH, JASON PAUL, pediatrician, director; b. Brisbane, Queensland, Australia, Sept. 8, 1968; s. Arthur Keith Acworth and Joy Elizabeth Walmsley; m. Nicola Jane Wyatt, Aug. 14, 1993; children: Elliott Luke, Lachlan James. MBBS (hon.), U. Queensland, St Lucia, 1991. Resident med. officer Royal Brisbane Hosp., 1992—94, Royal Children's Hosp., Brisbane, Queensland, Australia, 1994—95, paediatric registrar, 1995—98, paediatric emergency fellow, 1998—2000, Hosp. Sick Children, Toronto, Ont., Canada, 2000—01; staff specialist, paediatric emergency Royal Children's Hosp., Brisbane, Queensland, Australia, 2001—04, dep. dir., paediat. emergency, 2004—10; dir., paediat. emergency medicine Children's Health Svcs., Queensland Health, 2010—. Sr. lectr. U. Queensland, Faculty Medicine, 2002—; state chair tng. br. St John Ambulance, Queensland, 2004—08; nat. bd. mem. Advanced Paediatric Life Support Australia, 2006—09; sect. editor-paediatrics Emergency Medicine Australasia Jour., Australia, 2006—; inaugural vice chair Paediatric Rsch. Emergency Depts. Internat. Collaborative, Australia, 2004—08; chair Paediatric Rsch. Emergency Departments Internat. Collaborative, 2008—09; state pres., first aid svcs. St. John Ambulance, Queensland, 2008—, mem. nat. med. adv. group, Australia; found. mem. Internat. Pediatric Emergency Rsch. Network, 2009—. Recipient Australia Day Achievement Medallion, Queensland Health, 2006; Overseas Travelling fellowship, Royal Children's Hosp. Found., 2000, Rsch. Project grant, NHMRC, 2009—, Rsch. Program grant, Queensland Emergency Rsch. Found., 2010—. Fellow: Royal Australasian Coll. Physicians; mem.: Australian Med. Assn., Paediatric Emergency Medicine Soc. (found. mem. 2006—10), Australasian Soc. Simulation Healthcare (found. mem. 2006—10), Soc. Simulation Healthcare, Am. Coll. Emergency Physicians (internat. mem. 2008—10).

ADA, BILL, psychologist; b. Australia, Aug. 22, 1977; BSc in Psychology with honors, UNSW, 2000. Prin. psychologist iLead Psychology, 2003—. Mem.: Australian Psychol. Soc., Psychology Bd. Australia. Home: 7 Stanbrook St Fairfield Heights Sydney NSW 2165 Australia Personal E-mail: bill.ada@gmail.com.

ADACHI, KAZUHIDE, medical educator; b. Japan, Mar. 23, 1974; MD, Fujita Health U., 1999; PhD, Keio U., 2008. Lectr. Fujita Health U., 2010—. Recipient Tourin award, Keio U. Office: Fujita Health University 1-98 Kutsugak Toyoake Aichi 470-1192 Japan E-mail: kazu-adachi@rio.odn.ne.jp.

ADACHI, MASAZUMI, pathologist; DSc, MD, Keio U., Sch. Medicine, Tokyo, 1953, SUNY, 1971. Prof. pathology SUNY Downstate MC, Bklyn., 1980—; dir. labs. Kingsbrook Jewish Med. Ctr., 1980—97, cons. emeritus, 2006—. Contbr. scientific papers to profl. publs. Recipient award, Emperor Japan. Mem.: Coll. Am. Pathologists (mem. emeritus 1980—2008). Office: Kingsbrook Jewish Medical Ctr 585 Schenectady Ave Brooklyn NY 11203 Personal E-mail: madachi@kingsbrook.org.

ADACHI, SHINYA, surgeon, educator, Japanese government official; b. Oita, Japan, June 5, 1957; s. Tsugiya and Umeno (Goto) A.; m. Nahomi Toshimitsu, May 1, 1982; children: Kana, Kyosuke. MD, U. Tsukuba, 1982, D in Med. Sci., 1990. Resident Tsukuba U. Hosp., 1982-88; chief surgeon Kinu Med. Assn. Hosp., Mitsukaido, Japan, 1988-94; asst. prof. U. Tsukuba, 1994—2002, assoc. prof., 2003, Kasumigaura Nat. Hosp., 2003; mem. House of Councillors, 2004—. Contbr. articles to profl. jours. Mem. Internat. Gastric Cancer Assn. Avocations: golf, baseball, gardening. Office Phone: 81-36550 0613. Personal E-mail: info@adachishinya.com.

ADAIR, ELEANOR REED, environmental biologist; b. Arlington, Mass., Nov. 28, 1926; d. Kenneth Clarke and Margaret Reed; m. Robert Kemp Adair, June 21, 1952; children: Douglas, Margaret, James(dec.). BA, Mt. Holyoke Coll., 1948; MA, U. Wis., 1951, PhD, 1955. From rsch. asst. to lectr., sr. scientist Yale U., New Haven, 1960—. From asst. fellow to fellow John B. Pierce Lab., New Haven, 1966—96; cons. sci. adv. bd. EPA, 1983—89; sr. scientist Electromagnetic Radiation Effects, Air Force Rsch. Lab., Brooks AFB, Tex., 1996—2001, sr. scientist emeritus, 2001—. Editor: Microwaves & Thermoregulation, 1983; contbr. articles to profl. jours. Bd. dirs. Am. Himalayan Found., 1990—. Fellow: IEEE, APA, AAAS, N.Y. Acad. Scis., Am. Inst. Med. and Biol. Engring.; mem.: Bioelectromagnetics Soc. Avocations: birdwatching, gardening, Buddhism. Home: 200 Leeder Hill Dr Hamden CT 06517

ADAIR, STEFAN RENE, plastic surgeon; BA cum laude, Johns Hopkins U., 1988; MD, Tulane U., 1993. Diplomate Am. Bd. Plastic Surgery. Residency Santa Barbara Cottage Hosp., Calif., 1998; rotation Sherman Oaks Burn Ctr., Calif., 1994, Cedars-Sinai Hosp., LA, 1995, LA Children's Hosp., 1996, LA County Hosp., 1996;

fellowship in plastic surgery U. Calif. Irvine, 1998—2000; pvt. practice Beverly Hills, 2000—, Atlanta, 2005—, Macon, Ga., 2005—. Externship in reconstructive surgery Oxford Med. Sch., England, 1993; staff privileges Cedars Sinai Hosp., Century City Hosp. Contbr. articles to profl. jours. Lt. comdr. USNR. Fellow: ACS.

ADAM, PAULA, economist; b. Spain, Apr. 21, 1966; PhD in Economics, European U. Inst., 1996. Economist Orgn. Econ. Co-operation and Devel., 1998—2004; health scis. rschr. Catalan Agy. Health Info., Assessment and Quality, 2010—. Jr. Affiliate fellowship, Ctr. Econ. Policy Rsch. Mem.: Spanish Pub. Health Assn., Spanish Health Econ. Assn. Office: Roc Boronat 81-95 2 planta Barcelona 085005 Spain Business E-Mail: padam@aatrm.catsalut.net.

ADAMIAK, BEATA, microbiologist; arrived in Sweden, 2006; MS in Biology, U. Gdansk, 1998; PhD in Biochemistry, Med. U. Gdansk, Poland, 2008. Microbiologist Sahlgrenska U. Hosp., Sweden, 2008—. Performer (actress): Student Theater Group 'Russkaja Scena', 2007—. Vol. Caritas Gdansk, Poland, 1997—2000. Mem.: Soc. European Virology, Polish Biochemistry Soc. Achievements include research in function of proteins in virology. Avocations: travel, sports, dance, hiking, history. Office Phone: 46 31 3424619. Personal E-mail: beatada@yahoo.co.uk.

ADAMIS, DIMITRIOS, psychiatrist, researcher; b. Velina, Greece, Jan. 30, 1961; s. Anastasios Adamis and Danaeh Adami. Degree in dentistry, U. Athens, Greece, 1984; degree in medicine, Aristotle U., Thessaloniki, Greece, 1988; degrees in philosophy, pedagogy and psychology, Aristotle U., 1993; MS in Mental Health Studies, U. London, 1998; MS in Applied Stats., U. Oxford, 2006; MD, U. London, 2007. Med. specialisation in psychiatry Hellenic Republic. Trainee in psychiatry Aiginiteion U. Hosp., Athens, 1991—95; clin. rsch. fellow St. Thomas' Hosp., London, 2000—05; specialist registrar in old age psychiatry Oxleas NHS Trust, London, 2001—03; cons. in old age psychiatry Oxleas NHS Trust Meml. Hosp., London, 2004—. Vis. rsch. assoc. Inst. Psychiatry, U. London, 2002—. Contbr. articles to profl. jours. Grantee, Found. of Scholarships G.Mavroulias, 1979—84, rsch. grantee, Bosher Meml. Bequest, 2000—01; postgrad. scholar, Inst. State Scholarships, Greece, 1996—97. Fellow: Royal Statistical Soc. (life), Redwood Soc. (life); mem.: Gen. Med. Coun. (life), Hellenic Med. Assn. (life), Hellenic Psychiat. Assn (life). Achievements include research in biological markers in delirium. Office: Oxleas NHS Trust Meml Hosp Shooters Hill SE18 3RZ London England Personal E-mail: dimaadamis@yahoo.com. E-mail: dimitrious.adamis@oxleas.nhs.uk.

ADAMOPOULOS, DIMITRIOS A., physician, consultant; b. Corinth, Greece, Jan. 4, 1939; MD, Athens U. Med. Sch., 1963. Cert. clin. endocrinologist 1972, clin. andrologist 1992. Intern dept. internal medicine Laikon Hosp., Athens, 1964—67; mem. sci. staff med. rsch. coun. Cl. Endocrinology Res. Unit, Edinburgh, 1967—73; dir., cons. dept. endocrinology diabetes metabolism Elena Venizelou Hosp., Athens, 1974—2006. Chmn., co-chmn. more than 30 internat. congresses, invited spkr. Author (co-editor): (book) Basic Endocrinology, 1994; author: (editor) Emergencies in Endocrinology, 2003; editor-in-chief: jour. Anir; author: 320 sci. papers, articles, reviews and abstracts. Contbr. WWF, Green Peace Action Aid, Drs. Without Frontiers, 1995—2011. Lt. Med. Corps, Greek Army, 1963—64. Mem.: Am. Fertility Soc., European Acad. Andrology (treas. 1998—2002), Hellenic Acad. Andrology (pres. 1985—87), Am. Soc. Endocrinology, Brit. Soc. Endocrinology, Hellenic Soc. Endocrinology. Office: 98 Vas Sophias Ave 11528 Athens Greece Office Phone: 30210 7705394. Business E-Mail: adamdi@otenet.gr.

ADAMS, CHRISTOPHER D., pharmacist; b. Dighton, Mass., June 30, 1979; PharmD, Northeastern U., 2004. Clin. pharmacy specialist Brigham and Women's Hosp., 2004—. Adj. prof. Northeastern U. and Mass. Coll. Pharmacy and Allied Health Scis., 2005—11. Mem.: MSHP, ASHP, ACCP. Avocations: hiking, aviation. Office: 75 Francis St L2 Central Pharmacy Boston MA 02115 Business E-Mail: cdadams@partners.org.

ADAMS, CLINTON E., dean; BS in Chemistry, Baldwin-Wallace Coll., Ohio, 1972; DO, Chgo. Coll. Osteo. Medicine, 1976; MPA emphasis in Healthcare, U. Okla., 1998; LHD (hon.), Western U. of Health Sciences, 2005. Rotating internship Doctors Hosp., Columbus, Ohio, 1977; resident in family practice Naval Hosp., Charleston, SC, 1981; resident in anesthesiology George Washington U. Med. Ctr., Washington, 1991; physician to US Congress, Washington; commdg. officer US Naval Hosp., Beaufort, SC, Naples, Italy, Naval Med. Ctr., Portsmouth, Va.; sr. med. adv. Joint Forces Command, NATO, Norfolk, Va.; med. officer US Atlantic Fleet; rear admiral US Navy Med. Corps.; dean Coll. Osteo. Medicine of Pacific Western U., Calif., 2005—. Office: Coll Osteopathic Med of Pacific Western Univ 309 E Second St Pomona CA 91766-1854 Office Phone: 909-469-5423. E-mail: cadams@westernu.edu. *

ADAMS, CORLYN HOLBROOK, nursing facility administrator; b. Beloit, Kans., Sept. 28, 1926; d. Charles Benjamin and Hazel Marian (Brokaw) Holbrook; m. Henry Robert Adams, Oct. 28, 1961; 1 child, Charles Paul. Grad., U. Kans., 1948. Lic. nursing facility adminstr. Clk. bd. edn. Beloit City Sch., Kans., 1945-48; adminstr. Stanford Conv. Ctr., Ft. Worth, 1973-79; adminstr., owner Four Nursing Homes, Ft. Worth, 1979-84. Contbr.: Pioneer Women of Faith and Fortitude, Vol. IV; author: The Jose Family, 1994, Glen Elder Family History Book; contbr. Women of Faith and Fortitude, 1998, New England Ancestors, Vol. 3, No. 4; author: Family Chronicles, 1998; contbr. Family Chronicle, 2000; contbr.: Glen Elder History Book, contbr.: Journal of a Georgia Woman 1870-1872, rsch.: novels Jour. of a Ga. Woman, 1870-1872/ edited by S. Kitrell Rushing, contbr.: novel New England Ancestors, Negs vol. 3; co-author: The Brokaw-Smith Family Story; contbr. 500 Brickwall Solutions, 2003. Mem. Order of Ea. Star, DAR, Nat. Soc. New England Women (sec. 1975), Nat. Hugenot Soc., Gen. Soc. Mayflower Descendents, Daus. of Utah Pioneers. Republican. Avocations: genealogy, music-playing piano.

ADAMS, DAVID H., cardiac surgeon, educator; b. Jan. 29, 1957; BS, Duke U., Durham, NC, 1979, MD, 1983. Diplomate Am. Bd. Thoracic Surgery, Am. Bd. Surgery, lic. Mass., NY. Intern gen. surgery Brigham & Women's Hosp., Boston, 1983—84, resident gen. surgery, 1984—86, sr. resident, 1988—90, resident cardiothoracic surgery, 1990—92; clin. fellow surgery Harvard Med. Sch., Boston, 1983—86, 1988—92, rsch. fellow pathology, 1986—88, asst. prof. surgery, 1992—99, assoc. prof. surgery, 1999—2001; Marie-Josée & Henry R. Kravis endowed prof. cardiothoracic surgery Mt. Sinai Med. Ctr., NYC, 2002—, chmn. dept. cardiothoracic surgery, 2002—. Fellow cardiothoracic unit Harefield Hosp., London, 1992; hon. prof. surgery Capital U. Med. Scis., Beijing, 2000; sr. cons. Edwards Lifescis. Corp., Irvine, Calif., 2001—; co-dir. ann. heart valve summit Am. Coll. Cardiology. Mem. editl. bd. Graft, 1998—, Annals of Thoracic Surgery, 2002—, Jour. Heart Valve Disease, 2002—; contbr. articles to profl. jour. Vis. surgeon Chain of Hope Cardiac Surg. Prog., Kingston, Jamaica, 1997; med. dir. Project HOPE Coronary Artery Disease Edn. Prog., China, 1998—. Recipient Nat. Rsch. Svc. award, NIH, 1987; named one of Best Doc.'s for Thoracic Surgery, NY Mag., 2002—07, Top 100 Minimally Invasive Surgeons, 2006; scholar Internat. Coll. Surgeons, 1981; Paul Dudley White Rsch. fellow, Am. Heart Assn., 1986, Alton Ochner Rsch. scholar, Am. Assn. Thoracic Surgery, 1992. Mem.: ACS, AMA, NY Soc. Thoracic Surgery, Mass. Soc. Thoracic Surgery, Soc. Heart Valve Disease, Thoracic Surgery Directors Assn., Am. Assn. Thoracic Surgery, Transplantation Soc., Soc. Thoracic Surgeons, Am. Soc. Transplant Surgeons, Mass. Med. Soc., Internat. Soc. Heart & Lung Transplantation, Cardiac Surgery Biology Club, Alpha Omega Alpha. Achievements include 3 patents in field. Office: Mt Sinai Med Ctr Dept Cardiothoracic Surgery 1190 Fifth Ave New York NY 10029 Office Phone: 212-659-6820. Office Fax: 212-659-6818. E-mail: david.adams@mountsinai.org.

ADAMS, DONALD E., physiatrist; s. Robert Reith and Marlene Beth Adams; m. Theresa Ann Orturo, June 14, 1998; children: Jacob, Elizabeth, Jackson, Allison. BS in Biochemistry, Pacific Union Coll., Angwin, Calif., 1993; MD, Loma Linda U., Calif., 1997. Diplomate Am. Bd. Phys. Medicine and Rehab., Am. Bd. Electrodiagnostic Medicine. Internship San Bernardino County Med. Ctr., 1997—98; residency divsn. phys. medicine & rehab. U. Utah, 1998—2001, chief resident Slat Lake City, 2001—02; ptnr., attending Okla. Sports Sci. & Orhtop., Oklahoma City, 2003—. Asst. physician N. Pacific Union Conf., Mindinao, Philippines, 1997, med. dir., Zambia, 99; mem. exec. com. N.W. Surg. Hosp., Oklahoma City, 2005—. Mem.: Internat. Spine Intervention Soc., Am. Soc. Intervention Pain Physicians, Am. Acad. Phys. Medicine and Rehab. Seventh-Day Adventist. Office: Physicians Group 1616 S Kelly Edmond OK 73013

ADAMS, EDGAR HARVEY, epidemiologist; b. Meriden, Conn., Dec. 10, 1940; BS in Pharmacy, Fordham U., 1963; ScD, Johns Hiopkins Sch. Pub. Health, 1988; MS in Pharmacology, Purdue U., 1966. With Nat. Inst. Drug Abuse, 1974—87, dir. divsn. epidemiology and prevention rsch., 1987—90; v.p. to sr. v.p. Gordon S. Black Corp., 1991—99; sr. v.p. clin. rsch. and risk mgmt. Harris Interactive, 1999—2005; exec. dir. epidemiology Covance, 2005—. US rep., advisor Pompidou Group Experts Epidemiology, Coun. Europe, 1984—91; epidemiology expert Am. Del. UN Internat. Conf. Drug Abuse and Illicit Trafficing, Vienna, 1987; sci. adv. bd. Researched Abuse Diversion and Addiction Related Surveillance, Denver Health Sys., 2001—; faculty Pharm. Edn. and Rsch. Inst., Global Pharmacovigilance Course, 2009—; ret. commd. officer USPHS. Decorated Outstanding Svc. medal USPHS, Commendation medal, Unit Commendation medal. Mem.: Internat. Soc. Pharmacoepidemiology, Coll. Problems Drug Dependence, Commd. Officers Assn. Avocations: golf, bicycling, kayaking. Home: 218 Sayre Dr Princeton NJ 08540 Office Phone: 609-452-4827. Personal E-mail: ehadams@comcast.net.

ADAMS, FORREST H., retired pediatrician; b. Mpls., Sept. 20, 1919; s. Edward Forrest Adams and Helen Lea Anderson; m. Joan Bloch, Apr. 28, 1969; children: Judd, Scott, Mark, Gregg, Eric, Brent, Kurt, Lynn. Student, Johns Hopkins U., Balt., 1937—38; BA, U. Minn., Mpls., 1941, MB, 1943, MD, 1944, MS, 1949. Diplomate Am. Bd. Pediats., 1948. Intern pediats. U. Minn. Hosp., Mpls., 1943—44, resident pediats., 1944—46; fellow pediats. U. Minn. Nat. Rsch. Coun., Mpls., 1948—49; instr. pediats. U. Minn., Mpls., 1948—49, asst. prof. pediats., 1949—52, dir. pediat. heart clinic, 1951—52; asst. dir. Crippled Children's Program, St. Paul, 1949—50; physician-in-charge Sister Elizabeth Kenny Inst., Mpls., 1949—50; assoc. physician pediats. Mpls. Gen. Hosp., 1949—50, chief. pediats., 1950—52; assoc. prof. pediats. UCLA, 1952—58, acting chmn. dept. pediats., 1958—59, 1964—65, vice-chmn. dept. pediats., 1962—64, head divsn. cardiology, 1958—76, prof. pediats, 1958—78, emeritus prof. pediats., 1978—. Cons. cardiology State Bd. Pub. Health, Calif., 1963—78; cons. office surgeon gen. USPHS, 1965—69; mem. med. appraisal team Vietnam Pres. Lyndon Johnson, 1967; acad, senate UCLA, 1968—70; dir. rsch. and edn. Pediat. Caridology Med. Group Inc., San Diego, 1983—84; dir. rsch. Children's Hosp. and Health Ctr., San Diego, 1984—85; staff mem. Scripps Clinic and Rsch. Found., La Jolla, Calif., 1984—85; cons. North County Health Svcs., San Diego, 1992—99; lectr. in field. Goodwill amb. US State Dept. Cultural Exchange Program, 1964—71; mem. adv. com. Pub. Employees Retirement Sys. Calif., 1984—91, chmn., 1989—91; mem. bd. dirs. Fairbanks Ranch Cmty Svcs. Dist., 1992—96. Lt. med. corp USN, 1946—48. Recipient Career Rsch. award, US Pub. Health Svc., 1962—67, Vol. Svc. award, North County Health Svcs., San Diego, 1996, Diehl award, U. Minn. Med. Sch., 2009. Master: Am. Coll. Cardiology (chmn. sci. program 1966, mem. credentials com. 1966—70, trustee 1966—75, v.p. 1968—69, pres.-elect 1970—71, pres. 1971—72, Founder's award, Am. Acad. Pediat. 2000); fellow: Philippine Coll. Cardiology (hon.), Am. Heart Assn. (hon.; mem. exec. com. coun. rheumatic fever and congenital heart disease 1961—64, mem. adult and pediat. cardiology rsch. study com. 1967—69, coun. clin. cardiology); mem.: Assn. European Pediat. Cardiologists, Calif. Soc. Pediat. Cardiology, Am. Pediat. Soc., Spanish Soc. Cardiology (hon.), Venezuelan Soc. Cardiology (hon.), Peruvian Soc. Cardiology (hon.), Western Soc. Pediat. Rsch. (sec. 1953—54, coun. mem. 1954—57, v.p. 1961—62, pres. 1962—63), Soc. Pediat. Rsch. (coun. mem. 1960—62), Am. Acad. Pediats. (chmn. com. residency fellows 1961—63, coun. mem. section cardiology 1961—63).

ADAMS, H. RICHARD, dean; BS in Vet. Sci., Tex. A&M U., DVM in Vet. Medicine; PhD in Pharmacology, U. Pitts. Chmn. univ.-wide PhD grad. program in physiology area U. Mo., Columbia, 1986—90; prof. dept. pharmacology U. Mo.-Columbia Sch. Medicine, Columbia, 1986—98; assoc. dir. Dalton Rsch. Ctr. U. Mo.-Columbia, Columbia, 1989—92; chmn. dept. vet. biomed. scis. U. Mo.-Columbia Coll. Vet. Medicine, Columbia, 1984—92, interim dean, 1992—93, dean, 1993—98, Tex. A&M U. Coll. Vet. Medicine, 1998—. Contbr. articles to profl. jours. Recipient H. Richard Adams Conf. Ctr., U. Mo. named in his honor, Resolution of Appreciation, Mo. State Ho. Reps., 1998; named Hon. Diplomate in Emergency and Critical Care, Am. Coll. Vet. Emergency and Critical Care, 1998. Mem.: Am. Acad. Vet. Pharmacology and Therapeutics, Am. Assn. for Accreditation Lab. Animal Care, Am. Physiological Soc., Am. Soc. Vet. Pharmacology and Therapeutics, Am. Soc. Pharmacology and Exptl. Therapeutics, Am. Vet. Med. Assn., Am. Soc. Vet. Physiology and Pharmacology, Vet. Emergency and Critical Care Soc. (Robert Knowles lectr. and keynote spkr. 1994), Soc. for Exptl. Biology and Medicine (keynote spkr. ann. meeting 1985), Shock Soc. (pres.-elect, pres. 1993—94), Mo. Vet. Med. Assn. (Mo. Vet. of Yr. 1997), Am. Coll. Vet. Emergency and Critical Care (hon. diplomate in emergency and critical care 1998), Sigma Xi. Office: Tex A&M U Coll Vet Medicine Ste 101 VMA College Station TX 77843-4461

ADAMS, JAMES FREDERICK, psychologist, academic administrator, educator; b. Andong, Korea, Dec. 27, 1927; s. Benjamin Nyce and Phyllis Irene (Taylor) A.; m. Carol Ann Wagner, Jan. 17, 1980; children— James Edward, Dorothy Lee Adams Vanderhorst, Robert Benjamin. BA In Psychology, U. Calif.-Berkeley, 1950; Ed.M. in Counseling and Psychology, Temple U., 1951; PhD in Exptl. Psychology, Wash. State U., 1959. Cert. psychologist, Wash., Pa.; lic. psychologist, Pa. Psychometrician Measurement and Research Ctr., Temple U., Phila., 1951-52; asst. prof. psychology Whitworth Coll., Spokane, Wash., 1952-55; teaching and research asst. State U. Wash., 1955-57; research assoc. Miami U., Oxford, Ohio, 1957-59; asst. prof. psychology Coll. Liberal Arts, Temple U., 1959-62, assoc. prof., 1962-66, prof., 1966-80, chmn. dept. counseling psychology, 1969-72; vis. prof. psychology Coll. Soc. Scis., U. P.R., Rio Piedras, 1963-64, Coll. Scis., Cath. U., Ponce, PR, 1971-72; chmn. dept. counseling psychology Coll. Edn., Temple U., 1973-77, coord. divsn. ednl. psychology, 1974-76; grad. dean, prof. psychology Grad. Coll., U. Nev., Las Vegas, 1980-85; acad. (sr.) v.p. Longwood Coll., Farmville, Va., 1985-86. Author: Problems in Counseling: A Case Study Approach, 1962, Instructors Manual for Understanding Adolescence, 1969; (exhbn. catalogue with J. D. Selig) Colonial Spanish Art of the Americas, 1976; (comml. pamphlet with C. L. Davis) The Use of the Vu-graph as an Instructional Aid, 1960; editor: Counseling and Guidance: A Summary View, 1965, Understanding Adolescence: Current Developments in Adolescent Psychology, 1968, 4th edit., 1980, Human Behavior in a Changing Society, 1973, Songs that had to be Sung (by B. N. Adams), 1979; contbr. chpts., articles, tests and book revs. to profl. publs. Donor James F. Adams Endowment Wash. State U., Pullman, 2003. Served to cpl. USMC, 1945—46. Recipient Alexander Meiklejohn award AAUP, 1984; James McKean Cattell Rsch. Fund grantee Miami U., Oxford, Ohio, 1958, Bolton Fund Rsch. grant Temple U., 1960, 62, Faculty Rsch. grant Temple U., 1961, 63, Commonwealth of Pa. Rsch. grant Temple U., 1969-72, Summer Rsch. fellow Temple U., 1979; U. Munich scholar, 1955; named James F. Adams scholarship U. Nev., Las Vegas. Fellow Am. Psychol. Assn. (divs. 26, 17); mem. Eastern Psychol. Assn., Western Psychol. Assn., Interam. Soc. Psychology, Sigma Xi, Psi Chi

ADAMS, JAMES THOMAS, surgeon; b. Rochester, NY, Mar. 28, 1930; s. Thomas and Sarah A.; m. Jacqueline K. Stemmler, July 7, 1952; children: Pamela, Mark, Sari Lynn. AB, Washington U., St. Louis, 1951, MD, 1955. Intern, then resident in surgery Barnes Hosp., St. Louis, 1955-60; mem. faculty U. Rochester Med. Sch., 1962—, prof. surgery, 1977—. Author papers in field, chpts. in books. Served as officer M.C. USAR, 1960-62. Mem. Am. Surg. Assn., Soc. Internat. de Chirurgie, Soc. U. Surgeons, Central Surg. Assn., Soc. Vascular Surgery, Am. Gastroenterol. Assn., Soc. Surgery Alimentary Tract, Am. Assn. Surgery Trauma, Phi Beta Kappa, Sigma Xi, Alpha Omega Alpha. Clubs. Oak Hill Country (Rochester). Achievements include co-designing inferior vena cava clip. Office Phone: 585-275-2726. Personal E-mail: jadams06@rochester.rr.com. *

ADAMS, JENNIFER, medical products executive; MBA, Northwestern U., 1998. Office supplies sales; with Deerfield Med. Supplies, Chgo.; Joined Baxter International, Inc., Chgo., 1994, v.p., sales & transfusion therapies, 2002—. Named one of 40 Under Forty, Crain's Bus. Chgo., 2005. Avocations: running sprint triathlons, running marathons. Office: Baxter International Inc One Baxter Pky Deerfield IL 60015 Office Phone: 847-948-2000. Office Fax: 847-948-3642.

ADAMS, JULIAN TIMOTHY, psychologist; s. Julian and Bertha Ozella Adams; m. Sharlene Frances Bunge, Nov. 15, 1992; m. Martha Jo House, Mar. 22, 1975 (div. July 0, 1990); children: Julian Mclain, Thomas Daniel, Timothy James, Pamela Rose Bunge-Harrington, Todd Bunge. BS, Columbus Coll., Ga., 1974—76; MA, U. W. Fla., Pensacola, 1983—84; PsyD, Forest Inst. Profl. Psychology, Springfield, Mo., 1987—91; diploma, Naval War Coll., RI, 1987; diploma marine officer basic course, The Basic Sch., Va., 1976; cert. in Def. Ops., Nuc., Biol., Chem., Def. Staff and Officer, Camp Geiger, NC, 1977; cert. in Clin. Psychology Internship Program, Walter Reed Army Med. Ctr., Washington, DC, 1990. Diplomate Am. Bd. Forensic Examiners, Am. Bd. Forensic Medicine, 1996, in forensic neuropsychology Am. Bd. Psychol. Specialties, 1997, bd. cert. forensic examiner 1995; lic. clin. psychologist Ariz., 1991, Va., 1995. Clin. psychologist U.S. Army, 1989—94; CEO Psychol. Assessments, Interventions and Resources, Inc., Annandale, Va., 1994—2002; clin. psychologist Ednl. and Devel. Intervention Services, U. S. Army Hosp., Heidelberg, Germany, 2002—; rehab. psychologist Veterans Adminstrn., Washington, 2002. Adv. bd. mem. Am. Bd. Psychol. Specialties, 1996—99. Vol. Counselor FavorHouse, Pensacola, Fla., 1983—85; rape crisis counselor Lakeview Ctr. Inc., Pensacola, Fla., 1983—86, helpline counselor, 1983—86; auxillary police officer Fairfax County Police Dept., Va., 1996—99; vol. coord., elder Mission and Out Reach, Annandale, Va., 1997—98; mem. Shriners, 1992—. With USMCR, 1972—81, with USNR, 1981—89, with USAR, 1989—95. Fellow: Nat. Bd. Certified Clin. Hypnotherapists, Am. Coll. Forensic Examiners, Washington D.C. Area Geriatric Edn. Consortium. Avocations: outdoor activities, travel, theater, golf, fly fishing. Home: CMR 442 Box 214 AE APO 09042 Germany Personal E-mail: dr.juliantadams@mindspring.com.

ADAMS, JULIE KAREN, psychologist; b. Portland, Oreg., Dec. 12, 1955; d. Allen Hays and Susanna Angelina (Meyers) A. B, Willamette U., 1977; M, Ctrl. Wash. U., 1982; cert. bus. adminstrn., U. Wash., 1986; D, Pacific U., 1992; MS, Columbia U., 2000. Lic. clin. psychologist; cert. counselor, sch. psychologist, Wash. Sch. psychologist Highline Sch. Dist., Seattle, 1987—90; psychology intern Elmcrest Psychiat. Hosp., Portland, Conn., 1990, clinician, 1991; rsch. asst. Yale U., New Haven, 1991; clinician Advanced Clin. Svcs., Seattle, 1991—93; postdoctoral fellow U. Wash., Seattle, 1991—93; acad. counselor Johns Hopkins U., Balt., 1993; behavior intervention specialist Edmonds Sch. Dist., Wash., 1993—94, Marysville Sch. Dist., Wash., 1994—99; instr. Seattle U., 1995—99. Guest spkr. in field to profl. assns., also Pacific U., U. Wash., U. Oreg., 1989—. Freelance writer: Psychology Today Mag., reporter: Wash. Psychologist Newsletter; contbr. (book chpt.) Women in Communication; contbr. articles to profl. jours. Mem. tng. com., kids week com., nursing home com., pub. policy com. Jr. League Seattle, 1988—, bd. dirs. 2004-05; health care rsrch. Wash. State Legis., Olympia, 1993; campaigner Bush for Pres., Seattle, 1988, 92; rsch. asst. to state senator Oreg. State Legis., Salem, 1985; press page nat. conv. Rep. Nat. Com., Detroit, 1980; student grad. v.p., faculty rep. com. Pacific U. Sch. Profl. Psychology, 1989-90 Mem. APA (health psychology com. student rep. 1992-93), Wash. Psychol. Assn. (coun. reps.), Wash. State Psychol. Assn. Coun., Soc. Profl. Journalists, Willamette U. Alumni Assn. (bd. dirs. 1983-88), Vols. for Outdoor Wash. (bd. dirs. 1986-87), City Club Seattle (membership com. 1986-88), Psi Chi, Beta Alpha Gamma Avocations: writing, skiing, history, reading, travel. Home: 16116 Ash Way #405 Lynnwood WA 98037

ADAMS, LAVONNE MARILYN BECK, critical care nurse, educator; b. Bridgeport, Conn., Feb. 22, 1965; d. Adolf and Hazel B. (Henderson) Beck. ASN, Kettering Coll. Med. Arts, 1985; BSN, Wright State U., 1988; MSN, Andrews U., 1992, PhD, 2003. CCRN. Staff nurse Kettering Med. Ctr., Ohio, 1985-89, resource staff nurse, 1989-95, instr. in nursing, 1989-92; asst. prof. nursing Kettering Coll. Med. Arts, 1992—99, Southwestern Adventist U., Keene, Tex., 1999—2003, assoc. prof., 2003—04; asst. prof. nursing Harris Coll. Nursing and Health Scis. Tex. Christian U., Ft. Worth, 2004—10, assoc. prof., 2010—; PRN staff nurse Huguley Mem. Hosp., 2002—. Vol. Adventist Comty. Svcs.Disaster Response, 2004—, ARC, 2005—. Mem.: Am. Assn. Critical Care Nurses, Pi Lambda Theta, Sigma Theta Tau, Phi Kappa Phi. Avocations: music, travel. Home: 7000 Welch Ct Fort Worth TX 76133-6726 Office: Tex Christian U Harris Coll Nursing and Health Scis TCU Box 298620 Fort Worth TX 76129

ADAMS, REBECCA LOUISE CLAIRE, hematologist; b. Rockhampton, Australia, Feb. 1, 1977; MBBS, U. Queensland, 2004. Haematology registrar Pathology Queensland, 2007—. Grantee Registrar Clin. Cancer Rsch. Fellowship, Princess Alexandra Cancer Collaborative Group. Mem.: HSANZ (Registrar Travel grant). Avocations: reading, music, cooking. Home: 40 Cascade Dr Queensland Forest Lake 4078 Australia Home Phone: 0738798863. Business E-Mail: rebecca_l_adams@health.qld.gov.au.

ADAMS, RUSSELL LEE, neuropsychologist; b. Jefferson, Tex., Mar. 2, 1941; s. Irby Ray and Verda Mae Adams; m. Carolyn Sue Pulley, Aug. 8, 1964; children: David Lee, Scott Russell. BBA, Tex. A&M U., College Station, 1962; PhD, U. Tex., Austin, 1967. Diplomate Am. Bd. Clin. Neuropsychology. Assoc. prof. dept. psychiatry U. Tex. Health Scis. Ctr., San Antonio, 1969—78; assoc. prof. U. Okla. Health Scis. Ctr., Oklahoma City, 1978—82, prof., 1978—, dir. psychology internship program, 1978—, dir. postdoctoral neuropsychology fellowship program, 1982—. Co-author: Neuropsychology In Clinical Practice; mem. editl. bd numerous profl. jours., 1980—2006; contbr. articles to profl. jours. Adminstr. Scott Russell Adams Meml. Scholarship Baylor U., Waco, Tex., 1990—2006. Capt. US Army, 1967—69. Recipient Gordon Deckert award for Sustained Excellence In Edn., U. Okla. Health Scis. Ctr., 1989, 2002. Fellow: APA (various positions 1980—2006), Nat. Acad. Neuropsychology (com. chair 1980—2006). Baptist. Avocations: travel, reading. Office: U Okla Health Scis Ctr 920 Stanton L Young Blvd Oklahoma City OK 73104 Office Phone: 405-271-8801. Office Fax: 405-271-8802. Business E-Mail: russell-adams@ouhsc.edu.

ADAMS, SARAH VIRGINIA, psychotherapist, family counselor; b. San Francisco, Oct. 23, 1955; d. Marco Tulio and Helen (Jorge) Zea; children: Mark Vincent, Elena Giselle, Johnathan Richard. BA, Calif. State U., Long Beach, 1978, MS in Psychology, 1980; MA in Psychology, Fuller Sem., Pasadena, 1996, MA in Christian Leadership, 1997; PsyD in Clin. Psychology, Fuller Sem., 2000. Lic. marriage, family, child counseling; cert. EMDR, 2010. Tutor math. and sci., Montebello, Calif., 1979-82; behavioral specialist Cross Cultural Psychol. Corp., LA, 1979-80; psychol. asst. Legal Psychology, LA, 1980-82, Eisner Psychol. Assocs., LA, 1982-83; assoc. dir. Legal Psychodiagnosis and Forensic Psychology, LA, 1982-83; adminstrv. dir. Diagnostic Clinic, Calif., 1983-85; dir. Diagnostic Clinic of West Covina, Calif., 1985-87; owner Adams Family Counseling Inc., Calif., 1987—; with Health Group Psychol. Svcs., 1994—; domestic violence counselor Baldwin Park Counseling, 1996—2001; battered wives counselor Wings, 1996—2002; facilitator, vol., 1995—; facilitator in domestic violence Redlands, 2002—; program dir. Alternative Choices Together Batterers Counselor, 2002—. Tchr. piano, Montebello, 1973-84; ins. agent Am. Mut. Life Ins., Des Moines, 1982-84; DV counselor Baldwin Park Counseling, 1996-2001, Wings-Shelter for Battered Wives, 1996-, ALternatives Choices Together, Treatment Ctr. Batterers, 2002-. Fellow Am. Assn. Marriage and Family Therapists, Am. Psychol. Assn.; mem. NAFE, Calif. Assn. Marriage and Family Therapists, Calif. State Psychol. Assn., Calif. Soc. Indsl. Medicine and Surgery, Western Psychol. Assn., Psi Chi, Pi Delta Phi. Republican. Roman Catholic. Avocations: piano, creative writing, drawing, collecting coins. Office: 969 S Village Oaks Dr #201 Covina CA 91724 Home Phone: 626-331-1845. Personal E-mail: glenna@earthlink.net.

ADAMS, SHARON BUTLER, minister, philosopher, researcher; b. Chgo., Oct. 30, 1949; d. Lionel Augustus and Clara Bernice Butler; m. Vernon McFadden Jr., June 13, 1968 (div. Oct. 1977); children: Vernon McFadden III, Aleceia Marie McFadden. Ordained min. African-Am. Universal Ministry. Engring. technician Servitron, Baton Rouge, 1976—78; instr. Coml. Bus. Coll, Baton Rouge, 1978—80; project mgr. Minority Engrs. La., Baton Rouge, 1980—86; cleric adminstr. Baton Rouge African-Am. Cath. Cong., 1997—98, cleric adminstr., So. Region Baton Rouge, 1998—99; interim pastor Imani Temple, Baton Rouge, 1998—99; pastor Ch. of the Living God, Baton Rouge, 1999—2002, bus. cons., 2003—, cert. profl. counselor, 2004—. Advisor Kwanzaa celebration A-A Universal Apostolic Ministry, Baton Rouge, 1999—; dir. Females in Ministry, Baton Rouge, 1999—; spiritual adv. Jazz and Heritage Festival, New Orleans, 2001—; cons. NAACP, New Orleans, 2001; advisor La. Dept. of Environ. Quality, 1990; owner ADHD-Alarm, 2004—; lectr. in field. Author to newspapers and jours. Panelist New Orleans Jazz & Heritage Festival, 2002, Jazz Festival, 2003; bd. dirs. Cmty. Devel. Project, Baton Rouge, 1998, La. Dem. Project, Baton Rouge, 2000. Recipient Kwanazz Celebration award, Mayor & Metr. Coun. of Baton Rouge, 2001. Mem.: Internat. Black Environ. & Econ. Justice, Soc. Am. Music. Avocations: reading, sewing, music. E-mail: asharon@bellsouth.net.

ADAMS, THOMAS L., medical association administrator; AB in History, Lenoir Rhyne Coll., 1973, DHL (hon.), 2002; cert., U. Del., 1986. Staff asst. Senator Robert Morgan U.S. Senate, Washington, 1973—76; exec. asst. Congressman Lamar Gudger U.S. Congress, Washington, 1976—77; spl. asst. to the fed. co-chmn. Appalachian Regional Commn., Washington, 1977—78; dir. dept. govtl. affairs N.C. Med. Soc., Raleigh, 1978—83; dir. Office Govtl. Affairs Am. Soc. Anesthesiologists, Washington, 1983—86; exec. v.p., CEO State Med. Soc. Wis., Madison, 1986—96; pres., CEO Med. Group Mgmt. Assn., Denver, 1996—98, Washington, 1996—98; exec. dir. Am. Soc. Plastic Surgeons, Arlington Heights, Ill., 1999—2001; CEO Assn. Clin. Rsch. Profls., Washington, 2001—. Mem. adv. com. AMA Exec. V.p., 1993—96; mem. adv. com. human resource protections U.S. Sec. Office HHS, 2004—. Contbr. articles to profl. jours. Active U.S. Trade Mission to Japan, 1978; chair State Coun. on Health Programs for the Uninsured, Wis., 1989—92; mem. capital campaign cabinet Salvation Army, Madison, Wis., 1994; divsn. chair United Way Dane County, 1994; mem. furnishings com. Monona Terr. Conv. Ctr., 1995; mem. adv. bd. Hawaii Conv. and Visitor Bur., 2001—. With N.C. Air Nat. Guard, 1977. Named one of 25 most influential people in Wis., Madison Mag., 1995. Mem.: Profl. Conv. Mgmt. Assn., Assn. Forum Chgo., Am. Soc. Assn. Execs. (cert. assn. exec.), Am. Assn. Med. Soc. Execs. Office: ACRP Ste 800 500 Montgomery St Alexandria VA 22314 Home: 2015 Trout Valley Dr Champaign IL 61822-9775

ADAMS, WAYNE VERDUN, pediatric psychologist, educator; b. Rhinebeck, NY, Feb. 24, 1945; s. John Joseph and Lorena Pearl (Munroe) A.; m. Nora Lee Swindler, June 12, 1971; children: Jennifer, Elizabeth. BA, Houghton Coll., 1966; MA, Syracuse U., 1969, PhD, 1970; postgrad., U. NC, 1975. Diplomate Am. Bd. Profl. Psychology (hon.); lic. psychologist, NY, Oreg. Asst. prof. Colgate U., Hamilton, NY, 1970-75; chief psychologist Alfred I. DuPont Inst., Wilmington, Del., 1976-86; dir. divsn. psychology, dept. pediat. DuPont Hosp. for Children (formerly Alfred I. DuPont Inst.), Wilmington, 1987-99; mem. Del. Bd. Licensure in Psychology, 1983-86, bd. pres., 1986; assoc. prof. pediat. Thomas Jefferson Coll. Medicine, Phila., 1995-99; prof. psychology George Fox U., Newberg, Oreg., 1999—, chair grad. dept. clin. psychology, 2001—11. Grant reviewer NIH, 1999—2006; vis. prof. Wuhan U., China, 2004, 06, editl. bd. mem., psychological Assessment, 2010-. Cons. editor Jour. Pediatric Psychology, 1980-83, guest reviewer, 1984—; co-author 5 nationally used psychol. tests in field; contbr. over 25 articles to profl. jours. Scholar, Fulbright Found., 2006—07. Fellow APA, Nat. Acad. Neuropsychology; mem. Soc. Pediatric Psychology, Del. Psychol. Assn. (exec. com. 1979-82, pres. 1981-82), Oreg. Psychol. Assn. Office: George Fox U Grad Dept Clin Psychology Box 6141 414 N Meridian St Newberg OR 97132-2697

ADAMS, WILLIAM PETER, JR., plastic surgeon, educator; b. Feb. 14, 1965; BS with honors, Princeton U., NJ; MD, Vanderbilt U. Med. Sch., Nashville, 1991. Diplomate Am. Bd. Plastic Surgery. Intern gen. surgery U. Tex. Southwestern Med. Ctr., Dallas, 1991—92, resident gen. surgery, 1992—94, plastic surgery fellow, 1994—95, resident plastic surgery, 1995—97, asst. prof. dept. plastic surgery, 1997—2000, assoc. clin. prof. dept. plastic surgery, 2001—; pvt. practice Dallas, 2001—. Co-editor: (textbook) Dallas Rhinoplasty; editl. bd. Selected Readings in Plastic Surgery; contbr. articles to profl. jours., chapters to books. Recipient Excellence in Rsch. award, U. Tex. Southwestern Dept. Plastic Surgery, 1997, Excellence in Tchg. award, 1997, Faculty Excellence award, 2001, Faculty Tchg. award, 2005; named Clinician of Yr., 1998. Mem.: Dallas Soc. Plastic Surgeons, Tex. Soc. Plastic Surgery, Dallas County Med. Soc., Am. Soc. Aesthetic Plastic Surgery, Am. Soc. Plastic & Reconstructive Surgeons. Achievements include development of a new irrigant for use in clinical breast implant surgery that may make breast enlargement and breast reconstruction safer. Office: 2801 Lemmon Ave W Ste 300 Dallas TX 75204 also: 5600 W Lovers Ln Ste 212 Dallas TX 75209 Office Phone: 214-965-9885. E-mail: dr@dr-adams.com.

ADAMS-CAMPBELL, LUCILE L., epidemiologist, oncologist, educator; b. Washington; married; 2 children. BS in Biol. Sciences, Drexel U., 1977, MS in Biomedical Sci., 1979; PhD in Epidemiology, U. Pitts., 1983. Fellow U. Pitts., epidemiology dept.; dir. Howard U. Cancer Ctr., 1995—2008; assoc. dir. minority health and health disparities rsch. Georgetown U. Med. Ctr. Lombardi Comprehensive Cancer Ctr., Washington, 2008—, prof. oncology, 2008—. Primary investigator Boston U. Black Women's Health Study; adj. prof. epidemiology U. Pitts. Grad. Sch. Pub. Health; rsch. collaborator Gen. Hosp., Yaounde, Cameroon, U. Zimbobwe, U. Transkei, Caribbean Food and Nutrition Inst., Jamaica, Jamaica Cancer Soc., Med. Rsch. Coun., Cancer Assn. South Africa. Recipient Disting. Alumni Fellows award, U. Pitts., FDA Dep. Commr. Cmty. Svc. award, Searle Disting. Grad. award, McDonald's Black History Maker of Today award in Medicine; named Sigma Xi Nat. Lectr.; named to Washington DC Hall of Fame, 2009. Fellow: A. Coll. Epidemiology; mem.: Inst. Medicine.

ADAMSON, GEOFFREY DAVID, reproductive endocrinologist, surgeon; b. Ottawa, Ont., Can., Sept. 16, 1946; came to U.S., 1978, naturalized, 1986; s. Geoffrey Peter Adamson and Anne Marian Allan; m. Rosemary C. Oddie, Apr. 28, 1973; children: Stephanie, Rebecca, Eric. BSc with honors, Trinity Coll., Toronto, Can., 1969; MD, U. Toronto, 1973. Diplomate Am. Bd. Ob-Gyn., Am. Bd. Laser Surgery; cert. Bd. Reproductive Endocrinology. Resident in ob-gyn. Toronto Gen. Hosp., 1973-77, fellow in ob-gyn., 1977-78; fellow reproductive endocrinology Stanford U. Med. Ctr., Calif., 1978-80; practice medicine specializing in infertility Los Gatos, Calif., 1980-84; instr. Stanford U. Sch. Medicine, 1980-84, clin. asst. prof. Calif., 1984-92, clin. assoc. prof., 1992—, clin. prof., 1995—; assoc. clin. prof. Sch. Medicine U. Calif., San Francisco, 1992—; founder, chmn., CEO Advanced Reproductive Care Inc., Palo Alto, Calif., 1997—. Tech. adviser WHO, 2003—. Editor: (textbook) Endoscopic Management of Gynecologic Disease, 1996, Modern Management of Endometriosis, 2005, Single Embryo Transfer, 2009; mem. editl. bd. Can. Doctor mag., 1977—83, Jour. Am. Assn. Gynecol. Laparoscopists, 1996—, Fertility and Sterility, 2000—03, mem. editl. adv. bd. Mid. East Fertility Soc., 2004—, mem. editl. bd. others; assoc. editor: Mid. E. Fertility Soc., 2004—. Recipient Spl. Congl. Recognition cert., US Congress, 2006; McLaughlin fellowship, Ont. Ministry of Health, 1977—78. Fellow ACS, Royal Coll. Surgeons Can., Am. Coll. Ob-Gyns.; mem. AAAS, AMA, Am. Assn. Gynecol. Laparoscopists (adv. bd., bd. trustees, sec., treas. 2002-03, v.p. 2003-04, exec. com. 2002-06, v.p. 2003-04, pres. 2004-05, past pres. 2005-06), Am. Gynecol. and Obstet. Soc., Am. Soc. Reproductive Medicine (com. mem., bd. dirs. 1997-99, 2000-03, exec. com., 2002-04, v.p., 2005-06, pres. elect 2006-07, pres. 2007—08, past pres. 2008-10), Soc. Reproductive Endocrinologists (charter), Soc. Reproductive Surgeons (charter, bd. dirs., sec., treas., v.p., pres., past pres.), Soc. Assisted Reproductive Tech. (treas., dir., v.p., pres., past pres. bd. dirs. 1991-05), Nat. Coalition Oversight of Assisted Reproductive Techs. (vice-chair 2001-03, chair 2003-05), Internat. Com. Monitoring Assisted Reproductive Techs. (sec.-treas. 2005-11, chair, 2011-), Internat. Fedn. Fertility Socs. (audit com. 2001-07, bd. dirs. 2007—), Internat. Fedn. Ob-gyn. (chair reproductive medicine com., 2009-), Pacific Coast Reproductive Soc. (dir., sec., v.p., pres., past pres., bd. dir. 1991-2001), Pacific NW Ob-Gyn Soc. (hon. life), Pacific Coast Ob-Gyn. Soc., Soc. Gynecologic Surgeons, San Francisco Gynecol. Soc. (past pres.), Soc. for Gynecologic Investigation, Bay Area Reproductive Endocrinologists Soc. (founding pres., hon. life), Gynecol. Laser Soc., N.Y. Acad. Scis., Shufelt Gynecol. Soc., Peninsula Gynecol. Soc. (past pres.), World Endometriosis Rsch. Found. (founding bd. mem. 2005-, pres. 2010-), Calif. Med. Assn., San Mateo County Med. Assn., Santa Clara County Med. Assn. (Outstanding Achievement in Medicine award 2006), Am. Fedn. Clin. Rsch., Nat. Resolve (bd. dirs. 1991-01, sec., treas., Lifetime Svc. award 1999), Can. Assn. Interns and Residents (hon. life, pres. 1977-79, bd. dirs. 1974-79, rep. AMA resident physician sect. 1978-79, rep. Can. Med. Protective Assn. 1975-78, rep. Can. Med. Assn. 1975-78, Disting. Svc. award 1980), Profl. Assn. Interns and Residents Ont. (bd. dirs. 1973-76, v.p. 1974-75, pres. 1975-76), Royal Coll. Physicians and Surgeons Can. (com. exams. 1977-80), Ont. Med. Assn. (sec. interns and residents sect. 1973-74). Avocations: hiking, ice hockey, skiing. Office: Fertility Physicians University N Calif 540 University Ave Ste 200 Palo Alto CA 94301

ADAMSON, JOHN WILLIAM, hematologist; b. Oakland, Calif., Dec. 28, 1936; s. John William and Florence Jean Adamson; m. Susan Elizabeth Wood, June 16, 1960; children: Cairn Elizabeth, Loch Rachael; m. Christine Fenyvest, Sept. 1, 1989. BA, U. Calif., Berkeley, 1958; MD, UCLA, 1962. Cert. Am. Bd. Internal Medicine, 1970. Intern, resident in medicine U. Wash. Med. Ctr., Seattle, 1962-64, clin. and rsch. fellow hematology, 1964-67, faculty, 1969-90, prof. hematology, 1978-90, head divsn. hematology, 1981-89; pres. NY Blood Ctr., NYC, 1989-97; dir. Lindsley F. Kimball Rsch. Inst., NYC, 1989-98; exec. v.p. rsch., dir. Blood Rsch. Inst./Blood Ctr.Southeastern Wis., Milw., 1998—2007; prof., head, divsn. hematology Med. Coll. Wis.; clin. prof. medicine U. Calif. San Diego, 2007—. Josiah Macy Jr. Found. scholar, vis. scientist Nuffield dept. clin. medicine, U. Oxford, Eng., faculty medicine, 1976-77. Author papers in field, chpts. in books. With USPHS, 1967-69. Recipient Rsch. Career Devel. award NIH, 1972-77, Rsch. grant, 1976-95. Fellow AAAS; mem. Am. Soc. Hematology (pres. 1995-96), Soc. for the Advancement of Blood Mgmt. (pres. 2005-07), Assn. Am. Physicians, Am. Soc. Clin. Investigation, Western Assn. Physicians. Office: Moores UCSD Cancer Ctr 3855 Health Sciences Dr La Jolla CA 92093 also: UCSD Dept Medicine 9111-E 9500 Gilman Dr La Jolla CA 92093-9111 Office Phone: 858-822-6276. Office Fax: 858-822-6288. E-mail: jadamson@ucsd.edu.

ADAMSON, RICHARD HENRY, pharmacologist; b. Council Bluffs, Iowa, Aug. 9, 1937; s. Holger Nels and Mary Caroline (Dengle) A.; m. M. Charlene Denham, Oct. 25, 1963, (dec. 2002); children: Kristin, Kara. BA, Drake U., 1957; MS, U. Iowa, 1959, PhD, 1961; MA, George Washington U., 1968. Fellow U. Iowa Coll. Medicine, Iowa City, 1958-61; commd. officer USPHS, NIH, Bethesda, Md., 1961-63; sr. investigator lab. chem. pharmacology Nat. Cancer Inst., Bethesda, Md., 1963-69, head pharmacology and exptl. therapeutics sec., 1969-73, acting chief lab. chem. pharmacology, 1973-76, chief lab. chem. pharmacology, 1976-81, dir. divsn. cancer etiology, 1981-94; v.p. sci. and tech. affairs Nat. Soft Drink Assn. (now Am. Beverage Assn.), Washington, 1994—2004; sr. sci. cons. Am. Beverage Assn., Washington, 2004—05; CEO TPN Assocs., LLC, Germantown, Md., 2005—. Lectr. physiology George Washington U., Washington, 1963-70; Fulbright vis. scientist St. Mary's Hosp. Med. Sch., London, 1965-66; sr. policy analyst Office Sci. and Tech. Policy Exec. Office of Pres., 1979-80 Author: numerous publs. in field; mem. editl. bd.: Cancer Treatment Reports, 1972-75, Xenobiotica, 1971-84, Cancer Research, 1980-87, Jour. Biolchem. Toxicology, 1984—1990, Regulatory Toxicology and Pharmacology, 1994—, Health and Environment Digest, 1986—2000, Japanese Jour. Cancer Research (Gann), 1986-96, In Vivo, 1990—2000, Teratogenesis, Carcinogenesis and Mutagenesis, 1991—2000. Recipient USPHS Superior Svc. award, 1976, 82, Spl. Achievement award EEO, 1982, Presdl. Meritorious Exec. Rank award, 1989, Toxicology Forum Anderson award, 1990, PHS Spl. Recognition award, 1992, Leadership for Combined Fed. Campaign award NIH, 1993, 94, Shubik Disting. Scientist award, Toxicology Forum, 2006 Mem. AAAS, Am. Assn. Cancer Rsch., Biochem. Soc., Am. Soc. Pharmacology and Exptl. Therapeutics, Soc. Toxicology (Lehman award 1989), Japanese Cancer Assn. (hon.), Internat. Soc. Beverage Technologists, Assn. Food and Drug Ofcls. (tech. forum). Office: TPN Associates LLC 13625 Esworthy Rd Germantown MD 20874-3319 Office Phone: 301-869-0249.

ADAMSON, ROBERT M., medical association administrator; b. Salt Lake City, Utah, Nov. 14, 1953; BS, U. Utah, 1976, MD, 1980. Pres. Adamson and Dembitsky Med. Corp., 2003—. Avocations: tennis, surfing, music. Office: 8008 Frost St San Diego CA 92123 Personal E-mail: robandtl@aol.com.

ADAN, JOSEPH I., child and adolescent psychiatrist; MD, U. Ctrl. Del Este, Dominican Republic, 1986. Diplomate Am. Bd. Psychiatry and Neurology, 2003. Resident psychiatry St. Vincents Med. Ctr., NYC, 1990—93; fellow child and adolescent psychiatry Mt. Sinai Med. Ctr., NYC, 1994—95; psychiatric cons.; med. dir. Charter facility Largo, Fla., 1997—2000; designated health authority Eckerd Camp Challenge; staff A&M Psychiatric Svcs. P.A. Office: A&M Psychiatric Services P.A. 1938 Soule Rd Clearwater FL 33759 Office Phone: 727-726-7442. Office Fax: 727-288-1111.

ADASHI, ELI Y., obstetrician, gynecologist, educator, former dean; m. Toni Adashi. MD, U. Tel Aviv, Israel, 1972. Diplomate Am. Bd. Obstetrics-Gynecology, Am. Bd. Reprodn. Endocrinology. Intern Met. Gen. Hosp., Tel Aviv, 1972-73; resident ob.-gyn. Tufts U. Sch.

Medicine, Boston, 1974-77; fellow reprodn. endocrinology Johns Hopkins U., Balt., 1977-78; fellow reprodn.-endocrinology U. Calif. San Diego, La Jolla, 1978-81; mem. med. staff U. Md. Hosp., Balt., 1981-96; prof. ob.-gyn., physiology U. Md., Balt., 1981-96; pvt. practice in ob.-gyn. Balt., 1981-96; chair dept. ob-gyn. U. Utah Health Sciences Ctr., Salt Lake City, 1996—2005, John A. Dixon prof.; dean medicine and biological sciences Brown U. Med. Sch., Providence, 2005—08, prof. biology. Mem. Inst. Medicine ((in conjunction with NRC) mem. adv. com. Human Embryonic Stem Cell Rsch., 2006), ACOG, Am. Fedn. Surgeons, Endocrine Surgeons, Soc. Gastroenterology. Office: Brown Univ Med Sch Box G-A1 Providence RI 02912 Office Phone: 401-863-3330. E-mail: Eli_Adashi@brown.edu.

ADCOCK, DAVID FILMORE, radiologist, educator; b. Columbia, SC, Sept. 19, 1938; s. David Filmore and Eloise (Daniel) A. BS, U. S.C., 1958, MPH, 1986; MD, Med. Coll. S.C., 1962. Diplomate Am. Bd. Radiology, Am. Bd. Nuclear Medicine, Am. Bd. Preventive Medicine. Asst. prof. radiology U. N.C.-Chapel Hill, 1970-72, assoc. prof., 1972-73; dir. nuclear medicine Richard Meml. Hosp., Columbia, 1974-79; prof., chmn. dept. radiology U. S.C.-Columbia, 1979—. Cons. in field Contbr. articles to profl. jours. Served as capt. U.S. Army, 1963-66. Fellow Am. Coll. Preventive Medicine; mem. Radiol. Soc. N.Am., Assn. Univ. Radiologists, Soc. Chmn. Acad. Radiology Depts., Alpha Omega Alpha. Office: U SC Sch Medicine Dept Radiology Columbia SC 29208-0001 Office Phone: 803-733-3295. Business E-Mail: david.adcock@uscmed.sc.edu.

ADDISON, WINNIFRED ALLEN, gynecologist, educator; b. Toccoa, Ga., May 24, 1934; s. Allen Richard and Cordelia (McCurry) A.; m. Sally Bender, Aug. 28, 1959; children: Rebecca Dee, Cynthia Ann, Amy Sue. BA, Duke U., 1956, MD, 1960. Diplomate Am. Bd. Ob-Gyn (examiner). Prof., dir. div. gynecology, residency coord. Duke U., Durham, N.C., 1976—. Contbr. articles to scientific jours. Served to capt. U.S. Army, 1965-67. Fellow Am. Coll. Obstetricians and Gynecologists; mem. S. Atlantic Assn. Obstetricians and Gynecologists, Soc. Gynecologic Surgeons, Bayard Ctr. Assn. Obstetricians and Gynecologists, N.C. Soc. Obststricians-Gynecologists. Republican. Episcopalian. Avocation: horseback riding. Home: PO Box 727 Hillsborough NC 27278-0727 Office: Duke Univ Med Ctr PO Box 3296 Durham NC 27715-3296 Home Phone: 919-732-2206; Office Phone: 919-684-3866. E-mail: addisonsa@embergmail.com.

ADDUCCI, JOSEPH EDWARD, obstetrician, gynecologist; b. Chgo., Dec. 1, 1934; s. Dominee Edward and Harriet Evelyn (Kneppreth) A.; m. Mary Ann Tiertje, 1958; children: Christopher, Gregory, Steven, Jessica, Tobias. BS, U. Ill., 1955; MD, Loyola U., Chgo., 1959. Diplomate Am. Bd. Ob-Gyn., Nat. Bd. Med. Examiners. Intern Cook County Hosp, Chgo., 1959-60; resident in ob-gyn Mt. Carmel Hosp., Detroit, 1960-64; practice medicine specializing in obstetrics and gynecology Williston, ND, 1996—; chmn. dept. ob-gyn. Mercy Hosp., 1994—2004; councillor ND Med. Assn., 2004—; med. dir. Trenton Indian Sprial Area, 2008—, Trenton Indian Seruce Arks, Treton Indian Svc. Area. Chief staff, chmn. obstetrics dept. Mercy Hosp., Williston, gov. bd., 1996, chmn. dept. surgery; clin. prof. U. ND Med. Sch., 1973—; gov. bd. Mercy Hosp. Cath. Health Corp.; mem. coun. Accreditation Coun. for Gynecologic Endoscopy, 1999—. Mem. ND Bd. Med. Examiners, 1974—, past chmn., project dir. Tri County Family Planning Svc.; past pres. Tri County Health Planning Coun.; governing bd. Mercy Hosp., Williston, ND With Med. Corps, AUS, 1964-66. Fellow Am. Soc. Abdominal Surgeons, ACS (regent ND 1990—), Am. Coll. Obstetrics and Gynecologists (sect. chmn. ND), Internat. Coll. Surgeons (regent 1972-74, 88-89), Am. Fertility Soc., Am. Assn. Internat. Lazar Soc., Gynecol. Lataropists, ND Obstetricians and Gynecologists Soc. (pres. 1966, 76); mem. Am. Soc. for Colopscopy and Colpomicroscopy, Am. Soc. Cryosurgery, Am. Soc. Contemporary Medicine and Surgery, Am. Assn. Profl. Ob-Gyn., Pan Am. Med. Assn., ND State Med. Assn. (coun. 2004-), Kotana Med. Soc. (pres. 2003—), Elks. Home: 1717 Main St Williston ND 58801-4244 Office: Med Ctr Dept Ob-Gyn Williston ND 58801 Office Phone: 701-572-0316. Personal E-mail: jadducci@prodigy.net.

ADELMAN, ALAN M., family practice physician, educator; MD, Temple U., 1975. Diplomate Am. Bd. Family Practice, Am. Bd. Family Practice-geriatric medicine. Resident family medicine Kaiser Found. Hosp., LA, 1976—78; fellow family medicine Univ. of Iowa, 1981—83; prof. family and cmty. medicine Pennstate Hershey Coll. of Medicine. Co-author: (publs.) House call practices: a comparison by specialty, 1994, Abdominal pain in an HMO, 1995, and numerous others; author: (publs.) Using serology to detect H pylori infection, 1996, Treatment of croup with nebulized dexamethasone, 1996, Water precautions in children with tympanostomy tubes, 1996, and numerous others. Office: Penn State Hershey Medical Group 845 Fishburn Rd Hershey PA 17033 Office Fax: 800-243-1455, 717-531-8181. E-mail: aadelman@psu.edu.

ADELMAN, CHAZAN DANIEL, allergist, immunologist; MD, U. Calif., 1983. Diplomate Am. Bd. Internal Medicine, 1986, Am. Bd. Allergy and Immunology, 1999, lic. Calif., 1984. Intern Cedars-Sinai Med. Ctr., 1984, resident internal medicine, 1984—86; fellow allergy and immunology Ronald Reagan Univ. of Calif. Med. Ctr., 1988; hosp. affiliations include Nat. Cancer Inst., Alta Bates Summit Med. Ctr., Univ. Calif. Med. Ctr. Co-author: (publs.) Array comparative genomic hybridization-based characterization of genetic alterations in pulmonary neuroendocrine tumors, 2010, AMPK Regulates Metabolic Actions of Glucocorticoids by Phosphorylating the Glucocorticoid Receptor through p38 MAPK, 2010, Archival fine needle aspiration cytopathology (FNAC) samples: Untapped resource for clinical molecular profiling, 2010, and other numerous publications. Office: Alta Bates Summit Medical Center 350 Hawthorne Ave Oakland CA 94609-3100 Office Phone: 510-655-4000.

ADELMAN, MARK, vascular surgeon; Attended, NYU, 1985. Diplomate Am. Bd. Surgery, 1999, Am. Bd. Surgery-vascular surgery, 2001. Residency tng. NYU Med. Ctr., 1985—90, clin. fellowships, 1990—91; assoc prof. surgery dept. NYU; divsn. chief vascular surgery Langone Med. Ctr. Co-author: (publs.) The cause of perioperative stroke after carotid endarterectomy, 1994, Retroperitoneal caval filter as a source of abdominal pain, 1994, Long-term follow-up of patients undergoing carotid endarterectomy in the presence of a contralateral occlusion, 1995, The surgical management of carotid artery stenosis in patients with previous neck irradiation, 1996, and numerous others. Mem.: Assn. of Internat. Vascular Surgery (US rep.), NY Soc. for Vascular Surgery (pres.). Office: Langone Medical Center 530 1st Ave 6F New York NY 10016 Office Phone: 212-263-7311. Office Fax: 212-263-7722.

ADELMAN, MICHAEL D., academic administrator; m. Cheryl Adelman. DPM, Phila. Coll. Podiatric Medicine, 1977; DO, Coll. Osteo. Medicine and Surgery, 1981; postgrad., U. Toledo Coll. Law. Prof. Temple U., Phila., U. Toledo, Del. Valley Cmty. Coll., Doylestown, Pa.; assoc. dean for acad. affairs Ohio U. Coll. of Osteopathic Medicine, Athens, Ohio, 1998—2002; v.p. acad. affairs and dean W. Va. Sch. Osteo. Medicine, 2002—10, acting pres., 2010—11, pres., 2011—. Fellow: Am. Osteo. Coll. of Proctology (exec. dir. 1994—2000, Proctologist of the Year); mem.: W.Va. Soc. Osteo. Medicine (pres.). Avocations: magic, ventriloquism. Office: West Virginia School Osteopathic Medicine Office of President 400 N Lee St Lewisburg WV 24901 Office Phone: 304-647-6295. Office Fax: 304-645-4859. E-mail: madelman@osteo.wvsom.edu. *

ADELSON, JOEL W., physician, educator; b. Boston, Feb. 8, 1941; MD, PhD, U. Calif. San Francisco, 1978; MPH, U. SC, Columbia, 1978. Prof. social medicine, pub. health Inst Health & Aging, U. Calif. San Francisco, 2004—. Office: Inst Health and Aging Ste 340 3333 Caliornia St San Francisco CA 94118 Office Phone: 510-708-6355. E-mail: j.adelson@comcast.net.

ADELSTEIN, S(TANLEY) JAMES, radiologist, educator; b. NYC, Jan. 24, 1928; s. George and Belle (Schild) Adelstein; m. Mary Charlesworth Taylor, Sept. 20, 1957; children: Joseph Burrows, Elizabeth Dunster. BS, MS, MIT, Cambridge, 1949, PhD in Biophysics, 1957; MD, Harvard U., Cambridge, 1953. Med. house officer Peter Bent Brigham Hosp., Boston, 1953-54, sr. asst. resident physician, 1957-58, chief resident, 1959-60; fellow Howard Hughes Med. Inst., 1957-58, Henry A. and Camilus Christian fellow, 1959-60; Moseley travel fellow Harvard U. Med. Sch., Boston, 1958-59, instr. anatomy, then asst. prof., 1961-68, assoc prof. radiology, 1968-72, prof., 1972-89, Paul C. Cabot prof. med. biophysics, 1989-97, prof. pathology, Daniel S. Tosteson univ. prof., 1997—2003, Paul C. Cabot disting. prof. med. biophysics, 2003—, dean for acad. program, 1978-97. Dir. Nat. Coun. for Radiation Protection Measurements, 1980—2002, v.p., 1982—2002, hon. v.p., 2002—; cons. Med. Found. fellow, 1960—63; Walter Dandy lectr. Johns Hopkins U., 1996; John Cameron lectr. U. Wis., 1998; Lauristen Taylor lectr. Nat. Coun. for Radiatide Photection, 2000; radiation rsch. bd. NAS, 1999—2002, chair, 2002—05, nuc. and radiol. studies bd., vice chair, 2005—10; biol. and environ. rsch. adv. com. Dept. Energy, 2001—10; L. Taylor lectr. Nat. Coun. for Radiation Protection, 2000; rsch. coll. adv. bd. U. Tasmania, 2003—. Mem. editl. bd.: Investigative Radiology, 1972—80, Postgrad. Radiology, Radiology Rsch., 1990—94; editor (assoc. editor): Jour. Nuc. Medicine, 1975—81; contbr. articles to profl. jours. Trustee Am. Bd. Nuc. Medicine, 1972—78; mem. fellowship adv. com. Whitaker Found., 1991—97. Recipient Career Devel. award, NIH, 1965—68; fellow Nat. Found., MIT, 1953—57, Fogarty Sr. Internat., 1976. Fellow: AAAS, Am. Coll. Nuc. Physicians; mem.: Inst. Medicine, Boylston Med. Soc., Soc. Nuc. Medicine (trustee 1970—74, Blumgurt award 1983, Aebersold award 1986, Dr. Hevesy award 1999), Radiation Rsch. Soc. (councillor 1975—78), Assn. Radiation Rsch., Biophys. Soc., Am. Chem. Soc., Alpha Omega Alpha, Tau Beta Pi, Sigma Xi. Office: Harvard Med Sch 260 Longwood Ave Boston MA 02115-6027

ADESMAN, ANDREW, pediatrician; Attended, U. Pa. Sch. Medicine, Phila., 1981. Diplomate Am. Bd. Psychiatry and Neurology-neurodevelopmental disabilities, Am. Bd. Pediatrics-devel. behavior pediat., Am. Bd. Pediatrics. Intern Childrens Hosp. Nat. Med. Ctr., Wash., DC, resident in pediat., 1982—84; fellow Childrens Hosp., Phila., 1984—86; with North Shore Univ. Hosp., LI Jewish Med. Ctr.; pediatrician Steven and Alexandra Cohen Childrens Med. Ctr., NY. Author: (Book) BabyFacts: the Truth about Your Child's Health from Newborn through Preschool. Office: North Shore Long Island Jewish Medical Center 1983 Marcus Ave Ste 130 Lake Success New Hyde Park NY 11042 Office Phone: 516-802-6101. Office Fax: 516-616-5801.

ADHIKARI, MIRIAM, retired pediatrician, educator; b. Cape Town, South Africa, Jan. 17, 1945; MBChB, U. Cape Town, 1969; PhD, U. KWaZulu Natal, 1982. Assoc. prof. pediat. Dept. Pediat., Med. Sch. U. KwaZulu Natal, 1985—99, prof. head, 1996—2010; neonatologist pediat. nephrology U. KwaZulu Natal, 1988—2010, emeritus prof., 2011—. Chairperson postgrad. & rsch. com. Med. Sch. U. Kwa Zulu Natal, 1993—2005, mem. academic promotions com., 2001—05; mem. ministerial com. perinatal mortality Nat. Dept. Health South Africa, 2008—11. Recipient award, Soroptomist Orgn. South Africa, Lifeline award, Lancet; fellowship, U. Kwazulu Natal. Fellow: Colls. Medicine South Africa (edn. com. mem.). Achievements include research in stepdown and palliative care for children. Avocations: bicycling, reading, music. Office: Umbilo Rd Durban KwaZulu Natal 4013 South Africa Office Fax: 027 31 260 4359. Business E-Mail: adhikari@ukzn.ac.za.

ADHIKARI, SUBHENDU, soil scientist; b. Kolkata, Jan. 1, 1966; MSc with honors in Soil Sci., Calcutta U., 1988, PhD, 1995. Scientist Ctrl. Inst. Freshwater Aquaculture, 1992—2001, sr. scientist, 2001—. Cons. Tata Tea Pvt. Ltd., 2009—. Recipient Young Scientist award, CIFA (ICAR), Dr. B. C. Deb Meml. award, Indian Sci. Congress, award, ICAR, New Delhi, 2001—02; fellowship, Internat. Soc. Environ. Protection. Mem.: Indian Soc. Soil Sci. (XII Internat. Congress Commemoration award). Achievements include development of protocol for enhancement of pond productivity through efficient use of macronutrients for sustainable aquaculture production. Avocations: music, gardening. Home: Flat- A/202 Ashutosh Vihar Ravi Talkies Bhubaneswar Orissa 751002 India Personal E-mail: subhendu66@rediffmail.com.

ADHYA, SANKAR L., geneticist; BS, U. Calcutta, India, 1958, MS, 1960, PhD, 1963, U. Wis., 1967. Rsch. assoc., dept. biology U. Rochester, NY, 1966—68; rsch. assoc., dept. biol. sciences Stanford U., Calif., 1968—69; scientist, dept. biochemistry Bose Inst., Calcutta, 1969—70; vis. scientist, lab. molecular biology Nat. Cancer Inst., Bethesda, Md., 1971—75, geneticist, 1975—80, sr. investigator & chief, devel. genetics sect., 1990—. Mem. tenure and promotion rev. bd., divsn. cancer biology and diagnosis Nat. Cancer Inst., 1982—94; adj. prof., dept. genetics George Wash. U., Washington, 1990—. Assoc. editor: Virology, 1977—86, mem. editl. bd.: J. Bacteriology, 1988—93; contbr. scientific papers. Mem. sci. rev. bd. counselors US Dept. Energy Brookhaven Nat. Lab., 1985. Recipient Director's award, NIH, 1991. Fellow: Am. Acad. Microbiology, Indian Nat. Sci. Acad.; mem.: NAS, Genetics Soc. America, Am. Soc. Virologists, Am. Soc. Biochemistry and Molecular Biology, Am. Acad. Arts & Sciences. Achievements include patents in field; patents pending in field. Office: Nat Cancer Inst Bldg 37 Rm 5138 37 Convent Dr Bethesda MD 20892 Office Phone: 301-496-2495. Office Fax: 301-480-7687. Business E-Mail: sadhya@helix.nih.gov.

ADHYAPAK, SRILAKSHMI M., cardiologist, educator; b. India, Aug. 28, 1967; MBBS, Bangalore U., 1991; DNB in Cardiology, Narayana Hrudayalaya Inst. Med. Scis., 2006. Asst. prof. St. John's Med. Coll. Hosp., 2007—. Avocations: painting, creative writing. Home: 25 15th Cross 3rd Block Jayanagar Bangalore Karnataka 560011 India Personal E-mail: srili2881967@yahoo.com.

ADIGUZEL, OZKAN, dental educator; b. Diyarbakir, Turkey, Jan. 1, 1977; DDS, Dicle U., 1999, PhD, 2004. Asst. prof. Dicle U. Faculty Dentistry, 2006—. Mem.: European Endodontic Soc., Turkish Endodontic Soc. Office: Dicle University Faculty Dentistry Diyarbakir GD 21280 Turkey Personal E-mail: dentamania21@hotmail.com.

ADILOGLU, ALI KUDRET, microbiologist, director; b. Ankara, Feb. 10, 1967; MD, Hacettepe U., 1999. Assoc. prof. Suleyman Demirel U., 2006; dir., microbiology dept. Ankara Rsch. & Edn. Hosp., 2009—. Fellow: Clin. Microbiology Residency Soc.; mem.: Am. Soc. Microbiology, Turkish Microbiology Soc. Avocations: guitar, sports. Office: Ankara Egitim Hastanesi Mikrobiyolo Ankara 06230 Turkey Office Fax: 90312 3633396. Personal E-mail: aadiloglu@yahoo.com.

ADISESHIAH, MOHANKUMAR, surgeon, educator; b. Madras, Tamilnadu, India, May 20, 1941; s. Malcom Satyanandan and Helen Esther (Paranjoti) Adiseshiah; m. Maria Kilkelly; children: Emily, Charlotte. MB BS, King's Coll., London, 1965; MS, U. Coll. London, 1978; MA (hon.), U. Cambridge, Eng., 1979. Ho. officer Westminster Hosp., London, 1965—67; surg. registrar U. Coll. Hosp., London, 1968—76; rsch. fellow U. Toronto, Ont., Canada, 1975—76; cons. surgeon Addenbrookes Hosp., Cambridge, England, 1976—82; cons. vascular surgeon U. Coll. Hosp., London, 1982—; hon. sr. lectr. U. Coll., London, 1982—; hon. cons. surgeon St. Luke's Hosp., London, 1985—. Vice chmn. med. com. U. Coll. London, 1993—95; clin. dir. surgery U. Coll. Hosp., 1999—2001; chmn. med. com. St. Luke's Hosp. for Clergy, London, 2001—; mem. faculty Internat. Soc. Endovascular Surgery, Phoenix, 2000—02, Global Endovascular Technology, Monaco, 2001, Critical Endovascular Interventions, Netherlands, 2002. Author: Recent Advances in Surgery, 1999, Pathways in Surgery, 2002; actor: Nat. Youth Theatre, 1958—62. Mem. All Saint Parish Coun., London, 1999—. Fellow: Royal Coll. Physicians London, Royal Coll. Surgeons Eng.; mem.: Internat. Endovascular Therapists, Vascular Surg. Soc. Gt. Britain. Anglican. Achievements include patents for stainless steel balloon expandable stent. Avocations: skiing, reading, drama, music, rugby. Office: London Clinic 149 Harley Street W1G 6DE London England Office Fax: 0207 487 4808. Business E-Mail: m.achs@lonclin.co.uk.

ADLER, DALE STEVEN, internist, cardiologist; b. Cleve., July 31, 1953; m. Nancy Feins, Oct. 1985. AB in Biochemistry (magna cum laude), Harvard Coll., 1975; MD, Weill Med. Coll., Cornell U., 1979. Diplomate in internal medicine and cardiovascular diseases Am. Bd. Internal Medicine. Intern, medicine Brigham and Women's Hosp., Boston, 1979-80, jr. asst. resident, internal medicine, 1980—81, sr. asst. resident, internal medicine, 1981—82, clin. fellow, divsn. cardiology, 1982—83, clin. and rsch. fellow, divsn. cardiology, 1983—85, Henry J. Kaiser Rsch. Fellow, gen. internal medicine and clin. epidemiology, Harvard Med. Sch., 1983—85, Percutaneous Transluminal Coronary Angioplasty Fellow, divsn. cardiology, 1984—85, assoc. physician, 1984—85, vice chair medicine for network develop. and strategic planning, 2006—08, exec. vice chair, dept. medicine, 2007—; head, invasive cardiology Mt. Sinai Med. Ctr., Cleve., 1985, co-chief cardiology, acting co-chief, divsn. cardiology, 1987, co-chief, divsn. cardiology, 1988—97; chief, divsn. cardiology U. Hosps. Cleve., 1997; asst. prof. medicine Case Western Res. U., Cleve., 1985—99, assoc. prof. medicine, 1999—2003, prof. medicine, 2003, chief, divsn. cardiology, 1996—2004, vice-chair for clin. affairs, dept. medicine, 2004—06. Contbr. articles to profl. jours., chapters to books. Named Best Doctors-Cleve. Ohio, Cleve. Mag., 1987—88, 2002, 2004, 2006, Top Docs, Northeast Ohio Live Mag., 2000, 2001—06, Hon. co-chair gala, Am. Heart Assn., Northeastern Ohio, 2004, Boston Mag. Best Drs., 2007—08, Castle Connolly Top Drs., Mass., 2009. Mem. Am. Heart Assn. (mem. clin. cardiology coun., 1986-), Am. Profs. Cardiology, Alpha Omega Alpha, Phi Beta Kappa Office: Brigham and Women's Hosp Brigham Med Specialties 45 Francis St Boston MA 02115 Office Phone: 857-307-4026. Office Fax: 617-525-7752. Business E-Mail: dadler2@partners.org.

ADLER, FELICE C., physician, educator; b. NYC, July 17, 1967; BS, Duke U., 1989; MD, Vanderbilt U., 1993. Asst. clin. prof. U. Calif., Irvine, 2001—. Dir. outpatient svcs. infectious diseases CHOC Children's, 2010—. Office: CHOC Children's 455 S Main St Orange CA 92868

ADLER, KENNETH R., oncologist, hematologist; b. Bklyn., Sept. 22, 1947; BS, U. Pitts., 1968; MD, Albany Med. Coll., NY, 1973. Diplomate Am. Bd. Internal Medicine, Am. Bd. Hematology. Intern Albany Med. Ctr. Hosp., 1973—74, resident in internal medicine, 1974—76, resident in hematology and oncology, 1976—78; oncologist Carol G. Simon Cancer Ctr., Morristown (N.J.) Meml. Hosp. Clin. asst. prof. medicine N.J. Med. Sch. Named one of Top Drs. in N.Y. Met. Area, Castle Connolly, Top Drs. 2003, N.J. Monthly Mag., Top Drs. 2009, Top Drs., 2003—09. Office: Carol G Simon Cancer Ctr Morristown Meml Hosp 100 Madison Ave Morristown NJ 07960 Office Phone: 973-538-5210.

ADLER, NANCY ELINOR, psychologist, educator; BA, Wellesley Coll., 1968; MA, Harvard U., 1971, PhD, 1973. Asst. prof. psychology U. Calif., Santa Cruz, 1972-76, assoc. prof. psychology, 1976-77, assoc. prof. med. psychology dept. psychiatry and pediat. San Francisco, 1977-84, prof. med. psychology depts. psychiatry and pediat., 1984—, dir. health psychology program, 1988—, program dir. NIMH tng. program, 1991—, vice chair dept. psychiatry, 1994—, dir., Ctr. Health & Cmty., 1998—. Vis. asst. rsch. psychologist Inst. Personality Assessment and Rsch., U. Calif., Berkeley, 1975; mem. peer rev. panel Ad Hoc Sci. Study Sects., Nat. Inst. Child Health and

Human Devel., 1977—, Nat. Heart, Lung and Blood Inst., 1993; adv. com. for five-yr. plan Demographic and Social Scis. Br., Ctr. for Population RSch., Nat. Inst. Child Health and Human Devel., 1986-87, adv. com., 1991-2000; sr. rsch. scientist in psychology Yale U., New Haven. 1994-95; review com. Intramural Rsch. NIMH, 1997, sci. adv. bd. Ctr. Advancement Health, Washington, 1995-96, bd. trustees, 1996—; grant reviewer NSF, Social Scis. and Humanities Rsch. Coun. Can., Soc. Behavioral Medicine; March of Dimes, Ctrs. for Disease Control, Econ. and Social Rsch. Coun.; presenter in field. Author: (with others) Health Psychology-A Handbook: Theories, Applications, and Challenges of a Psychological Approach to the Health Car System, 1979, Preventing Preterm Birth: A Parent's Guide, 1988, SES & Health in Industrialized Nations, 1999; adv. bd. Ency. Mental Health, 1995—; assoc. editor Health Psychology, 1984-90, Women's Health: Research in Gender, Behavior and Policy, 1994-98; mem. editl. bd. Jour. Population and Environment, 1982-88, Health Psychology, 1994—; manuscript reviewer Jour. Personality and Social Psychology, Jour. Nervous and Mental Disease, Personality and Social Psychology Bull., Jour. Health and Social Behavior, Jour. Applied Social Psychology, Basic and Applied Social Psychology, Psychology Women Quarterly, The Western Jour. Medicine, Jour. Am. Med. Assn., Am. Jour. Pub. Health, many others; contbr. articles in field. Recipient Best Rsch. Paper award Soc. for Adolescent Medicine, 1984; NSF fellow, 1968-72, U. Calif. Regents Summer fellow, 1974; grantee in field. Fellow: APA (sec.-treas. divsn. 34 1975—78, pres. divsn. 34 1979—80, planning com. for nat. conf. on tng. in health psychology 1982—83, chairperson fellow com. divsn. 34 1982—86, participant Arden House conf. on edn. and tng. in health psychology 1983, chairperson nominations com. 1989—90, task force on promotion of population psychology 1992—97), Am. Psychol. Soc.; mem.: Am. Acad. Arts & Sciences, Inst. of Medicine, Soc. for Rsch. on Adolescence, Assn. Med. Sch. Profs. Psychology, Soc. Advancement Social Psychology, Internat. Assn. Applied Psychology, Soc. Exptl. Social Psychology, Phi Beta Kappa, Sigma Xi. Office: Ctr Health & Cmty 3333 California Ste 465 Campus Box 0844 San Francisco CA 94118 Office Phone: 415-476-7408. Office Fax: 415-502-1010. Business E-Mail: Nancy.Adler@ucsf.edu.

ADLER, ROBERT ALAN, endocrinologist; b. Somerville, NJ, Jan. 11, 1945; BA, Johns Hopkins, 1967, MD, 1970. Asst. chief, endocrinology and metabolism McGuire Veterans Affairs Med. Ctr., 1984—85; assoc. prof. internal medicine Va. Commonwealth U. Sch. Medicine, 1984—93, prof. epidemiology and cmty. health, 2002, prof. internal medicine, 1993; chief, endocrinology and metabolism McGuire Veterans Affairs Med. Ctr., 1985—. Recipient Irby-James award, Va. Commonwealth U. Sch. Medicine. Mem.: AAAS, Internat. Bone and Mineral Soc., Internat. Soc. Clin. Densitometry, Endocrine Soc., Am. Soc. Bone and Mineral Rsch. Office: McGuire Veterans Affairs Medical Ctr Richmond VA 23249 Office Fax: 804-675-5425. Business E-Mail: robert.adler@va.gov.

ADLER, RONALD S., radiologist, educator; MD, Wayne State U., 1984. Diplomate Am. Bd. Medical Examiners, 1985, Am. Bd. Radiology, 1988, lic. NY, Conn., Mich. Resident Univ. of Mich. Med. Ctr., Ann Arbor, 1984—88, fellow ultrasound and MRI, 1988—89; prof. radiology Weill Cornell Med. Coll., NYC; attending radiologist NY Presbyterian Hosp.; rsch. scientist Hosp. for Special Surgery, attending radiologist, chief ultrasound and body computed tomography divsn. Recipient 6th Annual Laurence A. Mack Rsch. award, Soc. of Radiologists in Ultrasound, Gen. Electric Found. award, 1976, Nat. Rsch. award, NIH, 1979, James A. Shannon award, HHS, 1990; named one of Best Doctors in NY, NY Mag., 2004—05, 2009—11; fellow Rackham Predoctoral fellowship. Fellow: Soc. of Radiologist in Ultrasound; mem.: Am. Coll. of Radiology, Radiol. Soc. of N.Am., Internat. Skeletal Soc., Soc. of Skeletal Radiologist, Sigma Xi. Office: Hospital for Special Surgery 3rd Fl Radiology 535 East 70th St New York NY 10021 Office Phone: 212-606-1635. Office Fax: 212-734-7475.

ADLERSBERG, JAY BEN, internist; b. Pitts., Nov. 25, 1944; s. Herman and Mathilda (Marshall) A.; 1 child, Zoe. BS magna cum laude, U. Pitts., 1965; MD, U. Pa., 1969. Diplomate Am. Bd. Internal Medicine, Nat. Bd. Med. Examiners. Intern in internal medicine NYU Med. Ctr., NYC, 1969-70, jr. asst. resident, asst. resident medicine Bellevue Hosp., 1970-72, NIH fellow in rheumatology/immunology, 1972-74; asst. prof. medicine divsn. rheumatic diseases/immunology Albert Einsteon Coll. Medicine, Bronx, 1974-80; assoc. attending physician Bronx Mcpl. Hosp. Ctr., NY, 1976-80; attending physician Beth Israel Med. Ctr., NYC, 1980—, Lenox Hill Hosp., NYC, 1986—; asst. prof. medicine Mt. Sinai Sch. Medicine, NYC, 1980—. Assoc. attending physician Hosp. for Joint Diseases/Orthopaedic Inst., N.Y.C., 1980—; attending physician Hosp. Albert Einstein Coll. Medicine, 1974-80, Montefiore Hosp. Med. Ctr., Bronx, 1974-76; teaching asst. in medicine NYU Med. Ctr., 1972-74; teaching fellow in rheumatology Bellevue Hosp., 1972-74; keynote speaker Jonas Salk Scholarship Awards CUNY, 1993. Contbg. corr. ABC News Now, 1992—; weekly med. corr. The Health Show, ABC News, 1987-90; med. reporter Eyewitness News, WABC-TV, NY, 1983—; co-host Arthritis Telethon, WOR-TV, NYC, 1982-86; guest host Healthline, WNYU-AM Radio, NYC, 1980;host Healthy Life, 2007; contbr. weekly health column Bridgehampton Sun, NY,1980-81. Master of ceremonies gala Cystic Fibrosis Found., 1990, S.I. Hospice Assn., 1990, Town Hall Arthritis Found., NYC, 2007, Castle Connelly Best Doctors Pubs., Awards for Achievement in Clin. Medicine, NYC, 2007; mem. med. and sci. com. NY chpt. Arthritis Found., 1985-88, bd. dirs., 2005-; elected dir. of bd. Arthritis Found., NY Chpt., 2005. Named One of Best Drs. in NY NY Mag., 1998, 05; included in How to Find the Best Doctors, NY, 1998-2008, George Foster Peabody award Excellence Journalism, 2001; citation NY City Coun., 2003; Am. Cancer Soc. grantee, 1977-79. Fellow Am. Coll. Rheumatology; mem. AMA, N.Y. Acad. Scis., Am. Rheumatism Assn., N.Y. Rheumatism Assn., Med. Soc. County of N.Y., Med. Soc. State of N.Y., Phi Beta Kappa. Avocations: road bicycling, skiing, tennis, reading, photography. Office: 220 E 69th St New York NY 10021-5737 Office Phone: 212-570-1800. Business E-Mail: drjay@medasso.com, drjay@medixmedia.com.

ADLY, AMIRA, pediatrician, educator; b. Cairo, Sept. 23, 1973; M in Pediat., 2002, MD in Pediat., 2005. Cons. diabetes pediat. clinic, Ain Shams U., 2005—, asst. prof. pediat., 2009—. Contbr. articles to profl. internat. jours. Recipient Pediat. award, Internat. Publ. Mem.: Egyptian Soc. Pediatric Allergy and Immunology, Egyptian Soc. Pediatric Hematology Oncology, Internat. Soc. Pediatric and Adolescents Diabetes. Avocation: computers. Home: 6 A-El sheshini St Saudia Bldg Cairo Shoubra 1136 Egypt Personal E-mail: amiradiabetes@yahoo.com.

ADOLPH, MICHAEL, medical educator; b. Cleve., Ohio, Dec. 7, 1962; MD, U. Cin., 1989; MBA, Ashland U., 2004. Asst. clin. prof. medicine and surgery James Cancer Hosp., Ohio State U. Med. Ctr., 2005—. Recipient Physician Excellence award, James Cancer Hosp. Office: Ohio State University 453 W 10th Ave Columbus OH 43210 Business E-Mail: michael.adolph@osumc.edu.

ADOLPHS, HANS-DIETER, retired urology educator; b. Raeren, Eupen, Germany, Aug. 7, 1942; s. Bernhard and Helene (Huppertz) A.; m. Heidel Pfennings, May 28, 1977; children: Julia,Claudia, Stephan. MD, U. Duesseldorf, 1968. Intern Univ. Hosps., Duesseldorf, Fed. Republic Germany, 1968-70, East Orange, N.J., 1968-70; asst. in internal medicine, surgery, immulology and urology Univ. Hosp., Aachen, Fed. Republic Germany, 1970-76; asst., then asst. prof. dept. urology U. Bonn (Fed. Republic Germany), 1976-83, assoc. prof., 1983—2007; chief dept. urology St. Ansgar Hosp., Hoexter, Germany, 1983—2007; ret., 2007. Contbr. over l00 articles on basic sci., exptl. immunology and urology to med. jours. Ministry Rsch. and Tech. grantee, 1979, 8l. Mem. German Cancer Assn., Assn. Immunology, German Assn. Urology, European Assn. Urology, Am. Urol. Assn., German TNM Com., Lions. Avocations: tennis, skiing, music, sailing. Business E-Mail: h-d.adolphs@gmx.de.

ADOLPHS, NICOLAI, maxillofacial surgeon; b. Leverkusen, Nordrheinwestfalen, Germany, Jan. 6, 1969; MD, Ludwig-Maximilians-Universität, München, 1990—96; D of Dental Medicine, Humboldt U., Berlin, 2002; DMD, FEBCMFS. Cert. maxillofacial surgery 2006. Resident in gen. surgery Kantonales Spital, Rorschach, KS Rorschach, St.Gallen, Switzerland, 1997—98; cons. maxillofacial surgery Klinik für MKG-Chirurgie, Charité Berlin, Berlin, 2003—. Rsch. fellow AO Found., Davos, Graubünden, Switzerland, 1998—2002; cons. in field. Achievements include research in distraction osteogenesis in the craniofacial skeleton; computer assisted surgery in craniomaxillofacial applications. Office: Klinik für MKG-Chirurgie Charité Berlin Augustenburger Platz 1 Berlin 13344 Germany Office Fax: 004930450555901. Business E-Mail: nicolai.adolphs@charite.de.

ADWAN, GHALEB MOHAMMAD, medical educator; b. Palestine, May 11, 1964; PhD, 1999. Asst. prof. An-Najah N. U., 2001—. Office: An-Najah N University Palesinian N Authority Nablus 00970 Israel Business E-Mail: adwang@najah.edu.

ADZICK, NICK SCOTT, surgeon, educator; b. Omaha, May 14, 1953; MD, Harvard Coll., 1975; postgrad., 1979. Resident gen. surgery Mass. Gen. Hosp., 1979-83, 85-86; resident surg. rsch. U. Calif., San Francisco, 1983-85; resident pediat. surgery Boston Children's Hosp., 1986-88; faculty U. Calif., San Francisco, 1988—; surgeon-in-chief The Children's Hosp., Phila.; C. Everett Koop prof. pediat. surgery U. Pa. Sch. Medicine, 1995—; pediat. surgery tng. program dir., dir. Ctr. for Fetal Diagnosis and Treatment. Fellow: ACS; mem.: AMA, Am. Acad. Pediat. (surg. sect.), Am. Coll. Physician Execs., Am. Pediat. Surg. Assn., Am. Surg. Assn., Assn. Acad. Surgery, Soc. Univ. Surgeons, Nat. Inst. Medicine, Internat. Fetal Medicine and Surgery Soc., Brit. Assn. Pediat. Surgery, Pacific Assn. Pediat. Surgeons, Wound Healing Soc, Coll. Physicians Phila., John Morgan Soc., Ravdin-Rhoads Surg. Soc. E-mail: adzick@email.chop.edu.

AEHLERT, BARBARA JUNE, health facility administrator; b. San Antonio, June 17, 1956; d. Bobby Ray and Ronella Su (Light) Mahoney; m. Dean A. Aehlert, Sept. 6, 1980; children: Andrea, Sherri. AA in Nursing, Glendale CC, Ariz., 1976; BS in Profl. Arts, St. Joseph's Coll., Windham, Maine, 1997. Cert. ACLS instr., BLS and PALS instr., emergency med. tng./paramedic instr. Gen. mgr. Hosp. Ambulance Svc., Phoenix, 1982-83; critical care nurse Samaritan Health Svcs., Phoenix, 1978-80, coord. patient transp., 1980-82, mgr. clin. programs, 1983-92; dir. emergency med. svcs. edn. EMS Edn. and Rsch., 1992-97; pres. S.W. EMS Edn. Inc., Glendale, Ariz., 1997—; dir. field tng. S.W. Ambulance, Mesa, Ariz., 2006—09. EMS coord., City of Mesa Fire Dept., 2001-04. Author: (book) Emergency Med. Technician: EMT in action, 2008, ACLS Study Guide, 3d edit., 2007, ACLS Quick Review Study Cards, 2003, PALS Study Guide, 3d edit., 2006, ECGs Made Easy, 4th edit., 2010, ECGs Made Easy Study Cards, 2003, Mosby's Comprehensive Pediatric Emergency Care, 2005, Paramedic Practice Today, 2009. Republican.

AFERZON, MARK, otolaryngologist; b. Kmelnitsky, Ukraine, July 7, 1971; arrived in US, 1979; s. Semyon and Bella Aferzon; m. Ruslana Aferzon, Aug. 5, 2000; 2 children. BA in Computer Sci., Brown U., 1993, MD, 1997. Diplomate Am. Bd. Otolaryngology. Resident otolaryngolgy Geisinger Health Sys., Danville, 1999—2002; active staff Griffin Hosp., Derby, Conn., 2002. Courtesy staff Milford Hosp., Conn., 2004. Contbr. articles to profl. jours., chapter to book. Clin. Rsch. grant, Geisinger Med. Ctr., 2000—02. Fellow: ACS; mem.: AMA, Am. Acad. Otolaryngology, New Haven County Med. Assn. Avocations: soccer, swimming, volleyball, tennis. Office: 2 Ivy Brook Rd Ste 110 Shelton CT 06484-6416

AFFELDT, JOHN ELLSWORTH, retired physician; b. Lansing, Mich., May 26, 1918; s. John Ferdin and Pearl Heald (Gardner) Affeldt; m. Nancy Faye Spomer, Sept. 2, 1942; children: John C., Elizabeth Affeldt Westberg, Cindy L. BS, Andrews U., Berrian Springs, Mich., 1939; MD, Loma Linda U., Calif., 1944. Intern Detroit Gen. Hosp., 1943—44; resident in internal medicine White Meml. Hosp., Los Angeles, 1946—49; fellow in pulmonary physiology Harvard Sch. Pub. Health, 1949—51; med. dir. Rancho Los Amigos Hosp., Downey, Calif., 1956—64, Los Angeles County Dept. Hosps., 1964—72, Los Angeles County Dept. Health Services, 1972—77; pres. Joint Commn. Accreditation Hosps., Chgo., 1977—86; med. advisor Beverly Enterprises, Fort Smith, Ark., 1986—97. With US Army, 1944—47. Mem.: ACP, AMA, Calif. Assn. Med. Dirs. (pres. 1993—94), Los Angeles County Med. Assn., We. Soc. Clin. Rsch., Ins. Medicine NAS, Am. Congress Rehab. Medicine. Home: 5140 Bareback Sq PO Box 8432 Rancho Santa Fe CA 92067-8432

AFIFI, RAAFAT YAHIA, surgeon, researcher; b. Cairo, June 30, 1960; s. Yahia Afifi and Anhar Mansour Farag; m. Maha Awny Abdel-Raouf, Oct. 9, 1987; children: Rana Raafat, Mohamed Raafat. MB, Cairo U., 1983, MSc in Gen. Surgery, 1987, DSc of Gen. Surgery, 1993. Ho. officer Cairo U. Hosp., Cairo, 1984—85, registrar gen. surgery, 1985—88, sr. registrar gen. surgery, 1988—89; asst. lectr. gen. surgery Cairo U., Cairo, 1989—93, lectr. in gen. surgery, 1993—99, assoc. prof. gen. surgery, 1999—2004, prof. gen. surgery, 2004—; registrar gen. surgery King's Coll. Sch. Medicine, London, 1989—90; clin. rsch. fellow U. Minn. Hosp., Minn., 1990—92; asst. prof. gen. surgery King's Khaled Sch. Medicine, Abha, Saudi Arabia, 2002. Cons. gen. surgery Cairo U., Cairo, Egypt, 1996—. Contbr. over 46 rsch. papers. Founder rsch. ethics com. Egyptian Med. Syndicate, Cairo, Egypt, 2004. Mem.: Am. Soc. Clin. Oncology, Egyptian Soc. Cancer, Egyptian Am. Soc., Egyptian Surgeon Soc., Egyptian Med. Syndicate, Bd. of dir. of SIS, Internat. Senology Soc., Egyptian Soc. of Surg. Oncology, Am. Soc. Breast Surgeons, Am. Soc. Breast Diseases, Kasr El-Aini Friends Soc. Muslim. Achievements include research in technique for repair of huge recurrent ventral hernias; classification of axillary lymph nodes; hypothesis for the mechanism of spread of breast cancer; simple triage scoring system for management of blunt abdominal trauma; diagnosis and management of Acute necrotizing fasciitis. Office: Faculty of Medicine Cairo Univ Handousa Basha St Cairo Egypt Home: 256, Building N0 8 Maadi Gadida 11435 Cairo Egypt Personal E-mail: raafatafifi@yahoo.com.

AFRICA, BRUCE, psychiatrist; b. Kane, Pa., Mar. 10, 1941; s. W. Beyer and Virginia Bell Africa; m. Martha Elizabeth Fay, Nov. 9, 1963 (div. Jan. 1997); children: Matthew, Julia. BS in Chemistry cum laude, Allegheny Coll., 1963; PhD in Biochemistry, U. Calif., Berkeley, 1968; MD, Duke U., 1973. Bd. cert. Am. Bd. Psychiatry and Neurology. Pvt. practice, Berkeley, 1977—97; staff psychiatrist Berkeley Mental Health, 1977—79; dir. consultation liaison psychiatry Herrick Hosp., Berkeley, 1979—83; active med. staff Alta Bates-Herrick Hosp., Berkeley, 1979—96; staff psychiatrist Napa (Calif.) State Hosp., 2003—. Asst. clin. prof. psychiatry U. Calif., San Francisco, 1978—89, assoc. clin. prof. psychiatry, 1989—97. Contbr. chapters to books. Activist Free Speech Movement, Berkeley, 1964. Named Outstanding Young Investigator, Soc. for Nuc. Medicine, 1970. Mem.: Am. Soc. for Clin. Psychopharmacology, Am. Psychiat. Assn., Phi Beta Kappa. Office Phone: 707-254-2570.

AFZAL, KHALID I., medical educator; b. Rawalpindi, Oct. 15, 1970; MD, Quaid-e-Azam U., 1995. Asst. prof. U. Chgo., 2010—. Recipient Excellence Rsch. award, Tech. U. Health Scis. Ctr., Paul L. Foster Sch. Medicine, El Paso, Tex., David F. Briones MD award, Chief Resident award, Instr. of Yr. award, Child & Adolescent Sect., Dept. Psychiatry & Behavioral Neurosci., U. Chgo., 2011. Mem.: Ill. Coun. Child & Adolescent Psychiatry, Acad. Psychosomatic Medicine, Am. Acad. Child & Adolescent Psychiatry (Outstanding Child & Adolescent Psychiatry Resident award). Avocations: writing, poetry. Office: 5841 S Maryland Ave MC 3077 Chicago IL 60637 Office Phone: 773-834-4093. Office Fax: 773-702-6649. Business E-Mail: khalid.afzal@uchospitals.edu.

AGALE, SHUBHANGI VINAYAK, medical educator; b. Murud, Maharashtra, India, Jan. 21, 1961; MBBS, Govt Med. Coll., Aurangabad, 1984; MD in Pathology, Mumbai U., 1989. Lectr. Grant Med. Coll., Byculla, Mumbai, 1990—2003, assoc. prof., 2003—. Exec. mem. Mumbai Hematology Group, 1996—2005, sec., 1997—98, organizing sec. cme and conf., 1997—98; joint organizing sec. CME, 2010; med. rep. to cmes Maharashahtra Med. Coun., Mumbai, 2011. Named one of Best Lectr., Grant Med. Coll. Mem.: Gastrointestinal Pathology Group (Mumbai), Assn. Med. Women India, Indian Assn. Pathologists & Microbiologists, Mumbai Hematology Group, Lymphoma Group and Endocrine Group (Mumbai), Gynecologic Group Pathologists. Avocation: yoga. Home: Dhanvantari Bldg- 02 Sir J J Hosp Mumbai Maharashatra 400008 India Personal E-mail: shubhagale@hotmail.com.

AGALLIANOS, DENNIS DIONYSIOS, retired psychiatrist; b. Galati, Romania, Jan. 1, 1923; arrived in U.S., 1957; s. Dionysios Nicholas and Eleni (Craciun) Agallianos; m. Georgia-Lee Virginia Foden, June 20, 1964 (dec. 2004); 1 child, Helen Penelope. BA, Classical Gymnasium, Galati, Romania, 1941; MD, Victor Babes Med. Sch., Cluj, Romania, 1948. Diplomate Am. Bd. Psychiatry and Neurology. Pvt. practice, Romania, 1948-49; preparator urol. dept. Victor Babes Med. Sch., 1949-51; intern. urol. dept. U. Athens Med. Sch., Greece, 1951-54; asst. prof. urology Med. Sch. U. Athens, Greece, 1956-57; staff physician Polikliniki Athinon, Athens, 1954-56; intern, resident French Hosp., NYC, 1957-58; resident in psychiatry Brattleboro Retreat, 1958-60; resident, staff psychiatrist Spring Grove State Hosp., Balt., 1960-64, chief of divsn., 1965-68; staff psychiatrist Brattleboro (Vt.) Retreat, 1969-76, chief of profl. svc., 1976-80, dir. older adult program, 1980-92; asst. prof. psychiatry Dartmouth Med. Sch., Hanover, 1978—95; pvt. practice, 1992—2000; locum tenens staff psychiatrist, 2000—11. Adj. asst. prof. clin. psychiatry Dartmouth Med. Sch., Hanover, 1995—2000. Contbr. articles to profl. jours. Pres. Parish Coun. St. George Greek Orthodox Ch., Keene, NH, 1985—86; sustaining mem. Greek Orthodox Archdiocese N. and S.Am., 1966—; founding father United Greek Orthodox Charities, 1967. Recipient Exemplary Psychiatrist award, Nat. Alliance Mentally Ill, 1994; grantee, NIMH. Fellow: Am. Psychiat. Assn. (life Disting. life fellow); mem.: AMA, Vt. State Med. Soc., Vt. Psychiat. Assn. Home: 101 W Windsor Rd Urbana IL 61802 Personal E-mail: dagallia@sover.net.

AGAMY, EMAD MOHAMED TOLBA, dental educator; b. Cairo, Jan. 19, 1967; B in Oral and Dental Medicine, Cairo U., 1989, PhD in Prosthodontics, 2005. Asst. prof. Faculty Dentistry Menia U., Egypt, 1988—, asst. lectr., dept. removable prosthodontics, 1998—2001, lectr., dept. removable prosthodontics, 2005—10; guest dentist, dept. prosthetic dentistry U. Cologne, Germany, 2001—04, guest dental surgeon, dept. oral, maxillofacial and plastic surgery, 2002—03. Dir. Menia U. Ednl. Dental Hosp., 2007—10; cons., continuing dental ednl. courses removable prosthodontics Ministry of Health, Egypt, 2009. Scholarship, Egyptian Ministry of Higher Edn. Mem.: Egyptian Dental Assn., Egyptian Dental Syndicate. Avocations: reading, poetry, walking. Office: Misr Aswan Agricultural Rd Menia 11606 Egypt Office Fax: 00286-2347767. Personal E-mail: emad_agamy@yahoo.com.

AGAR, BEATRICE ARLENE, nutritionist, educator; b. Phila., Nov. 24, 1963; d. Paul Berg and Martha Elaine Alexander; m. John R. Agar, Jr.; children: Rebekah A., Sarah L. BS, Drexel U., Phila., 1986; MA, Immaculata U., Pa., 1990; cert. of Proficiency, Del. County CC, Media, Pa., 2006. Cert. med. asst. Am. Assn. Med. Assts.; registered dietitian Am. Dietetic Assn., lic. dietitian-nutritionist Commonwealth of Pa. Clin. nutritionist Misericordia Hosp., Phila., 1986—88, Del. County Meml. Hosp., Drexel Hill, Pa., 1988—90; asst. chief dietitian The Lankenau Hosp., Wynnewood, Pa., 1990—91; clin. nutritionist Crozer Chester Med. Ctr., Upland, Pa., 1991—94, Springfield Hosp., Pa., 1994—97; instr. Del. County C.C., Media, Pa., 2003—; clin. nutritionist Fair Acres Geriatric Ctr., Lima, Pa., 2008—. Recipient Excellence in Tchg. award, Del. County CC, 2006. Mem.: Kappa Omicron Phi, Omicron Nu. Avocations: guitar, canoeing, drawing, painting, travel.

AGARD, EMMA ESTORNEL, psychotherapist; b. Bronx, NY; BA, Queens Coll., Flushing; MSW, Fordham U., Bronx, NY, 1962; cert. in Psychoanalytic Psychotherapy, Tng. Inst. for Mental Health, 1979; cert. in Child and Adolescent Psychotherapy, Postgrad. Ctr. for Mental Health, 1982. Cert. in supervision The Psychoanalytic Inst. Mental Health, 1982. Supr. social work Foster Care Div., NYC, 1968-72; asst. dir. Henry St. Settlement Urban Family Ctr., NYC, 1972-74; tng. analyst, sr. supr. Tng. Inst. for Mental Health, NYC, 1974—; pvt. practice psychotherapist NYC, 1974—. Lectr. social work Columbia U., NYC, 1977-90; adj. asst. prof. NYU, 1978-80; field instr. NYC Housing Authority, 1974-80; dist. dir., cons. Am. Consultation Ctrs., Bklyn. and NYC, 1985—, dir. Park Slope br.; field instr. Sch. Social Svc. Fordham U., 1985—. Mem. Albemarle-Kenmore Neighborhood Assn., Bklyn., 1974—99. Fellow NY State Soc. Clin. Social Work Psychotherapists (pres. Bklyn. chpt. 1988-91); mem. Profl. Soc. Tng. Inst. for Mental Health (sec.), Nat. Assn. Social Workers (diplomate), Acad. Cert. Social Workers, Nat. Coalition 100 Black Women, Delta Sigma Theta, Psychoanalytical Soc. Tng. Inst. Mental Health, Am. Assn. Psycho Analysis Clin. Social Work, Am. Bd. Examiners Clin. Social Work. Avocations: painting, tennis, yoga, swimming. Address: 109 E 36th St New York NY 10016-3447

AGARWAL, ARCHANA MISHRA, physician, researcher; d. Ramakant and Kamini Mishra; m. Neeraj Agarwal, Jan. 25, 1998; children: Ria, Ruchi. MBBS, Assam Med. Coll., Dibrugarh, 1995; MD, Maulana Azad Med. Coll., New Delhi, 2001. Diplomate Assam Med. Coll., Dibrugarh, India, 1995, in hematopathology Am. Bd. Pathology, 2009, in anatomic pathology Am. Bd. Pathology, 2009, in clinical pathology Am. Bd. Pathology, 2009. Postdoc. rsch. scholar U. Iowa, 2001—04; resident, pathology U. Utah, Salt Lake City, 2004—08, fellow, hematopathology, 2008—09, fellow, molecular genetic pathology, 2009—. Contbr. articles to profl.jours., chapters to books. Grant, Inst. Clin. & Exptl. Pathology, 2009. Fellow: Coll. Am. Pathologist; mem.: AMA, Utah Med. Assn., Am. Soc. Clin. Pathology, US & Can. Acad. Pathologist. Office: Med Dirs ARUP Labs 500 Chipeta Way Salt Lake City UT 84108 Business E-Mail: archana.agarwal@hsc.utah.edu. E-mail: archana.mishra@aruplab.com.

AGARWAL, BANKE, gastroenterologist, educator; b. New Delhi, Aug. 3, 1965; s. Nathmal and Vijaya Agarwal. MBBS, [illegible] Inst. for Med. Edn. and Rsch., India, 1989, MD, 1992. Diplomate in gastroenterology Am. Bd. Internal Medicine. Residency in internal medicine Columbia U., NYC, 1993—96, fellowship training in gastroenterology, 1996—99; fellowship in advanced gastrointestinal endoscopy Harvard Med. Sch., Boston, 1999—2000, instr. in medicine, 1999—2000; asst. prof. medicine MD Anderson Cancer Ctr., Houston, 2000—02, St. Louis U. Sch. Medicine, 2002—, dir. advanced gastrointestinal endoscopy, assoc. prof. medicine divsn. gastroenterology and hepatology, 2006—. Course dir. Ann. Symposia on Gastrointestinal Cancers, St. Louis, 2002—, David Jick Meml. Symposium Pancriato Biliary Disorders, 2006—. Recipient Charles Flood Rsch. prize, Columbia U. Coll. P&S, 1999, REGAL award (Rsch. Excellence in Gastrointestinal and Liver Disease), 2005, Hind Rattan award, 2010, Nav Rattan award, 2011; named one of Best Drs. in Am., 2005—, Am. Top Physicians, 2006—10. Mem.: Am. Assn. for Cancer Rsch., Am. Soc. Gastrointestinal Endoscopy, Am. Gastroenterology Assn. (Young Clinician award 1998). Hindu. Achievements include Conceived and developed the annual symposium on Gastrointestinal Cancers to promote their multidisciplinary management; development of one of nation's largest referral clinical practice specializing in diagnosis and staging of gastrointestinal cancers. Avocations: reading, running, tennis, swimming. Office: Saint Louis U Sch Medicine 3635 Vista Ave Saint Louis MO 63105 Office Fax: 314-577-8757. Personal E-mail: agarwalb@slu.edu.

AGARWAL, MANIKA, obstetrician, gynecologist, educator; b. Meerut, Jan. 25, 1972; MBBS, LLRM Coll., Meerut, 1994; MD in Ob-Gyn., MAMC, New Delhi, 1998. Ass. prof. ob-gyn. NEIGRIHMS, Govt. of India, 2007—. Cons. Apollo Clinic, Agra, 2004—05, Heritage Hosp., Agra, 2005—06. Recipient Gold medals, LLRM Coll. Mem.: MNAMS (India), SELSI (India), FOGSI. Avocations: music, reading. Office: Neigrihms Shillong Meghalaya 793018 India E-mail: drmanika89@yahoo.com.

AGARWAL, MANOJKUMAR, ophthalmologist, consultant; b. Sikar, Rajasthan, India, Oct. 19, 1963; s. Jagdishnarain and Indiradevi Agarwal; m. Suman Agarwal, May 5, 1992; 1 child, Shitij. MBBS with hons., Grant Med. Coll., Mumbai, India, 1987, MS, 1990, DNB, 1991. Lectr. Nair Hosp., Med. Coll., Mumbai, 1990—91, Grant Med. Coll., Mumbai, 1991—95, assoc. prof., 1995—2002; prof., head Dr. V. M. Med. Coll., Solapur, India, 2002; cons., dir. Shitij Eyecare Ctr., Mumbai, 2003—; cons. Pramukhswami Eye Hosp., Mumbai, 2003—. Cons. Gokuldham Med. Ctr., Mumbai, 2003—, Rotary Eye Hosp. Contbr. scientific papers to profl. jours. Recipient Farish scholarship, Sir Jamshedji Duggan prize for highest marks in ophthalmology, Dr. Menino Desouza prize for most outstanding student, Shirinji Mehtaji prize for best paper presentation, Assn. Med. Women in India. Fellow: Coll. Physician and Surgeons; mem.: Retina Found., Kandivali Med. Assn. (life), Vitreo-Retinal Soc. India (life), Maharashtra Ophthalmol. Soc. (life), All India Ophthalmol. Soc. (life), Bombay Ophthalmologists Assn. (life), Assn. Med. Cons. (life), Fedn. Coll. Ophthalmologists. Hindu. Avocations: sports, reading. Office: Shitij Eye Care Ctr Kaveri-D-002 Vasant Sagar Thakur Village Kandivali-E 400101 India Office Phone: 91 22 28855990.

AGARWAL, NIVEDITA, neurologist, radiologist; b. Tokyo, Jan. 28, 1975; MD, U. Cattolica del Sacro Cuore, Rome, 1999. Rsch. fellow Neuroimaging Ctr., McLean Hosp., 2008—09; adj. asst. prof. U. Utah, Sect. Neuroradiology, 2010—; postdoc. fellow U. Utah, Brain Inst., 2009—10; neuroradiologist Gen. Hosp. Trento 'Santa Chiara', 2010—; neurologist, radiologist U. Udine, Italy. Home: Via Zara 16 Trento 38122 Italy Personal E-mail: niveditaaga@gmail.com.

AGARWAL, PADAM KUMARI, pathologist, educator; b. Bulandshahar, India, Feb. 27, 1937; d. Triveni Sahai and Radha Devi Agarwal; m. Ramesh Chandra; 2 children. BSc, Meerut Coll., India, 1959; MBBS, S.N. Med. Coll., Agra, India, 1964; MD in Pathology, K.G. Med. Coll., Lucknow, India, 1969. Intern S.N. Med. Coll., Agra, 1964-65, resident, 1965-66; demonstrator King George's Med. Coll., Lucknow, 1966-69, lectr., 1970-75, reader, 1975-86, prof. pathology, 1986-97; sr. cons. pathology Vivekananda Poly. & Inst. Med. Scis., Lucknow, 2005—. Cons. G.M. & Assocs. Hosp., Lucknow, 1970-97. Commonwealth med. fellow Commonwealth U., London, 1977-78. Mem. Indian Assn Pathology and Microbiology (life), Indian Acad. Cytologists (life, Earnest Fernandes award 1982, Cipla-Acad. Oration 1995), Indian Soc. Oncology (life), Internat. Acad. Cytology (emeritus), N.Y. Acad. Scis. Avocation: reading and writing scientific papers. Home: A-15 Nirala Nagar Lucknow 226020 India Home Phone: 0522-2786721; Office Phone: 0522-2789680. Personal E-mail: madamagarwal@gmail.com. Business E-Mail: agarwal@sanekarnet.in.

AGARWAL, SANDEEP KRISHNA, physician, educator; b. Raliegh, NC, June 30, 1971; BA, U. Tex. Austin, 1993; MD, PhD, UTHSC-Houston Med. Sch., 2000. Asst. prof. UTHSC-Houston Med. Sch., 2007—. Office: UTHSC-Houston Med Sch 6431 Fannin Houston TX 77030 Office Fax: 713-500-0580. Business E-Mail: sandeep.k.agarwal@uth.tmc.edu.

AGARWAL, SHASHI KANT, cardiologist; b. Jullundur, Punjab, India, June 15, 1952; arrived in US, 1975; s. Vadhika Ram and Raj Aggarwal; children: Neil, Ayna. Bd. cert. internal medicine and cardiovascular diseases 1979, bd. cert. cardiovascular diseases 1981, bd. cert. managed care medicine and disability analysts 1999, isntr. fundamental critical care support Soc. Critical Care Medicine, 2000, bd. cert. disability analysts 2002, bd. cert. holistic medicine 2004, cert. hosp. physicians 2005, geriatrics 2005, ethical physicians 2005, diplomate anti-aging medicine 2006. Attending cardiologist Orange Meml. Hosp., NJ, 1985—97; pvt. practice Orange. Tchr. U. N.Mex., Albuquerque, St. Michael's Med. Ctr., Newark, 1979-81, asst. to chief of cardiology, 1980-81; dir. divsn. cardiology South Amboy Meml. Hosp., 1991; ofcl. physician India Festival Com.; lectr. in field. Author, editor: (monthly newsletter) Good Health Long Life; reviewer: Catheterization and Cardiovasc. Diagnosis; appeared on weekly TV show To Your Health, 1995-96; contbr. over 500 articles to profl. publs. Del. citizen amb. program People to People Internat., Med. Writers Del. to Russia and Estonia, 1997; gen. sec. Overseas Indian Congress, 1993-95; v.p. Asian Am. Heritage Coun., 1994-97; mem. nat. fin. com. Nat. Rep. Party, 1995-96; mem. Rep. Senatorial Trust, Nat. Rep. Congl. Com., Rep. Presdl. Legion of Merit; life mem. Rep. Presdl. Task Force; mem. steering com. Vedic Cultural Ctr. Project NY; pres. Asian Music Acad., 1997-98, Asian Am. Heritage Coun., 1997-99, chmn., 2000-01, Pragya Mission USA Inc; chmn. internat. adv. com. Physicians Panel of Sarvodaya Health Charitable Found., exec. dir. Sarvodaya Health Found., USA; judge MIss India Worldwide, Mumbai, India, 2004, 06, Miss Indian Can. Worldwide, Toronto, 2005, Miss India USA, Tampa, Fla., 2005, Miss Phillipine USA, Secaucus, NJ, 2005, Miss India UK, Leicester, 2005, several other beauty contests. Recipient Physician's Recognition award AMA, 1992-95, 95-98, 98-01, Rep. Presdl. award, 1994, Rep. Senatorial Medal of Freedom, 1994, News India Times Contbr.'s award, 1994, Rep. Presdl. Legion of Merit medal 1995, Key to West Orange, NJ, 1996, 98, Internat. Cultural Diploma of Honor, 1997, Med. Medal of Honor for Treatment of the Indigent, 1997, Chmn.'s Spl. award Asian Am. Heritage Coun., 1997, Hind Rattan award (Gem of India award) Indian Prime Minister Hon. I.K. Gural, 1998-2001. Fellow Am. Coll. Cardiology (cert.), Am. Coll. Chest Physicians, Am. Coll. Internat. Physicians, Internat. Coll. Physicians, Royal Soc. Medicine UK, Internat. Coun. Integrative Medicine Australia, Coll. Geriatric Cardiology, Acad. Medicine NJ; mem. ACP, Internat. Coll. Physicians (founder NJ chpt.), Am. Soc. Spiritual Medicine (founder), Am. Assn. Cardiologists of Indian Origin (life), Am. Assn. Physicians from India (patron), Am. Coll. Nuclear Physicians, Am. Sleep Disorders Assn., Am. Inst. Ultrasound Medicine, Am. Coll. Physician Execs., Soc. Critical Care Medicine, Heart Friends Around the World, Am. Acad. Family Physicians (supporting), Am. Philatelic Soc., Asian Am. Polit. Coalition (life), Mensa. Republican. Hindu. Avocations: flying, boating, singing, music.

AGARWAL, SHEELA, biology professor; b. Bangalore, Apr. 3, 1948; PhD, MS U. Baroda, 1973. Prof. J.N.V U., Jodhpur, Rajasthan, 1973—2008. Jr. Rsch. fellowship, U. Grants Commn. Mem.: Current Agr. Avocations: photography, mountain climbing, reading. Home: A-9 1004 Karishma Soc Kothrud Pune Maharashtra 411029 India Personal E-mail: sheelaagarwal@yahoo.com.

AGARWAL, SURESH, surgeon; b. Boston, Feb. 8, 1969; BA, U. Pa., 1991; MD, U. Pitts. Sch. Medicine, 1995. Chief, surg. critical care Boston Med. Ctr., 2003—; assoc. prof. surgery Boston U. Sch. Medicine, 2008. Fellow: ACS, Am. Coll. Chest Physicians, Am. Coll. Critical Care Medicine; mem.: Assn. Academic Surgery, Am. Assn. Surgery Trauma. Office: 850 Harrison Ave Dowling 2 S Ste 2508 Boston MA 02118 Business E-Mail: suresh.agarwal@bmc.org.

AGARWAL, UMBER, obstetrician, gynecologist, specialist registrar; b. Kanpur, Uttar Pradesh, India, Mar. 22, 1975; s. Balkishan and Raj Agarwal. MBBS, Baroda Med. Coll., Gujarat, India, 1998; MD, All India Inst. of Med. sciences, 2001. Diplomate Nat. Bd. of Exams., New Delhi, India, 2001, cert. neonaltal life support Resuscitation Coun. UK, 2003, mng. obstet. emergencies and trauma Advanced Life Support Group UK, 2003. Registrar in ob-gyn. Pt B.D.Sharma PGIMS, Rohtak, Haryana, India, 2001—03; specialist registrar in ob-gyn. Barnet Gen. Hosp., London, 2003—, specialist registrar, 2003—. Contbr. over 80 articles to profl. jours. Recipient Cert. of Merit and Book grant in physiology, biochemistry and microbiology, Baroda Charitable Edn. Fund, Baroda Med. Coll., 1992-1998; Nat. Merit and Scholarship Cert. in Physics and Biology, Govt. of India, Ministry of Edn., 1992. Fellow: Royal Coll. Ob-gyn. UK, Indian Coll. Maternal and Child Health; mem.: Nat. Acad. Med. Scis., Fedn. Ob-gyn. Soc. India (corr.), Nat. Assn. for Reproductive and Child Health India (life). Avocations: academic writing and research, travel, chess, music, poetry. Office: Barnet Gen Hosp Wellhouse Ln London EN5 3DJ England Office Fax: 0044(0)2082165221. E-mail: agarwalumber@yahoo.co.in.

AGARWAL, VIRENDRA KUMAR, dean, director medical education; s. Rameshwar Dayal and Bugali Devi Agarwal; m. Urmila Mittal, Mar. 1, 1954; children: Sujata Bhargava, Jyoti Bindal, Sanjiv Kumar. MBBS, MGM Med. Coll., Indore, 1953, MS, 1956. Lectr. surgery MGM Med. Coll., 1956—61, assoc. prof. cardio-thoracic surgery, 1961—67, dean, 1989—90; prof. and head, dept. surgery State Med. Colls., Gwalior, 1967—89, Bhopal, India, Indore; dir. med. edn. Govt. of M.P., Bhopal, 1990—91; med. dir. Sanjeevni Nursing Home, Indore, 1991—. Recipient Nat. Unity award, Govt. India, 1990; scholar, WHO, 1984; Commonwealth fellowship, U. Toronto, 1971. Fellow: ACS, Internat. Coll. Surgeons; mem.: Indian Med. Assn. (Charak award 2007), Asis Pacific Assn. Cardio-Thoracic Surgeons, Assn. Surgeons, India (Hari Om Ashram award 1984). Achievements include research in limb salvage and restoring vision in retinal degeration (Retinitis Pigmentosa), Agarwal technique of omental transplantation; breakthrough Established technique to restore vision in Retinitis Pigmentosa and Macular Deqeration. Home: 1 Phadnis Colony AB Rd Indore MP 452009 India Office: Sanjeevni Nursing Home 1 Phadnis Colony AB Rd Indore MP 452009 India Home Phone: 91-731-2542020; Office Phone: 91-731-2430033. Personal E-mail: dr_vkagarwal@rediffmail.com.

AGATSTON, ARTHUR STEPHEN, cardiologist, educator; b. NYC, Jan. 22, 1947; s. Howard James and Adell (Paymer) Agatston; m. Sari Agatston, Mar. 7, 1983; 1 child, Adam; 1 child, Evan. BA, U. Wis., 1969; MD, NYU, 1973. Diplomate Am. Bd. Internal Medicine, Am. Bd. Cardiovasc. Disease. Intern medicine Montefiore Hosp. Med. Ctr., Albert Einstein Coll. Medicine, NYC, 1973-74, resident, 1974-76; cardiology fellow NYU Med. Ctr., NYC, 1977-79; dir. noninvasive cardiology Mt. Sinai Med. Ctr., Miami Beach, Fla., 1980; assoc. prof. medicine U. Miami Miller Sch. Medicine; ptnr. pvt. practice South Fla. Cardiology Assocs., Miami. Pres. greater Miami chpt. Am. Heart Assn., 1992; bd. dirs. Am. Dietetic Assn. Found.; expert cons. Clin. Trials Com. NIH; founder Agatston Rsch. Found., Miami Beach, 2004—. Author: South Beach Diet: The Delicious, Doctor-Designed, Foolproof Plan for Fast & Healthy Weight Loss, 2003, South Beach Diet Cookbook, 2004, South Beach Diet Good Fats/Good Carbs Guide: The Complete & Easy Reference for All Your Favorite Foods, 2004, South Beach Diet Quick and Easy Cookbook: 200 Delicious Recipes Ready in 30 Minutes or Less, 2005, South Beach Diet Dining Guide, 2005, South Beach Diet Parties & Holidays Cookbook, 2006, South Beach Diet Taste of Summer Cookbook, 2007, South Beach Heart Health Revolution, 2007, The South Beach Diet Supercharged: Faster Weight Loss & Better Health for Life, 2008; contbr. articles to profl. jours., chapters to books. Fellow: Am. Coll. Cardiology; mem.: Soc. Atherosclerosis Imaging (founding mem. bd. dirs.), Am. Soc. Echocardiography. Achievements include development of (with others) the electron beam tomography scan (EBT), a screening method used to detect coronary artery disease and other diseases. Office: Agatston Rsch Found 1691 Michigan Ave Ste 500 Miami Beach FL 33139 Office Phone: 305-538-3828.

AGEWALL, STEFAN, physician, researcher, educator; b. Karlskrona, Sweden, Feb. 11, 1960; s. Bertil and Brita (Agewall) Andersson; m. Christina Bodehed, Oct. 20, 1993; children: Cecilia, Louise, John. MD, Goteborg U., Sweden, 1986, PhD, 1994. Intern Sahlgrenska U. Hosp., Goteborg, 1987-88, resident dept. medicine, 1988-92; internal medicine specialist and cardiologist Sahlgrenska U., Goteborg, 1992-99; vis. asst. prof. dept. medicine U. Auckland, New Zealand, 1997-98; cons., asst. prof. dept. cardiology Huddinge U. Hosp., Stockholm, 1999—, head of cardiac care unit, 2000—03, Karolinska Univ. Hosp., 2003—06; prof., cardiology Aker U. Hosp., 2006—10, Oslo U. Ullevil, 2011—. Edtl. bd. mem. European Heart Jour., 2006—; assoc. editor Atherosclerosis, 2007—. Contbr. articles to profl. jours. Recipient Internat. Rsch. Work award, Wenner-Gren Found., 1998; grantee, Goteborg Med. Soc., Swedish Heart and Lung Found., Swedish Med. Rsch. Coun.; fellow, European Soc. Cardiology. Fellow: European Soc. Cardiology (clin. hypertension specialist, nuc. mem. working group cardiovasc. pharmacology); mem.: European Soc. Hypertension, Swedish Med. Soc., Am. Soc. Hypertension (award 1992—98), Internat. Soc. Hypertension. Avocations: golf, squash. Office Phone: 47 22817512. Business E-Mail: stefan.agewall@medisin.u.oslo.nr, stefan.agewall@medisin.nio.no.

AGGARWAL, ANJALI, physician; b. Agra, India, Sept. 13, 1963; MBBS, Indore, India, 1987; MD, GMCH, Chandigarh, India, 2004. Cons. Postgrad. Inst. Med. Edn. & Rsch., Chandigarh, India, 2008, asst. prof., anatomy, 2008—. Mem.: ASI, EAS, AACA. Avocations: cooking, gardening. Office: Postgrad Inst Med Edn & Rsch Chandigarh 160012 India Office Fax: 91-172-2744401. Personal E-mail: anjli_doc@yahoo.com.

AGGARWAL, ARUN, neurologist, pain and rehabilitation specialist; b. New Dehli, India, Apr. 18, 1965; s. Niranjan and Veena Aggarwal; m. Ghauri Chandrasegaram, Apr. 13, 1990; children: Nisha, Ashwin. MBBS, U. Adelaide, Australia, 1989; PhD, U. Sydney, 1998—. Staff specialist in rehab. and pain medicine Royal Prince Alfred Hosp., Sydney, NSW, 1998—; clin. assoc. prof. Sydney Med. Sch. U. Sydney, 2010. Vis. med. officer neurology Strathfield Pvt. Hosp., Sydney, 1998—; vis. med. officer rehab. medicine Hunters Hill Pvt. Hosp., Sydney, 1998—; vis. med. officer neurology Concord Hosp., Sydney, 2000—. Recipient Rsch. grant, Motor Neurone Disease Rsch. Inst. Australia, 1999, 2000, 2002; named 58th winner of Challenge Cup, Brit. Med. Assn., 2001. Fellow: Royal Australian Coll. Physicians, Faculty Pain Medicine, Australasian Faculty of Rehab. Medicine; mem.: Australian Pain Soc., Australian Assn. Neurologists (Young Investigator award 1999), Royal Australasian Coll. Physicians. Avocations: golf, travel, wine. Home and Office: Ste 190 Victoria Rd Rozelle NSW 2039 Australia E-mail: arun@email.cs.nsw.gov.au.

AGGARWAL, GAURAV, medical educator; b. India, Jan. 15, 1976; MBBS, Govt. Med. Coll., 2002; MS, U. Utah, 2006. Instr. Coll. Medicine Mayo Clinic, Rochester, 2009—. Faculty mem. Faculty of 1000, 2010. Contbr. articles to jours. Recipient Investigator award, Internat. Assn. Pancreatology; Thomas D. Dee II fellowship, U. Utah. Mem.: Am. Pancreatic Assn. (Hirshberg award), Am. Gastroent. Assn., Am. Coll. Gastroenterology. Office: 200 1st St SW Rochester MN 55905 Personal E-mail: dr.gaurav.aggarwal@gmail.com.

AGGARWAL, PAKHEE, physician; b. New Delhi, Oct. 21, 1981; MBBS, Maulana Azad Med. Coll., 2004, MS, 2008. Sr. resident All India Inst. Med. Scis., 2008—. Pvt. practice. Recipient Mohan Lal Nayyar Gold medal, Maulana Azad Med. Coll. & Lok Nayak Hosp.,

2007; fellowship, Assn. Commonwealth U. Mem.: Indian Coll. Ob-Gyn., Indian Pub. Health Assn. Avocations: reading, writing. Home: Flat 4187 Sector B Pocket 5 & 6 Vasant New Delhi Delhi 110070 India Personal E-mail: pakh_ag@yahoo.com.

AGGARWAL, SANJEEV, cardiologist; b. New Delhi, Nov. 1, 1968; MD, Maulana Azad Med. Coll., 1992. Rsch. fellow Children's Hosp. Mich., 2005, cardiologist, 2006—11. Office: Children's Hosp Mich 3901 Beaubien St #4c19 Detroit MI 48201 Business E-Mail: ssanjeev@dmc.org.

AGHAJANIAN, GEORGE KEVORK, medical educator; b. Beirut, Apr. 14, 1932; (parents Am. citizens); s. Ghevont M. and Araxi (Movsessian) A.; m. Anne E. Hammond, Jan. 10, 1959; children: Michael, Andrew, Carol, Laura. AB, Cornell U., 1954; MD, Yale U., 1958. Asst. prof. psychiatry Sch. of Medicine Yale U., New Haven, 1965-68, assoc. prof. psychiatry Sch. of Medicine, 1968-70, assoc. prof. psychiatry and pharmacology Sch. of Medicine, 1970-74, prof. psychiatry and pharmacology Sch. of Medicine, 1974—, founds. fund prof. Sch. of Medicine, 1985. Contbr. more than 300 articles to profl. jours. Capt. US Army, 1963—65. Recipient Hoffheimer prize Am. Psychiat. Assn., 1981, Scheele medal Swedish Acad. Pharmacy, 1981, Merit award NIH, 1990-2000, Hillarp award Internat. Amine Group, 1996, Lieber prize NARSAD, 1998. Fellow Am. Coll. Neuropsychopharmacology (Efron award 1975, Axelrod award 2006); mem. Soc. for Pharmacology and Exptl. Therapeutics, Soc. for Neurosci., Internat. Brain Rsch. Orgn., Inst. of Medicine, Inst. of Medicine of NAS. Achievements include research in electrophysiological and pharmacological properties of brain serotonergic, noradrenergic, and dopaminergic neurons. Office: 34 Park St New Haven CT 06519-1109 E-mail: george.aghajanian@yale.edu.

AGIN, CAROLE, pain medicine physician, anesthesiologist, educator; MD, Rosalind Franklin U., 1986. Diplomate Am. Bd. Anesthesiology, Am. Bd. Anesthesiology-pain medicine. Resident anesthesiology Beth Israel Med. Ctr., NY, 1987—90; fellow in pain medicine Meml. Sloan- Kettering Cancer Ctr., NY, 1990—91; assoc. prof. in anesthesiology SUNY, 2002; physician Stony Brook Univ. Hosp. Office: Stony Brook University Hospital 3 Edmund D Pellegrino Rd Stony Brook NY 11794-9464

AGLAN, MONA SABRY, geneticist, educator, pediatrician; b. Cairo, Apr. 4, 1961; d. Sabry Ahmed Aglan and Amina Nosseir; m. Mohamed Gehad Marei, Jan. 19, 1984; children: Fouad Gehad Marei, Hadir Gehad Marei. MBBCh in Medicine with honors, Cairo U., 1984, MS, 1991, MD, 1999. House officer Cairo U. Hosp., 1985—86, resident, 1989—91; vis. scholar U. Sheffield, Children's Hosp., England, 1992—94; rsch. asst., human genetics dept. Nat. Rsch. Ctr., 1991—99, lectr., clin. genetics dept., 1999—2004, rschr. human genetics, 1999—2004, tchr., ministry health and population, 2000—, co-dir. skeletal dysplasia and limb malformations clinic, med. svc. unit, 2000—, supr., 2000—, asst. prof. clin. genetics, 2004—09, prof. clin. genetics, 2009—. Cons. Genetic Counselling Clinics, Ministry Health and Population, Cairo, 2004—; co-investigator Egyptian Team Leader, European Comm., 2006—07. Co-author: (book) 20 Q & A in Genetic Disorders, Simplified Approach For the Diagnosis of Genetic Diseases; contbr. chapters to books, articles to profl. jours. Orator Social Clubs, Cairo, 2000, organizer several pub. symposia increasing pub. awareness field human genetics, 2000; mem. offering free med. svc. different orphan socs. Religious Ctrs., Cairo, 1992; mem. Tree Lovers Assn., Cairo, 1994—98. Recipient Platinum award, 2003; grant, Nat. Rsch. Ctr., Acad. Sci. Rsch., 1998—. Mem.: Internat. Soc. Cmty. Genetics & Genomics, Nat. Soc. Human Genetics (founding mem.), European Soc. Human Genetics, Egyptian Soc. Med. Genetics, Arab Soc. Med. Rsch. (Appreciation Cert. 2005). Muslim. Achievements include research in rare genetic diseases including first reported cases from Egypt and emphasizing the effect of consanguinity in their inheritance and prevalence rates. Avocations: travel, reading, drawing, exercise. Office: Nat Rsch Ctr El-Buhouth St Dokki Cairo 12311 Egypt Office Phone: 20-101131203. Office Fax: 202-27538150. Personal E-mail: drmona_aglan@yahoo.com.

AGNEW, SAMUEL GERARD, orthopaedic traumatologist; b. New Orleans, Oct. 22, 1958; s. Thomas A. and Elizabeth (De la Houssaye) A.; m. Denise Kachler, May 3, 1986; children: Taylor Frances, Caroline Elizabeth. BS, U. S.C., 1980; MD, Tulane U., 1984. Diplomate Am. Bd. Orthopaedic Surgeons. Chief trauma orthopedic dept. orthopedics, asst. prof. U. Miss. Med. Ctr., Jackson, 1990-91; chief orthopedic trauma, asst. prof. U. Ark. for Med. Scis., Little Rock, 1991-95; chief orthopedic trauma, assoc. prof. U. Fla., Jacksonville, 1995—. Vis. lectr. Hennepin County Med., 1994, Pa. Orthopaedic, 1994. Author: Orthopedic Clinics of North America, 1992. Fellow Am. Acad. Orthopaedics; mem. ACS, Orthopedic Trauma Assn., Am. Assn. for Surgery of Trauma, Assn. for Advancement of Automotive Medicine. Office: Pee Dee Orthopaedic Associat 901 E Cheves St Ste 100 Florence SC 29506-2769

AGNIFILI, LUCA, physician, researcher; b. Lanciano, Italy, Oct. 7, 1973; MD, G. d'Annunzio U. Chieti-Pescara, 1999, PhD, 2009. Rschr. ophthalmic clinic G. d'Annunzio U. Chieti-Pescara, 2009. Office: Via dei Vestini snc Chieti Abruzzo 66100 Italy Office Fax: 390871358794. Business E-Mail: l.agnifili@unich.it.

AGRANOFF, BERNARD WILLIAM, biochemist, educator; b. Detroit, June 26, 1926; s. William and Phyllis (Pelavin) A.; m. Raquel Betty Schwartz, Sept. 1, 1957; children: William, Adam. MD, Wayne State U., 1950; BS, U. Mich., 1954. Intern Robert Packer Hosp., Sayre, Pa., 1950-51; lt. commd. surgeon USPHS, 1954—60; biochemist Nat. Inst. Neurol. Diseases and Blindness, NIH, Bethesda, Md., 1954-60; mem. faculty U. Mich., Ann Arbor, 1960—2005, prof. biochemistry, 1965—; R.W. Gerard prof. of neurosci. in psychiatry, 1991. Rsch. biochemist Mental Health Rsch. Inst., 1960—, assoc. dir., 1977-83, dir. 1983-95, dir. neurosci. lab., 1983-2000; vis. scientist Max Planck Inst. Zellchemie, Munich, 1957-58, Nat. Inst. Med. Rsch., Mill Hill, Eng., 1974-75; Henry Russel lectr. U. Mich., 1987; cons. pharm. industry, govt. Contbr. articles to profl. jours. Fogarty scholar-in-residence NIH, Bethesda, Md., 1989-95; named Mich. Scientist of Yr. Mus. of Sci., Lansing, 1992. Fellow AAAS, Am. Acad. Arts and Scis., N.Y. Acad. Sci., Am. Coll. Neuropsychopharmacology; mem. Am. Soc. Biochemistry and Molecular Biology, Am. Chem. Soc., Inst. Medicine of NAS, Internat. Soc. Neurochemistry (treas. 1985-89, chmn. 1989-91), Am. Soc. Neurochemistry (pres. 1973-75). Achievements include research in brain lipids, biochem. basis of learning, memory and regeneration in the nervous system, human brain imaging. Office: U Mich Molecular and Behavior Rsch Inst 205 Zina Pitcher Pl Ann Arbor MI 48109-5720 Office Phone: 734-764-4214. Personal E-mail: agranoff@umich.edu.

AGRAWAL, ALOK CHANDRA, orthopedist, educator; b. Nagpur, July 1, 1967; MBBS, Pt. J. N. M. Med. Coll., Raipur, Chhattisgarh, India, 1989, MS in Orthop., 1994; DNB in Orthop., NBE, India, 1993; PhD, PhD, RDVV, Jabalpur, Madhya Pradesh, India, 2004. Registrar, sr. registrar orthop. KMCH, Coimbatore, India, 1993—95; cons. orthop. surgeon Balaji Nursing Home, Raipur, 1995—97; asst. prof. orthop. NSCB Med. Coll., Jabalpur, 1997—2003, assoc. prof. orthop., 2003—11, Bundelkhand Med. Coll., Sagar, Madhya Pradesh, 2007—. Editor Ctrl. Zone Indian Orthop. Assn., 2009—. Mem.: MANIS (New Delhi), World Orthop. Concern (India), Indian Orthop. Assn. (Madhya Pradesh, Tamilnadu, Orissa, Chhattisgarh) (hon. sec. Madhya Pradesh chpt. 2009—, editor Madhya Pradesh chpt. 2000—07, assoc. editor Indian jour. orthop. 2007—10, exec. body mem. 2005—07, IOS UK Indo Brit. Travelling Orthop. fellowship 2008, Pres. Appreciation award, Chhattisgarh chpt. 2010, WOC-SICOT fellowship, Hong Kong 2008), Acad. Med. Scis. (India) (Sir Shriram Travel fellowship). Avocations: travel, violin. Home: NSCB Med Coll R-5 Doctor's Colony Jabalpur Madhya Pradesh 482003 India Personal E-mail: dralokcagrawal@yahoo.co.in.

AGRE, PETER COURTLAND, molecular biologist, educator; b. Northfield, Minn., Jan. 30, 1949; m. Mary Herbert Macgill, Mar. 29, 1975; children: Sara Macgill, Claire Coleman, Clarke Gambrill, Anne Carlyle. BA in Chemistry, with honors, Augsburg Coll., Mpls., 1970; MD, John Hopkins U. Sch. Medicine, Balt., 1974. Diplomate Am. Bd. Internal Medicine. Intern, resident internal medicine Case Western Res. U. & Hosp., Cleve., 1975—78; postdoc. fellow hematology/oncology divsn. U. NC, Chapel Hill, 1978—80, clin. asst. prof. medicine, 1980—81; from rsch. assoc., then instr. dept. medicine and cell biology/anatomy Johns Hopkins Sch. Medicine, 1981—83, asst. prof., 1984—88, assoc. prof., 1988—93, prof. dept. biol. chemistry and medicine, 1993—2005; prof. dept. cell biology and dept. medicine Duke U. Med. Ctr., Durham, NC, 2005—08, vice chancellor sci. and tech., 2005—08; dir. Malaria Rsch. Inst., Univ. prof. Johns Hopkins U. Bloomberg Sch. Pub. Health, 2008—. Sr. clin. rsch. scientist Wellcome Labs., Research Triangle Park, NC, 1980—81; vis. prof. dept. embryology Carnegie Instn., Washington, 1988—89; mem. adv. bd. Norwegian Rsch. & Tech. Forum US/Can.; mem. internat. sci. coun. Israeli-Palestinian Sci. Orgn.; mem. sci. rev. bd. Howard Hughes Med. Inst. Mem. editl. bd. Jour. Clin. Investigation, 1993—, Blood, 1993—97, Jour. Biol. Chemistry, 2003—; contbr. articles to profl. jours. Hon. mem. Internat. Raoul Wallenberg Found., 2004—. Recipient Clin. Investigator award, Nat. Heart, Lung & Blood Inst., 1981—85, Basil O'Connor award, March of Dimes Birth Defects Found., 1986—88, Established Investigator award, Am. Heart Assn., 1987—92, Young Investigator award, Am. Fedn. Clin. Rsch., 1991, Disting. Alumnus award, Augsburg Coll., 1995, Nobel prize for chemistry, 2003, Golden Plate award, Acad. Achievement, 2004, Karl Landsteiner award, Am. Assn. Blood Banks, 2005, Disting. Eagle Scout award, Boy Scouts America, 2005; co-recipient Biennial Spa Found. prize, 2003. Mem.: AAAS (pres. 2009—), NAS (com. on human rights 2003—08), Am. Philos. Soc., Am. Acad. Arts & Scis., Inst. Medicine, Am. Soc. Nephrology (Homer Smith award 1999), Am. Soc. Biochemistry & Molecular Biology, Am. Physiol. Soc., Am. Soc. Clin. Investigation, Am. Soc. Cell Biology, Interurban Clin. Club (hon.). Achievements include patents in field. Office: Johns Hopkins Bloomberg Sch Pub Health 615 N Wolfe St MD 21205 Baltimore MD 21205 Office Phone: 443-287-8745. Office Fax: 410-955-0105.

AGRESS, HARRY, JR., radiologist, nuclear medicine physician; s. Harry and June W. Agress. BA in Math., Tufts U., 1968, MD, 1972. Diplomate Am. Bd. Radiology, Am. Bd. Nuclear Medicine, Nat. Bd. Med. Examiners. Intern Mt. Sinai Med. Ctr., NYC, 1972—73; fellow NIH, Bethesda, Md., 1973—75; resident in diagnostic radiology Columbia-Presbyn. Med. Ctr., NYC, 1975—78; dir. divsn. nuc. medicine Hackensack U. Med. Ctr., NJ, 1978—; from asst. to attending physician Hackensack (NJ) U. Med. Ctr., 1980—96; asst. clin. prof. Columbia U. Coll. Physicians and Surgeons, NYC, 1980—88, assoc. clin. prof. radiology, 1988—2001; sr. attending radiologist Hackensack (NJ) U. Med. Ctr., 1996—; dir. Positron Emission Tomography Ctr., 1999—; clin. prof. Columbia U. Coll. Physicians and Surgeons, NYC, 2002—; chmn. dept. radiology Hackensack (NJ) U. Med. Ctr., 2005—. Bd. dirs. PET/CT, GE Med. Sys., Milw.; oral exam examiner Am. Bd. Radiology, Tucson, 1999—; nat. lectr., spkr., presenter in field. Contbr. chapters to books, articles to profl. jours. Bd. vis. Mary Inst. St. Louis Country Day Sch., 2003—07. Lt. comdr. USPHS, 1973—75. Named one of Castle Connolly Top Doctors, NY Metro Area Nuclear Medicine; fellowship, Am. Coll. Radiology, 2008. Mem.: AMA, Am. Roentgen Ray Soc., Radiol. Soc. NJ, NJ Med. Soc., Acad. Molecular Imaging, Radiol. Soc. N.Am., Soc. Nuclear Medicine, Am. Coll. Radiology (fellow 2008). Achievements include research in positron emission tomography detection of unexpected asymptomatic cancers. Avocations: piano, photography, golf. Office: Hackensack Univ Med Ctr Dept Radiology 30 Prospect Ave Hackensack NJ 07601 Office Phone: 201-996-2196.

AGRIMSON, LAURIE, nurse practitioner; b. Mpls., Jan. 3, 1956; MSN, U. Wis., Eau Claire, 2010. Nurse practitioner HealthEast Hosp., 1999—. Mem.: Phi Kappa Phi, Sigma Theta Tau. Avocations: music, bicycling. Home: 1077 Robert St S West Saint Paul MN 55118 Office Phone: 651-232-3819. Personal E-mail: agrihowell@aol.com, lagrimson@healtheast.org.

AGRUSS, NEIL STUART, cardiologist; b. Chgo., June 2, 1939; s. Meyer and Frances (Spector) A.; m. Janyce Zucker; children: David, Lauren, Michael, Joshua, Susan, Robyn, Bryan. BS, U. Ill., 1960, MD, 1963. Diplomate Am. Bd. Internal Medicine. Resident in internal medicine Cin. Gen. Hosp., 1964-65, 67-68, fellow in cardiology, 1968-70, dir. coronary care unit, 1971-74, dir. echocardiography lab., 1972-74; asst. prof. medicine U. Cin., 1970-74; dir. cardiac diagnostic labs. Ctr. DuPage Hosp., Winfield, Ill., 1974—; asst. prof. medicine Rush Med. Coll., 1976—. Chmn. coronary care com. Heart Assn. DuPage County, 1974-76. Author, co-author publs. in field. Active Congregation Beth Shalom, Naperville, Ill. Capt. M.C. U.S. Army, 1965-67. Fellow ACP, Am. Coll. Cardiology, Am. Coll. Chest Physicians, Coun. Clin. Cardiology, Am. Heart Assn.; mem. AMA, DuPage County Med. Soc., Ill. Med. Soc., Am. Fedn. Clin. Rsch., Chgo. Heart Assn. Office: 454 Pennsylvania Ave Glen Ellyn IL 60137-4418 Office Phone: 630-933-8100. Business E-Mail: hrtdoctor729@msn.com.

AGU, PATRICK ELUEMUNO, radiation technologist, nuclear medicine scientist; b. Onitsha, Nigeria, June 20, 1942; d. Simon Chukwuma and Keziah Udochukwu Agu; m. Mercy Ukamaka, Oct. 8, 1966. BSc in Radiation Tech., U. Vienna, Austria, 1975; MSc in Radiation Tech., U. Nigeria; PhD in Bus. Adminstrn., U. Calif., Glendale, 2000. Cert. radiation technologist. Chief radiology technologist Paterna X-Ray Clinics, Aba, Nigeria, 1979—. Author: Forensic Radiology in Nigeria, 2000 (award Inst. Bus. Execs. Nigeria, 2001). Pres. Help For All, Nigeria, 1970—2003; treas. Abia State Sickle Cell Assn., Aba, 1999—. Fellow in radiol. sci., Inst. Pub. Rels., Abuja, Nigeria, 1997, med. diagnostics, Inst. Sales Mgmt., Abuja, 1998, in med. radiology, Inst. Bus. Execs., Abuja, 2003. Mem.: Assn. Radiologists Nigeria, Internat. Soc. Radiographers and Radiology Technologists. Avocations: ping pong/table tennis, reading. Home: 162 Okigwe Rd Box 2679 Aba Nigeria Office: Paterna X-Ray Clinic 162 Okigwe Rd Aba Nigeria Office Fax: 08222406. Personal E-mail: mecidies@yahoo.com.

AGUAYO LEIVA, INGRID ROCÍO, dermatologist; b. Asunción, Paraguay, Sept. 11, 1977; Lic. U. Nat. Asunción, 2003. Dermatologist Hosp. Ramón y Cajal, 2007—. Home: Calle Riscos Polanco Madrid 28035 Spain Personal E-mail: ingridaguayo77@hotmail.com.

AGUILAR, DANIEL, immunologist, immunoallergist; b. Mexico, June 9, 1937; s. Aguilar Daniel and Bertha Angeles; m. Consuelo Flores, Feb. 5, 1970. MD, U. F. Medicine, Mexico. Pvt. practice, Mexico; specialist Gen. Hosp., Mexico City, Juarez Hosp., Mexico City. Author: Asthma Management, 1988; contbr. articles to profl. jours. Fellow Mexican Soc. Allergy and Immunology (past pres.), Am. Acad. Allergy and Immunology, Am. Coll. Allergy and Immunology, Acad. Mexicana de Cirugia. Office: Av Lindavista 251-501 Mexico City 07300 Mexico E-mail: primo65@prodigy.net.mx.

AGUILERA, SHINO BAY, dermatologist, educator, medical researcher; MD, Western U. of Health Sciences. Diplomate Am. Bd. of Dermatology, dermatologic surgeon. Internship Wellington Regional Med. Ctr., resident; fellow in osteopathic dermatology; asst. prof. dermatology NOVA Univ., L.E.C.O.M., Suncoast Univ., Universidad del Rosario; volunteer instr. dermatology Univ. Miami. Fellow: Am. Osteopathic Coll. of Dermatology; mem.: Broward Dermatol. Soc., Am. Soc. of Laser Medicine and Surgery, Am. Soc. for Dermatologic Surgery, Am. Acad. of Dermatology. Office: Shino Bay Cosmetic Dermatology and Laser Institute Ste 110 Ground Fl 350 Las Olas Blvd Fort Lauderdale FL 33301 Office Phone: 954-765-3005.

AGUINAGA, MARIA DEL PILAR, medical educator; b. Lima, Peru, Oct. 12; BSc in Biology, U. Peruana Cayetano Heredia, Lima, 1977; PhD, Kanazawa U. Med. Sch., 1984. Prof., dept. ob-gyn, assoc. dir., meharry sickle cell ctr. Meharry Med. Coll., Nashville, 1984—. Adj. assoc. prof. divsn. hematology/oncology Vanderbilt U. Med. Sch., 1997—; vis. prof. U. Peruana Cayetano Heredia. Recipient Dedicated Support award, YMCA Latino Achievers Program. Nashville, TN, Disting. Svc. Award, Dept. Ob-Gyn. Meharry Med. Coll.; named Mentor of the Yr., Nat. Ctr. Leadership Academic Medicine. Meharry Med. Coll. Mem.: Am. Soc. Clin. Pathology, EE Just Hematology Soc Minority Hematologists (LA) (pres.), Am. Soc. Hematology. Avocations: aerobics, travel, reading. Office: Meharry Med Coll Dr DB Todd B Nashville TN 37215 Office Fax: 615-327-6593. Business E-Mail: maguinaga@mmc.edu.

AGUREEV, ALEXANDER NIKITOVICH, medical researcher; b. Moscow, Aug. 25, 1943; Student in Med. Scis., Moscow Med. Inst., 1968. Lab. head SSC RF — IBMP RAS, 1968—. Decorated medal Govt. Office: Khoroshevskoye Shosse Moscow 123007 Russia Business E-Mail: aagureev@imbp.ru.

AGUS, DAVID BERNARD, oncologist, researcher, medical educator; b. Balt., Jan. 29, 1965; s. Zalman S. and Sondra L. (Lebow) A.; m. Amy Joyce Povich. BA cum laude, Princeton U., 1987; MD, U. Pa., 1992. Lic. NY, Calif., diplomate Nat. Bd. Med. Examiners, cert. in internal medicine, in med. oncology, Am. Urol. Assn., Soc. Basic Urol. Rsch. Fellow Rsch. Inst. of Scripps Clinic, La Jolla, Calif., 1988-90; physician scientist fellow NIH, Bethesda, Md., 1990-92, rsch. scholar Howard Hughes Med. Inst., 1990-92; Oster med. intern and resident, staff physician Johns Hopkins Hosp., Balt., 1992-94; fellow Meml. Sloan-Kettering Cancer Ctr., NYC, 1994-97, instr. lymphoma svc., 1997-99, head Lab. of Tumor Biology, 1997-2000; rsch. dir., Louis Warschaw Prostate Cancer Ctr. Cedars-Sinai Med. Ctr., LA, 2000—09; asst. prof. medicine UCLA Sch. Medicine, 2000—03, assoc. prof. medicine, 2003—09; prof. medicine U. Southern Calif. Keck Sch. Medicine, LA, 2009—, dir. ctr. applied molecular medicine, 2009—; dir. U. Southern Calif. Westside Prostate Cancer Ctr., Beverly Hills, 2009—. Instr. medicine Cornell U. Med. Ctr., 1997-99, asst. prof. medicine, 1999-2000; asst. mem. Meml. Sloan-Kettering Cancer Ctr., 1999-2000. Author: Interleukin-2: Cellular and Clinical Study, 1987; contbr. articles to Jour. Clin. Investigation, Cancer Cell, Jour. of Exptl. Medicine, Jour. Nat. Cancer Inst. Cancer Rsch.; founder oncology.com. Recipient Achievement award Am. Assn. Allergy and Immunology, 1988, John G. Clark award, 1991, Pioneer award Internat. Myeloma Found., 1995, Physician Rsch. Devel. award Am. Cancer Inst., 1996, Med. Rsch. award Stein Found, 1997-2003, Young Investigator award CaPCURE, 1998; grantee Nat. Cancer Inst., 1988, Ralph M. Parsons Found. 2001-03. Mem. AAAS, AMA, ACP, Am. Soc. Hematology, Am. Soc. Clin. Oncology, Am. Assn. for Cancer Rsch.

AGWUNOBI, JOHN ODERAH, retail executive, former federal agency administrator; b. Dundee, Angus, Scotland, Oct. 4, 1964; arrived in US, 1989; MB, BChir, U. Jos, Plateau State, Nigeria, 1987; MBA, Georgetown U., Washington, DC, 2000; MPH, Johns Hopkins U., Balt., 2004. Diplomate Am. Bd. Pediat. Resident in pediat. Howard University, Washington, 1990-93; attending pediatrician Hosp. for Sick Children, Washington, 1993-2000, med. dir., 1998—99, v.p. med. affairs & patient services, 1999—2000; dep. sec. Fla. Dept. Health, 2000—01, sec., 2001—05; asst. sec. for health US Dept. Health & Human Svcs., Washington, 2005—07; admiral US Pub. Health Svc. Commd. Corps, 2006—07; sr. v.p., pres. health & wellness. divsn. Wal-Mart Stores, Inc., Bentonville, Ark., 2007—. Chmn. US African Devel. Found., Washington, 2008—. Bd. dirs. Ct. Apptd. Spl. Advs., Montgomery County, Md., 1996. Fellow: Am.

Acad. Pediat.; mem.: AMA, Am. Coll. Physician Execs., Nat. Med. Assn. Office: Wal-Mart Stores Inc 702 SW 8th St MS0240 Bentonville AR 72716 also: US African Devel Found 1400 I St NW Ste 1000 Washington DC 20005

AHAD, MUHAMMAD ALI, ophthalmologist; s. Fiqhat and Arifa Khan. BA, Punjab U., 1991, MBBS, 1995. Basic specialist trainee ophthalmology, Lahore, Pakistan, 1996—99, England, 2000—02; rsch. fellow Moorfield's Eye Hosp., London, 2003—. Contbr. articles to profl. jours. Recipient Coll. Colour in Rowing, Allama Iqbal Med. Coll., Punjab U., 1993. Mem.: UK and Ireland Soc. of Cataract and Refractive Surgeons, Europeon Assn. of Vision and Eye Rsch., Assn. of Rsch. and Vision in Ophthalmology. Achievements include first to describe association of mutations in chemokine gene (CCR2) in uveitis; notice association between high serum levels of testosterone and central serous retinopathy; notice presence of Vitamin A defeciency in hemicolectomy; notice endophthalmitis in Lemierre's Syndrome. Office: Moorfields Eye Hosp City Rd London EC1V 2PD England Office Fax: 44-(0)207-251-9350. E-mail: m.ahad@ucl.ac.uk.

AHEARN, GERALDINE, medical/surgical nurse, writer, poet; b. Bklyn., Aug. 14, 1950; d. Louis Principessa and Patricia Donato; m. James J. Ahearn, Aug. 13, 1972 (div. June 4, 2001); children: Alicia Danielle, Katherine Ann. AA, Suffolk County CC, Selden, NY, 1971; diploma in nursing, Ctrl. Islip State Hosp. Sch. Nursing, 1974. LPN, NY, Ariz., RN NY, Ariz., cert. CCRN, Am. Heart Assn., EKG technician, Am. Heart Assn., med. claims and billing, med. coding. RN Bayshore Hosp., NY, 1970—83, Farmingville Clinic, NY, 1986—87, Sachem Schs., Farmingville, 1988—93; hosp. CCRN cardiac care NY, 1978—83; hosp. CCRN severely disabled children NY, 1989—90; freelance writer Mesa, Ariz., 1993—. Instr. CPR ARC, Coram, NY, 1986—90, instr. first aid, 1986—90, instr. CPR, Bohemia, NY, 1986—90. Author: (books) Inspirations, 2001, Words to Live By, 2001, Life's Poetic Journey, 2002, From America's Future Leaders, 2005, (series) The Nurse in the Purse, Vol. 1, 2001; contbr. poetry to anthologies. Leader Girl Scouts U.S., Farmingville, 1988—91; cmty. leader Am. Online, 2001—04; catechist Farmingville Ch., 1985—87. Recipient Internat. Peace Prize, United Cultural Convention, 2006; vis. scholar Poet fellow, Noble House, 2006. Mem.: ARC, Am. Heart Assn. Republican. Roman Catholic. Avocations: gardening, reading, walking, writing. Home: 4104 E Broadway Rd Apt 1137 Mesa AZ 85206-1985 Personal E-mail: hrt4angel@aol.com.

AHGREN, BENGT, healthcare educator, researcher; b. Sweden, June 7, 1950; s. Hugo and Ulla Ahgren; m. Eva Lundgren, Aug. 4, 1973; children: Martin Agren, Hanna Agren. Diploma in Health Mgmt., Cornell U., Ithaca, 1983; M in Polit. Sci., U. Lund, 1973, PhD in Pub. Health, Nordic Sch. Pub. Health, Gothenburg, 2007. Rsch. asst. Municipality Malmö, 1973—75; dep. mgr. dept. health care planning U. Hosp. Malmö, 1975—78, mgr. dept. health care planning, 1978—81; sr. mgmt. cons., area mng. dir. Sprikonsult, Ltd., 1981—90; sr. project mgr., office mgr., ptnr. SIAR-Bossard Mgmt. Cons., 1990—95; mng. dir. PUPRIMA Mgmt. Cons., 1995—97; ptnr., mgr. Bohlin & Strömberg Mgmt. Cons., 1997—2006; rsch. fellow health mgmt. Nordic Sch. Pub. Health, Göteborg, Sweden, 2007, sr. lectr., 2007—10, asst. prof., 2010—. Scholar, Swedish Assn. Authors Ednl. Material, 1999, 2002, 2005, 2008. Office: Nordic Sch Pub Health Box 12133 402 42 Gothenburg Sweden Office Phone: 46 (0)31 693919. Business E-Mail: bengt.ahgren@nhv.se.

AHLBERG, NORA LOUISE, psychology professor, director; b. Helsinki, Finland, Dec. 23, 1952, d. Hugo Wilhelm and Helene Louise Ahlberg; m. Svein Bjerke, Aug. 16, 1978; children: Ernst Hugo Ahlberg Bjerke, Mildrid Ahlberg Bjerke. Degree in Art Edn., Fria Målarskolan, Helsinki, 1975; degree in Clin. Psychology, U. Helsinki, 1977, Dr. Phil., 1990, PhD, 1982; degree in Psychology, U. Oslo, 1982. Cert. clin. psychologist Suomen Psykologiliitto, 1977. Assoc. prof. U. Helsinki, 1990—; prof., head dept. U. Tromsø, Norway, 1995—96, Norwegian U. Tech., Trondheim, 1996—2003; prof., dir. U. Oslo & Ullevål U. Hosp., 1996—; prof. Oslo U. Coll., 2003—06. Sec. Finnish Art Therapy Assn., Helsinki, 1976—78; com. mem. & cons. Norwegian & Finnish Rsch. Couns. & European Sci. Found., Oslo, Helsinki, Paris, 1990—2007; cons. Profl. & Govtl. Instns., Norway, 1990—2007; chief editor Norwegian Jour. Migration, Oslo, 2005—; editl. mem. Internat. Jour. Migration and Health, 2005—; bd. mem. Health and Social Care Migrants and Ethnic Minorities Europe, 2007. Contbr. scientific papers; exhibitions include painting, Helsinki, Lahtis, Oslo, Paris. Mem.: Norwegian Painters Assn. Office: Ullevål Univ Hosp Oslo N-0407 Norway Home: Holtegata 2 B 259 Oslo Norway Personal E-mail: noraahlberg@gmail.com. Business E-Mail: n.l.ahlberg@medisin.uio.no.

AHLEM, LLOYD HAROLD, psychologist; b. Moose Lake, Minn., Nov. 7, 1929; s. Harold Edward and Agnes (Carlson) A.; m. Anne T. Jensen, Dec. 29, 1952; children: Ted, Dan, Mary Jo, Carol, Aileen. AA, North Park Coll., 1948; AB, San Jose State Coll., 1952, MA, 1955; Ed.D., U. So. Calif., 1962. Tchr. retarded children Fresno County (Calif.) Pub. Schs., 1953-54; psychologist Baldwin Park (Calif.) Sch. Dist., 1955-62; prof. psychology Calif. State U., Stanislaus (formerly Stanislaus State Coll.), Turlock, Calif., 1962-70; pres. North Park U., Chgo., 1970-79, dir., 1966-70; exec. dir. Covenant Village Retirement Center, Turlock, 1979-89; dir. spl. projects Covenant Retirement Communities, Chgo., 1989-93; dir. Emanuel Med. Ctr., Turlock, Calif., 1984-99, Merced Mut. Ins. Co., Atwater, Calif., 1993—2005; chmn. Capital Corp. of West, Merced, Calif., 1995—2002; ret. Author: Do I Have To Be Me, 1974, How to Cope: Managing Change, Crisis and Conflict, 1978, Help for the Families of the Mentally Ill, 1983, Living and Growing in Later Years, 1992; columnist Covenant Companion, 1972-90. Decorated comdr. Order of Polar Star Sweden. Mem. Assn. Colls. Ill. (vice chmn. 1975-79) Mem. Covenant Ch. Club: Rotary (Paul Harris fellow 1987). Home: 2125 N Olive C-11 Turlock CA 95382 Personal E-mail: psygolf@att.net.

AHLGREN, JAMES DAVID, oncologist; b. Washington, Feb. 17, 1934; s. Charles David and Dorothy Elizabeth (Webb) A.; m. Barbara Elizabeth Donelko, Sept. 7, 1957 (div. Mar. 1978); children: Gillian Webb, Nils William; m. Alice Duong, Sept. 1978; 1 child, Mats Erik. BSEE, MIT, 1955; MD, Georgetown U., 1977. Diplomate Am. Bd. Internal Medicine, Am. Bd. Med. Oncology. Chief engr. McIntosh Electronics, Binghamton, N.Y., 1955-56; chief circuit design Reed Rsch., Washington, 1956-58; rsch. engr., asst. dir. R&D Page Comm. Engrs., Washington, 1958-63; v.p., acting pres. Telcom, Inc., McLean, Va., 1963-73; intern Georgetown U. Med. Ctr., Washington, 1977-78, resident in internal medicine, 1979-80, from instr. to assoc. prof., 1980-88; assoc. prof. George Washington U. Med. Ctr., Washington, 1988-94, prof. medicine, pharmacology, 1994—. Chmn. Mid-Atlantic Oncology Program, Silver Spring, Md., 1983-95, bd. dir. Ptnr. for Surgery. Author: Gastrointestinal Oncology, 1992. Chmn. Mid-Atlantic Cancer Rsch. Found., Silver Spring, 1989—. Recipient Edward B. Bunn award Georgetown U., Washington, 1977, Dept. Medicine award, 1977, Jonathan M. Wainwright award Moses Taylor Hosp., 1993, Elaine Snyder Cancer Rsch. award George Washington U., 1994. Mem. ACP, IEEE (sr. mem.), Am. Soc. Clin. Oncology, Am. Geophys. Union, Am. Meteorol. Soc. Republican. Lutheran. Avocations: amateur radio, piano, cooking. Office: George Washington U Med Ctr 2150 Pennsylvania Ave NW Washington DC 20037-3201 E-mail: jahlgren@mfa.gwu.edu.

AHLSTRÖM, HÅKAN K., radiologist, educator; b. Härnösand, Sweden, Apr. 26, 1953; s. Valter H. and Kerstin (Andersson) A.; m. Lena C. Randau, Aug. 6, 1983; children: Malin, Olle, Martin. MD, U. Uppsala, 1978, PhD, 1988. Cert. Nat. Bd. Health and Welfare, Sweden; cert. specialist in diagnostic radiology. Physician Dept. Radiology, Uppsala, 1981-88, asst. head physician, 1988-92, head physician, 1992—, head MR sect., 1993—, prof. radiology, 2002—. Assoc. prof. PET Ctr., Uppsala, 1992-93, prof. radiology 2002—; head MR, pediat., oncol., neurol. radiology, Uppsala, 1998-2005; chmn. KPS Oncology, Radiology, Clin. Immunology Instn., 2004—, head MRI, 2005—. Assoc. editor Acta Radiologica, 1993-2000; contbr. over 150 articles to sci. jours. Rsch. grantee Swedish Soc. for Cancer, 1991-95, 93, 98, Swedish Med. Rsch.Coun., 2000, 2002, and 2005; Sjogrens' award, 2002 Achievements include inventor of bone biopsy system. Home: Kåbov 11 75236 Uppsala Sweden Office: Dept Diagnostic Radiology Univ Hosp 75185 Uppsala Sweden Home Phone: +4618543445; Office Phone: +46186114771. E-mail: hakan.ahlstrom@akademista.se.

AHMAD, FEROZE, internist; b. Srinagar, Jammu & Kashmir, India, Nov. 28, 1975; MBBS, GMC, 2003; MD, SKIMS, 2005. Sr. resident Sheri Kashmir Inst. Med. Scis., 2008—. Master: SKIMS. Avocations: movies, cricket, reading. Office: Dept Internal Medicine Srinagar Jammu & Kashmir 190011 India Business E-Mail: fappy@operamail.com.

AHMAD, IRFAN, dental surgeon; b. Lahore, Punjab, Pakistan, Dec. 27, 1959; arrived in Eng., 1969; s. Mansur Ahmad and Bilqis Bibi; m. Samar Soulat, June 16, 2004; 1 child, Zayan. BDS, U. Liverpool, Eng., 1984. Pvt. practice, 1986—. Lectr. in field. Dir.: (audio-visual presentation) Surpassing Aesthetics: Guidelines for Prosthetic Dentistry, 2001; author: (book) Digital and Conventional Dental Photography A Practical Clinical Manual, 2004, A Clinical Guide to Anterior Dental Aesthetics, 2005, Protocols for Predictable Aesthetic Dental Restorations, 2006; contbr. articles to profl. jours. Mem.: European Acad. Esthetic Dentistry. Office: The Ridgeway Dental Surgery 173 The Ridgeway North Harrow Middlesex HA2 7DF England Office Fax: 020 8861 6181. Business E-Mail: iahmadbds@aol.com.

AHMAD, SHAMOON, hematologist, oncologist, consultant; b. Pakistan; arrived in U.S., 1988; MB, BChir, Dow Med. Coll., Karachi, Pakistan, 1987; law student, U. Nev., 2004—. Diplomate Am. Bd. Hosp. Physicians, Am. Bd. Hematology, Am. Bd. Oncology, Am. Bd. Internal Medicine, lic. physician Pa., Ala., N.Y., Nev. Resident in internal medicine Seton Hall U., NJ, 1989—92; fellow in hematology Mt. Sinai Sch. Medicine, NYC, 1992—93, 1995—96, fellow in neoplastic diseases, 1996—97, fellow in bone marrow transplant, 1997—98; dir. blood and marrow transplant program Comprehensive Cancer Ctrs. of Nev., Las Vegas, 1998—. Asst. med. dir. Jackson County (Ala.) Rural Health Project, Scottsboro, 1993—95; chair cancer com., sect. chief hematology/oncology Sunrise Hosp. and Med. Ctr., Las Vegas, 2001—02; part-time med. dir. therapeutic apheresis program United Blood Svcs., Las Vegas, 2002—; chair pain com. Sunrise Hosp. and Med. Ctr., 2002—, vice chmn. instnl. rev. bd., 2002—03; mem. gov.'s task force on prostate cancer State of Nev., 2004—; pres. Physician & Legal Consultants, Inc., 2004; lectr., presenter in field. Contbr. articles to profl. jours. Recipient Physician's Recognition award, AMA, 1992—2000, Curtsey Las Vegas award, C of C., Las Vegas, 2002; named to Who's Who in So. Nev., In Bus. Las Vegas mag., 2003. Fellow: ACP, Am. Bd. Hosp. Physicians; mem.: Am. Coll. Legal Medicine, Am. Coll. Physician Execs., Am. Soc. Blood and Marrow Transplantation, Clark County Med. Soc. (bylaws, policies and procedures com., profl. stds. coun. 2002—), Nev. State Med. Assn. (coun. on pub. health 2002—), Assn. Cmty. Cancer Ctrs. (ho. dels. 2003—), Am. Soc. Clin. Oncology (clin. practice com. 2003—), Nev. Oncology Soc. (pres. 2003—). Office: PO Box 60327 Las Vegas NV 89160 Office Phone: 702-363-2020. Fax: 702-458-2436. E-mail: shamoonahmad@yahoo.com.

AHMANN, ANDREW J., endocrinologist, educator; PharmM, ND State U., 1976; MD, U. Colo., 1980. Diplomate Am. Bd. Internal Medicine, 1983, Am. Bd. Internal Medicine-endocrinology, diabetes and metabolism, 1986, cert. Nat. Bd. Med. Examiners. Clin. pharmacy resident VA Palo Alto Health Care System, Stanford Univ.; resident internal medicine Fitzsimons Army Med. Ctr., Denver, 1980—83; fellow endocrinology Walter Reed Army Med. Ctr., Washington, 1983—86; prof. medicine Oreg. Health and Sci. Univ., hosp. affiliation includes. Co-author: (articles) Ultradian variation of blood glucose in intensive care unit patients receiving insulin infusions, 2007, The impact of diabetes and associated cardiometabolic risk factors on members: strategies for optimizing outcomes, 2008, Safety profile and metabolic effects of 14 days of treatment with DIO-902: results of a phase IIa multicenter, randomized, double-blind, placebo-controlled, parallel-group trial in patients with type 2 diabetes mellitus, 2008, Designing and implementing insulin infusion protocols and order sets, 2008, Treating to target: implementing an effective diabetes care paradigm for managed care, 2010, and numerous other articles. Recipient Portland Area Juvenile Diabetes Rsch. Found. Hope award, 2008. Mem.: Am. Thyroid Assn., Endocrine Soc., Am. Assn. of Clin. Endocrinologists, Am. Diabetes Assn. (pres. Portland area leadership bd. 2006—, mem profl. practice com. 2004—08). Avocations: golf, hiking, spending time with his two sons, daughters-in-law and grandson. Office: Oregon Health and Science University 3181 SW Sam Jackson Pk Rd Portland OR 97239 Office Phone: 503-494-8311.

AHMED, IQBAL, psychiatrist, consultant; b. Tumkur, Karnataka, India, Aug. 23, 1951; arrived in US, 1976, naturalized, 1982; s. Rahimuddin Ahmed and Arifa (Banu) Rahimuddin; m. Lisa Suzanne Rose, Oct. 9, 1983; children: Yasmin, Jihan. BS, MB, St. John's Med. Coll., 1975. Diplomate in gen. psychiatry, geriatric psychiatry and psychosomatic medicine Am. Bd. Psychiatry and Neurology. Intern St. Martha's Hosp., Bangalore, India, 1974-75; resident in psychiatry U. Nebr. Med. Ctr., Omaha, 1976-79; fellowship in consultation Boston U. Sch. Medicine, 1979-81; staff psychiatrist in consultation liaison psychiatry Boston City Hosp., 1981-87, staff psychiatrist, geriatric psychiatry, 1983-85, dir. geriatric neuropsychiatry unit, 1985-87, dir. geriatric psychiatry, 1988-92; assoc. dir. consultation liaison psychiatry New England Med. Ctr., Boston, 1989-92; faculty Assn. Med. Ctr. Honolulu, 1997—2010. Asst. prof. psychiatry Boston U. Sch. Medicine, 1981—87, Tufts U. Sch. Medicine, Boston, 1987—92; dir. med. student edn. in psychiatry Boston City Hosp., 1981—87; chief spl. svcs. Hawaii State Hosp., 1991—94, pres. med. staff, 1994—95, chief geriatric psychiatry, 1994—97; assoc. prof. dept. psychiatry U. Hawaii John A. Burns Sch. Medicine, 1992—97, prof. dept. psychiatry, 1997—2010; vice chmn. dept. psychiatry U. Hawaii, 1999—2001; cons. Tripler Army Med. Ctr., 1997—2010; program dir. gen. and geriatric psychiatry residency programs U. Hawaii, 1998—2004; dir. pyschopharm. Adult Dept. Mental Health State of Hawaii, Honolulu, 2003—10; cons. geriatric psychiatry Queens Med. Ctr., Honolulu, 2003—10, vice chmn. edn., dept. psychiatry, 1999—2004; oral examiner and mem. geriatric psychiatry cert. com. Am. Bd. Psychiatry & Neurology; clin. prof. psychiatry U. Hawaii, 2010; faculty Tripler Army Med. Ctr.; screening editor Am. Jour. Geridric Psychiatry. Author, co-editor: Spectrum of Psychotic Disorders-Neurobiology, Etiology amd Pathogenesis, 2007; mng. editor Psychiatry Sect. eMedicine; contbr. articles to profl. jours., chapters to books. Mem. Mass. State Dem. Party Minority Caucus, Boston, 1983. Recipient Irma Bland award, APA, 2005, Diversity award, AAGP, 2010, Outstanding Svc. award, Indo America Psychiatric Assn., 2010; finalist Parker Palmer Courage to Teach award, Accreditation Council Grad. Med. Edn., 2004. Fellow: Royal Coll. Psychiatrists; mem.: Am. Psychiatric Assn. (mem. sci. program com., dep. legis. rep., Hawaii), Am. Acad. Psychosomatic Medicine, Am. Coll. Psychiatrists, Internat. Coll. Geriatric Psychoneuropharmacology (founding mem.), Am. Assn. Geriatric Psychiatry (bd. dirs.), Am. Neuropsychiat. Assn., Alpha Omega Alpha (hon. elected hon. faculty mem. 2007). Office: Tripler Army Med Ctr 1 Jarrett White Rd Honolulu HI 96819 Personal E-mail: ahmedi.96822@gmail.com. Business E-Mail: ahmedi@dop.hawaii.edu.

AHMED, JAMIL, rehabilitation service physician; Grad., Karachin U.; MD, Sindh Med. Coll. Resident Maimonides Med. Ctr./Boston U. Med. Ctr.; attending physician, rehabilitation medicine Eric Country Med. Ctr., Buffalo, clin. instructor, rehabilitation medicine. Address: Eric County Med Ctr Rehabilitation Medicine G-217 462 Grider St Buffalo NY 14215 Office Phone: 716-898-5059, 716-898-6126. Business E-Mail: jahmed@ecmc.edu, ahmed7@buffalo.edu.

AHMED, MOHAMED RIFAAT, otolaryngologist; b. Sharkeya, Mar. 15, 1970; MD, Suez Canal U., 1993. Otolaryngologist Suez Canal U., 1996. Office: Suez Canal University Ismilia 002 Egypt E-mail: m_rifaat@hotmail.com.

AHMED, NASIYA N., geriatrician, medical educator; b. Edison, NJ, Nov. 17, 1976; MD, U. Tex., 2002. Resident U. Ariz. Coll. Medicine, 2002—05, fellow, 2005—07; asst. prof. U. Tex., 2007—. Office: 6431 Fannin MSB 5120 Houston TX 77004 Personal E-mail: nappio@hotmail.com.

AHMED, RISHAD, consultant physician, diabetologist, internist; b. India, Sept. 2, 1976; MBBS, AMCH, Karnataka, 2003, MD in Internal Medicine, 2007. Asst. prof. AMCH, 2007—10; cons. physician, cardiologist, diabetologist, mgr. dir. Don View Nursing Home, M.B.N.H, Desun Hosp., 2010—; cons. physician, diabetologist ESI Hosp., Kolkata, 2011—. Contbr. articles to profl. med. jours. Mem.: ACP, Assn. Physicians India (life). Avocations: reading, sports. Home: 26 Shamsul Huda Rd Third Fl Kolkata West Bengal 700017 India Office Phone: 33-22873671. Home Fax: 9830059214. Personal E-mail: rishad14@gmail.com.

AHMED, SHAIKH SULTAN, cardiologist, educator; b. Delh, Sept. 13, 1937; arrived in US, 1965; s. Mohammed Rafee and Sughra Jan (Yaseen) Ahmed; m. Shaheen K. Elley, Mar. 18, 1967; children: Salman, Sohaib. BSc, DJ Sci. Coll., Karachi, Pakistan, 1958; MBBS, Dow Med. Coll., Karachi, 1963. Diplomate Am. Bd. Internal Medicine, Royal Coll. Physicians Can., 1971. Registrar Dow Med. Coll., 1964—65; intern Samaritan Hosp., Troy, NY, 1965—66; resident Tucson Hosp. Med. Ednl. Program, 1966—68; cardiology fellow U. Medicine & Dentistry NJ-NJ Med. Sch., Newark, 1968—70, mem. faculty, 1970—, prof. medicine, 1980—. Co-dir. catheterization lab., 1976—93; dir. stress testing lab., 1975—; chief medicine Firm C., 1983—91; cons. cardiology St. Joseph Hosp., Patterson, NY, St. Michael's Hosp., Newark. Contbr. articles to med. jours., chapters to books. Sec., 1976—79; pres. Islamic Sch. Bergen County, Teaneck, NJ, 1980—81, Muslim CommunityBergen County, Teaneck. Recipient Exceptional Merit award, U. Medicine & Dentistry NJ, 1982, Nat. Civil award, Pres. Pakistan, 1993. Mem.: ACP, Soc. Cardiac Angiography & Intervention, Am. Coll. Angiology, Am. Coll. Cardiology, Am. Coll. Chest Physicians, Royal Coll. Physicians (Can.), Royal Soc. Medicine (U.K.). Islam. Office: U Medicine and Dentistry NJ Med Sch 100 Bergen St Newark NJ 07103-2407 Office Phone: 973-972-2574, 973-972-2573, 973-972-4736. Business E-Mail: ahmedss@umdnj.edu. *

AHN, BYEONG-CHEOL, medical educator; s. Seungsoo Ahn and Soshik Chun; m. Eun Joo Sohn, June 11, 1995; children: Gilhwan, Yeonghwan. D, Kyungpook Nat. U., Daegu, 1997. Diplomate Kyungpook Nat. U., 1990. Prof. Kyungpook Nat. U., Daegu, 2000—; physician Kyungpook Nat. U. Hosp., 1990—, prof. dept. nuc. medicine; vice assoc. dean rsch. affair Kyungpook Nat. U., Sch. Medicine. Capt. Med. Korean Army, 1997—2000. Mem.: Korean Soc. Nuc. Medicine, European Assn. Nuc. Medicine, Soc. Nuc. Medicine.

AHN, BYUNG HONG, retired nutritionist; b. Ham Yang, Gyeongsang nam-do, Republic of Korea, Jan. 26, 1942; s. Sung Sik Ahn and Hyung Soon Kang; m. Bok Ja Kim, Dec. 28, 1969; children: Joon Yung, Joon Kyu, Jang Kyu. PhD in Agr., Seoul Nat. U., Republic of Korea, 1981. Prof. animal nutrition faculty animal sci. Gyeongsang Nat. U., Jinju, Republic of Korea, 1969—2007, chmn. dept. dairy sci., 1989—92, dir. Inst. Agr. & Fishery Devel., 1996—98, dir. Inst. Devel. Livestock Prodn., 1999—2001, chmn. faculty animal sci., 2001—03; mem. Korean Soc. Animal Sci. & Tech., Seoul, 1968—; editor Korean Soc. Animal Sci., Seoul, 1981—84; vis. prof. Calif. U. Davis,

1986—87, Kyoto U., Japan, 1993. Mem. coun. Korean Buddhism Joge Sect., Seoul, 2004—. Recipient Best Paper award, Korean Fed. Sci. & Tech., 1993. Mem.: Asian-Australasian Assn. Animal Prodn. Socs., Korean Soc. Animal Nutrition & Feedstuffs (dir. 1991—99, editor 1987—91), Am. Soc. Animal Sci. Office: Gyeongsang Nat Univ 900 Gaja-dong Jinju Gyeongsang nam-do 660-701 Republic of Korea Home: 517-12 Chilam-Dong 660-988 Jinju Gyeongsangnam-do Republic of Korea Home Phone: 82-055-753-6202; Office Phone: 82-055-751-5410. Business E-Mail: bhahn@gnu.ac.kr.

AHN, BYUNG MOON, orthopedist; b. Republic of Korea, June 11, 1951; m. Mee Sook Lee Ahn, Nov. 6, 1982; children: Kyung Min, Ha Young. MD, Coll. Medicine, Seoul Nat. U., 1976; PhD in Biochemistry, Chung-Ang U., 1982. Cert. Splty. Bd., Orthop. Surgery, 1981; CEO Grad. Sch. Bus. Adminstrn., Yonsei U., 1996, Grad. Sch. Pub. Health, Yonsei U., 1999. V.p. Alumni Assn., Coll. Medicine, Seoul Nat. U., 1981; v.p. arbitration com. Incheon Dist. Ct., 2001—; chmn. Sungmin Gen. Hosp., 1993—; nat. del. sr. exec. adv. coun. HIMSS Analytic Asia, Tae-gu, Republic of Korea, 2011. Vis. prof., Coll. Medicine Hallym U., 1991, Seoul Nat. U., 1998—, Inha U., 1998—; pres. Incheon City Hosp. Assn., 2005—09; chmn. com. internat. affairs Spl. Task Team Health Care, Presdl. Coun. Future and Vision, 2010—, Nat. Forum for Digital Hosp., 2011—. Co-author: (textbook) Anti-Aging Medicine, 2006; contbr. articles to profl. jours. Maj. Korean Army. Recipient Humanitarian award, Choongwae Pharma. Corp. & Korean Hosp. Assn., 2008, Commendation award, Incheonn Dist. Prosecutor's Office, 2009, Healthcare Contbn. award, Ministry of Health & Welfare, 2010; named one of Govtl. Citation, 2010; named to Top 100 Health Profl., IBC, Eng., 2011. Mem.: Korean Hosp. Assn. (chmn.). Methodist. Avocations: reading, hiking, golf. Office: Sungmin Gen Hosp Seongnam-dong 522-1 Seo-gu Incheon 404-220 Republic of Korea Office Phone: 82-32-580-8700, 82 580 8690. Office Fax: 82-32-580-8577. Business E-Mail: bmahn@hanmail.net.

AHN, CHANG HOON, environmental scientist, educator; b. Seoul, Republic of Korea, June 1, 1968; PhD, U. Wis., Madison, 2004. Rsch. scientist Ctr. Environ. Biotech. ASU, 2005—08; rsch. prof. Seoul Nat. U., 2008—. Avocation: music. Home: Apt 102-1201 Raemian Seocho 7 Cha 1642-3 Seoul 137-880 Republic of Korea Personal E-mail: chahn68@yahoo.com.

AHN, DONGHYUN, medical educator; b. Incheon, Republic of Korea, Feb. 24, 1955; MD, Seoul Nat. U., 1979, PhD, 1992. Prof., dept. psychiatry Hanyang U. Med. Ctr., 1994—. Dir. Sungdong Cmty. Mental Health Ctr., 1998, Inst. Mental Health Hanyang U., 2006. Recipient Nat. medal, Pres. of Republic of Korea. Mem.: Korean Assn. Neuropsychaitry, Korean Assn. Child & Adolescent Psychaitry (Dr. Noh's Meml. award). Avocation: hiking. Office: Haengdang-dong 17 Sungdong-gu Seoul 133-792 Republic of Korea Office Fax: 82-2-2298-2055. Business E-Mail: ahndh@hanyang.ac.kr.

AHN, HEE BAE, medical educator; s. Si Young Ahn and Kyung Yeun Jeong; m. Seung Mi Lee, Jan. 21, 1995; children: Do Hyun, Ji Min. MD, Dong-A U. Med. Sch., Busan, Republic of Korea, 1991, PhD, 1998. Cert. physician Ministry of Health, Welfare and Family Affairs, Republic of Korea, 1991, ophthalmologist 1996. Intern Dong-A U. Hosp., Busan, 1991—92, resident, dept. ophthalmology, 1992—96, fellow, sect. oculoplastic, 1996—98; clin. fellow Seirei Hosp., Hamammatsu, Japan, 2002; clin. observer Cullen Eye Inst., Baylor Coll. Medicine, Houston, 2004; internat. fellow oculoplastic U. Wis, Madison, 2006—07, fellow eye pathology, 2007; chmn. ophthalmology Buckjae Integrated Army Hosp., Koyang, Republic of Korea, 1998—2000, Daejeon Integrated Army Hosp., Republic of Korea, 2000—01; asst. prof. Dong-A U., assoc. prof., 2008—. Reviewer Am. Ophthalmic Plastic and Reconstructive Surgery, Milw., 2008—. Contbr. articles to numerous clin. profl. jours., numerous sci. presentation to med. conf. Capt., med. officer Korean Army, 1998—2001, Seoul. Mem.: Wis. Oculoplastic Alumni (Madison), Asia-Pacific Soc. Ophthalmic Plastic and Reconstructive Surgery (Singapore), Korean Soc. Ophthalmic Plastic and Re-constructive Surgery (Seoul), Korean Ophthalmologist Soc. (Seoul) (Best Article award 2006), Korean Med. Assn. (Seoul). Office: Dong-A Univ Hosp Dept Ophthalmology 3-Ga Dongdaesin-Dong Seo-Gu 1 602-715 Busan Busan Republic of Korea

AHN, HYO HYUN, dermatologist; b. Seoul, Republic of Korea, Mar. 14, 1970; s. Ki Sung Ahn and Soo Bok Kim; m. Hyun Sook Lee, Mar. 20, 1999; children: Takmin, Nahyun, Nayoung. MD, PhD, Korea U., Seoul. Lic. med. Ministry Health and Welfare/Korea, 1995, medical specialist (Dermatology) Ministry of Health and Welfare/Korea, 2000. Intern Korea U. Guro Hosp., Seoul, 1995—96; resident Korea U. Anam Hosp., Seoul, 1996—2000, fellow, 2003—05, clin. asst. prof., 2005—07, asst. prof., 2007—09, assoc. prof., 2009—. Contbr. articles to jours. Mem.: Am. Acad. Dermatology, Internat. Soc. Biophysics and Imaging of Skin, Korean Dermatol. Assn. Avocation: photography. Office: Korea Univ Anam Hosp 126-1 Anam-dong 5ga Sungbuk-gu Seoul 136-705 Republic of Korea

AHN, HYUNG JOON, transplant and vascular surgeon; b. Seoul, Republic of Korea, Oct. 11, 1971; MD, Kyung Hee U., 1997, PhD, 2007. Asst. prof., dept. surgery Kwandong U. Coll. Medicine, 2007—08, Kyung Hee U. Coll. Medicine, 2008—. Grant, Kyung Hee U. Mem.: Korean Soc. Phlebology, Korean Soc. Vascular Surgery, Korean Soc. Transplantation (Overseas Tng. fellowship), Korean Surg. Soc., Transplantation Soc. Avocations: mountain climbing, skiing, tennis. Office: Hoegi-dong Dongdaemun-gu Seoul 130-702 Republic of Korea Office Fax: 82-2-966-9366. Business E-Mail: whipple@hanafos.com, whipple@khu.ac.kr.

AHN, JAE HOON, hydrologist, surgeon, educator; b. Busan, Republic of Korea, Aug. 26, 1964; s. Byung-Chul Ahn and Hye-Ok Yang; m. Eun-Jung Cho, Nov. 6, 1993; 1 child, Joon-Sung. MD, Seoul Nat. U., Korea, 1988, PhD, 1999. Lic. physician Korean Med. Assn, 1988, diplomate Korean Bd. of Orthopaedic Surgery, 1993. Resident of orthop. surgery Seoul (Korea) Nat. U. Hosp., 1989—93, clin. fellow of orthop. surgery, 1996—97, rsch. fellow of dept. of orthop. surgery, 1998—99; asst. prof. Eulji U. Coll. of Medicine, Daejon, Republic of Korea, 1999—2011; prof. Cath. U. Korea. Author: Textbook of Fractures. Mem.: Korean Orthopaedic Assn. (Best Paper award 2001). Office: Deptartment Orthopaedic Surgery St Mary's Hospital, Catholic University 505 Banpo-dong Seocho-gu Seoul 137-040 Republic of Korea Business E-Mail: jahn@catholic.ac.kr.

AHN, JAE SUNG, neurosurgeon, educator; b. Korea, Aug. 2, 1966; MD, Seoul Nat. U., 1990; PhD, U. Ulsan, 2003. Asst. prof. Asan Med. Ctr., U. Ulsan, 2001. Mem.: Korean Soc. Cerebrovasc. Surgeons, Korean Neurosurg. Soc. Office: 388-1 Poongnap-Dong Songpa-Gu Seoul 138-736 Republic of Korea Business E-Mail: jsahn@amc.seoul.kr.

AHN, KI YOUNG, plastic cosmetic surgeon; b. Daegu, South Korea, May 25, 1958; s. Sung Ju Ahn and Tae Sik Yang; m. Mee Young Park; 1 child, Jean Seo. B, Kyungpook Nat. U., Daegu, 1982, Master, 1985; PhD, YoungNam U., Daegu, 1992. Intern Kyungpook Nat. U. Hosp., Daegu, Republic of Korea, 1982, resident in plastic surgery, 1983—86; dir., prof. dept. plastic surgery Daegu Cath. U. Hosp., Republic of Korea, 1990—2005; dir. Dr. Ahn's Aesthetic & Plastic Clinic, Daegu, 2006—; v.p. Korean Assn. Plastic Surgeons, 2006—; pres. Betuinum Toxin; sr. fellow Study Group Korean Soc. Plastic & Reconstructive Surgeons, 2004—, bd. dirs., 2004—. Co-author: Botox Injection Technique, Cosmetic & Reconstructive Oculoplastic Surgery; author: The Plastic & Reconstructive Surgery Botox Injection Technique. Capt. Korean Army, 1987—90. Recipient Sci. award, Korean Microsurgery Soc., 1995, Daegu Soc. Korean Med. assn., 2001. Mem.: Oriental Soc. Aesthetic Plastic Surgery, Internat. Soc. Plastic Reconstructive Surgery, Korean Microsurgical Soc., Korean Soc. Aesthetic Plastic Surgery, Korean Soc. Plastic Reconstructive Surgeons (sec. 2003—). Office: Dr Ahn's Aesthetic & Plastic Clinic 24-6 Bong san-dong Jung-gu Daegu 700-822 Republic of Korea Office Phone: 82-53-422-6222. Personal E-mail: kyahn4585@hanmail.net.

AHN, MIN S., facial plastic surgeon; BA in Biology, Harvard Coll.; MD, George Wash. U. Diplomate Am. Bd. Otolaryngology, Am. Bd. Facial Plastic and Reconstructive Surgery. Resident facial plastic surgery Univ. Calif., San Francisco, fellow facial plastic surgery; dir. The Aesthetic Wellness Ctr. Co-author: (publs.) Exophytic brain tumors mimicking primary lesions of the cerebellopontine angle, 1997, Soft Tissue Augmentation, 1998, Temporal browlift using Botulinum Toxin-A, 2000, Calcium hydroxylapatite: Radiesse. Facial Plast Surg Clin North Am, 2007, Effect of homeopathic Arnica montana on bruising in face-lifts: results of a randomized, double-blind, placebo-controlled clinical trial, 2006, and numerous other publs. Mem.: AMA, Internat. Soc. of Hair Restoration Surgery, Am. Acad. of Otolaryngology-Head and Neck Surgery, Mass. Med. Soc., Calif. Soc. of Facial Plastic and Reconstructive Surgery, Am. Coll. of Surgeons, Am. Acad. of Facial Plastic and Reconstructive Surgery, Alpha Omega Alpha. Achievements include invention of sheathed protector for intranasal needle injection. Avocations: reading, golf, playing Jazz piano. Office: The Aesthetic Wellness Center Ste 2C 2 Connector Rd Westborough MA 01581 Office Phone: 508-366-2020.

AHN, SEONG KI, medical educator; s. Tae Young Ahn and Moon Ja Park; m. Mi Ae Kim, Oct. 24, 1993; children: Hyun Hee, Sang Hyun. MD, Gyeongsang Nat. U., Jinju, South Korea, 1992; PhD, Gyeongsang Nat. U., 2006. Lic. otolaryngologist Ministry Health & Welfare, 1992. Intern Gyeongsang Nat. U. Hosp., Jinju City, Republic of Korea, 1993—97, resident, 1997, prof., 2002—. Instr. U. Ulsan Coll. Medicine, Ulsan U. Hosp., 2002—. Pub. health physician Korean Army, 2000—01. Mem.: Assn. Rsch. Otolaryngology, Politzer Soc., Korean Audiological Soc., Korean Balance Soc., Korean Otolaryngology Soc. Home: 110 Hadae-dong Hyundai Apt 102-604 Jinju city 660330 Republic of Korea Office: Gyeonsang Nat Univ Hosp Chilam-Dong 90 660-702 Jinju Gyeongsangnam-do Republic of Korea Home Phone: 82557599525; Office Phone: 82557508176. Office Fax: 82557590613. Business E-Mail: skahn@gnu.ac.kr.

AHN, SOON CHEOL, microbiologist, educator; b. Jinju, Republic of Korea, May 30, 1961; m. Sun Hwa Sung; children: Jae Hyun, Jeong Bin, Cherrie. BS in Food Engring., Yonsei U., Seoul, Republic of Korea, 1985, MS in Food Engring., 1987; PhD in Life Sci., Korea Advanced Inst. Sci. & Biotech., Taejon, Republic of Korea, 1997. Rschr. Korea Rsch. Inst. Biosci. & Biotech., 1987—2003. Post-doctor U Tex. Health Sci. Ctr San Antonio, 1999—2001. Avocations: bowling, tennis, soccer, rock climbing. Office: Pusan Nat Univ 1-ga 10 Ami-dong Seo-gu Busan 602-739 Republic of Korea Home: 1st Sunkyoung Apt 4-1303 Guseo-dong Gumjeong-gu Busan Republic of Korea Home Phone: 82 51 514 8384; Office Phone: 82 51 240 7735. Office Fax: 82 51 243 2259. Business E-Mail: ahnsc@pusan.ac.kr.

AHN, TAI YOUNG, urologist; b. Ham An, Republic Of Korea, Apr. 15, 1953; s. Cha Se Ahn and Kyung Ae Lee; m. Yang Ki Min, Oct. 26, 1982; children: Jung Min, Yong Mo. MD, Seoul Nat. U., Republic Of Korea, 1977, MS, PhD, 1986. Diplomate Korean Bd. Urology. Staff urologist Nat. Police Hosp., Seoul, 1984—89, cons. urologist, 1995—; from asst. prof. to prof. Asan Med. Ctr., U. Ulsan, 1989—, chmn. dept. urology, 2000—04. Author: Text Book of Andrology, 2003. Lt. Med. Corps Reublic of Korea armed forces, 1977—80. Grantee, Pfizer Korea, Seoul, 2004. Mem.: Korean Urol. Assn. (exec. mem.), Am. Urol. Assn., Asia Pacific Soc. Sexual Medicine (chmn. local organizing com. 2005—, exec. mem.), Korean Andrological Soc. (pres. 2002—04). Avocations: golf, mountain climbing, swimming, skiing, tennis. Office: Asan Med Ctr Dept Urology 388-1 Poonjab-dong Songpa-gu Seoul 138-040 Republic of Korea Office Phone: 82-2-3010-3732. Business E-Mail: tyahn@amc.seoul.kr.

AHN, YOON-OK, medical educator, dean; b. Kimje, Jeonlabug-do, Korea, Mar. 11, 1948; s. Kil-Yong Ahn and Woo-Gon Kim; m. Jung-Hee Kim; children: Hyal-Sang, Seung-Joon. MD, Seoul Nat. U., 1972, MPH, 1974, PhD, 1977. Lic. med. Korean, 1972. Prof. Seoul Nat. U., Coll. Medicine, 1980—, chmn. dept. preventive medicine, 1993—2000; vice dean acad. affairs Coll. Medicine Seoul Nat. U., 2000—02. Rsch. assoc. Harvard Sch. Pub. Health, Boston, 1983—84; vis. scientist faculty medicine Nagoya U., Japan, 1984—85. Author: Manual for Medical Statistics, 1990, Understanding of Health Statistics, 1992, Methodological Introduction to Medical Research, 1997, Epidemiology: The Principles and Applications, 2005. Major, adv. surgeon doctor, 1977—80, Republic of Korea. Master: Korean Assn. Cancer Registries, Korean Assn. Cancer Prevention (pres. 2004—), Korean Epidemiol. Soc.; mem.: Asian Pacific Orgn. for Cancer Prevention (pres. 2002—04). Avocation: golf. Home: 6-403 Kaepo-Woosung Apt Daechi-dong Gangnam-gu 135-828 Republic of Korea Office: Seoul Nat U Coll Medicine 28 Yongon-dong Chongno-gu Seoul 110-799 Republic of Korea Home Phone: 82-2-569-8269; Office Phone: 82-2-740-8322. Office Fax: 82-2-747-4830. Business E-Mail: yoahn@plaza.snu.ac.kr.

AHUNBAY, ERGUN EMIN, medical educator; b. Ankara, Turkey, Aug. 21, 1970; PhD, Wayne State U., 2001. Asst. prof. Med. Coll. Wis., 2004—. Mem.: ASTRO, AAPM. Office: 9200 W Wisconsin Ave Milwaukee WI 53226 Business E-Mail: eahunbay@mcw.edu.

AIBIN, WU, medical educator; b. Jingzhou, China, Oct. 12, 1973; D, Yangtze U., 2010. Assoc. prof. Yangtze U., 2010—. Office: Nanhuan Rd 1 Jingzhou Hubei 434023 China Business E-Mail: abwu@yangtzeu.edu.cn.

AICH, RANEN KANTI, oncologist; b. Kolkata, West Bengal, India, Jan. 14, 1957; MBBS, Nilratan Sircar Med. Coll., Kolkata, 1983; MD in Radiation Oncology, U. Coll. Medicine, 1996. Cons. physician Dept. Radiotherapy, Nilratan Sircar Med. Coll., 1998—2005, assoc. prof., 2011; asst. prof. dept. radiotherapy Bankura Sammilani Med. Coll., West Bengal, 2006—10. Contbr. articles to profl. jours. Mem.: Assn. Radiation Oncologists India. Avocation: reading. Home: Simultala Agarpara N 24 Parganas Kolkata West Bengal 700109 India Personal E-mail: ranenaich@rediffmail.com.

AIELLO, WILLIAM PHILIP, plastic surgeon; b. Bklyn., May 22, 1952; Grad., SUNY, Binghamton; MD cum laude, U. Rome, 1980. Diplomate Am. Bd. Plastic Surgery. Intern gen. surgery Cabrini Med. Ctr., NYC, 1980—81; resident gen. surgery LI Jewish Med. Ctr., NY, 1981—82, Jersey City Med. Ctr., 1983; resident gen. & plastic surgery North Shore U. Hosp., LI, NY, 1983—84; resident plastic & reconstructive surgery St. Louis U., Mo., 1984—86; fellow hand & microvascular surgery Loma Linda U., Calif., 1986—87; founder, surgeon pvt. practice Ocean Plastic Surgery Ctr., Los Alamitos, Calif., 1987—; chief surgery Los Alamitos Med. Ctr., 1997—; also chief replantation svc. Long Beach Meml. Med. Ctr. Mem.: Am. Soc. Plastic & Reconstructive Surgeons. Office: Ocean Plastic Surgery Ctr 361 Hospital Rd Ste 324 Newport Beach CA 92663 also: Ocean Pacific Surgery Ctr 10921 Cherry St Ste 200 Los Alamitos CA 90720 Office Phone: 714-891-7288, 562-594-5996.

AIFANTIS, IOANNIS, pathologist, medical educator; b. Komitini, Thrace, Greece, Aug. 9, 1971; s. Alexander Aifantis and Magdalene Voulgaraki; m. Christine Elizabeth Borowski, Jan. 3, 2004. BS in Biology, U. Crete, Heraklion, Greece, 1994, MS, 1996; PhD in Immunology, U. Paris V-Rene Descartes, 1999. Rsch. fellow Harvard U., Boston, 1999—2003; asst. prof. U. Chgo., 2003—06; assoc. prof. pathology NYU, 2006—. Contbr. articles to profl. jours. Recipient Young Investigator award, Leukemia Rsch. Found., 2003, 2004, Cancer Rsch. Found., 2004, Scholar award, Sidney Kimmel Found., 2005, 2006, Rsch. Scholar award, V Found. Cancer Rsch., 2005, 2006, Early Career Scientist award, Howard Hughes Med. Inst., 2009; Marie Curie Biotechnology fellow, European Union, 1996—98, Eugenia Spanopoulou fellow, Irvington Inst. Immunological Rsch., 1999—2002. Achievements include research in the molecular mechanisms controlling hematopoietic stem cell (HSC) self-renewal, differentiation and transformation. Office: NYU Cancer Inst 550 1st Ave MSB 504 New York NY 10016 Office Phone: 212-263-5365. Office Fax: 212-263-8211. E-mail: Iannis.Aifantis@nyumc.org, iannis@aifantislab.com. *

AIGA, HIROTSUGU, epidemiologist; b. Kodaira, Tokyo, Japan, July 4, 1960; s. Junjiro and Sachiko Aiga; m. Mitsue Horino, Feb. 14, 1994; children: Taku, Ko, Ken. BSc, Waseda U., Tokyo, 1983; MPH, PhD, U. Tokyo, 1994. Cert. pub. health engr., WHO/Malaysia, 1994; statistician Ministry of Labor, 2000. Sci. tchr. Shinozaki Pub. H.S., Edogawa, Japan, 1983—88, Sunagawa Pub. H.S., Tachikawa, Japan, 1990—92; chmn., assoc. prof. Zorzor Rural Teachers' Tng. Inst., Fissebu, Lofa, Liberia, 1988—90; rsch. fellow WHO, Manila, Philippines, 1993; regional relief adminstrator Internat. Fedn. Red Cross and Red Crescent Socs., Khabarovsk, Russia, 1994—95, regional relief adminstr. Almaty, Kazakhstan, 1994; rsch. mgr., prin. rschr. Engring. Consulting Firms Assn., Minato, Japan, 1995—2004; pub. health specialist Ministry of Health, Accra, Greater Accra, Ghana, 1997—2000; adj. assoc. prof., rsch. fellow George Wash. U., Washington, 2002—; sr. programme adviser World Food Programme, Rome, 2004—; sr. adviser Japan Internat. Cooperation Agy., Shinjuku, Japan, 2006—. Vis. rschr. U. Tokyo, Bunkyo, Japan, 1997—; mem. reviewing panel Med. Sci. Monitor, Albertson, NY, 2005—, Jour. Pediat. Infectious Disease, Van, Turkey, 2006—; mem. editl. bd. Soc. Indicators Rsch., Netherlands, 2006—. Contbr. articles to profl. publs. Vol. sci. tchr. Accra Japanese Sch., 1997—2000; vol. lectr. Edn. Agy., Tokyo Met. Govt., Shinjuku-ku, 1990—90; vol. lectr. devel. assistance Tokyo Met. Govt., Shinjuku-ku, 1990—90. Grantee Internat. Devel. Rsch. Project, Mitsubishi Bank Found., 1992—93, Project Formulation Study Subsidy, Ministry Economy, Trade, and Industry, 2001—02; fellow Overseas Fellowship/Internship Program, U. Tokyo, 1993, Long-Term Rsch. Fellowship Program, Found. for Advanced Studies on Internat. Devel., Ministry Fgn. Affairs, 2002—03. Mem.: Japan Assn. Internat. Health, Japan Assn. Internat. Devel., Japan Assn. Pub. Health. Buddist. Achievements include research in reconsideration of definitin of access to safe water. Avocations: swimming, mountain climbing. Home: 4-31-7-219 ShimoTtakaido Tokyo Suginami 168-0073 Japan Personal E-mail: aiga.hirotsugu@j.ca.go.jp. Business E-Mail: hirotsugu.aiga@wfp.org. *

AIGEN, BETSY P., psychotherapist; b. NYC, Sept. 13, 1938; d. Abraham H. and Gertrude (Rosenblum) Wasserman; m. Ronald Aigen, Dec. 7, 1957 (div. Jan. 1979); m. Isadore Schumukler, June 20, 1982; children: Jennifer Loren, Samantha Devin. BA, New Sch. Social Research, 1971; MA, Columbia U., 1972; D of Psychology, Rutgers U., 1980. Group co-leader, asst. psychotherapist Inst. Rational Psychotherapy, NYC, 1967-72; asst. course instr. Columbia U., NYC, 1971-72; psychotherapist Mt. Carmel Guild, Englewood, NJ, 1980-82, SELF Edn. Learning and Feeling, NYC, 1982—; founder, dir. Childbirth Consultation Svcs. Surrogate Mother Program, NYC, 1985—. Cons. Police Chief Tng. Community Workshops Assn., N.Y.C., 1973-74, Richmond Fellowship Mental Health Halfway Houses, Eng. and U.S., 1970-75. Contbr. articles to profl. jours. Chmn. Tenants Com., N.Y.C., 1975-85; active Profl. Theatre, 1956-67. Mem. Nat. Orgn. Women, RESOLVE, Adoptive Parents Com., Am. Psychol. Assn., N.Y. St. Psychol. Assn., N.J. St. Psychol. Assn., N.Y. Assn. Feminist Therapists. (co-founder, charter), Am. Orgn. Surrogate Parenting Practitioners (founder, charter). Democrat. Jewish. Office Phone: 212-496-1070. Personal E-mail: newyorkaigen@aol.com.

AILAWADI, GORAV, medical educator; b. Germany, Dec. 26, 1973; MD, Northwestern U., 1998. Gen. surgery resident U. Mich., 1998—2005, surgical critical care fellow, 2001—02, Jobst vascular rsch. fellow, 2001—03; cardiothoracic surgery resident U. Va., 2005—07, asst. prof. surgery Divsn. Thoracic & Cardiovascular Surgery, 2007—. Contbr. articles to med. jours. Mem.: American Heart Assn., Southern Thoracic Surgical Assn., Soc. Thoracic Surgeons, American Coll. Surgeons. Office: University of Virginia Health System PO Box 800679 Charlottesville VA 22908-0679 Office Fax: 434-982-3885. Business E-Mail: ga3f@virginia.edu, ailawadi@virginia.edu.

AINSLIE, GEORGE WILLIAM, psychiatrist; b. Ithaca, NY, Sept. 19, 1944; s. George William and Elizabeth Lee Ainslie; m. Elizabeth Boyd Keeney, June 25, 1966; children: Matthew Forrest, Roger Scott, Eleanor Ruth. BA, Yale Coll., 1965; MD, Harvard Med. Sch., 1969. Diplomate Am. Bd. Psychiatry and Neurology; cert. adult psychiatry. Intern Mary Imogene Bassett Hosp., Cooperstown, NY, 1969-70; resident in psychiatry Mass. Mental Health Ctr., Boston, 1970-71, 73-75; fellow Harvard U. Health Svcs., Cambridge, Mass., 1975-76; asst. clin. dir. Mass. Mental Health Ctr., Boston, 1976-79; psychiatrist VA Med. Ctr., Coatesville, Pa., 1979-90, chief psychiatrist, 1990—. Asst. prof. Jefferson Med. Coll., Phila., 1979-85, assoc. prof., 1985-92; clin. prof. Temple U. Med. Coll., Phila., 1992-2006; rsch. assoc. Harvard Lab. Exptl. Psychology, Cambridge, Mass., 1967-78; hon. prof. U. Cape Town, South Africa, 2010-. Author: Picoeconomics: The Strategic Interaction of Successive Motivational States Within The Person, 1992, Breakdown of Will, 2001; contbr. articles on motivational conflict to profl. jours. Surgeon, USPHS, 1971-73. Mem. Players Club Swarthmore (stage dir.), Phi Beta Kappa. Avocation: theater. Office: Dept Psychiatry VA Med Ctr 116A Coatesville PA 19320 Home Phone: 610-328-5436; Office Phone: 610-383-0260. Business E-Mail: George.Ainslie@va.gov.

AISENBERG, ALAN C., physician, educator, researcher; b. NYC, Dec. 7, 1926; s. Jacob and Celia (Able) A.; m. Nadya Margulies, Oct. 2, 1952 (dec. Apr. 1999); children: James, Margaret. SB, Harvard U., 1945, MD, 1950; PhD, U. Wis., 1956. Diplomate Am. Bd. Internal Med. Internship and resident Presbyn. Hosp., NYC, 1950-53; instr. medicine Harvard Med. Sch., Boston, 1956-62, asst. prof., 1962-69, assoc. prof., 1969-84, prof., 1984—; asst. physician Mass. Gen. Hosp., Boston, 1959-69, assoc. physician, 1969-84, physician, 1984—. Mem. Clin. Trials Com. Nat. Cancer Inst., Bethesda, Md., 1977-82. Author: Glycolysis and Respiration of Tumors, 1961, Malignant Lymphoma: Biology, Natural History and Treatment, 1991; contbr. over 150 articles on rsch. in oncology to profl. jours. Recipient Guggenheim Fellowship, Guggenheim Found. Nat. Inst. for Med. Research, London, 1964-65. Mem. Am. Coll. of Physicians, Am. Soc. of Clin. Oncology, Am. Assn. Immunologists. Home: 124 Chestnut St Boston MA 02108-3318 Office: Mass Gen Hosp Fruit St Boston MA 02114-2620 Office Phone: 617-726-3677. Business E-Mail: aaisenberg@partners.org.

AISNER, JOSEPH, oncologist, medical educator; b. Munich, Jan. 5, 1944; came to U.S., 1948; s. Philip and Faye Aisner; m. Seena Feldman, Aug. 31, 1969; children: Dara Lianna, Leon Andrew. BS in Chemistry, Wayne State U., 1965, MD, 1970. Intern Sinai Hosp. Detroit, 1970-71; resident Georgetown U. Hosp., Washington, 1971-72; commd. med. officer USPHS, 1972, advanced through grades to rank 05, resigned, 1982; clin. assoc. Nat. Cancer Inst., Balt., 1972-75, sr. investigator, 1975-78, chief med. oncology, 1978-81, U. Md. Cancer Ctr., 1981-92, dep. dir. clin. affairs, 1982-88, ctr. dir., 1988-93; prof. medicine U. Medicine and Dentistry of N.J., New Brunswick, 1995—; prof. environ. and occupl. medicine U. Medicine and Dentistry of NJ, 1996; assoc. dir. clin. svcs. & chief med. officer Cancer Inst. NJ, 2007—. Prof. medicine U. Md., 1982-95, prof. oncology, 1982-95, prof. pharmacology, 1985-95, prof. clin. pharmacy, 1987-95, prof. epidemiology preventive medicine, 1993-95; mem. N.J. Legis. Commn. Pain Mgmt., 1998-2000, N.J. Com. to improve outcomes on cancer patients, 1999—. Editor books; contbr. numerous chpts. to books and articles and abstracts to profl. jours. Bd. dirs. Md. Chpt. Am. Cancer Soc., 1988-94, Am. Assn. Cancer Edn., 1990; exec. com. Md. Cancer Consortium, chmn. breast cancer sect., 1992-93, chmn., 1993-95,; mem. Gov.'s Coun. Cancer Prevention, 1991, exec. com., 1991-95; bd. dirs. Md. Children's Cancer Found., 1991-95. Named a Top Doctor, NY mag., 2000-10; Nat. Cancer Inst. grantee, 1982-95, 2000-. Fellow ACP; mem. Am. Fedn. Clin. Rsch., Am. Soc. Clin. Oncology (dir. edn. program 1985-86, bd. dirs. 1991-94), Am. Assn. Cancer Rsch., Cancer Leukemia Group B (bd. dirs. 1982-95, vice chair breast sect. 1980-86), Am. Radium Soc. (sci. program com. 1993-94), Ea. Cooperation Oncology Group (prin. investigator com. 1996—, data audit com. 1999—, sci. adv. com. 2000—, exec. com. 2003-, fin. oversight com. 2005—07). Office: Cancer Inst NJ 195 Little Albany St New Brunswick NJ 08903-2681 Office Phone: 732-235-7664. Personal E-mail: aisnerjo@verizon.net. Business E-Mail: aisnerjo@umdnj.edu.

AITHAL, JAIRAM K., cardiologist; b. Mumbai, July 28, 1974; MD in Internal Medicine, Seth G.S. Med. Coll., Mumbai, 2000; DM in Cardiology, Seth G.S. Med. Coll. and Kem Hosp., Mumbai, 2003. Fellow, interventional cardiology Geelong Hosp., Victoria, Royal Perth Hosp., Australia, 2007—09; fellow, peripheral interventions Pk. Hosp., Leipzig, Germany, 2009—10; specialist, interventional cardiology NMC Splty. Hosp., 2010—. Recipient Gold medal, Indian Pres. S. D. Sharma. Fellow: Cardiac Soc. (Australia and New Zealand); mem.: Cardiac Soc. India. Avocations: sports, painting, music. Office: Dept Cardiology 2nd Fl NMC Splty Hosp PO Box 6222 Abu Dhabi United Arab Emirates Personal E-mail: jairamaithal@hotmail.com.

AJITHDOSS, DHARANI K., veterinarian, educator; b. Ponnur, India, June 5, 1976; BVSc, TANUVAS, 2000; PhD, Tex. A&M U., 2009. Asst. lectr. Tex. A&M U., 2009—. Office: MS 4467 Veterinary Pathobiology Tex A College Station TX 77843 Business E-Mail: dajithdoss@cvm.tamu.edu.

AJLOUNI, RAED FAKHRY, dentist, educator; b. Mafraq, Jordan; s. Fakhry Mohammad Ajlouni and Naifeh Ali Shehabat. DDS, Jordan U. Sci. and Tech., Irbid, 1995; MS, U. Iowa, Iowa City, 2002. Cert. in clin. oral pathology U. Iowa, 2000, in oparetive dentistry U. Iowa, 2002, diplomate Am. Acad. Operative Dentistry, 2003. Asst. prof. Baylor Coll. Dentistry, Tex. A&M U. Sys. Health Sci. Ctr., Dallas, 2003—06; pres. DaVinci Dentistry, PA, Southlake, Tex., 2005—; assoc. prof. Baylor Coll. Dentistry, Tex. A&M U. Sys. Health Sci. Ctr., 2006—, clin. rsch. dir., 2009; v.p. Biomedical Ingenuity Inc., Southlake, Tex., 2006—. Mem. editl. bd.: Operative Dentistry Jour. Recipient Jordan Nat. Writing Contest award, Ministry Edn., 1987, Jordan Nat. Sci. Achievement award, 1989, Acad. Cosmetic Density Excellence award, 2007; scholar, Ministry Higher Edn., 1990—95, Jordan U. Sci. and Tech., 1999—2002. Mem.: Am. Bd. Operative Dentistry (Exec. coun. 2005), Am. Bd. Operative Dentistry, Am. Acad. Operative Dentistry, Omicron Kappa Upsilon. Achievements include research in clinical, laboratory and translational research on dental and biomedical materials, devices and technologies. Office: Baylor Coll Dentistry 3302 Gaston Ave Dallas TX 75246 Office Fax: 214-874-4543. E-mail: rajlouni@bcd.tamhsc.edu.

AJONUMA, LOUIS CHUKWUEMEKA, reproductive medical physician, researcher; s. Cyriacus Ihenmadu and Mary Joan Ajonuma; m. Mary Ann Alforque Bargamento, July 25, 1963; 1 child, Mary Joan Chinyere. B.Sc Med., M.D U., Rohtak, 1985; MD, Northwestern U., The Philippines, 1990; MMedSc in Ob-Gyn., U. Hong Kong, 2000; PhD in Reproductive Physiology, Chinese U. Hong Kong, 2004. Post doctoral fellow Inst. Biomed. Scis., Academia Sinica Taiwan, Taipei, 1993—94; fellow Epithelial Cell Biology Rsch. Ctr., Hong Kong, 2004—. Dir. Genius Internat. Co., 2000—. Editor, author (book) Infertility and Assisted Reproduction in the Tropics; contbr. over 40 articles to profl. jours. Head Eternal Sacred Order of Cherubim and Seraphim, Hong Kong, 2000. Fellow: Royal Soc. Health; mem.: Am. Soc. Reproductive Medicine, Inst. Biology, London. Achievements include discovery of the gene involved in ovarian hyperstimulation syndrome; patents pending for the pathogenesis of ovarian hyperstimulation syndrome; first to Cellular and molecular mechanisms of abnormal fluid formation in the female reproductive tract; research in Ultrastructure characterization of hydrosalpinx in infertile Chinese women.

AKAMA, HIDETO, pharmaceutical physician; b. Tokyo, Jan. 27, 1960; s. Kiyoto and Chikako Akama; m. Keiko Nakayama, July 21, 1991; 1 child, Kenta N. MD, Keio U., Tokyo, 1984, PhD, 1988. Instr. Keio U. Hosp., Tokyo, 1988—91; rsch. assoc. Washington U. Sch. Medicine, St. Louis, 1991—94; instr. Tokyo Women's Med. U., 1994—97, asst. prof., 1997, asst. prof. Inst. Rheumatology, 1999—2003; dir. Shimmatsudo Chuo Gen. Hosp., Matsudo, Japan, 1997—99; med. dir. Pfizer Japan Inc., Tokyo, 2003—06, Amgen Ltd., Tokyo, 2006—07; sr. dir. Eisai Co. Ltd., Tokyo, 2007—. Contbr. articles to profl. jours. Fellow: Japanese Soc. Allergology, Japan Soc. Infectious Diseases, Japan Endocrine Soc., Japan Rheumatism Assn.; mem.: ACP, Fellows Assn. Japanese Soc. Internal Medicine. Avocations: horseback riding, writing essays. Office: Eisai Co Ltd Japan Asia Clin Rsch Product Creation Sys Koishikawa Tokyo 112-8088 Japan Office Phone: 81338175360. Personal E-mail: akama@jb3.so-net.ne.jp. Business E-Mail: h-akama@hhc.eisai.co.jp.

AKANSU, BÜLENT, physician; b. Edremit, May 22, 1975; MD, Hacettepe U., 1999. Physician pathology and forensic medicine, 1999—. Office: Diyarbakir Egitim ve Arastirma Hastanesi Diyarbakir 21000 Turkey E-mail: bulentakansu@yahoo.com.

AKAPITO SKILLING, VITA, state agency administrator; MD, U. Hawaii; post grad., U. Otago, New Zealand. Residency in pediat. Fiji Sch. Medicine, Viti Levu; project dir. Kosrae Divsn. Pub. and Cmty. Health, Federated States of Micronesia; sec. Dept. Health and Social Affairs, Federated States of Micronesia, 2007—. Office: Federated States Micronesia Dept Health and Social Affairs PS 70 Palikir Pohnpei FM 96941 Office Phone: 691-320-2872. Office Fax: 691-320-5263.

AKAY, MEHMET HAKAN, thoracic surgeon; b. Burdur, Turkey, Aug. 22, 1968; MD, U. Istanbul, 1992; degree in Thoracic Surgery, Tex. Heart Inst., 2008. Surgeon Tex. Heart Inst., 2008—. Fellow: Am. Bd. Surgery. Home: 3838 North Braeswood Blvd Apt 145 Houston TX 77025 Personal E-mail: mhakay@hotmail.com.

AKBAR, SHEIKH MOHAMMAD FAZLE, medical educator; b. Faridpur, Bangladesh, Aug. 6, 1954; s. Sheikh Muizuddin Ahmed and Syeda Ashrafunnesa Nesa; m. Akbar Samsun Nehar, Mar. 7, 1985; 1 child, Tasmin. PhD in Medicine, Ehime U., Japan, 1993. Lic. doctor Bangladesh Med. Coun., 1980. Asst. prof. sch. medicine Ehime U., Toon, Japan, 1986—. PhD supr. Ehime U. Sch. Medicine, Shigenobu, 1997—. Contbr. over 100 articles to profl. jours. Recipient Kyoto Liver Forum award, Organising Com., 2000—03, 2003; grantee scientific rsch., Ministry of Edn, Japan, 2000—01, 2002—03. Mem.: Japanese Soc. Hepatology, Asia-Pacific Assn. for Study of the Liver, European Assn. for Study of the Liver, Am. Assn. Study Liver Diseases, Japanese Soc. Immunology. Home and Office: Toshiba Gen Hosp Higashi Oi6-3-22 Tokyo 1408522 Japan Office Fax: 8133764-8992. Business E-Mail: sheikh.akbar@po.toshiba.co.jp.

AKBARALI, HAMID INAYATALI, medical educator, researcher; b. Karachi, Pakistan, Feb. 14, 1957; BSc with honors, U. London, 1983; PhD, Meml. U. Nfld., 1988. Asst. prof. Harvard Med. Sch., 1993—2000; prof. U. Okla., 2000—05, Va. Commonwealth U., 2005—. Recipient Outstanding Clin. Achievement award, Am. Gastroenterology Inst., Genevieve and Roberta Colman Meml. award, Meml. U. Nfld. Mem.: Am. Gastroenterology Assn., Am. Physiol. Soc., Am. Soc. Pharmacology and Exptl. Therapeutics. Office: 1112 E Clay St McGuire Hall 317 Richmond VA 23298 Business E-Mail: hiakbarali@vcu.edu.

AKBARNIA, BEHROOZ A., orthopedist; b. Iran, Jan. 20, 1942; MD, Tehran U., 1966. Med. dir. San Diego Ctr. Spinal Disorders, 1990—2011. Recipient Life Time Svc. award, Western Orthop. Assn. Fellow: Am. Acad. Orthop. Surgeons; mem.: Pediat. Orthop. Soc. N.Am., Scoliosis Rsch. Soc. (pres. 2006, Humanitarian award). Avocation: skiing. Office: 4130 La Jolla Village Dr #300 La Jolla CA 92037 Office Fax: 858-678-0007. Business E-Mail: akbarnia@ucsd.edu.

AKELINA, YELENA, medical researcher; b. Moscow, July 17, 1965; DVM, Moscow Vet. Acad., MS, 1987. Assoc. rsch. scientist Columbia U., 1996—. Mem.: WSRM, LAWTE, AALAS. Office: 622W 168 St PH 1158 New York NY 10032 Business E-Mail: ya67@columbia.edu.

AKEMATSU, YUJI, research scientist; b. Japan, Dec. 21, 1981; PhD in Applied Informatics, U. Hyogo, 2007. Rsch. fellow Japan Soc. Promotion Sci. Grad. Sch. Economics Osaka U., 2011—. Office: 1-7 Machikaneyama Toyonaka Osaka 560-0043 Japan Personal E-mail: y_akematsu@yahoo.co.jp.

AKERA, TAI, retired pharmacologist; b. Tokyo, July 13, 1932; came to U.S., 1971; s. Jibusuke and Ayako (Omata) A.; m. Chiseko Masuda, Apr. 10, 1962; children— Atsushi, Yukako, Chikako MD, Keio U., Tokyo, 1958, PhD in Pharmacology, 1965. From instr. to asst. prof. Keio U., Tokyo, 1960-71; vis. asst. prof. dept. pharmacology Mich. State U., East Lansing, 1967-70, prof. dept. pharmacology and toxicology, 1974-87, chmn., 1986—87; dir. med. rsch. ctr. Nat. Children's Hosp., Tokyo, Japan, 1987-91; v.p. Merck Sharp and Dohme Rsch. Labs., Tokyo, 1991—; head, sr. v.p. R&D Banyu Pharm. Co., 1995—2001, exec. v.p., CTO, 2001—06. Vis. prof. Tokai U., Isehara, Japan, 1977, prof. Sch. Medicine, 1990-97; adj. prof. Sch. Medicine, Keio U., 1988-2008. Contbr. articles to profl. jours. Mem. Am. Soc. for Pharmacology and Exptl. Therapeutics, Japanese Pharm. Soc., Internat. Soc. for Heart Rsch. Home: 3-7-10 Jingumae Shibuya-ku Tokyo 150-0001 Japan Home Phone: 925-377-0117; Office Phone: +81-3-3270-8196. Personal E-mail: tai.akera@gmail.com.

AKERS, JAMES ERIC, commercial real estate broker; b. Jonesboro, Ark., Oct. 14, 1945; s. Ward Eldridge and Dorothy Catherine (Erb) A.; 1 child, William Eric; m. Marie Oreigr, Aug. 31, 1991. BA in Social Sci., Vanderbilt U., 1968; MDiv in Strategic Planning, Louisville Presbyn. Theol. Sem, 1971. Gen. mgr. TGI Fridays, Nashville, 1972-73, Annie Tigues Restaurant & Bar, Jacksonville, Fla., 1973-77; sales rep. Northwestern Mut. Life Ins. Co., Jacksonville, 1977-79, Peter Gregg Mercedes-Benz, Jacksonville, 1979-80; dir. life flight Bapt. Med. Ctr., Jacksonville, 1980-83, dir. spl. projects, 1983-84; dir. mktg. Jacksonville Faculty Practice Assn., 1984—98, v.p. planning, devel. and mktg., 1998; pres., CEO, Jim Akers and Assocs., Inc., Jacksonville. V.p. mktg. Profl. Biling Systems Inc. subs. JFPA, 1986—, Fin.-Med. Mgmt. Svcs., 1989—, Physician Bus. Svcs. Inc., 1990; pres. Healthcare Mktg. Cons., Jacksonville, 1990-2000; dir. of ops. Health Screen Am., 2000. Master of ceremonies Children's Miracle Network Telethon, Jacksonville, 1983, 84, 89, Am. Heart Assn., Jacksonville, 1988-90; chief auctioneer Sta. WJCT-TV, PBS, Jacksonville, 1983-98; campaign mgr. Senator Bill Bankhead, Jacksonville, 1984; pres. bd. dirs. Suicide Prevention Svcs., Jacksonville, 1983-89. Col. U.S. Army, 1966-96. Named Rotarian of Yr., Mandarin Rotary, 2001, Vol. of Yr., WJCT-TV (PBS), 2003. Mem. Med. Group Mgmt. Assn., Acad. Practice Assembly, Am. Soc. Hosp. Based Emergency Air Med. Svcs. (bd. dirs.), Am. Coll. Healthcare Mktg., Alliance for Healthcare Strategy and Mktg., Acad. Health Svcs. Mktg., N.G. Officers Assn., Ye Mystic Revellers (team leader), Rotary (pres. Mandarin, Fla. 2005-06, Paul Harris fellow 1990). Republican. Libertarian. Avocations: mountain climbing, flying, whitewater rafting. Home: 8629 Royalwood Dr Jacksonville FL 32256-8447 Office: Jim Akers and Assocs Inc 6817 Southpoint Pkwy Ste 1304 Jacksonville FL 32216 Office Phone: 904-281-8100. Personal E-mail: spoci@bellsouth.net.

ÅKERVALL, JAN A., otolaryngologist, educator; b. Linkoping, Sweden, Apr. 17, 1960; MD, Lund U., Sweden, 1983—89, PhD, 1993—98. MD Lund Univ., Sweden, temp. academic lic. Mich., 2000, permanent MD lic. Mich., 2002, cert. ear nose throat, head and neck surgery Sweden, 1998. Resident otolaryngology Univ. Hosp., Sweden, 1993—98; lectr. otolaryngology head and neck surgery Lund Univ., 1994—96, lectr. pathology, 1986—87, bd. dirs. ednl. med. faculty, 1996—97, ears nose throat specialist; intern Angelholm Hosp., 1991—92; fellow head and neck cancer surgery and reconstruction Univ. of Mich.; full time otolaryngologist, assoc. prof., dir. head and neck surgery divsn. dept. of otolaryngology Univ. Hosp., Lund, Sweden; ptnr. The Rontal Clinic; staff otolaryngologist William Beaumont Hosp., Royal Oak, 2004—, Detroit Med. Ctr., 2004—; clin. appointments include Vaxjo Hosp., 1989, Angelholm Hosp., 1990, Angelholm sjukhus, 1992—93, Malmoe Academic Hosp., 1992—93, 1994, dir. head and neck divsn., 2003. Head edn. program for ear nose throat specialists, Sweden, 1998—99, 2003. Editor: (jours.) Acta Otolaryngologica; reviewer (sci. studies) Clinical Cancer Research; co-author: (publs.) Are tumour necrosis factor (TNF) or Cortisol of value for the diagnosis of acute septicemia?, 1990, Chromosomalabnormalities involving 11q13 are associated with poor prognosis in squamous cell carcinoma of the head and neck, 1995, Amplification of cyclin D1 in squamous cell carcinoma of the head and neck and the prognostic value of chromosomal abnormalities and cyclin D1 overexpression, 1997, Complex karyotypes in flowcytometrically DNA-diploid squamous cell carcinomas of the head and neck, 1998, Pain treatment after tonsillectomy: Advantages for regularly given analgesics compared with given on demand, 2000, and numerous others. Recipient Best poster award, Swedish Soc. for Otorhinolaryngology, 1996, Tegger Found, Sweden, 1998, Teknibro Found., Lund Univ., Sweden, 1998, Mich. Technol. Tri-corridor Fund, 2004; nominee Buyers award, 6th Internat. Conf. on Head and Neck Cancer, Wash., 2004. Mem.: Am. Acad. of Otolaryngology — Head and Neck Surgery, Mich. Oto-Laryngol. Soc., Am. Assn. for Cancer Rsch., Scandinavian Soc. for Head and Neck Oncology. Office: Beaumont Hospital 3601 W Thirteen Mile Rd Royal Oak MI 48073 Office Phone: 248-898-5000.

AKGÜL, SINEM, pediatrician; b. London, Nov. 21, 1980; Degree in Medicine, Hacettepe U., 2004, degree in Pediat. Medicine, 2009. Pediat. resident Hacettepe U. Sch. Medicine, 2004—09, pediatrician, 2009—. Scholarship, Turkish Republic of Northern Cyprus Ministry of Edn. Fellow: Turkish Soc. Adolescent Health (exec. com. mem.). Avocations: reading, exercise. Office: Hacettepe University Sihhiye Ankara 06100 Turkey E-mail: sinemhusnu@yahoo.com.

AKHAVAN-HEIDARI, MEHDI, cardiothoracic surgeon; b. Tehran, Iran, Feb. 21, 1971; s. Reza Akhavan-Heidari and Sakineh Najmabadi; m. Naghmeh Khodabandeh Lou, Aug. 19, 1998; children: Ayeh children: Imaan. MD, U. Vienna, Austria, 1999—. Cert. Ednl. Commn. Fgn. Med. Grads., 2000. Resident family medicine Landeskrankenhaus Rohrbach, Oberoesterreich, Austria, 1999—2001; resident physician gen. surgery W.Va. U., Charleston, 2001—02; resident gen. surgery Marshall U., Huntington, W.Va., 2002—06; fellow cardiothoracic surgery Loyola U. Med. Ctr., Chgo., 2006—08, Wheeling Heart Inst., 2008—09, Wheeling Hosp., 2009—. Instr. med. software evaluation and med. tchg., faculty medicine U. Vienna, 1993—99; rep. acad. med. educators Marshall U., Huntington, W.Va., 2004—05, bd. mem., 2004—05, rep. internal resident affairs com., 2005—06; rep. Pediatric ICU Collaborative Practice Com., Huntington, 2005—06. Named Resident the Yr., Marshall U., 2004; scholar meritorious achievement, Vienna Med. Sch., 1993—99; Tchg. Resident scholar, Marshall U. Acad. Med. Educators, 2005. Mem.: Soc. Thoracic Surgeons, Am. Coll. Chest Physicians, So. Med. Assn., ACS, Am. Med. Assn., Austrian Coll. Surgeons.

AKHONDI, HOSSEIN, internist, researcher; b. Tehran, Iran, Nov. 16, 1968; s. Mahmood Akhondi and Parvaneh Espahbodi. MD, Iran U., Tehran, 1995. Diplomate Am. Bd. Internal Medicine. Instr. anatomy and neuroanatomy Iran U. Med. Scis., Tehran, 1990—95; hospitalist physician Police Hosp., Tehran, 1995—97; emergency room physician Day Gen. Hosp., Tehran, 1997—99; rsch. asst. Mercer U., Savannah, Ga., 1999—2001, internal medicine resident, 2001—. Mem. rsch. com. Mercer U. Meml. Hosp., Savannah, 2000—, mem. quality mgmt. resident liaison com., 2000—; presenter in field. Contbr. articles to profl. jours. Mem. nat. screening team for rheumatic heart diseases Ministry Health, Tehran, 1993—94. Recipient Continued Med. Edn. course prize, MAYO Clinic, 2000. Fellow: Iranian Med. Coun. (licentiate; young physicians 1995—97); mem.: AMA, Ga. Chpt. Physicians, ACP - Am. Soc. Internal Medicine (assoc. Second place for best original rsch. presentation 2002, Second place for an oral presentation award 2001), So. Med. Assn. (mem. resident adv. com. 2002—, First place for oral presentation 2002). Achievements include research in tongue piercing with infective endocarditis; role of positive pressure ventilation in treating patients with diastolic heart failure; role of illicit drug use in spinal cord infarct; ESR in Alzheimer and non-Alzheimer dementia; physicians using evidence based medicine in atrial fibrilation; discovery of the correlation of SPECT brain scan, Tau and Beta-42 protein with Alzheimer disease; development of antibody coated bacteria in UTI differentiation; presented first case of subclavian vein thrombosis after weigh lifting. Avocations: movies, reading, chess, tennis. Office: Suburban Hosp 8600 Old Georgetown Rd Bethesda MD 20814 Home: 1010 Massachusetts Ave NW Unit 904 Washington DC 20001-5413 Personal E-mail: h68akhond@hotmail.com.

AKHTAR, SALMAN, psychiatrist, educator; MD, Jawaharlal Nehru Med. Coll., India, 1968. Diplomate Am. Bd. Psychiatry and Neurology, cert. psychiatry. Resident Univ of Va., 1976; fellow psychoanalytic tng. Phila. Psychoanalytic Inst., 1986; prof. psychiatry and human behavior Thomas Jefferson Univ.; dir. adult outpatient svcs. dept. of psychiatry and human behavior Jefferson Univ. Hosp. Author: (publs.) The psychodynamic dimension of terrorism, The Immigrant, the Exile, and the Experience of Nostalgia, Visiting the father's grave, Mental pain and the cultural ointment of poetry, numerous publs. Office: 833 Chestnut St Suite 210 Philadelphia PA 19107 Office Phone: 215-955-2547. Office Fax: 215-503-2856.

AKHTER, MOHAMMAD NASIR, public health service officer; b. Jullandur, Punjab, India, June 6, 1944; came to U.S., 1970, naturalized, 1975; s. Mohammad and Fazal (Bibi) Sharif; m. Jeanette E. Easton, Sept. 26, 1970; 1 child, Sarah. F.Sc., Govt. Coll. Lahore, Pakistan, 1962; M.B.BS, King Edwards Med. Coll., Lahore, Pakistan, 1967; M.P.H., Johns Hopkins U., 1973. Diplomate: American Bd. Preventive Medicine. Resident and fellow Mt. Sinai Med. Sch., NYC, 1973-76; chief div. emergency med. service Ill. Dept. Pub. Health, Springfield, Ill., 1976-78, Mich. Dept. Pub. Health, Lansing, 1978-80; dir. health State of Mo., Jefferson City, 1980-82, dep. dir. med. affairs, 1982-84; pres. Mo. Patient Care Rev. Found., 1984-86, prof., 1987-90; dean Coll. Community Medicine, Lahore, Pakistan, 1990-91; commr. Commn. Pub. Health, Washington, 1991-94; sr. advisor Health Care Policy and Rsch. US Dept. Health & Human Services (HHS), Washington, 1994-97; exec. dir. American Pub. Health Assn. (APHA), Washington, 1997—2002; prof. Howard U. Coll. Medicine, 2002—11, sr. assoc. dean for pub. & internat. health, 2002—05; exec. dir. Nat. Medical Assn., 2007—11; dir. DC Dept. Health, 2011—. Office: DC Department Health 899 North Capitol St NE Washington DC 20002 Office Phone: 202-442-5955. Office Fax: 202-442-4795. *

AKIHO, HIROTADA, gastroenterologist; b. Kitakyushu, Fukuoka, Japan, Sept. 3, 1962; s. Hiromi and Tsutako (Oniki) A.; m. Namie Tashiro, May 17, 1997. MD, Kochi Med. Sch., Japan, 1989; PhD, Kyushu U., Fukuoka, Japan, 1997. Med. cert. Gastroenterologist Saga (Japan) Med. Sch. Hosp., 1989-90, Kyushu U. Hosp., Fukuoka, 1990-91, rschr., 1993-95; gastroenterologist Kyushu Rosai Hosp., Kitakyushu, Japan, 1991-93; rschr. Harasanshin Gen. Hosp., Fukuoka, 1995-99, McMaster U., 1999—2002; rschr. divsn. gastroenterology Aso Iizuika Hosp., Japan, 2002—04, Kyushu U. Hosp., Fukuoka, 2004—11, Kitakyushu Mcpl. Med. Ctr., Japan, 2011—. Contbr. articles to profl. jours. Mem.: Japanese Gastroent. Assn., Am. Gastroenterol. Assn., Can. Assn. of Gastroenterology, Japan Gastroenterol. Endoscopy Soc., Japanese Soc. Gastroenterology, Japanese Soc. Internal Medicine. Office: Kitakyushu Mcpl Med Ctr 2 1 1 Bashaku Kokura Kitaku Kitakyushu 802 0077 Japan

AKIL, HUDA, neuroscientist, educator, researcher; b. Damascus, Syria, May 19, 1945; came to U.S., 1968; d. Fakher and Widad (Al-Imam) A.; m. Stanley Jack Watson Jr., Dec. 21, 1972; children: Brendon Omar, Kathleen Tamara. BA, Am. U., Beirut, Lebanon, 1966, MA, 1968; PhD, UCLA, 1972. Postdoctoral fellow Stanford U., Palo Alto, Calif., 1974-78; from asst. prof. to Disting. Univ. Prof. and Quarton Prof. Neurosciences, Dept. Psychiatry U. Mich., Ann Arbor, 1979—, co-dir., rsch. prof., Molecular and Behavioral Neuroscience Inst. Mem. adv. bd. Neurex Corp., Menlo Park, Calif., 1986—, Neurobiol. Techs., Inc., 1994-97; sec. Internat. Narcotics Rsch. Conf., 1990-94. Editor: (jour.) Pain and Headache: Neurochemistry of Pain, 1990; contbr. articles over 300 articles to profl. jours., 1971—2001. Recipient Pacesetter award Nat. Inst. Drug Abuse, 1993, Pasarow award Pasarow Found., 1994, Bristol-Myers Squibb award, 1998, Edward Sachar award Columbia U., 1998; Rockefeller scholar, Beirut, 1963-66; Alfred P. Sloan fellow, Stanford, Calif., 1974-78; grantee Nat. Inst. Drug Abuse, Washington, 1978—, NIMH, Washington, 1980—, Markey Found., U. Mich., 1988-97. Fellow Am. Acad. Arts & Scis., Am. Coll. Neuropsychopharmacology (pres. 1997-98), U. Mich. Soc. Fellows; mem. Inst. Medicine (coun. mem.), NAS, Soc.for Neuroscience (pres. 2002-03, Mika Salpeter Lifetime Achievement award, 2007). Achievements include first to produce physiological evidence for existence of naturally occurring opiate-like substances (endorphins) in brain; described phenomenon of stress-induced analgesia; described functions and regulation of endorphins in brain and pituitary gland; contributed to understanding of biological mechanisms of morphine tolerance and physical dependence; (with colleagues) cloned two main types of opiate receptors, described critical brain circuits relevant to stress and depression. Office: Univ Michigan Molecular & Behavioral Neuroscience Inst 4137 Undergraduate Research Bldg 205 Zina Pitcher Pl 2064 MBNI Bldg Ann Arbor MI 48109-0720 Office Phone: 734-763-3770. E-mail: akil@umich.edu. *

AKIMOTO, MARTIN WAYNE, mental health services professional; b. Chgo., July 24, 1949; s. Ned E. and Emmy (Tsujimoto) Akimoto; m. Barbara Wendley, June 11, 1983; children: Emily, Ellen. BS in Psychology, U. Utah, 1972, MSW, 1974. Lic. social worker; cert. suicide intervention trainer Calif. Social worker Protective Svc. Davis County, Div. Family Svc., Utah, 1974; pvt. practice Simi Psychotherapy Group, Simi Valley, Calif., 1979-87; field work supr. U. So. Calif., 1983-85; sr. psychiat. social worker Simi Valley Mental Health, Ventura County Mental Health Dept, 1975-76, Conejo Valley Mental Health, 1976-87; coord. outpatient children's svc. Ventura County Mental Health, Thousand Oaks, 1987-88; regional supr. children's svcs. Ventura County Mental Health Dept., 1988-92, program supr. options program, 1992-2000; program mgr. Butte County Dept. Behavioral Health, Chico, 2000—04, sr. program mgr., 2004—06; pvt. practice cons. Chico, 2007—. Vol. lectr., rap session leader Planned Parenthood Utah, 1972—73. Office: 2571 Calif Park Dr Ste 210 Chico CA 95928 Home Phone: 530-893-2764; Office Phone: 530-345-4600. Personal E-mail: makimotolcsw@comcast.com. Business E-Mail: makimotolcsw@comcast.net.

AKIN, CEM, internist, allergist, medical researcher; b. Istanbul, Turkey, Nov. 25, 1964; came to U.S., 1989; s. Rifat and Ozden Akin. MD, Istanbul U., 1988; PhD, U. Louisville, 1995. Diplomate Am. Bd. Internal Medicine, Am. Bd. Allergy and Immunology. Intern, then resident U. Louisville Hosps., 1993-96; fellow in allergy and immunology NIH Clin. Ctr., 1996—; clin. assoc. NIH, Bethesda, Md., 1996—99, staff clinician, 2000—04; asst. prof. U. Mich., 2004—. Advisor European Competence Network on Mastocytosis, 2004—; med. adv. bd. Mastocytosis Soc., 2004—. Contbr. articles to profl. jours., chpts. to books. U. Louisville fellow, 1989-93. Mem. Am. Acad. Allergy, Am. Coll. Allergy Asthma and Immunology, Am. Soc. Hematology. Avocations: travel, photography, music. Office: U Mich 1150 W Med Ctr Dr 5520B MSRB1 Ann Arbor MI 48109 Home: 114 Westbourne Ter Brookline MA 02446-2234 Business E-Mail: cemakin@umich.edu.

AKINORI, OSUKA, surgeon; b. Aichi, Japan, Dec. 19, 1974; s. Hirossto and Eiko Osuka; m. Satoko Osuka, Oct. 20, 2004; 1 child, Hinata. MD, Nagoya U., Aichi Japan, 2000. Cert. in surgeon Japan Surg. Soc., 2006, emergency physician Assn. Acute Medicine, 2009. Staff surgeon Aichi Children's Health and Med. Ctr., Obu, Aichi, Japan, 2004—05, Osaka Prefectural Senshu Critical Care Med. Ctr., Izumisano, Osaka, Japan, 2005—09, Dept. Traumatology & Acute Critical Nedicine, U. Grad Sch. Medicine, 2009—. Disaster med. asst. team. Office: Osaka Univ Grad Sch Medicine Dept Traumatology & Acute Critical Medicine Yamadaoka 2-15 Suita Osaka 565 0871 Japan Office Phone: 06-6879-5111. Business E-Mail: akinori@sccmc.izumisano.osaka.jp, osukaakinori@hp-emerg.med.osaka-u.ac.jp.

AKINS, CARY WILLARD, cardiac surgeon; b. Eveleth, Minn., July 13, 1944; AB, Harvard Coll., Cambridge, Mass., 1966; MD, Harvard U. Med. Sch., 1970. Diplomate Am. Bd. Thoracic Surgery. Intern/resident cardiovasc. surgery Mass. Gen. Hosp., Boston, 1970—75, fellow cardiac surgery, 1975; cardiothoracic registrar Wessex Regional Cardiac Thoracic Ctr., Southampton, UK, England, 1974; cardiac surgeon Wilford Hall USAF Med. Ctr., 1975—77; cardiac surg. staff Mass. Gen. Hosp., 1977—; clinical prof. surgery Harvard U. Med. Sch., 1995—. Mem. internat. adv. bd. World-Heart Found. Contbr. articles to profl jours. Named one of America's Top Doctors, Castle Connolly Med. LTD, 2002—. Mem.: ACS, Soc. Thoracic Surgeons, Soc. Heart Valve Disease, Cardiothoracic Surgery Network, Am. Assn. Thoracic Surgery (ethics com.). Achievements include research in valve reconstruction and replacement. Office: Mass Gen Hosp Cox 648 55 Fruit St Boston MA 02114-2696 Office Phone: 617-726-8218. Office Fax: 617-726-3781.

AKIRA, SHIZUO, biomedical researcher, educator; b. Japan, Jan. 27, 1953; MD, Osaka U. Sch. Medicine, 1977; PhD, Osaka U. Grad. Sch. Medicine, 1984. Physician dept. internal medicine Sakai Mcpl. Hosp., 1978—80; rsch. fellow dept. microbiol. and immunology U. Calif., Berkeley, 1985—87; rsch. assoc. Osaka U. Inst. Molecular and Cellular Biology, 1985—87, assoc. prof., 1995; prof. biochemistry Hyogo Coll. Medicine, 1996—99; prof. dept. host def. Osaka U. Rsch. Inst. Microbial Diseases, 1999—; dir. Osaka U. World Premier Internat. Immunology Frontier Rsch. Ctr., 2007—. Rsch. head Solution Oriented Rsch. for Sci. and Tech. Japan Sci. and Tech. Corpn., 1996—2002, rsch. head Core Rsch. for Evolutional Sci. and Tech., 1996—2002, project dir. AKIRA Innate Immunity, Exploratory Rsch. for Advanced Tech., 2002—. Contbr. articles to profl. jours.; co-editor: Innate Immune Sys.: Strategies for Disease Control, 2005; mem. editl. bd.: Pub. Library of Sci. Biology, 2003—, BMC Immunology, assoc. editor: Internat. Immunology, 2002—, Jour. Immunology, 2003—, Microbes and Infection, 2003—, Immunity, 2005—. Recipient Inoue prize, 2000, Hideyo Noguchi Meml. award, 2001, Osaka Sci. prize, 2002, Takeda prize, 2003, Donnall E. Thomas award, 2004, Princess Takamatsu Cancer Rsch. Fund prize, 2004, Purple Ribbon medal, Japanese Cabinet Office, 2005, William B. Coley award, Cancer Rsch. Inst., NYC, 2006, Gairdner Internat. award, Gairdner Found., Can., 2011; co-recipient Robert Koch prize, Germany, 2004; named 2004-2005 Hottest Rschr., Thomson Sci. Mem.: Japanese Soc. Molecular Biology, Japanese Soc. Biochemistry, Japanese Soc. Molecular Cell Biology of Macrophages, Internat. Cytokine Soc., Internat. Endotoxin Soc., Am. Assn. Immunologists, Japan Soc. Immunology (bd. mem.). Office: Integrated Life Sci Bldg 10th Fl Osaka University 3-1 Yamadaoka Suita Osaka 565 0871 Japan *

AKIRA, TERAMOTO, neurosurgeon, educator, department chairman; b. Osaka, Japan, May 20, 1947; s. Hiroshi and Natsuko Teramoto; m. Haruko Teramoto, May 5, 1973; children: Reiko, Shinichiro. MD, U. Tokyo, 1973, D in Med. Sci., 1980. Intern, resident Tokyo U. Hosp., 1973—80; chief Tokyo Met. Police Hosp., 1982—90; asst. prof. Tokyo U., 1990—93; chief Toranomon Hosp., Tokyo, 1993—95; prof., chmn. Nippon Med. Sch., Tokyo, 1995—, dean, 2006—. Avocation: travel. Office: Nippon Med Sch Dept Neurosurgery 1-1-5 Sendagi Bunkyo-ku Tokyo 113-8603 Japan Home: 701 6 13 13 Honkomogome Bunkyo Ku Tokyo 113 0021 Japan Office Phone: 81-3 3822-2131.

AKISKAL, HAGOP SOUREN, psychiatric researcher, educator; b. Beirut, Jan. 16, 1944; U.S., 1969; s. Stephen Jacques and Vehanoushe Dickran (Bedrossian) A. MD, Am. U., Beirut, 1969; Dr honoris causa, U. Lisbon, 2003; Dr honoris causa (hon.), Aristotle U., Greece, 2005. Instr. U. Tenn., Memphis, 1972-73, asst. prof., 1973-77, assoc. prof., 1977-80, prof. psychiatry, dir. sect. affective disorders program, 1975—, dir. med. student edn., 1974-78. Co-dir. Sleep Disorders Ctr., Bapt. Meml. Hosp., Memphis, 1983—; Eli Robins lectr. Washington U., 1980; sr. sci. advisor Nat. Inst. Mental Health, 1990-94; prof. psychiatry, dir. Internat. Mood Ctr., Divsn. Internat. Health and Cross-Cultural Medicine, U. Calif. San Diego, 1994—, disting. prof., 2010-. Editor (editor-in-chief): Jour. of Affective Disorders, 1996—; editor: Psychopathology, 2010—. Recipient Anna Monika prize, 1999, Affective Disorders prize, NARSAD, 2001, Jean Delay prize, World Psychiat. Assn., 2002, Ellis Island medal of honor, 2003, Aristotle Gold medal, Brain & Behavior Soc., Greece, 2006. Fellow Am. Psychiat. Assn. (disting., life), Am. Med. Soc. Calif. (Lifetime Achievement award), Soc. Biol. Psychiatry (Gold medal 1995), Am. Coll. Psychiatrists, Internat. Coll. Neuropsychopharmacology, Royal Coll. Psychiatrists (hon.), French Nat. Academy Medicine (fgn. mem., Paris), Armenian Nat. Acad. Scis. (hon), Internat. Review Bipolar Disorders (Lifetime Achievement award), Mkhitar Herats: Gold Medal (Yerevan State Med. U.) Office: Univ Calif Psychiatary 0603 9500 Gilman Dr La Jolla CA 92093-5004 Office Phone: 858-552-8585 ext. 2226. Personal E-mail: hagopakiskal@yahoo.com. Business E-Mail: hakiskal@ucsd.edu.

AKIYAMA, KAYO, neuroscientist, researcher; b. Sapporo, Hokkaido, Japan, May 11, 1960; d. Kazumasa and Hisako (Shiota). BS, Hokkaido U., 1983; PhD in Health Sci., Kitasato U., Japan, 1991. Rschr. U. Tsukuba, Japan, 1983—, chief officer, 1996—. Cons. Nikon Corp., Tokyo, 1984-2010, Taisho Pharm. Co. Ltd., Tokyo, 1999-2010, Yamato Sci. Co. Ltd., Tokyo, 2000—. Author: Trends in Exercise and Health Research, 2005; contbr. articles to profl. jours. Grantee, Yamaha Music Found., Tokyo, 2005. Fellow Japanese Pharmacol. Soc., Japanese Soc. Neuropsychopharmacology; mem. AAAS, NY Acad. Scis., Japanese Music Therapy Assn. Avocations: classical music, bicycling, gardening. Office Phone: 81-29-853-3330. Business E-Mail: kayo@akiyama-ac.jp.

AKIYAMA, SHINICHIRO, oncologist, hematologist, researcher; b. Sapporo, Hokkaido, Japan, Mar. 18, 1965; s. Hideo and Toshi Akiyama; m. Keiko Kuribayashi, Sept. 16, 1989; 1 child, Manato. MD, Sapporo Med. U., Japan, 1989; PhD, Showa Med. U., Tokyo, 2005. Resident in internal medicine Nikko Meml. Hosp., Muroran, Hokkaido, Japan, 1989—90, Hakodate Red Cross Hosp., Hokkaido, Japan, 1990—92; fellow in oncology 4th dept. internal medicine Sapporo Med. U., Hokkaido, Japan, 1992—96; med. chief aerospace medicine Nat. Space Devel. Agy. Japan, Tsukuba, Ibaraki, Japan, 1996—98; physician-in-chief dept. internal medicine Saiyu Soka Hosp., Soka, Saitama, Japan, 1998—2007; exec. v.p. Mitsukaido Sakura Hosp., Jyoso, Ibaraki, Japan, 2007—09; dir. Kudan Clinic Immune Cell Therapy Ctr., Tokyo, 2009—; prof. LanZhou U. Second Hosp., China, 2010—. Cons. in field. Contbr. articles to profl. jours.; reviewer: Kidney Internat., AACR. Fellow: ACP (assoc.), Japanese Soc. Gastroenterology, Japan Gastroent. Endoscopy Soc., Japanese Soc. Internal Medicine (licentiate); mem.: Am. Chem. Soc (assoc.), Japan Soc. Clin. Oncology (assoc.), Japanese Soc. of Hematology (assoc.), Am. Soc. Clin. Oncology (assoc.), Japanese Soc. of Med. Oncology (assoc.). Shinto Seishinsukeikai. Achievements include discovery of Cu/Zn-SOD, human antioxidant enzyme is a new oxidative stress marker of hemodialysis patients; Cu/Zn-SOD is regulated by mRNA of leukocytes; ren-shen-yang-rong-tang, a chinese herbal drug that stimulates hematopoiesis; cyclic poly lactate and G-CSF enhances efficacy of dendritic cell therapy of cancer. Avocations: Karate, tennis, astronomy. Office: Kudan Clinic Immune Cell Therapy Ctr 1-11-4 Shinko Bldg 6F Kudankita Chiyoda Tokyo 102-0073 Japan Office Phone: 81-3-3263-0511. Personal E-mail: anc18271@nifty.com.

AKIYAMA, TOSHIO, cardiologist, educator, researcher, director, ambassador; b. Shimizu, Japan, Mar. 10, 1941; came to U.S., 1968; m. Akiko Okamura Akyama; children: Naoko, Sachiko. MD, Kyoto Prefectural U. Med., 1966. Cert. in internal medicine, specialty in cardiovasc. disease. Rotating intern U.S. Naval Hosp., Yokosuka, Japan, 1966—67; med. resident, 3d internal medicine dept. Kyoto Prefectural U. Medicine, 1967; staff physician Atomic Bomb Casualty Commn., Hiroshima, Japan, 1967—68; intern Rochester Gen. Hosp., 1968-69, resident in medicine, 1969-70, Strong Meml. Hosp.-U. Rochester, 1970-71, resident in cardiology, 1972-73; fellow in cardiology Emory U., Atlanta, 1971-72, U. Chgo., 1973-75; dir. heart sta. Strong Meml. Hosp., Rochester; prof. medicine with unltd. tenure U. Rochester Sch. Medicine, 1993—2006; co-dir. cardiovasc. scis. Covance, Reno, 2006—07. Reviewer NIH study sect. Biomed. Tech. Spl. Emphasis Panel; cons. Exec. com. for Japanese Med. Specialist Joint commn. Mem. editl. bd. Jour. Electrocardiology, Jour. Arrhythmia, Japanese Circulation Jour., Jour. Arrhythmia, Acta Medica Mem. Biologica; contbr. over 180 articles to profl. jours Chmn. Rochester Hamamatsu Sister City Com., chmn., 1998-2000. Fellow Am. Coll. Cardiology; mem. Am. Heart Assn., Japanese Med. Soc. (exec. com. joint commn. med. specialist sys.), Japanese Clin. Cardiology Soc., Japan Soc. Electrocardiology Achievements include appointed Hamamatsu Yaranaika Ambassador, november 2008. Office: 14531 Quail Rock Court Reno NV 89511 Personal E-mail: takiyama1558@charter.net.

AKIZUKI, SHAW, orthopedic surgeon, educator; b. Kyoto, Oct. 11, 1949; MD, Hirosaki U., Japan, 1975; PhD, Shinshu U., Matsumoto, Nagano, Japan, 1982. Resident Shinshu U., 1975-80, asst. prof., 1981-83, clin. assoc. prof., 1991-98, clin. prof., 1998—; rsch. assoc. Rensselaer Poly. Inst., Troy, NY, 1983-85; head orthopaedics Nagano Matsushiro Gen. Hosp., 1986-88, chmn. clin. divsn., 1989-92, exec. v.p., 1993—2007, pres., 2007—. Clin. assoc. prof. Tokyo Women's Med. Coll., Tokyo, 1991—. Contbr. papers to med. jours. Recipient 10th award Found. for Basic Rsch. of Joint Disease, 1983, John J. Joyce award Internat. Anthroscopy Assn., 1995. Fellow Japan Orthopedics Assn., Japan Rheumatism Assn. (trustee 1989—, traveling fellow 1983), Japan Rehab. Med. Soc.; mem. Japanese Soc. Rheumatism and Joint Surgery (trustee 1992—), Japan Clin. Biomechanical Soc. (trustee 1997—), Orthopedic Rsch. Soc., Internat. Rehab. Med. Assn., Internat. Soc. Orthopedics, Internat. Soc. Arthroscopy, Knee

Surgery, Orthopedic Sports Medicine. Avocations: canoeing, fishing, skiing. Home: 1427 Matsushiro Nagano 381-1231 Japan Office: Nagano Matsushiro Gen Hosp 183 Matsushiro Nagano 381-1231 Japan

AKKAN ÇETINKAYA, ZÜLEYHA, gastroenterologist; b. Istanbul, Turkey, Feb. 17, 1976; Degree in Gastroenterology; degree, Istanbul U. Med. Faculty, 1998. Gastroenterology specialist Kocaeli Derince Edn. and Rsch. Hosp., 2009—. Named one of Best Dr. in City, 2010. Mem.: Türk Gatsroenteroloji Dernegi, Türk Karaciger Arastirmalari Dernegi. Avocations: travel, reading, movies. Office: Ibn-i Sina Bulvari Tibb Kocaeli 41900 Turkey

AKKIZ, HIKMET, physician; b. Mersin, Apr. 25, 1954; MD, Cukurova Med. Faculty, 1978. Prof. Cukurova U., 1996; dir. Internal Medicine Dept., 2005—. Office: Cukurova Universty Balcali Hosp Adana 01336 Turkey Business E-Mail: hakkiz@superonline.com.

AKMAN, JEFFREY SCOTT, dean, psychiatrist; b. Balt., May 7, 1956; s. Alvin and Marion (Blumberg) A. BS, Duke U., 1977; MD, George Wash. U., 1981. Diplomate Am. Bd. Psychiatry and Neurology. Resident in psychiatry George Washington U., Washington, 1981-85, instr. chief resident in psychiatry, 1984-85, asst. prof. psychiatry and behavioral scis., 1985-90, assoc. prof. psychiatry and behaviorl scis., 1990-91, from asst. dean student ednl. policies to assoc. dean student and faculty devel. and policies, Sch. Medicine, 1991—2000, Leon M. Yochelson prof., chmn. dept. dept. psychiatry and behavioral sciences, 2000—10, interim vice provost health affairs and dean Sch. Medicine, 2011—. Prin. investigator AIDS edn. project NIMH/George Wash. U., 1986-89; dir. med. edn. George Washington U. Dept. Psychiatry. Contbr. articles to profl. jours. Cons. Whitman-Walker Clinic, Inc., Washington, 1986—, ARC, D.C. chpt., 1986—, D.C. Commn. of Pub. Health, 1986-89. Recipient Jr. Faculty Devel. award NIMH, 1985-86. Mem. Med. Soc. D.C., Washington Psychiat. Soc. (pres. D.C. chpt.), Med. Soc. D.C. (pres. psychiatry sect.), Am. Assn. Physicians for Human Rights, Am. Psychiat. Asns. (commn. on AIDS 1988—, C.A. Roeske award). Democrat. Jewish. Office: George Wash University Sch Medicine & Health Sciences 2300 Eye St NW Ste 713-W Washington DC 20037 Office Phone: 202-994-2987. Office Fax: 202-994-0926. *

AKSOY, BERNA, dermatologist; b. Mugla, Turkey, Apr. 11, 1975; m. Hasan Mete Aksoy; 1 child, Elifsu. MD, Hacettepe U., Ankara, Turkey, 1999. Cert. dermatologist Hacettepe U. Dermatology specialist Numune Tng. and Rsch. Hosp., Ankara, 2003—07, TDV 29 Mayis Pvt. Ankara Hosp., Turkey, 2007—09, Pvt. Konak Hosp., Kocaeli, Turkey, 2009—. Office: Pvt Konak Hosp Yenisehir Mh Donmez Sk 53 Izmit 41000 Kocaeli Turkey Office Phone: 002623187070/1146. Office Fax: 902623115544. Personal E-mail: bmaksoy@mynet.com, bernaaaksoy@gmail.com. Business E-Mail: baksoy@konakhastanesi.com.tr.

AKUKWE, CHINUA, public health physician, health service executive; b. Aug. 7, 1962; MD, U. Nigeria, Enugu, 1985; M in Pub. Health, Hebrew U., Jerusalem, Israel, 1991; cert. in Exec. Pub. Health Mgmt., Johns Hopkins U., 1998. Sci. coord. NIH, D.C. Initiative, Washington, 1993-97; sr. policy and planning advisor to dir. D.C Dept Health, Washington, 1997-98; prof. George Washington U. Sch. Pub. Health, Washington, 1998—. Coord. Global Health Seminars George Washington U. Med. Ctr., Washington, 1997—98, vice chmn. Nat. Coun. Internat. Health, Washington, 1997—98; workshop expert minority health Dept. Health, Columbia, SC, 1998; mem. tech. rev. panels for maternal and child health and health stats. U.S. Dept. HHS, 1995—; mem. com. on faculty support and profl. devel. George Washington U. Hosp. Ctr., 1999—2004, mem. exec. com., faculty senate, 2004—05, chair tech. adv. com., Africa Ctr. for Health and Security, 2005—10; bd. dirs. Constituency for Africa, Washington; mem. expert com. HIV/AIDS in Africa and governance UN Econ. Commn. Africa; tech. advisor, HIV/AIDS Internat. Labor Orgn., Geneva, 2003—04; tech. advisor Howard U., Washington, coord. global health com., 2004; chmn. bd. dirs. Africa Ctr. Epidemiology and Econ. Rsch., Abuja, Nigeria, 2006—; spkr. in field; exec. chmn. Union Africa Diaspora Health Initiative, 2008—. Author: (book) Healthcare in Africa, 2006, Development Issues in Africa, 2006, Healthcare Services in Africa, 2008; co-author: AIDS Orphans in Africa and Their Grandparents, 2006; editor-in-chief Jour. Pub. Health, Biotech. and Pharm. Products; editor: (spl. edit.) Africa Renaissance Jour. on Health Care Delivery in Africa, 2006, (book) Healthcare Svcs. in Africa, 2008; mem. editl. bd. Am. Jour. Pub. Health, 1999—2003, author, co-author 64 tech. monographs on various health issues; contbr. more than 100 articles on HIV/AIDS and health issues in Africa. Chmn., Health Forum World Bank Open House on African Diaspora, Washington, 2007; sr. fellow Nat. Med. Assn., Washington, 2007—08; bd. dirs. Christian Connections for Internat. Health, 1994—96, Peace Corps Nigeria Alumni Found., Washington, 2002—07. Fellow: Nat Acad. Pub. Adminstrn. DC, Am. Coll. Epidemiology, Royal Soc. Medicine London, Royal Soc. Health (Eng.), Am. Coun. Voluntary Internat. Action (Washington) (sr.); mem.: N.Y. Acad. Scis., Am. Pub. Health Assn. (co-chair 125th Ann. Conf. 1997). Achievements include development of the Communicable Diseases Guidelines for Africa Development Bank, 2003-04; HIV/AIDS, TB and Malaria Continental Implementation Plan for the African Union, 2006-07. Avocations: soccer, reading. Office: George Washington Univ Dept Global Health 2175 K St NW Ste 810 Washington DC 20037 Business E-Mail: cakukwe@gwu.edu. E-mail: cakukwe@att.net.

AKURA, JUNSUKE, ophthalmologist, researcher; b. Kurashiki, Japan, Dec. 2, 1954; s. Yasushi and Sachiko Akura; m. Kaori Akura, Apr. 5, 1998; children: Erika, Madoka. MD, Tottori U., Japan, 1980, PhD, 1987. Asst. prof. Faculty of Medicine, Tottori U., 1987—88; hosp. dir. Kushimoto (Japan) Rehab. Ctr., 1991—. Author: Letters from Birganj, 1991; patentee in field. Bd. dirs. Assn. for Ophthalmic Cooperation to Asia, Osaka, Japan, 1988—2002, chmn., 2002—. Recipient Film Festival award, Am. Soc. Cataract and Refractive Surgery, 1996, prize, Atsuhito Nakata Meml. Found. Charitable Trust, Japan, 1997, Prabal Gorkhadachhinbahu medal, King of Nepal, 2001. Achievements include development of new surgical methods of astigmatic keratotomy (FDAK); manual small incision cataract surgery (claw-vectis technique, quarter extraction); pterygium surgery (mini-flap technique); glaucoma surgery (Uveal shunt). Avocation: tennis. Office: Kushimoto Rehab Ctr 259-6 Kushimoto Kushimoto 649-3503 Japan Home: 1222-11 Kujinokawa Kushimoto 649-3511 Japan Home Phone: 81-735-62-0958; Office Phone: 81 735 62 3600. Office Fax: 81 735 62 3694.

AKUTSU, YASUSHI, cardiologist; b. Tokyo, Mar. 25, 1958; s. Takeo and Hideko Akutsu; m. Miyuki Ishida, Feb. 20, 1963; 1 child, Hitomi. MD, Showa U., Tokyo, 1986, PhD in Clin. Cardiology and Nuc. Medicine, 1994. Lic. Japan, 1986, diplomate Japanese Bd. Internal Medicine, 1991, Japanese Bd. Cardiology, 1995. Cardiologist-in-cochief third dept. internal medicine Showa U. Sch. Medicine, Tokyo, 1999—, asst. prof. third dept. internal medicine, 2002—. Instr. clin. cardiology Showa U. Sch. Medicine, Tokyo, 1996—2003, Showa U. Sch. Dental Medicine, Tokyo, 2001—03, Showa U. Nursing Sch., Tokyo, 2001—03. Contbr. articles to profl. jours. Mem.: ACP, Japanese Soc. Nuc. Medicine (assoc.), Japanese Coll. Cardiology (assoc.), Japanese Circulation Soc. (assoc.), Japanese Soc. Internal Medicine (assoc.). Achievements include research in usefulness of simultaneous evaluations of contractile reserve, perfusion, and metabolism during dobutamine stress for predicting the wall motion reversibility (myocardial stunning) after successful PT; evaluation of PTCA for acute myocardial infarction from long-term survival; quantitative measurement of regional myocardial blood flow with 13NH3 positron emission computed tomography; determination of regional myocardial blood flow with 13N-ammonia positron emission tomography during low-grade exercise for evaluating coronary artery stenosis; others. Office: Showa Univ Sch Medicine 1-5-8 Hatanodai Shinagawaku Tokyo 142-8666 Japan Office Fax: +81-3-3784-8622.

AL-ABDULJAWAD, KHAYRIA ABDULJAWAD, audiologist, educator; d. Abduljawad Jad Ab-Aduljawad; life ptnr. Abdullah Muhammed Al Qahtani, July 9, 1977 (dec. 1997); children: Samar Abdullah Al Qahtani, Iman Abdullah Al Qahtani, Sara Abdullah Al Qahtani, Ibrahem Abdullah Al Qahtani, Ahmed Abdullah Al Qahtani. PhD in Audiology, Nottingham U., 1998. Dir. Med. Rehab. Ctr. Ministry of Health, Abha, Saudi Arabia, 1981—83, head Unit Speech and Hearing Pathology Riyadh, Saudi Arabia, 1991—92, 1993—94, head Unit Speech and Hearing Pathology, cons. audiology, 1998—2000; prof., cons. audiology Coll. Applied Med. Scis. King Saud U., Riyadh, 2001—. Mem. nat. com. prevent and manage deafness and hearing loss Mnistry of Health, 1998—2003; cons. spl. edn. Ministry of Edn., Riyadh, 2001—04; mem. acad. com. King Saud U., 2001—04; prodr., pres. female com. Saudi Assn. Hearing Impairment, 2001—05; chmn. internship com. King Saud U., 2004—05; mem. Saudi Coun. for Health Specialties, Riyadh, 2005—; mem. editl. bd. Saudi Jour. Oto-Rhino-Laryngology Head and Neck Surgery; chair academic com. Coll. Applied Med. Scis., mem. employment com.; cons. Open U., Saudi Arabia. Contbr. articles to profl. and med. jours. Mem.: Saudi Assn. Hearing Impairment (pres. female com. 2001—05), Brit. Assn. Audiological Scientists (assoc.). Home and Office: Univ Coll Applied Med Scis Po Box 105595 11656 Riyadh Saudi Arabia Office Fax: 966 1 4455293; Home Fax: 00966 1 4455293. Personal E-mail: khayria_audio@hotmail.com.

ALAGKIOZIDIS, IOANNIS, physician; b. Thesssaloniki, Greece, Dec. 6, 1978; MD, Aristotle U., Greece, 2002. Resident physician U. Tex. Houston, 2007—. Recipient Med. Knowledge award, Aristotle U., 2000, U. Ioannina, Greece, 2000, Editor's Choice award, AAAS, 2009; scholarship, Ministry of Edn., Greek Govt., 2000. Mem.: HCMS, AAGL, ACOG, AOA, Honor Med. Soc. Avocations: running, reading, soccer. Home: 1800 EL PASEO Parqueview Apt 1308 Houston TX 77054 E-mail: ioannis.alagkiozidis@uth.tmc.edu.

AL-AHMADI, HAMID SULIMAN, ophthalmologist, consultant; b. Madina Al-Munwara, Saudi Arabia, Dec. 9, 1961; s. Suleman Hamid and Nora Ayed Al-Ahmadi; m. Najwa Saleh Al-Owrdi, May 6, 1986; children: Turky, Areej, Doaa, Raeed. Degree, Anas U., Madina, 1965, Obadh U., 1975, Ohud U., 1978. Lic. Ophthalmology Bd. King Saud U. Head continuous med. edn. Dammam Hosp., King Dom, Saudi Arabia, 1988—90; head quality assurance dept. Ohud Hosp., King Dom, 1992—99, cons. ophthalmologist, 1994—99, dep. head ophthalmology dept., 1994—99; dir. Spl. Eye Ctr. Ejlal Hosp., King Dom, 1999—2001; gen. mgr. Al-Ahmadi Hosp., King Dom, 2001—, head Spl. Eye Ctr., 2001—. Resident Dept. Ophthalmology, Dammam, 1986—88; gen. mgr. 4 brs. Optical Shops Ctr., Madina, 1994—; gen. mgr. Al-Ahmadi Hosp., Madina, 2001—. Author: (book) Care of Children's Eyes, 1988; contbr. papers to profl. symposia. Recipient opthalmology fellow, King Saud U., 1990—94. Mem.: Am. Assn. Eye Bank, Royal Coll. Ophthalmology U.K., Saudi Ophthalmic Soc. Assn. Office: Al Ahmadi Hosp PO Box 6476 Second Circle Rd X Rd Sayed El Shouhada Medina Saudi Arabia Office Fax: 00966 48363337. E-mail: dr._hamid_al_ahmadi@hotmail.com, sabir_991@hotmail.com.

AL AHMARI, ALI ABDULLAH, pediatrician; b. Abha, Sept. 13, 1969; MD, King Saud U., Med. Coll., 1996. Cons., pediat. hematology-oncology King Faisal Specialist Hosp. and Rsch. Ctr., 2005—, dir., histiocytosis program, 2008—. Mem.: European Group Blood and Marrow Transplantation, Eastern Mediterranean Blood and Marrow Transplantation, Saudi Soc. Blood and Marrow Transplantation, Saudi Arabia Pediat. Hematology/Oncology Soc. Avocations: swimming, reading. Office: PO Box 3354 Takhassusi Riyadh 11211 Saudi Arabia Office Fax: 96612055276. Business E-Mail: aahmari@kfshrc.edu.sa.

AL AHMARI, SAEED AWAD, cardiologist, consultant; b. Bahwan, Abha, Aug. 23; s. Awad Mohammed and Saleha Ali Al Ahmari; m. Jamellaha Abdullaha Al Ahmari, Mar. 10, 1995; children: Abdullelaha, Nada, Hatem, Riyadh. Degree, Abha Med. Sch., 1995. Diplomate Am. Bd. Echocardiography, Saudi Bd. Cardiology, Arab Bd. Cardiology. Intern Armed Forces Hosp., Riyadh, Saudi Arabia, 1995—96, resident, 1996—98; fellow Prince Sultan Cardiac Ctr., Riyadh, 1999—2001, cons., 2003—; fellow Mayo Clinic, Rochester, Minn., 2002. Contbr. articles to profl. jours. Mem.: Am. Coll. Cardiology, Royal Coll. Physicians (U.K.). Office: Prince Sultan Cardiac Ctr Al Sulemaniah PO Box 7897 Riyadh 11159 Saudi Arabia Home: Po Box 340301 11333 Riyadh Saudi Arabia Home Phone: 00966-1-4833065; Office Phone: 00966-1-4777714 ext 8840. Office Fax: 009661-4778771. Personal E-mail: naman45@hotmail.com.

ALAKI, SUMER MADANI, dental educator; b. Tuscon, Oct. 19, 1969; MS, U. Mich., 2002, DPH, 2006. Demonstrator jr. faculty Faculty Dentistry, King Abdulaziz U., 1994—97, asst. prof. preventive dentistry dept., 2006—10, asst. prof., 2010—. Active mem. Am. Acad. Pediat. Dentistry, 1997—2007. Mem.: Saudi Dental Soc. Avocations: reading, writing. Office: PO Box 80209 Jeddah 21589 Saudi Arabia Office Fax: 96626952847. E-mail: sumeralaki@msn.com.

AL-AKKAD, SALAH ABDULRAHMAN OMAR, neurosurgeon; b. Alkhobar, Saudi Arabia, July 4, 1968; s. Abdulrahman Omar Al-Akkad and Afaf Husni Kaki; m. Arwa Ruwaid Al-Akkad, 2006; children: Abdulelah Salah, Alhasan Salah. MBBS, King Faisal U., Dammam, Saudi Arabia, 1993. Gen. practice Saudi Aramco Med. Svcs. Orgn., Dhahran, Saudi Arabia, 1995—97, neurosurgeon, 2003—. Head neurospinal unit SAMSO, ARAMCO, Dhahran, 2005—. Fellow: Royal Coll. Surgeons Can.; mem.: Am. Assn. Neurol. Surgeons. Muslim. Achievements include first to use navigational technology. Avocations: walking, swimming, photography. Home: PO Box 9591 Dhahran 31311 Saudi Arabia Office: Saudi ARAMCO Med Svcs Dhahran Health Ctr Rm a-420 Box 76 Surg Divsn 31942 Dhahran Saudi Arabia Office Fax: 966 3 8773695. Personal E-mail: salah_alakkad@yahoo.com.

ALAM, MOHAMMED IQBAL, physiologist, educator; b. Kolkata, India, Jan. 10, 1968; MS, U. Calcutta, 1989, PhD, 1997. Rschr., tchr. M. M. Inst. Med. Sci. & Rsch., 1997—, prof. physiology, 2005—. Jr. Rsch. fellow, ICMR, New Delhi, Sr. Rsch. fellow, CSIR, New Delhi, Rsch. Assoc. fellow. Mem.: Indian Pharmacological Soc., Indian Sci. Congress Assn., Physiol. Soc. Avocations: reading, travel, soccer, cricket. Home: 3 Sir Syed Ahmed Rd Kolkata West Bengal 700014 India Personal E-mail: iqbalasc@yahoo.com.

AL-ANSI, SEHAM ABDULLAH, technologist; b. Riyadh, Feb. 12, 1980; BSc, King Saud U., 2004. Sr. med. technologist King Faisal Specialist Hosp. & Rsch. Ctr., 2004—. Application specialist ICP-MS. Contbr. to prfol. sci. publs. Office: Takassusi Riyadh 11211 Saudi Arabia Office Fax: 00966-1-4427231. Business E-Mail: salansi@kfshrc.edu.sa.

ALAQEEL, SINAA, medical researcher; b. Saudi Arabia, Jan. 14, 1971; BSc in Pharm. Scis., King Saud U., 1995; PhD, U. Manchester, 2004. Rschr. King Saud U., 1996—. Office: Coll Pharmacy Riyadh 11335 Saudi Arabia Office Fax: 009661-2913797. Business E-Mail: salageel@ksu.edu.sa.

AL-ARABI, YASSIR BABIKER, orthopedist; s. Babiker Abdelmahmoud Al-Arabi and Ihssan Ali Obeid; m. Marwa Osman Al-Arabi, Sept. 6, 2002; children: Omnia, Jude, Ali. MBBS, U. Khartoum, Sudan, 1998. Specialist registrar trauma and orthop. surgery Bristol Royal Infirmary, Avon, 2004—07; splty. registrar trauma & orthop. surgery Severn Inst., Severn and Wessex Deanery, Bristol, Avon, England, 2007—. Fellow: Royal Coll. Surgeons Eng. Trauma and Orthop. Surgery; mem.: RCS (London) (step course moderator 2006—08), Brit. Orthop. Assn. (assoc. mem. 2007—08, 1st prize Presentation, Brit. Assn. Surgery Knee Ann. Congress 2006). Muslim. Achievements include development of a new classification system for primary knee arthroplasty patients. Avocations: photography, computers. Personal E-mail: yassir6@hotmail.com.

AL-ARADI, IBRAHIM KHALIL, dermatologist, consultant; b. Kuwait City, Kuwait, Nov. 1, 1969; s. Khalil I. Al Aradi and Zahra A. Al-Eidani; m. Ghaida Mohammed Al-Sarraf, Aug. 6, 1996; children: Laila Ibrahim, Dalal Ibrahim, Ali Ibrahim. B in Basic Med. Scis., Kuwait U., 1992, MB, BChir, 1995. Intern Al-Adan/Mubarak Al-kabir Hosps., Kuwait, 1995—97; resident internal medicine U. Ottawa, Ontario, Canada, 1997—98, resident dermatology, 1998—2000, chief resident dermatology, 2000—01; clin. fellow dermatologic surgery U. Toronto, Ontario, Canada, 2001—02; sr. registrar dermatology Ministry Health Kuwait, 2001—05, cons. dermatologist, 2005—. Head dermatologic surgery unit As'ad Al-hamad Dermatology Ctr., Al-Sabah Hosp., Kuwait, 2002—; dir. hair clinic As'ad Al-hamad Dermatology Ctr., Kuwait, 2003—; clin. tutor dept. medicine faculty medicine and dentistry Kuwait U., 2003—; clin. tutor Kuwaiti Bd. Dermatology, Kuwait Inst. for Med. Subspecialities, Kuwait, 2004—; chmn. 1st Dermatologic Surgery Symposium, Kuwait, 2004. Contbr., co-founder: As' Ad Al-hamad Dermatology Center Health Journal; contbr. articles to profl. jours. Fellow: Am. Acad. Dermatology, Royal Coll. Physicians and Surgeons Can.; mem.: Internat. Soc. Dermatologic Surgery (corr.), Can. Soc. Dermatologic Surgery (corr.), Am. Soc. Dermatologic Surgery (corr. Silver award in pub. media 2003), Kuwait Dermatology Assn. (corr.), Can. Dermatology Assn. (assoc.). Avocations: swimming, walking, writing, reading.

AL-ARAJI, ADNAN, neurologist, consultant; b. Baghdad, Iraq, May 4, 1953; m. Wafaa Abdul Wahed, 1979; children: May, Rula, Sarmad. MBChB, U. Baghdad, 1977. Cons. neurologist, prof. Baghdad Med. Sch., Med. City Tchg. Hosp., 1997—2003; vis. assoc. prof. neurology U. BC, Vancouver, Canada, 2003—04; cons. neurologist U. Hosp. North Staffordshire, Stoke on Trent, Staffs, England, 2004—. Dir. Multiple Sclerosis Clinic, U. Baghdad, 1999—2003; chmn. sci. com. Iraqi Med. Assn., Baghdad, 2000—03; clin. lead North Staffordshire Regional Multiple Sclerosis Svc., Stoke on Trent, 2005—. Editor: (book) Multiple Sclerosis for the Practicing Neurologist; editor-in-chief: Iraqi Med. Jour., 2001—03; contbr. articles to profl. jours. Recipient Du Pre award, Internat. Fedn. Multiple Sclerosis Societies, 2003. Fellow: Royal Coll. Physicians, UK, Royal Coll. Physicians and Surgeons of Glasgow; mem.: Brit. Med. Assn., Assn. Brit. Neurologists. Achievements include development of Baghdad multiple sclerosis clinic; North Midland regional multiple sclerosis service. Office: U Hosp North Staffordshire Princess Rd Stoke-on-Trent ST4 7LN England

ALARCÓN DE LA LASTRA, CATALINA, pharmacologist, educator; b. Sevilla, Apr. 27, 1959; PhD in Pharmacy, 1985. Prof. U. Sevilla, 1988. Office: Profesor García González 2 Sevilla 41012 Spain

AL-ASHAAL, HANAN AL- HAY, medical researcher; b. Giza, Egypt, Jan. 5, 1959; MSc, Cairo U., 1987, PhD, 1995. Rsch. scientist Nat. Rsch. Ctr., 1995—. Contbr. scientific papers to profl. jours. publs. Mem.: Egyptian Soc. Clin. Chemistry, Egyptian Soc. Health And Environ. Legis. Avocations: reading, walking. Office: Al-Tahrir St El-Dokki Giza 123111 Egypt

ALAV, FARAMARZ, cardiologist, internist; b. Akstafa, Azerbaijan, Jan. 26, 1958; s. Ahmed Alav and Ashraf Abulmulla; m. Kristina Jalilova, Nov. 7, 2000; children: Leila, Emin children: Emil. MD, Azerbaijan State Med. Inst., Baku, Azerbaijan, 1974—80. Intern Rsch. Inst. Cardiology, Baku, Absheron, Azerbaijan, 1980—81; emergency unit physician Ctrl. Hosp. Emergency Unit, Baku, Azerbaijan, 1981—86; fellow Inst. Advanced Med. Studies, Baku, Azerbaijan, 1986—88; cardiologist Diagnostic Ctr., Baku, Azerbaijan, 1988—93; internist Bonab Ctrl. Hosp., Bonab, Iran, 1993—94; telemetry technician St. Joseph Hosp., Orange, 1995—98; resident in internal medicine Wayne State U. Sinai-Grace Hosp., Detroit, 1988—2001; physician in internal medicine United Family Care, Fontana, Calif., 2001—. Contbr. articles to profl. jours. Recipient award for Outstanding Performance and Svc. to the Cmty., State Bd., 1995. Mem.: Am. Soc. Internal Medicine, Am. Coll. Physicians. Office: PO Box 610 Rialto CA 92377-0610 Office Phone: 909-874-2371. Personal E-mail: falav@hotmail.com.

AL AWADI, YOUSEF ABDULLA, neurosurgeon, consultant; b. Kuwait, Kuwait, Feb. 11, 1957; s. Fatema Ahmed Haji and Abdulla Mohammed Al Awadi; m. Ludmilla Ivanovna Novitskaya, Oct. 10, 1978; children: Fatema Yousef, Aseel Yousef. MD, Minsk Med. Inst., Belarus, 1981; MD, PhD, Sofia Med. Acad., Bulgaria, 1988. Cert. Bulgarian Bd. Neurosurgery. Registrar Ministry of Health, Kuwait, 1981—83, Edinburgh Health Ministry, England, 1983—84; sr. registrar Rashid Hosp., Dubai, United Arab Emirates, 1990—91; asst. unit head, cons. Ministry of Health, Kuwait, 1991—94, sr. cons. neurosurgery, 1994—. Bd. advisor, adv. mem. His Highness Amir Cabinet, Kuwait, 1993—. Fellow: Skull Base Surgery (assoc.); mem.: Am. Assn. Neurosurgey, Kuwait Med. Assn. (hon.). Home: Al Rawda Kuwait P O Box 33580 Al Rawda 73456 Kuwait Office Fax: 965 4849226; Home Fax: 965 5348483. Personal E-mail: fatemay79@yahoo.com.

AL-BADAWI, EMAD A., dentist; b. Cairo, June 2, 1972; BDS, King AbdulAziz U., 1995; MS, Boston U., 2007; DSc. Cons. King Fahd Hosp., 1996. Mem.: Saudi Dental Soc. Office: Doaa Al-Ahsan Jeddah Al-Khalidia 02543 Saudi Arabia Business E-Mail: ealbadawi@aol.com.

AL-BADAWI, ISMAIL ABDUL RAHMAN, gynecologist; b. Cairo, Sept. 6, 1968; MBChB, King AbdulAziz U., 1991. Med. dir., Day Procedure Ctr. King Faisal Specialist Hosp. & Rsch. Ctr., 2002, dep. exec. dir., academic & tng. affairs, 2011, cons., sect. head, gynecology & gynecology oncology, 2011—. Assoc. prof. AlFaisal U., 2010. Recipient Pioneer Employee award, King Faisal Specialist Hosp. & Rsch. Ctr. Fellow: Royal Coll. Physician and Surgeons Can.; mem.: Gynecology Oncology Can. (Internat. mem.). Avocation: swimming. Office: Dept Obstetrics & Gynecology MBC Riyadh 11211 Saudi Arabia Office Fax: 966-1-442-7393. Personal E-mail: i_albadawi@yahoo.com.

AL-BAHRANI, ALI IHSAN, pathologist, department chairman; b. Edinburgh, Oct. 12, 1960; s. Ihsan Rouf Al-bahrani and Yousr Khalil Al-Bahrani; m. Ghada Jafar Al-Tamimi, Nov. 21, 1985; children: Noor Ali, Hassan Ali. MSc in Chem. Pathology, U. Surrey, Guildford, 1993. FRCPath Royal Coll. of Pathologists, UK, 2004. Cons., head dept. chem. pathology IOW Primary care Trust, Newport, Isle of Wight, England, 1992—. Contbr. scientific papers. Fellow: Royal Coll. Pathologists (London); mem.: Royal Coll. Pathologists, Assn. Clin. Biochemistry. Home: Lower St Cross Farm Dodnor Ln Newport Isle of Wight PO30 5TD England Office: Isle of Wight Primary Care Trust St Mary's Hosp St. Marys Hospital Parkhurst Road PO30 5TG Newport England Office Fax: 10983825437; Home Fax: 01983825437. Personal E-mail: aliihsanalbahrani@hotmail.com. Business E-Mail: ali.al-bahrani@iow.nhs.uk.

ALBALA, DAVID MOIS, urologist, educator; b. Chgo., Dec. 29, 1955; m. Francene Ann Salerno, Oct. 23, 1999; 1 child, Jack. BA in Geology, Lafayette Coll., Easton, Pa., 1978; MD, Mich. State U., 1983. Prof. urology Loyola U. Med. Ctr., Maywood, Ill., 1990—2000, Duke U. Med. Ctr., Durham, NC, 2000—10. Mem. editl. bd.: Jour. Endourology, Urology Index and Revs. Fellow, White House, 1995—96. Mem.: Am. Urol. Assn. Office: Associated Med Profls 1226 East Water St Syracuse NY 13210 Office Phone: 315-478-4178. Office Fax: 315-478-0840. Personal E-mail: albal002@mc.duke.edu. Business E-Mail: dalbala@ampofny.com. *

ALBANO, ANNE MARIE, clinical psychologist, educator; b. SI, NY, Aug. 18, 1957; d. Joseph James and Kathleen Anne (Duggan) A. AA, Broward Community Coll., Pompano, Fla., 1976; BS, Fla. State U., Tallahassee, 1979; MA, U. Richmond, 1983; PhD, U. Miss., 1991. Lic. in clin. psychology, NY. Substance abuse counselor Human Resources, Inc., Richmond, Va., 1981-82; psychologist Med. Coll. Va., Richmond, 1982-83; adolescent therapist Adolescents in Distress, Inc., Ft. Lauderdale, Fla., 1983-84; child and family therapist KIDS in Distress, Inc., Oakland Park, Fla., 1984-85; rsch. asst. U. Miss., Oxford, 1985-89, grad. instr., 1987-89; predoctoral intern Dept. Vets. Affairs Med. Ctr., Tufts U. Sch. Medicine, Boston, 1989-90; postdoctoral fellow Phobia and Anxiety Clinic, SUNY, Albany, 1990-92, asst. dir., 1992-95; asst. prof. dept. psychology U. Louisville, 1995—98, co-dir. Anxiety Rsch. and Treatment Ctr., 1995—98; asst. prof. psychiatry NYU, NYC, 1998—2004; assoc. prof. clin. psychology in psychiatry Columbia U., NYC, 2004—, dir. Clinic Anxiety and Related Disorders, 2004—. Program coord. Ctr. for Stress and Anxiety Disorders, Child and Adolescent Fear and Anxiety Treatment Program, Albany, 1990-95; adj. prof. psychology SUNY, Albany, 1991-95. Mem. APA (pres. divsn. 53 Soc. Clin. Child and Adolescent Psychology, 2011), Assn. Behavioral and Cognitive Therapies, Internat. Assn. Cognitive Therapy, Anxiety Disorders Assn. America, Soc. Rsch. in Child and Adolescent Psychopathology. Roman Catholic. Avocations: travel, diving, skiing, photography. Office: Divsn Child & Adolescent Psychiatry Columbia Univ Med Ctr Kolb Annex 2d Fl 722 W 168th St New York NY 10032 Office Phone: 212-543-5339. Business E-Mail: albanoa@childpsych.columbia.edu. *

ALBAQUMI, MAMDOUH NASSER, nephrologist, educator; b. Saudi Arabia, July 21, 1974; MD in Medicine, George Washington U., 2001. Cert. Nat. Bd. Med. Examiners, 2000, lic. NY State Medicine, 2004, diplomate Am. Bd. Internal Medicine, 2004, Am. Bd. Nephrology, 2008. Resident, internal medicine NY U. Med. Ctr., NY, 2001—04, fellow, nephrology, 2004—06, tchg. asst., dept. medicine, 2004, asst. rsch. scientist, nephrology divsn., 2006, clin. instr., nephrology divsn., 2006, adj. assoc. prof., dept. medicine, 2009; cons., nephrology sect. King Faisal Specialist Hosp. and Rsch. Ctr., Riyadh, Saudi Arabia, 2007. Recipient Young Investigator Forum award, Nat. Kidney Found., Orlando, Fla., 2007; nominee Tchr. of Yr., NY U. Med. Ctr., 2002; fellowship, Amgen Nephrology Inst., Thousand Oaks, Calif., 2005, NY Soc. Nephrology, 2006. Fellow: Am. Soc. Nephrology, Am. Coll. Physicians; mem.: Internat. Soc. Nephrology. Office: King Faisal Specialist Hosp and Rsch Ctr MBC-46 PO Box 3354 Riyadh 11211 Saudi Arabia Personal E-mail: albaqumi@gmail.com.

ALBARRACIN, DANIEL ESLAVA, nursing educator; b. Aguazul, Casanare, Feb. 2, 1966; Degree in Nursing, Javeriana U., 1987; PhD in Pub. Health, Sao Paulo U., 2001—01. Assoc. prof. Javeriana U., 1991—; dir. colective health dept. Sch. Nursing-Javeriana U., 2003—09, office dir. continue edn., 2010. Pres. Colombian Nat. Assn. Sch. Nursing, 2006—10, CTNE - Tech. Nat. Coun. Nursing, 2010—. Mem.: ACOFAEN (pres.), REDEVHIDA, Sigma Theta Tau (Colombia). Avocations: soccer, swimming. Home: Av Calle 80 23-86 apt 510 Bogota Cundinamarca 11001 Colombia Home Fax: 57-1-2886754. Business E-Mail: dgeslava@javeriana.edu.co.

ALBAYRAK, SEVIL, biologist, educator; b. Kayseri, Turkey, June 10, 1981; PhD, Erciyes U., 2008. Rsch. asst. Erciyes U., Sci. Faculty, Biology Dept., 2005—08, biologist, 2005—, rsch. asst. dir., 2008—09, asst. prof., rschr., 2009. Mem.: Soc. Botanique France. Avocations: music, sports, travel. Office: Melikgazi Kayseri 38039 Turkey Office Fax: 90 352 4374933. Business E-Mail: salbayrak@erciyes.edu.tr.

AL-BELASY, FOUAD AL-MAHDY, dental educator, department chairman, oral surgeon; b. Bany Obaid, Egypt, Mar. 31, 1957; s. Al-Mahdy Al-Belasy Mohammed and Ablah Hossein Shehata; m. Hanan Mansour Saleh, July 23, 1986; children: Nehal Fouad, Hadeel Fouad, Mohammed Fouad. BDS, Faculty of Dentistry Tanta U., Egypt, 1980; MSc, Faculty of Dentistry Mansoura U., Egypt, 1986, PhD in Oral Surgery, 1991. Clin. demonstrator pediatric dentistry Faculty of Dentistry Tanta U., Egypt, 1981—82; clin. demonstrator oral surgery Faculty of Dentistry Mansoura U., 1982—86, asst. lectr. oral surgery, 1986—91, lectr. oral surgery, 1992—99, assoc. prof. oral surgery, 1999—2004, prof. oral surgery, 2004—, vice dean grad. studies, rsch. and cultural affairs, 2006—, dean, 2008—, vice dean edn. & Students affairs, 2006—08; courtesy clin. asst. prof., dept. oral & maxillofacial surgery U. Fla., Coll. Dentistry, 2006—07. Com. mem. Faculty of Dentistry Mansoura U., 2000—05, head oral surgery dept., 2004—, dir. quality assurance and accreditation. With Med. Svc. Egyptian Army, 1985—86. Achievements include research in clinical research problems in oral surgery. Home: Shobra St Bany Ebeid Egypt Office: Mansoura Univ Faculty of Dentistry Al-Gomhoria St 35511 Mansoura Egypt Office Fax: 050 - 2260173; Home Fax: 050- 2260173. Personal E-mail: albelasy@netscape.net. Business E-Mail: falbelasy@mans.edu.eg.

ALBENSI, BENEDICT CHARLES, biomedical consultant, computer programmer, neuroscientist, educator; s. Benedict and Kathleen Helen (Owen) Albensi. BS in Gen. Sci., U. Oreg., 1982; MA in Biology, Sonoma State U., 1992; PhD in Neurosci., U. Utah, 1995; postgrad., Georgetown U., 1996—97, Sanders Brown Ctr. Aging, 1997—99; cert. mgmt., U. Utah. Analytical chemist Multi-Tech Labs., ETTC Corp., Rohnert Park, Calif., 1986—87; rsch. assoc., electrophysiologist NPS Pharms., Salt Lake City, 1987—92; clin. rsch. dept. Pfizer, Inc., Ann Arbor, Mich., 1999—2001; faculty dept. neurol. surgery Cleve. Clinic Found., 2001—04; assoc. prof. dept. pharmacology and therapeutics, divsn. neurodegenerative disorders U. Man./St. Boniface Rsch. Ctr., Winnipeg, Canada, 2004—. Adj. instr. Salt Lake C.C., 1994—95; cons. neurosci. U. Utah, Salt Lake City, 1990; grant reviewer study sect. NIH; chair Alzheimer's Assn., Alzheimer's Soc., FASEB, NSENC; adj. asst. prof. dept. biology Case We. Res. U., Cleve., 2004; online instr. DeVry U., 2009—. Contbr. articles to profl jours; manuscript ad hoc referee:; contbr. chapters to books. Adv. mental health Missoula Adv. Program, Mont. Recipient Achievement award, Multi-Tech Labs, 1987, 1st Pl. Best Poster award, U. Ky., 1998, Recognition award, Warner Lambert Colleague, 1999; grantee Surrey Med. Rsch. Travel, 1994, MMSF, 2007, CFI, 2005, MHRC, 2006—; fellow, U. Utah, 1993—94. Mem.: AAAS, Soc. Magnetic Resonance, Soc. Neurosci., Internat. Neural Network Soc., Nat. Stroke Assn., Internat. Brain Rsch. Orgn., Regulatory Affairs Profl. Soc., Cognitive Neurosci. Soc., Brain Injury Assn., Am. Epilepsy Soc., Soc. Tech. Comm., Drug Info. Assn., Am. Soc. Neurochemists, Am. Assn. Pharm. Scientists, Am. Chem. Soc. Avocations: painting, reading, camping, skiing, hiking. Office Phone: 204-235-3942, 204-782-3698. Personal E-mail: balbensi@sbrc.ca.

ALBERGATI, FRANCESCO, medical educator, vascular surgeon; s. Maria Celora. MD, U. Milan, 1980, postgrad. in surgery, 1984. Prof. U. Pavia, Italy, 1996—, U. Milan, 1998—; dir. cardiovascular dept. Nat. Rsch. Ctr., Italy, Smithkline, Phila., 1988—97; chief Gisem, Milan; chief Ctr. Microcirculation Policlinico di Monza, Italy, 1996—. V.p. Internat. Study Group on Extracellular Matrix, Milan, 2004. Author: Raynaud Phenomena, 2003, Elastocompression in CVI, 2004, Extracellular Matrix, 2004. Mem.: Italian Coll. Phlebology, Internat. Coll. Phlebology, Italian Soc. Andrology (mem. adv. bd. 1990), Italian Soc. Cardiology (mem. adv. bd. 1994). Avocations: sailing, fly fishing, golf. Home: via Fratelli Cervi 7 24042 Capriate San Gervasio Italy Office: Policlinico di'Monza Via Carlo Amati 111 20900 Monza MB Italy Office Phone: 390392810617. Home Fax: 390290961964. Business E-Mail: f.albergati@tiscali.it.

ALBERS, JAMES W., neurologist, educator; b. Detroit, Oct. 28, 1943; PhD, Mich., 1970, MD, 1972. Emeritus prof., neurology U. Mich., 1979—. Office: 1500 E Med Ctr Dr Neurology Ann Arbor MI 48109-0032 Business E-Mail: jwalbers@umich.edu.

ALBERT, DANIEL MYRON, ophthalmologist, educator; b. Newark, Dec. 19, 1936; s. Maurice I. and Flora Albert; m. Eleanor Kagle, June 26, 1960; children: B. Steven, Michael. BS, Franklin and Marshall Coll., Lancaster, Pa., 1958; MD, U. Pa., 1962; MA (hon.), Harvard U., Cambridge, Mass., 1976; D honoris causa, Louis Pasteur U., Strasbourg, 1992; MS, U. Wis., Madison, 1997. Diplomate Am. Bd. Ophthalmology. Intern Hosp. U. Pa., 1962-63, resident, 1963-66; surgeon USPHS, 1966-68; NIH spl. fellow in ophthalmic pathology Armed Forces Inst. Pathology, 1968-69; asst. prof. ophthalmology Yale U. Sch. Medicine, 1969-70, assoc. prof., 1970-75, prof., 1975-76; practice medicine specializing in ophthalmology; assoc. surgeon Mass. Eye and Ear Infirmary, 1976-86, surgeon, 1986-92, dir. David G. Cogan eye pathology lab., 1979-92; prof. ophthalmic pathology Harvard U. Med. Sch., 1976-84, David G. Cogan prof. ophthalmology, 1984-92; Frederick Allison Davis prof., dept. ophthalmology U. Wis., Madison, 1992—, chmn. dept. ophthalmology, 1992—2002, emeritus chmn., 2002—, Lorenz E. Zimmerman prof. dept. ophthalmology, 1999—, Emmett A. Humble disting. dir. Eye Rsch. Inst., 2002—. Author: (with Scheie) A History of Ophthalmology at the University of Pennsylvania, 1965, Textbook of Ophthalmology, 8th edit. 1969, 9th edit. 1977; co-author: Jaegar's Atlas of Ophthalmology, 1972, (with Puliafito) Foundations of Ophthalmology, 1979, Men of Vision, 1993, (with Jakobiec) Atlas of Clinical Ophthalmology, 1996; editor: Archives of Ophthalmology, 1994—, (with Edwards) The History of Ophthalmology, 1996, John Jeffres' Lectures on the Diseases of the Eye, 1998, Ophthalmic Surgery: Principles and Techniques, 1998, A Physician's Guide to Health Care Management, 2002, (with Polans) Ocular Oncology, 2003, (with Lucarelli) Clinical Atlas of Procedures in Ophthalic Surgery, 2003; co-editor (with Jakobiec) Principles and Practice of Ophthalmology, 1994, 2d edit., 1999, A Physician's Guide to Healthcare Management, 2002, Dates in Ophthalmology, 2002, (with Lucarelli) Clinical Atlas of Procedures in Ophthalmic Surgery, 2003, (with Polans) Ocular Oncology, 2003, (with Miller, Azar, and Blodi) Albert & Jakobiec's Principles and Practice of Ophthalmology, 3rd edit., 2008, (with Levin)Ocular Disease: Mechanisms And Management, 2010, (with Dubielzig, Ketring, McLellan) Veterinary Ocular Pathology: A Comparative Review, 2010; contbr. articles to profl. jours. Recipient Oliver Meml. medal, U. Pa., 1962, Friedenwald award, Assn. for Rsch. in Vision and Ophthamology, 1981, Gold Fellow, 2010, Von Sallmann award in vision and ophthalmology, Internat. Conf. for Eye Rsch., 1988, award, Humboldt Found., 1991, MacKenzie medal, Scottish Ophthal. Soc., 1992, Lighthouse Pisart Vision award, The Lighthouse Inc., 1997, Lorenz E. Zimmerman (WARF) professorship, 1999, Disting. Alumni award, U. Pa. Sch. Medicine, 2001, Weisenfeld award, Fight for Sight, 2003; William and Mary Greve scholar, 1978—79, Alcon Rsch. Inst. scholar, 1984—85. Fellow ACS; mem. Am. Assn. Ophthalmic Pathology (Zimmerman medal 1993), Am. Acad. Ophthalmology (Jackson Meml. lectr. 1996, Life Achievement Honor 2010), Am. Bd. Ophthalmology (dir. 1997-2005), Macula Soc. (W. Richard Green award 2003), Fight for Sight, New Eng. Ophthal. Soc. (Taylor Smith Gold medal 2004), Midwest Glaucoma Soc. (Albert C. Muse award 2006), Am. Ophthalmological Soc. (Howe medal 2007), Assn. Rsch. Vision & Ophthalology(Gold Lifetime fellow 2010). Jewish. Home: 1106 Wellesley Rd Madison WI 53705-2230 Office: Univ Wis Sch Medicine and Pub Health Dept Ophthalmology K6/412 CSC 600 Highland Ave Madison WI 53792-4673 Office Phone: 608-263-9798.

ALBERT, MARTIN LAWRENCE, behavioral neurologist, cognitive neuroscientist, writer, educator, researcher; b. Lawrence, Mass., Jan. 7, 1939; s. Benjamin and Alice (Kaminsky) A.; m. Phyllis Gloria Cohen, Dec. 25, 1960; children: David, Michael, Rachel. MD, Tufts U., 1963; PhD, U. Paris, France, 1971. Diplomate Am. Bd. Psychiatry and Neurology. Intern Maimonides Med. Ctr., Bklyn., 1963-64; resident in neurology Boston U. Med. Sch./Boston VA Hosp., 1966-69; fellow in behavioral neurology Boston U. Med. Sch., 1969-71, Laboratoire de Neuropsychologie, Hopital Ste-Anne, Paris, 1969-71; chief, clin. neurology Boston VA Med. Ctr., 1978-83; clin. dir., co-prin. investigator Aphasia Rsch. Ctr. Boston U., 1979-96, prof. neurology Sch. Medicine, 1980—, dir. behavioral neuroscis., dept. neurology, 1983-92, dir. Aphasia Rsch. Ctr., 1996—; dir. med. rsch. svc. Dept. of Veterans Affairs, Washington, 1992-95. Cons. in behavioral neurosci. WHO, Geneva, Switzerland, 1981—; cons. to Pres.' Office of Sci. and Tech. Policy, Washington, 1993-95; Sackler scholar Inst. Advanced Studies Tel Aviv U., 1996; vis. prof. neurology Hebrew U. Med. Sch., Jerusalem, 1993, Hosp. de la Salpetriere, Paris, France, 2001-02; nat. adv. coun. Program in Bioethics Dept. VA, Washington, 1995—; nat. adv. coun. Nat. Inst. Gen. Med. Scis. NIH, 1992-93. Author: Human Neuropsychology, 1978, The Bilingual Brain, 1978, Clinical Aspects of Aphasia, 1981, Language in the Aging Brain, 1981, Manual of Aphasia Therapy, 1991, Clinical Neurology of Aging, 1984, 2d edit., 1994, 3rd edit., 2010 Manual of Aphasia and Aphasia Therapy, 2004; contbr. over 200 articles to profl. jours. Mem. adv. bd. program in med. ethics Hebrew Coll., Boston, 1987; mem. adv. bd. U.S. Israel Mental Health Fedn., Worcester, Mass., 1991. Capt. U.S. Army, 1965-66. Grantee NIH, 1970—. Fellow Am. Acad. Neurology (co-founder, chmn. sect. geriatric neurology 1989-91); mem. Acad. Aphasia (bd. govs. 1986-88), Am. Neurol. Assn., Nat. Aphasia Assn. (v.p. 1988-2007). Jewish. Achievements include introduction of the concept subcortical dementia; development new treatment approaches for aphasia, including melodic intonation therapy and pharmacotherapy for aphasia; development of the study of language in aging and dementia, created popular diagnostic tests in behavioral neuroscience. Office: VA Boston Healthcare Sys 12A 150 S Huntington Ave Boston MA 02130-4817 Office Phone: 857-364-4774. Business E-Mail: malbert@bu.edu.

ALBERT, MICHAEL B., gastroenterologist, educator; MD, John Hopkins U., 1982. Diplomate Am. Bd. Internal Medicine-gastroenterology, 1985. Intern Mayo Clinic, Minn., 1983, resident, 1983—84, Duke Univ. Hosp., 1984—85; fellow George Washington Univ. Hosp., 1985—87; clin. prof. medicine George Washington Univ. Med. Sch. Author: (books) Clinical Nutrition for the House Officer. Mem.: Am. Gastroent. Assn. Office: The George Washington University Hospital 2141 K St NW 208 Washington DC 20037 Office Phone: 202-223-5544. Office Fax: 202-296-7631.

ALBERTI, LUIZ RONALDO, pediatric surgeon, gastroenterologist; b. Varginha, Brazil, Nov. 11, 1976; s. José Ronaldo and Alcione Bueno Alberti. MD, Fed. U. Minas Gerais, Belo Horizonte, 2001, MSc, 2003; DSc, Fed. U. Minas Ger, Belo Horizonte, 2005; degree in Pediatric Surgery, Fed. U. Minas Gerais, Belo Horizonte, 2007. Diplomate Faculty Med. Scis. Minas Gerais, 2001. Prof. Angloamerican Culture Ctr., Varginha, Brazil, 1992—94; rschr. coll. medicine dept. medicine Fed. U. Minas Gerais, Brazil, 1997—, postdoctoral rschr., 2006—07; trauma surgeon John XXIII Hosp. Minas Gerais State Hosps. Found., Belo Horizonte, 2003; gen. and pediatric surgeon Vila da Serra Hosp., Belo Horizonte, 2005—; trauma surgeon, gen. and pediatric surgeon Monsenhor Flávio D'Amata Mcpl. Hosp., Sete Lagoas, Brazil, 2005—; physician air critical care transp. Uniminas, Belo Horizonte, 2006—; gen. surgeon Santo Ivo Hosp., Belo Horizonte, 2006—; postgraduate prof. Providence Inst. Minas Gerais State, Belo Horizonte, 2006—; gen. and pediatric surgeon St. Lucy Hosp., Belo Horizonte, 2006—07; physician pre-hosp. care Unimed, Belo Horizonte, 2007—; gastroenterologist Biogastro, Belo Horizonte, 2006. Prof. coll. medicine Fed. U. Minas Gerais, 2007—; presenter in field. Contbr. articles to profl. jours. Recipient Best Paper in Sci. award, Fed. U. Minas Gerais, 2004, Lucas Machado award, Faculty Med. Scis. Minas Gerais, 1999, Third Lucas Machado award, 2001, Iracema Baccarini award, Faculty Medicine Fed. U. Minas Gerais, 1999, 2000, 2001, 2004, Best Exptl. Paper award, 2001, Best Clin. Paper award, 2001, Young Surgeon award, 2004, Mariano de Andrade award, Brazilian Coll. Surgeons, 2007; grantee, Nat. Coun. Sci. and Tech., Brazil, 2001, Albert Einstein Inst., Albert Einstein Hosp., Brazil, 2007; scholar Second Lucas Machado award, Faculty Med. Scis. Minas Gerais, 2000. Mem.: Brazilian Congress Gen.

Surgery (grantee 2000, Best Clin. Paper award 2005, Joao Batista Resende Alves award 2005, Best Exptl. Paper award 2005, Best Paper award 2006), Brazilian Soc. Clin. Pathology (Brazilian Congress Clin. Pathology award 2004), Nat. Medicine Acad. (Miguel Couto Best Paper award 2006, Best Exptl. Rsch. award 2004), Med. Assn. Minas Gerais (First Academic Congress award 2004), Brazilian Coll. Surgeons (assoc. grantee 2000, award 2004, José de Mendonca award 2004), Med. Residents Assn. Minas Gerais State (exec. sec. 2006—07), Residents Hosp. Clinics Assn. (pres. 2005—07). Avocations: travel, reading, writing, poetry. Home: Rua Prof Baroni 151/401 Minas Gerais Belo Horizonte 30 441 180 Brazil Office: Federal Univ Minas Gerais Rua Alfredo Balena 190 Minas Gerais Belo Horizonte Brazil Personal E-mail: luizronaldo@zipmail.com.br, luizronaldoa@yahoo.com.br.

ALBERTI-CHAPPELL, ROXANA DEARING, psychologist; b. LA, June 8, 1945; d. George Arthur and Ollie (McMurtrey) Dearing; m. Robert Brian Chappell, Mar. 23, 1998; children: Anthony Wyatt Alberti, Luke Alexander Enrique Alberti. BA in English, Calif. State U., 1967, MA in Ednl. Psychology, 1972; PhD in Counseling Psychology, U. So. Calif., 1996. Standard lifetime tchg. Calif., 1972, cert. pupil pers. svcs. Calif., 1987, bilingual cert. competence Calif., 1990. Sch. tchr. LA Unified Sch. Dist., 1967—87, bilingual sch. psychologist, 1987—. Sabbath sch. tchr Seventh Day Adventist Ch., Northridge, Calif., 1980—87, sec. bd., 1984—87. Avocations: bicycling, hiking, dance. Home: 3621 Dunkirk Dr Oxnard CA 93035-1293

ALBERTINI, DAVID FRED, biomedical scientist, educator; b. Hudson, Mass., Mar. 19, 1949; s. Edmund and Marguerite (Allen) A.; m. Susan Roni Misler, Aug. 27, 1972; children: Jennifer, Lauren. MS, U. Mass., 1972; PhD, Harvard U., 1975. Rsch. assoc. U. Conn. Health Ctr., Farmington, 1975-77; lectr. pathology Harvard U., Boston, 1977-83; staff scientist Lab. Human Reproduction/Reproduction Biology, Boston, 1977-83; from assoc. prof. to prof. anatomy and cellular biology and ob-gyn. Tufts U. Sch. Medicine, Boston, 1983—2004; prof. molecular and integrative physiology U. Kans. Med. Ctr., Kansas City, 2004—, Hall prof. molecular medicine, 2005—. Mem. cell biology study sect. NSF, Washington, 1979-82; adj. prof. U. Mass. Med. Ctr., Worcester, 1982-85. Contbr. articles to Jour. Cell Biology, PNAS, Biol. Reprodn., Devel. Biology. Cons. Boston Dept. Pub. Health, 1991. Recipient Lauro F. Cavazos Tchg. award, Tufts U., 1989, Outstanding Faculty Achievement award, 1996, Founders Lectr. award, Australian Soc. Reproductive Biology, 2001, Hammond medal, European Soc. Reproduction and Fertility, 2002; Colwin fellow, Marine Biol. Lab., 2003. Mem. Am. Soc. Cell Biology, NY Acad. Sci., Am. Assn. Anatomists, Soc. Study of Reproduction. Achievements include development of non-invasive fluroescence imaging techniques to evaluate viability of mammalian eggs and embryos, discovery of communication junctions in mammalian eggs. Office: U Kans Med Ctr 3088 Kans Life Sci Innovations Ctr 3901 Rainbow Blvd Kansas City KS 66160 Office Phone: 913-588-[illegible]

ALBERTS, BRUCE MICHAEL, cell biologist, former foundation administrator; b. Chgo., Apr. 14, 1938; s. Harry C. and Lillian (Surasky) A.; m. Betty Neary, June 14, 1960; children: Beth L., Jonathan B., Michael B. AB in Biochemical Scis. summa cum laude, Harvard Coll., 1960; PhD in Biophysics, Harvard U., 1965. Postdoctoral fellow NSF Institut de Biologie Moleculaire, Geneva, 1965-66; asst. prof. dept. chemistry Princeton U., NJ, 1966-73, assoc. prof. dept. biochemical scis. NJ, 1971-73, Damon Pfeiffer prof. life scis. NJ, 1973-76; prof., vice chmn. dept. biochemistry and biophysics U. Calif., San Francisco, 1976-81, Am. Cancer Soc. Rsch. prof., 1981-85, prof., chmn., 1985-90, Am. Cancer Soc. Rsch. prof. of biochemistry, 1990-93, prof., biochem. and biophysics dept., 2005—; pres. NAS, Washington, 1993—2005, pres.-emeritus, 2005—; chmn. NRC, Washington, 1993—2005. Trustee Cold Spring Harbor Lab., 1972-75; adv. panel human cell biology NSF, 1974-76; adv. coun. dept. biochemical scis. and molecular biology Princeton U., 1979-85; chmn. vis. com. dept. biochemistry and molecular biology Harvard Coll., 1983-86; chmn. mapping and sequencing the human genome Nat. Rsch. Coun. Com., 1986-88; bd. sci. couns. divsn. arthritis and metabolic diseases NIH, 1974-78, molecular cytology study sect. 1982-86, chmn. 1984-86; program adv. com. NIH Human Genome Project, 1988-91; sci. adv. bd. Jane Coffin Childs Meml. Fund for Med. Rsch., 1978-85, Markey Found., 1984—, Fred Hutchinson Cancer Rsch. Ctr., Seattle, 1988—; com. mem. corp. vis. dept. biology MIT, 1978—, dept. embryology Carnegie Inst., Washington, 1983—; faculty rsch. lectr. U. Calif., San Francisco, 1985; sci. adv. com. Marine Biological Lab., Woods Hole, Mass., 1988—; bd. dirs. Genentech Rsch. Found., Fed. Am. Socs. for Experimental Biology; adv. bd. Bethesda Rsch. Labs. Life Tech. Inc., Nat. Sci. Resources Ctr., Smithsonian Inst., 1990—; com. mem. adolescence and young adulthood/sci. standards, Nat. Bd. Profl. Teaching Standards, 1991—; co-chair InterAcademy Council, Amsterdam, 2000-09. Co-author: The Molecular Biology of the Cell, 1989; editor: Mechanistic Studies of DNA Replication and Genetic Recombination, 1980; editorial bd. Jour. Biological Chemistry, 1976-82, Jour. Cell Biology, 1984-87; assoc. editor Annual Reviews Cell Biology, 1984—; essay editor Molecular Biology of the Cell, 1991—; editor-in-chief, Science, 2008-; contbr. numerous articles to profl. jours. including Saunders Sci. Publ., Current Sci., Ltd. Trustee Gordon & Betty Moore Found., Carnegie Corp., NY; overseer Harvard U., 2001—07. Fellow NSF, 1960-65; recipient Eli Lilly award in biological chemistry Am. Chemical Soc., 1972, Baxter award for Disting. Rsch. in Biomedical Scis. Assn. Am. Med. Colls., 1992; named Lifetime Rsch. Prof. Am. Cancer Soc., 1980, Outstanding Vol. Coord. Calif. Sch. Vol. Partnership, 1993. Gairdner Found. Internat. award, 1995. Fellow AAAS; mem. NAS (commn. life scis. Nat. Rsch. Coun., chmn. 1988-93, adv. bd. Nat. Sci. Resources Ctr., Nat. Com. Sci. Edn. Standards and Assessment, com. mem. Nat. Edn. Support System for Tchrs. and Schs., U.S. Steel Found. award 1975), Am. Chemical Soc., Am. Soc. for Cell Biology (pres.-elect, pres. 2007), Am. Soc. for Microbiology, Genetics Soc. Am., Am. Soc. Biochemistry and Molecular Biology (councilor), Am. Philos. Soc., European Molecular Biology Orgn. (assoc.), Phi Beta Kappa. Office: UC San Francisco Dept Biochem & Biophysics 600 16th St San Francisco CA 94143 *

ALBERTS, DAVID SAMUEL, physician, pharmacologist, educator; b. Milw., Dec. 30, 1939; m. Heather Alberts; children: Tim, Sabrina. BS, Trinity Coll., Hartford, Conn., 1962; MD, U. Va., 1966. Dir. clin. pharmacology Ariz. Cancer Ctr., Tucson, 1975—89, prof. medicine and pharmacology, 1982—90, dir. cancer prevention and control, 1989—2005, dep. dir., 1989-96, assoc. dean rsch. Coll. Medicine, 1996—2002, acting chief hematology and oncology, 1998-99, Regent's prof. medicine, pharmacology, nutritional sci. pub. health, 2004—, dir., 2005—; v.p. bus. devel. AMPLIMED, Tucson, 2003—05. External advisor U. Chgo. Cancer Ctr., 1993-98, Tulane U. Cancer Ctr., New Orleans, 1993-96, M.D. Anderson Cancer Ctr., Houston, 1994—2004, Norris Cotton Cancer Ctr., Hanover, 1995-2000, Lee Moffit Cancer Ctr., Tampa, 2003-06, NJ Cancer Inst., 2005-2008; mem. bd. sci. counselors divsn. Cancer Prevention and Control, Nat. Cancer Inst., NIH, 1990-94, chmn. chemoprevention external com. divsn. cancer prevention, 1997-2001; chmn. gynecologic cancer com. S.W. Oncology Group, 1977-2001, co-chmn., 2007-; mem. monitoring and adv. panel Nat. Prostate Lung-Colon-Ovary Cancer Study, NCI-NIH, 1994—; mem. oversight com. NCI Nat. Lung Cancer Screening Trial, 2002—; chmn. cancer prevention com. Gynecologic Oncology Group, 1995—; chmn. oncologic adv. com. U.S. FDA, 1982-84, spl. cons., 1984-86; mem. bd. sci. adv., Nat. Cancer Inst., NIH, 1999-2006; bd. dirs., Cancer Rsch. and Prevention Found., 1992—. Co-editor-in-chief Cancer Epidemiology, Biomarkers and Prevention, 2002-08; assoc. editor Cancer Rsch., 1989-2002, Cancer Chemother. and Pharmacol., 1992—, Clin. Cancer Rsch., 1994-96, Neoplasia, 1998—; editor Fundamentals of Cancer Prevention, 2005, 2nd edit., 2008; contbr. articles to over 500 to profl. jours., 100 book chpts.; inventor azamitosene and anthracene anticancer agts., tumorimeter, hypodermic needle with automatic retracting point; topical DFMO; two step carcinogen/HIV chemical deactivation system; method and composition for deactivating HIV infected blood and anticancer drugs; amifostine reversal of platinum-induced neuropathy; measurement of lesion progression via mapping of chromatin texture features along progression curve. Grantee Nat. Cancer Inst., NIH, 1975—. Mem. Am. Soc. Clin. Pharmacology and Therapeutics, Am. Soc. Clin. Oncology (ACS Prevention award 1999), Am. Cancer Soc. Cancer Prevention, Am. Soc. Preventive Oncology (Disting. Achievement award 2004), Am. Assn. Cancer Rsch. (Jos. Burchenal clin. rsch. award 2003, Excellence in Cancer Prevention award 2004), Soc. Gynecologic Oncologists, Am. Assn. Cmty. Cancer Ctr.(Clin. Rsch. award, 2010), Am. Assn. Cancer Insts.(bd. dirs., 2010-) Achievements include Listed by Sci. June 15, 2001 as 3rd highest NIH peer reviewed funded clin. rschr. in U.S. Office: Ariz Cancer Ctr 1501 N Campbell Ave Tucson AZ 85724-0001

ALBERTS, MARION EDWARD, retired physician; b. Hastings, Nebr., Mar. 14, 1923; s. Eddie and Mary Margaret (Hilbers) A.; m. Jeannette McDaniel, Dec. 25, 1944 (dec. Dec. 2006); children: Kathryn (dec.), Brian, Deborah, Timothy. BA, U. Nebr., 1944, MD, 1948. Diplomate Am. Bd. Pediatrics. Intern Iowa Meth. Hosp., Des Moines, 1948-49; resident in pediatrics Raymond Blank Hosp. Children, Des Moines, 1949-50, 52-53; practice medicine specializing in pediatrics Des Moines, 1953-88; ret., 1988. Chief pediatrics Mercy Hosp., 1953-69, 74-78, chief med. staff, 1966; mem. med. staff Iowa Luth. Hosp., 1953-88, Iowa Meth. Hosp., 1953-88, Broadlawns Polk County Hosp., 1983-88; instr. clin. pediatrics Coll. Osteo. Medicine and Surgery, 1970-87. Author: History of the Polk County Medical Society 1951-2001, 2003; sci. editor Iowa Medicine, 1971—97, editl. com. mem. People's Health, 2005, William C. Page, Iowa Health Sys.; contbr. articles to profl. jours. Pres. Polk County Tb and Respiratory Diseases Assn., 1965, 66, 70. Comdr. USNR, 1943-45, 50-52 (ret.) 1983. Recipient Whitaker Interstate Teaching award Interstate Postgrad. Med. Assn., 1980; Service award Sisters of Mercy, 1978 Fellow Am. Acad. Pediatrics, AMA (recognition awards 1969—), Iowa Med. Soc.; mem. Masons, Kiwanis. Presbyterian (elder). Address: Edgewater Retirement Cmty #2209 9225 Cascade Ave West Des Moines IA 50266

ALBERTS, STEVEN ROBERT, oncologist; b. Seattle, Oct. 28, 1959; BA, Augustana Coll., Sioux Falls, SD, 1983; MD, U. Hawaii, Honolulu, 1985, U. Wash., Seattle, 1990. Cert. Am. Bd. Internal Medicine, in hematology, in med. oncology. Staff physician Mayo Clinic, Rochester, Minn., 1997—, med. dir. Cancer Ctr. Rsch. Office, 2004—. Chair GI com. North Ctrl. Cancer Treatment Group, Rochester, 2003—. Recipient Karis Award, Mayo Clinic, 2006; named one of Best Doctors, 2006—11. Mem.: Am. Soc. Advancement Sci., European Soc. Med. Oncology, Am. Soc. Clin. Oncology. Office: Mayo Clinic Divsn Med Oncology Go-10 200 First St SW Rochester MN 55905 Office Phone: 507-284-2511. Business E-Mail: alberts.steven@mayo.edu.

ALBERTSEN, PETER C., surgeon, educator; b. NYC, Jan. 8, 1953; s. Torkild and Else Albertsen; m. Pamela S. Stanton, Mar. 10, 1979; children: Kristen, Karl. BA in Biochemistry, Princeton U., 1974; MD, Columbia U. Coll. Physicians & Surgeons, NYC, 1978; MS in Med. Adminstrn., U. Wis., Madison, 1990. Diplomate Am. Bd. Urology. Resident New Eng. Deaconess Hosp., Boston, 1978—80, Brady Urol. Inst., Johns Hopkins Hosp., Balt., 1980—84, instr., 1984—86; asst. prof. surgery U. Conn. Health Ctr., Farmington, 1987—94, assoc. prof. surgery, 1994—2000, chief divsn. urology, prog. dir. urology residency, 1994—, prof., 2000—. Epidemiology and disease control study sect. NIH, 1986—89; tech. assessment panel Nat. Blue Cross/Blue Shield, 1997—; bd. mem. Drug Utilization Rev. State of Conn. Dept. Income Maintenance, 1991—95; cause of death com. Nat. Cancer Inst., 1999—. Mem. editl. bd. Urology, 1993—, Urology Times, 1993—, PDQ Screening and Prevention, 1997—, Prostate Jour., 1997—; contbr. articles to profl. jours., chapters to books. Trustee Am. Bd. Urology, 2000—07. Grantee, USPHS, 1991—93, Berlex Labs., 1991—94, Pfizer, Inc., 1991—95, Covance/Merck Rsch. Labs., 1991—99, NIH, 1994—2001, Dept. Pub. Health & Addiction Svcs., 1995—96, Conn. Dept. Pub. Health, 1996—2001, Agy. Health Care Policy & Rsch., 1998—. Mem.: Hartford Med. Soc. (bd. dirs. 1994—2000, sec.-treas. 1996—97, v.p. 1997—98, pres. 1998—99), Am. Assn. Clin. Urologists (bd. dirs. 1998—, pres. 2005—06, 2005—06), Am. Urol. Assn. (Conn. rep. to New Eng. sect. 1997—98, pres. New Eng. sect. 2004—05), Am. Coll. Genitourinary Surgeons. Office: U Conn Dept Surgery 263 Farmington Ave Farmington CT 06030-3955 Business E-Mail: albertsen@nso.uchc.edu. *

ALBERTY, ROBERT ARNOLD, chemistry professor; b. Winfield, Kans., June 21, 1921; s. Luman Harvey and Mattie (Arnold) Alberty; m. Lillian Jane Wind, May 22, 1944; children: Nancy Lou, Steven Charles, Catherine Ann. BS, U. Nebr., 1943, MS, 1944; PhD, U. Wis., 1947; DSc (hon.), U. Nebr., 1967, Lawrence U., 1967. Engaged in rsch. blood plasma fractionation for U.S. Govt., 1944—46; mem. faculty U. Wis., 1946—67, prof. chemistry, 1955—67, assoc. dean letters and sci., 1961—63, dean Grad. Sch., 1963—67; prof. chemistry MIT, 1967—91, dean Sch. Sci., 1967—82, prof. emeritus, 1991—. Cons. NSF, 1958—83, NIH, 1962—72; chmn. commn. on human resources NRC, 1974—77; dir. Colt Industries, 1978—88, Inst. for Def. Analysis, 1980—86; pres. phys. chemistry divsn. Internat. Union Pure and Applied Chemistry, 1991—93. Co-author: Experimental Physical Chemistry, 1970, Thermodynamics of Biochemical Reactions, 2003, Physical Chemistry, 2005. Recipient Eli Lilly award biol. chemistry, 1955; fellow Guggenheim, Calif. Inst. Tech., 1950—51. Fellow: AAAS; mem.: NAS, Am. Acad. Arts and Scis. (coun. 1991—94, 2003—), Am. Chem. Soc. (chmn. com. on chemistry and pub. affairs 1978—80), Inst. Medicine, Sigma Xi, Phi Beta Kappa. Home: 931 Massachusetts Ave Cambridge MA 02139-3171 Office: MIT 77 Massachusetts Ave Rm 6-215 Cambridge MA 02139-4307 Business E-Mail: alberty@mit.edu.

ALBERU, JOSEFINA MARÍA, surgeon, educator; b. La Habana, Cuba, Jan. 6, 1951; MD, U. Autónoma de Guadalajara, 1973; degree in Gen. Surgery and Transplant Surgery, Inst. Nacional de Ciencias Medicas y Nutricion Salvador Zubiran, 1979. Head transplantation dept. Inst. Nacional de Ciencias Medicas y Nutricion Salvador Zubiran, 1995—. Prof. U. Nacional Autonoma de Mex., 2000—. Recipient Academic Productivity award, Sociedad Mexicana de Trasplantes, 2007. Mem.: Sistema Nacional de Investigadores, Mex., Soc. Mexicana de Trasplantes (sec.), Soc. Trasplantes de Am. Latina y el Caribe (v.p.), Am. Soc. Transplantation, Transplantation Soc. Avocations: music, reading, cooking. Office: Vasco de Quiroga 15 Delegación Tlalpan Mexico City 14000 Mexico Office Fax: 52 55 56559471. Personal E-mail: josefinaalberu@hotmail.com.

ALBIS-DONADO, OSCAR D., ophthalmologist, educator; b. Barranquilla, Jan. 22, 1971; MD, Escuela Colombiana de medicina, 1995; degree in Ophthalmology, U. Nacional de Colombia, 1999. Glaucoma assoc. prof. Asociación para Evitar la Ceguera en Mex., 2006—. Mem.: Glaucoma Colombia, Colegio mexicano de glaucoma, Sociedad mexicana de oftalmologia, ARVO, Internat. Soc. Glaucoma Surgeons. Avocations: diving, ice skating. Office: Insurgentes Sur 1677 cons 903 Col Gua Mexico city 01020 Mexico E-mail: oalbis@msn.com.

ALBORES-SAAVEDRA, JORGE, pathologist, educator; b. La Concordia, Chiapas, Mex., Dec. 15, 1933; came to U.S., 1984; s. Enrique and Aurora (Saavedra) Albores; m. Blanca Gallo, Dec. 16, 1957; children: Lilia, Ruth. MD, Nat. U. Mex., Mexico City, 1957. Assoc. prof. pathology Nat. U. Mex., 1964-67, prof. pathology, 1968-84, U. Miami (Fla.) Sch. Medicine, 1984-90; prof. pathology, dir. divsn. anat. pathology U. Tex. Southwestern Med. Ctr., Dallas, 1990—2002; prof. pathology, divsn. anat. pathology La. State U. Health Scis. Ctr., Shreveport, 2002—. Chmn. dept. pathology Gen. Hosp. Mexico City, 1968-83, Nat. U. Mex., 1976-83, Hosp. Ctrl. sur de PEMEX, Mexico City, 1983-84. Author: Tumors of the Gallbladder and Extrahepatic Bile Ducts and Ampulla of Vater, 2000; co-author: Pathology of Incipient Neoplasia, 3d edit., 2001; contbr. more than 260 sci. papers to profl. publs., 44 chpts. to books. Office: Dept Pathology LSU Health Sci Ctr 1501 Kings Hwy Shreveport LA 71130 Home Phone: 318-798-7903. Business E-Mail: jalbore@hsc.edu.

AL BOUKAI, AHMAD AMER ABDULMUTTALEB, radiologist, educator; b. Damascus, July 7, 1958; MD, Damasus U., 1982; KSF-RD, King Saud U., 1992. Cons. radiologist & asst. prof. Coll. Medicine, King Saud U., 1997—, radiology postgrad. dir., 1999—2004, 2010—. Mem.: Saudi Bd. Tng. & Exam. Radiology Com. Avocations: swimming, reading. Office: King Abdullah St Riyadh 11472 Saudi Arabia Office Fax: 00966 1 467 1746. Personal E-mail: a_boukai@hotmail.com.

ALBRECHT, HEINZ, psychiatrist; b. Molln, Germany, Sept. 29, 1948; New Zealand, 1981; s. Werner A. and Irmgard Albrecht Schehl; m. Deborah Thomas, Jan. 26, 1986; children: Tessa, Bonnie. MD, U. Gottingen, Germany, 1976; diploma in Mental Health, U. Auckland, 1985. Psychiatrist Auckland Hosp. Bd., New Zealand, 1981—86, Regional Forensic Psychiatry Svcs., Auckland, 1986—98; pvt. practice Queensland, Australia. Sr. lectr. U. Auckland Med. Sch., 1989-98, asst. to dir., 1992-97; clin. dir. Acute Care/Crisis Cmty. Team, Gold Coast, Queensland, Australia, 1999-2002, Emergency Psychiatry, Gold Coast Hosp. clin. dir., emergency psychiatry svcs., Gold Coast, 2003—05; mem. adv. bd. criminology Bond U., Gold Coast; vis. adj. prof. Ctr. Applied Psychology and Criminology, 2001-; clin. tchr. Med. Sch. Bond U., Queensland, 2007-; mentor Med. Sch. Griffith U., Queensland, pvt. practice, Otsen Ave. specialist Clinic, Arundel, Australia, 2011. Asst. co-author: Caught Up with His Past, 1995; contbr. articles to profl. jours., chapter to books, moderator, presenter, Madigames Les Calmus Spain, 2011. Am Field Svc. Exch. Student scholar, 1969, Med. Rsch. grant, U Gottingen, 1977. Fellow: Australian and New Zealand Coll. Psychiatrists; mem.: Australian Coll. Medicine and the Law, World Med. Football. Fedn. (advisor 2008), Australian Coll. Legal Medicine (assoc.), Am. Acad. Forensic Scis. (assoc.), Medico-Legal Soc. Queensland (life), Am. Coll. Forensic Psychiatry (assoc.), Am. Acad. Psychiatry and Law (assoc.), Calif. Assn. Hostage Negotiators (assoc.), European Coll. Sports Sci., Nat. Australian Soccer Squad Med. Team (assoc.). Lutheran. Avocations: jogging, jet skiing, soccer. Office Phone: 07-5519-8211. Business E-Mail: Heinz_albrecht@health.qld.gov.au.

ALBRECHT, RONALD FRANK, retired anesthesiologist; b. Chgo., Apr. 17, 1937; s. Frank William and Mabel Dorothy (Cassens) A.; children: Ronald Frank II, Mark Burchfield, Meredith Ann. AB, U. Ill., 1958, BS, 1959, MD, 1961. Diplomate Am. Bd. Anesthesiology. Intern U. Cin. Hosp., 1961-62; resident in anesthesiology U. Ill. Hosp., Chgo., 1962-64, attending physician, 1966-73, 89—, chief dept. anesthesiology, 1989—2007, pres. med. staff, 1999-2001; clin. assoc. NIH, Bethesda, Md., 1964-66; practice medicine specializing in anesthesiology Chgo., 1966—; asst. prof. anesthesiology U. Ill., Chgo., 1966-70, clin. assoc. prof., 1970-73, prof. anesthesiology, 1989—2007, head dept. Coll. Medicine, 1989—2007, chief dept. anesthesiology, 1989—2007, prof. emeritus, 2007—. Chmn. dept. anesthesiology Michael Reese Med. Ctr., Chgo., 1971-2005; prof. anesthesiology U. Chgo., 1973-89. Contbr. articles to profl. jours. Served to lt. comdr. USPHS, 1964-66. Fellow Am. Coll. Anesthesiologists; mem. AMA, Internat. Anesthesia Rsch. Soc., Am. Soc. Anesthesiologists, Assn. Anesthesists Gt. Britain and Ireland, Am. Physiol. Soc., Soc. Acad. Anesthesiology Chairs, Assn. Anesthesiology Program Dirs. (pres. 1991-93), Ill. Soc. Anesthesiologists (pres. 1980-81), Ill. State Med. Soc., Chgo. Med. Soc., Chgo. Soc. Anesthesiologists (pres. 1986-90), Assn. Univ. Anesthesiologists. Presbyterian. Home: 1020 Chestnut Ave Wilmette IL 60091-1732 Office: U Ill Chgo Coll Medicine Dept Anesthesiology MC/515 1740 W Taylor St Ste 3200 Chicago IL 60612-7239 Business E-Mail: r.albrecht@att.net.

ALBRECHT, WILLARD HAROLD, retired medical educator; b. Elkhart, Ind., June 12, 1926; s. Aaron J. and Kathrine R. (Hooley) A.; m. Mary Ann McMahn, Sept. 6, 1959; children: Sharon, Grace, Clara, John, Douglas. BA in Natural Sci., Goshen Coll., 1954; MD, Northwestern U., Chgo., 1958. Diplomate Am. Bd. Anesthesiology. Asst. dir. dept. anesthesiology Wishard Hosp., Indpls., 1963-93; asst. prof. Ind. U. Med. Sch., Indpls., 1969-93, asst. prof. emeritus, 1993—. V.p. Dryden Corp., Indpls., 1970-87; dir. Paoli (Ind.) Peaks-Ski, 1992-98; dir. Global Gifts-Self Help, Indpls., 1994-2006, pres. 1999-2000; dir. Crroker Creek Multi-Svc. Ctr., 1998-2002. Contbr. articles to profl. jours. Recipient Disting. Svc. award, 2010. Avocations: woodworking, lawn and garden. Home: 421 Bent Tree Ln Indianapolis IN 46260 Personal E-mail: whalbrecht@comcast.net.

ALBRIGHT, BRITTANY BETH, physician, researcher; b. Ann Arbor, Oct. 11, 1984; BS, Emory U., 2007; MD, MPH, U. N.Mex. Med. rschr., co-investigator U. N.Mex., 2007—. Mem.: Alpha Omega Alpha (award), Phi Beta Kappa. Home: 11920 Oryx Pl NE Albuquerque NM 87111 Business E-Mail: balbright@salud.unm.edu.

ALBRIGHT, KAREN C., medical educator; b. Ames, Iowa, Oct. 23, 1973; DO, Des Moines U., MPH, 2005. Clin. instr. UAB, 2010—11. Office: RWUH M226 619 19th St S Birmingham AL 35249-3280 Office Fax: 205-975-6785. Business E-Mail: kca@uab.edu.

ALBRINK, MARGARET JORALEMON, medical educator; b. Warren, Ariz., Jan. 6, 1920; d. Ira Beaman and Dorothy (Rieber) Joralemon; m. Wilhelm Stockman Albrink, Sept. 16, 1944 (dec. July 1991); children: Frederick Henry, Jonathan Wilhelm, Peter Varick (dec. March 2003). BA in Psychology cum laude, Radcliffe Coll., 1941; MS in Physiol. Chemistry, Yale U., 1943, MD, 1946, MPH, 1951. Cert. Diplomate Am. Bd. Med. Examiners, Diplomate Am. Bd. Nutrition, Diplomate Am. Bd. Physician Nutrition Specialists. Intern New Haven (Conn.) Hosp., 1946—47; NIH postdoctoral fellow Yale U., New Haven, 1947—49, fellow pub. health, 1950—51, instr. medicine, 1952—58, asst. prof. medicine, 1958—61; assoc. prof. W.Va. U., Morgantown, 1961—66, prof. medicine, 1966—90, prof. emerita, 1990—, mem. grad. faculty, 1977—92; mem. med. and dental staff W.Va. U. Hosp., Morgantown, 1961—2000. Vis. scientist Donner Lab., U. Calif., Berkeley, 1993-2009; assoc. physician Grace-New Haven Cmty. Hosp., 1952-61; cons. nutrition study sect. NIH; vis. scholar U. Calif., Berkeley, 1977-78; established investigator Am. Heart Assn., 1958-63. Guest editor: Clinics in Endocrinology and Metabolism, 1976; guest editor Am. Jour. Clin. Nutrition, 1968, mem. editorial bd., 1963-68; mem. editorial adv. bd. Jour. Am. Coll. Nutrition, 1988-89; reviewer jours.; contbr. articles, chpts. and abstracts to profl. jours. Recipient Rsch. Career award Nat. Heart, Lung and Blood Inst., 1963-90. Fellow: ACP, Am. Coll. Nutrition, Am. Heart Assn. (emeritus, fellow arteriosclerosis coun., fellow coun. epidemiology); mem.: LWV, Am. Diabetes Assn. (epidemiology coun.), Am. Soc. Clin. Nutrition, Am. Soc. Clin. Investigation, Am. Fedn. Clin. Rsch., Phi Beta Kappa, Sigma Xi, Alpha Omega Alpha. Democrat. Avocations: music, archaeology, computers, nature conservation. Home: 817 Augusta Ave Morgantown WV 26501-6237 Office: WVa U Dept Medicine PO Box 9159 Morgantown WV 26506-9159 E-mail: mjalbrink@aol.com.

AL DAHOUK, SASCHA, internist, infectious diseases specialist; b. Stuttgart, Germany, Feb. 6, 1972; s. Khalil and Gabriele Al Dahouk; m. Stefanie von Oertzen, June 8, 2001; children: Benita Nasrin, Nicola Peer. Final univ. exam. in human medicine, Albert Einstein U., Ulm, Germany, 1998, doctorate magna cum laude, 1998. Registered Com. of Regional Govt., postgrad. cert. in emergency medicine Dist. Chamber of Medicine of South Wuerttemberg, postgrad. cert. in radiation protection Chamber of Medicine of Bavarian County. Major, med. corps. German Air Force, 1998—2007; surg. registrar dept. surgery Mil. Hosp. Ulm, 1998—99, med. registrar dept. internal medicine, 1999—2001; family practitioner Mil. Airbase, Fuerstenfeldbruck, Germany, 2001—02; med. registrar dept. internal medicine Aeromed. Ctr., Fuerstenfeldbruck, Germany, 2002—04; dep. head dept., head Brucella lab. dept. bacteriology Bundeswehr Inst. Microbiology, Munich, 2004—05; med. registrar, dept. internal medicine Ctrl. Mil. Hosp. Bundeswehr, Koblenz, Germany, 2006—07. Asst. lectr. dept. internal medicine, divsn. endocrinology U. Ulm, 1999—2001; asst. lectr. dept. bacteriology Bundeswehr Inst. Microbiology, Munich, 2001—06; invited spkr. 1st. Internat Meeting Treatment Human Brucellosis, Ioannina, Greece, 2006, Internat. Meeting Brucellosis SE European & Mediterranean Region, Struga, Macedonia, 2009; reviewer for Stds. for Surveillance and Control Brucellosis WHO, Geneva, 2005; vis. scientist Inst. Nat. de la Recherche Médicale, U. Montpellier II, France, 2005; master, sci. course epidemiology Inst. Med. Biostatistics, Epidemiology and Informatics, Johannes Gutenbery U. Mainz, Germany, 2006—07; med. registrar, asst. lectr. dept. internal medicine III RWTH Aachen U., 2007—10; sci. dir. divsn. hygiene and microbiology Fed. Inst. Risk Assessment, 2010—. Contbr. articles to profl. jours. Mem.: Soc. German Internists. Achievements include research activities with the topic epidemiology, diagnosis and pathogenesis of bacterial zoonoses. Avocation: exercise. Office: Federal Inst Risk Assessment Divsn Hygiene & Microbiology Diedersdorferweg 1 Berlin D-12277 Georgia Office Phone: 4930184121244. Office Fax: 4930184122000. Personal E-mail: sascha.al-dahouk@gmx.de.

ALDAMANHORI, BAHER KAMAL, urologist; b. Alexandria, Egypt, Sept. 5, 1953; Dr Ch Uro, Alexandria U., 1992. Prof. & chmn., dept. urology Dammam U., 1982—, dir. sci. coun., 2011; cons. & chmn., dept. urology King Fahd Hosp., 1993—. Fellow: Royal Coll. Surgeons; mem.: Am. Urol. Assn. Avocations: football, basketball. Office: PO Box 40036 Khobar Eastern 31952 Saudi Arabia Personal E-mail: drbaherkamal@yahoo.com.

ALDANA, PHILIPP ROQUE, neurosurgeon; b. Cebu, Philippines, July 3, 1966; s. Benigno Salcedo Aldana, Jr. and Estelita Roque Aldana; m. Carmina Montesa, Oct. 19, 1969; children: Carissa, Katrina. BS in zoology cum laude, U. Philippines, 1987; MD in rsch. with distinction magna cum laude, St. Louis U., 1994. Diplomate Am. Bd. Neurol. Surgery, 2005, Am. Bd. Pediatric Neurol. Surgery, 2007. Resident dept. surgery U. Miami, Fla., 1994—95; resident dept. neurosurgery U. Miami/Jackson Meml. Hosp., 1995—2001; pediatric neurosurgery fellow U. Utah, Primary Children's Hosp., Salt Lake City, 2001—02; asst. dir. divsn. neurosurgery, dir. comprehensive traumatic brain injury program Akron Children's Hosp., Ohio, 2002—06; clin. asst. prof. neurosurgery & pediat. U. Fla., Jacksonville, 2006—; chief svc. pediat. neurosurgery Wolfson Children's Hosp., Jacksonville, 2010—, med. dir. Pediatric Neurosurgery Ctr., 2010—; chief Divsn. Pediat. Neurosurgey, 2010—. Clin. asst. prof. neurosurgery Northeastern Ohio U. Coll. Medicine, Akron, 2002—06, U. Fla., Jacksonville, 2006—. Contbr. chapters to books, articles to profl. jours. Recipient Mo. State Med. Assn. award, St. Louis U., 1994, Resident Day Rsch. award, U. Miami Dept. Neurosurgery, 2001; named Top Surgeons in America, Consumers Rsch. Coun., 2009, Top Doctors Jacksonville, Jacksonville Mag., 2009; grantee Instl. grantee brain tumor rsch., Miami Children's Hosp., 1999; Akron Children's Hosp. Found. grantee for brain injury rsch., 2004, Faculty Enhancement Opportunity grant, U. Fla., 2010. Fellow: Am. Acad. Pediat.; mem.: Am. Soc. Pediatric Neurosurgery, Children's Oncology Group, Congress Neurol. Surgeons, Am. Assn. Neurol. Surgeons, Alpha Sigma Nu, Alpha Omega Alpha. Office: Lucy Gooding Pediatric Neurosurgery Ctr 836 Prudential Dr Ste 1005 Jacksonville FL 32207 Business E-Mail: philipp.aldana@jax.ufl.edu.

ALDEA, GABRIEL S., cardiothoracic surgeon, educator; b. Bucharest, Romania, Nov. 7, 1956; came to U.S., 1970; s. Adrian and Blanche (Fainaru) A.; m. Susan Arnold, May 8, 1988; children: Alexander, Daniel. BA in Biochemistry summa cum laude, Columbia Coll., 1977; MD, Columbia U., 1981. Diplomate Am. Bd. Surgery, Am. Bd. Thoracic Surgery, Nat. Bd. Med. Examiners. Resident in gen. surgery N.Y. Hosp., Cornell Med. Ctr., NYC, 1981—86, adminstrv. chief resident Dept. Surgery, 1985-86; cardiothoracic residency Dept. Cardiothoracic Surgery N.Y. Hosp., Cornell Med. Ctr. & Meml. Sloane Kettering Hosp., NYC, 1988-90; cardiovasc. rsch. fellowship Cardiovasc. Rsch. Inst.-U. Calif. San Francisco, 1986-88; asst. vis. surgeon in cardiothoracic surgery Boston U. Med. Ctr., 1990-98; assoc. vis. surgeon in thoracic surgery Boston City Hosp., 1990-98; thoracic surgeon Jamaica Plain VA Hosp., Boston; assoc. prof. cardiothoracic surgery Boston U. Sch. Medicine, 1990-98; chief adult cardiac surgery, prof. surgery U. Wash., Seattle, 1998—2002, prof. surgery, 2002—; cardiac surgeon N.W. Hosp., Seattle, 1998—, Puget Sound VA Hosp., Seattle, 1998—. Contbr. articles to profl. jours. and chpts. to books. Recipient Nat. Rsch. Svc. award in heart & vascular diseases NIH, 1986-88. Fellow New Eng. Oncologic Soc., Am. Surg. Assn.; mem. AAAS, AMA, ACS, Am. Coll. Chest Physicians, Am. Coll. Cardiology, Am. Heart Assn., Soc. for Thoracic Surgeons, Am. Assn. for Thoracic Surgery, Assn. Acad. Surgery, Mass. Med. Soc., Rsch. Assocs. Southwestern Oncology Group, Western Thoracic Assn, Am. Surgical Assn. Home: The Highlands Seattle WA 98177 Office: U Wash Dept Cardiothoracic Surgery PO Box 356310 Seattle WA 98195-6310 Office Phone: 206-543-3093.

ALDEN, ERROL R., medical association administrator; Dir. edn. then dep. exec. dir. Am. Acad. Pediat., Elk Grove Village, Ill., exec. dir., CEO, 2004—. Clin. prof. pediat. U. Chgo. Recipient Joseph St. Geme Jr. Leadership award, 1997. Fellow: Am. Acad. Pediat.; mem.: Internat. Pediat. Assn. (exec. com. Disaster Planning & Support Programs for Children). Office: AAP 141 NW Point Blvd Elk Grove Village IL 60007-1098 Office Phone: 847-434-4000. Business E-Mail: ealden@aap.org. *

ALDEN, INGEMAR BENGT, pharmaceuticals executive; b. Stockholm, Feb. 23, 1943; s. Bengt Erik and Agnes (Eriksson) Alden; m. Estelle Cuni Skrabanek, June 18, 1977; children: Lars, Sonja, Ingela. M in Social & Bus. Sci., Stockholm U., 1969. Field supr. Astra Lakemedel Sweden, Sodertalje, 1970—71, nat. sales mgr., 1971—72, mgr. mktg. & sales, 1973—74; internat. mktg. mgr. Astra Pharms., Sodertalje, 1975—76; dir. pharm. div. Astra Ltd., Watford, England, 1977—78; mng. dir. Merck Sharp & Dohme, Sweden, 1979—89; chief exec. officer Aldenco AB, 1989—91; dir. Pharma, Agro, Vet div. Svenska Hoechst AB, 1991—95; gen. mgr. Hoechst Marion Roussel AB, Stockholm, 1996; ceo Aldenco AB, Huddinge, Sweden. Chmn. Aldenco AB, Akinion Pharms. AB, IsiFer AB, Clanotech AB, LipoPeptide AB, SoftCure Pharms. AB, XSpray Microparticles AB. Mem.: Rotary. Office Phone: 46 8 774 2011. E-mail: ingemar.alden@aldenco.se.

ALDERDICE, JOHN THOMAS (LORD ALDERDICE), psychiatrist, educator, politician; b. Lurgan, No. Ireland, Mar. 28, 1955; s. David and Annie Margaret Helena (Shields) A.; m. Joan Margaret Hill, July 30, 1977; children: Stephen, Peter, Anna. MB, BCh, BAO, Queens U., Belfast, No. Ireland, 1978; DLitt (hon.), U. East London, 2008; LLD (hon.), Robert Gordon U., Aberdeen, 2009. Jr. house officer Lagan Valley Hosp., Lisburn, No. Ireland, 1978-79; sr. house officer Belfast City Hosp., 1979-80, sr. registrar in psychotherapy, 1983-87; registrar Whiteabbey and Holywell Hosps., Antrim, No. Ireland, 1980-81, Shaftesbury Square Hosp., Belfast, 1981-82, Lissue Child Psychiatry Hosp., Lisburn, 1982-83; registrar Windsor House Belfast City Hosp., 1983; sr. tutor in psychiatry Queens U., Belfast, 1983-87; cons. psychotherapist Albertbridge Rd. Day Hosp., Belfast, 1988-91, cons. psychotherapist Belfast Ctr. for Psychotherapy, 1991—2010; dir. No. Ireland Inst. of Human Rels., 1990-95; exec. med. dir. South and East Belfast Health and Social Svcs. Trust, 1994-97. From hon. lectr. to hon. sr. lectr. Queens U. of Belfast, 1990-99; hon. prof. Faculty Medicine U. San Marcos, Lima, Peru, 1999—; vis. prof. dept. psychiatry U. Va., 2006—10, pres. ARTIS(Europe), 2008- Contbr. articles on anorexia nervosa, ethics, psychotherapy and psychology of conflict and terrorism to academic jours., numerous polit. articles. Vice chmn. Alliance Party No. Ireland, 1987, party leader, 1987-98, leader Alliance del. to Brit.-Irish negotiations on future No. Ireland, 1991-98; leader Alliance del. at Forum for Peace and Reconciliation, Dublin Castle, 1994-96; led Alliance del. to All-Party Talks on future of No. Ireland, 1996-98; elected to No. Ireland Forum, 1996-98; Westminster candidate for Parliament, 1987, 92; councillor, City of Belfast, 1989-97; mem. exec. com. European Liberal Dem. and Reform Party, Brussels, 1987-93, mem. ctrl. coun., 1993-2003, treas., 1995-99, v.p., 1999-2003; v.p. Liberal Internat., 1991-99, chmn. human rights com., 1999-2005, dep. pres. 2000-05, pres. 2005—09; apptd. mem. Ho. of Lords, 1996; elected to No. Ireland Assembly, 1998-2003, spkr., 1998-2004; mem. Internat. Monitoring Commn., 2003—11; mem. Commonwealth Eminent Persons Group on Respect and Understanding, 2006-07; chmn. World Fedn. Scientists, Permanent Maintaining Panel Networking Terrorism, 2007-; joint chmn. Critical Incidents Analysis Group, U. Va., 2007-10. Decorated knight comdr. Order Francis I; recipient Galloway medal Nat. Schizophrenia Fellowship No. Ireland, 1987, John F. Kennedy Profiles in Courage award (USA), 1998, W. Averell Harriman award for Democracy (USA), 1998, Silver Medal of Congress (Peru), 1999, medal of honor Coll. Medicine Peru, 1999, award for extraordinary meritorious svc. to psychoanlysis Internat. Psychoanalytic Assn., 2005, Erice award World Fedn. Scientists, 2005; hon. citizen Balt., 1991. Fellow: Ulster Med. Soc., Brit. Psychoanalytical Soc. (hon.), Royal Coll. of Physicians of Ireland (hon.), Royal Coll. of Psychiatrists (hon.); mem.: No. Ireland Inst. Human Rels. (patron), Assn. for Psychoanalytic Psychotherapy, Peruvian Psychiatric. Assn. (hon.), Brit. Med. Assn., Ulster Reform Club (Belfast), Nat. Liberal Club (London) (trustee). Presbyterian. Avocations: music, reading, gastronomy. also: House of Lords London SW1A OPW England Office Phone: 02072195050. Business E-Mail: alderdicej@parliament.uk.

ALDERFER, CLAYTON PAUL, retired professor, organizational consultant, writer; b. Sellersville, Pa., Sept. 1, 1940; s. Joseph Paul and Ruth Althea (Buck) A.; m. Charleen Judith Frankenfield, July 14, 1962; children: Kate, Benjamin. BS with high honors, Yale U., 1962, PhD, 1966. Cert. Am. Bd. Profl. Psychology. Asst. prof. Cornell U., Ithaca, NY, 1966-68, Yale U., New Haven, 1968-70, assoc. prof., 1970-78, prof. Sch. Orgn. Mgmt., 1978-92, assoc. dean Sch. Orgn. Mgmt., 1982-84; prof. II Grad. Sch. Applied and Profl. Psychology Rutgers U., 1992—2006, dir. Orgnl. Psychology program, 1992—2004; prin. Alderfer and Assocs., 2006—. Author: Existence, Relatedness and Growth, 1972, Learning from Changing, 1975; mem. editl. bd. Jour. Applied Behavioral Sci., 1978-89, 2006, editor, 1990-2003; mem. editl. bd. Family Bus. Rev., 1987-2006, Jour. Orgnl. Behavior, 1988-92; mem. editl. bd. Consulting Psycology Jour., 2007; editor: Advances in Experiential Social Processes, vol. 1, 1979, vol. 2, 1980; contbr. articles to profl. jours. Bd. dirs. NTL Inst., Arlington, Va., 1975-78, DATA, New Haven, 1989-92. Grantee Office Naval Rsch., 1970-74, 79-80, 82-86; recipient Cattell award, 1972, McGregor award, 1979, Levinson award, 1997, Helms award, 1999, Tchr. of Yr., Rutgers GSAPP, 2006. Fellow Am. Psychol. Assn., Soc. Applied Anthropology, Am. Psychol. Soc.; mem. Sigma Xi, Tau Beta Pi. Independent. Lutheran. Office Phone: 908-281-6548. E-mail: claygray@aol.com.

ALDERMAN, AMY KATHLEEN, plastic surgeon, educator; b. Apr. 27, 1970; BA in Sociology, Birmingham-So. Coll., Ala., 1992; MD with honors, U. Ala. Sch. Medicine, Birmingham, 1996; MPH, U. Mich. Sch. Pub. Health, Ann Arbor, 2001. Lic. Mich., 1996, cert. Am. Bd. Plastic Surgery, 2005. Postdoctoral tng., clin. tng., plastic surgery integrated resident U. Mich., 1996—2000, 2002—04; rsch. tng., Robert Wood Johnson Clin. Scholar U. Mich. Sch. Medicine, 2000—02; asst. prof., dept. surgery, sect. plastic surgery U. Mich., Ann Arbor, 2004—; practicing plastic surgeon, health svcs. researcher U. Mich. Health Sys.; asst. prof., rsch. investigator Ann Arbor Veterans Adminstrn. Health Svcs. R&D. Fellow: ACS; mem.: Am. Soc. Plastic Surgeons (candidate), Alpha Omega Alpha Soc. Office: 2130 Taubman Ctr 1500 E Medical Center Dr Ann Arbor MI 48109-0340 Office Phone: 734-998-6022. Office Fax: 734-763-5354.

ALDERMAN, ELIZABETH, pediatrician, educator; MD, SUNY, Stony Brook, 1987. Clin. prof. pediat. Albert Einstein Coll. Medicine, Bronx, 2004—06. Office: 111 East 210 St Division of Adolescent Medicine Bronx NY 10467 *

ALDERMAN, MINNIS AMELIA, psychologist, educator, small business owner; b. Douglas, Ga., Oct. 14, 1928; d. Louis Cleveland Sr. and Minnis Amelia (Wooten) A. AB in Music, Speech and Drama, Ga. State Coll., Milledgeville, 1949; MA in Supervision/Counseling Psychology, Murray State U., Ky., 1960; postgrad., Columbia Pacific U., L.A., 1987. Tchr. music Lake County Sch. Dist., Umatilla, Fla., 1949—50; instr. vocal/instrumental music, dir. band, orch., choral Fulton County Sch. Dist., Atlanta, 1950—54; instr. English, speech, debate, vocal and instrumental music Elko County Sch. Dist., Wells, Nev., 1954—59, dir. drama, band, choral and orchestra, 1954—59; tchr. English and social studies Christian County Sch. Dist., Hopkinsville, Ky., 1960; instr. psychology, counselor critic prof. Murray State U., Ky., 1961—63, U. Nev., Reno, 1963—67; owner Minisizer Exercising Salon, Ely, Nev., 1969—71, Knit Knook, Ely, 1969—, Minimimeo, Ely, 1969—, Gift Gamut, Ely, 1977—; prof. dept. fine arts Wassuk Coll., Ely, 1986—91, assoc. dean, 1986—87, dean, 1987—90; counselor White Pine County Sch. Dist., Ely, 1960—68; dir. Child and Family Ctr. Ely Indian Tribe, 1988—93. Contbr. articles to profl. jours. Dir. Family Resource Ctr. (Great Basin Rural Nev. Youth Cabinet), 1996—; bd. dir. band Sacred Heart Sch., Ely, 1982-99; active Gov.'s Mental Health State Commn., 1963-65, Nev. Hwy. Safety Leaders Bd., 1979-82, Ely Shoshone Tribal Youth Camp, 1991-92, Elys Shoshone Tribal Unity Conf., 1991-92, Tribal Parenting Skills Coord., 1991, White Pine Overall Econ. Devel. Plan Coun., 1992-2005; bd. dir. White Pine County Sch. Employees Fed. Credit Union, 1961-68, pres., 1963-68; 2d v.p. White Pine Cmty. Concert Assn., 1965-67, pres., 1967, 85—, treas., 1975-79, dr. chmn., 1981-85; chmn. bd., 1984; bd. dir. United Way, 1970-76, White Pine chpt. ARC, 1978-82; mem. Gov.'s Commn. on Status Women, 1968-74, Gov.'s Nevada State Juvenile Justice Adv. Commn., 1992-94; dir. White Pine Cmty. Choir, 1962—, Ret. Sr. Vol. Program, 1973-74, White Pine Legis. Coalition, 2002—; sec.-treas. White Pine Rehab. Tng. Ctr. for Retarded Persons, 1973-75, White Pine County Juvenile Problems Cabinet, 1994—, Gt. Basin chpt. Nev. Employees Assn., 1970-76; chmn. adv. coun. White Pine Sr. Ctr., 2005—; mem. Gov.'s Commn. on Hwy. Safety, 1979-81, Gov's. Juvenile Justice Program; vice-chmn. Gt. Basin Health Coun., 1973-75, Home Ext. adv. Bd., 1977-80; vice-chmn. White Pine Coun. on Alcoholism and Drug Abuse, 1975-76, chmn., 1976-77, White Pine County Bus. Coun., 1998—; dir. White Pine Coalition; grants author 3 yrs. Indian Child Welfare Act, State Hist. Preservation, Fair and Recreation Bd. Centennial Fine Arts Ctr.; originator Cmty. Tng. Ctr. Retarded People, 1972, Ret. Sr. Vol. Program, 1973-74, Nutrition Program Sr. Citizens, 1974, Sr. Citizens Ctr., 1974, Home Repairs Sr. Citizens, 1974, Sr. Citizens Crafters Assns., 1976, Inst. Current World Affairs, 1989, Victims of Crime, 1990-92, grants author Family Resource Ctr., 1995; bd. dirs. Family coalition, 1990-92, Sacred Heart Parochial Sch., dir. band, 1982-2000; candidate diaconal ministry, 1982-93; invited performer Branson Jubilee Nat. Ch. Choir Festival, Mo., Ely Meth. Ch. Choir, 1960-84; choir dir., organist Sacred Heart Ch., 1984—; Precinct reporter ABC News, 1966; bd. dir. White Pine Juvenile Cabinet, 1993—, Ely/East Ely Bus. Coun., 1997—, Econ. Devel. Bd., 1998—; chmn. adv. coun. White Pine Sr. Ctr., 2005—; bd. White Pine C. of C., 2000—; bd. dirs. Whtie Pine Mus., 2006—, sec. 2009-; pres. White Pine Sr. Adv. Coun., 2005—. Recipient Recognition rose, Alpha Chi State Delta Kappa Gamma, 1994, Recognition Rose, 2002,

Perserving America's Treasures in the 21st Century, 2001; named scholar, Nat. Trust for Hist. Preservation, 2000; grantee, Nat. Trust for Historic Preservation, LA, 2000. Fellow Am. Coll. Musicians, Nat. Guild Piano Tchrs.; mem. NEA (life), UDC, DAR, Nat. Fedn. Ind. Bus. (dist. chair 1971-85, nat. guardian coun. 1985—, state guardian coun. 1987—), AAUW (pres. Wells br. 1957-58, pres. White Pine br. 1965-66, 86-87, 89-91, 93—, bd. dir. 1965-87, rep. edn. 1965-67, implementation chair 1967-69, area advisor 1969-73, 89-91), Nat. Fedn. Bus. and Profl. Women (1st v.p. Ely chpt. 1965-66, pres. Ely chpt. 1966-68, 74-76, 85—, bd. dir. Nev. chpt., 1st v.p. Nev. Fedn. 1970-71, pres. Nev. chpt. 1972-73, nat. bd. dir. 1972-73), White Pine County Mental Health Assn. (pres. 1960-63, 78—), Mensa (supr. testing 1965—), White Pine C. of C. (bd. dirs. 2000—), White Pine Nuc. Waste Assn., Lincoln Hwy. Assn. (bd. dirs., 2004—, sec. treas., 2011-), Bus. Area Network Group, Delta Kappa Gamma (chpt. pres. 1968-72, 94-99, 2008-, state bd. 1967—, chpt. parliamentarian 1974-78, 99—, state 1st v.p. 1967-69, state pres. 1969-71, nat. bd. 1969-71, state parliamentarian 1971-73, 95—, chmn. state nominating com. 1995-97, chmn. bylaws com. 2003—, workshop presenter aging, intelligence and learning, San Francisco, 1995), White Pine Knife and Fork Club (1st v.p. 1969-70, pres. 1970-71, bd. dirs.), Soc. Descs. Knights Most Noble Order of Garter, Nat. Soc. Magna Charta Dames, Delta Kappa Gamma (SW regional conf. workshop presenter 1995), Nat. Assn. Parliamentarians, 2005-. Office: 1280 E Aultman St Ely NV 89301 Office Phone: 775-289-2116. Fax: 775-289-5217.

ALDERSON, PHILIP OTIS, dean, educator, radiologist; b. San Francisco, Aug. 11, 1944; s. Lloyd I. and Helen A. (Boekemeier); m. Marjorie Jean Hawkins, June 13, 1970; children: Kelly Suzanne, Lisa Joanne. AB in Zoology, Washington U., St. Louis, 1966, MD, 1970. Cert. Diplomate Am. Bd. Nuclear Medicine, Am. Bd. Radiology (Diagnosis). Intern Jewish Hosp., Washington U. Med. Sch., St. Louis, 1970-71, resident in radiology and nuclear medicine, 1971-74; instr. in radiology Mallinckrodt Inst., Washington U. Med. Sch., St. Louis, 1974-75; from asst. to assoc. prof. dept. radiology Johns Hopkins Med. Inst., Balt., 1977-80; prof. radiology Columbia-Presbyn. Med. Ctr., NYC, 1980—2008, James Picker prof., chmn. dept. radiology, 1990—2008; dean St. Louis U. Sch. Medicine, 2008—. Trustee Am. Bd. Nuc. Medicine, 1989—95, Am. Bd. Radiology, 1998—2008, sec.-treas., 2002—04, pres.-elect, 2004—06, pres., 2006—; trustee NY Presbyn. Hosp., 2004—06, pres. med. bd., 2005—06. Author 4 books; contbr. articles to profl. jours. Maj. USAF, 1975—77. Recipient Alumni Achievement award, Washington U. Med. Sch., 1995; grantee, NIH, 1974—2001. Fellow: AAAS, Am. Inst. Med. and Biol. Engrs., N.Y. Acad. Medicine, Am. Coll. Radiology (bd. chancellors 1993—2000, v.p. 1999—2000), Am. Coll. Nuclear Physicians; mem.: Nat. Adv. Coun., Soc. Chmn. Acad. Radiology Depts. (rep. Coun. Acad. Socs. of Am. Assn. Med. Colls. 1990—95, pres. 1994—95), Acad. Radiology Rsch. (sec. 1998—99, v.p. 1999—2001, pres. 2001—03), Am. Roentgen Ray Soc. (chmn. exec. coun. 1997—98, v.p 2004—05, pres. elect 2005—06, pres. 2006—07), Assn. Residency Program Dirs. in Radiology (sec.-treas. 1996—97, pres. 1998—99), Assn. Univ. Radiologists (sec.-treas. 1994—95, pres. 1996—97), Soc. Nuclear Medicine (v.p. 1984—85, chmn. sci. program com. 1984—86), N.Y. State Radiol. Soc. (sec.-treas. 1991—93, pres. 1993—94), N.Y. City Roentgen Soc. (v.p. 1989—90, pres. 1991—92), Fleischner Soc. (sec. 1989—92, treas. 1996—99, pres. 2000—01), Omicron Delta Kappa. Office: St Louis University Sch Medicine 1402 S Grand Blvd Saint Louis MO 63104 Office Phone: 314-977-9870. *

ALDIGÉ, CAROLYN R. (BO ALDIGÉ), foundation administrator; Grad., Randolph Macon Women's Coll. Founder, pres. Prevent Cancer Found. (formerly Cancer Rsch. and Prevention Found.), Alexandria, Va., 1985—. Bd. mem. Nat. Coalition Cancer Rsch., past. pres.; com. mem. C-Change; v.p. Global Lung Cancer Coalition; mem. steering com. Internat. Digestive Cancer Alliance, Nat. Colorectal Cancer Roundtable. Recipient Pioneer in Prevention award, Nat. Cancer Inst., Yetta Rosenberg Humanitarian award, Gloria Heyison Breast Cancer Found., Belva Brissette Advocacy award, Breast Cancer Resource Com., Legacy of Leadership award, Howard U., Disting. Svc. award, Am. Soc. Preventive Oncology, 2006; named Washingtonian of Yr., 1996. Mem.: Am. Soc. Clin. Oncology (Pub. Svc. award), Am. Assn. Cancer Rsch. (Pub. Svc. award 2004). Office: Prevent Cancer Found 1600 Duke St Alexandria VA 22314 Office Phone: 703-836-4412. *

ALDRICH, CLARENCE KNIGHT, physician, educator; b. Chgo, Apr. 12, 1914; s. L. Sherman and Bessie A. (Knight) A.; m. Julie H. Murphy, Feb. 4, 1942; children— Carol K., Michael S., Thomas K., Robert F. BA, Wesleyan U., 1935; MD, Northwestern U., 1940. Faculty U. Minn. Med. Sch., 1947-55, asst. prof., 1947-52, assoc. prof., 1952-55; prof. psychiatry U. Chgo. Sch. Medicine, 1955-70, chmn. dept. psychiatry, 1955-64; prof., chmn. dept. N.J. Med. Sch., Newark, 1970-73; prof. psychiatry Sch. Medicine, U. Va., Charlottesville, 1973-77, prof. psychiatry and family medicine, 1977-84, prof. emeritus, 1984—, mem. Ctr. Advanced Studies, 1981-84. Vis. prof. psychiatry U. Edinburgh, 1963-64; dir. Blue Ridge Mental Health Ctr., 1973-75; Mayne guest prof. U. Queensland, Australia, 1986. Author: Psychiatry for the Family Physician, 1955, Introduction to Dynamic Psychiatry, 1966, (with C. Nighswonger) A Casebook for Pastoral Counseling, 1968, The Medical Interview: Gateway to the Doctor-Patient Relationship, 1993, Quest for a Star, 2003. Served from asst. surgeon to surgeon USPHS, 1940-46. Fellow Am. Coll. Psychiatrists, Am. Orthopsychiat. Assn., Am. Psychiat. Assn.; mem. Group for Advancement Psychiatry. Home and Office: 250 Pantops Mountain Rd Apt 5115 Charlottesville VA 22911 Home Phone: 434-972-2414. Business E-Mail: cka3f@virginia.edu. *

ALDRIGHETTI, LUCA ANTONIO, liver surgeon; b. Milan, May 25, 1963; s. Alessandro Aldrighetti and Adriana Ferri; m. Renata Clotilde Castellano; 1 child, Alessandro Liberatore. MD, U. Milan, 1989, PhD, 1995. Resident gen. surgery U. Milan, 1989—97; surg. fellow U. Pitts. Sch. Medicine, 1992—94; resident thoracic surgery Vita-Salute U., Milan, 1997—2002; staff surgeon San Raffaele Hosp., Milan, 1997—, chief hepatobiliary surgery unit, 2004—. Achievements include research in hepatobiliary surgery; treatment of liver neoplasms. Home: via Benedetto Marcello 20 Milan 20124 Italy Office: Sci Inst San Raffaele Via Olgettina 60 20132 Milan MI Italy Office Fax: 390226437807. Business E-Mail: aldrighetti.luca@hsr.it.

ALEA, JORGE ANTONIO, retired physician; b. Cuba; came to U.S., 1949; m. Barbara Chandler; children: Craig, Karen. BS in Chemistry, U. Ga., 1953; MD, Med. Coll. Ga., 1957. Diplomate Am. Bd. Internal Medicine, Am. Bd. Gastroenterology, Nat. Bd. Med. Examiners. Staff physician State Hosp., Raleigh, NC, 1957—58; intern City Meml. Hosp., Winston-Salem, NC, 1958—59; resident in internal medicine Henry Ford Hosp., Detroit, 1959—62; resident VA Hosp.- Med. Coll. VA, Richmond, Va., 1962—63; chief of gastroenterology VA Hosp., Buffalo, 1963—69; asst. prof. medicine SUNY, Buffalo, 1963—69; chief med. svc. and charter mem. Doctor's Hosp., Lake Worth, Fla., 1969—; mem. staff JFK Med. Ctr., Lake Worth, Fla., 1969—. Contbr. articles to profl. jours. Deacon First Bapt. Ch., West Palm Beach, Fla. Capt. USAR. Fellow ACP, Am. Coll. Gastroenterology; mem. Am. Gastroenterologic Soc., Am. Soc. Gastrointestinal Endoscopy. Avocations: bicycling, classical music, golf.

ALEDO, ALEXANDER, pediatrician, hematologist, oncologist; BA, NYU, 1980, MD, 1984. Cert. pediatric hematology-oncology. Resident NY-Presbyn. Hosp., 1984—87, assoc. attending pediatrician; chief fellow joint pediatric hematology-oncology program Weill Cornell Med. Coll., assoc. prof. clin. pediat.; chief fellow joint pediatric hematology-oncology program Meml. Sloan-Kettering Cancer Ctr., 1987—90; with Children's Oncology Group; dir. pediatric oncology program Komansky Center for Children's Health. Mem. instl. rev. bd. Weill-Cornell Med. Ctr. Recipient Children's Blood Found. award, 1998, The Creative Spirit award of The Creative Ctr., 2002; named one of NY Mag.'s Best Doctors, 2011. Office: Weill Cornell Medical College 525 E 68th St Payson Pavilion 659 New York NY 10065 Office Phone: 212-746-3400. Office Fax: 212-746-8609.

ALEGRIA, MARGARITA, psychologist; b. PR, Feb. 12, 1957; PhD, Temple U., 1989. Dir. Cambridge Health Alliance, Ctr. Multicultural Mental Health Rsch., 2002—. Bd. mem., chair, vice chair Academy Health Bd. Dirs., 2004—10; mem. Work Group on Child Mental Health, Harvard Ctr. on the Developing Child & Judge Baker Children's Ctr., 2006—07; com. mem. Inst. Medicine, 2008. Recipient Carl Taube award, APHA, Simon Bolivar award, Am. Psychiatry Assn., Harold Amos Diversity award, Harvard Med. Sch., Hispanic Mental Health awards, Mental Health Rsch. Advocacy and Leadership. Office: 120 Beacon St 4th fl Somerville MA 02143 Office Fax: 617-503-8430. Business E-Mail: malegria@charesearch.org.

ALEID, MILAD FALAH, cardiologist; b. Tisia, Damascus, Syria, Mar. 27, 1962; arrived in France, 1989; s. Falah Issa Aleid and Fauzich Souliman Rizik; m. Soizic Marcelle Ripoche, Dec. 29, 1992; children: Yann-Falah, Clarisse, Mikael. MD, Damascus U., 1986; emergency diploma, Reims U., France, 1991; cardiovasc. diploma, Angers U., France, 1995, diploma (hon.) in Coroscaner and Cardiac MRI, 2008. Medicine doctor Health Ministry, Damascus, 1986-89; emergency doctor Reims (France) Hosp., 1990-92; cardiologist Cholet (France) Hosp., 1992-93; rythmologist Angers (France) Hosp., 1993-94; interventional cardiologist Le Mans (France) Hosp., 1994-95, chief unit cardiology, 1995—. International cardiopediatrist Marie Lannelong Clinic, Paris, 1997-99; magnetic resonance imaging cardiologist Angers U. Hosp., 1999-2000. Med. officer Mil. Hosp., 1986-88, Syria. Fellow Am. Coll. Cardiology, Am. Heart Assn.; mem. Mediterranean Assn. Cardiology and Cardiosurgery, Franco-Syrian Med. Assn. Avocations: swimming, football, music, travel, reading. Office: Ctr Hosp du Mans Unite 71 194 Ave Rubillard 72037 Le Mans Cedex France Business E-Mail: maleid@ch-lemans.fr.

ALEKSIC, BRANKO, psychiatrist, educator; b. Belgrade, Yugoslavia, Mar. 4, 1976; s. Stevica and Sofija Aleksic; m. Yuko Mizoguchi, Jan. 29, 2001. MD, Belgrade U. Sch. Medicine, 2001. Lic. Republic of Serbia, 2001. Internship Emergency Ctr., Belgrade, 2001—02; physician, vol. Inst. Mental Health, Belgrade, 2002—03; rschr. Fujita Health U., Toyoake, Aichi prefecture, Japan, 2006—; asst. prof. Nagoya U. Grad. Sch. Medicine, Japan. Mem.: Japanese Soc. Biol. Psychiatry. Office: Nagoya Univ Grad Sch Medicine Showa Ku Tsurmai 65 Nagoya Aichi prefecture 466-8559 Japan Home: Naka-ku Chiyoda 5-8-12 Grand Court Tsurumai 202 Nagoya Japan Office Fax: +81 52 744 2293. Personal E-mail: branko_2010@hotmail.com. Business E-Mail: branko@med.nagoya-u.ac.jp.

ALEKSIEV, ASSEN ROMANOV, medical educator; b. Sofia, Bulgaria, Sept. 10, 1962; s. Roman Kirilov Aleksiev and Julia Aleksandrova Aleksieva; m. Elena Zdravkova Pampulova; 1 child, Silvia Aleksieva. MD, Med. U., Sofia, 1988, specialist in manual medicine, 1991, specialist in phys. medicine and rehab., 1993, PhD, 1994. Chief health dist., Milanovo/Svoge, Bulgaria, 1988—90; rsch. fellow Nat. Ctr. Phys. Medicine & Rehab., Sofia, 1992—94; postdoctoral vis. scholar U. Iowa, Iowa City, 1994—96; sr. asst. prof. Med. U., Sofia, 1997—99, chief asst. prof., 1999—, assoc. prof., 2004—; head clinic physical medicine rehab U. Hosp. Alexandrovska, 2008—. Cons. Med. Ctr. #8220 Lora & #8221, Sofia, 1997—, Clinic of Plastic Surgery #8220 Malinov & #8221;, Sofia, 2001—, Univ. Hosp. #8220 Aleksandrovska & #8221;, Sofia, 1997—; presenter confs. in field. Contbr. numerous articles to profl. jours., chpts. to books; patentee in field. Recipient Vienna award for phys. medicine and rehab., Austrian Soc. Phys. Medicine and Rehab., 1995, AcroMed award, European Spine Soc., 1995; fellow, NIH, Fogarty Internat. Ctr., 1994—96. Fellow: Bulgarian Soc. Manual Medicine, Bulgarian Soc. Phys. Medicine and Rehab.; mem.: AAAS, Bulgarian Soc. EMG, EEG and Clin. Neurophysiology, N.Y. Acad. Scis. Home: Svetlostrui St 13-B 1111 Sofia Bulgaria Office: Univ Hosp 8220 Alexandrovsk Sv G Sofiiski 8221 1 1431 Sofia Bulgaria Home Phone: 3592-9628484; Office Phone: 3592-9230637. Personal E-mail: assen_aleksiev@doctor.com. Business E-Mail: assen_aleksiev@hotmail.com.

ALEMANNO, FERNANDO, anesthesiologist, consultant; b. Scorzè-Venice, Italy, 1939; MD, U. Ferrara, Italy, 1966; M in Anesthesiology and Intensive Care, Padua U., Italy, 1970. With dept. anesthesiology and intensive care Padua U., Gen. Hosp. Treviso, Italy, 1970—78; chief anesthetist, dept. anesthesiology intensive care and pain therapy Gen. Hosp. Bolzano, Italy, 1978—97; anesthetist cons. Moro-Girelli Hosp., Don Carlo Gnocchi Found., Brescia, Italy, 1997—, S.Camillo Clinic, Brescia, Italy, 2007—. Prof. U. Verona, 1988—97, lectr., 1997—; spkr. in field. Contbr. articles to profl. jours., scientific papers. Achievements include research in new brachial plexus block technique; author of first Italian original technique of regional anesthesia. Home: Via Vivaldi 3 Peschiera Del Garda 37019 Verona Italy Office: San Camillo Hosp Via Filippo Turati 44 25123 Brescia BS Italy Office Fax: 0039030293369.

ALES, TICHY, pharmacist, educator; b. Liberec, Feb. 10, 1980; MSc, PharmD, Charles U., 2003, PhD, 2008. Tchg. asst. U. Def., 2005—. Recipient award, Faculty Medicine in Hraddec Kralove, Charles U. Mem.: Czech Med. Assn. J.E.Pukryne. Avocations: music, languages, mountain climbing. Office: Trebesska 1575 Hradec Kralove Kralovehradecky kraj 50001 Czech Republic Business E-Mail: tichy@pmfhk.cz.

ALEX, JAMES C., facial plastic surgeon; b. Boston; Attended, Phillips Acad., 1981, Dartmouth Coll., Hanover, 1985, MD, 1989. Diplomate Am. Bd. Facial Plastic and Reconstructive Surgery, Am. Bd. Otolaryngology. Intern in head and neck surgery SUNY Health Sci. Med. Ctr., Syracuse; intern in gen. surgery Syracuse Univ.; resident in head and neck surgery Med. Ctr. Hosp. of Vt., Burlington, resident in otolaryngology; resident in otolaryngology-head and neck surgery Univ. Vt.; fellow in facial plastic and reconstructive surgery Univ. of Ill., Chgo.; dir. in in facial plastic and reconstructive surgery Yale Univ., 1997—2004; joined otolaryngology dept. Lahey Clinic, 2003; pvt. practive Weston Ctr. for Cosmetic Surgery, Mass., 2009. Author: various publs. Recipient numerous awards. Fellow: Triological Soc., Am. Acad. of Otolaryngology-Head and Neck Surgery, ACS, Am. Acad. of Facial Plastic and Reconstructive Surgery; mem.: AOA Soc. Achievements include development of and 1st introduced the technique of Sentinel Node Radiolocalization for melanoma and breast cancer. Office: Weston Center for Cosmetic Surgery 158 Boston Post Rd Weston MA 02493 Office Phone: 781-899-3223.

ALEXANDER, DUANE FREDERICK, pediatrician, researcher, former federal agency administrator; b. Balt., Aug. 11, 1940; s. Fred Lucas and Christiana H. (Showacre) Alexander; m. Marianne Ellis, June 23, 1963; children: Keith Duane, Kristin Marianne. BS, Pa. State U., 1962; MD, Johns Hopkins U., Balt., 1966. Diplomate Am. Bd. Pediat. Intern Johns Hopkins Hosp., 1966—67, resident, 1967—68, fellow, 1970—71; commd. officer USPHS, 1968—2000, ret. rear adm.; clin. assoc. children's diagnostic & study br. Nat. Inst. Child Health & Human Devel. (NICHD), NIH, Bethesda, Md., 1968—70, asst. to sci. dir., 1971—74, asst. to dir., 1978—82, dep. dir., 1982—86, dir., 1986—2009; sr. scientific advisor on global maternal and child health rsch. emeritus NIH Fogarty Internat. Ctr., Bethesda, Md., 2009—. Contbr. articles to profl. jours., chapters to books. Recipient Meritorious Svc. medal, USPHS, 1985, Surgeon Gen.'s Exemplary Svc. medal, 1990, Pub. Svc. award, Am. Coll. Ob-Gyn., 1992, 2005, Fedn. Behavioral, Psychol. & Cognitive Scis., 1999, Disting. Pub. Svc. award, Am. Psychol. Assn., 1992, Am. Acad. Physical Medicine & Rehab., 1993, Disting. Svc. award, HHS, 1997, 1998, Disting Alumnus award, Pa. State U., 1999, Dr. Nathan Davis award for Outstanding Govt. Svc., AMA, 2004. Mem.: Am. Pediatric Soc., Soc. Devel. Pediat., Am. Acad. Pediat. (Excellence in Pub. Svc. award 1992, Arnold J. Capute award 2002). Methodist. Office: Fogarty International Center NIH 31 Center Drive - MSC 2220 Bethesda MD 20892-2220 Office Phone: 301-402-1112. Business E-Mail: duane.alexander@nih.gov. *

ALEXANDER, FREDERICK, pediatric surgery, educator; Attended, Columbia U., 1977. Diplomate Am. Bd. Surgery-pediatric surgery. Resident surgery Brigham-Womens Hosp., 1978—84; fellow pediatric surgery Childrens Hosp., 1984—86; clin. prof. surgery; affiliation Hackensack Univ. Med. Ctr. Office: Hackensack University Medical Center 30 Prospect Ave Hackensack NJ 07601 Office Phone: 201-996-2921. Office Fax: 201-996-4499.

ALEXANDER, HENRY RICHARD, JR., surgical oncologist; b. Washington, Nov. 17, 1953; BA, U. Colo.; MD, Georgetown U. Sch. Medicine, 1979. Diplomate Am. Bd. Surgery. Intern, resident gen. surgery Nat. Naval Med. Ctr., Bethesda, Md., 1979—85; surg. oncology fellow Meml. Sloan-Kettering Cancer Ctr., NYC, 1987—89; chief surg. metabolism sect., chmn. gastrointestinal malignancies sect. Nat. Cancer Inst., NIH, Bethesda, dep. dir. Ctr. Cancer Rsch.; assoc. chmn. clin. rsch., dept. surgery U. Md. Sch. Medicine, Balt., staff Marlene & Stewart Greenebaum Cancer Ctr. Mem. editl. bd. Jour. Clin. Oncology, Annals Surg. Oncology, reviewer New Eng. Jour. Medicine, Cancer Rsch., Clin. Cancer Rsch., Annals Surgery, Surgery; contbr. articles to profl. jours. Fellow: ACS, Soc. Surg. Oncology, Am. Surg. Assn.; mem.: Am. Assn. Endocrine Surgeons, Am. Assn. Cancer Rsch., Soc. Univ. Surgeons, Assn. Academic Surgery. Office: U Md Sch Medicine Dept Surgery 22 S Greene St S4B05A Baltimore MD 21201 Office Phone: 410-328-3828. E-mail: HRAlexander@smail.umaryland.edu. *

ALEXANDER, JAMES WESLEY, surgeon, educator; b. El Dorado, Kans., May 23, 1934; s. Rossiter Wells and Merle Lydia Alexander; m. Maureen L. Strohofer; children: Joseph, Judith, Elizabeth, Randolph, John Charles, Lori, Molly. Student, Tex. Technol. Coll., 1951-53; MD, U. Tex., 1957; ScD, U. Cin., 1958-64; postgrad., U. Minn., 1966-67. Diplomate Am. Bd. Surgery, Am. Bd. Thoracic Surgery, lic. physician Ohio. Intern Cin. Gen. Hosp., 1957-58; resident U. Cin.-Cin. Gen. Hosp., 1958-64; mem. faculty Coll. Medicine, U. Cin., 1962—64, 1966—2008, prof. surgery, 1975—2008, dir. transplantation div., dept. surgery, 1967-99, dir. surg. immunology lab., 1967—2000; dir. research Shriners Burns Inst., 1979-90; practice medicine and surgery Cin., 1966—2008; dir. Ctr. for Surg. Weight Loss, 2001—08. Mem. study sect. NIH, 1983—87, 1989—93, chmn, 1990—93, mem. ad hoc com., 1990—. Author (with R.A. Good): (immuno biology for surgeons) Fundamentals of Clinical Immunology, 1977; mem. editl. bd. Annals of Surgery, 1975—2009, Jour. Burn Care and Rehab., 1979—99, Burns, Including Thermal Injury, 1985—98, Graft, 1998—2009, Jour. Parenteral and Enteral Nutrition, 1991—99, Nutrition, 1991—2000, Transplantation Sci., 1991—94, (transplantation), 1994—98, Jour. Trauma, 1998—2005, (shock), 1994—2000; contbr. more than 670 articles to sci. jours. Capt. M.C. US Army, 1964—66. Mem.: ACS, AAAS, Am. Soc. Metabolic and Bariatric Surgeons, Mont Reid Surg. Soc., Shock Soc., Transplantation Soc., Surg. Infection Soc. (sec. 1981—84, pres.-elect 1985—86, pres. 1986—87), Soc. Univ. Surgeons, Ohio State Med. Assn., St. Paul Surg. Soc., Internat. Soc. Surgery, Halsted Soc., Am. Surg. Assn., Am. Soc. Parenteral and Enteral Nutrition, Am. Soc. Transplant Surgeons (sec. 1985—87, pres.-elect 1987—88, pres. 1988—89), Am. Burn Assn. (pres.-elect 1983—84, pres. 1984—85), Am. Assn. for Surgery of Trauma, Peruvian Acad. Surgery (hon.), Colombian Coll. Surgeons (hon.), Surg. Biology Club, Phi Eta Sigma, Alpha Epsilon Delta, Alpha Chi, Alpha Omega Alpha. Home: 757 Riverwatch Dr Crescent Springs KY 41017-4480 Office: Univ Cin Med Ctr 231 Albert Sabin Way Cincinnati OH 45267-0558 Office Phone: 513-558-6006. Business E-Mail: jwesley.alexander@uc.edu.

ALEXANDER, JOHN CHARLES, pharmaceutical executive, preventive medicine physician; b. Perth Amboy, NJ, Dec. 28, 1943; s. Charles John and Agnes (Maloney) A.; m. Margaret Ann Kohler, July 19, 1969; children: Laurel, Jennifer, Anna. BS, St. Francis Coll., Loretto, Pa., 1965; MD, St. Louis U., 1970; MPH, Johns Hopkins U., Balt., 1972. Intern Barnes Hosp./Washington U., St. Louis, 1970-71; resident in gen. preventive medicine State of Va./Med. Coll. Va., Richmond, 1974-76; clin. rsch. dir. Squibb Inst. Med. Rsch., Princeton, NJ, 1976—82, v.p. cardiovascular clin. rsch., 1982-86, sr. v.p. med. affairs, 1986-90; v.p. rsch. Bristol-Myers-Squibb Pharm. Rsch. Inst., Princeton, 1990-91; sr. v.p. med. rsch. Searle, Skokie, Ill., 1991-93, exec. v.p. med. rsch., 1993-99; pres. Daiichi Sankyo Pharma Devel., Edison, NJ, 1999—2009; global head R & D Daiichi Sankyo Co. Ltd., Tokyo, 2003—09; also. bd. dirs. Chmn. bd. Daiichi Sankyo, Inc., Parsippany, NJ, 2008—; mem. bd. trustees St. Fracis U., 2010—. Patentee in field. Lt. comdr. USN, 1972-74. Mem. Drug Info. Assn. (pres., bd. dirs.), Alpha Omega Alpha. Home: 86 Beech Hollow Ln Princeton NJ 08540-1235 Office: Daiichi Sankyo Pharma Inc 399 Thornall St Edison NJ 08837-2236 Home Phone: 609-924-9758; Office Phone: 732-590-5000. Business E-Mail: jalexander@dsi.com.

ALEXANDER, JONATHAN, cardiologist, consultant; b. NYC, Nov. 29, 1947; s. Josef and Hannah (Margolis) A.; m. Karen Deborah Einhorn, Aug. 8, 1971; children: Jessica Beth, Daniel Lewis, Benjamin Joel. BA, Harvard U., Cambridge, Mass., 1968; MD, Albert Einstein Coll. Medicine, 1973. MD. Intern, resident Yale-New Haven Hosp., 1973-76; fellow dept. cardiology Sch. Medicine Yale U., New Haven, 1976-78, asst. clin. prof. medicine, 1978-83, assoc. clin. prof., 1983-95, clin. prof., 1995—; attending physician West Haven Vets. Hosp., Conn., 1978—, New Milford Hosp., Conn., 1980, Danbury Hosp., Conn., 1978—, dir. cardiac rehab. unit and nuclear cardiology Conn., 1978—. Recipient Samuel Kushlan award Yale-New Haven Hosp., 1974, Revlon award 11th Internat. Congress Chemotherapy, 1983. Fellow: ACP, Found. for Cmty. Health Care, Conn. Hosp. Assn., Conn. chpt. Am. Coll. Cardiology (pres. 1993—96), Am. Coll. Cardiology (gov. Conn. 1993—96); mem.: Yale Cardiovascular Network. Jewish. Office Phone: 203-739-7155. Personal E-mail: jaheart1@aol.com. Business E-Mail: jonathan.alexander@danhosp.org.

ALEXANDER, JUDITH ELAINE, retired psychologist; b. Worcester, Mass., Nov. 30, 1948; d. Frank E. and Winnona V. (Tracy) A.; divorced; children: Kimberly, Jenniferlyn. BS, Worcester State Coll., 1981; MA, Assumption Coll., Worcester, 1986; PsyD, Antioch New Eng., Keane, NH, 1991. Lic. psychologist. Dir. mental health Indian Health Svc., Ft. Thompson, S.D., 1992-95; cons. self employed, 1995—99; psychologist VAMC, Dublin, Ga., 2001—03, Bur. Indian Affairs Ea. Navajo Agy., 2003—06, Yakoma Indian Health Svc., Toppenish, Wash., 2006—10. Adj. faculty Mt. Wachusett C.C., Gardner, Mass., 1996, Western New Eng. Coll., 1996-2001. Contbr. articles to profl. jours. Mem. Indian Health Svc. Home: 7100 Linden Ave N7 Seattle WA 98103 Personal E-mail: judialex@live.com. Business E-Mail: judith.alexander@ins.gov. E-mail: judithalexander@ins.gov.

ALEXANDER, PATRICK BYRON, hospital administrator; b. Texas City, Tex., May 11, 1950; s. Alvin Wesley and Mabel Bernice Alexander; m. Linda Graham, May 7, 1975. BA in Econs., George Mason Coll., U. Va., 1972; MLA, Oklahoma City U., 2006. Publs. dir. George Mason U., Fairfax, Va., 1973-75, U. Okla. Health Scis. Ctr., Oklahoma City, 1975-78, Presbyn. Hosp. Inc., Oklahoma City, 1978-79; mng. dir. Okla. Symphony Orch., Oklahoma City, 1979-88; exec. dir. Allied Arts Found., 1988-92, Okla. Zool. Soc., 1992—2001; exec. dir. advancement Oklahoma City U., 2001—03; planned giving dir. The Children's Ctr., 2003—. Bd. dirs. Okla. Philharm. Found. Recipient Gov.'s award for excellence in arts, 1987, Okla. Fundraiser of Yr. award, 1991; Kerr Found. fellow, 1981. Mem.: English Speaking Union, Rotary Club, Econ. Club of Oklahoma City. Home: 1515 Glenwood Ave Oklahoma City OK 73116-5206 Office: The Childrens Ctr 6800 NW 39th Expy Bethany OK 73008 E-mail: palexander@tccokc.org.

ALEXANDER, RICHARD, medical educator; b. Balt., Apr. 15, 1956; MD, Johns Hopkins Sch. Medicine, 1981. Prof. U. Md. Sch. Medicine, 1994—. Office: 29 S Greene St Ste 500 Baltimore MD 21201 Business E-Mail: ralexander@smail.umaryland.edu.

ALEXANDRE, GÉRARD-EUGENE, orthopedic surgeon; b. Paris, Jan. 13, 1930; s. Andrè-Maurice and Marcelle (Blum) A.; m. Liliane Martha Pierre, June 13, 1956; children: Fabienne-Jacqueline, Dominique Liliane. MD, U. Paris, 1963. Intern Hosp. of Paris, 1961-66, head surg. orthopedic clinic, 1966-69; cons. surgeon Nat. Inst. Disabled Ministry of War Veterans, 1963-74; asst. dept. child surgery St. Vincent-de-Paul Hosp., Paris, 1967; asst. dept. orthopedic surgery Hosp. Cochin, Paris, 1969-82; orthopedic surgeon Clinique de Marly, Marly le Roi, France, 1969-95, dir. massage, physiotherapy and chiropody sch., 1963—2004. Cons. orthopedic surgery Simone Veil Hosp. Eaubonne-Montmorency, 1997—; mem. Nat. Coun. Med. Formative, 2004—. Contbr. articles to profl. jours. Mem. Conseil Supérieur Professions Paramédicales, Health Ministry, 1973-81, 86-91, 2000—. Mem.: West Orthopedic Soc., Health Trade Assn. (Alliance v.p. 2002), Nat. Orgn. Dirs. Physiotherapy Schs. (sec. gen. 1969—89), French Soc. Surgical Orthopedy, Nat. Coll. Orthopedic Surgeons, French Assn. Artificial Limb Supply, Hand Study Group, Rotary. Avocations: skiing, windsurfing. Home: 59 avenue de Briens 78670 Villennes-sur-Seine France Personal E-mail: alexandregerard.e@wanadoo.fr.

ALEXANDRESCU, VLAD-ADRIAN, vascular surgeon; s. Mircea and Rodica Alexandrescu. MD 1st class with distinction, U. Louvain, Brussels, 1994. Diplomate in vascular and thoracic surgery 2000. Tng. in vascular and endovascular, vascular dept. U. Louvain, 1990—96, St. Joseph Hosp., Marseille, France, 1997—98, Royal Infirmary Hosp., Leicester, England, 1999, Princess Paola Hosp., St. Therese Hosp., Marche-en-Famenne, Belgium, 1999—2003, med coord., vascular dept., 2003—. Mem. med. coun. Princess Paola Hosp., St. Therese Hosp., 2008—. Contbr. articles to profl. jours. Mem.: Assn. Hosps., Royal Belgiun Soc. Surgery, European Soc. Surg. Oncology, Internat. Soc. Endovascular Specialists (award 2008), Internat. Soc. Vascular Surgery, Belgian Stroke Coun., Med. Coun. Hosp. (assoc.). Achievements include development of new techniques in carotid stenting and arterial angioplasty. Avocations: photography, tennis, travel. Office: Princess Paola Hosp Dept Vascular Surgery Rue du Vivier 21 Marche-en-Famenne 6900 Belgium Office Phone: 32 84 219111, 0113284219076. Office Fax: 32 84 316613.

ALEXANDROV, ANDREY, medical researcher; b. Volgograd, Russia, Oct. 26, 1968; MD, Volgograd State Med. U., 1985. Rsch. scientist Rsch. Inst. Clin. and Exptl. Rheumatology, Russian Acad. Med. Sci., 1992—. Office: Zemlyachki 76 Volgograd 400138 Russia Business E-Mail: imlab@mail.ru.

ALEXANIAN, RAYMOND, hematologist; b. NYC, June 8, 1932; s. Hagop and Eleeza (Bynderian) A.; m. Lois Abbott, Jan. 16, 1960; 1 dau., Jane. BA with honors, Dartmouth Coll., 1952; MD, Harvard U., 1955. Diplomate: Am. Bd. Internal Medicine. Intern King County Hosp., Seattle, 1955-56; successively asst. resident in medicine, research fellow in hematology, instr. medicine U. Wash. Med. Sch., 1958-64; mem. faculty U. Tex. M.D. Anderson Hosp., Houston, 1964—, prof. medicine, 1975—. Rsch. fellow in radiobiology Christle Hosp., Manchester, England. Contbr. numerous articles on myeloma and related disorders to med. jours. Served as capt. M.C. AUS, 1956-58. Mem. Am. Contract Bridge League(Bronze Life master) Home: 4082 Breakwood Dr Houston TX 77025-4033 Office: MD Anderson Hosp Dept Lymphoma-Myeloma 1515 Holcombe Blvd Houston TX 77030-4009 Office Phone: 713-792-2850.

ALEXIADES-ARMENAKAS, MACRENE RENEE, dermatologist, scientist, researcher, educator, consultant; d. Gregory and Sophia Alexiades; m. Noel Anthony Armenakas, Oct. 26, 1996; children: Sophia Stella Armenakas, Anthony Emmanuel Armenakas. BA, Harvard U., 1989; MD, Harvard Med. Sch., 1997; PhD, Harvard U., 1997. Cert. MD, PhD, lic. medicine & surgery N.Y., 1998, medicine and surgery Conn., 2004, Greece, 2004, credentialed in medicine and surgery European Union, 2004, diplomate Am. Bd. Dermatology, 2002, bd. cert. in dermatology 2009. Rschr. Harvard U., Cambridge, 1984—91, tutor supr., 1985—89, tchg. asst., 1990—97, doctorate rschr. Boston, 1991—97; intern medicine Lenox Hill Hosp., NYC, 1997—98; Fulbright scholar U. Heraklion, Crete, Greece, 1989—90; resident dermatology NYU Sch. Medicine, NYC, 1998—2000, chief resident dermatology, 2000—01; dir. rsch. & laser dermatology Laser & Skin Surgery Ctr. N.Y., 2001—03; attending physician Lenox Hill Hosp., NYC, 2001—; pres., dir. dermatology & laser surgery Macrene Alexiades-Armenakas, MD, PhD, PC, 2003—; asst. clin. prof. Yale U. Sch. Medicine, 2003—; attending physician Yale/New Haven Hosp., 2003, Yale Va. Hosp., 2006—; founder, owner NY Derm LLC, 2005—, Dr. Macrene Skin Results, 2009—. Tutor supr. Harvard Bur. Study Coun., 1985—89; mem. MD/PhD program steering com. Harvard Med. Sch., 1993—94, mem. MD/PhD program retreat com., 1992—94, mem. minority recruitment com., 1992—95, mem. advanced biomed. scis. com., 1993—95, admissions interviewer com., 2002—; cons. dermatologist L'Oreal, Paris, 2005—08; sci. advisor Archdiocese of N.Am., 2006—. Editor: The Harvard Polit. Rev., 1985—89; editor: (writer) The Biology Rev., 1986—89; mem. editl. bd.: The Harvard Crimson, 1985—89, columnist, editor: Jour. Drugs in Dermatology, 2005—, staff reviewer Jours.: Dermatologic Surgery, 2004—, Lasers in Medicine and Surgery, 2005—; staff reviewer Jours. J. Cos Laser Therapy, 2008—, J. Cos Dermatology, 2008—; author: abstracts, jour. articles, book chpts. Counselor rape crisis Response, Cambridge, 1988-89; counselor Harvard Med. Sch. peer counseling, 1990-92; yoga instr. Vanderbilt Hall Athletic Facility, Boston, 1990-92; vol. St. Francis House Soup Kitchen, 1990-94; solicitation coord. fundraising com. William Woodward Nursery Sch., 2001-02, chairperson, 2004-, bd. trustees, 2004-; mem. art com. The Chapin Sch., 2004-05, sci. and rsch. advisor, 2006—; mem. Parents Assn., 2004-05; bd. mem. Cathedral Sch., chair afternoon sch.; bd. dirs. Promenade Condo, 2008-, Primaeva Med., 2008-, Cutera, 2008-, Arthdiocesan Cathedral Holy Trinity, 2009-. Recipient Husik prize, 2001, First Pl. award, Jour. Drugs in Dermatology Rsch. Competition, 2004, Top Ten Rsch. Presentation, Am. Soc. Laser Medicine & Surgery, 2007, Top Five Treatments, NY Post, 2008, People's Choice award, 2009; grantee, Nat. Eye Inst., 1995; scholar, Fulbright Found., 1989—90; Paul Dudley White scholar, Harvard U., 1991. Fellow: Am. Soc. Laser Medicine and Surgery (faculty, dir. 2001—), Am. Acad. Dermatology (faculty 2008—), Hellenic Med. Soc.; mem.: CEW, Women's Dermatologic Soc., Dermatology Found., Harvard Hellenic Soc. (founder), Mass. Med. Soc., Am. Soc. Dermatologic Surgery (chmn. rsch. com. 2004—06, councilman edn. and rsch. com. 2002—06, editor), Harvard Greek Club. Greek Orthodox Christian. Achievements include numerous scientific discoveries, inventions, and patents. Avocations: sculpting, drawing, painting, skiing, tennis, yoga, photography. Home: 530 E 76th St #21HJ New York NY 10021 also: 955 Park Ave New York NY 10028 Office Phone: 212-570-2067. Office Fax: 212-861-7964. Business E-Mail: dralexiades@nyderm.org.

ALEXIS, ANDREW F., dermatologist; s. Nicholas and Mercy Alexis; m. Ama Gyekye, Sept. 21, 2002. MD, MPH, Columbia U., 1999. Diplomate Am. Bd. Dermatology. Resident in dermatology NY Presbyn. Hosp., Cornell U., NYC, 2003; rsch. fellow in dermatopharmacology, dept. dermatology NYU, NYC, 2003—04; assoc. dir. Skin of Color Ctr., St. Luke's-Roosevelt Hosp., NYC, 2004—05, dir., 2005—. Asst. clin. prof. dermatology Columbia U., NYC, 2004—. Contbr. articles to profl. jours. and book chpts. in field. Recipient Disting. Housetaff award, Weill Med. Coll., Cornell U., 2003; fellow Stanley scholar, Stanley Found. Rsch. Fund, 1996; Rudin scholar, Louis and Rachel Rudin Found., 1997, 1998. Fellow: Am. Acad. Dermatology; mem.: AMA, Skin of Color Soc., Soc. Investigative Dermatology, Nat. Med. Assn. Achievements include research in psoriasis, alopecia areata, acne, and skin of color. Office: Skin of Color Ctr 1090 Amsterdam Ave 11B New York NY 10025 Personal E-mail: andrew.alexis@columbia.edu.

ALEXIS, FRANK, engineering educator; b. Pointe-Noire, Oct. 9, 1976; PhD, Nanyang Technol. U., 2005. Postdoc. fellow Inst. Bioengring. and Nanotech., Singapore, 2003—; rsch. assoc. MIT, 2006—09; asst. prof., bioengring. Clemson U., 2009. Office: Clemson University Rhodes Research Ctr #201 Clemson SC 29634 Business E-Mail: falexis@clemson.edu.

ALFA, MICHELLE JOSEPHINE, microbiologist, educator; b. Winnipeg, Man., Canada, Dec. 9, 1953; d. Jim R. and Betty M. Foubert; m. Attahiru S. Alfa; children: Ismaila, Aisha. BSc, U. Man., 1975; MSC, U. NSW, Sydney, Australia, 1980; PhD, U. Alta., Edmonton, Can., 1986. Asst. prof. U. Man., 1989—96, assoc. prof., 1996—2000, prof., 2000—02; asst. dir. microbiology lab. St. Boniface Gen. Hosp., Winnipeg, 1989—2000, asst. dir., 2002—; assoc. prof. Wayne State U., Detroit, 2000—02. Contbr. articles to profl. jours. Bd. dirs., sec. Horace Patterson Found., Winnipeg. Studentship, Alta. Heritage Found., 1981—85, postgrad. fellow, Man. Health Rsch. Coun., 1986—88. Mem.: Assn. for Advancement of Med. Instrumentation, Am. Bd. Microbiology, Can. Coll. Microbiologists (mem. exec. com. 2003—, treas. 2003—). Achievements include invention of artificial test soil. Avocations: mentoring women in science, science education. Home: 51 Ravine Rd Winnipeg MB Canada R2M 5N4 Office: St Boniface Gen Hosp Microbiology Lab L4025 409 Tache Ave Winnipeg MB Canada R2H 2A6 Office Phone: 204-237-2105. Personal E-mail: malfa@dsmanitoba.ca. E-mail: malfa@sbgh.mb.ca.

ALFANO, MICHAEL CHARLES, university administrator; b. Newark, Aug. 8, 1947; s. Michael Ferdinand and Anne Marie (Barrington) A.; m. JoAnn Mary Coletta, Mar. 30, 1969; children: Michael Anthony, Kristin Lynn. Student, Rutgers U., 1967; DMD, U. Medicine and Dentistry of N.J., 1971; postgrad. in periodontics, Harvard U., 1974; PhD, MIT, 1975. Asst. prof. dentistry Fairleigh Dickinson U., Hackensack, NJ, 1974-77, assoc. prof., 1977-80, prof. with tenure, 1980-82, dir. Oral Health Rsch. Ctr., 1977-82, asst. dean grad. affairs and rsch., 1981-82; v.p. dental rsch. Block Drug Co., Inc., Jersey City, 1982-84, sr. v.p., Rsch. & Devel., 1987—98, bd. dirs., 1988-98, pres., dental products divsn., 1985—88, cons., office of chief exec., 1990—98; dean, Coll. Dentistry NYU, NY, 1998—2006, prof., basic sciencess & periodontology Coll. Dentistry NY, 1998—2006, exec. v.p., 2006—. Adj. prof. U. Medicine and Dentistry of N.J., Newark, 1985-2003; mem. sci. adv. coun. Office of Gov., State of N.J., 1981-84; bd. dirs., Dentsply Internat., 2001- Editor: Symposium on Nutrition, 1976; contbr. articles to profl. jours. and chpts. to books; patentee in field. Trustee Found. of U. Medicine and Dentistry of N.J., 1988-98, N.Y. State Dental Found., 2004-06; mem. adv. bd. Columbia U. Sch. Dental and Oral Surgery, 1990-98; mem. program com. Am. Fund for Dental Health, 1991-93; bd. overseers Forsyth Dental Ctr., Boston, 1992-99, U. Pa. Coll. Dental Medicine, 1992-2004; trustee Santa Fe Group, 1998—, YMCA Greater NY, 2010-, Delta Dental NY, 2010-; founding dir. Friends of Nat. Inst. Dental Rsch., 1998-2006; cons. Nat. Inst. Dental Rsch., Bethesda, Md., 1976-82; apptd. nat. adv. dental rsch. coun. NIH, Bethesda, 1994-98; apptd. vis. prof. Nat. Dairy Coun., Chgo., 1981; vis. sr. scientist Fairleigh Dickinson U., 1982-88 Recipient Leadership citation Newark YMCA, 1966, Disting. Alumnus award U. Medicine and Dentistry of N.J., 1986, Harvard U. Sch. Dental Medicine, 1998; NIH rsch. grantee, 1974-82; NIH postdoctoral fellow, 1971-74. Fellow Am. Coll. Dentists, Am. Coll. of Prosthodontists (hon. fellow), Internat. Congress Oral Implantologists (hon. life 2002-); mem. Am. Acad. Oral Med. (hon. mem., 2003), ADA (cons., Future of Dentistry Commn. 1999-2001, bd. govs. student clinicians 2000—07, Nat. Achievement award 1978), Internat. Assn. for Dental Rsch., Am. Assn. for Dental Rsch. (pres. N.J. chpt. 1985, Hein Pub. Svc. award 2004, Shils award 2004), Am. Dental Edn. Assn. (Gies award 2008), Am. Inst. Nutrition. Independent. Roman Catholic. Achievements include 8 patents; discovery of role of Vitamin C in mucous membrane barrier function. Home: 29 Washington Sq W Apt 5C New York NY 10011-9132 Office: New York University 70 Washington Sq S New York NY 10010 Office Fax: 212-995-4789. Business E-Mail: mca1@nyu.edu. *

ALFANO, ROBERT R., science and engineering educator; BS, Fairleigh Dickinson U., Teaneck, NJ, 1963, MS, 1964; PhD, NYU, NYC, 1972. Rschr. GTE, NYC, 1964-72; from asst. prof. to prof. CUNY, 1972—88, disting. prof. sci., 1987—; dir. N.Y. State Ctr. for Adv. Tech. in Ultrafast Photonics, 1992—2006, NASA Ctr. for Optical Sensing and Imaging, 2003—07, DOD Ctr. for Nanoscale Photonic Emitters and Sensors, 2003—09, Inst. Ultrafast Spectroscopy and Lasers, 1982—. Dir. Ctr. on Laser in Medicine, Dept. Energy, 1998-2002. Editor: Biological Events Probed by Ultrafast Laser Spectroscopy, 1982, Semiconductors Probed by Ultrafast Laser Spectroscopy, 1985, The Supercontinuum Laser Source, 1989, 2d edit., 2006, Photonics: Nonlinear Optics and Ultrafast Phenomena, 1990; contbr. 749 articles to profl. jours.; 107 patents in field. A.P. Sloan fellow, OSA fellow, APS fellow, OSA Charles Towres Award, 2008, Citation award. Fellow: NY Academic Sci., IEEE (leader, optical biopsy and mammography). Office Phone: 212-650-5531, 212-650-5533. Office Fax: 212-650-5530. Business E-Mail: ralfano@sci.ccny.cuny.edu.

ALFARO-RODRIGUEZ, ALFONSO, neurologist, researcher; b. Méx. City, Mar. 21, 1960; MD, U. Nat. Autónoma Méx., 1985, degree in Neurophysiology, 1990, PhD, 1995. Chief, dept. neurophysiology Nat. Inst. Rehab. Contbr. scientific papers to internat. publs. Fellow: Nat. Inst. Neurology and Neurosurgery. Achievements include research in neurophysiology and neurochemistry of neurodegenerative diseases. Avocations: reading, sports. Office: Calz México-Xochimilco 289 Col Arena México City 14389 Mexico Personal E-mail: alfa1360@yahoo.com.mx.

ALFIDI, RALPH JOSEPH, retired radiologist, educator, researcher, administrator; b. Rome, Apr. 20, 1932; s. Luca and Angeline (Panella) A.; m. Rose Esther Senesac, Sept. 3, 1956 (div. 1991); children: Suzanne, Lisa, Christine, Katherine, Mary, John; m. Mariella Boller, Aug. 29, 1992. AB, Ripon Coll., Wis., 1955; MD, Marquette U., Milw., 1959. Intern Oakwood Hosp., Dearborn, Mich., 1959-60; resident, chief resident, A.C.S. fellow U. Va., 1960-63; practice medicine, specializing in radiology Cleve., 1965-2000; staff mem. Cleve. Clinic, 1965-78, head dept. hosp. radiology, 1968-78; dir. dept. radiology Univ. Hosps., Cleve., 1978-92; prof. radiology U. N.Mex., Albuquerque, 2000—03. Cons. VA Hosp., Cleve.; chmn. dept. radiology Case Western Res. U. Sch. Medicine, 1978-92; chmn. staff Cleve. Clinic Found., 1975-76; co-founder Steris Corp. Author: Complications and Legal Implications of Special Procedures, 1972, Computed Tomography of the Human Body: An Atlas of Normal Anatomy, 1977; editor: Whole Body Computed Tomography, 1977; contbr. articles to radiology jours. Served to capt., M.C. U.S. Army Res., 1963-65 Picker Found. grantee, 1969-70; NRC grantee, 1969-70 Mem. Radiol. Soc. N. Am., Am. Roentgen Ray Soc., Am. Heart Assn., Soc. Cardiovascular Radiology, Soc. Gastrointestinal Radiology, Soc. Computed Body Tomography (pres. 1977-78), Eastern Radiol. Soc., Cleve. Radiol. Soc. (pres. 1976-77), Las Campanas Club. Roman Catholic. Achievements include discovery of renal splanchnic steal syndrome: aka Alfidi's Syndrome; patents for nitinol. Home: 81 Calle Ventoso W Santa Fe NM 87506-0141

ALFIERI, ALEX ALFIERI, neurosurgeon; b. Trento, Italy, May 5, 1971; m. Francesca Pagliani, May 14, 2000; children: Valentina, Ludovica, Edoardo. MD, U. Verona, 1996. Lic. physician European Assn. Neurol. Surgeons Bd., 2005. Resident Dept. Neurosurgery Azienda Sanitaria di Bolzano, Bolzano, Italy, 1998—2000, neurosurgeon, 2000—. Recipient Tagliapietra award, 2000. Mem.: Italian Assn. Neurological Surgeons (Tagliapietra award), Am. Assn. Neurological Surgeons (assoc.). Office: Neurochirurgia Ospedale di Bolzano Via Lorenz Boehler 5 39100 Bolzano BZ Italy Office Fax: +39 0471 908451. Business E-Mail: alex.alfieri@asbz.it.

ALFONSI, GRACE ANN, family practice physician, educator; MD, U. Pitts. Diplomate Am. Bd. Family Practice, Am. Bd. Family Practice-geriatric medicine. Resident Univ. of Colo. Health Sciences Ctr.; fellow Cook County Hosp.; asst. prof. family medicine Univ. Colo. Health Sciences Ctr.; attending physician Denver Metro Health (STD) Clinic. Office: Denver Health and Hospital Authority 777 Bannock St Denver CO 80204 Office Phone: 303-436-6000. E-mail: galfonsi@dhha.org.

ALFONSO, CALOGERO RINO, orthopedist; b. Palermo, Italy, Apr. 12, 1963; Degree in Medicine and Surgery, Bologna U., 1987, degree in Orthop. Surgery, 1992. Specialist in spinal disease Azienda Ospedaliera Policlinico S.Orsola, Malpighi, Bologna, 1996—. Mem.: Soc. Italiana Chirurgia Vertebrale. Avocation: gardening. Office: Via Albertoni 15 Bologna 40128 Italy Office Fax: 00390516362671. Personal E-mail: rinoalfonso@yahoo.it.

ALFONSO, CESAR A., psychiatrist, educator; BS, Yale U., New Haven, 1992, MD, NY Med. Coll., 1987, post-grad. studies in psychoanalysis, 1989—95. Cert. American Bd. Psychiatry and Geriatric Psychiatry. Residency in psychiatry NY Med. Coll., 1987—91, chief resident psychiatry, 1990—91, fellowship in consultation and liaison psychiatry, 1991—92; pvt. practice psychiatrist NYC; asst. prof. clin. psychiatry Columbia U. Med. Ctr., NYC. Psychiatric cons. Jewish Guild for Blind. Book rev. editor: Jour. of American Acad. Psychoanalysis; contbr. articles to profl. jours. Fellow: NY Acad. Medicine, American Acad. Psychoanalysis, American Coll. Psychoanalysis, American Acad. Psychoanalysis and Dynamic Psychiatry (pres. 2010—), Acad. Psychosomatic Medicine. Office: 262 Central Park W Ste 1B New York NY 10024 Office Phone: 212-595-7850. Office Fax: 888-910-5888. Business E-Mail: caa2105@columbia.edu. *

ALFORD, BOBBY RAY, otolaryngologist, academic administrator, educator; b. Dallas, May 30, 1932; s. Bryant J. and Edith M. (Garrett) A.; m. Othelia Jerry Dorn, Aug. 28, 1953; children: Bradley Keith, Raye Lynn, Alan Scott. AS, Tyler Jr. Coll., 1951; postgrad., U. Tex., 1951-52; MD, Baylor U., 1956. Diplomate Am. Bd. Otolaryngology (dir. 1972-90, pres. 1985-86, exec. v.p. 1986-90). Intern Jefferson Davis Hosp., Houston, 1956-57; resident Baylor U. Coll. Medicine Affiliated Hosps. Program, 1957-60; mem. faculty Baylor U. Coll. Medicine, 1962—, prof. otolaryngology, 1966—, chmn. dept., 1967-95, 96 , v.p. and dean acad. and clin. affairs, 1984-88, disting. service prof., 1985—, interim chmn. dept. surgery, 1983—84, exec. v.p., dean medicine, 1988—2004, chancellor, 2004—; pres., CEO BaylorMedCare, Houston, 1994-96; chmn., CEO Nat. Space Biomed. Rsch. Inst., 1997—. Rev. panel surgeon gen. on neurol. and sensory disease USPHS, 1965-67; cons. Nat. Inst. Neurol. Disease and Stroke, 1970-74; cons. to surgeon gen. U.S. Army, 1963-73; nat. adv. coun. Neurol. and Communicative Disorders and Stroke, NIH, 1977-80, Deafness and Other Communicative Disorders, 1991-95, NASA, 1992-95, chmn. aerospace medicine adv. com., 1993-94, chmn. life microgravity scis. and applications adv. com., 1993-95. Author: Neurological Aspects of Auditory and Vestibular Disorders, 1964, Electrophysiologic Evaluation in Otolaryngology, 1997; chief editor: A.M.A. Archives of Otolaryngology, 1970-79. Bd. dirs. Houston Acad. Medicine Tex. Med. Ctr. Libr., 1983-94. Recipient Herman Johnson award Baylor U. Coll. Medicine, 1956, NASA Disting. Pub. Svc. award, 1992, 95, Jeffries Aerospace Medicine and Life Scis. Rsch. award Am. Inst. Aeronautics and Astronautics, 2003, Bobby Alford award for Academic Clin. Professionalism Ben and Margaret Love Found., 2005; spl. NIH fellow Johns Hopkins Hosp., 1961-62. Fellow ACS (bd. govs. 1977-82); mem. AIAA (Jeffries Aerospace Medicine and Life Scis. Rsch. award 2003), NAS Inst. Medicine, Am. Laryngol. Assn., Soc. Univ. Otolaryngologists-Head and Neck Surgeons (sec. 1965-69), Am. Otol. Soc., Assn. Acad. Dept. Otolaryngology-Head and Neck Surgery, Am. Laryngol., Rhinol. and Otol. Soc., Am. Soc. Head and Neck Surgery (councillor 1978-80) Am. Acad. Otolaryngology-Head and Neck Surgery (pres. 1981), Am. Coun. Otolaryngology-Head and Neck Surgery (pres. 1980-81), Am. Bronchoesophagological Assn., Soc. Head and Neck Surgeons, Acoustical Soc. Am., Collegium Oto-Rhino-Laryngologicum Amicitiae Sacrum, Johns Hopkins U. Soc. Scholars, Univ. Space Rsch. Assn. (bd. dirs. 1991-95), Tex. Corinthian Yacht Club (bd. dirs. 1978-80, 94-95), Doctors Club (bd. govs. 1967-70, 91-93), Petroleum Club, Alpha Omega Alpha. Office: 6501 Fannin Ste NA102 Houston TX 77030 Office Phone: 713-798-5906. Business E-Mail: balford@bcm.tmc.edu. *

AL-GAZALI, LIHADH, clinical geneticist, educator; MB ChB, Baghdad Med. Coll., Baghdad U., 1973; DCH (Diploma in Child Health), Royal Coll. Physicians, 1979; MSc in Human Genetics, Edinburgh U., 1983. Clin. rsch. fellow, clin. genetics Edinburgh and Leeds U., 1986—90; asst. prof., clin. genetics, Faculty of Medicine & Health Scis. United Arab Emirates U., 1990—97, assoc. prof., clin. genetics, Faculty of Medicine & Health Scis., 1997—2003, prof. clin. genetics and pediat., sr. cons. clin. genetics, dept. pediat., Faculty of Medicine & Health Sciences, 2003—. Contbr. several articles to profl. jours., chapters to books; profiled for contbn. to clin. genetics and rsch. The Lancet, 2006. Recipient Disting. Performance award in Rsch. and Clin. Svcs., United Arab Emirates U., 2003, L'Oréal-UNESCO award for Women in Science, 2008, Sheikh Hamdan award, 2009. Fellow: RCS (Ireland), Royal Coll. Pediat. and Child Health (UK); mem.: Alpha Omega Alpha. Achievements include research in clinical and molecular delineation of recessive disorders in the Arab population. Office: Faculty of Medicine and Health Sciences Dept Pediatrics United Arab Emirates U PO Box 17666 Al Ain United Arab Emirates Office Phone: 971 3 7137 415. Office Fax: 971 3 7672022. Business E-Mail: l.algazali@uaeu.ac.ae.

AL GEZAIRY, HUSSEIN ABDEL-RAZZAK, international organization administrator; b. Mecca, Saudi Arabia, 1934; Grad. in medicine, Kasr El Aini Faculty Medicine, Cairo, 1957, diploma in surgery, 1960; D (hon.), Gezira U., Sudan, 1975; PhD in Surgery (hon.), Shendi U., Sudan, 1997; ScD (hon.), Khartoum U., Sudan, 2000; DSc (hon.), Baqai Med. U., Karachi, Pakistan, 2001. Staff mem. U. Riyadh, Saudi Arabia, 1960—65; fellow Royal Coll. Surgeons, England, 1965—69; founding dean King Saud U. Faculty Medicine, Riyadh, 1969—75; min. health Govt. Saudi Arabia, 1975—82; regional dir. Ea. Mediterranean WHO, Cairo, 1982—. Founding pres. Arab Bd. Med. Specializations Supreme Coun. and Exec. Bd. Bd. trustees Islamic Orgn. Med. Sciences; mem. higher steering com. Pan Arab Project Child Devel.; mem. Madinat-al-Hikmat Coun. and Com., Karachi. Decorated King Abdul-Aziz decoration, Grade II His Majesty King Khaled Bin Abdul Aziz, Leopold II medal His Majesty King of Belgium, State Knight decoration His Majesty Sultan Haj Ahmad-Shah, King of Malaysia, Independence decoration, Grade I His Majesty King Hussein of the Hashemite Kingdom of Jordan, Lebanese Health Golden Medal of Merit, Grade I Pres. Lebanon, Lebanese Medal of Merit, First Rank, First Grade TWO NILES medal Pres. Sudan, Nat. Medal Merit, First Rank Pres. Djibouti, Hilal-i-Azam Pres. Pakistan, Medal Order of Recognition Pres. Yemen. Fellow: Royal Coll. Physicians Faculty Pub. Health Medicine, Glasgow, UK (hon.), Sudanese Coun. Med. Specializations (hon.), Coll. Physician and Surgeons, Karachi, Pakistan (hon.). Office: WHO Ea Mediterranean Regional Office Abdul Razzak Al Sanhouri St PO Box 7608 Nasr City Cairo 11371 Egypt *

AL HAJ ZEN, AYMAN, physician-scientist; b. France, Dec. 30, 1973; MD, U. Aleppo, 1997; PhD, U. Paris 7 Diderot, 2005. Rsch. fellow Necker Med. Sch., Paris, 2000—05; postdoc. rsch. fellow London Rsch. Inst. Cancer Rsch., 2006—08; postdoc. rsch. assoc. U. Bristol, 2008—10; rsch. fellow U. Oxford, 2010—. Mem.: Brit. Soc. Cardiovasc. Rsch., European Soc. Cardiology. Office: Wellcome Trust Ctr Roosevelt Dr Oxford Oxfordshire OX3 7BN England Business E-Mail: aymanzen@well.ox.ac.uk. E-mail: aymanzen@aol.com.

AL-HALEES, ZOHAIR YOUSEF, surgeon; b. Ghazza, Mar. 6, 1954; MD, King Saud U. MedSch., 1976. Cons., cardiac surgery sect. King Faisal Heart Inst., King Faisal Specialist Hosp. & Rsch. Ctr., 1986—, chmn., dir., 1995—2005, advisor cardiovasc. svcs. to CEO, 2009. Recipient King Abdulaziz High Civilian award, 1ST Medal of Honor, King, Saudi Arabia, 2007, Al Moftaha award, Aseer, Saudi Arabia, 2009, Disting. Scientist award, Al Marai Co., 2003. Fellow: ACS, Royal Coll. Surgeons Can., Internat. Acad. Chest Physician & Surgeons Am. Coll. Chest Physicians, Am. Heart Assn., Am. Coll. Cardiology. Avocation: reading. Office: King Faisal Specialist Hosp & Rsch Ctr Riyadh 11211 Saudi Arabia Office Fax: 0096614427482. Business E-Mail: alhalees@kfshrc.edu.sa.

ALHELAIL, MOHAMMED, emergency physician; b. Riyadh, Saudi Arabia, Sept. 6, 1977; s. Abdulrahman Alhelail and Aljawhara Alhamdan; m. Lubna Alsultan, Aug. 2, 2005. MBBS, King Saud U., Saudi Arabia, Riyadh, 2001. Cert. Saudi Bd. Emergency Medicine. Dep. chief residents Saudi Bd. Emergency Medicine, Riyadh, 2004—05, chief residents, 2005—. Acls instr. King Faisal Specialist Hosp. & Rsch. Ctr., Riyadh, 2005—, pediat. advanced life support instr., 2005—; pre-hosp. trauma life support instr. King Abdulaziz Med. City, Riyadh, 2005—. Recipient Dr. Abdullah Al Hodaib award for Emergency Resident of Yr., Saudi Bd. Emergency Medicine, Emergency Medicine Residents' Appreciation Day, 2004-2005; named Emergency Medicine Resident of Yr., King Abdulaziz Med. City, 2004-2005. Mem.: Pan-Arab Soc. Emergency Medicine, Am. Acad. Emergency Medicine (resident rep. to Saudi Bd. Emergency Medicine 2005, mem. com. 2005), Am. Coll. Emergency Medicine, Emergency Medicine Residents' Assn. Achievements include design of emergency medicine academic activities' calender; research in comparison of bupivacaine and lidocaine with epinephrine for digital nerve block. Avocation: travel.

AL-HILALI, NABIEH, nephrologist; b. Mansoura, Egypt, June 2, 1949; s. El-Desouki Ahmed Al-Hilali and Aisha Abdelaziz Shehato; m. Maleka Serour; children: Mohammed Nabieh, Ahmed Nabieh. MBBCh, Mansoura U., 1975; MSc in Medicine and Nephrology, Ain Shams U., 1984. Intern Faculty of Medicine Mansoura (Egypt) U., 1975—76; med. officer Mil. Svc. and Ministry Pub. Health, Cairo, 1976—77, Ministry Pub. Health, Mansoura, 1976—79; resident in gen. medicine Al Ameri Hosp., Sharq, Kuwait, 1980—81, registrar nephrology, 1981—87; nephrologist Mubarak Al Kabeer Hosp., Jabriya, 1987—90, nephrologist in charge of dialysis unit, 1991—96, nephrologist in charge Dialysis Unit, 1996—. Trainer post-graduate students and dialysis staff Mubarak Al Kabeer Hosp., 1996—; nephrologist Health Ins. Ministry of Pub. Health, Cairo, 1990—91, Hamad Al-Esa Organ Transplant Ctr., Al-Shuweikh, Kuwait, 1996; presenter in field. Contbr. articles to profl. jours. Med. officer med. svc. Egyptian Army, 1976—77. Mem.: Kuwait Med. Assn., Egyptian Med. Syndicate, Arab Soc. Nephrology and Renal Transplantation (assoc.), Egyptian Soc. Nephrology (assoc.), Al-Ahly Sporting Club.

AL HOQAIL, IBRAHIM ABDULRAHMAN, medical educator, consultant; b. Riyadh, Ar-Riyad, Saudi Arabia, Feb. 26, 1970; s. Abdulrahman Ibrahim Al-Hoqail and Hessa Mohammad Nasser; m. Hessa Abdulrahman Abdullah. MB BChir, King Saud U., Riyadh, Saudi Arabia, 1994; MS in Health Adminstrn., Wash. U., St. Louis, 2008. Cert. Saudi Coun. Health Specialties, 1995, Licentiate Med. Coun. Can., 1996, in dermatology and venereology Arab Bd. Cert., 1999, bd. cert. Saudi Coun. Health Specialties, 1999; cert. exec. master in health adminstrn. Wash. U., St. Louis, 2008. Vice dean King Saud U., Buraydah, 2001—04, chmn. dermatology dept., 2002—04, dir. rsch. ctr., 2003—04; founding dean, assoc. prof. & cons. dermatology Faculty Medicine, King Fahd Med. City, Riyadh, Ar-Riyad, Saudi Arabia, 2004—. Parttime dermatology cons. King Fahd Specialist Hosp., Buraydah, 2001—04, Qassim Specialized Clinics, Buraydah, 2001—04; dir., outpatient clinics King Khalid Hosp., Majmaha, Ar-Riyad, Saudi Arabia, 2003—04. Contbr. articles to profl. jours. Mem. Saudi Soc. Dermatology And Dermatol. Surgery, Riyadh, 2000, Saudi Soc. Med. Edn., Riyadh, 2004, Saudi Soc. Med. Health Professions Ethics, Riyadh, 2004, Medico Legal Com., Ministry Health, Riyadh, 2002—05; exec. dir. mem. King Fahd Med. City, Riyadh, 2004. Fellowship in Dermatology, King Saud U., Riyadh, Saudi Arabia, 1995—99, fellowship in Dermatopathology, U. Bc, Vancouver, Can., 2000—01. Mem.: Health Com. On Nat. Commn. Academic Accreditation & Assessment, Saudi Soc. Health Professions Ethics, Saudi Soc. Med. Edn., Saudi Soc. Dermatology & Dermatol. Surgery (dir. of chair, health adminstrn. devel. rsch. 2009). Home: Dabab Riyadh Ar-Riyad 11525 Saudi Arabia Office: Faculty Medicine King Fahd Med C Dabab 11525 Riyadh Saudi Arabia Office Phone: 966 1 463 4551. Office Fax: 0096614634487. Personal E-mail: dermapath@yahoo.com. Business E-Mail: ialhoqail@kfmc.med.sa.

ALHOQAIL, ROLA ABDULLAH, consultant, medical educator; b. Alkhobar, Eastern, Saudia Arabia, Nov. 21, 1962; d. Abdullah Ibrahim and Sameera Mohammed (Ashmar) A. FRCS Glasg., Royal Coll. Physicians and Surgeons, UK, 1992; FRCS Ed., Royal Coll. Surgeons Edinburg, UK, 1992; CABS, Arab Bd. Surgical Specialties, Riyadh, Saudi Arabia, 1993; AO/ASIF, AO Internat., Basel, Switzerland, 1998. Dipomate Advanced Hand Surgery. Demostrator gen. surgery dept. King Faisal U., Alkhobar, Saudi Arabia, 1987-92, asst. prof. surgery, 1992—; visiting fellow plastic/reconstructive surgery Dept. Plastic Surgery U. Zurich, Switzerland, 1996, Dept. Plastic surgery U. Munich, Germany, 1996; cons. plastic surgery Divsn. Plastic Surgery Gen. Surgery Dept. Kings Faisal U., Alkhobar, 1992—; assoc. prof. surgery King Faisal U., Alkhobar, 2003—; visiting fellow Plastic/Maxillofacial Dept., Basel, Switzerland, 1998—. Eastern province reg. rep. GCC Assn. Plastic Surgeons, 1997—, sec. div. plastic surgery King Faisal U., Alkhobar, 1993—. Contbr. articles to profl. jours. in the field. Public writer health edn. surgical problems Public Newspapers ALyum and AL Riyadh, 1992-99. Recipient Merit award GCC Assn. Plastic Surgeons, 1999, Merit award Riyadh Military Hosp., 1999, Merit award The Assn. Plastic Surgeons in Kuwait, 1999, award Pan African Assn. Congress of Plastic Surgery in Libya, 2002. Mem. GCC Assn. Plastic Surgeons Kuwait, GCC Assn. Orthopaedic Surgeons, Saudi Assn. Plastic and Burns Surgery (ea. province rep. exec. bd. 2002—), Am. Soc. Plastic Surgeons (corr. mem.), WADEM, Mediteranean Club Burns and Fire Diabetes. Muslim. Avocations: swimming, painting, reading poetry, listening to music, collecting stamps. Home: PO Box 116 31952 Al-Khobar Saudi Arabia Office: King Faisal U Dammam Sea Rd Dammam Saudi Arabia

ALI, ARSHAD, cardiologist, medical researcher; MBBS, Rawalpindi Med. Coll., Pakistan, 1983. Diplomate Am. Bd. Internal Medicine, 1994, with subspeciality in cardiovascular disease Am. Bd. Internal Medicine, 1998, with subspeciality in interventional cardiology ABIM, 2002. Dir. cardiology rsch. St John Hosp., Detroit, 1998—2003; dir. interventional cardiology Guthrie Clinic, Sayre, Pa., 2003—06; med. dir. Heart and Vascular Inst. Williamsport Hosp., Williamsport, 2006—07. Scholar, Govt. of Pakistan, 1977—83. Fellow: Soc. Cardiovasc. Angiography and Interventions, Am. Coll. Cardiology (licentiate); mem.: Am. Heart Assn., Royal Coll. Physicians. Independent. Muslim. Achievements include research in thrombectomy in AMI. Office: KDMC Ste G10 Ashland KY 41101 Office Fax: 570-882-3507. Personal E-mail: mdali1992@aol.com.

ALI, A.T.M. MOBAROK, clinical pharmacologist, educator; b. Gaibandha, Bangladesh, May 31, 1944; s. Amiruddin and Morium (Begum) Mondal; m. Syeda Ali, May 13, 1973; children: Mustari, Jasmin, Nabeel. MBBS, U. Rajshahi, 1967; MPhil, U. Dhaka, 1973; PhD, U. Manchester, 1978; DPhT, CPhT, US, 2005. Asst. prof. Mymensing Med. Coll. U. Dhaka, Bangladesh, 1973-75, rsch. fellow clin. pharmacology U. London, 1978-82; sr. lectr. Maiduguri U., Nigeria, 1982-86; asst. prof. King Saud U., Riyadh, Saudi Arabia, 1986—91, assoc. prof., 1991—98, prof., 1998—2006, Bangladesh Med. Coll., Dhaka, Bangladesh, 2007—. Recipient Top 100 Health Prof. award, Internat. Biographical Ctr., Cambridge, Eng., 2007, 2010. Mem. Internat. Bee Rsch. Assn., Saudi Gastroenterol. Soc., Inst. Biology London, N.Y. Acad. Scis., Bangladesh Physiology & Pharms. Soc. Achievements include research in in molecular mechanism and therapeutic potential of honey. Avocations: football, reading, gardening. Home: Waterside Plz BL-3 Road 13/A House 28 Dhanmondi R/A Dhaka 1209 Bangladesh Office: Bangladesh Medical Coll Dept Pharmacology & Therapeutics Rd 14/A Dhanmondi R/A Dhkka 1209 Bangladesh Office Phone: 00788 01726203713. E-mail: mobarok2006@yahoo.com.

ALI, HAMMAD, medical educator; b. Pakistan, July 7, 1981; MPH, U. NSW, 2009. Program officer, rsch., monitoring, evaluation and tng. Contech Internat. Health Cons., 2006—08; pub. health cons. Ctrl. Sydney GP Network, 2008, Gen. Practice - NSW, 2008—09; sr. rsch. officer, Nat. Drug & Alcohol Rsch. Ctr. U. NSW, 2008—10, assoc. lectr., Nat. Ctr. HIV Epidemiology and Clin. Rsch., 2010—. Trainer Internat. Fedn. Med. Students Assn., Asian Med. Students Assn., 2006—09. Mem.: CAS Chlamydia Working Group, NSW Health, Australian Nat. BBV and STI Surveillance Com., World Med. Assn. Avocations: travel, reading. Office: 4/86 Alison Rd Randwick Sydney NSW 2031 Australia E-mail: drhammadali@gmail.com.

ALI, HASSAN REFAT HASSAN, research scientist; b. Assiut, Egypt, Mar. 11, 1974; PhD, U. Bradford, 2009. Rschr. Luleå U. Tech., 2010—. Office: Professorvägen 15 1306 Luleå Norbotten 97751 Sweden Personal E-mail: hareha11374@gmail.com.

ALI, NAEEM A., internist, educator; Grad., Williams Coll., Mass.; MD, Ohio State U. Coll. Medicine and Pub. Health. Cert. Am. Bd. Internal Medicine, Am. Bd. Internal Medicine-Pulmonary Diseases, Am. Bd. Internal Medicine-Critical Care Medicine, Am. Bd. Internal Medicine-Sleep Medicine. Intern, dept. internal medicine Ohio State U., 1996—97, residency, dept. internal medicine, 1997—99, chief med. resident, dept. internal medicine, 2000—01, fellow divsn. pulmonary, critical care and sleep medicine, 1999—2003; asst. prof. Ohio State U. Coll. Medicine, 2003—. Office: 201 Davis Heart and Lung Research Inst 473 W 12th Ave Columbus OH 43210 Office Phone: 614-247-7707.

ALIBRAHIM, AYMAN, allergist, immunologist; MD, Aleppo Med. Sch., 1986. Diplomate Am. Bd. Pediatrics, 2003, Am. Bd. Allergy and Immunology, 2007, lic. Fla., 2003. Resident pediat. Todd Children's Hosp., 1992—95; fellow allergy and immunology Children's Hospital Med. Ctr., 1995—97; hosp. affiliations include Brooksville Regional Hosp., Citrus Meml. Hosp., Oak Hill Hosp., Spring Hill Regional Hosp. Office: Citrus Memorial Hospital 502 W Highland Blvd Inverness FL 34452-4754 Office Phone: 352-726-1551.

ALIMOGLU, MUSTAFA KEMAL, physician, educator; b. Antalya, Turkey, Mar. 1, 1966; s. Hamdi and Suheyla Alimoglu; m. Emel Durmaz, June 27, 1992; children: Efe, Yigit. MD, Akdeniz U., 1991. Lic. specialist in family medician Ministry Health Ankara State Hosp., 1994, diplomate Ministry Health Ankara State Hosp., 1998. Gen. practitioner Emergency Rm. Burdur (Turkey) State Hosp., 1991—94; resident in family medicine Ministry Health Ankara State (Turkey) Hosp., 1994—98, family physician Family Planning and Mother and Child Health Care Ctr., 1998—2001; instr. Faculty Medicine Akdeniz

U., Antalya, Turkey, 2001—05, asst. prof. Faculty Medicine, 2005—. Tnr. clin. skills, cons., planner curriculum Faculty of Medicine Akdeniz U., 2001—. Editor: Bulletin of Medical Education; translator: Ankylosing Spondylitis, 2005; contbr. articles to profl. jours. Lt. Turkish AF, 1999—2000. Recipient Bursary award, Akdeniz U. Rsch. Unit, 2005; grantee, 2005. Mem.: Assn. Turkish Family Physicians, Assn. Med. Edn. Turkey (licentiate), Internat. Primary Care Respiratory Group (assoc.), European Respiratory Soc. (assoc. grantee 2003, 2004, 2005), Turkish Diabetes Assn. Islam. Avocations: travel, reading, music. Office: Akdeniz University Faculty of Medicine Department of Medical Education Antalya 07059 Turkey Office Fax: +902422274482. Business E-Mail: kalimoglu@akdeniz.edu.tr.

ALIVERTI, ALESSANDRO, biology professor; b. Milan, Mar. 15, 1960; M in Biol. Scis., U. degli Studi di Milano, 1986, PhD in Cell & Molecular Biology, 1990. Rsch. assoc. Ludwig-Maximilians U. Munich, 1987—88; rsch. scientist Ctr. Interuniversitario per lo Studio delle Macromolecole Informazionali, 1991—2000; asst. prof., biochemistry U. degli Studi di Milano, 2001—04; assoc. prof., biochemistry U. degli Studi di Milano Dept. Biomolecular Scis. & Biotech., 2005—. Bd. reviewers FEBS Jour., 2007, Biochimica et Biophysica Acta, 2008, Jour. Am. Chem. Soc., 2009, Archives Biochemistry and Biophysics, 2009, PROTEINS: Structure, Function, and Bioinformatics, 2009. Fellowship, Inst. Confalonieri, Italy. Mem.: Italian Soc. Biochemistry & Molecular Biology (Rsch. fellowship). Avocations: literature, jazz, hiking. Office: Via Celoria 26 Milan 20133 Italy Office Fax: 39-02-50314895. Business E-Mail: alessandro.aliverti@unimi.it.

ALIVIZATOS, VASSILIOS ANDREAS, surgeon; MD, U. Bologna, Italy, 1978. Dept. surgery St. Andrew Gen. Hosp., Patras, Greece, 1987—, dir. Artificial Nutrition Unit, 2004—. Artificial nutrition unit St. Andrew Gen. Hosp., Patras, Greece, 1993—. Soldier Greek Navy, 1979—81. Mem.: Greek Soc. Parenteral and Enteral Nutrition (gen. sec.). Office: St Andrew Gen Hosp Patras Greece Personal E-mail: valiviz@hol.gr.

ALIYU, MUKTAR, physician, educator; b. Kano, Nigeria, Mar. 27, 1970; MBBS, Ahmadu Bello U., 1993; DrPH, U. Ala., Birmingham, 2005. Asst. prof. preventive medicine Mayo Clinic Coll. Medicine, 2008—09, Vanderbilt U., 2009—. Asst. prof. family & cmty. medicine, assoc. dir., occupl. medicine residency program Meharry Med. Coll., 2009—11. Recipient Dean's award, Meharry Med. Coll., W.J. Summerskill Award, Mayo Found. Med. Edn. and Rsch. Mem.: Am. Coll. Occupl. and Environ. Medicine, Am. Coll. Preventive Medicine. Avocations: reading, travel, soccer. Office: 2525 W End Ave Ste 750 Nashville TN 37211 Business E-Mail: muktar.aliyu@vanderbilt.edu.

ALIZZI, ALI, surgeon, educator; b. Iraq, Sept. 9, 1965; MBChB, Almustansiriyah U., 1989; MSc, James Cook U., MD, 2005. Sr. med. officer, sr. rsch. fellow Townsville Hosp., 2000—04; cardiothoracic surgery fellow Royal Hobart Hosp., 2004—06; cardiothoracic surgery fellow, lectr. Flinders Med. Ctr., Ashford Hosp., Flinders U., 2009—. Lectr., clin. tutor, examiner, sr. rsch. fellow James Cook U., Townsville Hosp., Australia, 2001—04; lectr. Royal Hobart Hosp., Australia, 2004—06. Recipient Graeme Duffy Meml. prize, Royal Australasian Coll. Surgeons, Australia, 2004, Ethicon prize, 2004, 2006, Burns-Alpers award, Flinders U., Australia, 2010. Mem.: Nat. Geog. Assn., Iraqi Aviation Medicine Assn., Am. Heart Valve Assn. Avocations: martial arts, music, walking. Home: 1/10 Spence Ave Myrtle Bank Adelaide 5064 Australia

ALJABRI, KHALID SALIM, endocrinologist, director; b. Makkah, Saudi Arabia, Oct. 6, 1967; MD, UBC, Vancouver, Can. Cons. endocrinology KFAAFH, Jeddah, Saudi Arabia, 2001—08. Fellow: Royal College of Physicians of Canada, American College of Physicians. Personal E-mail: khalidsalim@yahoo.com.

ALJADHEY, HISHAM, medical association administrator; b. Riyadh, Saudi Arabia, Apr. 13, 1976; PhD, U. NC, 2008. Vice dean, academic affairs, dir., medication safety rsch. chair Coll. Pharmacy King Saud U., 2008—. Cons. Saudi Food and Drug Authority, 2008—11. Recipient Walid Kyiali award, Saudi Pharm. Soc.; named Best Reviewer, Annals Internal Medicine Jour.; Govt. scholarship, Saudi Ministry of Higher Edn. Mem.: Internat. Soc. Pharmacoepidemiology. Avocation: reading. Office: KSU Coll Pharmacy PO Box 2457 Riyadh 11451 Saudi Arabia Business E-Mail: haljadhey@ksu.edu.sa.

AL-JAHDALI, HAMDAN, pulmonologist, educator; b. Saudi Arabia, Dec. 19, 1961; MD, King Abdulaziz U., 1986. Diplomate Am. Bd. Internal Medicine, Am. Bd. Pulmonary, 1994, cert. Can. Bd. Internal Medicine, Can. Bd. Pulmonary. Assoc. prof., pulmonary head, dir. sleep ctr. King Saud U. Health Scis., 2002—. Recipient King Abdullah Internat. Rsch. award, King Abdullah Internat. Med. Rsch. Ctr., 2008—09. Fellow: RCP (Can.), Am. Coll. Chest Physicians. Office: King Saud University Health Scis Riyadh 11249 Saudi Arabia Personal E-mail: jahdali@yahoo.com.

ALJEBREEN, ABDULRAHMAN M., gastroenterologist, educator; s. Mohammed and Haya Aljebreen; m. Muneera Abdullah Aljebreen, Mar. 5, 1991; children: Mohammed A., A. Abdulmalik. MD, McGill U., Montreal, 2003. Diplomate Am. Bd. Medicine, 2003. Asst. prof. medicine King Saud U., Riyadh, Saudi Arabia, 2003—07, cons. gastroenterology, assoc. prof. medicine, 2007—. Head gastroenterology King Khalid U. Hosp., Riyadh, 2004—. Contbr. scientific papers. V.p. Saudi Gastroenterology Assn., Riyadh, 2006. Fellow: Royal Coll. Physicians in Gastroenterology, Am. Soc. Gastrointestinal Endoscopy. Achievements include research in clinical gastroenterology related diseases and endoscopy. Office: King Saud Univ 11321 Riyadh Saudi Arabia

ALKADHI, KARIM A., medical researcher, educator; b. Bagdad, Iraq, July 29, 1938; BSc, U. Bagdad, 1960; MSc, SUNY Buffalo Med Sch, PhD, 1972. Prof. pharmacology & neurosci. U. Houston, 1980—. Grants, Am. Heart Assn., Epilepsy Found., NIH. Mem.: Soc. Neurosci. Avocations: reading, travel, history. Office: University Houston Coll Pharma Houston TX 77204 Business E-Mail: kalkadhi@uh.edu.

ALKANDARI, JASEM RAMADAN, exercise physiology educator; b. Kuwait, Sept. 13, 1950; s. Ramadan Mohammad Alkandari and Fatma Mohammad Abdulrazzak; m. Haifa Abdulla Alrowaih, Oct. 30, 1960; children: Mohammad Jasem, Salah Jasem. PhD, La. State U., Baton Rouge, 1984. Prof. exercise physiology, faculty medicine Kuwait U., 1984—. Cons. & dir. Wellness and Fitness Ctr., Kuwait City, 2004—; coord. Kuwait Nat. Phys. Activity Com. Mem. Nat. Bd. Pub. Athority Youth and Sports, Kuwait, 1993—98. Office: Kuwait University Faculty Medicine PO Box 24923 13110 Kuwait City Kuwait Office Fax: 965 2533 8937. Business E-Mail: ramadan@hsc.edu.kw.

ALKHALDI, ABDULAZIZ A., cardiac surgeon; m. Eman S. Alrajhi, July 15, 1997; children: Fatima A., Razan A., Lian A. MD, King Saud U., Riyadh, Saudi Arabia, 1996; MSc, McGill U., Montreal, Que., Can., 2001. Clin. instr. Stanford U., Calif., 2004—06; cons. adult & pediatric cardiac surgery King Abdulaziz Med. City, Riyadh, 2006—. Asst. prof. King Saud U. Health Sci., Riyadh, 2007—. Contbr. scientific papers. Recipient Wilfred-Biglew Rsch. award, Terrence-Donnelly Heart Ctr., 2002, Resident Rsch. award, Can. Inst. Health Rsch., 2002; Postgrad. Tng. scholarship, Saudi Nat. Gaurd Health Affairs, 1998—2006, Cardiothorasic Transplantation fellowship, Stanford U., 2005, Pediatric & Adult Congenital Cardiac Surgery fellowship, 2006. Fellow: Royal Coll. Physician & Surgeons Can.; mem.: Internat. Soc. Heart & Lung Transplantation, Norman Shumway's Soc. Achievements include patents for utilization of genetically engineered stem cells for protien delivery in matrigel; first to Middle East for surgical reconstruction of pulmonary artery anomalies. Office: King Abdulaziz Cardiac Ctr PO Box 22490 MC 1413 Riyadh 11426 Saudi Arabia Office Fax: 966-1-2520088 ext.16700. Business E-Mail: khaldiab@ngha.med.sa.

ALKHARFY, KHALID M., pharmacist, educator; s. Mohammed I. Alkharfy and Moudi S. Almajhad; m. Ibtesam A. Alhendi; children: Marwah K., Addibah K., Luay K., Ghiadah K. B in Pharm. Scis., King Saud U., Riyadh, 1992; PharmD, U. Tenn., 1997; PhD, U. Pitts., 2002. Registered pharmacist Riyadh. Asst. prof., coord. pharmacokinetics/pharmacodynamics rsch. lab. King Saud U., Riyadh, 2002—; critical care medicine and anesthesia drug therapy specialist King Khalid U. Hosp., Riyadh, 2002—. Chmn. sci. and continuing edn. com. Saudi Pharm. Soc., Riyadh, 2005—. Recipient rsch. award, U. Pitts., 2001, Outstanding Contbn. award, Kuwait Pharm. Assn., 2004; grantee, King Saud U., 2005. Mem.: Saudi Pharm. Soc. (corr. Outstanding Contbn. award 2003), European Soc.Clin. Pharmacy (assoc.), Internat. Soc. for Study of Xenobiotics (assoc.), Am. Assn. Pharm. Scientists (assoc.). Muslim. Achievements include co-founding of "Society and Medications," the first TV show in Saudi Arabia to enhance public awareness of the use of medicines. Avocations: reading, travel.

AL-KHAWARI, HANAA, medical educator; d. Al-Khawari and Al-Yaqout. MBBCh, Faculty Medicine, Kuwait U., 1989. Registrar Ministry Health, Kuwait, 1994—95, sr. registrar, 1995—99, cons. radiologist, al-amiri hosp, 1999—, chairperson of al-amiri hosp, 2003—06, chairperson al-amiri hosp., 2008—; asst. prof., faculty medicine Kuwait U., 1999—2005, assoc. prof., faculty medicine, 2005—, chairperson radiol. sci. dept. faculty allied health, 2007—08. Chairperson of al-amiri hosp. Ministry of Health, Kuwait, Kuwait, Kuwait, 2003—06; chairperson radiol. sci. dept. Faculty of Allied Health, Kuwait U., Kuwait, Kuwait, Kuwait, 2007—08; chairperson al-amiri hosp. Ministry of Health, Kuwait, Kuwait, Kuwait, 2008—; cons. radiologist Ministry of Health, Al-Amiri Hosp., 1999—. Author: (book) MRI. Mem. health awareness Kuwait Med. Assn., 1999—2005. Grantee MRI, U. Coll. Hosp., UK, 1997, Pediatric Radiology, Gt. Ormond St. Hosp., UK, 1998. Fellow: FFR RCSI, Royal Coll. Surgeons, Dublin, Royal Coll. Radiologist. Achievements include research in MRI breast. Avocations: reading, travel. Personal E-mail: hkhawari@gmail.com.

AL-KHAYAT, JANAN QASSIM, consultant physician and gastrointestinal endoscopist; b. Mosul, Iraq, Apr. 14, 1953; arrived in United Arab Emirates, 2000; s. Qassim Muhildeen and Ramzy-iah Mahmoud Al-Khayat; m. Alaa Abid Yasin Al-Wizwazi, Sept. 12, 1996; children: Ula, Sali, Sama, Aya, Tabarak, Muhammad, Tuga. MB, BChir, Basrah Coll. Medicine, Iraq, 1978; Diploma in Medicine, Al-Mustansyriah Coll. Medicine, Baghdad, Iraq, 1990. Bd. cert. internal medicine Arab Bd. Coun. Jr. ho. physician Baghdad Main Hosp., 1978—79; gen. practitioner Rutba Hosp., Anbar, Iraq, 1985—86; sr. ho. physician Yarmouk Tchg. Hosp., Baghdad, 1986—90; physician in charge, mgr. Infectious Diseases Hosp., Tikrit, Iraq, 1990—92; cons. physician, hepatitis unit mgr. Tikrit Gen. Hosp., 1993—2000, endoscopy unit mgr., 1994—2000; lectr. dept. medicine Tikrit Coll. Medicine, 1995—98, asst. prof. dept. medicine, 1999—2000; cons. physician, gastroenterologist Nat. Hosp., Abu Dhabi, United Arab Emirates, 2000—04, Ruwais Hosp., Abu Dhabi, 2005—. Mem. nat. com. for hepatitis Ministry Health Iraq, Baghdad, 1993—2000; AIDS Ctr. mgr. Tikrit Gen. Hosp., 1998—2000; mem. allergy diploma bd. Tikrit U. Coll. Medicine, 1998—2000; head local med. com. Salahuddim Med. Authority, Tikrit, 1996; mem. infection control com. Ruwais Hosp., Abu Dhabi, 2005—, mem. morbidity and mortality com., 2005—, mem. theatre users com., 2005—, mem. pharmacy com., 2005—, mem.disaster com., 2005. Contbr. more than 20 articles to profl. jours. Lt. Iraqi Air Force, 1980—84. Mem.: ACP, Internat. Iraqi Doctors Assn. Sharjah, Iraq Doctors Assn. Muslim. Achievements include research in detection of know-how of the synthesis of Prednisolone; detection of know-how of the synthesis of Niclosamide. Avocations: reading, swimming, classical music, music, travel. Office: Ruwais Hosp PO Box 898 Abu Dhabi United Arab Emirates Office Phone: 9712 8027746. Business E-Mail: jmuhildeen@adnoc.com. E-mail: drjananqa@hotmail.com, drjananqa2005@yahoo.com.

ALKHOURI, NAIM, physician; b. Damascus, Syria, July 15, 1976; MD, Damascus U., 2000. Hepatologist Cleve. Clinic, 2010—. Recipient F. Merlin Bumpus Jr. Investigator award, Cleve. Clinic, 2009; Rsch. fellowship, North Am. Soc. Pediatric Gastroenterology, Hepatology, and Nutrition, 2010, grant, Salix Pharms. Inc., 2011. Mem.: Am. Coll. Gastroenterology, Am. Assn. for Study of Liver Diseases. Office: 9500 Euclid Ave A111 Cleveland OH 44195 Office Fax: 216-444-2974. Business E-Mail: alkhoun@ccf.org.

ALKIRE, MICHAEL T., anesthesiologist, researcher; s. Lloyd Gordon and Lydia Ann Alkire; m. Monica L. Brown; children: Erik, Claire. BS, U. Oreg., 1984; MD, UCLA, 1990. Diplomate Am. Bd. Anesthesiology. Asst. clin. prof. U. Calif., Irvine, 1995—99, asst. prof. residence, 1999—2006, assoc. prof., 2006—. Fellow ctr. neurobiology learning and memory U. Calif., 2004—. Grantee, NIH, 2002—. Mem.: Am. Soc. Anesthesiologists. Achievements include first to use PET-Fluoro-Deoxy-glucose brain imaging in volunteers for anesthesia research; discovery of role played by the amygdala in mediating anesthetic involved amnesia; role played by the thalamus in mediating anesthetic induced unconsciousness. Office: U Calif 101 City Dr S Orange CA 92868 Office Fax: 714-456-7702.

ALKON, ELLEN SKILLEN, physician; b. LA, Apr. 10, 1936; d. Emil Bogen and Jane (Skillen) Bogen Rost; m. Paul Kent Alkon, Aug. 30, 1957; children: Katherine Ellen (dec.), Cynthia Jane, Margaret Elaine. BA, Stanford U., 1955; MD, U. Chgo., 1961; MPH, U. Calif., Berkeley, 1968. Diplomate Nat. Bd. Med. Examiners, Am. Bd. Pediat., Am. Bd. Preventive Medicine in Pub. Health. Chief sch. health Anne Arundel County Health Dept., Annapolis, Md., 1970-71; practice medicine specializing in pediat. Mpls. Health Dept., 1971-73, dir. MCH, 1973-75, commr. health, 1975-80; chief preventive and pub. health Coastal Region of Los Angeles County Dept. Health Svcs., 1980-81; chief pub. health West Area Los Angeles County Dept. Health Svcs., 1981-85; acting med. dir. pub. health Los Angeles County Dept. Health, 1986-87, med. dir. pub. health, 1987-93; med. dir. Coastal Cluster Health Ctrs. L.A. County Dept. Pub. Health Svcs., 1993-96, CEO, 1996-98, med. dir., 1998-2000; dir. Pub. Health Edn. Physician, 2000—11. Adj. prof. UCLA Sch. Pub. Health, 1981—; adminstr. vis. nurses svc., Mpls., 1975-80. Fellow Am. Coll. Preventive Medicine, Am. Acad. Pediat.; mem. So. Calif. Pub. Health Assn. (pres. 1985-86, 04), Minn. Pub. Health Assn. (pres. 1978-79), Am. Pub. Health Assn., Calif. Conf. Local Health Officers (pres. 1990-91), Calif. Ctr. for Pub. Health Advocacy (pres. 2002-03), Calif. Acad. Preventive Medicine (pres. 1988-92, 2003-05), Delta Omega, Am. Assn. Pub. Health Physicians(v.p., 2010-) Office: LA County Dept Pub Health 313 N Figueroa St Rm 227B Los Angeles CA 90012 Office Phone: 213-250-8688. Business E-Mail: ealkon@ph.lacounty.gov.

ALLAHVERDIYEVA, LALA, pediatrician, educator; b. Baru, Azerbaijan, Dec. 28, 1950; d. Ismayil and Roza Yusufzade; m. Allahverdiyer Haley, Apr. 23, 1985; 1 child, Allahverdiyeva Aysel. BS, Azerbaija Med. U., 1974; MD, Azerbaijan Med. U., 2005. Docent Dept. Children Diseases Azerbaijan Med. U., Baku, Azerbaijan, 1993—2000, asst. prof., 2000—04, prof., 2005—. Cons. in field. Co-author. Jr. lt. Azerbaijan Army. Recipient medal, Encyclopedia of Famous Ladies of Azerbaijan, 2002. Mem.: European Acad. Allergy and Clin. Immunology, World Allergy Org. Avocations: tennis, swimming, reading, travel. Office: Azerbaijan Med Univ Bakikhanov str Baku Azerbaijan Home: Jaffarov Garda Shlari 21 Apt 17 Baku Azerbaijan

ALLAM, SALAH EL-DIN MAHMOUD, psychologist, educator; b. Cairo, Dec. 30, 1940; s. Mahmoud Ali Allam and Amina Ela Hassan; m. Kamilia Mohamed Abd-Elmageed; children: Ehab, Dalia. BSc in Math. and Edn., Ain Shams U., Cairo, 1960; Higher Diploma in Edn., Ain Shams U., 1964, MEd in Ednl. Psychology, 1971; PhD in Ednl. Measurement and Stats., U. Mich., 1980. Tchr., sr. tchr. math. various hs, Cairo, 1960—72; asst. lectr. Coll. for Women Ain Shams U., Cairo, 1972—77; rsch. assoc. U. Mich., Ann Arbor, 1974—80; lectr., assoc. prof. Coll. Edn. Al-Azhar U., Cairo, 1980—91, prof., 1991—. Lectr. Coll. Arts Kuwait U., 1983—87; vis. prof. Coll. Edn., Saudi Arabia, 1989, United Arab Emirates, 96, Bahrain, 2003; cons. Ednl. Bur. for the Gulf Arab States, Kuwait, 1984—87, UNESCO, Kuwait, 1985—87, Jordan, 1989—93, Ministry of Edn., United Arab Emirates, 1999—2001; head evaluation dept. Nat. Ctr. for Evaluation, Cairo, 1996—97; advisor to dir. gen. IBC, Cambridge, England, 2007; v.p. recognition bd. World Congress Arts and Scis., England, 2007. Author: Modern Advances in Educational and Psychological Assessment, 1986 (Kuwait U. award, 1986), Teacher's Manual for Developing Modern Achievement Tests, 1995 (award, Ministry Edn., Qatar, 1995), Data Analysis in Educational, Behavioral and Social Sciences, 2003 (award, 2003); translator: Educational Psychology, 2009; author: Item Response Models, 2005, Authentic Assessment, 2009, Item Response Theory: Undimensional & Multidimensional, 2005, Alternative Assessment, 2009, Educational Institutional Assessment, 2009; translator: Assessment of Students with Special Needs, 2009; author: Educational and Psychological Measurement & Evaluation, 2011, Inferential Statistics in Educational Research, 2011, Quality Education and Value Added Assessment, 2011; translator: Qualitative Research in Psychology, 2003, Educational Research: Competencies for analysis and application, 2011. Mem. Benevolent Soc., Cairo, 1990—. Recipient Recognition award, U. Mich., 1981, award, Dar Alfikr Alarabi Pub. Co., 2004, Cert. of Recognition, Emirates U., 1996, Nur-Al Hussein Assn., Jordan, 1996, Emirates Recognition award, Ministry Edn., 2000, World Lifetime Achievement award, ABI, 2008, Lifetime Sec. Gen. award, United Cultural Convention ABI USA; named 500 Greatest Genuises 21st Century, US ABI, 2009; named one of Outstanding Intellectuals of 21st Century, IBC, Eng., 2008, Cambridge Blue Book Formost Internat. Intellectuals, 2009; named to Internat. Biographical Dictionarie, US, Am. Hall of Fame, ABI, 2008. Mem.: People-to-People Amb. Programs(US), Arab Coun. for Gifted and Talented (founder), Jordan, Egyptian Psychol. Assn., Am. Ednl. Rsch. Assn. Avocations: reading, travel, sports. Home: 52 Al-Nozha St Rabaa Bldgs Madinet Nasr Cairo Egypt Office: Al Azhar Univ Coll of Edn Madinet Nasr Cairo Egypt Office Phone: 20224038956. Office Fax: 00 02 240389567. Personal E-mail: salaheldinallam@hotmail.com.

ALLAN, JANET D., dean, nursing educator; BSN, Skidmore Coll., Saratoga Springs, NY, 1964; MS in Cmty. Health Nursing, U. Calif., San Francisco, 1968; PhD in Med. Anthropology, U. Calif., San Francisco, Berkeley. Cert. adult nurse practitioner, ANA. Dean, prof. U. Tex. Health Sci. Ctr. Sch. Nursing, San Antonio, U. Md. Sch. Nursing, Balt., 2002—. Mem. Robert Wood Johnson Adv. Panel; mem. health adv. com., Rep. Ben Cardin US House of Reps. Contbr. articles to profl. jours., chapters to books. Pres. Nat. Orgn. Nurse Practitioner Facilities, Southern Nursing Rsch. Soc.; bd. dirs. Am. Acad. Nursing; bd. mem. Assn. Prevention Tchg. and Rsch. Recipient Disting. Rschr. award, Southern Nursing Rsch. Soc., 2001, Nursing Excellence award, Nurseweek mag., 2002; named one of Md. Top 100 Women, 2004, 2006. Mem.: Am. Assn. Colls. of Nursing (mem. healthy people curriculum task force 2004—, bd. dirs.). Office: Univ Md Sch Nursing Ste 505D SNB 655 W Lombard St Baltimore MD 21201-1579

ALLAN, SUSAN, academic administrator, former public health service officer; BA in Math., Seattle Univ., 1972; JD, Harvard Univ., Mass., 1977, MD, 1981; MPH, Johns Hopkins Univ., Balt., 1992. Cert. Am. Bd. Preventive Medicine. Public health physician & med. supr. Arlington County Dept. Human Svc., Va., dir. public health svc. Va., 1987—2004; pub. health dir., state health officer Oreg. Dept.

Human Svcs., Portland, 2004—07; dir., Northwest Ctr. Pub. Health Practice U. Wash., Seattle, 2008—. V.p. Coun. on Edn. Pub. Health; mem. bd. on population health and pub. health practice Inst. Medicine. Fellow: Am. Coll. Preventive Medicine. Office: Northwest Ctr Pub Health Practice Univ Wash 1107 NE 45th St Ste 400 Box 354809 Seattle WA 98195-4809 Office Phone: 206-685-1130. Business E-Mail: susallan@u.washington.edu.

ALLBRIGHT, KARAN ELIZABETH, psychologist, consultant; b. Oklahoma City, Jan. 28, 1948; d. Jack Gahnal and Irma Lolene (Keesee) Allbright. BA, Okla. City U., 1970, MAT, 1972; PhD, U. So. Miss., Hattiesburg, 1981. Cert. nat. sch. psychologist, psychometrist, lic. psychologist Okla., Ark. Psychol. technician Donald J. Bertoch, PhD, Okla. City, 1973-76; asst. adminstr. Parents' Assistance Ctr., Okla. City, 1976-77; psychology intern Burwell Psycho-ednl. Ctr., Carrollton, Ga., 1980-81; staff psychologist Griffin Area Psychoednl. Ctr., Ga., 1981-85; clinic dir. Sequoyah County Guidance Clinic, Sallisaw, Okla., 1985-88; psychologist Baker Psychiat. Clinic, Ft. Smith, Ark., 1988-90; cons. Harbor View Mercy Hosp., 1988-90, Integris Bethany Med. Ctr., 1992-99; pvt. practice Okla. City, 1990—, Mercy Health Ctr., 1996—. Cons. Family Alliance (Parents Anonymous) Sequoyah County, 1985-88; lectr. in field.; bd. dir. workshops. Mem. Task Force to Prevent Child Abuse, Fayette County, Ga., 1984-85, Task Force on Family Violence, Spalding County, Ga., 1983-85, Oklahoma County Child Abuse Task Force, 2006; assoc. bd. dir. Lyric Theatre. Named to Outstanding Young Women in Am., 1980. Mem. APA, Okla. Psychol. Assn. Nat. Register Health Svc. Providers in Psychology, Registry Oklahoma City (bd. dirs.), Okla. County Mental Health Assn., Okla. City Orch. League, Psi Chi, Delta Zeta (chpt. dir. 1970-72), Okla. City Mus. Art, Okla Zool. Soc. Republican. Presbyterian. Home: 3941 NW 44th St Oklahoma City OK 73112-2517 Office: Northwest Mental Health Assocs 3832 N Meridian Ave Oklahoma City OK 73112-2849 Office Phone: 405-949-9322.

ALLEGRA, EUGENIA, otolaryngologist, educator; b. Catania, Italy, Sept. 27, 1960; Degree in Biology, U. Catania, 1985, degree in Medicine, 1990, degree in Otolaryngology, 1994. Postdoc. rschr. U. Catania, 1999—2003; otolaryngologist Ospedale Garibaldi, Catania, 2004—08; aggregate prof. U. Catanzaro, 2008—. Cons. Med. Com. Disability Support Dept. Fin., 1997—2003. Grant, Ministry Health. Mem.: Italian Assn. Head and Neck Oncology, Italian Soc. Otolaryngology, Am. Assn. Otolaryngology- Head and Neck Surgery. Office: Magna Græcia University Catanzaro Viale Europa Catanzaro 88100 Italy

ALLEGRA, LUDWIG A., plastic surgeon; married; 2 children. MD, Tufts U., 1978. Diplomate Am. Acad. Facial Plastics and Reconstructive Surgery, Am Bd. Otolaryngology. Pvt. practice, Seattle, 1983—; resident in otolaryngology Univ. Wash. Med. Ctr.; resident in gen. surgery Rhode Island Hospital- Lifespan; founder Northwest Nasal Sinus Ctr; dir dept of otolaryngology Northwest Face med and aesthetic Ssvcs. Fellow: Am. Acad. of Sleep Medicine, ACS, Am. Acad. of Cosmetic Surgery. Office: Northwest Face Medical and Aesthetic Services 3100 Carillon Point Kirkland WA 98033 Office Phone: 425-576-1700.

ALLEN, HOWARD NORMAN, cardiologist, educator; b. Chgo., Nov. 19, 1936; s. Herman and Ida Gertrude (Weinstein) Allen; children: Michael Daniel, Jeffrey Scott. BS, U. Ill., Chgo., 1958, MD, 1960. Diplomate Am. Bd. Internal Medicine, Am. Bd. Cardiovasc. Disease, Nat. Bd. Med. Examiners. Intern Los Angeles County Gen. Hosp., LA, 1960—61; resident in internal medicine Wadsworth VA Med. Ctr., LA, 1961, 1964—66; fellow in cardiology Cedars-Sinai Med. Ctr., LA, 1966—67, dir. cardiac care unit Cedars of Lebanon Hosp. div., 1968—74, dir. Pacemaker Evaluation Ctr., 1968—89, dir. Cardiac Noninvasive Lab., 1972—88; Markus Found. fellow in cardiology St. George's Hosp., London, 1967—68; attending physician cardiology svc. Sepulveda (Calif.) VA Med. Ctr., 1972—86; program dir. Cardiology-Heart Inst. Grand Rounds, Cedars-Sinai Med. Ctr., 1978—2010; pvt. practice Beverly Hills, Calif., 1988—. Asst. prof. medicine UCLA, 1970—76, assoc. prof., 1976—84, adj. prof., 1984—88, clin. prof., 1988—; cons. Sutherland Learning Assocs., Inc., LA, 1970—75; cardiology cons. Occidental Life Ins. Co., LA, 1972—86. Contbr. articles to profl. jours., chapters to books. Commr. L.A. County Emergency Med. Svcs., 1989—91. Capt. M.C. US Army, 1962—63, Korea. Recipient Lou Liay Spirit award, U. Ill. Alumni Assn. at Chgo., 2005; fellow, NSF, 1958, NIH, 1966—67. Fellow: ACP, Am. Coll. Cardiology (Calif. chpt. dist. councilor 1999—2003, chmn. fellows in tng. com. 2006—); mem.: Shakespeare Globe 1000 Club, Am. Heart Assn. (bd. dirs. 1979—94, fellow coun. clin. cardiology, pres. Greater L.A. affiliate 1987—88, Disting. Svc. award 1988, Heart of Gold award 1994), U. Ill. Alumni Assn. (life; Loyalty award 1996, Lou Liay Spirit award 2005), Cedars-Sinai Alumni Assn. (exec. bd. 1999—, sec., treas. 2000, pres. 2001—02, Alumnus of Yr. 2008), Big Ten Club So. Calif. (bd. dirs.), Pi Kappa Epsilon, Alpha Omega Alpha. Office: 414 N Camden Dr Ste 1100 Beverly Hills CA 90210-4532 Office Phone: 310-652-4600. Business E-Mail: allen@cvmg.com.

ALLEN, HUGH DARYL, pediatric cardiologist, educator; b. Wadsworth, Ohio, 1940; MD, U. Cin., 1966. Diplomate Am. Bd. Pediat., cert. in pediatric cardiology. Intern pediat. Hennepin County Med. Ctr., Mpls., 1966—67; resident pediatric cardiology U. Minn. Hosp., Mpls., 1967—69, fellow, 1969—73; prof. pediat. U. Ariz.; chief pediatric cardiology divsn. Nationwide Children's Hosp., Columbus, Ohio, 1988—2001, physician-in-chief; prof. pediat. Ohio State U. Coll. Medicine, 1988—, exec. vice chair clin. affairs, dept. pediat., vice chair academic affairs. Editor: Moss and Adam's Heart Disease of Children and Adolescents 7th Edit.; contbr. articles to profl. jours., chapters to books. Maj. Med. Corps US Army. Recipient Disting. Educator award, Ohio State U. Coll. Medicine, 2007; named one of Best Doc.'s in America, Best Doctors Inc., 2005—08. Mem.: Am. Acad. Pediat. (mem. sub-bd. pediatric cardiology, mem. exec. com.), Am. Heart Assn. (v.p. councils, mem. exec. com., mem. bd. dirs.). Achievements include research in the effects of muscular dystrophy on the heart. Office: ED622 Childrens Hosp 700 Childrens Dr Columbus OH 43205 Office Phone: 614-722-2540. Business E-Mail: allen.13@osu.edu.

ALLEN, JANET, biomedical researcher; BS in Biochemistry, with honors, U. London, 1974; MD, Royal Free Hosp. Sch. Medicine. Postdoc. fellow Royal Postgrad. Med. Sch., London, Harvard Med. Sch.; faculty U. Cambridge, 1990—94; chair molecular medicine U. Glasgow, Scotland, 1994; dir. cell & molecular biology Pfizer Inc., Fresnes, France; dir. discovery biology Inpharmatica; dir. Univ. Coll. Dublin Conway Inst. Biomolecular & Biomed. Rsch., Ireland, 2005—08; dir. rsch. Biotech. & Biological Scis. Rsch. Coun., England, 2008—, chair Global Food Security Programme Devel. Bd. Vis. prof. Univ. Glasgow, 2002, Imperial Coll. Sch. Medicine, 2002. Contbr. scientific papers to profl jours. Fellow: Royal Soc. Edinburgh. Office: BBSRC Polaris House North Star Ave SN2 1UH Swindon England

ALLEN, JEFFREY A., neurologist, educator; b. Mich., Aug. 27, 1975; MS, Northwestern U., 1999; MD, Wayne State U., 2003. Resident New England Med. Ctr., 2007; fellow Brigham & Women's Hosp., Boston, 2008; asst. prof. Ken and Ruth Davee Dept. Neurology Northwestern U. Feinberg Sch. Medicine. Contbr. articles to med. jours. Office: Northwestern University Feinberg School of Medicine Abbott Hall Suite 1123 710 N Lake Shore Dr Chicago IL 60611 Office Phone: 312-908-5035. Business E-Mail: jallen1@nmff.org.

ALLEN, JEFFREY C., pediatric neurologist, educator; MD, Harvard U., 1969. Diplomate in child neurology Am. Bd. Psychiatry and Neurology, cert. in psychiatry and neurology. Intern U. Wash. Harborview Hosp., Seattle, 1969; resident in pediat. Montreal Children's Hosp., McGill U., 1969; resident in neurology Montreal Neurol. Inst., McGill U., 1969; dir. pediatric neuro-oncology program Meml. Sloan-Kettering Cancer Ctr., 1976—86; chmn. pediatric neurology dept. Beth Israel Med. Ctr., Singer Divsn., 1995—2004; prof. neurology NYU Med. Ctr., Otto and Marguerite Manley and Making Headway Found. prof. pediatric neuro-oncology, dir. pediatric neuro-oncology; founder, med. dir. Children's Brain Tumor Found. Prin. investigator NIH, 1992—95; various leadership positions Children's Cancer Study Group. Mem. editl. bd.: Jour. Neuro-oncology; contbr. articles to profl. jours. Fellow Royal Coll. of Physicians and Surgeons (Can.); mem. Child Neurology Soc., Am. Acad. Neurology. Office: NYU Med Ctr Hassenfeld Clinic 160 E 32nd St & 2nd Ave New York NY 10016 Office Phone: 212-263-9907. Office Fax: 212-263-8410.

ALLEN, JESSE OWEN, III, organizational behavior specialist; b. Albany, Ga., Apr. 7, 1938; s. Jesse Owen Jr. and Erma Hazel (Pearson) A.; children by previous marriage: Charlotte Renee, Garrett Owen, Cheryl Hazel; m. Barbara Joanna Smith Ozment, May 23, 1987; 1 stepchild, Pamela Ozment Cartee. LLB, LaSalle Law Sch., 1967; AS, U. State N.Y., Albany, 1978, BS in History, Lit. and Bus., 1986; MA in Philosophy, Calif. State U., 1987; PhD in Organizational Behavior, The Union Grad. Sch., 1991; postgrad., Oxford U., England, 1997. Founder, pres. Specific Action Corp., Greensboro, NC, 1971—; pres. Inst. Christian Studies, Inc., Greensboro, 1987—, Christian Family Online, Inc., 2001—; prof. mgmt. Laurel U., 1993; founder first dean Sch. Mgmt. John Wesley Coll., 2008, exec. v.p., 2010—. Lectr., cons. in field. Author: Weatherization Production Control, 1978, Personal Profile Labs 1980, Management Power: The Specific Action Way, 1985, Personality Power: The Specific Action Way, 1988, Master of Personal Excellence Program, 1994; contbr. articles to profl. jours., Specific Action Management System, 1996, Specific Action Personality System, 1996, Specific Action Team System, 1997, patentee Allen valve, 1967. With 40th Congressional Nat. Prayer Breakfast, 1992, Gallup Orgn., Washington, 2002, Carolina Presdl. Bus. Commn., 2004, 54th Congressional Nat. Prayer Breakfast, 2006. With USMC, 1955—64, capt. US Merchant Marines, 1993—99, with US Coast Guard Aux., 1993—95. Named to Hon. Order of Ky. Cols., Commonwealth of Ky., 1978, Hon. Adm. State of Nebr., 1978. Mem. High Point City Club, NC, Piedmont City Club, Winston-Salem, NC. Republican. Avocations: yachting, cruising, deep-sea fishing. Home: 520 Lindley Rd Greensboro NC 27410-4933 Office: Specific Action Corp PO Box 19125 Greensboro NC 27419-9125 Office Phone: 336-854-9494.

ALLEN, JULIAN LEWIS, pediatric pulmonologist, medical educator; b. Elizabeth, NJ, Oct. 7, 1952; s. Eugene Murray and Beatrice (Hyman) Allen; m. Debra Lynne Stoll, June 4, 1978; children: Eli, Jeremy. BA, Columbia U., NYC, 1974, MD, 1978. Diplomate Am. Bd. Pediat., cert. in pediatric pulmonology. Intern pediatric pulmonary medicine Columbia-Presbyn. Med. Ctr., NYC, 1978-79, resident pediatric pulmonary medicine, 1979-81; fellow pediatric pulmonology Boston Children's Hosp., 1981-84; instr. pediat. Harvard Med. Sch., Boston, 1984-86; asst. prof. pediat. Temple U. Sch. Medicine, Phila., 1986-90, assoc. prof., 1990-95, prof., 1995-97; prof. pediat. Allegheny Univ. Health Scis., Hahnemann Med. Sch., Pa., 1997-98; prof. pediat., Robert Gerard Morse chair pulmonary medicine U. Pa. Sch. Medicine, 1998—; attending physician, acting chief divsn. pulmonary medicine/cystic fibrosis ctr. Children's Hosp. Phila., 1998-99, chief, 1999—. Attending physician pulmonary disease Children's Hosp., Boston, 1984—86, St. Christopher's Hosp. Children, Phila., 1986—98, dir. pulmonary function lab., 1986—94, sect. chief pediatric pulmonary medicine, 1994—98; mem. sub bd. on pediat. pulmonology Am. Bd. Pediat., 2001—06, chmn., 2005—06. Author: The Children's Hospital of Philadelphia Guide to Asthma, 2004; mem. editl. bd. Pediat. Pulmonology, 2002—; contbr. articles to profl. jours., chapters to books. Recipient Sandoz award, Columbia U. Coll. Physicians & Surgeons, 1978; named a Top Doc for Kids, Phila. Mag., 2002; named one of Best Doc.'s in America, Best Doctors, Inc., 2001—02, 2005—08; fellow Parker B. Francis Found., 1982—86. Mem.: Soc. Pediat. Rsch., European Respiratory Soc. (joint com. on infant respiratory physiology 1990—, co-chmn. 1996), Am. Thoracic Soc. (program com. 1991—93, long range planning com. 1993—, chmn. 1996—98, pediat. assembly chmn. 1999—2001, bd. dirs. 1999—2001, rsch. advocacy com. 2000—02). Achievements include research in lung and chest wall development in infants. Avocation: violin. Office: Childrens Hosp Phila Divsn Pulmonary Medicine 34th St & Civic Ctr Blvd Philadelphia PA 19104 Office Phone: 215-590-3749. Business E-Mail: allenj@email.chop.edu.

ALLEN, MARILEE C., pediatrician, educator; b. Pittsfield, Mass., Dec. 14, 1950; BS with honors, Cornell U., 1972; MD, Johns Hopkins Sch. Medicine, 1976. Asst. prof., pediat. Johns Hopkins Sch. Medicine, 1983—90, assoc. prof., pediat., 1990—2002, prof., pediat., 2002—. Douglas Richardson meml. lectr. New Eng. Assn. Neonatologists; Ray Kroc vis. prof. James Whitcomb Riley Hosp. Children; co-dir., NICU follow-up clinic Kennedy Krieger Inst., 1988; co-editor-in-chief Devel. Disabilities Rsch. Reviews, 2002. Recipient Le JIM d'Or Gynecologie award, Le Jour. Internat. de Medicine. Fellow: Am. Acad. Pediat.; mem.: Am. Acad. Cerebral Palsy and Devel. Medicine (Richmond Cerebral Palsy Ctr. award), Soc. Pediatric Rsch., Am. Pediatric Soc. Office: Johns Hopkins Hosp Nelson 2-133 Baltimore MD 21287 Office Fax: 410-955-0398. Business E-Mail: mallen2@jhmi.edu.

ALLEN, PAMELA SMITH, retired psychologist, writer; b. Marianna, Fla., Dec. 19, 1943; d. Milton Clark Smith and Dora Bernadette Gordy; m. William Thomas Lassiter, Aug. 8, 1964 (div. 1972); 1 child, Kerry Lassiter Arnsten; m. George Young, 1974 (div. 1977); m. William Kelly, Jan. 11, 1979 (div. 1992); m. Lawrence Allen, Feb. 14, 2000 (div. Feb. 5, 2004); life ptnr. Lawrence Allen, 2005. BA, U. Fla., Gainesville, 1964; MEd, U. Fla., 1967, EdS, 1968; PhD, US Internat. U., San Diego, 1989. Lic. psychologist (inactive) Calif., marriage and family therapist (inactive) Calif., cert. pupil pers. svcs. plus psychology Calif., gen. elem. tchr. Calif. Spl. edn. tchr. Alachua County Schs., Gainesville, 1964—68, Duval County Schs., Jacksonville, Fla., 1969—70, sch. psychologist, 1970—72, spl. edn. tchr., 1972—73, Daniel Meml. Home, Jacksonville, 1973—74; 1st grade tchr. Valley Ctr. Schs., Valley Center, Calif., 1976—78; spl. edn. tchr. San Diego City Schs., 1978—79, sch. psychologist, 1979—2005; pvt. practice psychotherapist Escondido, Calif., 1990—92, Carlsbad, Calif., 1992—94. Adj. prof. US Internat. U., 1991—94; tchr. Camelrock Yoga Ctr., Valley Center, 2002—04; Tai Chi Chuan instr. Am. Universalist Temple Divine Wisdom, Valley Center, 2005—06, workshop presenter, 2004—05. Author: Enhancing Children's Creativity and Self Perceptions Through the Arts, 1989, Awakening to the Spirit Within: Eight Paths, 2004, (poetry) Unfolding, 1987; prodr.(with Barbara Morse): (game) Squnch Journey, 1993. Mem.: Assn. Rsch. and Enlightenment, Assn. Ret. Persons. Democrat. Personal E-mail: pmsmallen@yahoo.com.

ALLEN, PATRICIA JACKSON, pediatric nurse practitioner, educator; BA, U. Conn.; Master's degree in Maternal-Child Nursing, U. Calif., San Francisco. Cert. Pediatric Nurse Practitioner. Tng. Yale New Haven Hosp.; faculty mem. U. Calif., San Francisco, 1983—2003, dir., advanced practice pediatric nursing program; joined faculty Yale Sch. Nursing, 2003—, dir., pediatric nurse practitioner specialty; advanced practice registered nurse Yale U. Pediatric Primary Care Ctr. Author: Divsn. Nursing, Basic Nurse Edn. and Practice Program grant supporting edn. at Valencia Health Svcs., 2002—07; co-editor: (textbook) Primary Care of the Child with a Chronic Condition; contbr. articles to profl. jours. Recipient Outstanding Nurse Practitioner Educator award, Nat. Orgn. Nurse Practitioner Faculties, 2003, President's award for Outstanding Leadership for PNP's in Nontraditional Roles, Nat. Assn. Pediatric Nurse Practitioners, 2003. Mem.: Am. Acad. Nursing. Office: Yale Sch Nursing Rm 243 100 Church St S PO Box 9740 New Haven CT 06536 Office Phone: 203-737-2345. Office Fax: 203-785-6455.

ALLEN, RICHARD GARRETT, healthcare educator; b. St. Paul, July 8, 1923; s. John and Margaretta (Taggart) A.; m. Ida Elizabeth Vernon, July 5, 1944; children: Richard Garrett, Barbara Elizabeth, Julie Frances (dec.). BS cum laude, Trinity U., 1954; MHA, Baylor U., 1957; postgrad., Indsl. Coll. of Armed Forces, 1962, USAF Command and Staff Coll., 1962. Commd. 2d lt. Med. Svc. Corps USAF, 1948, advanced through grades to maj., 1961; served in U.S., Pacific, Germany; ret., 1964; asst. adminstr. U. Ala. Hosp. and Clinics; dir. Ctr. for Hosp. Continuing Edn., Sch. for Health Svcs., U. Ala., Birmingham, 1965-68; dir. edn. New Eng. Hosp. Assembly, Inc., New Eng. Ctr. for Continuing Edn., U. N.H., Durham, 1968-74; dir. Office Health Care Edn., 1970-74; exec. v.p. Edn. and Rsch. Found., San Francisco, 1974-77, Assn. West Hosps., 1974-77. V.p. health affairs M G & M Comm., Foster City, Calif.; pres. Calif. Coll. Podiatric Medicine; CEO Calif. Podiatry Hosp. and Outpatient Clinic, San Francisco, 1977-81; prof. health care adminstrn. St. Mary's Coll. of Calif., Moraga, 1982-85; cons. health care and edn., 1985—; owner Sleepy Hollow Books, 1985—; mem. Nat. Adv. Coun. on Vocat. Edn., 1969-71; also cons.; cons. Booz, Allen & Hamilton, Washington, Ops Rsch., Inc., Silver Spring, Md., Republic of Korea Air Force Med. Svcs., Seoul, Bio-Dynamics, Inc., Cambridge, Mass., HEALTHSAT-Appalachia Cmty. Svcs. Network, Washington, 1980—. Pub.: Hosp. Forum, San Francisco, 1974-77; contbr. articles to profl. jours. Decorated Air Force Commendation medal with oak leaf cluster. Fellow Am. Coll. Hosp. Adminstrs.; mem. Am. Soc. for Health Manpower Edn. and Tng., Am. Hosp. Assn., AAUP, Am. Soc. Hosp. Edn. and Tng. (pres. 1972), Am. Assn. Colls. Podiatric Medicine (pres. 1979-81), Sherlock Holmes Soc. London, Masons. Episcopalian. Home and Office: 96 Alicia Ct Marietta GA 30062-5173 Personal E-mail: dick78@earthlink.net.

ALLEN, ROBERT JOHNSON, plastic surgeon, educator; b. Florence, Mar. 19, 1951; s. James and Lucta Johnson Allen; m. Linda Truluck Perry Allen, June 5, 1976; children: Julia Marshall, Robert Johnson, James Perry, Celeste Blackwell. BS, Wofford Coll., Spartanburg, SC, 1972; MD, Med. U. SC, Charleston, 1976. Diplomate Am. Bd. Surgery, Am. Bd. Plastic Surgery, cert. in surgery of hand, lic. La., NY, SC. Intern/ resident gen. surgery La. State U. Med. Ctr., New Orleans, 1976—82, clin. instr. dept. surgery, 1983—88, clin. asst. prof., 1988—97, program dir. plastic surgery LSU Med. Ctr., 1987—98; microsurgery fellow NYU Med. Ctr., NYC, 1982—83; clin. assoc. prof. La. State U. Health Scis. Ctr., 1997—2004, clin. prof. plastic surgery, 2004—, chief plastic surgery, 1998—2005; staff Ctr. Microsurg. Breast Reconstruction, Charleston, NYC. Clin. prof. plastic surgery Med. U. SC, 2005—, NYU, 2007—. Editor: Seminars in Plastic Surgery, 2002; mem. editl. bd. Jour. Reconstructive Microsurgery, 1996—, Breast Diseases: A Yearbook, 1999—, Annals of Plastic Surgery, 2004; contbr. articles to profl. jours. Vol. celebrity waiter La. Breast Cancer Task Force, New Orleans, 2005. Recipient Spirit award, Am. Cancer Soc., 2003. Mem.: ACS, AMA, Am. Soc. Surgery of Hand, Southern Med. Assn. (sec.-elect 1993—97), New Orleans Surg. Soc., Am. Soc. Plastic & Reconstructive Surgeons, La. State Med. Soc., La. Surg. Soc., La. Soc. Plastic & Reconstructive Surgery (pres. 1990—91), Am. Soc. Reconstructive Microsurgery (edn. com. 1998—99), Southeastern Soc. Plastic Reconstructive Surgeons (bd. dir. 1998—2001), Am. Assn. Plastic Surgeons, World Soc. Reconstructive Microsurgery (coun. mem. 2001—03, sec. gen. 2003—06, founding mem.). Achievements include design of deep inferior episcastric perforator flap; superficial inferior episcastric artery flap; glutal artery perforator flap; first to complete breast reconstruction transplant in identical twins. Avocations: pottery, tennis, running, literature. Office: Ctr Microsurg Breast Reconstruction 125 Doughty St Ste 590 Charleston SC 29403-5744 also: 1776 Broadway Ste 1200 New York NY 10019 Office Fax: 843-727-3774. Business E-Mail: boballen@diepflap.com.

ALLEN, ROGER KENNEDY ABBOTT, thoracic and sleep physician, consultant, professor; b. Toowwoomba, Qld, Australia, Sept. 8, 1951; s. Lucius Allen and Lucy Elaine Allen née Gulbrandson; m. Linda Elena Stephenson, June 24, 1995; children: Victoria Claire, Samuel Kennedy Abbott, Roger Kennedy, Clarissa Jane, Lily Esther, Emlyn Rhys, Christian Hartley; m. Lorrene Karen Jackson, Oct. 21, 1978 (div. June 20, 1994). MMBS in Medicine and Surgery with 1st Class honors, U. Queensland, 1975; PhD, U. Melbourne, 1990. Intern Royal Brisbane Hosp., Qld, 1976—77; med. registrar Austin Hosp., Melbourne, Australia, 1977—78; thoracic med. registrar Repatriation Gen. Hosp., Melbourne, 1978—82; NH & MRC rsch. fellow Austin & Repatriation Hosp., Melbourne, 1982—85, vis. thoracic physician, 1985—87; clin. assoc. prof. Prince Charles Hosp., Brisbane, 1987—95, mem. sundry coms., 1987—2008, chmn., 1987—2008, sr. vis. thoracic & sleep physician, 1995—97, Redcliffe Hosp., Brisbane, 1995—2001; lt. col. RAAMC, Australian Army, Australia, 1987—2003; chmn. St. Andrew's War Meml. Hosp., Brisbane, 1987—2008, mem. sundry coms., 1987—2008, sr. cons. thoracic & sleep physician, 1995—2005, Wesley Hosp., Brisbane, 2005—, chmn., 1987—2008, mem. sundry coms., 1987—2008; apptd. prof. faculty health scis. & medicine Bond U., Gold Coast, Qld, 2009. Author: (novels) (autobiographic) A Ballina Boy; contbr. chapters to books, articles to profl. med. jours.;, author sundry poems. Expert witness, medicolegal Sundry Cts., Brisbane. Recipient U. medal, U. Queensland, 1976, Active Svc. medal, Australia; Rsch. grants, Prince Charles Hosp., 1987—95, Med. Rsch. grant, Wesley Rsch. Inst., 2007. Fellow: Am. Coll. Chest Physicians, Royal Australasian Coll. Chest Physicians; mem.: Société Pneumologie Langue Française, Queensland Thoracic Soc. (pres. 1998—99), Australasian Sleep Assn., World Assn. Sarcoidosis and Other Granulomatous Disorders, Australian Med. Assn., Brisbane Grammar Sch. Old Boys' Assn. Anglican. Avocation: yachting. Business E-Mail: rogerallen@sarcoidosis.com.au.

ALLEN, STEPHEN D(EAN), pathologist, microbiologist; b. Linton, Ind., Sept. 8, 1943; s. Wilburn and Betty Allen; m. Vally C. Autrey, June 17, 1964; children: Christopher D., Amy C. BA, Ind. U., 1965, MA, 1967; MD, Ind. U., Indpls., 1970. Diplomate Am. Bd. Pathology Anatomic and Clin. Pathology and Med. Microbiology. Intern in pathology Vanderbilt U. Hosp., Nashville, 1970-71, resident in pathology, 1971-74; clin. asst. prof. pathology Emory U., Atlanta, 1974-77; asst. prof. clin. pathology Ind. U., Indpls., 1977-79, asst. prof. pathology, 1979-81, assoc. prof. pathology, 1981-86, prof. pathology, 1986-92, prof. pathology and lab. medicine, 1992—, James Warren Smith prof. clin. microbiology, 2006—, assoc. dir. div. clin. microbiology, dept. pathology, 1977-92, dir. grad. progam pathology, 1986—, sr. assoc. chmn. dept. pathology, 1990-91, dir. divsn. clin. microbiology dept. pathology/lab. medicine, 1992-98, assoc. chair dept. pathology and lab. medicine & dir. labs., 1996-99; dir. disease control lab. divsn. Ind. State Dept. Health, Indpls., 1994—2004; dir. divsn. clin. microbiology dept. pathology/lab. medicine Clarian-Meth.-Ind U.-Riley Hosps., 1998—. Mem. residency rev. com. for pathology Accreditation Coun. for Grad. Med. Edn., 1996—2004, mem. residency rev. com. for molecular genetic pathology, 1999—2004, vice chmn., 2003—04, mem. molecular genetic pathology policy com., 1999—; trustee Am. Bd. Pathology, 1995—2006, life trustee, 2007—, chmn. microbiology test devel. and adv. com., 1995—2006, sec. bd., 2001—02, v.p., 2002, pres., 03, immediate past pres., 04. Co-author: Introduction to Diagnostic Microbology, 1994, Color Atlas and Textbook of Diagnostic Microbiology, 1997, 2006, Direct Smear Atlas, A Monograph of Gram-Stained Smear Preparations of Clinical Specimens, 2001, (CD-ROM) Direct Smear Atlas, 1998, Parasitology Image Atlas, 2003, Mycology Image Atlas, 2004, Bacteriology I Image Atlas, 2005; contbr. With USPHS, 1974—77. Fellow: Binford-Dammin Soc. Infectious Disease Pathologists, Infectious Diseases Soc. Am., Am. Acad. Microbiology, Coll. Am. Pathologists; mem.: Anaerobe Soc. Ams. (mem. coun. 1994—2002, pres. 2002—04), Am. Soc. Clin. Pathologists (coun. microbiology 1983—89), Masons (32d deg.), Shriners, Sigma Xi. Avocations: musicial instruments, fly fishing. Office: Ind U Sch Medicine Clarian Pathology Bldg Rm 6027 350 West 11th St Rm 6027 Indianapolis IN 46202

ALLEN, STEVEN LEE, hematologist, oncologist; b. Bklyn., Dec. 6, 1952; s. Morris and Ann A.; m. Barbara Helen Wolf, May 30, 1983; children: Jeremy Spencer, Peter Russell, Rebecca Rae. BS, CCNY, 1973; MD, Johns Hopkins U., 1977. Diplomate Am. Bd. Internal Medicine, 1980, cert. hematology 1982, med. oncology 1983. Intern NY Hosp. Cornell U., NYC, 1977-78, resident, 1978-80, fellow, 1980-83; instr. Cornell U. Med. Coll., NYC, 1982-84, asst. prof., 1984-90, assoc. prof. clin. medicine, 1990-96; asst. attending physician North Shore U. Hosp., Manhasset, NY, 1983-90, assoc. attending physician, 1990-95, attending physician, 1995—, assoc. chief, divsn. hematology, 2000—; assoc. investigator North Shore-LI Jewish Rsch. Inst., NY, 2000—. Prof. medicine Hofstra North Shore-LIJ Sch. Medicine, 2009-;prof. clin. medicine Albert Einstein Sch. Medicine,2007-; adj. assoc. prof. clin. medicine NYU Sch. Medicine, 2007-2010; assoc. prof. clin. medicine NYU Sch. Medicine, 1996—2007; adj. assoc. prof. clin. medicine N.Y. Coll. Osteo. Medicine, 1994—2011, adj. prof. clin. medicine, 2011-; prin. investigator Cancer and Leukemia Group B, 1989—. Contbr. articles to profl. jours. Jonas Salk scholar, 1973; W. Barry Wood Rsch. fellow, 1976, Jr. Faculty Clin. fellow, Am. Cancer Soc., 1984-86; Champion of Advocacy award, Am. Soc. Hematology, 2005; Outstanding Svc. award, Am. Soc. Hematology, 2006. Fellow ACP; mem. Am. Soc. Hematology, Am. Soc. Clin. Oncology, Am. Fedn. Med. Rsch., Phi Beta Kappa (Sci. medal 1973). Office: N Shore University Hosp Monter Cancer Ctr 450 Lakeville Rd Lake Success NY 11040 Office Phone: 516-734-8959. Business E-Mail: allen@nshs.edu.

ALLENDER, JULIE ANN, psychologist; b. Elmhurst, Ill., Feb. 27, 1950; d. Frank and Edith (Gluklick) A.; m. Louis Zivic, May 18, 1980 (div.); 1 child, Jonathan Ephriam Allender-Zivic. BS in Psychology, U. Ill., 1973; MEd in Psychoednl. Processes, Temple U., 1974, EdD in Psychoednl. Processes, 1978. Lic. psychologist, Pa., Mass.; cert. sch. psychologist, Pa. Asst. prin. Beth Or Congregation Religious Sch., Spring House, Pa., 1977-78; dir. Homebased Businesswomen's Network, Lebanon, Pa., 1983-88; pvt. practice psychologist Lebanon, 1980—2007, Sellersville, 2003—; staff cons. Good Samaritan Hosp., 1989—, Ranameo Abincton Hosp. Lansdale, 2004—. Former adj. faculty Community Coll. Phila., Temple U., Phila., Phila. Coll. Textile & Scis., Thomas Jefferson U. Med. Sch., Phila., Wheelock Coll., Boston, Pa. State U., Hershey, Reading; cons. med. staff Good Samaritan Hosp.; pvt. practice therapy, consultation and testing Pa. Coll. Optometry, Phila., Headstart, Chgo., Peabody (Mass.) Pub. Schs., Lynn (Mass.) Hist. Soc., Mich. Edn. Assn., Lansing, Dept. Agr. Extension Program, Lebanon, Pa., Lebanon Valley Coll., Annville, Pa., other orgns. Author: End of My Rope: Gender Cooperation Model, 1996, Chronic Illness: Healing the Wounded Heart, 1999, (ednl. program) Kids Concern, 1996; contbr. articles to profl. jours. and newspapers, chpts. to books; participant media programs Sta. WRKO, Boston, 1983, Sta. WVLV, Lebanon, 1983-84, Sta. WAHT, Lebanon, 1988-90. Active Potential Reentry Opportunities in Bus. and Edn., 1986-2003, Homebased Businesswomen's Network of the Lebanon Valley, 1983-88; mem. women in bus. com. Lebanon C. of C., 1985-87; bd. dirs. Assn. for Humanistic Edn., 1983-87; mem. women's pavilion adv. bd. Lebanon Valley Gen. Hosp., 1986-90; bd. dirs. Interagency Mental Health Coun., Inc., 1995-99; prof. PCRM Orthopsychiatric. Mem. APA, ASTD, Pa. Psychol. Assn., Lancaster-Lebanon Psychol. Assn. (treas. 1990-2000. pres. 1999-2000), Assn. Humanistic Psychology Jewish. Office Phone: 215-799-2220. Personal E-mail: jaallender@verizon.net.

ALLENDORF, JOHN D., surgeon, educator; b. NY, Apr. 13, 1971; BA, Johns Hopkins U., 1992; MD, Columbia U., 1997. Asst. prof. surgery Columbia U., NY Presbyn. Hosp., 2003—. Recipient Patients' Choice award, 2010, Allen O. Whipple Meml. prize, Columbia U. Surg. Housestaff; named one of Tchr. of Yr., 2010; grant, I.W. Found. Fellow: ACS; mem.: Soc. Surgery Alimentary Tract, Soc. Surg. Oncology, Am. Assn. Endocrine Surgeons, Am. Hepato Pancreato Biliary Assn., Phi Beta Kappa (Alpha chpt. Md.). Office: 161 Ft Washington Ave New York NY 10032 Business E-Mail: jda13@columbia.edu.

ALLEN-MEARES, PAULA G., academic administrator, social work educator; b. Buffalo, Feb. 29, 1948; d. Joe N. and Mary T. (Hienz) Allen; married; children: Tracey, Nikki, Shannon BS, SUNY, Buffalo, 1969; MSW Child Welfare, U. Ill., Urbana-Champaign, 1971, PhD Social Work and Ednl. Adminstrn., 1975; cert. mgmt., Harvard U., 1990; cert. mgmt. of mgrs., U. Mich., 1993. Lic. cert. social worker, Ill.; lic. clin. social worker, Ill. Rsch. asst. SUNY, Buffalo, 1966—69; child welfare worker Dept. Children and Family Svcs., Champaign, Ill., 1970—71; sch. social worker Urbana Sch. Dist. 116, Urbana, 1971—78; intern supr. Sch. Social Work Sch. Social Work, U. Ill., Urbana-Champaign, 1973—78, vis. lectr., 1977—78, asst. prof., 1978—83, chair Sch. Social Work Specialization, 1978—84, dir. doctoral program, 1985—89, assoc. prof., 1983—89, acting dean, 1989—90, prof., 1989—93, dean, prof., 1990—93, Sch. Social Work, U. Mich., Ann Arbor, 1993—2009, Norma Radin Collegiate prof. social work; prof. edn. Sch. Edn., U. Mich.; chancellor U. Ill., Chgo., 2009—. Scholars forum vis. lectr. U. Tex., Austin, 1992; vis. scholar Sch. Social Work, U. SC, 1994, U. Ga., Athens, 1997; manuscript and book reviewer; reviewer Social Casework, summers 1988-90; Children & Youth Svcs. Rev., 1988-90, Jour. Ethnic and Multicultural Concerns in Social Work, 1990, among others; cons. Ill. Office Edn., Pupil Pers. Svc. Unit, Springfield, 1977, Detroit Pub. Schs., 1979, Decatur (Ill.) Pub. Schs., 1979, Family Svcs. Champaign County, 1979, Dept. Pub. Instrn., State of N.C., 1979, Urbana Sch. Dist. 116, 1978-80, Ill. State Bd. Edn., 1979-81, Chgo. Pub. Schs., 1981, Champaign Pub. Schs., 1981, Vermillion County Spl. Edn. Coop., Danville, 1982, Pembroke Sch. Dist., Kankakee, Ill., 1982, Champaign Pub. Schs., 1982, Defferin-Pell Sch. Dist., Mississauga, Ont., Can., 1982, Mid-State Spl. Edn., 1983, Wis. Office Edn., Milw., 1983, D.C. Sch. Social Work, 1984, Ind. Office Edn. Pupil Pers. Divsn., Indpls., 1984, Glenbrook (Ill.) Sch. Dist., 1984-86, Kankakee Spl. Edn. Coop., 1985, N.J. State Dept. Edn. Office Cert., Trenton, 1985, Pub. Sch. Disvn., Mississauga, 1985, Budapest, Hungary, 1990, Dept. Def., 1991, Cath. Social Svcs., Indpls., 1991, Bd. Sch. Commrs., Indpls. Pub. Schs., 1991, Brown U. and Lilly Endowment, Indpls., 1992; external reviewer U. Mo., 1995, Columbia U., 2001, Wayne State U., 2002, U. Calif. Berkeley, 1995, Hunter U., 2006; keynote spkr. N.Mex., Ga., Mo. 1997; cons. in field. Author: Intervention with Children & Adolescents, 1995, (with others) Social Work Services in Schools, 1986, Controversial Issues in Social Work Research, 1995, Handbook of Social Work Direct Practice; co-editor: Methods and Issues-Evaluating Social Services in Education Settings, 1988, Adolescent Sexuality-An Overview and Principles of Intervention, 1986, Conducting Research: A Handbook For Schook Social Workers, 1988, The School Services Source Book: A Guide For School Based Professionals, 2006; mem. editl. bd. Jour. of Women in Social Work, 1990-93, Arete, 1989—, Sch. Jour. Social Work, 1986—, Ednl. and Psychol. Rsch., 1983-89, Jour. Social Svc. Rsch., 1993—, Children and Youth Svcs. Rev., 1991—, Jour. Tchg. Social Work, 1990—; cons. editor Social Work in Edn., 1978-84; editor-in-chief Social Work in Edn., 1989-93, Jour. of Social Work Edn., 1997—; tech. adv. com. Social Work in Edn. spl. edit., 1996—; mem. editl. adv. bd. Families in Contemporary Soc., 1991—; contbr. articles to profl. jours Human rels. dir. Urbana Edn., 1973-75; mem. regional adv. bd. Gifted, 1977-78; mem. planning com. Ill. March of Dimes, 1978; bd. dirs. Vol. Action Ctr. Champaign County, 1978-80, chair nomination com., ad hoc com. on bd. policy; mem. program com. Girls Club Champaign, 1978-81; mem. adv. bd. Ambulatory Care Ctr., Mercy Hosp., 1981-82; bd. dirs. devel. svcs. Champaign County, 1973-75; moderator black adoptions Children's Home and Aid Soc. Ill. and Dept. Children and Family Svcs., 1984; mem. policy com. Regional Ill. Children's Home and Aid Soc., 1980-84; bd. dirs. Family Svc. Champaign County, 1988-89; mem. Champaign county child placement rev. com. Champaign County Cir. Ct., 1985-93; trustee WT Grant Found., chair nomination com., 2004-2007. Recipient scholarship SUNY, 1966, Alumni of Yr. U. Ill., 1993, Human Rels. award Ill. Edn. Assn., 1975; fellow U. Ill., 1969-71; grantee Urban Sch. Dist. 116, 1976, Dept. Children and Family Svcs., 1983, Workshops on Prevention of Teenage Pregnancy, 1985, Dept. Edn., 1986, 89, U. Ill., 1986, Mich. Dept. Social Svcs., 1994 Mem. NASW (chair comm. com. 1993—, comm. bd. dirs., coun. editors bd. 1990—, cert., editor-in-chief Social Work in Edn. 1990—,jour. editl. bd. 1984-88, grantee 1988-92, Social Worker of Yr. Illini dist. 1992), Nat. Assn. Black Social Workers, Nat. Assn. Deans and Dirs. of Schs. of Social Work (v.p. 1993-95, v.p. 1993—, bd. dirs. 1991-93), Coun. on Social Work Edn. (treas. 1992—, bd. dirs. 1989-91, del. assembly 1988-89), Soc. Social Work Edn. and Rsch. (pres.-elect, 2001-2002, pres, 2002-2004, Padgett early career achievement award com.), NY Acad. Medicine (mem. steering com., chair, nat. adv. panel, social work leadership pub. policy com., trustee bd. trustees), Nat. Acads. Inst. Medicine (vice chair section X, mem. com., mem. health disparities interest group, com. future health care workforce older Ams.), Nat. Assn. Social Workers, An. Assn. Univ. Women, Rotary, Phi Delta Kappa, Delta Mu, Delta Kappa Gamma (Xi chpt.) Avocations: jogging, aerobics. Office: University of Illinois Office of Chancellor 2833 UH MC 102 601 S Morgan Chicago IL 60607-7128 Office Phone: 312-413-3350. Office Fax: 312-413-3393. E-mail: pameares@uic.edu. *

ALLEN-SCERBO, SUSAN LYNN, secondary education educator, counselor; b. Morristown, NJ, Apr. 15, 1950; d. Harry Moore and Rosemary (Griffin) A. BA, Monclair State U., 1972; MA, Fairleigh Dickinson U., 1978. Cert. drug and alcohol counselor; cert. tchr., N.J. Tchr. Bernards Twp. Bd. Edn., Basking Ridge, NJ, 1972—; mental health counselor St. Clares Hosp., Denville, NJ, 1987-93; pvt. practice counselor Mendham, NJ, 1991—. Mem. CORE team Ridge H.S., Basking Ridge, 1987—. Instr. ARC, Somerset County, N.J.; legis. chair Bernard Twp. Edn. Assn., Somerset County, N.J., 1994—, v.p., 1996-98, del., 1998, pres., 2001—. Gymnastics State Champion Tenn., 1970; named Counselor of yr., Somerset County, N.J., 1998. Mem. Nat. Assn. Alcohol and Drug Counselors, N.J. Assn. Alcohol and Drug Abuse Counselors. Avocations: softball, tennis, swimming, golf, gardening. Home and Office: 139 Mendham Rd E Mendham NJ 07945-3016 Fax: 973-543-1671.

ALLER, WAYNE KENDALL, psychologist, educator, computer company executive, property manager; b. Slyvia, Kans., Feb. 20, 1933; s. Alvin Ray and Florence Dorothy (Snowbarger) A.; m. Sharon Cecelia Forray, Aug. 21, 1962 (div.); children: Jay Ramzi, Joyce Amal; m. Sonia Y. Konialian, Apr. 8, 1969 BA in Physics, N.W. Nazarene Coll., Nampa, Idaho, 1955; MS in Psychology, U. Wash., 1960, PhD in Psychology, 1964. Asst. prof. psychology Pacific Lutheran U., 1962-64; asst. prof., chmn. divsn. behavioral scis. Beirut Coll. for Women, 1964-67; assoc. prof. Mankato State Coll., Minn., 1967-68, Ind. State U., Terre Haute, 1968—85, prof., 1985—, acting chair, psychology dept., 2001—02; pres. Learning Unlimited, 1983—, CompuLearn, 1983-87. Adj. prof. psychology Calif. State U., Northridge, 1984-2003; sr. rsch. adv. Ctr. Ednl. R&D, Ministry Planning, Republic Lebanon, Beirut, 1974-75; sr. rsch. assoc. Ctr. Behavioral Rsch., Am. U. of Beirut, 1974-75; vis. scholar dept. psychology UCLA, 1982-83; chair chpt. organizing America, North San Ferrnando Valley, 2009-; cons. English as fgn. lang. Vietnamese Affairs Ctr., Terre Haute, 1976-78; spkr. in field. Author: Readings and Experiments in General Psychology, 1970, rev. edit., 1971 Pres. Knollwood Property Owners Assn., 2002—07; sec. Earth Stewardship Ministry, Knollwood United Meth. Ch., 2009—; lay leader Santa Barbara Dist. United Meth. Ch., 2011—; mem. adv. bd. Cmty. Integration Svcs., 2007—09; chair Greater Granada Hills Organising America, 2009—, founder, dir., 2009—11; mem. Cantori Domina, 2007—; sec. City of LA Sunshine Canyon Landfill Citizens Advisory Com., 2002—09, mem. tech. adv. com., 2002—09; mem. LA County Sunshine Canyon Land Fill Cmty. Adv. Com., 2002—09, chmn., 2008—09; mem. adv. bd. United Campus Ministries, Calif. State U., Northridge, 2005—07, Knollwood United Meth. Ch., 2004—, chmn. bd. trustees, 2006—09, chmn. ch. coun., 2007—10; mem. leadership team United Meth. Ch. Calif. Pacific Annual Confs. Meth. for Social Action, 2008—10; bd. dirs. Granada Hills North Neighborhood Coun., 2002—06. Recipient LA Pearl award Outstanding Sr. Citizen, City of Atty., 2007; grantee Ford Found., 1974-75. Mem. Western Psychol. Assn., N.Y. Acad. Scis., Soc. Computers in Psychology, Computer Users Speech and Hearing, Wabash Valley Apple Byters Club (Terre Haute)(pres. 1981-82), LA Astronomical Soc., Sigma Xi, Psi Chi, Sigma Phi Iota. Methodist. Home: 12045 Susan Dr Granada Hills CA 91344-2642 Personal E-mail: wayneaIler07@hotmail.com.

ALLERTON, JEFFREY PAUL, oncologist; b. Catskill, NY, Mar. 22, 1960; s. Robert Stanley and Millie Allerton. BA in Chemistry and Biology, Coll. St. Rose, Albany, NY, 1982; MD Tufts U., 1986. Intern St. Elizabeth's Hosp., Boston, 1986—87, resident, 1987—89, fellow in hematology/oncology, 1989—92; chief oncology Wilford Hall Md. Ctr., San Antonio, 1995—98; staff physician Rockford (Ill.) Clinic, 1998—99; chief oncology Swedish Am. Hosp., Rockford, 1999—2001; corp. v.p. ACT Med. Group, Rockford, 2001—02; oncologist Blue Ridge Med. Specialists, Bristol, Tenn., 2002—04, McLeod Cancer and Blood Ctr., Johnson City, Tenn. Contbr. articles. Lt. col. USAF, 1992—98. Recipient Disting. Svc. award, SWOG, 1998, Physician's Recognition award, AMA, 1990. Fellow: ACP; mem.: Am. Cancer Soc., Am. Soc. Blood and Marrow Transplantation, Am. Soc. Hematology, Am. Soc. Clin. Oncology. Republican. Avocations: sports, reading. Office: McLeod Cancer and Blood Ctr Ste 401 310 N State of Franklin Rd Johnson City TN 37604 Office Phone: 423-926-3611. E-mail: docallerton@aol.com.

ALLEYNE, SIR GEORGE A.O., academic administrator, former public health service administrator; b. St. Philip, Barbados, Oct. 7, 1932; m. Sylvan I. Chen; 3 children. MB, U. London, 1957, MD, 1965; DSc (hon.), U. WI, McGill U., Montreal, Can., Queens U., Ont., Can., 2001. Researcher Univ. WI, West Indies, 1962—72, prof. medicine, 1972—76, chmn. dept. medicine, 1976—81, chancellor, 2003—; chief of rsch. promotion & coordination Pan Am. Health Org., 1981—85, dir., 1995—2003, dir. emeritus, 2003—; spl. envoy of sec.-gen. for HIV/AIDS in the Caribbean region UN, 2003—. Recipient Order of the Caribbean Community (O.C.C.), 2001; named Knight Bachelor, 1990. Office: University of WI Chancellor's Office Mona Campus Mona Jamaica

ALLGAYER, HEIKE, surgeon, educator, researcher; b. Lindenberg, Bavaria, Germany, June 12, 1969; d. Karlheinz and Hannelore Allgayer. MD, Ludwig Maximilians U., Munich, 1995, MD summa cum laude, 1996; PhD in Molecular Biology, U. Houston, 1999. Resident surgery Klinikum Grosshaden, U. Munich, 1995—97, 1999—2004, assoc. prof. exptl. surgery, 2001—04, head molecular oncology group dept. surgery, 2001—04; asst. prof. molecular oncology dept. surgery U. Munich, 1999—2001; postdoctoral fellow in cancer biology M.D. Anderson Cancer Ctr., Houston, 1997—99; prof. German Cancer Rsch. Ctr. Heidelberg and Ruprecht-Karls U., Germany, 2004—; head Dept. Exptl. Molecular Surgery Mannheim Ruprecht-Karls U., 2004—. Chair Internat. Congress on Molecular Staging of Cancer, Munich, 2001, Heidelberg, 06; assoc. editor Internat. Jour. Cancer, 2009—. Editor: Molecular Staging of Cancer, 2002, Hereditary Tumors, 2008; contbr. articles to profl. jours. Pianist, organist Civic Hosp., Lindenberg, Germany, 1987—93; mem. Mentors of the Ludwig Maximilians U., Munich, 1996—. Recipient Ferdinand-Sauerbruch Rsch. award, Surg. Soc. Berlin, 2001, Nussbaum Rsch. award, Bavarian Coll. Surgeons, 2002, Zimmerman Cancer Rsch. award for Outstanding Merits, Hanover Germany, 2003, Ingrid-zu-Solms Rsch. award, Frankfurt Germany, 2004, Rsch. award, Krupp Found., Essen, Germany, 2005, Hella Buehler award, 2006,

Walter Schulz award, 2008. Mem.: Ingrid Zu Solms Found. for Support of Excellent Women in Sci. Culture (Rsch. award 2004), Am. Soc. Clin. Oncology, European Assn. Cancer Rsch. (coun. mem., Lect. award 2005), German Coll. Surgeons (sect. molecular biology 1999—, Langenbeck Rsch. award 1999), Am. Assn. Cancer Rsch. (Rhone-Poulenc-Rorer award for young investigators 1999). Roman Catholic. Avocations: piano, art, music, literature, philosophy. Office: Univ Heidelberg Hosp Mannheim Theodor Kutzer Ufer 1-3 68135 Mannheim Germany Business E-Mail: heike.allgayer@umm.de.

ALLIS, C. DAVID, science educator; b. Mar. 22, 1951; B in Biology, U. Cin., 1973; MS & PhD in Biology, Ind. U., 1978. Postdoctoral rsch. U. Rochester, 1978—81, mem. faculty, 1995—98, Maria Currin Wilson and Joseph Chamberlain Wilson prof., Dept. Biology and oncology, 1997—98; asst. prof. Baylor Coll. Medicine, 1981—88, prof., 1988—90; mem. faculty Syracuse U., 1990—95; Harry F. Byrd, Jr. prof. biochemistry and molecular genetics, prof. microbiology, mem. Ctr. for Cell Signaling U. Va. Health Sciences. Ctr., Charlottesville, 1998—2002; Joy and Jack Fishman prof. Rockefeller U., NYC, 2003—, head, lab. chromatin biology and epigenetics, 2003—. Invited spkr. in field. Contbr. articles to profl. jours.; co-editor: Epigenetics. Recipient Baxter award for Disting. Rsch., Assn. Am. Med. Colleges, 2001, Massry prize, John Wiley prize in Biomedical Sciences, 2004, Gairdner Found. Internat. award, 2007. Mem.: Am. Soc. for Biochemistry and Molecular Biology, Harvey Soc., Am. Acad. Microbiology, NAS, Am. Acad. Arts Scis., Phi Beta Kappa. Achievements include research in chromatin via model systems such as protozoan Tetrahymena; clarification of how cells contain and protect DNA in protein-rich assemblies called chromatin. Office: Rockefeller U Allis Lab Box #78 1230 York Ave New York NY 10021 Office Phone: 212-327-7839. Office Fax: 212-327-7849. Business E-Mail: alliscd@rockefeller.edu. *

ALLISON, FRED, JR., internist, retired medical educator; b. Abingdon, Va., Sept. 8, 1922; s. Fred and Elizabeth Harriet (Kelly) A.; m. Clara Knox, Oct. 14, 1949; children: Rebecca Allison Parsley, Martha Allison Brown, Fred III, Robert Gardiner. BS, Ala. Poly. Inst., 1944; MD, Vanderbilt U., 1946. Diplomate: Am. Bd. Internal Medicine. Intern Vanderbilt Hosp., Nashville, 1946-47; resident Peter Bent Brigham Hosp., Boston, 1949-50; practice medicine specializing in internal medicine, 1946—; asst. prof. medicine Washington U., St. Louis, 1955; prof. medicine, head infectious disease divsn. U. Miss., Jackson, 1955—68; vis. scientist Rockefeller U., NYC, 1966-67; Edgar Hull prof. medicine, head dept. medicine La. State U., New Orleans, 1968-87; chief medicine La. State U. div. Charity Hosp., 1968—87; prof. medicine emeritus La. State U., 1987—; prof. medicine Vanderbilt U., Nashville, 1987-96, prof. medicine emeritus, 1996—, med. cons. Zerfoss Student Health Svc., 1996-99; physician-in-chief Met. Nashville Gen. Hosp., 1987-93; chief, divsn. gen. internal medicine Vanderbilt U., 1993-96. Bd. dirs. La. State U. Health Network, 1995-01; vice chmn. bd. trustees Hosp. Authority of Metro. Nashville and Davidson County, 1999—. With US Army, 1943-46, 47-49. Home: 418 Fairfax Ave Nashville TN 37212-4009

ALLISON, JAMES PATRICK, immunology educator, medical association administrator; b. Alice, Tex., Aug. 7, 1948; m. Malinda Bell. BS in Microbiology, U. Tex., 1969, PhD in Biol. Scis., 1973. Asst. biochemist and asst. prof. U. Tex., Smithville, 1977-83, asst. prof. biochemistry Grad. Sch. of Biomedical Scis., 1981-84, assoc. biochemist and assoc. prof. biochemistry, 1983-84; prof. immunology U. Calif., Berkeley, 1985—2004, dir. Cancer Rsch. Lab., 1985—2004, interim head Divsn. Immunology, 1987-89, head divsn immunology, 1989—97, co-chair and Howard Hughes prof. immunology; investigator Howard Hughes Med. Inst., 1997—; chmn. immunology prog. Meml. Sloan-Kettering Cancer Ctr., NYC, 2004—, dir. Ludwig Ctr. Cancer Immunotherapy, 2007—, David H. Koch chair immunologic studies. Adj. prof. zoology, U. Tex., 1979-84, spl. assoc. mem. grad. faculty, 1980-84; vis. scholar Dept. of Pathology, Stanford U., 1983-84; invited participant, Dahlem Workshop on Leukemia, 1983; faculty Advanced Course in Evolution of the Immune System Am. Assn. of Immunologists, 1985, Advanced Course in Regulation of the Immune System; mem bd. Midwinter Conf. of Immunologists, 1986-89; convener Indo-U.S. Short Term Course on The Molecular and Cellular Biology of the T Lymphocyte All India Inst. of Med. Scis., New Delhi, 1987; editorial bd. Devel. Immunology, 1989; cons. Becton-Dickinson Immunocytometry Systems, Inc., 1984. Reviewing editor Science, 1985-87; assoc. editor Journal of Immunology, 1987; transmitting editor International Immunology, 1988. Recipient Postdoctoral fellowship NIH, 1974-76, Dept. of Molecular Immunology Scripps Clinic and Rsch. Found., 1974-77; O.B. Williams award of the Tex. Branch Am. Soc. Microbiology, 1971, Centeon award for Innovative Breakthroughs in Immunology, 2001, William B. Coley award for Disting. Rsch., Cancer Rsch. Inst. Fellow: AAAS, Am. Acad. Microbiology; Mem.: NAS, Am. Assn. Immunologists (AAI-Dana Found. award in Human Immunology Rsch., 2008), Am. Assn. Cancer Rsch, Inst. Medicine. Office: Meml Sloan-Kettering Cancer Ctr 1275 York Ave New York NY 10065 Office Phone: 646-888-2332. Office Fax: 646-422-0618. E-mail: allisonj@mskcc.org.

ALLISON, JEFFERY CLAY, pharmacist, educator; b. Altoona, Pa., Sept. 27, 1948; s. John Wilmer and Charlotte Lorraine Allison; m. Nancy Wood Wood, Dec. 18, 1971; children: Scott Jeffery, Sharon Louise Gibson. BS in Pharmacy, Ohio No. U., Ada, 1971, PharmD, 1995. Registered pharmacist Ohio, 1971, Fla., 1986. Clin. pharmacist St. Rita's Med. Ctr., Lima, Ohio, 1973—88; pharmacist Gardners Drug Store, Ada, 1973—2000; prof. pharmacy practice Ohio No. U., 1995—. Cons. Blue Ridge Paper Co., Olmsted Falls, Ohio, 2003—07. Contbr. articles to profl. jours. Advisor Habitat for Humanity, Ada, 1996. Grantee, PSA3 Agy. Aging, 2002—07. Mem.: Ohio Pharmacists Assn. (mem. bylaws com. 2004—07), Am. Pharmacy Assn., Am. Assn. Health-Systems Pharmacists, NW Ohio Pharmacists Assn. (pres. 1992), Am. Assn. Colls. Pharmacy, Phi Kappa Phi, Phi Lambda Sigma, Omicron Delta Kappa. Methodist. Avocations: swimming, travel. Office: Ohio No U Coll Pharmacy 525 S Main St Ada OH 45810 Business E-Mail: j-allison@onu.edu.

ALLMAN, ANN LOWRANCE, counseling administrator; b. Carmel, Calif., June 2, 1938; d. Edward Walton and Rhoda Elizabeth (Patton) Lowrance; m. Jackie Howard Hamilton, Dec. 21, 1959 (div. May 1976); children: John Scott Hamilton, David Lee Hamilton, Dennis Lynn Hamilton; m. Jack Fredrick Allman, Dec. 22, 1977; stepchildren: John Frederick(dec.), James Paul, Jeffrey Lee. AA, Christian Coll., 1958; BA in Spanish, U. Mo., 1960, MEd, 1971, EdD, 1994. Tchr. Spanish Neosho (Mo.) HS, 1961-62, asst. prin., 1974-77; florist Wallflower Shop and Greenhouse, Joplin, Mo., 1962-69; dean girls Joplin Sr. HS, 1967-69; florist, bookkeeper Mueller's Garden Ctr., Columbia, Mo., 1969-71; instr. edn., asst. dean of students Columbia Coll., 1971-74; dir. guidance Am. Cmty. Sch., Buenos Aires, 1978-81; tchr. Spanish, psychology Ava (Mo.) HS, 1982-84; tchr. Spanish, social studies McDonald County HS, Anderson, Mo., 1984-88; counselor, acad. advisor Mo. So. State U., Joplin, 1988—2003. Cons. Mo. So. State Univ., 1990—; mem. internat. task force Mo. So. State Coll., 1994—96; mem. adv. bd. Adult Basic Edn., Joplin, 1992—2003; presenter Ctr. Applications Psychol. Type Internat. Conf., 1996. Elder First Christian Ch., Neosho, Mo. Recipient William D. Phillips Music award, 1st Christian Ch., Columbia, 1956; named to Outstanding Young Women Am., 1972. Mem.: Southwest Mo. Sch. Counselor Assn. (sec. 1994—97, v.p. 1992—94, 1999—2001, mem. governing bd., chmn. publs. and rsch. com. 1997—99), Mo. Sch. Counselor Assn., Phi Theta Kappa, Sigma Delta Pi, Phi Sigma Iota (romance lang., pres. 1959—60), Delta Eta Chi, Sigma Phi Gamma, Kappa Delta Pi. Avocations: music, writing, photography, sketch artist, needlecrafts, jewelry crafts. Home: 1214 Circle Dr Neosho MO 64850-1301 Office Phone: 417-451-7633. Personal E-mail: jfallman@sbcglobal.net.

ALLRED, KENDALL S., emergency physician; b. Safford, Ariz. m. Lisa Allred; 1 child. Pre-med, Ea. Ariz. Coll., Thatcher, 2000—01; BS, BA magna cum laude in Microbiology and Spanish, Ariz. State U., Tempe, 2004; MD, U. Ariz., Tucson, 2009, MPH in Health Policy and Mgmt., 2009. Emergency dept. lead technician Banner Health, 2001—05; emergency medicine resident U. Calif., San Francisco, 2009—. Commr. Med. Rep. Cert. Commn., 2009—. Recipient Disting. Svc. Award, Ariz. Med. Assn., 2008; named a Hero of Emergency Medicine, Am. Coll. Emergency Physicians. Mem.: AMA (vice chair Med. Student Sect. Governing Coun. 2006—07, bd. trustees 2008—09). Office: University Calif San Francisco Dept Emergeny Medicine 505 Parnassus Ave Rm M24 Box 0203 San Francisco CA 94143-0203 Office Phone: 415-353-1634. Office Fax: 415-353-1529. Business E-Mail: kendall.allred@ucsf.edu. *

ALLUMS, JAMES A., retired surgeon; b. Kountze, Tex., Sept. 28, 1937; m. Elizabeth Dee Walton, June 24, 1961; children: Ann Elizabeth, Sarah Dee, Benjamin Walton. BA, U. Tex., 1959; MD, U. Tex. Med. Br., 1962. Diplomate Am. Bd. Med. Examiners, Am. Bd. Surgery, Gen. Vascular Surgery, Am. Bd. Thoracic Surgery. Rotating intern Phila. Gen. Hosp., 1962-63; resident gen. surgery Med. Br. U. Tex., Galveston, 1963-66, 68-69; resident thoracic surgery Med. Branch U. Tex., Galveston, Tex., 1969—71; ptnr. Thoracic and Cardiovasc. Surg. Assocs., Beaumont, Tex., 1971-97; clin. asst. prof. dept. thoracic and cardiovasc. surgery U. Tex. Med. Br., Galveston, ret., 1997. Active physician St. Elizabeth Hosp., chief of staff 1976-77, 87-88; active Beaumont, Bapt. Hosp. of S.E. Tex., Beaumont, Beaumont Regional Med. Ctr., Beaumont Regional Med. Ctr., Park Place Hosp.; courtesy staff St. Mary Hosp., Port Arthur, Mid Jefferson Hosp., Nederland, Tex., cons. staff U. Tex. Med. Br. Hosp., Galveston; mem. cardiovasc. com. Bapt. Hosp., 1991-93, 1996, physician, nurse ad hoc com., 1992; clin. asst. prof. Dept. of Surgery U. Tex. Med. Br. Hosp., 1993-94; OR com. St. Elizabeth Hosp., Beaumont, 1990-91, 93-94, cardiovasc. quality assurance subcom., 1991-92, cardiovasc./coronary care com., 1990-91, 92-93, CCU quality assurance subcom. Contbr. articles to profl. jours. Capt. US Army, 1966-68. Recipient J.C. Crager award Am. Heart Assn., 1992, Mr. East Tex. award Tyler County Dogwood Festival, 1993. Fellow ACS (gov. 1989-94, pres. South Tex. chpt. 1987), Am. Coll. of Angiology, Am. Coll. of Cardiology, Am. Coll. of Chest Physicians, Beaumont Acad. of Medicine; mem. AMA, Assn. of Am. Physicians and Surgeons, Bapt. Hosp. P.H.O., Beaumont Regional P.H.O., Jefferson County Med. Soc., Singleton Surg. Soc., Soc. of Thoracic Surgeons, So. Assn. for Vascular Surgery, So. Med. Assn., So. Thoracic Surg. Assn., St. Elizabeth Hosp. P.H.O., Tex. Med. Assn. (coun. on med. edn. 1985-92), Tex. Surg. Soc., Alumni Assn. of the U. of Tex. Med. Br. (pres. 1984-85)Phi Eta Sigma, Alpha Epsilon Delta.

ALLWOOD, MICHAEL JOHN, retired clinical physiologist; b. Stoke-on-Trent, Eng., July 31, 1925; s. Edgar Henry and Florance (Nicholson) A.; m. Rosemary Marguerite Harrison, July 15, 1950 (dec. 1983); 5 children. MB BS, U. London, 1950, PhD, 1959, MD, 1970. Diplomate Eng. Bd. Med. Examiners. Rschr. Nat. Inst. Med. Rsch., London, 1951-53, Inst. Aviation Medicine, Farnborough, 1963-67; lectr. U. London, 1953-63; cons. Walsgrave Gen. Hosp., Coventry, 1967-90; ret., 1990. Hon. lectr. U. Birmingham, 1967-76. Contbr. articles to profl. jours. Served to surg. capt. Eng. Naval Res., 1949-82. Decorated Vol. Res. decoration with clasp. Mem. Interallied Confedn. Med. Res. Officers (UK rep. 1974-82, pres. 1980-82, cons. 1984), Midland Naval Officers Assn. (chmn. 1983-89), Res. Forces Assn. (coun. 1977-83), Naval Club. Mem. Ch. Eng. Home: 35 College House Pegasus Ct High Street NN13 7NR Brackley England Home Phone: 01280-706-967.

ALM, LIVIA, biomedical engineer; b. Cluj, Romania, Dec. 23, 1928; arrived in Sweden, 1945; d. Paul Mihalyi and Ella Sejavitz; m. Lars-Olof Alm, Apr. 6, 1957; children: Eva, Pia, Torsten. BS in Nutrition, Oslo U., 1969; D of Tech., KTH, 1978; Dr.med.sc., Karolinska Inst., 1982. Lab. asst. Royal Vet. U., Stockholm, 1952—58; food engr. Nat. Inst. Pub. Health, 1958—64; chief food. engr. Normalms A/S, 1964—67; prodn. devel. engr. Arla, 1970—86; sci. cons. Compact A/S, Bergen, Norway, 1990—94; prof. Shanghai Fisheries U., 1994—2000, Tianjin U., China, 1991—94. Author: Food Legislation, 1962; contbr. articles to profl. jours. Mem.: Internat. Water Resources Assn., Internat. Soc. Mushroom Biology, Soc. Microbial Ecology and Disease, Swedish Dairy Assn., Swedish Nutrition Soc., Swedish Soc. Microbiology, Swedish Soc. Food Engring, N.Y. Acad. Scis. Avocations: gardening, music, walking, writing, swimming.

AL-MAJED, ABDULRAHMAN AHMED, pharmacist, educator; b. Riyadh, Saudi Arabia, June 1, 1967; BSc in Pharm. Scis., King Saud U., 1990; PhD, U. Bradford, 1998. Prof., pharm. chemistry King Saud U., 1998—. Mem.: Saudi Pharm. Soc., Saudi Chem. Soc., Com. Health Edn., Chem. Pollution Protection Com., Housing Club Com. Avocations: football, reading, swimming. Home: King Saud University Riyadh 51564 Saudi Arabia Home Fax: 014677309.

ALMALEL, SUZANNE C., health facility administrator; b. Fairfax, Va., Mar. 5, 1962; BS, Strayer Coll., 1987. Pres. Dimensions Healthcare Sys. Found., 2005—. Bd. dirs. Prince George's County Crime Solvers, 2005—. Recipient Healthcare Exec. Leadership award, Dimensions Healthcare Sys. Mem.: Am. Coll. Healthcare Exec. Avocations: travel, horseback riding, surfing. Office: 3001 Hospital Dr Executive Ste Cheverly MD 20785 Office Fax: 301-618-2883. Business E-Mail: suzanne.almalel@dimensionshealth.org.

ALMANSA PASTOR, ANGEL F., chest physician; b. Sept. 12, 1934; s. Salvador Almansa de Cara and Paula Pastor Roda; m. Isabel Mendez Peña, May 16, 1970; children: Maria Isabel, Angel, Paloma. Student, Agustinos Coll., Malaga, 1943—47, Salesianos Coll., 1948—51; U.Grad. with honors, F. Medicine, Granada, 1957; specialist thoracic surgeon, 1965, specialist pneumologie, specialist cardiologie, 1980. Diplomate Spain Bd. Med. Examiners. Asst. Hosp. Princesa, Madrid, 1958—59, Speziallungenklinik Herner, Westfalhem, Germany, 1969—76, U. Chirurg Klinik, Dusseldorf, Germany, 1961—65; chief pneumology Hosp. Civil Privincial, Malaga, 1966—75; med. dir. Hosp. Torax, Malaga, 1975—. Prof. pneumologie Diputacion Provincial, Malaga, 1966, Valencia, 65. Author: International System of Measures in Medicine; patentee blood circulation activator; contbr. articles to profl. jours. With Spanish Mil. Svc., 1956—57. Fellow: Am. Coll. Chest Physicians; mem.: Found. Neumologia Cardiologia Andaluza (pres.), Assn. Med. Naturistas, Soc. Spain Geriatria, Soc. Andaluza Cardiologia, Soc. Spain Cardiologia, Soc. Spain Pathology A. Respiratorio, Coll. Internat. Angyologiae, Club Mediterraneo. Roman Catholic. Avocations: tennis, golf. Office: Calle San Lorenzo 2 29001 Malaga Spain Personal E-mail: info@angelalmansa.com. Business E-Mail: info@angelalmansa.es, aap@angelalmansapastor.es.

AL MARZOOQI, ALI HASSAN, public health service officer, director; b. Sharja, June 15, 1972; MBBS, RCS Ireland, 1997; MPH, Tulane Sch. Pub. Health, 2001. Dir., preventive medicine dept. Ministry of Health, United Arab Emirates, 2003—05, mem., Nat. Higher Immunization Com., 2006—, mem., Nat. HS Health Com., 2010—; dir., pub. health affairs dept. Dubai Health Authority, 2005—08, dir., pub. health and safety dept., 2008—. Recipient Shaikh Rashid Achievements award, Govt. of Dubai, UAE; grant, Ministry of Higher Edn., UAE Govt. Avocations: reading, sports. Office: Rashid Hosp Complex Dubai United Arab Emirates Mailing: PO Box 46000 Abu Dhabi United Arab Emirates E-mail: drzooqi@hotmail.com.

ALMAZOV, IRINA, neurologist, consultant; m. Valentin Gornik, 1965; 1 child, Anna Gulel. MD, PhD, I.M. Sechenov Moscow Med. Acad., 1956. Child neurologist Filatov Children's Hosp., Moscow, 1963—89, Meuhedet Healthcare, Natania, Israel, 1992. Mem.: Israel Neurology Soc. Achievements include research in tension type head ache in children is most probably post-infectious complication of streptococcal infections. Office: Meuhedet Healthcare Smilansky 20 Natania Israel Office Fax: 972-9-8872660; Home Fax: 972-9-7671952. Business E-Mail: almazov@netvision.net.il.

ALMEIDA, GIL LÚCIO, physical therapist, educator, researcher; b. Passos, Minas Gerais, Brazil, June 1, 1960; s. João Galdino Sobrinho and Judith Honorata Santos; m. Alba Chiesse da Silva, June 1, 1989 (div. 1999); 1 child, João Marcos Marconi Almeida (Nádia); m. Nádia Fernanda Marconi, Apr. 26, 2002; children: Gabriela Chiesse Almeida (Alba), Bárbara Marconi Almeida (Nádia). BS in Phys. Therapy, U. Fed. de Sao Carlos, Brazil, 1985, MS in Spl. Edn., 1988; PhD in Child Devel., Iowa State U., Ames, 1993; postdoc., U. Ill. at Chgo., Rush Med. Ctr., 1993—94. Lic. physical therapist Coun. Phys.l Therapy, São Paulo State, 1985. Prof. neurophysiology, Inst. Biology U. Campinas, São Paulo, 1987—2001; postdoc. fellow U. Ill., Chgo., 1993—94; prof., chmn. dept. phys. therapy U. Ribeirão Preto, São Paulo, 1999—2002, dir. grad programs in phys. therapy; prof., dir. Brazilian dept. phys. therapy NY Inst. Tech., NYC, 2005—; elected pres. Coun. Phys. Therapy São Paulo State, 2004—. Pres. União Mcpl. dos Estudantes de São Carlos, 1983, III Internat. Motor Rehability Congress, Brazil, 1998; pres. internat. com. Brazilian Nat. Meeting in Phys. Therapy, 2004, 06; co-pres. Progress in Motor Control, Brazil, 2007. Contbr. articles to profl. jours., chapters to books, scientific papers to profl. confs.; editl. mem. (numerous sci. jours.). Pres. Phys. Therapy and Occupl. Therapy Coun. São Paulo, 2004—; goodwill amb. Rotary Found., Ames, Iowa, 1988—94. Named São Paulo Citizen, Town Coun. São Paulo City, 2008; fellow, Rotary Found., 1988; scholar, Nat. Coun. Rsch., Brazil, 1988—93, 1996—98; Rsch. Productivity grantee, 1994—. Mem.: Internat. Soc. Motor Control, World Confederation Phys. Therapy, Latin Am. Confederation Phys. Therapy and Kinesiology, Brazilian Phys. Therapy Assn. Democrat. Roman Catholic. Avocations: travel, scuba diving. Home: Rafael de Barros St 336 Apt 161 São Paulo 04003-042 Brazil Office: Phys Therapy Coun São Paulo State 4th Fl Cincinato Braga St 59 São Paulo SP 01333-909 Brazil Office Fax: 55 11 55 91 22 34. Personal E-mail: gillucioalmeida@gmail.com. Business E-Mail: presidente@crefitosp.gov.br.

ALMEIDA, LUCIANA RODRIGUES, biomedical researcher; b. Bom Jardim, Brazil, Nov. 8, 1976; Degree in Vet., U. Fed. Rural do Rio de Janeiro, 1999, PhD, 2007. Vis. rschr., biomed. scis. Fundação Inst. Oswaldo Cruz, IOC-Fiocruz, 2008—. Homeopathy veterinarian Internat. Hosp. Bahrain, 2011. Avocation: hiking. Office: Avenida Brasil Rio de Janeiro 21040360 Brazil Personal E-mail: rodrigues_lu@yahoo.fr.

ALMEIDA, MARIA FERNANDA SOARES DE, biomedical engineer, researcher; b. São Paulo, Brazil, Dec. 6, 1984; PhD, Fed. U. Uberlândia, 2011. Postdoc. rschr. Fed. U. Uberlândia, 2011—. Avocations: music, movies. Home: Rua Francisco Vicente Ferreira 590 Apt Uberlândia Minas Gerais 38408102 Brazil Personal E-mail: nandasalmeida@yahoo.com.br.

ALMERS, WOLFHARD, physiology and biophysics educator; b. Helmstedt, W.Ger., May 29, 1943; came to U.S., 1966; s. Eberhard and Ute (Plathner) A.; m. Hilary M. Turnbull, May 17, 1967; children: Mattias, Lucy. Student, Free U. Berlin, 1963-66, Duke U., 1966-69; PhD in Physiology, U. Rochester, 1971. Postdoctoral fellow physiology Cambridge U., 1971-74; tutor Churchill Coll., Cambridge U., Eng., 1972-73; asst. prof. physiology biophysics U. Wash., Seattle, 1974-78, assoc. prof., 1978—84, prof., 1984—92; dir. dept. molecular and cellular rsch. Max-Planck Inst., Heidelberg, Germany, 1992—95; prof. biology U. Heidelberg, 1995—99; sr. scientist Vollum Institute, Portland, Oreg., 1999—; prof. biochemistry and molecular biology Oreg. Health and Sci. U., Portland, 1999—. Contbr. articles to sci. jours.; mem. editorial bd.: Jour. Physiology, 1981—, Am. Jour. Physiology, 1981—. NIH grantee, 1974—; Muscular Dystrophy Assn. grantee, 1981-84; Alexander von Humboldt award for sr. U.S.

scientists, 1984; Guggenheim fellow, 1984; recipient Merit award NIH, 1986. Mem. Soc. for Neurosci, Biophys. Soc., Physiol. Soc. Gt. Brit., NAS. Office: The Vollum Inst Oregon Health and Sci U 3181 SW Sam Jackson Park Rd Portland OR 97239-3098

AL-MEZAINE, HANI, ophthalmologist, educator; b. Riyadh, Saudi Arabia, Nov. 6, 1973; MD, Model Ednl. Schs., 1994. Asst. prof. King Saud U., 2004—08, assoc. prof., 2008—; cons. ophthalmologist King Abdulaziz U. Hosp., 2006. Mem.: European Soc. Cataract & Refractive Surgery, Saudi Ophthal. Soc. Office: King Abdulaziz University Hosp old PO Box 7805 Riyadh 11411 Saudi Arabia Business E-Mail: halmezaine@ksu.edu.sa.

ALMHANNA, KHALDOUN, internist; b. Damascus, Syria, Aug. 22, 1971; s. Najib and Allamah (Bahia) Almhanna. MD, Damascus U. Med. Sch., Damascus, Syria, 1994; MPH, Case Western Res. U., Cleve., 2001. Cert. ECFMG, 1995. Rsch. asst. Case Western Res. U., Cleve., 1997—2002; internal medicine resident Oakwood Health Care Sys., Dearborn, Mich., 2002—. Author: (paper) Medical Research (Intern of the yr., Resident rsch. Award, 2002). Mem.: Am. Coll. Physicians.

ALMODIN, CARLOS GILBERTO, obstetrician, researcher; b. Marialva, Paraná, Brazil, Oct. 29, 1955; s. José and Noemia Lidia Almodin; m. Edna Motta, Dec. 21, 1978; children: Juliana Motta, Flavia Motta, Paula Motta. MD, State U. N. Minas, Minas Gerais, Brazil, 1979; MSc. in Obstetrics, Fed. U. São Paulo, 1999, PhD in Medicine, 2003. Lic. ob-gyn Brazilian Med. Assn., Paraná, 1984. Prof. and rschr. Fed. U. São Paulo, Brazil, 2003—. Dir. Materbaby Human Reproduction and Genetics, Maringá, Brazil, 1995—. Author: Guidelines to the Pregnant Woman, 1995; contbr. chapters to books. Recipient Citzen of Paraná award, Cultural Ctr. Rsch. and Social Studies Brazil, 1995, Talent of Paraná, 2002, 500 Years of Brazil award, Cultural Ctr. Rsch. and Social Studies Brazil, 2002, Gente do Paraná, Cultural Ctr. Rsch. and Social Studies Brazil, 2003, Henrique Paraventi Sci. Prodn. award, Fed. U. São Paulo, 2002, Meritous Citzenship Relevant Svc. to Cmty., São Bernardo do Campo City Coun., 2004; named Gynecologist and Obstetrician of Yr., Braslopes Rsch. Inst., 1992, Profl. of Yr., Cultural Ctr. Rsch. and Social Studies Brazil, 1993, Best of Paraná State, Estado do Paraná Newspaper, 1993. Mem.: Brazilian Fedn. Gynecology and Obstetrics Societies (assoc.), L.Am. Soc. Human Reproduction (assoc.), European Soc. Human Reprodiction and Embriology (assoc.), Am. Soc. Reproductive Medicine (assoc. Best Video award Basic Sci. category 2002, Best Video Open category 2003), Brazilian Soc. Human Reproduction (assoc. Campos da Paz award 2002). Achievements include development of first gestation of a menopausal woman in L.Am; patents for trocar for intra-uterus fetal surgery; patents pending for cervical cerclage ring. Office: Materbaby - Human Reproduction Genetics Avenida 15 de Novembro 1232 87013-230 Maringá PR Brazil Office Fax: 55 44 3225 1162; Home Fax: 55 44 3225 1162. E-mail: almodin@materbaby.com.br.

ALMOND, CARL HERMAN, surgeon, physician, educator; b. Latour, Mo., Apr. 1, 1926; s. Hugh Herman and Sylvia (Morrison) A.; m. Nancy Ginn, June 18, 1964 (div. 1990); children: Carrie, Callie, Carl, Christopher. BS, Washington U., St. Louis, 1949, MD, 1953. Diplomate Am. Bd. Surgery, Am. Bd. Thoracic Surgery. Rotating intern Los Angeles County Gen. Hosp., 1953-54; resident surgery U. Mich., Ann Arbor, 1954-56, jr. clin. instr. surgery, 1956-57, sr. clin. instr., 1957-58; fellow surg. pathology Barnes Hosp.-Washington U., St. Louis, 1956; sr. surg. resident in urology Baylor U. Affiliated Hosps., 1958-59; resident thoracic surgery U. So. Calif., Los Angeles, 1959, fellow thoracic surgery, 1962-63; staff surgeon Univ. Hosp., Columbia, Mo., 1959-78, dir. thoracic and cardiovascular surgery, 1968-77, VA Hosp., Columbia; fellow Brompton Hosp., London, Eng., 1961; asst. prof. surgery U. Mo. Sch. Medicine, Columbia, 1959-64, asso. prof., 1964-69, prof., chief thoracic and cardiovascular surgery, from 1969; prof. and chmn. dept. surgery Sch. Medicine, U. S.C., Columbia, 1978-85, dir. gen. surgery residency program, 1979-85, assoc. dean clin. research and devel., 1986-90. Vis. prof. U. Geneva, Switzerland, 1972—73; mem. med. adv. panel FAA, 1970—75; mem. U.S. Commn. on UNESCO, 1983. Contbr. articles to profl. jours. With USNR, 1944—52. Fellow ACS; mem. AMA, Boone County Med. Soc., Columbia Med. Soc., S.C. Med. Assn., S.C. Thoracic Soc., Am. Assn. Med. Colls., Frederick H. Coller Surg. Soc., St. Louis Surg. Soc., Am. Coll. Cardiology, Am., S.C. heart assns., Am. Soc. Artificial Internal Organs, Soc. Med. Cons. to Armed Forces, Am. Coll. Chest Physicians, So. Thoracic Surg. Assn., Central Surg. Soc., Am. Assn. Thoracic Surgery, So. Surg. Assn., S.C. Surg. Soc., Chest Club, Soc. Surg. Chairmen, Marion S. DeWeese Surg. Soc., Southeastern Surg. Soc., So. Surg. Soc., Internat. Cardiovascular Soc., Soc. Thoracic Surgeons, Sigma Xi, Nu Sigma Nu, Sigma Chi. Home: 1829 Senate St 4E Columbia SC 29201 Office: University SC Sch Medicine Dept Surgery Two Medical Pk Ste 306 Columbia SC 29203 Office Phone: 803-254-4158.

AL-MOSLIH, MOSLIH IBRAHIM, microbiologist, educator, virologist; b. Baghdad, Iraq, June 1, 1948; s. Ibrahim Al-Moslih and Latifa Ibrahim; m. Muna Nori Yassin, Jan. 7, 1976; children: Ayad, Sura, Asil, Ayman. BSc, U. Baghdad, 1966; MSc, U. Nebr., Lincoln, 1968; PhD, U. Nebr., Omaha, 1972; cert. in med. edn., U. Dundee, Scotland, 2005. Assoc. prof. U. Nebr. Med. Ctr., Omaha, 1972—81; prof., chmn. microbiology dept. U. Baghdad Coll. Medicine, 1982—93; prof., cons., dir. U. Hosp. and Coll. Medicine, Sanaa, Yemen, 1994—97; prof., head Dubai Coll. Medicine, Dubai, United Arab Emirates, 1997—98; prof. U. Sharjah Coll. Health Scis., United Arab Emirates, 1998—2006, acting dean, 1998—, disting. prof., 2006—. Cons. in field. Mem. editl. bd.: Jour. Microbial World, 2004—, Jour. Univ. Sharjah, 2007; contbr. articles to profl. jours. Primary health svc. Sharjah Med. Dist. Diabetic Clinic, 2002—. Recipient Hemorrhagic Fever award, Ministry of Health, Baghdad, 1982, Hydatid Cyst award, U. Baghdad, 1982, Bosnian Health Conf. award, Bosnia Med. Assn., 2002, award, Sharjah Bank, 2006; Rsch. grant, Jour. Med. Virology and Clin. Microbiology, 2004—05. Mem.: Iraqi Microbiology Assn. (pres. 1982—85), Am. Soc. Microbiology. Achievements include research in treatment of hydatid cyst, hemorrhagic fever, viral hepatitis and hepato cellular carcinoma. Avocations: swimming, tennis. Home: Univ Sharjah Villa Q4 Sharjah 27272 United Arab Emirates Office Phone: 9716-5050805. Business E-Mail: mmoslih@sharjah.ac.ae.

AL-MOUTAWA, SAMIA ABDULQADER, ophthalmologist, consultant; b. Kuwait, Nov. 7, 1955; d. Abdulqader Bader Al-Moutawa and Radiya Mohammed Al-Quraishe; m. Yousef Saleh Al-Duwairi, Jan. 1, 1981; children: Sara Yousef Al-Duwairi, Saleh Yousef Al-Duwairi, Taiba Yousef Al-Duwairi, Hessa Yousef Al-Duwairi, Dalal Yousef Al-Duwairi. MB BCh, Cairo Med. U., Egypt, 1979; MD, Boston U. Med. Sch., PhD, 1990. Cons. & dir. Al-Bahar Eye Ctr., Opthalmology Lab., Sabah area, Shuwaikh, Kuwait, 1990—2007, Eye to Eye Clinic, Salmiya, Kuwait, 2007—. Author: (book) Inflammations of Uveal Tract:The Essentials. Mem., women rights com. Union of Kuwaiti Womens Assn., Kuwait, 1992—, cons. health com., 1992—. Mem.: Kuwait Med. Assn., Afro-Assian Med. Assn. Achievements include research in immune problems related to uveitis. Home: PO Box 44189 Kuwait Hawally 3205 Kuwait Office Fax: 0096522571295. Personal E-mail: sm_mtw@yahoo.com.

ALMQUIST, ADRIAN K., clinical cardiac electrophysiologist; b. Columbus, Nebr. Grad., Stanford U.; MD, U. Nebr., Omaha. Cert. Am. Bd. Internal Med., 1979, cardiovascular diseases 1985, clinical cardiac electrophysiology 1992. Intern U. Ore., Portland; resident internal med. Hennepin County Med. Ctr., Mpls.; fellow cardiology U. Minn.; fellow North Am. Soc. of Pacing and Electrophysiology; with U.S. Pub. Health Svc., 1973—76; internist Alexandria Clinic, Minn., 1980—82; med. cons. Dept. of Econ. Security, 1982—86; clinical cardiac electrophysiologist Marshfield Clinic, Wis., 1986—88, Mpls. Heart Inst., 1988—. Fellow: HRS, Am. Coll. Cardiology; mem.: AMA, ACP, Am. Autonomic Soc. Mailing: Minneapolis Heart Institute 920 E 28th St Ste 300 Minneapolis MN 55407 Office: Abbott Northwestern Hospital 800 E 28th St 2nd Fl Minneapolis MN 55407 also: Allina Medical Clinic 1400 Jefferson Rd Northfield MN 55057 Office Phone: 612-863-3900, 507-663-9000. Office Fax: 612-775-3199, 507-645-2096.

AL-MUHARRAQI, MOHAMMED ABDULLA, oral surgeon, educator; b. Bahrain, Dec. 21, 1974; BDS, U. Dundee, MBChB, 1998; MSc, 2007. Sr. cons. Royal Med. Svcs. Bahrain Def. Force, 2007—; sr. lectr. Royal Coll. Surgeons Med. U. Bahrain, 2008—. Fellow: Dental Surgery of Royal Coll. Surgeons Ireland; mem.: Royal Coll. Surgeons Glasgow, Faculty Dental Surgery Royal Coll. Surgeons Eng. Home: PO Box 33255 Isa Town Bahrain Home Fax: 973-17641100. Personal E-mail: mohammed@al-muharraqi.com.

AL-MULLA, FAHD, molecular pathologist, consultant; b. Kuwait, Kuwait, Aug. 28, 1966; s. Rashed Hamad and Layla Ibrahim (Kaaki) A.; m. Zsofia Victor, Oct. 1, 1969; children: Jaber, Yusef. BSc (Hons.) Molecular Biology, 1990, PhD, 1999. Asst. prof. Kuwait U., 1999—, dir. Shared Facility Lab., 2000—. Contbr. articles to profl. jours. Recipient Sir Alastair Currie prize Royal Pathol. Soc., 1998. Mem. Am. Soc. Biochemistry and Molecular Biology, Am. Assn. Molecular Pathology, Brit. Med. Assn., Glasgow Sch. of Cancer. Achievements include research on characterization of carbonyl reductase gene. Office: PO Box 24923 Safat Kuwait 13110 Kuwait Fax: (965) 5338905. E-mail: fahd@al-mulla.org.

AL-MURRANI, WALEED KHUDHAIR, geneticist, educator; b. Maysan, Iraq, June 16, 1938; m. Selma Z. Al-Sam; children: Samer, Sally, Sana, Sura Mandaean. BS in Vet. Medicine, Baghdad U., Iraq, 1961; diploma in Rsch., Bradford U., 1967; PhD, Edinburgh U., Scotland, 1973. Dept. head, prof. genetics and biostats. Coll. Vet. Medicine, Baghdad U., 1974—82, 1999—2004; prof. genetics and biostats. Inst. Genetic Engring. and Biotech. for Higher Studies, 2004—06. Tech. advisor Arab Orgn. for Agrl. Devel., 1982—86; mem. FAO Arab Agrl. Documentation Ctr., Sudan, 1982—84; dir. Higher Studies and Scientific Affairs, Baghdad U., 1986—90; prof. Plymouth U. Sch. Biomed. and Biol. Sci., 2006—07. Translator: numerous pubs.; contbr. chapters to books, over 100 articles to profl. jours. (Nat. First Class award and Golden medal for scientific achievements, 1999, 2003). 2d lt. Iraqi Army, 1961—62. Grantee, Min. Higher Edn. and Scientific Rsch., 2006. Mem.: Iraqi Acad. Sci. (mem. sci. com. 2006), Iraqi Assn. Translators, Iraqi Vet. Assn. Office: University of Plymouth Sch Biomedical and Biological Sciences Drake Circus Plymouth PL4 8AA England Business E-Mail: profmurrani@yahoo.com.

AL-MUSAWI, ALA, oral surgeon; b. London, Jan. 8, 1974; DDS, UMKC, 1999; degree in Oral and Maxillofacial Surgery, UIC, 2005. Asst. prof. Kuwait U., 2006. Home: Rumathia Kuwait City 13002 Kuwait E-mail: jaw@hsc.edu.kw.

AL MUTAIR, ANGHAM, endocrinologist; b. Riyadh, Saudi Arabia, Jan. 11, 1965; MD, King Saud U., 1991. Cons. endocrinologist, pediat. KAMC, 1991—. Home: Al Arbeen Riyadh 11426 Saudi Arabia Business E-Mail: mutaira@ngha.med.sa.

ALOLFE, MOHAMED ABDULLAH, biomedical engineer; b. Sanaa, Yemen, July 1, 1980; B, Cairo U., 2003, M in Biomedical Engring., PhD, 2009. Biomedical engr. Minsitry Pub. Health, 2003—. Cons. Med. Equipment Adminstrn., 2006. Office: Minstry Public Health-Alhasaba St Sanaa 299 Yemen Business E-Mail: al_olfe2001@k-space.org.

ALOMRANI, ADEEB NASSER, prosthodontist, consultant, research scientist; s. Nasser Alomrani; married; children: Nasser children: Norah. DMS in Oral Biology, Harvard U., 2001. Cert. Prosthodontics Harvard Sch. of Dental Medicine, 2001. Cons. prosthodontist, implantologist King Faisal Specialist Hosp. and Rsch. Ctr., Riyadh, Saudi Arabia, 2001—; implant rsch. fellow U. of Tex. Health Sci. Ctr. at San Antonio, 2002—03. Contbr. articles to profl. jours. Rsch. sci., Riyadh, Saudi Arabia, 1997—2005. Fellow: Internat. Congress Oral Implantologists (assoc.); mem.: Internat. Coll. Prosthodontists, European Assn. Osseointegration, Acad. Osseointegration, Am. Coll. Prosthodontics (assoc.). Achievements include research in Dental Implants. Personal E-mail: dradeeb@hotmail.com.

ALON, URI S., pediatrician, nephrologist; b. Haifa, Israel, June 30, 1946; MD, Hebrew U., Jerusalem, 1975. Cert. Pediat., 1998, Pediatric Nephrology, 2006. Intern in pediat. Rambam Med. Ctr., Haifa, 1971—72, resident in pediatric nephrology; fellow Med. Coll. Va., Richmond, 1981—83; prof. pediat. U. Mo.-Kansas City Sch. Medicine; pediatric nephrologist Children's Mercy Hosp., Kansas City. Office: Childrens Mercy Hosp and Clinics 2401 Gilham Rd Kansas City MO 64108 Office Phone: 816-234-3010.

ALONCI, ANDREA, physician; b. Messina, Feb. 8, 1957; MD, Messina U., 1982. Cert. specialist in hematology Messina U., 1985. Physician A.O.U. G. Martino Messina, 1991—, adj. prof., 2001. Adj. prof. A.O.U. G. Martino, 2001. Office: via C Valeria Messina Sicily 98100 Italy Business E-Mail: aalonci@unime.it.

ALONSO, ANTONIO, geneticist, educator; b. Zamora, Spain, Oct. 18, 1959; BSc, UAM, 1982, PhD, 1992. Facultative Inst. Nat. de Toxicologia y Ciencias Forenses, 1983—. Pres., GHEP Spanish and Portuguese Working Group ISFG, 1996—2000; sec., mem. Nat. Commn. Forensic Use of DNA, 2008. Contbr. articles to profl. jours. Mem.: Internat. Soc. Applied Biol. Scis., European Network Forensic Sci. Insts. DNA Working, Internat. Soc. Forensic Genetics. Office: José Echegaray Las Rozas Madrid 28232 Spain Business E-Mail: a.alonso@mju.es.

ALONSO, LUÍS GARCIA, medical geneticist, educator, medical researcher; b. São Paulo, Brazil, Dec. 6, 1969; s. Virginio Alonso Teijeiro and Maria Elena Garcia Alonso; m. Gláucia Somensi de Oliveira-Alonso, May 18, 2002. MD, Faculdade de Ciências Médicas da Santa Casa de São Paulo, Brazil, 1994; M in Morphology, Universidade Fed. de São Paulo-Escola Paulista de Medicina, 1997, D in Scis., 2002. Clin. Genetics Expert Sociedade Brasileira de Genética Clínica/Associação Médica Brasileira, 1997, Clin. Genetics/Dysmorphology Specialization Universidade Fed. de São Paulo-Escola Paulista de Medicina, 1996. Chief, clin. genetics/genetic counseling unit Sch. of Medicine, Universidade de Santo Amaro, São Paulo, 1998—2002; asst. prof. Sch. of Dentistry, Universidade de Santo Amaro, São Paulo, 1998—2002; prof. anatomy divsn. Sch. of Nursing, Hosp. Israelita Albert Einstein, São Paulo, 1999—, prof. genetics/evolution divsn., 1998—; chief, clin. genetics/genetic counseling divsn. Associação de Assistência à Criança Deficiente (AACD), São Paulo, 1999—; assoc. prof., morphology dept., topographic/descriptive anatomy divsn. Universidade Fed. de São Paulo-Escola Paulista de Medicina, São Paulo, 2002—. Chief clin. genetics/genetic counseling unit Clínica e Laboratório de Genética, São Paulo, 1997—; sci. methodology cons. Associação de Assistência à Criança Deficiente (AACD), São Paulo, 2002—, ethics in rsch. com. pres., 2002—; pres. paulista clin. genetics soc./clin. genetics dept. Paulista Med. Assn. (APM), São Paulo, 2002—. Roman Catholic. Avocations: swimming, chess, literature, tennis. Office: Depto de Morfologia UNIFESP-EPM Botucatu 740 - Edifício Leitão da Cunha São Paulo 04023-900 Brazil Home: Rua Itabaiana 657 - Apt 54 03171-010 São Paulo SP Brazil Office Fax: 55-11-5571-7597. Personal E-mail: lgalonso.ops@terra.com.br. E-mail: luisalonso.morf@epm.br.

ALONSO-LEJ, FERNANDO, cardiothoracic surgeon; b. Zaragoza, Spain, Jan. 27, 1927; s. Fernando Alonso-lej and Damiana De Las Casas; m. Madeleine Genty, May 20, 1955 (div. 1980); 1 child, Chantal; m. Mercedes Pascual, Oct. 3, 1983; 1 child, Raquel. BS, U. Zaragoza, 1945; MD summa cum laude, Zaragoza Med. Sch., 1951. Diplomate Am. Bd. Gern. Surgery, 1959, Am. Bd. Thoracic Surgery, 1960. Intern James Walker Meml. Hosp., Wilmington, NC, 1952-53; resident in surgery Balt. City Hosp., 1953-56; assoc. resident in surgery Mercy Hosp., Balt., 1956-57, chief resident, 1957-58; asst. resident thoracic surgery U. Md. Hosp., 1958-59, chief resident thoracic surgery, 1959-60, instr. thoracic surgery, 1960-61; chief thoracic and cardiovasc. surgery Hosp. Provincial Zaragoza, 1961-63; chief cardiothoracic surgery Hosp. Gen. Asturias, Spain, 1963-75; chief cardiovasc. surgery Hosp. Miguel Servet, Zaragoza, 1975-97; chief cardiac surgery Clinica Montpellier, Zaragoza, 1990—. Co-author: Recent Progess in Mitral Valve Disease, 1984; contbr. numerous articles to profl. jours. Mem. Soc. Thoracic Surgeons (founding mem.), Soc. Cardiosurgeons (pres. 1978-79), Aragonesa de Cardiologia (pres. 1984), Spanish Soc. Cardiovasc. Surgery, Spanish Soc. Cardiology. Home: Manuel Lasala 40-4 50006 Zaragoza Spain Office: Via Hispanidad 37 50012 Zaragoza Spain Personal E-mail: ralonsoly@hotmail.com.

ALOSZKO, AGNIESZKA DAGMARA, allergist; b. Gdansk, Poland, Apr. 18, 1972; d. Tadeusz and Hanna Maria Pruszko; m. Andrzej Aloszko, June 24, 2000. Med. studies, Med. U. Gdansk, Poland, 1997; Doctorate, Med. U. Bialystok, Poland, 2004; specialization in Internal Medicine, Poland, 2007, specialization in Allergology, 2010. Asst. Nova Med. Polska, Gdansk, 1997—2001, Dept. Allergology, Med. U. Gdansk, 2001—10; specialist in med. practice, 2011—. Contbr. articles various profl. jours. Mem.: Polish Soc. Internal Medicine, Polish Soc. Allergology.

ALPERIN, RICHARD MARTIN, social worker, psychoanalyst; b. Mt. Vernon, NY, Oct. 16, 1946; s. Israel and Sara A.; children: Heather Nicole, Alexander Scott. BBA, We. Mich. U., Kalamazoo, 1968; MSW, Fordham U., Bronx, NY, 1974; DSW, Columbia U., NYC, 1982; postdoctoral diploma in psychotherapy and psychoanalysis, Adelphi U., Garden City, NY, 1988. Lic. clin. social worker, NY, NJ; diplomate Am. Bd. Examiners in Clin. Social Work; cert. group psychotherapist Nat. Registry Cert. Group Psychotherapists. Cons. Mt. Vernon Youth Bd., 1972-76; adj. faculty Marymount Manhattan Coll., NYC, 1974-76; psychotherapist Riverdale Mental Health Clinic, Bronx, 1974-77; psychol. counselor, psychotherapist Ctr. Counseling and Psychol. Svcs. Ramapo Coll. of NJ, 1976-81, adj. faculty, 1977-86, moderator evening forums, 1978, 80; counselor, psychotherapist Ctr. Counseling and Psychol. Svcs. SUNY, Purchase, 1981-82, 84-85, acting dir., 1982-84; clin. cons. Westside Ctr. for Family Svcs., NYC, 1985-87; pvt. practice psychotherapy and psychoanalysis Riverdale, NY, 1977—, Teaneck, NJ, 1980—, NYC, 1984—. Lectr. Cabrini Med. Ctr., 1979; guest lectr. grand rounds dept. psychiatry, Brookdale Hosp. Med. Ctr., 1996; field instr. Grad. Sch. Social Work-Columbia U., 1983-85; adj. assoc. prof. Grad. Sch. Social Svc.-Fordham U., 1985-98; adj. asst. prof. Grad. Sch. Social Work-NYU, 1989-91; faculty, dean curriculum Rockland Inst. for Psychoanalysis and Psychotherapy, 1990-95; faculty Advanced Inst. Analytic Psychotherapy, 1992-95, Object Rel. Inst. Psychoanalysis and Psychotherapy, 1992—, Psychoanalytic Psychotherapy Study Ctr., 1994—, NJ Inst. for Tng. in Psychoanalysis, 1994—, chair curriculum com., 2005-08. Co-editor: The Impact of Managed Care on the Practice of Psychotherapy: Innovation, Implementation, and Controversy, 1996; contbr. articles to profl. jours.; rsch. on psychotherapy, suicide and provision of preventive svcs. Nat. Jewish Welfare Bd. fellow Fordham U., 1972-74. Trainee NIMH Columbia U., 1978. Mem.: NASW, Nat. Acads. Practice (disting. practitioner), NJ Coalition Mental Health Profls. and Consumers (mem. adv. bd.), Nat. Study Group on Social Work and Psychoanalysis, Alliance for Universal Access to Psychotherapy (founder, membership chair, mem. steering com. 1994-96 1994—96), Am. Assn. Psychoanalysis Clin. Social Work (treas. 1991—93, chair NY-NJ area 1992—94), Acad. Cert. Social Workers (cert.), Ea. Group Psychotherapy Soc., Am. Group Psychotherapy Assn., Adelphi Soc. Psychoanalysis and Psychotherapy, NY State Soc. Clin. Social Work (chair com. on psychoanalysis 1991—96, diplomate). Office: 175 Cedar Ln Teaneck NJ 07666-4315 Office Phone: 201-836-5050. Business E-Mail: ralperin@aol.com.

ALPERN, HARVEY L., cardiologist; b. LA, June 1, 1938; s. Sander A. and Rose K. Alpern; m. (div. 1972); 1 child, David. BA, Pomona Coll., 1960; MD, U. So. Calif., 1964. Diplomate Am. Bd. Internal Medicine, Am. Bd. Cardiovasc. Disease. Intern Cedars of Lebanon Hosp., LA, 1964-65; resident in internal medicine Cedars-Sinai Med. Ctr., LA, 1965-67, resident in cardiology, 1967-68; cardiology fellow St. Georges Hosp., London, 1968-69; pvt. practice Santa Monica, 1970—. Bd. dirs. Century City Hosp., L.A.; med. dir. Exec Fit Health, San Francisco, 1985-93. Contbr. articles to profl. jours. Bd. dirs. L.A. Bus. Coun., 1987-96, Nat. Health Found., L.A., 1985-95; active L.A.-Guangzhou Sister City Assn., 1994—. Capt. USAFR, 1965-70. Fellow Am. Heart Assn. (bd. dirs. L.A. chpt. 1974-75, coun. on clin. cardiology), Am. Coll. Cardiology, Am. Acad. Disability Evaluation Physicians (bd. dirs., pres.); mem. ACP, Calif. Soc. Indsl. Medicine (bd. dirs.). Jewish. Avocation: wine tasting. Office: 1223 Wilshire Blvd # 756 Santa Monica CA 90403 Office Phone: 310-829-4657. Personal E-mail: alpernh@aol.com. *

ALPERN, ROBERT J., dean, medical educator; b. Nov. 3, 1950; m. Patricia Ann Preisig; chilren: Rachelle, Kyle. BA in Chemistry with honors and highest distinction, Northwestern U., 1972; MD with honors, U. Chgo., 1976. Diplomate Am. Bd. Internal Medicine; bd. cert in nephrology. Intern in internal medicine Columbia U., NYC, 1976-77, resident in internal medicine, 1977-79; fellow in nephrology and renal physiology U. Calif. Cardiovascular Rsch. Inst., San Francisco, 1979-82, asst. prof. medicine divsn. nephrology, 1982-87; assoc. prof. medicine U. Tex. Southwestern Med. Ctr., Dallas, 1987-90, chief nephrology, 1987-98, prof. medicine, 1990—2004, Ruth W. and Milton P. Levy, Sr. chair in molecular nephrology, 1994—2004, dean, 1998—2004, Atticus James Gill M.C. Chair in Med. Sci., 2000—04; dean Yale U. Sch. Medicine, New Haven, 2004—. Max Martin Salick vis. prof., UCLA Sch. Medicine, 1994; mem. Med. Sch. Admissions com. U. Calif. San Francisco, 1985-87, general clin. rsch. ctr. adv. com. U. Tex. Southwestern Med. Ctr., 1987-91, search com. for chief of cardiology, 1989, search com. for chmn. urology, 1993, search com. for chief of hematology/oncology, 1997, Med. Sch. Admissions com., 1994-96, chmn. 1996-98; chmn. general clin. rsch. ctr. adv. com. U. Tex. Southwestern Med. Ctr., 1988-90, search com. for chief of infectious diseases U. Tex. Southwestern Med. Ctr., 1994-96; adv. coun. Nat. Inst. Diabetes and Digestive and Kidney Diseases; presenter, lectr. in field. Editl. bd: Kidney Internat., 1989-90, Renal Physiology and Biochemistry, 1989-95, Am. Jour. Physiology, 1992-94, Internat. Yearbook of Nephrology, 1989-92, Seminars in Nephrology, 1990—, Am. Jour. Kidney Diseases, 1991-96, Kidney and Blood Pressure Research, 1996—, Am. Jour. Med. Scis., 1996—, Am. Jour. Medicine, 1997—, cons. editor: Jour. Clin. Investigation, 1993-99, Kidney Internat., 1990—; editl. com. Jour. Clin. Investigation, 1988-93; assoc. editor Am. Jour. Physiology, 1989-92, Hospital Practice: Physiology in Medicine, 1991-94; section editor: Annual Review of Physiology, 1993-97, Current Opinion in Nephrology and Hypertension, 1997-99; contbr. papers, chaps., articles to profl. pubs. Recipient NSF award for rsch. in developmental biology, 1971, NIH Merit award, 1996-2003. Mem. Inst. Medicine, Am. Soc. Nephrology (mem. coun. 1995-2002, pres.-elect 2000, pres. 2001), Internat. Soc. Nephrology, Am. Physiological Soc., Am. Heart Assn., Am. Soc. Clin. Investigation, Assn. Am. Physicians, Alpha Omega Alpha, Sigma Xi, Phi Beta Kappa. Office: Yale U Sch Medicine Physicians Bldg 800 Howard Ave New Haven CT 06520 Office Phone: 203-785-4672. E-mail: robert.alpern@yale.edu. *

ALPERS, DAVID HERSHEL, gastroenterologist, educator; b. Phila., May 9, 1935; s. Bernard Jacob and Lillian (Sher) A.; m. Melanie Goldman, Aug. 12, 1977; children: Ann, Ruth, Barbara. BA, Harvard U., 1956, MD, 1960. Cert. Am. Bd. Internal Medicine, 1967. Intern Mass. Gen. Hosp., Boston, 1960-61, resident in internal medicine, 1961-62; instr. medicine Harvard U., 1965-67, assoc. in medicine, 1967-68, asst. prof., 1968-69; asst. prof. medicine Washington U., St. Louis, 1969-72, assoc. prof., 1972-73, prof., 1973—, William B. Kountz prof., 1997—, dir. gastrointestinal divsn., 1969-97, asst. dir. clin. nutrition rsch. unit, 1999—; sr. cons. R&D GlaxoSmith-Kline, 1999—2009. Author: (with others) Manual of Nutritional Therapeutics, 5th edit., 2008 assoc. editor: Textbook of Gastroenterology, 5th edit., 2008, Physiology of the Gastrointestinal Tract, 4th edit., 1997; assoc. editor: Jour. Clin. Investigation, 1977-82, Encyclopedia of Gastroenterology, 2003, Am. Jour. Clin. Nutrition, 2008-; editor: Am. Jour. Physiology, Gastrointestinal and Liver Physiology, 1991-97; mem. editl. bd.: Jour. Biol. Chemistry, 1998-2003; editor, Curr Opin Gastroenterol, sect. Small Intestine and Nutrition, 1995-; assoc editor, Am. Jours. Clin. Nutrition, 2008-; contbr. articles and revs. to profl. jours., chpts. to books. With USPHS, 1962—64. David H. Alpers Ann. lectureship, Wash. U., Sch. Medicine, 1999. Fellow Am. Soc. Nutrition; mem. Am. Soc. Clin. Investigation, Assn. Am. Physicians, Am. Gastroent. Assn. (chmn. tng. and edn. com. 1974-78, dir. undergrad. tchg. project 1974-99, pres. 1990-91, Julius Friedenwald medal 1997), Am. Soc. Biochem. Molecular Biology (editl. bd. 1998-2003), Am. Fedn. Clin. Rsch., Am. Physiol. Assn. (mem. gastrointestinal sect. steering com. 1991-97, Disting. Gastrointestinal Physiology Rsch. award 1998, mem. pubs. com. 1999-2001). Avocation: music. Office: Washington U Med Sch Dept Internal Medicine PO Box 8031 Saint Louis MO 63110-1010 Business E-Mail: dalpers@dom.wustl.edu.

ALPERT, BERNARD STEPHEN, plastic surgeon, educator; b. Potsdam, NY; BA cum laude, Amherst Coll., Mass.; MD, SUNY, Buffalo, 1974. Diplomate Am. Bd. Plastic Surgery. Intern plastic surgery U. Calif. San Francisco Med. Ctr., 1974—75, resident plastic surgery, 1975—80; fellow microsurgery Davies Med. Ctr., San Francisco, 1978—80; staff dept. plastic surgery Calif. Pacific Med. Ctr., 1980—; clin. asst. prof. to assoc. clin. prof. surgery U. Calif. San Francisco Sch. Medicine; pvt. practice San Francisco. Pres. Med. Bd. Calif., 2001—02. Contbr. articles to profl. jours. Mem.: ACS, Am. Soc. Plastic Surgery, Calif. Soc. Plastic Surgeons, Am. Soc. Aesthetic Plastic Surgery (chair legis. com.). Office: 45 Castro St Ste 150 San Francisco CA 94114 Office Phone: 415-626-6644. Business E-Mail: baipertmd@aol.com.

ALPERT, BRUCE S., cardiologist, educator; b. Albany, NY, Aug. 23, 1947; BA, Dartmouth Coll., Hanover, NH, 1969; MD, Johns Hopkins U., Balt., 1973. Prof. ULPS, 1984—. Co-chair AAMI Sphygmomanometer Com., 1987—. Recipient Plough Found. Chair of Excellence award, UTHSC. Master: NASPEM; fellow: AAP, ACC, AHA; mem.: ISHIB. Office: 50 N Dunlap St Rm 4610 Memphis TN 38103 Office Fax: 901-287-5107. Business E-Mail: bsalpert@uthsc.edu.

ALPERT, JOEL JACOBS, pediatrician, educator; b. New Haven, May 9, 1930; s. Herman Harold and Alice (Jacobs) A.; m. Barbara Ellen Wasserstrom, July 13, 1957; children: Norman, Mark, Deborah. AB, Yale U., 1952; MD, Harvard U., 1956. Diplomate Am. Bd. Pediatrics. Intern in medicine Children's Hosp. Med. Ctr., Boston, 1956-57, jr. asst. resident in medicine, 1957-58, chief resident for ambulatory svcs., fellow in medicine, 1961-62, from asst. to sr. assoc., 1962-72; exch. registrar St. Mary's Hosp. Med. Sch., London, 1958-59; from instr. to assoc. prof. Med. Sch., Harvard U., Boston, 1962-72, lectr., 1972—; pediatrician in chief Boston City Hosp., 1972-92; prof. pediatrics and pub. health Boston U. Sch. Medicine, 2002—02, chmn. dept. pediatrics, 1972-93, also prof. sociomed. scis. and pub. health law, 1980—2002, prof. emeritus pediats. cmty. medicine and sociomed. scis., chmn. pediats., 2002—, prof. emeritus pub. health and health law, 2002—; courtesy prof. pediat. U. Fla., Sainesville, 2007—. Dozer vis. prof. Ben. Gurion Sch. Medicine, Beersheva, Israel, 1979; Raine Found. vis. prof. U. Western Australia, Perth, 1983; James and Jean Davis Prestige visitor U. Otago, Dunedin, New Zealand, 1995; cons. USPHS, 1972—, Children's Hosp., Boston, 1972; spl. cons. pres. N.Y.C. Health and Hosps. Corp., 1989; vis. prof. pediatrics Columbia Coll. Phys. and Surg., NYU Sch. Medicine; mem. med. adv. com. N.Y.C. Health and Hosps. Corp., 1989; courtesy prof. U. Fla., Gainesville, 2007-; cons. Office Student Affairs Boston U. Sch. Medicine, 1995-, asst. dean, 2008-. Author books, including: The Education of Physicians For Primary Care, 1974; also numerous papers Mem. Town Meeting, Winchester, Mass., 1970-72; mem. exec. com. Mass. Com. for Children and Youth, Boston, 1975-82; chmn. adv. com. Mass. Poison Info. System, Boston, 1980-92; bd. dirs. Med. Found., Boston, 1992—; cons. Commonwealth Fund and MEM Assocs., 1996—. Capt. U.S. Army, 1959-61. Recipient lifetime achievement award Mass. Poison Info. System, 1992, Hon. Mention Pub. Health Svc. award Pew Found., 1999, Pew Found. award for Achievement in Primary Care Edn.; numerous grants, 1965—, spl. fellow Nat. Ctr. Health Svcs. Rsch., London, 1971. Fellow: Royal Coll. Pediat. and Child Health (hon. 2000, U.K.), Am. Acad. Pediat. (v.p. 1997—98, pres. 1998—99, Job Lewis Smith award 1992); mem.: Academic Pediat. Assn., Mass. Assn. Pediat. Dept. Chmn. (chmn. 1976—78, 1981—93), Ambulatory Pediat. Assn. (pres. 1989, George Armstrong medal 1989, Lifetime Career Achievement award 2000, Pub. Policy and Advocacy award 2002), Philippine Ambulatory Pediat. Assn. (hon.), Soc. Pediat. Rsch., Am. Pediat. Soc., Inst. Medicine NAS (mem. governing coun. 1993—95, mem. bd. families and children 1993—95, mem. task force on future of primary care 1994—96), St. Botolph Club, Aescalapian Club, Harvard Club, Yale Club, Lancet Club, Alpha Omega Alpha. Jewish. Home: 152 Orchid Cay Dr Palm Beach Gardens FL 33418 Office: Boston Univ Sch Medicine Boston Med Ctr 88 E Newton St Vose Hall 3 Boston MA 02118-2393

ALPERT, JOSEPH STEPHEN, cardiologist, educator; b. New Haven, Feb. 1, 1942; s. Zelly Charles and Beatrice Ann (Kopsofsky) A.; m. Helle Mathiasen, Aug. 6, 1965; children: Eva Elisabeth, Niels David. BA magna cum laude, Yale U., 1963; MD cum laude, Harvard U., 1969. Diplomate internal medicine and cardiovasc. disease Am. Bd. Internal Medicine. Successively intern, resident in internal medicine, fellow in cardiovascular disease Peter Bent Brigham Hosp.-Harvard U. Med. Sch., Boston, 1969-74, dir. Samuel A. Levine cardiac unit, asst. prof. medicine, 1976-78; prof., dir. divsn. cardiovascular medicine U. Mass. Med. Sch., Worcester, 1978-92, vice-chm. dept. medicine, 1990—, Edward Budnitz prof. of cardiovascular medicine, 1988-92; Robert W. and Irene P. Flinn prof. U. Ariz., 1992—, chmn. dept. medicine, 1992—2006, asst. to the dean Coll. Medicine, 2006—09; dir. Covonay Care, 2009—. Cons. West Roxbury VA Hosp., Boston, VA Med. Ctr., Tucson; sec., treas. med. staff U. Mass. Med. Ctr., 1979-81, pres. med. staff, 1981-82; bd. dirs. Am. Bd. Internal Medicine. Author: The Heart Attack Handbook, 1978, 3d edit., 1993, Cardiovascular Physiopathology, 1984; co-author: Manual of Coronary Care, 1977, 1980, 1984, 1987, 1993, 2000, Manual of Cardiovascular Diagnosis and Therapy, 1980, 1984, 1988, 1996, 2003, Valvular Heart Disease, 1981, 1987, 2000, Intensive Care Medicine, 1985, 2d edit., 1991, The Clinician's Companion, 1986, Modern Coronary Care, 1990, 2d edit., 1996, Diagnostic Atlas of the Heart, 1994, Cardiology for the Primary Care Physician, 1996, 3d edit., 2000, Primary Care of Native American Patients, 1999, American Heart Association's Clinical Cardiology Consult, 2001, 2006; editor-in-chief Current Cardiology Reports, 2001—05, Am. Jour. Medicine, 2005—; editor: Cardiology in Rev., 2001—05; assoc. editor Jour. History of Medicine and Allied Scis., 1977—80, editl. cons. Little, Brown & Co., Appleton-Century Crofts, mem. editl. bd. Am. Jour. Cardiology, 1985—, Archives Internal Medicine, 1987—, Heart and Lung, 1987—90, Geriatric Cardiovascular Medicine, 1988—89, Am. Jour. Noninvasive Cardiology, 1987—95, Am. Heart Jour., 1992—97, Internat. Jour. Cardiology, 1992—, European Heart Jour., 1995—, Heart Disease, 1999—2004, Cardiology, 1985—, assoc. editor, 1987—, editor-in-chief, 1991—2005, Am. Jour. Medicine, 2005—; contbr. articles to profl. jours. Lt. comdr. USNR, 1974—76. Recipient Gold medal U. Copenhagen, 1968, Edward Rhodes Stitt award San Diego Naval Hosp., 1976, George W. Thorn award Peter Bent Bingham Hosp., 1977, Outstanding Tchr. award U. Mass. Med. Sch., 1981, 86, 87, 90, U. Ariz. Med. Sch., 1995, 97-2002, 06; Fulbright scholar Copenhagen, 1963-64; USPHS-Mass. Heart Assn. fellow, 1971-72, NIH spl. rsch. fellow, 1972-73 Fellow and Master ACP, Fellow Am. Coll. Cardiology (jour. editl. bd. 1983-86, chmn. tng. dirs. com. 1991—, trustee 1996-2001, Gifted Tchr. award 2004), Am. Coll. Chest Physicians (gov. for Mass. 1983-85), European Soc. Cardiology; mem. AAAS, Am. Heart Assn. (fellow coun. clin. cardiology, vice chmn. 1991-92, chmn. 1993-95, exec. com. 1986—, Disting. Achievement award 2001), Am. Assn. History of Medicine, Am. Fedn. Clin. Rsch., Assn. Univ. Cardiologists, New Eng. Cardiovascular Club, Assn. Profs. of Medicine, Danish Cardiology Assn. (hon.), Argentine Heart Assn. (fgn. corr.), Israeli Heart Soc. (hon.), Am. Clin. and Climatological Assn., Aesculapian Club, Phi Beta Kappa, Sigma Xi, Alpha Omega Alpha. Office: U Az Coll Medicine 1501 N Campbell Ave Tucson AZ 85724-5017 Office Phone: 520-626-6138. Business E-Mail: jalpert@email.arizona.edu. *

ALPERT, MARTIN JEFFREY, chiropractor; b. NYC, Apr. 22, 1951; s. Sheldon Lee and Beatrice (Ostrager) Alpert; m. Gilberta Joachim, May 4, 2000; children: Chad, Mitchell, Eva. BA in Pre-Med. and History, Syracuse U., NY, 1972; DC in Chiropractic Medicine, NY Chiropractic Coll., 1976; MS in Biology and Nutrition, U. Bridgeport, Conn., 1979. Diplomate Am. Bd. Disability Analysts, Am. Acad. Pain Mgmt., Am. Bd. Profl. Disability Cons., Am. Acad. Experts Traumatic Stress, Am. Assn. Integrative Medicine, Coll. Pain Mgmt. Lt. col. ret. Signal Corps USAR, 1970—2005; pvt. practice Yonkers, NY, 1977—84, Hollywood, Fla., 1985, Coconut Creek, Fla., 1987—92, Miami, Fla., 1992—95, Ft. Lauderdale, Fla., 1985—2007, Orlando, Fla., 1994—2003, Palm Bay, Fla., 2008, Boca Raton, Fla., 2009—. Mil. acad. academic rep. & mil. liaison officer US Mil. Acad. West Pt., 1997—; adj. faculty US Army Command and Gen. Staff Col., Ft. Leavenworth, Kans., 1998—. Decorated Meritorious Svc. medal with Two Oak Leaf Cluster, Army Commendation medal with Five Oak Leaf Cluster, Army Achievement medal, Nat. Def. Svc. medal, Army Res. Component Achievement medal, Armed Forces Res. medal, Army Svc. Ribbon, Humanitarian Svc. medal. Fellow: Am. Assn. Integrative Medicine (diplomate mem.), Am. Acad. Experts Traumatic Stress, Am. Back Soc., Internat. Biog. Assn.; mem.: Palm Beach County Med. Rsch. Corps., US Sports Chiropractic Fedn., Fla. Chiropractic Assn., Fla. Chiropractic Soc., Am. Acad. Spine Physicians, Am. Acad. Chiropractic Physicians, Internat. Fedn. Sports Chiropractic, World Fedn. Chiropractic, Am. Pub. Health Assn., NY Acad. Scis., Am. Coll. Sports Medicine, Internat. Chiropractors Assn., Am. Chiropractic Assn., US Army Command and Gen. Staff Coll. Found., Army Hist. Found., Mil. Officers Assn. America, Res. Officers Assn. US, Assn. US Army, Signal Corps Regimental Assn., Naval War Coll. Found., Alpha Phi Omega (life), Nat. Svc. Frat. Democrat. Avocations: jogging, chess, basketball, piano. Home: 19674 Black Olive Ln Boca Raton FL 33498 Office: Boca Rehab Clin Ste B150 7601 N Federal Hwy Ste B150 Boca Raton FL 33487 Office Phone: 561-994-3113. Business E-Mail: doctorofchiropractic@hotmail.com.

ALPERT-DIANI, LINDA, psychologist; b. Phila., Mar. 6, 1945; d. David Martin and Annette Kravitz; m. Howard G. Sr. Diani, Feb. 26, 1996; stepchildren: Howard Jr., Marueen, Mike, Peter; children: Michael Weinstein, Stacey Weinstein. MHS, Lincoln U., 1995; PhD, Walden U., 2000. Registered hypnotherapist, cert. psychotherapist; addiction counselor, clin. supr. Pa., social worker N.J., addictions prevention specialist, bd. cert. adminstr., registered behavioral therapist; lic. profl. counselor. Client-liaison Achievement and Guidance Ctrs. Am., NYC and Bensalem, Pa., 1983—86, N.Y. adminstr., 1986—90; cons. Bucks County Drug and Alcohol Commn., Doylestown, Pa., 1990—91; acting dir. mental health svcs., dir. utilization rev. Mustard Seed Managed Care, Bensalem, 1990—93; psychotherapist, addiction counselor Riverside House Drug and Alcohol Rehab. Facility, Phila., 1993—9395; cons., outpatient counselor Kensington Project, Phila., 1993—94; pvt. practice substance abuse and mental health counseling Croydon, Pa., 1993—98; doctoral psychology intern Independence House, Phila., 1998—99; behavioral specialist cons. Lenape Valley Found., Doylestown, Pa., 1999—2006. ATOD specialist Mercer Coun. on Alcoholism and Drug Addiction, Trenton, NJ, 1994—95; outpatient therapist Penn Found., Inc., Sellersville, Pa., 1994—96, 2007—; psychiat. care mgr., social worker Allegheny U. Hosps., Bucks County Divsn., Warminster, Pa., 1995—97; outpatient therapist, addiction counselor Milestones Cmty. Healthcare, Inc., Roslyn, Pa., 1996—98. Cons. Cedar Ave. House, Croydon, 1993—97, bd. dirs., 1994—97. Fellow, Am. Bd. Forensic Counselors, Am. Coll. Mental Health Practitioners. Mem.: APA, Am. Coll. Profl. Mental Health Practitioners, Am. Physicians' Registrar Inc., Am. Coll. Advanced Practice Psychologists, Am. Coll. Forensic Examiners, Am. Acad. Drs. Psychology, Am. Coll. Forensic Counselors, Am. Assn. Behavioral Therapists, Am. Assn. Profl. Hypnotherapists, Nat. Assn. Addiction Prevention Specialists, Pa. Assn. Cert. Addiction Counselors, Pa. Psychol. Assn. Office: 807 Lawn Ave Sellersville PA 18960 Office Phone: 215-257-6551 ext. 385. Business E-Mail: lalpert@pennfoundation.org.

ALPHER, VICTOR SETH, clinical psychologist, consultant, researcher; b. Washington, Oct. 20, 1954; s. Ralph Asher and Louise Ellen (Simons) A. BA, U. Pa., Phila., 1976, MA; PhD in Clin. Psychology, Vanderbilt U., Nashville, Tenn., 1985. Diplomate in clin. psychology Am. Bd. Profl. Psychology, 1995. Grad. fellow Vanderbilt U., Nashville, 1981-85; asst. prof. U. Tex. Health Sci. Ctr., Houston, 1986-88, clin. asst. prof., 1989-96. Cons. Rsch. Inst. on Addictions, Buffalo, 1990—, Meml. Geriatric Evaluation and Resource Ctr., Houston, 1991-95 Cons. reviewer Jour. Cons. and Clin. Psychology, 1996; contbr. articles to profl. jours., including Radiations, The SPS Observer, APS News, Jour. Cons. and Clin. Psychology, Jour. Personality Assessment, Jour. Psychopathology and Behavioral Assessment, Psychotherapy, Jour. Applied Physiology, Operative Dentistry, The Submarine Rev., physics online ru Mem. AAAS, Am. Fedn. Musicians, Nat. Acad. Recording Arts Scis., Sigma Xi, Am. Phys. Soc, Internat. Naval Rsch. Orgn., Naval Submarine League, Historic Naval Ships Assn., Orgn. Am. Hists., Soc. Mil. Historians. Avocations: languages, music. Personal E-mail: alphervs@gmail.com. Business E-Mail: victor.s.alpher.85@alumni.vanderbilt.edu.

ALQAHTANI, JERMAN M., ophthalmologist, educator; b. Saudi Arabia, Dec. 8, 1962; MBBS, King Faisal U., 1988, degree in Ophthalmology, 1995. Rsch. fellow anterior segment King Faisal U., Dammam, 1995—97, asst. prof., 2002—10; rsch. fellow ophthalmic pathology Walter Reed Med. Army, Washington, 1997—99. Chmn. dept. ophthalmology King Fahd Hosp. U., 2003—07; dir. residency tng. program Eatern province, mem. sci. coun. Saudi Bd. Ophthalmology, 2006—10; mem. sci. coun. Arab Bd. Ophthalmology, 2006—10. Recipient Omani Ophthal. Soc. Sheild. Mem.: Am. Assn. Ophthalmic Pathologist, European Soc. Cataract and Refractive Surgeons, Am. Assn. Cataract and Refractive Surgery, Am. Acad. Ophthalmology (Internat. Scholar award, Internat. Ophthalmologist Edn. award). Office: King Faisal University Dept Ophthalmology P O Box 2114 Dammam 31451 Saudi Arabia Home Fax: 0096638944449. Personal E-mail: jalqahtany@yahoo.com.

ALQASOUMI, SALEH I., pharmacy professor, educator and researcher; b. Saudi Arabia, Feb. 16, 1972; BS in Pharm. Scis., King Saud U., Riyadh, 1996, MSc in Pharmacognosy, 1999, PhD in Pharmacognosy, 2007. Dean Coll. Pharmacy, Al-kharj U., 2008—. Stores mgr. & medicinal herbs cons. General Nutrition Ctrs., Saudi Arabia, 1997—99; dir. medicinal, aromatic and poisonous plants rsch. ctr. Coll. Pharmacy, King Saud U., 2007—09, supr. herbal & alternative medicine unit, 2004—07; cons. Riyadh Coll. Dentistry & Pharmacy, Saudi Arabia, 2007—. Recipient Disting. Rsch. & Publ. award, Riyadh, Saudi Arabia. Mem.: Herb Soc. America, Soc. Medicinal Plant Rsch., Am. Soc. Pharmacognosy, Saudi Pharm. Soc. Office: King Saud University Coll Pharmacy Riyadh 11451 Saudi Arabia Office Phone: 96614677278. Office Fax: 96614677245. Business E-Mail: sqasoumi@ksu.edu.sa.

AL-RABIAH, SAMI MAHMOUD, surgeon; b. Qebla, Kuwait, 1952; Ophthalmic surgeon Alrabiah Med. Ctr., Kuwait. CEO and owner Al-Deebaj Internat. Trading Co., Kuwait, 2004—. Mem.: Pan Arab African Coun. of Ophthalmology (pres. 2001), Pan Arab Coun. of Ophthalmology (pres. 2001), Ophthalmology Dept. (chmn. Kuwait 1990—2001). Achievements include establishment of the most equipped and largest eye clinics in Kuwait since 1988; renowned Dr. in ophthalmology and as an ophthalmic surgeon in Kuwait. Office: Alrabiah Medical Clinic Al Farwaniah 55 Airport Rd Kuwait Office Fax: 96524759394. *

AL-RUKBAN, MOHAMMED OTHMAN, dean; b. Riyadh, Saudi Arabia, Apr. 1, 1973; MBChB, King Saud U., Saudi Arabia, 1997; degree in Family Medicine, King Saud U., 2002. Assoc. prof. & cons. family medicine dean Majmaah U., Coll. Medicine Saudi Arabia, 2010—. Editl. bd. mem. Brit. Jour. Sports Medicine, Saudi Med. Jour.; family medicine bd. mem. Saudi Commn. Health Specialities, Majmaah U. Sci. Coun. Recipient Best Oral Presentation award, Internat. Conf. Med. Edn., Abu Dhabi, UAE, 2010; named Resident of Yr., Coll. Medicine, King Saud U., Saudi Arabia, 2001. Mem.: Saudi Soc. Med. Edn. Avocations: reading, swimming, travel. Home: PO Box 91678 King Abdel Aziz St Riyadh 11643 Saudi Arabia

ALS, HEIDELISE, psychology professor, director; b. Krumbach, Germany, Nov. 11, 1940; PhD, U. Pa., 1975. Assoc. prof. psychology, dir., neurobehavioral infant and child studies Harvard Med. Sch., Children's Hosp. Boston, 1984—. Office: 320 Longwood Ave Enders EN107 Child Boston MA 02115 Business E-Mail: heidelise.als@childrens.harvard.edu.

ALS, HEIDELISE, psychiatrist, educator; b. Krumbach, Schwaben, Germany; permanent resident; BS in Edn. summa cum laude, Friedrich-Maximilian U. Wurzburg & Padagogische Hochschule Eichstatt, Germany, 1963; MS in Edn., U. Pa., 1968, PhD in Devel. & Ednl. Psychology, 1975. Instr. Coll. Edn. U. Pa., 1970—71; vis. scientist, human ethology & devel. psychology Behavior Devel. Rsch. Unit St. Mary's Hosp. U. London, 1972—73; assoc., pediat. Harvard Med. Sch., 1975—77, postdoc. supr., fellow, clin. child psychology & child devel., Child Devel. Unit Children's Hosp. Boston, 1975—80, asst. prof., pediat., 1977—86, assoc. prof., psychology, 1986—. Rsch. assoc., pediat. Child Devel. Unit Children's Hosp. Med. Ctr., Boston, 1973—75, instr., pediat., 1974—79, assoc., divsn. child devel. & dept. psychiatry, 1975—84, dir., pediat. rsch., 1977—79, dir., clin. rsch., 1979—84; cons., advisor, infant devel. & care Brigham and Women's Hosp. Harvard Med. Sch. Newborn Svcs. Newborn Intensive Care Unit, Boston, 1979—; assoc., psychaitry Children's Hosp. Med. Ctr., 1984—98; investigator, neurology & psychiatry Children's Hosp., Boston, 1984—, dir., neurobehavioral infant & child studies, 1984—, sr. assoc., psychiatry, 1998—; rsch. assoc., newborn medicine Brigham & Women's Hosp., Boston, 1987—; consulting staff, pediatric psychology Spaulding Rehab. Hosp., Boston, 1988—. Mem. Nat. Ctr. Infant's Toddlers and Families Mental Health, Washington, 1975—84, Nat. Adv. Coun. Clin. Infant Programs NIMH Mental Health Study Ctr., Adelphi, Md., 1977—81, Nat. Adv. Com. Children and Youth Am. Found. for Blind, 1978—81, Consulting Bd. Nat. Inst. Edn. Funded Project Welcome Wheelock Coll., Boston, 1980—86, Nat. Consulting Bd. Nat. Inst. Edn. Funded Project Interact Oakland Children's Hosp., Calif., 1980—94, Nat. Consulting Bd. Nat. Inst. Edn. Funded Project NICU, Albuquerque, 1984—92, NICHD Spl. Study Sect., 1985, Task Force on Family-Centered Health Care Medically Fragile Children, 1987—88, NICHD Sudden Infant Death Adv. Bd. Panel, 1988—90, Expert Panel OSAP Nat. Resource Ctr. Prevention Perinatal Abuse of Alcohol and Other Drugs, 1992, SCRD Sci. Review Panel Soc. Rsch. Child Devel., 1992, Profl. Adv. Com. Phys. and Devel. Environment High-Risk Infant Nat. Resource Ctr. Study NICU Care Practices and Environ. Factors, 1993—2005. Mem.: Leadership Tng. Project U. Okla. Health Scis. Ctr. (sci. advisor), Boston Inst. for Devel. of Infants and Parents (faculty bd. mem.), Nat. NIDCAP Tng. Ctr. Children's Hosp. Boston and Brigham Women's Hosp. (founder, dir.). Office: Enders Pediatric Rsch Bldg EN-107 Children's Hosp Boston 320 Longwood Ave Boston MA 02115 Home: 1990 Commonwealth Ave 3 Boston MA 02135 Office Fax: 617-730-0224. Business E-Mail: heidelise.als@childrens.harvard.edu.

AL-SAATI, FAISAL ABDULKARIM, orthopedist, surgeon; s. Abdulkareem Abdul Allah Al-Saati and Lamia Rashed Al-Shek; m. Nahed Maed Ashek, June 28, 1978; children: Anoud, Ma'ad, Ghazal, Saud, Farah, Nouf, Hisham. MSc in Orthop., U. London, 1984; MD, U. Damascus, 1976. Intern King Faisal Specialist Hosp., U. London, 1984, Royal Coll. London; cons. orthop. surgeon; pres. Saati Med. Ctr. Fellow: ACS, Am. Acad. Orthop. Surgeons, Internat. Coll. Surgeons, Am. Acad. Orthop. Surgeons, Med. Soc. Vienna, Syrian Med. Assn., Internat. Coll. Surgeons; mem.: Med. Soc. Vienna. Achievements include development of distal femoral osteotomy for post polio patients; saati osteotomy for bone lengthening. Avocation: squash. Office: Saati Med Ctr Po Box 88591 Riyadh Saudi Arabia Office Phone: 0096614653789, 0096614614702. Personal E-mail: fsaati@yahoo.com.

AL-SARRAF, NAEL, surgeon; b. Kuwait, Nov. 13, 1976; s. Ahmed Al-Sarraf; m. Lamia Malek. MBBCh, Trinity Coll. Dublin, BAO, 2001. Intern St. James's Hosp., Dublin, 2002—03, sr. house officer-gen. surgery, 2003—04, sr. house officer-orthopeadics and trauma, 2004, sr. house officer-cardiothoracic surgery, 2005, rsch. registrar-thoracic oncology, 2005—07, Trinity Coll., Dublin, 2005—07; sr. house officer-emergency medicine Beaumont Hosp., Dublin, 2003; registrar-cardiothoracic surgery Chest Disease Hosp., Kuwait, 2007—. Master: RCS (Ireland). Democrat. Muslim. Office: Chest Disease Hosp Al-Sabah Kuwait Home: St 3 Block 11 House 5 718 Al-Jabriah Kuwait Personal E-mail: trinityq8@hotmail.com.

ALSASI, OMAI MOHAMMED, pediatric radiologist, consultant; b. Makkah, Saudi Arabia, May 24, 1967; d. Mohammed Abdullah Alsasi and Najat Hassan Alsindi; m. Mobarak Mohammed Alzahrani, 1993; children: Faisal Mobarak Alzahrani, Arwa Mobarak Alzahrani, Sara Mobarak Alzahrani, Reema Mobarak Alzahrani. MB, chB, King Abdulaziz U., 1990. MBBH Kingdom Of Saudi Arabia, 1990. Sr. registrar Riyadh Armed Forces Hosp., 1999—2004, pediatric radiologist, 2002—, cons., 2004—. Contbr. articles to profl. jours. Fellow, Riyadh Alkarj Hosp., 2000, 2002, 2004. Mem.: Royal Coll. Radiologists (assoc.; U.K. 1993—2005). Home: Prince Turki The First 365453 Riyadh 11393 Saudi Arabia Office: Riyadh Alkarj Hosp 7897 Riyadh 11159 Saudi Arabia Personal E-mail: dr_omaialsasi@hotmail.com.

AL SEBAI, MOHAMMED WASEF BADREDDIN, spinal surgeon; b. Homs, Syria, Feb. 18, 1954; s. Badreddin and Afaf Al Sebai; m. Zena AbdulRahim Al Sebai, Mar. 6, 1980; children: Afaf, Badr, Abdullah. MBBCh, Cairo U., 1978. Specialist spinal surgeon Riyadh Ctrl. Hosp., 1989—91, acting cons. spinal surgeon, 1991—94; clin. asst. prof. King Saud U., Riyadh, 1993—2004, clin. tutor, 1993—2004; cons., head spinal unit Riyadh Med. Complex, 1994—2000; cons. spinal surgeon Riyadh Armed Forces Hosp., 2000—04; cons. orthop. spinal surgeon Habib Med. Ctr., Riyadh, 2004—. Clin. tuto Arab Bd. and Saudi Bd. Tng. Program, Riyadh, 1993—2004; reviewer PanArab Neurosurgery Jour. and Saudi Med. Jour., Riyadh, 2000—; head standardization spinal units com. Ministry Def. and Aviation, Riyadh, 2002—04; organising com. mem. Riyadh Orthop. Club, 2004—. Author: (book) Tuberculosis; contbr. articles to jour. Fellow, Royal Coll. Physicians and Surgeons Glasgow, 1988. Fellow: ACS. Achievements include first to introduce and apply new systems of spinal fixation and spinal surgery in Saudi Arabia; research in spinal injuries in Saudi Arabia. Avocations: swimming, travel, walking, reading. Home: King Fahd Rd Riyadh Saudi Arabia Office: Po Box 300982 11372 Riyadh Saudi Arabia Office Fax: 0096614633582. Personal E-mail: wsebai@hotmail.com, wsebai@gmail.com.

AL-SHAMMARI, SULAIMAN ABDULLAH, medical educator, consultant; b. Arar, Saudi Arabia, Feb. 12, 1956; s. Abdullah Ibrahim and Meznah Saleh (Al-Goneaan) Al-S.; m. Inaam Saud Al-Helal; children: Meznah, Ali, Abdullah. MB, BS, King Saud U., Riyadh, Saudi Arabia, 1983, M of Family Medicine, 1986. Resident Dept. Family and Cmty. Medicine, King Saud U., 1985, demonstrator, 1985-86, lectr., 1986-88, asst. prof., 1988-92, assoc. prof., 1992-97, prof. family medicine, 1997—, chmn., 1996—. Coord. residency program Coll. Medicine, Riyadh, 1992-94; cons. Ministry of Health, Riyadh, 1992-93, 95-96; cons. family physician King Khalid and King Abdulaziz U. Hosp., Riyadh, 1991—; dir. primary care clinics, Riyadh, 1988-92. Contbr. articles to profl. jours. Recipient grant Ministry of Health, Riyadh, 1991, grant King Abdulaziz City for Sci. and Tech., Riyadh, 1992. Mem. Royal Coll. Gen. Practitioners, Saudi Soc. Family and Cmty. Medicine, World Orgn. Nat. Colls., Acads. and Acad. Assn. of Gen. Practitioners and Family Physicians, Am. Acad. Family Physicians. Muslim. Office: King Saud Univ PO Box 2925 Riyadh 11461 Saudi Arabia

AL SHAMMERY, FALAH, plastic surgeon; b. Iraq; MBCHB, Al-Jami'at Al-Mustansiriyah, Iraq, 2005. Plastic surgeon and owner Shammari Beauty Clinic, Baghdad, Iraq, 1987—. Office: Shammari Beauty Clinic Baghdad Al Mansour Iraq Personal E-mail: alshammery.beautyclinic@yahoo.com. *

AL-SHAMSAN, AWS IBRAHIM, pharmacist; b. Edmonton, Canada, Aug. 18, 1978; s. Ibrahim S. Al-Shamsan and Wasmiyah A. Almansour. BSc Pharm, King Saud U. Sch. Pharmacy, Riyadh, 2001. Pharmacist King Fahad Nat. Guard Hosp., Riyadh, 2001; tchg. asst. King Saud U., Riyadh, 2002; rsch. & tchg. asst. U. Alberta, Edmonton, Canada, 2003. Mem.: Can. Soc. Pharm. Scis., Am. Assn. of Pharm. Scientists, Saudi Pharm. Soc. Muslim. Office: Univ Alberta 3118 Dent Pharm Centre Edmonton AB Canada T5G 2N8 Office Phone: 780-492-6917. Business E-Mail: awsa@ualberta.ca.

AL-SHIBLI, KHALID IBRAHIM, pathologist, consultant; b. Baghdad, Iraq, Sept. 16, 1968; s. Ibrahim Mahdi Al-Shibli and Khawla Saleh Al-Ani; m. Hiba Mohammed Ahemd, Jan. 31, 2000; children: Mohammed Khalid, Dina Khalid. MBChB, Baghdad U., 1992. Cert. in pathology Jordan, 2002, European Bd. Pathology, in pathology Amsterdam, 2003, specialist in pathology Norway, 2003. House officer in medicine and surgery Med. City Tchg. Hosp., Baghdad, Iraq, 1992—94; pathology resident Jordan U. Sci. and Tech., Irbid, 1995—99, fellow in pathology, 1999—2000; asst. prof. Ajman U. Sci. and Tech., United Arab Emirates, 2000—01, dir. basic med. sci. courses, 2000—01; cons. pathologist Nordlnad Sykehuset, Bodo, Norway, 2002—. Contbr. rsch. papers in field. Vol. pathologist Pathology Mus. Human Diseases, 1999—2000. Recipient Best Student Rsch. prize, Baghdad Med. Coll., 1989. Mem.: Gen. Med. Coun. UK, Iraqi Med. Assn. Achievements include research in leucocytoclastic vasculitis; papular summer time dermatitis in childhood; sentinal lymph node in breast carcinoma, molecular profiling, the role of angiogenesis and the immune system in non-small cell lung carcinoma. Home: Sulithjelme veien 3a Bodo 8007 Norway Office: Nordland Sykehuset Pathology Dept Prinsens Gate 8092 Bodo Norway Office Fax: 47 75 53 40 74; Home Fax: 47 75 53 40 74. Personal E-mail: kshibli@hotmail.com.

AL-SHUNNAR, BUTHAINAH, surgeon; MBBCH with honors, Royal Coll. Surgeons, Dublin Ireland, 1991. Cert. Am. Bd. Plastic Surgeon. Admitting and oper. privileges Am. Hosp., Emirates Hosp., Internat. Modern Hosp.; gen surgery tng. Johns Hopkins Univ. Hosp., Balt., George Wash. Univ. Hosp., Washington; cons. plastic surgeon (pvt. practice) NY, Pa.; cons. plastic surgeon Sheikh Med. Ctr., Abu Dhabi; specialist plastic surgeon Al Shunnar Plastic Surgery, Jumeirah, United Arab Emirates. Mentor residents and fellows Hershey Med. Coll. Contbr. numerous articles on plastic surgery. Fellow: Am. Coll. Surgeons; mem.: Am. Med. Assn., Alpha Omega Aplpha Nat. Med. Honor Soc., Johns Hopkins Med. and Surg. Assn., Am. Soc. Plastic Surgeons. Office: Al Shunnar Plastic Surgery Villa Number 591 Jumeirah Rd Jumeirah 211821 United Arab Emirates Office Phone: 97143953033. Office Fax: 97143953034. *

ALSIDAWI, SAID, physician; b. Damascus, Syria, July 25, 1983; MD, U. Damascus, 2008. Physician U. Cin., 2009—; resident. Contbr. articles to profl. publs. Cardiology fellowship. Mem.: AMA, ACP, ACC. Home: 220 E ML King Dr B Cincinnati OH 45219 E-mail: alsidasd@ucmail.uc.edu.

ALSTRUP, AAGE KRISTIAN OLSEN, medical researcher; b. Denmark, Sept. 3, 1971; Degree in Vet, Royal Vet. & Agrl. U., Copenhagen, 1997, PhD, 2002. Rschr. Royal Vet. & Agrl., 1991—2001; rschr., dept. nuc. medicine & PET ctr. Aarhus U. Hosps., 2002—. Office: Nørrebrogade 44 10G Aarhus C 8000 Denmark Business E-Mail: aage@pet.auh.dk.

ALTAMURA, ALFREDO CARLO, psychiatrist, psychopharmacologist; b. Brindisi, Italy, Mar. 25, 1948; s. Teodoro Cosimo Altamura and Ines Maria Franco; m. Cristina Csopey; children: Carola, Edoardo. MD, U. Milan, 1972. Asst. prof. dept. psychiatry U. Milan, 1973, assoc. prof., 1982; prof. psychiatry U. Cagliari, 1992, U. Milan, Italy, 1997. Mem. editl. bd.: internat. sci. jours.; contbr. articles to profl. jours. Avocations: tennis, running, swimming. Office: Dept Psychiatry Polichinico Via F Storza 35 20122 Milan Italy Home: Viale Bianca Maria 41 20122 Milan MI Italy Personal E-mail: carlo.altamura@polichinico.mi.it.

ALTARAC, SILVIO, urological surgeon; b. Zagreb, Croatia, Dec. 30, 1958; s. Herman and Emilija (Gilica) A.; m. Lidija Lopicic, May 2, 1992; children: Filip, Silvia Max. MD, Sch. Medicine, Zagreb, 1983, PhD, 1989. Tchg. asst. dept. physiology and immunology Med. Faculty, Zagreb, 1985—89; resident urology U. Hosp. Rebro, Zagreb, 1989—93; clin. rsch. fellow U. Hosp., Pitts., 1990; mem. staff Royal Hallamshire Hosp., Sheffield, England, 1993—94, U. Hosp., Innsbruck, Austria, 1995, Brigham and Women's Hosp./Harvard U., Boston, 1995—96; urol. surgeon Gen. Hosp. Pula, Croatia, 1997—2000, Gen. Hosp. Zabok, 2001—, chief of staff, 2007. Columnist Salud (i) Ciencia, Buenos Aires; sci. assoc., 1993; sci. advisor, 2007. Contbr. articles to profl. jours. Mem.: Acad. Med. Scis. Croatia, Am. Urol. Assn., European Assn. Urology. Achievements include research in procedures for uro-genital trauma, urologic laparoscopy. Home: Bukovacka cesta 229 C Zagreb 10000 Croatia Home Phone: 011 385 1 561 4728; Office Phone: 011 385 49 204 643. Business E-Mail: silvio.altarac@vip.hr.

AL-TAWFIQ, JAFFAR A., infectious disease consultant; b. Qudaih, Saudi Arabia, Jan. 23, 1966; s. Al-Tawfiq and Khuwaildi; children: Zainab J., Kawthar J. Al-tawfiq, Mohammad J. MBBS, King Faisal U., Dammam, Saudi Arabia, 1991. Diplomate Am. Bd. internal medicine, 1998, cert. Diploma Tropical Medicine and Hygiene Royal Coll. Physicians London, 1998, Diploma Hospital Infection Control APL London Sch. Hygiene and Tropical Medicine, 2006. Head physician, internal medicine unit Saudi Aramco Med. Svcs. Orgn., Dhahran, Saudi Arabia, 2006—, acting chief, internal medicine svcs. divsn. Coord., continuous med. edn. Saudi Aramco Med. Svcs. Orgn., mem. editorial Bd., 2007. Contbr. articles more than 50 profl. jours. Recipient Outstanding Rsch. award, Dept. Medicine Fellows Rsch., 1999, Excellence award, Saudi Aramco Med. Svcs. Orgn., 2005—08. Fellow: ACP, Am. Coll. Chest Physician; mem.: Internat. Soc. Infectious Diseases. Achievements include research in an isogenic hemoglobin receptor-deficient mutant of haemophilus ducreyi. Office: Saudi Aramco Med Svcs Orgn Dhahran Health Ctr 31942 Dhahran Saudi Arabia Office Fax: +9663-877-3790. Personal E-mail: jaltawfi@yahoo.com.

ALTAY, BARIS, medical educator; b. Balikesir, Turkey, Dec. 5, 1966; Degree, Ege U., 1990. Prof. Ege U. Sch. Medicine, 2009—. Office: Ege University Sch Medicine Urology Bornova Izmir 35100 Turkey Office Fax: 902323746552. Business E-Mail: ahmet.baris.altay@ege.edu.tr.

ALTCHEK, DAVID WILSON, orthopedist, surgeon; b. NYC, Dec. 27, 1956; m. Anne Salmson, 1981; children: Charles, Christopher, Chloe, Sophie. MD, Cornell U., 1982. Cert. Am. Bd. Orthopaedic Surgeons. Resident gen. surgery NY Presbyn. Hosp., NYC; resident Hosp. Spl. Surgery, NYC, 1983—87, fellowship Sports Medicine and Shoulder Svc., 1987—88, attending orthopaedic surgeon. Team physician NY Mets, 2001—05, med. dir., 2005—; North America med. dir. Assn. Tennis Professionals (ATP); team physician US Davis Cup tennis team; assoc. prof. orthopaedic surgery Weill Medical Coll., Cornell U. Contbr. articles to med. jours. Recipient T. Campbell Thompson Award, Ea. Orthopaedic Assn. Fellowship Award, John Jay Award, Charles S. Neer Award, Am. Shoulder & Elbow Surgeons. Avocation: golf. Office: Hosp Spl Surgery 535 E 70th St New York NY 10021 Office Phone: 212-606-1909. Office Fax: 212-879-6526.

ALTENBURGER, KARL MARION, allergist; b. Coral Gables, Fla., Nov. 13, 1949; s. Karl and Carol Altenburger; m. Carol Bauer, May 25, 1974; children: Laura Alyson, Ashley Carolyn, Elizabeth Ann, Allison Nicole. BA in Zoology, U. South Fla., 1971, MD, 1974. Diplomate Am. Bd. Pediatrics, Am. Bd. Allergy and Immunology, Nat. Bd. Med. Examiners. Intern in pediatrics U. Colo. Med. Ctr., Denver, 1975-76, resident, 1976-78, fellow in allergy and immunology, 1978-81, Nat. Jewish Hosp. and Rsch. Ctr.-Nat. Asthma Ctr., Denver, 1978-81; pvt. practice, Ocala, Fla., 1981—2006. Instr. dept. pediatrics U. Colo. Sch. Medicine, 1980-81; pres. Fla. Med. Polit. Action Com., 1998-2001 Contbr. articles to profl. jours. Trustee Am. Lung Assn. Ctrl. Fla., 1985—93. Mem. AMA, Fla. Med. Assn. (bd. dirs. 2002-09, v.p. 2004-06, pres.-elect 2006-07, pres. 2007-08), Fla. Med. Assn. (Marion County del. 1990—), Fla. Allergy Asthma and Immunology Soc. (exec. com. 1990-96, pres. 1993-94), Marion County Med. Soc. (bd. dirs. 1983-88, pres. 1985-86, editor Bull. 1986-89), U. South Fla. Coll. Medicine Alumni Assn. (pres. 1983-87), Alpha Omega Alpha. Roman Catholic. Avocations: history, books. Personal E-mail: altenburge@aol.com.

ALTER, CRAIG A., pediatric endocrinologist; MD, Harvard Coll., Cambridge, Mass., 1987. Diplomate Am. Bd. Pediatrics, Am. Bd. Pediatrics-pediatric endocrinology, lic. Pa., 1990, NJ, 2000. Resident pediat. Children's Hosp. Boston, 1990; fellow pediatric endocrinology The Children's Hosp. Phila., 1993, clin. dir., attending physician; hosp. affiliations include Montgomery Hosp., Norristown, Pa., Doylestown Hosp., Pa. Named one of Top Doctors, Phila. Mag., 2011. Office: The Children's Hospital of Philadelphia 34th St and Civic Center Blvd Philadelphia PA 19104 Office Phone: 215-590-1000.

ALTER, GARY, plastic and reconstructive surgeon, urologist; Student, U. Calif., Berkeley; MD, UCLA, 1973. Diplomate Am. Bd.

Plastic Surgery, Am. Bd. Urology, lic. Calif., NY. Resident gen. surgery UCLA, 1973—75; resident urology Baylor Coll. Medicine, Houston, 1975—79; practicing urologist, 1979—89; resident plastic surgery Mayo Clinic, Rochester, Minn., 1990—92; fellow genital plastic reconstructive surgery Eastern Va. Grad. Sch. Medicine, Norfolk, Va., 1992; pvt. practice plastic & reconstructive surgery Beverly Hills, Calif., 1993—, Manhattan, NY, 1993—. Asst. clin. prof., plastic surgery UCLA Sch. Medicine. Co-editor: (med. textbook) Reconstructive and Plastic Surgery of the External Genitalia, 1999; contbr. articles to profl. jours.; regular appearances include Dr. 90210 (E-TV), Loveline (syndicated radio show). Mem.: Soc. Genitourinary Reconstructive Surgeons, Am. Urological Assn., Am. Assn. Plastic Surgeons, Am. Soc. Plastic Surgeons. Achievements include recognition as a leader in female genital surgery, labiaplasty or labia minora surgery, penis/scrotal surgery, penis enhancement and transsexual surgery. Office: 416 N Bedford Dr Ste 400 Beverly Hills CA 90210 also: 461 Park Ave S 7th Fl Ste New York NY 10016 Office Phone: 310-275-5566. Office Fax: 310-271-0521. Business E-Mail: altermd@earthlink.com.

ALTER, HARVEY J., hematologist, educator; b. NYC; BA, U. Rochester, MD, 1960. Internship, first-yr. resident Strong Meml. Hosp., Rochester, NY, 1960—61; clin. assoc. NIH, Bethesda, Md., 1961—64; second-yr. resident U. Wash. Hosp. Sys., Seattle, 1964—65; hematology fellow Georgetown U. Hosp., Wash., DC, 1965—66; instr. medicine Georgetown U. Sch. Medicine, Wash., 1966—68; dir. hematology rsch. Georgetown U. Hosp., Wash., 1966—69; asst. prof. medicine Georgetown U. Sch. Medicine, Wash., 1968—69, clin. asst. prof. medicine, 1969—71, clin. assoc. prof. medicine, 1969—71; sr. investigator NIH, Bethesda, Md., 1969—, chief infectious disease sect. clin. ctr., 1972—, assoc. dir. rsch. clin. ctr. dept. transfusion medicine, faculty clin. rsch., 1988—; clin. prof. medicine Georgetown U. Hosp., Wash., 1988—. Adj. prof. S.W. Found. Biomed. Rsch., San Antonio, 1986—. Contbr. articles to profl. jours. Recipient DSM, U.S. Pub. Health Svc., 1977, Karl Lansteiner award, Am. Assn. Blood Banks, 1992, Lab. Pub. Svc. Nat. Leadership award, 1999, World Health Day award, Am. Assn. World Health, 2000, Lasker-DeBakey Clin. Med. Rsch. award, Lasker Found., 2000, ACP award, 2004, Internat. award, Inserm French NIH, 2004. Master: ACP; fellow: Am. Soc. Internal Medicine; mem.: Nat. Acad. Scis., Inst. Medicine, Am. Bd. Pathology. Achievements include first to conduct work leading to the discovery of the virus that causes hepatitis C; development of screening methods that reduced the risk of blood transfusion-associated hepatitis in the U.S. from 30% in 1970 to virtually zero. Office: NIH Warren G Magunson Clin Ctr Dept Transfusion Medicine 10/1C711 10 Center Dr MSC-1184 Bldg 10 Room 1C711 Bethesda MD 20892 *

ALTER, MILTON, retired neurologist; b. Buffalo, Nov. 11, 1929; s. Samuel and Rose (Schaffer) Alter; m. Reina Rolnick, Aug. 31, 1952; children: David S., Daniel M., Michael A., Naomi T., Joel A. BA, U. Buffalo, 1951, MD, 1955; PhD, U. Minn., 1966. Diplomate Am. Bd. Psychiatry and Neurology. Intern U. Minn., Mpls., 1955-56; sr. surgeon USPHS, Bethesda, Md., 1956-62; fellow Med. Coll. S.C., Charleston, 1956-57, Dalhousie U., Halifax, 1957, Columbia U. Coll. Physicians and Surgeons, NYC, 1957-58, Hebrew U., Jerusalem, 1960-62; mem. faculty, chief neurology svc. U. Minn., Mpls., 1962—67, Mpls. VA Hosp., 1967-76; chmn. dept. neurology Temple U., Phila., 1976-87, prof. neurology, 1987—89; prof., dir. residency tng. Med. Coll. Pa., Phila., 1989-91; clin. prof. Drexel U., 1995—. Mem. sci. adv. bd. Nat. Multiple Sclerosis Soc., NYC, Dystonia Med. Rsch. Found., Alzheimer Disease Assn.; peer reviewer Epidemiology and Disease Control 1 and 2 NIH, Bethesda, Md.; adj. prof. Ctr. Clin. Epidemiology and Biostats. U. Pa., 1995—2004, Thomas Jefferson U., 1999—, adj. prof. epidemiology U. Pitts., 1985—; cons. mainline health stroke program Lankenau Inst. Med. Rsch., 1997—99, clin. prof. Guest editor: numerous profl. jours., editor-in-chief: Neuroepidemiology, 1989—96; editor emeritus Neuroepidemiology; contbr. articles to profl. jours., chapters to books. Capt. USPHS, 1962. Grantee, NIH, Multiple Sclerosis Soc. Mem.: AMA, World Fedn. Neurology (chair rsch. group epidemiology 1998—2001), Am. Epidemiology Soc., Am. Neurol. Assn., Am. Acad. Neurology. Democrat. Jewish. Home: 236 Indian Creek Rd Wynnewood PA 19096-3404 also: Prof Lankenau Med Rsch Ctr 100 E Lancaster Ave Wynnewood PA 19096-3404 Office Phone: 610-649-0686. Personal E-mail: malter5280@aol.com.

ALTER, MIRIAM J., epidemiologist, educator; b. Aug. 29, 1949; BS, U. Pa., 1971; PhD, Johns Hopkins U., MPH, 1981. Chief, viral hepatitis surveillance Ctrs. Disease Control and Prevention, 1981—89, chief, epidemiology br., divsn. viral hepatitis, 1990—2000, assoc. dir. epidemiologic sci., divsn. viral hepatitis, 2001—06; Robert E. Shope prof. infectious disease epidemiology U. Tex. Med. Br., 2006—. Fellow: Infectious Diseases Soc. America; mem.: APHA (Epidemiology Sect. John P. Snow award), Soc. Epidemiologic Rsch., Am. Soc. Epidemiology, Am. Assn. Study Liver Diseases. Office: 301 University Blvd Mail Route 0435 Galveston TX 77555-0435 Office Fax: 409-747-0220. Business E-Mail: mjalter@utmb.edu.

ALTIERE, RALPH J., dean, pharmacy educator; BS in Chemistry, Manhattan Coll.; MS in Chemistry, NYU; MS, PhD in Pharmacology, NY Med. Coll. Postdoc. rschr. Yale U., New Haven; asst. prof. U. Ky. Coll. Pharmacy; faculty U. Colo. Denver Sch. Pharmacy, 1987—, assoc. dean, 1995—2006, dean, 2006—, prof. cell biology, physiology, pathophysiology & health care ethics. Contbr. articles to profl. jours., chapters to books. Mem.: Am. Assn. Colleges of Pharmacy. Office: UCD Sch Pharmacy #C238-L15 Academic Bldg 1 12631 E 17th Ave Rm L15 Aurora CO 80045-2550 Home Phone: 303-724-2637; Office Phone: 303-724-2631. Business E-Mail: Ralph.Altiere@ucdenver.edu.

ALTMAN, BRIAN DAVID, pediatric ophthalmologist; b. Temple, Tex., Feb. 29, 1944; s. Harold and Alice A. BA, Adelphi U., 1965; MD, Yale Med. Sch., 1969. Diplomate Am. Bd. Pediatrics, Am. Bd. Opthalmologists. Pediatric ophthalmologist pvt. practice, Huntington Valley, Pa., 1976-98, Plymouth, Pa., 1976-98, Ocean City, NJ, 1992—, Cape May Courthouse, 1992—. Cons. in pediatric ophthalomogy several hosps. in Pa. and N.J., 1977—. Co-author: (with others) Medications in Pediatric Ophthalmology, 1975. Lt. cmmdr. USPHS, 1970-72. Fellow Am. Acad. Opthalmology, Am. Acad. Pediatrics, Am. Assn. Pediatric Ophthalmologists. Office: 315 Rt 9 S Cape May Court House NJ 08210 Office Phone: 609-398-1100.

ALTMAN, DREW E., foundation executive; b. Boston, Mar. 21, 1951; s. George and Harriet A.; m. Pamela Koch; children: Daniel, Jessica. BA magna cum laude, Brandeis U., 1973; MA, Brown U., 1974; PhD in Polit. Sci., MIT, 1983. Postdoctoral fellow, rsch. assoc. Harvard U. Sch. Pub. Health, Boston, 1975-76, 78-80; prin. rsch. assoc. Codman Rsch. Group, Boston, 1976-80; spl. asst. office of adminstr. Health Care Fin. Adminstrn. Dept. HHS, Washington, 1979-81; v.p. Robert Wood Johnson Found., Princeton, NJ, 1981-86; commr. N.J. Dept. Human Svcs., Trenton, 1986-89; program dir. health and human svcs. The Pew Charitable Trusts, Phila., 1989-90; pres., CEO Henry J. Kaiser Family Found., Menlo Park, Calif., 1990—. Contbr. articles to profl. jours. Mem. Inst. Medicine (coun. mem.), Nat. Acad. of Soc. Ins., Assn. for Health Svcs. Rsch. Office: Henry J Kaiser Family Found 2400 Sand Hill Rd Menlo Park CA 94025-6941 *

ALTMAN, GREGORY T., orthopaedic surgeon, educator; MD, Temple U. Cert. orthopaedic surgery. Intern Magee Womens Hosp. of Pitts.; resident Hamot Med. Ctr., Childrens Meml. Hosp.; fellow Mass. Gen. Hosp., Univ. Rochester; asst. prof. orthopaedic surgery Drexel Univ.; practice Allegheny Orthopaedic Assocs.; intern Allegheny Gen. Hosp., co-dir. divsn. orthopaedic trauma. Office: Allegheny General Hospital 320 E N Ave Pittsburgh PA 15212 Office Phone: 412-359-3131. Office Fax: 412-359-4108.

ALTMAN, IRWIN, psychologist, educator; BA, NYU, 1951; MA, U. Md., 1954, PhD, 1957. Asst. prof. psychology Am. U., Washington, 1957-58, sr. rsch. scientist, assoc. prof., 1960-62, adj. prof., 1962-69; rsch. scientist in human scis. Arlington, Va., 1958-60; rsch. psychologist Naval Med. Rsch. Inst., Bethesda, Md., 1962-69; adj. prof. U. Md., 1968-69; prof. U. Utah, Salt Lake City, 1969-79, chmn. dept. psychology, 1969-76, dean Coll. Social and Behavioral Sci., 1979-83, v.p. for acad. affairs, 1983-87, disting. prof., 1987—2005, disting. prof. emeritus, 2005—. Author: (with J.E. McGrath) Small Groups, 1966, (with D.A. Taylor) Social Penetration, 1973, Environment and Social Behavior, 1975; (with M. Chemers) Culture and Environment, 1980; (with J. Wohlwill) Human Behavior and Environment: Vol. I, 1976, Vol. II, 1977, Vol. III, 1978, Vol. IV, 1980, Vol. V, 1981, Vol. VI, 1983, Vol. VII, 1984, (with C. Werner) Vol. VIII, 1985, (with A. Wandersman) Vol. IX, 1987, (with E. Zube) Vol. X, 1989, (with K. Christensen) Vol. XI, 1990, (with S. Low) Vol. XII, 1992, (with A. Churchman) Women and the Environment, Vol. XIII, 1994; (with D. Stokols) Handbook of Environmental Psychology, Vols I and II, 1987; (with J. Ginat) Polygamous Families in Contemporary Society, 1996; mem. editl. bds.: Small Groups, 1970-79, Man-Environment Systems, 1969-73, Jour. Applied Social Psychology, 1973-85, Sociometry, 1973-76, Environment and Behavior, 1975, Jour. Personality and Social Psychology, 1974-83, Contemporary Psychology, 1975-86, Environ. Psychology and Nonverbal Behavior, Psychology, 1976-90, Am. Jour. Cmty. Psychology, 1978-81, Population and Environment, 1979, Jour. Environ. Psychology, 1982, Computers and Human Behavior, 1985, Internat. Jour. Applied Social Psychology, 1984, Communication Monographs, 1992-95; assoc. editor Am. Jour. Cmty. Psychology, 1988-92; co-editor Jour. Environ. Psychology, 1990-98; contbr. articles to profl. jours. 1st lt. Adj. Gen. Corps, AUS, 1954-56. Mem. APA (pres. divsn. population and environment), AAAS, Soc. Exptl. Social Psychology, Soc. Psychol. Study of Social Issues, Soc. Personality and Social Psychology (pres.), Environ. Design Rsch. Assn., Am. Psychol. Soc. Business E-Mail: irwin.altman@m.cc.utah.edu.

ALTMAN, LAWRENCE KIMBALL, physician, journalist; b. Quincy, Mass., June 19, 1937; s. William S. and Esther (Kimball) A. AB cum laude, Harvard U., 1958; MD, Tufts U., 1962. Diplomate: Am. Vet. Epidemiology Soc. Intern Mt. Zion Hosp., San Francisco, 1962-63; USPHS epidemic intelligence service officer CDC, Atlanta, 1963-66; med. resident, fellow U. Wash. Hosp., Seattle, 1966-69; med. corr., columnist The Doctors World New York Times, 1969—; clin. prof. medicine NYU, 1970—. Vis. physician Serafimer Hosp., Karolinska Inst., Stockholm, Sweden, 1973; vis. scientist U. Wash., 1971; Chancellor's Disting. Lecture for Pub. Understanding of Sci., U. Calif., San Francisco, 1989; Ida Beam Disting. vis. prof. U. Iowa, 2000, fellow Woodrow Wilson Internat. Ctr. for Scholars, Wash. Author: Science of The Times, 1981, Who Goes First? The Story of Self-Experimentation in Medicine, 1987, 98; contbr. chpts. to books, articles to profl. jours.; contbr. Ency. Brit., 1979, Grolier Ency., 1972-87. Recipient Claude Bernard award, Nat. Soc. Med. Rsch., 1971, 1974, Pub. Svc. award, Nat. Kidney Found., 1977, Walter C. Alvarez award, Am. Med. Writers Assn., 1980, journalism award, Am. Acad. Pediat., 1982, Pub. Svc. award, Nat. Kidney Found., 1983, Howard W. Blakeslee award, Am. Heart Assn., 1982—83, 1994, Journalism award, Coll. Am. Pathologists, 1985, George Polk award, 1986, Vincent Downing award, 1988, Med. Media Excellence award, Friends Nat. Libr. Medicine, 1993, Victor Cohn prize, Coun. for the Advancement of Sci. Writing, 2000, Howard Lewis Career award, Am. Heart Assn., 2001, medal, U. Calif., San Francisco, 2004, Walsh McDermott award, Associated Med. Schs. NY, 2004, Jonathan E. Rhoads medal, Am. Philos. Soc., 2008; fellow, Woodrow Wilson Internat. Ctr. Studies, 2010—. Master ACP; fellow Am. Coll. Epidemiology, NY Acad. Medicine, Kaiser Family Found.; mem. Inst. Medicine, NAS, Am. Soc. Tropical Medicine and Hygiene, Soc. Epidemiology, Am. Bd. Med. Spltys. (pub. 1986-88), Alpha Omega Alpha, Century Club (NYC), Harvard Club (NYC). Home: 140 W End Ave New York NY 10023-6131 Office: New York Times 620 8th Ave New York NY 10018-1405 Business E-Mail: altman@nytimes.com.

ALTMAN, ROBIN, pediatrician, educator; Attended, Robert Wood Johnson Med. Sch., 1983. Diplomate Am. Bd. Pediatrics. Intern Columbia Presbyn. Med. Ctr., resident in pediat., 1983—86; asst. prof. pediat. NY Med. Coll.; with Children's & Women's Physicians of Westchester LLP; pediatrician Westchester Med. Ctr. Office: Westchester Medical Center Chief General Pediatrics Munger Pavilion 312 Valhalla NY 10595 Office Phone: 914-493-7235. Office Fax: 914-594-3747.

ALTMAN, SIDNEY, biology professor; b. Montreal, Que., Can., May 7, 1939; s. Victor Altman and Ray Arlin; m. Ann Korner, 1972; children: Daniel, Leah. BS, MIT, 1960; PhD in Biophys., U. Colo., 1967; DSc (hon.), York U., Toronto, 1990, Conn. Coll., 1990, McGill U., Montreal, 1991, U. Colo., 1991, U. Montreal, 1991, U. BC, 1991, Dartmouth Coll., 1996. Tchg. asst. Columbia U., NYC, 1960—62; Damon Runyon Meml. Fund cancer rsch. fellow in molecular biology Harvard U., Cambridge, Mass., 1967—69; Anna Fuller Fund fellow Med. Rsch. Coun. Lab. Molecular Biology, England, 1969—71; asst. to assoc. prof. Yale U., New Haven, 1971—80, prof. molecular cellular and devel. biology, 1980—90, chmn. dept., 1983—85, dean Yale Coll., 1985—90, Sterling prof. molecular, cellular & devel. biology, 1990—. Tutor Radcliffe Coll., 1968—69. Contbr. articles to profl. jours. Recipient Nobel prize in chemistry, 1989, Merit award, NIH, 1989. Fellow: AAAS; mem.: NAS, Am. Philos. Soc. (Rosenstiel award 1989), Genetics Soc. America, Am. Soc. Biol. Chemists. Achievements include discovery that ribonucleic acid (RNA) can initiate some biological reactions, acting as a biocatalyst and seemingly playing the role of a protein enzyme, overturning the understanding that RNA acts only as a carrier of genetic information. Office: Yale U Dept Chemistry KBT 402 225 Prospect St New Haven CT 06520-8103 Office Phone: 203-432-3500. Office Fax: 203-432-5713. E-mail: sidney.altman@yale.edu.

ALTMAN, STUART HAROLD, economist, educator; b. NYC, Aug. 8, 1937; s. Sidney and Florence A.; m. Diane Kleinberg, June 7, 1959; children: Beth, Renee, Heather. BBA, CCNY; MA in Econs; PhD, UCLA. Assoc. prof. econs. Brown U., 1966-71; dep. asst. sec. for planning and evaluation/health HEW, 1971-76; dep. dir. for health Cost of Living Council, 1973-74; dean, Florence Heller Grad. Sch. Brandeis U., Waltham, Mass., 1977-92, interim pres., 1990—91, Sol C. Chaikin prof. Nat. Health Policy Waltham, 1992—. Mem. Nat. Bipartisan Commn. on the Future of Medicare; chmn. bd. Univ. Health Policy Consortium; chmn. U.S. Prospective Payment Assessment Commn.; co-chair of the Governor/Legislative Health Care Task Force for Commonwealth of Mass., 2000-02; independent dir. Lincare Holdings, Inc. 2001-; dir. Aveta, Inc. Author, editor govt. publs., reports. Bd. dirs. Beth Israel Hosp., Brookline, Mass., 1979—. Mem. Am. Public Health Assn., Inst. of Medicine, NAS. Office: Inst for Health Policy Heller Grad Sch PO Box 9110 Waltham MA 02454-9110 *

ALTMAN, WAYNE J., family practice physician; MD, U. Mass. Diplomate Am. Bd. Family Practice. Resident family medicine Univ. of Mass Memorial Med. Ctr., Boston, 1994—97. Office: Family Practice Grp 11 Water St Ste 1A Arlington MA 02476 Office Phone: 781-648-9700.

ALTMEYER, MARK P., pharmaceutical executive; BA, Middlebury Coll.; MBA, Harvard U. Mktg. assoc., group product analyst Bristol Labs; bus. devel. mgr. Cetus Corp., product mgr. oncology; sales rep. Bristol-Myers Squibb Co., product mgr., dir., sr. dir., v.p., gen. mgr. Turkey, sr. v.p. global commercialization; pres., CEO Otsuka America Pharm., Inc., 2009—. Mem. bd. dirs. Contact of Mercer County, Trinity Counseling Svc.; youth soccer coach Hopewell Valley Recreation Dept.; alumni recruiter Middlebury Coll. Office: Otsuka America Pharm Inc 2440 Research Blvd Rockville MD 20850 *

ALTORKI, NASSER KHALED, thoracic surgeon, educator; BChir, MB; MD, Cairo U., 1978. Diplomate Am. Bd. Thoracic Surgery, Am. Bd. Surgery. Intern Wash. Hosp. Ctr.; resident Univ. of Chgo. Med. Ctr., 1985, fellow in cardiothoracic surgery, 1987; prof. cardiothoracic surgery Weill Cornell Med. Coll., NY; dir. cardiothoracic surgery divsn. NY Presbyn. Hosp./Weill Cornell Med. Ctr. Author: (articles) Accuracy of surveillance computed tomography in detecting recurrent or new primary lung cancer in patients with completely resected lung cancer, 2006, Surgical resection for multifocal (T4) non-small cell lung cancer: is the T4 designation valid?, 2007, Risk factors for occult mediastinal metastases in clinical stage I nonsmall cell lung cancer, 2007, Long-term survival and recurrence in patients with resected non-small cell lung cancer 1cm or less in size, 2006, Positron emission tomographic scanning predicts survival after inducation chemotherapy for esophageal carcinoma, 2007. Fellow: ACS; mem.: Am. Assn. for Thoracic Surgery, Assn. Academic Surgery, Soc. for Surgery of the Alimentary Tract, Soc. of Thoracic Surgeons, Western Thoracic Surgical Assn. Office: New York-Presbyterian Hospital Weill Cornell Medical Center 525 E 68th St New York NY 10065 Office Phone: 212-746-5156. Office Fax: 212-745-8223.

ALTSCHULER, BRUCE ROBERT, research dentist; b. Bklyn., Feb. 17, 1947; s. Frank Philip and Sarah Gertrude (Cloder) A.; m. Ruth Phyllis Gass, Oct. 27, 1974; children: Joan Ellen, Wendy Karen, Cheryl Miriam. BA, Bklyn. Coll., 1967; DDS, Temple U., Phila., 1971. Lic. dentist Md., Pa., Conn., Maine, N.Y. Commd. capt. USAF, 1971, advanced through grades to col., 1986; project scientist dental holography Dental Scis. Br., Brooks AFB, Tex., 1971-74, chief dental consultation, 1975-76; chief dental laser holography USAF Dental Investigation Svc., Brooks AFB, Tex., 1976-80; chief dental computer/laser tech. USAF Aerospace Medicine, Brooks AFB, Tex., 1980-82; chief avionics advanced systems rsch. group Info. Processing Br., Wright-Patterson AFB, Ohio, 1982-84; dep. optical processing Systems Avionics Div., Wright-Patterson AFB, 1985; dental resident Advanced Clin. Dentistry Residence Program, Eglin AFB, Fla., 1985-86; Air Force rsch. liaison, chief laser imaging U.S. Army Inst. Dental Rsch., Ft. Meade, Md., 1986-94; chief imaging robotics lab. Walter Reed Army Inst. Rsch. Dental Rsch. Detachment, Ft. Meade, Md., 1995-97; dir. rsch. devel. Cobalt Rsch. LLC, 1997—2003, CEO, 2004—. Clin. asst. prof. dept. diagnosis/roentgenology U. Tex. Health Sci. Ctr., San Antonio, 1976-80, dept. dental diagnostic svc., 1980-82; mem. dental x-ray subcom. 26 Am. Nat. Standards Inst., Washington, 1980-85; reviewer NIH Computer Aided Dentistry, Washington, 1987; chmn. SPIE Robotics and Machine Perception Tech. Group, 2006. Editor 3-D Machine Perception; patentee in field. Bd. dirs. Am. Cancer Soc., Bexar County, Tex., 1980-82, mem. pub. edn. com., 1980-82; campaign coord. Avionics Lab. Combined Fed. Campaign, Dayton, Ohio 1984; spl. award judge Alamo Regional Sci. Fair, San Antonio, 1980-82. Mem. ADA, Internat. Assn. Dental Rsch., Air Force Assn., Armed Forces Communications, Electronics Assn., Amateur Radio Relay League, Nat. Def. Indsl. Assn., Md. State Dental Assn., Md. Profl. Vol. Corps., Soc. Photo Optical Instrumentation Engrs. (chmn. robotics and machine perception tech. group 2006), Tex. Dental Assn., Am. Mensa. Republican. Jewish. Avocations: photography, computers. Home: PO Box 458 Simpsonville MD 21150-0458 Office: Cobalt Rsch LLC PO Box 458 Simpsonville MD 21150-0458 Office Phone: 410-309-6085. Business E-Mail: cobalt-research@starpower.net.

ALTSCHULER, STEVEN M., health facility executive, pediatrician, gastroenterologist; m. Robin L. Altschuler. degree, MD, Case Western. Bd. cert. pediatrician, gastroenterologist. Pediat. residency tng. Children's Hosp., Boston; subspecialty tng., pediat. gastroenterology and nutrition Children's Hosp. Phila.; prof. pediat. U. Penn. Sch. Med., chmn. pediat. dept., 1997; fellow Children's Hosp. Phila., 1982, joined, 1985, physician-in-chief, chmn. dept. pediat., 1997, pres. & CEO, 2000—. Faculty mem. Harvard Med. Sch.; Leonard and Madlyn Abramson endowed chair, pediat. med. Children's Hosp. Phila., chmn. exec. com. Joseph Stokes Jr. Rsch. Inst.; spkr. in pediat. healthcare, gastroenterology, and rsch. Contbr. articles to med. jours., chapters to books. Recipient Janssen award, Janssen Pharmaceutica, 1999. Mem.: No. Am. Soc. Pediat. Gastroenterology, Am. Gastroent. Assn. Sect. on Motility and Nerve/Gut Interaction. Office: Children's Hosp Phila 34th St and Civic Ctr Blvd Philadelphia PA 19104-4399

ALTSHULER, DAVID MATTHEW, geneticist, endocrinologist; b. Ithaca, NY, Aug. 27, 1964; s. Alan Anthony and Julie Maller Altshuler; m. Jill Dara Suttenberg, Aug. 5, 1990; children: Zachary Miles, Jason Leonard. BS, MIT, 1986; PhD in Genetics, Harvard U., 1993; MD, Harvard Med. Sch., 1994. Diplomate Am. Bd. Internal Medicine, cert. in endocrinology, diabetes and metabolism. Intern Mass. Gen. Hosp., Boston, 1994—95, resident internal medicine, 1995—96, fellow in diabetes, endocrinology and metabolism, 1996—99, attending physician diabetes unit, prof. molecular biology,Ctr. Human Genetic Rsch.; asst., then assoc. prof. genetics and medicine Harvard Med. Sch., 2000—08, prof. genetics and medicine, 2008—. Co-chair 1000 Genomes Project, 2008—; founding mem., dir. program in med. and population genetics Broad Inst. of MIT & Harvard, 2003—, dep. dir., chief academic officer, 2009—. Contbr. articles to profl. jours. Trustee The Commonwealth Sch., Boston, 2002. Recipient Clin. Scientist award in translational rsch., Burroughs Welcome Fund, 2002, Steven Krane award, Mass. Gen. Hosp., 2002; Charles E. Culpeper scholar, Rockefeller Bros. Fund, 2002. Mem.: Am. Soc. Human Genetics (bd. dirs. 2010—), Assn. Am. Physicians, Am. Soc. Clin. Investigation. Office: Harvard Med Sch Dept Genetics Richard B Simches Rsch Ctr 185 Cambridge St Rm 6806 Boston MA 02114 Office Fax: 617-726-5937. Business E-Mail: altshuler@molbio.mgh.harvard.edu. *

ALTSHULER, KENNETH Z., psychiatrist, educator; b. Paterson, NJ, Apr. 11, 1929; s. Jacob and Altie (Freedman) A.; m. Gloria Seigel, June 14, 1952 (div. 1981); children: Steven, Lori, Dara; m. Ruth Collins Sharp, Dec. 5, 1987. BA, Cornell U., 1948; MD, U. Buffalo, 1952; DSc (hon.), Gallaudet Coll., 1972. Intern Kings County Hosp., Bklyn., 1952-53; resident NY State Psychiat. Inst., NYC, 1955-58; asst. in psychiatry Columbia U., 1958-59, instr., 1959-63, rsch. assoc., 1963-67, asst. clin. prof., 1967-71, assoc. clin. prof., 1971-75, prof., 1975-77; tng. analyst Columbia U. Psychoanalytic Clinic for Tng. and Rsch., 1969-77; project dir. Essential Aspects of Deafness, 1972-76, Trauma and Sleep Physiology, 1975-77; Stanton Sharp prof., chmn. psychiatry U. Tex.-Southwestern Med. Sch., Dallas, 1977-2000, Stanton Sharp prof. psychiatry, 2000—; tng. analyst New Orleans Psychoanalytic Inst., 1979-86, Dallas Psychoanalytic Inst., 1986—. Chief of deafness unit Rockland State Hosp., Orangeburg, NY, 1966-77; cons. to NIH; dir. Am. Bd. Psychiatry and Neurology, 1990-97, pres., 1996; mem. Nat. Bd. Med. Examiners, 1986-89, chmn. Part II psychiatry com., 1988-89; mem. Am. Assn. Chmn. Depts. Psychiatry, 1977-2000, pres. 1990-91. Co-author: Managing Sleep Complaints, 1982; co-editor: Family and Mental Health Problems in a Deaf Population, 1963, Comprehensive Mental Health Svc. for the Deaf, 1966, Psychiatry and the Deaf, 1968, Expanded Mental Health Care for the Deaf, 1970, Depression: Mechanisms, Diagnosis and Treatment, 1986; others.; Contbr. articles to profl. jour. Mem. governing bd. Tex. Sch. for the Deaf, 1986-90; bd. dir. Tex. Dept. Mental Health and Mental Retardation, 1999-2004, Shelter Ministries of Dallas, 2001-; bd. trustees, Callier Ctr. for Comm. Disorders 2005-; Phoenix Houses of Tex., board of advisors, 2001-; Gilda's Club of North Tex., adv. bd., 2001-. Recipient Wilson award in genetics and preventive medicine, 1961, Disting. Cmty. Svc. award Dallas County Mental Health Assn., 1986, Prism award, 1992, Disting. Alumnus award SUNY, Buffalo, 1993, 1st Trailblazer award named in his honor, Dallas County Mental Health and Retardation Ctr., 1996, Tex. Star award for Outstanding Cmty. Svc. Tex. Mental Health Assn., 1997; named Outstanding Psychiatrist, Tex. Soc. Psychiat. Physicians, 1996, Outstanding Alumnus of the 1960s Decade Columbia U., 1996; Kenneth Z. Altshuler Clinic named in honor by Dallas County Mental Health & Mental Retardation Ctr., 1997, Medical Leadership award Turtle Creek Manor, 2003; Cert. of Achievement Bd. of Hosp. Psychiatry, Cert. of Significant Achievement for Deafness Program, NY State, 1976, Cert. of Significant Achievement for Mental Health Connections Program, 1995. Fellow Am. Psychiat. Assn., Am. Coll. Psychiatrists, Am. Coll. Psychoanalysts; mem. AMA, Am. Psychoanalytic Assn., Assn. for Psychoanalytic Medicine (Merit award 1965), Tex. Med. Soc., Dallas County Med. Soc., Am. Psychopathol. Assn., Assn. Dir. Med. Student Edn. in Psychiatry (founder, v.p. 1976-77), So. Assn. Rsch. Psychiatry (pres. 1993-94). Office Phone: 214-648-5588. Business E-Mail: kenneth.altshuler@utsouthwestern.edu.

ALTSHULER, MARC, physician, educator; BS, U. Pa., 1995; MD, Jefferson Med. Coll., 2001. Diplomate Am. Bd. Family Practice. Intern Thomas Jefferson Univ. Hosp., resident family medicine, 2001—04, asst. prof. family medicine, asst. residency dir. Jefferson Family Medicine Residency program, program dir. departmental grand rounds, coord. weekly resident conf.; dir. The Ctr. for Refugee Health Dept. of Family and Cmty. Medicine, 2007—. Co-presenter Sixth Nat. Conf. on Quality Health Care for Culturally Diverse Populations, 2008, Ann. Spring Conf. for the Soc. for Tchrs. of Family Medicine, Childrens Hosp. of Phila. (CHOP): Global Health Symposium, 2009, Pa. Acad. of Family Physicians (PAFP) Rsch. Day, 43rd Soc. of Tchrs. in Family Medicine Ann. Spring Conf., 2010. Co-author: (publs., peer-reviewed) Iron Deficiency Anemia in Adults, Erythema multiforme after meningitis vaccine: patient safety concerns with repeat immunization, Review of the Key Clinical Issues in Colorectal Cancer Screening, 2006, The Management of Keloids: Hands-On Versus Hands-Off, Gardasil and Unilateral Lymphadenopathy, 2008, Can the Medical Home Reduce Cancer Morbidity and Mortality, 2009. Office: Thomas Jefferson University Hospital Department of Family and Community Medicine 833 Chestnut St Ste 301 Philadelphia PA 19107 Office Phone: 215-955-5561. Office Fax: 215-955-8600. E-mail: marc.altshuler@jefferson.edu.

ALTUN, ERSAN, radiologist; b. Istanbul, Turkey, Oct. 5, 1975; MD, Marmara U. Sch. Medicine, 1999. Radiologist Acibadem Kozyatagi Hosp., Istanbul, 2011—. Office: Acibadem Kozyatagi Hosp Istanbul 34744 Turkey Personal E-mail: altunersan@hotmail.com.

ALTUNOLUK, BULENT, medical educator; b. Nürnberg, Germany, Mar. 29, 1974; D, Inonu U., 2005. Asst. prof. Sutcu Imam U. Faculty Medicine, 2007—. Mem.: European Assn. Urology. Avocations: travel, photography, reading. Office: Kahramanmaras Sutcu Imam University Faculty Medicine Kahramanmaras 46050 Turkey Personal E-mail: drbulenta@yahoo.com.

ALTURA, BURTON MYRON, physiologist, educator; b. NYC, Apr. 9, 1936; s. Barney and Frances (Dorfman) A.; m. Bella Tabak, Dec. 27, 1961; 1 child, Rachel Allison. BA, Hofstra U., 1957; MS, NYU, 1961, PhD, 1964. Diplomate Am. Bd. Forensic Med., Am. Coll. Forensic Medicine, Am. Bd. Forensic Examiners, Coll. Pharm. and Apothecary Scis., Am. Assn. Integrative Medicine. Tchg. fellow in biology NYU, 1960—61, instr. exptl. anesthesiology Sch. Medicine, 1964—65, asst. prof. Sch. Medicine, 1965—66; rsch. fellow Bronx Mcpl. Hosp. Ctr., 1967—76; asst. prof. physiology and anesthesiology Albert Einstein Coll. Medicine, NYC, 1967—70, assoc. prof., 1970—74, vis. prof., 1974—78; prof. physiology SUNY Health Sci Ctr., Bklyn., 1974—, prof. medicine, 1992—; mem. Ctr. Cardiovasc. and Muscle Rsch., 1995—; prof. pharmacology SUNY Health Sci. Ctr., Bklyn., 1998—; mem. award comm. Golden Hippocrates Internat. Lending Physicians World, 2003—. Spl. study sect. on toxicology Nat. Inst. Environ. Health Scis., 1977—78; Alcohol Biomed. Rsch. Rev. Com. Nat. Inst. Alcohol Abuse and Alcoholism, 1978—83; vis. prof. Kyoto U. Sch. Medicine, 1979, U. Tokyo, 1979, U. Coll. London, 1980, U. Wurzburg, 1980; adj. prof. biology Queens Coll., CUNY, 1983—84; pres. (hon.) Internat. Symposium on Interactions of Magnesium and Potassium on Cardiac and Vascular Muscle, Montbazon, France, 1984; condr., chmn. Gordon Rsch. Conf. on Magnesium in Biochem. Processes and Medicine, 1984; v.p. Internat. Symposium on Magnesium, Blacksburg, 1985; adv. coun. Nat. Found. Addictive Drugs, 1986—; vis. prof. Harvard U. Med. Sch., 1988, Beijing Coll. Traditional Chinese Medicine, China, 1988, Yamaguchi U., Japan, 1988, Inst. Water, Soil and Air Hygiene, Fed. Health Inst., Berlin, 1991, Max Planck Inst., Dortmund, Germany, 1992, Yamaguchi U., 1993, U. Tokyo, 1993, Kyoto U. Sch. Medicine, 1993, Kumamoto U., 1993, Max Planck Inst., 1994, U. Copenhagen, 1994, U. Florence, 1994; pres. (hon.), lectr. (hon.) Hungarian Soc. Electrochemistry, Budapest, 1995; vis. prof. Humboldt Univ., Berlin, 1995, U. Tokyo, 1996, U. Birmingham, England, 1996, Self Med. Def. Coll., Japan, 1996; panel CNF bd. Inst. Med., NAS, 1996—97; vis. prof. U. Calif., Riverside, 1998, Fla. Atlantic U., 1998; spl. study sect. on toxicology Nat. Inst. Environ. Health Scis., 2001; spl. study sect. medications Nat. Inst. Alcohol Abuse and Alcoholism, 2002; vis. prof. British Min. Defense, Porton Down, Salisbury, England, 2004, Naval Med. Rsch. Ctr., Walter Reed Med. Ctr., Silver Spring, Md., 2004; vis. prof., lectr. Navy Med. Rsch. Ctr., Silver Spring Med. Ctr., 2004; panel grad. fellows NSF, 2004—07, cons.; vis. prof. U.S. Def. Threat Reduction Agy., Ft. Belvoir, Va., 2005; vis. prof., lectr. Def. Threat Reduction Agy., Ft. Belvoir, Va., 2005; vis. prof. The Defense Advanced Research Projects Agency, 2006, Emory U., 1973; guest lectr., vis. prof. Nat. Inst. Allergy and Infectious Diseases, 2006; cons. Nat. Heart, Lung, and Blood Inst., Nat. Inst. Allergy and Infectious Diseases, Nat. Inst. Drug Abuse; organizer, condr. symposia; founder, CEO, chmn. and chief sci. officer Bio-Defense Sys., Inc., Rockville Center, NY; spl. study section on radiation injury and nuclear accidents Nat. Inst. Allergy and Infectious Diseases, 2008; panel mem. NIH Challenge Rsch. Grants, 2009; mem., exe. editl. bd. Internat. Jour. Clin. Exptl. Medicine, 2008—; vis. prof. La. State U., 1974, Tulane U., 1974, U. Hawaii, Sch. Medicine, 1975, Yale U., 1975, U. Tex. San Antonio, 1979, Iowa State U., 1979, Columbia U., 1981; assoc. editor Internat. Jour. Med. & Clin. Rsch., 2010—, Jour. Clin. Exptl. Cardiology, 2010—, World Jour. Hypertension, 2010—, Brit. Jour. Pharm. Rsch., 2011—, Internat. Jors. Med. & Clin. Rsch., 2010—, Jours. Clin. Experimental Cardiology, 2010—, The World Jour. Hypertension, 2010—, British Jours. Pharm. Rsch., 2011—, Internat. Jour. Med. Clin. Rsch., 2010—, Jour. Clin. Experimental Cardiology, 2010—, World Jour. Hypertension, 2010—, British Jour. Pharm. Rsch., 2011—. Author: Microcirculation, 3 vols., 1977—80, Vascular Endothelium and Basement Membranes, 1980, Pathophysiology of the Reticuloendothelial System, 1981, Ionic Regulation of the Microcirculation, 1982, Handbook of Shock and Trauma, Vol. 1: Basic Science, 1983, Magnesium and the Cardiovascular System, 1985, Cardiovascular Actions of Anesthetic Agents and Drugs Used in Anesthesia, vol. I, 1986, vol. II, 1987, Magnesium, Stress and the Cardiovascular System, 1986, Magnesium in Biochemical Processes and Medicine, 1987, Magnesium in Clinical Medicine and Therapeutics, 1992, Unique Magnesium-Sensitive Ion Selective Electrodes, 1994; editor-in-chief: Physiology and Patho-physiology Series, 1976—81, Microcirculation, 1980—84, Magnesium: Exptl. and Clin. Rsch., 1981—89, Microcirculation, Endothelium and Lymphatics, 1984—, Magnesium and Trace Elements, 1990—, mem. editl. bd.: Jour. Circulatory Shock, 1973—85, Advances in Microcirculation, 1976—92, Jour. Cardiovasc. Pharmacology, 1977—84, Prostaglandins, Leukotrienes and Fatty Acids, 1978—2001, Substance and Alcohol Actions/Misuse, 1979—84, Alcoholism: Clin. and Exptl. Rsch., 1982—87; mem. exec. editl. bd. Internat. Jour. Clin. Exptl. Medicine, 2008; assoc. editor: Jour. Artery, 1974—, Microvasc. Rsch., 1978—85, Agts. and Actions, 1981—88, Biogenic Amines, 1985—88, Jour. Am. Coll. Nutrition, 1982—94, Frontiers in Biosci., 1996—, Internat. Jour. Cardiovasc. Medicine, Surgery and Biomechanics, 1997—; contbr. over 900 articles to profl. jours.; patentee in field. Recipient Rsch. Career Devel. award USPHS, 1968-72, Silver medal furthering French-U.S. sci. rels. Mayor of Paris, 1984, Medaille Vermeille, French Nat. Acad. Medicine, 1984, Travel awards NIH, 1968, Am. Soc. Pharm. and Exptl. Therapeutics, 1969, First Golden Hippocrates award, Haifa, Israel, 2002, Award Com., 2003-; Chancellor's Outstanding Inventor of Yr. award SUNY, 2002, medal Lifetime of Basic Med. Rsch. and Tchg., Haifa, Israel, 2002, Seelig award for lifetime of rsch. on magnesium in biochemistry and health processes Gordon Rsch. Conf. on Magnesium, 2005; grantee NIH, 1968—, NIMH, 1974-78, Nat. Heart Lung Blood Inst., 1974-86, Nat. Inst. Drug Abuse, 1979-83, Nat. Inst. Alcohol Abuse and Alcoholism, 1990-, US Naval Med. Rsch. Ctr., 2005—; Eminent fellow Wisdom Hall of Fame, 1999, Winston Churchill fellow Wisdom Hall of Fame, 2000, Golden Hippocrates Internat. award, Leading Physician of World, 2003-. Fellow: AAAS, Royal Soc. Medicine, Molecular Medicine Soc., Royal Australian Chem. Inst., Am. Soc. Angiology, Am. Coll. Nutrition (Seelig award 2002, hon. lectr.), Am. Inst. Chemists (hon. lectr., mem. editl. review bd.), Internat. Coll. Angiology, Am. Coll. Forensic Examiners (life), Am. Soc. Integrative Medicine (life), Am. Bd. Forensic Examiners (life), Am. Coll. Angiology (hon. lectr.), Am. Heart Assn. (coun. basic sci. 1969—, coun. on thrombosis 1971—, coun. on stroke 1973—, cardiovasc. A study sect. 1978—81, coun. on circulation 1978—, coun. on high blood pressure 1978—, coun. on cardiopulmonary circulation 1987—, coun. on arteriosclerosis, thrombosis, and vascular biology 1997—, coun. on cardiovascular basic scis. 2001—, fellow coun. on high blood pressure rsch. 2002, rsch. grants rev. com. N.E. 2004—07), Assn. Clin. Scientists, Am. Physiol. Soc. (circulation group 1971—, pub. info. com. 1980—84, hon. lectr.), Nat. Acad. Clin. Biochemistry, Anglo-Am. Acad. (hon. 1980); mem.: NSF, AAUP, APHA, Internat. Brain Injury Assn., Soc. Free Radical Biology and Medicine, Internat. Soc. Interferon and Cytokine Rsch., AHA NE Study Section, AM Physiol. Soc., Internat. Soc. Free Radical Rsch., Am. Soc. Biochemistry and Molecular Biology, Am. Inst. Biol. Sci., Internat. Soc. Police Surgeons, Am. Med. Writers Assn., Nat. Coun. Magnesium and Cardiovasc. Disease, Am. Assn. Pharm. Scis., Inter-Am. Soc. Hypertension, Am. Soc. Hypertension (founder), Internat. Soc. Hypertension, Internat. Anesthesia Soc., Coun. Biology Editors, NY Soc. Electron Microscopy, NY Heart Assn., NY Acad. Scis. (com. mem.), Am. Soc. Magnesium Rsch. (exec. dir. 1984—, founder, symposium chmn. and organizer, pres.), Am. Soc. Bone and Mineral Rsch., Am. Soc. Cell Biology, The Oxygen Soc., Am. Soc. Zoologists, Am. Microscopical Soc., Am. Assn. Lab. Animal Sci., Soc. Xenobiotics, Internat. Platform Assn., Soc. Scholarly Pub., Soc. Nutrition Edn., Soc. Parenteral and Enteral Nutrition, Liposome Soc., Internat. Soc. Exposure Analysis, Reticuloendothelial Soc. (hon. lectr., hon. lectr.), Soc. Cardiovasc. Pathology, Soc. Environ. Geochemistry and Health (hon lectr. and symposium organizer), Soc. Leukocyte Biology, Internat. Soc. Biorheology, Biomed. Optics Soc., Internat. Soc. Biomed. Rsch. on Alcoholism (founder), Am. Soc. Microbiology, Am. Inst. Nutrition (symposium chmn., organizer, hon. lectr.), Fedn. Am. Soc. Exptl. Biology (pub. info. com. and symposium organizer 1981—86), Internat. Anesthesia Rsch. Soc., Neurotrauma Soc., European Conf. Microcirculation (symposium organizer and hon. lectr.), Microscopy Soc. Am., Am. Fedn. Clin. Rsch., Shock Soc. (founder, symposium organizer, hon. lectr.), Soc. Neurosci., Am. Thoracic Soc., Soc. Critical Care Medicine, Am. Oil Chemists Soc., Rsch. Soc. on Alcoholism (hon lectr., symposium organizer), Am. Coll. Toxicology, Harvey Soc., Endocrine Soc., Am. Soc. Nutritional Scis. (hon. lectr., symposium organizer), Am. Soc. Pharm. and Exptl. Therapeutics (symposium organizer & hon lectr.), Am. Chem. Soc., Am. Soc. Headache, Am. Assn. Clin. Chemistry (hon. lectr. mem. editl. review bd.), Soc. Exptl. Biology and Medicine (editl. bd. 1976—83), Microcirculatory Soc. (nominating com. 1973—74, past exec. coun., hon. lectr.), Am. Soc. Investigative Pathology (hon. lectr.), Soc. Magnetic Resonance, Sigma Xi. Office: 450 Clarkson Ave Brooklyn NY 11203-2056 Office Phone: 718-270-2194. Business E-Mail: baltura@downstate.edu.

ALVARENGA, KÁTIA FREITAS, audiologist, educator; b. São Paulo, Brazil, Aug. 5, 1964; d. Pedro Pereira and Heloisa Ferreira de Freitas Alvarenga. Degree in Audiology and Speech Pathology, U. Sagrado Coração, Bauru, São Paulo, 1987; Specialization in Otoneurology, Fed. U. São Paulo, 1989, Specialization in Human Comm. Disorders, 1989, MS in Human Comm. Disorders Speech Pathology & Audiology, 1993, PhD in Human Comm. Disorders Speech Pathology & Audiology, 1997; Postdoc. degree in Audiological Assessment Children, U. Manchester, Eng., 2000; Postdoc. degree in Electrophysiology, U. Mich., Ann Arbor, 2000. Cert. in audiology and speech pathology U. Sagrado Coração, 1988. Prof., speech pathology and audiology dept. U. São Paulo, Bauru, 1992—, audiologist, cochlear implant team, 1994—, coord., profl. practice, 2003—, coordination com. mem., exch. agreement, 2005—, v.p., commn. internat. rels., 2007—. Mem. commn. Assn. Hearing Deficient Parents and Users Cochlear Implant, Bauru, 1998—2007; charter mem. Brazilian Acad. Audiology, São Paulo, 2001—, v.p., 2003—05, dir., 2007—. Contbr. articles. Mem. City Coun. Rights of Child and Adolescent, Bauru, 2002—04. Recipient award, Craniofacial Rehab. Hosp., U. São Paulo, 1994—2008; Rsch. grant, Auditory Health Model in Health Family Program, 2005. Achievements include research in proposal and indicators for quality evaluation of audiology services; newborn hearing health model; plasticity and development of central auditory system; electrical audiometry brainstem response in cochlear implant program; videoconference effectiveness in community health agents. Office: Faculdade Odontologia Bauru USP Al Dr Octávio Pinheiro Brisolla 9-75 Bauru São Paulo 17012-901 Brazil Office Fax: 55-14-32234679. Business E-Mail: katialv@fob.usp.br.

ALVAREZ, GABRIEL ELIAS, plastic surgeon, writer; s. Gabriel B. Alvarez Fuertes and Alicia Parra; m. Lynne Alvarez; children: Olivia, Lauren. Medico Cirujano, National Autonomous U. of Mexico, Mexico City, 1965—71. Cert. Mexican Board in Plastic Surgery 1979. Plastic surgeon Hosp. General de Mexico, Mexico City, 1979—82; assoc. specialist in plastic surgery The Royal Free Hosp., London, 1989—95; cons. plastic surgeon Princess Alexandra Hosp., Harlow, Essex, England, 1995—. Bd. dirs. GMED Ltd. Author: (CD-ROM) Multimedia Course in Minor Surgery, 2001. Fellow: Royal Coll. Surgeons England, Royal Soc. of Medicine. Office: U Coll Hosp PPW E G a Wing 25 Grafton Way WC1E 6DB London England Home Phone: 44 (0)289 07131; Office Phone: 44 (0)207 3837395. Home Fax: 44 (0)207 2660677. Business E-Mail: gabs@gmedltd.com.

ALVAREZ, MANUEL (MANNY ALVAREZ), hospital executive, medical educator and news correspondent; b. Cuba, Apr. 16, 1957; married; 3 children. MD. Cert. Am. Bd. Obstetrics and Gynecology, with subspecialty Bd. Fetal Medicine. Resident, obstetrics/gynecology and anesthesiology St. Joseph Hosp. and Med. Ctr., Paterson, NJ; fellow, maternal fetal medicine and critical care medicine Mount Sinai Hospital, NYC; assoc. prof. Mount Sinai School Medicine; vice-chmn., Dept. Obstetrics and Gynecology and Reproductive Sci. Mt. Sinai Med. Ctr.; chmn., Dept. Obstetrics and Gynecology and Reproductive Sci. Hackensack Univ. Med. Ctr., NJ, 1996—. Adj. prof., obstetrics and gynecology NYU Sch. Medicine; examiner Am. Bd. Obstetrics and Gynecology; spkr. in field. Former health sci. reportor Telemundo, developer (nightly news segment) A Dose of Health, med. contbr. FOX News Channel, including shows FOX & Friends and Dayside; contbr. articles to numerous publs. Mem. Celia Cruz Found.; bd. dir. Life Opportunities Unlimted. Named Man of Yr., NJ SEEDS, 2004. Mem.: Assn. Professors Gynecology and Obstetrics, Soc. Maternal Fetal Medicine, Am. Coll. Obstetrics and Gynecology, Am. Soc. for Blood and Marrow Trnsplantation, Am. Inst. Ultrasound and Medicine, Soc. Prenatal Care. Office: Hackensack University Medical Center Dept Obstetrics and Gynocology 30 Prospect Ave Hackensack NJ 07601 Office Phone: 201-996-2000. Fax: 201-487-8516. Business E-Mail: malvarez@humed.com. *

ALVAREZ, OFELIA AMPARO, pediatrician, hematologist; b. Havana, Cuba, Mar. 29, 1958; BS, U. Puerto Rico, 1978, MD, 1982. Diplomate Nat. Bd. Med. Examiners, Am. Bd. Pediat., Sub-bd. Pediatric Hematology-Oncology. Pediat. resident U. Children's Hosp., San Juan, 1982—85; fellow pediat. hematology, oncology Children's Hosp. L.A., 1985—88; asst. prof. pediat. Loma Linda U., Calif., 1988—95, assoc. prof., 1995—2000; prof. clin. pediats. U. Miami, 2001—, dir. pediat. sickle cell program. Chmn. instnl. rev. bd. U. Miami, 2004—. Contbr. articles to profl. jours. Clin. oncology fellow Am. Cancer Soc., 1985-86; named one of Best Doctors, 2005-10 Fellow: Am. Acad. Pediat.; mem.: Internat. Assn. Study Pain, Sickle Cell Disease Assn. America, Am. Soc. Hematology, Am. Soc. Pediat. Hematology/Oncology, Am. Soc. Clin. Oncology. Roman Catholic. Achievements include research in sickle cell disease. Office: Univ Miami Divsn Pediats Hematology Oncology Dept Pediats PO Box 016960 Miami FL 33101 E-mail: oalvarez2@med.miami.edu.

ÁLVAREZ-BORREGO, JOSUÉ, physics professor; b. Mazatlán, Sinaloa, Méx., May 10, 1957; PhD, Cicese, 1993. Prof. Cicese, 1986—. Recipient 2nd Pl. Nat. prize, 1994. Mem.: Rschrs. Nat. Sys., Scis. Mexican Acad., Plankton Mexican Soc., Mexican Acad. Optics. Avocations: tai chi, bicycling. Office: Carretera Ensenada-Tijuana 3918 Ensenada Baja Calif 22860 Mexico Business E-Mail: josue@cicese.mx.

ALVAREZ-DIAZ, JORGE ALBERTO, physician; s. Jose Angel Alvarez-Rodriguez and Maria Ester Diaz-Juarez; 1 child, Jeanette Aurora Alvarez-Lopez. MD, U. Autonoma Ciudad Juarez, Chihuahua, Mex., 1998; MSc in Bioethics, U. Nacional Mayor San Marcos, Lima, Perú, 2003; MSc in Human Sexuality, Akamai U., Hawai, 2004; MSc candidate in Molecular Biomedicine, Inst. Politecnico Nacional, Mex., 2004; PhD candidate, U. Complutense Madrid, 2006—. Cert. ultrasonographist U. Nacional San Luis Gonzaga de Ica, Lima, 2005, clin. sexologist L. Am. Fedn. Sexuality and Sex Edn., 2006. Tchr. U. Autonoma Ciudad Juarez, 2000—06; physician Inst. Reproduccion Asistida, Genetica y Embarazo de Alto Riesgo, Ciudad Juarez, 2000—02; physician primary care Inst. Medicina y Tecnologia Avanzada de la Conducta, Ciudad Juarez, 2002—06; tchr. continuous edn. U. Tex., El Paso, 2003—06; clin. sexologist Internat. Inst. Human Sexuality, Ciudad Juarez, 2004—06. Vol., Ciudad Juarez, 2006. Recipient Manuel Velasco-Suarez award, PAHEF PAHO/WHO, 2007; fellowship, U. Chile, Santiago de Chile, 2004, fellow, Fogarty, NIH, 2005. Mem.: Academia Nacional Mexicana de Bioetica. Office: Univ Complutense Madrid Ave Complutense Plaza Ramon y Cajal Madrid Spain Office Fax: (34-913) 941 803. Personal E-mail: bioetica_reproductiva@hotmail.com.

ALVAREZ-JIMENEZ, MARIO, psychiatrist; b. Pamplona, Spain, Mar. 26, 1977; BS in Psychology with honors, U. Salamanca, 1999; PhD, U. Cantabria, Spain, 2009. Intern clin. psychology Spanish Nat. Health Sys., 2001—04; lopez-albo internat. fellow Marques de Vadecilla Pub. Found. & Rsch. Inst., 2005—09; sr. rsch. fellow Centre Youth Mental Health, Orygen Youth Health Rsch. Centre, 2010—. Mem.: Internat. Early Psychosis Assn., Spanish Nat. Assn. Clin. Psychology. Office: 35 Poplar Rd Parkville Melbourne Victoria 3052 Australia Business E-Mail: malvarez@unimelb.edu.au.

ALVEGARD, THOR ANDREAS, retired medical educator; 1 child, Tatjana Merete. MD, Free U., Berlin, 1968; PhD, U. Lund, Skane, Sweden, 1989. Diplomate Lund U., 1991. Asst. prof. Lund U., 1991—. Dir., cancerepidemiolgy Lund U., 2000—08. Contbr. articles to profl. jours. Active CTOS, Chgo., 1999—2002. Mem.: EMSOS, CTOS, ASCO. Achievements include research in prognostic factors in soft tissue sarcoma, high dose chemotherapy and bone marrow transplantation, total body irradiation. Avocations: travel, swimming. Office Phone: 0046 46 177560. Office Fax: 0046 46 188143. Business E-Mail: thor.alvegard@med.lu.se.

ALVES, CAMILA ALOISIO, medical educator, researcher; b. Barra Mansa, Rio de Janeiro, Brasil, Oct. 30, 1980; Degree in Psychology, U. Fed. Fluminense, 2004; Master, Inst. Fernandes Figueira-Fiocruz, 2009. With mgmt. planning Inst. Fernandes Figueira-Fiocruz, 2009—10, rsch. scientist, 2010; prof. faculty medicine petrópolis, 2010; prof. U. Estado Rio de Janeiro, 2009—11. Jr. adminstr. level IV Ministério da Saúde, Brazil, 2007—09; rsch. scientist and devel. Escola Nat. Saúde Pública Sergio Arouca -Fiocruz, 2010—11. Grant, SOPERJ, Fiocruz, Brazilian Soc. Pediat. Avocations: reading, movies. Home: Rua das Palmeiras 93 Apt 603 Rio de Janeiro 22270-070 Brazil Personal E-mail: camila.aloisioalves@gmail.com.

ALVES, LEONARDO, cardiologist, educator; b. Rio Grande, Brazil, Nov. 12, 1971; MD, U. Fed. Rio Grande, 1995; MSc in Epidemiology, U. Fed. Pelotas, 2009. Cardiologist and interventional cardiologist Hosp. de Cardiologia do Rio Grande, 2004—. Prof. medicine sch. U. Fed. Rio Grande, 2010. Mem.: Brazilian Soc. Hemodynamics and Interventional Cardiology, Brazilian Cardiology Soc. Avocations: guitar, motorcycling, running. Home: Rua Aquidaban 639 Apt 201 Rio Grande 96200-480 Brazil Personal E-mail: leoalves@vetorial.net.

ALVES, LEONARDO SCHERER, biomedical researcher; b. Porto Alegre, Rio Grande do Sul, Brazil, Jan. 29, 1985; BS in Zoology, U. Okla., Norman, 2006. Grad. rschr. biochemistry U. Calif., Irvine, 2007—; predoctoral scholar Calif. Inst. Regenerative Medicine, San Francisco, 2009—. Vis. scientist Children Hosp. Phila., 2011. Participant 61st Internat. Workshop High Resolution Respirometry, 2011; active UNICEF, Irvine, 2009. Fellow Miguel Velez fellowship, 2011; HHMI tchg. fellowship, Howard Hewes Med. Inst., 2008. Mem.: Zool. Soc. (pres. 2004—05), PanAm. Student Assn. (with external affairs 2005—06), Alpha Lambda Delta Academic Honor Soc. Achievements include research in stem cell research with focus on regenerative medicine.

ALVIN, WILLIAM R., hospital administrator; BA, Thiel Coll., Greenville, Pa.; MPA, George Washington U. Past COO Hutzel Hosp.; CEO Maxicare/Independence Health Plan; sr. exec. Health Alliance Plan; CEO Henry Ford Wyandotte Hosp.; now pres., CEO Care Choices, Mich., 2001—07; exec. v.p. strategy devel. Detroit Med. Ctr., 2007—. Office: DMC Corp Offices 3990 John R Detroit MI 48201

ALVING, BARBARA MARIE, federal agency administrator, hematologist; BS with highest distinction, Purdue U., Ind., 1967; MD cum laude, Georgetown U., Washington, 1972. Intern internal medicine Georgetown U.; resident internal medicine, fellow hematology Johns Hopkins U. Hosp., Balt.; rsch. investigator divsn. blood & blood products FDA; various positions dept. hematology & vascular biology Walter Reed Army Inst. Rsch., Rockville, Md., 1980—92, chief dept. hematology & vascular biology, 1992—96; dir. med. oncology/hematology sect. Washington Hosp. Ctr., 1996—99; dir. extramural rsch. Nat. Heart, Lung & Blood Inst. (NHLBI), NIH, Bethesda, Md., 1999—2001, dep. dir. NHLBI, 2001—03, acting dir., 2003—05, dir. Women's Health Initiative, 2002—06, acting dir. Nat. Ctr. Rsch. Resources (NCRR), 2005—07, dir., 2007—. Prof. medicine Uniformed Svcs. U. Health Scis., Bethesda. Contbr. articles to profl. jours. Recipient Outstanding Svc. award, Am. Soc. Hematology. Master: ACP. Achievements include patents in field. Office: NCRR 6701 Democracy Blvd MSC 4874 Bethesda MD 20892-4872 Office Phone: 301-496-5793. Office Fax: 301-402-0006. E-mail: barbara.alving@nih.gov. *

ALWAN, ALA, international organization administrator; b. Iraq; MD, U. Alexandria, Egypt. Post-graduate tng. and qualifications, UK; med. practitioner Scotland; prof., dean Mustansiriya U. Faculty Medicine, Baghdad, Iraq; regional advisor non-communicable diseases, Eastern Mediterranean regional office WHO, rep. in Oman, dir., divsn. health systems devel. in the Eastern Mediterranean region, dir. non-communicable diseases prevention & dir., dept. non-communicable diseases mgmt. Geneva, 1998—2001, rep. in Jordan, 2001—03, rep. of the dir. gen., asst. dir. gen. health action in crises Geneva, 2005—08, asst. dir. gen. non-communicable diseases and mental health, 2008—; min. edn., min. health Govt. of Iraq, Baghdad, 2003—05. Office: WHO avenue Appia 20 1211 Geneva Switzerland *

ALWARD, RUTH ROSENDALL, nursing consultant; d. Henry Rosendall and Freda Jonkman, m. Samuel Alward, Jan. 17, 1976. RN, Butterworth Hosp. Sch. Nursing, Grand Rapids, Mich.; BSN summa cum laude, Hunter Coll./CUNY, NYC, 1980; MA Tchrs. Coll., Columbia U., 1982, EdM, 1983, EdD, 1986. Sr. clin. nurse Wadsworth VA Hosp., LA, 1966-68; exec. dir. nursing Care Corp, Grand Rapids, Mich., 1968-71; nursing cons. Humana Inc., Louisville, 1972-76; asst. prof., dir. nursing adminstrn. grad. prog. Hunter Coll., CUNY, NYC, 1986-90; pres. Nurse Exec. Assocs., Inc., Washington, 1990—; series editor Delmar Pubs. Inc., Albany, 1993-96. Co-author: The Nurse's Shift Work Handbook, 1993, The Nurse's Guide to Marketing, 1991; contbr. articles to profl. jours.; mem. editorial adv. bd. Jour. of Nursing Adminstrn. Bd. dirs., past pres. James Lenox House Assn.; bd. dirs. IONA Sr. Svcs., 1998-2004. Mem. Nat. League Nursing (treas. D.C. chpt.), Am. Orgn. Nurse Execs., Sigma Theta Tau. Home and Office: 2011 N St NW Washington DC 20036-2301 Home Phone: 202-728-2956; Office Phone: 202-728-2956. E-mail: ruthalward@aol.com.

ALWASEL, SALEH HAMAD, academic administrator; b. Saudi Arabia, Sept. 12, 1969; PhD, 2007; postgrad. in Academic Practice, King's Coll. London, 2010. Dir., attracting nobel laureate King Saud U., 2008, dir., fetal programming diseases rsch. chair, 2008—. Hon. vis. prof. Manchester U. Office: King Saud University Coll Sci PO Box 2455 Riyadh 11451 Saudi Arabia Office Fax: 0966-1-467-8514. Business E-Mail: salwasel@ksu.edu.sa.

ALY, AL SAID, plastic surgeon, otolaryngologist; b. Alexandria, Egypt, Oct. 6, 1956, MD, Georgetown U., Washington, 1983. Cert. Am. Bd. Plastic Surgery, Am. Bd. Otolaryngology. Intern surgery UCLA, Calif., 1983—84, resident Calif., 1984—85; resident otolaryngology-head & neck surgery Vanderbilt U., Nashville, 1988—92; fellow facial plastic & reconstructive surgery U. Calif., Irvine, 1992—93; resident plastic & reconstructive surgery U. Miami/Jackson Meml. Hosp., Fla., 1995—97; assoc. prof. plastic surgery U. Iowa, Iowa City, 1997—2004; pvt. practice Iowa City Plastic Surgery, LLC, Coralville. Author: (med. textbook) Body Contouring After Massive Weight Loss, 2006. Fellow: ACS; mem.: AMA, Iowa Soc. Plastic Surgeons (v.p., pres. 2007—08), Am. Soc. Aesthetic Plastic Surgery, Am. Soc. Plastic Surgeons (mem. task force on Post Massive Weight Loss Plastic Surgery). Office: Iowa City Plastic Surgery LLC Ste 102 501 12th Ave Coralville IA 52241 Office Phone: 319-337-3740. Office Fax: 319-337-7500. E-mail: mdplastic@aol.com.

AMACHER, ARTHUR LOREN, neurosurgeon; b. Saskatoon, Sask., Can., Oct. 22, 1938; came to U.S., 1983; s. Arthur Melvin and Johanna Martha (Niebergall) A.; m. Jane Elizabeth Tomlinson, Sept. 20, 1961; children: Scott, Jon, Marc. MD, U. Western Ont., London, Can., 1962. Intern Victoria Hosp., London, Ont., 1962-63, resident (jr.) surgery, 1963-64, resident neurosurgery, 1965-67, chief resident neurosurgery, 1969-70; fellow anatomy and neuroanatomy U. Western Ont., 1964-65; resident (sr.) surgery Vets. Hosp., London, 1965; fellow neuropathology U. Toronto, 1967; resident neurosurgery Childrens Hosp. Med. Ctr. and Peter Bent Brigham Harvard U., 1968, chief resident, teaching fellow surgery, 1969; from lectr. to assoc. prof. clin. neuro-sci., surgery U. Western Ont., London, Can., 1970-83; prof. neurosurgery U. Conn., Farmington, 1983-87; neurosurgeon Geisinger Med. Ctr., Danville, Pa., 1987-95, chief, 1995—2003; neurosurgeon Evangelical Med. Svcs. Found., 2003—; green rm. bd. Weis Ctr. Performing Arts, Bucknell U., 1995—. Cons. treatment alogitm USN, Washington, 1989, Via Cyometrics, Bel Air, Md. Author: Patient Care in Neurosurgery, 1990, Pediatric Head Injuries, 1988; contbr. over 130 articles to profl. jours., chpts. to books. Chorister Susquahanna Valley Chorale, Lewisburg, 1989—. Recipient Harriman award, Bucknell U., 1994, Svc. Cmty. and Univ. Backcourt award, Bison Club, Bucknell U., 2005. Fellow ACS, Royal Coll. Surgeons of Can.; mem. N.Y. Acad. Sci., Pa. Neurosurg. Soc. (exec. com., 1993-98, pres. 1997), Acad. Am. Poets, Pa. Med. Soc. (bd. trustees, 2002-) Avocations: poetry, writing, reading, fishing, sailing. Home Phone: 510-523-8686; Office Phone: 570-522-5033. E-mail: aljamach@ptd.net.

AMADA, GERALD, retired psychotherapist; b. Newark, Aug. 13, 1938; s. Samuel and Rose Amada; m. Marcia Rae Hirshberg, Aug. 9, 1962; children: Robin, Naomi, Laurie, Eric. BA, Rutgers U., Newark, 1960; MSW, Rutgers U., 1962; PhD, Wright Inst., Berkeley, Calif., 1977. Psychotherapist Mercer County Mental Health Clinic, Trenton, NJ, 1962—64, Dept. Mental Hygiene, Modesto, Calif., 1964—66, Homewood Terrace, San Francisco, 1966—68; staff devel. supr. Solano County Dept. Social Svcs., Vallejo, Calif., 1968—70; dir. Mental Health Program, City Coll. of San Francisco, 1970—2000; psychotherapist Mill Valley, Calif., 1980—2003; cons. colls. and univs., 1980—. Cons. KPIX-TV, San Francisco, 1980—82, Mass. Mutual Life Ins. Co., San Francisco, 1980—83; prof. Kittceman's Therapy, 2009. Author: Mental Health on the Community College Campus, 1977, Mental Health and Authoritarianism on the College Campus, 1978, A Guide to Psychotherapy, 1995, Coping with the Disruptive College Student, 1994, The Mystified Fortune and Other Tales from Psychotherapy, 1998, Coping with Misconduct in the College Classroom, 1999, The Power of Negative Thinking, 1999, Mental Health and Student Conduct Issues, 2001, Anker's Plight, 2006, Professor Kittleman's Therapy, 2009; reviewer Am. Jour. Psychotherapy, 1983—, contbr., reviewer Jour. Coll. Student Psychotherapy, 1988—; author: Mushu: A True Story, 2006; contbr. articles to profl. jours. Commr. Marin County Human Rights Commn.; facilitator Alzheimer's Orgn., San Rafael, Calif., 1998—2003. Recipient Award of Excellence, Nat. Assn. of Vocat. Edn. Spl. Needs Pers., 1984. Mem.: Am. Fedn. Tchrs., NASW, Freedom for Individual Rights in Edn. Avocations: tennis, writing, reading, travel, classical music. Mailing: 185 Mount Lassen Dr San Rafael CA 94903 Office Phone: 415-479-8889. Business E-Mail: mgamada@earthlink.com.

AMADA, NORITOSHI, surgeon; b. Takasaki, Gumma, Japan, Sept. 9, 1956; s. Masakazu and Kikuyo Amada; m. Noriko Nakamura, May 16, 1982; children: Hirohisa, Mizuho. MD, Tohoku U., Sendai, Japan, 1981, degree, 1989. Resident Mito Nat. Hosp. dept. surgery, 1981—85; dir. surgery Sendai Shakaihoken Hosp., 1991—2001, dir. transplant surgery, 2001—02, chief dir. transplant surgery, 2002—, vice dir., 2005—. Avocations: gardening, fishing. Office: Sendai Shakaihoken Hosp 3-16-1 Tsutsumimachi Aoba-ku Sendai Miyagi 981-8501 Japan Office Phone: 81-22-275-3111. Business E-Mail: amada-n@umin.ac.jp.

AMAECHI, BENNETT TOCHUKWU, dentist, prosthodontist; b. Obosi, Anambra state, Nigeria, Dec. 23, 1959; s. Christian and Henrietta Amaechi; m. Adaorah Ezife Adibe, Feb. 3, 1964; children: Chikaosolu, Adaiba, Chukwubinyelum, Chizaramepkere. BSc in Health Scis., U. Ife, Nigeria, 1983, B in Dental Surgery, 1986; MSc in Prosthodontics, U. London, 1993; PhD in Cariology, U. Liverpool, Eng., 1999. Cert. in dental implantology Guy's Dental Hosp., London and Branemark Inst., Gotenborg, Sweden. Dental house officer U. Ife Tchg. Hosp., Ile-Ife, Oyo, Nigeria, 1986—87; prosthodontics sr. house officer Guy's Dental Hosp., London, 1993—94; rsch. assoc. cariology U. Liverpool, 1995—2001; asst. prof. cmty. dentistry U. Tex. Health Sci. Ctr., San Antonio, 2001—, clin. tchr. in preventive dentistry, 2001—, dir. cariology, 2001—. Presenter in field. Contbr. book Tooth Wear and Sensitivity: Clinical Advances in Restorative Dentistry, 2000, articles to profl. jours. Recipient Rsch. in Prevention award, Internat. Assn. for Dental Rsch./Colgate-Palmolive, 1998. Mem.: CommonWealth Dental Assn., Am. Assn. for Dental Rsch., Internat. Assn. for Dental Rsch., European Orgn. for Caries Rsch. (Young Investigators Travel award 1998). Avocation: travel. Home: 2011 Encino Alto St San Antonio TX 78259 Office: Univ Tex Health Sci Ctr 7703 Floyd Curl Dr San Antonio TX 78229 Personal E-mail: amaechi2011@sbcglobal.net. Business E-Mail: amaechi@uthscsa.edu.

AMANKWAH, KWAME S., surgeon, educator; b. Ottawa, Ont., Sept. 23, 1967; MSc, U. Toronto, 1994; MD, Albany Med. Coll., 1997. Assoc. prof., surgery SUNY, Syracuse, 2004—. Mem.: Soc. Vascular Surgery. Office: University Hosp Ste 8801 750 East Syracuse NY 13210 Business E-Mail: amankwak@upstate.edu.

AMANO, YUJI, gastroenterologist, director; b. Japan, Mar. 13, 1957; Postgrad., Shimane Med. U., 1987. Dir. divsn. gastrointestinal endoscopy Shimane Med. U. Hosp., 2006—. Office: 89-1 Enya cho Izumo Shimane 693-8501 Japan Office Fax: 81-853-202187. Business E-Mail: amano@med.shimane-u.ac.jp.

AMARASINGHE, AMARASINGHE A.W., psychiatrist, consultant; b. Rajagiriya, Sri Lanka, Aug. 22, 1935; arrived in U.S., 1973; s. Podiappuhamy Amarasinghe and Bethmage Nona Perera; m. Nandawathy Rajapakse, Sept. 1, 1965; children: Charm Saumya, Shyly Saubhagya. B Medicine, U. Ceylon, Colombo, Sri Lanka, 1961, B Surgery, 1961; diploma in child health, Royal Coll. Physicians, London, 1971; grad., Command and Gen. Staff Coll., U.S. Army, 1995. Diplomate Am. Bd. Psychiatry, Am. Bd. Neurology. Med. officer Govt. Health Svcs., Sri Lanka, 1962—70; sr. house officer Nat. Health Svcs., England, 1970—72; resident in psychiatry Mount Sinai Hosp., NYC, 1973—76; psychiatrist VA Hosp., Augusta, Ga., 1976—97; cons. psychiatrist Ga. Dept. Corrections, 1998—. Assoc. clin. prof. Med. Coll. Ga., Augusta, 1992—97. Author: (novels) Tis Pe Tis Viya, 1992, Saudi Sat Sathiya, 1995, Ada Siya Wasa Diya, 2000. Pres. Assn. for Peace in Sri Lanka, Augusta, 1983. Col. USAR, 1991. Decorated Nat. Def. Svc. medal, Overseas Svc. ribbon; scholar A.E. Bennett scholarship, AMA on Alcoholism, 1980. Mem.: Assn. Mil. Surgeons of U.S. Buddhist. Avocations: meditation, travel. Home: 102 Bay Berry Hills Mcdonough GA 30253-4005 Personal E-mail: amareI@pol.net.

AMARO, HORTENSIA DE LOS ANGELES, health sciences professor, healthcare researcher; b. Cuba, Dec. 7, 1950; BA in Psychology, UCLA, 1975, MA in Psychology, 1977, PhD in Psychology, 1982; LHD (hon.), Simmons Coll., Boston, 1994. Rsch. psychologist, Alcohol Rsch. Ctr., UCLA, 1980—82; asst. prof. dept. social and behavioral scis. Boston U. Sch. Pub. Health, 1983—88, assoc. prof., 1989—93, prof., 1993—2001; disting. prof. Northeastern U. Bouve Coll. Health Scis., Boston, 2002—, dir. Inst. Urban Health Rsch., 2003—, assoc. dean urban health rsch., 2008—. Sr. vis. rsch. scientist Hispanic Health & Human Services Orgn., Washington, 1992; disting. vis. prof. Ben Gurion U., Beer Sheva, Israel, 2000. Assoc. editor Psychology of Women Quarterly, 1994—99, mem. editl. bd. American Jour. Pub. Health, 1997—2000, Perspectives Sexual & Reproductive Health, 2003—; contbr. articles to profl. jours. Founding mem. Latino Health Network Mass., 1986, pres. bd. dirs., 1988—91; bd. dirs. AIDS Action Com., Boston, 1986—87, Boston Med. Found., 1992—95, Pathways to Wellness, Boston, 2009—; vice chair bd. dirs. Boston Pub. Health Commn., 1996—. Recipient Alfred L. Frechette award, Mass. Pub. Health Assn., 1991, Rafael Tavares, M.D. Meml. award, NY Hispanic Mental Health Professionals Assn., 1998, Cmty. Leadership award, Whittier St. Health Ctr., Boston, 2002, Cmty. Health Rsch. award, Martha Elliot Cmty. Health Ctr., 2003, Humanitarian of Yr. award, Mass. Sch. Profl. Psychology, 2006, Susan Love award for women's health, Fenway Cmty. Health Ctr., Boston, 2006, Leadership award, Boston Latino Health Inst., 2007, Founder's award, Chgo. Human Resources Devel. Inst., 2007. Fellow: American Psychol. Assn. (Early Career award 1993, Dalmas Taylor Disting. Contbn. in Rsch. award 2001, Rsch. award 2006, James Jones Lifetime Achievement award 2009); mem.: APHA, Soc. Behavioral Medicine, Inst. Medicine, Nat. Hispanic Psychol. Assn. (founding mem., pres. Boston chpt. 1983—84). Achievements include contributions to improving behavioral health care in community-based organizations; research focused on alcohol and drug use and addiction among adolescents and adults; the development and testing of behavioral interventions for HIV/AIDS prevention, including innovative HIV prevention models targeted to Latina and African American women; substance abuse and mental health treatment for Latina and African American women and incarcerated men; alcohol and drug use among college populations; and behavioral interventions for HIV medications adherence. Office: Inst Urban Health Rsch Bouvé Coll Health Scis Northeastern U 310 International Village Boston MA 02115 Office Phone: 617-373-7601. Office Fax: 617-373-7309. Business E-Mail: h.amaro@neu.edu. *

AMARO, MIGUEL HAGE, physician; b. Brazil, Sept. 14, 1956; MD, Faculdade Medicina Estado Pará, 1980; degree, Fed. U. São Paulo, 2005. Fellow Vitreous Retona Macula Cons. NY, 1992—92. Office: Quintino Bocaiuva 516 Belem Para 66053-240 Brazil Office Fax: 55-91-32427067. Business E-Mail: amaro@amazon.com.br.

AMBALAVANAN, SIVA, nephrologist, educator; b. Madras, India, Nov. 26, 1962; arrived in U.S., 1993; d. A. and Sundari Sivasankaran; m. Geetha Ambalavanan, Aug. 22, 1991; children: Anita, Manoj. MB, BS, Madras Med. Coll., 1985. Cert. nephrology, internal medicine, Fed. Lic. Exam., Ednl. Commn. Fgn. Med. Grads. Tutor in medicine U. Aberdeen, Scotland, 1990—92; fellow Stanford U. Med. Ctr., 1993—95; physician VA Med. Ctr., Salt Lake City, 1996—97; resident Med. Ctr. U. Utah, Salt Lake City, 1996—97, asst. prof. medicine, cons. nephrologist Sch. Medicine, 1996—98. Asst. prof. medicine Wright State U., Dayton, Ohio, 1998—; adj. prof. U. Utah; mem. transfusion com. Fransiscan Med. Ctr., 1999—2000; mem. transplant com. Miami Valley Hosp. Contbr. articles to profl. jours. Active Hindu Cmty. Orgn., Dayton, Ohio, 1999. Recipient Trainee Investigator award for excellence in sci. rsch., Clin. Rsch. Meeting, 1995; grantee, Allan Evan. Fellow: Royal Coll. Physicians; mem.: AMA, ACP. Avocations: golf, travel, cooking, music. Office: Renal Physician Inc 1427 Business Ctr Dayton OH 45410

AMBORSKI, LEONARD EDWARD, retired chemist; b. Buffalo, Aug. 23, 1921; s. Nicholas Leon and Angeline (Laskowska) A.; m. Irene Kazmierczak, Oct. 3, 1944; children: Donna Marie, David Paul. BS, Canisius Coll., 1943; MA, SUNY, Buffalo, 1949, PhD, 1951. Cert. indsl. hygienist Am. Bd. Indsl. Hygiene; cert. EPA instr. in lead abatement and hazardous materials worker tng. Instr. physics Canisius Coll., 1943-44; physicist Carnegie Mellon Inst., Washington, 1944-45; with E.I. DuPont de Nemours & Co., Buffalo, 1945-90, staff scientist, 1973-90, environ. health cons., 1973-90; cons. in environ. health, 1990—. Rsch. assoc. Toxicoloty Rsch. Ctr., SUNY, Buffalo. Patentee in field. Bd. dirs. Am. Lung Assn. of N.Y. State, Buffalo, 1985—; chmn. Tonawanda (N.Y.) Citizen Pre-Treatment Program, 1985-86, Tonawanda Hazardous Materials Adv. Com., Buffalo, 1985-88; chmn. local emergency planning commn. Buffalo and Erie County, N.Y., 1988—; mem. citizens adv. com. Remedial Action Plan for Niagara River Recipient Indsl. and Hazardous Waste award N.Y. State Water Pollution Control Assn., 1989. Mem. Air Pollution Control Assn. (chmn. 1983-84, Svc. award 1984), Am. Chem. Soc., Am. Indsl. Hygiene Assn., Am. Bd. Indsl. Hygiene, Am. Pub. Health Assn., Am. Soc. Safety Engrs., Water Pollution Control Fedn. Republican. Roman Catholic. Avocations: photography, swimming, bicycling. Home: 1 Fox Run Ln Apt 219 Orchard Park NY 14127 Personal E-mail: lamborski@roadrunner.com. E-mail: lamborski@webtv.net.

AMBROS, VICTOR R., geneticist, educator; b. Hanover, NH, 1953; BS in Biology, MIT, Cambridge, 1975, PhD in Biology, 1979. Postdoc. fellow MIT, 1979—83; faculty mem. dept. cellular and devel. biology Harvard U., 1984—92; faculty mem., then prof. genetics Dartmouth Med. Sch., Hanover, NH, 1992—2007; prof. dept. molecular medicine U. Mass. Med. Sch., Worcester, Mass., 2008—. Co-dir. RNA Therapeutics Inst. Contbr. articles to sci. jours. Recipient Genetics Soc. Am. medal, 2006; co-recipient Newcomb Cleve. prize, AAAS, 2002, Lewis S. Rosenstiel award for disting. work in basic med. rsch., Brandeis U., 2005, Warren Triennial prize, Mass. Gen. Hosp., 2007, Benjamin Franklin medal in Life Sci., Franklin Inst., 2008, Gairdner Found. Internat. award, 2008, Albert Lasker award for basic med. rsch., Lasker Found., 2008, Louisa Gross Horwitz prize, 2009. Mem.: NAS. Achievements include along with the members of Ambros Lab, identifying the first microRNA, the product oflin-4, a heterochronic gene of C. elegans in 1993. Office: Univ Mass Med Sch Biotech II Ste 306 55 Lake Ave N Worcester MA 01655 E-mail: vrambros@gmail.com. *

AMBROSINO, GIOVANNI, surgeon, medical educator, department chairman; b. Pietradefusi, Italy, Jan. 1, 1959; s. Alessio Ambrosino and Anna Fiorini; m. Virginia Gubitosi Ambrosino, Mar. 21, 1992; children: Anna, Alessio. MD, U. Padova, Italy, 1984, specialist in gen. and emergency surgery, 1989, specialist in angiology, 1992; specialist in microsurgery, exptl. sugery, pediatric surgery, U. Milan, Italy, 1990. Cert. gen. and liver transplant surgeon. Clin. transplant fellow T. Starzi Transplant Inst., Pitts., 1985—87; asst. prof. surgery Padova U. Hosp., 1987—90; mem. liver transplant staff dept. surgery U. Padova, 1990—92, prof. surgery dept. surgery, 1992—. Mem. FIDH, Paris, 2002; v.p. Internat. Fedn. Human Rights, Italy, 1998—2000; expert in laparoscopic surgery, liver and pancreas surgery, acute liver failure treatment; chmn. dept. Gen. and Hepatobiciary, Pancreatic Surgery Regional Hosp., Vicenza. Patentee in field; dir.: (movie) The Old Age, 1982. Pres. Vita Film, Italy, 1987—88. Achievements include invention of bioartificial liver named "Alex"; first to perform a liver cell transplant on an awake 9 year old child. Avocations: guitar, piano, writing, painting, tennis. Office: Dept Chirurgia Generale I Viale Ferdinando Rodolfi 37 36100 Vicenza VI Italy Fax: 0444 993817.

AMBRUS, JULIAN LAWRENCE, JR., allergist, immunologist, educator; MD, Jefferson Med. Coll., 1979. Diplomate Am. Bd. Internal Medicine, 1982, Am. Bd. Allergy and Immunology, 1985, lic. NY, 1981. Intern State Univ. of NY Buffalo Affiliated Hosp., resident internal medicine, 1980—82; fellow allergy & immunology Nat. Inst. of Health Clin. Ctr., 1982—85; assoc. prof. med. State Univ. of NY; hosp. affiliations include Women & Children's Hosp. of Buffalo, Buffalo Gen. Hosp. Office: Buffalo General Hospital 100 High St Buffalo NY 14203-1154 Office Phone: 716-859-5600.

AMBRUS, MICHAEL JOHANN, surgeon; b. Glimboca, Banat, Romania, May 10, 1948; arrived in Germany, 1978; s. Peter and Tamara Ambrus; m. Denise Toader, Dec. 25, 1975; children: Patrick, Christian, Peter. Med. Dr., U. Medicine, Cluj-Napoca, Romania, 1972; MD, U. Düsseldorf, Germany, 1979; specialist in surgery, U. Koblenz, Germany, 1981, speciaist in traumatology, 1982. Physician 3d Surg. Clinic, Cluj-Napoca, 1972-75, hosp., Petrosani, Romania, 1975-76; intern Surg. Univ. Clinic, Bucharest, Romania, 1976-77; resident in surgery, tchg. asst. acad. tchg. hosp., Idar-Oberstein, Germany, 1977-80, fellow, tchg. asst., 1980-82; chief surg. and trauma dept., chief physician surg. dept. St. Anna Stift Hosp., Löningen, Germany, 1983—, cons. casualty ward, 1983—. Asst. prof. U. Bucharest, 1976-77; expert for accident ins. Contbr. articles to Romanian med. jours. Mem. German Assn. Surgeons, Culture Circle. Avocations: skiing, tennis, reading. Home: Gruener Weg 14 49624 Löningen Germany Office: St Anna Stift Hosp Annenstrasse 9 49624 Löningen Germany Fax: 05432/969696. E-mail: krankenhaus@loeningen.de.

AMBS, STEFAN, biochemist, researcher; MS in Biochemistry, U. Tubingen, Germany, 1988; PhD, U. Wuerzburg, Germany, 1992; MPH in Epidemiology, Johns Hopkins U., 2005. Asst. researcher Dept. Toxicology U. Wurzburg, 1988—92; fellow Lab. Human Carcinogenesis Nat. Cancer Inst., 1992—97, principal investigator, 2001—; rsch. scientist Megabios Corp., Burlingame, Calif., 1997—98; sr. rsch. scientist Cambridge Genomics Ctr., 1998—2001. Reviewer various industry jours. Mem.: Am. Assn. Advancement Sci., Am. Assn. for Cancer Rsch. Office: NIH Human Carcinogenesis Lab Bldg 37 Rm 3050B Bethesda MD 20892-4258 Office Phone: 301-496-4668. Office Fax: 301-496-0497. E-mail: ambss@mail.nih.gov.

AMEDEE, RONALD G., otolaryngologist, educator; MD, Louisiana State U. Sch. of Medicine, New Orleans, 1981. Diplomate Am. Bd. Otolaryngology, 1987. Resident Louisiana State Univ. Sch. of Medicine, New Orleans, 1986; fellow otology neurotology and skull base surgery Albert Ludwigs Univ., Freiburg, Germany, 1987; with dept. of otolaryngology - head and neck surgery Tulane Univ. Sch. of Medicine, 1988—, clin. prof. dept. of neurosurgery; Harold G. Tabb prof. and chair Tulane Otolaryngology Head Neck Surgery; assoc. dean grad. med. edn.; chief-of-staff Tulane Univ. Hosp. and Clinic, 2000—02. Recipient Disting. Svc. award, Am. Acad. of Otolaryngology-Head and Neck Surgery, Honor award, Physicians Recognition award, AMA, Disting. Clin. Tchg. award, Alpha Omega Alpha, Attending of the Yr. in Outpatient Surgery, Tulane Owl Club; named one of the Best Doctors in America, 1998, 1999, 2001—04. Office: Tulane University School of Medicine 1430 Tulane Ave New Orleans LA 70112 Office Phone: 504-988-5187.

AMEMIYA, HIROSHI, medical researcher; b. Hongo, Japan, Jan. 15, 1935; s. Miyoji Fukuda and Yoshiko Amemiya; m. Noriko Itakura, Mar. 25, 1961; children: Izumi, Megumi, Toru. MD, Chiba U., Japan, 1960, D in Med. Sci., 1965. Instr. Chiba Univ. Hosp., 1968—76, asst. prof., 1977—78; dir. exptl. surgery Nat. Cardiovasc. Ctr. Rsch. Inst., Suita, Japan, 1978—2000; gen. dir. Nat. Children's Med. Rsch. Ctr., Tokyo, 1992—2000, gen. dir. emeritus, 2001—. Dir. NPO/HAB Rsch. Orgn.; prof. Takarazuka U., Sch. Nursing, 2010—. Editor: Deoxyspergualin Immunosuppressive Properties, 1989; author: New Immunosuppressive Modalities and Anti-Rejection Approaches in Organ Transplantation, 1994, Immunosuppressive Drugs: Developments in Anti-Rejection Therapy, 1994. Recipient Asahi Sci. Bounty for 1970, Tokyo, 1970, Shiota Meml. prize Nat. Medical Congress of Nat. Hosp., 1988. Mem. Japan Soc. For Transplantation (hon. chmn., past insp., past dir., past chair), Asian Soc. Transplantation (adv. councilor), Japan Soc. Organ Preservation and Med. Biology (advisor, past pres.), Transplantation Soc., Internat. Soc. for Organ Sharing (councilor, past chair). Avocations: photography, sports. Home: Apt # 804 617 Nishiuoyacho Nakagyoku Kyoto 604-8142 Japan Office: Takarazuka University Sch Nursing 1-13-16 Shibata Kita-ku Osaka 530-0012 Japan

AMEND, WILLIAM JOHN CONRAD, JR., physician, educator; b. Wilmington, Del., Sept. 17, 1941; s. William John Conrad and Catherine (Broad) A.; m. Constance Roberts, Feb. 3, 1962; children—William, Richard, Nicole, Mark BA, Amherst Coll., 1963; MD, Cornell U., 1967. Diplomate Am. Bd. Internal Medicine and Nephrology. Asst. clin. prof. U. Calif. Med. Ctr., San Francisco, 1974-76, assoc. clin. prof., 1977-82, prof. clin. medicine and surgery, 1982—2005, prof. emeritus medicine, 2005—; chief divsn. nephrology U. Calif., San Francisco, 1998—2003; physician Falmouth Med. Assocs. Contbr. articles to med. jours. Chmn. med. adv. com. No. Calif. Kidney Found., 1987-88; mem. stewardship com. 1st Presbyn. Ch., Burlingame, Calif., 1983, 84, elder, 1982-85, 93-96. Maj. U.S. Army, 1969-71. Simpson fellow, 1963; recipient Gift of Life award No. Calif. Kidney Found., 1993, Gift Hope award, No. calif. Kidney Found., 2010. Fellow: ACP; mem.: Amherst Coll. Alumni Fund (class pres. 2003—08, class agt. 1973-83, reunion chmn. 2003). Avocations: golf, gardening, hiking. Home: 2860 Summit Dr Burlingame CA 94010-6257 Office: U Calif Med Ctr 3rd & Parnassus San Francisco CA 94143-0001 *

AMENTA, PETER SEBASTIAN, pathologist, dean; b. Middletown, Conn., Feb. 21, 1953; s. Sebastian Peter and Mary Veronica (Branciforte) Am. m. Edna A. Salvo, Aug. 26, 1978; children: Peter S., Katherine D. BS, Trinity Coll., 1975; MS, MD, Hahnemann U., 1980, PhD, 1984. Cert. anatomic and clin. pathologist. Asst. prof. pathology Hahnemann U., Phila., 1984-89, Robert Wood Johnson U. Hosp., New Brunswick, NJ, 1989—93, assoc. prof. clin. pathology, 1994—99, dir. residency program, 1994—2001, 2003—05, dir. assoc. residency program, 2001—03, chief pathology svc., 1994—2006, dir. assoc. residency program, 2001—03, chmn. pathology and lab. medicine, 1999—, interim chief of staff, 2002—05, interim sr. v.p. med. affairs, chief of staff, 2002—05, sr. v.p. med. affairs, chief staff, 2005—06; interim dean U. Medicine and Dentistry NJ, Robert Wood Johnson Med. Sch., 2006—08, dean, 2008—. Recipient Hahnemann Club award, 1980. Mem. Am. Soc. Cell Biology, US Can. Assn. Pathology, Can. Assn. Pathology, Hahnemann Club, Alpha Omega Alpha, US and Can. Assn. Pathologists, Coll. Am. Pathologists. Achievements include research in extracellular matrix pathobiology. Office: UMDNJ-Robert Wood Johnson Medical Sch One Robert Wood Johnson Pl New Brunswick NJ 08903 Office Phone: 732-235-8120. Business E-Mail: amenta@umdnj.edu. *

AMER, SAID EMAD EL DEIN, science educator; b. El Gharbia, Egypt, May 3, 1964; BSc, Tanta U., Egypt, 1986, PhD, 2000. Adj. prof. Kafr El Sheikh U., Egypt, 2007, assoc. prof., 2007—. Fellowship, Japan Soc. Promotion Sci. Avocation: football. Office: El Geish St Kafr El Sheikh 33516 Egypt Office Fax: 2-047-3215176. E-mail: mssamer5@yahoo.com.

AMES, ADELBERT, III, neuroscientist, educator; b. Boston, Feb. 25, 1921; MD, Harvard U., 1945. Intern, then resident in internal medicine Presbyn. Hosp., 1945-52; rsch. assoc. Med. Sch. Harvard U., Boston, 1955-69, prof. physiology, dept. surgery, 1969-91, Charles Anthony Pappas prof. neurosci. Med. Sch., 1983-91, prof. emeritus, 1991—; neurophysiologist in neurosurgery Mass. Gen. Hosp., Boston, 1983—. Recipient Rsch. Scientist award NIMH, 1968-80. Mem. Am. Physiol. Soc., Am. Soc. Neurochemistry, Soc. Neurosci., Internat. Soc. Neurochemistry. Home: 84 Jenckes Rd Brattleboro VT 05301-9258 E-mail: delames@sover.net.

AMES, RICHARD POLLARD, physician, educator, lecturer; b. Northampton, Mass., Aug. 4, 1932; s. Harold Leslie and Effie Melissa (Crowley) A.; m. Janet Ann Shaw, Oct. 7, 1961; children: Patricia Jean, Brian Shaw. BA cum laude, Williams Coll., 1954; MD, Columbia U., 1958. Diplomate Am. Bd. Internal Medicine, Am. Bd. Nephrology, Am. Bd. Med. Oncology, Am. Bd. Hematology, Am. Soc. of Hypertension Specialist in Clin. Hypertension. Intern Boston City Hosp., 1958-59, resident, 1959-61; fellow N.Y. Heart Assn. Presbyn. Hosp., NYC, 1961-63; clin. assoc. Nat. Cancer Inst., Bethesda, Md., 1963-65; investigator Nat. Inst. Arthritis Metab., Paris, 1965-66, Whitehall Found., NYC, 1967-70; nephrologist St. Luke's Roosevelt Hosp., NYC, 1970—, chief hypertension clinic, 1973-94, dir. phys. diagnosis, 1981-94, assoc. dir. nephrology, 1990-93; chief nephrology St. Clare's Hosp., NYC, 1998-2000. Dir. hypertension Am. Health Found., N.Y.C., 1972-82; clin. prof. Columbia U., N.Y.C., 1989—. Contbg. author: Topics in Hypertension, 1980, Frontiers in Hypertension Res., 1981, Clinical Cardiovascular Therapeutics, 1989, Laragh and Brenner's Hypertension, 1995, Messerli's Cardiovascular Drug Therapy, 1996; co-editor: Medical Symposium Drugs, 1988. Asst. surgeon USPHS, 1963-65. Named Top Metro Physician, Castle and Connally, 1997—, Consumers Rsch. Coun., 1998, Super Dr., NY, 2009—. Fellow ACP, AHA (mem. Coun. For High Blood Pressure Rsch., Kidney Coun.); mem. Am. Soc. Hypertension (charter mem.), Am. Soc. Nephrology, Phi Beta Kappa, Internat. Soc. Nephrology Office: 200 W 57th St New York NY 10019 Office Phone: 917-224-4270.

AMIDON, ROGER LYMAN, public health service officer, educator; b. Burlington, Vt., Apr. 8, 1938; s. Ellsworth L. and Mae (Liddle) A.; m. JoAnn Reiland, Aug. 1, 1968. BA, U. Vt., 1960; MA in Hosp. and Health Adminstrn., U. Iowa, 1965, PhD (USPHS trainee), 1968. Asst. prof. hosp. and health adminstrn. U. Iowa, 1968-73, asso. prof., 1973-77; prof., chmn. dept. health adminstrn. U. Okla., 1977-81; prof., chmn. dept. health svcs. policy and mgmt. U. S.C., 1981-88, on sabbatical, 1988-89, prof., grad. dir., 1989—2002, disting. prof. emeritus, 2002—. Exec. sec. Nat. Ctr. Health Svcs. Rsch., 1975-76; dir. Am. Indian Grad. Program in Health Adminstrn., U. Okla., 1977-81; cons. China Med. U. Hosp., 1999-2010, vis. scholar, Nat. Def. Med. Ctr., Taiwan, 2003. Contbr. articles to profl. jours. Chair S.C. Ctr. for Gerontology, 1999-01. Lt., M.S.C. US Army, 1961—62, exec. officer and platoon leader, 418 Med. Co. (Ambulance), XVIII Airborne Hdqs. Mem. APHA (emeritus), AARP (exec. coun. 2004-10), Am. Coll. Healthcare Execs., Am. Hosp. Assn. (life), Vermont Soc. Colonial Wars (gov. 2006-2011). Home: 234 Saluda Ave Columbia SC 29205-3031 Office: Arnold SPH U SC Health Svcs Policy and Mgmt Columbia SC 29208-0001 Home Phone: 803-252-8993. Personal E-mail: uvmer@sc.rr.com.

AMIEL, JONATHAN, physician; b. Israel, Nov. 24, 1979; BS, Yale U., 2001; MD, Columbia U., 2007. Asst. dean curricular affairs Columbia U. Coll. Physicians & Surgeons, 2011—. Mem.: AMA, Am. Psychoanalytic Assn., Am. Psychiat. Assn., Gold Humanism Honor Soc., Alpha Omega Alpha. Office: 630 W 168th St 3-401 New York NY 10032 Business E-Mail: jma2106@columbia.edu.

AMIN, AHMAD FAYEK, medical educator; s. Fayek Amin Mossa and Sonson Mohamed Khlaf; m. Ahmad Fayek Amin, Jan. 11, 1996; children: Mhmoud Ahmad, Malak Ahmad. MD, Assuit U., Egypt., 1995. Cert. prof. Assuit U., 2006. Asst. prof., ob-gyn. Assuit U., 2002—06, prof., ob-gyn., 2006—08, cons. Women's Health Ctr., AUH, 1966—. Contbr. articles to profl. publs. (IJGO Paper award for Best Clin. Article, 2003). Recipient Med. Scis. award, Assiut U., 2007. Mem.: Egyptian F&S Assn. Achievements include patents for treatment of unexplained Rpl, recurrent pregnancy loss; research in endoscopy, contraception, amnioinfusion, PCOS. Office: Assiut Univ Women's Health Ctr 71116 Assuit Egypt

AMIN, ALPESH N., internist; s. Navin and Harshila Amin; m. Sonali Amin; 1 child, Aanya. MD, Northwestern U., Chgo., 1994; MBA, U. Calif., Irvine, 2000. Physician U. Calif., Irvine Med. Ctr., Orange, 1997. Office: U Calif Irvine Med Ctr 101 The City Drive S Bldg 26 Rm 1005 Orange CA 92868 Office Phone: 714-456-3785. Office Fax: 714-456-7182. E-mail: anamin@uci.edu. *

AMIN, MOHAMMAD, urology educator; b. Sargodha, Pakistan, Jan. 1, 1942; came to U.S., 1964; s. Mohammad and Gulzar (Begum) Nawaz; m. Elizabeth Anne Howarth, May 25, 1973; children: Daniel, Omar. MB, BS, King Edward Coll., Lahore, Pakistan, 1963. Diplomate Am. Bd. of Urology. Intern Muhlenberg Hosp., Plainfield, NJ, 1964-65; resident in surgery Norton Hosp., Louisville, 1965-66; asst. prof. urology U. Louisville, 1971-74, assoc. prof., 1974-80, prof. urology, 1980—, resident in urology, 1966-69; med. officer Social Security, Pakistan, 1969-70; house officer urology Southmede Hosp., Bristol, England, 1970-71. Contbr. articles and book chpts. to profl. jours. Recipient Health Advancement award Nat. Kidney Found., 1981. Mem.: ACS, Soc. Internat. d'Urologie, Am. Urol. Assn. Democrat. Islamic. Address: VA Med Ctr 800 Zorn Ave Louisville KY 40206 Office Phone: 502-287-4000. Personal E-mail: maminlouky@yahoo.com.

AMIN, MUTAMAD AHMED, parasitologist, researcher; b. El Gietena, Sudan, Jan. 1, 1944; s. Ahmed Amin Hussin and Medinna Ahmed El Nasri; m. Reda Abdel Gadir El Amin, Sept. 20, 1963; children: Hani Mutamad, Hind Mutamad, Sarra Mutamad, Ebtihal Mutamad, Wael Mutamad, Rabah Mutamad, Tasneem Mutamad, Hamad Mutamad. BSc, U. Khartoum, Sudan, 1963; diploma in Parasitology & Entomology, London Sch. Hygiene & Tropical Medicine, 1965; PhD, London Sch. Hygien & Tropical Medicine, 1967. Charter, dir. Bilharzia sect. Ministry of Health, Khartoum, 1967—70; prof. Faculty Medicine Khartoum U., Sudan, 1970—81; regional min. health & social welfare Regional Govt., Medani, Sudan, 1981—85; primary health care & schistosomiasis control dir. Ministry of Health, Jazan, Saudi Arabia, 1985—2005; dir., rsch. & grants Ahfad U.

Women, Omdurman, Sudan, 2005—. Mem.: WHO (Geneva) (mem. adv. panel, parasitic diseases 1976—, fellow 1964—67). Achievements include relief of human suffering and prevention and control of serious diseases in Jazan region. Home: AL Mashtal PO Box 10105 Khartoum Sudan Office: Ahfad Univ Women AL Arda PO Box 167 Omdurman Sudan Office Fax: 249 187 579111. Personal E-mail: mutamadamin@hotmail.com.

AMIN, RAVINDRA NAVINCHANDRA, geriatric psychiatrist; MD, Baroda U., 1985. Diplomate Am. Bd. Psychiatry and Neurology, Am. Bd. Psychiatry and Neurology-addiction psychiatry, Am. Bd. Psychiatry and Neurology-geriatric psychiatry, registered NY, 1992. Resident in psychiatry Elmhurst Hosp. Ctr., 1992; hosp. affiliations include Mt. Sinai Hosp., LI Coll. Hosp., NY. Office: Long Island College Hospital University Hospital of Brooklyn 339 Hicks St Brooklyn NY 11201 Office Phone: 718-780-1065.

AMIN, TAREK TAWFIK, medical educator; b. Cairo, Jan. 27, 1963; d. Mohammed Tawfik Amin and Najia Hassan Ahmed; m. Hend Mohammed Abdullah, Feb. 11, 1993; children: Ahmed Tarek, Doha Tarek, Amr Tarek, Salma Tarek. MS, Cairo U., 1993, MS, 1996, MD, 2000; diploma, Am. U., Cairo, 2003. Resident neonatology Faculty Medicine, Cairo U., 1988—92, lectr. pub. health, epidemiology, 1993—2000, assoc. prof., 2005—, King Faisal U., Hofuf, Al Hassa, Saudi Arabia, 2003—, chmn. family and cmty. medicine dept., 2004—. Rsch. cons. Ministry Health, Cairo, 2000—03. Corpol Air Def., 1989—99, Egypt. Fellow: U. Calif., Irvine (assoc.). Muslim. Achievements include research in children and adolescent health. Home: Pyramids Hills 3rd Gate Mankaraa 104N Giza Greater Cairo 22133 Egypt Office: Cairo Univ Coll Medicine Kasr Al Aini Cairo 11559 Egypt Business E-Mail: amin55@myway.com.

AMINOFF, BECHOR ZVI, geriatrician, researcher; b. Samarkand, Uzbekistan, June 5, 1946; s. Michael Mashkobov and Osnat Aminoff; m. Rosa Rachel Gadaev, Oct. 14, 1973; children: Emanuel, Gabriel, Israel, Moshe. MD, Samarkand Med. Inst., 1970; PhD, Stavropol Med. Inst., 1974. Head geriatric D dept. Sheba Med. Ctr., Tel-Hashomer, Israel, 1983—, Human Suffering and Satisfaction Rsch. Ctr., Israel. Presenter in field. Contbr. articles to profl. jours. and monographs. Jewish. Achievements include development of and research in first objective tool for evaluation of suffering in end-stage dementia Mini Suffering State Examination scale and new theory and entropy definition of human suffering and satisfaction; measuring suffering in end stage dementia, overprotection phenomenon of dying dementia patients, refusal phenomenon appertaining to end stage dementia patients and new setting Suffering Relief units; research in measurement of suffering in end stage alzheimer's disease. Avocations: reading, travel. Office: Sheba Med Ctr Tel Hashomer 52621 Israel also: Human Suffering Satisfaction Research Ctr EL-Ad 40800 Israel Personal E-mail: bechorz@yahoo.com.

AMIRIKIA, HASSAN, obstetrician, gynecologist; b. Tehran, Iran, Dec. 10, 1937; came to U.S., 1966; d. Ahmad and Showkat (Asgari) Chefteaz; m. Minoo Vassigh Amirikia, Apr. 4, 1964; children: Arezo, Omid. MD, Tehran U., 1964. Cert. Am. Bd. Ob-Gyn. Intern Cook County Hosp., Chgo., 1966—67, resident Wayne State U., Detroit, 1967—71, fellow, 1971—72; practice reproductive endocrine specializing in infertility Detroit, 1972—; asst. prof. Wayne State U., Detroit, 1972—, dir. ob-gyn. tng. dept. family medicine, 1979—; dir. infertility and reproductive endocrinology St. Joseph's Hosp., Pontiac, Mich., 1990—93; chief staff Detroit Med. Ctr., 1993—, pres. med. staff, 1997—; chief staff Hutzel Hosp., 1996—2002; pres. Private Practise Physicians Corp., Detroit Med. Ctr., 2004—. Pres. med. staff Detroit Med. Ctr., 1998-2004, bd. trustees, 2002-2004, chair med. exec. com., 1997—, pres. Pvt. Practice Physician Corp.; alt. del. AMA 2003. Contbr. articles to profl. jours. Fellow ACS, ACOG (Mich. sect.), Royal Coll. Physicians and Surgeons, Wayne County Med. Soc. (pres. 1995-96); mem. AMA (life), Mich. State Med. Soc. (bd. dirs. 1996—, pres. 2003). Achievements include research in effects of androgens on the ovary. Home: 1435 Lone Pine Rd Bloomfield Hills MI 48302-2632 Office: 29877 Telegraph Rd Southfield MI 48034-1332 Business E-Mail: hamiriki@dmc.org.

AMIS, EDWARD STEPHEN, JR., radiologist, retired military officer; b. Baton Rouge, June 23, 1941; s. Edward Stephen and Annie Velma (Birdwhistell) Amis; m. Anne Schneider, Sept. 2, 1984. Student, U. Rochester, 1959-61; BS, U. Ark., 1963; MD, Northwestern U., 1967. Diplomate Am. Bd. Urology, Am. Bd. Radiology. Commd. ensign USN, 1966, advanced through grades to capt., 1980; resident in urology Naval Hosp., San Diego, 1968-72, resident in radiology, 1975-78, staff radiologist, 1978-80, 81-82, staff urologist Great Lakes, Ill., 1972-75; radiology fellow Mass. Gen. Hosp., Boston, 1980-81; chmn. radiology Naval Hosp., Bethesda, Md., 1982-84, exec. officer, 1984-85, comdg. officer, 1985-87; head sect. uroradiology dept. radiology Columbia U., NYC, 1987-91, vice chmn. dept. radiology, 1990-91; chmn. dept. radiology Albert Enstein Coll. Medicine and Montefiore Med. Ctr., Bronx, NY, 1991—. Co-author: Essentials of Uroradiology, 1990, Textbook of Uroradiology, 4th edit., 2008; contbr. chapters to textbooks. Leadership council Montgomery County Heart Assn., Bethesda, 1986-87. Bausch and Lomb scholar, 1959; recipient Disting. Radiologist award, NY Roentgen Soc., 2008. Mem.: Image Wisely (co-chair), Accreditation Coun. Grad. Med. Edn. (chair, radiology residency rev. com. 2007—11, chair coun. rev. com. 2009—11, bd. dirs. 2009—11, co-chair duty hours task force 2009—11), Coun. Med. Splty. Socs. (sec. 2008—10, bd. dirs. 2008—, pres. elect. 2010—), Nat. Coun. on Radiation Protection & Measurements, Am. Coll. Radiology (bd. chancellors 1995—, vice chair 2000—02, chair 2002—04, pres. 2004—05, Gold medal 2007), Am. Roentgen Ray Soc., Soc. Uroradiology (pres. 1995—97, Gold medal 2008), Assn. U. Radiologists, Radiol. Soc. N.Am. Democrat. Business E-Mail: e-stephen.amis@einstein.yu.edu.

AMLIE, JAN P., physician, educator; b. V. Toten, Norway, Sept. 23, 1940; s. Magnus and Bjørnhild Amlie; m. May L. Amlie, Nov. 16, 1963; children: Lars Peder, Lise Katrine, Julie Mathilde. Med. Sch., U. Oslo, 1965, MD, 1980. Med. authorization, 1969. Med. doctor Rikshospitalet, Oslo, 1973—, prof., 1990. Contbr. over 130 articles to profl. jours. Maj. Army, 1967. Fellow European Soc. Cardiology; mem. Norwegian Soc. Cardiology (pres. 1987-91), Union European Med. Specialists (pres. cardiology sect. 2002—06, mem. coun. 2006—). Office: Rikshospitalet 0027 Oslo Norway E-mail: jan.peder.amlie@rikshospitalet.no.

AMMAR, EL-SAYED MOHAMMAD, pharmacist, educator; b. Damietta, Egypt, July 15, 1940; s. Mohammad El-Sayed Ammar and W.A. Asal; m. Ahdab Mohammad Kamel Elmorshedy, July 13, 1974; children: Mohammad, Tarek, Moataz, Amr. BS in Pharmacy, Cairo U., 1961; PhD in Pharmacology & Toxicology, Coll. of Pharmacy, Moscow, Russia, 1969. Lic. Pharmacist for practice of Pharmacy Min. of Health, Egyptian syndicate of Pharmacists, 1961. Pharmacist Damietta Mcpl. Hosp., Damietta, Egypt, 1961—62; instr. Cairo U., Cairo, Giza, 1962—66; assoc. prof. Assiut U., Assiut, Egypt, 1970—74; prof. & chmn. dept. pharmacology & toxicology Mansoura U., 1976—2000, prof. emeritus coll. pharmacy, 2000—. Vis. prof. Khartoum U., Khartoum, Sudan, 1978—78; mem. of exec. bd. Gen. Syndicate of Pharmacists, Cairo, 1978—82; chmn. pharmacology faculty members promotion com. Supreme Coun. of U., Cairo, 1988—; coun. mem. coll. pharmacy Mansoura U., 1978—, sec. coun. of edn. and rsch., 1981—84; vis. prof. Ohio State U., Columbus, Ohio, 1979—81; vice dean coll. pharmacy Mansoura U., 1981—84; vis. prof. various Brit. U., England, 1983, various U., Germany, 1987, Japan, 98; cons. in field; vis. prof. UBC, Canada, 2004. Author: Toxicology, 1995; contbr. scientific papers seventy to profl. jours. Mem. Environ. Protection Com., Mansoura & Damietta, Egypt, 1984—90. Recipient Pharm. Achievements award, Egyptian Syndicate of Pharmacists, 1980, Pharm. Seminar award, Mansawa U., 2001, Merit award, Mansoura U., 2005. Fellow: Egyptian Acad. of Sci. (mem. nat. toxicology com. 1999). Muslim. Avocations: reading, walking, music. Home: 3 Alhasn st Cairo 12615 Egypt Office: Mansoura Univ College Pharmacy Algomhoria 35516 Mansoura Egypt Home Phone: 002-02-3376709; Office Phone: 002-050-2247496. Fax: 002-050-2247496. Business E-Mail: emammar@yahoo.com.

AMMIRATI, MARIO, neurosurgeon; b. Naples, Italy, Nov. 22, 1953; came to U.S., 1980; s. Giuseppe and Bianca (D'Elia) A.; 1 child, Giuseppe. MD, U. Naples, 1977. Diplomate Am. Bd. Neurol. Surgery. Resident, neurosurgery U. Naples, 1977-80; resident, neurosurgery Northwestern U., Chgo., 1980-87; post-doctoral fellow Nordstadt Krankenhaus, Hanover, Germany, 1987-89; asst. prof. divsn. neurosurgery UCLA Med. Ctr., LA, 1989-95; chief divsn. neurosurgery Olive View/UCLA Med. Ctr., LA, 1989-95; assoc. prof., chief sect. neuro oncology/skull base surgery U. Calif., Irvine, 1995—. Recipient Neurosurgery fellowship Alexander von Humboldt Found., Bonn, Germany, 1987-89. Fellow ACS. Home: 1 Miranova Pl Apt 705 Columbus OH 43215-7203

AMMON, HERMANN PHILIPP THEODOR, pharmacologist, educator; b. Nuremberg, Germany, Jan. 24, 1933; s. Theodor and Käthe (Schatz) A.; m. Helga Ursula Grummt, Aug. 3, 1963; children: Susanne, Christiane. MD, U. Erlangen-Nuremberg, Fed. Republic of Germany, 1963, privat dozent, 1968. Rsch. fellow U. Erlangen-Nuremberg, Germany, 1965-70; asst. prof. dept. pharmacology U. Erlangen, Nuremberg, Germany, 1971-74; instr. medicine Harvard Med. Sch., U. Harvard, Cambridge, Mass., 1970-71; assoc. prof. pharmacology Inst. Pharm. Scis., U. Tübingen, Germany, 1974-76, prof., 1976—2001, dir. Inst. Pharm. Scis., 1986-89, 95-98. Author, editor: (handbook) Arzneimittelneben und Wechselwirkungen, 1981, 86, 91, 2001; editor: Hunnius. Pharm. Wörterbúch, 9th ed. 2004, Diabetes in Frage und Antword, 2003,08, editor, co-editor over 26 sci. jours. and books, 30 rev. articles; contbr. 220 articles to profl. jours. Com. mem. Bundesgesundheitsamt, Berlin, 1978; bd. reviewers Deutsche Forschungsgemeinschaft, Bonn, Bad Godesbuerg, Fed. Republic of Germany, 1988, mem. Bs. Pharm. Scis., 2002 ; policy com. Fedn. Internat. de Pharmacy, 2002--. Recipient Gold Medal Chamber of Pharmacists Baden Wurttemberg, 1992, Verdienstorden der Bundesrepublik Deutschland am Band, 1999, Lesmuller-Medal, Arbeitsgemeinschaft Deutscher Apothekerverbaende, 2000, Dr. Buerger-Buesing Diabetes Rsch. award, 2011. Mem. German Soc. for Exptl. and Clin. Pharmacology, Toxicology, German Diabetes Assn. (bd. dirs. 1989, pres. 1994-95), German Pharm. Soc. (bd. dirs. 1986, pres. 1996-99), Am. Diabetes Assn., Endocrine Soc. (U.S.), European Soc. for Study Diabetes, Soc. Medicinal Plant Rsch., European Soc. Pharm. Scis., Lions (pres. Tuebingen 1983-84, gov. dist. IIISM 1992-93), Kuratorium German Diabetes Found., German Soc. Ayurveda (mem. sci. bd.), German Acad. Ayurveda (mem. sci. bd.), European Ayurvedic Med. Assn. Achievements include research in biochemistry of insulin secretion, antidiabetic drugs, pharmacology of caffeine, alcohol, B-blocker, nicotinic acid, central depressants, medicinal plants, boswellic acids (from francincense) with anti-inflamatory and antitumor activity. Home: Im Kleeacker 30 D-72072 Tübingen Germany Business E-Mail: sekretariat.ammon@uni-tuebingen.de, info@hptammon.de.

AMON, ANGELIKA, medical researcher; b. Austria, 1967; arrived in U.S., 1994; BSc in Biology, U. Vienna, PhD in Biology, 1993. Postdoctoral fellow Whitehead Inst. Biomedical Rsch., fellow; Howard S. and Linda B. Stern career develop. asst. prof., Ctr. Cancer Rsch. MIT, Cambridge, Mass., 1999, assoc. prof. biology, 1999, prof. biology and David Koch Inst. for Integrative Cancer Rsch. Assoc. investigator Howard Hughes Med. Inst., Chevy Chase, Md., 2000—. Recipient Alan T. Waterman award, NSF, 2003, Eli Lilly and Co. Rsch. award, Am. Soc. Microbiology, 2003, award in molecular biology, NAS, 2008, Presdl. Early Career award; co-recipient Paul Marks Prize for Cancer Rsch., Meml. Sloan-Kettering Cancer Ctr., 2007; fellow Helen Hay Whitney fellowship; Whitehead fellow, 1996. Mem.: NAS. Office: MIT Dept Biology 77 Massachusetts Ave Rm E17 233A Cambridge MA 02139 Office Phone: 617-258-8964. Business E-Mail: angelika@mit.edu. *

AMORIM, MELANIA M. R., obstetrician, educator; b. Campina Grande, Paraíba, Brazil, July 11, 1967; MD, U. Fed. Paraíba, 1989; PhD, Unicamp, 1998. Prof. ob-gyn. Inst. Medicina Integral, Fernando Figueira Fed & U. Campina Grande, 1992—. Achievements include research in humanization of childbirth, evidence-based medicine and high-risk pregnancy. Home: Rua Neuza Borborema de Souza 300 Campina Grande Paraíba 58406120 Brazil Personal E-mail: melania.amorim@gmail.com.

AMOROSO, RICHARD LOUIS, psychologist, educator; b. Medford, Mass., Apr. 24, 1946; s. Louis Raymond and Marjorie Lou (McCathie) Amoroso; m. Juliette Noble Sherer, Oct. 1982 (div. 1986); 1 child, Juliette Rachael. BS in Psychology, U. Mass., 1972; postgrad., Stanford U., 1972—74, Harvard U., 1980—82; PhD in Cosmology, Internat. Noetic U., 1992; MA in Consciousness Studies, J.F.K. U., 1994. Computer engr. Harvard Smithsonian Astrophys. Obs., Cambridge, Mass., 1980-82; instr. Peralta Coll., Oakland, Calif., 1987-88; dir. Mus. Robotics, Berkeley, Calif., 1989—, Noetic Advanced Studies Inst., Orinda, Calif., 1992—; pres. Cereroscopic Sys., Inc., Provo, Utah; CFO Elec. Corp., Oakland, 1992-94; prof. philosophy of mind Internat. Noetic U., Oakland, 1995—. Founding editor: Noetic Jour., 1997—; editor: Science and the Primary of Consciousness, 1998, The Scientific Origins of Sexual Preference, 2000, Gravitation and Cosmology: From the Hubble Radius to the Planck Scale, 2001, What is Conciousness? Introducing the Cosmology of Being, 2003, Shifting the Medical Paradigm, 2004, A Revolucao da Consciencia, 2005, Extending the Standard Model: The Search for Unity in Physics, 2005, Unified Theories, 2007, Rendezvous at The Temple of Love, 2007, Metatheory, 2007, The Complementarity of Mind and Body, 2008, The Holographic Anthropic Multiverse, 2008, Orbiting the Moons of Pluto, 2011. Recipient Telesio-Galilei Gold medal, 2010. Mem.: AAAS, N.Y. Acad. Sci., Romanian Acad. Sci. (hon.). Republican. Mem. Lds Ch. Achievements include having the 1st comprehensive theory of Cartesian dualism in history; research in an empirical method to surmount quantum uncertainty principle; patents for new class medical devices based on gerantion computing. Avocations: meditation, scuba diving, robotic sculpture, reading, sailing. Personal E-mail: noeticj@mindspring.com.

AMOS, CHRISTOPHER IAN, statistical geneticist; b. Buffalo, Aug. 25, 1957; s. Dennis Bernard and Solarge Marie A.; m. Julie E. McCarhin; children: Ryan Benjamin, Brendan Patrick. BA in Math., Reed Coll., 1980; MS in Biometry, La. State Univ. Med. Ctr., New Orleans, 1985, PhD in Biometry, 1988. Grad. asst., dept. medicine La. State U. Med. Ctr., New Orleans, 1983—88; vis. scientist, divsn. biostatics, rsch. informatics Internat. Agy. for Rsch. on Cancer, Lyon, France, 1989; asst. adj. prof., biostatistics and epidemiology dept., Howard Univ. Cancer Ctr., Washington, 1989—93; staff fellow, family studies sect. Environ. Epidemiology Br., Nat. Cancer Inst., NIH, Bethesda, Md., 1988—91; sr. staff fellow, genetics studies sect. Lab. Skin Biology, Nat. Inst. Arthritis and Musculoskeletal and Skin, NIH, Bethesda, Md., 1991—93; assoc. prof., epidemiology Univ. Tex. M.D. Anderson Cancer Ctr., Houston, 1993—96, prof., epidemiology and biomathematics, 1996—. Adj. prof. Univ. Tex. Sch. Pub. Health, Houston, 1993—; adj. prof., program in genetics U. Tex. Grad. Sch. for Biomedical Scis., Houston, 1994—; adj. prof., dept. statistics Rice U., Houston, 2001—; bd. dirs. Internat. Genetic Epidemnology Soc., 1997—, Genetic Analysis Workshop, San Antonio, Tex., 1997—. Contbr. articles to peer-reviewed jours. Recipient rsch. grants; named Ashbel Smith Prof., 2001. Mem.: Internat. Genetic Epidemiology Soc. (pres. 2002). Office: Univ Tex MD Anderson Cancer Ctr Dept Epidemiology 1515 Holcombe Blvd Houston TX 77030 Office Phone: 713-792-3020. Business E-Mail: camos@request.mdacc.tmc.edu.

AMOS, DANIEL PAUL, insurance company executive; b. Pensacola, Fla., Aug. 13, 1951; s. Paul Shelby and Mary Jean (Roberts) A.; m. Mary Shannon Landing, Sept. 12, 1972; children: Paul Shelby, Lauren Alyse. BS in Risk and Ins. Mgmt., U. Ga., Athens, 1973. Co-state mgr. Aflac (Am. Family Life Assurance Co.), Columbus, Ga., 1973-78, state mgr., 1978-83, pres., 1983-96, COO, 1987—90; CEO AFLAC, Inc., Columbus, Ga., 1990—, chmn., 2001—; dep. CEO Am. Family Corp., Columbus, Ga., 1996. Dir. Columbus Bank & Trust Co., Synovus Fin. Corp., So. Co. Bd. trustees Children's Healthcare of Atlanta, House of Mercy of Columbus. Recipient Dr. Martin Luther King Jr. Unity award, Torch of Liberty award, Anti-Defamation League. Methodist. Avocation: bridge. Office: Aflac Inc 1932 Wynnton Rd Columbus GA 31999 Office Phone: 706-323-3431.

AMOS, SHIRLEYANN, mental health therapist, social worker; b. Hampton, Va., Oct. 14, 1953; d. Pink Amos Jr. and Pauline Amos; 1 child, John David Taylor. AS, Commonwealth Coll., Va. Beach, Fla., 1991; BA in Psychology, U. Ctrl. Fla., Va. Beach, 1998, MSW, 2001; PhD, Canbourne U., 2005. Enlisted USN, 1973; substance abuse counselor USN and Fla. Keys Meml. Hosp., Key West, 1984—88; advanced through grades to yeoman 1st class petty officer (air warfare) USN, 1980, ret., 1994, administrv. supr. various duty stas, 1980—88, substance abuse counselor Norfolk, Va., 1988—90; asst. investigator Dept. Children and Families, DeLand, Fla., 1998; vol., protective svcs. Ctr. for Drug Free Living, Orlando, Fla., 1999—2000; mental health therapist House Next Door, Deland, Fla., 2000—01; co. comdr. Recruit Tng. Ctr., Orlando, 1979—82. Co-author: Conduct Disorder: DSM-IV-TR in Action, 2010, Childhood Disorder The Disruptive Behavior Disorders. Adv. GLBT, people with disabilities and the poor. Mem.: NASW, APA, Nat. Assn. Alcoholism and Drug Abuse Counselors, Disabled Am. Vets. Fla., Am. Legion, Psi Chi. Avocations: photography, art, singing. Home: 500 Rodeo Rd Apt 217 Santa Fe NM 87505-6353 Personal E-mail: dr_sam@comcast.net.

AMOS FRUMKIN, AMOS, geologist; b. Tel Aviv, Feb. 20, 1953; PhD, Hebrew U., 1992. Prof. Hebrew U. Jerusalem, 1995—. Dir. Israel Cave Rsch. Ctr., 1980. Recipient Outstanding Environ. Rsch. award, Robert Lewin awards. Mem.: Internat. Union Speleology. Avocations: hiking, spelunking. Office: Hebrew University Geography Dept Jerusalem 91905 Israel Office Fax: 972-2-5820549. Business E-Mail: msamos@mscc.huji.ac.il.

AMRANI, YASSINE, medical educator, researcher; married. PhD, U. Louis Pasteur, Strasbourg, France, 1995. Asst. prof. medicine U. Pa., Phila., 2003—07; assoc. prof. U. Leicester, England, 2007—. Recipient Career Investigator award, Am. Lung Assn., 2006—; grantee, NIH, 2003—08; Rsch. grant, Am. Lung Assn., 2002—04, PDF fellowship, Francis Families, 2002—05. Mem.: Am. Soc. Pharmacology and Exptl. Therapeutics. Achievements include research in TNF in airway hyper-responsiveness in asthma; molecular mechanisms of steroid resistance; role of IFNb in the pathogenesis of asthma. Office: Univ Leicester University Rd LE5 4DQ Leicester England Office Fax: 441162525030. Business E-Mail: ya26@le.ac.uk.

AMROL, DAVID, immunologist, educator, allergist; b. Alexandria, Va., Dec. 17, 1971; BA, U. Notre Dame, 1994; MD, U. SC, 1998. Dir., allergy and clin. immunology U. SC Sch. Medicine, 2003, assoc. prof. clin. medicine, 2003—. Pres. elect SC. Soc. Allergy, Asthma, and Immunology, 2010; chmn. internal medicine dept. Palmetto Health Richland Hosp., 2010. Fellow: Am. Acad. Allergy, Asthma, and Immunology. Avocations: tennis, soccer. Office: 2 Medical Pk Ste 506 Columbia SC 29203 Business E-Mail: damrol@sc.edu.

AMRON, DAVID M., plastic surgeon; b. Calcutta, India, Feb. 21, 1961; Student, Musicians Inst., LA, UCLA; BA in Biology, U. Calif., San Diego, 1982; MD, Albert Einstein Coll. Medicine, Bronx, NY, 1988. Diplomate Am. Bd. Dermatology. Resident dept. medicine

Cedars-Sinai Med. Ctr., LA, 1988-89; staff rsch. assoc., divsn. dermatology UCLA Sch. Medicine, Calif., 1989, rsch. fellow to asst. prof. dermatology LA, 1990, postgrad. rsch. fellow, divsn. dermatology Calif., 1991; resident, divsn. dermatology U. Calif. San Diego Med. Ctr., 1992-95; staff Sherman Oaks Hosp., Calif., 1995—; pvt. practice Mid Valley Dermatology, Sherman Oaks, 1995—99; co-owner Spalding Drive Cosmetic Surgery & Dermatology, Beverly Hills, Calif., 1999—. Beverly Hills Doctors Surgery Ctr., 1999—. Host (radio show) A Cut Above, KFWB 980 AM, appearances include Discovery Channel, Today Show, Good Morning America, CNN, BBC, KCBS Channel 2 News, Fox Good Day LA, Extra, Inside Edition, KCBS Women to Women, KCAL Channel 9 News, VHI, ABC News; contbr. articles to profl. jours., chapters to books. CPR instructor Am. Heart Assn.; vol. coach La Jolla Little Leaque, 1980—. Fellow: Am. Acad. Dermatology, Am. Soc. Liposuction Surgery, Am. Soc. Dermatologic Surgery, Am. Soc. Laser Medicine & Surgery; mem.: AMA, LA County Med. Assn. Achievements include performing his famous "mini liposuction" live, highlighting his impressive results while speaking with the patient during the entire procedure. Avocations: tennis, skiing, photography, theater, travel, acting. Office: Spaulding Drive Cosmetics Surgery & Dermatology 120 Spalding Dr Ste 315 Beverly Hills CA 90212 Office Phone: 310-275-2467. Office Fax: 310-275-6651.

AMTOWER, DEBRA LYNN, nursing consultant; b. Florence, Ariz., Sept. 19, 1965; d. M. L. and Catherine Louise Wisehart; m. Phil M. Amtower, June 11, 1993; children: Jessica Erin, Mark Allen, Christopher James. Degree in Nursing, St. John's U., 1994. Cert. EMT Mo., 1989. Nurse, EMT Cox Med. Ctrs., Springfield, 1989—97; correctional officer Dept. Justice Fed. Med. Ctr. Men, Springfield, 1997—98; coord. sr. svcs. Oxford Healthcare, Springfield, 1998—2001; RN Intelistaff Healthcare, Springfield, 2001—04; legal nurse cons. Strong Law Firm, Springfield, 2004—. Vol. emergency mgmt. EMA; firefighter Med. Tng. Office Vol. Fire Dept., EMT. Recipient Citizenship award, City Ozark, Mo., 1993. Mem.: Am. Assn. Legal Nurse Cons. Home: 919 Jasmine Rd Clever MO 65631-6646 Office: The Strong Law Firm 415 E Chestnut Expy Ste A Springfield MO 65802-3709 Office Fax: 417-887-4385; Home Fax: 417-743-2908. Personal E-mail: dlamtower@aol.com. Business E-Mail: dlamtower@stronglaw.com.

AMUNDSON, JOY A., pharmaceutical and health products executive; V.p. corp. hosp. mktg. Abbott Laboratory, Inc., Abbott Park, Ill., 1993-94, v.p. Abbott HealthSys., 1994-95, sr. v.p. chem. and agrl. products, 1995-98, sr. v.p. to pres. Ross Products, 1998—2004; corp. v.p., pres. Bioscience bus. Baxter International, Inc., Deerfield, Ill., 2004—. Office: Baxter Internat 1 Baxter Pkwy Deerfield IL 60015-4625

AMYLON, MICHAEL DAVID, physician, educator; b. Providence, Apr. 30, 1950; s. Sidney Robert and Mary Elisabeth (Alexander) A. AB, Brown U., 1972; MD, Stanford U., 1976. Diplomate sub-bd. hematology/oncology Am. Bd. Pediatrics. Resident physician Stanford U. Hosp., Calif., 1976-79; post-doctoral scholar Stanford U., Calif., 1979-81, acting asst. prof. Calif., 1981-82, asst. prof. pediat. Calif., 1982-89, assoc. prof. pediat. Calif., 1989-2001; prof. pediatrics Stanford U. Sch. Medicine, Palo Alto, Calif., 2001—03, prof. emeritus pediatrics hematology/oncology. Dir. marrow transplant svc. Children's Hosp. at Stanford, Palo Alto, Calif., 1986—2003; coord. nat. rsch. clin. trials in treatment pediatric leukemia and lymphoma Pediatric Oncology Group, St. Louis, Chgo., 1986—2001. Contbr. articles to profl. jours. Bd. dirs. Touchstone Support Network, Palo Alto, 1982-98, Robert J. Sturhahn Found., Novato, Calif., 1986-93, Okizu Found., Novato, 1993—, Parents Helping Parents, 1998—2005; med. dir. No. Calif. Oncology Camp, Nevada City, 1986—. Recipient For Those Who Care award Sta. KRON, 1990, "Ronnie" award Ronald McDonald House, 1992-93, Koshland prize Peninsula Cmty. Found., 1995, J.C. Penney Golden Rule award, 1996, Alwin C. Rambar-James B.D. Mark award for excellence in patient care Stanford U. Sch. Medicine, 2002. Mem. Am. Acad. Pediatrics, Am. Soc. Clin. Oncology, Am. Soc. Hematology, Am. Soc. Pediatric Hematology/Oncology, Am. Soc. Blood and Marrow Transplantation. E-mail: amylon@stanford.edu.

AN, BONG-JEUN, science educator; b. Pohang, Republic of Korea, Jan. 21, 1959; s. Ho-Yeun An and Kyung-Nam Jung; m. Jin-Sook Kim, Sept. 16, 1991; children: Jung-Yeun, Young-Ho. BSc, Yeungnam U., 1983, MSc, 1985, PhD, 1991. Mgr. rsch. Lotte Group Master Rsch. Inst., Seoul, Republic of Korea, 1987—92; prof. Daegu Haany U., Gyeongbuk, Republic of Korea, 1997—. Rschr. Kyushu U., Japan, 1989—91; investigator Korea FDA, Seoul, 2002—. Recipient Paragon award, Ministry Edn. Korea, 1984, Sci. Tech. award, Ministry Edn., Sci. and Tech., Korea, 2008. Achievements include invention of chewing gum designed to prevent tooth decay by blending a soluble extract of cacao husk; research in enzyme activities and the anti-wrinkle effect of polyphenol isolated from the persimmon leaf on human skin; physiological activity of irradiated green tea polyphenol on human skin; biological and anti-microbial activity of irradiated green tea polyphenols; development of natural cosmeceuticals. Isolation of skin activating substances from medicinal plants and their application as functional cosmetic ingredient; verification of biological activity of irradiated Sopoongsan, an oriental medinical prescription, for industrial application of functional cosmetic material; biological functions of a synthetic compound, octadeca-9,12-dienyl-3,4,5-hydroxybenzoate, from gallic acid-linoleic acid ester; antioxidant and cancer cell proliferation inhibition effect of citrus pecwtin-oligosaccharide prepared by irradiation. Home: 706 101 Apt Bumeadong Susunggu Daegu City 706-739 Republic of Korea Office: Daegu Haany Univ Yugok Dong 290 Gyeongbuk Gyeongsan Republic of Korea Office Phone: 82-53-819-1429. Business E-Mail: anbj@dhu.ac.kr.

AN, DUK KEUN, chemistry professor; b. Seoul, Republic of Korea, Feb. 28, 1967; PhD, Tokyo Inst. Tech., 1999. Prof. Kangwon Nat. U., 2002—. Mem.: Korean Chem. Soc. Office: Hoja-2-dong Chuncheon Kangwon-Do 200-701 Republic of Korea Business E-Mail: dkan@kangwon.ac.kr.

AN, YAN, medical educator; b. Yingkou City, Liaoning Province, China, Sept. 29, 1969; D, Jilin U. and Nihon U., 2001. Prof. dept. toxicology Sch. Radiation Medicine& Pub. Health, 2005—. Recipient Sci. & Tech. Advancement award, Ministry of Nuclear Industry China; scholarship, Japanese Govt. Office: Suzhou Industrial Pk 199 Renai Rd Suzhou Jiangsu Province 215123 China Office Fax: 0512-65884830. Business E-Mail: dranyan@126.com.

ANADIOTIS, GEORGE A., clinical geneticist; b. Athens, Greece; MD, Des Moines U., Iowa, 1993. Intern Mt. Clemens Gen. Hosp.; resident pediat. Univ. Nebraska Med. Ctr., 1994—97; fellow med. genetics Children's Hosp., Phila., 1997—2000; hospital affiliation include Legacy Emanuel Hosp. and Health Ctr. Office: Legacy Emanuel Hospital and Health Center 2801 N Gantenbein Ave Ste 2225 Portland OR 97227 Office Phone: 503-413-4505. Office Fax: 503-413-4719.

ANAGNOSTOU, THEODORE, urologist, surgeon, consultant; b. Athens, Attica, Greece, Jan. 6, 1970; s. George Anagnostou and Chrysoula Vitsadaki; m. Theodosia Theodoridon Anagnostou; children: Mathilde, George. PhD, U. Athens, Sch. Medicine, 2005. Diplomate in medicine U. Patras, Greece, 1994, cert. in urology Prefecture Ea. Attica, 2003, lic. Hellenic Ministry Health, 2004, cert. in advanced trauma and life support Am. Coll. Surgeons, 2007. Rsch. fellow urology U. Vienna, 2002, Western Gen. Hosp. NHS, Edinburgh, 2003; clin. fellow urology Royal Free Hosp. NHS, London, 2003—04; cons. urol. surgeon U. Thessaly, Larissa, Greece, 2005—. Trainee laparoscopic urology U. Linz, Austria, 2006—06. Designer (webpage) www.urology-uth.gr; co-author (with M. Melekos): (textbook) Contemporary Urology, author several papers in Medline cited jours., reviewer urology jours. Sponsor Actionaid Hellas, Athens, Greece, 2008. Sargent Gen. Air Force Hosp., 1996—97, Athens. Decorated Best cadet of Class Hellenic Air Force; recipient Best Abstract in Congress, Hellenic Urol. Assn., 2002, Best Student in Class, Secondary and High Schools of Piraeus, 1981-1987; scholar Rsch. Scholarship in Urology, European Assn. of Urology, 2002. Fellow: European Bd. Urology, Royal Coll. Surgeons; mem.: European Assn. Urology, Hellenic Urol. Assn. Achievements include special interests in urologic oncology, minimally invasive surgery, and laparoscopic urology. Office: Univ Thessaly Dept Urology Univ Hosp Larissa Mezurlo Larissa 41110 Greece Office Fax: 30-241-0670151. Personal E-mail: theoan@hotmail.com. Business E-Mail: theoan@otenet.gr.

ANAND, GIRISH, gastroenterologist, educator; MD, Christian Med. Coll., India. Diplomate Am. Bd. Internal Medicine. Intern Albert Einstein Med. Ctr., Pa., resident Pa., fellow Pa., Beth Israel Hosp., Boston; tchg. appointment includes Med. Sch. Thomas Jefferson Univ. Office: Albert Einstein Medical Center Klein Bldg Ste 202 5401 Old York Rd Philadelphia PA 19141 Office Phone: 215-456-8210. Office Fax: 215-456-2494.

ANAND, KANWALJEET SINGH, pediatrician, researcher; b. Ludhiana, Punjab, India, Nov. 29, 1957; s. Jaswant Singh and Tejinder Kaur Anand; m. Itinder Kaur Anand; children: Amrit K, Tejpartab S. MD, Mahatma Gandhi Meml. Med. Coll., Indore, India, 1980; PhD, Jesus Coll., U. Oxford, Eng., 1985. Diplomate Am. Bd. Pediat., cert. in pediatric critical care, pediatric advanced life support, lic. Ark. Rsch. fellow dept. pediat. U. Oxford, 1983—85; clin. fellow pediat. Harvard Med. Sch., Boston, 1988—91, 1991—93; asst. prof. pediat./anesthesiology Emory U. Sch. Medicine, Atlanta, 1993—97, asst. prof. psychiatry/behaviorial scis., 1994—97, dir. critical care rsch., 1994—97, interim dir. office rsch. promotion, dept. pediat., 1995—96; assoc. prof. pediat./anesthesiology U. Ark. for Med. Scis., Little Rock, 1997—2000, sect. chief pediat. critical care medicine, 1997—, assoc. prof. anatomy/neurobiology, 1998—2000, prof. pediat., anesthesiology, pharmacology & neurobiology, 2001—. Dir. pain neurobiology lab. Ark. Children's Hosp., Little Rock, 1999—; bd. dirs. Ark. Children's Hosp. Rsch. Inst., 1997—; Pfizer vis. prof. Wayne State U., Detroit, 2002; vis. prof. Baylor U., Waco, Tex., 2003. Contbr. articles to profl. jours. Mem. Rhodes scholarship selection com. (Ark. sec.), Little Rock, 1997—2003. Recipient Dr. Michael Blacow award, BPA, 1986, Pediat. Resident Rsch. award, AAP, 1992, Young Investigator award, IASP, 1994, Jeffrey Lawson award, Am. Pain Soc., 2000; grantee Rhodes Scholarship, India, 1982-1985, Ark. Ctr. Pain Rsch., 2001—03, Nat. Inst. Child Health & Human Devel., 1999—2003. Fellow: Am. Coll. Critical Care Medicine (Rsch. Com. 2003—06), Am. Acad. Pediat., Royal Coll. Pediat. & Child Health (Windermere Lectr. award 2004); mem.: Soc. Neurosci., Soc. Critical Care Medicine, Internat. Assn. Study of Pain, Soc. Pediatric Rsch., Am. Assn. Rhodes Scholars. Office: UAMS Pediat AR Childrens Hosp 1 Childrens Way Slot 512 12 Little Rock AR 72202-3500 Office Phone: 501-364-1845. Office Fax: 501-364-3188. E-mail: anandsunny@uams.edu.

ANAND, KISHLAY, cardiologist, researcher; b. Patna, Bihar, India, May 6, 1979; m. Preeti Singh. MBBS (hon.), All India Inst. Med. Sci., New Delhi, 2002; MS, Columbia U., NYC, 2004. Diplomate Am. Bd. Internal Medicine, 2007. Cardiology fellow Creighton U., Omaha, 2007—. Contbr. scientific papers. Dir. NRIhealth.com, Omaha. Health Sci. fellowship, Epilepsy Found. America, 2001. Achievements include research in RAAS inhibition decreases AF. Home: 6574 Dandelion Way San Diego CA 92130-5642 Personal E-mail: kishlay_anand@yahoo.com.

ANAND, MIRIAM K., physician, educator; b. Jan. 21, 1967; BA, U. Colo., Boulder, 1990; MD, George Washington Sch. Medicine, Washington, 1998. Lic. Ariz., diplomate Am. Bd. Internal Medicine, 2001, Am. Bd. Allergy and Immunology, 2003. Resident Mayo Grad. Sch. Medicine, Scottsdale, Ariz., 1998—2001; physician, pres. Allergy Assocs. & Lab. Ltd., Tempe, Ariz., 2003—. Clin. asst. prof. Ariz. Coll. Osteo. Medicine, Midwestern U., 2004—; coord. Phoenix Area Asthma Screening Program, 2007—; sponsor Am. Lung Assn. Ariz., 2008—09. Contbr. to profl. publs. Recipient Patient's Choice award, 2010; named one of Phoenix Mag. Top Drs., 2010; Allergy, Immunology fellowship, Nat. Jewish Med. Ctr., Denver, 2001—03. Fellow: Am. Coll. Allergy, Asthma & Immunology, Am. Acad. Allergy, Asthma & Immunology; mem.: AMA, ACS, Western Soc Allergy, Asthma, & Immunology, Ariz. Med. Assn. (dir. 2010—), Ariz. Assn. Physicians Indian Origin, Maricopa County Med. Soc. (v.p. 2009—11, sec. 2005—08), Ariz. Allergy and Asthma Soc. (sec., treas. 2007, v.p. 2008, pres. 2009, immediate past pres. 2010), Ariz. Found. Med. cure, Am. Coll. Chest Physicians. Avocations: hiking, yoga, travel. Home: 4440 E Camelback Rd #27 Phoenix AZ 85018 Mailing: 1006 E Guadalupe Rd Tempe AZ 85283 Office Fax: 480-820-1275. Personal E-mail: miriamanandmd@cox.net.

ANAND, PRAVEEN KUMAR, medical researcher; b. Agra, Uttar Pradesh, India, May 9, 1973; MBBS, S.N. Med. Coll., Agra, India, 2000; M in Applied Epidemiology, Nat. Inst. Epidemiology, ICMR, Chennai, India, 2009. Scientist-b Desert Medicine Rsch. Ctr., Indian Coun. Med. Rsch., Jodhpur, Rajasthan, India, 2002—07, scientist-c, 2007—. Office: Desert Medicine Rsch Ctr Jodhpur Rajasthan 342005 India Personal E-mail: ananddmrcjodhpur@gmail.com.

ANAND, RAJ (RK ANAND), pediatrician, hospital administrator; Former prof. BYL Nair Charitable Hosp. & Topiwala Nat. Med. Coll., Mumbai, India; head dept. pediatrics and neonatology Jaslok Hosp. and Rsch. Ctr., Mumbai, med. dir., 2005—. Author: Dr. RK Anand's Guide to Child Care. Fellow: Royal Coll. Physicians, Edinburgh, Indian Acad. Pediatrics; mem.: World Alliance for Breastfeeding Action (steering com.). Office: Jaslok Hosp and Rsch Ctr 15 Dr Deshmukh Marg Peddar Rd Mumbai 400 026 India Office Phone: 66573333. E-mail: ishanand@rediffmail.com. *

ANAND, SURESH CHANDRA, physician; b. Mathura, India, Sept. 13, 1931; arrived in U.S., 1957, naturalized, 1971; s. Satchit and Sumaran Bai Anand; m. Wiltrud Anand, Jan. 29, 1966; children: Miriam, Michael. MB, BS, King George's Coll., U. Lucknow, India, 1954; MS in Medicine, U. Colo., 1962. Diplomate Am. Bd. Allergy and Immunology. Fellow pulmonary diseases Nat. Jewish Hosp., Denver, 1957-58, resident in chest medicine, 1958-59, chief resident allergy-asthma, 1960-62; intern Mt. Sinai Hosp., Toronto, Ont., Can., 1962-63, resident in medicine, 1963-64, chief resident, 1964-65, demonstrator clin. technique, 1963-64, U. Toronto fellow in medicine, 1964-65; rsch. assoc. asthma-allergy Nat. Jewish Hosp., Denver, 1967-69; clin. instr. medicine U. Colo., Denver, 1967-69; internist Ft. Logan Mental Health Ctr., Denver, 1968-69; pres. Allergy Assocs. & Lab., Ltd., Phoenix, 1974—. Mem. staff Bapt. Hosp., chmn. med. records com., 1987; mem. staff Humana Hosp., John C. Lincoln Hosp., Phoenix Children's Hosp., Desert Samaritan Hosp., Mesa Luth. Hosp., Scottsdale Meml. Hosp., Chandler Regional Hosp., Ariz., Valley Luth. Hosp., Mesa, Ariz.; mem. med. com. Phoenix Meml. Hosp.; pres. NJH Fed. Credit Union, 1967—68; adj. assoc. prof. medicine Midwestern U., 2004—. Contbr. articles to profl. jours. Mem. citizens adv. bd. Camelback Hosp. Mental Health Ctr., Scottsdale, Ariz., 1974—80; mem. Phoenix Symphony Coun., 1973—90, Ariz. Opera co., Boyce Thompson Southwestern Arboretum, Ariz. Hist. Soc., Phoenix Arts Mus., Smithsonian Inst. Fellow: ACP, Am. Coll. Allergy and Immunology (pub. edn. com. 1991—94, aerobiology com., internat. com.), Am. Assn. Cert. Allergists, Am. Acad. Allergy (pub. edn. com.), Am. Coll. Chest Physicians (crit. care. com. past mem.); mem.: AMA, AAAS, Ariz. Found. Med. Care (bd. trustees 2009—), European Acad. Allergology and Clin. Immunology, Ariz. Thoracic Soc., Assn. Care of Asthma, Internat. Assn. Asthmology, World Med. Assn., NY Acad. Soc., Greater Phoenix Allergy Soc. (v.p. 1984—86, pres. 1986—88, med. adv. team sports medicine Ariz. State U.), West Coast Soc. Allergy and Immunology (editor-in-chief, Roundup Mag. M.C.M.S. 2003), Maricopa County Med. Soc. (bd. dirs. 1996—98, exec. com. 1996—98, pres.-elect 2002, pres. 2003, chmn. bd. census 2006), Ariz. Allergy Soc. (v.p. 1988—90, pres. 1990—91), Ariz. Med. Assn. (ctrl. dist. dir. 2006—), Internat. Assn. Allergy and Clin. Immunology, Scottsdalians Toastmasters, Nat. Geog. Soc., Phoenix Zoo, Ariz. Wild Life Assn., Village Tennis Club. Office: 1006 E Guadalupe Rd Tempe AZ 85283-3047 also: 4901 N 44th St Phoenix AZ 85018 also: 6553 E Baywood Ave Ste 201 Mesa AZ 85206-1754 also: 2248 N Alma School Rd Chandler AZ 85224-2488 Office Phone: 480-838-4296. Personal E-mail: sanand1@aol.com.

ANAND, VIJAY KRISHNAMURTHY, medical educator; b. Chennai, India, June 28, 1951; MD, Madras Med. Coll., Chennai, 1975. Clin. prof., otolaryngology Weill Cornell Med. Coll., NYC, 1983—. Recipient Outstanding Tchr. award, Am. Rhinologic Soc. Fellow: Am. Coll. Surgeons. Avocations: golf, travel, art. Office: 772 Park Ave New York NY 10021 Office Fax: 212-452-3660. Personal E-mail: vijayanandmd@gmail.com.

ANASTASAKOU, KORNILIA A., surgeon; b. Athens, Greece, Apr. 13, 1962; d. Aristoteles A. Anastasakos and Vassiliki A. Anastasakou; m. Michael A. Zazanis, Dec. 13, 1997; 1 child, Aristomenes M. Zazanis. MD, U. Munich, 1987, U. Berlin, 1987. Cert. general surgeon Hellenic Surg. Soc., U. Athens, 1996. Cons. breast surgeon,attending surgeon Athens Med. Ctr., Dept. Gen., Laparoscopic & Robotic Surgery, 2008—; surg. resident u. dept. Evangelismos Gen. Hosp., Athens, 1994—96; surg. resident Tzaneion Gen. Hosp. Piraeus, 1989—93; rural gen. practitioner Dist. Gen. Hosp. Kyparissia, Kyparissia- Peloponnes, Greece, 1988—89; vis. dr. Grosseto, Robotic Tng. Ctr., Grosseto, Italy, 2007; surg. trainee Instituto europeo di Oncologia, Milan; vis. surgeon dept. oncoplastic breast surgery Breast Ctr. Ruhr- Bethesdakrankenhaus, Tchg. Hosp. U. Duesseldorf, Duisburg, Germany, 2008—, Breast Ctr. St. Marienkrankenhaus, Tchg. Hosp. U. Frankfurt, 2005; vis. surg. resident dept.laparoscopic surgery Elisabethenkrankenhaus Frankfurt, Tchg. Hosp. Johann Wolfgang von Goethe U. Frankfurt, 1992, U. Hosp. Johann Wolfgang von Goethe U. Frankfurt, Germany, 1990. Consulting dr. ADAC, Athens, 1999—2006; contract physician Deutsche Lufthansa, 1995—. Contbr. scientific papers to profl jours. (European I.H.P.B.A Congress, 1995, Best Poster award, 2000, Poster Distinction award, 2007). Mem.: Minimal Invasive Robotic Assn., European Soc. Mastology, European Assn. Endoscopic Surgery, Soc. Am. Gastrointestinal Endoscopic Surgeons, Deutsche Gesellschaft fuer Senologie, Hellenic Soc. Robotic Surgery, Hellenic Soc. Laparoendoscopic Surgery, Hellenic Soc. Breast Surgery, IFSO, Hellenic Surg. Soc. Achievements include first to introduction of robotic surgery in Greece. Office: Athens Med Center Distomou 3-7 Athens 15125 Greece Office Phone: 00306944240898. Business E-Mail: kornilia@anastasakou.gr.

ANASTASIADIS, ANTONIOS P., orthopedist; b. Volos, Greece, May 12, 1964; MD, Nat. & Kapodistrian U. Athens, 1989, PhD, 2002. Resident orthop. surgery LAIKO Gen. Hosp. Athens, Greece, 1992—96; attending, orthop. surgeon Health Svcs. Found. Social Security, Greece, 1997—2001, Karditsa City Gen. Hosp., Greece, 2001—07, Amalia Fleming Gen. Hosp. Melissia, Athens, 2007—; shoulder fellow Royal Liverpool & Broadgreen U. Hosp., England, 2008. Recipient 1st prize, Amphiarion Found. Chemotherapeutic Studies, Athens; Fin. Support Tng. fellow, Hellenic Shoulder & Elbow Soc. Mem.: Hellenic Soc. Reconstructive Microsurgery, Hellenic Soc.

Surgery Hand, Hellenic Assn. Orthop. Surgery & Traumatology. Avocations: fishing, photography, soccer. Home: 27 Panagias Marmariotissas Halandri Athens GR15232 Greece Personal E-mail: a.p_anastasiadis@yahoo.gr.

ANCAR, VIRGILIU, physician; b. Pitesti, Romania, Feb. 24, 1944; s. Gheorghe Ancar and Ariadna Boghinschi-Ancar; m. Marcela Oprinescu; 1 child, Benedict. Degree, Nicolae Balcescu, 1950—61. Cert. Med. Diplomate 1968, specialist, Ob-gyn. 1972, primarium, Ob-gyn. 1981, Universitary Asst. 1971, Dr. of Med. Sciences 1983. Head of dept. Clin. Hosp., Bucharest, Ilfov, Romania, 1989—; prof. U. Of Medicine, Bucharest, Romania, 1992—; head, assisted human reproduction dept. Med. Ctr. "Medsana", Bucharest, Romania, 1996—. Editing advisor, Brookline, 1994—. Author: (textbook) Obstetrics, Romanian Academy Editions, 2001, Obstetrics and Gynecology, National Editions, 1997, Fetal hypotrophy, Amaltea Medical Editions, 1996; contbr. textbook Updates in Obstetrics and Gynecology, Medial Editions, 1985, textbook for students Obstetrics and Gynecology, University Library Editions, 1983. Recipient "Gheorghe Marinescu", Romanian Acad., 1980, Knight Of The "Steaua Romaniei" (Star Of Romania), Romanian Presidency, 2000. Mem.: Romanian Med. Acad., Romanian Nat. Soc. For Assisted Human Reproduction (pres. 1998), Nat. Romanian Soc. For Obstetrics And Gynecology (pres., bucharest br. 1995—2001), NY Acad. Of Sciences, Dist. 124-Romania, Internat. Assn. Of Lions Clubs (dist. gov. 2000—01, Governors Ext. Award 2001). Avocation: literature, history of religions, pipe collectionar. Office: Clinical Hospital 340 Sos Pantelimon 70000 Bucharest Romania Home Phone: 0040-0 1-2117733; Office Phone: 0040-0 1-2552177. Home Fax: +4012117733. Personal E-mail: vancar@arexim.ro. Business E-Mail: profancar@rol.ro.

ANCES, BEAU, medical educator; b. Feb. 20, 1970; MD, U. Pa., 2000. Asst. prof. Wash. U., St. Louis, 2007—. Office: Box 08111 660 South Euclid Ave Saint Louis MO 63110 Office Fax: 314-747-8427. Business E-Mail: bances@wustl.edu.

ANCES, BEAU M., neurologist; b. Balt., Md., Feb. 24, 1972; s. I.G. and Marlene Ances; m. Elizabeth Z. Wheeler, May 22, 2004. MSc, London Sch. of Economics, 1993—94; PhD, U. of Pa., 1994—2000, MD, 1994—2001, BA, 1989 93. Neurologist Hosp. of U. of Pa., 2001—. Editor Neurology. Achievements include research in Neuroimaging and NeuroAIDS. Office: Hosp of the Univ of Pennsylvan 3400 Spruce St Philadelphia PA 19103-4283 Personal E-mail: beau.ances@uphs.upenn.edu.

ANCES, I. G(EORGE), obstetrician, gynecologist; b. Balt., July 3, 1935; s. Harry and Fanny A.; m. Marlene Roth, Oct. 23, 1966; 1 son, Beau Mark. BS, U. Md., 1956, MD, 1959. Diplomate Am. Bd. Ob-Gyn. Intern Ohio State U. Hosp., 1959-60; resident in ob-gyn. Univ. Hosp., Balt., 1960-61, 63-65; faculty U. Md. Med. Sch., Balt., 1966— prof. ob-gyn., 1975-83, dir. labs. obstetrics and gynecol. rsch. and clin. labs., 1967-83, dir. divsn. adolescent ob-gyn. and family planning, 1981-83; prof. ob-gyn., chmn. dept. Rutgers U. Sch. Medicine, Camden, NJ, 1983—. Contbr. chpts. to books, articles to profl. jours. Capt. sustaining fund drive Balt. Symphony Orch., Opera Co. Phila.; med. adv. com. Fire Dept. Balt. City. With USAF, 1961-63. Recipient of Outstanding Tchg. and Edn. award Robert-Wood Johnson Sch. of Medicine-Cooper Hosp., 1989, 92, 96, 2000, 01, 02, o4, Appreciation Coverage award, 1999, 2000, 02, 04, Nat. Faculty award for excellence in resident edn., 1996, Douglass Soc. Faculty award for excellence in edn. and tchg., 2007. Fellow Am. Coll. Obstetrics and Gynecology; mem. Endocrine Soc., Soc. Gynecol. Investigation, Soc. Study Reprodn. (charter), Internat. Soc. Rsch. in Biology Reprodn. (charter), Md. Obstetrics and Gynecol. Soc. (sec. 1978-81, dir. 1979—), Med. and Chirurgical Soc. Md., Soc. Adolescent Medicine, Douglas Obstet. and Gynecol. Soc. (pres. 1984—), N.J. State Med. Soc. (chmn. neo-natal coop. So. Jersey 1986—), Phila. Ob-Gyn. Soc., English Speaking Union, Cooper Found., N.J. Conservation Coun., Harbour League Club, Md. Club, Towson Golf and Country Club, Sigma Xi. Clubs: Maryland, Towson Golf and Country. Home: 1 Lane Of Acres Haddonfield NJ 08033-3504 Office: Rutgers U Sch Medicine Dept Ob-Gyn 3 Cooper Plz Camden NJ 08103-1438 *

ANCOLI-ISRAEL, SONIA, psychologist, researcher; b. Tel Aviv, Dec. 25, 1951; came to U.S., 1955. m. Andrew G. Israel; 2 children. BA, SUNY, Stony Brook, 1972; MA, Calif. State U., Long Beach, 1974; PhD, U. Calif., San Francisco, 1979. Lic. psychologist, Calif. Staff psychologist U. Calif. San Diego, La Jolla, 1979-84, asst. adj. prof., 1984-88, assoc. prof., 1988-94; prof., 1994—; assoc. dir. Sleep Disorders Ctr., VA Med. Ctr., San Diego, 1981-92, dir., 1992—. Author: All I Want Is a Good Night's Sleep, 1996; contbr. numerous articles to profl. jours. Mem. exec. bd. Nat. Sleep Found., 1990-95. Recipient Robert E. Harris Meml. award U. Calif., San Franicsco, 1978, Lifetime Achievement award Nat. Sleep Found., 2007. Mem. Am. Acad. Sleep Medicine, Sleep Rsch. Soc. (bd. dirs. 1993-96, pres. 2004-05, Mary A. Carskadon Outstanding Educator award 2007), Soc. for Light Treatment and Biol. Rhythms (bd. dirs. 1994-97, pres. 2000—02), Gerontol. Soc. Am., Am. Geriatrics Soc., NY Acad. Sci. Business E-Mail: sancoliisrael@ucsd.edu.

ANCONA, GIUSEPPE FRANCESCO, financial consultant; b. Castellammare del Golfo, Italy, May 19, 1960; Degree in Economics, Turin U., 1988. Ptnr. Pricewaterhouse Coopers Adv., 2005—. Office: Corso Montevecchio Turin 10129 Italy Office Fax: 0039 (0)11 5773299. Business E-Mail: franco.ancona@it.pwc.com.

ANCU, EDWARD FLORIN, veterinarian; b. Galati, Romania, Oct. 14, 1969; s. Vasile and Haiganush Ancu-Gheorghiu; m. Jennifer Ann Marvel, Aug. 2, 2003; children: Evan Theodore-Joseph, Elise Agavni. BA in Biology, U. Calif. San Diego-Revelle, 1991; DVM, U. Wis., Madison, 1996. Intern small animal surgery and medicine Calif. Animal Hosp., LA, 1996—97; relief Dr. self-employed, 1997—2000; pvt. practice Big Tujunga Vet. Hosp., Calif., 2000—. Mem.: Lions Club (Tujunga chpt.). Avocations: travel, reading. Office: Big Tujunga Vet Hosp 6934 Foothill Blvd Tujunga CA 91042 Office Phone: 818-352-6085.

ANCUTA, EUGEN GIGEL, scientist, researcher; b. Iasi, Romania, Nov. 1, 1968; MD, Gr.T.Popa U. Medicine and Pharmacy, 1997, MSc, 2000, PhD, 2010. Adj. prof. Cuza Voda Hosp., 2000, asst. rsch. scientist, 2000—05, rsch. scientist, 2005—07, rsch. scientist iii, 2007—. Mem.: European Acad. Gynecol. Cancer, Internat. Soc. Against Pain, Internat. Soc. Ultrasound Ob-Gyn., European Calcified Tissue Soc., Romanian Soc. Ob-Gyn. Avocations: reading, sports, music. Home: 56 Ion Creanga St Iasi 700333 Romania Office Phone: 0040747555656. Home Fax: 40232244288. Personal E-mail: eugen01ro@yahoo.com.

ANDELIC, NADA, physiatrist, researcher; b. Trebinje, Bosnia-Herzegovina, July 3, 1956; d. Danilo and Jovanka Andjelic; m. Nebojsa Hadzic, Aug. 28, 1982; 1 child, Maria Hadzic. MD, Med. Faculty, U. Beograd, Serbia, 1982. Specialist in phys. medicine and rehab. Norway, 1996. Head dept. Sunnaas Rehab. Hosp., Askim, Norway, 2003—05; rschr. Oslo U. Hosp. Ulleval, 2005—. Reviewer. Contbr. scientific papers. Home: Valhallveien 17 Oslo 0196 Norway Office: Oslo Univ Hosp Ulleval Oslo 0407 Norway Office Phone: 472-211-8687. Business E-Mail: nada.andelic@ulleval.no.

ANDERBERG, EVA, medical researcher; b. Helsingborg, May 3, 1947; RNM, Barnmorskelätoanstalten Gothenburg, Sweden, 1970; PhD, Lund U., 2010, Skåne U. Hosp., 2010. Rschr. Skåne U. Hosp., Malmö, Sweden, 2004—10. Office: Skåne University Hos Ing 89A Malmö Skåne 20502 Sweden

ANDEROVA, MIROSLAVA, neuroscientist; b. Prague, Czech Republic, Apr. 4, 1958; Degree in Chem. Tech. Engring., 1983, PhD in Molecular Genetics and Microbiology, 1991. Dept. head Inst. Exptl. Medicine, 2010—. Mem.: Czech Physiol. Soc., Czech Med. Soc. J. E. Purkyne, Czech Neurosci. Soc., Soc. Neurosci. Avocations: skiing, swimming, hiking. Office: Videnska 1083 Prague 14220 Czech Republic Office Fax: 00420 241062783. Business E-Mail: anderova@biomed.cas.cz.

ANDERS, CLAUDIA, occupational therapist; d. Walter and Helen Anders; 1 child, Andrew T. Kiko. BS in Occupational Therapy with high honors, Va. Commonwealth U., 1973; postgrad., Ashland U., Ohio, 1984, Walsh (Ohio) Coll., 1985, Kent State U., Ohio, 1988-89, Colo. State U., 1991-92; MS, Clayton Coll., 2002, D in Naturopathy, 2003. Cert. traditional naturopath, occupl. therapist Ohio, bd. cert. pediat. occupl. therapist. With Children's Rehab. Ctr., Warren, Ohio, 1974-76; mem. transdisciplinary team Goodwill Rehab. Ctr., Canton, Ohio, 1976-78; pvt. practice, 1978-83; with Timken Mercy Med. Ctr., Canton, 1978-83; occupl. therapist adult tng. team Stark County Bd. Mental Retardation, Canton, 1983-85; developer occupl. therapy svcs. Stark County Local Schs., 1985-87; pediat. occupl. therapist home health care sch. and cmty. agys., 1985-91; owner Eagle Seminars and Therapy, 1998—. Presenter in field. Vol. Nat. Pk. Svc., Cleve. Metroparks; sec. Rocky River Trailsiders, 1993—95; rec. sec. Western Cuyahoga Audubon, 2005—06. Named Masters Clinician, based on training level and experience demonstrated, Integration, New Zealand, 2006—07; scholar, Rsch. Group Deerfield Beach, Fla., 2000, Cancun, 2006; A. D. Williams scholar, Va. Commonwealth U., 1972—73. Mem.: Am. Naturepathic Med. Assn., Ohio Occupl. Therapy Assn., Am. Occupl. Therapy Assn., Cuyahoya Valley Nat. Park Assn., Nature Conservancy. Avocations: gardening, birdwatching, hiking, sewing, needlecrafts. Office: Eagle Selminars and Therapy PO Box 604 Berea OH 44017

ANDERS, THOMAS F., psychiatrist, educator; AB, Stanford Univ., 1956, MD, 1960; grad. Program for Chiefs of Clin. Svcs., Sch. Pub. Health, Harvard Univ., 1989. Cert. gen. psychiatry Am. Bd. Psychiatry & Neurology, 1970, in child and adolescent psychiatry Am. Bd. Psychiatry & Neurology, 1976. Intern Mount Sinai Hosp., NYC, 1960—61; asst. resident, pediatrics Children's Hosp. Med. Ctr., Boston, 1961—62; asst. resident, sr. resident psychiatry Columbia Univ. Coll. Physicians and Surgeons and NY State psychiatric Inst., NYC, 1964—67; rsch. fellow Montefiore Hosp. and Albert Einstein Coll. of Medicine, Bronx, 1967—69; staff Columbia Univ. Psychoanalytic Clin. for Training and Rsch., NYC, 1965—70; prof., psychiatry Univ. Calif. Sch. Med., Davis, 1992—, acting chair, dept. psychiatry, 1992—94, chair, dept. psychiatry, 1994—98, exec. assoc. dean, 1998—. Mem.: Am. Acad. Child & Adolescent Psychiatry (pres. 2005—07). Office: MIND Inst Univ Calif 2825 50th St Sacramento CA 95817 also: Dept Psychiatry and Behav Sci 2230 Stockton Blvd Sacramento CA 95817 Office Phone: 916-703-0230, 916-734-2972. Business E-Mail: thomas.anders@ucdmc.ucdavis.edu. E-mail: tfanders@ucdavis.edu.

ANDERSEN, BURTON ROBERT, immunologist, educator, medical historian; b. Chgo., Aug. 27, 1932; s. Burton R. and Alice C. (Mara) A.; children: Ellen C., Julia A., Brian E. Student, Northwestern U., Evanston, Ill., 1950—51; BS, U. Ill., Chgo., 1953, MS, MD, U. Ill., Chgo., 1957. Intern Mpls. Gen. Hosp., 1957-58; resident and fellow U. Ill. Hosp., 1958-61; clin. assoc. NIH, Bethesda, Md., 1961-64; asst. prof. U. Rochester, NY, 1964-67; assoc. prof. Northwestern U., 1967-70; prof. medicine and microbiology U. Ill., Chgo., 1970—, chief infectious diseases, 1970—99, rsch. adv. clin. rsch. ctr., 2001—. Contbr. sci. rsch. articles to profl. jours. Served as sr. surgeon USPHS, 1961-63. Grantee Rsch. grantee, NEH, 2000—03. Fellow ACP; mem. Am. Assn. Immunologists, Am. Soc. for Clin. Investigation, Ctrl. Soc. for Clin. Rsch. Achievements include research in infectious diseases, white blood cells and ancient Mesopotamian medicine. Office: U Ill Sect Infectious Diseases 808 S Wood St Chicago IL 60612-7300 Business E-Mail: branders@uic.edu.

ANDERSEN, DONALD H., urologist; AB cum laude, Vassar Coll.; MD, Jefferson Med. Coll., 1989. Intern Univ. Va. Hosp., Charlottesville, resident urology; on staff Chester County Hosp., Brandywine Hosp., Paoli Hosp., 1995—; urologist Urology Ctr. of Chester County. Recipient Merck Clin. award in Surgery, E. Harold Hinman prize in Family Medicine; named Top Dr., Main Line Today, 2011, Phila. Mag., 2011. Fellow: ACS; mem.: Hobart Amory Hare, Alpha Omega Alpha, Phi Beta Kappa. Office: Urology Center of Chester County Bldg B Ste 202 915 Old fern Hill Rd West Chester PA 19380 Office Phone: 610-692-4270.

ANDERSEN, HOLLY SUE, cardiologist, educator; b. Jamestown, NY, Dec. 29, 1962; married; 2 children. Grad. in Neuroscience, Dartmouth Coll., 1985; MD with Honors, U. Rochester Sch. Medicine and Dentistry, 1989. Cert. Internal Medicine, Cardiovascular Disease. Rsch. fellow NIH; intern, resident and fellow NY Presbyn. Hosp., Cornell Med. Ctr., chief med. resident, dept. medicine, dir. edn. and outreach, Ronald O. Perelman Heart Inst., 2009—; asst. prof. clin. medicine Weill Cornell Med. Ctr.; asst. attending physician NY Presbyn. Hosp.; private practice NYC. Founder, chair David E. Rogers Meml. Rsch. award for Med. House Staff, NY Presbyn. Hosp.; invited spkr. in field. Expert panelist on internet webcasts, on air med. cons. ABC World News Tonight, CBS Evening News, NBC Evening News, Early Show, Fox TV Network, Fox News Channel, BBC, MTV Network. Bd. dirs. Michael J. Fox Found. for Parkinson's Rsch., President's Coun. for Internat. Women's Health Coalition; mem. nat. adv. bd. Women's Sports Found. Recipient Ernest T. Saeger Meml. award for outstanding work in premedical sci., Janet M. Glasgow Meml. Achievement award, Am. Med. Women's Assn.; named one of America's Best Doctors, 2001—, America's Top Cardiologists, Consumers Rsch. Coun. America. Fellow: Am. Coll. Cardiology; mem.: Screen Actors Guild, Arthur Ashe Athletic Assn. (past bd. dirs.), Am. Coll. Sports Medicine, Alpha Omega Alpha. Office: 125 E 72nd St New York NY 10021 Office Phone: 212-628-6100. Office Fax: 212-517-5468.

ANDERSEN, LARS FRANCH, gynecologist; b. Copenhagen, Apr. 20, 1952; MD, U. Copenhagen, 1981, PhD, 1998. Sr. cons., asst. prof. dept. ob-gyn. U. Copenhagen, Hilleroed Hosp., Denmark, 1997—. Mem.: DFS, ESHRE, NFOG, DSOG. Avocations: skiing, gardening, sailing. Home: Ole Olsens Allé 19 Hellerup Copenhagen DK2900 Denmark Home Fax: 45 48 29 36 10. Personal E-mail: lars.franch.andersen@dadlnet.dk.

ANDERSEN, LUBA, electrologist, electropigmentologist; b. Germany, Mar. 29, 1945; arrived in U.S., 1955; d. Osyp and Justyna Nahorniak; m. Roger A. Andersen, Dec. 9, 1989 (div. Oct. 2001). A in Bus. and Acctg., DePaul U., 1977; BS in Commerce and Social Studies, LaSalle U., 1978; postgrad., U. Mich., 1984; cert., Ariz. Inst. Electrolysis, 1993. Cert. profl. electrologist, clin. electropigmentologist. From analyst to contr. Fed. Home Loan Bank, Chgo., 1965-83, v.p., contr., 1985-92; owner The Electrolysis Connection, Tucson, 1993—. Mem. NAFE, Am. Soc. Women Accts. (chair bylaws com. 1981), Am. Electrology Assn., Electrologists Assn. Ariz., Internat. Guild Profl. Electrologists, Inc., Fin. Mgrs. Soc., Soc. Cosmetic Profls., Assn. Clin. Electropigmentologists. Republican. Roman Catholic. Avocation: creating tapestries. Office: Electrolysis Connection 11038 N Canada Ridge Dr Tucson AZ 85737-8796 Office Phone: 520-297-3919.

ANDERSEN, MARIANNE SINGER, psychologist; b. Baden nr. Vienna, Austria; came to U.S., 1940; naturalized, 1946; d. Richard L. and Jolanthe (Garda) Singer; 1 child, Richard Esten. BA, CUNY, 1950, MA, 1974; PhD, Fla. Inst. Tech., 1980. Rsch. assoc. Inst. for Rsch. in Hypnosis, NYC, 1974-76, fellow in clin. hypnosis, 1976, dir. seminars, 1978-82, dir. edn., 1982—2005; psychotherapist specializing in hypnotherapy Morton Prince Ctr. for Hypnotherapy, dir. clin. svcs., 1981-82; dir. adminstrn. Internat. Grad. U., NYC, 1974-77; pvt. practice psychotherapy, 1977—. Adminstrv. coordinator Internat. Grad. Sch. Behavior Sci., Fla. Inst. Tech., 1978; co-dir. Melbourne Group, 1983-90; clin. instr. hypnotherapy Mt. Sinai Sch. Medicine, NYC, 1996-2007; lectr. in field. Author: (with Louis Savary) Passages: A Guide for Pilgrims of the Mind, 1972; rsch. on treatment of obesity with hypnotherapy; book editor specializing in psychology and psychiatry including W.W. Norton Co., Sterling Pub. Co., E.P. Dutton Co., 1950-71. Fellow Soc. for Clin. and Exptl. Hypnosis; mem. APA, Internat. Soc. Clin. and Exptl. Hypnosis.

ANDERSEN, MARIT HELEN, surgeon, researcher; b. Bergen, Norway, Apr. 7, 1958; PhD, Oslo U., 2008. Postdoc. fellow Oslo U. Hosp., 2010—. Office. PO Box 4950 Nydalen Oslo 0424 Norway Office Fax: 4723072526. Business E-Mail: marit.andersen@ous-hf.no.

ANDERSEN, PETER, otolaryngologist, educator; married; 3 children. MD, Wash. U. Sch. of Medicine, St Louis, Mo., 1988. Diplomate Am. Bd. Otolaryngology, 1994. Resident otolaryngology, head and neck surgery Oregon Health and Sci. Univ., Portland, 1988—93; fellow head and neck surgery and oncology Meml. Sloane-Kettering Cancer Ctr., NY, 1993—95; dir. head and neck oncology, prof. otolaryngology Oregon Health And Sci. Univ. Fellow: ACS. Avocations: skiing, windsurfing. Office: Oregon Health and Science University 3181 S W Sam Jackson Pk Rd Portland OR 97239-3098 Office Phone: 503-494-8311.

ANDERSEN, POUL ERIK, radiologist, professor; b. Aarhus, Denmark, Nov. 15, 1948; s. Poul Erik and Margrethe (Von Barner) A.; m. Annette Bruhn, Dec. 26, 1969; children: Tina, Anne Marie. MD, U So. Denmark, Odense, 1974; specialist radiology, Denmark, 1982; PhD, U So. Denmark, 1987; Ednl. Coun. Fgn. Med. Grads., Copenhagen, 1975. Intern in gen. surgery Hobro, 1975-76, Varde, 1981; resident in internal medicine Hobro, 1976-77; chief radiologist dept. radiology cardiovascular sect. Odense U. Hosp., 1983; lectr. anatomy and radiology Odense U., 1979-85, asst. prof., 1985—2010; prof. European Bd. Interventional Radiology, 2011—. Author of 1 radiology book; editor of 1 radiology book; contbr. more than 100 articles to profl. jours., chpt. to books, more than 100 lectures. Grantee Siemens' Found., 1985, James Polack Found., 1987, Found. Congenital Diseases, 1987. Fellow Cardiovascular and Intervention Radiol. Soc. Europe, Denmark (local meeting chmn. annual meeting and postgrad. course); mem. Danish Radiol. Soc. (chmn. ann. postgrad. edn. courses 1988—99, 2008), Danish Soc. Interventional Radiology. Avocation: middle and long distance running. Office: Odense U Hosp Dept Radiology DK-5000 Odense Denmark Office Phone: 45 65412188.

ANDERSEN, RICHARD ALAN, physiologist; b. New Kensington, Pa., Oct. 27, 1950; s. John Nikoli and Norma Enid Andersen; m. Carol Louise Ahern, Sept. 11, 1979; children: Michael Blake, Kristen Nicole. BS, U. Calif., Davis, 1974; PhD, U. Calif., San Francisco, 1979. Postdoctoral fellow Johns Hopkins U. Med. Sch., Balt., 1981; asst. prof. Salk Inst., La Jolla, Calif., 1981—86, assoc. prof., 1986—87; adj. asst. prof. dept. neurosci. U. Calif., San Diego, 1982—; assoc. prof. dept. brain and cognitive scis. MIT, Cambridge, Mass., 1987—90, prof., 1990—94; James G. Boswell prof. neuroscience, Biology Divsn. Calif. Tech. Inst., Pasadena, 1994—, dir. Sloan-Swartz Ctr. Theoretical Neurobiology, 1994—2004; vis. prof. Coll. de France, 2005. Contbr. articles to profl. jours. Recipient Scholars award, McKnight Found., 1983—86, McKnight Tech. Innovation in Neuroscience award, 2000—02; fellow, Sloan Found., 1982—86; Abraham Rosenberg fellow, U. Calif., San Francisco, 1973, Regents' fellow, 1974—76. Mem.: AAAS, Inst. Medicine, NAS, Assn. Rsch. in Vision and Ophthalmology, Soc. Neurosci, Helmholtz Club. Office: The Andersen Lab Calif Tech Inst Divsn Biology 216-76 Pasadena CA 91125

ANDERSEN, RONALD MAX, health services researcher, educator; b. Omaha, 1939; s. Max Adolph and Evangeline Dorothy (Wobbe) Andersen; m. Diane Borella, June 19, 1965; 1 child, Rachel. BS, U. Santa Clara, 1960; MS, Purdue U., 1962, PhD, 1968. Rsch. assoc.

Purdue U., West Lafayette, Ind., 1962—63; assoc. study dir. Nat. Opinion Rsch. Ctr., Chgo., 1963—66; rsch. assoc. U. Chgo., 1963—77, from assoc. prof. to prof. Grad. Sch. Bus., 1974—90, dir. Program in Health Adminstrn. and Ctr. for Health Adminstrn. Studies, 1980—90; Wasserman prof. dept. health svcs. and sociology UCLA, 1991—, prof. emeritus, 2004—, chmn. dept. health svcs., 1993—96, 2000—03. Com. mem. Agy. for Health Care Policy and Rsch., Rockville, Md., 1970—. Mem. editl. bd.: Health Adminstrn. Press, 1980—83, 1988—98, Med. Care Rsch. & Rev., 1994—; author: A Decade of Health Services, 1967, Two Decades of Health Service, 1976, Total Survey Error, 1979, Health Services in the U.S., 1980, Ambulatory Care and Insurance Coverage in an Era of Constraint, 1987, Training Physicians, 1994, Changing the U.S. Health Care System, 1996, 2001. Grantee, Agy. for Health Care Policy and Rsch, 1982, Robert Wood Johnson Found., 1983, Kaiser Family Found., 1983, WHO, 1990; fellow, NIH, 1960—62. Mem.: APHA, Assn. for Health Svcs. Rsch. (dir. 1981—83, 1997—99, Disting. Career award 1996), Assoc. Univ. Program in Health Adminstrn. (Baxter Allegiance prize 1999), Inst. Medicine NAS, Am. Sociol. Assn. (chmn. med. sociology sect. 1980—81, Disting. Med. Sociologist 1994). Roman Catholic. Home: 10724 Wilshire Blvd Apt 312 Los Angeles CA 90024-4453 Office: UCLA Sch Pub Health Los Angeles CA 90024 Office Phone: 310-206-1810. Business E-Mail: randerse@ucla.edu.

ANDERSON, ALLAMAY EUDORIS, retired health educator, home economist; b. NYC, July 18, 1933; d. John Samuel and Charlotte Jane (Harrigan) Richardson; m. Edgar Leopold Anderson, Apr. 14, 1957 (div. Apr. 14, 1963); 1 child, David Lancelot; m. Diane Kay Swartz, July 19, 2003. BA, Queens Coll., CUNY, 1975; MS in Edn., Fordham U., 1984. Cert. profl. mgmt., Adelphi U., 1978. Staff sch. food svc. dietitian Bd. Edn., NYC, 1968—88; tchr. home and career skills Louis Armstrong Mid. Sch., 1988; spl. edn. tchr. Manhattan HS, NYC, 1989—95, coord AIDS resource, 1995, ret., 1995; profl. devel. cons. NYC, 1978—; ptnr. Masiba Bldg. Corp., Corona, NY, 1975—82; adj. lectr. home econs. Queens Coll., 1987; owner AEA Devel. Svc., 1987—97; exec. bd. Sch. Edn. Alumni Assn., Fordham U., 1997—2006. Leadership mem. Western Mich. U. Life Learning Acad. Ctr. Gerontology, 2011—. Vestry mem. youth ministries Grace Episcopal Ch., 1982—85, vestry mem., 1996—99; sch. coord. League Better Cmty. Life, Inc., 1977, treas. exec. bd., 1970—76; officer NYC Cmty. Devel. Agy., 1980—83; mem. Kwanzaa Adv. Com. Urban Coalition, PR, 1983, Ll 28 Episcopal Cursillo, 1991; asst. presiding ptnr. Dynamic Investors Club, 1996—2007; bridges chair Srs. Dorie Miller, 2003—06. Recipient Elmcor Cmty. Svc. award, Elmcor Youth and Adult Activities, Inc., 1989, Alumni Achievement award, Fordham U. Sch. Edn., 2000, Clergy award, 1996, 2006, Cmty. Svc. award, NY State United Tchrs., 2001, Concourse Village Br. Positive Image award, Key Women Am., Inc., 2005, Salutatorium, Inst. Sr. Action, 2005. Mem.: NAACP (local Women's History Month honoree 1996, health chair 2003—, silver life mem. 2007), United Fedn. Tchrs. (Ret. Tchrs. chpt.), Queens Coll. Home Econs. Alumni Assn. (v.p., chmn. bylaws com. 1982), Langston Hughes Libr. Action Com. (treas. 1989, Kwanza chair 1994—97, Appreciation award 2006), Nat. Assn. Investment Clubs (Award 2004), Assn. Fundraising Profls. (Greater NY chpt.), Joint Pub. Affairs Com. Older Adults (life), Negro Bus. and Profl. Women's Clubs (Profl. award 1998).

ANDERSON, ALLAN CROSBY, hospital executive; b. Jamestown, NY, Sept. 18, 1932; s. Emmons E. and Gertrude (Sweet) A.; m. Pauline Culver, June 24, 1956; children: Todd Culver, Emily Ann. BS, Syracuse U., 1954; MHA, U. Minn., 1956. Asst. adminstr. Highland Hosp., Rochester, N.Y., 1959-62, adminstr., 1965-68; asst. dir. Presbyn. Hosp., Phila., 1962-65; exec. dir. Strong Meml. Hosp., U. Rochester, 1968-79; pres. Lenox Hill Hosp., NYC, 1979-89; v.p., COO Milton S. Hershey Med. Ctr., dir. Univ. Hosps. Pa. State U., Hershey, 1990-96; asst. prof. health services U. Rochester Sch. Medicine and Dentistry. Mem. exec. com. Sub-Regional Adminstrs. Group, Adminstrs. Conf., Sub-Regional Exec. Conf.; chmn. bd. dirs. Rochester Regional Hosp. Assn., vice chmn. hosp. planning group; chmn. pub. rels. com., bd. dirs. Rochester Hosp. Svc. Corp., 1968-79; dir. Univ. Hosp. Consortium, 1990-96, mem. exec. com., 1994-96; mem. Accreditation Coun. for Grad. MEd. Edn., 1990-96, treas., 1992-94, mem. exec. com., 1992-96, chmn., 1995; bd. dirs. Capital Blue Cross, 1993-95, United Way of the Capital Region, 1993-98, mem. exec. com., 1995-98. Mem. blood program com. Rochester-Monroe County chpt. A.R.C.; mem. med. adv. com. Planned Parenthood of Rochester and Monroe County.; Bd. dirs. Rochester Presbyn. Home, 1967-70, Home Care Assn. Rochester and Monroe County, Health Council Monroe County. Served to 1st lt., Med. Service Corps USAF, 1957-59. Mem. Am. Coll. Health Care Execs., Assn. Am. Med. Colls. (assembly) Hosp. Assn. N.Y. State (dir., regional orgns. com., govt. rels. com., trustee 1980-84), Greater N.Y. Hosp. Assn. (gov. 1980-89, treas. 1982, sec. 1983, vice chmn. 1984, 85, 86, chmn. 1987, chmn. fiscal policy com. 1982-83, chmn. ambulatory care comm. 1980), Am. Hosp. Assn. (regional adv. bd. 1986-89, regional policy bd. 1992-95, trustee 1985-89, exec. com. 1987-89), League Vol. Hosps. (chmn.-elect 1983-86, chmn. 1986-88). Presbyterian (ruling elder). Home: 143 Gibbs St Rochester NY 14605

ANDERSON, BARBARA ALLEN, alcohol and drug abuse services professional, archivist; b. Atlanta, Aug. 15, 1956; d. Cliff Cole and Jeanne Tiller Allen; m. Richard Jefferson Anderson, Oct. 20, 1984. BA, Shorter Coll., 1978; MCM, S.B.T.S., Louisville, 1981. Cert. addictions counselor, master's level addiction counselor, clin. supr. Asst. creative dir. Trilogy Entertainment Corp., Atlanta, 1984—89; spiritual dir. Breakthru Ho., Decatur, Ga., 1989—92; continuing care therapist SAFE Recovery Campus, Atlanta, 1990—93; continuing care assoc. Talbott Recovery Campus, Atlanta, 1993—95, continuing care coord., 1996, dir. continuing care, 1996—2003, dir. continuing care, ref. liaison, 2004—08; southern regional mgr. Little Hill Alina Lodge, Bhairstown, NJ, 2009—. World svc. del. AFG of Ga., Inc., Atlanta, 1995—97, area office bd. chmn., 1998—2000, archivist, 2001—. Vol. writer, editor Paths to Recovery, 1997, editor (newsletter) Talbott Times, 1997—99; contbr. articles to Talbott Times. Mem.: NAFE, Ga. Addiction Counselors Assn., Nat. Employee Assistance Profls. Assn., Nat. Assn. Alcohol and Drug Abuse Counselors. Avocations: music, tennis, writing, movies, crafts. Home: 4380 Veterans Memorial Hwy Lithia Springs GA 30122-1707 Office: Little Hill Alina Lodge PO Box 1480 Austell GA 30168 Office Phone: 908-914-6465. Personal E-mail: pianobarb@aol.com.

ANDERSON, CORRIE T.M., pediatric anesthesiologist, educator; b. Minn., May 3, 1954; married; 2 children. AB in Biochemistry & Molecular Biology cum laude, Harvard Coll., Cambridge, MA, 1976; MD, Stanford U., 1982. Diplomate Nat. Bd. Med. Examiners, Am. Bd. Anesthesiology, 1994, Am. Bd. Anesthesiology-pain medicine, lic. Mass., Calif., Wash., DEA lic. Intern pediat. The Children's Hosp., Boston, 1982—83, resident pediat., 1983—85, fellow anesthesia, 1987—88; resident anesthesia The Brigham and Women's Hosp., Boston, 1985—87; asst. prof. anesthesiology UCLA Sch. of Medicine, LA, 1988—94, asst. prof. pediat., 1989—94, assoc. prof. anesthesiology, 1994—2001, assoc. prof. pediat., 1994—2001, prof. anesthesiology, 2001, Univ. Wash. Sch. of Medicine, Seattle, 2001—. Mem. scientific adv. bd. American Health Products, Inc., 1990—94; adjunct prof. pediat. Univ. Wash. Sch. of Medicine, Seattle, 2001—; pain mgmt. cons.; several administrative and hospital committee appointmens. Manuscripts in refereed journals; contbr. chapters to books. Bd. dirs. American Cancer Soc., Brookline, Mass., 1984—87; several vol. and cmty. service activities. Recipient Stanford Black Premedical Student Orgn. Appreciation award, 1980, 1981, Outstanding Physician of the Year award, UCLA Med. Ctr., Dept. of Nursing, 1992, Dillon award for Outstanding Tchg. by an Asst. Prof., UCLA Dept. of Anesthesiology, 1994, Cert. of Appreciation, UCLA, 1999—2000, Calif. State Univ., 1999, Adam Bischoff Sportsmanship award, Am. Youth Soccer Region, 1999; named Best Doctors in Seattle, Seattle Mag., 2002—07, Top Doctors, Seattle Metropolitan Mag., 2004—07, America's Top Pediatricians, Guide to America's Top Pediatricians, 2007; Fellow's Scholarship, Harvard Coll., 1972, Browne Scholarship, 1972, Dreyfus Fellowship for Biomedical Research, 1975, Merck, Sharp and Dohme Rsch. Fellowship, 1981—82. Mem.: Assn. of University Anesthesiologists, American Acad. of Pediatrics (sec.-treas. on the exec. com., sect. on anesthesiology & pain mgmt. 2006—), Washington State Med. Assn., Washington State Soc. of Anesthesiologists, NAACP, American Heart Assn., Nat. Med. Assn. (vice chair anesthesiology sect. 1996—98, chair anesthesiology sect. 1999—2001, immediate past chair anesthesiology sect. 2001—03), American Pain Soc., Soc. for Pediatric Anesthesia, Assn. University Anesthesiologists, Stanford Black Alumni Club, Stanford Alumni Contact Group, Stanford Alumni Assn., Harvard Alumni Assn. Achievements include patents in field. Office: Seattle Children's Hospital 4800 Sand Point Way NE Seattle WA 98105 Office Fax: 206-987-2704.

ANDERSON, DARLEEN SHIRCLIFFE, hospital administrator; b. Boston, Dec. 19, 1951; d. Albert Craycroft and Doreen Agnes (Newberg) Shircliffe; m. Billy Gray Anderson, June 9, 1973; children: Brandon, Brittany. Diploma in nursing, N.C. Bapt. Hosp., 1973; BSN, Old Dominion U., 1982; MS in Advanced Adult Nursing and Adminstrn., Hampton U., 1985. RN, Va.; cert. nursing adminstr. Staff nurse intensive and neuro ICU N.C. Bapt. Hosp., Winston-Salem, 1973-74, staff and charge nurse, 1974-76; staff nurse ICU Bapt. Meml. Hosp., Memphis, 1974; clin. coord. neuro ICU Sentara Norfolk (Va.) Gen. Hosp., 1977-79, quality assurance coord., 1979, critical care staff devel. coord., 1979-84, trauma program dir., 1984-89, adminstrv. advisor burn trauma ICU, 1988-89, DON, 1989-91, v.p., 1992—. Site reviewer Trauma Ctr. Designation, Va., 1983-91, EMS Designs Co., Calif., 1986; expert witness reviewer legal firms, Hampton Roads, Va., 1987-91 Mem. ACA, ANA (tri level 1983—), Am. Trauma Soc., Am. Orgn. Nurse Execs., Am. Assn. Neuro Sci. Nurses (treas. 1978, pres. 1980), Sigma Theta Tau. Baptist. Home: 1224 Heathcliff Dr Virginia Beach VA 23464-5848 Office: Sentara Leigh Hosp 830 Kempsville Rd Norfolk VA 23502-3920 *

ANDERSON, DAVID GREG, orthopaedic spine surgeon, educator; MD, Loma Linda U., Calif. Diplomate Am. Bd. Orthopaedic Surgery. Intern gen. surgery Univ. Calif., resident orthop. surgery; hosp. affiliations include Nazareth Hosp., Bucks County Splty. Hosp.; fellow spinal surgery Thomas Jefferson Univ., prof. orthop. surgery, clin. dir. spine sect. orthop. rsch. lab.; physician Rothman Inst. Co-author: (jours.) Harrop J. Correlation of C2 fractures and vertebral artery injury, 2010, Fibronectin Splicing variants in Human Intervertebral Disc and Association with Disc Degeneration, 2010, Complications in spine surgery, 2010, Transplantation of Goat Bone Marrow Stromal Cells to the Degenerating Intervertebral Disc in a Goat Injury Model, 2010, Trends in Epidemiology and Management of Type II Odontoid Fractures: 20-year Experience at a Model System Spine Injury Tertiary Referral Center, 2010, and numerous other jours. Named one of the Top Doctors, Phila Mag., 2011. Fellow: Am. Orthop. Assn. (ABC travelling fellow 2011); mem.: Scoliosis Rsch. Soc., Am. Spinal Injury Assn., North America Spine Soc., Cervical Spine Rsch. Soc., Am. Acad. Orthop. Surgeons, Minimally Invasive Spinal Surgery Soc. (founding mem. and pres.). Office: Rothman Institute 2630 Holme Ave 2nd Fl Philadelphia PA 19152 Office Phone: 800-321-9999. Office Fax: 215-992-4961.

ANDERSON, DAVID IAN, physiologist, educator; b. Australia, Dec. 21, 1965; PhD, Lo. State U., 1994. Prof. San Francisco State U., 1995—. Adj. prof. Inst. Human Devel., U. Calif., Berkeley, 1998—2011; bd. dirs. Ctr. Rsch. Human Devel., 2007—11; editl. bd. mem. Asian Jour. Sport Scis., 2010—11. Rsch. grant, NSF, NIH, Dept. Edn. Mem.: Internat. Soc. Infant Studies, Soc. Rsch. Child Devel., Am. Alliance Health, Phys. Edn., Recreation and Dance, N.Am. Soc. Psychology Sport and Phys. Activity. Avocation: sports. Office: 1600 Holloway Ave San Francisco CA 94132 Office Fax: 415-338-7566. Business E-Mail: danders@sfsu.edu.

ANDERSON, DEBORAH J., obstetrician, gynecologist, researcher; BA, Rice U., 1971; MS, U. Tex.-GSBS, PhD, 1976. Postdoctoral studies Oregon Health Sciences Ctr., 1976—80, Harvard Med. Sch., 1980—82; prof. ob/gyn. and microbiology Boston U. Sch. Medicine; lectr. in medicine Harvard Med. Sch. Contbr. articles. Recipient Ig Nobel prize, 2008. Office: Boston U Sch of Medicine 670 Albany St Ste 516 Boston MA 02118 Office Phone: 617-414-8482. Business E-Mail: Deborah.Anderson@bmc.org. *

ANDERSON, ERIC EDWARD, psychologist, consultant, healthcare executive, educator; b. Mpls., Jan. 24, 1951; s. Charles Eric and Elizabeth Blanche (Engstrand) A.; m. Florence Kaye, June 18, 1978; children: Cara Elizabeth, Evan Travis. BA summa cum laude, U. Minn., 1973; MA, Fuller Theol. Sem., 1977, PhD in Clin. Psychology, 1978. Lic. psychologist Minn., Pa.; cert. community coll. teaching credential in psychology and philosophy Calif. Postdoctoral intern U. Minn., Mpls., 1978-79, asst. prof., coord. tng. in aging, 1979-83; group v.p. Kiel Profl. Svcs., Inc., St. Paul, 1983-84; pres. Primary Mental Health Care, Inc., Bloomington, Minn., 1984-86, Anderson Health Strategies, LLC, 1996-97; sr. v.p. Treatment Ctrs. Am., Inc., Pasadena, Calif., 1986-88, LifeLink, Inc., Laguna Hills, Calif., 1988—91, chief operating officer, 1989-91; v.p., managed healthcare Columbia Gen., Laguna Hills, 1990-91; sr. v.p. managed health care Coll. Health Enterprises, Huntington Beach, Calif., 1991-94; exec. v.p. Medco. Behavioral Care/Merck Medco., 1994-96; pres., CEO Integra, Inc., 1997—2001, cons., exec. coach, 2001—06; chair health sci. and svcs. Immaculata U., 2006—, assoc. prof. Cons. Ebenezer Soc., Mpls., 1979-82, Wilder Found., St. Paul, 1981-84; rsch. advisor Walden U., Mpls., 1982-86; assoc. prof. Sch. Psychology, Fuller Theol. Sem., Pasadena, 1989; assoc. clin. prof. Widener U., 2000-; adj. prof. Chestnut Hill Coll., Phila., 2005-06. Contbr. articles to profl. jours. Sr. fellow, Sch. Population Studies, THomas Jefferson U., 2009—. Mem.: APHA, APA (conf. participant 1981), Am. Acad. Mgmt., Am. Coll. Healthcare Execs., Union League, Phi Beta Kappa. Avocations: tennis, gardening, bicycling, photography, golf. Address: 715 S Bryn Mawr Ave Bryn Mawr PA 19010-2005 Office Phone: 610-519-1973. Personal E-mail: eanderh@aol.com.

ANDERSON, ESTHER ELIZABETH, retired pediatrician, educator; b. Wabash, Ind., Aug. 6, 1924; d. William Earl Anderson and Marion Christine (Moore) Pelham. AB in Chemistry, Ind. U., Bloomington, 1945; MD, Ind. U. Sch. Medicine, Indpls., 1948. Cert. Am. Bd. Pediatrics, 1955. Intern Ind. U. Med. Ctr., 1948—49, resident in pediat., 1949—51; fellow pediatric tchg. and rsch. La. State U. Sch. Medicine, New Orleans, 1951—53, mem. faculty dept. pediat., subspecialty hematology, oncology, instr., asst. prof., assoc. prof., 1953—74; psychotherapist Primal Ctr., Denver, 1974—77; program mgmt. officer med. care evaluation Indian Health Svc., Aberdeen, SD, 1979—96; ret., 1996. Dir. hematology and oncology rsch. La. State U. Sch. Medicine, 1954—74, dir. heritable disease clinic, 1968—74. Fellow: Am. Acad. Pediatrics; mem.: Am. Coll. Physician Execs., Brown County Med. Soc., Am. Med. Soc., Alpha Omega Alpha. Avocations: music, art, literature, travel, sports. Home: 2023 3d Ave SE Apt 108 Aberdeen SD 57401

ANDERSON, EVA KLAUBER, psychologist, educator; b. Bratislava, Czechoslovakia, June 17, 1935; came to U.S., 1949; d. Gustav C. and Magda M. (Graber) Samak; m. Donald Woolfolk (div.); m. William F. Anderson; 1 child, Adam William. AB, Cornell U., 1957; MA, Syracuse U., 1959, PhD, 1965. Lic. psychologist, N.Y., Md.; Diplomate Am. Bd. Disability Analysts. Sch. psychologist Madison County Schs., N.Y., 1959-63; staff psychologist Children's Psychol. Ctr., Syracuse (N.Y.) U., 1963-65, asst. prof. spl. edn., 1965-66; pvt. practice, Syracuse, 1966-75, Salisbury, Md., 1975—; asst. prof. edn. Salisbury State U., 1975—2005; psychologist, psychiatry dept. Peninsula Regional Med. Ctr., Salisbury; trustee Salisbury Sch., 2005—. Mem. various coms. Md. Dept. Edn., 1975-83; grant evaluator U.S. Dept. Edn., Washington, 1984—. Bd. dirs. Dove Pointe Salisbury, 1984—; mem. parents coun. Wake Forest U., 1985-1989; mem. Mental Health Assn., Salisbury, 1987—. Fellow Md. Psychol. Assn.; mem. Am. Psychol. Assn., Coun. for Exceptional Children., Nat. Register of Health Svc. Providers in Psychology. Home: 715 Burning Tree Cir Salisbury MD 21801-7001 Office: Ste 2 540 Riverside Dr Salisbury MD 21801-5352 Office Phone: 410-548-7883.

ANDERSON, GARLAND D., dean, obstetrician, gynecologist, educator; b. Dec. 11, 1944; MD, U. Tenn. Intern Hermann Hosp., Houston, 1970—71; resident U. Tex. Health Sci. Ctr., Houston, 1971—74; fellow maternal fetal medicine U. Louisville, Ky., 1974—76, instr. ob-gyn. Ky., 1974—75, asst. prof. Ky., 1975—77, med. dir. Teen Alternative Parent Program Ky., 1975—77, assoc. prof. Ky.; dir. resident edn., div. chief Maternal and Fetal Medicine, prof. Dept. Obstetrics and Gynecology U. Tenn. Coll. Medicine, 1978—89; prof. ob-gyn. U. Tenn., 1983—89; prof., chmn. Dept. Ob-gyn. U. Tex. Med. Branch Sch. Medicine, Galveston, 1989—, Jennie Sealy Smith disting. chair ob-gyn., dean, 2006—. Steering com. chair Maternal-Fetal Units Network, Nat. Inst. Child Heath and Human Devel., 2003—06. Contbr. articles to profl. jours. Recipient Nicholas and Katherine Leone Award for Adminstrn. Excellence; named a Tex. Super Doc, Tex. Monthly; named one of Best Doctor for Women, Good Housekeeping mag.; named to Best Doctors in Am. Fellow: Am. Coll. of Obstetricians and Gynecologists (FACOG); mem.: Coun. of Univ. Chairs in Ob-gyn. (pres.), Soc. Maternal and Fetal Medicine (former bd. mem., pres., Award for Rsch. Excellence). Office: Office of Dean of Medicine 301 University Blvd 5 106 Adminstrn Bldg Galveston TX 77555-0133 Office Phone: 409-772-4797, 404-772-4579. Office Fax: 409-772-9598. E-mail: ganderso@utmb.edu. *

ANDERSON, GEORGE KENNETH, medical association administrator, physician, retired military officer; b. Providence, Feb. 17, 1946; s. George Raymond and Mildred (Caster) A.; m. Kimberly Kay Baker, May 18, 1968; children: George D., Ginger K. MD, U. Mich., 1971; MPH, Tulane U., 1973; postgrad., Nat. War Coll., Ft. McNair, Va., 1982-83. Diplomate Am. Bd. Preventive Medicine (chmn. 1991-95), Am. Bd. Med. Mgmt. (bd. dirs.). Intern Wilford Hall USAF Med Ctr., 1971-72; resident USAF Sch. Aerospace Medicine, 1973-75; commd. 2d lt. USAF, 1967, advanced through grades to maj. gen., 1993; comdr. USAF Hosp., Kunsan, Republic of Korea, 1975-76, 86th Tactical Hosp., Germany, 1976-79; mem. faculty USAF Sch. Aerospace Medicine, Brooks AFB, Tex., 1979-82; div. chief Office Surgeon Gen., Bolling AFB, Md., 1983-85, dep. dir., 1985-87; command surgeon Air Force Systems Command, Andrews AFB, Md., 1987-88; dir. med. inspection Air Force ISC, Norton AFB, Calif., 1988-90; comdr. Human Systems Ctr., Brooks AFB, 1990-94; dep. asst. sec. def. Health Svcs. Ops. and Readiness, Washington, 1994; ret. USAF, 1996; pres., CEO Koop Found. Inc., Rockville, Md., 1997-98; exec. v.p. Oceania Corp., Falls Church, Va., 1998-99; pres., CEO Oceania, Inc., Redwood City, Calif., 1999—2005; exec. dir. Assn. of Military Surgeons of U.S., Bethesda, Md. Bd. dir. New World Healthcare Solutions, Washington. Decorated Legion of Merit, Disting. Svc. medal; Koop Found. fellow. Fellow Am. Coll. Preventive Medicine (pres.), Am. Coll. Physician Execs. (disting.), Aerospace Med. Assn. (Julian Ward award 1975); mem. AMA, Air Force Assn. (life). Office: AMSUS 9320 Old Georgetown Rd Bethesda MD 20814-1653 *

ANDERSON, GWENEVERE WINIFRED, nursing educator, researcher; d. Gordon Edward Anderson and Mary Elizabeth Wheeler. PhD, Boston Coll., 1997. RN Alta. Assn. Registered Nurses, 1978. Postdoctoral fellow Stanford U., Ctr. Biomed. Ethics, Calif., 1999—2000; prof., rschr. San Diego State U., 2003—. Achievements include research in paradigm shift from cognitive decision making to holistic model of subjective decision making; international dissemination of genetic nursing practice and education; qualitative research into the cultural, social and ethical impact of genetic technologies on health care services and decision making. Avocation: meditation. Office: San Diego State Univ 5200 Campanile Dr San Diego CA Business E-Mail: gwen.anderson@ubc.ca.

ANDERSON, H. VERNON, medical educator; b. 1951; MS, Stanford U., 1975; MD, Emory U., 1980. Prof. medicine U. Tex. Health Sci. Ctr., Houston, 1990—. Fellow: Soc. Cardiac Angiography & Interventions, Am. Coll. Cardiology (Simon Dack award). Office: 6431 Fannin MSB 1246 Houston TX 77030 Business E-Mail: h.v.anderson@uth.tmc.edu.

ANDERSON, HARRISON CLARKE, pathologist, educator, biomedical researcher; b. Louisville, Sept. 2, 1932; married, 1961. BA in Zoology, U. Louisville, 1954, MD, 1958. Diplomate Am. Bd. Pathology. Pathology intern Mass. Gen. Hosp., Boston, 1958-59; NIH rsch. trainee U. Louisville, Ky., 1959-60; resident in pathology Sloan Kettering Meml. Hosp, NYC, 1960-62; postdoctoral fellow Sloan Kettering Inst., Rye, NY, 1962-63; from asst. prof., assoc. prof. to prof. pathology SUNY Downstate Med. Ctr., Bklyn., 1963-78; prof. pathology, chmn. pathology dept. U. Kans. Med. Ctr., Kansas City, Mo., 1978—90, Harrington prof. orthopedic rsch., 1990—; prof. emeritus pathology, 2002. Mem. study sect. NIH, Bethesda, Md., 1977—81, Bethesda, 1999—2005; chmn. Gordon Rsch. Conf. on Bone, Meriden, NH, 1981. Edit. bd. Am. Jour. Pathology, others, 1981—; contbr. articles to multiple profl. jours. Recipient Biol. Mineralization Research award Internat. Assn. Dental Research, 1985, Sr. Faulty Research award U. Kans. Med. Ctr., 1986, Kappa Delta Orthopedic Rsch. award Orthopedic Rsch. Soc., 1982, Higuchi Biomed. Rsch. award U. Kansas, 1991; NIH rsch. fellow Strangeways Lab., Cambridge, Eng., 1971-72, NIH sr. rsch. fellow in cell biology Yale U., New Haven,, 1984-85; grantee NIH, 1967-2007. Mem. Am. Soc. Investigative Pathologists, Assn. Pathology Chmn. (pres. 1988-90), Am. Soc. Cell Biology, Am. Soc. Bone and Mineral Research, Orthopaedic Research Soc. Clubs: Am. Yacht (Rye); Carriage (Kansas City). Avocations: tennis, skiing, sailing. Office: U Kansas Med Center Dept Pathology 39th & Rainbow Kansas City KS 66160-0001 Home Phone: 816-753-4116. Business E-Mail: handerso@kumc.edu.

ANDERSON, HENRY A., III, public health service officer, state official; b. Wis. MD, U. Wis. Medical Sch., 1972. Diplomate American Bd. Preventive Medicine. State health officer divsn. pub. health Wis. Dept. Health Svcs.; chief med. officer divsn. pub. health Wis. Dept. Health Services, 1980. Adj. prof. population health Univ. Wis. Fellow: American Coll. of Epidemiology. Office: Wisconsin Department of Health Services PO Box 2659 Madison WI 53701-2659 Office Phone: 608-266-9780. Office Fax: 608-267-2832. E-mail: henry.anderson@dhs.wisconsin.gov. *

ANDERSON, HOLLY GEIS, health facility administrator, educator, commentator; b. Waukesha, Wis., Oct. 23, 1946; d. Henry H. and Hulda S. Geis; m. Richard Kent Anderson, June 6, 1969. BA, Azusa Pacific U., 1970. CEO Oak Tree Antiques, San Gabriel, Calif., 1975-82; pres., founder, CEO Premenstrual Syndrome Med. Clinic, Arcadia, Calif., 1982—, Lake Forest, Calif., 2006—10, Irvine, Calif., 2010—, Breast Healthcare Ctr., 1986-89, Hormonal Treatment Ctrs., Inc., Arcadia, 1992-94; with Thyroid Ctr., 2001—. On-air radio personality Women's Clinic with Holly Anderson, 1990—; lectr. in field. Author: (audio cassette) What Every Woman Needs to Know About PMS, 1987, PMS Talk, 1989; (video cassette)The PMS Treatment Program, 1989. Mem. The Dalton Soc., Am. Hist. Soc. of Germans from Russia. Republican. Avocations: writing, genealogy, travel, hiking, boating. Office Phone: 626-447-0679. Personal E-mail: hra3@earthlink.net.

ANDERSON, JAMES ALFRED, cognitive science professor; b. Detroit, July 31, 1940; s. Courtney Alfred and Catherine (Bullock) A.; m. Diana De Vincent, Nov. 1, 1969; 1 child, Eric David; m. Marida Hollos, Dec. 21, 2008. BS, MIT, 1962, PhD, 1967. Postdoctoral fellow UCLA, 1967-71; research assoc. Rockefeller U., NYC, 1971-73; asst. prof. cognitive and linguistic scis. Brown U., Providence, 1973—78, assoc. prof., 1978-85, prof., 1985—, chmn. dept. cognitive and linguistic scis., 1993—2002. Chmn. cognitive functional neurosci. rev. panel NIMH, 1992-94; mem. adv. bd. Social, Behavioral and Econ. Scis. Directorate, NSF, 1996-99; founder Artemis Assocs., Inc., 1989-2004. Editor: (with G. Hinton) Parallel Models of Associative Memory, 1981, (with S. Lehmkuhle and W. Levy) Synaptic Modification, Neuron Selectivity and Nervous System Organization, 1985, (with E. Rosenfeld) Neurocomputing: Some Important Papers, 1988, (with E. Rosenfeld and A. Pellionisz) Neurocomputing 2, 1990, An Introduction to Neural Networks, 1995; (with E. Rosenfeld) Talking Nets, 1998. Recipient Info. Sci. award, Joint Conf. on Info. Sci., 2002; grantee, NSF, 1979, 1985, 1991, 1997, Office Naval Rsch., 1986, 1991, 1996, Def. Advanced Rsch. Projects Agy., 2002. Mem. Cognitive Sci. Soc., Psychonomic Soc., Soc. for Neurosci., Soc. for Math. Psychology, Internat. Neural Network Soc. (governing bd. 1987-95), Sigma Xi. Avocation: amateur radio. Office: Brown U Dept Cognitive & Linguistic Scis 190 Thayer St Providence RI 02912-9067 Home: 9 Creighton St Providence RI 02906 Home Phone: 401-273-2207; Office Phone: 401-863-2195. Business E-Mail: James_Anderson@Brown.edu.

ANDERSON, JAMES GEORGE, sociologist, educator, communications educator; b. Balt., July 24, 1936; s. Clair Sherrill and Kathryn Ann (Plovanich) A.; m. Marilyn Anderson, 1984; children: Robin Marie, James Brian, Melissa Lee, Derek Clair. B in Engring. Scis. in Chem. Engring, Johns Hopkins U., 1957, MSE in Ops. Rsch. and Indsl. Engring., 1959, MAT in Chemistry and Math., 1960, PhD in Edn. and Sociology, 1964. Adminstrv. asst. to dean Eve. Coll., Johns Hopkins U., 1964-65, dir. divsn. engring., 1965-66; rsch. prof. ednl. adminstrn. N.Mex. State U., 1966-70; mem. faculty Purdue U., Lafayette, Ind., 1970—, prof. sociology, 1974—, prof. com., 2004—; asst. dean for analytical studies Sch. Humanities, Social Sci. and Edn., Lafayette, Ind., 1975-78. Assoc. dir. AIDS Rsch. Ctr., Purdue U., 1991—, co-dir. Rural Ctr. for AIDS/STD Prevention, 1993-2006; adj. prof. med. sociology grad. med. edn. program Meth. Hosp. Ind., 1991—; dir. Social Rsch. Inst., Purdue U., 1995-98; cons. in field. Guest editor spl. issue on simulation in health sci.; spl. issues on modeling epidemics: spl. issue on simulation in med. informatics, Jour. the Am. Med. Informatics Assn., 2002, issue on simulation in health care mgmt., Health Care Mgmt. Sci., 2002, 07, issue on performance modeling and simulation in healthcare information systems, Simulation, 2007. Mem. Am. Assn. for Med. Systems and Informatics Del. to the Peoples Republic of China, 1985; mem., citizens amb. People to People Med. Informatics Del. to Hungary and Russia, 1993. USPHS grant; recipient award for outstanding paper Am. Assn. Med. Sys. and Informatics, 1983, Gov. award State of Ind., 1987, T. Hale New Investigators award Assn. Am. Med. Coll., 1988, Wyeth-Ayerst/William Campbell Felch, MD award Alliance for Continuing Med. Edn., 1995, Seeds of Excellence award, Purdue U., 2005. Fellow: Ctr. Edn. and Rsch. in Info. Assurance and Security, Am. Coll. Med. Informatics; mem.: APHA, AAAS (rep. soc. for computer simulation biol. scis. sect. 1992—99), AAUP, Social Sci. Computing Assn. (chair life scis. 1991—), Am. Sociol. Assn. (chair sect. sociology and computers 2000—01), Internat. Soc. Sys. Sci. in Health Care, Internat. Network for Social Network Analysis (chair life scis. 1997—), Soc. Modeling and Computer Simulation (sr.; assoc. v.p. simulation in health care 1992—), Am. Med. Informatics Assn. (internat. affairs com. 1993—96, chmn. sect. ethical, legal and social issues 1997—2000, mem. editl. bd. 2000—, guest editor 2002, chmn. sect. on quality improvement 2002—04, sci. program com. ann. conf. 1999, 2003, 2005, 2008, Best Theoretical Paper award 1997), Am. Ednl. Rsch. Assn. (treas. spl. interest group 1969—71), Am. Sociol. Assn., Assn. for Computing Machinery. Business E-Mail: andersonj@purdue.edu.

ANDERSON, JAMES LINWOOD, pharmaceutical sales official; b. Bangor, Maine, June 8, 1949; s. Linwood Lamont and Helena May (Armitage) A.; m. Susan Grace Hughey, Aug. 23, 1974 (div. Aug. 1994). BS in Biology and Premedicine, U. Maine, 1971, MS in Physiology, 1972. Narcotics officer Maine State Police/Drug Enforcement Agy., 1973-74; sales rep. Wallace Labs., 1974-76, Hoechst-Roussell, Somerville, N.J., 1976-84; pharm. sales rep. I Miles (Bayer) Pharms., New Haven, 1984-90, ter. sales specialist, 1990-91, hosp. sales specialist, 1991-93, pharm. sales rep. II, 1994—2004; sr. sales rep. Schering-Plough Pharms., 2005—09; owner E-Z Rider Limo Svcs. Inc., 2009—. Mem. academic coun. London (England) Diplomatic Acad., 2003—. Coord. pastoral affairs Calvary Bapt. Ch., Manchester, N.H., 1976-80; mem. acad. coun. London Diplomatic Acad., 2003—. Mem. USCG Aux. (flotilla comdr. New Bedford, Mass. 1992-94, divsn. capt. S.E. Mass. 1994-96, rear commodore Mass. and R.I. 1996-97, vice commodore for Maine, N.H., Mass., R.I. and part of Vt. 1998-99, dist. commodore 2000-2001, immediate past dist. commodore 2002-2003, chmn. dist. awards com. 2002-2003, coord. internat. search & rescue games adminstrn. logistics 2001, vice chair internat search & rescue adminstn. & logistics 2003-04, chmn. internat. search and rescue competition 2005-07), Order of DeMolay (master councilor 1965-66, state master councilor 1966-67, chevalier 1967—). Avocations: boating, gun collecting. Home: 877 Tucker Rd North Dartmouth MA 02747

ANDERSON, JAMES MILTON, securities trader; b. Chgo., Dec. 29, 1941; s. Milton H. and Eunice (Carlson) A.; m. Marjorie Henry Caldwell, Jan. 22, 1966; children: James Milton, Joseph H., Hilding F., Marjorie H. BA, Yale U., New Haven, Conn., 1963; JD, Vanderbilt U., Nashville, 1966. Bar: Ohio 1967. Assoc. firm Taft, Stettinius & Hollister, Cin., 1968-75, ptnr., 1975-77, 82-96, mem. exec. com., 1975-77, 91-96; pres. US ops., dir. Xomox Corp., Cin., 1977—82, sec. Access Corp., 1984-96; asst. sec. Carlisle Companies Inc., 1985-90; bd. trustee Cincinnati Children's Hospital Medical Center, 1979, chmn., 1991—96, pres., CEO, 1996—2009, spl. advisor to pres. Michael Fisher, 2009—; chmn. National Stock Exchange, Inc., 1980-89, 2007—. Bd. dirs. Command Sys. Inc., 1986—2002; trustee, chmn. Monarch Found., 1988—; assoc. sr. v.p. med. affairs U. Cin., 1997—; bd. adminstrs. Coun. Tchg. Hosps., 2000—04; dir. Nat. Assn. Children's Hosps. and Related Instns., 2002—08; bd. dirs. 3CDC Inc., 2003—, Uptown Consortium, 2004—, Union Ctrl. Life Ins. Co., 2002—06; chmn. bd. dirs. Cin. br. Fed. Res. Bank Cleve., 2005—; mem. US Medicaid Commn., 2005—06; bd. dirs. UNIFI Mutual Holding Co., 2006—, Inst. for Healthcare Improvement, 2007—, NSX Holdings, Inc., 2007—, Meridian Biosci., 2009—. Mem. Indian Hill Coun., 1981-89, vice-mayor, 1985-87, mayor, 1987-89; mem. Hamilton County Airport Authority, 1980-85; trustee The Children's Hosp. Found., 1990—, chmn. bd. trustees, 1990-93; trustee Cin. Ctr. for Devel. Disorders, 1969—2001, pres., 1974-80; trustee Dan Beard coun. Boy Scouts Am., 1982—, chmn., 1984-87, area pres. Ea. Ctrl. Region, 1989-91; trustee Cin. Mus. Natural History, 1984-87, Coll. Mt. St. Joseph, 1990-98; trustee Joy Outdoor Edn. Ctr., 1984-2000, pres., 1991-93, chmn., 1993-95. Capt. AUS, 1966-68. Decorated Bronze Star with two oak leaf clusters, Air medal; recipient Human Relations award, American Jewish Com. (Cin. Chapter), 2005. Mem. ABA, Ohio Bar Assn., Cin. Bar Assn., Valve Mfrs. Assn., Young Pres. Orgn., Camargo Club, Queen City Club, Commonwealth Club, Yale Club of N.Y., Cin. Yale Club, Order of Coif, Comml. Club. Avocation: sailing. Office: National Stock Exchange Inc 101 Hudson St Ste 1200 Jersey City NJ 07302 Office Phone: 201-499-3700. Office Fax: 201-499-0174. Personal E-mail: janderson@cincinnatichildrens.org. *

ANDERSON, JAMES WINGO, physician; b. Hinton, W.Va., Aug. 6, 1936; s. Fred Wingo and Georgia Lee (Whittaker) A.; m. Gay Veree Gilbert, June 7, 1957; children: Katherine, Steven. BS, W.Va. U., 1957; MD, Northwestern U., 1961; MS, Mayo Clinic, 1965. Intern Presbyn. Med. Ctr., Denver; resident, fellow Mayo Clinic, Rochester, Minn.; asst. prof. medicine U. Calif., San Francisco, 1968-73; prof. medicine, clin. nutrition U. Ky. Coll. Medicine, Lexington, 1973—; pres., founder HCF Nutrition Found., Lexington, 1979—. Author: Diabetes-A Practical Guide to Healthy Living, 1981, Dr. Anderson's High Fiber Fitness Plan, 1994, Dr. Anderson;s Antioxidant Antiaging, 1996. Trustee Georgetown (Ky.) Coll., 1988—, chmn. bd. trustees, 1994-96. Capt. U.S. Army, 1965-68. Fellow Am. Coll. Physicians. Republican. Baptist. Home: 913 Taborlake Ct Lexington KY 40502-3032 Home Phone: 859-269-6642; Office Phone: 859-422-4671.

ANDERSON, JEFFREY LANCE, cardiologist, educator; b. Salt Lake City, Oct. 27, 1944; s. Aldon Jr. and Virginia (Weilenmann) A.; m. Kathleen Tadje, Aug. 18, 1967; children: Russell, Nathan, Derek, Megan. BA magna cum laude, U. Utah, 1968; MD cum laude, Harvard U., 1972. Diplomate Am. Bd. Internal Medicine, Am. Bd. Cardiovascular Diseases, Am. Bd. Cardiac Electrophysiology. Resident in internal medicine Mass. Gen. Hosp., Boston, 1972-74; staff assoc. NIH, Bethesda, Md., 1974-76; fellow in cardiology Stanford U., Calif., 1976-78; asst. prof. medicine U. Mich., Ann Arbor, 1978-80, U. Utah, Salt Lake City, 1980-83, assoc. prof. medicine, 1983-89, prof. medicine, 1989—, prof., internal medicine; assoc. chief, cardiology LDS Hosp., Utah. Presenter in field. Author over several med./sci. papers in field; author, editor of several book chpts. and books in field; contbr. articles to profl. jours. Recipient numerous fed., local and indsl. grants, 1980—. Mem. ACP (gov. 1993—), Am. Coll. Cardiology (gov. 1986-88), Am. Heart Assn. (pres. Utah chpt. 1985). Mem. Lds Ch. Achievements include first randomized trial to show benefit of thrombolytic therapy in heart attacks, to show possible benefit of beta blockers in heart failure; investigation of land mark cardiac arrhythmia suppression trial; development of multiple pharmacologic agents to treat arrhythmias, heart attacks, heart failure. Home: 4474 Crest Oak Dr Salt Lake City UT 84124-3823 Office: LDS Hosp 8th Ave C St Salt Lake City UT 84143-0001

ANDERSON, JOAN BALYEAT, theology studies educator, minister; b. Cin., Apr. 14, 1926; d. Hal Donal and Myrtle (Skinner) Hukill Balyeat; m. Jerry William Anderson, Jr., Sept. 13, 1947: children: Katheleen, Diane. AA, Stephens Coll., 1946. Ordained Christian minister Ohio, 1988. Christian ch. bible tchr., Cin., 1944—; Christian counselor, advisor, 1964—; founder, pres., dir., ruling elder, and pastor Loving God Complete Bible Christian Ministries and First Ch., Cin., 1988—. Christian Bible tchr., preacher, pastor daily and Sunday radio throughout the east and midwest, 1988—, world wide internet, 2006—. Mem. Am. Conservative Cause, 1998—2001, Capitol His. Soc., 2000—; legacy leader supporter George Washington's Mt. Vernon, 2001—; coord., collector Heart Fund, T.B., 1948—90; civic assn. officer, rep. edn. com. to all Madeira Schs., 1960—62; co-founder, officer Grassroots, Inc., Cin., 1962—65; mem. Cin. Art Mus., 1972—, Cin. Zoo, 1974—, Colonial Williamsburg Found., 1979—, Nat. Right to Life, 1980—, MADD, 1985—, Heritage Found., 1996—, Am. Conservative Union, 1998, Ronald Reagan Presdl. Found., 1998—, Parents TV Coun., 1998—2001, Am. Policy Ctr., 1998—2001, US Justice Found., 1998—, Nat. Right to Work Legal Def. Found., 1998—, Nat. Security Ctr., 1998—, US Intelligence Ctr., 1998—, Jud. Watch, 1999—, Young Ams. Found., 2000—; supporter The Liberty Com., 2001—; lifelong activist for preservation of US Constn. and Bill of Rights; mem. US Rep. Senatorial Adv. Com., Washington, Cin., 1987—88, Rep. Senatorial Commn., Washington, Cin., 1996—2000, Am. Prayer Network, 1998—. Master: Blue Book of Cin. Avocation: travel. Home: 7208 Sycamorehill Ln Cincinnati OH 45243-2101 Office: Loving God Complete Bible Christian Mins/1st Ch PO Box 43404 Cincinnati OH 45243-2101 Office Phone: 513-271-0940.

ANDERSON, JOHN ALBERT, physician; b. Ashtabula, Ohio, Jan. 25, 1935; s. Albert Gunnard Anderson and Martha Anetta (Bieshline) White; m. Nicole Jeanne Anderson, July 10, 1963; children: Carole, John-Marc, Christopher B. BS, U. Ill., 1958, MD, 1960. Diplomate Am. Bd. Pediat., Am. Bd. Allergy and Immunology. Intern U. Ill., 1960-61, resident in pediat. Chgo., 1961-62, U.S. Naval Hosp., Bethesda, Md., 1964-65; fellow in allergy and immunology Children's Hosp., Washington, 1967-69; mem. sr. staff Henry Ford Hosp., Detroit, 1969-99, dir. pediat. allergy fellowship program, 1969-77, dir. allergy and immunology program, 1977-99, head divsn. allergy and immunology, dept. pediatrics, 1977-99, chmn. dept. pediatrics, 1982-90; physician Vivra Asthma and Allergy, Tucson, 1999-2000; with Vivra Asthma and Allergy, Inc., 2000—02; physician Allergy and Asthma Ctr. Ariz., Tucson, 2001—03, Aspen Med. Ctr., Fort Collins, Colo., 2003—05, Allergy and Asthma Care Ariz. PLLC, Yuma, 2006—. Clin. prof. U. Mich., Ann Arbor, 1985—94; prof. pediat. Case Western Res. U., 1994—99; dir. Am. Bd. Allergy and Immunology, 1990—96, sec., 1995—96. Contbr. articles Contbr. more than 60 articles to profl. jours. Lt. comdr. USN, 1962-66. Fellow Am. Acad. Allergy, Asthma and Immunology (pres. 1990-91), Am. Acad. Pediat. (chmn. allergy sect. 1979-82), Am. Coll. Allergy, Asthma & Immunology, Mich. Allergy Soc. (pres. 1978-79); mem. Asthma and Allergy Found. Am. (dir. 1992-99, v.p. med. affairs 1992-95, v.p. rsch. 1995-99), Coun. Med. Splty. Socs. (bd. dirs. 1992-94), Am. Bd. Med. Specialists, Sci. Advisors Internat. Life Scis. (allergy sect. 1990-2003). Home: 1609 S 42d Ave Yuma AZ 85365 Office: Allergy and Asthma Care Ariz PLLC 2110 W 24th Ste C Yuma AZ 85364 Office Phone: 928-344-2300.

ANDERSON, KATHRYN V., developmental biologist, educator; BA in biochemistry, U. Calif., Berkeley, 1973; MS in neurosciences, Stanford U., 1975; PhD in biology, UCLA, 1980. Postdoctoral fellow in devel. genetics Max Planck Inst., Germany, 1981—84; asst. prof. molecular and cell biology U. Calif., Berkeley, 1985—90, assoc. prof. molecular and cell biology, 1990—93, prof. molecular and cell biology, 1993—96; prof. Cornell U. Grad. Sch. Med. Sciences, 1996—; mem. molecular biology prog. Meml. Sloan-Kettering Cancer Ctr., NYC, 1996—2002, mem., chair develop. biology prog., 2002—. Genetics study sect. NIH, 1999—2003; mem. Searle Scholar Adv. Panel, 2003—, Damon Runyon Scholar Panel, 2003—. Fellow: AAAS, Am. Acad. Arts and Sciences; mem.: NAS, Soc. Devel. Biology (pres. 1998—99), Inst. Medicine, Phi Beta Kappa. Office: Meml Sloan-Kettering Cancer Ctr 1275 York Ave New York NY 10065 Office Phone: 212-639-6485, 212-639-6543. Office Fax: 646-422-2355. E-mail: k-anderson@ski.mskcc.org.

ANDERSON, KENNETH CARL, hematologist, educator; b. Worcester, Mass., Oct. 3, 1951; s. Kenneth R. and Helen L. Anderson; m. Cynthia Ellen Bird; children: Emily, David, Peter. BA summa cum laude, Boston U., 1973; MD, Johns Hopkins U., Balt., 1977. Diplomate Am. Bd. Internal Medicine, lic. Md., Mass. Intern medicine Johns Hopkins Hosp., 1977-78, resident, 1978—80; clin. fellow medicine Harvard Med. Sch., Boston, 1980-83, instr. medicine, 1983-84, asst. prof., 1985-91, assoc. prof., then prof., 1992—, Kraft Family prof. medicine, 2002—. Clin. fellow med. oncology Dana-Farber Cancer Inst., Boston, 1980—83, fellow tumor immunology, 1981—83, clin. assoc. med. oncology, 1983—85, med. dir. Blood Component Lab., 1984—, chief divsn. hematologic neoplasias, dir. Jerome Lipper Multiple Myeloma Ctr.; jr. assoc. physician Brigham and Women's Hosp., Boston, 1983—85, attending physician bone marrow transplantation, 1984—88; vis. prof. dept. pathology U. Pa. Sch. Medicine, 1991; Joseph R. Bove vis. prof. transfusion medicine Yale U. Sch. Medicine, 1994. Editor (with P.M. Ness): Scientific Basis of Transfusion Medicine: Implications for Clinical Practice, 1994; assoc. editor European Jour. Haematology, mem. editl bd. American Jour. Hematology, Transfusion Sci., Jour. Clin. Oncology, Blood, Jour. Clin. Investigation, European Jour. Cancer & Clin. Oncology, New Eng. Jour. Medicine; contbr. articles to profl. jours. Bd. dirs. Internat. Myeloma Found. Recipient Jr. Faculty Rsch. award, American Cancer Society, 1986—89, Robert A. Kyle Lifetime Achievement award, Internat. Myeloma Found., 2005. Mem.: AAAS, ACP, AMA (Physician's Recognition award), Inst. Medicine, Soc. Hemopheresis Specialists, Mass. Med. Soc., Mass. Assn. Blood Banks (Morten Grove-Rasmussen Meml. award 1994), American Assn. Blood Banks, American Soc. Hematology, Alpha Phi Omega, Phi Beta Kappa, Sigma Xi. Achievements include focus on translational research in multiple myeloma resulting in important new therapies for treatment; development of anti-tumor vaccines as well as ex vivo expansion of allogeneic and autologous antigen specific T cells, for allografting and autografting respectively; discovery of new treatment targets of the tumor cell and its bone marrow microenvironment. Office: Dana Farber Cancer Inst Mayer Bldg 557 44 Binney St Boston MA 02115-6084 Office Phone: 617-632-2144. Business E-Mail: kenneth_anderson@dfci.harvard.edu. *

ANDERSON, LINDA JEAN, critical care nurse, psychiatric nurse practitioner; b. Louisville, Ky., Mar. 28, 1956; d. James Phillip and Ellabelle Jean Anderson; children: Bradley, Vanessa, Frances, Joseph; m. Donald W. Goodman. BSN, U. Louisville, 1989, MSN, 2000; postgrad. in health care adminstrn., Kennedy Western U., 2005—. ARNP, Ky., Ind. Staff nurse Audubon Regional Med. Ctr., Louisville, 1989-90, Southwest Hosp., 1990-2000, Ctr. for Behavioral Health Bapt. East Hosp., 1996-2000; nurse clinician Vis. Nurses Assn. Louisville, 1990-95; rsch. coord. electrophysiology-cardiology U. Louisville, 1993-94, psychiat. clin. coord. Healthcare U. Hosp., 2000—02; pvt. practice Park View Psychiat. Svc., Jeffersonville, Ind., 2002—05, N.A. Saddiqui & Assocs., Louisville, 2005—07, Med. Staffing Resources, 2007, Humana Military Svcs., 2007—. Mem. alumni bd. govs. U. Louisville Sch. Nursing, 1988-97. Mem. ANA, Internat. Soc. Psychiatric Nursing, Kentuckiann Coun. Psychiatric Nursing, Am. Psychiat. Nurses Assn., Sigma Theta Tau. Avocations: watercolor painting, charcoal & pencil sketching.

ANDERSON, LINDA MARIE, nursing educator; b. Manly, NSW, Australia, July 5, 1963; Diploma in Edn., Curtin, 1985; BSN with honors, James Cook U., 2007. Specialist svc. officer Australian Army, 1990—2010, course mgr., army med. techician tng., 2011—. Recipient Nursing Excellence prize, James Cook U., 2006, medal, 2007. Mem.: Royal Australian Coll. Nursing, Golden Key. Office: Army Sch Health Army Logistic Training Ctr Latchford Barracks BONEGILLA VIC 3693 Bonegilla Victoria 3693 Australia Personal E-mail: andofam@hotmail.com.

ANDERSON, LLOYD LEE, physiologist, educator; b. Nevada, Iowa, Nov. 18, 1933; s. Clarence and Carrie G. (Sampson) A.; m. Janice G. Peterson, Sept. 7, 1958 (dec. Dec. 1966); m. JaNelle R. Hall, June 15, 1970; children: Marc C., James R. Student, Simpson Coll., 1951-52, Iowa State U., 1952-53, BS in Animal Husbandry, 1957, PhD in Animal Reproduction, 1961; DSc (hon.), Georgian Acad. Scis., Tbilisi, 2003. NIH postdoctoral fellow Iowa State U., Ames, 1961-62, asst. prof., 1961-65, assoc. prof., 1965-71, prof. animal sci., 1971—, Charles F. Curtiss Disting. prof. agr. & life scis., 1992—, sect. leader, animal physiology, 1974—2011, chmn. com. on coms., faculty senate, 2000—02, prof. biomed. sci., 2002—. Lalor Found. fellow Sta. Recherches Physiologie Animale, Inst. Nat. Recherche Agronomique, Jouy-en-Josas, France, 1963—64; rschr. physiology of reprodn. and ctrl. nervous sys.-pituitary regulation of growth for increased prodn. efficiency of farm animals; mem. reproductive biology study sect. NIH, 1984—88, NIH Reviewers Res. (NRR), 1988—92; vol. reviewer NIH Ctr. Sci. Review, 2010—; mem. peer rev. panel animal health spl. rsch. grants on beef and dairy cattle reproductive diseases USDA, 1986—88; Honor lectr. representing Iowa State U. Mid-Am. State Univs. Assn., 1989—90; mem. sustainable growth agrl. panel USDA, Agrl. Rsch. Svc., Nat. Program Staff to rev. rsch. projects, 1993; mem. referees panel for sponsored rsch. Kuwait U., 1998—; mem. Janice Peterson Anderson Excellence award and scholarship Coll. of Design Iowa State U., chair com. on coms., Faculty Senate, 2000—02; trustee Asian Inst. Nanobiosci. and Tech., Busan, Republic of Korea, 2002—; mem. selection com. for recipient of George E. Palade Gold Medal and Lecture award Wayne State U. Sch. Medicine, 2003—, mem. selection com. for recipient of Ahmed H. Zewail Gold Medal and Lecture award, 2008—; hon. mem. sci. coun. Georgian Inst. Physiology, 2003—; mem. competitive grants rev. bd. NSF, 2006—, Georgian NSF, 2006—; mem. Pres. Cir. Order Knoll Iowa State U. Found., 2006—. Mem. editl. bd. Biology Reprodn., 1968-70, 86-90, Jour. Animal Sci., 1982-87, 98-2001, Animal Reprodn. Sci., 1978—, Inst. for Sci. Info. Atlas of Sci., 1987-90, Domestic Animal Endocrinology, 1992-95, 2004-06, Endocrinology, 1993-97, Jour. Cellular and Molecular Medicine, 2005-; guest editor, Cell Secretion Rev. Series, 2006-, Basic & Clin. Pharm. & Toxicology, 2010-, Jour. Steroids & Hormonal Sci., 2010-; contbr. articles to profl. jours. Mem. 4-H Club, Pres. Circle, Order of the Knoll, Iowa State University Found., With Constrn. Engrs., U.S. Army, 1953-55, Germany, Signal Corps USAR, 1955-61, vol. reviewer NIH Ctr. Sci. Review, 2010-. Recipient Cert. Recognition, Cold War, 1991, Disting. Achievement award, Iowa State U. Alumni Assn., 2005, Golden Diploma in recognition of 50th anniversary of graduation, 2007, 50 Yrs. Mem., 25 Yrs. Club, 2009, dedication, Little N.Am. Livestock Show, 2006, Cert. Recognition, State of Iowa, House of Rep., 2008, Disting. Scientist award, Iowa Acad. Scis., 2011; grantee, USDA, 1978—, Nat. Pork Bd., 1992—; Iowa Biotech. grant, 1986—89. Fellow AAAS, Am. Soc. Animal Sci. (hon. Animal Physiology and Endocrinology award 1988, Nat Pork Prodrs. Coun. Innovation award in basic rsch. 1993, Outstanding Achievement in Rsch. award 2001, Animal Growth and Devel. award 2004, F.B. Morrison award 2007); mem. NRA, VFW (gold cir. mem. 2011), Endocrine Soc., Am. Physiol. Soc., Iowa Physiol. Soc., Am. Assn. Anatomists, Am. Soc. Cell Biology, Soc. Study of Reprodn., Soc. Exptl. Biology and Medicine (mem. coun. 1980-83), Brit. Soc. for Study of Fertility, Soc. Neurosci., Iowa Acad. Sci. (Disting. Iowa Scientist award 2011), Pituitary Soc., Asian Inst. of Nanobiosci. and Tech., Busan, Korea (trustee 2002—), Nano Bio Sci. Inst. Wayne State U. Sch. Med. Detroit(adv. bd. mem. 2004-), Am. Legion, Nat. Block and Bridle Club, Osborn Rsch. Club (chair 1994), Iowa Pork Prodrs. Assn., Nat. Pork Bd. Nutritional Efficiency Consortium, Sigma Xi (Recognition Golden Anniversary mem. 1960-2010), Gamma Sigma Delta (Mission award in rsch. 2002, Alumni Merit award 2004, Disting. Achievement in Agr. award 2008), Alpha Tau Omega (Gold Cir. award 2002), Internat. Atomic Energy Agy.(US Advisor expert 2008-), Global Alliance Internat. Advancement(round table group cons. 2008-, sci. adv. bd. mem. 2008-, cons. reuters insight team 2008-), Iowa State U. Meml. Union (life). Roman Catholic. Home: 2812 Valley View Rd Ames IA 50014-4506 Office: Iowa State U Dept Animal Sci 2356 Kildee Hl Ames IA 50011-3150 Office Phone: 515-294-5540. Business E-Mail: llanders@iastate.edu.

ANDERSON, MARGARET ELLEN, physiologist, educator; b. Omaha, June 17, 1941; d. Clarence Lloyd and Anita Emma (Kruse) A. BA, Augustana Coll., Sioux Falls, SD, 1963; PhD, Stanford U., 1967. NIH postdoctoral fellow Harvard U., 1968—70; rsch. assoc. Lab. Neurobiology, U. P.R., 1970—71; vis. asst. prof. Clark U., 1972; asst. prof. Bennington (Vt.) Coll., 1973, Smith Coll., Northampton, Mass., 1973—79, assoc. prof. dept. biol. scis., 1979—85, prof., 1985—, dean sr. class, 1993—96, acting dir. Office Grad Study, 1997—98. Mem. Bingham award selection com. Transylvania U., Lexington, Ky., 1987-94, 97-98. Assoc. editor Advances in Physiology Edn., 1988-92; contbr. articles to sci. jours., including Tissue and Cell, Jour. Gen. Physiology. NSF predoctoral fellow Stanford U., 1967; rsch. grantee NIH, 1974-86, NSF, 1989-90. Mem. Am. Physiol. Soc., Soc. for Neurosci., Soc. Gen. Physiologists, Biophys. Soc. Office: Smith Coll Dept Biol Sci Northampton MA 01063-0001 Business E-Mail: manderso@smith.edu.

ANDERSON, MARK E., cardiac electrophysiologist, educator; MD, U. Minn., 1989. Diplomate Am. Bd. Internal Medicine, 2005, Am. Bd. Internal Medicine-cardiovasc. disease, 2005. Resident internal medicine Stanford Univ. Med. Ctr., 1990—91; fellow cardiovasc. disease Stanford Univ., 1991—94, fellow cardiac electrophysiology, 1994—96; prof. medicine and physiology Univ. of Iowa, head dept. of internal medicine, assoc. dir. cardiovasc. rsch. ctr. Co-author: (publs.) Calmodulin kinase determines calcium-dependent facilitation of L-type calcium channels., 2000, Calmodulin kinase II is required for proarrhythmic defects in Timothy Syndrome., 2008, Calmodulin kinase II is required for fight or flight sinoatrial node physiology., 2009, numerous publs. Dir. Fondation Leducq Transatlantic Network. Mem.: Assn. of Am. Physicians, Am. Heart Assn. (established investigator), Am. Soc. of Clin. Investigation. Office: University of Iowa 200 Hawkins Dr rm SE308 GH Iowa City IA 52242-1081 Office Phone: 319-353-7101.

ANDERSON, MARTIN MATHEW, pediatrician, educator; b. Kingsburg, Calif., Dec. 14, 1953; m. Enid Gruber, Oct. 23, 1982; 1 child, Dane. BS in Genetics, with honors, U. Calf., Davis, 1976; MD, U. Calif., Davis, 1980; MPH, U. Calif., Berkeley, 1984. Diplomate Am. Bd. Pediat., cert. in adolescent medicine. Intern adolescent medicine Mott Children's Hosp./U. Mich., Ann Arbor, 1980—81, resident pediat., 1981—83; fellow adolescent medicine U. Calif., San Francisco, 1984-86; asst. prof. pediat. NY Med. Coll., Valhalla, 1986-88, asst. prof. preventive & cmty. medicine, 1987-88; asst. clin. prof. pediat. UCLA Med. Ctr., 1988-95, assoc. clin. prof. pediat., 1995—, adj. assoc. prof. pub. health, 1995—. Attending physician UCLA Matenal Child Immunology Clinic, 1992—. Fellow: Am. Acad. Pediat.; mem.: N.Am. Soc. Pediatric & Adolescent Gynecology, Soc. Adolescent Medicine, Am. Pub. Health Assn. Office: UCLA Childrens Health Ctr 200 Med Plaza Ste 265 Los Angeles CA 90095 Office Phone: 310-825-5744, 310-825-0867.

ANDERSON, MICHAEL ROBERT, pediatrician, educator; b. Detroit, Dec. 7, 1963; BS in Chemistry, cum laude, John Carroll U., Cleve., 1986; MD, Case Western Res. U., Cleve., 1990. Diplomate Am. Bd. Pediat., cert. in pediatric critical care medicine. Resident Children's Hosp. Mich., Detroit, 1990—93; fellow Rainbow Babies & Children's Hosp., Cleve., 1993—96, dir. pediatric critical care fellowship prog., 1997—; instr. pediat. Case Western Reserve U. Sch. Medicine, 1996—98, asst. prof. pediat., 1998—2007, assoc. prof. pediat., 2007—; v.p., assoc. chief med. officer Univ. Hosp.'s, Cleve., 2008—. Rsch. com. Rainbow Babies & Children's Hosp., 1997—2000, faculty adv. Rainbow residency, 1998—, pediatric resuscitation com., 1998—, intern recruitment com., 1998—, rsch. com., 2000—03, med. dir. PALS prog., 2002—, edn. com., 2003—; emergency svcs. com. Univ. Hosp.'s Health System, 1998—2000, PNT-Nutrition sub-com., 1999—2002; preceptor phys. diagnosis course Case Western Res. U., 1998—, mentor, 1998—2003; pediatric instl. review bd. U. Hosp. Cleve., 2001—03; chair pediatric resuscitation com. MetroHealth Med. Ctr., 2003—; regional physician's EMS adv. bd. Ohio State EMS Bd., Dist. 9, 2003—; mem. expert panel pediatric subspecialty capacity HHS, 2003; vice chair Nat. Commn. Children & Disasters, Washington, 2008—. Recipient Sanford Cohen Outstanding Resident award, Rainbow Babies & Children's Hosp., 1993, Pediatric Pearls Tchg. award, 2000, 2003, 2004, Tchg. award, MetroHealth Med. Ctr., 2004; named Clinic Resident of Yr., Children's Hosp. Mich., 1993. Mem.: AMA (RPS del. 1994—95), Am. Acad. Pediat. (ann. program chair young physicians sect. 1998—2002, mem. steering com. young physicians sect. 1998—, mem. com. pediatric workforce 1999—, chair com. pediatric workforce 2004—). Office: Rainbow Babies & Childrens Hosp Case Western Res U 11000 Euclid Ave Cleveland OH 44106 Office Phone: 216-844-3310. Office Fax: 216-844-5122. Business E-Mail: mxa35@case.edu.

ANDERSON, NORMAN B., health science association administrator, psychologist, educator; b. Greensboro, NC, 1955; m. P. Elizabeth Anderson, 1986. BA in psychology, NC Ctrl. U., 1976; MA in clin. psychology, U. NC, Greensboro, 1979, PhD in clin. psychology, 1983. Assoc. prof. psychiatry and psychology Duke U., 1991—93; assoc. dir. NIH, Bethesda, Md., founding dir., Office of Behavioral and Social Sciences Rsch., 1995—2000; prof. health and social behavior Harvard U. Sch. Pub. Health, 2000—02; CEO, exec. v.p. APA, Washington, 2003—. Co-author (with P. Elizabeth Anderson): Emotional Longevity: What Really Determines How Long You Live, 2003; co-editor: Expanding the Boundaries of Health and Social Sciences, 2003; editor: Encyclopedia of Health and Behavior, 2004. Fellow: AAAS, APA (CEO, exec. v.p. 2003—, Outstanding Contributions to Health Psychology award 1991), Assn. Psychol. Sci., Acad. Behavioral Medicine Rsch., Soc. Behavioral Medicine (pres. 1998—99). Office: APA 750 First St Washington DC 20002-4242 Office Phone: 202-336-5500. *

ANDERSON, PATRIK, hematologist; b. Uddevalla, Sweden, Sept. 16, 1963; children: Patricia, Alexandra. MD, U. Gothenburg, 1988. Cert. internal medicine Swedish Nat. Bd. Health and Welfare, 1998, hematology Swedish Nat. Bd. Health and Welfare, 2001. Physician hematology sect. Inst. Internal Medicine, Sahlgrenska U. Hosp. Ostra, Gothenburg, Sweden, 1997—2002; sr. physician internal medicine Hosp. So. Älvsborg, Skene, Sweden, 2002—. Contbr. articles to profl. jours. Mem.: European Hematology Assn., Swedish Soc. Medicine, Swedish Med. Assn., Swedish Soc. Palliative Medicine, Gothenburg Soc. Medicine, Swedish Soc. Hematology, Swedish Soc. History of Medicine, Am. Soc. Hematology, Swedish Soc. Internal Medicine. Home: Bjorkasgatan 6 Mölndal SE-43131 Sweden Office: Hosp Southern Älvsborg Dept Internal Medicine Skene SE-51181 Sweden Office Fax: +46-320-779069; Home Fax: +46-31-7034355. Personal E-mail: phacit@yahoo.com. Business E-Mail: patrik.anderson@vgregion.se.

ANDERSON, PAUL NATHANIEL, oncologist, educator; b. Omaha, May 30, 1937; s. Nels Paul E. and Doris Marie (Chesnut) A.; m. Dee Ann Hipps, June 27, 1965; children: Mary Kathleen, Anne Christen. BA, U. Colo., 1959, MD, 1963. Diplomate Am. Bd. Internal Medicine, Am. Bd. Med. Mgmt., Am. Bd. Med. Oncology. Intern Johns Hopkins Hosp., Balt., 1963-64, resident in internal medicine, 1964-65, fellow in oncology, 1970-72; rsch. assoc., staff assoc. NIH, Bethesda, Md., 1965-70; asst. prof. medicine, oncology Johns Hopkins U. Sch. Medicine, 1972-76; attending physician Balt. City Hosps., Johns Hopkins Hosp., 1972-76; dir. dept. med. oncology Penrose Cancer Hosp., Colorado Springs, Colo., 1976-86; clin. asst. prof. dept. medicine Colo. Sch. Medicine, 1976-90, clin. assoc. prof., 1990—. Dir. Penrose Cancer Hosp., 1979-86, chief dept. medicine, 1985-86; founding dir. Cancer Ctr. of Colorado Springs, 1986-95, Pikes Peak Forum for Health Care Ethics, 1996—, Rocky Mountain Cancer Ctr., Colorado Springs, 1995—; med. dir. So. Colo. Cancer Program, 1979-86; pres., chmn. bd. dirs. Preferred Physicians, Inc., 1986-92; mem. Colo. Found. for Med. Care Health Stds. Com., 1985, sec., exec. com., 1990, bd. dirs., pres., 1992-93; mem., chmn. treatment com. Colo. Cancer Control and Rsch. Panel, 1980-83; prin. investigator Cancer Info. Svc. of Colo., 1981-87; pres., founder Timberline Med. Assocs., 1986-87, Oncology Mgmt. Network, Inc., 1985-95. Editor Advances in Cancer Control; editl. bd. Jour. Cancer Program Mgmt., 1987-92, Health Care Mgmt. Rev., 1988—; contbr. articles to med. jours. Mem. Colo. Gov.'s Rocky Flats Employee Health Assessment Group, 1983-84; mem. Gov.'s Breast Cancer Control Commn. Colo., 1984-89; founder, dir. So. Colo. AIDS project, 1986-91; mem. adv. bd. Colo. State Bd. Health Tumor Registry, 1984-87; chmn., bd. dirs. Preferred Physicians, Inc., 1986-92; bd. dirs. Share Devel. Co. of Colo. Share Health Plan of Colo., 1986-90, vice chmn., 1989-91; bd. dirs., chmn. Preferred Health Care, Inc., 1991-92; mem. health care stds. com., trustee colo. Found. for Med. Care (PRO); mem. nat. bd. med. dirs. Fox Chase Cancer Ctr. Network, Phila., 1987-89; mem. tech. expert panel Harvard Resource-Based Relative Value Scale Study for Hematology/Oncology, 1991-92. With USPHS, 1965-70, chmn. Elpaso County Med. Soc. Med. Ethics Com., 2004, co-chmn. Colo. Med. Soc. Coun. Ethics & Legal Affairs, 2004-, mem. penrose Hosp. Credentials Com., 1984-, Picker Peak Forum Health Care, 1992- Mem. AMA (mem. practice parameters forum 1989-97, adv. com. to HCFA on uniform clin. data set), AAAS, Am. Coll. Forensic Examiners, Am. Soc. Clin. Oncology (chmn. subcom. on oncology clin. practice stds., mem. clin. practice com., rep. to AMA 1991—, mem. healthcare svcs. rsch. com., chmn. clin. guidelines subcom. 1993—), Am. Assn. Cancer Rsch., Am. Assn. Cancer Insts. (liaison mem. bd. trustees 1980-82), Am. Coll. Physician Execs., Am. Hospice Assn., Am. Soc. Internal Medicine, Nat. Cancer Inst. (com. for cmty. hosp. oncology program evaluation 1982-83), Colo. Soc. Internal Medicine, Assn. Cmty. Cancer Ctrs. (chmn. membership com. 1980, chmn. clin. rsch. com. 1983-85, sec. 1983-84, pres.-elect 1984-85, pres. 1986-87, trustee 1981-88), N.Y. Acad. Scis., Johns Hopkins Med. Soc., Colo. Med. Soc., Am. Mgmt. Assn., Am. Assn. Profl. Cons., Am. Soc. Quality, Am. Acad. Med. Dirs., Am. Coll. Physician Execs., El Paso County Med. Soc., Rocky Mountain Oncology Soc. (chmn. clin. practice com. 1989-94, pres.-elect 1990, pres. 1993-95), Acad. Hospice Physicians, Coalition for Cancer, Colorado Springs Clin. Club, Alpha Omega Alpha. Office: 32 Sanford Rd Colorado Springs CO 80906-4233 Home Phone: 719-471-4581, 719-312-3807; Office Phone: 719-577-2555, 719-577-2553. Personal E-mail: anderpna@aol.com. Business E-Mail: paul-anderson@usoncology.com.

ANDERSON, PORTER WARREN, JR., retired pediatrics educator; b. Corinth, Miss., Jan. 1, 1937; BA, Emory U., 1958; MA, Harvard U., 1962, PhD, 1967. Rsch. trainee Oak Ridge Nat. Lab., Tenn., 1957; asst. chemist tropical rsch. dept. Uited Fruit Co., Lima, Honduras, 1959-61; faculty mem. dept. chemistry Stillman Coll., Tuscaloosa, Ala., 1966-68; rsch. assoc. infectious diseases The Children's Hosp. Med. Ctr., Boston, 1968-77; asst. prof. microbiology & molecular genetics Harvard U., Cambridge, Mass., 1972-75, assoc. prof., 1975-77; assoc. prof. dept. pediatrics & microbiology U. Rochester (N.Y.) Sch. Medicine & Dentistry, 1977-87, prof., 1987-95, prof. emeritus, 1995-96; ret., 1996. Recipient Lasker-DeBakey Clin. Med. Rsch. award, Lasker Found., 1996. Mem.: NAS. *

ANDERSON, PRUDENCE FOX, Christian science practitioner; b. Wilkensburg, Pa., Apr. 9, 1943; d. Clarence Cole and Mildred Charlotte Ives. BA, Principia Coll., Elsah, Ill., 1965. Internat. negotiator NOAA, Washington, 1967—99; Christian Sci. practitioner Washington, 2004—; mem. Exec. Com. Assn. Pupils Herbert E. Rieke, CSB, 2010—. Bd. trustee Adams Morgan CS Ch., 2010—11. Recipient Bronze medal, U.S. Dept. of Commerce, 1999. Mem.: Principia Club (sec. 1995—2009). Achievements include aided in concluding agreements on international trade in endangered species, whale conservation through the Internationl Whaling Commission; elimination of foreign fishing in the U.S. 200 mile zone; conservation of fish and marine species and trade measures for conservation objectives. Home and Office: 219 Zodiac Ct Walkersville MD 21793 Personal E-mail: pruelewis@aol.com.

ANDERSON, RACHEL L., healthcare educator, researcher; life ptnr. Alba Nydia Quinones, June 12, 1999; 1 child, Isolina Catherine Quinones Anderson. BA in Psychology, Beloit Coll., Wis., 1987; MA in Human Devel. and Social Policy, Northwestern U., Evanston, Ill., 1995, PhD in Human Devel. and Social Policy, 1997. Post-doctoral fellowship in mental health and policy rsch. Rutgers U., New Brunswick, NJ, 1997—99; asst. prof. Coll. Pub. Health, U. Iowa, Iowa City, 1999—2005, assoc. prof., 2005—, Coll. Nursing, U. Iowa, Iowa City, 2000—; assoc. dir. Nat. Health Law and Policy Resource Ctr., U. Iowa, Iowa City, 2004—; assoc. prof. Coll. Law, U. Iowa, Iowa City, 2005—; dep. dir. Iowa Health and Disability Resource Ctr., Iowa City, 2005—07; dir. Mental Health Svcs. and Policy Collaborative, 2007—; editl. bd. Residential Treatment for Children & Youth, 2005—. Editl. bd. Open Area Studies Jour., 2008—, Open Pub. Health Jour., 2008—. Contbr. chapters to books, articles to profl. jours. Mem. psychiatric epidemiology/biochemistry tng. program steering com. U. Iowa, 2000—02; adv. bd. mem. strengthening cmtys. for youth U. Iowa Ctr. Addiction Rsch./Adolescent Health and Resource Ctr., 2003—06; Steering and comprehensive plan com. mem. Mental Health Transform Project, State Iowa, Divsn. Health Disability Svc., 2007—08; bd. mem. Women in Sci. and Engring., Iowa City, 2004—06, Johnson County Empowerment Bd., Iowa City, 2005—06; mem. consortium on comm. based outcomes Mgmt. Children Mental Health Northern U., Chgo., 2002—; adv. bd. mem. Romanian Health and Social Issues Ctr., 2007—08; mem. working group mental health and mental disorders State of Iowa, 2004—05, mem. lt govs. com. mental health and development disabilities, 1999—2003, bd. mem. mental health forum, 1999—2003. Recipient New Investigator Rsch. award, Coll. Pub. Health and Coll. Medicine, U. Iowa, 2000—01, Coll. Pub. Health Tchg. award, U. Iowa, 2002, Faculty Tchg. award, 2003; grantee, State of Iowa, 2002—, NIH, 2003—; fellow Mentoring and Edn. Program in Mental Health Svcs., Nat. Inst. Mental Health, 2001—03. Mem.: APA, Assn. Psychol. Sci. Avocations: kayaking, wine collection, travel, history. Office: Univ Iowa College Public Health 200 Hawkins Dr E 202 GH Iowa City IA 52242 Office Fax: 319-384-7095. Business E-Mail: rachel-anderson@uiowa.edu.

ANDERSON, RALPH ROBERT, endocrinologist, educator; b. Fords, NJ, Nov. 1, 1932; s. Harry Walter and Johanna Katherine (Damgaard) Anderson; m. LaVeta Ann Phillips, Jan. 28, 1961; children: Richard, Laura. BS, Rutgers U., 1953, MS, 1958; PhD, U. Mo., 1961. Rsch. asst. Rutgers U., 1957-58, U. Mo., Columbia, 1958-61, instr. dairy sci. (endocrinology), 1961-62, from asst. prof. to assoc. prof., 1965—72, prof., 1976—97, prof. emeritus, 1997—. Asst. prof. Iowa State U., Ames, 1962—64; rschr. in field. Editor, co-editor: 6 books; contbr. articles to profl. jours., chapters to books. With US Army, 1954—56. Recipient Grad. Tchg. Merit award, U. Mo. chpt. Gamma Sigma Delta, 1982, Rsch. award, 1994, Cook Disting. Alumni award, Rutgers U., 1997; NIH Endocrinology Postdoc. fellow, U. Wis., 1964—65, Fulbright-Hays Sr. Rsch. fellow, New Zealand, 1973—74. Mem.: Sigma Xi (sec.-treas. U. Mo. chpt. 1981—83, pres. 1984—85). Presbyterian. Office: University Mo Animal Sci Rsch Ctr Columbia MO 65211-0001

ANDERSON, RICHARD MCLEMORE, internist; b. Gainesville, Fla., Mar. 3, 1930; s. Montgomery Drummond and Myrtle (McLemore) A.; m. Leewood Shaw, Mar. 21, 1959; children: Richard McLemore Jr., Bruce Dexter. BS, U. Fla., 1951; MD, Emory U., 1958. Diplomate Am. Bd. Internal Medicine. Chief of staff Alachua Gen. Hosp., Gainesville, Fla., 1973-75; internist Gainesville, Fla., 1962—. Chmn. of bd. Santa Fe Health Care, Gainesville, 1984-91, bd. dirs. Pres. Rotary Club of Gainesville, 1980-81. Capt. USAF, 1951-54. Mem. AMA, ACP, Alachua County Med. Soc. (v.p. 1972), Fla. Med. Assn. Presbyterian.

ANDERSON, ROBERT E., diagnostic radiologist; MD, U. Minn., 1965. Diplomate Am. Bd. Radiology-diagnostic radiology, 1970. Intern Hennepin County Med. Ctr.; resident diagnostic radiology Univ. of Minn. Med. Ctr., Minneapolis, 1966—69; hosp. affiliation includes Orlando South Seminole Hosp. Office: Orlando South Seminole Hospital 1300 S Orange Ave Orlando FL 32806-2113 Office Phone: 407-423-2581.

ANDERSON, ROSS BARRETT, healthcare environmental services manager; b. Toronto, Ont., Can., Aug. 25, 1951; arrived in US, 1956; s. John Ross and Constance (Nielson) A.; m. Gladys Jeanette Vincent, Aug. 26, 1972; children: Christopher Matthew, John Ross II, Josiah Dan. Student, Boston U., 1970-73. Housekeeping supr. Parker Hill Med. Ctr., Roxbury, Mass., 1973-76; acct. mgr. Servicemaster Inc., 1973—; housekeeping mgr. Union Hosp., Lynn, Mass., 1976-77, Quincy (Mass.) City Hosp., 1977-78, St. Joseph's Hosp., Lowell, Mass., 1978-79, Waltham Weston Hosp. and Med. Ctr., Waltham, Mass., 1979-86, support services mgr., 1986-90, dir. environ. svcs., 1991-93, chmn. customer svcs. bd., 1992; asst. dir. clin. engring. Good Samaritan Med. Ctr., Stoughton/Brockton, Mass., 1993-95; dir. environ. svcs. Harrington Meml. Hosp., Southbridge, Mass., 1995—. Mem. Boston Latin Sch. Assn., Scots Charitable Soc. Boston, First Congl. Ch., Pomfret, Conn. Avocations: football, softball. Home: 133 Old Town Rd Ashford CT 06278-2020 Office: Harrington Meml Hosp 100 South St Ste 1 Southbridge MA 01550-4047 Business E-Mail: anderson-ross@aramark.com.

ANDERSON, SANDRA DOREEN, medical researcher; b. Sydney, Dec. 10, 1941; PhD, U. London, 1972, DSc, 1990. Prin. hosp. scientist Royal Prince Alfred Hosp., 1979—2009, part time prin. hosp. scientist, 2009—. Clin. prof. Sydney Med. Sch., 2008—11. Recipient Rsch. medal, Royal Prince Alfred Hosp.; Project grants, Nat. Health and Med. Rsch., 1986—2005. Fellow: Australia and New Zealand Soc. Respiratory Sci.; mem.: Am. Thoracic Soc., European Respiratory Soc., Thoracic Soc. Australia and New Zealand (Fisons medal). Achievements include research in asthma and exercise-induced asthma and a treatment to enhance clearance of secretions in patients with cystic fibrosis and bronchiectasis. Avocations: gardening, opera, theater. Home: PO Box 87 Balmain NSW 2041 Australia Business E-Mail: sandya@mail.med.usyd.edu.au.

ANDERSON, STEPHEN C., diagnostic radiology, educator; MD, U. Md., 1984. Diplomate Am. Bd. Radiology-diagnostic radiology, 1988. Fellow ultrasound, CT and MRI Duke Univ., Durham, 1988—89; resident diagnostic radiology Univ. South Fla., Tampa, 1984—88, asst. clin. prof. Coll. of Medicine. Office: University of South Florida School of Medicine 12901 Bruce B. Downs Blvd Tampa FL 33612

ANDERSON, STUART CHARLES, dean, educator; b. Birkenhead, Merseyside, Eng., Oct. 7, 1946; s. Eric Charles and Nora Anderson; m. Margaret Elizabeth Goodwill, Sept. 19, 1981; children: Claire Elizabeth, Richard Charles, Martin Stuart. BSc, U. Manchester, Eng., 1969; MA, U. London, 1983, PhD, 2000. Formulation pharmacist Beecham Rsch. Labs., Worthing, England, 1969—73; info. pharmacist Royal Alexandra Hosp., Rhyl, Wales, 1973—74; prin. pharmacist Aldey Hey Children's Hosp., Liverpool, England, 1974-78; chief pharmacist Westminster Hosp., London, 1978-83; dir. pharmacy svcs. St. George's Hosp., London, 1983-93; lectr. pharmacy practice Sch. Pharmacy U. London, 1993—95; rsch. fellow London Sch. Hygiene and Tropical Medicine, 1995-96, course dir. pub. health and policy, 1996-2000, dir tchg. programme, 2000—01, sr. lectr., 2001—05, assoc. dean studies, 2007—; academic dir. Nat. Coordinating Ctr. for NHS Svc. Delivery and Orgn. Rsch. Programme, London, 2005—07. Chair Soc. Social History Medicine, Oxford, England, 2001—05; pres. Brit. Soc. History Pharmacy, London, 2002—05, TropEd, European Network Edn. Internat. Health Tropical Edn., Berlin, 2004—05. Author: (book) Managing Pharmaceuticals in International Health, 2004; editor: (books) Studying the Organization and Delivery of Health Services, 2004, Making Medicines: A Brief History of Pharmacy and Pharmaceuticals, 2005. Recipient Merck Sharpe and Dohme award, Abbott Labs. award 1991, Evans Gold medal Guild of Hosp. Pharmacists, London, 1994; fellowship Baxter Travenol, 1984, ICI Travelling fellow Guild of Hosp. Pharmacists, Australia, 1986, med. fellow Coun. of Europe, Stockholm, 1991; Sonnedecker Residency fellow Am. Inst. History of Pharmacy, 1996, George Urdang medal, Am. Inst. History Pharmacy, 2011, Leslie Matthews medal, British Soc. History Pharmacy, 2011. Fellow Royal Pharm. Soc. (Eng.), Higher Edn. Acad.; mem. Soc. Social History Medicine (former chair 2001-05), Brit. Soc. History Pharmacy (former pres. 2002-05), Am. Inst. History Pharmacy, Internat. Acad. History Pharmacy (pres. 2005-). Office: London Sch Hygiene and Tropical Medicine Keppel St London WCIE 7HT England Office Fax: 02076366164. Business E-Mail: stuart.anderson@lshtm.ac.uk.

ANDERSON, THOMAS, orthopedist, consultant; s. Thea and Hans Anderson; children: Rebecka Anderson-Bodare, Max Anderson-Bodare. MD, Karolinska Institutet, Stockholm, 1982. Diplomate Nat. Soc. for Health and Welfare, 1989. Intern Sundsvall County Hosp., Sweden, 1983—84, resident dept. orthop., 1984—89, cons. dept. orthop., 1989—94; cons. Kalmar County Hosp., Sweden, 1994—99; cons. dept. orthop. Malmo U. Hosp., Malmo, Sweden, 1999—. Contbr. articles to profl. jours. Fellow: Swedish Foot Surgeons Soc. (sec. 1999—2003); mem.: Swedish Orthop. Soc. Avocations: golf, travel, wine and food, skiing. Office: Malmo University Hosp Dept Orthops 205 02 Malmö Sweden Office Fax: +46-40-33 62 00. E-mail: thomas.anderson@skane.se.

ANDERSON, URSULA M., retired pediatrician; b. Cheshire, Eng., 1929; MB BS, Liverpool U., Eng., 1953, diploma in Pub. Health, 1956; diploma in Psychol. Medicine, London U., 1958; diploma in Child Health, Royal Coll. Physicians, London. Diplomate Am. Bd. Pediats. Intern and resident Liverpool United Tchg. Hosps., 1953—57; fellow dept. pediatrics Yale U., New Haven, 1960—63; assoc. prof. pediats. SUNY, Buffalo; dir. maternal and child health Buffalo/Erie County; med. dir. interagy. programs for children, regional med. cons. U.S. Dept. Health, Edn. and Welfare; chief divsn. cmty. pediats., assoc. prof. pediats U. Toronto, Ont., Canada; disting. prof., rsch. prof. Forest Inst. Profl. Psychology. Cons. divsn. rsch. WHO, Geneva; cons. Nat. Perinatal Assn., National and Regional Head Start Programs; chmn. N.Y. State Task Force on Health Manpower, Albany, NY; mem. pediat. delegation to USSR People to People. Author: Reading Instruction, Dimensions and Issues, 1968, Weeds and Seedlings, 1992, The Psalms of Children, Their Songs and Laments, 1997, Immunology of the Soul, The Paradigm for the Future, 2000, Taking Out the Violence, 2003, Who and Where is God The Journey That Led Humanity to Violence; contbr. articles to profl. jours. Recipient Merit of Excellence award, UN Open U., Great Minds 21st Century award, Internat. Bio Ctr., Internat. Peace prize, United Cultural Convention, 2011; nominee Hon. award; grantee numerous grants for rsch. edn. and svc., U.S. and Can.; fellow, Royal Soc. Medicine, Great Britain. Fellow: Am. Acad. Pediats.; mem.: Royal Coll. Surgeons. Mailing: 8275 Crumb Hill Rd East Otto NY 14729-9748

ANDERSON, WAYNE KEITH, dean, educator; b. Pine Falls, Manitoba, Can., Apr. 1, 1941; s. Sigward Emmanuel and Verna Madelaine Anderson; m. Ellen Lorraine Robertson, Aug. 31, 1962; children: Brian Ross, Laura Elizabeth, Shari Lynn. BS in Pharmacy, U. Manitoba, 1962, MS, 1964; PhD, U. Wis., 1968. Asst. prof. to prof. medicinal chemistry SUNY Buffalo, 1968-81, prof. medicinal chemistry, 1981—, prof. chemistry, 1993—, assoc. chmn. medicinal chemistry, 1994-95, dean Sch. Pharmacy & Pharm. Scis., 1995—. Contbr. articles to profl. jours. Mem.: NY State Pharmacy Coun. (sec. 1997—98, chmn. 1998—2000), Pharmacists Assn. Western NY, Pharmacists Soc. NY, Am. Pharm. Assn., Am. Chemical Soc., Am. Assn. Colleges of Pharmacy. Achievements include patents for anticancer drugs. Avocations: genealogy, fishing, hockey, golf, travel. Office: SUNY Sch Pharmacy & Pharm Scis 126 Cooke Hall Buffalo NY 14260-1300 Office Phone: 716-645-2823. Office Fax: 716-645-3688.

ANDERSSON, GUNNAR BENGT JOHAN, orthopedist, educator; Student, U. Zurich, Switzerland; MD, U. Göteborg, Sweden, 1967, PhD, 1974. Diplomate Am. Bd. Orthopaedic Surgery, lic. Ill. Resident dept. orthopaedic surgery Boras Hosp., Sweden, 1968—69, Sahlgren Hosp., Göteborg, 1969—73; resident dept. gen. surgery Molndal Hosp., Sweden, 1974—75; assoc. prof. dept. orthopaedic surgery U. Göteborg, 1975—84, acting chmn. dept. orthopaedic surgery, 1980—81; prof. dept. orthopaedic surgery Rush Med. Coll., Chgo., 1985—, vice-dean surg. scis. & svcs., 2000—02, sr. v.p. med. affairs, 2002—04; William A. Hark & Susanne G. Swift prof. & chair orthopedic surgery Rush Univ. Med. Ctr., 1995—2008, Ronald L. DeWald prof. spinal deformities, 2008—. Fellow dept. orthopaedic surgery London Hosp., England, 1971; vis. assoc. prof. materials engring. U. Ill., Chgo., 1976—77; vis. asst. prof. orthopaedic surgery Rush-Presbyn.-St. Luke's Med. Ctr., 1976—77, disting. vis. prof., 1982—83, assoc. chmn. dept. orthopaedic surgery, 1986—94, acting chmn., 1994—95; ptnr. Midwest Orthopaedics, Chgo., 1985—, mng. ptnr., 1992—2002. Contbr. articles to profl. jours. Bd. dirs. Swedish Am. Mus. Ctr., 1987—93, bd. trustees, 1997—. Recipient SIROT award, Brazil, 1981, Hiker award, Cent. States Occupational Med. Assn., 1994, Russel S. Hibbs Basic Sci. award, Scoliosis Rsch. Soc., 2006; named a Top Doc., Chgo. Mag., 2009. Mem.: AAAS, AMA, Am. Coll. Physician Execs., MidAmerica Orthopaedic Soc., Spine Soc. Australia, Internat. Soc. Study of Lumbar Spine (pres. elect 1988—89, pres. 1989—90, Stryker Spine Lifetime Achievement award 2002), Am. Inst. Med. & Biological Engring., Swedish Orthopaedic Soc. (LIC award 1982), Scandanavian Orthopaedic Soc., Orthopaedic Rsch. Soc. (treas. 1992—95, program com. 1995—98, program com. chmn. 1998, pres. elect 1999, pres. 2000), N.Am. Spine Soc. (chmn. afilliate mem. com. 1992—95, chmn. sci. rsch. com. 1996—97, chmn. rsch. planning com. 1997—2002), Intradiscal Therapy Soc. (bd. dirs. 1990—92), Internat. Back Pain Soc., Internat. Soc. Biomechanics (Muybridge Medal 1989), Internat. Soc. Electrophysiological Kinesiology (sec. 1976—80, v.p. 1980—84, pres. 1985—89), Euro. Orthopaedic Rsch. Soc., Clin. Orthopaedic Soc., Clin. Orthopaedic Rsch. Soc., Assn. Am. Med. Colleges, Am. Acad. Disability Evaluating Physicians, Am. Soc. Biomechanics, Am. Orthopaedic Assn., Am. Acad. Orthopaedic Surgeons, Am. Orthopaedic Soc. Office: Rush Univ Med Ctr Dept Orthopedic Surgery 1471 Jelke 1653 W Congress Pkwy Chicago IL 60612 Office Phone: 312-942-4867. Office Fax: 312-942-2101. Business E-Mail: Gunnar_Andersson@rsh.net.

ANDERSSON, STEIN, psychologist; b. Mosvik, Norway, Apr. 27, 1958; Candidate in Psychol., U. Oslo, 1985, PhD, 2000. Neuropsychologist Sunnaas Rehab. Hosp., 1989—2003; head sect. neurocognition Oslo U. Hosp. Rikshospitalet, 2003—. Assoc. prof. U. Bergen, 2008. Fellow, Norwegian Rsch. Coun. Mem.: Norwegian Psychol. Assn., Norwegian Neuropsychiatric Assn., Norwegain Neuropsychol. Soc. Office: Oslo University Hosp Rikshospitalet Oslo 0424 Norway Office Phone: 47 23074164. Business E-Mail: stein.andersson@rikshospitalet.no.

ANDO, MIKAYO, psychologist; b. Shizuoka City, Shizuoka, Japan, 1966; d. Reiichi and Etsuko Sato; m. Shinichiro Ando. MA in Psychology, Chukyo U., Japan, 1991; MS in Devel. Psychology, Johns Hopkins U., 2000, MPH, 2002; PhD in Edn., Tokyo Gakugei U., 2005. Cert. Clin. Psychologist Japanese Cert. Bd. for Clin. Psychologist, 1993, Psychologist Japanese Psychol. Assn., 2004, Med. Psychologist Japanese Soc. for Psychosomatic Medicine, 2005. Clin. psychologist Fujieda Mcpl. Gen. Hosp., Fujieda, Shizuoka, Japan, 1989—97; rsch. fellow Prevention Rsch. Br., Divsn. of Epidemiology, Stats. and Prevention Rsch., Nat. Inst. of Child Health and Human Devel., Nat. Inst. of Health (NIH), Bethesda, Md., 2000—01; clin. psychologist Tokyo Met. Health and Med. Treatment Corp., Shinjuku, Tokyo, Japan, 2004—07; rsch. scientist Tokyo Gakugei U., Koganei, Tokyo, Japan, 2005—07; assoc. prof. Okayama U., 2007—. Recipient Seisho Sukemune, Bruce Bain Encouragement of Early Career Rsch. award, Internat. Coun. of Psychologists, 2005, Japanese Jour. Sch. Health award, Japanese Assn. Sch. Health, 2010; grantee, The United Grad. Sch. of Edn. Tokyo Gakugei U., 2002—03, Japan Soc. Promotion Sci., 2006, 2009—. Mem.: APA, Internat. Rorschach Soc., Internat. Assn. Applied Psychology, Assn. Japanese Sand Play Therapy, Assn. Japanese Psychosomatic Medicine, Assn. Japanese Drawing Test and Therapy, Assn. Japanese Criminal Psychology, Assn. Japanese Clin. Psychology, Assn. Japanese Child and Adolescent Psychiatry, Japanese Soc. Health Edn., Japanese Psychol. Assn., Japanese Assn. Sch. Health, Japanese Assn. of Ednl. Psychology, Japan Diabetes Soc., Internat. Soc. for Quality of Life Rsch. Achievements include development of psychoeducational program to prevent aggressive behavior among Japanese adolescents; psychoeducational intervention on patients with diabetes mellitus. Office: Okayama University Divsn Psychology & Clin Edn 3-1-1 Tsushimanaka Kita-ku Okayama 700-8530 Japan

ANDO, TETSUYA, physician, researcher; b. Fukuoka, Japan, May 23, 1960; MD, Kyushu U., 1986, PhD, 1995. Divsn. chief in stress rsch. NIMH, Nat. Ctr. of Neurology and Psychiatry, 1998—. Mem.: Japan Soc. Eating Disorders, Japanese Soc. Psychosomatic Medicine. Avocation: tennis. Office: 4-1-1 Ogawahigashi-cho Kodaira Tokyo 187-8553 Japan Office Fax: 042-346-1957. Business E-Mail: ando-t@ncnp.go.jp.

ANDRADE, FILIPE MOREIRA DE, thoracic surgeon, educator; b. Ubá, Minas Gerais, Brazil, June 30, 1979; MD, Fluminense Fed. U., 2005, PhD, 2011. Prof. Fluminense Fed. U., 2009—. Fellow, vis. prof. U. Ala. Avocation: running. Home: Rua Visconde do Rio Branco 755 Apt 812 Niterói RJ 24020-006 Brazil Personal E-mail: filipeandrade_torax@hotmail.com.

ANDRADE, JERUSA ALECRIM, medical doctor; b. Corumbá, Mato Grosso do Sul, Brazil, July 15, 1965; d. Ademar Araújo and Geny Alecrim Andrade. Medicine, Fed. U. Mato Grosso, Cuiabá - Mato Grosso - Brazil, 1991; MS, Autonomous U. Barcelona, 1995. Specialization in acupuncture U. Barcelona, 1993. Med. acupuncture specialist Alecrim Clinic, Campinas, São Paulo, Brazil, 1999—; voluntary rschr. State U. Campinas UNICAMP, 2000—05; predoc. fellow Autonomous U. Barcelona, 2000—. Contbr. articles to profl. jours. Mem.: Soc. Acupuncture Rsch., Internat. Headache Soc., Acupuncture Med. Coll., Brasilian Headache Soc. Achievements include research in acupuncture playing to prevent migraine attacks. Office: Clín Alecrim Rua Rafael Sampaio 428 Campinas São Paulo 13023-240 Brazil Office Phone: 55 19 3242 1492. Office Fax: 55 19 3242 1492. Business E-Mail: jerusa@alecrim.med.br.

ANDRAU, MAYA HEDDA, retired physical therapist; b. Digboi, Assam, India, Apr. 15, 1936; came to U.S., 1946; d. William Henry and Klara Irén Judit (Sima) Andrau; married, Sept. 1971 (div. July 1989); children: Francis Meher Traver, Darwin Meher Traver. BS Phys. Therapy, Columbia U., 1958; MA Social Anthropology, NYU, 1966. Lamaze cert. childbirth educator; lic. and phys. therapist. Phys. therapist Beekman-Downtown Hosp., NYC, 1959—60; physiotherapist Stamford Hosp., Conn., 1963—64, Benedictine Hosp., Kingston, NY, 1966—69; pvt. practice in phys. therapy and lamaze Woodstock, NY, 1968—71; chief phys. therapist No. Duchess Hosp., Rhinebeck, NY, 1970—71; phys. therapist Waccamaw Pub. Health Dist. S.C. Dept. Health, Myrtle Beach, 1982—84; pain clinic specialist Pain Therapy Ctr. of Columbia, Richland Meml. Hosp., SC, 1986—87; phys. therapist Comprehensive Med. Rehab. Ctr., Conway, SC, 1988—92; phys. therapist, instr. conditioning program Pawleys Island Wellness Inst., SC, 1993; phys. therapist Total Care, Inc., North Myrtle Beach, SC, 1993—97. Instr. phys. conditioning and therapeutic exercise courses, 1980—97; instr. conditioning program Health Focus Brief for TV, 1990; pvt. phys. therapist and instr. Conditioning-Wellness Program UNCA (Coll. for Srs.), Asheville, NC, 1998, Asheville-Buncombe Tech. C.C., Asheville, 1999, Blue Ridge C.C., Flat Rock, NC, 1999—2000, Elderhostel, Montreat, NC, 1999, 2001, 2003—06, 2007, 2008—10, Crescent View Retirement Cmty., Arden, NC, 2001; tchr. conditioning wellness, phys. therapist, Meherabad, India, 04, Meherabad, 06, Meherabad, 2009—10. Mem. Meher Spiritual Ctr., Inc., Alpha Kappa Delta. Follower of Avatar Meher Baba. Avocations: gardening, reading, walking, handwork, singing. Office Phone: 828-236-9196.

ANDRE, CLAUDE JACQUES, medical researcher, consultant; b. Arlon, Belgium, Feb. 6, 1942; m. Françoise Crismer. MD, Liege U. Belgium, 1966; diploma in Animal Physiology, DEA U., 1968, Claude Bernard U., Lyon, 1969, PhD, 1981. Med. sci. dir. Stallergenes, Antony, France, 1992—2005, sr. cons., 2006—. Home: 2 Le Mirabeau 69450 Saint-Cyr-au-Mont-d'Or France Office Phone: 33155592087. Personal E-mail: claude.andre23@orange.fr.

ANDRE, NICOLAS PIERRE MARIE, medical educator, consultant; b. Nancy, Oct. 11, 1969; MD, U. Marseille, 2000, PhD. Asst. prof. Faculté de Médecine de Marseille, 2007—; sr. cons. AP-HM, 2011—. Pres. Société Francophone de Recherche en Pédiatrie, 2009—; founder Metronomics Global Health Initiative, 2011. Mem.: Innovative Therapeutics Children Cancer, Societé Française de lutte contre les cancers de l'enfant. Office: Bd Jean Moulin Marseille Bouches du Rhone 13005 France E-mail: nicolas.andre@ap-hm.fr.

ANDRE, PIERRE, dermatologist; b. Paris, Feb. 10, 1949; m. Pascale Meyer, June 27, 1992; children: Raphael, Julia. Cert. in dermatology U. Paris, 1981, in internal medicine Paris U., 1984. Resident medicine Clermont U., France, 1975—81, chef clinique, 1983—85; resident medicine Laval U., Que., Canada, 1979—80; clin. rsch. fellow UCLA, 1982—83. Sci. dir. Anti-Aging World Congress. Mem.: SFD, ESLD, ESCAD, EADV, ISDS, AAD. Avocations: golf, skiing, painting. Office: Paris Univ Laser Skin Clinic 157 Rue de L Universite 75007 Paris France E-mail: pandre2@noos.fr.

ANDRE, SÉBASTIEN, medical educator; b. Paris, May 20, 1974; MS, U. Pierre & Marie Curie, 1999, PhD, 2002. Assoc. prof. U. Pierre & Marie Curie, 2009—. Recipient award, Assn. pour la Recherche contre le Cancer, 2003, CSL Behring Prof Heimburger award, 2008; scholarship, French Ministry, 1999—2002. Mem.: French Soc. Immunology. Avocation: mountain climbing. Office: UMRS872 Team 16 CRC 15 rue de l Ecol Paris 75006 France E-mail: sebastien.andre@crc.jussieu.fr.

ANDREACCHIO, ANTONIO, orthopedist, department chairman; b. Bari, Italy, Feb. 1, 1958; MD, U. Milan, 1984, degree in Orthop. Surgery, 1989. Chmn., paediatric orthop. dept. Regina Margherita Children's Hosp., 2007—. Rsch. fellow, paediatric orthops. Alfred I duPont Inst. Wilmington, Del., 1997; prof., paediatric orthop. Residency Program U. Turin, 2003—11. Mem.: Italian Sarcoma Group, Am. Acad. Cerebral Palsy and Devel. Medicine, Italian Paediatric Orthop. Soc., European Paediatric Orthop. Soc. Avocation: soccer. Office: Piazza Polonia 94 Torino 10126 Italy Office Fax: 39-011-3135092. Personal E-mail: a.andreacchio@libero.it.

ANDREANI, DOMENICO VINCENZO, endocrinologist, educator; b. Taranto, Italy, Mar. 5, 1925; s. Fortunato and Michelina Ligonzo Andreani; m. Elena Buccisano, Feb. 28, 1960; children: Paola, Cristiana, Emanuela, Saverio, Romana. MD, U. Pisa, Italy, 1948. Intern U. Pisa Clinica Medica, 1948-56; asst. prof. medicine U. Rome Clinica Medica, 1956-69; prof. therapeutics Cath. U., Rome, Italy, 1967-72; prof. endocrinology & metabolism La Sapienza U., Rome, Italy, 1972-2000, prof. emeritus, 2000—. Former editor-in-chief Diabetes/Metabolism Rev., 1991-95; co-editor book procs. Recipient Commendator of Merit Italian Republic, Rome, 1964, Commendator of Holy See, Order of St. Gregory the Great, 1964, M. Derot Prize Assn. Diabetologie Francaise, Paris, 1992, Claude Bernard Prize European Assn. Study Diabetes, London/Dusseldorf, 1993, Roma Europea prize, 1997, Gold Medal for Sci., Italian Govt., 2000. Fellow: Royal Soc. Medicine (London); mem.: Italian Soc. Diabetology, Dem. Found. (pres. Rome), Royal Acad. Medicine Belgium (corr.), Am. Soc. Endocrinology (hon.), European Assn. Study of Diabetes (hon.; pres. 1983—86), Am. Diabetes Assn. (hon.), European Thyroid Assn. (corr.), Italian Soc. Internal Medicine, Italian. Soc. Endocrinology (pres. 1988—90). Office: Foundation DEM Largo Marchiafava 1 00161 Rome Italy Home: Viale di Villa Grazioli 3 198 Rome RM Italy Personal E-mail: domenico.andreani@fastwebnet.it.

ANDREANO, RALPH LOUIS, economist, educator; b. Waterbury, Conn., Apr. 11, 1928; s. John and Loretta (Creasia) A.; m. Carol Jean Wessbecher, Sept. 5, 1955 (dec. 2003); children: Maria Carol, Nicholas George. AB, Drury Coll., 1952; MA, Washington U., St. Louis, 1955; MA Fulbright scholar, U. Oslo, Norway, 1952-53; PhD, Northwestern U., 1961. Instr. econs. Northwestern U., 1959-60; asst. prof. econs. Earlham Coll., 1961, asso. prof., chmn. dept., 1962-65; asst. prof. bus. adminstrn. Harvard Bus. Sch., 1961-62; Brookings Nat. Research prof., 1964-65; asso. prof. econs., dir. undergrad. program econs. U. Wis., 1965-67, prof., 1967—, dir. Health Econs. Research Ctr., 1969-87, chmn. dept. econs., 1980-83, dir. Ctr. for Devel.; emeritus prof. econs., 1994—. Ofcl. del. Am. Econ. Assn. to Am. Council Learned Socs., 1964-70; adminstr. Div. Health State of Wis., 1976-78; economist WHO, Geneva, 1973-74. Author: (with H.F. Williamson and others) A History of American Petroleum Industry, 2 vols., 1959, 63, No Joy in Mudville: The Dilemma of Major League Baseball, 1965, Student Economists Handbook, 1967, (with B.A. Weisbrod and others) Disease and Economic Development, 1973, (with B.A. Weisbrod) American Health Policy, 1973; editor, author: New Views on American Economic Development, 1965; editor: Economic Impact of the Civil War, 1963, rev., 1967, The New Economic History: Papers on Methodology, 1971, (with J. Siegfried) Economics of Crime, 1981, Essays on International Health, 2001, The International Health Policy Program: An Internal Assessment, 2001; editor, founder: Explorations in Entrepreneurial History, 2d series, 1963-71, Explorations in Economic History 1971-78; editor: Jour. Econ. History, 1974-75; sr. editor (econs.): Social Sci. and Medicine, 1983-87; contbr. articles to profl. jours. Ford Faculty Research fellow, 1968-69 Mem. Inst. Medicine of Nat. Acad. Scis. Democrat. Home: 1815 Vilas Ave Madison WI 53711-2231 E-mail: rlandrea@wisc.edu.

ANDREASEN, NANCY COOVER, psychiatrist, educator, neuroscientist; d. John A. Sr. and Pauline G. Coover; children: Robin, Susan. BA summa cum laude, U. Nebr., 1958, PhD, 1963; MA, Radcliffe Coll., 1959; MD, U. Iowa, 1970. Instr. English Nebr. Wesleyan Coll., 1960—61, U. Nebr., Lincoln, 1962—63; asst. prof. English U. Iowa, Iowa City, 1963—66, resident, 1970—73, asst. prof. psychiatry, 1973—77, assoc. prof., 1977—81, prof. psychiatry, 1981—82, Andrew H. Woods prof. psychiatry, 1992—97, Andrew H. Woods chair psychiatry, 1997—. Sr. cons. Northwick Park Hosp., London, 1983; acad. visitor Maudsley Hosp., London, 1986; dir. Mental Health Clin. Rsch. Ctr., 1987—. Author: The Broken Brain, 1984, Introductory Psychiatry Textbook, 1991; editor: Can Schizophrenia be Localized to the Brain?, 1986, Brain Imaging: Applications in Psychiatry, 1988, Brave New Brain: Conquering Mental Illness in the Era of the Genome, 2001, The Creating Brain: The Neuroscience of Genius, 2005, Am. Jour. Psychiat., 1988—, 1989—93; editor-in-chief:, 1993—2005; contbr. articles to profl. jours. Recipient Rhonda and Bernard Sarnat award NAS, 1999, C. Charles Burlingame award, 1999, Arthur P. Noyes award in schizophrenia, 1999, Lieber prize Nat. Alliance for Rsch. on Schizophrenia and Depression, 2000, Pres.'s Nat. Medal Sci., 2000, Interbrew Baillet-Latour Health prize, 2003, William K. Warren award Internat. Schizophrenia Congress, 2005, Vanderbilt prize in Biomedical Sci., Vanderbilt U. Sch. Medicine, 2006; Woodrow Wilson fellow, 1958-59, Fulbright fellow Oxford U., London, 1959-60. Fellow Royal Coll. Physicians Surgeons Can. (hon.), Am. Psychiat. Assn. (Adolf Meyer award 1999, Disting. Svc. award 2004, Judd Marmor award, 2007), Am. Coll. Neuropharmacologists, Royal Soc. Medicine; mem. Am. Acad. Arts and Scis., Am. Psychopathol. Assn. (pres. 1989-90), Inst. Medicine of NAS (coun. 1996—). Office: U Iowa Hosps and Clinics 200 Hawkins Dr Iowa City IA 52242-1057

ANDREEVA, HRISTINA DIMITROVA, immunologist, educator; b. Sopot, Bulgaria, Dec. 5, 1966; d. Dimiter Andreev Dimitrov and Kristina Penkova Dimitrova; 1 child, Dimitrii-Kamen Dimitrov Andreev. MD, St. Petersburg Acad. Pediatrics, Russia, 1986—92; PhD, Med. U., Pleven, 1998—2001. Cert. SPAP, Russia, 1992. Asst. prof., immunology Ctr. Clin. Immunology, VMI, Pleven, Bulgaria, 1993—. Mem.: DGLD (life), ICHS (life). Home: Drujba -424-V-10 Pleven 5800 Bulgaria Office: Ctr Clin Immunology Med U St Kliment Ochridski Str 1 Pleven 5800 Bulgaria Office Fax: 359/64/801603. Personal E-mail: hrdimitrova2003@yahoo.com. E-mail: immunelab@abv.bg.

ANDREOLI, KATHLEEN GAINOR, nurse, educator, dean; b. Albany, NY, Sept. 22, 1935; d. John Edward and Edmunda Elizabeth (Ringlemann) Gainor; children: Paula Kathleen, Thomas Anthony, Karen Marie. BSN, Georgetown U., 1957; MSN, Vanderbilt U., 1959; DSN, U. Ala., Birmingham, 1979. Staff nurse Albany Hosp. Med. Ctr., 1957; instr. St. Thomas Hosp. Sch. Nursing, Nashville, 1958—59, Georgetown U. Sch. Nursing, 1959—60, Duke U. Sch. Nursing, 1960—61, Bon Secours Hosp. Sch. Nursing, Balt., 1962—64; ednl. coordinator, physician asst. program, instr. coronary care unit nursing inservice edn. Duke U. Med. Ctr., Durham, NC, 1965—70; ednl. dir. physician asst. program dept. medicine U. Ala. Med. Ctr., Birmingham, 1970—75, clin. assoc. prof. cardiovasc. nursing Sch. Nursing, 1970—77, asst. prof. nursing dept. medicine, 1971, assoc. prof., 1972—, assoc. prof. nursing Sch. Pub. and Allied Health, 1973—; assoc. dir. Family Nurse Practitioner Program, 1976, assoc. prof. cmty. health nursing Grad. Program, 1977—79, assoc. prof. dept. pub. health, 1978—79; prof. nursing, spl. asst. to pres. for ednl. affairs U. Tex. Health Sci. Ctr., Houston, 1979—82, acting dean Sch. Allied Health Scis., 1981, v.p. for ednl. svcs., interdisciplinary edn., internat. programs, 1983—87; v.p. nursing affairs Rush-Presbyn.-St. Lukes's Med. Ctr., Chgo., 1987—; dean Rush U. Coll. Nursing, 1987—2005, Kellogg emeritus dean, 2005—. Mem. nat. adv. nursing coun. Veterans Health Adminstrn., 1992; adv. bd. Nursing Spectrum, midwest region, 1995—; cons. in field. Editor: Heart and Lung, Jour. Total Care, 1971; editl. bd. Nursing Consult, Elsevier Publs., 2004—05; contbr. articles to profl. jours.; author: Comprehensive Cardiac Care, 1983. Active Internat. Nursing Coalition for Mass Casualty Edn., 2002—05; mem. adv. bd. Robert Wood Johnson Clin. Nurse Sch. Program; mem. vis. com. Vanderbilt U. Sch. Nursing; mem. Leadership Ill., 1991; mem. nat. nursing adv. com. Voluntary Hosp. Am., 1991; mem. governing coun. Inst. for Hosp. Clin. Nursing Edn., Am. Hosp. Assn., 1993; bd. dirs. Ill. League for Nursing, 1994, Lyric Opera Chgo. Guild; bd. dirs., chair rsch. and edn. com. Rehab. Inst. Chgo., 2005—; adv. bd. Hospice Ptnrs. Recipient Founder's award, NC Heart Assn., 1970, Disting. Alumni award, Vanderbilt U. Sch. Nursing, 1985, Leadership Tex. award, 1985, Disting. Alumni award, U. Ala. Sch. Nursing, 1991, Henry Betts MD Employment Advocacy award, 2004, Sage Mentor award, Ill. Nursing Leadership Annual Conf., 2005, Critical Care Nursing Pioneering Spirit award, GE Healthcare Am. Assn., 2009. Fellow: Am. Acad. Nursing; mem.: ACNA, ANA, Inst. Medicine Interest Group Edn.Healthcare & Accurance Workforce (planning com. mem. 2009—), Internat. Nursing Coalition for Mass Casualty Edn., Inst. Medicine Chgo. (bd. govs. 2004—, sec. bd. 2005—), Nat. Nursing Adv. Coun. Hosps. Am., Am. Heart Assn. Coun. Cardiovasc. Nursing, Coun. Family Nurse Practitioners and Clinicians, Ala. Heart Assn., Nat. League Nursing, Inst. Medicine of NAS, Am. Assn. Colls. Nursing (dean emeritus 2005—), Rotary One Club Chgo., Phi Kappa Phi, Alpha Eta, Sigma Theta Tau (Dreher Outstanding Dean award 2003, Rehab. Inst. of Chgo. Henry Setts Disability Advocacy award 2004, U. Ill. Power Nursing Mentor award 2005, Sage Membership award Ill. Nursing Leadership Conf. 2005). Roman Catholic. Home: 1212 N Lake Shore Dr Apt 10AN Chicago IL 60610-2359 Office: 1212 N Lake Shore Dr Chicago IL 60610-2359 Office Phone: 312-266-8338. Business E-Mail: kathleen_g_andreoli@rush.edu.

ANDREONI, CASSIO RIBEIRO, urologist; b. Sao Paulo, Brazil, Dec. 15, 1970; s. Iraja Bernardino Ribeiro and Suely Ribeiro Andreoni; m. Danielle Macellaro Andreoni, May 12, 1999. Best resident in Gen. Surgery (hon.), Fed. U. Sao Paulo, Brazil, 1996; MD, Fed. Universty Sao Paulo, Brazil, 1993; Gen. Surgeon, Fed. U. Sao Paulo, Brazil, 1996, Urologist, 1998; Endourologist-laparoscopist, Wash. U. Sch. Medicine, St. Louis, 2000; PhD thesis, Fed. Univesity Sao Paulo, 2002. Med. Diplomate Fed. U. of Sao Paulo, 1993, Urologist Fed. U. of Sao Paulo, 1999, Laparoscopic Surgeon Brazilian Assn. for Laparoscopic Surgery, 2002. Rsch. fellow Wash. U. Sch. Med., St. Louis, 1999—2000; coord. residency in urology Fed. U. Sao Paulo, Divsn. Urology, Brazil, 2001—; urologist in chief Univ. Hosp. Vila Maria, Sao Paulo, Brazil, 2001—; sect. member, urooncology and urolithiasis Fed. U. Sao Paulo, Divsn. Urology, Brazil, 2001—; chief, sect. urol. exptl. surgery and robotics Fed. U. Sao Paulo, Divsn. Urology, Brazil, 2001—. Med. consulting ONG, Sao Paulo, Brazil, 2002—. Author: (pub., first description device) Jour. Urology, (invention new surgical technique) Jour. Endourology (Brazilian meeting award nominee, 2001); author: (first experience robotics brazil) (exhibition, podium presentation) Brazilian Jour. Urology (Brazilian Congress Highlight, 2001); author: (minimally invasive surgery developer) over 200 unedited procedures performed brazil. Mem. Cruz de Malta Charity Assn., Sao Paulo, Brazil, 2001—02. Lt. physician Brazilian Army, 1994—95, Sao Paulo/Brazil. Recipient Best Laparoscopic Paper award, World Congress on Endourology, 2002; Grants, CAPES-Brazilian Gov., 1999—2000. Mem.: Am. Urol. Assn. (corr.), Brazilian Urol. Assn. (assoc.), Internat. Soc. Computer Aided Surgery (assoc.), The Endourology Soc. (assoc.). Achievements include research in New surgical tech-intracorporeal renal shrinking. Avocations: golf, tennis. Home: R Jesuino Arruda 60 apt 201 São Paulo 04024-002 Brazil Office: Fed Univ Sao Paulo R Napoleao de Barros 715 2nd floor São Paulo 04532-080 Brazil Office Fax: 5511 3237 2758; Home Fax: 55 11 3071 0535. E-mail: c.andreoni@attglobal.net.

ANDREOTTI, LAMBERTO, pharmaceutical company executive; b. 1950; B in Engring., U. Rome; MS, MIT. Exec. Farmitalia Carlo Erba, Pharmacia AB; sr. v.p., pres. oncology divsn. Pharmacia & Upjohn; v.p., gen. mgr., European oncology, Worldwide Medicines Group Bristol-Myers Squibb Co., Paris, Fla., France, 1998—2002, Rome, 1998—2002, pres., Europe, Worldwide Medicines Group, 2000—02, sr. v.p., Europe, Asia-Pacific and Africa, pres. Internat., 2002—05, exec. v.p., COO, worldwide pharmaceuticals, 2005—08, exec. v.p., COO, 2008—09, pres., 2009—10, mem. exec. com., 2009—, CEO, 2010—. Bd. dirs. Bristol-Myers Squibb Co., 2009—. Office: Bristol-Myers Squibb Co 345 Park Ave New York NY 10154-0037 Office Fax: 212-546-4020. E-mail: lamberto.andreotti@bms.com. *

ANDRES, EMMANUEL, internist, researcher; b. Strasbourg, France, Aug. 23, 1966; s. Bertrand and Monique Andres; m. Muriel Hinderberger, Oct. 22, 1973; children: Maxime children: Frédéric. MD, Strasbourg U. Medicine, 1997. Intern, resident, physician Strasbourg U. Hosps., 1997—; rschr. Nat. Ctr. Sci. Rsch., Strasbourg, 1999—. Cons. Entomed, Strasbourg, 1999—, Laennext, Strasbourg, 2006, Infial, Strasbourg, 2009. Comdt. French Navy, 1992—2001. Recipient Prix Robert Zittoun, 2004. Mem.: French Soc. Hematology, French Nat. Soc. Internal Medicine (Prix Marcel Simon 2000). Achievements include development of managment of anemia drug-induced agranulocytosis, idiopathic thrombocytopenic purpura, cobalamin deficiencies, and medical sound analysis and e-auscultotim. Home: 2b rue de la Renaissance F-67000 Strasbourg France Office: Hosp Univs Strasbourg 1 place de L Hopital 67000 Bas-Rhin Strasbourg France Home Phone: 3 33 88 31 50 74; Office Phone: 3 33 88 11 50 66. Office Fax: 3 33 88 11 62 62. Business E-Mail: emmanuel.andres@chru-strasbourg.fr.

ANDRES, MARINA, radiologist; b. Spain, Feb. 17, 1977; MD, 2001. Radiologist Hosp., 2003—. Home: Delicias 28 Madrid 28045 Spain Personal E-mail: ambar_mir@hotmail.com.

ANDRES GARCIA, VICENTE, research scientist; b. Valencia, Spain, June 3, 1962; B in Biol. Sci., U. Barcelona, 1986, PhD in Biochemistry, 1990. Scientist, charge of animal facility IBV CSIC, Valencia, 1999—2009, rsch. scientist, 2003—05, chief, dept. molecular, cellular pathology and therapy, 2003—09, prof., 2005—09; pres., animal facility and transgenesis com. Spanish Nat. Cardiovasc. Rsch. Ctr., Madrid, 2009, sr. rsch. scientist, 2009—, mem., rsch. com., 2011. Asst., coordination team biomedicine area Nat. Agy. Evaluation of Grant Proposal & Fellowships, Spain, 2007; mem. subcom., tchg., tng. and mobility Red Temática de Investigación Cardiovasc. Inst. de Salud Carlos III, 2008, bd. mem., 08. Recipient award, Spanish Soc. Cardiology, 2001, 2nd prize, Pfizer Found., 2002, Dr. Leon Dumont prize, Belgian Soc. Cardiology, 2010; finalist New Eng. Cardiovasc. Rsch. award, Astra Merck. Mem.: European Soc. Cardiology, Am. Heart Assn. (coun. atherosclerosis, thrombosis and vascular biology), Spanish Soc. Cardiology, Spanish Soc. Atherosclerosis, Spanish Soc. Biochemistry and Molecular Biology, Frontiers Biosci. Soc. Scientists. Office: C Melchor Fernandez Almagro 3 Madrid 28029 Spain Office Fax: 34-91-453-12-65. Business E-Mail: vandres@cnic.es.

ANDREU-BALLESTER, JUAN C., emergency physician, researcher; b. Valencia, Spain, Apr. 14, 1956; m. Carmen Jaen; 1 child, Beatriz; 1 child, Alicia. BS in Medicine and Surgery, U. Valencia, Medicine, 1980, MD. Diplomate in methodology clin. rsch., family practice physician specialist, diplomate emergency medicine. Staff physician Hosp. Arnau de Vilanova, Emergency Dept. and Short-Med. Staying Unit, Valencia, 1983—, chief, 1997—2002, cons., 2005—. Reviewer Jour. Am. Geriat. Soc., Jour. Clin. Immunology; editl. bd. Jour. Open Access Surgery. Author, co-editor Algorithms of Emergency Medicine, Flow Diagrams in Emergency Situations. Mem.: Spanish Soc. Emergency Medicine, Rsch. Commn. Arnau de Vilanova Hosp. Achievements include research in diagnostic and therapeutic strategy of rectum cancer; immunology of the mucosal associated lymphoid tissues. Office Phone: 34963868500. Personal E-mail: jcandreu@ono.com.

ANDREUCCI, MICHELE, medical educator; b. Parma, Italy, Oct. 10, 1971; s. Vittorio Emanuele Andreucci and Maria Castelli; m. Teresa Faga; 1 child, Vittorio Emanuele. MD, Sch. Medicine, Naples, Italy, 1996; PhD, U. Parma, Italy, 2002. Diplomate nephrology specialist U. Messina, Italy, 2006. U. rschr., Catanzaro, Italy, 2001—06; rsch. fellow Harvard U., Boston, 2000—02; assoc. prof. medicine & surgery (nephrology) Magna Grecia U., Catanzaro, Italy; prof. medicine, surgery, nephrology U. Campobasso, Italy. Recipient award, Italian Soc. Nephrology, Rimini, Italy, 2010; grantee Travel grant, ERA-EDTA Copenhagen, 2002, ERA-EDTA/WCN Berlin, 2003. Home: Viale Tommaso Campanella n182/1 Catanzaro I-88100 Italy Office: Magna Graecia Univ Viale Europa 88100 Catanzaro CZ Italy Office Phone: 39-0961-3647301. Business E-Mail: andreucci@unicz.it.

ANDREW, CORNFORTH NIMITZ, research scientist; b. San Diego, Apr. 28, 1969; BS in Chemistry, U. Calif., Irvine, 1997, PhD, 2006. Sr. scientist Hoag Meml. Hosp., 2006—. Rschr. Cell Biology Lab, Cancer Ctr., 2006. Brython Davis fellowship, U. Calif., Irvine Grad. Divsn. Mem.: Soc. Biol. Therapy, Am. Assn. Cancer Rschrs. Avocations: sailing, camping, hiking, music. Home: 3 Windswept Way Mission Viejo CA 92692 Personal E-mail: acorn4th@gmail.com.

ANDREW, LOUISE BRIGGS, emergency physician, medical legal consultant; b. High Point, NC, May 6, 1951; d. Eugene Leroy Briggs Jr. and Maria Elizabeth (Brockmann) Miller; m. Clifford George Andrew, June 13, 1970 (div.); children: Galen Michael, Amalie Linnea; m. Theodore Edward Harrison, Oct. 26, 1987. MD, Duke U., Durham, NC, 1975; JD in Health Law, U. Md., 1991. Bar:; cert. in Emergency Medicine. Intern, fellow emergency medicine Duke U. Hosp., 1975—76; resident internal medicine Johns Hopkins Hosp., Balt., 1976—78, resident pulmonary intensive care, 1978; assoc. dir. emergency medicine Francis Scott Key Med. Ctr., Balt., 1976; assoc. dir. Ctr. Profl. Well Being, Durham; asst. prof. internal/emergency medicine Johns Hopkins U. Sch. Medicine, 1980—92; founder, consultant MDMentor.com, 1992—. Co-founder, past pres. Coalition & Ctr. for Ethical Med. Testimony, 2003. Contbr. articles to profl. jours., chapters to books; spkr. in field. Recipient Disting. Alumni award, Johns Hopkins Emergency Medicine Residency Prog., 2000. Fellow: Internat. Fedn. Emergency Medicine, Am. Coll. Emergency Physicians (life; sec. Md. chpt. 1982—86, mem. Med. Legal Com., Profl. Liability Task Force, chair Personal & Profl. Well-Being Com., Council Meritorious Svc. award 2002, James D. Mills Outstanding Contbn. to Emergency Medicine award 2005); mem.: ABA, AMA, AAUP, Emergency Medicine Residents' Assn. (charter mem.), Soc. Acad. Emergency Medicine, Soc. Internat. Advancement Emergency Medicine (co-founder 1989, sec. 1989—93, Founder's award 1995), Soc. Profl. Wellbeing, Nat. Health Lawyers Assn., Am. Med. Women's Assn., Am. Assn. Women Emergency Physicians (pres.

1987—89, bd. dirs. 1990—93, Leadership award 1989, Well-Being in Emergency Medicine award 1996). Achievements include being one of the first physicians in the country to be certified as a specialist in emergency medicine, and one of the first faculty members at Hopkins to teach this discipline. Avocations: piano, flute, singing, calligraphy, languages. Office: MDMentor 403 S Lincoln St Ste 4 51 Port Angeles WA 98362 Office Phone: 425-609-0039. Business E-Mail: mail@lbandrew.com.

ANDREWS, ANTHONY HUNTER, veterinary educator, writer, consultant; b. Swindon, Wiltshire, Eng., Aug. 16, 1942; s. Harold Edward and Alice Winifred (Hunter) Andrews; m. Joan Margaret Isle, Jan. 1, 1966 (div. Oct. 1972); 1 child, Michael John; m. Celia Josephine Tucker, Oct. 21, 1972 (div. Feb. 1977); 1 child, Mark Edward Alexander. B in Vet. Medicine, U. London, 1966, PhD, 1980. Diplomate European Coll. Small Ruminant Health Mgmt.; registered forensic practitioner Coun. Registration Forensic Practitioners, 2005. Vet. surgeon, Falmouth, Cornwall, England, 1966-67, Cranleigh, Surrey, England, 1967-68, 68-70, Isle of Wight, England, 1968; Royal Smithfield Club fellow Royal Vet. Coll., U. London, 1970-73, sr. lectr. farm animal medicine, 1979-97; ind. vet. cons., 1997—; sr. vet. officer Meat & Livestock Commn., Milton Keynes, England, 1973-79; recognized specialist cattle health and prod. Found. Diplomate European Coll., Bovine Health Mgmt., 2004. European vet. specialist in bovine health mgmt. Brit. Cattle Vet. Assn., sec., 1976—79, v.p., 1979—80, 1981—82, pres., 1980—81; vet. expert Social Econ. Com. EEC, Brussels, 1989—90, House of Lords Select Com. European Cmty., London, 1989; examiner U. London, U. Cambridge, U. Dublin, U. Edinburgh, Royal Coll. Vet. Surgeons; mem. Brit. Pharm. Commn., 1998—2007, mem. adv. com. antibiotics, 2005—09, mem. Min. Agr., Fisheries and Food, Beef Assurance Adv. Panel, 1999—2000, Food Stds. Agy., 2000—05; vet. cons. Food and Agrl. Orgn., Kosovo, 2001; vet. adviser Tubney Charitable Trust, 2001—07; vet. cons. Safeway Superstores Ltd., 2001—04; dir. Responsible Use of Medicines in Agrl. Alliance, 2003—09; chief exec. European Sch. Vet. Postgrad. Studies, 2004—; dir. Embryo Vet. Sch., 2005—. Author: Calf Management and Disease Notes, 1983, The Henston Veterinary Vade Mecum edits., 1984—2000, Growing Cattle Management and Disease Notes Management, 1985, 1986, Outline of Clinical Diagnosis in Cattle, 1990, Poisoning in Veterinary Practice, 1992; author, editor: Bovine Medicine, 1992, 2d edit., 2004, The Health of Dairy Cattle Blackwell Science, 2000; editor: The Expectant Cow, 2000; livestock editor UK Vet., 1995—, mem. editl. bd. Brit. Vet. Jour., 1988—2002, mem. exec. bd., 1995—98; asst. editor: Black's Veterinary Dictionary, 19th edit., 1998, 20th edit., 2001, 21st edit., 2005; contbr. articles to profl. jours. Recipient Bewicke award, Royal Vet. Coll., 1969, Centenary prize, Ctrl. Vet. Soc., 1987. Fellow: Vet. History Soc. (mem. com. 2007—), Royal Soc. Medicine, European Coll. Bovine Health Mgmt. (coun. mem. 1995—2006, vice chmn. 2002—04, chmn. accreditation com. 2005—07, bd. mem. 2008—11), Royal Coll. Vet. Surgeons, Brit. Inst. Agrl. Cons.; mem.: Goat Vet. Soc. (coun. mem. 1995—96, vice chmn. 1996—97, chmn. 1997—), Vet. Assn. Arbitration and Jurisprudence (coun. mem. 1994, vice chmn. 1996, chmn. 2002—04, sr. vice chmn. 2004—06), Brit. Cattle Vet. Assn. (sec. 1976—79, v.p. 1979—80, pres. 1980—81, sr. v.p. 1981—82, bd. mem. 1995—96, vice chair 1996—97, chmn. 1998—2000), Hertfordshire and Bedfordshire Vet. Soc. (v.p. 1993—95, pres. 1995—97, sr. 1997—99), Brit. Vet. Assn. (mem. coun. 1976—87, chmn. large animals com. 1983—84, chmn. sci. and edn. and mktg. com. 1984—87, mem. coun. 1990—, dir. Embryo Vet. Sch. 2005—, editl. bd. mem., 2nd opinion 2011—, mem. editl. working party for cattle practice 2011—, William Hunting award 1971), Farmers Club. Mem. Ch. Eng. Avocations: travel, gardening, reading, writing. Office Phone: 0044-1438-717900. Personal E-mail: andrewsah@talk21.com. Business E-Mail: andrewsah.t21@btinternet.com.

ANDREWS, AUDREY T., lawyer, healthcare service company executive; B in Govt., U. Tex., Austin, JD. Asst. gen. counsel M.A.P.A., Inc., 1995—98; hosp. ops. counsel Tenet Healthcare Corp., 1998, v.p., gen. counsel, v.p., chief compliance officer, 2006—08, sr. v.p., 2008, sr. v.p., chief compliance officer, 2009—. Mem. quality com. Fedn. of American Hosps., mem. legal & operational policy com. Named one of Top 25 Women in Healthcare, Modern Healthcare mag., 2011. Mem.: ABA, American Health Lawyers Assn., Tex. Bar Assn., Health Care Compliance Assn. Office: Tenet Healthcare Corp 1445 Ross Ave Ste 1400 Dallas TX 75202 Office Phone: 469-893-2200. Office Fax: 469-893-8600. Business E-Mail: audrey.andrews@tenethealth.com. *

ANDREWS, BERNARD A., medical educator; MD, U. Pitts. Diplomate Am. Bd. Internal Medicine. Practice Primary Care Northside; clin. asst. prof. medicine Drexel Univ.; intern Allegheny Gen. Hosp., resident. Named one of Top Doctors, Pitts. mag., 2011. Office: Allegheny General Hospital 320 E N Ave Pittsburgh PA 15212 Office Phone: 412-359-3131. Office Fax: 412-359-4108.

ANDREWS, BILLY FRANKLIN, pediatrician, educator; b. Graham, NC, Sept. 22, 1932; s. Dean Franklin and Arlee (Byers) A.; m. Faye Rich, Dec. 25, 1953; children: Ann Elizabeth Feigenbaum, Billy Franklin Jr., David Ashley. Student, Brevard Coll., NC, 1950, Elon Coll., 1951; BS cum laude, Wake Forest Coll., 1953; MD, Duke U., 1957. Diplomate Am. Bd. Pediat., 1963. Commd. 2d lt. U.S. Army, 1956, advanced through grades to maj., 1962; intern Ft. Benning U.S. Army Hosp., Ga., 1957—58; resident in pediat. Walter Reed Gen. Hosp., Washington, 1958—60; with mil. med. and allied scis. course Walter Reed Army Inst. Rsch., Washington, 1960—61; chief pediat. svc. Rodriguez U.S. Army Hosp., Ft. Brooke, PR, 1961—63; chief pediat. Tropical Med. Rsch. Lab., Ft. Brooke, 1963—64; ret. U.S. Army, 1964; dir. newborn svcs. U. Louisville, 1964—76, from asst. prof. pediat. to chmn., 1964—93, chmn. emeritus, 1993—, dir. neonatology tng. program, 1965—86, dir. doctors' and nurses tng. program and regional tng. programs, 1965—93, co-dir. genetic counseling unit, 1965—68, dir. Comprehensive Health Care Ctr. for High Risk Infants and Children, 1968—98, co-dir. health profls. spl. project grant for preceptorship tng., 1974—77; chief staff Kosair Children's Hosp., Louisville, 1969—93, chief-of-staff emeritus, 1993—. Cons. divsn. adult and child health Ky. Dept. Pub. Health, 1966—2003; AOA advisor U. LSM, 1970—79; lectr. Jour. Pediat. Found., 1972; Staley Disting. Christian scholar Mary Baldwin Coll., Washington and Lee U., Sch. Medicine of U.Va., 1990; vis. scholar in med. history and ethics Green Coll., Oxford (Eng.) U., 1993, vis. fellow med. history, ethics and humantities, 1998—2005. Author: Children's Bill of Rights, 1968; editor: Small-for-Date Infants, 1970, The Newborn, Pediatric Clinics of North America, 1977, Aphorisms, Tributes and Tenets of Billy F. Andrews: In Walls, M.E., 1986, Ideals and Inspiration (F.R. Andrews), 1993, Words to Live By (F.R. Andrews), 1993, A Statement on Transplantation and Organ Donors, 1994; contbr. numerous articles to profl. publs.; inventor, poet. Pres. Kornhauser Libr., Health Scis. Ctr., 1981-82, 90-91; mem., tchr., deacon, elder United Ch. of Christ; bd. dirs. Oak Ridge Mil. Acad., 2004-07. Recipient Helen B. Fraser award, 1978, Norton-Children's Hosp. award for leadership in neonatology, 1978, Award of Recognition, XVII Internat. Congress Pediat., Manila, 1983, Wisdom award of honor, eminent fellow The Wisdom Soc., 1991, The Billy F. Andrews, M.D. Endowed Chair in Pediat., U. Louisville, 1993, Winston Churchill medal of Wisdom Soc., Eminent Churchill Fellow of Wisdom Soc., 1993, Disting. Alumnus award Wake Forest U., 1983; Festschrift to Billy F. Andrews, M.D., Jour. of Perinatology, 1995; Billy F. Andrews, MD, scholarship at U. Louisville Sch. Medicine named in his honor, 1986, Billy F. Andrews, MD lectureship in neonatology, U. Louisville, 2002; Named Best Drs. In US, 1979 Fellow ACP, Am. Acad. Pediat., Royal Soc. Medicine (London); mem. AMA, Am. Pediat. Soc., Am. Osler Soc. (pres. 1996-97), Am. Soc. for Bioethics and Humanities, Soc. for Pediat. Rsch., So. Soc. Pediat. Rsch. (founding), Southeastern Perinatal Soc. (founding), Nat. Assn. Children's Hosps. and Related Instns. (founding), Ky. Med. Assn. (faculty Sci. Achievement award 1971, del. 1981-82, Ednl. Achievement award 1997), Greater Louisville Med. Soc., Ky. Pediat. Soc., Louisville Pediat. Soc., U. Louisville Sch. Medicine Alumni Assn. (bd. govs. 1972-75), Univ. Pediatric Found. Inc. (pres. 1982-93), Internat. Assn. Bioethics, Am. Soc. Law, Medicine and Ethics, Alpha Omega Alpha. Achievements include invention of infant oxygen hood, iontophoresis sweat induction apparatus, radiant open infant warmer, infant blood warmer, diagnostic and treatment table with warmer and position changes, head and extremities transeilluminator, infant transport incubator, others. Office: Kosair Charities Pediat Ctr 571 S Floyd St Ste 449 Louisville KY 40202-3830 Home Phone: 812-944-8087. Business E-Mail: bfandr01@louisville.edu.

ANDREWS, CHRIS THOMAS, orthopedist, surgeon; b. Newtownards, Northern Ireland, Nov. 30, 1963; s. Thomas Miller and Dianne Maureen Helen Andrews; m. Fiona Isabel Taylor, Nov. 18, 1989; children: Catriona, Elaine, Emma, Bethan. MBChB, Edinburgh U., Scotland, 1987. Registered trauma and orthop. Intercollegiate Bd., 1998. Jr. ho. officer Royal Infirmary, Edinburgh, Scotland, 1987—88; sr. ho. officer and demonstrator anatomy Glasgow U., Glasgow, 1988—89; surg. sr. ho. officer tng. Belfast Rotation, Northern Ireland, 1989—93, specialist registrar orthop. tng., 1993—98; limb reconstruction fellow Nuffield Orthop. Ctr., Oxford, England, 1998—99; cons. trauma and orthop. Royal Group Hosps., Belfast, Northern Ireland, 1999—. Examiner fellow orthop. Intercollegiate Bd. Royal Colls., 2006—, course rev. faculty; examiner Intercollegiate Splty. Bd. Trauma and Orthops. Contbr. scientific papers. Elder Non Subscribing Prebyn. Ch., Comber, Northern Ireland, 1999—. Fellow: Brit. Orthop. Assn., Royal Coll. Surgeons. Achievements include expert in trauma and adult and pediatric limb reconstruction using Ilizarov method. Avocations: sailing, skiing. Home: 8 Clattering Ford Comber BT23 59H Northern Ireland Office: Royal Victoria Hosp Wards 5 E-F Grosvenor Road BT12 6BA Belfast Northern Ireland Office Phone: 028 90634036. Business E-Mail: postmaster@ctandrews.plus.com.

ANDREWS, JAMES R., orthopedic surgeon; m. Jenelle Andrews; children: Andy, Amy, Archie, Ashley, Amber, Abby. Grad., La. State U., 1963, MD, 1967; LLD, Livingston U.; DSc, Troy State U., La. State U. Orthop. resident Tulane Med. Sch., 1972; surgical fellow in sports medicine U. Va. Med. Sch., 1972, U. Lyon, Lyn, France, 1972; founding mem. Andrews Sports Medicine and Orthopedic Ctr., Birmingham, Ala.; founder, med. dir. Am. Sports Medicine Inst., Birmingham, Ala.; med. dir. Andrews Inst. for Orthopaedics & Sports Medicine, Gulf Breeze, Fla., 2007—. Clin. prof. orthopedic surgery U. Ala. Birmingham Med. Sch., Ala. Med. Sch., U. Va. Sch. Medicine, U. SC Med. Sch.; med. dir., intercollegiate sports Auburn U.; sr. orthopedic cons., intercollegiate athletics U. Ala.; orthopedic cons. for athletic teams Troy State U., U. West Ala., Tuskegee U., Samtord U.; spl. med. cons., dept. athletics, Ala.; med. dir. Tampa Bay Devil Rays; sr. orthopedic cons. Washington Redskins; team physician Birmingham Barons Double A, affiliate Chgo. White Sox; med. dir. Ladies Profl. Golf Assn.; mem., sports medicine com. US Olympic Com.; served on NCAA Competitive Safeguards in Medical Aspects of Sports Com.; current mem. med. and safety adv. com. USA Baseball; bd. dirs. Fast Health Corp., Robins Morton Constrn. Co. Author numerous sci. articles and books. Bd. trustees Troy State U. Recipient Disting. Sportsman award, Ala. Sports Hall of Fame, 1992; named to Ala. Sports Hall of Fame, La. State U. Alumni Hall of Distinction, 1996. Mem.: Ladies Profl. Golf Assn., Internat. Knee Soc. (bd. dir.), Arthroscopy Assn. North America (bd. dir.), American Orthop. Soc. Sports Medicine (bd. dir., sec. bd. dir. 2004—05), American Acad. Orthop. Surgeons, American Bd. Orthop. Surgery. Widely recognized for his role in advancing the field of shoulder, knee and elbow surgery; mentored over 250 fellows throughout the course of his academic career; considered one of the foremost orthopedic surgeons and sports doctors in the world; and operated on a remarkable number of prominent athletes, including Troy Aikman, Roger Clemens, and Jack Nicklaus. Address: 805 St Vincent Dr Str 100 Birmingham AL 35205-1616 Office Phone: 205-581-7139.

ANDREWS, JOSEPH LYON, JR., internist, pulmonologist, medical educator, writer; b. NYC, Mar. 19, 1938; s. Joseph Lyon and Katherine Louise (New) A.; m. Margareta Langert, Apr. 18, 1969 (dec. Mar. 1994); children: Joe, Sara, Jennifer. BA cum laude, Amherst Coll., 1959; MD, U. Rochester, 1963. Diplomate Am. Bd. Internal Medicine, Am. Bd. Pulmonary Medicine. Intern, resident Boston City Hosp., 1963-65, Tufts Med. Sch., Boston, 1963-65; resident, fellow Harvard Med. Sch., Boston, 1967-70; pulmonary fellow Mass. Gen. Hosp., 1967-68; sr. resident Boston VA Hosp., 1968-69; cardiology fellow West Roxbury VA Hosp., 1969-70; internist, pulmonologist Lahey Clinic, Boston, Burlington, Mass., 1971-90; chief pulmonary dept. New Eng. Deaconess Hosp., Boston, 1972—82; dir. ambulatory care Bedford VA Med. Ctr., Mass., 1999-2000; internist Harvard Vanguard Health Care, Boston, 2003; internist, pulmonary cons. New Eng. Allergy, Asthma and Immunology PC, North Andover, 2004—05, Harbor Med. Group, Marblehead, Mass., 2006—07, Kaiser Permanente, Honolulu, 2008—09. Clin. tchg. staff Harvard Med. Sch., 1971-90, Tufts Med. Sch., 1971— Author: Revolutionary Boston, Lexington and Concord, The Shots Head Round the World, 1999; freelance writer Boston Globe Newspaper, 1971—; contbr. over 100 articles to profl. jours. Pres.'s social action. World Learning, Inc., Brattleboro, Vt., 1987—; mem., social action com. Temple Shalom, Newton, Mass., 1988-93; mem. Human Rights Com., Newton, 1983-88; bd. dirs. Am. Lung Assn. Boston, 1977-90; lic. guide Town Concord, 1995—; mem. Concord Mill Brook Task Force, 1995—99, Concord Hist. Commn., 1996-99; mem. social action com. Kerem Shalom, Concord, 1996—; mem. Am. Friends Neve Shalom, Israel, 1996—, Capt. USAF, 1965-67. Traveling fellow Am.Jewish Congress, Israel, 1959, Am. Cancer Soc., Mendoza, Argentina, 1962. Fellow Am. Coll. Physicians, Am. Coll. Chest Physicians; mem. AMA, Am. Thoracic Soc., Mass. Med. Assn., Mass. Thoracic Soc., Am. Jewish Hist. Soc., Sons Am. Revolution (surgeon 1996-, pres. Old Middlesex chpt. 2011-), Thoreau Soc., Concord Visitors Guide, Concord Guides and Press (founder, dir.). Avocations: writing, photography, swimming, hiking, tour guiding, travel. Home: 28 Center Village Dr Concord MA 01742-2900

ANDREWS, MITCHELL DEWAYNE, internist, dean, educator; b. Enid, Okla., May 24, 1944; s. Mitchell S. and Truel Eva (Melton) A.; m. Rebecca Ellen Meltzer, Aug. 26, 1984. BS, Baylor U., 1966; MD, U. Okla., 1970. Diplomate Am. Bd. Internal Medicine. Resident internal medicine Johns Hopkins Hosp., Balt., 1970-71, U. Okla. Health Sci. Ctr., Oklahoma City, 1971-72, 74-76; asst. prof., assoc. prof., dir. residency program dept. medicine U. Okla., Oklahoma City, 1976-84, vice chmn., chief gen. internal medicine, prof. dept. medicine, 1986—, assoc. dean grad. med. edn. Coll. Medicine, 1994—2000, sr. assoc. dean, 1996—2002, v.p. health affairs, exec. dean, 2002—; chief of medicine regional med. ctr., vice chmn. dept. medicine U. Tenn. Coll. Medicine, Memphis, 1984-86; chief of staff U. Hosp., Oklahoma City, 1992-94, med. dir., 1994-96. Bd. dirs. Nat. Commn. Certification Physician Assts., 1995—2003. Editor: Jour. Okla. State Med. Assn., 1991—; contbr. numerous articles to profl. jours. Bd. dirs. Chamber Orch. Oklahoma City, 1982-84, Lyric Theatre, Oklahoma City, 1996-2000, Oklahoma City Philharm. Found., 2003—; del. Okla. State Leadership Initiative to Soviet Union, 1988. Surgeon CDC, USPHS, 1972-74. Recipient Stollerman award U. Tenn., 1986, Aesculapian award U. Okla. Coll. Medicine, 1989; ACP tchg. and rsch. scholar, 1976-79. Master ACP (bd. govs. Okla. 1995-99); mem. AMA, Alpha Omega Alpha. Episcopalian. Avocation: photography. Office: U Okla Coll Medicine RM 357 BMSB PO Box 26901 Oklahoma City OK 73126-0901 *

ANDREWS, NANCY CATHERINE, dean, pediatrician, hematologist, educator; b. Syracuse, NY, Nov. 29, 1958; d. William Shankland and Virginia Helen (Rogers) A.; m. Bernard Mathey-Prevot, Aug. 10, 1985; children: Camille, Nicolas. BS in Molecular Biophysics and Biochemistry, MS in Molecular Biophysics and Biochemistry, Yale U., 1980; PhD in Biology, MIT, 1985; MD, Harvard Med. Sch., 1987. Intern Children's Hosp., Boston, 1987-88, resident, 1988-89; fellow in pediat. hematology/oncology Children's Hosp. and Dana-Farber Cancer Inst., Boston, 1989-92, instr., pediatrics Harvard Med. Sch., Boston, 1991—93, asst. prof., 1993—98, assoc. prof., 1998—2003, prof., 2003—07, dean, basic scis. and grad. studies, 2003—07; vice chancellor academic affairs, dean Duke U. Sch. Medicine, Durham, NC, 2007—. Investigator Howard Hughes Med. Inst., Boston, 1993-2006; dir. Harvard MD-PhD Program, Boston, 1999-2003. Author: (chpt.) Hematology of Infancy and Childhood, 1997; contbr. articles to Nature, others. Merck-AFCR Found. fellow, 1991-94; recipient Rosenthal award 1998. Fellow Molecular Medicine Soc., Am. Acad. Arts & Scis.; mem. Soc. Pediat. Rsch. (Young Investigator award 1994), Am. Soc. Hematology (membership com. 1994—), Am. Soc. Clin. Investigation, Inst. Medicine. Democrat. Achievements include being the first women to be appointed dean of Duke University School of Medicine and becomes the only women to lead one of the nation's top 10 medical schools. Avocations: travel, gardening, cooking. Office: Duke U Sch Medicine Box 2927 Med Ctr Durham NC 27710 Office Phone: 919-684-2455. Office Fax: 919-684-0208. E-mail: nancy.andrews@duke.edu. *

ANDREWS, PAUL S., research scientist; b. Wymouth, Mass., Apr. 16, 1969; BS, U. Mass., 2000; PhD, U. NC, Chapel Hill, 2005. Sr. scientist Amgen Inc., 2005—. Decorated SW Asia Svc. medal US Army. Avocations: boating, running. Office: 360 Binney St Cambridge MA 02142 Business E-Mail: psandrew@amgen.com.

ANDREY, LADISLAV GEORGE, research scientist; b. Vlaca, Czechoslovakia, July 15, 1948; s. George and Zuzana (Hermanovsky) Andrey; m. Helena Broulikova, Aug. 16, 1977; children: Margareta, Helena. Rerum Naturalium Dr, Charles U., Prague, Czech Republic, 1975, PhD, 1987; diploma, Japanese Lang. Sch., Osaka, Japan, 1978. Watchman Nat. Gallery, Prague, 1973-74; asst. prof. U. P.J. Safarik, Košice, Slovakia, 1974-78; rschr. Kyoto U., 1978-80; analyst Orgn. Selling Machines and Instruments, Prague, 1980—81; sr. scientist Acad. Scis., Prague, 1989—. Translator in field, Prague, 1981—89. Author: Biothermodynamics, 1980; contbr. articles to profl. jours. Named Am. Men of Sci., Bowker Ctr., Oldsmar, Fla., 1995. Mem.: Neurosci. Soc. Prague (com. mem. 1992), NY Acad. Scis., Am. Math. Soc. Avocations: chess, philosophy. Home Phone: 00 605822402; Office Phone: 004202 66052085. Business E-Mail: andre@cs.cas.cz, ladislav.andvey@gmail.com.

ANDRIANI, RUDY, urologist, educator; MD, NY Coll. of Medicine, 1981. Diplomate Am. Bd. Urology. Intern St. Vincent's Hosp. and Med. Ctr., NY, resident surgery, 1982—83; resident urology Duke Univ. Med. Ctr., 1983—87; urologist Stamford Hosp., Greenwich Hosp. Asst. clin. prof. urology Columbia Univ. Coll. of Physicians and Surgeons. Office: Greenwich Hospital 5 Perryridge Rd Greenwich CT 06830 Office Phone: 203-863-3000.

ANDRIEUX, KARINE, pharmacist, educator; b. Versailles, France, Jan. 8, 1972; PhD, U. Paris sud, 2000. Cert. pharmacist U. Paris sud, 1995. Asst. prof. UMR CNRS 8612, U. Paris sud, 2001—. Mem.: French Assn. Pharmacotech., APGI. Avocation: horseback riding. Office: Faculté de Pharmacie 5 rue JB Clément Chatenay Malabry 92296 France Business E-Mail: karine.andrieux@u-psud.fr.

ANDRIOLA, MARY REPOLE, neurologist, pediatrician; b. NYC, Sept. 13, 1942; d. Anthony Francis Repole and Florence Elizabeth Elliott; m. Micheal John Andriola, July 21, 1962 (div. Jan. 1982); children: Margaret Mary Danao, Joseph Anthony, James Michael; m. Jordan I. Levine, Feb. 24, 1990. Student, Vassar Coll., 1958-60; AB, Johns Hopkins U., 1962; MD, Duke U., 1965. Diplomate Am. Bd. Pediatrics, Am. Bd. Psychiatry and Neurology, with spl. competence in child neurology and added qualification in clin. neurophysiology, subspecialty neurodevel. disabilities, 2005. Resident in pediatrs. Duke U. Sch. Medicine, Durham, NC, 1965-66, U. Fla., Gainesville,

1966-67, resident in neurology, 1967-70; asst. prof. neurology and pediats. La. State U. Sch. Medicine, New Orleans, 1970-72; dir. electroencephalography and fellowship program U. Fla. Coll. Medicine, Gainesville, 1975-88, assoc. prof. neurology, 1975-88, assoc. prof. pediats., 1978-88; dir. pediat. neurology All Children's Hosp. U. S. Fla., St. Petersburg; assoc. prof. neurology SUNY, Stony Brook, 1988-98, dir. clin. neurophysiology, 1990-97, dir. divsn. clin. neurophysiology, 1997, prof. neurology and pediats., 1998—, dir. divsn. pediat. neurology, 2001—. Assoc. examiner Am. Bd. Qualification in EEG, 1976-85, Am. Bd. Psychiatry and Neurology, 1983—, Am. Bd. Clin. Neurophysiology, Inc., 1991—; mem. adv. com. Pinellas county Sch. Bd. Health, 1979-88; reviewer Neurology, 1997—; appeared in TV interviews; mem. People to People Women Specialist Med. Exch. to China, 1991; mem. profl. adv. bd. Epilepsy Found L.I., 1991—; mem. team to Russia, Physicians for Social Responsibility, 1992; lectr. in field. Author: Introduction to EEG and Evoked Potentials, 1983; contbr. articles to profl. jours., chpts. to books Grantee Abbott Labs., 1992, 96, Burroughs Wellcome, 1993, NIH, 1993, Parke-Davis, 1994, BECTS, 1995, Hoechst Marion Roussel, 1995, Warner Lambert, 1995, Cyberonics, 1998; named Best Dr. Child Neurology, NY Mag., 2005-10. Fellow: Am. Clin. Neurophysiology Soc. (program com. 1980—81, practice com. 1980—82, EEG lab. accreditation bd. 1980—90, liaison Child Neurology Soc. 1982—88), Am. Acad. Pediats.; mem.: So. Clin. Neurol. Soc. (bd. dirs.), Suffolk County Pediat. Soc., Tri-State Child Neurology Soc., Ea. Assn. Electroencephalographers, Child Neurology Soc., Am. Epilepsy Soc., So. EEG Soc. (sec.-treas. 1975—78, program chmn. 1979, pres. 1980, edn. chmn. 1981—89), Women's Am. Med. Assn. (sec.-treas. Suffolk County chpt. 1992). Office: SUNY Stony Brook Sch Medicine Dept Neurology Stony Brook NY 11794-0001 Home Phone: 631-751-1356; Office Phone: 631-444-2599. Business E-Mail: mandriol@notes.cc.sunysb.edu.

ANDRIOLE, JOSEPH G., diagnostic radiologist; MD, Howard U., 1980. Diplomate Am. Bd. Radiology-diagnostic radiology, 1985. Resident diagnostic radiology Case Western Univ. Hosps., Cleveland, 1981—84; hosp. affiliations include South Lake Meml. Hosp., Clermont, Fla., Health Ctrl. Hosp., Ocoee, Orlando Regional Healthcare, St. Cloud Regional Med. Ctr. Office: Medical Center Radiology Group 20 W Kaley St Orlando FL 32806 Office Phone: 407-423-5511. Office Fax: 407-423-1930.

ANDRONACHE, CONSTANTIN, physics professor; b. Ploiesti, Romania, Jan. 5, 1952; Degree in Physics, U. Bucuresti, 1975; PhD, U. Cluj-Napoca, 2008. Lectr., dept. sci. North U. Baia Mare, 1996—. Mem.: Romanian Physics Soc. Avocation: astrophysics, amateur radio. Office: Victoriei 48 Baia Mare Maramures 430000 Romania Personal E-mail: androtin03@yahoo.com.

AÑEZ, LUIS M., psychology professor; b. Caracas, Venezuela, Nov. 2, 1960; EdS, U. South Fla., 1992; PhD, Fla. Inst. Tech., 1996. Assoc. prof.; dir. Hispanic svcs. Yale U. Sch. Medicine, Conn. Mental Health Ctr., 1996—. Recipient Stephen Fleck award, Yale U. Sch. Medicine Dept. Psychiatry, 2010, Distinguish Faculty award, award, Office Minority Rsch., NIH, 2008—09; named one of Alumni of Yr., Fla. Inst. Tech., 2007; fellowship, APA, 1996. Mem.: Nat. Latino Psychol. Assn. Office: 35 Park St New Haven CT 06511 Office Fax: 203-974-5850. Business E-Mail: luis.aneznava@yale.edu.

ANG, CHONG LYE, hospital administrator; Grad., U. Singapore, 1979. Med. dir. Singapore Nat. Eye Ctr., 2000—08, clin. faculty, 1991—; asst. CEO clin. svcs. Singapore Health Svcs., 2008—; splty. tng. ophthalmology Singapore Gen. Hosp., CEO, 2008—. Chmn. specialist tng. com. Min. Health. Fellow Royal Coll. Surgeons Glasgow Ophthalmology, 1885, postgrad. tng., Min. Health, 1990, Royal Coll. Surgeons, Edinburgh, 2001, Asia Pacific Acad. Ophthalmology Outstanding award, 2001. Office: Singapore General Hospital Outram Rd 169608 Singapore Office Phone: 6562223322. Business E-Mail: ang.chong.lye@sgh.com.sg. *

ANG, JOCELYN, physician; b. Manila, Jan. 29, 1966; MD, Far Eastern U. NRMF, 1990. Staff attending physician, divsn. infectious diseases Children's Hosp. Mich., 2000—. Asst. prof. Wayne State U. Sch. Medicine, 2001—11. Recipient Coll. Tchg. award, Wayne State U. Sch. Medicine, Excellence Tchg. award, Children's Hosp. Mich.; named one of Leading Physician of World & Top Pediatrician, Internat. Assn. Pediatricians, 2010, 2011; grant, Nat. Inst. Health NCCAM. Fellow: Am. Acad. Pediat.; mem.: Pediatric Infectious Diseases Soc. America, Infectious Diseases Soc. America. Office: CHM 3901 Beaubien Blvd Detroit MI 48201 Business E-Mail: jang@dmc.org.

ANG, YENG SHONG, medical consultant; b. Sandakan, Sabah, Malaysia; s. Hon Wah and Get Lam Ang; m. Lai Fan Chan, Aug. 5, 1997; children: Joshua, Zoe. B of Medicine, U. Dublin, 1992, MD, 2001. Cons. physician, gastroent. Royal Albert Edward Infirmary, Manchester, England, 2002—. Examiner U. Manchester, 2003—. Mem. governing body Dublin Chinese Christian Ch., Chinese Gospel Ch. Dublin, 1992—2003. Grantee, Irish Soc. Gastroen., 1997—99. Fellow: European Bd. Gastroen.; mem.: Irish Soc. Gastroen., Brit. Soc. Gastroenterology, Royal Coll. Physicians Ireland. Avocations: history, soccer, travel. Office: Royal Albert Edward Infirmary Wigan Lane WN1 2NN Manchester England Office Phone: 01942-773119. Office Fax: 01942-822340. Business E-Mail: yeng.ang@wwl.whs.wk.

ANGEL, AUBIE, endocrinologist, academic administrator; b. Winnipeg, Man., Can., Aug. 28, 1935; BSc in Medicine, U. Man., 1959, MD, 1959; MSc, McGill U., 1963. Speciality resident in diabetes and endocrinology Montreal Gen. Hosp., 1961-62; postgrad. dept. exptl. medicine McGill U., 1962-63; asst. resident in medicine Royal Victoria Hosp., Montreal, 1963—64; asst. prof. pathology McGill U., Montreal, Que., Canada, 1965-68; staff physician Royal Victoria Hosp., Montreal, 1965-68; sr. physician and staff endocrinologist Toronto Gen. Hosp., 1968-90; asst. prof. medicine U. Toronto, Ont., Canada, 1968-72, assoc. prof., 1972-81, prof. medicine, 1981-90, dir. Inst. Med. Sci. and clin. scis. divsn., 1983-90; prof., head dept. medicine U. Man., Canada, 1991-95, sr. fellow Ctr. for Advancement ofMedicine, 2002—; physician in chief Health Sci. Ctr., Winnipeg, Man., 1991-95. Vis. scientist U. Calif., San Diego, 1977—78, Hammersmith Hosp., London, 1978; founding pres. Diabetes Rsch. and Treatment Ctr., Winnipeg, 1991—; founding pres., chmn. bd. dirs. Friends of CIHR, 1994—; scholar-in-residence MRC, Canada, 1996; pres. 7th Internat. Congress on Obesity, 1994; co-chair Internat. Conf. Diabetes and Cardiovascular Disease, 1999. Editor (with C.H. Hollenberg and D.A.K. Roncari): The Adipocyte and Obesity: Cellular and Molecular Mechanisms, 1983; editor: (with J. Frohlich) Lipoprotein Deficiency Syndromes: Advances in Experimental Medicine and Biology, 1986; editor: (with N. Sakamoto and N. Hotta) New Directions in Research and Clinical Works for Obesity and Diabetes Mellitus, 1991; editor: (with H. Anderson, C. Bouchard, D. Lau, L. Leiter, R. Mendels) Progress in Obesity Research, 1996; editor: (with N. Dhalla, G. Grant, P. Singal) Diabetes and Cardiovascular Disease, 2001. Project dir. Can. Internat. Devel. Agy., Toronto and Costa Rica, 1987-94. Recipient Outstanding Svc. award Heart and Stroke Found. Ont., 1985; U. Toronto Med. Rsch. Coun. scholar, 1965-71; Trinity Coll. fellow, Toronto, 1989—; sr. fellow Massey Coll. U. Toronto, 2005—. Fellow Royal Coll. Physicians and Surgeons Costa Rica (hon.), Royal Coll. Physicians Can., N.Am. Assn. Study Obesity (pres. 1986-87), Can. Soc. Clin. Investigation (councillor 1977-80), Am. Soc. Clin. Investigation, Can. Inst. Acad. Medicine (founding pres. 1990-92), Internat. Assn. Study Obesity (bd. govs. 1986—), Internat. Acad. Cardiovasc. Scis., Juvenile Diabetes Found. Internat. (hon. bd. dirs. 1987-90), Obesity Canada (founding bd. dirs. 1999-2001), Can. Acad. Health Scis. Office: Massey Coll Univ Toronto 4 Devonshire Pl Toronto ON Canada M5S 2E1

ANGEL, CARLOS ALBERTO, pediatric surgeon, urologist; b. Bogota, Colombia, Mar. 16, 1953; arrived in US, 1986; s. Carlos Eduardo and Margarita (De Greiff) A.; m. Claudia Malkun, 1987; children: Santiago, Catalina. BS, Presbyn. Coll., Clinton, SC, 1974; MD, Univ. del Rosario, Bogota, 1980. Resident in gen. surgery U. del Rosario, Bogota, 1983-86; fellow in pediat. surgery U. Tenn., Memphis, 1986-88, chief fellow pediat. surgery, 1988-89, fellow pediat. urology, 1990-91; fellow in pediat. oncologic surgery St. Jude's Children's Rsch. Hosp., Memphis, 1989-90; pediat. surgeon, pediat. urologist U. Tex. Med. Br., Galveston, Tex., 1993—2003; pediat. surgeon, pediat. urologist, assoc. prof. U. Tenn., Knoxville, 2003—. Contbr. articles to profl. jours., chpts. to books. Active vol. colombian Red Cross Surg. Brigades, Chocó, 1985, Meta, 1986; vol. Surg. Vols. Internat., Internat. Vols. Urology, 2005-. Mem. ACS, Am. Pediat. Surg. Assn., Singleton Surg. Soc., Brit. Assn. Pediat. Surgeons, Internat. Pediat. Endosurgery Group; fellow Am. Coll. Surgeons. Democrat. Roman Catholic. Avocations: tennis, jogging, reading, music, golf. Home: 4203 Towanda Trail Knoxville TN 37919 Office Phone: 865-546-2131. Business E-Mail: cangel@etch.com.

ANGELES, JORGE GIL CARINO, molecular biologist, researcher; b. Makati City, Philippines, Oct. 3, 1975; s. Jorge Sotelo and Lourdes Carino Angeles. MS in Molecular Biology and Biotech., U. The Philippines, 1997, BS in Biology, 1997, BS, 2002. Asst. to COO course developer, instr. STI Coll., Binan, Laguna, Philippines, 1997—2000; rschr. tissue culture lab. Internat. Rice Rsch. Inst., Los Banos, Laguna, Philippines, 1998—99; rschr. biochemistry lab. Inst. Plant Breeding, College, Laguna, Philippines, 2001—. Head servant St. Polycarp Chorale, Cabuyao, Laguna, Philippines, 1991—. Recipient Duty award, U. the Philippines Los Banos, 1994, Presdl. award, St. Polycarp Chorale, 2004, Ayala Found. award, Philippine Emerging Startups Open, 2005; named Most Outstanding Club Mem., De La Salle Santiago Zobel Sch., 1985—93; Coll. Scholar, U. the Philippines Los Banos. Mem.: Chem. Soc. the Philippines (assoc.), Philippine Soc. for Biochemistry and Molecular Biology (life), Gamma Sigma Delta (life Best MS Thesis award 2003). Achievements include research in coconut biochemistry, molecular biology, bioinformatics and biotechnology, control of ripening of papaya and mango through genetic engring. Office: Univ the Philippines Los Banos Inst Plant Breeding 4031 College Laguna Philippines

ANGELESCU, AMANDA GOSECO, pediatrician, endocrinologist; arrived in U.S., 1994; MD, U. of the East, Philippines, 1992. Diplomate Am. Bd. Pediat., 1997. Intern U. of the East, 1992—93; resident in pediat., 1994—97; chief resident in pediat. Westchester (NY) Med. Ctr., 1997—98; fellow in pediat. endocrinologiy N.Y. Presbyn. Hosp., NYC, 1998—2001; pediatric endocrinologist Driscoll Children's Hosp., Corpus Christi, Tex., 2002—05, U. Mass. Meml. Med. Ctr., Worcester, 2005—. Office: Univ Mass Meml Med Ctr 55 Lake Ave North Worcester MA 01655 Business E-Mail: angelesa@ummhc.org.

ANGELO, E. JOANNE, child, adolescent and adult psychiatrist; b. Boston, Feb. 11, 1936; d. Gaspar and Eda (Polcari) A. AB, Mt. Holyoke Coll., 1957; MD, Tufts U., 1961. Diplomate Am. Bd. Psychiatry and Neurology, 1972. Med. dir. Canarsie Mental Health Ctr., Bklyn., 1967—69; staff psychiatrist Cmty. Mental Health Svcs., Mass. Mental Health Ctr., Boston, 1969—73; psychiat. dir. Laboure Ctr., South Boston, Mass., 1974—78; pvt. practice Boston, 1969—. Cons. Chandler Sch. for Women, Boston, 1971-72, Kennedy Meml. Hosp., Boston, 1971-72, St. Margaret's Hosp., Boston, 1976-83, North Suffolk Health Ctr., Boston, 1978-79; mem. staff St. Elizabeth's Hosp., Boston, Good Samaritan Hospice Boston, 1985-1990. Mem. editl. bd. (Jour.) Nat. Cath. Bioethics Quar. Mem. Pontifical Acad. for Life (corr.). Office: 403 Commonwealth Ave Boston MA 02215-2326 Office Phone: 617-266-3093. E-mail: joanneangelo@massmed.org.

ANGELO, MARK, internist, educator; Grad., Temple U. Diplomate Am. Bd. Internal Medicine. Intern Temple Univ. Hosp., resident Phila.; physician Cooper Univ., Voorhees, NJ. Asst. prof. Cooper Univ. Hosp. Named one of the Top Doctors, Phila. Mag., 2011. Office: Cooper University Hospital Bldg 2 Ste 201 900 Centennial Blvd Voorhees NJ 08043 Office Phone: 856-325-6770. Office Fax: 856-673-4300.

ANGELOPOULOS, NICHOLAS G., endocrinologist, researcher; b. Athens, Greece, Apr. 1, 1972; s. George Angelopoulos and Maria Pantazi; m. Anastasia C. Goula, Jan. 19, 2002; children: Maria Angelopoulou, Constantine Angelopoulou. MD, Aristoteleion U., Thessaloniki, Greece, 1995. Cert. Greek Bd. Internal Medicine, Greek Ministry Health, 1995. Fellow internal medicine Gen. Hosp. Chalkis, Chalkida, Greece, 1997—2001; fellow endocrinology and metabolism Hippocration Hosp. Athens, 2002—06. Contbr. articles to profl. jours. Office: Hippocration Hosp Athens Vassilisis Olgas 108 11527 Athens Greece Office Fax: +44 210 7786889. Personal E-mail: drangelnick@hotmail.com. Business E-Mail: drangelnick@endo.gr.

ANGHELESCU, DORALINA LUCIA, anesthesiologist; b. Bucharest, Romania, Aug. 1, 1961; d. Liviu Veneriu and Aurelia Niculina (Arseni) Gontea; m. Mircea Vladimir Anghelescu, June 6, 1987 (div. July 1991); 1 child, Andrei. MD, Bucharest Sch. Medicine, 1985. Intern Elias Found. Hosp., Bucharest, 1985—87; staff physician in anesthesiology Inst. Endocrinology, Bucharest, 1987—93; resident in anesthesiology U. N.Mex., Albuquerque, 1993—97, fellow in pain mgmt., 1998—99; fellow in pediat. anesthesia Childrens Nat. Med. Ctr., Washington, 1997—98; pediat. anesthesiologist, dir. pain mgmt. svc. St. Jude Children's Rsch. Hosp., Memphis, 1999—. Co-author: The Pain Clinic Manual, 2d edit., 2000; contbr. articles to profl. jours. Grantee, Jenssen Found., 2001. Mem.: Internat. Assn. for the Study Pain, Am. Acad. Pain, Soc. Pediat. Anesthesia, Am. Soc. Anesthesiologists. Office: St Jude Childrens Rsch Hosp 332 N Lauderdale St Memphis TN 38105 Office Phone: 901-595-4034. Business E-Mail: doralina.anghelescu@stjude.org.

ANGINO, ERNEST EDWARD, retired geology and engineering educator; b. Winsted, Conn., Feb. 16, 1932; s. Alfred and Filomena Mabel (Serluco) A.; m. Margaret Mary Lachat, June 26, 1954; children— Cheryl Ann, Kimberly Ann. BS in Mining Engring., Lehigh U., Bethlehem, Pa., 1954; MS in Geology, U. Kans., 1958, PhD in Geology, 1961. Instr. geology U. Kans., Lawrence, 1961-62, prof. civil engring., 1971-99, prof. geology, 1972-99, prof. emeritus, 1999—, chmn. dept. geology, 1972-86, dir. water resources ctr., 1990-99; asst. prof. Tex. A&M U., College Station, 1962-65; chief geochemist Kans. Geol. Survey, Lawrence, 1965-70, assoc. state geologist, 1970-72. Cons. on water chemistry and pollution to various cos. and govt. agys. including Dow Chem. Co., Ocean Mining Inc., Envicon, Oak Ridge Lab., Fisheries Rsch. Bd. Can., Midwest Rsch. Inst., Coast and Geodetic Survey, U.S. Geol. Survey. Author: (with G.K. Billings) Atomic Absorption Spectrometry in Geology, 1967; author, editor: (with D.T. Long) Geochemistry of Bismuth, 1979; editor: (with R.K. Hardy) Proc. 3d Forum Geol. Industrial Minerals, 1967, (with G.K. Billings) Geochemistry Subsurface Brines, 1969; contbr. more than 125 articles to sci. and profl. jours. Sec. Geochem. Soc., 1970-76; mem. Lawrence City Police Rels. Commn., 1970-76, Lawrence City Commn., 1983-87, mayor, 1984-85; pres. Soc. Environ. Geochemistry and Health, 1978-79; treas. Internat. Assn. Geochemistry and Cosmochemistry, 1980-94; mem. Lawrence 2020 Planning Commn., 1992-94, Police Adv. Coun., 1994-06, Crimestoppers Bd., 1994-03, Lawrence Tax Abatement Commn., 2001-02, Lawrence-Douglas County Planning Commn. 2002-05, Health Care Access Bd., 1997-02, Lawrence-Douglas County Econ. Devel. Commn., 2006—. With U.S. Army, 1955-57. NSF fellow Oak Ridge Lab., 1963; recipient Antarctic Service medal Dept. Def., 1969; Angino Buttress in Antarctica named in his honor, 1967. Mem. Am. Philatelist Soc., Meter Stamp Soc., Forum Club (Factotum 1978-2008), Rotary (pres. 1993-95). Republican. Roman Catholic. Avocations: philately, Western history, Indian lore. Home: 4605 Grove Dr Lawrence KS 66049-3777 Office: U Kans Dept Geology Lindley 120 1475 Jayhawk Blvd Lawrence KS 66045-0001 Home Phone: 785-843-7503. Personal E-mail: rockdoc@sunflower.com.

ANGIOLILLO, DOMINICK J., cardiologist, director; b. NYC, May 19, 1971; MD, Cath. U. Rome, PhD, 1997. Dir., cardiovasc. rsch. U. Fla., 2004—. Home: 6766 Linford Ln Jacksonville FL 32217 Business E-Mail: dominick.angiolillo@jax.ufl.edu.

ANGIOLINI, MAURO, medicinal chemist; b. Bergamo, Italy, Mar. 21, 1970; s. Leonardo Salerno and Clorinda Angiolini; m. Paola Bandiera, Oct. 12, 2002; 1 child, Chiara. Degree in Chemistry, U. Degli Studi Milano, Italy, 1995, PhD in Medicinal Chemistry, 1998; postdoc., U. Montreal, Can., 2001. Jr. rschr. Pharmacia, Nerviano, Italy, 1998—2004; sr. rsch. scientist Nerviano Med. Scis., 2004—. Sci. jour. referee Springer Recover Diversity; edtl. bd. mem. Futuce Sci. Group; referee European Jour. Medicinal Chemistry, Jour. Medicinal Chemistry, Am. Chem. Soc. Contbr. articles to profl. jours. Named Top 100 Health Profl., Inst. Profl. Cambridge, 2011. Mem.: Am. Chem. Soc. Office: Nerviano Med Scis Viale Pasteur 10 Nerviano 20014 Italy Personal E-mail: mauro.angiolini@tin.it. Business E-Mail: mauro.angiolini@nervianoms.com.

ANGLADA-CURADO, FRANCISCO JOSÉ, surgeon; b. Sevilla, Spain, May 26, 1966; MD, Sevilla, 1992. Urologic surgeon Servicio Andaluz de Salud, 2000—. Master: Andalusian Urologic Assn.; mem.: Biomed. Investigation Inst. Córdoba. Avocations: reading, running. Office: Menendez Pidal sn Córdoba 14011 Spain Office Fax: 0034957011059. Business E-Mail: ancusr@ono.com.

ANGOFF, GERALD HARVEY, cardiologist; s. Nathan Robert and Evelyn (Kanter) A.; m. Rosalind Norma Tarko, Nov. 23, 1975; children: Elizabeth, Rebekah. AB, Harvard Coll., 1966; MD, Harvard U., 1970; MBA, U. Mass., 2006. Diplomate Am. Bd. Internal Medicine, Am. Bd. Cardiovascular Disease, Nat. Bd. Echocardiography; cert. physician exec. Resident internal medicine Cleve. Met. Gen. Hosp., 1970-72; fellow in cardiology Harvard Med. Sch., Peter Bent Brigham Hosp., Boston, 1975-77, Harvard Sch. Pub. Health, Boston, 1977-78; cardiologist The Heart Ctr., Manchester, NH, 1978-99, New Eng. Heart Inst., 1999—2005; dir. noninvasive cardiology New England Heart Inst., 1999—2002; physician exec. Cerner Corp., 2005—07; co-dir. Adult Congenital Heart, Disease Dartmouth-Hitchcock Med. Ctr., 2008—. Chief cardiology Elliot Hosp., Manchester, 1979-82, 86-93; instr. Harvard Med. Sch., Boston, 1978-96; pres. The Heart Ctr., 1995-99. Bd. dirs. Jewish Fedn. Greater Manchester, 1984-94; v.p. Temple Adath Yeshurun, Manchester, 1994-96, pres., 1996-98. Maj. Med. Corp US Army, 1972—75. Recipient award of acad. achievement in med. mgmt., Am. Coll. Physician Execs. Fellow Am. Coll. Cardiology, Am. Heart Assn. (Coun. on clin. cardiology), Adult Congenital Heart Assn., New England Congenital Cardiology Assn., Am. Coll. Physicinad Execs., Beta Gamma Sigma International Honor Soc. Avocations: computers, skiing. Office: Dartmouth-Hitchcock Med Ctr 100 Hitchcock Way Manchester NH 03104 Home Phone: 603-494-7334. Business E-Mail: gerry.angoff@cerner.com.

ANGOT, JEAN-LUC EUGENE ALBERT, veterinarian; b. Paris, Dec. 16, 1958; DVM, Nat. Vet. Sch., Toulouse, 1982. Dir. Meuse Vet. Svcs., 1993—95; codex alimentarius chief officer Prime Min. Svcs., 1996—98; dep. dir. French Agy. Meat and Livestock, 1998—2001; dep. dir. gen. World Orgn. Animal Health, 2001—09; chief vet. officer France, dep. dir. gen. food Ministry Agr., Food and Fisheries, 2009—. Exec. coun. Nat. Vet. Sch., Toulouse, 1978—82; bd. dirs. French Agy. Food Safety, 2009—11; exec. coun. Nat. Vet. Svcs. Sch., 2009—11. Contbr. articles to profl. med. jours. Recipient Agr. Merite award, Ministry Agr., Food and Fisheries, Silver medal, U. Toulouse; nominee Vet. of Yr., Le Point Vétérinaire. Master: French Vet. Practice Soc. (vice chmn.); mem.: High Com. Civil Def., French Vet.

Acad. Avocations: literature, running, movies. Office: 251 rue de Vaugirard Paris 75015 France Office Fax: 33 1 49 55 81 82. Business E-Mail: jean-luc.angot@agriculture.gouv.fr.

ANGOTTI, CATHERINE MARIE, occupational health director; b. Arlington, Va., Nov. 9, 1946; d. Frank William and Catherine Jeannette (Kolakoski) Poos; 1 child, Heather Jeannette. BS, James Madison U., 1968; RD, Med. Coll. Va., 1969. Home economist Washington Gas Light Co., 1968; clin. dietitian Fairfax (Va.) Hosp., 1969-73; pvt. practice as nutrition cons. Va., 1972-98; nutrition cons. Manassas (Va.) Manor Nursing Home, 1973-74, Bio-Tech., Inc., Falls Church, Va., 1977-78; nutrition surveyor JWK Internat., Annandale, Va., 1980-81; nutrition cons. NASA, Washington, 1977-92, program exec. occupl. health, 1992—2000, dir. occupl. health, 2000—, adminstrv. dept. to chief health and med. officer, 2003—. Pres. Nutrition Cons., Inc., 1980—98; nutrition lectr. Contbr. articles to profl. jours. Mem. com. Pub. Regional Diet Manual, 1971—73. Recipient Spl. Svcs. award, NASA, 1989, 1994, Exceptional Performance awards, 1996—2007, Space Flight Awareness award, 1996, Spl. Achievement award, 1997, Superior Accomplishment award, 2003, Exceptional Performance medal, 1999, Sr. Exec. Fellowship award, 2000, Outstanding Leadership medal, 2005. Mem.: NAFE, Cons. Nutritionists Chesapeake Bay Area (mem. nominating com. 1983, sec. 1986—87), Fairfax County Nutrition Com., No. Dist. Dietetic Assn. (exec. bd. 1977—86, treas. 1980—82, pres. 1983—84, chmn. nominating com. 1984—85, mem. awards com. 1988, exec. bd. 1988—95, Dietetic Appreciation award 1987), DC Dietetic Assn., Cons. Nutritionists (Va. state coord. 1976—79), Va. Assn. Allied Health Profls. (del. 1974—79, bd. dirs. 1975—77), Am. Dietetic Assn. (state rep. nutrition svcs. payment sys. 1984—87, del. 1987—90, chmn. dels. 1988—90, Recognized Young Dietitian of the Yr. award 1975, Outstanding Svc. award 1990, Occupation and Health award 1990, Disting. Dietitian award 1992), Va. Dietetic Assn. (del. Va. Coun. State Legis. 1974—76, exec. bd. 1974—76, legis. chmn. 1974—76, mem. nominating com. 1982—84, exec. bd. 1982—96, mem. licensure com. 1983—89, chmn. nutrition svcs. com. 1983—97, mem. payment sys. 1984—87, del., pres.-elect 1993—94, pres. 1994—95, chmn. nominating com. 1995—96, mem. disting. dietitian selection com. 2003—05, bd. dirs. 2004—, coord. outreach divsn. 2004—05, spl. advisor pub. policy 2005—). Home: 2727 Oak Valley Dr Vienna VA 22181-5339 Office: 300 E St SW Washington DC 20546 Business E-Mail: cangotti@hq.nasa.gov.

ANGOURAS, DIMITRIOS C., cardiologist, educator; b. Athens, Greece, Aug. 4, 1966, MD, Athens U. Sch. Medicine, 1990, PhD, 1996. Postdoc. clin. fellow, minimally invasive cardiac surgery Ohio State U., 2000—02; lectr. Dept. Cardiac Surgery, Athens U. Sch. Medicine, 2006—10, asst. prof., 2010—. Recipient Academic Excellence prize, Athens U. Med. Sch. Fellow: European Bd. Thoracic and Cardiovasc. Surgeons; mem.: Hellenic Soc. Thoracic and Cardiovasc. Surgeons (Best Exptl. Stu, 5th Nat. Congress, Best Study award, 4th Nat. Sci. Symposium), Zollinger Surg. Soc. (Ohio), Soc. Thoracic Surgeons, European Assn. Cardiothoracic Surgery. Avocations: basketball, theater. Office: 1 Rimini St Chaidari Athens Attica 12462 Greece Personal E-mail: dangouras@yahoo.com.

ANGRES, DANIEL H., psychiatrist, educator; MD, Autonomous U., Mexico, 1976. Diplomate Am. Bd. Psychiatry and Neurology-psychiatry, 1991, Am. Bd. Psychiatry and Neurology-addiction psychiatry, 2004. Resident neurology Univ. Ill. Med. Ctr., 1977—78, resident psychiatry Rush-Presbyn. St. Lukes Med. Ctr., Chgo., 1978—80, fellow psychiatry, 1987—88; assoc. prof. psychiatry coll. med. Univ. Ill.; hospital affiliations include St. Joseph Hosp., Rush Univ. Med. Ctr. Named one of Top Doctors, Chgo. Mag. Office: University of Illinois College of Medicine 1853 West Polk St Chicago IL 60612 Office Phone: 312-669-3500. Office Fax: 312-996-9006.

ANGUS, BEVERLEY MARGARET, retired parasitologist; b. Lautoka, Fiji, Nov. 18, 1934; arrived in Australia, 1964; d. David Arthur and Lily Kermeen (Lawson) Ewins; m. James Robert Beales Angus; children: Justine Robyn, Robert Gordon. BS, U. Queensland, Australia, 1979, BS with honors, 1980, PhD, 1994; grad. diploma in Edn., Queensland U. Tech., Australia, 1988. Sci. rschr. U. Newcastle, NSW, Australia, 1981-83; acting prin. Women's Coll. U. Queensland, Brisbane, Australia, 1984-85, prin. Grace Coll., 1985-87; dir. confs. and student residences Griffith U., Brisbane, 1988-89, rschr., 1990-94; cons., rsch. fellow Queensland Mus., Brisbane, 1997—2006, ret., 2006. Protocol officer VI internat. congress parasitology Australian Soc. Parasitology, Brisbane, 1985-86, guest lectr. Pathology, Sch. Hlth. Scis., Gold Coast Queensland, 1997-99. Author: Tick Fever and The Cattle Tick in Australia, 1998, 2nd edit., 2003; sect. editor Internat. Jour. Parasitology, 1995-97, A History of Parasitology in Queensland, 2007; contbr. From Many Nations, 1995, articles to profl. jours. Mem. U. Queensland Senate Com., 1984-88, gov., Internat. House U. Queensland, 1983-89, Cromwell Coll. coun., 1984-88. Mem. Australian Soc. Parasitology, Australian Soc. History Medicine. Australian Liberal Party. Anglican. Avocations: golf, swimming, weight training, history of science. Home: PO Box 4934 G C M C Bundall Queensland 9726 Australia Personal E-mail: bmangus@y7mail.com.

ANGUS, DEREK CALDER, internist; b. Glasgow, Aug. 13, 1962; MBChB, U. Glasgow, 1984; MPH, U. Pitts., 1992. Prof., tenure U. Pitts. Sch. Medicine, 2003, chair, dept. critical care medicine, 2009—. Recipient Disting. Investigator award, Am. Coll. Critical Care Medicine. Mem.: Am. Coll. Chest Physicians, Am. Thoracic Soc. (Citation award), Soc. Critical Care Medicine (Presdl. Citation award, Ednl. Healthcare Splty. award), Assn. Health Svcs. Rsch., European Soc. Intensive Care Medicine (Best Abstract award). Office: Scaife Hall Rm 614 3550 Ter St Pittsburgh PA 15261 Office Fax: 412-647-5258. Business E-Mail: angusdc@upmc.edu.

ANGUS, JAMES ALEXANDER, pharmacology educator; b. Sydney, NSW, Australia, Feb. 15, 1949; s. Stuart Douglas and Evelyn Simpson (Wilkie) A.; m. Helen Shirley Robinson, Dec. 28, 1971; children: Damien, Kirsten, Simon. BSc with honors in Pharmacology, U. Sydney, 1970, PhD in Pharmacology, 1974. Rsch. fellow dept. medicine Hallstrom Inst. Cardiology Royal Prince Alfred Hosp., U. Sydney, 1973, NHMRC sr. rsch. officer, 1974-75, Baker Med. Rsch. Inst., Prahran, Victoria, Australia, 1975-76, 80-81, NHMRC rsch. fellow, 1981-82, NHMRC sr. rsch. fellow, 1983-85, NHMRC prin. rsch. fellow, 1985, NHMRC sr. prin. rsch. fellow, 1989-92, dep. dir., 1990-92; personal chair pharmacology faculty medicine Monash U., Melbourne, Australia, 1992-93; chair pharmacology, head dept. Melbourne U., Australia, 1993—2003, pro-vice chancellor, 1999—2001, pres. acad. bd., 2000—01, dep. dean faculty medicine dentistry and health scis., 2002—03, dean faculty medicine dentistry and health scis., 2003—. NHMRC C.J. Martin traveling fellow dept. pharmacology U. Coll., London, 1977, Wellcome Rsch. Labs., Beckenham, Kent, Eng., 1978, Baker Med. Rsch. Inst., 1979; chair med. rsch. grants com. NHMRC, Canberra, Australia, 1991-93; mem. nat. com. pharmacology Australian Acad. Sci., 1994—; mem. sci. program com. 15th Sci. Meeting Internat. Soc. Hypertension, 1994; mem. nat. adv. bd. Internat. Soc. Cardiovascular Pharmacotherpy, Sydney, 1996; cons. panel Microsurgery Rsch. Ctr., St. Vincent's Hosp., 1990-2002. Editor (exec.): (jours.) Clin. and Exptl. Pharmacology and Physiology, 1993—98; editl. bd. Jour. Vascular Rsch., 1992—96, Endothelium, 1992—96, Brit. Jour. Pharmacology, 1991—95, mem. internat. adv. com. Pharmacology and Toxicology, 1993—2000. Bd. mem. Murdoch Inst. Birth Defects, Melbourne, 1991-97; coun. mem. Melbourne Grammar Sch., 1991-98; mem. poisons adv. com. Victorian Dept. Health & Cmty. Svcs., Melbourne, 1993-97; mem. bd. Queensland Pharm. Rsch. Inst., Griffith U., 1994—. Recipient Alfred Gottschalk medal Australian Acad. Sci., 1984; grantee Nat. Heart Found., 1979-80, 80-81, 88-89, 90-91, 91-93, NHMRC, 1982-92, Glaxo Australia and Pharmacology Lab. at Baker Inst., 1989-93, Glaxo Australia and Dept. Pharmacology, U. Melbourne, 1993-98. Fellow: Australian Acad. Sci. (coun. 2001—04); mem.: Internat. Union Pharmacology (coun. 1998—2002, 1st v.p. 2002—06), Internat. Soc. Heart Rsch., High Blood Pressure Rsch. Coun. Australia, Cardiac Soc. Australia and New Zealand, Brit. Pharmacol. Soc., Australian Soc. Clin. and Exptl. Pharmacology, Australian Physiol. and Pharmacol. Soc. Avocations: golf, fishing, sailing. Office: U Melbourne Faculty Med Parkville VIC 3010 Australia Business E-Mail: jamesaa@unimelb.edu.au.

ANGUS, ROBERT CARLYLE, JR., naturopathic physician, health administrator; b. Grand Rapids, Mich., July 23, 1946; s. Robert Carlyle Sr. and Vicki I. (Weidman) Deiters; m. Elizabeth T. Angus, May 1995; children: Tamra Ann, Robert M. BS, Donsbach U., Huntington Beach, Calif., 1985; PhD in Therapeutic Philosophy, World U., 1982. Registered cardiovasc. technologist, pulmonary technologist, cardiology technologist; cert. respiratory therapist; lic. respiratory care practitioner, Mich.; cert. occupl. hearing conservationist; bd. cert. naturopathic physician Am. Naturopathic Med. Assn.; nat. bd. cert. colon hydrotherapist advanced level; cert. thermographer. Dir. cardiopulmonary St. Mary's Hosp., Grand Rapids, Mich., 1970-74; Lectr. Muskegon (Mich.) Community Coll., 1974-76; dir. respiratory therapy Hackley Hosp., 1974-76; dir. cardiovascular, cardiopulmonary Am. Internat. Hosp., Zion, Ill., 1976-78; physician's asst. Dr. William J. Mauer; dir. med. svcs., clinic adminstr. Kingsley Med. Ctr., Arlington Heights, Ill., 1978-90; clinical dir., naturopathic physician Celebration of Health Assn., Inc., Bluffton, Ohio, 1990—. Edn. cons. Brookhaven Med. Care Facility; lectr., advisor Muskegon C.C., 1974-76; mem. Nat. Bd. Respiratory Care; bd. dirs. Nat. Bd. for Colon Hydrotherapy, 2000-04. Active Big Bros. Am., Muskegon, 1974-76. Mem. Am. Acad. Thermology, Nat. Bd. Cardiovascular Testing, Am. Cardiology Technologists Assn., Am. Assn. Respiratory Care, Am. Naturopathic Med. Assn., Nat. Soc. Cardiopulmonary Technologists, Coun. for Accreditation in Occupational Hearing Conservation, Internat. Assn. for Colon Hydrothrapy (bd. cert.), Soc. for Noninvasive Vascular Tech., Cardiovascular Credentialing Internat., Allen County Illicit Discharges Bd. Appeals. Avocations: canoeing, horses, antiques, old radios, reading.

ÁNGYÁN, LAJOS, physiologist, researcher; b. Böhönye, Somogy, Hungary, June 26, 1938; s. Lajos and Mária (Kalmár) A.; m. Éva Pados, Aug. 5, 1961; 1 child, Zoltán. MD, U. Pécs, Hungary, 1962; PhD, Hungarian Acad. Sci., Budapest, 1970, DSc, 1986. Cert. med. lab. examiner specialist; lic. physician. From asst. to lectr. Med. U. Pécs, 1962-95, prof., 1995—2008; ret., 2008. Rschr. lab. neurophysiol. faculty sci. U. Paris, 1969-70; vis. prof. sports physiology Janus Pannonius U., Pécs, 1990-98. Author: Basis of Sports Physiology, 1993, Manual of Sports Physiology, 1995, Introduction to Human Physiology, 1996, Essays in Physiology, 1997, 2001, (with Z. Ángyán) Arterial Blood Pressure: 100 Questions and Answers, 1999, Encyclopedia of Human Movement Sciences, 2000, Kinesiology of the Human Body, 2005; contbr. articles to profl. jours. Named Eminant Worker Edn., Min. Health, Budapest, 1973. Mem. Hungarian Physiol. Soc., Hungarian Neurosci. Soc., Hungarian Soc. Sport Sci., Internat. Brain Rsch. Orgn., European Sleep Rsch. Soc., European Brain and Behaviour Soc., European Neurosci. Assn. Achievements include research in neural control of human movements, and physiological manifestations of sports activities. Avocation: gardening. Home Phone: 36-72-516-637. E-mail: angyanlajos@freemail.hu.

ANIFANDIS, GEORGE M., embryologist; b. Athens, Greece, Dec. 20, 1974; BSc in Biology, 1999; PhD, Med. Sch. Athens, 2004. Clin. embryologist, human reproduction, IVF unit, dept. ob-gyn. Med. Sch. Larisa, U. Thessaly, 2004—. Contbr. articles to profl. jours. Mem.: ESHRE. Office: University Thessaly Medical Sch Larisa Larisa 41222 Greece Business E-Mail: ganif@med.uth.gr.

ANKERMANN, TOBIAS, pediatrician, pulmonologist, consultant; b. Rotenburg Wümme, Germany, Feb. 27, 1962; s. Ernst and Agnes Ankermann; m. Julia Jischa, May 23, 1997; children: Piet, Hannes, Torge, Rasmus. Student, Johann-Wolfgang-Goethe U., Frankfurt/Main, Germany, 1983—85, U. Kiel, Germany, 1985—89, MD, 1991. Lic. physician State Examination Bd., Germany, 1989. Intern kinderkardiologie U. Schleswig-Holstein, Kiel, Germany, 1989—92, resident klinik, 1992—99, cons. pediat. pulmonology, 1989—; pvt. practice, 2009—; asst. prof. pediat. & adolescent medicine, 2009. Author: Arzneimitteltherapie und Ernährung im Kindesalter, 1998, 2d edit., 2006. Handball trainer MTV Celle Germany, 1978—84. Lance cpl. amored infantryman Germany Army, 1981—82. Mem.: Deutsche Gesellschaft für Pädiatrische Pneumologie. Luth. Avocation: handball. Office: Universitätsklinikum Schleswig-Holstein Andel Hellow 1 St 3 Schleswig-Holstein Kiel 24105 Germany Office Fax: 49 431 597 1831. Business E-Mail: ankermann@pediatrics.uni-kiel.de.

ANKERST, JARO, medical educator, consultant; b. Loce, Slovenia, June 25, 1941; s. Erik and Ivanka Ankerst; m. Edith Marianne Ploss; 1 child, Kristina. MD, PhD, U. Lund, Sweden. Assoc. prof., tumorvirology U. Lund, 1972—82, assoc. prof., medicine, 1982—89, clin. tchr., medicine, 1989—91, sr. lectr., cons. med., 1991—2007; prof., sr. cons. U. Hosp. Lund, Sweden, 2007—. Mem.: Swedish Med. Assn. Catholic. Home: Bjeres v 14 Bjärred S-23734 Sweden Office: Univ Hosp Lund Dept Clin Scis Unit Med 221 85 Lund Sweden Office Fax: 46-46-184792. Business E-Mail: jaro.ankerst@med.lu.se.

ANKOLA, PRATIBHA ARUN, pediatrician, director; b. Mumbai, May 13, 1954; MBBS, Seth G. S. Med. Coll., 1978, MD in Pediat., 1980. Dir. neonatology, Met. Hosp. Ctr. NY Med. Coll., 1994—2010, prof. clin. pediat., 2009; med. dir., NICU Pediatrix Med. Group, Arnot Ogden Med. Ctr., 2011—. Named one of Best Tchr., Dept. Pediat. Fellow: NY Acad. Medicine, Am. Acad. Pediat.; mem.: NY Perinatal Soc. Avocations: travel, golf, music. Home: 35 Sprain Valley Rd Scarsdale NY 10583 Personal E-mail: pratibhaankola@yahoo.com.

ANLI, JIANG, nursing educator; b. Shanghai, Oct. 18, 1954; M, East China Normal U., 1993. Prof. Nursing Coll., Second Mil. Med. U., 1993—99, assoc. prof., 1999—, prof., 2003. Recipient Nat. Excellent Tchg. Achievement award, Ministry Edn., China, Excellent Tchg. Achievement award, Shanghai Commn. Edn., China, Mil. Excellent Tchg. Achievement award, PLA, China, Nat. Nursing Tech. Progress Award, Chinese Nursing Assn., Shanghai Nursing Tech. Progress award, Shanghai Nursing Assn., China. Master: Chinese Higher Nursing Edn. Assn. (vice dir.), Higher Nursing Edn. Appraisal Bd. Ministry Health (China), Higher Nursing Edn. Guidance Bd. Ministry Edn. (China) (vice dir.), Nursing Association. PLA (chief editor, vice chairperson). Avocations: reading, writing, travel. Office: 800 Xiangyin Rd Shanghai 200433 China Office Phone: 0086-21-81871501. E-mail: alj1018@yahoo.com.cn.

ANLIN, LV, medical educator; b. Shandong, Oct. 23, 1962; D, Fourth Mil. Med. U., 1998. Prof. Xijing Hosp., 2002—. Office: Changle West St Xi'an Shaanxi 710032 China Office Fax: 86-29-83210198. E-mail: lvanlin@yahoo.com.cn.

ANLYAN, WILLIAM GEORGE, surgeon, educator, academic administrator; b. Alexandria, Egypt, Oct. 14, 1925; s. Armand and Emmy (Nazar) A.; children: William George, John Peter, Louise. BS magna cum laude, Yale U., 1945, MD, 1949; DSc (hon.), Rush Med. Coll., 1973. Diplomate Am. Bd. Surgery, Am. Bd. Thoracic Surgery. Intern, resident, instr., assoc. in surgery Duke Hosp., Durham, NC, 1949-53, asst. prof. surgery, 1953-58, assoc. prof. surgery, 1958—61, prof. surgery, 1961-89; assoc. dean Duke U. Sch. Medicine, 1963, dean, 1964-69, v.p. health affairs, 1969-83, chancellor health affairs, 1983—89, exec. v.p., 1987—89; chancellor Duke U., 1989—90, chancellor emeritus, 1990—. Chmn, Durham VA Chancellor's Com., 1963—89; chmn. Pearle Health Svcs., Inc., 1983—85; surg. cons. Durham VA Hosp.; Markle scholar med. sci., 1953—58; bd. regents Nat. Libr. Medicine, 1971—72; trustee N.C. Sch. Sci. and Math., 1978—85, chmn. phys. facilities com., 1979, vice-chmn. bd. trustees, 1981—84; mem. bd. visitors The U. Tex. Health Sci. Ctr. at Houston, 1980—88, Stanford U., 1985—87; chmn. Yale U. Coun. Com. on Med. Affairs, 1985—93. Mem. editl. bd. Pharos, 1968-93. Trustee The Duke Endowment, 1990—, vice chmn., 2004-, Commn. Future Structure Vet. Health Care, 1990-92; chmn. Gov.'s Task Force Better Health NC in 2000, 1991-97; mem. White House Sci. Coun., 1988-89. Recipient Disting. Achievement award Modern Medicine, 1974; Gov.'s Disting. Meritorious Svc. award, 1978; Abraham Flexner award, 1980, Disting. Surgeon Alumnus award Yale U. Sch. Medicine, 1979, Award of Merit Duke U. Hosp. and Health Adminstrn. Alumni Assn., 1987, Lifetime Achievement award Duke U. Med. Alumni, 1995, Lifetime Achievement award Rsch. Am., 1997, Disting. Meritorius Svc. medal, Duke Univ., 2002, N.C. award in sci., presented by the gov., 2002, Lifetime Achievement award City of Medicine, 2003. Fellow ACS; mem. AMA (adv. com. med. sci. 1972—), Soc. Univ. Surgeons, Soc. Vascular Surgery, Internat. Cardiovasc. Soc., Soc. Clin. Surgery, Am. Heart Assn., Soc. Med. Adminstrs. (pres. 1983-85), Inst. Medicine of NAS, Coun. Deans (chmn. 1968-69), AAMC (exec. com. 1965-71, chmn. 1970-71), AAMC Coun. Deans (chmn. 1968-69), So. Med. Assn., Coord. Coun. Med. Edn. (chmn. 1973-74), Surg. Biology Club II, Am. Surg. Assn., So. Surg. Assn., Halsted Soc., Allen O. Whipple Surg. Soc., Assn. Am. Med. Colls. (chmn. 1970-71), Ind. Rsch. Roundtable NAS, Assn. Acad. Health Ctrs. (pres. 1975), Rsch. Am. (bd. dirs. 1989-2005, chmn. 1992-96), Rotary, Phi Beta Kappa, Sigma Xi, Alpha Omega Alpha. Home: 1516 Pinecrest Rd Durham NC 27705-5817 Office: Duke Med Ctr PO Box 3626 Durham NC 27710-0001 Home Phone: 919-489-3196; Office Phone: 919-684-3438. Business E-Mail: anlya001@mc.duke.edu.

ANNIS, JOSEPH P., anesthesiologist, educator; b. Tallahassee; m. Peggy Annis; 2 children. Grad., Marquette U., Milw.; MD, Med. Coll. Wis., Milw., 1969. Diplomate American Bd. Anesthesiology. Intern surgery Swedish Med. Ctr., Seattle, 1969—70; gen. med. officer US Air Force Med. Corps, Vietnam; resident anesthesiology Long Beach Meml. Hosp., Calif., 1972—73, Stanford U. Hosp., 1973—75; pres. med. staff, vice chair bd. dirs. St. David's Med. Ctr., Austin, Tex.; ptnr. Austin Anesthesiology Group. Bd. dirs. Preferred Physicians Med. Risk Retention Group (PPM), 1990—; adj. assoc. prof. Dartmouth-Hitchcock Med. Ctr./Dartmouth Med. Sch., Hanover, NH; assoc. examiner Am. Bd. Anesthesiology; bd. governers St. David's Health-Care Partnership; former asst. clin. prof. U. Tex. Med. Branch, Galveston, U. Fla. Coll. Medicine. Bd. dirs. Found. Anesthesia Edn. & Rsch. Mem.: AMA (bd. trustees 2006—, former chair Coun. on Med. Svc., sec. 2009—10), American Soc. Anesthesiologists (former mem. bd. dirs.), Tex. Soc. Anesthesiologists (past pres.). Office: Austin Anesthesiology Group Bldg 3, Ste 210 8140 N MoPac Expressway Austin TX 78759 E-mail: joseph.annis@ppmrrg.com. *

ANNWEILER, CÉDRIC, geriatrician, researcher; s. Marc and Josiane Annweiler. MS, U. Jean Monnet, St.-Etienne, France, 2007; MD, U. Med. Sch., St.-Etienne, France, 2007; diploma in Biostats., U. Lyon, France, 2009; PhD, U. Angers, France, 2011. Diplomate in gerontology and geriatric medicine Angers U. Hosp. and U. Angers, France, in biostatistics U. Lyon, France, 2009. Postgrad. jr. Angers U. Hosp., 2008—09, Alzheimer's rschr., 2009—. Master: Assn. des Jeunes Gériatres Hospitaliers (pres.); mem.: Aging Balance Cognition Rsch. Group, Internat. Soc. Posture and Gait Rsch., Soc. Française Gériatrie et Gérontologie. Achievements include research in implications of vitamin D in central nervous system and cognitive function; typology of gait and gait disorders in demented older adults. Office: Angers University Hosp 4 rue Larrey Angers 49933 France Office Fax: 33 2 41 35 48 94. Business E-Mail: ceannweiler@chu-angers.fr.

ANOOSH, FARHAD, surgeon; MD, Tabriz U. Med. Sci., Iran, 1991. Diplomate Am. Bd. Surgery, 2009, cert. Iranian Bd. Surgery, 2000, Am. Bd. Surgery. Surgeon U. Pitts. Med. Ctr., 2009—; gen. surgeon

NY Med. coll., 2003—; surgeon U. Pitts. Recipient first Prize, Surgery Bd., 2000, Top Surgeon award, Consumer's Rsch. Coun. Am., 2008. Fellow: ACS, Assn. Academic Surgery, Soc. Laproendoscopic Surgeons, Soc. Am. Gastrointestinal & Laproscopic Suregeons, Am. Bd. Surgery; mem.: Soc. Surgery Alimentor Tract, ASMBS. Home: 108 Scuddes Ln Glenwood Landing NY 11547

ANSBACHER, RUDI, physician; b. Sidney, NY, Oct. 11, 1934; s. Stefan and Beatrice (Michel) A.; m. Elisabeth Cornelia Vellenga, Nov. 19, 1965; children— R. Todd, Jeffrey N. Grad., Harvard Coll., 1951; BA, Va. Mil. Inst., 1955; MD, U. Va., 1959; MS, U. Mich., 1970. Diplomate Am. Bd. Ob-Gyn. Staff ob-gyn, chief clin. investigation Brooke Med. Ctr., San Antonio, 1971-75, asst. chief ob-gyn, 1975-77; chief dept. ob-gyn Letterman Army Med. Ctr., San Francisco, 1977-80; from prof. ob-gyn to prof. emeritus U. Mich., Ann Arbor, 1980—2001, prof. emeritus, 2002—. Cons. Biomed. Adv. Com. Population Resource Ctr., 1978-81; bd. dirs. Health Policy Internat. Contbr. articles to profl. jours., chpts to books; mem. editorial bds., reviewer jours. Served to col. U.S. Army, 1960-80. Named Disting. Mil. Grad. Va. Mil. Inst., Lexington, Va., 1955; NIH grantee, 1973-78 Fellow ACOG (Chmn.'s award 1970, Mentor award, Dist. V 2010), AAAS; mem. Am. Fertility Soc. (dir. 1979-82), Am. Soc. Andrology (sec. 1978-80, pres. 1984-85), Central Assn. Ob-Gyn, Assn. Mil. Surgeons U.S., Soc. for Study Reprodn., Mich. State Med. Soc. (bd. dirs. 1995-2005, sec. 2005-06), Mich. State Med. Soc. Found. (bd. dirs. 2003—), Physicians Rev. Orgn. Mich. (bd. dirs. 2000-), U. Mich. Med. Ctr. Alumni Soc. (bd. dirs. 2004-10, emeritus bd. mem. 2011-). Republican. Presbyterian. Avocations: tennis, softball, gardening, skiing. Home: 3755 Tremont Ln Ann Arbor MI 48105-3022 Home Phone: 734-665-2396; Office Phone: 734-763-4344. Business E-Mail: ansbache@med.umich.edu.

ANSCHEL, DAVID JOSEPH, neurologist, neuroscientist; b. Kingston, NY, Apr. 29, 1972; s. Morris and Dolores Anschel. BA in Biol. Scis. summa cum laude, SUNY, Buffalo, 1993; MD with honors in Physiology and Neurosci., NYU, 1998. Clin. fellow medicine, dept. medcine house officer Harvard U. Sch. Medicine, Boston, 1998—99, clin. fellow neurology, dept. neurology house officer Beth Israel Deaconess Med. Ctr., Boston Children's Hosp., 1999—2002; fellow in epilepsy and clin. neurophysiology Stanford U., 2002—04; asst. prof. neurology SUNY, Stony Brook, 2004—07; assoc. sci. Brookhaven Nat. Lab.; dir. clin. neurophysiology St. Charles Hosp., Port Jefferson, NY, 2007—. Rschr. Sch. Medicine and Biomed. Scis. SUNY, Buffalo, 1993; rschr. Lawrence Livermore (Calif.) Nat. Lab., Livermore, 1994—95, Japanese Nat. Inst. Neurosci., Tokyo, 1996, John F. Kennedy Space Ctr., Cape Canaveral, Fla., 1997, NYU Sch. Medicine, NYC, 1996—98, Beth Israel Deaconess Med. Ctr., Boston, 1999—, Boston Children's Hosp., 1999—; lab. instr. human nervous sys. and behavior Harvard Med. Sch., 2001—02; dir. Comprehensive Epilepsy Ctr., LI; clin. neurophysiologist St. Charles Hosp., Port Jefferson, NY. Contbr. articles to profl. publs., chpt. to book. Scholar, N.Y. State Regents Bd., 1990—94, Charles F. Wolf M.D. Found., 1994—98, Am. Neurol. Assn., 2001. Mem.: Boston Soc. Neurology and Psychiatry, Am. Acad. Neurology, Pi Eta Sigma, Alpha Epsilon Delta, Phi Beta Kappa. Avocations: rowing, scuba diving, bicycling, water polo. Office Phone: 631-474-6279.

ANSELL, JULIAN S., urologist, educator; b. Portland, Maine, June 30, 1922; s. Jacob M. and Anna Gertrude (Fieldman) A.; m. Eva Ruth Ballin, June 17, 1951; children: Steven, Jody, Carol, Ellen, Peter. BA, Bowdoin Coll., 1946; MD, Tufts U., 1951; PhD, U. Minn., 1959. Intern in surgery U. Minn. Hosps., Mpls., 1951-52, resident in urology, 1952-54; NIH fellow U. Minn., Mpls., 1954, instr., 1956-59; asst. prof., head urology U. Wash., Seattle, 1959-62, assoc. prof., head urology, 1962-64, prof., chair urology, 1965-87, prof. urology, 1987-92, prof. emeritus, 1992—. Contbr. scientific papers pub. to profl. jour. Chair Post Grad. Seminar Am. Urological Assn., 1978; pres. Soc. Univ. Urologists, 1979; med. quality assurance commn. Wash. State, 1992—2005, chair., 2001. With US Army, 1943—46. Mem. Am. Alpine Club. Achievements include development of neonatal closure of exstrophy of bladder; urology residency objectives; research in renal sparing surgery in bilateral renal cancer; total body potassium in patients with urinary diversion; smoking as a cause of bladder cancer; discordant urinary defects in monozygotic twins; wound healing in infected and irradiated tissues; reflux and renal failure. Office: 3827 49th Ave NE Seattle WA 98105-5233

ANSELMO, DEAN, surgeon, educator; b. Palo Alto, Calif., Oct. 13, 1972; BA, NYU, 1994; MD, UCLA, 1998. Pediatric surgeon Children's Hosp. LA, 2005—. Asst. prof. surgery Keck Sch. Medicine, U. SC, 2007. Mem.: Am. Pediatric Surg. Assn. Home: 7225 Crescent Pk West #401 Playa Vista CA 90094 Office Phone: 323-361-5193. Home Fax: 310 621-0665. Business E-Mail: danselmo@chla.usc.edu.

ANSON, GOESEL, plastic surgeon, educator; MD, U. Ill. Diplomate Am. Bd. Surgery, Am. Bd. Plastic Surgery. Resident in gen. surgery Univ. Ill., Cook County Hosp.; exec. chief resident Nat. Cancer Inst.; plastic and reconstructive surgery tng. NYU, fellow in microsurgery; hosp. affiliations include NYU Hosp., Bellevue Hosp., Manhattan Eye, Ear and Throat Hosp.; asst. prof. tng. next generation plastic surgeons Univ. N.Mex, Albuquerque; pvt. practice Dr Anson and Dr Higgins Plastic Surgery Assocs. Named Warren Cole Scholar award; named one of Best Doctors in America, Las Vegas Life, Las Vegas Mags. Mem.: Alpha Omega Alpha. Office: Dr Anson & Dr Higgins Plastic Surgery Associates 8530 W Sunset Ste 130 Las Vegas NV 89113 Office Phone: 702-822-2100. Office Fax: 702-822-2105.

ANTAL, ALBERT, gynecologist, anesthesiologist; b. Biharkeresztes, Bihar, Hungary, July 23, 1927; s. Albert and Julianna (Venyige) A.; m. Eva Beres, 1951 (dec. 1977); children: Albert, Eva. MD, U. Szeged, Hungary; diploma, Albert-Szent Gyorgy Med. Univ., Hungary, 2004. Asst. U. Szeged, 1953-54; from asst. to assoc. attending physician City Hosp. Szeged, 1954-75, attending ob-gyn. physician, 1957-90, oncology cons., 1986-92, ob-gyn. cons., 1992—. Author, co-author: Series of Studies on the Treatment of Bartholin-Cysta, 1965; contbr. over 50 articles to profl. jours.; co-author: (with A. Antal, L. Bodis, I. Boros, M. Sas) Annual Report of the Obstetrics and Gynecology, Szeged, 1995. Mem. Soc. for the Advancement of Sci., European Assn. Ob-Gyns. and Anesthesiologists, N.Y. Acad. Scis., Szeged Civil Club, Baross Alumni Assn., European Assn. Gynecologists, Ostetricians, Anesthesiologists. Avocations: fishing, swimming, literature, history.

ANTELL, DARRICK EUGENE, plastic surgeon, educator; b. Cleve., Feb. 22, 1951; s. E. James and Wanda H. (Kociecki) A.; m. Elizabeth Ann Sobottka, July 14, 1984; children: Gillian Elizabeth, Darrick Eugene Jr., Leslie Jane, Helen Greer, Meredith James. BS in Biology, Hobart Coll., 1973; DMD, Case Western Res. U. Dental, 1978; MD, The U. Toledo, Ohio, 1982. Diplomate Am. Bd. Plastic Surgery. Surgery intern Stanford (Calif.) U. Med. Ctr., 1982-83, surgery resident, 1983-85; plastic surgery resident N.Y. Hosp. Cornell, NYC, 1985-87; plastic and reconstructive surgeon St. Luke's/Roosevelt, NYC, 1987—; asst. clin. prof. plastic surgery Columbia U., Lenox Hill Hosp., NYC, 1989—; med. dir., founder Lenox Hill Ambulatory Surgery, PC, NYC. Author: Plastic Surgery, 1991; contbr. articles to profl. jours. Trustee East Side House Settlement, N.Y.C., 1991-2009, Hist. Soc. of the Town of Greenwich, 1999-2003, Univ. Sch. Cleve., 2000-10; trustee adv. Girl Scouts U.S.A., N.Y.C., 1991-95. Facial Proportions grantee Am. Soc. for Aesthetic Plastic Surgery, 1987; Maliniac fellow Plastic Surgery Edn. Found.; recipient Pres. Citizenship award N.Y. State Med. Soc., 1992. Fellow: ACS, Plastic Surgery Ednl. Found.; mem.: AMA, Lipoplasty Soc., Interplast, Am. Acad. Cosmetic Dentistry, Internat. Acad. Dental Facial Aesthetics (founding), Internat. Soc. for Aestheic Plastic Surgery, N.Y. Regional Soc. Plastic and Reconstructive Surgeons, Am. Soc. Maxillofacial Surgeons Parliamentarian, Am. Soc. Aesthetic Plastic Surgery, Am. Soc. Plastic and Reconstructive Surgeons, Univ. Sch. Alumni Adv. Coun., Herbert Conway Soc., Greenwich Skating Club, Mill Reef Club (Antigua, W.I.), Cleve. Skating Club, Fishers Island Yacht Club, Stanwich Country Club, Union Club. Avocations: squash, fly fishing, golf, skiing. Office: 850 Park Ave New York NY 10075-1845 Office Phone: 212-988-4040. E-mail: dea@antell-md.com.

ANTHONY, EVELYN Y., diagnostic radiologist, educator; BS, U. NC, 1985, MA, 1992; MD, Duke U., 1996. Diplomate Am. Bd. Radiology-diagnostic radiology, 2001. Resident diagnostic radiology Wake Forest Univ. Bapt. Med. Ctr., 1996—2001, fellow pediatric radiology, 2001—02; asst. prof. radiology Wake Forest Univ. Mem.: Am. Coll. of Radiology, Radiol. Soc. of N.Am., Soc. of Pediatric Radiology. Office: Wake Forest University 445 ICTAS Bldg Stanger St Blacksburg VA 24061 Office Phone: 336-716-6753. Office Fax: 336-716-2029. E-mail: eanthony@wakehealth.edu.

ANTHONY, VIRGINIA QUINN BAUSCH, medical association executive; b. Odessa, Tex., June 9, 1945; d. William Francis and Florence Elizabeth (Decker) Quinn; m. E. James Anthony; 1 child, Justin. BA, Mt. Holyoke Coll., 1967. Exec. dir. Am. Acad. Child and Adolescent Psychiatry, Washington, 1973—. Ex-officio mem. sci. adv. bd. The Klingenstein Third Generation Found. Recipient Spl. Presdl. citation Am. Psychiat. Assn., 1995, Exec. Achievement award AMA, 1999. Mem.: Asociacion Mexicana de Psiquiatria Infantil (hon.). Office: Am Acad Child & Adolescent Psychiatry 3615 Wisconsin Ave NW Washington DC 20016-3007 Office Phone: 202-966-7300 ext. 116. *

ANTHONY-PEREZ, BOBBIE COTTON MURPHY, retired psychology professor; b. Macon, Ga., Nov. 15, 1923; d. Solomon Richard and Maude Alice (Lockett) Cotton; m. Edward R. Murphy, Mar. 14, 1939 (dec.); 1 child, Freida; m. William Anthony, Aug. 22, 1959 (dec.); m. Andrew Silviano Perez, June 20, 1979 (dec.). BS, DePaul U., 1953, MS, 1954, MA, 1975; MS, U. Ill., 1959; PhD, U. Chgo., 1967. Tchr. Chgo. Pub. Schs., 1954-68; math. coord. U. Chgo., 1965; prof. Chgo. State U., 1968-95, coord. Black Studies Program, 1982-83, 90-94, prof. emeritus, 1995; with psychol. svcs. Chgo. Pub. Schs., 1971-72; rsch. coord. Urban Affairs Inst. Howard U., Washington, 1978; coord. higher edn., careers counseling, campus ministry Ingleside Whitfield Parish, 1978-84, comm. chmn., 1991-92, 95, comms. com., 2006—. Contbr. articles to profl. jours., chapters to books. V.p. Cmty. Affairs Chatham Bus. Assn., 1981-85, asst. sec., 1985-86, sec., 1986-87, directory com., 1987, 88; bus. rels. chmn. Chatham Avalon Pk. Cmty. Coun., 1984—, newsletter editor, 1993-2001; bd. dirs. United Meth. Found. at U. Chgo., 1980-84, Cmty. Mental Health Coun. Inc., 1979-83; pub. edn. chair Chatham Avalon unit Am. Cancer Soc., 1977-88, 90-97, pub. info. chair, 1988-94; pres. Aux. Chgo. chpt. Tuskegee Airmen, Inc., 1994-95, rec. sec., 1998-99, parliamentarian, 1991-95, newsletter feature writer, reporter Chgo. DODO chpt., 1999—, historian, 2006-. NSF fellow, 1957, 58, 59; recipient numerous awards religious, civic and ednl. instns. and assns. Mem. APA, Internat. Assn. Applied Psychology, Internat. Assn. Cross-Cultural Psychology, Internat. Assn. Ednl. and Vocat. Guidance, Assn. Black Psychologists (elder 1995—, pres. Chgo. chpt. 1995-96, past pres.), Chgo. Psychol. Assn., Nat. Coun. Tchrs. Math., Am. Ednl. Rsch. Assn., Midwest Ednl. Rsch. Assn., Am. Soc. Clin. Hypnosis, Midwestern Psychol. Assn., Chgo. Soc. Clin. Hypnosis. Methodist. Home: 7612 South St Lawrence Ave Chicago IL 60619

ANTIA, KERSEY H., industrial and clinical psychologist, consultant; b. Surat, Gujarat, India, Jan. 7, 1936; arrived in US, 1965; s. Homasji and Dinsi R. (Mistry) Antia; m. Dilshad K. Khambata, Dec. 18, 1966; children: Anahita, Mazda, Jimmy. AB with honors, U. Bombay, 1958; MS, Tata Inst. Social Scis., Bombay, 1960, NC State U., Raleigh, 1969; PhD, Ind. No. U., 1976. Lic. psychologist, Ill.; cert. social worker, Ill. Personnel mgr., welfare officer Tata Steel and Tata Chem., 1960-65; rsch. asst. psychology dept. NC State U., 1966-67, U. NC, 1967—69; project dir. Behavior Systems, Inc., Raleigh, 1969-70; dir. Midwest Inst. Human Resources, Tinley Park, Ill., 1972—. Lang. scholar U. Bombay, 1954-56. Assn. for the Advancement of Psychology, Am. Acad. Pain Mgmt., Am. Bd. Profl. Disability Cons. Zoroastrian. Avocations: photography, yoga, jogging, hiking, travel. Home: 8318 138th Pl Orland Park IL 60462-1746 Office Phone: 708-460-6060.

ANTMAN, ELLIOTT MARSHALL, cardiologist, educator; b. NYC, May 9, 1950; m. Karen Hamm Antman; children: Amy, David. MD, Columbia U. Coll. Physicians & Surgeons, NYC, 1974. Diplomate Am. Bd. Internal Medicine, Am. Bd. Cardiovasc. Disease. Intern medicine Columbia-Presbyn. Med. Ctr., NYC, 1974—75, resident cardiology, 1975—77; fellow cardiology Peter Bent Brigham Hosp., Boston, 1977—80; co-dir. coronary care unit Brigham & Women's Hosp., Boston, 1980; dir. Samuel L. Levine Cardiac Unit Brigham and Women's Hosp., Boston, 1980—; assoc. prof. to prof. medicine Harvard Med. Sch., Boston, 1989—, dir. postgrad. prog. clin. & translational sci., 2009—. Prin. investigator TIMI Trials (Thrombolysis in Myocardial Infarction), Boston, 1996—. Sr. assoc. editor Circulation; contbr. articles to profl. jours., chapters to books. Recipient A. Clifford Barger Excellence in Mentoring award, Harvard Med. Sch., 2001. Mem.: Am. Heart Assn., Am. Coll. Cardiology (Gifted Tchr. of Yr. 2003). Office: Brigham & Womens Hosp Cardiovasc Divsn 75 Francis St PBB 1 Boston MA 02115 Office Phone: 617-732-7149. Office Fax: 617-975-0990. Business E-Mail: eantman@partners.org.

ANTMAN, KAREN HAMM, oncologist, educator, dean; b. NJ, July 26, 1948; m. Elliot Antman; children: Amy, David. Grad. in Chemistry (magna cum laude), Muhlenberg Coll.; MD, Columbia U. Coll. Physicians and Surgeons, 1974. Diplomate Am. Bd. Internal Medicine, Am. Bd. Med. Oncology. Intern Columbia Presbyn. Med. Ctr., NYC, 1974—75, resident, 1975—77; clin. fellow, medicine Harvard Med. Sch., instr. medicine, 1979; clin. fellow, med. oncology Sidney Farber Cancer Inst., Boston, 1977—79; chief med. oncology Columbia U., NYC; clin. dir. Dana-Farber Cancer Inst./Beth Israel Solid Tumor Autologous Marrow Program, 1984; attending physician N.Y. Presbyn. Hosp., 1993; dir. Herbert Irving Cancer Ctr., Nat. Cancer Inst.; Wu prof., medicine & pharmacology, prof. medicine & pharmacology Columbia U. Coll. Physicians and Surgeons, NYC, 1993—2004; dep. dir. translation and clinical services Nat. Cancer Inst., 2004—05; provost, Med. Campus Boston U., 2005—, dean, Med. Sch., 2005—. Assoc. editor New England Journal of Medicine, mem. editl. of several med. jours.; contbr. articles to profl. jours. Bd. observer Muhlenberg Coll., 2007—. Mem.: Am. Soc. for Blood and Marrow Transplantation (past pres.), Am. Assn. for Cancer Rsch. (past pres.), Am. Soc. Clinical Oncology (past pres.). Avocations: backpacking, travel. Office: Boston Univ Medical Sch 715 Albany St L-103 Boston MA 02118 Office Phone: 617-638-5300. Office Fax: 617-638-5258. *

ANTON, JOHN, plastic surgeon; b. Seattle, Oct. 25, 1950; BS, U. Calif., Berkeley, 1973; MD, U. Vt., 1981. Bd. cert. Am. Bd. Plastic Surgery, diplomate Am. Bd. Plastic Surgery, Nt. Bd. Med. Examiners. Intern Baylor Coll. Medicine, Houston, 1981—82; jr. asst. resident in surgery Harvard Surg. Svc., New Eng. Deaconess Hosp., Boston, 1982—83, sr. asst. resident, 1983—84; resident in surgery Mass. Gen. Hosp., Boston, 1984—85, fellow in surgery, 1985—86; house surgeon Norwood (Mass.) Hosp., 1988—89; attending surgeon Southampton (NY) Hosp., 1989—, chmn. dept. surgery, 1996—; attending surgeon Ctrl. Suffolk Hosp., Riverhead, NY, 1989—. Mem. courtesy staff Ea. L.I. Hosp., Greenport, NY, 1990—, Brattleboro (Vt.) Meml. Hosp., 1996—; clin. fellow in surgery Harvard Med. Sch., 1982—85, clin., rsch. fellow in surgery, 1985—86; chmn. surg. peer rev. com. Ctrl. Suffolk Hosp., Riverhead, 1995—97. Contbr. articles to profl. jours. Police surgeon Southampton Village Police Dept., 2001—; dir. World Affairs Coun., Southampton, 1996—; trustee Southampton Hosp., 1998—99, Peconic Health Corp., Southampton, 1998—99. Named one of Best Drs. in NY, NY Mag., 1999, 2000, 2001, 2002, 2004, 2005—06. Fellow: ACS; mem.: Am. Bd. of Plastic Surgery, NY Regional Soc. Plastic Surgeons, Am. Soc. for Laser Medicine and Surgery Inc., New Eng. Soc. Plastic Surgeons, Northeastern Soc. Plastic Surgeons, Lipoplasty Soc. N.Am. Inc., Am. Assn. Hand Surgery, Am. Soc. Plastic and Reconstructive Surgeons, NY State Med. Soc., Internat. Soc. for Burn Injuries, Vt. State Med. Soc., Mass. Med. Soc. Office: 138 Old Town Rd Southampton NY 11968 also: Second Office 880 Fifth Ave St New York NY 10021 Office Phone: 212-283-9100.

ANTON, RAYMOND F., JR., psychiatrist, educator; b. USA, Jan. 9, 1951; BA in Biol. Sciences, Rutgers U., New Brunswick, NJ, 1972; MMS, Rutgers U., Piscataway, NJ, 1974, MD, 1976. Diplomate Am. Bd. Psychiatry and Neurology-psychiatry, 1982, Am. Bd. of Addiction Medicine, 2009, cert. Am. Bd. Psychiatry and Neurology-addiction psychiatry, 1997. Intern Greenwich Hosp. Assn., 1976—77; resident psychiatrist sch. medicine Yale Univ., 1977—80; resident psychiatrist Conn. Mental Health Ctr., 1977—80, resident psychiatrist and cons. the drug dependence unit methadone maintenace program, 1979, dir. Naltrexone high intervention program drug dependence unit, 1979—80; consulting psychiatrist Waterbury Gen. Hosp., Conn., 1978—79; asst. prof. dept. psychiatry and behavioral sciences Med. Univ. SC, 1980—85, assoc. prof. dept. psychiatry and behavioral sciences, 1985—91, dir. substance abuse fellowship dept. psychiatry and behavioral sciences, 1989—93, co-sci. dir. alcohol rsch. ctr., 1995—99, acting sci. dir. alcohol rsch. ctr., 1997, dir. alcohol medication studies ctr. for drug and alcohol programs, 1994—2000, sci. dir. rsch. ctr., 1998—2005, dir. rsch. ctr. for drug and alcohol programs, 1999—2000, co-dir. ctr. for drug and alcohol programs, 2000—01, prof. dept. psychiatry and behavioral sciences, 1991—2002, sci. dir. for clin. rsch. alcohol rsch. ctr., 2006—, dir. ctr. for drug and alcohol programs, 2001—, prof. dept. psychiatry and behavioral sciences, disting. univ. prof., 2002—; staff psychiatrist Veterans Adminstrn. Med. Ctr., Charleston, SC, 1980—88, dir. psychopharmacology rsch., 1984—88; dir. inpatient psychotic disorders program Inst. of Psychiatry, Charleston, SC, 1989—92, dir. clin. substance abuse rsch. dept. psychiatry and behavioral sciences, 1990—92, dir. clin.-neurobiology labs., 1988—. Editl. adv. bd. Alcohol Health and Rsch. World, 1996—99; assoc. editor alcoholism Clin. and Exptl. Rsch., 1997—98, editl. bd. alcoholism, 1999—2006, bd. of reviewing editors alcoholism, 2000—; editl. bd. Jour. of Studies on Alcohol, 1997—; guest editor CNS Spectrums, 1999. Co-author: (publs.) Multiple Family Therapy and Naltrexone in the Treatment of Opiate Dependence, Tricyclic Antidepressant Poisoning, 1981, Non-invasive Measurement of Cardiac Ejection Fraction During Desipramine Treatment, 1982, Inhibition of Prostaglandin Synthesis by Indomethacin does not Affect Alcohol Consumption in Inbred Mice, 1983, Efficacy of Amoxapine in Psychotic Depression, 1983, Amoxapine Elevates Serum Prolactin in Depressed Men, 1983, and numerous others. Recipient Disting. Alumni Award, UMDNJ-Robert Wood Johnson Med. Sch., 2000; named one of Best Doctors in America, 1997—98; nominee Golden Appple Award, Med. Univ. SC, 1984. Fellow: Am. Psychiat. Assn., Am. Coll. of Neuropsychopharmacology; mem.: Rsch. Soc. on Alcoholism, Internat. Soc. for Biomedical Rsch. on Alcoholism, Am. Soc. of Addiction Medicine (cert. 1996), Alpha Omega Alpha, Phi Beta Kappa. Office: Medical University of South Carolina Department of Psychiatry 67 President St Box 250861 Charleston SC 29425 Office Phone: 843-792-1226. Office Fax: 843-792-7353. E-mail: antonr@musc.edu.

ANTONINI, MARIO, anesthesiologist; b. Rome, May 30, 1954; MD, Rome U., 1980, degree in Anesthesia and Intensive Care, 1983. Resident Dept. Gen. Surgery & Transplant Anesthesia, Rome U. (formerly La Sapienza), 1985—2000, Regina Elena Tumors Nat. Inst. - ICU & Transplant Anesthesia, 2001—07; head - ICU & transplant anesthesia Nat. Inst. Infectious Disease L. Spallanzani, 2007—.

Mem.: Anaesthesia and Intensive Care Italian Soc. Achievements include first to liver transplant in Italy. Office: v Portuense 262 Roma Lazio 00149 Italy Business E-Mail: antoninima@libero.it.

ANTOSZEWSKA, JOANNA, orthodontist, educator; b. Walbrzych, Poland, Mar. 15, 1970; d. Andrzej Antoszewski and Barbara Owczarek-Antoszewska. Degree, Wroclaw Med. U., Poland, 1989. Cert. orthodontist Polish Orthodontic Bd., 2000. Asst. Wroclaw Med. U., 1995—2005, asst. prof., 2005—. Reviewer Recent Patents on Biomed. Engring., Poland; lectr. Kyung Pook Nat. U., Daegu, 2008—, Forestadent, Phorzheim, Germany, 2008—. Contbr. articles to profl. jours. Donator Tara-animal shelter, Fiona-animal shelter SOS Children Villiages, Poland, 2005. Mem.: European Orthodontic Soc., Polish Orthodontic Soc. Achievements include research in oral status in children and youth treated orthodontically. Avocations: skydiving, scuba diving. Office: Wroclaw Med University Orthod Dept Ul. Krakowska 26 50-425 Wroclaw Poland Personal E-mail: stomjan@gmail.com.

ANTOUN, MIKHAIL, medicinal chemistry and pharmacognosy educator; b. Khartoum, Sudan, Aug. 20, 1946; came to U.S., 1979; s. Daoud and Badia (Boulos) A.; m. Slavomira Kucerova, Sept. 14, 1973; children: Helena, David Emmanuel, Anna Maria. B in Pharm. with distinction, U. Khartoum, 1968; PhD, U. London, 1974. Asst. prof. pharm. U. Khartoum (Sudan), 1974—78, assoc. prof., 1978—81; sr. rsch. scientist Purdue U., West Lafayette, Ind., 1981—86; assoc. prof. medicinal chemistry and pharmacognosy U. P.R. Sch. Pharm., San Juan, 1986—92, prof. medicinal chemistry and pharmacognosy, faculty chair prof., 1993—, dept. head, 1993—2005. Vis. prof., rsch. assoc. Sch. Pharmacy and Pharm. Sci. Purdue U., West Lafayette, 1979-81. Contbr. articles to profl. jours. Sr. scholar U. Khartoum, 1968-69; teaching fellow U. London, 1969-73. Fellow Linnean Soc.; mem. Am. Assn. Colls. Pharmacy, Am. Soc. Pharmacognosy, Am. Assn. Pharm. Scientists, Sigma Xi. Avocations: piano, classical music, reading, chess, swimming. Personal E-mail: anto285@aol.com.

ANTSIFEROVA, YULIA, immunologist; b. Kursk, Russia, July 27, 1968; BD, Ivanovo's U., 2005. Sr. sci. worker Ivanovo's Rsch. Inst. Maternity and Childhood, 1998—. Grant, Russian Pres. Mem.: Russian Sci. Soc. Immunologists, Internat. Soc. Immunology Reproduction. Avocation: music. Home: Myakisheva 5-24 Ivanovo 153009 Russia Office Phone: 7-4932-37-13-97. Home Fax: 7-4932-33-62-56. Personal E-mail: niimid.immune@mail.ru.

ANTZ, MATTHIAS, cardiologist; b. Hamburg, Germany, Aug. 20, 1964; s. Ulrich and Christa Antz; m. Janna Schneider; children: Laurin, Josephine. MD, U. Hamburg, Germany, 1990. Physician U. Hosp. Hamburg, 1989—2004; rsch. fellow cardiology U. Hosp. Okla., Oklahoma City, 1995—96; physician electrophysiology,cardiology St. Georg Hosp., Hamburg, 1997—2007; chief electrophysiology Heart Ctr. Oldenburg, Germany, 2007—; prof. U. Hamburg, Germany, 2008. Contbr. scientific papers to profl. jours. Fellow: European Soc. Cardiology; mem.: European Heart Rhythm Assn., German Soc. Cardiology. Office: Oldenburg Heart Ctr Cardiology Rahel-Straus-Str 10 Oldenburg 26133 Germany Office Fax: +494414033077. Business E-Mail: antz.matthias@klinikum-oldenburg.de.

ANVERSA, PIERO, medical educator; s. Giuseppe Anversa and Maria Tolzani; m. Sandra Zanolli, Sept. 16, 1968; 1 child, Matteo. MD, Med. Sch., Parma, Italy, 1959—65; MD (hon.), Med. Sch., Bologna, Italy, 2002. Prof., medicine N.Y. Med. Coll., Valhalla, 1984—, v.chmn., medicine, 2000—; vis. prof. Albert Einstein Coll. Medicine, NYC, 1992—, Sacred Heart U., Rome, 1989—, U. Vita-Salute, Milan, 2003—, San Diego State U., 2003—. Fellow: Am. Heart Assn. (Rsch. Achievement award 2004, Disting. Scientist 2003). Achievements include research in the identification of stem cells and tissue regeneration death in the heart. Avocation: travel. Office: Brigham & Women's Hosp Dept Anesthesia & Medicine 20 Shattuck St Thorn Bldg Rm 1319A Boston MA 02115 Home: 42 Commonwealth Ave Unit 2 Boston MA 02116 Office Fax: 617-264-6320. Business E-Mail: panversa@zeus.bwh.harvard.edu, panversa@partners.org.

ANWAR, AMMAR IBNE, medical educator; b. Bijnor, India, June 6, 1976; MD, Aligarh Muslim U., 1999, MD, 2003. Asst. prof. unani medicine Aligarh Muslim U., 2005—. Recipient Academic Gem award, IIFS. Home: K78 Safina Apt Med Rd AMU Aligarh Uttar Pradesh 202002 India Personal E-mail: ammaramu@rediffmail.com.

ANWAR, KHURSHID, pathologist; b. Kohat, Pakistan, June 23, 1956; s. Dilawar Shah and Anjuman Sultan; m. Shahnaz Haque, Aug. 8, 1984; children: Saqib Khurshid, Sarah Khurshid. MBBS, Khyber Med. Coll., Peshawar, 1979; MPhil, BMSI, JMPC, Karachi, Pakistan, 1983; PhD, Fudan Med. Sch., China, 1993. Lectr. Khyber Med. Coll., Peshawar, Pakistan, 1980-85; from cons. histopathologist to assoc. prof. Postgrad. Med. Inst., Peshawar, 1986—. Cons. histopathologist Khurshid Clin. Lab., Peshawar, 1993—, Al-Shifa Clin. Lab., Peshawar, 1984-87. Mem. Pathologist Assn. Pakistan, Nat. Geog. Soc., N.Y. Acad. Scis. Muslim. Avocations: reading, travel, parenting. Home: Khurshid Clin Lab B2-B3 Auqaf Plz Dabgari Garden Peshawar Pakistan Office: Postgrad Med Inst Dept Path Lady Reading Hosp Peshawar Pakistan

ANYANE-YEBOA, KWAME, clinical geneticist; Grad., U. of Ghana Med. Sch., 1972. Cert. clin. genetics, diplomate Am. Bd. Pediatrics. Resident pediatrician Harlem Hosp. Ctr., 1976; fellowship Columbia Presbyterian Hosp, 1980; prof. clin. genetics Columbia Univ.; with NY-Presbyterian/Morgan Stanley Children's Hosp., St. Luke's - Roosevelt Hosp. Ctr. - Roosevelt Divsn. Office: NewYork-Presbyterian/Morgan Stanley Children's Hospital 3959 Broadway New York NY 10032 Mailing: St. Luke's - Roosevelt Hospital Center - Roosevelt Division 1000 Tenth Ave New York NY 10019 Office Phone: 212-305-6731. Office Fax: 212-305-9058.

ANYANWU, CHUKWUMA UCHENNA, clinical pharmacist, biomedical researcher; b. Owerri, Nigeria, Sept. 22, 1970; s. Max Uchechukwu and Stella Ugochi Anyanwu; m. Akudo Mmaulo Amaechi, 2004. BSc with honors, U. Nigeria, 1994; PharmD, Temple U., 2003; MPH in Epidemiology & Health Outcomes Rsch., U. Pa., 2008. Rsch. asst. epidemiology & preventative medicine Loyola U. Med. Ctr., Maywood, Ill., 1996—99; rsch. project coord. clin. cancer genetics U. Chgo. Med. Ctr., 1999; post-doctoral pharmacy practice resident Crozer-Keystone Health Sys., Upland, Pa., 2003; clin. and staff pharmacist Lankenau Hosp., Inst. Biomed. Rsch., Wynnewood, Pa., 2004—. Rsch. intern Temple U. Sch. of Medicine, Phila.; summer intern Bridging The Gaps, Phila., 2000; pharmacy extern Temple U. Hosp., 2000—03. Trustee, mem. of choir Second Bapt. Ch. of Germantown, Phila., 1999; vol., charity and hospice Public Health Edn. to Inner City Dwellers. Academic merit scholarship, Fed. Govt. of Nigeria, 1982—87. Fellow: Royal Inst. of Pub. Health; mem.: Drug Info. Soc., Am. Soc. of Health-Systems Pharmacy, Am. Coll. Clin. Pharmacy, Mbaitoli-Ikeduru Family Meeting. Independent. Achievements include research in the genetics of hypertension, obesity in blacks, cancer genetics and epidemiology studies, anticoagulation monitoring, drug safety. Avocations: music, chess, Scrabble, lawn tennis. Office: Lank Hosp and Lank Inst of Bmd Resc 100 Lancaster Ave Wynnewood PA 19096 Personal E-mail: chukky70@hotmail.com.

ANZIA, JOAN MEYER, psychiatrist; b. Evergreen Park, Ill., Mar. 1, 1950; d. William Nicholas and Loretta Ann (Hannifin) Meyer; m. Daniel Joseph Anzia, June 23, 1973; children: Carolyn, Sarah, Maura. BA, Stanford U., 1972; MD, Loyola U., Maywood, Ill., 1976. Resident psychiatry Northwestern U., Chgo., 1980-83, U. Ill., Chgo., 1991—2005, tchr. dept. psychiatry, 1991—2005; assoc. prof. psychiatry Northwestern U., Chgo., 2005—, dir. psychiatry and behavioral sciences, 2006—, dir. residency training; med. dir. ambulatory and cmty. programs Northwestern Meml. Hosp., Chgo., 2005—, med. dir. outpatient treatment clinic. Mem. admissions com. Loyola-Stritch Sch. Medicine, Ill., 1976-77. Author: Marital Intimacy, 1979. Recipient Richard Marohn Tchr. of Yr. award, Northwestern U., 2006. Mem. APA (coun. med. edn. and lifelong learning, 2005—, coun. advocacy and pub. policy), Ill. Psychiat. Soc. (pres., 2004-05), Assn. Academic Psychiatry (pres.), Assn. Women Psychiatrists (sec.). Roman Catholic. Avocations: painting, photography, gardening. Office: Northwestern U Feinberg Sch Medicine 446 E Ontario Chicago IL 60611 Office Phone: 312-695-5060. Fax: 312-695-5010. E-mail: janzia@nmh.org.

AOKI, HATSUO, pharmaceutical executive; PhD. Former pres., CEO Fujisawa Pharmaceutical; pres., CEO Astellas Pharma (merger of Fujisawa Pharmaceutical and Yamanouchi Pharmaceutical), 2005. Speaker NY Pharma Forum. Mem.: Japan Pharm. Manufacturers Assn. (chmn.), Internat. Federation of Pharmaceutical Mfrs. Office: JPMA Torii Nihonbashi Bldg 3-4-1 Nihonbashi-Honcho Chuo-Ku Tokyo 103-0023 Japan

AOKI, TAKESHI, surgeon, educator; b. Mito, Ibaraki, Japan, Nov. 16, 1968; s. Aoki Yukuo and Aoki Miwako; m. Hiroko Aoki; children: Kanon, Mone. MD, Showa U., Tokyo, 1993, PhD, 2008. Assoc. prof. Dept. Surgery, Divsn. Gastroent. and Gen. Surgery, Sch. Medicine, Showa U., Shinagawa, Tokyo, 2003—06, lectr., 2006—. Contbr. articles to profl. jours. Grants, Japan Soc. Promotion Sci., 2003—06. Office: Dept Surgery 1-5-8 Hatanodai Shinagawa-ku Tokyo 1428666 Japan Office Fax: 81-3-3784-5835. Business E-Mail: takejp@wb4.so-net.ne.jp.

AOKI, TAKUYA, medical educator; b. Hanishina, Nagano, Japan, Jan. 12, 1964; s. Akikazu Aoki; m. Masami Aoki. MD, Keio U. Sch. Medicine, Tokyo, PhD, 1997. Cert. Japanese Soc. Internal Medicine Bd., 2002. Postdoc. fellow Case Western Res. U., Cleve., 1999—2002, staff mem., sect. chief Saiseikai Ctrl. Hosp., Tokyo, 2002—04; head dept. Mito Red Cross Hosp., Japan, 2004—07; asst. prof. Tokai U. Sch. Medicine, Isehara, Kanagawa, Japan, 2007—. Contbr. scientific papers. Mem.: Am. Soc. Clin. Oncology, Am. Thoracic Soc. Home: 4-33-5 Numame Isehara Kanagawa 259-1126 Japan Office: Tokai Univ Sch Medicine 143 Shimokasuya Isehara Kanagawa 259-1193 Japan Office Fax: 81-463-93-0381; Home Fax: 81-463-91-4230. Business E-Mail: aokitaku@is.icc.u-tokai.ac.jp.

AONO, HIROYUKI, orthopedist; b. Toyonaka City, Osaka, Japan, Sept. 16, 1968; s. Toshihiro and Saeko Aono. MD, Okayama U., Japan, 1995. Cert. surgeon Japanese Orthopaedic Assn., 2005, Japanese Soc. Spine and Related Rsch., 2007. Physician Osaka Koseinenkin Hosp., 2003—06, Osaka Nat. Hosp., 2006—. Office: Osaka Nat Hosp 2-1-14 Hoenzaka Chuo-ku Osaka Osaka Prefecture 5400006 Japan Home: 1-7-25 #1202 Sagisu Fukushima W Osaka City Osaka 553000 Japan Office Fax: 81-6-6943-6467. Business E-Mail: h-aono@umin.ac.jp.

AOSHIBA, KAZUTETSU, physician, educator; b. Tokyo, Sept. 21, 1958; MD, Nippon Med. Sch., 1984. Assoc. prof. first dept. medicine Tokyo Women's Med. U., 2001, prof. pulmonary divsn., Grad. Sch. Med. Sci., 2007—. Mem.: Japan Respiratory Soc., Asian Pacific Soc. Respirology, European Respiratory Soc., Am. Thoracic Soc. Office: 8-1 Kawada-cho Shinjuku-ku Tokyo 162-8666 Japan Office Fax: 81-3-5379-5457. Business E-Mail: kaoshiba@chi.twmu.ac.jp.

APATOFF, BRIAN, neurologist, educator; MD, U. Chgo., 1984, PhD; med. tng., Harvard U. Diplomate Am. Bd. Psychiatry and Neurology, lic. NYC. Resident in neurology Columbia-Preesbyn. Med. Ctr., NY, 1987—90; fellow in multiple sclerosis Columbia Univ., 1990—92; assoc. prof. Cornell Univ.; dir. Multiple Sclerosis Inst. NY- Presbyn. Nosp.; clin. attendant NY- Presbyn. Hosp. Mailing: New York- Presbyterian Hospital 401 E 55th St New York NY 10022 Office Phone: 212-593-6262.

APFELBACH, GEORGE LEONARD, JR., urologist; b. Chgo., Mar. 10, 1931; s. George Leonard and Alice Clothilde (Hotz) Apfelbach; m. Claire Fleischmann Apfelbach, Aug. 8, 1955; children: Martha, Paul, Eric, Edward. AB, Harvard Coll., Cambridge, Mass., 1953; MD, Northwestern U., Chgo., 1957. Diplomate Am. Bd. Urology. Physician Mercy Hosp., Janesville, Wis., 1962—93, chief of staff, chief of surgery, pres. staff. Contbr. articles to profl. jours.; prodr.: (video-hist.) Tour Fish Creek, Wis., 2005. Mem.: Rock County Surg. Soc. (pres.), Rock County Med. Soc. (pres.), Rotary. Independent. Avocations: gardening, boating, theater, opera, symphony. Office Phone: 941-921-7006. Personal E-mail: lenapfelbach@yahoo.com.

APOSTOLODES, PAUL J., neurosurgeon; Studied, U. Mass., Worcester, 1987—91. Diplomate Am. Bd. Neurol. Surgery, Nat. Bd. of Med. Examiners. Intern Maricopa Med. Ctr., Phoenix, 1991—92; resident Barrow Neurol. Inst., 1992—98, fellow, 1998; with Coll. of Neurol. Surgeons, Stamford Hosp., Greenwich Hosp. Named one of NY Mag. Top Doctors, 2010—11, Greenwich Mag. Top Doctors, 2009—11, Conn. Mag. Top Doctors, 2009—10. Mem.: Spine Universe, AMA, North Am. Spine Soc., Joint Sect. on Disorders of the Spine and Peripheral Nerves, Greenwich Med. Soc., Fairfield County Med. Assn., Conn. State Med. Soc., Am. Acad. of Neurol. Surgeons. Office: Greenwich Hospital 6 Greenwich Office Park Greenwich CT 06831 Office Phone: 203-869-1145. Office Fax: 203-629-7606.

APOSTOLOPOULOS, ANASTASIOS, orthopedic surgeon; b. Athens, Apr. 30, 1962; s. Athanasios and Vasiliki Apostolopoulos; m. Sally Amanda Heath, Dec. 10, 1994; children: Isabelle, Nasos, Elizabeth, Stephania. Lauria of Medicine, U. Perugia, Italy, 1989, M of Traumatology, 1996. Resident Pilots Acad., Athens, Greece, 1989—90; resident in gen. surgery Airforce Hosp., Athens, 1990—91, resident in orthop., gen. surgery, 1991; resident in orthop. Edith Cavell, Peterborough, England, 1992, PDH, Peterborough, 1993, S. Tyneside, S. Shields, 1993—94, K and C, Canterbury, England, 1994; registrar in orthop. Buckland, Dover, 1994; resident in neurosurgery Brook Hosp., London, 1995; registrar in orthop. Alexandra Hosp., Redditch, 1995—96; registrar in plastic surgery, orthop. U. Hosp. Selly Oak, Birmingham, 1996; registrar orthop. Gen. Hosp., Northampton, England, 1996—97; cons. orthop. surgeon Athens Med. Ctr., 1998—. Lectr. in field. Recipient Gold medal, U. Birmingham, Eng., 1996. Fellow: Greek Arthroscopic Soc., Royal Coll. Surgeons Glasgow. Avocations: running, reading, Karate. Office: Amaelokipi Kalamon 21 and Slimon Sof 11526 Athens Greece

APPEL, ALBERT M., lawyer; b. NYC, May 26, 1945; s. Morris and Belle (Kaplan) A.; m. Irena Uhl, June 10, 1979; 1 child, Elliott. BS in Econs., U. Pa., 1966; JD, NYU, 1969. Bar: N.Y. 1969, U.S. Dist. Ct. (so. and ea. dists.) N.Y. 1971, U.S. Ct. Appeals (2d cir.) 1974, U.S. Ct. Appeals (4th cir.) 1979, U.S. Ct. Appeals (11th Cir.) 2002. Assoc. Spear and Hill, NYC, 1969-75, Webster & Sheffield, NYC, 1976-80, ptnr., 1981-91; spl. counsel Stroock & Stroock & Lavan LLP, NYC, 1991-97, ptnr., 1998—2009, of counsel, 2010—. Mem. Chartered Inst. Arbitrators (MCIArb), ABA, Am. Health Lawyers Assn., NY State Bar Assn., Assn. Bar City of NY, Beta Alpha Psi. Office: Stroock & Stroock & Lavan LLP 180 Maiden Ln New York NY 10038-4925 Office Phone: 212-806-6625. Business E-Mail: aappel@stroock.com.

APPEL, NORMAN, ophthalmologist, educator, real estate and import/export company executive; b. NYC, Dec. 4, 1945; s. Robert M. and Anne K. (Kleiner) A.; m. Rena Lee Moskovits, Sept. 2, 1973; m. Sheila Gail Popkin Wasserman, Aug. 16, 1984; children: Steven Mordechai, Ronit Danielle, James Moshe, Byron Dov. BA, U. Louisville, 1966, MD, 1970; postgrad., Harvard U., 1974. Diplomate: Am. Bd. Ophthalmology. Intern Maimonides Med. Ctr., Bklyn., 1970-71; resident in ophthalmology Strong Meml. Hosp. of U. Rochester, N.Y., 1973-76; fellow The Edward S. Harkness Eye Inst., Columbia-Presbyn. Med. Ctr., NYC, 1976; pvt. practice specializing in orbit, lacrimal and oculoplastic surgery and oncology NYC, 1977—; sr. clin. asst. ophthalmologist Mt. Sinai Hosp., 1977-86; asst. attending ophthalmologist Beth Israel Med. Ctr., 1977-85; assoc. attending ophthalmologist St. Clare's Hosp., 1977-86; asst. attending surgeon ophthalmology N.Y. Infirmary Beekman Downtown Hosp., 1977-84; attending ophthalmologist Bronx VA Hosp., 1977-86; asst. attending ophthalmologist Montefiore Hosp. and Med. Ctr., 1979—, Cabrini Med. Ctr., 1982-86, Westchester County Med. Ctr., 1983-86, St. Vincent's Hosp. and Med. Ctr. of N.Y., 1983-86; founder, dir. Orbit Clinic Mt. Sinai Hosp., 1977-78, Orbit and Oculoplastic Surgery Clinic Beth Israel Med. Ctr., 1977-79, St. Clare's Hosp., 1977-86, Bronx Va Hosp., 1977-86, North Central Bronx Hosp., 1980-86, Orbit Clinic N.Y. Infirmary Beekman Downtown Hosp., 1977-84; physician in charge orbit, lacrimal and oculoplastic surgery service Brookdale Hosp. Med. Ctr., 1982-84; founder, dir. Orbit, Lacrimal and Oculoplastic Surgery Clinic, 1982-84; dir. Orbit, Lacrimal and Oculoplastic Service Interfaith Med. Ctr., 1982-86; owner, dir. Appel Enterprises, Englewood, NJ, 1986—96, Appel Importers, Englewood, 1986—96; assoc. attending ophthalmologist L.I. Coll. Hosp., 2002—06, ophthalmologist The Stanley S. Lamm Inst. for Child Neurology and Devel. Medicine, 2002—05. Cons. Cabrini Med. Ctr., 1984-86, Jewish Hosp. and Med. Ctr. of Bklyn., 1978-83; mem. faculty Mt. Sinai Sch. of Medicne, 1977-87, Albert Einstein Coll. Medicine, 1979—, asst. clin. prof. ophthalmology and visual sci., 1993—; adj. asst. attending ophthalmologist Mt. Sinai Hosp., 1996--; lectr. ophthalmology Mt. Sinai Sch. Medicine, 1996--; cons. in field. Contbr. articles to med. jours. and book. Served with USAF, 1971-73, Vietnam. Named (with Sheila Appel) Parents of Yr., Yeshiva Ketana of Manhattan, 1995; N.Y. State Regents scholar, 1963. Fellow ACS; mem. Phi Delta Epsilon, Alpha Epsilon Delta. Office: 322 W 78th St New York NY 10024-6503

APPEL, STANLEY HERSH, neurologist, educator; b. Boston, May 8, 1933; married; 4 children. AB, Harvard U., 1954; MD, Columbia U., 1960. Diplomate Am. Bd. Psychiatry and Neurology. Intern medicine Mass. Gen. Hosp., 1960-61; resident neurology Mt. Sinai Hosp., 1961-62; rsch. assoc. Lab. Moleculat Biology NIH, 1962-64; chief rsch. assoc. Sch. Medicine U. Pa., 1965-66, asst. prof., 1966-67; assoc. of neurology Med. Ctr. Duke U., 1964-65, from assoc. prof. to prof. neurology, 1967-77, assoc. prof. biochemistry, 1968-77, chief divsn. neurology, 1969-77; prof. neurology Baylor Coll. Medicine, 1977—2004, prof., chmn. dept. neurology, 1977—2004, chmn. program neurosci., 1977-89, dir. Jerry Lewis Neuromuscular Disorder Rsch. Ctr., 1977—2004; dir. Vicki Appel MDA/ALS Ctr., 1977—2004; chair dept. neurology Meth. Hosp. Neurol. Inst., Houston, 2005—, dir. MDA/ALS Rsch. and Clin. Ctr., 2005—, Peggy and Gary Edwards disting. endowed chair for the treatment and rsch. of ALS dept. neurology, 2006—; prof. neurology Weill Med. Coll. Cornell U., NYC, 2005—; dir. Methodist Neurol. Inst., 2010—. Recipient Gold medal Columbia Coll. Physicians and Surgeons, 1997, Disting. Faculty award Baylor Coll. Medicine Alumni Assn., 2004, Lifetime Achievement award Tex. Neurol. Soc., 2005, Forbes Norris award Internat. Alliance ALS/MND Assn., 2005, John P. McGavern Compleat Physician award, 2008 Mem. Am. Acad. Neurology (Sheila Essey award, 2003), Am. Neurol. Assn., Soc. Neuroscience, Am. Soc. Neurochemistry. Achievements include research in etiology of amyotrophic lateral sclerosis, Parkinson's disease, and Alzheimer's disease. Office: Methodist Neurological Inst Dept Neurology 6560 Fannin St #802 Houston TX 77030 Office Phone: 713-441-3760.

APPEL, WILLIAM FRANK, pharmacist; b. Mpls., Oct. 8, 1924; s. William Ignatius and Elna Antonia (Mulzahn) A.; m. Louise D. Altman, Sept. 24, 1949; children— Nancy, Peggy, James, Elizabeth. BS in Pharmacy, U. Minn., 1949; D.Sc. (hon.), Phila. Coll. Pharmacy and Sci., 1978. Intern in pharmacy Northwestern Hosp., Mpls.; pres., pharmacist, mgr. Appel Com-Pharm, Inc., Mpls., 1949—; pres. Pharm. Cons. Services, P.A., St. Paul, 1960—. Mem. Minn. Bd. Pharmacy, 1960-65, pres., 1965; preceptor internship requirement program; chmn. Minn. Gov's. Commn. on Drug Abuse, 1971-73; mem. Mpls. Health Dept. Task Force on Pub. Health Approaches to Chem. Dependency; clin. instr. U. Minn. Coll. Pharmacy, 1970—; cons. HEW; long term care facilities; rep. Nat. Pharmacy/Industry Com. on Nat. Health Ins.; mem. revision com. U.S. Pharmacopeial Conv., 1980— Served with USN, 1942-46. Recipient Good Neighbor award, Sta. WCCO, Mpls., 1973. Mem. Twin City Met. Drug Assn., Minn. Pharm. Assn. (v.p., Harold R. Popp award 1974, mem. continuing edn. faculty 1970—), Am. Pharm. Assn. (pres. N.W. br., nat. pres. 1976-77, Daniel B. Smith award 1970, treas. 1979—) pharm. assns), Minn. Gerontol. Soc., U. Minn. Coll. Pharmacy Alumni Assn. (v.p., Distinguished Pharmacist award 1971) Home: 5251 Ashlar Dr Minneapolis MN 55437-3360

APPELBAUM, HEATHER, physician; b. Chgo., Mar. 19, 1970; MD, Emory U. Sch. Medicine, 1996. Physician Obstetrics and Gynecology, 2001—. Asst. prof. Albert Einstein Sch. Medicine, 2001—10, Hofstra Sch. Medicine, 2010; chief Divsn. Pediatric & Adolescent Gynecology, 2009; dir. Disorders Sex Devel. Program, 2010; med. adv. bd. CARES found., 2010. Recipient Excellence Tchg. award, CREOG. Fellow: Am. Coll. Obstetricians & Gynecologists; mem.: North Am. Soc. Pediatric & Adolescent Gynecology. Avocations: travel, cooking, bicycling. Office: 1554 Northern Blvd Manhasset NY 11559 Office Phone: 516-390-9242. Office Fax: 516-390-9251.

APPELBAUM, PAUL STUART, psychiatrist, medical educator, department chairman; b. Bklyn., Nov. 30, 1951; s. Isidore W. and Celia (Bressler) A.; m. Diana Muir Karter, Nov. 9, 1953; children: Binyamin, Yonatan, Avigail. AB, Columbia U., 1972; MD, Harvard U., 1976. Diplomate Am. Bd. Psychiatry and Neurology. Intern Soroka Med. Ctr., Beersheva, Israel, 1976-77; resident Mass. Mental Health Ctr., Boston, 1977-80; clin. fellow psychiatry Harvard Med. Sch., Boston, 1977-80; from asst. prof. to assoc. prof. psychiatry and law U. Pitts., 1980-84; assoc. prof. psychiatry Harvard Med. Sch., Boston, 1984-85; Zeleznik prof. psychiatry, dir. law and psychiatry program U. Mass. Med. Sch., Worcester, 1985—2005, chmn. dept., 1992—2005; vis. interdisciplinary prof. Law Ctr. Georgetown U., Washington, 1988-89; Dollard prof. psychiatry, medicine and law Columbia Coll. Physicians and Surgeons, NYC, 2006—. Mem. commn. on mentally disabled ABA, Washington, 1982-87; task force on involuntary civil commitment Nat. Ctr. for State Cts., Williamsburg, Va., 1984-89, Rsch. Network on Mental Health and Law, John D. and Catherine T. Macarthur Found., Chgo., 1988-96; fellow Ctr. for Advanced Study in the Behavioral Scis., Stanford, Calif., 1996-97; rsch. network on mandatory outpatient treatment John D. and Catherine T. MacArthur Found., Chgo., 2000-10; bd. dirs. neurosci. and behavioral health Inst. Medicine of NAS, 2001-04. Author: Clinical Handbook of Psychiatry and the Law, 1982 (M.F. Guttmacher award 1982), 4th edit., 2006, Informed Consent: Legal Theory and Clinical Practice, 1987, 2d edit., 2001, Paul Appelbaum on Law and Psychiatry, 1989, Almost A Revolution: Mental Health Law and Limits of Change, 1994 (M.F. Guttmacher award 1996), Trauma and Memory: Clinical and Legal Controversies, 1997, Assessing Patients' Capacities to Consent to Treatment, 1998 (M.F. Guttmacher award 2000), Rethinking Risk Assessment, 2001 (M.F. Guttmacher award 2002); contbr. articles to profl. jours. Nat. coord. Med. Mobilization for Soviet Jewry, Waltham, Mass., 1974-80; bd. dirs. Action for Soviet Jewry, Waltham, 1984-85, Torah Ctr., Sharon, Mass., 1987-88, Cmty. Health Link, Worcester, Mass., 1992-2005, Am. Psychiat. Press, 2001-03, Am. Psychiat. Inst. on Rsch. and Edn., 2001-03, Israel Healthcare Found., 2010-. Recipient Rsch. Scientist Devel. award NIMH, 1983, Bell/Hays award for leadership in med. ethics and professionalism, AMA, 2007; Rsch. grantee Pres.'s Commn. on Ethical Problems in Medicine, Washington, 1982, John D. and Catherine T. MacArthur Found., 1988, 2003, Nat. Human Genome Rsch. Inst.; fellow Ctr. for Advanced Study in Behavioral Scis., Palo Alto, Calif., 1996-97. Mem.: NAS (elected to Inst. Medicine 2000), World Psychiat. Assn. (standing com. ethics mem. 2008—11), Mass. Psychiat. Soc. (pres. 1992—93), Am. Soc. Law and Medicine, Am. Acad. Psychiatry and the Law (councillor 1987—90, pres. 1995—96, Seymour Pollock award 2001), Am. Psychiat. Assn. (chair commn. on jud. action 1984—90, joint reference com. 1984—94, chair coun. on psychiatry and law 1990—94, sec. 1997—99, bd. dirs. 1997—2006, v.p. 1999—2001, pres. 2002—03, chair coun. on psychiatry and law 2004—08, chair com. jud. action 2010—, Isaac Ray award 1990, Spl. Presdl. Commendation award 2011), Internat. Acad. Law and Mental Health (Philippe Pinel award 2000). Jewish. Avocation: writing for popular mags. Office: NY State Psychiat Inst 1051 Riverside Dr 122 New York NY 10032 Home Phone: 646-734-3684; Office Phone: 212-543-4184. Business E-Mail: psa21@columbia.edu.

APPENZELLER, OTTO, neurologist, researcher; b. Czernowitz, Romania, Dec. 11, 1927; came to U.S., 1963; s. Emmanuel Adam and Josephine (Metsch) A.; m. Judith Bryce, Dec. 11, 1956; children: Timothy, Martin, Peter. MBBS, Sydney U., Australia, 1957, MD, 1966; PhD, U. London, 1963. Diplomate Am. Bd. Psychiatry and Neurology. Prof. U. N. Mex., Albuquerque, 1970-90; vis. prof. McGill U., Montreal, Canada, 1977; hon. rsch. fellow U. London, 1983; vis. scientist Oxygen Transport Program Lovelace Med. Found., Albuquerque, 1990-92; pres. N.Mex. Health Enhancement and Marathon Clinics Rsch. Found., Albuquerque, 1992—; prof. exptl. neurobiology Bogomoletz Inst. Ukrainian Acad. Sci., Kiev, 1995-2000. U.S.-India exch. scientist NSF, 1992; Fogarty internat. exch. scientist, Kiev, Ukraine, 1993; rsch. com. UNESCO Internat. Coun. Sports and Phys. Edn., 1978-99; ref. Med. Rsch. Coun. New Zealand, 1986-99, reviewer, 1988-99; participant individual health scientist exch. program Fogarty Internat. Ctr., NIH to A.A. Bogomoletz Inst. Physiology, Kiev, 1993, PT Brookhaven Synchrotron Light Source, 2011. Author: The Autonomic Nervous System, 5th edit., 1997; co-author: Headache, 1984; editor: Pathogenesis and Management of Headache, 1976, Health Aspects of Endurance Training, 1978, Sports Medicine, 3rd edit., 1988, Jour. Headache, 1975-77, Annals of Sports Medicine, 1984-88; translator: Neurologic Differential Diagnosis (M. Mumenthaler), 2nd edit., 1992; vol. editor: Handbook of Clinical Neurology: The Autonomic Nervous System, Parts I and II, 1998-2000; mem. editl. bd. numerous med. jours. Grantee Diabetes Rsch. and Edn. Found., 1988, Inst. C. Mondino, U. Pavia, Italy, 1992, 95-96, 2000, NMHEMC Rsch. Found., 1992-, Dept. Pediat. UC San Diego, 2011. Fellow ACP (sr.), Am. Acad. Neurology (sr.), Royal Australasian Coll. Physicians (sr.). Achievements include discovery of disease affecting peripheral nerves of Navajo children, of release of opioids and endothelin in human circulatory system after exercise, of chronic neurodegenerative disease in human T-lymphotropic viral II (HTLV II) infection, of peptidergic innervation of blood vessels supplying blood to peripheral nerves in present day and ancient mummified tissues of neurologic dis. in mummy portraits, of neuropathy in chronic pulmonary disease and chronic mountain sickness of fossilized biological rhythm in ancient human teeth, and teeth of extinct archosaurs; of archived biologic rhythms in human and animal hair; of cerebral vasodilatation to nitric oxide as a measure of fitness for life at altitude, of Molecular Signature, of Chronic Mountain Sickness in the Andes and Himalayas; of biologic markers of susceptibility to chronic mountain sickness in healthy children of andean highlanders of gold deposition by bacteria on human hair of biologic rhythms in Siberian Mammoths' hair, leader of Mt. Everest rsch. expedition, 1987, Khachenjunga and Himalayas rsch. expedition, 1989, Stock Kangri rsch. expedition, 1992, Tso Moriri Lake (Ladakh) rsch. expedition, 1994, Cerro de Pasco rsch. expedition, 1997, 99-2000, 03, 2011, rsch. expedition Simen Mountains, Ethiopia, 2005, Korzok, Ladakh, 2006, 2007, Ethiopia, Bale Mountain, 2009. Business E-Mail: oarun@unm.edu. E-mail: ottoarun12@aol.com, o.appenzeller@comcast.net.

APPERSON, JEAN, psychologist; b. Durham, NC, June 8, 1934; d. James Harry and Dorothy Elizabeth (Johnson) Apperson; m. Calvin Adams Pope, Mar. 23, 1956 (div. 1967); 1 child, Richard Allan; m. Peter H. Amann, Sept. 4, 2004. BA, U. S. Fla., 1966; MA, Mich. State U., 1970, PhD, 1973. Cert. in psychoanalysis Mich. Psychoanalytic Coun., 1990. Teaching asst. Mich. State U., E. Lansing, 1968-69; psychiatric technician St. Lawrence Community Mental Health Ctr., Lansing, Mich., 1968-69, psychology intern, 1969-71, Mich. State U. Counseling Ctr., 1971-73; clin. psychologist U. Mich. Counseling Ctr., Ann Arbor, 1973-81; pvt. practice psychology and psychoanalysis Ann Arbor, 1974—. Mem., chmn. Mich. Bd. Psychology, Lansing, 1984-91. Contbr. articles to profl. jours.; cons. editor Am. Psychol. Assn. Catalog of Selected Documents, 1975-80. USPHS grantee, 1969-70; NIMH grantee, 1970-71. Fellow Mich. Psychol. Assn. (chmn. women's issues com. 1981-83); mem. APA (com. on sci. and profl. ethics and conduct 1977-80), Mich. Soc. Psychoanalytic Psychology (treas. 1982-86), Mich. Psychoanalytic Coun. (tchg. and supervising analyst, mem. at large 1991-93, tng. com. 1992-2001, pres. 1995-97, v.p. for edn. and tng. 1998-2001), Assn. for Advancement of Psychology, Am. Women in Psychology, Mich. Women Psychologists. Democrat. Unitarian Universalist. Avocations: french language and culture, gardening, nature study, music. Home: 7224 Chelsea Manchester Rd Manchester MI 48158-9443 Office: Ste 23E 555 E William St Ann Arbor MI 48104-2428 Office Phone: 734-428-9110. Personal E-mail: jeanatapp@aol.com.

APPLE, FRED S., medical educator, director; BS, Rensselaer Poly. Inst., Troy, NY, 1975; PhD in Bioorganic Biophys. Chemistry, U. Minn., Mpls., 1979. Cert. in chem. chemistry Am. Bd. Clin. Chemistry, 1985, in toxicological chemistry 1988. Vis. asst. prof., dept. chemistry U. Wis., River Falls, Wis., 1979; NIH rsch. tng. fellow clin. chemistry Washington U. Sch. Medicine, Barnes Hosp., St. Louis, 1980—82; asst. prof., dept. lab. medicine and pathology U. Minn. Med. Sch., Mpls., 1982—88, assoc. prof., dept. lab. medicine and pathology, 1988—95, prof., dept. lab. medicine and pathology, 1995—; assoc. prof., dept. kinesiology U. Minn., 1992—95, prof. dept. kinesiology, 1995—; assoc. dir.,dept. pathology residency program Hennepin County Med. Ctr., Mpls., 1993—2000; forensic toxicology cons. Hennepin County Med. Examiner's Office, 1982—; med. dir. Clin. Chemistry and Toxicology Lab., Hennepin County Med. Ctr., Mpls., 1982—, North Ctrl. (Formerly Regional Kidney Disease Program) Renal Lab. Total Renal Care (Davita), Mpls., 1992—2001, Point Care Testing, Hennepin County Med. Ctr., Mpls., 1995—, Clin. Lab., Hennepin County Med. Ctr., Mpls., 1996—, HFA Clin. Lab., Mpls., 2001—. Grad. sch. faculty mem., clin. lab. sci. U. Minn., 1985—, grad. sch. faculty mem., sch. kinesiology and leisure studies, 1992—; bd. dirs. Am. Bd. Clin. Chemistry, 1992—98; mem. FDA Clin. Chemistry and Clin. Toxicology Devices Panel of the Med. Devices Adv. Com. Ctr. for Devices and Radiological Health, 2004—05; mem. review bd. US Anti-Doping Agy., 2003—06; mem. Global Task Force for Redefinition of Myocardial Infarction, 2004—. Contbr. articles to profl.jours. Recipient Swedish Nat. Coun. Sports Rsch. award, Young Investigator award, Internat. Soc. Clin. Enzymology, 1983. Fellow: Am. Coll. Sports Medicine; mem.: Soc. Forensic Toxicology, Am. Acad. Forensic Sciences, Acad. Clin. Lab. Physicians and Scientists (pres. 2003—04, 2003—04), Am. Assn. Clin. Chemistry (assoc. editor 2001—), Global Task Force Redefination Myocardial Infarction, Internat. Fedn. Clin. Chemistry and Lab. Medicine (chair 2004—, mem. com. standardization of markers for cardiac damage 1998—, chair 2004—), Nat. Com. Clin. Lab. Stds. Clin. Chemistry, Am. Chem. Clin. Chemistry (Outstanding Spkr. award 1995—98, 2001—04), Canadian Soc. Clin. Chemists, Internat. Soc. Clin. Enzymology, Am. Chem. Soc. Office: Dept Lab Medicine and Pathology Univ Minn Medicine Sch Mayo Mail Code 609 420 Delaware St SE Minneapolis MN 55455 Office Phone: 612-873-3324. Office Fax: 612-626-2696. E-mail: apple004@umn.edu. *

APPLE, JERRY, diagnostic radiologist; MD, Duke U. Sch. of Medicine, 1978. Diplomate Am. Bd. of Radiology-diagnostic radiology. Resident Duke Univ. Med. Ctr., 1982, fellow, 1983. Named top dr., Phila. Mag., 2007, 2010, Inside Jersey Mag., 2010. Fellow: Am. Coll. of Radiology; mem.: West Jersey Med. Soc., Radiology Soc. of NJ, Med. Soc. of NJ, Camden County Med. Soc., Am. Roentgen Ray Soc., Radiol. Soc. of N. Am. Office: 100 Carnie Blvd Ste B5 Voorhees NJ 08043 Office Phone: 856-751-0123.

APPLEBAUM, EDWARD LEON, otolaryngologist, educator; b. Detroit, Jan. 14, 1940; s. M. Lawrence and Frieda Applebaum; m. Eva Redei; children: Daniel Ira, Rachel Anne. AB, Wayne State U., 1961, MD, 1964. Diplomate: Am. Bd. Otolaryngology. Intern Univ. Hosp., Ann Arbor, Mich., 1964-65; resident Mass. Eye and Ear Infirmary Harvard Med. Sch., Boston, 1966-69; practice medicine specializing in otolaryngology Chgo., 1972—2007; assoc. prof. Northwestern U. Med. Sch., 1972-79, prof. Chgo., 2000—06, chmn. dept. otolaryngology, 2000—06, prof. emeritus, 2007—; prof., head dept. otolaryngology, head and neck surgery Coll. Medicine, U. Ill., 1979-2000, prof. emeritus, 2000—. Mem. staff Northwestern Meml. Hosp. Author: Tracheal Intubation, 1976; editor: Am. Jour. Otolaryngology, 1982-87; mem. editl. bd. Am. Jour. Otolaryngology, Laryngoscope. Served as maj. U.S. Army, 1969-71. Recipient Anna Albert Keller Rsch. award Wayne State U. Coll. Medicine, 1964, Disting. Alumni award, 1989, William Beaumont Soc. Original Rsch. award, 1964, Disting. Faculty award, U. Ill. Coll. Medicine, 1996. Fellow ACS, Am. Soc. for Head and Neck Surgery, Surgery, Am. Acad. Otolaryngology, Head and Neck Surgery, Am. Laryngol., Rhinol. and Otol. Soc. (v.p. 1993, pres. 2000), Am. Laryngol. Assn., Am. Otol. Soc., Soc. Univ. Otolaryngologists, Head and Neck Surgeons (pres. 1988), Assn. Acad. Depts. Otolaryngology-Head and Neck Surgery (pres. 1995-96). E-mail: eapple@northwestern.edu.

APPLEBAUM, MICHAEL, medical association administrator; b. Chgo., Oct. 13, 1953; MD, U. Ill. Abraham Lincoln Sch. Medicine, 1979; JD, IIT-Kent Coll. Law, 1988. Cert. fitness trainer, specialist in performance nutrition & endurance fitness trainer 2003, specialist in fitness older adults, youth fitness trainer, fitness therapist 2003. Med. dir. FCLM Med. & Legal Consulting Svcs., 1988, Diagnostic Ultrasound, 1995. Prof. fitness scis., 2003; pres. FitnessMed, Inc., 2004; med. dir. Anabolic Clinic, SC, 2009. Fellow: Am. Coll. Legal Medicine. Office: 845 N Mich Ave Ste 935 E Chicago IL 60076 E-mail: aparticle@drapplebaum.com.

APPLEGATE, WILLIAM BROWN, medical educator, researcher; b. Louisville, July 28, 1946; s. Henry Lovelace and Margaret (Whitesides) A.; m. Gail Reekers, July 31, 1982; children: Elizabeth Marie, Jennifer Michelle. BA, U. Louisville, 1968, MD, 1972; MPH, Harvard U., 1973. Intern Boston City Hosp., 1973—74, resident in internal medicine, 1974—75; R.W. Johnson clin. scholar U. NC, Chapel Hill, 1975-77; asst. prof. medicine U. N.Mex., Albuquerque, 1977-79; chief divsn. geriatric medicine U. Tenn., Memphis, 1979-93, dir. gen. clin. rsch. ctr., 1993-99, chmn. dept. preventive medicine, 1994-99; chmn., prof. dept. internal medicine Wake Forest U., Winston-Salem, NC, 1999—2002, dean sch. medicine, sr. v.p. health scis., 2002—07; pres. Wake Forest U. Health Sciences, Winston-Salem, 2007—11; prof. geriatrics and gerontology Wake Forest Baptist Med. Ctr., Winston-Salem. Mem. coun. Nat. Inst. Aging, 1989-93, nat. adv. bd. Johnson Found. Clin. Scholars Program; bd. regents, ACP, 2002-. Contbr. articles to med. jours., including Jour. AMA, Archives Internal Medicine, others. Named Alumni fellow U. Louisville, 2003; grantee. Mem. ACP (bd. regents, chair bd. regents, 2008), Am. Geriat. Soc. (editor-in-chief jour. 1993-2000), Rotary. Democrat. Avocation: bicycling. Office: Wake Forest Bapt Med Ctr Medical Center Blvd Winston Salem NC 27157-0001 Office Phone: 336-713-8570. *

APPLEY, ALAN J., neurosurgeon; b. Long Beach, Calif., Mar. 2, 1958; s. Stephen N. and Arlene B. Appley; m. Cynthia C. Chicola, May 28, 1983; children: Maya A., Maxwell G. BA in Biology cum laude, Franklin and Marshall Coll., 1979; MD, Tulane U., New Orleans, 1983. Diplomate Am. Bd. Neurol. Surgery. Asst. prof. neurol. surgery Med. Coll., Richmond, Va., 1989—91, Orlando Neurol. Assocs., 1991—92, Fla. Neurosurgery, 1992—2001; neurosurgeon Neurol. Assoc. La., Lafayette, 2001—; clin. asst. prof. dept. neurosurgery Tulane U., New Orleans, 2003—. Chmn. dept. neurosurgery Fla. Hosp. Med. Ctr., Orlando, 1995—96; med. dir. Fla. Hosp. Gamma Knife Ctr., Orlando, 1996—2000, Terrebonne Regional Gamma Knife Ctr., Houma, La., 2002—04; chmn. sect. neurosurgery Winter Pk. Meml. Hosp., Fla., 1996—98; founding med. dir. Fla. Hosp. Neuroscience Inst., Orlando, 1998—2000; surg. dir. Cyberknife Ctr., Lafayette, La., 2007—. Active Am. Cancer Soc., Orlando, Fla., 1994—2001. Recipient Norman Rogers prize, Tulane U. Sch. Medicine, 1982; named one of Top Drs. in Orlando, Orlando Mag., 2001, La. Top Drs., La. Life Mag., 2009—10; fellow, Alpha Omega Alpha, 1982. Fellow: ACS; mem.: Leksell Gamma Knife Soc., La. Neurosurgical Soc., North Am. Spine Soc., Am. Soc. for Stereotactic and Functional Neurosurgery, World Soc. for Stereotactic and Functional Neurosurgery, Internat. Stereotactic Radiosurgery Soc., Congress Neurol. Surgeons, Am. Assn. Neurol. Surgeons, Cyberknife Soc. Office Fax: 337-235-7614. Personal E-mail: aappley@gmail.com.

APPLEY, MORTIMER HERBERT, psychologist, retired academic administrator; b. NYC, Nov. 21, 1921; s. Benjamin and Minnie (Albert) A.; m. Dee Gordon, June 5, 1942 (div. Oct. 1969); children: Richard Gordon, John Benton; m. Mariann B. Hundahl, Jan. 10, 1971; stepchildren: Scott, Eric, Heidi Hundahl. BS, CCNY, 1942; MA, U. Denver, 1946; PhD, U. Mich., 1950; DSc (hon.), York U., 1975; DHL (hon.), Northeastern U., 1983; LittD (hon.), Am. Internat. Coll., 1984; LLD (hon.), Clark U., 1984. Instr. U. Denver, 1945-47; instr. U. Mich., 1947-49; asst. prof. Wesleyan U., Middletown, Conn., 1949-52; prof., chmn. psychology Conn. Coll., New London, 1952-60, So. Ill. U., Carbondale, 1960-62, York U., Toronto, Ont., Canada, 1962-67, dean faculty grad. studies, 1965-68; prof., chmn. psychology U. Mass., Amherst, 1967-69; dean Grad. Sch., 1969-74, asso. provost, 1973-74; pres. Clark U., Worcester, Mass., 1974-84; vis. scholar psychology Harvard U., 1984-88, lectr., extension, 1985-95, vis. prof., 1985-86; exec. dir., Commn. on the Future of the Univ. U. Mass., Boston, 1988-89. Cons. NSF, NIMH, NRC of Can., Can. Council, VA., AAAS, MacArthur Found. Author: (with C.N. Cofer) Motivation: Theory and Research, 1964, (with R. Trumbull) Psychological Stress, 1967, (with J. Rickwood) Psychology in Canada, 1967, (with R. Trumbull) Dynamics of Stress, 1986, (with L. Lasagna) Who are the Elderly, 1986, (with W.B. Maher) Social and Behavioral Sciences, 1989, Learning to Lead, 1989; editor: Adaption Level Theory: A Symposium, 1971, Motivation and Emotion, 1976-88; assoc. editor Psychol. Abstracts, 1961-62; editor, contbr. Internat. Ency. Neurology, Psychology, Psychoanalysis and Psychiatry; contbr. articles to profl. jours. Chmn. bd. mgrs. Unitarian Fellowship, Toronto; vestryman King's Chapel, Boston; trustee Nantucket Atheneum. With USAAF, 1942-45. NSF Sci. Faculty fellow, 1959-60, Fulbright fellow, Germany, 1973-74. Fellow AAAS, APA (past chmn. edn. and tng. bd.), Can. Psychol. Assn. (bd. dirs.); mem. Conn. Psychol. Assn. (past pres.), New Eng. Psychol. Assn. (past pres.), St. Botolph Club (Boston, pres. 1997-2000), Worcester Econ. Club (pres. 1980-81), Wharf Rats (Nantucket), Sigma Xi, Psi Chi, Phi Sigma. Democrat. Unitarian Universalist. Home: Two Commonwealth Ave Boston MA 02116 Personal E-mail: mappley@comcast.net.

APPLEYARD, JENNIFER, allergist, immunologist; MD, Wayne State U. Cert. ABMS Bd. Internal Medicine, ABMS Bd. Allergy & Immunology. Resident St. John Hosp. Med. Ctr., chief allergy & immunology; fellow Henry Ford Hosp. Office: Lakeshore Ear, Nose & Throat Center 17770 Mack Ave Grosse Pointe MI 48230 Office Phone: 313-885-6367. Office Fax: 313-885-0586.

APPOLONOVA, SVETLANA A., chemist; b. Kazan, Russia, Feb. 25, 1973; BS, Kazan State U., 1995; PhD, Inst. Organic Chemistry, 1998. Sr. rsch. scientist Moscow Anti-Doping Ctr., 2000—05, dep. dir., 2005—07, head horsedoping dept., 2007—. Leading specialist Tatarstan Republic State Inspection, Dept. Lab. Analytical Investigation Alcoholic Products, 1998—2000. Sci. Investigation grant, Russian Fed. Agy. Sci. and Innovations, 2005, 2008, Russian Fed. Agy. Phys. Culture and Sport, 2008. Mem.: Russian Soc. Mass Spectrometry, Am. Soc. Mass Spectrometry, Assn. Ofcl. Racing Chemists. Avocations: travel, swimming. Office: Elizavetinskiy Per10 Moscow 105005 Russia Office Fax: 74992619943. Business E-Mail: appolosa@yandex.ru.

APT, LEONARD, pediatric ophthalmologist; AB with highest honors, U. Pa., 1942; MD with highest honors, Jefferson Med. Coll., Phila., 1945. Diplomate Am. Bd. Pediat., Am. Bd. Ophthalmology. Intern Jefferson Med. Coll. Hosp., 1945-46; rsch. fellow pathology-hematology, resident pediat. Children's Hosp. Detroit, 1946-49; resident pediat. Cin., 1949—50, Children's Med. Ctr., Boston, 1950-52, chief med. resident, 1952-53, asst. physician, 1953-55; resident ophthalmology Wills Eye Hosp., Phila., 1955-57, first fellow pediat. ophthalmology, 1959—61; first spl. fellow pediat. ophthalmology Children's Hosp., Washington, 1957—59, NIH, Bethesda, Md., 1957—59; asst. prof. to prof. ophthalmology UCLA Sch. Medicine, 1961—72, prof., 1972—, disting. prof., 1993—; attending surgeon Jules Stein Eye Inst., UCLA, founding dir. divsn. pediat. ophthalmology, 1961—81, founder, 1966, dir. emeritus, 1981—; co-dir. Ctr. to Prevent Childhood Blindness, 2005—. Pediat. tchg. fellow Harvard U. Med. Sch., Boston, 1950—52, instr. pediat., 1953—55; sr. physician, radioisotope unit Boston VA Hosp., 1953—55; cons. pediat. ophthalmology Cedars-Sinai Med. Ctr., LA, St. John's Hosp., Santa Monica, Calif., Dept. Pub. Health Calif., Dept. Health, LA, Bur. Maternal and Child Health. Author: Diagnostic Procedures in Pediatric Ophthalmology, 1963; mem. editl. bd.: numerous med. jours.:; contbr. articles to profl. jours., chapters to books. Founder LA Philharmonic Assn.; presdl. circle mem. LA County Mus. Art; v.p. fin. UCLA Grunwald Ctr. Graphic Arts, Hammer Mus.; bd. dirs. Royce Ctr. Cir., UCLA Performing Arts Dept., Cmty. Outreach Prog., UCLA Design for Sharing; founder John Wooden UCLA Athletic Ctr., UCLA Acosta Athletic Tng. Complex; judge Wines of America Ann. Competition; exec. coun. mem. UCLA Divsn. of Humanities. 1st lt. M.C. US Army, 1943—46. Recipient F.T. Stewart Surgery prize, Jefferson Med. Coll., 1945, Arthur J. Bedell Resident Rsch. prize, Wills Eye Hosp., Phila., 1957, Disting. Alumnus Achievement award, Jefferson Med. Coll., 1992, First Escalon Sci. award, 1992, Hall of Fame Distinction award, Cin. Pediat. Hist. Soc., 1994, First Disting. Alumni award, U. Pa. Sch. Arts & Scis., 1995, Alumni Univ. Svc. award, UCLA, 1996, William Feinbloom First Disting. Achievement award, 1999, Profl. Achievement award, UCLA Med. Alumni Assn., 1999, First Disting. Achievement award, Ethicon Inc./Johnson & Johnson Co., 1999, S. Rodman Irvine prize, Jules Stein Eye Inst., UCLA, 2005, Dickson Emeritus Prof. award, UCLA, 2009, Castle Connolly Nat. Physician of Yr. award, 2010. Mem.: AMA, Internat. Strabismol. Assn., Am. Med. Writers Assn., Pacific Coast Oto-Ophthal. Soc., Am. Assn. Pediat. Ophthalmology & Strabismus (First Disting. Achievement award 1996, Honor award 1995), Soc. Pediat. Rsch., Assn. Rsch. Ophthalmology, Am. Ophthal. Soc., Am. Acad. Pediats. (Lifetime Achievement award 2000, Ann. Leonard Apt Lectureship named in his honor 2000), Am. Acad. Ophthalmology (Honor award 1968), Confrerie de la Chaine des Rotisseurs, L'Ordre Mondial des Gourmets Degustaeurs, Internat. Wine & Food Soc., Shriner, Mason (32nd deg.), Alpha Omega Alpha. Avocations: sports, art, theater, gourmet food, oenology. Office: UCLA Jules Stein Eye Inst 100 Stein Plz Los Angeles CA 90095-7000 Office Phone: 310-825-3986. Office Fax: 310-206-3652.

APUZZIO, JOSEPH J., obstetrician, gynecologist; b. Elizabeth, NJ, 1947; MD, N.J. Med. Coll., 1973. Resident Martland Hosp., Newark, 1973-76; with U. Hosp., Newark, Clara Mass. Hosp., Belleville, N.J., Columbus Hosp., Newark, Trinitas (N.J.) Hosp. U. Hosp. fellow, Newark, 1980-82. Fellow ACOG, Maternal-Fetal Medicine; mem. Am. Coll. Ob-gyn. Office: Dept Ob-Gyn and Womens Health Med Sci Bldg E506 185 S Orange Ave Newark NJ 07103-2757 Office Phone: 973-972-5557. Business E-Mail: josephapuzzio@umdnj.edu.

APUZZO, MICHAEL LAWRENCE JOHN, neurological surgeon; b. New Haven, 1940; BA, Yale U., 1961; MD, Boston U., 1965. Intern in neurosurgery Yale U.; resident in surgery McGill U., 1966; resident in neurosurgery Yale U., New Haven, 1967-73; prof. neurol. surgery, radiation oncology, biology and physics U. So. Calif. Sch. Medicine, LA. Editor-in-chief World Neurosurgery; contbr. over 700 articles to profl. jours. Office: U So Calif Sch Medicine Ste 5046 1200 N State St Los Angeles CA 90033-1029 Office Phone: 323-442-3001. Business E-Mail: apuzzo@usc.edu.

AQUINO, JOSEPH MARIO, clinical psychologist; b. NYC, Nov. 21, 1947; s. Joseph and Rose (Nasi) A.; m. Kathleen Ann Ryan, Oct. 6, 1990; children: Joseph Patrick, Ryan Thomas, Erin Rose. BA in English, So. Ill. U., 1969, MS in Secondary Edn., 1976; PhD in Clin. Psychology, St. John's U., Jamaica, NY, 1987. Lic. psychologist, N.Y. Tchr. English Wappingers Cen. Schs., Wappingers Falls, NY, 1969-79; intern psychology Maimonides Med. Ctr., Bklyn., 1983-84; specialist in applied behavior sci. Builders for Family and Youth, Bklyn., 1984-85; trainee psychology and psychologist St. Vincent's Svcs., Bklyn., 1984-89; psychologist St. Christopher-Ottilie Svcs., Sea Cliff, NY, 1989-96; pvt. practice psychology NYC area, 1989—. Guest lectr. St. John's U., 1990. Co-author: Situational Leadership for Principals, 1983; mem. editl. bd. Jour. Urban Psychiatry, 1982-84; guest The Women's Line, WVOX 1460 AM, 1994; cited in newspaper articles; contbr. articles to profl. jours. Recipient citation VFW, Wappingers Falls, N.Y., 1977; Bethany House Achievement award Bethany House II, 1991; psychology teaching fellow St. John's U., 1981; cited in article Emergency mag., 1991. Mem. APA, N.Y. State Psychol. Assn., Westchester County Psychol. Assn., Nat. Register of Health Svc. Providers in Psychology, Am. Coll. of Advanced Practice Psychologists (founding fellow). Office: 10 Rye Ridge Plz Ste 214 Rye Brook NY 10573-2857 Office Phone: 914-253-9429. Personal E-mail: werpsyched@aol.com.

AQUINO, SIMONE, medical educator; b. São Paulo, Brazil, Aug. 6, 1966; PhD, U. São Paulo, 2007. Cert. in medicine vet. UNESP-Botucatu, 1990. Scientist rschr. Inst. Biológico São Paulo, 2007—11; prof. microbiology U. Nove de Julho, São Paulo, 2007—, adj. prof., 2010—. Avocation: scuba diving. Home: Rua Juréia 848 apto 23 São Paulo 04140-110 Brazil Personal E-mail: siaq06@hotmail.com.

ARABI, MANDANA, nutritionist; b. Tehran, Iran, July 31, 1974; MD, Tehran U. Med. Scis., 1999; PhD, Cornell U., 2010. Nutrition adviser UNICEF, 2007—. Home: 400 E71 St Apt 18F New York NY 10021 Business E-Mail: marabi@unicef.org.

ARABI, YASEEN, medical educator, consultant; b. Hama, Syria, Oct. 23, 1966; s. Mohammed Saeed and Hamidah Arabi; m. Amal Arabi, Aug. 7, 1993; children: Mohammed, Esraa, Obadah, Alaa, Anas. MD, Damascus U. Sch. Medicine, Syria, 1989. Diplomate pulmonary medicine Am. Bd., 1997, 2007, internal medicine 1995, 2005, critical care medicine 1998. Chief med. resident Harper Hosp. Detroit Med. Ctr., Wayne State U. Sch. Medicine, 1994—95, cons., 1998—; assoc. cons. Intensive Care Dept., King Abdulaziz Med. City, Riyadh, Saudi Arabia, 1998, program dir., 2001—06, dep. chmn., 2002—06, asst. prof., 2004—, acting chmn., 2006—07, chmn., 2007—. Attending physician Med. ICU, WS Middleton VA Hosp., Madison, Wis., 1996, Gen. Internal Medicine Clinic, U. Health Ctr., Detroit, 1994—95. Contbr. numerous articles and sci. rsch. papers to profl. jours. Recipient Presdl. Citation award, Soc. Critical Care Medicine, First Place award, Am. Coll. Chest Physicians, Can.; rsch. grant, King Abdulaziz City Sci. and Tech., Sanofi-Aventis. Fellow: Am. Coll. Chest Physicians, Am. Coll. Critical Care; mem.: Saudi Soc. Critical Medicine, U. Wis. Med. alumni Assn., Soc. Critical Care Medicine, Syrian Assn. Physicians. Achievements include first to receive plaque of appreciation in critical care management of human AI cases, 2nd Avian and Pandemic Influenza Training Workshop; internal medicine board review, international symposium in critical care medicine, King Abdulaziz Medical City, Riyadh; Hajj Emergency National Conference, Riyadh, Saudi Arabia; symposium on todays challenges in critical care practice, Security Forces Hospital, Riyadh, Saudi Arabia; 1st, 2nd, 3rd and 4th critical care conference, Syria; Ministry of Health, Syria Arab Republic. Office: ICU-MC 1425 King Abdulaziz Med City PO Box 22490 Riyadh 11426 KSA Riyadh 11426 Saudi Arabia Office Fax: 966-1-2520088 x18880.

ARAC, ZDENKO, dentist, educator; b. Mostar, May 31, 1966; Degree, Dental Sch., Zagreb, Croatia, 1994, degree, 2000. Asst. Med. faculty of Mostar, 2000—11; dr. oral surgery Home Health of Mostar, 1994—. Dir. Additional Pvt. Dental Practice, 2009—11. Mem.: Croatian Dental Soc., Croatian Implant Soc., Croatian Med. Assn. Avocation: football. Home: Kraljice Katarine 8/II Mostar 88 000 Bosnia-Herzegovina Home Phone: 00387 63 311 676.

ARAGÃO-NETO, ADELMO CAVALCANTI, surgeon; b. Recife, Brazil, May 28, 1979; Grad in Dentistry, Fed. U. Pernambuco, 2011. Voluntary rschr. Fed. U. Pernambuco, 2008—. Home: Prof Jose Candido Pessoa 1379 Olinda 53030020 Brazil Personal E-mail: ac.aragao.neto@gmail.com.

ARAGONA, PASQUALE, ophthalmologist, educator; b. Messina, Sicily, May 30, 1960; MD, U. Messina, 1985, Specialist in Ophthalmology, 1989; PhD, U. Padua, 1999. Asst. prof. U. Messina, 2002—08, prof., ophthalmology, head, ocular surface unit, 2007—. Recipient Rsch. award, Soc. Oftalmologica Italiana, 1996, Silver Amber medal, Polish Cornea Congress, 2011. Master: Italian Soc. Dacriology and Ocular Surface; fellow: Italian Soc. Uveitis and Ocular Inflammatory Diseases, Italian Med. Contact Lens Soc., Tear Film and Ocular Surface Soc., mem.: Soc. Oftalmologica Italiana. Avocations: music, painting, skiing. Office: Policlinico Universitario G Martino Messina ME 98125 Italy Office Fax: 39-090-221-3958. Business E-Mail: paragona@unime.it.

ARAI, AYAKO, hematologist, educator; b. Tokyo, Dec. 4, 1963; MD, Grad. Sch. Tokyo Med. & Dental U., PhD, 1999. Assoc. prof. Dept. Hematology, Tokyo Med. & Dental U., 2002—. Rep. Japanese Soc. Hematology; dir. Med-Learning Corp., 2011—. Recipient Ouchi prize, Tokyo Med. & Dental U.; Rsch. grant, Japan Leukemia Rsch. Found., Ministry of Edn., Culture, Sports, Sci. & Tech., Ministry of Health, Labour, & Welfare, Ichiro Kanehara Found. Mem.: Molecular Biology Soc. Japan, Japanese Cancer Assn., Japanese Soc. Hematology, European Hematology Assn., Am. Soc. Hematology. Avocations: ballet, tennis, piano. Office: 1-5-45 Yushima Bunkyo-Ku Tokyo 1138519 Japan Office Fax: 81358030131. Business E-Mail: ara.hema@tmd.ac.jp.

ARAI, MIDORI A., chemistry professor; b. Miyazaki, Apr. 2, 1972; PhD, U. Tokyo, 2000. Postdoc. fellow, dept. chemistry & chem. biology Harvard U., 2001—02; spl. postdoc. fellow RIKEN, 2003—04; asst. prof. Teikyo U., Sch. Pharm. Scis., 2004—06; assoc. prof. Chiba U., Grad. Sch. Pharm. Scis., 2006—; vis. assoc. prof. Kyoto U., Inst. Chem. Rsch., 2010—. Recipient Morita award, Japanese Assn. U. Women, 2011. Mem.: Synthetic Organic Chemistry Japan (Sankyo award), Chem. Soc. Japan, Pharm. Soc. Japan (Young Scientists award 2010), Am. Chem. Soc. Office: 1 8 1 Inohana Chuo Ku Chiba 260 8675 Japan Business E-Mail: marai@p.chiba-u.ac.jp, midori_arai@chiba.u.jp.

ARAI, MIKKI, ophthalmologist, researcher; b. Kyoto, Dec. 20, 1959; s. Motomichi and Tamako Arai; m. Naoko Takahashi; children: Chiaki, Yuki, Rikki, Taku. MD, Hyogo Coll. Medicine, Japan, 1985. Instr. Harvard Med. Sch., Boston, 1999—2000; assoc. prof. Kurume U. Sch. Medicine, Fukuoka, Japan, 2000—; adj. assoc. scientist Schepens Eye Rsch. Inst., Boston, 2002—. Mem.: Am. Acad. Ophthalmology (Achievement award 2007). Achievements include patents for optical guide fixture. Office: Arai Eye Clinic 2-10-43 Jiromaru Sawara-Ku Fukuoka 814-0165 Japan Office Phone: 81-92-401-3003. Office Fax: 81-92-401-3010; Home Fax: 81-92-847-2747.

ARAI, TOSHIHIKO, retired microbiology and immunology educator; b. Niigata, Japan, Sept. 12, 1937; s. Hachiro Sisido and Kazue Arai; m. Hatsue Aoki, Dec. 1, 1963; children: Masako, Tomoko, Kazuhiko. MD, Keio U., Tokyo, 1962; PhD, Keio U., 1968. Instr. dept. microbiology Keio U. Sch. Medicine, 1967-73, asst. prof., 1973-85, assoc. prof., 1985; prof. microbiology and immunology Meiji Coll. Pharmacy, Tokyo, 1985 97; ret., 1997. Rsch. assoc. U. Tex., Dallas, 1970—72; lectr. Ochanomizu U. Sch. Sci., Tokyo, 1978—79, Chiba U. Sch. Medicine, Japan, 1978—82, Josai Dental U., Sakado, Japan, 1978—87, Aoyama Gakuin U., Tokyo, 1988—2003; cons. Kitasato Inst., Tokyo, 1981—84. Author (15 books); contbr. Mem.: NY Acad. Scis., Am. Soc. Microbiology, Japan Soc. Ningen Dock, Japan Soc. Chemotherapy, Japan Soc. Bacteriology. Zen Buddhist. Home: 5-1-23 Yatsu Narashimo-shi Chiba 275-0026 Japan Office: St Maguerite Hosp 450 Kami-kouya Yachiyo-shi Chiba 276-0022 Japan Home Phone: 81 47 473 5768, 81 090 3689 4086; Office Phone: 81-47-485-5111. Business E-Mail: ya5-1-23@mxm.mesh.ne.jp.

ARAKAWA, HIROFUMI, medical scientist; b. Kumamoto, Japan, May 26, 1963; MD, Kumamoto U. Med. Sch., 1988; PhD, Kumamoto U. Grad. Sch. Medicine, 1995. Surgeon Kumamoto U. Hosp., 1988—95; postdoc. rsch. fellow Jefferson Med. Coll., Kimmel Cancer Ctr., 1995—98; asst. prof. U. Tokyo, Inst. Med. Sci., 1999—2001, assoc. prof., 2001—03; chief Nat. Cancer Ctr. Rsch. Inst., 2003—. Vis. prof. Tokyo Med. and Dental U., 2006—11; assoc. editor Sci. Jour. Cancer Sci., 2003—11. Rsch. grant, Princess Takamatsu Cancer Rsch. Mem.: Japanese Cancer Assn. (Incitement award), Am. Assn. Cancer Rsch. Avocations: travel, walking, music. Office: 5-1-1 Tsukiji Chuo-ku Tokyo 1040045 Japan Office Fax: 0335461369. Business E-Mail: harakawa@ncc.go.jp.

ARAKI, ISAO, urologist; married. MD, Gunma U., Japan; PhD, Kyoto U., Japan. Lic. med. Japan, 1980. Assoc. prof. dept. urology U. Yamanashi Interdisciplinary Grad. Sch. Medicine and Engring., Chuo, Yamanashi, Japan, 2001—, Shiga U. Med. Sci., Otsu, 2010. Contbr. articles to profl. jour. Sci. grants, Japan Ministry of Edn., Culture, Sports, Sci. and Tech., 1999—. Fellow: Japanese Neurogenic Bladder Soc., Japanese Urol. Assn. Achievements include patents for targeting materials for screening drugs for overactive bladder syndrome. Office: Shiga University Med Sci Dept Urology Seta Tsukinowa-cho Otsu Shiga 520-2192 Japan Business E-Mail: iaraki@belle.shiga-med.ac.jp.

ARANGO, PENELOPE COREY, psychologist, consultant; b. San Francisco, Oct. 10, 1943; d. George Raymond Corey Jr. and Katherine Barnard; m. Jorge Arango, Aug. 18, 1976. Diploma de cultura Española, U. Madrid, 1962; cert. de langue et litterature Francais, Universite de Grenoble, 1964; BA in art, U. Miami, Fla., 1965; MA in psychology, U. No. Colo., 1977. Psychol. asst. dept. clin. psychology U. Fla., 1966—68; asst. psychologist - Spanish Dade County Pub. Schs., Miami, 1968—76; dir., healthcare divsn. Helmsley-Spear of Fla., Miami, 1986—91; dir., CQI, tng. & devel. CAC-United Health-Care of Fla., Miami, 1991—98; faculty mem. Bayer Inst. Healthcare Comms., West Haven, Conn., 1995—; LAO continuing improvement facilitator Carrier Corp., Latin Am. Hdqs., 1998—2000; v.p. Arango Group, Quality Mgmt. Cons., Miami, 2000—. Quality adv. bd. mem. Coral Gables C. of C., Coral Gables, Fla., 1992—93. Mem.: APA. Office: Arango Group 5153 SW 71st Pl Miami FL 33155

ARANHA, GERARD V., surgeon; b. Bangalore, India, 1943; MB BS, Bangalore Med. Coll., 1969. Diplomate Am. Bd. Surgery. Intern Christ Hosp., Oak Lawn, Ill., 1970-71; resident in surgery Loyola Affiliated Hosp., Maywood, Ill., 1971-75; fellow in surg. oncology U. Minn. Hosps., Mpls., 1975-77; chief surg. oncology Loyola U.-Stritch Sch. Medicine, Maywood, 1990—, dir. breast care ctr., 1992—, prof. Fellow ACS, Royal Coll. Surgery; mem. Internat. Surg. Soc., Am. Surg. Assn., Assn. Acad. Surgery, Ctrl. Surg. Assn., Midwest Surg. Soc., Soc. Surgery Alimentary Tract, Soc. Surg. Oncology, Western Surg. Assn., Soc. Digestive Surgery, Am. Hepto-Pancreato-Biliary Assn., Internat. Hepto-Pancreato-Biliary Assn. Office: Loyola U Med Ctr Dept Surg EMS110-3236 2160 S 1st Ave Maywood IL 60153-3304 Office Phone: 708-327-3430. Business E-Mail: [illegible]

ARANZULLA, TIZIANA CLAUDIA, cardiologist, consultant; b. Catania, Italy, Aug. 31, 1976; d. Giuseppe Aranzulla. Diploma in Solfeggio and Singing, Acad. Music, Naples, 1995; degree in Medicine and Surgery cum laude, Alma Mater Studiorum U. Bologna, 2000; MS in Interventional Cardiology, U. Vita e Salute, San Raffaele Hosp., Milan, 2006. Cert. cardiology specialist U. Vita e Salute San Raffaele Hosp., 2005, acute coronary syndromes specialist "Alma Mater Studiorum", U. Bologna, 2001, in clin. practice 2001. Cons. cardiology & emergency Clin. Santa Rita, Milan, 2005—07; cons. & rschr. dept. cardiology San Raffaele Hosp., 2005—07, cons. & rschr. interventional cardiology, 2006—07, EMO Ctr. Cuore Columbus, Milan, 2006—07; cons. cardiology & interventional cardiology ASL2 Savonese, Savona, Italy, 2007—08; cons. interventional cardiology Azienda Ospedaliera Ordine Mauriziano di Torino, Turin, Italy, 2008—. Fellow, gen. surgery dept. U. Hosp. Tartu, Estonia, 1999—99; fellow, plastic surgery dept. U. Hosp. Campinas, Sao Paulo, Brazil, 2000—01; fellow dept. cardiology U. Hosp. Oulu, Finland, 2001, dr. Sparsholdt coll. Euro Master Studies, Winchester, 2001, dr., Kingstone Bridge House coll., London, 02. Contbr. scientific papers to profl. publs. Mem.: Nat. Soc. Hosp. Cardiologists, Italian Soc. Cardiology, Italian Soc. Interventional Cardiology. Independent. Roman Catholic. Avocations: languages, art, travel, music, reading. Personal E-mail: aratizi@hotmail.com.

ARAOZ, DANIEL LEON, psychologist, educator; b. Buenos Aires, Apr. 23, 1930; came to U.S., 1951, naturalized, 1967; s. Jose Daniel and Maria Lia (Suarez) A.; m. Marie Anne Carrese, July 27, 1991; m. Dorita Catherine Smyth, July 17, 1964 (div. 1984); children: Leon Daniel, Nadine Victoria. BA, Gonzaga U., 1953, MA, 1954; MST., U. Santa Clara, 1961; MA, Columbia U., 1964, EdD, 1969; Psychoanalysis Diploma, Am. Inst. for Psychotherapy and Psychoanalysis, 1972. Clin. psychologist, Ill., Pa. Diplomate in counseling psychology and family psychology Am. Bd. Profl. Psychology; diplomate in clin. hypnosis Am. Bd. Psychol. Hypnosis; lic. mental health counselor N.Y., 2006. Asst. chaplain Coll. Mt. St. Vincent, Bronx, N.Y., 1962-64; psychotherapist Cmty. Guidance Svc., NYC, 1965-72, supr., 1972-82; faculty Am. Inst. Psychotherapy and Psychoanalysis, NYC, 1972-82; assoc. prof. counseling L.I. U., 1973-82, prof., 1982—2008, chmn. dept. counseling and devel., 1995-97, sr. prof., 2008. Dir. L.I. Inst. Ericksonian Hypnosis, 1992-97. Editor-in-chief Am. Jour. Family Therapy, 1973-76, jour. adv., 1977—; author: Hypnosis and Sex Therapy, 1982, 98; Hypnosex, 1982; Self-Transformation Through the New Hypnosis, 1984; The New Hypnosis, 1985, 95, Spanish Edit., 2006, The New Hypnosis in Family Therapy, 1987; Selbst Hypnose: Kreative Imagination in Beruf und Alltag, 1992, Reengineering Yourself, 1994, 2d edit., 2003, Chinese edit., 1995, Solution-Oriented Brief Therapy for Adjustment Disorders, 1996, Japanese edit., 1999, Power Over Stress at Work, 1998, Autoreingeniería Para el nuevo Milenio, 2003, The Symptom is not the Whole Story, 2006; co-editor: Hypnosis Questions & Answers, 1986; contbr. articles to profl. jours. Named Hon. Prof. U. peruana Cayetano Heredia, Lima, Peru, Maestro Assn. Caribena de Hipnosis Terapeutica, Santo Domingo, 2008, Disting. Practitioner N&P Acads. Practice in Psychology, 2010; recipient LIU Excellence in Tchg., David Newton award, 2003. Fellow APA, Am. Inst. Psychotherapy and Psychoanalysis, Am. Soc. Psychosomatic Dentistry and Medicine, Acad. Counseling Psychology, Acad. Family Psychology, Soc. Clin. and Exptl. Hypnosis; mem. Am. Assn. Sexuality Educators, Counselors and Therapists (diplomate), Am. Assn. Marriage and Family Therapy (supr. 1973—2011), Nat. Assn. for Advancement of Psychoanalysis, Pa. Psychol. Assn., Ill. Psychol. Assn., NYS Psychol. Assn.(mem. emeritus), Nassau County

Psychol. Assn., Suffolk County Psychol. Assn., Distinguished Practioner Nat. Acad. of Practice, Am. Mgmt. Assn. (unit trainer 1987-94), N.Y. Soc. Clin. Hypnosis, N.Y. Mental Health Counselors Assn., Nat. Acad. Practice (Disting. Practitioner in Psychology), Nat. Alliance Profl. Psychology Providers, Sulfolk County Psychol. Assn. Home: 66 Gates Ave Malverne NY 11565-1912 Office: LI U CW Post Northern Blvd Greenvale NY 11548-1207 Office Phone: 516-599-5905, 516-299-2213. Business E-Mail: daniel.araoz@liu.edu, draraoz@optonline.net.

ARASHIRO, KEN, plastic surgeon; MD, Ehime U., Japan, 1984, PhD, 1996. Diplomate Japan Plastic Surg. Bd., 1991, Japanese Surg. Bd., 1989. Intern Okinawa Chubu Hosp., U. Hawaii Program, Gushikawa City, Japan, 1984, resident in gen. surgery, 1984—88; resident and fellow in plastic surgery Ehime U. Sch. Medicine, Toon City, Japan, 1988—94; chief divsn. plastic surgery Okinawa Chubu Hosp., Gushikawa, 1994—2004, Okinawa Naha Hosp., 2004—07; pvt. practice plastic surgery, 2007—. Mem.: Japanese Soc. Aesthetic Plastic Surgery, Internat. Soc. Plastic and Reconstructive Surgery, Japan Soc. Plastic and Reconstructive Surgery. Office: Plastic Surgery KC 2-7-11 Kumoji Naha Okinawa 900-0015 Japan

ARAUJO, ADERSON SILVA, hematologist, director; b. Recife, Brazil, Feb. 4, 1952; MD, Fed. U. Pernambuco, Brazil, 1976; PhD, State U. Sao Paulo, Brazil, 2003. Dir. hematology Hemope Found., 2007—. Sci. coord. anemias group Hemope Found., 1981; mem. bd. dirs. Multihemo Ltd., 1999; sci. advisor Brazilian Assn. Thalassemia, 2000; counselor Brazilian Assn. Hematology, 2009; sci. advisor Sickle Cell Disease International Orgn., 2004. Recipient Pernambuco Guararapes Merit medal, Pernambuco Govt. Master: Brazilian Assn. Hematology; mem.: Pernambuco Assn. Hereditary Anemias, Orgn. Internat. Lutte Contra La Drepanocytose Oild. Avocations: reading, swimming. Home: Rua Professor Edgar Altino 156 Rua Joa Recife Pernambuco 53061-300 Brazil Home Fax: 55 81 31824605. Personal E-mail: aderson.araujo@gmail.com.

ARAUJO JÚNIOR, EDWARD, obstetrician, gynecologist, researcher; b. Uberaba, Minas Gerais, Brazil, Feb. 12, 1976; s. Edward and Antonia Silva Araujo; m. Renata Marques Alves, Dec. 16, 2006. MS, PhD, Fed. U. São Paulo, Brazil, 2007. Diplomate Fed. U. Triângulo Mineiro, 2000. Physician asst. Fed. U. São Paulo, 2007—. Contbr. articles to numerous sci. jours. Assoc. mem. Brazilian Coll. Radiology, 2005—06, mem., 2006. Recipient Henrique Paraventi, Dept. Obstetrics Fed. U. São Paulo, 2005—07; CNPq scholar, Fed. U. São Paulo, 2005, CAPES scholar, 2006. Mem.: Paulista Soc. Gynecology and Obstetrics (Best Poster 2006), Brazilian Soc. Ultrasound. Achievements include development of establishment of a new constant for the measurement of fetal lung volume (J Matern Fetal Neonatal Med. Avocations: reading, movies, walking, travel. Office: Dept of Obstetrics Napoleão de Barros 875 São Paulo 04024-002 Brazil Home: Rua Carlos Weber 05303-000 São Paulo SP Brazil Home Fax: 55-11-3294-3220. Personal E-mail: araujojred@terra.com.br. Business E-Mail: mirian.toco@epm.br.

ARAVANIS, CHRISTOS IOANNIS, cardiologist, medical educator; s. Ioannis Savas and Sophia Stavrakas; m. Tula Theodos Aravanis, June 12, 1958; children: Ioannis, Eleni. Degree, U. Athens Med. Sch., 1948, PhD, 1959; degree, Jersey City Med. Ctr., 1953, Chgo. Med. Sch., 1959. Dir. lab ECG and phonocardiography U. Hosp. Athens, 1962—70, dir. program cardiovascular disease, 1960—75, sr. attending physician, 1972; assoc. prof. cardiology U. Athens, 1962; prof. physiology Chgo. Med. Sch., 1972; dir. cardiology Evangelisms Hosp., 1975—86, Athens Med. Ctr., 1986—. Vis. prof. Chgo. Med. Sch., 1969; vis. investigator various locations, vis. scientist, 1960—75. Contbr. articles in field; author: 3 books. Mem. Red Cross, 1970. Mem.: Greek Soc. Atherosclerosis (founder). Avocation: painting. Office: 21 Theseos St 15237 Filothei Greece Home: Vasilissis Sofias 47 106 76 Athens Greece

ARAYA, VICTOR R., gastroenterologist, educator; MD, George Washington U. Sch. of Medicine, 1985. Diplomate Am. Bd. Internal Medicine-gastroenterology, 2007, Am. Bd. Internal Medicine-transplant hepatology, 2008. Intern Temple Univ. Sch. of Medicine, resident; fellow Univ. of South Fl.; physician Albert Einstein Med. Ctr. Office: Albert Einstein Medical Center Klein Bldg Ste 101 5401 Old York Rd Philadelphia PA 19141 Office Phone: 215-456-8242. Office Fax: 215-456-8058.

ARBEIT, ROBERT DAVID, physician; b. Jersey City, Aug. 16, 1947; s. Sidney Robert and Marie A.; m. Susan Abelson, Dec. 20, 1970; children: Jeffrey, Miriam. BA, Williams Coll., 1968; MD, Yale U., 1972. Diplomate Am. Bd. Internat. Medicine, Am. Bd. Infectious Disease. Intern then resident Yale-New Haven Hosp., New Haven, 1972-74; clin. assoc. Nat. Cancer Inst., Bethesda, Md., 1974-76; fellow Sidney Farber Cancer Inst., Boston, 1976-79; staff physician VA Med. Ctr., Boston, 1979-2000, asst. chief med. svcs., 1989-91, dir. infectious diseases rsch., 1991-2000, assoc. chief of staff, rsch., 1991-2000; asst. prof. Sch. Med. Boston U., 1979-87, assoc. prof. Sch. Med., 1987-95, prof. Sch. Med., 1995-2000, adj. prof. Sch. Med., 2001—; dir. med. ops. Cubist Pharms., Lexington, Mass., 2001—02, exec. med. dir., 2002—03; exec. dir. clin. rsch. Paratek Pharms., Boston, 2003—07; v.p., clin. devel. Paratek, 2007—09, Idera Pharms. Inc., Cambridge, Mass., 2009—. Contbr. articles to profl. jours. and books. Fellow ACP, Infectious Diseases Soc. Am.; mem. Am. Soc. for Microbiology, Phi Beta Kappa, Alpha Omega Alpha. Avocation: personal computers. Office: Idera Pharms Inc 167 Sidney Cambridge MA 02139

ARBER, WERNER, microbiologist; b. Gränichen, Switzerland, June 3, 1929; married; 2 children. Grad., Swiss Fed. Inst. Tech. (ETH), 1953; PhD, U. Geneva, 1958. Asst. Lab. Biophysics, U. Geneva, 1953—58, docent, then extraordinary prof. molecular genetics, 1962—70; rsch. assoc. dept. microbiology U. So. Calif., 1958—59; vis. investigator dept. molecular biology U. Calif., Berkeley, 1970—71; prof. microbiology U. Basel, Switzerland, 1971—96, rector, 1986—88. Recipient Nobel prize for physiology/medicine, 1978. Mem.: NAS (assoc.), Pontifical Acad. Scis., Internat. Coun. Sci. (pres. 1996—99). Office: Biozentrum der Universität 70 Klingelbergstrasse CH 4056 Basel Switzerland E-mail: Werner.Arber@unibas.ch.

ARBESMAN, HARVEY, dermatologist; b. Buffalo, Feb. 10, 1954; MD, SUNY, Buffalo Sch. Medicine, 1980, MS, 1995. V.p. ArbesIdeas, Inc., 2002—. Clin. asst. prof., dept. dermatology, Sch. Medicine and Biomed. Scis. U. at Buffalo, 1986—2011, clin. asst. prof., dept. social and preventive medicine, Sch. Pub. Health and Health Professions, 1987—2011. Recipient ALS Biomarker Thought prize, Prize4Life, ALS Biomarker Challenge Discovery prize, Top Solver award, InnoCentive. Fellow: Am. Acad. Dermatology; mem.: Med. Soc. State of NY. Avocation: magic. Office: 19 Hopkins Rd Williamsville NY 14221 Personal E-mail: arbesman@roadrunner.com.

ARBOGAST, HELMUT P., surgeon, researcher; b. Zweibruecken, Rheinland-Pfalz, Germany, Mar. 31, 1959; s. Otto B. and Elsa Arbogast; m. Susanne C. Wirth; children: Fee S.C., Nikolaus M.A. MS, U. Minn., Mpls., 1984; MD, Tech. U. Munich, 1985; PhD, U. Munich, 1986. Vice dir. divsn. transplant surgery U. Munich, Grosshadern, Bavaria, 2001—04, mng. dir. transplant ctr., 2004—; fin. bd. mem. Eurotransplant Found., Leiden, Netherlands, 2006—. Treas. Deutsche Acad. Für Transplantationsmedizin, Munich, 2005—. Contbr. sci. exhbns. and posters (Best Sci. Exhbn. prize, Deutsche Gesellschaft für Chirurgie, 1988, Poster prize, 6th World Congress Microcirculation, 1996, DTG-Preis Zur Förderung Organspende, 2005). Mem. fin. bd. Eurotransplant Found., Leiden, Netherlands, 2006. With Sanitätsakademie, 1985—87, Munich. Decorated Ehrenmedaille Bundeswehr Deutsche Bundeswehr; grant, Fulbright Commn., 1983—84. Mem.: AIDPIT (bd. mem.), Fed. Chamber of Physicians (mem. standing commn., bus. adminstr. 2009—), German Transport Soc. (exec. bd. mem. 2010—, pres., pancreas commn. 2008—), Soc. Innate Immunity (councillor-at-large, founding mem. 2006), Deutsche Transplantationsgesellschaft, Deutsche Acad. Für Transplantationsmedizin (treas. 2005—), Deutsche Gesellschaft Für Allgemein Und Viszeralchirurgie, Arbeitsgemeinschaft Bayern Tätiger Notärzte, Berufsverband Der Deutschen Chirurgen, Deutsche Gesellschaft Für Angiologie, Deutsche Gesellschaft Für Chirurgie, Vereinigung Der Bayerischen Chirurgen. Achievements include research in proof of the thrombin paradox and its consequences for organ transplantation. Office: University of Munich - Grosshadern Marchioninistr 15 Bavaria Munich 81377 Germany Office Fax: 498970956577. Business E-Mail: helmut.arbogast@med.uni-muenchen.de.

ARBUCKLE, AVERIL DOROTHY (COOKIE ARBUCKLE), healthcare facility administrator; b. Bklyn., May 9, 1934; d. Arnold Drummond and Mildred (Engel) Lloyd; m. Robert V. Arbuckle (dec. Mar. 1990); children: Gregory, Jody, Leann, Kathleen, Mary. Student, Lamson Coll., Phoenix, 1968-71, Colo. State U., 1964-68, U. Ctrl. Okla., 1974, Okla. State U., Oklahoma City, 1976. Flight attendant Pacific Southwest Airlines, San Diego, 1952, Am. Airlines, Chgo., 1953; social worker Dept. Human Svcs., Oklahoma City, 1972-89; mem. task force Gov.'s Task Force on AIDS, Oklahoma City, 1987-88; exec. dir. Other Options, Inc., Oklahoma City, 1989—. Mem. adv. bd. Carter Hospice, Carter Home Health, Red Rock Mental Health Homeless Com., Okla. AIDS Coalition; cons. HIV-AIDS State of Okla., 1985—96; dir. Friends Food Pantry Okla. City. Author: Aids for HIV-AIDS, 4 edit. 1989 (award 1992), Accessing the System Directory, 1995, Physician Compassionate Use Directory, 1995. Bd. dirs. AIDS Support Program, 1986-88, Okla. Epilepsy Found., 1989-93; com. chmn. Cmty. Action Agy., Oklahoma City., 1994-95; bd. mem. Ven Cor Hosp. Ethics Com., 1998; HIV Care Consortium, Okla., 1998, 99, Okla. City Housing Com. HIV/AIDS, 1998, 99; Nat. Fin. Planning Bd. for Disabilities, 1998, 99; dir. fellowship award Okla. Lions Svc. Found., 2002; U.S. coord. Guatemala AIDS Medicine Program. Recipient Jefferson award Presbyn. Health Found., Oklahoma City, 1990, Jacqueline Kennedy award Am. Inst. Pub. Svc., Washington, 1990, Five Who Care award Gannett Found., Arlington, Va., 1992, merit award GLB Polit. Caucus, Oklahoma City, 1993, Book of Yr. award Woman's Front Page News, 1993, Friends of Libr. Book award City of Oklahoma City-Moore Libr., 1989, Cmty. Contbn. award, 1994, Individual award U. Okla. Coll. Pub. Health and Alumni Assn., 4th Annual Pub. Health award for excellence U. Okla. Health Scis. Ctr., 1999, Richard May Humanitarian award Okla. AIDS Care Found., 2006. Mem. Case Mgmt. Soc. Am., Case Mgmt. Soc. Ctrl. Okla. Lions (v.p. Bethany Helping Hands 2002. Lion of the Yr. 2002). Democrat. Avocations: writing, lecturing, consulting, horticulture, geology. Home: PO Box 36 Bethany OK 73008-0036 also: 3005 N May Ave Oklahoma City OK 73107-2120 Home Phone: 405-831-1225; Office Phone: 405-605-8020. E-mail: otheroptions@coxinet.net.

ARCANJO, FRANCISCO PLACIDO NOGUEIRA, medical educator; b. Sobral, Jan. 22, 1965; Degree, U. Fed. Ceara, 1988; PhD, U. Fed. Sao Paulo, 2008. Prof. U. Fed. Ceara, 2001, adj. prof. Home: Alameda Amazonas 120 Sobral Ce 62040300 Brazil Personal E-mail: placidoarcanjo@terra.com.br.

ARCE, A. ANTHONY, psychiatrist, educator; b. San Juan, June 13, 1923; s. Angel and Juana (Baez) A.; m. Malvene Balkind, Oct. 7, 1971; children: Alan I. Scheer, Judith Ann Scheer, Michael Anthony Arce. BS, Washington and Jefferson Coll., 1942; MD, Temple U., 1946. Diplomate: Am. Bd. Psychiatry and Neurology; certified in adminstrv. psychiatry. Intern Mercy Hosp., Bay City, Mich.; Frankford Hosp., Phila., 1946-47; dir. Aguadilla Dist. Hosp., PR, 1947-48; chief health officer Utuado, PR, 1950-51; physician US Mil. Acad., West Point, NY, 1951-52; med. officer Pa. R.R., 1952-53; practice medicine Yonkers, NY, 1953-59; resident psychiatrist Payne Whitney Clinic, NYC, 1959-62; assoc. dir. psychiatry Grasslands Hosp., Valhalla, NY, 1962-67; dir. psychiatry Lincoln Hall Sch., Lincolndale, NY, 1967-68; dir. Bur. Aftercare Svcs. NY State Dept. Mental Hygiene, 1968-71; dir. Manhattan Psychiat. Ctr., Ward's Island, NY, 1971-76, Hahnemann Cmty. Mental Health and Mental Retardation Ctr., Phila., 1976-84; pvt. practice medicine specializing in psychiatry, 1962—; prof. psychiatry, dep. chmn. dept. mental health svcs. Hahnemann U., 1976-85, prof., chmn., 1985-87, prof., dir. amb. svcs., 1987-91; prof., dep. chmn. dept. psychiatry Med. Coll., U. Pa., Phila., 1991-96; chmn. dept. behavioral medicine, med. dir. Girard Med. Ctr., Phila., 1996—. Mem. president's coun. NYU Sch. Social Work, 1963-66; bd. dirs. PR Family Inst., NYC, 1970-72. Served with AUS, 1943-46, 48-50. Mem. Am. Coll. Mental Health Adminstrs., Am. Coll. Psychiatrists, Am. Psychiat. Assn. (chmn. task force continuing care), Phila. Psychiat. Soc., Am. Assn. Psychiat. Adminstrs. (treas., pres.). Home: 1416 Academy Ln Elkins Park PA 19027-2515 Office: Girard Med Ctr 2ADC 8th St & Girard Ave Philadelphia PA 19122-9999

ARCE ROSS, GERMAN ALBERTO, psychologist, psychoanalyst; b. Lima, Peru, Oct. 27, 1957; arrived in France, 1983; s. Luis Alberto Arce Casas and Florence Graciela Ross Villaran; children: Flore, Caroline. Degree in Psychology, U. São Paulo, 1981; M in Psychoanalysis, U. Paris VIII, 1984, PhD in Psychoanalysis, 1989; PhD in Psychology, U. Rennes III, 1999. Cert. psychologist. Trainee Unibanco SA, São Paulo, Brazil, 1977—83; psychologist Psychiat. Hosp. Premontré, France, 1986—90; tchg. asst. Coll. Internat. Philosophie, Paris, 1986—90, U. Paris VIII, Paris, 1986—97; psychotherapist Métabole Assn., Paris, 1996—2000, Thélémythe Assn., Paris, 2000—06. Coord. clin. conf. U. Paris VIII, Paris, 1997—99; clin. supr. Main St. Prevention, Trappes, France, 2000—05; rsch. worker Lab. Psychoanalytical Psychopathology to tchr. U. Paris X. Author: (book) Mania, Melancholia and White Factors; editor: Beauchesne, 2009; contbr. chapters to books, articles to profl. jours. Mem.: World Psychoanalytical Assn., Assn. Franco Péruvienne of Psychiatry, Evolution Psychiatrique, Assn. Psychoanalyse et Recherches Univs., Ecole de la Cause Freudienne, World Assn. Psychoanalysis. Roman Catholic. Avocations: reading, sports, music. Home and Office: 6 Rue de L Abbe Gregoire 75006 Paris France Home Phone: 33-6-15378139, 33 1 7550 7749; Office Phone: 33-1-45448384. Business E-Mail: arce.ross@noos.fr.

ARCIERO, ROBERT, orthopedist, educator; b. El Paso, Tex., Dec. 8, 1954; BS in Biology, St. Bonaventure U., 1976; MD, Georgetown U. Sch. Medicine, 1980. Dir., orthop. sports medicine fellow US Mil. Acad., West Point, NY, 1987—2000, U. Conn. Health Ctr., prof., orthop. surgery, 2000—. Named to Conn. State Top Dr.'s List, Conn. Mag. Fellow: Am. Acad. Orthop. Surgeons; mem.: Herodicus Orthop. Sports Medicine Soc., Arthroscopy Assn. N.Am., Am. Shoulder and Elbow Soc., Am. Orthop. Soc. Sports Medicine (bd. mem., treas. 2007, George Rovere award, O'Donohue award, Hughston award, Asia-Pacific Traveling Orthop. Sports Medicine fellowship). Avocations: golf, motorcycling. Office: University Conn Health Ctr Farmington CT 06032 Business E-Mail: arciero@nso.uchc.edu.

ARDA, BERNA, medical educator, medical ethicist; b. Gaziantep, Turkey, May 28, 1964; d. Refik and Zübeyde Senel Özdinc; m. Tayfun Arda, Sept. 11, 1987; 1 child, Asli. MD, Ankara U., 1987. Fellow Ankara (Turkey) U. Sch. Medicine, 1987—90, asst. prof., 1990—93, assoc. prof., 1993—99, prof., 1999—. Assoc. editor: Turkish Jour. Med. Ethics, 1994—99, author, editor: books (in Turkish) in med. ethics, deontology, 1995—2001; contbr. articles to profl. jours. Founding mem. Human Rights Found. of Turkey, 2001; mem. Higher Coun. Health, Turkey, 2007—08; gov. WAML, 2006—. Nominee Avicenna prize for ethics in sci., UNESCO, 2003. Mem.: Bioethics Soc. Turkey, Turkish Med. Assn. Avocations: reading about cinema, visiting antique shops, paragliding. Office: Ankara U Sch Medicine Deontology Sihhiye Ankara Turkey Office Phone: +90-312 310 30-10. E-mail: arda@medicine.ankara.edu.tr.

ARDELEAN, IOAN, microbiologist, researcher; b. Arad, Romania, Mar. 10, 1957; s. Ioan and Victoria (Bulgar) Ardelean; m. Emilia Cornelia Axente, Mar. 11, 1989; children: Ioana, Maria-Alexandra, Ana-Valentina. Grad., Faculty Biology, Bucharest, Romania, 1981, MS, 1982, PhD, 1997. Biologist diplomate. Coll. tchr., Hârsova, Romania, 1982-84; jr. scientist Inst. Biology, Bucharest, 1984-90, scientist, 1990-95, sr. scientist, 1995-98, sr. scientist II, 2002—. Sec. Commn. Biology-Ministry Sci. and Tech., Bucharest, 1995-98; sec. Commn. Biology, Biotech.-Ministry of Edn. and Rsch., 2001—; prof. gen. Microbiology and Marine Microbiology Ovidius U., 2007-. Co-author: Research in Photosynthesis, 1992, Cyanobacterial Nitrogen Metabolism and Environmental Biotechnology, 1997; contbr. articles to sci. jours. Exec. dir. Civil Protection, Inst. Biology, Bucharest, 1990-94. Recipient Emil Racovitza prize Romanian Acad., 2000, award Am. Biog. Inst., 2011, Albert Einstein award, 2011. Mem. Romanian Soc. Biochemistry & Molecular Biology Avocations: jogging, gardening, cinema. Office: Inst Biology Spl Independ 296 POB 56-53 060031 Bucharest Romania Office Phone: 0728129144. Personal E-mail: ioan.ardelean57@yahoo.com. Business E-Mail: ioan.ardelean@ibiol.ro.

ARDELEAN, MIRCIA-AUREL, pediatrician, consultant; b. Borz, Austria, June 15, 1955; MD, Paracelsus Med. U., PhD, 1981. Physician SALK, Paracelsus Med. U., 1981—2011, cons., 2003—11. Fellow: EAPU, European Bd. Pediat. Surgery, European Pediat. Surgeons Assn., European Soc. Pediat. Urology. Office: Muellner Hauptstrasse Salzburg 5020 Austria Business E-Mail: m.ardelean@salk.at.

ARDEN, MARTHA R., pediatrician, educator; b. Dec. 21, 1958; BS cum laude, Yale U., 1976—80, MD, 1981—84. Diplomate Am. Bd. Pediatrics, 1988, cert. adolscent medicine 1994, recertified adolscent medicine 2002. Pediat. intern and resident Columbia- Presbyn. Hosp., 1984—87; sch. physician Franklin K. Lane High Sch., Brooklyn, NY, 1990—2008, med. dir., 1992—2008; project dir. Far Rockaway and MS 53 Sch.- Based Health Centers, 2000—08; fellowship adolescent medicine Schneider Children's Hosp., 1987—89, rsch. fellow atherosclerosis prevention, 1989—90, asst. attending pediatrician, 1990—2008, voluntary attending pediatrician, 2008—; asst. prof. pediat. Albert Einstein Coll., 1990—2000, assoc. prof. clin. pediat., 2000—. Recipient Women with Heart award, Long Island Heart Coun., 1993; named one of Best Doctors in NY, Castle Connoly Publishers, 1999—2008, NY Magazine, 0200—2004, 2006—07, numerous awards; scholar Long Island-Jewish Hosp. Rsch. Grant, 1988. Mem.: Instl. Rvw. Bd., Advocacy Com., Primary Care Com., Am. Acad. of Pediat., Soc. for Adolescent Medicine. Office: Schneider Children's Hospital 26901 76th Ave New Hyde Park NY 11040-1433 Office Phone: 718-470-3000.

ARDENGH, JOSÉ CELSO, gastroenterologist; b. São Paulo, Nov. 14, 1962; MD, Faculdade Medicina Bragança Paulista, 1987, PhD, Hosp. Clínicas Faculdade Medicina Ribeirão Preto U. São Paulo, 2009. Asst. physician, endoscopic svc. Hosp. 9 Julho, 2000; livre docente em cirurgia e anatomia Hosp. Clínicas Faculdade Medicina Ribeirão Preto U. São Paulo, 2002—, prof., 2002; médico pelo setor, endoscopia via biliar e pancreática Hosp. Ipiranga, Ctr. Treinamento SOBED, 2010, bd. drs., 2010. Recipient award, Brazilian Congress. Master: Brazilian Digestive Endoscopic Soc.; mem.: Am. Soc. Gastrointestinal Endoscopy. Avocations: tennis, swimming. Office: Alameda dos Arapanés 881- cj 111 São Paulo 04524-001 Brazil Office Fax: 55 11 50558942. Business E-Mail: jcelso@uol.com.br.

ARDIANSYAH, ARDY, food scientist; b. Japan, Oct. 18, 1975; PhD, Tohoku U., 2007. Postdoc. rsch. fellow Grad. Sch. Agrl. Sci., Tohoku U., Japan, 2007—. Monbukagakusho scholarship, Ministry of Edn., Culture, Sports, Sci., and Tech. Japan. Mem.: Indonesian Food

Technologist Assn., Japanese Soc. Nutrition and Food Sci., Am. Soc. Nutrition. Office: 1-1 Tsutsumidori-Amamiyamachi Aoba-ku Sendai Miyagi 981-8555 Japan Office Fax: 022-7178813. Business E-Mail: ardy@biochem.tohoku.ac.jp.

ARENA, SALVATORE, pediatrician; b. Messina, Italy, Mar. 23, 1977; MD, U. Messina, 2001, PhD, 2010. Specialist, pediat. surgery U. Messina, 2001—06; clin. fellow Royal Manchester Children's Hosp., 2011; rsch. fellow U. Manchester, 2011—. Recipient Travel award, 4th Internat. Conf. Aquaporins Genval Bruxell Belgium, 2005, Young Rschr. prize, U. Messina, 2007. Mem.: European Soc. Pediat. Urology, Italian Soc. Pediat. Video-Surgery, Italian Soc. Pediat. Urology, Italian Soc. Pediat. Surgery, European Pediat. Surgeons Assn. Home: Via Industriale 22 Messina 98123 Italy Personal E-mail: arenasal@inwind.it.

ARENBERG, IRVING KAUFMAN KARCHMER, otolaryngologist; b. East Chicago, Ind., Jan. 10, 1941; s. Harry and Gertrude (Field) Kaufman; divorced; children: Daniel Kaufman, Michael Harrison, Julie Gayle. BA in Zoology, U. Mich., 1963, MD, 1967. Diplomate Am. Bd. Otolaryngology. Intern Chgo. Wesley Meml. Hosp., 1967-68; resident Barnes and Allied Hosps., St. Louis, 1969-74; asst. prof. surgery U. Wis., Madison, 1976-80; chief otolaryngology VA Hosp., Madison, 1976-80; CEO Ear Ctr. PC, Englewood, Colo., 1989—96; chmn. bd., CEO IntraEar, Neurobiometrix Inc., Inc., 1994—99; pres., CEO, chmn. Arenberg and Assocs. Ltd., LLC, 2000—04. Dir., founder Internat. Meniere's Disease Rsch. Inst., Denver, 1971—; guest of honor 39th Chinese Nat. ENT Congress, Taipei, 1985, U. Antwerp, 1995, West German ENT Soc., 1996; vis. scientist Swedish Med. Rsch. Coun., 1975-76; vis. prof. U. Mich., Ann Arbor, 1988, 94, St. Mary's Hosp. and Med. Sch., London, 1988, U. Verona (Italy) Med. Sch., 1989, U. N.C., Chapel Hill, 1989, U. Wurzburg (Germany) Med. Sch., 1989, 90, 92, U. Ark., Little Rock, 1990, 95, U. Innsbruck, Austria, 1991, U. Sydney, Australia, 1992, U. Tex., Dallas, 1993. Editor: Meniere's Disease, 1983, Inner Ear Surgery, 1991, Dizziness and Balance Disorders, 1993; assoc. editor AMA Archives of Otolaryngology, 1968-81; mem. editorial bd. Am. Jour. Otology, 1978-91, Head and Neck Surgery Jour., 1992—; guest editor Otolaryngologic Clinics N.Am., 1980, 83, Neurologic Clinics N.Am., 1990; editor Inner Ear Surgery, 1991; mem. rev. bd. Rev. de Laryngologie et Otology (France), 1984—; contbr. over 400 articles to profl. peer-reviewed jours. Recipient Pietro Caliceti prize and Gold Medal Honor award U. Bologna, Italy, 1983, Spl. Tchr. Investigation Tng. award NIH, 1970-1975; fellow Barnes and Allied Hosps., 1968-69, 75, NIH, 1971-76, U. Uppsala-Royal Acad. Hosp., Sweden, 1975-76; grantee NIH, 1971-77, Deafness Rsch. Found., 1971-73. Fellow ACS, Am. Acad. Otolaryngology; mem. AMA, Am. Neurotology Soc., N.Y. Acad. Scis., Colo. Otologic Rsch. Ctr. (founder, pres., bd. dirs. 1980-88), Internat. Meniere's Disease Rsch. Inst. (dir. 1971—), Assn. Rsch. in Otolaryngology, Barany Soc., Triological Soc., Politzer Soc., Prosper Meniere Soc. (founder, exec. dir. 1981-99), Acoustical Soc. Am., [illegible] Soc., Sigma Xi. Achievements include 10 U.S. and foreign patents in field. Avocations: skiing, golf, biking, tennis.

AREND, PETER, retired biologist, physician, allergist, lab administrator; b. Lübeck, Germany, Dec. 21, 1932; m. Irmtraut Maria Arend; children: Werner, Stefanie, Lars. Diploma, Realgymnasium Barmbek-Uhlenhorst, Hamburg, Germany, 1954; MD in Biochemistry magna cum laude, U. Marburg, Germany, 1962. Cert. state boards U. Hamburg, 1960, Ednl. Coun. Fgn. Med. Grads. U. Ill., Chgo., 1970, habilitation U. Marburg, 1970. Fellow dept. biochemistry U. Hamburg, Germany, 1961—62; resident dept. internal medicine U. Marburg, 1963—68; fellow dept. immunochemistry rsch. Northwestern U., Evanston, Ill., 1969; guest rschr. Gastroenterology Rsch. Lab. U. Iowa Coll. Medicine, Iowa City, 1969—70; head dept. chemotherapy, dep. dir. rsch. Rsch. Labs. Chemie, Grünenthal, Aachen, Germany, 1972—78; lab. adminstr. Red Cross Blood Transfusion Svc., Hagen, Germany, 1978—80; allergist Olpe, Germany. Author: J. Immunogenetics, 1976, Immunobiology, 1977, 1980, Letters to Nature (London), 1977; contbr. articles to other profl. jours. Grantee, NIH, Paul-Martini-Stiftung, Deutsche Forschungsgemeinschaft. Mem.: ResearchGate: Biol. Scis. Forum. Lutheran. Achievements include discovery of human particulate leukocyte proteases modifying the autologous red cell receptor mosaic, loss of "N" and appearance of "H" as "HLe" in vitro, stimulating the mitogen-mediated proliferation of autologous lymphocytes in culture; research in phylogeny as mechanisms of natural immunity; detection and isolation of growth(age)-reflecting A-specific, water-soluble glycolipids in murine ovary and their specific association with production of the highly corresponding, autoreactive "natural" anti-A body; missing in the blood of early ovariectomized females, thus mirroring particular aminosugars binding lectins in gametogenesis of invertebrates (Helix pomatia) and higher plants (Dolichos biflorus), but produced as various qualities - from fish to man - wide spread in nature. Avocations: painting, classical music. Personal E-mail: parend@t-online.de.

ARENOWITZ, ALBERT HAROLD, psychiatrist; b. NYC, Jan. 12, 1925; s. Louis Isaac and Lena Helen (Skovron) A.; m. Betty Jane Wiener, Oct. 11, 1953; children: Frederick Stuart, Diane Helen. BA with honors, U. Wis., 1948; MD, U. Va., 1951. Diplomate Am. Bd. Psychiatry, Am. Bd. Child Psychiatry. With Coll. City NY, 1942—43; intern Kings County Gen. Hosp., Bklyn., 1951-52; resident in psychiatry Bronx (N.Y.) VA Hosp., 1952-55; postdoctoral fellow Youth Guidance Ctr., Worcester, Mass., 1955-57; dir. Ctr. for Child Guidance, Phila., 1962-65, Hahnemann Med. Service Eastern State Sch. and Hosp., Trevose, Pa., 1965-68; dir., tng. dir. Child and Adolescent Psychiat. Clinic, Phila. Gen. Hosp., 1965-67; asst. clin. prof. psychiatry Jefferson Med. Coll., Phila., 1974-76; exec. dir. Child Guidance and Mental Health Clinics, Media, Pa., 1967-74; med. dir. Intercommunity Child Guidance Ctr., Whittier, Calif., 1976—. Cons. Madison Pub. Schs., 1957-60, Dane County Child Guidance Ctr., Madison, 1957-62, Juvenile Ct., Madison, 1957-62; clin. asst. prof. child psychiatry Hahnemann Med. Coll., Phila., 1966-74; asst. clin. prof. psychiatry U. Wis., Madison, 1960-62, clin. asst. prof. psychiatry, behavioral scis. and family medicine U. So. Calif., L.A., 1976—; mem. med. staff Presbyn. Intercommunity Hosp., Whittier, 1976—. Pres. Whittier Area Coordinating Coun., 1978-80; chmn. ethics com. Presbyn. Intercommunity Hosp. Flight officer, navigator USAF, 1943-45. Decorated Air medal, POW medal. Fellow Am. Psychiat. Assn. (disting. life), Am. Acad. Child Psychiatry; mem. Los Angeles County Med. Assn., So. Calif. Psychiat. Soc., So. Calif. Soc. Child Psychiatry, Phila. Soc. Adolescent Psychiatry (pres. 1967-68), Peace Sci. Soc. Avocations: photography, music, travel. Office: Intercommunity Child Guidance Ctr 10155 Colima Rd Whittier CA 90603 Home Phone: 562-693-9805; Office Phone: 562-692-0383.

ARENSON, RONALD LEE, radiologist, educator; b. Richmond, Va., Sept. 16, 1943; BA, Duke U., 1965; MD, NY Med. Coll., 1970. Assoc. chair, clin. svcs., radiology U. Pa., 1976—92; Alexander R. Margulis disting. prof., chair, radiology and biomedical imaging U. Calif., San Francisco, 1992—. Bd. dirs. Radiol. Soc. N.Am., 2008. Home: 12 Dipsea Trail Mill Valley CA 94941 Business E-Mail: ronald.arenson@ucsf.edu.

AREPALLY, ARAVIND M., medical educator; b. Guntur, India, Sept. 7, 1966; married. BA in Math, Mercer U., Ga., 1989; MD, Emory U. Sch. Medicine, Ga., 1993. Lic. Md., Ga. Resident diagnostic radiology Emory U. Sch. Medicine, 1993—97; chief resident Emory U., 1995—96; fellow interventional radiology John Hopkins Med. Inst., 1997—99, chief fellow, 1998—99, clin. dir., Ctr. for Bioengineering Innovation & Design, 1999—; asst. prof. radiology and surgery, divsn. cardiovascular and interventional radiology John Hopkins Sch. Medicine, 1999—. Invited presenter in the field. Contbr. several articles to profl. jours. Mem.: Am. Roentgen Ray Soc., Radiological Soc. N.Am., Soc. Cardiovascular and Interventional Radiology, Internat. Soc. for Magnetic Resonance in Medicine, Am. Coll. Radiology, Am. Heart Assn. Avocations: sailing, astronomy, tennis, travel. Home: 263 The Prado NE Atlanta GA 30309-3335 Home Phone: 410-532-6035; Office Phone: 410-614-5183. Business E-Mail: aarepal@jhmi.edu.

ARETZ, STEFAN, medical geneticist; b. Marburg, Germany, Aug. 8, 1968; m. Diana Aretz; children: Lisa, Benedikt. Degree in Medicine, Philipps U., Marburg, 1995; MD, U. Cologne, Germany, 2001. Lic. Exam. Authority Hessen, 1997, cert. med. specialist human genetics Med. Assn. Nordrhein, 2006. Med. asst. Children's Hosp., U. Cologne, 1996—97, Dept. Pathology, Ruhr U., Bochum, Germany, 1998—2001, Inst. Human Genetics, U. Bonn, Germany, 2001—06, sr. physician, cons., 2006—, rsch. group leader, 2007—, postdoc. lectr., 2009. Contbr. scientific papers to profl. jours. Grantee, German Cancer Aid, 2008. Mem.: Internat. Soc. Gastrointestinal Hereditary Tumours, Gesellschaft Deutscher Naturforscher und Ärzte, Berufsverband Deutscher Humangenetiker, German Soc. Human Genetics. Achievements include research in hereditary gastrointestinal polyposis syndromes, adenomatous polyposis, hereditary cancer. Office: Inst Human Genetics Sigmund-Freud-Str 25 Bonn D-53127 Germany Office Fax: 004922828751011. Business E-Mail: stefan.aretz@uni-bonn.de.

ARGENT, VINCENT PATRICK, obstetrician, gynecologist, anesthesiologist, consultant; b. London, Eng., Dec. 4, 1947; s. Robert Joseph Argent and Ellen Gertude Newman; m. Yvonne Rhoda; children: James, Charlotte, Thomas, Katie. BA, Cambridge UNiv., 1971; MB, Cambridge Univ., 1976, MA, 1981; LLB, London Univ., 1985. Lic. gen. med. specialist Coun. Registrar. MRCOG examiner Royal Coll. OBY/GYN, London, 1995—2003; guideline rev. panel Nat. Inst. Clin. Excellence, London, 2002—03. Author: Safe Practice in Obstetrics and Gynecology, 2003; contbr. articles to profl. jour. Cmty. sports leader Hailsman Leisure Ctr., 1990—2003. Maj. RAMC, 1977—92, Eng. Recipient Ver Heyden De Lancey Prize, Cambridge Univ., 1982. Mem.: Pelvic Pain Spl. Interest Group (founder), Conscious Sedation Soc. (founder), Internat. Pelvic Pain Soc., East bound Soveriegn Rotary Club (past pres.). Avocations: sports, gardening, music, languages. Office: Eastbourne DGH King's Dr Eastbourne East Sussex BN212VD England Home: Little Friston Jevington Road BN20 0AG Friston England

ARGOW, MARY LOU, marriage and family therapist, educator, rehabilitation services professional; b. Oxford, NC, Nov. 12, 1941; d. Claude Van Burin and Mary Elizabeth (Britt) Morgan; m. Keith A. Argow, Apr. 12, 1969; children: Brittina Angevin, Kristen Morgan, Kenton Walter. BA in Sociology and Psychology, Meredith Coll., 1963; MEd in Counseling and Pers. Svcs., N.C. State U., 1969; postgrad., Va. Tech., 1990—92. Lic. profl. counselor, marriage and family therapist, substance abuse treatment practitioner Va. Bd. Counseling. Recreation aide ARC, Republic of Korea, 1963—65; youth dir. City of Raleigh, NC, 1966—68; dir. health careers N.C. Hosp. Assn., Raleigh, 1968—69, CPR Tng. Svcs., 1969—84; addictions counselor Fairfax Alcoholism Counseling & Treatment Svcs., Va., 1984—86; sr. counselor, supr. Beacon Recovery Svcs., Fairfax, 1987—93; pvt. practice Action Recovery, Fairfax, 1993—. Contbr. articles to profl. publs. Vol. Nat. Ski Patrol, 1968—2001, winter emergency care supr., 1986—91. Named Patroller of Yr., Nat. Ski Patrol, 1985, Outstanding Counselor of Yr., Va. Assn. Alcohol and Drug Abuse Counselors. Mem.: Va. Bd. Counseling & Bd. Health Professions, Am. Group Psychotherapy Assn., Nat. Coun. Sexual Addiction and Compulsivity, Am. Mental Health Counselors Assn., No. Va. Coun. Clin. Counselors, Va. Assn. Counselors, Am. Counselors Assn., Nat. Assn. Alcohol and Drug Abuse Counselors (cert. master addiction counselor, nat. cert. addictions counselor level II), Am. Assn. Marriage and Family Therapists. Unitarian. Avocations: skiing, hiking, conservation, travel, reading. Office: Action Recovery 10520 Warwick Ave # 2B Fairfax VA 22030 Office Phone: 703-273-5912.

ARIAS, ILEANA, federal agency administrator, psychiatrist, educator; AB, Barnard Coll., NYC; MA, PhD in Psychology, SUNY Stony Brook. From asst. prof. to clin. psychology prof. & dir. clin. tng. U. Ga., Athens, 1985—2000; chief etiology & surveillance br., divsn. violence prevention Nat. Ctr. Injury Prevention & Control, Atlanta, 2000—04, acting dir., 2004—05, dir., 2005—10; prin. dep. dir. Centers Disease Control & Prevention (CDC), 2010—. Mem. editl. bd. Jour. of Aggression, Maltreatment and Trauma, Rev. of Aggression and Violent Behavior, Violence and Victims; contbr. articles to profl. jours. Office: Centers for Disease Control 1600 Clifton Rd Atlanta GA 30333 Office Phone: 770-488-4696. Office Fax: 770-638-5501. Business E-Mail: iaa4@cdc.gov. *

ARICA, SEÇIL GUNHER, physician, educator; b. Eskisehir, Feb. 20, 1978; Degree, Uludag U. Med. Sch., 2002. Asst. prof. Mustafa Kemal U. Med. Faculty, 2010—. Office: Mustafa Kemal University Med Faculty Hatay Antakya 31100 Turkey E-mail: secilgunher@hotmail.com.

ARICA, VEFIK, pediatrician, educator; b. Siirt, Feb. 14, 1978; Degree, Istanbul U. Med. Sch., 2001. Pediat. clinic, asst. prof. Mustafa Kemal U. Med. Faculty, 2009—. Office: Mustafa Kemal University Med Faculty Hatay Antakya 31100 Turkey E-mail: vefikarica@hotmail.com.

ARICO', MAURIZIO, hematologist; b. Pavia, Italy, June 30, 1955; MD, Palermo U., Italy, 1979; degree in Pediat., Hematology, Pavia U., 1985. Head, dept. pediatric hematology oncology Azienda Ospedaliero-U. Meyer, 2008—. Mem.: Histiocyte Soc. (Nesbit prize), Italian Assn. Pediatric Hematology Oncology, Am. Soc. Hematology. Office: Vl Pieraccini 24 Florence 50139 Italy Business E-Mail: m.arico@meyer.it.

ARIDOGAN, IBRAHIM ATILLA, medical educator; b. Ankara, May 23, 1966; Degree, U. Çukurova, 1990. Assoc. prof. U. Çukurova, 1997—. Office: University Çukurova Faculty Medicine Adana 01330 Turkey Office Fax: 903223387087. Business E-Mail: aridogan@cu.edu.tr.

ARIJI, YOSHIKO, dentist, educator; m. Yoshiko Nakanishi, Feb. 11, 1988; children: Ryoichiro, Atsuko. DDS, Kyushu U., Fukuoka Prefecture, 1986; PhD in Med. Dentistry, Kyushu U. Faculty Dentistry, Fukuoka Prefecture, 1994. Instr. Kyushu U., 1991—93, Nagasaki U., Japan, 1993—96; asst. prof. Aichi-Gakuin U., Nagoya, Japan, 1997—. Office: Aichi-Gakuin Univ 2-11 Suemori-dori Chikusa-ku Aichi Prefecture Nagoya 464-8651 Japan Business E-Mail: yoshiko@dpc.agu.ac.jp.

ARILDSEN, RONALD, diagnostic radiologist, educator; MD, Columbia U., 1981. Diplomate Am. Bd. Radiology-diagnostic radiology, 1991. Resident diagnostic radiology St. Lukes Roosevelt Hosp. Ctr., 1987—91; fellow body imaging Vanderbilt Univ. Med. Ctr., Nashville, 1991—92; assoc. prof. radiology Vanderbilt Univ. Office: Vanderbilt University Medical Center N CCC-1121 1161 21st Ave S Nashville TN 37232 Office Phone: 615-322-3801.

ARIMA, EITOKU, surgeon; b. Kanoya City, Japan, Feb. 20, 1933; s. Tohemon and Ura (Kawabata) Tsurudome; adoptive s. Yuhjiro and Yasuko (Mesaki) Arima; m. Naoko Yamaguchi Arima, May 19, 1964; children: Jun-ichi, Yukie, Masae. Degree in Lit., 1954, MBBS, Keio U., 1958; BM in Broadcast Edn., Kagoshima U., Japan, 1958, DMS, 1964. Registered anesthetist, Japan, 1964; bd. cert. gastroenterologist and pediatric surgeon, sports physician and occupl. physician. Intern Nat. Sagamihara Hosp., Kanagawa, Japan, 1958-59; resident Kagoshima U. Hosp. Surgery, 1959-64; asst. in anesthesiology Kyushu U. Hosp. Anesthesiology, Fukuoka, Japan, 1964-65; rsch. fellow dept. surgery UCLA Sch. Medicine, 1971-73; asst. Kagoshima U. Hosp., 1966-74, lectr. 2d dept. surgery, 1974-80, lectr. dept. pediatric surgery, 1980-98, ret., 1998-2000; dir. Heim Berg Geriatric Health Svcs. Facility, Mizusawa, Japan, 1998-2001; vice dir. Miki Hosp, Iwate, Japan, 1998-2001; dept. surgery Nakajima Hosp., Shizuoka, 2001; dept surg & anesthesiology Atagawa Hot Springs Hosp., Shizuoka, 2001; dir. Kikyo-no-Sato Geriatric Health Care and Svcs. Facility, Fuji City, Shizuoka, Japan, 2001—03; surgeon Matsushita Hosp., Kagoshima, Japan, 2003—08, Tagami Meml. Hosp., Kagoshima, Japan, 2008—09; lectr. Jinshin Nursing Sch and Tachibana Nursing Sch., Hayato town Kirishima City, Japan, 2003—08; part time physician Shohnan Hosp., So-o City, Japan, 2005—08; dir. Mimata Hosp., Miyazaki, 2009; vice dir. Ohyama Hosp., Shibushi, Japan, 2009—. Vis. prof. sect. electron microscopy, histology, embryology and gastroenterol. surgery First Mil. Med. Coll. PLA, Guangzhou, China, 1993—, vis. prof. surgery Jinzhou Med. Coll., China, 1997—, lectr., surg. cons. Chinese Med. Assn., Beijing, 1984—, Electron Micros. Assn., 26 cities, 1984—; lectr. U. Sao Paulo Postgrad. Sch., Brazil, 1996—, UNIFE, Sao Paulo, U. Fed. Sao Paulo Postgrad. Sch., 1997—; keynote spkr. found. week celebration Nat. Rsch. Coun. of The Philippines, Manila, 2001; com. mem. for diagnostic criteria Japanese Study Group on Pancreaticobiliary Maljunction, Tokyo, 1983—98; local chmn. 9th Japanese Symposium on Scanning Electron Microscopy for Biomedicine, Ibusuki, Japan, 1980. Author: Guide Book on Pediatric Surgery for Citizens, 1969; co-author 16 books on surgery; contbr. articles to med. jours., including Jour. Pediatric Surge., Jour. Trace and Microprobe Techniques; editl. cons. Japanese Jour. Pediatric Surgery, 1977—; med. columnist Kagoshima Shinpo, 1969. Rescue physician, trainer Judo Assn. So. Calif., LA, 1971-73; rescue physician 5,000 kilometer Rally Raid Mongol Ulaanbaatar and others, 1995; condr. seminar on resuscitation, Kanoya City, 1989, 59th Peace Meets Gen. Voyages. Fellow Japan Surg. Soc. (diplomate), Japanese Soc. Pediatric Surgeons (diplomate, spl. mem.), Japanese Soc. Gastroent. Surgeons (diplomate, spl. mem.), Japanese Soc. Hepato-biliary-pancreatic Surgery (spl. mem.), Japanese Soc. of Pediatric Surgeons (diplomate, spl. mem., sr.); mem. Pacific Assn. Pediatric Surgeons (sr., diplomate), Haraldria Soc. Order of Peace Universal, Brit. Assn. Pediat. Surgeons, Orgn. Mondiale de Gastroenterologie, Japan Med. Assn. (cert. occupl. and sports physician). Avocations: mountain climbing, touring, fishing, judo (5th-dan), golf. Home: 6-33-19 Murasakibaru Kagoshima 890-0082 Japan Office: Ohyama Hosp Shibushi Kagoshima 899-7101 Japan Office Phone: 099-472-1400. Business E-Mail: ohyama-hp3303@chic.ocn.ne.jp, dr.sarima02.20.3391@softbank.ne.jp.

ARIMORI, KAZUHIKO, pharmacist, educator; b. Saga, Japan, Aug. 25, 1951; BS in Pharmacy, Kumamoto U., 1974, PharmM, 1976, PhD in Pharmacy, 1996; attended, St. Jude Children's Rsch. Hosp., Memphis. Assoc. prof., assoc. dir. Kumamoto U., 1993—99; prof., dir. U. Miyazaki Hosp., 1999—, head Ctr. clin. rschr. new drugs, 2004. Recipient award, Japanese Soc. Hosp. Pharmacists. Fellow: Pharm. Soc. Japan, Japanese Soc. Pharm. Palliative Care and Scis., Japanese Soc. Pharm. Health Care and Scis.; mem.: Japanese Soc. Clin. Pharmacology and Therapeutics, Japan Soc. Drug Delivery Sys. Office: 5200 Kihara Kiyotake-cho Miyazaki 889-1692 Japan Office Fax: 81-985-85-9429. Business E-Mail: arimori@med.miyazaki-u.ac.jp.

ARINGER, MARTIN, internist, researcher; b. Vienna, June 11, 1968; s. Waltraud and Irmfried A. Aringer; m. Gertrud Aringer, July 29, 1995; children: Johannes children: David. MD, U. Vienna, 1992. Cert. Bd. Internal Medicine Austria, Bd. Rheumatology Austria. Asst. in internal medicine Rheumatology, Internal Medicine III, U. Vienna, 1992—97, 1999—2003, assoc. prof. internal medicine, 2003—07; postdoctoral fellow NIAMS, NIH, Bethesda, Md., 1997—99; prof. medicine Carl Gustav Carus Tech. U., Dresden, Germany, 2007—, chief divsn. rheumatology, U. Med. Ctr., 2007—. Recipient Young

Investigator award, EULAR, 1993, Austrian Fed. award, Fed. Ministry Edn. and Sciences, 1994, Internat. Exch. award, ACR-EULAR, 2002; fellow, NIH, 1998—99, EULAR, 2002; Rsch. Exch. grant, Max Kade Found., 1997—98. Mem.: Soc. for Advances in Internal Medicine, German Soc. Internal Medicine, German Soc. Rheumatology, Am. Coll. Rheumatology, NY Acad. Sci., Austrian Soc. Rheumatology, Austrian Soc. Internal Medicine. Office: Univ Med Ctr Carl Gustav Carus Divsn Rheumatology Dept Medicine III Fetscherstrasse 74 01307 Dresden Germany Office Fax: 49-351-458-5801. Business E-Mail: martin.aringer@uniklinikum-dresden.de.

ARINIEGO, ROMEO PILOTIN, cardiologist; b. Vigan, Ilocos Sur, Philippines, Feb. 26, 1943; s. Felipe and Eleuteria (Pilotin) A. BS, Siliman U., Dumaquete City, 1967; MD, U. Philippines, Manila, 1972. Intern, resident in medicine U. Philippines-PGH Med. Ctr., Manila, 1971-76; fellow in cardiology Sahlgrenska Hosp./U. Gothenburg, Sweden, 1977-78; fellow non-invasive cardiology and cardiac rehab. medicine Lidcombe Hosp., N.S.W., 1979-82; prof. medicine Emilio Aquinaldo Coll. of Medicine, Dasmarinas, Cavite, Philippines, 1982-86, DLSU Coll. of Medicine, Dasmarinas, Cavite, Philippines, 1987—. Cons. physician U. Philippines-PGH Med. Ctr., 1977-78; part-time cons. Cardiovascular div. ASTRA Philippines, 1977-78; chmn. dept. medicine U. Med. Ctr. Desmarinas, Cavite, 1982-87, chief of clinics, 1985-87, hosp. tng. coord., 1982-87; asst. med. dir./chief of clinics De La Salle U. Med. Ctr., Desmarinas, Cavite, 1987—, chmn. dept. medicine, 1987—, also tng. coord., mem. pres.'s coun. and exec. coun., dir. med. svcs., 1993—, dean sch. medicine, 1999—. Contbr. articles to profl. jours. Mem. Peace and Order Found., Dasmarinias, 1987-93 Lederle scholar, 1972. Fellow and diplomate Philippine Heart Assn., Philippine Coll. of Cardiology, Philippine Coll. Physicians; mem. Philippine Coll. Emergency Medicine, Philippine Med. Assn., Cavite Med. Soc., U. Philippine Alumni Assn. (life), Nat. Rsch. Coun. of Philippines (assoc. mem.). Office: De La Salle Med Ctr Dasmarinas Philippines 4114

ARINZON, ZEEV, physician, researcher; m. Esphir Moshe Harah; 1 child, David. MD, U. Kishinev, 1985. Gen. physician, Kalarash, Moldova, 1985—90; family physician Meuhedet Healthcare Sys., Tel-Aviv, 1990—96, Kfar-Yona, Israel, 2003—; specialist in geriatric medicine Geriatric Med. Ctr., Dora, Netanya, Israel, 1996—2003; rschr., spinal unit Meir Med. Ctr., Kfar-Saba, Israel, 2000, rschr., dept. geriatric medicine, 2003—. Mem.: Geriatric Soc. (assoc.). Personal E-mail: arinzon@walla.co.il.

ARJMAND, ELLIS M., otolaryngologist, educator; MD, Northwestern U. Med. Sch. Resident Barnes-Jewish Hosp.; fellow Wash. Univ., St. Louis, asst. prof. surgery and pediat., 1994—99; hosp. affiliation includes Univ. Hosp.; postdoc. fellow Northwestern Univ., Evanston, Ill., 1986—87, 1988—89, Wash. Univ. Sch. of Medicine, St. Louis, 1989—93, asst. otolaryngology- head and neck surgery, 1992—93, chief resident tolaryngology- head and neck surgery, 1993—94; clin. instr. otolaryngology- head and neck surgery Univ. of Pitts. Sch. of Medicine, 1999—2004; asst. prof. otolaryngology and communication sci. and disorders Univ. of Pitts., 1999—2004; staff otolaryngologist Children's Hosp. of Pitts., 1999—2004, dir. The Hearing Ctr., 1999—2004, med. dir. cochlear implant program, 2001—04; dir. ear and hearing ctr. Cin. Children's Hosp. Med. Ctr., 2004—, med. dir. cochlear implant program, 2004—, staff otolaryngologist, 2004, dir. ctr. for hearing and deafness rsch, 2004—, dir. cochlear implant program, 2004—, med. dir. Liberty Campus, 2007—; assoc. prof. otolaryngology Univ. of Cin. Coll. of Medicine, 2004—; instr. otolaryngology- head and neck surgery Southern Ill. Univ. Sch. of Medicine, Springfield, Ill., 1994—99; staff otolaryngologist St. John's Hosp., 1994—99, Meml. Med. Ctr., 1994—99; consulting otolaryngologist Passavant Hosp., Jacksonville, 1997—99, St. Vincent's Hosp., Taylorville, 1997—99. Fellow: ACS, Am. Broncho-Esophagological Assn., Am. Acad. of Otolaryngology - Head and Neck Surgery; mem.: AMA, Pa. Acad. of Otolaryngology-Head and Neck Surgery, Allegheny County Med. Soc., Am. Acad. of Otolaryngic Allergy, Ill. State Med. Soc., Ill. Downstate Pediatric Soc. Newborn and Infant Hearing Screening Work Group, Sangamon County Med. Soc., Ill. Soc. of Ophthalmology and Otolaryngology, Am. Acad. Pediat., Am. Soc. of Pediatric Otolaryngology, Soc. for Ear, Nose, and Throat Advances in Children Inc., Assn. for Rsch. in Otolaryngology. Office: Cincinnati Children's Hospital Medical Center 3333 Burnet Ave Cincinnati OH 45229-3039 Office Phone: 513-636-4200.

ARK, NEBIL, surgeon, educator; b. Turkey, Jan. 8, 1967; MD, Hacettepe U., 1991. Vis. asst. prof. MD Anderson Cancer Ctr.; with dept. head & neck surgery U. Tex., 2007; asst. prof. otolaryngology head & neck surgery Fatih U., Sch. Medicine, 2008—. Mem.: Turkish Soc. Otolaryngology, Head & Neck Surgery. Avocation: basketball. Office: Alpaslan Turkes Cad 57 Ankara Bestepe 06510 Turkey Business E-Mail: nebilark@hotmail.copm.

ARKING, LUCILLE MUSSER, nurse, epidemiologist, consultant; b. Centre County, Pa., Jan. 26, 1936; d. Boyd Albert and Marion Anna (Merryman) Musser; m. Robert Arking, May 8, 1958; children: Henry David, Jonathan Jacob. BSN, U. Pa., 1968; MSN, Wayne State U., 1986; Doctoral Studies in Evaluation Stats., Wayne State U., Detroit, 1991—96. Psychiat. rsch. nurse Boston City Hosp., 1958; hosp. supr. Phila. Psychiat. Ctr., 1959-61; pub. health nurse Cmty. Nursing Svc., Phila., 1961-64; DON Green Acres Nursing Ctr., Phila., 1966-67; head nurse U. Va., Charlottesville, 1967-68; asst. DON U. Ky., Lexington, 1968-70; asst. dir. nursing edn. Rio Hondo Hosp., Downey, Calif., 1973-75; DON Bellwood Hosp., Bellflower, Calif., 1974-75; nurse epidemiologist Henry Ford Hosp., Detroit, 1975-84, dir. hosp. epidemiology, 1984-89, sr. clin. epidemiologist, 1990-94; v.p. clin. svcs. Great Lakes Rehab. Hosp., Southfield, Mich., 1994-96; adminstr. Cadillac Nursing Ctr., Detroit, 1997-99; exec. dir. St. Anthony Nursing Care Ctr., Warren, Mich., 1999—2001; with office of internat. affairs Pusan (South Korea) Nat. U., 2001; with St. James Nursing Ctr., Detroit, 2002—03, Arking Cons. Assocs., 2003—. Lectr. drug abuse Fountain Valley, Calif., 1970-75; instr. Santa Ana Coll., 1971-73. Contbr. articles to profl. jours. Co-founder Parents and Friends Learning Disabilities Orgn., 1968-70; den leader Cub Scouts, Fountain Valley and Troy, Mich., 1968-75; founding mem., bd. dirs. Wellness Networks, Detroit, 1982-86; mem. Mich. Gov. AIDS Task Force, 1985-86, Mich. Med. Soc. AIDS Task Force, 1986, chair religious affiliation social action com., 1984-90; sr. coun. mem. Oakland County, Mich., 2007. Women's Club of Centre County scholar, 1954-58; recipient edn. grant Phila. Cmty. Nursing Svc. Ednl., 1963-64; USPHS nursing trainee, 1965, Florence Nightingale award, Oakland U., 2009. Mem. APHA (mem. epidemiology sect. 1975-99), ANA, Mich. Nurses's Assn. (AIDS task force 1987-89, HIV adv. com. 1989-90), Assn. Practitioners Infection Control, Sci. Rsch. Soc., Assn. Women in Sci., Sigma Xi. Democrat. Jewish. Avocations: gardening, cooking, genealogy. Home and Office: 6450 Shagbark Dr Troy MI 48098-5233 Office Phone: 248-689-5286. Personal E-mail: brkac@aol.com. Business E-Mail: arkinglm@aol.com.

ARKING, ROBERT, geneticist, gerontologist, educator; b. Bklyn., July 1, 1936; s. Henry and Mollie (Levinson) Arking; m. Lucille Mae Musser, May 8, 1958; children: Henry David, Jonathan Jacob. BS, Dickinson Coll., 1958; PhD, Temple U., 1967. Sci. tchr. Phila. Public Schs., 1959—61; asst. prof. zoology U. Ky., Lexington, 1968—70; rsch. biologist Devel. Biology Ctr., U. Calif., Irvine, 1970—75; asst. prof. biology Wayne State U., Detroit, 1975—81, assoc. prof., 1981—83, prof., 1993, undergraduate officer, 1997—. Grant reviewer Fulbright Found., 2006—, AFAR Review Bd., 2004—; faculty assoc. Inst. Gerontology Wayne State U.; expert vis. prof. Pusan Nat. U., 2001; Fulbright disting. chair natural sci. U. Salzburg, Austria, 2006. Author: Biology of Aging: Observations and Principles, 1991, 2nd edit., 1998, 3rd edit., 2006; contbr. articles to profl. jours. Fellowship, NSF, 1964—66, NIH, 1967—68. Fellow: Gerontology Soc. America; mem.: AAAS, Sigma Xi. Home: 6450 Shagbark Dr Troy MI 48098-5239 Personal E-mail: arkingr@aol.com. Business E-Mail: aa2210@wayne.edu.

ARLAZOROFF, AHARON, neurologist; b. Wilno, Poland, Aug. 27, 1930; arrived in Israel, 1934; s. Eliyahu and Vera (Gordon) A.; m. Ritta Schaffer, July 3, 1966; children: Eliyahu, Amnon. MD, Hebrew U. Sch. Medicine, 1959. Intermed. dept. Govt. Hosp., Jaffa, Israel, 1959-61; intern, chief resident neurology dept. Ichilov Med. Ctr., Te Aviv, Israel, 1961-71; head dept. neurology Assaf Harofe Med. Ctr., Zerifin, Israel, 1971-95; sr. clin. lectr. Tel-Aviv U., 1971-95; assoc. clin. prof. Tel-Aviv U. Sch. of Medicine, 1996—. Mem. facultative coun. and inner coun. Tel Aviv U. Sch. Medicine, 1989-93; mem. high med. com. appeals Ministry of Defence, Israel, 1989—. Contbr. articles to profl. jours. Capt. Israeli Defence Forces, 1959-85. Israel Wechsler grantee, 1963; rsch. fellow Neurophysiology Lab. Hadassah Hosp., Jerusalem, 1963-64, Exptl. Neurophysiology Lab. Max Planck Inst., Munich, Germany, 1966-67. Mem. Israel Med. Assn., Israel Neurol. Assn., Israel Soc. Electroencephalography and Neurophysiology, Am. Acad. Neurology, The Movement Disorder Soc. Avocation: history of mid-east. Home: 27 Ahavat Zion St 62506 Tel Aviv Israel Office Phone: 03-6045783. Personal E-mail: arlazor@netvision.net.il.

ARLING, BRYAN JEREMY, internist; b. Mpls., Dec. 10, 1944; s. Leonard Swenson and Marion (Schroeder) A.; m. Donna Dickson; children: Elissa, Jeremy, Timothy. BA summa cum laude, U. Minn., 1965; MD, Harvard U., 1969. Diplomate Am. Bd. Internal Medicine. Intern Stanford Affiliated Hosp., Calif., 1969-70, resident in internal medicine Calif., 1970-71; spl. asst. to adminstr. health sci. mental health adminstrn. USPHS, Rockville, Md., 1971-73; instr., chief resident medicine George Washington U. Hosp., Washington, 1973-74, asst. prof. medicine, 1974-77; pvt. practice Washington, 1977—; clin. prof. medicine George Washington U., 1988—, Georgetown U., Washington, 1997—. Adminstrv. bd. Chevy Chase United Meth. Ch.; devel. com. Maret Sch., 1985-98, trustee, 1991-98, v.p., 1994-98; question relevance reviewer Am. Bd. Internal Medicine, 1991-92, com. on certifying and recertifying exam., 1992-93, reviewer, Pri Med. ACP Jeopardy Exam., 2011, White House Fellows Regional judge, 2011. Recipient Highest citation for Best Internist, Washington Consumers Checkbook, 2007, 2011; named one of Best Doctors in Town, Washington Mag., 1986, 1987, 1993, 1995, 1999, 2005, One of Best Pediatricians and Internists, 1987, Top Internists by other doctors, 1993, 1999, Best Doctors in Am., S.E. region, 1996, Top Internists by other doctors, 2005, Best Primary Care Physicians in Am., Town & Country Mag., 2000, Best Doctors in Am., Woodward & White, 2007, Naifen & Smith, 2001—07. Fellow ACP; adv. coun. on med. ed., Harvard Med. Sch., 2003-; mem. AMA, Am. Soc. Internal Medicine, DC Med. Soc., Acad. Medicine (mem. exec. com. 1995—), Acad. of Sci. of Washington DC (v.p. 2001—), Smithsonian Assocs., Friends of Kennedy Ctr., Harvard Club Washington (chmn. med. sch. alumni meetings 2007), Nat. Trust for Hist. Preservation, Friends of Nat. Zoo, Common Cause, ACLU, Physicians for Social Responsibility, Columbia Country Club, Bahamas Air-Sea Rescue Assn. Home: 3803 Taylor St Bethesda MD 20815-4117 Office: 2440 M St NW Ste 817 Washington DC 20037-1404 Office Phone: 202-833-5707. Personal E-mail: rhonda@arlingpat.com.

ARLING, DONNA DICKSON, social worker; b. Jersey Shore, Pa., July 8, 1945; d. Eugene Robert and Helen (Bardo) Dickson; m. Bryan Jeremy Arling, Aug. 28, 1969; children: Elissa, Jeremy, Timothy. BS, Pa. State U., 1967; MSW, Smith Coll., 1969; PhD, Clinical Social Work Inst., Wash., DC, 2003. Bd. cert. diplomate in clin. social work; cert. social worker, Md.; cert. ind. clin. social worker, D.C. Clin. social worker N. County Mental Health Ctr., Palo Alto, Calif., 1969-71, VA Hosp., Washington, 1971-77; pvt. practice clin. social work Washington, 1978—. Mem. Nat. Assn. Social Workers, Greater Washington Soc. Clin. Social Work, Smith Coll. Sch. Social Work Alumni Assn. (nat. exec. com. 1979-82, Washington exec. com. 1976-86) Home: 3803 Taylor St Chevy Chase MD 20815-4117 Office: 1015 33rd St NW Washington DC 20007-3523 Office Phone: 202-337-7115.

ARMADA, ANTHONY A., hospital administrator; B in Med. Tech., Mich. State U.; MHA, MBA, Xavier U., Cin. Pres. coun. Xavier Univ., with grad. program in health svcs. adminstrn. adv. bd.; with dean bd. advisors Coll. of Natural Sci. Mich. State Univ.; mentor Am. Coll. of Healthcare Execs.; chmn. healthcare mgmt. bd. dirs. Inst. for Diversity; sr. v.p. pres., area mgr. Kaiser Permanente's Met. LA Service Area, 2000—04; pres., CEO Henry Ford Hosp. and Health Network, Detroit, 2004—09; chmn. Asian Healthcare Leaders Assn., 2007; pres. Advocate Lutheran Gen. Children's Hosp., Advocate Lutheran Gen. Hosp.; bd. mem. Asian Health Care Leaders Assn. Named one of Top 25 Minority Execs., Modern Healthcare Mag., 2010. Fellow: Am. Colle. of Healthcare Execs.; mem.: Healthcare Exec.Study Soc. Office: Advocate Lutheran General Hospital 1775 Dempster St Park Ridge IL 60068 Mailing: Asian Health Care Leaders Association Ste 500 566 W Adams Chicago IL 60661 Office Phone: 847-723-2210, 877-485-0016. Office Fax: 312-533-2240.

ARMATO, UBALDO, anatomist, researcher, cell biologist, educator, histologist; b. Trieste, Italy, Apr. 30, 1943; s. Giuseppe and Rosalba (Pace) A.; m. Maria Grazia Cimmino, Aug. 20, 1970 (dec. Oct. 1993); children: Andrea, Federico; m. Ilaria Dal Pra, Oct. 24, 1998. Diploma Classical Letters, Liceo R. Franchetti, Venice, Italy, 1961; Degree (hons.) in Medicine and Surgery, U. Padua, Italy, 1967, Diploma in Hematology, 1969, Diploma (hons.) in Internal Medicine, 1975. Rsch. assoc. U. Padua, 1969-71, rsch. assoc. with tenure, 1971-80, assoc. prof. human anatomy, 1980-86; guest worker Can. Nat. Rsch. Coun., Ottawa, Ont., 1980, 96; prof. histology and embryology U. Verona, Italy, 1986—, dir. Tissue Culture and Human Proteomics Lab., 1986—, prof. exptl. oncology Sch. Dermatology, 1991—2006. Cons. Regione Veneto Ctr. Treatment and Prevention of Burns Injuries, 1989—; dir. histology & embryology unit Biomed. and Surg. Scis., 1998—2009, Life & Reproduction Scis., 2010. Contbr. chpts. to books, articles to sci. jours. Pres. funding com. U. Verona, 1989-96, mem. Atheneum's Com., 1990-93; mem. Atheneum's Linguistic Ctr. Directorate, 1994—, tech. com., 1995—. Recipient Sci. Productivity award U. Padua, 1971-73, Millipore Sci. Edn. award Millipore Ltd., Verona, 1987. Mem. Tissue Culture Assn., Am. Assn. Advancement Scis., Italian Anatomical Histological Soc. (T.L. Colonnello award 1976), European Tissue Repair Soc., European Acad. Scis. Avocations: swimming, jogging, cross country skiing, reading, anglo-saxon literary and historic authors. Home: 16 Via Giovanni XXIII 37059 Zevio Italy Office: U Verona Dept Biomed Surg Scis Strada le Grazie 8 37134 Verona VR Italy

ARMBRISTER, DOUGLAS KENLEY, retired surgeon; b. Emory, Va., Feb. 20, 1934; s. Victor Stradley and Naomi Lucile (Byrd) A.; m. Nancy Sheri Douglas, Apr. 30, 1960 (div. Sept. 1995); children: Valere Lynn, Victor Kenley, Christopher Douglas, Karen Leigh; m. Barbara Ann Atwell, Sept. 9, 2000. BA in English/German, BS in Chemistry/Biology, Emory and Henry Coll., 1955; MD, U. Va., Charlottesville, 1959, MS in Surg. Rsch., 1962. Diplomate Am. Bd. Surgery. Intern surgery U. Va., 1959—60, resident surgery, 1960—62, 1964—67; pvt. practice Marion, Va., 1967—2011. Regional adv. group Va. Regional Med. Program, 1971; subarea coun. chmn. Health Systems Agy.; bd. dirs. Va. Health Quality Ctr.; pres. Smyth County Cmty. Hosp. Med Staff, 1973, chair surg. svcs., 1978-2009. Bd. visitors Emory and Henry Coll., 1982—2006, trustee, 2006-. Capt. USAF, 1962-64. Fellow Am. Col. Surgeons: mem. Va. Surg. Soc. (malpractice review panel mem. 1972—), Med. Soc. Va. (review bd. dirs. 1985-95), Southwest Va. Med. Soc., Muller Surg. Soc., Nat. Eagle Scout Assn., Blue Key Nat. Honor Soc. (chpt. pres. 1953). Methodist. Avocations: tennis, classical music, singing, piano.

ARMENAKAS, NOEL ANTHONY, medical educator; b. Orange, NJ, Sept. 29, 1958; s. Anthony E. and Stella P. (Petroutsa) A.; m. Macrene R. Alexiades, Oct. 26, 1996; children: Sophie Stella, Anthony Emmanuel. MD, U. Athens, Greece, 1985. Diplomate Am. Bd. Urology. Intern surgery Lenox Hill Hosp., NYC, 1985-86; resident surgery Monmouth Med. Ctr., Long Branch, N.J., 1986-87; resident urology Lenox Hill Hosp., NYC, 1987-91; fellow trauma and reconstructive surgery U. Calif., San Francisco, 1991-92, clin. instr. dept. urology, 1991-92; clin. instr. dept. surgery Cornell U. Med. Coll., NYC, 1992-94; clin. asst. prof. dept. urology Cornell U. Med. Sch., NYC, 1994—2002, clin. assoc. prof. dept. urology, 2002—, assoc. program dir. sect. urology, 1992—2007, program dir. dept. urology, 2009—. Mem. oper. rm. com. Lenox Hill Hosp., 1990, outpatient clinic com., 1993—; mem. ChubbHealth Physician Adv. Panel, 1994-00; mem. scholarship com. Hellenic Med. Assn., bd. mem. Soc. Genitourinary Reconstructive Surgeons, 2006-; attending staff San Francisco Gen. Hosp., 1991-92; dir., physician-in-charge Outpatient Urologic Clinics Lenox Hill Hosp., 1992-05; attending staff NY Presbyn. Hosp., NYC, 1992—, Lenox Hill Hosp., NYC, 1992—, program dir. dept. urology, 2009-; lectr. in field. Contbr. chpts. to books and articles to profl. jours. Fellow ACS, NY Acad. Medicine; mem. Internat. Soc. Urology, Am. Assn. Clin. Urologists, Am. Urol. Assn., Hellenic Med. Assn., Soc. for Urology and Engring., Soc. Genitourinary and Reconstructive Surgeons. Avocations: skiing, tennis, travel. Office: New York Urological Assocs 880 5th Ave New York NY 10021-4951 Business E-Mail: drarmenakas@nyurological.com.

ARMSTRONG, CLAY, physiology educator; BA, Rice U., 1956; MD, Washington U., 1960. Postdoctoral fellow NIH, 1961—64, U. Coll., London, 1964—66; prof. Duke U., U. Rochester; prof. physiology U. Pa. Sch. Medicine, Phila., 1976—. Mem editorial bd. Journal of General Physiology, Journal of Neurophysiology. Recipient Louisa Gross Horwitz prize Columbia U., 1996, Jacob Javits Neuroscience Rsch. award, NIH, Albert Lasker award for Basic Med. Rsch., Lasker Found., 1999, Gairdner Found. Internat. award, 2001. Mem.: NAS, Soc. General Physiologists, Biophysical Soc., Am. Physiological Soc. Office: U Pa Dept Physiology C701 Richards Bldg/ 6085 Philadelphia PA 19104-6085 Office Phone: 215-898-7816. E-mail: carmstro@mail.med.upenn.edu. *

ARMSTRONG, DAVID LIGON, psychiatrist; b. Ontario, Calif., May 5, 1927; s. John Awdry and Ruth (Harrison) A.; m. Mary Meredith, Mar. 30, 1953 (dec. Feb. 13, 1997); children: Meredith Armstrong Richey, Paul, Adelaide Armstrong Butler. BS in Plant Sci., U. Calif., Berkeley, 1949; PhD in Genetics, U. Calif., Davis, 1956; MD, Creighton U., 1972. Diplomate Am. Bd. Psychiatry and Neurology. Dir. rsch. Armstrong Nurseries, Inc., Ontario, Calif., 1953—68; resident in psychiatry U. Calif., Irvine, 1972—75; staff psychiatrist Met. State Hosp., Norwalk, Calif., 1975—2005; ret., 2005. Pres. med. staff Met. State Hosp., Norwalk, 1985-88, 1997-2005 Pres. West End United Fund, Ontario, 1958-60, Chaffey Young Reps., Ontario, Upland, Chino, Calif., 1958-60, West End Coun. Cmty. Svcs., Ontario, Upland, Chino, 1960-64; chmn. Rep. Ctrl. Com., San Bernardino County, Calif., 1960-62. active USNR, 1945-46. Mem. Calif. State Employed Physicians Assn. (pres. 1984-86), Sigma Xi, Alpha Zeta. Republican. Achievements include patents for roses, peaches and nectarines. Avocations: politics, travel, gardening. Home: 2809 E Hillside Ave Orange CA 92867-8413 Home Phone: 714-998-2349. Personal E-mail: 1dla@att.net.

ARMSTRONG, DAVID WILLIAM, biotechnology entrepreneur, tissue engineer specialist, microbiologist; b. Ottawa, Ont., Can. s. Robert Crosby Armstrong and Margaret Theresa Shepherd; m. J. Elaine Robertson, June 10, 1978; 1 child, Laura Lynne. BSc with honors, U. Ottawa, Ontario, Can., 1978, MSc, 1980; postgrad., MIT, Cambridge, 1981; PhD, Carleton U., Ottawa, 1984. Rsch. scientist Nat. Rsch. Coun., Ottawa, 1979—99, sr. rsch. officer Tissue Regeneration Lab., 1985—99; pres., CEO IatroQuest Corp., Ottawa, 1999—2001, exec. v.p., 2001—04; v.p. clin. affairs and corp. devel. Canica, Inc., Almonte, Ont., Canada, 2004—06; co-CEO Converg Med. Corp., 2006—09; chief corp. devel. CRI Critical Care Edn. Network, 2009—10; exec. lead strategic devel. Royal Ottawa Health Care Group, Inst. Mental Health rsch., 2010—. Advisor Biotech. and Biomedicine, Canadian Space Agy., Ottawa, 1985-88; dir. Ottawa Life Scis. Coun., 2000-07, Ottawa Hosp. Rsch. Inst., 2005—08, VHA Health, 2006—, Inst. Mental Health Rsch., 2009-10. Named Ontario scholar, 1973; recipient Ontario Grad. scholarship, 1978-80. Mem. Can. Coll. Microbiologist (registered specialist) Mem. United Ch. Achievements include patents in field. Office: Converg Med Corp Ste 312 1411A Carling Ave Ottawa ON Canada K1Z 1A7 Business E-Mail: david.armstrong@criedunet.org.

ARMSTRONG, RICHARD, state agency administrator; Sr. v.p. sales and mktg. Blue Cross Idaho, 1990—2006; dir. Idaho Dept. Health and Welfare, 2006—. Office: Idaho Dept Health and Welfare 1720 Westgate Dr Boise ID 83704 Office Phone: 208-334-5500.

ARMSTRONG, SCOTT, hospital administrator; m. Sarah Armstrong; 2 children. BA, Hamilton Coll., Clinton, NY; MBA in Hosp. Adminstrn., U. Wis., Madison. Asst. v.p. hosp. Miami Valley Hosp., Dayton, Ohio; various positions ranging from asst. hosp. adminstr. to COO Group Health Cooperative, Seattle, 1986—2005, pres., CEO, 2005—. Commr. Medicare Payment Adv. Commn.; bd. chmn. Alliance Cmty. Health Plans; bd. mem. America's Health Ins. Plans, Pacific Sci. Ctr. Named one of 100 Most Influential People in Healthcare, Modern Healthcare, 2010, 2011. Fellow: American Coll. Healthcare Executives. Office: Group Health Cooperative 320 Westlake Ave N Ste 100 Seattle WA 98109-5233 Office Phone: 206-448-5600. *

ARN, PAMELA HAWKS, clinical geneticist, educator; MD, U. Va., 1983. Lic. Fla., 1989, diplomate Am. Bd. Pediatrics, 1987, cert. Am. Bd. Clin. Genetics-Med. Genetics, 1990, Am. Bd. Clin. Biochemical Genetics-Med. Genetics, 1990, Am. Bd. Clin. Molecular Genetics-Med. Genetics, 1990. Intern Children's Hosp., Pitts., 1984, resident pediatric surgery, 1983—86; fellow clin. genetics Johns Hopkins Hosp., 1986—89; asst. prof. pediat. Univ. Fla.; hosp. affiliation includes Nemours Children's Clinic, Wolfson Children's Hosp.; physician Baptist Med. Ctr. Office: Baptist Medical Center Division of Genetics 807 Children's Way Jacksonville FL 32207 Office Phone: 904-697-3586. Office Fax: 904-697-3565.

ARNAIZ-VILLENA, ANTONIO, immunologist, geneticist, ornithologist, educator, linguist, consultant; b. Madrid; s. Felipe Arnaiz and Etodia Villena. B, Inst. Ramiro Maeztu, Madrid, 1967; MD, U. Complutense, Madrid, 1971, PhD in Medicine and Biology, 1973. Postdoctoral fellow Middlesex Hosp. Med. Sch., London Hosp. Med. Coll., 1974—83; full prof., coord. r&d U. Complutense, Health Svc., Madrid, 1992—. Contbr. numerous articles to profl. jours. Achievements include research in immunology, genetics, linguistics, ornithology; discovery of first T lymphocite receptor molecular defect leading to immunodeficiency; molecular classification of Carduelinae Birds; first to discover genetics on Mediterranean and Amerindian populations. Office: Univ Complutense Madrid Health Svc Dept Immunology Regional Blood Ct Avda Complutense s/n Medicine Faculty Madrid 28040 Spain Business E-Mail: aarnaiz@med.ucm.es.

ARNDT, KENNETH ALFRED, dermatologist, educator; b. San Francisco, June 3, 1936; s. Sigmund Charles and Bernice Adele (Munter) Arndt; m. Anne Scolnick, Aug. 8, 1959; children: David Carl, Jennifer Anne. AA, U. Calif., Berkeley, 1957; MD, Yale U., New Haven, 1961. Diplomate Am. Bd. Dermatology. Intern dermatology Grace-New Haven Cmty. Hosp., 1961-62; resident dermatology Mass Gen. Hosp./Harvard Med. Sch., Boston, 1962-64, rsch. fellow, chief resident dermatology, 1964-65; instr. dermatology U. Cin. Coll. Medicine, 1965-67, Harvard Med. Sch., 1967-68, faculty, 1968-69, asst. prof. dermatology, 1969-73, assoc. prof. dermatology, 1973-86, clin. prof. dermatology, 1986—; also clin. prof. sect. dermatologic surgery/cutaneous oncology Yale U. Sch. Medicine; ptnr. SkinCare Physicians, Boylston, Mass. Surgeon USPHS, 1965—67; clin. assoc. dermatology Beth Israel Deaconess Med. Ctr., Boston, 1967—69, asst. dermatologist, 1969—70, assoc. dermatologist, 1970—71, dermatologist, 1972, chief divsn. dermatology, 1977—82, dermatologist-in-chief, 1982—2002; assoc. chief divsn. dermatology Children's Hosp. Med. Ctr., Boston, 1971—79, sr. assoc. dermatology, 1979; cons. dermatology Peter Bent Brigham Hosp., Boston, 1971—78, assoc. medicine/dermatology, 1978—84; dermatology cons. Dana-Farber Cancer Inst., Boston, 1978—84, Boston Hosp. Women, Mass. Gen. Hosp., VA Med. Ctr., Brockton, Mass., Brigham & Women's Hosp.; vis. prof. U. Calif., San Francisco, 1976, Ea. Maine Med. Ctr., Bangor, 1977, Columbia U., NYC, 1977, Johns Hopkins Med. Sch., Balt., 1978, Hershey Med. Ctr./Pa. State U., 1979, U. Miami Sch. Medicine, 1980, Brown U. Sch. Medicine, Providence, 1982, Washington U. Sch. Medicine, 1987; lectr. occupl. dermatology Harvard Sch. Pub. Health, 1981—; adj. prof. medicine Dartmouth Med. Sch., Hanover, NH. Author: Manual of Dermatologic Therapeutics, 1974 (translated into Spanish, Portuguese, Italian, Taiwan and Japanese lang.); co-author: Illustrated Cutaneous Laser Surgery: A Practitioner's Guide, 1990, Illustrated Cutaneous and Aesthetic Laser Surgery, 1999, Atlas of Cosmetic Surgery, 2002; co-editor: Cutaneous Laser Therapy: Principles and Methods, and Lasers in Cutaneous and Aesthetic Surgery, 1983, The Manual of Clinical Problems in Dermatology, 1992, Controversies and Conversations in Cutaneous Laser Surgery, 2002, others; contbr. articles to profl. jours., chapters to books; assoc. editor Jour. Investigative Dermatology, 1972—74, editor-in-chief Archives of Dermatology, 1984—2004, mem. editl. bd. Harvard Health Letter, Lasers in Surgery & Medicine, Jour. Cosmetic & Laser Therapy, Jour. Plastic & Oncologic Dermatology, Skin Therapy Letter. Recipient Presdl. Citation, William B. Mark Meml. award, Leon M. Goldman award for clin. excellence; named one of Nation's Leading Med. Specialists, Castle Connolly Med. Ltd., Best Doctors in America, Woodward/White Inc. Mem.: AMA, Am. Soc. Laser Medicine & Surgery (bd. dirs., Ellet H. Drake Lectureship award), Harvard-Mass. Gen. Hosp. House Officers. Assn. (pres. 1984—86), Mass. Med. Soc., Am. Venereal Disease Assn., Am. Dermatol. Assn, Mass. Acad. Dermatology, Dermatology Found., Soc. Investigative Dermatology (auditing com. 1971—74, pub. rels. com. 1973—76), New Eng. Dermatol. Soc. (pres. 1980—81), Am. Fedn. Clin. Rsch., Am. Acad. Dermatology (bd. dirs.), Fla. Soc. Dermatology (hon.), Boston Dermatol. Club (treas. 1970—75, v.p. 1979—80, pres. 1979—81), Alpha Omega Alpha. Office: Skincare Physicians 1244 Boylston St Ste 302 Chestnut Hill MA 02467 also: Yale U Sch Medicine Dermatology Dept PO Box 208059 New Haven CT 06520-8059 Office Phone: 617-731-1600. Office Fax: 617-731-1601.

ARNEDT, JOHN TODD, psychologist, educator; BA in Psychology (first class honors), Queen's U., 1991, MA in Clin. Psychology, 1994, PhD in Clin. Psychology, 2000. Lic. Psychologist, RI, 2001, cert. Behavioral Sleep Medicine, Am. Acad. Sleep Medicine, 2003. Intern, behavioral medicine Brown U. Clin. Psychology Tng. Consortium, Providence, 1999, postdoctoral fellow, behavioral medicine, 1999—2001; staff psychologist, dept. psychiatry RI Hosp., Providence, 2001—04; instr., dept. psychiatry and human behavior Brown Med. Sch., Providence, 2001—02, asst. prof. (rsch.), dept. psychiatry and human behavior, 2002—04; clin. asst. prof., dept. psychiatry U. Mich., 2004—, dir., Behavioral Sleep Medicine Program, 2004—. Tchg. asst., psychology of sleep, dept. psychology Queen's U., Canada, 1992—97, tng. coord., psychology tchg. assts., dept. psychology, Canada, 1997; intern rep. Brown U. Clin. Psychology Tng. Consortium Tng. Com., 1998—99; instr., sleep and chronobiology rsch. Brown U., Providence, 2001; lectr., psychiatry residency tng. program Brown Med. Sch., Providence, 2002, St. Elizabeth's Med. Ctr., Boston, 2002; lectr., gen. psychology Providence Coll., RI, 2003; lectr., pulmonary fellowship tng. program RI Hosp., 2004; invited presenter in field. Ad-hoc reviewer Jour. Sleep Rsch., 1999—2000, Neurology, 1999—2000, Jour. Physiology, 1999—2000, Jour. Applied Physiology, 2003—, Addiction, 2003—, Alcohol, 2003—, reviewer Sleep, 2000—, Behavioral Sleep Medicine, 2003—; contbr. several article to profl. publications. Mem.: Canadian Sleep Soc. (exec.), Soc. Behavioral Medicine, Am. Acad. Sleep Medicine, Am. Psychological Assn., Canadian Psychological Assn., Sleep Rsch. Soc., Canadian Sleep Soc. Office: U Mich Sleep Disorders Ctr Med Inn Bldg Fl 7 Rm C728 1500 E Medical Center Dr Ann Arbor MI 48109-5734

ARNELL, RICHARD ANTHONY, radiologist; b. Chgo., Aug. 21, 1938; s. Tony Frank and Mary Martha (Oberman) Yaki; m. Paula Ann Youngberg, June 28, 1964; children: Carla Ann, Paula Marie, Paul Anthony. BA, Grinnell Coll., 1960; MD, U. Iowa, 1964. Diplomate Am. Bd. Radiology, Am. Bd. Nuc. Medicine. With Moline Radiology Assocs., S.S., 1968—93; v.p. Innc., 1970-78, sec., 1978-90, pres., 1990—93, trustee pension profit plan, 1979-2000; pres. Moline Radiology Assocs., S.C., 1990-93, Advanced Radiology, S.C., 1993-2001, Radiology Assocs., LLC, 2000—01, Advanced Radiology Diagnostic Ctrs., LLC, 2000—01; with Moline Radiology SC; major Med. Coop., USAR, 1964—70. Mem. staff Luth. Hosp., Moline, 1968-88, dir. continuing mem. edn. prog. for physicians, 1979-83, bd. dirs., 1977-83; mem. staff Moline Pub. Hosp., 1968-88, Hammond Henry Dist. Ill., Geneseo, Ill., mem. staff United Med. Ctr., 1989-92, chmn. radiology dept., 1992-94, med. dir. radiology dept., 1992-99; pres. Moline Radiology Assocs., S.S., 1990-93; mem. med. staff Mercer County Hosp., 1994-2003, Ill. Hosp., 1995-2003, Trinity Med. Ctr., 1992-2003, ret., 2003; trustee Midstate Found. for Med. Care, 1976-79, mem. exec. com., 1976-79, v.p. Quad City HMO Health Plan, 1979; clin. lectr. U. Iowa. Pres. Moline Mgmt. Assocs., S.S., 1990—; chmn. mng. com. Metro MRI Ctr., Ltd. Partnership, 1990--; supt. Sunday Ch. Sch. St. John's Ch., Rock Island, Ill., 1974-79, mem. ch. cabinet, 1975-76, del. Chs. United of Scott and Rock Island counties, Ill., 1977; mem. nat. exec. com. Augustana Coll., Rock Island, 1977-81; assoc. chmn. profl. div. United Way, 1985; bd. dirs. Luth. Hosp. Found., 1981-84, pres. 1982-84; bd. dirs. Quad Cities Health Care Resources, Inc., 1984-88; chmn. Luth. Health Care Found., 1984-88, United Health Care Found., 1989-91. Maj. med. USAR, 1964—70. Recipient David Theophillus trophy for outstanding athlete Grinnell Coll., 1960, Dr. of Distinction award Rock Island Med. Soc. Alliance, 1998. Mem. Am. Coll. Radiology, Ill. Radiol. Soc., Am. Coll. Nuc. Medicine, Soc. Nuc. Medicine, AMA, Ill. Med. Soc. (ho. of dels., 1974-79), Rock Island County Med. Soc. (exec. com. 1974-79, peer rev. com. 1975-79), Iowa-Ill. Ctrl. Med. Soc. (pres. 1978), Ctrl. Ill. Med. Assn. (v.p. 1977, pres. 1978), Ind. Physicians Assn. Western Ill. (dir. 1984-86, v.p. 1985, pres. 1986), World Med. Assn., Am. Coll. Med. Imaging, Short Hills Country Club., TPC (Silvis, Ill.). Office: 615 Valley View Dr Ste 101 Moline IL 61265 E-mail: rarny@aol.com.

ARNETT, DONNA K., epidemiologist, educator; MSPH in in Biostatistics & Epidemiology, U. South Fla.; PHD in Epidemiology, UNC, Chapel Hill, 1991. Prof. epidemiology U. Minn., 1994—2004; prof. epidemiology & dept. chmn. U. Ala. Sch. Pub. Health, Birmingham, 2004—. Contbr. scientific papers. Mailing: UAB School of Public Health Dept Epidemiology 1530 3rd Ave S RPHB 217C Birmingham AL 35294-0022 Office: 1665 University Blvd RPHB Rm 220 Birmingham AL 35294-0022 Office Phone: 205-934-7066. Office Fax: 205-975-3329. E-mail: arnett@uab.edu.

ARNETT, FRANK COUCHMAN, JR., retired rheumatologist, educator; b. Salyersville, Ky., Mar. 8, 1942; s. Frank Couchman Arnett and Edna Carol Salyer; m. Lynne Anne Whetstone, Aug. 29, 1965. BA, U. Cin., 1964, MD, 1968. Cert. in internal medicine ABIM, 1972, in rheumatology 1976, in diagnostic immunology 1990. Resident, medicine Johns Hopkins Hosp., Balt., 1968—70, fellow, rheumatology, 1970—72, asst., assoc. prof., medicine, 1975—84; chief, rheumatology Wilford Hall USAFMC, San Antonio, 1972—74; instr., medicine Johns Hopkins U., Balt., 1974—75; dir., divsn. rheumatology U. Tex. Med. Sch., Houston, 1984—2001, prof., internal medicine, 1984—2011, chmn., dept. internal medicine, 2001—04. Mem. PI-NIH CTSA Grant, Houston, 2006—08. Contbr. chapters to books, articles to numerous profl. jours. Adv. com. mem. Arthritis Found., Sjogrens Syndrome Found., Scleroderma Found., Lupus Found. Recipient Best Drs. America award, 2000—, Pres. Scholar Tchg. award, U. Tex. Med. Sch., Houston, 2005, 2009, Disting. Educator award, TIAA-CREF, 2006. Master: ACP, Am. Coll. Rheumatology.

ARNOLD, ANTHONY C., ophthalmologist, educator; MD, UCLA, 1975. Diplomate Am. Bd. Ophthalmology. Prof. ophthalmology Jules Stein Eye Inst., L.A., 1986—, chief neuro-ophthalmology divsn., 1986—, dir. residency program, 1995—; dir. UCLA Optic Neuropathy Ctr., 1991—. Lt. col. USAF, 1971—86. Mem.: Am. Bd. Opthalmology (dir. 2008—), N.Am. Neuro-Oph. Soc. (pres. 2008—), Am. Acad. Ophthalmology. Office: Jules Stein Eye Inst 100 Stein Plz Los Angeles CA 90095

ARNOLD, BARRY RAYNOR, philosophy educator, medical ethicist, counselor; b. Mooresville, NC, Sept. 29, 1951; s. Adrian Leicester and Cleo Agnes (Fisher) A.; m. Margaret Elizabeth Morelock, Aug. 15, 1984. AB cum laude, Davidson Coll., 1973; MDiv magna cum laude, Emory U., 1976, PhD, 1986. Ordained to ministry Presbyn. Ch.; trappist Lay Cistercians of Gethsemani Abbey, cert. Christian clin. counselor Am. Counseling Assn.; lic. mental health counselor, Ind. Min. various parishes, Ga., Fla., 1976—; instr. religion, assoc. chaplain The Lovett Sch., 1980-82; prof. Andrew Coll., Cuthbert, Ga., 1983-84; from asst. prof. to prof. emeritus U. West Fla., Pensacola, 1986—2007, prof. emeritus, 2007—; pvt. practice clin. counseling, Pace, Fla., 1996—; acting chmn. dept. philosophy/religion U. West Fla., Pensacola, 1997—, chmn. dept. interdisciplinary humanities, philosophy, relig., 2000—, exec. dir. Univ. Office for Applied Ethics, 2000—, joint prof. biology and philosophy divsn. life and health scis., 2003—; prof. Bioethics and Philosophy, dir. Ctr. for Health Care Ethics U. West Fla./Sacred Heart Hosp., Pensacola, 2003—; supr. interns in palliative care and bioethics Sacred Heart Hosp., 2004—; dir. Ctr. for Health Care Ethics U. West Fla./Sacred Heart Hosp., 2003—; prof. emeritus biology, allied health U. West Fla., Pensacola, 2007—. Counselor Pace Counseling Ctr., 1996-97; bd. dirs. Unif Ctr. Aging; reviewer med. edn. Coun. Pensacola Fla., 2006—; spkr. in field. Author: The Pursuit of Virtue, 1989; editor: Essays in American Ethics, 1992; gen. editor (11 vols.) The Reshaping of Psychoanalysis, 1992-2002; assoc. editor Explorations: Jour. Adventurous Thought, 1999—; featured as med. ethicist on CBS Radio, 2006; contbr. articles to profl. jours. Bd. dirs. Sacred Heart Hosp., Pensacola, Bapt. Hosp.; mem. instl. rev. bd. U. West Fla., 2006—; bioethicist, bd. dirs. Sacred Heart Hosp., 2003—, com. on palliative care, com. on blood products, com. on intravenous immunoglobulon, 2006—, keynote spkr. geriatric ethics, ann. symposium on best clin. practice, 2009; pres., bd. dirs. Assn. for Retarded Citizens, Albany, Ga., 1978—79; bioethicist, bd. dirs. West Fla. Regional Med. Ctr., Pensacola, 1990—, Bapt. Hosp., 2003—; adv. bd. mem. McGraw Hill Publs. Bioethics, 2010. Recipient Disting. Tchg. award UWF and Fla. State Legislature, 1988, 90, 95, 6 awards UWF, 1986-2007; fellow Rice U., 1973-75, Emory U., 1975-76, 79-82, U. Glasgow, 1976. Fellow: Am. Coll. Counselors (cert. Christian clin. counselor, chair examiners for cert.), Am. Assn. Integrative Medicine (chair nat. bd. 2002—03, diplomate, nat. bd. dirs.), Am. Bd. Child Mental Health Providers; mem.: APA, ACA, APA, Am. Assn. Hospice & Palliative Medicine (acad. adv. bd. bioethics), Assn. for Cognitive Behavioral Therapists (cert. cognitive forensic therapist, cert. anxiety disorders specialist), So. Soc. Philosophy and Psychology, Am. Acad. Religion, Internat. Thomas Merton Soc., Rotary (sgt.-at-arms 1982—83), Phi Beta Kappa, A£D (hon.), Alpha Epsilon Delta, Phi Kappa Phi (sec. 1988). Democrat. Avocation: birdwatching. Home: 5820 Kirkland Dr Milton FL 32570-8251 Office: Univ West Fla 11000 University Pkwy Pensacola FL 32514-5750 Home Phone: 850-626-7556. Business E-Mail: barnold@uwf.edu.

ARNOLD, DAMON THEODORE, state agency administrator, public health service officer; b. Bklyn., Mar. 21, 1957; s. Charles William and Dorothy Sinclair Arnold; m. Sharon Elizabeth Johnson-Arnold, Sept. 6. BS, Howard U., Washington, 1980; MD, U. Ill., Chgo., 1987, MPH, 1992; Massage Therapist, Chgo. Sch. Massage Therapy, 2002. Lic. physician and surgeon Ill. Resident in internal medicine Cook County Hosp., Chgo., 1987—90, resident in occupl. medicine, 1990—92; med. dir. occupl. health svcs. and staff physician St. Francis Hosp. and Health Ctrs., Blue Island, Ill., 1992—96; med. dir. for LTV Steel Co. Corporate Health Dimensions, East Chicago, Ind., 1996—97; med. dir. employee health svc., med. and sci. staff Mercy Hosp. and Med. Ctr., Chgo., 1997—2007; dir. bioterrorism and preparedness Chgo. Dept. Pub. Health; dir. Ill. Dept. Pub. Health, 2007—. Med. rev. officer Med. Rev. Officers Cert. Coun., 1995—. Contbr. articles toprofl. jours. Col. US Army, 1984—, state surgeon, comdr. Army Nat. Guard, Ill. Decorated Army Commendation medals; named Military Hero of Yr., Am. Red Cross, 2007. Mem.: AMA, Ill. State Med. Soc., N.G. Assn. Ill., Chgo. Med. Soc., Am. Legion (life), Soc. of U.S. Army Flight Surgeons (life), Assn. Mil. Surgeons U.S. (life), Am. Massage Therapy Assn., Japanese Karate Assn. (Black Belt). Avocations: oil painting, sculpting, photography, martial arts, poetry. Office: Ill Dept Pub Health 535 W Jefferson St Springfield IL 62761 Office Phone: 217-782-4977. Office Fax: 217-782-3987. Business E-Mail: d.arnold@us.army.mil.

ARNOLD, DIRK, physician, educator; MD, Humboldt U., Berlin, 1995. Cert. oncologist Bd. Berlin, 2002. Physician Charité, Berlin, 1998—2002; asst. prof. Martin Luther U., Halle, Germany, 2003—10, prof. oncology, 2010; med. dir. U. Hamburg-Eppendorf, U. Cancer Ctr., 2010—. Mem.: ESMO, ASCO. Office: University Hamburg-Eppendorf University Cancer Ctr Hamburg Partivistrasse 52 Hamburg 20246 Germany Office Fax: 4940741040190. Business E-Mail: d.arnold@uke.de.

ARNOLD, FRANCES HAMILTON, chemistry educator; b. Pitts., July 25, 1956; d. William Howard and Josephine Inman (Routheau) A.; children: James Howard, William Andrew, Joseph Inman. BS magna cum laude, Princeton U., 1979; PhD in Chem. Engring., U. Calif., Berkeley, 1985. Postdoctoral U. Calif., Berkeley, 1985, Calif. Inst. Tech., Pasadena, 1986, asst. chem. engring., 1987-92, assoc. prof., 1992—96, prof. chem. engring & biochemistry, 1999, Dick and Barbara Dickinson prof. chemical engring. and biochemistry. Vis. assoc. chemistry U. Calif., Berkeley, 1986—87; William Rauscher Lectr. in Chemistry Rensselaer Polytechnic Inst., 1996; Purves Lectr. in Chemistry McGill U., 1998; Lindsay Disting. Lectr. Tex. A&M, 2003; Merck-Frosst Invited Lectr. Biochemistry U. Alberta, 2003; Sir Robert Price Lectr. CSIRO, Melbourne, 2003; Lewis lectr. MIT, 2006; Walker lectr. Pa. State U., 2006; Kelly lectr. Purdue U., 2006; Cruickshank lectr. Gordon Rsch. Confs., 2008; Linnaeus lectr. Uppsala U., 2008; Steenbock lectr. U. Wis., 2008; elec. mem. Nat. Acad. Engring., 2000, Inst. Medicine, 2004, Nat. Acad. Scis., 2008. Contbr. articles to profl. jours. Decorated Garvan Olin medal Am. Chem. Soc.; recipient Office Naval Rsch. Young Investigator award, 1988, NSF Presdl. Young Investigator award, 1989, Van Ness Award, Rensselaer Polytechnic Inst., 1994, Profl. Progress Award, AIChE, 2000, Food Pharms., and Bioengring. Divsn. award, 2005, Enzyme Engring. award, 2007, Excellence in Sci. award, Fedn. Am. Socs. for Exptl. Biology, 2007, award, Tech. Review TR10, 2008, Enzyme Engring. award, Engring. Found., 2007, FASEB Excellence Sci. award, 2007, Walker Lectr., Penn. State U., 2006, Food harm & Bioengring. Divsn. award, AIChE, 2005; named Parr Lectr., Chem. Engring. U. Ill., 2009, Wilhelm Lectrs., Chem. Engring. Princeton U., 2008, Alexander M. Cruickshank Lectr., Gordon Rsch. Confs.,· 2008, Linnaeus Lectr., Uppsala U., 2008, Five Coll. Chemistry Lectr., U. Mass., 2007, Kewaunee Lectr., Duke U. Bioengring., 2007, Lewis Lectrs., Mass. Inst. Tech., 2006, Kelly Lectr., Purdue U., 2006, Dodge Lectr., Chem. Engring. Yale U., 2005, Britton Chance Lectr., Chem. & Bioengring.

U. Penn., 2005, Berkeley Lectrs., Chem. Engring. U.C. Berkeley, 2005; nominee, Nat. Acad. Scis., 2008; grantee David and Lucile Packard fellow, 1989; fellow, Am. Acad. Microbiology, 2009. Mem.: NAS, NAE (Charles Stark Draper prize 2011), AAAS (Sci. Innovation Topical Lectr.), Inst. Medicine, Santa Fe Inst. (Sci. Bd.), Am. Inst. Medical and Biological Engring., Am. Soc. Microbiology, Protein Soc., Am. Inst. Chem. Engrs., Am. Chem. Soc. (David Perlman Lectr. Award, ACS Biochemical Tech. 2003, Carothers award, ACS Del. divsn. 2003, Francis P. Garvan-John M. Olin medal 2005), Tau Beta Pi, Phi Beta Kappa. Achievements include research in protein engineering, directed evolution, biocatalysis, biological circuit design, bioenergy, and evolutionary design methods applied to biological systems; only woman to have been elected to all three membership organizations of the National Academies. Office: Calif Inst Tech Div of Chem & Chem Engring 228B Spalding MC 210-41 Pasadena CA 91125-0001 Office Phone: 626-395-4162. Office Fax: 626-568-8743. E-mail: frances@cheme.caltech.edu. *

ARNOLD, JAMES E., pediatrician, educator; b. East Liverpool, Ohio, Oct. 27, 1947; BS in Pre-medicine, Pa. State U., 1969; MD, U. Tex., San Antonio, 1977. Diplomate Am. Bd. Otolaryngology, lic. Wash., Mass., Ohio. Intern Walter Reed Army Med. Ctr., Washington, 1977—78; resident otolaryngology Fitzsimons Army Med. Ctr., Aurora, Colo., 1978—82; fellow pediatric otolaryngology Children's Hosp., Boston, 1986—87; chief divsn. pediatric otolaryngology Rainbow Babies & Children's Hosp., Cleve., 1987—2000; assoc. prof. otolaryngology - head & neck surgery & pediat. Case Western Res. U. Sch. Medicine, Cleve., 1994—99, prof., 1999—, Julius W. McCall prof. & chmn. otolaryngology - head & neck surgery, 2000—; vice chmn. otolaryngology - head & neck surgery Univ. Hospitals, Cleve., 1994—2000, dir. otolaryngology - head & neck surgery, 2000—, prof. pediat., 2000—. Clin. instr. dept. otolaryngology U. Wash. Sch. Medicine, Seattle, 1982—86, Harvard Med. Sch., Boston, 1986—87; med. profl. adv. com. Achievement Ctr. for Children, Cleve., 1990—98. Contbr. articles to profl. jours., chapters to books. Medic, med. lab. technician, instr. med. lab. procedures US Army, 1970—73, staff otolaryngologist, asst. chief otolaryngology - head & neck surgery svc., 1982—86, Madigan Army Med. Ctr., Tacoma, Wash., acting chief svc., 1985—86, Madigan Army Med. Ctr. Recipient Samuel S. Horowitz award for clin. excellence, Rainbow Babies & Children's Hosp.; named to Best Doctors in America, Woodward/White, Inc. Fellow: Am. Acad. Pediat., Am. Acad. Otolaryngology - Head & Neck Surgery (mem. com. infections disease 1992—98, mem. com. sleep disorders 1992—98); mem.: Am. Broncho-Esophagological Assn., Am. Soc. Pediatric Otolaryngology, Inc. (mem. audit com. 1992—95, mem. nominating com. 1992, 1998), Northern Ohio Otolaryngology - Head & Neck Soc. (pres. 1993—94), Northern Ohio Pediatric Soc. Office: UH Case Med Ctr 11100 Euclid Ave Cleveland OH 44106 also: UH Chagrin Highlands Health Ctr 3909 Orange Pl Beachwood OH 44122 also: UH Westlake Health Ctr 960 Clague Rd Westlake OH 44145 Office Phone: 216-844-5031. Office Fax: 216-844-5727. Business E-Mail: james.arnold@uhhs.com.

ARNOLD, JAMES H., cosmetic dentist; m. Sarah Arnold, 1998; children: Julia, Sophia, Ethan, Matthew. BS in Biology, Ind. U., Bloomington, 1992; DDS, Ind. U., Indpls., 1996. Clin. mentor Hornbrook Group; owner Smiles By Arnold & Assocs. Advanced tng. Dawson Acad., Esthetic Epitome, LAs Vegas Inst. for Advanced Dental Studies, Pacific Aesthetic Continuum, The Hornbrook Group, The Pankey Inst., World Clin. Laser Inst.; chmn. Northwest Ind.'s Dental Peer Rev. Com. Bd. dir. Northwest Ind. Dental. Found., 2003—; vol. Hilltop Neighborhood House. Named Cosmetic Dentistry Expert, Med. News Now Inc., 2004. Fellow: Pierre Fauchard Acad., Am. Acad. Cosmetic Dentistry (PArtners in Peace award 2008); mem.: Ind. Dental Assn. (strategic planning com., coun. new dentists), Northwest Ind. Dental Soc. (bd. dirs. 1999—), Porter County Dental Soc. (v.p. 1996—98), Acad. Comprehensive Esthetics (bd. dirs. 2004—09, internat. fellowship com. chmn. 2006—08), ADA, Acad. Gen. Dentistry, Crown Coun., Mensa Soc. (life). Office: Smiles By Arnold & Associates 1830 S 11th St Chesterton IN 46304 Office Phone: 219-926-5445. Office Fax: 219-921-1234.

ARNOLD, JANET NINA, health facility administrator, consultant; b. Poughkeepsie, NY, Apr. 23, 1933; d. Paul Dudley and Pauline Katherine (Board) Bartram; m. Robert William Arnold, Dec. 19, 1954; children: Paul Dudley, Janet Elizabeth. AB cum laude, Vassar Coll., 1955; postgrad. Sch. Med. Tech., Albany Med. Coll., 1955—56; MS Microbiology cum laude, Vassar Coll., 1963; MHSM, Webster Coll., 1981. Rsch. asst., med. technologist H. Aird Boswell, M.D., Troy, NY, 1956—59; tchg. supr., adminstrv. cons. Vassar Bros. Hosp., Poughkeepsie, 1959—69; asst. adminstr., lab. mgr. Boulder Meml. Hosp., Colo., 1975—80; cons. hosp. planning Mercy Med. Ctr., Denver, 1981—82; clin. lab. dir., adminstr. Humana, Denver, 1982—85, dir. MRI, 1985—2006. Cons. health care mgmt. Humana, Inc., 1982-96, Columbia/HCA Health Sys., 1992-96; pres. Arnold and Assocs., 1988—; acad./adminstrv. cons. U. Guam, Vassar Coll., Boulder Cmty. Hosp., Humana Int., 1990-97; adj. faculty Vassar Coll., adv. to med. lab., lectr. med. mycology, 1961-66, tchg. fellow 1961-63, chmn. unrestricted fund raising, 1989-96, co-chair major gifts, 2000-05; sec., bd. dirs. Sanitas Fed. Credit Union, 1977-78, pres., 1979-82 Assoc. editor Am. Jour. Med. Tech., 1980-88; contbr. articles to profl. jours Contbr. NMC, 1988-92 NSF rsch. fellow, 1960-62 Mem. Am. Acad. Microbiology, Soc. for Gen. Microbiology, Am. Soc. Med. Technologists, Colo. Pub. Health Assn., Soc. Women Environ. Profls., Med. Mycological Soc. Ams Republican. Episcopalian. Office Phone: 717-464-8536. Personal E-mail: r-j-arnold-assoc@att.net.

ARNOLD, JEAN ANN, health science facility administrator; b. Coronado, Calif., Nov. 17, 1948; d. Scott Crittenden Daubin and Barbara Jean (Spooner) Annowada; m. Lonnie Lea Arnold, July 14, 1973; children: Danielle Louise and Casey Jean (twins). Student, Santa Barbara City Coll., Calif., 1966—67, U. Wyo., Laramie, 1968—69; BS in Allied Health Scis./Health Svcs. Adminstrn., Weber State U., 1995. Registered Technol., LIc. Technol., Calif., Wash. Staff technol. x-ray Mt. Auburn Hosp., Cambridge, Mass., 1971-72, Victor Valley Hosp., Victorville, Calif., 1972-74, Fairfield Hosp., Calif., 1974-76; chief technol. Oakridge Med. Group, Roseville, Calif., 1976-78; staff technol. radiation therapy U. Cancer Ctr., U. Hosp., Seattle, 1979-84; staff technol. Providence Med. Ctr., Seattle, 1984; relief technol. UCSD Med. Ctr., San Diego, 1984-85; staff technol. Scripps Meml. Hosp., La Jolla, Calif., 1984-87, dir. radiation oncology, 1987—95; mgr. radiation oncology Deaconess Med. Ctr., Spokane, 1995—98, St. Alphonsus Regional Med. Ctr., Boise, Idaho, 1999—. Clin. coord., instr. San Diego Radiation Therapy Tech. Edn. Program. Producer Video, Occpl. Radiation Safety 1988. Mem. Soc. for Radiation Oncology Adminstrs., Calif. Soc. Radiologic Technologists, Am. Soc. Radiologic Technologists, Am. Registry Radiologic Technologists (job analysis adv. com., radiation therapy exam. com., item writer Therapy Tech.). Republican. Baptist.

ARNOLD, PHILLIP GORDON, plastic surgeon; b. Lincolnton, NC, Sept. 14, 1941; s. A.F. and Geneva Arnold; m. Susan BonDurant; children: Phillip, Peter. BS, Davidson Coll., NC, 1962; MD, U. NC, 1967. Diplomate Am. Bd. Plastic Surgery. Intern, resident NC Meml. Hosp., Chapel Hill, 1971-74; resident Emory U. Affialiated Hosps., Atlanta, 1974-76; pvt. practice medicine, plastic surgery Rochester, Minn., 1976—. Assoc. prof. plastic surgery Mayo Clinic, Rochester, 1983—, chief emeritus, dept. plastic surgery. Contbr. articles to profl. jours. Served with US Army, 1969—71, Vietnam. Decorated Bronze Star, Svc. Cross. Fellow: ACS; mem.: Northwestern Soc. Plastic Surgeons, Internat. Assn. Plastics Surgeons, So. Surg. Assn., Am. Assn. Plastic Surgeons, Am. Soc. Plastic & Reconstructive Surgeons. Avocations: fishing, hunting. Office: Mayo Clinic Dept Plastic Surgery 200 1st St SW Rochester MN 55905

ARNOLD, ROBERT M., internist; b. Vancouver, Wash., Nov. 12, 1957; s. Stanley Arnold and Joan (Gleitsman) Huber; m. Nancy Levine, Dec. 5, 1996; children: Hillel, Shula, Brandon, Kirsten. Cert. med. ethics practicum, U. Tenn., Memphis, 1980; student, U. Tenn., Knoxville, 1981; BA in Biology and Philosophy, U. Mo., Kansas City, 1983, MD, 1983. Lic. physician, Pa.; diplomate Am. Bd. Internal Medicine, Hospice Palliative Medicine Bd., Am. Acad. Hospice and Palliative Medicine. Gen. internal medicine resident R.I. Hosp., Providence, 1983-86; Robert Wood Johnson Found. clin. scholar U. Pa., Phila., 1986-88; fellow in pub. and health policy Kellogg Found., 1987; dir. clin. ethics tng. program U. Pitts. Sch. Medicine, 1988—, dir. fellowship in med. ethics, 1988—, asst. prof. divsn. gen. internal medicine, 1988-93, clin. coord. primary care internal medicine residency, 1990-93, asst. prof. dept. psychiatry, 1990—, assoc. dir. edn. Ctr. for Bioethics and Health Law, 1992—, dir. Primary Care Residency Tng. Program, 1993-96, assoc. prof. medicine divsn. gen. internal medicine, 1994—, dir. ambulatory edn. divsn. gen. medicine, 1994-96, chief sect. palliative care and med. ethics. Staff physician Pitts. AIDS Ctr. for Treatment; co-instr. U. Mo., Kansas City Sch. Medicine, 1980-81; grad. asst. U. Tenn., Knoxville, 1981; instr. Brown U. Program in Medicine, 1985; founder, co-dir. curriculum in med. ethics gen. internal medicine residency program R.I. Hosp., 1984-86; co-organizer, instr. ethics component of introduction to clin. medicine Brown U. Program in Medicine, 1985-86; instr. seminar in med. ethics U. Pa. Sch. Medicine, 1986-88; mem. data safety and monitoring bd. peripheral arterial disease-pilot study Nat. Heart, Lung and Blood Inst., 1993; abstractor APDIM Ednl. Clearinghouse Tchg. Med. Ethics, 1989—, Miles Annotated Bibliography Doctor-Patient Comm.-Med. Ethics, 1992; lectr. various univs., orgns., hosps.; mem. cons. ethics and human rights com. Presbyn. U. Hosp., 1988—, ethics cons., 1991—; preceptor summer premed. acad. enrichment program, 1991—; mem. faculty Ctr. for Bioethics and Health Law Continung Edn. Program, 1992—; staff physician Rainbow Free Care Clinic, Pitts., 1992—. Author: (with C.W. Lidz and L. Fischer) The Erosion of Autonomy in Long-Term Care, 1992; mem. editl. bd. Jour. Gen. Internal Medicine, 1990-94; reviewer Am. Jour. Hosp. Pharmacy, Am. Jour. Medicine, Annals Internal Medicine, Archives Internal Medicine, Chest, Clin. Rsch., Digestive Diseases and Scis., Hastings Center Report, Jour. AMA, Jour. Am. Geriatrics Soc., Jour. Clin. Ethics, Jour. Gen. Internal Medicine, Kennedy Inst. Jour. Ethics, Milbank Meml. Quart., Oxford U. Press, Social Sci. and Medicine; contbr. articles to profl. jours., chpts. to books. Pres. SHHV, 1996; Am. Acad. Hospice and Palliative Medicine, 2005. Recipient Vice Chancellor award for outstanding cmty. svc., 1983, Mosby Book award, 1983; grantee Brown U., Providence, R.I., 1984-85, Pub. Health Svcs., DHHS, Washington, 1984, AIDS Commn., Phila., 1988, Richard K. Mellon Found., 1990, McArthur Found., 1989-90, Agy. for Health Care Policy Rsch., 1990-93, Nat. Ctr. for Nursing Rsch., 1992-95, HRSA, 1992, Greenwall Foudn., 1992, Agy. for Health Care Policy Rsch., 1993-97. Mem. ACP, APHA, Am. Acad. on Doctor and Patient, Am. Geriatric Soc. (legis. affairs com. Pa. chpt. 1992), Am. Fedn. Clin. Rsch., Am. Med. Women's Assn., Assn. Practical and Profl. Ethics, Carol F. Reynolds Hist. Soc., Physicians for Human Rights, Physicians for Nat. Health Program, Physicians for Social Responsibility (nat. bd. dirs. 1986-90, nat. treas. exec. com. 1989-90, mem. Pitts. steering com. 1988-91, chmn. 1990-91), Soc. Bioehtics Consultation, Soc. Gen. Internal Medicine (co-chmn. ethics com. 1994-95), Soc. Health and Human Values (resident interest group 1985-88, 91-94, reviewer nat. meeting 1988-89, nat. program coord. 1991-92, treas., sec. 1990-92, mem. coun. 1989-92, pres.-elect 1996, pres. 1997), Phi Kappa Phi, Omega Delta Kappa. Office: U Pitts Div Gen Int Med Pitts AIDS Ctr for Treatment 3601 Fifth Ave Pittsburgh PA 15213 also: Ctr Med Ethics Med Arts Bldg Ste 300 3708 5th Ave Pittsburgh PA 15213-3415 Office Phone: 412-647-7228.

ARNON, RUTH, immunologist, educator, researcher; b. Tel Aviv, June 1, 1933; MS, Hebrew U., Jerusalem, 1955, PhD, 1960. Rsch. assoc. Rockefeller Inst., NYC, 1960-62, Weizmann Inst. Sci., Rehovot, Israel, 1963—66, sr. scientist, 1966-71, assoc. prof. immunology, 1971-75, prof., 1975—. Vis. prof. microbiology UCLA, 1977—78. Contbr. articles to profl. jours. Decorated Legion of Honor France; recipient Robert Koch prize, 1979, Jimenez Diaz Gold medal, 1979, Wolf Round. prize in medicine, Israel, 1998, Rothschild prize in biology, 1998, Israel prize in medicine, 2001; Fogarty scholar, NIH, 1996—98. Mem.: Am. Philosophical Soc. (elected. mem. 2009), Assn. of Acads. Scis. Asia (pres. 2004—06), European Molecular Biology Orgn., Internat. Union Immunological Socs. (sec. gen. 1989—92), European Fedn. Immunological Socs. (pres. 1983—86), Israel Acad. Scis. & Humanities (chmn. sci. divsn. 1995—2001, v.p. 2004—), Israel Biochem. Soc. (pres. 1981—83), Israel Soc. Immunology (sec. 1972—77). Achievements include development of the multiple sclerosis drug Copaxone. Office: Weizmann Inst Sci Wolfson Bldg Rm 431A 76100 Rehovot Israel Home: 9 Shine Residence 76100 Rehovot Israel Office Phone: 972 8 934 4017. Fax: 972 8 947 4141. Business E-Mail: ruth.arnon@weizmann.ac.il. *

ARNON, STEPHEN S., physician, research scientist; b. Oakland, Calif., Oct. 14, 1946; s. Daniel I. and Lucile S. Arnon; m. Joyce M. Meissinger, Aug. 24, 1985; children: Eric, Christina. AB, Harvard U., 1968, MPH, 1972, MD, 1973. Lic. physician Calif. Resident physician U. Colo. Hosps., Denver, 1973—75; med. epidemiologist Ctrs. for Disease Control, Atlanta, 1975—76, Berkeley, Calif., 1976—77; founder, chief infant botulism treatment and prevention program Calif. Dept. Public Health, Berkeley and Richmond, 1977—. Contbr. articles and book chpts. to profl. publs. Bd. dirs. Orinda (Calif.) Pks. and Recreation Found., Orinda, 1992—. Lt. comdr. USPHS, 1975—77. Recipient Jens Aubrey Westengard and John Houghton Taylor scholarships, Harvard Med. Sch., 1968—73, Wiley medal, U.S. Pub. Health Svc., 1998, Therapeutic Achievement award, Nat. Orgn. for Rare Disorders, 2004. Fellow: Am. Coll. Epidemiology, Infectious Disease Soc. Am. Achievements include creation and development of public service orphan drug Botulism Immune Globulin Intravenous (Human) BabyBIG (registered) for treatment of infant botulism; research in orphan drug development; medical and public health management of botulinum toxin if used as bioweapon. Office: Calif Dept Public Health 850 Marina Bay Pkwy Richmond CA 94804 Office Phone: 510-231-7600. Business E-Mail: stephen.arnon@cdph.ca.gov.

ARNOTT, HOWARD JOSEPH, biology professor, dean; b. LA, Mar. 9, 1928; s. Andrew Hugh and Evelyn Leonore (Donnelly) A.; m. Wanda Jean Cross, Jan. 28, 1950; children: John Joseph, Catherine Jean Arnott-Thornton, Susan Leonore Arnott Garrett, Virginia Anne Arnott Scott. AB, U. So. Calif., 1952, MS, 1953; PhD, U. Calif., Berkeley, 1958. Asst. prof. biology Northwestern U., Evanston, Ill., 1958-64; assoc. prof. dept. botany U. Tex., Austin, 1965-68, prof., 1968-72, acting chmn. dept., 1970-71; prof., chmn. dept. biology U. So. Fla., Tampa, 1972-74; dean Coll. Sci. U. Tex., Arlington, 1974-90, prof. biology, 1974-91, Ashbel Smith prof. biology, 1991-96, dir. Ctr. for Electron Microscopy Coll. Sci., 1984—, Jenkins Garrett prof. biology emeritus, dean sci. emeritus, 1996—. Vis. mem. dept. biology Tex. A&M U., 1971-75; cons. Ency. Brit. Films, NASA, Alcon Labs., Frito-Lay; bd. dirs. Ft. Worth Nature Ctr., 1985-91; chmn. 2nd Gordon Conf. Calcium Oxalate, 1989, main spkr. 4th Conf., 1993; vis. prof. Purdue U., 1990-91; Bessey lectr. Iowa State U., 1993; visitor Lab. Tree-Ring Rsch., U. Ariz., Tucson, 2006, 07. Advisory editor: Protoplasma; Contbr. articles, abstracts to sci. jours., chpts. to books. With USN, 1946-48. Recipient award for disting. and continued research U. Tex. at Arlington, 1984; postdoctoral fellow U. Tex., NIH, 1964-65; NSF grantee, 1963-65, NIH grantee, 1989. Mem. Am. Soc. Plant Physiology, Bot. Soc. Am., Mycol. Soc. Am., Microscopy Soc. Am., Tex. Soc. Microscopy (hon., pres. 1988-89), Sigma Xi (bd. dirs. S.W. region 1984-91), Phi Sigma (Spl. award 2005). Office Phone: 817-272-2413. Business E-Mail: arnott@uta.edu.

ARNSTEIN, NELSON BARRITT, nuclear medicine physician, educator; s. Benjamin Simon and Vera Daphne (Barritt-Vane) Arnstein. BA, Pomona Coll., 1975; MD, Mt. Sinai, 1979. Diplomate Am. Bd. Nuc. Medicine. Intern L.I. Jewish Med. Ctr., 1979—80; resident in radiation oncology Johns Hopkins, 1980—81; resident in nuc. medicine Georgetown U., 1982—83; fellow nuc. medicine U. Mich., 1984—85; asst. prof. U. So. Calif., LA, 1985—92, assoc. prof., 1992—95; med. officer FDA, Rockville, Md., 1996—2002; chief nuc. medicine Kaiser Permanente, Bellflower, Calif., 2002—. Area radiation safety officer Kaiser, Bellflower, 2002—. Contbr. articles to profl. jours. Mem.: Soc. Nuc. Medicine. Avocations: photography, astronomy, maritime and aerospace history, track and field. Office: 9333 Imperial Havy Downey CA 90242 Home Phone: 562-437-2243; Office Phone: 562-657-7302. Personal E-mail: Arnstein4@aol.com. Business E-Mail: nbarnstein@kp.org.

ARON, ALAN MILFORD, pediatric neurology educator; b. White Plains, NY, Oct. 15, 1933; s. Henri Jordan and Rosalind (Weinstein) A.; m. Sarah Deborah Bornstein, Dec. 29, 1963; children: Alexandra, Abigail, Adam. BS, Tufts U., 1954; MD, Columbia U., 1958. Diplomate Am. Bd. Pediatrics, Am. Bd. Psychiatry and Neurology with spl. competence in child neurology. Intern Grace New Haven Hosp. and Yale Med. Ctr., 1958-59; resident in pediatrics Babies Hosp. Columbia Presbyn. Med. Ctr., NYC, 1959-61; Fellow Columbia Presbyn. Med. Ctr. and Neurologic Inst., NYC, 1961—64; pediatric neurologist Mt. Sinai Hosp., NYC; dir. child neurology Mt. Sinai Sch. Medicine, NYC, 1975—, prof. pediatrics and neurology, 1982—. Pres. N.Y. Pediatric Soc., N.Y.C., 1980-81. Contbr. articles to profl. jours. Recipient Lucy Moses award Clin. Research Neurologic Inst., N.Y.C., 1964. Mem. AMA, Am. Acad. Pediatrics, Am. Acad. Neurology, Child Neurology Soc., Tri-State Child Neurology Soc. (pres. 1990-91), Profs. Child Neurology, Phi Beta Kappa. Democrat. Jewish. Avocations: music, piano, opera, antiques, art. Office: Mt Sinai Sch Medicine 5 E 98th St New York NY 10029-6501 Home Phone: 914-834-4881; Office Phone: 212-831-4393. E-mail: amaronmd@aol.com.

ARONCHICK, CRAIG, gastroenterologist; MD, Temple U. Diplomate Am. Bd. Internal Medicine, 1981, cert. gastrointestinal medicine 1984. Intern Temple Univ. Hosp., resident; fellow Pa. Univ. Hosp.; hosp. affiliation includes Pa. Hosp.; gastroenterologist Pa. Hosp. Gastrointestinal Assocs. Ltd. Named recognized, Best Doctors in America, 2003—04, 2005—06; named one of the Top Doctors, Phila. Mag., 2004—07, 2009—11, the Top Doctors in America, 2007—08, 2010. Mem.: ACP, Am. Gastroenterology Assn. Office: Pennsylvania Hospital Gastrointestinal Associates Limited Washington Square Endoscopy Center 4th Fl W Washington Square Philadelphia PA 19106 Office Phone: 800-789-7366.

ARONEY, CONSTANTINE NICHOLAS, cardiologist, researcher; b. Brisbane, Australia, Oct. 18, 1956; s. Nicholas and Chryssa Aroney; m. Patricia Aroney; children: Chris-Anne, NIcholas, Elizabeth, Stephanie. MB, BS, U. Queensland, Brisbane, 1979, MD, 1991. Cert. cardiologist Queensland Med. Bd., 1986. Cardiology registrar Royal Hobart Hosp., 1984, Royal Brisbane Hosp., 1985, Prince Charles Hosp., 1986; cardiology fellow Mass. Gen. Hosp., Boston, 1987—89; dir. coronary care unit Prince Charles Hosp., Brisbane, 1991—2005; dir. cardiology Holy Spirit Northside Hosp., Brisbane, 2001—. Contbr. chapters to books, articles to profl. jours. Named Queensland Whistleblower of Yr., Whistleblowers Action Group Queensland, 2005, Mem. Order Australia, Commonwealth Australia, 2007; Overseas Clin. fellow, Heart Found. Australia, 1987. Mem.: Heart Found. Australia (chmn. clin. issues com. 2001—04, chmn. writing group guidelines mgmt. acute coronary syndrome), Cardiac Soc. Australia and New Zealand (mem. sci. com. 1996—, chmn. interventional working group 1995—2001). Achievements include first to describe a new disease Familial Restrictive Cardiomyopathy 1988; performed world's youngest reported angioplasty on a 3 year old girl in 1997; performed first balloon valvuloplasty, percutaneous ASD closure, alcohol septal ablation in Queensland; established linearity of the end-systolic pressure-volume relation in patients with severe heart failure. Home: 18 Rosanne St Brisbane QLD 4034 Australia Office: Holy Spirit Northside Hospital Rode Rd 4032 Brisbane QLD Australia Personal E-mail: conar@bigpond.net.au.

ARONIN, JEFFREY S., pharmaceutical executive; b. 1967; BS in Mktg., Northern Ill. U., 1989; MBA, DePaul U. Mktg. and bus. devel. leadership positions Carter-Wallace, Inc.; v.p. bus. devel. and v.p. mktg. Am. Health Products Corp.; chmn., pres., CEO PhytoMedical Technologies, Inc.; pres., CEO RxMarketing; chmn., CEO MedCare Technologies; founder, pres., CEO Ovation Pharmaceuticals, Inc., 2000—09; pres., CEO Lundbeck Inc., 2009; chmn., CEO Paragon Pharmaceuticals, Inc., 2009—. Bd. dirs. Discover Fin. Svcs., 2007—; lectr. De Paul U., Northwestern U., U. Chgo. Grad. Sch. Bus.; spl. advisor Merrick Ventures, LLC. Mem. Hillary Clinton for Pres., Young Presidents' Orgn.; bd. dirs. The Pharm. Rsch. and Mfrs. of America (PhRMA), The Chgo. Entrepreneurial Ctr., The Mus. of Sci. and Industry, Juvenile Diabetes Rsch. Found., Epilepsy Found. of America. Named 100 Most Inspiring People in the Life-Sciences Industry, PharmaVOICE Mag., 40 Most Influential People Under 40, 2004, Who's Who in Healthcare, Crain's Chgo. Bus., 2007; recipient Chgo. Entrepreneurship Hall of Fame, 2005, Entrepreneur of the Yr., Ernst & Young, 2006. Office: Paragon Pharmaceuticals Inc 9 Parkway N Deerfield IL 60015 Office Phone: 224-515-3500. Office Fax: 224-515-3510. *

ARONNE, LOUIS J., internist; b. Bklyn., Sept. 8, 1955; Grad., Trinity Coll.; MD, Johns Hopkins U., 1981. Cert. Internal Medicine, 1984. Resident in internal medicine Albert Einstein Coll. Medicine, NYC; Henry J. Kaiser Family Found. fellow in gen. internal medicine Cornell U. Med. Coll. and the NY Hosp., 1984—86; clin. prof. medicine, attending physician NY-Presbyn. Hosp./Weill Cornell Med. Ctr., NYC, founder, dir. Comprehensive Weight Control Prog., 1986—; adj. prof. medicine Columbia U. Coll. Physicians and Surgeons, NYC. Recipient Davidoff prize, Albert Einstein Coll. Medicine, Elliot Hochstein award, Weill Cornell Med. Coll.; named one of Best Doctors, NY Mag., 2009. Fellow: ACP; mem.: N.Am. Assn. for the Study of Obesity (pres. 2004—08), Phi Beta Kappa, Alpha Omega Alpha. Office: 1165 York Ave New York NY 10065 Office Phone: 212-583-1000. Office Fax: 212-832-9495.

ARONOFF, GEORGE RODGER, medicine and pharmacology educator; b. Peoria, Ill., Mar. 6, 1950; BA in Chemistry with distinction, Ind. U., 1972; MD with honors, Ind. U., Indpls., 1975, MS in Pharmacology, 1984. Diplomate Am. Bd. Internal Medicine; diplomate Am. Bd. Internal Medicine Nephrology. Intern in internal medicine Ind. U., Indpls., 1975-76, resident, 1976-77, clin. fellow div. nephrology, 1977-78, chief resident in internal medicine Wishard Meml. Hosp., 1978-79, rsch. fellow div. nephrology, 1979-80, instr. phys. diagnosis, 1977-78, instr. medicine, 1978-79, from asst. prof. to assoc. prof. medicine, 1980-87, assoc. prof. pharmacology, 1985-87; prof. medicine, prof. pharmacology U. Louisville, 1987—; mem. staff Univ. Louisville (Ky.) Hosp., 1987—. Fellow in clin. pharmacology Eli Lilly & Co., Indpls., 1979-80. Contbr. numerous articles and abstracts to profl. jours. Fellow ACP; mem. Am. Soc. Nephrology, Cen. Soc. Clin. Rsch., Ky. State Med. Assn., Jefferson County Med. Soc. (editorial bd. Louisville Medicine 1989-92, editor 1990), Renal Physicians Assn., Nat. Kidney Found., Phi Eta Sigma, Phi Lambda Upsilon, Phi Beta Kappa, Alpha Omega Alpha, Sigma Xi. Office: U Louisville Kidney Disease Program 615 S Preston St Louisville KY 40202-1715

ARONOW, WILBERT SOLOMON, physician, educator; b. NYC, Oct. 30, 1931; s. Simon and Bella (Safrin) A.; m. Ina Gloria Brody, Sept. 20, 1958; children: Michael Steven, Janice Susan. BS, Queens Coll., Flushing, 1953; MD, Harvard U., Cambridge, Mass., 1957. Diplomate Am. Bd. Internal Medicine. Intern Michael Reese Hosp. and Med. Ctr., Chgo., 1957-58, resident, 1958-61; practice medicine specializing in internal medicine and cardiology; cardiologist, chief Noninvasive Cardiovascular Lab., Long Beach VA Hosp., Calif., 1964-72, chief cardiovascular diseases Calif., 1973-82, asst. chief medicine for rsch. Calif., 1975-80; asso. prof. medicine U. Calif., Irvine, 1972-75, prof. medicine, 1975-82, prof. cmty. and environ. medicine, 1975-82, prof. pharmacology and therapeutics, 1976-82, vice chief cardiovascular divsn., chief cardiovascular rsch., 1974-82; prof. medicine, chief cardiovascular rsch. Creighton U., Omaha, 1982-84; chief Cardiology Clinic Westchester Med. Ctr./NY Med. Coll., Valhalla, NY, 2001—, sr. assoc. program dir., Cardiology Fellowship Program, 2001—, sr. assoc. program dir., rsch. mentor, Pediology Fellowship Program, 2004—, sr. assoc. dir., Ctr. Ednl. Internship Project Quality Rsch., 2009—; vis. prof. med. U. Calif., 2008, U. Ala., Birmingham, 2008. Vis. prof. U. Tex. Southwestern Med. Sch., Dallas, 1976, U. Man., 1979, U. Toronto, 1979, Tex. Tech U. Sch. Medicine, Lubbock, 1983, U. Medicine and Dentistry of NJ-Rutgers Med. Sch., 1983; vis. prof. geriat. U. Rochester Sch. Medicine, 1999; staff cardiology svc. St. Joseph Hosp., Omaha, 1982—84; mem. ad hoc sci. ad. coms. FDA, 1970—72, mem. cardiovascular and renal adv. com., 1973—76; chmn. spl. rev. com. Nat. Cancer Inst., 1980; mem. subcom. smoking, co chmn. Am. Heart Assn., 1980—83; med. dir. Hebrew Hosp. Home, 1984—2001; adj. prof. geriat. and adult devel. Mt. Sinai Sch. Medicine, 1992—; clin. prof. medicine NY Med. Coll., 2001—; chief cardiology clinic Westchester Med. Ctr./NY Med. Coll., 2001—, sr. assoc. program dir., rsch. mentor residency fellowship programs dept. medicine, 2003—; cons. in field. Mem. editl. bd. Jour. Pharmacology an Exptl. Therapeutics, guest field editor, 1981, mem. editl. bd. Am. Jour. Cardiology, 1980—82, Jour. Circulation, 1980—83, E R Reports, 1981—84, Physician's Drug Alert, 1982—, Jour. Cardiovascular and Pulmonary Technique, 1983—86, Clin. Pharmacology and Therapeutics, 1977—83, Jour. ACC, 1982—83, Drugs and Aging, 1990—, Am. Jour. Noninvasive Cardiology, 1986—95, Jour. Cardiovascular Diagnosis and Procedures, 1992—, Preventive Cardiology, 1998—2010, Jour. Am. Med. Dirs. Assn., 1999—2004; mem. editl. bd.: Jour. Am. Med. Dirs. Assn., 2006—; mem. editl. bd. Caring for the Ages, 1999—2001, Jour. Gerontology: Med. Scis., 2000—08, Heart Disease, 2000—03, Geriatrics, 2001—09, Cardiology in Rev., 2006—, Jour. Cardiac Failure, 2007—10, Comprehensive Therapy, 2006—10, Jour. Ger Cardiol, 2007—, Arch Med. Sci., 2007—, Open Aging Jour., 2007—, Integrated Blood Pressure Control, 2008—, Jour. Heart Disease, 2007—, Open Longevity Scis., 2008—, Open Jour. Cardiology, 2009—, World Jour. Cardiology, 2009—, Am. Jour. Medicine, 2009—, Modern Medicine Com., 2009, Cardiovasc. Continuum, 2010—, Open Geriat. Medicine Jour., 2010—, Jour. Clin. Exptl. Cardiology, 2010—, Jour. Surg. Sci., 2010—, Jour. Biol. Medicine, 2010—, Jour. Surg. Heart, 2010—, Jour. Aging Health, 2010—, Internat. Scholarly Rsch. Network Cardiology, 2010—, Jour. Allergy and Therapy, 2011—, Jour. Diofetes & Metabolism, 2011—; contbr. articles to profl. jours. Served to capt., M.C. AUS, 1961-63. Fellow: ACP, Soc. Geriatric Cardiology (chmn. program com. 1993—2003, bd. dirs. 1994—2000), Coun. Clin. Cardiology, Am. Coll. Chest Physicians (gov. So. Calif. 1977—83, vice chmn. coronary disease sect. 1978—79, chmn. coronary disease sect. 1979—81, mem. exec. coun. 1979—81, chmn. forum on cardiovasc. disease 1980—81, sec. coun. on govs. 1981—82, vice chmn. gov.'s coun.), Gerontol. Soc. Am., Am. Geriatrics Soc., Am. Coll. Cardiology (co-chair); mem.: Am. Heart Assn., Am. Coll. Cardiology (Expert Consensus Document on Hypertension Elderly 2009—11), Am. Heart Assn. (co-chair), Am. Soc. Preventive Cardiology (mem. bd. dirs.), Orange County Heart Assn. (dir. 1979—81), Long Beach Heart Assn. (dir. 1972—75), Assn. VA Cardiologists (pres. 1975—77), Am. Fedn. Med. Rsch., Am. Soc. Clin. Pharmacology and Therapeutics (chmn. cardiovasc. and pulmonary diseases sect. 1973—74, 1975—77), Phi Beta Kappa. Jewish. Achievements include patents for cardiovascular drug discovery. Home: 23 Pebbleway Rd New Rochelle NY 10804-3914 Office: Westchester Med Ctr/NY Med Coll Cardiology Divsn Macy Pavilion Rm 138 Valhalla NY 10595 Office Phone: 914-493-5311. Personal E-mail: wsaronow@aol.com.

ARONSON, CARL EDWARD, pharmacology and toxicology educator; b. Providence, Mar. 14, 1936; s. Carl Ivar and Ruth (Workman) A.; m. Marjorie Peck Boutelle, Dec. 17, 1960; children— Linda J., Kristen L. AB, Brown U., Providence, 1958; PhD, U. Vt., Burlington, 1966; MA, U. Pa., Phila., 1973. Asst. prof. pharmacology U. Pa. Sch. Medicine, Phila., 1971-75, assoc. prof. pharmacology, 1975-92; asst. prof. pharmacology and toxicology dept. animal biology U. Pa. Sch. Vet. Medicine, Phila., 1971-73, head labs. of pharmacology and toxicology, 1972-86, assoc. prof. pharmacology and toxicology, 1973-96; retired to emeritus status, 1996; instrument specialist, dept. chemistry Haverford (Pa.) Coll., 1996—. Editor Veterinary Pharmaceuticals and Biologicals, 1978-83, 85-86; contbr. chpts. to books, articles to profl. jours. Active local sch. dist. coms. and other civic assns. 1st lt. USAFR, 1958-65 Recipient Norden award U. Pa. Sch. Vet. Medicine, 1982, Legion of Honor, Chapel of the Four Chaplains, 1984. Fellow: Am. Acad. Vet. and Comparative Toxicology, Am. Acad. Vet. Pharmacology and Therapeutics (newsletter editor 1982—2001, pres. 1983—85, Svc. award 1994, L.E. Davis Career Achievement award 2001); mem.: AAUP, Am. Soc. Pharmacology and Exptl. Therapeutics, Bay Region Mariners Sailing Assn. (treas. 1981—83, vice commodore 1986, commodore 1987), The Haven Yacht Club (charter), Masons, Sigma Xi. Lutheran. Avocations: sailing, photography, woodworking. Office: Haverford Coll Dept Chemistry 370 Lancaster Ave Haverford PA 19041-1392

ARONSON, JEFFREY KENNETH, pharmacologist; b. Glasgow, Scotland, Aug. 31, 1947; s. Samuel and Sybil (Solomon) A.; m. Renée Elaine Wellins, Aug. 20, 1973; children: Simon, Natalie. B in Medicine, B Surgery, U. Glasgow, 1970; DPhil, U. Oxford, 1977, MA, 1984, FFPM (hon.), 2007. Clin. lectr. U. Oxford (England), 1980-84, reader, 1984—, cons. physician Oxfordshire Health Authority, 1990—. Vis. prof. U. Ceara, 1991, U. Ky., 1997, U. Colombo, 2000; vice-chmn. Medicines Commn., U.K., 2002—05. Author: An Account of the Foxglove and Its Medical Uses, 1785-1985, 1985; co-author: The Oxford Textbook of Clinical Pharmacology and Drug Therapy, 3rd edit., 2003, ABC of Monitoring Drug Therapy, 1994, Oxford Handbook of Practical Drug Therapy, 2005, 2nd edit., 2010; editor: Meyler's Side Effects of Drugs, 15th edit., 2006; co editor: Evidence-based Medical Monitoring-From Principles to Practice, 2008, editor Side Effects of Drugs Annuals, 1991—, European Jour. Clin. Pharmacology, 1985-93, reviews editor, 1994—2002; editor-in-chief Brit. Jour. Clin. Pharmacology, 2002-07; contbr. articles to profl. jours. Formulary com. Brit. Nat. Formulary, 2003—, Brit. Nat. Formulary for Children, 2003—. Recipient Paul Martini prize, 1980; fellow Green Coll., Oxford, 1985—2008, Green Templeton Coll., 2008-. Fellow: Brit. Pharmacol. Soc. (pres. 2008—09, pres. emeritus), Royal Coll. Physicians; mem.: Assn. Physicians Gt. Britain and Ireland (sr.). Achievements include research in ion transport, cardiac glycosides, adverse drug reactions and monitoring drug therapy. Avocations: reading, writing, cricket, movies, arithmetic. Office: Univ Dept Primary Health Care 23-38 Hy the Bridge St OXI2ET Oxford England E-mail: jeffrey.aronson@clinpharm.ox.ac.uk.

ARONSON, NEAL IRWIN, neurosurgeon, medical educator; b. Bklyn., July 22, 1926; s. Gustave Coburn and Lillian Aronson; m. Shirlee Rose Friedman, Nov. 8, 1949; children: Rita Jane Joseph, Andrew Charles. MD, U. Cin., 1949. Cert. neurosurgery 1956. Chief neurosurgery Sinai Hosp. Balt., Inc., 1966—95; assoc. prof. neurosurgery Johns Hopkins U., Balt., 1980—. Bd. mem. JCC, Balt., 1989—95. A.S.V-12 USNR, 1944—46, lt. USNR, 1954—56. Recipient Cert. of Merit, AMA, 1971; grantee, NIH, Nat. Inst. Neurol. Diseases and Blindness, 1957—61. Fellow: ACS; mem.: Harvey Cushing Soc., Walter Dandy Soc., Cervical Spine Rsch., Congress Neurol. Surgeons, Assn. Neurol. Surgeons (life). Achievements include design of instrumentation for cervical fusion. Avocations: swimming, golf. Home: 4 Swanhill Dr Baltimore MD 21208-1927 Office: Mid-Atlantic Neurosurgical Associates 2411 W Belvedere Ave Baltimore MD 21215 Home Phone: 410-484-1269. Office Fax: 410-601-9974.

ARONSON, PETER SAMUEL, physiologist, researcher; b. Bklyn., Feb. 3, 1947; s. Harry and Sydelle Aronson; m. Marie Louise Landry, Sept. 25, 1977; children: Paul L., William L. AB, U. Rochester, NY, 1967; MD, NYU, 1970; MA (hon.), Yale U., New Haven, Conn., 1987. Diplomate Nat. Bd. Med. Examiners; diplomate in internal medicine and nephrology Am. Bd. Internal Medicine. Intern and resident in internal medicine U. NC Sch. Medicine, Chapel Hill, 1970-72; clin. assoc. Gerontology Rsch. Ctr., NIH, Balt., 1972-74; fellow in nephrology Yale U. Sch. Medicine, New Haven, 1974-77, asst. prof. medicine and physiology, 1977-81, assoc. prof. medicine and physiology, 1981-87, prof. medicine and cellular and molecular physiology, 1987—, C.N.H. Long prof. internal medicine, 1995—. Chief sect. nephrology Yale U. Sch. Medicine, New Haven, 1987-2002; established investigator Am. Heart Assn., 1981-86. Mem. editl. bd. Am. Jour. Physiology, 1982-86, 87-90, 96-2000, Kidney Internat., 1990-94, Jour. Biol. Chemistry, 1995-2000; cons. editor Jour. Clin. Investigation, 1993-98; contbr. rsch. articles to profl. jours. With USPHS, 1972-74. Recipient Solomon Berson Med. Alumni Achievement award NYU, 1996; co-recipient Charles W. Bohmfalk Tchg. prize in basic sci., Yale U., 2005. Fellow: AAAS, Am. Acad. Arts & Scis.; mem.: Soc. Gen. Physiologists, Internat. Soc. Nephrology, Am. Heart Assn. (exec. com. coun. on the kidney 1986—90), Am. Soc. Nephrology (councillor 2002—06, pres. 2007—08, past pres. 2008—09, Young Investigator award 1985, Homer Smith award 1994), Am. Soc. Clin. Investigation (councillor 1986—88, editl. com. 1993—98), Am. Physiol. Soc., Am. Fedn. Med. Rsch., Am. Assn. Physicians, Salt and Water Club (sec. 1985—87), Alpha Omega Alpha, Phi Beta Kappa. Office: Yale Sch Medicine Dept Medicine/Nephrology PO Box 208029 New Haven CT 06520-8029

ARONSON, STANLEY MAYNARD, physician, educator; b. NYC, May 28, 1922; s. Eliuh and Lena (Hassner) A.; m. Betty Ellis, June 3, 1947; children: Susan, Lisa, Sarah; m. Gale Matheson Holmes, Oct. 12, 2003. BS, CCNY, 1943; MD, NYU, 1947; MA, Brown U., 1971; MPH, Harvard U. Sch. Pub. Health, 1981; DSc (hon.), Tougaloo Coll., 2005; LHD (hon.), RI Coll., 2006; D in Med. Sci. (hon.), Brown. U., 2007. Diplomate Am. Bd. Pathology, Am. Bd. Neuropathology. Resident Bellevue Hosp., Sydenham Hosp., Meml. Sloan-Kettering Ctr. for Cancer, VA Med. Ctr., NYC, 1946-51; fellow Mt. Sinai Hosp., NYC, 1951-54; faculty Armed Forces Inst. Pathology Columbia Coll. Physicians and Surgeons, 1951-54; prof. pathology, asst. dean SUNY, Bklyn., 1954-70; prof. med. sci., dean medicine Brown U., 1970-81, Univ. prof. med. sci., 1981-87, dean medicine emeritus, 1987—. Dir. labs. Kings County Hosp. Ctr., Bklyn., 1965-70; pathologist-in-chief Miriam Hosp., Providence, 1970-75; vis. prof. cmty. medicine Dartmouth Coll. Med. Sch., 1982-; lectr. Yale Sch. Medicine, 1964-65; lectr. pathology Tufts U. Sch. Medicine, 1978-; profl. lectr. Bklyn. Health Ctr., SUNY, 1970—; cons. physician neuropathology Jewish Chronic Disease Hosp., Bklyn., 1951-, NIH, 1962-, RI Hosp., Roger Williams Hosp., Meml. Hosp., Miriam Hosp., Providence VA Hosp., Butler Hosp., Providence, RI Med. Ctr., Luth. Med. Ctr., NYC. Author: (with B.W. Volk) Cerebral Sphingolipidoses, 1962, Inborn Disorders of Sphingolipid Metabolism, 1966, Sphingolipids, Sphingolipidoses and Allied Disorders, 1972, (with A. Sahs and E Hartman) Guidelines for Stroke Care, 1976; (with Adachi and Hirano) The Pathology of the Myelinated Axon, 1985, Tapestry of Medicine, 1999, Worms, Germs and Wayward Physicians, 2000, Smallpox in Colonial America, 2002, (with R. Shield), Aging in Today's World, 2003, Perilous Encounters, 2009; also numerous articles; mem. editl. bd. Jour. Submicroscopic Cytology, Jour. Neuropathology and Exptl. Neurology; editl. bd., editor-in-chief RI Med. Jour.; weekly columnist Providence Jour.-Bull. Commr. US Commn. Control of Huntington's Disease, 1976-79; chmn. Legis. Commn. Dementia Related to Aging; vice chmn. RI Bd. of Med. Licensure and Discipline, 1993-2003; pres. Hospice RI, 1989—, Interfaith Health Care Ministries, 1989-91; mem. Nat. Adv. Commn. on Multiple Sclerosis, 1973-74, NIH Perinatal Rsch. Commn., Joint Commn. on Stroke Facilities, med. adv. bd. Nat. Multiple Sclerosis Soc., Dysautonomia Found., Nat. Tay-Sachs Assn., Nat. Fund for Med. Edn.; trustee Finch Univ. Health Sci., Chgo.; cons. for internat. epidemiology programs The Rockefeller Found., 1990—; chmn. bd. trustees Jewish Home for Aged, RI, 1993-94; pres. Shalom Housing for Elderly, 1993-94. With U.S. Army, 1942-46. Named to R.I. Hall of Fame, 1997. Mem. AMA, Am. Neurol. Assn., Am. Assn. Neuropathology (pres. 1971-72), NY Acad. Medicine, Am. Acad. Neurology, Am. Assn. Pathologists and Bacteriologists, Internat. Soc. Neuropathology, Assn. Am. Med. Coll., NY Neurol. Soc., APHA, Am. Osler Soc., Am. Coll. Epidemiology, NAS (com. on nutrition in med. edn. 1983-85, com. on dietary guidelines implementation 1988-90). Achievements include research on genetics, epidemiology, pathology and diagnostic features of cerebral degenerative diseases, population dynamics, pathology and epidemiology of cerebral vascular disease and organic dementia. Home: 530 Blackstone Blvd Providence RI 02906 Office: Brown U Office Med Affairs Providence RI 02912-0001 Home Phone: 401-383-0060. Personal E-mail: smamd@cox.net.

ARORA, BRIJ BALA, physician; b. Jalandur, Mar. 4, 1947; MBBS, MAMC, New Delhi, 1970; MD in Pathology, PGIMS, Rohtak, 1975. Prof., pathology PGIMS, Rohtak, 1972—92, sr. prof. & head pathology, 1992—2009, SGT Med. Coll., Gurgaon, 2010—. Advisor UPSC, New Delhi, 1992—2009, HPSC, Chandigarh. Contbr. 172 rsch. articles to profl. jours. Recipient Internat. Gold Star award, Indo- Thai Entrepreneurs Summit Bangkok, 2010, Bharat Jyoti award, Scroll, hon., MAMC, New Delhi. Mem.: Patient Welfare Com. PGIMS Rohtak, Chairperson, Clinicopathological Confs., PGIMS, Patient Welfare Com., PGIMS, Paraclinical Scis. Animal Ethical Com., PGIMS, Indian Acad. Cytologists, Indian Assn. Pathologists & Microbiologists. Avocations: reading, writing. Office: House 1161 Sector 1 Rohtak Haryana 124001 India Personal E-mail: drarorab@rediffmail.com.

ARORA, DES RAJ, medical educator; b. Jhang, Pakistan, May 3, 1944; MD in Microbiology, PGIMS, Rohtak, 1973, PhD in Microbiology, 1983. Prof. SGT Med. Coll., Gurgaon, 2010—. Vis. prof. U. Mauritius; faculty Postgrad. Inst. Med. Scis., Rohtak, 1971—94, prof., head, 1994—2004. Contbr. numerous articles to profl. jours. Recipient Smt. Kunti Mehrotra award, Indian Assn. Pathologists and Microbiologists, Drs. Day Honor award, Indian Med. Assn.; WHO fellowship. Mem.: Indian Assn. Med. Microbiologists, Indian Assn. Pathologists and Microbiologists, Nat. Acad. Med. Scis. (India). Avocations: reading, writing, music. Home: House 1161 Sector 1 Rohtak Haryana 124001 India Home Fax: 00191242278183. Personal E-mail: draroradr@redimail.com.

ARORA, PREM, researcher, pediatrician, neonatologist, educator; b. Rode, Punjab, India, Dec. 31, 1977; MBBS, Maulana Azad Med. Coll., New Delhi, 2002; MD in Pediat., Children's Hosp. Mich., 2010. Med. officer Chacha Nehru Bal Chikitsalaya, New Delhi, 2004—07; resident Detroit Med. Ctr., Children's Hosp. Mich., 2007—10, rsch. fellow, neonatal-perinatal medicine, 2010—. Recipient Neonatology Resident Research award, Dept. Neonatal-Perinatal Medicine, Children's Hosp. Mich., 2010; The Deepak Kamat MD PhD Fellow of the Yr. award, Children's Hosp. Mich., 2011. Fellow: Am. Acad. Pediat.; mem.: Nat. Perinatal Assoc., Mich. State Med. Soc. Avocations: movies, travel. Home: 3737 Beaubien Str Apt # 908 Detroit MI 48201 Personal E-mail: premarora96@yahoo.com.

ARORA, SARIKA, medical educator, researcher; d. Prem Lal and Satya Bansal; m. Dheeraj Arora, Jan. 25, 2000; 1 child, Naman. MBBS, Lady Hardinge Med. Coll., Connaught Pl., New Delhi, 1997; MD in Biochemistry, Delhi U., 2002. Sr. resident Lady Hardinge Med. Coll., New Delhi, 2002—05; asst. prof. G.B. Pant Hosp., New Delhi, 2006—09. Contbr. articles profl. internat. jours. Recipient Hari Mirchandani Meml. Silver medal, Lady Hardinge Med. Coll., 1994. Office: Lady Hardinge Med Coll New Delhi 110001 India Personal E-mail: sarikaarora08@rediffmail.com.

ARQUES, STEPHANE, cardiologist; b. Reims, France, Apr. 18, 1970; s. Pierre-Yves and Janine Arques. MD, U. Mediterranee, France, 1998. Intern, resident Univ. Hosp., Marseille, France, 1994—98; asst. cardiology dept. Aubagne Hosp., France, 1999—2003, dir. cardiology dept., 2003—. Mem. editl. bd. Jour. Cardiac Failure, 2009—. Contbr. articles to profl. jours. Mem.: French Soc. Cardiology (mem. echocardiography and heart failure working groups). Roman Catholic. Achievements include research in heart failure. Avocations: classical music, French literature, swimming. Home: Rue Gorde 13010 Marseilles France Office Fax: 33 442 847153. E-mail: sarques@ch-aubagne.fr.

ARREDONDO, JENNA DOLORES, speech pathology/audiology services professional; m. Hector Javier Arredondo, Aug. 5, 1995 (dec.); children: Kayleigh Marie, Noelia Elena children: James Ray Velasquez. AA, Tex. Southmost Coll., 1992; BA, U. Tex.-Pan Am., 1997, MA in Comm. Disorders, 1999; CALT, 2008; MEd, So. Meth. U., 2010. Certificate of Clinical Competence, Am. Speech Hearing Assn., 2000. Staff speech lang. pathologist Milestones Therapeutic Assocs., McAllen, Tex., 2000—. Mem.: Tex. Speech Hearing Assn. (assoc.), Am. Speech Hearing Lang. Assn. (assoc.). Office: Milestones Therapeutic Assocs 3300 N McCall St Ste A Mcallen TX 78501 Office Phone: 956-661-0475. Business E-Mail: jenna@milestonestx.com.

ARROW, KENNETH JOSEPH, economist, educator; b. NYC, Aug. 23, 1921; s. Harry I. and Lillian (Greenberg) Arrow; m. Selma Schweitzer, Aug. 31, 1947; children: David Michael, Andrew. BS in Social Sci., CCNY, 1940; MA, Columbia U., 1941, PhD, 1951, DSc (hon.), 1973; LLD (hon.), U. Chgo., 1967, CUNY, 1972, Hebrew U. Jerusalem, 1975, U. Pa., 1976, Washington U., St. Louis, 1989, Ben-Gurion U. of the Negev, 1992, Harvard U., 1999, Hitotsubashi U., 2004, Waseda U., 2009; D in Social Scis. (hon.), Yale U., 1974; D (hon.), U. René Descartes, Paris, 1974, U. Aix-Marseille III, 1985, U. Cattolica del Sacro Cuore, Milan, Italy, 1994, U. Uppsala, 1995, U. Buenos Aires, 1999, U. Cyprus, 2000; MA (hon.), Harvard U., 1968; DLitt, Cambridge U., Eng., 1985; PhD (hon.), Tel Aviv U., 2001. Rsch. assoc. Cowles Commn. Rsch. in Economics, Chgo., 1947—49; asst. prof. economics U. Chgo., 1948—49; acting asst. prof. economics and stats. Stanford U., Calif., 1949—50, assoc. prof., 1950—53, prof. economics, stats. and ops. rsch., 1953—68, exec. head dept. economics, 1954—56, Joan Kenney prof. economics and prof. ops. rsch., 1979—91, prof. emeritus, 1991—; prof. economics Harvard U., Cambridge, Mass., 1968—74, James Bryant Conant Univ. prof., 1974—79. Economist US Coun. Econ. Advisers, 1962; cons. RAND Corp., 1948—; overseas rsch. fellow Churchill Coll., Cambridge, 1963—64, Cambridge, 1970; guest prof. Inst. Advanced Studies, Vienna, 1964, 71; Fulbright prof. U. Siena, 1995. Author: Social Choice and Individual Values, 1951, Essays in the Theory of Risk Bearing, 1971, The Limits of Organization, 1974, Collected Papers, Vols. I-VI, 1983—85; co-author: Mathematical Studies in Inventory and Production, 1958, Studies in Linear and Nonlinear Programming, 1958, Time Series Analysis of Inter-industry Demands, 1959, Public Investment, The Rate of Return and Optimal Fiscal Policy, 1971, General Competitive Analysis, 1971, Studies in Resource Allocation Processes, 1977, Social Choice and Multicriterion Decision Making, 1985. Weather officer, capt. US Army Air Corps, 1942—46. Recipient Nobel prize in economics, 1972, U. Paris medal, 1998, Nat. Medal Sci., 2004; fellow, Ctr. Advanced Study in Behavioral Scis., 1956—57, John Simon Guggenheim Meml. Found., 1972—73. Fellow: AAAS, NAS (mem. coun. inst. medicine 1990—93), Am. Fin. Assn., Am. Econ. Assn. (exec. com. 1967—69, pres. 1973, John Bates Clark medal 1957), Internat. Soc. Inventory Rsch. (pres. 1983—90), Econometric Soc. (v.p. 1955, pres. 1956), Am. Acad. Arts and Scis. (v.p. 1979—81, 1991—93), Am. Statis. Assn., Inst. Math. Stats.; mem.: Royal Soc. (fgn.), Game Theory Soc., Brit. Acad. (corr.), Pontifical Acad. Social Scis., Soc. Social Choice and Welfare (pres. 1991—93); Western Econ. Assn. (pres. 1980—81), Finnish Acad. Scis. (fgn. hon.), Inst. Ops. Rsch. and Mgmt. Sci. (pres. 1963, chmn. coun. 1964, Von Neumann prize 1986, Fellows' award), Am. Philos. Soc., Internat. Econs. Assn. (pres. 1983—86). Office: Stanford University SIEPR Economics Bldg Stanford CA 94305-6072 Office Phone: 650-723-9165. Office Fax: 650-725-5702. Business E-Mail: arrow@stanford.edu.

ARSLAN, HALIL, radiologist, educator; b. Yayladagi, Hatay, July 15, 1967; Degree, U. Cerrahpasa, 1990; PhD, Yüzüncü Yil U., 1994. Chief physician Ankara Atatürk Edn. and Rsch. Hosp., 2011—. Head radiology dept. Med. Sch. Yüzüncü Yil U., 1994—2011. Mem.: Turkish Soc. Radiology, European Assn. Radiology. Avocations: reading, travel, swimming. Office: Bilkent Rd Ankara Bilkent 06800 Turkey E-mail: drhalilarslan@hotmail.com.

ARSLANIAN, SILVA A., pediatrician, pediatric endocrinologist; MD, Am. U. of Beirut Med. Ctr., 1978. Diplomate Am. Bd. Pediatrics, cert. pediatric endocrinology. Intern Am. Univ. of Beirut Med. Ctr., 1978, resident, 1980; fellow Children's Hosp. of Pitts., 1983; hosp. affiliations include Magee-Womens Hosp. of Univ. of Pitts. Med. Ctr. (UPMC), Children's Hosp. of Pitts. of UPMC. Office: Children's Hospital of Pittsburgh University of Pittsburgh Medical Center Penn Ave 3rd Fl Pittsburgh PA 15224 Office Phone: 412-692-5170.

ARSLAN ÖZKAN, ILKAY, nursing educator, researcher; b. Turkey, May 21, 1979; PhD, Dokuz Eylül U., 2011. Rschr., educator dept. ob-gyn. nursing Akdeniz U., Antalya Sch. Health, 2005—11. Office: Akdeniz University Antalya Sch Health Dept Nursing Mgmt Antalya 07058 Turkey Office Phone: 90 5054678789. Business E-Mail: ilkayarslan@akdeniz.edu.tr.

ARTHUR, DONALD C., retired career military officer; b. Northampton, Mass., Jan. 4, 1950; MD, Coll. Medince & Dentistry NJ, 1978. Advanced through grades to vice admiral USN Med. Corps, 2003, flight surgeon, diving med. officer, then sr. med. officer USS Kitty Hawk, head emergency medicine Naval Hosp. San Diego, head spl. products divsn., then dir. med. programs USMC, Naval Aerospace Med. Inst. Washington, dep. commdr. (COO) Naval Med. Ctr. San Diego, commdg. officer (CEO) Naval Hosp. Camp Lejeune, NC, various positions including asst. chief health care ops. and vice chief (COO), Bur. Medicine & Surgery Washington, 1998—2002, comdr. Naval Med. Ctr. Bethesda, Md., 2002—04, surgeon gen., chief Bur. Medicine & Surgery, 2004—07, ret., 2007. Decorated Navy Disting. Svc. Medal, four Legions of Merit, three Meritorious Svc. Medals, three Navy Commendation Medals, Navy and Marine Corps Achievement Medal, others; recipient U.S. Outstanding Fed. Healthcare Exec. award, Assn. Military Surgeons, 2002. Fellow: Aerospace Med. Assn. (past pres.), Am. Coll. Healthcare Execs. (Fed. Excellence in Healthcare Leadership award 2002); mem.: Alpha Omega Alpha.

ARUL, VENKATESAN, biotechnologist, educator; b. Melavanniyur, India, Jan. 18, 1959; MSc in Integrated Biology, Madurai Kamaraj U., 1981, PhD, 1989. Tchr., rschr. Pondicherry U., 1992—, assoc. prof., 2007—. Vis. prof. JSPS, Nagoya U., Japan. Mem.: Biotech. Rsch. Soc. India. Avocations: stamp collecting/philately, coin collecting/numismatics, music. Office: Dept Biotech Pondicherry University Pondicherry 605014 India E-mail: varul18@yahoo.com.

ARUNACHALAM, SANKARALINGAM, chemistry professor; b. Tamil Nadu, India, Dec. 9, 1954; MS, PhD, Govt. Sch., 1985. Prof. Sch. Chemistry, Bharathidasan U., 1986—. Mem.: Chem. Rsch. Soc. India. Office: Sch Chemistry Bharathidasan University Tiruchirappalli Tamil Nadu 620024 India E-mail: arunasurf@yahoo.com.

ARUNAKARAN, J., endocrinologist, biotechnologist, educator; b. Tirunelveli, India, Jan. 15, 1956; s. Jagadeesan and Sornapackiam Arunakaran; m. Kumudha Arunakaran, Nov. 14, 1986; children: J.A. Ganesh, A. Sucitra. MSc, Madurai Kamaraj U., India, 1978; MPhil, U. Madras, India, 1983, PhD, 1986; DCA, Nat. Inst. Nutrition, Hyderabad, India, 1999. Temporary lectr. U. Madras, Chennai, India, 1986—2000, lectr., 2000—04, sr. prof., 2004—. Bd. studies U. Madras, 2005—, Bharathidasan U., Trichurappalli, India, 2007—08. Contbr. articles to profl. jours. Officer welfare assn. post-grad. inst. basic. med. scis. U. Madras, convener Faculty Club. Mem.: Indian Assn Biomed. Scientists (life), Soc. Reproductive Biology and Comparative Endocrinology (treas., Mem. in Reproduction and Endocrinology award 1995), Soc. Andrology (life). Avocations: reading, gardening, bookkeeping. Office: U Madras Dept Endocrinology 600 113 Chennai India Personal E-mail: j_arunakaran@hotmail.com.

ARUNY, JOHN E., vascular and interventional radiologist; MD, Autonomous U. Guadalajara, Mex., 1983. Diplomate Am. Bd. Radiology-diagnostic radiology, 1989, Am. Bd. Radiology-vascular and interventional radiology, 2009. Fellow NYU, 1984; chief resident NY Med. Coll.-Met. Hosp. Ctr., 1988; resident NY Med. Coll., 1989; fellow Harvard Med. Sch., Brigham and Women's Hosp., 1991; assoc. prof. of diagnostic radiology and surgery (vascular) Yale Univ., co-sect. chief, vascular and interventional radiology, dir., vascular and interventional radiolgy; hosp. affiliation includes Yale-New Haven Hosp. Office: Yale-New Haven Hospital 2nd Fl 20 York St New Haven CT 06510 Office Phone: 203-785-7026. Office Fax: 203-737-1077. E-mail: john.aruny@yale.edu.

ARUSHANIAN, EDWARD BENIAMINOVICH, pharmacologist, researcher; b. Vladivostock, Russia, Jan. 18, 1934; s. Beniamin Andreevich and Serafima Davidovna (Baratova) A.; m. Ludmila Gavrilovna Dvinina, Oct. 7, 1967; children: Helena, Arsen. MD, 1st Med. Inst., Leningrad, Russia, 1957; PhD, Inst. Physiology, Leningrad, 1962; MD, Acad. Med. Scis., Moscow, 1969. Asst. dept. pharmacology Med. Inst., Chita, Russia, 1957—65, 1965—69, docent, 1969—83, prof., 1969—83, head dept. pharmacology Stavropol, Russia, 1983—. Author: Caudate Nucleus, 1976, Nigrostrionigral System, 1989 (Pavlov award, 1994), Chronopharmacology, 2000, Antidepressant Drugs, 2002, Psychostimulant Drugs, 2003, Nootropic Drugs, 2004, Psychopharmacology, 2008, more than 700 publs. Recipient Kravkov's award USSR Acad. Med. Scis., 1976; named Honoured Scientist of Russia, 1993. Avocations: stamp collecting/philately, mineralogy. Home: L Tolstoy str 17 fl 15 355003 Stavropol Russia Office: Med Acad Dept Pharmacology Mira str 310 355017 Stavropol Russia

ARVYSTAS, MICHAEL GECIAUSKAS, orthodontist, educator; b. Vilnius, Lithuania, Dec. 18, 1942; arrived in U.S., 1949, naturalized, 1961; s. Mykolas and Antanina (Kleiza) Arvystas; m. Jane Grannis, 1969 (div. 1978); m. Mary Ruth Buchness, Nov. 2, 1992. BA, Colgate U., 1965; DMD, Tufts U., 1969. Cert. Columbia U., 1973, diplomate Am. Bd. Orthodontics. Chief orthodontic sect. Morrisania City Hosp., Bronx, NY, 1973—76; dir. orthodontics ctr. for craniofacial disorders and cleft palate ctr. Montefiore Hosp. and Med. Ctr., 1973—; chief orthodontic sect. North Ctrl. Bronx Hosp., 1976—83; clin. prof. N.J. Dental Sch., Newark, 1974—, dir., lectr. undergrad. and postgrad. students, 1974—. Vis. prof. Albert Einstein Coll. Medicine, Bronx; lectr. in field. Author: Orthodontic Management of Agenesis and Other Complexitues: An Interdisciplinary Approach to Functional Aesthetics, 2003; contbr. articles to profl. jours., chpts. to books. Capt. Dental Corps USAF, 1969—71. Mem.: ADA, Am. Acad. Esthetic Dentistry (orgn. com. Greater N.Y. Dental Meeting), N.Y. Acad. Dentistry, Northeastern Soc. Orthodontists, Am. Assn. Orthodontists, Dental Soc. N.Y.C., N.Y. County Dental Soc. (bd. dirs., pres.), Sigma Xi, Colgate U. Alumni Assn., Orthodontic Alumni Soc. Columbia U., Tufts U. Dental Alumni Assn. Office: 24 Washington Sq N New York NY 10011-9168 Office Phone: 212-777-9977. Personal E-mail: marvystas@optonline.net.

ARYA, LILY A., gynecologist, obstetrician; MB, BChir, Calcutta U., 1987; MD in Obstetrics and Gynecology, Postgrad. Inst. of Med. Edn. and Rsch., Chandigarh, India, 1990; MS in Epidemiology, U. Ariz., 1993. Diplomate Am. Bd. Ob-Gyn. Intern Columbia Univ., resident; fellow Brown Univ.; assoc. prof. ob-gyn Univ. Pa.; chief divsn. urogynecology and pelvic reconstructive surgery Univ. Pa. Hosp., fellowship program dir. Author: Urinary Incontinence in Women, Risk of new onset urinary incontinence in primiparous women following forceps and vacuum deliveries, 2001, Office screening test for intrinsic urethral sphincter deficiency: pediatric foley catheter test, 2001, GAX Collagen for female stress urinary incontinence: where are we now?, 2001, Pelvic anatomy for Obstetrics and Gynecology residents: An experimental study using clay models, 2001, Treating Interstitial Cystitis in Women, 2001, Diagnosing interstitial cystitis in women with chronic pelvic pain, 2002, Treating urinary symptoms in women with Parkinson's Disease, 2002, Pessaries and Prostheses for Pelvic Organ Prolapse and Urinary Incontinence, 2002, Vaginal Erosion after pubovaginal sling procedures using dermal allografts, 2003. Named one of Top Doctors, Phila. mag., 2010, 2011. Mem.: Am. Urogynecologic Soc., ACOG. Office: Hospital of the University of Pennsylvania Department of Obstetrics and Gynecology 3400 Spruce St 5 Pennsylvania Tower Philadelphia PA 19104 Office Phone: 215-615-7514, 215-662-7929.

ARZHANNIKOV, ANDREI VASIL'EVICH, education educator, researcher; b. Shelobolikha, Russia, Aug. 25, 1948; s. Vasilii Petrovich Strel'nikov and Anna Mikhailovna Arzhannikova; m. Irina Yur'evna Vil'kovskaya, Nov. 3, 1970; children: Zhanna Andreevna Arzhannikova, Sophia Andreevna Arzhannikova. Technician, Novosibirsk Radiotechnikal Sch., 1964—68; M, Novosibirsk State U., 1968—73; PhD, Budker Inst. of Nuc. Physics, 1976—79; DSc (hon.), Budker Inst. of Nuc. Physicsk, 1994. Cert. Prof. Ministery of Edn., 1998. Jr. scientist Budker Inst. of Nuc. Physics, Novosibirsk, Russia, 1978—80, sr. scientist, 1980—93, sr. prin. scientist, 1993—2000, chief rschr., 2000—; assoc. prof. Novosibirsk State U., 1991—95, prof., 1995—2000, dean of faculty, 2000—. Cons. Sci. Coun. of Novosibirsk State U., 2000—, Vis. Com. on Physics for Russian Universities, Moscow, 2000—; directorships Assn. of Siberia Universities on Physics Edn., Novosibirsk, 2000—. Grant, ISTC, 1998—2001, CRDF, 2001—, INTAS, 2003—. Mem.: Sigma Xi. Achievements include invention of increasing ecological safety and healthcare of people oriented in 3 directions; research in powerful microwave synthesis and modification of solids in connection with new drugs, for cleaning the atmosphere, restoring ozone layer, and taking out radionuclides at nuclear power stations; giving lecture courses for student physicists on the problems of ecology and human healthcare, organizing the chair of biomedical physics at Physics Faculty being responsible for educational; component of the project molecular design and ecologically safe technologies supported by the BRHE program; organizing and giving popular lectures children and school teachers on ecology, medicine, healthy life-styles, publications in newspapers and participation in radio and TV programs on these topics. Home: Polevaya 14-7 Novosibirsk 630128 Russia Office: Novosibirsk State Univ ul. Pirogova 2 630090 Novosibirsk Novosibirskaya obl. Russia Office Fax: 73832397801. Personal E-mail: arzhannikov@inp.nsk.su.

ASAD, MOHAMMED, pharmacist, educator; b. Bangalore, Karnataka, India, Apr. 2, 1972; PharmM, Bangalore U., 1997; PhD, Pondicherry U., 2002. Assoc. prof. Shaqra U., 2010. Mem.: Assn. Pharm. Tchrs. India. Home: 16 Mosque Ln Kumbarpet Bangalore Karnataka 560002 India Personal E-mail: mohammedasad@rediffmail.com.

ASAHINA, KINJI, medical researcher; b. Tokyo, Sept. 10, 1970; PhD, Hiroshima U., Japan, 1999. Rschr. Hiroshima Prefectural Inst. Indsl. Sci. and Tech., Higashihiroshima, Japan, 1999—2002; rsch. assoc. Med. Rsch. Inst., Tokyo Med. and Dental U., Chiyoda-ku, Japan, 2002—. Contbr. articles to profl. jours. Recipient Best Presentation award, Japanese Soc. Regenerative Medicine, 2004. Achievements include demonstration of hepatocyte differentiation from embryonic stem cells.

ASAI, EMIKO, plastic surgeon; b. Niigata, Japan, Oct. 25, 1975; MD, Fukushima Med. U., 2001. Specialist Japan Soc. Plastic Surgery, 2001. Mem.: Japan Soc. Reconstructive Microsurgery, Japan Soc. Facial Nerve Rsch., Japan Soc. Surg. Wound Care, Japanese Cleft Palate Assn. Avocations: reading, sports. Office: 1 Hikarigaoka Fukushima 960-1295 Japan Office Fax: 08-024-548-9700. Personal E-mail: smilingchild1025@yahoo.co.jp.

ASAI, MASATO, medical educator; b. Gifu, Japan, Nov. 30, 1970; MD, Nagoya U., 1995, PhD, 2004. Lectr., dept. pathology Nagoya U., 2009. Home: 1302-1 Miyukiyama D-Granse 707 Tenpaku Nagoya Aichi 468-0075 Japan

ASAKA, TADAYOSHI, physical therapist, educator; b. Japan, July 19, 1956; PhD, Muroran Inst. Tech., 1996. Assoc. prof. Hokkaido U., 2006—. Mem.: World Congress Phys. Therapy, Internat. Soc. Posture & Gait Rsch., Internat. Soc. Motor Control. Avocation: exercise. Office: Kita 12 Nishi 5 Kita-Ku Sapporo Hokkaido 060-0812 Japan Business E-Mail: ask-chu@hs.hokudai.ac.jp.

ASAKURA, HIROYUKI, medical educator, physician; arrived in U.S., 1990; MD, Kyoto U., Japan, 1986; Diploma, Japan Soc. Fertility and Sterility, 2004; Diploma in Reproductive Endocrinology and Infertility, Am. Bd. Ob-Gyn, 2001. Diplomate in ob-gyn., reproductive endocrinology and infertility Am. Bd. Ob-Gyn. Clin. asst. prof. U. Wis., Milw., 1997—2001, clin. assoc. prof., 2001—05; clin. asst. prof. Kyoto U., 2004—. Fellow: Am. Coll. Ob-Gyn. Office Phone: 81 6-6311-2511.

ASAKURA, HITOSHI, medical educator; b. Yokohama, Kanagawa, Japan, Feb. 21, 1937; s. Takeshi and Kito Asakura; m. Hiroko Suzuki, May 18, 1975; children: Tomoko, Makoto. Student, Keio Gijuku U., Tokyo, 1963; MD, Keio Gijuku U., 1968, postgrad., 1964-68. Diplomate Japan. Intern Keio Gijuku U. Hosp., Tokyo, 1963-64, med. dr., 1968-73; asst. prof. internal medicine Keio Gijuku U. Sch. Medicine, Tokyo, 1973-88; prof. Niigata (Japan) U. Sch. Medicine, 1988—2002, prof. emeritus, 2002—. Fellow: Am. Gastroent. Assn., Internat. Coll. Angiology; mem.: Japanese Soc. Internal Medicine, Japanese Soc. Gastroenterology, N.Y. Acad. Sci. Home: 7-26-14 Koonandai Koonan-ku Yokohama Kanagawa 234-0054 Japan Office: Dir Koukan Clinics 1-2-3 Koukantori Kawasaki-ku Kawasaki 210-0852 Japan Office Phone: 81443668900. Business E-Mail: hitoshi-asakura@koukankai.or.jp.

ASAMOA-BAAH, ANARFI, international organization administrator; b. Ghana; MB ChB, Ghana Med. Sch., 1983; MCommH, Liverpool Tropical Sch., UK, 1989; degree in health planning, U. Keele, UK, 1990; PhD in Health Econs., Aberdeen U., UK, 1991; degree in health policy, U. Wis., Madison, 1992. Med. administr., Ghana; primary health care coord. Cath. Ch. in Ghana; dist. med. dir. Ghana Health Services, provincial dir. health services, dir. policy, planning, monitoring and evaluation, dir. gen. health services; primary health care cons. WHO, Geneva, 1988—98, sr. policy advisor to the dir. gen., 1998—2000, exec. dir. external rels. and governing bodies, 2000—02, exec. dir. health, tech. and pharmaceuticals, 2002—03, asst. dir. gen. communicable diseases, 2003—05, asst. dir. gen. HIV/AIDS, tuberculosis, and malaria, 2005—06, dep. dir. gen., 2007—. Office: WHO avenue Appia 20 1211 Geneva Switzerland *

ASAMOAH, ERNEST OPOKU, endocrinologist; b. Ghana, Dec. 24, 1960; MD, U. Ghana, 1989. Cons. endocrinologist Diabetes & Endocrinology Cons., 1999—. Named one of Top Drs., Indpls. Monthly. Fellow: ACP, Am. Coll. Clin. Endocrinologist, RCS (London); mem.: Endocrine Soc., Am. Thyroid Assn. Avocations: sports, reading. Office: 8435 Clearvista Pl Ste 101 Indianapolis IN 46256 Office Fax: 317-621-1010. Business E-Mail: eoasamoah@pol.net. E-mail: easamoah@ecommunity.com.

ASANO, KATSURA, biology professor; b. Yokosuka, Japan, Sept. 16, 1965; BSc, U. Tokyo, 1989, PhD, 1994. Assoc. prof. Kans. State U., 2006. Mem.: ASBMB. Office: 258 Chalmers Hall Manhattan KS 66506 Business E-Mail: kasano@ksu.edu.

ASANO, MAKISHIGE, medical educator; b. Gunma, Japan, Aug. 1, 1928; s. Harusuke and Shima (Amagawa) A.; m. Tetsuko Sakai, Dec. 3, 1957. MB, Tokyo Med. and Dental U., 1955, MD, 1962. From rschr. to prof. emeritus Nat. Inst. of Pub. Health, Japan, 1956—98, prof. emeritus, 1998—, hon. rschr., 1990—2005, guest rschr., 2005—; prof. Tokyo Med. and Dental U., 1990-94, dean Sch. Allied Health Scis., 1993-94; prof. Japan Women's U., Tokyo, 1994-97; adviser Promotion Com. for Healthy Cities, 2006—. Author: Circulatory Physiology, 1976, Health Science of Smoking, 1985. Chmn. Promotion Com. for Healthy Cities, Tokyo, 1999—2006. Grantee, WHO, 1968. Fellow: Internat. Coll. Angiology; mem.: Japanese Soc. Biorheology (dir. 1975—2010, hon. advisor 2010—, OKA Syoten. prize 2006), NY Acad. Scis., Japanese Soc. Microcirculation (hon.), European Soc. Microcirculation, Internat. Soc. Biorheology. Avocations: fishing, playing piano, reading. Office: Nat Inst Pub Health 3-6 Minami 2 chome Wako 351-0197 Japan Home Phone: 81-3-3756-2045; Office Phone: 81-48-458-6260. Business E-Mail: asano@niph.go.jp.

ASANO, SATOSHI, pathologist; s. Takeshi and Kazuko Asano; m. Yoko Nakamoto, July 3, 2004; 1 child, Yuki. MS in Pharmacology, Toyama Med. and Pharm. U., Japan, 1986; PhD, Yokohama City U., Japan, 1995. Diplomate Japanese Soc. Toxicologic Pathology, 1999. Rschr. pathology safety rsch. dept. Teijin Ltd., Tokyo, 1986—95, group mgr. pathology & reproductive toxicology safety rsch. dept., 1997—2002; guest rschr. Lecm, Niehs, Research Triangle Park, NC, 1995—97; sect. head pathology, imaging & biomarker pharmacology dept. GlaxoSmithKline, Tsukuba, Ibaraki, Japan, 2002—06, sect. head pathology & imaging, pharmacology dept. Tokyo, 2006—. Contbr. articles to profl. jours. including Molecular Biology. Achievements include patents for inhibitor of aggregation of beta-amyloid. Business E-Mail: satoshi.asano@gsk.com.

ASAO, KEIKO, internist, researcher; MD, Tohoku U., Sendai, Japan, 1993; MPH, Johns Hopkins U., Balt., 2001, MHS, 2004, PhD, 2007, Jikei U., Tokyo, 2004. Fellow U. Mich., Ann Arbor, Mich., 2009—. Mem.: ACP, Endocrine Soc., Am. Diabetes Assn. Office: PO Box 482 24 Frank Lloyd Wright Dr Ann Arbor MI 48106 Business E-Mail: kasao@med.umich.edu.

ASASHIMA, MAKOTO, biology professor, educational association administrator; b. Niigata, Sado, Japan, Sept. 6, 1944; m. Yoshiko Hasei, Nov. 24, 1975; children: Nobuko, Hiromitsu. BS, Tokyo Univ. Edn., 1967; MS, U. Tokyo, 1969, PhD, 1972. Rsch. asst. Rsch. Inst. Molecular Biology, Free U., Berlin, 1972-74; assoc. prof. Yokohama City U. Coll. Humanities & Scis., Japan, 1976—86, prof., 1986—93, head dept., mem. univ. coun., 1989-92; prof. U. Tokyo, 1993—, spl. asst. dean Grad. Sch. Arts & Scis., 2001—03, dean faculty, dean Grad. Sch. Arts & Scis., 2003—07, mng. dir., exec. v.p., 2007—09. Mem. adminstrv. bd. Internat. Assn. Universities, 2008—; mem. com. on internat. prize biology Japan Soc. Promotion of Sci. Author: Mechanism of Development, 1983, Modern Biology, 1985; editor: Fundamentals of Space Biology, 1990, Development Growth Difference, 1991, Zoology Science, 1994. Recipient Eto Acad. Found. prize, 1990, Zool. Soc. Japan prize, 1990, Inoue Acad. Found. prize, 1991, Kihara Meml. Life Sci. Found. prize, 1994, Siebold prize Humboldt Found. (Germany), 1994. Mem. Zool. Soc. Japan (councilor 1986—), Japanese Soc. Devel. Biologists (councilor 1986—), Internat. Soc. Devel. Biologists (editor Devel. Growth Differences 1993—, Zool. Sci. 1993—). Avocations: collecting stamps, collecting fossils. Office: U Tokyo Dept Biology 3-8-1 Komaba Meguro-ku Tokyo 153 Japan Office Phone: 81 3 5454 6632. Business E-Mail: asashi@bio.c.u-tokyo.ac.jp.

ASBURY, ARTHUR KNIGHT, neurologist, educator; b. Cin., Nov. 22, 1928; s. Eslie and Mary (Knight) Asbury; m. Carolyn Holstein, May 17, 1980; children from previous marriage: Dana, Patricia Knight, William Francis. Grad., Phillips Acad., Andover, Mass., 1946; student, Stanford, 1947—48; BS, U. Ky., 1951; MD, U. Cin., 1958; MA (hon.), U. Pa., 1974. Intern in medicine Mass. Gen. Hosp., Boston, 1958—59, resident, 1959—63, fellow, 1963—65, staff neurologist, 1965—69; chief neurology San Francisco VA Hosp., 1969—74; prof. dept. neurology U. Pa., Phila., 1974—, chmn. dept. neurology, 1974—82, Van Meter prof. neurology, 1983—97; acting dean, exec. v.p. U. Pa. Sch. Medicine, 1988—89, vice dean for rsch., 1990—93, vice dean for faculty affairs, 1993—97, interim dean, 2000—01; tchg. fellow Harvard Med. Sch., 1958—65, instr., 1965—68, assoc., 1968—69; assoc. prof. neurology U. Calif. at San Francisco, 1969—73, vice-chmn., 1969—74, prof., 1973—74. Mem. nat. adv. neurol. disease & stroke coun. NIH, 1990—93; hon. prof. med. scis. Hebei Med. Coll., China, 1995. Sr. editor: Blue Books of Practical Neurology, 1980—2004, assoc. editor: Archives of Neurology, 1975—76, Annals of Neurology, 1976—81, chief editor:, 1985—93, mem. editl. bd.: Muscle and Nerve, 1977—89, Neurology, 1981—85, Jour. Neuropathology and Exptl. Neurology, 1981—83, Jour. Neurol. Scis., 1989—2001; contbr. chpts. to med. textbooks, articles to med. jours. V.p., bd. dirs. Forest Retreat Farms Inc., Carlisle, Ky., 1970—92. With US Army, 1951—53. Recipient Daniel Drake medal, U. Cin., 1988, IS Ravdin Master Clinician award, U. Pa., 1999, Lindback Tchg. award, 2000, Disting. Almuni award, U. Cin. Coll. Medicine, 2008; grantee, UPHS, 1967—93, Muscular Dystrophy Assn., 1974—82. Fellow: AAAS, Royal Coll. Physicians London, Am. Acad. Neurology (v.p. 1977—79, hon. 2003); mem.: Coll. Physicians Phila. (pres. 2004—06, Meritorious Svc. award 2006), World Fedn. Neurology (v.p. 1989—93, chair rsch. group on neuromuscular diseases 2001—05, Lifetime Achievement award for work in neuromuscular diseases 2002), Assn. Univ. Profs. Neurology (pres. 1980—82, Meritorious Svc. award 2006), Am. Assn. Neuromuscular and Electrodiagnostic Medicine (hon.; hon.), European Neurol. Soc. (hon.), Assn. Brit. Neurologists (hon.), Soc. Neurosci., Am. Assn. Neuropathologists (v.p. 1983—84), Am. Neurol. Assn. (councillor 1976—81, pres. 1982—83, hon. 1995), Inst. Medicine. Achievements include Arthur K. Asbury Ann. award for faculty mentoring established at University Pennsylvania School of Medicine in 2004. Home: 408 S Van Pelt St Philadelphia PA 19146-1233 Office: U Pa Hosp Dept Neurology 3400 Spruce St Philadelphia PA 19104-4283 Home Phone: 215-790-4882; Office Phone: 215-662-2629. Business E-Mail: asbury@mail.med.upenn.edu.

ASBURY, CAROLYN, medical drug policy researcher; SCmPH, John Hopkins Bloomberg Sch. Pub. Health, 1980; PhD, Wharton U. Pa., 1982. Former dir. Pew Charitable Trusts' Health & Human Svcs. Program, 1991—97; formerly with Robert Wood Johnson Found., 1984—90; sr. fellow Leonard Davis Inst., Univ. Pa.; sr. cons. Dana Found., NYC. Chair Nat. Orgn. Rare Disorders, Danbury, Conn., Treatment Rsch. Inst.; bd. mem. US Pharmacopeia, 2005—, Coll. Physicians Phila., 2010—. Author: Orphan Drugs, Medical Versus Market Value, 1985. Office: Dana Found Ste 900 745 Fifth Ave New York NY 10151 Business E-Mail: casbury@dana.org.

ASCH, DAVID ALAN, economist, educator, healthcare educator; b. NYC, Apr. 5, 1958; AB, Harvard U., 1980; MD, Cornell U., 1984; MBA, Wharton Sch., U. Pa., 1989. Cert. Internal Medicine, 1987. Resident U. Pa., Phila., 1984—87, fellow, 1987—89, assoc. dir. Robert Wood Johnson Clin. Scholars Prog., 1992—96, dir. Robert Wood Johnson Health and Soc. Scholars Prog., 2002—, prof. medicine, health care mgmt., ops, and info. mgmt. and med. ethics; chief health services rsch. Phila. VA Med. Ctr., 1992—, chief gen. internal medicine, 1993—96; Robert D. Eilers prof. health care mgmt. and economics Wharton Sch., U. Pa., Phila., 1998—, exec. dir. Leonard Davis Inst. Health Economics, 1998—. Recipient John M. Eisenberg Tchg. award, 1995, Young Investigaor award, Acad. Health Services Rsch., 1997, Nellie Westerman prize, Am. Fedn. Med. Rsch., 1998, Outstanding Investigator in Clin. Sci., 1999, Samuel P. Martin award in Health Services Rsch., 2000, Robert C. Witt Rsch. award, Am. Risk and Ins. Assn., 2000, Christian R. and Mary F. Lindback award for Disting. Tchg., 2006. Mem.: Inst. Medicine, Assn. Am. Physicians. Office: Leonard Davis Inst Health Economics 3641 Locust Walk Philadelphia PA 19104 Office Phone: 215-746-2705. Office Fax: 215-898-0229. E-mail: asch@wharton.upenn.edu.

ASCH, SUSAN MCCLELLAN, pediatrician; b. Cleve., Dec. 31, 1945; d. William Alton and Alice Lonore (Heide) McClellan; m. Marc Asch, Sept. 10, 1966; children: Marc William, Sarah Susan, Rebecca Janney. AB, Oberlin Coll., Ohio, 1967; MA, Mich. State U., 1968, PhD, 1975; MD, Case Western Res., 1977, AOA, 1976. Diplomate Nat. Bd. Med. Examiners, Am. Bd. Pediatrics, Am. Bd. Emergency Pediatrics. Instr. sociology Mich. State U., East Lansing, 1971-73; resident in pediatrics Children's Nat. Med. Ctr., Washington, 1977-80, chief resident in ambulatory and emergency pediatrics, 1979-80; asst. to dir. Office for Med. Applications of Rsch. NIH, Bethesda, 1980-81; pvt. practice in pediatrics Millinocket (Maine) Regional Hosp., 1981-84; assoc. dir. emergency Akron (Ohio) Children's Hosp., 1984-87; asst. prof. pediatrics Northeastern Ohio U. Coll. Medicine, 1984-87; dir. emergency St. Paul Children's Hosp., 1987-91; asst. prof. pediatrics U. Minn., 1987-93, clin. asst. prof., 1993—; pvt. practice pediatrics Stillwater, Minn., 1992—; sec. exec. com. med. staff Lakeview Meml. Hosp., 1999—2001, vice chief of staff, 2001—03, chief of staff, 2003—05, past chief of staff, 2005—07, chair pediatrics, 2005—07. Nat. faculty PALS Am. Heart Assn., Mpls., Dallas, 1987—94, regional PALS faculty, 1994—2007, training ctr. faculty, 2008—, state bd. dirs. Minn. affiliate, 1988—92; mem. task force, sub-bd. emergency pediat. Am. Bd. Pediat., 1987—91, mem. sub-bd. emergency pediat., 1991—93; chmn. SIDS task force Minn. Dept. Maternal and Child Health, St. Paul, 1990—92. Assoc. editor Pediatric Emergency Medicine, 1992, contbr., 1992, 96; author various publs., 1970—. Mem.: Minn. Med. Assn. (emergency svcs. com. 1990, ho. of dels. 1994), Am. Acad. Pediat. (exec. com. sect. on emergency pediat. 1988—90, chair Minn. emergency pediat. com. 1989—91, nat. faculty advanced pediat. life support 1989—, regional faculty neonatal resuscitation program 1994—, nat. svc. commendation 1991), Alpha Omega Alpha. Democrat. Mem. Soc. Of Friends. Avocation: horseback riding. Home: 34 N Oaks Rd North Oaks MN 55127-6325 Office: Stillwater Med Group 1500 Curve Crest Brd Stillwater MN 55082-5935 Office Phone: 651-439-1234. Business E-Mail: sasch@lakeview.org.

ASCHAUER, CHARLES JOSEPH, JR., retired health products executive; b. Decatur, Ill., July 23, 1928; s. Charles Joseph and Beulah Diehl (Kniple) A.; m. Elizabeth Claire Meagher, Apr. 28, 1962; children: Karen A. Vorwald, Thomas Arthur, Susan A. Baisley, Karl Andrew. BBA, Northwestern U., 1950. Cert. internat. bus. adminstr. Centre d'Etudes Industrielles, 1951. Prin. McKinsey & Co., Chgo., 1955-62; v.p. mktg. Mead Johnson Labs. div. Mead Johnson & Co., Evansville, Ind., 1962-67; v.p., pres. automotive group Maremont Corp., Chgo., 1967-70; v.p., group exec. Whittaker Corp., Los Angeles, 1970-71; v.p., pres. hosp. products div. Abbott Labs., North Chicago, Ill., 1971-76, v.p., group exec., 1976—89, exec. v.p., dir., 1979-89, ret., 1989. Lt. Supply Corps. USNR, 1951—55. Mem.: Shadow Wood Country Club, Sunset Ridge Country Club, Econs. Club Chgo., Univ. Club Chgo. Home Phone: 847-251-3699.

ASCHER, JAMES JOHN, pharmaceutical executive; b. Kansas City, Mo., Oct. 2, 1928; s. Bordner Fredrick and Helen (Barron) A.; m. Mary Ellen Robitsch, Feb. 27, 1954; children: Jill Denise, James John, Christopher Bordner Student, Bergen Jr. Coll., 1947—48, U. Kans., 1946—47, student, 1949—51. Rep. B.F. Ascher & Co., Inc., Memphis, 1954-55, asst. to pres. Kansas City, Mo., 1956-57, v.p., 1958-64, pres., 1965—2001, chmn. bd., 2001—. Bd. dirs. Childrens Cardiac Ctr., 1964-70, pres., 1968-70; mem. cen. governing bd. Children's Mercy Hosp., 1968-80; bd. dirs. Jr. Achievement of Middle Am., 1970-90, pres., 1973-76, chmn., 1979-81; edn. chmn. Young Pres.'s Orgn. 6th Internat. Univ. for Pres., Athens, 1975. 1st. lt. inf., U.S. Army, 1951-53, Korea Decorated Bronze Star, Combat Infantryman's Badge Mem.: VFW, Consumer Health Care Products Assn., Am. Mgmt. Assn. (pres.'s assn.), Chief Execs. Orgn., World Pres.'s Orgn., Lenexa City C. of C., Indian Hills Country Club, Kansas City Club, Lotos Club, N.Y. Athletic Club, Mercury Club, Delta Chi. Home: 6706 Glenwood St Shawnee Mission KS 66204-1451 Office: 15501 W 109th St Lenexa KS 66219-1307

ASCHERMAN, JEFFREY ALAN, plastic and reconstructive surgeon; b. Erie, Pa., Mar. 19, 1962; s. Herbert Stanley and Dorothy Rose A.; m. Corinne Fortunee Rouah, June 9, 1988; children: Jeremy, Benjamin, Jonathan, Sarah. Student, Am. U. Paris, 1983; BA, Harvard U., 1984; MD, Columbia U., 1988. Diplomate Am. Bd. Plastic Surgery. Resident in gen. surgery Columbia-Presbyn. Med. Ctr., NYC, 1988-91, rsch. fellow, 1991-92, resident in plastic surgery, 1992-94; fellow in craniofacial and pediat. plastic surgery Hôpital Necker-Enfants Malades, Paris, 1994-95; instr. clin. surgery Columbia U., NYC, 1995-97, asst. prof. surgery, 1998—2006, chief divsn. plastic surgery, 2004—, assoc. prof. clin. surgery, 2006—11, prof. clin. surgery, 2011—. Assoc. adj. N.Y. Eye and Ear Infirmary, N.Y.C., 1995-2001, adj. surg., 2001—; asst. attending physician N.Y. Presbyn. Hosp., N.Y.C., 1995—; adj. asst. prof. surgery Cornell Univ., 2002-08, adj. asst. prof. clin. surgery, 2008-. Patentee palatal distractor; contbr. articles to profl. jours. Active local synagogues Kehilath Jeshurun, N.Y.C., 1996—. Palatal Distraction Rsch. grantee Columbia U., 1996, Plastic Surgery Edn. Found., 1997; Cranial Ossification Rsch. grantee Columbia U., 1997; Retention Suture Rsch. grantee Columbia U., 1998; Hydroxyapatite Resin Rsch. grantee Columbia U., 1999; Cranial bone rsch. grantee, 2000, Cranial Reossification Rsch. grantee, 2001, Wound Healing Rsch. grantee, 2002, 05, Craniofacial Outcomes Study grantee, 2004, Wound Angiogenesis rsch. grantee, 2004; grantee NIH, 2005, 2009, Rsch. grant, 2009, Neointimal Hyperplasia Rsch. grant, 2010. Mem. AMA, ACS, Am. Soc. Plastic Surgeons, Am. Assn. Plastic Surgeons, Am. Cleft Palate-Craniofacial Assn., Am. Soc. for Aesthetic Plastic Surgery, Am. Soc. Peripheral Nerve, Med. Soc. State N.Y., Assn. Academic Surgery, N.Y. County Med. Soc., N.Y. Regional Soc. Plastic and Reconstructive Surgery, Plastic Surgery Rsch. Coun., No. Soc. Plastic Surgeons, Alpha Omega Alpha. Republican. Avocations: tennis, travel, skiing. Office: Columbia Univ Med Ctr 161 Fort Washington Ave New York NY 10032-3713 Office Phone: 212-305-9612. Business E-Mail: jaa7@columbia.edu. *

ASCHER-WALSH, CHARLES J., obstetrician, gynecologist, educator; BA in History cum laude, Amherst Coll., 1986—90; MD, SUNY, 1991—95; M in Biostatistics, Columbia U., 2000—02. Diplomate Am. Bd. Ob-Gyn. Resident ob-gyn. NY Presbyn. Hosp., 1995—99, adminstrv. chief resident, 1998—99, fellowship advanced pelvic surgery/urogynecology, 1999—2000, asst. clin. prof. ob-gyn.; mem. divsn. urogynecology Columbia Univ., 2003—06, co-dir. divsn. minimal access surgery, 2003—06; dir. NY Fibroid Ctr., 2003—; mem. med. adv. bd. obstetric fistula repair Internat. Fund for Women and Devel., Niger, 2004—; asst. clin. prof. Mt. Sinai Sch. Med.; dir. divsn. gynecology Mt. Sinai Med. Ctr., 2006—. Office: Mount Sinai Medical Center 5 E 98th St New York NY 10029 Office Phone: 212-241-7952.

ASCHNER, JUDY LYNN, pediatrician, educator; b. Troy, NY, June 9, 1955; d. Herman and Roselyn Arbit; m. Michael Aschner, Aug. 5, 1979; children: Yael, Eitan, Nadav, Amir. BS summa cum laude, Union Coll., Schnectady, NY, 1977; MD, U. Rochester Sch. Medicine, Rochester, NY, 1981. Diplomate Nat. Bd. Med. Examiners, 1984, bd. cert. Am. Bd. Pediat., 1989, cert. in ABP neonatal-perinatal medicine subboard 1991. Asst. prof. pediat. Albany Med. Coll., Albany, NY, 1988—94; assoc. prof. pediat. Wake Forest U. Health Scis. Ctr., Winston-Salem, NC, 1994—2003, prof. pediat., 2003—04, Vanderbilt U. Med. Ctr., Nashville, 2004—, dir. neonatology, 2004—. Vice-chairperson and mem. exec. bd. IPOKRaTES Internat., Munich, 2002—. Founder Tenn. Initiative Perinatal Quality Care, Nashville, 2008. Recipient Lee Wrubel Meml. prize, Union Coll., 1977, Best Dr. Am., 2005—08; Rsch. grants, NIH, 1999, 2005—06. Fellow: Am. Acad. Pediat.; mem.: Perinatal Rsch. Soc., Am. Bd. Pediat. (neonatal-perinatal subboard 2007—), Tenn. Perinatal Adv. Com., AAP Sect. Perinatal Pediat. (exec. com. liaison ontpd 2003—08, strategic planning com. 2003—08), Orgn. Neonatology Fellowship Tng. Dir. (chair 2003—07), Am. Heart Assn. (cardiopulmonary & critical care coun. leadership & program com. 2004—08), Soc. Pediatric Rsch., Tenn. Initiative Perinatal Quality Care (exec. com. 2008), Am. Pediatric Soc. Achievements include research in basic research in perinatal pulmonary vascular biology, clinical research in neonatology. Office: Vanderbilt Univ Med Ctr 2200 Children's Way Nashville TN 37232 0034

ASCIERTO, PAOLO ANTONIO, physician, director; b. Solopaca, Benevento, Italy, Nov. 8, 1964; s. Domenico Ascierto and Cesira Maria Fasano; m. MariaTeresa Melucci, Sept. 2, 1995; children: Marco, Luca. Diplomate U. Federico II Napoli, 1990, in oncology U. Federico II Napoli, 1994. Prof. dermatology Second Sch. Medicine, U. Napoli, 2008; vice dir. unit clin. immunology Inst. Nat. Tumori Pascale, Napoli, 1993—2007, dir. unit med. oncology & innovative therapy, 2008—. Cons. Alleanza Nat., Rome, 2003—07. Recipient Knight Italian Republic award, 2005, Citation award, 2007, Comdr. Italian Republic award, 2011. Mem.: Nat. Oncology Com., Italian Melanoma Intergroup (pres. 2005—07), European Soc. Med. Oncology, Am. Soc. Clin. Oncology. Roman Catholic. Avocations: soccer, horseback riding. Office: Inst Nat Tumori Pascale via Mariano Semmola Napoli 80131 Italy Office Fax: 390815903841. Business E-Mail: pasciert@tin.it.

ASCIONE, FRANK JOSEPH, dean, pharmacy educator; b. Detroit, Nov. 12, 1946; s. Salvatore Enrico and Anne Nelse (Wagman) Ascione; children: Wendy, Mark; m. Nancy A. Grand, July 22, 2004 (dec.). BS, U. Mich. Coll. Pharmacy, Ann Arbor, 1969, PharmD, 1973; MPH, U. Mich. Sch. Pub. Health, 1977, PhD, 1981. Lic. pharmacist Mich. Staff pharmacist St. Joseph Mercy Hosp., Ann Arbor, 1969-73; prog. dir. Am. Pharm. Assn., Washington, 1973-76; asst. then assoc. prof. pharmacy U. Mich. Coll. Pharmacy, 1976—2001, prof. social and adminstrv. scis., 2001—, assoc. dean, 1996—2004, dean, 2004—. Author: Principles of Scientific Literature Evaluation: Critiquing Clinical Drug Trials, 2001; co-author: Principles of Drug Information and Scientific Literature Evaluation, 1994; contbr. articles to profl. jours., chapters to books. Mem. Am. Pharm. Assn. (chmn. econ. and adminstrv. sci. sect. 1990-91, Acad. fellow 1994), Mich. Pharmacy Assn. (task force on patient edn. 1983-86, exec. bd. medal 1986), Am. Pub. Health Assn., Drug Info. Assn., Rho Chi. Office: U Mich Coll Pharmacy 428 Church St Ann Arbor MI 48109-1065 Home Phone: 734-747-8483; Office Phone: 734-763-0100, 734-764-7144. Office Fax: 734-764-2022. Business E-Mail: fascione@umich.edu.

ASERO, RICCARDO SALVATORE, physician; b. Milan, Feb. 27, 1956; s. Biagio Antonino and Vanna (Carnevali) Asero; m. Luisa Faravelli, July 4, 1987; 1 child, Sergio. MD, U. Milan, 1982, Specialist in Allergy/Clin. Immunology, 1985. Postdoctoral fellowship in Allergy and Clin. Immunology U. Milan, 1982—85; head allergy unit Ospedale Caduti Bollatesi, Bollate, Milan, 1990—2002; head allergy divsn. Clinica San Carlo, Paderno Dugnano, Italy, 2002—. Cons. Pirelli Spa, Milan, 1988—; vol. rschr. Allergy and Clin. Immunology Sch., U. Milan, 1985—88. Contbr. articles to profl. jours.; mem. editl. staff The Lancet, 1983—96. Mem. World Wildlife Fund, 1988—. Mem.: Italian Soc. Allergy Immunology, European

Acad. Allergy Immunology. Avocations: sports, music, travel, art. Office: Clinica San Carlo Via Ospedale 21 20037 Paderno Dugnano MI Italy Office Phone: +39 02 99038470. Business E-Mail: r.asero@libero.it.

ASFOURY, ZAKARIA MOHAMMED, physician; b. Port Said, Egypt, Aug. 5, 1921; arrived in Eng., 1946; s. Mohammed El Asfoury; m. Fadia Katamesh BSc distinction and specialization, Cairo U., 1942, BSc honors, 1944, MB BCh, 1946; MSc, London U., 1952; PhD, Heliopolice & Georgia U., 1965. Hon. demonstrator medicine Liverpool U., England, 1946—49; hon. demonstrator, rsch. fellow London U. Medicine, 1949—52; curator mus., asst. lectr. Cairo U., 1952—55; pvt. practice Cairo, 1952—69, London, 1969—2002. Owner Brislington Pvt. Nursing Home and Hosp., Bristol, Eng.; rep. London Hosp., London U. 5th Internat. Anatomical Congress-Oxford, 1950; head dept. medicine and tropical diseases Schs. Hosp., Cairo; physician in charge various hosps.; lectr. Oxford, Cambridge; chmn. Egyptian Scholars Ann. Conf. concerning Suez Canal; expert in field of petrol pollution in Alaska, Ebola virus in Africa, WHO, successful ancient herbal treatments; mem. Internat. Religions Conf., N.J.; spkr, lectr. in field Author: Sympathectomy and the Innervation of the Kidney, 1971; contbr. articles to profl. jours.; translator books: Fine Whole Vision, 1934, Clothes from Feethers, 1935, Silent Aircrafts, 1940, Fertilizers from Insects, 1950, Diabetes in Animals, 1951, A New Fungicide, 2005, Save our Seas, 2006. Mem. Royal Coll. Physicians London (lic.), Royal Coll. Surgeons Eng., Brit. Med. Assn., Royal Soc. Medicine, Renal Assn. Britain, Anatomical Soc. U.K., Geriat. Soc. Britain, Hunterian Soc. Britain, Internat. Cultural Exch., Egyptian Med. Union in World (chmn.), Ea. Carpet Soc., Egyptian Scholars Abroad (chmn.), Egyptian Scholars (chmn.), Port Said Scholars (hon. chmn.), Cardiac Assn Achievements include discovery of 1st motor working by water in 1937 and new cars work by water, the cause of appendicitis, 1st renal transplant(kidney) 1949; first use of ultraviolet microscopy to discover details of central nervous system; first demonstration of detailed innervation of whole kidneys, of microscopic details of sympathetic and Vagus nerve distributions above and below the diaphragm in human embryos, 1950; use of electric treatments for bronchitis, asthma, renal stones, severe pain and neuritis; pioneer in breaking of kidney, 1st in world before 1953, stones by very high frequency currents; treatment of bilharzia, amoeba and malaria by daithermy; treatment of heart ischemia by very high frequency currents; treatment of psoriasis; treatment of a 40 year old resistant eczema by natural elements; treatment of diabetic children by very high frequency currents; liquification of natural gases in Kuwait and solving water shortage in Kuwait, 1969; reduction of human sperm and different forms of renewable energy; discovery of collagenase enzyme and anticollagenase in man and animals; discovery that ants protect plants from green flies. Office Phone: 02 7274 6877.

ASHAMALLA, HANI L., radiation oncologist, educator; b. Aug. 11, 1960; Grad., Ain Shams U.; M in Pulmonary Med., Ain shams U., 1989. Diplomate Am. Bd. Radiology, 1995, lic. Calif., 1990, NY, 1994, Pa., 1994. Co- prin. investigator; prin. investigator; med. supr. Maimonides Med. Ctr., Brooklyn, NY; fellow Am. Coll of Chest Physicians, 1998, Am. Coll. Radiation Oncology, 2004; med. intern NY Meth. Hosp., 1990—91, chief resident, 1993—94, radiation oncology resident, 1991—94, asst. attending radiation oncologist, 1995—2002, assoc. attending radiation oncologist, 2002—, vice chmn. cancer activities com., 1997—99, vice chmn. rsch. and devel., 1999—, chmn. cancer activities com., 1999—2002, chmn. ethics com., 2004—05, chmn. credentials com., 2002—03, 2005—; asst. attending radiation oncologist Maimonides Med. Ctr., 1995—, Coney Island Hosp., 1997—, victory Meml. Hosp., Kingsbrook Med. Ctr., 2003—; asst. clin. prof. in radiology Cornell Med. Ctr., 1997—; pulmonary medicine resident Ain Shams Univ., Cairo, 1986—89; pediatric oncology fellow Pa. Univ., 1994. Author: Treatment Related Morbidity in Prostate Cancer-Impact of Technique, Role of Gold Grain Implant in Cancer Palliation, Role of Gold grain Implant in the Palliation of Recurrent Locally Advanced Head and Neck Cancers, Correlation between Back Pain and MRI Findings in Neurologically Intact Patients with Spinal Metastasis, 87 Gold grain implants in resistant tumors- a useful modality in difficult head and neck sites, Mitotic arrest, cell death and increased p53 Immunofluorescence in Taxol Treated Cells, Hyperbaric Oxygen Therapy for the Treatment of Radiation Sequelae in Children, Comparative Study and Significance of Measured and Calculated Doses Delivered to the Rectum in Different Plans for Treatment of ProstaticCancer, Phase I/II Trial of Hyperfractionated Radiation Therapy with Taxol in Locally advanced/unresectable pancreatic cancer, Primary Hodgkin's Disease of the Thyroid. Case Report and Literature Review, Interstitial Hyperthermia as a Radiosensitizer in Resistant and Recurrent Tumors - the Pelvic Lesions, various publs. Mem.: Am. Brachytherapy Soc., Am. Radium Soc., Soc. of Neuro-Oncology, Children's Cancer Study Group, Pediatric Oncology Group, Internatio. Soc. of Radiosurgery, Am. Soc. of Clinical Oncology, European Soc. of Therapeutic Oncology, Radiological Soc. of North America, Assn. of Residents in Radiation Oncology, Am. Coll. of Radiation Oncology, Am. Soc. of Chest Physicians, Am. Soc. of Therapeutic Radiology and Oncology. Office: New York Methodist Hospital 506 Sixth St Brooklyn NY 11215

ASHER, VALERIE, otolaryngologist; MD summa cum laude, Yale Coll., 1985. Diplomate Am. Bd. Otolaryngology. Intern UMDNJ — Robert Wood Johnson Hosp., NJ; resident otolaryngology-head and neck surgery Yale New Haven Hosp.; hosp. affiliation includes Drs. Hauck and Bianchi, 1999, Wash. Adventist Hosp. Tchg. fellow Yale — China Assn. Named one of the Top Doctors, Washingtonian Mag., 2011. Fellow: Am. Acad. of Otolaryngology-Head and Neck Surgery. Avocations: travel, fencing, languages. Office: Hauck, Bianchi & Driscoll PA Number 203 2415 Musgrove Rd Silver Spring MD 20904 Office Phone: 301-989-2300. Office Fax: 301-236-5357.

ASHFAQ, RAHEELA, pathologist, educator; arrived in U.S., 1985; m. M. Hossein Saboorian; children: Nina Saboorian, Amir Saboorian. MB, BChir, Fatima Jinnah Med. Coll., Pakistan, 1976; degree (hon.), Govt. Coll., Rawalpindi, Pakistan. Diplomate Am. Bd. Pathology, 1992. Staff surg. pathologist Zale-Lipshy U. Hosp., Dallas, 1992—; dir. cytopathology Parkland Meml. Hosp., Dallas, 1993—2005; program dir. cytology fellowship U. Tex. Southwestern Med. Ctr., Dallas, 1994—, prof. pathology, 2002—; dir. oncodiagnostic lab. Parkland Health & Hosp. Sys., Dallas, 1996—. Mem. pathology rev. com. Gynecology Oncology Group, 1995—; grant reviewer Susan G. Komen Breast Cancer Found., Dallas, 2003—; jour. reviewer Obs & Gyn, Cancer, Cancer Cytopathology, Diagnostic Cytopathology, JAMA, 1998—. Founding mem. bd. trustees Breast Cancer Risk Stratification Assn., Dallas, 2003—05. Mem.: U.S. and Can. Acad. Pathology, Coll. Am. Pathologists, Am. Soc. for Clin. Pathology, Am. Soc. Cytopathology. Achievements include research in prognostic and predictive tumor markers; evaluation of new technologies in cancer diagnosis and prognosis; makers for targeted therapies. Office: UT Southwestern Medical Center at Dallas 5323 Harry Hines Blvd EE4-206 Dallas TX 75390-9073

ASHINOFF, ROBIN, dermatologic surgeon; b. Bklyn., May 31, 1960; d. Melvin and Ava Joan Ashinoff; m. Jeffrey Keith Steuer, May 14, 1988; children: Alexa Beth, Justin Eric. BA, Johns Hopkins U., 1981; MD, NYU, 1985. Intern N.Y. Hosp., NYC, 1985-86, resident, 1986-89; fellow Rockefeller U., NYC, 1988-89; Mohs fellow, laser fellow N.Y. Skin and Cancer Unit, NYC, 1989-91; chief of dermatologic and Mohs surgery, cosmetic and laser surgery Hackensack (N.J.) U. Med. Ctr. Avocations: reading, swimming. Office: Hackensack U Med Ctr 360 Essex St Hackensack NJ 07601 Office Phone: 201-336-8660. Personal E-mail: rashinoffmd@aol.com. Business E-Mail: rashinoff@humed.com.

ASHIZAWA, NAOKI, pharmacologist, researcher; b. Kawanehoncho, Shizuoka, Japan, Aug. 1, 1961; s. Tomio and Rin Ashizawa; m. Masumi Kato. B in Pharmacy, Shizuoka Coll. Pharmacy, Japan, 1984, MS in Pharmacy, 1986; PhD, U. Shizuoka, 1994. Rschr. Sapporo Breweries Co., Ltd. R&D Divsn., Yaizu, Shizuoka, 1986—93; sr. rsch. scientist Grelan Pharm. Co., Ltd. R&D Divsn., Hamura, Tokyo, 1993—99, Fujiyakuhin Co., Ltd. Med. R&D Divsn., Saitama, Japan, 1999—. Sci. councilor Japanese Pharmacol. Soc., 1996—. Author: (book) Brain and Blood Pressure Control; contbr. articles to profl. jours. Achievements include discovery of a novel, potent xanthine oxidoreductase inhibitor, FYX-051, which is currently under development. It has contributed to the determination of the structure and catalytic mechanism of the enzyme; patents in field. Avocation: running. Office: Fuji Yakuhin Co Rsch Labs 2 636-1 Iidashinden Nishi-ku Saitama 3310068 Japan Personal E-mail: ashiza@dianet.ne.jp. Business E-Mail: 12-26899@fujiyakuhin.co.jp.

ASHMAWY, MAGDY MAHMOUD, dermatologist, consultant; b. Alexandria, Egypt, May 14, 1955; s. Mahmoud Mohammed and Fatma Ibraheem Ashmawy; m. Mervat Mahmoud Abulela, Aug. 2, 1985; children: Abdelrahman Magdy, Nouran Magdy. B, U. Alexandia, 1979; MD, U. Tanta, 1987. Head physician, trainer Magdy Ashmawy Dermatology Ctr. Ministry Health, Alexandria, 1987—. Cons. dermatologist, Alexandria, 1999—. Fellow: Am. Acad. Dermatology (assoc.); mem.: Egyptian Soc. Dermatology and Venerology (assoc.), Internat. Soc. Dermatology (assoc.), European Acad. Dermatology and Venerology (assoc.). Muslim. Avocations: travel, reading. Home: 18 Tawneyat Smouha 21321 Alexandria Egypt Office: Private Clinic 10, Kenna St Ibrahimeya 21321 Alexandria Egypt Office Fax: +2 034250109. E-mail: magdyeshmawy@yahoo.com.

ASHOUR, MOHAMED MOTEE, pharmacist; b. Jizan, Saudi Arabia, Jan. 1, 1963; BS in Pharmacy, King Saud U., 1987, PharmM, 1992. Pharmacy asst. King Faisal Hosp., 1987—88, pharmacist 2, 1988—90, clin. pharmacist, 1993—2005; pharmacist 1 King Faisal Specialist Hosp., 1991—92, mgr., 2005—. Rschr. King Saud U., 1987—. Mem.: Saudi Pharm. Soc. Avocation: swimming. Office: Takhassusi St PO Box 3354 Riyadh 11211 Saudi Arabia Office Fax: 00966-1-4427608. Business E-Mail: ashour@kfshrc.edu.sa.

ASHRAF ALI, MOHAMED, pharmacist; b. Elangakurichy, Jan. 15, 1980; PhD, Jamia Hamdard U., 2006. Rsch. dir. Alwar Pharmacy Coll., 2006—. Fellow U. Sainsmalaysia. Postdoc. Fellowship, U. Sains Malaysia. Mem.: Indian Pharmacy Coun. Avocations: tennis, reading, cricket. Office: Alwar Pharmacy Coll Mia-Alwar Alwar Rajasthan 301030 India E-mail: asraf80med@rediffmail.com.

ASHTON, DIANE MARIE, health charity association administrator; b. NYC, Sept. 10, 1957; d. Lorimer and Josephine Ashton; m. Michael William Geffrard, May 15, 2004. BA in Biology, NYU, 1979; MD, Weil Cornell Med. Coll., NYC, 1983; MPH, Cornell U. Sch. Pub. Health, 1990. Diplomate Am. Bd. Ob-Gyn. Resident in obstetrics & gynecology St. Luke's-Roosevelt Hosp. Ctr., NYC, 1983—87; attending physician Harlem Hosp., 1989—96; dir. women's health services King's County Med. Ctr., Bklyn., 1998—2004; dep. med. dir. March of Dimes Found., White Plains, NY, 2003—. V.p. bd. dirs. Heartbeats of the World,Inc., NYC. Contbr. articles to profl. jours. Office: March of Dimes Nat Office 1275 Mamaroneck Ave White Plains NY 10605 Office Phone: 914-997-4488. Business E-Mail: dashton@marchofdimes.com. *

ASHWELL, JONATHAN D., medical researcher; MD, Columbia U., 1978. Resident in internal medicine Columbia Presbyn. Hosp., NYC; postdoctoral fellow in immunology Nat. Inst. Allergy and Infectious Diseases, NIH; prin. investigator Nat. Cancer Inst., NIH, 1985—92, chief Lab. Immune Cell Biology, Ctr. Cancer Rsch., 1992—. Office: Lab Immune Cell Biology Nat Inst Cancer Ctr Cancer Rsch 9000 Rockville Pike Bldg 37 Rm 3002C Bethesda MD 20892-4259 Office Phone: 301-496-4931. Office Fax: 301-402-4844. E-mail: jda@pop.nci.nih.gov. *

ASHWORTH, RONALD BROUGHTON, health facility executive, accountant; b. San Francisco, Apr. 19, 1945; s. Robert William and Tracy Marie (Parks) Ashworth; m. Carol Lynn Heaps, Oct. 2, 1970; 1 child, Christina Ann. BBA, U. Mo., Columbia, 1967; MA, U. Mo., 1968. CPA Mo., NC, Ill., La. With Peat Marwick Mitchell & Co., 1968—91, ptnr., 1975—91, in charge St. Louis Office health care practice, 1975—77, nat. dir. health care practice, 1978—91, Chgo., 1979—91; exec. v.p., COO Sisters of Mercy Health Sys., 1991—99, pres., CEO, 1999—. Bd. dirs. Chgo. Lung Assn., Mid-Am. chpt. ARC. Recipient Haskins and Sells award, 1967, award, Fin. Execs. Inst., 1967; scholar, Alpha Kappa Psi, 1967. Mem.: Ill. Soc. CPAs, Am. Hosp. Assn., Fedn. Am. Hosps., Am. Inst. CPAs, Healthcare Fin. Mgmt. Assn., Country Club Mo., Medinah Country Club, Tavern Club. Office: Sisters of Mercy Health System 14528 S Outer Forty Chesterfield MO 63017

ASIMACOPOULOS, PANAYIOTIS JOHN, cardiovascular and thoracic surgeon, consultant, researcher; s. John Athanasios Asimacopoulos and Eleni Emmanuel Kapetanakis; m. Vivian Joan Gettas, July 16, 1983; children: Eleni, Anastasia, John. DDS, U. Athens, 1959, MD, 1967, PhD, 1978; cert. in biomed. engring., MIT, 1975. Diplomate Am. Bd. Surgery, European Bd. Thoracic and Cardiovasc. Surgeons, Greek Bd. Surgery, Greek Bd. Thoracic Surgery, Greek Bd. Vascular Surgery, lic. physician Greece, Maine, Tex. Resident in gen. surgery, 1st surg. svc., U. Athens Med. Sch., 1960—61, prof., chmn. cardiac surgery, 1994—2001; intern Tufts Surg. Svc., Boston, 1971—72; resident in gen. surgery Harvard Surg. Svc., Boston, 1972—77, chief resident in gen. surgery, 1977—78; clin. fellow Harvard U., Cambridge, Mass., 1977—78; resident in cardiovasc.-thoracic surgery Med. Coll. Wis., Milw., 1978—79, chief resident in cardiovasc.-thoracic surgery, 1979—80; postdoctoral fellow in cardiovasc. surgery Baylor Coll. Medicine, Houston, 1980—82, instr. surgery, 1982—83, asst. prof. surgery, 1983—85, clin. asst. prof. surgery, 1988—92, clin. assoc. prof. surgery, 1993—95; dir. cardiothoracic surgery Henry Dunant Hosp., Athens, 2001—04; cardiovasc. surgeon IASO Hosp., Athens, 2004—. Rsch. fellow in surgery Harvard Med. Sch., Boston, 1969—71, 1973—74; fellow MIT, Boston, 1974—75; vis. prof. U. Athens Med. Sch., 1991, St. Mary's Hosp., London, 1998; staff physician Meth. Hosp., Houston, 1982—94, Athens Med. Ctr., 1994—98, Apollonion Hosp., Athens, 1998—2001; prof., chmn. dept. cardiac surgery Red Cross Hosp., Athens, 1998—2001; mem. spl. adv. com., chmn. extra-corporeal circulation com. Ctrl. Health Coun., Ministry of Health, Athens, 1996, mem. spl. com. for evaluation pacemaker ctrs., chmn. examiners of Greek Bds. of Thoracic Surgery; spkr., lectr. in field. Author (with others): Elements of Cardiac Surgery, 1999; contbr. articles to profl. jours, chapters to books. 2d lt. med. corps Greek Air Force, 1959—61. Recipient plaque, 1st Hellenic Congress Angiology and Vascular Surgery, 1993, 3d Symposium of Greek Friends of Meth. Hosp., 1994. Fellow: ACS, Am. Coll. Cardiology, European Soc. Cardiology, Internat. Coll. Surgeons in Cardiovasc. Surgery, Am. Coll. Angiology, Am. Coll. Cardiology (assoc.), Am. Coll. Chest Physicians (assoc.); mem.: AMA (Physician's Recognition award in continuing med. edn. 1982—91), Greek Coll. Cardiology and Cardiac Surgery, European Soc. Vascular Surgery, European Assn. Cardiothoracic Surgery, Hellenic Soc. Biomed. Rsch. and Lab. Animals, Soc. Critical Care Medicine, Internat. Soc. Endovascular Surgery, Hellenic Vascular Surg. Soc., Hellenic Soc. Thoracic and Cardiovasc. Surgery, Internat. Assn. Surgery of Trauma and Surg. Intensive Care, Internat. Soc. Surgery, Hellenic Profl. Soc. of Tex., European Soc. Vascular Surgery, N.Am. Soc. Pacing and Electrophysiology, Am. Thoracic Soc., Houston Cardiology Soc., Am. Heart Assn., Southea. Surg. Congress, Am. Fedn. Clin. Rsch., Houston Surg. Soc., Tex. Med. Found., Hellenic (Greek) Surg. Soc. (honorary plaque 1993), Southwestern Surg. Congress, Internat. Union Angiology (internat. adv. com. jour. 1992), Tex. Med. Assn., Harris County Med. Soc., Michael E. DeBakey Internat. Surg. Soc., Assn. Advancement of Med. Instrumentation, Internat. Soc. Artificial Organs, N.Y. Acad. Scis., Athens Med. Assn., Internat. Microsurg. Soc., Am. Soc. Artificial Internal Organs, Brotherhood of Friends of Patriarchate of Jerusalem, Greek Red Cross, Soc. of Greek Friends of Meth. Hosp., Med. Coll. Wis. Marquette Med. Alumni Assn., Harvard Med. Alumni Assn., Assn. Alumni and Alumnae of MIT. Achievements include patents for intraluminal vascular or visceral of variable diameter removable stent; patents pending for radiolabeling of white blood cells using liposomes. Office: Krimeas 19-21 Neo Psychiko Athens Greece also: IASO Gen Hosp 264 Meeogion St Cholargos Athens Greece Home: Valaoritu 10 154 52 Athens Greece Office Phone: (01) 2106502655. Office Fax: (01) 2106925950, (01) 2106925950, (01) 2106502654. E-mail: panas1@otenet.gr.

ASIMAKOPOULOS, ANASTASIOS D., urologist; b. Pyrgos, Greece, Jan. 15, 1980; Degree in Medicine & Surgery, U. Rome Tor Vergata, 2004; PhD in Robotics Surgery. Urology specialist U. Rome Tor Vergata, 2005—. Contbr. scientific papers to profl. jours. Grant, Alexander S. Onassis Found. Fellow: Clinique St. Augustine Com. (Bordeaux, France) (mem. dept. urology). Achievements include research in minimally invasive urology in terms of laparoscopy and robotics, the prostate carcinogenesis and HIFU. Avocation: sports. Home: Via Todi 60 Rome 00181 Italy Home Fax: 390620902975. Personal E-mail: tasospao2003@yahoo.com.

ASKANAS-ENGEL, VALERIE, neurologist, educator, researcher; b. Poland, May 28, 1937; came to U.S., 1969, naturalized, 1975; d. Marian and Leontyne Hornik; m. W. King Engel; 1 dau., Eve Monique Kerr. MD, Warsaw Med. Sch., Poland, 1960, PhD, 1967; Doctor honoris causa, U. d'Aix-Marseille, France, 1987. Rotating intern Univ. Hosp. Warsaw Med. Sch., 1960-61, resident in neurology, 1961-64, fellow in neuromuscular diseases, 1964-65; asst. prof. neurology Warsaw Med. Sch., 1965-69; assoc. mem. Inst. Muscle Diseases, NYC, 1969-73; asst. prof. NYU Med. Sch., 1973-77; sr. investigator NIH, Bethesda, Md., 1977-81; prof. neurology and pathology U. So. Calif., LA, 1981—; co-dir. Neuromuscular Ctr. at Hosp. Good Samaritan, 1981—, Muscular Dystrophy Assn. Clinic, 1981—, The Jerry Lewis ALS Clin. and Rsch. Ctr., 1988—; editl. bd. mem. Neuromuscular Disorders, 2004—; acta Neuropathologica, 2008—. V.p. 6th Internat. Congress on Neuromuscular Diseases, 1986, 7th, 1990, 8th, 1994;pres. sci. program com. XII Internat. Jour Neuromuscular Diseases, Naples, Italy, 2010, vis. prof. internat. congresses, Europe, S.Am., Can., Far East; hon. lectr. Royal Coll. Physicians and Surgeons, 1999. Contbr. numerous articles, chpts., abstracts to med. publs.; sr. editor: (book) Inclusion-Body Myositis and Myopathies, 1998; assoc. editor Acta Myologia, 2002—. Recipient Dean's prize for outstanding rsch., 1967, NIH Merit award, 1999—, Gaetano Conti Gold Medal for Basic Rsch., Napoli, 1999; Premio Associazione Stampa Medica Italiana Di Giurnal ItalianaIsmo Medico, 1980; grantee NIH, 1974-77, 83—, NIH Merit award, 1999—, Muscular Dystrophy Assn., 1969-77, 81—. Fellow Am. Acad. Neurology, L.A. Acad. Medicine; mem. Soc. for Neurosci., Am. Neurol. Assn., d'Honneur de la Soc. Francaise de Neurologie, Am. Soc. Cell Biology, Am. Assn. Neuropathology, Histochem. Soc., Uruguayan Neurological Assn. (hon. mem.), L.A. County Med. Assn., Polish Neurol. Assn. (hon.). Office: U So Calif Neuromuscular Ctr Good Samaritan Hosp 637 Lucas Ave Los Angeles CA 90017-1912 Office Phone: 213-975-9951, 213-977-2265. Business E-Mail: askanas@usc.edu.

ASKENASY, JEAN JACQUES, neurologist; b. Sofia, Bulgaria, Nov. 13, 1929; arrived in Israel, 1972; s. Marcel Jacov and Roza Josef (Capon) Eskenasy; m. Hermina Nathan Stroe, 1956 (div. 1977); 1 child, Nadir; m. Rita Adolf Lupu Askenasy, Dec. 1, 1977; 1 child, Ran. MD, U. Cluj, Romania, 1954; PhD, C.I. Parhan U., Bucharest, Romania, 1969; sleep specialist, Albert Einstein U., 1981. Registration as specialist in neurology U. Bucharest, 1956. Resident U. Hosp. #9, Bucharest, 1957-62; chief resident Neurol. Inst., Bucharest, 1963-64; chmn. dept. U. Hosp. #9, Bucharest, 1965-72; sr. neurologist Souraski Med. Ctr., Tel Aviv, 1973-76; dep. chmn. Soroka Hosp.,

Beersheba, Israel, 1976-78; head neurology unit Ein-Shemer Psychiat. Hosp., Hadera, Israel, 1978-80; sr. neurologist Appeals Commn. Ministry of Health, Jerusalem, 1978—. Sr. neurologist Loewenstein Hosp. and Sackler Sch. Medicine, Tel Aviv, 1978-93, sr. lectr. Sackler Sch. Medicine, 1985-95, assoc. prof. neurology, 1995—; vis. assoc. prof. Mt. Sinai Sch. NYU, 1980-81; med. counselor Health Dept., Ministry of Edn., Jerusalem, 1985—; sr. neurologist and chmn. High Commn. Govt. Employees, Ministry of Health, Jerusalem, 1985—; assoc. prof. Pierre et Marie Curie U., Paris, 1986; dir. Inst. Sleep Medicine, Sheba Med. Ctr., Tel Hashomer, Israel, 1989—; mem. coun. Faculty Medicine, Tel Aviv U., 1994—. Author (book): Violence, 1995, The Grey Third of Life, 1995, The Brain and His Universe, 2007, Consciousness, 2007, The Enigmas of Sleep, 2008, File No. 148074, 2008, Emotions Humor, Smile, Laughter and Crying, 2010, Yawning and sighing, 2011; patentee in field. Pres. Israeli Assn. for Helping Immigrant Physicians, 1994—. Decorated officer Mono Order of Togo Republic, Gheorge Marinescu Order; recipient first prize Journées Internationales de Medicine, Grenoble, France, 1970, Acad. Merit of Academia Romana, 2003; named Notable of City, Mcpl. Coun., Yerucham, Israel, 1978. Mem. Asian Sleep Rsch. Soc. (pres. 1994—, chmn. sci. com. 1997—), Israeli Sleep Medicine Assn. (chmn. 1994—), Romanian Acad. Med. Scis. (hon.), Romanian Acad. Men of Sci. (hon.). Avocations: classical music, popularization of science, helping immigrants. Home: 79, Ben Yehuda 46403 Herzliya Israel Home Phone: 972-99543242; Office Phone: 972 54428558. E-mail: ajean@post.tau.ac.il.

ASLLANI, IRIS, medical educator; b. Tirana, Albania, Dec. 26, 1966; M. U. Wash., 1998, PhD, 2002. Asst. prof. clin. radiology Columbia U., 2007—. Fulbright scholar. Mem.: Soc. Neurosci., Human Brain Maping, Internat. Soc. Magnetic Resonance Medicine. Home: 2700 Broadway Apt 2L New York NY 10025 Personal E-mail: irelas@gmail.com.

ASMA, EVREN, medical imaging researcher; b. Ankara, Turkey, Aug. 5, 1978; s. Tahir and Muzeyyen Asma. BSc, Bilkent U., Ankara, 1999; MSc, U. Southern Calif., LA, 2000; PhD, U. Southern Calif., 2004. Rsch. asst. U. Southern Calif., 1999—2004, postdoctoral rsch. assoc., 2004—; mem. staff GE Global Rsch. Ctr., 2005—. Mem.: IEEE. Avocation: swimming. Office: 1 Research Circle KWC-1311 Niskayuna NY 12309 Home: 30 Captions Blvd Waterford NY 12188 Office Phone: 518-387-7909.

ASMIS, LARS M., hematologist; b. Berlin, Nov. 7, 1964; Eidgenossische Maturität - Typus B Latein, Feusi Ruedi Schule, Berne, Switzerland, 1984; MD in Medicine, U. Berne, 1990; habilitation, U. Zurich, 2010. Cert. in internal medicine FMH, 1998, in hematology FMH, 2000, FAMH, 2005. Mem. postgrad. course exptl. medicine & biology U. Zurich & U. Hosp., Berne, 1991—93; mem. clinic internal medicine & divsn. hematology U. Hosp., 1993—95; mem. clinic internal medicine 1 & divsn. hematology U. Hosp. Geneva, 1995—2002; vis. scientist Johns Hopkins U., Balt., 2002—04; head, coagulation lab. U. Hosp. Zurich, Divsn. Hematology, 2004—10. Contbr. articles to profl. jours. Fellowship, Swiss Found. Med.-Biol. Grants, 2002. Mem.: Schweizerische Gesellschaft Innere Medizin, Schweizerische Gesellschaft Hämatoloie, Gesellschaft Thrombose- und Hämostaseforschung, Am. Soc. Hematology, Internat. Soc. Thrombosis & Haemostasis. Home: Winterthurerstrasse 97A 8610 Uster Switzerland Personal E-mail: lars_asmis@yahoo.com.

ASOLA, MARKKU RAFAEL, nephrologist, director; b. Turku, Finland, Sept. 29, 1957; s. Rafael and Raili Asola; m. Raija Anita Altis; children:. MD, Turku U., 1982. Cert. specialist in nephrology Bd. Specialist Exams., Helsinki, Finland, 1991, specialist in internal medicine Turku U., 1988. Head dept. nephrology Satakunta Ctrl. Hosp., Pori, Finland, 2002—10; med. dir. Baxter Renal Europe, Stockholm, 2010—. Mem.: Finnish Soc. Nephrology. Office Phone: 358400209889.

ASPERILLA, MARIANITO O. (MARK), epidemiologist; b. Manila, Philippines, Dec. 21, 1954; MD, U. Santo Tomas, Manila. Intern internal medicine Frankford Hosp., 1982—83; resident infectious disease Atlantic City Med. Ctr., 1983—86; fellow infectious disease Chgo. Med. Sch., 1986—87; fellow Albany Med. Coll., NY, 1988—90; physician St. Joseph's Hosp., Fla., 1990—93, Fawcett Hosp., Fla., 1990—93. Vol. physician Red Cross, 1985, Charlotte County Med. Soc., 1990; founder SW Fla. Disability Found., 1993, Free HIV Clinic, Charlotte, 1994; co-founder ACCESS Care, Inc., 1994; founder Charlotte County Disaster Preparedness Assessment Team, 2001. Recipient Presdl. Volunteer Svc. award, Leadership award (Internat. Med. Grad. Physician), AMA Found., 2006, Pride in the Profession award, AMA Found., 2006; April 12, 2005 named Mark O. Asperilla Day in Charlotte County, Fla. Office: Charlotte Regional Med Ctr Ste 102-A 3300 Tamiami Trail Port Charlotte FL 33952 Office Fax: 941-624-0212.

ASPINALL, MARA GLICKMAN, medical diagnostic company executive; b. NYC, Aug. 14, 1962; d. Alvin and Betty Glickman. BA in Internat. Rels., Tufts U., 1983; MBA, Harvard U., 1987. Assoc. First Boston Corp., NYC, 1986; cons. Bain & Co., Inc., Boston, 1987-90; dir. mktg., client services Hale & Dorr LLP, Boston, 1990-97; v.p. corporate devel. Genzyme Corp., Cambridge, Mass., 1997-2000; pres. Genzyme Pharmaceuticals, Cambridge, Mass., 1997—2003, Genzyme Emerging Technologies, 2000-01, Genzyme Genetics, Westborough, 2001—08; chmn. bd. DentaQuest Ventures, 2002—04; pres., CEO On-Q-ity, Inc., Waltham, Mass., 2008—11; pres. Ventana Medical Systems, Inc., Tucson, 2011—. Bd. dirs. Delta Dental Plan Mass., 2000-03, Tufts U., Coll. Citizenship & Pub. Svc., 2000-03; mem. biotech project adv. group Radcliffe Pub. Policy Inst. Mem. editl. bd.: Rainmaker's Quar., 1996. Chmn. American Cancer Soc., Mass., 1996-99; bd. dirs. Arts Boston, 1996-1999, Dana-Farber Cancer Inst., Boston, 1998—; dir. Success by 6 Leadership Coun., United Way, 1998-99; co-chmn. Early Edn. for All, 2000—. Recipient Woman of Vision award Mass. Prevent Blindness Assn., 1995, Pinnacle award for Emerging Exec. of Yr. Greater Boston C. of C., 1997; named one of The Forty under Forty Top Bus. Execs., Boston Bus. Jour., 1999, Ten Outstanding Young Leaders Boston Jaycees, 1999, Acad. of Women Achievers YWCA, 1999. Mem. Nat. Assn. Law Firm Mktg. (pres. New Eng. 1992-94), Assn. Tufts Alumnae (pres. 1988-90, 92-94, alumni trustee rep. bd. trustees), Harvard Bus. Sch. Assn. (chairperson reunion com.), Harvard Bus. Sch. Network for Women (dir. 1995-98), WGBH Corp. Exec. Coun. (dir. 1997-99), The Children's Mus. Boston (trustee 1996—), Greater Boston C. of C. (bd. dirs. 1999—). Office: Ventana Medical Systems Inc 1910 E Innovation Park Dr Tucson AZ 85701 Office Phone: 520-887-2155. *

ASSAF, AHMED ABDEL-RAHMAN, ophthalmic surgeon, consultant, educator; b. BeitNabala, Lod, Palestine, July 19, 1947; arrived in the U.K., 1973; s. Abdel-Rahman Sulieman Assaf and Hanieh Mohamed Safi; m. Tahani Ghalib Jarrar, Aug. 5, 1982; children: Noor Dawn, Sarah. MB, BChir, Coll. Medicine, Baghdad, Iraq, 1971; diploma in ophthalmology, Royal Colls., London, 1975; MD, U. Sheffield, Eng., 1984. Sr. house officer ophthalmology St. Pauls Eye Hosp., Liverpool, Eng., 1974-75; registrar in ophthalmology Sheffield U. Hosps., 1976-78; lectr. in ophthalmology Coll. Medicine, U. Sheffield, 1978-86; cons. pediat. ophthalm & strabismus King Khaled Eye Hosp., Riyadh, 1988-93; cons. ophthalmologist Milton Keynes NHS Trust/Stoke Mandeville Hosp., Buckinghamshire, England, 1994—2010; clin. dir. head and neck directorate Milton Keynes NHS Trust, 2002—05; regional advisor Coll. Ophthalmologists, Oxford Region, 2004—07; chmn. ophthalmology tng. com. Oxford Deanery, 2004—07. Asst. prof. ophthalmology Coll. Medicine, U. Kuwait, 1981-82, Coll. Medicine, King Saud U., Riyadh, 1987-90, assoc. prof., 1990-93; dir. residency tng. in ophthalmology King Saud U.-King Khaled Eye Hosp., Riyadh, 1990-94. Contbr. articles to profl. jours.; inventor in field. Scholar U. Baghdad, 1965-71. Fellow Royal Coll. Surgeons Edinburgh (cert. higher surg. tng. 1980), Royal Coll. Ophthalmologists London (examiner 1996—2007); mem. Internat. Strabismological Assn., European Strabismological Assn. Avocations: computer programming, chess, ping pong/table tennis, tennis. Office: Milton Keynes NHS Trust Standing Way Milton Keynes MK6 5LD England Personal E-mail: a3.assaf@gmail.com.

ASSAI ARDAKANI, MOHAMMAD, physician; b. Tehran, Iran, Feb. 11, 1956; MBBS, Dow Med. Coll., Karachi, 1981; MPH, Dundee U., 1991. Adviser dep. min., health Ministry of Health and Med. Edn., Iran, 1995—2000; with med. office PHC WHO, Pakistan, 2000—04, regional adviser Cmty. Based Initiatives, 2004—. Avocation: football. Office: Abdul Razak Al-Sanhouri Nasr City Cairo 11371 Egypt Office Phone: 202-2276-5029. Office Fax: 202-2670-2492. Business E-Mail: assaim@emro.who.int.

ASSANTACHAI, PRASERT, internist, geriatrician; b. Bangkok, June 1, 1957; s. Jitr Sudnoreekul; m. Malee Jungsupong, June 15, 1960; children: Kanin, Krit. MD with honors, Mahidol U., Bangkok, Thailand, 1981; BS (hon.), Mahidol U., 1980. Dep. head dept. preventive & social medicine Siriraj Hosp. Med. Sch., Bangkok, 1998—2008, asst. to dean, 1998—2005. Guest lectr. Thammasat U., Bangkok, 1995—. Author: The Comprehensive Study of Nutritional Survey in the Thai Elderly, 1999 (Chalermprakiat Fund, Faculty of Medicine Siriraj Hospital, 1995); contbr. articles to profl. jours.; author: Fall Prevention in the Thai Elderly, 2002. Fellow: Royal Coll. Physicians Thailand, Royal Coll. Physicians London; mem.: Thai Soc. Atherosclerosis (sci. com. 2001—), Med. Coun. Thailand (life). Buddhist. Avocations: stamp collection, jogging, travel, reading. Home: 30/32 Moo 8 Saibangwak Rd Bangkok 10160 Thailand Office: Siriraj Hosp Prannok Rd 10700 Bangkok Bangkok Thailand Home Phone: 662-4105625; Office Phone: 662-4197284. Office Fax: 662-4115034; Home Fax: 662-8657481. Business E-Mail: SIPUS@MAHIDOL.AC.TH.

ASSENZA, MARCO, research scientist, educator; b. Rome, Nov. 18, 1960; Degree in medicine, U. Sapienza, 1985, degree in Gen. Surgery, 1990. Rsch. scientist U. Sapienza Rome Policlinico Umberto I, 1991—, prof., 2001— Cons. Azienda U. Policlinico Umberto I, 1991—. Mem.: Soc. Italiana di Chirurgia. Avocation: running. Office: Azienda Policlinico Umberto I Via del P Rome 00100 Italy Office Fax: 39676901756. E-mail: marcomonica.assenza@libero.it.

ASSIRI, ADEL MOHAMMAD ALI, clinical biochemistry professor, department chairman; b. Jeddah, Saudi Arabia, June 19, 1964; s. Mohammad Ali Assiri and Fawziah Mohammad Kamal; m. Dalal Sayel Al-Harthy, Feb. 11, 1999; children: Lolwah Adel, Saud Adel. PhD, Faculty Medicine, Sheffield, Eng., 1995. Asst. prof. Dept. Clin. Biochemistry, U. King Saud, Abha, Saudi Arabia, 1995—2000; asst. prof. Dept. Biochemistry Umm Al-Qura U., Makkah, Saudi Arabia, 2000—03, dir. Med. Rsch. Ctr., Faculty Medicine, 2000—03, assoc. prof., 2003—, chmn. Dept. Biochemistry, Faculty Medicine, 2003—. Dir. clin. biochemistry lab. Faculty Medicine, Makkah, 2001—. Islam. Avocations: swimming, gardening, reading, travel.

ASSUMPCAO, FRANCISCO BAPTISTA, JR., psychiatrist, educator; b. Sao Paulo, Brazil, Sept. 7, 1951; s. Francisco Baptista and Lybia (Felice) A.; children: Tatiana, Thais MD, Med. Sch. ABC U., S. Andre, Brazil, 1974; M Psychology, Cath. U. Sao Paulo, 1985, D Psychology, 1988. Dir. rehab. ctr. Parents Assn. Handicapped Children, Sao Paulo, 1981—88; dir. rsch. Parents & Friends Assn. Exceptional Children, Sao Paulo, 1988—91; dir. psychology svc. med. sch. Sao Paulo U., 1994—96, dir. child psychiatry svc. fac. med., 1996—2003, prof. child psychiatry faculty medicine, 2003—04, prof. psychopathology psychology inst., 2005—. Author: Psiquiatria Infantil Brasileira, 1995, Psiquiatria Da Infancia E Adolescencia, 1994, Autismo, 1996, Adolescence, 1999, Handbook of Child and Adolescent Psychiatry, 2003, Sexuality and Mental Retardation, 2005, Psicopalolofia Evolutica, 2008; contbr. articles to profl. jours Mem. Brazilian Psychiatry Soc. (pres. child psychiatry dept. 1996-98), Child Psychiatry Soc., LatinoAm. Psychiatry Assn. (sec. child psychiat. dept. 1999-2001) Avocations: music, books, comics, drawing. Home: Al Lorena 105/83 01424-000 São Paulo Brazil Office: R Otonis 697 V Clementino 04025-002 Sao Paulo Brazil Home Phone: 55-11-30514794; Office Phone: 55-11-55792762. Office Fax: 55-11-55797195. Personal E-mail: cassiterides@bol.com.br.

ASSUMPÇÃO, FRANCISCO BAPTISTA, JR., psychology professor; b. São Paulo, Sept. 7, 1951; Degree in Medicine, Med. Sch. ABC, 1974, PhD in Psychology. Prof. Med. Sch. Sao Paulo U., 1991; assoc. prof. Psychol. Inst. São Paulo U., 2005—. Dir. child psychiatry svc. Clin. Hosp. São Paulo U., 1996—2001. Master: Brazilian Assn. Neurology Child Psychiatry; mem.: Psychology Acad. São Paulo. Avocations: music, art. Home: Al Lorena 105 Apt 83 São Paulo 01424-000 Brazil Home Fax: 55-11-55797195. Personal E-mail: cassiterides@bol.com.br.

ASSY, NIMER, physician; b. Fassouta, Galilee, Israel, Sept. 10, 1961; s. Najib Habib and Zakiya (Moussa) A.; m. Mary Nassib Khoury, July 20, 1985; 5 children. MD, U. Louvain, Brussels, 1987. Residency in internal medicine Rambam Hosp., Haifa, Israel, 1990-94, sr. physician, 1994-95, hepatology cons., 1996-99; dep. head internal medicine Zefat Hosp., 1999—, head Liver Clinic, 1999—. Asst. prof. Technion U., Haifa, 2000-01. Contbr. articles to profl. jours. including Jour. Hepatology, Hepatology. Hepatology fellow, Can., 1995-96. Mem Israeli Assn. Law and Medicine, Israel Assn. Study Liver Disease (awards 1998, 99). Roman Catholic. Avocations: poetry, jeep racing, chess, horse racing, politics. Home: Fassouta Village Box 428 25170 Upper Galilee Israel Office: Zefat Hosp 13100 Zefat, Upper Galilee Israel Office Phone: 927-4-9870-080, 972-4-6828-442. Office Fax: 972-4-9870-338. Personal E-mail: assy.nimer@gmail.com.

ASTON, SHERRELL JERONE, plastic surgeon, educator; b. Suffolk, Va., July 14, 1942; s. Walter Mathew Aston, Jr. and Mary Louise (Bracy) Aston; m. Michelle Sykes, Nov. 24, 1967 (dec. July 1995); children: Walter Mathew III, Sherrell Jerone, Bradford Sykes; m. Miriam (Muffie) Isabelle Potter, Dec. 27, 1996; children: Ashleigh Tatiana, Bracie Potter. BA, U. Va., Charlottesville, 1964, MD, 1968. Diplomate Am. Bd. Plastic Surgery, lic. Va., Calif., NY, Fla. Surgical intern UCLA Med. Ctr., 1968—69, surgical resident, 1969—70, surgical/chief resident, 1971—73; Halsted fellow in surgery John Hopkins Hosp., Balt., 1970; plastic surgery resident/chief resident Inst. Reconstructive Plastic Surgery, NYU Langone Med. Ctr., 1973—75, asst. prof. plastic surgery, 1975—82; assoc. prof. plastic surgery NYU Sch. Medicine, 1982—97, prof. plastic surgery, 1997—; assoc. attending surgeons Manhattan Eye, Ear & Throat Hosp., NY, 1975—79, attending surgeon NY, 1979—92, surgeon dir. NY, 1989—, chmn., dept. plastic surgery NY, 1992—. Chmn. plastic surgery svc. Manhattan Vet.'s Hosp., 1975—79; asst. attending plastic surgeon Bellevue Hosp. Ctr., NYC, 1975—80, assoc. attending plastic surgeon, 1980—97, attending plastic surgeon, 1997—, Lenox Hill Hosp., NYC, 2005—, bd. trustees, 2006—. Mem. editl. bd. Aesthetic Plastic Surgery, 1984, Annals of Plastic Surgery, 1985; contbr. articles to profl. jours., chapters to books. Recipient Merit award, LA Surgical Soc., 1972, Edn. Svc. award, NYU, 1998, Lifetime Achievement award, Inst. Reconstructive Plastic Surgery, 2005; named one of NY's Top Doctors, NY Mag., 1982—2008, America's Top Doctors, Castle Connolly Med. Ltd., 1996—. Fellow: ACS, Internat. Coll. Surgeons Plastic Surgery, Am. Soc. Plastic & Reconstructive Surgeons, Inc. (interprofl. rels. com. 1978—80, fund raising com. 1979—82, pub. edn. com. 1981—82, mem. speaker's bur. 1981—82, comm. commn. vice. commr. 1982—83, mem. pub. edn. com. 1985—88, mem.-at-large, bd. dirs. 1988—89, chmn. strategic planning com. 1990—92), NY Acad. Medicine; mem.: AMA (Physician's Recognition award 1977—79), Aesthetic Soc. Edn. & Rsch. Found. (bd. dirs. 1992—95, founding mem.), Pan-Pacific Surgical Soc., Royal Soc. Medicine Eng., NY Regional Soc. Plastic & Reconstructive Surgeons (pub. rels./info. com. 1980—81, chmn. constitution & by-laws com. 1980—82, ethics com. 1981, parliamentarian 1987), Assn. Academic Surgeons, Internat. Soc. Aesthetic Plastic Surgery, Am. Assn. Plastic Surgeons, Sociedade Brasileira De Cirurgia Plastica (hon.), Australian Soc. Aesthetic Plastic Surgeons (hon.), British Assn. Aesthetic Plastic Surgeons (hon.), Brazilian Soc. Plastic & Reconstructive Surgery (corr.), Am. Assn. Accreditation Ambulatory Plastic Surgery Facilities (sec. 1980, founding mem.), Am. Soc. Aesthetic Plastic Surgery, Inc. (asst. sec. 1987—89, v.p. 1991—92, pres. 1993—94, chmn. bd. trustees 1994—95, bd. dirs. 1995—97, bd. trustees 2002, chmn. nom. com. 2004—06, Walter Scott Brown award 1981, 2007, Simon Fredricks award 1993), Brazilian Plastic Surgery Soc., Pan Am. Med. Assn., Soc. Academic Surgeons, NY County Med. Soc., NY State Med. Soc. Achievements include developing the FAME (finger-assisted malar elevation) facelift technique, which repositions not only the skin, but also the soft tissue of the face; organization of an annual aesthetic surgery symposium in NY that is attended by several hundred plastic surgeons from more than 50 countries. Office: Pvt Practice 728 Park Ave New York NY 10021 also: NYU Langone Med Ctr 550 First Ave New York NY 10016 Office Phone: 212-249-6000. Business E-Mail: sjaston@sjaston.com.

ÅSTRAND, BENGT, pharmacist; b. Linköping, Sweden, Mar. 20, 1955; MSc in Pharmacy, Uppsala U., Sweden, 1978; PhD, Linnaeus U., Kalmar, 2007. Pharmacy mgr., regional pharmacy dir. Apoteket AB, 1978—2009. Adj. lectr. Linnaeus U., 2009. Office: Länssjukhuset Kalmar 391 85 Sweden Business E-Mail: bengt.astrand@lnu.se.

ÅSTRAND, PER-OLOF, retired physiologist; b. Svenarum, Sweden, Oct. 21, 1922; s. Karl and Martha (Thunander) Åstrand; m. Irma Ryhming, July 14, 1956; children: Elin Kristina, Per Gustaf. Tchr. exam., Coll. Phys. Edn., Stockholm, 1946; MD, PhD, Karolinska Inst., Stockholm, 1952; D (hon.), U. Grenoble, France, 1968, U. Jyväskylä, Finland, 1971, Czechoslovak Med. Soc. J.E., Purkyne, 1985, U. Libre de Bruxelles, 1987, U. Tech., Loughborough, Eng., 1991, Aristoteles U., Thessaloniki, Greece, 1992, U. Exeter, Eng., 2000, U. Bologna, Italy, 2002; D, U. Athens, Greece, 2002, Norwegian Sch. Sport Scis., Norway, 2008. Rsch. asst. Coll. Phys. Edn., 1946-70, prof. physiology, 1970-77; prof. physiology, physiol. dept., mem. Nobel Prize Assembly, Karlinska Inst., Stockholm, 1977-88; prof. emeritus Karolinska Inst., Stockholm, 1989—. Co-author: (book) Textbook of Work Physiology, 1970, 4th edit., 2003; co-editor: Endurance in Sports, 2000. Decorated officer Ordre des Palmes Académiques (France); recipient Eleanor Naylor Dana award for preventive medicine, Am. Health Found., 1974, Philip Noel Baker Rsch. prize, 1975, Disting. Svc. award, U.S. Sports Acad., 1982, cert. of merti, Govt. of Can., 1984. Fellow: AAAS (hon.); mem.: Am. Coll. Sports Medicine (hon.; Joseph B. Wolffe Meml. lectr. 1991, Honor award), European Coll. Sport Sci. (hon.), Spanish Fedn. Sports Medicine (hon.), Am. Phys. Therapy Assn. (hon.), Hong Kong Assn. Sports Medicine and Sports Scis. (hon.), Swedish Soc. Cardiology (hon.), Hungarian Soc. Sports Medicine (hon.), Australasian Coll. Rehab. Medicine (hon.), Internat. Fedn. Sports Medicine (hon.), Internat. Fedn. Phys. Edn. (hon.), Swiss soc. Cardiology (hon.), Am. Coll. Cardiology (hon.; Louis F. Bishop lectr. 1970), Internat. Union Physiol. Scis. (hon.), Rotary (hon.). Home: Orrspelsvagen 6 S-183 57 Täby Sweden Office: Karolinska Inst PO Box 5626 S-114 86 Stockholm Sweden Business E-Mail: per-olof.astrand@gih.se.

ASTROW, ALAN B., oncologist, hematologist; MD, Yale U. Resident Boston City Hosp.; fellow NYU Med. Ctr.; assoc. med. dir. Comprehensive Cancer Ctr. St. Vincent's Hosp., chief clinical oncology; dir. hematology & med. oncology Maimonides Cancer Ctr. Fellow: Am. Coll. Physicians. Office: Maimonides Cancer Center 6300 Eighth Ave 2nd Fl Brooklyn NY 11220 Office Phone: 718-765-2600. Office Fax: 718-765-2630. E-mail: aastrow@maimonidesmed.org.

ASTWOOD, WILLIAM PETER, psychotherapist; b. NYC, May 18, 1940; s. Henry Kenneth and Rose Margit (Eastby) A.; m. Sharon Lisa Sprung, June 10, 1979; 1 child, Jesse Jack. BA, CUNY, 1962; MA, NYU, 1967, PhD, 1975. Case worker, supr. dept. social services City N.Y., 1964-67; community orgn. trainer Block Communities, Inc., NYC, 1967-68; field rep. Office Econ. Opportunity, NYC, 1968-70, U.S. Dept. Health, Edn., Welfare, NYC, 1970-71; pvt. practice Bklyn., 1971—; dir. family therapy div. DiMele Ctr. for Psychotherapy, NYC, 1990—. Bd. dirs. South Beach Psychiat. Ctr., Bklyn., 1976-78, N.Y. Group for Comprehensive Family Therapy, Mineola, 1988—; exec. bd. Met. Ctr. for Psychotherapy, N.Y.C., 1969-72. Co-author: Practicing Psychotherapy, 1980. Exec. bd. Social Service Employees Union, N.Y.C., 1965-67. Staff sgt. USANG, 1963-69. Mem. N.Y. Acad. Scis., Assn. for Humanistic Psychology, Am. Assn. Marriage and Family Therapy (clin.). Home: 394 Atlantic Ave Brooklyn NY 11217-1703 Office: 116 Clinton St Brooklyn NY 11201 Home Phone: 718-625-3872; Office Phone: 718-522-2842. Personal E-mail: drbastwood@aol.com.

ATAL, BISHNU SAROOP, retired speech research executive, educator; b. Kanpur, Uttar Pradesh, India, May 10, 1933; came to U.S., 1961; s. Jagannath Prasad and Lakshmi Devi (Lakshmi) A.; m. Kamla Atal, July 3, 1959; children: Alka, Namita. BS with honors, U. Lucknow, India, 1952; elec. engring. degree, Indian Inst. Sci., Bangalore, 1955; PhD in Elec. Engring., Poly. Inst. Bklyn., 1968. Sr. rsch. asst. Indian Inst. Sci., Bangalore, 1955-56, lectr., 1957-60; sr. rsch. fellow Cen. Elec. Engring. Rsch. Inst., Pilani, Rajasthan, India, 1960-61; mem. tech. staff AT&T Bell Labs., Murray Hill, N.J., 1961-85, head acoustics rsch., 1985-90, head speech rsch., 1990-97; tech. dir. AT&T Labs., Florham Park, NJ, 1997—2002; affiliate prof. U. Washington, Seattle, 2002—. Contbr. articles to various publs. Fellow Acoustical Soc. Am., IEEE (Acoustics, Speech and Signal Processing Sr. Tech. Achievement award 1975, ASSP Sr. award 1980, Centennial medal 1984, Morris N. Liebman Meml. Field award 1986); mem. NAE, NAS (Franklin medal 2003). Home: 6226 95th Pl SW Mukilteo WA 98275-3533 E-mail: catchall@bishnu.net.

ATALA, ANTHONY JOHN, surgeon; b. July 14, 1958; m. Katherine Atala, May 13, 1985. BA, U. Miami, 1984; MD, U. Louisville, 1985. Cert. Am. Bd. Urology. Intern in surgery U. Louisville Sch. Medicine, 1985-86, resident in surgery, 1985—87, resident in urology, 1987-89, chief resident in urology, 1989-90; rsch. fellow dept. surgery Children's Hosp., Harvard Med. Sch., Boston, 1990-91, clin. fellow dept. surgery, 1991-92, instr., 1992-93, asst. prof., 1993—2003, mem. investigations rev. bd., 1994—; dir. lab. tissue engring. and cellular therapeutics Children's Hosp. and Harvard Med. Sch., 1993—2004; W.H. Boyce prof., chair dept. urology, dir. Wake Forest Inst. for Regenerative Medicine Wake Forest Univ. Baptist Med. Ctr., 2004—. Mem. study sect. NIH, 1996; editor-in-chief Current Stem Cell Rsch. and Therapy, Therapautic Avances in Urology. Cons. Jour. Urology, 1993-, editor investigative urology sect., editor, Lancet, 1994, editor: Jour. Rejuvenation Rsch., Tissue Engring. and Regenerative Medicine, Nanotech. in Engring. and Regenerative Medicine; editor investigative urology sect., Urology, Current Reviews in Urology, The Scientific World: Cell Biology; mem. editl. bd. Expert Opinion on Biol. Therapy; contbr. articles to profl. jours. Rsch. award ACS, 1990, Am. Acad. Pediat., 1993, 94, 96, Am. Soc. Plastic Surgery, 1994, Christopher Columbus Found. award, Gold Cystoscope award, Number 1 Top Sci. Story of Yr., Discover Mag., 2007; named Med. Treatments Leader of the Yr., Scientific American, 56th Most Influential Person of Yr., Time Mag., 2007; named one of 50 People, Fast Co. Mag., 2006, 100 Most Creating People, 2009. Mem. AMA, AAAS, Am. Urol. Assn. (program com. 1995), Soc. for Basic Urol. Rsch. (program com. 1995), Soc. of Regenerative Medicine (bd, dir., v.p.), Tissue Engring. Soc. (bd. gov.), Tissue Engring. and Regerative Medicine Internat. Soc. (chair N.Am. chpt.). Achievements include patents in field, inventions in area of tissue engineering and medicine. First to build a functioning organ from scratch-a bladder made cell by cell. Office: Wake Forest Univ Baptist Med Ctr Dept Urology Medical Ctr Blvd Winston Salem NC 27157 Office Phone: 336-716-4131. Office Fax: 336-716-9042. Business E-Mail: cmontgom@wfubmc.edu, aatala@wfubmc.edu. *

ATANASOV, DIMITAR TODOROV, oral and maxillofacial surgeon, consultant; b. Dobrotitza, Bulgaria, July 25, 1946; s. Todor Dimitrov and Dimitra Petrova Atanasov; m. Tzvetana Kirilova Bratoeva, June 12, 1972; 1 child, Teodor Dimitrov. M of Stomatology, Med. Acad. Sofija, 1974, diploma in oral surgery, 1978, diploma in maxillofacial surgery, 1982; D of Stomatology, Med. U. Plovdiv, 1987, cert. in periodontology, 2001, cert. in gen. dentistry, 2005. Asst. oral and maxillofacial surgery Stomatological Faculty, Plovdiv, Bulgaria, 1974—82, sub dean, 1989—92, assoc. prof. oral and maxillofacial surgery, 1989—2005, dean, 2003, prof. oral and maxillofacial surgery, 2005—; vice rector Med. U., Plovdiv, 1999—2003. Cons. in field. Author: Periodontal Surgery, 1995, Tumours of Oral and Maxillofacial Region, 1997, Urgent Stomatology, 2002, Pharmaceuticals in the Urgent Stomatology, 2003. Fellow: Soc. Periodontology and Implantology in Bulgaria; mem.: Assn. Dentists in Bulgaria (v.p. 1999—2002). Avocations: basketball, skiing, computers, travel. Home: Coml Trakija bl127 vh Z ap19 Plovdiv 4023 Bulgaria Office Fax: 35932632687. Personal E-mail: dtatanasov2004@yahoo.com.

ATAR, DAN, cardiologist, educator, medical researcher; b. Jan. 12, 1959; arrived in Denmark, 1998, arrived in Norway, 2002; MD, U. Basel, Switzerland, 1985, habilitation, 1996. Bd. cert. internal medicine and cardiology. Intern surgery U. Hosp. Copenhagen, Gentofte, Denmark, 1986; Swiss Nat. Rsch. Foun. postdoctoral rsch. fellow Hagedorn Rsch. Lab., Steno Meml. Hosp., Gentofte, 1986-88; intern, resident dept. medicine U. Basel Med. Ctr., 1988-89; resident Bispebjerg U. Hosp., Copenhagen Sch. Medicine, 1989-90, State U. Hosp., Copenhagen, 1990-91, cardiology fellow divsn. cardiology, 1991-92; postdoctoral rsch. fellow, cardiology fellow U. Md. Med. Ctr., Balt., 1992-93; postdoctoral rsch. fellow divsn. cardiology Johns Hopkins U. Sch. Medicine, Balt., 1993-94; cardiology fellow dept. medicine, divsn. cardiology Basel U. Hosp., 1994-97; staff, faculty mem. interventional cardiology Zürich (Switzerland) U. Hosp., 1997-98; prof. head cardiology Oslo U. Hosp., 2010—; head cardiology Oslo Univ. Hosp. Ulleval, 2002—. Sr. registrar Heart Ctr., Nat. U. Hosp., Copenhagen, 1998—2000; vis. assoc. prof. Johns Hopkins U., Balt., 1998—; assoc. prof. Zürich U., 1999—2002; chief physician divsn. cardiology Frederiksberg Hosp., Copenhagen, 2001—; presenter in field. Contbr. articles to profl. jours.; assoc. editor: Cardiology. Fellow: Am. Coll. Cardiology, Am. Heart Assn. (inaugural, basic sci. coun.), European Soc. Cardiology (chmn. working group cardiovascular pharmacology); mem.: Norwegian Soc. Cardiology, Internat. Soc. Heart Rsch., Danish Soc. Internal Medicine, Swiss Soc. Cardiology, Danish Soc. Cardiology. Home: Nils Lauritssonsv 25 0854 Oslo Norway Office: Oslo University Hosp Dept Cardiology Kirkeveien 166 Oslo N-0407 Norway Office Phone: 47 2289 4808.

ATAR, MICHAEL, pediatric dentist; b. Basel, Switzerland, Oct. 25, 1973; m. Daphna Regina Atar-Zwillenberg; children: Akiva Oscar children: Jemima Tiffany, Ophra Allegra, Leo Chananya. DDS, U. Basel, Switzerland, 1998; PhD, U. Basel, 2002; MClinDent, Queen Mary U., London, 2005. Lic. pediatric dentist U. London, 2005. Postdoctoral rsch. fellow U. Basel, 2002—03; clin. lectr. pediatric dentistry Queen Mary's Sch. Medicine & Dentistry, London, 2005—07; head Swiss Smile Kids Pvt. Clinic Child Oral Health, Mayfair, England, 2008—, Zurich, Switzerland, 2008—; assoc. prof. pediat. dentistry NY U., 2009—. Found. govt. Hasmonean Primary Sch., London, 2006. Recipient Rudolf Hotz Meml. award, Swiss Assn. Pediatric Dentistry, 2003, Bengt Magnusson Meml. award, Internat. Assn. Pediatric Dentistry, 2003, Young Scientist Rsch. prize, European Acad. Pediatric Dentistry, 2006, Found. Rsch. award, Am. Acad. Pediatric Dentistry, 2007; grantee Young Investigator Career Advancement grant, Swiss Nat. Found., 2003, Novartis Found., 2003. Mem.: Swiss Dental Soc., Brit. Dental Assn., Gen. Dental Coun. Gt. Britain, Swiss Assn. Pediatric Dentistry, Internat. Assn. Pediatric Dentistry, Am. Acad. Pediatric Dentistry, Alpha Omega Internat. Dental Frat. Achievements include internationaly acclaimed research the influence of diabetes mellitus and other systemic diseases on developing dental hard tissues. Office Phone: 442072901180.

ATARASHI, HIROTSUGU, cardiologist, educator; b. Fukaya-shi, Saitama, Japan, Aug. 19, 1949; s. Jonosuke and Chizuko Atarashi. MD, Nippon Med. Sch., Tokyo, 1974. Asst. prof. Nippon Med. Sch., Tokyo, 1992-97, assoc. prof., 1997—, prof., 2003—. Mem. Internat. Soc. Cardiovascular Pharmacotherapy, Am. Heart Assn., Heart Rhythm Soc. Office: Nippon Med Sch 1st Dept Int Med Tama-Nagayama Hosp Tokyo 206-8512 Japan Office Phone: 81 42 371 2111.

ATAY, DIDEM, physician; b. Istanbul, Oct. 15, 1973; MD, Istanbul U., 1997. Physician Istanbul medicine faculty pediat. hematology oncology bone marrow transplant unit Istanbul U., 2003—. Mem.: Turkish Pediat. Hematology Soc. Home: Kartaltepe Mah Dost Sok Motif apt 5/11 Istanbul 34414 Turkey Personal E-mail: didematay@hotmail.com.

ATHANASOPOULOS, CONSTANTIN BASIL, physician, consultant; b. Athens, Greece, June 27, 1935; s. Basil Constantin and Andromache Constantin (Sakellare) A.; m. Sophie Leonidas Papaconstantinou, Dec. 1, 1973; children: Andromache, Leonidas. MD, U. Athens, 1960, MS, 1972. Diplomate Am. Bd. Internal Medicine, Greek Bd. Internal Medicine, Greek Bd. Cardiology. Intern Swedish Covenant Hosp., Chgo., 1968-69; resident internal medicine U. Ill., Chgo., 1969-70; fellow cardiology U. Chgo., Chgo., 1970-72; instr. internal medicine U. Athens, 1967-68; assoc. in cardiology Michael Reese Hosp. Med. Ctr., 1972, Columbus-Cuneo Med. Ctr., 1972-73, Evangelismos Med. Ctr., Athens, 1978-84; cardiology instr. Gen. State Hosp., Athens, 1974-76, dir. dept. cardiology, 1976-78; asst. prof. cardiology U. Athens, 1985—; cons. cardiologist Athens Med. Ctr., 1985—. Vis. prof. cardiology SUNY, Stony Brook, 1985—. Med. lt. Greek Air Force, 1960-63. Fellow Am. Coll. Cardiology, Am. Coll. Angiology, Am. Coll. Chest Physicians; mem. Internat. Acad. Chest Physicians (gov. 1989—), N.Y. Acad. Scis. Avocations: classical music, reading. Office: 23 Ypsilantou St 10675 Athens Kolonaki Greece Personal E-mail: athan_const@hotmail.com.

ATHANASOPOULOS, LEONIDAS VASILEIOS, medical researcher; b. Athens, Greece, Dec. 18, 1978; s. Constantin and Sofia Athanasopoulos. MD, U. Athens, 2004, PhD with honors, 2009. Cert. ECFMG, 2007. Rsch. fellow cardiology dept. Onassis Cardiac Surgery Ctr., Athens, 2005—09; postdoc. rsch. fellow cardiovascular divsn. Brigham & Women's Hosp., Harvard Med. Sch., 2009—10, postdoc. rsch. fellow cardiac surgery divsn., 2010—. Mem.: Athens Med. Assn., Am. Heart Assn. Avocations: piano, classical music, jazz, reading. Home: 23 Ypsilantou St Kolonaki Athens 10675 Greece Personal E-mail: athanleon@hotmail.com.

ATIBA, JOSHUA OLAJIDE OLUWABUNMI, internist, philanthropist, oncologist, educator, pharmacologist; b. Enugu, Nigeria, July 6, 1956; arrived in US, 1983, naturalized, 1995; s. Joseph Ojo and Abigail Olayo A.; m. Stella N. Mordi, June 26, 1981; children: April, Annamarie, Joseph. MD, U. Lagos, Nigeria, 1979; MHA, St. Mary's Coll., Moraga, Calif., 1999. Diplomate Am. Bd. Internal Medicine, Am. Bd. Oncology. Rotating intern Ahmadu Bello U. Tchg. Hosp., Kaduna, Nigeria, 1979-80; resident in internal medicine Lagos U. Tchg. Hosp., 1981-83; fellow in med. oncology Cancer Control Agy., Vancouver, B.C., Can., 1988-90; fellow in clin. pharmacology Stanford U. Med. Ctr., Palo Alto, Calif., 1983-86; pvt. practice Irvine, Calif.; med. oncologist Drs. Pomeroy, Choate and Atiba, Soquel and Watsonville, Calif., 2004—05, Cancer and Blood Inst. Lucy Curci Cancer Ctr., Rancho Mirage, Calif., 2005—06. Dir. clin. investigation U. Calif., Irvine, 1991-95; mem. U. Calif. Irvine Med. Ctr., Orange, North Bay Med. Ctr., Fairfield, Calif., Vaca Valley Hosp., Vacaville, Calif.; asst. prof. medicine, pharmacology U. Calif., Irvine; med. dir. N. Bay Hosp., 1997-99; pres. NOAH Med. Svc. Corp.; med. dir. NOAH, Inc.; rancher. Med. dir. North Bay Hospice, Fairfield, Calif.; pres. Newport Oncology and Healthcare Found. Fellowship in clin. pharm., Merck Internat., 1984—86, PHARMA Jr. Faculty fellowship award, 1991—95, Dean's Fellowship award, Stanford U., 1983. Fellow Royal Coll. Physicians Can.; mem. ACP, AMA, Am. Fedn. for Clin. Rsch., Am. Soc. of Clin. Pharmacology and Therapeutics, Am. Soc. Clin. Oncology, Calif. Med. Assn., Solano County Med. Soc. (sec./treas., pres.-elect, pres.), Physician Peer Rev. Orgn. (dir.), KC (knight 1997). Republican. Roman Catholic. Home (Winter): 15 Spyglass Cir Rancho Mirage CA 92270 Office Phone: 707-631-0921. Home Fax: 831-536-1767. Personal E-mail: jatiba@yahoo.com.

ATICHARTAKARN, VICHAI, physician; b. Nakornpathom, Thailand, Feb. 11, 1946; s. Yimmeng Lee and Suda (Ung) A.; s. Vilai Vongsiridej, 1980; 2 children. MD, Faculty Medicine and Siriraj Hosp., Bangkok, 1969. Diplomate Am. Bd. Internal Medicine, Diplomate Sub. Specialty Bd. Hematology. Instr. med. dept. medicine, faculty of medicine Ramathibodi Hosp., Bangkok, 1977-79, asst. prof. medicine, 1979-82, chief divsn. hematology dept. medicine, 1980—2006; assoc. prof. medicine Faculty of Medicine and Ramathibodi Hosp., Bangkok, 1982-88, prof. medicine, 1988—. Contbr. articles to profl. jours. Fellow Am. Coll. Physicians; mem. Med. Assn. Thailand, Hematology Soc. Thailand, Am. Soc. Hematology, Internat. Soc. of Thrombosis and Haemostasis. Avocations: tennis, listening to music, reading. Office: Faculty Med/Ramathibodi Hosp Rama VI Rd Bangkok 10400 Thailand Home: 228 Soi Yen Ahgaad 2 Bangkok 10120 Thailand Office Phone: 662-201-1392. Business E-Mail: ravtc@mahidol.ac.th.

ATIEH, MO'MEN AHMAD, oral surgeon, researcher; b. Amman, Jordan, June 22, 1972; s. Ahmad Hasan Atieh and Feryal Mohammad Abu Omar; m. Hadeel Mohammad Ibrahim, Nov. 2, 2000; children: Ahmad Mo'men, Yasmeen Mo'men. BDS, U. Jordan, Amman, 1995; MSc in Oral and Maxillofacial Surgery, Sch. Dentistry, U. Manchester, Eng., 1998. Gen. dentist Ministry of Health, Shobak, Jordan, 1996—97; oral surgeon Dammam Med. Ctr.-SECERB, Saudi Arabia, 1999—2008; rschr. Sir John Walsh Rsch. Inst., Faculty Dentistry, U. Otago, Dunedin, New Zealand, 2008—. Contbr. articles to profl. dental jours. (Best Poster for Yr., 2008);, author in multiple systematic revs. in the field of oral implantology. Handsearcher Cochrane Collaboration Worldwide Hand Search Program, Manchester. Mem.: Internat. Team for Implantology, Am. Coll. Oral and Maxillofacial Surgeons, New Zealand Dental Assn., Saudi Dental Soc., Jordan Dental Assn. Avocations: travel, writing, puzzles. Office: Sir John Walsh Rsch Inst Sch Dentistry P O Box 647 Dunedin 9054 Dunedin New Zealand Home: 7 Balmoral St Opoho Dunedin 9010 New Zealand Home Phone: 64 3 4739971; Office Phone: 64 211 878327. Personal E-mail: maatieh@gmail.com.

ATIK, EDMAR, physician; b. Sao Paulo, Brazil, Sept. 16, 1942; s. Elias Demian and Evelin Assali Atik; m. Mariana Antibas Atik, June 15, 1968; children: Fernando, Guilherme, Carolina. Grad in medicine, U. Brazil, 1966; M in Cardiology, U. Sao Paulo, 1978. Intern in cardiology Santa Casa de Misericordia, Rio de Janeiro, 1966; fellow in pediatric cardiology St. Christopher's Hosp. Children, Temple U., Phila., 1968—69; cardiologist Hosp. do Servidor Publico Estudual Francisco Mora to de Oliveira, Sao Paulo, 1971—79; pediatric cardiologist Hosp. das Clinicas de Faculdade de Medicina da U. de Sao Paulo, 1969—; in charge neonatal cardiac service, 1972—; chief pediatric cardiology svc. Hosp. Matarazzo de Sao Paulo, 1979—84. Cons. congenital heart diseases to various hosps.; mem. faculty congenital heart disease courses Inst. do Coracaodo Hosp. das Clinicas da Universidade de Sao Paulo. Contbr. articles to med. jours. Pres. Pediatric Cardiology dept. Sociedade Brasileira de Cardiologia, 1983—85. Recipient award, Pero Vas de Caminha, Instituto Historica e Cultural Pero Vaz de Caminha, 1982. Mem.: Sociedade Brasileira de Pediatria, Associacao Medica Brasileira, Associacao Paulista de Medicina (mem. editl. staff 1979—), Sociedade Brasileira de Cardiologia, Esporte Clube Sirio (Sao Paulo). Democrat. Roman Catholic. Office: 1954 Treze de Maio Sãa Paulo 01327 Brazil

ATIK, FERNANDO A., cardiac surgeon; b. Sao Paulo, Brazil, Apr. 19, 1970; s. Edmar and Mariana Antibas Atik; m. Lilian Mendes Sousa, Apr. 6, 2003; children: Gustavo Mendes children: Lucas Mendes. MD, Faculdade de Medicina do ABC, Santo Andre, Brazil, 1994. Diplomate Bd. Brazilian Soc. Cardiovasc. Surgery, 2008. Gen. surgery resident Fed. U. Sao Paulo, 1996—98; cardiovasc. surgery resident U. Sao Paulo Med. Sch., 1998—2001; pediat. and congenital heart surgery fellow Cleve. Clinic Found., 2002—03, cardiothoracic surgery fellow, 2003—06; vice chmn. cardiovasc. surgery Heart Inst. Fed. Dist., Brasilia, Brazil, 2006—, co-dir., 2008—, med. ethics bd. pres., 2008—, hosp. mgmt., 2008. Reviewer Annals Thoracic Surgery, Phila., 2003—, Internat. Jour. Cardiology, Melbourne, Australia, 2006—. Contbr. articles to profl. med. jours. Recipient Renee Favaloro Internat. award, Cleve. Clinic, 2005, Rsch. Team award, 2005. Democrat. Avocations: travel, movies, art.

ATKIN, J MYRON, science educator; b. Bklyn., Apr. 6, 1927; s. Charles Z. and Esther (Jaffe) A.; m. Ann Spiegel, Dec. 25, 1947; children— David, Ruth, Jonathan. BS, CCNY, 1947; MA, NYU, 1948, PhD, 1956. Tchr. sci. Ramaz H.S., NYC, 1948—50; tchr. elem. sch. sci. Great Neck Pub. Schs., NY, 1950—55; prof. sci. edn. Coll. Edn., U. Ill., Urbana, 1955—79, assoc. dean, 1966—70, dean, 1970—79; prof. Sch. Edn., Stanford U., Calif., 1979—2004, prof. emeritus, 2004—, dean, 1979—86. Cons. OECD, Paris, Nat. Inst. Edn.; mem. edn. adv. bd. NSF, 1973-76, 84-86, vice-chmn., 1984-85, sr. advisor, 1986-87; mem. Ill. Tchr. Certification Bd., 1973-76; Sir John Adams lectr. U. London Inst. Edn., 1980, vis. scholar com. scholarly commn. Nat. Acad. Scis., People's Republic China, 1987; math. sci. edn. bd. NRC, 1985-89, nat. com. sci. edn. standards and assessment, 1992-96, com. on sci. edn. K-12, 1996-2002, vice chair, 1998, chair, 1999-2002; invited lectr. Nat. Sci. Coun., Taiwan, 1989—; resident Rockefeller Found., Bellagio Ctr., 1999; nat. assoc., Nat. Acads. of Sci., 2001-. Author children's sci. textbooks. Served with USNR, 1945-46. Fellow: AAAS (v.p. sect. Q 73 1974); mem.: NAS (assoc.), Nat. Assessment Ednl. Progress (planning com. mem. 2009), Am. Ednl. Rsch. Assn. (exec. bd. 1972—75, chmn. govt. and profl. liaison com.), Coun. Elem. Sci. Internat. (pres. 1969—70), Sigma Xi (chmn. com. on sci., math. and engring. edn.). Office Phone: 650-450-3514. Business E-Mail: atkin@stanford.edu.

ATKINS, DIANNE L., pediatrician, educator; b. Balt., Mar. 11, 1952; Student, Goucher Coll., Balt., 1974; BA in Human Biology, Johns Hopkins U., Balt., 1974, MD, 1977. Diplomate Am. Bd. Pediat., cert. in pediatric cardiology. Resident pediat. U. Ky., Lexington, 1977—80; fellow pediatric cardiology U. Iowa, Iowa City, 1980—83, asst. prof., 1986—92, assoc. prof., 1992—2002, prof. pediat., 2002—. Achievements include research in ventricular fibrillation in children; pharmacokinetics of anti-arrhythmic drugs in children. Office: U Iowa Dept Pediat 2633 Carver Pavilion Iowa City IA 52242 Office Phone: 319-356-3540. Business E-Mail: dianne-atkins@uiowa.edu.

ATKINSON, ARTHUR JOHN, JR., pharmacologist, educator, consultant; b. Chgo., Mar. 22, 1938; s. Arthur John and Inez (Hill) Atkinson; m. Mary Jo Yunker, May 12, 1984. AB in Chemistry, Harvard U., 1959; MD, Cornell U., 1963. Intern, asst. resident medicine Mass. Gen. Hosp., Boston, 1963-65; chief resident, Howard Carroll fellow medicine Passavant Meml. Hosp., Chgo., 1967-68; fellow clin. pharmacology U. Cin., 1968-69, asst. prof. pharmacology, 1969; vis. scientist dept. toxicology Karolinska Inst., Stockholm, 1970; from asst. prof. to assoc. prof. medicine and pharmacology Northwestern U., Chgo., 1970—76, prof., 1976-94; corp. v.p. clin. devel. and med. affairs Upjohn Co., 1994-95; v.p. clin. R & D worldwide clin. pharmacology Pharmacia & Upjohn, Inc., 1995-96;

adj. prof. pharmacology Ctr. for Drug Devel. Sci., Georgetown U., 1996—2003. With NIH, USPHS, 1965—67; sr. advisor clin. pharmacology to dir. clin. ctr. NIH, 1998—2005; vice chair safe medication use expert com. U.S. Pharmacopeia, 2000—05; cons. in field. Recipient Faculty Devel. award in clin. pharmacology, Pharm. Mfrs. Assn., 1970—72, award of excellence in clin. pharmacology, 2002; scholar Burroughs Wellcome, 1972—77. Master: ACP; mem.: Assn. Am. Physicians, Am. Soc. Clin. Pharmacology and Therapeutics (pres. 1995—96, Rawls Palmer award 1983, Henry W. Elliott award 2004, Oscar B. Hunter award 2005), Am. Soc. Pharmacology and Exptl. Therapeutics (Harry Gold award 1989), Gibson Island Club, Chgo. Yacht Club, Alpha Omega Alpha. Home: 6176 Hidden Lake Cir Richland MI 49083 Personal E-mail: art_atkinson@msn.com.

ATKINSON, BARBARA F., academic administrator, dean, medical educator; b. Mpls., Oct. 19, 1942; BS, Coll. Wooster; MD, Jefferson Med. Coll., Thomas Jefferson U., 1974. Diplomate Am. Bd. Anatomic and Clin. Pathology, Am. Bd. Cytopathology. Intern Hosp. U. Pa., Phila., 1974—75, resident in pathology, 1975—78; dir. cytopathology lab. U. Pa. Sch. Medicine, Phila., 1978—87; prof., chair Dept. Pathology and Lab. Medicine Med. Coll. of Pa. / MCP Hahnemann, Phila., 1987—96; dean MCP Hahnemann Sch. Medicine, Phila., 1996—99; prof., chair Dept. Pathology and Lab. Medicine U. Kans. Sch. Medicine, 2000—02, dir. resident program, 2000, exec. dean, 2002—, exec. vice chancellor, 2005—; interim chancellor U. Kans., 2009. Assoc. scientist Wistar Inst. Anatomy and Biology, 1983—87; dir. Del. Valley Regional Lab. Svcs., Med. Coll. Hosps. and St. Christopher's Hosp. for Children, 1991—96; trustee Am. Bd. Pathology, 1992—95, pres., 1998. Mem. editl. bd. Lab. Investigation, 1988—94, Modern Pathology, 1990—94, Human Pathology, 1992—94, manuscript reviewer Cancer, Diagnostic Cytopathology, Modern Pathology, 1988—94, abstract rev. bd. U.S. and Can. Acad. Pathology, 1989—92, rev. panel Am. Soc. Clin. Pathology Abstract, 1991—96; contbr. articles to profl. jours., chapters to books. Bd. dirs., treas. Laennec Soc. Phila., 1979—81; bd. dirs. Thyroid Soc. Phila., 1982—84; exec. com., bd. dirs. Med. Coll. Pa., 1994—96; bd. trustees Hahnemann U., 1994—96. Recipient Golden Apple Tchg. award for excellent sci. tchg., 1994; grantee, NIH, 1985—88, Takeda-Abbott R&D, 1989—94, NIA, 1991—94. Fellow: ASIM, Coll. Am. Pathologists; mem.: NAS (mem. Inst. Medicine), US and Can. Acad. Pathology, Am. Soc. Clin. Pathology (Janet M. Glasgow Meml. scholarship 1974), Am. Soc. Cytopathology. Office: U Kans Med Ctr Mail Stop 2015 3901 Rainbow Blvd Kansas City KS 66160 Office Phone: 913-588-1440. Business E-Mail: batkinson@kumc.edu. *

ATKINSON, HOLLY GAIL, physician, journalist, educator, human rights activist, writer; b. Detroit, Oct. 20, 1952; d. John S. and Patricia Atkinson; m. Galen Jay Guengerich, Nov. 18, 2000. BA in Biology magna cum laude, Colgate U., 1974; MD, U. Rochester, NYC, 1978; MS in Journalism, Columbia U., NYC, 1981. Diplomate Nat. Med. Bds. Intern in internal medicine Strong Meml. Hosp., Rochester, NY, 1978-79; rsch. Walter Cronkite's Universe show CBS News, NYC, 1981-82; med. reporter CBS Morning News, NYC, 1982-83; on-air co-host Bodywatch health show PBS, 1983-88; contbg. editor and health columnist New Woman mag., 1983-88; on-air corr., med. editor, sr. v.p. programming/med. affairs Lifetime Med. TV, 1985-93; assoc. editor Journal Watch, 1986-90; med. corr. Today Show NBC News, NYC, 1991-94; editor HealthNews, 1994—2006; exec. v.p. Reuters Health, NYC, 1994-98, pres., CEO, 1998-2000; CEO New Media Health Answers Inc., 2000; pres. allHealth.com (iVillage health), 2000—01; med. editor-in-chief, columnist Everydayhealth-.com, 2006—08; chief med. officer HealthiNation, 2008—. Lectr. dept. pub. health Cornell U. Med. Coll., 1997-2003, asst. prof., 2003—; asst. prof. medicine, co-dir. advancing idealism in medicine program Mt. Sinai Med. Sch., 2006—. Author: Women and Fatigue, 1986. Vol. nat. and local level Am. Heart Assn., 1984-91, bd. dirs., chmn. nat. comms. com. Am. Heart Assn., 1987-91; bd. dirs. Interstitial Cystitis Assn., 2009-, bd. dirs. Womens eNews, 2010-,bd. dirs., Phys. Human Rights, 1994—2010, pres. 2002-07, bd. dirs., NOW Legal Def. and Edn. Fund, 1996-2006, Soc. Advancement Women's Health Rsch., 1997-99, Am. Lyme Disease Found, 1997-98. Recipient Young Achievers award Nat. Coun. Women, 1986, Achievement award Soc. Advancement Women's Health Rsch., 1995, Health and Human Rights award Physicians for Human Rights, 2006, UU UNO Health and Human Rights award, 2009. Mem. Phi Beta Kappa.

ATKINSON, RICHARD CHATHAM, academic administrator, cognitive scientist; b. Oak Park, Ill., Mar. 19, 1929; s. Herbert and Margaret Atkinson; m. Rita Loyd, Aug. 20, 1952; 1 dau., Lynn Loyd. Ph.B., U. Chgo., 1948; PhD, Ind. U., 1955. Lectr. applied math. and stats. Stanford (Calif.) U., 1956—57, assoc. prof. psychology, 1961—64, prof. psychology, 1964—80; asst. prof. psychology UCLA, 1957—61; dep. dir. NSF, 1975—76, acting dir., 1976, dir., 1976—80; chancellor, prof. cognitive sci. and psychology U. Calif., San Diego, 1980—95; pres. U. Calif. Sys., 1995—2003, pres. emeritus, 2003—. Author: (with others) Introduction to Psychology, 14th edit., 2003, Computer Assisted Instruction, 1969, An Introduction to Mathematical Learning Theory, 1965, Contemporary Developments in Mathematical Psychology, 1974, Mind and Behavior, 1980, Stevens' Handbook of Experimental Psychology, 1988. With AUS, 1954—56. Guggenheim fellow, 1967; fellow Ctr. for Advanced Study in Behavioral Scis., 1963; recipient Disting. Rsch. award Social Sci. Rsch. Coun., 1962, Vannevar Bush award, 2003. Fellow APA (Disting. Sci. Contbn. award 1977, Thorndike award 1980), AAAS (pres. 1989-90), Am. Psychol. Soc. (William James fellow 1985), Am. Acad. Arts and Scis.; mem. NAS, Soc. Exptl. Psychologists, Am. Philos. Soc., Nat. Acad. Edn., Inst. of Medicine, Cosmos Club (Washington), Explorers Club (N.Y.C.). Home: 6845 La Jolla Scenic Dr S La Jolla CA 92037-5738 Office: U Calif San Diego Rm 5320 Atkinson Hall La Jolla CA 92093-0436 Business E-Mail: RCA@ucsd.edu.

ATKINSON, RICHARD LEE, JR., internal medicine educator; b. Petersburg, Va., May 15, 1942; s. Richard Lee and Ruth (Scarborough) A.; m. Susan Stayner Hume, Aug. 13, 1966; children: Catherine Crane, Barbara Hill, Deborah Gildea. BA, VA Mil. Inst., 1964; MD, Med. Coll. Va., 1968. Divsn. surgeon 101st Airborne Divsn., 1973; chief, dept. medicine Ft. Campbell Army Hosp., Ft. Campbell, 1973—74; liaison endocrinologist Vanderbilt U., Nashville, 1973-74; instr. UCLA, 1975-77; asst. prof. internal medicine U. Va. Sch. Medicine, Charlottesville, 1977-83; assoc. prof. internal medicine U. Calif., Davis, 1983-87; prof. internal medicine Ea. Va. Med. Sch., Norfolk, 1987-93; assoc. chief staff for rsch. and devel. VA Med. Ctr., Hampton, Va., 1987-93; prof. medicine and nutritional scis., dir. Beers-Murphy Clin. Nutrition Ctr. U. Wis., Madison, 1993—2002; emeritus prof. medicine and nutritional scis. U. Wis., Madison, 2002—; dir. Obesity Inst. Medstar Rsch. Inst., Washington, 2002—04; pres. Obetech, LLC, Richmond, Va., 2004—, dir. Obesity Rsch. Ctr., 2004—. Clin. prof. pathology Va. Commonwealth U., Richmond, 2005—; vis. prof. molecular medicine Karolinska Inst., Stockholm, 2009-; nutrition study sect. NIH, 1991-95, chair, 1993-95; chair subcom. on obesity in the mil. NAS, 1999-2003; chair USDA Intramural Peer Rev. Com., 2003-04, USDA Retrospective Rev. Panel on Human Nutrition Rsch., 2006-07. Contbr. articles to profl. jours. Maj. US Army, 1970—74. Decorated Army Commendation medal; recipient Richard L. Atkinson-Judith S.Stern award, 2006. Mem. N.Am. Assn. Study Obesity (pres. 1990-91), Am. Soc. Clin. Nutrition (pres. 1994-95), Am. Obesity Assn. (pres. 1995-2006), Internat. Assn. Study Obesity (regional v.p.), Obesity Soc. (regional v.p.). Home: 6077 Barkers Mill Rd Mechanicsville VA 23111 Office: Obetech LLC Va Biotech Rsch Pk 800 E Leigh St Ste 50 Richmond VA 23219 Office Phone: 804-344-5360. Business E-Mail: ratkinson2@vcu.edu.

ATKISSON, DEBRA, physician; d. Thomas and Patricia Atkisson; m. Roger Geer, June 22, 2002; 1 child, Katherine Kowalski. MD, Tex. Tech U. Sch. Medicine, Lubbock, 1986. Cert. Am. Bd. of Psychiatry and Neurology, 1991, in child and adolescent psychiatry Am. Bd. of Psychiatry and Neurology, 1993. Assoc. med. dir. Cook Children's Med. Ctr., Ft. Worth, 1992—96; med. dir. The Excel Ctr., Ft. Worth, 1996—2001, Sundance Behavioral Health Care, Ft. Worth, 2005—. Cons. CorpHealth, Ft. Worth, 1999—, Early Childhood Intervention, Ft. Worth, 2000—, Childhood Mental Health, 2001—08. Tchr. Tex. Girl's Choir, Ft. Worth, 2006, Elem. Sunday Sch. Class, Ft. Worth, 2005—06; cons. Early Childhood Mental Health Com., Ft. Worth, 2005; troop leader Girl Scouts, Ft. Worth, 2001—06. Named one of Ft. Worth Tex. Top Drs., Tarrant County Med. Soc., 2002—04, 2006—09, 2009—10, Tex. Super Drs., Tex. Monthly, 2006—10; Seeley fellowship, Karl Menninger Sch. of Psychiatry, 1991. Fellow: Am. Psychiat. Assn. (rep. public affairs com. 2003); mem.: Tex. Soc. Psychiat. Physicians (sec., treas. 2010—, pres. elect 2011). Avocations: travel, cooking, reading. Office: 6410 Southwest Blvd Ste 205 Fort Worth TX 76109 Office Fax: 817-735-4565.

ATLAN, HENRI, biologist, philosopher; b. Blida, Algeria, Dec. 27, 1931; s. Benjamin and Anna (Chiche) A.; m. Liliane (div. 1977); children: Mireille, Michael; m. Bela Rachel Kohn, July 7, 1977. MD, U. Paris, 1958, PhD, 1973; D.h.c., U. Montreal, 2000. Prof. biophysics Med. Sch., Rouen, France, 1966-73, Univ. Hosp. Broussais-Hotel Dieu, Paris, 1973—98. Rsch. assoc. NASA, Moffett Field, Calif., 1966-68; vis. prof. Weizmann Inst., Rehovot, Israel, 1970-73, Johns Hopkins U., Balt., 2007; prof., head biophysics dept. Hadassah Univ. Hosp., Jerusalem, 1975-96, scholar in residence in philos. and ethics of biol., 1992—, dir. Human Biology Rsch. Ctr., 1992—; head biophysics & nuclear medicine Hotel Dieu Hosp., Paris, 1991-97; dir. rsch. Ecole des Hautes Etudes en Scis. Sociales (EHESS), Paris, 1995—. Author: Theory of Self-Organization and Complex Systems, 1972, 79, 82, 92, 2006, Philosophy of Knowledge based on Intercritique of Science and Myth, 1986, 91, 99, 2005, Questions of Life Between Science and Opinion, 1994; co-author: Magnetic Resonance Imaging: Basis for Interpretation, 1988; co-editor: Theories of Immune Networks, 1989, T-cell Immunotherapy of HIV-Infected Patients, 1993-94, 2004-05, 2007; contbr. articles to profl. jours. French Nat. ethics com. Life and Health Scis., 1983—2000. Mem. N.Y. Acad. Sci., European Acad. Arts., Sci. and Humanities, Universal Acad. of Cultures. Jewish. Avocation: jewish studies. Office: EHESS 54 Blvd Raspail 75006 Paris France also: Human Biology Rsch Ctr Hadassah Univ Hosp Ein Karem Jerusalem Israel Office Phone: 972-2-6777653. E-mail: henri.atlan@ehess.fr.

ATLANTIS, EVAN, medical researcher; b. Australia, Jan. 24, 1969; PhD in Exercise & Sport Sci., U. Adelaide, 2005. Rsch. fellow U. Adelaide, 2009—. Mem.: Dialogue Diabetes & Depression. Avocations: cooking, winemaking. Home: 1/374 Seaview Rd Henley Beach 5022 Australia Business E-Mail: e.atlantis@usyd.edu.au.

ATLAS, MARK P., pediatrician, educator; b. May 16, 1963; BA, Brown U., 1985; MD, Albert Einstein Coll. Medicine, 1989. Asst. prof. pediat. Columbia U., 1998—2001; assoc. chief, education-pediatric hematology, oncology, asst. prof. Cohen Children's Med. Ctr., 2001—, chief, childhood brain and spinal cord tumor program, 2002—. Dir., fellowship tng. program Pediatric Hematology, Oncology CCMC, 2005—11. Fellow: Am. Soc. Blood and Marrow Transplantation; mem.: Soc. Neuro-oncology, Am. Soc. Hematology. Office: 269-01 76th Ave 255 Apt 3C New Hyde Park NY 11040 Office Fax: 718-470-3132. Business E-Mail: matlas@nshs.edu.

ATLEE, JOHN LIGHT, physician, consultant; b. Lancaster, Pa., Feb. 22, 1941; s. John Light Jr. and Ann (Stevens) A.; m. Barbara Sheaffer, June 20, 1964 (dec. Apr. 14, 1967); m. Barbara Sanford, Feb. 3, 1968; children: Sarah Sanford Mann, John Light Jr. BA, Franklin and Marshall Coll., 1963; MD, Temple U., 1967, MS in Pharmacology, 1971; DSc, 2008, MS in Med. Sci., 1978. Diplomate Am. Bd. Anesthesiology. Intern Germantown Hosp., Phila., 1967-68; resident in anesthesiology Temple U. Hosp., Phila., 1968-70; postdoctoral rsch. fellow pharmacology Temple U. Grad. Sch. Medicine, 1970-71; staff anesthesiologist U.S. Naval Hosp, Bethesda, Md., 1971—74; asst. prof. anesthesiology U. Wis., Madison, 1973-78, tenured assoc. prof. anesthesiology, 1978-85, prof. anesthesiology, 1985-88; tenured prof. anesthesiology Med. Coll. Wis., Milw., 1988—2005; ret., 2005; sr. v.p. sci. & tech. Esophageal Techs. Inc., Middleton, Wis., 2008—; prof. anesthesiology U. Wis. Madison, 1973—88, Med. Coll. Wis. Milw., 1988—2005. Founder, sr. v.p. sci. and tech., prin.-owner Eso_Techs., Inc., Middleton, Wis., 2007—; inventor Eso_Techs. Tech. in Human Trials; cons. in field. Author: Perioperative Cardiac Arrhythmias, 1985, 2d edit., 1990, Arrhythmias and Pacemakers, 1996; editor: Perioperative Management of Pacemaker Patients, 1992, Complications in Anesthesia, 1999, 2d edit., 2007, Critical Care Cardiology in the Perioperative Period, 2001, 2d edit., 2007 (in English and Spanish), Complicanze in Anestesia (Italian), 2001; past mem. editl. bd. Anesthesia & Analgesia, Am. Heart Jour., Am. Jour. Physiology, Anesthesiology, Med. and Biol. Engring. and Computing, Jour. Cardiothoracic and Vascular Anesthesia, A Jolly Good Old Fellow; contbr. articles to profl. jours. Lt. comdr. USN, 1971—74. Grantee, NIH, 1978—98. Fellow: Phila. Coll. Physicians, Am. Heart Assn., Am. Coll. Cardiology and Anesthesiology; mem.: Am. Soc. Exptl. Pharmacology and Therapeutics, Soc. Register Assn., Heart Rhythm Soc., Assn. Univ. Anesthesiologists, Am. Soc. Anesthesiologists, Sigma Xi. Republican. Episcopalian. Achievements include patents in field. Personal E-mail: jatlee@wi.rr.com.

ATMACA, MURAD, medical educator, researcher; b. Elbistan, Turkey, Aug. 12, 1971; s. Recep and Hadiye Atmaca; m. Nukhet Bulut, Aug. 10, 1976; 1 child, Ahmet Tuluhan. MD, Cukurova U., Turkey, 1994. Assoc. prof. Firat U. Sch. Medicine, Elazig, Turkey, 2004—. Bd. dirs. Firat Tip Merkezi Psikiyatri Abd, Elazig, Turkey. Contbr. articles to profl. jours. Achievements include research in neurobiologics. Home: Firat Tip Merkezi Psikiyatri Abd Elazig 23119 Turkey Office: Firat Tip Merkezi Psikiyatri Abd Universite Cad 23119 Elazig Turkey Office Fax: 90 424 2388096. Personal E-mail: matmaca_p@yahoo.com.

ATSUHIRO, TANABE, research scientist; b. Sendai, Japan, Oct. 2, 1971; PhD, Grad. Sch. Pharm. Scis. Osaka U., 2001. Rsch. assoc. Kitasato U., 2003—. Mem.: Pharm. Soc. Japan, Japanese Biochem. Soc. Office: 5-9-1 Shirogane Minato Tokoyo 108-8641 Japan Office Fax: 81-3-3442-3875. Business E-Mail: tanabea@pharm.kitasato-u.ac.jp.

ATTARD, FRANK A., molecular biologist, writer; BS, U. Md., Coll. Pk., 1986, MS, 1991, PhD, 1995. Postdoc. fellow Armed Forces Radiobiology Rsch. Inst., Bethesda, Md., 1995—97; nat. rsch. svc. award fellow Johns Hopkins U. Sch. Medicine, Balt., 1997—2000; rsch. assoc. Uniformed Svcs. U. Health Sci., Bethesda, Md., 2000—04; sci. writer Henry M. Jackson Found. Advancement Military Medicine Inc., Rockville, Md., 2004—. Med. database author Exam Master Corp., Newark, 1995—2000; participant Howard County Assn. for Gifted and Talented Youth, 1980—81; v.p. Poutry Sci. Club, U. MD, 1988—89; senator Campus Senate U. Md., 1990—91; election judge Howard County Bd. Elections, 1992—2002; with Am. Men & Women Sci., 1995—; trustee Knights Columbus Columbia Coun., 2010—. Contbr. articles to profl. jours. Recipient Merit award, Howard County, Md., 1981, Shaffner Academic Excellence award, 1990, Superior Performance award, Henry M. Jackson Found. Advancement Mil. Medicine, Inc., 2002, Cert. Appreciation, 2010. Mem.: KC, Sigma Xi. Office: Henry M Jackson Found 1401 Rockville Pike Ste 600 Rockville MD 20852 Personal E-mail: molecular.biologist@yahoo.com. Business E-Mail: fattard@hjf.org.

ATTAS, LEWIS MICHAEL, medical oncologist; BA in Biochemistry cum laude, U. Pa.; MD, Mt. Sinai Sch. of Medicine, NY. Diplomate Am. Bd. Internal Medicine, Am. Bd. Internal Medicine-med. oncology, Am. Bd. Internal Medicine-hematology, registered NY, 1983, lic. NJ, 1988, Fla., 1988. Intern Montefiore Med. Ctr., Bronx, NY, 1982—83, resident, 1983—85; fellow in hematology North Shore Univ. Hosp., Manhasset, 1985—86, fellow in oncology, 1986—87, rsch. fellow in hematology/oncology, 1987—88; hosp. affiliations include Englewood Hosp. and Med. Ctr., NY, Holy Name Hosp. Named one of Top Doctor, Inside Jersey, 2010. Office: Englewood Hospital and Medical Center 350 Engle St Englewood NJ 07631 Office Phone: 201-568-5250. Office Fax: 201-568-5358.

ATTATIPPAHOLKUN, WATCHAREE HIRUNYAVASASIT, medical educator; b. Supan Buri, Thailand, June 22, 1955; BSc in Biochemistry, 1977, PhD in Biochemistry, 1983. Assoc. prof. Mahidol U., Faculty Med. Tech., 1999—. Recipient award, NIH. Mem.: Soc. Biotech. Thailand, Assn. Med. Technologist Thailand, Genetic Soc. Thailand, Sci. Soc. Thailand Under Patronage His Majesty King, Soc. Advancement Sci. Avocations: golf, tennis. Office: Prannok Rd Bangkok 10700 Thailand Office Fax: 66-02-4124110.

ATTEBERRY, LINDA ROSE, surgeon, retired military officer; b. Indpls., Oct. 8, 1951; d. Carlysle L. and Marjorie Elizabeth Atteberry. MD, Wake Forest U., 1991. Diplomate Am. Bd. Surgery. Commd. pvt. 1st class U.S. Army, 1972, advanced through grades to col.; resident Health Sci. Ctr. U. Fla., Jacksonville, 1991—97; chief of surgery Irwin Army Hosp., Ft. Riley, Kans., 1998—99, fellow critical care, 2006—07; chief of surgery 10th Combat Support Hosp., Tuzla, Bosnia-Herzegovina, 1999, Winn Army Hosp., Ft. Stewart, Ga., 1999—2001; divsn. surgeon 24th Infantry Divsn., Ft. Riley, Kans., 2001—03; surgeon 250th Forward Surg. Team, Kirkuk, Iraq, 2003—04, comdr. Ft. Lewis, Wash., 2003—05; asst. prof. surgery Sect. Trauma, Medical Coll. Ga. Contbr. articles to profl. jours. Decorated Legion of Merit, Legion of Merit with one oak leaf cluster. Fellow: Am. Coll. Surgeons; mem.: So. Surg. Congress, Eastern Assoc.Surgery Trauma, Assn. Mil. Surgeons of U.S., Alpha Omega Alpha. Home: 1276 Kings way Augusta GA 30904 Personal E-mail: linda.atteberry@us.army.mil. *

ATTILI, ADOLFO FRANCESCO, gastroenterologist, educator; b. Terni, Mar. 15, 1948; MD, U. Rome La Sapienza, 1972, PhD, 1976. Assoc. prof. gastroenterology U. L'Aquila, 1977—2000; prof. gastroenterology U. Rome La Sapienza, 2000—. Mem.: Italian Assn. Study of Liver, Italian Soc. Gastroenterology. Office: Via Ruggero Fauro 66 Rome Lazio 00197 Italy Business E-Mail: adolfo.attili@uniroma1.it.

ATWELL, ROBERT, psychologist; BS in Psychology, Temple Univ., MS in Counseling Psychology; PhD in Clin. Psychology, Univ. Denver. Clin., forensic psychologist, Denver & Boulder, Colo., 1973—. Mem.: Assn. Black Psychologists (pres. 2005—07). Office: 17235 S Logan Denver CO 80210-3123 Office Phone: 303-698-0446. Office Fax: 303-722-2557. Business E-Mail: robert@afrikanholistichealth.com.

ATWOOD, KAREN, insurance company executive; BS in Fin., U. Ill., Urbana-Champaign, 1978; MBA in Acctg., De Paul U., Chgo., 1982. Mgr. accounts receivable and collections Health Care Svc. Corp., 1990—95, nat. account underwriting officer, 1995—2001, v.p., chief underwriter, 2001—06; sr. v.p. nat. accounts Blue Cross Blue Shield Ill., 2006—09, pres., 2009—. Corp. sponsor Ill. State Coun. SHRM, 2008—10, Fin. Executives Internat. Chgo. Chpt., 2010. Bd. trustees De Paul Univ.; bd. dirs. Silk Rd. Theatre Project, Chgo. Office: Blue Cross Blue Shield Ill 300 E Randolph St Chicago IL 60601 *

AU, OTTO YUM-TO, plastic surgeon, educator; b. Hong Kong, Dec. 1, 1925; s. Lum and Hor Kun (Tse) A.; m. Pauline Lau, Apr. 24, 1953; children: Anthony, Victor, Karen. MD, Jefferson Med. Coll., 1957. Diplomate Am. Bd. Plastic Surgery. Intern Hosp. Good Samaritan, LA, 1957-58, surg. resident, 1958-61; plastic surgery resident St. Joseph Hosp., Ann Arbor, Mich., 1961-63; cons. plastic surgery Hong

Kong Ctrl. Hosp., 1964—, Canossa Hosp., Hong Kong, 1964-97, Hong Kong Sanitorium & Hosp., 1999—. Clin. prof. plastic surgery Chinese U., Hong Kong, 1997—. Mem. Hong Kong Acad. Medicine, Hong Kong Soc. Plastic Surgery (pres. 1967-68), Brit. Med. Assn. (Hong Kong br. pres. 1969-70), Oriental Soc. of Aesthetic Plastic Surgery (pres. 1999—). Avocations: swimming, bridge, horse racing. Office: 407 New World Tower Hong Kong Hong Kong Home Phone: (852) 94607439; Office Phone: (852)25229365. Office Fax: 25244218. Personal E-mail: ottoau@biznetvigator.com.

AU, RHODA, neurologist, educator; b. Chgo., Sept. 30, 1960; PhD, U. Calif., Riverside, 1985; MBA, Boston U., 1995. Assoc. prof. neurology Boston U. Sch. Medicine, 1986—. Advisor ViaCLIX, 2009. Office: 72 E Concord St Boston MA 02118 Office Fax: 617-638-8086. Business E-Mail: rhodaau@bu.edu.

AU, WING LOK, neurologist; married. MBBS, Nat. U. Singapore, 1994. House officer Ministry of Health, Singapore, 1994—95, med. officer, 1995—2000; registrar Nat. Neuroscience Inst., Singapore, 2000—03, assoc. cons., 2003—05, cons., 2005—, coord. Parkinson's Disease and Movement Disorders Ctr., 2007—; asst. prof. Dukenus Grad. Med. Schs., Singapore, 2009—. Clin. tutor, faculty of medicine Nat. U. Singapore, 2002—05, clin. tchr. Yong Loo Lin Sch. Medicine, 2005—07, clin. lectr. Yong Loo Lin Sch. Medicine, 2007—; mem. Parkinson's Disease Clin. Practice Guidelines Workgroup, Singapore, 2005—07, Specialist Accreditation Bd. Rsch. Com., Singapore, 2007—. Contbr. articles to profl. jours. Mem. Conf. Amb. Programme, Singapore, 2007—08. Fellow Health Manpower Devel. Programme, Ministry of Health, 2004, Med. Rsch. Fellowship, Nat. Med. Rsch. Coun., Singapore, 2005, Melvin Yahr Meml. Fellowship, Internat. Fedn. Parkinson's Disease Found., 2005; Outreach Grant, Nat. Parkinson Found., USA, 2007—. Fellow: RCP, Acad. Medicine; mem.: Clin. Neuroscience Soc. (exec. mem. 2008—), Coll. of Physicians, Movement Disorders Soc., Parkinson's Disease Soc. (editor, Parkinson's news 2007—). Office Phone: 65-6357 7171. Business E-Mail: wing_lok_au@nni.com.sg.

AUDICANA, MARÍA TERESA, allergist, consultant; b. Nürnberg, Germany, Dec. 16, 1961; d. Miguel Audicana and Margarita Berasategui; m. Miguel Angel Mendigutxia, Apr. 15, 1989; children: Jon Mendigutxia, Maialen Mendigutxia. BS, Basque Country U., 1985. Resident Santiago Apostol Hosp., Vitoria-Gasteiz, Spain, 1987—91, physician, 1994—; cons. Galdakaoko Hosp., Bilbao, Spain, 1991—94. Mem.: Medicus Mundi, Spanish Soc. Allergy and Clin. Immunology (assoc.). Achievements include research in Anisakis allergy. Avocations: mountain climbing, skiing. Office: Santiago Apostol Hosp Calle Olaguibel 29 1004 Vitoria-Gasteiz Spain Office Fax: 945 00 76 08. Business E-Mail: taudicana@hsan.osakidetza.net.

AUDUS, KENNETH L., dean, pharmaceutical researcher; b. Watertown, SD, Nov. 11, 1954; BS in Chemistry, U. SD, Vermillion, 1980; PhD in Pharmacology, U. Kans. Sch. Medicine, Kansas City, 1984. Postdoc. fellow dept. pharm. chemistry U. Kans., Lawrence, 1984—85, asst. to assoc. prof. pharm. chemistry, 1986—98, prof., chmn. pharm. chemistry, 1998—, dean. Sch. Pharmacy, 2004—, also courtesy prof. pharmacology & toxicology; prof. molecular & integrative physiology U. Kans. Med. Ctr. Mem. sci. adv. bd. Genzyme Pharm., 2001—. Mem. editl. bd. Internat. Jour. Pharmaceutics, Jour. Pharmacy & Pharmacology, Biol. & Pharm. Bulletin, Jour. Pharm. Scis.; contbr. articles to profl. jours., chapters to books. Recipient Life Scis. Contacts award, Lilly Rsch. Labs., 1987. Fellow: Am. Assn. Pharm. Scientists; mem.: Am. Heart Assn. (pres. Kans. affiliate 1997—98). Achievements include research in the application of endothelial and epithelial cell and tissue culture systems to study mechanisms of drug transport, metabolism, and tissue permeability regulation. Office: U Kans Sch Pharmacy 1251 Wescoe Hall Dr 2056 Malott Lawrence KS 66045 also: KU Med Ctr 3901 Rainbow Blvd Kansas City KS 66160 Business E-Mail: audus@ku.edu.

AUERBACH, ANITA L., clinical psychologist; d. Ben and Gussie Weiss; m. Steven Miles Auerbach, May 25, 1969. BA cum laude, SUNY, Buffalo, 1968, MA, 1970; PhD, George Washington U., 1977. Diplomate Am. Bd. Med. Psychotherapists, Internat. Acad. Behavioral Medicine. Chief rsch. Youth Crime Control Project D.C. Dept. Corrections, 1970-74; intern clin. psychology No. Va. Tng. Ctr., Fairfax, 1974-75, staff psychologist, then chief psychol. svcs., 1975-79; pvt. practice clin. psychology Commonwealth Psychol. Assocs. PLC, McLean, Va., 1979—; founder,dir. Commonwealth Psychol. Assocs., 1979—, pres., 1979—. Lectr. Washington Tech. Inst., 1972-74, George Mason U., 1978—82; clin. prof. psychology George Washington U., 2004—; chair RXP Task Force Va. Acad. Clin. Psychologists, 2006-; cons. in field. Contbr. articles to profl. jours. Mem. adv. bd. World Children's Choir, 2000—02; mem. family edn. project Joseph P. Kennedy Jr. Found., 1977—79; mem. regional appeals bd. No. Va. Pub. Sch. Sys., 1977—79; mem. adv. bd. Value Options Behavioral Health, 2001—03. Fellow N.Y. State Regents 1968-70; recipient N.Y. State Scholar Incentive award, 1969. Mem. APA, Am. Soc. Clin. Hypnosis (approved cons.), Va. Acad. Clin. Psychologists (exec. com. mem.), Va. Psychol. Assn., No. Va. Soc. Clin. Psychologists, Washington Soc. Study Clin. Hypnosis, Assn. Advancement Applied Sports Psychology, Psi Chi, Alpha Lambda Delta. Office: 1479 Chain Bridge Rd Mc Lean VA 22101-5730 Office Phone: 703-734-0787.

AUERBACH, ETHEL LOUISE, retired healthcare facility administrator; BS in Edn. for the Exceptional Students, Barry U., 1960; M in Guidance and Counseling for the Exceptional Students, Barry U., 1966, Specialist Degree in Guidance and Counseling for the Exceptional Students, 1971; D in Edn./Adminstrn. and Leadership, Nova Southeastern U., 1981. Cert. adminstrn. and supervision grades K-12 Fla., guidance and counselling grades pre K-12 Fla., mental retardation Fla., mentally handicapped pre K-12 Fla., supervision in exceptional student edn. K-12 Fla., varying exceptionalities grades K-12 Fla., exceptional child supervision grades K-12. Counselor South Fla. Hosp., Thomas Jefferson Middle Sch.; tchr. Roosevelt Elem. Sch., Sunland Tng. Ctr., Ft. Myers, Fla., 1960—62; tchr. elem. level students with challenges, 1960; tchr. educable class Santa Clara Elem., 1962—65; intern Riviera Middle Sch., 1960; intern in mid. sch. students having challenges, 1966; tchr./counselor exceptional student program Riviera Middle Sch., 1966—70, counselor, chairperson exceptional student program, 1971—75; intern in hosp. with students having emotional challenges, 1971; asst. prin. Redland Middle Sch., 1976—77; asst. prin. exceptional student program Sylvania Heights Elem. Sch., 1977—80, Kensington Elem. Sch., 1980—88; asst. adminstr. Miami Cerebral Palsy Residential Svcs., Inc., Fla., 1989—92, adminstr., 1992—2007, assoc. dir., 2007. Adj. instr. exceptional student edn. Barry U., Miami, 1991—93; mem. Coun. Exceptional Children. Recipient Esteemed Employees with Disabilities award, 1995; named a Profl. Recognized Spl. Educator, Coun. for Exceptional Children; named to Barry U. Alumni Hall of Fame, 1994; nominee Adminstr. of Yr., Coun. for Exceptional Children, 1980, Final Rsch. Study award, 1981. Mem.: CEC, Phi Gamma Sigma, Phi Delta Kappa, Kappa Delta Pi.

AUERBACH, JOHN M., state agency administrator, public health service officer; MBA. With Uhpham's Corner Health Ctr., Dorchester, Mass.; linked city's health centers with Boston City Hosp. City of Boston, 1986—88; chief of staff state commr. public health Mass Dept. Pub. Health, 1988—90; dir., AIDS bur. and asst. commr. Mass. Dept. Pub. Health, 1990—97; exec. dir. Boston Pub. Health Commn., 1998—2007; commr. Mass. State Dept. Pub. Health, Boston, 2007—. Office: Mass Dept Pub Health 250 Washington St Boston MA 02108 Office Phone: 617-624-6000.

AUFF, EDUARD, neurologist, educator; b. Wien, Austria, Nov. 20, 1951; MD, U. Wien, 1975. Prof. Med. U. Vienna, 1991—. Head, sect. neurorehabiltation, dept. neurology, 1991—2006; dir., dept. neurology, 2000. Mem.: Movement Disorder Soc., Austrian Soc. Parkinson's Disease, Austrian Soc. Neurorehabilitation, Austrian Soc. Neurology. Office: Waehringer Guertel 18-20 Wien 1090 Austria Office Fax: 431404006215. Business E-Mail: eduard.auff@meduniwien.ac.at.

AUFSES, ARTHUR HAROLD, JR., surgeon, educator; b. NYC, Feb. 8, 1926; s. Arthur Harold and Beatrice (Hauser) A.; m. Harriet Whitman, Dec. 28, 1947; children: Arthur Harold III, Carolyn Aufses Blashek. Student, Columbia U., 1942-43; BS, Union Coll., 1944; MD, Columbia U. Coll. Physicians and Surgeons, 1948. Diplomate Am. Bd. Surgery. Intern Presbyn. Hosp., NYC, 1948-49, resident in surgery, 1950-51, 53-54, Mt. Sinai Hosp., NYC, 1954-56; practice medicine specializing in surgery NYC, 1956-97; prof. Mt. Sinai Med. Ctr., NYC, 1974—; chmn. dept. surgery Mt. Sinai Sch. Medicine, NYC, 1974-96, L.I. Jewish Med. Ctr., 1971-74; prof. surgery SUNY-Stony Brook, 1971-74; surgeon-in-chief Mt. Sinai Hosp., NYC, 1974-96. Contbr. articles to med. jours. Bd. dirs. 92d St. YMHA, 1974—. 1st lt. U.S. Army, 1951-53. Recipient Jacobi medallion Mt. Sinai Med. Ctr., 1979; recipient Gold Headed Cane award Mt. Sinai Med. Ctr., 1982 Fellow ACS (2nd v.p. 1996-97), Am. Surg. Assn. (2nd v.p. 1995-96), Am. Coll. Gastroenterology (pres. 1986-87), Assn. of Program Dirs. Surgery (pres. 1989-91), N.Y. Acad. Medicine; mem. Soc. Surg. Oncology, Am. Gastroent. Assn., N.Y. Surg. Soc. (pres. 1979-80), Soc. Surgery Alimentary Tract, Brazilian Coll. Surgeons, Chilean Congress Surgeons, Portuguese Soc. Gastroenterology. Jewish. Home: 1185 Park Ave New York NY 10128-1308 Office: Mt Sinai Sch Medicine Box 1077 1 Gustave L Levy Pl New York NY 10029-6500 Home Phone: 212-410-6056; Office Phone: 212-659-9560. Business E-Mail: arthur.aufses@mssm.edu.

AUGUST, GILBERT PAUL, pediatrician, educator; b. NJ, Sept. 18, 1936; m. Bernice Ide, Apr. 27, 1938; children: Sharon Michal, Lauren Joelle. BS, CCNY, 1958; MD, NYU, 1962. Diplomate Am. Bd. Pediat., cert. in pediatric endocrinology. Intern pediatric endocrinology & metabolism Bellevue Hosp., NYC, 1962—63, resident, 1963—65; fellow U. Calif. San Francisco Med. Ctr., 1967—67; pediatric endocrinologist Children's Nat. Med. Ctr., Washington, 1969; prof. emeritus pediat. George Washington U., 1983—. Contbr. articles to profl. jours. Mem.: Endocrine Soc., Soc. Pediatric Rsch., Am. Pediatric Soc., Lawson Wilkins Pediatric Endocrine Soc.

AUGUSTIN, ALBERT J., ophthalmologist, department chairman; b. Wuerzburg, Germany, Sept. 16, 1959; s. Berthold and Regina Augustin; m. Christel M. Burckhardt, Dec. 3, 1983; children: Constanze M.A., Victor A. Abitur, AKG, 1979. Cert. Landes-Ärztekammer, 1995. Head retina sect. Dept. Ophthalmology, Mainz, Germany, 1998—2001, prof. Karlsruhe, Germany, 2001—, chmn., 2001—. Recipient Gedenkjahresstiftung, U. Wuerzburg, Bavaria, 1990. Achievements include first to combination therapy in AMD and establishment of the theoretical basis for new treatment strategies of retinal diseases. Office: Dept Ophthalmology Moltkestrasse 90 Karlsruhe 76133 Germany Home: Raiffeisenstrasses Sulzfeld am Main 97320 Switzerland Office Phone: 497219742001. Office Fax: 497219742009. Personal E-mail: albertjaugustin@googlemail.com.

AUGUSTIN, EWA ANNA, research scientist; b. Gdynia, June 11, 1963; PhD, U. Gdansk, 1998. Rsch. scientist Gdansk U. Tech., 1986—. Mem.: Polish Cytometry Soc., European Cell Death Orgn. Avocations: gardening, swimming. Office: Narutowicza 11/12 Gdansk 80-233 Poland Office Fax: 4858 347 15 16. Business E-Mail: ewa.augustin@pg.gda.pl.

AUGUSTINE, NORMAN RALPH, not-for-profit and business executive, educator, retired federal agency administrator; b. Denver, July 27, 1935; s. Ralph Harvey and Freda Irene (Immenga) A.; m. Margareta Engman, Jan. 20, 1962; children: Gregory Eugen (dec.), René Irene. BSE magna cum laude, Princeton U., 1957, MSE, 1959; DEng (hon.), Rensselaer Poly. Inst., 1988; DSc (hon.), U. Colo., 1989; DEng (hon.), McDaniel Coll., 1990, U. Md., 1992; D in Mgmt. (hon.), Embry Riddle U., 1992; DEng (hon.), Stevens Inst., 1993; HHD (hon.), Wheeling Jesuit U., 1994; DSc (hon.), SUNY, 1994; DEng (hon.), U. Ctrl. Fla., 1995; LHD (hon.), U. Denver, 1996; DEng (hon.), Worcester Polytech., 1996; LHD (hon.), Georgetown U., 1997, Trinity Coll., 1997; DEng (hon.), U. Ariz., 1997; LLD (hon.), Duke U., 1997; DEng (hon.), Milw. Sch. Engring., 1998, Colo. Sch. Mines; DSc (hon.), Arcadia U., 1998; D in Nat. Security Affairs (hon.), Nat. Def. U., 2005; D in Bus. Adminstrn. (hon.), Drexel U., 2006; DEng (hon.), Princeton U., 2007; DEng, George Mason U., 2008; DSc (hon.), Carnegie Mellon U., 2008; LHD (hon.), Marymount U., 2010; PhD (hon.), Pa. State U., 2010; DSc. in Engring., Mich. Technol. U., 2011; DSc., McGill U., 2011. Rsch. asst. Princeton U., 1957-58; program mgr., chief engr. Douglas Aircraft Co., Inc., Santa Monica, Calif., 1958-65; asst. dir. rsch. & engring. US Dept. Def., Washington, 1965-70; v.p. advanced systems Missiles and Space Co., LTV Aerospace Corp., Dallas, 1970-73; asst. sec. Dept. Army, US Dept. Def., Washington, 1973-75, under sec., 1975-77; v.p. ops. Martin Marietta Aerospace Corp., Bethesda, Md., 1977-82; pres. Martin Marietta Denver Aerospace Co., 1982-85, sr. v.p. info. systems, 1985, CEO, 1987—95; pres. Lockheed Martin Corp., Bethesda, 1995, chmn., CEO, 1995—97. Chmn. exec. com. Lockheed Martin Corp., Bethesda, Md., 1998-2004; bd. dirs. Procter & Gamble Co., 1989-2007, Phillips Petroleum Co., 1989-2002, Black & Decker, 1997-, Conoco-Phillips Co., 2002-; US adv. bd. Deutches Bank, 2006-; cons. office Sec. of Def., 1971—, Nat. Security Coun., Exec. Office Pres., 1971-73, Dept. Army, Dept. Air Force, Dept. Navy, FAA, Dept. Energy, Dept. Transp., Dept. Homeland Security, Dept. Commerce; mem. USAF Sci. Adv. Bd.; chmn. Def. Sci. Bd., 1997—; mem. NATO Group Experts on Air Def., 1966-70, NASA Rsch. and Tech. Adv. Coun., 1973-75, chmn. Space Sys. and Tech. Adv. Bd., 1985-89; mem. Chief of Naval Ops. Exec. Bd., 1989-92; chmn. def. policy adv. com. on trade, 1988-91, 93—; lectr. with rank of prof. Princeton U., 1997-99; chaired NRC study panels such as the Com. on the Orgn. and Mgmt. of Rsch in Astronomy and Astrophysics; served on Com. on the Orgnl. Structure, NIH, co-chair NIH Panel on Conflicts of Interest; chmn. Nat. Acads. Competitiveness Com., Aerospace Industry Assn.; mem. Pres.'s Com. Advisors on Sci. and Tech.; mem. adv. bd. Dept. Homeland Security., Sec. of Energy, 2010; mem. Hart/Rudman Commn. on Nat. Security. Author: Augustine's Laws, Augustine's Travels, 1997; co-author: The Defense Revolution, 1990, Shakespeare in Charge, 2001; mem. adv. bd. Jour. Def. Rsch., 1970—; assoc. editor Def. Systems Mgmt. Rev., 1977-82; mem. editl. bd. Astronautics and Aerospace. Trustee Johns Hopkins U., Princeton U., MIT; mem. bd. govs. Colonial Williamsburg, 1996-2006; mem. bd. trustees Callaway Gardens Found.; chmn. White House/NASA Adv. Com. on Future of US Space Program, 1991, Nat. Security Telecomm. Adv. Com., US Antarctic Program Rev. Com., 1996-97; nat. program evaluation com., coun. v.p. Boy Scouts Am., pres., 1993-95; chmn., prin. officer ARC, 1993-2002. Recipient Meritorious Svc. medal US Dept. Def., 1979, 5 Disting. Civilian Svc. medals Dept. Def., Nat. Engring. award Am. Assn. Engring. Socs., 1991, Am. Acad. Achievement Golden Plate award, 1995, James Madison medal Princeton U., 1995, Blumenthal award Johns Hopkins U. Sch. Engring., 1996, Gold Eagle award Soc. Am. Mil. Engrs. Acad. of Fellows, 1996, Ralph Coates Roe medal ASME, 1996, M. Eugene Merchant Mfg. medal, 1997, Nat. Medal of Technology, 1997, Nat. Indsl. Rsch. Inst. medal, 2009, NAS award in aeronautical engring., 2010; named Personality of Yr., Flight Internat. Aerospace, 1996, 05 AAAS Philip Hauge Abelson prize, 2006, Pub. Welfare medal, NAS, 2006, Bower award for Bus. Leadership, Franklin Inst., 2007, Vannevar Bush award Nat. Sci. Found., 2008. Fellow IEEE (Founders' award 1996), AIAA (hon., bd. dirs. 1978-85, pres. 1983-84, Goddard medal 1988), Am. Astron. Soc., Am. Helicopter Soc. (dir. 1974-75), Royal Aero. Soc., Explorers Club; mem. NAE (chmn. 1994-96, Arthur M. Bueche award 1991), Am. Acad. Arts and Scis., Am. Philos. Soc., Internat. Acad. Astronautics, Assn. US Army (pres. 1980-84, chmn. 1990—, George C. Marshall medal), Nat. Security Indsl. Assn. (Forrestal medal 1988), Indsl. Coll. Armed Forces (Eisenhower award 1990), Armed Forces Comm. and Electronics Assn. (Sarnoff medal 1990), Hart Rudman Commn., US Mil. Acad. (Thayer medal, A.F. Acad. Thomas White award), Nat. Space Club (Goddard Trophy 1991), Rotary (Nat. Space Trophy 1992), Planetary Soc. (bd. dirs.), Phi Beta Kappa, Sigma Xi, Tau Beta Pi. Presbyterian. travelled extensively around the world, including dogsledding in the Arctic, exploring volcanoes in Antarctica, canoeing the Boundary Waters of Canada, snorkeling on the Great Barrier Reef, Trans-Siberian Railroad and Silk Route, and stood on both poles of the Earth. Personal E-mail: norm.augustine@lmco.com.

AUKLAND, ELVA DAYTON, retired biologist; b. Arlington, Va., Apr. 25, 1922; d. William A. and Helen Gertrude (Rollins) Dayton; m. Merrill Forrest Aukland Aukland, June 18, 1949; children: Bruce Michael, Duncan Dayton, Rebecca Elizabeth. AB cum laude, Wheaton Coll., 1943; MS, U. Minn., 1946. Tchg. asst. U. Minn., 1943—46; instr. botany Ohio Wesleyan U., Del., 1946—49; instr. zoology & microbiology Ohio U., Athens, 1949—50; bacteriologist E.R. Squibb & Sons, New Brunswick, NJ, 1951—53; tchr. chmn. sci. dept. Washington-Lee HS, Arlington, 1962—78, T.C. Williams HS, Alexandria, Va., 1978—87, biology coord., 1978—87, 1980—85; lectr. biology Marymount U., 1987—97; dir. Insect Zoo, Smithsonian Instn., 1972, Va. Sci. Talent Search, 1980—82; ret., 1994. Editor sci. tchrs. sect. Va. Jour. Sci., 1971—76; mem. exec. com. Com. on Housing Arlington. Commr. Arlington Parks & Recreation Commn., 1971—77; mem. Environ. Improvement Commn. Arlington County, 1977—83, Arlington Com. 100, Com. Housing in Arlington; bd. dirs. Northern Va. Conservation Coun. Named Outstanding Tchr. Sci. & Math., Washington Acad. Sci., 1966, exec. bd., Arlington United Way, 1989—92. Mem.: NEA, LWV, Audubon Soc., Va. Edn. Assn., Arlington Edn. Assn., Nat. Sci. Tchrs. Assn., Va. Jr. Acad. Sci. (bd. dirs., task force quality edn. 1983—86, Outstanding Tchr. award 1975), Nat. Assn. Biology Tchrs., Phi Theta Kappa, Delta Kappa Gamma. Home: 3623 Falls River Ave Raleigh NC 27614-7089

AULD, FRANK, psychologist, educator; b. Denver, Aug. 9, 1923; s. Benjamin Franklin and Marion Leland (Evans) A.; m. Elinor James, June 29, 1946 (dec. June 1990); children: Mary, Robert, Margaret; m. Elinor Leah Levine, Dec. 8, 1996 (dec. Dec. 2004). AB, Drew U., 1946; MA, Yale U., 1948, PhD, 1950. Cert. psychologist, Mich., Ont. Instr. psychology Yale U., New Haven, 1950-52, asst. prof., 1952-59; assoc. prof. Wayne State U., Detroit, 1959-61, prof., 1961-67, dir. clin. psychology tng. program, 1960-66; prof. U. Detroit, 1967-70, dir. psychol. clinic, 1967-69; prof. U. Windsor, Ont., Canada, 1970—91, prof. emeritus, 1992—. Cons. in field. Author: Steps in Psychotherapy, 1953, Scoring Human Motives, 1959, Resolution of Inner Conflict, 1991, 2d edit., 2005; contbr. articles to profl. jours. Chmn. Dearborn CC, Mich., 1962; mem. adv. com. on coll. work Episcopal Diocese Mich., 1962-71. Recipient Alumni Achievement award Drew U., 1965 Fellow APA (evaluation com. 1961-66); mem. Ont. Psychol. Assn. (edn. and tng. bd. 1976-91, Lifetime Achievement award 1998), Conn. State Psychol. Soc. (pres. 1958), Soc. Psychotherapy Research, Phi Beta Kappa, Sigma Xi. Home: 200 Chester St Apt 306 Birmingham MI 48009-1428 Home Phone: 248-433-1886. Business E-Mail: frankauld@aya.yale.edu.

AULD, JAMES S., educational psychologist; Grad., U. Nebr. Cert. sch. counselor, profl. counselor. Dir. testing, asst. prof.; K-12 dir. guidance; kindergarten-12 dir. psychol. svcs. Author: Real Personality. Mem. APA, AACD, ASCD, Can. Psychol. Assn., Nebr. Profl. Counselors, Gold Key, nat. Disting. Svc. Registry for Counselors, Phi Delta Kappa. Office: PO Box 6228 Lincoln NE 68506-0228

AULD, ROBERT HENRY, JR., biomedical engineer, educator, consultant, writer; b. Akron, Ohio, Sept. 19, 1942; s. Robert Henry Sr. and Elsie Mae (Rollans) A.; children: Sheila Kay, Jason Craig; stepson: Christopher William Weiss. BSBA, Biomed. Engr., U. San Francisco, 1978. Registered profl. engr., Calif.; cert. clin. engr. Reg.

svc. mgr. scientific products div. AHSC, Sunnyvale, Calif., 1963-68; founder, gen. mgr. Lab. Instrument Svc., Campbell, Calif., 1968-77; nat. mgr. Biomed. Svcs. Group Pilot Project Honeywell, Inc., Denver, 1977-79; internship Stanford U. Med, Ctr., 1976, UCSF, 1978; profl. engr. Robert Auld Enterprises, San Jose, Calif., 1979-86; dir. clin. engring. St. Louis Reg. Med. Ctr., 1987-89; engring. mgr. Robert Auld Engring.-West, Imperial, Mo., 1989—, biomedical engr. cons. Santee, Calif., 1989—; nat. svc. mgr. R.C. Network, Cleveland, OH, 1990-99; expert examiner State of Calif. Bd. Registration for Profl. Engrs., Sacramento, 1995-99. Seminar dir. ASMT, Phoenix, Ariz., 1968-79; instrument workshop seminar coordinator, Stanford U. Med. Ctr., 1980-84; engring. advisor St. Louis Reg. Career Access Ctr., 1987-89, U. Mo., Rolla and St. Louis. Author: The Clone Factory (A True Story About Police), 1992; contbr. articles to profl. jours. Apptd. hazardous waste com. State of Mo., 1988—90; del. at large Rep. Legion of Merit, Imperial, Mo., 1990—93; registrar of voters, precinct inspector San Diego County, 2004, 2005, 2006; precinct rep. San Diego, 2006—. Recipient Govs. Golden Spike award, Calif., 1986. Mem. IEEE, NY Acad. Scis., Am. Soc. Hosp. Engrs., NSPE, Mo. Soc. Profl. Engrs. (chmn. 1988-89, chmn. minority Math Counts pilot project 1987-89), Order Demolay (life). Republican. Achievements include development of device for equilibrating gases in a liquid or blood for measurement of gases in blood; patent pending for dual halogen colormetric light source; Innovator "Single Source Service", "Parts Banks" for Clinical Equipment for Health Care Facilities. Mailing: PO Box 40541 San Diego CA 92164 Office: Robert Auld Engring West 525 14th St Ste 423 San Diego CA 92101 Office Phone: 619-379-8206, 619-379-2272.

AULISI, EDWARD FIORE, neurosurgeon; b. Nov. 10, 1961; married; 3 children. BA, Princeton U., NJ, 1984; MD, George Washington U., 1988. Diplomate Nat. Bd. Med. Examiners, lic. DC, Md. Physician Neurol. Surgery Group, Washington, 1995; surgeon Washington Brain & Spine Inst.; med. dir. neurosciences Washington Hosp. Ctr. Fellow: ACS; mem.: AMA, AAAS, Am. Assn. Neurol. Surgeons, Congress of Neurological Surgeons, Soc. Neuroscience, Internat. Brain Rsch. Orgn., William Beaumont Med. Soc., Sigma Xi. Office: Washington Hosp Ctr 110 Irving St NW Washington DC 20010

AULL, SUSAN, physician; b. NYC; d. Eugene and Ines Aull. BA, Vassar Coll., 1981; MD, N.Y. Med. Coll., 1986. Diplomate Am. Acad. Phys. Medicine and Rehab., Am. Acad. Pain Mgmt. Intern L.I. Coll. Hosp., Bklyn., 1986-87; phys. medicine and rehab. PGY II, III Westchester County Med. Ctr., Valhalla, NY, 1987-89; phys. medicine and rehab. PGY IV Lincoln Hosp., Bronx, NY, 1989-90, Ctrl. Fla. Physicians Rehab., Orlando, 1990-91; med. dir. dept. phys. medicine and rehab. Halifax Med. Ctr., Daytona Beach, Fla., 1992-99; med. dir. 21st Century Rehab. and Wound Mgmt. Ctr., Maitland, Fla., 1992; staff dept. internal medicine Winter Park (Fla.) Meml. Hosp., 1991-96; pvt. practice WWPM&R, Winter Park and Sarasota, 1991—2002; multi-specialty group practice, dir. phys. medicine and rehab. Ctrl. Fla. Physicians Rehab., Orlando, 1990-91; physician Advanced Sports Medicine Ctr., 2002—04, S. Aull MD PA Phys. Medicine Rehab. Pain Mgmt. Electrodiagnostic Consultation, 2002—, IOM Svcs. Inc., 2004—07. Electrodiagnostic cons. SEA Med. Svcs., PA, Goldenrod, Fla., 1990-96; adj. clin. prof. U. Ctrl. Fla., Orlando, 1991-96. Author: (with others) Strength Conditioning for Preventive Medicine, 1992, ISC Control Points - New Generation of Pressure Points, 1993. Recipient Leadership award Defensive Tactics Newsletter, 1993; grantee PPCT Mgmt. Systems, Inc., 1992. Fellow Am. Acad. Phys. Medicine and Rehab.; mem. AMA, Am. Acad. Pain Mgmt., Am. Coll. Sports Medicine. Office: 5535 Marquesas Cir Sarasota FL 34233 Office Phone: 941-487-7244.

AUNER, HOLGER WERNER, hematologist; b. Graz, Austria, Dec. 10, 1971; MD, Karl-Franzens U. Graz, Austria, 1997; PhD, Imperial Coll. London, 2009. Resident internal medicine, hematology Med. U. Graz, 1999—2004; clin. rsch. fellow MRC Clin. Scis. Ctr., 2004—08; stem cell transplant coord. Imperial Coll. NHS Trust, 2008—10; clin. rsch. fellow Imperial Coll. London, 2010—. Recipient Value People award, Wellcome Trust/Imperial Coll. London, ASH Travel award, UK Myeloma Forum, Supporting award, Styrian Cancer Soc.; Jr. Rsch. fellowship, Kay Kendall Leukaemia Fund. Mem.: Internat. Myeloma Soc., European Hematology Assn. Office: Du Cane Rd Hammersmith Hosp Camp London W12 0HS England Business E-Mail: holger.auner@csc.mrc.ac.uk.

AUNG, LELE, pediatrician, educator; b. Rangoon, Burma, Oct. 22, 1800; MD, Meharry Med. Coll., 1995; degree in Pediatric Hematology-Oncology, Meml. Sloan-Kettering Cancer Ctr., 2002. Pediatric hematologist-oncologist K K Women's and Children's Hosp., 2010. Asst. prof. Duke-NUS Grad. Med. Sch., 2010. Recipient Young Investigator award, NHG. Avocations: running, cooking. Office: K K Women's and Children's Hosp Singapore 229899 Singapore Business E-Mail: aung.lele@kkh.com.sg.

AURITI, ANTONIO, cardiologist, director; b. Rome, Oct. 28, 1956; Degree in Medicine, U. Rome, 1981, degree in Cardiology, 1985. Physician, dir., Echocardiography Lab. Hosp. S. Filippo Neri, Rome, 1985—. Contbr. scientific papers to rsch. publs. Mem.: European Assn. Echocardiography, Am. Soc. Echocardiography, Italian Soc. Echocardiography, Italian Fedn. Cardiology. Avocation: piano. Home: via Attilio Friggeri 19 Rome 00136 Italy Business E-Mail: a.auriti@sanfilipponeri.roma.it.

AUSTEN, W(ILLIAM) GERALD, surgeon, educator; b. Akron, Ohio, Jan. 20, 1930; s. Karl and Bertl (Jehle) Austen; m. Patricia Ramsdell, Jan. 28, 1961; children: Karl Ramsdell, William Gerald Jr., Christopher Marshall, Elizabeth A. BS, MIT, 1951; MD, Harvard U., 1955; HHD (hon.), U. Akron, 1980; DSc (hon.), U. Athens, 1981, U. Mass., 1985, Northeastern Ohio U. Coll. Medicine, 1996. Diplomate Am. Bd. Surgery, Am. Bd. Thoracic Surgery. Intern, then resident in surgery Mass. Gen. Hosp., Boston, 1955—61, chief surg. cardiovasc. rsch. unit, 1963—69, chief surgery, 1969—97, surgeon-in-chief, 1989—97, surgeon-in-chief emeritus, 1997—; surgeon clinic surgery Nat. Heart Inst., 1961—62; CEO, pres. Mass. Gen. Physicians Orgn., Boston, 1994—98, CEO, chmn., 1998—99, chmn., 1999—2000, hon. trustee, chmn. emeritus, 2000—. Assoc. in surgery Harvard Med. Sch., 1963—65, assoc. prof. surgery, 1965—66, prof. surgery, 1966—74, Edward D. Churchill prof. surgery, 1974—2011, Churchill disting. prof., 2011—; mem. residency review com. surgery Accreditation Coun. Grad. Med. Edn., 1988—93; bd. dirs. Abiomed, Inc., The Smithers Group, Inc. Author, editor: med. textbooks; contbr. articles to profl. jours. Mem. corp. MIT 1972-2005, life mem. corp., 1982-2005, life mem. corp. emeritus, 2005—, mem. exec. com. corp., 1986-98; trustee John S. and James L. Knight Found., 1986-2010, vice chmn., 1991-96, chmn., 1996-2010, chmn. emeritus, 2010-; bd. dirs. Found. Biomed Rsch., 1988-2000; trustee Mass. Eye and Ear Infirmary, 1991-2010, Ptnrs. HealthCare System Inc., 1994-97, Mass. Gen. Hosp., 1997-99, Dana Farber/Ptnrs. Cancer Care Inc., 1999-, Mass. Taxpayers Found., 2000—, North Shore Med. Ctr., 2001—; hon. trustee Mass. Gen. Hosp., 1999—; hon. trustee Akron Art Mus., 2004— Markle scholar, 1963-68. Fellow AAAS, Royal Coll. Surgeons Eng. (hon.), Am. Acad. Arts and Scis.; mem. NAS Inst. Medicine, Am. Heart Assn. (pres. 1977-78, Gold Heart award 1980), Am. Surg. Assn. (sec. 1979-84, pres. 1985-86), Am. Assn. Thoracic Surgery (v.p. 1987-88, pres. 1988-89), Am. Bd. Surgery (mem. bd. 1969-74, sr. mem. 1974-), Am. Bd. Thoracic Surgery (bd. dirs. 1984-90), ACS (regent 1982-91, chmn. bd. regents 1989-91, pres. 1992-93), Assn. Acad. Surgery (pres. 1970), Soc. Univ. Surgeons (sec. 1967-70, pres. 1972-73), New Eng. Surg. Soc. (Disting. Svc. award 2002), New Eng. Cardiovasc. Soc. (pres. 1972-73), Mass. Heart Assn. (pres. 1972-74, Paul Dudley White Cardiac medal 1981). Home: 330 Beacon St Apt C66 Boston MA 02116-1190 Office: Mass Gen Hosp BUL 3 Boston MA 02114-2696 Office Phone: 617-726-2050. E-mail: wgausten@partners.org.

AUSTGARD, KITT IRENE BERG, nursing educator; b. Harstad, Norway, Oct. 2, 1946; d. Nils Berg Austgard and Kelsy Ingvarda Nilsen; children: Marianne Wollan, Camilla Julie Wollan. BS in History Art, U. Oslo, 1994; Candidata Sanitatis, Faculty Medicine, U. Oslo, 1999. RN Bærum Sykehus, Norway, 1985—87, Martina Hansens Hosp., Asker, Norway, 1987—99, ednl. adviser, 1987—99; asst. prof. Lovisenberg Diaconal Coll., Oslo, 1999—. Contbr. articles to profl. nursing jours.; author: (book) Omsorgsfilosofi i praksis. Avocations: philosophy, art, skiing. Home: Eckersbergsgt 13 Oslo 0266 Norway Office: Lovisenberg Diakonale Høgskole Lovisenberggt 15B Oslo 0456 Norway Office Fax: 4722374934. Business E-Mail: kitt.austgard@ldh.no.

AUSTGULEN, RIGMOR, pediatrician, educator; b. Bergen, Norway, Sept. 11, 1949; d. Ingolf and Judith Sandø Austgulen; children: Kamilla Austgulen Westin, Johanna Austgulen Westin, Andreas Austgulen Westin. MD, U. Bergen, 1975; PhD, U. Trondheim, 1988. Pediatrician St. Olavs U. Hosp., Trondheim, Norway, 1979—96; prof. medicine Norway U. Sci. Tech., Trondheim, 1993—, vice dean, 1993—96, vice rector, 1996—99, bd. mem., 2003—. Mem., leader rsch. program Norwegian Rsch. Coun., Oslo, 1994—97, bd. mem., 2000—02, leader, Norway, 2001—03, 2nd leader nat. com., 2007—, bd. mem. ethics rsch. programme, 2007—; bd. mem. St. Olavs U. Hosp., Trondheim, 2001—03, Norwegian bd. Tech., 2002—04, Ctrl. Norway Health Authorities, 2003—07. Recipient Gender equality price, Norwegian U. Sci. & Tech., 2002, Dissemination prize, 2003. Mem.: Am. J Ob-Gyn., Royal Norwegian Soc. Sci. & Letters, Norwegian Soc. Sci. & Tech. Home: Jacob Rollsgate 11 Trondheim 7016 Norway Office: Norway Univ Sci & Tech Kvinne Barn Senteret 7006 Trondheim Norway Office Fax: 47 72574704. Business E-Mail: rigmor.austgulen@ntnu.no.

AUSTIN, CLAUDE LIDELL, retired surgeon; b. Winona, Miss., Jan. 4, 1919; s. Luther Barksdale Austin and Cora Claudine Carter; m. Elizabeth Hightower, Sept. 2, 1944 (dec. Mar. 1990); children: Larry, Richard; m. Merry Cobb Lowry, Feb. 1, 1991. BA, U. Miss., 1940, BS, 1944; MD, Jefferson Med. Sch., 1946. Pvt. practice, Hattiesburg, Miss., 1947—91; ret., 1992. Pres. med. staff Hattiesburg Hosp., 1969—80; established vol. med. office and ongoing med. care Home of Grace, 1997—. Pres. Belle Fontaine Beach Assn., Ocean Springs, Miss., 1995; bd. dirs. Rotary Club, Hattiesburg, 1947. Fellow: Internat. Coll. Surgeons; mem.: AMA, Miss. State Med. Assn. Republican. Methodist. Avocation: deep sea fishing. Office: Home of Grace 14200 Jericho Rd Ocean Springs MS 39565 Home: 200 Greenwood Pl Hattiesburg MS 39402-2315

AUSTIN, DAVID GEORGE, dentist; b. Dayton, Ohio, Sept. 11, 1951; s. Donald Edward and Mary Josephine (Thompson) A.; children: Jonathon David, Jennifer Mary; m. Sharon Margaret Livingston, July 21, 2001; 2 children, Jack Daniel and David George Jr. BA, Ohio Wesleyan U., 1973; DDS, Ohio State U., 1977; MS, U. Med. Dentistry N.J., 1992. Diplomate Am. Bd. Orofacial Pain, Am. Bd. Dental Sleep Med., Am. Acad. Pain Mgmt. Sr. assoc. dentist Dr. Deeds and Assocs., Inc., Columbus, Ohio, 1980-82, clinic dir., 1982-85; gen. practice dentistry Columbus, 1981-88; fellow TMJ/Orofacial Pain Ctr. Univ. Med. Dentistry N.J., 1988-90; clin. asst. prof. neurology Coll. Medicine Ohio State U., Columbus, 1992-98, asst. dir. dept. neurology headache clinic, 1994-98; clin. asst. prof. dept. spec. med. Ohio U. Coll. Osteopath Med., 2010—. Dental cons. Franklin County Dept. Human Svcs., Columbus, 1982-88; bd. dirs. Found. Pedodontique d'Haiti, Port-au-Prince; pres. Brineserve, Inc., Columbus, 1985-88; adj. assoc. prof. Coll. Dentistry Ohio State U., 1986-88; chmn. Coll. Dentistry Almni Assn. Class Reunion Ohio State U., 1997. Patents in apparatus/method for processing oil well brine, 1988; in apparatus and method for measuring human mandibular movement, 1990; in apparatus and method for craniovertebral imbalance and headache during sleep, 1992. Mem. pub. rels. com., chmn. cmty. ctr. project Upper Arlington Leadership Program, 1999; bd. dirs. Upper Arlington Friend of the Arts, 2002-05; pres., founder Vol. Health Svcs. Found., Columbus, 1982—2010; bd. dirs. ctrl. Ohio chpt. Arthritis Found., 2004-05. Capt. U.S. Army, 1977-80. Mem.: ADA (Fgn. Vol. Svc. award 1988), Am. Pain and Sleep Disorder Found. (founder 2010—, pres.), Pierre Fauchard Hon. Dental Acad., Ohio Acad. Gen. Dentistry (bd. dirs. 2005—, v.p. 2010—), Acad. Gen. Dentistry (alt. del. 2005—07, del. 2009), Ohio Pain and Sleep Disorders Assn. (founder 2005, pres.), U. Med. Dentistry N.J.-TMJ Alumni Soc., Columbus Dental Assn. (spkrs. bur. 1982—88, pub. rels. coun. 1984—88, vice chmn. radio com. 1985—88), Ohio Dental Assn. (alt. del. 1994—96, 1998, 2002—04, Humanitarian of Yr. 1986), Ohio Headache Assn., Am. Acad. Pain Mgmt., Am. Assn. for Study of Headache, Am. Acad. Orofacial Pain (bd. dirs. 2000—04, splty. status com., chmn. external rels. com., chmn. found. com.), Am. Pain Soc., Ohio Xi Psi Phi Alumni Assn. (pres. 2001—), Sigma Xi, Xi Psi Phi (pres. Kappa chpt. 1976—77). Office: 3600 Olentangy River Rd Ste B1 Columbus OH 43214-3437 Office Phone: 614-451-3600. E-mail: drdavidgaustin@hotmail.com.

AUSTIN, DENISE, dietician; b. San Pedro, Calif. m. Jeff Austin; 2 children. Attended, U. Ariz.; BA in Phys. Edn., Calif. State. U., Long Beach, 1979. Co-host The Jack LaLanne Show, 1981; fitness expert NBC Today Show, 1984—88; host ESPN Getting Fit, Denise Austin's Daily Workout. Spokeswoman Idaho Potatoes, Nature Made; coun. mem. Pres. Coun. on Physical Fitness & Sports, 2002—. Performer: (films) Rock Aerobics, Rock Hard Abs, Denise Austin Body Burn, Dance With Pilates, Denise Austin Get Fit Daily Dozen. Recipient Red Dress award, AHA, 2008. Office: Waterfront Media 345 Hudson St Ste 1601 New York NY 10014-7119 Office Phone: 718-797-0722. Office Fax: 718-797-0582. E-mail: Questions@DeniseAustin.com.

AUSTIN, JOHN RILEY, surgeon, educator; b. St. Louis, Feb. 19, 1960; s. Thomas L. and Barbara (Riley) A.; children: Claire Frances, Emily Grace, John Michael. BS with highest honors, U. Wyo., 1982; MD, U. Utah, 1986. Diplomate Am. Bd. Facial Plastic and Reconstructive Surgery, Am. Bd. Otolaryngolgy, Nat. Bd. Med. Examiners. Surg. intern U. So. Calif., L.A. County Med. Ctr., LA, 1986-87, resident otolarynogology, head and neck surgery dept., 1987-91; fellow in head and neck surg. oncology M.D. Anderson Cancer Ctr. M.D. Anderson Cancer Ctr. U. Tex., Houston, 1991-92; asst. surgeon, clin. instr. U. Tex., Houston, 1992-93; asst. prof., asst. surgeon M.D. Anderson Cancer Ctr. U. Tex., Houston, 1993-95, clin. asst. prof., 1995—; adj. asst. prof. dept. otorhinolaryngology/comm. disorders Baylor Coll. Medicine, 1993-95. Otolaryngologic cons. dept. infectious diseases U. So. Calif., 1988-91; mem. utilization com. M.D. Anderson Cancer Ctr., U.Tex., 1993-95, mem. laser com., 1993-95; presenter in field. Cons. editor Head and Neck, Laryngoscope, Otolaryngology-Head and Neck Surgery, Cancer, 1993—, Archives of Otolaryngology; contbr. articles to profl. jours. Mem. Graduate Edn. com. U. Tex., 1994. Fellow ACS, Am. Acad. Otolaryngology (human resource com.), AMA, Am. Acad. Facial Plastic and Reconstructive Surgery (mem. publs. com.), Tex. Med. Assn. (mem. physician oncology edn. program 1993—, mem. com. cancer 1993—), M.D. Anderson Assocs., Soc. Univ. Otolaryngologists, N.Am. Skull Base Soc., Tex. Assn. Otolaryngology, Sir Charles Bell Soc. (founding), Travis County Med. Soc. (jour. com.), Salerni Colegium, Phi Kappa Phi, Phi Beta Kappa, Sigma Nu. Meth. Avocations: photography, fishing, golf, skiing, reading. Office: 3705 Medical Pkwy Ste 310 Austin TX 78705-1028 Office Phone: 512-458-6391. Personal E-mail: jraustin98@aol.com.

AUSTIN, MATTHEW S., orthopaedic surgeon; MD, Temple U., 1998. Lic. Pa., 2000, NJ, 2003, diplomate Am. Bd. Orthopaedic Surgery. Intern Thomas Jefferson Univ. Hosp., resident, fellow, physician. Author: (jours.) Image-guided spine surgery, 2002, Stability and leg length in total hip arthroplasty, 2003, The effect of tibial polyethylene insert design on range of motion, 2004, Hematoma causing late sciatic nerve palsy after total hip arthroplasty, 2004, Passing the Boards: Can USMLE and Orthopaedic-In-Training Scores Predict Passage of the ABOS Part I Examination?, 2004. Named one of the Top Doctors, Phila Mag., 2010—11. Mem.: Pa. Orthopaedic Soc., Am. Assn. Hip and Knee Surgeons, Am. Acad. Orthopaedic Surgeon. Office: Thomas Jefferson University Hospital 925 Chestnut St 5th Fl Philadelphia PA 19107 Office Phone: 267-339-3500.

AUSTIN, SANDRA IKENBERRY, nursing educator, consultant; b. Lexington, Va., Dec. 22, 1941; d. William Peters and June Virginia (Blackwell) Ikenberry; m. Joseph M. Austin, Apr. 10, 1965; children: Joseph M. Jr., Susan C., Christopher M. BSN, U. Va., 1963; MSN, U. Calif., LA, 1967; EdD, U. Mass., 1997. RN, Mass. Pub. health nurse Dept. Health, Waynesboro, Va., 1963-64; instr. U. Va., Charlottesville, 1964-65; staff nurse Santa Monica (Calif.) Hosp., 1965-66; faculty nursing Boston U., 1968-69, Quinsigamond C.C., Worcester, Mass., 1969-70, Fitchburg (Mass.) State Coll., 1973-96; assoc. prof. nursing Framingham (Mass.) State Coll., 1997—; project dir., sr. health edn. cons. HealthCo Consulting Inc., Shrewsbury, Mass., 1996—. Mem. Shrewsbury Town Meeting, 1992—95; chair steering com. Framingham State Coll. Nursing Honor Soc., 1998, faculty counselor/advisor, 1999—, pres., 1999—; people to people ambassador program delegate China Healthcare Info., 2004. HBO and Co. Nurse scholar, 1995. Mem.: Assn. Critical Care Nurses, Nat. League Nursing (awards com. 1999—2001), Assn. Women's Health, Obstet. and Neonatal Nurses, Am. Ednl. Rsch. ASsn., Sigma Theta Tau (Epsilon Beta edn. chair 1993—95, Rho Phi chpt. pres. 2002—04, chpt. pres. 2005, faculty counselor 2000—, rsch. grant 1996), Pi Lambda Theta. Republican. Congregationalist. Avocations: computer multimedia production, reading, walking. Home: 100 Harrington Farms Way Shrewsbury MA 01545-4081 Office: Framingham State Coll Nursing Dept Framingham MA 01701 Office Phone: 508-626-4715. Business E-Mail: sanaustin@aol.com.

AUTERI, JOSEPH S., thoracic surgeon; MD, Thomas Jefferson U., Phila., 1986. Diplomate Am. Bd. Thoracic Surgery, lic. NY, 1989, Pa., 2007. Intern gen. surgery Columbia Presbyn. Med. Ctr., NY, 1987, resident gen. surgery NY, 1992, fellow cardiothoracic surgery NY, 1994; hosp. affiliations includes Doylestown Hosp., Pa. Named one of Top Doctors, Phila. Mag., 2010—. Fellow: ACS; mem.: Western Thoracic Surg. Assn., Soc. of Thoracic Surgeons, Am. Assn. for Thoracic Surgery. Office: Doylestown Hospital 595 West State St Doylestown PA 18901 Office Phone: 215-345-2200. Office Fax: 215-345-2110.

AUVIN, STÉPHANE, child neurologist, epileptologist, researcher; b. Douai, France, May 29, 1975; s. Michel Auvin and Michèle Caretti. MD, Lillle Sch. Medicine, France, 1999; PhD, Lillle Sch. Medicine, 2007. Cert. pediatrician France, 2004, child neurologist France, 2004. Chef de clinique asst. Lille U. Hosp., 2005—08; with epilepsy program Robert Debré Children Hosp., Paris, 2008—. Contbr. articles to profl. jours. Expert French Medicine Agy. Mem.: Soc. Française Neurologie Pédiatrique, Ligue Française Contre l'epilepsie, Soc. Neurosci., Am. Epilepsy Soc. Office: Pediatric Neurology Dept CHU Robert Debre 48 Bd Serrurier Paris 75019 France

AUWAERTER, PAUL GISBERT, physician, educator; b. East Patchogue, NY, Mar. 3, 1962; s. Gisbert Paul and JoAnn Elizabeth Auwaerter; m. Karen M. Manzo, May 23, 1992; children: Alec, Bennett. AB, Columbia U., 1984, MD, 1988; MBA, John Hopkins U. Sch. Profl. Studies in Bus. and Edn., Balt., 2003. Diplomate Am. Bd. Internal Medicine, Am. Bd. Infectious Diseases. Intern, infectious disease Johns Hopkins Hosp., Balt., 1988-89, resident, internal medicine, 1989-91, chief resident, medicine, 1991-92; fellow, infectious diseases Johns Hopkins U. Sch. Medicine, Balt., 1992-96, asst. prof., assoc. prof., medicine (gen. internal medicine and infectious diseases), chief med. officer, Point of Care-Info. Tech. Ctr., Lighthouse Point, dir., gen. internal medicine, Green Spring Station. Mng. editor John Hopkins Antibiotic Guide. Office: John Hopkins

Greenspring Station 10753 Falls Rd Ste 325 Lutherville Timonium MD 21093 Office Phone: 410-583-2774. Office Fax: 410-583-2883. Business E-Mail: pauwaert@jhmi.edu.

AU-YEUNG, PETER KAR KIT, anesthesiologist; b. Hong Kong, Feb. 19, 1961; BSc, U. London King's Coll., 1982; MBBS, U. London King's Coll. Sch. of Medicine, 1985; MA, U. Manchester, 2010. Trainee in medicine Wolverhampton Hosps., England, 1987—89; trainee in anaesthesia Bromley Group of Hosps., England, 1989—90, U. Coll. and Middlesex Hosps., London, 1990—92; vis. lectr. in anaesthesia Chinese U. Hong Kong, 1992—94; staff specialist in anaesthesia Yan Chai Hosp., Tsuen Wan, Hong Kong, 1994—. Chmn., medication incident reporting programme Yan Chai Hosp., Tsuen Wan, 1995—, mem., rsch. ethics com., 1998—2002; mem., ctrl. transfusion com. Hosp. Authority, Hong Kong, 1998—, co-chmn., Hong Kong, 2006—10; mem., rsch. ethics com. Kowloon West Cluster of Hosps., Hosp. Authority, Hong Kong, 2003—09. Chmn. diocesan com. on bioethics Cath. Diocese of Hong Kong, 2005—. Master: Guild of Cath. Doctors Hong Kong; mem.: Asian Fedn. Cath. Med. Assns. (v.p. 2004—), New Medico-Legal Soc. Hong Kong (coun. 2003—08), Birthright Hong Kong (vice-chmn. 2002—05, chmn. 2006—), Hong Kong Soc. Sleep Medicine (founding treas. 1993—2001), Guild of Cath. Doctors UK (coun. 1984—92), Hong Kong Oratorio Soc. (hon. sec. 1997—2005, vice chmn. 2005—08). Office: Department of Anaesthesia Yan Chai Hospital New Territories Tsuen Wan Hong Kong Office Fax: (852)24167277. Personal E-mail: peter.auyeung@hotmail.com.

AVAKOFF, JOSEPH CARNEGIE, medical and law consultant; b. Fairbanks, Alaska, July 15, 1936; s. Harry B. and Margaret Avakoff; m. Teddy I. Law, May 7, 1966; children: Caroline, Joe E., John. AA, U. Calif., Berkeley, 1956, AB, 1957; MD, U. Calif., San Francisco, 1961; JD, Santa Clara U., 1985. Bar: Calif. 1987; diplomate Am. Bd. Surgery, Am. Bd. Plastic Surgery. Physicist U.S. Naval Radiol. Def. Lab., San Francisco, 1957, 59; intern So. Pacific Gen. Hosp., San Francisco, 1961-62; resident in surgery Kaiser Found. Hosp., San Francisco, 1962-66; resident in plastic surgery U. Tex. Sch. Medicine, San Antonio, 1970-72; pvt. practice specializing in surgery Sacramento, 1966-70; pvt. practice specializing in plastic surgery Los Gatos and San Jose, Calif., 1972-94; cons. to med. and legal professions, 1994—. Clin. instr. Sch. Medicine U. Calif., Davis, 1967—70; chief dept. surgery Mission Oaks Hosp., Los Gatos, 1988—90; chief divsn. plastic surgery Good Samaritan Hosp., San Jose, 1988—91; expert med. reviewer Med. Bd. Calif., 1995—2001; spl. cons. Calif. Dept. Corps., 1997—2002; presenter numerous med. orgns. Contbr. articles to profl. jours. Mem. San Jose Adv. Commn. Health, 1975—82; bd. govs. San Jose YMCA, 1977—80. Mem.: AMA, Union Am. Physicians and Dentists, Santa Clara County Med. Assn., Calif. Med. Assn., Phi Beta Kappa, Phi Eta Sigma. Republican. Presbyterian. Avocations: music, photography, computer programming. Home: 6832 Rockview Ct San Jose CA 95120-5607.

AVANT, PATRICIA KAY, nursing educator; b. Dallas, Aug. 15, 1941; d. Lem Barrett and Georgia Evelyn Coalson; m. Gayle R. Avant, Sept. 6, 1963; children: Samantha Gay Foss, Celia Kay Drews. RN, Meth. Hosp., Dallas, 1962; BSN, Tex. Christian U., Ft. Worth, 1963; MSN, U. N.C., Chapel Hill, 1965; PhD, Tex. Woman's U., Denton, 1978. Chair internat. program sch. nursing U. Tex. Health Sci. Ctr., San Antonio, 2005—. Co-author: (book) Strategies for Theory Construction in Nursing. Fellow Am. Acad. Nursing; mem. Royal Coll. Nursing (Australia), ANA (pres. Dist. 10 1983-84), Nat. League Nursing, (1st v.p. Tex. 1985-89), N.Am. Nursing Diagnosis Assn. (taxonomy chair 1994-98, pres. 2000-02, bd. mem., chair informatics com.). Democrat. Baptist. Home: 7601 Tallahassee Rd Waco TX 76712-3814 Office: U Tex Health Sci Ctr 7703 Floyd Curl Dr San Antonio TX 78229-3900 Office Phone: 210-567-5881. Business E-Mail: avantk@uthscsa.edu.

AVANZI, GIAN CARLO, internist, educator; b. Torino, Italy, July 13, 1954; s. Lino Avanzi and Maria Giovanna Abate Daga; m. Laura Azzoni, June 3, 2003; 1 child, Riccardo. MD, U. Torino, 1984. Diplomate U. Torino, 1985. Asst. prof., internal medicine U. Turin, Novara, Italy, 1994—2000; assoc. prof., internal medicine Ea. Piedmont U., Novara, Italy, 2000—05, prof., internal medicine, 2005—, directorships allergology and immunology unit, 2005—. Mem. Slow Food, Novara, 1998—2008. With Air Force, 1982—83. Mem.: Società Italiana Di Medicina D'emergenza-urgenza, Am. Coll. Emergency Physicians, Società Italiana di Medicina Interna (Rome). Avocations: fishing, travel. Office: Dept Clin & Experimental Medicine Via Generale Paolo Solaroli 17 28100 Novara NO Italy Office Fax: 3903213733841. Business E-Mail: avanzi@med.unipmn.it.

AVCI, REMZI, ophthalmologist, educator; b. Mudanya, Oct. 1, 1963; Grad. in Medicine, Uludag U., 1986. Prof. pathology med. faculty Uludag U., 1990—2011. Recipient 3rd Best Video award, Internat. Ocular Trauma Soc., 2006. Mem.: European VitreoRetinal Soc., EURETINA (3rd Best Video award, 7th Euretina Congress, Montecarlo), Am. Acad. Ophthalmology, Turkis Ophthalmology Soc. (Best Video award, 42th Turkish Nat. Ophthalmology Congress, Best Video award, 44th Turkish Nat. Ophthalmology Congress), Gonin Jules Gonin. Avocation: tennis. Office: Esentepe Mah Mudanya Yolu Cad 171 Nil Bursa 16120 Turkey Office Fax: 90 224 2402400.

AVERY, ROBERT LOGAN, ophthalmologist; s. Thomas and Frances Avery; m. Kelly Elhatton, July 1, 1994; children: Olivia Nicole, Logan Patrick, Georgia Michelle, Kincade Jackson. BA, Rice U., Houston, 1982; MD, Johns Hopkins U., Balt., 1987. Cert. ophthalmologist Am. Bd. Ophthalmology, 1992. Intern Santa Barbara Coll. Hosp., 1987—88; ophthalmology resident Johns Hopkins U., Balt., 1988—91, asst. chief svc., ophthalmology dept., 1992—93; retina fellow Duke U., Durham, NC, 1991—92; rsch. biologist U. Calif., Santa Barbara, 1993—; CEO Calif. Retina Cons., Santa Barbara, Calif., 1995—. Dir. Calif. Retina Rsch. Found., Santa Barbara, 2000—; assoc. editor Retina Today, 2008—. Fellow, Ronald G. Michels Found., 1993. Fellow: Am. Acad. Ophthalmology (Achievement award 2006); mem.: Calif. Med. Assn., Calif. Assn. Ophthalmology, Assn. Rsch. in Vision and Ophthalmology, Am. Soc. Retina Specialists, Phi Beta Kappa. Achievements include patents for retinal drug delivery devices. Office: Calif Retina Cons 515 E Micheltorena St Ste C Santa Barbara CA 93103 Office Fax: 805-965-5214. Personal E-mail: avery1@jhu.edu.

AVIDAN, ALON Y., physician; b. Jerusalem, May 13, 1966; s. Kami and Tova Avidan. BS, UCLA, 1988; MD, MPH, George Washington U., 1994. Diplomate in neurology Am. Bd. Psychiatry and Neurology, cert. Am. Bd. Sleep Medicine. Dir. sleep disorders clinic U. Mich., Ann Arbor, Mich., 2002—06; dir. UCLA Sleep Ctr. Disorders, 2005—; dir. outpatient neurology clinic Reed neurol. rsch. ctr. UCLA, 2005—, assoc. prof. neurology David Geffen sch. medicine, 2007—; dir. UCLA Neurology Residency Program. Office: UCLA Dept Neurology Rm 1-145 Reed Bldg 710 Westwood Plz Los Angeles CA 90095-1769 Office Fax: 310-825-6956. Business E-Mail: avidan@mednet.ucla.edu. E-mail: alonavidan@gmail.com.

AVILA, ELI NARCISO, public health service officer, state official; b. 1959; BS in Biology, Brown U., 1981, MD; JD cum laude, St. John's U., 2003; MPH with honors, NYU. Diplomate American Bd. Legal Medicine. Sr. exam. occupl. medicine physician NY Dept. Health, NY; sr. exam. occupl. medicine physician Fed. Occupl. Health Svc. US Dept. Health & Human Services (HHS), NY; clin. faculty ophthalmology dept. Columbia's Coll. Physician & Surgeons; chief dep. health services Suffolk County, NY, 2010—11; sec. Pa. Dept. Health, Harrisburg, 2011—. Fellow: Am. Coll. of Legal Medicine (ad hoc com. legis. and exec. affairs); mem.: NY State Legislature's Health Com., Health Law Sec. (exec. com.), NY State Bar Assn. (co-chair med. rsch., biotechnology subcommittee). Office: Pennsylvania Department of Health Health and Welfare Bldg 8th Fl W 625 Forster St Harrisburg PA 17120 Office Phone: 877-724-3258. *

AVILES, ALAN D., lawyer, insurance company executive; b. NYC, 1951; BA, Columbia U., 1973; JD, Rutgers U., 1977. Past sr. v.p. Ryan Cmty. Health Network; from assoc. exec. dir. managed care to dep. exec. dir. Elmhurst Hosp. Ctr., 1997—2001; gen. counsel Health and Hosp. Corp., NYC, 2001—04, sr. v.p. Queens Health Network, 2004—05, dir., pres., CEO NYC, 2005—. Past gen. counsel NYC Housing Authority; past dep. chief pub. advocacy divsn. NY State Atty. Gen. Office; past dep. bureau chief Charities Bureau, NYC; bd. dirs. Greater NY Hosp. Assn., Healthcare Assn. of NY State, Primary Care Devel. Corp., Pub. Health Solutions; regional policy coun. American Hosp. Assn.; fellow NY Acad. of Medicine.; adv. coun. United Hosp. Fund Health Policy Forum. Adv. coun. NY State Health Found. Recipient CEO IT Achievement award, Modern Healthcare mag., 2007; named one of 100 Most Powerful People in Healthcare, 2007, Top 25 Minority Execs. in Health Care. Office: NYC Health and Hospital Corporation 125 Worth St New York NY 10013 Office Phone: 212-788-3321. Office Fax: 212-788-0040. *

AVILES, ALICE ALERS, psychologist; b. NYC; d. Jose Oscar and Pauline (Irizarry) Alers; m. Jose A. Aviles, Aug. 13, 1954 (div. Oct. 1981); children: Jeffrey (dec.), Brian, Gregory; m. Clifford M. Goldman, June 29, 1997. BS magna cum laude, SUNY, Oswego, 1955; MA, Queens Coll., 1978; PhD, Yeshiva U., 1984; postdoctoral diploma in psychoanalysis and psychotherapy, Adelphi U., 1991. Lic. psychologist, N.Y. Tchr. elem. schs., Spring Valley, NY, 1955, Erlangen Am. Sch., Germany, 1955—56, Uniondale, NY, 1956, Freeport, NY, 1957—58, Island Park, NY, 1973—75; psychology clk. Fifth Ave. Ctr. for Counseling and Psychotherapy, NYC, 1978—80; psychology intern St. Vincent's Hosp. and Med. Ctr., NYC, 1980—81; psychologist Kingsboro Psychiat. Ctr., Bklyn., 1981—84; psychologist to assoc. psychologist South Beach Psychiat. Ctr., Bklyn., 1984—86; pvt. practice North Woodmere, NY, 1985—. From staff psychologist to sr. psychologist Luth. Med. Ctr., Bklyn., 1986-95; cons. Beach Terrace Care Ctr., Long Beach, N.Y., 1995-97; mem. adv. com. Hispanic Counseling Ctr. of Family Svc. Assn. of Nassau County, Hempstead, N.Y., 1978-80; cons. Nassau County Extended Care Ctr., Hempstead, 1997-99, Resort Nursing Home, Far Rockaway, N.Y., 1998-2000, Woodmere (N.Y.) Rehab. and Health Care Ctr., 1999-2000. Ford found. grad. fellow, 1978-81. Mem. APA, NY State Psychol. Assn., Nassau County Psychol. Assn. (mem. pvt. practice com. 1992-93). Office Phone: 516-791-8326.

AVOGO, WINFRED AWEYIRE, sociologist, educator; b. Ghana, Sept. 18, 1974; MA in Demography, U. Ghana, 2002; PhD in Sociology, Ariz. State U., 2008. Demographer, rsch. officer Ghana Health Svc., 2002—04; asst. prof. Ill. State U., 2008—. Mem.: Am. Sociol. Assn., Population Assn. America. Office: Dept Sociology and Anthropology Campus Box 4660 Normal IL 61790-4660 Office Fax: 309-438-5378. E-mail: winnyavogo@hotmail.com.

AVORN, JERRY L., epidemiologist, educator; b. NYC, Feb. 13, 1948; m. Karen Avorn; 2 children. BA, Columbia U., 1969; MD, Harvard Med. Sch., 1974. Lic. Mass., 1974, cert. Nat. Bd. Med. Examiners, 1974, diplomate Am. Bd. Internal Med., 1977, cert. Geriatric Med. Am. Bd. Internal Med., 1988. Intern Cambridge Hosp., Boston; clinical fellow Harvard Med. Sch., instr. preventive & social med., 1977—79, asst. prof. social med. & health policy, 1979—85, assoc. prof. social med., 1985—90, assoc. prof. med., 1990—; attending physician Beth Israel Hosp., 1977—81, asst. in med., 1977—84, attending physician, 1981—92, asst. physician, 1984—87, assoc. physician, 1987—89, physician, 1989—94; assoc. physician Brigham & Women's Hosp., 1986—92, attending physician, 1992—, chief div. pharmacoepidemiology & pharmacoeconomics, 1998—. Dir. Brigham & Women's Hosp. Program for the Analysis of Clinical Strategies. Author: Powerful Medicine: The Benefits, Risks, and Costs of Prescription Drugs, 2004; contbr. scientific papers. Mem.: Soc. Pharmaco-Epidemiology (former pres.). Mailing: 1620 Tremont St Ste 3030 Boston MA 02120 Office Phone: 617-278-0930. Office Fax: 617-232-8602. E-mail: pharmacoepi@partners.org.

AVRAM, MARC R., dermatologist; b. Bklyn., June 27, 1963; MD, Suny Downstate, 1989. Residency Harvard Med. Sch., 1994; pvt. practice, 1995—. Fellow: Am. Soc. Lasers Medicine; mem.: Am. Soc. Dermatologic Surgery, Am. Acad. Dermatology. Office: 905 Fifth Ave New York NY 10021 Office Fax: 212-734-4321. Business E-Mail: mavram@dravram.com.

AVRAMI, SHIRLEY, social worker; children: Sharon, Yuval, Alon. PhD, Haifa U., Israel, 2003. Cert. occupl. therapist Orgn. Occupl. Therapist. Occupl. therapist Youth Rehab. Ctr., Jerusalem, 1985—89; advisor to min. labor and social affairs Ministry Labor and Social Affairs, Jerusalem, 1993—97; dir. parliamentary com. labor, social affairs and health Israeli Parliament (Knesset), Jerusalem, 1997—2003; head rsch. and info. ctr. Israeli Parliament, Jerusalem, 2003—. Sargent ARMOUR, 1979—81. Office: Knesset (Israeli parliament) 3 Kaplan 91010 Jerusalem Israel Home Phone: 972-2-6784230; Office Phone: 972-2-6408240. Business E-Mail: avrami@knesset.gov.il.

AVSAR, FATIH MEHMET, surgeon, researcher; b. Turkey, June 12, 1959; s. Kerem and Ayten Avsar; m. Ayse Filiz Yavuz, Sept. 10, 1987; children: Gokturk Burak, Pamir Zeynep. BEE, Mid.-East Tech. U., Ankara, 1979; MD, Ankara U. Faculty of Medicine, 1985; diploma in Anesthesiology and Reanimation and Algology, Istanbul U. Istanbul Med. Faculty, 1987. Cert. Internat. Gastric Cancer Assn., Japan, 1997, European Soc. Surg. Rsch., Belgium, 2003, Internat. Fedn. Surgery of Obesity, Can., 2003. Rsch. fellow Istanbul U. Med. Faculty, Turkey, 1985—87; rsch. fellow dept. surgery Ankara U. Faculty of Medicine, Turkey, 1987—94; cons. surgeon and rschr. 1st surg. dept. Ankara Numune Tng. And Rsch. Hosp., Turkey, 1994—2001, clin. chief of surgery 1st surg. dept., 2001—. Vice chief of med. staff Ankara Numune Tng. And Rsch. Hosp., Turkey, 2002—. 2d lt. Army Med., 1992—93, Ankara. Achievements include research in Intraabdominal Adhesions; Hernia Formation; Surgical Oncology; Pancreatitis; Advanced Laparoscopic Surgery; Obesity Surgery; Vascular Surgery. Office: Ankara Numune Training & Rsch Hosp Talat Pasa Bulvari - Opera Ankara 06100 Turkey Home: Mesrutiyet Cd No28/6 6640 Ankara Ankara Turkey Office Fax: +90 312 310 34 60; Home Fax: +90 312 418 27 60. Personal E-mail: avsar59@hotmail.com.

AW, CHEN WEE DERRICK, dermatologist; b. Singapore, Nov. 7, 1971; MBBBS, Nat. U. Singapore, 1997. Cons. dermatologist Nat. U. Hosp., Singapore, 2006—, asst. prof., 2009. Named Best Tchr., Nat. U. Singapore. Fellow: Royal Coll. Physicians, Acad. Medicine Singapore; mem.: Med. Protection Soc. Avocations: piano, travel, reading. Office: 1E Kent Ridge Rd Tower Block NUHS Singapore 119228 Singapore Office Fax: 6567794112. Business E-Mail: derrick_aw@nuhs.edu.sg.

AWAD, MOHAMED ABDEL-GHANI, medical educator; b. Bani-ebaid, Jan. 24, 1967; BSc, Mansoura U., 1988; PhD, Wagningen U., 2001. Assoc. prof. Mansoura U., 2007—. Recipient Prof. A. Soenen-Found. award, Ghent U., Belgium, 2003. Office: Al-Gamaa St Gehan El-Mansoura El-Dakahlia 35516 Egypt Office Fax: 00-20-50-2221688. Business E-Mail: mawad@mans.edu.eg.

AWAD, SAWSAN MOKHTAR MOSTAFA, pediatrician, educator; d. Mokhtar Mostafa Awad and Naeema Mohamad Awaad; m. Khaled Mohamed Abdelhady, Feb. 10, 1997. MBBCh, U. Cairo, 1992, MSc, 1997. Cert. physician ECFMG, 2002, diplomate Am. Bd. Pediat., 2006. Clin. assoc., pediat. cardiology U. Chgo., 2007; asst. prof., pediat. Rush U. Med. Ctr., Chgo., 2008—, asst. fellowship program dir., 2009—. Mem.: AMA, Am. Coll. Cardiology, Am. Acad. Pediat. Achievements include research in balloon dilation of right ventricular outflow tract in patients with tetralogy of fallot; T-cell deficiency in dual infection with cytomegalovirus and pneumocystis jiroveci; current and future therapy for pulmonary hypertension in patients with right and left heart failure; conotruncal anomalies and craniofacial abnormalities; spectrum of multifocal atrial tachycardia in infants; intracardiac echocardiography for the guidance of percutaneous procedures; left ventricular accessory chamber; reversible cardiomyopathy in an adolescent with idiopathic aortic cusp ventricular tachycardia. Avocations: travel, languages, reading. Office: Rush University Med Ctr 1653 W Congress Pky Chicago IL 60612 Office Fax: 312-942-5360. Business E-Mail: sawsan_m_awad@rush.edu.

AWAIS, GEORGE MUSA, obstetrician, gynecologist; b. Ajloun, Jordan, Dec. 15, 1929; arrived in U.S., 1951; s. Musa and Meha (Koury) A.; m. Nabila Rizk, June 24, 1970 AB, Hope Coll., 1955; MD, U. Toronto, 1960. Diplomate Am. Bd. Obstetrics and Gynecology. Intern U. Toronto Hosps., Ont., Canada, 1960—61, resident in ob-gyn, 1961—64, chief resident, 1965, Harlem Hosp., Columbia U., NYC, 1967; instr. ob-gyn Case We. Res. U., Cleve., 1967—70, asst. prof., 1970, asst. clin. prof. dept. reproductive biology, 1971; mem. staff, dept. gynecology Cleve. Clinic Found., 1975. Chmn. dept. ob-gyn. King Faisal Specialist Hosp. and Rsch. Ctr., Riyadh, 1975-76; cons. panel mem. Internat. Corr. Soc. Obstetricians and Gynecologists, 1971; emeritus staff Cleve. Clinic Found., 1991; pres. Task Force on Humanitarian Aid and Relief Inc., 1997. Contbr. articles to publs. in field, papers, reports to confs., TV appearances, Saudi Arabia Named Grand Officer of Order of Independence His Majesty King Hussein of Jordan, 1992. Fellow ACS, Am. Coll. Obstetricians and Gynecologists, Royal Coll. Surgeons Can.; mem. AMA, AAAS, Am. Infertility Soc., Arab Am. Med. Assn. (pres. 1991—, chmn. humanities relief 1996), Acad. Medicine of Cleve. Office: Cleve Clinic Found Emeritus Office AC 334 Beachwood OH 44122 Office Phone: 216-448-2000. Business E-Mail: emeritus@ccf.org, awaisg@ccf.org.

AXEL, RICHARD, neuroscientist, educator; b. NYC, July 2, 1946; AB magna cum laude, Columbia U., NYC, 1967; MD, Johns Hopkins U. Sch. Medicine, Balt., 1970. Intern dept. pathology Columbia U. Coll. Physicians & Surgeons, 1970-71, vis. fellow dept. pathology, 1971-72; rsch. assoc. USPHS, NIH, 1972-74; asst. prof. dept. pathology Columbia U., 1974-78, prof. pathology and biochemistry, 1978—, Univ. prof., 1999—. Investigator Howard Hughes Med. Inst., 1984—. Recipient Johns Hopkins Med. Soc. Rsch. award, 1969, Irma T. Hirschl Career Scientist award, 1976, Young Scientist award, Passano Found., 1979, Ely Lilly award, 1983, NY Acad. Scis. award in biol. & med. scis., Unilever Sci. award, NYC Mayor's award for excellence in sci. & tech., 1997, Bristol-Meyers Squibb award for disting. achievement in neurosci. rsch., 1998, Alexander Hamilton award, Columbia U., 1999, Medal for Disting. Contbn. in Biomed. Scis., NY Acad. Medicine, 2001, Gairdner Found. Internat. award, 2003, Nobel Prize in Physiology/Medicine, The Nobel Found., 2004. Mem.: NAS (Richard Lounsbery award 1989), American Philos. Soc., American Acad. Arts & Sciences, Phi Beta Kappa. Achievements include discovery of odorant receptors and the organization of the olfactory system. Office: Columbia U Hammer Health Scis Ctr 701 W 168th St Rm 1016 New York NY 10032-2704 Office Phone: 212-305-6915. Office Fax: 212-923-7249. E-mail: ra27@columbia.edu. *

AXÉLL, TONY, dentist, consultant; b. Ljungby, Sweden, Oct. 21, 1939; s. Verner and Gulli Axéll; children: Anna, Karin, Göran. DDS, Malmö Sch. Dentistry, Sweden, 1954; PhD, Lund U., Sweden, 1977. Assoc. prof. Sch. Dentistry, Malmö, 1977—93; prof. Oslo U., Faculty Dentistry, 1993—2003; sr. cons. Maxillofacial Unit, Halmstad, Sweden, 2003—. Author: (text books) Oral Mucosal Lesions - Diagnosis and Treatment (Forssbergs dental award, 1991). Advisor & expert

WHO, Geneva, 1988—; expert European Union, Brussels, 2006—08; examinator Swedish Oral Medicine Soc., Gothenburg, Sweden, 1998—. Mem.: Brit. Soc. Oral Medicine (hon.), Swedish Orofacial Medicine Soc. (hon.). Achievements include CD-ROM of educational material. Avocations: travel, golf, bridge. Home: Junivägen 4B Halmstad SE-302 60 Sweden Office: Halmstad Hosp Lasarettsvägen Halmstad SE-301 85 Sweden Personal E-mail: tony.axell@telia.com.

AXELROD, EVAN M., psychologist, educator; s. David and Carrie Axelrod; m. Michelle Axelrod; children: Sam children: J. T. BA in Psychology, U. Puget Sound; D of Psychology, U. Denver. Bd. cert. traumatic stress expert Am. Acad. Experts Traumatic Stress, 2004. Clin. police psychologist Nicoletti-Flater Assocs., Lakewood, Colo., 2000—. Adj. prof. U. Denver Grad. Sch. Profl. Psychology. Contbr. text book. Grantee, U. Puget Sound, 1996—97. Mem.: APA, Colo. Psychol. Assn., Soc. Police and Criminal Psychology, Am. Acad. Experts Traumatic Stress, Internat. Assn. Chiefs of Police, Colo. Assn. Peer Support (hon.), Psi Chi. Achievements include research in Interpersonal Violence on the Internet and Cyber-Terrorism; Impact of Divorce on the Adjustment of College Students. Office: Nicolettii-Flater Assocs 3900 S Wadsworth Blvd Denver CO 80235 Personal E-mail: e2axe@aol.com.

AXELROD, RITA S., oncologist, educator; MD, NYU, 1970. Diplomate Am. Bd. Internal Medicine, Am. Bd. Internal Medicine-med. oncology, Am. Bd. Internal Medicine-hematology. Intern St. Luke's/Roosevelt Hosp., NY; resident Med. Coll., Ga.; fellow Lankenau Hosp., Ardmore, Pa., Phila. Gen. Hosp.; assoc. prof., dept. med. oncology Thomas Jefferson Univ.; hosp. affiliations include Thomas Jefferson Univ. Hosp., Methodist Hosp. Divsn. of Thomas Jefferson Univ. Hosp. Named one of Top Docs, Phila. Mag., 2010. Office: Thomas Jefferson University Hospital Ste 220A 925 Chestnut St Philadelphia PA 19107 Office Phone: 215-955-8874. Office Fax: 215-503-7697. E-mail: Rita.Axelrod@jefferson.edu.

AYACHE, STÉPHANE, surgeon; b. Neuilly sur Seine, France, Mar. 2, 1969; s. Louis and Jeanne Ayache; m. Severine Dejean, July 13, 2004; children: Noa, Leane. B, Antibes, France, 1987; MA in Lang. and Voice, 2001; MD, U. Amiens, Marseille, Nice, 2003; degree med. studies, Medicine U., Nice France, 1994. Lic. head and neck surgeon Amiens, 1999, cert. facial plastic surgery Lyon, France, 2001, lic. middle ear Paris Sud, France, 2003, highly specialized in ear diseases and surgery, endoscopy of ear and sal'vary glands, thyroid surgery. Intern abdominal surgery dept. Tchg. Hosp., 1994—95, intern, dept. head and neck surgery, 1995, intern, maxillo facial and reconstructive surgery dept., 1997—98, intern, dept. head and neck surgery, 1998—2001, tchr., med. staff, dept. head & neck surgery, 2001—03, cons. ENT dept., 2003—05; residency U. Hosp. Amiens, 1994—96; intern, dept. head and neck surgery Military Gen Hosp., 1996—97; intern, abdominal surgery dept. Gen. Hosp., 1995—96, cons., dept. head & neck surgery, 2005—07, cons. dept. head & neck surgery, 2001—03, residency U. Hosp. Amiens, 1990—99, General Hosp. Senlis, 1995, Army Hosp. Toulouse, 1997; head-neck surgeon Pvt. Hosp, Clinique du Palais, Grasse, France, 2001—07, head, dept. head and neck surgery, 2008—; chmn. IWGEES, 2008—, head, Internat. Working Group on Endoscopic Ear Surgery. Med. rschr. Tchg. Hosp., Marseille, France, 1998—2000; dir. head and neck surgery dept. Palais Pvt. Hosp., Grasse, 2008—; chmn. Internat. Working Group Endoscopic Ear Surgery, 2008—. Contbr. articles to profl. jours. Mem.: Internat. Working Group on Endoscopic Ear Surgery (chmn. 2008—), European Acad. Otology and Neurotology. Achievements include research in otologic and thyroid surgery otologic surgery & earendoscopy thyroid surgery & salivery gland surgery and endoscopy. Office: Palais Pvt Hosp Ctr Dept Head and Neck Surgery 25 avenue Chiris 6130 Grasse France Office Phone: 33 0 493 40 50 50. Office Fax: 33 4 93 77 29 83.

AYAD, IHAB, anesthesiologist, educator; b. Cairo, Sept. 23, 1968; MD, Cairo U., 1991. Assoc. clin. prof. UCLA, 2001—, asst. chief pediat. anesthesia, 2009—. Fellow: Am. Bd. Anesthesiology; mem.: Am. Soc. Anesthesia, Soc. Pediat. Anesthesia. Home: 757 Westwood Plz Ste 3325 Los Angeles CA 90095 Business E-Mail: iayad@mednet.ucla.edu.

AYADE, BENEDICT BENGIOUSHUYE, biotechnologist; b. Obudu, Nigeria, Mar. 1968; BSc, U. Ibadan, 1988, MSc, 1990, PhD, 1994; MBA, Edo State U., Nigeria, 2001. Asst. lectr. U. Ibadan, 1993—94, lectr. II, 1995—97, lectr. I, 1998—2000. Exec. dir. Internat. Inst. for Environ. Rsch., 2000—; chmn./CEO Global Environ. Cons., Houston. Co-author: (jour.) Jour. of Water Environmental and Technology, 1992. Grantee $140,000., Internat. Inst. for Environ. Rsch., 2000. Fellow: Nigerian Environ. Soc.; mem.: N.Y. Acad. Scis. E-mail: Ngayi12@yahoo.com.

AYALA, FRANCISCO JOSÉ, geneticist, educator, evolutionary biologist; b. Madrid, Mar. 12, 1934; came to U.S., 1961, naturalized, 1971; s. Francisco and Soledad (Pereda) A.; m. Hana Lostakova, Mar. 8, 1985; children by previous marriage: Francisco José, Carlos Alberto. BS, Universidad de Madrid, 1954; MA, Columbia U., 1963, PhD, 1964; D honoris causa, Universidad de León, Spain, 1982, Universidad de Barcelona, 1986, Universidad de Madrid, 1986, U. Athens, Greece, 1991, U. Vigo, Spain, 1996, U. Islas, Baleares, Spain, 1998, U. Valencia, Spain, 1999, U. Bologna, Italy, 2001, U. Vladivostok, Russia, 2002, Masaryk U., Czech. Rep., 2003, U. Padua, Italy, 2006, Nat. U. de la Plata, Argentina, 2007; D, U. Warsaw, Poland, 2009, U. Salamanca, Spain, 2009, U. Buenos Aires, Argentina, 2009, U. Pais Vasco, Spain, 2009, U. South Bohemia, Czech Republic, 2010, Ohio State U., 2010, U. Nat. Santiago Chile, 2010. Research assoc. Rockefeller U., 1964-65; asst. prof. Providence Coll., 1965-67, Rockefeller U., 1967-71; assoc. prof. to prof. genetics U. Calif., Davis, 1971-87, disting. prof. biology Irvine, 1987-89, Donald Bren prof. of Biol. Sciences, Ecology & Evolutionary Biology, 1989—, univ. prof., 2003—, prof. philosophy, prof. logic and the philosophy of sci., logic & philosophy of sci. Bd. dirs. basic biology NRC, 1982-91, chmn., 1984-91, mem. commn. on life scis., 1982-91; mem. nat. adv. coun. Nat. Inst. Gen. Med. Scis.; mem. exec. com. EPA, 1979-80; mem. adv. com. directorate sci. and engring. edn. NSF, 1989-91; mem. nat. adv. coun. for human genome rsch. NIH, 1990-93; mem. Pres. com. advisors sci. and tech., 1994-2001. Author: Am I A Monkey? 2010, Human Evolution. Trails from the Past, 2007, Darwin's Gift to Science and Religion, 2007, Systematics and the Origin of Species. On Ernst Mayr's 100th Anniversary, 2006, Variation and Evolution in Plants and Microorganisms. Toward a New Synthesis 50 Years after Stebbins, 2000, Evolutionary and Molecular Biology: Scientific Perspectives on Divine Action, 1998, Population and Evolutionary Genetics, 1982, Modern Genetics, 1980, 2d edit., 1984, Evolving: the Theory and Processes of Organic Evolution, 1979, Evolution, 1977, Molecular Evolution, 1976, Studies in the Philosophy of Biology, 1974. Recipient medal Coll. de France, 1979, Mendel medal Czech Republic Acad. Scis., 1994, Hon. Gold medal Acad. Nat. dei Lincei, Rome, 2000, Nat. Medal of Sci., The White House, 2001, gold medal Stazione Zoological Naples, 2003, Templeton prize, John Templeton Found, 2010; Guggenheim fellow, Fulbright fellow. Fellow AAAS (Sci. Freedom and Responsibility award 1987, bd. dirs. 1989-93, pres.-elect 1993-94, pres. 1994-95, chmn. of bd. 1995-96, chmn. com. on health of sci. enterprise 1991—, mem. nat. coun. for sci. and edn. for phase II, project 2061 1990—), Am. Acad. Microbiology; mem. NAS (sect. population biology evolution and ecology chmn. 1983-86, councillor 1986-89, bd. dirs. Nat. Acad. Corp. 1990—), Am. Acad. Arts and Scis., Am. Soc. Naturalists (sec. 1973-76), Genetics Soc. Am., Am. Genetic Assn. (hon. life, Wilhelmine E. Key award), Ecology Soc. Am., Am. Philos. Soc., Soc. Study Evolution (pres. 1979-80), Royal Acad. Scis. Spain (fgn. mem.), Russian Acad. Natural Scis. (fgn. mem.), Mex. Acad. Scis. (fgn. mem.), Acad. Nat. dei Lincei (Rome) (fgn.), Soc. for Molecular Biology and Evolution, Serbian Acad. Scis. & Arts (fgn. mem.), Sigma Xi (William Proctor prize 2000, pres. 2003). Home: 2 Locke Ct Irvine CA 92617-4034 Office: U Calif Dept Ecology & Evolutionary Biology 321 Steinhaus Hall Mail Code 2525 Irvine CA 92697 Office Phone: 949-824-8293. Office Fax: 949-824-2474. Business E-Mail: fjayala@uci.edu.

AYAN, ERHAN, surgeon; b. Balikesir, Oct. 10, 1972; Degree, Med. Faculty, 1995. Physician thoracic surgery Med. faculty, 1997. Office: Mersin University Med Faculty Mersin Akdcniz 33100 Turkey Business E-Mail: erhanayan@mersin.edu.tr.

AYANIAN, JOHN Z., internist, educator; BA summa cum laude, Duke U., Durham, NC; MD, Harvard Med. Sch., Boston; MA of Pub. Policy, Harvard U. Kennedy Sch. Govt. Prof. medicine and health care policy Harvard Med. Sch., dir. Fellowship in General Medicine and Primary Care; prof. health policy and mgmt. Harvard Sch. Pub. Health. Med. dir. Ctr. Surgery & Pub. Health, Brigham & Women's Hosp., Boston. Mem. editl. bd. Jour. Clin. Oncology; contbr. articles to profl. jours. Recipient Generalist Physician Training award, Robert Wood Johnson Found., Alice Hersh Young Investigator award, AcademyHealth, Clifford Barger award for excellence in mentoring, Harvard Med. Sch. Fellow: ACP; mem.: American Soc. Clin. Investigation, Assn. American Physicians, Inst. Medicine. Achievements include research in quality of care for people with colorectal cancer, lung cancer or breast cancer; this research focuses on the effect of patients' race, ethnicity, gender, insurance coverage and socioeconomic characteristics on access to care and clinical outcomes, and the impact of physicians' specialty and organizational characteristics on the quality of care. Office: Harvard Med Sch Dept Health Care Policy 100 Longwood Ave Boston MA 02115 Office Fax: 617-432-3455, 617-432-0173. E-mail: ayanian@hcp.med.harvard.edu.

AYDELOTTE, MYRTLE KITCHELL, retired nursing administrator; b. Van Meter, Iowa, May 31, 1917; d. John J. and Larava Josephine (Gutshall) Kitchell; m. William O. Aydelotte, June 22, 1956; children: Marie Elizabeth, Jeannette Farley. BS, U. Minn., 1939, MA, 1947, PhD, 1955; postgrad., Columbia U. Tchrs. Coll., 1948. Head nurse Charles T. Miller Hosp., St. Paul, 1939—41; surg. tchg. St. Mary's Hosp. Sch. Nursing, Mpls., 1941—42, ARMY Nurse Corps., 1942—46; instr. U. Minn., 1945—49; dir., dean State U. Iowa Coll. Nursing, 1949—57, prof., 1957—62; assoc. chief nurse VA Hosp. Rsch. for Nursing, Iowa City, 1963—64, chief nursing rsch., 1964—65; prof. U. Iowa Coll. Nursing, 1964—76, 1982—88; exec. dir. ANA, 1977—81; ret., 1988. Dir. nursing U. Iowa Hosps. and Clinics, 1968—76; mem. sci. adv. bd. Ctr. Health Rsch. Wayne State U., 1972—76, Inst. Medicine, 1973—; cons. U. Minn., 1970, 82, 90, U. Rochester, 1971, U. Mich., 1970, 73, U. Colo., 1970—71, U. Hawaii, 1972—73, Ariz. State U., 1972, U. Nebr., 1972—73. Mem. editl. bd.: Nursing Forum, 1969—72, Jour. Nursing Adminstrn., 1971; contbr. articles to profl. jours. Mem., v.p. Iowa City Libr. Bd., 1961—67; mem. Johnson County Bd. Health, 1967—70; mem. adv. com. family living courses Iowa City Bd. Edn., 1970—72. With Nurse Corps. US Army, 1942—46. Mem.: ANA, Am. Acad. Nursing, Inst. Medicine, Sigma Theta Tau (rsch. com. 1968—72). Home: 111 Thackery Rd Rochester NY 14610-3359

AYDIN, OSMAN NURI, physician, educator; b. Trabzon, Turkey, Jan. 1, 1959; MD, Karadeniz Tech. U., 1983; degree, Erciyes U., 1994. Prof., physician chief, algology dept. Adnan Menderes U., Medicine Faculty, 2010—. Fellowship, Interventional Pain Practice. Fellow: IPP; mem.: WIP, IASP. Avocations: tennis, football, swimming. Office: Adnan Menderes University Medicine Faculty Aydin 09100 Turkey Office Fax: 0902562120146. Business E-Mail: onaydin@superonline.com.

AYERS GIBSON, ELIZABETH, medical technician; b. Seattle, Apr. 30, 1975; B in Diagnostic Med. Sonography, Rochester Inst. Tech., 1998; MS in Secondary Edn., Nat. Tech. Inst. Deaf, Rochester Inst. Tech., 2002. Ultrasonographer Rochester Gen. Hosp., Rochester Radiology Assoc. PC, 1998—2002, Va. Mason Fed. Way, 2002—. Nat. adv. group mem. Nat. Tech. Inst. Deaf, Rochester Inst. Tech., 2009—. Vol. advocate ADWAS. Named Employee of Yr., Va. Mason Med. Ctr. Mem.: Soc. Diagnostic Med. Sonographers, Am. Registry Diagnostic Med. Sonographers. Office: 33501 1st Way S Federal Way WA 98003 Personal E-mail: elizsono@comcast.net.

AYES, KHALID AHMED MOHAMED, medical consultant; b. Barakat, Al-Neel Al-Azraq, Sudan, Sept. 20, 1962; s. Ahmed Mohamed Ayes and Asia Hussain Abdel-Rahman; m. Manal Abdemajeed Yassin, Oct. 25, 1969; children: Ammar Khalid, Mariam Khalid. BS in Medicine and Surgery, U. Khartoum, Sudan, 1989. Registrar in medicine West Midlands Tng. Scheme, Birmingham, West Midlands, England, 1997—2003; lead stroke clinician Kettering Gen. Hosp., Kettering, Northamptomshire, England, 2003—. Mem.: Royal Coll. Physicians, Brit. Assn. Stroke Physicians. Achievements include development of a stroke service. Office: Kettering Gen Hosp Rothwell Rd Northamptonshire Kettering NN16 8UZ England Home: 10 Southfield Drive NN15 5YQ Barton Seagrave NN15 5YQ England Office Fax: 00441536492296; Home Fax: 01536492296. Personal E-mail: khalidayes@yahoo.com. Business E-Mail: khalid.ayes@kgh.nhs.uk.

AYLOO, SUBHASHINI, surgeon; b. June 16; MD, Rosalind Franklin U. Medicine & Sci., Chgo. Med. Sch., 1999. Dir. bariatric surgery, asst. prof. surgery U. Ill. Chgo., 2005. Recipient Ann. Resident Rsch. award, 2009. Mem.: Am. Bd. Surgeons. Office: 840 S Wood St #435E Chicago IL 60612 Business E-Mail: arhoward@uic.edu.

AYLWARD, BRUCE, international organization administrator; b. St. John's, Newfoundland, Can. Med. tng., Meml. U., Newfoundland; specialist tng. in internal medicine, Vancouver, BC; diploma in tropical medicine and hygiene, London Sch. Hygiene and Tropical Medicine; MPH summa cum laude, Johns Hopkins Sch. Pub. Health. Physician and epidemiologist; med. officer expanded programme on immunization WHO, 1992—93, mem. field level nat. immunization programs, 1993—97, mem. global polio eradication initiative, 1997—98, dir. global polio eradication initiative Geneva, 1998—2011, asst. dir.-gen. polio, emergencies and country collaboration, 2011—. Office: WHO avenue Appia 20 1211 Geneva Switzerland *

AYOUB, JEAN MOHAMED, medical educator; b. Cap de l'Eau, Nador, Morocco, Nov. 15, 1957; s. Chadli and Habiba (Faïz) A.; m. Francoise Ayoub-Mancuso, July 23, 1987 (div. July 1996); 1 child, Louisa; m. Sour Ouafae, Feb. 2002; 1 child, Wallim. MSc, Montpellier U., France, 1991, PhD, 1997; MD, Faculty of Medicine, Rabat, Morocco, 1987. Ho. physician Hosp. St. Amaud, Montrond, France, 1985-90; ultrasonographist Hosp., Bourges, France, 1990-91; physiologist, ultrasonographist Univ. Hosp., Nîmes, France, 1991-95, asst. faculty mem. Faculty of Medicine, 1996—; head ultrasound dept. Trousseau U. Hosp. of Tours. Co-author (CD-rom-CDI) Pneumologic, 1995; contbr. articles to med. jours. Mem. Soc. Ultrasound, Tchg. Coll. Biophysics. Avocations: painting, history, travel, sports. Office: Trousseau Univ Hosp France 37044 Tours France Home Phone: 33-2-47376220; Office Phone: 33-2-47478814. E-mail: ayoub.jean@wanadoo.fr, j.ayoub@chu-tours.fr.

AYOUB, MOSTAFA AHMED, orthopedist, educator; b. Menoufia, Egypt, Apr. 16, 1966; MSc in Orthop. Surgery, Tanta U., Egypt, 1994, MD in Orthop. Surgery, 2002. Cons., orthop. surgery Tanta U., 2005—06, asst. prof., orthop. surgery and traumatology, 2008—. Fellowship, Ministry of High Edn., Egypt. Mem.: Egyptian Orthop. Assn. Avocations: basketball, football. Home: 20 Taha Hussein St Al Haram Giza 00202 Egypt Personal E-mail: maayoub@yahoo.com.

AYOUB, NAKHLÉ MICHEL, dermatologist, researcher; b. Beirut, Feb. 27, 1973; s. Michel Nakhlé Ayoub and Dunia Deeb Rizkalla. BS, Notre Dame de Jamhour, 1990; MD, St. Joseph U., 1997, dermatologist, 2003. Resident Etranger des Hosp. de Paris, 2002; dermatologist Hôtel-Dieu de France Hosp., Beirut, 2003—. Author: (clin. rsch.) Protein Z deficiency in Sneddon's syndrome (Best clin. rsch., 48th congress of the French Soc. of Internal Medicine, 2003) (clin. study) Circumcision in a multiethnic social setting (Best original communication, 7th panarab congress of dermato-venereology, 2000); contbr. articles to profl. jours. Raising funds for cath. schools scholarships Lebanus, Beirut, Lebanon, 2000—01. Fellow Pitié Salpêtrière Hosp., Collège de Médecine des hôpitaux de Paris, 2001—02; Clin. rsch. grant, Société Française de Dermatologie, 2001—02. Mem.: League of French speaking dermatologists, Lebanese Order Physicians. Roman Catholic. Office: Hôtel-Dieu de France Hospital Bvd Alfred Naccache Achrafieh Beirut Lebanon Office Fax: 00961-1616160. E-mail: nakhleayoub@yahoo.com.

AYO-YUSUF, OLALEKAN ABDULWAHAB, dental surgeon, educator; b. Lagos, Lagos, Nigeria, May 11, 1969; s. Ayo-Ola Saliu and Risikat Olakitan Yusuf; m. Imade Joan Aghedo, Nov. 22, 1995; children: Kolade, Laolu. BDS, U. Benin, Nigeria, 1992; MSc in Odontology with distinction, U. Pretoria, South Africa, 1998, Diploma Health Systems Mgmt., 2000, MPH, 2003; PhD, U. Maastricht, 2008. Dental ho. officer U. Benin Tchg. Hosp., Nigeria, 1992—94; dental officer Randle Ctr. Lagos State Health Mgmt. Bd., Lagos, 1994—95; sr. dental officer F. H. Odendaal Hosp., Nylstroom, South Africa, 1995—98, supt. and mgr., 1999—2002; head clin. unit, asooc. prof. U. Pretoria, 2002—; regional dir. Global Bridge Africa Network Treatment Tobacco Dependence. Prin. dir. F.H. Odendaal Hosp., Nysltroom, South Africa, 1999—2002; mem. internat. adv. bd. African Jour. Oral Health, Ile-Ife, Nigeria, 2004—; sci. reviewer Tobacco Control Jour., Sydney, 2005—, Nat. Rsch. Found., Pretoria, South Africa, 2005—. Contbr. scientific papers to profl. jours. (Travel award best rsch. in oral disease prevention Africa and Middle-East region, 2005). Recipient Best Cmty.-Based Rsch. Paper, IADR Congress South Africa, 2000; grantee, Cancer Assn. South Africa, 2004, Med. Rsch. Coun. South Africa, 2005—; scholar Travel award, Nat. Cancer Inst. U.S., 2002; grant, Am. Cancer Soc., 2011—. Fellow: Internat. Union Against Cancer, Assn. UICC fellows; mem.: Internat. Soc. Rsch. on Nicotine and Tobacco, Internat. Assn. Dental Rsch., GlobaLink Internat. Tobacco Control Network. Achievements include design of Sixteen sense of coherence scale - a psychometric measure of ability to cope with stress - was used for the first time on African adolescent population and found to be predictor of their risk behaviours; first dentist to be appointed as principal director and hospital manager in the Limpopo health department; first to report on nicotine content of smokeless tobacco products in South Africa; report on fluoride content of bottled-waters and inacurate labelling, which saw the enactment of relevant regulation of these products in South Africa; research in quantitative measure of the extent of hospital management decentralisation in South Africa. Avocations: playing soccer, exploring new environments, travel. Office: Mond Hospl Univ Pretoria Dr Savage Rd PO Box 1266 1 Pretoria 0001 South Africa Home: 18 Oakmont St Silverlake Gantence Pretoria 0054 South Africa Office Fax: +27 123237616. E-mail: lekan.ayoyusuf@up.ac.za.

AYRES-DE-CAMPOS, DIOGO, obstetrician and gynecologist; b. Oporto, Portugal, Nov. 2, 1962; s. Nuno and Maria da Paz (Matos Graça) A.; m. Maria João Cardoso, June 19, 1993. MD, Oporto Faculty Medicine, 1988, PhD, 2001. Resident Hosp. São João, Oporto, Portugal, 1989-97, staff ob-gyn., 1997—. Contbr. articles to profl. jours. Rsch. grantee Portuguese Ministry of Health, 1995, Junta Nacional Investigação Cientifica Tecnológica, 1996, Fundação Calouste Gulbenkian, 1997. Mem. European Soc. Reproductive Medicine, European Soc. Gynecology, Portuguese Soc. Obstetrics and Gynecology. Avocations: music, tennis, squash. Office: Hosp São João Dept Obstetrics Gynecology 4200 Oporto Portugal E-mail: d.decampos@mail.telepac.pt, sisporto@med.up.pt.

AYUS, JUAN CARLOS, nephrologist; b. Buenos Aires, Feb. 25, 1941; arrived in U.S., 1973; s. Jose and Matilde A.; m. Linda Maria Giudici; children: Sebastian, Mariana. BS, Nat. Coll., 1959; MD, U. Buenos Aires, 1967. Diplomate Am. Bd. Internal Medicine, Am. Bd. Nephrology. Resident in internal medicine U. Buenos Aires, 1968-71, fellow in nephrology, 1971-72; resident in internal medicine U. Mass., Worcester, 1973-74, U. Minn., Mpls., 1974-75; fellow in nephrology U. Calif., San Francisco, 1975-77; chief renal svc. Ben-Taub Regional hosp., Houston, 1977-84; from assoc. prof. to prof. medicine Baylor Coll. Medicine, Houston, 1984—2001; prof. medicine U. Tex. Health Sci. Ctr., San Antonio, 2001—. Recipient Gold Insignia, Spanish Soc. Nephrology, 1999. Fellow ACP; mem. L.Am. Soc. Nephrology (sec.-treas. 1993-96, v.p. 1996-99), Argentine Soc. Critical Care (founder). Home: 2412 Westgate Houston TX 77019 Office Phone: 713-502-0543. Personal E-mail: carlosayus@yahoo.com.

AYYAGARI, RADHA, ophthalmologist, medical educator; b. India, Jan. 1, 1990; BS in Biology and Chemisty, Andhra U., 1979, MS in Biochemistry, 1982; PhD, Nat. Inst. Nutrition, 1987. Postdoctoral assoc. Ophthalmic Genetics and Clin. Svc. Br. Nat. Eye Inst., NIH, Bethesda, Md., 1991—96; rsch. investigator Dept. Ophthalmology and Visual Sciences U. Mich., Ann Arbor, 1996—2002, asst. rsch. scientist, 2002—04, asst. prof., 2004—07, asst. prof. Ctr. Human Genetic and Genomic Medicine, 2006—07; assoc. prof. Dept. Ophthalmology U. Calif. at San Diego, La Jolla, 2007—, assoc. prof. Dept. Pathology, 2008—. Office: Shiley Eye Center #227, Jacobs Retina Center 9415 Campus Point Dr San Diego CA 92130 Office Phone: 858-534-9029. Office Fax: 858-534-8293. Business E-Mail: rayyagari@ucsd.edu.

AZAD, AHMED ABDULLAH, biotechnologist, educator; b. Bangladesh, Nov. 17, 1945; BSc (hon.), Dhaka U., MSc, 1968; PhD, U. Toronto, 1973. Postdoc. fellow U. Toronto, 1973—75; rsch. fellow Australian Nat. U., 1975—80; chief rsch. scientist Coun. Sci. & Indsl. Rsch., Australia, 1980—99; dir. rsch. & prof. med. biotech. U. Cape Town, 2000—05; hon. prof. biotech. advisor Dhaka U. Ctr. Advanced Rsch. Scis., 2006—. Mem., coun. sci. advisors Internat. Ctr. Genetic Engring. & Biotech., 1999—2008; bd. dirs. South African Med. Rsch. Coun., 2005—08. Recipient Chmn. Gold medal, CSIRO, Australia. Fellow: Royal Soc. South Africa, Islamic-World Acad. Sci., Bangladesh Acad. Sci., TWAS Acad. Sci. Developing World; mem.: South African Acad. Sci. Avocations: music, reading, travel. Home: 4 Chapel Ct Doncaster Melbourne Victoria 3108 Australia Personal E-mail: a_azad05@yahoo.com.au.

AZANZA, MARÍA JESÚS, medical educator, department chairman; b. Pamplona, Navarra, Spain, Sept. 7, 1944; d. Gonzalo Azanza and Ruiz Adoración; m. Agustin Del Moral; children: Nerea Del Moral, Victoria Del Moral. PhD in Biology, U. Navarra, Pamplona, Spain, 1972. Lic. in biology U. Complutense, Madrid, 1966. Ayudante microbiology U. Navarra, 1966—67, ayudante pharmacology, 1967—69, lectr. biology, 1969—75, Spain, 1977—81, U. Zaragoza, Aragon, Spain, 1981—85, titular biología, 1985—95, head, Inst. Bioelectromagnetism Alonso Santa Cruz, 1993—, head dept. morphological scis., 1995—99, chair prof. cell biology and magnetobiology, 1995—; lectr. biology U. Malaga, Spain, 1977—81. Rschr. Inst. Pasteur Lille, France, 1967; vis. rschr. U. Southampton, England, 1971, 73, 79, 82, 91; sec. faculty scis. U. Malaga, Spain, 1978—80; conseiller sci. club jeune biologists Inst. Goya, Zaragoza, 1990—91; mem. comm., pub. health and electromagnetic fields Ministry of Health, Madrid, 2000—05; mem. action cost emerging info. and communication techs. electromagnetic fields and health European Union, 2001—. Contbr. to 100 sci. papers. Grantee, Brit. Coun. Spanish Govt., 1979, 1982, 1991, Spanish Ministry Sci. and Edn., 1997, Bilateral Exch. Program Poland-Spain, 1999—2000. Roman Catholic. Office: Univ Zaragoza Faculty Medicine Domingo Miral S/N 50009 Zaragoza Spain Office Fax: 34 076 761754. Business E-Mail: mjazanza@unizar.es.

AZAR, DIMITRI T., medical educator, department chairman; b. Beirut; m. Nathalie Azar. BS, AM, U. Beirut, 1979, MD, 1983. Lic. in components I and II NY, 1985, registered in medicine Mass., 1987, lic. Bd. Physician Quality Assurance, 1997, Am. Bd. Ophthalmology, 2006. Instr. ophthalmology Harvard Med. Sch., Boston, 1990—91; asst. prof. opthalmology John Hopkins U., Balt., 1991—96, assoc. prof. opthalmology, 1996—96; assoc. prof. ophthalmology Harvard Med. Sch., Boston, 1996—2003; assoc. clin. scientist Schepens Eye Rsch. Inst., Harvard Med. Sch., 1999—2003; prof. opthalmology Harvard Med. Sch., 2003—06; BA Field chair ophthalmologic rsch., physician surgeon, prof., head dept. ophthalmology and visual sciences U. Ill., Chgo., 2006—, interim dean coll. medicine, 2011—. Recipient Tchr. of Yr., Wilmer Inst., Johns Hopkins U., 1993, Resident Tchg. Recognition award, 1996, Honor award, Am. Acad. Ophthalmology, 1997, Sr. Achievement award, Boston Hearld Supplement and Am. Acad. Ophthalmology, 2004, Sr. Scientist Rsch. award, Alcon Inst.; named Tchr. of Yr., Mass. Eye and Ear Infirmary, 1991; named one of Top 10 US Refractive Surgeons, Ophthalmology Times, 1996, Top 50 Opinion Leaders, Cataract and Refractive Surgery Today, 2005, Top 10 Ophthalmologists in Grater Boston Area, Boston Herald Supplement, 2005; named to Top Doctors Ophthalmology and Refractive Surgery, Boston Mag., 1991—2001, Top Doctors, Balt. Mag., 1994—96, Boston Mag., 2003. Fellow: Am. Academy Ophthalomolgy; mem.: AMA, Mass. Eye and Ear Alumni Assn., Assn. U. Profs. Opthalmology (chair mentoring program), New Eng. Ophthal. Soc., Internat. Soc. Optical Engring., Am. Soc. Cataract and Refractive Surgery, Internat. Soc. Refractive Keratoplasty, Mass. Med. Soc., Intenat. Soc. Refractive Surgery, Eye Transplantation Found., UIC Fight for Sight, Chgo. Ophthamological Soc., Assn. Rsch. Vision and Ophthalmology, Lions Club. Achievements include patents for excimer laser ablation within Bowman's; photochemical tissue bonding; bi-manual phacoemulsification; accommodating IOL; automated lasek device. Office: Univ Ill Chgo Dept Ophthalmology and Visual Sciences 1855 W Taylor Ste 3138 M/C 648 Chicago IL 60612 Office Fax: 312-996-7770. Business E-Mail: dazar@uic.edu. *

AZAR, RIAD R., gastroenterologist, educator; b. Lebanon, July 5, 1969; MD, St. Joseph U., 1994. Assoc. prof., dir. endoscopic ultrasound program Wash. U. St. Louis, 2002—. Fellow: Am. Soc. Gstrointestinal Endoscopy. Office: 660 S Euclid Ave Campus Bos 8124 Saint Louis MO 63108 Office Fax: 314-454-5005. Business E-Mail: razar@dom.wustl.edu.

AZARI, KODI, surgeon, educator; b. London, May 27, 1968; BS, U. Conn., 1990; MD, East Carolina U., 1997. Asst. prof. plastic surgery U. Pitts. Sch. Medicine, 2004—08, dir. hand surgery fellowship, 2005—08; dir., hand transplantation program David Geffen Sch. Medicine, UCLA, 2008, assoc. prof. orthop. surgery and plastic surgery, 2008—. Chief hand surgery UPMC Mercy Hosp., 2006—08. Recipient Outstanding Rsch. Plastic Surgery award, Carnegie Mellon U., Charles C. Moore award, U. Pitts. Sch. Medicine, Faculty Tchg. award, U. Pitts. Divsn. Plastic Surgery. Fellow: ACS; mem.: Am. Soc. Reconstructive Transplantation, Am. Soc. Surgery Hand (plastic surgery vis. prof., Young Members Leadership Program fellowship), Am. Assn. Hand Surgery, Am. Soc. Plastic Surgeons. Avocations: bicycling, hiking, skiing. Office: 10945 Le Conte Ave Ste 3355 Los Angeles CA 90095 Office Fax: 310-206-0063. E-mail: kodiazari@yahoo.com.

AZARINFAR, ANDRÉ, dentist; m. Parisa Azarinfar. Grad., Karolinksa Inst., Stockholm; DDS, Royal Caroline Medico-Surgico Univ., 1992. Private practice dentist, San Francisco. Mem.: Am. Acad. Cosmetic Dentistry, Am. Acad. Gen. Dentistry, San Francisco Dental Soc., Calif. Dental Assn., Am. Dental Assn. Office: Embarcadero Dental 10 De Silva Island Dr Mill Valley CA 94941-3004 Fax: 415-362-5912.

AZARNOFF, DANIEL LESTER, pharmaceutical executive, consultant; s. Samuel J. and Kate (Asarnow) A.; m. Joanne Stokes, Dec. 26, 1951; children: Rachel, Richard, Martin. BS, Rutgers U., 1947, MS, 1948; MD, U. Kans., 1955. Asst. instr. anatomy U. Kans. Med. Sch., 1949—50, rsch. fellow, 1950—52, intern, 1955—56, resident, Nat. Heart Inst. research fellow, 1956—58, asst. prof. medicine, 1962—64, assoc. prof., 1964—68, dir. clin. pharmacology study unit, 1964—68, assoc. prof. pharmacology, 1965—68, prof. medicine and pharmacology, 1968, dir. Clin. Pharmacology-Toxicology Ctr., 1967—78, Disting. prof., 1973—78, also prof. medicine, 1965—67, pres. Sigma Xi Club, 1968—69, clin. prof. medicine, 1982—96, prof. medicine, 1997—2007; Nat. Inst. Neurol. Diseases and Blindness spl. trainee Washington U. Sch. Medicine, St. Louis, 1958—60; asst. prof. medicine St. Louis U. Sch. Medicine, 1960—62; sr. v.p. worldwide R&D, G.D. Searle & Co., Skokie, 1978; pres. Searle R&D, Skokie, 1979—85, Azarnoff Assocs., Inc., Evanston, Ill., 1986—87, D.L. Azarnoff Assocs., So. San Francisco, Calif., 1987—; prof. pathology, clin. prof. pharmacology Northwestern U. Med. Sch., 1978—85; sr. v.p. clin. regulatory affairs Cellegy Pharms., San Francisco, 1998—2003; sr. v.p. clin. devel., pharmacology Congentus Pharms., 2006—07; commr. Nat. Commn. on Orphan Diseases, 1985—87; chmn. bd. dirs. Alpha RX Corp., South San Francisco, Calif., 1992—94; clin. prof. med. Stanford U. Sch. Med., 1998—2002. Professorial lectr. U. Chgo., 1978-86; dir. Second Workshop on Prins. Drug Evaluation in Man, 1970; chmn. com. on problems of drug safety NRC-NAS, 1972-76; chmn. bd. dirs. Oread, Inc., Lawrence, Kans., 1998-99; CEO Cibus Pharms., Burlingame, Calif., 1996-97; cons. numerous govt. agys.; chmn. bd. dirs. Cibus Pharm., Inc., 1996-97; CEO, chmn. bd. dirs. Vitalsensor, Inc., 2004-05. Editor: Devel. of Drug Interactions, 1974-77, Yearbook of Drug Therapy, 1977-79; series editor: Monographs in Clin. Pharmacology, 1977-84; mem. editl. bd. Drug Investigation, Brit. Jour. Clin. Pharmacology, Clin. Pharmacol. Therapy, Clin. Pharmacokinetics, Clin. Drug Investigation, 1989—, others. Served with U.S. Army, 1945-46. Recipient Ginsburg award in phys. diagnosis U. Kanas. Med. Ctr., 1953, Outstanding Intern award, 1956, Ciba award for gerontol. rsch., 1958, Rectors medal U. Helsinki, 1968, Nathanial T. Kwit Meml. Disting. Svc. award Am. Coll. Clin. Pharmacology, 2002; named Disting. Med. Alumnus, U. Kans. Coll. Health Sci., 1995; John and Mary R. Markle scholar, 1964, William N. Creasy vis. prof. clin. pharmacology Med. Coll. Va., 1975; Bruce Hall Meml. lectr. St. Vincents Hosp., Sydney, 1976, 7th Sir Henry Hallett Dale lectr. Johns Hopkins U. Med. Sch., 1978; Fulbright scholar Karolinska Inst., Stockholm, 1968. Fellow ACP, N.Y. Acad. Scis., Am. Assn. Pharm. Scientists (Rsch. Achievement award in clin. scis. 1995), AAAS (chmn. elect pharm. sect. 2001, chmn. pharm. divsn. 2002-03); mem. AMA (vice chmn. coun. on drugs 1971-72, editl. bd. jours.), Am. Soc. Clin. Nutrition, Am. Nutrition Instn., Am. Soc. Pharmacology and Exptl. Therapeutics (chmn. clin. pharmacology divsn. 1969-71, mem. exec. com. 1966-73, 78-81, del. 1975-78, bd. publ. trustees), Am. Soc. Clin. Pharmacology and Therapeutics (Oscar B. Hunter Meml. award 1995), Am. Fedn. Clin. Rsch., Brit. Pharmacol. Soc., Ctrl. Soc. Clin. Rsch., Royal Soc. for Promotion Health, Inst. Medicine of Nat. Acad. Scis., Soc. Exptl. Biology and Medicine (councillor 1976-80), Internat. Union Pharmacologists (sec. clin. pharmacology sect. 1975-81, internat. adv. com. Paris Congress 1978), GPIA (blue ribbon com. on generic medicine 1990), Sigma Xi. Office: DL Azarnoff Assoc 610 Edgewood Dr Rio Vista CA 94571 Office Phone: 707-374-2715. Business E-Mail: dan@azarnoffassociates.com.

AZEN, STANLEY PAUL, medical educator; s. Shirley Azen; m. Joyce Niland, May 22, 1993; 1 child, Matthew. PhD, UCLA, 1969; Dr., U. Salerno, 2006. Prof. U. So. Calif., LA, 1970—. Composer: (films) The World Outside, (plays) Ubu Roi; founding editor-in-chief: Computational Stats. and Data Analysis, 1994—; contbr. over 300 articles to profl. jours. Recipient Assoc. award Excellence Tchg., U. So. Calif., 1997, Alumni Hall of Fame, UCLA Sch. Pub. Health, 1998. Fellow: Internat. Statis. Inst., Am. Statis. Assn. Office: Univ So Calif 1540 Alcazar CHP222 Los Angeles CA 90033 Office Fax: 323-442-2993. Personal E-mail: sazen@usc.edu.

AZENABOR, ANTHONY AJAYI, immunologist, researcher; s. Caxton Ailojie and Grace Azenabor; m. Sarah Omonsose Inojie, June 6, 1962; children: Esesose Eminehi, Izodose Osose, Andrew Ainose, Violet Adaze. PhD, U. Benin, Benin City, Nigeria, 1992. Lectr. U. of Benin, Benin City, Edo State, Nigeria, 1993—97; rsch. scientist McMaster U. Regional Virology and Chlamydiology Laboratories, Hamilton, Ontario, Canada, 1997—98, U. Waterloo, Ontario, Canada, 1998—99, U. Wis., Madison, 2000—01, prof. Milw., 2001—. Dir. Zetalab Ltd, Benin City, Edo State, Nigeria, 1988—97. Recipient Shaw Scientist award, Greater Milw. Found., 2003—. Mem.: Internat. Soc. for Infectious Diseases, Am. Heart Assn., Am. Soc. Clin. Pathology (assoc.). Achievements include patents for Treatment of Chronic Intracellular bacterial Infection. Office: U Wis-Milwaukee 2400 E Hartford Ave Milwaukee WI 53211 E-mail: aazenabo@uwm.edu.

AZER, NIGEL MERRIETT, orthopedic surgeon, researcher; b. Anniston, Ala., Aug. 21, 1970; s. Rida and Valerie Azer; m. Elizabeth Ann Frye, Dec. 15, 1970; 1 child, Josefine. MD, U. Va., Charlottesville, 1996. Lic. physician Va., Md., DC, Mass., 2003. Residency U. Va., Charlottesville, 1996—2002; fellowship Harvard Med. Sch., Boston, 2002—03; surgeon-in-chief Wash. Orthop. Ctr., Washington, 2003—. Arthroplasty and biol. reconstruction fellow Brigham and Woman's Hosp., Boston, 2002—03. Author: (textbook chapters) Painful Total Knee Arthroplasty. Mem.: Royal Soc. Medicine U.K., Med. Soc. Va., Aerospace Med. Assn. Achievements include research in Cell Based Gene Therapy enhances bone repair. Avocations: tennis, motorsports, physical fitness, music, travel. Office: Washington Orthop Ctr 2112 F St NW Ste 804 Washington DC 20037 Home: 7730 Lee Ave Alexandria VA 22308-1003

AZER, SAMY AZIZ, gastroenterologist, medical educator; b. Cairo, Mar. 28, 1953; s. Aziz Azer and Sania Sedrak; m. Mary Azer; children: Sarah, Diana. B in Medicine and Surgery, Ain Shams U., Cairo, 1977, M in Medicine, 1983; MEd, U. New South Wales, 1993, MPH, 2005; PhD, U. Sydney, 1995. Resident in internal medicine Govt. of Health, Egypt, 1979-80, cons. in medicine, 1983-84, Saudi Arabia, 1984-89; vis. med. officer Ain Shams U. Hosps., 1980-83; postdoctoral fellow U. Kans. Med. Ctr., 1994; sr. lectr. med. edn. U. Melbourne, Australia, 1999—2006, U. Sydney, Australia, 1997—98; dir. problem-based learning tng. program faculty medicine, dentistry and health scis. U. Melbourne, 2001—06, chair semesters 1 - 5, faculty medicine, dentistry and health scis., 2002—06, chair faculty excellence in tchg. awards comm., faculty of medicine, dentistry, and health scis., 2003—04, anti-discrimination advisor, 2004—; prof. med. edn., unit head Sch. Medicine, U. Teknologi MARA, Malaysia, 2007—09; prof. med. edn. Coll. Medicine, King Sand U., Saudi Arabia, 2010—. Cons. NIHS, Australia, 1995; lectr. spkrs. bur. ACG, Australia, 1996; instr. pathology and grad. med. program, faculty medicine U. Sydney, 1997, sr. lectr. in med. edn., 1998—99; vis. prof. med. edn. Sch. Medicine, U. Toyama, Japan, 2006; chair, prof. med. edn., faculty of medicine U. Teknologi MARA, Malaysia; assoc. editor BMC med. Edn., 2009—; editor MedEd World, 2009—; mem. policy com. Assn. Study Med. Edn., 2009—. Author: Core Clinical Cases in Basic Biomedical Science, 2006, Navigating Problem-based Learning; co-author: Our Children, 1987; writer med. column El-Telegraph, Australia, 1996-97; contbr. chpts. to books, articles to profl. jours. Mem. ch. coun. Fairfield Anglican Chs., Australia, 1994, 95; elder Presbyn. Ch. of Australia, South Yarra, Victoria, 2002. Scholar Ministry of Edn., Egypt, 1968-71, undergrad. scholar, 1972-77, postgrad. scholar U. Sydney, 1993-94. Fellow Am. Coll. Gastroenterology, Royal Soc. of Health; mem. ASME (mem. policy com. 2009-), U. New South Wales Union (life), Gastroenterol. Soc. Australia, Am. Assn. for Study Liver Disease, Am. Coll. Gastroenterology. Presbyterian. Avocations: painting, soccer, history of medicine. Office: King Saud University Coll Medicine Dept of Medical Education Riyadh Saudi Arabia Business E-Mail: azer2000@optusnet.com.au.

AZEVEDO, JULIANA DE SOUZA, research scientist; b. Rio de Janeiro, Oct. 15, 1978; PhD, U. São Paulo, 2008, postdoc., 2011. Rschr. Inst. Rsch. and Nuc. Energy, 2009—. Substitute prof. Cederj, 2002—04. Home: R Prof Vicente Peixoto 37 São Paulo SP 05587-160 Brazil Personal E-mail: julianaazevedo_1978@yahoo.com.br.

AZHER, MOHAMMED, internist, consultant; b. Sahiwal, Pakistan, Nov. 30, 1953; arrived in England, 1981; s. Anwar Mohammed Choudhry and Mukhtar Begum; m. Izzah Azher, Mar. 23, 1986; children: Anum, Amal, Saad. MBBS, 1977. Cons. physician Armed Forces Hosp., Riyadh, Saudi Arabia, 1991—2000, Kettering Hosp., Northants, England, 2000—01; cons. chest physician Bedford Hosp., 2002—. Pres. Pakistan Drs. Group, Riyadh, 1998—2000; program dir. Found. Tng. Program, Bedford, 2005; clin. tchr. Cambridge U. Med. Sch., Cambridge, England, 2005—. Fellow: Royal Coll. Physicians Edinburgh, Royal Coll. Physicians London (coll. tutor 2007). Avocations: travel, music. Home: 195 Kimbolton Rd Bedford MK41 8DR England Office: Bedford Hosp South Wing Kempston Road MK42 9DJ Bedford England

AZIZI, S. AUSIM, neurologist, psychiatrist, educator; Attended, U. Tex., Austin, 1978; MD, Southwestern Med. Sch., Dallas, 1990. Diplomate Am. Bd. Psychiatry and Neurology, 1998. Intern Yale Univ. New Haven Hosp., Conn., 1991, resident, 1994; chairperson dept. neurology Temple Univ. Sch. Medicine. Author: Brain to music to brain!, 2009, Of sleep, seizures and networks, 2011; co-author: Successful elimination of non-neural cells and unachievable elimination of glial cells by means of commonly used cell culture manipulations during differentiation of GFAP and SOX2 positive neural progenitors (NHA) to neuronal cell, 2008, A population of human brain cells expressing phenotypic markers of more than one lineage can be induced in vitro to differentiate into mesenchymal cells, 2009, Bone marrow-derived mesenchymal stem cells undergo JCV T-antigen mediated transformation and generate tumors with neuroectodermal characteristics, 2010, various others. Mem.: Am. Heart Assn., Phila. Neurol. Soc., Am. Soc. Experimental Neurotherapeutics (founding mem.), Am. Soc. Neurotransplantation and Repair, Internat. Brain Rsch. Orgn., Am. Acad. Neurology, Soc. Neuroscience. Office: Temple University Hospital 3401 N Broad St Parkinson Bldg 5th Fl Philadelphia PA 19140 Office Phone: 215-707-5953. Office Fax: 215-707-8235.

AZMI, HOOMAN, neurosurgeon; BS, Stony Brook U.; MD, NY Med. Coll. Neurosurgical resident NJ U. Medicine & Dentistry; fellow Ctr. for Neurological Restoration, Cleveland Clinic; founder Ctr. for Functional & Restorative Neurosurgery Hackensack U. Med. Ctr., dir. movement disorders; physician Valley Hosp., Pascack Valley Hosp., Holy Name Hosp. Mem.: Bergen County Med. Soc., NJ Med. Soc., Am. Assn. Stereotactic & Functional Neurosurgery, Am. Assn. Neurological Surgeons, Congress Neurological Surgeons, Alpha Omega Alpha. Home: 680 Kinderkmack Rd Ste 300 Oradell NJ 07549-1500 Office Phone: 201-342-2550. Office Fax: 201-342-7171.

AZOULAY, CATHERINE, gynecological endocrinologist, consultant; b. Neuilly Sur Seine, France, Sept. 25, 1962; d. Yves and Josette Azoulay; 1 child, Jean-Élie Barjonet. BSc, Lycée Marcelin Berthelot, France, 1980; M, Université Pierre & Marie Curie, Paris VI, 1990. Board Certified Endocrinologist Université de Créteil-Paris XII, 1991. Assoc. prof. Hosp. Intercommunal, Créteil, France, 1992—2007; project mgr. govtl. agy. Haute Autorité de Santé, Paris, 1994—. Cons. Pharm. Industries, 2003—; editor in chief Reflexions en Gynecologie. Recipient Silver medal, Med. Sch. of Paris, Université de Créteil, Paris XII, 1992. Office: Ctr de Sante MGEN 178 Rue de Vaugirard Paris 75738 France Office Fax: 33144492812.

AZRIA, DAVID, radiation oncologist, researcher; b. Castres, France, Apr. 30, 1971; s. Raphael and Danielle Azria; m. Isabelle Esclassan, Nov. 10, 1998; children: Elise, Colin, Cloe. MD, U. Montpellier, France, 2001, PhD, 2004. Laureate med. faculty; resident U. Montpellier, 1996—2000; radiobiologist Inst. Gurie, Paris, 2000—01, Montpellier and Lausanne, Switzerland, 2001—02; assoc. prof. Val D'Aurelle Cancer Inst., Montpellier, 2002—. Cons. on various sci. bds., Paris, 2002. Recipient prize, Lilly Oncologie, 2002. Mem.: Am. Soc. Radiotherapy and Oncology (corr.), French Fedn. Digestive Oncology (assoc.), French Soc. Radiotherapy (assoc.), European Orgn. Rsch. and Treatment of Cancer Radiotherapy Group (assoc.). Achievements include research in bispecific antibodies and radiotherapy. Office: Crlc Val D'Aurelle Rue de la Croix Verte 34298 Montpellier France Office Fax: + 33 4 67 61 31 35. E-mail: azria@valdorel.fnclcc.fr.

AZUARA, HÉCTOR FERNÁNDEZ, pediatric surgeon; b. Mexico City, Sept. 19; s. Hector Gutierrez Azuara and Gloria de Azuara Fernández; m. Maria del Carmen Galdeano de Azuara; children: Maricarmen, Héctor, Federico, Marisol, Pedro. MD, La Salle U., Mexico City, 1978. Intern Hosp. Especial, Mexico City, 1975—76; postgrad. intern Hosp. ABC, Mexico City, 1978—79; resident in pediat. Inst. Pediat., Mexico City, 1979—80, resident in pediat. surgery, 1980—83, chief resident, 1983—84; chief pediat. surgery Hosp. Maria Inmarulada de Guadalupe, 1986—. Mem. adminstrv. coun. Hosp. MIG, 1990—. Co-editor (in Spanish): Principles of Pediatric Surgery, 1990; assoc. editor Mex. Rev. Pediat. Surgery, 2005, mem. editl. bd. Pediat. Endosurgye and Immunotech., 1997—2005. Vol. surgeon kidney transplant program INP Hosp., 1994—. Fellow: ACS (pres. Mex. chpt.); mem.: Mex. Soc. Pediat. Surgery (pres. 2001—03). Roman Catholic. Avocation: golf. Home: Cali 878 Col Lindavista Str 07300 Mexico City Mexico Office: Pediat Surgery Group Riobamba 776 Pb 7300 Mexico City Mexico Office Phone: (55) 51191637. Fax: (55) 51191638. E-mail: azuara@prodigy.net.mx.

AZUMA, JUNICHI, medical educator; s. Sumimasa and Sayoko Azuma; m. Kimiko Azuma; children: Junya, Lisa Takemoto, Junji. MD, Osaka U. Prof. clin. evaluation of medicines and therapeutics Osaka U., Suita, Japan, 1995—. Exec. dir. PharmacoGene TipTop Inc, Osaka, 2003—. Contbr. numerous articles to profl. jours. Office: Osaka U Yamadaoka 1-6 Suita 565-0871 Japan Office Fax: 06-6879-8259. E-mail: azuma@phs.osaka-u.ac.jp.

AZUMA, NORIYUKI, ophthalmologist, director; b. Tokyo, Oct. 21, 1954; MD, Keio U., 1980, PhD, 1986. Dir. ophthalmology Nat. Ctr. Child Health and Devel., 2002—. Pres. Assn. Japanese Pediatric Ophthalmology, 2011. Recipient award, Pfizer Inc. Office: 2-10-1 Okura Setagaya-ku Tokyo 157-8535 Japan Office Fax: 81-3-3416-2222. Business E-Mail: azuma-n@ncchd.go.jp.

AZZALIS, LIGIA AJAIME, biology professor; b. Sao Paulo, Brazil, Apr 3, 1968; PhD USP 2001. Adj. prof. Unifesp - Campus Diadema, 2010. Home: Rua Francisco Leitao 115 - Apto 506 Sao Paulo 05414025 Brazil

AZZAZI, ALAA MOHAMED, neurosurgeon, consultant; b. Cairo, Aug. 11, 1968; s. Mohamed Mostafa Azzazi and Fayza Ali Shendi; m. Nervana Mohamed Edrees, children: Yousef Alaa, Mariam Mohamed. MB, Cairo U., 1991; D in Neurosurgery, Carir U., 1999. Asst. prof. Cairo U., 1993—. Cons. Internal Affair Hospitals, Giza, Giza, Egypt, 2003—, Wadi Elneel Hosp., Cairo, 2001—. Recipient Rsch. award, Egyptian Soc. Low Back Pain, 2004. Mem.: Egyptian Soc. Neurol. Surgeons, Congress Neurol. Surgeons, Am. Assn. Neurol. Surgeons, Egyptian Soc. MIN, Internat. Spine Intervention Soc. (assoc.). Democrat-Npl. Muslim. Achievements include research in uses of endoscopes in neurosurgery; minimal invasive techniques in neurosurgery. Avocations: swimming, tennis. Office: Private Clinic 106 Gamet Eldwal Elarabia St Mohandesen Cairo 1234 Egypt Home: 28, Mansora St 1234 Cairo Cairo Egypt Personal E-mail: alaaazzazi@yahoo.com.

BAAN, JAN, physiologist, researcher; b. Rotterdam, Netherlands, Mar. 24, 1939; s. Jan Baan and Geertruida J. Eykman; m. Jozina M. Baan-Luteyn, May 27, 1964; children: Jan, Marc, Matthijs I. BS in Physics and Math., U. Utrecht, Netherlands, 1962, MS in Physics, 1965; PhD in Biomed. Engring., U. Pa., 1970. Postdoctoral fellow in cardiopulmonary med. U. Pa. Med. Sch., Phila., 1970—71, rsch. assoc., 1971—73, asst. prof. bioengineering in medicine, 1973—74; assoc. prof. in cardiac physiology Leiden (Netherlands) U. Med. Ctr., 1974—82, prof. cardiovasc. dynamics, 1982—. Reviewer sci. jours., 1974—; referee of grants Netherlands Heart Found., The Hague, Netherlands, 1990—2002, European Cmty.-Euromed 1, Brussels, 1994—95. Editor: Cardiovascular System Dynamics, 1978, Cardiac Dynamics, 1980, Cardiac Mechanics adn Function in the Normal and Diseased Heart, 1989, Systolic and Diastolic Funtion of the Heart, 1996, Vascular Medicine: from Endothelium to Myocardium, 1997; contbr. articles to profl. jours. Advisor Cardio-Dynamics Inc., Zoetermeer, Netherlands, 1991—2003. Recipient C.J.Kok award, Leiden U., 1978; grantee, Found. for Tech. Scis., 1980—88, Netherlands Heart Found., 1982—2003, Hirosaki U. Med. Sch., Japan, 1984; fellow, NIH, 1970—71. Mem.: Dutch Soc. for Physiology, Dutch Soc. Cardiology, Leycom Found. (chmn. 1980—2003), Cardiovasc. Sys. Dynamics Soc. (hon.; pres. 1982—84), Rotary Internat. (pres. local chpt. 2002—03). Achievements include development of cardiac conductance catheter. Avocations: photography, literature, bicycling, travel, music. Office: Leiden Univ Med Ctr POBox 9600 2300 RC Leiden Netherlands Personal E-mail: j.m.baan@freeler.nl. Business E-Mail: j.baan@lumc.nl.

BABA, TAKEO, neurosurgeon; b. Sapporo, Hokkaido, Japan, July 31, 1967; s. Masao Baba; m. Naoko Furukawa, Aug. 15, 2004; children: Yukino, Sotaro. MD, Grad. Sch. Medicine, Sapporo Med. U., 1996, PhD. Diplomate Japan Neurosurg. Soc., 1998, Japanese Soc. NeuroEndovascular Therapy, 2004, Japan Stroke Soc., 2005. Asst. prof. dept. neurosurgery Sapporo Med. U., 2004—07; chief physician, dept. neurosurgery Shinsapporo Neurosurg. Hosp., Sapporo, 2007—. Contbr. scientific papers to profl. jour. articles. Office: Shinsapporo Neurosurg Hosp 1-2-1-10 Kaminopporo Atsubetsu-ku Sapporo Hokkaido 004-0031 Japan Office Fax: 81-11-891-5100. Business E-Mail: baba@snh.or.jp.

BABA, TSUYOSHI, gynecologist, director; b. Hokuto, Hokkaido, Japan, Aug. 3, 1971; married. PhD, Sapporo Med. U., Hokkaido, Japan, 2001. Asst. prof. Sapporo Med. U., 2007—08; dir. gynecology Hakodate City Hosp., Hakodate, 2008—. Office: Sapporo Med Univ South 1 West 16 Sapporo Hokkaido 060-8543 Japan Office Fax: 81-11-614-0860. Business E-Mail: tbaba@sapmed.ac.jp.

BABACAN, HASAN, orthodontist; b. Ankara, Oct. 28, 1974; D in Dental Sci., Hacettepe U., 1997; MS, Cumhuriyet U., 2002. With Cumhuriyet U., 1998, assoc. prof., vice dean, 2008. Mem.: Am. Assn. Orthodontics. Office: Cumhuriey University Faculty Dentistry Sivas 58140 Turkey E-mail: babacanhasan@yahoo.com.

BABAO, DONNA MARIE, retired community health and psychiatric nurse, educator; b. St. Louis, May 6, 1945; d. Wilbert C. and Cecelia (Hogan) Bremer; widowed; 1 child, Tonya J. Diploma, Henry Ford Hosp. Sch. Nursing, Detroit, 1966; BSN, Calif. State U., Sacramento, 1978, MS in Nursing, 1990; MA in Edn., Calif. State U., Chico, 1985. Cert. pub. health nurse; master tchr. cert.; cert. clin. use of interactive guided imagery. Staff nurse U. Calif. Med. Ctr., San Franicsco, 1968-72; staff and charge CCU nurse Children's Hosp. of San Francisco, 1972-78; pub. health nurse II Sutter-Yuba Health Dept., Yuba City, Calif., 1979-81; prof. nursing Yuba Coll., Marysville, Calif., 1981-2000; psychiat. charge nurse Sunridge Hosp., Yuba City, 1994-96; RN case mgr. Home Health Care Mgmt. Inc., Chico, Calif., 2004—05; office nurse, case mgr. First Care Med. Clinic, Oregon House, 2005—. Mem. exam. item writing panel NCLEX-RN, 1998. Writer health column, 1986-90; chpt. to textbooks; reviewer nursing textbooks and jour. articles; contbr. articles to profl. jours. 1st lt. Nurse Corps, U.S. Army, 1966-68. Mem. Vietnam Vets. Am., Imagery Internat., Henry Ford Hosp. Alumni Assn. Nursing. Personal E-mail: dbabao@hotmail.com.

BABAZONO, AKIRA, physician, researcher; b. Kagoshima, Japan, Mar. 31; s. Tatsumi and Noriko Babazono; m. Tsuneko Babazono, Sept. 8, 2000; children: Koh, Kei, Soh, Rei. MD, Kyushu U., 1984; PhD, Okayama U., 2000. Resident in internal medicine Okinawa Chubu Hosp., Gushikawa city, Japan, 1984—86; asst. prof. Okayama U., Japan, 1990—94; assoc. prof. Inst. Health Sci. Kyushu U., 1994—2005, prof. Dept. Healthcare Adminstrn. and Mgmt. Grad. Sch. Med. Scis., 2005—. Editor: Japanese Jour. Health Promotion. Home: 5-2-15 Minamigaoka Fukuoka Oonojo City 816-0964 Japan Office: Grad Sch Med Sci Kyushu Univ Dept Healthcare Adminstrn & Mgmt 3-1-1 MaidashiHigashi-ku Fukuoka 812-8582 Japan Office Fax: 81-92-642-6961; Home Fax: 81-92-595-8952. Personal E-mail: babazonoa@yahoo.co.jp. Business E-Mail: babazono@hcam.med.u.ac.jp.

BABB, JOSEPH DOLBY, physician; b. Columbus, Ohio, Apr. 16, 1939; s. Joe A. and Dorothe (Dolby) B.; m. Anne Tanner Hammerlund, Sept. 2, 1969 (div. Apr. 1985); children: Elizabeth Anne, Peter Dolby; m. Margo Tregenza, Oct. 6, 1990. BA magna cum laude, Kenyon Coll., Gambier, Ohio, 1961; MD, Johns Hopkins U., Balt., 1966. Diplomate in internal medicine and cardiovasc. diseases, internat. cardiology, Am. Bd. Internal Medicine; cert. physician, Pa., Conn., NC. Intern Mass. Gen. Hosp., Boston, 1966-67, resident in internal medicine, 1967-68, clin. and rsch. fellow, 1970-72; teaching fellow Harvard Med. Sch., Boston, 1970-72; asst. prof. med. cardiology Pa. State U. Sch. Medicine, Hershey, 1972-76, assoc. prof., 1976-80; chief of cardiology Bridgeport Hosp., Conn., 1980-95; clin. assoc. prof. medicine (cardiology) Yale U., New Haven, 1980-95; prof. medicine (cardiology) East Carolina U. Sch. Medicine, Greenville, 1995—, Bd. dir., pres. Alcohol and Drug Dependency Coun., Westport, Conn., 1987-95. Maj. US Army, 1968—70, Vietnam. Fulbright fellow, Utrecht, Netherlands, 1961-62. Fellow Am. Coll. Cardiology (gov. 1987-90, 2002-05), Am. Heart Assn. (coun. clin. cardiology), Soc. Cardiac Angiography and Intervention (trustee 1993-99, pres. 2001-02), Coalition Cardiovasc. Orgns. (pres. 2004-05). Avocations: fishing, hiking. Office: East Carolina Univ Sch Med 115 Heart Dr Rm 3231 Greenville NC 27834 Business E-Mail: babbj@ecu.edu.

BABCOCK, MARGUERITE LOCKWOOD, psychiatric treatment therapist, educator, writer; b. Jacksonville, Fla., Jan. 1, 1944; d. Allen Seaman and Emilie (Lockwood) B. BA in Art History, Am. U., Washington, DC, 1965; M in Counselor Edn., U. Pitts., 1982. Lic. profl. counselor, Pa.; cert. nat. cert. counselor, nat. cert. master's addiction counselor. Addictions therapist South Hills Health Sys., Pitts., 1979—81; addiction therapist, clin. supr., clin. dir. Alternatives Turtle Creek Mental Health/Mental Retardation/D&A Ctr., Pitts., 1981—86; addictions therapist, coord. Ligonier Valley Treatment Ctr., Stahlstown, Pa., 1986—88; addictions clin. supr., unit dir. Ctr. for Substance Abuse Mon-Yough, McKeesport, Pa., 1988—96; quality assurance Mon-Yough, McKeesport, 1996—97; clin. supr. Sojourner House, Pitts., 1997—2000; co-founder, addictions consulting Outcomes Builders, 2000—; therapist Persoma PC, Manroeville, Pa., 2009—. Adj. instr. in addictions courses Seton Hill Coll., Greensburg, Pa., 1989-91, C.C. Allegheny County, West Mifflin, Pa., 1989-91, Pa. State U., McKeesport, 1993-97; pvt. trainer, writer, Acme, Pa., 1985—. Co-author, co-editor: Challenging Codependency: Feminist Critiques, 1995; mem. editl. bd. Jour. Tchg. in Addictions, 2000—; contbr. articles to profl. jours. Fellow Andrew Mellon Found., 1966-68, NSF, 1967. Mem.: Alpha Lambda Delta. Office Phone: 724-593-7139.

BABE, GREGORY S., pharmaceutical executive; b. W.Va. married; 4 children. BS in Mech. Engring., W.Va. U., 1980. Joined as an intern in the polyurethanes group Bayer Corp., 1976, mgr. Brunsbuttel facility Germany, dir. & gen. mgr. Hennecke Machiner, polymers divsn. Pa., v.p. corp. quality, dir. nat. program to implement Bayer's enterprise resource planning sys., sr. v.p. info. svcs., 1999—2004, pres., CEO Bayer Corp. & Bus. Svcs. LLC, 2003—04, pres., CEO Bayer MaterialScience LLC, 2004—, pres., CEO, sr. rep. for US & Can., 2008—. Chmn. Bayer Polit. Action Com., Bayer USA Found.; exec. sponsor Bayer Diversity Adv. Coun.; bd. dirs. Matthews Internat. Corp. Bd. dirs. W. Va. U. Found.; mem. bd. dirs. & exec. com. Allegheny Conf. on Cmty. Devel., Nat. Assn. Mfrs.; mem. bd. dirs., exec. com., responsible care bd. com., chem. mgmt. com. and bd. rsch. com. American Chemistry Coun. Office: Bayer Corp 100 Bayer Rd Pittsburgh PA 15205-9741 Office Phone: 412-777-2000. Office Fax: 412-777-3883. Business E-Mail: gregory.babe@bayerbms.com.

BABICH, YURI F., research scientist, director; b. Nikolaev, Sept. 14, 1941; PhD, KPI, 2001. Head lab. Inst. Applied Problems Physics and Biophysics, 1991—2001; sci. dir. Ctr. Biomed. Electroengring., 2002—. Achievements include development of new method for breast cancer diagnosis STCU. Avocations: piano, tennis, skiing. Home: Kurska 12A Kiev 03049 Ukraine Personal E-mail: babich@ua.fm.

BABIUK, LORNE ALAN, virologist, immunologist, researcher; b. Canora, Sask., Can., Jan. 25, 1946; s. Paul and Mary Babiuk; m. Betty Lou Carol Wagar, Sept. 29, 1973; children: Shawn, Kimberley. BSA, U. SK, Saskatoon, 1967, MSc, 1969, DSc, 1987; PhD, U. BC, Vancouver, 1972; DSc in Infectious Diseases, Colo. State U., Ft. Collins, 2007; DSc (hon.), U. Guelph, 2008. Postdoctoral fellow U. Toronto, Ont., Canada, 1972-73; asst. prof. Western Coll. Vet. Medicine, Saskatoon, SK, 1973-75, assoc. prof., 1975-79, prof., 1979—2007; v.p. U. Alberta, 2007—. Cons. Molecular Genetics, Mpls., 1980—84, Genentech, San Francisco, 1981—84, Ciba Geigy, Basel, Switzerland, 1984—91; assoc. dir. rsch. Vet. Infectious Disease Orgn., Saskatoon, 1984—93, dir., 1993—2007; v.p. rsch. U. Alberta, 2007—. Contbr. chapters to books, articles to profl. jours. Recipient award, Can. Soc. Microbiology, 1990, Am. Vet. Immunology, 1992, Xerox-Can. Forum, 1993, Emerging Sci. and Tech. award for innovation, 1995, Pfizer award in animal health, 1998, Nat. Merit award, 1998, Bill Snowden Meml. award, 2000, Saskatchewan Order of Merit, 2004, Saskatchewan Centennial medal, 2005, Officer of Order of Can., 2005, Centennial medal, Province of Saskatchewan, 2005, Prix Galien Can. Rsch. award, 2005, McLaughlin medal, 2009. Fellow: Can. Acad. Health Scis., Royal Soc. Can., Infectious Disease Soc. Am. (Can. rsch. chair in vaccinology and biotech. 2001—07), Royal Coll. Physicians and Surgeons Can. (hon.); mem.: Internat. Soc. Antiviral Rsch., Soc. Gen. Microbiology, Can. Soc. Microbiology, Am. Soc. Virology, Am. Soc. Microbiology, Internat. Soc. Interferon Rsch. Achievements include 35 patents in field. Office: Vice Pres Rsch 3-7 University Hall Edmonton AB Canada T6G 2J9 Home: 2130 Haddow Dr NW Edmonton AB T6R 3C9 Canada Office Phone: 780-492-5353.

BABIZHAYEV, MARK ARKADJEVICH, biophysicist; b. Moscow, Sept. 25, 1959; s. Arkadii M. Goldman and Serafima Ch. Babizhayeva; m. Olga V. Vasil'eva, July 15, 1982 (div. Feb. 1990); 1 child, Olesya M. PhD, Moscow Helmholtz Inst. Eye Dis, 1983. Young sci. rschr. Moscow Helmholtz Rsch. Inst., 1983-89, sci. rschr., 1989-94, sr. sci. rschr., 1994-95; sci. cons. EXSYMOL SAM, Monte Carlo, Principaute de Monaco, 1992—; sr. investigator, scientific cons. Bruschettini S.r.l., Genoa, Italy, 1994—; exec. dir. Innovative Vision Products Inc., Del., 1998. Editor-in-chief Recent Patents on Drug Delivery & Formulation, 2011—. Contbr. articles to profl. jours.; patentee in field. Exec. dir. Chernobyl Workers Goodwill Union, 1992. Recipient Oka Meml. award, Yokohama, Japan, 1992; grantee Internat. Sci. Found., 1994. Mem. N.Y. Acad. Sci. Avocations: launching of scientific and indsl. projects. Home: Ivanovskaya 20 74 Moscow 127434 Russia Office: Moscow Helmholtz Inst 14/19 Sadovaya-Chernogryazs Moscow 103064 Russia Personal E-mail: markbabizhayev@yahoo.com.

BABJAK, PATRICIA M., medical association administrator; Grad., U. Ill., Chgo.; MLS, Dominican U. Asst. coord. of Commn. on Dietetic Registration Am. Dietetic Assn., Chgo., 1975—78, dir. of Commn. on Dietetic Registration, 1978—98, interim CEO, 1997, exec. v.p. strategic mgmt., 1998—2009, CEO, 2009—. Mem.: Am. Dietetic Assn. (hon.). Office: Am Dietetic Assn Ste 2000 120 S Riverside Plz Chicago IL 60606 Office Phone: 800-877-1600 ext. 4856. E-mail: pbabjak@eatright.org.

BABU, ABRAHAM SAMUEL, physical therapist, educator; b. Tiruvalla, India, Sept. 10, 1982; BPT, Christian Med. Coll., Vellore, 2005; MPT, Manipal Coll. Allied Health Scis., 2010. Chief phys. therapist CSI Mission Hosp., 2006—08; lectr., dept. physiotherapy, 2010—. Academician, clinician and rschr. Manipal Coll. Allied Health Scis., 2010. Mem.: Am. Thoracic Soc., Soc. Clin. Trials, Pulmonary Vascular Rsch. Inst., Indian Assn. Physiotherapists, Am. Heart Assn. Avocation: music. Office: Manipal Coll Allied Health Scis Dept Physiotherapy Manipal Karnataka 576104 India

BABUS, VLADIMIR, epidemiologist, educator; b. Mali Raven, Croatia, June 24, 1932; s. Marko and Marija (Busija) B.; m. Branka Markusic, Dec. 8, 1961. MD, U. Zagreb, Croatia, 1962; DPH, A. Stampar Sch. Pub. Health, Zagreb, 1971; MS, U. Zagreb, 1975, DSc, 1983. Gen. practitioner Health Sta., Orehovec, Croatia, 1962-65; chief preventive svcs. Health Ctr., Ivanić-Grad, 1965-69; epidemiologist Inst. Pub. Health Croatia, Zagreb, 1969-79; lectr. Med. Sch., U. Zagreb, 1979-93, asst. prof., 1993—. Author: Epidemiological Methods; editor: Epidemiology, 1987; 3d edit., 1997; contbr. articles to profl. jours. Home: Kraljevec 16 10000 Zagreb Croatia Office: A Stampar Sch Pub Health Rockefellerova 4 10000 Zagreb Croatia

BACAL, FERNANDO, cardiologist; b. Sao Paulo, Feb. 28, 1966; MD, U. Santo Amaro, 1989; PhD, U. Sao Paulo, 1999. Physician Heart Inst., U. Sao Paulo, Med. Sch., 1991—. Editor in chief Brazilian Archives Cardiology, 2008—10. Mem.: Brazilian Soc. Cardiology (pres. heart failure dept.). Avocation: soccer. Home: Ave Divino Salvador 395 apt 201 Sao Paulo 04078-011 Brazil Home Phone: 55-11-30442618. Home Fax: 55-11-30695419. Business E-Mail: fbacal@uol.com.br.

BACA NEGLIA, HILDA ZORAIDA, dean; b. Callao, Lima, Peru, May 31, 1949; d. Máximo Baca León and Dora Neglia Donayre; m. Donato Venegas Olivares, Aug. 28, 1970; children: Godwin David Venegas Baca, Rafael Alfonso Venegas Baca. B in Edn., San Martin de Porres U., Lima, 1991, M in Edn., 1994; B in Obstetrics, San Marcos Nat. U., Lima, 1999; Hon. Prof. (hon.), Tumbes Nat. U., Peru, 2001; PhD in Edn., San Martin de Porres U., Lima, 2002, M in Obstetrics, 2002. Chmn. profl. obstetrics sch. San Martin de Porres U., Lima, 1990—92, dean, obstetrics faculty, 1992—, dean, obstetrics/nursing faculty, 2003—. Obstetrics asst. Peruvian Health Ministry, Lima (South Lima), 1976—87, chmn. nat. obstetrics assn., Lima, 1981, chief, obstetrics unit - dept. unit of health, 87, nat. dep. dir., family planning program, 1988—92. Author: (rsch.) The Future of Edn. in Obstetrics, (book) Principles of Strategic Mgmt. in Health, Guidebook for the Cmty. Health Course, Prospective Analysis in Tchg. of Reproductive Health; author: (co-author) Profile of the Peruvian Women. Specialist in devel./nat. def. Ctr. of Nat. High Studies, Lima, 1997—98; hon. mem. civic def. Jesus Maria Town Coun., Lima, 2003. Recipient, Recognition Award-Sub-Regional Dept. of Health, 1994. Mem.: Peruvian Soc. in Obstet. Psychoprophilaxis (hon.), Latin Am. Rsch. Assn. in Human Reproduction (hon.), San Martin de Porres U. (professors assn. 1992). Roman Catholic.

Avocations: reading, cooking, gardening, decoration. Office: San Martin de Porres Univ Salaverry 1136 - 1144 Lima 11 Peru Home: Vesalio 565 Lima Peru Office Fax: +51-1-4716791; Home Fax: +51-1-2259658. E-mail: hbaca@usmp.edu.pe.

BACCARINI, ENRICO, journalist; b. Florence, Italy; s. Franco Baccarini and Maria Novella Elvira Aurora Biava. Student, U. Florence, 2001—04; cert. giornalista pubblicista, Ordine dei Giornalisti, Rome, 2003. Directive counsil CUN, Florence, 2000—04; chief redactor CIRPET-Archeomisteri, Florence, 2001—04; counselor pub. rels. Marucelliana Libr., Florence, 2002. Author: Italia Esoterica, 2004; co-editor: Archeomisteri, 2000. Mem.: AIAA, Cohitato Interdisciplinare Ricerche Prestostoriche and Tradizionali (dir. commn. 1999—2004, co-founder), Italian Soc. for Modified State of Consciousness (hon.), Rotary (sostenitore 2003). Avocations: astronomy, travel, tennis, photography, informatics.

BACCASH, EMIL, geriatrician; Grad., Universita di Roma La Sapienza Facolta di Medicina e Chirurgia, Rome, Italy, 1978. Lic. NY, diplomate Am. Bd. of Internal Medicine-geriatric medicine. Tng. internal medicine Methodist Hosp., with. Office: New York Methodist Hospital 506 6th St Brooklyn NY 11215 Office Phone: 718-780-3000.

BACCHUS, HAROLD MUSTAPHA, physician; b. New Amsterdam, Guyana, June 19, 1946; arrived in US, 1964; s. H. M. Bacchus Sr. and Saira Bacchus; children: Timothy, Lisa, Jamy; m. Fazia Deen, 1985 (div.); children: Jannah, Jibril, Maryam. BA, MA, Minn. State U., Mankato, 1970; BS in Med., U. Iowa, 1974; MD, Am. U. Caribbean, 1981. Diplomate Am. Assn. Physician Specialists. ER physician part time; med. dir. family practice Med-I-Qwik, Inc., Ft. Wayne, Ind. Lt. col., chief flight surgeon USAFR, 1985—2006, Grissom AFB. Fellow: Am. Assn. Physician Specialists (officer 2006, pres., F.P. Acad. 1999—2011, bd. cert. F.P. officer 1991—, named F. P. Physician of Yr. 2010), Am. Acad. Family Physicians; mem.: Lions, Jaycees. Democrat. Islam. Avocations: music, dance, travel, singing. Home: 12002 Woodbourne Ct Fort Wayne IN 46845 Office: Med-I-Qwik Inc 1719 Cremer Ave Fort Wayne IN 46818 Office Phone: 260-490-9150. Business E-Mail: mediqwikinc@yahoo.com.

BACCIAGALUPPI, MARCO, psychiatrist, educator; b. Bolzano, Italy, Oct. 22, 1932; s. Giuseppe Bacciagaluppi and Audrey Partridge Smith; m. Laura Bertolucci; children: Guido, Claudio; m. Maria Mazza, June 24, 1963 (dec. Jan. 16, 1993). Degree in Medicine, U. Med. Sch., Milan, 1957. Cert. U. di Ferrara, Italy, 1958, specialist in psychiatry U. Sch. Specialization, Milan, 1965. Tchr. Sch. Specialization Psychiatry, Milan, 1978—81. Pres. Orgn. di Psicoanalisti Italiani, Firenze, 1996—2001. Contbr. scientific papers. Organizer Assn. Italiana Fulbright, Milan, 1977—81. 2nd lt. Med. Officer Italian Army, 1959—61, Monza. Fellowship, Dept. Psychiatry, NY Med. Coll., 1963—64, Fulbright-Hays Travel grant, US Govt., 1983. Fellow: Am. Acad. Psychoanalysis & Dynamic Psychiatry; mem.: World Psychiat. Assn. (sect. psychotherapy), Internat. Erich Fromm Soc. Home: Via Eugenio Pellini 4 20125 Milan MI Italy Home Fax: 0039.02.66716895. Personal E-mail: bacciagaluppi@iol.it. E-mail: m.bacciagaluppi@marcobacciagaluppi.com.

BACH, BERNARD R., JR., orthopedist, educator; b. Ann Arbor, Mich., Dec. 10, 1952; m. Elizabeth King Ingle, 1982; children: David, Laura. AB, Harvard Coll., Cambridge, Mass., 1975; MD, U. Cin. Coll. Med., 1979. Diplomate Am. Bd. Orthopaedic Surgery. Intern gen. surgery New Eng. Deaconess Hosp., Boston, 1979—80, resident gen. surgery, 1980—81; resident orthopedic surgery Mass. Gen. Hosp., Boston, 1981—84, chief resident trauma svc., jr. attending asst. dept. orthopedic surgery, 1985—86; dir. sports medicine sect. Rush Presbyn. St. Luke's Med. Ctr., Chgo., 1986—, fellowship dir. orthopedic sports medicine, 1988—; asst. prof. dept. orthopedics Rush Med. Coll., 1986—93, assoc. prof. orthopaedic surgery, 1993—96, prof. orthopaedic surgery, 1996—, dir. divsn. sports medicine, 2003—, Claude N. Lambert &Helen S. Thomson chair orthopedic surgery, 2004—. Clin. fellow surgery Harvard Med. Sch., 1979—81, clin. fellow orthopedic surgery, 1981—84; orthopedic cons. Harvard U. Health Svc., 1983; rsch. asst. Biomechanics Gait Lab. Children's Hosp. Med. Ctr., Boston, 1983; jr. attending orthopaedic surgeon, dept. sports medicine Hosp. Spl. Surgery, NYC, 1985—86. Mem. edtl. bd. Am. Jour. Knee Surgery, 1987—, Advances in Orthopaedic Surgery, 1990—, Sports Medicine Digest, 1996—, Orthopedics Today, 1997—, mem. editl. bd. Sports Medicine & Arthroscopy Review, 2001—04, reviewer Am. Jour. Sports Medicine, 1991—, Jour. Bone & Joint Surgery, 1996—, editor-in-chief Jour. Knee Surgery, 2003—; contbr. articles to profl. jours. Mem.: AMA, Am. Assn. Orthopaedic Surgeons, Acad. Orthaepedic Soc., Arthroscopy Assn. N.Am., Am. Acad. Orthopaedic Surgeons (com. sports medicine 1995—2001, surg. skills edn. com. 1999—2002), Assn. Sports Medicine Fellowship Directors, Herodicus Sports Medicine Soc. (nom. com. 1994—95, exec. com. 1994—97, sec. 1999—2000, pres. elect 2004—05, prog. chmn. 2004—05, pres. 2005—06), Am. Coll. Sports Medicine, Nat. Athletic Trainers Assn., Ill. Athletic Trainers Assn., Chgo. Orthopedic Soc., Thomas B. Quigley Sports Medicine Soc., Ill. State Med. Soc., Chgo. Med. Soc., Profl. Baseball Team Physicians Assn. Office: Midwest Orthopedics Rush Med Ctr 1725 W Harrison St Ste 1063 Chicago IL 60612 Office Phone: 312-432-2353. Office Fax: 312-942-1517.

BACH, RICHARD GORDON, internist, cardiologist, educator; b. 1956; BS in Biology, Georgetown U., 1977; MD, NYU, 1984. Resident internal medicine NYU Med. Ctr., NYC, 1984-87, fellow cardiology, 1987-91; dir. CCU St. Louis U. Hosp., 1997—99, Barnes-Jewish Hosp., St. Louis, 1999—. Assoc. prof. medicine St. Louis U. Hosp., 1996-99, Washington U. Sch. Medicine, St. Louis, 1999—. Fellow Am. Coll. Cardiology, Soc. for Cardiac Angiography and Interventions; mem. ACP, Am. Fedn. Clin. Rsch. Office: Box 8086 660 S Euclid Ave Saint Louis MO 63110 Office Phone: 314-362-1963. E-mail: rbach@wustl.edu. *

BACHE, ROBERT JAMES, physician, educator; MD, Harvard U. Diplomate Am. Bd. Internal Medicine, Am. Bd. Cardiovasc. Disease. Resident in internal medicine Duke U., Durham, NC, assoc. prof. medicine; prof. medicine U. Minn., Mpls. Contbr. articles to profl. jours. Fellow Am. Coll. Cardiology; mem. Am. Soc. for Clin. Investigation, Assn. of Am. Physicians, Assn. Univ. Cardiologists, Am. Heart Assn. Office: U Minn Med Sch Med Box 508 Mayo 420 Delaware St SE Minneapolis MN 55455-0374 Office Phone: 612-624-8970. Business E-Mail: bache001@umn.edu.

BACHICHA, JOSEPH ALFRED, physician, educator; b. Rock Springs, Wyo. s. Alfred and Helen B BA, Stanford U., Calif., 1977; MD, Boston U., 1982. Diplomate Am. Bd. of Ob-Gyn. Intern St. Luke's-Roosevelt Hosp., NYC, 1982—83; resident ob-gyn Stanford U. Hosp., Palo Alto, Calif., 1983—86; pvt. practice Chgo., 1986—95; asst. prof. ob-gyn U. Calif., San Francisco, 1996—97, assoc. prof., 1997—99; med. dir. Pacific Occupl. Health Med. Assocs., South San Francisco, 1999—2003; sr. physician Kaiser Permanente, 2000—, chief, patient edn. and health promotion Hayward, Calif., 2004—. Cons. WHO, UN Family Planning Assn.; asst. prof. Northwestern U., Chgo., 1986-95; Gen. Hosp., 1996-99, dir. student edn. dept. ob-gyn., San Francisco, 1995-99, dir. obstetrics, 1998-99; dir. Excelsior Group Health Care for Women and Children, San Francisco, 1995-99; dir. low-risk obstetrics, coord. undergrad. med. edn. Prentice Women's Hosp., Chgo., 1990-95; mem. Liaison Com. on Med. Edn.; physician, educator Carnegie Found., Ghana, 1989, Project Hope, Nicaragua, 1992, World Surgical Found. Ethopia, 2009 Contbr. articles to profl. jours. Mem. Chgo. Coun. Fgn. Rels Grad. fellow Rotary Found., 1980; mem. Harvard Macy Scholars Inst. Fellow ACOG, Am. Coll. Surgeons, Assn. Profs. Gynecology and Obstetrics, Internat. Coll. Surgeons (US State sect. pres. 2010, N.Am. Fedn. sec. 2011, Red Team Releif Internat. Haiti Mission, 2010), Royal Soc. Medicine; mem. AMA, APHA, Nat. Bd. Med. Examiners (bd. dirs.), Am. Assn. Maternal and Neonatal Health, Am. Fertility Soc., Chgo. Gynecol. Soc., San Mateo County Med. Soc., Stanford U. Alumni Assn., Boston U. Sch. Medicine Alumni Assn., Commonwealth Club Calif Roman Catholic. Avocations: mystery books, cross country skiing, weight training, running, aerobics. Office: 27400 Hesperian Blvd Hayward CA 94545 Business E-Mail: joseph.bachicha@kp.org.

BACHMAN, DAVID CHRISTIAN, orthopedic surgeon; b. Peoria, Ill., Apr. 11, 1934; s. Leland Alvin and Elsie May (Springer) B.; m. Betty June Foster, Sept. 9, 1956; children: Lynne Allison, Laura; m. Karen Jean McDaniel, Oct. 21, 2006. BA, Goshen Coll., 1958; MD, Northwestern U., 1962. Intern Cook County Hosp., Chgo., 1962-63; resident in orthopaedic surgery Northwestern U. Med. Sch., 1963-67; practice medicine specializing in orthopaedic surgery Chgo., 1967-80; practice specializing in ski injuries, 1980-93; with Mountain Med. Services, Telluride, Colo., 1982-87, Ouray Mountain Rescue Team, Inc., Ouray Med. Ctr., Ouray, Colo.; coroner Ouray County, Colo., 1982-93; mem. staffs Northwestern Meml. Hosp., Children's Meml. Hosp., Grant hosp., Chgo., 1967-80, Montrose Meml. Hosp., Colo., 1984-93; med. cons. Western Area U.S. Postal Svc. Dir. Ctr. for Sports Medicine, Northwestern U. Med. Sch., 1978-80; team physician Chgo. Bulls, Nat. Basketball Assn., 1967-80; asst. prof. dept. orthop. surgery Northwestern U. Med. Sch., 1967-80; syndicated columnist on sports medicine Dr. Jock, 1976-90; cons. Western area U.S. Postal Svc., 1996-97; sr. area med. dir. Western Area U.S. Postal Svc., 1997-2002, Pacific Arae U.S. Postal Svc., 2002-06, nat. med. adminstr. U.S. Postal Svc., 2006—. Author: (with Marilyn Preston) Dear Doctor Jock... The Peoples Guide to Sports and Fitness, 1980, (with others) The Diet That Lets You Cheat, 1983, (with Tod Bacigalupi) The Way it Was, 1990, (with Robert Pickering) The Use of Forensic Anthropology, 1st edit., 1996, 2nd edit., 2009. Elder Presbyn. Ch., 1965—; rsch. assoc. anthropology dept. Denver Mus. Natural History, 1994-99. Mem. ACS, Am. Acad. Orthop. Surgery, Am. Orthop. Soc. for Sports Medicine, Phi Rho Sigma. Presbyterian. Home and Office: 849 W Golf Course Pl Green Valley AZ 85622 Office Phone: 520-388-5202. Business E-Mail: david.c.bachman@usps.gov.

BACHMAN, SISTER JANICE, healthcare executive, religious order administrator; b. Coshocton, Ohio, Oct. 25, 1945; d. Edward Michael and Kathryn Elizabeth (Norris) B. Student, Ohio Dominican Coll., 1963-67; BS in Pharmacy, Ohio State U., 1971; MBA in Mgmt., Xavier U., 1976; MA in Christian Spirituality, Creighton U., 1989. Joined Dominican Sisters, 1963. Staff pharmacist St. George Hosp., Cin., 1971-73, dir. pharmacy svcs., 1973-76; instr. pharmacology and related courses Coll. Mt. St. Joseph, Cin., 1973-74; instr. pharmacology Sch. Nursing Bethesda Hosp., Cin., 1975; adminstrv. resident St. Joseph Hosp., Mt. Clemens, Mich., 1976-77, adminstrv. asst., 1977-78, asst. adminstr., 1978-79; corp. dir. religious programs St. Francis-St. George Hosp., Inc., Cin., 1979-80, asst. v.p. hosp. support svcs., 1980-82, v.p. therapeutic and diagnostic svcs., 1983-89; dir. exec. affairs Benedictine Health Sys., Inc., Duluth, Minn., 1989-90; vicaress Dominican Sisters St. Mary of the Springs, Columbus, Ohio, 1990-96. Editor: Guidelines for Developing an IV Admixture, 1976. Trustee Ohio Dominican Coll., 1980-96, mem. devel. com., 1984-94, physical facilities com., 1994-96; mem. radiologic tech. adv. bd. Xavier U., Cin., 1983-89; mem. MLT adv. bd. Coll. Mt. St. Joseph, 1983-85; trustee Program for Medically Underserved dba Health Moms and Babes, 1986-91, co-founder, chair, 1986-89; bd. dirs. Franciscan Health Sys. Cin., 1990-92; chmn. bd. dirs. Nazareth Towers, Columbus, 1990-94; bd. dirs. Dominican Acad., N.Y.C., 1990-95; trustee St. Mary of the Springs Montessori Sch., Columbus, 1990-95; trustee Milford (Ohio) Spiritual Ctr., 1993-99, vice chair, 1993-94, chair, 1994-98; mem. fin. com. Dominican Leadership Conf., 1994-96; bd. dirs. Westwood Civic Assn., Cin., 1979-86, past sec., past 1st v.p., past pres.; mem. steering com. Cong. Neighborhood Groups, Cin., treas., 1981-84; mem. planning divsn. bd. Cmty. Chest and Coun., Cin., 1981-88, chair single parent task force study, 1983-85; mem. rev. bd. City of Cin. Commercial/Indsl. Revolving Loan Fund, 1982-84; bd. dirs. Cin. Area Chpt. ARC, 1982-89, chair nursing and health com., 1983-87, bd. exec. com., 1987-89; bd. dirs. SW Ohio Residences, Cin., 1983-89, vice chair, 1984-87, chair, 1987-89; trustee Providence Fund, Franciscan Sisters of Stella, Niagara, N.Y., 1996—, C.G. Jung Assn. Ctrl. Ohio, co-chair program com., 1996-99; trustee Las Casas (Ministry to Cheyenne and Arapaho Native Ams.), Canton, Okla., 1996-2003, treas., 1997—2002. Recipient Cmty. Leadership award United Appeal and Cmty. Chest, 1985, 9th Ann. Living Faith award Columbus Met. Area Ch. Coun., 2000. Fellow Am. Coll. Healthcare Execs.; mem. Spiritual Dirs. Internat. Avocations: swimming, cross country skiing, biking. Office: St Mary of the Springs 2320 Airport Dr Columbus OH 43219-2098

BACHMAN, LEONARD, physician, educator, retired federal official; b. Balt., May 20, 1925; m. Sarah Jaffe (dec. May 2005); children: Emily, L. Joseph, Daniel, Jacob. BS, Franklin and Marshall Coll., 1946; MD, U. Md., 1949; MS (hon.), U. Pa., 1969; LHD (hon.), Pa. Coll. Podiatric Medicine, 1975, Hahnemann Med. Coll., 1977. Diplomate Am. Bd. Anesthesiology (assoc. examiner 1965). Asst. resident in anesthesiology U.S. Naval Hosps., Bethesda, Md. and Chelsea, Mass., 1950-52; resident Children's Med. Ctr., Boston, 1952-53; fellow in anesthesiology N.E. Deaconess Hosp., Boston, 1952-53; anesthesiologist, instr. anesthesiology, pharmacology and exptl. therapeutics Johns Hopkins U. Med. Sch., 1953-55; dir. div. anesthesiology Children's Hosp., Phila., 1955-72; dir. health svcs. Commonwealth of Pa., 1972-75, chmn. Gov.'s health care task force, 1971, sec. of health, 1975-79; dir. div. hosps. and clinics HEW, Washington, 1979-83; med. dir. NOAA, Washington, 1983-88; dir. med. affairs, Office Surgeon Gen. USPHS, Washington, 1988-90, dir. med. svcs., 1990-94, ret. Washington, 1994. Asst. prof. anesthesiology U. Pa., 1955-61, assoc. prof., 1961-66, prof., 1966-72; vis. anesthesiologist VA Hosp., Loch Raven, Balt., 1953-55; cons. VA Hosp., Phila., 1961—; hon. vis. prof. U. Iowa, 1964, Einstein Coll. Medicine, N.Y.C., 1970; clin. prof. anesthesiology George Washington U. Sch. Medicine, 1982—. Campaign chmn. Delaware County Dem. Com., 1965; bd. dirs. Cen. Phila. Reform Dems., 1967, pres. 1968; chmn. Health Profls. for Humphrey/Muskie, 1968; mem. Urban Coalition Phila.; bd. dirs. Society Hill Civic Assn., 1968; active Boy Scouts Am. With USNR, 1943-46, lt. M.C., 1950-52. Fellow Am. Acad. Pediatrics, Am. Coll. Chest Physicians, Am. Coll. Anesthesiology; mem. Am. Soc. Anethesiologists, Pa. Soc. Anesthesiologists (pres. 1968-69), Phila. Soc. Anesthesiologists (pres. 1965-67), AMA, Pa. Med. Soc., Balt. City Med. Soc., Phila. County Med. Soc., N.Y. Acad. Scis., Physiol. Soc. Phila., Sigma Xi. Home: 8100 Connecticut Ave Apt 1512 Chevy Chase MD 20215 Personal E-mail: lbach77243@aol.com.

BACHMANN, CHRISTINE ELFRIEDE, orthopedist, surgeon, researcher; b. Donauwoerth, Germany, Aug. 16, 1963; d. Helmut Josef and Ella Babette Bachmann; life ptnr. C. S. Alimi-Jahn; 1 child, Louis E. MD, Tech. U., 1990. Intern in traumatology and orthopaedic surgery The U. NSW, Sydney, Australia, 1989—89; jr. ho. officer gen. surgery Dist. Hosp. Simbach/Inn, Germany, 1990—91; sr. ho. officer Dept. Orthopaedics Baumrainklinik, Bad Berleburg, Germany, 1991—92, Klinikum Landshut, Landshut, Germany, 1993—96; head Shock Wave Ctr. Orthopaedic Practice and Shock Wave Ctr., Germany, 1996—97, med. dir. Germering, Germany, 1998—2004; med. cons. Dornier Med Tech Europe, Munich, 1997; med. dir. Orthopaedic Concept 216, Munich, 2005—. Rschr. Dornier Med Tech., Atlanta, 1990—93. Author: Extracorporal Shockwave Therapy. Master: Acad. Neural Therapy; mem.: Dachverband Osteologie, Bayerische Landes Aerzte Kammer, Deutsche Gesellschaft für Ernährungsmedizin, Verband Süddeutscher Orthopäden, Bundesverband Orthopädei. Achievements include research in effectiveness of extracorporal shock waves in orthopaedic indications. Office: Orthopädie Concept 216 Wolfratshauser Str 216 Bavaria Munich 81479 Germany Office Fax: 004989750769 25. Personal E-mail: christine.bachmann@t-online.de.

BACHMANN, FEDOR WOLFGANG, hematology educator, scientist; b. Zurich, Switzerland, May 23, 1927; naturalized, 1968; s. Theodor E. and Maria (Isler) B.; m. Edith I. Derendinger, Oct. 17, 1957; 1 child, Christian M. MD, U. Zurich, 1954. Diplomate Swiss Bd. Internal Medicine and Hematology. Intern, resident Med. Sch. U. Zurich, 1955-61; trainee USPHS Med. Sch. Washington U., St. Louis, 1961-64, asst. prof. Med. Sch., 1964-68; assoc. prof. Med. Sch. Rush-Presbyn.-St. Luke's Hosp., Chgo., 1968-73; dir. med. rsch. Schering Corp., USA, Lucerne, Switzerland, 1973-76; prof. medicine Med. Sch. U. Lausanne, Switzerland, 1976-92, prof. emeritus, 1992—. Dir. hematology labs. U. Lausanne Med. Ctr., 1976-92, acting chmn. dept. medicine, 1980-81, provost, 1987-91; sci. coord. Thrombosis Rsch. Inst., London, 1995-98; vis. scholar pathology dept. Stanford (Calif.) U., 1986; vis. prof. U. Paris VI, 1991-95; internat. dir. Thrombosis/Vascular Tng. Ctr. Programme, 1994—2005. Editor: Progress in Fibrinolysis, vol. 6, 1983, Fibrinolytics and Antifibrinolytics, 2000; assoc. editor Fibrinolysis; contbr. over 200 articles to profl. jours.; editl. bd. Clin. and Lab. Haematology, 1979-98, Thrombosis and Haemostasis, 1986-88, Schweizerische Medizinische Wochenscrift, 1986-88, Internat. Jour. Haematology, 1990—, CVD Prevention, 1997-2001. Chmn. med. adv. bd. Nat. Hemophilia Found., Greater St. Louis chpt., 1966-68; chmn. nursing svcs. com. Dept. Health and Hosps., City of St. Louis, 1967-68; mem. manpower com. Bi-State Regional Health Program, St. Louis, 1968-69; vice chmn. med. adv. bd. Nat. Hemophilipa Found., Midwest chpt., Chgo., 1971-73, med. adv. bd., Nat. Hemophilia Soc., Switzerland, 1977-85; mem. sci. coun. Swiss Nat. Blood Transfusion Svc., 1978-82; mem. sci. coun. Swiss Cancer Inst., 1980-88; pres. Rsch. Found. on Atherosclerosis and Thrombosis, Lausanne-Le Mont, 1983-2003; pres. Sci. Coun. "Aging and Cardiovascular Disease" of the French Ministry of Industry and Rsch., 1985-86; mem. sci. coun. European Sch. Haematology, 1986—; mem. sci. coun. on biomaterials German Ministry of Tech., 1986-92. Capt. Swiss Army Med. Corps, 1955-56. Recipient prize Internat. Com. of Fibrinolysis, Amsterdam, 1988, Disting. Career award Internat. Soc. Thrombosis and Haemostasis, 1997; grantee NIH/USPHS, 1961-73, Swiss Nat. Sci. Found., 1977-92, Emil Barrell Found., 1955-57, Sandoz Found., 1981-84, Roche Found., 1979-80, Swiss Cancer League, 1979-84, Thrombosis and Atherosclerosis Found., 1983-2003, Swiss Cardiology Found., 1986-87. Fellow ACP; mem. Internat. Soc. Thrombosis and Haemostasis (exec. coun. 1988-94), Am. Heart Assn. (coun. on thrombosis), N.Y. Acad. Scis., Internat. Soc. Haematology, Internat. Soc. Fibrinolysis and Thrombolysis (exec. coun. 1992-93), Am. Fedn. Clin. Rsch., Am. Soc. Hematology, Am. Physiol. Soc., Ctrl. Soc. Clin. Rsch., Swiss Med. Soc., Swiss Hematol. Soc. (pres. 1986-88), Soc. of Medicine Vaudois, Swiss Soc. Internal Medicine, German-Austrian Soc. Thrombosis and Haemostasis (exec. coun. 1989-93), Argentinian Med. Soc. (hon.), Med. Soc. Vienna (corr.), European Thrombosis Rsch. Assn. (hon.), World Heart Fedn. (coun. on thrombosis, pres. 1994-98), Sigma Xi. Avocations: reading, music. Home: Chemin de praz-Mandry 20 1052 Le Mont Switzerland

BACHRACH, CHRISTINE A., social demographer; MS in Sociology, Georgetown U., Washington, 1974; PhD in Population Dynamics, John Hopkins U. Sch. Hygiene & Pub. Health, Balt., 1978. Formerly with Nat. Ctr. Health Statistics, Ctr.'s Disease Control & Prevention; statistician/demographer Ctr. Population Rsch., Nat. Inst. Child Health & Human Devel. (NICHD) NIH, Bethesda, Md., 1988—92, chief demographic & behavioral scis. br., 1992—2008, acting dir. Office Behavioral & Social Scis. Rsch. (OBSSR), 2008—10; rsch. prof. Md. Population Rsch. Ctr., College Park, 2010—. Mem. editl. bd. Jour. Marriage & Family. Mem.: Am. Sociological Assn., Population Assn. of America (past v.p.). Office: Md Population Rsch Ctr 0124 Cole Student Activities Bldg College Park MD 20742 E-mail: chrisbachrach@gmail.com. *

BACIC VRCA, VESNA, pharmacist, researcher; b. Split, Croatia, Sept. 19, 1957; d. Luka and Marija Bacic; m. Andelko Vrca, June 16, 1984; children: Mirna Vrca, Ivan Vrca. Degree in clin. pharmacy, U. Ljubljana, Slovenia, 1989; PhD, U. Zagreb, 2003. Head clin. pharmacy dept. Dubrava U. Hosp., Zagreb, 1992—; asst. prof. clin. pharmacy Sch. Pharmacy, U. Zagreb, 2005—. Fellow, Tex. Heart Inst., 1995. Mem.: Croatian Pharm. Soc, Tex. Soc. Health-System Pharmacists (hon. hon. membership 1995). Home: Korculanska 12 Zagreb 10 000 Croatia Office: Dubrava Univ Hosp Avenija Gojka Suska 6 10-000 Zagreb Croatia Office Fax: 386 1 286 3695.

BACK, ERNST WALTER, pathologist; b. Erbach/Odenwald, Hessen, Germany, Aug. 21, 1960; s. Peter Walter and Elisabeth Back; m. Kirsten Neudeck; children: Justus, Magdalene. MD, U. Heidelberg, 1985; facharzt in pathology, Landesarztekammer, 1991; habilitation pathology and pathol. anatomy, U. Heidelberg, 2004. Sci. asst. U. Heidelberg, Baden-Wuerttemberg, Germany, 1993—98; Leitender Oberarzt pathology dept. U. Clinics, Mannheim, 1998—2008; Inst. Pathology Bremerhaven, 2008—. Bd. dirs. Practical Nephropathology. Mem. quality control in gynecol. cytology com. Landesaerztekammer Baden-Wuerttemberg, Stuttgart, Baden-Wuerttemberg, Germany, 2001—08. Stabsarzt Bundeswehrzentralkrankenhaus, 1991—92, Koblenz, Germany. Recipient Internat. Travel award, ADHF, 1996. Mem.: Internat. Acad. Pathology, German Soc. for Pathology. Lutheran. Achievements include research in unravelling the gene responsible for Peutz-Jeghers syndrome. Avocations: string instruments, classical music. Office: Inst Pathology Bremerhaven Postbrookstrasse 101 27574 Bremerhaven Germany Home: Jierweg 9 27619 Schiffdorf Germany Office Phone: 49-4719-29890. Business E-Mail: back@pathologie-bremerhaven.de.

BACK, JENIFER C., dentist; Grad, U. Ky., Lexington, 1995. Dentist Sarasota Smile Design. Instr. Nash Inst. Author: (publ.) Woman Dentist Journal. Mem.: Seattle Study Club Saragator Chpt., Sarasota Dental Assn., West Coast Dental Assn., Acad. of Gen. Dentistry, ADA, Fla. Assn. of Cosmetic Dentistry, Am. Acad. of Cosmetic Dentists. Office: Sarasota Smile Design 3800 Clark Rd Sarasota FL 34233 Office Phone: 941-927-5411.

BACK, ROBERT WYATT, investment company and pharmaceutical executive, consultant; b. Omaha, Dec. 22, 1936; s. Albert Edward, Jr. and Edith (Elliott) Back; m. Linaya Gail Hahn, Aug. 30, 1964; children: Christopher Frederick, Gregory Franklin. BA, Trinity Coll., 1958; postgrad., London Sch. Econs. and Polit., 1959-60, Harvard U., 1960-61; MA, Yale U., 1960. CLU; CFA, ChFC. Head equity trader, reinsurance rep., security analyst Lincoln Nat. Life Ins. Co., Fort Wayne, Ind., 1964—69; sr. investment analyst Allstate Ins. Co., Northbrook, Ill., 1969-72; investment adv. acct. mgr. Brown Bros. Harriman & Co., Chgo., 1972-74; asst. v.p., investment analyst Harris Trust & Savs. Bank, 1974-82; v.p. instnl. rsch. Prescott Ball & Turben, 1982-83, Blunt, Ellis & Loewi, Inc., 1983-84; v.p. instnl. equity sales Rodman & Renshaw, Inc., 1984-87; v.p. instnl. rsch. ins. Legg, Mason, Wood & Walker, Inc., 1987-89; mng. dir. instnl. dept. J.E. Liss & Co., 1989-92; sr. v.p., sales mgr. SNC Capital Mgmt., 1991—; CEO Iposite.com, Inc.; mng. dir. Your Fundraising Options. Mng. dir. investor pub. rels. CCR Assocs., sr. advisor Ivy Coll. Privileges; mng. dir. Ivy Coll. Privileges Ltd. Liability Cos., Revenyouniverse, dir. devel.; arbitrator NY Stock Exchange, 2002—04; expert witness Nat. Assn. Security Dealers, 2004; exec. chmn. Skull and Bones Coll. Presenters; mng. dir. Sarbanes-Oxley Nat. Pub. Awareness Forum, cons. exec. Pension Protection Act, 2006; sec. 12 Walker Garden Condominium Assn., 2006—; lectr. in field; advisor families and employee groups 401K Adv. Svcs. Co-author: Yale in the Modern World: The Yale Presidential Succession, Bush/Clinton/Bush, Big Money and the Presidential Elections, Adult Authors: Big Money Hurting Yale's Future; contbr. articles to profl. jours. Active founding coun. Nat. Edn. Access Fund, 1992; pres. Buffalo Grove Police Pension Fund, 1973—90; mem. long-range planning com. Adlai Stevenson HS, Prairie View, Ill., 1980—82; chmn. investments Ill. Police Pension Fund Assn., Chgo., 1985—87, fund mgr. AIDS/HIV Select Fund, 1992—; mem. corp. Scholarships for Ill. Residents; vice chmn. Wheaton Cmty. Media Commn., 1996—2007; deacon Presbyn. Ch. Capt. USAFR, 1958—67. Woodrow Wilson fellow, Yale U., 1958, English-Speaking Union fellow, London Sch. Econs., 1959, Russian Rsch. fellow, Harvard U., 1960—61. Fellow: Fin. Analysts Fedn. (internat. del. 1974—); mem.: Cantigny Am. Legion, Am. Coll. CLUs and ChFCs (bd. dirs. 1986—87), Inst. CFAs (sec., bd. dirs. Chgo. chpt. 1980—84, lectr.), Am. Assn. Individual Investors (life), Soc. First Divsn. (life), Yale Club Ft. Wayne (pres., alumni bd. mem.), Yale Club Chgo. (bd. dirs. alumni assn. del. 1972—, founding coord. grad. and profl. alumni, Assn. Yale Alumni founding coord. grad. and profl. programs), Trinity Club (mem. scholarship Ill. residents inc. 1973—, mem. exec. com. Chgo. chpt. 1987—90, fin. com.), Harvard Club Chgo. (schs. com.), Am. Legion, Phi Beta Kappa, Pi Gamma Mu. Independent. Avocations: skiing, travel, homeland security. Home and Office: Ivy College Privileges Ltd Liability Cos 545 Belmont Ln #204 Carol Stream IL 60188 Office Phone: 630-745-0885. Personal E-mail: backfocus_bob2002@yahoo.com.

BACKLUND, ERIK-OLOF, neurosurgeon; b. Skellefteå, Sweden, May 7, 1931; s. Gustaf Birger and Elsa Elisabet (Jernberg) B.; m. Margareta Hernvald, Oct. 14, 1960; children: Stina, Erika, Britta. MD, Karolinska Inst., Stockholm, 1959, PhD, 1972. Diplomate Swedish Bd. Medicine. Resident in neurosurgery Karolinska Inst., 1960-65, mem. staff neurosurgery, 1965-72, assoc. prof. neurosurgery, 1972-83, dir. Gamma Knife and Stereotactic Surg., 1975-83; prof. neurosurgery U. Bergen, Norway, 1983-93; dir. dept. neurosurgery U. Linköping, Sweden, 1993—96. Guest lectr. in field. Contbr. articles and columns to profl. publs. and public press; ad hoc referee (various profl. jours.);, author published collection poetry; reviewer sci. jours. Mem. Soc. Neurol. Surgeons (hon.), Europa India Found. (hon.), Sociedad Luso-Espanola de Neurocirugia (hon.), Am. Assn. Neurol. Surgeons. Avocations: music, art, cooking, outdoor life.

BACOLLA, ALBINO CLAUDIO, molecular biologist, researcher; b. Turin, Piedmont, Italy, Oct. 14, 1951; s. Luigi and Romana Bacolla. PhD in Biology, U. Turin, Italy, 1976. Fellow Nat. Ministry Internal Affairs Mauriziano Hosp. Ctr. for Endemic Goiter, Turin, 1976—79; tech. dir. screening for congenital hypothyroidism Mauriziano Hosp., Turin, 1979—84, biologist, 1986—87; fellow of Commn. of European Cmtys. Free U., Brussels, 1984—86; fellow SUNY, Stony Brook, 1987—90; rsch. assoc. Boehringer Ingelheim Pharms., Ridgefield, Conn., 1990—92; sr. rsch. assoc. Tex. A&M U. System Health Sci. Ctr., Houston, 1992—2006, asst. rsch. scientist, 2006—08; rsch. scientist dept. carcinogenesis MD Anderson Cancer Ctr., Smithville, Tex.; contractor NIH, Nat. Cancer Inst., Advanced Biomed. Computing Ctr., NCI-Frederick, Md. Author: Thyroid Cancer, 1985, Results and Problems in Cell Differentiation, 1998, Genetic Instabilities and Hereditary Neurological Diseases, 1998, 2d edit., 2006, Encyclopedia of Molecular Medicine, 2002, Encyclopedia of Biological Chemistry, 2004, Genomic Disorders: The Genomic Basis of Disease, 2006, Mechanisms of Chromosomal, Translocations, 2009, Intrinsic Genomic Instability from Natutally Occuring in DNA Sequences, 2009. Home: 401 Quail Run Smithville TX 78957-8405 Office Phone: 512-495-3039. Business E-Mail: bacollaac@mail.nih.gov.

BACON, BRUCE RAYMOND, physician; b. Amherst, Ohio, Nov. 7, 1949; s. Raymond Clifford and Cathryn E. (Fowell) B.; children: Jeffrey Dale, Laurie Katherine. BA in Chemistry, Coll. Wooster, 1971; MD, Case We. Res. U., 1975. Diplomate Am. Bd. Internal Medicine and Gastroenterology. Asst. prof. medicine Case We. Res. U., Cleve., 1982—87, assoc. prof. medicine, 1987—88; assoc. prof. medicine, chief gastroenterology sect. La. State U., Shreveport, 1988—90; prof. internal medicine, dir. gastroenterology divsn. St. Louis U. Sch. Medicine, 1990—2010. Chair subsplty. bd. gasteroenterology Am. Bd. Internal Medicine, 1999-2003, chair subsplty. bd. transplant hepatology, 2004-10. Co-author: Essentials of Clinical Hepatology, 1993; co-editor: Liver Disease: Diagnosis and Management, 2000, Comprehensive Clinical Hepatology, 2006; contbr. numerous articles to profl. jours. Fellow ACP, Am. Coll. Gastroenterology, Am. Soc. Clin. Investigation; mem. Am. Assn. Study Liver Disease (pres. 2004). Presbyterian. Avocation: photography. Office: St Louis U Health Sci Ctr 3635 Vista Ave PO Box 15250 Saint Louis MO 63110-0250 Office Phone: 314-577-8764. Business E-Mail: baconbr@slu.edu.

BACON, GEORGE EDGAR, retired pediatrician; b. NYC, Apr. 13, 1932, s. Edgar and Margaret Priscilla (Anderson) B.; m. Grace Elizabeth Graham, June 30, 1956; children: Nancy, George, John BA, Wesleyan U., 1953; MD, Duke U., 1957; MS in Pharmacology, U. Mich., 1967. Diplomate Am. Bd. Pediatrics, subsplty. Bd. Pediatric Endocrinology. Intern in pediatrics Duke Hosp., Durham, NC, 1957-58; resident in pediatrics Columbia-Presbyn. Med. Ctr., NYC, 1961-63; from instr. to prof. emeritus U. Mich., Ann Arbor, 1963—86, prof. emeritus, 1986—, chief pediatric endocrinology svc., dept. pediatrics, 1970-83, dir. house officer programs, dept. pediatrics, 1981-86, assoc. chmn. dept. pediatrics, 1983-86, mem. senate assembly, 1978-80; vice chmn. dir.'s adv. coun. Univ. Hosp., Ann Arbor, 1981-82; prof. pediatrics Tex. Tech U., Lubbock, 1986—90, chmn. dept., 1986—90, chmn. med. practice income plan, 1989; chief staff pediatrics Lubbock Gen. Hosp., 1986—90; dir. med. edn. and rsch. Butterworth Hosp., Grand Rapids, Mich., 1990-91, med. dir. dept. pediatrics, 1991—95; prof. pediatrics Mich. State U., East Lansing, 1990—95; pediatric endocrinologist Univ. Mich. Hosp., Ann Arbor, 1995—2007, Detroit Med. Ctr., Southfield, Mich., 1996—2001. Coord. profl. svc. C.S. Mott Children's Hosp., 1973-83, mem. exec. com. for clin. affairs, 1975-76, 77-79, assoc. vice chmn. med. staff, 1978-79; chmn. exec. com. Women's Hosp., Holden Hosp., Ann Arbor, 1973-82. Author: A Practical Approach to Pediatric Endocrinology, 1975, 3d edit., 1990; contbr. articles to profl. jours. Capt. U.S. Army, 1958-61. Fellow Am. Acad. Pediat. (treas. Mich. chpt. 1983-86, alt. at-large 1995-2001, coun. Tex. chpt. 1986-89, Pediatrician of Yr. Mich. chpt. 2002); mem. Am. Pediat. Soc., Pediat. Endocrine Soc., Soc. Pediat. Rsch. Home: 3911 Waldenwood Dr Ann Arbor MI 48105 3008 Personal E-mail: gbacon4999@aol.com.

BADALA, FEDERICO, ophthalmologist; MD in Surgery, 1999. Cert. ophthalmology specialist U. Genoa, 2003, glaucoma specialist U. Calif., LA, 2005, cornea & retractive surgery specialist Wills Eye Hosp., Thomas Jefferson U., 2006. Reviewer Am. jour. ophthalmology, 2007—. Contbr. to numerous publs. Mem.: Soc. Italiana Superficie Oculare Cellule Staminali, Soc. Oftalmologica Italiana, Assn. Rsch. Vision and Ophthalmology, Am. Acad. Ophthalmology. Office: Via A Brofferio 7 Rome 00195 Italy Personal E-mail: febadal@yahoo.com.

BADALYAN, RAFAEL ROBESPIER, urologist, educator; b. Yerevan, Armenia, Jan. 8, 1976; MD, Yerevan State Med U., PhD, 1997; Md, NIH, 2004. Asst. prof. NIH, 2004—. Fellow: European Urology Assn. Office: Saryan 40-39 Yerevan 0001 Armenia Office Fax: 37410589810. Personal E-mail: rbadalyan@hotmail.com.

BADDOURA, RASHID JOSEPH, emergency physician; b. Beirut, Aug. 4, 1947; came to U.S., 1974; s. Joseph and Renée Baddoura; m. Rola Tohme, July 15, 1989; children: Joseph, Philip, Karen. BS, Am. U. Beirut, 1970, MD, 1974. Diplomate Am. Bd. Emergency Medicine (examiner 1984-89), Am. Bd. Internal Medicine, Am. Bd. Pulmonary Diseases. Intern Am. U. Med. Ctr., Beirut; resident in internal medicine St. Joseph's Hosp. & Med. Ctr., Paterson, NJ, 1974-76; fellow in pulmonary and critical care Duke U., 1976-79; dir. emergency dept. Meml. Hosp., Danville, Va., 1981-84; corp. med. officer, mem. med. adv. bd. Coastal Healthcare Group, Durham, NC, 1981-86; assoc. dir. emergency dept. Valley Hosp., Ridgewood, NJ, 1986-90, dir. emergency dept., 1990—2000; ptnr., bd. dirs. Valley Emergency Assocs., 1986—, Valley Regional Emergency Group, 1999—2005; pres. Valley Emergency Assocs., 2002—; ptnr., bd. dirs. Bergen Regional Emergency Group, 1998—2003; trustee Valley Hosp. Found., 2006—. Mem. bd. Coastal Found. for Med. Edn., Durham, 1984-89; clin. asst. prof. emergency medicine Georgetown U., Washington, 1986-89; exec. com. bd. trustees Valley Hosp. Found., 2008. Reviewer: Journal of Critical Care Medicine, 2004—. Fellow: Am. Coll. Chest Physicians, Am. Coll. Emergency Physicians; mem.: Soc. Critical Care Medicine. Avocations: hunting, fishing, philosophy, classical music, architecture. Office: Valley Hosp Dept Emergency Medicine Ridgewood NJ 07451 Office Phone: 201-447-8318.

BADEER, HENRY SARKIS, physiology educator; b. Mersine, Turkey, Jan. 31, 1915; arrived in US, 1965, naturalized, 1971; s. Sarkis and Persape Hagop (Koundakjian) B.; m. Mariam Mihran Kassarjian, July 12, 1948; children: Gilbert H., Daniel H. MD, Am. U., Beirut, Lebanon, 1938. Gen. practice medicine, Beirut, 1940—51; asst. instr. Am. U. Sch. Medicine, Beirut, 1938—45, adj. prof., 1945—51, assoc. prof., 1951—62, prof. physiology, 1962—65, acting chmn. dept., 1951—56, chmn., 1956—65; rsch. fellow Harvard U. Med. Sch., Boston, 1948—49; prof. physiology Creighton U. Med. Sch., Omaha, 1967—91, emeritus prof., 1991—, acting chmn. dept., 1971—72. Vis. prof. U. Iowa, Iowa City, 1957-58, Downstate Med. Center, Bklyn., 1965-67; mem. med. com. Azounieh Sanatorium, Beirut, 1961-65; mem. research com. Nebr. Heart Assn., 1967-70, 85-88. Author textbook Spanish translation; contbr. chpts. to books, articles to profl. jours. Recipient Golden Apple award Students of AMA, 1975, Disting. Prof. award, 1992; Rockefeller fellow., 1948-49; grantee med. research com. Am. U. Beirut, 1956-65 Mem. Internat. Soc. Heart Rsch., Am. Physiol. Soc., Internat. Soc. for Adaptive Medicine (founding mem.). Home: PO Box 147 Panama NE 68419-0147

BADEN, MICHAEL M., pathologist, educator; b. Bronx, NY, July 27, 1934; s. Harry and Fannie (Linn) B.; m. Judianne Densen-Gerber June 14, 1958 (div. 1997); m. Linda Kenney, 2000; 4 children. BS, CCNY, 1955; MD, NYU, 1959. Diplomate Am. Bd. Pathology. Intern, first med. div. Bellevue Hosp., NYC, 1959-60, resident, 1960-61, resident in pathology, 1961-63, chief resident in pathology, 1963-64, fellow in pathology, 1964-65; pvt. practice in pathology NYC, 1965—; asst. med. examiner City of NY, 1961-65, jr. med. examiner, 1965-66, assoc. med. examiner, 1966-70, dep. chief med. examiner, 1970-78, 79-81, 83-86, chief med. examiner, 1978-79; dep. chief med. examiner, dir. labs. Suffolk County, NY, 1981-83; dep. chief med. examiner NYC, 1983-86; dir. forensic scis. unit NY State Police, 1986—; instr. in pathology NYU, NYC, 1964-65, asst. prof. pathology, 1966-70, assoc. prof. forensic medicine, 1970-89; private practice. Adj. prof. law NY Law Sch., NYC, 1975-88, John Jay Coll. Criminal Justice, NYC, 1989-90, 93; vis. prof. pathology Albert Einstein Sch. Medicine, NYC, 1975—; lectr. pathology Coll. Physicians and Surgeons, Columbia U., NYC, 1975—, adj. prof. pathology and lab. medicine, 1993—; asst. vis. pathologist Bellevue Hosp., NYC, 1965-75; adj. prof. pathology and lab. medicine Albany (NY) Med. Sch.; lectr. Drug Enforcement Adminstrn., Dept. Justice, 1973—; vis. lectr. Fairleigh Dickinson Dentistry, Hackensack, NJ, 1968-70; spl. forensic pathology cons. NY State Organized Crime Task Force, 1971-75; chmn. forensic pathology panel US Ho. of Reps. select coms. on assassinations of Pres. John F. Kennedy and Dr. Martin Luther King, Jr., 1977-79; mem. med. adv. bd. Andrew Menchell Infant Survival Found., 1969-74; mem. cert. bd. Addiction Svcs. Agy., NYC, 1966-69; preceptor health research tng. program NYC Dept. Health, 1968-79; v.p. Coun. for Interdisciplinary Communication in Medicine, 1967-69; forensic pathology cons. NY State Police, 1985-; involed as an expert in several cases including the examination of the remains of Czar Nicholas and his family, death of John Belushi, second autopsy of the civil rights leader Medgar Evers, and the autopsies of victims of TWA Flight 800; expert in criminal cases, including O.J. Simpson, Claus Von Bulow and Marlon Brando's son, Christian. Author: Alcohol, Other Drugs and Violent Death, 1978, Unnatural Death, 1989 (with Marion Roach) Dead Reckoning: New Science of Catching Killers, 2001, (novels with Linda Kenney) Remains Silent, 2005; contbr. articles on forensic medicine to profl. jours.; mem. editorial bd. Am. Jour. Drug and Alcohol Abuse, 1973—, Internat. Microfilm Jour. Legal Medicine, 1969-73, Contemporary Drug Problems, 1971; host, HBO series, Autopsy, 1995-; forensic sci. contbr., Fox National News. Active NY adv. bd. Odyssey House, Inc., 1966-76; bd. dirs. NY Coun. on Alcoholism, sec., 1969-79; bd. dirs. Belco Scholarship Found., Inc., 1971-87. Recipient Great Tchr. award NYU, 1980 Fellow Coll. Am. Pathologists (chmn. toxicology subcom. 1972-74), Am. Soc. Clin. Pathologists (mem. drug abuse task force 1973—), Am. Acad. Forensic Scis. (program chmn. 1971-72, sec. sect. pathology and biology 1970-71, exec. com. 1971-74, v.p. 1982-83); mem. Med. Soc. County NY (mem. pub. health com. 1966-76), Soc. Med. Jurisprudence (corr. sec. 1971-78, v.p. 1979-81, pres. 1981-85, chmn. bd. 1985—), Nat. Assn. Med. Examiners, NY Path. Soc., NY State Med. Soc., AMA, Internat. Royal Coll. Health Home: 15 W 53 St New York NY 10019 Office Phone: 212-397-2732.

BADEN, THOMAS JAMES, dermatologist; b. Coral Gables, Fla., Dec. 29, 1951; s. Thomas Benjamin and Helen (Threadgill) B.; m. Sandra Louise Bradley, June 22, 1974; children: Craig, Scott, Michael. AB in Chemistry, Duke U., 1973; MD cum laude, Emory U., 1977. Diplomate Am. Bd. Internal Medicine, Am. Bd. Dermatology. Internal medicine resident N.C. Meml. Hosp., Chapel Hill, 1977-80, dermatology resident, 1983-86; internist Toe Valley Med. Assn., Spruce Pine, NC, 1980-83; dermatologist West Piedmont Dermatology Assn., Morganton, NC, 1986—. Consulting dermatologist Western Carolina Ctr., Broughton Hosp., Morganton, 1986—; staff dermatologist Grace Hosp., Morganton, 1986—. Contbr. articles to profl. jours. Deacon First Bapt. Ch., Morganton. Fellow ACP, Am. Acad. Dermatology, Am. Soc. Dermatology Surgeons; mem. AMA, Christian Med. Soc. Avocations: music, hiking, photography. Home and Office: West Piedmont Dermatology 111 Foothills Dr Morganton NC 28655-5152

BADER, ROBERT SMITH, biology and zoology educator, researcher; b. Falls City, Nebr., June 18, 1925; s. Ray Jay and Grace (Smith) B.; m. Joan Larson; children: Douglas, Jonathan, Eric, Joel. BS, Kans. State U., 1949; PhD, U. Chgo., 1954. From instr. to asst. prof. biology U. Fla., 1952-56; from asst. prof. to prof. zoology U. Ill., Urbana, 1956-68; prof. biology, dean Coll. Arts and Scis., U. Mo., St. Louis, 1968-83, rsch. prof., 1983-85; rsch. assoc. dept. history U. Kans., 1985-91. Adj. prof. history Kans. State U., 1986-91. With USNR, 1943-45. Achievements include research on Kansas history, prohibition history, Biblical theology. Home: 2165 Squirrel Rd Neosho Falls KS 66758-7122 E-mail: jlbader@terraworld.net.

BADER, THOMAS J., gynecologist, obstetrician; M in Govtl. Adminstrn., U. Pa.; MD, Georgetown U. Diplomate Am. Bd. Ob-Gyn. Resident ob-gyn. Univ. Pa. Hosp.; fellow ob-gyn. Univ. Pa., fellow biostatistics and epidemiology; chmn. Crozer- Chester Med. Ctr. Office: Crozer- Chester Medical Center One Medical Center Blvd Chester PA 19013 Office Phone: 610-447-2000.

BADETTI, ROLANDO EMILIO, health science facility administrator; b. Istanbul, Turkey, Mar. 25, 1947; s. Umberto and Iole (Bianchi) B.; m. Emanuela Ponte, Oct. 29, 1973; children: Barbara, Fabiana. PhD in Pharmacy, U. Padua, Italy, 1971. Mfg. supr. Gruppo Lepetit, El Jadida, Morocco, 1971-76, plant mgr., 1977-79, quality assurance mgr. Milan, 1980-81, material mgr., 1982-83; tech. dir. Lirca Synthelabo, Milan, 1983-91; gen. mgr. asst. Arval, Milan, 1991-92; tech. dir. UCB Pharma, Turin, 1992—96, ATP Avant-Garde Techs. & Products, Vacallo, Switzerland, 1997—2002; R&D dir. Rivopharm, Manno, Switzerland, 2002—04, DPB, Lugano, Switzerland, 2004—05, Qualified Person Evultis, Lugano, 2005—09.

BADLANI, GOPAL, medical educator; Degree in internal sci., Bombay U., 1968; MD, T.N. Med. Coll. Bombay U., 1972. Resident L.I. Jewish Med. Ctr., NY, 1975, 1980, St. Agnes Hosp., Balt., 1976; fellow Baylor U. Sch. Medicine, Houston, 1983; clin. asst. Queen Mary Hosp., Sidcup, England, 1975; pvt. practice East Nassau Med. Group, NY, 1980—83; attending physician L.I. Jewish Med. Ctr.,

1983—, chief neurology and prosthetics, dept. urology New Hyde Park, NY, 1990—; attending physician dept. urology Queens Hosp. Ctr., Jamaica, NY, 1983—, chief dept. urology, 1983—96; assoc. prof. dept. urology Albert Einstein Coll. Medicine, Bronx, 1992—96, prof. dept. urology, 1996—; program dir., assoc. chmn. dept. urology North Shore L.I. Jewish Med. Ctr.; prof., vice chair rsch. affairs, dir. uro-gynecology regenerative medicine program, dept. urology Wake Forest U., Winston-Salem, NC, 2007—. Contbr. articles various profl. jours. Recipient Essay Contest award, Urological Soc., 1979, 1st prize Movie, Am. Urology Assn., 1990. Mem.: Queens Urol. Soc., Bklyn. Urol. Soc., N.Y. Acad. Medicine (chmn. 1995—96), Soc. for Minimally Invasive Therapy, L.I. Urol. Soc. (pres. 1990—92), Urodynamic Soc., Assn. Indian Urologists in N.Am., Endourology Soc. (treas.), N.Y. State Med. Soc., Nassau County Med. Soc., Am. Urol. Assn. (sec. elect 2011—). Achievements include patents for vesicovaginal ambulatory monitor, 1992. Office: Wake Forest University Medical Center Blvd Winston Salem NC 27157-1094 Office Phone: 336-716-4131. Business E-Mail: gbadlani@wakehealth.edu.

BADR EL-DIN, NARIMAN KAMAL, biologist, educator; m. Galal El-Din Hassan Thabet; children: Yasmine Galal El-Din Thabet, Ahmed Galal El-Din Thabet. BSc in Chemistry & Zoology (hon.), Cairo U.; MSc in Radiobiology, Mansoura U.-Nat. Cancer Inst. Cairo U., Egypt; PhD in Cancer Biology, Nat. Cancer Inst. Prof. faculty sci. U. Mansoura, Egypt. Asst. prof. Coll. Medicine and Med. Scis. King Fasal U., El-dammam, Saudi Arabia, 1989—94; vis. postdoc. scientist Dept. Nutrition, U. Nev., Reno, 2002. Contbr. scientific papers. Referee mem. Egyptian Univs. Promotion Com. Recipient Sci. Distinction award, U. Mansoura, 2009. Mem.: Am. Assn. Cancer Rsch., Am. Chem. Soc., Zool. Soc. (A.R.E.), Egyptian Soc. Biochemistry & Molecular Biology, Am. Assn. Cancer Rsch. Achievements include research in several novel potential anticancer agents derived from natural product that showed amazing effect in the treatment of solid tumors such as MGN-3/Biobran and the Baker's yeast; MGN-3/Biobran compound was introduced into the potential groups of natural antitumor agents with no toxic effect that showed potential treatment of solid tumor in experimental animal models; in vivo effect of the Baker's yeast Sacchromyces cerevisia as a potent anticancer agents was highly significant. Avocations: travel, photography, walking. Office: Univ Mansoura Faculty Sci Mansoura 35516 Egypt Office Fax: 2-050-2246781. Business E-Mail: na_ri_eg@yahoo.com.

BAE, CHANG HOON, otolaryngologist, educator; b. Daegu, Republic of Korea, Feb. 19, 1970; s. Sang Chul and Sul Ja Bae; m. Hye Gyoung Kang, Nov. 15, 1997; children: Joo Hyoung, Jin Ho. MD, Yeungnam U., Daegu, Republic of Korea, 1994, PhD, 2002. Lic. Min. Health, Welfare and Family Affairs, Republic of Korea, 1994, cert. otolaryngologist 1999. Rotating intern Yeungnam U. Med. Ctr., 1994—95, resident, 1995—99, clinician, 1999—2001, instr., dept. otorhinolaryngology-head & neck surgery, coll. medicine, 2005—07; asst. prof., dept. otorhinolaryngology-head & neck surgery Coll. Medicine, Yeungnam U., 2007—11, assoc. prof., dept. otorhinolaryngology-head & neck surgery, 2011—. Practitioner Dr. Bae's Otorhinolaryngology-Head & Neck Surgery Clinic, Gyeongsan, Gyeongsangbuk-Do, 2001—04. Contbr. articles to profl. jours. Mem.: Korean Audiological Soc., Korean Balance Soc., Korean Otologic Soc., Korean Rhinologic Soc. Home: #101-701 Jungwha Woobang Palace Apt Daegu 706-775 Republic of Korea Office: Yeungnam University Med Ctr 317-1 Daemyeong 5-Dong Nam-Gu 705-717 Daegu Daegu Republic of Korea Office Fax: 82-53-628-7884. Business E-Mail: baech@ynu.ac.kr.

BAE, DUK SOO, obstetrician, gynecologist, researcher; b. Seoul, Republic of Korea, Sept. 18, 1955; s. Won Keun Bae and Moon Rang Jung; m. Hye Sook Shim; children: Jung Won, Jung Min, Sung Jae. MS, Seoul Nat. U., Korea, 1988, PhD, 1991. Lic. doctor Ministry Health and Welfare, Republic of Korea, 1980. Intern Seoul (Korea) Nat. U., 1983—84, resident, 1985—88; chief dept. ob-gyn. Seoul (Korea) Redcross Hosp., 1988—92; prof. Sungkyunkwan U., Soowon, Republic of Korea, 1992—. Rsch. assoc. Med. Ctr. Duke U., Durham, NC, 1992—94. Contbr. articles to profl. jours. Lt, Korean Navy, 1980—83. Grantee, Insung Med. Sci. Found., 2003—05, 2005—. Mem.: Korean Soc. Gyn. Endoscopy (dir. 2004—05), Korean Soc. Gyn. Oncology and Colposcopy (dir. 2004—05), Korean Soc. Ob.-gyn. (dir. 2004—05), Korean Assn. Ob.-gyn. Home: 213-1402 Sibum Woosung apartment Seohyun-Dong Bundang-Gu Sungnam 463-050 Republic of Korea Office: Samsung medical center 50 Ilwon-Dong Kangnam-Gu Seoul 135-710 Republic of Korea Office Fax: 02-3410-0630. Business E-Mail: dsbae@smc.samsung.co.kr.

BAE, HAN-IK, medical educator, director; b. Daegu, Dec. 28, 1956; MD, Kyungpook Nat.U. Sch. Medicine, 1980; PhD, Kyungpook Nat. U., Daegu, Republic of Korea, 1987. Assoc. prof. Dongguk U. Hosp., Kyong-Ju, Kyungpook, Republic of Korea, 1993—96; prof. Kyungpook Nat. U. Sch. Medicine, 1997—. Dir. Nat. Biobank Korea, 2008—. Recipient Minister award, Ministry of Health, Welfare & Family Affairs. Office: 101 Dongin 2Ga Jung-gu Daegu 700-422 Republic of Korea E-mail: baehi@knu.ac.kr.

BAE, JANGHO, cardiologist, educator; b. Daegu, Kyungsangbuk-Do, Republic of Korea, Mar. 28, 1967; s. Hyojoon Bae and Eunja Jeong; m. Sohyoung Park, Sept. 25, 1993; children: Jeeweon, Jeesoo. PhD, Keimyung U., Daegu, 1995—98. Diplomate 1991. Intern DongSan Med. Ctr., Daegu, Kyungsangbuk-Do, Republic of Korea, 1991—92, resident, 1992—96, fellow, 1996—99; clin. dir. Andong (Korea) Presbyn. Hosp., 1999—2000; dir. divsn. cardiology Konyang Univ. Hosp., Daejeon, Choongcheong-Do, Republic of Korea, 2000—. Contbr. articles to profl. jours. and publs., 2001. Mem.: Basic Cardiovascular Sci. Coun., Korean Soc. of Circulation (Seoul 1997—now). Home: Daejayeon Apt 107 1105 Gwanjeo-Dong Daejeon Republic of Korea Office: Cardiology Dept Konyang Univ Hosp 685 Gasoowon-Dong Seo-Gu Choongcheong-Do Daejeon 302-718 Republic of Korea Office Phone: 82-42-600-9400. Office Fax: 82-42-600-9420. Personal E-mail: janghobae@yahoo.co.kr. Business E-Mail: jhbae@kyuh.co.kr.

BAE, JEOUNGWON, surgeon, educator; s. Pan Dong Bae and Ul Saek Jung; m. Ok Hee Han; children: Soo Yean children: Jae Yean. MD, Korea U. Coll. Medicine, Seoul, 1977; MS, Postgrad. Sch. Korea U., Seoul, 1980; PhD, Chung Ang U., Seoul, 1991; degree in Advanced Mgmt. Procedure, Korea U. Bus. Sch., Seoul, 2007. Lic. in medicine Ministry of Health and Welfare, 1977, cert. Korean Surg. Soc. Nat. Bd., 1982. Rotating intern and resident Korea U. Hosp., Seoul, 1977—82; instr. Korea U., 1985—87, asst. prof., 1987—91, assoc. prof., 1991—96, prof., 1996—; rsch. fellowship NY Med. Coll., NYC, 1989—90; head, med. sci. Korea U. Coll. Medicine, 1995—96, academic vice dean, 2001—03. Adv. bd. mem. Roche Korea, Seoul, 2005—, Kyunghyang Newspaper Co., Seoul, Global Breast Cancer Conf., Seoul, 2007. Author: (book) The Breast, Self Management of Lymphedema after Breast Cancer Operation. Capt. Med., 1982—85, Korea. Recipient Pres. award, Korea U., 1977. Mem.: Korean Soc. Clin. Oncology, Korean Assn. Endocrine Surgeon (exec. bd. 1999—), Am. Soc. Clin. Oncology, Am. Soc. Breast Disease, Korean Cancer Soc., Korean Surg. Soc., Korean Med. Assn., Korean Breast Cancer Soc. (exec. bd. 1999—2006, vice and elected pres. 2007—, DongA 2007). Office: Korea Univ Hosp 5th St Anam-Dong Sungbuk-gu Seoul 136-705 Republic of Korea Office Phone: 82-2-920-5305. Office Fax: 82-2-928-9231. Business E-Mail: kujwbae@korea.ac.kr.

BAE, KWANG-HAK, dental educator; b. Milyang, Kyoungsangnando, Republic of Korea; s. Bong-Han Bae and Suhn-Yi Lee; m. Hyang-Sun Kim, Nov. 5, 2000; 1 child, Sung-Hyoun. DDS, Seoul Nat. U., Republic of Korea, 1997, MDS, 2000, PhD, 2005. Lic. in dental Dept. Health, Republic of Korea, 1997. Tchg. asst. Seoul Nat. U., 1997—2001, asst. prof., 2006—10, assoc. prof., 2010—; lectr. Pusan Nat. U., Republic of Korea, 2004—06. Recipient Commendation award, Min. Health & Welfare, 2010. Avocations: swimming, reading. Office: Seoul National University School Dentistry Dept Preventive Public Health Dentistry 28-22 Yeongeon-Dong Seoul Jongno 110-749 Republic of Korea Business E-Mail: baekh@snu.ac.kr.

BAE, KYUNGDONG, immunologist, researcher, vaccine specialist, educator; b. Yousu, Republic of Korea, May 19, 1966; PhD, Inha U., Incheon, Republic of Korea, 2004. Rschr. Hani group Hanhyo Inst., DaeJon, Republic of Korea, 1992—98; dir. Crucell Korea, Inchen, 1998—. Adj. prof. Inha U., Incheon, 2006—. Contbr. articles to profl. jours. With Korean Mil., 1990—92. Achievements include research in characterization of HBsAg, detoxification of various toxins, vaccine development, fermentation and purification technology; patents in field. Home: 504-103 Kolong Apt Kugal-Dong Kiheung-gu Yongin 449-903 Republic of Korea Office: Berna Biotech Korea Crucell Korea 13-42 Songdo-dong Yeonsu-gu Incheon 406-840 Republic of Korea Office Phone: 82-10132-290-8602. Office Fax: 82-(0)32-232-3029. Personal E-mail: csbae0@empal.com. Business E-Mail: kyungdong.bae@crucell.kr.

BAE, YONG CHAN, plastic surgeon, educator; b. Busan, Republic Of Korea, Dec. 4, 1963; s. Jeong Ho Bae and Si Ja Jeong; m. Ji Young Park; children: Hyun Tai, Jin Whan. BS, Pusan Nat. U., Busan, 1987; MS, Pusan Nat. U., 1990, PhD, 1999. Lic. Ministry Health, 1987. Chmn. Dept. Plastic Surgery, Pusan Nat. U. Hosp., 1998—2008, head prof., 1998—2002, assoc. prof., 2002—07, prof., 2007—; clin. rsch. fellow U. Toronto, Canada, 2000—01. Author: (book) Plastic Surgery, Cleft Lip & Palate. Mem.: The Korean Soc. Plastic & Re Constructive Surgeons, Busan. (chmn. bd dirs. 2007—). Avocations: golf, swimming, running. Office: Pusan Nat Univ Hosp 1-10 Ami-Dong Seo-Gu Busan 602-739 Republic of Korea Home Phone: 82-51-628-1990; Office Phone: 82-51-240-7269. Office Fax: 82-51-243-9405. Business E-Mail: baeyc2@hanmail.net.

BAEK, GOO HYUN, hand surgeon, educator; b. Seoul, Republic of Korea, Aug. 29, 1957; s. Suk Ki and Sun Sook (Shin) B.; m. Jae Min Lee, Mar. 15, 1961; children: Seung Yoon, Seung Youb. MD, Seoul Nat. U., 1982; PhD, 1993. Diplomate Bd. Orthopedic Surgery. Sr. staff surgeon Korea Cancer Ctr., Seoul, 1990-92; asst. prof. orthopedic surgery Seoul Nat. U. Hosp., 1993-2001, assoc. prof. orthopedic surgery, 2001—06, prof. orthpredic surgery, 2006—. Contbr. articles to profl. jours. Mem.: Am. Soc. for Surgery of the Hand, Soc. Internat. Chirurgie Orthopedique et the Traumatologie, Internat. Fedn. Socs. Surgery of the Hand (program chmn., gen. sec. 11th congress 2010, mem.-at-large, nominating com.), Korean Microsurg. Soc., Korean Med. Assn., Korean Soc. Surgery Hand (gen. sec. 2000, jour. editor 2000), Korean Orthopaedic Assn. (life; Manrye award 1999, Best Clin. Paper award 2000, gen. sec., treas. 2003—04, SICOT 93 award 2004). Avocations: travel, hiking, skiing, skating, movies, golf. Office: Seoul Nat University Hosp Orthop Surgery Daehak-ro 101 Jongno-gu Seoul 110-744 Republic of Korea Home: Samsung Chervill 1st A-3603 Sinjeong-6-dong 318-10 Yangchon-gu Seoul 158-762 Republic of Korea Office Phone: 82-2-2072-3787. Office Fax: 82-2-764-2718. Business E-Mail: ghbaek@snu.ac.kr.

BAEK, HAN JOO, rheumatologist; Cert. med. specialist Ministry Health & Welfare, South Korea, 1997, in rheumatology Korean Assn. Internal Medicine, 1999. Assoc. prof. Gachon U. Medicine & Sci., Incheon, Republic of Korea, 1999—; head divsn. rheumatology Gachon U. Gil Med. Ctr., Incheon, 1999—. Contbr. articles to profl. jours. Mem.: Assn. Physicians for Humanism, Korean Rheumatism Assn. Office: Gachon Univ Gil Med Ctr Kuwol-Dong Namdong-Gu 1198 405-760 Incheon Incheon Republic of Korea Business E-Mail: baekhj@gilhospital.com.

BAEK, JONG-RYOON, orthopedist, educator; b. Seoul, Republic Of Korea, Aug. 6, 1969; s. Sung-Yong Baek and Ai-Wan Song; m. Moon-Jung Yoon; children: Chae-Won, Hyo-Won. PhD, Korea U., Republic of Korea, 2004. Cert. orthop. specialist Ministry Health and Welfare, 1999, specialist Korean Soc. Surgery Hand, 2006. Clin. asst. prof. Korea U. Hosp., 2004—06; asst. prof. Gacheon U. Medicine, Gil Med. Ctr., Incheon, Republic of Korea, 2006—. Contbr. articles to profl. med. jours. Capt. Korean Army, 1999—2002. Mem.: Korean Soc. Surg. Hand, Korean Soc. Microsurg., Korean Soc. Fractures, Korean Orthop. Assn. Achievements include research in clinical and basic science of orthopaedics. Office: Gachon Univ Medicine Kuwol-Dong Namdong-Gu 1198 405-760 Incheon Incheon Republic of Korea Office Fax: 82-32-468-5437. Business E-Mail: bjr-88@hanmail.net.

BAEK, JU-YEOUL, biomedical engineer, physicist; b. Hwaseong, Gyeonggi-do, Republic of Korea, Nov. 28, 1969; s. Jong-Hwa Baek and Mi-Sun Hong; m. Hey-Ran Lee, Apr. 13, 1976; children: Seo-Bin, Gyu-Bin. BS, Dankook Univ., 1992, MS, 1994, PhD, 1999. Cert. tchr. physics HS Ministry Edn., Korea, 1992. Rschr. agy. for tech. and standards Ministry Commerce, Industry, and Energy, Kwachon, Gyeonggi-do, 2001; sr. rschr. dept. biomed. engring. Dankook U. Coll. Medicine, Choenan, Chungnam, 2001—05; rsch. prof. dept. biomed. engring. Korea U. Coll. Medicine, Seoul, 2006—07, Yonsie U. Coll. Health Sci., Wonju, 2008—09; dept. phys. therapy Korea U. Coll. Health Sci., Seoul, Republic of Korea, 2009—10; se. mem. engring. staff tech. commercialization divsn. Cooperation Team, ETRI, Daejeon, Republic of Korea, 2010—. Author: articles in profl. jours. Sgt. Republic of Korea Spl. Warfare Command, 1998—2000. Recipient scholarship, Korea Sanhak Found., 1989—91; grantee Young Investigator, Korea Sci. and Engring. Found., 2004, Prin. Investigator, Korea Atomic Energy Rsch. Inst., 2006. Mem.: Rehab. Engring. and Assitive Tech. Soc. Korea (corr.), Korean Inst. Elec. Engrs. (corr.), Korean Sensors Soc. (corr.), Korea Soc. Med. Biol. Engring. (corr.). Achievements include research in motion analysis and etc. for the proof of improve by physical therapy; design and development of polymeric BioMEMS devices such as microvalve, micropump, and the flexible microelectrode for the biomedical applications. Office: Electronics and Telecomm Rsch Inst Tech Commercialization Divsn Gajeong-dong Yuseong-gu Daejeon 305 700 Republic of Korea Office Phone: 82-31-299-3820. Business E-Mail: dr100@etri.re.kr.

BAEK, KWANG-HYUN, medical educator; b. Suwon, Kyunggi, Republic of Korea, May 29, 1964; s. Lin-Kee Baek and Choon-Ja Park. BS, Kyung-Hee U., Seoul, Republic of Korea, 1987; MS, U. So. Miss., 1989; PhD, Iowa State U., 1995. Rsch. assoc. Harvard Med. Sch., Boston, 1996—99; prof., dir. Grad. Sch. Life Sci. and Biotech. CHA U., CHA Gen. Hosp., Seoul, Republic of Korea, 1999—. Vice-dir Cell and Gene Threrapy Rsch. Inst., CHA U., 2003—. Author: Human Genetics, 2000, The Prenatal Prescription, 2003. Grantee, Korea Rsch. Found., 1999-2001, Korea Sci. Engring. Found., 1999—2004, Korea Ministry of Health & Welfare, 2001—, Korea Inst. S & T Evaluation and Planning, 2002—. Mem.: European Soc. Human Reproduction Embryology, Am. Soc. Hematology. Home: Hangang Hyundai Apt 111-Dong 703 Ho Heuksesk-Dong Seoul Dongjak-Gu 156-792 Republic of Korea Office: 606-16 Yeoksam 1-Dong Gangnam-gu Seoul 135-081 Republic of Korea Home Phone: 822-816-3324; Office Phone: 82-2-3468-3197. Personal E-mail: genedr@yahoo.com.

BAEK, NAM-IN, chemistry professor, researcher; b. Seoul, Republic of Korea, Sept. 30, 1956; s. Nak-Soo Baek and Ock-Chun Lee; m. Jung-Hwa Kim, Nov. 12, 1983; children: Kon, Bin. BS in Agrl. Chemistry, Seoul U., 1979, M in Plant Physiology, 1983; PhD in Pharm. Scis., Osaka U., Japan, 1989; postgrad., U. Ill., Chgo., 2002—03. Rschr. Nongshim Foods Mfg. Co. Ltd, Seoul, Seoul, 1979—81; sr. rschr. Korea Ginseng & Tobacco Rsch. Inst., Taejeon, 1983—97; prof. Kyung Hee U., Suwon-Si, Kyunggi-Do, 1997—. Dir. Sunkwang Meth. Ch., Seoul, 1993—2005. Recipient Excellent Treatise award, Korean Soc. Ginseng, 1997, Korean Fedn. Sci. & Tech. Socs., 1998; scholar, Adminstrn. Ednl. Affairs Japan, 1985—89. Fellow: Korean Soc. Medicinal Crop Sci. (corr.), Korean Soc. Pharmacognosy (corr.), Korean Soc. Ginseng (assoc.), Korean Soc. Applied Biol. Chemistry (assoc.); mem.: Pharm. Soc. Korea (assoc.), Japan Soc. Pharmacognosy (assoc.). Green Party. Achievements include research in chronological changes in pyridoxine-5'-phosphate oxidase immunoreactivity in the seizure-sensitive gerbil hippocampus; 5-(Hydroxymethyl)-2-furfuraldehyde, Anticonvulsant Furan; development of biologically active compounds from edible plant sources XIV. cyclohexylethanoids from the flower of campsis grandiflora K. Schum. J; research in quantitative analysis of t-cinnamaldehyde of cinnamomum cassia by 1H-NMR spectrometry; development of biologically active compounds from edible plant sources-XII. Flavonol glycosides from trigonotis peduncularis benth and its hACAT1 inhibitory activity; research in agrobacterium-mediated transformation of lettuce with a Amorpha-4, 11-dienes ynthase gene; screening and analysis of transcriptional inhibitors for human CC chemokine CKB8 gene; polyacetylenes and sterols from the aerial parts of chrysanthemum coronarium L.(Garland), Atta-ur-Rahman(Ed.) frontier in natural product chemistry; triterpenoids from the flower of campsis grandiflora K. Schum. as human acy-CoA: cholesterol acyltransferase inhibitors; erogosterol peroxide from flowers of erigeron annuus L. as an anti-atherosclerosis agent; inhibitory activity of isorhamnetin from persicaria thunbergii on farnesyl protein transferase; aceriphyllic acid A, a new ACAT inhibitory triterpenoid; production of a new sucrese derivative by transglycosylation of recombinant sulfolobus shibatae B-glycosidase; accumulation of crude lipids, phenolic compounds and iron in rusty ginseng root epidermis; isolation of a glycoside compound from the aerial parts of garland chrysanthemum (chrysanthemum coronarium L). Home: Ssangyong Apt 104/2001 Mangpo-Dong Suwon-Si Republic of Korea Office: Kyung Hee U Seochun-Ni 449-701 Yongin-Si Republic of Korea Office Fax: +82-31-201-2157. Business E-Mail: nibaek@khu.ac.kr.

BAEK, SEUNG HWA, chemistry professor; b. Nonsan, Republic of Korea, Sept. 26, 1948; s. Sung Heum and Bong Soo (Chung) Baek; m. Hwa Yop Lee, Oct. 8, 1981; children: Jong-Min, Jean-Ha. BSc, MSc, Hannam U., Daejeon, Republic of Korea, 1978; PhD, Hebrew U., Jerusalem, 1986. Assoc. prof. Wonkwang U., Iksan, Republic of Korea, 1989—95, chmn. dept. chemistry, 1990—92, prof., 1999—. Vis. prof. Otago U., Dunedin, New Zealand, 1996—98, Sydney U., 2000, 2006—, Pune U., India, 2002—04. Editor: Oriental Pharmacy and Exptl. Medicine, 2005—; contbr. articles to profl. jours. Recipient Rsch. Sci. award, Wonkwang U., 2002; fellow, Uppsala U., Sweden, 1989—90, Hebrew U., Jerusalem, 1991—92. Mem.: Pharm. Soc. Korea, Korean Chem. Soc., Soc. Cosmetics and Pub. Health (pres. 2005—). Avocations: mountain climbing, reading. Office: Wonkwang Univ 344-2 570-749 Iksan Jeollabuk-do Republic of Korea Office Phone: +82-63-850-6225.

BAEK, SEUNG-HOON, medical educator; s. Yong-Hyun Baek and Young-Chang Choi; m. Bo-Young Chun; 1 child, Kun-Woo. BS in Med. Sci., Kyungpook Nat. U., Daegu, Republic of Korea, 1998, MS in Med. Sci., 2001; MBA, Grad. Sch. Bus. Adminstrn., Kyunghee U., Seoul, Republic of Korea, 2006. Cert. Korean Med. Assn., 1998, lic. Nat. Bd. Orthop. Surgery, Korean Orthop. Assn., 2003, cert. clin. trial specialist Kyungpook Nat. U. Hosp., 2006. Intern Dept. Orthop. Surgery, Kyungpook Nat. U. Hosp., Daegu, 1998—99, resident, 1999—2003, clin. fellow, 2006—07, clin. instr., 2007, clin. asst. prof., 2007—08; instr. Sch. Medicine, Daegu Cath. U., 2008—. Contbr. numerous articles to profl. jours. Capt., mil. physician Korean Army, 2003—06, Yeongi. Mem.: Korean Arthoscopy Soc. (Seoul) (Sci. Paper award 2002), Korean Soc. Sports Medicine (Seoul), Korean Knee Soc. (Seoul), Korean Soc. Fractures (Seoul), Korean Orthop. Assn. (Seoul), Korean Med. Assn. (Seoul), Daegu Med. Soc. Achievements include research in effect of pamidronate. Office: Daegu Cath Univ Med Ctr 3056-6 Dae-myung-4-dong Nam-gu Daegu 705-718

Republic of Korea Home: 102/3401 Centropalace Apt Daebong 1 dong Daegu Jung-gu 700-810 Republic of Korea Office Fax: 82-53-626-4272; Home Fax: 82-53-650-4272. Personal E-mail: insideme@paran.com.

BAEK, WAN KI, surgeon; s. Woon Song Baek and Eun Ae Lee; m. Jung Hyun Lee, Oct. 31, 1990; children: Min Jung, Min Kyong, Min Zhu. MD, Seoul Nat. U., Seoul, 1983; MS, Coll. of Medicine, Seoul Nat. U., Seoul, 1993, PhD; MSc, Seoul Nat. U., Seoul, PhD, 1996. Lic. Physician's Korean Ministry of health & welfare, 1983, Korean Board of Thoracic & Cardiovascular Surgery Soc. of Korean Thoracic & Cardiovasc. Surgery, 1991. Intern Seoul Nat. U. Hosp., Seoul, Republic of Korea, 1983—84; army physician Korean Army, Republic of Korea, 1984—87; thoracic & cardiovasc. surg. resident Seoul Nat. U. Hosp., Seoul, Republic of Korea, 1987—91, surg. fellow, cardiac surgery, 1991—92; chief Sejong Gen. Hosp., Bucheon, Kyonggi-do, Republic of Korea, 1992—94; prof. Coll. of Medicine, Inha U., Incheon, Republic of Korea, 1995—; chief Coll. of medicine, Inha U., Incheon, Republic of Korea, 2002—. Dir., heart ctr. Inha U. Hosp., Incheon, Republic of Korea, 2002—04. Contbr. scientific papers pub. to profl. jour. Mem.: Asian Soc. for Cardiovasc. Surgery, Korean Soc. of Vascular Surgery, Soc. of Korean Thoracic & Cardiovasc. Surgery. Office: Inha Univ Hosp 7-206 Shinheungdong 3-Ga Jung-Gu 400-711 Incheon Incheon Republic of Korea Office Fax: 032-890-3099. Business E-Mail: wkbaek@inha.ac.kr.

BAEK, YONGHYEON, health science association administrator, director, medical educator; b. Hamyang, Kyungsangnamdo, Republic of Korea, Apr. 5, 1970; s. Byungki Baek and JungSoon Cha; m. SangHee Song, Nov. 24, 2001; children: SeungJu Ryan, SuhnJu Christie. BS, KyungHee U., Seoul, Republic of Korea, 1999, MS, 2003, MD, 2006. Cert. oriental med. dr. Korean Ministry Health and Welfare, 1999, in acupuncture & moxibustion Korean Ministry Health and Welfare, 2003. Dir. Korean Acupuncture and Moxibustion Soc., Seoul, 2006—, Korean Oriental Spine and Articular Soc., Seoul, 2006—, Facial Palsy Ctr., KyungHee EW Neo Med. Ctr., Seoul, 2006—; acupuncturist Arthritis & Rheumatism Ctr., KyungHee EW. Neo Med. Ctr., Seoul, 2006—; prof. Coll. Oriental Medicine, KyungHee U., Seoul, 2006—; chief rschr. KyungHee E.-W. Med. Rsch. Inst., 2007—; chief, dept. acupuncture & moxibustion KyungHee U. Hosp., Gangdong, 2010; chief dept. acupuncture & maxibustion Kyung Hee U. Hosp., Gangdong, 2010; assoc. mem. Korea oriental Medicine Edn. & Evaluation Inst. Contbr. articles to profl. jours. With inf. divsn. Korean Army, 1992—93. Recipient Rsch. award, KyungHee U., 2007, 2009. Fellow: Korean Oriental Spine and Articular Soc., Korean Acupuncture and Moxibustion Soc. Achievements include patents for herbal medicine in arthritis, fracture healing, angiogenesis; research in acupunctural mechanism in rheumatoid arthritis, osteoarthritis & herbal medication in bone and joint disease. Avocations: golf, soccer, travel, reading. Office: KyungHee University Hosp Gangdong # 149 Sangildong Gangdong Seoul 134-727 Republic of Korea Office Fax: 82 2 440 6295. Business E-Mail: byhacu@khu.ac.kr.

BAEK, YUNMI, medical researcher; b. Seoul, Sept. 9, 1968; PhD, Ewha Womans U., 2005. Sr. rschr. Korea Hydro & Nuc. Power Co., Ltd., 2005—, rschr., mgmt. and co. evaluation, 2006—. Mem.: Korean Diabetes Assn. Office: 388-1 Ssangmoon-dong Dobong-gu Seoul 132-703 Republic of Korea Office Fax: 82-2-3499-6622. Business E Mail: ympaek2000@hanmail.net.

BAENA TAMARGO, JACINTA, orthopedist; b. Barcelona, Oct. 18, 1974; Degree in Traumatology and Orthops., 2001. Cons. Barcelona U., 1998; traumatology and orthops. specialist Fremap Barcelona, 2001—. Office: Madrazo 8-10 Barcelona Catalonia 08006 Spain Business E-Mail: jacintabacna@fremap.es.

BAER, FRANK M., internist, cardiologist, educator; s. Rudolf and Gabriele Baer; m. Hannelore Krings; children: Matthias, Christian, Julia. MD, PhD, U. Köln, Germany, 1984. Intern, rschr. U. Natal, Durban, South Africa, 1983—85; rschr. Deutsche Sporthochschule Köln, Physiologisches Inst., 1985—87; clin. rschr. U. Köln, 1989—; rschr. U. Dusseldorf, Germany, 1988—89; prof. cardiology U. Köln, 2002—. Author, editor: Circulation, Jour. Am. Coll. Cardiology, Am. Heart Jour., New Eng. Jour. Medicine. Mem.: Am. Coll. Cardiology, Am. Heart Assn., European Soc. Cardiology (sec. working group magnetic resonance imaging 1995—96). Office: Univ Köln Joseph-Stelzmann-Str 9 50924 Koeln Germany

BAER, MARIA RENÉE, hematologist, researcher; b. NYC, Jan. 6, 1952; d. George Bernard and Evelyn Joan (Mandl) Schless; m. Alan Nathaniel Baer, June 4, 1978; children: Tamara, Nicholas. BA, Harvard U., 1973; MD, Johns Hopkins U., 1979. Assoc. prof. dept. pharmacology and therapeutics Roswell Park Cancer Inst., SUNY, Buffalo, prof., 1986—2007; prof. medicine U. Md. Sch. Medicine, Balt., 2007—; dir. hematologic malignancies program U. Md. Greenebaum Cancer Ctr., Balt., 2007—. Contbr. articles to profl. jours. Recipient Nat. Rsch. Svc. award, Divsn. Hematology Vanderbilt U., Nashville, 1984-86. Fellow ACP; mem. Am. Soc. Hematology, Am. Assn. Cancer Rsch., Am. Soc. Clin. Oncology, Cancer and Leukemia Group B, Divsn. Hematology Vanderbilt U., Nashville, 1982-84. Office: U Md Greenebaum Cancer Ctr 22 S Greene St Baltimore MD 21201 Office Phone: 410-328-8708. Business E-Mail: mbaer@umm.edu.

BAER, RICHARD N., lawyer, insurance company executive; b. Glen Cove, NY, Mar. 30, 1957; m. Anne Baer; children: Jane, Carson. BA, Columbia U., NYC, 1979; JD, Duke U., Durham, NC, 1983. Bar: NY 1984, Colo. Asst. dist. atty., Bklyn., 1983—88; staff atty. Securities & Exchange Commn. (SEC), Washington, 1988; assoc. Rosenman & Colin, NYC, 1988—92; chmn. litig. dept. Sherman & Howard, Denver, 1992—2000; spl. legal counsel to chmn. and CEO Richard C. Notebaert Qwest Communications International, Inc., Denver, 2001—02, exec. v.p., gen. counsel, 2002—11, chief adminstrv. officer, 2008—11; exec. v.p., chief legal officer UnitedHealth Group, Inc., Minnetonka, Minn., 2011—. Chmn. Colo. Workforce Devel. Coun. Bd. mem. Nat. Jewish Med. Ctr., Colo. Campaign for Inclusive Excellence. Mem.: Colo. Legal Aid Found. Office: UnitedHealth Group Inc 9900 Bren Rd E Minnetonka MN 55343 also: UnitedHealth Group Inc PO Box 1459 Minneapolis MN 55440-1459 *

BAEZ-TORRES, AXEL ALBERTO, anatomist, pathologist; b. Ponce, PR, Sept. 13, 1963; s. Jose Wigberto Baez-Torres and Osdila Torres-Lugo; m. Raquel Lugo-Diaz, May 20, 1989; children: Axel Manuel, Frances Marie. BS, U. PR, 1985; MD, U. PR Sch. Medicine, 1990; degree in anatomic and clin. pathology, U. Dist. Hosp., Rio Piedras, 1995. Diplomate Am. Bd. Pathology, Nat. Bd. Med. Examiners. Chief resident U. Dist. Hosp., Rio Piedras, 1994; staff pathologist San Pablo Pathology Group, Bayamon, PR, 1996; med. dir. So. Pathology Svc., Ponce, 1996—2000; dir. pathology dept. Hosp. La Conception, San German, PR, 2000—. Asst. clin. prof. Ponce Sch. Medicine, 1996—, senator-acad. senate, 1997—2003; dep. commr. for PR Coll. Am. Pathologists, 1997—. Contbr. articles to profl. jours. Fellow: Am. Soc. Clin. Pathologists, Coll. Am. Pathologists; mem.: Internat. Acad. Pathology, PR Coll. Physicians. Roman Catholic. Avocation: reading. Home: Mansion Real 232 Isabel St Coto Laurel PR 00780 Office: Hosp La Conception Pathology Dept Highway #2 KM 173.4 San German PR 00683 E-mail: fablar@prtc.net.

BAFI, AMMAR S., cardiovascular surgeon; BS, Fordham U., Bronx, 1983; MD, George Wash. U., 1987. Cert. Nat. Bd. Medical Examiners, diplomate Am. Bd. Surgery, Am. Bd. Thoracic Surgery. Resident surgery George Wash. Univ. Med. Ctr., 1988—90, 1991—93, resident cardiothoracic surgery, 1993—95; clin. assoc. fellow dept. of thoracic and cardiovascular surgery Cleve. Clin. Found. Finalist Ralph G. DePalma award, George Wash. Univ. Med. Ctr. Mem.: ACS, AMA, Soc. of Thoracic Surgeons, Am. Med. Polit. Action Com., Chief Residents Com. Office: Washington Hospital Center 110 Irving St NW Washington DC 20010 Office Phone: 202-877-7000.

BAGAN, MERWYN, neurological surgeon; b. Phila., Jan. 25, 1936; s. Frank and Shirley (Lindenbaum) B.; m. Carol Augusta Joseph, Nov. 14, 1964; children: Eric, Seth, Karin. AB, Dartmouth Coll., 1957; MD, Boston U., 1962, MPH, 1995. Diplomate Am. Bd. Neurol. Surgery. Neurol. surgeon Surg. Neurology Profl. Assn., Concord, NH, 1970-93; chmn. Healthsource, Inc., Hooksett, 1985 97. Chmn., pres. Healthsource N.H., Concord, 1985-93; adj. asst. prof. clin. surgery (neurosurgery) Dartmouth Med. Sch., 1981-88; vis. prof. dept. surgery Tribhuvan U. Inst. Medicine, Kathmandu, Nepal, 1997-2000. Chmn.deans adv. bd. Boston U. Sch. Medicine; mem. bd. overseers Boston U. Lt. comdr. USPHS, 1963—65. Recipient Disting. Alumnus award Boston U. Sch. Medicine, 1993, alumni award Boston U., 1999, Suprabal Gorkha Dakshina Bahu award, 2000. Fellow ACS; mem. AMA, Am. Assn. Neurol. Surgeons (pres. 1992-93, humanitarian award 2000), N.H. Med. Soc. (pres. 1983), Congress of Neurol. Surgeons (Disting. Svc. award 1990), Found. Internat. Edn. Neurol. Surgery (chmn.), Alpha Omega Alpha. Home: 173 School St Concord NH 03301-2568

BAGGISH, MICHAEL SIMEON, obstetrician; b. Hartford, Conn., July 22, 1936; BS in Chemistry, U. Louisville, 1957, MD, 1961. Prof. ob-gyn. U. Cin., Sch. Medicine, 1993—2011, Wright State U. Sch. Medicine, Dayton, 2008—11, U. Calif., San Francisco, 2011—. Chmn. dept. ob-gyn. Good Samaritan Hosp., Cin., 1993—2010; dir. residency tng. ob-gyn. TriHealth, Good Samaritan and Bethesda North Hosps., 2006—10; dir. Vulvar Vaginal Clinic, St. Helena Women's Ctr. St. Helena Hosp., Adventist Health Sys., 2010. Contbr. chapters to books, scientific papers. Mem.: Am. Soc. Laparoendoscopic Surgeons. Fellow: Am. Coll. Obstetrics and Gynecology; mem.: AMA. Avocation: historian. Home: 1576 Voorhees Cir Saint Helena CA 94574 Home Fax: 707-963-5641. Personal E-mail: mbaggish@gmail.com.

BAGHIROVA, RAFIGA MAZAHIR, physiologist, researcher; b. Baku, Azerbaijan, Azerbaijani, Aug. 14, 1955; s. Baghirov Mazahir Ismi and Baghirova Gulustan Nobatali; m. Gadjiev Arif Allahyar, Mar. 21, 1997. Student in Human & Animal Psysiology, Baku State U., Azerbaijan, 1974—80; student in Biol. Scis., 1985; postgrad., Acad. Sci., Baku, 1980—84. Sr. lab. asst. A.I. Karayev Inst. Physiology Acad. Scis., Baku, 1977, jr. rschr., 1985, sr. sci. rschr., 1994; docent, faculty gen. & sport physiology Azerbaijan State Acad. Phys. Edn. & Sport, 2002, asst. prof., 2002, prof., 2008. Active Sci. Symposiums and Internat. Congress, 25th Congress Turkish Physiol. Soc., Elazig, 1999, 26th Congress Turkish Physiol. Soc., 2000, Internat. Symposium IBRO, Moscow, 2003, 2nd Internat. Disciplinary Congress, Neurosci. Medicine & Psychology, Sudak, Crimea, Ukraine, 2006, Internat. Congress Neurosci. Medicine & Psychology, Sudak, 2010. Author: Central Nervous System, 2002, Analizatory Sistem, 2005, Psysiological Characteristics of Movement Properties, 2010, Psysiology of Central Nervous and Sensor Systems, 2010, Human Physiology, 2010. Recipient many certs. physiological sci. Mem.: I.P. Pavlov's Nat. Physiol. Soc. Office: Azerbaijan State Acad Phys Edn & Sport Xoyski St 98 Baku Azerbaijan Home: Mir-Jalal St 121 a Flat 9 Baku Azerbaijan Office Phone: 99412 564-92-64. Business E-Mail: rafiga_bagirova1@mail.ru.

BAGNELL, PHILIP C., dean, pediatrician, educator; b. Nova Scotia, Can. Residency Izaak Walton Killam Hosp. Children, Halifax, NS, Canada, Children's Hosp. Med. Ctr., Cin., fellowship in pediatric gastroenterology and nutrition; faculty mem. dept. pediat. Ea. Tenn. State U. Quillen Coll. Medicine, Johnson City, 1991—, dir. pediatric residency tng. program, 1996—98, exec. assoc. dean academic and faculty affairs, chief academic officer, 2000—06, dean medicine, 2006—; v.p. med. affairs Johnson City Med. Ctr., 1998—2000. Fellow: Royal Coll. Physicians and Surgeons Can., American Acad. Pediat.; mem.: AMA, N.Am. Soc. Gastroenterology and Nutrition, American Gastroenterol. Assn., American Acad. Pediat., Tenn. Chpt., Tenn. Med. Assn., Alpha Omega Alpha. Office: ETSU Quillen Coll Medicine Stanton Gerber Hall Ste C-200 Box 70694 Johnson City TN 37614-1710 Office Phone: 423-439-6315. Office Fax: 423-439-8090. Business E-Mail: deanofmedicine@etsu.edu. *

BAGNI, URSULA VIANA, nutritionist; b. Brazil, Sept. 19, 1982; Degree in Nutrition, State U. Rio de Janeiro, 2003; PhD, Fed. U. Rio de Janeiro, 2011. Nutritionist rschr. Fundação Oswaldo Cruz, 2008. Mem.: Internat. Soc. Advancement Kinantropometry. Home: Presidente João Pessoa 197/1902 - Icaraí Niterói Rio de Janeiro 24220-330 Brazil Personal E-mail: ursulaviana@gmail.com.

BAGO, JOSIP, gastroenterologist; b. Imotski, Apr. 18, 1952; MD, U. Zagreb Sch. Medicine, 1976, DSc, 1994. Chief divsn. gastroenterology and pancreatology Clin. Hosp. Sveti Duh, 1979—. Sr. rsch. fellow U. Zagreb Sch. Medicine, 2006—. Mem.: Croatian Soc. Gastroenterology. Avocation: writing. Home: Ladi'ina 9 Zagreb Grad Zagreb 10000 Croatia

BAGSHAW, MICHAEL, medicine educator; b. Formby, UK, July 9, 1946; s. Robert and Alice Bagshaw; m. Penelope Margaret Isaac, Aug. 15, 1970; children: Caroline, Elizabeth. MB, BCh, Welsh Nat. Sch. Medicine, Cardiff, 1973; D in Aviation Medicine, RAF Inst. Aviation Medicine, 1980. Cert. airline pilot lic. Squadron leader Royal Air Force, 1970-86, unit med. officer Lyneham, Wiltshire, U.K., 1974-75, mil. pilot, 1975-79, med. officer test pilot Farnborough, U.K., 1980-86; gen. med. practitioner Nat. Health Svc., Crowthorne, U.K., 1987-90; establishment med. officer Royal Aerospace Establishment, Farnborough, 1990-92; head med. svcs. Brit. Airways, London, 1992—2004; prof. aviation medicine Sch. Biomed. Health Scis. King's Coll., London, 2004—08. Author: Human Performance and Limitations in Aviation, 1991; contbg. author: Aviation Medicine, 2006; contbr. articles to profl. jours. Recipient award of merit Guild Air Pilots and Air Navigators, 1997. Fellow Royal Aero. Soc. (vice chmn. aviation medicine group 1998, Buchanan Barbour award 1984), Aerospace Med. Assn. (chmn. air transport medicine com. 1999, v.p. 2001, pres. 2005-06); mem. Royal Coll. Surgeons, Internat. Acad. Aviation and Space Medicine (sci. com. 1999). Achievements include research in military and civilian aviation medicine.

BAGSHAWE, KENNETH DAWSON, oncologist; b. Marple, Eng., Aug. 17, 1925; s. Harry and Gladys (Dawson) B.; m. Ann Alice Kelly, Dec. 26, 1946 (div. Jan. 1977): children: Janita Marie, James Adrian; m. Sylvia Dorothy Corben, Jan. 29, 1977 (dec. Jan. 1996); m. Surinder Kanta Sharma, July 20, 1998. Student, London Sch. Econs., 1942-43; MB, BS, St. Mary's Hosp. Med. Sch., London, 1952, John Hopkins Hosp., 1956; MD, Charing Cross Hosp. Med. Sch., London, 1961. Fellow Royal Coll. Physicians of London. Sr. registrar St. Mary's Hosp. Med. Sch., 1956-60; sr. lectr. Charing Cross Hosp. and Med. Sch., 1961-63, cons. physician, 1963—, prof. med. oncology, 1975-90, prof. emeritus, 1990-2000. Bd. dirs. Kemble Instrument Co., Eng.; chmn. scientific com. Cancer Rsch. Campaign, Eng., 1983-88, exec. com., 1988-90; mem. Gen. Motors Cancer Awards Assembly, 1985-89. Author: Choriocarcinoma, 1969; contbr. 300 articles to profl. jours.; editorial bd. several cancer rsch. jours.; inventor and patentee in field. Lt. Royal Navy, 1943-46. Decorated comdr. Order of Brit. Empire, 1990 Fellow Royal Coll. Ob-Gyn, Royal Coll. Radiology, Royal Soc., Royal Soc. Medicine (pres. oncology section 1974-75), British Assn. Cancer Rsch. (pres. 1989-94), Assn. Cancer Physicians (pres. 1985-94), Athenaeum. Office: Imperial Coll Charing Cross Campus Lab Block London W6 8RF England Home: 115 George Street W1H 7HF London England Personal E-mail: k.bagshawe@googlemail.com.

BAHADO-SINGH, RAY OLIVER, obstetrician, medical educator; b. Kingston, Jamaica, Aug. 13, 1954; MBBS, U. West Indies, MD, 1979; MBA, U. Tenn., Knoxville, 2008. Prof. ob-gyn. sch. medicine Wayne State U., 2005—, assoc. chmn. edn., 2005—, dir. divsn. obstetric imaging, 2006—. Recipient Pres. Presenter award, Soc. Gynecologic Investigator, America's Top Obstetrician and Gynecologist award, Consumer Rsch. Coun. America; named one of Detroit Super Drs., Soc. Gynecologic Investigator, America's Top Drs., 10th Edit. Maternal-Fetal Medicine, Castle Connolly Med. Ltd., Best Drs. in America, 2011—. Mem.: Soc. Maternal-Fetal Medicine, Am. coll. Med. Genetics, Am. Inst. Ultrasound in Medicine, Am. Coll. Ob-Gyn. Avocations: reading, running. Office: 3990 John R St / Brush N Detroit MI 48201 Office Fax: 313-993-1379. Business E-Mail: mthigpen@med.wayne.edu, rbahados@med.wayne.edu.

BAHCALL, SAFI R., pharmaceutical executive; s. John N. and Neta A. Bahcall. BA summa cum laude, Harvard U.; PhD in Theoretical Physics, Stanford U., 1995. Post-doctoral fellow, theoretical physics U. of Calif., Berkeley, 1995—97; cons. McKinsey & Co., NYC, 1997—2001; co-founder, dir., CEO Synta Pharmaceuticals, Lexington, Mass., 2001—, pres., 2003—. Contbr. articles to profl. jours. Finalist New Eng. Young Entrepreneur the Yr. award, Ernst & Young, 2007; fellow, NSF, 1988—91, ARCS Fellowship, Stanford U., 1991—93, Miller Post-Doctoral Fellowship, U. of Calif. Berkeley, 1995—97. Achievements include the establishment of an integrated drug discovery and development organization. Office: Synta Pharmaceuticals Corp 45 Hartwell Ave Lexington MA 02421 Office Phone: 781-274-8200. Office Fax: 781-274-8228.

BAHK, WON-MYONG, psychiatrist, educator; b. Seoul, Republic of Korea, Oct. 25, 1959; s. Yong-Whee Bahk and Yeon-Soo Cho; m. Seung-Im Son, June 5, 1963; children: Ji-Hun, Soo-Hyun. MD, Cath. U. Korea, 1984, M of Med. Sci., 1987, PhD in Med. sci., 1996. Cert. Korean Nat. Bd. Cert. med. dr. Korean Med. Assn., Korean Nat. Bd. Cert. psychiatrist Korean Neuropsychiat. Assn. Chief dir. exec. com. Korean medication algorithm project for bipolar disorder Korean Coll. Neuropsychopharmacology, Seoul, 1999—; prof. dept. neuropsychiatry Cath. U. Korea, Med. Coll., Seoul, 2005—. Vis. prof. McLean Hosp., Harvard Med. Sch., Boston, 1998—99. Author: (exhbn.) Effect of Amantadine on Weight Gain Induced by Olanzapine, 2002 (Superior Poster award 2002 Korean Neuropsychiat. Assn. Ann. Meeting, 2002), (novels) Korean Medication Guideline for Bipolar Disorders, 2002 (1st Sci. award Korean Coll. Neuropsychopharmacology, 2002). Capt. Capital Armed Forces, 1988—91. Fellow: CINP (Collegium Internat. Neuro-Psychopharmaculogium), Internat. Soc. Affective Disorders (London); mem.: Korean Soc. for Depressive and Bipolar Disorders, Korean Coll. Neuropsychopharmacology (mem. editl. com. bd. 1999—, gen. sec. 2001—), Korean Neuropsychiat. Assn (mem. sci. com. and editl. com. bd. 2001—05). Office: St Mary's Hosp Dept Psychiatry # 62 Youido-Dong Youngdungpo-Ku Seoul 150-713 Republic of Korea Office Fax: 82-2-780-6577. E-mail: wmbahk@catholic.ac.kr.

BAHK, YONG-WHEE, radiologist, nuclear physician, educator, researcher; b. Yongsanpo (Naju), Chonnam, Korea, Sept. 11, 1930; s. Jang-Joo and Gye-Ryun (Son) B.; m. Yeun-Soo Cho, Apr. 19, 1975; children: Won-Jong, Won-Myung, Kyung-Lim, Won-June. MD, Chonnam Nat. U., Kwangju, Korea, 1953; PhD in Med. Sci., Cath. U. Med. Coll., Seoul, Korea, 1965. Lic. physician, Korea; diplomate Korean Bd. Radiology and Nuc. Medicine. Clin. lectr. radiology Jonnam U., Gwangju, 1957-62; resident Boston City Hosp., 1959-60; instr. Cath. U., Seoul, 1962-64, asst. prof., 1964-67, assoc. prof., 1967-69, prof. radiology, 1969—, dir. and chmn. dept. radiology, 1967-92, dean grad. sch., 1986-90, prof. emeritus med. coll., 1996—; chief dept. nuc. medicine Sung Ae Gen. Hosp., Seoul, 1994, 2000, 2007. Lectr. in field; cons. radiologist Armed Forces Gen. Hosp., Seoul, 1980-82. Author: X-Ray Diagnosis of the Chest, 1979, X-Ray Diagnosis of the Abdomen, 1980, X-Ray Diagnosis of Alimentary Tract, 1984-85, Imaging Diagnosis of the Chest, 1990, Combined Scintigraphic and Radiographic Diagnosis of Bone and Joint Diseases, 2000; editor: Radioaerosol Imaging of the Lung, 1994, Nuclear Imaging of the Chest, 1997, Human Radiographic Anatomy, 2000, Molecular Nuclear Medicine, 2003; reviewer and editl. assoc. Jour.

Nuclear Medicine (N.Y.), European Jour. Nuclear Medicine (Heidelberg), Nuclear Medicine Comms. (London), Radiologe (Heidelberg), Jour. Korean Med. Sci. (Seoul), JAMA (Hong Kong), others; contbr. more than 370 articles to profl. jours. Chmn. Yangjae Scholarship Found., Seoul. Capt. Med. Corps Korean Army, 1953-57. Recipient 7 sci. awards including Korean Nat. Acad. Scis. prize, 1995, medal for disting. civil svc. Govt. Republic of Korea, 1996; named Most. Disting. Grad., Chonnam Nat. U., 1997; grantee IAEA, Vienna, 1984-94, Ministry of Edn., Seoul, 1970-72, Cath. U. Coll., 1984-95. Fellow Korean Acad. Sci. and Tech. (sr.); mem. N.Y. Acad. Scis., Asian Fedn. Cath. Med. Assns. (pres.), Internat. Fedn. of Cath. Med. Assns. (v.p.), Korean Radiol. Soc. (Acad. award 1966), Korean Med. Assn. (former dir. acad. award 1971, award of med. book pub. 1984), Korean Soc. Nuc. Medicine (hon. pres., acad. awards 1988, 91), Korean Assn. Radiation Protection (pres.), Am. Soc. Nuc. Medicine, European Soc. Nuc. Medicine, Japanese Soc. Nuc. Medicine, Internat. Skeletal Soc. (faculty), Korean Cath. Physicians Guild (hon. pres.). Avocations: tennis, travel. Home: 201-24 Donggyo-dong Mapo-ku 121-200 Seoul Republic of Korea Office: Sung Ae Gen Hosp PET Ctr Shingil-1-Dong Youngdungpo Seoul 150-031 Republic of Korea Fax: 82 2 2277-8598. E-mail: ywbahk@hanmail.net.

BAHL, SAROJ MEHTA, nutritionist, educator; b. New Delhi, Apr. 4, 1946; came to U.S., 1972; d. L.D. and G.D. Mehta; m. Vishwa Mittar Bahl; children: Rahul, Ragini. BS in Home Sci., Delhi U., 1965, MS in Nutrition, 1967, PhD in Nutrition, 1973. Lectr. Lady Irwin Coll., New Delhi, 1970-71; instr. U. N.D., Grand Forks, 1972-74; from rsch. assoc. med. sch. to assoc. prof. dental sch. U. Tex., Houston, 1976—2002, tenured assoc. prof. dental sch., 2002—; experts Am. Dietet. Assoc. Program dir. Peace Corps, Houston, 1984. Author: Nutritional Management of the AIDS Patient; contbr. articles to profl. jours. Den leader Boy Scouts Am., Houston, 1983; mem. ednl. com. March of Dimes, Houston, 1986—; mem. exec. bd. Indo-Am. Charity Found. of Houston, 1995-98. Recipient several awards for tchg. excellence including John P. McGovern award, 1992, 95; named Outstanding Dietetic Educator Tex. Tex. Dietetic Assn., 1995; nominated for U.S. Prof. of Yr., 1993, 94. Mem. Am. Inst. Life Threatening Illness (assoc.), Am. Dietetic Assn. (work group mem., evidence based guidelines for HIV/AIDS), Soc. Nutrition Edn. (editor newsletter), Minority Faculty Assn. (pres. 1996-97), Vivekananda Vedanta Soc. (pres. 1993-1998). Avocations: painting, music, reading. Office: U Tex Dental Sch Rm B-30 6516 MD Anderson Blvd Houston TX 77030 Home Phone: 281-265-3459; Office Phone: 713-500-4586. Business E-Mail: saroj.m.bahl@uth.tmc.edu.

BAHN, DUKE K., diagnostic radiologist, educator; MD, Cath. Medicine Coll., Korea, 1970. Diplomate Am. Bd. Radiology-diagnostic radiology, 1978. Resident diagnostic radiology Wayne State Univ. Med. Ctr., Detroit, 1975—78; clin. prof. radiology; hosp. affiliations include Hosp. for Special Surgery, New York-Presbyn. Univ. Hosp. of Columbia and Cornell, Prostate Inst. of America. Named one of the Top Doctor, US News, 2011. Office: Prostate Inst. of America Ste 402 168 N Brent St Ventura CA 93003 Office Phone: 805-585-3082.

BAHN, REBECCA S., endocrinologist, educator; BA in Pre-med., U. Minn.; MS in Anatomy, U. Louisville; MD, Mayo Med. Sch., Minn., 1981. Diplomate Am. Bd. Internal Medicine, 1985, Am. Bd. Internal Medicine-endocrinology, diabetes and metabolism, 1987. Trainee immunology/endocrinology Mayo Clinic, trainee endocrinology, resident internal medicine, 1982—84, fellow immunology/endocrinology, 1984—86, hosp. affiliation includes Rochester, Minn.; prof. medicine Mayo Med. Sch., Rochester, Minn. Co-author: (articles) Speed mentoring: an innovative method to facilitate mentoring relationships, 2010, Relationships between thyroid function and lipid status or insulin resistance in a pediatric population, 2010, A stimulatory TSH receptor antibody enhances adipogenesis via phosphoinositide 3-kinase activation in orbital preadipocytes from patients with Graves' ophthalmopathy, 2011, Approach to the patient with nontoxic multinodular goiter, 2011, Hyperthyroidism and other Causes of Thyrotoxicosis: Management Guidelines of the American Thyroid Association and American Association of Clinical Endocrinoloigists, 2011, and numerous other articles. Mem.: Am. Thyroid Assn. (pres. 2007—08). Office: Mayo Clinic 200 First St SW Rochester MN 55905 Office Phone: 507-284-2511. Office Fax: 507-284-0161.

BAHR, GERALD S., critical care specialist, educator; MD, NYU, 1972. Diplomate Am. Bd. Internal Medicine, 1976, Am Bd. Internal Medicine- critical care medicine, 2009, lic. NY. Assoc. clin. prof. Sch. Medicine NYU; resident in internal medicine Lenox Hill Hosp., NYC, 1973—76; chief resident in internal medicine Lenox HIll Hosp., 1975—76; Schwerfeger fellow in internal medicine Lenox Hill Hosp., 1975—76, dir. critical care medicine. Fellow: ACP; mem.: Soc. of Critical Care Medicine. Office: Lenox Hill Hospital Department of Medicine 110 E 59th St 9A New York NY 10022 Office Phone: 212-583-2878. Office Fax: 212-644-2111.

BAHRA, RANBIR S., pulmonologist; b. India, Sept. 25, 1962; MBChB, Aberdeen Med. Sch., 1987. Sr. med. adviser, pharmacology physician Pfizer Ltd., 1996—98; global med. dir. Pfizer Inc., NY, 1998—2002; med. dir. Pfizer Hellas, Athens, Greece, 2002—06; med. dir. team leader Europe cardiovasc., metabolic Pfizer, 2006—09, European head med. affairs, pulmonary vascular disease, 2009—. Avocations: tennis, travel. Home: Braeside Reiagte Surrey RH2 9RE England Personal E-mail: ranbir_bahra@hotmail.com.

BAHRAMI, HOSSEIN, epidemiologist, physician; s. Abdolazim and Mahboobeh Bahrami. MD, Tehran U., 2001; MPH, Johns Hopkins U., 2004. Lic. physician 2001. Intern Tehran U., 1999—2001; methodolgist, epidemiologist Digestive Disease Rsch. Ctr., Trauma Rsch. Ctr. Cardiovasc. Rsch. Ctr., Daryani GI Clinic, 1999—; rsch. fellow cardiology divsn. and Wilmer Eye Inst. Johns Hopkins U., Balt., 2003—. Mem. Sci. Adv. Bd., Arlington, Md.; physician, rschr. Iranian Charity Hepatic Patients Support. Author: (book) Nutrition in Digestive Diseases, Hepatitis; contbr. articles to profl. jours. Vol. physician Iranian Charity Hepatic Patients Support; mem. Hurricane Katrina Relief Com., JHSPH-SA; councilor APHA Governing Coun., 2005—; bd. mem. Sci. Bd., Washington, 2005—. Recipient Ruth Rice Puffer award, Johns Hopkins U., 2005, Eskridge award, 2005, Silverman award, 2005, Dyar Mem. award, 2006, Jay S. Drotman Mem. award, APHA, 2006. Mem.: APHA (mem. governing coun. 2005—, Jay Drotman Meml. award 2006), Soc. Epidemiologic Rsch., Assn. Rsch. Vision and Ophthalmology, Am. Heart Assn., Amercian Coll. Epidemiology (assoc.), Delta Omega. Achievements include invention of New Methods for Improving Scientific Papers; research in New Treatment of Hepatitis B; New PC-Based Eye Tests; Finding different patterns of Fatty Liver in developing countries. Avocations: travel, music, swimming, dancing, camping, hiking. Office: Johns Hopkins Hosp 110 D Nelson 600 N Broadway Baltimore MD 21205 Personal E-mail: nbahrami@gmail.com.

BAHU, MARWAN M., cardiac electrophysiologist; Grad. in Chemistry, U. Calif., Berkeley, MD, U. Mich., Ann Arbor, 1990. Diplomate Am. Bd. Internal Medicine-cardiovasc. disease, 2007, Am. Bd. Internal Medicine-clin. cardiac electrophysiology. Resident internal medicine Univ. of Mich. Med. Ctr., 1992—94, fellow cardiovasc. disease, 1994—97; hosp. affiliations include Banner Good Samaritan Regional Med. Ctr., St. Joseph's Hosp. and Med. Ctr., Ariz. Heart Hosp., Select Splty. Hosp. Phoenix, Casa Grande Regional Med. Ctr. Office: Baltimore Cardiology 4444 N 32nd St Ste 175 Phoenix AZ 85018 Office Phone: 602-952-0002.

BAI, JIANFA, biology professor; b. Xi'an, Shaanxi, China, Feb. 24, 1960; BS, NW Agrl. U., China, 1982; PhD, Kans. State U., 2000. Asst. prof. Kans. State U., 2007—. Mem.: Am. Soc. Microbiology. Avocation: photography. Office: L222 Mosier Hall 1800 Denison Ave Manhattan KS 66506 Office Fax: 785-532-4481. Personal E-mail: jfbai@yahoo.com.

BAI, YUJIE, medical geneticist, director; b. Xingtai, Hebei, Apr. 26, 1965; D, 4th Mil. Med. U., 1996. Vice dir. Zhejiang U., Adinovo Rsch. Ctr. Genetic and Genomic Medicine, 2007—; CTO Beijing Adinovo Gene Tech. Co., Ltd., 2009—. Home: #3 Rd Hainan Med Coll Haikou Hainan 571101 China Personal E-mail: yujiebai@163.com.

BAICY, JANET KAREN, nursing executive; b. Tulsa, Oct. 2, 1944; d. David Alexander Sr. and Helen Marie (Oliver) Simons; John Williamson Baicy, Jan. 20, 1968 (div. 1974); 1 child, Eric Simons. BSN, U. Md., 1967; M in Nursing, UCLA, 1971. Staff nurse Univ. Hosp., Balt., 1967-68; staff/triage nurse emergency dept. Children's Hosp., Hollywood, Calif., 1968-69; writer, rschr. Career Devel. Corp., Glendale, Calif., 1970-72; asst. clin. dir. Deer Park (U. Calif.-San Diego Dept. Psychiatry Inpatient Narcotic Treatment Program, 1971-72; instr. nursing Idaho State U., Boise, 1972-74; coord. activity therapies Dept. Health and Welfare, Boise, 1975; assoc. prof. nursing program Boise State U., 1975-79; clin. specialist VA Med. Ctr., Boise, 1979, nursing supr., 1979-80, assoc. chief nursing svc. for edn., 1981-84, staff nurse, 1984-86; dir. nursing Intermountain Hosp., Boise, 1986-87; head nurse neuropsychiat. and chem. dependency unit West Valley Med. Ctr., Caldwell, Idaho, 1987-89, chief nursing officer, 1989-93; assoc. adminstr. patient care svcs. Coronado Hosp., Pampa, Tex., 1993-94, chief nursing officer, 1993-94; assoc. adminstr. patient care svcs. McMinneville Cmty. Hosp., Oreg., 1993—; nursing cons. Bd. of Nurse Examiners, Austin, Tex., 1995-96; chief of staff, patient care officer Columbus Bayview Psychiat. Hosp., Corpus Christi, Tex., 1996—. Mem. adj. faculty Boise State U., 1991-93, cons., 1994—. Active United Meth. Ch., Caldwell, Idaho, Speakers' Bur., Paint the Town, 1991-92. Mem. ANA, AAUW, Tex. Nurses Assn., Tex. Orgn. Nurse Execs., Idaho Orgn. Nurse Execs., Alpha Phi (Delta Zeta chpt.), Sigma Theta Tau. Democrat. Methodist. Avocations: travel, swimming, reading, music, horse-back riding, dance. Office: Bayview Hosp 6226 Saratoga Blvd Corpus Christi TX 78414-3421 Address: 3701A S Harvard Ave # 319 Tulsa OK 74135-2265 *

BAIK, HYOUNG SEON, orthodontist, educator; b. Seoul, Republic of Korea, Feb. 16, 1952; s. Eun Sin (Lee) Baik; m. Young Jin Kim, Mar. 2, 1956; children: Yoon Jae, Min Jae. MSD, Yonsei U., Seoul, 1980, PhD, 1986. Cert. dentist Ministry Health and Welfare, 1977. Vis. asst. prof. U. N.C., Chapel Hill, 1988—89; chmn. orthodontic dept. Yonsei Univ., Seoul, 1996—, edn. dir. Dental Hosp., 1998—, lectr., asst. prof., assoc. prof., prof. Coll. Dentistry, 1984—, assoc. dean for student affairs Coll. Dentistry, 2000—02; pres. Korean Assn. Orthodentists, 2004—06. Vis. prof. U. So. Calif., LA, 2000; vice dir. Dental Hosp. Yonsei U., 2004—, gen. dir., 2008—. Author: (book) Contemporary Removable Orthodontics, 1999, Contemporary Cephalometrics, 1999, Orthodontics in the 21st Ccentury, 2002, Guide of Orthodontic Treatment, 2002, Surgico-Orthodontics, 2003; referee: Korean Jour. Orthodontics, 1992—, referee, cons.: Am. Jour. Orthodontics and Dentofacial Orthopedics, 1997—, mem. editl. bd.: World Jour. Orthodontics, 1999—; contbr. articles to profl. jours. Overseas dental svc. for mission Upper Rm. Evangelistic Assn., Seoul, 1992—2003; elder Sarang Cmty. Ch., Seoul, 1999; dir. internat. student fellowship ISF, Seoul, 0200; dir. Korean World Missionary Assn., Seoul, 2002. Recipient Best Rsch. award, Korean Fedn. Sci. and Tech. Soc., 1998. Mem.: Korean Assn. Orthodontists (life; v.p. 2000—, pres. 2004—06). Achievements include research in maxillary protraction in Class III children and 3-D image in craniofacial complex. Home: Seocho ku Seocho dong Samho Apt4-803 Seoul 137-074 Republic of Korea Office: Yonsei Univ Coll Dentistry Seodaemunku Shinchondong 134 Seoul 120-752 Republic of Korea Office Phone: 822 2228-3102. Office Fax: 822 363-3404. Business E-Mail: baik@yuhs.ac.

BAIK, SOON KOO, hepatologist; b. Seoul, Republic of Korea, July 29, 1964; s. Chi Kon Baik and Doo Il Park; m. Min Hee Lee; children: Seung Yeon, Seung Min. PhD, Korea U., 2003. Diplomate Korean Med. Assn., 1994. Assoc. prof., chmn. Gastroenterology and Hepatology Wonju Med. Coll., Wonju, Republic of Korea, 2004—. Mem.: Korean Assn. for the Study of Liver (assoc. Rsch. grant 2003). Avocations: golf, mountain climbing. Office: Yonsei Univ Wonju Med Coll San Dong 162 IL 220-701 Wonju Gangwon-do Republic of Korea Office Fax: 82-33-745-6782. E-mail: baiksk@medimail.co.kr.

BAIK-HAN, WON H., pediatrician, educator, consultant; b. Seoul, Jong Ro Gu, Republic of Korea, July 22, 1956; arrived in U.S., 1983; d. Hong In Baik and Ok Hee Chang; m. Muyol Han, Nov. 15, 1986; children: Jeffrey J. Han, Steven J. Han. MD, Ewha Woman's U., Seoul, 1981. Diplomate Am. Bd. Pediat. Intern Soon Chun Hyang U. Hosp., Seoul, Republic of Korea, 1981—82, resident in pediat., 1982—83; pediat. externship St. Elizabeth Hosp. Ctr., Youngstown, Ohio, 1983—84; vol. pediat. physician Flushing (N.Y.) Hosp. Med. Ctr., 1984—86, resident in pediat., 1986—89; fellow in allergy and clin. immunology St. Luke's/Roosevelt Hosp. Ctr., NYC, 1989—91; clin. fellow in allergy & immunology and medicine Columbia U., NYC, 1989—91; dir. pediat. allergy and immunology Flushing (N.Y.) Hosp. Med. Ctr., 1991—, dir. pediat. allergy and asthma clinic, 1991—, consulting physician medicine and pediat., 1991—, com. mem. pharmacy therapeutic com., 1999—. Dir. pediat. allergy Wyckoff Heights Med. Ctr., Bklyn., 1995—99; consulting physician pediat., allergy and immunology N.Y. Hosp. Queens, Flushing, 1997—2000; dir. pediat. allergy clinic Jamaica (N.Y.) Hosp. Med. Ctr., 2000—; asst. prof. pediat. Albert Einstein Coll. Medicine, Bronx, 1994—96, asst. clin. prof. pediat., 1999—; clin. asst. prof. pediat. Cornell U. Med. Coll., NYC, 1997—99; regional spkr. allergy immunology Schering Plough Pharm. Co., NJ, 2001—. Author (with D.M. Rubin): Pediatric Emergency Medicine-Self Assessment and Review, 1994; author: (with A. Stock) Allergic & Immunologic Disease: Pediatric Emergency Medicine-Self Assessment and Review, 2nd edit., 1998. Consulting physician The Korean Am. Nail Assn. N.Y., Inc., Flushing, 1998—, The Korean Sr. Citizen Ctr., Corona, NY, 1999—. Recipient Presentation award for allergy and asthma, Soon Chun Hyang U. Hosp., Seoul, 1992, Physicians Recognition award, AMA, 1999—, Contbn. award for Korean Health Fair, Korean-Am. Nail Assn. N.Y., Inc., Flushing, 1999. Fellow: Am. Acad. Pediat.; mem.: Coalition for Asian Am. Children and Families (com. mem.), N.Y. Allergy, Asthma and Immunology Soc., Am. Acad. Allergy, Asthma and Immunology (Travel Grand award for rsch. project 1991), Hunter Coll. H.S. Korean-Am. Parents Assn. (pres. 2002—). Avocations: drawing and painting, playing pingpong and tennis, singing, collecting coins, stamps and collectibles, collecting antiques. Office: 1st Fl 143-20 Sanford Ave Flushing NY 11355 Home Phone: 516-487-7977; Office Phone: 718-460-3943.

BAIL, KASIA SIOBHAN, nursing educator; b. Switzerland, Nov. 6, 1980; BSN, U. Canberra, 2002. Grad. cert. in higher edn. U. Canberra, 2009. Asst. prof. U. Canberra, 2007—. RN ACT Health, 2003. Recipient Vice-Chancellor's award, U. Canberra. Mem.: Australian Assn. Gerontology, Australian Coll. Nurse Practitioners, Royal Coll. Nursing Australia. Avocations: skiing, drums, Kung Fu. Office: University Canberra Ctr Research and Action in Pub Health Canberra ACT 2611 Australia Business E-Mail: kasia.bail@canberra.edu.au.

BAILAR, JOHN CHRISTIAN, III, retired public health educator, physician, statistician; b. Urbana, Ill., Oct. 9, 1932; married; 4 children. BA, U. Colo., 1953; MD, Yale U., 1955; PhD in Stats., Am. U., 1973. Intern U. Colo. Med. Ctr., Denver, 1955-56; field investigator, biometry br. Nat Cancer Inst., NIH, Bethesda, Md., 1956-62, head demography sect., 1962-70, dir. 3d nat. cancer survey, 1967-70, dep. assoc. dir. for cancer control, 1972-74; editor-in-chief JNCI, 1974-80; dir. research service VA, Washington, 1970-72; lectr. in biostats. Harvard U., Cambridge, Mass., 1980-87; prof. McGill U., Montreal, 1987-95, chair dept. epidemiology and biostats., 1993—95; sr. scientist Office Disease Prevention and Health Promotion, Dept. HHS, Washington, 1983-92; chair dept. health studies U. Chgo., 1995—99, prof. dept. health studies, 1995—2001, assoc. faculty Harris Sch. Pub. Policy, 1999-2000, prof. emeritus, 2001—. Sr. scientist health and environ. rev. divsn. EPA, 1980-83; lectr. epidemiology and pub. health Yale U., New Haven, Conn., 1958-83; mem. faculty math. and stats. USDA Grad. Sch., Washington, 1966-76; vis. prof. stats. SUNY, Buffalo, 1974-80; professorial lectr. George Washington U., Washington, 1975-80; cons. in biostats. and epidemiology Dana-Farber Cancer Inst., Boston, 1977-83; vis. prof. Harvard U., 1977-79; spl. appointment grad. faculty U. Colo. Med. Ctr., Denver, 1979-81; scholar in residence NAS, 1992-96, 2002—. Mem. editl. adv. bd. Cancer Rsch., 1968-72; statis. cons. New Eng. Jour. Medicine, 1980-91; mem. bd. editors New Eng. Jour. Medicine, 1992-96; contbr. numerous articles to profl. jours. John D. and Catherine T. MacArthur Found. fellow, 1990-95. Fellow AAAS (chair sect. U 2000-01), Am. Coll. Epidemiology, Am. Statis. Assn. (chair-elect and chair biometric sect. 1979-81, founding chair sect. stats. and environment 1990); mem. Am. Med. Writer's Assn. (hon.), Inst. of Medicine, Internat. Statis. Inst., Coun. Biology Editors (chair publishing policy com. 1983-89, pres.-elect, pres., past pres. 1986-89), Soc. Risk Analysis (founding chair Boston chpt. 1985-86). Office: Apt 8 2101 Connecticut Ave NW Washington DC 20008 Business E-Mail: jcbailar@midway.uchicago.edu.

BAILEY, CARLA LYNN, nursing administrator; b. Balt., June 4, 1957; d. Carlton L. and Helen P. (Wales) B. BSN, U. Md., Balt., 1979; MS in Health Sci., Towson U., Md., 1987; PhD in Healthcare Mgmt., Century Brentwick U., 2000. Nurse clinician I, charge nurse, clin. nurse U. Md. Med. Systems, Balt., 1981—87; maternal transport coord. U. Md. Med. Systems Hosp., Balt., 1979—96; rsch. nurse Tokos Med. Corp., Balt., 1988—91; perinatal care coord. U. Md. Med. Systems/Hosp., 1993—99; perinatal programs dir. Md. Inst. Emergency Med. Svcs. Sys., 1999—. Mem. assoc. faculty U. Md. Sch. Nursing, 1993-95; mem. fetal and infant mortality rev. bd. Healthy Start; mem. State Commn. on Infant Mortality Prevention. Mem. Assn. Women's Health, Obstetric and Neonatal Nurses, Md. Nurse's Assn., Nat. Perinatal Assn. (bd. dirs.) Office Phone: 410-706-3931. E-mail: cbailey@miemss.org.

BAILEY, HAROLD RANDOLPH, surgeon, educator; b. Palestine, Tex., Jan. 20, 1943; m. Kelly Curry Bailey. BA in Biology summa cum laude, Rice U., 1964; MD, U. Tex., Dallas, 1968. Diplomate Am. Bd. Surgery, Am. Bd. Colon and Rectal Surgery. Intern straight surg. Parkland Hosp., Dallas, 1968-69; resident gen. surgery U. Tex. Med. Sch./Hermann Hosp., Houston, 1969-73; fellow colon and rectal surgery Ferguson-Droste-Ferguson Hosp., Grand Rapids, Mich., 1973-74; clin. faculty U. Tex. Med. Sch., Houston, 1974—, dir. residency tng. program colon and rectal surgery, 1984—2005, clin. prof. surgery, 1986—; clin. faculty Baylor Coll. Medicine, 1986—, clin. prof., 1999—2005; chief div. colon rectal surgery Methodist Hosp., Houston, 2006—; clin. prof. surgery Weill Med. Coll., Cornell U., 2007—. Assoc. examiner Am. Bd. Colon and Rectal Surgery, 1985—89, bd. mem., 1988—97, chmn. exam. com., 1995—97, pres., 1996—97, sr. examiner, 1997—; chief staff Park Plaza Hosp., Houston, 1988—90. Bd. dir. Am. Cancer Soc., Greater Houston unit, 1989-93, v.p., 1991-93, pres., 1993-95; mem. vestry Palmer Meml. Episcopal Ch., Houston, 1979-83, 84-86, chmn. fin. com., 1984-86; mem. fund coun. Rice U., Houston, 1993-95, class fund drive chmn. 1993-95). Recipient George Waldron award Hermann Hosp., 1970, Violet Keller award, 1973; named to Good Housekeeping mag. 400 Best Doctors in U.S., 1991, Good Housekeeping mag. Best Cancer Doctors in U.S., 1993; named Disting. Alumnus, Rice U., 2000. Fellow ACS (chmn. adv. coun. colon and rectal surgery 1996-2001, chmn. membership svcs. com. 2005-08, bd. govs. 2002-04, bd. regents 2003—), Am. Surg. Assn., Internat. Soc. Univ. Colon and Rectal Surgeons (program com. 1986), Am. Soc. Colon and Rectal Surgeons (treas., exec. coun. 1993-99, pres. 1999-2000), Tex. Surg. Soc.; mem. AMA, Tex. Soc. Colon and Rectal Surgeons (pres. 1981, exec. sec. 1982-88, exec. sec. 2007-), Tex. Med. Assn., Tex. Soc. Gastrointestinal Endoscopy, Harris County Med. Soc., Houston Surg. Soc., Phi Beta Kappa, Alpha Omega Alpha. Office: Colon & Rectal Clinic 6550 Fannin St Ste 2307 Houston TX 77030-2723 Office Phone: 713-790-9250. Personal E-mail: hrbailey@swbell.net. Business E-Mail: h.randolph.bailey@uth.tmc.edu.

BAILEY, HOWARD H., medical educator; b. ND, June 7, 1959; MD, U. ND Sch. Medicine, 1985. Prof. medicine U. Wis., 1994—. Recipient Career Devel. award, Am. Cancer Soc., Scientist award, NIH; Rsch. grant. Office: K4/650 CSC 600 Highland Ave Madison WI 53792 Business E-Mail: hhb@medicine.wisc.edu.

BAILEY, LEONARD LEE, surgeon; b. Takoma Park, Md., Aug. 28, 1942; s. Nelson Hulburt and Catherine Effie (Long) B.; m. Nancy Ann Schroeder, Aug. 21, 1966; children: Jonathan Brooks, Charles Connor. BS, Columbia Union Coll., 1964; postgrad., NIH, 1965; MD, Loma Linda U., Calif., 1969. Diplomate Am. Bd. Surgery, Am. Bd. Thoracic Surgery. Intern Loma Linda U. Med. Ctr., 1969-70, resident in surgery, 1970-73, resident in thoracic and cardiovasc. surgery, 1973-74; resident in pediatric cardiovasc. surgery Hosp. for Sick Children, Toronto, Ont., Canada, 1974-75; resident in thoracic and cardiovasc. surgery Loma Linda U. Med. Sch., 1975-76, asst. prof. surgery, 1976-86, prof. surgery, 1986—2005, disting. prof. surgery, 2005—, dir. pediatric cardiac surgery, 1976—, chief divsn. cardiothoracic surgery, 1988-92, chair dept. surgery, 1992—2008, disting. prof. pediat., 2009—; surgeon in chief Loma Linda U. Children's Hosp., 2008—. Mem. ACS, Am. Assn. Thoracic Surgery, Am. Surg. Assn., Am. Coll. Cardiology, Western Thoracic Surg. Assn., Soc. Thoracic Surgery, Western Soc. Pediatric Rsch., Internat. Soc. for Heart Transplantation, Am. Heart Assn., Internat. Assn. for Cardiac Biol. Implants, Am. Soc. for Artificial Internal Organs, Pacific Coast Surg. Assn., Western Assn. Transplant Surgeons, Internat. Soc. for Cardiovasc. Surgery, United Network for Organ Sharing, The Transplant Soc. Democrat. Adventist. Office: Loma Linda U Med Ctr and Children's Hosp 11175 Campus St Ste 21120 Loma Linda CA 92350-1700 Office Phone: 909-558-8744. Business E-Mail: lbailey@llu.edu.

BAILEY, MARY BEATRICE, retired health science association administrator; b. Pitts., Dec. 24, 1933; d. Harry Chantler and Beatrice Iseli (Koenig) B. Diploma in Nursing, Allegheny Gen. Hosp., Pitts., 1956; BSNE, Chatham Coll., Pitts., 1956; MSN, Duke U., Durham, 1967. Cert. nursing adminstr., advanced. Staff nurse, head nurse, nursing supr. Allegheny Gen. Hosp., Pittsburgh, 1956-60; nursing instr. pediatrics Duke U. Sch. Nursing, Durham, N.C., 1960-61; nursing instr. med. surg Rex Hosp. Sch. Nursing, Raleigh, N.C., 1962-63; nursing supr. Rex Hosp., Raleigh, 1964-71, patient care coord., 1972-86, clin. dir., 1987, dir. nursing info. system, 1987-95. Author: The Role of the Mother with her Hospitalized Child, 1966. Vol. Rn open door clinic, Raleigh, 1987-88, Meals on Wheels, Wake Co., 1996—2006, Raleigh Little Theatre, 1993—2000; mem. elected N.C. Bd. of Nursing, 1991-93, 94-96. Named to The Great 100 N.C. Nurses, 1992. Mem. N.C. Nurses Assn. (life, treas. 1977-79), Great 100 (charter treas. 1989), Zonta Club of Raleigh (charter treas.). Democrat. Episcopalian. Avocations: reading, theater, music, sports. Home: 311 Furches St Raleigh NC 27607-4015

BAILEY, PATRICIA, surgeon; MD, U. Mass. Resident Hosp. of the Univ. of Pa.; chief resident Temple Univ. Hosp.; clin. assoc. prof. surgery Hosp. of the Univ. of Pa., joined Chestnut Hill Hosp., 2006, with women's ctr.; med. dir. Chestnut Hill Women's Ctr. Office: Chestnut Hill Surgical Associates Ste 2 8200 Flourtown Ave Wyndmoor PA 19038 Office Phone: 215-836-5120.

BAILEY, PHILIP D., JR., medical educator; b. NY, June 27, 1972; BS, Siena Coll., 1993; DO, UNECOM, 1997. Asst. prof. anesthesiology & critical care medicine Children's Hosp., Phila., 2008—. Office: 34th & Civic Ctr Blvd Philadelphia PA 19104 Business E-Mail: baileyp@email.chop.edu.

BAILEY, RAHN KENNEDY, psychiatrist; b. Beaumont, Tex., Aug. 18, 1964; BS, Morehouse Coll., Atlanta, Ga., 1986; MD, U. Tex. Med. Br., Galveston, Tex., 1990. Staff psychiatrist Whiting Forensic Inst., 1994—95; asst. clin. dir. La. State U., Tulane U., 1995—97; med. dir., CEO Bailey Psychiat. Assoc., 1997—2008; psychiatrist Clearlake Regional Hosp., Houston, 2004—08; chair, dept. psychiatry & behavioral scis., exec. dir. Lloyd C. Elam Mental Health Ctr., Meharry Med. Coll., 2008. Spkr. Nat. Med. Assn., 2009—11, bd. trustees, Cobb Found., 2009—11; pres. elect Tenn. State Psychiat. Assn., 2011; dep. rep. Black Caucus, Am. Psychiatry Assn., 2010; splty. chief editor Frontiers Forensic Psychiatry, 2010. Recipient Issac Slaughter, Meml. Leadership award, Black Psychiatrists Am., Inc. Mem.: Instl. Setting Com. Liaison Com. Med. Edn., Mental Health Coop. Found. Tenn., Am. Acad. Psychiatry and Law. Avocations: golf, travel, sports. Home: 84 Governors Way Brentwood TN 37208 Home Fax: 615-327-5661.

BAILEY, ROBERT CONVERSE, epidemiologist, anthropologist, educator; b. NYC, Sept. 27, 1946; s. Charles Wesley and Katharine (Palmer) B.; m. Nadine Ruth Peacock, Sept. 6, 1985; children: Nathan T., Alexander Morgan Peacock. AB, Harvard U., 1969, PhD, 1985; MPH, Emory U., 1997. Resident biologist Tarpon Zoo, Inc., Amazonas, Colombia, 1972-74; field dir. Ituri Project, Zaire Harvard U., Cambridge, Mass., 1980-84; acting asst. prof. anthropology UCLA, 1984-85, asst. prof. anthropology, 1985-91, assoc. prof. anthropology, 1991-96, prof. anthropology, 1996-97; prof. epidemiology U. Ill. Sch. Pub. Health, Chgo., 1996—; adj. prof. anthropology U. Ill., Chgo., 1996—. NIMH Nat. Rsch. fellow HIV/AIDS Rsch. Tng. Program, Emory U. Rollins Sch. Pub. Health and Nat. Ctrs. Disease Control, Atlanta, 1994-96; invited spkr. and presenter in field.; co-organizer, co-chair symposia on tropical forest ecology, Washington, 1989, 90; cons. to World Bank Environ. Sect., 1990; rsch. assoc. Nat. Ctr. Human Nutrition, Kinshasa, Zaire, 1980-90; mem. scientific com. UNESCO Symposium on Food and Nutrition in the Tropical Forest, 1991; mem. Population Rsch. Ctr., Harbor-UCLA Med. Ctr., 1988-92; cons. Global Environ. Fund World Bank, 1992, 93; co-chair exec. com. and adv. bd. Ituri Fund/Cultural Survival, 1989—; co-dir. Ituri Project, 1980—; dir. Project MenSH, Uganda, 1997—; reviewer manuscripts and proposals NSF, Nat. Ctrs. Disease Control, Wenner Gren Found. Rsch. and Exploration, Swan Fund, numerous other instns. and orgns; dir. Ituri Forest Peoples Fund, Dem. Republic of Congo, 1989—. Author: The Behavioral Ecology of Efe Pygmy Men in the Ituri Forest, Zaire, 1991; co-author: The Time Allocation of Efe Pygmies in the Ituri Forest, Zaire, 1989, Efe: Investigating Food and Fertility in the Ituri Rain Forest, 1994; co-editor: Tropical Deforestation: The Human Dimension, 1996; co-editor spl. issue (jour.) Human Ecology, Human Foragers in Tropical Rain Forests, 1991; contbr. over 60 articles and papers to profl. jours. and conf. procs.; book rev. editor (jour.) Ethology and Sociobiology, 1985-89. Rsch. grantee USPHS/Ctr. Disease Control Coop. Agreement, 1996-98, other agys. and instns., 1973-96. Fellow Am. Anthropol. Assn.; mem. APHA, Am. Assn. Phys. Anthropologists (rev. bd. 59th-67th Ann. Meetings 1988-96), Human Biology Assn., Human Behavior and Evolution Soc., Internat. Soc. Human Ethology, Internat. Epidemiol. Soc. Avocation: birding. Home: 907 N Euclid Ave Oak Park IL 60302-1319 Office: UIC Sch Pub Health 959 Sphpi M/C 923 1603 W Taylor St Chicago IL 60612 Office Phone: 312-355-0440. E-mail: rcbailey@uic.edu.

BAILEY, ROBERT S., JR., ophthalmologist; BA in Biology, Lafayette Coll.; MD, Hahnemann Med. Coll. Diplomate Am. Bd. Ophthalmology. Intern Crozer-Chester Med. Ctr.; resident Wills Eye Hosp., chief cataract and primary eye svc., 2000; chief ophthalmology divsn. Chestnut Hill Hosp. Instr. Jefferson Med. Coll. Author of numerous publs. presentations and lectures focus on cataract and anterior segment surgery and their complications. Fellow: ACS. Office: Wills Eye Hospital 840 Walnut St Philadelphia PA 19107 Office Phone: 215-928-3000.

BAILEY, ROBIN KEITH, medical educator; b. St. Petersburg, Fla., Jan. 8, 1951; s. Albert Hugh and Kathleen Elizabeth (Badgley) B.; m. Patricia Celeste Bailey. AA, St. Petersburg Jr. Coll., 1973; BS in Pub. Rels. in Criminal Justice, U. Fla., 1976, B Health Sci., 1981; cert., Newark Beth Israel Med. Ctr., 1990; Masters in Physician Assts. Studies, U. Nebr., 1998; MD, USAT, Mass., 2010. Cert. physician Nat. Cert. Commn. of Physician Assts. Paramedic Alachua County Emergency Med. Svc., Gainesville, Fla., 1972-78; perfusionist U. Fla./VA Med. Ctr., Gainesville, 1980-96; physician asst. U. Fla., 1984-96; chief perfusionist, physician asst. U. South Fla.-VA Med. Ctr., Tampa, 1996—2002; prof. otolaryngology-head and neck surgery U. South Fla. Coll. Medicine, 2005—. Air ambulance medic/perfusionist Shands Hosp., Gainesville, 1995-97; cons. in field. Contbr. articles to profl. publs. Lt. col. U.S. Army, 1978-81, USAFR, 1981-2002. Mem. Am. Acad. Physician Assts., Fla. Acad. Physician Assts. (v.p. 2007-), Assn. Mil. Surgeons, Am. Heart Assn. (exec. com., ACLS instr., BCLS instr./trainer). Avocations: golf, fishing. Home: 2944 Sunset Point Rd Clearwater FL 33759-1614 Personal E-mail: RKBaileypa@yahoo.com, rkbaileypa@gmail.com.

BAILEY, SUSAN RUDD, allergist, immunologist, pediatrician; b. Louisville, Dec. 25, 1955; BS, Tex. A&M U., 1979, MD, 1981. Diplomate American Bd. Pediat., American Bd. Allergy & Immunology. Intern, resident pediat. Mayo Clinic, Rochester, Minn., 1981—84, fellow pediatric allergy & immunology, 1984—86; pvt. practice Ft. Worth Allergy & Asthma Associates, 1986—. Mem. editl. bd. Annals Allergy, Asthma, & Immunology, 1997—2003, asst. editor Allergy Watch; contbr. articles to profl. jours. Treas. Mayo Assn. Fellows, 1984—85; trustee Minn. Med. Assn., 1984—85; bd. visitors Scott & White Clinic, Temple, Tex., 1991—; mem. adv. bd. MD Anderson Physicians Network, 1992—94; bd. regents Tex. A&M U. Sys., 1999—2005. Fellow: American Acad. Pediat., mem.: AMA (chair com. women in medicine 1987—89, mem. House Dels. 1988—, mem. Coun. Med. Edn. 2001—10, chair Tex. del. 2006—11, chair adv. com., Coun. Med. Edn. 2009—10, bd. trustees 2011—, vice spkr. House Dels. 2011—), American Coll. Allergists (Leon Unger award 1985), Tarrant County Med. Soc. (bd. dirs. 1990—, v.p. 1994—95, pres. elect 1995—96, pres. 1996—97, trustee 1998—2001), American Coll. Allergy & Immunology (bd. regents 1994—97), American Assn. Cert. Allergists, Tex. Med. Assn. (vice spkr. 1997—2001, spkr. 2001—05, pres. 2010—11), Alpha Zeta, Alpha Omega Alpha. Office: Fort Worth Allergy & Asthma Associates 5929 Lovell Ave Fort Worth TX 76107-5029 Office Phone: 817-315-2550. E-mail: susanruddbailey@yahoo.com. *

BAILIE, DAVID, orthopedist, consultant; BS in Biology, Physiology, U. Mich., 1986; MD, Indiana U. Sch. Medicine, 1990. Lic. Ariz. Med. Bd., cert. Tex. Med. Bd., Ill. Med. Bd., Am. Bd. Orthop. Surgery, in orthop. sports medicine 2010. Residency dept. orthop. surgery Northwestern U., Mcgaw Med. Ctr., Chgo., 1990—95; fellow dept. orthopaedic surgery sports medicine and arthroscopic surgery Baylor Coll. Medicine, 1995—96; orthop. physician, surgeon Ctr.For Sports Medicine and Orthop., 1996—98; clin. program cons. Glendale Cmty. Coll., 1996—; clin. faculty dept. physician asst. & physical therapy Ariz. Sch. Health Sci., 1996—; clinical asst. prof. Arizona Coll. Osteopathic Medicine, 1996—; orthop. cons. Grand Canyon U., 1996—2003, Phoenix Coll., 1996—2003, Seattle Mariners Baseball Club, 1996—98; asst. team orthop. surgeon Phoenix Suns, 1996—98, orthop. cons., 1996—, Phoenix Coyotes, 1996—98; head team orthop. surgeon Arizona Rattlers, 1996—98; co-team physician Women's Nat. Basketball Assn., 1996—98, team orthop. cons., 1998—; orthop. cons. Arizona Rattlers, 1998—2009; orthop. physician, surgeon, ptnr. Orthop. Clinic Assn., Phoenix, 1998—, v.p., 2002—07; team orthop. surgeon Ariz. State U., Tempe, 1998—2000, orthop. cons., 2001—, US Women's Olympic Gymnastics Team, 1998—2005; physician Shadow Mountain HS, 1998—2010; team physician Justin Sports Medicine Team-PRCA Circuit, 1998—; physician Mesquite HS, 1999—2003; orthop. cons. Elite Care/Desert Mountain Med, 1999—; physician Dobson HS, 1999—2009; surgery cons. Umpire Med. Svcs., 2000—01; physician Higley HS, 2001—; chmn., orthop. surgery Scottsdale Healthcare Shea Hosp., 2001—05; orthop. cons. Milw. Brewers Baseball Club, 2002—09; v.p., bd. Dirs. The Orthop. Clinic Assn. (TOCA), 2002—07; orthop. cons. PGA Tour, 2004—; chmn. dept surgery Scottsdale Healthcare Shea Hosp., 2005, mem. med. exec. com., 2005; med. dir. The Orthop. Surgical Ctr. Ariz., 2006; clinical orthop. faculty dept internal medicine/family medicine Mayo Clinic Scottsdale, 2004—06; cons. Breg Orthop. Products, San Diego, 2005—08; med. consultant to the bd. Chaparral Firebirds Found., 2009—, United States Fed Cup Team, 2009. Med. advisor Bodyl.Com, 2001—, Shoulderl.Com, 2001—; bd. dirs. Arizona Jr. Sports Found, 2001—; orthop. cons. Smith & Nephew Orthops., 2002—, Biomet Orthop.S Warsaw, 2002—, principal investigator, 2009—; editl. bd. mem. World Jour. Orthoep., 2011—. Contbr. articles to numerous pubs.

BAILLET, GILLES PIERRE, orthodontist; b. Paris, Dec. 6, 1948; s. Lucien Pierre and Madeleine Alphonsine (Champoix) B.; m. Daniele Luce Floch, Dec. 6, 1980; 1 child, Victoire. DS, Paris U., Paris, 1974; MS, Nantes U., Nantes, 1980; diploma in Orthodontist, Paris U., Paris, 1978; diploma in oral dental survey, Montpellier U., France, 1992; diploma in behavioral and cognitive therapies, Paris, 2001. Cons. Helio-Marin Ctr., Roscoff, 1978-83; clin. asst. Gen. Hosp., Morlaix, 1980-82; asst. prof. Dental U., Brest, 1980-82, prof. orthodontic dept., 1982-86; assoc. prof. Gen. Hosp., 1988-91; pvt. practice Morlaix, 1977—. Asst. med. psychology Brest U., France. Contbr. articles to profl. jours. Mem. ADA, Am. Assn. Orthodontists, European Orthodontic Soc., Coll. European Orthodontists, European Assn. Behavioral and Cognitive Therapies, Psychol. Odontostomatology and Maxillofacial Soc. (pres.). Avocation: motorcycle biker. Office: 8 Ter Place Du Pouliet 29600 Morlaix France Office Phone: 0298887978. Personal E-mail: gbaillet003@cegetel.rss.fr.

BAILLIE, THOMAS A., dean, former pharmaceutical executive; BS in Chemistry, U. Glasgow, Scotland, 1970, PhD in Organic Chemistry, 1973, DSc in Chemistry, 1992; MS in Biochemistry, U. London, 1978. Postdoc. rsch. fellow dept. physiological chemistry Karolinska Inst., Stockholm, 1973—75; lectr. analytical chemistry, dept. clin. pharmacology U. London, 1975—78; asst. prof. pharm. chemistry U. Calif., San Francisco, 1979—81; asst. prof. medicinal chemistry U. Wash. Sch. Pharmacy, Seattle, 1981—83, assoc. prof., 1983—88, prof., 1988—94, dean Sch. Pharmacy, 2008—; exec. dir. preclin. drug metabolism Merck & Co., Inc., 1994—96, v.p. drug metabolism, 1996—2007, v.p., global head drug metabolism & pharmacokinetics, 2007—08. Sci. adv. FDA San Francisco Regional Labs., 1980—81; cons. Procter & Gamble Co., 1987—94. Contbr. articles to profl. jours. Mem.: Am. Chem. Soc., Internat. Isotope Soc. (pres. 1991), Internat. Soc. Study of Xenobiotics (councillor 1991—93, sec. elect 1996—97, sec. 1998—99), Am. Soc. Mass Spectrometry (sec. 1993—95), Royal Soc. Chemistry. Office: U Wash Coll Pharmacy Box 357631 H364 Health Scis Bldg Seattle WA 98195 Office Phone: 206-543-2030. Office Fax: 206-685-9297. Business E-Mail: tbaillie@u.washington.edu.

BAILYN, LOTTE, psychologist, educator; b. Vienna, July 17, 1930; came to U.S., 1937; d. Paul Felix Lazarsfeld and Marie (Jahoda) Albu; m. Bernard Bailyn, June 18, 1952; children: Charles, John. BA in Math. with high honors, Swarthmore Coll., 1951; MA in Social Psychology, Harvard U., 1953, PhD in Social Psychology, 1956; PhD (hon.), U. Piraeus, Greece, 2000. Rsch. assoc. Grad. Sch. Edn., Harvard U., Cambridge, Mass., 1956-57, rsch. assoc. dept. social rels., 1958-64, lectr., 1963-67; instr. dept. econs. and social sci. MIT, Cambridge, 1957-58, rsch. assoc. Sloan Sch. Mgmt., 1969-70, lectr., 1970-71, from sr. lectr. to prof., 1971-91, T Wilson prof. mgmt., 1991—2005, prof. mgmt., 2005—, chair MIT faculty, 1997-99; acad. visitor Imperial Coll. Sci., Tech. and Medicine, London, 1991, 1995—, 2000; disting. vis. prof. Radcliffe Coll., 1995-97. Trustee Cambridge Savs. Bank, 1975-98, mem. adv. coun. Suffolk U. Mgmt. Sch., Boston, 1983-86; mem. sr. coun. Leadership Devel. Inst., Rutgers U., 1986-89; panel mem. NAS, NRC, Washington, 1988-90; mem. task force in career devel. and maintenance IEEE, Washington, 1982-90; vis. scholar Imperial Coll. Sci. and Tech., London, 1982, New Hall, Cambridge (Eng.) U., 1986-87; scholar-in-residence Rockefeller Found. Study and Conf. Ctr., Bellagio, Italy, 1983; vis. fellow U. Auckland, N.Z., 1984. Author: Mass Media and Children, 1959, Living with Technology, 1980, Breaking the Mold: Women, Men, and Time in the New Corporate World, 1993, Breaking the Mold: Redesigning Work for Productive and Satisfying Lives, 2006; co-author: Working with Careers, 1984, Relinking Life and Work: Toward a Better Future, 1996, Beyond Work-Family Balance: Advancing Gender Equity and Workplace Performance, 2002; mem. editl. bd. Cmty., Work and Family, Human Rels.; contbr. chpts. to books and articles to profl. jours. Trustee Radcliffe Coll., 1974-79, Cambridge Fin. Group, Inc., 1998-2005; bd. dirs. Families and Work Inst., 1995—2011, emeritus trustee, 2011-, Cambridge Savings Bank, 1998-2005; adv. group, Creating Options: Models for Flexible Faculty Career Pathways, Office of Women in Higher Edn., Am. Coun. Edn., 2003-06; com. Women in Sci. and Engring., Nat. Acad. Sci., 2004—06, Women in Acad. Sci. and Engring., Nat. Acads., 2005-2006; internat. bd. sci. adv. Proctising Gender Equality Sci., Rome, 2009-10, Assn. Rsch. in Astronomy Com. Workforce & Diversity, 2009-, European Commn., 2010-11. Recipient Grad. Soc. medal Radcliffe Coll., 1998, Everett Cherrington Hughes award for careers scholarship Acad. of Mgmt., 2003, Work Life Legacy award, Families and Work Inst., 2005, Gordon Y. Billard award, MIT, 2009. Fellow APA, APS; mem. Acad. Mgmt., Am. Sociol. Assn. Home: 170 Clifton St Belmont MA 02478-2604 Office: MIT Sloan Sch Mgmt 100 Main St Cambridge MA 02142-1347 Business E-Mail: lbailyn@mit.edu.

BAIM, HOWARD M., otolaryngologist, educator; MD, U. of Ill. Coll. of Medicine, Chicago, Ill., 1969—73. Diplomate Am. Bd. Otolaryngology, 1978. Resident gen. surgery Univ. of Ill., 1973—75, resident eye and ear infirmary, 1975—78; asst. clin. prof. otolaryngology U. of Ill. Coll. of Medicine; hosp. affiliation includes Advocate Ill. Masonic Med. Ctr. Office: Advocate Illinois Masonic Medical Center 836 West Wellington Ave Chicago IL 60657 Office Phone: 773-975-1600.

BAINS, MANJIT SINGH, thoracic surgeon; MBBS, All India Institute of Med. Sciences, New Delhi, 1963. Diplomate Am. Bd. Thoracic Surgery, Am. Bd. Surgery. Intern Queens Hosp. Ctr., 1965, resident, 1966, Rochester Gen. Hosp., 1970; fellow NY Presbyn. Hosp./Weill Cornell Med. Ctr., Meml. Sloan-Kettering Cancer Ctr., NY, thoracic surgeon. Author: (articles) Pulmonary resection in metastatic carcinoma, 2009, Predictors of outcomes after surgical treatment of synchronous primary lung cancers, 2010, Nael Martini: a leader in thoracic surgical oncology, 2010, TI-CE high-dose chemotherapy for patients with previously treated germ cell tumors: results and prognostic factor analysis, 2010, Computed Tomography-Guided Access to the Cisterna Chyli: Introduction of a Technique for Direct Lymphangiography to Evaluate and Treat Chylothorax, 2010. Office: Memorial Sloan-Kettering Cancer Center 1275 York Ave New York NY 10065 Office Phone: 212-639-7450.

BAINTON, DOROTHY FORD, pathologist, educator; b. Magnolia, Miss., June 18, 1933; d. Aubrey Ratcliff and Leta (Brumfield) Ford; m. Cedric R. Bainton, Nov. 28, 1959; children: Roland J., Bruce G., James H. BS, Millsaps Coll., 1955; MD, Tulane U. Sch. of Medicine, 1958; MS, U. Calif., San Francisco, 1966. Postdoctoral rsch. fellow U. Calif., San Francisco, 1963-66, postdoctoral rsch. pathologist, 1966-69, asst. prof. pathology, 1969-75, assoc. prof., 1975-81, prof. pathology, 1981—, chair pathology, 1987-94, vice chancellor acad. affairs, 1994—2004; ret. Mem. Inst. of Medicine, NAS, 1990—.

Grantee, NIH, 1968—98. Fellow AAAS, Am. Acad. Arts & Scis.; mem. FASEB (bd. dirs.), Am. Soc. for Cell Biology, Am. Soc. Hematology, Am. Soc. Histochemists and Cytochemists, Am. Assn. of Pathologists. Democrat. Address: 50 Ventura Ave San Francisco CA 94116 E-mail: dbainton@mac.com.

BAIR, WILLIAM J., retired radiobiologist; b. Jackson, Mich., July 14, 1924; s. William J. and Mona J. (Gamble) B.; m. Barbara Joan Sites, Feb. 16, 1952; children: William J., Michael Braden, Andrew Emil. BA in Chemistry, Ohio Wesleyan U., 1949; PhD in Radiation Biology, U. Rochester, 1954. NRC-AEC fellow U. Rochester, 1949-50, rsch. assoc. radiation biology, 1950-54; biol. scientist Hanford Labs. of GE, Richland, Wash., 1954-56, mgr. inhalation toxicology sect., biology dept., 1956-65, Battelle Meml. Inst., 1965-68; mgr. biology dept. Pacific Northwest Nat. Labs., Richland, 1968-74, dir. life scis. program, 1973-75, mgr. biomed. and environ. rsch. program, 1975-76, mgr. environ. health and safety rsch. program, 1976-86, mgr. life scis. ctr., 1986-93, sr. advisor health protection rsch., 1993—2002; ret., 2002. Lectr. radiation biology Joint Ctr. Grad. Study, Richland, 1955-75; cons. to adv. com. on reactor safeguards Nuc. Regulatory Commn., 1971-87; mem. com. on plutonium toxicology; subcom. inhalation hazards, com. pathologic effects atomic radiation NAS, 1957-64, ad hoc com. on hot particles of subcom. biol. effects ionizing radiation NAS-NRC, 1974-76, vice-chmn. com. on biol. effects of ionizing radiation, BEIR IV Alpha radiation, 1985-88, battlefield radiation exposure com., 1997-99; chmn. task force on biol. effects of inhaled particles Internat. Commn. on Radiol. Protection, 1970-79, com. 2 on permissible dose for internal radiation, 1973-93, chmn. task group on respiratory tract models, 1984-93; mem. Nat. Coun. on Radiation Protection and Measurements, 1974-92, hon. mem., 1992-, com. on maximum permissible concentration of radionuclides for occupl. and nonoccupl. exposure, 1970-74, com. basic radiation protection criteria, 1975-93, chmn. ad hoc com. on hot particles, 1974, chmn. ad hoc com. internal emitter activities, 1976-77, com. on internal emitter stds., 1977-92, chmn. com. mgmt. of persons contaminated with radionuclides, 2004-10, Lauriston S. Taylor lectr., 1997; radiation adv. com. and sci. adv. bd. EPA, 1993-99; founder, pres. Herbert M. Parker Found., 1987-94, bd. trustees, 1994-; cons. in field, 2002-. Author 200 books, articles, reports, chpts. in books. Mem. cmty. concerts bd. Kiwanis Internat.; mem. bd. mid-columbia Woodturners, South Ctrl. Washington Orchid Soc., Columbia Basin Flycasters, Ctrl. United Protestant Ch. With US Army, 1943—46. Decorated Bronze Star; recipient Combat Infantry Badge US Army, E.O. Lawrence Meml. award AEC, 1970, cert. of appreciation AEC, 1975, Alumni Disting. Achievement citation Ohio Wesleyan U, Tribute of Appreciation US Environ. Protection Agy., 1999, Robley D. Evans Commemorative medal, 2010. Fellow AAAS (life), Health Physics Soc. (life, bd. dirs. 1970-73, 83-86, pres. elect 1983-84, pres. 1984-85, J.N. Stannard lectr. No. Calif. chpt. and Sierra Nev. chpt. 2004, Disting. Sci. Achievement award 1991, Robley D. Evans Commemorative medal, 2010, Robley D. Evans Commemorative medal, 2010, Herbert H. Parker award Columbia chpt. 1998); mem. Internat. Commn. Radiological Protection, Radiation Rsch. Soc., Soc. Exptl. Biology and Medicine (vice chmn. N.W. chpt. 1967-70, 74-75), Sigma Xi. Achievements include research in developing methods for studying health effects of inhaled radioactive aerosols; discovery of different behaviors of inhaled plutonium-238 and 239 oxides; research in deposition, retention and translocation of inhaled aerosols showing relevance of particle size to pulmonary dynamics; demonstrated carcinogenic effects of inhaled plutonium; and led international commission on radiological protection task group in developing a human respiratory tract model for inhaled radioactive materials. Avocations: wildlife photography, woodcarving, fly fishing, orchids, wood turning. Home: 578 Clermont Dr Richland WA 99352-1966

BAIRD, PATRICIA ANN, physician, educator; b. Rochdale, Eng. arrived in Can., 1955; d. Harold and Winifred (Cainen) Holt; m. Robert Merrifield Baird, Feb. 22, 1964; children: Jennifer Ellen, Brian Merrifield, Bruce Andrew BSc in Biol. Sci. with honors, McGill U., 1959, MD, CM, 1963; DSc (hon.), McMaster U., 1991; D (hon.), U. Ottawa, 1991; LLD (hon.), Wilfrid Laurier U., 2000; PhD (hon.), Queen's U., 2010. Intern Royal Victoria Hosp., Montreal, Que., Canada, 1963-64; resident, fellow in pediat. Vancouver Gen. Hosp., B.C., Canada, 1964-67; instr. pediat. U. B.C., Vancouver, 1968-72, from asst. prof. to prof., 1972-94, Univ. Killam Disting. prof., 1994—; head dept. med. genetics Grace Hosp., Vancouver, 1981-89, Children's Hosp., Vancouver, 1981-89, Health Scis. Centre Hosp., 1986-89. Med. cons. B.C. Health Surveillance Registry, 1977-90; chmn. genetics grants com. Med. Rsch. Coun., Ottawa, Ont., Can., 1982-87, mem. coun., 1987-90; mem. Nat. Adv. Bd. on Sci. and Tech. to Fed. Govt., 1987-91; genetic predisposition study steering com. Sci. Coun. Can., 1987-90; chair Royal Commn. on New Reproductive Technologies, 1989-93, Premier's Coun. on Aging Sr. Issues, 2005-06; co-chair Nat. Forum Sci. and Tech. Couns., 1991; v.p. Can. Inst. for Advanced Rsch., 1991-2002, vice chmn. bd., 2002-10; bd. dirs. Biomed. Rsch. Centre, 1986-89; bd. govs. U. B.C., 1984-90; temporary cons. WHO, 1999-2001, human genetics ELSI planning group, 2000-02, expert adv. panel on human genetics, 2002—10. Contbr. articles to med. jours. Decorated officer Order of Can., 2000, Order of B.C., 1992; recipient Commemorative medal for Confedn. of Can., 1992, Queen's Golden Jubilee medal, 2002. Fellow RCP Can., Royal Soc. Can., Can. Coll. Med. Geneticists (v.p. 1984-86); mem. Am. Soc. Human Genetics (chair nominating com. 1987-89), B.C. Med. Assn., Can. Med. Assn., Genetics Soc. Can., Genetic Epidemiology (adv. bd. 1991-94), Internat. Fedn. of Gyn. and Obs. (mem. ethics com. 1997-99). Avocations: skiing, bicycling, music. Address: 3267 Point Grey Rd Vancouver BC V6K 1B3 Canada Office Phone: 604-822-6115. Business E-Mail: pbaird@interchange.ubc.ca.

BAJORY, ZOLTÁN, urologist, andrologist; b. Szeged, Hungary, Sept. 19, 1970; s. Zoltán Bajory and Klára Forgács; m. Éva Zsók Bajory, 2009; children: Hanna children: András. MD, U. Szeged, 1995, PhD, 2003. Urologist in tng. Hosp. Orosháza, Hungary, 1995—98; urologist U. Szeged, 1998—, asst. prof., 2009—. Advisor higher edn. com. Ministry of Health, Budapest, 1999—2002. Contbr. articles. Mem.: Hungarian Acad. Sci., European Bd. Urology, European Assn. Urology (fellow 2001), Hungarian Assn. Urology (cert.). Roman Catholic. Avocations: travel, cars, tennis. Office: Dept Urology Univ Szeged Kálvária sgt 57 Szeged 6725 Hungary Personal E-mail: bajory@freemail.hu.

BAJTAI, ATTILA, pathologist; b. Temesvar, Romania, July 12, 1933; came to Hungary, 1940; s. John and Louise (Csehalik) B.; m. Eva Toóth, Feb. 15, 1958; 1 child, Zoltán. MD, Med. Sch. Budapest, 1958. Asst. physician Town Coun. Hosp., Budapest, 1958-60; cons. Med. Sch. Budapest, 1960-68; cons., lectr., asst. prof. Postgrad. Med. Sch., Budapest, 1968-89, hon. prof. pathology, 1991; head dept. pathology Town Coun. Hosp., Budapest, 1989-2000, cons., 2000—10. Profl. insp. pathology Capital of Budapest, 1992—2005. Contbr. articles to profl. jours., chpts. to books. Recipient József Baló's award, Hungarian Assn. Pathology, 1995, Town Council award, Jászberény, 1999, Batthyány-Strattmann award, 2000, Lege Artis Medicinae award, Budapest, 2005, 2009, Hungarian Med. medals, numerous grants, Ödön Krompecher award, Hungarian Soc. Oncology, 1993, Hetényi Géza award, Hungarian Soc. Gastroenterology, 1994, Standing award, Dr. Antal Genersich Found., 2010. Mem.: Internat. Acad. Pathology, Hungarian Soc. Pathologists (sec.-gen. 1990—95), Hungarian Soc. Gastroenterology (hon.; perpetual hon. bd. mem., Pro Optimo Merito Gastroenterologia award). Avocations: music, records, stamp collecting/philately, travel. Personal E-mail: bajtai.attila@mail.eol.hu.

BAKALCZUK, SZYMON, gynecologist; b. Cheăm, June 29, 1949; MD, U. Medicine Lublin, Poland, 1973, PhD, 1986. Head, dept. reproduction & andrology Ovum, 2003—. Fellow: Polish Andrology Soc.; mem.: ESHRE. Home: Obywatelska 14/68 Lublin Lubelskie 20-092 Poland Personal E-mail: szymon.bakalczuk@am.lublin.pl.

BAKAN, MEFKUR, anesthesiologist; b. Bursa, Turkey, Jan. 5, 1970; MD, Istanbul U., 1993, degree in Anesthesiology, 2001. Anesthesiologist, anesthesiology dept. Bezmialem Vakif U. Med. Faculty, 2010; cons. anesthesiologist Bezmialem Vakif U., 2010. Office: Vatan Caddesi Istanbul Fatih 34093 Turkey Personal E-mail: mefkur@yahoo.com.

BAKAR, ÖZGÜR, medical educator; b. Ankara, Turkey, Sept. 12, 1975; D, Hacettepe U. Sch. Medicine, 1998. Assoc. prof. dermatology Acibadem U. Sch. Medicine, 2004—. Office: Acibadem Kozyatagi Hosp Inonu Cad Istanbul Kozyatagi 34742 Turkey Office Fax: 90216588455. Personal E-mail: ozgurtimurkaynak@hotmail.com.

BAKARDJIEV, ANGEL GEORGIEV, medical educator, researcher; b. Pazardzik, Bulgaria, Dec. 12, 1947; s. George Angelov Bakardjiev and Violet Hristova Bakardjieva; m. Kirilka Ilieva Jeliazkova, Oct. 31, 1971; children: Violet Angelova Bakardjieva, George Angelov. M in Med. Sci., Nat. Commn., 1992. Oral surgeon Nat. Commn., Sofia, 1982, maxillofacial surgeon Nat. Commn., Sofia, 1987. Physician State Policlinic, Pazardjik, 1972—75; asst. prof. Med. U., Plovdiv, Bulgaria, 1975—81, prof., 2003—. Editor (editor in chief): (journal) Synthesis; author: (book) Oral Surgery in Dental Practice, Apicoectomy in Dental Practice. Mem.: Bulgarian Dental Assn. (v.p. 1994—97, mem. coun. 1997—, co-pres. 1991—94), European Assn. Cranio-Maxillofacial Surgery (assoc.), Rotary. Achievements include research in dental implantology. Avocations: swimming, flowers. Home: Jr Trakia bl 96 entry B Plovdiv 4023 Bulgaria Office: Medical Univ 24 Veliko Tirnovo Plovdiv 4000 Bulgaria Office Fax: +35932632697. Personal E-mail: abakardjiev@netscape.net.

BAKAY, ROY ARPAD EARLE, neurosurgeon, educator; b. Chgo., Mar. 5, 1949; s. Archie Joseph and Marjory (Jordahl) B.; m. Joann P. Feiertag; children: Mark, Scott, Candace, Jacqueline. BS, Beloit Coll., 1971; MD, Northwestern U., 1975. Diplomate Nat. Bd. Med. Examiners, Am. Bd. Neurol. Surgery. Intern U. Mich., Ann Arbor, 1975-76; resident in neurosurgery U. Wash., Seattle, 1976—81; acting instr., asst. in neurosurgery U. Wash. Med. Sch., Seattle, 1980-82, NIH fellow, 1981-82; asst. prof. sect. neurol. surgery Emory U. Med. Sch., Atlanta, 1982-88, dir. neurol. surgery resident rsch., 1984-2000, assoc. prof., 1988-93, prof., 1993-2000; mem. R & D Com. VA Med. Ctr., Decatur, Ga., 1982-86, sect. chief neurol. surgery, 1982-95; affiliate scientist neurobiology Yerkes Regional Primate Rsch. Ctr., Atlanta, 1982—2000, vice chmn. dept. neurol. surgery, 1995-2000; prof., vice chmn. Rush U. Med. Ctr., Chgo., 2000—, dir. Movement Disorder Surg. Ctr., 2000—, A. Watson Armour III and Sarah Armour presdl. prof., 2003—; with Chgo. Inst. Neurosurgery and Neurorsch., 2000—06; faculty dept. pharmacology, 2009. Author: (with others) Yearbook of Science and Technology, 1989; mem. editorial bd. Jour. Contemporary Neurosurgery, 1987-93; mem. editorial rev. bd. Neurosurgery, 1994—; contbr. articles to profl. jours., chpts. to books. Chmn. profl. adv. bd. Ga. chpt. Epilepsy Found. Am., 1987-88; mem. adv. panel U.S. Congl. Office Tech. Assessment, Washington, 1988-90; profl. rep. Am. Cancer Soc., Atlanta, 1987-90. Recipient Resident Rsch. award Western Neurosurgery Soc., 1979, No. Pacific Soc. Neurology and Psychiatry, 1979, Soc. Neurology Anesthesists and Neurology Supportive Care, 1981; named one of Outstanding Athletes of Am., 1971, Best Drs. in America, 1994—, World Tech. award, 2000, Healthcare Heroes Atlanta, 1998, Chgo.'s Top Drs. 2004-11, World Tech. award, 2002. Mem. AAAS, Soc. Neurosci., Am. Stereotactic and Functional Neurosurgeons (v.p. 1988-91, pres. 1991-93), Am. Assn. Neurol. Surgeons (chmn. GRAFT Registry Com. 1987-95), Congress Neurol. Surgeons (v.p. joint com. 1988-91, sect. pres. 1991-93), Am. Soc. Neural Tranplantation and Repair (founding 1992, counsilor, 1992-99, pres.-elect 1999, pres. 2000, Molly & Bernard Sandberg award 2011). Presbyterian. Avocations: hiking, camping, skiing, fishing, team sports. Office: Rush University Med Ctr 1725 W Harrison St Ste 970 Chicago IL 60612 Home: 2025 S Indiana Ave Apt 201 Chicago IL 60616

BAKER, ANDREW HARTILL, health facility administrator; b. London, Dec. 7, 1948; came to U.S., 1976; s. Charles David and Isobel Joyce (Taylor) B.; m. Susan Nancy Spector, Oct. 24, 1986; children: Laura, Sally, Thomas; 1 stepchild, Jason Fredson. Attended, Framlingham Coll., Suffolk, Eng., 1966; diploma in Accountancy, City of London Polytechnique, 1968. Pres. SciCor Inc., Hazleton Corp., G.H.Besselaar Assocs.; auditor Touche Ross, London, 1968-73; contr. Corning, Inc., Essex, 1974-76, div. contr., 1977-79, asst. contr., 1980-82; sr. v.p. Metpath Inc., Teterboro, 1982-85, pres., CEO, 1985—92; pres. Corning Lab Svcs., Inc., Teterboro, 1990—92; chmn., CEO Unilabs Corp., Hackensack, 1989-97, chmn. emeritus, 1998; exec. chmn. Huntingdon Life Sciences Ltd., 1998—; chmn., CEO Life Sciences Research, Inc., 2002—. Founder, dir. Med. Diagnostic Mgmt., Inc.; proprietor, chmn. Hartill Ltd. Investment Co.; chmn. Unilabs (UK) Ltd.; sr. ptnr. Focused Healthcare Ptnrs. Treas. United Way of Steuben County, Corning, N.Y., 1978-82; trustee Wayne Gen. Hosp., N.J., 1982-87. Fellow Inst. Chartered Accts. in Eng. and Wales, Honourable Arty. Co. Club (London). Mem. Ch. Eng. Avocations: duck hunting, motor racing. Home: 1521 Alton Rd Apt 211 Miami Beach FL 33139 Office: Life Sciences Research Inc Mettlers Rd East Millstone NJ 08875-2360 Office Phone: 201-525-1819. E-mail: abaker@lsrinc.net. *

BAKER, BRUCE EDWARD, orthopedic surgeon, consultant; b. Oswego, NY, Mar. 22, 1937; s. Elbert J. and Reatha (Hartranft) B.; m. Patricia Therese Gormel, Aug. 19, 1961; children: Brett, Clayton, Sean, Reatha BSME, Syracuse U., 1959; MD, SUNY Syracuse, 1965. Intern State U. Iowa, Iowa City, 1965—66, asst. resident, 1966—67; resident orthop. SUNY Upstate Med. Ctr., Syracuse, 1969—72, NIH orthop. rsch. fellow, 1972—73, asst. prof. orthop. surgery, 1973—79, assoc. prof., 1979—86, prof., 1986—89. Dir. univ. sports medicine svc. divsn. dept. orthop. surgery 1980-89; team physician, dir. sports medicine athletic dept., Syracuse U., 1973-93, orthop. cons. Student Health Ctr., 1973-93, staff SUNY Hosp., Syracuse, 1973-89, Syracuse VA Hosp., 1973-89, A.C. Silverman Pub. Health Hosp., 1973-77, Crouse-Irving Meml. Hosp., 1973—; cons. in field Contbr. numerous articles to profl. jours Capt. M.C. USAF, 1967—69. Recipient Bronze medal Am. Roentgen Ray Soc., 1980, Gold medal Sound Slide Prodn. Conditioning, 1977; Syracuse U. scholar, 1955; N.Y. State Regents scholar, 1955-59; grantee USPHS, 1973-74, Hendricks Rsch. Fund, 1973-75, NIH, 1974-77 Fellow ACS, Am. Acad. Orthop. Surgeons; mem. AMA (Physicians Recognition award 1978), Med. Soc. State N.Y., Onondaga County Med. Soc., Orthop. Rsch. Soc., Am. Coll. Sports Medicine, N.Y. Soc. Orthop. Surgeons, Royal Soc. Medicine, Internat. Soc. Arthroscopy, Knee Surgery and Orthop. Sports Medicine, Am. Orthop. Soc. Sports Medicine, European Soc. Sports Trauma, Knee Surgery and Arthroscopy, Arthroscopy Assn. N.Am Office: 600 E Genesee St Ste 117 Syracuse NY 13202-3108 Home: 2910 Ave E PO Box 38 Holmes Beach FL 34217-0038 Home Phone: 315-655-2220; Office Phone: 315-476-2670.

BAKER, CARLETON HAROLD, physiology educator; b. Utica, NY, Aug. 2, 1930; s. Harold George and Loretta (Darling) B.; m. Sara Frances Johnson, July 20, 1963; children: Elizabeth Ann Bradshow, Janet Lee Howele. BA, Utica Coll. Syracuse U., 1952; MA, Princeton U., 1954, PhD, 1955. Asst. instr. Princeton U., NJ, 1952—54, asst. rsch., 1954—55; asst. prof. Med. Coll. Ga., Augusta, 1955—61, assoc prof., 1961—67, prof., 1967; prof. physiology and biophysics U. Louisville Health Scis. Ctr., 1967—71; prof., founding chmn. dept. physiology and biophysics U. South Fla. Coll. Medicine, Tampa, 1971—92, dep. dean rsch. and grad. studies, 1980—82, prof surgery, physiology and biophysics, dir. surg. rsch., 1992—95; prof. emeritus U. South Fla., 1995—. Rsch. com. mem. Am. Heart Assn., Louisville, 1969-71; rsch. com., bd. dirs. Am. Heart Assn. Fla., Tampa, 1971-85; NIH program project site visit team, 1982-84, mem. LCME Accreditation Survey Team, 1980-81; cons. U. Louisville Grad. Sch., East Carolina U. Grad. Program; rsch. prof. physiology U. S.C. Coll. Medicine, Columbia, 1994-2001 Editor: Microcirculatory Technology, 1986; mem. numerous editl. bds.; contbr. numerous articles in field Pres. Augusta Choral Soc., 1963; v.p. Blount Rd. Homeowners Assn., Lutz, Fla., 1986-93; bd. dirs. Friends of Augusta; tech., math & physics to young people. Grantee NIH, 1960-92, Am. Heart Assn., 1968-97; recipient Svc. awards Am. Heart Assn. Fla., 1974, 77, Disting. Scientist award U. South Fla. Coll. Medicine, 1981, Dean's Citation, 1991, Founder award, 1992, Outstanding Artist/Scholar award Phi Kappa Phi, 1991 Fellow: Am. Heart Assn., Am. Physiol. Soc. (fellow cardiovasc. sect.); mem.: Shock Soc. (program coms.), European Microcirculatory Soc., Microcirculatory Soc., Torch Club Internat. Republican. Avocations: golf, fishing, music. Home: 4039 Old Waynesboro Rd Augusta GA 30906-9254 Personal E-mail: microves@bellsouth.net.

BAKER, CHARLES DUANE, JR., former health insurance company executive, venture capital firm executive, board member; b. Nov. 13, 1956; m. Lauren Baker; children: Charlie, AJ, Caroline. BA in English, Harvard Coll., 1979; MBA, Northwestern U., 1986. Co-founder The Pioneer Inst. for Pub. Policy Rsch., 1988—91; State Under Secretary of Health and Human Services Gov. William Weld, Mass., 1991—92; Mass. Sec. of Health and Human Services, 1991—94; Mass. sec. of Adminstrn. and Fin. Gov. William Weld and successor Paul Cellucci, 1994—98; budget chief rep. administrn. to former Gov. William F. Weld; pres., CEO Harvard Vanguard Med. Assocs., 1998, Harvard Pilgrim Health Care, Quincy, Mass., 1999—2009; Republican candidate for 2010 Mass. Gubernatorial race, 2009—10; entrepreneur-in-residence Gen. Catalyst Ptnrs., 2011—. Media relations dir. New Eng. Coun.; corp. comm. dir. Mass. High Tech. Coun.; bd. trustee Natixis Funds; governing bd. mem. HealthView Services, Danvers, Mass., Kenneth B. Schwartz Ctr. for Compassionate Healthcare, Boston; bd. dirs. Tremont Credit Union, Med Ventive Inc., Waltham, Mass., 2010—, America Health Ins. Plans; bd. trustee IXIS Advisor Funds, Loomis Sayles Funds. Bd. mem. Greater Boston C. of C.; bd. trustee Rose Kennedy Greenway Conservancy; bd. selectman Swampscott, 2004—07. Recipient Disting. Svc. award, Nat. Gov.'s Assn., 1998. Mem.: Mass. Assn. of Health Plans (bd. chair). Republican. Office: Med Ventive Inc 400 5th Ave Ste 200 Waltham MA 02451-8706 also: General Catalyst Partners 20 University Rd 4th Fl Cambridge MA 02138 Office Phone: 781-290-2500. Office Fax: 781-290-2501. *

BAKER, DANIEL CLIFTON, III, plastic surgeon, educator; b. NYC, Dec. 11, 1942; s. Daniel Clifton Jr. and Geraldine Baker; m. Nina Griscom, Dec. 8, 1990 (div.). MD, Columbia U. Coll. Physicians & Surgeons, NYC, 1968. Diplomate Nat. Bd. Med. Examiners, Am. Bd. Plastic Surgery. Intern gen. surgery San Francisco Gen. Hosp., 1968—69; resident plastic surgery U. Calif., San Francisco, 1969—70, 1973—75; resident, head & neck surgery NYU Langone Med. Ctr., 1975—77; clin. fellow NYU/St. Vincent's Hosp./Columbia Presbyn. Med. Ctr., 1977—78; assoc. prof. plastic surgery NYU Sch. Medicine, NYC; surgeon dir. Manhattan Eye, Ear & Throat Hosp. Recipient Disting. Achievement award, Farleigh Dickinson U.; named one of Top Doctors in NY Metro Area, Castle Connolly Med. Ltd., 1999—2008, America's Top Doctors, 2002—08. Mem.: Am. Soc. Aesthetic Plastic Surgeons, Am. Soc. Plastic and Reconstructive Surgeons. Office: Pvt Practice 65 E 66th St New York NY 10021 Office Phone: 212-734-9695. Office Fax: 212-744-5410. E-mail: daniel.baker@med.nyu.edu.

BAKER, DAVID, biochemist; BA, Harvard U.; PhD in Biochemistry, U. Calif., Berkeley. Prof. biochemistry U. Wash., Seattle. Sci. adv. bd. Codon Devices, Cambridge, Mass.; investigator Howard Hughes Med. Inst., 2000—. Contbr. articles to sci. jours. Recipient Irving Sigal Young Investigator award, Protein Soc., 2000, Overton prize, Internat. Soc. Computational Biology, 2002, Feynman prize, Foresight

Inst., 2004, Newcomb Cleveland prize, AAAS, 2004, Raymond and Beverly Sackler Internat. prize in biophysics, Tel Aviv U., 2008. Mem.: NAS, Am. Acad. Arts & Sciences. Office: U Wash Dept Biochemistry J Wing Health Scis Bldg Box 357350 Seattle WA 98195

BAKER, DAVID A., obstetrician, gynecologist, educator; s. Milton and Sonia Baker; children: Dara A., Dawn G., Erica J. BS, Bklyn Coll., 1967; MS, U. Rochester, 1969; MD, SUNY, Bklyn., 1973. Diplomate Am. Bd. Ob-Gyn. Instr. ob-gyn U. Vt. Med. Ctr., Burlington, 1977—79; asst. prof. ob-gyn SUNY, Stony Brook, 1979—85; assoc. prof. dept. ob-gyn. SUNY Health Sci. Ctr., Stony Brook, 1985—98, prof. dept. ob-gyn., 1998—; assoc. prof. SUNY Dental Sch., Stony Brook, 1985—; hon. rsch. assoc. NY Bot. Garden's Cullman Program. With Best Drs. NY Mag., 2009; hon. rsch. assoc. NY Bot. Garden Cullman Prog., 2010—. Contbr. articles to profl. jours. Cons. LI HELP group, Beth Page, NY. Grantee Westat, NIAID, 1992—2003. Fellow: ACOG. Achievements include research in management and treament of Herpes virus infections. Avocation: gardening. Office: Dept Ob-gyn Health Scis Ctr SUNY Stony Brook NY 11794-8091 E-mail: dbaker@notes.cc.sunysb.edu.

BAKER, EDWARD L., JR., public health physician; b. Chattanooga, Nov. 18, 1946; s. Edward Lamar and Sue B. Baker; m. Pamela Taylor, June 21, 1969; children: Justin, Ryan, Lindsay. BA, Vanderbilt U., 1968; MD, Baylor U., 1972; MPH, Harvard U., 1979, MS, 1980. Diplomate Am. Bd. Internal Medicine, Am. Bd. Occupational Medicine. Commd. USPHS, 1974—2003, asst. surgeon gen.; dep. dir. Nat. Inst. for Occupational Safety; asst. prof. Harvard U. Sch. Pub. Health, Boston, 1980-82, assoc. prof., 1982-85; asst. dir. Nat. Inst Occupl. Safety and Health Ctr. Disease Control, Atlanta, 1985-88, dep. dir. Nat. Inst. Occupl. Safety and Health, 1988-90, dir. Pub. Health Practice Program Office, 1990—2003; dir. NC Inst. Pub. Health, Gillings Sch. Global Pub. Health U. NC, Chapel Hill, 2003—, prof. Dept. Health Policy and Mgmt. Bd. dirs. Internat. Commn. on Occupl. Health, 1986-92. Author, editor 100 sci. articles and book chpts. Fellow Am. Coll. Epidemiology; mem. APHA, Am. Coll. Occupl. and Environ. Medicine (authorship award 1988), Soc. Occupl. and Environ. Health, Royal Soc. Medicine (London, vis. fellow). Office: NC Inst Public Health Univ North Carolina Campus Box 8165 Chapel Hill NC 27599-8165 Office Phone: 919-966-1069. Office Fax: 919-966-0478. Business E-Mail: ed_baker@unc.edu.

BAKER, FLOYD WILMER, surgeon, retired military officer; b. Leavenworth, Kans., May 25, 1927; s. Floyd Winfield and Lolita Clare (Somers) B.; m. Darlene Marie Fulk, Apr. 10, 1949; children: Linda Marie, Diane Louise, Barbara Jayne. BA, U. Kans., 1950, MD, 1953; grad., Army Command and Gen. Staff Coll., 1964, Indsl. Coll. Armed Forces, 1967. Diplomate: Am. Bd. Surgery. Commd. 1st lt. U.S. Army, 1953, advanced through grades to maj. gen., 1980; intern Madigan Gen. Hosp., Tacoma, 1953-54; resident in gen. surgery Fitzsimons Army Hosp., Denver, [illegible] dir. personnel and [illegible] Office of Surgeon Gen., 1970-71; comdg. gen. Brooke Army Med. Center, Ft. Sam Houston, Tex., 1974-78; Letterman Army Med Center, Presidio of San Francisco, 1978-81; chief surgeon U.S. Army, Europe; comdg. gen. U.S. Army 7th Med. Command, 1981-83, U.S. Army Health Services Command, Ft. Sam Houston, 1983-86; retired U.S. Army, 1986. Served with USNR, 1945-46. Decorated Legion of Merit (2), Meritorious Service medal, Army Commendation medal (3), Air medal (2), Disting. Service medal. Fellow Am. Coll. Physician Execs.; mem. AMA, Soc. U.S. Army Flight Surgeons. Republican. Baptist. Home and Office: 1413 Wiltshire Ave San Antonio TX 78209-6050 E-mail: fbaker1@satx.rr.com. *

BAKER, HERMAN, medical educator, writer; b. NYC, Jan. 22, 1926; s. Harry and Fannie Baker; m. Shirley Levitz, Nov. 15, 1952; children: Elliott Robert, Joel Martin. BS, CCNY, 1946; MS, Emory U., 1948; PhD, NYU, 1956. Cert. specialist human nutrition Am. Bd. Nutrition. Research asst. Columbia U., NYC, 1949-50; research assoc. Mt. Sinai Hosp., NYC, 1950-60; assoc. prof. medicine N.J. Med. Sch., Jersey City, 1960-70, prof. medicine and preventive medicine Newark, 1970—. Author: Clinical Vitaminology: Methods and Interpretation, 1968; contbr. articles to profl. jours. Fellow: Am. Coll. Nutrition. Avocation: music. Home: 27 Wilk Rd Edison NJ 08837-2726 Office: NJ Med Sch ADMC 1618A 30 Bergen St Newark NJ 07107-3001 Office Phone: 973-972-4664. Business E-Mail: bakerhe@umdnj.edu.

BAKER, J. DENNIS, surgeon; b. Flint, Mich., 1938; MD, Columbia U., 1966. Diplomate Am. Bd. Gen. Vascular Surgery. Intern Bellevue Hosp. Ctr., NYC, 1966-67; resident in surgery Tufts U.-New Eng. Med. Ctr., Boston, 1969-73; resident in vascular surgery Henry Ford Hosp., Detroit, 1973-74; fellow in surgery Tufts U., Boston, 1972-73; chief sect. vascular surgery VA Med. Ctr., Sepulveda, Calif., 1974-94; attending surgeon UCLA Med. Ctr., LA, 1974—; staff surgeon West L.A. VA Med. Ctr., 1994—; acad. faculty UCLA Sch. Medicine, 1974—. Fellow ACS; mem. Am. Heart Assn., Am. Surg. Assn., Soc. Clin. Vascular Surgery, Soc. Vascular Surgery, Western Vascular Surgery. Home Phone: 310-475-5682; Office Phone: 310-825-3684. E-mail: jbaker@mednet.ucla.edu. *

BAKER, JAMES L., JR., plastic surgeon, educator; b. Somerville, NJ, 1936; MD, U. Amsterdam, 1964. Diplomate Am. Bd. Plastic Surgery. Intern Monmouth Med. Ctr., Long Branch, NJ, 1964—65, resident gen. surgery, 1965—69; resident plastic surgery Orlando Regional Med. Ctr., Fla., 1969—71; fellow hand surgery U. Louisville, 1971; clin. prof. plastic surgery U. South Fla., Tampa, 1991—; pvt. practice Winter Park, Fla. Prof. surgery, dept. med. edn. U. Ctrl. Fla. Coll. Medicine, Orlando; past chmn. dept. plastic surgery Fla. Hosp. Sys. Contbr. articles to profl. jours., chapters to books. Mem.: Fla. Soc. Plastic & Reconstructive Surgeons (pres. 1984), Am. Soc. Aesthetic Plastic Surgery (pres. 1995—96). Office: Pvt Practice 400 W Morse Blvd Ste 203 Winter Park FL 32789-4280 Office Phone: 407-644-5242. Office Fax: 407-644-0236. E-mail: jlbakerjr@msn.com.

BAKER, JAMES RUSSELL, JR., allergist, immunologist, educator; MD, Loyola U., 1978. Diplomate Am. Bd. Internal Medicine, 1981, Am. Bd. Internal Medicine-diagnostic lab. immunology, 1986. Intern Walter Reed Army Med. Ctr., 1979, resident internal medicine, 1979—81, fellow allergy & immunology, 1981—84; prof. internal medicine dept. Univ. Mich. Med. Sch., prof. pathology dept.; ruth dow doan prof. Biologic Nanotechnology; divsn. chief allergy and clin. immunology Univ. of Mich. Hosps. and Health Centers. Office: University of Michigan Hospitals and Health Centers 1500 E Medical Center Dr Ann Arbor MI 48109 Office Phone: 734-936-4000.

BAKER, JEFFREY HOPKINS, physician; b. Bellefonte, Pa., Apr. 7, 1956; BS, Pa. State U., 1978; MD, Pa. State Coll. Medicine, 1982. Diplomate Am. Bd. Med. Acupuncture, Am. Bd. Integrative Holistic Medicine. Physician Family Practice Assocs. State Coll., PC, 1985—89; family medicine physician Geisinger Clinic, 1989—99; pvt. practice in family medicine, 2000—. Fellow: Am. Acad. Family Physicians; mem.: Pa. Med. Soc., Am. Bd. Integrative Holistic Medicine, Am. Acad. Med. Acupuncturists, Am. Bd. Med. Acupuncturists. Avocations: piano, bicycling. Office: 724 S Atherton St Ste 200 State College PA 16801 Office Fax: 814-867-0464. Personal E-mail: jhbaker56@verizon.net.

BAKER, JULIEN STEVEN, medical researcher; b. South Wales, Wales, United Kingdom; s. Milton and Jose Baker; m. Olivia Gair, Sept. 11, 1999; children: Alyn, Fay, Morgan, Oliver. PhD, U. Glamorgan, Pontypridd, 1997—2000; MSc, Loughborough U., Loughborough, 1989—90; BA(Hons), U. Wales, Inst., Cardiff, 1986—89. Reader in applied physiology U. of Glamorgan, South Wales, Wales, United Kingdom, 1997—. Fellow, Royal Soc. of Medicine, 2001. Mem.: Am. Physiological Soc., Physiological Soc. Great Britian. Achievements include research in over 100 peer reviewed small papers and full publications. Office: Applied Sci U Glamorgan Llantwit Rd Pontypridd Wales South Wales CF37 1DL England Office Fax: 01443 482285. E-mail: jsbaker@glam.ac.uk.

BAKER, K. SCOTT, pediatrician, educator; MD, U. Nebr. Coll. Medicine, Omaha, 1988; MS in Clin. Rsch., U. Minn., Mpls., 2002. Diplomate Am. Bd. Pediat., cert. in pediatric hematology/oncology. Intern pediat. U. Nebr. Med. Ctr., resident pediat.; hematology-oncology fellow Children's Hosp. Med. Ctr., Cin., 1994; prof. pediatric hematology-oncology & bone marrow transplant U. Nebr. Coll. Medicine; assoc. prof., physician pediat. blood & marrow transplantaion U. Minn. Med. Sch., 1997—2008, dir. outpatient blood & marrow transplant clinic, dir. pediatric hematology-oncology/blood & marrow transplant fellowship program; dir. survivorship prog. Fred Hutchinson Cancer Rsch. Ctr., Seattle Children's Hosp. & Rsch. Found., 2009—; prof. pediat. U. Wash., Seattle, 2009—. Named to Best Doctors in America, 2007—08. Office: Seattle Childrens B 6553 Hematology Oncology 4800 Sand Point Way NE Seattle WA 98105 also: Fred Hutchinson Cancer Rsch Ctr FHCRC Box 358080 MS D5 283 PO Box 19024 Seattle WA 98109 Office Phone: 206-987-2106.

BAKER, LEE EDWARD, biomedical engineering educator; b. Springfield, Mo., Aug. 31, 1924; s. Edward Fielding and Oneita Geneva (Patton) B.; m. Jeanne Carolyn Ferbrache, June 20, 1948; children: Carson Phillips, Carolyn Patton. BEE, U. Kans., 1945; MEE, Rice U., 1960; PhD in Physiology, Baylor U., 1965. Registered profl. engr., Tex. Asst. prof. electrical engring. Rice U., Houston, 1960-64; asst. prof. physiology Baylor U. Coll. Medicine, Houston, 1965-69, assoc. prof., 1969-75; prof. biomed. engring. U. Tex., 1975-82, Robert L. Parker Sr. Centennial Prof. Engring, Austin, 1982-2000, prof. emeritus, 2000—. Co-author: Principles of Applied Biomedical Engineering, 1968, 3d edit., 1989; author, co-author scientific papers. Served to lt. USN, 1943-46, PTO, 1951-53. Spl. research fellow NIH, 1964-65. Fellow Am. Inst. Med. and Biol. Engring., Royal Soc. Medicine; mem. IEEE (sr.), Biomed. Engring. Soc. (sr.), Am. Physiol. Soc. Office: Univ Tex Biomed Engring Dept Austin TX 78712 Business E-Mail: leb@mail.utexas.edu.

BAKER, PHILIP STEVEN, dentist, educator; m. Jacqulyn Bennett, June 25, 1995. BS in Biology, Regis Coll., 1974; DDS, Loyola U., 1978. Diplomate Am. Bd. Prosthodontics, 2005. From clin. instr. to asst. prof. Sch. Dentistry Loyola U., Chgo., 1978—85; from asst. prof. to assoc. prof. Coll. Dentistry U. Fla., Gainesville, Fla., 1987—98; assoc. prof. Coll. Dental Medicine, Ga. Health Scis. U., 1998—. Interim dir. grad. prosthodontics. Recipient Tchg. Excellence award, Coll. Dental Medicine, Ga. Health Scis. U., 2008; named Outstanding Tchr. of Yr., U. Fla. Coll. Dentistry, 1989. Fellow: Am. Coll. Prosthodontists (pres. Ga. sect. 2003—04). Office: Ga Health Scis University Coll Dental Medicine 1120 15th St Augusta GA 30912 Office Phone: 706-721-2261.

BAKER, R. ROBINSON, surgeon; b. Balt., Dec. 30, 1928; s. Henry Scott and Frances (Robinson) B.; m. Jean Harvey, Sept. 12, 1953; children: Susan, Scott, Robert, Jean. AB, Johns Hopkins U., 1950, MD, 1954. Diplomate Am. Bd. Surgery, Bd. Thoracic Surgery. Intern Johns Hopkins U., 1954-55; sr. asst. surgeon Nat. Heart Inst., 1955-57; asst. resident Johns Hopkins Hosp., 1957-58, resident, 1958-61, chief surg. resident, 1961-62; surgeon-in-charge Johns Hopkins Hosp. (Breast Clinic), 1970—, Johns Hopkins Hosp. (Oncology Center), 1976; prof. surgery Johns Hopkins U., 1967—, prof. oncology, 1975—, Warfield M. Firor perf. surgery, 1991—; mem. (Coop. Lung Cancer Detection Group), 1971—. Recipient grants Am. Cancer Soc., 1966-71, grants John A. Hartford Found., 1968-73, grants Upjohn Co., 1973, grants Sterling-Winthrop Rsch. Inst., 1975—; named hon. fellow Royal Coll. Surgeons of Ireland. Fellow ACS, Royal Coll. Surgeons (hon.); mem. Soc. Univ. Surgeons, Am. Assn Thoracic Surgery, So. Thoracic Surg. Assn., Soc. Head and Neck Surgeons, AMA, Am., So. Surg. Assns., Elkridge (Balt.) Club, Fishers Island (N.Y.) Club, Hay Harbor Club (Fishers Island). Home: 8717 Mcdonogh Rd Baltimore MD 21208-1021 Office: 600 N Wolfe St Baltimore MD 21287-0005 E-mail: rrbaker@jhmi.edu.

BAKER, RAYMOND CHARLES, pediatrician, educator; b. Elkhart, Ind., Jan. 19, 1945; s. Ruth Abigail and Albert Easton Baker; m. Patricia Ann Rhine, Oct. 23, 1976; children: Katherine Ruth Thomas, Brandon Heath, Aimee Alexa, Zachary Justin. BSc, Ohio State U., Columbus, 1967, MD, 1971; MEd, U. Cin. Coll. Edn., 2001. Prof. pediat. U. Cin. Coll. Medicine, 1979—; med. educator Cin. Children's Hosp., 1979—. Contbr. articles to profl. jour. on pediatric primary care. Surgeon USPHS, 1972—74, Balt. Grantee, HRSA Bur. Health Professions, 1997—. Fellow: Am. Acad. Pediat.; mem.: Acad. Pediatric Assn. (Ann. Tchg. award 2007), Am. Pediatric Soc. Avocations: classical music, reading. Office: Cincinnati Children's Hosp ML 2011 3333 Burnet Ave Cincinnati OH 45229-3039

BAKER, ROBERT DENIO, pediatric gastroenterologist; BA in English cum laude, Harvard Coll., 1968; MD, Temple U. Sch. of Medicine, 1972; PhD in Nutritional Biochemistry and Metabolism, Mass. Inst. of Tech., 1984. Diplomate Am. Bd. of Pediatrics-pediatric gastroenterology. Intern Children's Hosp. of Buffalo, 1973, resident pediatrics, 1975; fellow gastroenterology Children's Hosp. of Boston, Mass. Gen. Hosp.; exec. bd. gastroenterology, nutrition and hepatology sect. Am. Acad. of Pediatrics; co-dir. Digestive Disease Nat. Coalition, 2000—. Prof. pediatrics SUNY Buffalo; physician Women & Childrens Hosp. of Buffalo. Author: (articles) Diagnosis and prevention of iron deficiency and iron-deficiency anemia in infants and young children (0-3 years of age), 2010, Role of alcohol metabolism in non-alcoholic steatohepatitis, 2010, Treatment with high-dose proton pump inhibitors helps distinguish eosinophilic esophagitis from noneosinophilic esophagitis, 2010, and several others. Named top dr., Buffalo Spree Mag. Office: Women and Children's Hospital of Buffalo 239 Bryant St Buffalo NY 14222 Office Phone: 716-878-7793. Office Fax: 716-888-3842. E-mail: rbaker2@buffalo.edu.

BAKER, ROBERT FRANK, molecular biologist, educator; b. Weiser, Idaho, Apr. 9, 1936; s. Robert Clarence and Beulah (Hulet) B.; m. Mary Margaret Murphy, May 29, 1965; children: Allison Leslie, Steven Mark. BS, Stanford U., 1959; PhD, Brown U., 1966. Postdoctoral rsch. assoc. Stanford (Calif.) U., 1966-68; asst. prof. dept. biol. scis. U. So. Calif., LA, 1968-72, assoc. prof., 1972-83, prof., 1983—, dir. molecular biology div., 1978-80, mem. Comprehensive Cancer Ctr., 1984—. Vis. assoc. prof. Harvard U. Med. Sch., Boston 1975-76; mem. genetic study sect. NIH, Bethesda, Md., 1977-79, 82 Contbr. articles to profl. jours. Grantee NIH, NSF, 1968—. Mem. Am. Soc. Zoologists, Am. Soc. Microbiology, Sigma Xi. Avocation: amateur radio. Home: 607 Almar Ave Pacific Palisades CA 90272-4208 Office: U So Calif Dept Molecular Biology Mc 1340 Los Angeles CA 90089-1340 Office Phone: 213-740-5565. Business E-Mail: baker@molbio.usc.edu.

BAKER, SUSAN P., public health educator; b. Atlanta, May 31, 1930; d. Charles Laban and Susan (Lowell) Pardee; m. Timothy Danforth Baker, June 23, 1951; children— Timothy D., David C., Susan L. AB, Cornell U., 1951; MPH, Johns Hopkins U., 1968; ScD (hon.), U. N.C., 1998. Rsch. assoc. Office of Chief Med. Examiner, Balt., 1968-81; rsch. assoc. Sch. Hygiene and Pub. Health, Johns Hopkins U., Balt., 1968-71, asst. prof., 1971-74, assoc. prof., 1974-83, prof. health policy and mgmt., 1983—, assoc. chmn. dept. health policy and mgmt., 1997-99, joint appointment in environ. health scis., 1975—, joint appointment in pediatrics, 1983—, dir. Injury Prevention Ctr., 1987-88, co-dir., 1988—94, acting head div. pub. health, 1988-90, joint appointment emergency medicine Sch. Medicine, 1991—. Vis. prof. U. Minn. Sch. Pub. Health, 1975-87; chmn. nat. rev. panel for nat. accident sampling sys. Dept. Transp., Washington, 1976-81; vice chmn. com. on trauma rsch. Nat. Rsch. Coun., Washington, 1984-85; mem. adv. com. on injury control CDC, 1989-95; mem. Armed Forces Epidemiol. Bd., 1996-2000, 04-06; commr. West Latir Ditch Assn., N.Mex., 1990—; vis. lectr. in injury prevention Harvard Sch. Pub. Health, 1984-87; John T. Law meml. lectr. U. Calgary, Alta., 1984; expert panel Age 60 rule FAA, 1991-93; cons. and lectr. in field. Author: (monograph) Fatally Injured Drivers, 1970 (Prince Bernhard medal 1974), The Injury Fact Book, 1984, 2d edit., 1992, Saving Children: A Guide to Injury Prevention, 1991, Injury Prevention: An International Perspective, 1998; contbr. articles to books and articles to profl. jours. Recipient Charles A. Dana award for pioneering achievements in health, 1989, Johns Hopkins U. Disting. Alumnus award, 1996, APHA Excellence award, 1999, Stebbins award Johns Hopkins Bloomberg Sch. Pub. Health, 2006, Calderone prize Columbia U., 2010; named to Md. Women Hall of Fame, 2006. Fellow Am. Assn. Automotive Medicine (bd. dirs. 1971-76, pres. 1974-75, award of merit 1985, Abe Mirkin Svc. award 2002), Aerospace Med. Assn. (editl. bd. 1994—, John Stapp award 2005, Moseley award 2010), Soc. Advancement Violence and Injury Rsch. (Champion award, 2006); mem. APHA (governing coun. 1975-77, jour. bd. 1983-87, award for excellence 1999), Am. Trauma Soc. (bd. dirs., Disting. Achievement award 1981, Stone lectr. 1985), Am. Assn. for Surgery of Trauma (hon., Fitts oration award 1996), Phi Beta Kappa, Delta Omega. Office: Johns Hopkins U Bloomberg Sch Pub Health 624 N Broadway Baltimore MD 21205-1900 Business E-Mail: sbaker@jhsph.edu.

BAKER, SUSAN S., pediatric gastroenterologist; BS, U. of Pitts.; MD, Temple U. Sch. of Medicine, 1972; PhD, Mass. Inst. of Tech. Diplomate Am. Bd. Pediatrics, 1978, Am. Bd. Pediatrics-pediatric gastroenterology, 2005. Intern Women and Children's Hosp. of Buffalo, 1973, resident, 1975, lab. dir. gastroenterology; fellow MIT, 1978—81, Harvard Univ., 1981—84; with Univ. of Mass. Med. Ctr., Univ. of SC, Inst. of Medicine, USDA, FDA; chairperson Am. Acad. of Pediatrics, Am. Bd. of Pediatrics. Dir. Pediatric GI Fellowship program. Named top dr., Buffalo Spree Mag. Office: Women and Childrens Hospital of Buffalo 219 Bryant St Buffalo NY 14201-2099 Office Phone: 716-878-7793.

BAKER, THOMAS J., JR., plastic surgeon; b. Clay, Ky., Nov. 8, 1925; MD, U. Ind., 1949. Diplomate Am Bd. Surgery, Am. Bd. Plastic Surgery, cert. of advanced edn. in cosmetic surgery Am. Soc. Aesthetic Plastic Surgery. Intern plastic surgery Jackson Meml. Hosp., Miami, 1949—50, resident, 1951—55, U. Tex., 1955—57; pvt. practice Miami; clin. prof. plastic surgery U. Miami Sch. Medicine, 1997—. Staff Mercy Hosp., Miami; clin. prof. plastic surgery U. Tex. Med. Ctr., Galveston. Mem.: Am. Assn. Plastic Surgeons (Disting. Fellow award 2000), Am. Soc. Plastic & Reconstructive Surgeons (Spl. Achievement award 1999), Am. Soc. Aesthetic Plastic Surgeons (Disting. Svc. award 1990), Plastic Surgery Ednl. Found. (Disting. Svc. award 1989), Internat. Soc. Aesthetic Plastic Surgery (ednl. found. prof.). Achievements include development of the Baker-Gordon phenol peel which has been used successfully for over 40 years for deep chemical peeling producing reliable results. Office: Pvt Practice 9155 S Dadeland Blvd Miami FL 33156 Office Phone: 305-670-9995.

BAKER, TIMOTHY DANFORTH, physician, educator; b. Balt., July 4, 1925; s. Frank A. and Alice Elizabeth (Chandler) Baker; m. Susan Lowell Pardee, June 23, 1951; children: Timothy, David, Susan. BA, Johns Hopkins U., 1948, MPH, 1954; MD, U. Md., 1952. Intern U. Md. Hosp., Balt., 1952-53; resident pub. health N.Y. State Dept. Pub. Health, Albany, 1953-56; health officer Syracuse, NY, 1958-59; asst. and acting chief health USAID, India, 1956-58; assoc. prof. Johns Hopkins U. Sch. Pub. Health, Balt., 1959-67, asst. dean, 1959-77, prof. internat. health, health svcs. adminstrn., and environ. health, 1967—, pres. faculty gen. assembly, 1987—, dir. Hubert H. Humphrey scholars program, 1987—. V.p., dir. Univ. Assocs., 1973-77; vis. prof. epidemiology U. Minn., 1976; dir. Intermed., 1982—; external examiner U. Singapore; vis. prof. Am. U., Armenia, 1999, U. Sao Paulo, Brazil; mem. Surgeon Gen.'s Com. on Global Health, 2004; mem. Md. Gov.'s Commn. on Minority Health, Md. Gov.'s

Task Force on Violence; cons., 27 countries Inst. Medicine, 2007. Author: Health Manpower in a Developing Economy, Assessment of Health Status and Needs, International Health Perspectives; contbr. articles to profl. publs. First vice chmn. Balt. com. Rep. Party; del., nominating com. Rep. party; bd. dirs., treas. Pan Am. Health Edn. Found. With USAF, 1943-45; USPHS, 1956-58. Recipient Disting. Grad. award, Balt. Poly. Inst., Heritage award, Johns Hopkins U. Fellow: AAAS; mem.: APHA (chmn. epidemiology sect., internat. health sect., Lifetime Achievement award 1994), Balt. Med. Soc. (chmn. med. care com.), Md. Pub. Health Assn. (pres., H.P. & M.P. Laughlin Disting. Author-Editor award 2007), Md. Med. Soc. (chmn. health manpower com., ho. of dels., editl. bd., guest editor Md. Medicine), Delta Omega, Omicron Delta Kappa. Republican. Home: 13801 York Rd E6 Cockeysville MD 21030 Office: Johns Hopkins U Sch Hygiene 615 N Wolfe St Baltimore MD 21205-2103 Office Phone: 410-614-3819. Business E-Mail: tbaker@jhsph.edu.

BAKIRCIOGLU, MUSTAFA EMRE, urologist; s. Mehmet and Huriye Bakircioglu; m. Fatma Dilek Bakircioglu, Aug. 20, 2000; children: Mehmet, Zeynep. MD, U. Istanbul, Cerrahpasa Med. Sch., 1990. Urology resident Haydarpasa Numune Hosp., Istanbul, 1992—97; postdoc. fellow U. Calif., San Francisco, 1996—2000. Recipient Hon. Mention award, Lapides Essay Contest, 1996, Second prize, 2000, Physician Essay Contest First prize, Joseph F. McCarthy and Circon ACMI, 1998, Basic Sci. Sect. Second prize, Internat. Bladder Symposium, 1999. Mem.: Soc. Male Reproduction and Urology, Turkish Soc. Urology, Turkish Soc. Andrology, Am. Soc. Reproductive Medicine, Am. Urology Assn. (Best Abstract award 2000). Office: German Hosp Siraselviler Cad No 119 Istanbul Turkey Personal E-mail: emre@emrebakircioglu.com.

BAKRIS, GEORGE L., nephrologist, educator, clinical researcher, hypertension specialist; b. Athens, June 15, 1952; arrived in U.S., 1952; s. Louis George Bakris and Athena Petros Marolias; m. Demetria Mary Arges, Nov. 26, 1983; children: Athena, Louis. BA in Biology/Psychology, Ind. U., 1974; MA in Human Devel., U. Chgo., 1975, MD in Medicine, 1981. Diplomate Am. Bd. Internal Medicine, Am. Bd. Nephrology, bd. cert. specialist in clin. hypertension Am. Soc. Hypertension. Staff nephrologist Ochsner Clinic, New Orleans, 1988-91, dir. renal rsch., 1988—91; asst. prof. medicine U. Tex. Health Sci. Ctr., San Antonio, 1991-93, dir. nephrology fellowship program, 1991—93; assoc. prof. preventive medicine and internal medicine Rush U. Med. Ctr., Chgo., 1993-98, prof. preventive medicine and internal medicine, 1998—2006, vice chmn. dept. preventive medicine and internal medicine, 1998—2006, dir. Hypertension Clinic Rush. Ctr., 1998—2006; prof. medicine, Hypertension Ctr. U. Chgo. Sch. Medicine, 2006—, dir. Hypertensive Diseas Ctr., 2006—. Adj. asst. prof. medicine Tulane U. Sch. Medicine, New Orleans, 1988—91; cons. cardiorenal divsn. FDA, Rockville, Md., 1993—2003; chmn. hypertension exec. coun. Nat. Kidney Found., NYC, 1998—2000. Editor: (book) Hypertension: A Clinician's Guide to Diagnosis and Treatment, 2d edit., 2000, The Kidney in Hypertension, 2004; co-editor: Hypertension: Practice and Principles, 2004; jour. guest editor: Jour. Mineral and Electrolyte Metabolism, 1998; contbr. articles to profl. jours.; editor: Am. Jour. Nephrology, 2002. Grantee, Nat. Inst. Diabetes and Digestive Diseases, 1994—2001, 2002—, heart, lung and blood divsn. NIH, 1996—2001, Clin. Rsch. Tng., prin. investigator, 1999—. Fellow: ACP, Am. Heat Assn. Coun., Am. Heart Assn. (coun. high blood pressure rsch. 1992—), Am. Coll. Clin. Pharmacology (pres. 2000—02); mem.: Am. Soc. Hyper Tension (pres. 2010—). Greek Orthodox. Avocations: writing music, guitar, golf, bowling. Office: Univ Chgo Sch Medicine 5841 S Maryland Ave MC1027 Rm P328A Chicago IL 60637 Office Phone: 773-702-7936. Office Fax: 773-834-0486. Personal E-mail: gbakris@gmail.com.

BAK-ROMANISZYN, LEOKADIA, gastroenterologist, educator, pediatrician; b. Mielec, Poland, Apr. 14, 1957; d. Michał and Janina (Kozioł) Bak; m. Mirosław Stanislaw Romaniszyn, Oct. 17, 1992. MD, Med. U., Łódź, Poland, 1982, 1st degree in pediatrics, 1986, 2d degree in pediatrics, 1992; PhD, Mil. Med. U., Łódź, 1996, 3d degree in gastroenterology, 1998. Jr. asst. dept. pediatrics Hosp. TB and Pulmonary, Łódź, 1982-83; asst. Inst. Mother's and Children's Diseases, Łódź, 1983-88; lectr., rschr. assoc. Polish Mother's Meml. Hosp., Łódź, 1988-89; sr. lectr., rsch. assoc. Mil. Med. U., Inst. Polish Mother's Meml. Hosp., 1989-96, asst. prof. dept. pediatrics, 1996—. Contbr. articles and abstracts to profl. publ. Grantee Polish. Sci. Found., 1992-95, Environ. Protection Fund for Province of Łódź, 1995-98, 99-2000, Polish Acad. Scis., 2000—; recipient 1st award sci. com. 25 Congress of Polish Pediat. Sci., 1997. Mem. Polish Pediat. Soc., Polish Gastroenterologic Soc. (1st award sci. com. congresses 1994, 1997, 2000, 06), NY Acad. Sci. Avocations: embroidery, travel. Office: Med U Inst Polish Meml Rzgowska Str 281 93-338 Lodz Poland Home: Ul. Trwala 3 93-535 Lodz Poland Personal E-mail: lbrmr@neostrada.pl. Business E-Mail: pinklinika@gmail.com, leokadia.bak-romaniszyn@umed.lodz.pl.

BAKSHI, JAIMANTI, otolaryngologist, educator, consultant; b. Renuka, India, Nov. 19, 1969; d. Sannu Ram and Dwarka Devi Chauhan; m. Navdeep Bandhu Bakshi, Feb. 6, 1998; 1 child, Aarushi. MBBS, Indira Gandhi Med. Coll., Shimla, 1994; MS in Otolaryngology, Postgrad. Inst. Med. Edn. and Rsch., Chandigarh, 1997. Diplomate Nat. Bd. Examinations Otolaryngology, 1998. Resident Postgrad. Inst. Med. Edn. & Rsch., Chandigarth, India, 1994—97, sr. resident in otolaryngology, 1997—2000, asst. prof., 2001—. Cons. surgeon Postgrad. Inst. Med. Edn. & Rsch., 2001—. Contbr. 65 articles to profl. jours. Recipient Rashtriya Gaurav award, India Internat. Friendship Soc., 2007, award, IBC, 2007, Best Citizen of India, 2008; named Internat. Health Profl. of Yr.; fellow, Postgrad. Inst. Med. Edn. & Rsch., 2000—01. Mem.: Internat. Rotary Assn. (vol.), Brit. Assn. Head and Neck Oncology Surgeons, Cochlear Implant Group India, Indian Med. Assn., Rhinology Soc. India, Am. Head and Neck Soc. (active mem. 2009—), Assn. Otolaryngologists of India, Postgrad. Inst. Alumni Assn., Indian Soc. Otology, Found. for Head and Neck Oncology India, Nat. Acad. Med. Scis., Assn. Otolaryngologists India, Indira Gandhi Med. Coll. Alumni Assn. Hindu. Achievements include research in injection snoreplasty, a painless cure for snoring; role of screening unilateral tonsillectomy in unknown primary with secondary neck; Misoprostol; a promising therapy for Tinnitus; oral cancer. Avocations: swimming, reading, music, writing. Office: Postgrad Inst Med Edn & Rsch Sector 12 Chandigarh 160012 India Office Phone: 09914209764, 09855827931. Personal E-mail: drjayabakshi@ymail.com.

BALABAN, YASEMIN HATICE, gastroenterologist; d. Mustafa and Ayse Semihan Balaban. MD, Hacettepe U., Ankara, 1996. Specialization in internal medicine Hacettepe U., 1996—2000, specialization in gastroenterology, 2000—04. Mem.: European Soc. Gastrointestinal Endoscopy (award 2006). Personal E-mail: ybalaban@superonline.com. Business E-Mail: ybalaban@hacettepe.edu.tr.

BALACHANDRAN, INDRA, cytologist; b. Coimbatore, India, Oct. 13, 1946; MS, Syracuse U., 1993, PhD, 1994. Staff cytotechnologist, instr., asst. prof. SUNY Upstate Med. U., 1976—90; assoc. prof., cytotech. Thomas Jefferson U., Phila., 1998—2006; program dir., cytotech. Albany Coll. Pharmacy & Health Scis., 2006—. Recipient Disting. Tchg. award, Lindbeck Found. Fellow: Internat. Acad. Cytology; mem.: Upper NY Soc. Cytology, Am. Soc. Cytotech., Am. Soc. Clin. Pathology, Am. Soc. Cytopathology. Avocations: reading, music, movies. Office: Albany Coll Pharmacy & Health Sci Albany NY 12208 Office Fax: 518-694-3437. Business E-Mail: indra.balachandran@acphs.edu.

BALACHANDRAN, KANARATH PAYATTIYATH, cardiologist; b. Mannamangalam, India, July 24, 1969; s. Ambat and Shanti Balakrishnan; m. Vandana Menon, May 5, 2001; 1 child, Ariyan. MBBS, Madras Med. Coll., 1993, MD, 1996. Sr. ho. officer Govt. Gen. Hosp. and Madras Med. Coll., Chennai, India, 1993—96; registrar Malar heart Found., Chennai, India, 1997—98, Hairmyres Hosp., East Kilbride, Lanarkshire, United Kingdom, 1998—99, Stobhill Hosp., Glasgow, Scotland, 1999—2000; rsch. fellow Hairmyres Hosp., East Kilbride, Lanarkshire, United Kingdom, 2000—02; specialist registrar Bristol Royal Infirmary, Bristol, South Gloucestershire, 2002—. Spkr. in cardiology Bristol Royal Infirmary, Bristol, South Gloucestershire, 2002—. Contbr. articles to profl. jours. Recipient Edmund Chalke Lerede award, Madras Med. Coll., 1995, Young Investigators award, European Soc. of Cardiology, 2002. Mem.: Scottish Soc. of Exptl. Medicine, Brit. Soc. of Interventional Cardiology, Brit. Soc. of Echocardiography, Brit. Cardiac Soc., Royal Coll. of Physicians (UK). Achievements include research in relevance of coronary pressure and collateral estimation in acute myocardial infarction; feasibility of coronary angioplasty in hospitals without on-site cardiac surgery. Office: Bristol Royal Infirmary Marlborough St South Gloucestershire Bristol BS2 8HW England Office Fax: 0044 117 9282666. Personal E-mail: kpbala@msn.com.

BALACUMARASWAMI, LOGNATHEN, cardiothoracic surgeon, researcher; s. Swamiappan Lognathen and Lognathen Gnanambadevi; m. Sindhuja L B Swami, June 1, 2001. MBBS, Madras Med. Coll., 1993. Specialist registrar cardiothoracic surgery SW Cardiothoracis Ctr. Derriford Hosp., Plymouth, Devon, England, 1997—99, Bristol Royal Infirmary, Bristol, Avon, 2000—01; rsch. fellow cardiac surgery Nuffield Dept. Surgery U. Oxford, John Radcliffe Hosp., Oxford, Oxfordshire, 2002—03; specialist registrar cardiothoracic surgery Papworth Hosp., Cambridge, England, 2004—05; specialist registrar Norfolk and Norwich U. Hosp., Noriwch, England, 2006. Contbr. articles to profl. jours. Grantee Med. Rsch. Fund, U. Oxford, 2003. Fellow: Royal Coll. Surgeons Edinburgh; mem.: Soc. Cardiothoracic Surgeons Gt. Britain and Ireland. Avocations: long distance running, swimming, music. Office: John Radcliffe Hospital Cardiothoracic Surgery Headley Way Headington Oxfordshire Oxford OX3 9DU England Personal E-mail: bala1log@yahoo.co.uk. E-mail: bala1log@doctors.org.uk.

BALADY, GARY, cardiologist, educator; MD, Robert Wood Johnson Med. Sch., New Brunswick, 1979. Diplomate Am. Bd. Internal Medicine, 1982, Am. Bd. Internal Medicine-cardiovasc. disease, 1985. Resident internal medicine Boston Univ. Med. Ctr., 1980—82, fellow cardiovasc. disease, 1982—85; prof. medicine Boston Univ. Sch. of Medicine, asst. dean admissions; dir. non invasive cardiovasc. labs. Boston Med. Ctr., dir. preventive cardiology cardiovasc. ctr. Assoc. editor (jour.) Circulation, editor-in-chief Journal of Cardiopulmonary Rehabilitation;, editor. Fellow: Am. Assn. of Cardiovasc. and Pulmonary Rehab. (past chmn. coun. on clin. cardiology), Am. Coll. of Cardiology, Am. Heart Assn. (past pres. Greater Boston divsn., immediate past pres. bd. dirs. founders affiliate). Office: Boston Medical Center Preston Family Bldg 3rd Fl 732 Harrison Ave Boston MA 02118

BALAGUÉ, FEDERICO, rheumatologist, director; b. Barcelona, Feb. 20, 1950; m. Gertrude Liechti; children: Nicolas, Olivier, Cecilia. MD, Sch. Medicine U. Barcelona, 1973. Assoc. dir. dept. rheumatology, phys. medicine & rehab. HFR Fribourg-Hôsp. cantonal, Switzerland, 1988—. Recipient Grammar award, Spine Soc. Europe, 2003. Mem.: Swiss Soc. Rheumatology (sci. com. 2005), Eurospine- Spine Soc. Europe (pres. 2008—09), Internat. Soc. Study Lumbar Spine (pres. 2009—10), Am. Acad. Phys. Medicine Rehab. Office: HFR Fribourg-Hôpital cantonal Bertigny Fribourg 1708 Switzerland Home Phone: +41264131908; Office Phone: +41264267380. Office Fax: +41264267387. E-mail: balaguef@h-fr.ch.

BALAMURUGAN, SENTHILNAYAGAM, pathologist, educator; b. Coimbatore, Oct. 9, 1969; MBBS, Stanley Med. Coll., Madras U., 1993; MD, Dr. ALM Postgrad. Inst., Madras U., 1997. Asst. prof. pathology Sree Ramchandra Med. Coll., 1997—2000; assoc.prof., asst. prof. pathology Madras Med. Coll., 2000—07; prof. pathology Chettinad Med. Coll. & Rsch. Inst., 2007—. Cons. pathologist, academician Chettinad Med. Coll., 2007—11. Recipient award, Tata Meml. Trust. Mem.: Indian Assn. Pathologists and Microbiologists. Avocations: reading, music, travel. Office: Chettinad Med. Coll & Rsch Inst IT Hwy Kancheepuram Tamil Nadu 603103 India Personal E-mail: ambikayal@yahoo.co.in.

BALARATNA, ASOKA, cardiologist; BA in Biochemistry cum laude, Case Western Res. U., 1987—91, MD, 1991—95. Diplomate Am. Bd. Internal Medicine, Am. Bd. Internal Medicine-interventional cardiology, 2002, Am. Bd. Internal Medicine-cardiovascular diseases, 2001. Resident intern medicine Univ. Hosps. of Cleve. Case Western Res. Univ., 1995—98, fellow cardiology Univ. Hosps. of Cleve., 1998—99; fellow cardiology Temple Univ. Hosp., Phila., 1999—2001, fellow interventional cardiology, 2001—02; staff cardiology divsn. Pila Heart Ctr. Abington Meml. Hosp., Abington, Pa., 2003—. Recipient numerous awards for vol. works. Office: Abington Medical Specialists Ste 222 Levy Medical Plz 1235 Old York Rd Abington PA 19001 Office Phone: 215-517-1000. Office Fax: 215-517-1049.

BALART, LUIS ANTONIO, JR., gastroenterologist; MD, La. State U. Sch. of Medicine, 1973. Diplomate Am. Bd. Internal Medicine-gastroenterology, 1981. Intern Charity Hosp., 1973—74; intern internal medicine La. State Univ., 1974—76; resident internal medicine Naval Regional Med. Ctr., Phila., 1974—76; fellow gastroenterology Ochsner Med. Instns., 1979—81; fellow hepatology Univ. of Southern Calif., 1981—82; physician Tulane Univ. Hosp. and Clinic, Chief Tulane gastroenterology and hepatology. Prof. medicine Tulane Univ. Sch. of Medicine. Office: Tulane University School of Medicine 1415 Tulane Ave Fl 6 New Orleans LA 70112 Office Phone: 504-988-5800.

BALAWY, SALEH DAKHEEL, surgeon, consultant; s. Dakheel Mohmmad and Hamdah Daroom Balawy; m. Abeer Mohmmad Karman; children: Tala, Danah, Raad. MB, BChir, Dow Med. Coll., Karachi, 1975. Diplomate Saudi Bd. Surgery. Cons. surgeon Armed Forces Hosp., Jeddah, Saudi Arabia, 1988—92, dep. clin. dir. surgery, 1992—93, clin. dir. surgery, 1993—97, sr. cons., transplant surgeon, 1997—; fellow transplant surgeon Royal Infirmary, Manchester, England, 1989—90. Tng. supr. Saudi Bd. Surgery, Saudi Arabia. Fundraiser Internat. Islamic Relief, Jeddah, 1995; physician Mecca Relief, Saudi Arabia, 2004. Govt. scholar, 1968—87. Fellow: ACS, Royal Coll. Surgeons Edinburgh, Royal Coll. Surgeons Glasgow; mem.: Saudi Transplant Soc., Brit. Transplant Soc. Avocations: reading, poetry, gardening.

BALCER, LAURA J., neurologist, neuro-ophthalmologist, educator; b. Baltimore, MD; m. David Lynch; 1 child, Abby. Grad. in Biology with higest honors, Coll. William and Mary, Williamsburg, Va.; MD, John Hopkins Sch. Medicine; MSCE, U. Pa., Phila. Diplomate Am. Bd. Psychiatry and Neurology, 1996. Fellow Hosp. of the Univ. Pa. Scheie Eye Inst.; intern Hosp. of the Univ. Pa., resident neurology, 1995, clin. fellow neuro-ophthalmology, assist. prof. neurology and ophthalmology Penn faculty, 1997, assoc. prof. neurology Penn faculty. Program dir. Neurologic Clin. Epidemiology T32 Tng. Grant. Named one of Top Docs, Phila. Mag., 2010, 2011, Best Doctors in America, 2005—06, 2007—08, 2009—10. Mem.: North Am. Neuro-Opthalmology Soc., Am. Acad. Neurology. Office: Hospital of the University of Pennsylvania 3400 Spruce St Philadelphia PA 19104 Office Phone: 215-662-3606.

BALCERZAK, STANLEY PAUL, retired hematologist, oncologist, director, medical educator; b. Pitts., Apr. 27, 1930; BS, U. Pitts., 1953; MD, U. Md., 1955. Diplomate Am. Bd. Internal Medicine, Am. Bd. Hematology, Am. Bd. Oncology. Instr. medicine U Chgo., 1959-60, U. Pitts., 1962-64, asst. prof., 1964-67; assoc. prof. medicine Ohio State U., Columbus, 1967-71, prof., 1971-99, prof. emeritus, 1999—, dir. div. hematology and oncology, 1969-94, dep. dir. Ohio State U. Comprehensive Cancer Ctr., 1984-97, assoc. chmn. dept. medicine, 1984-98, dir. Hemophilia Ctr., 1975-79, 1981-99. Mem. clin. rev. com. Am. Cancer Soc., N.Y.C., 1976-82 Contbr. chpts. to books, numerous articles to profl. jours. Served to capt. U.S. Army, 1960-62 Recipient numerous grants Fellow ACP; mem. Central Soc. for Clin. Research (chmn. subsplty. council in hematology 1980-81, councillor 1980-83), Am. Soc. for Clin. Oncology, Am. Assn. for Cancer Research, Am. Soc. Hematology, Phi Beta Kappa, Alpha Omega Alpha Home: 3113 N 3 Bs And K Rd Sunbury OH 43074-9582 Office: Ohio State U Divsn Hematology Oncology 320 W 10th Ave Columbus OH 43210-1240 Home Phone: 740-524-7191; Office Phone: 614-293-8729. Business E-Mail: balcerzak.1@osu.edu.

BALCH, CHARLES M., surgeon, educator; b. Milford, Del., Aug. 24, 1942; m. Carol Mitchell; 4 children. BS cum laude, U. Toledo, 1963; MD, Columbia U., 1967. Diplomate Am. Bd. Surgery (bd. dirs. 1986-1992). Intern in surgery Duke U. Med. Ctr., Durham, N.C., 1967-68; resident in gen. surgery U. Ala., Birmingham, 1970-71, 73-75, asst. prof. to assoc. prof. dept. surgery, 1975-81, prof, 1981-85, chief sect. surg. oncology, 1979-85, asst. to assoc. prof. dept. microbiology, 1975-82, prof., 1982-85; assoc. scientist to sr. scientist, sr. investigator cellular immunobiology unit Comprehensive Cancer Ctr., U. Ala., 1975-85, assoc. dir for clin. studies, 1979-85, acting dir., 1982-83; head div. surgery and anesthesiology U. Tex.-M.D. Anderson Cancer Ctr., Houston, 1985-94, v.p. hosp. and clinics, 1993-94, chmn. dept. surgical oncology, 1985-94, prof. surgery, 1993-96, exec. v.p. health affairs, 1994-96; pres., CEO City of Hope, 1996—98; exec. v.p. Am. Soc. Clinical Oncology, Alexandria, Va. Assoc. chmn. dept. surgery U. Tex., 1985-94; staff surgeon, chief oncology rsch. VA Hosp., Birmingham, 1975-85; vis. prof., Eleanor Roosevelt internat. fellow U. Sydney, Australia, 1983; chmn. nat. intergroup melanoma com., Nat. Cancer Inst., NIH, 1981—, mem. subcom. bd. sci. counselors, 1980-86, mem. bd. sci. counselors, 1987-1991, other coms., 1978—; mem. Kettering selection com. GM Cancer Rsch. Found., Inc., 1986, vice chmn., 1987-88, mem. awards assembly, 1988—; prof. surgery & oncology, Johns Hopkins Med. Institutions, 2000-. Author, editor-in-chief: (with G.W. Milton) Cutaneous Melanoma: Clinical Management and Treatment Results Worldwide, 1985, 98, 2003, 09; author, editor: Surgical Approaches to Cutaneous Melanoma, 1985; author over 100 book chpts. including Hardy's Textbook of Surgery, 1988, The Physiologic Basis of Modern Surgical Care, 1988, Textbook on Clinical Oncology, 1991, Advances in Surgery, 1991, Cancer: Principles and Practice of Oncology, 1989, Current Surgical Therapy, 3d edit., 1989; author over 280 jour. articles, abstracts; mem. editorial bds. Practical Rev. in Cancer Mgmt., 1979-85, Ala. Jour. Med. Scis., 1979-81, Jour. Biol. Response Modifiers, 1981—, Am. Jour. Clin. Oncology, 1981-84, Jour. Surg. Rsch., 1982-88, Jour. Immunology, 1982-85, Cancer Treatment Reports, 1984— (also adv. bd.), Jour. Clin. Oncology, 1986—, Archives Surgery, 1986—, Surgery, 1986—, European Jour. Cancer, 1989—, Melanoma Rsch., 1990—, Postgrad. Gen. Surgery, 1991—, many others; editor The Melanoma Letter, 1986-93, Breast Diseases: A Year Book Quarterly, 1990—, Annals of Surgical Oncology, 1993—; assoc. editor Advances in Surgery, 1986—, Cancer Rsch., 1989—. Program specialist USPHS, 1968-70. Immunology fellow Lab. Dr. J. Feldman, La Jolla, Calif., 1971-73; NIH grantee, 1980-84, 83-85, 84-87, 84-86,87-1993, VA, 1981-84, 84-89, CEP grantee, 1990-92, NCI grantee, 1987-94. Fellow ACS (various coms. on commn. on cancer, 1980—, chmn. edn. com. 1981-84, chmn. cancer mgmt. course con. 1981-83, assoc. Internat. Fedn. Surg. Colls. 1988—, mem. surg. forum 1985-91, grantee 1984-88, 85-91); mem. AMA, Am. Cancer Soc. (bd. dirs. Ala. divsn. 1983-85, exec. bd. Bay Area chpt. Houston 1986—, clin. fellowship nat. divsn. 1985-87, mem. profl. edn. subcom. clin. fellowship 1988), Am. Radium Soc. (chmn. publs. com. 1982-84), Am. Soc. Clin. Oncology (sci. and publs. coml 1987-90, bd. dirs.), Assn. Acad. Surgery (sec.-treas. 1981-83, pres.-elect 1983-84, pres. 1984-85, exec. coun. 1982-86), Assn. Surg. Edn., Conjoint Coun.

Surg. Edn. (cancer com. 1985—), Soc. Biol. Therapy, Soc. Surg. Oncology (sec. 1986-88, v.p. 1989-90, chmn. membership com. 1986-89, clin. rsch. and govt. rels. com. 1983-85, pres. elect 1990-91, pres. 1991-92), Soc. Univ. Surgeons (councilman 1982-85), Southeastern Cancer Study Group (chmn. surg. com. 1978-85, exec. com. 1979-85, chmn. melanoma/sarcoma com. 1983-85), Am. Soc. Clin. Investigation, Am. Assn. Cancer Edn., Am. Assn. Cancer Rsch., Am. Assn. Immunologists, Am. Assn. Transplant Surgeons, Am. Surg. Assn., European Soc. Surg. Oncology, Harris county Med. Soc., Houston Surg. Soc., Jefferson County Med. Soc., John Kirklin Soc., Pan-Pacific Surg. Assn., Reticuloendothelial Soc., Soc. Internat. de Chirurgie, Soc. Surg. Chmn., Tex. Surg. Soc., WHO Melanoma Group, others. Office: Johns Hopkins Med Institutions 1550 Orleans St Rm 509 Baltimore MD 21231 Business E-Mail: balchch@jhmi.edu.

BALCI, BAHATTIN, cardiologist, researcher; b. Samsun, Turkey, Aug. 20, 1964; s. Ismail and Rabiye Balci; m. Belma Karsli, July 15, 1996; children: Aylin Ece, Ozgur Kagan. MD, Cerrahpasa Med. Sch., Istanbul, 1990. Physician Diyarbakir and Samsun, Turkey, 1990—92; fellow cardiology Ataturk U., Erzurum, 1993—97; specialist Mugla and Samsun, 1997—99; asst. prof., rschr. Ondokuz Mayis U., Samsun, 1999—. Contbr. articles to profl. publs. Achievements include research in hypertension and interventional cardiology. Home: Istasyon Mh Saadet Cd Baris Ap No=101 Samsun 55060 Turkey Personal E-mail: bahattinbalci@ttnet.net.tr.

BALCI, BIRGUL DONMEZ, medical researcher; b. Cyprus, Jan. 27, 1979, PhD, Dokuz Eylul U., 2009. Rsch. asst. Sch. Physiotherapy and Rehab., Dokuz Eylul U., 2001—. Office: Dokuz Eylul University Sch Physiotherapy and Rehab Izmir Inciralti 35330 Turkey Personal E-mail: birguldonmez@gmail.com.

BALCIUNAS, MINDAUGAS, surgeon; b. Vilnius, Sept. 13, 1974; MD, Vilnius U., 1999. Head cardiac surgery ICU Vilnius U. Hosp. Santariskiu Klinikos, 2003—. Office: Santariskiu 2 Vilnius 08661 Lithuania Business E-Mail: mindaugas.balciunas@santa.lt.

BALDERSTON, RICHARD A., orthopaedic surgeon, educator; MD, U. Pa., 1977. Lic. Pa., 1978, NJ, 1998, diplomate Am. Bd. Orthopaedic Surgery, 1985. Intern gen. surgery Main Line Hosp., 1978; fellow Univ. Minn. Health System, 1983; hosp. affiliations include Grad. Hosp., Main Line Health System, Virtua West Jersey Hosp.; resident orthop. surgery Pa. Hosp., 1982, clin. prof. orthop. surgery, surgeon, chief spine surgery. Recipient Best Doctor, Best Doctors in America, 2008—10; named one of America's Top Doctors, 2007—08, 2010, the Top Doctors, Phila. Mag., 2008—11. Office: Pennsylvania Hospital 1 Cathcart 800 Spruce St Philadelphia PA 19107 Office Phone: 215-829-2222.

BALDI, ALFONSO, pathologist; b. Salerno, Italy, Feb. 22, 1968, s. Feliciano Baldi and Amalia Rinaldi; m. Nicoletta Onori, May 15, 1999; children: Feliciano, Giulio Diploma medicine, U. Federico II, Naples, Italy, 1992. Resident pathology U. Federico II, Naples, 1992—96; asst. prof. pathology Second U. Naples, 2001—05, assoc. prof. pathology, 2006—; postdoctoral fellow Temple U., Phila., 1993—94 Thomas Jefferson U., Phila., 1994—96, U. Navarra, Pamplona, 1997; rschr., tutor U. Campus Biomedico, Rome, 1997—99; rschr. Regina Elena Cancer Inst., Rome, 2000—01. Chief Lab. Molecular Diagnostic Centro Diagnostico, 1998—99. Mem.: AAAS, Am. Assn. for Clin. Rsch., N.Y. Acad. Scis., Soc. Neurosci. Roman Catholic. Achievements include patent for Human Retinoblastoma-Related Genomic DNA and Methods for Detecting Mutations Therein; discovery of Retinoblastoma-related gene; involvement of Simian Virus 40 in the pathogenesis of human mesothelioma; prognostic role of the CDK-Inhibitor P27 in lung cancer; definition of a software for the analysis and comparison of dermoscopic images; definition of an equipment for electrochemotherapy. Office: Second U Naples Dept Biochemistry Via L Armanni 80100 Naples Italy Office Phone: +390815666003. E-mail: alfonsobaldi@tiscali.it.

BALDRICK, PAUL, toxicologist; b. Londonderry, Northern Ireland, Feb. 27, 1962; s. Matthew and June (Galbraith) Baldrick; m. Lynda Margaret Crighton; children: Camilla Elizabeth, Clarissa Alice. BSc in Zoology with honors, Durham U., Eng., 1983, PhD, 1987. Cert. biologist; registered toxicologist. Rschr. Durham U., 1983-87; study dir. Huntingdon Life Scis., England, 1988-92; sr. toxicologist Fisons Pharms., Loughborough, England, 1993—96; head toxicology UCB Pharma, Braine l'Alleud, Belgium, 1996—98. Contbr. articles to numerous profl. jours., chapters to books; mem. editl. bd.: Jour. Applied Toxicology and Food Chemical Tox. Mem. Inst. Biology, Brit. Toxicology Soc., Org. Profl. Regulatory Affairs, Drug Info. Assn., Toxicokinetics Discussion Group, Assn. Inhalation Toxicologists, Biologics Expert Working Group, Round Table Office: Head Regulatory Affairs-Pharm Sci & Regulatory Consultancy Otley Road HG3 1PY Harrogate England

BALDRIDGE, ALAN, pediatric gastroenterologist educator; Attended, Med. Coll. Va. Diplomate Am. Bd. Pediatrics, Am. Bd. Pediatrics-Pediatric Gastroenterology & Nutrition. Intern Boston City Hosp., resident; fellow Children's Hosp., Boston; asst. prof. pediat. Cooper Univ. Hosp., head divsn. pediatric gastroenterology/nutrition. Named Top Pediatric GI Physician, SJ Mag., Phila. Mag. Mem.: Phila. GI Tng. Dirs. Soc., North Am. Soc. for Pediatric GI. Office: Cooper University Hospital 6400 Main St Voorhees NJ 08043 Mailing: Cooper University Hospital Ste 200 Three Cooper Plz Camden NJ 08103 Office Phone: 856-751-9339, 856-342-2001.

BALDWIN, BONNIE, physician; b. Dallas, Dec. 18, 1954; d. Eugene and Mary Ellen Jericho; m. Robert Talbot Baldwin, May 28, 1985; children: Robert, Ryan. AB, Duke U., Durham, NC, 1977; MD, Baylor Coll. Medicine, 1985. Gen. surgery resident U. Tex.-Houston, 1985-88; plastic surgery resident Baylor Coll. Medicine, Houston, 1988-91; asst. prof. M.D. Anderson Cancer Ctr., Houston, 1991-97; physician pvt. practice, Houston, 1997—. Med. advisor Reach for Recovery, Houston, 1999, cons. M.D. Anderson, 1998—. Contbr. articles to profl. jours. Named Best Scientific Exhibit Am. Soc. Aesthetic Plastic Surgery, 1997. Fellow ACS; mem. Am. Soc. Plastic Surgery, Soc. Surg. Oncology, Am. Soc. Aesthetic Plastic Surgery. Office: Cons in Plastic Surgery 7737 Southwest Fwy Ste 201 Houston TX 77074-1865 Office Phone: 713-791-1975. Business E-Mail: bjb@bonniebaldwinmd.com.

BALDWIN, DAVID SHEPARD, physician; b. Rochester, NY, Sept. 5, 1921; s. Jacob and Anna B.; m. Halee Morris, June 24, 1945; children: Neil, Andrew, Daniel, James. BA, U. Rochester, 1943, MD, 1945. Intern Barnes Hosp., St. Louis, 1945-46; resident in medicine Bellevue Hosp., NYC, 1946-48; renal fellow in medicine and physiology NYU Sch. Medicine, 1948-50, mem. faculty, 1950—, prof. medicine, nephrology, 1972—2004, prof. emeritus, 2004—. Attending physician Bellevue Hosp.; hon. attending physician NYU Hosp.; mem. coun. high blood pressure rsch. AHA. Author papers in med. jours., chpts. in books. Served as officer M.C. AUS, 1953-55. Mem. AHA, Harvey Soc., Am. Soc. Nephrology, Am. Soc. Clin. Investigation, Internat. Soc. Nephrology, N.Y. Soc. Nephrology (pres. 1974-75), N.Y. Heart Assn. Home: 333 E 69th St New York NY 10021-5560 Office: NYU Sch Medicine 550 1st Ave OBV CD679 New York NY 10016-6402 Office Phone: 212-263-5635.

BALDWIN, DEWITT CLAIR, JR., physician, educator; b. Bangor, Maine, July 19, 1922; s. DeWitt Clair and Edna Frances (Aikin) B.; m. Michele Albre, Dec. 27, 1957; children: Lisa Anne, Mireille Diane. BA, Swarthmore Coll., 1943; postgrad. Div. Sch., Yale U., 1943-45, MD, 1949; ScD (hon.), Northeastern Ohio U. Coll. Medicine, 2003; D in Human Letters (hon.), Rosalind Franklin U. Medicine and Sci., Chgo., 2011; DHL (hon.), Rosalind Franklin U. Medicine & Sci., Chgo., 2011. Diplomate Am. Bd. Med. Examiners, Am. Bd. Pediatrics, Am. Bd. Family Practice. Intern, then resident in pediatrics U. Minn. Hosps., Mpls., 1949-51; rsch. fellow Yale Child Study Ctr., New Haven, 1951-52; instr., asst. prof. pediatrics U. Washington Sch. Medicine, Seattle, 1952-57; resident in psychiatry Met. State Hosp., Waltham, Mass., 1957-58; chief resident in psychiatry Mass. Meml. Hosps., Boston, 1958-59; fellow in child psychiatry Boston City Hosp., 1959-61; asst. prof. pediatrics Harvard Med. Sch., Boston, 1961-67; prof., chmn. behavioral scis. and community health U. Conn. Health Ctr., Farmington, 1967-71; prof. chmn. behavioral scis. U. Nev. Sch. Medicine, Reno, 1971-73, dir. health scis. program, 1971-81, prof. psychiatry and behavioral scis., 1971-83, asst. dean rural health, 1977-83, prof. emeritus psychiatry and behavioral scis., 1983—; pres. Earlham Coll. and Earlham Sch. Religion, Richmond, Ind., 1983-84, Connor Prairie Pioneer Settlement Mus., Noblesville, Ind., 1983-84; dir. office edn. rsch. AMA, Chgo., 1985-88, dir. divsn. med. edn., rsch., info., 1988-91, scholar-in-residence, 1991—2002, sr. assoc. Inst. Ethics, 1991—2002, scholar-in-residence Accreditation Coun. for Grad. Med. Edn., 2002—; adj. prof. psychiatry and behavioral scis. Northwestern U. Med. Sch., Chgo., 1986—; adj. prof. med. edn. U. Ill. Coll. Medicine, Chgo., 1988-93; pres. Med. Edn. and Rsch. Assocs., Inc., Chgo., 1992—. Trustee Friends World Coll., Huntington, N.Y., 1980-83; bd. dirs. Nat. League Nursing, N.Y.C., 1981-83, Gt. Lakes Colls. Assn., 1983-84, Am. Rural Health Assn., 1985-87; mem. Nat. Bd. Med. Examiners, 1979-88, Nat. Adv. Coun. Nursing Tng., 1978-82; mem. coun. acad. socs. AAMC, Washington, 1987-94. Author: (with others) Behavioral Sciences and Medical Education, 1983, other books; author, editor: (with others) Interdisciplinary Health Care Teams in Teaching and Practice, 1981, Interdisciplinary Health Team Training, 1978; contbr. over 200 articles to scholarly publs. Recipient Rsch. Career Devel. award USPHS, 1961-67, Louis Gorin award in rural health, 1991, John P. McGovern award Health Scis., 1997, John C. Gienapp award, 2010, Pellegrino medal, 2010; Commonwealth Fund fellow, 1951-52, Milbank Fund fellow, 1968, Rural Health fellow WHO, 1976. Mem. Assn. Behavioral Scis. and Med. Edn. (pres. 1978-79, 90-91), Nev. Bd. Oriental Medicine (pres. 1976-83). Democrat. Mem. Soc. Of Friends. Office: RCGME Ste 2000 515 State St Chicago IL 60654 also: ACGME 515 N State St Ste 2000 Chicago IL 60610 Business E-Mail: dbaldwin@acgme.org.

BALDWIN, H SCOTT, cardiologist; b. Honolulu, Dec. 22, 1954; BA, U. Va., 1977, MD, 1981. Prof. pediat., cell and devel. biology Vanderbilt, 2001; vice chair lab. scis. Monroe Carell Jr. Children's Hosp. at Vanderbilt, 2002—07, chief pediat. cardiology, 2004—. Grant, NHLBI, NIH. Fellow: Am. Heart Assn. (mem. coun. on cardiovasc. disease in young, program com. 1998—2001, mem. nominating com. 2001—03); mem.: Academic Pediat. Soc., Stanley Sarnoff Found. Cardiovasc. Rsch. (sci. bd. mem. 2004), Am. Coll. Cardiology. Office: 5230 Children's Way Nashville TN 37232-9119 Office Fax: 615-322-2210. Business E-Mail: scott.baldwin@vanderbilt.edu.

BALDWIN, HAROLD SCOTT, pediatrician, educator; b. Honolulu, Dec. 22, 1954; MD, U. Va. Sch. Medicine, 1981. Diplomate Am. Bd. Pediat. Intern U. Rochester/Strong Meml. Hosp., NY, 1982—86, resident in pediat. NY; assoc. prof. Children's Hosp., Phila.; fellow in pediatric cardiology U. Iowa Coll. Med., Iowa City, 1986—90; prof. pediatrics, cell and devel. biology, prof. pediat. Vanderbilt U. Med. Ctr., Nashville; chief divsn. pediatric cardiology Vanderbilt Children's Hosp., Nashville. Recipient Established Investigator award, Am. Heart Assn., 1995. Office: Vanderbilt U Med Ctr 2204 Childrens Way Ste 5230 Nashville TN 37232 Office Phone: 615-322-7447. Business E-Mail: scott.baldwin@vanderbilt.edu.

BALDWIN, PETER ARTHUR, psychologist, educator, author, minister; b. Andover, Mass., Apr. 7, 1932; s. Alfred Graham and Katherine (Ashworth) B.; m. Carolyn Whitmore, Sept. 3, 1955; children: Sarah MacDonald Baldwin-Welcome, Judith Helen Baldwin-Gleason, Robert Henry. BA, Middlebury Coll., 1955; S.T.B., Boston U., 1959, PhD, 1964; student, New Coll., U. London, 1957-58. Lic. psychologist, N.H.; approved cons. in clin. hypnosis, Am. Soc. Clin. Hypnosis. Ordained to ministry Unitarian-Universalist Ch., 1959; assoc. pastor 2d Ch., Boston, 1955—57, in Dighton, Mass., 1958—62; religious counselor M.I.T., 1959-63; exec. dir. Liberal Religious Youth, Unitarian Universalist Assn., 1963-66; asst. prof. Crane Theol. Sch., Tufts U., 1965-67, Meadville Theol. Sch., U. Chgo., 1967-73; pastor All Souls 1st Universalist Soc., Chgo., 1971-73; assoc. prof. psychology New Eng. Coll., Henniker, NH, 1973-74; vis. assoc. prof. psychology Colby-Sawyer Coll., New London, NH, 1974-76; assoc. prof., dir. clin. psychology Antioch U. New Eng., Keene, NH, 1976—; pvt. practice, 1976—2011. Dir. Sr. High and Family Insts., Rowe, Mass., 1967-74; Nat. Edn. Conf. lectr. Williston Acad., 1967; Judy lectr., Omaha, 1970, Hon. Brother St. Benedicitine Ctr., Madison, 1972; invited speaker 5th Internat. Congress on Gestalt Therapy, Valencia, Spain, 1993. Recipient; Disting. Svc. Antioch New Eng. Grad. Sch., 1994, New Hampshire Psychological Assn., Margaret M. Riggs Disting. Contribution award, 1995. Fellow: ISDF, N.H. Psychol. Assn. (pres. 1980—81, 1988—90); mem.: APA, Unitarian- Universalists Mins. Assn., Liberal Religious Youth (life). Democrat. Home and Office: 113 Pancake Hill Rd Gilmanton NH 03237

BALDWIN, ROBERT LESH, biochemist, educator; b. Madison, Wis., Sept. 30, 1927; s. Ira Lawrence and Mary (Lesh) B.; m. Anne Theodora Norris, Aug. 28, 1965; children: David Norris, Eric Lawrence. BA, U. Wis., 1950; D.Phil. (Rhodes scholar), Oxford U., Eng., 1954. Asst. prof., then asso. prof. biochemistry U. Wis., 1955-59; mem. faculty Stanford, 1959—, prof. biochemistry, 1964-98, prof. emeritus, 1998—, chmn. dept., 1989-94. Vis. prof. Collège de France, Paris, 1972, Tsinghua U., Beijing, 2002; mem. adv. panel biochemistry and biophysics NSF, 1974—76; mem. NIH study sect. molecular and cellular biophysics, 1984—88. Assoc. editor Jour. Molecular Biology, 1964-68, 75-79; mem. editl. bd. Trends Biochem. Sci., 1977-84, Biochemistry, 1984—2008, Protein Sci., 1992-97. Mem. award panel Searle Scholars, 1993—96, 1997—98; mem. adv. panel in biophysics Burroughs-Wellcome, 1995—2001. Recipient Wheland award U. Chgo., 1995, Merit award NIH, 1988; Guggenheim fellow, 1958-59. Fellow Am. Biophysics Soc. (coun. 1977-81, Founder's award 1999); mem. NAS, Am. Soc. Biol. Chemists (Merck award 1999), Am. Chem. Soc., Am. Acad. Arts and Scis., Protein Soc. (coun. 1993-95, Stein and Moore award 1992). Home: 1243 Los Trancos Rd Portola Valley CA 94028-8125 Office: Stanford Med Sch Dept Biochemistry Beckman Ctr Stanford CA 94305-5307 E-mail: baldwinb@stanford.edu.

BALDWIN, WILLIAM RUSSELL, optometrist, foundation administrator; b. Danville, Ind., July 29, 1926; s. Edward Claire and Letha Verona (Russell) B.; m. Honey Esther Fisher, Aug. 16, 1947; children: Linda Marie Smith (dec.), Leslie Ann Baldwin Bloom. BS, Pacific U., 1949, OD, 1951, ScD (hon.), 1991; MS, Ind. U., 1956, PhD, 1964; LHD (hon.), New Eng. Coll., 1982; D.S. (hon.), SUNY, 1998; DS (hon.), Pa. Coll. Optometry, 2003. Pvt. practice, Beech Grove, Ind., 1951-54; dir. optometry clinic Ind. U., Bloomington, 1959-63; dean Coll. Optometry Pacific U., Forest Grove, Oreg., 1963-69; pres. New England Coll. Optometry, Boston, 1969-79; dean Coll. Optometry U. Houston, 1979-90; pres. River Blindness Found., 1990-96, chmn. bd. dirs., 1996—2001. Author: (with C.R. Shick) Corneal Contact Lenses, Fitting Procedures, 1962, (with others) The Refractive State of the Eye, 1969, Pediatric Optometry, 1988; editor Vision Science Symposium, Ind. U., 1988, (with others) Refractive Anomalies, 1991, Borish, 2005. Chmn. arts, scis. divsn. Ind. Reps., 1961-63; mem. Bloomington Hosp. Bd., 1961-63, bd. dirs. Am. Optometric Found., 1998-2003. Named to Nat. Optometric Hall of Frame, 2011, recipient Disting. Alumni Svc. award Ind. U., 1977, Pacific U., 1995, Gold Medal award Beta Sigma Kappa, 1968, Lifetime Achievement award Prevent Blindness Am., 1995, Disting. Svc. award USPHA Vision Sect., 1998, Social Justice Action award New Eng. United Meth. Conf., 1999, Disting. Svc. award World Coun. Optometry, 2000; named Man of Vision Prevent Blindness Mass., 1994, Disting. scholar Nat. Acad. Practice, 1994, Disting. Svc. award, Vis. Section Am. Pub. Health Assn., 1998. Fellow AAAS, Am. Acad. Optometry (life mem, chmn. sect. on edn. 1984-87); mem. working group Nat. Rsch. Coun. Com. Vision of NAS, Am. Optometric Assn. (chmn. com. on rsch. 1964-69, chmn. task force on manpower 1968, Disting. Svc. award 1992), Assn. Schs. Colls. Optometry (pres. 1974-76, chmn. internat. optometric edn.), Tex. Soc. to Prevent Blindness (v.p. 1985-90), Nat. Soc. to Prevent Blindness Am. (bd. dirs. 1988-96, chm. 1st World Conf. on Optometric Edn. 1990), Optometric Rsch. Inst. (bd. dirs. 1995-2001), Rotary, Sigma Xi, Sigma Nu Home Phone: 812-361-9782; Office Phone: 812-333-2013. Personal E-mail: bilbald@comcast.net.

BALESTRA, COSTANTINO, physiologist, researcher; b. Udine, Italy, Feb. 13, 1964; s. Antonio Balestra and Jeannine Dutillieux; m. Anne Marie Esmeralda Fontana; children: Marine Noemi, Ambre Gemma, Adrien Elio. PhD, U. Libre de Bruxelles, Brussels, 1990. Prof. physiology Haute Ecole Paul Henri Spaak, Auderghem, Belgium, 1990—; v.p. rsch. and edn. DAN Europe, Roseto degli Abruzzi, Italy, 1994—. Dir. environ. and occupl. lab. Haute Ecole Paul Henri Spaak, Auderghem, Belgium, 2000—. Contbr. over 100 articles to profl. jours. Recipient Diving for Disabled People award, PADI Europe, 2001, Dan Europe Advancement of Sci. award, Dan Internat., 2002; grantee, Fondation Van Goethem Brichant, 1990, Région Bruxelles Capital, 2007—. Fellow: European Baromedical Soc. (Per Zetterström award 2005). Avocations: saxophone, gymnastics, trampoline, scuba diving. Office: Haute Ecole Paul Henri Spaak Avenue Charles Schaller Brussels 1160 Belgium Home: Chemin des Voiturons Brabant Wallon 1420 Braine l'Alleud Belgium Home Fax: 3223873714. Personal E-mail: balestra@daneurope.org.

BALFOUR, DONALD C., physician, director; b. Rochester, Minn., Jan. 15, 1945; Degree in Economics, Yale U., 1966; MD, Northwestern U., 1970. Maj., chief outpatient dept. USAF, 1973—75; physician, internal medicine hematology oncology Sharp Rees Stealy Med. Group, 1977—93, chief, divsn. internal medicine, 1981—83, pres., 1985—2011, pres., med. dir., 1993—. Bd. dirs. Sharp HealthCare, 1985. Fellow: ACP; mem.: Coun. Accountable Physician Practices (founding mem.), Calif. Assn. Physician Groups Exec. Com., Am. Med. Group Assn. (past pres.), Anthem Blue Cross Physicians Rels. Com. Avocations: golf, sailing, travel. Office: 2001 Fourth Ave San Diego CA 92101 Office Phone: 619-446-1530. Office Fax: 619-233-4730. Business E-Mail: donald.balfour@sharp.com.

BALFOUR, HENRY HALLOWELL, JR., medical educator, researcher, physician, writer; b. Jersey City, Feb. 9, 1940; s. Henry Hallowell and Dorothy Kathryn (Dietze) B.; m. Carol Lenore Pries, Sept. 23, 1967; children: Henry Hallowell III, Anne Lenore, Caroline Dorothy. BA, Princeton U., 1962; MD, Columbia U., 1966. Diplomate Am. Bd. Pediatrics. Attending pediatrician Wright-Patterson AFB, Ohio, 1968-70; asst. prof. U. Minn., Mpls., 1972-75, assoc. prof., 1975-79, prof. lab. medicine, pathology and pediatrics, 1979—, dir. div. clin. virology, 1974—. Mem. Nat. AIDS Clin. Trials Group NIH, 1987-2008, chmn. virology com. Nat. AIDS Clin. Trials Group, 1989-92, exec. com., 1992-94; vice chmn. ACTG exec. com., 1994; prin. investigator Internat. Ctr. Antiviral Rsch. and Epidemiology, 1995—. Author: (with Ralph C. Heussner) Herpes Diseases and Your Health, 1984; mem. editl. bd. Jour. Infectious Diseases, 2006—, Jour. Clin. Virology, 2006—; contbr. sci. articles to profl. jours. Recipient Clin. Virology award, Pan Am. Soc. Virology, 2007, Excellence award in Health Rsch., U. Minn. Acad. Health Ctr., 2008. Mem. Am. Soc. Microbiology, Infectious Disease Soc. Am. Lutheran. Avocations: oenology, fishing, travel. Home: PO Box 100 Annandale MN 55302-

0100 Office: U Minn Health Sci Ctr MMC 437 Mayo 420 Delaware St SE Minneapolis MN 55455-0392 Home Phone: 320-274-7467; Office Phone: 612-625-3998. Business E-Mail: balfo001@umn.edu.

BALGEMAN, RICHARD VERNON, radiology administrator, alcoholism counselor; b. Berwyn, Ill., Dec. 25, 1929; s. Vernon Ernest and Regina Marie (Fitzgerald) B.; m. Wauneta Frances Laird, Nov. 15, 1952; children: Marcia, Kathleen, Barbara, Daniel. Student, Chgo. Art Inst., 1944; radiology technician, Cook County Grad. Sch. of Med., 1951; BA in Health Svc., Governor State U., 1976, MA in Sci., 1978. Cert. technologist; ordained Deacon Roman Cath. Ch., 1997. Radiology adminstr. Manteno (Ill.) Mental Health Ctr., 1951-84; adminstrv. asst. bus. office Shapiro Devel. Ctr., Kankakee, Ill., 1984-88; with St. James Hosp., Chicago Heights, Ill., 1990-99; bd. dirs. Manteno Golf Course. Inventor DuPont Cronex Tech. Aid, 1965; artist: exhbn. Chgo. Culture Ctr. Trustee Village of Manteno, 1969-72, chmn. planning commn., 1985-93; pres. Village View TV Channel 4; vol. Rialto Theater, Joliet, Ill. With USNG, 1948-56. Gov.'s award Ill. Dept. Mental Health, Manteno, 1971; named Citizen of Yr. Manteno Hist. Soc., 1996. Mem. Am. Legion, Rotary. Roman Catholic. Avocations: camping, making miniature furniture, writing, art. Home: 555 Park St Manteno IL 60950-1045 Home Phone: 815-468-8063.

BALI, KAMAL, orthopedist; b. Barnala, Punjab, India, Sept. 12, 1981; MBBS, All India Inst. Med. Scis., New Delhi, 2005; MS in Orthops., PGIMER, Chandigarh, India, 2009. Jr. resident PGIMER, 2006—09, sr. resident, 2009—10; fellow orthops. Concord Pub. Hosp., NSW, Australia, 2011—. Reviewer Jour. Bone and Joint Surgery America, 2010, Jour. Arthroscopy, 2011. Contbr. articles to numerous profl. jours. Travelling fellowship, D S Grewal Soc., Chandigarh. Mem.: Asian Assn. Dynamic Osteosynthesis, Nat. Acad. Med. Scis. (New Delhi), Indian Orthop. Assn., SICOT (Brussels) (SIROT award). Avocations: swimming, travel, chess. Home: 6/60 Victoria St Ashfield NSW 2131 Australia Personal E-mail: kamalpgi@gmail.com.

BALIGA, RADHAKRISHNA, pediatrician, educator, nephrologist, director; b. Bombay; naturalized, U.S. m. Mithra Baliga; children: Priya, Divya. Degree, Loyola Coll, Madras, India, 1962, Kasturba Med. Coll., Manipal, 1968; MB, BS, Mysore U., 1968; diploma in Child Health, Madras U., 1973. Lic. DC, 1976, Calif., 1979, La. La., 1982, Miss., 1993, Am. Bd. Pediat. Nephrology, 1982. Internship Govt. Gen. Hosp. Madras U., 1969—70, sr. house surgency, 1970—71; postgrad. pediat. Inst. Child and Health and Hosp. for Sick Children, Madras U., 1971—73; pediat. level I Jewish Hosp and Med. Ctr. Bklyn., 1974—75; pediat. level 2 St. Vincent's Med. Ctr., Staten Island, 1975—76; fellow pediat. nephrology Children's Hosp Mich. Wayne State U., Detroit, 1976—78; pediatrician New Ctr. Med. Plz. Groups, 1978—80; staff pediatrician South La. Med. Ctr., Houma, 1980—82; clin. asst. prof. pediat. Tulane U., New Orleans, 1980—82, instr. pediat., 1982—83, clin. asst. prof. pediat., 1986—92, asst. prof. pediat., 1985—86, rsch. assoc., 1989—90, clin. asst. prof. pediat., 1985—87, clin. assoc. prof. pediat., 1992—96, clin. prof. pediat., 1996—; clin. asst. prof. pediat. La. State U., 1985—87, asst. prof. pediat., 1986—92, assoc. prof. pediat., 1992—93; prof. pediats. U. Miss., 1993—. Cons. in pediat. nephrology Handicapped Children Svcs. Program, New Orleans, 1985—93; vis. asst. prof. dept. pediat. U. Calif., San Francisco, 1986—87. Contbr. numerous presentations, articles to profl. jour. Grantee Biomedical Rsch. Support Grant, 1991—92, Dept. grant, 1997—98, Dept. Rsch. grant, 2001—03. Fellow: Am. Soc. Nephrology; mem.: Internat. Soc. Pediat. Nephrology, Am. Heart Assn., North Am. Pediat. Renal Transplant Cooperative Study Kidney Coun., Southest Pediat. Nephrology Study Group, Internat. Soc. Nephology, Internat. Soc. Pediat. Nephrology, Am. Soc. Pediat. Nephrology. *

BALIGA, RAGAVENDRA RAMAKRISHNA, cardiologist, researcher; b. Mangalore, India, Mar. 17, 1960; s. Ram Krishna and Shanthi Baliga; m. Jayashree Baliga, May 1, 1990; children: Anoop, Neena. MBBS, St. John's Med. Coll., Bangalore, India, 1984; MD, Bangalore Med. Coll., 1988; MBA, U. Mich., Ann Arbor, 2004. Diplomate Nat. Bd. Medicine, New Delhi, 1988; mem. Royal Coll. Physicians, Eng., 1991. Intern, resident St. John's Med. Coll. Hosp., Victoria Hosp., Bangalore, 1983-87; sr. house officer Nat. Spinal Injuries Ctr., Stoke Mandeville, England, 1988-89; clin. rsch. fellow St. Mary's Hosp. Med. Sch., London, 1989-90; clin. tutor U. Aberdeen, Scotland, 1990-92; registrar in cardiology Hammersmith Hosp., London, 1993-95; scientist Harvard Med. Sch./Brigham & Women's Hosp., Boston, 1995-97; heart failure fellow Boston U. Med. Sch., 1997-98; heart transplant fellow U. Tex. Southwestern Med. Sch., Dallas, 1998-99; asst. prof. medicine U. Mich., Ann Arbor, 1999—2005; dir. Cardiology Sect. Ohio State U. Hosp. East, 2005—. Clin. prof. internal medicine Ohio State U., Columbus, Ohio, 2005—. Editor-in-chief St. John's Jour. Medicine, 1988; author: 200 Short Cases in Clinical Medicine, 1993, Multiple Choice Questions in Clinical Medicine, 1994, 250 Short Cases in Clinical Medicine, 3d edit., 2003; editor University of Michigan Cardiology Textbook, 2003; mem. editl. bd. Current Journal Review of American College of Cardiology, 2003. Recipient Nat. Rsch. Svc. award NIH, 1995-97, Astra Found. travel award, Eng., 1995. Fellow: Royal Coll. Physicians Edinburgh, Am. Coll. Cardiology; mem.: Soc. Authors Great Britain, Royal Coll. Surgeons and Physicians Glasgow. Avocations: photography, travel.

BALISTRERI, WILLIAM FRANCIS, pediatric gastroenterologist, educator; b. Geneva, NY, June 24, 1944; s. Francis William and Mary (Yannotti) Balistreri; m. Rebecca Ann McLeod, May 31, 1969; children: Anthony, Jennifer, William Phillip. Student, St. Bonaventure U., NY, 1962; BA, SUNY, Buffalo, 1966; MD, U. Buffalo Sch. Medicine, 1970. Diplomate Am. Bd. Pediat., cert. in pediat. gastroenterology. Intern Children's Hosp. Med. Ctr., Cin., 1970-71, resident, 1971-72, fellow pediatric gastroenterology, 1972—74, Dorothy M. Kersten prof. pediat., 1984—, med. dir. pediatric liver care ctr., assoc. chair subspecialty tng., dept. pediat.; asst. prof. pediat. U. Pa. Sch. Medicine, 1976-78; assoc. prof. pediat. to prof. medicine U. Cin. Coll. Medicine, 1978-91, prof. pediat., 1983—, prof. medicine, 1991—. Rsch. fellow gastroenterology Mayo Clinic, Rochester, Minn., 1973—75; staff pediatrician US Naval Hosp., Phila., 1974—76; bd. dirs. Am. Bd. Pediat., 1991—97, chmn. sub-bd. pediatric gastroenterology, 1991—93; vis. prof. Chgo. Children's Hosp., 2003, U. Mich., Ann Arbor, 2004, Phoenix Children's Hosp., U. Arizona, 2005, Buffalo Children's Hosp., 2005, U. Tex. Southwestern Med. Ctr., Dallas, 2005, U. Rochester, NY, 2005, U. Vt., Burlington, 2006. Editor: Jour. Pediat., 1995—, (med. text) Liver Disease in Children, 2001; mem. editl. bd. Liver, 1998—1004, Jour. Hepatology, 1999—2003; contbr. articles to profl. jours., chapters to books. Lt. comdr. USN, 1974—76. Recipient Disting. Alumnus award, U. Buffalo Sch. Medicine, 1993, Disting. Leadership award, Crohn's & Colitis Found. America, 1995, Andrew Sass-Kortsak Meml. award, Canadian Liver Found. /Canadian Assn. Study of Liver, 1998, Murray Davidson award, Am. Acad. Pediat., 1999, Daniel Drake award, U. Cin. Coll. Medicine, 2006; named Outstanding Pediatrician of Yr., Am. Acad. Pediat. (Ohio chpt.), 2001; named one of Best Doctors in America, Cin. Mag., 2004, 2005. Mem.: Children's Digestive Health & Nutrition Found. (pres. 2005—08), Am. Assn. Study Liver Disease (pres. 1999—2000, Disting. Svc. award 2008), N.Am. Soc. Pediatric Gastroenterology, Hepatology & Nutrition (pres. 1985—86, Harry Shwachman award 1999), Am. Liver Found. (bd. dirs. 1980—83). Roman Catholic. Avocations: skiing, hiking. Office: Children's Hosp Med Ctr 3333 Burnet Ave Cincinnati OH 45229-3026 Office Phone: 513-636-4594. Office Fax: 513-636-7805. Business E-Mail: william.balistreri@cchmc.org.

BALKHY, HANAN HASSAN, physician; d. Hassan Omar Balkhy and Rugaya Alawi Malki; m. Ayman Sameeh AlKhadra, Apr. 8, 1993; children: Mohammad Ayman Alkhadra, Omar Ayman Alkhadra. MBBch, King Abdulaziz Med. Sch., Jeddah, Saudi Arabia, 1985—91. Cert. Am. Bd. Pediatrics Mass. Gen. Hosp., 1996, in pediat. infectious diseases Cleve. Clinic Found., 1999, Rainbow Babies and Children's Hosp., 2003. Dir. infection prevention and control dept. King Khalid N.G. Hosp., Jeddah, Saudi Arabia, 1999—2001; cons. pediatric infectious diseases King Fahad N.G. Hosp., Riyadh, Saudi Arabia, 2001—; hosp. infection control and epidemiology King Abdulaziz Med. City, Riyadh, Saudi Arabia, 2001—, chmn. pediatric rsch. com., 2003—. Mem.: Am. Acad. Pediat., Infectious Disease Soc. Am., Pediatric Infectious Disease Soc. Achievements include research in publishing local data on clinical topics pertinent to Saudi Arabia, such as Brucellosis and Hajj related infections; development of a comprehensive well baby clinic to follow the well-being of newborn babies up to the age of 2 years. Avocations: hiking, skiing, reading. Office: King Abdul Aziz Med City Khashm AlAan Riyadh 22490 Saudi Arabia Office Fax: 966-1-2520437. E-mail: balkhyh@hotmail.com.

BALL, CARROLL RAYBOURNE, anatomist, researcher, medical educator; b. Hillman, Miss., Oct. 11, 1925; s. Marvin Hugh and Elizabeth (Hillman) B.; m. Jannie Vee Brooks, Sept. 5, 1947 (dec. 1954); children: Hugh Brooks, Peter Stephen; m. Sally Ann Montgomery, Mar. 22, 1963 (div. 1976); 1 child, Lou Ellen. BA, U. Miss., 1947, MS, 1948, PhD, 1963. Grad. asst. in zoology U. Miss., Oxford, 1946-48; instr. Duke U., 1948-51; instr. anatomy Med. Sch. W.Va. U., 1951-57; asst. prof. biology U. So. Miss., 1957-60; asst. prof. U. Miss. Med. Ctr., Jackson, 1963-66, assoc. prof., 1966-71, prof., 1971-99. Contbr. numerous articles to profl. jours. Pres. Jackson Civil War Round Table, 1983-84; chmn. Hist. Coker House Restoration Project, 1984-99; v.p. Magnolia chpt. Nat. Assn. Watch and Clock Collectors, 1980-82; bd. dirs. Miss. Hist. Soc., 1976-79, 85-88, 93-96. Lt. comdr. USNR, 1944-71, PTO. NIH predoctoral trainee, 1960-63; Miss. Heart Assn. grantee, 1963-66 Mem. Am. Assn. Anatomists, Soc. Exptl. Biology and Medicine, Am. Assn. Pathology, So. Assn. Anatomy, Miss. Acad. Sci., Hattiesburg Jr. C. of C. (sec. 1959-60), Order of First Families of Miss. (Gov. Gen. 2001-2003), Sigma Xi, Alpha Epsilon Delta, Theta Nu Sigma, Beta Beta Beta (pres. 1947-48), Omicron Delta Kappa, Pi Kappa Alpha (sec. 1943-44) Methodist.

BALL, DOUGLAS W., endocrinologist, educator; MD, George Wash. U. Diplomate Am. Bd. Internal Medicine, 1987, Am. Bd. Internal Medicine-endocrinology, diabetes and metabolism. Resident internal medicine Univ. Pitts., 1984—87; fellow endocrinology, diabetes and metabolism Johns Hopkins Hosp., 1987—91, hosp. affiliation includes; assoc. prof. medicine and oncology Johns Hopkins Univ. Office: Johns Hopkins University Division of Endocrinology and Metabolism Suite 333 1830 E Monument St Baltimore MD 21287 Office Phone: 410-502-4926. Office Fax: 410-955-8172.

BALL, EDWARD DAVID, hematologist, oncologist; b. Syracuse, NY, Mar. 15, 1950; s. Edward and Della Lucille (Koehler) B.; m. Elizabeth Kate Rath, June 20, 1970 (div. 1975); 1 child, David; m. Susan Elaine Blonder, Jan. 15, 1977; children: Brian, Lindsey. BS in Biochemistry, U. Md., 1972; MD, Case Western Res. U., 1976. Resident Hartford Hosp., 1976-79; fellow in hematology and oncology Univ. Hosps. Cleve., 1979-81, Dartmouth-Hitchcock Med. Ctr., 1982-83; asst. prof. Dartmouth Coll., Hanover, NH, 1982-86, assoc. prof., 1986-91; prof. U. Pitts., 1991-98; prof. medicine, chief divsn. bone marrow transplant U. Calif., San Diego, 1998—. Co-founder Medarex, Inc., Princeton, NJ, 1987; dir. bone marrow transplant program Pitts. Cancer Inst., 1993-98, co-dir. leukemia/lymphoma program, 1991-98; mem. staff Montefiore U. Hosp., Pitts., 1991-98, Presbyn. U. Hosp., Pitts., 1991-98; assoc. mem. Hitchcock Clinic, Hanover, NH, 1983-91; mem. clin. staff Mary Hitchcock Meml. Hosp., Hanover, 1983-91; mem. sr. staff Norris Cotton Cancer Ctr., Hanover, 1983-91. Contbr. articles to profl. jours., chpts. to books. Bd. dirs. Leukemia Soc. Am., Pitts., 1991-98. Scholar Leukemia Soc. Am., 1986-91, Stolhman award; Tiffany Blake fellow Hitchcock Found., 1982-83. Mem. AAAS, Am. Soc. Hematology, Am. Soc. Clin. Oncology, Am. Assn. Immunologists, Am. Assn. Cancer Rsch., Am. Soc. for Blood and Marrow Transplantation (bd. dirs. 2001-2004, 2008-), Am. Soc. for Clin. Investigation, Internat. Soc. for Exptl. Hematology (councilor 2003—), Assn. Subsplty. Profs., Assn. Hematology/Oncology Program Dirs. (pres. 1998-2000), Phi Beta Kappa, Phi Kappa Phi. Avocations: running, skiing, hiking, bicycling, surfing. Office: U Calif San Diego Bone Marrow Transplant Divsn 200 West Arbor Dr San Diego CA 92103 Office Phone: 858-822-6600. Business E-Mail: tball@ucsd.edu.

BALL, F. MICHAEL, pharmaceutical executive; b. Can., 1955; BS, MBA, Queen's U., Can. Pres. Syntex Inc., Can.; sr. v.p. Syntex Laboratories USA; corp. v.p., pres., N.Am. region, Rx Bus. Global Eye, 1998; sr. v.p., US Eye Care Allergan, Inc., Irvine, Calif., 1995, exec. v.p., pres., pharmaceuticals, 2003—06, pres., 2006—11; CEO Hospira, Inc., Lake Forest, Ill., 2011—. Bd. dirs. STEC, Inc., Hospira, Inc., 2011—. Office: Hospira Inc 275 N Field Dr Lake Forest IL 60045 *

BALL, JOHN ROBERT, healthcare executive; b. Opelika, Ala., July 16, 1944; s. John Cooper Jr. and Ellen Beverly (Williams) B.; m. Cornelia Anne Phillips, Aug. 13, 1966 (div. 1983); children: Kristen Anne, John Robert; m. Pamela Preston Reynolds, Jan. 9, 1988 (div. 2006). AB, Emory U., 1966; JD, Duke U., 1971, MD, 1972. Rsch. assoc. Duke U. Sch. Medicine, Durham, NC, 1971—72, resident in medicine, 1972-74; asst. to dir. office asst. sec. for health USPHS, Rockville, Md., 1974-76; chief med. audit br. bur. quality assurance HEW, Rockville, 1976-77; sr. policy analyst Office Sci. and Tech. Policy Exec. Office of Pres., Washington, 1978-81; assoc. exec. v.p. ACP, Phila., 1981-86, exec. v.p., 1986-94, also master; sr. scholar Assn. Acad. Health Ctrs., Washington, 1994-95; exec. v.p., acting pres., CEO Pa. Hosp., Phila., 1995-96, pres., CEO, 1996-99; sr. v.p. The Lewin Group, Falls Church, Va., 2000; exec. v.p. master Am. Soc. Clin. Pathology, Chgo., 2002—10. Robert Wood Johnson clin. scholar George Washington U., Washington, 1977-79; bd. mgrs. Pa. Hosp., 1988-97; bd. dirs. Milbank Meml. Fund, Holy Cross Hosp. Assoc. editor Jour. Am. Geriatrics Soc., 1984-86; mem. editorial bd. Internat. Jour. Tech. Assessment in Health Care, 1986-89, European Jour. Internal Medicine, 1988-94, Duke U. Law Jour., 1969-71; contbr. articles to profl. jours. Sr. surgeon USPHS, 1974-77. John Gordon Stipe scholar, Nat. Merit scholar, Emory U., 1962. Mem. Inst. Medicine of NAS, N.C. Bar Assn., Am. Clin. and Climatol. Assn., Soc. Med. Adminstrs. Democrat. Personal E-mail: johnrball@hotmail.com.

BALL, MELVYN, medical educator; b. Toronto, Canada, Aug. 30, 1940; s. Louis and Rose Ball; m. Elaine Kagan; children: Lawrence, Tamara, Robert. MD, U. Toronto, Canada, 1963. Prof. neuropathology Oreg. Health and Sci. U., Portland, 1990—2003, prof. emeritus, 2003—. Dir. Oreg. Brain Bank, Portland, 1990—2003. Vol. music therapist oncology ward Oreg. Health Scis. U. Hosp., Portland. Recipient Nicholas Munk award in geriatrics, Baycrest Ctr. U. Toronto, 1978. Fellow: Royal Coll. Physicians Can. Business E-Mail: ballm@ohsu.edu.

BALLANTYNE, REGINALD MALCOLM, III, hospital administrator; b. Columbus, Ga., Oct. 2, 1943; s. Reginald Malcolm and Constance Aimee (Martin) B.; m. Cynthia Sue Truair, Mar. 28, 1987; 1 child, Steven Truair. BS, Coll. Holy Cross, 1965; MBA, Cornell U., 1967. Adminstrv. resident Glen Cove (N.Y.) Cmty. Hosp., 1966; asst. adminstr. St. Luke's Hosp. Med. Ctr., 1970-73; adminstr. Meml. Hosp., 1973-74, exec. v.p., adminstr., 1974-76; pres. Phoenix Meml. Hosp., 1976-84, PMH Health Resources, Inc., 1984—2001; joined Vanguard Health Sys., Inc., 2001, sr. v.p., market strategy & govt. affairs, 2002—. Bd. dirs. Preferred Health Network, Ariz. Healthcare Fedn., Ariz. Healthcare Alliance, Premier Healthcare; pres. Phoenix Regional Hosp. Coun.; chmn. Florence Crittendon Svcs. Ariz.; preceptor Cornell U., Ariz. State U.; mem. adv. bd. Bayer Diagnostics Econs.; mem. editl. adv. bd. Healthcare Briefings; bd. dirs. Superior Cons. Holdings Corp.; speaker in field. Edit. adv. bd. Bus. Jour.; contbr. articles to profl. jours. Health Care Cost Containment and Regulation com. Ariz. Legis. Coun.; Hosps. svc. agys. unit chmn. Phoenix-Scottsdale United Way Campaign; emergency med. svcs. coun. Ariz. Dept. Health Svcs.; bd. dirs. Greater Phoenix Leadership; Ariz. Statewide Health Coord. Coun.; chmn. Ariz. Affordable Health Care Found., Valley Emergency Med. Svcs., Ariz. Emergency Med. Svcs., Phoenix Revitalization Corp.; adv. bd. Sun Angel Found., Jr. League Phoenix; pres. Hosp. Shared Svcs. Ariz.; bd. dirs., exec. com. Mountain States Shared Svcs. Corp.; bd. dirs. Cmty. Orgn. Drug Abuse Control, Ariz. C. of C., Phoenix Cmty. Alliance, Phoenix Civic Plz. Bldg. Corp., Ariz. Coalition for Tomorrow, Phoenix C. of C. Health Care Coun., Citizens Com. Better Health; chmn. anti-crime com. Greater Phoenix Leadership. Healthsvcs. officer, pub. health advisor Commn. Corps USPHS, 1967-70. fellow Am. Coll. of Healthcare Execs., chmn., com. commrs. Am. Hosp. Assn., 1992-1995, chmn., Am. Hosp. Assn., 1997, nat. bd. commrs. Joint Commn. on Accreditation of Healthcare Orgns., chmn.elect Ariz. C. of C. & Industry Recipient N.Y. State Scholar Incentive award Cornell U., Hope award Nat. Multiple Sclerosis Soc.; Alfred P. Sloan scholar, fellow Cornell U., Recipient The Goldmedal award American College of Healthcare Executives 1995. Fellow Am. Coll. Healthcare Execs. (ad hoc com. role hosp. CEO, Gold medal award); mem. APHA (Commd. Officers Assn.), Am. Hosp. Assn. (ins. resource inc., chmn. com. of commrs., regional policy bd. 8, bd. trustees), Joint Commn. on Accreditation of Healthcare Orgns. (bd. commrs.), Ariz. Hosp. Assn. (past chmn.), Am. Acad. Med. Adminstrs. (state chmn.), Assn. Western Hosps. (ho. dels., nominating com.), Ariz. Coop. Purchasing Assn. (bd. chmn.), Ariz. Pub. Health Assn., Comprehensive Health Planning Coun. Maricopa County (steering com.), Soc. Pub. Health Edn., Phoenix Sunrise Rotary (pres.) Roman Catholic. Home: 3266 E Valley Vista Ln Paradise Valley AZ 85253-3738 Office: Vanguard Health Systems Inc 20 Burton Hills Blvd Ste 100 Nashville TN 37215 Office Phone: 615-665-6000. Business E-Mail: rballantyne@vanguardhealth.com. *

BALLARD, DAVID EUGENE, anesthesiologist; b. Carlsbad, N.Mex., July 30, 1949; s. Samuel Lafayette and Kathleen (Krebs) B.; m. Patricia Ann Lafferty, June 11, 1972; 1 child, Leslie Christine. BA, U. Kans., 1971; MD, U. N.Mex., 1975. Diplomate Am. Bd. Anesthesiology. Intern and resident N.C. Meml. Hosp., U. N.C., Chapel Hill, 1975-78; pvt. practice Anesthesia Cons. Associated, El Paso, Tex., 1978-86; chief anesthesia sect. VA Med. Ctr., Albuquerque, 1986-88; chmn. dept. anesthesiology Lovelace Med. Ctr., Albuquerque, 1988-98; dir. anesthesiology West Mesa Med. Ctr., Albuquerque, 2003—04; clin. assoc. prof. anesthesiology U. NC, Chapel Hill, 2007—. Clin. asst. prof. anesthesiology, U. N.Mex., 1986-88, mem. resident selection com., 1986-88; clin. asst. prof. anesthesiology U. NC, Chapel Hill, 1991-96. Mem. Am. Soc. Anesthesiologists (alt. del. 1988-91, mem. com. on physician resources 1993-94), AMA, Internat. Anesthesia Rsch. Soc., Anesthesia Patient Safety Found., Soc. Ambulatory Anesthesia, Tex. Soc. Anesthesiologists (alt. del. dist. 5, 1986), Greater Albuquerque Anesthesia Soc. (pres., v.p. 1987-89), N.Mex. Med. Sch. Alumni Assn. (bd. dirs. 1984-92, exec. com. 1988-90). Avocation: golf. Office: N2201 UNC Hosps CB #7010 Chapel Hill NC 27599-7010 Home: 1215 Country Ln Durham NC 27713-6448 Office Phone: 919-966-5136. Business E-Mail: davideballard@mac.com, dballard@aims.unc.edu.

BALLDIN, ULF INGEMAR, medical researcher; b. Malmö, Sweden, Apr. 5, 1939; arrived in U.S., 1992, naturalized, 2002; s. Anton and Ebba T. (Engholm) B.; m. Susanne Ploman, June 29, 1974 (dec. Apr. 2003); children: Carl H., B. Christian, Fredrik J. BA, U. Lund, Sweden, 1959, MD, 1967, PhD, 1973; D (hon.), State Scientific Rsch. Inst., Moscow, 1995. Lic. physician, Sweden. Instr. physiology U. Lund, Sweden, 1964-67, rsch. physician, 1968-73; resident U. Hosp., Lund, Sweden, 1974; acting assoc. prof. U. Lund, 1975; rsch. flight surgeon Nat. Defense Rsch., Linköping, Sweden, 1976; sr. rsch. med. officer Nat. Defense Rsch. Establishment, Stockholm, 1977-86; rsch.

dir. Nat. Def. Rsch. Establishment, Stockholm, 1987-99, dir. Inst. Aviation Medicine Sweden, 1987-92; sr. scientist aerospace medicine Wyle, Brooks City-Base, Tex., 2000—10; chief scientist Wyle Integrated Sci. & Engring., 2011—. Adj. prof., head dept. aerospace medicine Karolinska Inst. Med. Sch., Stockholm, 1982-91; liaison scientist Brooks AFB, USAF, San Antonio, 1992-98; clin. asst. prof. U. Tex. Med. Br., Galveston, 1997-07, clin. assoc. prof., 2008-. Contbr. chpt. to book, about 90 sci.articles to profl. jours. Sr. Rsch. Flight Surgeon Swedish Air Force, 1976-99. Fellow Aerospace Med. Assn. (v.p., coun. mem.); mem. Royal Swedish Acad. War Scis., Internat. Acad. Aviation and Space Medicine (dir. 1993-97, 2d v.p. 1997-99, 1st v.p. 1999-2001, pres. 2001-2003). Achievements include improving inert gas elimination for decreasing risk of decompression sickness in divers and during extravehicular space activity, improved G-tolerance in fighter pilots with balanced pressure breathing during G and extended coverage anti-G suit. Home: 14227 Parkhurst St San Antonio TX 78232-4733 Office: Wyle Wyle Integrated Science & Engring 2485 Gillingham Dr Brooks City-Base TX 78235 Home Phone: 210-490-9565. Business E-Mail: ulf.balldin@wyle.com.

BALLEN, ANN E., ophthalmologist; b. Geneva, NY, Dec. 2, 1952; 2 children. MD, Tufts U., Medford, Mass., 1979. Diplomate Am. Bd. Ophthalmology. Intern dept. pediat. Montefiore Hosp. Med. Ctr., NYC; fellow in pediatric ophthalmology Nat. Med. Ctr., Washington; ophthalmologist MedEye Lasik, Miami, 1995—; pediatrician Miami Children's Hosp. Office: MedEye Lasik 5950 Sunset Dr South Miami FL 33143 also: Miami Childrens Hosp 3100 SW 62nd Ave Miami FL 33155 Office Phone: 500-883-7866, 305-661-8588.

BALLENGER, JAMES C., psychiatrist, researcher; b. Raleigh, NC, Mar. 2, 1944; s. Stanley Thomas and Flossie Jane (Caudell) Ballenger; m. Martha Dantzler, June 28, 1969 (div. July 1990); m. Susan I.B. Ballenger, June 13, 1992; children: James Scott, Matthew Thomas, Pleasant Woodfin. BS, U. N.C., 1966; MD, Duke U., 1970. Med. intern Duke U. Med. Ctr., 1970—71; resident in psychiatry Harvard Med. Sch., Mass. Gen. Hosp., Boston, 1971—74, Nat. Naval Med. Ctr., Bethesda, Md., 1974—76; clin. rsch. psychiatrist NIH, Bethesda, 1976—79; dir. rsch., dept. psychiatry U. Va. Sch. Medicine, Charlottesville, 1979—83; chair dept. psychiatry Med. U. S.C., Charleston, 1983—2000. Author: 16 books; contbr. over 400 articles to profl. jours. Office: 192 E Bay St Ste 204 Charleston SC 29401 Office Phone: 843-937-5950. Personal E-mail: ballengerjc@aol.com.

BALLENTINE, RON, pharmacist, educator; b. New Carlisle, Ohio, Nov. 27, 1947, s. Rollin E. and Margaret L. Ballentine; m. Lydia S. Prather, June 23, 1984; 1 child, Susan Margaret. BS in Pharmacy, U. Cin., 1971; PharmD in Clin. Pharmacy, U. Mich., Ann Arbor, 1973. Lic. pharmacist Ohio, 1971, Calif., 1971, Tex., 1974, Va., 1988. Resident, hosp. pharmacy U. Mich., 1972—74; drug info. specialist U. Tex. M.D. Anderson Cancer Inst., Houston, 1974—85; asst. prof. U. Houston, 1974—81, assoc. prof., dept. chair, 1981—85; dir. profl. resources Owen Healthcare, Houston, 1985—87; sr. mgr., pharmacy ops. VCU Health Sys., Richmond, 1987—2001, coord., pharmacy residency programs, 1991—2000, interim dir., pharmacy, 1995—96, 1998; assoc. prof., pharmacy VCU/MCV Sch. Pharmacy, Richmond, Va., 1987—, coord., experiential edn., 2001—07, asst. dir. admissions and student svc., 2007—; clin. specialist Ambulatory Care, Primary Care, 2001—. Included in Guide to America's Top Pharmacists, 2006. Mem., past pres. Am. Cancer Soc., Richmond, Va., 1997—; mem., past pres., com. mem. Instructive Vis. Nurse Assn., Richmond, 1995—2010. Recipient Lederle Pharmacy Faculty Rsch. award, U. Houston, 1977, George Wash. Honor medal, Freedoms Found. Valley Forge, 1965; scholar, Squibb, Inc., 1974. Mem.: Am. Assn. Colls. Pharmacy (assoc.), Am. Soc. Health Sys. Pharmacists (assoc.). Independent. Avocations: travel, skiing. Office: VCU/MCV Sch Pharmacy Box 980581 Richmond VA 23298-0581 Business E-Mail: rlballen@vcu.edu.

BALLOW, MARK, immunologist, educator; b. Harrisburg, Pa., Sept. 8, 1943; m. Molly Ballow, June 25, 1967; children: Sarah, Mara, Andrew. BA, Rutgers U., 1965; MD, U. Chgo., 1969. Diplomate Nat. Bd. Med. Examiners, Am. Bd. Pediatrics, Am. Bd. Allergy and Immunology, Diagnostic Lab. Immunology. Intern, resident Yale-New Haven Hosp., 1969-71; fellow U. Minn., 1971-73; chief clin./exptl. immunology U. Conn. Health Ctr., Farmington, 1975-79, assoc. prof. pediatrics, 1979-85, prof. pediatrics, 1985—; prof., chief allergy and immunology divsn. Children's Hosp. Buffalo, SUNY at Buffalo, 1988—. Dir. Am. Bd. Allergy and Immunology, 1993-99., pres. Am. Acad. Allergy, Asthma & Immunology, 2010-2011. Fellow Am. Acad. Allergy and Immunology (Carl Arbesman Meml. lectr. 1994), Am. Coll. Allergy, Asthma and Immunology; mem. Soc. Pediatric Rsch., Clin. Immunology Soc., Am. Pediatric Soc., Phi Beta Kappa. Avocation: tennis. Office: SUNY-Buffalo/Childrens Hosp Dept Allergy & Immunology 219 Bryant St Buffalo NY 14222-2006 Office Phone: 716-878-7105, 716-878-7258. Business E-Mail: ballow@buffalo.edu. *

BALLUERKA, NEKANE, psychology educator, researcher; b. Ordizia, Spain, Dec. 5, 1966; d. Iñaki Balluerka and Rosario Lasa; m. Víctor Herrarte; children: Amaia Herrarte, Eider Herrarte. Degree in Psychology, U. Basque Country, San Sebastián, Spain, 1989, PhD in Psychology, 1992. Full prof. U. Basque Country, rsch. dir. Mem. editl. bd. Uztaro Jour., Bilbao, Spain, 1994—, Jour. Metodología de las Ciencias del Comportamiento, Murcia, Spain, 2000—. Author: (book) How to Improve the Study and Learning of Scientific Texts, 1995 (Doctorate Award of the U. of the Basque Country, 1995), Experimental Designs and Data Analysis in Behavioral Sciences, 1995, Validity of Experimental and Quasi-experimental Designs in Psychology, 1996, Psychology as Science: Main Paradigmatic and Methodological Changes, 1998, The Planning of the Research. The Validity of the Design, 1999, The Concept of Nation in Basque Children, 2001, Experimental Research Designs in Psychology, 2002, Research in Psychology, 2003; contbr. articles to profl. jours., chpts. to books. Mem.: Spanish Assn. Methodology in Behavioral Scis. (assoc.), Summer Basque U. (assoc.). Achievements include invention of inventory to measure social use of Basque and Spanish; inventory to measure level of adaptation of the foster child to the foster family; inventory to measure the history of acquisition of Basque and Spanish. Avocations: running, travel, reading. Home: Urdaneta 44 Gipuzkoa Ordizia 20240 Spain Office: Univ Basque Country Avenida Tolosa 70 20018 San Sebastian 20018 Spain Home Phone: 34943087265; Office Phone: 34943018339. Office Fax: 3443015670. Personal E-mail: nekane.balluerka@ehu.es.

BALM, ALFONSUS JACOBUS MARIA, otolaryngologist, head and neck surgeon; b. Haarlem, Netherlands, Dec. 8, 1950; s. Aloysius and Maria Henriette (Van Schie) B.; m. Gea Eunice Boeijinga, Aug. 29, 1974; children: Thomas, Rachel, Norbert. MSc, Free U., Amsterdam, 1975, MD, 1976, PhD, 1982. Med. diplomate. Asst. prof. Free U. Hosp., Amsterdam, 1982-89; vis. rsch. scientist U. Mich., 1984; staff head and neck surgeon Netherlands Cancer Inst., Amsterdam, 1989—; chmn. head and neck cancer coop. group Netherlands Cancer Inst./Acad. Med. Ctr., 1990—. Mem. med. bd. Netherlands Cancer Inst., 1995-2003, chmn. divsn. surg. oncology, 1995—; staff dept. ORL Acad. Med. Ctr., 2002—, prof. head and neck oncology and surgery, 2003—. Contbr. articles to profl. jours. 1st lt. Med. Svc. Dutch Army, 1977-78. Fellow ACS, Royal Coll. Surgeons of Eng.; mem. Am. Soc. Head and Neck Surgery (corr.), Soc. Head and Neck Surgeons (corr.), Netherlands Soc. Otorhinolaryngology (first sec. exec. com. 1996-99), Royal Netherlands Med. Soc. (mem. ctrl. coll. 1999—). Avocations: reading, classical music, sailing. Office: Netherlands Cancer Inst Plesmanlaan 121 1066CX Amsterdam Netherlands Office Phone: +31-20-5122550. E-mail: a.balm@nki.nl.

BALMASOVA, IRINA PETROVNA, dental educator; b. Astrakhan, Russia, May 11, 1945; MD, Samara Med. U., 1968, PhD, 1975. Prof. Russian U. People's Friendship, 2004, Moscow State U. Medicine and Dentistry, 2006—. Mem.: CIS Soc. Allergy and Immunology, Russian Assn. Allergy and Clin. Immunology. Avocation: jazz. Home: Krasnoyarskaya St 5/36 - 71 Moscow 107589 Russia Home Fax: 7-495-365-9855. Business E-Mail: immunolab@mail.ru.

BALÓ-BANGA, JOSEPH MATHIAS, dermatologist, educator; b. Budapest, Hungary, Feb. 28, 1947, s. Joseph Baló and Ilona Banga; m. Elisabeth Pinter, May 16, 1972; 1 child, Timea. MD, Semmelweis Med. Sch., 1971. Rsch. asst. Semmelweis Med. Sch., Budapest, 1972—73, resident, 1973—75, adj. prof., 1977—90, sr. lectr., 1990—97; asst. prof. Ind. U./Purdue U. Indpls., 1976—77; chief dermatologist, head dept. Ctrl. Hosp. Hungarian Army, Budapest, 1998—2007, State Med. Ctr., Budapest, 2007—09, sr. chief dermatologist, head dept., 2009—. Editor: DNA Repair with Clinical Aspects, 1984. Mem.: Internat. Soc. Dermatologic Surg. Congress (Budapest) (chmn. 1995), German-Hungarian Dermatologic Soc. (v.p. 1995—98, 2002—06, pres. 2006—10), Hungarian Dermatologic Soc. (bd. dirs. 1979—, sec. gen. 1992—96, Mór Kaposi award 1996, Home Defense award 2008). Achievements include patents for diagnostic procedure for invitro determination of the extent of drug or chemical allergy, including test kits. Avocations: antique books, painting. Home: 21 Németvölgyi H-1126 Budapest Hungary Office: Ministry Def State Health Ctr Róbert Károly Krt 44 Budapest H-1126 Hungary Office Phone: 361-475-2628. Office Fax: 361-239-2915.

BALOGH, LÁSZLÓ, educational psychologist; b. Debrecen, Hungary, July 15, 1944; s. Sándor Balogh and Kornélia Bánhidi; m. Júlia Zsoldos, Aug. 26, 1967; children: Zuzsa, Ágnes, Tamás. MA in Hungarian lang. and edn. psychology, Kossuth U., Debrecen, 1967, D in Psychology, 1972; Candidate in Psychology, Hungarian Sci. Acad., Budapest, 1980. Cert. tchr. and psychologist. Tchr. Indsl. Secondary Sch., Debrecen, 1967—71; lectr. Kossuth U., Debrecen, 1971—73, assoc. prof., 1973—83, prof., head dept., 1983—, vice-dean Faculty Arts and Social Scis., 1989—93, dean Faculty Arts and Social Scis., 1998—2001. Mem. tchg. tng. subcom. Hungarian Acad. Arts and Scis., 1993—; assoc. expert World Bank Ednl. Devel. Projects, Budapest, 1994—98; consulting editor High Ability Studies, Bonn, Germany, 1998—; pres. tchr. tng. reform com. Hungarian Ministry Edn., 2001—; mem. gen. com. European Coun. for High Ability, Bonn, 2000—. Author: The Complex-Task Teaching System and Development of Thinking, 1987, (postgrad. tchr.-tng. program in Hungary) Gifted Education Expert, 1997; editor: Gifted Development at Schools: Research and Practice, 2001; editor-in-chief: Applied Psychology in Hungary, 1999—. Mem. com. Nat. Coun. for the Children Program, Budapest, 1995—98; pres. Hungarian Assn. for Children, Budapest, 1997—98. Recipient Nobel prize, United Cultural Conf., Raleigh, N.C., 2002, Apaczai prize, Min. Hungarian Edn., Budapest, 2002. Mem.: Tchr. Trainer's Assn. (pres. psychology sect. 1992—), Hungarian Assn. for Gifted Children (v.p. 2001—05, pres. 2005—). Avocations: skiing, tennis, music, dance. Office Phone: 36-52-422-402. E-mail: l_balogh@tigris.klte.hu.

BALOGUN, RASHEED ABIODUN, physician and medical educator; s. Ishaq Ayinde and Morinat Bisi Balogun; m. Seki A. Balogun; children: Aisha Ayodele, Zainab Ayoade, Ishaq Opeyemi. MBBS, U. Ibadan, Nigeria, 1991. Diplomate Am. Bd. Internal Medicine, Am. Bd. Nephrology. Assoc. prof. medicine U. Va., Charlottesville, 2001—, asst. dean student affairs, 2010—. Chmn. med. adv. bd. Nat. Kidney Found. of the Virginias, Richmond; asst. dean student affairs U. Va., Sch. Medicine. Recipient Willem J. Kolff Young Investigator award, ASAIO, 2002, Cmty. Svc. award, U. Va. Health Systems, 2007; named to Acad. Disting. Educators, U. Va. Sch. Medicine, 2005. Fellow: ACP, Am. Soc. Nephrology; mem.: Am. Soc. for Artificial Internat. Organs. Avocations: bicycling, tennis. Office: U VA Nephrology Divsn 1215 Lee St Box 800133 Charlottesville VA 22911 Office Fax: 434-948-2458.

BALOH, ROBERT HARRIS, neurologist, educator; b. Dec. 22, 1972; ScB in Neuroscience with honors, Brown U., 1995; MD, PhD, Washington U., 2001; PhD, Wash. U. Sch. Medicine, 2001. Resident neurology Mass. Gen. Hosp. / Brigham and Women's Hosp., Boston, 2004; fellow neuromuscular disease Washington U. Sch. Med., St. Louis, 2006, asst. prof. neurology Divsn. Adult Neurology, 2007. Recipient S. Weir Mitchell Award, American Acad. Neurology, 2007. Office: Washington University School of Medicine 660 S Euclid Campus Box 8111 Saint Louis MO 63110 Office Phone: 314-362-6981. E-mail: rbaloh@wustl.edu.

BALOYANNIS, STAVROS JOANNIS, neurologist, educator, researcher; b. Thessaloniki, Macedonia, Greece, Aug. 24, 1944; s. Joannis K. and Maria (Stefanidou) B.; m. Heleni G. Bozini, 1965; children: Joannis, Maria, Georgia, Angeliki. MD, Aristotelian U., Thessaloniki, 1968, PhD, 1975, Docent, 1980; MSc in Theology, Thessaloniki, Thessaloniki, 1979. Postdoctoral fellow London U., Nat. Hosp., Inst. Neurology, 1974-75, U. Catholique de Louvain, Belgium, 1975-76; fellow in neuropathology U. Pa., Phila., 1977-78; docent Aristotelian U., Thessaloniki, 1980-83, asst. prof., 1983-87, assoc. prof., 1987-2000, head 1st dept. neurology, 1992—, dir. lab. of neuropathology, 1993, prof., 2000—. Vis. prof. Tufts U., Boston, 1986, Democritean U., Alexandroupolis, Greece, 1989-90, Sch. Philosophy, Aristotelian U., Thessoloniki, 1993—. Author: Clinical Neuropathology, vols. I-III, 1984—88, Diseases of the Muscles, 1991, Neurology, Vols. I-VII, 1996, Pastoral Psychiatry, 1986, Psychology, Via Psychology, 1984, Andreas Vesalius on the Human Brain, 1995, The Role of Calcium in the Life and Death of the Nerve Cell, 1995, The Receptors of Excitatory Amino Acids, 1996, Introduction to Neurosciences, 1996, From Andreas Vesalius to Santiago Ramon y Cajal, 2000, The Brain in the Manuscripts of Leonardo da Vinci, 2001; contbr. more than 560 articles to sci. and med. jours. Mem. EECC Com. on Bioethics; pres. com. on bioethics Orthodox Ch. 2s lt. Greek Air Force, 1968—72. Recipient Gold medal of St. Demetrius, Orthodox Ch., Thessaloniki, 1984, Gold medal of St. Paul, 1988, Gold medal of Holy Theotokos, 1989, 91, Gold medal Greek Red Cross, 1994, Gold medal of St. Cyrillus and Methodius, Gold medal St. Gregorius, Thessaloniki, 1997, Gold Cross of St. Paul of first rank, Veria, 2000, Gold Cross of Justinian; named Archon Actuarius of Oecumenical Patriachate, 2003. Fellow: Royal Soc. Medicine London; mem.: Soc. Orthodox Med. Missionary (pres.), Internat. Coll. Psychogeriatric Pharmacology (founder), Internat. Coll. Neuropsychopharmacology (founding), Am. Acad. Neurology, Internat. Soc. for Quality of Life of Chronic Neurologic Patients (pres.), European Soc. Psychogeriatrics (hon. life mem.), N.Y. Acad. Scis., Acad. Hellenic Air Forces (hon.), Hellenic Neuropathol. Soc. (pres. 1986—97), European Neuropathol. Soc. (founding mem.), Internat. Soc. Neuropathology, Am. Assn. Neuropathology, Collegium Orl, Internat. Brain Rsch. Assn. Orthodox Ch. Avocations: philosophy, painting, poetry, classical music, linguistics-glossology, history of neurology. Home: Angelaki 5 Thessaloniki Greece 54621 Office: Aristotelian Univ 1st Dept Neurology Neuropathol & Exptl Neurol 540 06 Thessaloniki Greece Home Phone: 302310270434; Office Phone: 302310994661. Personal E mail: sibh844@otenet.gr.

BALSER, JEFFREY R., dean, medical educator; MD, PhD in Pharmacology, Vanderbilt U., 1990. Resident anesthesiology, fellow critical care medicine Johns Hopkins U., faculty mem., 1995—98; assoc. dean physician scientists Vanderbilt U., 1998, James Tayloe Gwathmey prof., chair anesthesiology, 2001; assoc. vice chancellor for rsch. Vanderbilt Med. Ctr., 2004; assoc. vice chancellor health affairs, dean Vanderbilt U. Sch. Medicine, 2008—. Contbr. articles to med. jours. Mem.: NAS (mem. Inst. of Medicine), Assn. of Am. Physicians, Am. Soc. Clin. Investigation. Office: Vanderbilt U Sch Medicine D-3300 MCN 2104 215 Light Hall Nashville TN 37232 Office Phone: 615-936-3030. E-mail: jeff.balser@vanderbilt.edu. *

BALSHI, THOMAS J., dentist, educator; b. Bethlehem, Pa., Mar. 23, 1946; m. Joanne Balshi, 1969; children: Anne Kristen, Thomas Christopher, Stephen Francis. BA in Social Sci., Villanova U., Pa., 1968; DDS, Temple U., Phila., 1972, postdoc., 1976; tng. in Surgery and Prosthesis, U. Toronto; DSc (hon.), Cabrini Coll., Radnor, Pa., 2010. Diplomate Am. Bd. Prosthodontics, lic. to practice dentistry Pa., 1972. Clin. practice assoc. office of George J. Capaldi DDS, Phila., 1972—73; pres. Fort Washington Dental Assocs., Pa., 1973—86; asst. prof. dept. fixed partial prosthodontics sch. dentistry Temple Univ., Phila., 1974—77, assoc. clin. prof. dept. fixed partial prosthodontics sch. dentistry, 1984—91; lecturing prosthodontist dental hygiene dept. Montgomery County Cmty. Coll., 1975—; pres. Fort Washington Dental Lab Inc., Pa., 1977—99, chmn. bd. advisors Pa., 1977—99; pres. Inst. for Facial Esthetics Inc., Fort Washington, Pa., 1984—, founding dir., 1984—; pres. Prosthodontics Intermedia, Fort Washington, Pa., 1986—; bd. dirs. Fort Washington Surg. Ctr., Pa., 1997—; staff mem. dept. surgery gen. dentistry Holy Redeemer Hosp., Meadowbrook, Pa., 2000—07. Part-time faculty dept. fixed partial prosthodontics sch. dentistry Temple Univ., Phila., 1971—74; bd. dirs. Prosthodontics Intermedia Found., 2001—. Co-author: (publs.) Osseointegration Treatment of Transverse Root Fractures in the Region of the Alveolar Crest, 1998, Dental Implants in the Diabetic Patient: A Retrospective Study, 1999, Pterygomaxillary Implants in Edentulous Arches for Fixed Prosthesis Anchorage, 1999, A New Protocol for Immediate Functional Loading of Dental Implants, 2001, Treatment of Congenital Ectodermal Dysplasia with Zygomatic Implants: A Case Report, 2002, and numerous others. Capt. US Army, 1972—74. Recipient Outstanding Documentation and Presentation in Restorative Dentistry, Temple Univ. Sch. Dentistry, Stomatognathic Soc., J.M. Ney Co., 1971, Outstanding Achievement in Fixed and Removable Prothetics, Temple Univ. Sch. Dentistry, Fixed Partial Prosthodontic Faculty, 1972, Excellence in Restorative Dentistry, Temple Univ. Sch. Dentistry, 1972, US Army Commendation Medal, Mills Army Dental Clinic, 1974, Cert. of Appreciation, Am. Coll. of Prosthodontists, 1983, Citation of Recognition, The Commonwealth of Pa., House of Representatives, 1994, George Wash. Honor Medal for Excellence and Individual Achievement in the Dental Field, Freedom's Found., 1995; named The Student Demonstrating the Most Understanding in the Art and Sci. of Fixed Partial Prosthodontics, Temple Univ. Sch. Dentistry, Fixed Partial Prosthodontic Faculty and the Stomatognathic Soc., Star Dental Mfg. Co., 1971, Disting. Practitioner, Nat. Academics of Practice, 1999, Citizen of the Week, Prosthodontics Intermedia Found., 2002, America's Top Dentist, Consumer's Rsch. Coun. of America, 2007; named one of The Best Dentists in America, 2004; fellow, Am. Coll. of Dentists, 1986. Master: Am. Acad. of Implant Prosthodontics; fellow: Am. Acad. of Implant Prosthodontics, Acad. of Osseointegration (charter mem.); mem.: Am. Assn. for the Advancement of Sci., Found. of Dentistry for the Handicapped, Internat. Soc. for Clin. Densitometry, Osteoporosis Found., Spl. Care in Dentistry, Am. Soc. for Geriatric Dentistry, Am. Soc. of Aging, Inst. for Facial Esthetics, Joseph E. Ewing Dental Study Group, Phila. County Dental Assn., ADA, Am. Coll. of Dentists, Del. Valley Acad. of Osseointegration, Am. Soc. for Bone and Mineral Rsch., Pa. Prosthodontics Assn. (founding mem.), Internat. Coll. of Prosthodontics, Am. Coll. of Prosthodontics Ednl. Found., Osseointegration Study Club, Omicron Kappa Upsilon, PSI Omega Frat. Office: Prosthodontics Intermedia 467 W Pennsylvania Ave Ste 201 Fort Washington PA 19034 Office Phone: 215-646-6334, 215-643-1149.

BALSTER, ROBERT LOUIS, alcohol/drug abuse educator researcher; b. St. Cloud, Minn., Oct. 12, 1944; s. Louis and Marion Balster; m. Sandra Kay Herwig, June 25, 1966; 1 child, Sarah Elizabeth. BS, U. Minn., Mpls., 1966; PhD, U. Houston, 1970. Postdoctoral fellow in psychiatry and pharmacology U. Chgo., 1970-72; rsch. assoc. in psychiatry Duke U., Durham, NC, 1972-73; asst. prof. pharmacology Med. Coll. Va., Richmond, 1973-78, assoc. prof., 1978-84, prof. pharmacology, 1984—2003, Luther A Butler prof. pharmacology, 2003—; dir. Inst. for Drug and Alcohol Studies, 1993—; coord. Humphrey Fellowship Program in Substance Abuse, 2006—; founder co dir. Internat. Program Addiction Studies, 2008—.

Chmn. Drug Abuse Adv. Com., FDA, Rockville, Md., 1983-84; mem. Robert Wood Johnson Rsch. Network on Etiology of Tobacco Dependence, 1997-2006; mem. adv. bd. Partnership for Drug Free Am. Editor-in-chief Drug Alcohol Dependence, 1998—2010; contbr. 277 articles to profl. jours. Recipient NIH Merit award, 1993-2004, Va. Commonwealth U. Faculty award of Excellence, 1999, Mentoring award Coll. Problems Drug Dependence, 2000, Nathan B. Eddy award, 2009, Faculty Tchg. Excellence award Va. Commonwealth U. Sch. Medicine, 2003, Mentoring award NIDA Internat. Program, 2006. Fellow Coll. on Problems of Drug Dependence (charter fellow, pres. 1995-96), Am. Coll. Neuropsychopharmacology, APA (pres. psychopharmacology divsn. 1989-90, chair bd. sci. affairs 1995-96, Disting. Svc. to Psychol. Sci. award, 2006, Brady-Schuster award 2007, bd. mem. 1994-96, 2008-); mem. European Behavioral Pharmacology Soc. (coun. mem. 1986-94). Achievements include development of laboratory methods for studying the behavioral effects of drugs of abuse and procedures for drug abuse potential evaluation and the management of international training programs in addiction. Office: Va Commonwealth U PO Box 980310 Richmond VA 23298-0310 Business E-Mail: balster@vcu.edu. *

BALTARO, RICHARD J., pathologist, medical educator; came to the U.S., 1964; s. Dimitri and Maria Silvana Baltaro; m. Laura E. Neece, 1972; children: Elizabeth B., John C. BA, Earlham Coll., 1972; PhD summa cum laude, U. Rome, Italy, 1977; MD magna cum laude, Cath. U., Rome, 1983. Bd. cert. anatomic and clin. pathology Am. Bd. Pathology, cert. immunopathology Am. Bd. Pathology. Pathology resident Brown U., Providence, 1983-87; clin. pathology fellow George Washington U. Hosp., Washington, 1987-88; asst. in pathology George Washington Med. Sch., Washington, 1987-88; sr. staff fellow NIH Clin. Ctr. Immunology, Bethesda, Md., 1988-90; jr. active staff NIH Clin. Ctr., Bethesda, 1988-90; asst. prof. Marshall U. Sch. Medicine, Huntington, W.Va., 1990-93, dir. pathology residency program, 1991-93; staff pathologist lab. svc. VA Med. Ctr., Huntington, 1990-93; pathologist Med. Arts Lab., Oklahoma City, 1993-98; assoc. clin. prof. Med. Ctr. U. Rochester, 1999—2001; assoc. prof. Creighton U., Omaha, 2001—. Stockholder Med. Arts Lab., 1994-98; ptnr. Med. Arts Pathologists, 1995-98; adj. assoc. prof. U. Okla. Health Sci., Oklahoma City, 1993-99; spkr. in field. Contbr. articles to profl. jours. Recipient NIH grant, 1991. Fellow Coll. Am. Pathologists (lab. insp. 1985—), Am. Soc. Clin. Pathologists, Internat. Acad. Pathology, Acad. Clin. Lab. Physicians and Scientists, Am. Coll. Internat. Physicians, Assn. Clin. Scientists; mem. AMA, AAAS, Am. Soc. Microbiology, Am. Assn. for Clin. Chemistry, Assn. Med. Lab. Immunologists. Avocations: gardening, reading, dance, child raising. Office: Creighton Univ Med Ct Path Dept 601 N 30th St Omaha NE 68131

BALTIMORE, DAVID, virologist, educator, former academic administrator; b. NYC, Mar. 7, 1938; s. Richard I. and Gertrude Baltimore; m. Alice S. Huang, Oct. 5, 1968; 1 child, Teak. BA in Chemistry, with high honors, Swarthmore Coll., Pa., 1960; PhD, Rockefeller U., NYC, 1964. Postdoc. fellow Albert Einstein Coll. Medicine, Bronx, NY, 1964—65; rsch. assoc. Salk Inst. Biol. Studies, La Jolla, Calif., 1965—68; assoc. prof. microbiology MIT, Cambridge, Mass., 1968—72, prof. biology, 1972—90, founding dir., Whitehead Inst. Biomed. Rsch., 1982—90; pres. Rockefeller U., NYC, 1990—91, prof., 1990—94; pres. Calif. Inst. Tech., Pasadena, 1997—2006, pres. emeritus, 2006—, Robert Andrews Millikan prof. biology, 2006—. Co-chmn. Commn. Nat. Strategy of Aids, 1986; mem. AIDS rsch. adv. coun. NIH, 1996, chair vaccine adv. com., 1997—2002; bd. dirs. MedImmune, Inc., 2003—07. Mem. editorial bd. Jour. Molecular Biology, 1971-73, Jour. Virology, 1969-90, Sci., 1986-98, New Eng. Jour. Medicine, 1989-94; contbr. articles to profl. jours. Bd. governers Weizmann Inst. Sci., Israel; bd. dirs. Life Sci. Rsch. Found. Recipient Gustav Stern award in virology, 1970, Warren Triennial prize, Mass. Gen. Hosp., 1971, Eli Lilly and Co. award in microbiology, 1971, Gairdner Found. Internat. award, 1974, Nobel prize in physiology/medicine, 1975, Nat. Medal Sci., 1999, Warren Alpert Found. prize, 2000. Fellow: AAAS (pres. 2007, chmn. bd. dirs. 2008—09), Am. Acad. Mircobiology, Am. Med. Writers Assn. (hon.); mem.: NAS, French Acad. Scis. (fgn. assoc.), Royal Soc. (fgn.), Pontifical Acad. Scis., Am. Philos. Soc., Inst. Medicine, Am. Acad. Arts & Scis. Office: Calif Inst Tech Divsn Biology Mail Code 156 29 1200 E California Blvd Pasadena CA 91125-0001 *

BALTIMORE, ROBERT SAMUEL, pediatrician, epidemiologist; b. NYC, Nov. 3, 1942; s. Richard Irving and Gertrude (Lipshitz) B.; m. Nancy Virginia Ward, June 16, 1967 (dec. Aug. 1977); 1 child, Gwen; m. Katalin Rachel Radnay, Sept. 24, 1978; 1 child, Richard. AB, U. Chgo., 1964; MD, SUNY, Buffalo, 1968. Diplomate in pediatrics and pediatric infectious diseases Am. Bd. Pediatrics. Intern U. Chgo. Hosps. and Clinics, 1968-69, resident in pediatrics, 1969—71; postdoctoral fellow Walter Reed Army Inst. Rsch., Washington, 1971-74; postdoctoral fellow, instr. Harvard Med. Sch., 1974-76, asst. prof. pediats. and epidemiology, 1976-81; assoc. prof. pediatrics and epidemiology Yale U. Sch. Medicine, New Haven, 1981—95, prof. pediatrics, epidemiology, pub. health, 1995—. Assoc. editor Jour. Watch Infectious Diseases; editl. bd. mem. Current Opinion Pediat. Co-editor: Topics in Critical Care Pediatrics, 1984, Pediatric Infectious Diseases: Principles and Practice, 1995, 2d edit., 2002. Asst. dir. health Town of Orange, Conn., 1990—. Maj. U.S. Army, 1971-74. Rsch. grantee NIH, 1981-84, Cystic Fibrosis Found., 1988-90, Ctrs. for Disease Control and Prevention, 1990—. Fellow Infectious Diseases Soc. Am., Pediatric Infectious Diseases Soc., Soc. for Pediatric Rsch., Am. Acad. Pediatrics (mem. com. infectious diseases 2001-07), Am. Pediat. Soc., Soc. for Healthcare Epidemiology, Am. Heart Assn. (mem. com. Rheumatic Fever, Endocarditis and Kawasaki disease 2001-). Democrat. Jewish. Avocations: gardening, hiking, canoeing. Home: 188 Crocker Ct Orange CT 06477-3025 Office: Yale Univ Sch Medicine 333 Cedar St New Haven CT 06520-8064 Office Phone: 203-785-4655. E-mail: robert.baltimore@yale.edu.

BALTZ, RICHARD JAY, healthcare company executive; b. Kingston, NY, June 6, 1952; s. Harold H. and Virginia K. (Luedtke) B.; m. Mary Melissa White, May 26, 1974; 1 child, Christopher Jay. BS, St. Lawrence U., 1974; MA, George Washington U., 1978. Lic. nursing home adminstr. Adminstr. Hudson Valley Sr. Residence, Kingston, N.Y., 1974-76; adminstr. resident/asst. Buffalo VA Med. Ctr., 1977-80, asst. chief Med. Adminstrv. Svc., 1980-83; chief Med. Adminstrv. Svc. Syracuse (N.Y.) VA Med. Ctr., 1984-86; assoc. dir. trainee Albany (N.Y.) VA Med. Ctr., 1987; assoc. med. ctr. dir. Togus (Maine) VA Med. Ctr., 1988-90, VA Med. Ctr., Jackson, Miss., 1990-97, dir., 2000—, Fayetteville, NC, 1997—2000. Adj. prof. dept. health care adminstrn. U. Ala., Birmingham, 1990-94. Bd. dirs. Kennebec, Maine unit Am. Cancer Soc., 1988-90, pres., 1989, 90, Maine divsn., 1988-90. Fellow Am. Coll. Healthcare Execs. Address: 527 Northwind Dr Brandon MS 39047 Home: 527 Northwind Dr Brandon MS 39047-8688 *

BALZ, JEAN ARLYNN, physician assistant; b. Wausau, Wis., Dec. 17, 1955; d. Clarence Louis and Althea Virginia (Bloch) B. Cert. operating rm. asst., Mid-State Tech. Inst., 1975; student physician asst. program, U. Wis., 1981-84; cert. surgeon asst., Cornell U., 1986. Rsch. asst. U. Wis., Madison, 1984; physician asst. Fargo (N.D.) Clinic-MeritCare, 1987-92, Gundersen Clinic, La Crosse, Wis., 1992-99, Marshfield Clinic, Wis., 1999—2011. Author rsch. papers in field. Youth advisor Pilgrim Luth. Ch., Bethesda, Md., 1978-81; advisor St. Luke's Med. Explorers Post, Boy Scouts Am., Fargo, 1989-92, bd. dirs., 1989-92; mem. Fargo-Morehead City Disaster Bd., 1989-92; mem. com. Robert Wood Johnson Grant Project, Fargo, 1989-91; bd. dirs. Habitat for Humanity, 1999-2001, Good Shepherd Luth. Ch. Coun., 2000-06. With USN, 1975—81, with Res. USN, 1981—2001. Mem.: Am. Legion Post 4, Aid Assn. for Luths. (treas. 2001—03). Lutheran. Avocations: photography, sewing, private pilot. Office: Marshfield Clinic Dept Gen Surgery 1000 N Oak Ave Marshfield WI 54449-5702 E-mail: jabhmcm@aol.com.

BAMEZAI, RAMESHWAR NATH KOUL, academic administrator; b. Srinagar, Jammu & Kashmir, India, Dec. 26, 1951; PhD, All India Inst. Med. Scis., New Delhi, 1979. Rsch. assoc. All India Inst. Med. Scis., New Delhi, 1979—80; lectr. Inst. Med. Scis., Benaras Hindu U., Varanasi, 1980—89; assoc. prof. Jawaharlal Nehru U., New Delhi, 1989—96, prof., 1996, coord. Nat. Ctr. Applied Human Genetics, 2002—; vice chancellor Shri Mata Vaishno Devi U., Katra, Jammu & Kashmir, 2010—. Adj. prof. Manipal U., Inst. Life Scis., 2009; mem. plan & expert com. U. Grants Commn., 2000—; mem. expert com., dept. biotechnology Govt. India, 2008—. Recipient Hari Om Ashram-Jagdish Chander Bose award, U. Grants Commn., 2000, Acharya Abinavgupta Samman, G.M.Coll. Edn., H.E.Soc., Kashmir, 2003, KECSS award, Kashmir Edn. and Culture and Sci. Soc., New Delhi, 2009; Monbusho fellow, Govt. Japan, 1985. Fellow: INSA, Internat. Med. Scis. Aced., Nat. Acad. Med. Scis. (India), Indian Nat. Sci. Acad., NAS (India); mem.: Internat. Assn. Environ. Mutagen Soc. Avocations: music, reading, writing. Home: Jawaharlal Nehru University Campus New Delhi 110067 India Personal E-mail: bamezai@hotmail.com. Business E-Mail: bamezai@ncahg.org.

BAMFORD, JOSEPH CHARLES, JR., gynecologist, obstetrician, educator, medical missionary, author; b. Paterson, NJ, Oct. 23, 1930; s. Joseph Charles and Luise (Whitehead) Bamford; m. Susan Jane Hall, Apr. 13, 1951; children: Joseph Charles III, Elizabeth Ann. BS, Rutgers U., 1952; MD, NY Med. Coll., 1956. Diplomate Am. Bd. Ob-Gyn. Intern U. Vt., 1956—57; resident in ob-gyn NY Med. Coll., NYC, 1957—60, asst. clin. instr. dept. ob-gyn, 1960—64, clin. instr., 1964—65, asst. prof., 1965—70, assoc. prof., 1970—72, asst. dean, 1966—68, assoc. dean, 1968—72, acting v.p. hosp. affairs, 1971—72; sect. chief psychosomatic ob-gyn Met. Hosp. Ctr., NYC, 1963—72, chief svc., 1971—72; practice medicine specializing in ob-gyn Paterson, NJ, 1962—66; practice medicien specializing in ob-gyn St. Johnsbury, Vt., 1972—76; asst. obstetrician and gynecologist Flower and Fifth Ave. hosps., NYC, 1960—66, asst. attending, 1966—70, attending, 1970—72; asst. vis. obstetrician and gynecologist Met. Hosp. Ctr., NYC, 1960—66, assoc., 1968—70, vis., 1970—72; vis. ob-gyn Indian Health Svc. Hosp., Ft. Defiance, Ariz., 1981; clin. asst. ob-gyn Paterson Gen. Hosp., 1962—64, assoc. attending, 1964—66, attending, 1966—67; cons., 1967; attending obstetrician and gynecologist Northeastern Vt. Regional Hosp., St. Johnsburg, 1972—76, cons., 1976—85. Vis. obstetrician and gynecologist St. Jude Missions Hosp., St. Lucia, 1986; med. officer Tumutumu Mission Hosp., Kenya, 1987—88; cons. Beatrice D. Weeks Meml. Hosp., Lancaster, NH, 1972—80; vol. program steering com. for retired physicians Vt. Med. Soc., 1996—2001; chmn. subcom. for fact finding Mayor's Com. for Hosp. Facilities Planning, Paterson, 1964—66. Contbr. articles to profl. jours. Chmn. med. adv. com. Passaic County (NJ) Com. for Planned Parenthood, 1965—67; mem. NJ Com. on Med. Edn., 1965—66; trustee Greater Paterson Gen. Hosp., 1966—2000, So. Vt. Art Ctr., 1997—2002; pres. Lyndon State Coll. Found., 1980—84, Kagando Mission Hosp. Found., 2003—. Lt. comdr. USNR, 1960—62. Fellow: ACOG (mem. com. on course coord. 1977—79); mem.: Caledonia County Med. Soc. (v.p. 1974—75), Vt. Med. Soc. (mem. jud. com. 1975—77), Ob-Gyn. Soc. NY Med. Coll. (mem. exec. com. 1963—66), No. New England Acad. Medicine. Home: Box 724 Myrickview Vlg Dorset VT 05251

BAMGBOLA, OLUWATOYIN FATAI, pediatric renal physician, researcher; MD, U. Ilorin, Nigeria, 1986. Diplomate Am. Bd. Pediat., 2001. Registrar West African Postgraduate Med. Coll., ABU Hosp., Zaria, Nigeria; sr. registrar Nat. Postgraduate Med. Coll., ABU Hosp., Zaria, 1993—96; asst. prof. pediat. U. Okla. Health Sci. Ctr., Oklahoma, 2003—. Contbr. articles to profl. jours. Exec. mem. Full Gospel Bus. Men's Fellowship Internat., NYC, 1997—2003. Grantee, Nat. Kidney Found., 2001; fellow, West African Postgraduate Med. Coll., 1989, Nat. Postgraduate Med. Coll., Lagos, Nigeria, 1989, Albert Einstein Coll. Medicine, Bronx, Am. Soc. Transplantation, 2001—03; scholar, Amgen, 2002. Mem.: Am. Soc. Transplantation, Internat. Pediatric Nephrology Assn. (licentiate), Am. Soc. Pediatric Nephrology (licentiate), Am. Soc. Nephrology (licentiate), Renal Physician Assn. (assoc.).

BANACH, TOMASZ ARKADIUSZ, cardiologist; b. Tarnow, Aug. 4, 1972; MD, Jagiellonian U., 1997, PhD, 2003. Asst., adj. prof. dept. pathophysiology Jagiellonian U., 1997—2007, rsch. fellow dept. integrative biology and pharmacology Tex. U., Med. Sch., Houston, 2001—02; physician, specialist dept. cardiology Ludwik Rydygier Specialist Hosp., 2008—. Mem.: Polish Cardiol. Soc. Avocations: travel, skiing, exercise, jogging, reading. Home: ul Grzegorzecka 67 C / 17 Krakow Malopolska 31-559 Poland Personal E-mail: tombanach@poczta.onet.pl.

BANAS, JOHN STANLEY, obstetrician, gynecologist; b. Chgo., May 27, 1955; s. Edward Thomas and Stephanie Victoria (Gatz) B.; m. Kerry Jeanine Keenan, June 7, 1981; children: Melissa, Kevin, Daniel, Amanda. BS in Biology cum laude, Loyola U., Chgo., 1977; MD, Loyola U., Maywood, Ill., 1981. Diplomate Am. Bd. Ob-Gyn. Resident in ob/gyn. SUNY, Buffalo, 1981-85; pvt. practice Ft. Wayne, Ind., 1985-88, Racine, Wis., 1988-90, Rock Island, Ill., 1990—. Fellow ACOG; mem. AMA, Ill. Med. Soc., Rock Island Med. Soc. Roman Catholic. Avocations: swimming, running, bicycling, gardening, reading. Home: 2130 Nathan Ct Bettendorf IA 52722-2100 Office: Trinity Med Ctr 2570 24th St Ste 122 Rock Island IL 61201-5394 Office Phone: 309-779-3868.

BANDLER, MARTIN, physician; b. Vienna, Oct. 2, 1930; came to U.S., 1954; s. Sidney and Sara (Feinsinger) B.; m. Frances Feffer; children: Bruce, Gail, Ruth. MD, Dalhousie U., 1954. Diplomate Am. Bd. Internal Medicine. Intern Victoria Genl. Hosp., Halifax, N.S., Canada, 1953-54; resident in medicine Jewish Hosp., Bklyn., 1954-56, fellow in gastroenterology, 1956-57; physician-in-charge divsn. gastroenterology U.S. Naval Hosp., Phila., 1957-59; pvt. practice Bklyn., 1959—; clin. instr. SUNY, 1959-70, clin. asst. prof. medicine, 1970—. With USN, 1957-59. Fellow ACP, Am. Coll. Gastroenterology; mem. AMA, Kings County Med. Soc., N.Y. Med. Soc., Am. Soc. Gastrointestinal Endoscopy, Bklyn. Gastroenterol. Soc. (v.p. 1972-73, pres. 1973-74), N.Y. Soc. for Gastrointestinal Endoscopy. Office: 954 President St Brooklyn NY 11215-1604 Home Phone: 718-859-7377; Office Phone: 718-783-6364. E-mail: fmbandler@aol.com.

BANDURA, ALBERT, psychologist, educator; b. Mundare, Alta., Can., Dec. 4, 1925; arrived in U.S., 1949, naturalized, 1956; m. Virginia Varns; 2 children. BA, U. B.C., 1949, D.Sc. (hon.), 1979; MA in Psychology, U. Iowa, 1951, PhD in Psychology, 1952. Prof. psychology Stanford U., 1953—2010, David Starr Jordan prof. social sci. in psychology, 1973—2010. Author: (with R.H. Walters) Adolescent Aggression, 1959, (with R.H. Walters) Social Learning and Personality Development, 1963, Principles of Behavior Modification, 1969, Aggression, 1973, Social Learning Theory, 1977, Social Foundations of Thought and Action: A Social Cognitive Theory, 1986; editor: Psychological Modeling: Conflicting Theories, 1971, Self-Efficacy in Changing Societies, 1995, Self-Efficacy: The Exercise of Control, 1997. Recipient Disting. Lifetime Contbn. award, Soc. for Advancement of Behavior Therapy, 2001, Disting. Achievement Alumni award, U. Iowa, 2005, Lifetime Achievement award, Am. Acad. Health Behavior, 2006, Evertt M. Rogers award, Norman Lear Ctr., 2007, Grawemeyer award, 2007, Lifetime Achievement award, Stanford U., 2011;, Guggenheim Found. fellow, 1972. Fellow: Ctr. Advanced Study in Behavioral Sci., Am. Acad. Arts and Scis.; mem.: APA (pres. 1974, Disting. Scientist award divsn. 12 1972, Disting. Sci. Contbn. award 1980, Outstanding Lifetime Contbn. award 2004), Am. Psychol. Found. (Gold medal award 2006), Can. Psychol. Assn. (hon. pres. 1999), Internat. Soc. Rsch. on Aggression (Disting. Contbn. award 1980), Western Psychol. Assn. (pres. 1980, Lifetime Achievement award 2003), Calif. Psychol. Assn. (Disting. Scientist award 1973, Lifetime Disting. Contbr. award 1998, Healthtrac award for disting. contbns. to health promotion 2002, McGovern medal for disting. contbn. to health promotion sci. 2004, Lifetime Achievement award for health promotion rsch. 2006), Inst. Medicine NAS, Am. Psychol. Soc. (William James award 1989, James Cattell award 2003, Inter-Am. Psychology award 2009). Office: Stanford U Dept Psychology Stanford CA 94305-2130 Office Phone: 650-725-2409, 650-857-9355. Business E-Mail: bandura@stanford.edu.

BANDYOPADHYAY, PRABIRKUMAR, endocrinologist; b. Kolkata, India, Jan. 1, 1952; arrived in Eng., 1997; d. Umapada and Pravati Banerjee; m. Saliamma Kuriakose Bandyopadhyay, Feb. 4, 1990; children: Prithu Banerjee, Sruti Banerjee. MBBS, Bankura Sammilani Med. Coll. and Hosp., Bankura, India, 1977; diploma in Tropical Medicine and Hygiene, Sch. Tropical Medicine, Kolkata, 1980; diploma in Cardiology, Inst. Postgrad. Med. Edn. and Rsch., Kolkata, 1980; MD, Postgrad. Inst. Med. Edn. and Rsch., Chandigarh, India, 1984; DM in Diabetes and Endocrinology, Postgrad. Inst. Med. Edn. and Rsch., 1986. Rotating house officer Bankura Sammilani Med. Coll. and Hosp., Bankura, 1976—77, sr. house officer internal medicine, 1977; sr. house officer cardiology SSKM Hosp., Kolkata, 1977—78; family practice in medicine Rupnarayanpur, Burdwan, 1978—81; jr. resident in internal medicine Postgrad. Inst. Med. Edn. and Rsch., Chandigarh, 1981—83, jr. rsch. fellow in internal medicine, 1983—84, rsch. assoc. internal medicine, 1984, sr. resident in diabetes and endocrinology, 1985—88, pool officer in diabetes and endocrinology, 1988; specialist in diabetes and endocrinology Oleya Poly. Ctr., Riyadh, Saudi Arabia, 1988—90, Medicare, Asansol, India, 1991—92; sr. registrar in diabetes and endocrinology Salmaniya Med. Ctr., Manama, Bahrain, 1992—97; sr. house officer in diabetes and endocrinology St. Mary's Hosp., Newport, England, 1997—98, sr. house officer in internal medicine, 1998—2000; staff grade in diabetes and endocrinology Caerphilly Dist. Minors Hosp., Caerphilly, Wales, 2000—01; staff grade in diabetes and endocrinology, co-investigator Sandwell Gen. Hosp., West Bromwich, England, 2001—03, assoc. specialist diabetes and endocrinology, 2003—. Contbr. articles to profl. jours. Fellow: ACP; mem.: Royal Coll. Physicians U.K., Indian Med. Assn. (life), Endocrine Soc. India (life), Assn. Physicians India (life). Achievements include research in in andromeda - comparing rosuvastatin and atorvastatin; includes diabetes and heart failure, heart and renal protection, diabetes and cardiovascular disease, diabetes and retinopathy, viagra in diabetes. Avocations: sports, reading, travel, movies. Home: 22 Raven Rd Walsall WS5 3PZ England Office: Sandwell Gen Hosp Lyndon West Bromwich B71 4HJ England Office Phone: 0044-121-6073324. E-mail: prabirbanerjee@yahoo.co.uk.

BANERJEE, BHASKAR, gastroenterologist, medical educator; m. Mousumi Ganguly, Feb. 18, 1992; children: Shoujit, Romit. MBBS, U. London, 1983. Diplomate in internal medicine and gastroenterology Am. Bd. Internal Medicine. House surgeon Ashford Hosp., England, 1983; house physician St. Peters Hosp., England, 1983—84; internal medicine intern U. Conn., 1984—85, resident in internal medicine, 1985—87, fellow in gastroenterology, 1987—89; asst. prof. medicine U. Ark., Little Rock, 1989—94; dir. Biliary-Pancreatic Ctr. Winthrop-U. Hosp., Mineola, NY, 1994—95; assoc. prof. medicine U. Mo., Columbia, 1995—99, Washington U. Sch. Medicine, St. Louis, 1999—2006; prof. medicine Wash. U. Sch. Medicine, St. Louis, 2007—09; prof. medicine optical scis. biomed. engring. U. Ariz., Tucson, 2008—; dir. gastroenterology fellowship program Ariz. Cancer Ctr., 2009—. Presenter in field. Contbr. chapters to books, articles to profl. jours.; editl. bd. mem. reviewer Sci. Manuscript; author: (book) Nutritional Management of Digestive Disorders. Fellow: ACP (life), Am. Coll. Gastroentrology (life), Am. Gastroent. Assn. (life); mem.: Optical Soc. America, SPIE (mem. internat. soc. optics photonics). Achievements include patents for method of detecting early cancer using a beam of light; development of fiber-optic instrument to detect cancer using a beam of light; research in optial detection of cancer cancer and other disorders using light scattering, confocal microscopy, spectroscopy, in disease detection using nano bubbles and nano particles; high contrast imaging methods in gastroenterology and endoscopy. Office: PO Box 245028 1501 N Campbell Ave Tucson AZ 85724 Business E-Mail: bbanerjee@deptofmed.arizona.edu.

BANERJI, JOHN SAMUEL, medical educator; b. Kolkata, Aug. 19, 1974; MBBS, Christian Med. Coll., Vellore, 2000, MS, MCh in Urology, 2009. Asst. prof. Christian Med. Coll., 2009—10, assoc. prof., 2010—. Mem.: South Zone-Urol. Soc. India, Assn. Southern Urologists, Tamil Nadu and Pondicherry Assn. Urologists. Avocations: piano, violin, reading, gardening. Office: Christian Med Coll Dept Urology Ida Scudder Rd Vellore Tamil Nadu 632004 India Office Phone: 416-2282055. E-mail: johnsbanerji2002@yahoo.co.in.

BANERJI, PRASANTA, homeopathic physician; b. Jamalpur, Bihar, India, Oct. 17, 1933; s. Pareshnath and Ava Banerji; m. Krishna Chatterji, Jan. 30, 1958; children: Nabanita, Pratip. Intermediate in Sci., Calcutta U., 1951. Registered homeopathic physician India. Med. cons., examiner Hosp. Mihijam Coll. of Homeopathy, India, 1956—60; homeopathic physician Charitable Dispensary of Late Dr. Pareshnath Banerji, Bihar, India, 1956—60; pvt. practice homeopathic medicine Calcutta, India, 1961—. Mng. trustee P.B. Homeopathic Rsch. Found., Calcutta, 1992—; lectr. homeopathy All India Radio, Calcutta; mem. program adv. com. Nat. Cancer Control Program, Govt. India; appointed mem. key adv. group experts to Hon. Minister for Health and Family Welfare Govt. India; lectr. in field to various confs.; cancer rschr. U. Kansas. Contbr. articles to profl. jours. Fellow Instn. fellow, Mihijam Inst. Homeopathy, 1956. Mem.: AAAS, N.Y. Acad. Scis., Calcutta Club, Tollygunge Club. Achievements include research in treatment of diseases such as cancer; tumors of the brain; osteomyelitis; osteosarcoma; acromegaly; rental failures; nephritis, others. Avocations: reading, photography. Personal E-mail: pbhrf@vsnl.com. Business E-Mail: prasanta@pbhrfindia.org.

BANEY, RICHARD NEIL, retired physician, internist; b. Phila., Apr. 13, 1937; s. Robert Emmet and Mary Elizabeth (Hedges) B.; m. Carolyn Vern Kurey, Feb. 17, 1962; children: Richard N. Jr., Michael D., Marisa V., Brian E. BS, Georgetown U., 1958; MD, U. Pitts., 1963. Diplomate Am. Bd. Internal Medicine, Am. Bd. Rheumatology. Intern VA & Parkland Hosp., Dallas, 1963—64; resident U. Pitts., 1967—70; internist Jess Parrish Hosp., Titusville, Fla., 1971—76, chief med. staff, 1974—76; internist Melbourne (Fla.) Internal Med. Assocs., Holmes Regional Med Ctr., 1976—95; sr. v.p. med. affairs Holmes Regional Med. Ctr., Melbourne, Fla., 1995—96; CEO Health First Physicians, 1995—98; med. officer M.S. Nat. Geog. Endeavor, 1999—2011; ret., 2011. Trustee Holmes Regional Med. Ctr., Melbourne, 1984-95; founding dir., chmn. bd. dirs. Reliance Bank Fla., Melbourne, 1985-95; founding dir., chmn. bd. Bank Brevard, 1996-2004, dir., 2004-08. Trustee Fla. Inst. Tech., Melbourne, 1985—, mem. exec. com., 1987—, vice chmn. bd. trustees, 1991—2002; pres. Canaveral chpt. Am. Heart Assn., Rockledge, Fla., 1973—74; chmn. bd. trustees Sea Pines Rehab. Hosp., Melbourne, 1992—94. Lt. comdr. USN, 1964—67. Fellow ACP; mem. Royal Soc. Medicine, Am. Coll. Rheumatology, Brevard County Med. Soc. (pres. 1977-78), Navy League U.S., Eau Gallie Yacht Club (commodore 1985-86), Coast Club (bd. dirs. 1985-91, chmn. bd. 1989-91). Republican. Avocations: bicycling, travel, collecting antique maps, golf. Personal E-mail: rnbaney@aol.com.

BANFALVI, GASPAR, biochemist, researcher, biologist; b. Nemesnadudvar, Hungary, Oct. 8, 1943; s. Karoly and Ilona (Tokobi) B.; m. Judith Iren Csukas, June 20, 2003; children: Judith, George. MS in Pharmacy, Med. U. Szeged, Hungary, 1968, PhD, 1972; Cand. Sci., Med. U. Budapest, Hungary, 1981, DSc, 1989, D.Med.Habil., 1994; D.Habil. in Biology, U. Sci., Szeged, 1994. Lic. pharmacist, specialist of pharmacology and toxicology. Asst. prof. Med. U. Szeged, 1970-72; staff scientist Drug Rsch. Inst., Budapest, 1972-74; assoc. prof. Med. U. Budapest, 1974-2000; prof. U. Debrecen, 2000—. Rsch. fellow Harvard Med. Sch., Boston, 1981-82, vis. scientist, 1983-84, vis. lectr., 1987-88, vis. prof., Harvard U., 1994; staff fellow Boston Biomed. Rsch. Inst., 1980-82, rsch. fellow, 1983-84, vis. scientist, 1987-88, Fulbright fellow, 1994; rsch. faculty U. Sci. Szeged, 1991-96; vis. prof. Weizman Inst., Rehovot, 1998-99, vis. prof. Teikyo U., 2003, Szecheroji prof., 1997—2001. Author: (book) Molecular Biology, 1995, Molecular Cell Biologgy, 2005, Comparative Physiology 2006, Apoptotic Chromatic Changes, 2009, Effects of Heavy Metals, 2011, Cell Cycle Synchronization, 2011; contbr. articles to profl. jours.; inventor in field; editl. bd. DNA and Cell Biology, Apoptosis, Toxicology in Vitro; sr. editor Bio Nanotoxicology. Pres. Trade Union of Hungarian Med. Univs., Budapest, 1993. Soros fellow Leiden U., Holland, 1988; ORISE/ORAU fellow, 1996. Avocations: building molecular models, book reviews. Office: Dept Microbial Biotech & Cell Biology 1 Egyetem ter 4010 Debrecen Hungary Home: 7 Doczy St Debrecen 4032 Hungary E-mail: bgaspar@delfin.klte.hu.

BANG, JANG SEOK, dermatologist; s. Cho Won Bang and Kae Seon Kang; m. Jung Lin Yoo; children: Sung, Hyun. MD, Dongguk U. Medicine, Republic of Korea, 1993, D in Dermatology, 2002. Cert. Korean Nat. Bd. Dermatology. Head pub. health physician Nat. Pub. Health Ctr., Kyeong ju, Republic of Korea, 1994—97; physician Dongguk U. Hosp., Kyeong ju, Republic of Korea, 1997—2002; pres. Leejihan Skin Clinic, Seoul, 2002—03; head prof. Gachon U. Medicine, Incheon, Republic of Korea, 2003—05, prof., 2003—; pres. Laser Inst., Meline Skin Clinic, Seoul, Republic of Korea, 2005—. Dir. dermatology divsn. Gil Hosp., Inchen, 2003—05; acad. dir. Korean Acad. Anti-Aging Medicine, Seoul, 2003—04, Korean Acad. Integrated Medicine, Seoul, 2004—. Author: Essential Surgical Skill, 2005; translator: Handbook of Obesity Treatment, 2004; contbr. articles to profl. jours. Physician Nat. Pub. Health Care Com., Republic of Korea, 1994—97; head Truth Med. Care, Republic of Korea, 2000. Mem.: Internat. Acad. Cosmetic Dermatology, Korean Acad. Dermatology, Am. Acad. Dermatology. Avocations: movies, travel. Office: Meline Skin Clinic Jump Milano BD Yuksam Dong Seoul 135-080 Republic of Korea Office Phone: 82 2 6440 5588. Business E-Mail: skindoctor@freechal.com.

BANGA, AMIT, medical educator; b. New Delhi, Dec. 2, 1973; MBBS, GR Med. Coll., India, 1997; MD, All India Inst. Med. Scis., New Delhi, 2000. Asst. prof. medicine Mich. State U., 2011—. Sr. med. rsch. specialist Pfizer, 2004—08. Recipient Young Scientist Fgn. Travel award, CSIR, Govt.of India, DST, Govt. of India, INSA, Govt. of India; Rsch. Mini grants, Grad. Med. Edn. Inc., Mich. State U. Fellow: Am. Coll. Chest Physicians (Chgo.) (Young Investigator award). Avocations: travel, chess. Home: 2380 Club Meridian Dr B3 Okemos MI 48864 Personal E-mail: amit.banga@gmail.com.

BANGS, SCOTT, physician; b. Blue Earth, Minn., Sept. 21, 1972; s. Keith and Marian Bangs; m. Rebecca Bulver, July 26, 1997; children: Michael, Lindsay. MD, Med. Coll. of Wis., 1995—99. Bd. Cert. Family Practice Minn., 2002. Resident physician UT Valley Family Practice Residency Program, 1999—2002; family physician Owatonna Clinic - Mayo Health Sys., Owatonna, Minn., 2002—. Contbr. articles to profl. jours. Recipient Andrew W. Mayberry Excellence In Tchg. award, UT Valley Family Practice Residency Program, 1999—2002. Fellow: ACP; mem.: Am. Acad. of Family Physicians. Lutheran. Avocations: sports, music, golf. Office: Owatonna Clinic - Mayo Health System 2200 26th St NW Owatonna MN 55060 Business E-Mail: bangs.scott@mayo.edu.

BANICH, FRANCIS EDWARD, retired surgeon; b. Chgo., Aug. 30, 1932; BS, Loyola U., 1953, MD, 1957. Diplomate Am. Bd. Surgery. Intern Cook County Hosp., Chgo., 1957-58, resident in surgery, 1958-63; attending surgeon Elmhurst Meml. Hosp., Ill., Good Samaritan Hosp., Downers Grove, Ill., 1970; clin. assoc. prof. surgery Stritch Sch. Medicine-Loyola Med. Ctr., 1985—2010, emeritas assoc. prof., 2011—. Mem. ACS, Soc. Surgery Alimentary Tract. Personal E-mail: FEBI@aol.com. *

BANI-HANI, KAMAL E., surgeon, educator, researcher; b. Irbid, Jordan, Dec. 5, 1958; s. Hussein A. Bani-Hani and Jawaher S. Bataineh; m. Golzar O. Karim; children: Salar K., Ahmad K., Bayan K., Mohammed K., Dana K. MB, Faculty Medicine, Baghdad, 1984; FRCS, Royal Coll. Surgeons, Glasgow, 1991; MD, Leeds U., UK, 1998. Cert. Jordanian Bd. Surgery, 1991. Asst. prof. surgery Jordan U. Sci. and Tech., Irbid, 1998—2002, assoc. prof. surgery, 2002—05, prof. surgery, 2005—. Chmn. accident and emergency dept. Jordan U. Sci. and Tech., 2000—03, chmn. dept. surgery, 2003—06; chmn. Pan-Arab gastrointestinal cancer group Med. Arab Assn. Against Cancer, Cairo, 2004—; chmn. med. rsch. com. King Abdullah U. Hosp., Irbid, 2004—06; program dir. Arab Bd. Surgery, Damascus, Syria, 2006—. Contbr. scientific papers to profl. jours. Local cmty. educator Jordanian Med. Assn., Irbid, 1998. Recipient Best Rsch. plaque, Pan-Arab Cancer Congress, 2004, Best Clin. Tchr. prize, Jordan U. Sci. & Tech., 2005. Mem.: Jordanian Med. Coun. (mem. sci. com. 2003). Muslim. Achievements include research in cyclin D1 as a useful early marker in the process of malignant progression from columnar metaplasia to esophageal adenocarcinoma. Avocations: poetry, music, reading. Home: Yarmouk area-Husen Irbid 22110 Jordan Office: Jordan U Sci and Tech Faculty of Medicine 22110 Irbid Jordan Office Fax: 00962-2-7060200; Home Fax: 00962-2-7060200. Personal E-mail: banihani60@yahoo.com.

BANIK, SAMBHU NATH, psychologist; b. Joypara, India, Nov. 7, 1935; s. Padma L. and Kadambini B.; m. Promila (Roy), Nov. 16, 1968; children: Sharmila, and Kakali. BS, Calcutta U., 1956, MS, 1958; PhD, Bristol U., 1964. Staff psychologist Des Moines Child Guidance Ctr., 1965; sr. psychologist, dir. internship tng. Univ. Hosp., Saskatoon, Sask., Canada, 1965-69, dir. psychol. svcs., 1969-71; asst. chief mental health svc. Glenn Dale Hosp. and DC Village, 1971-81; chief South Cmty. Mental Health Ctr., Washington, 1981-84, chief child and youth svc., 1984-88; clin. adminstr. NE SE Family Ctr., Washington, 1988—. Pres. Family Diagnostic and Therapeutic Ctr., Washington, 1993—; exec. dir. President's Com. on Mental Retardation HHS, Washington, 1990-93, cons. psychologist, 1993—; pres. Banik and Assoc. Family Diagnostic and Therapeutic Ctr., 1993—; v.p. devel., chmn. Third World Found., 1993—; asst. prof. U. Sask., 1965-71; vis. prof. Bowie State Coll. Md., 1972-81, prof. psychology, 1993; vis. prof. Thakur Hariprasad Inst., India, 1994. Contbr. articles to profj. jours. Mem. nat. adv. coun. on drug abuse, 1987-90; mem. adv. bd. ARC, Washington, 1987-90; founder, pres. Prabashi, Inc., 1974-78, Assn. Indians in Am., 1980-84; pres. E.S.-Asia Found., 1995—; v.p. India Cultural Coordinating Com., 1979-80, Indian Am. Forum for Polit. Edn., 2000; sec. gen. Asian Pacific Am. Cultural Heritage Coun., 1981-82; treas. Asian Pacific Am. Heritage Coun., 1982-84; mem. spl. com. 3d Conv. Asian Indians in N.Am., 1984, chmn. Indian Am. Forum Polit. Edn., Md., 1986-88, 94—; chmn. Third World Found., 1993—; adv. bd. Ednl. India Found., Inc., 1993—, Commonwealth Assn. for the Mentally Handicapped and Developmental Dis., 1992—, Md. com. on diversity, 2000; chmn. Internat. Cooperation and Coordinating Com. 11th World Congress on Mental Retardation, 1993-94; bd. trustees Woodley House, Washington; pub. mem. Svc., Personel, Rev. Bd., Wash., 1996; commr. Commn. People with Disabilities, Montgomery County, Human Rights Commn., 2004—, State Md. Human Rels. Commn., 2005; elected Md. Bush-Cheney del. Rep. Nat. Conv., 2004. Recipient Dept. Humanitarian Svc. Award D.C., 1986; Cmty. Svc. Award U.S. Asia Found., 1995, Disting. Profl. Svc. Award Ariz. Brain Injury Assn., 1999, Mother Teresa Internat. Millennium Award, 2002, Lifetime Achievement award World Bus. Forum, 2004; elected Bush del. to Rep. Nat. Conv. Mem. APA, Am. Group Psychotherapy Assn., DC Psychol. Assn.; Internat. Acad. Forensic Psychology; Nat. Health Svc. Providers in Psychology, Pres.'s Com. People with Intellectual Disabilities. Home: 8606 Bradmoor Dr Bethesda MD 20817-3633 Office Phone: 202-342-3832. Personal E-mail: sbanik7539@comcast.net.

BANK, ARTHUR, physician; b. NYC, Apr. 20, 1935; s. Abraham and Yetta (Slovis) B.; m. Rona King, June 14, 1960; children: David, Michael. BA, Columbia Coll., 1956; MD, Harvard U., 1960. Diplomate Am. Bd. Internal Medicine, Am. Bd. Hematology. Intern II and IV Harvard Med. Svc. Boston City Hosp, 1960-61, asst. resident II and IV Harvard Med. Svc., 1961-62; rsch. assoc. US Pub. Health Svc. NIH, Bethesda, Md., 1962-64; fellow dept. medicine Coll. Physcians and Surgeons Columbia U., NYC, 1964-66, assoc.dept. medicine Coll. Physicians and Surgeons, 1966-67, asst. prof. dept. medicine Coll. Physicians and Surgeons, 1967-71, acting chair dept. genetics and devel. Coll. Physicians and Surgeons, 1980-81, prof.dept. medicine, dept. genetics and devel., 1975—, dir. divsn. hematology dept. medicine Coll. Physicians and Surgeons, 1980—; asst. attending physician Columbia-Presbyterian Med. Ctr., NYC, 1967-71, dir. dept. clin. pathology, 1970-93, assoc. attending physician, 1971-75, attending physician, 1975—; emeritus prof. medicine & genetics & devel Columbia U. Adj. prof. dept. cell biology and anatomy Grad. Sch. Med. Scis., Cornell U., N.Y.C., 1984-88; founder, cons. Genetix Pharms., Cambridge. Mass., 1990—; Rachford lectr. U. Cin., 1984; Dean's Disting. lectr. Coll. P&S, Columbia U., 1984; Mark Falcon Lesses vis. prof. Harvard Med. Sch., Beth Israel Hosp., Boston U., 1988; active NHLBI, NIH. Author: Book Turning Blood Red The Fight For Life In Cooley's Anemia., Assoc. editor: Jour. Exptl. Biology and Medicine, 1975-80; mem. editl. bd.: Blood, 1975-85; contbr. 200 articles to profl. jours Mem. merit review bd. Hematolgy V.A., 1975-80; senator Columbia U. Senate, 1979-81; mem. med. adv. bd. Cooley's Anemia Found., 1980—, chair med. adv. bd., 1983-88, v.p. med. affairs, 1983-88; mem. adv. com. personnel rsch. Am. Cancer Soc., 1985-88; mem scientific adv. bd. N.Y. Blood Ctr., 1983-90. Scholar Leukemia Soc., 1966-71; recipient Faculty Rsch. award, Am. Cancer Soc., 1971-76, MERIT award Nat. Inst. Diabetes and Digestive and Kidney Diseases, 1988—95 Fellow AAAS, ACP, Molecular Medicine Soc., Royal Soc. Medicine; mem. Am. Soc. Hematolgy (mem. fin. affairs com. 1991-95), Am. Fedn. Clin. Rsch. Am. Soc. Biol. Chemists, Am. Assn. Cancer Rsch., Am. Soc. Human Genetics, Am. Soc. Biochemistry and Molecular Biology, Assn. Am. Physicians, Harvey Soc., Soc. Study of Blood, Assn. Hematology and Oncology Program Dirs., N.Y. State Soc. Med. Oncologists and Hematologists. Avocations: writing, swimming. Home: Hayden-on-Hudson 4465 Douglas Ave Bronx NY 10471-3525 Business E-Mail: ab13@columbia.edu.

BANKS, DALIA A., anesthesiologist; b. Egypt, July 19, 1966; MD, Cairo U., 1990; degree in Anesthesiology, Yale U., New Haven, 2000. Program dir. cardiac anesthesia fellowship U. Calif. San Diego, 2007, chief cardiac anesthesia, 2009—, chief Sulpizio cardiovasc. anesthesia, 2011. Grant, U. Calif. San Diego. Fellow: Am. Soc. Echocardiography; mem.: Am. Soc. Anesthesiologist, Soc. Cardiovasc. Anesthesiologist. Avocations: travel, music, reading. Office: 3350 La Jolla Village Dr # 125A San Diego CA 92161-5085 Office Fax: 858-822-5009. Business E-Mail: dabanks@ucsd.edu.

BANKS, HENRY H., orthopedist, educator, dean; b. Boston, Mar. 9, 1921; s. Isaac and Bessie B.; m. Judith Epstein, June 1945; children: Nancy (Mrs. Curt Civin), Betsy (Mrs. David Epstein), Steven. AB cum laude, Harvard U., 1942; MD, Tufts U., 1945. Diplomate Am. Bd. Orthopedic Surgery (pres. 1978-79, exec. dir. 1979-86). Surg. intern Beth Israel Hosp., Boston, 1945-46, asst. resident in surgery, 1947-49; asst. resident orthopedic lab. and pathology Children's Hosp., Boston, 1949-50, asst. resident orthopedic surgery, 1950-51, Mass. Gen. Hosp., Boston, 1951-52, chief resident orthopedic surgery Peter Bent Brigham Hosp., Boston, 1952, Children's Hosp. Med. Center, Boston, 1952-53; practice medicine, specializing in orthopedic surgery Boston, 1953—; prof. Tufts U. Sch. Medicine, 1970-90, prof. emeritus, 1990—, chmn. dept. orthopedic surgery, 1970-84, assoc. dean, 1972-82, sr. assoc. dean med. affairs, 1982, acting med. dean, then med. dean, 1983-90, dean emeritus, 1990—; dir. orthopedic surgery Boston City Hosp., 1970-74; orthopedic surgeon-in-chief New Eng. Med. Center Hosps., 1970-84. Orthopedic surgeon children's Hosp. Med. Ctr., 1953-70, Peter Bent Brigham Hosp., 1953-70, chief orthopedic surgery, 1968-70. Author: A Century of Excellence: The History of Tufts University School of Medicine, 1893-1993, 1993, Orthopaedic Surgery at Tufts University School of Medicine, 1893-1998, 1998; editor: The Pediatric Clinics of North America-Musculoskeletal Disorder I, 1967; guest editor: Clinical Orthopedics and Related Research, 1968, Orthopedic Clinics of North America, 1976, 78; contbr. articles to profl. jours. With M.C. AUS, 1945-47. Mem. AMA, ACS, Am. Orthopedic Assn. (v.p. 1986-87), Am. Acad. Orthopedic Surgeons, Am. Acad. Cerebral Palsy (pres.), Eastern Orthopedic Assn., Mass. Med. Soc., Internat. Soc. Orthopedic Surgery and Traumatology, Boston Orthopedic Club (pres.), Pediatric Orthopedic Soc., Am. Bd. Orthopedic Surgery (sec., pres. 1973-79). Home: 54 Commonwealth Ave Boston MA 02116-3043 Office: 136 Harrison Ave Boston MA 02111-1817

BANKS, SONJA L., medical association administrator; BA in Polit. Sci., U. Ala., 1991; MPA, Jacksonville State U., Ala., 1996. Leadership positions United Way Ctrl. Ala. and City of Birmingham; state dir. Ala. & Miss. and regional dir. United Negro Coll. Fund, Inc., 2000—07; dir. cmty. svc., outreach and adult indigent services St. Vincent's Health Sys., Birmingham, Ala., 2007—10; nat. pres., COO Sickle Cell Disease Assn. America, Inc., Balt., 2010—. Recipient Coca-Cola Women Who Care award, 2003, Outstanding Cmty. Svc. award, 2009; named one of 30 Leaders 30 and Under, Ebony mag., 1998; finalist Adminstr. of Yr. award, ASPA, 2005. Mem.: Alpha Kappa Alpha Sorority, Inc. Office: Sickle Cell Disease Assn America Inc 231 E Baltimore St Ste 800 Baltimore MD 21202 Office Phone: 410-528-1555. Office Fax: 410-528-1495. Business E-Mail: sbanks@sicklecelldisease.org. *

BANNASCH, PETER, pathologist, researcher; b. Biebergemund, Hessen, Germany, Apr. 14, 1934; s. Hans and Ruth (Trebst) B.; m. Helga Wende; children: Christoph, Bettina, Daniel. MD, U. Freiburg, Germany, 1960. Sci. asst. U. Würzburg, Germany, 1963-68, lectr. pathology, 1968-73; prof. pathology U. Heidelberg, Germany, 1973—; head divsn. cell pathology German Cancer Rsch. Ctr., Heidelberg, 1973-99, chmn. sci. coun., 1981-84, 87-88, trustee, 1996-99. Guest prof. U. Xi'an, China, 2000; chmn. Alumni DKFZ, Heidelberg, 2002-10; vis. prof. U. Wuhan, China, 2005. Editor: Liver Cancer, 1978, 89, Cancer Risks, 1987, Cancer Treatment, 1989, Cancer Diagnosis, 1992, Pathology of Neoplasia and Preneoplasia in Rodents, 1994, 97, Cell Growth and Oncogenesis, 1998; author: The Cytoplasm of Hepatocytes During Carcinogenesis, 1968; contbr. numerous articles to sci. and profl. jours. Mem.: Soc. for Histochemistry, Soc. for Toxicol. Pathology, Am. Assn. for Cancer Rsch., German Soc. for Cancer, German Soc. for Cell Biology, German Soc. for Pathology, European Assn. Pathology, European Assn. Cancer Rsch. (pres. 1987—93). Office: Deutsches Krebsforschungsz Postfach 101949 69120 Heidelberg Germany Office Phone: 49 6221 423202. Business E-Mail: p.bannasch@dkfz.de.

BANNISTER, SIR ROGER GILBERT, neurologist, academic administrator; b. Harrow, Middlesex, England, Mar. 23, 1929; s. Ralph and Alice Bannister; m. Moyra Elver Jacobsson; 4 children. BA with honors in Physiology, Exeter Coll., Merton Coll., Oxford U., 1950; MSc, St. Mary's Hosp., 1952; MB BCh, Oxford U., 1954, DM, 1963; LLD (hon.), U. Liverpool, 1972; DLitt (hon.), U. Sheffield, 1978; doctorate (hon.), Jyvaskyla U., Finland, 1983, U. Bath, 1984, Imperial Coll., London, 1984, Grinnell Coll., Iowa, 1984, U. Wales, Cardiff, 1995, U. Loughborough, 1996, U. East Anglia, 1997, Cranfield U., 2002, Royal Coll. Surgeons, Edinburgh, 2002. Cons. neurologist Western Opthalmic Hosp., 1963—85, St. Mary's Hosp., London, 1963—85, Nat. Hosp. for Neurology and Neurosurgery, London, 1963—90; now hon. cons. neurologist; v.p. St. Mary's Hosp. Med.

Sch., 1985-88; master Pembroke Coll., Oxford, 1985-93; gov. Nat. Hosp. Neurology and Neurosurgery, 1994-96; trustee St. Mary's Hosp. Med. Sch. Devel. Trust, 1994—2006, chmn., 1998. Chmn. Sports Coun. of Great Britain, 1971—74; pres. Internat. Coun. for Sport and Phys. Recreation, 1976—83; chmn. editl. bd. Clin. Autonomic Rsch. jour., 1990—. Author: (autobiography) First Four Minutes (reprinted as Four Minute Mile), 1955, 50th Anniversary edit., 2004; editor: Brain's Clinical Neurology (retitled Brain and Bannister's Clinical Neurology, 1990), 1969; co-editor (with C.J. Mathias): (textbook) Autonomic Failure, 1982, 5th edit., 2009. Created knight, 1975; recipient Pears Silver Trophy, 1954, Freedom of Borough of Harrow award, Freedom City Oxford, Acad. Neurology award; hon. fellow Exeter, Merton, Pembroke and Harris Manchester Colls., Oxford U. Fellow Royal Coll. Physicians; mem. Royal Coll. Surgeons, Oxford U. Athletic Club (pres. 1948), Athenaeum. Achievements include Brit. Mile Champion, 1951, 53, 54; finalist in 1500m, 1952 Olympic Games, Helsinki; ran first sub-4-minute mile in 3:59.4 at Iffley Road Track, Oxford U., May 6, 1954. Office: 21 Bardwell Rd Oxford OX2 6SU England

BANNO, YOSHIKO, medical educator, researcher; b. Iida, Nagano, Japan, Feb. 28, 1946; d. Yoshio and Imae Hiraguri; m. Yoshiko Hiraguri, Apr. 28, 1971; 1 child, Yoshifumi. PhD, Gifu Pharm. U., 1968. Asst. Sch. Medicine Gifu U., 1968—71, asst. prof. Sch. Medicine, 1980—97, lectr. Sch. Medicine, 1998—99, assoc. prof. Sch. Medicine, 1999—; asst. Sch. Medicine Tokushima U., Japan, 1971—79. Lectr. Gifu Uman Jr. Coll., 1998—. Avocations: gardening, climbing. Office: Gifu Univ Grad Sch Medicine 1-1 Yanagido Gifu 501 1194 Japan

BANNON, MARY, insurance company executive, lawyer; Grad., Smith Coll.; attended, Trinity Coll., Hartford; LLB, Harvard Law Sch. Healthcare lawyer Carmody & Torrance LLP, Robinson & Cole LLP, Cigna; cons. Human Resource Consortium; gen. counsel ConnectiCare Inc., 1994—99, now sr. v.p. and gen. counsel; dep. gen. counsel Horizon Blue Cross Blue Shield of NJ, 2003—07; gen. counsel Health Net of the NE, 2007—08. Office: ConnectiCare Inc. PO Box 4050 175 Scott Swamp Rd Farmington CT 06034-4050 Office Phone: 860-674-5757. Office Fax: 860-674-2215.

BANO, SHAHINA, radiologist; b. Allahabad, Mar. 6, 1972; MBBS, N.S.C.B. Med. Coll., Jabalpur, India, 2002, MD in Radiodiagnosis, 2006. Sr. resident Dr. R.M.L. Hosp. & PGIMER, 2007—; asst. prof., radiodiagnosis G.B. Pant Hosp. & Maulana Azad Med. Coll., New Delhi, 2010. Referee, reviewer Am. Jour. Neuroradiology, Indian Jour. Radiology & Imaging, 2009—. Mem.: Indian Soc. Neuroradiology, Indian Radiol. & Imaging Assn. Avocations: gardening, travel. Office: Dept Radiodiagnosis New Delhi 110002 India Personal E-mail: dr_shahinaindia@yahoo.com.

BANSAL, VIPUL, biotechnologist, educator; b. Chandausi, India, Feb. 7, 1980; arrived in Australia, 2006, permanent resident, 2010; s. Anil and Anshu Agarwal; m. Priyanka Gupta, Dec. 3, 2009. BS in Plant and Agrl. Sci., Allahabad Agrl. U., India, 2001; MS in Biotechnology, Tamil Nadu Agrl. U., Coimbatore, India, 2003; PhD in Nanobiotechnology, Nat. Chem. Lab., Pune, India, 2007. Cert. CSIR Indian Inst. Mgmt. Fellow RMIT U., 2006—07, Melbourne U., 2007—08, sr. lectr., 2010—. APD fellow Australian Rsch. Coun., 2009—; hon. fellow Melbourne U., 2008—. Recipient Emerging Rschr. award, RMIT, 2008, Keerthi Sangoram Best Rsch. Scholar award, NCL India, 2006, Gold medal, AAI India, 2001; grant, ARC Industry Linkage, 2010. Fellow: Australian Tech. Network, Australian Rsch. Coun.; mem.: Australian Rsch. Coun. Nanotechnology Network. Avocations: reading, travel, badminton, cooking. Office: RMIT University 003 01 004 Sch Applied Scis 3001 Melbourne VIC Australia Office Phone: 61 3 99252121. Office Fax: 61 3 99253747. Business E-Mail: vipul.bansal@rmit.edu.au.

BANTA, JAMES ELMER, epidemiologist, educator, dean; b. Tucumcari, N.Mex., July 1, 1927; s. James Elmer and Edna Mae (Murnahan) B. MD, Marquette U., 1950; M.P.H., Johns Hopkins U., 1954; diploma, U.S. Naval Med. Sch., 1952. Med. officer USN, 1950-60; capt. med. officer USPHS, 1960-69; dir. med. program Peace Corps, 1963-65; dir. Office Internat. Health, HEW, 1967-68; med. officer WHO, 1968-70; prof. public health U. Hawaii, 1970-73; dep. dir. Office Health, AID, State Dept., Washington, 1973-75; dean, prof. Sch. Public Health and Tropical Medicine, Tulane U., New Orleans, 1975-87; prof. Sch. Pub. Health U. Hawaii, Honolulu, 1987-88; clin. prof. dept. community and family medicine Georgetown U., Washington, 1990-99. Adj. prof. sch. pub. health and health scis. George Washington U., Washington, 1992-2006. Co-author: How to Travel the World and Stay Healthy, 1969, Year-round Travelers' Health Guide, 1978; Contbr. articles on epidemiology, microbiology and health to profl. jours. Served with USN, 1944-46. Recipient Outstanding Service award Georgetown U., 1965 Fellow AAAS, Am. Coll. Preventive Medicine, Am. Public Health Assn., Am. Heart Assn., Am. Coll. Epidemiology, Coll. Phys. Phila.; mem. ACLU, Common Cause, Environ. Action, Assn. Schs. Public Health (pres. 1979-81), Sigma Xi, Phi Sigma, Delta Omega. Personal E-mail: jebanta@erols.com.

BANUELOS, BETTY LOU, rehabilitation nurse; b. Vandergrift, Pa., Nov. 28, 1930; d. Archibald and Bella Irene (George) McKinney; m. Raul, Nov. 1, 1986; children: Patrice, Michael. Diploma, U. Pitts., 1951; cert., Loma Linda U., 1960. RN, Calif.; cert. chem. dependency nurse, addictions treatment specialist; ordained to ministry Ch. of God. Cons. occupl. health svc. Bd. Registered Nurses, 1984—. Lectr., cons. in field. Recipient Scholarship U. Pitts. Mem. Dirs. of Nursing, Calif. Assn. Nurses in Substance Abuse. Home and Office: 15 Oak Spring Ln Laguna Hills CA 92656-2980 Office Phone: 949-831-1767. Personal E-mail: BettyB8@hotmail.com.

BAPTIST, ALLWYN J., healthcare consultant; b. India, July 10, 1943; came to U.S., 1971; s. Peter L.G. and Trescilla (Lobo) B.; m. Anita Lobo, Sept. 8, 1973; children: Alan, Andrew, Annabel, Arthur. BCS, U. Calcutta, India, 1962; cert. mgmt., U. Chgo., 1978. CPA, Ill; chartered acct., India. Divisional acct. Rallis India Ltd., Bombay, 1967-71; mgr. Chgo. Blue Cross, 1972-79; sr. mgr. Price Waterhouse, Chgo., 1979-84; v.p., dir. Truman Esmond and Assocs., Barrington, Ill., 1984-86; ptnr. Laventhol and Horwath, Chgo., 1986-90, BDO Seidman, Chgo., 1991-2000; pres. Baptist Cons. Inc., 2000—. Mem. adv. bd. St. Mary of Nazareth Hosp., 1989—, mem. gov. bd., 1992-94, 96-98, lifetime trustee. Contbr. articles to profl. jours. Mem. fin. com. St. James Ch., Arlington Heights, Ill., 1987; mem. AICPA Health Care Com., 1991-94. Mem. Healthcare Fin. Mgmt. Assn. (dir., sec. 1983-85, pres. 1988-89, recipient William J. Follmer award 1984, Reeves award 1989, Muncie Gold award 1992, founders medal of honor 1998), India Cath. Assn. Am. (treas. 1980, 87, pres. 1988). Avocations: travel, reading, tennis, golf. Office: Bapt Cons Inc 126 E Wing St Arlington Heights IL 60004

BAPTISTA-SILVA, JOSE CARLOS COSTA, medical educator; s. Francisco Baptista-Silva and Oliria Baptista-Costa; m. Marcia Seiscento; children: Thales Seiscento Baptista, Talita Seiscento Baptista. MD, Faculdade Medicina Marilia, Sao Paulo, 1976. Prof. surgery U. Fed. Sao Paulo, Brazil, 1985—, rschr., 1990—. With Med. Hosp., 1983—84, Sao Paulo. Mem.: SBACVSP (Alexis Carrel 2007). Home and Office: Univ Federal Sao Paulo Rua Borges Lagoa 564 CJ 124 São Paulo 04038000 Brazil Office Fax: 55 11 55718419. Personal E-mail: jocabaptista@uol.com.br.

BAR, MICHAEL, hematologist, educator, oncologist, internist; Grad., Columbia U., NYC, 1983. Diplomate Am. Bd. Internal Medicine, Am. Bd. Internal Medicine-med. oncology, Am. Bd. Internal Medicine-hematology. Resident internal medicine Columbia-Presby Med. Ctr., NYC, 1984—86; fellow hematology and oncology Univ. Calif. San Francisco Med. Ctr., 1987—90; asst. clin. prof. medicine Columbia Univ., NYC; with Stamford Hosp., Conn. Office: Stamford Hospital 30 Shelburne Rd Stamford CT 06904 Office Phone: 203-276-1000.

BARAB, PATSY LEE, nutritionist, realtor; b. Indpls., Sept. 24, 1934; 1 child, Gregory (dec.); m. John D. Barab Jr., Apr. 8, 1995 (dec. Dec. 4, 2007). BS, Mich. State U., 1956, MA, 1970. Asst. prof. Med. Coll. Ga., Augusta, 1972-82; nutrition cons., 1982—. Assoc. Meybohm Realty, Inc., Augusta, 1987—. Docent Morris Mus. Art, 1992—; mem. program com. Gertrude Herbert Art Inst., 1992—94, Imperial Theater, bd. dirs., 2001—03. Mem.: CRS, GRI, Nutritionists in Nursing Edn. (nat. chmn. 1983—84), Nutrition Today Soc. (charter), Soc. Nutrition Edn., Ga. Dietetic Assn., Am. Dietetic Assn., Million Dollar Club (life), Pi Beta Phi, Omicron Nu. Home and Office: 3051 Walton Way Augusta GA 30909 Personal E-mail: patsypink3@aol.com.

BARABÁS, JÓZSEF LAJOS, maxillofacial surgeon; b. Kántorjánosi, Hungary, Apr. 9, 1951; MD, Semmelweis Med. U., Budapest, Hungary, 1975, PhD, 1985. Surgeon Hosp. Sümeg, Hungary, 1975—77; maxillofacial surgeon Semmelweis Med. U., 1977—2004, head dept. oro-maxillofacial surgery, 2004, mem. faculty coun., faculty dentistry. Recipient Ministerial award, Hungarian Ministry Health, award, Ferenczi Erzsébet Found., Disting. Lectr. award, Semmelweis Med. U. Mem.: Internat. Assn. Oral and Maxillofacial Surgery, European Assn. Cranio-Maxillofacial Surgery, Hungarian Assn. Oro-Maxillofacial Surgery & Stomatology (exec. com. mem.), Hungarian Assn. Dentists (presdl. bd. mem.). Office: Dept Oro-Maxillofacial Surgery and Stomatology 52 Maria St Budapest 1085 Hungary Office Fax: 36-1-266-0456. Business E-Mail: barabas@fok.usn.hu.

BARAC, BOSKO ANTUN, neurologist, educator; b. Zagreb, Croatia, Sept. 11, 1930; s. Antun Mate and Nevenka Mihovil Barac; m. Dragica B. Sokacic, Sept. 21, 1963; children: Iva, Ana, Mirna. MD, U. Zagreb, 1956, Dr. Med. Sc., 1965. Neuropsychiatrist Hosp. Vinogradska Str., Zagreb, 1959-62; clin. asst. dept. neurology Med. Faculty U. Zagreb, 1965-68, asst. prof. neurology, 1968-75, leader postgrad. study in neurology, 1972-84, assoc. prof., 1975-77, prof., 1977-95, founder, 1st head neurol. ICU, 1970-79, chief neurology, 1979-87; prof. neurology, head dept. neurology Osijek U. Sch. Medicine, 1995—2001. Organizer symposia on cerebrovascular disease, 1971, 74, 79, 85, 89; trustee Internat. Neuropsychiat. Pula Congresses, Croatia, 1974—, sec.-gen. 1985—; v.p. Assembly for Sci. Work Croatia, Zagreb, 1982, pres., 1985-87; hon. pres. Kuratorium INPC; hon. mem. CROMBES, 2001; chmn. rsch. group on orgn. of neurology World Fedn. Neurology, 1985—, mem. rsch. group on neurology edn. Author: Neurology, 1978, 79, Fundamentals of Neurology, 1979, Neurology, 1989, 2d rev. edit., 1992; editor: Neurology in Developing Countries, 1991; pres. editorial bd. Neurologija, Zagreb; contbr. over 250 articles to profl. jours. Dep. Parliament Croatia, 1978-82. Fellow Intensive Care Soc. of Brit. Med. Assn.; mem. Assn. Neurology and Psychiatry Yugoslavia (sec. gen. 1965-68), Yugoslav Neurol. Assn. (trustee 1984-91), Croatian Neurol. Soc. (pres. 1979-88), Soc. E.E.G. and Clin. Neurophysiology Croatia (pres. 1972-81), Croatian Med. Acad. Zagreb, N.Y. Acad. Scis., Am. Acad. Neurology (hon. corr.), Am. Neurol. Assn., World Fedn. Neurology (Yugoslav del. 1984-91), World Fedn. Neurology (mem. rsch. coun.), South-East European Soc. for Neurology and Psychiatry, Rsch. Group for Orgn. and Delivery of Neurol. Svcs. E-mail: bosko.barac@zg.ht-com.hr.

BARAD, MARK GORDON, psychiatrist, educator; b. Providence, Oct. 10, 1952; AB, Harvard Coll., 1979; MD, Yale U., PhD, 1991. Intern, internal medicine Yale New Haven Hosp., 1991—92; postdoc. fellow, Dr. Eric Kandel Columbia U., 1992—96, resident, psychiatry, 1996—99; assoc. clin. prof. UCLA, 1999—; psychiatrist, pvt. practice, 1999—; attending psychiatrist West LA Vets. Health Adminstrn., 2005—. Office: 1554 S Sepulveda Blvd Ste 101 Los Angeles CA 90025 Office Fax: 310-919-3666. Business E-Mail: mbarad@mednet.ucla.edu.

BARAKAT, AMIN J., pediatrician, pediatric nephrologist; b. Beirut, Nov. 2, 1942; s. Yousef and Mabel Barakat; m. Amal Nassar; children: Rana, Nadim, Zena. MD, Am. Univ. Beirut, 1960—67. Pediat. Johns Hopkins Hosp.; clin. prof. pediat. and pediat. nephrology Georgetown U., Washington, 1989—; clin. prof. pediat. George Wash. U., 2009—. Vis. prof. dept. pediat. U. Va., Charlottesville, 1996—; pres. Am. Found. St. George Hosp., Washington, 1999—; mem. ALSAC, St. Jude Leadership Coun., St. Jude Children's Rsch. Hosp. Author: Renal Disease in Children, 1990, The Kidney in Genetic Disease, 1986, Pediatric Nephrology for Primary Care, 2009; editor: Arabic edit. Caring for Your Baby and Young Child, 2007, Arabic edit. A Parents Guide to Childhood Obesity, 2010. Recipient Ellis Island Medal of Honor, NECO, 2000; named one of Best Doctors in Am., 2005—10; named to, America's Top Pediatricians, 2002—09. Mem.: Am. Acad. Pediatrics, Alpha Omega Pi. Achievements include first to describe the Barakat Syndrome in 1977. Office: No Va Pedia Assoc 107 N Virginia Ave Falls Church VA 22046 Office Phone: 703-532-4446.

BARAK-SHINAR, DEGANIT, medical association administrator; b. Israel, Dec. 19, 1972; PhD, Tel-Aviv U., 2005. V.p. clin. affairs WideMed Ltd., 2005—. Office: 10 Hasadnaot St Herzliya 46733 Israel Office Fax: 971-9-9514158. Business E-Mail: deganit@widemed.com.

BARAN, XIAOLEI YU, physician, psychiatry professor; d. Tian Shou and Ai Fu (Yang) Yu; m. Mark Richard Baran, Dec. 21, 2002. MD, Shanghai Second Med. Coll., 1983. Med. resident Shanghai Med. Coll., 1983—85, NY Med. Coll., Valhalla, 1991—92; rsch. fellow Am. Health Found., Valhalla, 1990—91; psychiat. resident NY Hosp.-Cornell Med. Ctr., White Plains, 1992—95; psychiat. fellow Cornell Med. Coll., 1995—96, instr. in psychiatry, 1995—98; attending psychiatrist NY Presbyn. Hosp., White Plains, 1996—; asst. prof. psychiatry Weill Cornell Med. Coll., NYC, 1998—2005, asst. prof. clin. psychiatry, 2005—. Mem.: Am. Assn. Geriatric Psychiatry, Am. Psychiat. Assn. (gen. mem. 1992). Office: NY Presbyn Hosp 21 Bloomingdale Rd White Plains NY 10605 Office Phone: 914-997-4358. Office Fax: 646-962-1998. Business E-Mail: xyu@med.cornell.edu.

BARANETSKY, NICHOLAS, endocrinologist, educator; Attended, NY Med. Coll., 1974. Diplomate Am. Bd. of Internal Medicine, Am. Bd. of Internal Medicine-endocrinology, diabetes & metabolism. Resident Stanford Hosp., 1975—77; fellow Va. Med. Ctr., 1977—79; prof. medicine Seton Hall Univ.; chmn. dept. of medicine St. Michael's Med. Ctr. Office: Saint Michael's Medical Center 111 Central Ave Newark NJ 07102 Office Phone: 973-877-5000.

BARANGAN, CAROLINE J., pediatrician, educator; MD, Mt. Sinai sch. of Medicine, 1996. Diplomate Am. Bd. Pediatrics, 2003, Am. Bd. Pediatrics-adolescent medicine, 2005. Resident pediat. Arnold Palmer Hosp., Orlando, 1997—2000; fellow adolescent medicine Montefiore Med. Ctr., Bronx, 2000—03; assoc. residency program dir. Univ. Nev. sch. of medicine, chief sect. adolescent medicine, asst. prof. pediat.; physician Children's Hosp. of Nev. Mem.: Am. Acad. of Pediat., Soc. for Adolescent Medicine. Office: University of Nevada School of Medicine 3006 S Maryland Pkwy Ste 315 Las Vegas NV 89109 Office Phone: 702-992-6868. Office Fax: 702-671-2231.

BARANNIK, ALLA PETROVNA, biologist; b. Moscow, Feb. 14, 1967; MSc in Biology, Moscow State U., 1992. Rsch. scientist Shemyakin-Ovchinnikov Inst. Bioorganic Chemistry Russian Acad. Scis., 1992—, Civilian R & D Found. grant, Russian Fedn., Russian Found. Basic Rsch. grant. Office: Ul Miklukho-Maklaya 16/10 Moscow 117997 Russia Office Fax: 74997934611. Business E-Mail: abarannik@mx.ibch.ru.

BARANOV, PAVEL ANDREEVICH, quality assurance professional; b. Moscow, June 13, 1984; PhD in Clin. Pharmacology, State Found. Inst. Pharmacology, 2010. Tech. specialist Moscow Antidoping Ctr., 2005—06, sr. tech. specialist, 2006—09, scientist, dept. horse doping, 2009—10, sr. scientist, dept. horse doping, 2010, head quality assurance dept., 2010—. Avocations: sports, snowboarding, music. Home: Marshala Timoshenko 34-80 Moscow 121359 Russia Business E-Mail: qualitydoping@yandex.ru.

BARANOWSKI, WOJCIECH JANUSZ, vocational school educator; b. Lodz, Poland, Jan. 4, 1971; MD, Med. U. Lodz, 1996; PhD, U. Sch. Phys. Edn. Poznan, Poland, 2006. Lectr. Lodzka Korporacja Oswiatowa, 1999—; sr. lectr. Higher Vocat. Sch. LKO, Lodz, 2004—. Cons. UNIQA Towarzystwo Ubezpieczen Spólka Akcyjna, 2000—; grader - external examiner Okregowa Komisja Egzaminacyjna w Lodzi, 2005—. Mem.: Polish Pediat. Soc. Office: Lodzka 87 Powiat Pabianicki Konstantynow Lodzki Województwo Lodzkie 95050 Poland Office Phone: 48502063567. Business E-Mail: kosmetologia@wp.pl.

BARANSKI, JAMES, medical association administrator; Ind. mgmt. cons.; mng. ptnr. Coleman, Epstein, Berlin & Co., Chgo.; pres., CEO Nat. Stroke Assn., 2003—. Office: Nat Stroke Assn 9707 E Easter Ln Centennial CO 80112 Office Phone: 303-754-0904. Business E-Mail: jbaranski@stroke.org. *

BARAO, VALENTIM ADELINO RICARDO, dentist, researcher; b. Olimpia, Sao Paulo, Brazil, Oct. 18, 1983; DDS, Sao Paulo State U., UNESP, Aracatuba Dental Sch., 2005, MSc, PhD student, Sao Paulo State U., UNESP, Aracatuba Dental Sch., 2008—. Rsch. scholar U. Ill. Chgo., Coll. Dentistry, 2009—10. Recipient Prof. Jose Marcondes Santini award, Sao Paulo State U., Prof. Enyr Geraldo Arcieri award; finalist Arthur R. Frechette New Investigator award, Internat. Assn. Dental Rsch., 2011. Mem.: ADA, Brazilian Soc. Dental Rsch., Internat. Assn. Dental Rsch. Avocation: gymnastics. Home: Alameda Garibaldi 102 Olimpia Sao Paulo 15400-000 Brazil Office Phone: 55 18 8807 4249. Personal E-mail: ricardo.barao@hotmail.com.

BARATZ, MARK E., orthopaedic surgeon, educator; MD, U. Pitts. Cert. orthopaedic surgery, orthopaedic surgery- surgery of the hand. Intern Univ. Pitts. Med. Ctr., resident, fellow; prof. orthopaedic surgery Drexel Univ.; fellow Allegheny Gen. Hosp., dir. divsn. hand and upper extrmity surgery, vice chmn. dept. orthopaedic surgery, divsn. dir. upper extremity surgery, dir. orpthpaedic residency and fellowship programs. Named one of Top Doctors, Pitts. mag., 2011. Office: Allegheny General Hospital 320 E N Ave Pittsburgh PA 15212 Office Phone: 412-359-3131. Office Fax: 412-359-4108.

BARBARINI, GIORGIO, medical researcher; b. Voghera, Pavia, Italy, Aug. 27, 1951; s. Felice Barbarini and Clelia Cognolato; m. Sandra Ferrari, Apr. 20, 1985; 1 child, Daniel. MD, U. Pavia, 1976. Profl. qualification Med. Order Pavia Italy, 1977. Infectious disease physician U. Pavia, 1977—80, gastroenterologist, 1982—85, chief outpatients structure dept. infection and tropical diseases Inst. Ricovero Cura Carattere Sci. S. Matteo, 1987—; vis. sci. NIAID NIH, Bethesda, Md., 1993. Contbr. over 200 sci. publications to profl. jours.; co-author: (book) Cardiology in AIDS. Recipient U. award of Infectious and Tropical Diseases, 1977. Mem.: Italian Soc. Infectious and Tropical Diseases, Internat. Soc. Infectious and Tropical Diseases, Internat. AIDS Soc. Freedom Socialist. Achievements include research in the clinical and therapeutic aspects of HIV, HBV, and HCV infections. Avocations: climbing, travel. Office: IRCCS Polyclinic SMatteo-Univ Taramelli st 27100 Pavia Italy Home: Via Leonardo da Vinci 13 27058 Voghera PV Italy Office Fax: 0039(0)382-529730. Personal E-mail: giorgio.barbarini@libero.it.

BARBATO, ANTHONY L., hospital administrator, medical educator; BA, U. Windsor; MD, Stritch Sch. Medicine, Loyola U. Chgo. Cert. bd. cert. Am. Bd. Internal Medicine, Am. Bd. Endocrinology and

Metabolism. Asst. prof. Stritch Sch. Medicine, Loyola U., Maywood, Ill., 1976—81, assoc. prof., 1981—86, prof. medicine, 1986—; dean Stritch Sch. Medicine, Maywood, Ill., exec. dean, asst. chmn., medicine for post-grad. edn., program dir., internal medicine residency; exec. v.p., health affairs Loyola U. Health Sys., Maywood, Ill., provost, health affairs, chief admin. officer, health affairs, v.p., health affairs, pres., CEO, 1995—. Chmn. Assoc. Academic Health Ctrs., 2000; sr. health policy adv. com. Rep. Danny Davis. Office: 2160 S First Ave Maywood IL 60153

BARBE, DAVID O., physician, healthcare executive; m. Debbie Barbe; 2 children. B in Microbiology with honors, U. Mo., Colombia, MD, M in Health Adminstrn. Cert. in family medicine. Residency in family medicine U. Kans.-St. Joseph's Hosp., Witchita, Kans.; pvt. practice in traditional family medicine Mountain Grove, Mo., 1984—; med. dir. dept. obstetrics Tex. County Meml. Hosp., Houston, Mo., 1986—2007, chief med. staff, Mercy Hosp., Mansfield, Mo.; pres. regional divsn. St. John's Clinic, Inc., Mountain Grove, 1999—. Mem. med. exec. com. & bd. dirs. St. John's Hosp., Mo.; bd. mem. St. John's Health Plans. Fellow: American Acad. Family Physicians; mem.: AMA (Mo. del. 1997—2009, chmn. coun. on med. svc. 2008—09, bd. trustees 2009—, sec. 2011—), Mo. Acad. Family Physicians, Mo. State Med. Assn. (chmn. 2003, pres. 2005, bd. dirs.). Office: St Johns Clinic 120 W 16th St Mountain Grove MO 65711-1039 Office Phone: 417-926-6111. Office Fax: 417-926-6115. Business E-Mail: david.barbe@mercy.net. *

BARBER, BYRON, II, plastic surgeon; m. Henrietta Barber; 3 children. Grad. magna cum laude, Wofford Coll., Spartanburg, SC; MD, Med. U. SC, Charleston. Diplomate Am. Bd. Plastic Surgery. Gen. surgery residency Bethesda Naval Hosp.; plastic surgery residency Duke Med. Ctr.; chief plastic surgery Moses Cone Hosp. Sys. Christine Kleinert fellow Univ. of Louisville. Contbr. Greensboro News & Record column on Ask the Doctor. Named Top Surgeon, Rrsch. Coun. of America; named one of One of the country's leading plastic surgeons, New Beauty Mag. Fellow: Am. Coll. of Surgeons; mem.: Am. Soc. for Aesthetic Plastic Surgery, Southeastern Soc. of Plastic and Reconstructive Surgeons (v.p.), NC Soc. of Plastic Surgeons (former pres.), Triad Plastic Surgery (former pres.), NC Med. Soc., Guilford County Med. Soc., Am. Soc. of Plastic Surgeons. Office: Barber Center for Plastic Surgery Ste 100 1591 Yanceyville St Greensboro NC 27405 Office Phone: 336-275-3430. Office Fax: 336-275-3420.

BARBER, JERRY RANDEL, retired medical device company executive; b. Killarney, W.Va., Sept. 23, 1940; s. Edward Clay and Nora (Mullins) B.; m. Carrolyn Rae Acree, June 9, 1964; 1 child, Alyssa Rae. BSChemE, W.Va. U., 1962; MSChemE, Ohio State U., 1964, PhD, 1968. Rsch. engr. Union Carbide Corp., South Charleston, W.Va., 1968-73, group leader rsch., 1973-77, assoc. dir. rsch., 1977-81, dir. rsch., Tarrytown, NY, 1981-89, dir. new bus. and tech. devel., Danbury, Conn., 1989-93; gen. mgr. Medisyn Techs., Corp., Las Vegas, Nev., 1993-94; mng. dir. Medisyn Techs. Ltd., Arklow, Ireland, 1994-97; exec. v.p. techs. McGhan Med. Corp., Santa Barbara, Calif., 1997-98; v.p. R&D, Mentor Corp., Irving, Tex., 1998-2000, Santa Barbara, Calif., 1999—2000, v.p. advanced devel., 2000—05, v.p. rsch., 2005—06. Mem. AIChE, AAAS, Sigma Xi. Democrat. Methodist. Home: 2785 Poli St Ventura CA 93003-1556 Office Phone: 805-218-8419. Personal E-mail: jrbarber7@aol.com.

BARBER, ROBERT BRIAN, physician; b. Mishawaka, Ind., Apr. 9, 1968; MD, St. Matthews U. Sch. Medicine, 2002; degree in Family Medicine Residency, Mayo Clinic Coll. Medicine, 2006. Family medicine physician St. Vincent Med. Group, 2010—. Staff physician Operation Renewed Hope, 2007; founder & exec. dir. S.O.M.E. Ministries Med. Mission Team, 2011; medical missionary & mission team dir. Fellow: Am. Profl. Wound Care Assn.; mem.: AMA, IAFP, AAFP. Office: 350 JH Walker Dr Ste 100 Pendleton IN 46064 Office Fax: 765-778-8388. Personal E-mail: barbersforlife@yahoo.com.

BARBO, DOROTHY MARIE, obstetrician, gynecologist, educator; b. River Falls, Wis., May 28, 1932; d. George William and Marie Lillian (Stelsel) B. BA, Asbury U., 1954, DSc (hon.), 1981; MD, U. Wis., 1958. Diplomate Am. Bd. Ob-Gyn. Resident Luth. Hosp. Milw., 1958-62; instr. Sch. Medicine Marquette U., Milw., 1962-66, asst. prof., 1966-67; assoc. prof. Christian Med. Coll. Punjab U., Ludhiana, India, 1968-72; assoc. prof. Med. Coll. Pa., Phila., 1972-87, prof., 1988-91, U. N.Mex., Albuquerque, 1991-99, prof. emerita, 1999—; med. dir. Women's Health Ctr., Albuquerque, 1991-99. Acting dept. chair Christian Med. Coll., Punjab U., 1970; dir. Ctr. for Mature Woman Med. Coll. Pa., 1983-91; examiner Am. Bd. Ob-Gyn, 1984-97; bd. dirs. Ludhiana Christian Med. Coll. Bd., choir mem., 2005—; bd. dirs. Colorado Springs., Colo., chair, 2005, Svc. Master Co. Ltd., Downers Grove, Ill., 1982-91; bd. trustees Asbury U., 1996-2006, vice chair bd. trustees, chair acad. com., chair presdl. search com., 2007. Co-author: Care of Post Menopausal Patient, 1985; editor: Medical Clinics of N.A., vol. 71, 1987; assoc. editor, contbg. author: Textbook of Women's Health, 1998; contbr. chpt. to book. Student chpt. sponsor Christian Med. and Dental Soc., Phila., 1973-93, trustee, 1991-95, pres., chair bd. trustees, 1997-99, chair com. for continuing med. and dental edn.; tchr., elder Leverington Presbyn. Ch., Phila., 1988-91; interviewer Readers Digest Internat. fellowships, Brunswick, Ga., 1982—; bd. dirs. Phila. chpt. Am. Cancer Soc., 1980-86, vol., 1984; leadership St. Stephens UMC, 2007-, lay leader, 2008. Recipient Ralph Hawley Disting. Svc. award U. Wis. Med. Alumni Assn., 2009, Disting. Asbury A award Asbury U. Alumni Assn., 2009; named sr. clin. trainee USPHS, HEW, 1963-65, one of Best Woman Drs. in Am. Harper Bazaar, 1985. Fellow ACS (sec. Phila. chpt. 1990), ACOG, Am. Fertility Soc.; mem. Obstet. Soc. Phila. (pres. 1989-90), Phila. Colposcopy Soc. (pres. 1982-84), Philadelphia County Med. Soc. (com. chmn. 1989-90), Alpha Omega Alpha. Avocations: gardening, travel, collecting antiques.

BARBON, CHRISTINE M., medical researcher; b. Mass., Dec. 20, 1970; BS in Biology, Worcester State U., 1993, MS in Biotechnology, 2004. Profl. rsch. tech UMASS Med. Ctr., Worcester, 1990—98; sr. rsch. assoc. Zycos, Inc., 1998—2001; staff scientist Genzyme, 2001—05; sr. scientist MGI Pharm. Inc., 2005—09; staff scientist Dana Farber Cancer Inst., 2009—. Home: 415 Main St Groton MA 01450 Business E-Mail: christinem_barbon@dfci.harvard.edu.

BARBOSA, PAULO BENCHIMOL, biomedical researcher; b. Rio de Janeiro, Nov. 12, 1961; s. José Barbosa de Medeiros Gomes Filho and Eliana Benchimol Barbosa Gomes; m. Consuelo Loayza Benchimol Barbosa, July 19, 1969; children: Paola Loayza Benchimol, Ana Carolina Loayza Benchimol, Eduarda Loayza Benchimol. MD, State U. of Rio de Janeiro, 1985; MS in Biomed. Engring., Fed. U. of Rio de Janeiro, 1997, ScD in Biomed. Engring., 2003. CCU med. staff State U. of Rio de Janeiro Meml. Hosp., Rio de Janeiro, 1988—; head of the lab. on electrocardiology rsch. Nat. Inst. of Cardiology, Rio de Janeiro, 1998—; lt. col. fireman cardiologist Fire Dept. of the State of Rio de Janeiro, 2000—; chief of cardiology Fire Dept. of the State of Rio de Janeiro Ctrl. Hosp., 2001—; chief of the sect. of non-invasive eletrocardiology, chief diagnostic methods in internal medicine Dept. of Cardiology - State U. of Rio de Janeiro, Rio de Janeiro, 2001—; prof. of medicine Gama Filho U., Rio de Janeiro, 1998—. Supr. of med. undergrad. rsch. Gama Filho U., Rio de Janeiro, 2002—. Recipient Motion of Congratulation, Praise and Applause, Town Coun. of the City of Rio de Janeiro, 2002, Cuidados com a Vida award, Nat. Acad. Medicine of Brazil, 1999, Young Scientist prize, Internat. Soc. Electrocardiology, 2001, Priza Cardeos, Non-Invasive Electro Cardiology, 2001, prize for best sci. study at 18th Congress of State of Rio de Janeiro, Coll. of Cardiology, 2001, Nelson Botelho prize, Instituti Estadual de Cardiologia Aloisio de Castro-Procardio, 1998, Sci. and Tech. award, Health Ministry Brazil and UNESCO. Master: Internat. Soc. Drs. for the Environment Brazil; fellow: Brazilian Soc. Cardiology (life); mem.: IEEE (life), Heart Rhythm Soc., Am. Heart Assn., Brazilian Soc. Biomed. Engring. Office: State Univ of Rio de Janeiro 2d Fl dept Cardiology Boulevard Vinte e Oito de Setembro 77 Rio de Janeiro 20551-030 Brazil Personal E-mail: ecgar@yahoo.com. E-mail: ecgar@uerj.br.

BARBOSA, PAULO CESAR RIBEIRO, medical educator; b. Sao Paulo, Brazil, Nov. 13, 1968; PhD, UNICAMP, 2008. Prof. adjunto U. Estadual de Santa Cruz, 2002—11. Home: Ave Moraes Sales 1610 Apt 144 Campinas Sao Paulo 13010002 Brazil Personal E-mail: pcesarr@yahoo.com.br.

BARBOSA, WAGNER LUIZ RAMOS, pharmacist, educator; b. Rio de Janeiro, Mar. 26, 1956; PhD, UniBonn, Germany, 2009. Pharmacist UFRJ, Brazil, 1982. Assoc. prof. UFPA, 1997—; vice-dir. UFPA-NUMA, 2005—. Mem.: SBPC. Office: Faculdade Farmacia UFPA - Campus Gua Belem Para 66075110 Brazil Office Fax: 559132017204. Business E-Mail: barbosa@ufpa.br.

BARBOZA, EDUARDO, surgeon, educator; b. Ica, Peru, May 2, 1943; s. Luis E. and Julia (Besada) Barboza; m. Rosa C. Beraún, May 30, 1970; children: Eduardo Jr., Gustavo, Aurelio L., Sergio R. MD, Cayetano Heredia U., Lima, Peru, 1969. Intern Johns Hopkins Hosp. /Mt. Sinai Med. Ctr., 1971—75; prof. surgery Cayetano Heredia U., Lima, 1982—, chief surgery, 1990—93. Editor: Principles and Practice of Surgery (1st prize Hipolito Unanue Found., 2000). Pres. Peruvian Acad. Surgery, Lima, 2000—02. Recipient Roussel prize, Roussel Lab., 1998, Comendador award, Cayetano Heredia U., 2000, Extraordinary Merit award, Peruvian Coll. Medicine, 2005; Gov. Peruvian Chpt. grant, ACS, 2005—. Mem.: Peruvian Gastroenterology Soc. (assoc.). Roman Catholic. Avocation: tennis. Home: [illegible]selvas 345 Casuarinas Baja - Surco Lima 33 Peru Office: Clinica San Felipe Gregorio Escobedo 676 Ste 411 J MarÈa Lima Peru Office Fax: 511-4614779; Home Fax: 511-4614779. Personal E-mail: ebarbozab@terra.com.pe. Business E-Mail: edbarboza@qnet.com.pe.

BARBOZA, MARCELLO COLOMBO, ophthalmologist; b. Santos, Feb. 4, 19[illegible]; MD, Santa Casa Sao Paulo, 2003. Head Hosp VisãoLaser, 2003—. Mem.: Am. Acad. Ophthalmology. Avocation: travel. Office: Ave Conselheiro Nebias 355 Santos SP 11015001 Brazil Office Fax: 551321045000.

BARBOZA-CLARK, FRANCES EMILY, retired technologist; b. Jersey City, June 22, 1938; d. Lawrence and Clementina Frances (Lopes) Barboza; div.; children: Donald, Renee, Edward. Diploma med. tech., Coll. Medicine and Dentistry N.J. Rutgers U., NJ, 1970. Chem. lab. technician, 1956-57; histology technician Coll. Medicine and Dentistry N.J.-Rutgers U. Med. Sch., 1969-72, rsch. asst., 1972-75, med. technologist, 1975-81, sr. med. technologist, 1981-86, chief technologist, vivarium supr., 1986-89, mgr. rsch. animal facility vivarium, 1989-2000, ret., 2000. Tchr., trainer students, supr. histology lab. Mem. Am. Soc. Clin. Pathologists (registered assoc.), Am. Soc. for Clin. Lab. Sci., Nat. Soc. Histotech., Am. Assn. Lab. Animal Sci. (N.J. br.), N.J. Soc. Histotech. (charter), NOW (chpt. coord. 1979-81, 88-89, bd. dirs. 1983-86, polit. action com. 1983-86).

BARBUTO, JOHN E., JR., agricultural studies educator, director; b. Melrose, Mass., July 10, 1968; MBA, Bentley U., 1993; PhD, U. RI, 1997. Assoc. prof., leadership U. Nebr., Lincoln, 1997—2011; dir. Ctr. Leadership Studies Calif. State U., Fullerton, 2011—. Rsch. scientist Internat. Life Scis. Com. Mental Energy. Contbr. numerous articles to profl. publs. Recipient Hollings Family award, U. Nebr., Excellence Rsch. award, U. Nebr. Coll. Agrl. Scis. Mem.: Internat. Life Scis. Inst. Office: Dept Management PO Box 6848 Fullerton CA 92834-6848 Business E-Mail: barbuto@nebrr.com.

BAR-CHAMA, NATAN, urologist, educator; MD, Albert Einstein Coll. Med., 1987. Diplomate Am. Bd. Urology. Resident urology Montefiore Med. Ctr., Bronx, 1988—93; fellow male infertility Baylor Coll. Med., Houston, 1993—94; dir. ctr. of male reproductive health Reproductive Medicine Assocs., NY; dir. male reproductive medicine and surgery Mount Sinai Hosp. Assoc. prof. urology Mount Sinai Sch. of Medicine. Office: Mount Sinai Medical Center One Gustave L Levy Pl New York NY 10029 Office Phone: 212-241-6500.

BARCHET, STEPHEN, obstetrician, gynecologist, retired military officer; b. Annapolis, Md., Oct. 25, 1932; s. Stephen George and Louise (Lankford) B.; m. Marguerite Joan Racek, Aug. 9, 1965. Student, Brown U., 1949—52; MD, U. Md., 1956. Diplomate Am. Bd. Ob-Gyn.; cert. physician exec. Commd. ensign M.C. USN, 1955, advanced through grades to rear adm., 1978; intern Naval Hosp., Chelsea, Mass., 1956-57, resident in ob-gyn., 1958-61, resident in gen. surgery Portsmouth, Va., 1957-58; fellow Harvard Med. Sch., 1959-60; obstetrician-gynecologist Naval Hosp., Naples, Italy, 1961-63, Portsmouth, NH, 1963-64, Beaufort, SC, 1964-66, Bremerton, Wash., 1967-70, chief ob-gyn. Boston, 1970-73; asst. head, tng. br. Bur. Medicine and Surgery, Washington, 1973, head, 1973-75; dep. spl. asst. to surgeon gen. USN, 1975; assoc. dean Sch. Medicine, Uniformed Svcs. U. Health Scis., Bethesda, Md., 1976-77, exec. sec. bd. regents, 1976-77; spl. asst. to surgeon gen. for med. dept. edn. and tng. Bur. Medicine and Surgery, Navy Dept., Washington, 1977-79, insp. gen., 1979-80; comdg. officer Naval Health Scis. and Edn. and Tng. Command, Nat. Naval Med. Ctr., Bethesda, 1977-79; asst. chief planning, resources BUMED, 1980-82; dep. surg. gen., dep. dir. naval medicine Dept. Navy, 1982-83; ret., 1983; with Pacific Med. Ctr., Seattle, 1985-91; cons. Mil. Health Care, Seattle, 1987—; prin. MSA Programs, Seattle, 1995—; mng. ptnr. Benefit Payment Solutions, 1998—2011; coord. Health Plan for Life, 2003—; corp. officer Abrige Co., Bellingham, Wash., 2007—. Clin. asst. prof. Boston U. Sch. Medicine, 1971—; alt. regent Nat. Libr. Medicine, Bethesda, 1977-79; asst. prof. health care scis. George Washington U. Sch. Medicine and Health Scis., Washington, 1978—; ex officio mem. grad. med. edn. nat. adv. com. HEW, 1978-79; chmn. med.-dental com. Intersvc. Tng. Rev. Orgn., Washington, 1977-79; chmn. Washington Med. Savs. Accounts Project, 1994; bd. dir. Hope Heart Inst., chmn. edn. com., 2004-06; Policy Coun. Wash. Health Found., 2006-10. Contbr. articles to med. jours. Sec. The Rainier Club, 1992—93; bd. dir. North Seattle C.C. Found., 1992—95. Decorated Bronze Star, others. Fellow Am. Coll. Obstetricians and Gynecologists, Am. Coll. Physician Execs.; mem. AMA, Assn. Mil. Surgeons U.S., Soc. Med. Cons. Armed Forces, Wash. State Med. Assn., King County Med. Assn., N.W. Mil. Health Benefit Assn. (exec. dir. 1991-94). Home and Office: 18601 SE 64th Way Issaquah WA 98027-8616

BARD, DAVID ROY, medical researcher; b. London, Aug. 23, 1946; m. Sarah Judith Yarrow Eccles, Aug. 21, 1982; children: Deborah, Jonathan. BSc, U. Bath, UK, 1969; MSc, U. Surrey, UK, 1970, PhD, 1974; BA, Open U., UK, 2003. Postdoctoral rschr. Strangeways Rsch. Lab., Cambridge, Eng., 1973-79, sr. scientist, 1979-92, head cancer rsch. group, 1992—96, Open U., 1996—. Vis. prof. Teikyo U., Sagamiko, Japan, 1989; com. mem. Cancer Rsch. Campaign, Targeting Trials Group, London, 1992—2000; med. rsch. adviser Nat. Lottery Charities Bd., 1998-99. Editorial bd.: Drug Delivery Jour., 1993—; inventor in field; contbr. articles to profl. jours. Elected mem. South Cambridgeshire Dist. Coun., Cambridge, 1987—, chmn. fin. com., 1993—2001; portfolio holder ICT Comms., 2001-03, planning and econ. devel., 2003-07, Portfolio Holder Sustainable Cmtys., 2007-11, vice chmn. coun., 2011-; chmn. Icknield County Primary Sch. Govs., Cambridge, 1997—04. Recipient rsch. grants Cancer Rsch. Campaign, 1986, 89, 92, CRC Tech., 1991. Mem. Biochem. Soc., NY Acad. Sci., Brit. Soc. History Sci., History Sci. Soc. Home: 15 Huddleston Way CB22 3SW Cambridge England Business E-Mail: cllr.bard@scambs.gov.uk.

BARDACH, JOAN LUCILE, clinical psychologist; b. Albany, NY, Oct. 3, 1919; d. Monroe Lederer and Lucile May (Lowenberg) B. BA, Cornell U., 1940; AM in Psychology, NYU, 1951; PhD in Clin. Psychology, 1957; cert. in psychoanalysis and psychotherapy, NYU, 1970. Supr. clin. psychologist NYU Rusk Inst. Rehab. Medicine, 1959-61; asst. chief and acting chief psychologist Rusk Inst. Rehab. Medicine, 1962-65, dir. psychol. services, 1965-82; research psychologist, mem. faculty N.Y. Med. Coll., 1961-62; prof. rehab. medicine, psychology NYU Med. Ctr., 1976—; supr. postdoctoral program psychoanalysis and psychotherapy NYU, 1978—; pvt. practice clin. psychology and psychoanalysis NYC, 1957—2010. Nongovtl. orgn. rep. to UN Internat. Ctr. Sociol., Penal and Penitentiary Rsch. and Studies, Messina, Italy, 1985—; prin. investigator NIMH, 1976-81; mem. adv. bd. Coalition Sexuality and Disability, Planned Parenthood, 1983-89; cons. in field. Contbr. articles to profl. jours., chpt. to books. Recipient 3 awards for ednl. film, Choices: In Sexuality With Physical Disability, Internat. Film Festivals, Pioneer award for Sexual Attitude Reassessment Workshops The Coalition on Sexuality and Disability, 1989; NIMH fellow Inst. Sex Rsch., U. Ind., 1976. Fellow Am. Orthopsychiat. Assn.; mem. APA, Sex Info. and Edn. Council U.S., Nat. Register Health Service Providers in Psychology. Home: Pennswood Village 1382 Newtown Langhorne Rd Apt 113A Newtown PA 18940-2418

BARDAJÍ-PASCUAL, CARLOS, pediatric surgeon; b. Barcelona, June 6, 1954; s. Carlos Bardaji-Gimenez and Rosa Pascual-Bacchini; m. Maria Luisa De Prado-Marcilla, Dec. 27, 1996; children: Beatriz Bardaji, Alberto Bardaji, Juan Bardaji, Carla Bardaji. Licentiate in medicine and surgery, Autonomous U. Barcelona, 1978, specialization in pediatric surgery, 1984, degree, 1991. Phisician Doctor Autonomous U., 1991, cert. European Bd. Pediatric Surgery, in pediatric health Health Ministry Spain, in cmty. health Health Ministry Spain. Resident in surgery Nacional Health Svc., Zaragoza, Spain, 1978—79; resident in pediatric surgery Nat. Health Svc., Barcelona, 1980—84, pediatric surgeon Pamplona, Navarra, Spain, 1985—92, Sabadell, Barcelona, 1992—93, chief pediatric surgery Tarragona, 1994—; assoc. prof. pediatric surgery U. Rovira I Virgili, Reus, Spain, 1999—. Chief pediatric surgery Nat. Health Svc., Tarragona, 1994—; assoc. prof. pediatric surgery U. Rovira I Virgili, Reus, Tarragona, 1999—. Contbr. articles to profl. jours. Recipient award, Portuguese Soc. Pediatric Surgery, 1989. Mem.: Catalan Acad. Med. Scis., Spanish Soc. Pediat., Spanish Soc. Pediatric Surgery (assoc. award 1984). Achievements include design of orthesis for treatment of thorax deformities; device for surgical treatment of thoracic deformities. Office: Hosp Univ Joan Xxiii Calle Doctor Mallafre Guasch 4 43005 Tarragona Spain E-mail: cbardaji@hjxxiii.scs.es.

BAR-DAYAN, YARON, internist, educator; b. Petah Tiqua, Israel, Apr. 10, 1963; s. Meir Bar-Dayan and Eva Bar-dayan; m. Yosefa Koifman, Sept. 1, 1988; children: Yaniv, Yuval, Yair. MD (hon.), Tel Aviv U., 1988; MHA, Ben Gurion U., Beer Sheva, Israel, 2001. Sr. physician Meir Hosp., Kfar Saba, Israel, 2008—. Head, med. br. Isreli Air Force, Ramat Gan, 2002—04. Chief med. officer, home front command Supreme Health Authority, Tel Aviv, 2004—07. Achievements include research in world leading research in reverse ageing, cancer auto immunity, disaster planning, terrorism, explosions, triag, mass casualty incidents and military medicine; building network of qr primary care clinic for IOF career personel; establishment of the military faculty of medicine in Israel. Home: 16 Dolev St Or Yehuda 60411 Israel Office: Ben Gurion Univ Beer Sheva Israel Home Fax: 0097236341039. Business E-Mail: bardayan@netvision.net.il.

BARDEHLE, DORIS ILSE SILVIA, public health service officer, educator; b. Breslau, Silesia, Germany, Nov. 27, 1941; d. Paul and Frieda Bardehle; m. Klessen, June 1967 (div. Dec. 1989); 1 child, Sylvia Klessen. Diploma, Med. Inst., Charkov, Ukraine, 1967; MD, Med. Acad., Magdeburg, Germany, 1970; D in Med. Sci. habilitation (hon.), Acad. for Further Med. Qualification, Berlin, 1981. Specialist in social hygiene Berlin, 1972. Med. asst. gynecology Hosp., Magdeburg, Germany, 1967—68; head dept. Mcpl. Authority, Berlin, 1969—79; sci. employee, head dept. stats. and data processing Inst. Health, Berlin, 1979—90; head dept. Inst. Pub. Health, Bielefeld, 1990—2006. Sr. lectr. pub. health U. Bielefeld, Germany,

1995—2003, prof., 2003—; project leader European Commn., Luxembourg, 1995—2002, WHO/Europe, Bielefeld, 1996—2000; project mgr. Common Minimum Indicators Set for South Eastern European Countries, 2002, Indicator Set Health Reporting in German States, 2003, 05. Author: Indicators on Health Status of the Former GDR Population, 1993, Structure and Indicators on Dental Care in Former GDR, 1993; contbr. articles to profl. jours. Advisor pub. health Stability Pact for South Ea. Europe, 2000—07; project coord. Metq Net. Mem.: Chamber Physicians, German Soc. for Social Medicine. Avocations: swimming, piano. Home: Hudeweg 17 33607 Bielefeld Germany Office: Univ Bielefeld Faculty Health Scis Universitaetstr 25 Bielefeld 33615 Germany Office Phone: 495211063891. Personal E-mail: doris.bardehle@t-online.de. Business E-Mail: doris.bardehle@uni-bielefeld.de.

BARDELAS, JOSE ANTONIO, allergist; b. Havana, Cuba, Feb. 3, 1948; came to U.S., 1961; s. Jose A. and Georgina (Leyva) B.; m. Sallie Young, July 3, 1971; children: Joseph, Mary. BA in Human Biology, Johns Hopkins U., 1970, MD, 1973. Intern, then resident in pediats. Johns Hopkins Hosp., Balt., 1973-75; fellow in allergy and immunology Nat. Jewish Ctr., Denver, 1975-77; pvt. practice Greensboro, NC, 1977—. Asst. clin. prof. pediats. U. N.C., Chapel Hill, 1979—. Named one of Best Doctor, Am., 1996—. Fellow Am. Acad. Allergy and Immunology; mem. AMA, N.C. Soc. Allergy and Immunology (pres. 1982), N.C. Med. Soc. (mem. exec. coun. 1990, 91), High Point Med. Soc. (pres. 1989). Roman Catholic. Avocations: golf, reading. Home: 400 Edgedale Dr High Point NC 27262-2908 Office: 100 Westwood Ave High Point NC 27262-4320 Office Phone: 336-883-1393. Personal E-mail: sybardelas@aol.com, j.bardelas@northstate.net.

BARDFIELD, STEVEN, orthopedist; MD, Loyola U. Stritch Sch. Med., Maywood, Ill., 1993. Diplomate Am. Bd. Physical Medicine & Rehabilitation. Intern, resident Med. Coll. Wis., Milw.; pvt. practice outpatient care/patient rehabilitation Chgo.; physician Hinsdale Orthopaedic Assoc., S.C., Ill., 2001—; med. dir. Hinsdale Orthopaedic Therapy Ctr., 2002—. Staff physician Edward Hosp., Naperville, Ill., Good Samaritan Hosp., Downers Grove, Ill., Silver Cross Hosp., Joliet, Ill., Salt Creek Surgery Ctr., Westmont, Ill., Hinsdale Hosp. Mem.: AMA, Internat. Spine Intervention Soc., Ill. State Med. Soc. Office: Hinsdale Orthopaedic Assoc 550 W Ogden Ave Hinsdale IL 60521 Office Phone: 630-323-6116, 630-323-6169.

BARDIN, CLYDE WAYNE, biomedical researcher; b. McCamey, Tex., Sept. 18, 1934; s. James A. and Nora Irene (Barnett) Bardin; m. Bonnie Lambdin, June 24, 1958 (div.); children: Charlotte E., Stephanie F.; m. Dorothy Kreiger, Aug. 11, 1978 (dec. Apr. 2, 1985); m. Beatrice MacDonald, June 12, 1987. BA in Biology, Rice U., 1957; MS with honors, MD with honors, Baylor U., 1962; Docteur (hon.), U. de Caen, France, 1990, U. Pierre et Marie Curie, Paris, 1997, U. Helsinki, Finland, 2000. Lic. physician Tex., 1962, N.Y., 1963, Pa., 1970. Resident in medicine N.Y. Hosp., NYC, 1962-64; clin. assoc. NIH, Bethesda, Md., 1964-67; sr. investigator NCI, Bethesda, Md., 1967-70; assoc. prof. Milton S. Hershey Med. Ctr., Pa. State U., Hershey, 1970-72, prof. medicine, 1972—78; v.p. The Population Coun., NYC, 1978-95; pres. Bardin LLC, NYC, 1996—; pres., CEO Thyreos Corp., Newark, 1997—2003. Adj. prof. Rockefeller U., NYC, 1978-2004, Cornell Med. Ctr., NYC, 1985-2004; cons. WHO, 1972-73; chmn. bd. sci. counselors Nat. Inst. Child Health and Human Devel., Bethesda, 1982-83; chmn. endocrine study sect. NIH, Bethesda, 1977-79; nat. prostate cancer task force Nat. Cancer Inst., 1973-78; endocrinologist Nat. Inst. Child Health and Human Devel., NIH, 1996-97; bd. dirs. Harris and Harris Group, Inc. Editor 18 books on medicine and endocrinology; mem. editl. bd. 16 sci. jours.; contbr. over 500 articles to profl. jours. Advisor internat. divsn. Ford Found., NYC, 1975-79; bd. dirs. Internat. Assn. Axel Munthe Awards, 1982-92; chmn. bd. dirs. Hormone Found., 1997-98. Decorated comdr. Order of Lion (Finland); recipient Transatlantic medal Brit. Endocrine Socs., 1988; fellow Josiah Macy Jr. Found., 1976-77; named Disting. Alumnus Rice U., 1994, Disting. Alumnus N.Y. Hosp.-Cornell Med. Ctr., 1992, Baylor Coll. Medicine, 2010. Mem. Am. Assn. Physicians, Am. Soc. Clin. Investigation, Am. Soc. Andrology (coun., v.p., pres. 1984-89, Serono award 1984, Disting. Andrologist award 1992), Endocrine Soc. (coun. 1976-79, pres. 1993-94, Sidney H. Ingbar Disting. Svc. award 1996), Internat. Soc. Andrology (exec. coun. 1981-85), Internat. Com. Contraception Rsch. (chmn. 1978-95), Inst. Medicine. Democrat. Achievements include studies of male reproduction, hormone action; maturation of germ cells and inhibition of cancer growth as well as direction of a team of scientists that developed seven contraceptives and treatments for menopause and cancer. Home Phone: 212-876-1830. Personal E-mail: cwbardin@aol.com.

BARDIS, JOHN A., information technology executive; BS in Bus., U. Ariz. With Am. Hosp. Supply; various positions including v.p., Operating Room Divsn., gen. mgr., Eastern zone Baxter International, Inc.; with Kinetic Concepts, 1987, pres., 1992; pres., CEO TheraTx, Inc., 1992—97; chmn., pres., CEO MedAssets, Inc., 1999—. Bd. dirs. TheraTx, Inc.; bd. adv. High Bar Capital. Team leader, U.S. Greco-Roman Wrestling Team Beijing Olympics, 2008; team leader, team USA World Championships, 2007; bd. dirs. USA Wrestling, Heart for Africa, The Health Careers Found.; chmn. Atlanta Fire Youth Hockey Club. Recipient Entrepreneur of the Year award, INC mag., 1995. Office: MedAssets Inc 100 N Point Ctr E Ste 200 Alpharetta GA 30022 Office Phone: 678-323-2500. Office Fax: 678-323-2501. Business E-Mail: johnbardis@medassets.com. *

BAREIS, DONNA LYNN, biochemist, pharmacologist, executive; b. Abington, Pa., May 1, 1954; d. Walter Charles and Doris (Cameron) B.; m. Paul Joseph Amico, Jan. 24, 1981. BS in Biochemistry, Pa. State U., 1975; PhD in Pharmacology, Duke U., 1979. Staff fellow NIH, Bethesda, Md., 1979-81; pharmacologist U.S. Army Med. Rsch. Inst. Chem. Def., Aberdeen Proving Ground, Md., 1981-82; program mgr. U.S. Army C.E., Washington, 1982-83; sr. scientist Sci. Applications Internat. Corp., Joppa, Md., 1983-87, div. mgr., 1987-89, asst. v.p. Frederick, Md., 1989-94, v.p., 1994—2006, dep. mgr. biomed. scis., 1997—2006, mgr. vaccine and drug devel. program, 2003—06; COO. Social and Sci. Systems, Md., 2006—; bd. dirs. Tech. Coun. Md., 2008—. Contbr. articles to profl. jours. Lighting designer Rockville (Md.) Musical Theater, 1980—; pres. Swan Point Condominium Assn., Columbia, Md., 1982-84. Mem.: AAAS, Soc. for Risk Analysis, Am. Chemical Soc., Cattail Creek Country Club (bd. dirs. 1995—96), Porsche Club Racing (nat. scrutineer 2000—, chief nat. scrutineer 2001—05, tech. and rules chair 2005—10), Sigma Xi. Home: 8805 Blue Sea Columbia MD 21046-1412

BARGAGLIOTTI, LILLIAN ANTOINETTE, nursing educator; b. Millington, Tenn., Dec. 29, 1949; d. Benard Wood and Georgeanne (Lowe) McIllwain; m. Ronald M. Prentice, Apr. 24, 1970 (div. 1975); m. bill L. Bargagliotti, July 8, 1978; 1 child, William Benard. RN, Tacoma Gen. Hosp., 1971; BSN, U. Tenn., 1976; MS, U. Calif., San Francisco, 1978; D in Nursing Sci., U. Calif., 1984. Staff nurse Tacoma (Wash.) Gen. Hosp., 1971, St. Joseph's Hosp., Tacoma, 1971-75, City of Memphis Hosp., 1975-76; instr. N.W. Miss. Jr. Coll., Senatobia, 1976-78; inservice coord. Eden Hosp., Castro Valley, Calif., 1978-79; instr. Ohlone Coll., Fremont, Calif., 1979-84; assoc. prof. nursing San Francisco State U., 1984-85; assoc. dean, prof. nursing U. San Francisco, 1985-89, interim dean, prof. nursing, 1989-91; assoc. DON Davies Med. Ctr., 1992; dean, prof. nursing Loewenberg Sch. Nursing, U. Memphis, 1992—2005, prof., 2005—. Clin. evaluator SUNY Western Performance Assessment Ctr., Long Beach and Palo Alto, Calif., 1982-85; program evaluator Collegiate Commn. for Nursing Edn. Contbr. articles to profl. jours. Capt. USAR, 1976-78. Fellow Acad. Nursing Edn.; mem. ANA, Tenn. Nurses Assn., Assn. Oper. Rm. Nurses (mem. jour. editl. bd. 1987-90), Nat. League for Nursing (program evaluator, pres. 2005-07, bd. govs. 2003-07, trustee found. bd.), Tenn. Assn. Deans/Dirs. Nursing (pres. 1997-99, 99-2001), Coun. on Grad. Fgn. Nursing Schs. (mem. exam. com. 2008-), Sigma Theta Tau. Republican. Mem. Ch. of Christ. Home: 7423 Wood Rail Cv Memphis TN 38119-9007 Office: U Memphis 308 Admin Bldg Memphis TN 38152 Office Phone: 901-678-5926. Business E-Mail: tbargagl@memphis.edu.

BARGER, RICHARD LEE, JR., radiologist; b. Lorain, Ohio, Dec. 30, 1979; BA, Coll. Wooster, 2002; MD, U. Toledo Coll. Medicine, 2006. Musculoskeletal radiology fellow William Beaumont Hosp., 2011—. Recipient Rsch. award, Radiol. Soc. N.Am. RSNA Rsch. & Edn. Found. Wilhelm Conrad Roentgen, Ralph Riddall Dobelbower award, U. Toledo Coll. Medicine Dept. Radiation Oncology. Mem.: Am. Bd. Radiology, Am. Roentgen Ray Soc., Am. Coll. Radiology, Radiol. Soc. N.Am., Phi Beta Kappa. Avocations: hiking, computers. Office: 3601 West 13 Mile Rd Royal Oak MI 48073 Business E-Mail: richard.barger@beaumont.edu.

BARGMANN, CORI (CORNELIA ISABELLA BARGMANN), neurobiologist, science educator; b. Va., 1961; m. Richard Axel. BS in Biochemistry, U. Ga., 1981; PhD, MIT, 1987. Postdoc.l rschr. MIT; asst. to assoc. prof. U. Calif., San Francisco, 1991—98, prof., 1998—2004, vice chair dept. anatomy, 1999—2004; Torsten N. Wiesel prof. Rockefeller U., NYC, 2004—, assoc. dir. Shelby White & Leon Levy Ctr. Mind, Brain & Behavior. Investigator Howard Hughes Med. Inst., 1995—. Mem. editl. bd. Neural Devel.; contbr. numerous articles to profl. jours. Recipient Lucille P. Markey award, 1990—95, W. Alden Spencer award, Columbia U., 1997, Takasago award for olfaction rsch., 1997, Charles Judson Herrick award, American Assn. Anatomists, 2000, Dargut & Milena Kemali Found. Internat. prize for rsch. in basic and clin. neuroscience, 2004; Searle scholar, 1992—95. Fellow: American Acad. Arts & Scis.; mem.: NAS (Richard Lounsbery award 2009). Achievements include using caenorhabditis elegans, a worm with just 302 neurons to study how environment, experience and the biology of the brain interact to shape an animal's behavior; research in how genetic variation between individuals can cause them to behave differently from one another. Office: Rockefeller U 1230 York Ave New York NY 10065 Business E-Mail: Cori.Bargmann@rockefeller.edu. *

BARI, SANJAYKUMAR BABURAO, pharmacist; b. Jalgaon, Maharashtra, India, May 20, 1971; BS in Pharmacy, Govt. Coll. Pharmacy, Karad, 1994; PharmD, U. Coll. Pharm. Scis., Warangal, Andhra Pradesh, India, 2006. Lectr. Anuradha Coll. Pharmacy, Chikhli, MS, India, 1996—2004; adj. prof. R.C.Patel Inst. Pharm. Edn. & Rsch., Shirpur, 2004—06, asst. prof., 2004—, prof., 2006—10, vice-prin., 2010—. Nat. Merit scholarship, Ctrl. Govt. India. Mem.: Indian Chem. Soc., Indian Soc. Pharmacognosy, Indian Soc. Tech. Edn., Assn. Pharm. Tchrs. India, Indian Pharm. Assn. Avocations: travel, music, sports. Office: Karvand Naka Shirpur Maharashtra 425 405 India Office Fax: 02563-255189. E-mail: sbbari71@rediffmail.com.

BARIL, NANCY ANN, gerontological nurse practitioner, consultant; b. Paterson, NJ, May 10, 1952; d. Kenneth Gerald and Jeanette Elenore (Girodet) Keiser; m. Joel Mark Baril, Apr. 15, 1984; children: Jason Kenneth, Jennifer Jean. AA, Gulf Coast C.C., Panama City, Fla., 1976; BSN, Fla. State U., Tallahassee, 1978; MSN, UCLA, 1983. Registered pub. health nurse, Calif.; ANA cert. gerontol. nurse practitioner. Charge nurse, nurse preceptor Cedar Sinai Med. Ctr., LA, 1979-83; nurse Nursing Svcs. Inc., Sherman Oaks, Calif., 1980-83; nurse practitioner Santa Monica (Calif.) Peer Counseling Ctr., 1983; nurse cons., gerontol. nurse practitioner Summit Health Ltd., Burbank, Calif., 1983-85; nurse cons. Geriatric Assocs., Granada Hills, Calif., 1983-85; nurse cons., gerontol. nurse practitioner ARA Living Ctrs., Glendale, Calif., 1986-87; DON, gerontol. nurse practitioner Astoria Convalescent Hosp. Sign of the Dove, Sylmar, Calif., 1988-91; gerontol. nurse practitioner Balboa Plz. Med. Group, 1991-98, Absolute Health Care, Mission Hills, Calif., 1998-2000, Ctr. Sr. Health, Akron, Ohio, 2000—01, Health Strata, Nashville, 2001—03, Dr. Martin Freimer, East Stroudsburg, Pa., 2003—. Mem. PTA, Granada Hills, 1985. Mem. ANA, Calif. Coalition Nurse Practitioners, Calif. Nursing Assn., Gerontol. Soc., Sigma Theta Tau (rec. sec. 1983-85). Democrat. Episcopalian. Home: 115 Ledgeview Dr Hawley PA 18428 Office: 254 B Mountain Ave Ste 306 Hackettstown NJ 07840 Home Phone: 570-685-2963; Office Phone: 908-684-0401. Personal E-mail: nannynp@aol.com.

BARILLA-LABARCA, MARIA-LOUISE, rheumatologist, educator; b. NY, Mar. 7, 1968; MD, SUNY StonyBrook, 1994. Asst. prof. Hofstra North Shore LIJ Sch. Medicine; program dir., rheumatology fellowship North Shore LIJ Health Sys., Divsn. Rheumatology, 2003—, dir., housestaff & med. student edn., 2003, dir., ctr. performing arts medicine, 2004, dir., rheumatology fellowship, 2008, dir., gout & crystalline arthritis ctr., dir., musculoskeletal ultrasound program, 2011. Recipient Tchg. award, NSLIJ; fellowship, Internat. League Against Rheumatism. Fellow: Am. Coll. Rheumatology (Innovative Tchg. grant); mem.: North Shore Symphony Orchestra. Office: 2800 Marcus Ave Ste 200 New Hyde Park NY 11040 Office Fax: 516-708-2597. Business E-Mail: mbarilla@lij.edu.

BARILLI, ELOMAR CASTILHO, medical researcher; b. Rio de Janeiro, Dec. 31, 1958; M, Fed. U. RJ, 1994, D, 2007. Rschr. pub. health Oswaldo Cruz Found., 1983—. Rschr. & prof. Nat. Sch. Pub. Health Oswaldo Cruz Found., 1983. Fellowship, Profl. Edn. Health. Home: R Gen Espírito Santo Cardoso 139/501 Rio de Janbeiro 20530500 Brazil Personal E-mail: barilli@ead.fiocruz.br.

BARISH, CHARLES FRANKLIN, internist, gastroenterologist, researcher; b. Franklin, NJ, Jan. 5, 1955; s. Philip and Laura (Freedman) Barish; m. Debrah Lee Kaufman, Aug. 13, 1977; children: Philip, Stefanie, Jacob. BS in Chemistry with honors, U. Fla., 1976, MD, 1980. Diplomate in internal medicine and gastroenterology Am. Bd. Internal Medicine. Resident, fellow Wake Forest U. Sch. Medicine, Winston-Salem, NC, 1980-85; physician Wake Gastroenterology Divsn. Wake Internal Medicine Cons., Raleigh, NC, 1985—; founder, pres. Wake Rsch. Assocs., Raleigh, 1985—2011; clin. asst. prof. medicine U. NC Sch. Medicine, Chapel Hill, 1985—. Chmn. nutritional care com. Rex Hosp., Raleigh, 1987—97; thought leader & cons. Study Design & Protocol Development for Pharmaceutical & Biotech. Industry. Contbr. numerous articles to med. jours., chapters to books. Pres. Jewish Cmty. Ctr., Raleigh, 1995—97; v.p. Jewish Fedn. Greater Raleigh, 1993—97; bd. dirs. Raleigh-Cary Jewish Fedn., 1990—2006. Fellow: ACP, Am. Gastroenterology Assn., Am. Coll. Gastroenterology; mem.: AMA, NC Soc. Gastroenterology, Crohn's and Colitis Found. (bd. dirs.), Wake County Med. Soc., N.C. Med. Soc., Am. Soc. Gastrointestinal Endoscopy, Alpha Epsilon Delta, Phi Kappa Phi, Alpha Omega Alpha. Avocations: gardening, golf, travel. Office: Wake Gastroenterology 3100 Blue Ridge Rd Ste 300 Raleigh NC 27612-8035 also: Wake Rsch Assocs 3100 Duraleigh Rd Ste 304 Raleigh NC 27612 Office Phone: 919-781-7515. Business E-Mail: CFBGastro@aol.com.

BARISIONE, CHIARA, medical researcher; b. Genoa, Italy, July 22, 1974; Degree in Biology, 2001, PhD in Medicine, 2007; attending, U. Genova, 2009. Postdoc. rschr. U. Genova Sch. Medicine, 2007—. Vis. scholar, U. Ky., Gill Heart Inst., 2005—06. Home: Sal Montebello 15/9 Genova 16126 Italy Home Fax: 39 353 7990. Personal E-mail: cbari@libero.it.

BARKER, BARBARA ANN, ophthalmologist; b. Paterson, NJ, Nov. 10, 1943; d. Earle Louis and Dorothy Louise (Williamson) Barker; m. Joel Ira Papernik, July 28, 1972; children: Deborah Papernik, Ilana Papernik. BA magna cum laude, Conn. Coll., 1965; BS, Yale U., 1967; MA, Rutgers U., 1974; MD, Mt. Sinai Sch. Medicine, 1976. Diplomate Am. Bd. Ophthalmology. Intern Beth Israel Med. Ctr., 1977; resident Mt. Sinai Sch. Medicine/Beth Israel Med. Ctr., 1980, fellow in glaucoma, 1980-81, fellow cornea, refractive surgery, 1981-82; pvt. practice medicine specializing in ophthalmology, NYC, 1983—. Rsch. technician The Rockefeller U., NYC, 1965—66; tchr. Riverdale Country Sch., NYC, 1967—68; rsch. asst. Sloan Kettering Inst., NYC, 1969—72; asst. clin. prof. Mt. Sinai Sch. Medicine, NYC, 1982—; mem. staff N.Y. Eye and Ear Hosp., Beth Israel/St. Luke's/Roosevelt Hosp. Recipient Resident Best Paper award, Beth Israel Med. Ctr., 1989, Honor award, Am. Acad. Ophthalmology, 1955; grantee Beth Israel Rsch. grant, 1983, NSF, 1966. Fellow: ACS, N.Y. Acad. Medicine; mem.: AMA, N.Y. County Med. Assn., Women's Med. Soc. NYC, Am. Med. Women's Assn., Phi Beta Kappa. Home: 11 E 86th St New York NY 10028-0501 Office: 70 E 96th St New York NY 10028 Office Phone: 212-289-2244. Personal E-mail: bbarkermd@aol.com.

BARKER, CLYDE FREDERICK, surgeon, educator; b. Salt Lake City, Aug. 16, 1932; s. Frederick George and Jennetta Elizabeth (Stephens) B.; m. Dorothy Joan Bieler, Aug. 11, 1956; children: Frederick George II, John Randolph, William Stephens, Elizabeth Dell. BA, Cornell U., 1954, MD, 1958. Diplomate Am. Bd. Surgery. Intern Hosp. U. Pa., Phila., 1958-59, resident in surgery, 1959-64, fellow in vascular surgery, 1964-65; fellow in med. genetics U. Pa. Sch. Medicine, Phila., 1965-66, assoc. in surgery, 1964-68, assoc. in med. genetics, 1966-72; attending surgeon Hosp. U. Pa., Phila., 1966—; chief div. transplantation U. Pa. Sch. Medicine, Phila., 1966—2001, asst. prof. surgery, 1968-69, assoc. prof. surgery, 1969-73, prof. surgery, 1973—, J. William White prof. surg. research, 1978-82, chief div. vascular surgery, 1982—2001, Guthrie prof. surgery, 1982—, John Rhea Barton prof. surgery, 1983—2001, chmn. dept. surgery, 1983—2001; chief surgery Hosp. U. Pa., Phila., 1983—2001. Dir. Harrison dept. surgery rsch. U. Pa., Phila., 1983-2001; immunobiology study sect. NIH; chmn. clin. practices U. Pa., 1987-89; v.p. United Network for Organ Sharing, 2001-02, pres., 2002-03. Mem. editl. bd. Jour. Transplantation, 1977-2001, Clin. Transplantation, 1988—, Jour. Surg. Rsch., 1979-85, Jour. Diabetes, 1981-86, Archives of Surgery, 1987-96, Transplantation Procs., 1990-2001, Surgery, 1991-95, Cell Transplantation, 1991—, Postgrad. Gen. Surgery, 1991-95, Jour. ACS, 1994—, Annals of Surgery, 1995—; contbr. articles to profl. jours. and textbooks. Markle Found. Scholar, 1968-74; NIH grantee, 1974-2001; recipient Merit award NIH, 1987-95, Lifetime Achievement award Soc. U. Surgeons, 2009, Thomas E Starzll prize, 2009, Medawar prize, Internat. Transplantation Soc., 2010, Henry Alan Moe prize, Humanities Am. Phil. Soc., 2009. Fellow AOA, NAS (Inst. Medicine), ACS (com. Forum on Fundamental Surg. Problems 1983-88, vice chmn. 1987-88, bd. govs. 1994-2001, pres. Phila. chpt. 1991-92), Coll. Physicians Phila., Royal Coll. Surgeons Eng. (hon.), Royal Coll. Surgeons Ireland (hon.); mem. AMA, Royal Coll. Surgeons of Ireland (hon.), Assn. Acad. Surgery, Am. Diabetes Assn., Am. Soc. Artificial Internal Organs, Am. Fedn. Clin. Rsch., Juvenile Diabetes Found., Soc. Univ. Surgeons, Am. Surg. Assn. (recorder 1991-96, pres. 1996-97, medallion for sci. achievement 2003), Soc. Clin. Surgery (chmn. membership 1984-85), Halsted Soc. (chmn. membership 1984-85, v.p. 1985-86, pres. 1986-87), Surg. Biology Club II, Soc. Vascular Surgery, Internat. Cardiovascular Soc., Internat. Surg. Group (treas. 1988-94, pres. 1994-95), Internat. Soc. Surgery (v.p. U.S. chpt. 1995-97, pres. 1997-99), Transplantation Soc. (councilman 1978-84, 94—), Am. Soc. Transplant Surgeons (chmn. membership 1980-81, treas. 1988-91, pres. 1992-93), Unitd Network for Organ Sharing (v.p. 2001-02), (pres. 2002-03), Am. Acad. Arts and Scis., Assn. Am. Physicians, Phila. Acad. Surgery (program chmn. 1984-86, v.p. 1986-88, pres. 1988-89), Greater Delaware Valley Soc. Transplant Surgeons (pres. 1978-80), Am. Philos. Soc. (coun. 2003—, v.p. 2005—) Home: 3 Coopertown Rd Haverford PA 19041-1012 Office: Hosp Univ Pa Dept Surgery 3400 Spruce St Philadelphia PA 19104-4206

BARKER, HAROLD GRANT, surgeon, educator; b. Salt Lake City, June 10, 1917; s. Frederick George and Elizabeth Jennetta (Stephens) B.; m. Kathleen Butler, July 29, 1949; children: Janet Stephens, Douglas Reid. AB, U. Utah, 1939, postgrad., 1939-41; MD, U. Pa., 1943. Diplomate Am. Bd. Surgery. Intern. Hosp. U. Pa., 1943-44, asst. resident in surgery, 1947-51, sr. resident in surgery, 1951-52, asst. attending surgeon, 1952-53; also asst. instr., research fellow U. Pa., 1946-51, instr., research fellow, 1951-52, assoc. in surgery, 1952-53; asst. prof. surgery Columbia U., 1953-57, assoc. prof., 1957-68, prof., 1968-82, prof. emeritus, 1982—. Asst. attending surgeon Presbyn. Hosp., 1953-57, assoc. attending surgeon, 1957-69, attending surgeon, 1969-89, cons. surgeon, 1989—, dir. med. affairs, 1974-82; pvt. practice, Phila., 1952-53, N.Y.C., 1953-88. Contbr. articles med. jours. Served from 1st lt. to capt., M.C. AUS, 1944-46, ETO. Fellow ACS; mem. Soc. U. Surgeons, N.Y. Surg. Soc., Am. Physiol. Soc., Soc. Exptl. Biology and Medicine, AMA, Halsted Soc., N.Y. State (chmn. surg. sect. 1961-62), N.Y. County med. socs., Am. Surg. Assn., N.Y. Gastroent. Assn., Société Internationale de Chirurgie, Soc. Surgery Alimentary Tract, Allen O. Whipple Surg. Soc., Am. Assn. History Medicine, Collegium Internationale Chirurgiae Digestivae, Century Assn., Am. Yacht Club. Home: 717 Jacoby Rd Xenia OH 45385-9459

BARKER, SAM L., pharmaceutical executive; BS, Henderson State Coll., 1964; MS, U. Ark., 1966; PhD, Purdue U., 1969. Rsch. scientist Squibb Pharmaceuticals, 1969—75, various exec. positions in rsch. and develop., mfr., fin., bus. develop., sls. and mktg.; former pres., gen. mgr. E.R. Squibb Diagnostics; pres. intercontinental commercial ops. Bristol-Myers Squibb Co., 1990—92, pres. US pharmaceuticals, 1992—97, exec. v.p. worldwide franchise mgmt. and strategy, 1998; co-founder, pres., CEO Clearview Projects, Inc., 2003—04. Bd. dirs. Lexicon Pharms. (formerly Lexicon Genetics), The Woodlands, Tex., 2000—, bd. chmn., 2005—. Office: Lexicon Pharms 8800 Technology Forest Pl The Woodlands TX 77381-1160 *

BARKER, VIRGINIA LEE, nursing educator; Diploma, Ind. U. Sch. Nursing, 1952, BS, 1955, MS, 1961, EdD, 1969. Dean sch. nursing, prof. Alfred (N.Y.) U., 1969-78; prof., dean nursing U. Louisville, 1978-81; dean Mary Black Sch. Nursing, prof. U. S.C., Spartanburg, 1981-90; dean profl. studies, prof. nursing SUNY, Plattsburg, 1990-98, prof. nursing Plattsburgh, 1990—. Cons. nursing program NY Regents Coll., 1972—91; dir. federally funded telenursing project rural upstate NY, 1993—2005; dir. project to develop virtual reality simulations edn. physicians, nurses, allied health pers. SUNY, Plattsburgh, 1995—; advisor to students in RN-BSN program over no. NY, 2000—. Contbr. articles to profl. jours., papers nat. and internat. confs. Mem. ARC. Grantee Disting. Practitioner, N.Y. State Nurses Assn. Mem.: AAUW, ANA, Internat. Coun. of Nurses, S.C. Deans and Dirs. Nursing Fedn. (chmn. 1989), Am. Assn. Higher Edn., S.C. League Nursing, Nat. League Nurses (com. mem. 1976—77), N.Y. State Nurses Assn. (pres. 1976—77), Ind. U. Sch. Nursing Alumni Assn. (pres. 1960), Kappa Delta Pi, Phi Kappa Phi, Sigma Theta Tau. Business E-Mail: barkervl@educ.psu.edu.

BARKER, WILEY FRANKLIN, surgeon, educator; b. Santa Fe, Oct. 16, 1919; s. Charles Burton and Bertha (Steed) Barker; m. Nancy Ann Kerber, June 8, 1943; children: Robert Lawrence, Jonathan Steed, Christina Lee. BS, Harvard U., Cambridge, Mass., 1941, MD, 1944. Diplomate Am. Bd. Surgery (bd. dirs. 1964-70). Intern, then resident Peter Bent Brigham Hosp., Boston, 1944-46; Arthur Tracy Cabot fellow Harvard Med. Sch., 1948-49; from asst. chief surg. svc. to chief surg. sect. Wadsworth VA Hosp., LA, 1951-54, attending physician, 1951—; mem. faculty UCLA Med. Sch., 1954—, prof. surgery, 1964-86, prof. emeritus, 1986—, chief div. gen. surgery, 1955-77; cons. Sepulveda VA Hosp., 1966-78, chief of staff, 1978-83; chair vascular surgery UCLA, 2010. Mem. com. trauma NRC, 1964—68; mem. bd. advisors UCLA Med. Ctr., 1982—. Author: Surgical Treatment of Peripheral Vascular Disease, 1962, Peripheral Arterial Disease, 1966, 2d edit., 1976, Clio Chirugica: The Arteries, vols. I and II, 1992; contbr. articles to profl. jours., chapters to books. Lt. (j.g.) M.C. USNR, 1946—47. Harvard Nat. scholar, 1937—44. Fellow: ACS (2d v.p. 1986—87); mem.: AMA, Los Angeles County Med Assn., Calif. Med. Assn., Pan Pacific Surg. Assn. (pres. 1986—88), Pacific Coast Surg. Assn. (pres. 1982—83), So. Surg. Assn., Internat. Cardiovasc. Soc. (v.p. N.Am. chpt. 1964—85, pres. 1979—80), Soc. Vascular Surgery (pres. 1972—73), Soc. Univ. Surgeons, Soc. Clin. Surgery (pres. 1972—74), Am. Surg. Assn., Sigma Xi, Phi Beta Kappa, Alpha Omega Alpha. Republican. Episcopalian. Address: 29129 Paiute Dr Agoura Hills CA 91301-2938 *

BARKER, WILLIAM DANIEL, hospital administrator; b. New Orleans, July 21, 1926; s. William Daniel and Ada (Will) B.; m. Nancy Pool, Sept. 23, 1949; children: Nancy Louise, Julia Ann, William Daniel III, Marion DeVilbiss. B in Bus. Adminstrn., Emory U., 1949; M in Hosp. Adminstrn., Ga. State U., 1966. Bus. office mgr. Emory U. Hosp., Atlanta, 1949-50; asst. adminstr. Griffin (Ga.) Spalding County Hosp., 1950-51; adminstr. Winder-Barrow (Ga.) Hosp., 1951-52; hosp. field rep. Ga. Dept. Pub. Health, Atlanta, 1952-54, hosp. cons., 1954-55; asst. adminstr. Tri-County Hosp., Ft. Oglethorpe, Ga., 1955-60; asst. dir. Crawford Long Hosp. Emory U., Atlanta, 1960-73, adminstr., 1973-84, dir. hosps., 1984-90, exec. dir. hosp., 1987-90; ret., 1991; prof. Emory U., Atlanta, 1988-93. Bd. dirs. Ga. Fed. Bank, Atlanta, Blue Cross Blue Shield Ga., Inc.; provider affairs com. Blue Cross Blue Shield Assn., United Network for Organ Sharing, bd. dirs., 1991—; bd. govs. SunHealth, Charlotte, N.C., chmn., 1988-89; bd. commrs. Joint Commn. on Accreditation of Healthcare Orgns., 1981-86; v.p. Greater Atlanta Coalition on Health Care, 1983-84; mem. Gov.'s Coun. Malpractice Ins., 1975-83, Medicaid Adv. Com. Ga. Dept. Human Resources, 1973-77, Health Facilities Planning Com. Met. Atlanta Coun. for Health, 1971-74, Atlanta Regional Commn. Emergency Med. Task Force 1969-73, Gov.'s Commn. on Nursing, 1970-71, adv. commn. Internat. Implant Registry, 1989—, vice-chmn., 1991, chmn., 1992; pres. Health Careers of Ga., Inc., 1969-70, Ga. Coun. Paramed. Edn., 1968. Contbr. articles to profl. jours. With U.S. Army, 1944-46. Recipient R.C. Williams award Ga. State U., 1966, Disting. Alumni award, Ga. State U., 1979, Disting. Svc. award. Ga. Med. Assn. Atlanta, 1980; Disting. Guest Lectr. Ga. State U., 1978. Fellow Am. Coll. Healthcare Execs. (regent 1972-75); mem. Am. Hosp. Assn. (chmn. 1979, Speaker of Ho. 1980, Disting. Svc. award 1987), Ga. Hosp. Assn. (pres. 1966-79, Gold Honor award of Excellence 1980), Ansley Golf Club. Baptist. Home: 50 S Prado NE Atlanta GA 30309-3309 Personal E-mail: dbarker@emory.edu.

BARKIN, JAMIE STEVEN, gastroenterologist, educator; b. Miami, Fla., June 1, 1943; s. Mazie Barkin; m. Faith Eileen Block; 1 child, Jodie. Grad., U. Miami, 1965, MD, 1970. Diplomate Am. Bd. Internal Medicine, Am. Bd. Gastroenterology. BS magna cum laude U. Miami, Fla., 1970-71, jr. resident in medicine Fla., 1971-72, sr. resident in medicine Fla., 1972-73, jr. fellow in gastroenterology Fla., 1973-74, sr. fellow in gastroenterology Fla., 1974-75, asst. prof. dept. medicine Fla., 1975-80, assoc. prof. dept. medicine Fla., 1980-87, prof. dept. medicine Fla., 1987—. Asst. prof. dept. oncology U. Miami, 1978-81, assoc. prof., 1981-86, prof., 1987—, assoc. prof. dept. pediatrics, 1983-87, prof., 1987—; coord. endoscopy Miami VA Hosp., 1975-85; chief divsn. gastroenterology Mt. Sinai Med. Ctr., 1985—; active attending staff Jackson Meml. Hosp., Miami, 1975—, VA Med. Ctr., Miami, 1975-85, U. Miami Hosps. & Clinics, 1975—, Mt. Sinai Med. Ctr., Miami Beach, 1985—; cons. VA Med. Ctr., 1986; mem. coms. U. Miami Hosps. & Clinics, 1977-84, Jackson Meml. Hosp., 1977-80, VA Med. Ctr., 1977-85, U. Miami Sch. of Medicine, 1982-85, Mt. Sinai Med. Ctr., 1985-90; lectr., cons. in field. Editor: (with A.I. Rogers) Difficult Decisions in Digestive Diseases, 1988, 2d edit., 1994, (with C.A. O'Phelan) Advanced Therapeutic Endoscopy, 1990, 2d edit., 1994; mem. editorial bd. Internat. Jour. Pancreatology, 1985-91, Current Concepts in Gastroenterology, 1985—, Endoscopy Around the World, 1987, Postgrad. Medicine, 1989, Am. Jour. Gastroenterology, 1986-93, Cirugia, Gastro & Ginecologia, 1989, Romanian Jour. Gastroenterology, 1993, Digestive Diseases, 1993; mem. bd. assoc. editors Pancreas, 1993—; contbr. articles and revs. to profl. jours, chpts. to books. With U.S. Army Res., Brigadier Gen. Commdr, 322nd Med. Brigade, Nashville Tenn. Recipient Rorer Pharm. Corp. award Am. Coll. Gastroenterology, 1989; Grantee AGA Clinicians Postgrad. Support Program, 1989, Women's Cancer League of Miami Beach, 1990. Fellow ACP (chmn. pub. rels. com. Fla. chpt. 1988-93, MKSAP adv. com. 1990-92, MKSAP planning sub-com. 1991-93, gov.-elect Fla. chpt. 1995-96, gov. 1996—); mem. AMA, Am. Coll. Gastroent. (pres.-elect 1988-89, pres. 1989-90), Am. Gastroent. Assn. (abstract selection com. 1988-90, tng. and edn. com. 1988-91), Am. Soc. Gastrointestinal Endoscopy (mem. various coms. 1980-87), Am. Pancreatic Assn., Am. Fedn. Clin. Rsch., Am. Assn. History Medicine, Am. Soc. Laser Medicine and Surgery Inc., Assn. Mil. Surgeons of the U.S., Internat. Biliary Assn., Internat. Assn. Pancreatology, Internat. Gastro-Surg. Club, Bockus Internat. Soc. Gastroenterology (fellowship com. 1983-89, constn. and bylaws com. 1987-89, treas. 1985-93, v.p. 1993, pres. 1996—), So. Med. Assn., Fla. Gastroent. Soc. (pres. elect 1993-94, pres. 1994-95), Gastroenterology Rsch. Group, Alpha Omega Alpha. Office: 4300 Alton Rd Miami FL 33140-2800

BARKMEIER, WAYNE W., dentist, administrator, researcher, educator; b. Friend, Nebr., Mar. 29, 1944; m. Carolyn A. Johnsen; children: Kimberly, Jennifer, Wayne Jr. Postgrad., U. Nebr., Lincoln, 1962—65; DDS, U. Nebr. Med. Ctr. Coll. Dentistry, 1965—69; MS, U. Tex. Health Sci. Ctr., Houston, 1973—75. Asst. prof., oral surgery Creighton U., 1978—79; pvt. practice Omaha, 1978—82; asst. prof., operative dentistry Creighton U., 1979—82; rsch. dentist L.D. Caulk Divsn., Dentsply Internat., Milford, Del., 1982—85, intramural rsch. mgr., 1985; asst. dean rsch. and assoc. prof. operative dentistry, Sch. Dentistry Creighton U., 1985—87, dir., Ctr. Oral Health Rsch., 1986—95, assoc. dean rsch., Sch. Dentistry, 1991—94, prof., operative dentistry, Sch. Dentistry, 1991—2000, prof. gen. dentistry, Sch. Dentistry, 2000—, dean, Sch. Dentistry, 1994—2005, 2009—11, dean emeritus, 2006—. Cons. on dental materials Nat. Bd. Test Constrn. Com. for Joint Commn. on Nat. Dental Exams.; past mem. Am. Dental Assn. Coun. on Dental Rsch. Mem. editl. bd. Operative Dentistry, article rev. cons. Jour. Am. Dental Assn., Am. Jour. Dentistry, Dental Materials, Jour. Dentistry, Quintessence Internat., Jour. Dental Edn., Mil. Medicine; contbr. more than 150 articles to profl. jours. Active duty USAF, 1969—78, brig. gen. USAFR, 1991—94. Office Phone: 402-280-5061.

BARKSDALE, EDWARD METZ, JR., pediatrician, educator; b. Lynchburg, Va., July 6, 1958; BS in Biology, with honors, Yale U., New Haven, 1980; MD, Harvard Med. Sch., Boston, 1984. Diplomate Am. Bd. Surgery, Am. Bd. Pediatric Surgery. Intern, resident gen. surgery Mass. Gen. Hosp., Boston, 1984—91, chief resident surgery, 1991—92; fellow pediatric surgery Children's Hosp. Med. Ctr., Cin., 1992—94; asst. prof. pediatric surgery U. Pitts., 1994—2001, assoc. prof. pediatric surgery, 2001—07; pediatric surgery staff, dir. nutrition Children's Hosp., Pitts., 1994—2007; prof. & chief divsn. pediatric surgery, Robert J. Izant, Jr. MD chair pediatric surgery Rainbow Babies & Children's Hosp., Cleve., 2007—; vice-chmn. dept. surgery Univ. Hosp./Case Med. Ctr., Cleve., 2007—. Co-dir. Fetal Diagnosis & Treatment Ctr. Magee Women's Hosp., Pitts. Active Project Focus to Reduce Urban Violence, Cleve.; co-founding bd. mem., chmn. Every Child Inc. Recipient Robert Wood Johnson Career Devel. award, 1996—2000, Michael E. Miller Young Investigator award, Children's Hosp. Pitts., 2000, Health Care Hero award, Pitts. Bus. Times, 2001, Chancellor's Disting. pub. svc. award, U. Pitts., 2002, Edgar B. Jackson Jr. Faculty Mentor award for outstanding svc., Univ. Hosp./Case Med. Ctr., 2008; named a Top Doc., Cleve. Mag., 2008; named one of Dozen Making a Difference, Pitts. Post-Gazette, 2003, Americas Leading Doc.'s, Black Enterprise Mag., 2008. Mem.: Soc. Univ. Surgeons, Soc. Black Academic Surgeons, Assn. Academic Surgeons, Am. Pediatric Surgery Assn. Office: Rainbow Babies & Childrens Hosp Dept Pediatric Surgery 11100 Euclid Ave Cleveland OH 44106 Office Phone: 216-844-3015. Office Fax: 216-844-8687.

BARLOW, ANNE LOUISE, pediatrician, medical researcher; b. Skipton-in-Craven, Eng., Jan. 28, 1925; came to U.S., 1951, naturalized, 1954; m. Howard Cadwell, May 19, 1951; children: Barbara Anne, John James Stewart; m. Alastair Ramsay, Dec. 19, 1969. MB BS, London Sch. Medicine for Women, U. London, 1948; diploma in child health, Royal Colls. Eng., 1950; MPH with honors, Yale U., 1952. House physician North Lonsdale Hosp., Barrow-in-Furness, Lancashire, Eng., 1948-49; house surgeon Royal Infirmary (Glasgow), Scotland, 1949; resident to profl. unit of child health Royal Hosp. for Sick Children, Glasgow, 1949-50; jr. hosp. med. officer Knightswood Infectious Diseases Hosp., Glasgow, 1950; Rotary Found. Internat. fellow U. Toronto Med. Sch., Ont., Canada, 1950-51; research asst. Yale U. Sch. Pub. Health, New Haven, 1952-53; clinic physician in cancer prevention Arlington, Va., part-time 1953-54; resident, staff physician William H. Maybury Tb Sanatorium, Northville, Mich., 1954-56; research dir. Detroit Feeding Study with the Detroit City Health Dept., 1954-56; research asst., instr. sch. health U. Pitts. Grad. Sch. Pub. Health, 1957-62; pvt. practice medicine specializing in pediatrics Pitts., 1959-62; mem. courtesy staff St. Margaret Hosp., Pitts., 1959-62; research assoc. Tice Lab for Tb research, Cook County Hosp., Chgo., 1962; med. writer product info. Abbott Labs., North Chicago, Ill., 1963-66, med. specialist antibiotic medicine, 1966-68; mgr. clin. devel. pharm. products div. Abbott Lab., North Chicago, Ill., 1968-71, asst. med. dir., 1971-72, mgr. parenteral nutrition hosp. products div., 1972-73, med. dir., 1973-80, v.p. med. affairs hosp. products div., 1980-84; pres. Albamed, Inc., 1985—2005; asst. clin. prof. Med.Coll. Pa., 1988. Cons. maternal, child and sch. health, dir. well baby clinic Lake County (Ill.) Health Dept., 1963-76; pres. Tb Sanatorium Bd. Lake County Health Dept., Ill., 1976-79; dir., pres. Lake County Bd. Health, 1979-82; health officer Village of North Barrington, Ill., 1964-67; physician-adviser Head Start Lake County Community Action Project, 1970-84; chmn. profl. adv. com. Lake County Health Dept., 1972-84; preceptor Pediatric Nurse Assoc. Program; chmn. bd. Sutton Place Behavioral Health Inc., 2000-05. Contbr. articles on maternal and infant care, pediatrics and nutrition; patentee high calorie solution of low molecular weight glucose polymer mixtures useful for intravenouse adminstrn. Bd. dirs. Heart Assn. of Lake County, 1979-84, chmn. nutrition com. 1980-82, v.p. 1982-83, pres., 1983-84; mem. sch. bd. Grant Twp. Cmty. H.S. (Ill. Dist. 124), 1973-79; sec. to governing bd. Spl. Edn. Dist. of Lake County, 1977-79; assoc. Nat. Coll. Edn., Evanston, Ill., 1976-84; chmn. Am. Women's Hosp. Svc., 1986-95, 2004-; vol. Guardian ad Litem, 1989-2004. Recipient award of merit for outstanding contbns. to pub. health, Ill. Pub. Health Assn., 1975, award of merit for outstanding cmty. svc., Lake County Cmty. Action Project, 1976, award for outstanding and dedicated svc. as pres., Lake County TB Sanatorium Bd., 1979, TWIN award, YWCA, 1983, Charlotte Danstrom award for excellence, Women in Mgmt., 1984, award for volunteering in medicine, AMA Found., 2006. Mem. AAAS, NOW, LWV, AMA (chair sr. physician gov. com. 1996-2005), Am. Med. Women's Assn. (councilor for orgn. and mgmt. 1977-79, treas. 1980, 1st v.p. 1981, pres. 1983, chair found. 1992-95, chair Am. Women's Hosps. Svcs. com. 2004-, Elizabeth Blackwell medal 1992), Fla. Med. Assn. (vice chair Internat. Med. Grad. sect. 1998-2004, coun. on pub. health 2000-05), Med. Women's Internat. Assn. (v.p. N. Am. 1993-95), Pan-Am. Med. Women's Alliance (pres. 2000), Nassau County Med. Soc. (pres. 2002-03). Home and Office: 20 S 19th St Fernandina Beach FL 32034-2767 Personal E-mail: czardaska@bellsouth.net.

BARLOW, HORACE BASIL, physiologist; b. Chesham Bois, Eng., Dec. 8, 1921; s. James Alan and Emma Nora Barlow; m. Miranda Weston-Smith, June 28, 1980; children: Oscar Hugh, Ida Lucy, Pepita Elizabeth; children by previous marriage: Rebecca Nora, Natasha Helen, Naomi Jane, Emily Anne. BA, Cambridge U., Eng., 1943; MD, Harvard U., 1946; MBB, Univ. Coll. Hosp. of London, 1947. Fellow Trinity Coll., 1950-54; demonstrator, asst. dir. rsch. physiology lab. King's Coll., 1954-63; Royal Soc. rsch. prof. Cambridge U., 1973-87; prof. physiol. optics U. Calif., Berkeley, 1963-73. Editor Jour. of Physiology, 1972-77; contbr. articles to profl. jours. Recipient Edward D. Tillyer award Optical Soc. Am., 1992, Crook medal Worshipful Co. of Spectacle Makers, 1993, Australia prize, 1993, Royal medal Royal Soc. London, 1993, Karl Spencer Lashley award Am. Philos. Soc., 2003. Mem. Physiol. Soc., Exptl. Psychology Soc., Brain Rsch. Assn. Avocations: walking, music. Home: 9 Selwyn Gardens Cambridge CB3 9AX England Office: U Cambridge Physiol Lab Downing St Cambridge CB2 3EG England Office Phone: 1223 333867. E-mail: hbb10@cam.ac.uk.

BARLOW, PAULA C., nurse; b. New Albany, Ind., May 27, 1952; d. Chester Joseph and Bonnie Faye Stiller; m. Rick Keith Barlow, Nov. 17, 1984; 1 child, Laura Elise. BSN, U. Louisville, 1982. RN Ga., Ky., Fla. Nurse St. Anthony Hosp., Louisville, 1972—82, St. Vincent's Hosp., Jacksonville, Fla., 1985—97; sch. nurse Camden Bd. Edn., Kingsland, Ga., 1997—. CPR instr. ARC. Mem.: Sight for Students Orgn., Ga. Assn. Sch. Nurses, Nat. Assn. Sch. Nurses. Avocations: reading, cooking, travel. Home: 6465 Chariot St NE Atlanta GA 30328-4298

BARLOW- RADEMEYER, IRENE MARY, physical therapist; b. Johannesburg, Mar. 3, 1952; BS in Phys. Therapy, U. Witwatersrand, 1973. Cert. specialist in orthop. Am. Phys. Therapy Assn. Dir. clin. edn. Columbia Health Care, 1993—96; dir. phys. therapy Fla. Spine Inst., 1996—2008; dir. phys. therapy, dir. clinic Laser Spine Inst., 2008—10, sr. dir. clinic ops., 2010—, v.p. clinic ops. & diagnostic svcs., 2011—. Clin. lectr. phys. therapy USF, 1997—2000, selection faculty lectrs. phys. therapy, 1997—98; part-time editor & selection CME courses. Dynamic Learning, 2000—10. Avocations: yoga, kayaking, hiking, travel. Home: 1945 Barcelona Dr Dunedin FL 34698 Personal E-mail: irademeyer@laserspineinstitute.com, irenem100@aol.com.

BARNES, BETTY RAE, retired counselor; b. Wichita, Kans., June 24, 1932; d. Henry Charles and Vivian Augusta (Lamberth) Archer; m. Orland Eugene Barnes, Mar. 18, 1953; children: Terry Lee, Steven Gregory. BA, Our Lady of the Lake, 1986, MS in Counseling Psychology, 1989. Lic. profl. counselor, marriage and family therapist; cert. profl. sec. Info. specialist S.W. Rsch. Inst., San Antonio, 1975—96; counselor Cmty. Clinic, Inc., San Antonio, 1989—91, counselor, counseling coord., 1991—2001, supr. interns; counselor supr. Am. Assn. Marriage & Family Therapists, 2001—11. Counselor Cmty. Counseling Ctr. Our Lady of the Lake U., San Antonio, 1989—91; pvt. practice, San Antonio; cons. in field. Asst. editor, data collection, conversion and entry (CD) Abstracts on Radio Direction Finding, 2d edit., 1996. Past chair Life After Loss com. Am. Cancer Soc. Recipient Outstanding Achievement award, Sch. Bus. and Pub. Adminstrn., Our Lady of the Lake U., 1984. Mem.: ACA, South Tex. Counseling Asso., San Antonio Assn. Marriage and Family Therapy (past pres.), Tex. Counseling Assn., Tex. Assn. Marriage and Family Therapists (past bd. dirs.), Am. Mental Health Counselors Assn., Am. Assn. Marriage and Family Therapists (clin., approved supr.), San Antonio Mus. Assn., Delta Mu Delta. Avocations: piano, reading. Home Phone: 210-673-8156. Personal E-mail: bbarnes@satx.rr.com.

BARNES, DAVID SHIELDS, gastroenterologist; MD, U. of NC Sch. of Medicine, 1981. Diplomate Am. Bd. Internal Medicine-gastroenterology, 1987, Am. Bd. Internal Medicine-transplant hepatology, 2006. Intern UMass Meml. Med. Ctr., 1982, resident, 1984; fellow Univ. Hosps. Case Med. Ctr., 1985; with Cleveland Clinic, adminstrv. vice chmn. gastroenterology and hepatology dept. Author: (articles) Scents and sensibilities: disgust and the meanings of odors in the late nineteenth-century Paris, 2005, Pegylated interferon alpha-2b, ribavirin and amantadine for chronic hepatitis C, 2005, Methotrexate (MTX) plus ursodeoxycholic acid (UDCA) in the treatment of primary biliary cirrhosis, 2005, and several others. Named top dr., Cleveland; named one of Castle Connolly America's Top Doctors, 2011. Office: Cleveland Clinic 9500 Euclid Ave MC A-51 Cleveland OH 44195 Office Phone: 216-444-1764.

BARNES, GRAHAM, psychotherapist, consultant; b. Creswell, NC, Oct. 24, 1936; arrived in Sweden, 1983; naturalized, 1996; s. Will Mitchell and Wilma (Norman) Barnes; m. Ethel Dale McBride, 1959 (div. 1978); children: Christopher David, James McBride; life ptnr. Stephanos Giotas, 1983 (div. 2009). BA, Mid-Atlantic Christian U., 1959; MA, Abilene Christian U., 1964; STB, Harvard U., 1967; PhD, Royal Melbourne Inst. Tech., 2002. Diplomate Redecision Therapy Assn.; lic. psychotherapist, Swedish Nat. Bd. Health & Welfare; cert. group psychotherapist. Founder, dir. Fellowship for Racial and Econ. Equality, Lynchburg, Va., 1969-73; founder, pres., faculty S.E. Inst., Chapel Hill, NC, 1973-78; lectr., supr. Psychotherapy Insts. & Univs. in 12 European Countries, 1979—89; head sch. for cybernetics of psychotherapy, dept. psychiatry U. Zagreb, Croatia, 1990-97; chmn. Inform AB, Stockholm, 1991—. Adj. lectr. dept. psychiatry U. NC, Chapel Hill, 1973—78; lectr. Sch. Pub. Health, U. NC, 1976; cons. Norwegian Sport Fedn., Oslo, 1979—83, Corp. Strategic Planning Team, Pharmacia AB, Uppsala, Sweden, 1981—83, Hydro Aluminum A/S, Oslo, 1984—96, Swedbank, Stockholm, 1995—2002, IRIS Devel. Ctr., Stockholm, 1991—2001; vis. lectr. dept. psychiatry U. Zagreb, 1990—; assoc. cons. Nextwork AB, Stockholm, 1998—2005; advisor Found. 2020, Zagreb, 1999—2008; editl. adv. bd. mem. Kairos-Slovenian Jour. Psychotherapy, 2007—. Author: Justice, Love and Wisdom Linking Psychotherapy to Second-Order Cybernetics, 1994; editor: Transactional Analysis After Eric Berne, 1977; mem. editl. bd. Transactional Analysis Jour., 1997-99, Hypnos-Swedish and European Jour. Hypnosis, 2000-05; contbr. articles to profl. jours. Mem. adv. bd. Tällberg Found., 2003-08; life mem. Disciples of Christ Hist. Soc. Fellow: Royal Soc. Encouragement Arts, Mfrs. and Commerce, Am. Soc. Cybernetics; mem.: Redecision Therapy Assn. (charter mem.), Riksföreningen Psykoterapi Centrum, Latin Am. Assn. Transactional Analysis (hon.), Am. Group Psychotherapy Assn. (life; clin. mem.), Assn. Psychol. Sci., Swedish Soc. Clin. and Exptl. Hypnosis (bd. dirs. 2001—02), Internat. Transactional Analysis Assn. (tchg. mem. 1972—, trustee 1973—77, v.p. 1976—77, trustee 1982—84, Eric Berne Meml. award 2005), Harvard Club Sweden (bd. mem. 2008—). Home: Drottninggatan 73C LGH 1402 SE-111 36 Stockholm Sweden Office Phone: 46 70 582 2021. Business E-Mail: graham.barnes@inform.se.

BARNES, JOHN D., health science association administrator; BSBA, Creighton U., 1982. Dir. govt. and pub. affairs Steel Tank Inst.; spl. asst. to US Senator Charles E. Grassley US Senate; chief of staff to US Rep. Greg Ganske US Ho. of Reps.; assoc. exec. dir. govt. rels. and health policy Am. Acad. Dermatology Assn., Am. Acad. Dermatology, 1999—2005, dep. exec. dir., 2005—07; CEO Am. Phys. Therapy Assn., Alexandria, Va., 2007—. Office: Am Physical Therapy Assn 1111 N Fairfax St Alexandria VA 22314-1488 Office Phone: 703-684-2782. Office Fax: 703-684-7343. E-mail: johnbarnes@apta.org. *

BARNES, MAGGIE LUE SHIFFLETT, retired nurse; b. Redmond, Tex., Mar. 29, 1931; d. Howard Eldridge and Sadie Adilene (Dunlap) Shifflett; m. T.C. Fagan, Jan. 1950 (Dec. Feb. 1952); 1 child, Lawayne; m. Lawrence Barnes, Sept. 2, 1960. Student, Cogdell Sch. Nursing, 1959—60, Western Tex. Coll., 1972—76; postgrad., Meth. Hosp. Sch. Nursing, Lubbock, Tex., 1975; BSN, West Tex. State U., Canyon, 1977; cert. legal nurse cons., Kaplan Coll., 2001. Cert. gerontol. nurse, RN Tex., Ruth Hosp. Sch. Nursing, Lubock. Floor nurse D.M. Cogdell Meml. Hosp., Snyder, Tex., 1960-64, medication nurse, 1964-76, asst. evening supr., 1976-78, charge nurse, after 1978, evening nursing supr., 1980; nursing supr. for 5 counties West Ctrl. Home Health Agy., Snyder, 1983—89; emergency rm. evening supr. Mitchell County Hosp., 1983-89; dir. nurses Snyder Oak Care Ctr., 1989-91, Mountain View Lodge, Big Spring, Tex., 1991-92, Med. Arts Hosp. Home Health, Lamesa, 1992—93, Metplex Home Health Svcs., Snyder, 1993-94, ret., 1994; weekend RN Snyder Oaks Care Ctr. CNA Sch. instr.; leader Bible study, 1997—; vol. Helping Children Read Sch., Bible study at nursing homes; regional coord. home health svcs. Beverly Enterprises, 1983; legal nurse cons. Grad. Kaplan Coll., Boca Raton, Fla., 2001. Den leader Boy Scouts Am., Holliday, Tex., 1960-61; active PTA, Snyder, 1960-69; adviser Sr. Citizens Assn.; mem Tri-Region Health Sys. Agy., 1979—; adv. bd. Scurry County Diabetes Assn., 1982—; vol. reading program, tchr. quilting Kent County Nursing Home, 2007-, former, County Quality Club; ch. sec.-treas. Apostolic Faith Ch., 1956-58 Mem.: DAR, Emergency Dept. Nursing Assn., Vocat. Nurses Assn. Tex. (bd. dirs. 1963—65, divsn. pres. 1967—69), Rock and Roll Quilting Club (coord.). Home: 2006 31th St Apt 33 Snyder TX 79549 *

BARNES, STUART ROBERT, physician assistant; b. Wilkes-Barre, Pa., July 11, 1952; s. Stanley Fenton and Arlene Violet Barnes; m. Dawn Marie Barnes, Oct. 24, 1992; children: Patricia Ann, Rebecca Paige. Paramedic cert., St. Petersburg Jr. Coll., 1974; physician asst. cert., King's Coll., 1983. Cert. physician asst. King's Coll., ACLS, lic. physician asst. Md., Fla.; cert. firefighter Fla. State Fire Coll., 1973, smoke diver Fla. State Fire Coll., 1973. Firefighter/EMT New Port Richey Fire Dept., 1972-74; EMT/paramedic Pasco County Emergency Svcs., Newport Richey, Fla., 1974-76; paramedic Manatee County Emergency Svcs., Bradenton, Fla., 1976-80; physician asst. Ariz. State Dept. of Corrections, Florence, 1984-87, Caroline Health Svcs., Denton, Md., 1988-90, Genessis Physician Svcs., Salisbury, Md., 1990—2002, Breton Med. Group/Shah Assocs., California, Md., 2002—06, Medero Med., Ocala, Fla., 2006—07, Workers Med. Compcare, Ocala, Fla., 2007—08, Beverly Hills Medicine Ctr., Fla., 2008—. Contbr. articles to profl. jours. Pres. Chestnut Hill Civic Assn., Delmar, Md., 1996, Leonard's Mill Pond Assn., Delmar, 1999. Disting. fellow, Am. Acad. Physician Assts. Fellow Md. Acad. Physician Assts., Fla. Acad. Physician Assts., Assn. Family Practice Physician Assts., Am. Coll. Clinicians; mem. N.Am. Fishing Club (life), Masons, Cooking Club of Am.(life) Avocations: music, fishing, woodworking, collecting old medical books. Office: Beverly Hills Medicine Ctr 3745 N Lecanto Hwy Beverly Hills FL 34465 Business E-Mail: knothead6888@embarqmail.com.

BARNESS, LEWIS ABRAHAM, retired physician; b. Atlantic City, July 31, 1921; s. Joseph and Mary (Silverstein) B.; m. Elaine Berger, June 14, 1953 (dec. Jan. 1985); children: Carol, Laura, Joseph; m. Enid May Fischer Gilbert, July 5, 1987; stepchildren: Mary, Elizabeth, Jennifer, Rebecca. AB, Harvard U., 1941, MD, 1944; MA (hon.), U. Pa., 1971; DS U. Wis. (hon.), 2002. Intern Phila. Gen. Hosp., 1944-45; resident Boston Children's Hosp., 1947-50; asst. chief, then chief dept. pediatrics Phila. Gen. Hosp., 1951-72; vis. physician U. Pa. Hosp., 1952-57, acting chief, then chief, 1957-72. Mem. faculty U. Pa. Sch. Medicine, 1951-72, prof. pediat., 1964-72; chmn. dept. U. So. Fla. Med. Sch., Tampa, 1972-88, prof. pediat., 1988—, Disting. Univ. prof., 2000—; vis. prof. Univ. Wis., 1987-92, prof. emeritus, 1993—. Author: Pediatric Physical Diagnosis Yearbook, edits. 1-6, 1957—; editor: Advances in Pediatrics, 1976-2004, Pediatric Nutrition Handbook, 3d edit., 1991; asst. editor Pediatric Gastroenterology and Nutrition, 1981-91; editl. bd. Cons., 1960-84, Pediatrics, 1978-83, Core Jour. Pediatrics, 1980-96, Contemporary Pediatrics, 1984—, Jour. Clin. Medicine and Nutrition, 1985-95, Nutrition Rev., 1985-87. Served to capt. AUS, 1945-46. Recipient Lindback Teaching award U. Pa., 1963; Borden award nutrition, 1972; Noer Disting. Prof. award, 1980, Joseph B. Goldberger award in clin. nutrition, 1984, Joseph St. Geme Leadership award 7 pediatric socs., 1991, U. So. Fla. Svc. award, 1997, President's Award, U. So. Fla., 2000, Distinguished Prof. award, 2000; inductee Phila. Pediat. Soc. Hall of Fame, 1996. Fellow Am. Inst. Nutrition; mem. AAAS, Am. Pediatric Soc. (recorder-editor 1964-75, pres. 1985-86, John Howland award 1993), Soc. Pediatric Rsch., Am. Acad. Pediatrics (chmn. com. on nutrition 1974-81), Abraham Jacobi award 1991, Hon. Internat. disting. fellow pediatric soc. Thailand, 2004, Med. Edn. Lifetime Achievement award, 1995, Sigma Xi, Alpha Omega Alpha. Home: 3301 Bayshore Blvd Unit 403 Tampa FL 33629-8841 Office: U South Fla Dept Pediat 17 Davis Blvd Tampa FL 33606 Home Phone: 813-837-9357; Office Phone: 813-259-8711. E-mail: eglbert@tgh.org.

BARNET, ROBERT JOSEPH, cardiologist, philosopher; b. Port Huron, Mich., Apr. 27, 1929; s. John A. and Ruth Elizabeth (Wittliff) B.; m Carol R. Taylor; children: Benedict, Maria, Antonia, Peter, Elizabeth, Rebecca, Christina, Jacqueline, Ann. Student, Port Huron Jr. Coll., summers 1947, 49; MD, Loyola U., Chgo., 1951; BS in Chemistry magna cum laude, U. Notre Dame, Ind., 1954, MA in Philosophy, 1988; MA in History, U. Nev., Reno, 1986. Diplomate Am. Bd. Internal Medicine, Nat. Bd. Med. Examiners. Intern Boston City Hosp., 1954—55; rotating intern Mercy Hosp., Chgo., 1955; asst. resident in medicine Boston City Hosp., 1958-59; clin. and research fellow in cardiology Children's Med. Center and House of the Good Samaritan, Boston, 1959-60; cons. fellow in rheumatic fever pediatric service Boston City Hosp., 1959-60; research fellow in pediatrics Harvard U., Boston, 1959-60; clin. fellow in cardiology Mass. Meml. Hosps., Boston, 1960-61; physician-in-charge St. Francis Mission Hosp., Solwezi, No. Rhodesia, 1961-62; dir. clinics, assoc. in medicine Stritch Sch. Medicine, Loyola U., Chgo., 1962-65; physician-in-charge Cardiac Clinic, Loyola U., Chgo., Fantus Outpatient dept. Cook County Hosp., Chgo., 1962-65, Hypertension Clinic, Fantus Outpatient dept. Cook County Hosp., 1962-65; assoc. attending physician dept. medicine Cook County Hosp., 1962-63, attending physician, 1963-65; practice medicine specializing in cardiology Reno, 1965-87; med. staff Washoe Med. Center, 1965—2006, St. Mary's Hosp., 1965—2006; assoc. clin. prof. cardiology U. Nev.; also assoc. dir. Lab. Environ. Patho-Physiology, Desert Research Inst., U. Nev., Reno, 1965-68; dir. Cardiac Care unit Washoe Med. Center, 1965-83, exec. com., 1967-71, 73-77, vice chief dept. medicine, 1969, chief, 1970-71, 78, chief dept. emergency services, 1973-77. Vis physician Solwezi Boma Rural Hosp., 1961-62; cons. in cardiology disability determination unit State of Nev., 1966-87, Crippled Children's Svc., 1966-76, Reno VA Hosp., 1967-80; asst. clin. prof. med. edn. U. Utah, 1968-71; cons. Churchill Pub. Hosp., Fallon, Nev., 1969-87, Pershing Gen. Hosp., Lovelock, Nev., 1969-87; clin. assoc. U. Nev., Reno, 1971-72, assoc. clin. prof. medicine, 1973-77, prof., 1978-2006; vis. scholar U. Notre Dame, 1989-90, 96-97; prof. med. ethics St. Louis U., 1993-95; med. reviewer, cons. Nev. State Bd. Med. Examiners, 1994-2007; sr. scholar-in-residence Ctr. Clin. Bioethics, Georgetown U., Sch. Medicine, 2000—, adj. prof. dept. medicine, 2010-; lectr. in electrocardiography and cardiology Loyola U., Chgo., 1962-65. Contbr. articles to profl. jours. Served with US Army, 1955-58. Recipient Clin. Faculty Honor award Loyola U., 1963-64. Fellow A.C.P. (bd. govs. 1980-85), Am. Coll. Cardiology (bd. govs. 1974-77), Am. Coll. Chest Physicians; mem. Nev. Heart Assn. (bd. dirs., exec. com., pres. 1974-75) Office: Georgetown U Ctr Clin Bioethics Box 571409 Washington DC 20057-1409 Office Phone: 202-687-9385. Personal E-mail: phbobmd@aol.com.

BARNETT, BENJAMIN LEWIS, JR., retired physician, educator; b. Woodruff, SC, July 22, 1926; s. Benjamin Lewis and Mattie Bernice (Skinner) B.; m. Annalyne Louise Hall, Oct. 25, 1958; children: Benjamin Lewis III, Jane Kristen. BS, Furman U., 1946, LLD, 1978; MD, Med. U. S.C., 1949. Diplomate Am. Bd. Family Practice. Intern Protestant Episcopal Hosp., Phila., 1949-50; pvt. practice Woodruff, 1950-70; from assoc. prof. family practice to asst. dean and prof. Med. U. S.C., Charleston, 1970—75, asst. dean for student affairs, 1975—77; clin. staff Med. U. Hosp., Charleston County Hosp., 1970-77; from prof. to prof. emeritus U. Va. Med. Sch., 1977—2000, prof. emeritus, 2000—; family medicine physician-in-chief U. Va. Med. Ctr. Hosp., 1977-96. Admissions com. U. Va. Med. Sch., 1997-99; Stoneburner lectr. Med. Coll. Va., 1975; Daniel Drake lectr. U. Cin., 1976; Robert P. Walton lectr. Med. U. SC, 1978; Goodlark prof. U. Tenn., 1979; Roy J. Gerard lectr. Mich. State U., 1992; vis. scholar U. Mich. Med. Sch., 1984; vis. lectr. Med. Coll. of Ga., 1982; vis. prof. Case Western Res. Sch. Medicine, 1984, U. Vt., 1988, U. N.Mex., 1991, U. SC Sch. Medicine, 1999; spkr. baccalaureate address U. Va., 1986, 2000; Mack Lipkin vis. prof. U. Oreg., 1987, U. Utah, 1989; Donald J. Welter Meml. lectr. Med. Coll. Wis., 1989; Frederick Lytel Meml. lectr., Abington, Pa., 1989; Bradford Strock lectr. Harrisburg (Pa.) Gen. Hosp., 1989; 7th Leland Blanchard Meml. lectr. Soc. Tchrs. Family Medicine ann. meeting, Nashville, 1985; health officer, Town of Woodruff, 1950-54; keynote speaker Assn. Depts. Family Medicine, Clearwater, Fla., 1991; commencement speaker U. Va. Med. Sch., 1992, 97; Grand Prof. Rounds St. Margaret's Hosp., Pitts., 1993; Julian Keith lectr. Bowman Gray Sch. Medicine, 1993; keynote speaker leadership conf. Fla. Med. Assn., Ponta Vedra, 1994, AHEC conf. SC Family Practice, Myrtle Beach, 1994; B. Leslie Huffman lectr. Med. Coll. Ohio, Toledo, 1994; lectr. Atlanta Med. Ctr., 2000—; grad. speaker McLennan County Med. Edn. and Rsch. Found., Waco, Tex., 1995; Inaugural Buck Crockett lectr., Roanoke, Va., 2000; founder's prof. U. Okla. Health Scis. Ctr., Tulsa, 2000; Harlan Thomas Meml. lectr.; Hiram B. Curry Meml. lectr. MUSC, 1990, 2001; lectr. and cons. in field. Author: Between the Lines (Reflections of a Family Physician), 1989, Pebbles in the Water, 2003, Between the Lines Silver edit., 2008, Weaving of Threads, 2008; editor: S.C. Family Physician, 1973—74; contbr. articles to med. jours. and chpts. to textbooks. Mem. Spartanburg County Bd. Edn., 1968-70, sec. 1969-70; trustee Bethea Bapt. Home for Aged, Darlington, S.C., 1972-73; mem. bd. trustees Furman U., 1994-99; dir. Marietta-Lost Mtn. Kiwanis, 2003-05; mentor character curriculum Kennesaw Mountain HS, 2002-2006. Physican USN, 1954—56. Named Citizen of Year Woodmen of World, 1968; recipient Golden Apple award for clin. teaching Student AMA, 1973; Thomas W. Johnson award Am. Acad. Family Physicians, 1976, Disting. Alumnus award Med. U. S.C., 1993; endowed Barnett Professorship in Family Medicine established U. Va. Bd. Visitors, 1997; Thomas Jefferson award U. Va., 1997. Mem. AMA (mem. residency rev. com. for family practice 1974-79), Am. Bd. Family Practice (exam. bd. 1975-81, dir. 1976-81, exec. com. 1979-81, pres. 1980-81), Va. Med. Soc., Albemarle County Med. Soc., Soc. Tchrs. Family Medicine (v.p. 1974, sec.-treas. 1975, dir. 1981-85, Cert. of Excellence 1983, F. Marian Bishop award 1996), Am. Acad. Family Physicians, S.C. Acad. Family Physicians (v.p. 1973, pres. 1975-76), Spartanburg County Med. Soc. (v.p. 1968), Am. Philatelic Soc., Coun. Acad. Socs., Furman U. Alumni Assn. (dir. 1972-77), U. Va. Raven Soc., Kiwanis (dir.), Alpha Omega Alpha (faculty councilor, vis. prof. U. S.C. Sch. Medicine 1999), Alpha Kappa Kappa (pres. 1948), Kappa Alpha (v.p. 1944), Loyal Order. Baptist (deacon, chmn. bd.).

BARNETT, CARLTON, oncologist, director; b. Englewood, Colo., Jan. 28, 1966; BS, Baylor U., 1988; MD, U. Colo. Health Scis. Ctr., 1992. Attending physician Parkland Meml. Hosp., Dallas, 2004—08, St. Paul U. Hosp., Dallas, 2004—08, Zale Lipshy U. Hosp., Dallas, 2004—08, Vets. Adminstrn. Med. Ctr., Dallas, 2004—08; dir., surg. oncology Denver Health Med. Ctr., 2008—. Recipient Covidien Resident Edn. award; grant, Am. Cancer Soc., U. Colo. Denver Health Academic Enrichment Funds, Northfield Labs. Inc. Office: Denver Health Med Ctr 777 Bannoc Denver CO 80204 Office Fax: 303-436-6572. Business E-Mail: carlton.barnett@dhha.org.

BARNETT, CRAWFORD FANNIN, JR., internist, educator, cardiologist, travel medicine specialist; b. Atlanta, May 11, 1938; s. Crawford Fannin and Penelope Hollinshead (Brown) B.; m. Elizabeth McCarthy Hale, June 6, 1964; children: Crawford Fannin III, Robert Hale. Student, U. Minn., Mpls. Campus, 1957; AB magna cum laude, Yale U., New Haven, Conn., 1960; postgrad., Oxford U., Eng., 1963; MD, Duke U., Durham, NC, 1964. Intern in internal medicine Duke U. Med. Ctr., Durham, NC, 1964-65, resident, 1965; resident in internal medicine Wilmington Med. Ctr., Del., 1965-66; dir. Tenn. Heart Disease Control Program, Nashville, 1966-68; pvt. practice medicine in internal/travel medicine Atlanta, 1968—. Dir. Travel Immunization Ctr., Atlanta; mem. staff Crawford Long Hosp., Atlanta, Northside Hosp., Atlanta, Grady Meml. Hosp., Atlanta, West Paces Hosp., Atlanta, Piedmont Hosp., Atlanta, North Fulton Hosp., Atlanta; mem. tchg. staff Vanderbilt Med. Ctr., Nashville, 1966-68, Crawford Long Meml. Hosp., 1969—; clin. instr. internal medicine, dept. medicine Emory U. Med. Sch., Atlanta, 1969—. Contbr. articles to profl. publs. Bd. councillors Carter Ctr., 2009-, Bd. govs. Doctors Meml. Hosp., 1971-80; bd. dir. Atlanta Speech Sch., 1976-80, 92—, Hist. Oakland Cemetery, 1976-86, So. Turf Nurseries, 1977-92, Tech Industries, 1978-92; bd. dirs. Am. Chestnut Found., 1990; trustee Mary Brown Found. Atlanta, 1998—, Woodward Found., 2001—, George M. Brown Fund Atlanta, 2006-. Surgeon USPHS, 1966-68. Fellow Am. Geog. Soc., Royal Soc. of Tropical Medicine and Hygiene, Royal Geog. Soc., Royal Soc. Medicine, Explorers Club (life, NYC); mem. Am. Soc. Tropical Medicine and Hygiene, Am. Fedn. Clin. Rsch., Coun. Clin. Cardiology, AMA, Ga. Med. Assn., Atlanta Med. Assn., Am. Heart Assn., Ga. Heart Assn., Am. Soc. Internal Medicine, Am. Assn. History Medicine, Ga. Hist. Soc., Atlanta Hist. Soc. (bd. govs. 1976-84), Ga. Trust for Hist. Preservation, Nat. Trust Hist. Preservation, Internat. Hippocratic Found. Soc. (Greece), Faculty of History of Medicine and Pharmacy Worshipful Soc. Apothecaries of London, Atlanta Com. on Fgn. Rels. (chmn. exec. com. 1972-88), So. Coun. Internat. and Pub. Affairs, Newcomen Soc., Atlanta Clin. Soc., Wilderness Med. Soc., Internat. Soc. Travel Medicine (founding), Travelers Century Club, Circumnavigators Club, South Am. Explorers Club, Victorian Soc. Am. (bd. advisers Atlanta chpt. 1971-86), Mensa, Gridiron, Piedmont Driving Club, Yale Club (dir. 1970-74), Nine O'Clocks Club, Pan Am. Drs. Club, Phi Beta Kappa. Episcopalian. Home: 2739 Ramsgate Ct NW Atlanta GA 30305-2817 Office: Ste 302 3193 Howell Mill Rd NW Atlanta GA 30327-2100 Home Phone: 404-351-1372; Office Phone: 404-262-1414. Personal E-mail: cfbarne@comcast.net.

BARNETT, JOEY VICTOR, pharmacologist, research scientist, educator; b. Evansville, Ind., June 18, 1958; s. Victor Alan and Judy Kay (Kohlmeyer) Barnett. BS in Biology, U. So. Ind., 1980; PhD in Pharmacology, Vanderbilt U., 1986. Rsch. intern Argonne (Ill.) Nat. Lab., U.S. Dept. Energy, 1981; rsch. fellow Brigham & Women's Hosp., Harvard Med. Sch., Boston, 1986-89, instr. medicine, 1989-92; asst. prof. medicine and pharmacology Vanderbilt U., Nashville, 1992-99, assoc. prof., 1999—, dir. grad. studies pharmacology, 2001—05, vice chair pharmacology, 2005—. Rsch. investigator Tenn. affiliate Am. Heart Assn., 1993—95, established investigator, 1996—; mem. devel. mechanisms panel NSF, 1995—98; mem. dev-1 panel NIH, 2003—; chmn. organizing com. Nat. Meeting for Dirs. of Grad. Studies in Pharmacology, 2005—. Co-author: Heart Failure: Basic Science and Clinical Aspects, 1993; contbr. articles to profl. jours. Co-chair cardiovasc. devel. panel Nat. Am. Heart Assn., 1997—98, chair, 1999—2000; founding bd. dirs. Dismas House Ctrl. Mass., Worcester, 1987—90. Recipient Nat. Rsch. Svc. award, Nat. Heart Lung and Blood Inst./NIH, Boston, 1988—90, Disting. Alumni award, U. So. Ind., 1991; Mass. affiliate fellow, Am. Heart Assn., 1986—88. Mem.: AAAS, Am. Soc. for Pharmacology and Exptl. Therapeutics (chmn. grad. edn. com. 2007—), Am. Heart Assn. (basic rsch. coun., vice-chmn. rsch. com. greater southeast affiliate 2007), Ind. Acad. Sci., N.Y. Acad. Scis., Sigma Xi, Sigmz Zeta. Roman Catholic. Achievements include research in molecular mechanisms that regulate development of the cardiovascular system. Office: 460 Prb 2220 Pierce Ave Nashville TN 37232-6600 Business E-Mail: joey.barnett@vanderbilt.edu.

BARNHART, MARY C., health facility administrator; b. Milw., Mar. 7, 1951; d. Zenon and Olga Soblewski; m. Clayton F. Barnhart, Feb. 22, 1997 (dec.); children: Clayton D., Lucille. BA, U. Wis. - Milw., 2002; MA in Bioethics, Med. Coll. Wis., 2004. Certified IRB Mgr. Nat. Assn. of IRB Managers, 2001, Certified IRB Profl. Pub. Responsibility in Medicine, 2002. Sec. Milw. County Children's Ct., 1986—96; mgr. instl. revenue bd. programs Oakwood Healthcare Sys., Dearborn, Mich., 1996—2005; coord. instl. rev. bd. St. John

Hosp. and Med. Ctr., Detroit, 2005—; dir. ethics, edn., policy, compliance U. Chgo. Contbr. newsletter articles Nat. Assn. of IRB Managers Newsletter, newsletter articles Med. Ethics Rsch. Network of Mich.; editor: (jour.) Oakwood Healthcare Rsch. Quar., (newsletter) Ch. Newsletter, author short stories, poetry. Ministry leader Twin Oaks Christian Ch., Mich., 1996—. Mem.: Nat. Assn. Internal Rev. Bd. Mgrs. (assoc. program dir. 2001—). Baptist. Avocations: reading, poetry, music, travel, graphic design. Home: 1117 Leavitt Ave Apt 210 Flossmoor IL 60422-1545 Office: Univ Chgo 5835 S Kimbark Ave Judd 335 Chicago IL 60637 Office Phone: 773-702-5064, 773-834-8700. Business E-Mail: mbarnhart@uchicago.edu.

BARNUM, BARBARA STEVENS, retired nursing educator, writer; b. Johnstown, Pa., Sept. 2, 1937; d. William C. and Freda Inzes (Claycomb) Burkett; m. H. James Barnum (dec.); children: Lauren, Elizabeth, Catherine, Anne (dec.), Shauna, Sallee, David. AA in Nursing, St. Petersburg Jr. Coll., 1958; BPh, Northwestern U., 1967; MA, DePaul U., 1971; PhD, U. Chgo., 1976. RN, Ill., N.Y. Dir. nursing svcs. Augustana Hosp. and Health Care Ctr., Chgo., 1970-71; dir. staff edn. U. Chgo. Hosps. and Clinics, 1971-73; prof. U. Ill., Chgo., 1973-79; dir. div. health svcs., sci. and edn. Columbia U. Tchrs. Coll., NYC, 1979-87; editor Nursing & Health Care Nat. League for Nursing, NYC, 1989-91; editor div. nursing Columbia-Presbyn. Med. Ctr., Columbia U., NYC, 1991-95; prof. Sch. Nursing Columbia U., NYC, 1995-98; ret., 1998; adj. prof. Coll. Nursing, NY U., NYC, 2009—. Chmn. bd. Barnum & Souza, N.Y.C., 1989-92; civilian cons. to surgeon gen. USAF, 1980-87. Author: Nursing Theory, Analysis, Application and Evaluation, 4th edit., 1994, Writing for Publication: A Primer for Nurses, 1995; author: (with K. Kerfoot) The Nurse as Executive, 4th edit., 1995; author: Spirituality and Nursing: From Traditional to New Age, 1996, 2d edit., 2003, Teaching Nursing in the Era of Managed Care, 1999, The New Healers: Minds and Hands in Complementary Medicine, 2002, (fiction) The Haunting of Lisa Tilden, 1999; editor: Nursing Leadership Forum, 1994—98. Mem. governing bd. Nurses House, 1979-86, Nat. Health Coun., 1981-90, others. Fellow Am. Acad. Nursing (governing bd. 1982-84); mem. Sigma Theta Tau (Founders' award 1979). Home: 80 Park Ave Apt 15G New York NY 10016-2547 Personal E-mail: barbbarnum@aol.com.

BAROFF, GEORGE STANLEY, psychologist, educator; b. Bronx, NY, Nov. 27, 1924; s. Irving and Ida (Herman) B.; m. Rose Kislin, June 15, 1952 (dec. May 1992); children: Marina Binet, Roy James. BS in Zoology, George Washington U., 1948, MA in Psychology, 1950; PhD in Clin. Psychology, NYU, 1955. Research psychologist dept. med. genetics N.Y. State Psychiat. Inst., 1952-60; chief clin. psychologist Vineland (N.J.) Tng. Sch., 1960-63; asso. prof. psychology U. N.C., Chapel Hill, 1963-67, prof., 1967-2000, prof. emeritus, 2000—, dir. devel. disabilties tng. inst., 1964-2000. Forensic psychologist with criminal defendants who may be mentally retarded, 1987—. Author: Mental Retardation: Nature, Cause and Management, 1974, 3d edit. (with J.G. Olley), 1999, Developmental Disabilities: Psychosocial Aspects, 1991, Does Got Exist: A Primer For the Perplexed, 2009; contbr. articles to profl. jours. With US Army, 1943—45. Mem. APA, Assn., Am. Assn. Mental Retardation. Jewish. Home: 417 Granville Rd Chapel Hill NC 27514-2723 E-mail: gbaroff@bellsouth.net.

BARON, DAVID A., neuropsychiatric researcher, educator; b. Mt. Pleasant, Iowa, Feb. 16, 1953; s. Ned and Ada Paula (Badman) B.; m. Patricia Eileen Strong, July 17, 1954; children: D. Adrew, Shawn M. Student, Emory U., 1971-72, Temple U., 1972-74; DO, Phila. Coll. Osteo. Medicine, 1978; MSEd, U. So. Calif., 1987. Am. Bd. Psychiatry and Neurology, cert. Am. Coll. Psychiatrists. Intern Del. Valley Med. Ctr., Bristol, Pa., 1979; residency U. So. Calif. Sch. Medicine, LA, 1982, fellow, 1983, assoc. prof., 1985-89; dep. clin. dir. Nat. Inst. Mental Health, Bethesda, Md., 1987-92; assoc. prof. pharmacology NY Inst. Tech., LI, 1987—; med. dir. Horsham Clinic, Ambler, Pa., 1992-94; pres., med. dir. First Rsch. Found., Ambler, 1993—; prof. psychiatry and behavioral sci. Temple U. Sch. Medicine, Phila., 1993—, chmn. dept. psychiatry and behavioral sci., 1998—; exec. v.p., med. dir. Neuro-Core Rsch. Ctr., Phila., 1997—. Chmn. dept. psychiatry Found. Advancement Edn. in Scis., Bethesda, 1989—. Editor-in-chief JACN jour., 1988-; contbr. several artucles to profl. jours. Youth sports coach Wissehickon Recreation Assn., Blue Bell, Pa., 1993—. Fellow Am. Psychiat. Assn. (Roesnick award 1992), Am. Coll. Neuropsychiatrists (pres. 1991-92), Phila. Coll. Physicians; mem. AMA, AAAS, Am. Osteo. Assn., Am. Coll. Psychiatrists, World Psychiatric Assn., Nat. Bd. Osteopathic Med. Examiners, Am. Coll. Osteo. Neurologists and Psychiatrists, Acad. Sports Medicine, Avocations: skiing, scuba diving; photography. Office: Temple Univ Sch Medicine Dept Psychiatry and Behavioral Sci 3420 N Broad St Philadelphia PA 19140 Business E-Mail: dbaron@temple.edu.

BARON, JACQUELINE MARIE, psychologist, educator; b. Toledo, 1980; PhD, U. Fla., 2011. Rschr. U. Fla., 2003—, rsch. cons., survey rsch. ctr., 2008, undergrad. advisor, 2008—10, instr., dept. psychology, 2010. Recipient Gerber Devel. Rsch. award, U. Fla., Leighton E. Cluff Aging Related Rsch. award. Mem.: APA (Rsch. Proposal award), Gerontol. Soc. Am. Avocations: travel, yoga. Home: 6022 NW 37th Dr Gainesville FL 32653 Personal E-mail: jacquelinembaron@gmail.com.

BARON, JEFFREY, retired pharmacologist; b. Bklyn., July 10, 1942; m. Judith Carol Rothberg, June 27, 1965; children: Stephanie Ann, Leslie Beth, Melissa Leigh. BS in Pharmacy, U. Conn., 1965; PhD in Pharmacology, U. Mich., 1969. Rsch. fellow in biochemistry U. Tex. Southwestern Med. Sch., Dallas, 1969-71, rsch. asst. prof. biochemistry and pharmacology, 1971-72; from asst. prof. pharmacology to prof. emeritus U. Iowa, Iowa City, 1972—2002, prof. emeritus, 2002—. Mem. chem. pathology study sect. NIH, Bethesda, Md., 1983—87, mem. environ. health scis. rev. com., Nat. Inst. Environ. Health Scis., Research Triangle Park, NC, 1990—94. Contbr. chapters to books, articles to profl. jours. Recipient Rsch. Career Devel. award, NIH, 1975—80. Mem.: Internat. Soc. Study Xenobiotics, Soc. Toxicology, Am. Assn. Cancer Rsch., Am. Soc. Biochem. and Molecular Biology, Am. Soc. Pharmacology and Exptl. Therapeutics. Jewish. Achievements include discovery of the role of heme synthesis in regulating the induction of cytochrome P450 in liver; participation in the discovery of oxygenated cytochrome P450; research in immunohistochemical localization of cytochromes P450 and other xenobiotic-metabolizing enzymes in liver and extrahepatic tissues. Personal E-mail: jeffrey-baron@uiowa.edu.

BARON, JEROME, research scientist, educator; b. Paris, June 19, 1972; BSc in Neurosci., Sussex U., 1994; DPhil in Physiology, Oxford U., 2000. Scientist Max-Planck Inst. Brain Rsch., Germany, 1999—2002; prof. Fed. U., Minas Gerais, Brazil, 2004—. Avocation: farming. Office: Av Antônio Carlos 6627 Pampulha UFMG Belo Horizonte Minas Gerais CEP 31270-901 Brazil E-mail: jbaron@icb.ufmg.br.

BARON, JOSEPH MANDEL, hematologist; b. Oak Park, Ill., 1938; BS in BioChemistry, U. Chgo., 1958; MD, U. Chgo. Pritzker Sch. Medicine, 1962; MS in Pharmacology, U. Chgo., 1962. Diplomate Am. Bd. Internal Medicine, Am. Bd. Hematology, Am. Bd. Med. Oncology. Intern U. Chgo. Hosps., 1962—63, resident internal medicine, 1963—64, 1966—68, fellow hematology, 1967—68, assoc. prof. medicine, hematology and oncology, 1975—. Office: Univ Chgo MC 2115 5841 S Maryland Ave Chicago IL 60637 Office Phone: 773-702-6114.

BARON, MELVIN FARRELL, pharmacy educator; b. LA, July 29, 1932; s. Leo Ben and Sadie (Bauchman) B.; m. Lorraine Ross, Dec. 20, 1953; children: Lynn Baron Friedman, Ross David. PharmD, U. So. Calif., 1957, MPA, 1973. Lic. pharmacist, Calif. Pres. Shield Health Care Ctrs., Van Nuys, Calif., 1957-83; dir. externship program U. So. Calif., LA, 1991—; v.p. Shield Health Care Ctrs., Inc. (C.R. Bard, Inc. subsidiary), 1983-86; pres. Merit Coll., 1988-92, Pharma-Com., LA, 1990—; assoc. prof. clin. pharmacy U. So. Calif., LA, 1991—, asst. dean pharm. care programs, 1995—97, dir. PharmD/MBA program, asst. dean programmatic advancement, 1998—; prin. New Horizon Pharmacy Cons. Adj. asst. prof. U. without Walls, Shaw U., Raleigh, NC, 1973; project dir. Haynes Found. Drug Rsch. Ctr., U. So. Calif., LA, 1973; assoc. dir. Calif. Alcoholism Found., 1973—75; adj. asst. prof. clin. pharmacy Sch. Pharmacy, U. So. Calif., 1981—91; cons. Topanga Terr. Convalescent Hosp., 1970—80, Calif. Labor Mgmt. Plan of alcoholism programs and coords., 1974, Office of Alcoholism, State of Calif., Nat. In-Home Health Svc., 1975, Continuity of Life Team, 1975, Triad Med., Longs Drug Stores, HealthTek, others; vis. prof. Tokyo Coll. Pharmacy, 1994, Sandoz Pharm. Co., 1995, Clin Oscar Romero, 2000; lectr. Meijo U., Nagoya U., Japan, 1994; presenter Nat. Pharmacy Dir. Conf., 1995; cons., mem. sci. adv. bd. Leiner Health Products, 1998—; cons. Prime Care Pharmacy, 1998—, Jackson Meml. Hosp., 1998, New Horizon Pharmacy, Avalon Hosp., Queenscare Family Clinics; cons., mem. adv. bd. Medpin, 2001; chair nominating com. CPHA, 1998; co-developer Trends in Healthcare Svcs.; presenter in field. Adv. bd. Pharmacist Newsletter, 1980—. Chmn. Friends of Operation Bootstrap, 1967-77; svc. chmn. tng. coord. Am. Cancer Soc., San Fernando Valley, Calif., 1980; mem. adv. bd. L.A. VNA, 1982; bd. dirs. pres. QSAD, 1987-88; pres. bd. Everywoman's Village, 1988-89; bd. dirs. Life Svcs., 1988-94; pres. bd. counselors, U. So. Calif., 1988-92, co-chmn. good neighborhood campaign Sch. Pharmacy, 1998; mem. Calif. Bd. Pharmacy Com. on Student/Preceptor Manual, 1991-92, Named Disting. Alumnus of Yr., U. So. Calif., Sch. of Pharmacy Alumni Assn. 1983, U. So. Calif. Torchbearer, 1990-91, Hon. Tchr. of Yr. U. So. Calif. Sch. Pharmacy, 1997, Top Pharmacist of Yr.; recipient Outlook award, 2008, AACP Inaugural award, Transformative Cmty. Svc., 2008. Fellow Am. Coll. Apothecaries, Calif. Pharmacist Assn. (chair edn. com., named Pharmacist of Yr., Ca. State Legis. Resolution, 2007-08); mem. Am. Pharmacist Assn. (Found. Pinnacle award, USC Cmty. Pharmacy Group, 2007), Am. Soc. Health Sys. Pharmacists (Best Practices award, USC Cmty. Pharmacy Group, 2008), Am. Soc. Pub. Adminstrn., Am. Assn. Colls. of Pharmacy (spkr. ann. meeting 2000), Phi Kappa Phi, Phi Lambda Sigma (hon., faculty advisor), Rho Chi. Home: 1245 Wellesley Ave Apt 201 Los Angeles CA 90025-1170 Office: 1985 Zonal Ave Los Angeles CA 90089-0105 Office Phone: 323-442-2686. Business E-Mail: mbaron@usc.edu.

BARON, REBECCA, physician; b. Chgo., Sept. 14, 1968; MD, Harvard Med. Sch., 1994. Physician Brigham and Women's Hosp., 2002. Office: 75 Francis St Boston MA 02115 Business E-Mail: rbaron@partners.org.

BARON, REBECCA M., critical care specialist, educator; MD, Harvard U., 1994. Diplomate Am Bd. Internal Medicine- critical care medicine, 2001, Am. Bd. Internal Medicine, 2007, Am Bd. Internal Medicine- pulmonary disease, 2009. Instr. in medicine Med. Sch. Harvard Univ.; resident in internal medicine Brigham and Women's Hosp., Boston, 1995—97, resident in pulmonary critical care medicine, 1999—2000, fellow in pulmonary critical care medicine, 1997—99, 2000—02, critical care specialist. Co-author: IFN regulatory factor-1 regulates IFN-gamma-dependent cathepsin S expression, 2002, Constitutive and cytokine-induced expression of the ETS transcription factor ESE-3 in the lung, 2002, High-mobility group-I/Y proteins: Potential role in the pathophysiology of critical illnesses, 2002, DNA sequence variants in epithelium-specific ETS-2 and ETS-3 are not associated with asthma, 2002, Cyclooxygenase-2-deficient mice are resistant to endotoxin-induced inflammation and death, 2003, Elk-3 is a transcriptional repressor of nitric-oxide synthase 2, 2003. Office: Brigham and Women's Hospital 15 Francis St Boston MA 02115-7750 Office Phone: 617-732-6770.

BARON, RICCARDO, computational chemistry researcher; b. Milan, Aug. 25, 1977; PhD, ETH Zurich, 2006. Asst. prof. medicinal chemistry U. Utah, Sch. Pharmacy, 2011; postdoc. rsch. assoc. HHMI, UC San Diego, 2006—. Editor Humana Press, Springer, 2010—11. Recipient Premio Alfredo di Braccio prize, Accademia Nat. Lincei, Italy, 2010; Socrates/Erasmus fellowship, U. Cambridge, Eng., EU Cmty. Mem.: Swiss Chem. Soc., Am. Chem. Soc. (Postdoc. Rsch. award 2010). Avocations: sailing, piano. Office: L S Skaggs Pharmacy Physical Chemistry Divsn 30 S 2000 E Salt Lake City UT 84112-5820 Office Phone: 801-585-7117. Business E-Mail: rbaron@ucsd.edu, r.baron@utah.edu.

BARONDES, SAMUEL HERBERT, psychiatrist, educator; b. Bklyn., Dec. 21, 1933; s. Solomon and Yetta (Kaplow) B.; m. Ellen Slater, Sept. 1, 1963 (dec. Nov. 22, 1971); children: Elizabeth Francesca, Jessica Gabrielle; m. Louann Brizendine, Sept. 14, 2002. AB, Columbia U., 1954, MD, 1958. Intern, then asst. resident in medicine Peter Bent Brigham Hosp., Boston, 1958-60; sr. asst. surgeon USPHS, NIH, Bethesda, Md., 1960-63; resident in psychiatry McLean and Mass. Gen. hosps., Boston, 1963-66; asst. prof., then assoc. prof. psychiatry and molecular biology Albert Einstein Coll. Medicine., Bronx, NY, 1966-69; prof. psychiatry U. Calif., San Diego, 1969-86, prof., chmn. dept. psychiatry, dir. Langley Porter Psychiat. Inst. San Francisco, 1986-94, dir. Ctr. Neurobiology and Psychiatry, 1994—, Jeanne and Sanford Robertson Prof. Neurobiol. and Psychiatry, 1996—. Pres. McKnight Endowment Fund for Neurosci., 1989-98; sci. adv. com. Rsch. Am.; governing coun. Internat. Brain Rsch. Orgn., 1994-2000; bd. sci. counselors NIMH, 1997-2002, chair, 2000-02. Author: Molecules and Mental Illness, 1993, Mood Genes, 1998, Better Than Prozac, 2003; mem. editl. bd. profl. jours.; contbr. articles to profl. jours. Recipient Rsch. Career Devel. award USPHS, 1967, Elliott Royer award, 1989, P.H. Stillmark medal Estonia, 1989; Fogarty Internat. scholar NIH, 1979; J. Robert Oppenheimer lectr., 2000. Fellow AAAS, Am. Psychiat. Assn., Am. Coll. Neuropsychopharmacology; mem. Inst. Medicine Nat. Acad. Sci., Am. Acad. Arts & Scis. Office: U Calif-San Francisco Langley Porter Psychiat Ins 401 Parnassus Ave San Francisco CA 94143-0984 Business E-Mail: barondes@cgl.ucsf.edu.

BARONDESS, JEREMIAH ABRAHAM, physician; b. NYC, June 6, 1924; s. Benjamin and Dora (Greenberg) B.; m. Sue Kaufman, Nov. 22, 1953 (dec. 1977); 1 child, James Joseph; m. Linda Hiddemen, Dec. 10, 1982. MD, Johns Hopkins U., Balt., 1949; DSc (hon.), Albany Med. Coll., Union U., 1978; LittD (hon.), NY Inst. Tech., Old Westbury, 1992; DMedSci (hon.), Med. Coll. Pa., 1993; DSc (hon.), NY Med. Coll., 1998. Diplomate Am. Bd. Internal Medicine (bd. govs., council gen. internal medicine 1975-81). Intern, then asst. resident in medicine Osler Med. Svc. Johns Hopkins Hosp., 1949-51; asst. medicine Johns Hopkins U. Med. Sch., 1950-51; staff virology sect., rsch. divsn. Children's Hosp., Phila.; rsch. fellow virology U. Pa. Med. Sch., 1951-53; asst. resident, then chief resident in medicine NY Hosp.-Cornell U. Med. Center, 1953-55; faculty Cornell U. Med. Coll., 1953—, clin. prof. medicine, 1971-78, prof. clin. medicine, 1978-87, Irene F. and I. Roy Psaty disting. prof. clin. medicine, 1987-89, William T. Foley Disting.prof. clin. medicine, 1989-90, adj. prof. clin. medicine, 1990, prof. emeritus, 1993—, prof. clin. pub. health, 2006—; staff NY Hosp., 1953—, attending physician, 1971—, chief pvt. med. svc., 1971-92, hon. staff mem., 1992—, assoc. chmn. dept. medicine, 1983-90; asst. vis. physician Bellevue Hosp., 1960-67; cons. medicine Meml. Hosp. Cancer and Allied Diseases, 1972-90; Alpha Omega Alpha vis. prof. U. P.R. Med. Sch., 1972; Meyerowitz meml. lectr. U. Rochester Sch. Medicine, 1980. Disting. lectr. U. NC, 1982; vis. prof. medicine U. Ill. Med. Sch., 1974, U. Va. Med. Sch., 1976, Mayo Clinic and Med. Sch., 1978, U. Iowa Sch. Medicine, 1979, U. Tex. Med. Ctr., 1986, 90, U. Pa., 1986, U. Va., 1989, NY Med. Coll., 1990, Alpha Omega Alpha vis. prof. medicine, 2006; vis. prof. medicine SUNY Health Sci. Ctr., Bklyn., 1992; mem. nat. resources com. Johns Hopkins U., 1965—, trustee, 1977—94, trustee emeritus, 1994—, chmn. vis. com. Sch. Medicine, 1978—92. Author: (with A.M. Harvey and J. Bordley) Differential Diagnosis, (with J. McGovern and C. Roland) The Persisting Osler, 1985, (with A.H. Samiy and R.G. Douglas) Textbook of Diagnostic Medicine, 1987, (with C. Roland) The Persisting Osler II, 1994, (with C. Roland) The Persisting Osler III, 2002; editor: Diagnostic Approaches to Presenting Syndromes, 1971; co-editor Differential Diagnosis, 1994, mem. editl. bd. Forum on Medicine, Pharos, Internat. Jour. Technol. Assessment in Health Care, Jour. Royal Soc. Med.; contbr. articles to profl. jours. Bd. dirs. Am. Fedn. Aging Rsch., 1996-2001. With AUS, 1943-46, USPHS, 1951-53 Recipient Wiggers award Albany Med. Coll. Union U., 1978, Alfred Stengel award ACP, 1983; named Hon. Alumnus Cornell U. Med. Coll., 1974. Fellow AAAS, Am. Acad. Arts and Scis., Royal Coll. Physicians London, ACP (chmn. bd. govs. 1973-75, bd. regents 1975—, pres. 1978-79, pres. emeritus 1988), Federated Coun. Internal Medicine, Royal Soc. Medicine (hon. 2005), Royal Soc. Health, Royal Coll. Physicians Ireland (hon.); mem. Am. Clin. and Climatol. Assn. (coun. 1973-78, pres. 1994), Am. Osler Soc. (pres. 1983-84), Am. Fedn. Clin. Rsch., APHA, Assn. Am. Physicians, Harvey Soc., NY Heart Assn., Inst. Medicine NAS (coun. 1979-81, co-chair coun. on health care tech., chair com. on managed care and chronic disease 1996, chair com. on musculoskeletal disorders and the workplace 1999-01, mem. com. on spinal cord injury, 2004-05), The NY Acad. Scis., The NY Acad. Medicine (pres. 1990 2006, pres. emeritus 2006—), Internat. Soc. Internal Medicine, Phi Beta Kappa, Alpha Omega Alpha (dir. 1978-79, pres. 1987-89), Century Assn-.(NYC), Cosmos Club (Washington). Jewish. Home: 544 E 86th St New York NY 10028-7536 Office: NY Acad Medicine 1216 5th Ave New York NY 10029-5202 Business E-Mail: jbaronde@nyam.org.

BAROODY, FUAD, pediatrician, educator; b. Beirut; MD, Am. U., Beirut, 1984. Diplomate Am. Bd. Pediat., cert. in otolaryngology. Intern Am. U. Beirut Med. Ctr., 1983—86, resident, 1986—88; fellow Johns Hopkins U., Balt., 1988—92; asst. prof. Johns Hopkins Sch. Med., 1992—94, U. Chgo. Med. Ctr., 1994—2001, prof. surgery/pediat., 2001—, dir. pediatric otolaryngology. Contbr. articles to profl. jours., chapters to books. Mem.: ACS, Chgo. Laryngological & Otological Soc., Am. Soc. Pediatric Otolaryngology, Am. Acad. Otolaryngology-Head & Neck Surgery, Am. Acad. Otolaryngic Allergy, Am. Acad. Allergy Asthma & Immunology. Office: U Chgo Med Ctr 5841 S Maryland Ave MC 1035 Chicago IL 60637 Office Phone: 773-702-4790. Office Fax: 773-702-6809. Business E-Mail: fbaroody@surgery.bsd.uchicago.edu.

BAROUCH, DAN HUNG, physician, scientist, educator; b. Gottingen, Germany, Feb. 4, 1973; s. Eytan and Winifred Wendy B.; m. Fina Canas, May 15, 1999. BA summa cum laude, Harvard U., Cambridge, Mass., 1993, MD summa cum laude, 1999; PhD, Oxford U., Eng., 1995. Diplomate in internal medicine and infectious diseases Am. Bd. Internal Medicine. Rschr. HIV immunology and vaccines Oxford U., 1993-95; rschr. Beth Israel Deaconess Med. Ctr., Boston, 1995—; resident in internal medicine Mass. Gen. Hosp., Boston, 1999—2001; fellow infectious diseases Mass. Gen. Hosp./Brigham Women's Hosp., Boston, 2001—04; staff physician infectious diseases Brigham and Women's Hosp., Boston, 2004—, Beth Israel Deaconess Med. Ctr., 2004—, chief Divsn. Vaccine Rsch., 2009—; clin. fellow in medicine Harvard Med. Sch., Boston, 1999—2002, instr. in medicine, 2002—04, asst. prof., 2004—06, assoc. prof., 2006—10, prof. medicine, 2010—. Investigator HIV Vaccine Trials Network, Boston, 2000—. Contbr. rsch. articles to profl. jours. and textbooks. British Marshall scholar Marshall Commn., 1993-95, Barry M. Goldwater scholar U.S. Govt., 1991-93, USA Today Coll. scholar, 1993; recipient Ptnrs. in Excellence award Mass. Gen. Hosp., 2002, Maxwell Finland Investigator award Mass. Infectious Diseases Soc., 2004. Mem.: AAAS, ACP, AMA, Am. Soc. Clin. Investigation, Am. Assn. Immunologists, Am. Soc. for Microbiology, Mass. Med. Soc., Infectious Diseases Soc. Am., Mass. Infectious Diseases Soc. Avocations: calligraphy, violin, skiing, travel. Office: Beth Israel Deaconess Med

Ctr E/CLS 1047 Divsn Vaccine Research 330 Brookline Ave Boston MA 02215 Home: 115 Willard St Newton Highlands MA 02461 Office Phone: 617-735-4485. Business E-Mail: dbarouch@bidmc.harvard.edu.

BAROUCH, LILI, cardiologist, educator; b. Boston, June 28, 1971; BA, Harvard U., 1992; MD, Johns Hopkins U., 1996. Asst. prof. Johns Hopkins U. Sch. Medicine, 2003—. Fellow: Am. Coll. Cardiology, Am. Heart Assn. Avocations: violin, running. Office: 720 Rutland Ave Ross 1050 Baltimore MD 21205 Business E-Mail: barouch@jhmi.edu.

BAROUDY, BAHIGE MOURAD, biochemist, researcher; b. Beirut, July 1, 1950; came to U.S., 1973, naturalized, 1988; s. Mourad Bahige and Ludmila Adelheid (Obermuller-Haddad) BSc, Am. U. of Beirut, 1972; PhD, Georgetown U., 1978. Teaching asst. Wesleyan U., Middletown, Conn., 1973-74; rsch. asst. Georgetown U., Washington, 1974-78, fellow, 1982, rsch. assoc. prof., 1985-89; dir. molecular virology div. James N. Gamble Inst. Med. Rsch., Cin., 1989-95; assoc. dir. antiviral therapy Schering-Plough Rsch. Ins., Kenilworth, NJ, 1996-2000, dir., 2000—01, group dir., 2001—02, group dir. antiviral and antimicrobial therapy, 2002—03; v.p. drug discovery Avance Pharma, Laval, Que., Canada, 2003—05; pres. CSO Millenia Hope Inc., Montreal, Quebec, 2006—; CSO Millenia Hope Biopharma, Kirkland, 2006—, pres., 2007—. Vis. fellow scientist NIH, Bethesda, Md., 1979-81, vis. assoc. scientist, 1982-85. Contbr. articles to profl. jours., chpts. to books. Mem. Am. Assn. for Study of Liver Diseases, Am. Chem. Soc., Am. Soc. Biochemistry and Molecular Biology, Am. Soc. for Microbiology, Am. Soc. for Virology, N.Y. Acad. Scis., NIH Alumni Assn., Sigma Xi. Lutheran. Avocations: fencing, viola, skiing. Address: Millenia Hope Inc 1250 Rene Levesque W Ste 2200 Montreal PQ H3B 4WB Canada Business E-Mail: bahige.baroudy@mh-b.com.

BARQAWI, ALBAHA Z., urologist, educator, researcher; m. Dina A. Abu-Hilal, Dec. 9, 1995; children: Natasha A., Zuhair A., Sandra Jean. B of Medicine, Med. Acad., Sofia, Bulgaria, 1990. Resident in surgery Royal Coll. Surgeons, Dublin, 1993—98; registrar in gen. surgery/urology Portlaoise Gen. Hosp., Laois, Ireland, 1998—99; hon. fellow Leicester Gen. Hosp., 1999—2000; specialist registrar Worthing Gen. Hosp., West Sussex; clin. instr. dept. oncology and urology U. Colo., Denver, 2000—. Prin. investigator U. Colo. Health Sci. Ctr., Denver. Contbr. articles to profl. jours. Fellow: Royal Coll. Surgeons, Royal Acad. Medicine in Ireland (life). Avocation: travel. Office: Univ Colo Health Sci Ctr 4200 E 9th Ave C-319 Denver CO 80262 Home: 8940 E Berry Ave Greenwood Village CO 80111 Office Phone: 720-848-0568. Business E-Mail: al.barqawi@ucdenver.edu.

BARR, CHARLES C., medical educator; b. Louisville, Feb. 14, 1949; MD, Johns Hopkins U., Balt., 1975. Prof. U. Louisville Sch. Medicine, 1991—. Recipient Sr. Honor award, Am. Acad. Ophthalmology. Mem.: Retina Soc. Avocation: golf. Office: 301 E Muhammad Ali Blvd Louisville KY 40202 E-mail: ccbarr@pol.net.

BARR, MARTIN, science educator, academic administrator; b. Phila., Nov. 11, 1925; s. Louis and Bella (Moskowitz) B.; m. Nancy Lipschutz, July 15, 1951; children: Lawrence Allen, Richard Andrew, Debra Ann, Steven Bruce. B.Sc. in Pharmacy, Temple U., 1946; M.Sc. in Pharmacy, Phila. Coll. Pharmacy and Scis., 1947; PhD, Ohio State U., 1950. Grad. asst., then instr. Ohio State U. Coll. Pharmacy, 1947-50; from asst. prof. pharmacy to prof. phys. pharmacy and pharm. research Phila. Coll. Pharmacy and Sci., 1950-61; prof. pharmaceutics Wayne State U. Coll. Pharmacy, 1961-87, prof. emeritus, 1987—, chmn. dept., 1961-63, dean, 1963-72, v.p. spl. assignments, 1972-76, v.p., sec. to bd. govs., 1976-78, sec. to bd. govs., acting v.p. for health affairs, 1978-80, v.p., dep. provost, 1980-82, dean Coll. Pharmacy and Allied Health Professions, 1982-87; exec. v.p. corp. bus. and med. devel. Mich. Health Care Corp., Detroit, 1987-90, v.p. bd., profl. rels., 1990-92, v.p. continuous quality improvement, 1992-95. Cons. HEW, 1964-69 Contbg. author: Pharmacy, Compounding and Dispensing, 2d edit, 1956, Remington's Practice of Pharmacy, 11th edit, 1956, 12th edit., 1965; Profl. editor: Mid-Atlantic Apothecary, 1953-64, Apothecary, 1953-64, Central Pharm. Jour, 1961-64. Chmn. Mayor's Com. Rehab. Narcotics Addiction, Detroit, 1971-73; pres. Oakland County unit Mich. Heart Assn., 1970-72; chmn. Spectrum Cmty. Svcs., 2003-04; chmn. task force health care costs, del. pers. health svcs. Comprehensive Health Planning Adv. Coun., Mich., 1971. Recipient Disting. Service award, Disitng. Alumnus award Alumni Assn. Coll. Pharmacy, Temple U., 1957, Disting. Alumnus award Temple U., 1964, Alpha Zeta Omega award, 1979, Meritorious Service award Wayne State U. Pharm. Alumni Assn., Ann. Alumus award Phila. Coll. Pharmacy and Sci., 1983, John H. Webster award Met. Detroit Pharmacist Assn., 1985, Disting. alumnus award Pharmacy Alumni Assn., 1987, Jack L. Beal Postbaccalaureate award Ohio State U. Coll. Pharmacy Alumni Assn., 1989, Disting. Svc. award Wayne State U. Pharmacy Alumni Assn., 1993, Advocate award Detroit Occupl. Therapy Assn., 1995; named Mich. Med. Assistance Program Counselor of Yr., 2006. Fellow Am. Coll. Apothecaries, Acad. Pharm. Scis.; mem. Am. Pharm. Assn. (pres. Phila. br. 1954-55, chmn. sci. sect. 1959-60, Ebert medal 1956), Am. Soc. Hosp. Pharmacists, Mich. State Pharm. Assn. (pharmacist of yr. 1971), Am. Assn. Colls. Pharmacy (chmn. sect. tchrs. pharmacy 1959-60, chmn. conf. tchrs. pharmacy 1961-62), Inst. Ret. Profls. (lectr. 2001-), Vis. Nurse Assn. S.E. Mich. (chmn. 1999-2002), Vis. Nurse Assn. Inc. (life, chmn. 2004-06, elected hon. bd. dirs.), Sigma Xi, Rho Chi., Presbyn. Village Mich. (ethics com. mem. 2008-). Home: 7430 Tall Timbers West Bloomfield MI 48322-1082 Personal E-mail: mbarr@nshore.net, martinbarr1111@gmail.com.

BARR, RONALD JEFFREY, dermatologist, pathologist; b. Mpls., Jan. 5, 1945; s. Maxwell Michael and Ethel Deana (Ring) B.; m. Ulla Elisabet Edstam; children: Anna, Jessica, Sara. BA, Johns Hopkins U., 1967, MD, 1970. Diplomate Am. Bd. Pathology, Am. Bd. Dermatology. Intern U. Calif., San Diego, 1970-71, resident in pathology, 1971-75, resident in dermatology Irvine, 1975-78, fellow in dermatopathology, 1975-78, asst. prof. dermatology, 1977-83, assoc. prof. dermatology and pathology, 1983-86, prof. dermatology and pathology, 1987—2005, dir. Dermatopathology Lab., 1979—2005, prof., chmn. dept. dermatology Davis, 1986-87, emeritus prof. dermatology and pathology. Bd. dirs. Am. Bd. Dermatology, 1989-1998, pres., 1997. Contbr. more than 10 chpts. to books. more than 140 articles to profl. jours. Lt. USN, 1971-73. Fellow Am. Soc. Dermatopathology (pres. 1988-89); mem. Internat. Soc. Dermatopathology, Internat. Com. for Dermatopathology (sec.-treas. 1987-91, pres. 1992-93). Office: Laguna Pathology Med Group Mission Hosp Laguna Beach 31872 Coast Hwy Laguna Beach CA 92651 Office Phone: 949-499-7288. E-mail: rjbarr@uci.edu. *

BARR, SANFORD LEE, dentist; b. Chgo., Jan. 18, 1952; s. Mike and Bernice (Kaplan) B.; m. Randy Joyce Briskman, Dec. 24, 1973; children: Shelby Paige, Blake Jared, Taylor Ashley. BS, U. Ill., 1972; DDS, Northwestern U., 1976. Resident gen. practice VA Hosp., Chgo., 1976-77; gen. practice dentistry Chgo., 1977—. Attending dentist Rush Med. Coll., Chgo., 1977—; asst. prof. Presbyn.-St. Luke's Hosp., Chgo., 1977—, Northwestern U. Sch. Dentistry, Chgo., 1977-83; cons. VA Hosp., Chgo., 1978—. Mem. adv. bd. Homehealth of Ill. Chgo., 1984—. Fellow Acad. Gen. Dentistry, Acad. Facial Aesthetics; mem. ADA, Acad. Hosp. Dentistry, Chgo. Dental Soc., Alpha Omega (treas. 1984, pres. elect 1988), Tau Delta Phi. Lodges: B'nai B'rith (v.p. Chgo. chpt. 1984—). Jewish. Avocations: computers, photography, golf, baseball. Home: 632 Dauphine Ct Northbrook IL 60062-2256 Office: 25 E Washington St Chicago IL 60602-1708 Office Phone: 312-372-4844. Business E-Mail: drsbarr@sanfordbarr.dds.com.

BARRA, ENRIQUE, psychology professor; b. Concepción, Chile, Sept. 30, 1949; Degree in Psychology, U. Chile, 1973; MA, U. Mo., 1988. Assoc. prof. U. Concepción, 1978—. Mem.: APA. Home: Paicavi 521 Dp 202 Concepción Octava 403 0432 Chile Business E-Mail: ebarra@udec.cl.

BARRA, JULIEN, psychology professor; b. France, Feb. 20, 1978; PhD, U. Grenoble 2, 2007. Assoc. prof. U. Paris 5, 2009—. Office: 71 Ave Edouard Vaillant Boulogne-Billancourt 92774 France Business E-Mail: julien.barra@college-de-france.fr.

BARRABES, JOSE A., cardiologist; b. Huesca, Spain, June 13, 1962; MD, U. de Zaragoza, 1986; PhD in Medicine, U. Autonoma de Barcelona, 2000. Resident, cardiology Hosp. U. Vall d'Hebron, 1988—92, med. staff, 1993—. Assoc. editor Cardiovasc. Rsch., 2003; assoc. prof., dept. medicine U. Autonoma de Barcelona, 2006; vice chmn. Working Group Ischemic Heart Disease Spanish Soc. Cardiology, 2006—09, chmn., 2009. Recipient prize, Spanish Soc. Cardiology; grant, Inst. de Salud Carlos III Spanish Health Ministry, Spanish Soc. Cardiology. Fellow: European Soc. Cardiology; mem.: Am. Coll. Cardiology, Spanish Soc. Cardiology. Office: PG Vall d'Hebron 119 Barcelona 08035 Spain Business E-Mail: jabarrabes@vhebron.net.

BARRASSO, JOHN ANTHONY, United States Senator from Wyoming, orthopedic surgeon; b. Reading, Pa., July 21, 1952; s. John A. and Louise M. (DeCisco) Barrasso; m. Linda D. Nix, May 6, 1978 (div.); children: Peter, Emma, Hadley; m. Bobbi Brown, Jan. 1, 2008. BS, Georgetown U., Washington, 1974, MD, 1978. Diplomate Am. Bd. Orthopaedic Surgeons. Resident Yale-New Haven Hosp., 1978-83; orthopedic surgeon Casper Orthopedic Associates, Wyo., 1983—2007; chief of staff Wyo. Med. Ctr., 2003—05; mem. Dist. 27 Wyo. State Senate, 2003—07, mem. minerals, bus. & econ. devel. com., labor, health & social services com., 2003—05, chmn. transp., highways & mil. affairs com., 2005—07; US Senator from Wyo., 2007—; vice chmn. US Senate Indian Affairs Com., 2009—, US Senate Republican Conf., 2011—. Treas. Republican Nat. Com., 1991—92; del. Republican Nat. Conv., 1992, 2004, leader, delegation to Rep. of China, 1994. Pres. United Way Natrona County, Wyo. Health Fairs; emcee Jerry Lewis Labor Day Telethon, Wyo.'s K-2 TV. Recipient Ken Alvord Cmty. Svc. award, Nat. Assn. Medical Communicators, 1992, Wyo. Physician of the Yr. award, Medal of Excellence, Wyo. Nat. Guard, Legis. Svc. award, Veterans Fgn. Wars, Congressional award, Small Bus. Coun. of America, 2010, Friend of Farm Bur. award, Wyo. Farm Bur. Fedn., 2010; named one of The 10 Members to Watch in the 112th Congress, Roll Call, 2011. Mem.: Nat. Assn. Physician Broadcasters (pres. 1988—89), Wyo. Med. Soc. (pres.). Republican. Office: US Senate 307 Dirksen Senate Office Bldg Washington DC 20510 also: 100 E B St Ste 2201 Casper WY 82601 Office Phone: 202-224-6441. Office Fax: 202-224-1724. *

BARREDO, JULIO C., physician, educator; b. Lima, Peru, Nov. 19, 1953; MD, U. Miami Miller Sch. Medicine, 1981. Prof. U. Miami Miller Sch. Medicine, 2006—, dir. pediat. oncology, 2006. Office: 1611 NW 12th Ave R-131 Miami FL 33136 Office Phone: 305-585-5635. Business E-Mail: jbarredo@med.miami.edu.

BARREDO, RONALD DE VERA, physical therapist, educator; b. Quezon City, Philippines, Apr. 24, 1969; s. Rodolfo Garcia and Josefina De Vera Barredo; m. Maria Adora Simpas, Aug. 7, 2001; children: Rubric Michael children: Ryan Christopher. BS in Phys. Therapy, U. of the Philippines, Manila, 1990; MA in Orgnl. Mgmt., Trevecca Nazarene U., Nashville, 1995, EdD in profl. Practics, 2002. Diplomate Am. Bd. Phys. Therapy Specialties; lic. physical therapist Tenn., Okla., Ark. Program dir., phys. therapist asst. and massage therapy programs Kaskaskia Coll., Centralia, Ill., 2000—05; assoc. prof. grad. program in physical therapy Ark. State U., State University, 2005—. Vis. faculty mem. phys. therapy program Langston (Okla.) U., 2003—; bd. dirs. Fgn. Credentialing Commn. in Phys. Therapy, Alexandria, Va., 2002—, Christian Phys. Therapists Internat., NJ, 2000—. Recipient President's Disting. Pub. Svc. Award, Tenn. State U., 1999. Mem.: Am. Phys. Therapy Assn. (chmn. awards com. 2003—04), Toastmasters Internat. (dist. gov. 1999—2000, Select Disting. Dist. Gov. 2000, Disting. Toastmaster award 1997). Office: Ark State Univ Grad Program in Phys Therapy PO Box 910 State University AR 72467 Business E-Mail: rbarredo@nstate.edu.

BARRER, STEVEN J., neurosurgeon, director; Attended, U. Pa.; MD, Drexel U., Phila., 1972—76. Diplomate Am. Bd. Neurol. Surgery. Intern in surgery Univ. Chgo. Hosp. and Clinics, 1976—77; resident in neurosurgery Hosp. Univ. Pa., 1977—82; fellow in pediatric neurosurgery Children's Hosp. Phila., 1980—81; asst. surgeon Abington Meml. Hosp., Pa., 1986—90, assoc. surgeon, 1990—98, sr. surgeon, 1998—, chief neurosurgery divsn., 2000—, dir. neurosciences inst., 2009—. Author: various publs. Named one of Top Doctors, Phila. Mag., 2010—11. Fellow: Am. Cancer Soc., ACS; mem.: Pediatric Neurol. Surgery, Brain Attack Coalition, Montgomery County Med. Soc., Am. Assn. of Neurol. Surgeons. Office: Abington Memorial Hospital 1200 Old York Rd Abington PA 19001 Office Phone: 215-657-5886. Office Fax: 215-657-9996.

BARRERA, ELVIRA PUIG, retired counselor, academic administrator, educational program evaluator; b. Alice, Tex., Dec. 11, 1943; d. Carlos Rogers and Delia Rebeca (Puig) B.; 1 child, Dennis Lee Cheatham, Jr. BA, Incarnate Word Coll., 1971; M Counseling and Guidance, St. Mary's U., San Antonio, 1978; specialist degree marriage and family therapy, St. Mary's U., 1989. Lic. profl. counselor, marriage & family therapist, lic. chem. dependency counselor. Tchr. Edgewood Ind. Sch. Dist., San Antonio, 1965—74, Dallas Ind. Sch. Dist., 1971—72, Northside Ind. Sch. Dist., San Antonio, 1974; ednl. cons. Region 20-Edn. Svc. Ctr., San Antonio, 1974—79; coord. career edn. San Antonio Ind. Sch. Dist., 1979—84, counselor, 1984—91, vice prin., 1998—2005; ret., 2005; program evaluator AOC Solutions, Inc., Chantilly, Va., 2006—. Cons. SBA, 1981, U.S. Office Edn., Washington, 1981-82, Tex. Edn. Agy., Austin, 1979-80; cons., writer San Antonio Ind. Sch. Dist. and Tex. Edn. Agy., 1985; cons. various edn. publs.; family coord. CATCH project U. Tex. Health Sci. Ctr., Houston, 1991-94; counselor Austin Ind. Sch. Dist., 1994-97, dist. transition counselor, 1997-98 Chairperson career awareness exploring divsn. Boy Scouts Am., 1982-87. Named Disting. Alumna, Incarnate Word Coll., 1983, Hall of Fame Internat. Profl. and Bus. Women, 1995; recipient Spurgeon award Boy Scouts Am., 1985, Merit award, 1986, Growth award, 1986 Mem. Am. Assn. Marriage and Family Therapy, San Antonio Hash House Harriers (treas. 1990-91), Incarnate Word Coll. Alumni Assn. (adv. bd. 1990—95), St. Mary's U. Alumni Assn. (v.p. Austin alumni chpt. 2003-10), The Harp and Shamrock Soc. Tex., Delta Kappa Gamma (Kappa Beta chpt. 2d v.p. 1982-84, 1st v.p. 1986-88, sec. 2005-06, pres. 2006-10, parliamentarian 10-), Tex. State Orgn. (area 6 coord. 2011-), Pan Am. League. Roman Catholic. Avocation: running. Home: 13711 Oak Cabin San Antonio TX 78232-5427 *

BARRE-SINOUSSI, FRANÇOISE, virologist, researcher; b. Paris, July 30, 1947; d. Roger and Jeanine (Fau) Sinoussi; m. Jean-Claude Barre, Oct. 7, 1978. MS in Biochemistry, U. Paris, 1972; PhD in Virology, Inst. Pasteur, Paris, 1975. Rsch. fellow Inst. Pasteur, Garches, France, 1971-75, rsch. asst. Paris, 1975—80, asst. dir. virology dept., 1978-82, asst. prof., 1980-86, rsch. dir., 1986—, head Retrovirus Biology Lab., 1986—91, prof., head Regulation of Retroviral Infections Unit, 1996—, dep. dir. sci. affairs, 2001—05; post-doctoral fellow NIH, Bethesda, Md., 1975-76. Mem. sci. com. Nat. Inst. Health & Med. Rsch. (INSERM), Paris, 1987—90; mem. virology com. French Agy. AIDS Rsch., 1989—91, pres. virology com., 1993—96, pres. HIV vaccine programme, 1999—2001, mem. adminstrv., 2003—; bd. dirs. World Found. AIDS, 1998—. Recipient European Sci. award, Germany, 1986, French Acad. Medicine award, 1988, King Faisal Internat. prize of medicine, Saudi Arabia, 1993, Nobel prize in physiology/medicine, 2008; named to Women in Tech. Internat. Hall of Fame, 2007. Mem.: French Soc. Microbiology, Am. Soc. Microbiology, Internat. AIDS Soc. Achievements include co-discovery of the human immunodeficiency virus (HIV). Office: Institut Pasteur 25,28 rue du Docteur Roux 75724 Paris France *

BARRETT, BERNARD MORRIS, JR., plastic and reconstructive surgeon; b. Pensacola, Fla., May 3, 1944; s. Bernard Morris and Blanche (Lischkoff) B.; m. Sandra Neal Barrett; children: Beverly Frances, Julie Blaine, Audrey Blake, Bernard Joseph. BS, Tulane U., 1965; MD, U. Miami, 1969. Diplomate Am. Bd. Plastic Surgery. Surg. intern Meth. Hosp. and Ben Taub Hosp., Houston, 1969-70; resident in gen. surgery Baylor Coll. Medicine, Houston, 1970-71, UCLA, 1971-73; resident in plastic surgery U. Miami (Fla.) Affilated Hosps., 1973-75, chief resident in plastic surgery, 1975; fellow in plastic surgery Clinica Ivo Pitanguy, Rio de Janeiro, 1973; instr. surgery Baylor Coll. Medicine, 1970-71, clin. instr. plastic surgery, 1977-80, clin. asst. prof., 1980-90, clin. assoc. prof., 1991-97, clin. prof. surgery, 1997—; instr. surg. emergencies L.A. County Paramedics, 1972-73; plastic surgery coord. for jr. med. students Sch. Medicine U. Miami, 1975; practice medicine specializing in plastic and reconstructive surgery Houston, 1976—. Pres., chmn. bd. dirs. Plastic and Reconstructive Surgeons, P.A., 1978—; chmn. Tex. Inst. Plastic Surgery, Houston; assoc. chief plastic surgery St. Luke's Episcopal Hosp., Houston, 1991—; attending physician Jr. League Clinic, Tex. Children's Hosp., Houston, 1977—; active staff St. Luke's Hosp., Houston, Meth. Hosp., Houston; clin. assoc. in plastic surgery U. Tex. Med. Sch., Houston, 1976—; instr. surg. emergencies Harris County C.C.; dir. Am. Physicians Ins. Exch., Austin, 1976-2003, vice chmn., bd. dirs., 1995—; bd. dirs. Advocate M.D. Ins., Austin, 2004—; past chief of staff, chief plastic surgery Travis Centre Hosp., Houston, 1985—; dir. Physicians for Peace, Norfolk, Va., 1991—; cons. physician Houston Oilers, 1978-97; attending physician Ontario Motor Speedway, Calif., 1972-73. Author: Patient Care in Plastic Surgery, 1982, 2nd edit., 1996, Manuel de Ciudados en Cirugia Plastica, 1985, Atencion al Paciente de Cirugia Plastica, 1998; contbg. editor: Plastic Surgery Obsession: Brazil's Dr. Ivo Pitanguy Triggered It All, 2011; Professional Adviser: Surgeon: The Man Behind the Mask, Richard H. German, MD, 2011; contbr. articles to med. publs., presentations to profl. confs.; inventor Barrett sterling surgigrip. Bd. dirs. Plastic Surgery Ednl. Found., Chgo.; mem. Fed. Coun. on Aging, Washington, 1991-93, Pres.'s Coun. U. Miami, 1997—; adv. bd. Johnson & Johnson, New Brunswick, N.J. Lt. comdr. M.C., USNR, 1969-74. Recipient Outstanding Tchg. Plastic Surgeon award Baylor Coll. Medicine, 2003; Surg. exch. scholar to Royal Coll. Surgeons, London, 1968; hon. dep. sheriff Harris County, Tex. Fellow ACS; mem. Am. Assn. Plastic Surgery, Am. Soc. Plastic Surgeons, Royal Soc. Medicine, Michael E. DeBakey Internat. Cardiovascular Surg. Soc., Am. Soc. for Aesthetic Plastic Surgery, Denton A. Cooley Cardiovascular Surg. Soc., Tex. Med. Assn., Tex. Soc. Plastic Surgery, Harris County Med. Soc., Houston Soc. Plastic Surgery, D Ralph Millard Plastic Surg. Soc. (pres. 1993-94, v.p. 1977-79, sec., treas. 1975-77, historian 1980—), U. Miami Sch. Medicine Nat. Alumni Assn. (bd. dirs. 1975-77, pres. coun. 1997—), Houston City Club, Houstonian Club, Royal Biscayne Racquet Club, Commodore Club, Coral Beach and Tennis Club, Sweetwater Country Club, Alpha Kappa Kappa (pres. 1968-69). Office: 25 West Ln Houston TX 77019-1007 Office Phone: 713-626-4747. Personal E-mail: bbarrettmd@gmail.com.

BARRETT, CONOR D., physician, educator; MB, BChir, BAO, Nat. U. Ireland, Cork, BMedSc, 1999. Fellow Cleve. Clinic Found., 2006—08; attending physician Mass. Gen. Hosp., Boston, 2008—; instr., medicine Harvard Med. Sch., Boston, 2008—. Contbr. chapters to books, articles to profl. jours. Recipient Jansen medal, Cork U. Hosp., 2000. Mem.: Royal Coll. Physicians Ireland, Am. Heart Assn., Heart Rhythm Soc., European Echocardiographic Assn., European Heart Rhythm Assn., European Soc. Cardiology. Achievements include research in ablation of cardiac arrhythmias. Office: Mass Gen Hosp 55 Fruit St GRB 109 Boston MA 02114

BARRETT, DAVID M., urologist; b. Detroit, Mar. 25, 1942; B, Albion Coll.; MD, Wayne State U., 1968. Diplomate Am. Bd. Urology. Intern Detroit Gen. Hosp., 1968-69; resident in gen. surgery Mayo Clinic, Rochester, Minn., 1969-70, resident in urology, 1972-75, staff, dept. urology, 1975-99, chair, dept. urology, 1991—99; faculty Mayo Med. Sch., Rochester, Minn., 1986-99, chair, dept. urology, 1991-99, Anson L. Clark prof. urology, 1997; CEO Lahey Clinic, Burlington, Mass., 1999—, chmn. bd. gov., bd. trustees; prof. urology Tufts U. Sch. Medicine. Bd. govs. Mayo Clinic, 1988-96, trustee, 1991-97; pres. Am. Bd. Urology, 1999; bd. trustees Healthcare Leadership Coun.; bd. dirs. Mass. High Tech. Coun., C.R. Bard, Inc., 2009-; sec. Mass. Hosp. Assn. Flight surgeon USAF, 1970—72, US & Vietnam. Recipient Jordanian Medal of Independence of First Order, King Hussein of Jordan, 1996. Mem.: Am. Coll. Healthcare Executives, Am. Urologic Assn., ACS. Office: Lahey Clinic 41 Mall Rd Burlington MA 01805-0002 Business E-Mail: david.barrett@lahey.org. *

BARRETT, ELIZABETH ANN MANHART, psychotherapist, consultant, nursing educator; b. Hume, Ill., July 11, 1934; d. Francis J. and Grace C. (Manhart) Fridy; children: Joseph B., Jeffrey F., Paula G. Brown, Pamela M. Temple, Scott D. BSN summa cum laude, U. Evansville, 1970, MA, 1973, MSN, 1976; grad., Gestalt Assocs. Psychotherapy, 1982; PhD in Nursing, NYU, 1983; grad., Am. Inst. for Mental Imagery, 1995. From instr. to asst. prof. nursing U. Evansville, Ind., 1970-76; staff nurse Welborn Bapt. Hosp., Evansville, 1975-76, Bellevue Psychiat. Hosp., NYC, 1976-79; clin. tchr. CUNY, 1977-82; asst. prof. Adelphi U., 1979-80; group practice Nurse Healers, 1979-82; pvt. practice psychotherapy, 1980—. Nurse rschr. Mt. Sinai Med. Ctr., N.Y.C., 1982-86, asst. dir. nursing, 1983-86; assoc. prof. Hunter Coll., N.Y.C., 1986-89, prof., 1994-2001, prof. emerita, 2001—, dir. grad. studies, 1989-92, coord. Ctr. for Nursing Rsch., 1993-2001; cons. Internat. Soc. Univ. Nurses; co-chair adv. com. Martha E. Rogers Ctr. for Study of Nursing Svc., 1994-96; sec., treas. Am. Inst. for Mental Imagery, 2002—; com. mem. Regional Health Planning Coun., Evansville, 1974-77. Mem. editl. bd. Alt. Therapies in Health and Medicine, 1995—. Recipient Disting. Nursing Alumnus award NYU, 1994, Disting. Nurse Rschr. award Found. N.Y. State Nurses Assn., 1995. Fellow Am. Acad. Nursing; mem. ANA (cert. psychiat.-mental health), NOW, Nat. League Nursing, Ea. Nursing Rsch. Assn. (charter), Ea. Nursing Rsch. Soc., Soc. Rogerian Scholars (co-founder, 1st pres. 1988-90), Phi Kappa Phi, Sigma Theta Tau (Uspilon chpt. pres. 1986-88), Alpha Tau Delta, Sigma Xi. Home: 415 E 85th St Apt 9E New York NY 10028-6358 Office: 16 E 96th St Ste 1 A New York NY 10128 Office Phone: 917-371-7269. Personal E-mail: eambarrett@nyc.rr.com. Business E-Mail: elizabeth@dailybrobarrett.com.

BARRETT, EUGENE JOSEPH, physician, educator, researcher; b. Jersey City, May 22, 1946; s. Joseph Francis and Margaret (Harney) B.; m. Paue Marie Quiricani, Jan. 31, 1976, children: Nora, Matthew. BS in Physics, St. Peters Coll., Jersey City, NJ, 1960, MD, U. Rochester, 1975, PhD in Biophysics, 1975. Intern in medicine Strong Meml. Hosp., Rochester, NY, 1975-76, asst. resident in medicine, 1976-77; fellow in endocrinology and metabolism Yale U. Sch. Medicine, New Haven, 1977-80, asst. prof. medicine, 1980-85, assoc. prof. medicine, 1985-91, chief diabetes unit, 1988-91, prof. internal medicine and pediats. U. Va. Sch. Medicine, Charlottesville, 1991—; dir. U. Va. Diabetes Ctr., 1991—. Dir. diabetes unit Yale U. Sch. Medicine, 1987-91; dir. diabetes ctr. U. Va., 1991— Contbr. over 150 articles to profl. jours. Recipient Rsch. Career award NIH, 1981-85, Mem. NIH (mem. metabolism study sect. 1993-96), Am. Diabetes Assn. (bd. dirs. Va. affiliate 1993-96, v.p. 2002, pres.-elect 2002, pres. 2003-04, mem. nat. profl. practice com., rsch. award 1996), Am. Heart Assn. (Established Investigator 1987-92, mem. Conn. affiliate grant rev. panel 1985-90, mem. grant rev. panel New Eng. region 1986-91, chair 1991), Am. Fedn. Clin. Rsch., Am. Soc. Clin. Investigation. Roman Catholic. Avocations: sailing, tennis. Office: U Va Sch Medicine Diabetes Rsch Ctr PO Box 801410 Charlottesville VA 22908 Business E-Mail: ejb8x@virginia.edu.

BARRETT, GEORGE S., health products executive; b. 1955; Bachelor's degree, Brown U., 1977; MBA, NYU, 1988. Various positions NMC Lab., 1981—91; pres. NMC Lab. (acquired by Alpharma Inc.), 1988—94, Alpharma US Pharm. group, 1994—97, Barre Nat., subs. Alpharma Inc., 1991—94; pres., CEO Diad Rsch., 1999, Teva Pharm. USA, 1999—2004; group v.p. N.Am., CEO Teva N.Am., 2005—08; vice-chmn., CEO healthcare supply chain services Cardinal Health, Inc., Dublin, Ohio, 2008—; several positions Teva Pharmaceuticals Industries, Ltd., pres., CEO, Teva N.Am., mem., Office of CEO, exec. v.p., Global Pharm. Markets, pres., Teva USA, 1998—2005, group v.p., N.Am., 2005—06, pres., CEO, Teva N.Am., 2006—08; chmn., CEO Cardinal Health, Inc., 2009—. Bd. dir. Eaton Corp., 2011—. Mem. bd. ambassadors Project Restore, John Hopkins Sch. Med.; dir. Am. Found. for Pharm. Edn., U. Md. Sch. Pharmacy, Nationwide Children's Hosp.; mem. Pres. Leadership Coun. Brown Univ.; trustee Healthcare Leadership Coun. Mem.: Generic Pharm. Industry Assn. (past chmn., bd. dir.). Office: Cardinal Health Inc 7000 Cardinal Pl Dublin OH 43017 Office Phone: 614-757-5000. Office Fax: 614-757-6000. Business E-Mail: george.barrett@cardinal.com. *

BARRETT, HARRISON H., optical engineer, imaging scientist, educator; b. Springfield, Mass., July 1, 1939; BS in Physics, Va. Poly. Inst., 1960; MS in Physics, MIT, 1962; PhD in Applied Physics, Harvard U., Cambridge, Mass. Rsch. scientist, med. electronics rsch. divsn. Raytheon Co., Waltham, Mass., 1962—68, sr. rsch. scientist, 1968—73, project leader, 1971—74, prin. rsch. scientist, 1973—74; assoc. prof. radiology, assoc. prof. optical scis. U. Ariz., Tucson, 1974—76, prof., 1976—90, acting dir. Optical Scis. Ctr., 1983, prof. applied math., 1986—, Regents prof. radiology & optical scis., 1990—, dir. Ctr. Gamma-Ray Imaging, 1999—, vice chair radiology, 2005—09. Vis. prof. Weizmann Inst., Rehovot, Israel, 1980, U. Erlangen-Nuernberg, Germany, 1980—81, Nankai U., Tianjin, China, 1982, Tokyo Inst. Tech., 1998, Nat. U. Ireland, Galway, 2005; vis. scientist Nat. Inst. Environ. Health Scis., 1992. Mem. editl. bd. Rev. Sci. Instruments, 1974—76, Optics Letters, 1978—81, editor, 1985—91; contbr. articles to profl. jours. Vice-chair Gordon Rsch. Conf. Coherent Optics & Holography, Santa Barbara, Calif., 1978, chmn., 1980; mem. US nat. com. Internat. Commn. Optics, 1983—86; bd. dirs. Internat. Conf. Info. Processing in Med. Imaging, 1993—; founding mem. bd. dirs. Ariz. Coun. Econ. Conversion, 1988—91. Recipient IR-100 award, Indsl. Rsch. Mag., 1973, Humboldt Prize, Alexander von Humboldt Found., 1980, MERIT award, Nat. Inst. Biomedical Engrng. & Bioengineering, 2003, Founders Day Faculty Sci. award, U. Ariz. Coll. Medicine, 2006, Paul Capp award, 2010; E.T.S. Walton Fellowship, Sci. Found. Ireland, 2004. Fellow: IEEE (Med. Imaging Scientist award 2000, Medal for Innovations in Healthcare Tech. 2011), Optical Soc. America (C.E.K. Mees Medal 2005), American Inst. Med. & Biol. Imaging, American Phys. Soc.; mem.: AAAS, Soc. Indsl. & Applied Math., Acad. Molecular Imaging, Internat. Soc. Optical Engrng. (Soc. Gold Medal 2011), Soc. Nuclear Medicine, Hupmobile Club America, Sigma Xi, Phi Kappa Phi, Sigma Pi Sigma. Office: Univ Arizona Coll Optical Sciences Meinel Bldg 1630 E University Blvd Tucson AZ 85721 Office Phone: 520-626-6815. *

BARRETT, JANET TIDD, academic administrator; b. Crystal City, Mo., Nov. 29, 1939; d. Lewis Samuel and Mamie Lou (Hulvey) Tidd; m. David Clark Barrett, June 3, 1961; children: Barbara, Pam. Diploma in nursing, St. Lukes Hosp. Sch. Nursing, 1960; BSN with honors, Washington U., St. Louis, 1964, MSN, 1979; PhD, St. Louis U., 1987. Assoc. prof. Maryville Coll., St. Louis, 1979-89; acad. dean Barnes Coll., St. Louis, 1989-91; dir. BSN program Deaconess Coll. Nursing, St. Louis, 1991-2000, acad. dean, 2000—02; nursing cons., 2002—. Contbg. author to Beare and Meyers: Principles of Medical-Surgical Nursing; dancer with St. Louis Strutters, 2003-. St. Lukes Hosp. scholar; recipient Sister Agnita Claire Day Rsch. award St. Louis U.; named Ms. Mo. Sr. Am., 2005. Mem.: Mo. League Nursing, Nat. League Nursing, St. Luke's Alumni Assn., Pi Lambda Theta, Sigma Theta Tau. Personal E-mail: barretjan@hotmail.com, jtbarrett02@charter.net.

BARRETT, MICHAEL JOHN, anesthesiologist; b. Milw., Feb. 27, 1954; s. Walter Joseph and Valerie Clara (Wisniewski) Baclawski, m. Joan Marie Rowley, May 28, 1983; children: Michael J. Jr., Jessica Marie, Monica Jane. BS in Math. with honors, U. Wis., 1974; MD, Med. Coll. Wis., 1981; MBA, U. Toledo, 1998. Diplomate Am. Bd. Anesthesiology, Nat. Bd. Medicine and Surgery, Nat. Bd. Med. Examiners, Am. Acad. Pain Mgmt., Am. Bd. Anesthesiology Pain Mgmt. Intern Med. Coll. Wis. Affiliated Hosps., Milw., 1981, resident in anesthesiology, 1982—84; dir. anesthesiology Putnam Cmty. Hosp., Palatka, Fla., 1984—92, dir. Putnam Pain Ctr., 1985—92; clin. asst. prof. anesthesiology Ohio U. Coll. Osteo. Medicine; chief dept. anesthesia Putnam Cmty. Hosp., Palatka, 1984—92. Pres. Putnam Anesthesia Assocs., Palatka, 1985-92, Associated Anesthesiologists Toledo, 2005—; staff anesthesiologist St. Vincent Med. Ctr., Toledo, 1992—, vice chmn. dept. anesthesia, 2001-05 dir. Pain Mgmt. Ctr., 1994—; ptnr. Assn. Anestheseologists of Toledo, 1993—, fiduciary pension plan, 1999—. Bd. dirs. Round Lake Park Homeowners Assn., Palatka, 1986-88. Walter Zeit fellow; recipient St. Vincents Physician Excellence award, 1996. Mem. AMA, Internat. Anesthesia Rsch. Soc., Am. Soc. Anesthesiologists, Am. Soc. Regional Anesthesiologists, Ohio Med. Assn., Acad. Medicine of Toledo and Lucas County, Am. Neuromodulation Soc., Ohio Soc. Anesthesiologists, Assoc. Anesthesiologists Toledo, Putnam County Med. Soc. (pres. 1989-91), Phi Delta Kappa, Phi Kappa Phi. Independent. Avocations: boating, private pilot, swimming. Home: 8646 Plum Hollow Pt Holland OH 43528-8487 Office: Assoc Anesthesiologists 2409 Cherry St Ste 305 Toledo OH 43608-2600 Office Phone: 419-251-4715. Business E-Mail: mjhjmb@ameritech.net.

BARRETT, O'NEILL, JR., medical educator; b. Baton Rouge, Mar. 21, 1929; s. O'Neill and Hazel (Lohman) B.; m. Elois Stone; children: Deborah Ann, Michael, William. BS in Biology, La. State U., 1949; MSc in Medicine, Baylor U., 1958; MD, La. State U., New Orleans, 1953. Diplomate Am. Bd. Internal Medicine, Am. Bd. Med. Oncology, Am. Bd. Hematology. Commd. 2d lt. U.S. Army, 1953, advanced through grades to col., 1968; intern Brooke Army Med. Ctr., San Antonio, 1953-54, med. resident, 1955-58; chief gen. medicine Madigan Army Hosp., Tacoma, 1960-62; asst. chief medicine Letterman Army Hosp., San Francisco, 1963-68; chief dept. medicine Tripler Army Med. Ctr., Honolulu, 1968-71, Walter Reed Army Med. Ctr., Washington, 1971-73, ret., 1973; chmn. dept. comprehensive medicine U. So. Fla. Sch. Medicine, Tampa, 1973-76; dir. div. gen. medicine U. S.C. Sch. Medicine, Columbia, 1976-86, chmn. dept. medicine, 1987-92, dir. clin. curriculum, 1992-94, disting. prof. emeritus, 1994—. Assoc. counselor So. Med. Assn. Editor: Internal Medicine in Vietnam, 1982; mem. editorial bd. Med. History Vietnam-U.S. Army, 1972—, Archives of Internal Medicine, 1980-91; asst. editor Southern Med. Assn. Jour.; contbr. articles to profl. jours. Recipient 5 Outstanding Tchr. of Yr. awards U. S.C. Sch. Medicine. Fellow ACP, Am. Coll. Clin. Pharmacology; mem. Am. Soc. Hematology, Am. Soc. Clin. Oncology. Avocations: sailing, birding. Office: U SC Sch Medicine Med Libr Bldg Garver's Ferry Rd Ste 316 Columbia SC 29201

BARRETT, REGINALD HAUGHTON, wildlife management educator; b. San Francisco, June 11, 1942; s. Paul Hutchison and Mary Lambert (Hodgkin) Barrett; m. Katharine Lawrence Ditmars, July 15, 1967; children: Wade Lawrence, Heather Elizabeth. BS in Game Mgmt., Humboldt State U., 1965; MS in Wildlife Mgmt., U. Mich., 1966; PhD in Zoology, U. Calif., Berkeley, 1971. Rsch. biologist U. Calif., Berkeley, 1970—71, acting asst. prof., 1971—72; rsch. scientist divsn. wildlife rsch. Commonwealth Scientific and Indsl. Rsch. Orgn., Darwin, Australia, 1972—75; from asst. prof. to prof. U. Calif., Berkeley, 1975—, George and Wilhelmina Goertz disting. prof. wildlife mgmt., 2002—. Author (with others): Report on the Use of Fire in National Parks and Reserves, 1977, Research and Management of Wild Hog Populations, Proceedings of a Symposium, 1977, Sitka Deer Symposium, 1979, Symposium on Ecology and Management of Barbary Sheep, 1980, Handbook of Census Methods for Birds and Mammals, 1981, Wildlife 2001: Populations, 1992; contbr. abstracts, reports to profl. jours. Recipient Outstanding Achievement award, Humboldt State U. Alumni Assn., 1986, Bruce R. Dodd award, 1965, Howard M. Wight award, 1966; Undergrad. scholar, Nat. Wildlife Fedn., 1964, NSF Grad. fellow, 1965—70, Union Found. Wildlife Rsch. grantee, 1968—70. Fellow: Calif. Acad. Sci., Explorers Club; mem.: AAAS, Orgn. Wildlife Planners, Calif. Bot. Soc., Am. Inst. Biol. Scis., Internat. Union Conservation Nature (life), Am. Soc. Mammalogists (life), Soc. Range Mgmt. (life), Australian Mammal Soc., Soc. Am. Foresters, Ecol. Soc. Am. (cert. sr. ecologist), Wildlife Soc. (pres. Bay Area chpt. 1978—79, pres. western sect. 1997—98, cert. wildlife biologist, R. F. Dasmann Profl. of the Yr. award western sect. 1989), Sigma Xi, Xi Sigma Pi. Episcopalian. Avocations: hunting, fishing, photography, camping, backpacking. Office: U Calif 130 Mulford Hall Berkeley CA 94720-3114 Office Phone: 925-286-9269. Business E-Mail: rbarrett@berkeley.edu.

BARRETT, WILLIAM LANNON, oncologist, educator; b. Cin., Mar. 18, 1960; MD, U. Cin., 1987. Prof. & chmn., dept. radiation oncology U. Cin., 1999—; med. dir. Barrett Cancer Ctr., 2010. Mem. U. Cin. Curriculum Com., 1995, U. Cin. Alumni Coun., 2001, U. Cin. Residency Program Dirs. Com., 2006—08, U. Cin. Physicians Exec. Com., 2011; bd. mem. Precision Radiotherapy INC, 2002—. Recipient 9th Ann. Martin Luther Ling, Jr. 'Keep the Dream Alive' award, St. Mark's Ch., Cin., Cmty. Achievement award, Am. Cancer Soc., Black Tie Gala; named Best Doctors, Cin. Mag., 1998, 2000, 2007—10. Mem.: Cin. Acad. Medicine, Am. Assn. Cancer Edn., Am. Brachytherapy Soc., Ohio Med. Assn., Am. Soc. Therapeutic Radiology & Oncology. Office: UC Barrett Cancer Ctr 234 Goodman St Cincinnati OH 45267-0757 Office Fax: 513-584-4007. Business E-Mail: william.barrett@uchealth.com.

BARREY, CEDRIC YVES, research scientist; b. Calais, France, Feb. 1, 1975; MD, U. Claude Bernard, Lyon, France, PhD, 2004. Rschr. Hospices Civils de Lyon, 2004—. Rschr., biomechanics Lab. Biomechanics, Paris, 2007; dir., sci. bd. French Soc. Spine Surgery, 2010. Recipient Rsch. prize, French Lang. Soc. Neurosurgery. Mem.: French Soc. Neurosurgery, French Soc. Spine Surgery. Avocations: jogging, skiing, travel. Office: 59 Blvd PINEL Hosp Wertheimer Lyon-Bron Rhone 69003 France Office Fax: 04-72-35-72-62. E-mail: c.barrey@wanadoo.fr.

BARRI, YOUSRI M. H., nephrologist; b. Sudan, Mar. 10, 1955; MBBS, U. Khartoum, 1979. Diplomate Am. Bd. Internal Medicine, 2007. Transplant nephrologist Dallas Nephrology Assoc., 2002—. Master: RCP; fellow: FASN. Office: 3601 Swiss Ave Dallas TX 75204 Office Fax: 214-366-6341 Personal E-mail: ymbarri@aol.com.

BARRICKMAN, LES L., psychiatrist; b. Centerville, Iowa, Nov. 2, 1953; s. Bob and Margie Barrickman. BA, William Penn Coll., 1976; DO, Kirksville Coll. Osteopathic, 1982. Diplomate in adult psychiatry and in child and adolescent psychiatry Am. Bd. Psychiatry and Neurology. Intern Des Moines Gen. Hosp., 1982-83; resident adult psychiatry U. Iowa Coll. Medicine, Iowa City, 1983-86, resident child/adolescent psychiatry, 1986-88, assoc. faculty, 1989-90, instr., 1990-93, asst. prof., 1991-93; clin. asst. prof. U. N.Mex., Iowa City, 1995; dir. child/adolescent edn. tng. program U. Iowa, 1991-93; assoc. prof. U. Hawaii, Honolulu, 1996-98; clin. assoc. prof. dept. psychiatry Coll. Medicine, 1999—; pvt. practice Honolulu, 1998—. Mem. Am. Psychiat. Assn., Am. Acad. Child and Adolescent Psychiatry, Hawaii Assn. Osteo. Physicians and Surgeons (pres. 2005-11), Hawaii Bd. Med. Examiners (bd. mem. 2011-), Alpha Omega Alpha.

BARRICKS, MICHAEL ELI, retinal surgeon; b. Chgo., Feb. 22, 1940; s. Arthur Goetz and Ruth (Zuckerman) B.; m. Zondra Dell Natman, Jan. 18, 1992; 1 child, Charleigh Ruth. BA, Harvard Coll., 1961; MD, U. Chgo., 1965; PhD, Stanford U., 1973. Diplomate Nat. Bd. Med. Examiners, am. Bd. Ophthal., 1976; lic. physician, Calif. Intern then resident in surgery Stanford (Calif.) U., 1965-67, postdoctoral fellow, 1967-72; resident, fellow in ophthalmology Bascom Palmer Eye Inst., Miami, Fla., 1972-76; fellow in retinal surgery U. Calif., San Francisco, 1976-77; asst. prof., dir. retina svc. U. Tex., San Antonio, 1977-78; retinal surgeon, dir. retina svc. Permanente Med. Group., Oakland, Calif., 1979—. Asst. clin. prof. U. Calif., San Francisco, 1980-92, assoc. clin. prof., 1993-2001, clin. prof., 2001--. Contbr. articles to profl. jours. Recipient Gold award Am. Acad. Pediatrics, Outstanding Physician award Kaiser Hosp., 1982, Cert. of Appreciation for Outstanding Teaching, U. Calif, San Francisco;; Nat. scholar Fisher Body Craftsmans Guild, USPHS fellow Stanford U., 1967-70, Atholl McBean fellow Stanford Rsch. Inst., 1970-71. Fellow Am. Acad. Ophthalmology; mem. Permanente Ophthalmologic Soc. (pres. 1981), Vitreous Soc., Harvard Varsity Club, Crimson Key Soc. E-mail: michael.barricks@worldnet.att.net, mbarricks@comcast.net.

BARRIE, JOSEPH ROLLIN, retired surgeon; b. Bklyn., Aug. 22, 1935; s. David Joseph and Bertha (Rollin) Barrie; m. D. Christine Pilkington, June 20, 1981; children from previous marriage: John Rollin, Susan Smith. BS, Yale U., New Haven, Conn., 1956; MD, Harvard U., Boston, 1960. Diplomate Am. Bd. Surgery. Intern to first asst. resident surgery Mass. Gen. Hosp., Boston, 1960—65; sr. resident surgery Meml. Sloan-Kettering Cancer Ctr., NYC, 1967—69; staff surgeon Emerson Hosp., Concord, Mass., 1969—2004, ret., 2004. Clin. assoc. surgery Mass. Gen. Hosp., 1969—2003. Contbr. articles to profl. jours. Lt. comdr. USNR, 1965—67. Fellow: ACS; mem.: AMA, Boston Surg. Soc., Mass. Med. Soc., Soc. Surg. Oncology, Am. Soc. Clin. Oncology, Yale Club N.Y.C., Harvard Club Boston. Home and Office: 79 Whitney Rd Harvard MA 01451-1406 Office Phone: 978-621-0283. Business E-Mail: joseph.barrie@aya.yale.edu. *

BARRIENTOS, RUTH M., medical researcher; b. Cochabamba, Bolivia, Nov. 13, 1969; BS, George Mason U., 1992; PhD, George Wash. U., 2000. Predoctoral fellow NIH, NIMH, 1995—2000; post-doc. fellow U. Colo., 2000—05, sr. rsch. assoc., 2005—. Recipient Intramural Rsch. Tng. award, NIH-NIMH; grant, NIH-NIA, NIH-NIMH. Mem.: Psychoneuroimmunology Rsch. Soc., Soc. Neurosci. Achievements include research in understanding the mechanisms involved in age-related cognitive declines following an immune challenge, and to develop effective therapies to prevent and/or reverse these detrimental neurological and behavioral outcomes. Avocations: hiking, soccer. Office: University Colo UCB 345 Boulder CO 80309 Business E-Mail: ruth.barrientos@colorado.edu.

BARRINGER, JOAN MARIE, counselor, educator, artist, writer; b. Washington, Sept. 30, 1955; d. John Thomas and Maria Reginia Barringer. BA in Latin Am. Studies, George Mason U., 1981; grad. in Creating and Selling Short Stories, Inst. Childrens Lit., 1995; MA in Edn. and Counseling, George Mason U., 1999. Cert. in clin. hypnotherapist 2006. Translator and receptionist Brazilian Embassy, Cultural Inst., Washington, 1975—83; dir. and founder day care Rainbow City Army-Navy Country Club, Arlington, Va., 1983—; visitors svcs. Nat. Gallery Art, Washington, 1991—94; workshop and leadership conf. asst. Women's Ctr., Vienna, Va., 1996—2000; career counselor Dept. Rehab. Svcs., Alexandria, Va., 1998—99, Ind. Art. Bus. Studio of Nat. Arts, 2002—. Presenter in field; ordained reverend Universal Life Ch., 2004; chmn. lib. com. Unity. Author: (poetry) Metronome, 1979; designer CD cover, singer Gift of Love; Fairfax (Va.) Jour., 1992, Montgomery (Va.) Jour., 1992, one-woman shows include Vienna Arts Soc., 2006, exhibitions include Graffiti Gallery, 2002, Greenbelt Cmty. Ctr., 2003, Joanne Rose Gallery, 2003, Rehoboth Art League, 2004, Angel Eyes, 2004, Mimi's American Bistro, 2004—05, Represented in permanent collections Inova Hosp., Unity Fairfax and Vero Beach & Melbourne, Fla., 2008—10, presentation, Nutrition & Lifestyle Changes, Leisure Worlds, Md., 2009; author: Magic Manifesting, 2010—11, Heaven on Earth & Professional Dreamer Unity of Melbourne, 2010. Pres. Hampton Roadrunners, 2004—06; leader Internat. Essential Tremor Found. support group Georgetown Hosp., Washington, 2005—; election officer U.S. Govt., Va., 2001; fundraiser Unity Ch.; translator, missionary work Softly Internat., Peru; with Lobbying Congress IETF, 2009. Recipient award, Vienna Photo Show, 2004, 2005. Mem.: Vienna Photog. Soc., Assn. Rsch. and Enlightenment (wayshower 2001—), Women's Caucus for Art (editor, lay out designer, writer, photographer newsletter 1999—2001), Sigma Pi Alpha. Avocations: genealogy, travel, interior decorating, yoga, photography, Oceanography. Home: 11107 Hampton Rd Fairfax Station VA 22039 Personal E-mail: joanmarie5@aol.com.

BARRON, SUSAN, clinical psychologist; b. Chgo., May 13, 1940; d. Earl and Trixie (Chernoff) B.; m. Eugene Pratt, Jan. 18, 1975 (div. 1983). BBA, CCNY, 1960, MA, 1963; PhD, CUNY, 1973. Lic. psychologist, diplomate Am. Bd. Psychol. Specialties, bd. cert. fellow Am. Coll. Advanced Practice Psychologists, cert. alcohol and related substance abuse APA Coll. Profl. Psychology. Intern psychologist Bellevue Psychiat. Hosp., NYC, 1964-65, psychologist, 1966-67; thcg. fellow CUNY, 1965-66; staff psychologist Lighthouse, N.Y. Assn. for the Blind, NYC, 1968-71, sr. clin. psychologist, 1971-74; dir. psychol. counseling svcs. Peninsula Ctr. for the Blind, Palo Alto, Calif., 1974-75; cons. psychologist N.Y. State Commn. for Blind and Visually Handicapped, NYC, 1975-78, 86—; dir. psychol. svcs. Thoms Rehab. Hosp., Asheville, NC, 1978-79; state coord. psychol. svcs. N.Y. State Office Vocat. Rehab., Albany, 1979-85; founder, dir. Family Support Program ICU N.Y. Infirmary-Beekman Downtown Hosp., NYC, 1982-84; cons. clin. psychologist N.Y. Hosp. Cornell U. Med. Ctr., 1987—; pvt. practice, 1987—; behavioral scientist diabetes control/complications trial NIH Cornell U. Med. Ctr., NYC, 1987—; cons. clin. psychologist Joslin Ctr. for Diabetes St. Luke's-Roosevelt Hosp. Ctr./Columbia U. Phys. and Surg., NYC, 1994-95. Cons. clin. psychologist Joslin Ctr. Diabetes, St. Lukes-Roosevelt Hosp. Ctr., U. Hosp. of Columbia U. Coll. of Physicians and Surgeons, N.Y.C., 1994-95, Health Psychology Assocs., Calif., 1997—, N.Y.C., 1997—; mem. Nat. Human Svcs. Adv. Bd.-Retinitis Pigmentosa Found., Balt., 1975-82; cons. Del. State Commn. for Blind, 1975-78, Am. Found. Blind, 1974-82, Calif. Dept. Rehab., 1974-82, Hawaii State Svcs. Blind, 1974-82, Ariz. State Svcs. Blind, 1974-82, Nev. State Svcs. Blind, 1974-82; spkr. Nat. Multiple Disabilities Conf., 1982, NAS, 1981; mem. adv. bd. doctoral psychology internship program Rusk Inst. of Rehab. Medicine, NYU Med. Ctr., 1979-84; behavioral scientist Diabetes Control and Complications Trial NIH-Cornell U. Med. Ctr., 1987—; mem. mended hearts NYU Med. Ctr., Cardiac Prevention and Rehab. Ctr.; group leader nat. tele-support network Parents of Blind and Visually Impaired Children, Jewish Guild for Blind, NYC, 2006—, parents & Blind & Autistic Children, 2010-. Contbr. articles to profl. jours. Recipient Leadership award Alumni Assn. CCNY, 1960, 62, Rsch. award Retinal Dystrophy Soc., Australia, 1975, Charles H. Best medal for disting. svc. Am. Diabetes Assn., 1994. Fellow Am. Coll. Advanced Practice Psychologists (bd. cert.), Am. Orthopsychiat. Assn. (life); mem. APA, AAAS, Am. Coll. Forensic Examiners, Calif. State Psychol. Assn., N.Y. Acad. Scis., Mended Hearts. Achievements include patents for autistic and blind children. Office: 347 5th Ave Rm 603 New York NY 10016-5010 Office Phone: 212-686-7270.

BARROS, CAMILA DE GIACOMO CARNEIRO, physician, educator; b. Bauru, Dec. 27, 1973; Degree in Medicine, Sch. Medicine Ribeirao Preto - U. Sao Paulo, Brazil, 1998; PhD, U. Sao Paulo Sch. Medicine, 2011. Prof. Sch. Medicine Ribeirão Preto - U. Sao Paulo, 2009—. Avocations: cello, travel. Office: Ave Bandeirantes 3900 Ribeirão Preto São Paulo 14049900 Brazil Business E-Mail: cgcbarros@fmrp.usp.br.

BARROS, COLLEEN F., federal agency administrator; BS, U. Md.; MPA, Am. U., Washington. With NIH, 1979—, budget analyst, 1979, sr. adminstrv. officer Office of Dir., assoc. dir. adminstrn., Nat. Inst. Aging, 1995—2004, acting dep. dir. mgmt., 2004, dep. dir. mgmt., CFO, 2004—. Recipient PHS Superior Svc. award, 1995, Presdl. Rank award, 2003, 2008. Office: NIH Office Mgmt Shannon Bldg Rm 102 1 Center Dr Bethesda MD 20892 Office Phone: 301-496-3271. Office Fax: 301-480-4689. Business E-Mail: colleen.barros@nih.gov. *

BARROW, DANIEL LOUIS, neurosurgeon; b. Jacksonville, Ill., Jan. 19, 1955; s. Warren Coultas and Elvera (Pessina) B.; m. Mollie Ann Winston, Oct. 4, 1986; children: Emily, Jack, Tom. BA in Biology, Westminster Coll., 1976; MD, So. Ill. U., 1979. Diplomate Am. Bd. Neurol. Surgeons. Asst. prof. Emory U. Sch. Medicine, Atlanta, 1985-89, assoc. prof., vice chmn. dept. neurosurgery, 1990-95; MBNA/Bowman prof., chmn. neurosurgery, 1995—. Mem. adv. bd. Ga. Regional Organ and Tissue Pricurement Agy., 1987-89; mem. editorial bd. Clin. Neurosrgery, 1988-92, Neurosurgery, 1988—. Author: Disorders of the Pituitary, 1986; editor: Intracranial Vascular Malformations, 1990, Neuroendocrinology, 1992, Complications & Sequelae of Head Injury, 1992; editor: Surgery of Cranial Nerves of the Posterior Fossa, 1993, Duval Arteriovenous Malformations, 1993, Cavernous Malformations, 1993, Giant Intracranial Aneurysms, 1995, Dialogues in Neurological Surgery, 1995, The Practice of Neurosurgery, 1995. Fellow Am. Coll. Surgeons, Stroke Coun. Am. Heart Assn.; mem. AMA (Physician Recognition award 1990), Am. Assn. Nuerological Surgeons, Am. Acad. Neurological Surgeons, Neurosurg. Soc. Am., Med. Assn. Ga., Ga. Neurosurg. Soc. (former pres.), Med. Assn. Atlanta, Med. Assn. Atlanta, So. Neurosurg. Soc., Soc. Univ. Neurosurgeons, Congress Neurol. Surgeons (sec. 1992-95, pres. 1999-2000), Am Bd. Neurol. Surgery (sec. 2008-11, chmn. 2011—). Avocations: hunting, fishing, rock-climbing, skiing, sports. Home: 859 Lullwater Pky NE Atlanta GA 30307-1233 Office: The Emory Clinic 1365 B Clifton Rd NE Atlanta GA 30322-1013 Office Phone: 404-778-5770. Business E-Mail: daniel.barrow@emory.org. *

BARRY, HERBERT, III, psychologist, educator; b. NYC, June 2, 1930; s. Herbert and Lucy Manning (Brown) Barry. BA, Harvard U., 1952; MS, Yale U., 1953, PhD, 1957. USPHS-NIMH rsch. fellow Yale U., 1957-59, asst. prof. psychology, 1960-61, U. Conn., Storrs, 1961-63; rsch. assoc. prof. pharmacology Sch. Pharmacy U. Pitts., 1963-70, prof., 1970-87, prof. pharm. scis., 1995—2001, prof. emeritus, 2001—, prof. pharmacology and physiology Sch. Dental Medicine, 1987-94. Mem. alcohol rsch. rev. com. Nat. Inst. Alcohol Abuse and Alcoholism, 1972—76; mem. sociobehavioral subcom. AIDS rsch. rev. com. Nat. Inst. Drug Abuse, 1988—89. Author (with H. Wallgren): (book) Actions of Alcohol, 1970; author: (with A. Schlegel) Adolescence: An Anthropological Inquiry, 1991; field editor: jour. Psychopharmacology, 1974—91; contbr. articles to profl. jours. Bd. dirs. Schalkenbach Found., 1996—2004, 2005—11, Ctr. Study Econs., 1988—; mem. Allegheny County Dem. Com., 1984—2010. Recipient Rsch. Scientist Devel. award, NIMH, 1967—77. Fellow: APA (coun. reps. 1975—76, pres. divsn. psychopharmacology 1980—81), AAAS; mem.: Am. Coll. Neuropsychopharmacology, Psychonomic Soc., Am. Name Soc. (mem. exec. com. 2000—03), Sigma Xi, Phi Beta Kappa. Unitarian Universalist. Avocation: chess. Home: 552 N Neville St Apt 83 Pittsburgh PA 15213-2830 Office: Univ Pitts 534 Salk Hall Pittsburgh PA 15261-1905 Home Phone: 412-621-6934. Business E-Mail: barryh@pitt.edu.

BARRY, JOHN MAYNARD, urologist; b. Winona, Minn., Mar. 14, 1940; MD, U. Minn., 1965. Intern SUNY, Syracuse, 1965-66; resident U. Oreg. Med. Sch., Portland, 1969-73; prof., urology Oreg. Health Sci. U., Portland, 1980—, dir. renal transplantation, 1976—2009, chmn. urology, 1979—2008, chmn. abdominal organ transplantation, 2000—02, prof. emeritus of surgery, 2010. Office: Oreg Health Sci U Divsn Urology 3303 SW Bond Ave Portland OR 97293 Office Phone: 503-346-1500. Business E-Mail: barruj@oshu.edu.

BARRY, JOYCE ALICE, dietician, consultant; b. Chgo., Apr. 27, 1932; d. Walter Stephen and Ethel Myrtle (Paetow) B. Student, Iowa State Coll., 1950—52, Loyola U., 1952—58; BS, Mundelein Coll., 1955; postgrad., Simmons Coll., 1963—64, U. Ga., 1979, Calif. We. U., 1980. Registered dietitian. Prodn. supr. Marshall Field & Co., Chgo., 1955-59; dir. food svcs. Women's Ednl. and Indsl. Union, Boston, 1959-62, Wellesley Pub. Schs., Mass., 1962-70; regional dietitian Canteen Corp., Chgo., 1970-83; gen. mgr. bus. devel. Plantation-Sysco, Orlando, Fla., 1983-87; dir. product devel., corp. quality assurance, procurement Marriott Internat. Hdqrs., Washington, 1987-95; owner food svc. cons. svc., 1995—. Cons. Stokes Food Svcs., Newton, Mass., 1960-70; vis. lectr. Affiliate Produce for Better Health Found. Mem.: AAUW, Nutrition in Complementary Care, Nat. Assn. Female Execs., Nat. Hist. Trust, Sch. Nutrition Svcs., Am. Dietetics Assn. (career adv. cons.), Food and Culinary Profls., Dietitians in Bus. and Comm., Smithsonian Instn. (assoc.), Washington Opera Guild, Met. Opera Guild. Republican. Roman Catholic. Home and Office: 1009 Pearce Dr Apt 101 Clearwater FL 33764-1107 Office Phone: 727-669-6454. Personal E-mail: joyce4374@yahoo.com.

BARSAM, ALLON, surgeon; b. London, May 5, 1977; MA; MBBS, Cambridge U., 1999; MRCOphth, Royal Coll. Ophthalmologists, 2003. Fellow Ophthalmic Cons. LI, 2010—. Office: Ste 402 Ryan Med Arts Bldg Rockville Centre NY 11570 Personal E-mail: abarsam@hotmail.com.

BARSAN, WILLIAM GEORGE, emergency physician; b. Akron, Aug. 1950; m. Mary Barsan. MD, Ohio State U., 1975. Diplomate Am. Bd. Emergency Medicine. Intern U. Va. Hosp., Charlottesville, 1975-76, resident in radiology, 1976-77; resident in emergency medicine U. Cin. Hosp., 1977-79; resident coordinator U. Cincinnati, 1981—92; prof., chair dept. emergency medicine U. Mich., Ann Arbor, 1992—, dir. surgery, 1992—. Mem. AMA, Soc. Tchrs. Emergency Medicine, U. Assn. Emergency Medicine, Am. Bd. Emergency Medicine (pres. 1998), Am. Coll. Emergency Physicians, Assn. Acad. Chairs of Emergency Medicine (pres. 2005-2006), Inst. Medicine. Office: Taubman Health Care Ctr Rm B1 354 1500 E Med Ctr Dr Ann Arbor MI 48109-0303 Home: 6281 Cobblestone Ln Dexter MI 48130-8422 Office Phone: 734-936-6020. Office Fax: 734-763-7228.

BARSANO, CHARLES PAUL, internist, medical educator; BS in Biology, Loyola U., Chgo., 1969; PhD in Pathology, U. Chgo., 1974, MD, 1975. Diplomate Am. Bd. Internal Medicine. Resident internal medicine Barnes Hosp./Washington U., St. Louis, 1975-77; fellow endocrinology U. Chgo. Sch. Medicine, 1977-79, rsch. assoc. endocrinology, 1979-80; asst. prof. medicine Northwestern U. and Lakeside VA Med. Ctr., 1980-85, U. Health Scis./Chgo. Med. Sch. and North Chgo. VA Med. Ctr., 1985-87, assoc. prof., 1987-92, prof. medicine, 1992-98, assoc. prof. pharmacology and molecular biology, 1992-94, prof. pharmacology and molecular biology, 1994-98, acting dean Med. Sch., 1998—99, sr. assoc. dean for clin. affairs, vice-chmn. dept. medicine, 1999—2001, interim dean, 2001—03; staff physician med. svc., endocrinology sect. North Chgo. VA Med. Ctr.; with clin. affairs Chgo. Med. Sch. Rosalind Franklin U. Medicine and Sci.; physician Capt. James A. Lovell Fed. Health Care Ctr., Chgo. Mem. editl. bd. Thyroid, 1990-95; mem. adv. bd. Toxic Substance Mechanisms, 1993-99. Recipient Bausch and Lomb Nat. Sci. award, 1965, Individual Nat. Rsch. Svc. award, 1979-80. Mem. Internat. Coun. for Control of Iodine Deficiency Disorders, Assn. Am. Med. Colls. (group on ednl. affairs sect. on resident edn.), Am. Assn. Clin. Endocrinologists, Am. Thyroid Assn. (fiscal com. 1982-85, pub. health com. 1986-88, membership com. 1990-93, chmn. membership com. 1993, local organizing com. 1994, bylaws com. 1995—), Endocrine Soc., Chgo. Endocrine Club (pres. 1984-85), Sigma Xi, Alpha Omega Alpha. Office: Capt James A Lovell Fed Health Care Ctr 3001 Breen Bay Rd North Chicago IL 60064 Office Phone: 847-688-1900. *

BARTASEVICIUS, ALGIMANTAS, mathematics professor; b. Radviliskis, Lithuania, May 26, 1941; Magister in Mechanics, Moscow U. M. Lomonosov, 1965, D in Math. Sci., 1969. Asst. prof., dept. informatics & math. Lithuanian U. Agr., 1972—, cons., 1972—. Mem.: Lithuanian Royal Union Nobility, Lithuanian Soc. Math. Home: Pilenu str 3 - 38 Akademija Kaunas LT-53361 Lithuania Personal E-mail: mik@lzuu.lt.

BARTECCHI, CARL EDWIN, physician, educator; b. Scranton, Pa., Apr. 29, 1939; BS, U. Scranton, 1960; MD, U. Pa. Sch. Medicine, 1964. Founding ptnr., 1st mng. ptnr. Southern Colo. Clinic, 1970—2001; chief, dept. medicine Family Practice Residency Program, 1975—95; disting. clin. prof., medicine U. Colo. Sch. Medicine, 1999—; founder, vol. physician Los Pobres Migrant Worker Clinic, 2005—; sunday health columnist Pueblo Chieftain, 2010—. Paul Harris fellow Rotary Internat., 1975; vis. prof., critical care medicine Bach Mai Hosp., Vietnam, 1997—; dir. Bach Mai Hosp. Project, Vietnam, 1997—; hon. prof. Hanoi Med. U., 2010—; founding fellow Inst. Sci. in Medicine, 2010—. Contbr. articles to profl. jours. Recipient Health medal, Ministry of Health, Vietnam, Florence Rena Sabin award, U. Colo. Sch. Medicine, Frank O'Hara Alumni award, U. Scranton. Master: ACP (Ralph O. Claypoole Meml. award, Colo. Disting. Internist award); mem.: U. Scranton Alumni Soc., U. Pa. Alumni Soc., Alpha Sigma Nu Honor Soc. Avocations: running, tennis, photography, writing, mountain climbing. Home: 615 Dittmer Ave Pueblo CO 81005 Personal E-mail: ckbartecchi@gmail.com.

BARTELS, BRUCE MICHAEL, health facility administrator; b. Chgo., Oct. 13, 1946; s. John Phillip Frederick and Margaret Florine (Michael) B.; children: Sarah, Jennifer, Rebecca. BA, U. Wis., 1969; MBA, U. Chgo., 1975. Adminstrv. asst. U. Chgo. Hosp., 1975-77; asst. adminstr. Meth. Hosp., Indpls., 1977-81; exec. v.p. Med. Ctr. Hosp. Vt., Burlington, 1981-88; pres. York (Pa.) Hosp. and Found., 1988-95, York Health Sys., 1995-99, WellSpan Health, York, 1999—. Contbr. articles to profl. jours. Bd. dirs. York County chpt. YMCA, York, 1989-98, chmn., 1994-96; bd. dirs. ARC, 1990-96, 2003—, United Way, 1991-96, WITF, Inc., Ctrl. Pa. Pub. Broadcasting, 1994-2002, chmn., 1999-2001; bd. dirs. Pa. Trauma Systems Found., Mechanicsburg, 1990-2003, chmn., 1997-99; bd. dirs. Novation, Inc., 2003—09, Alliance Ind. Acad. Med. Ctrs., 2005—. With U.S. Army, Korea. Fellow Am. Coll. Healthcare Execs. (membership com. 1990-93); mem. Am. Hosp. Assn., Hosp. Assn. Pa. (bd. dirs., chmn.), York C. of C., U. Chgo. Health Adminstrn. Alumni Assn. (exec. com. 1991-95), Rotary. Avocations: reading, running, travel. Office: WellSpan Health 45 Monument Dr Ste 200 York PA 17403-3676 Office Phone: 717-851-2121. Business E-Mail: bbartels@wellspan.org. *

BARTELS, JEAN ELLEN, nursing educator; b. Two Rivers, Wis., July 15, 1949; m. Terry D. Bartels, Aug. 14, 1971; children: Justin Dean, Ashlee Jill. Diploma, Columbia Hosp. Sch. Nursing, 1970; BSN with honors, Alverno Coll., Milw., 1981; MSN, Marquette U., Milw., 1983; PhD in Nursing, U. Wis., Milw., 1990. Staff nurse ICU Columbia Hosp., Milw., 1970-76; prof. nursing Alverno Coll., Milw., 1983-99, dean nursing, 1990-99; chair Sch. Nursing Ga. So. U., Statesboro, 1999—, prof. nursing, 1999, clin. nurse leader, 2007—; chair Sch. Nursing, 1999—2010, Coll. Health & Human Scis., 2010; v.p. Academic Affairs & Provost, 2010—. Contbr. articles to profl. jours. Mem.: AACN (past pres.), ANA, Am. Ednl. Rsch. Assn., Am. Assn. Colls. Nursing, Internat. Soc. for Sci. Study Subjectivity, Mu Kappa, Sigma Theta Tau. Home: 912 Brittany Ln Statesboro GA 30461-4499 Office: Ga So U PO Box 8158 Statesboro GA 30460-1000 Office Phone: 912-478-5455. E-mail: jbartels@georgiasouthern.edu.

BARTH, ROLF FREDERICK, pathologist, educator; b. NYC, Apr. 4, 1937; s. Rolf L. and Josephine Barth; m. Christine Ferguson, Oct. 30, 1965; children: Suzanna, Alison, Rolf, Christofer. AB, Cornell U., 1959; MD, Columbia U., 1964. Diplomate Am. Bd. Pathology. Surg. intern Columbia-Presbyn. Med. Ctr., NYC, 1964-65; postdoctoral fellow Karolinska Inst., Stockholm, 1965-66; rsch. assoc. Nat. Inst. Allergy and Infectious Diseases, NIH, Bethesda, Md., 1966-68; resident pathology br. Nat. Cancer Inst., 1966-68, Nat. Inst. Health, 1968-70; Prof. dept. pathology and oncology U. Kans. Med. Ctr., Kansas City, 1970-77; clin. prof. dept. pathology Med. Coll. Wis. and U. Wis., Madison, 1977-79; prof. dept. pathology Ohio State U., Columbus, 1979—. Contbr. articles to profl. jours. Sr. asst. surgeon USPHS, 1966-70, inactive Res., 1970-. Grantee NIH. Mem. Am. Assn. Cancer Rsch., Internat. Soc. for Neutron Capture Therapy, Sigma Xi, Phi Kappa Phi; fellow Am. Assn. Adv. Sci. Office: Ohio State U Dept Pathology 165 Hamilton Hall 1645 Neil Ave Columbus OH 43210-1218 Office Phone: 614-292-2177. Business E-Mail: rolf.barth@osumc.edu.

BARTHELEMY, JEAN-PAUL FRANCOIS, orthopedic surgeon; b. Uzerche, Correze, France, Sept. 13, 1947; s. Maurice Barthelemy and Suzanne Croizet; m. Marie-Christine Bourgeais; children: Laurent, Olivier, Julien, Manon. BA, Coll. Gregoire, Tours, France, 1966; MD, Inst. Medicine Tours, 1976. Intern Tours Hosp., 1972-76, resident in plastic surgery, 1972, gen. surgery, 1972-74, resident in gen. surgery, 1972-74, fellow in orthopedic surgery, 1974-76, asst. in orthopedic surgery, 1976-78; orthopedic surgeon Clin. des Dames Blanches, Tours, 1976-86, Clinic St. Gatien, Tours, 1986—. Contbr. articles to profl. publs. Mem.: Heroicus Soc., Am. Orthop. Soc. Sports Medicine, Internat. Soc. Arthroscopy, Knee Surgery, Sports Medicine, Soc. Invennavionale Chirurgie Orthopiedique, European Soc. Sports, Trauma, Knee Surgery, and Arthroscopie, Soc. Francaise Arthroscopie. Roman Catholic. Home: La Martiniere 37230 Fondettes France Office: Clinic St Gatien 8 Place de la Cathedrale 37000 Tours France Personal E-mail: jpbarthelemy@aol.com.

BARTHOLD, JULIA SPENCER, urologist, researcher; b. Parkersburg, W.Va., Apr. 6, 1957; d. R. Donald and Janina R. Spencer; m. Steve Jensen Barthold, July 3, 1993; children: Christopher, Laura. BA, Northwestern U., 1979, MD, 1981. Resident in surgery McGaw Med. Ctr. Northwestern U., 1981—84, resident in urology McGaw Med. Ctr., 1984—88; fellow pediat. urology Children's Hosp. Mich., 1988—89; fellow rsch. Med. Coll. Cornell U., 1989—91, asst. prof. Med. Coll. NY, 1991—92; attending urologist N.Y. Hosp., 1991—92; pediat. urologist Ark. Children's Hosp., Little Rock, 1992—95, Children's Hosp. Mich., Detroit, 1995—99; assoc. chief urology A. I. duPont Hosp., Wilmington, Del., 2000—; prof. urology & pediat. Thomas Jefferson U., 2011—. Asst. prof. U. Ark. for Med. Scis., Little Rock, 1992—95; assoc. prof. Wayne State U., Detroit, 1995—99, Thomas Jefferson U., Phila., 2000—; mem. pediatric editl. bd. Jour. Urology, 2007—11. Contbr. articles to profl. jours. Fellow: Soc. for Pediat. Urology, Am. acad. Pediat. (exec. com. Mid-Atlantic sect. 2002—); mem.: Am. Urol. Assn. (exec. com. mem. Mid-Atlantic sect. 2002—06). Avocations: swimming, skiing, music. Office: A I duPont Hosp for Children Box 269 1600 Rockland Rd Wilmington DE 19899

BARTHOLDSON, LENNART OSKAR, plastic surgeon; b. Kodaikanal, India, Apr. 11, 1935; MD, U. Hosp. Gothenburg, 1966, PhD, 1981. Sr. cons., mentor Founder Art Clinic AB, Sweden, 1999—. Mem.: European Acad. Facial Surgery, Internat. Soc. Aesthetic Plastic Surgery, Am. Acad. Facial Plastic and Reconstructive Surgery. Avocation: art. Home: Mölndalsvägen 1 Gothenburg 412 63 Sweden

BARTHOLOMEW, LINCOLN EDWIN, physician; b. Oct. 12, 1954; MD, U. Pa., 1981; MPH, Columbia U., 1999. Dir. primary care St. Albans (N.Y.) VA Med. Ctr.; med. dir. Montefiore Rikers Island Health Svcs.; dir. NY Harbor Health Care Sys., 1998—. Home: 179th St Linea Blu Jamaica NY 11425 Office Phone: 718-526-1000, 718-298-8400. Business E-Mail: lincoln.bartholomew@va.gov. *

BARTHOLOMEW, LLOYD GIBSON, physician; b. Whitehall, NY, Sept. 15, 1921; s. Emerson F. and Minnie (Swinton) B.; m. Elisabeth Thrall, Dec. 27, 1943; children: Suzanne, Lynne, Lloyd

Gibson, Deborah, Douglass Thrall. AA, Green Mountain Jr. Coll., 1939; BA, Union Coll., Schenectady, 1941; MD, U. Vt., 1944; MS in Internal Medicine (fellow), U. Minn., 1952; LHD (hon.), Green Mountain Coll., 1984. Diplomate Am. Bd. Internal Medicine, subsplty. bd. gastroenterology. Intern Mary Hitchcock Meml. Hosp., Hanover, NH, 1944-45, resident, 1945-46, 48-49; asst. internal medicine Dartmouth, 1948-49; 1st asst. div. internal medicine Mayo Clinic, Rochester, Minn., 1949-52, asst. to staff div. internal medicine, 1952-53; practice medicine, specializing in gastroenterology Rochester, 1952—; instr. internal medicine Mayo Found., U. Minn., 1952-58, asst. prof., 1958-63, assoc. prof. internal medicine, 1963-67, prof. medicine, 1967—, Mayo Med. Sch., 1973—. Attending physician St. Mary's, Meth. hosps., Rochester, 1952; mem. adv. bd. to surgeons gen. of armed forces and asst. sec. def., 1978-86; mem. policy bd. Bush Found., 1978-87. Contbr. articles profl. publs. Trustee Green Mountain Coll. Poultney, Vt., 1991—, chmn. bd. trustees, 1997-2003, trustee emeritus, 2003—. Capt. M.C. AUS, 1946-47; col. M.C., 1960-86, ret. Recipient Woodbury prize in medicine, 1944, Carbee prize in obstetrics, 1994, disting. svc. award U. Vt. Coll. Medicine, 1977, Henry J. Plummer disting. clinician award Mayo Found. Internal Medicine, 1992, disting. svc. award Green Mtn. Coll. Alumni Assn., 1995; named to Green Mtn. Coll. Athletic Hall of Fame, 2006. Mem. AMA (sec. gastroenterology sect. 1962-68, vice chmn. gastroenterology sect. 1968-69, chmn. 1969-70, mem. council sci. assembly 1969, chmn. program planning com. 1971-75, chmn. council sci. assembly 1974-76, chmn. council continuing physician edn. 1976-77), Minn. Med. Assn. (del. ho. dels. 1964—, chmn. scholarship and loan com. 1967—, alt. del. to AMA 1974-77, 85—, del. to AMA 1978-83, Pres.'s award 1983, Disting. Service award 1987), So. Minn. Med. Assn. (pres. 1963-64), Zumbro Valley Med. Soc. (sec.-treas. 1969-70, v.p. 1970-71, pres. 1971-72), Soc. Med. Cons. to Armed Forces (mem. governing council 1980-86, pres. 1984, del. to AMA 1984-92), Am. Gastroent. Assn. (com. on procedures 1970-72, presdl. commn. on future of assn. 1973-74, com. on constn. and by-laws 1980-85), Minn. Soc. Internal Medicine, Sigma Xi. Mailing: 211 2nd St NW Apt 1214 Rochester MN 55901-2897

BARTKEVICIENE, ALDONA, cardiologist; b. Ukmerge, Lithuania, May 12, 1959; PhD, Kaunas Med. U., 1982, MD, 2009, MD, 1982. Cardiologist Klaipeda Children Hosp., 1983—2010, Klaipeda U. Hosp., 2010—. Cons. Klaipeda Med. Ctr. Salvija, 1996—. Mem.: Assn. European Pediat. Cardiology, Assn. European Children Cardiologist. Avocations: travel, theater, music. Home: Kanto 17-6 Klaipeda 92241 Lithuania Personal E-mail: aldonabar@yahoo.com.

BARTLETT, ALICE BRAND, psychoanalyst, educator, researcher; b. Carrollton, Mo., Oct. 27, 1950; d. Daniel Arthur and Nellie May (Farmer) Brand; m. Thomas Sidney Bartlett, Aug. 12, 1989. BA, U. Mo., 1972, MLS, 1973; postgrad., Topeka Inst. Psychoanalysis, 1979-96; PhD, Fielding Grad. U., 2008. Dir. libr. Mo. Inst. Psychiatry, St. Louis, 1973-74; chief libr. Menninger Clinic, Topeka, 1975—2001, psychotherapist, 1984—2001, assoc. dean info./media Karl Menninger Sch. Psychiatry, 1988—2001, E. Greenwood prof., 1990—2001, prin. investigator Child and Family Ctr., 1995—2001; pvt. practice tng. supr., psychoanalyst Greater Kans. City Psychoanalytic Inst., 2001—. Cons. C.F. Menninger Meml. Hosp., Topeka, 1987-2001; bd. dirs. Psychoanalytic Rsch. Consortium, N.Y.C. and Topeka, 1989-; bd. dirs. Psychoanalytic Electronic Pub. Contbr. articles to profl. publs. Interfuture scholar, 1971-72. Mem. Am. Psychoanalytic Assn. (Liddle grantee 1985), Topeka Psychoanalytic Soc. (recorder 1983-86, program chair 1993-97, pres. 2000-04), Greater Kansas City & Topeka Psychoanalytic Ctr. (pres. 2006-08). Office: 3649 SW Burlingame Rd Topeka KS 66604 Office Phone: 785-234-3873, 785-266-6751. Business E-Mail: dralicebartlett@sbcglobal.net.

BARTLETT, DAVID L., surgeon, educator; b. Ann Arbor, Mich, Nov. 5, 1961; BA, Rice U., Houston, 1979—83; MD, U. Tex., Houston, 1983—87. Diplomate Am. Bd. Surgery. Rsch. fellow dept. of devel. therapeutics M.D. Anderson Hosp., 1984—87; resident surgery Hosp. of the Univ. of Pa., Phila., 1987—93, dept. surgery, Harrison Dept. of surg. rsch., 1989—91; surgery fellow Meml. Sloan-Kettering Surg. Cancer Ctr., NYC, 1993—95; spl. expert surgery br. Nat. Cancer Inst., 1995—96, sr. investigator surgery br., 1996—2001; asst. prof. Univ. of Health Svcs. Uniformed Svcs., 1996—2001; chief divsn. surgical oncology surgery dept. Univ. of Pitts.; dir. David C. Koch Regional Perfusion Cancer Therapy Ctr. Univ. of Pitts. Cancer Inst.; Dr. Bernard Fisher prof. surgery Univ. of Pitts. Sch. of Medicine, 2006—. Vis. assoc. prof. surgery dept. Univ. of Pitts. Fellow Clin. Oncology, Am. Cancer Soc., 1994—95. Mem.: AMA, Am. Soc. of Gene Therapy, Soc. of Surg. Oncology. Office: University of Pittsburgh Physicians Division of Surgical Oncology 5150 Centre Ave Pittsburgh PA 15232 Mailing: University of Pittsburgh Medical Center Cancer Center Ground Fl 9100 Babcock Blvd Pittsburgh PA 15237 Office Phone: 412-692-2852, 412-367-6454.

BARTLETT, DIANE SUE, counselor; b. Laconia, NH, Dec. 6, 1947; d. Fred Elmer and Dorothy Pearl (Wakefield) Davis; m. Josiah Henry Bartlett, Aug. 23, 1980; 1 stepchild, Juliet; 1 child from previous marriage, Fred Louis Hacker. AA, Plymouth State Coll., 1982, MEd, 1988; B in Gen. Studies summa cum laude, U. N.H., 1984. Lic. clin. mental health counselor. Mental health counselor, Ossipee, NH, 1995—; police comm. specialist Divsn. Motor Vehicles, Concord, NH, 1970-76, br. office mgr., 1976-83, coord. motor vehicle registrations, 1983-84; tax collector City of Dover, NH, 1984; intern Lakes Region Mental Health Divsn., Laconia, NH, 1985; counselor Latchkey Pastoral Counseling, Laconia, 1984-87; family therapist Children's Best Interest, Laconia, 1988—. Mental health counselor Carroll County Mental Health Svcs., Wolfeboro, NH, 1988—95; participant N.H. Ann. Conf. Status and Role Women, Concord, 1985—87. Mem. Moultonboro (N.H.) Sch. Feasibility Study Commn., 1978, Carroll County Domestic Violence Coun., 1997—, Friends of Families Carroll County, 1995—; mem. bd. dirs. Child Advocacy Ctr. Carroll County, 2008—; mem. adminstrv. bd. dirs., chmn. pastor-parish rels. com. United Meth. Ch., Moultonboro, 1983—94, mem. adminstrv. bd. dirs. N.H. ann. conf., 1986—88. Grantee, N.H. Charitable Found., 1985. Mem.: ACA, Am. Mental Health Counselors Assn. Avocations: skiing, swimming, reading, writing. Home: PO Box 14 Moultonborough NH 03254-0014 Office: Mountainside Bus Ctr 127 Route 28 Ossipee NH 03864-7300 Office Phone: 603-539-3333. *

BARTLETT, JACQUELINE A., child and adolescent psychiatrist, educator; MD, U. Cin., 1971. Diplomate Am. Bd. Psychiatry and Neurology-child and adolescent psychiatry, 1981, Am. Bd. Psychiatry and Neurology, 1983. Intern pediat. Albert Einstein Coll. Montefiore Hosp., Bronx, NY, 1971—72; resident psychiatry Albert Einstein Coll. Columbia Presbyn. Med. Ctr., 1972—73, fellow child & adolescent psychiatry, 1977—79; assoc. prof. clin. psychiatry NJ Med. Sch. Univ. Medicine and Dentistry NJ. Office: University of Medicine and Dentistry New Jersey Medical School 183 S Orange Ave Ste E1546 Newark NJ 07107 Office Phone: 973-972-2977. Office Fax: 973-972-2979.

BARTLETT, MARK R., insurance company executive; BSBA, U. Mich.; MDiv, Moddy Theol. Sem. (formerly Mich. Theol. Sem.); grad. in Leadership Mich. program, Mich. Chamber of Commerce. CPA. Audit mng. Detroit acctg. firm; dir. fin. acctg. Blue Cross Blue Shield of Mich., Detroit, 1989, sr. v.p., exec. v.p.,pres. emerging markets, CFO. Bd. dirs. Detroit Investment Fund, Accident Fund Ins. Co. of America, Blue Venture Fund, Blue Care Network of Mich. Inc., His Mansion; bd. govs. Van Andel Inst., Spectrum Human Svcs.; adv. bd. mem. Moody Theol. Sem.-Mich.; bd. treas. Ctr. for Healthcare Rsch. and Transformation. Named one of the 40 Under 40, Crain's Detroit Bus. Mem.: Chartered Property Casualty Underwriters Soc., Mich. Assn. Cert. Pub. Accountants, American Inst. of Cert. Pub. Accountants. Office: Blue Cross Blue Shield of Michigan 600 E Lafayette Blvd Detroit MI 48226 Office Phone: 313-225-9000. Office Fax: 313-225-6239. *

BARTLETT, SCOTT PAUL, plastic surgeon; m. Kimberly Ruhanen, Feb. 26, 1983; children: Alexandra Wright, Natalie Paxton. MD, Wash. U., St Louis, 1975. Cert. Am. Bd. Surgery, 1985, Am. Bd. Plastic Surgery, 1987. Assoc prof of surgery Univ. Pa. Sch. Medicine, Phila., 1986—, surgeon, 1986—, dir. craniofacial program, and prof., plastic surgery; also, chief, divsn. plastic surgery Children's Hosp. Phila.; resident in tng. MGH Howard Med. Sch., 1975—86. Dir. craniofacial program U. Of Pa, Phila., 2001—; past pres. Northeastern Soc. of Plastic Surgeons; assoc. editor Plastic Rsch. Surgery, 2005—, Yearbook of Plastic and Aesthetic Surgery, 1998—. Named a Top Doc, Phila. mag., 2002, 2004—. Mem.: Northeastern Soc. Plastic Surgeons (past pres. 2001), Am. Soc. Of Plastics Surgeons (licentiate; com. chmn. 2003—). Achievements include research in craniofacial biology. Office: U Pa 10 Penn Tower 3400 Spruce St Philadelphia PA 19104 also: Children's Hosp Phila Wood Bldg 34th E Civic Ctr Blvd Philadelphia PA 19104 E-mail: scott.bartlett@uphs.upenn.edu.

BARTLEY, GEORGE B., ophthalmologist, oculoplastic, surgeon; b. Warren, Ohio, Nov. 12, 1955; B in Zoology, Miami U., Oxford, OH; MD, Ohio State U., 1981. Intern Riverside Methodist Hosp., Columbus, Ohio, 1981—82; resident in ophthalmology Mayo Clinic, Rochester, Minn., 1982—85, chmn. ophthalmology, 1992—2001, prof. ophthalmology Coll. Medicine, 1996—; fellow, ophthal. plastic orbital surgery Wright State U. Sch. Med., Dayton, 1985—86. Mem. bd. trustees Mayo Found., Rochester, Minn.; dir. Am. Bd. Opthalmology, 1999—2006; CEO Mayo Clinic, Jacksonville, Fla., 2002—08. Office: Mayo Clinic 200 First St SW Rochester MN 55905 Office Phone: 507-284-3340.

BARTLEY, JAMIE M., urologist; b. Lansing, Mich., Nov. 10, 1978; BS, U. Mich., 2001; DO, Mich. State U. Coll. Osteo. Medicine, 2006. Urology resident Botsford Hosp., 2006—. Mem.: Am. Osteo. Assn., Am. Coll. Osteo. Surgeons, Am. Urologic Assn. Avocations: running, movies, exercise. Home: 10415 Hart Ave Huntington Woods MI 48070 Home Fax: 517 896 5231. Personal E-mail: bartley.jamie.78@gmail.com.

BARTO, DEBORAH ANN, physician; b. West Chester, Pa., July 27, 1948; d. Charles Guy and Jeannette Victoria (Golder) B. BA, Oberlin Coll., Ohio, 1970, MD, Hahnemann U., Phila., 1974; Reiki III, N.W. Sch. Healing, Redmond, Wash., 2003. Cert. Reiki master. Intern, resident Kaiser Permanente Hosp., San Francisco, 1974-77; dir. med. oncology Evergreen Hosp., Kirkland, Wash., 1980-85, head oncology quality assurance, 1992-94; med. dir. Cmty. Home Health Care Hospice, Seattle, 1981-84. Hosp. ethics com. Evergreen Hosp., 1995-98, integrative care com., 1996-2001. Recipient Leading Health Profl. award, IBCP's, 2009; named America's Top Physicians, 2009, Top Dr., IAI, Kirkland, Wash., 2010; named one of Top Primary Care, Puget Sound's, 2009. Mem. Evergreen Women's Physicians, Reiki III. Democrat. Buddhist. Avocation: horseback riding. Office: 13115 121st Way NE Ste C Kirkland WA 98034

BARTOLEK, DUBRAVKA, anesthesiologist, researcher; b. Varazdin, Croatia, Mar. 3, 1963; d. Franjo and Ljubica Bartolek. BS, Med. Sch. U. Zagreb, Croatia, 1988, MS, 2000. Cert. specialist anesthesiology and intensive medicine Med. Sch. U. Zagreb, 1996, subspecialist critical care medicine 2008, hemodynamic monitoring Croatian Soc. Aesthesiology and Intensive Care Medicine, 1996, evoked potential NYU Med. Ctr., Dept. Anesthesiology, 1996, infection control U. Zagreb, Med. Sch., 1998, clin. pharmacology and toxicology U. Zagreb, Med. Sch., 2000, EU diploma Fondation Europeenne d'Enseignement Anaesthesiologie, 2001, cert. Obstetric Anesthetists Assn., London, 2001, cert. enteral and parenteral nutrition therapy ESPEN, Izvorani, Romania, 2003, mech. ventilation U. Zagreb, Med. Sch., Dubrovnik, 2004, sepsis and multiorgan dysfunction Deutsche Sepsis Gesellschaft, Weimar, Germany, 2005, preoperative intensive medicine Osterreichische Innere Medizin Gesellschaft, Wien, Austria, 2007, beatmungstherapie intensivmedicin Osterreichische Gesellschaft Internistische Intensivmedizine, 2007. Internship Gen. Hosp., Varazdin, 1989—90; gen. practitioner Cmty. Health Ctr., Varazdin, 1990—91; trainee anesthesia and intensive care medicine U. Hosp. Ctr. Rebro, Zagreb, 1992—96. Lectr. regional anesthesia U. Zagreb, Med. Sch., 2000—; leader anesthesiology ENT dept. U. Clinic, Zagreb, 2003—05; leader substitute anesthesiology U. Clinic Traumatology, Zagreb, 2005—07. Contbr. chapters to books, scientific papers to profl. jours. articles. Healthcare vol. Mercy Ships, Human Resources, Internat. Operations Ctr., Canada, 2008. Recipient award, Croatian Soc. Anesthesiology and Intensive Medicine, 2000, Croatian Soc. Critical Care Medicine, 2006. Mem.: Croatian Soc. Traumatology, Croatian Soc. Critical Care Medicine, Croatian Soc. Anaesthesiology and Intensive Medicine, Croatian Soc. Regional Anesthesia and Analgesia, Internat. Anesthesia Reasrch Soc., Obstetric Anaesthesia Assn., European Soc. Anesthesiology, European Soc. Regional Anaesthesia and Pain Therapy, Croatian Montain-climbing Soc. Matica, Zagreb. Roman Catholic. Avocations: skiing, painting, music, gardening, diving, mountain climbing. Office: Univ Clinic Traumatology Draškoviceva 19 Zagreb 00385 Croatia Home: Kuhaceva 18 00-385 Zagreb Croatia Office Fax: 385 1 46 10 365. Business E-Mail: dubravka.bartolek1@zg.t-com.hr.

BARTOLOZZI, ARTHUR R., orthopaedic surgeon, educator; MD, U. Calif., San Diego, 1981. Lic. ret. Calif., 1986, NJ, 1991, diplomate Am. Bd. Orthopaedic Surgery, 1989. Fellow sports medicine Ronald Reagan UCLA Med. Ctr., 1987; intern gen. surgery Pa. Hosp., 1982, resident orthop. surgery, 1986, clin. assoc. prof. orthop. surgery, surgeon, chief sports medicine. Recipient Best Doctor, Best Doctors in America, 2008—10; named one of America's Top Doctors, 2007—08, 2010, the Top Doctors, Phila. Mag., 2008—11. Office: Pennsylvania Hospital 1 Cathcart 800 Spruce St Philadelphia PA 19107 Office Phone: 215-829-2222.

BARTON, EVERARD NATHANIEL, medical educator, consultant nephrologist; b. Scarborough, Tobago, Jan. 29, 1948; arrived in Jamaica, 1989; s. Daniel Marcus Barton and Cislyn Priscilla (Chapman) Romeo; m. Joycelyn Anderson, Oct. 18, 1995. BSc with honors, U. W.I., Trinidad and Tobago, 1974; MBBS, U. Ibadan, Nigeria, 1980; DM in Internal Medicine, U. W.I., Kingston, Jamaica, 1992. Med. cert. Nigeria, 1980, Trinidad & Tobago, 1983, Jamaica, 1989. Intern Univ. Coll. Hosp., Ibadan, 1980-81; med. officer Osogbo (Nigeria) State Hosp., 1981-83; sr. ho. officer Port-of-Spain (Trinidad) Hosp., 1983-89; resident Univ. Hosp. of W.I., Kingston, Jamaica, 1989-92, cons. physician, 1992—. Lectr. U. W.I., 1992-93, Commonwealth rsch. fellow in nephrology Nottingham (Eng.) City Hosp. renal unit, 1993-94, lectr. dept. medicine U. W.I., 1994-95, sr. lectr., 1996-2001, prof. medicine and nephrology, 2001, chair head dept. medicine, 2004, campus coord. for accreditation med. program, 2006; mem. various coms., Univ. Hosp. W.I., mem. splty. bd. in medicine, 1995—; founder, chmn. Caribbean Inst. Nephrology, 2003. Editor-in-chief West Indian Med. Jour., 1999—, chmn. dept. medicine, 2004—; contbr. articles to profl. med. jours. Resource person Ch. of God 7th Day, Kingston, 1995—; welfare and edn. mem. Renal Support Found., Kingston, 1994—; exec. mem. Kidney Found., Kingston, 1993—; mem. resource pers. Lupus Found., Kingston, 1995—; del. People to People Internat., South Africa, 1996, Egypt, 1998; founder, chmn. Caribbean Inst. Nephrology. Recipient Cert., People to People Amb. Programs, 1998, Unsung Hero Jamaica, 2010; ACP fellow, 1997; Renal Care grantee Renal Support Found., 1997; nephrology fellow Commonwealth Med. Fellowship, Eng., 1993. Fellow Royal Coll. Physicians Edinburgh; mem. AAAS, N.Y. Acad. Scis., Internat. Soc. Nephrology. Mem. Ch. of England. Avocations: poetry, chess, swimming, community work. Office: U of WI Dept Medicine Mona Kingston 6 Jamaica Office Phone: 876-9471271. Fax: 876-977-0691. Business E-Mail: everard.barton@uwimona.edu.jm.

BARTON, FRITZ ENGEL, JR., plastic surgeon, educator; b. Ft. Worth, Tex., Mar. 5, 1942; BS, So. Meth. U., Dallas, 1963; MD, U. Tex. Southwestern Med. Sch., Dallas, 1967. Diplomate Am. Bd. Surgery, Am. Bd. Plastic Surgery, lic. Tex. Intern gen. surgery NC Meml. Hosp., Chapel Hill, 1967-68; resident plastic reconstructive surgery Parkland Meml. Hosp./U. Tex., 1970-74; resident plastic surgery Inst. Reconstructive Plastic Surgery, NYU, NYC, 1974-76; prof., chmn. divsn. plastic surgery U. Tex. Southwestern Med. Sch., 1977—91, clin. prof. plastic surgery, 1991—; pvt. practice Dallas Plastic Surgery Inst., Dallas, 1976—. Bd. dirs. Am. Bd. Surgery, 1988—95; attending staff Baylor U. Med. Ctr., Dallas, Presbyn. Hosp. Dallas, VA Med. Ctr. Dallas, Zale Lipshy U. Hosp. Contbr. articles to profl. jours., chapters to books. Served with US Army, 1968—70, Vietnam. Recipient Tattinger award, Susan G. Komen Found. Breast Cancer Rsch., 1996. Fellow: ACS; mem.: AMA, Assn. Academic Chmn. of Plastic Surgery (pres. 1991—92), Tex. Med. Assn., Dallas Soc. Plastic Surgeons (pres. 1983—84), Tex. Soc. Plastic Surgery (pres. 1988), Plastic Surgery Ednl. Found. (pres.-elect 1991—92, pres. 1992—93), Am. Soc. Plastic & Reconstructive Surgery (bd. dirs. 1988—91), Am. Soc. Aesthetic Plastic Surgeons, Am. Soc. Aesthetic Plastic Surgery (parliamentarian 1993, v.p. 1997—98, pres. 1999—2000, Simon Fredricks award 1989, 1998), Am. Assn. Plastic Surgeons (trustee 1991), Alpha Omega Alpha. Achievements include development of the high "SMAS" facelift technique which uniquely produces natural, long lasting facial rejuvenation. Office: Dallas Plastic Surgery Inst Pyramids Med Ctr 9101 N Central Expy Ste 600 Dallas TX 75231-5956 Office Phone: 214-821-9355.

BARTON, JEAN MARIE, psychologist, educator; b. Pitts., Mar. 24, 1945; d. Joseph Paul and Jean Marie (Anderson) Adamchic; m. Robert L. Barton, Jr., Aug. 14, 1965; children: Robert Joseph, Katherine Anne. BS summa cum laude, U. Pitts., 1965; MEd, Boston U., 1969; CAGS, Cath. U. Am., 1985, PhD in Ednl. Psychology, 1988. Cert. sch. psychologist, Md., nationally cert. sch. psychologist. Tchr./curriculum Wellesley Pub. Schs., Mass., 1965—69; lectr. U. R.I./R.I. Coll., Providence, 1969—72; curriculum specialist/tchr. St. Jane DeChantal Sch., Bethesda, Md., 1977—83, dir. computer prog., 1982—84; psychology assoc. Long Assocs., Bethesda, 1988—; psychol. cons. gifted unit Montgomery County Pub. Schs., Rockville, Md., 1985—99; sch. psychologist various schs. Archdiocese Washington, Md., 1987—; adj. mem. faculty Cath. U. Am., Washington, 1989—2004. Mem. evaluation team Cath. Schs. Studies, 1987-92; dir. Profl. Devel. Inst., Cath. U. Am., 1985-86; mem. adv. com., chairperson identification com. Jacob Javits Grant, Montgomery County Pub. Schs., 1989-92, project coord. Jacob Javitz grant, 1992-95, supt. adv. com. on Edn. of Gifted, 1992-96, on Spl. Edn.; assoc. dir. Ctr. for Advancement Cath. Edn. at Cath. U. Am., 1998-2004; mem. adv. com. on gifted edn. Md. State Dept. Edn., 1999-2000. Contbr. articles to profl. jours. U. Pitts. scholar, 1962-65. Mem. APA, NASP, Md. Sch. Psychologists Assn. Home: 5008 Benton Ave Bethesda MD 20814-2804 Personal E-mail: docjeanbarton@yahoo.com.

BARTON, JOHN JOSEPH, obstetrician, gynecologist, administrator, educator, researcher; b. Rockford, Ill., Mar. 19, 1933; s. L. David and Helen M. (Fox) B.; m. Lois Maltby, 1959 (div. 1965); children: Mary Katherine, Karen Ann. BA in History, U. Ill., 1957; BS in Medicine, U. Ill., Chgo., 1959, MD, 1961; student Law, Loyola U., Chgo., 1966-69. Diplomate Am. Bd. Ob.-Gyn.; cert. Advanced Cardiac Life Support. Rotating intern Cook County Hosp., Chgo., 1961-62, resident in ob.-gyn., 1962-65; fellow gynecologic pathology Northwestern U., Chgo., 1963, clin. asst. ob.-gyn., 1963-64, clin. instr. ob.-gyn., 1964-65, assoc. in ob.-gyn., 1965-71; prof. ob.-gyn. Cook County Grad. Sch. of Medicine, Chgo., 1965—; dir. ob.-gyn. rsch. and edn. Cook County Hosp., Chgo., 1965-69; chmn. ob.-gyn. Ill. Masonic Med. Ctr., Chgo., 1970—2001; assoc. prof. ob.-gyn. U. Ill. Coll. Medicine, Chgo., 1971-83, prof., 1983-93, lectr. in ob.-gyn., 1993—;

prof. ob.-gyn. Rush Med. Coll., Chgo., 1993—; chmn. emeritus ob-gyn Ill. Masonic Med. Ctr., 2002—. Clin. clerkship subcom. U. Ill. Coll. Medicine, 1974-90, acad. senate 1977-91, 85-87, perinatal steering com., 1977-92, admissions com. 1985-91, screening subcom. 1988-89; ad hoc com. on rules for governance, Rush Med. Coll., Chgo., 1993—, curriculum com. 1993, com. on student evaluation and promotions, 1994—, core ckerkship subcom. of curriculum com. 1995—; editl. bd. Jour. Obstetrics and Gynecology, Am. Jour. Obstetrics and Gynecology, Internat. Jour. Obstetrics and Gynecology Contbr. numerous articles to profl. jours., chpts. to books. including Laparoscopy in Gynecologic Practice, 1972, Guidelines for Perinatal Care, 1983, Antepartum HIV Screenings: A Comparison of Methodologies, 1990. Vol. cons. Ob.-Gyn. Claremore (Okla.) Indian Hosp., 1979-80, 86, Fort Defiance (Ariz.) Indian Hosp., 1981, Red Crescent Soc., Heliopolis, Cairo, Egypt, 1987; vol. surgeon Internat. Red Cross and Red Crescent Soc. Vols., West Beirut, Lebanon, 1982; mem. Ill. Gov.'s AIDS adv. coun.; advisor, expert witness Atty. Gen. State of Ill. on Standards of Practice in Ob.-Gyn.; mem. com. formation of outcome-oriented surveillance systems for Ill. Dept. of Pub. Health, adv. com. to Health Planning Com. for Chgo., perinatal adv. com. Ill. Dept. Health, steering com. Mayor Washington's Infant Mortality Reduction Initiative and others. Sgt. USMC, 1950-55, Korea. Fellow Am. Coll. Obstetricians and Gynecologists (adv. coun. 1977-81, adv. coun. dist. VI 1977-81, chmn. Ill. sect. 1977-78, com. on profl. liability 1989-92, Jr. Fellow Rsch. prize award 1991), Ctrl. Assn. Obstetricians nd Gynecologists (ctrl. travel club, sci. awards com. 1985-89. chmn. 1987-89, Ann. prize award 1988), Chgo. Gynecol. Soc. (exec. com. 1994—, pres. 1995-96), Am. Coll. Surgeons, Soc. Contemporary Medicine and Surgery, Am. Soc. Clin. Hypnosis, Chgo. Inst. Medicine, Royal Soc. Medicine (London); mem. Ill. Assn. Maternal and Child Health, Assn. Profs. Gynecology and Obstetrics, Am. Pub. Health Assn., Phi Kappa Phi, Nu Sigma Nu. Home: Bar T Ranch 20516 Bunker Hill Rd Marengo IL 60152-8003 Office: Ill Masonic Med Ctr 836 W Wellington Ave Chicago IL 60657-9224 Office Phone: 815-943-6823. Personal E-mail: barthandz@aol.com.

BARTON, JÓZSEF, retired physician, dentist; b. Villány, Baranya, Hungary, July 31, 1937; s. József and Mária (Herr) B.; m. Éva Gerenday, Apr. 24, 1968; children: József Gábor, Balázs. MD, Med. U., Pécs, Hungary, 1961, DD, 1965; Sports Physiology Diploma, OTKI, Budapest, Hungary, 1979. Surgeon City Hosp., Komló, Hungary, 1961-62; dentist Stomatology Clinic, Pécs, Hungary, 1962-65; sports dr. Janus Pannonius U., Pécs, 1965-86; biomechanists U. Phys. Edn., Budapest, 1986-93; vice-dir. faculty health scis. Med. U. Pécs, Zalaegerszeg, Hungary, 1993-97; ret., 1998. Author: (textbook) Biomechanics, 1984; contbr. articles to profl. jours. Scholar TEMPUS, 1991, TEMPUS-PHARE, 1997, Soros Found., 1997. Mem. Hungarian Sports Medicine Soc. Avocations: travel, swimming, skiing, photography. Home: Siklósi 80 7632 Pécs Baranya Hungary

BARTON, MATTHIAS, physician; b. Wolfsburg, Germany, Aug. 6, 1964; s. Erich and Anna Elisabeth Barton. MD, Hannover Med. Sch., Germany, 1994. Diplomate German Med. Assn. Intern Hannover Med. Sch., 1994—95; fellow in cardiology U. Hosp. Bern, Switzerland, 1995—97, U. Hosp. Zurich, Switzerland, 1997—99, attending physician dept. medicine, 2000—, dir. rsch., med. policlinic, 2001—06; assoc. prof. U. Zurich, 2001—06, prof. medicine, cardiology, 2007—; dir. Molecular Internal Medicine, 2001—. Contbr. articles to profl. jours. With German Air Force. Fellow: Am. Heart Assn. (assoc.). Achievements include research in atherosclerosis and related diseases. Office Fax: 41-1-255-8747. Personal E-mail: barton@gmx.ch. Business E-Mail: barton@usz.ch.

BARTSCH, ERNST KARL, medical products executive; s. Kurt and Rosemarie Bartsch. Diploma in engring., Fachhochschule Regensburg, Germany, 1997; MS, U. Hull, Eng., 1998; PhD, U. Cambridge, Eng., 2003; Dr h. c., Yorker Internat. U. Mgmt. Trainee Adaptive Broadband Ltd., Cambridge, 1989, Siemens VDO Automotive AG, Regensburg, Germany, 1996; pre-doctoral rsch. asst. U. Cambridge, 1999; product mgr. Siemens Med. Solutions, Erlangen, Germany, 2003—04, innovation mgr., 2004—06, version mgr., 2006—08, project dir., 2008—, bus. mgr. Contbr. articles various profl. jours. Fellow, Cambridge European Soc., 1999, Bursary, 2002. Mem.: IEEE (assoc.), Inst. Elec. Engrs. (assoc.). Avocations: windsurfing, mountain biking, photography, football, skiing. Office: Siemens Healthcare Dept CS M BM Hartmann Str 16 91052 Erlangen Germany Business E-Mail: ernst.bartsch@cantab.net, ernst.bartsch@siemens.com.

BARTZATT, RONALD LEE, research biochemist, consultant; b. Lincoln, Nebr., Dec. 18, 1953; s. Frank Wright and Lorretta (Warta) B.; m. Patricia Ann Dockham, July 30, 1979 (div. Oct. 1983). BS, U. Nebr., 1978, MS, 1980, PhD, 1982. Cert. med. lab. technician. Research biochemist U. Nebr., Lincoln, 1983-84, Eppley Cancer Ctr., Omaha, 1984-85, Theodor Gildore Ctr., San Diego, 1985, U. Calif., San Diego, 1985-88; rsch. biochemist Eppley Cancer Ctr., 1988—. Cons. IRCS Med. Sci., Lancaster, England, 1985—. Author: Proceedings of ACS Symposia on Computer Data Analysis and Optimization; contbr. articles to profl. jours. Deacon Luth. Ch., San Diego. Served with U.S. Army, 1973-76. Towle Scholar U. Nebr., 1973; NIH fellow, 1984; grantee Nebr. Water Co., 1981. Mem. Am. Soc. Clin. Pathologists, Phi Lambda Upsilon. Republican. Avocations: kayaking, ice skating, skiing, music. Business E-Mail: bartzatt@mail.unomaha.edu.

BARUZAIG, ALI SALEH, pharmacologist, educator; b. Yemen, Sept. 5, 1970; M, Suez Canal U., 2009. Lectr., faculty medicin pharmacology dept. Hadramout U., 2009—. Office: Hadramout University Sci & Tech Dept Pharmacology Mukalla PO Box 8892 Shehir Yemen Home Fax: 009675327366. Personal E-mail: alhadramy@hotmail.com.

BARUZZI, AGOSTINO, neurologist, educator; b. Bologna, June 16, 1946; Maturità Liceo Classico, Liceo Luigi Galvani, Bologna, 1965; Laurea Medicina e Chirurgia, U. di Bologna, 1971. Rschr., assoc. prof. neurology U. di Bologna, 1974—94, prof. neurology, 1994—, prof., dir. inst. neurol. clinic, 1998—2002, prof., dir. dept. neurol. scis., 2002—08, 2011—. Recipient "Amb. Epilepsy", IBE-ILAE. Avocations: reading, music, gardening. Office: Clinica Neurologica via U Foscolo 7 Bologna Emilia-Romagna 40123 Italy E-mail: agostino.baruzzi@unibo.it.

BARZILAY, JOSHUA ISRAEL, endocrinologist, educator; b. NYC, May 11, 1951; s. Isaac and Helly Barzilay; m. Sarah Gilda Goldszer, June 22, 1982; children: Simon David, Aliza. MD, SUNY Downstate, Bklyn., 1976. Cert. in medicine Nat. Bd. Med. Examiners, 1976. Endocrinologist Kaiser Permanente, Tucker, Ga., 1990—; clin. prof. Emory U. Sch. Medicine, Atlanta, 1991—. Author: (book) The Water We Drink. Physician Jewish Health Care Internat., Atlanta, 2000—08. Capt., 1984—86, Israel Air Force. Fellow: Am. Coll. Physicians.

BASAK, SURAJIT, physician; b. Kolkata, Dec. 24, 1975; MSc, Calcutta U., 2000; PhD, Bose Inst., 2007. Physician NICED, 2008—. Avocations: reading, travel. Office: P33 CIT Rd Kolkata West Bengal 700010 India Business E-Mail: basaksurajit@gmail.com.

BASARAN, NURSEN, toxicologist, educator; b. Ankara, Mar. 8, 1955; MS, Hacettepe U., 1987, D, 1992. Asst. prof. Hacettepe U., 1992—99, prof., 1999—, head pharmaceutic toxicology dept., 2009. Recipient award, Dr. Ibrahim Etem Ilaç Fabrikasi, 1990, Hacettepe Ü., 1991. Mem.: EUROTOX & IUTOX, Commns. Ministry of Health, Turkish Soc. Toxicology, Editl. Bd. Internat. Toxicology, Editl. Bd. Human & Exptl. Toxicolgy. Office: Hacettepe University Faculty Pharmacy Ankara Altindag 06100 Turkey Office Fax: 00903123052178. Business E-Mail: nbasaran@hacettepe.edu.tr.

BASCONES-MARTINEZ, ANTONIO, dentist, educator; b. Madrid, Aug. 7, 1944; MD, DDS, PhD, MSc, Dental Sch., 1961; PhD (hon.), Cayetano Heredia U., Chile U. Prof., head Complutense U., 1962—. Exvice dean Dental Sch.; ex pres. Dental Assn. Madrid. Recipient Gold medal, Spanish Soc. Avocations: reading, writing. Office: Boix y Morer 6-1° Madrid 28003 Spain Office Fax: 34-915345860. Business E-Mail: antbasco@odon.ucm.es.

BASGUT, BILGEN, pharmacologist; b. Eskisehir, May 20, 1977; PhD, Gazi U., 2005. Lectr. dept. pharmacology Gazi U. Faculty Pharmacy, 2006—. Recipient Women Sci.' awards, L'Oreal, 2008—09; Postdoc. Rsch. grant, U. Fla., Dept. Pharmacology and Therapeutics, Gainesville, TUBITAK. Mem.: Internat. Soc. Heart Rsch., Turkish Pharmacological Soc. Office: Gazi University Faculty Pharmacy Ankara 06330 Turkey Business E-Mail: bilgenbasgut@gmail.com.

BASHA, FAYEZ, surgeon; MB, Damascus Univ., Syria UK, M in Surgery. Higher gen. surg. and advanced laparoscopic tng., England; fellowship Royal Coll. Surgeons, Ireland, 1998; specialist gen. surgeon Mil. Hosp., Damascus; chief surgery King Khalid Hosp.; specialist gen. / laparoscopic surgeon and chief surgery Emirates Hosp., Dubai. Mailing: c/o Emirates Hospital PO Box 73663 Jumeirah Beach Rd Dubai United Arab Emirates Office Phone: 97143496666. Office Fax: 97143496664. *

BASHORE, THOMAS MICHAEL, cardiologist, educator; b. Paulding, Ohio, Apr. 9, 1946; s. Raymond Earl and Bertha Gladys (Smith) B.; m. Jill Eickhoff; children: Todd Thomas, Tiffany Lynn, Blake William. AB in Zoology, Miami U., 1968; MD, Ohio State U., 1972. Intern, resident U. N.C., Chapel Hill, 1972-75; fellow in cardiology Duke Med. Ctr., Durham, N.C., 1975-77, from asst. prof. to prof., dir. cardiac cath. lab., dir. fellowship tng., prof., 1980-85; asst. prof., dir. nuc. cardiology Ohio State U., Columbus, 1980-85; prof. Duke Med. Ctr., Durham, NC, 1985—, vice chief divsn. cardiology, 2007—. Assoc. editor Am. Heart Jour., 1996—; mem. editl. bd. Am. Jour. Cardiology, 1987—, Catheterization and Cardiovasc. Diagnosis, 1990—, Emergency Medicine, 1992-2002, Circulation, 1995-2001, Duke Med. Update, 1996, Cardiology Today, 1998—, Jour. Am. Coll. Cardiology, 2002—; contbr. articles to profl. jours., chpts. to books; author 3 books on cardiology Recipient endowed professorship, 2008. Fellow Am. Coll. Cardiology. (mem. coms. cardiac catheterization 1996-2001, cardiac imaging 1997-2000, adult congenital heart disease com. 2003—, mem. bd. rev. CD ROM 1996-2002, author ACCSAP & CATHSAP questions, mem. com. workforce & tng., chmn. com. on cardiac cath. lab. guidelines 1998-2000, 2009-), Am. Heart Assn., Alpha Omega Alpha. Avocations: fly fishing, basketball, painting, computers. Home: 3825 Westchester Rd Durham NC 27707-5072 Office: Duke Med Ctr PO Box 3012 Durham NC 27715-3012 Office Phone: 919-684-2407. *

BASINGER, KAREN LYNN, renal dietitian; b. Mechanicsville, Md., July 4, 1955; d. Leonard Marcus and Mary Jane (Harding) Brookbank; m. Joseph Andrew Basinger, Nov. 17, 1984; 1 child, James Marcus. BS, U. Md., 1977; MS, Hood Coll., 1987. Lic. nutritionist. Libr. technician Bowie (Md.) State Coll., 1973-79; instr. St. Mary's County Adult Edn., Leonardtown, Md., 1979-80; home economist Zamoiski Co., Balt., 1977-83; nutritionist/WIC coord. South County Health Plan, Prince Frederick, Md., 1979-80; nutritionist Walter Reed Army Med. Ctr., Washington, 1980-82; renal dietitian Mid Atlantic/BMA, Camp Springs, Md., 1982-87, Kidney Care Ctr., Landover, Md., 1987-99; instr. dietary intern program Andrews AFB, 1988-91; renal dietitian Silver Spring (Md.) Artificial Kindey Ctr., 1998—; outpatient dietitian Holy Cross Hosp., Silver Spring, 1999-2000; renal dietitian DaVita-Wheaton, Md., 1999—. Cons. Leisure World Med. Ctr., 2002—; adj. prof. Montgomery Coll., Rockville, 2004—; lectr. in field. Profl. adv. bd. Nat. Kidney Found./NCA, 1989-94; chair coun. on renal nutrition Nat. Kidney Found., 1993-94, program chair, 1990-92. Recipient Spl. Recognition Nat. Kidney Found./NCA, 1990, 92, Recognized Renal Dietitian/NCA, 1991, 94. Mem.: Washington Met. Coun. on Renal Nutrition (chair 1986—94, 1986—94, nutrition symposium chair 1989, chair 2001—02), Am. Dietetic Assn. (legis. chair, reimbursement chair, renal practice group 2003—, Renal Practise Group Outstanding Svc. award 2008), Md. Home Econs. Assn. (bylaws chair 1982—94), Am. Home Econs. Assn., U. Md. Aumni Assn. Democrat. Lutheran. Avocation: cross-stitch.

BASKARA, ARUNKUMAR, surgeon; b. Sivakasi, India, Dec. 24, 1976; MD, Stanley Med. Coll., 2001. Physician Mercy Cath. Med. Ctr., 2007—. Recipient Dulees Travel grant, MII Course, 2011. Mem.: ACS, RCS (Edinburgh), SAGES. Home: 51-7 Revere Rd Drexel Hill PA 19026 Personal E-mail: abaskara24@yahoo.co.uk.

BASKIN, LAURENCE SETH, pediatrician, educator; BS in Biophysics, U. Calif., Berkeley, 1982; MD, UCLA, 1986. Cert. Am. Bd. Urology. Intern gen. surgery U. Calif., San Francisco, 1986—88, resident, 1988—91, asst. prof. dept. urology, 1993—98, assoc. prof. dept. urology & pediat., 1998—2004, prof. dept. urology & pediat., 2004—, founder Ctr. Treatment & Study of Hypospadias; chief pediatric urology U. Calif. San Francisco Children's Hosp., 1998—; fellow pediatric urology Children's Hosp. Phila., 1991—93. Contbr. articles to profl. jours. Fellow: ACS; mem.: Am. Urol. Assn., Asian Pacific Assn. Pediatric Urology (pres.), Soc. Fetal Urology (pres.), Soc. Pediatric Urology, Am. Acad. Pediat. Office: UCSF Med Ctr 400 Parnassus Ave Ste A-610 San Francisco CA 94143-0330 also: UCSF Med Ctr Dept Urology Box 0738 San Francisco CA 94143-0738 Office Phone: 415-353-2200, 415-476-1611. Office Fax: 415-353-2480, 415-476-8849. Business E-Mail: lbaskin@urology.ucsf.edu.

BASNET, NARAYAN BAHADUR, pediatrician, researcher, cardiologist; b. Sotang Village, Nepal, Aug. 25, 1960; arrived in Japan, 1995; s. Khadga Bahadur and Nanda Basnet; m. Sangeeta B. Basnet, Nov. 19, 1992; children: Abhilasha, Abhishek. MPA, Tribhuvan U., Kathmandu, Nepal, 1985, MBBS, 1990, cert. in gen. medicine, 1979, diploma in pub. adminstrn., 1981; PhD, U. Tokyo, 2000. Registered physician Nepal Med. Coun., 1991. Clin. clerk U. Lund, Sweden, 1990; clin. intern Tribhuran U. Tchg. Hosp., Kathmandu, 1990—91; house officer pediat. Tribhuran U. Tchg. Hosp. and Kanti Children's Hosp., Kathmandu, 1991—93; med. officer pediatric surgery Kanti Children's Hosp., Kathmandu, 1993—94; med. coord. Assn. Med. Drs. Asia, Phnom Penh, Cambodia, 1994—95; vis. rschr. dept. pediat. U. Tokyo, 2000—01, JSPS postdoctoral fellow dept. pediat., 2001—03; freelance rschr. Nepal and Japan, 2003—04; vol. pediat. cardiologist Kanti Children's Hosp., Nepal, 2004—05; founder, dir., cons. Children's Med. Diagnosis Ctr., Kathmandu, 2005—; pediatrician, pediat. cardiologist Durga Bhawani Polyclinic, Kathmandu, 2006—; med. escort Internat. Orgn. Migration, Kathmandu, 2008—. Chairperson Health Info. Ctr. Nepal, Kathmandu, 1991—94; med. officer, co-investigator Acute Respiratory Infection Project, Kathmandu, 1993—94. Contbr. articles to profl. jours. Adviser Nepalese Assn. in Japan, 1996—2003. Recipient rsch. award, Grad. Sch. Medicine, U. Tokyo, 1999, 2001. Mem.: AAAS, Asian Soc. Pediatric Rsch., Japan Pediat. Soc., Pediat. Cardiol. Soc. India (life), Nepal Pediatric Soc. (life), Cardiol. Soc. India (life), Assn. Med. Drs. Asia (life), Nepal Family Planning Assn. (life), Nepal Med. Assn. (life). Achievements include research in normal value of pulmonary arterial compliance in children and its variation in septal defects; common heart problems in Nepali children, situation of pediatric manpower in Nepal; development of basic INFANT health care package (I=immunization, N=nutrition, F=feeding, A=adult support, N=neonatal care, T=treatment of common conditions) recommended to improve infant health care in Nepal; research in on child raising issues in Japan; pediatric heart problems/pediatric heart health Nepal. Avocations: reading, writing, travel, social service. Home: Chunderi Kathmandu 4 Nepal Address: GPO Box 1563 Kathmandu Nepal Office Phone: (977) 98510 84273. Personal E-mail: nbbasnet777@hotmail.com.

BASRA, MOHAMMAD KHURSHID AZAM, dermatologist, researcher; b. Lahore, Punjab, Pakistan, Jan. 10, 1969; s. Muhammad Azam Choudhry and Nasim Azam; m. Zarqa Mansoor, Dec. 23, 1994; 1 child, Sarah Khurshid. MBBS, U. Punjab, Pakistan, 1994; DDSc, U. Wales Coll. Medicine, Cardiff, Wales, 2004; MD, Cardiff U., 2007. Lectr. dept. dermatology Cardiff. U., Cardiff, England. Mem.: European Acad. Dermatology and Venereology (corr.). Achievements include first to development of outcome measure for the measurment of dermatology patients' families quality of life. Office: Cardiff Univ Dept Dermatology Heath Park Cardiff CF14 4XN England Home: 73 The Hawthorns Cardiff CF23 7AQ England Office Fax: 44(0)2920744312; Home Fax: 44(0)2920744312. Personal E-mail: drkhurshid69@hotmail.com. Business E-Mail: basramk@cardiff.ac.uk.

BASS, HAROLD NEAL, pediatrician, medical geneticist; b. Chgo., Apr. 14, 1939; s. Louis A. and Minnie (Schachter) B.; m. Phyllis Appell, June 25, 1961; children: Laura Renee, Alana Suzanne. Student, U. Ill., 1956—59; MS in Pharmacology, U. Chgo., 1963, MD, 1963. Diplomate Am. Bd. Pediat., Am. Bd. Med. Genetics, Nat. Bd. Med. Examiners. Intern Children's Meml. Hosp., Chgo., 1963-64, resident, 1964-65, chief resident, 1965-66, fellow in med. genetics, 1965-66; chief pediat. and profl. svcs. Norton AFB Hosp., Calif., 1966-68; attending pediatrician/med. geneticist Kaiser Permanente Med. Ctr., Panorama City, Calif., 1968—; dir. med. genetics prog. Kaiser Permanente Med. Care Program So. Calif., 1987—2003; clin. prof. pediat. and human genetics UCLA Med. Sch., 1970—. Pres. med. staff Kaiser Permanente Med. Ctr., 1989-90; bd. dirs. So. Calif. Permanente Med. Group, 1998-04; adj. prof. biology Calif. State U., Northridge, 1995—. Contbr. articles to profl. jours. Mem. mayor's adv. com. San Fernando Valley, City of L.A., 1973-78. Capt. USAF, 1966—68. Founding Fellow Am. Coll. Med. Genetics, Western Soc. Pediat. Rsch., Brady Handgun Control, ACLU, Am. Soc. Human Genetics, Amnesty Internat. Democrat. Jewish. Avocations: civic affairs, music, writing. Home: 11922 Dunnicliffe Ct Porter Ranch CA 91326-1324 Office: Kaiser Permanente Med Ctr 13652 Cantara St Panorama City CA 91402-5497 Home Phone: 818-360-0154; Office Phone: 818-375-2073. Business E-Mail: harold.n.bass@kp.org.

BASSET-SEGUIN, NICOLE, medical educator; b. Neuilly-sur-Seine, France, Feb. 15, 1957; MD, Lariboisiere St Louis, PhD, 1986. Prof. U. Paris, 1997—. Avocations: art, drawing, sports, travel. Office: 1 Ave Claude vellefaux Paris 75010 France Office Fax: 33142385310. Business E-Mail: nicole.basset-seguin@sls.aphp.fr.

BASSETT, CLIFFORD WAYNE, allergist and immunologist; b. NY, Dec. 29, 1957; MD, SUNY, 1985. Diplomate Am. Bd. Allergy and Immunology. Intern, internal medicine NY Hosp. Queens, Valhalla, NY, 1985—86; resident, allergy and immunology Hackensack Med. Ctr., 1986—89; fellow LI Coll. Hosp., 1991—93; med. dir. Allergy and Asthma Care of NY, NY; asst. clin. prof. medicine SUNY-Health Sciences Ctr., Bklyn.; faculty mem. NYU Sch. Medicine. Mem. med. adv. bd. Allergy and Asthma Found. of America; mem. exec. com. NY Allergy & Asthma Soc. of Greater NY; police surgeon, peace officer NY State; hosp. appointment LI Coll. Hosp., NYU Med. Ctr., NYU Downtown Hosp., Cabrini Med. Ctr., 1994—2002, St. Vincent's Hosp., NY, 2002; investigator in clin. trials. Published papers in Journal of Allergy and Clinical Immunology, Annals of Allergy, Chest; contbr. chapters to books; contributed to articles in NY Daily News, NY Newsday, Time, NY Post, Baby Talk, Prevention, Bottom Line Health Newsletter, Journal of the AMA, Women's World, Self & USA Today, frequently contributes to medical information websites, interviewed on several radio and TV programs including Today Show, Early Show, CBS Evening News, World News Tonight, CNBC, Good Day New York, NBC Nightly News, MSNBC, Telemundo, and Bloomberg Radio Network. Fellow: Am. Acad. Allergy, Asthma and Immunology. Office: 150 Broadway Ste 1601 New York NY 10038 also: 381 Park Ave S Ste 1020 New York NY 10016 also: 115 E 57th St 10th Fl New York NY 10022

BASSETT, LAWRENCE W., diagnostic radiologist, educator; MD, U. of Calif., Irvine, 1968. Diplomate Am. Bd. of Radiology-diagnostic radiology, 1975. Intern Northwestern Univ. Hosps. and Clinics, Chgo., 1968—69; resident UCLA Radiol. Sciences, 1971—74, clin. instr. radiology, 1974—75, asst. prof. radiology, 1975—82, assoc. prof. radiology, 1982—88, dir. residency tng. program, 1978—83, 1985—90, vice chair edn., 1986—90, vice chair academic affairs and dir. breast imaging fellowship, 1990—; Iris Cantor prof. breast imaging and asst. dean student affairs David Deffen Sch. of Medicine UCLA; hosp. affiliation includes Ronald Reagan UCLA Med. Ctr. Co-author: (publs.) The ACR BI-RADS experience: learning from history, 2009, The positive predictive value of BI-RADS microcalcification descriptors and final assessment categories, 2010, Influence of annual interpretive volume on screening mammography performance in the United States, 2011, and numerous others. Recipient Distinguished Tchg. award, UCLA Alumni Assn., 1987, The Excellence in Diagnostic Imaging award, RSNA, 2000, Sherman M. Mellinkoff Faculty award, UCLA Sch. of Medicine, 2004, STAR award, UCLA Healthcare, 2005, Edie and Perry Grant Ptnrs.s in Caring award, 2006, and numerous others. Office: UCLA David Geffen School of Medicine Le Conte Ave & Westwood Blvd Los Angeles CA 90024 Office Phone: 310-825-6373.

BASSINGTHWAIGHTE, JAMES BUCKLIN, physiologist, educator, medical researcher; b. Toronto, Sept. 10, 1929; s. Ewart MacQuarrie and Velma Emeline B.; m. Joan Elizabeth Graham, June 18, 1955; children: Elizabeth Anne, Mary, Alan, Sarah, Rebecca. BA, U. Toronto, 1951, MD, 1955; postgrad., Med. Sch. London, 1957-58; PhD, Mayo Grad. Sch. Medicine U. Minn., Rochester, 1964. Intern Toronto Gen. Hosp., 1955-56; physician Internat. Nickel Co., Sudbury and Matheson, Ont., 1956-57; house physician Hammersmith Hosp., London; postgrad. Med. Sch. London, 1957-58; teaching asst. physiology U. Minn., Mpls., 1961-62; fellow Mayo Grad. Sch. Medicine, Rochester, Minn., 1958-64, instr., 1964-67, asst. prof., 1967-69, assoc. prof., 1969-72; vis. prof. Pharmacology Inst., U. Bern, Switzerland, 1970-71; asso. prof. bioengring. U. Minn., 1972-75; prof. physiology Mayo Grad. Sch. Medicine, 1973-75, prof. medicine, 1975; prof. bioengring., radiology and biomath U. Wash., Seattle, 1975—; dir. Ctr. for Bioengring., 1975-80; vis. prof. medicine and physiology McGill U., 1979-81, affiliate prof. physiology Limburg U., Maastricht, Netherlands, 1990—. Mem. study sect. NIH, 1970-74, 80-83, chmn., 2004; chmn. Biotech. Resources Adv. Com., 1977-79, chmn. 1st Gordon Rsch. Conf. on Water and Solute Transport in Microvasculature, 1976; chmn. workshop on metabolic imaging Nat. Heart, Lung and Blood Inst., 1985; bd. dirs. Nat. Space Biomed. Rsch. Inst., NASA, 2002—; adv. bd. mem. Steps Towards European Physione, 2004-06, Virtual Physiol. Human, 2006-; Lewellen-Thomas lectr., U. Toronto, 1991; Coulter lectr. U. NC, 1995; Oxford lectr. Internat. Soc. Magnetic Resonance Medicine, 1996; mem. ednl. materials com. Whitaker Found., 1995-2005, Kline lectr. U. Cin., 2010; CASI award com. Burrough Wellcome Fund 2004—11, chair, 2007—8. Author: (with L.S. Liebovitch and B.J. West) Fractal Physiology, 1994; contbr. over 280 articles to profl. publs. Recipient NIH Rsch. Career Devel. award, 1964-74, Louis and Artur Lucian award McGill U., 1979, Witzig award Cardiovasc. Sys. Dynamics Soc., 1982, Faculty Achievement award for outstanding rsch. U. Wash. Coll. Engring., 1993; Edmund Hustinx chair Maastricht U., 1999. Fellow Internat. Fedn. Med. & Biograhical. Engring., Biomed. Engring. Soc. (dir. 1971-74, pres. 1977-78, Alza award 1988, editor-in-chief Annals of Biomed. Engring. 1993-2001, assoc. editor 2002—, Disting. Svc. award 1999); mem. AAAS, NAE, Am. Heart Assn. (coun. on circulation 1976—), Biophys. Soc. (assoc. editor Biophys. Jour. 1980-83), Microcirculatory Soc. (mem. coun. 1975-78, 80-83, pres. 1990-91, Landis award 1995), Am. Physiol. Soc. (mem. circulation group, editl. bd. 1972-76, 79-83, mem. edn. com., chair cardiovasc. sect. 1995-96, Wiggers award 2005), Internat. Union Physiol. Scis. (U.S.A. nat. com. 1978-86, U.S. del. to assembly 1980, 83, 86, chmn. 1983-86, chmn. Commn. on Bioengring. and Clin. Physiology 1986-97, chmn. satellite to 30th Congress on Endothelial Transport 1986, co-chmn. satellite on microvascular networks 1989, chmn. satellite on Physiome Project 1997, com. on physiome 1997—), Nat. Acad. Engring. (mem. peer com. 2005—, chair 2006—, Russ award com. 2006-07). Achievements include research in cardiovascular physiology and bioengineering, biomathematics and computer simulation with emphasis on ion and substrate exchange in heart, fractals in physiology, integrative biology and originator of the Physiome Project. Home: 3150 E Laurelhurst Dr NE Seattle WA 98105-5333 Office: University Wash Dept Bioengring N210G Foege Bldg 3720 15th Ave NE PO Box 35-5061 Seattle WA 98195-5061 Office Phone: 206-685-2012. Business E-Mail: jbb2@u.washington.edu.

BASSIR, IYABO BOLA, psychologist, academic administrator; d. Olumbe Abdul and adopted d. Constance Enid Bassir. PhD, U. Ibadan, 1989. Postdoctoral rsch. fellow Internat. Ctr. Insect Physiology and Ecology, Nairobi, Kenya; lectr. grade 1 Ladoke Akintola U. of Tech., Ogbomoso, Nigeria, 1994—96, sr. lectr., 1996—2002; freelance cons. Ibadan, 2002—04; dir. univ. advancement U. Ibadan, 2004—. Cons. UNICEF, Lagos, Nigeria, 2001—02. Patron Youth Of Africa, Ogbomoso, 1998—2001. Rsch. grantee, Ford Found., 1988. Mem.: APA (assoc.), Assn. African Women in Rsch. for Devel., Brit. Psychol. Soc. (licentiate; chartered psychologist), Zonta. Office: U Ibadan Oyo Rd Ibadan 200002 Nigeria Personal E-mail: ibassir@hotmail.com. E-mail: admin@uiadvance.org.

BASSLER, BONNIE L., molecular biologist; BS with high honors, U. Calif., Davis, 1984; PhD, Johns Hopkins U., 1990. Head tchg. asst. Johns Hopkins U, 1985—86; postdoctoral fellow Agouron Inst., La Jolla, Calif., 1990—93, rsch. scientist, 1993—94; asst. prof. dept. molecular biology Princeton U., NJ, 1994—2000, assoc. prof., 2000—03, prof., 2003—. Assoc. faculty mem. Princeton Environ. Inst., 1996—; mem. com. academic standing Princeton U., 1996—99; instr. Cold Spring Harbor Lab., NY, 1996—2000; mem. sci. adv. bd. Quorex Pharms., 1999—, Cumbre, 2002—, Damon Runyon Cancer Rsch. Found., 2003; Burroughs Wellcome Fund vis. prof. La. State U., 2001; dir. grad. studies dept. molecular biology Princeton U., 2003—; investigator Howard Hughes Med. Inst., 2005—; internat. lectr. Contbr. articles to profl. jours.; mem. (editl. bd.) Molecular and Cellular Proteomics, 2001—, Jour. Bacteriology, 2001—, assoc. editor Genetics, 2001—04; editor: Molecular Microbiol., 2003—. Recipient Thomas Edison Patent award, NJ Rsch. & Devel. Coun., 2003, Waksman award, Theobald Smith Soc., 2003, Inventor of the Yr., New York Intellectual Property Law Assn., 2004; grantee W.R. Grace & Co. fellowship, 1988; fellow, Am. Acad. Microbiol., 2002, MacArthur Found., 2002. Fellow: Am. Acad. Arts & Scis.; mem.: Internat. Union of Microbiological Socs., Am. Soc. Cell Biology, Am. Soc. Biochemistry and Molecular Biology, Soc. Bioluminescence and Chemiluminescence, NAS (planning com. 2005, Richard Lounsbery award 2011), Am. Soc. Microbiology (conferences com. 2002—), Phi Kappa Phi, Phi Beta Kappa. Achievements include research in quorum sensing. Office: Princeton U Dept Molecular Biology 329 Lewis Thomas Lab Princeton NJ 08544 *

BASSOLS, ANGEL CARLOS, emergency physician; s. Angel Bassols and Maria Ricardez; m. Maria De Jesus Sanchez, Aug. 30, 2000; children: Francisco Javier, Karla. MD, UNAM, Mexico City, 1978. Diplomate in critical care Acad. Nat. Medicina, 1996. Physician IMSS, Guadalajara, Mexico, 1984—; med. staff Grupo Angeles Servicios De Salud, Guadalajara, 2000—. Election staff IFE, Zapopan, Mexico, 1999—2006. Mem.: SCCM. Home and Office: Hosp Angeles Del Carmen Tarascos St 3435 44670 Guadalajara Jalisco Mexico Office Phone: 3338130042. Personal E-mail: acbassols@gmail.com. Business E-Mail: angel.bassols@saludangeles.com.

BASSUK, ELLEN LINDA, psychiatrist; b. NYC, Feb. 8, 1945; d. Irving and Molly (Pakarow) B.; children: Daniel, Sarah. BA, Brandeis U., 1964; MD, Tufts U., 1968; Dr.P.S. (hon.), Northeastern U., 1993. Diplomate Am. Bd. Psychiatry. Intern Mt. Auburn Hosp., Cambridge, Mass., 1968-69; resident psychiatry Univ. Hosp., Boston, 1969-70, Boston State Hosp., Boston, 1970-71, Beth Israel Hosp., Boston, 1971-73, dir. psychiat. emergency svcs., 1974-82; fellow Bunting Inst., Cambridge, Mass., 1982-84; assoc. prof. psychiatry Harvard Med. Sch., Boston, 1983—. Founder, pres. Nat. Ctr. on Family Homelessness, Newton, Mass., 1988—, Manger Inst. Homelessness and Trauma, Newton, Mass.; mem. Com. on Health Care of Homeless Persons Inst. of Medicine, Washington, 1986-88. Editor: The Practitioners Guide to Psychoactive Drugs, 1977, 83, 91, 97; editor-in-chief Am. Jour. Orthopsychiatry, 1994-98; contbr. numerous articles to profl. jours. Fellow: Am. Psychiat. Assn. (life); mem.: Mass. Psychiat. Soc. Home: 70 Montvale Rd Newton MA 02459 Office: Nat Ctr Family Homelessness 200 Reservoir St Ste 200 Needham Heights MA 02494-3146 Office Phone: 617-964-3834 14. E-mail: ellen.bassuk@familyhomelessness.org.

BAST, ROBERT CLINTON, JR., medical researcher, educator, physician; b. Washington, Dec. 8, 1943; s. Robert Clinton and Ann Christine (Borland) Bast; m. Blanche Amy Simpson, Oct. 21, 1972; 1 child, Elizabeth. BA cum laude, Wesleyan U., Middletown, Conn., 1965; MD magna cum laude, Harvard Med. Sch., Boston, 1971. Diplomate Am. Bd. Internal Medicine, cert. Med. Oncology, Hematology, lic. Tex., NC. Predoctoral fellow dept. pathology Mass. Gen. Hosp., Boston, 1967-69; intern Johns Hopkins Hosp., Balt., 1971-72; rsch. assoc. biology br. Nat. Cancer Inst., NIH, Bethesda, Md., 1972-75; asst. resident Peter Bent Brigham Hosp., Boston, 1975-76; fellow med. oncology Sidney Farber Cancer Inst., Boston, 1976-77; asst. prof. medicine Harvard Med. Sch., 1977-83, assoc. prof., 1983-84; prof. Duke U. Med. Ctr., Durham, NC, 1984-92, Wellcome clin. prof. medicine, 1992-94, co-dir. divsn. hematology-oncology, 1984-94, dir. divsn. med. oncology U. Tex. Health Sci. Ctr., Houston, 1994-2000; head divsn. med. U. Tex. M.D. Anderson Cancer Ctr., 1994-2000, dir., Harry Carothers Wiess chair cancer rsch., 1994—2004, v.p. translational rsch., 2000—, Harry Carothers Wiess disting. Univ. chair, 2004—. Surgeon USPHS, 1972—75; jr. assoc. medicine Brigham & Women's Hosp., Boston, 1977—82; cons. oncologist Boston Women's Hosp., 1978—80; dir. clin. rsch. progs. Duke U. Comprehensive Cancer Ctr., 1984—87; mem. biol. response modifiers decision network com. Nat. Cancer Inst., 1984—87; mem. grant rev. com. Leukemia Soc. Am., 1985—87, Am. Cancer Soc., 1987; lectr. Am. Cancer Soc., Soc. Gyneacologic Oncologists. Contbr. articles to profl. jours., chapters to books. Recipient Dominus award, 1984, Robert C. Knapp award, 1990, Outstanding Leadership and Advocacy award, Nat. Coalition Cancer Rsch., 1995, Smith Kline Beecham Clin. Labs. award, Clin. Ligand Soc., 1996, Abbott award, Internat. Soc. Oncodevel. Biology & Markers, 2001; named Disting. Spkr., Chao Family Comprehensive Cancer Ctr. Symposium, U. Calif., Irvine, 2002, Best Drs. in America, 1992, Americas Toop Physicians, 2003, Americas Top Drs., 2009; named an Edward G. Waters Meml. lectr., 1987, John Ohtani Meml. lectr., 1991, D. Nelson Henderson lectr., 1991, Stolte Meml. lectr., 1992, Robert C. Knapp lectr., 1996, Alan Dembo Meml. Keynote lectr., 1997, George Willbanks lectr., 2000; scholar, Leukemia Soc. Am., 1978—83. Fellow: AAAS, ACP; mem.: Am. Clin. & Climatological Assn., Am. Soc. Hematology, Soc. Biol. Therapy (bd. dirs. 1984—86), Internat. Soc. Immunopharmacology, Am. Soc. Clin. Investigation, Am. Fedn. Clin. Rsch., Am. Soc. Clin. Oncology, Assn. Am. Physicians, Am. Assn. Immunologists, Am. Assn. Cancer Rsch., Am. Soc. Microbiology, Reticuloendothelial Soc., Internat. Gynecol. Cancer Soc. (coun. 1997—2002), Soc. Gynecol. Oncology (assoc.; trustee Helene Harris Meml. trust). Achievements include development of techniques for selective elimination of tumor cells from human bone marrow; monoclonal antibodies to react with human ovarian cancer; discovery of molecular changes associated with malignant transformation of ovarian epithelium. Office: 1400 Pressler St Unit 1439 Houston TX 77030 Office Phone: 713-792-7743. Office Fax: 713-792-7864. Business E-Mail: rbast@mdanderson.org.

BASTIAN, ROBERT W., otolaryngologist; BA magna cum laude, Greenville Coll., 1974; MD, Washington U. Sch. Medicine, 1978. Lic. Ill., cert. Nat. Bd. Med. Examiners, Am. Bd. Otolaryngology, Royal Coll. Physicians and Surgeons Can. (Otolaryngology). Fellow, laryngology, Paris, 1983, Lyon, France, 1983, Erlangen, Germany, 1983, Marburg, Germany, 1983; chief resident, otolaryngology Washington U. Hosp., 1982—83, resident, otolaryngology, 1979—82; resident, surgery Jewish Hosp. of St. Louis, Washington U., 1978—79; attending staff Foster G. McGaw Hosp., Loyola U. Med. Ctr., Maywood, Ill., 1987—2003; asst. prof., otolaryngology Washington U. Sch. Medicine, 1984—87, Loyola U. Sch. Medicine, 1987—91; consulting staff Hines VA Hosp., Loyola U. Med. Ctr., 1987—2003; assoc. prof., otolaryngology Loyola U. Sch. Medicine, 1991—2000, prof., otolaryngology, 2000—03; attending staff Good Samaritan Hosp., 2003—; pres., dir. Bastian Voice Inst., Downers Grove, Ill., 2003—. Med. advisor Nat. Spasmodic Dysphonia Assn., 1998—; bd. advisor Voice Care Network, 2000—, VASTA, 2000—; invited spkr. in field. Referee for several profl. publications; contbr. chapters to books, articles to profl. jours. Named one of Top Doctors in Chgo., Chgo. Mag.; named to America's Registry of Outstanding Professionals, 2002, America's Top Physicians, 2003. Mem.: Ill. Soc. Opthalmology & Otolaryngology (pres. 2002, mem.-at-large 1999—2000), Chgo. Laryngologic and Otologic Soc., Ill. Laryngologic and Otologic Soc., Am. Acad. Otolaryngology (Head and Neck Surgery Honor award 1995). Office: Bastian Voice Inst 3010 Highland Pkwy Ste 550 Downers Grove IL 60515 Office Phone: 630-724-1100. Office Fax: 630-724-0084.

BASTIDAS, JOSÉ-MARÍA, research scientist, educator; b. Zujar, Granada, Spain, Sept. 25, 1949; s. Antonio Bastidas and Adelaida Rull. PhD in Chem. Scis., U. Madrid, 1981. Prof. Nat. Ctr. Metall. Rsch. Spanish Coun. for Sci. Rsch., Madrid, 1989—, dept. head, 2001—. Recipient 1st Prize Co-Winner Corrosion Award, Fedn. of Societies for Paint Tech., USA, 1990, Extraordinary Award for Ph.Thesis, Complutense U. of Madrid, 1995, 2001; fellow RAMSAY meml. Fellowship Trust, UK, UMIST, 1984-1986, Predoctoral and Postdoctoral Fellowship, CSIC, 1978-1983. Mem.: Spanish Soc. of Indsl. Chemistry, Spanish Nat. Assn. of Chemistry (ANQUE), Spanish Royal Soc. of Chemistry, The Electrochem. Soc. Achievements include research in more than 170 papers in international scientific journals; 90 communications presented in congresses; patents in field of corrosion science and technology; leader of more than 30 international research projects on environmental and materials engineering, materials for medical applications, electrochemistry and bioimpedance; supervisor of 20 Ph.D thesis. Avocation: Spanish mastiff breeding. Office: CENIM-CSIC Avda Gregorio d' Amo 8 Madrid 28040 Spain Office Fax: +34 91 5347425. E-mail: bastidas@cenim.csic.es.

BASU, PARTHA SARATHI, oncologist; b. Kolkata, India, Oct. 13, 1964; MBBS, Med. Coll., Kolkata, 1988; MD, Indira Gandhi Med. Coll., Shimla, 1993. Specialist gynecol. oncology Chittaranjan Nat. Cancer Inst., Kolkata, 1996—97, head dept. gynecol. oncology, 1998—; clin. asst. Hammersmith Hosp., London, 1997—98. Cons. UN Populations Fund, WHO; mem. Asian Cervical Cancer Prevention Adv. Bd. Recipient Bharat Jyoti award, India Internat. Friendship Soc.; Travel grants, Internat. Union Against Cancer, fellowship, Commonwealth U., UK. Mem.: Asia Oceania Rsch. Orgn. on Genital Infection & Neoplasia. Office: Chittaranjan Nat Cancer Inst Kolkata West Bengal 700026 India Office Fax: 91 3324851558. E-mail: basupartha@hotmail.com.

BASU, SOMPRAKAS, surgeon, consultant; b. Kolkata, West Bengal, India, Dec. 26, 1967; s. Satya Prokas and Kalpana Bose; m. Sriparna Mukhopadhyay, June 5, 1994; 1 child, Saurodeep. ISC, St. Joseph's Coll., Kolkata, 1985; MBBS, Calcutta U., 1990; MS, Delhi U., 1998. Jr. resident Lady Hardinge Med. Coll., New Delhi, 1995—98, sr. resident, 1998—2000; clin. tutor North Bengal Med. Coll., Siliguri, West Bengal, India, 2000—02; asst. prof. West Bengal Med. Edn. Svc., Siliguri, 2002—03, Manipal Coll. Med. Scis., Pokhara, Nepal, 2003—04; lectr. Dept. Surgery, IMS, BHU, Varanasi, Uttar Pradesh, India, 2004—. Cons. surgery S.S. Hosp. BHU, Varanasi, Uttar Pradesh, India, 2004—. Stetch and painting. Mng. editor Indian Soc. Wound Mgmt., Varanasi, Uttar Pradesh, India, 2006—08. Recipient Dr. A.D. Sehgal best poster award, Internat. Coll. Surgeons-Indian sect., 2008, Maj. Sudhir Dutta Medal, R.G. Kar Med. Coll., 1989, Lt. Col. S.P. Sarbadhikary Gold Medal, 1990, Anuka Banerjee Meml. Medal, Assn. Surgeons India, West Bengal Chpt., 1990, Raja Laxmi Trophy, Lady Hardinge Med. Coll., 1997, Dr. V. Mahadevan best rsch. paper award, Internat. Coll. Surgeons-Indian Sect., 2006; fellow Dr. A.K. Basu Traveling fellowship, Assn. Surgeons India, 2008; Bimalananda Saha scholarship in Anatomy, R.G. Kar Med. Coll., 1986, Nat. Acad. Med. Sci. fellowship, 2002. Fellow: Royal Soc. Medicine, Internat. Coll. Surgeons (life); mem.: Assn. Colon and Rectal Surgeons India (life), Indian Med. Assn. (life), Assn. Surgeons India (life). Office: Banaras Hindu Univ Dept Surgery IMS 221 005 Varanasi India E-mail: sombasu@hotmail.com.

BASU, SOUMYAVA, ophthalmologist; b. West Bengal, India, Nov. 21, 1976; MBBS, Seth Gordhandas Sunderdas Med. Coll., Mumbai, 2000; MS, Topiwala Nat. Med. Coll., Mumbai, 2004. Head, retina-vitreous svc. LV Prasad Eye Inst., Bhubaneswar, Orissa, India, 2006—. Office: LV Prasad Eye Inst Patia Bhubaneswar Orissa 751024 India Business E-Mail: basu@lvpei.org.

BATAGOL, RONALD PETER, pharmacy and drug information consultant and health journalist; s. Isaac Batagol and Millicent Feldman; m. Irene Marks, Apr. 4, 1962; children: David Michael, Paul Graeme, Mark Andrew. Degree in Pharmacy, Victorian Coll. Pharmacy, Parkville, 1961; diploma in Journalism, Internat. Correspondence Schos., Sydney, 1972; degree, Inst. Chartered Secretaries, Melbourne, 1981. Postgrad. fellow Soc. Hosp. Pharmacists Australia, Melbourne, 1973—77; dep. dir. pharmacy Royal Women's Hosp., Carlton, Victoria, 1977—88, dir. pharmacy and therapeutic svc., co-ordinator obstetric drug info. svc., 1977—93; cons. pharmacist Batagol Consulting Svcs., Nunawading, Victoria, 1993—97; pharmacist-in-charge ambulatory svcs. Southern Health Clayton Campus, Clayton, 2002—08. Lectr. and co-ordinator ob-gyn. sect., grad. diploma in hosp. pharmacy Victorian Coll. Pharmacy, Melbourne, 1992—94; asst. editor Micromedex, Denver, 1993—2004; rsch. officer epidemiology Murdoch Rsch. Inst., Parkville, Victoria, 1993—96; lectr. drugs and teratogenicity, pharmacology dept. U. Melbourne, 1994—95; mem., adec medicines in pregnancy subcom. Australian Drug Evaluation Com., Canberra, A.C.T, Australia, 1995—2002; keynote lectr. drugs in pregnancy and breast-feeding Pharm. Soc. NSW, Sydney. Contbr. articles to profl. jours. Fellow: Soc. Hosp. Pharmacists Australia (chmn. drug info. com. spity. practice 1979—88, state br. sec. 1978—81). Home Fax: 61398849201. Personal E-mail: rbatagol@optusnet.com.au.

BATAI, ISTVAN, anesthesiologist, consultant; b. Pecs, Hungary, May 31, 1959; s. Istvan Batai and Ilona Varnai; m. Monika Kerenyi, Mar. 19, 1983; children: Reka Angela, Andras Akos, Istvan Zoard. Diploma, U. Pecs, 1983, PhD, 2000, med. habil, 2009. Registrar anaesthesia U. Liverpool, England, 1991—92; cons. anaesthetist U. Pecs, 1995—, head dept. anaesthesia, 1999—. Part-time cons. anaesthetist GMSC, Manchester, England, 2005—. Roman Catholic. Avocation: mountain climbing. Home: Martirok 6 Pecs H-7623 Hungary Office: Dept Anaesthesia Univ Pecs Ifjusag 13 Pecs H-7624 Hungary Personal E-mail: ibatai@gmail.com.

BATAVIA, MITCHELL, physical therapist, educator; b. Bklyn., Nov. 8, 1959; s. Gabriel and Renée (Hyman) Batavia; m. Evgenia Yakovleva, Aug. 12, 2001; 1 child, Michael Andrew. BS, U. of Del., 1978—81; MA, Columbia U., 1986; PhD, N.Y. U, 1994—97; PG diploma, U. London, 2008. Lic. Physical Therapist N.Y. State, 1981.

Staff phys. therapist Inst. for Rehab. Medicine, NY U. Med. Ctr., 1981—84; home care phys. therapist Vis. Nurse Svc. of NY, 1984—86; pediatric phys. therapist NY Foundling Hosp., 1986—91; phys. therapy cons. Terence Cardinal Cooke Health Care Ctr., NYC, 1989—97; adj. lectr. Hunter Coll. Phys. Therapy Program, NYC, 1992—93, 1996; asst. prof. of phys. therapy NYU, 1998—2004, assoc. prof. phys. therapy, 2004—. Manuscript reviewer Neurology Sect., Am. Phys. Therapy Assn., Alexandria, Va., 2000—; manuscript reviewer for book submissions Butterworth-Heinemann, Boston, 1999—2001; editl. bd. mem. Jour. Neurologic Phys. Therapy; referee Cochrane Injuries Group. Author: The Wheelchair Evaluation: A Practical Guide, 1998, Clinical Research for Health Professionals: A User Friendly Guide, 2001, Contraindications in Physical Rehabilitation, 2006, The Wheelchair Evaluation: A Clinician's Guide, 2010; manuscript reviewer: Perceptual-Motor Skills, 2006; contbr. articles to profl. jours. Vol., food distbr. Coalition for the Homeless, NYC, 2002. Recipient NY U. Arch award, NY U., 1997; DeWitt Wallace Reader's Digest fellow, Inst. for Rehab. Medicine; NY U. Med. Ctr., 1978, Trainee for Phys. Therapy Clin. Rsch. in Doctoral Studies, Nat. Inst. for Disabilities Rsch. in Rehab., NY U., 1993—97, Robert Salant Post Doctoral fellow, Dept. of Phys. Therapy, NY U., The Inst. for Rehab., NY U. Med. Ctr., 1997—98, Rsch. Challenge fund, NY U., Sch. of Edn., 2000. Mem.: Neurology Sect. of the Am. Phys. Therapy Assn., Am. Phys. Therapy Assn. Avocation: music. Office: New York U 380 Second Ave 4th floor New York NY 10010 Business E-Mail: mitchell.batavia@nyu.edu.

BATE, MARILYN ANNE, psychologist; b. Dillonvale, Ohio, May 23, 1939; d. Louis Edward and Veronica (Koval) Dezera; m. Brian Richard Bate, Sept. 7, 1968 (div. Apr. 1976); children: Jennifer, Julia. BSc, Ohio State U., Columbus, 1961; MA, Case Western Res. U., Cleve., 1965, PhD, 1974. Lic. psychologist. Elem. tchr., sch. psychologist Cleve. City Schs., 1961-67; sch. psychologist, spl. edn. coord. Cleveland Heights, U. Heights, Ohio City Schs., Ohio, 1967-70; sch. psychologist Mayfield City Schs., Ohio, 1970-71, Cleve. City Schs., 1971-79, North Olmsted Schs., Ohio, 1979-82; instr. Cuyahoga C.C., Cleve., 1967-82; pvt. practice Cleve., 1967-82; psychologist Dept. Def. Dependent Schs., Aviano, Italy, 1982-86; pvt. practice Columbus, Ohio, 1986—2000; ct. psychologist Franklin County Ct. Common Pleas, Columbus, 1987—2000; sch. psychologist Montgomery County Pub. Schools, Silver Spring, Md., 2000—. Mem. adv. bd. Eastpark Elem. Sch., Middleburg Heights, Ohio, 1985; vol. Son of Heaven, Columbus, 1989; HOA bd. mem. Cameron Homeowners Assn., 2005-09. Mem. APA, Am. Correctional Assn., Nat. Sch. Psychology Assn. (charter mem.), Ohio Psychol. Assn. (mem. ethics com. 1986-92, exec. bd. 1992-2000), Ctrl. Ohio Psychol. Assn. (exec. bd. 1986-2000, pres. 1993), European Sch. Psychology Assn. (treas. 1985), Ohio Sch. Psychology Assn. (co-chmn. ethics com. 1976-86, exec. bd. 1992-2000), Cleve. Sch. Psychology Assn. (pres. 1969-71), Md. Sch. Psychology Assn., Montagomery County Sch. Psychologists Assn., Cameronhill Home Owners Assn. (sec.), Kennedy Ctr., OSU Alumni Assn., Strathmore Arts Ctr., Am. Film Inst., Smithsonian Residents Assn. Avocation: crafts. Home: 8706 Ramsey Ave Silver Spring MD 20910-3469 Office: 600 E Wayne Ave Silver Spring MD 20901 Personal E-mail: marilynbate@hotmail.com.

BATES, DAVID WESTFALL, internist, educator, medical researcher; b. Madison, Wis., June 5, 1957; s. Robert and Patricia Bates; m. Carol Kurtz; children: Michael, Sarah. BS, Stanford U., 1979; MD, Johns Hopkins U., 1983; MSc, Harvard U., 1990. Diplomate Am. Bd. Internal Medicine. Intern and resident internal medicine Oreg. Health Scis. U., Portland, 1983-86; house physician Vancouver (Wash.) Vets. Hosp., 1984-87, Kaiser Sunnyside Hosp., Portland, 1984-86; assoc. physician Oreg. Health Scis. U. Hosp., Portland, 1986-87; rsch. fellow medicine Harvard Med. Sch., Boston, 1988-90; rsch./clin. fellow medicine Brigham and Women's Hosp., Boston, 1988-90, assoc. physician, 1989-91, attending physician holding unit, 1990-95, attending physician med. consultation svc., 1990-97, attending physician Brigham Internal Medicine Assocs., 1990—, mem. Ctr. for Applied Med. Info. Sys. Rsch., 1993—, chief divsn. of gen. internal medicine, 1998—; med. dir. clinical and quality analysis information systems Partners Healthcare Systems, Inc. Physician Wallace Med. Concern, Portland, 1985-87, Tumu-Tumu Hosp., Karatina, Kenya, 1987-88; instr. medicine Oreg. Health Scis. U., 1986-87, Harvard Med. Sch., 1990-93, asst. prof. medicine, 1993-97, assoc. prof. medicine, 1997—; joint appt. Harvard Sch. Pub. Health, Dept. Health Policy and Mgmt., 2000—; house physician St. Luke's Hosp., New Bedford, 1989-91; mem. program project grant com. Nat. Cancer Inst. Can., 1996; mem. quality care coun. Ptnrs. Cmty. Health Care Inc., 1996—, mem. coronary disease prevention task force, 1996-98, mem. drug therapy team, 1996-98, mem. med. mgmt. com., 1996—; med. dir. Brigham and Women's Physician Hosp. Orgn., 1996-97, Ptnrs. Clin. Data Warehouse, 1997-99; med. dir. clin. and quality analysis Ptnrs. Healthcare Sys., 1997—; mem. Nat. Acad. Clin. Biochemistry, Stds. for Lab. Practice, 1997, Improving Prescribing Practices Initiative, Inst. for Health Care Improvement, 1997-98; chief divsn. Gen. Internal Medicine, 1998—; sci. advisor SCRIPT project Health Care Financing Adminstrn. and Joint Commn. for Accreditation of Healthcare Orgns., 1998—; chair abstract selection com. SGIM N.E. Region, 1999; mem. Consensus Devel. Panel on the Safety of Intravenous Drug Delivery Sys., Latiolais Leaderhip Program, 1999; trustee Inst. for Safe Medication Practices, 2000; mem. steering com. Nat. Quality Forum, 2000—; mem. safe medication use expert com. U.S. Pharmacopeia, 2000—; mem. Harkness Fellows in Health Care Policy, The Commonwealth Fund, 2000—, Inst. Medicine, 2005; presenter in field; many others. Mem. editl. bd. Jour. Evaluation in Clin. Practice, 1997—, The Joint Commn. Jour. on Quality Improvement, 1997—; contbr. numerous articles to profl. jours. Recipient Nat. Rsch. Svc. award Agy. for Health Care Policy and Rsch., 1990, Young Investigator of the Yr. award Soc. for Med. Decision-Making, 1993. Fellow ACP; mem. AMA (mem. medication error reducation initiative 1996-98), Am. Soc. for Clin. Pharmacology and Therapeutics, Am. Med. Informatics Assn. (mem. editl. bd. jour. 1997—, awards com. 2000—), Am. Fedn. Clin. Rsch. (Henry Christian award for excellence in rsch. 1992), Assn. for Health Svcs. Rsch., Soc. for Med. Decision Making, Soc. for Gen. Internal Medicine (Clin. Investigator of Yr. award N.E. region 1993), Inst. Medicine. Office: Brigham and Womens Hosp 75 Francis St Boston MA 02115

BATES, ERIC RANDOLPH, physician, educator; b. Ann Arbor, Mich., Apr. 10, 1950; s. Richard Chester and Signe (Hegge) Bates; m. Nancy Joanne Fortino, Sept. 25, 1976; children: Andrew, Alexis, Evan. AB, Princeton U., NJ, 1972; MD, U. Mich., Ann Arbor, 1976. Diplomate Am. Bd. Internal Medicine, cert. in cardiovasc. disease, interventional cardiology. Intern internal medicine U. Mich. Health Sys., Ann Arbor, 1976—79, fellow cardiovasc. disease, 1979—81, instr. internal medicine, 1981-84, asst. prof. internal medicine, 1984-89, assoc. prof. internal medicine, 1989-95, prof. internal medicine, 1995—. Fellow: ACP, Am. Heart Assn.; mem.: Am. Coll. Cardiology. Achievements include research in acute ischemic syndromes and coronary revascularization. Office: U Mich Cardiovasc Ctr 1500 E Med Ctr Dr Rm 2A398 Ann Arbor MI 48109-5869 Office Phone: 734-936-5840, 734-232-4276. Office Fax: 734-936-7026, 734-764-4142.

BATES, GEORGE WILLIAM, obstetrician, gynecologist, educator; b. Durham, NC, Feb. 15, 1940; s. George W. and Lillian M. (Streete) B.; m. Susanne Rayburn, Oct. 18, 1969; children: Jonathan Rayburn, Jeffrey William, Robert Wiser. BS, U. N.C., 1962, MD, 1965; SM, MIT, 1984. Diplomate Am. Bd. Ob-Gyn. (examiner 1984-93). Intern U. Ala., Birmingham, 1965-66; resident ob-gyn U. N.C., Chapel Hill, 1966-70; prof., chmn. ob-gyn U. Tenn., Knoxville, 1972-76; fellow reproductive endocrinology U. Tex., Dallas, 1976-78; prof., dir. reproductive endocrinology U. Miss. Med. Ctr., Jackson, 1978-86; prof. ob.-gyn. Coll. Medicine, Med. U. S.C., Charleston, 1986-90, dean, 1986-89; v.p. med. edn. Greenville (S.C.) Hosp. System, 1990-96; exec. v.p., chief med. officer Prin.Care, Inc., Brentwood, Tenn., 1996-98; v.p. devel. Vanderbilt U. Med. Ctr., Nashville, 1998—. CEO digiChart, Inc. Co-author: Obstetrics and Gynecology for Medical Students, 1992, 95; editor: Manual of Clinical Problems in Obstetrics and Gynecology, 1982, 86, 90; contbr. numerous articles to profl. publs. Commr. coun. Boy Scouts Am., 1989-90, v.p. adminstrn., 1992, pres., 1993-94, bd. dirs. Mid. Tenn. Coun., 2002--; elder Mt. Pleasant Presbyn. Ch., Westminster Presbyn. Ch.; mem. pres.'s adv. coun. Mars Hill Coll., Presbyn. Coll., Nat. Devel. Coun., U. N.C. Maj. USAF, 1970-72. Morehead scholar, 1958; NIH rsch. trainee, 1976-78; Sloan fellow, 1983; recipient Eagle Scout award, 1955, Henry Fordham award, 1966, Golden Apple award, 1987, Silver Beaver award, 1989, Hon. Alumnus award Med. U. S.C., 1990, Disting. Eagle Scout award, 1991; named Prof. of Yr., U. Miss., 1980, Top 100 Healthcare Exec., 2002. Mem. ACOG (chmn. fin. com. 1990-94, health care commn. 1994-97, Jr. Fellow Profl. of Y. award dist. IV 1991), AMA, AAAS, Assn. Profs. Ob-Gyn. Found. (bd. dirs. 1993), Am. Gyn.-Ob. Soc., Nat. Bd. Med. Examiners, Gynecol. Investigation, Am. Fertility Soc. (bd. dirs. 1991-94, treas. 1994-96), Soc. Gynecol. Surgeons, Accreditation Coun. Grad. Med. Edn., So. Atlantic Assn. Obstetricians and Gynecologists, Ctrl. Assn. Obstetricians and Gynecologists, Endocrine Soc., Rotary, Alpha Omega Alpha. Office: digiChart Inc 100 Winners Cir N Ste 450 Brentwood TN 37027-1004 Office Phone: 615-777-2727.

BATES, JONATHAN R., hospital administrator; BA, Reed Coll.; MD, U. Mo. Pediatric residency Children's Hosp. Med. Ctr., Boston, chief med. resident, med. dir. Emergency Dept.; sr. v.p. Children's Hosp. and Health Ctr., San Diego; adminstr. Meml. Miller Children's Hosp., Long Beach, Calif.; pres., CEO Ark. Children's Hosp., 1993—. Bd. dirs. Nat. Initiative for Children's Healthcare Quality. Office: Ark Children's Hosp 800 Marshall St Little Rock AR 72202

BATES, JOSEPH HENRY, internist, educator; b. Little Rock, Sept. 19, 1933; s. Henry Ermer and Susan Elizabeth (Wallis) B.; m. Patsy McGinnis, Aug. 6, 1955 (dec. 2007); children— Patricia, Susan Elizabeth, Joseph Henry, III, Elisabeth Lee; m. Donna Dudney McNair, 2008. BS, MD, U. Ark., 1957, MS, 1963. Diplomate in internal medicine and pulmonary diseases Am. Bd. Internal Medicine, also mem. exam. bd. Med. intern U. Ark. Med. Center, 1957-58, resident in internal medicine, 1958-61, fellow in infections diseases, 1961-63; clin. investigator Little Rock VA Med. Ctr., 1963-66; mem. faculty U. Ark. Med. Ctr., Little Rock, 1967—, prof. medicine, 1973—, vice chmn. dept., 1978-98; assoc. dean U. Ark. Coll. Pub. Health, 2001—, Coll. Pub. Health, U. Ark. for Med. Sci., 2001—. Chief med. service Little Rock VA Hosp., 1970-98, dep. state health officer, chief sci. officer, Ark. Dept. Health, 1998—. Author research papers in field, chpts. in books. Chmn. Ark. chpt. NCCJ, 1980; chmn. biracial commn. Little Rock public schs., 1977-79; bd. dirs. Am. Lung Assn., 1972-90. Served as officer M.C. AUS, 1956-65. Grantee USPHS, 1961-63; Grantee NIH, VA, also pvt. founds. and corps., 1963— Mem. ACP (gov.), Am. Coll. Chest Physicians (gov.), Am. Fedn. Clin. Rsch., Am. Thoracic Soc. (pres. 1988-89), Infectious Disease Soc., So. Soc. Clin. Rsch., Am. Lung Assn. (pres. 1994-95), Assn. Am. Physicians, Assn. Profs. Medicine. Presbyterian. Office: 4815 W Markham St Little Rock AR 72205-3866 Home: 5 Timberlake Dr Little Rock AR 72207-1609 Home Phone: 501-224-3033; Office Phone: 501-661-2412. Personal E-mail: joseph.bates@arkansas.gov.

BATISTA, ERALDO LUIZ, dentist, educator; b. Porto Alegre, Rio Grande do Sul, Brazil, Sept. 26, 1967; DDS, Pontificia U. Cath. do Rio Grande do Sul, 1988; DSc, Boston U., 2005. Adj. prof. Pontificia U. Cath. do Rio Grande do Sul, 2005—. Mem.: Internat. Team Implantology. Office: Av Ipiranga 6681 Bldg 06 Porto Alegre Rio Grande do Sul 91530-000 Brazil Business E-Mail: eraldo.junior@pucrs.br.

BATJER, H. HUNT (HENRY HUNTINGTON BATJER III), neurosurgeon; b. Burlington, Vt., Nov. 2, 1951; s. Henry Huntington Betjer, Jr. and Eleanor Mae (Thomas) Stanlis; m. Sharon Keller; 1 child, John Templer Batjer; m. Janet Eileen, May 20, 1989; children: Hannah Alden, Devon Julianna, Victoria Huntington, Ashley Shannon. MD, U. Tex. Southwestern Med. Sch., 1977. Diplomate Am. Bd. Neurol. Surgery. Intern gen. surgery U. Tex. Southwestern Med. Ctr., Dallas, 1977-78, resident neurol. surgery, 1978-82; hon. house staff physician The Nat. Hosp., U. London, 1981; clin. fellow U. Western Ont., London, Can., 1981-82; asst. prof. U. Tex. Southwestern Med. Ctr., Dallas, 1983-89, assoc. prof., 1989-93, prof., 1993-95; Michael J. Marchese prof., chief divsn. neurol. surgery Northwestern U. Med. Sch., Chgo., 1995—. Bd. trustees Found. for Internat. Edn. in Neurosurgery, 1994—; exec. coun. Joint Sect. Cerebrovascular Surgery, 1990—; co-chmn NFL Head, Neck, & Spine Medical Com., 2010- Co-author: (book) Intracranial Aneurysm Surgery: Techniques, 1990, Spontaneous Intracerebral Hemorrhage, 1992; co-editor Techniques in Neurosurgery, 1995. Mem. Congress of Neurol. Surgeons (exec. com. 1990—, sec. 1995, pres. 1998-99), Am. Assn. Neurol. Surgeons, Am. Heart Assn., N.Y. Acad. Scis. Republican. Episcopalian. Office: Northwestern U Med Sch Dept Neurol Surgery 233 E Erie St Ste 614 Chicago IL 60611-5934 also: 675 N St Clair Galter 20-250 Chicago IL 60611 E-mail: hbatjer@nmff.org. *

BATOCCHI, ANNA PAOLA, neurologist; b. Macerata, Feb. 5, 1959; Degree in Medicine, Surgery, Cath. U. Rome, 1984. Resident neurology Cath. U. Rome, 1988, assoc. prof. neurology, 2007—. Office: largo Gemelli 8 Rome 00168 Italy Office Fax: 00390635501909. Business E-Mail: annapaola.batocchi@rm.unicatt.it.

BATRA, RAJIV BHUSHAN, pathologist, educator; b. Dehradun, Aug. 3, 1962; MBBS, Armed Forces Med. Coll., 1984; MD in Pathology, Delhi, 1992. Sr. pathologist Command Hosp. Kolkata, 2001—06; assoc. prof. pathology Armed Forces Med. Coll., 2006—. Mem.: Indian Soc. Histocompatibility & Immunogenetics, Indian Acad. Cytology, Indian Soc. Pathologists & Microbiologists. Avocations: reading, travel. Home: SAKET 15/3 Circular Rd Dalanwala Dehradun Uttarakhand 248001 India Personal E-mail: rajivbbatra@rediffmail.com.

BATSAKIS, JOHN GEORGE, pathology educator; b. Petoskey, Mich., Aug. 14, 1929; s. George John and Stella (Vlahkis) B.; m. Mary Janet Savage, Dec. 28, 1957; children: Laura, Sharon, George. Student, Va. Mil. Inst., 1947, Albion Coll., Mich., 1948-50; MD, U. Mich., 1954. Diplomate Am. Bd. Pathology. Intern George Washington Univ. Hosp., Washington, 1954-55; resident in pathology U. Mich. Hosp., Ann Arbor, 1955-59; prof. pathology U. Mich., Ann Arbor, 1969-79; chmn. dept. pathology M.D. Anderson Hosp. U. Tex., Houston, 1981-96, chm. and prof. emeritus dept pathology, 1996—. Ruth Legett Jones prof. U. Tex., Austin, 1982-96; adj. prof. oral pathology U. Tex. Dental Br., Houston; cons. Armed Forces Inst. Pathology, 1972—, VA Hosp., Ann Arbor, 1968-79; Hayes Martin lectr. Am. Soc. for Head and Neck Surgery, 1994; Gunnar Holmgren lectr. Swedish Nat. Ear, Nose, Throat Meeting, 1994; William Christopherson lectr. U. Louisville Dept. of Pathology, 1995; external examiner U. Hong Kong Dental Sch., 1995—; Francis A. Sooy lectr. dept. otolaryngology, head and neck surgery U. Calif., San Francisco, 1997; 2d Matthews lectr. dept. pathology Emory U., 1997; spkr. in field. Author: Tumors of the Head and Neck, 2d edit., 1979; co-author: Surgical Pathology of the Head and Neck, 2000; editor: Clin. Lab. Ann., 1981—86; co-editor: Advances in Anatomic Pathology, 1994—98; editor-in-chief Advances in Anatomic Pathology, 1998—2000; co-editor: Oral Cancer, 2003, Comprehensive Management of Head and Neck Tumors, 1999; mem. editl. bd. 13 jours., 1974—; contbr. articles to profl. jours. Bd. trustees, v.p. Mike Hogg Found., Houston, 1991—; trustee George C. Marshall Found., Lexington, Va., 1995-00, emeritus trustee, 2000—. Capt. U.S. Army, 1959-61. Recipient William H. Rorer award Am. Coll. Gastroenterology, 1972, Disting. Alumnus award Albion Coll., 1987, Reviewer of the Decade award AMA Archives Orolaryngology Head Neck Surgery, 1990, Presdl. award Am. Soc. Head and Neck Surgery, 1991, Harlan Spjut award Houston Soc. Clin. Pathologists, 1992, Honor award Am. Laryngologic Assn., 1995; Spl. Honored Guest of Am. Soc. for Head and Neck Surgery, 1993. Fellow ACP, Am. Soc. Clin. Pathologists, Coll. Am. Pathologists (Disting. Svc. award 2002), Am. Acad. Otolaryngology (assoc., honor award 1994), Royal Soc. Medicine. Republican. Episcopalian. Home: 1701 Hermann Dr Unit 1401 Houston TX 77004-7373

BATSFORD, WILLIAM P., cardiac electrophysiologist; MD, Albany Med. Coll., 1969. Diplomate Am. Bd. Internal Medicine, 1972, Am. Bd. of Internal Medicine-cardiovasc. disease, 1976. Fellow US PHS Hosp., Yale Univ. Sch. of Medicine; resident Univ. of Pennsylvania Hospital, 1972; prof. medicine Yale Univ. Office: Yale Medical Group Yale Physicians Building 800 Howard Ave 2nd Fl New Haven CT 06519 Office Phone: 203-785-4126. Office Fax: 203-785-6506.

BATSHAW, MARK LEVITT, pediatrician, director; b. Montreal, Que., Canada, Sept. 19, 1945; s. Manuel G. and Rachel (Levitt) B.; m. Karen N. Korman, June 29, 1969; children: Elissa, Michael, Andrew. BA, U. Pa., 1967; MD, U. Chgo., 1971. Diplomate Am. Bd. Pediatrics. Resident in pediatrics Hosp. for Sick Children, Toronto, 1971-73; fellow in developmental pediatrics Kennedy Kreiger Inst., Johns Hopkins U. Sch. Medicine, 1973-75; instr. Johns Hopkins U. Sch. Medicine, Balt., 1975-76, asst. prof., 1976-80, assoc. prof. pediatrics, 1980-88; W.T. Grant prof. pediatrics and neurology U. Pa. Sch. Medicine, Phila., 1988-98; chief div. child devel. and rehab. Children's Hosp. of Phila., 1988-98; physician-in-chief Children's Seashore House, Phila., 1988-98; chief acad. officer Children's Nat. Med. Ctr., Washington, 1998—; dir. Children's Rsch. Inst., Washington, 1998—; chmn. pediats. George Washington U. Med. Ctr., Washington, 1998—; and assoc. dean, academic affairs George Washington U., Washington, 2001—. Mem. NIH study NICHD, 1991-95. Author: Children with Disabilities, 6th edit., 2007, Your Child Has a Disability, 2001. Johns Hopkins U. fellow, 1973-75; Kennedy scholar, Kennedy Inst., 1983-86. Fellow Royal Coll. Physicians; mem. Am. Pediatric Soc. Office: Children's Nat Med Ctr 111 Michigan Ave NW Washington DC 20010-2916

BATTAFARANO, DANIEL FRANCIS, rheumatologist; b. Darby, Pa., Jan. 17, 1956; s. Nicholas C. and Margaret Rose (Maguire) B.; m. Karen Susan Pietryka, Apr. 27, 1985; children: Margaret, Claire, Monica, Vincent. BS, U. Scranton, 1977; MA, Bryn Mawr Coll., 1979; DO, Phila. Coll. Osteo. Medicine, 1983. Diplomate Am. Bd. Internal Medicine, 1987, sub-bd. Rheumatology, 1992, 2002. Intern, resident Brooke Army Med. Ctr., Ft. Sam Houston, Tex., 1983-87; internist, chief dept. medicine Nuernberg Hosp., Germany, 1987-90; fellow in rheumatology, then rheumatologist Fitzsimmons Army Med. Ctr., Aurora, Colo., 1990-93; asst. chief rheumatology Brooke Army Med. Ctr., 1993-97, dir. internal med. resident rsch., 1993-97, dir. transitional year residency and intern coord., 1994-97; dep. dir. med. edn. US Army Med. Command, Ft. Sam Houston, Tex., 1997-98; dir. continuing med. edn. US Army, 1997-98; chief dept. med. sci. Acad. Health Scis., Ft. Sam Houston, Tex., 1998-2000; dir. med. edn. Brooke Army Med. Ctr., Ft. Sam Houston, Tex., 2000—04, dir. continuing med. edn., 2000—04; chief Brooke Army Med. Ctr., Dept. Hosp. Edn., 2002—04, chief rheumatology svc., 2004—, key faculty in internal medicine residency, 2005—; key faculty in rheumatology fellowship, 2007—. Affil. clin. faculty dept. medicine Brooke Army Med. Ctr., Ft. Sam Houston, Tex., 1997—2000; adj. prof. phys. therapy Baylor U. Grad Sch., Waco, Tex., 1998—; assoc. dean San Antonio Uniformed Svcs. Health Edn. Consortium, 2000—04; assoc. prof. medicine Uniformed Svcs. U. Health Scis., Bethesda, Md., 1998—; clin. prof. medicine U. Tex. Health Sci. Ctr., San Antonio, 2008—. Reviewer of numerous profl. jours., 1994—; mem. adv. bd. U.S. Army Med. Dept. Jour., 1998-2000; contbr. articles to med. jours. Med. adv. bd. Lupus Found. Am., San Antonio, 1994-2000. Emcee

San Antonio Arthritis Walk 2005; med. oversight of vol. Listeners Program, Brooke Army Med. Ctr. 2003-08; physician vol Seton Home Clinic, San Antonio, 2010. Col. US Army Med. Corps, 1983—2004. Decorated Legion of Merit, Meritorious Svc. medal, Army Commendation medal, Army Achievement medal, Nat. Def. Svc. medal, Armed Forces Res. medal, Army Svc. Ribbon, Overseas Ribbon, Order of Mil. Med. Merit, 1998; recipient Outstanding Internal Medicine Resident Tchr. Brooke Army Med. Ctr., 1987, A Designator in Rheumatology from the US Army Surgeon Gen. 1998, Outstanding Faculty San Antonio Uniformed Svc. Health Edn. Consortium, 2007, Outstanding Clin. Faculty U. Tex. Health Sci. Ctr. San Antonio, 2006, 2008, 2011, Dept. Medicine, Brooke Army Med. Ctr., 1997; named Most Valued Tchr., Uniformed Svc. U. Health Scis., 2007, 2009, 2010, Best Drs., 2010, 11, Recognition award Arthritis Found., 2010, Best Tchg. Svc. award San Antanio Mil. Med. Ctr., 2009, Best Tchg. Seaning, 2011, Outstanding Clin. Educator award, Dept. Medicine San Antonio Mil. Mediator Ctr., 2011. Fellow ACP (Laureate award, 2007), Am. Coll. Rheumatology; mem. Assn. Mil. Surgeons US Assn., Inst. Noetic Scis. Independent. Achievements include education conference room dedicated in name of col. Daniel Francis Battafarano in 2004. Avocations: exercise, gardening, birdwatching, writing. Office: Brooke Army Med Ctr MCHE-MDR 3851 Roger Brooke Dr San Antonio TX 78234-6272 Office Phone: 210-916-0797. Business E-Mail: daniel.battafarano@amedd.army.mil.

BATTERMAN, STEVEN CHARLES, engineering mechanics and bioengineering professor, consultant; b. Bklyn., Aug. 15, 1937; s. Jacob and Anna (Abramowitz) B.; m. Judith Wilpon, Mar. 29, 1959; children: Scott David, Risa Karen, Daniel Adam. BCE, Cooper Union, 1959; ScM (NSF fellow), Brown U., 1961, PhD, 1964; MA (hon.), U. Pa., 1971. Diplomate Internat. Bd. Forensic Engring. Scis. Mem. faculty U. Pa., 1964-97, prof. mech. engring. and applied mechanics, 1974-79; assoc. prof. orthopaedic surgery rsch. U. Pa. Sch. Medicine, 1972-74, prof. orthopaedic surgery rsch., 1974-97; prof. biomechanics in vet. medicine U. Pa Sch. Vet Medicine, 1975-84, prof. bioengring., 1974-97; emeritus prof. Sch. Engring. and Applied Sci., Sch. Medicine U. Pa., 1997—; mng. ptnr. Batterman Engring., LLC, Cherry Hill. Forensic enring. and biomechanics cons. to govt., industry, ins. cos., attys.; mem. adv. bd. Cyril H. Wecht Inst. Forensic Sci. and Law, Duquesne U., adj. prof. Coll. Medicine, Drexel U., 2006-11. Contbr. numerous articles to profl. jours. Recipient S.R. Warren Disting. Teaching award, U. Pa., 1982. Fellow ASME; mem. ASCE, Am. Acad. Mechanics, Am. Soc. Engring. Edn., Biomed. Engring. Soc., Soc. Exptl. Mech., Soc. Automotive Engrs., Am. Soc. Safety Engrs., Am. Acad. Forensic Scis. (Founder's award 1992, 2004, pres.-elect 1993-94, pres. 1994-95, Disting. Fellow 2001), Assn. for Advancement Automotive Medicine, Sigma Xi, Tau Beta Pi, Chi Epsilon. Jewish. Achievements include patents for apparatus for acoustically determining periodontal health; method and system for determining occurrence of slips leading to falls. Home: 109 Charlann Cir Cherry Hill NJ 08003-2906 Home Phone: 856-424-3701; Office Phone: 856-795-3993. E-mail: batterman@aol.com.

BATTEY, JAMES F., JR., federal agency administrator, neurologist; BS in Physics, with honors, Calif. Inst. Tech.; MD, PhD, Stanford U., Calif. Resident pediat. Stanford U.; postdoc. fellow Harvard Med. Sch.; sr. staff fellow to sr. investigator Nat. Cancer Inst., NIH, 1983—88, head molecular structure sect., Lab Biol. Chemistry, 1992—95, chief molecular neurosci. sect., Lab. Neurochemistry, Nat. Inst. Neurol. Disorders & Stroke, 1988—92, dir. intramural rsch., Nat. Inst. Deafness & Other Comm. Disorders (NIDCD) Bethesda, Md., 1995—98, chief Lab. Molecular Biology, 1996, dir. NIDCD, 1998—. Chmn. Stem Cell Task Force NIH, 2002—; adj. prof. George Washington U. Sch. Medicine. Contbr. articles to profl. jours. Recipient PHS Commendation medal, 1990, Outstanding Svc. medal, 1994. Office: NIDCD 31 Center Dr Msc 2320 Bethesda MD 20892 2320 Office Phone: 301-402-0900. Office Fax: 301-402-1590. E mail: james.battey@nih.gov. *

BATTIN, R. RAY (ROSABELL HARRIET RAY), audiologist, neuropsychologist; b. Rock Creek, Ohio; d. Harry Walter and Sophia (Boldt) Ray; m. Tom C. Battin, Aug. 27, 1949. AB, U. Denver, 1948; MS, U. Mich., 1950; PhD, U. Fla., 1959; postgrad., U. Miami Sch. Medicine, Fla., 1957, U. Iowa, 1958. Diplomate Am. Bd. Forensic Medicine, Am. Bd. Profl. Disability Cons., Am. Bd. Psychol. Specialties, Am. Bd. Forensic Examiners (cert. forensic examiner, cert. med. examiner), forensic neuropsychology, devel. psychology, psychol. assessment, lic. psychologist Tex., audiologist Tex., speech pathologist Tex. Instr. in speech pathology U. Denver, 1949-50; audiologist Ann Arbor (Mich.) Sch., 1950-51, Houston Speech and Hearing Ctr., 1954-56; clin. fellow divsn. Clin. Svcs. U. Fla., Gainesville, 1952-54; dir. speech pathology/psychology Hedgecroft Hosp. and Rehab. Ctr., Houston, 1956-59; audiologist Drs. Guilford, Wright and Draper, Houston, 1959-63; pvt. practice psychology, audiology, and neuropsychology Houston, 1959—. Clin. instr. dept. otolaryngology U. Tex. Sch. Medicine, Galveston, 1964-80; dir. of audiology vestibulography and speech pathology lab. Houston Ear, Nose and Throat Hosp. Clinic, 1963-73; adj. clin. instr. U. Houston, 1981-86; lectr. The First Word program Sta. KUHT-TV, 1959; v.p. Behavioral Perceptual Ctr., 1986-90; neuropsychol. cons. edn. divsn. Environ. Health Screening Lab., 1989-99, adv. bd., 1989-99; lectr. in field in U.S., So. Am., and Europe. Author: (with C. Olaf Haug) Speech and Language Delay, 1964, Vestibulography, 1974, Private Practice: Guidelines for Speech Pathology and Audiology, 1971; editor (with Donna R. Fox) Private Practice in Audiology and Speech and Language Pathology, 1978; contbg. author: Seminars in Speech, Language, Hearing (Northern), Auditory Disorders in School Children (4th edit. Roeser and Downs), Current Therapy of Communications Disorder (Perkins); editor Jour. Acad. Pvt. Practice in Speech Pathology and Audiology, 1981-84; contbr. articles in field to profl. jours.; author: (with Irvin A. Kraft) The Dysynchronous Child (film), 1971, Symposium Brain Plasticity As it Relates to the Remediation of Attention, Auditory Processing, Language and Reading Disorders, 1999; The Battin Clinic Language Learning Screening Test for Preschool Children, 1985, The Battin Scale of Parent's Attitude Toward Family Experience and Need for Child Cochlear Implant Candidates. Bd. dirs. Juvenile Ct. Vols., 1980—83, Children's Resource and Info. Ctr., 1981—85, Dyslexic Adult Support Svcs., 1986—90, Musicfest, 1990—2002, Houston Repretory Theater, 1993—98; mem. adv. bd. Caring Adoptions, 1993—, HISD for the Performing and Visual Arts Friends, 1998—, Bayou City Concert Musicals, 2006—. Counselor Women's Army Corps, 1945—46. Recipient Gold award for Ednl. Exhibit, Am. Acad. Pediats., 1969, Lifetime Achievement award Houston Psychol. Assn., 1996, Leadership award Sci. Learning Corp., 2000. Fellow: Am. Acad. Audiology, World Acad. Inc., Am. Speech and Hearing Assn. (profl. svcs. bd. 1967—70, com. on pvt. practice 1971—74); mem.: APA, Soc. Ear Nose and Throat Advances in Children, Tex. Biofeedback Soc., Internat. Assn. Logopedics and Phoniatrics, Acad. of Aphasia, Harris County Biofeedback Soc. (pres. 1984), Houston Psychol. Assn., Tex. Acad. Audiology, Tex. Psychol. Assn., Tex. Speech and Hearing Assn. (v.p. 1968), Am. Acad. Pvt. Practice in Speech Pathology and Audiology (pres. 1968—70), Am. Coll. Forensic Examiners, Internat. Assn. Applied Psychology. Home: 3837 Meadow Lake Ln Houston TX 77027-4029 Office: Battin Clinic Inc 4545 Post Oak Place Dr Ste 375 Houston TX 77027-3121 Office Phone: 713-621-3072. Personal E-mail: rhrb@aol.com. E-mail: rhrb@pdq.net.

BATTLE, ALLEN OVERTON, JR., psychologist, educator; b. Memphis, Nov. 19, 1927; s. Allen Overton and Florence Louise (Castelvecchi) B.; m. Mary Madeline Vroman, June 14, 1952; 1 son, Allen Overton, III. BS, Siena Coll., 1949; MA, Cath. U. Am., 1953, PhD, 1961; certificate in clin. psychology, U. Tenn. Coll. Medicine, 1953. Diplomate: in clin. psychology Am. Bd. Profl. Psychology, 1971. Instr. dept. psychiatry U. Tenn. Coll. Medicine, 1956-61, asst. prof., 1961-67, asso. prof., 1966-72, prof., 1972—; chief clin. psychologist U. Tenn. Mental Health Center, 1971-78, chief div. clin. psychology, 1974—. Vis. lectr. Southwestern U. at Memphis, 1962-84; vis. prof. Rhodes Coll., 1984—2001. Author: Clinical Psychology for Physical Therapists, 1975, Suicide and Crisis Intervention Training Manuals, 1978, The Psychology of Patient Care: A Humanistic Approach, 1979; contbr. articles to profl. jours. Cons. USPHS, Suicide and Crisis Intervention Svc.; mem. Mayor's Commn. on Alcohol and Drug Abuse, 1974-77; bd. dirs. Runaway House, St. Peter's Home for Children, De Neuville Heights Sch. Family Svc. Decorated knight Russian Imperial Order; knight Order St. John of Jerusalem; recipient Disting. Svc. award Tenn. Dept. Mental Health, 1971, Jefferson award, Am. Inst. for Pub. Svc., 2001. Mem. Am., Tenn. psychol. assns., Am. Anthrop. Assn., N.Y. Acad. Sci., AAAS, Brit. Soc. Projective Techniques, Sigma Xi. Home: 2220 Washington Ave Memphis TN 38104-3025 Office: 920 Madison Ave Memphis TN 38103 Home Phone: 901-726-5641.

BATTRELL, ANN, dental association administrator, dental hygienist, educator; 2 children. BS in Dental Hygiene, Northwestern Univ., Chgo.; postgrad. work, Univ. Mo., Kansas City. Dental hygienist, 1979—; strategic planning cons. Am. Dental Hygientists' Assn., Chgo., pres., 1996—97, mgr. cdn. to dir. edn., 2000—04, asst. exec. dir. strategic planning, 2004—05, exec. dir., 2005—. Dental hygiene faculty Northwestern Univ. Dental Sch., Palm Beach (Fla.) Cmty. Coll. Mem.: Am. Dental Hygientists' Assn. Office: ADHA Ste 3400 444 N Michigan Ave Chicago IL 60611 Office Phone: 312-440-8900. *

BATU, SEMA E., special education educator; b. Izmir, Turkey, Jan. 1, 1970; BA in Spl. Edn., Anadolu U., 1987, PhD, 1998. Assoc. prof. Anadolu U., 1998—, vice dir. Rsch. Inst. Handicapped, 1998. Mem.: CEC. Office: Anadolu Universitesi Engelliler Arastirma Eskisehir Tepebasi 26470 Turkey Business E Mail: esbatu@anadolu.edu.tr.

BAUCUS, MAX SIEBEN, United States Senator from Montana; b. Helena, Mont., Dec. 11, 1941; s. John and Jean (Sheriff) Baucus; m. Ann Geracimos (div. 1982), 1 child, Zeno; m. Wanda Minge, Apr. 23, 1983 (div. 2009); m. Melodee Hanes, July 2, 2011. BA in Economics, Stanford U., Calif., 1964, LLB, 1967. Bar: DC 1969, Mont. 1972. Staff atty. Civil Aeronautics Bd., Washington, 1967-68; atty. SEC, Washington, 1968-71, legal asst. to chmn., 1970-71; atty. George & Baucus, Missoula, Mont., 1971—74; mem. Mont. House of Reps., 1973-74, US Congress from 1st Mont. Dist., 1975—78; US Senator from Mont., 1979—; chmn. US Senate Environment & Pub. Works Com., 1993—95, US Senate Finance Com., 2001—03, 2007—, vice chmn. Joint Com. on Taxation, 2007—09, chmn., 2009—; mem. Joint Select Com. on Deficit Reduction, 2011—. Bd. dirs. Congl. Award Found. Recipient Guardian of Small Bus. award, Nat. Fedn. Ind. Bus., 1983—84, Bronze Symbol Svc. award, Nat. Pork Producers Coun., 1997, Legis. award, Nat. Rural Health Assn., 1999, American Fin. Leadership award, Fin. Services Roundtable, 2001, Wheat Leader of Yr. award, Nat. Assn. Wheat Growers, 2003, Cyber Champion award, Bus. Software Alliance, 2005; named one of The 50 Most Powerful People in DC, GQ mag., 2009. Mem.: Mont. Bar Assn., DC Bar Assn. Democrat. Avocation: motorcycling. Office: US Senate 511 Hart Senate Bldg Washington DC 20510-0001 also: District Office Ste 100 222 North 32nd St Billings MT 59101 Office Phone: 202-224-2651, 406-657-6790. Office Fax: 202-224-0515. *

BAUE, ARTHUR EDWARD, retired surgeon, educator, health facility administrator; b. St. Louis, Oct. 7, 1929; s. Arthur Christian and Viola (Wegener) B.; m. Rosemary Dysart, Nov. 24, 1956; children: Patricia Sage Baue Nizen, Arthur Christian II, William Dysart. AB summa cum laude, Westminster Coll., 1950; MD cum laude, Harvard, 1954; M Honoris Privatum, Yale U., 1975; MD honoris causa, Ludwig Maxmillian U., Munich, Germany, 2000. Diplomate Am. Bd. Surgery (dir.), Am. Bd. Thoracic Surgery (dir.). Cpt. asst. chief of surgery USAF Hosp., Philippine Islands, 1955-57; from intern to chief resident surgery Mass. Gen. Hosp., Boston, 1954-61; asst. prof. surgery U. Mo. Sch. Medicine, 1962-64; sr. registrar in thoracic surgery Bristol, Eng., 1961-62; from asst. prof. to assoc. prof. surgery U. Pa. Sch. Medicine, Phila., 1964-67; Harry Edison prof. surgery Washington U. Sch. Medicine, St. Louis, 1967-75; surgeon-in-chief, dir. dept. surgery Jewish Hosp., St. Louis, 1967-75; chief of surgery Yale-New Haven Hosp., 1975-85; prof., chmn. dept. surgery Yale U., 1975-85, Donald Guthrie prof. surgery, 1977-85; assoc. dean for clin. affairs St. Louis U. Sch. Medicine, 1985-86; v.p. for the med. ctr. St. Louis U., 1986-90, prof. surgery, 1986-97, prof. emeritus, v.p. emeritus for the med. ctr., 1997—2008. Dir. surg. edn. St. Mary's Health Ctr., 1990-97; cons. surgery Nat. Bd. Med. Examiners; cons. to chief of staff VAMC, St. Louis, 1994-97; chmn. NIH surgery B study sect., 1978-82; bd. dirs., med. dir. Healthcare Mgmt., Inc.; vis. prof. various colls.; hon. pres., Internat. Symposium Critical Care Medicine, Trieste, 2003, 04, 05; honored chmn. emeritus dept. surgery Yale U. Sch. Medicine, 2007; lectr., spkr. in field. Author: Doctor, Can I Ask You A Question? 2005; chief editor: Archives of Surgery, 1977-88, sr. cons. editor, 1989-93; editor: Thoracic and Cardiovascular Surgery, 4th edit., 1983, The Pathophysiology and Clinical Management of Shock, 1984, Parameters of Health Care, 1986-90, Multiple Organ Failure, Patient Care and Prevention, 1990, Glenn's Thoracic and Cardiovascular Surgery, 5th edit., 1990, 6th edit., 1996, Multiple Organ Failure, 2000, Sepsis and Organ Dysfuntion-Epidemiology and Scoring Systems, 1009, Sepsis and Organ Dysfunction-From Basics to Clinical Approaches, 1999, Sepsis and Organ Dysfunction: The Challenge Continues, 2000, Sepsis and Organ Dysunction-Bad and Good News on Prevention and Management, 2000, Sepsis and Organ Dysfunction-From Chaos to Rationale, 2002; mem. editl. bd. JAMA, 1977-88, Circulatory Shock, Am. Jour. Physiology, 1975-87, Postgrad. Gen. Surgery, Jour. Shock, 1994—; sr. editor: Glenn's Thoracic and Cardiovascular Surgery; contbr. over 630 articles to profl. jours. Life trustee Westminster Coll.; trustee Nat. Commn. for Quality Health Care, 1986-92, Health Care Leadership Coun.; bd. dirs. United Way; chmn. bd. deacons Union Chapel F.I. Capt. USAF, 1959-69. John and Mary R. Markle scholar, 1963; recipient Rsch. Career Devel. award USPHS, 1965-68, Arthur E. Baue award, Munich, 2007; named Scientist of Yr., Sigma Xi, 1991, Honored Chmn. award, Yale Surg. Soc., 2007, Internat. Health Prof. of Yr., 2005, Lifetime Achievement award, Soc. Crit. Care Medicine, 2008. Mem. ACS, AMA (trustee jour., editl. bd. jour.), Assn. Am. Med. Colls. (coun. acad. socs.), Am. Assn. Thoracic Surgery, Am. Coll. Cardiology, Am. Coll. Chest Physicians (Pres.'s citation), Assn. Acad. Surgery, New Eng. Surg. Soc., New Eng. Vascular Soc., Internat. Cardiovasc. Soc., Soc. Thoracic Surgeons, Soc. Univ. Surgeons, Soc. Vascular Surgery, Shock Soc. (Scientific Achievement award 2003), Internat. Fedn. Shock Socs. (pres. 1992-95), Internat. Vascular Soc. Surgery, Am. Assn. for Surgery Trauma, Am. Assn. Artificial Internal Organs, Organ Failure Acad. (Trieste, Italy, hon. pres. 1983-2005), Surg. Biol. Club, Soc. U. Surgeons, Am. Physiol. Soc., Sr. Physiol. Commn., Soc. Critical Care Medicine (Lifetime Achievement award 2007), Am. Surg. Assn., Ctrl. Surg. Assn., Halsted Soc., Soc. Internat. Surgery, Soc. Clin. Surgery, Surg. Infection Soc., James IV Assn. of Surgeons, Southern Thoracic Surg. Soc., Soc. for Surgery Alimentary Tract, St. Louis Surg. Soc. (hon.), Soc. Grad. Surgeons LA County-U. SC Med. Ctr. (hon.), Assn. VA Surgeons (hon.), Colombia Surg. Soc. (hon.), Chgo. Surg. Soc. (hon.), LA Surg. Soc. (hon.), Mpls. Surg. Soc. (hon.), Fla. Assn. Gen. Surgeons, (hon.), Indonesian Shock Soc. (hon.), Organ Failure Soc. (hon. pres.), Alpha Omega Alpha.

BAUER, A(UGUST) ROBERT, JR., surgeon; b. Dec. 23, 1928; s. A(ugust) Robert and Jessie Martha-Maynard (Monie) Bauer; m. Charmaine Louise Studer, June 28, 1957; children: Robert, John, William, Anne, Charles, James. BS, U. Mich., 1949, MS, 1950, MD, 1954; M in Med. Sci.-Surgery, Ohio State U., 1960. Diplomate Am. Bd. Surgery. Intern Walter Reed Army Med. Ctr., 1954—55; resident in surgery Univ. Hosp., Ohio State U., Columbus, also instr., 1957—61; pvt. practice medicine, specializing in surgery Mt. Pleasant, Mich., 1962—74; chief surgery Ctrl. Mich. Cmty. Hosp., Mt. Pleasant, 1964—65, vice chief of staff, 1967, chief of staff, 1968; clin. faculty Mich. State Med. Sch., East Lansing, 1974; mem. staff St. Mark's Hosp., Salt Lake City, 1974—91; pvt. practice surgery Salt Lake City, 1974—91. Clin. instr. surgery U. Utah, 1975—91; rschr. surg. immunology. Contbr. articles to profl. publs. Trustee Rowland Hall, St. Mark's Sch., Salt Lake City, 1978—84; mem. Utah Health Planning Coun., 1979—81. With M.C. US Army, 1954—57. Fellow: ACS, Southwestern Surg. Congress; mem.: AAAS (affiliate), AMA, Zollinger Surg. Soc., Pan Am. Med. Assn. (affiliate), Salt Lake Surg. Soc., Utah Med. Assn. (various coms.), Salt Lake County Med. Soc., Phi Rho Sigma, Sigma Phi Epsilon. Episcopalian. Office: PO Box 17533 Salt Lake City UT 84117-0533 Address: 1366 Murray Holladay Rd Salt Lake City UT 84117-5050

BAUER, JOEL J., surgeon, educator; b. NYC, Aug. 16, 1942; s. David W. and Toby B.; m. Judy Bauer (Siegel), Dec. 3, 1967; children: Dana, Ross. BS, U. Vt., 1963; MD, NYU, 1967. Lic. physician, N.Y.; cert. Am. Bd. Surgery. Intern in surgery Mt. Sinai Hosp., NYC, 1967-68, resident in surgery, 1968-72, chief resident in surgery, 1972-73, clin. asst. surgery, 1973-77, asst. attending surgeon, 1977-81, assoc. attending surgeon, 1981-88, attending surgeon, 1988—; instr. surgery to asst. clin. prof. to clin. prof. surgery Mt. Sinai Sch. Medicine, NYC, 1972—; vice chmn., dept. surgery Mt. Sinai Hosp., 2001—08. Presenter in field. Contbr. articles to profl. jours. Named Physician of Yr., Crohn's and Colitis Found., 2003. Fellow Am. Coll. Surgeons; mem. AMA, Assn. Acad. Surgery, Am. Coll. Gastroenterology, Am. Coll. Colon & Rectal Surgery, Soc. for Surgery for the Alimentary Tract, N.Y. Acad. Scis., N.Y. County Med. Soc., N.Y. Acad. Gastroenterology, N.Y. Soc. Colon & Rectal Surgeons, N.Y. Surg. Soc., N.Y. Acad. Medicine (sec. surg. sect. 1986-87, pres. surg. sect. 1987-88), Soc. Pelvic Surgeons, Soc. Laparoscopic Surgeons, Soc. Am. Gastrointestinal Endoscopic Surgeons Office: 25 E 69th St New York NY 10021-4925 Office Phone: 212-517-8600. Business E-Mail: joel.bauer@mssm.edu.

BAUER, JOY, nutritionist, consultant; m. Ian Bauer; 3 children. BS in Kinesiological Sciences, U. Md.; MS in Nutrition, NYU. Cert. nutrition NY. Dir. nutrition & fitness Heart-Smart Kids Program Mt. Sinai Med. Ctr., clinical nutritionist; prof. anatomy, physiology, sports nutrition NYU Sch. Continuing Edn.; nutrition cons. Columbia Presbyterian Med. Ctr.; nutrition & health expert Today Show, Yahoo Inc.; nutritionist NY City Ballet, America Ballet Theatre. Nutrition expert & contbg. editor Parade Mag., Parade Healthy Style; contbg. editor & columnist Self Mag. Author: Joy's LIFE Diet, 2008, Joy Bauer's Food Cures, 2007. Mem.: Am. Dietetic Assn. Office: 116 E 63rd St New York NY 10065 Office Phone: 212-759-6999. Office Fax: 212-759-7766.

BAUER, MICHAEL, nursing educator, researcher; M in Gerontology, BA, PhD, diploma in Edn. RN Nurses Bd. Victoria. Lectr. La Trobe U., Bundoora, Australia, 2000—; rschr. Australian Ctr. Evidence Based Aged Care, Bundoora, 2004—. Contbr. articles to profl. jours., chapters to books. Grant, JO & JR Wicking Trust, Alzheimer's Australia Rsch., Windermere Found., Dept. Health and Ageing. Mem.: Royal Coll. Nursing Australia, Australian Assn. Gerontology. Office: La Trobe Univ Plenty Rd 3086 Bundoora VIC Australia

BAUER, MISLEN STOL, clinical geneticist; MD, Pontifical U., 1976. Lic. Fla., 1983, diplomate Am. Bd. Pediatrics, 2006, cert. Am. Bd. Clin. Genetics-Med. Genetics, 2010. Intern San Ignacio Hosp., 1976, resident pediat., 1977—80; fellow clin. genetics Univ. Miami Hosps., 1986—88; clin. genetics cons. Genzyme Genetics, Miami, Fla.; med. dir. and pediat. cons. Children's Med. Svcs.; hosp. affiliation includes South Miami Hosp., Plantation Gen. Hosp., Joe Dimaggio Children's hosp., Broward Gen. Hosp. Med. Ctr., Baptist Hosp.; resident pediat. Miami Children's Hosp., 1981—84, dir.

neurofibromatois ctr., clin. geneticist. Mem.: Am. Acad. Pediat. Office: Miami Children's Hospital 3100 SW 62 Ave Number 301 Miami FL 33155-3009 Office Phone: 305-663-8595. Office Fax: 305-669-6443.

BAUER, URSULA E., public health service officer; married; 2 children. M in Polit. Sci., Rutgers U., NJ; PhD in Epidemiology, Yale U., New Haven; MPH in Family Health, Columbia U., NYC. Epidemic intelligence officer La. Office Pub. Health; chronic disease epidemiologist Fla. Dept. Health; asst. prof. U. South Fla. Coll. Pub. Health; dir. tobacco control program NY State Dept. Health, 2001—08, dir. divsn. chronic disease and injury prevention, 2008—09; dir. Nat. Ct. Chronic Disease Prevention and Health Promotion Centers Disease Control and Prevention, Atlanta, 2010—. Contbr. articles to profl. jours. Office: Centers Disease Control and Prevention NCCDPHP 1600 Clifton Rd Atlanta GA 30333 *

BAUJAT, BERTRAND, surgeon; b. Pertuis, France, Jan. 26, 1968; MD, Paris U., 1999, PhD, 2005. Physician Hosp. Foch, Suresnes, 2002—11; prof. Hosp. Tenon, Paris, 2011—. Master: Réseau d'Expertise Français sur les Cancers ORL Rares; mem.: Groupement d'Etude sur les Tumeurs de la Tête Et du Cou, Société Française de carcinologie cervicofaciale, European Assn. Cranio Maxillo Facial Surgery, Société Française d'ORL. Office: 4 rue de la Chine Paris 75020 France Office Fax: 33156017010. Business E-Mail: b.baujat@hopital-foch.org.

BAULCOMBE, SIR DAVID C., plant scientist; b. 1952; BSc in Botany, Leeds U., 1973; PhD, U. Edinburgh, 1977. Postdoctoral fellow McGill U., Montreal, 1977—78, U. Ga., Athens, 1978—80; higher sci. officer Plant Breeding Inst., Cambridge, UK, 1980—86, prin. sci. officer, 1986—88; joined The Sainsbury Lab., Norwich, UK, 1988, sr. rsch. scientist, head of lab., 1990—93, 1999—2003, prof. U. East Anglia, 2002—07; Regius prof. botany, Royal Soc. rsch. prof., head dept. plant sciences U. Cambridge, 2007—. Recipient Prix des Cerealiers de France, 1990, Kumbo Sci. Internat. award in plant molecular biology and biotechnology, 2002, Ruth Allen award, Am. Phytopathology Soc., 2002, Wiley prize biomedical rsch., 2003, Massry Prize, Massry Found., 2005, Royal Soc. London Medal, 2006, Wolf Prize in Agriculture, Wolf Found., Israel, 2010; co-recipient Benjamin Franklin medal in Life Sci., Franklin Inst., 2008, Albert Lasker award for Basic Med. Rsch., Lasker Found., 2008. Fellow: Royal Soc. London; mem.: European Molecular Biology Orgn., NAS (fgn. assoc. 2005). Office: University Cambridge Dept Plant Sciences Downing St Cambridge CB2 3EA England Office Phone: 440 1223 333958. Office Fax: 440 1223 333953. Business E-Mail: david.baulcombe@plantscicam.ac.uk. *

BAUM, BRUCE J., dentist, medical geneticist; BA, U. Va., 1967; DMD, Tufts U., 1971; PhD, Boston U., 1974. Chief gene transfer sect. NIH Nat. Inst. Dental and Craniofacial Rsch., Bethesda, Md. Mem.: Inst. Medicine, Internat. Assn. Dental Rsch. (Oral Medicine and Pathology Rsch. award 2007). Office: NIH/NIDCR Bldg 10 Rm N113 10 Ctr Dr MSC 1190 Bethesda MD 20892-1190 Office Phone: 301-496-1363. Office Fax: 301-402-1228. E-mail: bruce.baum@nih.gov.

BAUM, JULES LEONARD, ophthalmologist, educator; b. NYC, Mar. 13, 1931; children from previous marriage: Jeffrey Stuart, Alison Rachel; m. Laura Klabin, 1990; stepchildren: Alexander Matthew, Samantha Merrill. AB, Dartmouth Coll., 1952; MD, Tufts U., 1956. NIH fellow in rsch. in ophthalmology NYU, 1958-59, rschr. in ophthalmology, 1961-62; asst. prof. NYU Med. Sch., 1965-68; resident in ophthalmology Bellevue Hosp., NYC, 1962-64; mem. faculty Tufts U. Med. Sch., 1968—, prof. ophthalmology, 1974-91; sr. surgeon New Eng. Med. Ctr. Hosp., Boston, 1973-91; rsch. prof. Tufts U. Med. Sch., 1991—2002, prof. ophthalmology emeritus, 2002—. Assoc. editor Ophthalmic Lit., 1967-85; mem. editl. bd. Investigative Ophthalmology and Vision Sci., 1978-82, Survey of Ophthalmology, 1970-79, Am. Jour. Ophthalmology, 1985-91, Ophthalmic Surgery, 1985-95, Cornea Jour., 1989-98; contbr. articles to profl. jours. Served to capt. M.C. AUS, 1959-61. Recipient William Warner Hoppin award N.Y. Acad. Medicine; Alcon Rsch. Inst. award, 1991, Lifetime Achievement award Poly Prep, 2008; NIH fellow, 1958-59, 64-65; Nat. Eye Inst. grantee. Fellow: Royal Coll. Ophthalmologists; mem.: Ocular Microbiology Immunology Group (pres. 1990—91, Thygeson lecture 2001), Mass. Ophthalmology Soc. (sec. 1974—76), Cornea Soc. (exec. sec., treas. 1979—87, v.p. 1987—89, pres. 1989—91, Castroviejo Corneal medalist 1997), Assn. Rsch. in Vision and Ophthalmology (trustee 1981—86, v.p. 1986, Gold fellow 2010), Am. Acad. Ophthalmology (bd. councillors 1981—83, honor award 1979, sr. honor award 1990), Confrerie des Chevaliers du Tastevin, Internat. Wine and Food Soc., Phi Beta Kappa. Jewish. Home Phone: 781-237-5558. Personal E-mail: julesbaum@verizon.net.

BAUM, STANLEY, radiologist, educator; b. NYC, Dec. 26, 1929; s. Herman and Fannie (Harris) B.; m. Jeanne Masch, June 29, 1958; children: Richard Arthur, Laura Dianne, Carol Lisa. BA, NYU, 1951; MD, U. Utrecht, Holland, 1957. Intern Kings County Hosp., NYC, 1957-58; resident in radiology Grad. Hosp., U. Pa., Phila., 1958-61; trainee Nat. Cancer Inst., Bethesda, Md., 1958-61; fellow cardiovascular radiology Stanford (Calif.) U., 1961-62; instr. radiology U. Pa., Phila., 1962-63, asst. prof., 1963-66, assoc. prof., 1966-70, prof., 1970—, Eugene P. Pendergrass prof. radiology, 1977-96, chmn. dept. radiology, 1975-96; chmn. med. bd. Hosp. of U. Pa., 1983-86; chief cardiovascular radiology Mass. Gen. Hosp., Boston, 1971-75; prof. radiology Harvard Med. Sch., Boston, 1971-75. Cons. Radiation Effects Research Found., Hiroshima, Japan, 1975-76; mem. cardiovasc. rev. bd. Am. Heart Assn., 1970-90. Editorial bd.: Investigative Radiology, 1970-80, New Eng. Jour. Medicine, 1975-76, Radiology, 1975-85, Gastrointestinal Radiology, 1975-79, Jour. Continuing Edn., 1978-80, Postgrad. Radiology, 1980-90; editor-in-chief: Acad. Radiology, 2000—. Fellow Am. Coll. Radiology, Am. Coll. Cardiology; mem. Inst. Medicine Nat. Acad. Sci., Soc. Cardiovascular Radiology (pres. 1974-76), Soc. Chmn. Acad. Radiology Depts. (pres. elect 1985-86, pres. 1986), Acad. Radiol. Rsch. (pres. 1997-2000, editor-in-chief Acad. Radiology 2000—). Home: 401 W Moreland Ave Philadelphia PA 19118-4207 Office: U Pa 3400 Spruce St Philadelphia PA 19104-4206 Home Phone: 215-242-2367; Office Phone: 215-662-2028. Business E-Mail: baum@oasis.rad.upenn.edu.

BAUMAN, JERRY L., dean, pharmacy researcher, educator; b. Rutland, Ill., Aug. 15, 1953; s. Ronald H. and Wilma J. Bauman; m. Judith M. Hicks, July 26, 1975; children: Gregory L., Tracy J., Kevin M. BS, U. Ill. Chgo. Coll. Pharmacy, 1976; PharmD, U. Mo., Kansas City, 1978. Lic. pharmacist Ill., cert. pharmacotherapy specialist. Asst. head rsch. U. Ill. Chgo. Coll. Pharmacy, 1983—98, prof. pharmacy practice, head dept. pharmacy practice, 1998—, prof. pharmacy dept. medicine, cardiology sect., 1998—, dean, 2006—. Recipient Alumni Loyalty award, U. Ill. Chgo. Coll. Pharmacy, 1989, Rsch. award, Am. Heart Assn. Met. Chgo., 1991; named Outstanding Tchr. of Yr., U. Ill. Chgo. Coll. Pharmacy, 1984, 1988. Fellow: Am. Coll. Cardiology, Am. Coll. Clin. Pharmacy (sec. 1985—87, bd. regents 1987—90, pres.-elect 1996—97, pres. 1997—98, Russell Miller award for sustained rsch. 1994); mem.: Am. Soc. Health Sys. Pharmacists, Cardiac Electrophysiology Soc., Am. Assn. Colleges of Pharmacy. Achievements include research in the side effects of antiarrhythmic drugs; electrophysiology of cocaine with implications of mechanisms of arrhythmic death and treatments for cocaine-induced arrhythmias; development of clinical pharmacy (pharmacotherapy) as a specialized discipline within pharmacy; a training program in cardiovascular drug research for clinical pharmacists. Office: U Ill Coll Pharmacy MC 866 833 S Wood St Chicago IL 60612 Office Phone: 312-996-3267. Office Fax: 312-996-0379. E-mail: jbauman@uic.edu.

BAUMAN, PHILLIP A., orthopedist; b. NYC, Aug. 4, 1955; BA, Harvard Coll., MA, 1977; MD, Columbia Coll. Physicians and Surgeons, 1981. Physician Orthop. Assocs. NY, 1987—. Sr. attending physician, orthop. surgery St. Lukes-Roosevelt Hosp. Ctr., 1987—2011, mem., exec. com. med. bd., 2000—11; bd. dirs. Harris and Harris Group, 1998—2011; orthop. cons. NYC Ballet, 1995—2011, Am. Ballet Theatre, 1995—2011. Named one of Best Drs. in America, Consumer Rsch. Coun. America, Castle-Connelly, Best Drs. in NY. Fellow: Am. Bd. Orthop. Surgery; mem.: Internat. Soc. Dance Medicine, Am. Orthop. Foot and Ankle Soc., Am. Orthop. Soc. Sports Medicine, Am. Acad. Orthop. Surgeons. Office: 343 W 58th St New York NY 10019 Office Fax: 212-265-0739. Personal E-mail: pabaumanmd@yahoo.com.

BAUMAN, WILLIAM ALLEN, pediatrician, educator, health systems consultant; b. NYC, Nov. 23, 1923; s. Louis and Stella (Kraus) B.; m. Joan Vivian Carlsen, June 28, 1952; children: William Carlsen, Phillip Allen, Pamela Joan Pitasi. Student, Harvard U., 1942-43, 46; MD, Columbia U., 1947; postgrad. in biostats., Sch. Pub. Health, 1960-63. Intern L.I. divsn. Kings County Hosp., Bklyn., 1947-48; resident The Babies Hosp., NYC, 1948-50, practice medicine specializing in pediatrics, 1953-75; chief pediatric clinic Vanderbilt Clinic, NYC, 1954-65; dir. med. data processing Presbyn. Hosp., NYC, 1966-74, assoc. attending pediatrician, 1973-93, emeritus staff, 1994—. V.p. med. adminstrv. svcs. Group Health Inc., N.Y.C., 1974-77; chmn. bd. govs. Hillcrest Gen. Hosp.-Group Health Inc., 1975-79, attending pediatrician, 1975-79; sr. v.p. Health Svcs. Group Health Inc., 1977-79; v.p. med. affairs Danbury Hosp., Conn., 1979-90; mem. faculty dept. pediatrics Columbia U., 1952-73, assoc. clin. prof. pediatrics, 1973—; mem. med. bd. Maternity Ctr. Assn., 1969-95; chmn. faculty-student adv. bd. P&S Club, Coll. Physicians and Surgeons, Columbia U., 1970-90; chmn. com. on data processing N.Y. County Health Rev. Orgn., 1976-79; mem. exec. com. Babies Hosp. Alumni Assn., 1998—. Contbr. articles to profl. jours. Mem. data protection rev. bd. N.Y. State Dept. Health, 1993-2009. With M.C. USAF, 1951-52. Fellow Am. Coll. Med. Informatics, N.Y. Acad. Medicine; mem. Am. Acad. Pediatrics, N.Y. County Med. Soc., AMA, Med. Soc. State N.Y. (chmn. com. info. tech. in medicine 1967-93), Assn. Ambulatory Pediatrics, Assn. Computing Machinery, Soc. Computer Medicine (bd. dirs.), Bioengring. Inst., Am. Soc. Info. Scis., N.Y. Acad. Scis., N.Y. State Assn. Professions, Am. Assn. Med. Systems and Infomatics (pres. 1983). Home and Office: 887 Heritage Hls Somers NY 10589-4053 Personal E-mail: drgmd@aol.com.

BAUMANN, DONALD PETER, plastic surgeon, educator; b. NY, Aug. 8, 1969; BA, NYU, 1991; MD, SUNY, 1998. Faculty surgeon LI Plastic Surgery Group, 2004—05; assoc. prof. MD Anderson Cancer Ctr., U. Tex., 2005—. Fellow: ACS; mem.: Am. Soc. Reconstructive Microsurgery (Best Microsurgery Case of Yr. award 2011), Am. Soc. Plastic Surgeons. Avocations: sailing, piano, skydiving. Office: MD Anderson Cancer Ctr 1515 Holcombe Houston TX 77005 Business E-Mail: dpbauman@mdanderson.org.

BAUMANN, PETER, medical educator; b. Emden, Germany, Mar. 7, 1954; MD, U. Essen, 1982. Assoc. prof. Wayne State U. Sch. Medicine, 2007—. Office: 3990 John R 7 Brush North Detroit MI 48201 Business E-Mail: pbaumann@med.wayne.edu.

BAUMANN, SHELLY, diagnostic radiologist, educator; MD, Tulane U., 1982. Diplomate Am. Bd. Radiology-diagnostic radiology, 1986. Resident diagnostic radiology Univ. South Fla. Affiliated Hosps., Tampa, 1983—86; asst. clin. prof. radiology Coll. of Medicine Univ. South Fla.; hosp. affiliation includes Tampa Gen. Hosp. Office: University of South Florida 2700 University Sq Dr Tampa FL 33612 Office Phone: 813-253-2721.

BAUMERT, BRIGITTA GERTRUD, oncologist, researcher; b. Dortmund, Germany, Sept. 25, 1961; d. Ruth Josefine Baur and Norbert Baumert. MD, Albert-Ludwigs U. Freiburg, Germany, 1987; PhD, U. Maastricht, 2004. Cert. approbation Baden-Wuerttemberg, Germany, 1987. Residency Dept. Surgery, Kantonsspital Olten, Switzerland, 1989—90; residency spl. interest internal medicine and rheumatology Heilbadzentrum St. Moritz, Switzerland, 1990—91. Vis. fellow stereotactic radiotherapy Joint Ctr. Radiation Therapy, Boston, 1997—97; residency diagnostic radiology Limmattalspital Zurich, Switzerland, 1993—94; residency gynaecology U. Hosp. Zurich, 1996—96, staff mem. radiation oncology, 1996—99; vis. fellow stereotactic radiotherapy Royal Marsden Hosp., Neuro-Oncology Unit, London, 1997; clin. rsch. fellow neuro-oncology unit Royal Marsden Hosp. NHS Trust, Sutton, London, 1999—2000, clin. rsch. fellow paediatric unit; staff mem. radiation-oncology U. Hosp. Zurich, 2000—01, MAASTRO clinic, U. Hosp. Maastricht, Netherlands, 2002—10, assoc. prof. Musician concerts. Founding and active mem. Organ bldg. soc., Gundelfingen, Breisgau, Germany, 1987—92. Recipient Travel award, DAAD, 1985; named Outstanding Article of Yr., Internat. Soc. Quality Life Rsch., 2006; grant, Cancer League, Canton Zürich, Switzerland, 2000—02, Radium found. U. Zurich, 2000—01, Schering-Plough, 2005—, MAASTRO Found., 2009. Mem.: Swiss Inst. Applied Cancer Rsch. (founding mem. neurooncology spl. interest group 1999—2001), Dutch Working Group Neuro-Oncology, Comprehensive Cancer Centre Limburg (cons. 2002), Nederlandse Vereniging voor Radiotherapie en Oncologie, European Assn. Neuro-Oncology, European Orgn. Rsch. and Treatment Cancer (chair, Radiation-Oncology Group & Brain Tumor Working party 2003—09, brain tumor group sec. 2009—), Sci. Assn. Swiss Radiation Oncology, Am. Soc. Therapeutic Radiation and Oncology, Swiss Soc. Med. Radiology, Eur. Soc. Therapeutic Radiatiion Oncologgy (mem., editl. bds. different cancer releted jours.). Roman Catholic. Avocations: music, opera, skiing, hiking, antiques, art.

BAUMGAERTNER, MICHAEL R., orthopedist, surgeon, educator; m. Baumgaertner Irene; children: Sarah, Emily, Benjamin, Geoffrey. Attended, Stanford U.; MD, U. Calif., 1982. Diplomate Am. Bd. of Orthopaedic Surgery. Resident surgery and orthopaedic surgery Univ. of Calif., 1983—87; fellow plastic surgery Univ. of Mass. Med. Ctr., 1987—88; fellow orthopaedic trauma AO Found., Switzerland, 1989; prof. orthopaedic surgery Yale Univ.; prof. orthopaedics and rehab.; chief orthopaedic trauma svc.; with Yale Med. Group, Yale-New Haven Hosp. Office: Yale-New Haven Hospital 1st Fl Yale Physicians Bldg 800 Howard Ave New Haven CT 06520 Office Phone: 203-737-5667.

BAUMGART, DANIEL C., physician, researcher; B summa cum laude, Max Planck Sch., Berlin, 1986; MD, Humboldt U., Berlin, 1994, PhD magna cum laude, 1994. Med. resident Charité Med. Ctr., Berlin, 1994—96; postdoctoral rsch. fellow U. Pa., Phila., 1996—98; med. resident Georgetown U., Washington, 1998—2000; staff physician, investigator Charité Med. Ctr. Humboldt U., Berlin, 2000—. Cons. Berlin Internat. Studies Network, 2000, Univs. Future Project, Berlin, 2002. On site rep. New Traditions Network U.S. Dept. of State, Berlin, 2000. Rsch. fellow, German Acad. Exch. Svc., 1996—97, German Rsch. Coun., 1997—98, Rsch. grantee, 2001—02, Internat. Faculty Devel. Program fellow, Georgetown U., 1998—2000, Bonus Rsch. grantee, Humboldt U., 2001, 2002, 2004, 2005, 2006, 2007, Rsch. grantee, Eli & Edythe L. Broad Found., 2003—05, Hewlett Packard Tech. for Tchg. grantee, 2006. Fellow: Friends and Promoters of the German Acad. Exch. Svc.; mem.: AMA, Tsas atlantic Forum, World Young Leaders Forum, Am. Soc. Gastrointestinal Endoscopy, Am. Gastroenterological Assn., Berlin-Brandenburg Soc. Hepatology and Gastroenterology, Berlin Bd. Physicians, German Med. Assn., German Inflammatory Bowel Disease Task Force Group (life). Achievements include research in involvement of intestinal epithelial cells and dendritic cells antigen presenting cells in the pathogenesis of inflammatory bowel disease; evaluation and development of novel immunomodulatory therapies for Crohn's disease and ulcerative colitis. Office: Humboldt-U Berlin Charité Med Ctr Augustenburger Platz 1 D-13353 Berlin Germany Office Fax: +49-30-450-553983.

BAUMGART, STEPHEN, pediatrician, educator; b. Chgo., Ill., May 23, 1949; MD, Northwestern U., 1975. Fellowship neonatal perinatal medicine Childrens Hosp. Phila., 1977—80, assoc. prof. pediat. neonatology, 1980—99; prof. pediat. neonatology Thomas Jefferson U. Med. Sch., 1992—99, SUNY Stony Brook, 1999—2004, Childrens Nat. Med. Ctr., 2004—, sr. staff physician, 2004—11, dir. neonatal neuroprotection program, 2006—11. Dir. ecmo program Childrens Hosp. Phila., 1990—92, Thomas Jefferson U. Med. Sch., 1992—99, vice chmn. pediat., 1997—99. Recipient Residency Fellows Faculty Tchr. of Yr. award, SUNY Stony Brook, CHOP & CNMC. Fellow: Am. Acad. Pediat.; mem.: Neonatal Resuscitation Program, Soc. Pediatric Rsch. Avocations: swimming, bicycling, guitar. Office: 111 Michigan Ave NW West Wing 3-600 Washington DC 20010 Office Fax: 202-476-3459. Business E-Mail: stbaumga@cnmc.org.

BAUMGARTEN, CLIVE M., biology professor; b. NYC, July 14, 1949; BA, Northwestern U., 1970, PhD, 1976. Physiology & biophysics prof. Va. Commonwealth U., 1979—. Office: Va Commonwealth University Dept Physiology & Biophysics Richmond VA 23298-0551 Business E-Mail: baumgart@vcu.edu.

BAUMGARTNER, CRAIG ALLEN, physician assistant, healthcare consultant, researcher, clinical assistant professor; s. Gerald and Gloria (Klopfenstein) B.; m. Jeanine Marie; children Siera, Jackson. BHS, U. Fla., 1985; MBA, Jacksonville U., Fla., 1989; MPAS, U. Nebr., 1999. Bd. cert. physician asst., Nat. Comm. Cert. Physician Assistants, in healthcare mgmt., Am. Coll. Healthcare Execs. Sr. physician asst. Shands, Jacksonville, 1985—92; adminstrv. dir. Dominique Engel MD, 2000—02; physician asst. Evanston Northwestern Healthcare, 1992—2001, NW Cmty. Hosp., 2002—06; physician asst. co chair advanced practitioner rsch. coun. North Shore U. Health Sys., 2006—. Clin. asst. prof. Rosalind Franklin U. Vice chmn. Mayor's Disability Coun., Jacksonville, 1990. Disting. fellow, Am. Acad. Physician Assts. Fellow Am. Coll. Healthcare Execs. Office Phone: 847-477-8885.

BAUMGARTNER, HANS RUDOLF, retired pharmaceutical researcher, educator; b. Basel, Switzerland, June 10, 1934; s. Johann Jakob and Lina (Keller) B.; m. E. Regula Morf, Apr. 24, 1962; children: Meret, Matthias, Maja. Grad., U. Basel, 1961, MD, 1963; postgrad., U. Paris, 1958-59, U. Vienna, Austria, 1959-60, Roche, Basel, 1961-63. Resident dept. pathology U. Basel, 1963-64, resident dept. internal medicine, 1964-66; rsch. fellow Royal Coll. Surgeons, London, 1967; rsch. assoc. Montefiore Hosp. and Med. Ctr., NYC, 1968-70; group leader thrombosis rsch. Roche, Basel, 1970-81, head thrombosis and atherosclerosis rsch., 1982-86, head cardiovascular rsch., 1987-97; prof. U. Bern, Switzerland, 1988-99. Contbr. articles to med. jours. Recipient Theodor Naegeli prize Naegeli Found., 1987. Mem. Internat. Soc. on Thrombosis and Hemostasis (coun. 1972-78, com. mem. 1973-79, sr. adv. coun. 1980—, Disting. Career award 1997), European Thrombosis Rsch. Orgn. (exec. com. 1980-88), European Atherosclerosis Soc. (exec. com. 1982-96), Am. Heart Assn. (corr. fellow arteriosclerosis coun. 1986, mem. thrombosis coun. 1986). Avocations: mountain climbing, mountain farming and gardening, arts, music, exercise. E-mail: hr.rbm@datacomm.ch.

BAUMGARTNER, LISA, education educator; b. Phillips, Wis., May 28, 1964; BA, Augsburg Coll., 1986; EdD, U. Ga., 2000. Asst. prof. Buffalo State Coll., SUNY, 2000—03; assoc. prof. dept counseling, adult & higher edn Northern Ill. U., 2003—. Mem.: Am. Assn. Adult and Continuing Edn. (Cyril O Houle Award). Avocation: running. Office: Northern Ill University Dept Counseling, Adult & Higher Edn 200 Gabel Hall Dekalb IL 60115 Business E-Mail: lbaumgartner@niu.edu.

BAUMGARTNER, WILLIAM ANTHONY, cardiac surgeon; b. Covington, Ky., Apr. 18, 1947; s. Nicholas Raymond Baumgartner and Rosemary Jones; m. Betsy Reik; children: Bill Jr., Amy, Mark.

BS, Xavier U., 1969; MD, U. Ky., 1973. Cert. Am. Bd. Thoracic Surg. Intern surgery Stanford (Calif.) U. Med. Ctr., 1973—74, asst. resident gen. surgery, 1974—75, asst. resident cardiothoracic surgery, 1975—76, asst. resident cardiovasc. surgery, 1976—77, chief resident cardiovasc. surgery, 1977—78, chief resident thoracic surgery, 1978, asst. resident gen. surgery, 1978—80, chief resident, 1980—81; Vincent L. Gott prof. Johns Hopkins U. Sch. Medicine, Balt., chief cardiac surgery, 1992—2009; exec. dir. Am. Bd. Thoracic Surgery, 2009—. Editor: (book) Heart and Heart Lung Transplantation, 1990, 2001. Grantee, NIH, 1988, 1992, 1995, 2000, 2008; Javits Neurosci. Rsch. Investigator awardee, 2000. Mem.: ACS, Clin. Practice Assn. (pres., vice dean clin. practice 1999—), Soc. Univ. Surgeons, Am. Assn. Thoracic Surgery, Am. Soc. Transplant Surgeons, Internat. Soc. Heart and Lung Transplantation (pres. 1997—98), Soc. Thoracic Surgeons (pres. 2002—03), Am. Surg. Assn. Avocation: golf. Office: Johns Hopkins Hosp 600 N Wolfe St # 618 Baltimore MD 21287-0005 Office Phone: 410-955-5248. Business E-Mail: wbaumgar@csurg.jhmi.jhu.edu. *

BAUMRIND, DIANA, research psychologist; b. NYC, Aug. 23, 1927; AB, Hunter Coll., 1948; MA, U. Calif., Berkeley, 1951, PhD, 1955. Cert. and lic. psychologist, Calif. Project dir. psychology dept. U. Calif., Berkeley, 1955-58; project dir. Inst. of Human Devel., 1960—, also rsch. psychologist and prin. investigator family socialization and devel. competence project. Lectr. and cons. in field; referee for rsch. proposals Grant Found., NIH, 1970—, NSF, 1970—. Contbr. numerous articles to profl. jours. and books; author 2 monographs; mem. editorial bd. Devel. Psychology, 1986-90, Parenting: Science and Practice, 2000—. Recipient Rsch. Scientist award, NIMH; grantee NIMH, 1955-58, 60-66, Nat. Inst. Child Health and Human Devel., 1967-74, MacArthur Found., Grant Found., 1967—. Fellow Am. Psychol. Assn., Am. Psychol. Soc. (G. Stanley Hall award 1988), Soc. Research in Child Devel. Office: U Calif Inst of Human Devel 1217 Tolman Hall Berkeley CA 94720-1690 Office Phone: 510-642-3603.

BAUSE, GEORGE STEPHEN LONERAVEN, anesthesiologist; b. Chester, Pa., Nov. 22, 1955; BS in Biophysics cum laude, Ursinus Coll., Collegeville, PA, 1973—77; MPH in Epidemiology, Johns Hopkins U., 1980—81, MD, 1977—81. Diplomate Am. Bd. Anesthesiology. Intern Johns Hopkins Hosp., Balt., 1981-82, resident in anesthesiology, 1982-84; fellow geriatric anesthesiology Johns Hopkins Hosp.-Nat. Inst. Aging, Balt., 1984-85; attending physician Yale-New Haven Hosp., 1985-92, dir. geriatric anesthesia, 1987-92; chief dept. anesthesia West Haven (Conn.) VA Med. Ctr., 1990-92; Whitacre dir. anesthesia edn. Meridia Health Sys. of Cleve. Clinic, Ohio, 1992-96; asst. prof. Yale U., New Haven, 1985-91, assoc. prof., 1991-92; clin. assoc. prof. anesthesiology, perioperative medicine Case Western Res. U., Cleve., 1993—, clin. assoc. prof. oral and maxillofacial surgery, 2009—. Hon. curator USA's Wood Libr.-Mus. Anesthesiology, 1987—; curator George and Ramona Bause Collection, USA's Wood Libr. Mus., 2002; assoc. curator Living Hist. Anesthesiology Interviewee, 2005; lectr. Hektoen Inst. Medicine, 2007. Contbr. scientific papers in field. Pres. Yale Assn. Native Americans, 1988—90; assoc. curator United Ch. Christ Archives, 1999—2009, Berman Art Gallery Curator of Images and Energies of Freud and Einstein, 2005. St. Andrews Scholar, U. Edinburgh, 1975. Fellow: Royal Inst. Great Britain, Am. Indian Sci. and Engring. Soc., Royal Soc. Medicine, Coll. Physicians Phila., Internat. Coll. Anesthetists (hon.), Soc. Pithotomists (life; pres. 1980—81), Am. Acad. History of Dentistry (life), Internat. Coll. Surgeons (hon. William Halsted prize in Anesthesiology 1993); mem.: AMA, History Anaesthesia Soc., Mensa, Am. Osler Soc., Soc. Advancement Geriatric Anesthesia (life), Anesthesia History Assn. (named Roderick Calverley Lectr. 2004), Soc. Cardiovasc. Anesthesiologists, Internat. Anesthesia Rsch. Soc., Am. Soc. Regional Anesthesia, Am. Soc. Anesthesiologists, Am. Geriat. Soc., Acad. Anesthesiology, Nat. Eagle Scout Assn. (life), Triple Nine Soc., Phi Beta Kappa (scholar 2004), Alpha Phi Omega (life). Democrat. Congregationalist. Office: 5247 Wilson Mills # 282 Cleveland OH 44143-3016 Business E-Mail: ujyc@aol.com.

BAUTISTA, ABRAHAM PARANA, immunologist; b. Davao, Philippines, Mar. 15, 1952; s. Eufronio Bernardo and Loreto (Parana) B. BS in Biology, Far Eastern U., Manila, Philippines, 1972; Diploma in Microbiology, U. Tokyo, 1978; MS, Aberdeen U., Scotland, 1981, PhD in Immunology, 1984. Sr. rschr. lectr. U. Santo Tomas, Manila, 1976-81; rsch. scholar U. Aberdeen, 1979-84; rsch. assoc. East Carolina U., Greenville, N.C., 1984-89; asst. prof. La. State U. Med. Ctr., New Orleans, 1989-93, assoc. prof., 1993-2001, prof., 2001—02; adminstr. Ctr. Sci. Review, NIH, 2002—06; chief, Extramural Project Review Br. NIAAA, NIH, 2006—08, acting dir., Office Extramural Activities, 2008—, dir. office extramural activities, 2009—. Cons. Jefferson Trust/NationsBank, 1993-2001, prof., 2001—; reviewer, mem. NIH-Nat. Inst. Environ. Health Scis. Study Sect. for spl. program project, 1997—; sci. rev. adminstr. NIH, 2002—; mem. study sect. Alcohol and Toxicology #2, NIH, 1997—, adhoc mem. #1, 1997—; mem. study sect. molecular and cellular biology Am. Heart Assn., 1998—; mem. study sect. VA, reviewer, cons., 1998—; mem. study sect. for spl. program project NIDDKD, 2000—; mem. study sect. on program project, Nat. Inst. on Diabetes, Digestive and Kidney Disease, 2000—; mem. study sect. Fla. State Dept. Health, 2001—; reviewer Wellcome Trust, London, 2001—, Ky. Sci. and Tech. Found., 2001—. Guest editor, reviewer Jour. Leukocyte Biology, 1988—, Circulatory Shock, 1991—, Am. Jour. Physiology, 1991—, Alcohol, 1992—, Alcoholism Clin. and Exptl. Rsch., 1992—, Hepatology, 1993—, Gastroenterology, 1994—, Biochem. Pharmacol, 1995—, Internat. Jour. Cancer, 1995—, Alcohol Health & Rsch. World, 1997—, Critical Care Medicine, 2003; assoc. reviewing editor Alcoholism: Clin. and Exptl. Rsch., 2000—; mng. editor Frontiers in Biosci., 2001—; mem. editl. bd. Hepatology, 2004-; contbr. numerous articles to profl. jours. NIH-NIAAA grantee, 1995—; travel fellow Am. Assn. for Study Liver Disease, 1990; Internat. scholar Brit. Coun., 1979; recipient Rsch. award in Medicine, U. Aberdeen, 1981-84, F.I.R.S.T. award/Rsch. grantee NIH, 1991—; named Internat. UNESCO, 1978; named Philippine Med. Tech. Bd. Exam. Topnotcher, 1972. Mem. AAAS, Internat. Cytokine Soc., Am. Assn. Immunology, N.Y. Acad. Scis., Inst. of Biology, Soc. for Leukocyte Biology, Rsch. Soc. of Alcoholism, Shock Soc., Sigma Xi. Achievements include first demonstration that endogenous or exogenous interleukin-1 regulates insulin biosynthesis in vivo and that hepatic immune response is suppressed in chronic alcoholics with hepatitis; first to demonstrate that chemokines (e.g. macrophage inflammatory protein-2) are involved in liver injury during alcohol intoxication. Home: 13929 Highstream Pl Germantown MD 20874-6164 Office: NIAAA-NIH Office Extramural Activities 5635 Fishers Ln Rockville MD 20852 Business E-Mail: bautista@mail.nih.gov.

BAUTISTA, JIMMY MARTIN, physician, consultant; b. Baguio City, Benguet, Philippines, Nov. 18, 1970; s. Ang Min Po and Teresita Martin Bautista; m. Ma. Teresa Tricia Guison-Bautista, Jan. 26, 2002; children: Justine Therese, Jillian Triana. BS in Med. Tech., St. Louis U., Baguio City, 1991, MD, 1995. Diplomate Philippine Coll. Physicians, 2001. Chief resident, Dept. Medicine Baguio Gen. Hosp. and Med. Ctr., 2000—01; med. dir. St. Theodore's Hosp., Sagada, Mountain Province, Philippines, 2001; fellow, neuroenteric clin. rsch. group Southern Ariz. Vets. Health Care Sys., Tucson, 2003—04; fellow, gastrointestinal motility U. Ariz. Health Scis. Ctr., 2003—04; fellow, gastroenterology U. Santo Tomas Hosp., Manila, 2002—03, med. cons., internal medicine & gastroenterology, 2005—, mem., com. on hosp. infection control, 2008—, mem., dept. medicine rsch. com., 2008—; med. cons., internal medicine & gastroenterology Quirino Meml. Med. Ctr., Quezon City, Metro Manila, Philippines, 2005—, Lung Ctr. Philippines, Quezon City, 2007—; coord., motility unit Jose R. Reyes Meml. Med. Ctr., Manila, 2005—. Med. mgr. Janssen Pharm., Divsn. Johnson & Johnson, Paranaque City, Metro Manila, 2008—. Contbr. scientific papers to numerous sci. publs. Mem. Christian Family Movement, Quezon City, 2006—. Mem.: Philippine Soc. Exptl. and Clin. Pharmacology, Philippine Coll. Pharm. Medicine, Am. Neurogastroenterology & Motility Soc. Avocation: travel. Home: 42 Fordham St White Plains Quezon City Metro Manila 1110 Philippines Office: Univ Santo Tomas Hosp Espana Blvd Manila Metro Manila 1008 Philippines also: Johnson & Johnson Janssen Divsn Edison Rd Barrio Ibayo Paranaque City 1700 Philippines Office Phone: 632-824-8969. Office Fax: 632 7126348; Home Fax: 632 7769819. Personal E-mail: jimmy_bautista@hotmail.com.

BAVA, ANTONIO E., human physiology professor, researcher; b. Catania, Italy, Mar. 5, 1940; s. Michele F. Bava and Anna M. Maag; m. Maria A. Maricchiolo (div.); children: Michele S., Carlo E.; m. Mary L. Artero-Bava, Nov. 14, 1991. MD, U. Catania, 1965. Asst. prof. med. faculty U. Catania, 1967—80, asst. prof. gen. physiology sci. faculty, 1972—76; asst. prof. human physiology med. faculty U. Trieste, Italy, 1977—80, prof. human physiology med. faculty, 1980—, dir. Inst. Physiology, 1977—97, dir. Specialization Sch. Sport Medicine, 1997—. Author: Funzioni del Sistema Nervoso e Linguaggio, 1984, Asimmetrie dell' Encefalo Umano: Filogenesi ed Ontogenesi, 1990, The Cerebellum and the Reading Process, 2003; editor: Prospettive Nello Studio dei Primati, 1991; contbr. articles to numerous sci. jours. Fellow, NATO Coun. Nat. Rsch., 1976—78. Mem.: AAAS, NY Acad. Scis., Assn. Primatologica Italian, Italian Physiology Soc. Roman Catholic. Avocations: history, human evolution, ancient civilization, astronomy, poetry. Home: Via Commerciale 50 34134 Trieste Italy Office: U Trieste Dept Physiology and Pathology Via Alexander Fleming 22 34127 Trieste TS Italy Office Phone: 040-558-71-80. Business E-Mail: bava@univ.trieste.it.

BAXI, LAXMI V., obstetrician, gynecologist, educator; b. India; came to the U.S., 1976; d. Ishwardas Bhatia; m. Vibhakar K. Baxi, 1969. MBBS, Seth G. S. Med. Coll., Bombay U., 1962; MD, King Edward Meml. Hosp., Bombay, 1966. Diplomate Am. Bd. Ob Gyn and maternal fetal medicine sub-specialty, 1998-04. Rotating intern, resident ob/gyn King Edward Meml. Hosp., Nowrosjee Wadia Maternity Hosp., Bombay, 1962-69; sr. registrar ob-gyn. King Edward Meml. Hosp., Bombay, 1969-72; asst. prof. ob-gyn. Lokmanya Tilak Med. Coll., Bombay, 1972-76; chief resident ob-gyn. C.M.D.N.J., Rutgers Med. Sch., St. Peter's Med. Ctr., N.J., 1976 77; fellow in maternal fetal medicine Coll. Physicians and Surgeons Columbia U., 1977-79; asst. prof. clin. ob-gyn. Columbia U. Coll. Physicians & Surgeons, NYC, 1979—, asst. prof. ob-gyn., 1980-87, assoc. prof. ob-gyn., 1987-91, prof. clin. ob-gyn., 1992—, assoc. chair ob gyn., 1997, vice chair ob-gyn., 1998—2003. Asst. attending ob-gyn. Sloane Hosp. for Women, Presbyn. Hosp., NYC, 1979-87, assoc. attending, 1987-91; vis. prof. dept. ob-gyn. King Edward Meml. Hosp., Bombay, 1986; co-dir. obstet. svc. Sloane Hosp. for Women, Columbia Presbyn. Med. Ctr., NYC, 1991-92, dir., 1992-96, attending ob-gyn., 1992—, assoc. chair ob/gyn, 1997, vice chair ob-gyn., 1998-2003, acting dir. maternal-fetal medicine & maternal-fetal medicine fellowship program, 1995-96, 98-99; mem. NY State Bd. Profl. Conduct Dept.; senator Columbia U., 2005—07; presenter in field. Reviewer: Obstetrics and Gynecology, Jour. Maternal Fetal Medicine, Jour. Perinatal Medicine, Am. Jour. Ob-Gyn., Soc. for Perinatal Obstetricians, Jour. Gynecol. Investigation, Jour. Reproductive Medicine; co-editor: Jour. Assn. Med. Women in India, 1974-75; cons. internat. bd. editors: Jour. Ob-Gyn. India; contbr. articles to profl. jours Mem. fin. com. City NY Dept. Health, Bur. Maternity Svcs. and Family Planning; Health; diplomate Am. Bd. ob-gyn amd Maternal-Fetal Medicine, 1981, 1987, 1995, 2009 Grantee Diabetic Found., 1990-91, Newborn Lung Ctr., 1979, 80, 81. Fellow Coll. Physicians and Surgeons; mem. Soc. for Gynecol. Investigation, Am. Coll. Ob-Gyn., N.Y. Obstet. Soc., N.Y. Acad. Medicine (sec. divsn. ob-gyn. 1985-86, chairperson divsn. ob-gyn. 1986-87), Indian Coll. Ob-Gyn. (founding mem.), Soc. Maternal Fetal Medicine, Assn. Med. Women India (life), Assn. Profs. Ob-Gyn., Jacob's Inst. Women's Health (founding mem.), Sloane Alumni Assn. (pres. 1992-93). Avocation: indian classical music and dancing. Office Phone: 212-305-5899. Business E-Mail: lvb1@columbia.edu.

BAXTER, RICHARD ALAN, plastic surgeon, educator; b. Covina, Calif., Oct. 10, 1955; MD, U. Calif., San Diego, 1983. Cert. Am. Bd. Plastic Surgery, 1992. Intern surgery Swedish Med. Ctr., Seattle, 1983—84, resident surgery, 1984—88; fellowship plastic surgery Oreg. Health Scis. U., Portland, 1988—90; pvt. practice Mountlake Terrace, Wash.; chief med. officer Calidora Skin Clinic. Clin. instr. plastic surgery U. Wash. Sch. Medicine. Fellow: ACS; mem.: King County Med. Soc., Wash. State Med. Assn., N.W. Soc. Plastic Surgeons, Internat. Soc. Aesthetic Plastic Surgery, Am. Soc. Aesthetic Plastic Surgery, Am Soc. Plastic Surgeons, Wash. Soc. Plastic Surgeons (past pres.). Office: Plastic Surgery Clinic 6100 219th St SW Ste 290 Mountlake Terrace WA 98043 Office Phone: 425-776-0880. E-mail: drbaxter@drbaxter.com.

BAXTER, SHEILA R., career military officer; b. Franklin, Va., Apr. 4, 1955; B in Health and Phys. Edn., Va. State Coll., 1977; disting. mil. grad., Reserve Officer's Training Corps; M in Health Svcs. Mgmt., Webster U. Med. svcs. offficer U.S. Army, 1978, advanced through grades to brigadier gen., 2004, asst. surgeon gen., dep. chief of staff for force sustainment med. command US Army Med. Services Corp. Ft. Sam Houston, Tex., 2004—05; comdr. Madigan Army Med. Ctr., Tacoma, 2005—. Evangelist Ch. of God and Christ. Decorated Legion of Merit, Bronze Star, Meritorious Svc. Medal with four oak leaf clusters, Army Commendation Medal with two oak leaf clusters, Army Achievement Medal with two oak leaf clusters, Kuwait Liberation Medal, Expert Field Med. Badge, others; recipient Hon. Silver award for excellence in cmty svc., Lord Mayor of Pirmasens, Germany, Executive of Year, 2008, Mil. Highest award, Disting. Svc. medal; named Powerful Women in America, Newsweek Mag., 2005. Mem.: Nat. Scholars Hon. Soc.

BAY, BOON-HUAT, medical educator; s. Khim-Yong Bay and Siang-Eng Seet; m. Alice Heah; children: Noel, Nigel. MBBS, Nat. U. Singapore, 1982, PhD, 1992. Sr. lectr., dept. anatomy Nat. U. Singapore, 1996—98, asst. prof., 1998—99, assoc. prof., 1999—2007, prof. anatomy, 2008—, chair, dept. anatomy, 2008—. Contbr. articles to profl. jours. Chmn. Salem day Rehab. Ctr. for Elderly, Singapore, 1995—2005. Fellow Commonwealth Med. Fellowship, Assn. of Commonwealth Universities, 1. Mem.: Microscopy Soc., Singapore (pres. 1998—2002). Office: Nat Univ Singapore 4 Med Dr BLK Md10 117597 Singapore Singapore Office Fax: 656778 7643. Business E-Mail: antbaybh@nus.edu.sg.

BAYAR, HEXIG, research scientist, educator; b. Inner Mongolia, Apr. 1, 1972; PhD, Tokyo Inst. Tech., 2005. Rschr. Nat. Inst. Health Sci., 2005—07; asst. prof. Tokyo Inst. Tech., 2007—. Mem.: Japanese Soc. Biomaterials, Japanese Soc. Regenerative Medicine. Avocation: hockey. Home: 304 Rm 18 B 1-13-4 Ogawa Machida Machida Tokyo 194-0003 Japan Home Fax: 81-42-796-5077. Personal E-mail: bhexig@bio.titech.ac.jp.

BAYDIN, AHMET, medical educator; b. Artvin, Turkey, Aug. 20, 1965; D, Ondokuz Mayis U., 1989. Assoc. prof., dept. emergency medicine Ondokuz Mayis U., 2003—. Office: Kurupelit Samsun Atakum 55139 Turkey Office Fax: 0362 4576041. Business E-Mail: abaydin@omu.edu.tr.

BAYER, JORDANA, clinical psychologist, researcher; b. Adelaide, South Australia, Apr. 8, 1969; BA in Psychology with honours, U. Adelaide, South Australia, 1991; M in Clin. Psychology, Flinders U. South Australia, Adelaide, 1994; PhD, U. Melbourne, Australia, 2003. Cert. in coll. clinical psychologists Australian Psychol. Soc. Australia, 1995. Clin. child psychologist Child Protection Svc. Flinders Med. Ctr., Adelaide, South Australia, 1995—96; rsch. fellow Centre Cmty. Child Health and Murdoch Childrens Rsch. Inst., Royal Children's Hosp., Melbourne, Victoria, Australia, 2003—11; expert cons. for children's mental health Centre Cmty. Child Health, Royal Children's Hosp., Melbourne, 2004—11; lectr. U. Melbourne, Parkville, Victoria, Australia, 2008—; assoc. prof. clin. psychology LaTrobe U., 2011—. Contbr. articles to profl. jours. Mem. Australian Rsch. Coun., 2009—, equity trustees, 2009—, Grantee Rsch., VicHealth, 1999—2001, Telstra Cmty. Devel. Fund, 2004—07, William Buckland Found., 2007—08; scholar, U. Melbourne, 1997—2000; Commonwealth Postgrad. Coursework scholarship, Australian Govt., 1993—94, NHMRC, 2010—, Inaugural Colin Dodds Postdoct. fellowship, Australian Rotary Health Rsch. Fund, 2007—09, Postdoc. fellowship, Australian Nat. Health & Med. Rsch. Coun. Mem.: Australian Clin. Psychology Assn., Australian Psychol. Soc. (coll. mem. 1995—2009). Achievements include research in aetiology and prevention programs for children's mental health problems. Office: Royal Children's Hosp Ctr Cmty Child Health Flemington Rd 3052 Parkville VIC Australia Business E-Mail: jordana.bayer@mcri.edu.au.

BAYLESS, BETSEY, health facility administrator; b. Phoenix; BA in Latin Am. Studies and Spanish, U. Ariz., 1966; MPA, Ariz. State U., 1974; DHL (hon.), U. Ariz., 2001. V.p. pub. fin. Peacock, Hislop, Staley & Given, Inc., Phoenix; asst. dir. Ariz. Bd. Regents; acting dir. dept. revenue State of Ariz., dir. dept. adminstrn., sec. of state, 1997—2003; dir. Ariz. Dept. Adminstrn., 2003—05; CEO Maricopa Integrated Health System, 2005—. Bd. suprs. Maricopa County, 1989-97, chmn. bd., 1992, 94, vice chair, 1997; mem. Ariz. Bd. Investment, 2003—; bd. dirs. Child Help Ariz.; mem. Nat.bd. dirs. U. Ariz. Coll. of Bus. and Pub. Adminstrn.; adv. bd. Ariz. State U. West. Bd. dirs. Xavier Coll. Preparatory Found., Charter 100, Valley Leadership Class VI, Ariz. Rep. Caucus, Ariz. Women's Forum, 4-H Found., Ariz. Cmty. Found.; mem. leadership bd. U. Ariz. Health Svcs.-Phoenix Campus. Named to Hall of Fame, Ariz. State U. Coll. Pub. Programs; recipient Disting. Citizen award U. Ariz. Alumni Assn., Woman of Yr. award Capitol chpt. Bus. and Profl. Women, Disting. Achievement award NEH Fellowship, Achievement award Nat. Assn. Counties, 1993, Citizen award Bur. Reclamation, 1993, Woman of Achievement award Xavier Coll. Preparatory, 1995. Mem. Phi Beta Kappa (Freeman medal 1966). Republican. Office: 2601 E Roosevelt St Phoenix AZ 85008 *

BAYLESS, THEODORE M(ORRIS), gastroenterologist, educator, researcher; b. Atlantic City, Apr. 14, 1931; s. David N. and Fan (Halpern) B.; m. Janet M. Nides, June 22, 1954; children: Jeffrey, Andrew, Neal. BS, Bucknell U., 1953; MD, Chgo. Med. Sch., 1957. Intern Cornell div. Bellevue Hosp., also Meml. Cancer Ctr., NYC, 1957-58, 58-60; fellow gastroenterology Johns Hopkins U., Balt., 1960-62, prof., 1981—; physician Johns Hopkins Hosp., Balt., 1964—; dir. emeritus Meyerhoff Inflammatory Bowel Disease Ctr. Johns Hopkins U.; Sherlock Hibbs prof. IBD, 2006. Co-author: NOD2 Gene in Crohn's Disease, 2001; editor: Advanced Therapy of Inflammatory Bowel Disease, 2011, Advanced Therapy-Gastroenterology and Liver Disease, 2004. Capt. USAR, 1962-64. Recipient Corson Nutrition medal Franklin Inst., Phila., 1987, Johns Hopkins Mentoring award, 2003, Edn. award Johns Hopkins U. Alumni Assn., 2004. Fellow ACP (Md. chpt. Clin. Investigation award 1996); mem. Am. Soc. Clin. Investigation, Am. Gastroenterology Assn. (dir. immunology, microbiology and inflammatory bowel disease 1991-96, Disting. Educator award 1987, Disting. Clinician award 2004), Alpha Omega Alpha. Jewish. Home: 2206 South Rd Baltimore MD 21209-4428 Office: Johns Hopkins Hosp 600 N Wolfe St Baltimore MD 21287-0005 Office Phone: 410-955-4916. Business E-Mail: tbayless@jhmi.edu.

BAYSAL, EROL, geneticist, educator; b. Nicosia, Cyprus, Dec. 17, 1960; s. Ahmet and Letafet Baysal; m. Emine Baysal, May 12, 1988; children: Ahmet Sacit, Inci. BSc with honors, U. London, 1983, PhD, 1987. Rsch. scientist NY U. Med. Ctr., NYC, 1987—89; asst. prof. Med. Coll. Ga., Augusta, 1989—95, head DNA labs., 1989—95, mem., grad. faculty adv. com., 1990—95, mem. dean's student rsch.

com., 1990—95, mem., admissions com., 1990—95, faculty senator, 1991—94, mem., academic admissions com., 1992—95; head molecular genetics dept. Dubai Genetic and Thalassemia Ctr., United Arab Emirates, 1995—, dir. DNA diagnostics, 1995—, cons. molecular geneticist, 1995—; sr. lectr. Dubai Med. Coll., 1996—. Mem., editl. rev. bd. Hemoglobin, Am. Jour. Hematology, Brit. Jour. Haematology, Molecular Therapy and Genomics, 1989; mem. sci. rev. bd. NATO Collaborative Rsch. Programs, Brussels, 1990—95; cons. UN Tokten Program, Istanbul, Turkey, 1993—94; sci. advisor Glaxo-SmithKline, Pa., 1994—95; mem., grant rev. bd. Terry Fox Rsch. Grant, Al Ain, United Arab Emirates, 1999—2000; acting asst. dir. Al Wasl Hosp., Dubai, 2000—02; exec. founding bd. mem. Ctr. Arab Genomic Studies, Dubai, 2004—; sci. advisor to pres. Govt. Northern Cyprus, Nicosia, 2005—07; dir. UAE Genetic Diseases Assn., Dubai, 2005—06. Co-author: Syllabus of Thalassemia Mutations, 1997; contbr. articles to numerous sci. jours. Grantee Rsch. grants, NATO, 1995; Postgrad. scholarship, Govt. Cyprus, 1983, Rsch. grants, Med. Coll. Ga., 1995, NIH, 1993, 1996, 1998, Rsch. grant on Novel Rapid Diagnostic Methods, Sheikh Hamdan Awards Med. Scis., 2002. Fellow: RCP (London); mem.: Emirates Hematology Soc. (hon.), NY Acad. Scis. (life). Achievements include discovery of novel method for detection of alpha-thalassemia, the most common single gene disorder in the world by polymerase chain reaction; established DNA diagnostic laboratories for genetic diseases in UK, USA, UAE, Turkey, Cyprus. Home: PO Box 9115 Dubai UAE United Arab Emirates Office: Dubai Genetic & Thalassemia Ctr PO Box 9115 Dubai United Arab Emirates Office Fax: 971 4 3352569. Business E-Mail: emerinah@eim.ae.

BAZ, MAHER AFIF, internist, educator, medical director lung transplant program; b. Monrovia, Liberia, Aug. 3, 1964; s. Afif Salem and Sana Baz. MD, Am. U. of Beirut, 1989. Resident internal medicine Duke U., Durham, NC, 1989—92, pulmonary fellow, 1992—95; asst. prof. of medicine U. of Fla., Gainesville, 1996—2002, assoc. prof. of medicine, 2002—. Med. dir. lung transplant program U. of Fla., Gainesville, 1996—; thoracic com. United Network for Organ Sharing. Named one of Young Leaders in Pulmonary Medicine, Boehringer-Ingelheim Pharmaceuticals, 2001. Mem.: Internat. Soc. of Heart and Lung Transplantation, Am. Thoracic Soc. Achievements include research in biology and immunosuppressive therapy of airway rejection. Office: U Fla 1600 SW Archer Rd PO Box 100395 Gainesville FL 32610 Business E-Mail: bazma@medicine.ufl.edu.

BAZ, RACHID, hematologist; b. Beirut, Jan. 1, 1976; MD, Am. U. Beirut, 2000. Assoc. staff, dept. hematologic malignancies Cleve. Clinic, 2007—08; asst. mem., dept. malignant hematology H. Lee Moffitt Cancer Ctr. and Rsch. Inst., 2008—. Asst. prof., dept. oncologic scis. U. South Fla., 2008—. Mem.: Am. Soc. Clin. Oncology, Internat. Myeloma Soc., Am. Soc. Hematology. Office: 12902 Magnolia Dr FOB3 Tampa FL 33612 Office Fax: 813-745-3071. Business E-Mail: rachid.baz@moffitt.org.

BAZELL, ROBERT JOSEPH, health and science correspondent; b. Pitts., Aug. 21, 1945; s. Irving and Beatrice (Robb) B.; m. Ilene Tanz, Sept. 11, 1966 (div.), m. Margot Weinshel, July 31, 1979; children: Rebecca, Joshua, Stephanie. BA, U. Calif., Berkeley, 1967; student, U. Sussex, Eng., 1968-69; postgrad., U. Calif., 1971. Writer Sci. Mag., Washington, 1971-72; reporter NY Post, NYC, 1972-76; sci. and health corr. WNBC-TV, NBC News, NYC, 1976—. Author: HER-2: The Making of Herceptin, a Revolutionary Treatment for Breast Cancer, 1998; contbr. articles to mags. Recipient over 2000 various journalistic awards. Mem. Phi Beta Kappa Office: NBC News 30 Rockefeller Plz Fl 3 New York NY 10112-0002 *

BEACH, MARY CATHERINE, internist, educator; b. May 26, 1969; BA, Barnard Coll., NYC, 1991; MD, Mt. Sinai Sch. Medicine, NYC, 1995; MPH, Johns Hopkins U. Sch. Hygiene & Pub. Health, 1999. Diplomate Am. Bd. Internal Medicine, cert. Nat. Bd. Med. Examiners. Intern, resident dept. medicine Mt. Sinai Med. Ctr., 1995—98; fellowship divsn. gen. internal medicine Johns Hopkins U. Sch. Medicine, Balt., 1998—2002, asst. prof. dept. medicine, 2002—08, faculty Phoebe R. Berman Bioethics Inst., 2002—, faculty Welch Ctr. Prevention, Epidemiology & Clin. Rsch., 2003—, assoc. prof., 2008—. Greenwall fellowship in bioethics & health policy Kennedy Inst. Ethics, Georgetown U., Washington, 2000—02; Congl. fellow in health policy US Senate, Washington, 2001. Assoc. editor Jour. Gen. Internal Medicine, 2001—04; contbr. articles to profl. jours. Recipient Robert Wood Johnson Generalist Physician Faculty Scholars award, 2003, K-08 award, Agy. Healthcare Rsch. & Quality, 2003; grantee Oxford Fellowship, Mt. Sinai Sch. Medicine, 1995. Mem.: ACP, Am. Acad. Communication in Healthcare, Am. Soc. Bioethics & Humanities, Soc. Gen. Internal Medicine. Achievements include research on the theoretical foundations of respect and the impact of physician attitudes and patient-physician communication on patients in the primary care setting, in the treatment of HIV, and in the treatment of sickle cell disease. Office: Johns Hopkins U Sch Medicine 2024 E Monument St Ste 2 500 Baltimore MD 21287 Office Phone: 410-614-1134. Office Fax: 410-614-0588. E-mail: mcbeach@jhmi.edu. *

BEACHLEY, MICHAEL CHARLES, radiologist; b. Harrisburg, Pa., Nov. 14, 1940; s. Kenneth Gumbert and Carolyn Elizabeth (Jones) B.; m. Deborah Rowe Samson, July 27, 1963; children: Kenneth, Barbara, William; m. Barbara Ann Giba, 2003. AB, Dartmouth Coll., 1962, B.MS, 1963; MD, Harvard U., 1965. Diplomate Am. Bd. Radiology. Intern in surgery Med. Coll. Va., Richmond, 1965-66, resident in radiology, 1966-69, instr. radiology, 1970, faculty, 1972—, acting chmn. dept. radiology, 1976, prof., 1977-87, chmn. dept. radiology, 1977-82, prof. radiation scis., 1981-87, prof. biophysics, 1980-82, prof. physiology and biophysics, 1982-87, clin. prof., 1987—2009; clin. prof. radiology U. Pitts., 1988—2009; chmn. Dept. Radiology St. Margaret Meml. Hosp., Pitts., 1987-97; pres. Three Rivers Imaging Cons., Ltd., 1993-94, Duquesne Imaging Ltd., 1994-2001; med. dir. Radiology Ptnrs.; chmn. dept. radiology U. Pitts. Med. Ctr., Saint Margaret, 1997-99. Cons. McGuire VA Hosp., 1977—; fellow in radiol. pathology Armed Forces Inst. Pathology, Washington, 1969. Contbr. articles to profl. jours., chapters to books. Major US Army, 1970—72. Recipient Commendation medal, US Army. Fellow Am. Coll. Radiology (pres. Va. chpt. 1982-83, chmn. com. on stds. and accreditation 1998-2004); mem. AMA, Am. Heart Assn., Radiol. Soc. N.Am. (chmn. bylaws com. 1994-96), Am. Roentgen Ray Soc., Pitts. Roentgen Soc. (chmn. com on fellowship nomination 1998-99), Pa. Radiol. Soc., Pa. Med. Soc. (alt. del., mem. med.-legal com.), Allegheny Med. Soc. (peer rev. bd. 1997-99), Pa. Radiol. MSO, Dartmouth Club Western Pa., Harvard Club Western Pa. Home: PO Box 331 Bakerstown PA 15007-0331 Personal E-mail: beachley.m.c@gmail.com.

BEADLE, BETH MICHELLE, oncologist; b. 1975; BS in Chemistry, Northwestern U., 1996, Ph.D in Structural Biology & Biochemistry, 2002, MD, 2004. Surgical resident, McGaw Med. Ctr. Northwestern U., 2004—05; radiation oncology resident U. Tex. MD Anderson Cancer Ctr., 2005—09, asst. prof. radiology. Recipient Centennial prize, Phi Betta Kappa, 1996, Marple-Schweitzer award for Disting. Chemistry Undergraduate, 1996, Northwestern U. Med. Student Rsch. award, 1997, Drug Discovery Program Symposium Outstanding Poster award, 1998, Finn World Travel Grant award, 2001, Eli Lilly award for Outstanding Poster, 2001, Eleanor Montague Disting. Resident award in Radiation Oncology, Am. Assn. Women Radiologists, 2008, Outstanding ASTRO Presentation award, 2008, Young Oncologist Essay award, Am. Radium Soc., 2008. Office: U Tex MD Anderson Cancer Ctr Unit 097 1515 Holcombe Blvd Houston TX 77030 Office Phone: 713-563-2308. Office Fax: 713-563-2331.

BEAGRIE, GEORGE SIMPSON, dentist, educator, retired dean; b. Peterhead, Scotland, Sept. 14, 1925; emigrated to Can., 1968, naturalized, 1973; s. George and Eliza Lawson (Simpson) B.; m. Marjorie McVie, Sept. 30, 1950; children: Jennifer, Lesley, Ailsa, Elspeth. LDS, Royal Coll. Surgeons, Edinburgh, Scotland, 1947; DDS, U. Edinburgh, 1966; DSc (hon.), McGill U., Can., 1985; DDS (hon.), U. Edinburgh, 1987; D, U. Montreal, Can., 1991. Prof., chmn. dept. restorative dentistry U. Edinburgh Dental Sch., 1963-68; prof., chmn. dept. clin. scis. U. Toronto Dental Sch., 1968-78, dir. postgrad. div., 1974-78; dean faculty dentistry U. B.C., Vancouver, Canada, 1978—88, dean emeritus, 1989—. Sci. officer grants com. dental scis. Med. Rsch. Coun. Can., 1971-76, dir. dental tng. grants programme, 1971-78; mem. Nat. Dental Examining Bd. Can.; chmn. written exams com. Nat. Dental Examining Bd., Can., 1984-93; cons. WHO, 1976-1996, in field. Contbr. over 100 articles to dental jours. Mem. United Ch. Can. Served to flight lt. RAF, 1948-50. Fellow Nuffield Found., 1957-58; grantee Med. Research Council U.K., 1962-64; grantee Med. Research Council Can., 1968; grantee Commonwealth Found., 1973 Fellow Royal Coll. Dentists Can. (pres. 1977-79), Am. Coll. Dentists, Internat. Coll. Dentists; fellow in dental surgery Royal Coll. Surgeons Edinburgh and Eng.; mem. ADA (hon.), Internat. Assn. Dental Research (pres. 1977-78), Fedn. Dentaire Internat. (chmn. commn. on dental edn. and practice 1981-87), Can. Dental Assn. (editor tape cassette program 1972-76, coord. Self-Learning, Self-Appt. C-E program for gen. practitioners, 1986-), Omicron Kappa Upsilon.

BEAL, JOHN M., surgeon, medical educator; b. Starkville, Miss., 1915; m. Mary Lucinda Phemister, Feb. 20, 1943 (dec. July 2005); children: John M., Bruce Phemister, Margaret Anne MD, U. Chgo., 1941. Diplomate Am. Bd. Surgery. Intern N.Y. Hosp., NYC, 1941-42, asst. resident surgery, 1942-44, 46-47, surgeon, 1947-48, attending surgeon, 1953-63; chmn. tumor bd. and staff surgeon Wadsworth Gen. Hosp., West Los Angeles, 1949-50, chief surg. service, 1950-53; cons. staff St. John's Hosp., Santa Monica, Calif., 1950-53; instr. surgery Cornell U., Ithaca, N.Y., 1948-49, assoc. prof. clin. surgery, 1953-63; instr. surgery UCLA, 1949-50, asst. prof., 1950-53; J. Roscoe Miller disting. prof. Northwestern U., 1981-84, prof. emeritus, 1984—, chmn. dep. surgery, 1963-82; clin. prof. surgery U. N.C., Chapel Hill, 1984-88; chmn. dept. surgery Chgo. Wesley Meml. Hosp., 1963-69, Northwestern Meml. Hosp., 1973-82; chief surgery Passavant Meml. Hosp., Chgo., 1963-73. Chmn. Am. Bd. Surgery, 1970-71. Served to capt. M.C. AUS, 1944-46. Fellow ACS (bd. regents 1973-83, pres. 1982-83); mem. Council of Med. Splty. Socs. (sec. 1978-80), Soc. Univ. Surgeons, Soc. Clin. Surgery, AMA, Am. Surg. Assn. Address: 432 Georgetown Cir Valdosta GA 31602-4114

BEAL, M. FLINT, neurologist; b. London, Nov. 6, 1950; s. Myron C. and Esther (Delong) B.; m. Judy A. Ahlheim, June 12, 1976; children: Bradley, Emily. BA, Colgate U., 1972; MA, U. Va., 1976. Diplomate Am. Bd. Psychiatry and Neurology, 1982. Med. resident N.Y. Hosp. Cornell, NYC, 1976—78; neurology resident Mass. Gen. Hosp., Boston, 1978—81, neurology fellow, 1981—83, asst. prof. neurology, 1983—87, assoc. prof. neurology, 1987—95, prof., 1995—98; Ann Parrish Titzell prof., chmn. dept. neurology Cornell U. Weill Med. Coll., NYC, 1998—; neurologist-in-chief N.Y. Presbyn. Hosp., NYC, 1998—. Editl. bd.: Annals of Neurology and Jour. of Neurochemistry; contbr. articles to profl. jours. Fellow Stroke Coun. Am. Heart Assn., Am. Acad. Neurology, NY Acad. Sci., Soc. Neurosci., Internat. Soc. Cerebral Blood Flow and Metabolism, Alpha Omega Alpha; mem. AAAS, Inst. Medicine, Am. Neurol. Assn. (v.p., Derek Denny-Brown award). Achievements include delineation of postmortem neurochemistry of neurodegenerative diseases improved animal models of neurodegenerative diseases and new therapy for neuro protection in neurodegenerative diseases. Office: NY Hosp-Weill Cornell Med Ctr Dept Neurology and Neurosci 525 E 68th St New York NY 10021 Office Phone: 212-746-6575.

BEAL, MYRON CLARENCE, osteopath; b. NYC, Dec. 4, 1920; s. Clarence Joseph and Birdice Elvira (Flint) Beal; m. Esther Naomi DeLong, Sept. 11, 1948; children: Rebecca Johnson, Myron Flint, Shelley Rees, Julie Wilson, Christina Beal Bailey. AB, U. Rochester, 1942; D.O., Chgo. Coll. Osteo. Medicine, 1945; MS in Physiology, U. Chgo., 1949. Asst. dir. clinics Chgo. Coll. Osteo. Medicine, 1946-49; instr. London Coll. Osteopathy, 1949-51; pvt. practice osteo. medicine Rochester, N.Y., 1951-74; prof. biomechanics Coll. Osteo. Medicine, Mich. State U., East Lansing, 1974-81, prof. family medicine, 1981-89, prof. emeritus, 1989—, acting chmn. biomechanics, 1975-77. Mem. Nat. Bd. Examiners Osteo. Physicians and Surgeons, 1960—84, cons., 1984—89; mem. N.Y. State Bd. Medicine, 1961—73. Trustee Chgo. Coll. Osteo. Medicine, 1969—93, chmn. bd. dirs., 1985—91. Fellow: Am. Acad. Osteopathy (editor 1987—2005); mem.: Chgo. Osteo. Health Sys. (bd. dirs. 1986—90), Mich. Assn. Osteo. Physicians and Surgeons, N.Y. State Osteo. Soc., Am. Osteo. Assn. Congregationalist. Office: 110 Ferris Hills Canandaigua NY 14424-3202

BEALE, MARK DOUGLAS, psychiatrist, educator; b. Richmond, Va., May 11, 1962; BA, U. Va., 1984; MD, Ea. Va. Med. Sch., 1989. Diplomate Am. Bd. Psychiatry and Neurology; lic. S.C. State Bd. Med. Examiners. Intern Med. U. S.C., Charleston, 1989-90, resident in psychiatry, 1989-93, fellow in electroconvulsive therapy, 1992-93, instr. dept. psychiatry and behavioral scis., 1993-94, asst. prof. dept. psychiatry and behavioral scis., 1994—98, assoc. prof., 1999—; owner, pres. Charleston Psychiat. Assocs., 2000—. Cons. electroconvulsive therapy, attending psychiatrist Inst. Psychiatry, Med. U. SC, Charleston, 1993—2000, Ralph Johnson VA, Charleston, 1996—; cons. electroconvulsive therapy Charleston Meml. Hosp., 1993-96; lectr. in field. Author: (with others) Handbook of ECT, 1996, (book chpts.) Handbook of Child and Adolescent Psychiatry, 1996, Textbook of Consultation-Liaison Psychiatry, 1996, (jours.) Convulsive Therapy, Psychosomatics, Neuropsychiatry/Neuropsychology & Behavioral Neurology; book reviewer: Clinical Gerontologist. Recipient Young Investigator award Nat. Alliance Rsch. on Schizophrenia and Depression, 1998; named to Am.'s Top Psychiatrists, 2004-09. Fellow Am. Psychiat. Assn.; mem. SC Psychiat. Assn. Avocations: guitarist in the psychodymanics band, painting, guitar building. Office: Charleston Psychiatric Associates 669 St Andrews Blvd Charleston SC 29407

BEALE, SUSAN YATES, social worker; b. Saginaw, Mich., Nov. 17, 1943; d. William Miller and Dorothy LaVerne (Langdon) Yates; m. Henry B.R. Beale, Aug. 27, 1966; children: Andrew, Nathaniel. AB cum laude, Oberlin Coll., 1966; MA, U. Chgo., 1969. Social worker West Side VA Hosp., Chgo., 1969-70, DC Dept. Human Resources, Washington, 1970-72, DC Pub. Schs., Washington, 1972-73; pvt. practice Washington, 1973-74; dir. social svc. Capitol Hill Hosp., Washington, 1974-80; social worker No. Va. Dialysis Ctr., Alexandria, 1982-87, Vis. Nurse Assn., Rockville, Md., 1987-89; sr. social worker Hospice of Washington, 1989-95; sr. social svcs. analyst Microeconomic Applications, 1982—; pres. Coping Ptnrs., Washington, 1996—2004; social worker Capital, Falls Church, Va., 1999—2007; social worker, educator Capital Hospice, Washington, 2007—10; social worker IV Capital Caring, Washington, 2010—. Tchr. Royal Scottish Country Dance Soc. Mem.: NASW. Avocations: singing, gardening. Office: Capital Hospice 50 F St NW Ste 3300 Washington DC 20001

BEALER, JOHN FREDRIC, pediatrician, colon and rectal surgeon; b. St. Louis, July 2, 1962; MD, U. Mo., Kans. City, 1986. Ptnr. Rocky Mountain Pediat. Surgery, PC, 1997—2007; assoc. prof. U. Colo., Denver, 2007—. Dir. bariatric surgery Children's Hosp. Colo., 2007—11, dir. colorectal program, 2008—. Fellow: ACS, Am. Acad. Pediat.; mem.: Denver Med. Soc., Am. Soc. Bariatric Surgery, Am. Pediat. Surg. Assn. Office: Anschutz Med Campus 13123 E 16th Ave Aurora CO 80045 Office Fax: 720-777-7271. Personal E-mail: john.bealer@comcast.net.

BEALL, ROBERT JOSEPH, foundation executive; b. Washington, May 19, 1943; s. William Joseph and Louise Rachel (Tayman) B.; m. Mary Ellen O'Connor, June 24, 1967; children: Thomas Joseph, Robert Andrew. BS, Albright Coll., 1965; MA, PhD, SUNY, Buffalo, 1970. Asst. prof. dept. physiology Case-Western Reserve U., Cleve., 1971-74, asst. prof., Sch. Dentistry, 1972-74; grants assoc. divsn. rsch. grants NIH, 1974-75; program dir. metabolic diseases program Nat. Inst. Arthritis, Metabolism & Digestive Diseases, 1975-79; med. dir. Cystic Fibrosis Found., Rockville, Md., 1980-93, nat. dir. Bethesda, Md., 1981-84, exec. v.p., 1984-93, pres., CEO, 1994—. Bd. trustees Albright Coll.; bd. dirs. Multiple Myeloma Rsch. Consortium. Recipient Merit award NIH, 1980 Mem. AAAS, N.Y. Acad. Scis., Am. Soc. Human Genetics, Sigma Xi. Presbyterian. Office: Cystic Fibrosis Found 6931 Arlington Rd Bethesda MD 20814-5231 Office Phone: 301-907-2541. *

BEAR, GERALDINE M., nursing assistant, poet; b. Spartanburg, SC, Mar. 6, 1926; d. Clarence Lee and Lucy Bell Hayes; m. Samuel Sidney Bear, Apr. 8, 1945; children: Diana L., Russell M., Joseph J. Student, Edgecombe Acad., 1943. Cert. nursing asst., CPR, RN home health aide. Author: (poems) Dedications of Love, 1974, The Poetry Seed, 1991, (book) Soft Reflections. Deacon, mem. choir Grace Presbyn. Ch., Springhill, Fla., 1975—79. Avocations: painting, sewing, decorating. Home Phone: 352-860-0683.

BEARB, MICHAEL EDWIN, anesthesiologist; b. Beaumont, Tex., June 30, 1956; s. Edwin and Ella Lou (Broussard) B.; children: Emily, Renee. BS in Psychology with highest honors, Lamar U., 1978; MD, U. Tex., Dallas, 1984. Diplomate Am. Bd. Anesthesiology. Intern St. Paul Hosp., Dallas, 1984-85; resident in anesthesiology Parkland Meml. Hosp., Dallas, 1985-87; fellow in cardio-thoracic anesthesiology The Cleve. Clin. Found., Cleve., 1987-88; instr. in anesthesiology Georgetown U. Hosp., Washington, 1988-90, asst. prof. anesthesiology, 1990-93, chmn. resident selection com., 1990-93, coord. cardiovasc. lectr. series, 1990-91, attending intensivist cardiovasc. ICU, 1989-93; staff cardiac anesthesiologist Jackson (Tenn.)-Madison County Gen. Hosp., 1993—. Author: (with others) Trauma Patients with Hemoglobinopathies in Textbook of Trauma Anesthesia and Critical Care, 1993. Fellow Am. Coll. Angiology; mem. AMA, Internat. Anesthesia Rsch. Soc., Soc. Cardiovascular Anesthesiologists, Am. Soc. Anesthesiologists, Civil War Soc., Smithsonian Inst., Phi Kappa Phi. Avocations: military history, presidential history, photography, astronomy, short wave radio. Office: Cardiac Anesthesia Group 810 W Forest Ave Jackson TN 38301-3942 Home: 144 Southwind Dr Jackson TN 38305-3962 Business E-Mail: michaelbearb@eplus.net.

BEARD, ELIZABETH LETITIA, physiologist, educator; b. New Orleans, Apr. 2, 1932; d. Howard Horace and Irene (Handley) Beard. BA in Biology, Tex. Christian U., Ft. Worth, 1952, BS in Med. Tech., 1953, MS in Med. Tech., 1955; postgrad., Smith Coll., Northampton, Mass., 1953-54, Vanderbilt U., Nashville, 1954-55; PhD in Animal Physiology, Tulane U., New Orleans, 1961. Instr. dept. biol. scis. Loyola U., New Orleans, 1955-58, asst. prof., 1958-62, assoc. prof., 1962-68, prof., 1969—, chmn. premed. com., 1978—; rsch. assoc. dept. physiology Sch. Medicine Tulane U., New Orleans, 1960-63, prof. biology med. reinforcement and enrichment program, 1968-94. Vis. prof. dept. physiology and biophysics Med. Sch. Harvard U., 1983-84, dept. neuropharmacology Scripps Rsch. Inst., La Jolla, Calif., spring 2001; vis. scientist Am. Indian Rsch. Opportunities Programs at Mont. State U., 1994. Contbr. articles on rsch. in physiology to profl. publs. Project rev. com. New Orleans Health Planning Coun., 1974-77, bd. dirs., 1975-78; soprano soloist Holy Name of Jesus Ch., 1978—, pres. sch. bd., 1976-79; grad. rsch. com. La. chpt. Am. Heart Assn., 1970-72, 81-83, undergrad. rsch. com., 1978-81, 89-93; active Met. Mus. Art, New Orleans Mus. Art. NIH grantee, 1962-64, 67-69, La. Heart Assn. grantee, 1966-67, Edward Schleider Found. grantee, 1974-77, New Orleans Cancer Assn. grantee, 1962-63; Libby Rsch. fellow Sch. Medicine Tulane U., 1961.

Mem. AAUP, AAAS, Am. Physiol. Soc., Soc. Exptl. Biology and Medicine, Christian Med. and Dental Soc. (participant internat. med. missions 1993—), Sigma Xi. Office: 6363 St Charles Ave New Orleans LA 70118-6143 Home: # 22 6363 Saint Charles Ave New Orleans LA 70118-6143 Office Phone: 504-865-2768. Business E-Mail: Beard@Loyno.edu.

BEARD, JOHN MARK, family practice physician, educator; MD, U. Mo., 1986. Diplomate Am. Bd. Family Practice, 1989. Intern providence family practice Swedish Med. Ctr., resident providence family practice; fellow family medicine dept. Univ. of Washington, assoc. prof. family medicine; hosp. affiliation includes Univ. of Washington Med. Ctr. Co-author: (selected pub.) "Clinical inquiries. What treatment works best for tennis elbow?" The Journal of Family Practice, 2009. Avocations: scuba diving, sporting events, hiking. Office: Family Medical Center at UWMC-Roosevelt UW Medical Center-Roosevelt II 4245 Roosevelt Way NE Seattle WA 98105 Office Phone: 206-598-4055.

BEARD, LILLIAN B. MCLEAN, pediatrician, consultant; b. NY; d. Johnie Wilson and Woodie (Durden) McLean; m. Delawrence Beard. BS, Howard U., 1965, MD, 1970. MD, 1970. Pvt. practice pediat. Lillian M. Beard, Washington, 1973—; assoc. prof. pediat. George Washington U., 1983—; asst. prof. cmty. medicine Howard U., 1983—; contbg. editor Good Housekeeping Mag., NYC, 1989-95; health adv. WUSA-TV, Washington, 1993-95; health and med. contbr. ABC-TV, Washington, 2000—04. Comm. cons. to industry including: Nestle Nutritional Products; mem. bd. dirs. Nat. Women's Econ. Alliance, 1993-2000, Children's Hosp., 1993-2002. Author: Salt in Your Sock and Other Tried and True Home Remedies. Recipient Disting. Leadership award Nat. Assn. Equal Opportunity in Higher Edn., 1993, Disting. Svc. award Nat. Med. Assn., 1990, Hall of Fame in Medicine award, 1994, Healthy Babies Project "Making a Difference" award, 1995, Howard U. Alumni Achievement award, 1996. Fellow Am. Acad. Pediat.; mem. Nat. Med. Assn., Am. Acad. Pediat. (physician recognition awards 1993—). Home: 10517 Alloway Dr Potomac MD 20854-1662 Office: 10801 Lockwood Dr Ste 230 Silver Spring MD 20901

BEARDSLEY, RICHARD L., family practice physician, educator; MD, Ind. U. Diplomate Am. Bd. Family Practice, Am. Bd. Family Practice-geriatric medicine. Resident family medicine St. Francis Hosp., Indpls., 1979—82; hosp. affiliations include St. Francis Hosp. and Health Ctrs., Franciscan St. Francis Health; asst. dir. St. Francis Family Medicine Residency; assoc. prof. clin. medicine Ind. Univ. Named Family Physician of the Year, Ind. Acad. of Family Physicians, 2006; named one of Top Doctors, Indpls. Monthly Mag., 2005, Top Doctors in Geriatrics, 2009, Top Doctors, 2010. Avocations: poetry, ceramics, glass blowing, running, photography. Office: Saint Francis Medical Group Beech Grove Family Medicine 2030 Churchman Ave Beech Grove IN 46107 Office Phone: 317-786-9285. Office Fax: 317-781-2793.

BEARE-ROGERS, JOYCE LOUISE, retired research and development executive; b. nr. Pickering, Ont., Can., Sept. 8, 1927; d. Frederick John and Sarah May (Michell) Beare; m. Charles Graham Rogers, Dec. 30, 1961; 1 child, Anne Catherine. BA, U. Toronto, Ont., 1951, MA, 1952; PhD, Carleton U., Ottawa, Ont., 1966; DSc (hon.), U. Man., Winnipeg, Can., 1985, U. Guelph, Ont., 1993. Rsch. assoc. U. Toronto, 1952-54; instr. Vassar Coll., Poughkeepsie, 1954-56; chemist Food, Drug Directorate, Ottawa, 1956-65; rsch. scientist Health Can., Ottawa, 1965-75, rsch. mgr. Bur. Nutritional Scis., Ottawa, 1975-91. Adj. prof. U. Ottawa, 1980-92; cons. Food and Agrl Orgn. UN, 1992-94; Hilditch lectr. U.K., 1994; trustee Nat. Inst. Nutrition (Can.), 1997-99. Editor: Methods for Nutritional Assessment of Fats, 1985, Fat Requirements for Development and Health, 1988; contbr. articles on dietary fats to profl. jours. Decorated Order of Can.; recipient Queen's Jubilee medal Govt. of Can., 1977, Medaille Chevreul award Inst. Corps Gras, 1984, Crompton award McGill U., 1986, Normann medal German Assn. for Fat Rsch., 1987, Commemorative medal for 125th Anniversary of Fedn. of Can., 1992, Queen's Golden Jubilee medal 2002. Fellow: Am. Inst. Nutrition, Royal Soc. Can. (panelist on food biotechnology 2000—01, hon. treas. 2000—04, chair com. awards and medals 2004—06); mem.: Can. Biochem. Soc., Can. Soc. for Nutrition Scis. (pres. 1984—85, Bordon award 1971, McHenry award 1993), Internat. Soc. Fat Rsch. (pres. 1991—92), Am. Oil Chemists Soc. (pres. 1985—86, Lifetime Achievement award Can. sect. 1995). Avocations: hiking, canoeing, cross country skiing, reading, bridge. Home: 41 Okanagan Dr Ottawa ON Canada K2H 7E9 E-mail: jbrogers@sympatico.ca.

BEART, ROBERT W., JR., colon and rectal surgeon, educator; b. Kansas City, Mo., Mar. 3, 1945; s. Robert Woodward and Helen Elizabeth (Wamsley) B.; m. Cynthia Anne, Jan. 23, 1971; children: Jennifer, Kristina, Amy. AB, Princeton U., 1967; MD, Harvard U., 1971. Diplomate Am. Bd. Surgery, Am. Bd. Colon and Rectal Surgery. Intern U. Colo., 1971-72, resident, 1972-76; prof. surgery Mayo Clinic, Scottsdale, Ariz., 1976—87, U. So. Calif., LA, 1992—. Maj. USMC, 1972-83. Fellow Am. Soc. Colon and Rectal Surgery (pres. 1994). Office: 1441 Eastlake Ave Ste 7418 Los Angeles CA 90033 Office Phone: 323-865-3690.

BEARY, JOHN FRANCIS, III, rheumatologist, clinical pharmacologist, naval officer; b. Melrose, Iowa, 1946; s. John F. and Dorothy (McGrath) B.; m. Bianca E. Mason, 1972; children: John Daniel, Vanessa, Webster, Nina. BS summa cum laude, U. Notre Dame, Ind., 1969; MD, Harvard U., Cambridge, Mass., 1973; MBA, Georgetown U., Washington, DC, 1988. Diplomate Am Bd. Internal Medicine, Am. Bd. Rheumatology, Am. Bd. Clin. Pharmacology. Flight surgeon 89th Mil. Airlift Wing (Air Force One), 1974—77; Osler medicine resident Johns Hopkins Hosp., Balt., 1977—78; rheumatology rsch. fellow Cornell-Hosp. Spl. Surgery, NYC, 1978—80; from asst. prof. to clin. prof. Sch. Medicine Georgetown U., Washington, 1980—2005; prin. dept. asst. sec. health affairs Dept. Def., Washington, 1981—83, appropriations task force for USNS Mercy and USNS Comfort, 1982; assoc. dean strategic planning Georgetown U. Sch. Medicine, Washington, 1984—87; sr. v.p. regulatory and sci. affairs Pharm. Rsch. and Mfg. Assn., Washington, 1988—97; sr. med. dir. bone and arthritis rsch. Procter and Gamble Pharma, Cin., 1997—2008. Steering com. Internat. Conf. on Harmonization of Pharm. Stds., 1990-97; clin. prof. rheumatology and immunology U. Cin., 1997—; mem. OMERACT Rheumatology Rsch. Com., 1998-2003; sci. com. Arthritis Found., Ohio, 1998-2011. Editor: Manual of Rheumatology, 1981, 5th edit., 2005; mem. editl. bd. Jour. Pharm. Medicine, 1990—2010, Drug Devel. Rsch., 1992-2000. Bd. dirs. Scleroderma Found., Washington, 1982—92. Served to capt. USNR, 1984—99. Recipient Disting. Mil. Grad. award, 1969, Rsch. award NY Arthritis Found., 1979, Disting. Pub. Svc. medal Dept. Def., 1983, Albia H.S. Career Achievement award, 1992, Navy and Marine Corps Commendation medal, 1997, Georgetown Med. Vicennial medal, 2003, 6th Naval Beach Bn. Normandy award, 2004. Fellow: ACP, Am. Coll. Rheumatology; mem.: Am. Soc. Clin. Pharmacology and Therapeutics, Am. Geriat. Soc., Weller-Brown Assn., US Naval Inst., Mil. Officers Assn., Johns Hopkins Med. and Surg. Assn., Harvard Club, Notre Dame Monogram Club, Chevy Chase Club. Office: Univ Cin Rheumatology Divsn 231 Albert Sabin Way Cincinnati OH 45267-0563 Office Phone: 513-558-4701.

BEASLEY, KAREN, dermatologist, educator; B with magna cum laude, Loyola Coll.; MD, U. Md. Diplomate Am. Bd. Dermatology. Intern internal medicine Pa. State Univ.; specialized dermatology tng. Univ. of NC, Chapel Hill; clin. asst. prof., dermatology U. Md.; founder Resident Cosmetic Dermatology; physician Md. Laser, Skin, and Vein Inst. Fellow: Am. Coll. of Phlebology, Am. Soc. of Dermatologic Surgery, Am. Acad. of Dermatology; mem.: Nat. Botox® Edn. Faculty, Alpha Omega Alpha. Office: Maryland Laser, Skin, and Vein Institute, LLC 54 Scott Adam Rd Ste 301 Aspen Mill Profl Bldg Hunt Valley MD 21030 Office Phone: 410-666-3960. Office Fax: 410-666-3981.

BEATRICE, RUTH HADFIELD, hypnotherapist, retired elementary school educator, financial administrator; b. Phila., Feb. 6, 1931; d. Claude and Alice Elizabeth (Smith) Hadfield; m. Michael Joseph Beatrice, May 29, 1954 BS, West Chester State U., 1953; MS, Marywood Coll., 1978; postgrad., Temple U., Pa. State U., 1978-80; cert. clinl. hypnotherapist, Phila. Hypnosis Union Inst., 1980. Cert. hypno-anaesthesia therapist Nat. Bd. Hypnotherapy and Hypnotic Anaesthesiology, 1991. Educator Bristol Twp. (Pa.) Sch. Dist., 1953-54, Phila. Sch. Dist., 1954-55; recreation dir. Phila. Dept. Recreation, 1953-57; educator Worcester (Pa.) Sch. Dist., 1958-59, Springford (Pa.) Joint Sch. Dist., 1960-61, Souderton (Pa.) Sch. Dist., 1961-63, Ctrl. Bucks Sch. Dist., Doylestown, Pa., 1970-1993; ret., 1993; clin. hypnotherapist in pvt. practice Perkasie, Pa., 1980—; clin. hypnotherapist, pvt. practice Avalon, NJ, 1980—, Port St. Lucie, Fla., Perkasie, Pa. Bus. adminstr. Beatrice Adminstrs. Co-author books on tutoring for Ptnrs. at Learning Series, 1978, 1979, 1983. Bd. mem. Pierce Free Libr., Hilltown, Pa., 1970-75; union del. Office and Profl. Employees Internat. Union Internat. Conv., Vancouver, B.C., Can., 1995; treas. Newcomers Civic Assn., Perkasie, 1964-85; mc. Avalon (N.J.) Civic Assn., avalon Sr. Assn. Mem. NEA (life), AAUW, Nat. Assn. Profl. Therapists, Am. Legion Aux., Pa. State Edn. Assn. (life), Hypnotism Soc. of Pa. (v.p. Phila. br. 1993-95), Phila. Hypnosis Union Local 476 (v.p. 1993-95), Nat. Guild of Hypnotists, Nat. Bd. for Hypnotherapy and Hypnotic Anaesthesiology, Womens Assn., Ballanlfae's Angler Assn., Ballanlfrae Gulf & Yacht Club, Jupiter Lighthouse Hypnosis Group. Democrat. Presbyterian. Avocations: biking, fishing, golf, tennis, walking, camping. Home and Office: 3192 Carrick Green Ct Port Saint Lucie FL 34952 also: 273 52d St Avalon NJ 08202 Office Phone: 772-337-1469, 609-368-3256. Personal E-mail: rudibea@yahoo.com.

BEATTY, CHARLES W., otolaryngologist, educator; MD, U. Iowa. Diplomate Am. Bd. Otolaryngology, 1982. Resident Grad. Sch. of Medicine Mayo Clinic, Rochester, Minn.; prof. otolaryngology Mayo Med. Sch.; hosp. affiliations include Rochester Meth. Hosp., St. Mary's Hosp. Mem. edn. com. Triological Soc., 2009—11, v.p. mid. sect., 2010. Co-author: (pubs.) Antrochoanal polyps in children, 2001, Psychologic profile of tinnitus patients using the SCL-90-R and Tinnitus Handicap Inventory, 2003, Retrospective analysis of outcomes after stapedotomy with implantation of a self-crimping Nitinol stapes prosthesis, 2007, A hemorrhagic vestibular schwannoma presenting with rapid neurologic decline: a case report, 2010, Implications of minimizing trauma during conventional cochlear implantation, 2011, and numerous others. Recipient Disting. Svc. award, Luther Coll., 2008. Office: Mayo Clinic 200 First St S W Rochester MN 55905 Office Phone: 507-284-2511. Office Fax: 507-284-0161.

BEATTY, RANDALL L., ophthalmologist; MD, Albany Med. Coll. Diplomate Am. Bd. Surgery-ophthalmology. Intern Denver Health Med. Ctr., Phila. Coll. of Osteopathic Medicine; resident Univ. Pitts. Med. Ctr., Siloam Christian Aid Mission Hosp.; fellow Med. Coll. Wis.; practice Allegheny Opthalmic and Orbital Assocs.; dir. divsn. opthalmic, plastic and orbital surgery Allegheny Gen. Hosp. Named one of Top Doctors, Pitts. mag., 2011. Office: Allegheny General Hospital 320 E N Ave Pittsburgh PA 15212 Office Phone: 412-359-3131. Office Fax: 412-359-4108.

BEATY, JAMES HAROLD, pediatric orthopaedic surgeon; b. Atlanta, Feb. 3, 1952; s. James Harold and Stella Cater B.; m. Teresa Stewart, Apr. 8, 1978; children: Eric Christopher, Meredith Ann. BA magna cum laude, Washington and Lee U., 1973; MD, U. Tenn. Coll. Medicine, 1976. Diplomate Am. Bd. Orthop. Surgery. Intern Baptist Meml. Hosp., Memphis, 1977, resident, 1978, U. Tenn.-Campbell Clinic, Memphis, 1979-81, staff mem., prof. orthop. and pediatric trauma, chief-of-staff Germantown, Tenn., 1982—; fellow, pediatric orthop. Alfred I. DuPont Inst., Wilmington, Del., 1982; from instr. to prof. orthop. U. Tenn., Memphis, 1982-96, prof., 1995. Chief Tenn. Crippled Children's Svc., 1984; dir. pediat. orthop. fellowship U. Tenn. Campbell Clinic, Memphis, 1990, program dir. orthop. residency, 1992-99; chief of surgery, 1992-94, med. dir. 1993-; active staff Baptist Meml. Hosp., Regional Med. Ctr., Memphis, VA Hosp.; former pres. Orthop. Learning Ctr.; cons. Meth. Hosp.; lectr. in field. Co-editor: Operative Pediatric Orthopaedics, 1991, 2d edit., 1995, Fractures in Children, 4th edit., 1996; cons. editor Jour. Bone and Joint Surgery, 1994—, editl. cons., 1996—; editl. cons. Jour. Pediat. Orthop., 1991—, Clin. Orthop. and Related Rsch., 1993—, Orthop. Rsch., 1996; editl. bd. Jour. Ped. Ortho., 1997-; editor, Orthop. Knowledge Update VI; contbr. several articles and abstracts to profl. jours., several textbooks. Bd. dirs. Mid-South Down Soc., 1983-89, United Cerebral Palsy, 1983-89, Spina Bifida Found., 1984-89, Safe Kids Coalition, Memphis, 1991—, Children's Mus., Memphis, 1993-98; profl. adv. bd. Nat. Down Syndrome Congress, 1986-89, assoc. bd., 1990-94; sponsor Boy Scouts Am., Memphis, 1994—. J.W. Warner Acad. scholar, 1971-73, Gooch Acad. scholar, 1975-76; named one of Golf Digest Top 250 Golfer Doctors in Am. Fellow Am. Acad. Orthop. Surgeons (evaluation com. 1990-95, com. pediat. orthop. 1992-95, chmn. com. pediat. orthop. 1995—, past chmn. com. on continuing med. edn., bd. dirs. 1993-94, editl. bd. 1996-, pres. 2007-08), Am. Bd. Orthop. Surgery (bd. dirs. 1997-, pres. 2003-04); mem. AMA, Am. Acad. Pediat., Am. Acad. Cerebral Palsy and Devel. Medicine (edn. com. 1988-89), Orthop. Rsch. and Edn. Found. (state solicitor Tenn. 1989-92, state chmn., med. dir. 1993—), Pediat. Orthop. Soc. N.Am. (long range planning com. 1991-92, com. healthcare policy 1994-95, sec. 1995, pres. 2000-01), Am. Orthop. Assn. (traveling fellow 1984, ABC-Traveling Fellow 1991), Orthop. Trauma Assn., Mid-Am. Orthop. Assn. (program com. 1993-96, chmn. program com. 1996, pres. 2002-03), So. Med. Assn., So. Orthop. Assn., Tenn. Med. Assn., Tenn. Orthop. Soc. (chmn. membership com. 1988-89, pres. 1990-91, bd. dirs. 1992-94), Memphis Orthop. Soc., Memphis-Shelby County Med. Soc., Memphis Jour. Club, So. Internat. Chirurgie Orthop. Trauma, Soc. Argentenia Orthop. Trauma Infantil (hon.), Soc. Brazil Orthop. Trauma Infantil (hon.), Soc. Peru Orthop. Trauma Infantil (hon.), Interurban Club, Willis C. Campbell Club, Phi Beta Kappa, Omicron Delta Kappa. Avocation: golf. Office: Campbell Clinic 1400 S Germantown Rd Germantown TN 38138

BEAUCHAMP, JAMES L., family practice physician; MD, U. Kans., 1963. Diplomate Am. Bd. Family Practice. Hosp. affiliation includes Eden Med. Ctr. Office: Eden Medical Center 20103 Lake Chabot Rd Castro Valley CA 94546 Office Phone: 510-537-1234, 510-351-2100. Office Fax: 510-889-6506.

BEAUCHAMP, ROBERT DANIEL, surgeon, educator; b. San Antonio, Apr. 17, 1956; m. Shannon Riordan; 1 child, Bryn Henefield-Ree. BS with high honors, Tex. Tech. U., 1978; MD with highest honors, U. Tex., Galveston, 1982. Diplomate Am. Bd. Surgery with qualifications in surg. critical care; lic. physician, Tex., Tenn.; cert. advanced trauma life support instr. Intern surgery U. Tex. Med. Br., Galveston, 1982-83, resident gen. surgery, 1983-87; rsch. asst. prof. dept. cell biology, asst. prof. surgery Vanderbilt U. Sch. Medicine, Nashville, 1987-89; assoc. prof. surgery dept. human biol. chemistry & genetics Tex. Med. Br./Shriners Hosps. for Crippled Children, Galveston, 1989-94; grad. faculty Grad. Sch. Biomed. Scis. U. Tex. Med. Br., Galveston, 1989-94; assoc. prof. surg. oncology, surgery & cell biology depts. Vanderbilt U. Sch. Medicine, Nashville, 1994-97, John L. Sawyers prof. of surgery, cell biology, chief divsn. surg. oncology, 1997-2001, J.C. Foshee prof., chmn. sect. surg. scis., 2001—; surgeon-in-chief Vanderbilt U. Med. Ctr., 2001—. Ad hoc reviewer granting agys. NIH and VA. Mem. editorial bd. Jour. Parenteral and Enteral Nutrition, 1991-1999, Jour. Surg. Tsch., 1995—; ad hoc reviewer Cancer Rsch., Exptl. Gerontology, Gastroenterology, Gut, Jour. Clin. Investigation, Jour. Parenteral and Enteral Nutrition, Jour. Surg. Rsch., Molecular Carcinogenesis, Molecular Endocrinology; contbr. articles to profl. jours., chpts. to books. Recipient Physician Scientist award NIH, 1987-92; grantee Shriners Hosps. for Crippled Children, 1991-94, NIH, 1991—, John Sealy Meml. Endowment Fund., 1992-94. Fellow ACS; mem. AMA, ASA, Am. Assn. Cancer Rsch., Am. Gastroenterol. Assn., Am. Surg. Assn., Am. Pancreatic Assn., Am. Soc. Cell Biology, Am. Soc. Parenteral and Enteral Nutrition, Am. Soc. Clin. Investigation, Assn. Acad. Surgery, Endocrine Soc., Galveston County Med. Soc., Singleton Surg. Soc., Soc. Critical Care Medicine, Soc. Surgery Alimentary Tract, Soc. Univ. Surgeons (pres. 1999-2000), Surg. Infection Soc., So. Surg. Assn., Southeastern Surg. Congress, Southwestern Surg. Congress, Tex. Med. Assn., Tex. Med. Found., Alpha Omega Alpha, Mu Delta, Phi Beta Pi. Office: Vanderbilt University Med Ctr 116 21st Ave South D-4316 MCN Nashville TN 37232-2730 Office Phone: 615-322-2363.

BEAUCHET, OLIVIER, geriatrician, researcher; s. Henri and Monique Beauchet; m. Samantha Beauchet; children: Emilie, Arthur, Alice. MD, PhD, U. Angers, France, 2007. Bd. cert. prof. medicine Angers U. Hosp., France, 2007. Chief dept. geriat. Angers U. Hosp., 2007—. Cons. Korian, Paris, 2007—. Cons. CETAF, St. Etienne, 2005—08. Captain Navy, 1994—95, Lorient. Office: Angers Univ Hosp Larrey Angers 49933 France Office Phone: 00 33 41 35 47 25. Office Fax: 00 33 41 35 48 94. Business E-Mail: olbeauchet@chu-angers.fr.

BEAUDRY, DIANE FAY, medical quality management executive; b. Manitowoc, Wis., Mar. 6, 1947; d. Ruben William and Gertrude Katherine (Novak) Puta. BSN, Alverno Coll., 1971; MS in Ednl. Adminstrn., U. Wis., Milw., 1979, PhD in Urban Edn., 1991. Staff nurse St. Mary's Hosp., Milw., 1971-72, St. Anthony's Hosp., Milw., 1972-74; nurse coord. Pvt. Initiative in PSRO, Wis., 1974-75; insvc. instr. Deaconess Hosp., Milw., 1975-77, insvc. coord., 1977-81; dir. nursing staff devel./quality assurance Good Samaritan Med. Ctr., Milw., 1981-84, dir. quality assurance, 1984-85, dir. utilization mgmt., 1985-88; mgr. quality mgmt. Sinai Samaritan Med. Ctr., Milw., 1988-89, dir. med. staff svcs. and quality mgmt., 1989-97, dir. quality mgmt., 1997—2008, Aurora St. Luke's Med. Ctr., 1997—2008, dir. accreditation, 2008—10. Author: (with others) Interdisciplinary QA: Issues in Collaboration, 1991 Mem. Nat. Assn. for Healthcare Quality, Alverno Coll. Alumnae Assn., U. Wis. Alumni Assn., Delta Epsilon Sigma, Kappa Gamma Pi. Avocations: ballroom dancing, motorcycle riding. Home: 11047 N Riverland Ct # 36W Mequon WI 53092-4900 Office: Aurora St Luke's Med Ctr PO Box 2901 Milwaukee WI 53201-2901 Office Phone: 414-649-7138.

BEAUREGARD, ARTHUR, research scientist; b. Albany, NY, Apr. 30, 1978; PhD, U. Albany, 2009. Rsch. support specialist - lab dir. Ctr. Nanoscale Sci. and Engring., 2010; rsch. scientist Wadsworth Ctr., 2010—. Consulting rsch. scientist U. NC, Chapel Hill, 2009—. Recipient Rsch. Excellence award, U. Albany, Travel award, NE Mobile Genetic Element Meeting, Arthur M. Sackler Colloquia NAS. Mem.: AAAS, Am. Chem. Soc., Am. Soc. Microbiology. Home: 389 Washington Ave Albany NY 12206 Personal E-mail: arthurbeauregard@hotmail.com.

BECEREN, GÖKBEN NESRIN, emergency physician; b. Antalya, Turkey, Aug. 30, 1974; MD, Akdeniz U. Med. Sch., 1998. Cert. emergency medicine specialist Süleyman Demirel U. Med. Sch., 2005. Vice chief pyhsician Süleyman Demirel U. Practice and Rsch. Hosp., 2009; asst. prof. Süleyman Demirel U. Med. Sch., 2005—. Asst. mgr. Isparta Health Svcs. Vocat. Sch. Süleyman Demirel U., 2007—09. Mem.: Emergency Medicine Physicians Assn. (Turkey), Emergency Medicine Assn. (Turkey). Avocation: scuba diving. Office: Süleyman Demirel University Medical Sch Isparta Cünür 32260 Turkey Office Fax: 00902462370240. Personal E-mail: gokbencetin@hotmail.com.

BECERRA IBANEZ PELLIZA, JULIO C., psychologist, consultant; s. Matias Becerra y Bustos and Irma Soledad Ibanez de Pelliza; m. Elida Elena Vivot, Nov. 27, 2004. Licenciate in Psychology, U. Buenos Aires, 1985; MA in Psychology, Sierra U., Costa Mesa, Calif., 1992; D in Psychology, Calif. Coast U., Santa Ana, 1998; MA in Derecho Nobiliario y Premial, UNED, Madrid, MA in Genealogia y Heraldica, 2008. Lic. psychologist Ministry Pub. Health, Argentina, 1985. Cons. dept. medicine Hosp. and Clinic Jose de San Martin U. Buenos Aires, 1985—88; master facilitator batterers intervention dept. criminal justice sys. Per Probation Dept., Calif., 1989—; psychotherapist and counsellor El Nido Family Ctr., Mission Hills, 1990—2009. Contbr. scientific papers. Mem. San Fernando Child Abuse Coun. & Batterers Intervention Programs, San Fernando & Long Beach, Calif., 1990. Pilot cadet Argentine Navy, 1964—66. Mem.: Royal House Bourbon Parma (Sir, Knight of Columbus, Calif., Knight of Merit, Sacred Mil. Constantinian Order St. George, Madrid). Roman Catholic. Avocations: history, genealogy, Heraldry.

BECHAMPS, GERALD JOSEPH, surgeon; b. Flushing, NY, 1937; MD, Georgetown U., 1963. Diplomate Am. Bd. Surgery. Intern Meadowbrook Hosp., East Meadow, NY, 1963-64, resident in surgery, 1964-65; fellow surgery Mayo Clinic-Found., Rochester, 1965-69; clin. instr. U. Va. Sch. Medicine, 1971—; pvt. practice Winchester Surg. Clinic, Ltd., 1971—; asst. clin. prof., dept family medicine Va. Commonwealth U., 2003—09, clin. prof. surgery, dept. surgery, 2009—. Past pres. Fedn. State Med. Bds. of U.S.; surgeon Winchester Med. Ctr., Surgi-Ctr. of Winchester; mem. Va. State Bd. Medicine, pres., 1985-86, 87-88. Mem. ACS (past pres. Va. chpt.), So. Soc. Clin. Surgeons. Office: Winchester Surg Clinic Ltd 20 S Stewart St Winchester VA 22601 Office Phone: 540-536-0130. Office Fax: 540-536-0135.

BECHER, JULIE ROBIN, medical researcher, educator; b. Jamaica, NY, Queens, NY, Apr. 29, 1969; d. Laurence Ira and Marjorie Ann Kraut; m. David Alon Becher, May 26, 2002. BS, Pa. State U., University Park, 1991, PhD, 1998. Postdoctoral fellow U.S. Ctrs. Disease Control and Prevention, Atlanta, 1998—2000; asst. prof. No. Ill. U., DeKalb, 2000—03; rschr. U. Pa., Phila., 2003—; vis. prof. econs. Swarthmore Coll., Pa., 2003—05; vis. prof. Haverford Coll., Pa., 2006—. Adj. prof. Haverford Coll., 2006—10. Contbr. articles to profl. jours. Workshop organizer Expanding Your Horizons Conf., Swarthmore College, Pa., 2006. Recipient Outstanding Tchg. Asst. award, Pa. State U., 1993, 1996—97; grantee, No. Ill. U., 2001, 2003; Internat. Faculty Devel. grantee, 2001. Mem.: APHA, Am. Sexually Transmitted Diseases Assn., Population Assn. Am., Am. Econ. Assn., Alpha Eta. Personal E-mail: djbecher@yahoo.com.

BECHTOLD, ROBERT, diagnostic radiologist, educator; MD, Wash. U., 1979. Diplomate Am. Bd. Radiology-diagnostic radiology, 1983. Intern Vanderbilt Univ. Med. Ctr., Nashville, 1980, resident, 1983; fellow NC Baptist Hosp., 1984; prof. radiology Wake Forest Univ. Office: Wake Forest University Medical Center Radiology Department Medical Center Blvd Winston Salem NC 27157 Office Phone: 336-716-2471.

BECICH, RAYMOND BRICE, healthcare consultant, mediator, trainer, educator; b. Chgo., Jan. 9, 1945; s. Nicholas Gabriel and Rose Christina (Spillar) B. BA, Ind. U., 1966; MS, Columbia U., 1968. Adminstrv. officer, then hosp. dir. Indian Health Svc., Harlem, Mont., 1968-72, hosp. dir. Rapid City, S.D., 1972-78; hosp. adminstr. St. Elizabeth's Hosp., Washington, 1979-82, exec. officer, 1983-86, NIH Clin. Ctr., Bethesda, Md., 1986-94; healthcare cons., mediator, trainer, educator, 1994—. Adj. faculty Univ. Coll., U. Md., College Park, U. N.Mex., Albuquerque and Los Alamos, Coll. Santa Fe, Ctrl. Mich. U., Mt. Pleasant, U. St Francis, Joliet, Ill., 1995—; adj. instr. Bus. Sch., U. Portland, Oreg. Bd. dirs. Ronald McDonald House, Washington, 1986-89; vol. Whitman-Walker Clinic, 1987-95. Fellow Am. Coll. Healthcare Execs. (life). Democrat. Episcopalian. Personal E-mail: rbecich31@gmail.com.

BECK, AARON TEMKIN, psychiatrist, educator; b. Providence, July 18, 1921; s. Harry S. and Elizabeth (Temkin) B.; m. Phyllis Whitman, June 4, 1950; children: Judith, Daniel, Alice, Roy. BA, Brown U., 1942, Dr.Med.Sci. (hon.), 1982; MD, Yale U., 1946; LHD (hon.), Assumption Coll., 1995; DSc (hon.), U. Pa., 2007. Mem. faculty U. Pa. Med. Sch., 1954—, prof. psychiatry, 1971—, Univ. prof. (now prof. emeritus), 1983—, dir. Ctr. for Treatment and Prevention of Suicide; dir. Center Cognitive Therapy, 1965-94; pres. Beck Found. for Cognitive Therapy, 1995—. Mem. rev. panel NIMH, 1965-80, chmn. task force suicide prevention, 1969-80; bd. dirs. West Philadelphia Community Mental Health Consortium, 1975-77. Author: Depression: Causes and Treatment, 1967, Diagnosis and Management of Depression, 1973, Prediction of Suicide, 1973, Cognitive Therapy and the Emotional Disorders, 1976, Cognitive Theory of Depression, 1979, Anxiety Disorders and Phobias: A Cognitive Perspective, 1985, Love is Never Enough, 1988, Cognitive Therapy of Personality Disorders, 1990, 2nd edit., 2004; co-author: Cognitive Therapy in Clinical Practice, 1989, Cognitive Therapy with Inpatients, 1992, Cognitive Therapy of Substance Abuse, 1993, The Integrative Power of Cognitive Therapy, 1997, Scientific Foundations of Cognitive Theory and Therapy of Depression, 1999, Prisoners of Hate, 1999, Bipolar Disorder: A Cognitive Perspective, 2001, Cognitive Therapy for Chronic Pain, 2003, Cognitive Therapy for Suicidal Patient, 2008, Cognitive Therapy of Personality Disorders, 2004, Anxiety Disorders and Phobias: A Cognitive Perspective, 2nd edit., 2005, Schizophrenia: Cognitive Theory Research, and Therapy, 2009, Depression: Causes and Treatments, 2nd edit., 2009. Served as officer M.C. U.S. Army, 1952-54. Recipient rsch. award, R.I. Med. Soc., 1948, ann. award, Phila. Soc. Clin. Psychologists, 1978, Am. Psychopathol. Assn., 1983, Soc. for Psychotherapy Rsch., 1995, Calif. Psychol. Soc., 1996, Belmont Hosp. award, 1996, Disting. Sci. award, APA, 1989, rsch. award, Am. Assn. Suicidology, 1985, Am. Suicide Found., 1991, Albert Einstein Sch. Medicine award, 1992, Nathaniel Winkelman award, 1996, Heinz Found. award, 2001, Grawemeyer award, 2004, Lasker-DeBakey Clin. Med. Rsch. award, Lasker Found., 2006, Albert Lasker award, 2006, Salmon medal, NY Acad. Sci., 2007. Fellow Royal Coll. Psychiatry, NY Acad. Medicine (Thomas Salmon award 1992), APA (rsch. award 1993), Am. Acad. Arts & Scis.; mem. Calif. Psychol. Assn. (lifetime svc. award 1996), So. Psychotherapy Rsch. (pres. 1975-76), Am. Psychiat. Assn. (prize rsch. psychiatry 1979, Adolf Meyer award, 2006, Disting. Svc. award, 2008), Am. Assn. Suicidology (rsch. prize 1985), Assn. Advancement of Behavior Therapy (Lifetime Contbn. award 2001), Inst. Medicine (Rhoda and Bernard Sarnat Internat. Prize in Mental Health, 2003, Gustav O. Lienhard award, 2006), Internat. Acad. Suicide Rsch. (Morselli medal, 2005), Am. Found. Suicide Prevention (Lifetime Achievement award, 2006), ACP (Lifetime Achievement award, 2007), Am. Counselling Assn. (Presdl. award 2007). Office: 3535 Market St Rm 2032 Philadelphia PA 19104-2641 Office Phone: 215-898-4102. Business E-Mail: abeck@mail.med.upenn.edu. *

BECK, DAVID EDWARD, surgeon; b. Geneva, Ill., May 1, 1953; s. George R. and Gloria M. (Zesch) B.; m. Sharon Mieir, Aug. 30, 1983; children: Allison, Lauren, John. BS, USAF Acad., 1975; MD, U. Miami, Fla., 1979; postgrad., USAF Aerospace Medicine Primary Course, Brooks AFB, Tex., 1978, Combat Casualty Care Course, Ft. Sam Houston, Tex., 1980, Hyperbaric Oxygen CourseB, Brooks AFB, 1982, ATLS Instr. Course, Ft. Sam Houston, 1986, Squadon Officers Sch., 1987-88, Mgmt. for Chief of Hosp. Svcs., Sheppard AFB, Tex., 1988, Sch. Pub. Health, Harvard U., 1990. Diplomate Am. Bd. Colon and Rectal Surgery. Lt. Col. USAF, 1975-93; resident in gen. surgery Wilford Hall USAF Med. Ctr., Lackland AFB, Tex., 1979-84, chief colorectal surgery, 1986-92, staff surgeon, chief colorectal surgery svc., 1986-92, asst. chmn. dept. gen. surgery, 1988, chmn. dept. gen. surgery, residency program dir., 1988-92; staff gen. surgeon Patrick AFB Hosp., Fla., 1984-85; fellow in colorectal surgery Cleve. Clinic Found., 1985-86; residency program dir. gen. surgery Joint Mil. Med. Command, San Antonio, 1989-91; clin. assoc. prof. surgery U. Tex. Health Sci. Ctr., San Antonio, 1990-92, F. Edward Herbert Sch. Medicine, U. Health Scis., Bethesda, Md., 1992—; chief surgery 870 USAF Contingency Hosp., RAF Little Rissington, England, 1993; staff colorectal surgeon Ochsner Clinic, New Orleans, 1993—, chmn. dept. colon and rectal surgery, 1994—; med. dir. Ochsner Endoscopy Ambulatory Surgery Ctr., 2003—06. Cons. USAF Surgeon Gen., Washington, 1986-92. Author chpts. to books; co-editor (textbooks); (with David R. Welling) Patient Care in Colorectal Surgery, 1991, (with Steven D. Wexner) Fundamentals of Anorectal Surgery, 1992, 2nd edit., 1998, (with T.C. Hicks, F.E. Opelka, A.E., Timmcke) Complications of Colon and Rectal Surgery, 1996; editor: Handbook of Colorectal Surgery, 1997, 2d edit., 2002, ASCRS Textbook of Colon and Rectal Surgery, 2007; mem. editl. bd. Current Surgery, 1990-2006; reviewer Diseases of the Colon and Rectum, 1990—, mem. editl. bd., 1992-98, So. Me. Jour., 1988-92; mem. editl. bd. Perspectives in Colon and Rectal Surgery, 1997-2000; editor-in-chief Clinics in Colon and Rectal Surgery, 2001—, Ochsner Jour.; contbr. articles to profl. jours. Decorated Air Force Achievement medal with oak leaf cluster, Air Force Meritorious Svc. medal with oak leaf cluster; recipient Pres. award United Ostomy Assn., 2000. Fellow ACS; mem. AMA, Am. Soc. Colon and Rectal Surgeons (mem. socioecon./legis. com. 1991-94, pub. rels. com. 1993-99, chmn. 1996-99, mem.-at-large exec. coun. 2004-07, pres.-elect 2009-, Outstanding Young Investigator award, 1992), Assn. Mil. Surgeons U.S., La. State Med. Soc., Soc. Air Force Clin. Surgeons (treas. 1989-90, v.p. 1990-92, pres. 1992-93, Excalibur award 1992), Soc. Surgery of Alimentary Tract, So. Med. Assn. (mem. colon and rectal sect., sec. 1988-91, v.p. 1990-91, pres. 1991-92), Soc. Med. Cons. to Armed forces, St. Tamminy Parish Med. Soc., Tex. Soc. Colon and Rectal Surgeons (sec. 1991-93), Air force Assn., USAF Acad. Assn. Grads. Avocations: fishing, wood working, gardening. Home: 127 Deloaks Rd Madisonville LA 70447-9597 Office: Oschner Clin Found 1514 Jefferson Hwy New Orleans LA 70121-2429 Home Phone: 985-845-1063; Office Phone: 504-842-4060. Personal E-mail: dbeckmd@aol.com. Business E-Mail: dbeck@oschner.org.

BECK, JAMES M., internist, researcher; b. Allentown, Pa., Mar. 19, 1958; s. Irwin Yale and Carole (Rosner) B. BS, Tufts U., 1980; MD, U. Pa., 1984. Diplomate Am. Bd. Med. Examiners; cert. Am. Bd. Internal Medicine and Pulmonary Diseases. Resident U. Pa. Hosp., Phila., 1984-87; pulmonary fellow U. Calif., San Francisco, 1987-89, asst. prof. Medicine, 1990—. Assoc. investigator Dept. Vet. Affairs Med. Ctr., San Francisco, 1990-92, staff physician, 1993—. Contbr. articles to profl. jours. including Jour. Clin. Investigation, Clin and Exptl. Immunology. Recipient Career Devel. award Dept. Vet. Affairs, 1990—, Young Investigator award Am. Lung Assn. Calif., 1990-92. Fellow Am. Coll. Chest Physicians; mem. AAAS, Am. Fedn. Clin. Rsch., Am. Thoracic Soc. Office: VA Med Ctr 4150 Clement St San Francisco CA 94121-1598

BECK, JOHN CHRISTIAN, physician, educator; b. Audubon, Iowa, Jan. 4, 1924; s. Wilhelm and Marie (Brandt) Beck. MD, McGill U., 1947, MSc, 1951, DSc (hon.), 1994; PhD (hon.), Ben Gurion U. of Negev, 1981. Diplomate Am. Bd. Internal Medicine (chmn., dir.). Intern Royal Victoria Hosp., Montreal, 1947—48, sr. asst. resident, 1948—49, physician-in-chief, endocrinologist, 1964—74; chmn. dept. medicine and dir. Univ. Clinic McGill U., 1964—74; prof. medicine U. Calif., San Francisco, 1974—79; dir. Robert Wood Johnson Clin. Scholars Program, 1973—78; prof. geriat. medicine and gerontology UCLA, 1979—, dir. academic geriat. resource ctr., 1984—90; dir. long term car gerontology ctr. UCLA/U. So. Calif., 1980—85; dir. Calif. Geriatric Edn. Ctr., 1987—97, emeritus dir., 1993—; dir. multicampus program in geriat. medicine and gerontology UCLA, 1979—93; Froehlich Vis. prof. Royal Soc. Medicine, 2006. Pres. Am. Bd. Med. Spltys.; vis. prof. numerous univs.; Simeone lectr. Brown U., 1977; John McCreary Meml. lectr. U. B.C., 1985; Bruce Hall Meml. lectr. Garvan Inst. Med. Rsch., U. NSW, Sydney, 1989; Allen T. Bailey Meml. lectr. U. Sask., Canada, 1989; delivered Chaikin Oration, Australian Acad. Tech. Scis. and Engring., 2004—; Froehlich vis. prof. Royal Soc. Medcine, England, 2006. Editl. bd. Jour. Clin. Endocrinology and Metabolism, Current Topics in Exptl. Endocrinology, Psychiatry in Medicine, Health Policy and Edn., Jour. Am. Bd. Family Practice, cons. editor Roche Lab. Series on Geriatrics and Gerontology. Recipient Lifetime award, Ben Gurion U. of Negev, Israel, 1985, Ann. Gerontology award in edn., Jewish Homes for the Aging, 1994, commendation, City of L.A., 1994, Ignatius Nascher award, Vienna City, 2006, Philips award, Am. Coll. Physicians ASIM, 2003, Ignatius Nascher award, Vienna, 2006. Master: ACP (Philips award 2003); fellow: AAAS, Am. Fedn. on Aging Rsch. (Irving S. Wright award 1991), Gerontol. Soc. Am. (mem. editl. bd. jour., Joseph T. Freeman award 1990, Donald P. Kent award 2001), Western Assn. Physicians, Am. Geriat. Soc. (Milo F. Leavitt Meml. award 1988), Soc. Exptl. Biology and Medicine (mem. editl. bd. jour.), Can. Med. Protective Assn., Am. Clin. and Climatol. Assn., Laurentian Hormone Conf. (bd. dirs.), Montreal Physiol. Soc., Inst. Medicine, Internat. Soc. Endocrinology (sec.-gen.), Can. Soc. Clin. Investigation (pres.), Endocrine Soc. (v.p., chmn. postgrad. assembly), Am. Fedn. Clin. Rsch. (coun. East divsn.), Can. Med. Assn. (postgrad. edn. com.), Am. Diabetes Assn., Can. Diabetes Assn., McGill Osler Reporting Soc. (sec.), Royal Coll. Physicians Can. (mem. coun., Duncan Graham award 1990), Royal Coll. Physicians London, Royal Soc. Can., Can. Physiol. Soc., Can. Assn. Profs. Medicine (Ronald V. Christie award 1987), Assn. Am. Med. Colls., Internat. Soc. Neuroendocrinology, Alpha Omega Alpha, Sigma Xi; mem.: Israel Nat. Inst. Health Policy and Health Svcs. Rsch. (chmn., internat. adv. bd. 1995—2007, chmn. emeritus 2008), Australian Acad. Technol. Scis. and Engring. (Chaikin Oration 2004), Assn. for Gerontology in Higher Edn. (Disting. Svc. Recognition award 2001). Office: 1562 Casale Rd Pacific Palisades CA 90272-2714 Fax: 310-454-1944. Business E-Mail: egebjcb@ucla.edu.

BECK, JOHN ROBERT, pathologist, information scientist; b. Cleve., Sept. 8, 1953; s. John Edward and Maralyn Janet (Smith) Beck; children: John Benjamin, Stefan Andrew, Meredith Louise; m. Marjorie Callahan Ritchie, July 20, 2002. AB, Dartmouth Coll., 1974; MD, Johns Hopkins U., 1978. Diplomate Am. Bd. Pathology. Intern, then resident in pathology Dartmouth-Hitchcock Med. Ctr., Hanover, NH, 1978-80, dir. bloodbank, 1984-89, dir. clin. pathology, 1987-89; fellow, clin. decision making New Eng. Med. Ctr., Boston, 1981; from asst. to assoc. prof. pathology Dartmouth Med. Sch., Hanover, 1982-89; prof., dir. biomed. info. communication ctr. Oreg. Health Scis. U., Portland, 1989-92; prof., v.p. info. tech. Baylor Coll. Medicine, Houston, 1992—2001; exec. dir. Houston Acad. Medicine-Tex. Med. Ctr. Libr., 1999—2001; sr. mem., v.p. Infotech Fox Chase Cancer Ctr., Phila., 2001—07, sr. v.p., chief acad. officer, 2007—, chief med. officer, 2009—. Mem. healthcare tech. and decision scis. rev. panel Agy. Healthcare Rsch. and Quality, 2005—, chair, 2008—; prof. Temple U. Sch. Medicine, 2009—. Editor-in-chief: Med. Decision Making, 1989—94. Recipient Rsch. Career Devel. award, Nat. Libr. Medicine, 1986, Cancer Biomed. Informatics Grid award, Nat. Cancer Inst., 2006; Endowed Chair grant, H.O. West and J.R. Wike Chair in Cancer Rsch., 2011—. Fellow: Coll. Am. Pathologists (com. vice-chair 1997—2000), Am. Coll. Med. Informatics; mem.: Am. Assn. Cancer Rsch., Leadership of Phila., Group on Info. Resources (exec. com. 1997—2000), Am. Assn. Med. Colls., Soc. for Med. Decision Making (sec.-treas. 1985—87, v.p. 1987—88, pres. 1995—96). Republican. Avocations: golf, bridge, trumpet, scuba diving. Office: 333 Cottman Ave Philadelphia PA 19111 Office Phone: 215-214-1490. Business E-Mail: j.robert.beck@fccc.edu.

BECK, MORRIS, allergist; b. Miami, Fla., Oct. 12, 1927; s. Max and Anna (Luks) B.; m. Hollis Schwartz, Aug. 6, 1960; children: Gayle Beck Finan, Anne Lin. BA, UCLA, 1949; MD, U. Zurich, Switzerland, 1957. Diplomate Am. Bd. Allergy and Immunology, Am. Bd. Pediatrics. Intern Queens Hosp. Ctr., 1958, resident in pediatrics, 1959-60; preceptor in allergy U. Miami (Fla.) Med. Sch., 1961-77; pvt. practice pediatrician Miami, 1961—78; pvt. practice allergist, 1979—; chief dept. allergy Miami Children's Hosp., 1986—2003; clin. prof. pediatrics Nova U. Southeastern Med. Sch., 1998—; clin. asst. prof. U. Miami Med. Sch. With U.S. Army, 1950-52. Fellow: Am. Assn. Cert. Allergists, Am. Acad. Pediatrics, Am. Acad. Asthma, Allergy and Immunology, Am. Coll. Allergy and Immunology; mem.: Am. Coll. Chest Physicians. Republican. Jewish. Avocations: photography, fishing, travel. Office: 7800 SW 87th Ave # C-340 Miami FL 33173-3570 Home Phone: 305-667-3090. E-mail: beckmd123@aol.com.

BECK, ROBIN A., medical educator; b. Killee, Tex., Aug. 10, 1969; MD, Ind. U., 1995. Assoc. prof. clin. medicine Ind. U. Sch. Medicine, 1999—. Office: 1001 West 10th St Indianapolis IN 46202 Business E-Mail: robeck@iupui.edu.

BECKEMEYER, SHAWN DAVINE, physician; b. Belleville, Ill., May 11, 1970; BS, St. Louis U., 1991; MD, SIU, 1995. Physician Sparta Cmty. Hosp., 1998—, chief staff, 2010—. Assoc. clin. prof. SIU Sch. Medicine, 2000—; clin. instr. St. Louis U. Family Medicine Residency, 2000—; bd. dirs. Randolph County Bd. Health, 2009—. Mem.: AMA, Girl Scouts US, AAFP. Avocations: horseback riding, sports, camping. Office: 203 East Grant Coulterville IL 62237 Office Fax: 618-758-2180. Business E-Mail: beckemey@spartahospital.com.

BECKER, BRUCE CARL, II, physician, educator, health facility administrator; b. Chgo., Sept. 8, 1948; s. Carl Max and Lillian (Podzamski) B.; m. Irene Stepien-Thibault, 1991; 1 child, Joseph. BS in Aero. and Astron. Engring., U. Ill., 1970; MSME, Colo. State U., 1972; postgrad., Wright State U., 1973—74; MD, Chgo. Med. Sch., 1978; MS in Health Svcs. Adminstrn., Coll. St. Francis, Joliet, Ill., 1984; diploma in Spanish, U. Chgo., 1988; diploma in Polish, Coll. Du Page, 1989. Diplomate Am. Bd. Med. Mgmt., cert. physician exec. Resident in surgery U. N.C., Chapel Hill, 1978—79; resident in family practice St. Mary of Nazareth Hosp. Ctr., Chgo., 1979—81, chmn., program dir. dept. family practice, 1985—90, asst. dir. med. edn., 1981—82, dir. family practice residency, 1983—90, chief Family Practice Ctr., 1983—85, chmn. dept. family practice, 1985—90, med. dir. home health svc., 1985—2001, med. dir. HMO-Ill., 1985—2001, mem. planning and devel. com. governing bd., 1987—91, v.p. med. affairs, 1989—2001; clin. instr. Chgo. Med. Sch., 1982, affiliate instr., 1982—83, asst. prof., 1983, vice chmn. dept. family medicine, 1983—91; chief med. officer Med. Ctr. Hosp., Odessa, Tex., 2002—, chief quality officer, 2008—; mem. High Reliability Orgn. Program Health Sys., 2011—, Healthcare Coalition Tex. Phys. Leadership Network, 2009—. Pres. ProCare, 501a Profl. Corp., 2005-08; adminstr. Family Health Ctr., 2005-08; pres. Permian Basin Health Care Network PHO, 2005-08; mem. family practice residency act Adv. Com. Ill. Dept. Pub. Health, 1991-02; mem. Vol. Hosp. Assn. S.W. Physician Quality and Patient Safety Coun., 2003-08, VHA SW Physleadership Network, 2009-, Tex. Hosp. Assn. Physical Exec. Coun., 2008-, Coun. Policy Devel., 2009- Mem. editl. rev. bd. Postgrad. Medicine, 1987-89; contbr. articles to med. jours. Mem. pub. health adv. network HHS, 1990-91; bd. dirs. Midwest region Inn Care Am., 1991—; mem. dinner com. Ill. chpt. Lupus Found. Am., 1991, St. Elizabeth Ann Seton. Parish Coun., 2004-07. Capt. USAFR, 1970—75. Fellow Am. Acad. Family Physicians (rep. to accrediation rev. com. for physician assts. 1989-94, chmn., 1991-93), Am. Coll. Physician Execs., Am. Coll. Health Care Execs. (regents adv. coun. 1996-2000), Inst. Medicine Chgo.; mem. AMA, Ill. Acad. Family Physicians (commn. on internal affairs 1986, commn. pub. and govt. policy 1987-89, chmn. 1989-90, bd. dirs. 1988-92, chmn. pub. rels. and info. com. 1988-92, state rep. family practice res. act com. 1990-92, vice spkr. 1991-92), Tex. Acad. Family Physicians (commn. on pub. health clin. affairs 2003-06, com. on acad. affairs 2004-07), Tex. Med. Assn. (processes com.), Permian Basin Regional Citizen Corps, Soc. Tchrs. Family Medicine, Assn. Am. Med. Colls., Alliance Continuing Med. Edn., Am. Coll. Occupl.

Medicine, Am. Acad. Med. Adminstrn., Chgo. Med. Soc. (councilor for Chgo. Med. Sch. 1986-91, alt. councilor 1991-95, physicians stress ad hoc com. 1989-90, vice chmn. 1990-91, adv. com. on pub. health policy 1990-2001, presdl. adv. com. 1991-2001), Ill. Med. Soc. (coun. on edn. and manpower 1986-96, chmn. com. on CME activities 1991-96, chmn. subcom. physician placement and practice issues 1986-90, third party payment and processes com., Ill. Acad. Family Physicians rep. 1990-92), Ector County Med. Soc., Phi Delta Epsilon. Roman Catholic. Office Phone: 432-640-1059. Personal E-mail: bbeckerii@netscape.com. E-mail: bbecker@echd.org.

BECKER, DANIEL GRANT, physician, consultant; s. William Howard and Merle Skoler Becker; m. Madeleine Anne Spatola. BA (magna cum laude), Harvard U., 1986; MD, U. Va. Med. Sch., 1990. Cert. Am. Bd. Otolaryngology, 1996, Am. Bd. Facial Plastic and Reconstructive Surgery, 1999. Asst. prof. U. Pa., 1997—2000, assoc. prof., 2000—03, clin. assoc. prof., 2003—. Cons. Linvatec Corp., Largo, Fla., 1993—2003; dir. facial plastic surgery U. Pa., 1997—; med. dir. Becker Nose and Sinus Ctr., Sewell, NJ, 2003—. Author: (textbook) Rhinoplasty Disection Manual, 1999; editor: (med. jour.) Facial Plastic Surgery, 2001—. Telemedicine Grant, Phila. Antique Show, 1999. Mem.: Am. Acad. Facial Plastic Surgery, Am. Rhinologic Soc. (cons. to bd. 1999—2002). Achievements include design of multiple new instruments for surgery; research in description of new operations. Office: Becker Nose and Sinus Ctr 400 Med Ctr Dr Ste B Sewell NJ 08080 Office Phone: 856-589-6673. E-mail: beckermailbox@aol.com.

BECKER, DAVID KENNETH, pediatrician, educator; b. Jan. 23, 1967; MD, U. NC Chapel Hill, MPH in Maternal & Child Health, 1996. Cert. Am. Bd. Pediat. Intern U. NC Chapel Hill, resident, 1996—99; asst. clinical prof. dept. pediat. U. Calif. San Francisco, 2001—. Fellow, U. Ariz. Program in Integrative Medicine; Bravewell fellow, U. Calif. San Francisco Osher Ctr. Integrative Medicine. Mem.: Doctors Without Borders (vol.). Office: Dept Pediat Mt Zion U Calif San Francisco Box 1660 2330 Post St 320 San Francisco CA 94143-1660 Office Phone: 415-885-7478. Office Fax: 415-885-3790. Business E-Mail: beckerda@peds.ucsf.edu.

BECKER, DIETRICH WALTER PIUS, surgeon; b. Gleiwitz, Germany, Jan. 3, 1938; s. Willy Gerhard Julius and Editha Anastasia (Kern) B.; m. Helge Winkler (div. 1968); m. Karin Elisabeth Rudolph, Nov. 4, 1989; children: Marcus, Klaus-Joachim, Tanya Editha, Wiebke-Saskia. Med. asst., Justus Liebig U., 1964, medicus, 1966, MD, 1978; Humboldt prof., U. Berlin, 1998. Med. asst. Divers Hosp., U. Giessen, Hessen, Germany, 1964—66; asst, chmn. Landesarztekammer, Hessen, 1966—84, med. trauma leader, 1964—, Leitender Notarzt, 1991—; sub-chief physician Acad. Tng. Hosp. Emergency Surgery, Bad Hersfeld, Hessen, Germany, 1971—99; med. dir. IFBE Med. Sch., Bad Hersfeld, 1999—; extraordinary prof. U. Teuffen, Switzerland, 2006. Specialist joint and ligament surgery; mem. U. Louisville. Author: Reconstruction des Kreuzbandes durch prothetische Versorgung mit dem Stryker-Dacron-Ligament, 1996, (video) The Robinson Drainage: A New Principle of Drainage in Emergency Surgery, 1980; co-author: New Trends in Bone Grafting, 1992, Regulations und Repairmechanismen, 1994, Wound Dressing in Burns with Fresh, Sterile Porcine Skin, Annals of Mediterranean Club for Burns and Fire Disasters, 1999, The Burn Disease, 2001, Tratamiento De Quemados A Bordo En Catastrofes Maritimas, 2002, co-author: Medical Ship Guide No 3, 2006, The Aidadiva-A State of the Art Cruise Ship with New proven Progress in Fire Safety Devices Annals of Burn and Fire Disaster, 2008; contbr. articles to profl. jours. Med. sub. comdr. German Navy, 1984. Recipient hons. and awards, Polish Sect. of Internat. Coll. of Surgeons, 1990, Medaille of merits, German Red Cross-Sect. Hessen, 1998, Cross of Honour in Gold, German Red Cross, 1994, Medaille of Merit, Austrian Assn. of Vets. "Fedmarschall Radetzky", 1996, Bundesvedienstkreuz in Silver, Austrian Vet. Assn. "Fedmarschall Radetzky", 1999, Great Cross of Honour in Gold, Necktie Austrian Vet. Assn. "Feldmarschall Radetzky", "Cross of Honour of the Bundeswehr in Gold", 1999, Chirurgus et Medicus Honoris Causae, Koeniglich-Preussisches Infantrieregiment NR.25 v. Möllendorf, 1998; fellow, Mediterrean Coun. Burns and Fire Disasters, 1990. Fellow: Austrian Hunting Assn., Hungarian Hunting Assn., Mediterranean Club for Burns and Fire Disasters; mem.: Henolic Med. Assn. (hasso rhenania glessen adolphiana fulda salia silesia gleimitz gov. 2008), German Assn. for Search and Rescue in Sea, Foderverein Rahsegler Greif e.V., Internat. Maritime Health Assn. (bd. mem.), Polish-German Assn. for Med. Coop., German Assn. for Militerian Medicine and Pharmacy, Assn. Orthop. Rsch., German Assn. Disaster Medicine, German Assn. Sports Medicine, European Burn Assn., Internat. Fedn. Sports Medicine, Hunting Club Germany. Achievements include research of biodegradable implants in treatment of bone fractures; research in psychic lesions after disasters in the high seas. Home: Berberitzenweg 34 36251 Bad Hersfeld Hessen Germany Office: IFBE Sch Hainstr 7 36251 Bad Hersfeld Hessen Germany Home Phone: 0049 6621 62426; Office Phone: 0049 6621 77892. Personal E-mail: dokterdb@t-online.de.

BECKER, DOREEN DORIS, medical/surgical nurse; b. Elgin, ND, May 22, 1944; d. Carl Ruff and Dorothy Buttmann; m. Glenn Alan Watson, Jan. 19, 2002; m. Roy Ernest Becker, June 5, 1964 (dec. Sept. 6, 1993); 1 child, Allen Roy. Degree in Nursing, U. Chgo., 1963. Cert. coding assoc. Am. Health Info. Mgmt. Assn., 2005. Nurse Columbia Hosp., Grand Forks, ND, 1976—77, surg. nurse, 1977—90; surg. nurse supr. Columbia HCA, Plano, Tex., 1990—92, med. records coder, 1993—2001, Baylor Hosp., Richardson, Tex., 2001—02, Med. City, Dallas, 2002—05, Med. Ctr., Rowlett, Tex., 2005—07; cert. coder for Presby/Rockwall Tex., 2007—. Instr. HCA Med. Ctr., Plano, 1990—92. Instr. Red Cross, Braddock, ND, 1966. Recipient Medicorp award, Mott HS, 1962. Avocations: marathon running, bicycling, fishing, fossils, rocks. Home: 616 Buffalo Bend Plano TX 75023

BECKER, FERDINAND F., facial plastic surgeon, otolaryngologist, educator; MD, Tulane U. Sch. of Medicine, La. Diplomate Am. Bd. Otolaryngology, 1972, cert. Am. Bd. Facial Plastic and Reconstructive Surgery. Intern, resident Charity Hosp., La.; asst. clin. prof. otolaryngology Univ. Of Fla. Coll. of Medicine; hosp. appointment includes Indian River Med. Ctr. Nat. tng. ctr. physician Botox Cosmetic Network Perceptorship Tng. Program. Supporter Samaritan Ctr., Women's Refuge, The Ctr. for the Arts, Riverside Theatre. Recipient Guide to America's Top Physicians, Consumer Rsch. Coun. of America, William Wright award, Am. Acad. Facial Plastic and Reconstructive Surgery; named Guest of Honor at the ann. conv., Fla. Soc. of Dermatol. Surgeons, Amateur Outdoor Photographer; named one of The Best Doctors in America, 1992, America's Top Doctors, Castle Connolly, America's Cosmetic Doctors and Dentists, Orlando's Top Doctors, Orlando Mag., the foremost facial plastic surgeon in Fla., Fla. Soc. of Dermatol. Surgeons. Avocation: walking. Office: Indian River Medical Center 1000 36th St Vero Beach FL 32960 Office Phone: 772-567-4311.

BECKER, GARY J., medical association administrator, radiologist, educator; b. Chgo. BA, Indiana U., 1974; MD, Indiana U. Sch. Medicine, 1977. Joined faculty to prof., chief of vascular section Indiana U. Sch. Medicine, 1981—90; medical dir. Miami Cardiac & Vascular Inst., 1990—2004; asst. medical dir. Baptist Cardiac & Vascular Inst. Miami, 1998—2004, medical director of research and outcomes, 1998—2004; branch chief image guided intervention, Cancer Imaging Program Nat. Cancer Inst., Washington, 2004—05; prof. vascular and interventional medicine U. Ariz. Coll. Medicine, 2005—; exec. dir. American Bd. Radiology, 2008—. Founding editor Jour. Vascular & Interventional Radiology, editor-in-chief, 1990—95. Fellow: American Coll. Radiology; mem.: Soc. Interventional Radiology (Gold medal 2008), American Bd. Radiology (bd. trustees 2000—, assoc. exec. dir. diagnostic radiology and subspecialties 2006—07), Radiological Soc. North America (bd. dirs. 2001—10, chmn. 2007—08, pres. 2009—10). Office: University Ariz Sch Medicine PO Box 245017 Tucson AZ 85724 *

BECKER, JAMES MURDOCH, surgeon, educator; b. Cleve., Jan. 7, 1949; s. Norman O. and Mildred Edith (Murdoch) B.; m. Christine Louise Lohmann, Dec. 30, 1972; children: Alexander, Selby, Catherine, Anne. BA in Biology, Yale U., 1971; MD, Case Western Res. U., 1975. Diplomate Nat. Bd. Med. Examiners, Am. Bd. Surgery; lic. surgeon, Minn., Utah, Mo., Mass. Intern in surgery U. Utah Hosps., Salt Lake City, 1975-76, resident in gen. surgery, 1976-79, chief resident in surgery, 1979—80; research fellow in surgery U. Utah Sch. Medicine, 1977-78, asst. prof. surgery, 1982-86; NIH rsch. fellow digestive diseases Mayo Clinic, 1980-82; mem. surg. staff VA Hosp., Salt Lake City, 1982-86, chief green service, 1983-86, head nutritional support team, 1983-86; mem. cons. staff Intermountain Unit Shriners Hosps. for Crippled Children, Salt Lake City, 1984-86; assoc. prof. surgery, dir. gastrointestinal surgery Washington U. Sch. Medicine, 1986-89; assoc. prof surgery, chief divsn. gen. and gastroint. surg. Harvard Med. Sch./Brigham and Women's Hosp., Boston, 1989-94; James Utley prof. and chmn. surgeon-in-chief Boston U. Sch. Medicine/Boston Med. Ctr., 1994—. Contbr. articles to profl. jours., chpts. to books. NIH fellow, Mayo Clinic, 1980-82; grantee Johnson & Johnson Products, Inc., 1985, NIH, 1985—, Sandoz Corp., 1985-87, Ethicon, Inc., 1985-86. Mem. ACS, AMA, Am. Gastroenterol. Assn., Am. Motility Soc., Am. Pancreatic Assn., Assn. Acad. Surgery, Am. Soc. Parenteral and Enteral Nutrition, Internat. Biliary Assn., Collegium Internat. Chirurgiae Digestivae (Grassi prize 8th World Congress 1984), Soc. for Surgery Alimentary Tract, Soc. Univ. Surgeons, Yale U. Alumni Assn., Am. Coll. Surgeons, Am. Surg. Assn., We. Surg. Assn., Cen. Surg. Assn., New Eng. Surg. Assn., Am. Soc. Colorectal Surgeons, Soc. Internat. Chirugiae, Soc. Surg. Oncology, Alpha Omega Alpha. Office: Boston Med Ctr 88 E Newton St Boston MA 02118-2308 Office Phone: 617-638-8600.

BECKER, LANCE B., medical educator; B in Gen. Studies, U. Mich., 1975; MA in Biochemistry, U. Ill., 1977; MD, 1981. Cert. internal medicine, emergency medicine, critical care medicine. Founder, dir. Emergency Resuscitation Ctr. at U. Chicago in Chicago and Argonne Nat. Lab; prof. U. Chicago Dept. of Medicine; prof. emergency medicine U. Pa., 2006—, dir. Ctr. Resuscitation Sci., 2007—. Nat. Conf. dir. Am. Heart Assn. Emergency Cardiac Care Evidence Evaluation Conf., 1999; past chmn. Cardiopulmonary, Perioperative, and Critical Care Coun. of Am. Heart Assn., Basic Life Support Com.; chmn. Internat. AHA Guidelines Conf. for daily Controversial Topics, 2005; co-direct Resuscitation Sci. Symposium of Am. Heart Assn.; rep. Internat. Liaison Com. on Resuscitation; mem. Food and Drug Adminstrn. Device Evaluation panels, Nat. Am. Heart Assn. Basic Life Support Com. and Advanced Life Support subcommittees. Co-author numerous scientific publications. Recipient Time, Feeling, and Focus award, Am. Heart Assn., Chairman's award for excellence in volunteering, leadership awards, Nat. Emergency Cardiac Care Com. of American Heart Assn.; named Attending Physician of Yr., Emergency Medicine, 1997. Mem.: IOM. Office: Translational Research Laboratory 125 South 31st Street Suite 1200 Philadelphia PA 19104-3403 Office Phone: 215-746-3625. Office Fax: 215-746-1224. E-mail: lance.becker@uphs.upenn.edu.

BECKER, LORNE ARTHUR, family physician; b. Kitchener, Ont., Can., Mar. 6, 1945; s. Percy Lorne Becker and Katie Klassen; m. Elizabeth Joy Wonnacott, June 1, 1968; children: Andrew James, Doug Scott, Lynn Marie. MD, U. We. Ont., 1969. Diplomate Am. Bd. Family Practice. Asst. prof. U. Rochester, NY, 1977—79; assoc. prof. Temple U., Phila., 1979—83, U. Okla., Oklahoma City, 1983—88, dir. family health program, 1983—88; assoc. prof. U. Toronto, Ont., 1988—94, chief family medicine, 1988—93; prof. dept. family medicine SUNY, Syracuse, 1994—2004, chair dept. family medicine, 1997—2004; prof. emeritus family medicine SUNY Upstate Med. U., Syracuse, 2004—. Founding bd. mem. Family Practice Inquiries Network; mem. steering group Cochrane Collaboration, 2004—10, co-chair steering group, coord. pub. policy group, 2006—10; mem. panel Gulf war and health Inst. Medicine, 2002—03; mem. working group on hearing loss in children US Dept. HHS, 2004—; coord. Cochrane Primary Health Care Field, 1998—2006; mem. rsch. com. World Orgn. Nat. Acads. and Colls. of Gen. Practice/Family Medicine, 2004—; dir. Cochrane Trading Co., 2010—; co-convenor Cochrane Multiple Interventions Methods Group, 2010—. Assoc. editor: Family Practice, 2004—06, mem. editl. bd.: Evidence Based Child Health, 2005—; contbr. chapters to books. Fellow Coll. Family Physicians Can., Am. Acad. Family Physicians; mem. Soc. Tchrs. Family Medicine (chair rsch. com. 1985-89, Curtis Hames Rsch. award 2001), Ambulatory Sentinel Practice Network (bd. dirs. 1979-93), advisory bd., Guidelines Internat. Network, 2008- Avocations: sailing, handheld computers. Office: SUNY Dept Family Medicine 475 Irving Ave Ste 200 Syracuse NY 13210-1529 Business E-Mail: beckerla@upstate.edu.

BECKER, MATTHEW LEONARD, chemistry professor; b. Iowa, Oct. 6, 1975; BS, NW Mo. State U., 1998; PhD in Organic Chemistry, Wash. U., 2003. Assoc. prof. U. Akron, 2009—. Project leader Nat. Inst. Standards and Tech., 2003—09. Fellow Postdoctoral Fellowship, NRC, Chemistry-Biology interface Tng. Fellowship, NIH. Mem.: Soc. Biomaterials, Am. Chem. Soc. Office: University Akron Dept Polymer Sci 170 University Ave Akron OH 44325-3909 Office Fax: 330-972-5290. Business E-Mail: becker@uakorn.edu.

BECKER, MICHAEL ALLEN, internist, rheumatologist, educator; b. NYC, Oct. 3, 1940; s. David S. and Sylvia M. (Salomon) B.; m. Mary E. Baim; children: David, Jonathan, Abigail, Arielle, Daniel. BA, U. Pa., Phila., 1961, MD, 1965. Diplomate Am. Bd. Internal Medicine, Am. Bd. Rheumatology. Intern Barnes Hosp., Washington U., St. Louis, 1965-66, resident, 1969-70; asst. prof. U. Calif., San Diego, 1972-77, assoc. prof., 1977-80; prof. medicine U. Chgo. Pritzker Sch. Medicine, 1980—. Mem. biochemistry study sect. NIH, Bethesda, Md., 1991-95. Contbr. numerous rsch. articles to med. publs. Sr. asst. surgeon USPHS, 1966-69, Pres. Purine and Pyrimidine Soc. Fellow, John Simon Guggenheim Meml. Found. Master Am. Coll. Rheumatology; mem. Am. Soc. Clin. Investigation, Assn. Am. Physicians. Office: U Chgo Med Ctr MC0930 Chicago IL 60637 Home Phone: 312-640-8801; Office Phone: 773-702-6899. Business E-Mail: mbecker@medicine.bsd.uchicago.edu.

BECKER, MICHAEL HANNS-JOACHIM, plastic surgeon, consultant; b. Lingen, Europe, Germany, Dec. 25, 1958; s. Hans-Joachim Paul and Waltraud Becker; m. Regina Thanheiser, Dec. 27, 1992; m. Michaela Hofmeister, Dec. 18, 1986 (div. July 8, 1991); children: Johann Paul Anton, Jakob Fritz Martin. Degree, Med. U. Hannover, Germany, 1977, MD, 1987; PhD, Med. U. Witten/Herdecke, Germany, 2002. Registrar in plastic surgery Med. U. Hannover, 1991—97; sr. registrar plastic surgery Med. U. Aachen, Germany, 1997—2000, Med. U. Wuppertal, Germany, 2000—02; cons. Plastic Surgery, Aachen, Germany, 2003—. Mem.: German Soc. Reconstructive Microsurgery, Am. Soc. Peripheral Nerve, World Soc. Reconstructive Microsurgery. Avocations: music, woodworking. Office: Plastic Surgery Boxgraben 56 D-52064 Aachen Germany Office Fax: 0049-241-9008595. Personal E-mail: becker.pch@gmx.de.

BECKER, NANCY MAY, nursing educator; b. Reading, Pa., July 28, 1949; d. Theodore R. and Minerva M. (Deiseroth) B. Diploma, Reading Hosp. Sch. Nursing, 1970; BS, Albright Coll., 1979; MS, U. Del., 1981. RN Pa., Del. Nurse mgr. Cmty. Gen. Hosp., Reading, 1974-76; nurse educator Albright Coll., Reading, 1980-87; clin. nurse specialist Polyclinic Med. Ctr., Harrisburg, Pa., 1987-89, asst. prof. Lehigh Carbon C.C., Schnecksville, Pa., 1989-95, dir. nursing programs, 1995-97, dean allied health/dir. nursing, 1998—2001, dean profl. accreditation and curriculum, dir. nursing, 2001—06, interim v.p. acad. and student affairs, 2001—02, v.p. academic student affairs, DON, 2006—08; assoc. prof. Reading Area Cmty. Coll., 2008—. Mem. Nat. League Nursing, Sigma Theta Tau.

BECKER, PETER H., biologist; b. Köln, Germany, Oct. 31, 1949; s. Karl and Liselotte Becker; m. Gabriele Göpfert, Apr. 2, 1976; children: Kristin, Andreas, Birgit. Abitur, U. Cologne, 1968, Diploma in Biology, 1973, PhD, 1976. Sci. mem. Inst. Avian Rsch., Wilhelmshaven, Germany, 1978—92, sci. dir., 1992—. Prof. biology U. Oldenburg, Germany, 1997—. Editor: Jour. Ornithology; contbr. articles to profl. jours., chapters to books. Curator Cath. Found. St, Johannes, Varel, Germany, 1996— Fellow, MPI Verhaltensphysiologie, Germany, 1977—78. Mem.: European Ornithologists Union (treas. 2005—09), Waterbird Soc., Seabird Group, German Ornithologists' Soc. (assoc.; sec. 1982—85, bd. mem. 1986—95), Internat. Ornithol. Com. (life). Roman Catholic. Avocations: woodworking, travel. Office: Institute of Avian Research An der Vogelwarte 21 Wilhelmshaven 26386 Germany Business E-Mail: peter.becker@ifv-vogelwarte.de.

BECKER, QUINN HENDERSON, orthopedic surgeon, military officer; b. Kirksville, Mo., June 11, 1930; s. Quinn Henry B. and Sarah Lucille (Henderson) Finley; m. Gladys Marie Roussell, Aug. 11, 1951; children: Quinn E., Terri K., Paul Eric. Grad., N.E. La. State Coll., 1952; MD, La. State U., 1956; student, Armed Forces Staff Coll., 1969-70, Command and Gen. Staff Coll., 1971, U.S. Army War Coll., 1974-75. Diplomate Am. Bd. Orthop. Surgery. Commd. 2d lt. U.S. Army, advanced through grades to lt. gen., 1985; intern Tripler Gen. Hosp., 1956-57; resident in orthopedic surgery Confederate Meml. Med. Ctr., Shreveport, La., 1958-61; orthopedic surgeon Ft. Gordon, Ga., 1962-63; chief orthopedic service Ft. Rucker, Ala., 1963-64; comdg. officer 5th Surg. Hosp. (Mobile Army), Heidelberg, W. Ger., 1964-65; surgeon 3d Inf. Div., Wurzburg, W. Ger., 1965-66; chief orthpedic surgery 33d Field Hosp., Wurzburg, 1965; asst. chief orthopedic service Walter Reed Gen. Hosp., 1966-69; chief profl. services 85th Evacuation Hosp., Vietnam, 1970; div. surgeon and bn. comdr. 15th Med. Bn. 1st Cavalry Div., Vietnam, 1970-71; chief orthopedic service and orthopedic residency tng. Tripler Army Med. Ctr., 1971-74; surgeon 18th Airborne Corps., Ft. Bragg, 1975-77; comdr. Med. Activity Womack Army Hosp., Ft. Bragg, 1976-77; dir. health care ops. Office Surgeon Gen., 1977-80; comdt. Acad. Health Scis., U.S. Army, Ft. Sam Houston, Tex., 1980-81; dep. surgeon gen. Washington, 1981-83; comdr. 7th Med. Command, Heidelberg, 1983-85; Surgeon Gen. Dept. Army, 1985-88, ret., 1988. Asst. prof. orthopedic surgery Howard U., Washington, 1967-69; clin. assoc. prof. Sch. Medicine U. Hawaii, Honolulu, 1973-74; chief of staff VA Hosp., Asheville, N.C., 1989-92, ret. 1992; mem. Congl. Commn. on Svc. Mems. and Vets. Transition Assistance, 1998; mem. adv. bd. Ind.-Ohio Ctr. Traumetic Amputation Rsch. Vietnam, 2006-. Contbr. papers to publs. and confs. in field. Pres. ARC Golden K- Kiwanis Club, 2007—08; team tchr. Ramp Project San Antonio Br., 2007—; chmn. bd. Army Med. Mus. Found. Ft. Sam, Houston, 2005—08. Decorated Legion of Merit, Meritorious Service medal, Bronze Star, Air medal, Disting. Service medal. Fellow Am. Acad. Orthopedic Surgeons (chmn. mil. affairs com. 1981-85), ACS, Am. Coll. Physician Execs. (disting.); mem. AMA (ho. of dels.), Am. Orthopaedic Assn., Masons (33d degree, Grand Cross 1993), Civitan (pres. Asheville club 1992, chmn. internat. rsch. com. 1996-98). Home: 2111 Peninsula Dr San Antonio TX 78239-3085

BECKER, STEPHAN W. J., surgeon; b. Edenkoben, Germany, July 20, 1962; s. Günter and Irene Becker; m. Silke Becker; 1 child, Simon. Bachelor's, Kurfürst Ruprecht Gymnasium, Neustadt /Weinstrasse, Germany, 1981; MD, Karl-Ruprecht U. Heidelberg, Germany, 1989. Cert. orthop. surgery Med. Coun. Germany, 1997, sports medicine German Assn. Sports Medicine, 1995, chirotherapy German Soc. Manual Medicine, 1999, emergency medicine Med. Coun. Germany, 1991. Intern U. Birmingham, Dudley Rd. Hosp., England, 1989—90, Royal Naval Hosp., Portsmouth, England, 1990, Caritashospital, Bad Mergentheim, Germany, 1991; resident Lord Mayor Treloar Hosp.,

Alton, England, 1991—92, BG Trauma Ctr., Ludwigshafen, Germany, 1992—95, Halle, Saale, Germany, 1995—98, Friedrich-Schiller-U., Eisenberg, Germany, 1998—2002, Orthop. Hosp. Vienna-Speising, Vienna, 2002—09; adj. prof. U. Sherbrooke, Sherbrooke, Que., Canada, 2008; dir. orthop. Spine Inst. Musculoskeletal Analysis Rsch. Therapy, Vienna, 2009—. Advising surgeon AO Biomaterials Bd., Frankfurt, Germany, 2003; invited lectr. sports medicine Leopold Franzens U., Innsbruck, Austria, 2002—06; invited lectr. Ivan Franco U., Ukraine, 2005; cons. surgeon French Consulate, Leipzig, Germany, 1997—99; presenter in field; dir., orthop. and spine Inst. Musculoskeletal Analysis, Rsch. and Therapy, Vienna. Contbg. author: Biological Monitoring, 1990, Reconstructive Surgery of the Anterior Cruciate Ligament, 1995, Orthopaedic Year Book, 1996, Paraplegia, 2000; editor: Aspects in Physical and Rehabilitative Medicine, 2001; contbg. author: Instructional Course Orthopaedics and Traumatology 10, 2004; editor: Balloonkyphoplasty, 2006; contbr. articles to profl. jours. Formula one/superbike racing surgeon Internat. Racing Assn., Hockenheim, Germany, 1992—95; helicopter rescue svc. German Ministry Internal Affairs, Ludwigshafen, Germany, 1992—95; rescue svc. German Red Cross, Ludwigshafen, Neustadt, Jena, Germany, 1992—98. Med. officer Royal Naval Hosp., 1990—91, Portsmouth. Recipient Sci. award, U. Vienna, 2004; grantee, Am. Paraplegia Soc., 2000; European Traveling fellow, European Fedn. Orthops. and Traumatology, 1997, Clin. fellow, German and French Assns. Orthops. and Traumatology, 1999. Master: World Endoscopic, Neuronavigation and Minimal Invasive Spine Soc. (licentiate; gen. sec. 2004—05, v.p. 2005—); fellow: European Bd. Orthops. and Traumatology; mem.: German Soc. Traumatology (licentiate), European Spine Assn. (licentiate), AO Spine (licentiate), Internat. Med. Soc. Paraplegia (licentiate), Asian Pacific Orthop. Assn. (licentiate), Can. Orthop. Assn. (licentiate), German Assn. Orthop. Practitioners (licentiate), Austrian Soc. Orthops. (licentiate), Austrian Spine Soc. (licentiate), German Soc. Orthops. (licentiate). Achievements include patents for artificial bone matrix. Avocation: languages. Business E-Mail: stephan.becker@medimpuls.at.

BECKERMAN, JAMES GREGG, cardiologist; b. Nov. 4, 1971; married; 2 children. Grad. summa cum laude, Harvard Coll.; MD, Harvard Med. Sch., 1999. Cert. internal medicine, cardiovascular diseases, nuclear cardiology. Resident Mass. Gen. Hosp.; fellow Stanford Hosp. & Clinics; invasive cardiologist Columbia Cardiology Assocs., 2006—, Providence Heart & Vascular Inst. Columnist USA Today. Fellow: Am. Coll. Cardiology. Office: 9427 SW Barnes Rd Ste 498 Portland OR 97225 Office Phone: 503-297-6234. Office Fax: 503-297-3121.

BECKETT, VICTORIA LING, physician; m. Peter G.S. Beckett, 1954 (dec. 1974); 1 child, Paul T. (dec.); m. Joseph C. Sharp, 1996. BA, Mt. Holyoke Coll., 1945; MD, U. Mich., 1949; MA, St. Mary's U., 1995. Intern Mpls. Gen. Hosp., 1949-50; fellow Mayo Grad. Sch., 1951-55; clin. instr. Wayne State U. Sch. Medicine, Detroit, 1956-67; staff cons. internal medicine oncology svc. Henry Ford Hosp., Detroit, 1957-60; rsch. physician Darling Meml. Ctr., Detroit, 1965-69; rsch. assoc. rheumatology Trinity Coll. Dublin U., 1970-72, postgrad. tutor, 1972-73, dir., 1973-76; cons. physician in rheumatology Federated Dublin Vol. Hosps., 1973-76; staff cons. rheumatology Mayo Clinic, 1976-90, emeritus staff, 1990—; asst. prof. medicine Mayo Med. Sch., 1976-90; med. dir. Rochester Health Care Ctr., Minn., 1985—90. Author: Living Medicine: Memoir Snap Shots, 2004, Six Years in Shanrila: Life in a Retirement Complex, 2008. Fellow: ACP; mem.: Mayo Med. Alumni Assn., Am. Coll. Rheumatology (ret. mem.), Minn. State Med. Assn., Zumbro Valley Med. Soc., Phi Beta Kappa, Sigma Xi. Methodist. Office Phone: 507-284-2691.

BECKHOLT, ALICE, clinical nurse specialist; b. NYC, Aug. 7, 1941; d. Julius and Mary (Katz) Kalkow; m. Richard H. Polakoff, Aug. 12, 1962 (div. 1984); children: Katherine, Michael, Matthew; m. Kenneth Eugene Beckholt, Feb. 3, 1990. BA, Syracuse U., 1962; ADN, El Centro Coll., 1977; BSN, U. Tex., Arlington, 1980; MS, Tex. Women's U., 1988. RN Tex., Ohio. Staff nurse, outpatient mgr. Irving (Tex.) Cmty. Hosp., 1977—86; staff nurse Meth. Hosp., Dallas, 1986—89, U. Tex. S.W. Med. Ctr., Dallas, 1989—90; pediat. home care nurse various agys., Columbus, Ohio, 1990—94; advanced practice nurse, pub. speaking, preceptor Columbus Health Dept., 1994—. Adj. faculty Ohio State U., 2007—09. Sec., 2nd v.p., 1st v.p., pres. Am. Cancer Soc., 1971-76, bd. dirs. Irving, Tex., 1971-90, BSE instr., nurse's com., 1990-97, triple touch coord., 1991-97, BSE faculty, 1986-90; vol., auction subchair Sta. KERA-TV, Dallas, 1972-84; CPR instr. Am. Heart Assn., 1984-98; med. adv. Ohio Support HELP. Recipient Outstanding Svc. award Am. Cancer Soc. Columbus chpt., 1992-93; named Outstanding Vol., Am. Cancer Soc., Irving, Tex., 1973, 74, 76. Mem.: APHA, Ohio Assn. Advanced Practice Nurses, Ohio Pub. Health Assn., Sigma Theta Tau. Avocations: gourmet cooking, classical music, travel. Home: 1444 Bexton Loop Columbus OH 43209-2904 Office: Columbus Dept Health 240 S Parsons Ave Columbus OH 43215-4022

BECKMANN, CHARLES HENRY, cardiologist, educator; b. NYC, July 18, 1930; s. William and Margaret (Wellershaus) Beckmann; m. Ardith Clara Kuehm, June 9, 1956; children: Eric, Eric, Diana. BS, MIT, Cambridge, 1952; MD, Cornell U., Ithaca, NY, 1956. Diplomate Am. Bd. Internal Medicine, Am. Bd. Cardiology. Entered USAF, 1957, advanced through grades to col., 1971; asst. chief cardiology USAF Willford Hall Med. Ctr., San Antonio, 1965-70; chmn. dept. medicine Clark AFB Hosp. USAF, Philippines, 1970-73, chief cardiology Wilford Hall Med. Ctr. San Antonio, 1973-83; dir. med. ctr. San Antonio State Hosp., 1983-84; cardiologist Skinner Clinic, San Antonio, 1984—; clin. prof. medicine U. Tex., San Antonio, 1983—; prof. medicine Uniformed Svcs. U. Health Scis., Bethesda, Md., 1982-83. Nat. cons. to surgeon gen., USAF, 1979-83, chief cardiology Bapt. Meml. Hosp. System, San Antonio, 1992-93, chmn. dept. medicine, mem. exec. bd., 1993-94; chmn. ethics com. Baptist Meml. Hosp., 1993-94,; chmn. dept. cardiology Bapt. Hosps. Sys., San Antonio, 1996-98. Mem. editl. bd. Heart Smart mag., contbr. articles to Am. Jour. Cardiology, Jour. Nuclear Medicine, Archives Internal Medicine, Jour. Cardia Rehab., Circulation, Jour. Allergy and Clin. Immunology. Pres. Helotes Park Civic Assn., Tex., 1965-67, Helotes Elem. PTA, 1968-70; mem. exec. bd. So. Region Boy Scouts Am., Atlanta, 1989—; bd. dirs. San Antonio divsn. Am. Heart Assn., 1989-92. Recipient Award of Merit Boy Scouts of Am., San Antonio, 1976, Silver Beaver medal, 1977. Fellow ACP, Am. Coll. Cardiology (bd. govs. 1979-83), Am. Coll. Preventive Medicine, Coun. Clin. Cardiology, Am. Heart Assn., N.Y. Acad. Sci., San Antonio Cardiology Soc. (pres. 1989-90), Am. Fed. Clin. Rsch. (sr.), Masons, Shriners. Lutheran. Home: 14802 Circle A Trl Helotes TX 78023-4023 Office: Skinner Clinic 124 Dallas St San Antonio TX 78205-1288

BECKMEYER, HENRY ERNEST, anesthesiologist, pain management specialist, educator; b. Cape Girardeau, Mo., Apr. 13, 1939; s. Henry Ernest Jr. and Margaret Gertrude (Link) B.; m. Deborah Beckmyer; children: Henry IV, James, Martha, Leigh, Hillary. BA, Mich. State U., 1961; DO, Des Moines U., 1965. Diplomate Am. Bd. Med. Examiners, Am. Acad. Pain Mgmt.; cert. Am. Osteo. Bd. Anesthesiology. Chief physician migrant worker program and op. head start Sheridan (Mich.) Community Hosp., 1967-69; resident in anesthesia Bi-County Community Hosp./DOH Corp., Detroit, 1969-71, chief resident, 1968-69; staff anesthesiologist Detroit Osteo. Hosp./BCCH, 1971-75; founding chmn. dept. anesthesia Humana Hosp. of the Palm Beaches, West Palm Beach, Fla., 1975-79; assoc. prof. Mich. State U., East Lansing, 1979-88, prof. anesthesia, 1988—, chmn. dept. osteo. medicine, 1985-96; chmn. dept. osteo. surg. specialities, 1996-97; chief staff Mich. State U. Health Facilities, 1988-90, chmn. med. staff exec. and steering coms., 1988-90; chmn. of anesthesia St. Lawrence Hosp., Lansing, Mich., 1984-90, adminstrv. dir. dept. anesthesia and pain mgmt., 1994-98. Chief of staff Sheridan Cmty. Hosp., 1968-69; adminstrv. coun. Mich. State U., 1988-97, acad. coun., 1992-96, faculty coun., 1992-96, U. hearing bd., 2000-02, bylaws com., 2000-04, clin. practice bd., bd. dirs. sports medicine, athletic coun., 2003-05, pres.'s adv. com. on disability issues, 2007-; internal mgmt. com. Mich. Ctr. for Rural Health; cons. Ministry Health, Belize, Calif., 1993-97; amb. Midwestern U. Consortium Internat. Activities, 1993; chmn. com. student performance, 2002-03, COSE, 2002-05, com. on acad. policy, 2000-05, admission com., 2000-06, 2010-, chmn. admissions com., 2003-07, MOA-MSUCOM liaison com. chair 2005-08; adv. com. on pain mgmt. State of Mich., 1999-2001; program chmn. Am. Russian Med. Exch., 1993-97; bd. dirs. Belize Med. Partnership; internat. studies and programs advisive and consultive com. MSU, 2008-10; adv. com. Internat. Studies Programs, 2008-, advisor, Internat. Health Programs MSU, Anthesia Interest Group, Generate Help Heal Generations. Spkr. Sta. WKAR, Mich. State U.; bd. dirs. Boy Scouts Am., W. Bloomfield, Mich., 1973-74, Palm Beach Mental Health, 1977-79, Care Choices HMO, Lansing, 1987-88; mem. ISP MSU, 2008-; mem. athletic coun. Mich. State U., 2003-05, self study subcom. NCAA, 2004-05. Fellow Am. Coll. Osteo. Anesthesiologists; mem. AMA, Am. Osteo. Coll. Anesthesiology (chmn. commn. on colls. 1988-89), Soc. Critical Care Medicine, Internat. Anesthesiology Rsch. Soc., Am. Coll. Physician Execs., Am. Osteo. Assn. (spkr., mem. evaluators registry), Am. Acad. Pain Mgmt., Am. Arbitration Assn., Mich. State Med. Soc., Mich. Pain Soc., Mich. Peer Rev. Orgn., Mich. Osteo. Assn. (chmn. edn. com. 2002-08), Ingham County Med. Soc. (edn. com.), Am. Soc. Regional Anesthesia, Soc. Security Disability Evaluation, Soc. Internat. Scholars; Phi Beta Delta. Office: Mich State U West Fee Hall East Lansing MI 48824 Office Phone: 517-353-8470. Business E-Mail: beckmey1@msu.edu.

BECKSON, MACE, psychiatrist; b. NYC, Aug. 6, 1959; s. Karl and Estelle Beckson; m. Ann Marie Davis, June 16, 1989. AB magna cum laude, Harvard U., 1980; MD, Cornell U., 1985. Diplomate forensic psychiatry and addiction psychiatry Am. Bd. Psychiatry and Neurology, Am. Bd. Addiction Medicine, lic. Physician State of Calif., diplomate forensic suicidologist Am. Assn. Suicidology. Intern N.Y. Hosp.-Payne Whitney Clinic, NYC, 1985—86; resident, chief resident UCLA Neuropsychiatric Inst., 1986—89; neurobehavior fellow UCLA Sch. Medicine, 1989—91; rsch. psychiatrist NIDA-VA Med. Devel., LA, 1991—97; program chief alcohol and drug treatment VA Med. Ctr., LA, 1992—95, chief intensive OPT treatment of addictions, 1995—97; med. dir. PICU VA Greater L.A. Healthcare Sys., 1998—, forensic psychiatrist, expert witness, 1998—; clin. prof. dept. psychiatry UCLA, 2005—, tng. supr. psychiatry residents, 1988—. Contbr. articles and chpts. to profl. jours. Recipient VA Innovations of Care Recognition award, Dept. Vet. Affairs, Dir.'s Recognition award, VA Spl. Contbn. award, Oskar Diethelm prize, Cornell U. Med. Coll., 1985. Fellow: Am. Psychiat. Assn. (disting. fellow); mem.: Calif. Psychiat. Assn. (jud. action com.), Am. Assn. Suicidology, Internat. Soc. Traumatic Stress Studies, Am. Acad. Psychiatry & Law (chmn. addiction psychiatry com. 2004—09). Office Phone: 310-966-1907. Business E-Mail: becksonmd@becksonmd.com.

BECKWITH, CHARLES ALLAN, healthcare administrator, consultant; b. LA, Feb. 15, 1940; s. Harry Spencer and Mary Dorothy (Riley) B.; m. Roberta Louise Sommerdorf, Nov. 27, 1963 (dec. Jan. 1966); m. Susan Ann Robinson, Aug. 24, 1969; 1 child, Mary Aileen. BS in Psychology, Loyola-Marymount U., 1962; cert., George Washington U., 1989; M of Profl. Studies: Hosp. and Health Svcs. Adminstrn., Cornell U., 1976. Adminstr. Grover M. Hermann divsn. Comty. Gen. Hosp. Sullivan County, Callicoon, N.Y., 1976-77, assoc. dir. Harris, N.Y., 1977-78; adminstr. for ambulatory care USPHS Hosp., Balt., 1978-81; program cons. Office Ambulatory Care Bur. Med. Svcs., Hyattsville, Md., 1981; adminstr. area contract health svcs., program/internal auditor Albuquerque Area Indian Health Svc., 1981-84, internal auditor Office of Area Dir., 1984; sr. internal auditor Calif. Area Indian Health Svc., Sacramento, 1984-89, spl. adminstrv. asst., 1989—. Mem. health svcs. adminstrn. adv. bd. Sch. Pub. Adminstrn., U. So. Calif., 1988-93; adminstrv. residency preceptor for M. of Healthcare Adminstrn. students Sacramento campus U. So. Calif., 1992-94; presenter profl. papers ann. meeting USPHS Profl. Assn., Scottsdale, Ariz., 1988, 93; mem. Sloan Program Hosp. and Health Svcs. Adminstrn., Grad. Sch. Bus. and Pub. Adminstrn., Cornell U., 1976; presenter in field. Contbr. articles to profl. publs. Alumni admissions interviewer Johnson Grad. Sch. Mgmt., Cornell U., 1985—; co-master of ceremony duties for commemorative awards Indian Health Svcs. Honor Awards Ceremony, Rockville, Md., 1989, 91. Capt. USPHS, 1978—. Decorated Bronze Star medal; recipient Calif. Area Dir.'s award for Managerial Excellence for leadership in advancement of healthcare adminstrn., 1994, award of appreciation Combined Fed. Campaign Coord., 1993, award for Area Office with Best Overall Performance, U.S. Savs. Bond Campaign Coord., 1994, PHS Outstanding Svc. medal, 2 PHS Commendation medals, PHS Citation and Unit Citation. Fellow Am. Coll. Healthcare Execs. (membership examiner); mem. Commd. Officers Assn. Roman Catholic. Achievements include initiation and coordination of first epidemiology study of California Indian health status. *

BECKWITH, JONATHAN ROGER, geneticist; b. Cambridge, Mass., Dec. 25, 1935; s. Manuel and Mildred B.; m. Barbara Shutt, Dec. 26, 1960; children— Benjamin Hunter, Anthony Rhys. AB in Chemistry, Harvard U., 1957, PhD in Biomedical Sciences, 1961; LHD (hon.), U. Mass., Lowell, 2005. Tchg. asst. U. Ill., Urbana, 1960; mem. faculty Harvard Med. Sch., 1965—, assoc. dept bacteriology and immunology, 1965, asst. prof. dept. bacteriology and immunology, 1966—68, assoc. prof. dept. bacteriology and immunology, 1968—69, prof. dept. bacteriology and immunology, 1969—, prof. dept. microbiology and molecular genetics, 1969—, Am. Cancer Soc. prof., dept. microbiology and molecular genetics, 1971—, chmn. dept. microbiology and molecular genetics, 1971—73, dir. genetics training grant, 1975—2000; American Cancer Soc. rsch. prof., 1980—. Mem. scientific adv. bd. New England BioLabs, Beverly, Mass., 1981—91, Internat. Inst. of Genetics and Biophysics, Naples, Italy, 1986—90, Ctr. for Microbial Sciences, San Diego, 2002—; vis. prof. U. Calif., Berkeley, 1985; mem. adv. bd. Coun. for Responsible Genetics, 1985—, Eritrean Relief Com., 1985—, Program in Science, Technology and Soc. Program, Kennedy Sch. Govt., Harvard U., 2002—; mem. Working Group on Ethical, Legal and Social Implications of the Human Genome Project, Nat. Ctr. for Human Genome Rsch., NIH, 1989—95; pres. bd. dirs. Science for the People, 1990—93; Samuel Rudin vis. prof. Columbia U. Coll. of Physicans & Surgeons, 1991; cons. Genentech Corp., 1994—98; mem. Behavioral Genetics Working Group, Hastings Ctr., 2000—02; spkr. in field. Published Genetic Discrimination as a Consequence of Genetic Testing, 1992, The Responsibilities of Scientists in the Genetics and Race Controversies, 1997, (memoir) Making Genes, Making Waves: A Social Activist in Science, 2002;, author scientific publs.; contbr. articles to profl. jours.; mem. of several editl. bds. NIH postdoctoral fellow 1961-65, Guggenheim Fellowship, 1970; recipient Eli Lilly award for Outstanding Achievements in Microbiology, 1970, Merit award, NIH, 1986, Edinburgh medal, 2009 Fellow AAAS, Am. Acad. of Microbiology; mem. NAS (Selman A. Waksman award in microbiology, 2009), Am. Acad. Arts and Scis., European Molecular Biology Orgn. (assoc.), Am. Soc. Exptl. Biologists, Am. Soc. Microbiology (Abbott-ASM Lifetime Achievement award, 2005), Genetics Soc. Am. (medal, 1993), Phi Beta Kappa (hon.) Achievements include research and publs. in bacterial genetics and social implications of genetics; made history in 1969 as the first researcher to isolate a single gene. Home: 8A Appleton Rd Cambridge MA 02138 Office: Dept Microbiology and Molecular Genetics Harvard Med Sch 200 Longwood Ave Boston MA 02115 Office Phone: 617-432-1920, 617-432-1788. Office Fax: 617-738-7664. Business E-Mail: jbeckwith@hms.harvard.edu, jon_beckwith@hms.harvard.edu.

BEDIGUIAN, MARIAMIG JINX, operating room nurse; b. Neptune, NJ, July 13, 1956; d. Haig Leon and Mary (Durna) B. BSN, George Mason U., 1979. RN, Va., N.J.; cert. nurse operating room, 1983. Operating room staff nurse Jersey Shore Med. Ctr., Neptune, 1979—, clinical scholar, svc. leader gynecology and laser, 1992-94, svc. leader gen., gynecology and genitourinary endoscopy, 1994-98; operating rm. staff nurse Monmouth Med. Ctr., Long Branch, N.J., 1994-96. Focus panel mem., oper. rm. cons. Ansell Med. Corp., Eatontown, N.J., 1993; oper. rm. cons. Armenian Gen. Benevolent Union, Saddle Brook, N.J., Plastic and Reconstructive Surgery Ctr., Yerevan, Armenia, 1992. Recipient Chief Residents award Jersey Shore Med. Ctr. Obs.-Gyn. Residency Program, 1993, Florence Nightingale award, Jersey Shore Med. Ctr., 2001, United Surgical Ptnrs., Inc. Nursing Clin. Excellence award, 2004. Mem. Assn. Oper. Rm. Nurses (product fair co-chair 1987-90, 93, chair seminar com. 1985, chair program com. 1985-88, 99-2002, v.p. 1983-85, 2009-, bd. dirs. 1985-89, 95-97, audit com. 1987-88, Congress del. 1984-, 2009, 11, alt. del. 1987, chair 2009, 11), Nat. Assn. Orthopaedic Nurses (bd. dirs. 1994-2009, chair program com. 1998—), Am. Nurse Assn., N.J. State Nurses Assn., Va. State Nurse Assn., George Mason U. Coll. Nursing Alumni Assn., George Mason U. Alumni Assn., U. Mary Washington Alumni Assn., Armenian Students Assn., Armenian Am. Health Profls. Orgn., Armenian Am. Nurses Assn., Phi Mu (rec. sec. 1977-78), Sigma Theta Tau Hon. Nursing Soc. Avocations: music, languages, travel, dance. Home: 12 Inlet Ter Belmar NJ 07719-2142 Office: Operating Rm Jersey Shore Med Ctr 1945 Corlies Ave Neptune NJ 07753-4896

BEDNAREK, DANIEL R., medical physicist, educator; b. Buffalo, Mar. 22, 1947; PhD, U. Chgo., 1978. Prof. SUNY, Buffalo, 1978—. Med. physicist Erie County Med. Ctr., 1978—2011. Recipient Lifetime Svc. award, Am. Bd. Radiology, 1st prize, Blue Ribbon, Soc. Photo-Optical Instrumentation Engrs., 1999, 2000, Merit award, Radiol. Soc. N.Am., 1993, 1995, 1996, 1997, 1998, 2000, 2001, 2002; Tng. grant, Nat. Inst. Health. Fellow: Am. Assn. Physicists Medicine; mem.: Upstate NY Assn. Physicists Medicine, Soc. Imaging Informatics Medicine, Soc. Photo-Optical Instrumentation Engrs., Am. Coll. Radiology. Avocation: gardening. Office: Erie County Medical Ctr Radiology 462 Grider St Buffalo NY 14215 Business E-Mail: bednarek@buffalo.edu.

BEDNAREK, PIOTR TOMASZ, molecular biologist, chemist; s. Zenon and Iwonna Bednarek; m. Ewa Romanczuk-Bednarek; 1 child, Artur. PhD, Lomonosov Moscow State U., 1991. Sr. prof. asst. Bot. Garden, CBDC, PAS, Warsaw, 1993—2004; sr. prof. asst., Plant Breeding & Acclimatization Inst., Blonie, Poland, 2003—. Translator tech. transl. (pl, gb, ru). Achievements include patents pending for PCT PCT/PL05/000083. A molecular marker based system was developed to give qualitative and quantitative characteristics of tissue culture induced and somaclonal variation. Office: Plant Breeding & Acclimatization Inst Radzików Blonie 05-870 Poland Personal E-mail: p.t.bednarek@gmail.com. Business E-Mail: p.bednarek@ihar.edu.pl.

BEDNOFF, STUART LEON, obstetrician, gynecologist, educator; b. NYC, Aug. 31, 1936; MD, SUNY, 1961. Diplomate Am. Bd. Ob/gyn. Intern L.I. Jewish Hosp., NYC, 1961-62; resident in ob/gyn. North Shore U. Hosp., Manhasset, N.Y., 1962-66, mem. staff, 1965; pvt. practice, Gt. Neck, N.Y., 1968. Clin. assoc. prof. dept. ob-gyn. NYU Sch. Medicine. Fellow ACOG, ACS; mem. Nassau Obstetricians/Gynecologists. Office Phone: 516-482-8741. *

BEDWORTH, DAVID ALBERT, health educator; b. Cortland, NY, Mar. 31, 1949; s. Albert Ernest and Agnes Sheldon (Franklin) B.; children: Jodi Michele, Michael David. BS, Butler U., 1971; MS, U. Ill., 1972, PhD, 1976. Instr. Russell Sage Coll., Troy, NY, 1973-75; asst. prof. SUNY, Brockport, 1976-78; program coord. Heart Health Edn. R.I., Pawtucket, 1978-79; prof. SUNY, Plattsburgh, 1979—.

Cmty. edn. cons. STOP Ctr. for Domestic Violence, Plattsburgh, 1982; drug edn. cons. Federal Correction Instn., Ray Brook, N.Y., 1982, Ticonderoga (N.Y.) Ctrl. Sch. Dist., 1985. Author: (with Albert E. Bedworth) Health Education: A Process for Human Effectivess, 1978, Health for Human Effectiveness, 1982, The Profession and Practice of Health Education, 1992; contbr. articles to profl. jours., chpts. to books, The Dictionary of Health Education, 2009 Task force on youthful alcohol abuse N.Y. State Dept. Mental Hygiene, 1977; profl. edn. com. Am. Lung Assn., 1980-84, exec. com., 1981-82. Mem. APHA, ASCD, N.Y. State Fedn. Profl. Health Educators (pres. 1977). Democrat. Avocations: antiques, travel. Office: SUNY Plattsburgh NY 12901 Home Phone: 518-293-7228. Business E-Mail: david.bedworth@plattsburgh.edu.

BEECHER, LEE HEWITT, psychiatrist; b. Mpls., Feb. 18, 1939; s. James Morrison and Ruth Eleanor (Borgendale) Beecher; m. Mary Jane Heinen, June 10, 1978; children: James Arthur, Lynn Ruth. BA, Carleton Coll., 1961; MD, U. Minn., 1965. Lic. md State of Minn.; cert. in psychiatry ABPN, 1971, in addiction psychiatry ABPN, 2009. Resident U. Chgo., 1966—69; psychiatrist Mpls. Clin. Psychiatry and Neurology, Golden Valley, Minn., 1972—73; self employed Lee H. Beecher, St. Louis Park, Minn., 1973—. Bd. dir. Alliance for the Mentally Ill, Minn., 1982—91; assoc. med. dir. Preferred One, Golden Valley, Minn., 1991—95; adj. prof. U. Minn., Dept. Psychiatry, 2006. Contbr. articles numerous profl. jours. Lcdr USN, 1969—72, Hawaii. Recipient Pres. award, Minn. Med. Assn., 2004; named one of Top 100 Minn. Healthcare Leaders, Minn. Physician, 2004; Dist. Life fellow, Am. Psychiatric Assn., 2001. Fellow: Am. Soc. Addiction Medicine; mem.: Clin. Psychiatry News (edtl. adv. bd.), Minn. Physician Patient Alliance (pres. 1998—), Minn. Psychiatric Soc. (pres. 1987—89), Minn. Med. Assn. (trustee 1998—2005). Avocations: philosophy, travel. Home: 7574 Mariner Pt Maple Grove MN 55311-2617 Office: Lee H Beecher MD PA 6600 Excelsior Blvd Ste 121 Saint Louis Park MN 55426-4746 Office Phone: 952-935-7116. Office Fax: 952-935-0687.

BEER, JOHN VINCENT, pathologist, consultant; b. Newbury, Eng., May 3, 1928; s. Harold Vincent and Henrietta Elizabeth B. BSc, U. Reading, UK, 1948, Diploma in Gen. Bacteriology, 1950; PhD, U. Bristol, UK, 1960. Applied microbiologist Howards of Ilford Ltd., England, 1949-53; microbiologist Boots Ltd., Nottingham, England, 1953-54; pathologist Wildfowl Trust, Slimbridge, England, 1954-69; rsch. dir. Oiled Seabird Rsch. Unit, Newcastle, England, 1969-70; sr. pathologist The Game Conservancy Trust, Fordingbridge, England, 1971-93; cons. Gamebird Consultancy, Chard, England, 1993—. Hon. mem. Game Conservancy Trust. Author: Diseases of Gamebirds and Wildfowl, 1988, Egg Production and Incubation, 1982. Fellow The Wildfowl and Wetlands Trust, Zool. Soc. London; mem. Soc. Biology, World Assn. Wildlife Vets. (assoc.), Incubation and Fertility Rsch. Group, World Pheasant Assn., People to People. Avocations: photography, amateur dramatics, hill walking, natural history, amateur radio, travel, astronomy.

BEER, KARL THOMAS, radiation oncologist, consultant; b. Tegernsee, Germany, July 26, 1958; s. Karl and Johanna Beer; m. Marion Meister; children: Lukas Robert Thomas, Léon Jonathan Thomas. MD, Technische U., Munich, 1986. Bd. cert. in radiation oncology Foederatio Medicorum Helveticorum, Switzerland, cert. med. mgmt. Pvt. Hochschule Wirtschaft, Switzerland. Jr. dr. Inst. Strahlentherapie and Nuc. Medicine, Kilinkum Bayreuth, Germany, 1989—90, 1990, Kantonsspital Aarau, Switzerland, 1990—92, Inst. Röntgendiagnostik, 1989—90; resident Clinic Radio Oncology Inselspital U. Hosp. Bern, Switzerland, 1992—97, mem. staff, 1994—2005, sr. resident, 1997—2005; cons. Inselspital U. Hosp. Bern, 1995—2005, mem. Dept. Mgmt. Team, 2001—04, assoc. Working Group Enteral/Parental Nutrition, 2001—05, assoc. ecology commn., 2001—05; head dept. Ctr. Radio-oncologie, Biel-Bienne, 2005—. Cons. Burgerspital Solothurn, Switzerland, 2002—05. Contbr. articles to profl. jours. Office: Ctr de Radio-Oncologie Chemin des vignes 2503 Bienne Switzerland Home: Juraweg 3053 Berne Switzerland Office Fax: 0041323668112. Personal E-mail: familybeer@gmail.com. Business E-Mail: karl.beer@radioonkologie.ch.

BEER, KENNETH ROBERT, dermatologist; b. May 7, 1963; BS in Zoology magna cum laude, dean's list and honors, U. Oxford; AB, Duke U., 1981—85; MD, U. Pa., 1985—89. Diplomate Am. Bd. of Dermatology, 1993, Am. Bd. of Dermatology-Dermatopathology, 1995, cert. recertified in dermatology with specialization in dermatologic surgery and dermatopathology 2001, lic. Fla. Bd. of Health, Calif. Bd. of Medicine, Ill. Dept. of Profl. Regulation, NY State Dept. of Medicine. Internship in internal medicine Grad. Hosp., Pa., 1989—90; resident in dermatology Univ. Chgo., 1990—93, fellow in dermatopathology, 1993—94; fellow Am. Soc. for Laser Medicine and Surgery, Am. Soc. for Dermatologic Surgery, Am. Soc. for Mohs Surgery; founder & dir. Cosmetic Bootcamp LLC; founder Dermsoftware; voluntary assoc. prof. dermatology Univ. Miami, 1995—; consulting assoc. dept. of medicine Duke Univ., 1998—; section chief dermatology Good Samaritan Med. Ctr., mem. exec. bd. Instr. Am. Acad. of Dermatology, 2001—; preceptor Am. Soc. for Dermatologic Surgery, 2002—; instr. allergan Medicis, Sanofi Aventis, Stiefel, 2004—. Mem.: Assn. for the Study of Lung Cancer, Am. Soc. of Cosmetic Dermatology & Aesthetic Surgery, Am. Soc. for Dermatopathology, Am. Acad. of Dermatology, Phi Beta kappa, Duke Univ., Assn. of Clin. Rsch. Professionals. Office: Kenneth Beer MD. PA. Suite 305 1500 North Dixie Hwy West Palm Beach FL 33401 Office Phone: 561-655-9055. Office Fax: 561-655-9233.

BEER, TOMASZ M., physician; b. Warsaw, 1965; MD, Johns Hopkins U., 1991. Diplomate Am. Bd. Internal Medicine. Intern Oreg. Health Scis. U., Portland, 1991-92, resident internal medicine, 1992-94, chief resident, medicine, 1995—96, fellow, hematology and med. oncology, 1996—99, prof., medicine oncology, 2009—, dir., prostate cancer program, Grover C. Bagby Endowed Chair for Prostate Cancer Rsch., dep. dir. Knight Cancer Inst., 2009—. Mem. ACP, Oreg. Med. Assn., Am. Soc. Clin. Oncology, Am. Soc. Hematology, Am. Assn. Cancer Rsch., SW Oncology Group. Achievements include patents for Vitamin D and its analogs in the treatment of tumors and other hyperproliferative disorders. Office: Oreg Health Scis Univ 3303 SW Bond Ave CHI4R Portland OR 97239 Office Phone: 503-494-6594.

BEERING, STEVEN CLAUS, academic administrator, medical educator; b. Berlin, Aug. 20, 1932; arrived in U.S., 1948, naturalized, 1953; s. Steven and Alice (Friedrichs) Beering; m. Catherine Jane Pickering, Dec. 27, 1956; children: Peter, David, John. BS summa cum laude, U. Pitts., 1954, MD, 1958, ScD (hon.), 1998; DSc (hon.), Ind. Cen. U., 1983, U. Evansville, Ind., 1984, Ramapo Coll., 1986, Anderson Coll., 1987, Purdue U., 2000; ScD (hon.), Ind. U., 1988; LLD (hon.), Hanover Coll., 1986, Tex. Wesleyan, 2001, Notre Dame U., 2009. Intern Walter Reed Gen. Hosp., Washington, 1958—59; resident Wilford Hall Med. Center, San Antonio, 1959—62, chief internal medicine, edn. coordinator, 1967—69; prof. medicine Ind. U. Sch. Medicine, Indpls., 1969—, asst. dean, 1969—70, assoc. dean, dir. postgrad. edn., 1970—74, dir. statewide med. edn. system, 1970-83, dean, 1974—83; chief exec. officer Ind. U. Med. Center, Indpls., 1974—83; pres. Purdue U. and Purdue U. Rsch. Found., West Lafayette, Ind., 1983—2000, pres. emeritus, 2000—; dir. emeritus Purdue Rsch. Found., West Lafayette, 2006—. Prof. pharmacology and toxicology Purdue U.; bd. dirs. NISource, Inc.; chmn. Med. Edn. Bd. Ind., 1974—83, Liaison Com. Med. Edn., 1976—81, Ind. Commn. Med. Edn., 1978—83; mem. Nat. Sci. Bd., NSF, 2002—, chmn., 2006—10. Contbr. articles to sci. jours. Sec. Ind. Atty. Gen.'s Trust, 1974—83; regent Nat. Libr. Medicine, 1987—91; trustee U. Pitts., 2000—. Lt. col. M.C. USAF, 1957—69. Fellow: ACP, Royal Soc. Medicine; mem.: Nat. Sci. Bd., Ind. Acad., Nat. Acad. Sci. Inst. of Medicine, Assn. Am. Univs. (chair 1995—96), Coun. Med. Deans (chmn. 1980—81), Assn. Am. Med. Colls. (chmn. 1982—83), Endocrine Soc., Am. Diabetes Assn., Am. Fedn. Med. Rsch., Meridian Hills Club, Skyline Club, Phi Rho Sigma (US v.p. 1976—85), Alpha Omega Alpha, Sigma Xi, Phi Beta Kappa. Presbyterian. Home: 10487 Windemere Dr Carmel IN 46032 Office: Purdue U Office Pres Emeritus Rm 218 Memorial Union West Lafayette IN 47906-3584 Home Phone: 317-581-1414; Office Phone: 765-496-7555. Personal E-mail: sbeering@indy.rr.com. Business E-Mail: scb@purdue.edu.

BEERMAN, LEE BANKIN, pediatric cardiologist, educator; MD, U. of Pitts., 1974. Diplomate Am. Bd. Pediatrics, Am. Bd. Pediatrics-pediatric cardiology, lic. Nat. Bd. Med. Examiners. Resident Children's Hosp. of Phila., 1977, fellow, 1979; dir. electrophysiology svcs. Children's Hosp. of Pitts. of UPMC, dir. pediatric arrhythmia program; prof. pediatrics Univ. of Pitts. Co-author of numerous publications. Recipient Fellowship award, Western Pa. Heart Assn., Excellence in Education award; named one of Best Doctors in America, America's Top Doctors, Castle Connolly Group. Fellow: Am. Coll. of Cardiology, Am. Acad. of Pediatrics; mem.: Heart Rhythm Soc., N. Am. Soc. of Pacing and Electrophysiology, Med.Alumni Assn. of Children's Hosp. of Pitts., Soc. of Pediatric Electrophysiology, Am. Heart Assn. Coun. on Cardiovasc. Disease in the Young, Soc. of Pediatric Echocardiography, Pitts. Pediatric Soc., Midwest Pediatric Cardiology Soc., Am. Coll. of Cardiology, Am. Heart Assn. (Western Pa. Chapt.). Office: Childrens Hospital of Pittsburgh of UPMC 1 Childrens Hospital Drive 4401 Penn Ave Pittsburgh PA 15224 Office Phone: 412-692-5540. E-mail: lee.beerman@chp.edu.

BEESER, HEINZ PETER, hematologist, educator; b. Meerbusch, North Rhine Westfalia, Germany, Sept. 8, [illegible] Maria Elisabeth (Hermes) B.; m. Maria Anna Davids, July 29, 1959; children: Jutta Maria, Markus Maria, Beate Maria. Degree in pharmacy, U. Bonn, Germany, 1960, MD, 1965, PhD, 1970. Pharmacist pub. pharmacy, Meersbusch, Fed. Republic Germany, 1960-62; asst. prof. physiology U. Bonn, 1962-74, assoc. prof. exptl. hematology, 1974-82; head dept. transfusion and coagulation U. Freiburg, Germany, 1983—. Bd. dirs. Inst. Standardization in the Med. Lab., Düsseldorf, Germany, 1980—; head com. on hemostasis German Stds. Com., Berlin, 1978—, mem. various other standards coms., 1974—, head standards area com. on lab. medicine, 1994—; dir. Inst. Quality Mgmt. and Standardization in Hemostaseology and Transfusion Medicine, Teningen, Germany, 1999—. Author: Prothrombin, Biochemistry, Physiology, Pathology, 1970, Hematology, 1991; editor: Liver and Hemostasis, 1973, Deutsches Institut für Normung Standard Procedures in the Hemostasis Lab., 1994;: 2d edit., 2002. Mem. Internat. Soc. Thrombosis and Hemostasis, Internat. Soc. Blood Transfusion, Am. Assn. Blood Banks, World Fedn. Hemophilia, German Assn. for Plasmapheresis (chmn. 1995—). Roman Catholic. Avocations: sailing, diving, trekking, travel. Office: Inst for Quality Mgmt Klausenstrasse 13 D-79331 Teningen Germany Office Phone: 49 7663 3346.

BEESON, MONTEL EILEEN, retired human services administrator, gerontologist; b. El Dorado, Ark., Dec. 22, 1939; d. Waymon Willett and Myrtle May (Roach) B. BS Recreation, Calif. State U., Hayward, 1963; MA Edn. and Human Devel., Holy Names Coll., Oakland, Calif., 1979. Lic. nursing home adminstr.; cert. cmty. coll. instr.; cert. in gerontology. Dist. exec. Ariz. Cactus-Pine coun. Girl Scouts U.S.A., Phoenix, 1963—66, dist. exec. San Francisco Bay coun. Oakland, Calif., 1966—68, bus. mgr., 1968—71, exec. dir. Shabonee coun. Moline, Ill., 1971—73, exec. dir. Tongass-Alaska coun. Ketchikan, 1973—74, exec. dir. Muir Trail coun. Modesto, Calif., 1974—78; asst. adminstr. Beulah Home, Inc., Oakland, 1980—86; exec. dir. Cmty. Adult Day Health Svcs., Oakland, 1987—88, Greenhills Retirement Ctr., Millbrae, Calif., 1988—99; elder care cons., 1986—. Mem.: Am. Soc. on Aging. Avocations: history, travel, reading, music. Personal E-mail: maxandm@sbcglobal.net.

BEETON, ALFRED MERLE, lab administrator, director, biologist, educator, environmentalist; b. Denver, Aug. 15, 1927; s. Charles Frederick and Edna F. (Smith) B.; m. Mary Eileen Wilcox, July 20, 1945; children: Maureen Ann, Heather Ann, Celeste Nadine; m. Ruth Elizabeth Holland, June 4, 1966; children: Jonathan Eugene, Daniel Paul. BS, U. Mich., 1952, MS, 1954, PhD, 1958; DSc (hon.), U. Wis., Milw., 1996. Fishery biologist U.S. Bur. Comml. Fisheries, Ann Arbor, Mich., 1957—65, chief environ. research, 1960—65; prof. zoology U. Wis.-Milw., 1966—76, asst. dir. Ctr. for Gt. Lakes Studies, 1966—69, assoc. dir. Ctr. for Gt. Lakes Studies, 1969—73; assoc. dean U. Wis.-Milw. (Grad. Sch.), 1973—76; dir. Gt. Lakes and Marine Waters Ctr., Mich. Sea Grant; prof. engrng. and natural resources U. Mich., Ann Arbor, 1976—86; dir. Gt. Lakes Environ. Research Lab., Nat. Oceanic and Atmospheric Adminstrn. Dept. Commerce, Ann Arbor, 1986—96, emeritus, 2002—, acting chief scientist Nat Oceanic & Atmospheric Adminstrn. Washington, 1996—97, sr. sci. advisor, 1998—2002. Instr. biology Wayne State U., 1956—57, lectr. biology, 1957—61; lectr. civil engrng. U. Mich., 1961—65; U.S. chmn. Sci. Adv. Bd. Internat. Joint Commn., 1986—91; mem. Mich. Toxic Substance Control Commn., 1987—89; mem. rsch. adv. coun. Wis. Dept. Natural Resources; mem. water quality criteria com. Nat. Acad. Scis.; cons. U.S. Army C.E., 1967—73, Met. San. Dist. Chgo., 1968—76, EPA, 1973—83; adviser on projects in Ghana, Laos and Yugoslavia Smithsonian Instn., 1972—82; adviser WHO/Pan Am. Health Orgn., Venezuela, 1978; mem. environ. program com. NRC, 1976—82, internat. environ. program com., 1977—82, mem. environ. studies bd.; adj. vis. prof. Oreg.State U., 1982; mem. Coun. Great Lakes Rsch. Mgrs., 1995—97; chmn. sci. adv. bd. NOAA, 1998—2002; mem. Ocean Rsch. Adv. Panel/Nat. Oceanographic Partnership Program, 2000—02; adj. prof. Sch. Pub. Health U. Mich., 1999—2009; bd. dirs. Ecology Ctr., 2006—, pres., 2010—. Contbr. chpts. to books; articles Ency. Brit. Mem.: Gt. Lakes Observing Sys. (bd. dirs. 2006—09), Mich. Acad. Sci., Arts and Letters, Internat. Assn. Gt. Lakes Rsch., Am. Soc. Limnology and Oceanography (treas. 1962—81), Internat. Assn. Theoretical and Applied Limnology (nat. rep. for U.S. 1976—95), Detroit Audubon Soc. (bd. dirs. 2002—04), Mich. Sierra Club (exec. com. 2006—). Home: 2761 Oakcleft St Ann Arbor MI 48103-2247 Personal E-mail: beeton@att.net.

BEEVER, JAMES WILLIAM, III, biologist; b. Balt., Aug. 17, 1955; s. James William, Jr. and Virginia Irene (Ruhlmann) Beever; m. Lisa Britt Dodd, May 26, 1990. BS, Fla. State U., 1977, MS, 1979; postgrad., U. Calif., Davis, 1984. Environ. specialist Fla. Dept. Environ. Regulation, Ft. Myers, 1984—88; coord. resource mgmt. and rsch. S.W. Fla. Aquatic Preserves, Bokeelia, 1988—90; biol. scientist III Fla. Game and Fresh Water Fish Commn., Punta Gorda, 1990—98; biol. scientist IV Fla. Fish and Wildlife Conservation Commn., Punta Gorda, 1998—2006; prin. planner S.W. Fla. Regional Planning Coun., 2006—. Mem. tech. adv. bd. Sarasota Bay and Tampa Bay Nat. Estuary Program; mem. policy com. and tech. adv. com. Charlotte Harbor Nat. Estuary Program, 1989—2006; chair sci. com. on Mangrove Tech. Adv. Com. Fla. Dept. Environ. Protection, 1994—95; coord. Conservation Plan Hillsborough River Greenway Area, 1995; founder Frog Listening Network, 1997; chair Estero Bay Agy. on Bay Mgmt., 1999—2006; expert witness in field, 1986—. Author: (book) Lemon Bay Aquatic Preserve Management Plan, 1988, The Cedar Point Study, 1992, Hydric Pine Flatwoods of Southwest Florida, 1994, (database) Resource Inventory of Species in S.W. Fla., Coastal Conservation Corridor Plan, Climate Change Vulnerability Assessment For SW Florida, 2009; contbr. articles to profl. jours. Recipient Grad. Rsch. award, 1982—83, Outstanding Profl. Achievements award, Fla. DNR, 1989, Spl. Chmn.s award, Fla. Wildlife Fedn./Nat. Wildlife Fedn., 2000, Guy Bradley award, 2001; Regents fellow, U. Calif., 1983—84. Mem.: Ecol. Soc. Am., Soc. Conservation Biology, Soc. Wetland Scientists, Estuarine Rsch. Fedn., Fla. Acad. Sci., Sigma Xi, Phi Beta Kappa. Achievements include research in mangrove tree crab and arboreal folivores; mangrove cutting; endangered species protection; red cockaded woodpeckers; hydric pine flatwoods; xeric oak scrub; salt marshes regional wildlife habitat/wildlife corridor planning; designation Florida ecosystems; hydrogeomorphic method for the Everglades; coastal methods functional assessment, climate change vulnerability resiliency and adaptation in SW Florida. Office: SW Fla Regional Planning Coun 1926 Victoria Ave Fort Myers FL [illegible] Office Phone: 239-338-2550, ext. 224. Personal E-mail: jlbeever@aol.com. Business E-Mail: jbeever@swfrpc.org.

BEGGS, WILLIAM H., microbiologist, researcher; b. Ft. Dodge, Iowa, Feb. 19, 1935; s. Harold William and Bliss Jewel (Swanstrom) Beggs; m. Nancy Florence Ost, Sept. 14, 1957 (dec. June 1995); children: John W., Margaret B. BA, U. Minn., 1956; PhD, U. Cin., 1964. Rsch. microbiologist Dept. Vets. Affairs Med. Ctr., Mpls., 1965—. Bd. dirs. Minn. Vets. Rsch. Inst., Mpls. Contbr. articles to profl. jours. and conf. procs. 1st lt. US Army, 1956—58, Tex., Kans., La. Mem.: Am. Soc. Microbiology. Achievements include research in chemical properties, biological activities, modes of action and chemotherapeutic potentials of antituberculosis and antifungal drugs. Avocations: tennis, travel, hiking, music.

BEGHI, MASSIMILIANO, psychiatrist; b. Legnano, Italy, Jan. 2, 1979; Degree in Medicine and Surgery, U. Milano-Bicocca, 2003, degree in Psychiatry, 2008. Psychiatrist G. Salvini Hosp., Garbagnate Milanse, Milan, 2009—. Avocations: tennis, chess. Home: via Cairoli 14 Legnano Milan 20025 Italy Personal E-mail: massibeghi@libero.it.

BEGLEY, CHRISTOPHER B., pharmaceutical executive; b. Chgo., Apr. 13, 1952; married; 3 children. BBA, Western Ill. U.; MBA, No. Ill. U. V.p. mktg. V. Mueller Divsn., Am. Hosp. Supply Corp.; various positions Abbott Laboratory, Inc., Abbott Park, Ill., 1986—90, divisional v.p., gen. mgr. hosp. products bus. sector, 1990—93, v.p. hosp. products bus. sector, 1993—96, v.p. MediSense, Inc., 1996—98, v.p. Abbott HealthSystems, 1998—99, sr. v.p. chem. and agrl. products, 1999—2000, pres. hospital products div., 2000—04; CEO Hospira, Inc., Lake Forest, Ill., 2004—07, chmn., CEO, 2007—11, exec. chmn., 2011—. Bd. dir. Children's Meml. Hosp., Chgo.; mem. Healthcare Leadership Council, AdvaMed; mem. civic com. Comml. Club Found. Mem.: Econ. Club Chgo., Executives Club Chgo. Office: Hospira Inc 275 North Field Dr Lake Forest IL 60045 *

BEHBEHANI, RAED, ophthalmologist; MD, Kuwait Faculty Medicine, 1996. Diplomate Am. Bd. Ophthalmology, 2004, cert. Royal Coll. Physicians Surgeons Can., 2003. Residency in ophthalmology Dalhousie U., Canada, 1998—2003; fellowship neuro-ohthalmology Wills Eye Hosp., Phila., 2003—05; cons. ophthalmologist, neuroophthalmologist Ibn Sina Hosp., Kuwait Ministry Health, 2005—. Fellow: Royal Coll. Physicians and Surgeons of Can.; mem.: Am. Acad. Ophthalmology, N. Am. Neuro-ophthalmology Soc. Avocations: reading, drawing. Office Phone: 968-2563-6988. Personal E-mail: rsbehbehani@gmail.com.

BEHBEHANIAN, MAHIN FAZELI, surgeon; b. Kermanshah region, Iran; arrived in U.S., 1959; d. M Jaafar and Ozra (A.) B.; m. Abolfath H. Fazeli, Sept, 4, 1969; children: Pouneh, Pontea. BS, Wilmington Coll., Ohio, 1961; MD, Med. Coll. Pa., Phila., 1965. Diplomate Am. Bd. Surgery. Gen. surgeon Lankenan Hosp., Phila., 1970; chief surgery, pres. med. staff Imperial Ct. Hosp., Teheran, Iran, 1971-79; gen. surgery Riddle Meml. Hosp., Media, Pa., 1980—; pvt. practice Phila., Chester, Media, Pa., 1984—. Chief subdivsn. gen. surgery Riddle Meml. Hosp., Media, 1998—. Editor-in-chief Behkoosh Jour. of Medicine, Teheran, 1976-79. Named Top Doctor, Main Line Mag., 2006-07, Top Surgeon, 2008; recipient Gilson Colby Engel award, 1966. Fellow: ACS; mem.: Del. County Med. Soc., Pa. Med. Soc., Am. Hernia Assn., Am. Soc. Breast Surgeons, Am. Women Surg. Soc. Office: Riddle Meml Health Care Ctr 1088 W Baltimore Pike Media PA 19063-5136 Office Phone: 610-565-6625. Personal E-mail: mahinmd@aol.com.

BEHLMAR, CINDY LEE, medical association administrator, management consultant; b. Smyrna, Tenn., July 4, 1959; d. James Wallace and Barbara Ann (Behlmar) Gribble. BBA, Coll. William and Mary, 1981; MBA, Old Dominion U., 1995. Cert. mgmt. acct.; gen. mediator. Adminstrv. extern Hampton Gen. Hosp., Va., 1981-82; from mktg. rep. to supr. mktg. svcs. PruCare of Richmond, Va., 1983-85; exec. dir. PhysicianCare, Inc., Newport News, Va., 1986-89; provider rels. cons. Va. Health Network, Richmond, 1989-91; ind. cons. Tidewater Health Care, Virginia Beach, Va., 1991-92; COO Tidewater Phys. Therapy, Inc., Newport News, 1993-95; ind. cons. Yorktown, Va., 1996-97; contract mgr. Sentara Health Mgmt., Virginia Beach, 1998-99; state mgr. managed care Va. Oncology Assocs., 1999—2004; adminstr. Peninsula Emergency Physicians, Inc., 2004—10. Sec., bd. dirs. Greater Peninsula Area Med.-Bus. Coalition, Newport News, 1987-89; symposium faculty mem. Am. Hosp. Assn., Orlando, Fla., 1987, Washington, 1988; profl. spkr. in field. Mem. ch. coun. St. Mark Luth. Ch., Yorktown, Va., 1988-91, Trinity Luth. Ch., Newport News, Va., 2008-10. Fin. Exec. Inst. scholar, 1993. Mem. Inst. Mgmt. Accts., Toastmasters Internat. (club pres. 1997-98, area gov. 1998-99, Club Toastmaster of Yr. 1997-98, Dist. Spirit Success award 1998, Dist. Area Gov. of Yr. 1998-99, Disting. Toastmaster 1999), Phi Kappa Phi, Beta Gamma Sigma. Avocations: reading, art, fashion, music, piano. Home: 922 Hanson Dr Newport News VA 23602-8910

BEHM, DUTSI, physician; b. Uzhgorod, Ukraine, Aug. 2, 1948; came to U.S., 1978; d. Aron and Rose Akerman; m. Ernest Behm, Aug. 20, 1972; 1 child, Thomas. MD with honors, Uzhgorod State U., 1973. Resident in medicine N.Y. Meth. Hosp., Bklyn., 1980-83; physician in pvt. practice, Bklyn., 1983—. Mem. ACP. Jewish. Avocation: music (opera). Home: 2364 E 66th St Brooklyn NY 11234-6326

BEHNEY, CLYDE JOSEPH, health policy association administrator, researcher; b. Williamstown, Pa., May 19, 1946; s. Clyde J. Behney and Gladys Yvonne (Host) Williams; children: Lindsay, Fletcher, Taylor. BS, Lehigh U., 1968; MBA, U. Md., 1972; postgrad., George Washington U., 1975—82. Staff asst. US Dept. Health, Edn., & Welfare, Washington, 1972-74, mgmt. intern, 1974-77; analyst/project dir. Office Tech. Assessment US Congress, Washington, 1977-81, health program mgr. Office Tech. Assessment, 1981-93, asst. dir. Office Tech. Assessment, 1993-96; dir. divsn. health care svcs. Inst. Medicine, NAS, 1996-97, dep. dir., 1997—, interim exec. officer, 1998, 2007, acting dir. healthcare svcs. bd., 2005—06, 2006—07, dep. exec. officer. Exec. dir. Sorcerer's Apprentice Network, Washington, 1981—85, 1998—; mem. steering com. Nat. Health Policy Forum, 1998—2000; adv. com. mem. George Washington Univ. Pub. Health Program, 1999—; mem. tech. adv. bd. Millbank Meml. Fund, NYC, 1998—2002; liaison mem., bd. dirs. Nat. Quality Forum, 2005—07. Co-author: Toward Rational Technology in Medicine, 1981; editor: (newsletter) The Sorcerer's Apprentice, 1981-85; mem. editl. bd. Internat. Jour. Tech. Assessment in Health Care, 1985-98; contbr. articles to profl. jours.; chpts. to books. Treas. Glebe Elem. PTA, Arlington, Va., 1990—94, Swanson Mid. Sch. PTSA, Arlington, 1994—96, Yorktown H.S. PTA, 2001—02, 2005—06. Sgt. US Army, 1969—71. Home: 2515 N Vermont St Arlington VA 22207-4125 Office: Institute of Medicine 500 Fifth St NW Keck 838 Washington DC 20001 Business E-Mail: cbehney@nas.edu.

BEHNKE, MARYLOU, pediatrician, educator; b. Orlando, Fla., Sept. 1, 1950; d. Ernest Edmund and Elizabeth (Kolb) Behnke. BS in Chemistry, U. Fla., 1972, MD, 1976. Diplomate Am. Bd. Pediatrics, Am. Bd. Neonatology-Perinatology. Intern dept. pediat. Coll. Medicine U. Fla., Gainesville, 1976-77, resident, 1977-79, chief resident, 1979-80, fellow in neonatology, 1981-83, asst. prof., 1979-81, 83-89, assoc. prof., 1989-99, prof., 1999—, adj. asst. prof. Coll. Nursing, 1988-89, adj. assoc. prof., 1989-99, mem. senate-at-large, 1984-89, 2004—10, mem. grad. studies faculty, 1988-2000. Presenter nat. and internat. meetings, 1981—; med. dir. ICU Shands Hosp., Gainesville, 1983—89, neonatal devel. follow-up program, 1989—; ad hoc mem. spl. rev. com. human devel. rsch. NIH, 1991—96, chair, 1993, 94, mem. human devel. and aging-3 study sect., 1998—99; mem. BBBP-6 study sect., 1999—2002. Mem. editl. bd.: Death Studies, 1983—94; mem. editl. bd. Jour. Addiction Medicine, 2007—; contbr. chpts. to books, articles to profl. jours. Grantee, NIH, 1984—87, 1991—, Nat. Inst. Drug Abuse, 1991—, Ctr. Substance Abuse Treatment, 1993—95. Fellow: Am. Acad. Pediat. (sect. perinatal pediat. com. substance abuse 2003—09); mem.: Soc. Rsch. in Child Devel., Fla. Pediat. Soc., Am. Pediatric Soc., Soc. Pediatric Rsch., Southern Soc. Pediat. Rsch., Fla. Med. Assn. Mem. Ch. Of Christ. Avocation: reading. Home: 426 SW 40th St Gainesville FL 32607-2749 Office: J Hillis Miller Health Ctr Dept Pediatrics PO Box 100296 Gainesville FL 32610-0296 Business E-Mail: behnkem@peds.ufl.edu.

BEHRENS, ASHLEY, physician, ophthalmologist, researcher; b. Caracas, Distrito Capital, Venezuela, May 27, 1964; s. Aquiles Anibal and Bethy Behrens; m. Nathalie Morales, Nov. 28, 1997; children: Ashley Aquiles, Nicole Nathalie, Jessica. MD, Ctrl. U. Venezuela, Caracas, 1990. Chmn. dept. Ophthalmology Friends Blinds Soc., Caracas, Distrito Capital, Venezuela, 2002—03; asst. prof. ophthalmology Johns Hopkins U., Baltimore, 2003—. Editor-in-chief Venezuelan Ophthal. Jour., Caracas, 2001—. Mem. Sci. Edn. Ctr., Caracas, Distrito Capital, 2000—03. Recipient Fellowship Award, German Academic Exch. Svc., 1996, Prof. Dr. Eugen Schreck, U. Erlangen-Nuremberg, 2000, Travel award, Eye Bank Assn. Am., 2000. Fellow: Venezuelan Soc. Ophthalmology (licentiate; sci. com. 2000—02, diplomate 1994); mem.: Assn. Rsch. and Vision in Ophthalmology (assoc.), Am. Acad. Ophthalmology (assoc.). Achievements include research in microkeratome technology. Office: Wilmer Eye Inst Johns Hopkins Hosp 600 N Wolfe St Baltimore MD 21287 Home: 400 N Broadway Baltimore MD 21231-1104 Personal E-mail: ashleybehrens@verizon.net. E-mail: abehrens@jhmi.edu.

BEHRENS, M. KATHLEEN, medical researcher; PhD in Microbiology, U. Calif., Davis. Gen. ptnr., mng. dir. Robertson Stephens Mgmt. Co., 1983—96; mng. dir. RS Investments, San Francisco, 1996—. Bd. dirs. Abgenix Inc., HealthTrio, AVI BioPharma, Inc., 2009—; dir. Bd. Sci., Tech. and Econ. Policy (STEP) Nat. Rsch. Coun., 1993—2000; mem. President's Coun. Advisors on Sci. and Tech. (PCAST), 2001—09, chair Subcommittee on Personalized Medicine. Mem.: Nat. Venture Capital Assn. (former dir., pres., chair and past chair). Office: RS Investments 388 Market St San Francisco CA 94111 also: Abgenix Inc 7601 Dumbarton Cir Fremont CA 94555-3616

BEHRMAN, RICHARD ELLIOT, pediatrician, dean; b. Phila., Dec. 13, 1931; s. Robert and Vivian (Keegan) Behrman; m. Ann Nelson, Aug. 14, 1954; children: Amy Jane, Michael Jameson, Carolyn Ann, Hillary. AB, Amherst Coll., 1953; JD, Harvard U., 1956; MD, U. Rochester, 1960; DSc (hon.), Med. Coll. Wisc., 2000. Diplomate Am. Bd. Pediat. (examiner). Intern Johns Hopkins Hosp., Balt., 1960—61, resident in pediat., 1963—65; asst. prof. pediat. U. Oreg. Sch. Medicine, Portland, 1965—67, assoc. prof., 1967—68; prof. U. Ill. Coll. Medicine, Chgo., 1968—71; prof., chmn. dept. pediat. Columbia U. Coll. Physicians and Surgeons, NYC, 1971—76; prof., chmn. dept. Case Western Res. U. Sch. Medicine, Cleve., 1976—81, dean Sch. Medicine, 1980—89; prof. clin. pediat. Stanford U., 1989; v.p. med. affairs Case Western Res. U. Sch. Medicine, Cleve., 1987—89; dir. dept. pediat. Rainbow Babies and Children's Hosp., Cleve., 1976—81; dir. Ctr. for Future of Children, 1989—99; sr. v.p. med. affairs Lucile Packard Found. for Children's Health, Palo Alto, Calif., 1999—2002, chmn. bd., 1996—99; dir. Lucile S. Packard Children's Hosp./Stanford Health Svcs., Stanford, UCSF-Stanford Health Care; exec. chair pediat. edn. steering com. Fedn. Pediat. Orgns., 2002—06; exec. dir. Non-Profit Healthcare and Ednl. Cons., 2006—. Author: Neonatology: Diseases of the Fetus and Infant, 1973, Neonatal-Perinatal Medicine, 1977; editor: Nelson's Textbook of Pediatrics, 1978, 1983, 1987, 1992, 1995, 2000, 2004, 2007, Essentials of Pediatrics, 1989, 1993, 1997, 2001, 2005; editor-in-chief: The Future of Children, 1990—2005, mem. editl. bd., sect. editor fetal and neonatal medicine: Jour. Pediat., 1970—85, assoc. editor, mem. editl. bd., cons. editor: Pediat. Rsch. Jour., 1971—80. With USPHS, 1961—63; mem. Century Assn., 1976—2007. Fellow, Wyeth pediat., 1963—65; scholar, Whipple, 1960—61, Univ., U. Rochester, 1960. Fellow: Am. Acad. Pediat.; mem.: Soc. Gynecol. Investigation, Perinatal Rsch. Soc. (coun. 1970—73), Inst. Medicine of NAS, Soc. Pediat. Rsch. (v.p. 1976—77), Sigma Xi. Episcopalian. Home: PO Box 4446 Santa Barbara CA 93140 Office Phone: 805-565-2953. Business E-Mail: behrmannon-profitconsult@nphec.org.

BEHRMANN, MARLENE, psychology professor, speech pathology/audiology services professional; BA in Speech & Hearing Therapy, U. Witwatersrand, Johannesburg, 1981, MA in Speech Pathology, 1984; PhD in Psychology, U. Toronto, 1991. Speech pathologist pvt. practice, 1982—; clinical supr. dept. speech pathology & audiology U. Witwatersrand, 1983—85; staff scientist Rotman Rsch. Inst. Baycrest Centre, 1990—93; asst. prof. dept. psychology & medicine U. Toronto, 1991—93, prof. dept. psychology, 2006—; asst. prof. dept. comm. sci. & disorders U. Pitts., 1994—97, adj. assoc. prof. dept. neuroscience & comm. disorders, 1997—; asst. prof. dept. psychology Carnegie Mellon U., 1993—97, assoc. prof. dept. psychology, 1997—2002, prof. dept. psychology, 2002—, prof. cognitive neuroscience. Recipient Justine & Yves Sergent award, U. Montreal, 2006. Fellow: Am. Psychological Soc.; mem.: Soc. Experimental Psychologists, Vision Sciences Soc., Am. Psychological Assn., Psychonomic Soc., Soc. for Neurosciences, Cognitive Neuroscience Soc. Office: Carnegie Mellon University Center for Neural Basis of Cognition 4400 Fifth Ave Ste 115 Pittsburgh PA 15213 Office Phone: 412-268-2790. Office Fax: 412-268-2798. E-mail: behrmann@cmu.edu.

BEIERWALTES, WILLIAM HOWARD, physiologist, educator; b. Ann Arbor, Mich., Oct. 6, 1947; s. William Henry and Mary-Martha B.; m. Patricia Sue Olson, July 11, 1982; children: William N., Peter L., Nora R. BA, Kalamazoo Coll., 1969; PhD, U. N.C., 1978. Instr. Mayo Med. Sch., Rochester, Minn., 1979-81; sr. staff scientist Henry Ford Hosp., Detroit, 1981—. Prof. Wayne State U. Sch. Medicine, Detroit, 2004—. Contbr. articles to profl. jours. With US Army, 1971—72. Mem. Am. Physiol. Soc., Am. Heart Assn. (fellow coun. on high blood pressure 1992, honor roll coun. on kidney 1988, chair rsch. fellowship com. Mich. chpt. 1987-90, 92-94, established investigator 1983-88), Am. Soc. Nephrology, Inter-Am. Soc. Hypertension, Mich. Soc. Med. Rsch. (bd. dirs. 1988-94, pres. 1992-94), Nat. Kidney Found. Mich. (rsch. rev. com. 1984-85, 88, 2004-09). Presbyterian. Avocation: collecting antique toy soldiers. Home: 750 Lakepointe St Grosse Pointe Park MI 48230-1706 Office: Henry Ford Hosp 2799 W Grand Blvd Detroit MI 48202-2689 Office Phone: 313-916-7494. Business E-Mail: wbeierw1@hfhs.org.

BEIL, RICHARD J., plastic surgeon, educator; married; 3 children. MD, Ohio State U. Diplomate Am. Bd. Plastic Surgery, lic. Mich. Rsch. fellow Johns Hopkins Hosp.; resident in plastic and reconstructive surgery Univ. of Mich. Med. Ctr.; chief resident SUNY Health Sci. Ctr., Syracuse; plastic surgeon Ctr. for Plastic and Reconstructive Surgery, Mich. Author: various publs. Recipient Hyde Tchg. award. Office: Center for Plastic and Reconstructive Surgery PO Box 994 5333 McAuley Dr Suites 5001 and 5008 Ann Arbor MI 48106 Office Phone: 734-712-2323. Office Fax: 734-712-2312.

BEILOCK, SIAN LEAH, psychology professor; BS in Cognitive Sci., U. Calif., San Diego, 1997; MA in Psychology, Mich. State U., 2000, PhD in Kinesiology and Psychology, 2003. Asst. prof. dept. psychology Miami U. Ohio, 2003—05, U. Chgo., 2005—08, assoc. prof., 2008—. Author: Choke: What the Secrets of the Brain Reveal about Success and Failure at Work and at Play, 2010; mem. editl. bd. Frontiers in Cognition, American Jour. Psychology, Cognition, Jour. Sport & Exercise Psychology; contbr. articles to profl. sci. jours. Recipient CAREER award, NSF, 2008; named a Rising Star, Chronicle Higher Edn., 2005; named one of 25 Women to Watch, Crain's Chgo. Bus., 2007. Fellow: Midwestern Psychol. Assn., Assn. Psychol. Sci.; mem.: AAAS, North American Soc. Psychology of Sport & Physical Activity (Early Career Disting. Scholar award 2008), Internat. Soc. Sport Psychology (Young Scholar award 2005), American Ednl. Rsch. Assn., Soc. Rsch. Ednl. Effectiveness, Soc. Personality & Social Psychology, Psychonomic Soc., Soc. Cognitive Neurosci. Achievements include research in attention and executive control of complex cognitive and sensorimotor skills; performance under pressure and stereotype threat and individual differences in executive functioning. Office: Univ Chgo Dept Psychology 5848 S University Ave Chicago IL 60637 Office Phone: 773-834-3713. Office Fax: 773-702-0886. E-mail: beilock@uchicago.edu. *

BEIRNE, OWEN ROSS, dental educator, researcher; b. Santa Maria, Calif., Jan. 18, 1947; s. Owen and Thelma Beirne; m. Sheryl Martha Schochet; children: Samuel, Deborah. BA, U. Calif., Berkeley, 1968; DMD, Harvard U., 1972; PhD, U. Calif., San Francisco, 1979. Cert. in oral and maxillofacial surgery, diplomate Am. Bd. Oral and Maxillofacial Surgery, Nat. Dental Bd. Anesthesiology. Asst. prof. U. Calif., San Francisco, 1979—85, assoc. prof., 1985—85; assoc. prof. Sch. Dentistry U. Wash., Seattle, 1985—93, prof., 1993—, dir. residency tng. dept. oral and maxillofacial surgery, 1985—99, chmn. dept. oral and maxillofacial surgery, 1999—2009. Mem. oral biology and medicine II study sect. Nat. Inst. Dental Rsch., Bethesda, Md., 1988—91; abstract reviewer Internat. Jour. Oral and Maxillofacial Implants, 1988—2008, cons., 1989—2008, assoc. editor, 2008—; cons. ADA Commn. Dental Accreditation, Chgo., 1997—2003; mem. examination com. Am. Bd. Oral and Maxillofacial Surgery, 1997—2001; vis. prof. Otago Cmty. Trust, Otago U., Sch. Dentistry, 2009. Sect. editor Principles of Oral and Maxillofacial Surgery, 1992; contbr. articles to profl. jours., chpts. to books; assoc. editor: Jour. Oral Implantology, 1992—2008; mem. editl. bd. Jour. Evidence Based Dental Practice, 2001—. Mem. editl. bd. Anesthesia Progress, 2003—; mem. boundary com. Northshore Sch. Dist., Bothell, 1996—98. Recipient Distinction in Tchg. award, U. Calif.-San Francisco, 1984. Fellow: Am. Coll. Dentists, Am. Dental Soc. Anesthesiology (pres. Wash. State 1996—2006); mem.: Osseointegration Found. Rsch. Grant Com., Nat. Dental Bd. Anesthesia (pres.), Oral Maxillofacial Surgery Found. (rsch. com. 2002—, chair 2007—), Am. Assn. Oral and Maxillofacial Surgeons (chmn. adv. com. on rsch. and tech. assessment 1999—2000), Am. Assn. Dental Rsch. (councilor 1992—2009), Phi Beta Kappa, Omicron Kappa Upsilon (pres. Supreme chpt. 2000—01, William J. Gies Ann. award 2008). Office: Univ Washington Oral Maxillofacial Surgery Box 357134 Seattle WA 98195-7134 Office Phone: 206-543-7722. Business E-Mail: slsb@u.washington.edu.

BEISWANGER, CHRISTINE M., biomedical researcher; PhD in Neurophysiology, SUNY, Albany. Postdoctoral rsch. U. Ky. Sch. Biological Sciences; rschr. Marine Biological Lab., Woods Hole, Mass.; asst. prof. Dept. Zoology Ariz. State U.; dir. quality control AgResearch, Inc., Chandler, Ariz.; rschr. Worchester Found. Exptl. Biology, Mass.; rschr. Neutoxicology Lab. Rutgers U. Coll. Pharmacy, Piscataway, NJ; supr. Cell Culture and Cryogenic Lab. Coriell Inst. Med. Rsch., NJ, 1996—97, assoc. prof. NJ, asst. dir. Coriell Cell Repositories NJ, 1997—. Recipient Rsch. Svc. award, NIH; Grass Found. fellow. Office: Coriell Inst Med Rsch 403 Haddon Ave Camden NJ 08103 Office Phone: 854-757-9694. Office Fax: 854-964-0254, 854-757-9737. E-mail: cbeiswan@coriell.org.

BEKELIS, KIMON, neurosurgeon; b. Athens, Greece, June 19, 1984; MD, U. Athens Med. Sch., 2008. Postdoc. fellow in neurosurgery Johns Hopkins Hosp., 2008—09; resident in neurosurgery Dartmouth-Hitchcock Med. Ctr., 2009—. Rsch. asst. U. Athens Med. Sch., 2003—04; rsch. assoc. U. Medicine and Dentistry NJ, 2006—07; vol. rschr. Harvard Med. Sch., 2007. Recipient Dean's award, U. Athens Med. Sch., Pantia Ralli award, Nat. Found. Fellowships, Greece; CNS Dandy fellowship, Congress of Neurol. Surgeons, Med. Sch. fellowship, Nat. Found. Fellowships, Greece, Dimitrios Mavrokordatos fellowship. Mem.: Greek Med. Assn., Am. Assn. Neurol. Surgeons, Congress of Neurol. Surgeons. Avocations: swimming, ping pong/table tennis, travel. Home: 5 Shadow Brook Dr Hanover NH 03755 Personal E-mail: kimon.bekelis@hitchcock.org.

BEKTAS, FIRAT, emergency physician; b. Turhal, Sept. 3, 1974; Asst. prof. Akdeniz U., 1991, physician, emergency medicine, 1998—. Office: Akdeniz Universitesi Tip Fakultesi Aci Antalya Merkez 07059 Turkey Business E-Mail: fbektas@akdeniz.edu.tr.

BELAKOVSKIY, MARK, biomedical researcher; b. Russia, Jan. 30, 1947; PhD, First Moscow Med. Inst., 1972. Head dept. State Sci. Ctr. Russian Fedn. Inst. Biomed. Problems Russian Acad. Scis., 1988—. Office: Khoroshevskoye Shosse 76A Moscow 123007 Russia Office Fax: 7 499 195 15 00. Business E-Mail: supermb@yandex.ru.

BELANI, CHANDRA PRAKASH, oncologist; b. Ajmer, India, May 29, 1954; MB, BChir, Rajasthan U. Sawai Man Singh Med. Coll., Jaipur, India, 1978, MD, 1981. Diplomate Am. Bd. Internal Medicine, cert. in hematology, oncology. Intern Sawai Man Singh Med. Coll., 1977-78, resident internal medicine, 1978-81; intern Good Samaritan Hosp./U. Md. Hosp., Balt., 1982-83, resident medicine, 1983-84; fellow hematology/med. oncology U. Md. Cancer Ctr., Balt., 1985-88; instr. medicine U. Md. Sch. Medicine, 1988-89, asst. prof. medicine and oncology, 1989-94, assoc. prof., 1994-95; assoc. prof. to prof. medicine, dir. Lung Cancer Prog. U. Pitts. Cancer Inst., 1995—2007; Miriam Beckner disting. prof. medicine Pa. State U. Coll. Medicine, 2007—. Mem. patient care policy com. U. Md. Med. System, 1988—94, pharmacy and therapeutics com., 1990—94, credentials com., med. sch. coun., 1991—94; dir. thoracic oncology U. Md. Cancer Ctr., 1989—94, mem. ambulatory care com., 1991—94; co-dir. experimental therapeutic program U. Pitts. Cancer Inst.; consulting med. dir. Internat. Oncology Network, 2001—; dep. dir. Pa. State Cancer Inst., Milton S. Hershey Med. Ctr., 2007—. Contbr. articles to profl. jours. Recipient Lung Cancer Rsch. award, Cora & John Davidson Found., 1990. Mem.: AMA, Multinat. Assn. Supportive Care in Cancer, Internat. Assn. Study of Lung Cancer, Am. Soc. Clin. Oncology. Office: Pa State Cancer Inst 500 University Dr Hershey PA 17033 Office Phone: 717-531-4995. Office Fax: 717-531-5076. *

BELARMINO, JAMES MICHAEL, urologist; b. Cleve., Jan. 5, 1973; MD, Loyola U., 1999. Diplomate Am. Bd. Urology. Urologist Urology Tyler, PA, 2008—, Watson Clinic, LLP, 2011—. Mem.: Tex. Med. Assn., Endourology Soc., Am. Urol. Assn. Avocations: weightlifting, golf. Home: 8517 Castleton Way Tyler TX 75703 Personal E-mail: jimmyb_md992001@yahoo.com.

BELCASTRO, PATRICK FRANK, pharmacist, researcher; b. Italy, June 3, 1920; came to U.S., 1927, naturalized, 1943; s. Samuel and Sarah (Mosca) B.; m. Hanna Vilhelmina Jensen, July 6, 1963; children— Helen Maria, Paul Anthony. BS, Duquesne U., 1942; MS (Am. Found. Pharm. Edn. fellow), Purdue U., 1951, PhD in Pharmacy and Pharm. Chemistry (Am. Found. for Pharm. Edn. fellow), 1953. Instr. pharmacy Duquesne U., 1946-49; asst. prof. pharmacy Ohio State U., 1953-54; prof. indsl. pharmacy Purdue U., 1954-90, prof. emeritus, 1990—. Author: Physical and Technical Pharmacy, 1963; contbg. editor: (with others) Pharm. Tech, 1977—; contbr. to: (with others) Jour. Pharm. Scis. Served with U.S. Army, 1942-46. Mem. Am. Pharm. Assn., Rho Chi, Phi Lambda Upsilon. Roman Catholic. Home: 327 Meridian St West Lafayette IN 47906-2603 Office: Purdue U Sch Pharmacy and Pharm Scis West Lafayette IN 47907 E-mail: pbelcas1@purdue.edu.

BELCASTRO, VINCENZO, neurologist; b. Reggio Calabria, Italy, May 28, 1976; married. Cert. vincenzo belcastro Italy. Physician Neurology Clinic, Perugia, Italy, 2007—. Office: Neurology Clinic S Andrea delle Fratte Perugia 06100 Italy Office Phone: 39 075 5784228. Office Fax: 39 075 5784229. Business E-Mail: vincenzobelcastro@libero.it.

BELDA, JOSE I., ophthalmologist; b. Valencia, Spain, Mar. 31, 1968; MD, U. de Alicante, 1992; PhD, U. de Valencia, 1998. Staff physician Clinica Baviera, 1986—99, Hosp. de la Ribera, 1989, Vissum Corp., 1999—2011; resident tng. physician Hosp. U. La Fe, 1993—96; dept. head Hosp. de Torrevieja, 2006—. Hon. prof. Miguel Hernández U., 1999—2011. Mem.: Spanish Glaucoma Soc., Spanish Soc. Ophthalmology, European Soc. Cataract and Refractive Surgeons, Am. Acad. Ophthalmology. Avocations: running, mountain climbing, sailing. Office: Hosp de Torrevieja Servicio de Torrevieja Alicante 03180 Spain E-mail: ji.beldas@coma.es.

BELDA, WALTER JUNIOR, dermatologist; s. Walter and Anna Luongo Belda; m. Walter Junior Belda, Oct. 22, 1981; children: Walter Malta, Rodrigo Malta. Degree in Medicine, UNISA, Sao Paulo, 1980; PhD student, Campinas U., Sao Paulo, 2006—. Cert. dermatologist Brazilian Dermatology Soc., Sao Paulo, 1982. Physician Sao Paulo U., 1982—2006, dir., 2006—. Contbr. articles to profl. jours. (Clin. Dermatology award, 2008). Home Fax: (11)50511921. Personal E-mail: walterbelda@uol.com.br.

BELDEN, WILLIAM A., cardiac electrophysiologist; MD, Case Western Res. U., 1999. Diplomate Am. Bd. Internal Medicine, 2001, Am. Bd. Internal Medicine-cardiovasc. disease, 2004, Am. Bd. Internal Medicine-clin. cardiac electrophysiology, 2005. Intern Univ. Hosp. of Cleve., resident internal medicine, 1999—2002; fellow cardiopulomary disease Allegheny Gen. Hosp., 2002—03, hosp. affiliation include; fellow cardiac electrophysiology Cleve. Clin. Found., 2003—04. Office: Allegheny General Hospital 320 E North Ave Pittsburgh PA 15212 Office Phone: 412-359-6444.

BELDNER, STEVEN, orthopedist, surgeon; b. Paramus, NJ, June 5, 1965; BS magna cum laude in Biology, Seton Hall U., 1987; MD, U. Medicine and Dentistry of NJ (UMDNJ), 1991. Cert. Am. Bd. Orthop. Surgery, 1999. Gen. surgery internship NYU Med. Ctr., Bellevue Hosp., NYC, 1991—92, orthopaedic surgery residency, 1992—96, hand surgery fellowship, 1996—97; attending orthopaedic surgery Pascack Valley Hosp., Ridgewood, NJ, 1997—98, Barnert Hosp., Paterson, NJ, 1997—98; faculty practice Divsn. Hand Surgery Beth Israel Med. Ctr., NYC, 1998—, attending orthop. surgery, 1998—2000, 2000—, Roosevelt Hosp., NYC, 2004—. Asst. clin. instr. NYU Med. Ctr., 1997—99; hand cons. NJ Nets, 1999—; asst. prof. orthop. surgery Albert Einstein Coll. Medicine, 2001—, supr. Dept. Plastics Surgery Fellows in Hand Surgery Edn., 2003—; dir. edn. Albert Einstein Coll. Medicine, Beth Israel Hand Fellowship, 2001—; cons. hand injuries related to boxing NY Athletic Commn., 2001—03; spkr. in field. Contbr. articles to med. jours. Recipient Lillian Luskin Tchg. Award; named a Super Doc, NY Times, 2008. Fellow: Am. Acad. Orthop. Surgeons; mem.: AMA (Physician's Recognition Award 2002), WebMD Physicians Insight Panel, Am. Soc. for Surgery of Hand, NY Soc. Surgery of Hand, Ea. Orthop. Assn., NY County Med. Soc., NY Hand Soc. (sec. 2008—), Alpha Omega Alpha. Office: 321 E 34th St New York NY 10016 Office Phone: 212-340-0000.

BELENKY, WALTER, otolaryngologist; MD, U. of Mich. Med. Sch., 1963. Diplomate Am. Bd. Otolaryngology, 1970. Resident gen. surgery William Beaumont Hosp., 1965; resident otolaryngology Wayne State Univ. Sch. of Medicine, 1968; hosp. affiliation includes Children's Hosp. of Mich. Office: Children's Hospital of Michigan 3901 Beaubien Blvd Detroit MI 48201-9985 Office Phone: 313-745-5437.

BELFIGLIO, VALENTINE JOHN, political science professor; b. May 28, 1934; s. Edmond Liberato and Mildred Elizabeth (Sherwood) B.; 1 child by previous marriage, Valentine Edmond; m. Ellie K. Belfiglio; stepchildren: Andy, Kevian Navid. BS, Union U., 1956; MA, U. Okla., Norman, 1967; PhD, U. Okla., 1970. Registered pharmacist, Fla., Okla., Tex.; cert. cons. pharmacist., pharmacy based immunization delivery, sterile pharmaceutical compounding. Grad. asst., instr. U. Okla., 1967-70; prof. polit. sci., instr. drug law and policy Tex. Woman's U., Denton, 1970—; cons. pharmacist Whitaker Med., Ltd. Lectr. in field to Great Britain, Spain, Italy and Greece. Contbr. textbooks in the practice of pharmacy Holbrook Press, Boston, 1973-75. With USAF, 1959—67, ret. col. tex. State Guard, mem. Dept. DEf. ESGR. Decorated knight Order of Merit, Republic of Italy; recipient Guido Dorso prize U. Naples, 1985, C.K. Chamberlain award East Tex. Hist. Assn., 1990, Cornaro award Tex. Woman's U., 2003, Faculty Devel. leave, Rome, 2001, Cornaro award Tex. Woman's U., 2003, Counseling Excellence award in pharmacy Pharmacy Today, 2006, One-to-One award in pharm. counseling Am. Pharm. Assn., 2006; Instnl. Rsch. grantee Tex. Woman's U., 1973-74, 76-77, Faculty Devel. fellow, Rome, 2001. Fellow Am. Soc. Cons. Pharmacists; mem. AAUP, Internat. Studies Assn. (sec.-treas. region 1974-76), Am. Polit. Sci. Assn., Am. Italian Hist. Assn. (col., ret.), Tex. State Def. Forces, US Dept. Def. (ESGR Com. mem. 2009-), Fourth degree Knight of Columbus, Mensa, Kappa Psi Republican. Roman Catholic. Avocations: chess, dance, gourmet cooking. Office: Tex Woman's Univ PO Box 425889 Denton TX 76204-5889 Home: 11505 Sonnet Dr Dallas TX 75229-2629 Office Phone: 940-898-2144. Business E-Mail: vbelfiglio@twu.edu.

BELGOROD, BARRY MILES, surgeon, educator; b. NYC, Mar. 27, 1953; s. Howard H. and Madeline (Bloom) B. BA summa cum laude, Queens Coll., 1973; MD, U. Pa., 1977. Diplomate Am. Bd. Ophthalmology, Nat. Bd. Med. Examiners. Intern in internal medicine Pa. Hosp., 1977-78; resident in ophthalmology Manhattan Eye, Ear and Throat Hosp., NYC, 1978-81, assoc. attending surgeon, 1981—; asst. attending ophthalmologist N.Y. Hosp., 1982—. Clin. instr. dept. ophthalmology Cornell U. Med. Coll., NYC; pres. BMB Patent Holding Corp.; med. coun. U. Pa., 1973-76; cons. in field. Bd. dirs. Soc. Salk Scholars, 1983—88. Fellow NSF, 1972; recipient Ira M. Goldin award, 1973, Charles A. Oliver Meml. prize in ophthalmology, 1977; scholar N.Y. States Regents, 1969-73, Jonas Salk Found., 1973-77. Fellow ACS, Am. Acad. Ophthalmology, NY Acad. Medicine, NY State Ophthal. Soc.; mem. U. Pa. Alumni Assn., Phi Beta Kappa, Sigma Xi, Beta Delta Chi. Achievements include patents for electronic photocromic lens. laser corneal surgery, analgesics. Office: 115 E 61st St New York NY 10021-8183 Office Phone: 212-753-2020.

BELHOCINE, TARIK ZINE, nuclear medicine physician, researcher; b. Algiers, Algeria, Aug. 8, 1967; s. Saad Belhocine and Leila Oussedik. B Math. and Physics, French Sch., Algiers, 1985; MD, U. Algiers, 1993; PhD, U. Liège, Belgium, 2002. Resident in nuc. medicine U. Algiers, 1994—98, specialist in nuc. medicine faculty medicine, 1994—98; specialist in nuc. medicine (md,phd) - rschr. U. Hosp. of Liège, 1998—. IAEA fellow, 1998—99, rschr. divsn. nuc. medicine, 1999—2002. Mem.: AAAS (assoc.), European Soc. of Urogenital Radiology (assoc.), Algerian Soc. of Nuc. Medicine (assoc.), Belgian Soc. of Nuc. Medicine (assoc.), French Soc. of Biophysics and Nuc. Medicine (assoc.), European Assn. of Nuc. Medicine (assoc.), Am. Soc. of Nuc. Medicine (assoc.), Advisory Bd. of the Scientist (assoc.). Achievements include development of new radiophamaceutical for the imaging of the apoptosis in human cancers; research in better management of uterine cancers (cervical cancers and endometrial cancers) using fluorodeoxyglucose positron emission tomography); rational management of malignant melanoma using sentinel node biopsy and fluorodeoxyglucose positron tomography; better clinical and imaging management of carcinoïd tumors; mechanisms of 18F-fluorodeoxyglucose uptakein Horton's disease. Home: 49 Boulevard D'Avroy 4000 Liège Belgium E-mail: tarik.bel@swing.be.

BELKNAP, JAMES KENNEDY, surgeon, educator; b. Denver, Jan. 17, 1961; DVM, Colo. State U., 1985, PhD, 1992. Prof. equine surgery Ohio State U., 2004—. Recipient Equine Vet. Jour. Open award, Brit. Equine Vet. Assn. Mem.: Am. Coll. Vet. Surgeons. Avocation: fly fishing. Office: 601 Vernon Tharp St Columbus OH 43210 Office Fax: 614-688-5642. Business E-Mail: belknap.16@osu.edu.

BELL, ANTHONY J., emergency physician, director; b. Australia, Sept. 12, 1970; MBBS, UWA, 1994. Dir., emergency medicine Q Health QE II Jubilee Hosp., 2009—. Sr. lectr. U. Queensland, 2003—11; clin. chair Statewide ED Network, 2011—. Rsch. grant, QEMRF. Fellow: Australasian Coll. Emergency Medicine. Office: Kessels Rd Troughton Rd Coopers Plains Queensland 4108 Australia Personal E-mail: dr.aj.bell@gmail.com.

BELL, BETH P., public health service officer; BA, Brown U., Providence; MD, Yale U., New Haven; MPH, U. Rochester Sch. Medicine, NY. Epidemic intelligence officer Wash. State Dept. Health; mem. hepatitis br., divsn. viral and rickettsial diseases Centers Disease Control an Prevention, Atlanta, chief epidemiology br., divsn. viral hepatitis, leadership positions during fed. responses to major pub. health events including 2001 anthrax attacks, Hurricane Katrina and 2009 H1N1 flu response, acting dep. dir. then acting dir. Nat. Ctr. Immunization and Respiratory Diseases, 2008—09, assoc. dir. epidemiol. sci. Nat. Ctr. Immunization and Respiratory Diseases, 2009—10, dir. Nat. Ctr. Emerging and Zoonotic Infectious Diseases, 2010—. Contbr. articles to profl. jours. (Alexander Langmuir prize, Iain Hardy award). Fellow: Infectious Disease Soc. America, American Acad. Family Medicine, American Acad. Preventive Medicine; mem.: American Epidemiol. Soc. Office: Centers Disease Control and Prevention NCEZID 1600 Clifton Rd Atlanta GA 30333 *

BELL, CARL COMPTON, psychiatrist, researcher; b. Chgo., Oct. 28, 1947; s. William Yancy and Pearl Louise (Debnam) Bell; m. Joanne Scott, Jan. 1, 1969 (div. Apr. 1971); 1 child, Cristin Carol; m. Dora Dixie, Dec. 1984 (div. May 1989); m. Tyra Taylor, Mar. 19, 1991 (div. Oct. 2003); children: Briatta Honore, William Yancy Bell IV; m. Phyllis West, Mar. 18, 2005. BS Biology, U. Ill.-Chgo., 1967; MD, Meharry Med. Coll., 1971. Diplomate Am. Bd. Psychiatry and Neurology (examiner). Intern Ill. State Psychiat. Inst., Chgo., 1971—72, resident, 1972—74; pvt. practice medicine specializing in psychiatry Chgo., 1974—; dir. psychiat. emergency svcs. Jackson Park Hosp., Chgo., 1976—77, assoc. dir. divsn. behavioral and psychodynamic medicine, 1979—82, mem. staff, 1972—; staff psychiatrist Human Correctional and Svcs. Inst., Chgo., 1977—78, Chgo. Bd. Edn., 1977—79, Chatham Avalon Mental Health Ctr., Chgo., 1977—79, Cmty. Mental Health Coun., Chgo., 1977—79, med. dir., 1983—87, exec. dir., 1987—; pres., CEO Cmty. Mental Health Coun. and Found., 1993—; assoc. prof. to prof. clin. psychiatry U. Ill., 1983—, prof. pub. health, 1993—, dir. dept. psychiatry Inst. Juvenile Rsch. Chgo., 2009; with Nat. Rsch. Coun., Nat. Acad. Sci. Com. Law Justice. Cons. Cmty. divsn. Lilly Endowment; cons. editl. bd. Jour. Prison and Jail Health, 1990-92, Cmty. Mental Health Jour., 1989—, Jour. Hosp. and Cmty. Psychiatry, 1990-94, Jour. Nat. Med. Assn., 1994-98, Psychiat. Svcs., 1994-98, Jour. Correctional Health Care, 1997-2000, Jour. Health Care to Poor and Underserved, 1991—, Jour. Infant, Child and Adolescent Psychotherapy, 1997—, Clin. Psychiat. News, 2000—; mem. editl. bd. Ill. Child Welfare, 2004-08; appointed mem., Nat. Rsch. Coun. Com. Assessing Juvenile Justice Reform, Divsn. Behavioral & Social Scis., 2010-, mem., Nat. Acad. Scis., Inst. Medicine Bd. Children, Youth & Families & Bd. Health Care Svcs. Com., Prevention Mental Disorders & Substance Abuse Children, Youth and Young Adults., Rsch. Advances & Promising Interventions, 2010. Prodr.(creator animation): Book Worm, 1984; author: Psychiatric Aspects of Violence: Issues in Prevention and Treatment, 2000, Sanity of Survival: Reflections on Community Mental Health and Wellness, 2004; co-author: Suicide and Homicide Among Adolescents, 1994; contbr. articles to profl. jours.; prodr.(creator): (video) Eight Pieces of Brocade, 2000—; mem. editl. bd.: Am. Psychiat. Pub., Inc., 2001—; talk show host: Sta. WVON-AM, 1987—90; Sta. WJPC-FM, 1992—93; co-editor: Psychiatric Clinics of N.Am. Prevention in Psychiatry, 2011. Profl. adv. panel Mental Health Assn. Greater Chgo., 1983—; adv. com. funded grant on Aggressors, Victims and Bystanders, 1989-92; bd. dirs. Ill. Coun. Against Handgun Violence, Nat. Commn. on Correctional Health Care, chmn., 1992, 2011; lectr. U. Chgo., 1986—, Chgo. Med. Sch., 1987—; co-dir. Interdisciplinary violence Prevention Ctr. U. Ill., 2006—; tchr. martial arts, 1973—; apptd. to violence against women adv. coun., 1995-2000; mem. White House strategy session on Children, Violence and Responsibility, 1999; mem. surgeon gen. report on mental health-Culture, Race and Ethnicity Working Group, 2000-01; mem. Surgeon Gen. report on youth violence working group, 2000-01; mem. Chgo. Bd. Health, 2002—; apptd. adv. group. strengthening families Joint Learning Initiative on Children and HIV/AIDS Human Scis. Rsch. Coun., South Africa, 2007-09; mem. nat. mental health adv. coun. NIMH, 2008-. Lt. comdr. USN, 1974-76. Recipient plaque in recognition and appreciation, Chatham-Avalon Mental Health Ctr., 1979, Div. Behavioral Medicine, 1982, Social Action award, Chgo. chpt. Black Social Workers, 1988, Mental Health award, Englewood Cmty. Health Orgn., 1988, Scholastic Achievement award, Chgo. chpt. Nat. Assn. Black Social Workers, 1980, Ellen Quinn Meml. award, 1986, Monarch award, Alpha Kappa Alpha, 1986, Alumnus of Yr. award, Meharry Med. Coll., 1991, Cmty. Psychiatry award, Am. Assn. Cmty. Psychiatrists, 1992, Lifetime Achievement award, Black Psychiatrists of Am., 1994, Freddye Smith award, Cmty. Mental Health Coun., 1997, Blanche F. Ittleson award Lifetime Contbns., Am. Ortho Psychiatric Assn., 2000, Lifetime Achievement award, Cmty. Behavioral Healthcare Assn. Ill., 2001, Living Legacy award, Provident Found., 2001, Dr. Jeanne Spurlock Lectr. award, Am. Acad. Child and Adolescent Psychiatrists, 2002, George B. Nash, Sr. Pub. Edn. award, Nat. Alliance for Mentally Ill, Chgo., 2003, Disting. Psychiatrist Lecture Award Outstanding Achievement in Psychiatry, Am. Psychiat. Assn., 2003, Minority Mental Health award, Am. Psychiat. Found., 2003, Minority Svcs. award, 2004, Welcome Back award, Eli Lily Co., 2003, From Whence We Came award, Allstate Ins. Co., 2004, Recognition plaque, Ill. Mental Health and Adv. Coun., 2005, Graduating Class of Hyde Pk. Acad., 2005, Health Warriors award, Ga. Doty Mental Health Edn. Fund, 2005, Pub. Svc. award, Inst. Medicine Chgo., 2006, Lloyd C. Elam MD Meml. Lifetime Achivement award, Francis J. Bonner award, Mass. Gen. Hosp., Dept. Psychiatrist, Dept. Diversity Coms., Harvard U., 2011; named Top Doctor, Chgo. mag., 1997, 2001, 2007, Internat. fellow Inst. Philosophy, Diversity and Mental Health, Ctr. Ethnicity and Health U. Ctrl. Lancashire, Eng., 2007—08; named to Guide To Am.'s Top Psychiatrists, Consumers Rsch. Coun. Am., 2004—05; grantee, NIMH, 2001—07; fellow, Inst. Medicine Chgo., 2004; Goldberger fellow, 1969, Dr. Martin Luther King Jr. fellow, 1970—71. Fellow Am. Coll. Psychiatrists (com. Laughlin fellows 1989-92, fin. com. 1993-96, pub. edn. com. 1994-96, com. membership devel. 1996-00, com. strategic planning 2000—, bd. regents 2006—09, Bowis Disting. Svc. award 2002), Am. Psychiat. Assn. (disting.; Falk fellow 1972-73, task force-delivery psychiat. svcs. to proverty areas 1972-73, com. black psychiatrists, 1988-90, chmn. black caucus 1990-92, vice chair task force psychiat. aspects of violence 1997—, joint commn. on pub. affairs 2000-04, psychiat. diagnosis and assessment com. 2003—, personality disorders work group task force on the Diagnostic and Statis. Manual of Mental Disorders 5th edit., 2007-, Spl. Presdl. Commendation 1997, Disting. Psychiatrist Lecture award 2003, apptd. to presdl. task force on biopsychosocial consequences of early childhood violence, 2005, vice chair coun. advocacy and pub. policy, 2006-07, Solomon Carter Fuller award, 2011); mem. Nat. Med. Assn. (local chmn. sect. on neurology and psychiatry 1983, conv., nat. chmn. sect. on psychiatry and behavioral scis. 1985-86, E.Y. Williams Disting. Sr. Clin. scholar psychiatry sect. 1992), Am. Psychiat. Assn. (chmn. coun. social issues and pub. psychiatry 2007—), Black Psychiatrists Am. (editor Bottom Line newsletter 1977-82, v.p. 1980-82), Cook County Physicians Assn., Prairie State Physicians, Ill. Psychiat. Soc., Am. Assn. Cmty. Mental Health Ctr. Psychiatrists (bd. dirs. 1985-89), Am. Coll. Psychiatry, Nat. Coun. Cmty. Health Ctrs. (sec. bd. dirs. 1986, sec., treas. 1987), Underwater Explorers Soc., Shorei Goju Karate Soc. (7th degree Black Belt), Martial Arts Karate Assn., Alpha Omega Alpha, Am. Psychiat. Assn.(life)(Administrative Psychiat. award), NRC, Nat. Acad. Scis. Com. on Law & Justice, Nat. Strategy Suicide Prevention Task Force. Office: Community Mental Health Coun 8704 S Constance Ave Chicago IL 60617-2756 also: Inst Juvenile Rsch 1747 West Roosevelt Rd Rm 155 Chicago IL 60608-1264 Office Phone: 773-734-4033 204, 773-908-0076. Business E-Mail: carlcbell@pol.net.

BELL, DAVID ROBERT, physiologist, educator; b. Detroit, Aug. 16, 1952; BS, Mich. State U., MS, 1974, PhD, 1983. Assoc. prof. cellular and integrative physiology Ind. U. Sch. Medicine, 1989—. Textbook author, editl. rev. Little, Brown and Co., McGraw Hill, 1991—2000; mem. instl. rev. bd. Parkview Meml. Hosp. Sys., 1997—2003; pres., bd. dirs. Am. Heart Assn. NE Ind., 1998—99; text book editor, author Lippincott, Williams and Wilkins, 2005; cons. Welch's Inc., 2006—07. Recipient Rsch. Star award, Am. Heart Assn. NE Ind., Excellence Tchg. award, Ind. U., Nat. Rsch. Svc. award, NIH. Mem.: Am. Med. Writers Assn., Am. Physiol. Soc. Avocations: reading, politics, sports. Home: 4704 Collbran Ct Fort Wayne IN 46835 Home Fax: 260-481-6401. Business E-Mail: bell@ipfw.edu.

BELL, DELORIS WILEY, physician; b. Solomon, Kans., Sept. 30, 1942; d. Harry A. and Mildred H. (Watt) Wiley; children: Leslie, John. BA, Kans. Wesleyan U., 1964; MD, U. Kans., 1968. Diplomate Am. Bd. Ophthalmology. Intern St. Luke's Hosp., Kansas City, Mo., 1968-69; resident U. Kans. Med. Ctr., Kansas City, 1969-72; practice medicine specializing in ophthalmology Overland Park, Kans., 1973—. Mem. AMA, Kans. Med. Soc. (pres. sect. ophthalmology 1985-86, spkr. house 1994-97), Am. Acad. Ophthalmology (councillor 1988-93, chmn. state govtl. affairs 1993-97, bd. trustees 2000-03), Kans. Soc. Ophthalmology (pres. 1985-86), Kansas City Soc. Ophthalmology and Otolaryngology (sec. 1984-86, pres.-elect 1988, pres. 1989). Avocations: photography, travel. Office: 7000 W 121st St Ste 100 Shawnee Mission KS 66209-2010 Office Phone: 913-498-2015. Personal E-mail: cd2cdb@gmail.com.

BELL, DEREK, medical educator; b. Dundee, Scotland, Mar. 24, 1955; BSc with 1st class honors, U. Edinburgh, Scotland, 1977, MB BChir, 1980, MD. Lectr. U. Edinburgh, 1983—88; sr. registrar Cen. Middlesex, London, 1988—90, cons. physician, 1990—96, Royal Infirmary, Edinburgh, 1996—2006; assoc. med. dir. Lothian U. Hosp., London, 2005—06; prof. acute medicine Imperial Coll. London, 2006—. Chmn. Emergency Med. Admissions, Scotland, 2001—. Editor: (jour.) Acute Medicine, 2000. Fellow: Royal Coll. Physicians London, Royal Coll. Physicians Glasgow, Royal Coll. Physicians Edinburgh; mem.: Soc. for Acute Medicine (pres. 2000—03). Office Phone: 020 874 68114. E-mail: d.bell@imperial.ac.uk.

BELL, DON ANTONIO, neurointerventional surgeon; b. Yadkinville, NC, Feb. 11, 1958; s. Joseph Luther and Jeanette (Bruner) B.; m. Amelia Fort, May 19, 1984; children: Ryan Tierney, Riley Katherine, Joseph Regan. BS, U. N.C., 1980, MD, 1984. Diplomate Am. Bd. Internal Medicine, Am. Bd. Diagnostic Radiology. Instr. radiology U. Utah, Salt Lake City, 1993-94; asst. prof. radiology Wake Forest U., Winston-Salem, NC, 1994-97; clin. prof. radiology U. NC, Chapel Hill, 1997-2000, Med. U. SC, Charleston, 2000—03. Mem. sci. adv. bd. Cordis Endovasc. Sys., Miami, 1999—2003, Datascope, Inc.,

Islen, NJ, 1998-03, Siemens Med. Sys., Erlangen, Germany, 1999-04, GE Med. Sys., Milw., 1996-98. NSF fellow, 1978-80, Nat. Cancer Inst. fellow, 1986-87. Mem. World Fedn. Intvl. Neuroradiology, Radiol. Soc. N.Am., Am. Roentgen Ray Soc., Am. Soc. Neuroradiology, Soc. Neurointerventional Surgery. Independent. Avocations: running, golf, gardening. Office: St Luke's Hosp Dept Radiology 190 E Bannock St Boise ID 83712 Office Phone: 208-381-2094. Business E-Mail: bellt@slhs.org. E-mail: tonybell1@gmail.com.

BELL, GRAEME I., biochemistry and molecular biology educator; BSc in Zoology, U. Calgary, 1968, MSc in Biology, 1971; PhD in Biochemistry, U. Calif., San Francisco, 1977. Sr. scientist Chiron Corp.; prof. dept. biochemistry and molecular biology U. Chgo., 1986—, Louis Block prof. biochemistry and molecular biology, 2006—, prof. human genetics and medicine. Investigator Howard Hughes Med. Inst., 1986—2005. Contbr. articles to profl. jours. Recipient Outstanding Sci. Achievement award Am. Diabetes Assn., Rolf Luft award Swedish Med. Soc., Gerold and Kayla Grodsky Basic Rsch. Scientist award Juvenile Diabetes Found. Internat., Disting. Alumni award, U. Calgary, Naomi Berri award for Outstanding Achievement in Diabetes Rsch., Columbia U., J. Allyn Taylor Internat. prize in Medicine. Fellow: Am. Acad. Arts & Scis.; mem.: Inst. Medicine of the Nat. Acad. Sciences. Office: U Chgo AMB N237 (MC1028) 5841 S Maryland Ave Chicago IL 60637-1463 Office Fax: 773-702-9237. E-mail: g-bell@uchicago.edu.

BELL, JULIE MARIE, health facility administrator, consultant; b. Mt. Clemens, Mich., Aug. 21, 1974; d. John and Helen Mary Bell. BA in Psychology and Bus., Siena Hts. U., Adrian, Mich., 1997; MS in Psychology, U. Detroit Mercy, 2000; PhD in Psychology. Cert. Baldridge examiner, green belt Six Sigma, master change agt. Constrn. asst. Triangle Elec., Madison Hts., Mich., 1996—98; human resource cons. Aero Svcs., Internat., Troy, Mich., 1998—2000; sr. orgnl. cons. St. John Health, Warren, Mich., 2000—; sr. mgr. orgnl. devel. DaimlerChrysler, internal cons. Auburn Hills, Mich.; dir. talent mgmt. Goodyear Tire & Rubber, Akron, Ohio, 2008—10; chief learning officer Cleve. Clinic Health Sys., Cleve., 2010—. Cons. in field; mem. adv. bd. U. Detroit-Mercy, 2001—. Girl's athletic coach St. Anne Cath. Sch., Warren, 2004—; care ptnr. Providence Hosp., Southfield, Mich., 2004—; donor ASPCA, Humance Spciety & Compassion Internat.; mem. Nothside Christian Ch., Wadsworth, Ohio; Shoes for Children vol. Little Rock Bapt. Ch., 2003—. Scholar McCracken scholar, McCracken Basketball Camps, Ind., 1999. Democrat. Roman Catholic. Avocations: reading, travel, home decorating. Office: Saint John Health 28000 Dequindre Rd Warren MI Business E-Mail: jmb179@dcx.com.

BELL, NORMAN HOWARD, retired endocrinologist, educator; b. Gainesville, Ga., Feb. 11, 1931; s. Kenneth Rush and Henrietta Maria (Howard Rankin) Bell; m. Claude Handy Bell, June 27, 1959 (dec. 1967); children: Douglas Howard, Julianne Rankin; m. Mary Virginia Baughman, Aug. 24, 1968 (div. July 1972); m. Ledlie Laird Dinsmore, Dec. 16, 1972; 1 child, Bayard Gardiner. AB, Emory U., 1951; MD, Duke U., 1955. Intern Duke U. Med. Ctr., Durham, NC, 1955-56, resident, 1956-57; clin. assoc. Nat. Inst. Allergy and Infectious Diseases, NIH, Bethesda, Md., 1957-59; mem. staff clin. endocrinology br. Nat. Heart, Lung and Blood Inst., NIH, Bethesda, 1959-63, assoc. in medicine, 1963-65; asst. prof. medicine Northwestern U. Sch. Medicine, Chgo., 1965-68; assoc. prof. Ind. U. Med Sch., Indpls., 1968-71, prof., 1971-79; prof. medicine and pharmacology Med. U. SC, Charleston, SC, 1979—2006, disting. univ. prof., 1998. Mem. gen. medicine B study sect. NIH, Bethesda, 1982—86, chmn., 1985—86, mem. spl. grants rev. com. Nat. Inst. Arthritis, Musculo-Skeletal and Skin Diseases, 1990—95, chmn., 1993—94. Mem. editl. bd. Calcified Tissue Internat., 1978—83, 1994—2002, Jour. Clin. Endocrinology and Metabolism, 1982—87, Jour. Bone and Mineral Rsch., 1989—93, Italian Jour. Mineral and Electrolyte Metabolism, 1990—, Current Drug Targets-Immune, Endocrine and Metabolic Disorders, 2000—06, Reviews in Endocrine & Metabolic Disorders, 2000—05. Trustee Nat. Osteoporosis Found., Washington, 1984—88, chmn. sci. adv. bd., 1985—88. With USPHS, 1957—63. Recipient Career Devel. award, USPHS, 1965—68, VA Med. Investigator award, 1979, 1981—87, Thomas A. Roe Found. award, S.C. Med. Assn., 1982, William S. Middleton VA award, 1983, Frederic C. Bartter award, Am. Soc. Bone and Mineral Rsch., 1992, Career Recognition award, Vitamin D Workshop, 1997. Mem.: Endocrine Soc., Assn. Osteobiology (councillor 1997—98, sec.-treas. 1999, pres. 2000—02), Assn. Am. Physicians, Am. Soc. Pharmacology and Exptl. Therapeutics, Am. Soc. Bone and Mineral Rsch. (sec.-treas. 1978—85, pres. 1986—87, Shirley Hohl Svc. award 1998), Am. Soc. Clin. Investigation, Alpha Omega Alpha. Democrat. Episcopalian. Home: 1 Johnson Rd Charleston SC 29407-7514 E-mail: belln@musc.edu.

BELL, R. BRYAN, oral surgeon, educator; b. Houston, Dec. 17, 1965; MD, U. NC, Chapel Hill, 1997; DDS, Creighton U., 1995. Attending surgeon, trauma svc., oral and maxillofacial surgery svc. Legacy Emanuel Med. Ctr., 2000—; ptnr. Head and Neck Surg. Assocs., 2001; assoc. prof. Oreg. Health and Sci. U., 2001; med. dir., oral head and neck cancer program Providence Cancer Ctr., 2010—. Bd. trustees Med. Soc. Met. Portland, 2009. Recipient Presdl. award, Oreg. Soc. Oral and Maxillofacial Surgeons. Fellow: ACS, Am. Coll. Oral and Maxillofacial Surgeons (bd. regents 2006—11), Am. Skull Base Soc., Am. Head and Neck Soc., Am. Assn. Oral and Maxillofacial Surgeons (editor in chief, oral and maxillofacial surgery updates 2009, Daniel M. Laskin award). Avocations: fishing, hunting, scuba diving. Office: 1849 NW Kearney Ste 300 Portland OR 97209 Business E-Mail: bellb@hsna1.com.

BELL, RICHARD M., critical care surgeon, educator; BS, Ctr. Coll. Ky., Danville; MD, U. Ky., 1979. Diplomate Am. Bd. of Surgery, 1980. Resident gen. surgery Univ. Ky. Coll. Medicine/Chandler Med. Ctr., Lexington, 1979; faculty mem. Univ. Ky.; flight surgeon 123rd Tac Hosp., Ky., 1977; prof. surgery dept. Sch. Medicine Univ. SC, 1985—, chmn. surgery dept. Sch. Medicine, 1998; critical care surgeon Palmetto Health Richland. Chmn. subcommittee Advanced Trauma Life Support. Lt. col. USAF, chief aeromedical svcs. Blytheville Air Force, Ark., chief aeromedical svcs. Ky. Air Nat. Guard, Louisville. Recipient Meritorious Svc. award, Advanced Trauma Life Support, Dean's medal, Univ. SC Sch. Medicine. Mem.: ACS (trauma com. mem.), Assn. Surg. Edn. (pres.). Office: Palmetto Health Richland 5 Richland Medical Park Dr Columbia SC 29203 Office Phone: 803-256-2657.

BELL, ROBERT LLOYD, retired neurosurgeon; b. McKeesport, Pa., Sept. 3, 1923; s. Samuel Lowry and Nellie Pearl Bell; m. Helen Louise Matthews, Oct. 13, 1951; children: Robert Matthews, Louise Helen. BS, Washington and Jefferson Coll., 1944; MD, U. Pitts., 1947. Jr. intern Shady Side Hosp., Pitts., 1945—47; intern Western Pa. Hosp., Pitts., 1947—48; resident in surgery Aspin Wall Pa. Hosp., Pitts., 1948—49; resident in neurosurgery Bklyn. Hosp., 1949—50, Kings County Hosp., Bklyn., 1950—51, chief neurosurg. resident, 1953—54; chief neurosurgery 98th GH Hosp., Munich, 1951—53; from instr. to assoc. prof. SUNY, Bklyn., 1954—59; chief neurosurgery Wadsworth (Kans.) VA Hosp., 1959—64, Coatesville (Pa.) VA Hosp., 1964—69, Chester County Hosp., West Chester, Pa., 1969—83; chair nuc. medicine VA Hosp. Coatesville, 1983—91. 1st lt. col. USMC, 1951—53. Fellow: ACS, Am. Coll. Nuc. Medicine (gold medal 1989); mem.: AMA, SAR (compatriot), Chester County Med. Soc., Pa. Med. Soc., Am. Legion. Presbyterian. Home: 51 S 12th St Coatesville PA 19320

BELL, RODNEY DONALD, medical educator; b. Nampa, Idaho, Jan. 16, 1946; AB, NW Nazarene Coll., 1968; MD, Oregen Health Sci. Ctr., 1972. Prof., neurology Med. Coll. Thomas Jefferson U., 1985—. Recipient Master Clinician award, Thomas Jefferson U.; named to Phila. Top Drs., Castle Connelly. Fellow: Am. Heart Assn.; mem.: Am. Acad. Neurology. Avocations: running, bicycling, cooking. Office: 900 Walnut Ste 200 Philadelphia PA 19107 Office Fax: 215-923-6792. Business E-Mail: rodney.bell@jefferson.edu.

BELL, SUSAN JANE, nurse; b. Columbus, Ohio, July 24, 1946; d. Donald Richard Bell and Martha Jane (McDowell) Nichols; m. Robert Earlin Ward, Oct. 24, 1964 (div. 1984); children: Duane Allen Ward, Melissa Jane Ward, Bryan Thomas Ward. Grad., Columbus Sch. Practical Nursing, 1985; diploma in Nutrition & Fitness, Stanford Career Inst., 2005; student, Coll. Music Educ. Ohio State U., 1964; student in Healthcare Admin., Franklin U., 1993; A in Nursing, Columbus State CC, 1989; diploma in Forensic Sci., Palm Forth Coll., 2008. Diploma with distinction North HS, 1964; lic. practical nurse, State of Ohio, 1986, valedictorion, Columbus Sch. Practical Nursing, 1985, RN State of Ohio, 1989, Nat. Dean's List, 1989; Healthcare provider CPR cert. Am. Heart. Assn., 2011, cert. Notary State of Ohio, 2007, in child psychology Pa. Foster Coll., 2010, Penn Foster Coll., 2010. Nurse's asst. Riverside Meth. Hosp., Columbus, 1970-80, Norworth Convalescent Ctr., Columbus, 1980-86; nurse, charge nurse Heartland Thurber Care Ctr., Columbus, 1986-89; staff nurse Am. Nursing Care, Columbus, 1989—; medicare home visitation, staffing and pvt. duty nurse Telemed, Columbus, 1989—; asst. head nurse Northland Terr., Columbus, 1989; supr. Elmington Manor, Columbus, 1989; staff nurse cardiac step down unit Grant Hosp., Columbus, 1989—90; nurse med. ICU, CCU and pediatric ICU, 1990—92; charge nurse skilled unit First Cmty. Village Health Care Ctr., Columbus, 1992—2001; supr., charge nurse St. Rita's Home; unit nurse & supervisor Mother Angeline McCrory Manor, 2005—11; mem. Mestuin Pistol Shooting Am. Rifle Assn., 1979. Pvt. duty ALS ventilator patients Med. Pers. Poole, ptnrs. Cir. HSUS, ptnr., hon. team captain, 2010, USA Olympics. Sponsor Childreach; ptnr. Spl. Olympia, 2011. Mem. NAFE, ASPCA, World Wildlife Found., AARP, Nature Conservancy, Environ. Def. Fund, Nat. Wildlife Fedn., Humane Soc. U.S., Am. Coun. on Exercise, Columbus Met. Mus. Art, Sierra Club, Wexner Ctr. Arts, St. Josephs Legacy Club, John Wayne Found. (life), Nat. Notary Assn., Artifacts of Hist. Significance Ohio Hist. Soc. (contbr. 1983), Ctrl. Assn. Miraculous Medal (life), Metrofittness World Gym, Law CE for Pharmacologists & Nurses Soc., The Mother Angeline Soc., Shrine of the Holy Innocents (founding contbr.), Save the Manatee Club, COSI Avocations: bodybuilding, power lifting, swimming, music, crocheting, reading, travel. Personal E-mail: bellcanine@aol.com.

BELLANGER, BARBARA DORIS HOYSAK, biomedical researcher; b. Syracuse, NY, Oct. 24, 1936; d. Edward George and Bernardine Elizabeth (Blaney) Hoysak; m. Ronald Patrick Bellanger, July 1, 1961; children: Laura Jeanne, Andrea Lynne, Janis Anne. BS, Syracuse U., 1958. Tech. asst. Bur. of Labs., Syracuse, 1958; rsch. scientist Bristol Labs., Syracuse, 1958-63; chief rsch. assoc., facility supr. Syracuse Cancer Rsch. Inst., 1973—. Pres. CNS Northstars Band Parents, Inc., Cicero-North Syracuse, N.Y., 1986-87. Mem. Am. Assn. Lab. Animal Sci. (cert. and registered lab. animal technician, sec. Upstate N.Y. br. 1990-2007, Technician of Yr. award 1992, Harlan Teklad award 1998, 2005, Charles E. Schadler award 2000), NY Acad. Scis., Alpha Gamma Delta (pres. Alpha alumnae chpt. 1959-60, treas. 1989-2011). Home: 410 David Dr North Syracuse NY 13212-1929 Office: Syracuse Cancer Rsch Inst Presdl Plz Med Bldg 600 E Genesee St Syracuse NY 13202

BELLANTUONO, CESARIO, psychiatrist, director; b. Monopoli, Apr. 27, 1947; Degree in Medicine, U. Bari, 1971, degree in Psychiatry, 1976. Dir. psychiat. dept. U. Ancona, 2007—. Mem.: Italian Soc. Neuropsychopharmacology. Home: via San Giovanni Lupatoto 57 Verona 37134 Italy Personal E-mail: c.bellantuono@univpm.it.

BELLE, GERALD, pharmaceutical executive; BSBA Mktg., cum laude, Xavier U., Cin., 1968; MBA, Northwestern U., 1969. Mem. staff Merrell-Nat. Labs., Cin., 1969-77, mem. sales and mktg. staff U.S. and Philippines Manila, 1978-82; East Asia regional mgr. pharms. Dow Chem. Pacific Ltd., Hong Kong, 1982-83; product group dir. Merrell-Nat. Labs., Cin., 1983-85; dir. product planning and promotion Lakeside Pharms., Cin., 1985-87; dir. mktg. Merrell Dow Pharms. KK, Tokyo, 1987-90; v.p. mktg. and sales Marion Merrell Dow Europe AG, Zurich, Switzerland, 1990-95; pres. Hoechst Marion Roussel Can., Montreal, Que., 1995-97; pres., N.Am., CEO Hoechst Marion Roussel, Inc. Hoechst Marion Roussel, Kansas City, Mo., 1997—99; pres. Aventis, N. Am. Pharm. (from merger of Hoechst Marion Roussel and Rhône-Poulenc Rorer), 1999—2004; exec. chmn. Merial Ltd., Duluth, Ga., 2004—07. Bd. dirs. Nat. Pharm. Coun., Mid-Am. Coalition on Health Care. Mem. Civic Coun. Greater Kansas City. Office: Merial Ltd Bldg 500 3239 Satellite Blvd Duluth GA 30096 Office Phone: 678-638-3000.

BELLEI, NANCY, medical educator; b. Sao Paulo, Brazil, June 22, 1962; PhD, Fed. U. Sao Paulo, 1987, PhD, 1998. Prof. Fed. U. Sao Paulo, 2001—. Office: Rua Pedro De Toledo 980 Cj 144 Sao Paulo 04039002 Brazil Office Fax: 55 11 55798610. Business E-Mail: nbellei@uol.com.br.

BELLEMARE, SARAH, surgeon, educator; MD, Laval U., 1996. Diplomate Am. Bd. Surgery. Resident in surgery Montreal Univ. Med. Ctr., Can., 1996—2001; fellow in hepatobiliary surgery NY Presbyn.-Columbia Med. Ctr., 2002—03, fellow in transplant surgery, 2003—04; asst. clin. prof. surgery Yeshiva Univ.; surgeon Jack D. Weiler divsn. Montefiore Med. Ctr. Office: Montefiore Medical Center 111 E 210th St Rosenfeld 2 Bronx NY 10467 Office Phone: 718-920-4321. Office Fax: 718-920-6321.

BELLER, GEORGE A., cardiologist, educator; b. NYC, Dec. 23, 1940; children: Michael, Amy, Leslie, Ray Wadlow, Jeff Wadlow. B in Philosophy, Dartmouth Coll., Hanover, NH; MD, U. Va., 1966. Diplomate Am. Bd. Cardiovascular Disease, Am. Bd. Internal Medicine. Internship in internal medicine U. Wis. Hosp., Madison; sr. resident in internal medicine Boston City Hosp.; clin. fellow in cardiology Harvard U. Med. Sch.; rsch. fellow in cardiovascular diseases, asst. prof. Mass. Gen. Hosp.; prof. cardiology and internal medicine, chief cardiovasc. divsn. U. Va. Health Sys., Charlottesville, 1977—2004, pres. clin. staff, U. Va. Med. Ctr., 1999—2005, Ruth C. Heede prof. cardiology and prof. internal medicine. Editor-in-chief: Jour. Nuc. Cardiology, 2003—; contbr. articles to profl. jours. Maj. US Army, 1970—73. Recipient Disting. Achievement award, Am. Heart Assn., Herrick award, 2000, Walter Reed Disting. Achievement award, U. Va., 2006, Lifetime Achievement award, Paul Dudly White Soc., Mass. Gen. Hosp., 2006, Disting. Scientist award, Am. Coll. Cardiiology, 2010. Mem. Am. Soc. Clin. Investigation, Am. Fedn. Clin. Rsch., Assn. Am. Physicians, Am. Coll. Cardiology (chmn. bd. govs. 1994-95, pres. 2000-01, trustee), Assn. Profs. Cardiology (pres. 1995). Office: U Va Health Sys Box 800158 Charlottesville VA 22908 Business E-Mail: gbeller@virginia.edu.

BELLER, MARTIN LEONARD, retired orthopaedic surgeon; b. NYC, Apr. 30, 1924; s. Abraham Jacob and Ida (Fishkin) B.; m. Wilma Gertrude Kjelgaard, June 29, 1947; children: Alan Lewis, Beatrice Ann Beller Foreman Heck, Peter James. AB with honors, Columbia U., 1944, MD, 1946. Diplomate Am. Bd. Orthopaedic Surgery. Intern Mt. Sinai Hosp., NYC, 1946-47; resident in orthopaedic surgery Hosp. Joint Diseases, NYC, 1949-52; pvt. practice Phila., 1952-87; asst. prof. orthopaedic surgery U. Pa. Sch. Medicine, Phila., 1967-72, assoc. prof., 1972-80, clin. prof., 1980-87; ret., 1987. Attending orthopaedic surgeon Hosp. U. Pa., 1963-87; assoc. attending orthopaedic surgeon Albert Einstein Med. Ctr., Phila., 1960-70; chmn. dept. orthopaedic surgery Albert Einstein Med. Ctr. (Daroff divsn.), 1970-79. Author (with I. Stein and R. O. Stein): Living Bone in Health and Disease, 1955; author: (with I. Stein) Clinical Densitometry of Bone, 1970. Vestryman Episcopal Ch., 1966—87, 1990—93, 1996—99, 2002—05, 2007—10; trustee St. Paul's Episcopal Ch., Wellsboro, Pa., 1999—. Am. Orthopaedic Assn. exchange fellow, Gt. Britain, 1963. Fellow ACS, Am. Acad. Orthopaedic Surgeons (bd. councilors 1978-81, Pa. rep. commn. on trauma 1984-87), Internat. Soc. Orthopaedic Surgery and Traumatology; mem. Am. Orthopaedic Assn., Pa. Orthopaedic Soc. (pres. 1975-77), Orthopaedic Rsch. Soc., Am. Coll. Rheumatology, NY Acad. Sci., Phi Beta Kappa, Alpha Omega Alpha, Phi Delta Epsilon (nat. pres. 1975-76, chmn. bd. trustees 1984-85, assoc. exec. sec. 1991-95, exec. com. 1995—2010), Union League Phila. (life), Tyoga Country Club (Wellsboro, Pa.). Republican. Home: 2415 Rt 6 Gaines PA 16921-9505 Home Phone: 814-435-6607.

BELLIS, CARROLL JOSEPH, surgeon, educator; b. Shreveport, La. s. Joseph and Rose (Bloome) B.; m. Mildred Darmody, Dec. 26, 1939; children: Joseph, David. BS summa cum laude, U. Minn., 1930, MS in Physiology, 1932, PhD in Physiology, 1934, MD, 1936, PhD in Surgery, 1941. Diplomate Am. Bd. Surgery, cert. Internat. Bd. Proctology, Internat. Bd. Surgery. Fellow in physiology U. Minn., Mpls., 1930-34; resident in surgery U. Minn. Hosps., Mpls., 1937-41; pvt. practice surgery Long Beach, Calif., 1945-95. Prof., chmn. dept. surgery Calif. Coll. Medicine, 1962—; surg. cons. to surgeon gen. U.S. Army; adj. prof. surgery U. Calif. Author: Fundamentals of Human Physiology, A Critique of Reason, Lectures in Medical Physiology; contbr. numerous articles on surgery and physiology to profl. jours. Served to col. M.C. AUS, 1941-46. Recipient Charles Lyman Green prize in physiology, 1934, prize Mpls. Surg. Soc., 1938, ann. award Mississippi Valley Med. Soc., 1955; Alice Shevlin fellow U. Minn., 1932-34. Fellow: ACS, Peripheral Vascular Soc. Am. (founding), Internat. Acad. Proctology, Nat. Cancer Inst., Phlebology Soc. Am., Gerontol. Soc., Am. Med. Writers Assn., Internat. Coll. Surgeons, Royal Soc. Medicine, Am. Coll. Gastroenterology, Internat. Coll. Angiology (sci. coun.), Am. Soc. Abdominal Surgeons; mem.: AAAS, Pan Am. Med. Assn. (diplomate), Indsl. Med. Assn., Pan Pacific Surg. Assn., Am. Assn. History Medicine, Irish Med. Assn., Am. Geriatrics Soc., Hollywood Acad. Medicine, N.Y. Acad. Scis., Miss. Valley Med. Soc., Am. Assn. Study Neoplastic Diseases, Alpha Omega Alpha, Sigma Xi, Phi Beta Kappa. Home: PMB 808 904 Silver Spur Rd Rolling Hills Estates CA 90274 Office Phone: 310-377-6343.

BELLISOLA, GIUSEPPE, research scientist; b. Vicenza, Feb. 1, 1955; Laurea, U. Padova, 1981. Rsch. scientist Azienda Ospedaliera U. Integrata Verona, 1989—. Office: Policlinico G Rossi Ple LA Scuro 10 Verona 37134 Italy E-mail: giuseppe.bellisola@ospedaleuniverona.it.

BELLM, JOAN, civic worker; b. Alton, Ill., June 20, 1934; d. Harvey Jacob and Alma Lorene (Roberts) Goldsby; m. Earl David Bellm, Oct. 1, 1955; children: David, Lori, Michael. Bd. dirs. Drug Watch Internat., 1991-02, lifetime hon. dir., 1998—; exec. dir. Ctr. for Drug Info., 1998—. Editor Best of IDEA newsletter, 1991-96, Drug Watch World News, 1996-02; chmn. Drug Watch Internat. editl. rev. com., 1996-02; columnist weekly newspaper, 1998—. Organist, dir. jr. choir St. Mary's Cath. Ch., 1958-78; mem. adv. bd. Carlinville (Ill.) Area Hosp., 1981-86; trustee Blackburn Coll., Carlinville, 1983-86; bd. dirs. Cath. Children's Home, Diocese of Springfield, Ill., 1986—; founder, bd. dirs., state networker Ill. Drug Edn. Alliance, 1982-86, pres., 1987-89; bd. dirs., nat. networker Nat. Fedn. Parents for Drug-Free Youth, Washington, 1984-86; mem. Ill. Gov.'s Adv. Coun. on Alcoholism and Substance Abuse, 1989-93; dir. Ctr. for Drug Info., 1998—; founder Drug Watch Internat., 1991, Internat. Drug Strategy Inst., 1993, invited participant Internat. Private Sector Conf. on Drugs, Seville, 1993, advisor U.N. Internat. Drug Ctrl. Program, 1994; numerous others. Recipient letter of endorsement Pres. of U.S., 1981, citation of recognition Ill. Dept., Am. Legion, 1981, Meritorious Svc. award, 1982, award Ill. Drug Edn. Alliance award, 1984, Southwestern Ill. Law Enforcement Commn., 1984, Carlinville Sch. Bd., 1985, Outstanding Svc. award Nat. Fedn. Parents, 1986, award Ill. Alcohol and Drug Dependence Assn., 1986, Optimist Internat., 1987, Ill. Drug Edn. Alliance, 1988, Outstanding Citizen award Blackburn U., 1989, Citizen of Yr. award, Carlinville, 1990; Leadership award Drug Watch Internat., 2001. Office Fax: 217 854 8472.

BELLO, BRAIMOH, epidemiologist; b. Nigeria, July 21, 1974; BSc with honors, U. Benin, Nigeria, 1998; MSc in Medicine, U. Witwatersrand, South Africa, 2005. Rschr., tchr., supr. U. Witwatersrand, epidemiologist, 2009—. Named one of 200 Young South Africans, Mail and Guardian. Mem.: Pub. Health Assn. South Africa, Golden Key (life). Avocation: soccer, reading, table tennis. Office: Corner Klein and Esselen Johannesburg Gauteng 2000 South Africa E-mail: braimohbello@yahoo.com.

BELLOHUSEN, RONALD MICHAEL, orthodontist, educator; b. McKeesport, Pa., July 25, 1947; s. Michael and Ann (Montrenes) B.; m. Gail Jean Davies, Nov. 22, 1969; children: Michael, Beth. BS, U. Pitts., 1968, MS in Organic Chemistry, 1974, DMD, 1978. Cert. in splty. of orthodontics. Rschr. NIH/Nat. Cancer Inst., Bethesda, Md., 1971-72; clin. instr. Eastman Dental Ctr., Rochester, N.Y., 1994—; orthodontist Orthodontic Assocs. of So. Tier, Elmira, N.Y., 1994—. Lt. USN, 1969-72. Recipient Pierre Fauchard Acad. award, 1992; NESO rsch. grantee on asymmetry in cleft palate, 1993. Fellow Internat. Coll. Dentists; mem. ADA, Am. Assn. Orthodontists, Am. Bd. Orthodontists (bd. cert.). Avocations: flying, sailing, kayaking, skiing. Office: Orthodontic Assoc So Tier 440 E Water St Elmira NY 14901-3411 Office Phone: 607-733-7163. E-mail: ortho1@stny.rr.com.

BELLOLIO, FELIPE, medical educator; b. Santiago, Chile, Mar. 12, 1976; MD, U. Catolica de Chile, 2001. Asst. instr. U. Catolica de Chile, 2008—. Office: Marcoleta 367 Santiago Region Metropolitana Chile Business E-Mail: fbelloli@med.puc.cl.

BELLO-SILVA, MARINA STELLA, dentist, educator, medical researcher; b. São Paulo, Brazil, May 27, 1983; DDS, U. São Paulo, 2005, PhD, U. Aachen, Germany, 2010. Prof., rsch. scientist U. Nove Julho, 2010—. Collaborator Spl. Lab. Lasers in Dentistry, U. São Paulo, 2004, Soc. Laser in Dentistry, 2009; internat. collaborator Aachen Dental Laser Inst., 2005; with, communication and website S.Am. Dlvsn., World Fedn. Laser Dentistry, 2009. Recipient 1st award, III Internat. Congress for Laser Dentistry, APCD; David B. Scott fellowship, Internat. Assn. Dental Rsch. Mem.: Brazilian Assn. Laser in Dentistry, World Fedn. Laser Dentistry, Brazilian Soc. Dental Rsch. Avocation: basketball. Home: Rua Abilio Soares 760 Apt 111 São Paulo 04005-003 Brazil Personal E-mail: marinastella@hotmail.com.

BELLUCK, PAM, journalist; B in Internat. Rels., Princeton U., 1985. Reporter The Atlanta Jou.-Constitution, Atlanta, 1987—89, The Phila. Inquirer, Phila., 1989—95, New York Times, NYC, 1995—97, midwest bur. chief Chgo., 1997—2001, new eng. bur. chief Boston, 2001—09, science and health writer, 2009—. Musician compositions. Fulbright scholar, 1986, Knight Journalism Fellow, Harvard and MIT, 2007—08. E-mail: belluck@nytimes.com. *

BELO, VICTORIA G., plastic surgeon, dermatologist; b. Jan. 25, 1956; B in Psychology, UP, Diliman, 1978; MD, U. Sto Tomas, 1985; diploma in Dermatology, Inst. of Dermatology, Bangkok, Thailand, 1990; tng. in Dermatologic Surgery, Scripps Clinic, San Diego Calif.; tng in Cultaneous Laser Surgery, Harvard Med. Sch., Boston, Mass., 1993, studied Skin Rejuvenation and Laser Surgery, St. Francis Meml Hosp. U. Calif., San Francisco, 1995; studied Advanced Techniques in Phlebology, Pauline Raymond-Martimbeau Vein Inst., Texas, studied Liposuction & Laser Assisted Liposuction, San Juan Capistrano, Calif. Med. dir. Belo Med. Group. Mem. Found. for Facial Plastic Surgery, New Port Beach, Calif. Mem.: Philippine Liposuction Surgery (Founding Officer), Internat. Soc. of Dermatologic Surgery, Internat. Soc. of Cosmetic Laser Surgeons (ISCLS), Am. Soc. of Hair Restoration Surgery, Am. Soc. of Lipoplastic Surgery, Am. Acad. of Cosmetic Surgery, Am. Soc. of Dermatologic Surgery, Am. Acad. of Dermatology. Office: Belo Medical Group Ste 901 Medical Plaza Makati Amorsolo Corner Dela Rosa Streets Makati 1229 Philippines Office Phone: 8441182. Office Fax: 8179777. *

BELSHÉ, KIMBERLY (SHARON KIMBERLY BELSHE), public health service officer, former state official; b. 1959; AB, Harvard Coll.; MA, Princeton U. Legis. asst. to Rep. Norm Shumway US House of Reps., Washington, 1988—89; legis. asst. to Senator Pete Wilson US Senate, Washington, 1989—90; dep. sec. Calif. Health & Welfare Agy., 1991—93; dir. Calif. Dept. Health Services, 1993—99; prog. dir. The James Irvine Found., 1999—2003; sec. Calif. Dept Health & Human Services, Sacramento, 2003—11; sr. policy adv. Pub. Policy Inst. Calif., Sacramento, 2011—. Mem. Atty. Gen.'s Violence Prevention Policy Coun.; exec. com. mem. Women in State Govt., Nat. Acad. State Health Policy; bd. mem. Calif. Health Decisions; appointee Managed Risk Med. Ins. Bd., 1994; founding commr., vice chmn. Calif. Children & Families Commn. Bd. mem. Great Valley Ctr., Crocker Art Mus. Office: Public Policy Institute of California Senator Office Bldg 1121 L St Ste 801 Sacramento CA 95814 Office Phone: 916-440-1132. Office Fax: 916-440-1121. E-mail: belshe@ppic.org. *

BELSHE, ROBERT, epidemiologist, educator; MD, U. Ill. Chgo. Med. Ctr. Intern Saint Louis U. Hosp.; resident U. Ill. Hosp.; fellow Nat. Inst. Health; dir. Ctr. for Vaccine Devel. Saint Louis U., prof. infectious diseases. Office: St Louis University School of Medicine Division of Infectious Diseases 1100 S Grand Blvd Saint Louis MO 63104

BELSKY, JOSEPH L., endocrinologist; b. Newark, Mar. 14, 1927; m. Jane Belsky; 4 children. BA in Chemistry, cum laude, Drew U., 1949; MA in Chemistry, Wesleyan U., 1951; MD, Albany Med. Coll., 1955. Diplomate Am. Bd. Internal Medicine, Am. Bd. Endocrinology and Metabolism, cert. advanced achievement in internal medicine 1987. Intern Tufts Med. Svc., Boston City Hosp., 1955—56; asst. resident Boston City Hosp., 1956—57; asst. resident, internal medicine (metabolism) VA Hosp., Boston, 1957—58, resident, internal medicine, 1958—59, staff physician, med. svc., 1959—61; pvt. practice Ridgefield, Conn., 1961—64; dir. med. edn. Danbury Hosp., Conn., 1964—69; chief of medicine Atomic Bomb Casualty Commn., Hiroshima/Nagasaki, Japan, 1969—72; chief of medicine, program dir. internal medicine Danbury Hosp., 1972—80, chief of endocrinology and metabolism, 1980—96, part-time endocrinologist, 1994—. Vis. staff, internal medicine Yale New Haven Hosp., 1962—; attending physician, medicine Danbury Hosp., 1961—, asst. attending physician, lab. medicine, 1968—, cons. pediat., 1981—; tchg. fellow to clin. instr. medicine Tufts U. Sch. Medicine, 1957—61; clin. asst., medicine Harvard Med. Svc., Boston City Hosp., 1958; clin. instr. to assoc. clin. prof. medicine Yale U. Sch. Medicine, 1962—86, clin. prof. medicine, 1986—. Spkr. Med. Town Meetings; participant regular health broadcasts local radio, Ridgefield, 1966—95; mem. Bd. Edn. Town of Ridgefield, 1965—69, sch. bldg. com., 1964—69, bd. ethics, 1994—2004. Served USN, 1945—46. Recipient Alumni Achievement award, Drew U. Master: ACP (sec.-treas., v.p., pres. 1975—82, gov.'s coun. Conn. chpt. 1975—93, gov. for Conn. 1985—89, chmn. assocs. subcom. 1988—89, Laureate award Conn. chpt. 1990); mem.: Am. Diabetes Assn. (bd. dirs. Conn. affiliate 1981—84), Am. Soc. Internal Medicine, Nat. Bd. Med. Examiners (adv. com. 1976), Lawson Wilkins Pediatric Endocrine Soc., Conn. Endocrine Soc. (v.p. 1975—77, 1980—83, pres. 1983—85), Endocrine Soc., ACGME (residency rev. com. internal medicine 1989—92, appeals panel 1993—96), Am. Fedn. Clin. Rsch., Alpha Omega Alpha, Sigma Xi (assoc.). Office: 25 Germantown Rd Danbury CT 06810 Office Phone: 203-794-5620. Business E-Mail: joseph.belsky@danhosp.org. *

BELTRAN, MARCELO A., surgeon; b. Cochabamba, Bolivia, Aug. 6, 1968; M.D., U. Mayor De San Simon, 1994; degree in Gen. Surgery, U. Chile, 2001. Chief surgery Hosp. de La Serena, Coquimbo, Chile, 2008—. Adj. prof. U. Catolica Del Norte, 2007. Recipient Excellence prize, Fedn. L.Am. de Cirugia. Mem.: Soc. Chilena De Cirugia, Internat. Gastric Cancer Assn., Soc. Surgery Alimentary Tract, Internat. Surg. Soc. Avocation: motorcycling. Home and Office: Hosp de La Serena Dept Surgery Manuel Antonio Caro 2629 La Serena Coquimbo 170000000 Chile Personal E-mail: beltran_01@yahoo.com.

BELTRAO, HERNANI TEIXEIRA, retired surgeon; b. Marinha Grande, Portugal, May 29, 1937; s. Henrique Teixeira and Francine (Azevedo) B.; m. Maria Luizete Sousa, Dec. 28, 1963; children: Paulo, Cristina. MD, Coimbra Medicine Faculty, Portugal, 1962. Intern Coimbra U. Hosp., Portugal, 1963-70, resident, 1970-72; dir. urgency dept. Leiria Hosp., Portugal, 1979-86, dir. surgery dept., 1981-99, oncology registry coord., 1988-98. Contbr. articles to profl. jours. Fellow Internat. Coll. Surgeons; mem. Portuguese Soc. Surgery, Assn. Surgeons, Internat. Soc. Surgery. Avocations: bicycling, bricolage, home made video. Office: Clinigrande R D Joao Pereira Venancio 2430 Marinha Grande Portugal Home: L Ilidio Carvalho 15-1 2430-259 Marinha Grande Portugal Business E-Mail: beltraohernani@sapo.pt.

BELZ, GABRIELLE THERESE, veterinary surgeon; d. Mervyn Bernard and Mary Rose Belz. BVBiol, U. Queensland, 1990, BS in Vet. Sci., 1993, PhD, 1997. Postdoc. fellow WEHI, Memphis, 1997—2002, SJCHR, Memphis; fellow ARC QEII, WEHI, Melbourne, Victoria, Australia, 2002—03, HHMI, Melbourne, Victoria, 2005—, Wellcome Trust, Melbourne, Victoria, 2003—07; lab. head WEHI, Melbourne, Victoria, 2008—. Recipient Burnet award, 2007, Gottschalk medal, 2008; Viertel fellowship, 2008 . Office: WEHI 1G Royal Parade Melbourne 3052 Australia Office Phone: 61-3-9345-2544. Office Fax: 61-3-9347-0852. Business E-Mail: belz@wehi.edu.au.

BELZBERG, ALLAN JOEL, neurosurgery educator; b. Montreal, Que., Can., July 1, 1956; came to U.S., 1990; s. Sam Isadoer and Dorothy (Chetner) B., m. Lorinda Gayle Sproule, May 29, 1988; children: Micah, Adam. BSc in Physiology with honors, U. B.C., Vancouver, Can., 1978, postgrad., 1978-79; MD, U. Calgary, Alta., Can., 1982. Mixed surg. and med. intern McGill U. Tchg. Hosps., Montreal, 1982-83; jr. resident in neurosurgery Foothills Hosp.-U. Calgary, 1984-85, 86, 87, sr. resident, 1988, resident in neuroradiology, sr. resident in neurology, 1986, resident in neuropathology, 1988; jr. resident, then sr. resident in neurosurgery Calgary Gen. Hosp., 1985, 87, chief resident, 1989; sr. resident Alta. Children's Hosp., 1988; rsch. fellow in neurosurgery U. Calgary, 1989-90, clin. asst. dept. neurosci., 1989-90; tng. in pain dept. neurosurgery, instr. Johns Hopkins U. Sch. Medicine, Balt., 1990-92, asst. prof., 1992, assoc. prof. Attending neurosurgeon Johns Hopkins Hosp., 1990—, Bay View Hosp., Balt., 1990—; lectr., vis. prof., presenter in field. Contbr. articles to med. jours., chpts. to books. Fellow Royal Coll. Surgery Can.; mem. Am. Assn. Neurol. Surgeons, Am. Soc. for Neurosci., Am. Soc. for Peripheral Nerve, Am. Pain Soc., Internat. Assn. for Study Pain, Can. Neurosurg. Soc., Can. Neurosci. Soc., Md. Neurosurg. Soc. Office: Johns Hopkins Hospital 600 N Wolfe St Baltimore MD 21287-0005

BELZBERG, SAMUEL, investment professional; b. Calgary, Alta., Can., June 26, 1928; s. Abraham and Hinda (Fishman) B.; m. Frances Cooper; children: Cheryl Rae, Marc David, Wendy Jay, Lisa. B.Comm., U. Alta., Edmonton, 1948; doctorate (hon.), Simon Fraser Univ. Chmn. Balfour Holdings, Inc., 1992-97; pres. 1st City Fin. Corp. Ltd., Vancouver, B.C., Can., 1970-83, 86-91, chmn., 1983-91; pres. Gibralt Capital Corp., Vancouver, 1995—, Bel-Fran US Inc., 1997—. Bd. dirs. chmn. bd. trustees & founder, Simon Wiesenthal Ctr., LA, chmn. Second City Capital, dir. chmn., Rockford Coorp., chmn., Action Canada. Recipient Order of Can., 1989, Officer of Order of Can., 2002, Gov. Gen. Canada, 1998. Mem.: Can. Dystonia Med. Rsch. Found. (founding chmn.), Am. Dystonia Med. Rsch. Found. (founding chmn.). Office: Dystonia Med Rsch Found Canada Ste 106 8 King St East Toronto M5C 1B5 Canada

BENA-BOUPDA, NICOLE FRANCOISE, nuclear medicine physician, pediatrician; b. Douala, Littoral, Cameroon, Mar. 9, 1972; d. Jean-Paul and Esther Boupda; m. Andre Bena, Mar. 22, 2000; children: Noor-Cella Bena, Mee Malaika Bena, Norabelle Iken Bena, Al Joe Bena Jr. MD, Med. Sch. Heidelberg, Germany, 1998. Diplomate in cmty. health and tropical medicine German Found. Internat. Devel., 1997, specialist in nuc. medicine Landesärztekammer Hessen, 2003, specialist in pediat. 2010. Chief insp. German Authority Quality Assurance, Eschborn, Germany, 2004—. Contbr. articles to profl. jours. Mem.: German Soc. Pediat., German Soc. Nuc. Medicine.

BENAGIANO, GIUSEPPE PINO, medical association administrator, medical educator; b. Rome, Oct. 15, 1937; s. Andrea and Maria Luisa (Piergili) Benagiano; m. Orietta Bianchini, Oct. 4, 1965 (div. 1984); children: Marisa, Andrea; m. Stephanie Canwell, June 29, 1985. MD, U. Rome, 1961, specialist in Ob-gyn., 1965. Supranumerary asst. prof. U. Rome, 1962—67, from asst. to assoc. prof., 1968-73; Ford Found. fellow Karolinska Inst., Stockholm, 1964-67; rsch. specialist Population Coun., NYC, 1967; med. officer WHO, Geneva, 1973-80, dir. spl. program rsch. in human reproduction, 1993-97; prof., dir. Inst. Ob-Gyn. U. la Sapienza, Rome, 1981-93, dean Postgrad. Sch. Ob-gyn., 2002—09; dir.-gen. Italian NIH, Rome, 1997-2001; assoc. prof. ob-gyn. U. Geneva, 1997—2003. Hon. prof. U. Peking, 2003; cons. U.S.AID, Washington, 1982, 90, UNFPA, 1995, 2002; hon senator U. Szeged, 2008. Editor: Progestogens in Therapy, 1982, Endocrine Mechanisms in Fertility Regulation, 1986, Immaginario Erotico e "Realta" Pornografica, 1989, Trattato di Fisiopatologia della Riproduzione Umana, 1993, The Evolution of the Meaning of Sexual Intercourse in the Human, 1996. Fellow: ACOG (hon.), Royal Coll. Ob-gyn. (hon.); mem.: E&S Diczfalusy Found. (v.p. 2007), Internat. Com. Rsch. in Reproduction (founding mem., bd. dirs. 1981—96), Internat. Fedn. Gynecologists and Obstetricians (jour. assoc. editor 1989—2011, sec.-gen. 1997—2003), Soc. Advancement of Contraception (pres. 1992—95), Soc. Italiana di Sessuologia Clinica (pres. 1986—89), Spanish Soc. Ob-gyn. (hon.), Swiss Soc. Ob-gyn. (hon.), Chilean Soc. Ob-gyn. (hon.), Lebanese Soc. Ob-gyn. (hon.), Taiwan Assn. Ob-gyn. (hon.), Chinese Soc. Ob-gyn. (hon.), Romanian Soc. Ob-gyn. (hon.), Brazilian Soc. Ob-gyn. (hon.), Argentine Soc. Ob-gyn. (hon.), Italian Soc. Ob-gyn. (hon.). Roman Catholic. Avocation: gardening. Office: Policlinico Umberto I Viale Regina Elena 269 00161 Rome Italy Home: Chemin des Massettes 28 1218 Grand-Saconnex Geneva Switzerland Personal E-mail: gbenagiano@libero.it. Business E-Mail: giuseppe.benagiano@uniroma1.it, pinoingeneva@sunrise.ch.

BENAZZI, LUCIANE ELOISA BRANDT, medical educator; b. Santa Cruz Do Sul, Rio Grande Do Sul, Brasil, May 11, 1972; Grad., U. Luterana Do Brasil, 2003, M, 2007. Tchr. U. Luterana Do Brasil, 2002—. Home: Rua Édalo Michelin 182 Bento Gonçalves Rio Grande Do Sul 95700000 Brazil Personal E-mail: lubenazzi@terra.com.br.

BENCKART, DANIEL H., cardiologist, educator; MD, Georgetown U. Diplomate Am. Bd. Surgery-vascular surgery. Practice McGinnis Thoracic & Cardiovascular Surgical Assocs.; intern Vanderbilt Univ. Med. Ctr., residnet; fellow NYU Med. Ctr.; assoc. prof. cardiovascular and thoracic surgery Drexel Univ.; assoc. dean acad. affairs Allegheny Gen. Hosp. Named one of Top Doctors, Pitts. mag., 2011. Office: Allegheny General Hospital 320 E N Ave Pittsburgh PA 15212 Office Phone: 412-359-3131. Office Fax: 412-359-4108.

BENDARDAF, RIYAD AHMAD, medical researcher; b. Benghazi, Libya, Mar. 10, 1971; s. Ahmad Othman Bendardaf and Salima Rafaa El Ghwail; m. Hanan Lamlum, Jan. 5, 2002. MB, BChir, Al Arab Med. U., Benghazi, 1997; PhD, Turku U., Finland, 2003. Sr. ho. officer in orthopaedic surgery Al Jalla Trauma and Emergency U. Hosp., Benghazi, 1998—99; sr. ho. officer in gen. surgery Seventh of Oct. U. Hosp., Benghazi, 1999—2000; clin. rsch. fellow Turku U. Ctrl. Hosp., 2000—. Muslim.

BENDAVID, CLAUDE, biochemist, educator; b. Angers, France, Sept. 27, 1969, MD, Rennes1 U., PhD, 2001. Asst. prof. Rennes U. Med. Ctr., 2007—10, prof., rschr., 2010—. Office: CHU de Rennes Pontchaillou 2 Rue Henri Rennes Bretagne 35000 France Business E-Mail: claude.bendavid@univ-rennes1.fr.

BENDER, HARVEY A., biology professor; b. Cleve., June 5, 1933; m. Eileen Adelle Teper, June 16, 1956; children: Leslie Carol, Samuel David, Philip Michael. AB in Chemistry, Case Western Res. U., 1954, student, 1954-55; MS, Northwestern U., 1957, PhD, 1959. Diplomate Am. Bd. Medical Genetics (founding). Post-doctoral fellow USPHS U. Calif., Berkeley, 1959-60; asst. prof. biology U. Notre Dame, Ind., 1960-64, assoc. prof. Ind., 1964-69, prof. Ind., 1969—. Adj. prof. law U. Notre Dame, 1974-; dir. No. Ind. Regional Genetics Ctr., Meml. Hosp. South Bend (Ind.), 1979-2000, Gt. Lakes Regional Genetics Group, 1991-, Cancer Genetics Ctr., St. Joseph Regional Med. Ctr., 2000—, Cancer Genetics & Risk Assessment Ctr., St. Joseph Med. Ctr., South Bend, Ind.; NSF In-Svc. Inst. prof., fall term 1962-63; vis. prof. human genetics, rsch. assoc. Yale U., 1973-74; vis. prof. zoology So. Ill. U., Carbondale, summer 1978; adj. prof. medical genetics Ind. U., 1979—; vis. prof. natural scis. Washington Coll., Chestertown, Md., 1984; cons. Ednl. Rsch. Coun. Am., 1967-69, Pres.'s Com. on Mental Retardation, 1973, N.J. Inst. Tech., 1975-76, Ind. State Bd. Health, 1991—, mem. sickle cell commn., 1987—, chronic disease commn., 1989—; genetics cons. Ind. State Bd. Health, 1991-. Editorial reviewer various profl. jours. Bd. dirs. Internat. Rels. Coun., 1961-69, v.p., 1962-64, pres., 1964-65; bd. dirs. Coun. for Retarded of St. Joseph County, 1964-76, 1st v.p., 1967-76; chmn. human rights com. No. Ind. State Hosp., 1980—. Pre-doctoral fellow USPHS, 1957-59, Cross-disciplinary fellow Yale U., 1973-74, Carnegie fellow, 2001-, KANEB fellow U. Notre Dame, 2002—; grantee NIH, 1961-67, DOE, 1961—, United Health Svc., 1963-73, NSF, 1978-81, HEW, HHS, others; Carnegie Found. scholar, 2001—; named Disting. Hoosier, Govt. of Ind. 2006. Fellow AAAS; mem. AAUP, Am. Assn. Mental Deficiency, Am. Inst. Biol. Scientists, Am. Soc. Human Genetics, Genetics Soc. Am., Ind. Acad. Sci., Radiation Rsch. Soc., Soc. Devel. Biology, Soc. for Values in Higher Edn., Sigma Xi (regional lectr. 1977—, mem. nat. com. on sci. and society 1978-89, chmn. 1981-89, mem. nat. com. awards, 1981-86, chmn. 1981-83, dir.-at-large 1980-86, bd. dirs. nat. exec. com. 1983-84, long range planning com. 1986—). Office: U Notre Dame Dept Biol Scis Notre Dame IN 46556 Office Phone: 574-631-7075, 574-231-6477. Business E-Mail: bender@nd.edu.

BENDO, JOHN A., orthopedist, surgeon, educator; Attended, CUNY, 1985—89. Diplomate Am. Bd. of Orthopaedic Surgery, 2008. Intern gen. surgery Mt. Sinai Med. Ctr., 1989—90, resident orthopaedics, 1990—94; clin. fellow spinal surgery NY Univ. Hosp. for Joint Diseases, 1994—95, dir. spine svc. clin. affairs, 2010—; asst. prof. orthopaedic surgery NY Univ. Sch. of Medicine; with NY Univ. Langone Med. Ctr. Co-author: (publs.) Systematic review of cohort studies comparing surgical treatments for cervical spondylotic myelopathy, 2010, The lumbar facet joint: a review of current knowledge: part 1: anatomy, biomechanics, and grading, 2011, The lumbar facet joint: a review of current knowledge: Part II: diagnosis and management, 2011, and numerous other publications. Office: New York University Hospital for Joint Diseases Ste 400 301 E 17th St New York NY 10003 Office Phone: 212-598-6625.

BENDOK, BERNARD R., neurosurgeon, researcher; b. Grosse Pointe, Mich., Feb. 4, 1971; s. Riad and Mountaha Bendok; m. Karen Bendok; 1 child, Michael. BS in Biology summa cum laude, Wayne State U., 1991; MD, Northwestern U., 1995. Diplomate Am. Bd.

Neurol. Surgeons, lic. physician Ill., NY. Intern Northwestern U., Chgo., 1995—96, resident in neurol. surgery, 1996—2001, fellow in neuroendovascular surgery, 2000; mullan neuroendovascular surgery fellow SUNY, Buffalo, 2001—03; asst. prof. dept. neurol. surgery, dept. radiology Northwestern Meml. Hosp., Chgo., 2003—. Clin. instr. SUNY, Buffalo, 2001—03; lectr., presenter in field. Contbr. chapters to books, articles to profl. jours. Grantee, Am. Assn. Neurol. Surgeons/Congress Neurol. Surgeons Jt. Sect., 2001—02; Merit scholar, Wayne State U., Student Rsch. grantee, Alpha Omego Alpha, 1992. Mem.: AMA, Neurocritical Care Soc., Am. Heart Assn., Am. Soc. Interventional and Therapeutic Neuroradiology, Ill. State Neurosurg. Soc., Congress Neurol. Surgeons (sgt.-at-arms com. San Antonio 2000, sgt.-at-arms com. Seattle 1998), Am. Assn. Neurol. Surgeons (sgt.-at-arms com. Chgo. 2002), Alpha Omega Alpha. Avocations: tennis, travel. Office: Bernard Bendok 676 N Saint Clair St Ste 2210 Chicago IL 60611-2922 Business E-Mail: bbendok@nmff.org.

BENENATI, SUSAN VENTO, allergist, immunologist; MD, U. South Fla., 1984. Diplomate Am. Bd. Internal Medicine, 1988, Am. Bd. Allergy and Immunology, 1999, lic. Fla., 1990. Intern internal medicine Ind. Univ. Hosp., 1985, resident internal medicine, 1987, fellow hematology, 1988; fellow allergy and immunology Johns Hopkins Hosp., 1990; hosp. affiliations include Doctors Hosp., Meml. Regional Hosp., Miami Children's Hosp., South Miami Hosp., Baptist Hosp. of Miami. Office: Baptist Hospital of Miami 8900 North Kendall Dr Miami FL 33176-2197 Office Phone: 786-596-1960.

BENES, FRANCINE M., neuroscientist, psychiatrist; b. NYC, May 8, 1946; d. Joseph William and Emma Mary B. BA in Biology, St. John's U., 1967; PhD in Cell Biology, Yale U., 1972, MD, 1978. Lectr. in neuroanatomy Yale Sch. of Medicine, New Haven, 1975-77; asst. prof. psychiatry Harvard Med. Sch., Boston, 1982-87, assoc. prof., 1987-97, prof., 1997—, test prof. psychiatric, neuroscience, 2007—; dir. program in structural and molecular neurosci. lab. McLean Hosp., Belmont, Mass., 1992—, dir. Harvard Brain Tissue Resource Ctr., 1996—; dir. clin. neurosci. tng. program in psychiatry Harvard Med. Sch., 1994-99. Mem. bd. sci. counselors Nat. Inst. Mental Health, Bethesda, Md., 1994-98; mem. sci. adv. bd. Internat. Congress Schizophrenia Rsch., 1994—, Schizophrenia Bull., Calif. Neuro-Aids Tissue Network, San Diego, 2000—; cons. WHO, Paris, 1999. Neuropsychiatry editor Current Opinion in Psychiatry, 2000—; mem. editl. bd. Biotechniques, 1990-96, Devel. and Psychopathology, 1991—, Synapse, 1995—, Neuropsychopharmacology, 1997-2001, Schizophrenia Rsch., 1998—.; contbr. articles to profl. jours. Bd. dirs. Waldon Pond Reservation Trust, Concord, Mass., 2001—; mem. Nat. Wildlife Fedn., Humane Soc. of US; chair affirmative action com., McLean Hosp., Belmont, 1993-94. Recipient Shervert S. Frazier Lifetime Achievement award, 1999, Merit award NIMH, 2000-02, Lifetime Achievement award in mentoring, 2006, Kempf award Am. Psychiat. Assn. Mem. Inst. Medicine, Nat. Acad. Sci., Soc. for Neurosci., Am. Coll. Neuropsychopharmacology, World Fedn. Socs. of Biol. Psychiatry (co-chair task force on brain pathology 2001—), Nat. Assn. for Rsch. on Schizophrenia and Depression (mem. sci. adv. bd., Lieber prize 2002), Schizophrenia Forum (sci. adv. bd. mem. 2009-), Pathology & Lab. Medicine (dept. neuropsychopharm. mem. 2008-, editl. bd. mem. 2009-), J. Care Death Epigenetics and Genetyics (hon. editl. bd. mem. 2008-). Avocations: sailing, reading, creative writing. Office: McLean Hosp 115 Mill St Belmont MA 02478 E-mail: benesf@mclean.harvard.edu.

BENES, JAN, anesthesiologist, educator; b. Plzen, Czech Republic, Mar. 2, 1979; MD, Charles U., Prague, 2004. Anesthesia and intensive care specialist Charles U., Prague, 2004—, lectr., rsch. specialist, faculty medicine, 2006—. Recipient 2nd Pl, NY State Soc. Anesthesiologists, 2009; named one of Best Spoken Lectr., Czech Soc. Anesthesiology, Resuscitation and Intensive Care Medicine. Mem.: Czech Soc. Intensive Care Medicine, Czech Soc. Anesthesiology, Resuscitation and Intensive Care Medicine, European Soc. Anesthesiology. Avocations: swimming, skiing, mountain climbing, sculpting, literature. Home: Predni Cesta 18 Plzen West Bohemia 32600 Czech Republic Personal E-mail: benesj@fnplzen.cz.

BENET, LESLIE ZACHARY, pharmacologist, educator; b. Cin., May 17, 1937; s. Jonas John and Esther Racie (Hirschfeld) Benet; m. Carol Ann Levin, Sept. 8, 1960; children: Reed Michael, Gillian Vivia. AB in English, U. Mich., 1959, BS in Pharmacy, 1960, MS in Pharm. Chemistry, 1962; PhD in Pharm. Chemistry, U. Calif., San Francisco, 1965; PhD (hon.), Leiden U., Netherlands, 1995, U. Athens, 2005; PharmD (hon.), Uppsala U., Sweden, 1987; DSc (hon.), U. Ill., Chgo., 1997, Phila. Coll. Pharm. and Sci., 1997, LI U., 1999; PhD (hon.), Cath. U., Leuven, Belgium, 2010. Asst. prof. pharmacy Wash. State U., Pullman, 1965—69; asst. prof. pharmacy and pharm. chemistry U. Calif., San Francisco, 1969—71, assoc. prof., 1971—76, prof., 1976—, vice chmn. dept. pharmacy, 1973—78, chmn. dept. pharmacy, 1978—96, dir. drug studies unit, 1977—, dir. drug kinetics and dynamics ctr., 1979—98, chmn. dept. biopharm. scis., 1996—98. Mem. pharmacology study sect. NIH, Washington, 1977—81, chmn., 1979—81, 1986—88, mem. pharmacol. scis. rev. com., 1984—88; mem. generic drugs adv. com. FDA, 1990—94; mem. Sci. Bd., 1992—98; chair external rev. com. CBER, 1998, chair expert panel on individual equivalence, 1998—2000; mem. sci. adv. bd. SmithKline Beecham Pharms., 1989—92, Pharmetrix, 1989—92, Alteon, Inc., 1993—2003, TheraTech, Inc., 1993—96, Roche Biosci., 1998—2001, Pain Therapeutics, Inc., 1999—2003, UMD, Inc., 1999—2008, Silico Insights, Inc., 2000—, InforMedix, 2001—06, LifeCycle Pharma, 2004—08, Hurel Corp., 2004—, CoMentis, 2004—09, Savient Pharm., 2004—07, Limerick BioPharma, 2005—, Panacea Biotech Ltd., 2006—, CNS Bio Pty Ltd., 2007—, Auspex Pharm., 2008—09, Optivia Biotech., 2008—, Viral Genetics, 2009—; chmn. bd. AvMax, Inc., 1994—2008, Medicines 360, 2009—; bd. dirs. Impax Pharmas., One World Health, 2001—09. Assoc. editor Pharmacology and Therapeutics, 1995—2000, editor Jour. Pharmacokinetics and Biopharmaceutics, 1976—98, mem. editl. bd. The Effect of Disease States on Drug Pharmacokinetics, 1976, Pharmacology, 1979—, Pharmacy Internat., 1979—82, Pharm. Rsch., 1983—95, Pharmacokinetic Basis for Drug Treatment, 1984, Pharmacokinetics: A Modern View, 1984, ISI Atlas of Sci.: Pharmacology, 1988—89, Integration of Pharmacokinetics, Pharmacodynamics and Toxicokinetics in Rational Drug Development, 1992, Clinical Applications of Mifepristone (RU486) and Other Antiprogestins, 1993, Pharm. News, 1994—98, AAPS Jour., 1999—, Molecular Interventions, 2000—, Chemistry and Pharm. Bull., 2000—, Drug Metabolism and Pharmacokinetics, 2002—, Current Drug Metabolism, 2004—, Giving Full Measure to Counter Measures, 2004, Expert Opinion on Drug Metabolism and Toxicology, 2005—; contbr. more than 500 articles to profl. jours. Apptd. Forum on Drug Devel. and Regulation, 1988. Recipient Disting. Tchr. award, 1972—73, Outstanding Faculty Mentorship award, 2001, Rsch. Achievement award in pharm. scis., Pharm. Sics. World Congress, 2004, Career Achievement award in oral drug delivery, Controlled Release Soc., 2004, Disting. Clin. Rsch. award, 2007; named ISI Highly Cited Rschr., 2003. Fellow: AAAS (mem.-at-large exec. com. pharm. scis. sect. 1978—81, 1991—95, chair 1996—97), Am. Assn. Pharm. Scientists (pres. 1986, treas. 1987, bd. dirs. 1988—93, Disting. Pharm. Scientist award 1989, Disting. Svc. award 1996, Wurster rsch. award in pharmaceutics 2000), Acad. Pharm. Scis. (chmn. basic pharmaceutics sect. 1976—77, mem.-at-large exec. com. 1979—83, pres. 1985—86, Rsch. Achievement award 1982); mem.: ISSX (councillor 1992—96, treas. 1998—99), AAUP, Japanese Soc. for Study of Xenobiotics (internat. hon. mem. 2007), Pharm. Scis. World Congress (Rsch. Achievement award 2004), Inst. Medicine of NRC (devel. & acquisition med. countermeasures against biol. warfare agts. 2002—04, mem., standing com. biodef. 2007—, chmn. com. accelerating rsch.), Am. Assn. Colls. Pharmacy (bd. dirs. 1992—95, pres. 1993—94, Volwiler Rsch. Achievement award 1991), Am. Coll. Clin. Pharmacy, Drug Info. Assn., Internat. Pharm. Fedn. (bd. pharm. scis. 1988—, chair 1996—2000, chmn., Found Edn. & Rsch. 2008—, Host-Madsen medal 2001), Generic Pharm. Industry Assn. (mem. blue ribbon com. on generic medicines 1990), Am. Soc. for Pharmacology and Exptl. Therapeutics, Am. Soc. Clin. Pharmacology and Exptl. Therapeutics (Rawls-Palmer award and lectureship 1995, Oscar B. Hunter Meml. award 2010), Am. Pharm. Assn. (Higuchi Rsch. prize 2000), Am. Coll. Clin. Pharmacology (Disting. Svc. award 1988), Am. Found. for Pharm. Edn. (bd. dirs. 1987—, Disting. Svc. "Profile" award 1993), Inst. Medicine of NAS (forum on drug devel. and regulation 1988—94, chmn. com. on antiprogestins 1993, membership com. 1994—97, chmn. other health profns. sect. 1995—97, chmn. com. pharmacokinetics and drug interactions in elderly 1996—97, mem. Round Table R & D Drugs, Biologics & Med. Devices 1997—2000, bd. on health scis. policy 1999—2005, mem. forum on drug discovery, devel. and transl. 2005—), Sigma Xi, Phi Lambda Sigma, Rho Chi (Ann. Lecture award 1990). Office: University Calif San Francisco Dept Bioengrng and Therapeutic Scis 533 Parnassus Rm U68 San Francisco CA 94143-0912 Office Phone: 415-476-3853. Business E-Mail: leslie.benet@ucsf.edu.

BENEYTO, MONICA, neuroscientist, educator; b. Alicante, Spain, Sept. 15, 1972; MSc, U. Alicante, 1995; PhD, U. Miguel Hernandez, 2000. Postdoc. fellow U. Mich., Mental Health Rsch. Inst., 2001—04, rsch. investigator, 2004—06; asst. prof. U. Ala., 2006—07, U. Pitts., 2007—11; lectr. U. Vt., 2011—. Instr. CC Vt., 2011. Recipient Young Investigator award, Nat. Alliance Rsch. Schizophrenia and Depression, Mich. Investigator award, II prize, U. Mich.; Postdoc. fellowship, Molecular Biology Ctr., Fgn. Rsch. Ctrs. Collaboration Program grant, U. Berkeley, U. London, NIH, Generalitat Valenciana. Mem.: Soc. Neurosci., Biol. Psychiatry Assn., Fed. European Neuroci. Soc., Spanish Assn. Neurosci. Avocations: travel, mountain climbing. Home: 27 German Hill Farm Rd North Chittenden VT 05763 Business E-Mail: beneytom@upmc.edu.

BENFER, DAVID WILLIAM, hospital administrator; b. Toledo, May 28, 1946; s. Wilson L. and Marjorie (Baringer) B.; m. Mary Sturner, Sept. 5, 1970; children: Emily, Matthew, Andrew. BA, Wittenberg U., 1968; MBA in Hosp. Adminstrn., Xavier U., 1970. Asst. admintrn. Med. Coll., Ohio Hosp., Toledo, 1971-76, exec. dir., CEO, 1976-81, Bon Secours Hosp., Grosse Pointe, Mich., 1982-84, Henry Ford Hosp., Detroit, 1985-92; pres., CEO, St. Joseph Med. Ctr., Joliet, Ill., 1992-99; CEO St. Raphael Healthcare System, New Haven, 1999—2010; chair The Benfer Group LLC, 2010—; advs. healthcare supplier, ptnr., 2010—. Dir. Merchants and Mfrs. Bank, Stereotaxis, Inc.; fellow Berkeley Coll. Yale U., 2002—. Co-author: Issues in Health Care Management, 1982; contbg. author: Sisters of Bon Secours Centennial, 1982. Trustee, chmn. Family Svcs., Detroit and Wayne County, 1982-92; chmn. AIDS Consortium Southeastern Mich., Toledo, 1988-921 v.p. Med. Value Plan, Inc., 1986-91; chmn. S.E. Mich. Hosp. Coun.; bd. dirs. U. St. Francis, Joliet, 1993-2002; vice chmn. New Ctr. Area Coun., 1991-92; mem. Mich. Tastefest, 1996; bd. dirs., chmn. Ctr. Econ. Devel., Will County C. of C., Ill., New Haven Symphony, v.p. bd. Recipient Commendation 114th Ohio Gen Assembly, 1981, Torch of Liberty award Anti Defamation League, 2005. Fellow Am. Coll. Health Care Execs. (coun. regents 1989-92, bd. govs. 1992—2000, Robert S. Hudgens award 1982, chair 1998-99); mem. Am. Hosp. Assn. (regional policy bd.), Conn. Hosp. Assn. (bd. dirs. 2003-09), Cath. Health Assn. (bd. dirs. 2003-09), Quinnipiack Club (New Haven), Country Club Detroit (Grosse Pointe), New Haven Country Club. Roman Catholic. Avocations: jogging, golf. Home: 7618 Silver Wood Ct Bradenton FL 34202

BENFIELD, JOHN RICHARD, surgeon, educator; b. Vienna, June 24, 1931; arrived in U.S., 1938, naturalized, 1945; s. Richard and Charlotte Lola Benfield; m. Joyce A. Cohler, Dec. 22, 1963; children: Richard L., Robert E., Nancy J. AB, Columbia U., 1952; MD, U. Chgo., 1955. Diplomate Am. Bd. Surgery, Am. Bd. Thoracic Surgery. Intern Columbia-Presbyn. Hosp., NYC, 1955-56; E.H. Andrews fellow in thoracic surgery U. Chgo., 1956-57; chief resident and instr. in surgery U. Chgo. Clinics, 1962-64, resident in surgery, 1956-57, 59-63; asst. prof. surgery U. Wis., 1964-67; asst. prof. UCLA, 1967-69, assoc. prof., 1969-73, prof., 1973-77, clin. prof., 1978-88; prof. surgery, chief cardiothoracic surgery, vice chmn. surgery U. Calif. Davis Med. Ctr., Sacramento, 1988-95, prof. surgery, chief thoracic surgery, 1995-98, prof. emeritus, 1998—; attending surgeon V.A. Martinez Med. Ctr., 1988-98; courtesy staff Kaiser Permanente Med. Ctr., Sacramento, 1988-98. James Utley prof. surgery, chmn. dept. surgery Boston U., 1977; chmn. surgery City of Hope Nat. Med. Ctr., Duarte, Calif., 1978-87; bd. dirs. Am. Bd. Thoracic Surgery, 1982-88; cons. U.S. Naval Med. Ctr., San Diego, 1968-88; mem. sr. staff VA Wadsworth Med. Ctr., LA, 1978-88. Editor Current Problems in Cancer, 1975-86; mem. editl. bd. Annals Thoracic Surgery, 1979-2001, assoc. editor, 1987-2001; mem. editl. bd. Annals Surg. Oncology, 1994-2000; contbr. articles to profl. jours., chpts. to books. Sec., trustee Univ. Synagogue, LA. Served as capt. M.C. U.S. Army, 1957-59, Korea. Grantee Life Ins. Med. Rsch., 1962-66, Am. Heart Assn., 1968-71, USPHS, 1971-92. Mem. ACS (bd. govs. 1982-88, 92-98), Am. Surg. Assn., Am. Assn. Thoracic Surgery, Am. Assn. Cancer Rsch., Am. Med. Writers Assn., Internat. Assn. Study Lung Cancer, Internat. Soc. Surgery, Calif. Med. Soc., Ctrl. Surg. Assn., LA Acad. Medicine, The Royal Soc. Medicine (Gt. Britain), The Transplantation Soc., Soc. Thoracic Surgeons (v.p. 1994-95, pres. 1995-96), Soc. Univ. Surgeons, Pacific Coast Surg. Assn. (v.p. 1995-96), Soc. Surg. Oncology, Am. Coll. Chest Physicians (pres. Calif. chpt. 1996-97), Western Thoracic Surgeons Assn. (pres. 1989-90), Internat. Surg. Soc., Thoracic Surgery Dirs. Assn. (pres. 1995-97), Thoracic Surgery Found. Rsch. and Edn. (pres. 2003-06). Office Phone: 310-294-7333. Personal E-mail: j.benfield@verizon.net.

BENG, ARTHUR KIAN LAM, physician; b. Singapore, Apr. 24, 1949; MBBS, U. Singapore, 1973; MMed in Pub. Health, Nat. U. Singapore, 2005; FAMS. Pres., ceo Overseas Med. Svcs. Pte Ltd, 1979—; coun. chmn. Nat. Cadet Corps, Singapore, 1987—2011; IT 2000 master plan, chmn. healthcare sector Nat. Computer Bd., Singapore, 1989—90; advisor to ceo sars, Indonesia, Vietnam & China Temasek Holdings, 2003—05; sr. cons., Army-hr Ministry of Defence, 2009—11. Founding ptnr. Ooi Clinic Group Med. Practice, Singapore, 1979—2000; mp, govt. parl c'ttee law & home affairs Parliament, Rep. of Singapore, 1984—96; exec. chmn. kindergarten c'ttee; restructuring nat. pre sch. curriculum, ngo PAP Cmty. Found., Singapore, 1986—96; founding ptnr. med. centre indsl. pk., Batam, Indonesia Batamindo Pk. Klinik, 1990; founding ptnr. indsl. pk., China Suzhou Singapore Internat. Sch., 1994—2000. Recipient State award, Pres. Singapore, BBM. Fellow: Acad. Medicine, Singapore. Office: Blk 164 Kallang Way 06-28 S349248 Singapore S349248 Singapore Office Fax: 6562549789. Business E-Mail: bengkla@pacific.net.sg.

BENGTSON, ANN BIRGITTA, nursing educator; b. Vastervik, Sweden, May 20, 1947; d. Bertil Bengt and Maj Birgit Bengtson; 1 child, Viktor. RN, Gothenburg U., Sweden, 1970, RNT, 1990, PhD, 1996. Head nurse Coronary Care, Sweden, 1970—81; rsch. nurse Gothenburg U., 1981—87, sr. lectr., 1996—. Mem. ethics com. Gothenburg U., 1999—. Home: Vallsjovagen 23 SE 43543 Pixbo Sweden Office: Gothenburg U The Sahlgrenska Acad Box 457 SE 405 30 Gothenburg Sweden

BENIRSCHKE, KURT, retired pathologist, educator; b. Glueckstadt, Germany, May 26, 1924; arrived in US, 1949, naturalized, 1955; s. Fritz Franz and Marie (Luebcke) B.; m. Marion Elizabeth Waldhausen, May 17, 1952; children: Stephen Kurt, Rolf Joachim, Ingrid Marie. Student, U. Hamburg, Germany, 1942, 45-48, U. Berlin, 1943, U. Wuerzburg, 1943-44; MD, U. Hamburg, 1948; DVM (hon.), U. Zürich, 2004. Resident, Teaneck, NJ, 1950-51, Peter Bent Brigham Hosp., Boston, 1951-52, Boston Lying-in-Hosp., 1952-53, Free Hosp. for Women, Boston, 1953, Children's Hosp., Boston, 1953; pathologist Boston Lying-in-Hosp., 1955-60; tchg. fellow, assoc. Med. Sch. Harvard, 1954-60; prof. pathology, chmn. dept. pathology Med. Sch. Dartmouth, Hanover, NH, 1960-70; prof. reproductive medicine and pathology U. Calif., San Diego, 1970-94, ret., 1994; chmn. dept. pathology U. Calif. at San Diego Sch. Med., La Jolla, 1976-79. Dir. rsch. San Diego Zoo, 1975-86, trustee, 1986-00, pres., 1998-00; cons. NIH, 1957-70. Served with German Army, 1942-45. Mem. Am. Soc. Pathology, Internat. Acad. Pathology, Am. Coll. Pathology, Am. Acad. Arts and Scis., Teratol. Soc., Am. Soc. Zool. Vets. Home: 8457 Prestwick Dr La Jolla CA 92037-2023 Office: Univ Calif San Diego Med Ctr 200 W Arbor Dr San Diego CA 92103-8321 Office Phone: 619-543-2618. Business E-Mail: kbenirsc@ucsd.edu.

BEN-ISHAY, OFFIR, physician; b. Afula, Israel, July 21, 1973; MD, U. Rome Tor Vergata, 2005. Physician Rambam Health Care Campus, 2007—. Lectr. surgery Technion Inst. Tech., 2009—11. Mem.: Israeli Pediat. Surgery Assn., Israeli Surgeons Assn., Israeli Med. Assn. Avocations: scuba diving, travel. Home: Rashi St Haifa 33271 Israel Personal E-mail: o_ben-ishay@rambam.health.gov.il.

BENITEZ, JOHN GRISWOLD, medical toxicologist; b. St. Louis, July 1, 1957; s. Vicente and Jane (Griswold) B.; m. Linda Gail (Allison), May 2, 1982. BA, So. Ill. U., 1978, MD, 1981; MPH, U. Pitts., 1995. Diplomate Am. Bd. Med. Toxicology, Am. Bd. Emergency Medicine, Am. Bd. Preventive Medicine (with spl. qualifications in med. toxicology), Am. Bd. Preventive Medicine in occupl. medicine. Intern surgery S.W. Mich. Area Health Edn. Ctr., Kalamazoo, 1981-82; fellow in hyperbaric medicine St. Luke's Hosp., Milw., 1988; emergency med. svc. project med. dir. Bromenn Med. Ctr., Normal, Ill., 1988-89; instr., fellow in clin. toxicology Vanderbilt Univ. Med. Ctr., Nashville, 1989-91; chmn. adverse drug reaction com. U. Pitts. Med. Ctr., 1991-95; clin. toxicology fellowship dir., asst. prof. U. Pitts., 1991-2000; med. dir. Pitts. Poison Ctr., 1993-2000; intox project internat. program on chem. safety WHO, 1995—2000; dir. toxicology treatment program U. Pitts., 1996-99; dir. multidisciplinary MPH and MD/MPH programs Grad. Sch. Pub. Health, U. Pitts., 1997-2000; mng. dir., assoc. med. dir. Ruth A. Lawrence Poison and Drug Info. Ctr., NY, 2000—11; assoc. prof. U. Rochester, NY, 2000—08; assoc. dir. Ctr. Disaster Medicine and Emergency Preparedness, 2004—08, chair preventive medicine adv. com., 2007—08; mng. dir. Tenn. Poison Ctr., 2008—; assoc. prof. Vanderbilt U., 2008—. Emergency medicine edn. chmn. St. John's Hosp., Springfield, Ill., 1984-88; clin. assoc., Dept. Surgery So. Ill. Sch. Medicine, 1986-89; affiliate faculty mem. AHA Ill. affiliate, Normal, 1988-89; asst. state dir. basic trauma life support, Normal, Ill., 1988-89; cons. pub. health and disaster preparedness, 2003—. Med. cons. disaster svc. ARC, Springfield, Ill., 1987-88, patroller, National Ski Patrol Genesee Valley Nordic Ski Patrol, Rochester, NY, 2001-2008, active mem. Monroe County Amateur Radio Emergency Svc., NY, 2001-08, County Amateur Radio Emergency Svc., Tenn., 2008-, med. cons. Bristol Mountain Ski Patrol, NY, 20002-08, Genessee Valley Nordic Ski Patrol, Rochester, 2008-. Recipient Am. Acad. Clin. Toxicology Rsch. Award, 1990; fellow Legis. Office of Rsch. Liaison, Ho. of Reps., Commonwealth Pa., 1998. Fellow Am. Coll. Med. Toxicology, Am. Coll. Preventive Medicine, Am. Acad. Emergency Medicine, Soc. Acad. Emergency Physicians; Am. Acad. Clin. Toxicolog; Wilderness Med. Soc.; mem. Am. Acad. Clin. Toxicology, Soc. Toxicology Avocations: astronomy, sailing, cross country skiing, backpacking, amateur radio, photography. Office: TN Poison Ctr 501 Oxford House 1161 21St Ave South Nashville TN 37232-4632 Office Phone: 615-936-0760. Business E-Mail: john.g.benitez@vanderbilt.edu.

BENITEZ-MACIAS, JUAN F., physician; b. Cadiz, Spain, Dec. 13, 1975; Degree in Medicine, Cadiz U., 1999; degree in Internal Medicine, Puerta del Mar U. Hosp., Cadiz, 2006. Specialist, internal medicine, staff physician Puerto Real U. Hosp., Cadiz, 2007—. Office: Carretera Nacional IV Km 665 Puerto Real Cadiz 11510 Spain Business E-Mail: juanbema@ono.com.

BENJAMIN, BONNS G., pediatrician; b. Pitts., June 1, 1047; BS, Grove City Coll., Pa., 1969; MD, U. Pitts. Sch. Medicine, 1973. Prof. pediat., surgery Tex. Tech U. HealthSci. Ctr., 2005, regional chair dept. pediat., asst. dean quality improvement, 2007—. Fellow: AAP, APSA. Avocations: swimming, reading. Home: 4 Carnoustie Ln Amarillo TX 79124 Home Fax: 806-354-5436. Business E-Mail: bonna.benjamin@ttuhsc.edu.

BENJAMIN, BRUCE NEIL, otolaryngologist, educator; b. Wagga Wagga, NSW, Australia, Dec. 20, 1931; s. Neil Fernandez and Lena Procter Benjamin; m. Nellie Marjory Forbes; children: Gregory Bruce, Susanne Jane. MBBS, Sydney U., Australia, 1956, DLO, 1961. Otolaryngologist Sydney Hosp., 1961—83, Royal Alexandra Hosp. for Children, Sydney, 1961—98, St. Lukes Hosp., Sydney, 1971—99, Royal North Shore Hosp., Sydney, 1983—99; clin. prof. otolaryngology Sydney U., 1993—. Mem. med. subcom. Royal Flying Dr. Svc. of Australia, 1972—86; chmn. Bd. Otolaryngological Studies, 1995; pres. Australasian Soc. Paediatric Otolaryngology, Australia and New Zealand, 1993—96. Author: (textbooks) Atlas of Paediatric Endoscopy, 1981, Diagnostic Laryngology, 1990, Endolaryngeal Surgery, 1998; co-author: Colour Atlas of Otorhinolaryngology, 1995; sr. editor Internat. Jour. Pediatric Otorhinolaryngology, 1979—, mem. editl. bd. Medicine Today, 1981—, Jour. of Otolaryngol. Soc. Australia, 1989—, Jour. Otolaryngology, 1990—, Ear Nose and Throat Jour., 1992—, Laryngoscope, 1998; contbr. articles to profl. jours. Recipient Order of Brit. Empire, Queen Elizabeth, 1964; named Officer, Order of Australia, 2003. Fellow: ACS (hon.), Royal Australian Coll. Surgeons, Am. Acad. Pediat.; mem.: Australian Soc. Otolaryngology/Head and Neck Surgery, Internat. Bronchoesophagological Assn., Collegium Oto-Rhino-Laryngologicum, Otolaryngol. Soc. South Africa, Am. Triologic Soc., Am. Soc. for Pediatric Otorhinolaryngology, Am. Laryngol. Assn., Am. Broncho-Esophagological Assn. Achievements include design of surgical instruments for endolaryngeal microsurgery. Avocations: golf, photography, philately. Home: 19 Prince Rd Killara NSW 2071 Australia Home Phone: 02 9498 3638. Personal E-mail: brucebenjamin@optusnet.com.au.

BENJAMIN, ERNEST, critical care specialist, educator; MD, U.Claude Bernard, 1971. Diplomate Am. Bd. Anesthesiology, 1988, Am. Bd. Anesthesiology- critical care medicine, 1989. Resident in anesthesiology Mt. Sinai Hosp.; resident in critical care Univ. Lyon; resident in internal medicine North Gen. Hosp.; resident in anesthesiology Univ. Claude Bernard; prof. in surgery Mt. Sinai Sch. of Medicine, prof. in anesthesiology; critical care specialist Mt. Sinai Med. Ctr. Author: Continuous venovenous hemofiltration with dialysis (CVVHD) and lactate clearance in critically ill patients, 1997; co-dir.: transesophageal echocardiography performed by intensivists to assess left ventricular function: comparison with pulmonary artery catheterization, 1999; co-author: Diagnostic Dilemma: An unexpected intracardiac mass, 1998, Multicenter clinical trial of recombinant human insulin-like growth factor I in patients with acute renal failure, 1999, Multicenter experience using a new prototype transnasal transesophageal echocardiography probe, 1999, Gastrointestinal complications of intensive care, 1999, Neurological complications of intensive care, 1999, Hemodynamic waveform detection from pulmonary artery catheters in the ICU, 1999, Neurological complications in the intensive care unit, 2001, Intravenous iloprost increases mesenteric blood flow in experimental acute nonocclusive mesenteric ischemia, 2002. Office: Mount Sinai Medical Center 1 Gustave L. Levy Pl. New York NY 10029-6574 Office Phone: 212-241-6500. E-mail: ernest.benjamin@mountsinai.org.

BENJAMIN, GEORGES CURTIS, medical association administrator, emergency physician, consultant; b. Chgo., Sept. 28, 1952; s. George and Tessie Cozie (Edwards) Benjamin; m. Yvette Josphanie Janisse; children: Stephanie, Kali. BS, Ill. Inst. Tech., 1973; MD, U. Ill. Coll. Medicine, 1978. Diplomate Am. Bd. Internal Medicine, Am. Bd. Med. Examiners. Intern, resident internal medicine Brooke Army Med. Ctr., San Antonio, 1978-81; dept. emergency medicine Madigan Army Med. Ctr., Tacoma, 1981-83; chief emergency medicine Walter Reed Army Med. Ctr., Washington, 1983-87; chair. dept. cmty. health & ambulatory care DC Gen. Hosp., 1987-90; acting commr. pub. health Dist. Columbia, 1990-91; emergency physician Holy Cross Cmty. Hosp., Silver Spring, Md., 1991-95; dep. sec. pub. health State of Md., Balt., 1995-99; sec. Md. Dept. Health & Mental Hygiene, Balt., 1999—2002; exec. dir. APHA, 2002—. Emergency physician Nisqually Clinic, Yelm, Wash., 1981—82, Allenmore Cmty. Hosp., Tacoma, 1981—82, Patuxent Naval Air Station, Patuxent River, Md., 1989; asst. prof. medicine Uniformed Svcs. U. Health Scis., Bethesda, Md., 1984—87; internist Greater Southeast Cmty. Hosp., Washington, 1985—87; clin. instr. emergency medicine Georgetown U., 1988—95, adj. prof. health care scis., 1993. Mem. editl. bd. Jour. Nat. Med. Assn., 1986—93, reviewer Mil. Medicine, 1983—87, Am. Jour. Emergency Medicine, 1986—94; contbr. articles to profl. jours. Mem. DC Emergency Med. Svcs. Com., 1990—91, DC State Health Coord. Coun., 1990—91; mem. adv. bd. Montgomery County HIV/AIDS Citizens, Md., 1992—93, DC Commn. Pub. Health Disability & Injury Prevention, 1993; mem. adv. com. on pub. health preparedness HHS; mem. adv. com. to dir. Ctrs. Disease Control; bd. trustees Am. Cancer Soc.; bd. dirs. Regan-Udall Found., Rsch!America, Partnership for Prevention. Served with USAR, 1974—78, US Army, 1978—87. Decorated Eisenhower Proclamation medal 1970, Comdrs. award 1981, Army Commendation medal 1983; recipient Best Friends of DC cert. appreciation, 1991. Fellow: ACP, Am. Coll. Emergency Physicians (DC chpt. v.p. 1988—90, DC chpt. pres. 1989—90, nat. health policy com. 1992—93, govt. affairs com. 1993, emeritus fellow); mem.: AMA, Inst. Medicine, Assn. State Territorial Health Ofcls. (sec.-treas. 1999—2000, pres. 2001—02), Am. Coll. Physicians Execs., Nat. Med. Assn. (nat. co-chmn. 1985—86, nat. chmn. 1987, emergency medicine nat. chmn. 1990—93). Office: APHA 800 I St NW Washington DC 20001-3710 Office Phone: 202-777-2534, 202-777-2430. Business E-Mail: georges.benjamin@apha.org. *

BENJAMIN, IVOR J., cardiologist, educator; Attended, CUNY: Hunter Coll.; MD, Johns Hopkins U. Sch. of Medicine, 1982. Diplomate Am. Bd. Internal Medicine, 1985, Am. Bd. Internal Medicine-cardiovasc. disease, 1989. Resident internal medicine Yale-New Haven Hosp., New Haven, 1983—85, fellow cardiology rsch., 1985—88; clin. fellow Michael Reese Hosp./Univ. of Chgo., Chgo., 1988—89; postdoc. rsch. Duke Univ. Med. Ctr.; fellow Univ. of Tex. Southwestern Med. Ctr. at Dallas; prof. medicine Univ. of UT. Co-author: (publs.) Learning from failure: congestive heart failure in the postgenomic age, 2005, Mouse HSF1 disruption perturbs redox state and increases mitochondrial oxidative stress in kidney, 2005, Small heat shock proteins: a new classifcation scheme in mammals, 2005, CRYAB and HSPB2 deficiency increases myocyte mitochondrial permeability transition and mitochondrial calcium uptake, 2006, Heat shock response: lessons from mouse knockouts, 2006, Unmasking different mechanical and energetic roles for the small heat shock proteins CryAB and HSPb2 using genetically modified mouse hearts, 2007, Genetic Models of HSF Function, 2007, Heart Failure in the Era of Genomic Medicine. In: Handbook of Genomic Medicine, 2007, CRYAB and HSPB2 deficiency alters cardiac metabolism and paradoxically confers protection against myocardial ischemia in aging mice, 2007, Human alpha B-crystallin mutation causes oxido-reductive stress and protein aggregation cardiomyopathy in micc, 2007. Office: University of Utah School of Medicine Health Sciences Center 30 N 1900 E Rm 4A100 Salt Lake City UT 84132 Office Phone: 801-585-2341. Office Fax: 801-581-7735. Business E-Mail: ivor.benjamin@hsc.utah.edu.

BENJAMIN, REGINA MARCIA, federal official, physician; b. Mobile, Ala., Oct. 26, 1956; d. Clarence and Millie Benjamin. BS in Chemistry, Xavier U., New Orleans, 1979; MD, U. Ala., Birmingham, 1984; MBA, Tulane U., New Orleans, 1991; DSc (hon.), Dartmouth Coll., Hanover, NH, 2010; PharmD (hon.), Albany Coll. Pharmacy & Health Scis., NY, 2010; LHD (hon.), Rensselaer Poly. Inst., Troy, NY, 2011. Diplomate American Bd. Family Medicine. Intern, resident Med. Ctr. Ctrl. Ga., Macon; pvt. med. practice Bayou La Batre, Ala.; assoc. dean rural health U. South Ala. Coll. Medicine, Mobile; founder, CEO Bayou La Batre Rural Health Clinic, Inc., 1990—2009; surgeon gen. US Dept. Health & Human Services, 2009—. Mem. Kaiser Commn. Medicaid & Uninsured; past v.p. Ala. Governor's Commn. Aging. Bd. dirs. Physicians for Human Rights. Recipient Nelson Mandela award for health & human rights, Kaiser Family Found., 1997, Nat. Caring award, Caring Inst., 2000, President's award, U. Ala. Birmingham, 2001, Pro Ecclesia et Pontifice Disting. Svc. medal, Pope Benedict XVI, 2006, NAACP Chairman's award, 2011; named Woman of Yr., CBS This Morning, 1996; named a MacArthur Fellow, The John D. and Catherine T. MacArthur Found., 2008; named one of The Nation's 50 Future Leaders Age 40 and Under, TIME mag., 1995, America's Best Leaders, US News & World Report, 2008; Kellogg Nat. Fellow, 1993—96, Next Generation Leadership fellowship, Rockefeller Found. Fellow: American Acad. Family Physicians; mem.: NAS, AMA (Women in Medicine Panel 1986—87, pres. Edn. & Rsch. Found. 1997—98, bd. trustees 1995—, Found. Leadership award 2009), Med. Assn. State of Ala. (pres. 2002—03). Achievements include featured in Nat. Libr. Medicine exhibit Changing the Face of Medicine honoring women physicians, 2003. Office: Office Surgeon Gen 5600 Fishers Ln Rm 18-66 Rockville MD 20857 Office Phone: 301-443-4000. Office Fax: 301-443-3574. *

BENJAMIN, THERESA MARY, retired psychotherapist; b. Boston, July 27, 1920; d. Vincenzo James and Maria (Morelli) Cardinale; children: Richard, Lorri, Denise. PhD, 1982; BA, Internat. Coll., 1978, MA, 1979; PhD, Profl. Sch. for Humanities Studies, 1982. Pvt. practice, Carlsbad, Calif., 1988—. Cons. Mgmt. Plus, Oceanside; lectr. U. So. Calif., LA, Carlsbad (Calif.) HS, Carlsbad. Author: What's The Meta, 1982, I'd Rather Be Right Than Happy, 1995, The Priest is in the Parlor, 2004. Grantee, Social Work Advancement Assn., 1997. Mem.: Sierra Club. Home and Office: 1809 Kelly Drive Carlsbad CA 92008 Home Phone: 760-434-6444; Office Phone: 760-434-6444. E-mail: drtmbenjamin@msn.com.

BENJAPONPITAK, SUWAT, allergist; b. Songkhla, Songkhla, Thailand, Mar. 1, 1960; s. Chuajui Sae-chua and Saikee Sae-eung; m. Amporn Sae-lee, Mar. 10, 1966; 1 child, Thaddeaus Thad. MD (hon.), Prince Songkhla U., 1985; speciality in Pediat. Allergy and Clinical Immunology, Stanford U., 1998. Assoc. prof. pediat. Faculty of Medicine Ramathibodi Hosp., Mahidol U., Ratchataevee, Bangkok, Thailand, 1995—. Mem.: World Allergy Orgn. (corr.), Pediat.Soc. Thailand (life), Royal Coll. Pediatricians Thailand (life), Med. Coun. Thailand (life), Allergy and Immunology Soc. Thailand (life; faculty of medicine Siriraj hosp. 1984—2005, sci. dir. 1999). Achievements include research in allergy and immunology. Office: Ramathibodi Hosp Rama 6 Rd Bangkok Ratchataevee 10400 Thailand Home: Sir-Ayuthaya Rd 10400 Ratchataevee Bangkok Thailand Office Fax: 662-2011850.

BEN-MENACHEM, TAMIR, gastroenterologist, educator; MD, Ben-Gurion U., Israel, 1989. Diplomate Am. Bd. Internal Medicine, 1993, Am. Bd. Internal Medicine-gastroenterology, 1997. Intern surgery St. Joseph Hosp., Ann Arbor, Mich., 1989—90; resident internal medicine Henry Ford Hosp., Detroit, 1990—93, chief resident, 1993—94, fellow gastroenterology, 1994—97; assoc. prof. medicine Robert Wood Johnson Med. Sch., New Brunswick, NJ, dir. gastrointestinal endoscopy; gastroenterology Robert Wood Johnson Univ. Hosp. Office: Robert Wood Johnson Medical School Clinical Academic Bldg 125 Paterson St Ste 5100B New Brunswick NJ 08901 Office Phone: 732-235-7784. Office Fax: 732-235-7792. Business E-Mail: benmenta@umdnj.edu.

BENNETT, ANDREW DAVID, alcohol and drug abuse services professional; b. Bklyn., Apr. 21, 1947; s. Reginald and Thelma Bennett; m. Deborah Vitale, Aug. 12, 1984 (div. 1997). BS in Cmty. Svc. and Social Welfare, SUNY, 1977. Cert. alcohol and drug counselor Calif. Cert. Bd. Alcohol and Drug Counselors. Alcoholism counselor Cortland (N.Y.) County Mental Health Ctr., 1977—82; employee counseling rep. Hughes Aircraft Co., El Segonda, L.A., 1982—85; founder Counselor's Recovery Group, La Mesa, San Diego, 1989—91; chem. dependency counselor Broad Horizons, Ramona, San Diego, 1991—97; program dir. LaPosta Substance Abuse Ctr.-So. Indian Health Coun., Boulevard, Calif., 1997—99; counselor, trainer Phoenix House Found., Descanso, San Diego, 2001—03. Contbr. articles to profl. jours. Chmn. youth adv. subcom. Cortland County Youth Bur., 1978—80. Recipient Eagle Feather for contbns. to Native Am. Recovery, 2000. Avocations: body surfing, free diving, surf casting, jazz/Afro-Cuban percussion. Office: Multi Seruce Ctr San Diego CA 92128 also: Axis Residential Treatment Indian Wells CA 92210 Office Phone: 760-346-8032. Personal E-mail: cloudedb@aol.com.

BENNETT, ARLIE JOYCE, clinical social worker; b. Central Lake, Mich., Nov. 22, 1921; d. Charles Herbert and Bernice Evelyn (Miller) B. Student, Alma Coll., Mich., 1946-48; BA, U. Mich., 1950, MSW, 1955. Bd. cert. diplomate emerita Am. Bd. Examiners in Clin. Social Work. Social worker Ypsilanti (Mich.) State Hosp., 1950-54; staff social worker Kalamazoo Child Guidance Clinic, 1955-67, chief social worker, 1967-71; clin. social worker State Tech. Inst. Rehab. Ctr., Plainwell, Mich., 1971-90; pvt. practice, Kalamazoo, 1991-92. Field instr. Mich. State U., 1959-76, Western Mich. U. Sch. Social Work, Kalanazoo, 1971-90, U. Mich., 1967-71. Author: Pie Is in the Eye of the Beholder, 1980, War and Memory, 1991; editor newsletter Late Show Connection, 1993—; contbr. articles to profl. jours. Vol. record reviewer Cath. Family Svcs. Agys., Kalamazoo; bd. dirs. Youth Opportunities Unltd., Kalamazoo, 1968—1980; bd. mem. Juvenile Home Found., 2004—. Tech. sgt. WAC, AUS, 1944-46, ETO. Mem. NASW (past chmn. and officer), AAUW (legis. chmn. Kalamazoo br. 1985-89, 93-95, pres. 1991-93, pub. policy chmn. 1999-2002), Mensa (local coord. 1990—), Loners Am. (pres. Mich. chpt. 1990-92, 97-98), U. Mich. Alumnae Club (past pres. and officer), Phi Kapa Phi. Avocations: poetry, camping, seat weaving. Home: 1110 W Maple St Kalamazoo MI 49008-1846

BENNETT, BETSY D., medical association administrator; MD, Vanderbilt U. Sch. Medicine, Nashville. Asst. prof. and dir. clin. chemistry Vanderbilt U./Nashville Veterans Affairs Med. Ctr.; joined faculty U. South Ala. Coll. Medicine, Mobile, 1981, univ. disting. prof., 1995—2003, vice dean student affairs & med. edn., 1999—2003; exec. v.p. American Bd. Pathology, Tampa, 2003—. Office: American Bd Pathology 4830 W Kennedy Blvd Ste 690 Tampa FL 33609-2571 Office Phone: 813-286-2444. Office Fax: 813-289-5279. Business E-Mail: bdbennett@abpath.org. *

BENNETT, CATHERINE MARIE, epidemiologist, educator; b. Melbourne, Victoria, Australia, Apr. 22, 1961; d. Marie Margaret Pietzsch and John Raymond Bennett. BS with honors, La Trobe U., Melbourne, 1985, PhD, 1995; MS in Applied Epidemiology, Australian Nat. U., Canberra, 2000. Olympic pub. health coord. NSW Health, Sydney, 2000—01; lectr. epidemiology U. Melbourne, 2001—03, sr. lectr. epidemiology, 2003—08, assoc. prof., 2008—. Program dir. Pharmwiz Internat., Sydney, 2005—. Editor: Applied Environmental Science & Public Health. Recipient award, Melbourne Sch. Population Health, 2004, Excellence Tchg. & Learning award, 2007, award, Australian Learning and Tchg. Coun., 2008, David White award, U. Melbourne, 2008. Fellow: Capacity Bldg. Indigenous Policy-Relevant Health Rsch. Program; mem.: Australian Network Academic Pub. Health Insts. (exec. mem. 2008), Australasian Soc. Human Biology (com. mem. 2004—08), Am. Soc. Microbiology, Pub. Health Assn. Australia, Australian Soc. Antimicrobials, Australasian Epidemiol. Assn.

BENNETT, JAMES TOLIVER, pediatric orthopedist; b. New Orleans, Nov. 29, 1953; s. Joseph Walter and Alberta (Toliver) B.; m. Susan Pardue, Oct. 20, 1972; children: James Jr., Robert Clifton. BS in Engring., Tulane U., 1974, MD, 1978. Cert. Am. Bd. Orthopedic Surgery., Am. Bd. Spine Surgeons. Resident U. NC, Alfred Dupont Inst.; fellow Scottish Rite Hosp./ Emory, Atlanta; prof. orthopaedics; chief pediatric orthopaedics Tulane U., New Orleans. Contbr. articles to profl. jours. Bd. dirs. United Cerebral Palsy, New Orleans. Mem. Am. Acad. Orthop. Surgery, Am. Acad. Pediat., Scoliosis Rsch. Soc., Pediatric Orthop. Soc. N.Am. Republican. Presbyterian. Avocation: sailing. Office: Tulane U 1430 Tulane Ave New Orleans LA 70112-2699 also: Tulane University Hospital Clinic 129 New Camellia Blvd Covington LA 70433-7813

BENNETT, JEAN, ophthalmologist, educator; BS in Biology (with honors), Yale U., 1976; PhD in Cell & Develop. Biology & Zoology, U. Calif., Berkeley, 1980; MD, Harvard Med. Sch., 1986. Prof. ophthalmology, cell & devel. biology U. Pa. Sch. Med. Contbr. scientific papers. Mem.: Inst. Medicine. Office: FM Kirby Center for Molecular Ophthalmology 310 Stellar-Chance Labs 422 Curie Blvd Philadelphia PA 19104-6069 Office Phone: 215-898-0915, 215-898-0163. Office Fax: 215-573-7155. E-mail: jebennet@mail.med.upenn.edu.

BENNETT, JOAN WENNSTROM, biology educator; b. Bklyn., Sept. 15, 1942; d. John Anton and Kerttu L. (Johnson) Wennstrom; m. David L. Peterson; 3 children. BS, Upsala Coll., 1963; MS, U. Chgo., 1964, PhD, 1967; Litt.D (hon.), Upsala Coll., 1990; Sci.D (hon.), Bethany Coll., 2005. NSF postdoctoral rsch. assoc. U. Chgo., 1967-68; NRC rsch. assoc. So. Reg. Rsch. Labs., New Orleans, 1968-70; NSF postdoctoral rsch. assoc. Tulane U., New Orleans, 1970-71, asst. prof. biology, 1971-76, assoc. prof. biology, 1976-81, prof. biology, 1981-89, prof. cell and molecular biology, 1991—2006; prof. II, plant biology and pathology, assoc. v.p. Rutgers U., New Brunswick, NJ, 2006—; hon. prof. Chinese Acad. Scis., Beijing, 2008—. Vis. scientist dept. plant molecular biology Leiden (The Netherlands) U., 1991-92; NRC postdoctoral fellow So. Regional Rsch. Lab., 1968-70, collaborator, 1982-2006. Editor: (with K.I. Abroms) Genetics and Exceptional Children, 1981, (with A. Ciegler) Differentiation and Secondary Metabolism in Fungi, 1983, (with L. Lasure) Gene Manipulations in Fungi, 1985, More Gene Manipulations in Fungi, 1991; editl. bd. Mycol. Rsch., 1991-94, Applied and Environ. Microbiology, 1978-85, Jour. Indsl. Microbiology, 1985-89, Mycopathologia, 1984-94, Applied Microbiology and Biotechnology, 1985-94, Ann. Rev. Microbiology, 1996-2001, editor-in-chief Mycologia, 2000-04; contbr. articles to profl. jours. Bd. dirs. Newcomb Found., 1988-89. Recipient Mortar Board award of excellence in Teaching, 1974-75, others; named Honors Prof. of Yr., Tulane U., 1991. Fellow Soc. for Indsl. Microbiology (bd. dirs. 1986-89, pres. 2001-02); mem. AAAS (biology sect. chair 2005-06), NAS (elect 2005), Am. Soc. Microbiology (pres. 1990-91), Brit. Mycol. Soc. (v.p. 1988-89), Mycol. Soc. Am., Soc. Gen. Microbiology, Czech Microbiology Soc. (hon.), Torrey Bot. Club, Sigma Xi (pres. Tulane chpt. 1986-89), Internat. Union Microbiol. Socs. (v.p. 2005-). Avocations: photography, jogging. Office: Dept Plant Biology & Pathology Sch Environmental Biological Sci Rutgers U 59 Dudley Rd New Brunswick NJ 08901

BENNETT, JOHN EUGENE, clinician, researcher; b. El Centro, Calif., Mar. 6, 1933; s. Ray Crawford and Helene Thomas Bennett; m. Shirley Kendrick Bennett, Aug. 30, 1958; children: Byard John, Colin Craig. MD, Johns Hopkins U., Balt., 1959. Diplomate Am. Bd. Internal Medicine, 1972. Dir., infectious disease tng. progrm & chief, clin. mycology sect. NIAID, NIH, Bethesda, Md., 1995—; co-dir. Infectious Disease Bd. Rev., LLC, Potomac, 2009—. Bd. sci. councilors Ctrs. Disease Control & Prevention, Atlanta, 1983—; pres. Infectious Diseases Soc. America, 1997. Editor (author): (book) Principles and Practice of Infectious Diseases (RR Hawkins award, 1979). Elder Presbyn. Ch., Bethesda, 1975—. Capt. US Pub. Health

Svc., 1961—98, Bethesda. Recipient Outstanding Svc. award, US Pub. Health Svc., 1994, Lucille George award, Internat. Soc. Human & Animal Mycology, 2000. Master: Am. Coll. Physicians; fellow: Am. Acad. Microbiology; mem.: Am. Soc. Clin. Investigation, Internat. Soc. Human & Animal Mycology, Assn. Am. Physicians. Presbyterian. Avocations: jogging, piano. Home: 10913 Candlelight Ln Potomac MD 20854 Office: Nat Inst Health 9000 Rockville Pike Bethesda MD 20892 Office Fax: 301-480-0050. Business E-Mail: jbennett@niaid.nih.gov.

BENNETT, MICHAEL H., medical educator; b. Perth, Australia, Mar. 30, 1956; MBBS, UNSW, 1979, MD, 2007. Sr. staff specialist Prince Wales Hosp., 1994—2008; conjoint assoc. prof. U. NSW, 2008—. Med. dir., dept. hyperbaric, diving medicine POWH, 1995—2007, dir. oper. theatres, anaesthesia, 2008—10; pres. South Pacific Underwater Medicine Soc., 2009—. Recipient Albert Behnke award, UHMS. Fellow: Royal Coll. Surgeons Ireland, Australia & New Zealand Coll. Anaesthetists; mem.: Undersea & Hyperbaric Med. Soc. Avocations: diving, skiing, winemaking. Office: Prince Wales Hosp Barker St Randwick NSW 2031 Australia Business E-Mail: m.bennett@unsw.edu.au.

BENNETT, PAUL WILLIAM, nurse; b. Darwin, Mar. 13, 1958; MS in Primary Health Care, Flinders U., 2002; diploma, U. Adelaide, 2000. Health edn. officer, lectr. nurse academic U. Sydney, 2004—. Decorated Australian Svc. medal Australian Defence Force, medal. Mem.: Australian Nursing Fedn., Coun. Remote Area Nurses Assn., Royal Coll. Nursing (Australia), Royal Agrl. & Hort. Soc. SA (life). Avocations: sculpting, walking. Office: Dept Rural Health Broken Hill NSW 2880 Australia Business E-Mail: pbennett@gwahs.health.nsw.gov.au.

BENNETT, PETER BRIAN, medical researcher, educator; b. Portsmouth, Hampshire, Eng., June 12, 1931; s. Charles Risby and Doris Isobel (Peckham) B.; m. Margaret Camellia Rose, July 7, 1956; children: Caroline Susan, Christopher Charles BSc, U. London, 1951; PhD, U. Southampton, 1964, DSc, 1984; Dr. honoris causa, U. de la Mediterranean, France, 2001. Asst. head surg. sect. Royal Navy Physiol. Lab., Alverstoke, England, 1953-56, head inert gas narcosis sect., 1953-66; dep. dir., prin. sci. officer, head pressure physiology sect. Royal Naval Physiol. Lab., Alverstoke, 1968-72; head pressure physiology group Can. Def. and Civil Inst. for Environ. Rsch., Toronto, Ont., 1966-68; prof. biomed. engring. Duke U., Durham, NC, 1972-75, assoc. prof. physiology, 1975—80, prof. anesthesiology, 1972—2007, founder, pres. Nat. Divers Alert Network, 1980—2003, dir. rsch. dept. anesthesiology, Duke Med. Ctr., 1980, 2007; dep. dir. F.G. Hall Lab. Environ. Rsch., 1973-74; co-dir. F.G. Hall Lab. Environ. Research, 1974-77, dir., 1977-88; sr. dir. Hyperbaric Ctr., 1988—2007; exec. dir. Underseas and Hyperbaric Med. Soc., 2007—. Cons. in field Author: The Aetiology of Compressed Air Intoxication and Inert Gas Narcosis, 1966; author, editor: The Physiology and Medicine of Diving and Compressed Air Work, 1969, Russian edit., 1987, 4th edit., 1993, (autobiography) To The Very Depths, 2008; contbr. over 200 articles to profl. jours. With RAF, 1951-53. Recipient Letter of Commendation, Pres. Ronald Reagan, 1981, Sci. award Underwater Soc. Am., 1980, Leonard Greenstone Safety award Nat. Assn. Underwater Instrs., 1985, 1st Prince Tomohito of Mikasa Japan prize, 1990, Craig Hoffman Meml. award, 1992, Dan Seap Mentor award, 1998, Ernst & Young Entrepreneur of Yr. in Life Scis. award, NC and SC, 2002, Reaching Out award Diving Equipment Mfrs., 2002, Colin McLeod award Brit. Sub Aqua Jubilee Trust, 2011. Fellow Nat. Underwater Explorers Club; mem. Undersea Med. Soc. (pres. 1975-76, mem. exec. com. 1972-75, editor jour. 1976-79, 1st Oceaneering Internat. award 1975, Albert R. Behnke award 1983), Am. Physiol. Soc., European Undersea Biomed. Soc., Russian Acad. Sci. (fgn. mem., Pavlov medal 2001), Aerospace Med. Soc., Marine Tech. Soc., Croatian Undersea and Hyperbaric Med. Soc. (hon.), Nat. Acad. Scuba Educators (Meritorious Svc. award 1997). Avocations: gardening, swimming, boating. Home: 213 Lancaster Dr Chapel Hill NC 27517-3430 Home Phone: 919-932-5879; Office Phone: 919-490-6161. Business E-Mail: peterbennett@uhms.org. E-mail: pbennett25@nc.rr.com.

BENNETT, STEPHEN, medical association administrator; b. Lubbock, Tex. BA in Polit. Sci., Pepperdine Univ. CEO AIDS Project LA, 1989—92; pres. nat. health care cons. practice, 1992—2001; pres. TeamWorks, 2001—02; exec. dir., LA and Ventura Counties United Cerebral Palsy, 1978—86, pres., CEO Washington, 2003—. Adj. faculty Anderson Sch. Mgmt., UCLA, Pepperdine Univ. VISTA vol. Peace Corps, S. Ctrl. LA. Office: United Cerebral Palsy Research 1660 L St NW Ste 700 Washington DC 20036-5638 Business E-Mail: stephen@ucp.org. *

BENNETT, WILLIAM MICHAEL, internist, educator, nephrologist; b. Chgo., May 6, 1938; s. Harry H. and Helen A. (Kaplan) B.; m. Sandra S. Silen, June 12, 1977; four children. Student, U. Mich., 1956-59; BS, Northwestern U., 1960, MD, 1963. Diplomate Am. Bd. Internal Medicine, Am. Bd. Nephrology, Am. Bd. Clin. Pharmacology. Intern U. Oreg., 1963-64; resident Northwestern U., 1964-66; practice medicine specializing in internal medicine Portland, Oreg., Boston; mem. staff Mass. Gen. Hosp., 1969-70; asst. prof. medicine U. Oreg. Health Scis. Center, 1970-74, assoc. prof., 1974-78, prof. medicine and pharmacology, 1978-2000, ret., 2000. Author: Pharmacology and Management of Hypertension, 1994, Manual of Nephrology, 1990, Drug Therapy in Renal Failure, 1994; contbr. articles to med. jours. Served with USAF, 1967-69. Master ACP; mem. Am. Soc. Nephrology (pres. 1998-99), Transplantation Soc., Internat. Soc. Nephrology, Am. Soc. Pharmacology and Exptl. Therapeutics. Office: Legacy Good Samaritan Hosp Transplant Svcs 1040 NW 22d Ave Ste 480 Portland OR 97210 also: NW Renal Clinic 1130 NW 22d St Ste 640 Portland OR 97210 Office Phone: 503-413-6555. E-mail: bennettw@lhs.org.

BENNETZEN, JEFFREY L., molecular biologist; BA in Biology, U. Calif., San Diego, 1974; PhD in Biochemistry, U. Wash., 1980; postdoctoral study, Wash. U., 1980—81, Stanford U., 1980—81, U. Calif., Berkeley, 1980—81. Rsch. scientist Internat. Plant Rsch. Inst., 1981—83; asst. to full prof. Purdue U., 1983—99, Umbarger prof. genetics, 1999—2003; Norman Giles Eminent Scholar chair in molecular biology and functional genetics U. Ga., 2003—. Vis. prof. U. Calif., Davis, 1998. Mem. editl. bd. Current Opinion in Plant Biology, Ency. Life Scis. Recipient McKnight Found. award, Plant Biology, 1986, Fulbright award, 1990, Faculty Rsch. award, Sigma Xi, 1995, Nehru Centenary Professorship, U. Hyderabad, 2002. Fellow: AAAS; mem.: NAS. Office: U Ga C426A Life Sci Bldg Athens GA 30602 Business E-Mail: maize@uga.edu.

BENNINK, JACK RICHARD, microbiologist, researcher; b. Corry, Pa., Feb. 18, 1953; s. Ivan Guy and Mary Lou (Hurlbert) B.; m. Cindi Sue Merkle, May 29, 1976; children: Nathanael Scott, Tara Susanne. BA, Asbury Coll., 1975; PhD, U. Pa., 1978. Staff mem. Basel (Switzerland) Inst. for Immunology, 1980-82; asst. prof., assoc. prof. Wister Inst., Phila., 1982-87; sr. investigator NIH, Bethesda, Md., 1987—. Contbr. articles to profl. jours. Recipient Pub. Health Svc. award, 1990, 94, 95, 96, 99, 2000. Fellow: Am. Acad. Microbiology; mem.: Am. Soc. Virology, Am. Assn. Immunologists. Office: NIH Rm 2E13C Bldg 33 Bethesda MD 20892-3209 Business E-Mail: jbennink@nih.gov.

BENOIT, MARILYN B., psychiatrist, consultant; b. Trinidad & Tobago, 1943; MD, Georgetown U., 1973; M in Health Svcs. Adminstrn., George Washington U., 1993. Diplomate Am. Bd. Psychiatry and Neurology with subspecialty in child and adolescent psychiatry. Resident in psychiatry Georgetown U., Washington, 1973—75, resident in child psychiatry, fellow in child psychiatry, 1975—77, clin. assoc. prof. psychiatry; med. dir., exec. dir. Devereux Children's Ctr., 1993—98; pvt. practice, cons. Washington, 1998—. Pvt. practice psychiatry. Fellow: Am. Acad. Child and Adolescent Psychiatry (past pres. 2001—03); mem.: AMA, Am. Psychiat. Assn. Office: 141 Log Canoe Cir Stevensville MD 21666 also: 141 Log Canoe Cir Stevensville MD 21666-2127 Office Phone: 202-607-3032. Personal E-mail: bartolom@aol.com, mbbenoitmd@gmail.com.

BENOMRAN, FAWZI, forensic specialist, educator; b. Elmarje, Libya, Apr. 6, 1953; s. Abdussalam Benomran and Mofida Basim; m. Eman Sharsher, Sept. 2, 1979. B Medicine B Surgery, U. Garyounis, Benghazi, Libya, 1977; DCh, U. Coll. Dublin, Ireland, 1980; MSc in Medicine, U. Glasgow, Scotland, 1983, U. Colombo, Sri Lanka, 1991. Sr. house officer Our Lady's Hosp. for Sick Children, Dublin, 1979—80; forensic pathologist med. dept. U. Glasgow, 1980—83; sr. forensic med. examiner Ministry of Justice, Benghazi, 1983—97, Dubai (United Arab Emirates) Police Gen. Hdqrs., 1997—, dir. dept. forensic medicine, 2001—; asst. prof. forensic medicine U. Garyounis, 1989—97, head dept. forensic medicine, 1989—97; prof. forensic dentistry Ajman (United Arab Emirates) U., 2001—; prof. forensic medicine Dubai Police Acad., Dubai, 2001—. Dir. medico-legal ctr. Ministry of Justice, Benghazi, 1983—97. Contbr. articles to profl. jours. Mem. coun. Libyan Med. Syndicate, Benghazi, 1994—97; dir. Ctr. for Health and Drug Rsch., Benghazi, 1995—97; pres. Univ. Staff Assn., Benghazi, 1996—97. Recipient Nat. Pioneer in Forensic Medicine award, Ministry of Justice, Libya, 1984; grantee, Ministry High Edn., Libya, 1978—83. Mem.: Am. Acad. Forensic Scis., Brit. Assn. Forensic Medicine, Pan Arab Union Forensic Medicine and Sci., Indo Pacific Assn. Med. Sci. Law. Avocations: tennis, squash, writing. Home: Al Maktoom Twr Al Maktoom St Dubai PO Box 39844 United Arab Emirates Office: Dubai Police Gen Hdqrs PO Box 1493 Dubai United Arab Emirates Fax: +971-4-2014551. E-mail: benemran@hotmail.com.

BENOWITZ, JOEL, surgeon; b. Bklyn., Oct. 3, 1950; s. Albert and Miriam Benowitz; m. Joan Ellen Broder, Nov. 24, 1976; children: Lauren, Alison, Jacqueline. BA, Long Island U., 1971; MD, Autonomous U., Mex., 1975. Diplomate Am. Bd. Surgery, cert. breast ultrasound Am. Soc. Breast Surgeons. Resident, chief resident surgery Brookdale Hosp. Med. Ctr., Bklyn., 1975—81, attending surgeon, 1981—87, Long Beach (N.Y.) Med. Ctr., 1982—, dir. surgery, 2000—, chmn. med. staff, 2002—; attending surgeon S. Nassau Cmty. Hosp., 1996—, N. Shore Univ. Hosp., Syosset, NY, 1999—. Bd. trustees Congregation Beth Shalom, Long Beach, 1990—, Long Beach Med. Ctr., 2000—, pres. med. bd., 2005—06; clin. asst. prof. NY Coll. Osteo. Medicine, 1999—. Named Profl. of Yr., St. James of Jerusalem, Long Beach, 2002. Fellow: Am. Coll. Surgeons. Avocations: boating, travel, reading, horseback riding. Home: 978 Gerry Ave Lido Beach NY 11561 Office: 206 W Park Ave Long Beach NY 11561 Office Phone: 516-889-9100. Personal E-mail: jbenowitz@aol.com.

BENSCH, KLAUS GEORGE, pathology educator; b. Miedar, Germany, Sept. 1, 1928; married; 3 children. MD, U. Erlangen, Germany, 1953. Diplomate: Am. Bd. Pathology. Intern U. Hosps. of Erlangen, 1953-54; resident in anat. pathology U. Tex./M.D. Anderson Hosp., Houston, 1954—56; instr. pathology Yale Med. Sch., 1958-61, asst. prof., 1961-64, assoc. prof., 1964-68; prof. pathology Stanford Med. Sch., 1968—, acting chmn. dept. pathology, 1984-85, chmn. dept. pathology, 1985-99, prof. emeritus, 2001—. Office: Stanford U Med Sch Dept Pathology 300 Pasteur Dr Palo Alto CA 94304-2203 E-mail: kbensch@stanford.edu.

BEN SHAUL, YOCHANAN MENASHSHEH See MISHLER, JOHN

BENSHOFF-LUDICK, DIXIE LEE, psychologist, educator; b. Ravenna, Ohio, Apr. 11, 1950; d. Roy O. and Pauline G. Benshoff; m. Timothy David Ludick, Mar. 21, 1992; 1 child, David Grant Benshoff Ludick. BA, Hiram Coll., Ohio, 1968—72; MEd, Kent State U., Ohio, 1972—73, PhD, 1973—77; postgrad, Case Western Reserve U., Cleve., 1988. Lic. psychologist Ohio State Bd. Psychology; cert. tchr. Ohio State Bd. Edn. Psychologist Bedford City Sch. Dist., Ohio, 1997—; student personal advisor Northeastern Ohio Univs. Colls. Medicine & Pharmacy, 2000—. Contbr. chapters to books; author: (book) David Was a Pirate, 2001. Mem.: Internat. Assn. in Behavioral Medicine, Counseling and Psychology. Office Phone: 330-325-6756.

BEN SIMON, GUY JONATHAN, ophthalmologist; b. Haifa, Israel, Dec. 31, 1969; MD, Hebrew U., 1993. Pvt. practice, 2003—. Home: 18/5 Perluk St Tal Aviv 62631 Israel Home Fax: 97236401228. Personal E-mail: guybensimon@gmail.com.

BENSINGER, DAVID AUGUST, dentist, dean; b. St. Louis, May 14, 1926; s. William and Esther (Lissner) B.; m. Myra Blass, Dec. 24, 1944 (div. June 1972); children: Judith Ann (Mrs. William Thomas Haynes), Scott David; m. Susan Cohn Hartman, May 31, 1975. BA, Washington U., 1944; DDS, St. Louis U., 1948; postgrad. health systems mgmt, Harvard U. Sch. Bus. Adminstrn., 1977. Mem. faculty, adminstrn. Sch. Dentistry Washington U., St. Louis, 1949—, assoc. prof. dept. periodontics, 1956-76, prof., 1976-90, assoc. dean, 1970-76, acting dean, 1976-83, exec. assoc. dean, 1983-87; dean Washington U. Sch. Dental Medicine, 1987-90, dean, prof. emeritus, 1990; practice dentistry, specializing in periodontics St. Louis, 1949-90; mem. staff Barnes, Jewish hosps., both St. Louis; mem. deans com. VA Hosp.; mem. nat. adv. com. Dental Edn. Rev. Com., NIH, 1969-72. Cons. Scott AFB, St. Louis, 1956-62; mem. adv. coun. SBA, 1975. Editor: Jour. Greater St. Louis Dental Soc, 1963-70; asso. editor: Jour. Mo. Dental Assn, 1966-73. Mem. exec. bd. Ladue (Mo.) Sch. Sys., 1964-67; chmn. bd. counselors U. Calif. Med. Ctr., San Francisco, 1995-98; chmn. regional cabinet Wash. U., San Francisco, 1996—; elected trustee Coll. of Notre Dame, Belmont, Calif., 1998—, chmn. fin. and investment com. Lt. M.C., U.S. Army, 1948-49, capt. med. dept. USAF, 1955-56. Fellow Am. Coll. Dentists, Internat. Coll. Dentists; mem. ADA (ho. of dels.), Mo. Dental Assn. (pres. 1973-74, jud. coun.), Greater St. Louis Dental Soc. (bd. dirs. 1963-70, Svc. award 1971), Am. Acad. Peridontology, Internat. Assn. Dental Rsch., Midwest Soc. Peridontology (pres. 1972-73), Pierre Fouchard Acad., Royal Soc. Medicine (Eng.), Inst. Internat. Edn. (vice chmn. bd. dirs., chmn. exec. com. 1996-98), Washington U. Alumni Assn. (Alumnus of Yr. 1968), Univ. Club (St. Louis), St. Louis Club, Harvard Club (Boston and N.Y.C.), Omicron Kappa Upsilon. Home: 2100 Pacific Ave San Francisco CA 94115-1585

BENSINGER, THOMAS A., oncologist, hematologist; Grad., Georgetown U.; MD, George Wash. U. Diplomate Am. Bd. Internal Medicine-hematology. Intern hematology Duke Univ. Med. Ctr., fellow hematology; resident Walter Reed Army Med. Ctr., Wash., DC; fellow City of Hope Nat. Med. Ctr., Duarte, Calif.; established and pres. Hematology Oncology Consultants P.A. (former Bensinger & Weltz, MD, PA), 1980—. Fellow: ACP; mem.: Am. Soc. of Hematology (exec. com.). Office: Hematology-Oncology Consultants PA Ste 205 7525 Greenway Center Dr Greenbelt MD 20770 Office Phone: 301-982-9800. Office Fax: 301-982-2420.

BENSON, AL BOWEN, III, oncologist, educator; b. Buffalo, Dec. 23, 1950; BA, SUNY, 1972; MD, SUNY, Buffalo, 1976. Diplomate Am. Bd. Internal Medicine, cert. med. oncology Am. Bd. Internal Medicine, diplomate internal medicine 1979, med. oncology 1983. Intern U. Wis. Hosps., Madison, 1976—77, resident medicine, 1977—79; co-dir. medicine Nat. Pub. Health Svc., Ill., 1979—81; fellow oncology U. Wis. Hosps., Madison, 1981—84; attending physician Northwestern Meml. Hosp., Chgo., 1984—, Lakeside VA Med. Ctr., Chgo., 1984—. Prof. medicine U. Ill., 1979—81, Northwestern U., 1984—, assoc. dir. clin. investigations, 1995—. Office: Northwestern Univ 676 N St Clair Ste 850 Chicago IL 60611-2998

BENSON, HOLLY, company executive; Grad., Dartmouth Coll., Hanover, NH; LLB, U. Fla., Gainesville. Sec. Fla. Agy. Health Care Adminstrn., Fla. Dept. Bus. and Profl. regulation; mem. House of Representatives, chair health care coun.; practicing municipal bond law Miller, Canfield, Paddock and Stone P.L.C.; sr. v.p. health policy Centene Corp., 2011—. With Mary Brogan Mus. of Art Bd. Recipient Recognized Outstanding Efforts in Health Care Policy, Fla. Assn. Health Plans, Fla. Med. Assn., Associated Industries Fla. Mem.: Fla. Coun. of 100, Tallahassee Chamber Commerce. Office: Centene Corporation Centene Plaza 7700 Forsyth Blvd Saint Louis MO 63105 Office Phone: 314-725-4477.

BENSON, JOHN ALEXANDER, JR., internist, educator; b. Manchester, Conn., July 23, 1921; s. John A. and Rachel (Patterson) B.; children: Peter M., John Alexander III, Susan Leigh, Jeremy P. BA, Wesleyan U., Middletown, Conn., 1943; MD, Harvard Med. Sch., Boston, 1946. Diplomate Am. Bd. Internal Medicine (mem. 1969-91, sec.-treas. 1972-75, pres. 1975-91, pres. emeritus 1991—), Subsplty. Bd. Gastroenterology (mem. 1961-66, chmn. 1965-66). Intern Univ. Hosps., Cleve., 1946-47; resident Peter Bent Brigham Hosp., Boston, 1949-51; fellow Mass. Gen. Hosp., Boston, 1951-53; rsch. asst. Mayo Clinic, Rochester, Minn., 1953-54; asst. in medicine Mass. Gen. Hosp., 1954-59; instr. medicine Harvard U., 1956-59; head divsn. gastroenterology U. Oreg. Med. Sch., Portland, 1959-75, prof. medicine, 1965-93; prof. emeritus Oreg. Health & Sci. U., Portland, 1993—, interim dean Sch. Medicine, 1991—93, dean emeritus, 1993—, asst. dir. Ctr. for Ethics in Health Care, 1992—2003; prof. internal medicine U. Nebr. Coll. Medicine, Omaha, 2003—. Cons. VA Hosps., Madigan Gen. Army Hosp., John A. Hartford Found. Editorial bd.: Am. Jour. Digestive Diseases, 1966-73, The Pharos, 2000—; contbr. articles to profl. jours. Mem. Oreg. Med. Ednl. Found., 1967-73, dir., 1967-73, pres., 1969-72; bd. dirs. N.W. Ctr. for Physician-Patient Comm., 1994-99, Am. Acad. on Physician and Patient, 1994-99, chmn., 1995-98, Found. Med. Excellence, 1996-2003, pres., 1998-2000; trustee Oreg. Health and Sci. U. Found., 1999-2003. With USNR, 1947-49. Mem. AAS, AMA, ACP (master), Am. Gastroenterol. Assn. (sec. 1970-73, v.p. 1975-76, pres.-elect. 1976-77, pres. 1977-78), Am. Clin. and Climatol. Assn. (v.p. 1997), Am. Soc. Internal Medicine, Western Assn. Physicians, North Pacific Soc. Internal Medicine, Am. Fedn. Clin. Rsch., Federated Coun. for Internal Medicine, Am. Assn. Study Liver Disease, Western Soc. Clin. Investigation, Soc. Health and Human Values, Assn. Health Svcs. Rsch., Inst. Medicine NAS, Phi Beta Kappa, Sigma Xi, Alpha Omega Alpha. Office: 985520 Nebr Med Ctr Omaha NE 68198-5520 Office Phone: 402-559-4887. Business E-Mail: jabenson@unmc.edu.

BENSON, JOHN RUSSELL, surgeon, researcher; b. Kingston-upon-Hull, Eng., Nov. 8, 1959; s. George Samuel and Elsie May (Bell) B. BA with honours, Oxford U., Eng., 1981, BM, BCh, 1984, MA (hon.), 1985, DM, 1997. Sr. house officer Hammersmith Hosp., London, 1988; dept. demonstrator, dept. anatomy U. Oxford, England, 1986; sr. house officer Radcliffe Infirmary, Oxford, 1987; registrar Newham Gen. Hosp., London, 1989-92; clin. rsch. fellow Inst. Cancer Rsch., London, 1992-94; sr. registrar Royal Marsden Hosp., London, 1994-96, Chelsea and Westminster Hosp., London, 1996-2000; cons. breast surgeon Addenbrookes Hosp., Cambridge, England, 2000—; dir. clin. studies and fellow Selwyn Coll., Cambridge, 2000—. Author: TGFB and Cancer (RG Landes Co.); co-editor: Oncoplastic and Reconstructive Surgery of the Breast, 2004, Management Options in Breast Cancer, Informa Healthcare, 2007, Early Breast Cancer, The Lencet, 2009; co-editor: Oncoplastic and Reconstructive Surgery of the Breast and Early Breast Cancer - form screening to multidisciplinary management, 2006; mem. editl. adv. bd. Lancet Oncology; contbr. articles to med. jours., including Lancet, Brit. Jour. Cancer. Grad. scholar St. Peter's Coll., Oxford U., 1983-84; grantee Brit. Oncological Assn., 1995, Ethicon Found. Fund, 1998; Travel fellow Royal Coll. Surgeons, Inc., NY, 1996. Fellow Royal Coll. Surgeons (Eng.), Royal Coll. Surgeons (Edinburgh), Brit. Breast Group; mem. Am. Assn. for Cancer Rsch. (corr., travel grantee 1994), Brit. Assn. Surg. Oncologists, Oxford Union Soc. (life), NY Acad. Scis., NY met. Breast Group, Panel Examiners. Avocations: piano, travel, collecting bric-a-brac. Office: Cambridge Breast U Addenbrooke's Hosp Cambridge CB2 2QQ England E-mail: john.benson@addenbrookes.nhs.uk.

BENSUSSAN, ARMAND, biologist, researcher, immunologist; b. Casablanca, Morocco, Sept. 10, 1954; s. Léon and Rosa (Abitan) B.; m. Elisabeth Eugenie Larbi, Nov. 21, 1981; 1 child, Florian Adrien. M Biochemistry, M Human Biology, U. Paris 7, 1979, D State in Human Biology, 1987. Rsch. assoc. Harvard U. Med. Sch., Boston, 1982-85; in charge rsch. Nat. Inst. Health and Med. Rsch. (INSERM), Paris, 1985-90, dir. rsch., 1991—; dir. rsch. unit U. Paris 12, Creteil, France, 1996—2008, U. Paris 7, 2009—. Mem. sci. coun. INSERM, 2004—07, U. Paris 12, 2006—08. Contbr. articles to profl. jours. including Jour. Exptl. Medicine, Nature, Blood, Jour. Immunol. Recipient Bernard Halpern prize, Paris, 1995, French Acad. Scis. prize, Paris, 1986, 2003, prize Med. Rsch. Found., Paris, 1988, Cancer Rsch. prize Val de Marne Region, Creteil, 1998 Mem. AAAS, Am. Assn. Imunologists, French Assn. Immunologists (past pres.), Orega Biotech (founder biotech. co. 2010). Office: St Louis Hosp Skin Rsch Ctr Paris France Home Phone: 06 09 69 77 38; Office Phone: 33-1-49-81-35-13. Personal E-mail: a.bensussan@free.fr.

BENSUSSAN, DENIS, radiologist; b. Marseille, Bouches du Rhone, France, Mar. 31, 1951; s. Roger Pierre B. and Jeanine Coulomb; m. Claudia Husson, July 7, 1983; children: Pierre-Brice, Marie-Albane, David-Edouard, Anne-Sophie. Baccalaureat Sci. Mention AB, Lycée Périer, Marseille, France, 1969; MD, Faculté Medecine Marseille, 1977. Nat. Diploma Radiology, Paris, 1982; Diplôme d'Univ. Réparation Juridique Dommage Corporel, Marseille, 1995. Asst. vascular radiology svc. CHU Timone, Marseille, France, 1978-82, attaché consultation hosps., 1982-92; vascular and interventional radiologist Ctr d'Angiographie Diagnostique et Thérapeutique. V.p. Assn. Pour la Promotion de la Radiologie Interventionnelle, Marseille, France, 1984. Contbr. article to med. jour. Medecin prin., comdr. French Navy, 1978-79. Mem. Assn. Eleveurs Chevaux de Sang du Sud-Est (pres. 1997—), Lions Club (pres. Marseille-Doyen 1997-98), RSNA, CIRSE, French Radiology Soc., Soc. Francaise d'Imagerie Cardiovasculaire, Fed. des Counsels du Sud Est (v.p. 2007-), Counsels Mgmt. Cheever P.A.C. (pres. 2004-08). Home: 408 Rue Paradis 13008 Marseille France Office: Ctr Angiographie Therapeut Clinique Bouchard 77 Rue Dr ESCAT 13006 Marseille France Home Phone: 33491763898; Office Phone: 33-607520650, 33 491159077. Office Fax: 33442961955. Business E-Mail: denisbensussan@numericable.fr.

BENTLEY, GEORGE, orthopedics educator, orthopedic surgeon, researcher, consultant; b. Rotherham, Eng., Jan. 19, 1936; s. George and Doris (Blagden) B.; m. Ann Gillian Hutchings, June 4, 1960; children: Sarah, Paul, Stephen. MB, ChB, U. Sheffield, 1959, M in Surgery, 1972, DSc, 2002. Cert. orthopaedic surgeon. Ho. surgeon, ho. physician Royal Infirmary, Sheffield, England, 1959—60, sr. ho. officer in orthop., 1960—61, lectr. in anatomy U. Birmingham, England, 1961—62; sr. ho. officer in surgery Manchester Royal Infirmary, England, 1962—63; rotating surg. registrar Sheffield Royal Infirmary and Children's Hosp., 1963—65; registrar in orthop. Orthopaedic Hosp., Oswestry, England, 1965—67; sr. registrar in orthopaedics Nuffield Orthocentre and Radcliffe Infirmary, Oxford, England, 1967—69; instr. orthop. U. Pitts., 1969—70; lectr., sr. lectr., clin. reader U. Oxford, England, 1970—76; prof. orthop. and accident surgery U. Liverpool, England, 1976—82; prof. orthop. Univ. Coll., London. Hon. cons. orthopaedic surgeon Royal Nat. Orthopaedics and Middlesex Hosp., London, 1982—. Editor, author: Mercer's Orthopaedic Surgery, 1996, Robb & Smiths Operative Orthopaedics, 1991, European editor-in-chief: Jour. Arthroplasty, 2001—; contbr. 300 articles to profl. jours. Fellow: Orthop. Rsch. Soc., European Fedn. Nat. Assns. Orthops. and Traumatology (exec. com. 1995—, v.p. 2002—03, pres. 2004—), Brit. Orthop. Assn. (pres. 1991—92), Royal Coll. Surgeons Edinburgh, Acad. Med. Scis., French Soc. Orthop. Surgery and Traumatology (hon.), Royal Soc. Medicine (hon.), Royal Coll. Surgeons of Eng. (coun. 1982—2004, v.p. 2003—04, Robert Jones lectr. 2007), Brit. Orthop. Rsch. Soc. (pres. 1986—87); mem.: Oxford Med. Soc. Avocations: golf, tennis, music, horology. Office: Royal Nat Orthopaedic Hosp Brockley Hill Stanmore Middlesex HA7 4LP England Office Phone: 0044-0-208-909-5532. Personal E-mail: profgbentley@talktalk.net. Business E-Mail: rosemary.radland@rnoh.nhs.uk.

BENTLEY, KENNETH CHESSAR, oral and maxillofacial surgeon, educator; b. Montreal, Que., Can., Sept. 22, 1935; s. Albert Edwin and Lilian Beatrice (Hoare) B.; m. Jean Wadsworth, Aug. 19, 1961; children: Douglas, Margaret. DDS, McGill U., 1958, MD, CM, 1962. Intern, then resident Montreal Gen. Hosp. and Bellevue Hosp., NY, 1962-66; from asst. prof. to assoc. prof. McGill U., 1966-67, prof. dentistry, 1975-98, prof. emeritus, 1998; dean McGill U. Sch. Dentistry, 1977-87; jr. asst. dental surgeon Montreal Gen. Hosp., 1966, assoc. dental surgeon, assoc. dir. dentistry, 1968, dental surgeon-in-chief, 1970-2000. Pres. Thistle Coun. Quebec; pres., bd dirs. Griffith McConnell Residence Nursing Home, 2003-08. Co-author: Advanced Oral Radiographic Interpretation, 1979. Recipient Queen's Golden Jubilee medal, 2002; named Decorated Hospitaller, Order St. John Jerusalem. Fellow Am. Coll. Dentists, Internat. Coll. Dentists, Royal Coll. Dentists Can., Pierre Fauchard Acad., Academie Dentaire Du Quebec; mem. Assn. Oral and Maxillofacial Surgeons Que., Bellevue Soc. Oral Surgeons, Can. Dental Assn. (hon.; chmn. coun. hosp. svcs. 1971-75, coun. edn. 1982-85), Can. Assn. Oral and Maxillofacial Surgeons (sec.-treas. 1970-71), Internat. Assn. Oral Surgeons, Montreal Dental Club (sec. 1968, pres.1992), Nat. Dental Exam. Bd. Can., Order Dentists Que., Found. for Continuing Edn. and Rsch. (sec.-treas. 2002), St. Andrew's Soc. Montreal (pres. 2007—09) Avocations: music, pipe organ, scottish country dancing. Home Phone: 450-246-2285. E-mail: kcb@total.net.

BENTZ, BRANDON G., medical educator; b. Nurnberg, Germany, Dec. 7, 1964; MD, U. Pitts., 1987. Assoc. prof. U. Utah Sch. Medicine, 2002—. Chief, otolaryngology head & neck surgery George E. Wahlen Vets. Adminstrn. Hosp., 2009—11. Recipient Young Investigator award, AAO-HNSF/AHNS, Career Devel. award, Triological Soc., Henry Christian award, Am. Fedn. Clin. Rsch.; grant, Else U. Pardee Found. Fellow: ACS; mem.: Soc. Surg. Oncology, Am. Soc. Clin. Oncology (Young Investigator award), Am. Acad. Otolaryngology-Head & Neck Surgery Found. Inc., Am. Head & Neck Soc. Avocations: skiing, fly fishing, camping. Office: 3C120 SOM 50 N Med Dr Salt Lake City UT 84132 Business E-Mail: brandon.bentz@hci.utah.edu.

BENUM, PÅL SVERRE, medical educator; b. Verdal, Norway, Aug. 3, 1935; MD, U. Bergen, 1961; PhD, U. Oslo, 1974. Assoc. prof. Norwegian U. Sci. and Tech., Trondheim, 1976—82, prof., 1982—2005. Tng. positions Ullevål U. Hosp., Crown Princess Märthas Inst., Sophie Meml. Orthopaedic Hosp. and Rikshospitalet, Oslo, 1964—76; chmn. Norwegian Orthop. Assn., 1976—79; cons. Orthop. Dept. Trondheim U. Hosp., 1976—85, chmn., 1985—2005, Nordic Orthop. Fedn., 1985—86. Recipient Knight of Royal Norwegian St. Olavs Order, King Harald VI Norway. Mem.: Internat. Soc. Tech. Arthroplasty, European Hip Soc., Norwegian Surg. Assn. (hon.), Nordic Orthop. Fedn. (hon.), Norwegian Orthop. Assn. (hon.). Avocations: history, cross country skiing. Home: Inge Krokanns vef 6 Trondheim 7024 Norway Business E-Mail: pal.benum@ntnu.no.

BENUSIGLIO, LEON NICK, medical doctor; b. Munich, Mar. 2, 1947; s. Raoul E. and Sarah (Ribstein) B.; m. Sonia Licha; children: Serge, Patrick. B in Math., Paris U., 1963; diploma in medicine, Geneva U., 1969, MD, 1976. Med. dr. U. Geneva, Geneva, Switzerland, 1976-80; attending physician Univ. Hosp. Geneva, Geneva, 1980—. Mem.: British Thoracic Soc., Am. Thoracic Soc., Alpina Swiss Lodge. Jewish. Avocations: photography, literature. Home and Office: Chemin tour-de-Champel 10 1206 Geneva Switzerland Business E-Mail: leon.benusiglio@bluewin.ch.

BENUSKOVA, LUBICA, neuroscientist, educator; b. Bratislava, Slovak Republic, Feb. 20, 1958; d. Jozef Benuska and Edita Bogyayova. RNDr in Phys. Electronics, Comenius U., Bratislava, Slovakia, 1982; PhD in Biophysics, Comenius U., 1994; MA in Psychology, Vanderbilt U., Nashville, 1993. Rsch. asst., dept. psychiatry Med. Sch. Hosp., Bratislava, Slovakia, 1982—88; rsch. fellow Slovak Acad. Scis., Inst. Animal Biochemistry & Genetics, Ivanka pri Dunaji, Slovakia, 1988—94; sr. rsch. fellow Slovak Tech. U., Sch. Informatics & Info. Technologies, Bratislava, 1994—2001; assoc. prof., dept. applied informatics Comenius U., Bratislava, 2001—; sr. rsch. fellow Auckland U. Tech., Knowledge Engring. & Discovery Rsch. Inst., Auckland, New Zealand, 2003—07; sr. lectr. U. Otago, Dunedin, New Zealand, 2008—. Vis. scientist Brown U., Providence, 1992—96, Internat. Sch. Advanced Studies, Trieste, Italy, 1995—98, Vanderbilt U., Nashville, 1996—99, U. Otago, Dunedin, New Zealand, 2003; guest lectr. U. Vienna, 2002. Author: (books) Computational Neurogenetic Modeling, 2007, Artificial Intelligence, 2006, Introduction into Theory of Neural Networks, 1997; editor: Quest for a Common Language in Cognitive Sciences, 2000, Cognitive Sciences, 2002; contbr. chapters to books. Theory of cortical plasticity grantee, U.S.-Slovak Sci. and Tech. Program, 1996—99. Mem.: IEEE, Royal Soc. New Zealand. Lutheran. Achievements include development of computational models of neural plasticity; computational neurogenetic models; research in pattern recognition by neural networks; synaptic plasticity and antidepressants; introduced cognitive science in universities in Slovakia; popularization of neuroscience and cognitive science in Slovakia. Avocations: music, literature, astronomy, drawing, travel. Home: 71 Mayfield Rd Andersons Bay 9013 Dunedin New Zealand Personal E-mail: luba.benuskova@gmail.com.

BENVENISTY, ALAN I., vascular surgeon; MD, Union Coll., Schenectady, NY, B in Biology (summa cum laude); grad., Columbia U., 1978. Diplomate Am. Bd. Surgery-gen. surgery, Am. Bd. Surgery-vascular surgery, registered vascular technologist. Internship in gen. surgery Columbia Univ., resident gen. surgery, fellowship in vascular and transplant, dir. St. Luke's-Roosevelt surgical clerkship; joined Presbyterian Hosp., faculty coll. of physicians and surgeons, prof. clin. surgery. Named Super-Chief; named one of NY's Top Doctor, Castle Connolly, America's Top Doctors. Mem.: Am. Soc. of Transplant Surgeons, NY Soc. for Vascular Surgery (past pres.). Office: St. Luke's-Roosevelt Hospital Center Ste 2B 1000 Tenth Ave New York NY 10019 Office Phone: 212-523-4706.

BEN-YEHUDA, YORAM, pediatrician, director; b. Afula, Israel, Mar. 12, 1954; MD, Technion, Israel Inst. Tech., 1987. Dir. pediat. emergency medicine Wolfson Med. Ctr., 1999—2006; dir. pediat. emergency medicine, chmn. child protection com. Hadassah Ein Kerem U. Hosp., 2006—. Bd. dirs. Nat. Coun. Children, 2007—; adv. bd. mem. Haruv Inst. Child Maltreatment, 2007—. Mem.: Israel Assn. Pediat., Israel Assn. Emergency Medicine. Avocations: kayaking, sailing. Office: Hadassah Ein Kerem Jerusalem Israel Office Fax: 972-153507874304. Business E-Mail: yoramby@haruv.org.il.

BENYUNES, ABRAHAM JOSEPH, pediatrician; b. NYC, June 30, 1938; MD, Georgetown U., Washington, DC, 1963. Cert. Am. Acad. Pediatrics; conservative Mohel Jewish Theological Seminary America (cert. by Rabbinical Assembly). Intern pediatrics Downstate NY Sch. Medicine, Kings County Hosp., Bklyn., 1963—64, resident pediatrics, 1964—65; resident Mt. Sinai Hosp., NYC, 1965—66; sr. attending pediatrician Miami Children's Hosp., Baptist Hosp.; clin. assoc. prof. pediatrics U. Miami Sch. Medicine, Fla.; with South Dade Pediatrics, Miami. Chief pediatrics US Pub. Health Svc. Hosp., Baltimore, Md. Fellow: Am. Acad. Pediatrics. Office: 7800 SW 87th Ave Miami FL 33173 Office Phone: 305-271-4711. Office Fax: 305-271-8732.

BENZ, EDWARD JOHN, SR., clinical pathologist; b. June 11, 1923; s. Henry John and Gertrude Nora (Heffernan) B.; m. Verna Marie Cuddyre, June 20, 1945; children: Edward John, Thomas James, Gregory Paul, Mary Louise. BS, U. Pitts., 1943, MD, 1946; MS, U. Minn., 1952. Intern St. Joseph's Hosp., Pitts., 1946-47; resident, fellow Mayo Found., Mayo Clinic, 1949-53; pathologist, dir. labs. St. Luke's Hosp., Bethlehem, Pa., 1953-84, v.p. med. affairs, 1984-89; med. dir. utilization rev. Sacred Heart Hosp., Allentown, Pa., 1990-98. Adj. prof. microbiology Lehigh U., Bethlehem, 1956-64; pres. Lab. Clin. Pathology, Bethlehem, 1956-88, ret., 1988; cons. Palmerton (Pa.) Hosp., Allentown (Pa.) State Hosp.; past dir. Miller Meml. Blood Bank, Bethlehem Mem. adv. com. Pa. Sec. Health on Clin. Labs., 1973-89; mem. health sci. adv. com. Lehigh U., 1973-89. Contbr. articles to profl. publs. Trustee St. Luke's Hosp., 1968-71; pres. Pa. Assn. Clin. Pathologists, 1966-67. Capt. M.C., AUS, 1947-49. Fellow Coll. Am. Pathologists (past chmn. anat. path. commn., past del. from Pa.), Am. Soc. Clin. Pathologists; mem. Internat. Acad. Pathology, Am. Assn. Pathologists and Bacteriologists, Am. Assn. Blood Banks, Am. Coll. Physician Execs., Saucon Club, Valley Country Club, Sigma Xi, Alpha Omega Alpha. Home and Office: 10 Devon Dr Apt 314 Acton MA 01720-5859

BENZ, EDWARD JOHN, JR., hematologist, educator, health facility administrator; b. Pitts., May 22, 1946; s. Edward John and Verna Marie (Cuddyre) Benz; m. Margaret A. Vettese; children: Timothy Edward, Jennifer Kirsten. AB in Biology, cum laude, Princeton U., NJ, 1968; MD magna cum laude, Harvard U., 1973. Diplomate Am. Bd. Internal Medicine, Am. Bd. Hematology. Resident Peter Bent Brigham Hosp., Boston, 1973-75; fellow pediatric hematology Children's Hosp. Med. Ctr., Boston, 1974-75; fellow adult hematology Yale U. Sch. Medicine, New Haven, 1978-79, asst. prof. internal medicine, 1979-82, assoc. prof. internal medicine, human genetics, 1982-87, prof. internal medicine, human genetics, 1987-92, chief sect. hematology, 1987-92, chmn. dean's curriculum task force, 1987-88, assoc. chmn. dept. internal medicine, 1988-92; Jack D. Myers prof., chmn. dept. medicine U. Pitts. Sch. Medicine, 1993-95; prof. molecular biology & genetics Johns Hopkins U. Sch. Medicine, 1995-2000, Sir William Osler prof., dir. dept. medicine, 1995-2000; physician-in-chief Johns Hopkins Hosp., Balt., 1995-2000; Richard & Susan Smith prof. medicine, prof. pediat. and genetics Harvard Med. Sch., Boston, 2000—; pres., CEO Dana Farber Cancer Inst., Boston, 2000—. CEO Dana Farber Ptnrs. CancerCare, Boston; dir. Dana Farber/Harvard Cancer Ctr., Boston; trustee Dana Farber/Children's Hosp. Cancer Care; surgeon USPHS, 1975—78; rsch. assoc. molecular hematology Nat. Heart, Lung & Blood Inst., Bethesda, Md., 1975—78; adj. prof. biol. scis. Carnegie Mellon U., Pitts., 1993—95; prof. pro-tem, hon. vis. chief svc. Brigham & Women's Hosp., Boston, 1997; Howard Hiatt vis. prof. Harvard Med. Sch., 1998; Clement Finch prof. U. Wash., 1998; Litchfield lectr. Oxford U., 1999; Bulfinch vis. prof. medicine Mass. Gen. Hosp./Harvard Med. Sch., 2000; Haynes disting. vis. prof. medicine Duke U., 2000; Franz Inglefinger vis. prof. Boston U., 2001. Author: Molecular Genetics Methods, 1987; co-editor: Hermatology, Principles and Practice, 1990—2010 (First prize Brit. Med. Soc.), Oxford Textbook of Medicine, 2002 (First prize Royal Soc. Authors); mem. editl. bd. Blood, 1988—94; assoc. editor: New Eng. Jour. Medicine; contbr. articles to profl. jours. Pres. Friends Nat. Inst. Nursing Rsch., 2005—06; trustee Rockefeller U., 2004—. Recipient Career Devel. award, NIH, 1982, Basil O'Connor award, March of Dimes, 1980, Edward Paradiso Rsch. award, Cooley's Aemia Found., NYC, 1985, Disting. Eagle Scout award, Boy Scouts of America, 2003, James N. Lowell award, 2008, Am. Soc. Hematology Mentor award, 2008, Margaret L. Kripke Legends award, 2011. Fellow: AAAS, ACP, Am. Acad. Arts & Scis.; mem.: Am. Assn. Cancer Institutes (v.p. 2005—06, pres. 2007—08), Inst. Medicine, Am. Soc. Human Genetics, Am. Clin. & Climatol. Soc. (pres. 2011), Am. Soc. Hematology (exec. coun. 1994, v.p. 1998, pres. 2000), Am. Fedn. Clin. Rsch., Assn. Am. Physicians, Am. Soc. Clin. Investigation (nat. coun. 1987—91, pres. 1991—92), Princeton Elm Club, Interurban Clin. Club, Alpha Omega Alpha, Sigma Xi, Phi Beta Kappa. Office: Dana Farber Cancer Inst 44 Binney St Boston MA 02115 Office Phone: 617-632-2159, 617-632-4266. Personal E-mail: ebenz@comcast.net. Business E-Mail: edward_benz@dfci.harvard.edu.

BEN-ZE'EV, AVRI, molecular and cell biologist, scientist; b. Tirgu-Mures, Romania, Feb. 11, 1947; arrived in Israel, 1960; s. Zvi and Hana (Apfelbaum) B.-Z.; m. Sylvia Shalom, Aug. 7, 1975; children: Tal, Rony. BSc, Hebrew U., Jerusalem, 1970, MSc, 1972, PhD, 1977. Postdoctoral fellow MIT, Cambridge, 1976-79; rsch. assoc. Weizmann Inst., Rehovot, Israel, 1979-81, sr. scientist, 1981-84, assoc. prof. biology, 1985-99, prof. biology, 2000—. Vis. prof. Med. Sch. Harvard U., Boston, 1986-87, La Jolla (Calif.) Cancer Rsch. Found., 1992-93, Curie Inst., Paris, 1999, Albert Einstein Coll. Medicine, N.Y., 2000. Contbr. articles to profl. jours. With Israel Def. Forces, 1965-67. Mem. Am. Soc. for Cell Biology, Am. Assn. for Cancer Rsch., Israeli Soc. for Cell Biology. Office: Weizmann Inst Dept Molecular Cell Biology 76100 Rehovot Israel Business E-Mail: avri.ben-zeev@weizmann.ac.il.

BERAKA, GEORGE JOSEPH, plastic surgeon; b. Buenes Aires, Argentina, Nov. 21, 1942; s. David and Esther Rossi Beraka; m. Judith Chestman, Sept. 5, 1980; children: Scott, David, Michael. BS, Columbia U., 1965, MD, 1969. Diplomate plastic surgery Am. Bd. Plastic Surgery. Surgery resident Johns Hopkins Hosp., Balt., 1969—73; plastic surgery resident Cornell NY Hosp., NYC, 1973—75; pvt. practice Princeton, 1975—77, NYC, 1977—. Asst. prof. surgery Rutgers Med. Sch., New Brunswick, NJ, 1975—79, Cornell NY Hosp., 1985—; preceptor cosmetic surgery fellowship Lenox Hill Hosp., 1997—. Author: The Breast, 1977, Aesthetic Facial Surgery, 2002; contbr. articles various profl. jours.; mem. editl. bd.: Plastic Surgery Practice Advisor, 2004—. Tutor E. Harlem Sch., NYC, 2000—. Recipient Annual award, Artists for Breast Cancer, 2001, Outstanding Med. Student Roche award, Columbia U., 1969. Mem.: ACS, Am. Soc. Aesthetic Plastic Surgery, U. Club, Metropolitan Opera Club, Phi Beta Kappa. Republican. Episcopalian. Avocations: sailing, opera, persian rugs, biblical scholarships. Office: 875 Pk Ave New York NY 10075 Office Phone: 212-288-1122. Business E-Mail: info@drberaka.com.

BERAL, VALERIE, epidemiologist; b. Sydney, New South Wales, Australia; arrived in Eng., 1970; children: Richard, Stephen. BS, MB, U. Sydney, Australia, 1969, MD, 2000, FRS, 2006, DBE, AC, U. Sydney, Australia, 2010. House officer, jr. Royal Prince Alfred Hosp., Sydney, 1969—70; house officer, sr. Hammersmith Hosp., London, 1970—71; epidemiologist Under Sch. Hygiene & Tropical Med., London, 1971—88; dir., cancer epidemiologist unit U. Oxford, England, 1989—, prin. investigator internat. Million Women Study. Contbr. articles to profl. jours. Fellow: Royal Coll. OB/GYN, Royal Coll. Physicians. Office: Cancer Epidemology Unit Richard Doll Bldg Roosevelt Dr OX3 7LF Oxford England Office Phone: 01865 289 600. Office Fax: 01865 289 610.

BERAN, ROY GARY, neurologist, accredited sleep physician; b. Sydney, Mar. 6, 1950; s. Frederick and Erica (Grosner) B.; m. Maureen Elizabeth Riley, Oct. 18, 1944; children: Ruth Elizabeth, Rachel, Esther, Joshua Robert. MBBS, U. New South Wales, Australia, 1972, MD, 1984; diploma of tertiary edn., U. New Eng., Australia, 1982; diploma further edn., Adeliade CAE, Australia, 1982; B in Legal Studies, Macquarie U., Sydney, 1992, M in Health Law, 2001; postgrad., Sydney U., 2000—. Training St. Vincents Hosp., Sydney, 1973-75; gen. practice Sydney, 1976-77; neurology trainee Public Hosp., Adelaide, Australia, 1978-80, Prince of Wales/Prince Henry Hosp., Sydney, 1980-82; neurologist Prince Henry Hosp., Sydney, 1982—; prof. Sch. Medicine, Griffith U., Queensland, Australia; cojoint assoc. prof. U. NSW. Vis. neurologist Royal Rehab. Ctr., Sydney, 1982—; cons. neurologist Royal Australian Navy, 1982—; vis. neurologist South Western Health Area, Sydney, 1983— Contbr. numerous articles to profl. jours.; presenter in field; editor books. Rep. ACROD, 1990—2001; v.p. WAML, 2004-08, sec. gen., 2008-; gov.

bd. mem. World Assn. Medicine Law, 1996—. Comdr. RANR, 2009-. Recipient Public Health prize Univ. New South Wales, 1972; Francis Hardy Fauldings Meml. rsch. fellow, 1981, Winston Churchill Meml. Trust fellowship, 1982. Fellow Royal Coll. Physicians (London) (hon., Faculty Forensic & legal medicine), Australasian Coll. of Legal Medicine (exec. councilor 1995-97, v.p. 1998—2002, bd. editors jour. 1998—, censor in chief 1999—2002, pres. 2002-), Am. Acad. Neurology, Australian Faculty Pub. Health Medicine, Royal Australian Coll. Gen. Practitioners, Royal Coll. Physicians UK, Australian Coll. Biomed. Scientists; mem. Epilepsy Soc. Australia (bd. dirs. 1980-93, 99—2000), Epilespy Assn. of NSW, Australian and New Zealand Assn. of Neurologists, Australasian Mil. Assn. Jewish. Avocations: surfing, skiing, travel, studying, writing. Office: 12 Thomas St Ste 5 6th fl Chatswood 2067 Australia Home: PO Box 598 1560 North Bridge NSW Australia

BERANEK, RANDY, foundation administrator; B, U. Iowa, Iowa City, 1984. Affiliate mgmt. cons. Am. Heart Assn., 1990—95; exec. dir., San Diego chpt. Am. Diabetes Assn., sr. exec. dir., Greater Bay Area chpt., 2005—08; pres., CEO Nat. Psoriasis Found., 2008—. Bd. dirs. Nat. Health Coun., 2010—. Office: Nat Psoriasis Found 6600 SW 92d Ave Ste 300 Portland OR 97223-7195 Office Phone: 503-244-7404. Office Fax: 503-245-0626. *

BERANOVA-GIORGIANNI, SARKA, biomedical researcher, educator; b. Brno, Czech Republic, June 22, 1966; d. Zdenek Beran and Eva Beranova; m. Francesco Giorgianni, Apr. 23, 1963; children: Francesca Eva, Gino Martin. MS, Prague Inst. Chem. Tech., Czech Republic, 1989; PhD, U. Akron, Ohio, 1995. Rsch. assoc. U. Tenn. Health Sci. Ctr., Dental Rsch. Ctr., Memphis, 1996—2000, asst. prof., 2000—02, 2003—. Contbr. over 24 scientific papers. Grantee Rsch. grant, NIH, 2002—06, Dept. of Def., 2003—. Mem.: Am. Assn. Pharm. Scientists, Am. Soc. Mass Spectrometry. Office: Univ Tenn Health Sci Ctr 874 Union Ave Rm 5P Memphis TN 38163 Office Fax: 901-448-6940. E-mail: sberanova@utmem.edu.

BERARDI, ROSSANA, oncologist, educator; b. Senigallia, AN, Italy, Mar. 14, 1973; MD, U. Politecnica delle Marche, Italy, 1997, postgrad, 2001. Lectr. med. oncology, cons. med. oncologist U. Politecnica delle Marche, 2005—. Expert evaluator projects in oncology European Cmty., 2009—. Recipient Best Lectr. award, U. Politecnica delle Marche; Internat. Cancer Tech. Transfer fellowship, Internat. Union Against Cancer. Mem.: Assn. Internat. Union Against Cancer Fellows, Italian Assn. Med. Oncology (mem. Ind. rsch. working group 2009—), European Soc. Med. Oncology (grants 2002—03, 2005, 2010), Am. Soc. Clin. Oncology (Merit awards 2000—01). Office: UNIVPM-Via Conca 71 Ancona 60126 Italy Business E-Mail: r.berardi@univpm.it.

BERCHUCK, ANDREW, gynecologic oncologist, educator; married; 3 children. MD, Case Western Reserve U., Ohio, 1980. Resident, ob-gyn. Case Western Reserve U., Cleve., 1980—84; rsch. and clin. tng. gynecologic oncology U. Tex. Southwestern, Dallas, Meml. Sloan-Kettering Cancer Ctr., NYC, 1985—87; with Duke U. Med. Ctr., 1987—, F. Bayard Carter Disting. Professorship; dir., gynecologic cancer rsch. prof. gynecologic oncology, dept. ob-gyn. Duke Comprehensive Cancer Ctr. Chair scientific adv. com. Ovarian Cancer Rsch. Fund. Contbr. several articles to profl. jours.; editor of several books. Recipient award for best scientific presentation, Internat. Gynecologic Cancer Soc., Barbara Thomason Ovarian Cancer Rsch. Professorship, Am. Cancer Soc., 2006. Mem.: Soc. Gynecoligic Oncologists (pres. 2007—08). Office: Duke U Med Ctr DUMC 3079 Durham NC 27710 Office Phone: 919-684-3765. Office Fax: 919-684-8719.

BERCU, BARRY BERNARD, pediatric endocrinologist; b. Montreal, Aug. 10, 1944; m. Sandra Bercu, 2 children. BS, U. Md., 1965, MD, 1969. Diplomate Nat. Bd. Med. Examiners, Am. Bd. Pediatrics, Am. Bd. Pediatric Endocrinology; lic. physician, Mass., Md., Fla. Med. intern V and VI Med. Svc. Boston City Hosp., 1969—70; asst. and sr. resident pediat. Mass. Gen. Hosp., Boston, 1970—72; clin. and rsch. fellow pediatric endocrinology & metabolism Harvard Med. Sch., Boston, 1974—77; clin. and rsch. fellow endocrinology dept. internal medicine Tufts U. Med. Sch., New Eng. Med. Ctr., Boston, 1974—77; clin. assoc. Nat. Inst. Child Health and Human Devel., NIH, Bethesda, Md., 1977—79, head pediatric endocrine unit neonatal & pediatric med. br., 1979—82, head pediatric endocrine unit, pregnancy rsch. br., 1982—84; assoc. prof. pediat. Uniformed Svcs. U., Bethesda Naval Ctr., 1980—84; assoc. rsch. prof. child health and devel. George Washington U. Sch. Medicine and Health Scis., Washington, 1983—84; prof. pediat., biochemistry and molecular biology, pharmacology and therapeutics U. South Fla. Coll. Medicine, Tampa, 1984, pres. faculty coun., 1998—99. Grant reviewer various orgns.; chmn. U. IRB Com.; mem. Dir.'s Conf. on Uses and Abuses of Growth Hormone in Children, Nat. Inst. Child Health and Human Devel., NIH, 1983-; mem. med. adv. bd. Parent Coun. Growth Normality, 1985—; mem. pediatric clin. oncology group Clin. Oncology Program, 1989—, MAGIC Found., 1995—; mem. staff All Children's Hosp., St. Petersburg, 1984-, Shriner's Hosp., Tampa, 1985-, Tampa Gen. Hosp., 1986-, others; instr. online courses Bioethical Considerations in Human Subject Rsch., Therapeutic Interventions in Aging-Growth Hormone, 2004; chmn. numerous internat. and nat. symposia, 1985—. Mem. editl. bd. Jour. Clin. Endocrinology and Metabolism, 1986-89, Jour. Anti-Aging Medicine, 1998—, Internat. Jour. Integrative Medicine, 2003—, Jour. Evidence Based Integrative Medicine, 2003—, Jour. Rejuvenation Medicine, 2004—, Jour. Clin. Intervention Into Aging, 2005—; editl. manuscript reviewer Acta Endocrinologica, Am. Jour. Nutrition, Biol. Psychiatry, Biology of Reprodn., Clin. Endocrinology, Clin. Pediatrics, Endocrine Jour., Endocrine Revs., Endocrinology, European Jour. Pediatrics, Hormone and Metabolic Rsch., Jour. AMA, Jour. Clin. Endocrinology and Metabolism, Jour. Clin. Investigation, Metabolism, Advances in Pituitary Disease: Metabolic, New England Jour. Medicine, Neuroendocrine and Psychosocial Issues, 2001, others; contbr. articles to profl. jours.; patentee in field. Bd. dirs. Birth Defects Found., Fla. Bay Area chpt., 1991—, chmn. med. adv. com., 1991; mem. expert divsn. vaccine injury compensation and mem. bd. dirs. USF Divsn. Sponsored Rsch., 1994-95. Grantee NIH, NIDA, BioNebr., Eli Lilly and Co., Genentech Corp., Daniel Pharm. Corp., Serono Labs., Am. Cancer Soc. Fla., ICN Pharms., Merck & Co., Novo Nordisk, Pfizer, Pharmacia Peptides, Inc., Pharmacia & Upjohn, Wyeth-Ayerst, Alkermes, Astra Zeneca, Infimed, BioPtnrs. and LG Bioscis. Mem. AMA, Am. Acad. Pediatrics (endocrinology sect.), Am. Assn. Clin. Endocrinologists, Am. Fedn. Clin. Rsch., Am. Pediatric Soc., Am. Pituitary Assn., Endocrine Soc., Fla. Endocrine Soc., Fla. Med. Assn., Hillsborough County Med. Assn., Hillsborough County Pediatric Soc., Lawson Wilkins Soc. Pediatric Endocrinology, Soc. Pediatric Rsch., So. Soc. Pediatric Rsch., Tampa Bay Area Soc. Neurosci.

BERDAI, DRISS, physician, consultant; b. Rabat, Morocco, Oct. 15, 1964; MD, U. Bordeaux, 1990. Sr. cons. U. Hosp. Bordeaux, 2009—. Home: 3 Rue Du Dr Schweitzer Martignas 33127 France Personal E-mail: driss.berdai@u-bordeaux2.fr.

BEREK, JONATHAN SAMUEL, surgeon, gynecologic oncologist, writer; b. Sioux City, Iowa, Apr. 21, 1948; s. Samuel I. and Janet (Graetz) Berek; m. Deborah L. Jones, June 6, 1970; children: Micah, James, Jessica. AB, Brown U., 1970, MMS, 1973; MD, Johns Hopkins U., 1975; postgrad., Harvard U., 1979. Diplomate in ob-gyn. and gynecol. oncology Am. Bd. Ob-Gyn. Intern and resident Brigham and Women's Hosp. Harvard U. Med. Sch., Boston, 1975-79; fellow UCLA Sch. Medicine, 1979-81, prof., 1981—2005, prof., exec. vice-chair dept. ob-gyn., chair gynecologic oncology, 1986—2005, chair Coll. Applied Anatomy, 1999—2005; prof., chair dept. ob-gyn Stanford U. Sch. Medicine, Calif., 2005—. Author: Berek & Hacker's Gynecologic Oncology, 5th edit., 2009, Berek & Novak's Gynecology, 14th edit., 2006; contbr. over 400 articles to profl. jours. Fellow: ACOG, ACS. Office: Stanford U Sch Medicine 300 Pasteur Dr HH333 Stanford CA 94305-5317

BERENBOM, LOREN DAVID, cardiologist; b. Kansas City, Kans., Mar. 15, 1953; s. Max and Doreen Sybil (Katz) B.; m. Merilyn Kay Krigel, June 17, 1975; children: Anne, Michael, Katie. BS with honors, Northwestern U., 1975, MD with honors, 1977. Diplomate Am. Bd. Internal Medicine, Am. Bd. Cardiology; cert. clin. cardiac electro physiology. Intern, resident in internal medicine Barnes Hosp. Wash. U., St. Louis, 1977-80, fellow cardiology, 1980-82, rsch. instr. cardiology, 1982-83; cons. cardiologist Mid Am. Heart Inst., Kansas City, 1983—2001; clin. assoc. prof. med. U. Mo., Kansas City, 1983—; dir., Bloch Heart Rhythm Ctr. Univ. Kans. Hosp. Named a Kans. City Super Doctor, Kans. City mag., 2007. Fellow Am. Coll. Cardiology, Kans. ACC, (Gov., 2005-08); mem. AMA, Alpha Omega Alpha., Heart Rhythm Soc. Office: 3901 Rainbow Blvd Ste G600 Kansas City KS 66160 Office Phone: 913-588-9600.

BERENCSI, GYORGY, III, retired virologist; b. Budapest, Dec. 4, 1941; s. Gyorgy Berencsi and Klara Matthes; m. Eva Horvath, Apr. 21, 1980; children: Gyorgy IV, Zoltan, Marton, Klara Borbala. MD, PhD, Karacs Ferenc HS, Puspokladany, 1959. Med. diploma U. Med. Sch., Debrecen, 1965. Lab. virologist Pub. Health Sta. County Hajdú-Bihar, Debrecen, Hungary, 1965—67; sci. staff mem. NIH, Budapest, 1968—73. Head, dept. and divsn. Nat. Ctr. Epidemiology, Divsn. Virlogy, Budapest, 1988—2006. Pres. Soc. Environ. Health, Budapest, 2006. Recipient Fodor József Medaillon, Hungarian Soc. Hygiene, 2001, medal, 2010, Johan Bela medal, 2010; named Golden Cross Excellence, Hungarian Republic, 2004. Mem.: Hungarian Soc. Microbiology (gen. sec. 1988—93, Manninger Medaillon 1994). Achievements include discovery of intracellular neutralization of polioviruses, restriction endonuclease maps of adenovirus DNA and alternative secondary structure of the non-translated region of enteroviral RNA; development of leading of the reconstruction of the BSL4 laboratory at the institution; discovery of presence of herpes- and papillomaviruses in the amniotic fluvid of healthy newborns born at term; role of transplcental transmission of anti-idiotypes. Office: Nat Ctr Epidemiology Gyali u 2-6 Budapest 1097 Hungary Home Phone: (361)340-1352; Office Phone: (361)476-1264. Office Fax: (+361)476-1368. Business E-Mail: berencsi.gyorgy@gmail.com.

BERENSON, GERALD SANDERS, physician; b. Bogalusa, La., Sept. 19, 1922; s. Meyer A. and Eva (Singerman) B.; m. Joan Seidenbach, Mar. 7, 1951; children— Leslie, Ann, Robert, Laurie. BS, Tulane U., 1943, MD, 1945. Intern U.S. Navy Hosp., Great Lakes, Ill., 1945-46; practice medicine specializing in cardiology New Orleans; mem. staff Charity Hosp., U. Hosp.; instr. dept. medicine Tulane U., 1948—52, prof. epidemiology Sch. Pub. Health, 1992—; asst. prof. medicine La. State U. Med. Sch., 1954-58, assoc. prof., 1958-63, prof., 1963-92, disting. Boyd prof., 1988-92, prof. emeritus, 1992—; prof. medicine, biochemistry and pediatrics Tulane U. Sch. Medicine, New Orleans, 1992—. Dir. Specialized Ctr. Rsch. Arteriosclerosis, New Orleans, 1972-87, Nat. Rsch. and Demonstration Ctr. in Arteriosclerosis, 1984-87, Nat. Ctr. Cardiovascular Health, Sch. Pub. Health and Tropical Medicine Tulane U., 1992—; sr. vis. physician Charity Hosp. La., New Orleans, 1948—; cons. Touro Infirmary, 1967—. Contbr. articles to profl. jours. Served with USNR, 1945-48. USPHS fellow U. Chgo., 1952-54 Mem. Am. Coll. Cardiology (gov. La. 1985-88, trustee 1988, chmn. prevention com. 1990-93), So. Soc. Clin. Investigation (pres. 1969), La. Heart Assn. (pres. 1971), New Orleans Acad. Internal Medicine (pres. 1966), Musser-Burch Soc. (pres. 1981), Soc. Geriatric Cardiology (pres. 1999-00), Sigma Xi, Alpha Omega Alpha. Office: Tulane Sch Pub Health Nat Ctr Cardiovascular Health 1440 Canal St Ste 1838 New Orleans LA 70112-2750 Office Phone: 504-988-7197. Business E-Mail: berenson@tulane.edu.

BERENZON, SHOSHANA, medical researcher; b. Costa Rica, Dec. 27, 1969; PhD, U. Nat. Autónoma Méx., 2003. Med. rschr. Inst. Nat. Psiquiatria, 1994—. Prof. U. Nat. Autónoma Méx., 2004. Rsch. grant, Nat. Coun. Sci. and Tech. Avocations: films, bicycling, reading. Office: Calzada Mexico-Xochimilco 101 Tlalpan Mexico City 14370 Mexico Business E-Mail: berenz@imp.edu.mx.

BERG, BRITT, writer, editor; m. John Berg; 2 children. BA, Emory U., Atlanta, 1998; MS in Counseling Psychology, 2004. Writer, editor Deb Bruce PhD, Consulting, 1998—; rsch. supr., dept. ednl. psychology Ga. State U., Atlanta, 1999—2001; project manager, dept. psychiatry and behavioral sciences Emory Sch. Medicine, 2004—06; sr. rsch. specialist, dept. psychology Emory Coll., 2006—. Contbg. med. writer/editor for several published books, peer-reviewed publications and presentations, contbg. writer/editor of scientific content for publications, grants, manuscripts, newsletters, websites, and other communications. Vol. work Emory Rsch. Staff Assn., 2005—, Glenn Sch. Bd. Dirs., 2008—. Office: Emory U Psychology Dept 36 Eagle Row Atlanta GA 30322 Office Phone: 404-727-2979. Business E-Mail: britt.berg@emory.edu.

BERG, CHARLES G., health products executive, lawyer; m. Casey Wiggins; 3 children. Degree in Law, Georgetown U.; BA in Polit. Sci., Macalester Coll., St. Paul, Minn., 1978. Founder, CEO Health Ptnrs., Inc.; exec. v.p., med. delivery Oxford Health Plans, Inc., 1998—2000, exec. v.p., med. delivery and tech., 2000—01, pres., COO, 2001—02, pres., CEO, 2002—04; CEO, Northeast region UnitedHealth Group, Inc., 2004—05, exec., 2005—06; sr. adv. Welsh, Carson, Anderson & Stowe, 2007—09; exec. chmn. WellCare Health Plans, Inc., Tampa, Fla., 2008—10, non-exec. chmn., 2011—. Bd. dirs. America's Health Ins. Plans, DaVita, Inc. Office: WellCare Health Plans Inc 8725 Henderson Rd Renaissance 1 Tampa FL 33634 Office Phone: 813-290-6200. Office Fax: 813-262-2802. Business E-Mail: charles.berg@wellcare.com. *

BERG, DANIEL, science and technology educator; b. NYC, June 1, 1929; s. Jack and Hattie (Tannenbaum) B.; m. Frances Helena Ely, Aug. 18, 1956; children: Brian, Laura, Meredith. BS, CCNY, 1950; MS, Yale U., 1951, PhD, 1953; grad. execs. program, Carnegie-Mellon U., 1972. With Westinghouse Electric Corp., Pitts., 1953-77, research div. mgr., then tech. dir., 1976-77; prof. sci. and tech. Carnegie-Mellon U., 1977-83, dean Mellon Coll. Sci., 1977-81, univ. provost, 1981-83; v.p. acad. affairs, provost, Inst. prof. sci. and tech. Rensselaer Poly. Inst., Troy, NY, 1983-85, pres., 1985-87, Inst. prof., 1987—. Bd. dirs. Hy-Tech. Machine Co., Inc.; chmn. bd. Crystek Inc.; mem. Pa. Sci. and Engring. Found., 1975-76; mem. vis. coun. sci. and engring. CCNY, 1980-84; mem. vis. coun. Sch. Computer Sci., Carnegie-Mellon U., 1992—; mem. Yale U. Coun., 1981-85; assoc. fellow Jonathan Edwards Coll., 1982—; cons. to industry and govt. Author, editor, patentee in field. Fellow IEEE, AAAS, INFORMS, Am. Inst. Chemists, N.Y. Acad. Scis.; mem. Nat. Acad. Engring. (coun. 1985-88), Am. Chem. Soc., Cosmos Club of Washington, Rivers Club of Pitts., Phi Beta Kappa, Sigma Xi, Alpha Chi Sigma, Tau Beta Pi. Home: 12 The Crossways Troy NY 12180-7263 Office: Rensselaer Poly Inst 5015 CII Troy NY 12180-3522 Home Phone: 518-272-7611. Business E-Mail: bergd@rpi.edu.

BERG, HOWARD C., biology professor; b. Iowa City, Mar. 16, 1934; s. Clarence P. and Esther M. (Carlson) B.; m. Mary E. Guyer, Dec. 19, 1964; children— Henry G., Alexander H., Elena C. BS in Chemistry, Calif. Inst. Tech., Pasadena, 1956; AM in Physics, Harvard U., 1960, PhD in Chem. Physics, 1964. Jr. fellow Harvard Soc. Fellows, Cambridge, Mass., 1963-66; asst. prof. dept. biology Harvard U., Cambridge, 1966-69, assoc. prof. dept. biochemistry and molecular biology, 1969-70, prof. dept. molecular and cellular biology, 1986—; prof. physics, 1997—; assoc. prof. to prof. dept. molecular, cellular and developmental biology U. Colo., Boulder, 1970-79; prof. div. biology Calif. Inst. Tech., Pasadena, 1979-86. Mem. Rowland Inst., Cambridge, 1986—. Author: Random Walks in Biology, 1983, revised edit., 1993, E. coli in Motion, 2004; contbr. articles to profl. jours. Fulbright fellow, 1956-57, Guggenheim fellow, 2000-01; NSF Sci. Faculty Devel. awardee, 1978-79. Mem. AAAS, Am. Phys. Soc. (Biol. Physics prize 1984), Biophys. Soc. (Single Molecule Biology prize 2007), Am. Soc. Microbiol., NAS, Am. Acad. Arts and Scis., Am. Philos. Soc. Office: Harvard U Biology Labs 16 Divinity Ave Cambridge MA 02138-2020 also: Rowland Inst 100 Edwin H Land Blvd Cambridge MA 02142 Office Phone: 617-495-0924. Business E-Mail: hberg@mcb.harvard.edu.

BERG, JEREMY MARK, academic administrator, biochemist, researcher; BS in Chemistry, MS in Chemistry, Stanford U., Calif., 1980; PhD in Chemistry, Harvard U., Cambridge, Mass., 1985. Vis. rsch. assoc. Charles F. Kettering Rsch Lab., Yellow Springs, Ohio, 1979; NSF predoc. fellow Harvard U., 1980—83; Jane Coffin Childs Meml. Fund postdoc. fellow, Sch. Medicine Johns Hopkins U., Balt., 1984—86, asst. prof. dept. chemistry, 1986—90, prof., dir. dept. biophysics & biophysical chemistry, Sch. Medicine, 1990—2003, prof. chemistry, 1992—2003; dir. Nat. Inst. Gen. Med. Scis. (NIGMS), NIH, Bethesda, Md., 2003—11, sr. investigator, Nat. Inst. Diabetes and Digestive & Kidney Diseases, 2008—11; assoc. sr. vice chancellor sci. strategy and planning in the health sciences U. Pitts., 2011—. Dir. Markey Ctr. Macromolecular Structure & Function Johns Hopkins U. Sch. Medicine, 1990—2003, dir. Inst. Basic Biomedical Scis., 2001—03, co-dir. Keck Ctr. Rational Design Biologically Active Molecules, 2002—03. Contbr. articles to profl. jours., chapters to books. Recipient Disting. New Faculty in Chemistry award, Camille & Henry Dreyfus Found., 1986, Eli Lilly award for fundamental rsch. in biol. chemistry, 1995, W. Barry Wood Tchg. award, Johns Hopkins U. Sch. Medicine, 1995, 1996, Prof.'s Tchg. award for preclin. scis., 1997, NIH Director's award, 2008, Disting. Svc. award, Biophysical Soc., 2009; named Md. Outstanding Young Scientist of Yr., 1995; Searle Scholar, 1987—90, Alfred P. Sloan Found. fellow, 1988. Fellow: AAAS; mem.: American Soc. Biochemistry and Molecular Biology (pres.-elect 2011—, Howard K. Schachman Pub. Svc. award), Inst. Medicine, Am. Chem. Soc. (Pure Chemistry award 1993, Harrison Howe award 1997), Phi Beta Kappa. Office: University Pitts Scaife Hall S304 3550 Terrance St Pittsburgh PA 15213 Office Phone: 412-624-1223. Business E-Mail: jberg@pitt.edu. *

BERG, PATRICIA ELENE, molecular biologist; b. Dubuque, Iowa, Sept. 17, 1943; d. Clifford Jay and Dorothy Ruth (McKibben) Emerson; 1 child, Bridget K. Mora; m. Robert S. Weiner. SB in Math., U. Chgo., 1965; PhD in Microbiology, Ill. Inst. Tech., 1973. Postdoctoral fellow U. Chgo., 1973-78; dir. genetic engring. Bethesda Rsch. Labs., Rockville, Md., 1978-80; expert NIH, Bethesda, 1980-82, sr. staff fellow, 1982-85, Nat. Inst. Digestive Diseases and Kidney, 1985-91; assoc. prof. divsn. of pediatric hematology/oncology Sch. Medicine U. Md., Balt., 1991-98; assoc. prof. dept. biochem. and molecular biology George Washington U. Med. Sch., 1999—2008, prof., dept. biochem and molecular biology, 2008—. Contbr. articles to profl. jours. and to NY Times, Washington Post, L.A. Times, AP, Reuters; reported on CNN, Fox, CBS, 160 TV stas., U. Chgo. scholar, 1961—65. Mem. AAAS, Am. Soc. Microbiology, Am. Soc. Hematology, Am. Assn. Cancer Rsch., Sigma Xi. Achievements include discovery of BP1, gene expressed in over 80 percent of breast cancer patients and 70% of prostate cancer patients. Office: George Washington U Med Sch Dept Biochem/Molecular Biol 2300 Eye St NW Washington DC 20037-2336 Home Phone: 301-283-0821; Office Phone: 202-994-2810. Business E-Mail: bcmpeb@gwumc.edu.

BERG, PAUL, biochemist, educator; b. Bklyn., June 30, 1926; s. Harry and Sarah (Brodsky) Berg; m. Mildred Levy, Sept. 14, 1947; 1 child, John. BS, Pa. State U., 1948; PhD, Case Western Res. U., Cleve., 1952; DSc (hon.), U. Rochester, 1978, Yale U., 1978, Washington U., St. Louis, 1986, Oreg. State U., 1989, Pa. State U., 1995. Postdoc. fellow Inst. Cytophysiology, Copenhagen, 1952—53, Washington U. Sch. Medicine, 1953—54, Am. Cancer Soc. scholar in cancer rsch., dept. microbiology, 1954, asst. to assoc. prof. microbiology, 1955—59; assoc. prof. biochemistry Stanford U. Sch. Medicine, Calif., 1959—60, prof., 1960—69, chmn. dept. biochemistry,

1969—74, Sam, Lulu & Jack Willson prof. biochemistry, 1970—94, Vivian K. & Robert W. Cahill prof. biochemistry & cancer rsch., 1994—2000, Cahill prof. biochemistry emeritus, 2000—. Fellow Salk Inst., La Jolla, Calif., 1973—83; dir. Beckman Ctr. Molecular & Genetic Medicine, Stanford U., 1985—2000, dir. emeritus, 2000—; bd. sci. advisors Jane Coffin Childs Found. Med. Rsch., 1970—80; chmn. sci. adv. com. Whitehead Inst. Biomed. Rsch., Cambridge, Mass., 1984—90; bd. dirs. Nat. Found. Biomed. Rsch., 1994—; mem. internat. adv. bd. Basel Inst. Immunology, Switzerland. Mem. editl. bd.: Molecular Biology, 1956—69; contbr. to profl. jours. Trustee Rockefeller U., 1990—92. Lt. USNR, 1943—46. Recipient Eli Lilly prize biochemistry, 1959, Henry J. Kaiser award for excellence in teaching, 1969, V.D. Mattia award, Roche Inst. Molecular Biology, 1972, Disting. Alumnus award, Pa. State U., 1972, Gairdner Found. ann. award, 1980, Lasker Found. award, 1980, Nobel prize for chemistry, 1980, NY Acad. Sci. award, 1980, Nat. Medal Sci., 1983, Nat. Libr. Medicine Medal, 1986, 7th Ann. Biotechnology Heritage award, Chem. Heritage Found., 2005; named Calif. Scientist of Yr., Calif. Mus. Sci. & Industry, 1963. Fellow: AAAS (Sci. Freedom & Responsibility award 1982); mem.: NAS, Royal Soc. (fgn.), French Acad. Sci. (fgn.), Japan Biochem. Soc. (fgn.), Internat. Soc. Molecular Biology, Am. Philos. Soc., Am. Soc. Microbiology, Am. Soc. Cell Biology, Am. Soc. Biol. Chemists (pres. 1974—75), Am. Acad. Arts & Scis., Inst. Medicine. Office: Stanford Sch Medicine Beckman Ctr B 062 Stanford CA 94305-5301

BERG, STACEY LYNN, pediatric oncologist; b. Pitts., Apr. 17, 1960; AB, Harvard U., 1981; MD, U. Pitts., 1985. Diplomate Am. Bd. Pediatrics, Am. Bd. Pediatric Hematology-Oncology. Resident Children's Hosp. Pitts., 1985-88; fellow pediatric hematology-oncology pediatric br. Nat. Cancer Inst., Bethesda, Md., 1988-91, biotech. fellow, 1991-94; asst. prof. pediatrics Uniformed Scis. U. Health Scis., Bethesda, 1993-94, Tex. Childrens Hosp., Baylor Coll. Medicine, Houston, 1994—. Recipient travel award Am. Soc. Clin. Oncology, Washington, 1990. Mem. Am. Assn. Cancer Rsch., Am. Soc. Clin. Oncology, Children's Oncology Group, Pediatric Brain Tumor Consortium, Phi Beta Kappa. Office: Tex Childrens Cancer Ctr 6621 Fannin St # Mc33320 Houston TX 77030-2303 Business E-Mail: sberg@txccc.org. *

BERG, WENDIE, radiologist; Former prof. radiology U. Md., former dir. breast imaging; diagnostic radiologist & breast imaging cons. Am. Radiology Svcs. Johns Hopkins Green Spring. Chmn. & prin. investigator Am. Coll. Radiology Imaging Network's Screening Breast Ultrasound in High-Risk Women Study. Co-author over 50 peer reviewed articles. Mem.: RSNA, ARRS, Md. Radiation Soc. Office: 10755 & 10753 Falls Rd Lutherville MD 21093 Mailing: 21 Crossroads Dr Ste 100 Owings Mills MD 21117 Office Phone: 410-583-2700. Office Fax: 410-583-2710.

BERGA, SARAH L., obstetrician, gynecologist, educator; b. San Benito, Tex., May 22, 1954; d. John Orrin and Nancy Estelle (Michael) B.; m. Frederick S. Sherman, Sept. 26, 1981 (div. 1994); children: Alexis Estelle, Nathaniel Abbott; m. Lockwood Hoehl, Oct. 28, 1995. BA, U. Va., Charlottesville, 1976, MD, 1980. Diplomate Am. Bd. Ob-Gyn., Am. Bd. Reproductive Endocrinology and Infertility. From asst. to assoc. prof. U. Pitts., 1988-2001; dir. reproductive endocrinology and infertility divsn. U. Pitts. Sch. Medicine, 2000; prof. U. Pitts., 2001—03; prof., chair, dept. gynecology and obstetrics Emory U., Atlanta, 2003—. Mem.: Am. Soc. Reproductive Medicine (bd. dirs. 2002—04), Soc. Gynecologic Investigation (coun. mem. 1999—2002, pres. elect 2011—). Office: Emory U Sch Medicine Dept GYNOB Atlanta GA 30322 Home: 21 Palisades Road NE Atlanta GA 30309 Office Phone: 404-727-8600. Business E-Mail: sberga@emory.edu.

BERGAMINI, ETTORE, pathologist; b. Ferrara, Italy, Oct. 2, 1937; s. Aldo and Laura (Pasquali) B.; m. Zina Gori, June 8, 1975; 1 child, Laura. MD, U. Pisa, Italy, 1962; PhD, Scuola Normale Superiore, Pisa, 1965. Asst. prof. U. Messina, Italy, 1964-66, U. Siena, Italy, 1966-73, U. Pisa, Italy, 1974-80, prof., 1980—. Dir. Ctr. Gerontological Rsch., Pisa, 1989-95, 2001-07; vice chmn. Gordon Rsch. Subcom. Europe, 1991-93, ad-hoc com., 1994; chair biogerontology sect. Italian Soc. Gerontology and Geriatrics, 1995-2003; chair Italian Nat. Program on Biomarkers of Aging, 1995-2005; pres. 3rd European Congress Biogerontology, 2002; chair biology sect. Gerontological Soc. Am., 2005. Editor: General Pathology and Pathophysiology of Aging, 1993; co-editor: Protein Metabolism in Aging, 1990; guest editor: Molecular Aspects of Medicine, 2006. Mem. Rotary. Roman Catholic. Avocations: music, farming. Office: Inst Patologia Generale via Roma 55 56126 Pisa Italy

BERGEN, DORIS, psychologist, educator; b. St. Louis, Feb. 11, 1932; m. Joel S. Fink; m. James Sponseller (div.); children: Ellen Creager, Holly Andrecheck, Gail Burnett. Student, Heidelberg Coll., 1949—51; BS, Ohio State U., 1953; MA, Mich. State U., 1970, PhD, 1974. From instr. to assoc. prof. Oakland U., Rochester, Mich., 1970—80; dean grad. sch. Wheelock Coll., Boston, 1980—84; dean grad. studies and rsch. Pittsburg State U., Pittsburg, Kans., 1984—88; prof., chair ednl. psychology dept. Miami U., Oxford, Ohio, 1988—98, prof., dir. ctr. for human devel., learning and tech., 1998—. Assoc. dean Oakland U., Rochester, 1979—80; vis. scholar Com. Scholarly Comm. with China NAS, 1989—91; cons. Fisher-Price, Inc., 2006—08; trainer Heads Up Network, 1998—99; disting. prof. ednl. psychology, 2007. Author: Assessment Methods for Infants and Toddlers: Transdisciplinary Team Approaches, 1994, 2003, Human Development: Traditional and Contemporary Theories, 2007; co-author (with J.M. Coscia): Brain Research and Childhood Education: Implications for Educators, 2001, 2006; co-author: (with R. Reid, L. Torelli) Educating and Caring for Very Young Children: A Comprehensive Curriculum, 2000; co-author: 2d edit., 2008; editor: Play as a Learning Medium, 1974, Play as a Learning Medium, 2d printing, 1976, Play as a Learning Medium, 3d printing, 1978, Play as a Learning Medium, 4th printing, 1982, Play as a Medium for Learning and Development: A Handbook of Theory and Practice, 1988, Readings from Play as a Medium for Learning and Development, 1998; co-editor (with D. Fromberg): Play from Birth to Twelve, Perspectives and Meanings, 1998, 2nd edit., 2006; contbr. chpts. in books, articles to profl. jours., parent brochures, book reviews, curriculum manuals, govt. booklets; presenter at scholarly meetings; author: (book) Harris, Y & Bergen D. Children & Families of African Origin, 2008, Bergen D, Reid R, & Torelli, L. Educating & Caring Very Young Children, 2d edit., 2008. Grantee Rsch. on Rescue Heroes, Laugh and Learning, Fisher-Price, Inc., 2001—02, Evaluation of Dragonfly Sci. Inquiry Tng., Eisenhower Grant, 1996—99, Evaluation of Oxford/Talawanda Family Resource Ctr., Oxford/Talawanda Cmty. Svcs., 1999, Evaluation of RISE Winning Teams Early Childhood Tng., Ohio Dept. Edn., 1996—98, Evaluation of Butler County Early Intervention Tracking Program, Civitan Svc. Club, 1996—98, Instl. Devel. Grant, U.S. Dept. Edn., 1986—89, Birth through Seven: Early Intervention and Preschool Spl. Needs, U.S. Dept. Spl. Edn., 1981—84, Day Care Policy: Views of Parents and Practitioners in Mich., NSF, 1979—80. Fellow: AERA, Am. Orthopsychiatric Soc., Assn. Psychological Sci.; mem.: Nat. Assn. Early Childhood Tchr. Educators (sec. 2000—02, founding bd. dirs.), Jean Piaget Soc., Coun. Exceptional Children (divsn. early childhood), Am. Evaluation Soc., Assn. for Study of Play, Nat. Assn. for Edn. Young Children, Soc. Rsch. in Child Devel., Am. Ednl. Rsch. Assn. (bd. dirs. 1998—2000, early childhood sect.), Assn. Childhood Edn. Internat., Internat. Humor Soc., Phi Delta Theta, Phi Kappa Phi. Office: Miami Univ 100G McGuffey Hall Oxford OH 45056 Office Phone: 513-529-6622. Business E-Mail: bergend@mohio.edu. *

BERGER, ALLAN SIDNEY, psychiatrist, educator; b. NYC, Nov. 26, 1931; s. Nathan and Ida (Masor) B.; m. Lois Harriet Blumfield, Dec. 27, 1953; children: Karen, Gary, Jonathan. AB magna cum laude, Syracuse U., 1951; MD, SUNY, Bklyn., 1955. Diplomate Am. Bd. Psychiatry and Neurology, 1962; additional qualification in geriatric psychiatry cert., 1991. Intern L.I. Coll. Hosp., NYC, 1955-56; resident Yale U. Sch. Medicine, New Haven, 1956-58, fellow Yale Child Study Ctr., 1958-59; pvt. practice Silver Spring, Md., 1961—; asst. chief D.C. Gen. Hosp., Washington, 1961-62. Clin. prof. Georgetown U. Sch. Medicine, Washington, 1986—; cons. NIH, 1987-88; command cons. Nat. Naval Med. Ctr. Bethesda, 1990-97; mem. physician expert panel VA, 1993-96; mem. peer rev. com. on behalf of Md. Med. Licensing Bd., 1992-2003. Contbr. articles to profl. jours. Cons. Peace Corps, 1962, Hebrew Home for the Aged, Rockville, Md., 1962-72. Recipient Vicennial Medalist award Georgetown U. Sch. Medicine, 1981. Mem. AMA, Mid-Atlantic Group Psychotherapy Soc. (bd. dirs. 1977-78), Metro. Washington Soc. Adolescent Psychiatry (treas. 1979-80, pres. 1982-83), Med. and Chirurgical Faculty Md., B'nai B'rith. Independent. Avocations: tennis, swimming, gardening. Home and Office: 1302 Midwood Pl Silver Spring MD 20910-1645 Office Phone: 301-589-1443.

BERGER, BONNIE G., sport psychologist, educator; b. Champaign, Ill., May 20, 1941; d. Bernard G. and Mildred W. Berger; 1 child, Stephen Casher. BS, Wittenberg U., Springfield, Ohio, 1962; MA, Columbia U., NYC, 1965, EdD, 1972. Cert. cons. Assn. Applied Sport Psychology. Tchr. George Rogers Clark Jr. H.S., Springfield, Ohio, 1962-64; supr. phys. edn. Agnes Russell Elem. Sch., NYC, 1964-65; asst. prof. SUNY, Geneseo, 1965-66, Dalhousie U., Halifax, N.S., Can., 1969-71, Bklyn. Coll., 1971-77, assoc. prof., 1978-82, prof., 1982-93, dir. Sport Psychology Lab., dep. chair dept. phys. edn., 1989-93; prof., assoc. dean Sch. Phys. and Health Edn. U. Wyo., Laramie, 1993-96, prof., assoc. dean Coll. Health Scis., 1996-99; prof., dir. Sch. Human Movement, Sport and Leisure Studies, Bowling Green State U., Ohio, 1999—2009. Cons. in field. Author: Free Weights for Women, 1984, Foundations of Exercise Psychology 2d edit., 2007; editl. bd. mem. Jour. Applied Sport Psychology. Fellow Am. Acad. Kinesiology; contbr. chapters to books, articles to profl. jours. Fellow Assn. for Advancement of Applied Sport Psychology (exec. bd.) Am. Acad. Kinesiology and Phys. Edn.; mem. APA, AAHPERD, Internat. Soc. Sports Psychology, N.Am. Soc. Psychology and Phy. Activity, Assn. Applied Sport Psychology (pres. 2009-10, pres. elect 2010-). Avocations: travel, skiing, swimming. Home: 640 Pine Valley Dr Bowling Green OH 43402 Business E-Mail: bberger@bgnet.bgsu.edu, bberger@bgsu.edu.

BERGER, GERT ALEXANDER, neurologist; b. Gunzenhausen, Bavaria, Germany, Dec. 12, 1943; s. Raimund and Hanne (Thurn) B.; m. Martina Pfister (div. 1987); 1 child, Florian; m. Saskia Carissima Nöggerath, Dec. 9, 1988; children: Oliver, Carolin. BS, MD, U. Erlangen, 1969. Cert. epileptologist, neurologist, psychiatrist. Resident Klinikum, Nürnberg, Germany, 1970-76; sr. house officer Neurol. Klinik, Nürnberg, 1976—2008. Contbr. articles to profl. jours. Fellow neurology and psychiatry Bayer. Landesärztekammer, Germany, 1974—. Mem. Internat. Liga gegen Epilepsie (Deutsche sect.), Internat. Fedn. Clin. Neurophysiology (German assn. supr. EEG edn. 1975—, supr. EMG edn. 1987—), German Assn. Ultrasound in Medicine (supr. UDS edn. 1988—). Avocations: riding, tennis. Office: Neurologic Kaiserhof Konig Str 39 Nurmberg D90402 Germany Business E-Mail: info@neurologic-kaiserhof.de.

BERGER, HARVEY JAMES, pharmaceutical executive, physician, educator; b. NYC, June 6, 1950; s. Howard H. and Edith E. (Muskat) B.; children: Eric Michael, Mark Phillip, Nicole Elizabeth, Isabella Grace. Grad., The Hotchkiss Sch., 1968; AB magna cum laude, Colgate U., 1972; MD, Yale U., 1977. Diplomate Am. Bd. Nuclear Medicine. Resident Yale-New Haven (Conn.) Hosp., 1977-81, dir. cardiovascular imaging, 1981-84; asst. prof. radiology and medicine Yale U., New Haven, 1981-83, assoc. prof., 1983-84; prof. radiology and assoc. prof. medicine Emory U., Atlanta, 1984-86; dir. Divsn. Nuclear Medicine Emory U. affiliated hosps., Atlanta, 1984-86; sr. v.p. med. affairs Centocor, Inc., Malvern, Pa., 1986—87; sr. v.p., R&D Centacor, Inc., Malvern, Pa., 1987—89; pres. R&D div., exec. v.p., med. dir. Centocor, Inc., Malvern, Pa., 1989-91; chmn., chief exec. officer, founder ARIAD Pharmaceuticals, Inc., Cambridge, Mass., 1991—; chmn., CEO, founder ARIAD Gene Therapeutics, Inc., Cambridge, Mass., 1993—2008; chmn. ARIAD Inst. BioMedical Research, 1993—. Bd. dirs. Centocor Devel. Corp. I, PTC Therapeutics, Inc.; lectr. divsn. health scis. and tech. MIT, 1992-97, Harvard Med. Sch., 1992-97; adj. prof. U. Pa., Phila., 1986-92; mem. adv. study sects. Nat. Heart, Lung and Blood Inst., Washington, 1984-90; advisor Office of Dir. NIH, Washington, 1984-87; mem. panel on govt. role in civilian tech. NRC/NAS, 1989-92; mem. Dean's Coun. Yale Sch. Medicine, New Haven, 2007-. Founding editor Am. Jour. of Cardiac Imaging, 1985-89; editor Nuclear Medicine Communications, 1985-88; mem. editl. bd. Investigative Radiology, 1984-88; contbr. numerous articles to profl. jours.; patentee in field. Cline Fixott award Am. Acad. Dental Radiologists, 1984, Symbol of Caring award Sarcoma Found. Am., 2005 Mem. ACP, Soc. Nuclear Medicine (com. chmn., nat. trustee, Tetalman award 1982), Am. Coll. Cardiology (editl. bd. jour. 1983-88), Am. Coll. Chest Physicians, Am. Heart Assn. (established investigator 1981, cardiovascular radiology/circulation couns.), Am. Coll. Radiology, Am. Fedn. Clin. Rsch., Assn. Univ. Radiologists (Young Investigator award 1979), N.Am. Soc. Cardiovascular Radiology, Soc. Thoracic Radiology, Soc. Exptl. Biology and Medicine, Harvard Club of Boston, Yale Club of N.Y., Phi Beta Kappa. Office: ARIAD Pharmaceuticals Inc 26 Landsdowne St Cambridge MA 02139-4216

BERGER, JERRY J., anesthesiologist, educator; MD, Duke U., 1977. Diplomate Am. Bd. Anesthesiology, 1981, Am. Bd. Anesthesiology-pain medicine, 2004, lic. Fla., 1979, Colo., 2005. Intern Shands Hosp. at Univ. Fla., 1978, resident anesthesiology, 1981; intern St. Vincent's Hosp, 2005; hosp. affiliation includes Malcom Randall VA Med. Ctr.; assoc. prof. anesthesiology Univ. Fla. Coll. of Medicine, Gainesville, Fla. Office: Shands at the University of Florida 1600 SW Archer Rd Gainesville FL 32608 Office Phone: 352-265-0943.

BERGER, JOSEF, biologist; b. Czech Republic, July 24, 1949; s. Josef Berger and Vera Bergerova; m. Ruzena Suchomelova; children: Josef, Zdenek. MSc, Charles U., Prague, 1973, Doc, 1994; RNDr, 1978, PhD, 1983. Head, haematological lab. Inst. Biochemistry & Pharmacy, Pardubice, Czech Republic, 1976—87, U. Hosp. H. Kralove, 1989—92; prof. U. South Bohemia, Ceske Budejovice, Czech Republic, 1996—; founder U. Pardubice, 1991; clin. biol. Czech Republic. Editor-in-chief Jour. Applied Biomedicine, 2003—. Contbr. more than 100 original articles and 17 books. Bd. mem. Czecho-Slovak Biol. Soc., 1996—2002. Office: Univ South Bohemia Emy Destinove Ceske Budejovice 37005 Czech Republic Home: Na Tresnovce 4 373 71 Rudolfov Czech Republic Business E-Mail: berger@jcu.cz.

BERGER, KARIN ULRIKE, pharmacist; b. Berlin, June 16, 1967; d. Kurt Peter and Rosemarie Anna Elisabeth Bonfert; m. Hans-Martin Berger, Apr. 21, 1995; 1 child, Lisann. Degree in pharmacy, Freie Univ., Berlin, 1992; MPH, Technische Univ., Berlin, 1998. Cert. NLP-Practitioner Germany. Cmty. pharmacist Apotheke am Heckerdamm, Berlin, 1993—2003; pharm. care referent Fed. Union German Assns. of Pharmacists, Berlin, 2003—. Cons. pharmacist BKK-Landesverband Nord, Hamburg, Germany, 1999—2002. Chair parent's orgn. Hermann-Löns-Grundschule, Berlin, 2003—06. Home: Am Laubwald 8 Berlin 13629 Germany Office: Abda Jaegerstrasse 49/50 Berlin 10117 Germany Office Fax: 0049/30/40004253; Home Fax: 0049/30/38306774. Personal E-mail: k.berger@mailberlin.net. E-mail: k.berger@abda.aponet.de.

BERGER, MARVIN, medical educator; b. Bronx, NY, July 22, 1936; BA, Ohio U., 1957; MD, Chgo. Med. Sch., 1961. Diplomate Am. Bd. Internal Medicine, 1969, Am. Bd. Cardiovasc. Disease, 1977, Am. Bd. Echocardiography, 2009. Intern Beth Israel Med. Ctr., NYC, 1961-62, resident in internal medicine, 1962-64, dir. echocardiography lab., 1975—, assoc. chief cardiology, 1981—2003; fellow in cardiology Mt. Sinai Med. Ctr., NYC, 1964-65; asst. prof. clin. medicine Mt. Sinai Sch. Medicine, NYC, 1976-81, assoc. prof., 1982 90, assoc. prof. medicine, 1990-94; assoc. prof. Albert Einstein Coll. Medicine, Bronx, 1994—, prof. clin. medicine, 1999—. Editor: Doppler Echocardiography in Heart Disease, 1987; contbr. articles to profl. jours. Capt. US Army, 1965—67. Fellow: ACP, Am. Soc. Echocardiography, Am. Coll. Cardiology, NY Cardiol. Soc.; mem.: AMA, Am. Heart Assn. Avocations: reading, classical music, jazz, sports. Office: Beth Israel Med Ctr 1st Ave and 16th St New York NY 10003 Business E-Mail: mberger@bethisraelny.org.

BERGER, NATHAN ALLEN, medical educator, academic administrator; b. Phila., July 8, 1940; s. Meyer and Lillian (Salko) B.; m. Sosamma John, June 23, 1968; children: Joshua S., Ravi B., Sarina H. AB, Temple U., 1962; MD, Hahneman U., 1966. Intern Michael Reese Med. Ctr., Chgo., 1967-68; rsch. assoc. NIH, Balt., 1968-71; assoc. prof. Washington U. Sch. Medicine, St. Louis, 1971-82; prof. medicine, biochemistry, and oncology Case Western Res. U., Cleve., 1983, Hanna Payne prof. experimental medicine, 1983—95, dir. cancer ctr., 1985 95, interim dean, v.p. med. affairs, 1995-96, dean, v.p. med. affairs, 1996—2002, dir. Ctr. Sci., Health and Soc., 2002—, dir. Sci. Enrichment and Opportunity Program, 2003—; med. dir. Case Mini Med. Sch., 2005—. Bd. trustees Edison Biotech. Am. Cancer Soc., U. Hosp. Cleve., Henry Ford Health System, Montefiore, Ohio Biomed. Rsch. and Tech. Task Force. Contbr. articles to profl. jours.; mem. editl. bd. Jour. Clin. Investigation, Jour. Biol. Chemistry, Cancer Rsch.; others. Lt. comdr. USPHS, 1968—71. Fellow Washington U. Sch. Medicine, 1971-82, Frank & Dorathy Hummel Havana prize, 2007, named Hon. Med. Alumnus of Yr., CWRU Sch. Medicine, 2009, Disting. prof., 2011; Leukemia Soc. Am. scholar; named to Am. Cancer Soc. Hall of Fame, Cleve. Med. Hall of Fame. Mem. Am. Soc. Hematology, Am. Soc. Biol. Chemists, Am. Soc. Clin. Oncology, Am. Soc. Cancer Rsch., Am. Soc. Clin. Investigation, Am. Assn. Physicians, Alpha Omega Alpha. Office: Case Western Res U 10900 Euclid Ave Cleveland OH 44106-4971 Office Phone: 216-368-4084, 216-368-2059. Business E-Mail: nab@case.edu.

BERGER, RICHARD, obstetrician and gynecologist; b. Augsburg, Germany, Sept. 3, 1960; s. Richard and Maria (Brunner) B.; m. Carmen Prassler, July 15, 1988; children: Georg, Franziska. MD, U. Munich, 1987; PhD, U. Bochum, Germany, 1996. Rsch. fellow Inst. for Surg. Rsch., U. Munich, 1984-87; rsch., clin. fellow dept. gynecology Univ. Hosp. Giessen, Germany, 1987-94; rsch. fellow Max-Planck Inst. for Neurol. Rsch., Cologne, 1994-95; cons. dept. gynecology Univ. Hosp. Bochum, 1995—; chair dept. ob-gyn. Marienhaus Klinikum, Neuwied, Germany, 2003—. Co-author: Fetus and Neonate, The Circulation, Vol. 1, 1993, Giessener Gynaekologische Fortbildung, 1993, Vom Accouchierhaus fur Frauenklinik, 1989, Geburtshilfe in Hessen, 1992, Emergency Surgery, 1986, Microcirculation - an update, Vol. 2, 1987; contbr. articles to profl. jours. Mem. Cartellverband (CV), Munich, 1981—. Recipient award European Congress of Anesthesiology, 1985, Sci. award Mittelrheinische Soc. Gynecology and Obstetrics, 1990, Sci. award German Soc. Perinatology, 1997; grantee Deutsche Forschungsgemeinschaft, 1993—, Max-Planck Soc., 1995—, U. Bochum, 1996—. Mem. German Soc. for Gynecology and Obstetrics (Sci. award 1992), German Soc. Physiology (sec. developmental physiology), Med. Faculty of U. Bochum. Roman Catholic. Avocations: modern art and history, hiking, skiing, guitar playing, cooking. Office: Marienhaus Klinikum Frauenklinik Friedrich-Ebert-Strasse 55 56564 Neuwied Germany E-mail: r.berger@mhk.st-elisabeth.de.

BERGER, RICHARD A., orthopedist; BS in Mech. Engring., Mass. Inst. Tech., 1985; MD, Tufts Univ., 1989. Lic. Pa., cert. Ill. Intern, dept. gen. surgery Univ. Health Ctr. Hosp., Pitts., 1989—90; orthopaedic resident U. Pitts., 1990—94, clin. instr., dept. orthopaedic surgery, 1994—95; adult reconstruction fell. Rush U. Med. Ctr., Chgo., 1995—96, asst. prof., orthopaedic surgeon. Contbr. articles to numerous profl. jours. Recipient Charles A. Moore Tchg. award, 1990, Upjohn Young Investigator award, 1990, Resident/Fell. award, Eastern Orthopaedic Assn., 1992, First Place award, Penn. Orthopaedic Soc., 1993, Founder's award, Ea. Orthopaedic Assn., 1994, Resident's Rsch. award, Pitts. Resident's Rsch. Day, 1995. Mem.: AMA, Mass. Med. Soc., Pa. Med. Soc., Pi Tau Sigma. Office: Midwest Orthopaedics Ste 240 One Westbrook Corp Ctr Westchester IL 60154

BERGER, RONALD D., cardiac electrophysiologist, educator; Grad., MIT; MD, Harvard Coll., 1987. Diplomate Am. Bd. Internal Medicine-cardiovasc. disease, 2004, Am. Bd. Internal Medicine-clin. cardiac electrophysiology, 2006. Resident internal medicine Brigham and Women's Hosp., 1987—90; fellow cardiovasc. disease John Hopkins Hosp., 1990—93, prof. medicine, prof. biomedical engring., dir. cardiac electrophysiology tng. program. Co-author: (publs.) Response to cardiac resynchronization therapy: substrate matters., 2011, End-Stage Renal Disease Predicts Complications in Pacemaker and ICD Implants., 2011, Gaps in the ablation line as a potential cause of recovery from electrical isolation and their visualization using MRI., 2011, numerous publs. Office: Johns Hopkins Outpatient Center 601 N Caroline St Baltimore MD 21287

BERGER, SEYMOUR MAURICE, social psychologist; b. Bklyn., Jan. 7, 1928; s. Leo and Bessie Ida (Okun) Berger; m. Sara Marilyn Nappen, Sept. 7, 1952; children: Evelyn Joyce, Nancy Faith. BS, Okla. A&M Coll., 1949; MA, Columbia U., 1950; PhD, Cornell U., 1959. Instr. Trinity Coll., Hartford, Conn., 1958-59; from instr. to assoc. prof. Ind. U., Bloomington, 1959-69; prof. social psychology U. Mass., Amherst, 1969-95, prof. emeritus, 1995—, acting dean social and behavioral scis., 1991-92, dean social behavioral scis., 1992-95. Contbr. articles on social psychology to profl. jours.; mem. editorial bd. Jour. Personality and Social Psychology. Served with USNR, 1945-46; served with USAF, 1951-55. Fulbright sr. research scholar, 1975-76,83; spl. fellow NIH, 1965-66 Democrat. Jewish. Home: 459 Flat Hills Rd Amherst MA 01002-1219 E-mail: berger@psych.umass.edu.

BERGER, THOMAS, cardiologist, researcher; s. Siegfried Berger and Berta Bergsmann; life ptnr. Katharina Wienerroither. MD, Vienna Med. U., 1999. Cert. med. dr. Austrian Med. Soc., 1999, in sports medicine 2005. Rschr. Divsn. Cardiology, Innsbruck, Austria, 2001—08; cons. dept. internal medicine III Med. U. Innsbruck, 2001—. Cons. Gerson Lehrman Group, NYC, 2006—08. Officer Med. Svc., 2000, Austria. Recipient Rsch. award, Med. U. Innsbruck, 2004, Stefan Schuy award, Austrian Soc. Biomed. Engring., 2007; fellow, ÖGIM, ÖKG, OEGBMT, 2007. Achievements include research in noninvasive imaging of cardiac electrophysiology. Home: Heiliggeiststrasse 35 Innsbruck 6020 Austria Office: Dept Cardiology Anichstraße 35 Innsbruck 6020 Austria Business E-Mail: thomas.berger@uki.at.

BERGER, THOMAS GEORG, dermatologist; b. Wiesbaden, Germany, May 10, 1966; s. Fritz Georg and Brigitte Berger; m. Halveig Spiekermann, Dec. 11, 1998; children: Linn Kristin, Lovis Malte, Lotte Mia. Diploma in Tropical Medicine and Med. Parasitology, Bernhard-Nocht Inst., Hamburg, Germany, 1997. Cert. in med. Johannes Gutenberg U., 1994; in paramedic Dublin, 1994, in internship Trinity Coll. Med. Sch., U. Cape Town Med. Sch., South Africa, 1994, lic. Landesamt Rheinland Pfalz, 1995, cert. in dermatology and venereology Bavarian Physicians Coun., 2001, in allergology and clin. immunology Bavarian Physicians Coun., 2004, lic. in med. laser treatment German Dermatol. Acad., 2004, in med.-dermatological cosmetology German Dermatol. Acad., 2004, cert. in dermato-oncology Bavarian Physicians Coun., 2005. Physician in tropical medicine Eberhard-Karls U., Tübingen, Baden-Württemberg, Germany, 1995—96; dermatologist Johannes-Gutenberg U., Mainz, Rheinland-Pfalz, Germany, 1996—97, U. Hosp. Erlangen, Bavaria, Germany, 1997—2001, asst. prof., dept. head, divsn. exptl. immunotherapy, 2001—04; head divsn. dermatology Tawam Hosp., Johns Hopkins Medicine, Al Ain, Abu Dhabi, United Arab Emirates, 2004—09, assoc. prof., faculty medicine and health sci., 2008—; cons. dermatologist German Med. Ctr., 2009—, head dept. dermatology Abu Dhabi, 2009—. Mem. drug adv. bd. Health Authority, Abu Dhabi, 2005—, laser and cosmetic treatment safety com., 2006—. Contbr. articles to profl. jours. Fellow: Am. Acad. Dermatology; mem.: European Laser Acad. (hon.), German Japanese Soc. Dermatology (assoc.), German Cancer Soc. (assoc.), European Acad. Dermatology and Venereology (assoc.). Achievements include patents pending for production of clinical grade dendritic cells for immunotherapy of cancer; treatment of metastatic retinal melanoma with artesunate. Avocations: travel, scuba diving, mountain biking, snowboarding. Home and Office: German Med Ctr PO Box 61822 Abu Dhabi United Arab Emirates Office Fax: 00971 02-6520299. Business E-Mail: bergerts@web.de.

BERGERON, CHRISTINE, pathologist; b. Clermont-Ferrand, July 21, 1955; MD, U. Paris VI, 1984; PhD, McGill U. Montreal, 1989. Assoc. dir. papillomavirus unit Inst. Pasteur, 1992—2002; head pathology dept. Lab. Cerba, 1992—, chief exec. officer, 2005—09. Sec. French Soc. Colposcopy, 2005—11; pres. elect French Soc. Cytology, 2011—, European Fedn. Colposcopy, 2010—; chair ednl. com. Internat. Fedn. Cervical Pathology And Colposcopy, 2008—11. Mem.: Internat. Agy. Rsch. on Cancer (mem. cervical working group), Union Internat. Cancer Control Cervical Cancer (mem. initiative adv. group). Avocation: reading. Home: 163 Rue De Grenelle Paris 75007 France Personal E-mail: bergeron.ch@gmail.com.

BERGERON, WILTON LEE, physician; b. Scott, La., Feb. 13, 1933; s. Lee and Ida (Duhon) B.; m. Juanita Marie Landry, Aug. 3, 1957; children: David, Marcel, René, Jeanne. BS, U. South La., 1956; MD, La. State U., 1958. Diplomate Am. Bd. Allergy and Immunology. Intern Confederate Meml. Med. Ctr. (now La. State U. Med. Sch.), Shreveport, 1958-59; resident Lafayette (La.) Charity Hosp., 1959-60; fellow in allergy Tulane U. Med. Sch., New Orleans, 1968-70; pvt. practice Lafayette and Scott, La., 1960—; allergist, 1970—. Pres. Secular Franciscan Order, 1990-93. Mem. La. Allergy Soc. (former pres.). Republican. Roman Catholic. Avocations: fishing, computers. Home and Office: PO Box 98 # 90 Scott LA 70583-0098

BERGERS, GABRIELE, medical educator; b. Munich, Aug. 19, 1963; MS, U. Munich LMU, 1989; PhD, U. Vienna, 1993. Prof. U. Calif., San Francisco, 1994—. Office: 1450 3rd St San Francisco CA 94158-9001 Office Fax: 415-476-0388. Business E-Mail: gabriele.bergers@ucsf.edu.

BERGGREN, RONALD BERNARD, surgeon, retired educator; b. SI, NY, June 13, 1931; s. Bernard and Florence (Schmidt) B.; m. Mary Beth Griffith, Nov. 25, 1954; children: Karen Berggren Murray, Eric Griffith. BA, Johns Hopkins U., 1953; MD, U. Pa., 1957. Diplomate Am. Bd. Surgery, Nat. Bd. Med. Examiners, Am. Bd. Plastic Surgery (bd. dirs. 1982-88, chmn. 1987-88). Asst. instr. surgery U. Pa., 1958-62, instr., 1962-65; gen. surg. resident Hosp. U. Pa., 1958-62, resident plastic surgery, 1963-64, chief resident plastic surgery, 1964-65; sr. resident surgery Phila. Gen. Hosp., 1962-63; asst. prof. surgery Ohio State U. Sch. Medicine, 1965-68, dir. div. plastic surgery, 1965-85, assoc. prof. surgery, 1968-73, prof. surgery, 1973-86, emeritus prof. surgery, 1986—; attending staff Ohio State U. Hosps., chief of staff, 1983-85, hon. staff, 1986—. Attending staff, dir. div. plastic surgery Children's Hosp., Columbus, Ohio, 1965-90; v.p. Plastic Surgery Ednl. Found., 1984-85, pres., 1986-87; sec. Plastic Surgery Tng. Program Dirs., 1981-83, chmn., 1983-85; mem. med. adv. bd. Ohio Bur. for Children with Med. Handicaps, 1974-2004, mem. emeritus, 2004. Trustee Mid Ohio Health Planning Fedn., 1979-82, 84, PSRO, 1980-84, Scioto Valley Health Systems Agy., 1985-87; del. Coun. Med. Splty. Socs., 1982-90, dir., 1988-90. Recipient Disting. Svc. award Plastic Surgery Edn. Foun., 1990. Fellow: ACS (gov. 1996—2001, chair gov.'s com. on ambulatory surg. care); mem.: AMA, Coun. Plastic Surgical Orgn. (convenor 1996—2000), Coun. Med. Specialty Socs. (dir. 1989—90, sec. 1991—92, pres.-elect 1993, pres. 1994), Accreditation Coun. for Grad. Med. Edn. (rev. com. for plastic surgery 1983—90, mem. exec. com. 1987—90, designate chmn. 1988, chmn. 1989, mem. exec. com. 1994, chmn. 1994, institutional rev. com. 1996—2004, chair 2002—04, John C. Gienapp award 2005), Am. Soc. Maxillofacial Surgery, Am. Soc. Aesthetic Plastic Surgery (parliamentarian 1992—93), Am. Trauma Soc., Am. Burn Assn., Assn. Acad. Surgery, Am. Assn. Surgery Trauma, N.Y. Acad. Scis., Plastic Surg. Rsch. Coun. (chair 1975—76), Franklin County Med. Soc. (pres.-elect 1982—83, pres. 1983—84), Am. Assn. Plastic Surgeons (treas. 1982—85, v.p. 1988—89, pres.-elect 1989—90, pres. 1990—91), Am. Cleft Palate Assn., Ohio Valley Plastic Surg. Soc., Am. Soc. Plastic and Reconstructive Surgeons (spl. hon. citation 1995, Trustees award for spl. achievement in plastic surgery 2000), Columbus Surg. Soc., Ctrl. Surg. Soc., Alpha Kappa Kappa, Phi Kappa Psi, Sigma Xi. Office: 9787 Windale Farms Cir Galena OH 43021-9609 Personal E-mail: rbergg@aol.com.

BERGHOLM, ULLA IRENE ELISABET, retired surgeon; b. Stockholm, Dec. 19, 1948; d. Helge and Ida (Holmgren) Johansson; m. Lars Bergholm (div. 1976; children: Daniel, Gustav Athos. MD, Karolinska U. Hosp., Stockholm, 1975; Dr. Med. Sci., Univ. Hosp. Uppsala, Sweden, 1989. Surgeon Löwenströmska Hosp., Stockholm, 1974-80, Univ. Hosp. Uppsala, 1980-90; sr. surgeon Visby Hosp., Sweden, 1990-91; cons. surgeon Med. Products Agy., Uppsala, 1991-96; pvt. practice Uppsala, Stockholm, 1991-99; rschr. Inst. Cancer Epidemiology, Uppsala, 1985-97, Karolinska Inst. Med. Epidem, Stockholm, 1997—2003; sr. surgeon Kalmar Hosp., 2000—03; ret., 2003. Avocations: reading, music, golf. Home: Berghemsvägen 34 177 70 Järfälla Stockholm Sweden also: Väringavägen 14 Sigtuna 19335 Sweden Personal E-mail: ulla.bergholm@telia.com, ullabergholm@gmail.com.

BERGHOLZ, GEORGE, clinical psychologist; b. Chgo., May 13, 1963; s. Bernard Bengholz Jr. and Sobumnessa (Bonita) Ali. BFA, Sch. of Art Inst., Chgo., 1986; MAAT, Sch. of Art Inst., Rush-Presbyn-St Lukes MedCtr., Chgo., 1990; PsyD, Argosy U., Hawaii, 2005. Child psychiatrist IV Kellogg Rush Presbyterian-St. Luke, Chgo., 1991—94, Rush Day Sch., Chgo., 1992—94, Old Orchard Hosp., Skokie, Ill., 1994—96; activity dir. Nursefinders, Honolulu, 1997, Hoahana Inst., Honolulu, 1997—99, Loveland Acad., Honolulu, 1999—2004; asst. dir. VA Med. Ctr., North Chgo., 2004—05; psychology intern Dept. Edn., Honolulu, 2005—. Vol. John Howard and Assocs., Honolulu, 1998, Na Kolea Homeless Solutions, Honolulu, 1998. Named Outstanding Young Men in America, 1988—89. Avocations: weightlifting, bicycling, running, writing, drawing. Office: Convalescent Ctr Honolulu 1900 Bachelot St Honolulu HI 96817-2487 Home and Office: 60 N Nimitz Hwy Apt 1906 Honolulu HI 96817-5343 Personal E-mail: georgebergholz@yahoo.com.

BERGIN, ALLEN ERIC, clinical psychologist, educator; b. Spokane, Wash, Aug. 4, 1934; s. Bernard F. and Vivian Selma (Kullberg) B.; m. Marian Shafer, June 4, 1955; children: David, Sue, Cyndy, Kathy, Eric, Ben, Patrick, Daniel, Michael. BS, Brigham Young U., 1956, MS, 1957; PhD, Stanford U., 1960. Diplomate Am. Bd. Profl. Psychology, 1969. Postdoc. fellow U. Wis., Psychiatric Inst., Madison, 1960-61; prof. psychology and edn. Tchr. Coll., Columbia U., NYC, 1961-72; prof. psychology Brigham Young U., Provo, Utah, 1972-99, prof. emeritus, 1999—, dir. Values Inst., 1976-78, dir. clin. psychology, 1989-93. Assessment officer Peace Corps, Washington, 1961-66; cons. NIMH, Rockville, Md., 1969-75, 90, sr. rsch. fellow Nat. Inst. Healthcare Rsch., 1992-2000; former pres. Soc. Psychotherapy Rsch., Assn. Mormon Counselors. Co-author: Changing Frontiers in Psychotherapy, 1972, A Spiritual Strategy for Counseling and Psychotherapy, 1997, 2d edit., 2005; co-editor: Handbook of Psychotherapy, 1971, 4th edit., 1994 (citation classic 1979), Handbook of Pyschotherapy and Religious Diversity, 2000, Casebook for a Spiritual Strategy, 2004; author: Eternal Values and Personal Growth, 2002. Bishop LDS Ch., Emerson, NJ, 1970-72, Provo, 1981-84, stake pres., 1992-1995, Church Ed. Mission, San Diego, 2002-03; mem. steering com. Utah Gov.'s Conf. on Families, 1979-80. Recipient Biggs-Pine award Am. Assn. Counseling and Devel., 1986, Maeser rsch. award Brigham Young U., 1986, exemplary paper award Templeton Found., 1996, Pfister award Am. Psychiat. Assn., 1998, Disting. Profl. Contbr. to Knowledge award Am. Psychol. Assn., 1998, Rsch. Disting. Career award Soc. for Psychotherapy Rsch., 1998, Wm. James award, 1990, Disting. Svc. award Utah Acad. Scis, Arts & Letters, 1998. Republican. Avocations: writing, travel.

BERGLIN, EVA ELISABET, cardiothoracic-heart transplant surgeon, educator; b. Gothenburg, Sweden, Jan. 2, 1947; d. Tore Magnus and Ingrid Elisabet (Cederberg) B.; m. Göran Enar William William-Olsson, May 22, 1976; 1 child, Peter Filip. BM, BS, Gothenburg U., 1975, PhD, 1978. Intern Sahlgren's Hosp., Gothenburg, 1975-76, resident in cardiothoracic surgery, 1976-81, mem. organ transplantation staff, 1981-83, mem. cardiothoracic surgery staff, 1984-86, head arrythmia surgery, 1986—, asst. prof. cardiothoracic surgery, 1987—, head cardiac transplantation, 1988—98, also cons. on cardiothoracic surgery, 1982—; rsch. fellow Gothenburg U., 1972-76. Prof. cardiothoracic surgery, 2001. Contbr. articles to profl. jours. Mem. Swedish Transplant Soc. (mem. mgmt. 1988—), European Soc. Heart Transplantation (sec. 1989-91, pres. 1992-94), European Soc. Organ Transplantation, European Assn. Cardiothoracic Surgery, Soc. Thoracic Surgeons. Achievements include research in cardiothoracic surgery. Avocations: sailing, skiing, horseback riding. Office: Sahlgren's Hosp Dept Cardiothoracic Surgery S-41345 Gothenburg Sweden Personal E-mail: eva_berglin@hotmail.com.

BERGLUND, JOHAN, research scientist; b. Linköping, Sweden, May 19, 1983; MSc, attending, Uppsala U., 2008—. Rsch. fellow Uppsala U., 2008—. Office: MRT Entrance 24 Uppsala University Hosp Uppsala 751 85 Sweden Business E-Mail: johan.berglund@radiol.uu.se.

BERGLUND, ROBIN G., child and adult psychiatrist; b. Milw., Oct. 12, 1945; s. Gunnar E. and V. June (Huebsch) B.; children: Victoria S., Christopher F.; m. Akiko Haraguchi, Oct., 2000; 1 child, Liri. BS in Biochemistry magna cum laude, Mich. State U., 1967; MBA, Harvard U., 1971; MD, Med. Univ. S.C., 1995. Engr. Eastman Kodak Co., Rochester, NY, 1967-69; v.p. The First Nat. Bank of Chgo., 1971-75, Wells Fargo Bank, N.A., LA, 1975-77; exec. v.p. Ponderosa Homes, Newport Beach, Calif., 1977-84; chmn., CEO Glenfed Devel. Corp., Encino, Calif., 1984-88; pres. Lowe Enterprises Northwest, Seattle, 1988-89, Met. Homes Inc., Portland, Oreg., 1989-90; pediatrician UCLA-Cedars Sinai Med. Ctr., LA, 1995-96; psychiatrist UCLA Neuropsychiatric Inst. and Hosp., 1996-98, child psychiatrist, 1998-2000; pvt. practice child and adult psychiatry, 2000—. Bd. dirs. United Svc. Orgn., Hollywood, Calif., 1975-80, Am. Youth Soccer Orgn., Newport Beach, Calif., 1980-84, Waring Libr. Soc., Charleston, 1992-95; scoutmaster Boy Scouts of Am., San Marino, Calif., 1984-89; vol. Children's Hosp., Seattle, 1990-91. Nat. Merit and Nat. Honor Soc. scholar, Mich. State U., 1964-67. Mem. Am. Psychiat. Assn., Am. Acad. Child and Adolescent Psychiatry, Young Pres.'s Orgn., Blue Key, Phi Kappa Phi, Phi Eta Sigma, Delta Phi Epsilon, Omicron Delta Kappa. Avocations: travel, sailing. Office Phone: 818-784-4706.

BERGLUND, TORSTEN LARS, epidemiologist; b. Nacka, Stockholm County, Sweden, Feb. 24, 1965; s. Lars E.G. Berglund and Ingalill K. Runnby. BSc, Stockholm U., 1992; PhD in Epidemiology, Karolinska Inst., Stockholm, 2006. Counsellor HIV & STI Clinic Venhälsan, Södersjukhuset, Stockholm, 1992—2000; epidemiologist Swedish Inst. Communicable Disease Control., Solna, Sweden, 1997—2006, sr. program officer, 2011—; sr. advisor Nat. Bd. Health and Welfare, Stockholm, 2006—11. Mem. steering com. European Surveillance STIs, 2002—06; expert and rsch. officer Govtl. Com. Inquiry HIV/Aids, Ministry Health and Social Affairs, Sweden, 2003—04. Contbr. articles to profl. jours. Mem. editl. bd. Swedish Family Register (Svenska Släktkalendern), Sweden, 2002—. Recipient Sci. Poster, EpiDay 1st prize, Karolinska Inst., 2002. Avocation: genealogy. Office: Swedish Inst for Communicable Disease Control Solna 17182 Sweden

BERGMAN, DONALD ARTHUR, endocrinologist, educator; b. Bklyn., Apr. 6, 1946; s. Joseph and Clara Bergman; m. Susan Menin, June 23, 1970; 1 child, Melissa. AB, Dartmouth Coll., 1967; MD, Jefferson Med. Coll., 1971. Diplomate Am. Bd. Internal Medicine, Am. Bd. Internal Medicine. Ob-gyn. resident Mt. Sinai Hosp., NYC, 1971—72; med. intern NYU Hosps., NYC, 1972—73; med. resident Mt. Sinai Hosp., NYC, 1973—75, endocrinology fellow, 1975—77; pvt. practice NYC, 1977—; asst. clin. prof. medicine Mt. Sinai Sch. Medicine, NYC, 1984—97, assoc. clin. prof., 1997—2004, clin. prof., 2004—. Co-author: Mount Sinai Book of Nutrition, Clinical Practice Guidelines for Physicians-Thyroid Cancer, 2000; co-editor: Guide to Physical Activity, 2006; contbr. articles to profl. jours.; assoc. editor: Endocrine Practice, 1996—99; contbg. editor: The Complete Guide to Lifelong Nutrition, 2011. Bd. dirs. N.Y. Menopause Ctr., 1997—99. Capt. USAR, 1971—77. Master: Am. Coll. Endocrinology (sec.-treas. 2000—01, trustee 2000—01, chancellor 2004—05, pres. 2006—07, immediate past pres. 2007—08); fellow: ACP; mem.: Endocrine Soc., Am. Assn. Clin. Endocrinologists (bd. dirs. 1993—, chair practice stds. com. 1995—97, state chpts. chair 1997—2002, sec. 1999—2000, treas. 2000—01, v.p. 2001—02, co-chmn. corp. adv. bd. 2002—03, pres.-elect 2002—03, co-chmn. ann. meeting 2003, pres. 2003—04, chair power prevention com. 2004—). Office: 1199 Park Ave Apt (1f) New York NY 10128-1713

BERGMAN, IRA, child neurologist; Grad., U. Chgo. Resident Mass. Gen. Hosp.; hosp. affiliation includes Magee-Womens Hos. of UPMC; interim chief child devel. unit. Children's Hosp. of Pitts. of UPMC, chief child neurology divsn. Co-author: (publs.) Treatment of meningeal breast cancer xenografts in the rat with an anti-p185/Her2 antibody, 2001, Preferential targeting of Vesicular Stomatitis Virus to breast cancer cells, 2004, Treatment of implanted mammary tumors with recombinant vesicular stomatitis virus targeted to Her2/neu, 2007, Recombinant vesicular stomatitis virus targeted to Her2/neu combines with anti-CTLA4 antibody eliminates implanted mammary tumors, 2009, and numerous others. Named one of the Top Doctors, Pitts. Mag., 2011. Office: Children's Hospital of Pittsburgh of UPMC Child Neurology Division 2nd Fl 4401 Penn Ave Pittsburgh PA 15224 Office Phone: 412-692-5520. Office Fax: 412-692-6787.

BERGMAN, MICHAEL I., pulmonologist, educator; Attended, Albert Einstein Coll. Medicine, 1978. Diplomate Am. Bd. Internal Medicine, Am. Bd. Internal Medicine-pulmonary disease, Am. Bd. Internal Medicine-critical care medicine. Resident in internal medicine Brookdale Hosp., Brooklyn, NY, 1979—81; fellow in pulmonary disease Mt. Sinai Hosp., NY, 1982—84; asst. prof. medicine SUNY Health Sci. Ctr.; pulmonologist univ. hosp. brooklyn LI Coll. Hosp. Named one of the Top Doctors - NY Metro Area, Castle Connolly, 2009. Office: SUNY Downstate Medical Center Long Island College Hospital 339 Hicks St Brooklyn NY 11201 Office Phone: 718-780-1416. Office Fax: 718-780-1256.

BERGMAN, RICHARD ISAAC, health information executive; b. Bklyn., Jan. 18, 1934; s. Joseph and Clara (Menchel) Bergman; m. Judith Hyman, June 24, 1956 (div. 1974); children: Deborah Jill, Susan Bergman Hackett; m. Victoria Smalley, June 9, 1987. SB, MIT,

Cambridge, 1955, SM, 1956. Devel. engr. Exxon Rsch., Linden, NJ, 1956-60; mem. adj. faculty NJ Inst. Tech., Newark, 1957-58; dir. engring. Princeton Chem. Rsch., NJ, 1960-67; exec. v.p. Systemedics, Inc., Princeton, 1967-80; pres. Savant Assocs., Inc., Princeton, 1980-98; exec. dir. White House Task Force on Workplace Safety and Health, Washington, 1977-78; pres. Project Masters, Inc., Princeton, 1980—. Mem. vis. com. med. dept. MIT, Cambridge, 1973—83, 1986—88, Whitaker Coll., 1979—85; dir. Response Analysis Corp., Princeton, 1970—77; pres. MIT Club of Princeton, 1988—90, CWW, Inc., Princeton, 1998—2007, dir., 1998—. Contbr. articles to profl. jours. Mem.: AIChE (past chmn. NJ sect.), NY Acad. Scis., Am. Chem. Soc., MIT Alumni/ae Assn. (bd. dirs. 2000—03, class sec. 2010—). Achievements include patents in field. Home: 134 Leabrook Ln Princeton NJ 08540-3622 Office: Project Masters Inc PO Box AG Princeton NJ 08542-0872 Office Phone: 609-921-0749. Personal E-mail: richard.bergman@verizon.net.

BERGMAN, STANLEY M., health products executive; CPA NY. Exec. v.p. Henry Schein, Inc., Melville, NY, 1985-89, bd. dir., 1982—, v.p. fin. and adminstrn., 1980-85, chmn., CEO, pres., 1989—2005, chmn., CEO, 2005—. Mem.: Forsyth Inst., Am. Inst. CPAs, Am. Dental Assn. (hon.). Office: Henry Schein Inc 135 Duryea Rd Melville NY 11747 *

BERGMANN, LEIGH SCOTT, urologist; BA, Brandeis U., 1978—82; MD, U. Pa., 1982—86. Diplomate Am. Bd. Urology, 1999, lic. Pa., 1981, Fla., Conn., NY. Intern New Britain Gen. Hosp., 1986—90, resident; transplant fellow Univ. Conn., Farmington, 1991—93; resident urology Univ. Conn. Health Ctr., Farmington, 1993—97; transplant fellow Hartford Hosp., Conn., 1991—93; with Thomas Jefferson Univ.; on staff Bryn Mawr Hosp., 1997—, surg. rep. grad. med. edn. com., cancer com., chief Clin. Decision Support Physician Coun., dir.; on staff Lankenau Med. Ctr., 1998—, Paoli Hosp., 1998—; urologist Bryn Mawr Urology Group. Physician adv. com. Main Line Health Info. Sys. Co-author: Expanded Uses of Teflon Sheaths in Interventional Uroradiology, 1986, Grover Cleveland's Secret Surgery, 1987, Cystadenomas of the Pancreas, 1988, Malignancy Arising in Colorectal Endometriosis, 1991, The Need for Biopsies in Gastrointestinal Cytomegalovirus Infection in Organ Transplant Recipients, 1991; author and co-author various publs. Recipient Rishon M. Bialer Meml. award, Brandeis Univ., 1982, Class of 1955 Endowment Fund award, 1982, Howard Levine MD Sci. award for Clin. Rsch. in Kidney Transplantation, Univ. Conn. Affiliated Hosps., 1992. Fellow: ACS; mem.: AMA, Pa. Med. Soc., Montgomery County Med. Soc., Am. Urol. Assn. (Mid-Atlantic sect. mem.). Office: Bryn Mawr Urology Group Bldg 1 Ste 300 919 Conestoga Rd Bryn Mawr PA 19010 Office Phone: 610-525-6580. Office Fax: 610-525-3664.

BERGMARK, TORD, psychiatrist, psychotherapist; b. Skellefteå, Sweden, Dec. 9, 1941; s. Kjell and Gunnel (Flodmark) Bergmark; m. Christina Anderson, Aug. 14, 1982 (div.); children: Agnes, Gustav, Anders, Emma. MD, Karolinska Inst., Stockholm, 1977. Sr. clinician, dept. psychiatry Söder Hosp., Stockholm, 1991-92; gen. practitioner Stockholm, 1992-93; head Cognitive Psychiatry Stockholm, 1993—. Bd. dirs. support group for people with schizophrenia, Stockholm, 1992-95; creator Care Burden Scale for Relatives, 1988, Self-Confidence Scale, 1995; supr. Pain Clinic Sankt Göran's Hosp., 2007-08. Contbr. articles to profl. jours., co-editor Empathy, 1992-94; creator introduction to TV program Living with Schizophrenia, 1992. Mem. Am. Psychiat. Assn. (Internat.), Swedish Assn. Psychiatrists, Internat. Assn. Cognitive Therapy, Internat. Assn. for Study of Personality Disorders. Avocation: kayaking. Office: Cognitive Psychiatry Stockholm St Eriksgatan 43 112 34 Stockholm Sweden Office Phone: 46-8-6439520.

BERGSMA, JURRIT, medical psychologist; b. Oldeberkoop, The Netherlands, Sept. 3, 1934; s. Meindert Jelles Bergsma and Jeke Schaap; m. Gea Harmina Sypkes, Jan. 16, 1960; children: Meindert G., Maricke E.S. PhD in Psychology, State U. Groningen, The Netherlands, 1963, State U. Leiden, 1965. Lic. psychologist, psychotherapist. Pvt. practice, 1960—98; clin. psychologist Psychiat. Hosp., Zeist, 1961—66; lectr. in psychology De Horst Acad., Driebergen, 1966—70; med. psychologist Gen. Hosp., Alkmaar, 1969—74; lectr. in health psychology Tilburg U., 1973—80; prof. chmn. med. psychology State Univ., Utrecht, 1980—89; prof. Loyola U. Chgo. Guest vis. prof. med. psychology Med. Sch., Loyola U., Chgo., 1990—98; chmn. hosp. bd. Utrecht Hosp., 1988—96. Author: a.o Psychosocial Dimensions of Health Care, 1980, Doctors and Patients, 1997, Choice, 2008; editor: (book series) International Library of Ethics, Law, Medicine, 1990—2003. Capt. Dutch Army, 1959—62. Grantee, Yale Med. Sch.; Fulbright grantee, 1978. Mem.: Dutch Psychother. Assn. (bd. dirs.). Avocations: sculpting, painting, writing, travel, photography.

BERGSTRESSER, PAUL RICHARD, dermatologist, educator; b. Ottawa, Kans., Aug. 24, 1941; s. Karl Samuel and May (Holmes) B.; m. Rebecca Louise Baird, Jan. 4, 1969; children: Daniel Baird, Laura Suzanne. AB, Coll. of Wooster, 1963; MD, Stanford U., 1968. Diplomate Am. Bd. Dermatology (bd. dirs. 1996-2005, v.p. 2003-05). Asst. prof. dept. dermatology U. Miami, 1975-76; asst. prof. to prof. Southwestern Med. Ctr. U. Tex., Dallas, 1976—, chmn. dept., 1984—2007. Mem. dermatologic drugs adv. com., FDA, 1986-88; mem. gen. medicine study sect. GM1A, NIH, 1989-93; mem. adv. coun. Nat. Inst. Arthritis and Musculoskeletal and Skin Disease, 1999-2003. Editor Photodermatology, Photoimmunology and Photomedicine, 1990-99; editor Jour. Investigative Dermatology, 2007-; contbr. numerous articles to profl. jours. Odland lectr., Dept. Medicine Dermatology, U. Wash., 2011. Maj. U.S. Army, 1970-72. Recipient John Lathrop award, Coll. Wooster, 1963, Hopkins award, Stanford U. Sch. Medicine, 1968, Dermatitis Rsch. award, Am. Skin Assn., 1994, Marion B. Sulzberger Meml. award, 2000, Dohi Lecture award, Japanese Dermatological Soc., 2008, Fogarty Sr. Internat. fellowship, Dept. Dermatology, U. Vienna, 1993—94. Fellow AAP, AAAS, ACP, Am. Acad. Dermatology; mem. Am. Assn. Immunologists, Assn. Am. Physicians, Soc. Investigative Dermatology (bd. dirs. 1987-92, sec.-treas. 1999-2004), Am. Assn. Tissue Banks, Am. Dermatol. Assn., Assn. Profs. Dermatology (bd. dirs. 1990-95, pres.-elect 1998-2000, pres. 2000-02), Polish Dermatological Assn. (hon.), Finnish Dermatol. Assn. (hon.), Austrian Dermatol. Assn. (hon.), Norwegian Dermatol. Assn. (hon.), Japanese Dermatol. Soc. (hon.), Chinese Dermatology Soc. (internat. fellow mem. 2008), Philippine Dermatol. Soc. (hon.). Democrat. Methodist. Avocations: choral music, running. Home: 3758 Pallos Verdas Dr Dallas TX 75229-2740 Office: U Tex Southwestern Med Ctr Dept Dermatology 5323 Harry Hines Blvd Dallas TX 75390-9069 Business E-Mail: paul.bergstresser@utsouthwestern.edu.

BERK, PAUL DAVID, internist, research scientist, educator; b. Bklyn., Apr. 3, 1938; s. Charles and Helen (Goell) B.; m. Aviva Ancona, July 4, 1965 (div. Aug. 1990); children: Claire, Philip, Edward; m. Nicole Polak, 1991; 1 child, David. BA, Swarthmore Coll., 1959; cert., U. St. Andrews, Scotland, 1960; MD, Columbia U., 1964. Diplomate Am. Bd. Internal Medicine, Am. Bd. Hematology. Intern Columbia-Presbyn. Med. Ctr., NYC, 1964-65, resident, 1965-66, fellow in hematology, 1969-70; clin. assoc. metabolism br. Nat. Cancer Inst., Bethesda, Md., 1966-69, sr. investigator, 1970-73; clin. asst. prof. medicine Georgetown U., Washington, 1971-75, clin. assoc. prof., 1975-77; chief sect. on diseases of the liver Nat. Inst. Arthritis, Metabolism and Digestive Diseases, NIH, Bethesda, 1973-77; prof. medicine Mt. Sinai Sch. Medicine, NYC, 1977—2004, Albert and Vera List prof. medicine, 1980-89, prof. biochemistry, 1987-99, Henry and Lillian Stratton prof. molecular medicine, 1989—2004, chief divsn. hematology, 1977-89, acting chief, 1989-90, chief divsn. liver disease, 1989-01; prof. dept. medicine Columbia U. Coll. Physicians and Surgeons, NYC, 2004—. Prof. biochemistry and molecular biology Mt. Sinai Sch. Medicine, 1999-2004; adj. prof. Rockefeller U., 1987-89; cons. in liver disease NIH, 1977-80, mem. adv. coun. Nat. Inst. Diabetes and Digestive and Kidney Diseases, 1990-94. Editor: (with others) Chemistry and Physiology of the Bile Pigments, 1977, Frontiers in Liver Disease, 1981, Myelofibrosis and the Biology of Connective Tissue, 1984, Hans Popper: A Tribute, 1992, Hepatic Transport and Bile Secretion, 1993, Polcythemia Vera, 1994; editor-in-chief Seminars in Liver Disease, 1981-90, 96—, Hepatology, 1991-96; mem. editorial bd. Artificial Organs, 1979-92, Liver, 1980-93; contbr. articles to profl. jours. Served as sr. surgeon USPHS, 1966-69, 75-77. Recipient Honorable Mention, Westinghouse Sci. Talent Search, 1955; Ivy Medal, Swarthmore Coll., 1959; Mosby Award, 1963, Merck Award, 1964, Spl. award, 1992, Columbia U. Coll. Physician & Surgeons; Distin. Svc. award, Am. Assn. Study Liver Disease, 2003; George Jamieson Humanitarian Award, Am. Liver Foun., 2004. Fellow ACP, Am. Coll. Gastroenterology; mem. Am. Liver Found. (chmn. bd. dirs. 2000-04), Am. Physiology Soc., Soc. Clin. Investigation, Assn. Am. Physicians, Am. Assn. Study of Liver Disease (councillor 1985-93, v.p. 1988, pres. 1989), Internat. Assn. Study of Liver (councillor 1988-91), Am. Soc. for Hematology, Am. Clin. and Climatological Assn., Nat. Polycythemia Vera Study Group (vice chmn. 1978-95), Soc. Exptl. Biol. Medicine (councillor 1993-96), N.Y. Soc. Study of Blood (pres. 1982-83), Sigma Xi, Phi Beta Kappa, Alpha Omega Alpha. Office: Columbia University Med Ctr William Black Med Rsch Bldg Rm 1002 650 West 168th St New York NY 10032 Home Phone: 212-860-3728; Office Phone: 212-305-4491. Business E-Mail: pb2158@columbia.edu. *

BERK, STEVEN LEE, dean, internist, educator; b. NYC, Mar. 12, 1949; s. Sidney and Frelda (Blank) B.; m. Shirley Anne Holtzclaw, Oct. 10, 1981; children: Jeremy Charles, Justin Lee. BS, Brandeis U., 1971; MD, Boston U., 1975. Diplomate Am. Bd. Internal Medicine, Am. Bd. Infectious Disease, Am. Bd. Geriatrics. Intern Boston City Hosp., 1975-76, resident, 1976-78; chief of infectious disease VA Med. Ctr., Johnson City, Tenn., 1979-83, chief of medicine, 1982-88; chief of infectious disease East Tenn. State U., Johnson City, 1982-88, dir. clin. clerkships in medicine, 1981—99, prof. medicine, 1986—99, chmn. dept. internal medicine, 1988—99, dir. internal medicine residency program, 1988—99; regional dean, prof. medicine Tex. Tech U. Health Sci. Ctr. Sch. Medicine, Lubbock, 1999—2006, Mirick-Myers endowed chmn. in geriatric medicine, 2001—06, dean, 2006—, v.p. med. affairs, 2006—10, exec. v.p., provost, 2010—. Author: Infections in the Nursing Home, 1990, Manual of Clinical Infectious Diseases, 1994; contbr. articles to profl. jours. Recipient Tchr. of Yr. award students East Tenn. State U. Coll. Medicine, 1982-93. Fellow ACP, Am. Coll. Chest Physicians, Am. Geriatric Soc., Infectious Disease Soc. Am.; mem. Alpha Omega Alpha, Am. Osler Soc., Phi Beta Kappa. Avocations: medical history, tennis. Office: Tex Tech University Sch Medicine Office of Dean 3601 4th St Stop 6207 Lubbock TX 79430-6207 Office Phone: 806-743-3000. Business E-Mail: steven.berk@ttuhsc.edu. *

BERKELHAMER, JAY ELLIS, pediatrician; b. Tuscaloosa, Ala., Apr. 8, 1942; s. Louis H. and Belle F. B.; m. Jacqueline Beth Colman, June 12, 1966; children: Beth Carolyn, Sara Kay, Adam Colman. BS, U. Mich., 1963, MD, 1967. Resident U. Chgo., 1967-70, asst. prof., 1972-78, assoc. prof., 1978-84, prof., 1984-93, assoc. chair, dir. residency program, 1986-93, assoc. dean ambulatory care, 1983-88; chair pediatrics Henry Ford Health Sys., Detroit, 1993-99. Prof. pediatrics Case Western Res. U., Cleve., 1994-99; clin. prof. pediatrics and communicable diseases U. Mich., Ann Arbor, 1994-2006; sr. v.p. for med. affairs Children's Healthcare of Atlanta, 1999—2007; clin. prof. pediats. Emory U., Atlanta, 1999—; sr. v.p. academic affairs Children's Healthcare Atlanta, 2007-10, sr. physician advisor, 2010-; adj. clin. prof. Morehouse Sch. Medicine. Lt. comdr. USPHS, 1970-72. Robert Wood Johnson Health Policy fellow NAS, Washington, 1978-79. Mem. Am. Acad. Pediatrics (pres. Ill. chpt. 1992, pres. 2006-07), Chgo. Pediatric Soc. (pres. 1987, Archibald L. Hoyne award 1993), Ambulatory Pediatric Assn. (pres. 1986). Office Phone: 404-785-7005. Personal E-mail: javeb@att.net.

BERKLEY, SETH FRANKLIN, epidemiologist, international health specialist; b. NYC, Oct. 18, 1956; s. William and Ruth (Kutik) Berkley. BSc, Brown U., Providence, 1978, MD, 1981. Diplomate Am. Bd. Internal Medicine, Nat. Bd. Med. Examiners, lic. physician Mass., Ga., NY. Intern, resident in primary care internal medicine Harvard U./Beth Israel Hosp., Boston, 1981-84; preventive medicine resident USPHS/CDC, Atlanta, 1985-87; med. epidemiologist Mass. Dept. Pub. Health, Jamaica Plains, 1986-87, Task Force for Child Survival, Carter Presdl. Ctr., Entebbe, Uganda, 1987-89; assoc. dir. health scis. divsn. The Rockefeller Found., NYC, 1989—96; adj. asst. prof. pub. health Columbia U., NYC, 1990-93, adj. assoc. prof. pub. health, 1993—; clin. asst. prof. medicine NYU, 1993—; pres., CEO Internat. AIDS Vaccine Initiative, 1996—. Vis. physician U. Sri Lanka, Colombo, 1984; cons. US Dept. State Bur. Refugee Programs, Western Sudan, 1985; sec. of health, Sao Paulo, Brazil, 86; fellow The Salsburg Seminars, 1988; content expert Internat. Clin. Epidemiology Network. Co-author: (books) Investing in Health: The 1993 World Development Report, 1993, Infectious Diseases, 1999; contbr. numerous articles to profl. jours., chapters to books. Lt. comdr. USPHS, 1984—87, res., 1987—. Recipient Surgeon Gen.'s Cert. of Appreciation, USPHS, 1989; named one of The World's Most Influential People, TIME mag., 2009. Fellow: ACP, Mass. Med. Soc., Infectious Diseases Soc. America, Coun. Fgn. Rels.; mem.: Network AIDS Researchers of Ea. & So. Africa (founding mem.). Avocations: squash, flying, travel, scuba diving, skiing. Office: Internat AIDS Vaccine Initiative 110 William St Fl 27 New York NY 10038-3901 E-mail: sberkley@iavi.org.

BERKMAN, CLAIRE FLEET, psychologist; b. New Orleans, Dec. 5, 1942; d. Joel and Margaret Grace (Fishler) Fleet; m. Arnold Stephen Berkman, Apr. 27, 1975; children: Janna Samantha, Micah Seth Siegel. BA, Boston U., 1964; EdM, Harvard U., 1966; EdD, Boston U., 1970. Asst. prof. Counseling Ctr. Mich. State U., East Lansing, 1971-75, assoc. prof., 1975-78, assoc. prof. dept. psychiatry, 1975-82, clin. assoc. prof., 1986-87; pvt. clin. practice, 1975—. Cons. Cath. Family Social Service, Lansing, 1979-83; mem. adv. bd. Cir. Ct. Family Counseling Program, 1982-88. V.p. Kehillat Israel Synagogue, 1975-76, pres., 1992-94; bd. dirs. Jewish Welfare Fedn., Lansing, 1974-75, 84-87; mem. children's task force State Bar Mich., 1993-95. NDEA fellow, 1968-70. Mem. APA, Mich. Psychol. Assn., Mich. Soc. Forensic Psychologists, Nat. Soc. Arts and Letters (pres. Mid-Mich. chpt. 2000-02). Office: 4084 Okemos Rd Okemos MI 48864-3258

BERKO, BARBARA ANN, cardiologist; b. Charlottesville, Va., Sept. 10, 1952; BA, Brandeis U., 1973; MD, Tufts, 1977. Asst. prof. medicine Thomas Jefferson U., 2001—, cardiologist, 2001—11. Named Best Doctors in Am. Fellow: Am. Soc. Echocardiography, Am. Coll. Cardiology; mem.: Am. Heart Assn. Office: 925 Chestnut St Jefferson Heart Inst Philadelphia PA 19107 Office Phone: 215-955-5050. E-mail: barbara.berko@jefferson.edu.

BERKOFF, CHARLES EDWARD, pharmaceutical and biotech consultant; b. London, Sept. 29, 1932; arrived in US, 1963, naturalized, 1975; s. Maurice and Dora (Landy) B.; children: Timothy, David, Kevin; m. Heide-Gisela Triesch, 1997. BS in Chemistry (1st class honors), U. London, 1956; DIC, PhD, Imperial Coll., U. London, 1959. Chartered chemist. Dir. GlaxoSmithKline, Phila., 1964-83; exec. v.p. ImuTech, Inc., Huntingdon Valley, Pa., 1983-84; pres., CEO Antigenics, Inc., Horsham, Pa., 1984-89, Creative Licensing Internat., Inc., Sarasota, Fla., 1987—, CEBRAL, Inc., 1987—. Research fellow Johns Hopkins U., Balt., 1959-60; sr. research fellow Southampton U., Eng., 1960-61; mem. Adv. Council Smithsonian Sci. Info. Exchange, Washington, 1976-82. Contbr. articles to profl. jours.; patentee numerous U.S. and fgn. patents. Monsanto Research fellow Imperial Coll. Sci. and Tech., 1956-59; Fulbright scholar, 1959-60; recipient Statue of Victory World Culture prize Centro Studi e Ricerche Delle Nazioni, 1985. Fellow Am. Chem. Soc., Royal Soc. Chemistry; mem. Am. Arbitration Assn., Entomol. Soc., Am. Inst. Chem. Engrs., Licensing Execs. Soc. Clubs: Engrs. Club of Phila. Republican. Unitarian Universalist. Avocations: writing, tennis, guitar, bridge, swimming. E-mail: cebral@verizon.net.

BERKOVSKAYA, MARINA ARONOVNA, endocrinologist; b. Moscow Region, Nov. 16, 1981; MD, Sechenov Moscow Med. Acad., 2005; PhD, Endocrine Rsch. Ctr., 2011. Endocrinologist Endocrine Rsch. Ctr., 2005—, Med. Ctr., 2011—. Avocations: reading, music, sports. Home: Novogireevskaya Moscow 111397 Russia Personal E-mail: abaita@rambler.ru.

BERKOW, SUSAN, nutritionist, educator; b. Blkyn., Sept. 19, 1949; BS, U. Md., 1971, PhD, 1982. Pres. SEB Assocs., 1990—. Postgrad rsch. fellow Georgetown U. Med. Sch., Dept. Pediat., 1982—84; program officer Food and Nutrition Bd., Nat. Acad. Scis., 1984—90; v.p. sci. and regulatory affairs Am. Frozen Food Inst., 1990—91; dir., sci. and regulatory affairs Nat. Food Processors Assoc., 1991—95; adj. prof. George Mason U., 2005—. Recipient Faculty Devel. award, U. Mary Wash. Mem.: Wash. Soc. Study Eating Disorders and Obesity, Am. Soc. Nutrition, Am. Dietetic Assn., Inst. Food Technologist. Avocations: cooking, bicycling, tennis, reading. Office: 1211 Tatum Dr Alexandria VA 22307 Business E-Mail: susan@susanberkow.com.

BERKSON, RICHARD ALAN, endocrinologist, educator; married; 4 children. MD, SUNY, 1972. Diplomate Am. Bd. Internal Medicine, 1975, Am. Bd. Internal Medicine-endocrinology, diabetes and metabolism, 1977. Resident internal medicine SUNY, Buffalo, 1973—75; fellow endocrinology, diabetes and metabolism Joslin Clinic, Boston, 1975—76, Univ. Calif. Med. Ctr., LA, 1976—77; asst. clin. prof. medicine Univ. Calif., LA; hosp. affiliations include St. Mary Med. Ctr., Long Beach Meml. Med. Ctr. Avocation: walking. Office: Long Beach Memorial Medical Center 1868 Pacific Ave Long Beach CA 90806 Office Phone: 562-595-4718.

BERLAN, ELISE DEVORE, pediatrician, educator; MD, U. Iowa, 2000. Diplomate Am. Bd. Pediatrics, 2003, Am. Bd. Pediatrics-adolescent medicine, 2008. Resident pediat. Children's Hosp., Phila., 2001—04, fellow adolescent medicine Boston, 2004—07; with faculty Ohio State Univ., 2007; asst. prof. clin. pediat. Ohio State Univ. Coll. of Medicine; mem. sect. of adolescent health Nationwide Children's Hosp. Author: (publ.) Adolescent Health, Medicine and Therapeutics, 2009, Expert Review of Obstetrics and Gynecology, 2009, The Pediatric Resident's Perspective, 2010, (jour.) Sexual orientation and bullying among adolescents in the Growing Up Today Study, 2010, various publs. including Screening Tool for Type II Diabetes Mellitus, Obesity Quality Improvement in Adolescent Clinic and Jour. of Adolescent Health; co-author: (publ.) Update on Sexually Transmitted Infections in Adolescents, 2010. Mem.: Soc. for Adolescent Medicine, Am. Acad. of Pediat. Office: Nationwide Children's Hospital 700 Children's Dr Columbus OH 43205 Office Phone: 614-722-2458. Office Fax: 614-355-3583.

BERLIN, CHESTON MILTON, JR., pediatrician, educator; b. Pitts., Mar. 28, 1936; s. Cheston Milton and Gladys Irene (Vance) B.; m. Anne Risher, July 9, 1960; children: Jean Vance, Douglas Cheston, Alexander Lindsay, Gordon Johnston. BA, Haverford Coll., Pa., 1958; MD, Harvard U., 1962. Intern Boston Children's Hosp., 1962-63, resident in pediatrics, 1965-67; asst. prof. pediatrics U. Ala. Sch. Medicine, Birmingham, 1967-68, George Washington U. Sch. Medicine, Washington, 1968-71; assoc. prof. pediatrics Pa. State U. Coll. Medicine, Hershey, 1971-75, prof. pediatrics and pharmacology, 1975-86, univ. prof. pediatrics, prof. pharmacology, 1986—. Pediat. panel U.S. Pharmacopeia, Rockville, Md., 1970—75, Rockville, 1980—2000. Contbr. articles to profl. jours. Sr. asst. surgeon USPHS, 1963-65. Markle Found. scholar, 1969, 74; recipient Cheston M. Berlin Alumni Svc. award Pa. State U. Coll. Medicine, 1987. Mem. Am. Acad. Pediatrics, Am. Soc. Exptl. Pharmacology and Therapeutics, Am. Soc. Clin. Pharmacology and Therapeutics, Am. Pediatric Soc., Am. Soc. Nutrition Sci., Phi Beta Kappa, Alpha Omega Alpha, Alpha Epsilon Delta. Office: MS Hershey Med Ctr Dept Pediatrics PO Box 850 Hershey PA 17033-0850 Office Phone: 717-531-8006. Business E-Mail: cmb6@psu.edu.

BERLIN, HEATHER AYN, neuroscientist, philosopher, educator; b. East Meadow, NY, June 20, 1975; d. Leonard Arthur Berlin and Beth Judy Scneider; m. Michiel Visser, Aug. 28, 2006. BS, SUNY, Stony Brook, 1997; MA, New Sch. for Social Rsch., NYC, 2000; PhD, U. Oxford, Eng., 2003; MPH, Harvard Sch. of Pub. Health, Boston, Mass., 2004. Intern Bellevue Hosp., NYC, 1996—96; rsch. coord. Cornell U. Med. Ctr./N.Y. Presbyn. Hosp., NYC, 1997—97; rsch. asst. Applied Behavioral Medicine Rsch. Inst., SUNY, Stony Brook, 1998—98, project dir. dept. psychiatry and behavioral sci., 1998—99; clin. rsch. NYU Med. Ctr., NYC, 1999—2000, Inst. of Psychiatry/Bethlem Royal Hosp.; Radcliffe Infirmary/John Radcliffe Hosp.; Rivermead Rehab. Centre, London/Oxford, 2001—03; psychiat. mgmt. practicum Harvard U. Health Svcs., Cambridge, Mass., 2004—04; nimh post-doctoral fellow Mt. Sinai Sch. of Medicine, NYC, 2004—, asst. prof. psychiatry, 2008—. Vis. asst. prof. Vassar Coll., 2005—06; vis. lectr. Hebrew U., 2007, Swiss Fed. Inst. Tech. U. Zurich, 2007; lectr. in field. Contbr. articles to profl. jours. Recipient Young Investigator award, Nat. Edn. Alliance Borderline Personality Disorde, 2005, Travel award, CDI, 2007; fellow, New Sch. for Social Rsch., 2000, NY Acad. Scis., 2007, Health Emotions Rsch. Inst., 2008; scholar, New Sch. for Social Rsch., 1998—2000, Brit. Coun., 2000-2003; Oppenheim scholarship, Magdalen Coll., Oxford, Eng., 2002-2003. Fellow: NY Acad. Scis.; mem.: AAAS, APA, Soc. Neurosci., Assn. for the Sci. Study of Consciousness, Internat. Soc. for Rsch. on Impulsivity and Impulse Control Disorders, Nat. Acad. of Neuropsychology, Am. Psychopathological Assn., Am. Neuropsychiatric Assn. (Young Investigator award 2005), Brit. Neuropsychological Soc., Internat. Neuropsychological Soc., Psi Chi, Sigma Beta, Golden Key Honor Soc. Office: Mt Sinai Sch of Medicine Box 1230 One Gustave L Levy Pl New York NY 10029 Home: PO BOX 645 East Meadow NY 11554-0645

BERLIN, JORDAN D., gastrointestinal oncologist, healthcare educator; MD, U. Ill., 1989. Resident U. Wis. Hosp. & Clinics, U. Cincinnati Hosp.; assoc. prof. med. Vanderbilt U.; clinical dir. gastrointestinal oncology Vanderbilt-Ingram Cancer Ctr. Editorial bd. mem. Internat. Jour. GI Cancer; editor-in-chief Colorectal Cancer Index & Reviews. Office: 1903 The Vanderbilt Clinic Nashville TN 37232-5536 also: Vanderbilt-Ingram Cancer Center 777 Preston Bldg Nashville TN 37232-6307 Office Phone: 615-322-6053, 615-322-4967. Office Fax: 615-343-8668, 615-343-7602.

BERLINER, ALLEN IRWIN, dermatologist; b. NYC, Apr. 18, 1947; s. Joseph Benjamin and Ruth (Kaplan) B.; m. Edwina BA, Queens Coll., 1967; MD, SUNY, Buffalo, 1971. Diplomate: Am. Bd. Dermatology. Intern Nassau County Med. Ctr., East Meadow, NY, 1971-72; resident in dermatology Boston U. Med. Ctr., 1974-76, chief resident, 1976-77; practice medicine specializing in dermatology Norwood, Mass., 1977—; asst. clin. prof. Tufts U., 1980-90, assoc. clin. prof., 1990—; chief dermatology sect. Steward Norwood Hosp., 1986—; assoc. staff Tufts Med. Ctr. Bd. dirs. Mass. Acad. Dermatology. Served as surgeon USPHS, 1972-74. Mem. Am. Acad. Dermatology, New Eng. Dermatol. Soc., New Eng. Dermatology Soc. (coun. mem. 2006-08, v.p. 2008-09, pres. 2009-), Mass. Acad. Dermatology (pres. 1994-95). Office: 95 Chapel St Norwood MA 02062-3161 Home Phone: 508-359-6171; Office Phone: 781-762-5858.

BERLINER, NANCY, hematologist, medical professor; b. May 17, 1954; BA summa cum laude, Yale Coll., New Haven, 1975; MD cum laude, Yale U. Sch. Medicine, 1979. Diplomate Am. Bd. Internal Medicine, cert. in hematology. Intern medicine Brigham & Women's Hosp., Boston, 1979—80, resident, fellow hematology, 1980—85, chief med. resident, 1986, sr. attending physician, chief hematology, 2007—; asst. prof. internal medicine Yale U. Sch. Medicine, 1986—91, assoc. prof., then prof. medicine and genetics, 1991—2007; prof. medicine Harvard Med. Sch., Boston, 2007—. Contbr. articles to profl. jours. Recipient Jr. Faculty Rsch. award, American Cancer Soc.; Stohlman Scholar, Leukemia Soc. America, 1997. Fellow: AAAS; mem.: Assn. American Physicians, American Soc. Hematology (sec. 2001—04, pres. 2009), Inst. Medicine, American Soc. Clin. Investigation (v.p. 1995), Interurban Clin. Club. Office: Brigham & Womens Hosp Divsn Hematology 75 Francis St Boston MA 02115 E-mail: nberliner@partners.org. *

BERMAN, BRIAN WILLIAM, pediatrician, educator; b. Phila., Jan. 19, 1950; s. Milton and Estelle (Resnick) Berman; m. Nora Krasney; children: Elizabeth, Jared, Amanda. BS with high distinction, Pa. State U., 1971; MD, Temple U., 1975. Diplomate Am. Bd. Pediatrics, cert. Pediat. Hematology-Oncology. Intern pediat. St. Christopher's Hosp. for Children, Phila., 1978, resident pediat., 1976—78; fellowship pediat. hematology-oncology Yale U. Sch. Medicine, New Haven, 1978—80; dir. Rainbow Sickle Cell Anemia Ctr. Rainbow Babies and Children's Hosp., Cleve., 1989—, med. staff Dept. Pediat., 1980—, acting chief Genetics Ctr. Cleve., 1990—92, dir. Pediat. consultation and referral svc., 1993—, chief divsn. gen. acad. pediat., 1993—, vice chmn. cmty. physician affairs, 1998—, acting chief divsn. pediat. hematology/oncology, 2002—05, interim co-chair dept. pediat., 2008—10. Clin. instr. Case Western Reserve U. Sch. Medicine, 1980—89, clin. asst. prof., 1989—91, asst. prof., 1991—93, assoc. prof., 1993—2001, prof., 2001—. Contbr. articles to med. jours. Bd. dirs. Children's Rsch. Found. of Cleve., 1995—2007. Fellow: Am. Acad. Pediat.; mem.: Ambulatory Pediatric Assn., Am. Soc. Pediat. Hematology and Oncology, Am. Soc. Hematology. Office: Rainbow Babies & Childrens Hosp 11100 Euclid Ave Cleveland OH 44106-6019 Office Phone: 216-844-3752. Office Fax: 216-844-8444. E-mail: brian.berman@uhhospitals.org.

BERMAN, CAROL WENDY, psychiatrist; b. NYC, Sept. 14, 1951; d. Irving and Dora (Adler) B.; m. Martin Farber, Feb. 5, 1994. BA, U. Calif., Berkeley, 1972; MD, NYU, 1981. Diplomate Am. Bd. Psychiatry and Neurology. Intern, resident in psychiatry St. Lukes-Roosevelt Hosp., NYC, 1982-85; rsch. fellow in psychiatry NYU Med. Ctr., NYC, 1986-87, mem. attending staff, 1987—; pvt. practice, NYC, 1988—. Author: (book) 100 Questions and Answers About Panic Disorder, 2005, Personality Disorders, 2009, (plays) Under the Dragon, Sunshine Sally, Professional Misconduct, Brownstone Breakdown, Huffington Post Mental Health; contbr. numerous articles to med. jours.; patentee device to prevent drunk driving. Active legal problems of mentally ill, Bar Assn. City N.Y., 1993-95. Recipient writing prize Psychiat. Annals, 1987. Mem. Am. Psychiat. Assn.

BERMAN, CLIFF, lawyer, retail executive; BS in Pharmacy, U. Mich., Ann Arbor; JD, Loyola U., Chgo.; MBA, U. Chgo. Various positions including v.p. legal services Caremark, Inc.; sr. v.p., gen. counsel, chief privacy officer Allscripts; divsn. counsel legal regulatory and compliance Abbott Laboratories; sr. v.p., gen. counsel, corp. sec. SXC Health Solutions, Corp., 2008—. Mem. Ill. State Bd. Pharmacy, 1994—99. Mem.: Pharm. Care Mgmt. Assn. (past pres.). Office: SXC Health Solutions Corp 2441Warrenville Rd Ste 610 Lisle IL 60532-3642 *

BERMAN, DAVID A., ophthalmologist; Attended, SUNY, 1982. Diplomate Am. Bd. of Ophthalmology. With Bklyn. Hosp. Ctr., Long Island Coll. Hosp., Wyckoff Heights Med. Ctr. Office: SUNY Downstate Medical Center 450 Clarkson Ave Brooklyn NY 11203 Office Phone: 718-270-1000.

BERMAN, DAVID ALBERT, pharmacologist, educator; b. Rochester, NY, Nov. 4, 1917; s. Sam Moses and Anna (Newman) B.; m. Miriam Goodman, July 13, 1945; children: Shelley, Judith. BS, U. So. Calif., 1940, MS, 1948, PhD, 1951. Instr. U. So. Calif. Med. Sch., LA, 1952-54, asst. prof., 1954-58, assoc. prof., 1958-63, prof., 1963—93, Disting. emeritus prof., 1993. Contbr. articles to profl. jours. Mem. Calif. Rsch. Adv. Panel, San Francisco, 1970-82. Recipient Elaine Stevely Hoffman Achievement award, 1971, Merit award Am. Heart Assn., 1979, Faculty Achievement award Burlington No. Found., 1988, Tchg. award Kaiser Permanente, 1993, Kaiser Permanente Tchg. award, 1971, 75, 77, 79, 81, 83, 85, 87, 89, 90-93, 96-99, 03. Mem. Am. Soc. Pharmacology and Exptl. Therapeutics, Sigma XI, Phi Kappa Phi. Home: 3304 Scadlock Ln Sherman Oaks CA 91403-4912 Office: 2025 Zonal Ave Los Angeles CA 90089-0110 Office Phone: 323-442-1791. Business E-Mail: daberman@usc.edu.

BERMAN, HARRIS A., dean, medical educator; AB cum laude, Harvard Coll., Cambridge, Mass., 1960; MD, Columbia U., NYC, 1964. Resident Harvard Med. Svc. of Boston City Hosp., Tufts-New Eng. Med. Ctr., fellowship in infectious disease; exec. dir., co-founder Matthew Thornton Health Plan, Nashua, NH, 1971—86; CEO Tufts Health Plan, 1986—2003; clin. prof. medicine Tufts U. Sch. Medicine, 1986—2008, chmn. dept. pub. health and cmty. health, 2003—08, dean pub. health and profl. degree programs, 2004—08, vice dean academic and clin. affairs, 2008—09, prof. pub. health and cmty. medicine, 2008—, interim dean, 2009—. Physician Peace Corps; cons. US Agency Internat. Devel.; chmn. of bd. Mass. Assn. HMOs, Bank American Celebrity Series; bd. dirs. American Assn. Health Plans, Tufts Med. Ctr. Commr. Group Ins. Commn.; bd. dirs. AvMed Health Plan, Fla., Tufts Health Care Inst., New Eng. Healthcare Inst., The Wolfson Found., Hebrew Sr. Life. Fellow: American Coll. Physicians. Office: Tufts University Sch Medicine 136 Harrison Ave Boston MA 02111 Office Phone: 617-636-6555. Office Fax: 617-636-4017. Business E-Mail: harris.berman@tufts.edu. *

BERMAN, LAURA, sex and relationship therapist; BA in anthropology, U. Vt., 1990; MA in health edn., NYU Sch. Edn., 1992; MSW, NYU, 1994, PhD in Health Edn. specializing in human sexuality, 1997. Fellow in human sexual therapy NYU Med. Ctr., 1997; former co-dir. (with sister Jennifer) Women's Sexual Health Clinic, Boston U. Med. Ctr.; co-dir. (with sister Jennifer) Network Excellence Women's Sexual Health; clinical asst. prof. ob-gyn. and psychiatry Feinberg Sch. Medicine Northwestern U.; dir. Berman Ctr., Chgo., 2004—; co-host (with sister Jennifer) Berman & Berman: For Women Only, Discovery Health Channel, 2004. Co-author (with sister Jennifer): For Women Only: A Revolutionary Guide to Overcoming Sexual Dysfunction and Reclaiming Your Sex Life, 2001, Secrets of the Sexually Satisfied Woman: 10 Keys to Unlocking Ultimate Pleasure, 2005; actor: (TV series) Sexual Healing, 2006; author: The Passion Prescription, 2006, Talking to Your Kids About Sex, 2009, It's Not Him, It's You: How to Take Charge of Your Life and Create the Love and Intimacy You Deserve, 2010, Real Sex for Real: Intimacy, Pleasure, and Sexual Wellbeing, 2010, The Book of Love: Every Couple's Guide to Emotional and Sexuak Intimacy, 2010, Loving Sex: The Book of Joy and Passion, 2011; host DrLauraBerman.com, Dr. Laura Berman Show, Oprah Radio on XM 111 and SIRIUS 204, In the Bedroom with Dr. Laura Berman, OWN Network (Oprah Winfrey Network), contbr. to Oprah.com, New York Times and USA Today, regular guest Oprah Winfrey Show, The Dr. Oz Show, weekly columnist for Chicago Sum Times, guest appearances on Fox News and CNN, contbr. of articles to every women's magazine. Found. bd. mem. Soc. Sci. Study Sexuality (SSSS). Recipient Rising Star Yr., Nat. Assn. Women Bus. Owners, LA, 2002, Women Action award, Israel Cancer Rsch. Fund, 2002, Gracie award for Outstanding Talk Show, Alliance for Women in Media, 2011; named one of 40 Under 40, Crains' Chicago Business, 2005. Mem.: American Urologic Soc., Internat. Soc. for the Study of Women's Sexual Health, Am. Assn. Sex Educators, Counselors, and Therapists, Internat. Soc. Study Women's Sexual Health, Am. Assn. Social Workers. Office: Berman Ctr Inc 211 E Ontario Ste 800 Chicago IL 60611 Office Phone: 800-709-4709, 312-255-8088. Office Fax: 312-255-8007. *

BERMAN, MICHAEL ALLEN, hospital administrator, pediatric cardiologist; b. Bklyn., Sept. 11, 1942; MD, SUNY, Syracuse, 1967; postgrad in pediatrics, Johns Hopkins Sch. Medicine. Pediatrics resident Johns Hopkins U. Sch. Medicine, 1967—68; fellowship, pediatric cardiology Yale U., 1970—76; pediatric cardiologist Nat. Inst. of Health; chief, clinical pediatric cardiology, dir., cardiac catheterization lab. Yale U.; joined U. Maryland, 1976; dir., pediatric cardiology, dept. pediatrics U. Maryland Sch. Medicine, 1976—84, chmn., dept. pediatrics, 1984—97; sr. v.p., chief med. officer NY Presbyterian Hosp., 1997—99, exec. v.p., bd. dirs., 1999—. Achievements include development of Berman Angiographic Catheter device, used to diagnose cardiac problems in pediatric patients. Office: NewYork Presbyterian Hospital 622 W 168th St New York NY 10032 Office Phone: 212-305-2500. Business E-Mail: mberman@nyp.org.

BERMAN, MICHAEL LEONARD, gynecologic oncologist; BS in Phys. Scis., U. Md., 1963; MD, George Washington U., 1967. Diplomate Am. Bd. Obstetrics and Gynecology; lic. physician, Calif. Resident in ob-gyn. George Washington U., Washington, 1968-69, Harbor Gen. Hosp., Torrance, Calif., 1971-74; NICHD clin. assoc. UCLA Sch. Medicine, 1969-71, acting asst. prof. ob-gyn., 1974-75, asst. prof. ob-gyn., 1975-77; asst. prof. and dir. divsn. gynecologic oncology U. Pitts./Magee Women's Hosp., 1977-81; assoc. prof. U. Calif.-Irvine Coll., Orange, 1981-90; prof. divsn. gynecologic oncology U. Calif.-Irvine Coll. Medicine, Orange, 1990—; dir. divsn. gynecologic oncology U. Calif.-Irvine Med. Ctr., Orange, 1981—90; clin. assoc. prof. U. Nev., Las Vegas, 1983-99. Cons. med. staff Saddleback Meml. Hosp., Laguna Hills, Calif., 1988—, U. Nev., Las Vegas, 1985-99, City of Hope Nat. Med. Ctr., Duarte, Calif., 1983-94; fellow in gynecologic oncology City of Hope Nat. Med. Ctr., Duarte, and UCLA Med. Ctr., 1974-76; attending physician Long Beach Meml. Med. Ctr./Women's Hosp., 1981—; lectr. in field; mem. carrier adv. com. Medicare, State of Calif., 1993—; cons. Health Care Fin. Adminstrn., others. Co-editor: Med. Tribune News, 1994—99; mng. editor: SGO Issues, 1990—91; reviewer Am. Jour. Obstetrics and Gynecology, Cancer, Gynecologic Oncology, Obstetrics and Gynecology, reviewer PDQ External Adv. Bd NIH, Nat. Cancer Inst., 1994—96; co-author: Bibliography of Chemical Kinetics and Collision Processes, 1969; contbr. numerous articles and abstracts to profl. jours., chapters to books. Recipient Physician's Recognition award AMA, 1990-93; Am. Cancer Soc. 2d yr. faculty clin. fellow, 1977-78, 1st yr. faculty clin. fellow, 1976-77, 2d yr. fellow, 1975-76, 1st yr. fellow, 1974-75; rsch. grantee NIH, 1987-90, 89-94, U.S. Biosci., 1989-91, Cetus, 1989-92, Gynecologic Oncology Group, 1989-94, Nat. Cancer Inst., 1991—. Fellow: ACOG (health econs. com. 1992—, mem. com. on coding and nomenclature 1997—99, chair com. coding and nomenclature 1999—2001); mem.: AMA, ACS, Gynecologic Oncology Group, Long Beach Obstetrics and Gynecology Soc., Internat. Gynecologic Cancer Soc., Am. Soc. Clin. Oncology, Am. Radium Soc., Western Assn. Gynecologic Oncologists (sec.-treas. 1981—86, pres. 1987), Soc. Gynecologic Oncologists (chair com./govt. rels. com. 1991—94, chair govt. rels. com. 1994—97, chair coding com. 1997—2000, pres.-elect 1999—2001, pres. 2001—02, past pres. 2002—), Dan Morton Soc., Phi Delta Epsilon, Alpha Omega Alpha. Office: Univ of Calif-Irvine Med Ct Dept Ob-Gyn 101 The City Dr S Bldg 23 Orange CA 92868-3201 Office Phone: 714-456-7974. E-mail: mberman@uci.edu. *

BERMAN, ROBERT FARR, neuroscientist, educator; b. Salt Lake City, Feb. 16, 1948; PhD, U. Utah, 1977. Postdoc U. NC Chapel Hill, 1979; prof. dept. psychology Wayne State U., 1979—97; prof., vice chair rsch. dept. neurol. surgery U. Calif. Davis, 1997—, prof. Ctr. Neurosci., 1998—, prof. M.I.N.D. Inst., 2001—, mem. adv. com. Ctr. Children's Environ. Health, 2001—11, mem. steering com. Neurotherapeutic Rsch. Inst., 2007—. Chair Life Scis. Rev. Panel, NRC, 2000—05. Grant, NAS, NRC. Mem.: Nat. Neurotrauma Soc., Rsch. Soc. on Alcoholism, Am. Assn. Neurochemistry, Soc. Neurosci. Avocation: skiing. Office: University California Davis 1515 Newton Ct Davis CA 95616 Office Fax: 530-754-5125. Business E-Mail: rfberman@ucdavis.edu.

BERMAN, RUSSELL SCOTT, surgical oncologist, medical educator; m. Susan B. Berman. BS summa cum laude, Sophie Davis Sch. Biomed. Edn., NYC, 1988; MD, NYU Sch. Medicine, NYC, 1990. Diplomate Am. Bd. Surgery. Resident gen. surgery NYU, Bellevue Hosp., 1990—92, 1994—97; rsch. surg. oncology fellow Meml. Sloan-Kettering Cancer Ctr., 1992—94; fellow in surg. oncology, jr. faculty assoc. M.D. Anderson Cancer Ctr., Houston, 1997—2000; asst. prof. surgery NYU Sch. Medicine Faculty, 2000—. Editl. bd. mem. Nat. Cancer Inst. PDQ Adult Treatment, 2002—; editor Soft Tissue Surgery- UpToDate; program dir. surg. residency NYU Sch. Medicine, Langone Med. Ctr., Bellevue Hosp. Ctr. Mem. health commn. Village of East Hills, NY, 2001—. Fellow: ACS; mem.: NY Surg. Soc., Assn. Program Dirs. in Surgery, Assn. Surg. Edn., Am. Assn. Cancer Rsch., Assn. Academic Surgery, Americas Hepatopancreatobiliary Assn., Am. Soc. Clin. Oncology, Soc. Surg. Oncology (tng. com. chmn.). Office: NYU Sch Medicine 423 E 23rd St # 15 New York NY 10010-5011 Business E-Mail: bermar01@nyumc.org. *

BERMAN, STANLEY ZISSMAN, allergist, immunologist, educator, internist, author; b. New Orleans, June 17, 1941; s. Herman Zissman and Golda (Kleinfeldt) Feir, Leo Berman (Stepfather); m. Leslie Dale Miller, July 7, 1968; children: Jason Lee, Laura Elizabeth. Student, Tulane U., 1959-62; BSM, Northwestern U., Evanston, Ill., 1963; MD, Northwestern U., Chgo., 1966. Diplomate Am. Bd. Internal Medicine, Am. Bd. Allergy and Immunology, Nat. Bd. Med. Examiners. Intern Chgo. Wesley Meml. Hosp., 1966-67; med. resident Mayo Grad. Sch. Medicine, Rochester, Minn., 1969-71; fellow in allergy and immunology Scripps Clinic and Rsch. Found., La Jolla, Calif., 1971-73; chmn. allergy Lovelace Clinic now Lovelace Health Sys., Albuquerque, 1973—99, ret., 1999; clin. asst., assoc. prof. dept. medicine U. N.Mex. Sch. Medicine, Albuquerque, 1973—98, clin. prof. dept. medicine, 1998—2000; adj. prof. U. St. Francis, Albuquerque, 2003—. Spkr. in field. Co-author, reviewer, contbr.: articles to profl. jours. Lt. comdr. M.C. USNR, 1967—73, with Navy Submarine Svc., 1967—69. Fellow: ACP, Am. Coll. Physicians, Am. Acad. Allergy, Asthma & Immunology (emeritus), Am. Coll. Chest Physicians; mem.: Am. Thoracic Soc. (pres. N.Mex. chpt. 1977—78), N.Mex. Lung Assn. (bd. dirs. 1977—78). Avocations: jogging, travel, history. Office: 7416 Vista Del Arroyo Ave NE Albuquerque NM 87109-2941

BERMAN, STEPHEN ALAN, neurologist; b. Oak Park, Ill., Mar. 15, 1948; s. Edward and Esther Ruby Berman; m. Sherry Bursztajn. BS, U. Ill., Champaign-Urbana, 1970; MD, U. Ill., 1974, PhD in Biochemistry; MBA, U. Tenn., 2008. Diplomate Am. Bd. Psychiatry and Neurology, Am. Bd. Clinical Neurophysiology. Intern Greater Balt. Med. Ctr., 1976—77; resident in neurology Baylor Coll. Medicine, Houston, 1977—80, fellow in genetics and muscle disease, 1980—83; asst. prof. neurology U. Chgo., 1983—89, U. Tex. and MD Anderson Cancer Ctr., Houston, 1989—90; instr. neurology Harvard Med. Sch., Boston, 1990—92, asst. prof., 1992—96; prof. neurology La. State U., Shreveport, 1996—2000; prof. medicine neurology Dartmouth Med. Coll., Hanover, NH, 2000—; chief neurology White River Junction Vets. Med. Ctr., White River Junction, Vt., 2000—. Med. dir. lab. clinical neurophysiology La. State U., Shreveport, 1997—2000. Contbr. articles to profl. jours.; mem. editl. bd. E-Medicine, 1999. Med. adv. com. Multiple Sclerosis Soc., Shreveport, La., 1997—2000. Recipient Rsch. award, Clarence A. Hawkinson Meml. Fund, 1983—84, Brain Rsch. Found., 1984—87, Tchr. Investigator Devel. award, NIH, 1985—89, Physician Scientist award, Nat. Inst. Aging, 1992—96; grantee, Alzheimer Found., 1984—85, Louis Bloch Fund grant, 1984—87; fellow, Muscular Dystrophy Assn., 1981—83. Mem.: Soc. for Neurorehabilitation (cert.), Am. Acad. Neurology (quality stds. subcom., therapeutics and tech. assessment subcom. 1998), Alpha Omega Alpha (v.p. Ill. chpt.

1973—74), Phi Beta Kappa. Jewish. Office: University Central Fla Coll Medicine 6850 Lake Nona Blvd Orlando FL 32827 Office Phone: 407-266-1190. Business E-Mail: stephen.berman@ucf.edu.

BERMEJO-MARTIN, JESUS F., immunologist; b. Miranda de Ebro, Spain, Mar. 23, 1974; MD, Sch. Medicine, Valladolid, Spain, 1998; PhD, U. Complutense de Madrid, 2005. Prin. investigator Infection & Immunity Med. Investigation Unit, Hosp. Clínico U.-IECSCYL, 2008—. Fellowship clin. immunology Hosp. Gen. U. Gregorio Marañón de Madrid, 1999—2003; assoc. editor Jour. Infection Developing Countries. Recipient Correspondant Academist, Royal Acad. Medicine, Valladolid. Mem.: Spanish Soc. Respiratory Medicine, Spanish Soc. Immunology. Office: Avda Ramón y Cajal 3 Valladolid 47005 Spain Office Phone: 00 34 983 420 000-20974. Personal E-mail: berinmuno@hotmail.com.

BERMEJO-VELASCO, PEDRO E., neurologist; b. Toledo, Spain, May 9, 1978; MD, Autonoma U. Madrid, 2002, PhD, 2011. Neurologist Hosp. U. La Paz, 2009—10, Hosp. U. Puerta de Hierro, 2010—. Recipient Best Resident Curriculum award, Hosp. U. Puerta de Hierro. Master: Spanish Assn. Neuroeconomics (pres. 2009—11); mem.: Soc. Neuroeconomics, Spanish Soc. Neurology, European Neurol. Soc. Home: Calle Isla de Arosa 37 2B Madrid 28035 Spain Home Phone: 34609894124. Personal E-mail: pedro_bermejo@hotmail.com.

BERMES, ROBERT JOEL, physician; b. Oran, Algeria, Jan. 19, 1932; s. Marcel Julien and Germaine Eloise (Blanchard) B. D in Medicine, U. Lyon, France, 1962. Various activities with Edouard Herriot Hosp. and Hôtel Dieu, 1952-60; ancien externe Hopitaux de Lyon, Roquebrune sur Argens, 1962—. Inventor rotary pump for artificial heart, 1979, with electric motorization and electronic computer assited management (sphygmocircular motor), 1987. Mem.: Aero Club Grasse (Cannes, France). Home and Office: 1 Ave Jean Giono 83520 Roquebrune sur Argens France

BERMUDEZ, OVIDIO B., adolescent medicine physician, eating disorders specialist; b. Havana, Cuba, June 11, 1960; MD, Eastern Ctrl. U., Dominican Republic, 1985. Diplomate Am. Bd. Pediat., cert. in adolescent medicine, cert. eating disorders specialist. Intern, resident pediat. Med. Coll. Pa., Phila., 1985—88; fellow adolescent medicine U. Ala., Birmingham, 1988—90; dir. adolescent medicine Miami Children's Hosp., Fla., 1990—99; med dir. eating disorders program Laureate Psychiat. Clinic & Hosp., Tulsa, Okla.; med. dir. child & adolescent svcs. Eating Recovery Ctr., Denver, 2010—. Co-founder, hon. bd. mem. Eating Disorders Coalition Tenn., 1999—; adj. assoc. prof. pediat. Vanderbilt U. Sch. Medicine, Nashville, 2000—09; clin. prof. psychiatry and pediat. U. Okla. Coll. Medicine. Mem. nat. bd. dirs. Students Against Destructive Decisions (SADD). Fellow: Am. Acad. Pediat., Soc. Adolescent Medicine, Acad. Eating Disorders (past chair Hispano Latino Am. chpt., chair Med. Care Spl Interest Group); mem.: Internat. Assn. Eating Disorders Professionals, Okla. Eating Disorders Assn. (bd. dirs. co-founder), Nat. Eating Disorders Assn. (past chmn. bd. dirs.). Office: Eating Recovery Ctr 8140 E 5th Ave Denver CO 80230

BERN, HOWARD ALAN, biologist, researcher, science educator; b. Montreal, Que., Can., Jan. 30, 1920; m. Estelle Bruck, 1946; children: Alan, Lauren. BA, UCLA, 1941, MA, 1942, PhD in Zoology, 1948; D (hon.), U. Rouen, France, 1996; LLD (hon.), U. Hokkaido, Japan, 1994; DPhil (hon.), Yokohama City U., 1997; DSc (hon.), Toho U., Japan, 2001. Nat. Rsch. Coun. predoctoral fellow in biology UCLA, 1946—48; instr. in zoology U. Calif., Berkeley, 1948-50, asst. prof., 1950-56, assoc. prof., 1956-60, prof., 1960-89, prof. integrative biology, 1989-90, prof. emeritus, 1990—; rsch. endocrinologist Cancer Rsch. Lab., U. Calif., Berkeley, 1960—; chair group in endocrinology U. Calif., Berkeley, 1962-90, faculty rsch. lectr., 1988. Rsch. prof. Miller Inst. for Basic Rsch. in Sci., 1961, vis. prof. pharmacology U. Bristol, 1965-66, U. Kerala, India, 1967, Ocean Rsch. Inst., U. Tokyo, 1971, 86, U. P.R., 1973-74, U. Tel Aviv, 1975, Nat. Mus. Natural History, Paris, 1981, Toho U., Funabashi, Japan, 1982-84, 86-89, U. Hawaii, 1986, 91-93, Hokkaido U., 1992, 94, U. Fla., 1991-92; James vis. prof. St. Francis Xavier U., Antigonish, N.S., 1986; Walker-Ames prof. U. Wash., 1977; disting. visitor U. Alta., Edmonton, Can., 1981; John W. Cowper Disting. vis. lectr. SUNY, Buffalo, 1984; Watkins vis. prof. Wichita (Kans.) State U., 1984; vis. scholar Meiji U., Tokyo, 1986; internat. guest prof. Yokohama City U., Japan, 1988, 95; adv. com. on instl. rsch. grants Am. Cancer Soc., 1967-70; adv. com. Nat. Cancer Inst., 1975-79; adv. com. in endocrinology and metabolism NIH, 1978-79; mem. GM Cancer Rsch. Found., Sloan Medal Selection Com., 1984-85, Japan Internat. Prize in Biology Selection Com., 1987, 92, 96; guest of honor Internat. Symposium Amphibian and Reptilian Endocrinology and Neurobiology, Camerino, Italy, 2001, Jeju, Korea, 2003; lectr., spkr. in field Mem. editl. bd. Endocrinology, 1962-74, Gen. and Comparative Endocrinology, Revs. in Fish Biology and Fisheries, Jour. Exptl. Zoology, 1965-69, 86-89, Internat. Rev. Cytology, Neuroendocrinology, 1974-80, Cancer Rsch., 1975-78, Jour. Comparative Physiology B, 1977-84, Am. Zoologist, 1978-83, Acta Zoologica, 1982-96, Zool. Sci., Tokyo, 1984-2002; contbr. articles to profl. jours. Assoc. Nat. Mus. Natural History, Paris, 1980; adv. com. Contra Costa Cancer Rsch. Fund, 1984-98, Stazione Zoologica Anton Dohrn di Napoli, 1987-92. Recipient Disting. Tchg. award U. Calif., Berkeley, 1972, The Berkeley Citation, 1990, Disting. Svc. award Soc. Adv. Chicanos and Native Americans in Sci., 1990, Hatai medal Sci. Coun. Japan, 1998, Beverton medal Fisheries Soc. Brit. Isles, 2001, Outstanding Achievement award Am. Inst. Fishery Rsch. Biologists, 2003; Guggenheim fellow, 1951-52, NSF fellow U. Hawaii, 1958-59, fellow Ctr. for Advanced Study in Behavioral Scis., Stanford, 1960, NSF fellow Stazione Zoologica, Naples, 1965-66, Japan Soc. Promotion of Sci. Rsch. fellow U. Toyama, Japan, 1993. Fellow NAS, AAAS, Am. Acad. Arts and Scis., Indian Nat. Sci. Acad. (fgn.), Società Nazionale di Scienze Lettere e Arti Napoli (fgn.), Calif. Acad. Sci., Accademia Nazionale dei Lincei (fgn.), Am. Inst. Fishery Rsch. Biologists (hon.), Fisheries Soc. Brit. Isles (hon.); mem. Soc. Integrative Comparative Biology (hon.; pres. 1967, Howard A. Bern Disting. Lectureship in comparative endocrinology 2002—), Am. Assn. Cancer Rsch., Am. Physiol. Soc., Endocrine Soc., Internat. Soc. Neuroendocrinology (coun. 1977-80), Exptl. Biology and Medicine (coun. 1980-83), Am. Soc. Molec. Marine Biol. Biotech., Western Soc. Naturalists, Japan Soc. Zootech. Sci. (hon.), Am. Fisheries Soc., Japan Soc. Comparative Endocrinology (hon.), Cosmos Club. Home: 1010 Shattuck Ave Berkeley CA 94707-2626 Office: University Calif Dept Integrative Biology Berkeley CA 94720-3140 Office Phone: 510-642-2940, 510-524-3480. Fax: 510-643-6264. Business E-Mail: bern@berkeley.edu.

BERN, MURRAY MORRIS, hematologist, oncologist; b. Montgomery, Ala., Feb. 26, 1944; s. Hymie and Ruth Edith (Schaeffer) B.; m. Nancy Frazee, Nov. 23, 1967; 1 child, Alan. BA, Vanderbilt U., 1966; MD, Tulane U., 1970. Diplomate Am. Bd. Internal Medicine, Am. Bd. Hematology, Am. Bd. Oncology. Intern, then resident New Eng. Deaconess Hosp., Boston, 1970—72; resident medicine Boston City Hosp., 1972—73; fellow hematology & oncology New Eng. Deaconess Hosp.; Am. Cancer Soc. fellow Ctr. for Blood Rsch., Boston, 1973—75; sect. chief hematology New Eng. Deaconess Hosp., Boston, 1975—86; co-founder Cancer Ctr. Boston, 1986, lab. dir. bone marrow transplantation Boston and Plymouth, 1986—90; chmn. transfusion com., chmn. cancer care com., sect. chief hematology, oncology New Eng. Bapt. Hosp., 1999—2004; clin. asst. prof. medicine Harvard Med. Sch., 2004—. Dir. Cancer Ctr. Boston and its stem cell support care, 1990-97, 2007—08, med. dir., 2007—; asst. prof. medicine Harvard U., 1987-94, asst. clin. prof. medicine, 1978-87, 2004—, instr. medicine, 1999-2004. Author, editor: Urinary Track Bleeding, 1985, Hematologic Disorders in Maternal and Fetal Medicine, 1990; contbr. articles to profl. jours. Bd. med. advisors Am. Cancer Soc., Mass., 1976-80, fellow, 1973-75; mem. med. adv. com. N.E. region ARC, 1994-2004; bd. dirs. assocs. Ctr. Blood Rsch. Recipient Tullis award rsch., 2004, DaVinci Diamond award, 2004. Fellow: ACP (jr. faculty fellow 1973—77), Internat. Acad. Clin. Applied Thrombosis and Hemosthsis; mem.: Mass. Soc. Clin. Oncologists (bd. dir. 2003—05), Am. Soc. Clin. Oncology, Am. Soc. Hematology (clin. practice com. 1996—2000, govt. affairs com. 2000—05, comm. com. 2004). Avocations: camping, fishing. Office: 99 Lincoln St Framingham MA 01702 Office Phone: 508-875-7104. E-mail: mbern@cancercenterofboston.com, murraybern@aol.com.

BERNARD, LOUIS JOSEPH, surgeon, educator; b. Laplace, La., Aug. 19, 1925; s. Edward and Jeanne (Vinet) B.; m. Lois Jeannette McDonald, Feb. 1, 1976; children: Marie Antonia, Phyllis Elaine. BA magna cum laude, Dillard U., New Orleans, 1946; MD, Meharry Med. Coll., 1950. Diplomate: Am. Bd. Surgery. Instr. surgery Sch. Medicine, Meharry Med. Coll., Nashville, 1958-59, prof., 1973-90, chmn. dept. surgery, 1973-87, dean, 1987-90, v.p. for health svcs., 1988-90; practice medicine specializing in surgery, 1959-69; mem. clin. faculty U. Okla., 1959-69, assoc. prof., vice chmn. dept. surgery, 1969-73, chmn. dept. surgery, 1973-87, disting. prof. emeritus, 1990—. Dir. Drew-Meharry Morehouse Consortium Cancer Ctr., 1990-96. Contbr. articles in field to profl. jours. Mem. Okla. State Bd. Corrections, 1968-69. With M.C. U.S. Army, 1951-53. USPHS research fellow NCI, U. Rochester, 1953-54 Fellow ACS, Southeastern Surg. Congress; mem. Soc. Surg. Oncology, Internat. Surg. Soc., Am. Assn. Cancer Edn., Alpha Omega Alpha. Democrat. Roman Catholic. Home: 156 Queens Ln Nashville TN 37218-1826

BERNARD, RICHARD MONTGOMERY, retired physician; b. Long Beach, Calif., Feb. 21, 1925; s. Francis M. and Irma V. (Phillips) B.; m. Virginia Marie Thompson, Sept. 19, 1946 (div. Mar. 1971); children: Richard Jr., David, Mary, Danielle; m. Nancy Johnston, Nov. 18, 1971; stepchildren: Vivienne Kouba, N. Catherine Thompson. BS in Chemistry, U. Calif. Berkeley, 1945; MD, U. Chgo., 1950. Charter Diplomate Am. Bd. Family Practice. Pvt. practice Westslope, Portland, Oreg., 1954-60, Beaverton, Oreg., 1960-86; assoc. with Dr. D. Graham, Beaverton, 1986-90; family practitioner St. Vincent Tanesbourne Med. Plz., Beaverton, 1990-91; locum tenens Oreg., 1991-92; family practitioner Providence Health Sys., Wilsonville, Oreg., 1992-98. Prof. emeritus clin. medicine dept. family practice Oreg. Health Sci. U., Portland, 1994. Mem. transp. adv. commn. City of Wilsonville, 1994 96, mem. long range planning commn., 1996-98; healthcare ombudsman Portland Metro Elders in Action, 2000—; v.p., bd. dirs. Oreg. Medications Edn. Program, 2001-03. vol. staff, bd. dirs. Wilsonville Publ. Libr. Found., 2003-05. Capt. USNR, WWII, 1942-46, Korea, 1950-53, ret., 1985. Recipient Meritorious Achievement award Oreg. Health Science U., 1988. Mem. Oreg. Med. Assn. (ho. of del. 1975—), Charbonneau Country Club (bd. dirs. 2000-06). Republican. Avocations: fishing, travel, photography, genealogy, painting in acrylics. Home: 31530 SW Village Green Ct Wilsonville OR 97070-8426

BERNARD, ROBERT WILLIAM, plastic surgeon; b. NYC, Aug. 18, 1942; Student, U. Mich., 1959-60; BA in Zoology with honors, U. Vt., 1963, MD cum laude, 1967. Diplomate Am. Bd. Surgery, Am. Bd. Plastic Surgery. Intern U. Pa. Hosp., Phila., 1967-68; resident in gen. surgery NYU Med. Ctr., 1968-72, resident in plastic surgery, 1972-74; asst. prof. plastic surgery NYU Med. Sch., 1972—86; chief plastic surgery No. Westchester Hosp., Mt. Kisco, NY, 1982-87, 96—, White Plains (NY) Hosp., 1979-86, United Hosp., Port Chester, NY, 1986-94. Author, editor: book Aesthetic Restoration of the Aging Face, 1997; editor: Aesthetic Surg. Jour., 1993—98; contbr. articles to profl. jours. Fellow: ACS; mem.: AMA (Recognition award 1983, 1984, 1986, 1988, 1990, 1992, 1995, 1998, 2001, 2004, 2007), Am. Cancer Soc., Westchester County Med. Soc., NY Regional Soc. Plastic and Reconstructive Surgery (chair sci. program com. 1984—85, pres. 1986—87, mem. exec. com. 1987—88), NY State Med. Soc. (pres. plastic surgery sect. 1983—84), Am. Soc. Aesthetic Plastic Surgery (pres. 2003—04). Office: 10 Chester Ave White Plains NY 10601-5112 also: 91 Smith Ave Mount Kisco NY 10549-2810 Office Phone: 914-761-8667.

BERNARD, SALLIE, non-profit organization executive; married; 3 children. Grad. with honors, Radcliffe U., Harvard U., 1979. Founder, pres. ARC Rsch., 1986—2004; former exec. dir., NJ chpt. Cure Autism Now; chmn. Cure Autism Now (now merged with Autism Speaks); co-founder, exec. dir. SafeMinds, Tyrone, Ga., 2000—. Mem., Founders Forum Autism Ctr., Univ. Medicine and Dentistry NJ; presenter in field. Published several rsch. papers and letters in sci. jours. Co-founder, pres. Extreme Sports Camp, Aspen, Colo., 2001—. Office: SafeMinds 254 Trickum Creek Rd Tyrone GA 30290

BERNARD, STEPHEN ALAN, oncologist; b. High Point, NC, 1947; MD, U. N.C., 1973. Diplomate Am. Bd. Internal Medicine, Am. Acad. Internal Medicine, Am. Bd. Oncology, Am. Bd. Hospice & Palliative Medicine, 2008. Intern Colum-Presbyn. Med. Ctr., 1973-74, resident in medicine, 1974-76; fellow in hematol. oncology Washington U. Hosps., St. Louis, 1976-78; mem. staff U. N.C. Hosp., Chapel Hill, 1981—; prof. U. NC Sch. Medicine, Chapel Hill, 1990—. Mem. ACP, Am. Soc. Clin. Oncology. Office: U NC Sch Medicine Cb # 7305 Chapel Hill NC 27599-0001 *

BERNARDINO, CARLO ROBERTO, ophthalmologist; b. Manilla, July 15, 1971; s. Vitaliano B. and Evelina Abuel Bernardino. Student, U. Alicante, Spain, 1991—91; BA in Biology, Lehigh U., 1993; MD, Jefferson Med. Coll., 1997. Cert. Del., 2001, Commonwealth Pa., 2002, Commonwealth Mass., 2003, Ga., 2007. Intern Crozer-Chester Med. Ctr., Upland, Pa., 1997—98; resident in ophthalmology Wills Eye Hosp., Phila., 1998—2001, chief resident, 2000—01; oculoplastics fellow Mass. Eye and Ear Infirmary, Boston, 2001—03; asst. prof. Emory U. Sch. Medicine, 2003—07; assoc. prof. Yale U. Sch. Medicine, 2007—10; with oculoplastics and aesthetic surgery Vantage Eye Ctr., 2010—. Contbr. numerous articles and sci. papers to profl. publs. Dir. Esperanza, Free Ophthalmology Clinic Northern Phila., Pa., 2000—01; mem. Surg. Mission Healing the Children, Guaranda, Ecuador, 2006, Med. Edn. Mission Port au Prince, Haiti, 2010, Surg. and Med. Edn. Mission, Da Nang, Vietnam, 2010, Ga. Soc. Ophthalmology, 2003—07, Am. Med. Assn., 1998—2009, Conn. Soc. Eye Physicians, 2007—10, Assn. Philippine Ophthalmologists in America, 2006—10, Assn. U. Profs. Ophthalmology, 2007—10, Most Venerable Order of Hosp. St. John, Jerusalem, 2009—10; hon. cons. Bahamas Med. Coun., Nassau, 2009—. Recipient Am. Med. Assn. Physician Recognition award, 2001—04, Achievement award, Am. Acad. Ophthalmology, 2006, Secretariat award, 2007, Top Drs. award, NY Metro Area Castle Connolly Med. Ltd., 2009, 2010, 1st Pl. award, Conn. Chpt. Am. Coll. Surgeons, 2009; named one of Best Drs. in America, 2009, 2010; nominee Alice Bohmfalk Tchg. award, 2009; Bausch & Lomb Young Investigators grant, 2000—01. Fellow: ACS, Am. Acad. Ophthalmology; mem.: Am. Eye Study Club. Office: Vantage Eye Ctr 2 Upper Ragsdale Dr Ste B130 Monterey CA 93940 Office Phone: 831-771-3900. Business E-Mail: rbernardino@vantageeye.com. *

BERNARDINO, ELIZABETH V., child and adolescent psychiatrist; MD, Philippines, 1980. Diplomate Am. Bd. Psychiatry and Neurology, 1991, Am. Bd. Psychiatry and Neurology-child and adolescent psychiatry, 1994. Resident psychiatry Loyola Univ. Med. Ctr., Maywood, Ill., 1985—88; fellow child & adolescent psychiatry Boston Univ. Med. Ctr., 1990—92; med. dir. child & adolescent psychiatry program Hinsdale Hosp., 1993—2003; pvt. practice Cypress Prof. Group LLC. Office: Cypress Professional Group LLC 7055-C Veterans Blvd Burr Ridge IL 60527 Office Phone: 630-325-4899. Office Fax: 630-325-4811.

BERNARDO, JOHN, critical care specialist, educator; MD, U. Ill., 1973. Diplomate Am. Bd. Internal Medicine, 1976, Am. Bd. Internal Medicine- pulmonary disease, 1982, Am. Bd. Internal Medicine-critical care medicine, 1989. Resident in internal medicine NY Hosp., 1974—76, Boston City Hosp., 1975—76; fellow in pulmonary disease Nat. Heart, Lung and Blood Inst., 1976—79; assoc. prof. Sch. of Medicine Boston Univ.; staff Boston Med. Ctr., Lemuel Shattuck Hosp. Office: BostonMedical Center 725 Albany St 9th Fl Ste 9B Boston MA 02118 Office Phone: 617-639-8748, 617-522-8110. Office Fax: 617-638-7486.

BERNAT, JAMES LAWRENCE, neurologist, educator; b. Cin., May 23, 1947; s. Mitchell Joseph and Ruth Claire (Betagole) B.; m. Judith Elaine Lenzner, June 8, 1969; children: Deborah Eden, David Clare. BA, U. Mass., Amherst, 1969; MD, Cornell U., NYC, 1973. Diplomate Nat. Bd. Med. Examiners, 1974, Am. Bd. Psychiatry and Neurology, 1978. Resident in medicine Dartmouth-Hitchcock Med. Ctr., Hanover, NH, 1973-74, resident in neurology, 1974-77, staff neurologist Lebanon, 1995—, assoc. chmn. neurology sect., 1999—2002; staff neurologist VA Med. Ctr., White River Junction, Vt., 1977-94; prof. neurology and medicine Dartmouth Med. Sch., Hanover, 1991—, asst. dean, 1995—99, dir. program in med. ethics, 1995—, Louis & Ruth Frank prof. nuerosci., 2011—. Author: Neurology: Problems in Primary Care, 1987, 2d edit., 1993, Ethical Issues in Neurology, 1994, 3d edit., 2008; editor (editl. bd.): Neurocritical Care; co-editor: Palliative Care in Neurology, 2004. Bd. dirs. Vt. Ethics Network, Montpelier, 1995-2000, New Eng. Organ Bank, 1999-2006, Hospice V.N.H., 1999-2002; mem. Dana Alliance Brain Initiatives. Fellow ACP, Am. Acad. Neurology (chair ethics, law & humanities com. 1993-03, exec. bd. 1993-97), Am. Neurological Assn., Hastings Ctr. Office: Neurology Dept Dartmouth-Hitchcock Med Ctr Lebanon NH 03756 Office Phone: 603-650-5104. Business E-Mail: bernat@dartmouth.edu.

BERNE, PATRICIA HIGGINS, psychologist, writer, educator; b. Indpls., Feb. 21, 1934; d. Edward Robert and Esther Josephine (Maschino) Higgins; m. John Henry Berne, June 19, 1957 (div. May 1979); children: Suzanne, Eve, Serena; m. Louis M. Savary, Oct. 11, 1992. Student, Am. U., 1970-72, George Washington U., 1974; MA, Goddard Coll., 1976; PhD, Union Inst., Cin., 1978. Lic. clin. psychologist, Washington, mental health counselor, Tampa, Fla., specialization in trauma, anxiety, grief, death and dying, transitations, depression and stress using CBT, hypnosis and EMDR; specialization in hypnosis for sleep, pain, management, anxiety and confidence regarding testing, performances, interviewing, pregnancy and healing for surgery, IBS and other health issues. Counselor Campus Ministry Georgetown U., 1978-80; dir. Counseling Ctr. Trinity Coll., Washington, 1979-81; pvt. practice Washington, 1982—; pvt. practice, therapist The Life Ctr., Tampa, Fla., 1992—. Co-dir. Inner Devel. Assocs., Washington, 1990—, adj. prof., 1981—; adj. faculty at numerous colls. and univs., 1978—; lectr. at confs. internationally, 1980—. Co-author: Prayerways, 1980, Building Self-Esteem in Children, 1981, Dreams and Spiritual Growth, 1984, Prayer Medicine, 1986, Kything, 1988, Dream Symbol Work, 1991, In Process The Spirituality and Evolution of Relationship. Mem. APA, ACA, ASCH, Eye Movement Desentization and Reprocessing Internat. Assn., Round Table Group Psychotherapists (consulting experts), Inst. for Noetic Sci., DC Psychol. Assn., Am. Soc. Clin. Hypnosis. Roman Catholic. Achievements include research in the use of metaphor & suggestion in healing&hynosis IBS, sleep, anxiety, confidence pre-surgery, pain management, pregnancy, test & performance anxiety or enhancement relaxation & peace of mind and support in Illness and death. Avocations: travel, theater, mentoring, kayaking. Office Phone: 813-494-0220. Personal E-mail: lousavary@yahoo.com.

BERNE, ROBERT, academic administrator; BS in Indsl. Engring. and Ops. Rsch. with distinction, Cornell U., Ithaca, NY, 1970, MBA in Fin., 1971, PhD in Bus. and Pub. Adminstrn., 1977. Asst. to the dir.

planning U. Saskatchewan, Saskatoon, 1971—73; asst. prof. pub. adminstrn. NYU Robert F. Wagner Grad. Sch. Pub. Svc., NYC, 1976—79, assoc. prof. pub. adminstrn., 1979—85, prof. pub. adminstrn., 1985—, assoc. dean, 1988—94, dean, 1994—97; co-dir., Inst. Edn. and Social Policy NYU, 1994—96, v.p. academic devel., 1996—2000, v.p. academic and health affairs, 2000—02, sr. v.p. health, 2002—. Dir. policy rsch. NY State Temporary Commn. on the Distbn. State Aid to Local Sch. Dists., 1988; exec. dir. NY State Temporary Commn. on NYC Sch. Governance, 1989—91; cons. in field. Author: The Measurement of Equity in School Finance, 1984, The Relationships between Financial Reporting and the Measurement of Financial Condition, 1992; co-author (with R. Schramm): The Financial Analysis of Governments, 1986; co-author: (with C. Ascher, N. Fruchter) Hard Lessons: Public Schools and Privatization, 1996; co-editor (with S. Jacobson): Reforming Education. The Emerging Systemic Approach, 1994; co-editor: (with L. Picus) Outcome Equity in Education, 1994; contbr. articles to profl. jours., chapters to books. Bd. dirs. Univ. Settlement House, NYC, 1987—2001, treas., 1988—98. Recipient Great Tchr. award, NYU Alumni Fedn., 1986. Mem.: Am. Acad. Arts and Sciences, Assn. Pub. Policy Analysis and Mgmt., Nat. Tax Assn., Am. Soc. Pub. Adminstrn. (mem. exec. com., budgeting and fin. mgmt. sect. 1985—89, Outstanding Academic award 1987), Am. Edn. Fin. Assn. (bd. dirs. 1985—88, Outstanding Svc. award 1999), Am. Econ. Assn. Office: NYU Elmer Holmes Bobst Libr Rm 1223 70 Washington Sq S New York NY 10012-1091 Office Phone: 212-998-2283. Office Fax: 212-995-4601. Business E-Mail: Robert.Berne@nyu.edu.

BERNHAGEN, LILLIAN FLICKINGER, retired school health consultant; b. Cleve., Oct. 1, 1916; d. Norman Henry and Bertha May (Rogers) Flickinger; m. Ralph John Bernhagen, Sept. 2, 1940; children: Ralph, Janet Elizabeth Darling, Penelope Anne Braat. Student, Ohio Wesleyan U., 1934—37; BS in Edn., Ohio State U., 1940, MA, 1958; postgrad., LaVerne Coll., 1972—73, BSEd. Cert. health edn. specialist; cert. holistic coach Journeys of Wisdom Inst.; RN. Asst. dir. Kiwanis Health Camp for Underprivileged Children, Steubenville, Ohio, summer 1940; asst. dir. nurses Jefferson Davis Hosp., Houston, 1940-41; ARC instr. Ohio State U., 1943, 63, elem. edn. lectr., 1970, health edn. instr., 1976-77; dir. health svcs. Worthington City Schs., Ohio, 1951-76; spl. cons. venereal disease and sex edn. Ohio Dept. Health, 1976-82; sch. health cons. Ohio Dept. Edn., 1976—82; vice chmn. medicine, edn. com. on sch. and coll. health AMA, 1976-78, chmn., 1978-80; mng. editor Self Growth Wisdom.com, 2006—. Author: Sex Education: Understanding Growth and Social Development, 1968, What A Miracle You Are-Boys, 1968, 3d rev. edit., 1986, What A Miracle You Are-Girls, 1968, 3d rev. edit., 1986, Toward a Reverence for Life, 1971, Personality, Sexuality and Stereotyping, 1974, (with others) Growth Patterns and Sex Education: A Suggested Curriculum Guide K-12, 1967; contbr. articles to profl. jours. & mags. Bd. dirs. Hearing and Speech Ctr. of Columbus and Franklin County, 1954-57, sec., 1957; mem. nat. adv. com. Nat. Ctr. for Health Edn., 1978-82; sec.-tres. Ohio Wesleyan U. Class of 38, 1968-78, 83-88; bd. dirs. V.D. Hotline Columbus and Franklin County, 1974-87, bd. expansion chmn., 1978-85, pres., 1985-86; mem. profl. adv. com. Ptnrs. Home Health Inc., 1991-97; mem. Worthington Hist. Soc., Doll Docent, 1982—; mem King Ave. United Meth. Ch., 1938—, mem. marriage counseling com., 1997-98, mem. choir, 1950—2004, pres., 1961-63, pastor/parish rels. com., 1985-88, bd. trustees, 1989-92, adminstrv. coun., 1992-98, homosexual study com., 1998-99, edn. commn., 1982-85, nominations and pers., 1992-94; treas. Franklin County Women's Golf Tournament, 1992. Recipient Outstanding Alumna award Ohio State U. Coll. Nursing, 1964, Legend in Nursing award, 2008, Centennial award Ohio State U., 1970, Disting. Svc. award Mich. Sch. Nurses Assn., 1972, Alumni Hon. award Ohio Wesleyan U., 1998; hon. mention La Sertoma Internat. Woman of Yr., 1972, named Legend in Nursing, Ohio State Coll., 2008. Fellow Am. Sch. Health Assn. (v.p. 1974, U. pres. 1976, governing coun. 1973-88, chmn. health guidance in sex edn. com. 1963-67, 71-77, chmn. sr. adv. coun. 1983-89, Disting. Svc. award 1969, Howe award 1979, cert. of merit, 1985, mem. awards com. 1986-89, mem. hist. com. 1989-95, constn. and bylaws com. 1997-99), APHA (chmn. com. on urban health problems 1972); mem. NEA (life, ret.), Sex Edn. and Info. Coun. of U.S., Worthington Edn. Assn. (v.p. 1961-62, Tchr. of Yr. 1972-73), Ctrl. Ohio Tchrs. Assn. (chmn. sch. health svcs. sect. 1963), Ohio State U. Women's Golf Assn. (chmn. 1973, parliamentarian 1988—), Ohio Wesleyan U. Alumni Assn. (bd. dirs., chmn. alumni recognition com. 1994-95, chmn. bylaws revision com. 1991-96, mem. orgn. com. 1994-95), Columbus Women's Dist. Golf Assn. (treas. 1985, sec. 1987, v.p. 1989, pres. 1990, adv. bd. 1991-98, parliamentarian 1996-98), Chi Omega (pres. Columbus Alumnae chpt. 1947-49, fin. adv. Ohio Wesleyan U. 1964-76, Outstanding Alumna of Yr. State of Ohio 1986), Ohio State U. Nursing Alumni Soc. (Disting. Alumni award, 2004), Pi Lambda Theta (citation award 1971, mem. program com. 1986-89, chmn. by laws revision com. 1990-2000, parliamentarian), Journeys of Wisdom, Monnett Club, Worthington Women's Club, Sigma Theta Tau, Phi Delta Kappa, Pi Lamda Theta. Home and Office: 5916 Linworth Rd Worthington OH 43085-3357 Personal E-mail: lfbern@aol.com.

BERNHARD, JEAN-CHRISTOPHE, urologist; b. Toulouse, June 14, 1978; MD, U. Bordeaux II, 2010; M, U. Paris XI, 2009. Clin. dir., asst. U. Hosp. Ctr. Bordeaux, 2010—. Adminstrn. bd. mem. Assn. Française Urologues en Formation, 2008—10; editl. bd. mem. Correspondances en Onco-Urologie - Edimark, 2009. Recipient 1st Award, BAYER; named Chirurgien de l'avenir en Cancérologie, Académie Nat. Chirurgie - Fondation l'Avenir, 2009; Bourse grant, Assn. Française Urology, grant, Inst. Nat. Cancer. Mem.: Assn. pour la Rsch. ur les Tumeurs du Rein, Endouurol. Soc., European Assn. Urology, Assn. Urologues Formation d'Aquitaine (pres. 2007—10), Assn. Française Urolouès Formation. Office: University Hosp. Ctr Bordeaux Pl Amélie Raba Léon Bordeaux 33076 France Personal E-mail: jcb31000@hotmail.com.

BERNHARD, JEFFREY DAVID, dermatologist, educator, editor; b. Buffalo, Oct. 31, 1951; AB, Harvard Coll., 1973; MD, Harvard Med. Sch., 1978. Diplomate Am. Bd. Dermatology. Knox fellow St. John's Coll. Cambridge U., England, 1973—74; chief resident dermatology Mass. gen. Hosp., Boston, 1982; fellow photomedicine Mass. Gen. Hosp., 1983; mem. faculty Med. Sch. U. Mass., Worcester, 1983—86, chief dermatology, assoc. prof. Sch. Medicine, 1986—2002, assoc. dean for admissions Med. Sch., 1989—95, prof. Med. Sch., 1992, prof. medicine and physiology, 2005, acad. chief dermatology, 2002—07, prof. emeritus, 2007—. Arthur Curtis vis. prof. U. Mich., 2007; T. B. Fitzpatrick lectr. Harvard Med., 2007; EP Cawley vis. prof. U. Va., 2009. Author: Itch: Mechanisms and Management of Pruritus, 1994; asst. editor Jour. Am. Acad. Dermatology, 1993-98, editor, 1998—2008, Britsh Jour. Dermatology Sect. editor, 2008-; mem. editl. bd. Jour. European Acad. Dermatology and Venereology, Yearbook of Cancer, 1981-88, Yearbook of Dermatology, 1988-97, Internat. Jour. Dermatology, Jour. Geriat. Dermatology, 1993-97. Bd. dirs. Internat. Forum Study Itch., 2008—. Named J. Graham Smith, Jr., hon. lectr., 2000, Narins Meml. Lectr., 2001, Novy lectr., U. Calif., Davis, 2002, Lorincz lectr., Chgo. Derm. Soc., 2002, Luscombe lectr., Jefferson Med. Coll., 2003, Sydney Watson Smith lectr., Royal Coll. Physicians Edinburgh, 2004, Ervin Epstein lectr., Pacific Dermatol. Assn., 2004; named an hon. mem., Czech. Soc. Dermatol, 2002. Fellow: Royal Coll. Physicians (Edinburgh), Royal Soc. Medicine, Am. Dermatol. Assn.; mem.: Coun. Sci. Editors, European Soc. History of Dermatology, History Dermatology Soc., Quinsigamond Dermatol. Soc., French Soc. Dermatology and Venereology (corr.), British Assn. Dermatologists (hon.), Austrian Soc. Dermatology and Venerology (corr.), New Eng. Dermatol. Soc. (pres. 1990—91), Assn. Profs. Dermatology, Sir James Saunders Soc., European Acad. Dermatology and Venereology, Soc. for Investigative Dermatology (bd. dirs. 1981—83), Am. Acad. Dermatology (Presdl. citation 2000, 2008), James C. White Club, Aesculapian Club Boston, Sigma Xi, Alpha Omega Alpha, Phi Beta Kappa. Office: 24 Julio Dr Shrewsbury MA 01545 *

BERNHARD, WILLIAM FRANCIS, thoracic and cardiovascular surgeon; b. Bklyn., Dec. 11, 1924; s. William and Helen (Conroy) B.; m. June Horne, Sept. 17, 1948; children: Susan, William Francis, Christine, Margaret, Catherine, John, Ann, James, Robert, Peter. BA, Williams Coll., 1946; MD, Syracuse U., 1950; MS (hon.), Harvard U., 1990. Intern Syracuse U. Hosp., 1950-51; asst. resident Children's Hosp. Med. Center, Boston, 1951-52; dir. surg. research lab. Children's Hosp., Boston, 1960—, assoc. surgeon, 1962-66; sr. assoc. in cardiovascular surgery Children's Hosp. Med. Center; asst. resident Peter Bent Brigham Hosp., Boston, 1952—57, attending staff cardiovascular surgery, 1973—, attending staff, 1974—; resident Bellevue Hosp., Columbia div., NYC, 1957-58; resident in surgery Columbia-Presbyn. Hosp., NYC, 1959; attending surgeon thoracic and cardiovascular surgery VA Hosp., West Roxbury, Mass., 1960—; Harvey Cushing fellow Harvard Med. Sch., 1954—55, clin. assoc. surgery, 1962-66, asst. clin. prof. surgery, 1966-68, assoc. clin. prof. surgery, 1968-71, prof. surgery, 1971—, prof. surgery emeritus, 1994; sr. surgeon Brigham and Woman's Hosp., Boston, 1987. Cons. in cardiothoracic surgery Beth Israel Hosp., Boston, 1986. Ensign USNR, 1944-46. Harvey Cushing fellow, Harvard Med. Sch., 1954—55. Mem. ACS., New Eng. Surg. Soc. (sr.), Am. Heart Assn., Mass. Med. Soc., Am. Assn. Thoracic and Cardiovasc. Surgery, Soc. Thoracic Surgery, Soc. Univ. Surgeons, Am. Acad. Pediatrics, New Eng. Cardiovasc. Soc., Internat. Soc. Heart Transplantation, Soc. Vascular Surgery, Am. Soc. Artificial Internal Organs, Am. Surg. Assn. Home: 58 Singletary Ln Framingham MA 01702-6161 Office: Children's Hosp 300 Longwood Ave Boston MA 02115-5737

BERNHARDT, INGOLF GÜNTER, biophysicist, educator; b. Wurzen, Saxony, Germany, Sept. 18, 1952; s. Günter and Istrid (Andrä) B.; m. Rita Ruth Arlt, Sept. 13, 1974; 1 child, Tilo. Diploma, Moscow Lomonosov State U., 1977; PhD, Humboldt U., Berlin, 2000, DSc, 1986. Jr. scientist Humboldt U., 1977-82, sr. scientist, 1982-87, reader biophysics, 1987-2000, U. Saarland, 2000—02, prof., 2002—. Author: Cell Electrophoresis, 1994, Red Cell Membrane Transport in Health and Disease, 2003; contbr. articles to sci. jours. including Jour. Membrane Biology, Jour. Physiology, Biophys. Jour. Recipient Humboldt prize, 1982. Avocations: mountain climbing, classical music. Office: U Saarland Faculty Scis Postfach 151150 66041 Saarbrücken Germany Office Phone: 49-681-3026689. E-mail: i.bernhardt@mx.uni-saarland.de.

BERNHARDT, MARCIA BRENDA, mental health counselor; b. Jersey City, Aug. 22, 1938; d. Jerome and Mitzie (Cohen) B. BA, Fairleigh Dickinson U., 1960; MA, Columbia U., 1960-63, postgrad., 1968-70, Hunter Coll., 1973-74. Nat. cert. counselor. Rsch. asst. Tchrs. Coll., Columbia U., NYC, 1963-64; counselor JOIN, NYC, 1965-66; project assoc. Bd. Higher Edn. N.Y., NYC, 1966-68, Tchrs. Coll, Columbia U., NYC, 1968-70; counselor Nassau Community Coll., Garden City, N.Y., 1970-72; rsch. scientist Div. for Youth, NYC, 1972-73; rsch. assoc. Family Svc. Assn., NYC, 1974-76; counselor Div. Blind Svcs., West Palm Beach, Fla., 1984-96. Sec., chairperson adv. bd. com. Lighthouse for the Blind, West Palm Beach, 1984-90. Mem. AAUW, Am. Mental Health Counselors Assn., Am. Soc. for Handicapped Children in Israel. Democrat. Jewish. Avocations: theater, ballet, opera, art, swimming. Home: 40 Chatham B West Palm Beach FL 33417-1807 Personal E-mail: marciabrend@aol.com.

BERNHOFT, FRANKLIN OTTO, psychotherapist, psychologist; b. Fargo, ND, Aug. 12, 1944; s. Otto and Irene Bernhoft; m. Dorothy Ann Larsen, Aug. 11, 1973; children: Kimberley, Brady, Heather. BA in English, N.D. State U., 1966; MA in Counseling Psychology, U. N.D., 1970; MA in English, Calif. State U., 1978; PhD in Counseling Psychology, Brigham Young U., 1985. Cert. therapist, hypnotherapist, counselor, secondary tchr.; lic. psychologist, marriage, family and child counselor, ednl. psychologist. Instr. Chapman Coll., Brigham Young U., U. N.D., U. S.I.U.; staff trainer Sacramento County Office Edn., 1977—82; therapist Lodi and Stockton, Calif., 1985—; devel. capable people trainer U. Pacific Behavioral Medicine Clinic, 1979—84, master trainer systematic helping skills, 1981—88, therapist, family fitness trainer, 1988—. Co-founder prevention/intervention project, Sacto County, 1977; presenter in field. Contbr. articles to profl. jours. Lt. U.S. Army, 1967-69. H.H. Kirk R. Askanase scholar, 1962-66; cert. achievement Ft. Carson, 1967; decorated Bronze star, combat med. badge Nat. Def. Svc. Vietnam, 1968-69; named Support Person of Yr. Phi Delta Kappa, 2000-2001. Mem. ACA, Children with Attention Deficit Disorders, Nat. Assn. Sch. Psychologists, Assn. Mormon Counselors and Psychotherapists, Calif. Assn. Marriage and Family Therapists, Calif. Psychol. Assn., Sacramento Area Sch. Psychologists Assn., Calif. Continuation Edn. Assn. (past treas.), Calif. Assn. Lic. Edn. Psychologists, Mensa, Eye Movement Desensitization and Reprocessing Internat. Assn., Calif. Assn. Psychologists, Am. Assn. Christian Counselors, Internat. Critical Incident Stress Found. Office: Creative Therapy 2000 W Kettleman Ln Ste 103 Lodi CA 95242-4334 Office Phone: 209-366-1516.

BERNIER, JACQUES RENÉ FERNAND, radiologist; b. Courcelles, Belgium, Nov. 11, 1950; arrived in Switzerland, 1988; s. Pol and Odette (Souply) B.; m. Lesire Anne, Jan. 15, 1975; children: Caroline, Geraldine. MD, U. Liege, 1974, degree in radiotherapy, 1978, degree in nuclear medicine, 1980; PhD (hon), U. Geneva, 1995. Resident Inst. Curie, Paris, 1977-78; sci. cons. dept. radioimmunology U. Liege, 1983-87; dep. chmn. Civil Hosp., Charleroi, Belgium, 1983-88; chmn. Cantonal Dept. Radiation Oncology and Nuclear Medicine, Tessin, Switzerland, 1988—2006. Bd. dirs. Ospedale San Giovanni, Bellinzona, Switzerland, 1994-2006, Swiss Genolier Med. Network Dept. Radio-Oncology, 2006—, Tessin Found. Against Cancer; prof. a.c. U. degli Studi, Faculty of Medicine, Perugia, Italy, 1997-99; mem. editl. office Annals of Oncology, Lugano, Switzerland, 1989-2000; mem. protocol rev. com. European Orgn. Rsch. and Treatment of Cancer, Belgium, mem. quality assurance com., chmn. quality assurance in radiotherapy, 1988-1999; mem. sci. coun. Centro Nazionale di Adronterapia Oncologica, Milan, 1988-1997; chmn. Com. for the Centenary of the X-Ray Discovery, European Soc. Therapeutic Radiology and Oncology, 1995-96; chmn. Head and Neck Group, European Orgn. Rsch. and Treatment of Cancer, Belgium, 1998-2006; pres. Tessin League Against Cancer, Bellinzona, Switzerland, 1998-2006; bd. mem., Swiss League of Senology, Baden, 1998—, pres., 2002-2003; lectr. European Sch. of Oncology, 1988—, bd. mem., 2001—; pres., Found. Advancement of Radio-Oncology, Geneva, Switzerland, 2001—; mem. scientific coun. Ctr. Antoine LaCassagne, Nice, France, 2003—; chmn. Internat. Conf. Translational Rsch. in Radiation Oncology, 2000—; adv. bd. Cancerworld Mag., 2004; coord. SenoNetwork, 2007-; mem. editl. bd. Jour. Clin. Oncology, 2007-. Contbr. over 250 articles and chpts. to profl. jours. and books; mem. editl. bd. Future Drugs, Internat. Jour. Radiation Biology, Oncology, Physics, 2001, Head & Neck, 2004, Revista de Oncologia, 2004; editor Annals Oncology, 1990-2000, Revista de Oncologia, 2004—, assoc. editor, Jour. Clin. Oncology, 2009-, Annals Oncology, 2010-, Oral Oncology, 2011-. Recipient award Fondazione San Salvatore, Lugano, Switzerland, 1989, Croix de Chevalier de l'Ordre de la Couronne, Belgium. Mem. AAAS, N.Y. Acad. Scis., Gilbert Fletcher Soc. (Houston), Am. Radium Soc., Am. Soc. Clin. Oncology, Am. Soc. Therapeutic Radiology and Oncology, Swiss Proton User's Group, French Cancer Soc., French Soc. Radio-Oncology, Tessin League Against Cancer (bd. dirs. 1996-99), Sci. Assn. of Swiss Radio-Oncology (bd. dirs.), Swiss Assn. Rsch. on Cancer (bd. dirs., 1988-2000), European Soc. Therapeutic Radiology and Oncology (bd. dirs. 1992-98), Head and Neck Coop. Group (chmn.), Swiss Soc. Senology (chmn.), Oncology Inst. Switzerland (vice-chmn.) Office: Swiss Genolier Med Network 1272 Genolier Switzerland Business E-Mail: jbernier@genolier.net.

BERNS, JEFFREY SCOTT, nephrologist, educator; MD, Case Western Res. U. Diplomate Am. Bd. of Internal Medicine, 1984, Am. Bd. of Internal Medicine-renal/nephrology, 1986. Intern Univ. Hosp. of Cleve., resident; fellow Yale Univ. Sch. of Medicine; prof. medicine Univ. Pa.; assoc. chief renal electrolyte and hypertension Hosp. of the Univ. of Pa., dir. renal fellowship program, assoc. dean grad. med. edn. Named one of Top Docs, Phila. Mag., 2002, 2005, 2010, 2011. Office: Hospital of the University of Pennsylvania 3400 Spruce St Philadelphia PA 19104 Office Phone: 215-662-4000.

BERNS, KENNETH IRA, physician; b. Cleve., June 14, 1938; s. Charles and Delnet (Cohn) Berns; m. Laura Louise Lawless, June 26, 1964; children: Jonathan Charles, Deborah Louise. Student, Harvard U., 1956—59; AB, Johns Hopkins U., 1960, PhD, 1964, MD, 1966. Intern Johns Hopkins Hosp., 1966—67; asst. prof. microbiology Johns Hopkins U. Sch. Medicine, 1970—74, asst. prof. pediat., 1970—76, asso. prof. microbiology, 1974—76; dir. Johns Hopkins U. Sch. Medicine (Yr. I program), 1973—76; prof., chmn. dept. immunology and med. microbiology, prof. pediat. U. Fla. Coll. Medicine, Gainesville, 1976—84, disting. prof., 2006—, dean, 1997—2002, v.p. health affairs, 2000—02; R.A. Rees Pritchett prof., chmn. dept. microbiology Cornell U. Med. Coll., 1984—97; pres., CEO Mt. Sinai Med. Ctr., NYC, 2002—03; dir. U. Fla. Genetics Inst., 2003—. Howard Hughes med. investigator, 1970—75; mem. microbiology test com. Nat. Bd. Med. Examiners, 1979—82, chmn., 1983—86, mem. exec. bd., 1986—95; mem. Recombinant DNA adv. com. NIH, 1980—83, chmn., 1982—83, mem. virology study sect., 1985—89; mem. genetic biology panel NSF, 1981—84; Fogarty sr. internat. fellow virology dept. Weizmann Inst. Sci., Rehovot, Israel, 1982—83; ad hoc mem. Bd. Sci. Counselors Nat. Inst. Allergy and Infectious Diseases, 1982, permanent mem., 1992—96; del. U.S.-Japan Coop. Program on Recombinant DNA, 1981; mem. Internat. Com. Taxonomy of Viruses, 1981—98; mem. virology and microbiology adv. com. Am. Cancer Soc., 1985—89, mem. liaison com. on med. edn., 1989—92; mem. composite com. U.S. Med. Licensing Exam., 1995—98; nat. adv. coun. Nat. Ctr. Rsch. Resources, 1999—2003. Bd. trustees Johns Hopkins U., 2000—06; bd. dir. Rosalind Franklin Soc., 2007—. With USPHS, 1967—70. Recipient Faculty Rsch. award, Am. Cancer Soc., 1975—76, Disting. Svc. award, Nat. Bd. Med. Examiners, 1995; named Disting. Svc. Mem., Assn. Am. Med. Coll., 2003; grantee Am. Cancer Soc., 1970—72, NIH, 1970—76, 1980—2005, NSF, 1973—75, 1979—80; fellow Shell Oil, 1963—64; Fogarty Sr. Internat. Fellowship, 1982—83. Fellow: AAAS; mem.: NAS, Inst. Medicine of NAS, Internat. Union Microbiol. Socs. (v.p. 1990—94), Soc. Pediatric Rsch., Soc. Gen. Microbiology, Am. Soc. Virology (pres. 1988—89), Assn. Med. Sch. Microbiology Chairmen (chmn. com. pub. policy 1979, counselor 1980—83, pres. 1985), Am. Soc. Microbiology (chair Public and Scientific Affairs Bd. 1990—96, pres. 1996—97), Am. Soc. Biol. Chemists, Am. Acad. Microbiology (bd. govs. 2003—), Alpha Omega Alpha, Sigma Xi, Phi Beta Kappa. Office: Univ Fla Coll of Medicine PO Box 103610 Gainesville FL 32610-3610 Office Phone: 352-273-8100. Business E-Mail: kberns@ufl.edu.

BERNS, SVETLANA ALEXANDROVNA, cardiologist, educator; b. Russia, May 19, 1969; MD, Kemerovo Med. Acad., 1993. Prof. Kemerovo Med. Acad., 2005, Moscow Stomatology U., 2010—; head dep., rsch. inst. Rsch. Inst. Integrated Problem Cardiovasc. Diseases RAMS Siberian Br., 2006—10. Mem.: European Assn. Percutaneous Cardiovasc. Interventions, Heart Failure Assn., ECS. Home: Denisa Davidova Moscow Moscow Region 121293 Russia Personal E-mail: svberns@yandex.ru.

BERNSON, MARCELLA S., psychiatrist; b. NYC, Aug. 24, 1952; d. Maxwell Isaac and Priscilla Edith (Zuckerman) Bernson; m. Robert A. Foster, Aug. 7, 2001. BA in Biology summa cum laude, Hofstra U., 1973; MD, Albert Einstein Coll. Medicine, 1976. Diplomate Am. Bd.

Psychiatry and Neurology. Resident in psychiatry Bronx (N.Y.) Mcpl. Hosp. Ctr., 1976—79; assoc. dir. med. student edn. in psychiatry U. Medicine and Dentistry N.J.-N.J. Med. Sch., Newark, 1979—81; pvt. practice psychiatry Westfield, NJ, 1981—86; cons. psychiatrist Healthwise EAP, Elizabeth, NJ, 1985—86; staff psychiatrist Elizabeth Gen. Med. Ctr., 1985—88, 1992—95, med. chief adult ambulatory svcs. dept. psychiatry, 1986—87, asst. dir. dept. psychiatry, 1987—88; dir. tng. psychiat. svc. VA Med. Ctr., East Orange, NJ, 1988—89; med. dir. partial care Occupl. Ctr. Union County, Roselle, NJ, 1989—92; cons. psychiatrist Union County Ednl. Svcs. Commn., Westfield, 1992—95; med. dir. Richard Hall CMHC, Bridgewater, NJ, 1995—99, staff psychiatrist, 2003—; with devel. disabilities ctr. Morristown (N.J.) Meml. Hosp., 1999—2003. Instr. U. Medicine and Dentistry N.J.-N.J. Med. Sch., Newark, 1979—81, asst. prof. clin. psychiatry, 1988—89; mem. human rights com. Divsn. Devel. Disabilities, State of N.J. Mem.: N.J. Psychiat. Assn. (Union County rep. 1989—90, Morris County rep. 2000—02), Am. Psychiat. Assn. Avocation: short fiction. Office: Richard Hall CMHC 500 N Bridge St Bridgewater NJ 08807

BERNSTEIN, ALAN, research scientist, global scientific organization executive; PhD in Med. Biophysics, U. Toronto, 1972. Post doc Imperial Cancer Rsch. Fund Lab., London, 1972—74; mem. staff Ontario Cancer Inst., Canada, 1974—85; from mem. staff to prof. U. Toronto, 1974—84, prof. molecular & med. genetics Canada, 1984—; head molecular & develop. biology, Samuel Lunenfeld Rsch. Inst. Mount Sinai Hosp., 1985—88, assoc. dir., 1988—94, dir., 1994—2002; founding pres. Canadian Inst. Health Rsch., Ottawa, Ontario, Canada, 2002—07; inaugural exec. dir. Global HIV Vaccine Enterprise, NYC, 2007—. Anne Tanenbaum chair in molecular and develop. biology Lunenfeld Inst., 1990—2000; mem. scientific bd. Grand Challenge in Global Health; cons. in field. Contbr. articles several articles to profl. jours; mem. editl. bd.: Science mag. Recipient Award of Excellence, Genetics Soc. Can., Robert L. Noble award, Nat. Cancer Inst. Can., McLaughlin medal, Royal Soc. Can., Henry Friesen award, Canadian Soc. Clin. Investigation and Royal Coll. Physicians and Surgeons, 2000, medal, Australian Soc. Med. Rsch., 2001, Order of Can., 2002, Merit medal, Inst. Clin. Rsch. Montreal, 2007, Wightman award, Gairdner Found., 2008. Office: Global HIV Vaccine Enterprise 200 Park Ave S Ste 1501 New York NY 10003 Office Phone: 212-461-3692.

BERNSTEIN, CAROL, molecular biologist; b. Paterson, NJ, Mar. 20, 1941; d. Benjamin and Mina (Regenbogen) Adelberg; m. Harris Bernstein, June 7, 1962; children: Beryl, Golda, Benjamin. BS in Physics, U. Chgo., 1961; MS in Biophysics, Yale U., 1964; PhD in Genetics, U. Calif.-Davis, 1967. NIH fellow zoology dept. U. Calif.-Davis, 1967—68; rsch. assoc. Dept. Microbiology to rsch. assoc. prof. U. Ariz., Tucson, 1968—2004, rsch. assoc. prof. cell biology and anatomy Coll. Medicine, 2004—. Proposal reviewer NSF, 1978—87, VA, 1983, Wellcome Trust, 2001—03, Michael Smith Found. for Health Rsch., Canada, 2003, Associazione Italiana Per La Ricerca Sul Cancro, 2003; exec. bd. Patient Quality Care Project; spkr. in field. Author (with Harris Bernstein): Aging, Sex and DNA Repair, 1991; mem. editl. bd.: Electronic Jour. Biotech.; contbr. articles to profl. jours. and encys. Panel mem. grad fellow rev. NSF, 1984—86, NAS, 1991—94, NSF, 1998, 1999, 2004. Grantee NSF, 1975—79, Nat. Found., 1975—76, NIH, 1979—81, 1982—87, 1997—, Ariz. Disease Control, 1986—89, 1991—, Vets. Affairs Merit Review, 2007—09; grant, Ariz. Biomed. Rsch. Commn., 2007—10. Mem. AAUP (pres. Ariz. state conf. 1983-86, 90-2004, 2007-08, Ariz. chpt. 1983, del. nat. coun. 1986-89, treas. nat. assembly state conf. 1990-92, designated lobbyist 1990—2007), Am. Assn. Cancer Rsch., Genetics Soc. Am., Whistleblower Week Wash. (treas. 2007-09). Democrat. Jewish. Achievements include research in molecular basis for the existence of sex, the cause of aging and the basis for high level of bile acids to lead to colon cancer; led the passage of an Arizona faculty governance law for the American Association of University Professors. Office: U Ariz Coll Med Dept Cellular Molecular Medicine Tucson AZ 85724-5044 Home: 2639 E 4th St Tucson AZ 85716-4417 Home Phone: 520-324-0275. Personal E-mail: bernstein3@earthlink.net. Business E-Mail: bernstei@u.arizona.edu.

BERNSTEIN, DAVID, gastroenterologist; b. NYC; BA, Johns Hopkins U., 1984; MD, SUNY, Stony Brook, 1988. Attending hepatology U. Miami (Fla.) Sch. Medicine, 1994-96; chief clin. gastroenterology Winthrop Univ. Hosp., Mineola, N.Y., 1996-99; chief gastroenterology North Shore Univ. Hosp. and LI Jewish Med. Ctr., Manhasset, NY, 2005—. Mem. sci. adv. bd. Am. Liver Found., N.Y.C., 1996—. Fellow ACP, Am. Coll. Gastroenterology, Am. Assn. Study of Liver Disease, Am. Gastrointestinal Assn.; mem. Am. Soc. Gastrointestinal Endoscopy, NY Gastrointestinal Assn. Office: North Shore Univ Hosp 300 Community Dr Manhasset NY 11030-3801 Fax: 516-562-2683.

BERNSTEIN, ERIC FERENC, dermatologist, educator; b. Washington, June 3, 1959; m. Mindy G. Schuster, July 21, 1991. BS summa cum laude, Duke U., 1981; MD, Yale U., 1986. Diplomate Am. Bd. Dermatology. Assoc. prof. Thomas Jefferson U., Phila., 1992—96; clin. assoc. prof. U. Pa., Phila., 1998—. Bd. dirs. Candela Laser Corp., Wayland, Mass. Med. Staff fellow, NIH, 1987—89. Fellow: Am. Acad. Dermatology (fellow 1993—2005).

BERNSTEIN, HENRY H., pediatrician, educator; b. Perth Amboy, NJ, 1954; BS in Math & Biology, Union Coll., Schenectady, NY; DO, Univ. Medicine & Dentistry NJ-Sch. Osteo. Medicine, Stratford, 1982. Diplomate Am. Bd. Pediat. Intern, resident pediat. St. Christopher's Hosp. Children, Phila., 1982—85; assoc. prof. pediat. Harvard Med. Sch.; assoc. chief divsn. gen. pediat. Children's Hosp. Boston; chief sect. gen. academic pediat. Dartmouth-Hitchcock Med. Ctr., NH, 2005—; vis. prof. pediat. Dartmouth Med. Sch. Editor Pediatrics in Practice: A Health Promotion Curriculum for Child Health Professionals, 2005; contbr. articles to profl. jours. Fellow: Am. Acad. Pediat. (com. infectious diseases). Office: Dartmouth Hitchcock Med Ctr Dept Pediat One Medical Center Dr Lebanon NH 03756 Office Phone: 603-653-9663. Office Fax: 603-650-0910. Business E-Mail: Henry.H.Bernstein@Dartmouth.edu. *

BERNSTEIN, JONATHAN ABRAM, allergist, immunologist, educator; MD, U. Cin., 1985. Diplomate Am. Bd. Internal Medicine, 1988. Resident internal medicine Cleve. Clinic, 1986—88; fellow allergy & immunology Northwestern Meml. Hosp., 1988—90; prof. clin. medicine internal medicine dept. Univ. of Cin. Med. Ctr., prof. divsn. immunology/allergy sect.; dir. Veterans Adminstrn. Hosp. Allergy Clinic and Allergy Lab.; dir. clin. rsch. immunology divsn.; hosp. affiliations include Bethesda North Hosp., Cin. Children's Hosp. Med. Ctr., Jewish Hosp., Univ. Hosp. Assoc. editor Jour. of Asthma, Jour. of Allergy and Clin. Immunology, reviewer, Annals of Allergy, Asthma and Immunology, Jour. of Asthma and Chest. Mem.: Am. Acad. of Asthma, Allergy and Immunology (vice chmn. environ. and occupl. respiratory disease interest sect.). Office: University Hospital 234 Goodman St Cincinnati OH 45219-2316 Office Phone: 513-584-1000.

BERNSTEIN, LARRY HOWARD, clinical pathologist; b. Highland Park, Mich., Dec. 28, 1941; s. David Mordecai and Lillian Cecilia (Schwartz) B.; m. Audrey Jean Mellen, Dec. 20, 1969; children: Rachel Laura, Naomi Beth. BS, Wayne State U., 1963, MS, 1966, MD, 1968. Intern pathology Kans. U. Med. Ctr., Kansas City, 1968-69; resident and fellow in pathology U. Calif.-San Diego, La Jolla, 1970-73; pathologist Armed Forces Inst. Pathology, Washington, 1973-75; asst. prof. pathology U. South Fla., Tampa, 1975-77; assoc. prof. pathology U. South Ala., Mobile, 1977-78; dir. chemistry Iowa Meth. Med. Ctr., Des Moines, 1979-80, United Health Svcs., Binghampton, N.Y., 1981-82; dir. chemistry and blood bank Bridgeport (Conn.) Hosp., 1983—. Cons. Beckman, Boehringer Mannheim, Eastman Kodak, Brea, Calif., Rochester, N.Y. and Indpls., 1985-95; Nat. Com. Clin. Lab. Scis. rev. com., Chgo., 1988-92. Contbr. articles to Nutrition, Clin. Chemistry, Cancer, Arch. Pathol. Lab. Medicine, Jour. Biol. Chemistry, Brit. Jour. Cancer, Jour. Molecular Cellular Cardiology. Bd. dir. Nat. Accrediting Agency for Clin. Laboratory Scis. Lt. cmdr. USNR. Fellow Am. Assn. Clin. Chemistry (lectr., program chmn. nat. mtgs. 1985—, Labbe-Garry award), Coll. Am. Pathologists, Am. Coll. Nutrition; mem. ASTM, Clin. Lab. Mgmt. Assn. (lectr., nat. mtgs. 1985), AHSR, others. Democrat. Jewish. Achievements include patents for lactate dehydrogenase method, malate dehydrogenase mthod; rsch. in effect of nutritional states; rsch. in determining decision values for laboratory tests using truth-table comprehension and quality management using data classification and analysis; rsch. in diagnosis of acute myocardial infarction (heart attack), and in cancer markers in serum and body fluids. Home: 232 Fitch's Pass Trumbull CT 06611-5602 Home Phone: 203-261-3655; Office Phone: 203-261-8671. Business E-Mail: plbern@yahoo.com.

BERNSTEIN, MICHAEL O., surgeon, educator; MD, Pa. State U., 1983. Diplomate Am. Bd. Surgery, Am. Bd. Surgery-surgical critical care. Resident in surgery SUNY- Kings Co. Hosp., Bklyn., 1983—88; asst. prof. surgery SUNY Downstate; surgeon Long Island Coll. Hosp. Office: Long Island College Hospital 339 Hicks St Brooklyn NY 11201 Office Phone: 718-780-1000. Office Fax: 718-780-1256.

BERNSTEIN, ROBERT M., dermatologic surgeon; b. NYC, July 13, 1952; BS in Psychology, Tulane U., New Orleans, 1973; MD, U. Medicine and Dentistry of N.J., 1978. Lic. N.Y., N.J., Calif., diplomate Nat. Bd. Med. Examiners, Am. Bd. Dermatology, Am. Bd. Hair Restoration Surgery. Resident in internal medicine U. Medicine and Dentistry of N.J., 1978—79; resident in dermatology Albert Einstein Coll. Medicine, NYC, 1979—81, chief resident in dermatology, 1981—82; pvt. practice dermatology, 1982—95; pvt. practice hair restoration surgery NYC, 1995—; founder Bernstein Med.-Ctr. Hair Restoration, 2005—. Asst. in clin. dermatology Coll. Physicians and Surgeons, Columbia U., NYC, 1982—85, instr. clin. dermatology, 1985—90, assoc. in clin. dermatology, 1990—95, asst. clin. prof. dermatology, 1995—2000, assoc. clin. prof. dermatology, 2000—; asst. attending dermatologist Manhattan Eye, Ear and Throat Hosp., NYC, 1982—2000; attending, dept. dermatology Englewood Hosp., NJ, 1982—, pharmacy and therapeutics com., NJ, 1982—88, chmn. quality assurance and compliance com., dept. dermatology, NJ, 1990—94; asst. dermatologist Presbyn. Hosp., NYC, 1982—90, assoc. dermatologist, 1990—96; asst. attending dermatology svc. N.Y. Presbyn. Hosp., 1996—2000, assoc. attending dermatology svc., 2000—; examiner Am. Bd. Hair Restoration Surgery, 2000—; mem. Almay Stress Info. coun. Almay Cosmetics, NYC, 1990—92, mem. Almay Health Watch Coun. adv. bd., 1992—96; evaluation com. World Hair Soc., Scientific Workshop, Orlando, Fla., 1999—2000; lectr. in field. Contbg. editor: Dermatologic Surgery, 1998—, Jour. Aesthetic Dermatology and Cosmetic Dermatologic Surgery, 1998—2000; contbr. articles, editorial reviews, book and textbook chapters; guest appearances ABC, CBS, and Fox 5 News, featured on Good Morning America, The Discovery Channel. Recipient Continuing Med. Edn. award, Am. Acad. Dermatology, 1982—99, Platinum Follicle award for Outstanding Achievement in Scientific and Clin. Rsch. in Hair Restoration, Internat. Soc. of Hair Restoration Surgery, 2001; named Surgeon of the Month, Hair Transplant Forum Internat., The Best Doctors in NY, 2000, 2001, Top Doctors: NY Metro Area, 2001, America's Top Doctors 2001-Surgical Hair Restoration; Tulane Scholar. Fellow: Am. Acad. Dermatology; mem.: Am. Hair Loss Coun., Am. Soc. for Dermatologic Surgery, Am. Acad. Aesthetic and Restorative Surgery, World Soc. of Hair Restoration Surgeons, North Jersey Dermatologic Soc., N.Am. Acad. Cosmetic and Restorative Surgery, Internat. Soc. Hair Restoration Surgery (mem. scientific and edn. com. 1999—2001, mem. certification com. 2002, ad hoc preceptorship com. 2001), Am. Laser Medicine and Surgery, Am. Soc. Hair Restoration Surgery, Am. Acad. Cosmetic Surgery (mem. Am. hair loss coun.). Address: 2150 Center Ave Fort Lee NJ 07024 Office: Bernstein Medical 110 E 55TH ST FL 11 New York NY 10022-4551 Office Phone: 212-826-2400, 201-585-1115. Office Fax: 201-585-0464. Business E-Mail: contact@bernsteinmedical.com.

BERNSTEIN, SOL, cardiologist, educator; b. West New York, NJ, Feb. 3, 1927; s. Morris Irving and Rose (Leibowitz) B.; m. Suzi Maris Sommer, Sept. 15, 1963; 1 son, Paul. AB in Bacteriology, U. So. Calif., 1952, MD, 1956. Diplomate Am. Bd. Internal Medicine. Intern Los Angeles County Hosp., 1956-57, resident, 1957-60; practice medicine specializing in cardiology LA, 1960—; staff physician dept. medicine Los Angeles County Hosp./U. So. Calif. Med. Ctr., LA, 1960—, chief cardiology clinics, 1964, asst. dir. dept. medicine, 1965-72, med. dir., 1974-94; med. dir. central region Los Angeles County, 1974-78; dir. Dept. Health Svcs., Los Angeles County, 1978; assoc. dean Sch. Medicine, U. So. Calif., LA, 1986-94, assoc. prof., 1968—; med. dir. Health Rsch. Assn., LA, 1995—2005. Cons. Crippled Childrens Svc. Calif., 1965—. Contbr. articles on cardiac surgery, cardiology, diabetes and health care planning to med. jours. Served with AUS, 1946-47, 52-53. Fellow ACP, Am. Coll. Cardiology; mem. Am. Acad. Phys. Execs., Am. Fedn. Clin. Research, NY Acad. Sci., Am. Heart Assn., LA Soc. Internal Medicine, LA Acad. Medicine, Sigma Xi, Phi Beta Kappa, Phi Eta Sigma, Alpha Omega Alpha. Home: 4966 Ambrose Ave Los Angeles CA 90027-1756 Home Phone: 323-666-8547. Business E-Mail: sol@hsc.usc.edu.

BERNTHAL, HAROLD GEORGE, health products executive, director; b. Frankenmuth, Mich., June 11, 1928; s. Wilfred Michael and Olga Bertha (Stern) B.; m. Margaret Hrebek, Jan. 25, 1958; children: Barbara Anne, Karen Elizabeth, James Willard. BS in Chemistry, Mich. State U., 1950. Pres. Am. Hosp. Supply Corp., Evanston, Ill., 1974-85; chmn. Cobern Inc., Lake Forest, Ill., 1986—. Life trustee Northwestern Meml. Hosp., Chgo.; hon. bd. dirs. Valparaiso (Ind.) U.; former chair Wheat Ridge Ministries; former governing mem. Chgo. Symphony Orch. Served with AUS, 1950-52. Recipient Lumen Christi medal Valparaiso U., 1988. Mem. Health Industries Assn. (past pres.), Health Industry Mfr.'s Assn. (past mem. exec. com.), Pharm. Mfrs. Assn. (past chmn. med. device com., Knollwood Club, Old Elm Club, The Reserve, Bigfoot Country Club.

BERNTORP, KERSTIN ELISABETH, endocrinologist, educator; b. Malmö, June 15, 1950; MD, Lund U., 1976, PhD, 1987. Head physician, assoc. prof. Dept. Endocrinology, 1994—. Mem.: IDF, EASD. Avocation: sailing. Home: Krankajen 6 Malmö Skåne 21112 Sweden Personal E-mail: kerstin.berntorp@med.lu.se.

BERNTSON, GARY GLEN, psychiatry, psychology and pediatrics educator; b. Mpls., June 16, 1945; s. Edward Mathias and Meryle Berntson; m. Susan Berntson, July 11, 2002. BA, U. Minn., 1968, PhD, 1971. Postdoctoral fellow Rockefeller U., NYC, 1971-73; asst. prof. dept. psychology Ohio State U., Columbus, 1973-77, assoc. prof., 1977-81, prof., 1981—, prof. dept. pediatrics, 1983—, prof. of psychiatry, 1988—. Affiliate scientist Yerkes Regional Primate Rsch. Ctr., Emory U., Atlanta, 1984-95; mem. initial rev. group ADAMHA, Washington, 1989-91, NIMH, Washington, 1991-93, NIH, 2004—; mem. fellowship rev. panel NSF, Washington, 1991-95. Contbr. over 150 articles to profl. jours., 20 chpts. to books; co-editor: Handbook of Psychophysiology. Fellow NSF, 1969, USPHS, 1972. Mem. Soc. for Neurosci., Soc. for Psychophysiol. Rsch. (pres. 2010-11); fellow AAAS. Achievements include novel concepts of control of the autonomic nervous system and psychosomatic relations. Office: Ohio State U Dept Psychology 1835 Neil Ave Columbus OH 43210-1222 Office Phone: 614-292-1749. *

BERNTSSON, MATILDA, dermatologist; b. Gothenburg, Sept. 13, 1968; MD, Gothenburg U., 1995, PhD, 2011. Physician Frölunda Specialistsjukhus, Dermatovenereological Dep, 2008—. Head Venereological Clinic, Sahlgrenska U. Hosp., 2005—08. Contbr. articles to sci. profl. jours. Office: Hudmottagningen Frölunda Specialistsju V Frolunda Gothenburg 42122 Sweden Business E-Mail: matilda.berntsson@vgregion.se.

BERRETTINI, STEFANO, otolaryngologist, educator; b. Lucca, June 21, 1956; Degree, U. Pisa, 1982. ENT specialist U. Pisa, 1985. Assoc. prof., otolaryngology U. Pisa, 1985—. Office: Via Paradisa 2 Pisa 56124 Italy Office Fax: 39050997495. Business E-Mail: s.berrettini@med.unipi.it.

BERRIDGE, SIR MICHAEL JOHN, cell biologist; b. Gatooma, Zimbabwe, Oct. 22, 1938; s. George Kirton Berridge and Stella Elaine Hards; m. Susan Graham Winter, 1965; 2 children. BSc in Zoology and Chemistry, U. Rhodesia & Nyasaland, Salisbury, Zimbabwe, 1960; PhD, U. Cambridge, Eng., 1965. Postdoc. fellow U. Va., 1965-66, Case Western Reserve U., Cleve., 1966-69; prof. dept. zoology U. Cambridge, 1969—90; dep. chief sci. officer, head cell signalling Babraham Inst., Cambridge, 1987—2003, emeritus Babraham fellow, 2003—. Recipient Feldberg prize, 1984, King Faisal Found. Internat. prize for sci., 1986, Louis Jeantet Found. prize for medicine, 1986, Gairdner Found. Internat. award, 1988, Albert Lasker award for basic med. rsch., 1989, Dr. H.P. Heineken prize for biochem. & biophysics, Royal Netherlands Acad. Arts & Scis., 1994, Ernst Schering prize, 1999, Shaw prize in life sci. & medicine, 2005; co-recipient Wolf Found. prize in medicine, Israel, 1995. Fellow: Royal Soc., Am. Physiological Soc. (hon.), Japanese Biochem. Soc. (hon.), Soc. Exptl. Biology (hon.), Biochem. Soc. (hon.); mem.: NAS, Acad. Med. Scis. (founding mem.), European Molecular Biology Orgn. Avocations: golf, gardening. Office: Babraham Inst Lab Molecular Signalling CB2 4AT Cambridge England E-mail: michael.berridge@bbsrc.ac.uk.

BERRY, GAIL W., psychiatrist, educator; b. Kalamazoo, Nov. 7, 1939; BA, Kalamazoo Coll., 1960; MD, NYU, 1964; cert. in psychoanalysis, N.Y. Med. Coll., 1976. Lic. Am. Bd. Psychiatry and Neurology. Clin. instr. psychiatry Mt. Sinai Sch. Medicine, NYC, 1969—76, asst. clin. prof. psychiatry, 1976—2008; tng. and supervising psychoanalyst Psychoanalytic Inst. N.Y. Med. Coll., Valhalla, NY, 1980—; assoc. attending psychiatrist Mt. Sinai Hosp., NYC, 1981—2008. Adj. prof. psychiatry N.Y. Med. Coll., Valhalla, 1984—. Fellow: Am. Psychiat. Assn. (life; disting.); mem.: Am. Acad. Psychoanalysis (asst. editor jour. 1984—2002), Am. Acad. Psychoanalysis and Dynamic Psychiatry (consulting editor jour. 2002—11, editl. bd. mem. 2011—).

BERRY, SHARON, medical/surgical nurse, legal nurse consultant; b. Manila, Philippines, Nov. 22, 1973; d. Reynaldo and Henrietta Dingcong; m. Jason Brad Berry, Apr. 10, 2000; children: Jake Ryan, Harley Lynn. ADN, No. Va. C.C., 1998. RN Commonwealth Va. Bd. Nursing, 1998. Nurse Sibley Meml. Hosp., Washington, 1998—99; travel nurse post-partum unit CrosscountryTravcorps, Boca Raton, Fla., 1999—2005; nurse post-partum, gynecology unit Meml. Med. Ctr., New Orleans, 1999—2001, nurse labor and delivery, 2001—03; nurse ICU Ochsner Clinic Found., 2003—05; nurse home health INOVA VNA Home Health, Springfield, Va., 2005—. Legal nurse cons. pvt. practice, Springfield, 2005—. Mem.: Am. Assn. Legal Nurse Cons., Am. Assn. Critical Nurses, Assn. Women's Health, Obs., and Neonatal Nurses. Avocations: violin, hiking, camping. Personal E-mail: sberry12002@yahoo.com.

BERS, DONALD MARTIN, physiology educator; b. NYC, Dec. 13, 1953; s. Harold Theodore and Penny (Wall) B.; m. Kathryn Eileen Hammond, July 17, 1976; children: Brian Alexander, Rebecca Ann. BA, U. Colo., 1974; PhD, UCLA, 1978. Postdoctoral research fellow UCLA, 1978-79, asst. research physiologist, 1980-82, adj. asst. prof., 1981-87; postdoctoral research fellow Edinburgh (Scotland) U., 1979-80; asst. prof. U. Calif., Riverside, 1982-86, assoc. prof., 1986-89, prof., 1989-92, divisional dean, dir. biomed. scis. program, 1991-92; prof., chmn. dept. physiology Loyola U., Chgo., 1992—. Author: Excitation-Contraction Coupling and Cardiac Contractile Force, 1991, 2001; assoc. editor News in Physiol. Sci.; mem. editl. bd. Am. Jour. Physiology, Circulation Rsch., Jour. Pharm. and Exptl. Therapeutics, Jour. Molecular Cell Cardiology; contbr. articles to profl. jours. Bd. dirs. Am. Heart Assn., Riverside, 1985-92, pres., 1989-91. Fellow Am. Heart Assn., L.A., 1978-80, Brit.-Am., Am. Heart Assn., 1980-81; recipient New Investigator Rsch. award NIH, 1982-85, Rsch. Career Devel. award NIH, 1985-90. Fellow: Internat. Soc. Heart Rsch. (mem. coun.), Am. Heart Assn.; mem.: AAAS, Biophys. Soc. (mem. coun., mem. exec. bd.), Am. Physiol. Soc., Soc. Gen. Physiology. Office: Univ Calif Davis Dept Pharmacology Genome Bldg Rm 3513 Davis CA 95616

BERSCHEID, ELLEN S., psychology professor, writer, researcher; b. Colfax, Wis., Oct. 11, 1936; d. Sylvan L. and Alvilde (Running) Saumer; m. Dewey Mathias Berscheid, Nov. 21, 1959. BA, U. Nev., 1959, MA, 1960; PhD, U. Minn., 1965. Market rsch. analyst Pillsbury Co., Mpls., 1960-62; asst. prof. psychology and mktg. U. Minn., Mpls., 1965-66, asst. prof. psychology, 1967-68, assoc. prof., 1969-71, prof., 1971-88, Regents' prof. psychology, 1988—2010, Regents' prof. psychology emeritus, 2010—. Mem. NRC Assembly Behavioral and Social Scis., 1973-77. Co-author: Interpersonal Attraction, 1969, 78, Equity: Theory and Research, 1978, Close Relationships, 1983, Psychology of Interpersonal Relationships, 2005, also numerous articles; mem. numerous editl. bds., past editorships. Recipient Disting. Scientist award Soc. Exptl. Social Psychology, 1993. Fellow APA (Donald T. Campbell award 1984, editor Contemporary Psychology Jour. 1985-91, Disting. Sci. Contbn. award 1997, Presdl. Citation 2003), Soc. Personality and Social Psychology (pres. 1985), Soc. for Psychol. Study Social Issues, Am. Acad. Arts and Scis.; mem. Internat. Soc. for the Study Personal Relationships (pres. 1990-92), Soc. Exptl. Social Psychology (exec. bd. 1971-74, 77-80, 85-89, Disting. Scientist award 1993). Lutheran. Avocation: interior design. Home: 329 Park Cir Menomonie WI 54751 Office: U Minn Dept Psychology N309 Elliott Hall Minneapolis MN 55455 Business E-Mail: bersc001@umn.edu.

BERSON, ELIOT LAWRENCE, ophthalmologist, medical educator; b. Boston, Mass., 1937; MD, Harvard U., 1962. Intern Calif. Hosp., San Francisco, 1962-63; resident in ophthalmology Barnes and McMillan Hosps., St. Louis, 1963-66; clin. assoc. ophthalmologist Nat. Inst. Neurol. Diseases and Blindness, Bethesda, Md., 1966-68; asst. Mass. Eye and Ear Infirmary, Boston, 1968-73, asst. surgeon, 1974-78, dir. Berman-Gund Lab. for Study of Retinal Degenerations, Harvard Med. Sch., 1974—, assoc. surgeon in ophthalmology, 1979-84, surgeon in ophthalmology, 1984—. Instr. Harvard U. Sch. Medicine, Boston, 1968-70, asst. prof., 1971-76, assoc. prof. ophthalmology, 1976-82, Chatlos prof. ophthalmology, 1982—. Surgeon USPHS, 1966-68. Mem. AMA, Assn. for Rsch. in Vision and Ophthalmology, Am. Acad. Ophthalmology, Am. Ophthal. Soc. Office: Berman-Gund Lab Mass Eye and Ear Infirmary 243 Charles St Boston MA 02114-3002

BERTAGNOLI, RUDOLF, spine surgeon; b. St. Pölten, Austria, Apr. 19, 1957; s. Rudolf Bertagnoli and Berta Harrer; m. Christina Bertagnoli, Jan. 28, 1987; children: Adrian, Laura. MD, U. Vienna, Austria. Dr. W. Firbas prof. Inst. of Anatomy, U. Vienna, 1984—85; Dr. J. Poigenfürst prof. Emergency Hosp. Lorenz Böhler, Vienna, 1985; Dr. R. Streli primary dir. Emergency Hosp. Linz, Linz, Austria, 1985—86; Dr. K. Zielke dir. German Ctr. of Spine Surgery, Bad Wildungen, Germany, 1986—89; Dr. H.G. Willert prof. dir. asst. prof., chief spinal dept. Orthop. Univ. Hosp., Georg Aug. U. Göttingen, Germany, 1989—94; chief spine dept. Klinikum St. Elisabeth, Straubing, Germany, 1994—2010; chief St. Wolfgang Spine Ctr., St. Wolfgang Klinik, Bad Griesbach, Germany, 1994—; chief Spine Ctr. Johannesbadklinik, Bad Füssing, Germany, 1994—, Pro Spine, Bogen, Germany; CEO First European Ctr. Spine Arthroplasty and Associated Non Fusion Techs.; prof. U. Pitesti, 2010. Adv. bd. Spine Solutions Inc., New York, Sp Iii, I.S.T., NuVasive Inc., San Diego; bd. dirs. Spinemark. Author (with others): (book) El dolor de espalda, 1996; author: Technique, Indications and Results of L5-S1 Arthrodeses Using Carbon Cages, 1999, Review of Modern Treatment Options for Degenerative Disc Disease, 2002, Interbody Carbon Fiber, 2003; author: (with others) Total Disc Replacement for degenerative disc disease in the lumbar spine, 2003, Minimally Invasive Spine Surgery, 2d edit., 2005, Dynamic Reconstruction of the Spine, 2005; author: Motion Preservation Surgery of the Spine, 2008; author: (editor) Bewegungserhaltende Wirbelsäulenchirurgie; contbr. articles to profl. jours.; author: (film) Anterolateral Transpsoatic Approach for the Prosthetic Disc Nucleus Replacement (ALPA)., PRODISC: Total Disc Replacement., Progress in Spinal Fixation. International Symposium with Live Surgery. Bern, Switzerland, 21-22.06.2002. Recipient Cert., Cleve. Spine and Arthritis Ctr., Luth. Med. Ctr., 1991, Isola Systems, 1992, Barrow Neurol. Inst., 2002, Med. Edn. Activity Course, 2002, Cert. for outstanding and impressive lecture, Hirosaki U. Sch. of Medicine, Japan, 1995, Prize for best lecture, 1st Internat. Symposium on Prosthetic Disc Nucleus, Jeddah, Saudi Arabia, 2000, Physician's Recognition award, AMA, 2000, Cert. of Achievement award, Surgeon Edn. Program Bordeaux, 2001, Acknowledgement of gt. contbn., Internat. Spine Course Davos, Switzerland, 2001, Lyman-Smith award for Best Presentation, Williamsburg, Va., 2000. Mem.: Berufsverband der Fachärzte für Orthopädie e.v., Deutscher Orthopäden-Verband, Soc. Nuc. Arthroplasty, AO Spine Internat., Spine Soc. Europe, North Am. Spine Soc., Internat. Meeting on Advanced Spine Techniques, Groupe Internat. Cotrel-Dubousset, Deutschen Wirbelsäulengesell Schaft, Spine Evolution Nucleus Europe (pres.), Internat. Soc. for Minimal Intervention in Spinal Surgery, Spine Arthroplasty Soc. (founding mem., past pres). Achievements include patents for fixedly adjustable intervertebral prosthesis; patents in field. Avocations: golf, horse back riding, skiing, motorsports. Office: Med Consulting Kay 2a Straubing 94315 Germany Business E-Mail: bertagnoli@pro-spine.com.

BERTARELLI, ERNESTO, corporate financial executive, yachtsman; b. Sept. 22, 1965; s. Fabio Bertarelli; married; 2 children. BS, Babson Coll.; MBA, Harvard U. Joined Serono SA, 1985, dep. CEO, 1991—95, CEO, chmn. exec. com. Geneva, 1996—2006, vice chmn. bd. dirs., 1991—2006. Bd. dirs. UBS AG, Switzerland, 2002—, PHARMA, United States, BIO, United States; founder, navigator, pres. Team Alinghi, 2000—. Co-founder, bd. dir. Bertarelli Found., 1999—; mem. adv. coun. Harvard Med. Sch. Biol. Chemistry and Molecular Pharmacology. Recipient Bol d'Or Lake Geneva, 1997, 2000, 2001, 2002, 2003, Sardinia Cup, 1998, 12M JI World Championship, South Australia, Team Alinghi, 2001, Farr 40, Team Alinghi, 2001, Swedish Match Cup Marstrand, 2002, Am. Cup, Team Alinghi, 2003, Louis Vuitton Cup, Team Alinghi, 2003; named one of World's Richest People, Forbes Mag., 1999—. Avocations: sailing, running, skiing, squash. Office: UBS AG Bahnhofstr 45 Po Box 8098 Zurich Switzerland

BERTAZZONI MINELLI, ELISA, pharmacologist, educator; b. Mantova, Italy, Dec. 18, 1945; Degree in Pharmacy, U. Bologna, Italy, 1968. Asst. prof., Inst. Pharmacology Med. Sch., U. Padova, 1970—72, asst. prof. toxicology, 1972—73, asst. prof. chemotherapy, U. Verona, Med. Sch., Italy, 1973—81, assoc. prof. chemotherapy, 1982—85, prof. pharmacology, chemotherapy, 1986—, dir., cert. lab. UNI EN, 2010—. Mem. pharmacological-toxicological adv. group Hosp. Verona, 1973—77; mem., bioethical com. Ordine dei Medici e Chirurghi di Verona, 2000—; expert referee, nat. ednl. courses in medicine Ministry of Health, 2002—; ofcl. expert evaluator, internat. projects European Cmty., 2004—11. Recipient award, Academic Autorities U. Padova Operosità Scientifica. Mem.: Italian Coll. U. Pharmacologists, European Soc. Clin. Microbiology and Infectious Diseases, Italian Pharmacological Soc., Italian Soc. Chemotherapy (exec. com. v.p.), Soc. Microbial Ecology and Disease (exec. bd. councillor). Avocations: travel, art. Office: Policlinico GB Rossi Piazza Ludovic Scuro Verona 37134 Italy Office Fax: 39 045 8027452. Business E-Mail: elisa.bertazzoni@univr.it.

BERTH-JONES, JOHN, consultant dermatologist, educator; b. London, Oct. 23, 1955; s. Harold Berth-Jones and Elizabeth Beesley. MB, BS, St. Bartholomews Hosp. Med. Sch., 1979. Sr. house officer in dermatology Univ. Hosp. Wales, Cardiff, 1986-87; registrar in dermatology Leicester Royal Infirmary, 1987-89, rsch. fellow in dermatology, 1989-91; sr. registrar in dermatology Leicestershire Hosps., 1991-94; cons. in dermatology Walsgrave Hosp., Coventry, 1994—. Editor: Treatment of Skin Disease Comprehensive Therapeutic Strategies 3rd edit., 2010; past editor Clin. and Exptl. Dermatology; contbr. articles on dermatology, atopic dermatitis and psoriasis to med. jours Surg. lt. comdr. Royal Navy, 1979-86. Fellow Royal Coll. Physicians, Brit. Assn. Dermatologists, European Acad. Dermatology and Venereology, Am. Acad. Dermatology. Office: Walsgrave Hosp Dept Dermatology Coventry CV2 2DX England Personal E-mail: johnberthjones@aol.com.

BERTHOUX, FRANCOIS CLAUDE, nephrologist; b. Mervans, Saône et Loire, Jan. 19, 1942; MD, U. Lyon, 1971. Prof., nephrology head dept. U. Hosp., St. Etienne, 1976—2008, sr. cons. nephrology dept., prof. nephrology, 2008. Recipient Palmes Académiques award, French Pub. Recognition. Mem.: Am. Soc. Nephrology, European Renal Assn., Internat. Soc. Nephrology, Internat. Soc. Transplantation. Avocations: reading, crafts, walking. Home: 27 Rue Max de Saint-Genest Veauche Loire 42340 France Personal E-mail: francois.berthoux@wanadoo.fr.

BERTI, GIOVANNI, diagnostics company executive; b. Marsciano, Perugia, Italy, Sept. 18, 1935; s. Ercole and Sofia (Bianconi) B.; m. Serenella di Marsciano, Dec. 11, 1965 (dec. 1991); children: Daniele, Lucia. D, U. Bologna, Italy, 1959. Cert. indsl. chemist. Mgr. Montedison Spa., Terni, Italy, 1960-70; exec. Bayer Diagnostici Spa., Cavenago Brianza, Italy, 1970-93, ret., 1994. Contbr. articles to profl. jours. Mem. Am. Assn. Clin. Chemistry, Internat. Soc. Clin. Enzymology, Royal Soc. Chemistry, N.Y. Acad. Scis. Roman Catholic. Achievements include patents in field. Home: Via Provinciale 34 23864 Malgrate LC Italy

BERTI, PHYLLIS MAE, retired health information management specialist; b. Blue Island, Ill., Jan. 27, 1941; d. Louis J. and Helen Beatrice (Smola) Hankus; m. Jerome Leon Berti, May 27, 1967; children: James Louis, Jeffrey Jerome, Joseph Gregory, Cynthia Ann. AS Health Info. Mgmt., Stark Tech. Coll., 1992. Claims processor Mass. Mut. Ins. Co., Hazel Crest, Ill., 1981—84; physician billing rep. Ingalls Meml. Hosp., Harvey, Ill., 1984—87; coder, abstractor Timken Mercy Med. Ctr., Canton, Ohio, 1987—89, Wooster Cmty. Hosp., Ohio, 1989—92; coord. clin. records Quest Recovery Svcs., Canton, 1992—93; health info. mgmt. specialist So. Health Care Ctr., Southaven, Miss., 1994—99, Bapt. Progressive Care Ctr., Southaven, 1999—2002, cons., 2002—03; mgr. health info. mgmt. Brookewood Nursing Ctr., De Queen, Ark., 2003—08, cons., 2008—. Mem.: Ark. Health Info. Mgmt. Assn., Am. Health Info. Mgmt. Assn. (long term care sect., registered health info. technician). Avocations: crafts, gardening, fishing, swimming, boating. Home: 111 Country Club Estates De Queen AR 71832

BERTINI, LUCA, radiologist; b. Rome, Dec. 29, 1975; Degree in Medicine, U. Sapienza Rome, 2000, degree in Radiology, 2004. Radiologist Umberto I Hosp. Rome, 2005—. Avocations: fishing, running. Office: Vle del Policlinico 155 Rome 00160 Italy Business E-Mail: l.bertini@tiscali.it.

BERTLES, JOHN FRANCIS, physician, educator; b. Spokane, Wash., June 8, 1925; s. John Francis and Henrita Swart (Brown) B.; m. Jeannette Winans, 1948 (div. 1978); children: Mark Dwight, Jacquelyn Eve, John Francis; m. Lila Rodriguez, 1981. BS, Yale U., 1945; MD, Harvard U., 1952. Diplomate Am. Bd. Internal Medicine. Intern Presbyterian Hosp., NYC, 1952-53, asst. resident in medicine, 1953-55; research fellow in hematology U. Rochester and Strong Meml. Hosp., 1955-56; research fellow in immunohematology Harvard U. Med. Sch. and Mass. Gen. Hosp., Boston, 1956-58, research fellow in hematology, 1958-59; instr. in medicine Harvard U. Med. Sch. at Mass. Gen. Hosp., 1959-61; dir. hematology-oncology div. St. Luke's Hosp. Center, NYC, 1962-95, asst. attending physician, 1962-64, assoc. attending physician, 1964-71, attending physician, 1971-95; dir. transfusion services St. Luke's Roosevelt Hosp. Ctr., 1981-95; sr. research asso. dept. biol. scis. Columbia U., 1970-71, asst. clin. prof. medicine, 1962-67, assoc. clin. prof., 1967-71, assoc. prof., 1971-74, prof., 1974-95, prof. emeritus of medicine, 1995—; attending physician Montefiore Med. Ctr., NYC, 1995-97; clin. prof. medicine Albert Einstein Coll. Medicine, NYC, 1995-97. Vis. prof. medicine Nuffield dept. clin. medicine Radcliffe Infirmary, U. Oxford, Eng., 1977-78; cons. to various govt. agys., including hematology study sect. NIH, 1972-76, 82-84, blood rsch. rev. group, 1978-82; mem. dirs. coun. N.Y. Heart Assn., 1974-90; mem. basic rsch. adv. com. Nat. Found. March of Dimes, 1977-80. Contbr. articles to profl. publs. Ensign USNR, 1945-46. Fellow ACP; mem. Am. Soc. Clin. Investigation, Am. Physiol. Soc., Am. Soc. Hematology, Am. Fedn. Clin. Rsch., Am. Chem. Soc., Alpha Omega Alpha. Office: 72 Pondfield Rd W Apt 3K Bronxville NY 10708

BERTOL, LICIANE SABADIN, research scientist; b. Passo Fundo, Passo Fundo, Dec. 6, 1982; Degree in Engring., Fed. U. Rio Grande do Sul, Brazil, 2005, MSc, 2008. Rsch. scientist Laboratório Design Seleção Materiais, 2005—. Cons. Promm Indústria Materiais Cirúrgicos Ltda, 2006; mem. bd. dirs. Jahr Bioceramicas, 2009, Jomon Ceramicas Avançadas, 2010; rsch. scientist Lehrstuhl Konstruktionstechnik/CAD Tech. U. Dresden, 2010—11. Avocations: movies, sports. Home: Rua Felipe de Oliveira 842/204 Porto Alegre Rio Grande do Sul 90630000 Brazil

BERTOLINI, MARK T., insurance company executive; b. 1956; BS in Bus. Adminstrn., Wayne State U.; MBA in Fin., Cornell U. CEO, previously COO SelectCare, 1992—95; exec. v.p. NYLCare Health Plans; sr. v.p., nat. sales & delivery Cigna Corp., 2000—02, sr. v.p., regional & middle market, 2002—03; sr. v.p., splty. products Aetna, Inc., Hartford, Conn., 2003—05, sr. v.p. specialty group, 2005, sr. v.p. regional bus., 2005—06, exec. v.p. regional bus., 2006—07, exec. v.p. bus. ops., 2007, pres., 2007—10, pres., CEO, 2010—11, chmn., pres., CEO, 2011—. Bd. dirs. Aetna Inc., 2010—. Bd. dirs. U. Conn. Health Ctr., Conn. Bus. & Ind. Assn.; chmn. ops. com. Assn. Health Ins. Plans; mem. advisory bd. Cornell U. Sch. Human Ecology. Office: Aetna Inc 151 Farmington Ave Hartford CT 06156 *

BERTOLONE, SALVATORE J., pediatric medicine educator; b. Bronx, NY, July 31, 1944; BS in Biology, Fordham U., 1966; MD, U. Louisville, 1970. Med. lic., Ky.; cert. Am. Bd. Pediatrics, Supspecialty Bd. Pediatric Hematology/Oncology. Pediatric intern U. Louisville (Ky.) Sch. Medicine, 1970-71, pediatric resident, 1971-72; fellow dept. pediatrics U. Colo., Denver, 1972-74; asst. clin. prof., dept. pediatrics, dept. neurosurgery U. Colo., Sch. Medicine, Denver, 1974-76; asst. prof. pediatrics, dept. pediatrics U. Louisville (Ky.) Sch. Medicine, 1976-82; assoc. in oncology U. Louisville (Ky.), James Graham Brown Cancer Ctr., 1977; assoc. prof. pediatrics, dept. pediatrics U. Louisville (Ky.) Sch. Medicine, 1982-92, prof. pediatrics, dept. pediatrics, 1992—, dir. pediatric Hematology, Oncology, 1998—. Cons. Crippled Children's Svcs., State of Ky., 1976—, State of Ind., 1976, Hemophilia Clinic, Kosair Children's Hosp., Louisville, 1979—, Dept. Pediat. Ireland Army Hosp., Fort Knox, Ky., 1979—, Jefferson County Dept. Health, Lead Poisoning Program, Louisville, 1983—; founder, bd. dirs. Pediat. Hospice Louisville, 1979—, med. dir., 1979-84; com. mem. U. Louisville Sch. Medicine and Kosair Children's Hosp., others; asst. chief pediat. clinic Fitzsimons Army Med. Ctr., Denver, 1974-76, chief pediatric hematology/oncology, 1974-76; active med. staff Kosair Children's Hosp., Louisville, 1976—, Humana Hosp., Audubon, Louisville, 1979—, U. Gen. Hosp., Louisville, 1979—, Humana Hosp., U., Louisville, 1986—, Meth. Evang. Hosp., Louisville, 1987-93; med. staff Home of Innocents, Louisville, 1980-83; courtesy staff Humana Hosp. Suburban, Louisville, 1981—, Jewish Hosp., Louisville, 1982—. Mem. editl. bd. Jour. Cancer Edn., 1986—; contbr. chpts. in books and numerous articles to profl. jours. Adv. com. on childhood cancer Am. Cancer Soc., Louisville, 1979-80; mem. med. adv. com. ARC, Louisville, 1979—; bd. dirs. Help Our Parents Endure, Parent Support Group, Louisville, 1980-85; med., bd. dirs. Ronald McDonald House, Louisville, 1980—, chmn. planning com., 1980-82; co-chmn. Affiliate Instn. Com., Children's Cancer Group, 1984—; others. Maj. U.S. Army, 1972-76. Recipient WLKY Bell award, 1991, Nat. Jefferson award, Washington, 1992; grantee Nat. Cancer Inst., 1977-82, Crusade for Children, 1978, 80, 82, 86, 90, 91, 92, Ky. Adv. Bd. on Hemophilia, State of Ky., 1981, 82, 83-85, 86-90, 91, Am. Cancer Soc., 1982, Louisville and Jefferson County Bd. of Health, 1983-90, 91, Children's Cancer Group, 1984-87, 87, 88, 89, 90, 91, 92, 93, Cabinet for Human Resources, 1988, 89, 90, Alpha Therapeutic Corp., 1991, others. Fellow Am. Acad. Pediatrics; mem. Am. Soc. Clin. Oncology, Am. Soc. Pediatric Hematology/Oncology, Am. Assn. Cancer Eductors, So. Soc. for Pediatric Rsch., Ky. Chpt. Am. Acad. Pediatrics, Ky. Med. Assn., Jefferson County Med. Soc., Louisville Pediatric Soc., Alpha Omega Alpha. Office: Dept Pediats Hemtology/Oncology 601 S Floyd St Ste 403 Louisville KY 40202-1837

BERTOLUCI, MARCELLO CASACCIA, medical educator; b. Porto Alegre, Brazil, Oct. 15, 1960; MD, U. Fed. do Rio Grande do Sul, 1983, DSc, 1994. Assoc. prof. U. Fed. do Rio Grande do Sul, 1999—, prof., med. scis., 2004—11. Mem.: Soc. Brasileira de Diabetes. Avocations: tennis, chess, travel. Office: Ave Palmeira 18 Sala 602 Porto Alegre 90470-300 Brazil Office Fax: 5551-33349925. Personal E-mail: mbertoluci@uol.com.br.

BERTONI, CARMEN, biologist; PhD, U. Perugia, Italy, 1999. Postdoc. fellow Stanford U., Palo Alto, Calif., 1999—2004, instr., 2004—06; asst. prof. UCLA, 2006—. Bd. mem. and reviewer Instl. Rev. Bd. Office Protection of Human Subjects, UCLA, 2008—09. Grantee, Italian Govt., Muscular Dystrophy Assn., 1995—2009. Mem.: Am. Soc. Gene Therapy. Achievements include research in muscle diseases using oligonucleotide-mediated gene correction. Office Phone: 310-825-6387. Business E-Mail: cbertoni@ucla.edu.

BERTOZZI, MIRKO, surgeon; b. Rimini, Italy, Dec. 11, 1970; MD, U. Bologna, Italy, 1997, PhD in Pediat. Surgery, 2005. Surgeon, cons. pediat. surgery Ospedale S. Maria della Misericordia, Perugia, 2004—, with pediat. endoscopy and pediat. minimally invasive surgery program, 2010—11, dep. dir. pediat. surgery dept., 2011—. Mem.: Italian Soc. Pediat. Videosurgery, Italian Soc. Pediat. Surgery. Avocations: windsurfing, surfing, motorcycling. Office: Ospedale S Maria della Misericordia Perugia Umbria 06100 Italy Office Fax: 39 075 5783376. E-mail: mirkobertozzi@hotmail.com.

BERTRAND, BETTY HARLEEN, nurse; b. Little Rock, Ark., July 17, 1960; d. Harley Walter and Joyce Elaine (Bryant) Baker; m. Robert K. Bertrand, June 13, 1980; children: Mary, Jessie, Alyssa, Jared. AA, Cerro Coso C.C., 1981; ADN, Texarkana Coll., 1989; BSN, U. Ark. Med. Sch., 1994. RN, Tex.; lic. vocat. nurse; cert. low risk neonatal care. Nurse asst. Ridgecrest (Calif.) Cmty. Hosp., 1982-85; lic. vocat. nurse Wadley Regional Med. Ctr., Texarkana, Tex., 1986-89, RN, 1989-92; field supervising nurse HealthCor Home Health, Texarkana, 1992-93; nurse Blankenship Dialysis Ctr., Texarkana, 1993-95; clin. instr. Texarkana Coll., 1995-97, instr. vocat. nursing program, 1997—2008; nurse St. Michael Health Care Ctr., 1995—. Baptist. Avocations: reading, cross stitching, crochet, parenting, piano. Home: 2007 Presley Rd Texarkana TX 75501

BERTUZZI, FRANCESCA, ophthalmologist; b. Asola, Mantova, Italy, Oct. 27, 1974; MD, Università degli Studi di parma, 1999, specialist in Ophthalmology, 2003. Ophthalmology cons. Clinica

Oculistica- Università Milano Bicocca, 2004—. Mem.: Associazione Italiana Studio Glaucoma, Am. Acad. Ophthalmology, Società Oftalmologica Italiana. Avocations: singing, swimming, reading. Office: Via Amati 111 Monza Brianza 20900 Italy Office Fax: 390392810332. Business E-Mail: francyhoney@libero.it.

BERWICK, DONALD MARK, federal agency administrator; b. NYC, Sept. 9, 1946; m. Ann Greenberg; children: Ben, Dan, Jessica, Rebecca. BA, Harvard Coll.; MA of Pub. Policy, Harvard U. John F. Kennedy Sch. Govt.; MD cum laude, Harvard Med. Sch., 1972. Intern pediat. Mass. Gen. Hosp., Boston, 1972—73; resident pediat. Children's Hosp., Boston, 1973—76; v.p. quality-of-care measurement Harvard Cmty. Health Plan, 1983—87; clin. prof. pediat. & health care policy Harvard Med. Sch.; prof. health policy & mgmt. Harvard Sch. Pub. Health; pediatrician, adj. staff dept. medicine Boston Children's Hosp.; pres., CEO Inst. Healthcare Improvement, Boston, 1991—2010; adminstr. Centers Medicare & Medicaid Services (CMS), US Dept. Health & Human Services, 2010—. Co-founder, co-prin. investigator Nat. Demonstration Project Quality Improvement in Health Care, 1987—91; vice-chmn. US Preventive Services Task Force, 1990—96; chair health svcs. rsch. rev. study sect. Agy. Health Care Policy & Rsch., 1995—99; apptd. mem. Adv. Commn. Consumer Protection & Quality in Healthcare Industry, 1997—98; chair nat. adv. coun. Agy. Healthcare Rsch. & Quality, 1999—2001. Mem. editl. bd. Brit. Med. Jour., Jour. AMA; contbr. articles to profl. jour. Mem. judges panel Malcolm Baldrige Nat. Quality Award Program, 1989—91; ind. mem., bd. trustees Am. Hosp. Assn., 1996—99. Recipient Ernest A. Codman award, Joint Commn. Accreditation of Healthcare Organizations, 1999, Alfred I. DuPont award for excellence in children's health care, Nemours Found., 2001, Award of Honor, American Hosp. Assn., 2002, John M. Eisenberg Patient Safety & Quality award, Nat. Quality Forum/Joint Commn. Accreditation of Healthcare Organizations, 2006, William B. Graham prize for health svcs. rsch., Assn. Univ. Programs in Health Adminstrn., 2007, Heinz award for pub. policy, Heinz Family Found., 2007, Civic Ventures Purpose prize, 2007. Fellow: Royal Coll. Physicians London; mem.: NAS, Inst. Med. (mem. governing coun. 2002—07), Internat. Soc. Med. Decision-Making (pres.). Office: Centers for Medicare & Medicaid Services 7500 Security Blvd Baltimore MD 21244 *

BERWICK, MARIANNE, epidemiologist, educator; BA in English, UCLA, 1963; MPH in Environ. Health, Yale U., 1979, PhD in Epidemiology, 1987. Grad. asst. rsch. J.B. Pierce Found., New Haven, 1984—85; assoc. rsch. scientist, dept. epidemiology & pub. health Yale Sch. Medicine, New Haven, 1986—91; epidemiologist, rsch. scientist Cancer Prevention Rsch. Inst., NY, 1991—93, dir. epidemiology NY, 1993—94; rsch. asst. prof. Inst. Environ. Medicine, NYU, 1991—97; rsch. affiliate Yale U., New Haven, 1993—; asst. attending epidemiologist Meml. Sloan-Kettering Cancer Ctr., NY, 1994—97, assoc. attending epidemiologist NY, 1997—2003, attending epidemiologist NY, 2003; assoc. prof. epidemiology in pub. health Cornell U. Med. Coll., NY, 2001—03; prof. epidemiology U. N.Mex., 2004—, chief divsn. epidemiology and biostatistics, dept. internal medicine, 2004—; sr. leader for population sci. program U. N.Mex. Cancer Ctr., 2004, co leader program in population health and cancer control, 2004 , assoc. dir. population health. Mem. Nat. Cancer Inst.-SubE, 2003—; mem. steering com. Melanoma Rsch. Found., 2004—. Contbr. several articles to peer-reviewed publs. Recipient Wilbur Downs Internat. Travel award, Yale U., Sch. Medicine, 1978, Hull award, 1988, Melanoma Rsch. Found. award, 1988, LILAC award for Cancer Rsch., 1996, Byrne Fund award, 1997—99, David Klein Found. award, 2001. Mem.: Am. Assn. for Cancer Rsch./Molecular Epidemiology Group (chmn. 2004—05), Soc. for Melanoma Rsch. (mem. steering com. 2003—, Established Researcher award 2006). Office: U NMex Cancer Ctr MSC08 4630 1 University of New Mexico Albuquerque NM 87131-0001

BERZOFSKY, JAY A., medical researcher; b. Balt., Apr. 13, 1946; AB summa cum laude, in chemistry, Harvard U., 1967; PhD in biochemistry/biophysics, Albert Einstein Coll. Medicine, 1971, MD, 1973. Rsch. asst. rediat. rsch. unit Sinai Hosp., Balt., 1962—65; rsch. asst. dept. pharmacology, organic synthesis lab. Johns Hopkins Sch. Medicine, Balt., 1966; vis. scientist Ctr. Nat. de la Recherche Sci., Lab. d'Enzymologie, Gif-sur-Yvette, France, 1967; med. intern Mass. Gen. Hosp., Boston, 1973—74; rsch. assoc. Nat. Inst. Arthritis, Metabolism, and Digestive Diseases, NIH, Lab. Chem. Biology, Bethesda, Md., 1974—76; investigator metabolism br. Nat. Cancer Inst., NIH, Bethesda, 1976—79, sr. investigator, 1979—87, head molecular immunogenetics and vaccine rsch. sect., Ctr. Cancer Rsch., 1987—, chief Vaccine Br., 2003—. Hollister-Stier's Disting. lectr. Washington State U., 1986; McLaughlin vis. prof. U. Tex. Med. Sch., Galveston, 1992. Assoc. editor: Jour. Immunology, 1980—84, adv. editor: Molecular Immunology, 1985—88, mem. editl. bd.: Jour. Human Virology, 1997—, consulting editor: Jour. Clin. Investigation, 1998—. Recipient Superior Svc. Award, USPHS; named Disting. Alumnus of Yr., Albert Einstein Sch. Medicine, 2007. Fellow: AAAS (chair med. scis. sect. 2007—); mem.: Assn. Am. Physicians, Am. Soc. for Clin. Investigation (sec.-treas. 1989—92, pres.-elect 1992—93, pres. 1993—94), Am. Soc. Biol. Chemists (coun. mem. 1989—94), Am. Fedn. for Clin. Rsch., Am. Assn. Immunologists, N.Y. Acad. Scis., Assn. Harvard Chemists, Phi Beta Kappa. Achievements include research in T-lymphocyte recognition of antigens and applications; regulation of tumor immunosurveillance. Office: Ctr Cancer Rsch Vaccine Br Bldg 10 Rm 6B-04 10 Center Dr Bethesda MD 20892-1578 Office Phone: 301-496-6874. Office Fax: 301-480-0681. Business E-Mail: berzofsk@helix.nih.gov. *

BERZUINI, ALESSANDRA, hematologist; b. Bolzano, Jan. 6, 1957; Degree in Medicine, U. Pavia, 1983. Cert. in hematology, internal medicine U. Pavia, 1991. Physician, dept. transfusion medicine and hematology Ospedale Maggiore Policlinico, Milan, 1986—94, Ospedale A. Manzoni, Lecco, 2006—; physician, lab. and pathology dept. Ospedale Valduce, Como, 1994—2006. Master: Soc. Italiana Medicina Trasfusionale. Home: Via Prudenziana 2 Como 22100 Italy Home Fax: 390341489875. Personal E-mail: a.berzuini@ospedale.lecco.it.

BESCH, EMERSON LOUIS, physiologist, educator, retired dean; b. Hammond, Ind., June 9, 1928; s. Ernest Henry and Carolyn (Dieckmann) B.; m. H. Jean Whitstine, May 28, 1955; children: Karen J., Kevin D., Kathleen L., Kristine A. BS in Biology/Chemistry, S.W. Tex. State U., 1952, MA in Biology/Chemistry, 1955; PhD in Physiology, U. Calif., Davis, 1964. Grad. instr. biology dept. S.W. Tex. State U., San Marcos, 1954-55; research asst., NIH trainee U. Calif., Davis, 1960-64, research physiologist, lectr., 1964-67; research assoc. Pacific Missile Range, USN, Point Mugu, Calif., 1960-64; from assoc. to full prof., head dept. physiology Kans. State U., Manhattan, 1967-74, from assoc. to full prof. mech. engring., 1967-74; prof. mech. engring. U. Fla., Gainesville, 1974-93; prof. physiology U. Fla. Coll. Vet. Medicine, Gainesville, 1974-93, assoc. dean, 1974-87, acting dean, 1980-81, exec. assoc. dean, 1987-88, prof. emeritus, 1993—. Served to capt. USNR. Fellow Aerospace Med. Assn. (exec. council 1985-88, profl. excellence award 1987); mem. Am. Physiology Soc., Soc. for Exptl. Biology & Medicine, Aerospace Physiologist Soc. (pres. 1984-86), Am. Soc. Heating, Refrigerating & Air Conditioning Engring. Achievements include research in environmental physiology and acceleration biology. Home: 15207 Rompel Trail Dr San Antonio TX 78232-4255 Office: U Fla Coll Vet Medicine PO Box 100144 Gainesville FL 32610-0144 Office Phone: 352-392-2246. E-mail: ebesch@satx.rr.com.

BESCHNIDT, SVEN MARCUS, dentist; b. Aalen, Baden-Wuerttemberg, Germany, Jan. 2, 1969; s. Reinhard and Hannelore B. DDS, U. Freiburg, Germany, 1995, DMD, 1997. Asst. prof. U. Freiburg, 1995-98, sr. lectr., 1999—2001, 2005, lectr., 2001—; pvt. dentistry practice, 2001—. Clin. assoc. U. Freiburg, 2004—, st. lectr., 2005. Contbr. articles to profl. jours. Mem. German Assn. Prosthodontics and Dental Materials (specialist of prosthodontics 2001—), German Assn. Implantology (specialist of implantology 2004-), European Acad. Esthetic Dentistry. Avocations: bicycling, music, private pilot. Address: Brenner's Parkhotel Lichtentaler Allee 1 76530 Baden-Württemberg Germany Office Phone: 49 7221 3939719. Business E-Mail: s.marcus@beschnidt.com.

BESHARA, MATTHEW N., gynecologist, obstetrician; MD, Wayne State U. Diplomate Am. Bd. Ob-Gyn. Asst. prof. clin. ob-gyn. Univ. Pa.; intern Univ. Pa. Hosp., resident, physician. Named one of Top Doctors, Phila. mag., 2010, 2011. Fellow: ACOG; mem.: Pa. Med. Soc. Office: University of Pennsylvania Hospital 3400 Spruce St Philadelphia PA 19104 Office Phone: 215-662-6035.

BESIER, JAMES LOUIS, pharmacist, educator; b. Waukegan, Ill., Feb. 23, 1954; s. Louis Clark and Jessie Olive Besier; m. Janice Lynn Halloran, Nov. 2, 1979; children: Matthew, Christopher, Robert. BS, U. Cin., 1977, MS, 1990; PhD, Union Inst. & U., 2004. Lic. pharmacist Ohio, Ky. Staff pharmacist Children's Hosp. Med. Ctr., Cin., 1977—89; svc. chief pediat. Strong Meml. Hosp., Rochester, NY, 1989—90; staff pharmacist U. Cin. Hosp., 1990—91; pharmacy mgr. U. Hosp., Cin., 1991—97; asst. dir. pharmacy St. Luke Hosps., Ft. Thomas, Ky., 1997—2004, adminstr. bar code medication adminstrn., 2005—, dir. health alliance pharmacy residency program, 2005—. Adj. asst. prof. Coll. Pharmacy U. Cin., 1991—2004, adj. assoc. prof. Coll. Nursing, 2004—; spkr. Glaxo Pharm. Rsch., Triangle Park, NC, 1994—97; lectr. Coll. Nursing, U. Cin., 1998—; adv. coun. Gateway Cmty. & Tech. Coll., Edgewood, Ky., 2002—04. Contbr. articles to profl. jours. Bus. edn. cons. Jr. Achievement, Cin., 1995—99. Mem.: Am. Assn. Coll. Pharmacy, Am. Soc. Health Sys. Pharmacists. Office: Dept Pharmacy Services Alliance Business Ctr 3 South Cincinnati OH 45229 Home: 4439 Hillcrest Oaks Owensboro KY 42303-1967

BESSA, SAHAR SAAD EL-DIN, medical educator; b. Tanta, Egypt, Nov. 3, 1965; MSc, Tanta U., 1994, MD, 2002. Lectr. Faculty Medicine, Tanta U., 2002—07, asst. prof., 2007—. Avocations: reading, travel. Office: Al-Geish St Tanta Al Gharbia 31527 Egypt Office Fax: 202 0403419831. Personal E-mail: saharbessa@yahoo.com.

BESSELL, ERIC MICHAEL, medical practitioner, clinical oncology consultant; b. Stony Stratford, Eng., Dec. 17, 1946; s. William Henry and Doris Mabel (Willson) B.; m. Deborah Jane Lloyd, July 31, 1971; children: Laura Elizabeth, Andrew Thomas. BSc, U. Bristol, Eng., 1967; PhD, U. London, 1970; MB BS, St. Mary's Hosp. Med. Sch., London, 1978. Registrar in clin. oncology Royal Postgrad. Med. Sch./Hammersmith Hosp., London, 1980-83; sr. registrar Royal Marsden Hosp., London, 1983-85; cons. Nottingham (Eng.) Health Authority, 1985—. Cons. Kings Mill Hosp., Sutton-in-Ashfield, Eng., 1985—, The Park Hosp., Nottingham; clin. dir. dept. clin. oncology Nottingham City Hosp., 1986-96, 2003—2007. Contbr. articles to profl. jours. Fellow Royal Coll. Physicians, Royal Coll. Radiologists (examiner London and Hong Kong 1993-2000); mem. Brit. Oncol. Assn., European Soc. for Therapeutic Radiology and Oncology, Nat. Cancer Rsch. Inst. (lymphoma clin. studies group U.K. 2003-05), Radiotherapy Club (pres. 1998-99). Anglican. Avocations: mountain walking, piano playing, opera. Office: Nottingham City Hosp Clin Oncol/Hucknall Rd Nottingham NG5 1PB England Home: 13 Dovedale Road NG2 6JB Nottingham England Business E-Mail: eric.bessell@nuh.nhs.uk.

BESSER, MICHAL J., immunologist, educator; b. Tel Aviv, Dec. 4, 1971; PhD in Immunology, U. Munich, 1999. Chief scientist Ella Inst. Melanoma, Sheba Med. Ctr., 2004—. Lectr. U. Tel Aviv, 2009—. Rsch. grant, Pfizer Inc. Mem.: Israeli Assn. Cancer Rsch., Orgn. Biochemist and Microbiologist (Israel), Am. Assn. Cancer Rsch., European Assn. Cancer Rsch. Office: Sheba Medical Ctr Ramat Gan 52621 Israel Business E-Mail: michal.besser@sheba.health.gov.il.

BESSER, RICHARD ERIC, television personality, pediatrician; b. Aug. 28, 1959; m. Jeanne Besser; children: Alex, Jack. BA in Economics, Williams Coll., Williamstown, Mass.; MD, U. Pa., 1986. Cert. Am. Bd. Pediat. Resident, chief resident, pediat. John Hopkins U. Hosp., Balt.; Epidemic Intelligence Svc. officer, Enteric Diseases Br., Divsn. Bacterial and Mycotic Diseases Nat. Ctr. for Infectious Disease, 1991, epidemiology sect. chief, respiratory diseases br., acting chief meningitis and spl. pathogens br.; dir., Coordinating Office for Terrorism Preparedness and Emergency Response (COTPER) Centers for Disease Control & Prevention (CDC), US Dept. Health & Human Services, 2005—09, acting dir., 2009, acting adminstr., Agy. for Toxic Substance and Disease Registry, 2009; chief health and med. editor ABC News, 2009—. Founder, med. dir. Get Smart: Know When Antibiotics Work; presenter in field. Contbr. several articles to profl. jours., chapters to books. Avocations: baseball, tennis. Office: ABC News 7 W 66th St New York NY 10023 *

BESSEY, PALMER QUINTARD, surgeon; BA, Williams Coll., 1967; MA in Chemistry, U. Oregon, 1970; MD, U. Vt., 1975; MS in Epidemiology and Public Health, Columbia U., 2006. Diplomate Am. Bd. Surgeons, Am. Bd. Critical Care Surgery. Intern U. Ala. Hosp., Birmingham, 1975-76, resident in surgery, 1976-81; fellow metabolism and nutrition Brigham and Women's Hosp., Boston, 1981-83; assoc. dir. Burn Ctr. N.Y. Presbyterian Hosp., 2000—; prof. surgery Weill Med. Coll. Cornell U., 2000—. Mem. ACS (region chief), Assn. Acad. Surgery, Soc Univ. Surgeons, Am. Assn. Surgery Trauma, ASPEN, Soc. Critical Care Medicine, Ctrl. Surg. Assn., Am. Surg. Assn., Am. Bd. Surgery (bd. dirs.), Am. Burn Assn. (com. on trauma). Office: Dept Surgery Box 137 P-703 525 E 68th St New York NY 10021

BESSLER, MARC, surgeon, educator; b. NYC, Oct. 21, 1964; BA cum laude, Yeshiva U., NYC, 1985; MD, NYU Sch. Medicine, 1989; Advanced Operative Laparoscopy for Gen. Surgery, Advanced Laparoscopy Tng. Ctr., Marietta, Ga., 1991; Course in Laparoscopic Suturing, Anastomosis and Intracorporeal Knot Tying, Microsurgery and Operative Endoscopy Tng. Inst., San Francisco, Calif., 1992; Basic Microsurgery Course, Columbia U. Coll. Physicians and Surgeons, NYC, 1992; Endosurgical Techniques of the Foregut and Hindgut, U. So. Calif., LA, 1993; Vertical Banded Gastroplasty and Mgmt. of Morbid Obesity, U. Iowa, Iowa City, 1996; Gastric Bypass and Mgmt. of Morbid Obesity, Med. Coll. Va., Richmond, Va., 1996. Cert. Am. Bd. Surgery. Resident, gen. surgery NY-Presbyn. Hosp./Columbia U. Med. Ctr., NYC, 1989—96, fellow, surgical endoscopy, 1993—94, asst. attending surgeon, 1997—, dir., NY Presbyn. Ctr. for Obesity Surgery, 1997—, dir., laparoscopic surgery, 1997—, dir., network relationships, divsn. gen. surgery, 2005—, dir. minimal access surgery ctr., 2008—; instr. clin. surgery Columbia U. Coll. Physicians and Surgeons, NYC, 1996—97, asst. prof. surgery, 1997—. Presenter in field. Contbr. articles to profl. jours. Recipient Blackmore award for Surgical Rsch., 1992, 1993, 1996, Soc. Laparoendoscopic Surgeons Resident Achievement award, Best Resident Presentation, SAGES, 1995. Fellow: ACS (assoc.); mem.: Soc. for Surgery Alimentary Tract, Am. Soc. for Bariatric Surgery, Assn. Academic Surgery, Soc. Am. Gastrointestinal Endoscopic Surgeons. Achievements include patents for Gastrointestinal Staplescope, 1993; Gastrointestinal Tissue Approximating and Attaching Device, 1995; Device and Method for Performing Laproscopic Vertical Banded Gastroplasty; Device and Method for Percutaneous Removal and Replacement of Cardiac Valves; Bessler Treat Laparoscopic Suturing Assistant Forreps. Office: NY Presbyn Hosp Columbia U Med Ctr Irving Pavilion Rm 6-620 161 Fort Washington Ave New York NY 10032 Office Phone: 212-305-9506. Office Fax: 212-305-5992.

BESSMAN, ALICE NEUMAN, internist, educator; b. Washington, Nov. 7, 1922; d. Lester and Janet (Nusbaum) Neuman; m. Samuel P. Bessman, July 3, 1945; children: Joel David, Ellen. BA, Smith Coll., 1943; MD, George Washington U., 1949. Am. Bd. Internal Medicine. Intern, resident George Washington U. Hosp., 1949-51, fellow in medicine, 1951-52,53-54; fellow in pediatrics Harvard U. and Mass. Gen. Hosp., Boston, 1952-53; instr. medicine Johns Hopkins Balt. City Hosp., 1955-68; assoc. prof. medicine U. So. Calif., LA, 1969-79, prof. medicine, 1979-94; prof. emeritus, 1993. Chief Rancho Los Amigos Med. Ctr., 1968-93, diabetes endocrine svc.; attending physician, instr. diabetes clin. Wadsworth VA Hosp.; attending physician Rancho Los Amigos Med. Ctr.; cons. Calif. State Bd. of Corps.; lectr. in field. Contbr. over 100 articles to profl. jours. and chpts. to books. Mem. Am. Fedn. for Clin. Rsch., AMA, Am. Diabetes Assn. (diabetes clinician of yr. award 1993), L.A. County Med. Assn., L.A. Soc. Internal Medicine, So. Calif. Diabetes Assn. Jewish. Avocation: music. Office: Rancho Los Amigos Med Ctr 7601 Imperial Hwy Rm 145 Downey CA 90242-3456 *

BESSON, NICOLE MARIE ARCHAMBAULT, speech pathology/audiology services professional; b. Anaheim, Calif., Nov. 24, 1973; d. Guy Rene and Donna Jean Archambault; m. Peter Besson; 1 child, Tenée Marie. BA in Speech and Hearing Scis., Wash. State U., 1996; MS in Speech and Hearing Scis., U. N.Mex, 1999; EdS in Brain Rsch. and Concentration Instrnl. Leadership, Nova Southeastern U., 2007. Cert. lactation educator, counselor U. Calif., San Diego, 2009; clin. competence speech-lang. pathology Am. Speech-Language Hearing Assn., 2000, lic. speech-lang. pathologist Calif. Speech-Language Pathology and Audiology Bd., 2000, Nev. Bd. of Examiners for Audiology and Speech Pathology, 1999, cert. Hanen Centre, 2002, interior decorator Decorator Tng. Inst., 2005, speech-lang. pathologist orofacial myofunctional therapist exec., infant massage instr. Internat. Loving Touch Found., ind. instr. Baby Signs Inst., 2007. Speech-language pathologist The Continuum, Reno, 1999—; pediatric speech-language pathologist Cedars Sinai Med. Ctr., LA; owner, dir. Minds In Motion (formerly Talk For Tots), Santa Monica. Cons. Benjamin Links; sr. cons. Little Lima Bean Prodns.; co-owner Kids Places & Spaces Integrative Develop. Design Co., 2005—07; owner, founder Room To Grow - An Integrative Devel. Design Co. Recipient ACE award, Am. Speech Lang. Hearing Assn., 2005, 2008; Maynard Lee Daggy scholar, Wash. State U., 1995, All-Am. scholar, U.S. Achievement Acad., 1996. Mem.: Children's Book Writers & Illustrators, Internat. Soc. for Devel. Neurosci., Internat. Assn. Orofacial Myology, Internat. Mind, Brain and Edn. Soc., Nat. Coalition Auditory Processing Disorders, Calif. Speech and Hearing Assn., Am. Speech-Lang. Hearing Assn. (Am. Continuing Edn. award 2003, 2005, 2006), Acad. Neurological Comm. Disorders and Sci. (assoc.), Golden Key Nat. Honor Soc. Office: Minds In Motion 1218 Sixth St Ste 2 Santa Monica CA 90401 Office Phone: 310-936-3020. Business E-Mail: nicole@mindsinmotiontherapy.com.

BEST, BROOKIE MANNING DUGAN, pharmacist; d. Michael Patrick Dugan and Vicky Lynnette Manning; m. William Gainey Best, III, July 31, 1999; children: Alexander Jacob children: Noah Gainey. BS in Chemistry, U. Calif., La Jolla, Calif., 1994; PharmD, U. of Calif., San Francisco, Calif., 1999; cert., U. of Calif., La Jolla, CA, 2002; student in Advanced Studies, Clin. Rsch., U. of Calif., La Jolla, Calif., 2003—. Lic. pharmacist Bd. Pharmacy, Calif., 1999. Resident in pharmacy practice San Diego (Calif.) Med. Ctr. U. of Calif., 1999—2000, asst. clin. prof. San Francisco (Calif.) Sch. of Pharmacy, 2000—, pharmacokinetic specialist San Diego (Calif.) Med. Ctr., 2000—, rsch. fellow San Diego (Calif.) Pediat. Pharm. Rsch. Unit, 2001—04. Asst. prof. San Diego (Calif.) Sch. Pharmacy and Pharm. Scis. U. Calif., 2004—; admissions interviewer San Diego (Calif.) Sch. Pharmacy and Pharm. Scis. U. of Calif., 2002—; mem. therapeutic drug monitoring com. NIH Pediatric AIDs Clin. Trials Group, 2001—02; mem., ednl. policy and academic oversight com. San Diego (Calif.) Sch. Pharmacy and Pharm. Scis. U. of Calif., 2003—, mem., residency adv. com. San Diego (Calif.) Med. Ctr., 2003—; lectr. San Diego (Calif.) Sch. Pharmacy and Pharm. Scis. U. Calif., 2003—. Reviewer: Jour. Pediats., 2000; reviewer Antimicrobial Agts.

and Chemotherapy, 2003—; contbr. articles to profl. jours. Vol. pharmacist attending U. Calif. San Diego Student -Run Free Med. Clinic Project, 1999—; judge Greater San Diego (Calif.) Sci. & Engrng. Fair, 2001. Recipient Baker Appreciation award, Baker Elem. Sch., San Diego Unified Sch. Dist., 1998; fellow Nat. Rsch. Svc. award, Nat. Inst. for Child Health and Human Devel., 2001—04; scholar Nat. Merit scholarship, U. of Calif., San Diego, 1990, Julian Weiss Clin. Pharmacy Rsch. scholarship, U. of Calif., San Francisco Sch. of Pharmacy, 1998. Mem.: Am. Coll. Clin. Pharmacy, Calif. Soc. Health Systems Pharmacists (co-chmn. cmty. outreach com. 2001—02), Calif. Pharm. Assn., Am. Soc. of Health Systems Pharmacists, Am. Pharm. Assn., Rho Chi. Avocations: snow-boarding, water-skiing. Office: U Calif San Diego 9500 Gilman Dr MC 0719 La Jolla CA 92093-0719 E-mail: brookie@ucsd.edu.

BEST, CHARLES, urologist, educator; b. Oakland, Calif., Oct. 6, 1965; BA in Biology, UC San Diego, 1988; MD, USC, 1992. Asst. prof., urology and surgery USC Inst. Urology, 2000—. Svc. chief, urology LAC & USC County Med. Ctr., 2001—11. Fellow: ACS, AAST; mem.: GURS, WSAUA, AUA. Avocations: martial arts, camping, fishing. Office: 1441 Eastlake Ave Ste 7416 Los Angeles CA 90089 Office Fax: 323-226-7927. Business E-Mail: cbest@usc.edu.

BEST, ULRICH-PETER, physician, director; s. Karl Friedrich and Helma Margarete Best; m. Doris Renate Hellmuth, Dec. 4, 2003; 1 child, Daniel. MD, Johannes Gutenberg U., Mainz, 1984. Cert. cons. in ophthalmology Free-Lance Specialist Christoffel-Blindenmission, specialist in tropical ophthalmology Christoffel-Blindenmission. Project dir., Eye Care Programme Surigao Christoffel-Blindenmission, Surigao City, Surigao del Norte, Philippines, 1994—97; co dir. Augenklinik und Augenlaserklinik Mainfranken, Schweinfurt, Bavaria, Germany, 1998—; med. dir. ophthalmology Leopoldina-Hosp., Schweinfurt, 1998—. Contbr. scientific papers. Developing helper Christoffel-Blindenmission, Kano, Kano State, Nigeria, 2000—08. Capt. med. corps Gen. Surgery and Traumatic Surgery, 1997—98, German Armed Forces Hosp. Bad Zwischenahn. Fellow: German Com. Prevention Blindness. Office: Augenklinik Mainfranken Am Oberen Marienbach 1 Schweinfurt 97421 Germany Office Phone: 49 9721 4742390.

BEST, WILLIAM ROBERT, internist, educator, retired dean; b. Chgo., July 14, 1922; s. Gordon and Marian Burton (Shapland) B.; m. Ruth Johanna Stuchlik, Sept. 2, 1944; children: Barbara Ann Best Mulch, Patricia Marian Best Williams. BS, U. Ill., 1945; MD, U. Ill., Chgo., 1947, MS, 1951; postgrad. math. biology, U. Chgo., 1964-65. Diplomate Am. Bd. Internal Medicine, Am. Bd. Hematology. From intern to fellow in hematology then to resident U. Ill. Hosp., 1947-51; asst. prof., assoc. prof. medicine U. Ill. Coll. Medicine, Chgo., 1953-67, prof., assoc. dean, 1972-81; chief Midwest Rsch. Support Ctr., VA Hosp., Hines, Ill., 1967-72, chief staff, 1981-92, sr. health svcs. rschr., 1992—2008; prof. medicine, assoc. dean for VA affairs Loyola U. Stritch Sch. Medicine, Maywood, Ill., 1981-92; chief staff U. Ill. Hosp., Chgo., 1976-81. Contbr. numerous articles to sci. jours. 1st lt. US Army, 1951—53. Named Alumnus of Yr., U. Ill. Med. Alumni Assn., l980. Fellow ACP; mem. AMA (br. pres. l985), Am. Statis. Assn., AAAS. Episcopalian. Avocations: sailing, computers. Home: 1712 Waverly Cir Saint Charles IL 60174-5869 Personal E-mail: w.and.r.best@sbcglobal.net.

BESUSCHIO, SANTIAGO CESAR, pathologist, epidemiologist; b. Buenos Aires, Oct. 12, 1931; s. Santiago and Carmen (Otero) B.; m. Isabel Casado, July 17, 1959; children: Susana, Adrian; m. Alicia Bonvino, July 19, 2003. MD, U. Buenos Aires, 1958, grad. hygienist, 1960; grad. pathologist, Pub. Health Dept. Sch., Buenos Aires, 1960. Intern, resident Pirovano Hosp., Buenos Aires, 1961-64; chief pathology dept. Inst. Microbiology/U. Buenos Aires, 1963-68, Inst. Cardiology/Nat. Acad. Medicine, Argentina, 1967-73, French Hosp., Buenos Aires, 1968—; dir. collaborating ctr. WHO Internat. Classification Tumors, Geneva, 1970-76; chief pathology dept. Inst. Hematological Rsch./Nat. Acad. Medicine, Buenos Aires, 1972-94; prof. pathology U. Buenos Aires, 1986—; assoc. prof. pathology U. Paris VI Pierre et Marie Curie, France, 1993-94. Cons. pathologist Cancer Ctr. Buenos Aires Province, Gonnet, Argentina, 1985-93, Club Pathologie Hematologique, Paris, 1988—; hon. coord. nat. sci. and tech. dept. Nat. Program Health, Buenos Aires, 1989—; organizer Nat. Registry Cancer, Abidjan, Ivory Coast, 1969-70; assoc. rschr. epidemiology unit IARC/WHO, Lyon, France, 1969; coord. continuing edn. program Pub. Health Dept.; commn. study AIDS Nat. Acad. Medicine and Pub. Health Ministry, 1985, 90; vis. prof. Kiel U., Germany, 1970, 88. Author: Chronic Hydroarsenicism Regional Endemic, 1982, Argentine Hemorrnagic Fever, 1982 (Nat. Dept. Culture award 1990), General Pathology, 1992, Pathological Anatomy, 1993. Mem. Nat. Comm. Against Hemorrnagic Fever, 1971-74; OAS rep. UN Conf. on Tech. Coop. between devel. countries, Buenos Aires, 1978; v.p. Argentine br. Soc. Ingenieurs Scientifiques France, Paris, 1980—; pres. Hematol. Pathology Club, Buenos Aires, 1981. Decorated officer Order Acad. Palmes (France); recipient Sci. award Nat. Acad. Medicine, Buenos Aires, 1966, 72, 82, 91, Faculty Medicine-U. Buenos Aires, 1967-79, 70-71, 71-73, 73; Sci. Merit award Severo Vaccaro Found., Buenos Aires, 1990-91. Fellow OAS, Leukemia and Lymphomas Epidemiology, Leukemia and Lymphomas; mem. Soc. Anatomique, European Acad. Scis., Arts and Humanities (corr. mem.), N.Y. Acad. Sci., Argentinian Soc. Med. Humanism (pres. 2002—). Home: Parera 90 1014 Buenos Aires Argentina Office: Inst Pathology Laprida 1708 1425 Buenos Aires Argentina Fax: 54-1-1-4824-0829. E-mail: besuchio@ciudad.com.ar.

BETHEA, LOUISE HUFFMAN, allergist; b. Jackson, Miss., Mar. 27, 1947; d. Theodore G. and Frances (Allen) Huffman; m. Henry L. Bethea, Sept. 15, 1946; children: Mary, Samuel, Sarah. BS, Miss. Coll., Clinton, 1968; MD, U. Miss., 1974. Diplomate Am. Bd. Allergy and Immunology, Am. Bd. Pediatrics. Resident pediatrics U. Miss., Jackson, 1973-75; fellow allergy and immunology U. Fla., 1977-79; pvt. practice Houston, 1983—. Instr. pediatrics U. Miss., 1975-77, U. Fla., 1979-80; active staff Houston Northwest Med. Ctr., 1983—, Meml. Hermann Hosp. The Woodlands, St. Luke's Hosp. The Woodlands; cons. in field. Fellow Am. Acad. Allergy, Asthma and Immunology, Am. Coll. Allergy, Am. Acad. Pediatrics. Republican. Episcopalian. Avocations: photography, travel, arts and crafts. Home: 92 Hollymead Dr The Woodlands TX 77381-5121 Office Phone: 281-298-8132. Office Fax: 281-298-8213. Business E-Mail: bethea@dbmed.net.

BETHOUX, FRANÇOIS ANDRE, physiatrist, researcher; b. Paris, May 31, 1964; arrived in U.S., 1997; s. Pierre Andre and Janine Gabrielle (Monin) Bethoux; m. Sandrine Christine Delclaud, Apr. 9, 1988; children: Nicolas, Ambre. MD, A. Carrel Med. Sch., Lyon, France, 1990; Bd. Phys. Med. and Rehab., J. Monnet U., St. Etienne, France, 1994; DEA Handicap and Rehab., Bourgogne U., Dijon, France, 1994. Diplomate specializing in physical med and rehab. Resident U. Hosps., St. Etienne, France, 1991-94, acad. physiatrist, 1995-97; rsch. fellow Case We. Res. U., Cleve., 1994-95; fellow in neuroimmunology Mellen Ctr. Multiple Sclerosis, Cleve., 1997-2000, clin. assoc., 2001—02, staff physician, dir. rehab. svcs., 2003—. Rschr. Jean Monnet U., St. Etienne, 1992—97, tchr., 1995—97, Sch. Phys. Therapy, St. Etienne, 1992—97, Inst. Social Scis., St. Etienne, 1996—97; assoc rschr. Page Ctr Outcomes Rsch. Cleve. Clin, 2000—. Contbr. chapters to books, articles to profl jours; co-editor: Guide of Evaluation and Measurement Tools in Physical Medicine and Rehabilitation, 2003. Grantee, French Assn. Paralyzed People, 1994, Nat. Multiple Sclerosis Soc., 2002. Mem.: Am Acad Neurology, Int Soc Quality Life, French Soc Physical Med and Rehab. Avocations: music, reading, bicycling. Office: Cleve Clin Found 9500 Euclid Ave Cleveland OH 44195-0001 Business E-Mail: bethouf@ccf.org.

BETSON, LANCE, gynecologist; b. Newport Beach, Sept. 6, 1964; BS, U. Southern Calif., 1989; DO, Des Moines U., 1993. Asst. prof. Harbor-UCLA Med. Ctr., 2000—. Fellow: Am. Coll. Obstetricians and Gynecologists. Office: 361 Hospital Rd Ste 324 Newport Beach CA 92663 E-mail: lhallatlv@aol.com.

BETTA, PIER-GIACOMO, pathologist; b. Alessandria, Piedmont, Italy, Dec. 24, 1949; s. Mario and Caterina (Balbi) Betta; m. Patrizia Longo, Sept. 7, 1990; 1 child, Beatrice. Degree in medicine, U. Turin, Italy, 1975; specialist in anatomic pathology, U. Parma, 1979; specialist in oncology, U. Turin, 1982; specialist in exptl. pathology, U. Genoa, Italy, 1986. Asst. unit pathology City Hosp., Alessandria, 1976-82, dep. chief unit pathology, 1982-89, chief pathology unit, 1997—2009; co-dir. Asbestos Regional Ctr. Casale Monferrato, 2009—; chief svc. pathol. anatomy and cytopathology Santo Spirito Hosp., Casale Monferrato, Italy, 1989-97. Mem. asbestos group Nat. Oncology Commn., Ministry of Health; mem. oncology com. Piedmont Region; sci. com. mem. Regional Asbestos Ctr., biomed. programme mgr. Mem.: Italian Soc. Pathologic Anatomy and Cytopathology, NY Acad. Scis., Am. Soc. Clin. Oncology, Italian League Against Cancer (pres. Alessandria sect., coord. nat. com. profl. and environ. carcinogenesis 2002—05), Internat. Mesothelioma Interest Group. Office: City Hosp Via Venezia 16 15100 Alessandria Italy Office Phone: 39-0131-206205. Personal E-mail: pgbetta@libero.it. Business E-Mail: pgbetta@ospedale.al.it.

BETTELLI, GABRIELLA, anesthesiologist; m. Maurizio Costantini, June 1, 1985. Degree in Medicine, U. Modena, 1973; PhD in Anaesthesia and Intensive Care; PhD in Cardiology, U. Bologna, Italy. Cert. internal quality sys. auditor Certimedica, 1998. Cons. Azienda Ospedaliero U. Policlinico di Modena, 1974—2008; head Anaesthesia and Intensive Care dept. INRCA, Ancona, Italy, 2008—, head dept. surgery, 2010. Chair Safety in Soc. Italiana Anestesia Analgesia Rianimazione e Terapia Intensiva; head, geriatric anaesthesia subcommittee Soc. Italiana Anestesia Analgesia Rianimazione e Terapia Intensiva, 2009—; assoc. prof. anaesthesia U. Politecnica delle Marche, Ancona, 2009—. Author: (novel) L'eunuco del tempo, 2007 (Nat. Lit. award, 1999), (scientific movie) Perché non resti un brutto ricordo (nat. award Andrea Alesini). Mem.: SIAARTI (head anaesthesia intensive care sub com.), Soc. Ambulatory Anaesthesia, SICADS, European Soc. Anaesthesia (mem. geriat. anaesthesia subcom.). Avocations: literature, cooking, languages. Office: INRCA Italian Nat Res Centres Aging Via Della Montagnola Ancona 60100 Italy Office Phone: 390718003400. Business E-Mail: g.bettelli@inrca.it.

BETTERIDGE, D. JOHN, medical educator; b. Ashby-de-la Zouch, Eng., Sept. 24, 1948; s. Winston and Annie-Elizabeth Betteridge; m. Christine Martin, May 20, 1985; children: Tom, Sally. BSc in Biochemistry with honors, Guy's Hosp. Med. Sch., London, 1969; MBBS, King's Coll. Hosp. Med. Sch., London, 1972; MD, London U., 1980; PhD, Bath, 1982. Prof. endocrinology and metabolism U. Coll. London, 1981—. R.D. lawrence rsch. fellow Diabetes UK, 1976—79; chmn. HEART UK, 1995—98; pres. sect. on lipids Royal Soc. Medicine, London. Author: (books) Lipoproteins in Health and Disease; contbr. scientific papers. Fellow: RCP (London), Internat. Atherosclerosis Soc. (Disting. fellow 2006), Am. Heart Assn. Office: Univ Coll Hosp 250 Euston Road NW1 2PG London England Business E-Mail: j.betteridge@ucl.ac.uk.

BETTS, EUGENE KOHLER, pediatric anesthesiologist; b. Boston, June 2, 1942; MD, Wake Forest U., 1968. Diplomate Am. Bd. Anesthesiology. Intern N.C. Bapt. Hosp., Winston-Salem, N.C., 1968-69, resident in anesthesiology, 1969-72; fellow in pediat. anesthesiology Childrens Hosp., Phila., 1971, assoc. in chief anesthesiology, 1974—98; staff anesthesiology Hosp. U. Pa., 1979—98; assoc. prof. anesthesiology U. Pa.; prof. anesthesiology and pediats., vice chair anesthesiology Med. Coll. Ga., Augusta. Mem. Am. Soc. Anesthesiologists, Soc. Pediat. Anesthesia, Assn. Univ. Anesthesiologists, Ga. ANES Soc. Office: Med Coll Ga Children's Med Ctr 1446 Harper St Augusta GA 30912-2700 Home Phone: 706-738-7124; Office Phone: 706-721-9519.

BETZ, A. LORRIS, academic administrator, medical educator, pediatrician; b. LaCrosse, Wis., Feb. 9, 1947; s. Alert L. and Charlotte M. (Kopp) B.; m. Ann C. Doyle, Aug. 30, 1968; children: Jennifer A., Bryan L. BS, U. Wis., 1969, MD., PhD, 1975. Intern pediatrics U. Calif., San Francisco, 1975, resident in pediatrics, 1975-79; asst. prof. pediatrics and neurology U. Mich., Ann Arbor, 1979-83, assoc. prof. pediatrics and neurology, 1983-87, prof. pediatrics, surgery, neurology, 1987—99, dir. neurosurg. rsch., surgery, 1987—99, assoc. dean for faculty affairs, 1993-97, interim dean Med. Sch., 1997—99; dean, sr. v.p. health sci. U. Utah Med. Sch., Salt Lake City, 1999—, sr. v.p.; interim pres. U. Utah, 2004, 2011—. Cons. NIH, Bethesda, Md., 1985—. Editorial bd.: Jour. Neurochemistry, 1986-94; contbr. articles to Sci., Brain Rsch., Sci. Am., Stroke, Am. Jour. Physiology. Grantee, NIH, Univ. Mich., 1980—; named Established Investigator, Am. Heart Assn., Univ. Mich., 1981. Mem. Internat. Soc. Cerebral Blood Flow and Metabolism (bd. dirs. 1991—, sec. 1995—), Internat. Soc. Neurochemistry, Am. Physiol. Soc., Soc. for Pediatric Rsch., Am. Pediatric Soc., Phi Beta Kappa, Sigma Xi, Alpha Omega Alpha. Achievements include research in basic mechanisms that are responsible for moving nutrients and electrolytes between the blood and the brain of mammals, processes that produce brain injury following a stroke. Office: University fo Utah Office of President 201 S Presidents Circle, Room 203 Salt Lake City UT 84112 also: Heath Science Center Moran Eye Ctr Fl 5 50 N Med Dr Salt Lake City UT 84132-0001 Office Phone: 801-581-7480. E-mail: lorris.betz@hsc.utah.edu. *

BETZ, RANDAL R., orthopedist; MD, Temple U. Fellow pediatric orthopaedics Alfred I duPont Inst.; Am.-Brit.-Can. traveling fellow Can. Orthopaedic Assn., North Am. traveling fellow; Berg-Sloat traveling fellow Orthopaedic Rsch. and Edn. Found.; intern gen. surgery Temple Univ. Hosp., resident orthopaedic surgery; prof. orthopaedic surgery Temple Univ. Sch. Medicine; staff Temple Univ. Children's Med. Ctr.; chief staff Shriners Hosps. for Children, med. dir. spinal cord injury unit. Editl. bd. Jour. Pediatric Orthopaedics, SpineUniverse, assoc. editor Spinal Frontiers, reviewer Jour. of Bone And Joint Surgery, Jour. Pediatric Orthopaedics, Spine. Mem.: Spinal Deformity Edn. Group, Internat. Functional Elec. Stimulation Soc., Brit. Scoliosis Soc., Am. Spinal Injury Assn., Am. Paraplegia Soc., Am. Orthopaedic Assn., Am. Acad. Orthopaedic Surgeons, Am. Acad. Cerebral Palsy and Devel. Medicine, Am. Orthopaedic Soc., Alpha Mega Alpha. Office: Shriners Hospitals for Children 2900 Rocky Point Dr Tampa FL 33607 Office Phone: 813-281-0300.

BETZ, RONALD PHILIP, pharmacist; b. Chgo., Nov. 26, 1933; s. David Robert and Olga Marie (Martinson) B.; m. Rose Marie Marella, May 18, 1963; children: David Christian, Christopher Peter. BS, U. Ill., 1955; MPA, Roosevelt U., 1987. Asst. dir. pharmacy U. Ill., Chgo., 1959-62; dir. pharmacy Mt. Sinai Hosp., Chgo., 1962-2001; pres. Pharmacy Systems, Inc., 1982-89; teaching assoc. Coll. Pharmacy, U. Ill., Chgo., 1977-88. Adj. clin. asst. prof. pharmacy, U. Ill., 1988-2001; pres. Pharmacy Svc. and Systems, 1972-81; dir. Ill. Coop. Health Data Systems, 1976-80. Contbr. articles to profl. jours. Bd. dirs. Howard/Paulina Redevel. Corp., 1983-92. With U.S. Army, 1956-58. Mem.: No. Ill. Soc. Hosp. Pharmacists (pres. 1966), Ill. Acad. Preceptors in Pharmacy (pres. 1972), Ill. Pharm. Assn. (pres. 1975), Am. Soc. Health Sys. Pharmacists, Kappa Psi. Democrat. Lutheran. Home: 1021 Sussex Dr Northbrook IL 60062-3328 E-mail: rbetznb@aol.com.

BETZER, SUSAN ELIZABETH BEERS, physician, geriatrician; b. Evanston, Ill., Aug. 24, 1943; d. Thomas Moulding and Mary Ella (Waidner) Beers; m. Peter Robin Betzer, June 18, 1965; children: Sarah Elizabeth, Katherine Hannah. AB in Biol. Scis. magna cum, Mount Holyoke Coll., 1965; PhD in Oceanography, U. R.I., 1972; MD, U. Miami, 1978. Diplomate Am. Bd. Family Practice, Am. Bd. Geriat. Rsch. assoc. dept. marine sci. U. South Fla., St. Petersburg, 1973-74, rsch. scholar, scientist, 1975-76; resident in family practice Bayfront Med. Ctr., St. Petersburg, 1978-81; clin. asst. prof. dept. family medicine U. South Fla., Tampa, 1982—2007; pvt. practice St. Petersburg, 1982—. Cons. physician Fed. Employee Health Clinic, Honolulu, 1981-82. Contbr. articles to profl. jours. Adv. com. St. Petersburg H.S., 1996-2002; bd. dir. Fla. Orch., St. Petersburg, 1983-86, 88-, pres., 1985-86, mem. exec. com., 1988-, vice-chair bd. trustees 1996-2002, sec., 2002-, founder, chair audience devel. com., St. Petersburg, 1990-94; bd. dirs. Suncoast Ctr. Cmty. Mental Health, St. Petersburg, 1992-93; trustee Bayfront Health Found., 1996-2004, chmn., 2001-03; trustee Bayfront Health Svcs., 1992-96, vice-chair, 1993-96; vol. physician St. Petersburg Free Clinic, 1979-2003. Recipient Golden Baton award, St. Petersburg Fla. Orch. Guild, 1994, Chmns. award, Fla. Orch., 1997, Svc. award, Pinellas County Med. Soc., 1999, Philanthropy Vol. of Yr., Tampa Bay chpt. Assn. Fundraising Profls., 2003, Humanitarian Physician of Yr., Tampa Bay Area, Fla. Med. Bus., 2004; named Woman of Distinction, Suncoast coun. Girl Scouts U.S., 1994; named one of Best Doctors in Am., 1996—. Mem.: Mt. Holyoke Coll. Campaign Steering Com., Fla. Acad. Family Physicians (Dr. of the Day, Fla. Legislature 1995, 1996), Am. Med. Women's Assn., Am. Acad. Family Physicians (Mead Johnson award 1980), Mount Holyoke Alumnae Assn. (alumnae honor rsch. com. 1988—91, alumnae devel. com. 1996—2003, pres. 2003—06, Alumnae medal of honor 2000), Phi Beta Kappa. Avocations: symphony, birding, cooking, reading. Home: 1830 7th St N Saint Petersburg FL 33704-3322 Office: 461 7th Ave S Saint Petersburg FL 33701-4818 Office Phone: 727-823-0402.

BEUTLER, BRUCE A., geneticist, immunologist; b. Chgo., Dec. 29, 1957; s. Ernest and Brondelle May Beutler; children: Daniel Edward, Elliot Karl, Jonathan David. BA, U. Calif., San Diego, 1976; MD, U. Chgo. Pritzker Sch. Medicine, 1981; MD (hon.), Tech. U. Munich, 2007. Med. tng. U. Tex. Southwester Med. Ctr., Dallas, 1981—83, asst. prof., 1986—90, assoc. prof., 1990—96, founding dir., Ctr. Genetics of Host Defense, 2011—, prof., 1996—2000; fellow Rockefeller U, NY, 1983—85, asst. prof., 1985; assoc. physician Rockefeller U. Hosp., 1984—86; prof. dept. immunology Scripps Rsch. Inst., La Jolla, Calif., 2000—11, chmn. dept. genetics, 2007—11. Investigator Howard Hughes Med. Inst., 1986—2000. Recipient Young Investigator award, American Fedn. Clin. Rsch., 1994, Charles-Léopold Mayer prize, French Acad. Scis., 2006, William B. Coley award, Cancer Rsch. Inst., 2006, Will Rogers Inst. Ann. prize for rsch., 2009; co-recipient Robert Koch prize, Germany, 2004, Internat. Balzan Found. prize, 2007, Albany Med. Ctr. prize, 2009, Shaw Found. prize for Life Sci./Medicine, Hong Kong, 2011. Mem.: NAS, Inst. Medicine, Assn. American Physicians, American Soc. Clin. Investigation, European Molecular Biology Orgn. (assoc.; fgn. assoc.). Achievements include first to isolate mouse tumor necrosis factor-alpha (TNF) and to demonstrate the inflammatory potential of this cytokine, proving its important role in endotoxin-induced shock; invention of recombinant molecules expressly designed to neutralize TNF used extensively in the treatment of rheumatoid arthritis, Crohn's disease, psoriasis, and other forms of inflammation. Office: UT Southwestern Med Ctr 5323 Harry Hines Blvd Dallas TX 75390 Office Phone: 858-784-2037. Business E-Mail: bruce@scripps.edu. *

BEUTLER, LARRY EDWARD, psychologist, educator; b. Logan, Utah, Feb. 14, 1941; s. Edward and Beulah (Andrus) B.; children: Jana, Kelly, Ian David, Gail. BS, Utah State U., 1965, MS, 1966; PhD, U. Nebr., 1970. Diplomate Am. Bd. Clin. Psychology. Asst. prof. psychology Duke U., Ashville, NC, 1970-71; asst. prof. Stephen F. Austin State U., Nacogdoches, Tex., 1971-73; assoc. prof. Baylor Coll. Medicine, Houston, 1973-79; prof. U. Ariz., Tucson, 1979-90, U. Calif., Santa Barbara, 1990—, Pab Alto U., Stanford U., Palo Alto, Calif., 2002—. Co-author: Systematic Treatment Selection, 1990, Guidelines for the Systematic Treatment of the Depressed Patient,

2000, Integrative Assessment of Adult Personality, 2003, Principles of Therapeutic Change That Work, 2006, others; editor Jour. Cons. Clin. Psychology, 1990-96, Psychology of Terrorism, 2007; editor Jour. Clin. Psychology, 1997—2004. Fellow APA (pres. divsn. psychotherapy, 1997, pres. divsn. clin. psychology, 2002), Am. Psychol. Soc.; mem. Soc. Psychotherapy Rsch. (pres. 1986-88). Home: 2620 Piedra Verde Ct Placerville CA 95667 Office: Pacific Grad School Of Psychology 1791 Arastradero Rd Palo Alto CA 94304-1337 Home Phone: 530-642-1353. Business E-Mail: larrybeutler@yahoo.com. *

BEVAN, WILLIAM ARNOLD, JR., emergency physician; b. Sault St. Marie, Mich., June 23, 1943; s. William Arnold and Syneva Lois (Martin) B.; m. Martha Lynn Peterson, Dec. 29, 1973; children: Terry Eugene, Brian William, Patrick Jon. BS, U. Minn., 1966, MD, 1970. Diplomate Am. Bd. Family Practice, Am. Bd. Emergency Medicine. Intern U. Utah, 1970—71; family practitioner Vail Mountain Med. Profl. Corp., Vail, Colo., 1972—83; emergency physician Vail Valley Emergency Physicians, 1983—; dir. Vail Valley Med. Ctr., 1990—. Dir. Vail Valley Emergency Dept., 1992—, pres. med. staff, 1977; adviser Western Eagle County Ambulance Dist., 1983—. Trustee Shattuck St. Mary's Sch., Faribault, Minn., 1977—; football coach Battle Mountain H.S., Vail, 1978—; trustee, bd. dirs. Vail Christian H.S., 1998—, football coach; Eagle Scout. Named Man of Yr. Boy Scouts Am., 1966, 77, Physician of Yr. Vail Valley Med. Ctr., 2007. Fellow Am. Coll. Emergency Physicians; mem. AMA, Rocky Mountain Med. Soc., Colo. Med. Soc., U. Minn. Alumni Assn. (life). Republican. Lutheran. Home: 25 Cottonwood Rd Eagle CO 81631 Office: Vail Valley Emergency Dept 181 W Meadow Dr Vail CO 81657-5058 Mailing: Box 1143 Avon CO 81620 Home Phone: 970-949-7093; Office Phone: 970-476-8065. E-mail: williambevan@comcast.net.

BEVERLEY, CORDIA LUVONNE, gastroenterologist; b. Jamaica, W.I., Oct. 19, 1950; d. Hurdley Aston and Joyce Ruby (Baker) Beverley. BA, Hunter Coll., 1971; MD, NYU, 1975. Diplomate Am. Bd. Gastroenterology, Am. Bd. Internal Medicine. Intern Columbia U., Harlem Hosp. Ctr., 1975—76, resident in medicine, 1976—78; clin. fellow divsn. gastroenterology NY Hosp./Cornell U. Med. Coll., 1979—82; asst. physician Rockefeller U. Hosp., 1978—81; pvt. practice gastroenterology, 1981—; assoc. med. staff mem. Lenox Hill Hosp., 1985—. Fellow Postdoctoral fellow, Nat. Inst. Alcohol Abuse and Alcoholism, 1980—82. Mem.: Women's Med. Assn. N.Y.C. Office: 1085 Park Ave New York NY 10128-1168 Office Phone: 212-876-1886.

BEVERSDORF, DAVID QUENTIN, neurologist, researcher; b. Bloomington, Ind., May 28, 1965; s. Samuel Thomas and Norma (Beeson) B., m. Shelley Catherne Beversdorf. BS, Ind. U., 1987; MD, Ind. U., Indpls., 1992. Med. resident Meth. Hosp. Ind., Indpls., 1992-93; neurology resident Dartmouth-Hitchcock Med. Ctr., Lebanon, N.H., 1993-96; behavioral neurology fellow U. Fla. Coll. Medicine, Gainesville, 1996-98; asst. prof. neurology Ohio State U. Med. Ctr., Columbus, 1998—2008; assoc. prof. radiology, neurology, psychology Thompson Ctr. U. Missouri, Colo., 2008—. Contbr. articles to profl. jours. including Procs. Nat. Acad. Scis., Lancet, Neurology, Psychiatry Rsch.-Neuroimaging, Jour. Neurology, Jour. Cognitive Neurosci., Neurosurgery and Psychiatry, and Physiology and Behavior. Rsch. grant Stallone Fund, L.A., 1994, grantee Nat. Inst. on Drug Abuse, 2002, Nat. Inst. Neurol. Diseases and Stroke, 2002, Nat. Alliance for Autism Rsch., 2005, Health Resource Service Admin, 2009. Mem. Internat. Neuropsychol. Soc., Am. Acad. Neurology, Soc. for Neurosci., Cognitive Neurosci. Soc., Phi Beta Kappa. Office: Univ Missouri Thompson Ctr Dept Radiology Neurology & Psychology 205 Portland St Rm 130E Columbia MO 65211 Home: 14120 Hwy BB Rocheport MO 65279 Office Phone: 573-882-6081. Business E-Mail: beversdorfd@health.missouri.edu.

BEYER-MEARS, ANNETTE, physiologist; b. Madison, Wis., May 26, 1941; d. Karl and Annette (Weiss) Beyer. BA, Vassar Coll., 1963; MS, Fairleigh Dickinson U., 1973; PhD, Coll. Medicine and Dentistry NJ, 1977. NIH fellow Cornell U. Med. Sch., 1963-65; instr. physiology Springside Sch., Phila., 1967-71; teaching asst. dept. physiology Coll. Medicine & Dentistry NJ, NJ Med. Sch., 1974-77, NIH fellow dept. ophthalmology, 1978-80; asst. prof. dept. ophthalmology U. Medicine and Dentistry NJ., NJ Med. Sch., Newark, 1979-85, asst. prof. dept. physiology, 1980-85, assoc. prof. dept. physiology, 1986—, assoc. prof. dept. ophthalmology, 1986—. Vis. assoc. prof. dept. ophthalmology and vision sci. U. Wis., Madison, 1995—; cons. Alcon Labs. Contbr. articles in field of diabetic lens and kidney therapy to profl. jours. Chmn. admissions No. NJ, Vassar Coll., 1974-79; mem. minister search com. St. Bartholomew Episcopal Ch., NJ, 1978, fund-raising chmn., 1978, 79; del. Episc. Diocesian Conv., 1977, 78; long range planning com. Christ Ch., Ridgewood, NJ, 1985-87, vestry, 1994-95. Recipient NIH Nat. Rsch. Svc. award, 1978-80, Found. CMDNJ Rsch. award, 1980; grantee Juvenile Diabetes Found., 1985-87, NIH, NEI grantee, 1980-95, Pfizer, Inc. grantee, 1985-89, 93—. Mem. Am. Physiol. Soc., NY Acad. Scis., Soc. for Neurosci., Am. Soc. Pharmacology and Exptl. Therapeutics, Assn. for Rsch. Vision & Ophthalmology, Internat. Soc. for Eye Research, AAAS, The Royal Soc. Medicine, Internat. Diabetes Found., Am. Diabetes Assn., European Assn. Study of Diabetes, Aircraft Owners and Pilots Assn., Sigma Xi. Home: 120 Ely Pl Madison WI 53726-4015

BEZKOROVAINY, ANATOLY, medical educator, retired biochemist; b. Riga, Latvia, Feb. 11, 1935; s. Ignatius and Olga (Solovey) Bezkorovainy; m. Marilyn Grib, June 14, 1964; children: Gregory, Alexander. BS, U. Chgo., 1956; PhD, U. Ill., 1960; JD, Ill. Inst. Tech., 1977. Bar: Ill. 1977. Rsch. assoc. Oak Ridge Nat. Lab., Tenn., 1960—61; chemist USDA, Ames, Iowa, 1961—62; mem. faculty Rush-Presbyn. St. Luke's Med. Ctr., Chgo., 1962—, asst. prof., 1962—67, assoc. prof., 1967—73, prof. biochemistry, 1973—2004, emeritus prof., 2004, assoc. chmn., dir. ednl. programs biochemistry dept., 1980—2000. Lectr. Dr. Scholl Coll. Podiatric Medicine, North Chgo., Ill., 2000—08. Author: Basic Protein Chemistry, 1970, Biochemistry of Nonheme Iron, 1980, All Was Not Lost, 2008; co-author (with Rafelson and Hayashi): Basic Biochemistry, 1980; co-author: (with Miller-Catchpole) Biochemistry and Physiology of Bifidobacteria, 1989; co-author: (with Rafelson) Concise Biochemistry, 1995; contbr. articles to profl. jours. Numerous grants, NSF, NIH, Am. Heart Assn., indsl. instns., 1962. Mem.: Am. Soc. Biol. Chemists, Am. Dairy Sci. Assn. Eastern Orthodox. Home: 4 Northbend Ln Galena IL 61036 Home Phone: 815-776-0175. Personal E-mail: marilynb38@hotmail.com.

BEZOLD, GUNTRAM DIETRICH, physician, dermatologist; b. Stuttgart, Germany, Sept. 28, 1966; s. Gunter and Hermine Bezold; m. Petra Gottloeber, May 8, 1999. MD, Ludwig-Maximilians-U., Munich, Germany, 1993. Resident dept. dermatology Ludwig-Maximilians-U., 1994, resident, 1996-97; postdoctoral fellow Brigham and Women's Hosp./Harvard U., Boston, 1994-96; resident dept. dermatology U. Ulm, Germany, 1997—2002; sci. leader Lab. Molecular Dermantology, Neu-Ulm, Germany, 2002—. Contbr. articles to profl. jours. Deutsche Forschungsgemeinschaft grantee, 1994-96. Mem. German Dermatol. Soc., German Alpine Club. Avocations: skiing, mountain climbing. Office: Lab Molecular Dermatology Augsburger Strasse 6 89231 Neu-Ulm Germany Home Phone: +49-7309-929180; Office Phone: +49-731-75556.

BEZUIDENHOUT, DEON, medical educator; b. Cape Town, July 20, 1965; MSc, Stellenosch U., 1993, PhD, 2001. Sr. lectr. U. Cape Town, 1986—. Cons. 180 Degrees, 2004—08; bd. dirs. Southern Acces Tech., 2009—11. Recipient award, Nat. Rsch. Found., South Africa; Bue Sky grant, grant, Nat. Rsch. Found., Sweden, NIH. Mem.: Internat. Soc. Applied Cardiovasc. Biology, South African Heart Assn., Biomaterials Assn. South Africa, Am. Soc. Artificial Internal Organs, Soc. Biomaterials. Avocations: travel, guitar, reading. Office: University Cape Town 203 Cape Heart Ctr FHS Anzio RD Cape Town Western Cape 7925 South Africa Office Fax: 27 (0)21 448 5935. Business E-Mail: deon.bezuidenhout@uct.ac.za.

BHAGAT, GOVIND, biology professor; b. New Delhi, Dec. 23, 1968; MBBS, U. Coll. Med. Scis., New Delhi, 1992. Prof. clin. pathology & cell biology Columbia U. Med. Ctr. & NY Presbyn. Hosp., 2001—, dir., divsn. hematopathology. Mem.: Soc. Mucosal Immunology, Am. Soc. Hematology, US & Canadian Acad. Pathology. Office: VC14-228 630W 168th St New York NY 10032 Office Phone: 212-305-6719. Office Fax: 212-305-2301. Business E-Mail: gb96@columbia.edu.

BHAGAT, NEELAKSHI, surgeon, educator; b. India, May 17, 1968; BS, CUNY, 1990, MPH; MD, SUNY, Stonybrook, 1994. Dir., vitreo-retinal surgery Inst. Ophthalmology and Visual Sci., 2001—. Assoc. prof. ophthalmology NJ Med. Sch., 2001. Recipient Top Dr's in NJ City, Castle Connoly, 2010; named one of Best Dr's in Am., Best Doctors, Inc., 2003—11, Top Dr's in NJ City, Castle Connoly, 2009, Top Dr's in NY Metro Area, 2010, 2011. Fellow: ACS, Am. Acad. Ophthalmology; mem.: Am. Soc. Retina Specialists, Retina Soc., Macula Soc. Office: Inst Ophthalmology and Visual Sci DOC-6100 90 Bergen St Newark NJ 07103 Office Phone: 973-972-2032. Business E-Mail: bhagatne@umdnj.edu.

BHAGIA, VASDEV, pediatrician, consultant; b. India, July 28, 1943; s. Shewakram Pahlajrai Bhagia and Parpati Thawani; m. Veena Gopi Hingorani, June 7, 1972; children: Vijay, Vinita. MBBS, All India Inst. Med. Scis., New Delhi, 1965. Diplomate Am. Bd. Pediatrics. Intern All India Inst. Med. Scis., New Delhi, 1965, house surgeon, 1966; sr. house officer pediats. England, 1967; sr. resident in pediats. Meadowbrook Hosp., LI, NY, 1968; chief resident NY Med. Coll., NYC, 1969; fellow in pediats. Harvard Med. Sch. Children's Hosp., Mass., 1970; gen. mgr., head dept. med. svcs. Indian Airlines, New Delhi, 1973—2001. Fellow: Internat. Med. Scis. Acad., Inst. Aero-Space Medicine; mem.: Indian Acad. Pediats., Med. Club (sec. gen. 1984—86). Avocation: travel. Home: 806 Shady Bend Friendswood TX 77546 Office: Bayshore Pediat 4024 Brookhaven Pasadena TX 77504 Office Phone: 713-944-2324.

BHAKDI, SUCHARIT PUNYARATABANDU, microbiology educator; b. Washington, Nov. 1, 1946; arrived in Germany, 1963; citizen of Thailand. s. Luang Dithakar and Tanpuying Saiyude (Gengradomying) B.; m. Birgit Elfriede Lehnen, Mar. 9, 1973 (div. 1999); children: Sebastian Chakrit, Johannes Suriya, Benjamin Suchinda, Jeremias Ramet; m. Verena Gerl, May 25, 2000; children: Lara Sudawadee, Julian Suranat. MD, Bonn U., 1970. Diplomate in Med. Microbiology. Postdoctoral Max-Planck Inst., Freiburg, Germany, 1972-76, Copenhagen (Denmark) Univ., 1976-77, Giessen (Germany) Univ., 1977-82, asst. prof., 1982-87, assoc. prof., 1987-90; prof., head dept. Mainz (Germany) Univ., 1990—. Advisor Ctr. for Molecular Medicine, Siriraj Hosp., Bangkok Univ., 1991—. Editor Med. Microbiology and Immunology, 1990—; contbr. numerous articles to profl. jours. Recipient Justus-Liebig award U. Giessen, 1979, Constance award U. Constance, 1980, German Soc. for Microbiology award German Soc. for Microbiology, 1987, Dr. Sasse award U. Berlin, 1988, Robert-Koch award Clausthal-Zellerfeld, 1989, Schunk award, 1989, Alexander-von Humboldt award Alexander von Humboldt-Stiftung, 1991, Schettler award 1999, German Soc. Angiology award, 1999, Aronson award, 2001, award Soc. Atherosclerosis Rsch., 2005, Rudolf Schonheimer medal German Atherosclerosis Soc., 2009. Avocations: sports, music, history medicine and science. Office: U Mainz Inst Med Microbiology Augustusplatz 55101 Mainz Germany Home Phone: 6136 81256; Office Phone: 6131 3937341. Business E-Mail: sbhakdi@uni-mainz.de.

BHANDARI, SUMAN, cardiologist; b. Bhiwani, Haryana, India, Oct. 9, 1955; s. Bharat Kumar and Bimla (Kohli) B.; m. Nita Chawla, Feb. 16, 1982; 1 child, Sonakshi. MBBS, Rohtak Med. Coll., Haryana, 1977, MD in Gen. Medicine, 1981; DM in Cardiology, All India Inst. Med. Scis., New Delhi, 1983. Med. diplomate, India. Sr. resident medicine All India Inst. Med. Scis., New Delhi, 1981-82, sr. resident cardiology, 1982-84, pool officer cardiology, 1985-86; cons. cardiologist Sir Ganga Ram Hosp., New Delhi, 1986-88; prin. cons. cardiologist Escort's Heart Hosp., New Delhi, 1988—. Editor: Indian Heart Jour., 2006—; contbr. articles to profl. jours. Mem. Cardiol. Soc. India, Panchshila Club (New Delhi), New Friends Club Avocations: reading, music, hockey, squash. Office: Escorts Heart Hosp New Delhi India Home: B-10 110 048 New Delhi India Office Phone: 91-11-26825000. Personal E-mail: sumanbhandari@yahoo.com.

BHANDARI, SUNIL, physician, educator, researcher; s. Joginder Paul B.; m. Elizabeth Morris, May 19, 1996; children: Sara, Alisha. MBChB, U. Edinburgh, Scotland, 1990, MRCP, 1993; PhD, U. Leeds, Eng., 1999; dipl. in Med. Edn., U. Newcastle, 2006. ECDL and advanced ECDL Brit. Computing Soc., 2002; CCST JCHMT, 2000. Jr. ho. physician Nat. Health Svc., Edinburgh, 1990-91, sr. med. physician, 1991-92, registrar, 1993-94, Leeds, Eng., 1994-96; rsch. fellow Nat. Kidney Rsch. Found., Leeds, 1996-99; advanced trainee Sydney, 1999—2000; hon. clin. reader, cons. Hull and East Yorkshire NHS Trust, 2000. Dir. clin. studies Hull York Med. Sch. Contbr. articles to profl. jours. Kaberry tng. fellow NHS Trust, Leeds, 1996, Nat. tng. fellow Nat. Kidney Rsch. Found., 1996; Victor-Wallace scholar, U. Edinburgh, 1989. Fellow Royal Coll. Physicians Scotland; mem. Brit. Renal Assn. Achievements include research in Contributions To The Field Of Basic And Clinical Nephrology. Avocations: scuba-diving, skiing, cricket. Office: Hull and East Yorkshire NHS Trust East Yorkshire HU3 2JZ England Office Phone: 44 01482 674566. Office Fax: 44 014826 74998. Business E-Mail: sunil.bhandari@hey.nhs.uk.

BHANDARI, VINEET, pediatrician; s. Jagdish and Rajni Bhandari; m. Anita Narula, Dec. 14, 1991; children: Shreya, Esha. Indian Sch. cert., St. Columba's Sch., New Delhi, India, 1981; MBBS, Armed Forces Med. Coll., Pune, India, 1985; MD, Post Grad. Inst. of Med. Edn. and Rsch., Chandigarh, India, 1990. Diplomate Am. Acad. Pediat., Am. Bd. Neonatal-Perinatal Medicine. Sr. registrar in neonatology Postgrad. Inst. of Med. Edn. and Rsch., Chandigarh, Punjab, India, 1990—92; instr. clin. pediat. (neonatology) U. Conn. Sch. of Medicine, Farmington, Conn., 1996—97, asst. clin. prof., pediat. (neonatology), 1997—98; asst. prof. pediat. (neonatology) Temple U. Sch. of Medicine, Phila., 1998—2001; assoc. rsch. scientist Yale U. Sch. of Medicine, New Haven, 2001—. Dir., neonatal respiratory rsch. lab. Albert Einstein Med. Ctr., Phila., 2000—01. Rsch. grantee, Einstein Soc., 1999—2000, NIH/NICHD, 1999—2002, NIH/NHLBI, 2003—. Fellow: Am. Acad. of Pediat.; mem.: AAAS, AMA, Soc. Pediatric Rsch., Nat. Neonatology Forum (life), Indian Acad. of Pediat. (life). Home: 95 Nichole Ct Cheshire CT 06410

BHARATH, CHALAVADI, medical educator; b. Bellary, India, Jan. 5, 1963; s. Bate Basavanappa Chalavadi and Chalavadi Kenchamma; m. Annapoorna Bharath, June 8, 1990; children: Mohan, B. Savan Kumar. MBBS, Govt. Med. Coll., 1986, MD in Pathology, 1995. Lic. physician Karnataka Med. Coun., Bangalore, cert. pathologist Gulbarga U., 1995. Intern Med. Coll. Bellary, 1986—88, resident in pathology, 1991—95; lectr. Siddartha Med. Coll, Tumkur Karnataka, 1988—91; asst. prof. Psginisr Coimbatore, Tamil Nadu, India, 1995—97; from lectr. Coll. Medicine to assoc. prof. Vijayanagar Inst. Med. Scis., Bellary-Karnataka, India, 1997—2004; prof. pathology Med. Coll. Bellary, 2004—. Sec. Med. Edn. Cell, Bellory-Karnataka, 2003—05; pres. Kannada Sangha, Bellory-Karnataka, 2004—05, chmn. sports com., 2004. Contbr. articles to profl. jours. Recipient Rastriya Ratan award, Internat. Study Ctr., 2004, Med. Excellence award, 2004, Gold medal, 2004. Mem.: Indian Assn. Pathologists, Indian Med. Assn., Karnataka Sahitya Parishad (life). Avocations: photography, singing, sports, painting, literature. Office: Med College VIMS Cantonment Bellary 583104 India Personal E-mail: bhar5anu@yahoo.co.in.

BHARGAVA, DARPAN, oral surgeon; b. Bhopal, Madhya Pradesh, India, Apr. 20, 1982; MDS, Meenakshi Ammal Dental Coll., 2011, MOMSRCPS; postgrad. diploma in Hosp. mgmt., postgrad. diploma in Clin. Rsch. Surgeon Meenakshi Ammal Dental Coll., Chennai, 2001—11. Named Best Outgoing Oral and Maxillofacial Surgeon, Meenakshi Acad. Higher Edn. & Rsch., Chennai, 2011. Home: H-3/2 BDA Colony Nayapura Lal Ghati Bhopal Madhya Pradesh 462001 India Personal E-mail: drdarpanbhargava@gmail.com.

BHASIN, NEERAJ, surgeon, researcher; b. Farnborough, England, Aug. 27, 1975; s. Bharat and Priti Bhasin; m. Victoria Percival. BSc with hons., United Med. and Dental Schs. Guys and St. Thomas's Hosps., 1999, MB BS, 1999; MD, U. Leeds, Eng., 2007. House officer gen. surgery Maidstone Hosp., England, 1999—2000; house officer in elderly medicine and cardiology St. Thomas's Hosp., London, 2000; sr. house officer accident and emergency Halifax Royal Infirmary, England, 2000—01; sr. house officer orthop. and trauma Calderdale Royal Hosp., Halifax, 2001, sr. house officer gen. surgery, 2002, specialist registrar gen. surgery, 2006—07, Calderdale and Huddersfield Hosp., Dewsbury, 2007—08; sr. house officer intensive care medicine St. James's U. Hosp., Leeds, 2001—02, sr. house officer vascular surgery, 2002—03, sr. house officer urology, 2003; sr. house officer gen. surgery Bradford Royal Infirmary, England, 2003; clin. rsch. fellow Academic Unit Molecular Vascular Medicine U. Leeds, 2003—05; specialist registrar vascular surgery Leeds Gen. Infirmary, 2005—06, Airedale Gen., 2008—09, Hull Royal Infirmary, 2010; specialist registrar Bradford Royal Infirmary, 2009—10. Physician The Galpharm Stadium, Huddersfield, England, 2001—09. Contbr. articles to profl. jours. Fellow, Brit. Heart Found., 2003—05. Fellow: RCS (Eng.). Achievements include research in the fibrin clot structure and function in the first degree relatives of subjects with peripheral vascular disease. Home: 39 Quarmby Fold Huddersfield HD34YT England

BHASIN, SHALENDER, endocrinologist, educator; MD, All India Inst. Med. Sciences, 1976. Diplomate Am. Bd. Internal Medicine, 1981, Am. Bd. Internal Medicine-endocrinology, diabetes and metabolism, 2008. Resident internal medicine Northwestern Univ. Med. Ctr., Chgo., 1979—81; fellow endocrinology, diabetes and metabolism Harbor-UCLA Med. Ctr., Torrance, Calif., 1981—84; prof. medicine Boston Univ.; chief sect. endocrinology, diabetes, and nutrition Boston Med. Ctr. Assoc. editor Jour. of Clin. Endocrinology and Metabolism. Recipient Fellow of the Year award, Harbor-UCLA Med. Ctr., 1984, Richard Weitzman Meml. Young Investigator award, 1990, Disting. Tchg. award, 1990, Gen. Clin. Rsch. Ctr. (GCRC) award, UT Southwestern Med. Sch., 2000, Pharmacia award, Jour. of Clin. Endocrinology and Metabolism (JCEM), 2003; named one of Best Doctors in Boston, 2006. Mem.: Endocrine Soc. (chair expert panel on androgen deficiency syndromes in men). Office: Boston Medical Center One Boston Medical Center Pl Boston MA 02118 Office Phone: 617-638-8000.

BHAT, BAL KRISHEN, geneticist, plant breeder; b. Srinagar, India, May 3, 1940; came to U.S. 1989; s. Justice Janki Nath and Dhanwati (Kaul) B.; m. Sarla Kaul, Sept. 23, 1966; children: Arun Bhat, Anupama Bhat. MSc, Indian Agrl. Rsch. Inst., New Delhi, 1963; PhD, I.A.R.I., New Delhi, 1967. Rsch. assoc. Rockefeller Found., New Delhi, 1967; plant breeder in charge of rsch. Birla Inst. of Sci. Rsch., Rupar, Punjab, India, 1967-68; scientist C Reg. Rsch. Lab. Coun. of Sci. and Indsl. Rsch., Srinagar, India, 1968-74, head, 1972-79, 87-89, scientist E I, 1974-79, scientist E II, 1981-85, deputy dir., 1985-89; v.p., dir. rsch. Bot. Resources, Inc., Independence, Oreg., 1989—95; cons., 1995—. Rsch. fellow U. Tasmania, Hobart, Australia, 1979-81, sr. rsch. fellow, 1981-86; cons. in field. Contbr. over 110 articles to profl. jours. Named Scientist of the Yr., Reg. Rsch. Lab., Srinagar, 1976. Fellow: Indian Soc. Genetics and Plant Breeding; mem.: Am. Botanical Coun., Coun. for Agrl. Sci. and Tech., Soc. for Advancement of Breeding Rsch. in Asia and Oceania, Crop Sci. Soc. Am., Am. Soc. Agronomy. Achievements include introduction and organization of commercial production of crops to new lands such as hops in India, pyrethrum in Australia, others; evolved a number of new cultivars in hops, pyrethrum, and medicinal and aromatic plants.

BHAT, DEEPTI PAGARE, physician; b. New Delhi, Aug. 19, 1973; MBBS, Mysore Med. Coll., 1999; MD in Pediat., Case Western U., 2010. Physician preventive and social medicine Maulana Azad Med. Coll., New Delhi, 2001—04; physician pediat. Hull Royal Infirmary, 2005—06, Case Western Res. U., Metrohealth Campus, 2008—10; physician pediat. cardiology Leeds Gen. Infirmary, 2007. With WHO, UNICEF. Recipient Gold medal, Mysore U., 1999, Sr. Resident Tchg. award, Dept. Pediat., Metrohealth Med. Ctr., 2010. Mem.: Am. Acad. Pediat. Avocations: reading, travel, poetry. Home: 11230 Navajo Ln Apt 201 Parma Heights OH 44130 Personal E-mail: drdeeptibhat@yahoo.com.

BHAT, VIKRAM K., otolaryngologist, educator; b. Manipal, Karnatak, India, Aug. 22, 1970; s. Vasudeva T.K. and Vanajakshi K. Bhat; m. Roopa S. Bhat, Apr. 9, 2000. MBBS, Mysore Med. Coll., India, 1993; MS, Kasturba Med. Coll., India, 1998; DNB, NAt. Bd. Exams., New Delhi, 1999; PhD in ENT, Karnataka Inst. Med. Scis., Hubli, India, 2008. Registrar Manipal Hosp., Bangalore, India; assoc. prof., dept. ear, nose, and throat Karnataka Inst. Med. Scis., Hubli. Author: Instruments in Ear, Nose, and Throat; contbr. articles to profl. jours. Fellow head and neck oncology, Indian Nat. Sci. Acad., 2002; vis. fellow, Indian Soc. Otology, 2005. Mem.: Indian Med. Assn., Neurotological and Equillibriometric Soc. India, Indian Soc. Otology, Assn. Otolaryngologists India. Avocations: cooking, music. Office: Karnataka Inst Med Scis Dept Ear Nose and Throat Hubli Karnataka 580021 India Home: No 102 Arvind Apts 580 031 Hubli India Personal E-mail: vikram.ent@gmail.com, entvikram@rediffmail.com.

BHATIA, SMITA, epidemiologist, researcher, pediatric oncologist, educator; b. Jalandhar, Punjab, India, May 6, 1961; U.S, 1989; d. Raghubir Chand and Pramila Arora; m. Ravi Bhatia, Feb. 10, 1985; children: Devika, Shweta. MD, All India Inst. Med. Scis., New Delhi, 1989; MPH, U. Minn., 1994. Intern All India Inst. Med. Sci., New Delhi, 1984, resident in pediat., 1985—87, chief resident in pediat., 1988—89; rsch. assoc. U. Minn., 1989—90, postdoc. fellow pediat. epidemiology and clin. rsch., 1994—96; prof., chair, population scis. City of Hope Nat. Med. Ctr., Duarte, Calif., 2001—. Contbr. articles to profl. jours. Recipient Translational Rsch. award, Leukemia/Lymphoma Soc., 2001—, Scholar award in Clin. Rsch., Leukemia/Lymphoma Soc, 2001—; named to Am. Soc. Clin. Investigators, 2006; grantee, Nat. Cancer Inst., 2000—; Divsn. Blood Banking fellow, U. Minn., 1990—91, pediat. hematology/oncology and bone marrow transplant fellow, 1991—94. Mem.: Children's Oncology Group (chair late effects com. 2000). Hindu. Avocation: reading. Office: City Hope Nat Med Ctr 1500 East Duarte Rd Duarte CA 91010 Business E-Mail: sbhatia@coh.org.

BHATNAGAR, DEEPAK, biochemist, researcher; b. Ratlam, India, Oct. 19, 1951; s. Mahavir Prasad and Pushpa Bhatnagar; m. Sadhna Bhatnagar, Apr. 4, 1982. BSc, U. Jodhpur, India, 1971; MSc, Maharaja Siyajirao U. Baroda, India, 1973; PhD, Banaras Hindu U., Varanasi, India, 1981. Lectr. Govt. Med. Coll., Faridkot, India, 1974-77; rsch. fellow Banaras Hindu U., Varanasi, 1978-81; lectr. Govt. Med. Coll., Patiala, India, 1982-88; sr. lectr. Devi Ahilya U. Indore, India, 1989-91, reader, 1991—99, prof., 1999—. Contbr. articles to profl. jours. Recipient award U. Grants Commn. Rsch. Project, New Delhi, 1991-94, 2004-, Madhya Pradesh Coun. Sci. and Tech., Bhopal Rsch. Project, 1991-96. Avocations: reading, writing, sports, social activities. Office: Devi Ahilya Univ Dept Biochemistry Khandwa Rd Indore 452017 India Personal E-mail: dbhatnagar1@rediffmail.com.

BHATNAGAR, SUSHMA, physician; d. Jagmohan and Satya Bhatnagar; m. Naresh Bhatnagar; children: Tigmanshu, Khagol. MD, Sms Med. Coll., Rajasthan, 1991; MBBS, Rajasthan. Physician Dr. BRAIRCH, AIIMS, New Delhi, 1999—. Contbr. scientific papers. Mem.: ISCC, IASP, ISO, IAHPC, IAPC. Achievements include first to pain and palliative care services at Irch, AIIMS; worked to spread the awreness about cancer pain management. Office: RNO242 DrBRAIRCH AIIMS New Delhi New Delhi 110029 India Home: 27 N Ave 110 016 New Delhi India Office Fax: 91-11-26588227. Personal E-mail: shumob@yahoo.com.

BHATOE, HARJINDER SINGH, neurosurgeon; b. Mhow, Madhya, India, Nov. 16, 1956; s. Kartar Singh and Harbans Kaur B.; m. Kulwant Kaur Saini, Sept. 11, 1981; 1 child, Puneeta Singh. BS, Govt. Coll., Mhow, India, 1974; MBBS, Armed Forces Med. Coll., Pune, India, 1978; M Surgery, Army rsch. and Referral Hosp., Delhi, 1986; Magister Neursurgery, Postgrad. Inst. of Med. Edn., and Rsch., Chandigarh, India, 1991. Med. officer Armed Forces, India, 1978-86, gen. surgeon, 1987-89, resident in neurosurgery, 1990-91, neurosurgeon, 1992—; med. officer The Pres.'s Bodyguard, India, 1983-87. Author: Craniospinal Missile Injuries, 2003; contbg. author: Modern Concepts in the Management of Neurotrauma, 1994; contbr. articles to profl. jours. Lt. col. Army Med. Corps, India, 1979—. Mem. Neurotrauma Soc. India, Congress Neurol. Surgeons, Neurol. Soc. of India, Indian Soc. of Pediatric Neurosurgery. Avocation: qualified paratrooper.

BHATT, ROHIT V, gynecologist, consultant; b. Ahmedabad, Gujarat, India, Dec. 6, 1931; s. Vijayshanker M and Dhanlaxmi V Bhatt; m. Minaxi R Minaxi, Mar. 9, 1962; 1 child, Amit R. MD, DCH, G.S. Med. Coll., Mumbai, India, 1958. Cert. in laparocopy & microsurgery John Hopkins Med. Sch., 1982. Chief, ob-gyn. Med. Coll., Vadodara, Gujarat., India, 1961—84, BD Amin Gen. Hosp., Vadodara, 1984—. Vis. prof. Edinburgh U. WHO, Geneva, 1965, cons., 88; past pres. FOKOSI, NARCHI & ISOPARB Assoc.; editor in chief ISLFO, India; hon. fellow AOFOK. Contbr. articles to med. jours. (Dr. Rajam Oration Award, 2008). Cons. Baroda Citizens Coun., Vadodara, 1986—89. Fellow: ICOG, AMS; mem.: Trim Line Club (nil). Office: BD Amin Gen Hosp Gorwa Rd Vadodara Gujarat 390007-21 India Home: 1 Shivani Societyvasna Road 390007-21 Vadodara. India Personal E-mail: gabt@satyam.net.in.

BHATTACHARYA, DEBASHISH, environmental scientist, educator; s. Bonaj Bhushan and Sujata Bhattacharya; m. Susanne Elisabeth Ruemmele, Sept. 23, 1995; children: Lydia Sanjana, Ashim Alexander. BS with honors, Dalhousie U., Halifax, NS, Can., 1981, M in Environ. Sci., 1983; PhD, Simon Fraser U., Burnaby, B.C., Can., 1989. Asst. prof. U. Iowa, Iowa City, 1997—2003, assoc. prof., 2003—, dir. genetics program, 2004—. Assoc. editor: Jour. Molecular Evolution, 2003—; contbr. articles to profl. jours. Grantee, NASA, 1994—97, NSF, 1994—99, 2001—04, 2001—05, 2002—05, 2004—05; Postdoctoral fellow, Alfred P. Sloan Found., 1989—91, Humboldt scholar, Alexander von Humboldt Found., Germany, 1991—93. Achievements include playing critical role in elucidating how photosynthesis originated in plants and algae through endosymbiosis; clarifying the evolutionary history of catalytic RNAs (ribozymes).

BHATTACHARYA, RAHUL, statistician, educator; b. Kolkata, India, Jan. 8, 1977; MSc in Stats., U. Calcutta, 2000, PhD, 2007. Rsch. scholar, dept. stats. U. Calcutta, 2001—05; lectr. Asutosh Coll., Kolkata, 2005—09; reader West Bengal State U., Barasat, India, 2009—. Recipient R.C. Bose Meml. prize, Dept. Stats., U. Calcutta, 2007, Haldane Meml. prize, Indian Statis. Inst., Kolkata, 2007—08; scholarship, Ministry Human Resource Devel., India, 1998. Mem.: Calcutta Statis. Assn. Avocations: reading, music, chess. Home: 28 Anandasri 2nd Ln PO-Garia Kolkata West Bengal 700084 India Personal E-mail: rahul_bhattya@yahoo.com.

BHATTACHARYA, SUJIT KUMAR, physician, educator; b. Howrah, West Bengal, India, Apr. 23, 1944; MBBS, Banaras Hindu U., 1966, MD, 1971. Asst. prof. medicine Banaras Hindu U., 1973—79, assoc. prof. medicine, 1979—89, prof. medicine, 1989—2006, chmn., dept. medicine, 1995—98, dean, inst. med. scis., 2004—06; pvt. practice Varanasi, 2006—. Mem. Govt of Nepal, Physician Selection Com., 1996—2006, Govt of Saudi Arabia, Physician Selection Com., 1996—2006; cons. Govt. of Botswana, NGR Hosp., 1998—2001. Recipient Best Intern award, Banaras Hindu U. Mem.: Indian Rheumatoid Assn., Assn. Physicians India, Indian Soc. Clin. Pharmacology and Therapeutics, Internat. Soc. Heart Rsch. Avocations: writing, gardening. Home: B 15/41 A2 Faridpura Varanasi Uttar Pradesh 221001 India Personal E-mail: sujitbhatt@rediffmail.com.

BHATTACHARYA, VISWESWAR, plastic surgeon, educator; b. London, Apr. 22, 1950; MBBS, MS, Inst. Med. Scis., India, MCh, 1978, PhD, 1994. Asst. prof. Inst. Med. Scis., Banaras Hindu U., Uttar Pradesh, 1978—90, assoc. prof., 1990—97, prof., head, dept. plastic surgery, 1997—. Fellow: Internat. Coll. Surgeons (Indian Sect., Mahadevan Best Rsch. award, Indian Sect.); mem.: Nat. Acad. Med. Scis., Nat. Assn. Burns, Assn. Surgeons India (Hari Om Ashram Best Rsch. award), Assn. Plastic Surgeons India (elected pres. 2008, Kilner award, Peet Prize, Gold medal). Avocations: music, writing, travel, cricket, swimming. Home: B33/14-16 Gandhi Nagar Naria Varanasi Uttar Pradesh 221005 India Personal E-mail: vishweswar1@rediffmail.com.

BHATTACHARYYA, SHALMOLI, medical educator; b. India, Apr. 11, 1972; PhD, PGIMER, 2003. Asst. prof. PGIMER, 2008—. Tchr. Panjab U., 2005—08. Recipient Young Scientist award, Indian Sci. Congress; Nat. scholarship, Ctrl. Bd. Secondary edn., Govt. of India, 1988, Sr. Rsch. fellow, CSIR, Govt. of India, Travel fellowship, Hellenic Soc. Nuc. Medicine. Fellow: Interant. Soc. Biotech.; mem.: Indian Biophys. Soc., Indian Sci. Congress Assn. Avocations: music, reading, cooking. Office: PGIMER Sector 12 Chandigarh 160012 India E-mail: shalmoli2007@yahoo.co.in.

BHATTI, ASIF ZUBAIR, plastic surgeon; b. Lahore, Punjab, Pakistan, Apr. 13, 1973; s. Muhammad Zubair and Zareena Zubair Bhatty; m. Saima Amin, Mar. 2, 2003; children: Arfa Asif, Areesha Asif. MBBS, King Edward Med. Sch., Lahore, 1995. Trainee med. officer orthop. Lahore Gen. Hosp., 1997—99; registrar gen. surgery Jinnah Hosp., Allama Iqbal Med. Coll., Lahore, 1999—2001; fellow adult reconstructive surgery Nat. U. Hosp., Singapore, 2001—02; registrar plastic surgery Wellington Regional Plastics Unit, Hutt, Lower Hutt, New Zealand, 2002—03; specialist registrar plastic surgery St. Helens & Knowsley NHS Trust, Liverpool, Merseyside, England, 2004; registrar plastic surgery Plymouth Hosp. NHS Trust, Devon, England, 2004—06; clin. fellow hand surgery Mid Yorkshire NHS Trust, Wakefield, West Yorkshire, England, 2006—07; registrar plastic surgery U. Coll. Hosp., Galway, Ireland, 2006—07; sr. hand surgery fellow Mid Essex NHS Trust, Chelmsford, Essex, England, 2007—08; sr. clin. fellow Barts and London NHS Trust, London, 2008—. Fgn. prof. Higher Edn. Commn., Islamabad, Punjab; editor, sub editor lang. sect., literary KEMCOL, 1994. Contbr. articles to profl. rsch. jours. Mgr. Wanganui Mosque, New Zealand, 2002—03. Fellow Adult Reconstruction Surgery, Nat. U. Hosp., Singapore, 2001—02; Hand & Microsurgery fellowship, Christine Kleinert Inst. Hand & Microsurgery, Ky. Fellow: Royal Coll. Surgeons (Glasgow); mem.: Med. Def. Union, Brit. Med. Assn., Brit. Assn. Hand Surgery, Brit. Assn. Plastic Reconstructive and Aesthetic Surgery. Islam. Achievements include first to devise the grading and scoring of the prominent ears; registrar in plastic surgery in 3 different continents; research in double blind randomized trial comparing two methods of inguinal hernia repair; youngest person to complete the specialist surgical examination in Pakistan. Avocations: travel, Web surfing, cricket, reading. Home: 96-Temple Ave London Dagenham RM8 1LS England Office: Barts and London NHS Trust Whitechapel St London WhiteChapel E1 1BB England Personal E-mail: asif1025@yahoo.com. Business E-Mail: asifbhatti@bartsandthelondon.nhs.uk, asifbhatti@qvh.nhs.uk.

BHAVSAR, ABDHISH RAMAN, ophthalmologist, researcher; s. Raman N. and Meena R. Bhavsar; m. Mary A. Bhavsar; children: Nirayudh, Atreyus, Niharika. MD, Wayne State U., Detroit, 1991. Lic. Nat. Bd. Med. Examiners, 1991, diplomate Am. Bd. Ophthalmology, 1996, recertification 2006, lic. Minn., 2007. Opthalmology resident Ill. Eye Ear Infirmary, Chgo., 1992—95; retina surgery fellow UCLA Jules Stein Eye Inst., LA, 1995—97, assoc. attending ophthalmologist, 1995—97; exec. com. Diabetic Retinopathy Rsch. Network, National, Minn., 2006—. Chair Phillips Eye Inst., Mpls., 2004—, dir. clin. rsch., National, Minn.; adj. asst. prof. U. Minn., Mpls., 2004—, adj. assoc. prof., 2007; dir. retina rsch. Phillips Eye Inst.; hon. chair Visionwalk, Mpls., 2007—11. Author: Retina and Vitreous Surgery; contbr. articles to profl. jours., chapters to books. Co-founder Raman Narandas Bhavsar and Bhartibala Raman Bhavsar Internat. Scholarship Fund Dartmouth Coll., Hanover, NH. Mem.: ARVO (assoc.), Am. Soc. Retina Specialists (assoc. Rhett Buckler award 2001, honor award 2001, sr. honor award 2003), Am. Acad. Ophthalmology (assoc.; chair 2004—, web task force 2004—, innovation award 2002, hon. award 2006, comm. secretariate award 2006). Achievements include research in oxygen metabolism of the retina; macular degeneration and diabetic retinopathy. Avocations: art, painting, sculpting, auto racing, hockey. Office: Retina Center PA 710 E 24th St Minneapolis MN 55404 Office Fax: 612-871-0195.

BHOPAL, RAJ SINGH, epidemiology and public health educator, physician; b. Moga, India, Apr. 10, 1953; s. Jhanda Singh and Bhagwanti Kaur (Rakhra) B.; m. Roma Mazumdar, June 21, 1981; children: Sunil, Vijay, Anand, Rajan. BSc with honors, Edinburgh U., Scotland, 1975, MB, BChir, 1978, MD, 1991; MPH, Glasgow U., Scotland, 1985; DSc (hon.), Queen Margaret U. Coll., 2005. House officer in medicine City Hosp., Edinburgh, 1978-79; house officer in surgery St. Bernard's Hosp., Gibralter, 1978-79; trainee gen. practitioner Edinburgh, 1980-81; sr. house officer in medicine Neville Hall Hosp., Abergavenny, Wales, 1981-82, East Birmingham Hosp., 1982; registrar then sr. registrar cmty. medicine Greater Glasgow Health Bd., 1983-85; lectr., hon. sr. registrar in cmty. medicine Glasgow U., Glasgow, 1985-88; sr. lectr. and cons. cmty. medicine U. Newcastle Upon Tyne, 1988-91; head dept. epidemiology, prof. chair epidemiology & pub. health Newcastle Med. Sch., U.K., 1991-99; non-exec. dir., vice-chmn. Newcastle and North Tyneside Health Authority, 1992-96; Bruce and John Usher prof. pub. health Edinburgh Med. Sch., 1999—; hon. cons. in pub. health medicine Lothian Health Bd., 1999—; head Dept. Cmty. Health Scis., 2000—03. Respiratory infection task force Schering Plough Internat., 1993-96; non-exec. dir. Health Edn. Authority of Eng. and Wales, 1996-99. Author: Concepts of Epidemiology, 2002, 2nd edit. 2008; co-editor: Coronary Heart Disease in South Asians: Causes and Consequences, 2004; co-editor: Public Health: Past, Present and Future, 2004; Ethnicity, Race and Health in Multicultural Socs., 2007; mem. editl. bd. Jour. Epidemiology-Community Health, 1993-98; contbr. more than 200 articles to profl. jours. Gov. Coquet Park First Sch., Whitley Bay, U.K., 1992-96; mem. health panel Racial Equality Coun., Newcastle, 1990-93. Decorated CBE; recipient J.W. Starkey Silver medal, Royal Soc. Promotion Health, 2000, award, Sikh Heritage Scotland, 2007. Fellow: Royal Coll. Physicians, Faculty of Pub. Health Medicine (Littlejohn Gairdner prize 1987), Soc. of Pub. Health (Maddison prize 1993, Neech prize 1995); mem.: South Assn. Health Found. (award 2008), Brit. Assn. Physicians Indian Origin (award 2008), Internat. Epidemiology Assn., Soc. for Social Medicine, Brit. Med. Assn. Avocations: chess, reading, walking, photography, golf. Office: Ctr Population Health Sci Univ Edinburgh Med Sch Teviot Pl Edinburgh EH89AG Scotland Office Phone: 00 44 131 6229 7023.

BHUSHAN, SHASHI, agriculturist; b. Hamirpur, Himachal Pradesh, India, Jan. 10, 1971; BSc, Dr. YS Paramr, U. Horticulture and Forestry, Soaln, Himachal Pradesh, 1994, PhD, 2002. Asst. prof. Ctrl. Agrl. U., 2006—07; scientist Inst. Himalayan Bioresource Tech., 2007—. Mem.: Internat. Assn. Plant Biotech. Avocations: gardening, music, travel. Office: Food and Nutraceutical Lab Divisn Palampur Himachal Pradesh 176061 India Office Fax: 01894230411. Business E-Mail: sbhushan@ihbt.res.in.

BI, HONGSHENG, dean; b. Jinan, Shandong, China, Feb. 3, 1960; D, Shandong U. TCM, 2011. Dean Affiliated Eye Hosp. Shandong U. TCM, 1996—. Mem.: Am. Acad. Ophthalmology. Office: 48 Ying Xiong Shan Rd Jinan Shandong 250001 China Office Fax: 86-531-82432074. Personal E-mail: 18653129365@163.com.

BIAGIOTTI, GUY A., urologist, medical association administrator, director; b. Cleve., June 20, 1927; s. Eliseo Biagiotti and Rose Coreno; m. Gloria J. Buccieri, June 1, 1963; children: Victoria, Guy Rocco. BS in Chemistry, Adelbert Coll., Cleve., 1949; MA in Physiology, Oberlin Coll., Ohio, 1950; MD, Ohio State U., Columbus, 1955. Cert. Am. Bd. Urology, 1965. Intern Orange County Hosp., Calif., 1955—56; resident gen. surgery Crile VA Hosp, Western Res. UN Hosp. Cleve., 1956—57; resident urology UN Hosp., Western Res. and Crile Hosp., Cleve., 1957—60; pvt. practice urology Orange County, 1960—; med. dir. Orange County Litho Ctr., Garden Grove, Calif., 1986—; ass. clin. prof. urology U. Calif. Med. Ctr. Orange County, Irvine, 1969—2006; med. dir. Orange County Kidney Stone and Oclitho Ctr., Garden Grove, 1986—. Chmn. urology Children's Hosp., Orange, 1969, 75, 78; staff St. Joseph Hosp., Orange, 1967, 75, 78; chief urology, mem. exec. com. Drs. Hosp., Santa Ana, Calif.; head urology Canyon Gen. Hosp., Anaheim, Calif., 1974—78; staff AMI Garden Grove Hosp.; past. med. dir. Mobile Lithotripters, Inc., 1990—93; design cons. Calumet Coach Co., Chgo., 1991. Contbr. articles to profl. jours. Charter mem. Orange County Urol. Soc., 1986; vol. tchg. staff U. Calif., Irvine, 1969—2006. Cpl. med. corp US Army, 1945—46, Colo. Grantee, Am. Coll. Surgens. Mem.: AMA, Am. Lithotripter Soc., Am. Urol. Assn., Orange County Med. Assn., Calif. Med. Assn., Orange County Urol. Soc. Achievements include development of techniques in treating lower ureteral stones and presacral ureteral stone on the dornier HM3 lithotripter.

BIALASIEWICZ, ALEXANDER ARTHUR, ophthalmologist, educator; b. Palembang, Sumatra, Indonesia, May 4, 1956; s. Arthur and Helga Bialasiewicz; m. Katharina Breidenbach, Dec. 11, 2005; 1 child: Alexandra, Nicholas. MD, Hannover U., Germany, 1978, PhD, 1981. Fellow Wilmer Ophthal. Inst. Johns Hopkins U., Balt., 1979-80; resident in ophthalmology U. Eye Hosp., Erlangen, 1982-85, asst. prof. ophthalmology, 1986-89, Münster, 1990-92, prof. Hamburg, 1993-2001; prof., head dept. ophthalmology U. Oman, Muscat, 2001—. Mem. nat. and European adv. bds. Ophthalmic Antiinfectives, 1990. Author: Chlamydial Infections, 1989, Infectious Diseases of the Eye, 1994, Manual of Laboratory Diagnosis in Ophthalmology, 1994, Quality Management in Ophthalmology, 2002; editor: Ophthalmic Rsch. Mem.: Internat. Orgn. Against Trachoma, Internat. Uveitis Study Group, German Ophthalmol. Soc., Am. Soc. for Microbiology, N.Y. Acad. Sci., Assn. for Rsch. in Vision and Ophthalmology, Am. Acad. Ophthalmology. Avocations: tennis, skiing, scuba diving. Office Phone: (00974) 572-6886. Personal E-mail: bialasiew@aol.com.

BIANCHI, DAVID A., otolaryngologist, educator; 4 children. Grad. with honors, George Wash. U., 1984. Diplomate Am. Bd. Otolaryngology. Resident otolaryngology-head and neck surgery US Navy Naval Med. Ctr., Bethesda, Md., 1989; faculty Uniformed Univ. of the Health Sciences, George Wash. Univ.; clin. appointment divsn. of otolaryongloy/head and neck oncology Nat. Inst. on Deafness and Other Communication Disorders. Named one of the Top Doctors, Washingtonian Mag., 2011. Fellow: Am. Acad. of Otolaryngology — Head and Neck Surgery; mem.: ACS. Office: Hauck, Bianchi & Driscoll PA Number 203 2415 Musgrove Rd Silver Spring MD 20904 Office Phone: 301-989-2300. Office Fax: 301-236-5357.

BIANCHI, DIANA WILLA, clinical geneticists, educator; MD, Stanford U., Calif., 1980. Lic. Mass., 1985, diplomate Am. Bd. Pediatrics, 1985, cert. Am. Bd. Neonatal-Perinatal Medicine-Pediatrics, 1987, Am. Bd. Med. Genetics, 1987. Intern Children's Hosp. Boston, 1981, resident pediat., 1981—83, fellow, 1984—86; fellow neonatal and perinatal medicine Harvard Med. Sch., 1986—87; prof. pediat. Tufts Univ.; hosp. affiliation include Tufts med. Ctr. Co-author: (jours.) Microchimerism and HLA-compatible relationships of pregnancy, and scleroderma, 1998, Microchimerism of presumed fetal origin in thyroid specimens from women: a case-control study, 2001, Fetal cell microchimerism in tissues from multiple sites in women with systemic sclerosis, 2001, Maternal cell microchimerism in newborn tissues, 2003, Pregnancy-associated fetal progenitor/stem cells (PAPCs) differentiate into epithelial cells and hepatocytes in maternal organs, 2004. Recipient Top Dr., Boston Mag., 2009. Mem.: Perinatal Rsch. Soc. (past pres.), Internat. Soc. Prenatal Diagnosis (pres.). Office: Tufts Medical Center Mailbox 394 800 WA St. Boston MA 02111 Office Phone: 617-636-9122. Office Fax: 617-636-1469.

BIANCHI, MARIA, critical care specialist, acute care nurse practitioner, consultant; b. Springfield, Mass. B in Nursing, Catherine Laboure Sch. Nursing, Boston, 1979; BSN, Fitchburg State Coll./U. Mass., Amherst, 1985; MS in Critical Care and Nursing Adminstrn., Nat. Medicine, Russell Sage Grad. Coll., Troy, NY, 1993. Cert. post-anesthesia care nurse; critical care clin. specialist; expert witness, Mass., Conn. Recovery as mgmt. educator; mktg. and recruitment cons.; cons. in critical care nursing; clin. faculty Am. Internat. Coll., Springfield; adminstr. dept. spl. svcs., mgr. critical care Baystate Med. Ctr., Springfield, Mass., 1980-89; recruitment adminstrn. and sr. faculty St. Francis Med. Ctr. Sch. of Nursing, Hartford, Conn., 1989-92; grad. faculty U. Mass. Med. Ctr., Worcester, 1995-97; asst. prof. Grad. Sch. U. Mass., Amherst, 1998-99; faculty U. Mass. Sch. of Nursing, Amherst, per diem nurse practitioner dept. surgery Worcester, 1995—97, 1999—; CS/NP Mass Gen. Hosp., Boston; nurse dept. emergency medicine St. Francis Hosp. and Med. Ctr., Hartford, Conn., 2006—; critical care specialist adminstrn. program Sage, Troy, NY; nat. cons., lectr., expert legal; pvt. practise; expert investigation nursing practice Medicu-Legal-Clin.; clin. preceptor NP-MGH Students; mem. govt. com. APROS. Pres. ProLase Medi-Spa & Clinic, Worcester and Springfield, Mass., TI Healthcare; nat. cons. critical care/post anesthesia issues; medicolegal cons.; laser med. provider; lectr. critical care and post anesthesia issues, empowerment, acute pain, holistic techniques, medicological documentation, trauma; lectr. cardiac and non-cardiac chest pain issues. Invited amb. del. People's for People's, Fed. Govt. Mem. AACN, Am. Soc. Post-Anesthesia Nursing (Boston chpt. editl. cons.), Soc. Critical Care Medicine, Conn. APRN Govt. Com., Soc. Laser Surgery Medicine, Mass. Gen. Hosp. Alumni Assn., Catherine Laboure Alumni Assn., Sigma Theta Tau. Achievements include research in pain, burn trauma, stress reduction, holistic methods for high risk individuals in maximum security penitentiary and critical care patients and burn trauma patients. Office: PO Box 614 Suffield CT 06078 0614 Office Phone: 1 888 750 5273. Personal E-mail: mariatih@comcast.net.

BIANCHI, UMBERTO ANGELO, obstetrician, gynecologist; m. Giuseppina Marinella Dolci. MD, U. Pavia, Italy, 1959; PhD in Ob-gyn., U. Milan, Italy, 1968; PhD in Normal and Pathol. Hystochemistry, U. Pavia, 1975. Dir. ob-gyn. divsn. U. Brescia, Italy, 1986—2006, dir. sch. splty. in ob-gyn, 1996—2006, pres. course for midewifes, 1996—2006, dir. maternal-pediat.-biotech. dept, 2003—06, prof., 2007—. Cons. Spedali Civili Gen. Hosp., Brescia, 2007—. Mem.: Italian Gyn Obs. Soc., Univ. Gyn Ital. Assn., European Soc. Gyn. Oncology, Internat. Gyn Cancer Soc. (assoc.). Home: Via Taramelli 19 Brescia 25133 Italy Office: U Brescia Viale Europa 11 Brescia 25125 Italy Office Fax: 00390303384460; Home Fax: 003903042264. Personal E-mail: u.a.bianchi@virgilio.it. E-mail: bianchiu@med.unibs.it.

BIANCHIN, MARINO MUXFELDT, physician, educator; b. Tapejara, Rio Grande do Sul, Brazil, Oct. 14, 1968; s. Avelino and Esmeralda Bianchin. MD, Universidade Fed. do Rio Grande do Sul, Brazil, 1991, PhD, 1999. Prof. Med. Sch. UFRGS, Porto Alegre, Rio Grande do Sul, Brazil, 2005—. Contbr. scientific papers to profl. jours. Achievements include research in basic mechanisms of learning and memory. Office: Hospital de Clinicas de Ribeirao Preto Avenida Bandeirantes 3900 14048-900 Ribeirão Preto SP Brazil Office Fax: 55 16 36330760. Business E-Mail: mmbianchin@rnp.fmrp.usp.br.

BIANCO, PIERO RINALDO, medical educator; b. South Africa, Dec. 23, 1965; BS, ACU, 1987; PhD, UT Houston GSBS, 1993. Assoc. prof. U. Buffalo, 2001. Office: 321 Cary Hall Dept Microbiology Buffalo NY 14221 Business E-Mail: pbianco@buffalo.edu.

BIAS, VAL, foundation administrator; Attended, Calif. State U., Hayward. Assoc. exec. dir. Berkley/Albany YMCA; cons., lobbyist MARC Associates; cons. Ctrs. Disease Control and Prevention; mng. cons. The Bias Group; CEO, co-founder Compass Non-Profit Consulting Services; exec. dir. Hemophilia Coun. Calif.; CEO Nat. Hemophilia Found., NYC, 2008—. Vol., cons., advocate Nat. Hemophilia Found., bd. chmn., 1992—94, legis. coord., 1994—98; co-dir., Camp Hemotion Hemophilia Found. Northern Calif., bd. pres. Office: Nat Hemophilia Found 116 W 32nd St 11th Fl New York NY 10001 Office Phone: 212-328-3700. Office Fax: 212-328-3777. *

BIBB, SANDRA C., nursing educator; b. Mobile, Ala., Aug. 7, 1954; PhD in Nursing, U. San Diego, 1999. Assoc. prof. Uniformed Svc. U., Bethesda, Md., 2004—. Home: P O Box 849 Silver Spring MD 20918 Home Fax: 301-625-8623. Business E-Mail: sbibb@usuhs.mil.

BIBBINS-DOMINGO, KIRSTEN BEATRICE, internist; b. Nov. 24, 1965; AB, Princeton U.; PhD, U. Calif., San Francisco, MD, 1999, MCR. Cert. Internal Medicine, 2003. Resident in internal medicine U. Calif., San Francisco, asst. prof. in residence medicine, epidemiology and biostatistics. Office: U Calif San Francisco Box 1364 San Francisco CA 94143 Office Phone: 415-206-4464. E-mail: bibbinsk@medicine.ucsf.edu.

BIBBO, MARLUCE, physician, educator; b. Sao Paulo, Brazil, July 14, 1939; d. Domingos and Yolanda (Ranciaro) Bibbo. MD, U. Sao Paulo, 1963, ScD, 1968. Intern Hosps. das Clinicas, U. Sao Paulo, 1963, resident in morphology, 1964-66; instr. dept. morphology and ob-gyn. U. Sao Paulo, 1966-68, asst. prof., 1968-69; fellow in cytology U. Chgo., 1969-70, asst. prof. sect. cytology dept. ob-gyn., 1971-73, assoc. prof., 1973-77, assoc. prof. pathology, 1974-77, prof. ob-gyn. and pathology, 1978-92; assoc. dir. Cytology Lab., Approved Sch. Cytotech and Cytocybernetics, AMA-Am. Soc. Clin. Pathologists, 1970-91; dir. Cytology Lab., Phila., 1992—; prof. pathology and cell biology Thomas Jefferson U., Phila., 1992—, Warren R. Lang prof. pathology & cell biology, 1993—. Mem. rsch. com. Ill. divsn. Am. Cancer Soc., 1976-91. Contbr. numerous articles to profl. jours.; editor: Comprehensive Cytopathology, 1991, 1997, 2008. Fellow Internat. Acad. Cytology (pres.-elect, v.p. 1987, pres. 1992, dep. editor Acta Cytologica, editor 1995—), Am. Soc. Clin. Pathologists (coun. on cytopathology); mem. Am. Soc. Cytology (exec. com., pres. 1982-83), U.S. Acad. Pathology, Can. Acad. Pathology, Soc. Analytical Cytology, Coun. Cytopathology. Home: 250 S 9th St Philadelphia PA 19107-5734 Office: Cytology Lab Rm 260 Main Bldg 132 S 10th St Philadelphia PA 19107-5244 Office Phone: 215-955-1197. Business E-Mail: bibbo@cytology-iac.org, marluce.bibbo@jefferson.edu.

BIBEL, DEBRA JAN, medical scientist, editor, artist; b. San Francisco, Apr. 6, 1945; d. Philip and Bassya (Maltzer) B. AB, U. Calif., Berkeley, 1967, PhD, 1972. Rsch. microbiologist Letterman Army Inst. Rsch., San Francisco, 1972-79; tech. writer Hoefer Sci. Inst., San Francisco, 1979; rsch. assoc. Kaiser Found. Rsch. Inst., San Francisco, 1981-83, 87-95; product mgr. Tago Inc., Burlingame, Calif., 1983-85; dir. Elie Metchnikoff Meml. Library, Oakland, Calif., 1977—2004, historian, 1986; staff rsch. assoc. dept. dermatology U. Calif., San Francisco, 1987-88, faculty rsch. assoc. dept. dermatology, 1994—99; editor AMUR Pharms., Inc., Belmont, Calif., 1997; comm. coord., exec. assoc. Alcohol Rsch. Group, Pub. Health Inst., Emeryville, Calif., 1999—2006; artist Studio Lone Mountain, Oakland, Calif., 2006—. Lectr. U. Calif., Berkeley, 1975, Antioch Coll. West, San Francisco, 1975. Author: Milestones in Immunology, A Historical Exploration, 1988, Freeing the Goose in the Bottle: Discovering Zen Through Science, Understanding Science Through Zen, 1992, A Collection of Clouds. Zen Haiku and Other Poetry, 1997, Microbial Musings: A History of Microbiology, 2001; columnist Rummagings Along the Dusty Shelf, 1982-2006; contbr. articles to profl. jours; solo exhbns. include ProArts Quar. Latham Sq., Oakland, Calif. Instr. Berkeley Cmty. Health Project, 1971-75. Capt. U.S. Army, 1972-76. Mem. AAAS, ACLU, No. Calif. Am. Soc. Microbiology. Buddhist. Avocations: painting, photography, Asian philosophy, music. Home: 230 Orange St Apt 6 Oakland CA 94610-4139 Studio: Studio Lone Mountain 230 Orange St Oakland CA 94610-4319 Business E-Mail: bibel@lonemountain-art.com.

BIBERTHALER, PETER, trauma surgeon, orthopedic surgeon, medical researcher; b. Germany, June 14, 1968; MD, Ludwig-Maximilians-Univ., Munich, 1996. Intern Ludwig-Maximilians-Univ., Munich, 1996—97, postdoctoral fellow Inst. Surg. Rsch., 1998—2000, resident, 1997—2002, cons. dept. trauma and orthopaedic surgery, 2003—, asst. prof. traumatology and orthopedic surgery, 2005—; orthopedic surgeon, 2003—; trauma surgeon, 2003—. Instructor Advanced Trauma Life Support (ATLS), 2003. Assoc. editor (Journal) Der Unfallchirurg, Springer, NY, 2003. Recipient Innovation award, German Soc. Traumatology, 2002, Otto Goetze award, Bavarian Soc. Surgery, 2004, Travel award, German Endoprosthesis Soc., 2005; scholar, Soc. Critical Care Medicine, 2005. Office: Ludwig-Maximilians-University-Innenstadt Nussbaumstrasse 20 Bavaria Munich 80336 Germany Office Phone: 0049-89-5160-2511. Office Fax. 0049-89-5160-2585.

BICAL, OLIVIER MICHEL, cardiac surgeon, consultant; b. Neuilly, France, June 9, 1948; s. Robert Emile Bical and Lydia Marcelle Pochon; m. Françoise Jeannine Granger, Oct. 8, 1982; children: Antoine David, Alexis David. MD, Pitie-Salpetriere, Paris, 1977. Cert. cardiac surgeon France. Chief cardiac surgery dept. Found. Hosp. St. Joseph, Paris, 1994—. Mem.: European Assn. Cardiothoracic Surgery. Achievements include research in mini extra corporeal circulation. Office: Found Hosp Saint Joseph 185 Rue Raymond Losserand 75014 Paris France Fax: 0033/144123383. E-mail: ombical@hopital-saint-joseph.org.

BICANIC, GORAN, orthopedist; b. Zagreb, July 23, 1975; MD, Zagreb U., 2000, PhD, 2009. Orthop. surgeon Clin. Hosp. Ctr. Zagreb, 2008—. Sr. asst. Sch. Medicine, U. Zagreb, 2011. Mem.: Croatian Orthop. and Trumatology Assn., EFORT. Office: Salata 6 Zagreb 10000 Croatia Business E-Mail: gbic@mef.hr.

BICHSEL, HANS, physicist, consultant, researcher; b. Basel, Switzerland, Sept. 2, 1924; came to U.S., 1951; s. Paul and Anna Maria Bichsel; m. Sue O. Greenwalt, Sept. 12, 1959; children: Elizabeth Christine, Joseph Oliver. MA, PhD, U. Basel, 1951. Rsch. asst. Princeton (N.J.) U., 1951-55; rsch. assoc. Rice U., Houston, 1955-57; asst. prof. physics U. Wash., Seattle, 1957-59; affiliate prof. physics U. Wash., Seattle, 1992—; assoc. prof., prof. radiology U. Wash., Seattle, 1969-80; asst. prof., assoc. prof. physics U. So. Calif., LA, 1959-68; assoc. prof. U. Calif., Berkeley, 1968-69. Cons. Internat. Commn. on Radiation Units, Bethesda, Md., 1970—, Los Alamos (N.Mex.) Nat. Lab., 1978-83, IAEA, Vienna, Austria, 1990—; vis. scientist Nat. Inst. Radiol., Scis., Chiba, Japan, 1991-96, U. Sherbrooke Med. Sch., Que., Can.; rschr. Relativistic Heavy Ion Collider, Brookhaven Nat. Lab., 1999—; referee Phys. Rev., Nuclear Instruments and Methods, Physics in Medicine and Biology, also others. Contbr. articles to profl. jours. Fellow Am. Phys. Soc.; mem. Swiss Phys. Soc. Achievements include research in heavy ion radiation therapy and statistics of interactions of radiations with matter. Home and Office: 1211 22nd Ave E Seattle WA 98112-3534 Home Phone: 206-329-2792; Office Phone: 206-543-4054. Personal E-mail: hbichsel@scientist.com. Business E-Mail: hbichsel@uw.edu.

BICHSEL, RUTH J., psychologist, educator; d. Edwin John Bichsel and Doris May Dickinson. BS in Psychology, U. Oreg., Eugene, 1980; MS in Counseling, U. Oreg., 1990, PhD in Counseling Psychology, 1997. Lic. psychologist Oreg., 1998. Faculty U. Oreg., 1995—97; instr. Lane Cmty. Coll., Eugene, 1995—. Vol. Animal Rescue and Rehab., Eugene, 1998—2007. Recipient Social Interest award, Oreg. Soc. Individual Psychologists, 2003; named Instr. of Yr., Lane CC, 1995-1996, Outstanding Instr., 2005. Fellow: Am. Coll. Forensic Examiners; mem.: Am. Hort. Therapists Assn., Am. Fedn. Police and Concerned Citizens (Citizenship award 1993). Avocation: animal training. Office: Lane Cmty Coll 4000 E 30th Ave Eugene OR 97405

BICK, KATHERINE LIVINGSTONE, neuroscientist, educator, researcher; b. Charlottetown, Can., May 3, 1932; came to U.S., 1954; d. Spurgeon Arthur and Flora Hazel (Murray) Livingstone; m. James Harry Bick, Aug. 20, 1955 (div.); children: James A., Charles L. (dec.); m. Ernst Freese, 1986 (dec. 1990). BS with honors, Acadia U., Can., 1951, MS, 1952; PhD, Brown U., 1957; DSc (hon.), Acadia U., 1990. Rsch. pathologist UCLA Med. Sch., 1959-61; asst. prof. Calif. State U., Northridge, 1961-66; lab. instr. Georgetown U., Washington, 1970-72, asst. prof., 1972-76; dep. dir. neurol. disorder program Nat. Inst. Neurol. and Communicative Disorders and Stroke, NIH, Bethesda, Md., 1976-81, acting dep. dir., 1981-83, dep. dir., 1983-87; dep. dir. extramural rsch. Office of Dir. NIH, 1987-90; sci. liaison Centro Studio Multicentrico Internazionale Sulla Demenza, Washington, 1990-95. Cons. Nat. Rsch. Coun., Italy, 1991-97, The Charles A. Dana Found., N.Y.C., 1993-98, Edn. Commn. of the States, 1996-99. Editor: Alzheimer's Disease: Senile Dementia and Related Disorders, 1978, Neurosecretion and Brain Peptides, Implications for Brain Functions and Neurol. Disease, 1981, The Early Story of Alzheimer's Disease, 1987, Alzheimer Disease, 1994, 2d edit., 1999, Alzheimer Disease: The Changing View, 2000; contbr. articles to profl. jours. Pres. Woman's Club, McLean, Va., 1968-69; bd. dirs. Fairfax County (Va.) YWCA, 1969-70; pres. Avenel Homeowner's Assn., 1998; pres. Emerson Unitarian Ch., 1964-66; mem. Bethesda Pl. Cmty. Coun., 1992-95, pres., 1993-94; mem. Dana Alliance for Brain Initiatives, 1993—; bd. dirs. Wilmington NC Child Advocacy Commn., 1998-2002; mem. vol. guild St. John's Mus. Art, Wilmington; chair Vol. Guild Cameron Art Mus., Wilmington, 2002-03, Cameron Art Mus. Bd., 2003-06; vestry St. Andrew's on the Sound, Wilmington, 2004-06. Recipient Can. NRC award Acadia U., 1951-52, NIH Dir.'s award, 1978, Spl. Achievement award NIH, 1981, 83, Superior Svc. award USPHS, 1986, Presdl. Rank award meritorious sr. exec., 1989, Genesis award Alzheimer's Assn., 2005; Universal Match Found. fellow Brown U., 1956-57, Fed. Exec. Inst. Leadership fellow, 1980 Fellow AAAS, Internat. Brain Rsch. Orgn., World Fedn. Neurology Rsch. Group on Dementias (exec. sec. Am. region 1984-86, chmn. 1986-93), Alzheimer's Disease Internat., Soc. for Neurosci. (emeritus), Acad. of Medicine Washington (emeritus), Dana Alliance for Brain Initiatives. Home: 528 Cedar Club Cir Chapel Hill NC 27517

BICKEL, JANET, healthcare educator; b. St. Louis, May 14, 1949; MA, Brown U., 1976. Coord., admissions and fin. aid Brown U. Med. Sch., 1972—76; assoc. v.p. Med. Sch. Affairs, Assn. Am. Med. Colls., 1977—2003; faculty and selection com. mem. exec. leadership Academic Medicine Fellowship Program, 1995—; adj. asst. prof., med. edn. George Washington U. Sch. Medicine, 2003—. Contbr. articles to sci. profl. jours. Recipient Spl. Recognition award, Johns Hopkins Dept. Medicine, Am. Med. Women's Assn. Pres. Fellow: Relationship Centered Health Care; mem.: Soc. Exec. Leadership Academic Medicine Internat. (Excellence award), Am. Acad. Communication Healthcare, Assn. Women Surgeons (hon.), Soc. Gen. Internal Medicine. Avocations: mountain climbing, birdwatching. Office: 7407 Venice St Falls Church VA 22043 Business E-Mail: janetbickel@cox.net.

BICKERS, DAVID RINSEY, dermatologist, educator, department chairman, health facility administrator; b. Richmond, Va., Sept. 23, 1941; s. William McKenzie and Helen Virginia (Fitzpatrick) B.; m. Melinda Lee Jarger, May 30, 1970 (div. 2003); 1 child, McKenzie Winchester; m. Sara Hurlburt Patterson, Nov. 13, 2004. AB, Georgetown U., 1963; MD, U. Va., 1967. Intern in medicine U. Iowa Hosps., Iowa City, 1967-68; resident in dermatology skin and cancer unit N.Y.U. Med. Center, 1970-73; NIH tng. fellow, guest investigator Rockefeller U., 1971-73, R.J. Reynolds scholar in clin. medicine, asst. prof., asso. physician, 1976-77; asst. prof. dermatology Columbia U. Coll. Physicians and Surgeons, 1973-76; asst. attending dermatologist Presbyn. Hosp., NYC, 1973-76; prof. dermatology, chmn. dept. Case Western Res. U. Med. Sch., 1977-93, assoc. dean, 1990-93. Dir. dermatology svc. U. Hosps., 1977-93, sr. v.p. med. program planning, 1977-89, chief staff, sr. v.p. med. affairs, 1990-93; dir. dermatology svc. Cleve. VA Hosp., 1977-89; mem. gen. medicine A study sect., NIH, 1980-84, chmn., 1982-84; adv. coun. Nat. Inst. Arthritis, Musculoskeletal and Skin Diseases, NIH, 1988-92; Carl Truman Nelson prof. dermatology, chmn. Dept. Coll. Physicians and Surgeons, Columbia U., 1994—; dir. dermatology svc. NY Presbyn. Hosp. Columbia Divsn., 1994—, pres. med bd. Author: (with L.C. Harber) Photosensitivity Diseases: Principles of Diagnosis and Treatment, 1981, 2d. edit., 1989, (with Hazen and Lynch) Clinical Pharmacology of Skin Disease, 1984, (with T. Krieg and Y. Miyachi) Therapy of Skin Disease, 2008; mem. editorial bd. Jour. Am. Acad. Dermatology, 1979-85, Physicians Drug Alert, 1982—, Today's Therapeutic Trends, 1983-2004, Photodermatology, 1983-88; assoc. editor Jour. Investigative Dermatol., 1987-97. Served as officer M.C. USAF, 1968-70. Decorated Air Force Commendation medal. Mem. Assn. Am. Physicians, Am. Soc. Clin. Investigation, Am. Soc. Pharmacology and Exptl. Therapeutics, Am. Fedn. Clin. Rsch., Am. Soc. Photobiology, Am. Acad. Dermatology (hon.), Am. Dermatol. Assn., Soc. Investigative Dermatology (bd. dirs. 1985-89, sec.-treas. 1989—, pres. 2003), Pasteur Club (Cleve.), Med. Strollers, Skin Pharmacology Soc. (sec. 1985-87, pres. 1987-89), Dermatology Found. (sec.-treas. 1984, chmn. bd. 1987-88), Bicontinental Assn. Edn. and Rsch. in Dermatology (founding mem.), German Dermatol. Soc. (hon.), Am. Univ. Beirut (bd. trustees, 1996-, chair health sci. com., 2005-), Austrian Dermatol. Soc. (hon.), Commanderie De Bordeaux, Confrérie des Chevaliers du Tastevin, Expert Panel Rsch. Inst. for Fragrance Materials, 1996 (chair, 2002-2005), Am. Bd. Dermatology (bd. dirs. 1997-2005, pres. 2005) Office: Columbia Univ Med Ctr IP-1214 161 Fort Washington Ave New York NY 10032-3713 Office Phone: 212-305-5565. Business E-Mail: drb25@columbia.edu.

BIDEL, SIAMAK, medical researcher; b. Kermanshah, Iran, Sept. 13, 1962; s. Mohamad Jafar Bidel and Pari Sedaghat; m. Giti Khalighi-Sikaroudi, Sept. 6, 1981; children: Ali, Kamran. BS in Nat. Scis., Italian Don Bosco Coll., Tehran, Iran, 1980; MD, U. Med. Scis., Iran, 1993; PhD, U. Helsinki, Finland, 2007. Lic. dr. Ministry Health and Med. Edn. Lectr. Kurdistan U. Med. Scis., Sanandaj, Iran, 1993—95; gen. practitioner Ministry Health Hosps. & Health Ctrs., Sanandaj, 1994—96; rschr. Pulmonary Disease and Tuberculosis Rsch. Ctr., Rasht, Iran, 1996—98; freelance rschr. Finland, 1998—2000; med. tng. Helsinki U. Ctrl. Hosp., Finland, 2000—01, rschr., 2001—03, dept. health promotion & chronic disease prevention, Nat. Pub. Health Inst., Helsinki, 2003, dept. pub. health, U. Helsinki, 2004—. Lit. reviewer Elsevier Pub., Helsinki, Finland, 2006. Contbr. articles to profl. jours. Grantee Rsch. grant, Juho Vainio Found., 2005—07. Mem.: Angiology Assn. Finland, Radiology Assn. Finland, Diabetes Assn. Finland. Achievements include research in The role of coffee consumption in prevention of type-2 diabetes and its complications; the role of coffee consumption in developement of

Parkinson's disease; the effects of coffee consumption on markers of glycemia; the effect of the ulcerogenic agents on actin cytoskeleton and cell motility in cultured rat gastric mucosal cells. Avocations: walking, bicycling. Home: Pykäläitie 5 B Helsinki 00690 Finland Office: Nat Pub Health Inst Mannerheimintie 166 Helsinki 00300 Finland Office Phone: 358919127340. Office Fax: 358919127313. Personal E-mail: siamak.bidel@helsinki.fi. Business E-Mail: siamak.bidel@ktl.fi.

BIDIC, SEAN MICHAEL, plastic surgeon, orthopedist; b. Vineland, NJ, May 29, 1970; s. Reiner Paul and Christine Angela Bidic; m. Gretchen Ann Hays; children: Emma Gretchen, Leyna Raine. BA, U. Pa., Phila., 1992, BS in econ., 1992; MD, Columbia U., NYC, 1996; MFA, Carnegie Mellon U., Pitts., 2002. Cert. Am. Bd. Plastic Surgery, 2006, added qualification in hand surgery 2007. Resident in gen. surgery U. Pitts. Med. Ctr., 1996—99, resident in plastic surgery, 2002—04; fellow in bone substitutes, robotic hands and human computer interfaces Carnegie Mellon U., 1999—2001; fellow in hand and microsurgery UCLA Dept. Orthopaedic Surgery, 2004—05; asst. prof. U. Tex. Southwestern, Dallas, 2005, dir. hand surgery fellowship, 2007—. Video, In The Absence Of Voyeurism. Mem.: Dallas Soc. Plastic Surgeons, Am. Soc. Plastic Surgeons. Office: Univ Tex Southwestern Med 1801 Inwood Rd Dallas TX 07530 Office Fax: 214-645-3105. Business E-Mail: sean.bidic@utsouthwestern.edu.

BIDWELL, ROGER GRAFTON SHELFORD, biologist, educator; b. Halifax, NS, Can., June 8, 1927; came to U.S., 1965; s. Roger Edward Shelford and Mary B.; m. Shirley Mae Rachael Mason, July 1, 1950; children— Barbara, Alison, Roger, Gillian. B.Sc., Dalhousie U., 1947; BA, Queen's U., 1950, MA, 1951, PhD, 1954. Tech. officer Canadian Def. Research Bd., Kingston, Ont., 1951-56; asst. research officer Nat. Research Council, Halifax, 1956-59; assoc. prof. biology U. Toronto, Ont., 1959-65; prof. biology Case Western Res. U., Cleve., 1965-69, chmn. dept., 1966-68; prof. biology Queen's U., Kingston, Ont., Canada, 1969-79, prof. emeritus, 1979—; I.W. Killam research prof. Dalhousie U., Halifax, 1980-85; sr. ptnr. Atlantic Research Assocs. Ltd., Wallace, N.S., 1980-91; exec. dir. Atlantic Inst. Biotech., Halifax, 1985-88. Vis. prof. Cornell U., 1961-63; vis. scientist Atlantic Regional Lab., NRC, Halifax, 1966, 76; cons. Faculty Edn., Simon Fraser U., 1966; Can. Sci. Exch. visitor to People's Republic of China, 1975, 77; participant Dark Skies Symposium, Ecology of the Night, Muskoka, Ont., 2003. Author: Plant Physiology, 1974, 79; co-editor: Plant Physiology: A Treatise, 1978-90; contbr. over 160 articles to profl. jours., chpts. books. Active Crime Stoppers, Cumberland region, 1993-97, chmn., 1994-97; com. mem. Anglican Diocese N.S.; pres., chmn. bd. Pugwash Coop. Ltd., 1995-2000; warden Parish of Pugwash/River John, 1998-2002, parish treas., 2004-05; mem. diocesan coun. Diocese of N.S. and P.E.I., 1999-2001; active Pugwash and Area Cmty. Health Bd., 2001-2005 Recipient Queen Elizabeth II Silver Jubilee medal, 1977. Fellow AAAS, Royal Soc. Can.; mem. Canadian Soc. Plant Physiologists (founder, past sec.-treas., pres. 1972-73, Gold medal 1979), Biol. Council Can. (sec. 1973-76), Am. Soc. Plant Biology. Achievements include research in biochem. mechanisms in plants, protein metabolism, CO2 metabolism in leaves, photosynthesis and metabolism in marine algae; global climate change and the discovery and development of the science of scotobiology, the biology of darkness, active in the campaign against light pollution. Avocations: bicycling, walking, skiing, birdwatching. Personal E-mail: roger01@xplorent.ca.

BIEBER, FREDERICK ROBERT, medical geneticist; b. Regina, Sask., Can., Feb. 9, 1950; s. Frederick John and Marjorie (Davidson) B.; m. Jane Marie McNamara, June 23, 1973. BA, SUNY, Oswego, 1972; MS, U. Rochester, 1976; PhD, Med. Coll. Va., 1981. Diplomate Am. Bd. Med. Genetics. Asst. prof. Harvard Med. Sch., Boston, 1985-91; assoc. prof. pathology Brigham Womens Hosp., Boston, 1992—. Mem. DNA adv. bd. FBI, Royal Can. Mounted Police, U.S. Dept. Def. Author: The Malformed Fetus and Stillbirth, 1988; mem. editl. bd. Clin. Genetics; contbr. articles to profl. jours. Bd. dirs. Greyhound Friends, Hopkinton, Mass., 1992. Capt. US Army Res., 2001—. Office: Brigham & Women's Hosp Dept Pathology 75 Francis St Boston MA 02115-6106

BIEBUYCK, JULIEN FRANCOIS, physician, anesthesiologist, medical administrator, educator; b. South Africa, Feb. 2, 1935; arrived in US, 1971, naturalized, 1985; s. Lucien Jean and Drix J. B.; m. Jeanette A. Sumner, May 10, 1961; children: Gavin L., Richard M., Clare E. Karpinksi. MB, ChB in Medicine and Surgery, U. Capetown, South Africa, 1959; DPhil in Biochemistry and Pharmacology, Oxford U., Eng., 1971. Diplomate Am. Bd. Anesthesiology, 1985, fellow faculty of anaesthetists Coll. Medicine South Africa, 1969, fellow Australian and New Zealand Coll. Anaesthetists 1992, fellow Faculty of Anaesthetists, Royal Australasian College of Surgeons 1987, fellow Royal Coll. Anaesthetists, 1996. Nuffield scholar Oxford U., Eng., 1969-71; asst. prof. anesthesiology Harvard Med. Sch., Mass. Gen. Hosp., Boston, 1971-76; Eric A. Walker prof., chmn. dept. anesthesia Pa. State U. Coll. Medicine, Hershey, 1977-97, assoc. dean, 1991-97, sr. assoc. dean for acad. affairs, 1997—2000; Robert G. Petersdorf scholar-in-residence Assn. Am. Med. Coll., Washington DC, 2001—02, sr. cons. acad. mgmt. programs, 2003—. Pres. Soc. Acad. Anesthesiology Chairs, 1985—86; chair clin. scis. com. Am. Physiological Soc., 1987—90; rep. Assn. U. Anesthesiologists, Coun. Academic Socs., Assn. Am. Med. Colls., 1991—97; mem. anesthetic and life support drugs adv. com. FDA, 1995—97; chair com. rsch. Am. Soc. Anesthesiologists, 1995—98; sr. cons. academic mgmt. programs Assn. Am. Med. Colls., DC, 2003—. Editor, Jour. Anesthesiology, 1985-94, Clin. Sci. Pubs., Am. Physiol. Soc., 1987-1990, editor-in-chief Current Opinion in Anaesthesiology, 1993-99; editor sci. books, contbr. chpts. to books, articles to med. and sci. jours. Bd. dirs. Found. for Anesthesia Edn. and Rsch., Rochester, Minn., 1993—97. Recipient Ellis Gillespie Hon. Lectr., Royal Australasian Coll. Surgeons, Australia, 1987, Ninth Martin Helrich Hon. Lectr., U. Md., Balt., 1996, Disting. Svc. award, Pa. Soc. Anesthesiologists, 1999; named 8th E.M. Papper Hon. lectr., UCLA, 1985; rsch. fellow, Med. Found. Boston, 1972—76, Nuffield scholar, Oxford U., Eng., 1969—72, Robert G. Petersdorf Scholar in Residence, Assn. Am. Med. Colls., 2001—02. Fellow: Royal Coll. Anaesthetists London; mem. AMA, Assn. Univ. Anesthesiologists, Am. Soc. Anesthesiologists (chair com. on rsch. 1994-97), Am. Physiol. Soc., Soc. Acad. Anesthesia Chmn. (past pres.), Coun. Acad. Socs., Assn. Am. Med. Colls., Biochem. Soc., Soc. Parenteral Nutrition, Soc. Neurosci., Soc. Neurosurg. Anesthesia, Pa. Med. Soc., Trinity Coll. Oxford Soc., Cosmos Club, Alpha Omega Alpha. Democrat. Avocations: art, gardening, golf. Office Phone: 717-583-2679. Personal E-mail: jbiebuyck@comcast.net.

BIEGEL, DAVID ELI, social worker, educator; b. NYC, July 3, 1946; s. Jack and Estelle (Lentin) B.; m. Margaret S. Smoot, Jan. 31, 1976 (div.); 1 child, Geoffrey S.; m. Ronna Kaplan, Oct. 26, 2003. BA, CCNY, 1967; MSW, U. Md., 1970, PhD, 1982. Field coord. United Farm Workers, AFL-CIO, Balt., 1971; exec. dir. Junction, Inc., Westminster, Md., 1971—72; dir. office planning and program devel. Cath. Charities, Balt., 1973—76; ctr. assoc., dir. neighborhood and family svcs. project U. So. Calif., Washington Pub. Affairs Ctr., 1976—80; asst. prof. social work U. Pitts., 1980—85, assoc. prof., 1985—86; Henry L. Zucker prof. social work practice Mandel Sch. Applied Social Scis., Case Western Res. U., 1987—, prof. psychiatry and sociology, 1987—, assoc. dean rsch. & tng., 2008—, co-dir. Ctr. for Practice Innovations, 1991—97, chair doctoral program, 1998—2001, 2005; bd. dirs. Alcohol, Drug Addiction & Mental Health Svc., Bd. Cuyahoga County, 2011—. Co-dir. Cuyahoga County Cmty. Mental Health Rsch. Inst., 1994—2002; pres. Inst. for the Advancement of Social Work Rsch., 1999—2002; dir. rsch. and evaluation Ohio Substance Abuse and Mental Illness Coord. Ctr. Excellence, 2000—05; co-dir. Ctr. Substance Abuse and Mental Illness, 2002—. Co-editor: Evidence-Based Practices Series, Innovations in Practice and Service Delivery with Vulnerable Populations Series, Family Caregiving Applications Series; editor Practice Concepts sect., The Gerontologist, 2002-04; co-author: Neighborhood Networks for Humane Mental Health Care, 1982, Community Support Systems and Mental Health: Practice, Policy and Research, 1982, Building Support Networks for the Elderly: Theory and Applications, 1984, Social Networks and Mental Health: An Annotated Bibliography, 1985, Social Support Networks: A Bibliography 1983-1987, 1989, Aging and Caregiving: Theory, Research and Policy, 1990, Family Preservation Programs: Research and Evaluation, 1991, Family Caregiving in Chronic Illness: Alzheimer's Dsiease, Cancer, Heart Disease, Mental Illness, and Stroke, 1991, Family Caregiving: A Lifespan Perspective, 1994, The Jewish Aged in the U.S. and Israel: Diversity, Programs and Services, 1994, Innovations in Practice and Service Delivery with Vulnerable Populations Across the Lifespan, 1999; contbr. articles to profl. jours., chpts. to books. Cons. Vol. VISTA, Raton, N.Mex., and Balt., 1967-70; active Big Bros. Am., Balt., 1974-77, mem. bd. dirs., Alcohol Drug, bd. mem., Mental Health Scis.Cuyahoga County, 2010-, pres. bd. trustees Bridgeway, Inc., 2004-07; sec. bd. trustees Cmty. Care Network, Inc., 2006-07—. N.Y. State Incentive scholar, 1963-64; VISTA Fellows Program fellow, 1968-70. Fellow Gerontol. Soc. Am.; mem. NASW, Acad. Cert. Social Workers, Soc. Social Work Rsch. Democrat. Jewish. Home Phone: 216-371-3108; Office Phone: 216-368-2308. Business E-Mail: david.biegel@case.edu.

BIEÍK, VÍTÌZSLAV, biologist, educator, research scientist; b. Neplachovice, Czechoslovakia, Dec. 26, 1937; s. Oldrich and Anna (Benšova) Bieík; m. Ludmila Doleželová, Jan. 5, 1963; 1 child, Kamila Bičiková. MSc, Palacky U., Olomouc, Czechoslovakia, 1961; D in Natural Scis., Komensky U., Bratislava, Czechoslovakia, 1967, PhD, 1977. Asst. Palacky U., Olomouc, 1963-65, lectr., 1965-80, assoc. prof., 1980-87, prof. zoology, 1987—, head dept. zoology, 1985—91. Cons. Pedagogical Faculty, Ostrava, Czech Republic, 1983—88, Pardubice (Czech Republic) U., 1993—96, Komensky U., Bratislava, 1995—; organizer Internat. Biology Olympiad, 1992; chmn., mem. jury Internat. Biology Olympiads; founder Olomouc, 1990. Author: (book) An Introduction to Zoopsychology, 1985 (Min.'s award, 1987), Comparative Physiology of Animals, 2004, numerous univ. textbooks, films and videos; exec. editor: Acta U. Palacki Olomuc Jour., 1988—95, editor-in-chief:, 1996—; contbr. articles to profl. jours. Recipient 1st prize, Nat. Competition Rsch. Works, Bratislava, 1961, medal, Chulalongkorn U., Bangkok, 1995, Gold medal, Palacky U., 1997, New Memory medal, 2002, Memory medal, Kiel U., 1998, Laureate prize, Town Olomouc2; named Hon. Citizenship Neplachovice, 2007. Mem.: Czech Biol. Soc., Czech and Slovak Ethological Soc., Czech Zool. Soc. (Northmoravian office chmn. 1994—). Avocations: poetry, mycology, diving, ping pong/table tennis, stamp collecting/philately. Home: U Kovarny 3 779 00 Olomouc Czech Republic Office: Palacky U Dept Zoo & Ornitogical Lab Tr. Svobody 26 779 00 Olomouc Czech Republic Business E-Mail: bicikv@seznam.cz.

BIELORY, LEONARD, allergist, immunologist, medical school administrator; b. Neptune, NJ, Nov. 17, 1954; s. Max and Bessie (Spielberg) B.; m. Marilyn Miriam Gilan, July 5, 1981; children: Brett Phillip, Barry Mark, Amy Beth BS, MS, Lehigh U., 1976; MD, NJ Med. Sch., 1980. Intern, resident U. Md. Hosp., Balt., 1980-82; clin. assoc. NIH, Bethesda, Md., 1982-85; dir. divsn. allergy, immunology & rheumatology NJ Med. Sch., Newark, 1985—, co-dir. immuno-ophthalmology svcs., prof. medicine, pediats. and ophthalmology, 1992—2002, dir. devel. & clin. rsch. dept. medicine; pres. med. staff U. Medicine and Dentistry NJ-U. Hosp., 1993-95; pres., chmn. U. Physician Assocs., 1996-2000. Pres. med. staff ex-oficio mem. NIH Safety and Data Mgmt. Bd., 1993-98; bd. dirs. Univ. Health Care Corp., acting med. dir., 1995-97; dir. Asthma and Allergy Rsch. Ctr., 1992—; prof. medicine, pediat. and ophthalmology, 2002—; chmn. clin. treatment study sect. NIH, 1993; prin. investigator Nat. Ctr. for Complementary and Alternative Medicine, NIH, 2002-04. Assoc. editor: Annals of Allergy, Asthma & Immunology, 1996-; contbr. rsch. papers to profl. jours., chpt. to books. Bd. dirs. Congregation Israel, Springfield, NJ, 1988, pres., 1999-01; v.p. Kushner Yeshiva, pres. 2005-07, chmn. bd., 2007—; bd. dirs. St. John's Cmty. Svc., 2002-. Recipient Young Investigator award Am. Acad. Allergy and Immunology, 1985; Schering Corp. Travel grantee, 1985. Fellow ACP, Am. Acad. Allergy and Immunology; mem. Med. Soc. NJ Jewish. Avocations: skiing, camping, rafting, bicycling. Home Phone: 973-972-2768; Office Phone: 973-912-9817. E-mail: dr1bielory@gmail.com.

BIER, JEAN-CHRISTOPHE, neurologist; b. Bruxelles II, Belgium, Aug. 28, 1970; s. Johannes Paolus Bier and Yvonne Marechal; life ptnr. Patricia Klein; children: Alexandre Delvaux, Samuel, Noah. MD, ULB, Bruxelles, 1995. Resident, neurology, Erasme Hosp. ULB, 1995—2000, neurologist, Erasme Hosp., 2000—. Contbr. articles to profl. jours. Office: Erasme route de Lennik 1070 Bruxelles Belgium Office Fax: 32 2 555 39 42; Home Fax: 32 2 277 86 13. Business E-Mail: jbier@ulb.ac.be.

BIER, LOUIS HENRY GUSTAV, minister; b. Chgo., Jan. 12, 1933; s. Louis Wilfred and Ethel Lea (Laue) Bier; m. Helene Mueller, July 29, 1962; children: Richard Allen, Karen Elizabeth, Lisa Anne. BE, Chgo. Tchrs. Coll., 1954; B in Theology, Concordia Sem., 1959, MDiv in Theology, 1959; MEd, Boston State Coll., 1962; DRE, Smith Bapt. U., 1987, DD, 1986. Ordained ministry Luth. Ch., 1959; lic. social worker; 40 yr. cert. Va., 2007. Vicar Redeemer Luth. Ch., Phila., 1957, 1st Luth. Ch., Holyoke, Mass., 1957—58; pastor St. Paul's Luth. Ch., West Frankfort, Ill., 1959—61, Trinity Luth. Ch., Boston, 1961—98, emeritus, 1999—; chaplain VA New Eng. Health Care Sys., Boston, 1965—2007; instr. psychology Boston State Coll., 1967—81; mem. adj. faculty Holy Cross Greek Orthodox Sem., Brookline, Mass., 1998, citation, 2007; bd. dirs. Health Planning Coun. Greater Boston, 1972; cons., 2007. Chaplain German Home Elderly, Boston, 1962, also trustee, clk. corp., 1971—; chaplain Arbour, Boston, 1969, West Roxbury VA Hosp., 1978—86; circuit counselor Luth. Ch. Mo. Synod; trustee Chapel Four Chaplains, Valley Forge, Pa., 2000; cons. Slavik Rsch. Inst.; mem. animal studies com. Beth Israel-Deaconess Hosp., Havard Med. Sch., 2000; bd. dirs. Interfaith Bible Readings, Inc.; seved to lt. col. CAP, 1975—. Editor: New England Lutherian Cultures. Active Boy Scouts Am., Boston, 1970—; mem. USO Coun. New Eng.; bd. mgrs. Sophia Snow Ho.; br. pres. A.A.L., 1982. Col. chaplain Mass. State Def. Fort, mem., 1997. Recipient Honored Citizen award, Kennedy VFW, 1973, Cmty. Svc. award, Greater Boston Assn. Retarded Citizens, 1974, Lamb award, Luth. Coun., 1975, George Meany Youth Svc. award, AFL-CIO, 1983, Dist. Eagle Scout award, Boy Scouts Am., 1993, Recognition award, Slovik Rsch. Inst., 1999, Svc. award, Concordia Seminary, Ft. Wayne, Ind., 1999, 30 Yr. citation, CAP, 2005, St. Herman of Alaska award, 2007, 1967, St. Martin Tours award, 1993, 50th Anniversary Cert. award, N.E. Luthar Hist. Soc., Shovak Resear Inst., 2009, Ret. Chaplain Yr. award, APC Fin. Com., 2010; co-recipient 40 Yr. award, Friends of Old Sturbridge Village, 2005; West fellow, Boy Scouts Am., 1999, Emerson fellow, Mil. Chaplains Assn. USA, 1999. Mem.: APC, Am. Assn. Mental Retardation (20 Year Citation 2002, Humanitarian award Northeast region 2002), Concordia Sem. (Servus Ecclesia Christi award), Mass. Chaplains Assn., German Aid Soc. Boston (trustee), Alumni Assn. (life), Assn. Profl. Chaplains (life; cert., 25th Anniversary citation 2000), Mil. Chaplains Assn. (life; treas., v.p., pres.), Luth. Edn. Assn. (life), Friends of Jackson Lab. of Bar Harbor, New Eng. Luth. Hist. Soc. (life), Franklin County Hist. Soc. (Ill.) (life), Nat. Eagle Scout Assn. (life), Slovik Assn. (life), Bar Harbor Hist. Soc. (Maine) (life), Westwood Hist. Soc., Vanderbilt Club. Avocations: swimming, golf, reading. Home Phone: 781-326-5774; Office Phone: 617-232-9500 ext. 45065.

BIERIG, JACK R., lawyer, educator; b. Chgo., Apr. 10, 1947; s. Henry J. and Helga (Rothschild) B.; m. Barbara A. Winokur; children: Robert, Sarah. BA, Brandeis U., 1968; JD, Harvard U., 1972. Bar: Ill. 1972, US Dist. Ct. (no. dist.) Ill. 1972, US Ct. Appeals (1st-3d, 5th-11th and DC cirs.) 1974, US Supreme Ct. 1980. Ptnr. Sidley Austin, LLP, Chgo., 1972—; prof. Ill. Inst. Tech.-Chgo. Kent Coll. Law, 1974-95; lectr. law. U. Chgo. Law Sch. and Harris Sch. Pub. Policy, 2000—. Chmn. legal sect. Am. Soc. Assn. Execs., 1994-95. Contbr. articles to profl. jours. Pres. Neighborhood Justice Chgo., 1983-87; pres. Jewish Vocat. Svc., 1997-99. Mem. Ill. Assn. of Hosp. Attys. (pres. 1991), Chgo. Bar Assn. (bd. govs., 1982-84). Clubs: Standard (Chgo.). Jewish.

BIERING-SORENSEN, FIN, physiatrist; b. Denmark, Oct. 21, 1948; s. Knud and Ellen (Carstensen) B.-S.; m. Maja Stellerova, Jan. 6, 1973; children: Bo, Jes, Tor, Ida. MD, U. Copenhagen, 1975. Registrar dept. surgery Municipality Hosp., Copenhagen, 1975; registrar dept. neurology Rigshospitalet, Copenhagen, 1976; registrar dept. internal medicine Sundby Hosp., Copenhagen, 1976-77; registrar dept. physiatry Orthop. Hosp., Copenhagen, 1977; rsch. fellow Glostrup County Hosp. and Rigshospital, Copenhagen, 1977-79; registrar dept. orthop. surgery Bispebjerg Hosp., Copenhagen, 1981; registrar to sr. registrar dept. physiatry Rigshospitalet, Copenhagen, 1979-80, sr. registrar dept. physiatry and rheumatology, 1981-86, chief physician dept. phys. medicine and rehab. Copenhagen, Hornbaek, 1986—97; chief physician Clinic for Spinal Cord Injuries Rigshospitalet, Copenhagen, 1986—, med. dir., 1992—. Danish rep. epidemiologic com. European League Against Rheumatism, 1983—94, Sect. Monospécialisée Medicine Physique et Readaptation Union Europeene des Medicins Spécialites, 1988, Internat. Fedn. Phys. Medicine and Rehab., 1989—2000, Internat. Soc. Phys. and Rehab. Medicine, 2000—; Danish dep. rep. Rehab. Internat., 1996—2001; asst. prof. U. Copenhagen, 1999—2002; vice chmn. Med. Commn., 2000—01; mem. neurol. stds. com. Am. Spinal Injury Assn., 2001—; exec. chmn. com. internat. spinal cord injury data sets Am. Spinal Injury Assn./Internat. Spinal Cord Soc., 2002—; Lars Sullivan Meml. lectr. Nordic Spinal Cord Soc., Bergen, 2005; prof. neuro rehabilitation U. Copenhagen, 2008—. Author: Africa for the Hitchhiker, 4th edit., 1976, Health and Social Service, 1977; assoc. editor: Rehab. Scis., 1992-98; mem. adv. bd. SPINE, 1993-2003; mem. editl. bd. Spinal Cord, 1990—, asst. editor, 2007-; mem. adv. bd. Jour. Rehab. Medicine, 1999—; referee 25 jours.; contbr. over 230 articles to profl. jours., 55 chpts. to books. Chmn. or mem. various coms. Danish sports orgns. for disabled, 1978—, Internat. Sports Orgn. for Disabled, 1980-92; internat. coord. com. of World Sports Orgns. for Disabled, 1985-86, 88-89, Seoul Paralympics, 1988, Internat. Paralympic Com., 1992-2000. Recipient Volvo award Internat. Soc. for Study of Lumbar Spine, Cambridge, Eng., 1983, rsch. award Soc. Poliomyelitis, Skive, Denmark, 1984, Danish Soc. Manual Medicine, 1984, Golden pin Internat. Sports Orgn. for Disabled, Arnhem, Holland, 1989, rsch. award Danish Disability Found., 1995, Lars Sullivan Spinalis award as co-author, Atlanta, 1996, Paraplegia prize as co-author, Innsbruck, Austria, 1997. Fellow: Internat. Med. Soc. Paraplegia (Iguassu, Brazil); mem.: Danish Soc. Neurorehab. (vice chair 2005—), Danish Soc. Rheumatology (exec. com., hon. sec. 1988—91, v.p. 1991—92), Danish Soc. Rehab. (exec. com., hon. sec. 1988—90, v.p. 1991—96, pres. 1996—2000, v.p. 2000—), Internat. Spinal Cord Soc. (coun. 1992—, v.p. 1997—2003, pres. 38th sci. meeting Copenhagen 1999, chmn. sci. com. 2002—08, elect pres. 2008—10, pres. 2010—, Silver medal 2007), Danish Paraplegic Assn. (hon.), Romanian Acad. Med. Scis. (hon.), Scandinavian Med. Soc. Paraplegia (adv. coun. 1987, pres. 2d sci. meeting Copenhagen 1991, exec. com. hon. sec. and treas. 1991—93, pres. 1993—99, pres. 6th sci meeting Copenhagen 1999), European Assn. for Rsch. into Adapted Phys. Activities (Danish key person 1987—92), Soc. for Back Pain Rsch. (exec. com. 1983—85). Avocation: swimming.

Office: Rigshospitalet Copenhagen U Hosp Havnevej 25 DK-3100 Hornbaek Denmark Home: Oster Farimagsgade 30 2100 Copenhagen Denmark Office Phone: 45 35 45 19 10. Business E-Mail: finbs@rh.regionh.dk.

BIERMAN, ARNOLD, optometrist; b. NYC, May 6, 1943; s. William Leonard and Dora Bierman; m. Carol F. Bierman, Dec. 26, 1965; 1 child, Julie Elise. BS, OD, Pa. Coll., 1968. Pvt. practice, Lansdale, Pa., 1968—. Clin. instr. Pa. Coll. Optometry, Phila., 1968—72, asst. prof., 1972—79; visual cons. Montgomery County Intermediate Unit, Norristown, Pa., 1976—87; mem. eyecare quality assurance com. U.S. Healthcare, Blue Bell, Pa., 1992—99. Editor: Jour. Pa. Optometrist, 1979—81. Chmn. Jaycees Amblyopia Clinic, Lansdale, Pa., 1969—70. Mem.: Am. Optometric Assn., Pa. Optometric Assn., Am. Acad. Optometry (pres. ea. Pa. chpt. 1980—82), Beta Sigma Kappa. Achievements include expertise in remediating reading and/or learning problems in children and adults. Avocations: art, music, bowling, photography. Office: 2302 N Broad St PO Box 1369 Lansdale PA 19446-0749 Office Phone: 215-822-1365. Personal E-mail: arnoldbierman@comcast.net.

BIERMAN, FREDRICK, pediatric cardiologist, educator; BS, Union Coll., Schenectady, NY; MD, SUNY, 1973. Diplomate Am. Bd. Pediatrics, Am. Bd. Pediatrics-pediatric cardiology. Dir. pediatric echocardiography lab. Columbia-Presbyterian Med. Ctr., Manhattan, NY; resident pediatrics Mt. Sinai Med. Ctr., NYC, 1974—76; fellow pediatric cardiology Harvard Children's Hosp., Boston, 1976—79; prof. pediat. Albert Einstein Coll. Medicine, 1992—; chmn. pediat. Steven and Alexandra Cohen Children's Med. Ctr., NYC, 2006, chief pediatric cardiology, 1991—, assoc. chmn. pediat., 1992—2006; pediatric cardiology Taylor Care Ctr. Westchester Med. Ctr. Office: Westchester Medical Center 100 Woods Rd Valhalla NY 10595 Office Phone: 914-493-7000.

BIERMANN, MARTIN, nuclear medicine physician, educator; b. Recklinghausen, Germany, Nov. 13, 1963; s. Rudolf Biermann and Gerda Schmidt; m. Helene Sanden, Dec. 12, 2002; children: Johanne, Niels. Physician, U. Münster, Germany, 1991, MD, 1994. Cert. specialist nuc. medicine Westphalian Med. Bd., Germany, 2002, specialist med. informatics Westphalian Med. Bd., Germany, 2003. Rsch. fellow cardiology Münster U. Hosp., Münster, Germany, 1991—93, physician cardiology, 1993—95, physician nuc. medicine, 1997—2003, registrar nuc. medicine, 2003—05; rsch. fellow Krannert Inst. Cardiology, Indpls., 1995—97; cons. physician nuc. medicine Haukeland U. Hosp., Bergen, Norway, 2005—; assoc. prof. U. Bergen, 2006—. Study coord. Multicenter Trial Differentiated Thyroid Carcinoma, Münster, 2000—. Grantee, German Rsch. Coun., 1995. Mem.: Soc. Nuc. Medicine N.Am., German Soc. for Endocrinology (thyroid sect.), German Soc. for Nuc. Medicine, European Assn. for Nuc. Medicine. Office: Haukeland U Hosp NM/PET Ctr Dept Radiology Jonas Lies Vei 5021 Bergen Norway Business E-Mail: martin.biermann@kir.uib.no.

BIERUT, LAURA J., psychiatrist, educator; BA, Harvard Radcliffe Coll., Cambridge, 1982; MD, Washington U., St. Louis, 1987. Lic. Mo. Resident Washington U. Barnes Hosp., 1991; prof. psychiatry Washington U. Med. Sch., mem. epidemiology & prevention rsch. group. Recipient Sidney I. Schwab prize, Washington U., Book award, Internat. Brain Research Org. award. Office: Washington University School of Medicine 40 N Kingshighway Ste 4 Saint Louis MO 63108 Office Phone: 314-286-2261. Office Fax: 314-286-2265.

BIESTER, DORIS J., hospital administrator; BS, U. Iowa; MS in Pediatric Nursing, U. Wis.; PhD in Nursing and Comty. Orgn., U. Colo., 1994. Pediat. staff nurse U. Iowa Hospitals and Clinics, 1963—65, head nurse, pediatrics nursery and spl. care clinic, 1969—72, clin. nursing specialist, adminstr. pediat.; asst. dir. pediatric and obstetric nursing Women and Infants Hosp., RI; with Children Hosp., Denver, 1979—, sr. v.p., dir. nursing, sr. v.p. patient care svc., exec. v.p., COO, pres., CEO, 1998—. Mem. Am. Acad. of Nursing, Urban Peak Assn. (bd. dirs. 1996-98), Denver Metro C. of C. Office: The Childrens Hospital 13123 E 16TH AVE Aurora CO 80045-7106

BIFFIGNANDI, PAOLO MARIA, biomedical researcher, consultant; b. Torino, Italy, Sept. 10, 1953; s. Giorgio and Giulia (Cossa) B.; m. Lorella Carletto, Sept. 29, 1992; children: Virginia, Elisa. MD, U. Torino, 1980, PhD in endocrinology, 1983; PhD in pharmacology, U. Napoli, Italy, 1988. Dir. Delalande Rsch. Ctr., Torino, 1984-88; dir. scientific affairs ABC Farmaceutici, Torino, 1988-89; pres. Pharmacon, Torino, 1988—. Dir. scientific affairs Vi.Rel Plasma, S.E.M.T., s.a.s., 1989—; mem. editl. com. ESRA, London, 1992-96, mem. edn. com., 1993-95, 98—; mem. exec. com. SIAR, Milano, 1994-96; prof. in ethics and mgmt. of clin. trials Faculty of Medicine, U. Torino, 1996—. Editor Clinica e Terapia, 1990—; contbr. articles to profl. jours. Mem. Am. Fertility Soc., Regulatory Affairs Profl. Soc., Drug Info. Assn., N.Y. Acad. Sci. Avocations: golf, horses. Office: Pharmacon Via Vadone 22/6 Vinovo 10048 Italy Office Phone: 39-011-0014838. E-mail: pbiffignandi@virelpharma.it.

BIGGAR, PATRICK HENRY, nephrologist, consultant; b. Eastham, Cheshire, Eng., Dec. 21, 1956; s. Patrick Robert and Caecilie Biggar; m. Ingeborg Olbert, Oct. 2, 1997; children: Helena, Emily. Cert. D Darmstadt Govt., Hesse, Germany, 1983, med. practitioner Brit. Gen. Med. Coun., 1985, Arzt fuer Innere Medizin Landesaerztekammer Hesse, Germany, 1994, nephrologist Landesaerzekammer Hesse, Germany, 1997, specialist Gen. Medicine Brit. Gen. Med. Coun., 1994, German Med. Univs. Asst. internal med. D Hanau City Hosp., Hesse, 1984—92, KfH Dialysis Ctr. Hanau, Hesse, 1992—95; cons. nephrologist KfH Dialysis Ctr., Norderney, 1997; asst. nephrology cons. Kassel City Hosp., Hesse, 1995—97; cons. nephrologist Klinikum Coburg gGmbH, Bavaria, Germany, 1997—. Cons. Various pharm. cos., Germany, 2002—. Contbr. scientific papers. Mem.: Landesaerztekammer Bavaria, Germany, Landesaerztekammer Hesse, Germany, KfH Curatorium Dialysis & Transplantation, Brit. Med. Assn. Achievements include research in renal anemia care and calcium/phosphate/vitamin D control in CKD-mineral and bone disease. Home: Hinterer Glockenberg 18 Bavaria Coburg 96450 Germany Office: Klinikum Coburg gGmbH Ketschendorfer Strasse 33 Bavaria Coburg 96450 Germany Business E-Mail: patrick.biggar@klinikum-coburg.de.

BIGLIANI, LOUIS U., orthopedist, surgeon, educator; AB in Sociology, Coll. of the Holy Cross, 1964—68; attended, Loyola U., 1968—72. Diplomate Am. Bd. of Orthopaedic Surgery, 1979. Intern surgical Roosevelt Hosp., 1972—73, resident gen. surgery, 1973—74; resident orthopaedic surgery, NY Orthopaedic Hosp., 1974—76, jr. Annie C. Kane fellow and sr. resident, 1976—77, chief resident and sr. Annie C. Kane fellow shoulder and implant surgery, 1977—78; Frank E. Stinchfield prof. Columbia Univ., chmn. orthopaedic surgery, chief shoulder, elbow and sports medicine; dir. orthopaedic surgery svc. NY-Presbyn. Hosp. Mem. Orthopaedic Rsch. and Edn. Found., 1985. Recipient Upjohn Achievement award, Loyola Univ., 1972, Outstanding Student award, 1972. Fellow: Am. Acad. of Orthopaedic Surgeons; mem.: S.I.C.O.T., Sociedad de Ortopedia y Traumatologia de Cordoba, Columbia Shoulder Soc. (founder 2001), S.E.C.E.C. (corr. mem. 2000), Sociedade Brasilleira de Cirurgia de Ombro e Cotovelo (hon. mem. 2000), Korean Shoulder and Elbow Soc. (hon. mem. 1999), Argentine Orthopaedic Soc. (hon. mem. 1988), Am. Shoulder and Elbow Surgeons (founding mem. 1982), New England Orthopaedic Soc., Arthroscopy Assn. of N. Am., Soc. for Tennis Medicine and Sci., 20th Century Orthopaedic Soc., Italian Shoulder and Elbow Soc., Acad. Orthopaedic Soc., NY Acad. of Medicine, Assn. of Bone and Joint Surgeons, Orthopaedic Rsch. Soc., NY State Orthopaedic Soc., Greater Met. Sports Medicine Soc., AMA, Med. Soc. of NY County, Med. Soc. of the State of NY, Am. Orthopaedic Assn. (pres. 2008). Office: NewYork-Presbyterian Hospital HIP 2nd Fl 161 Fort Washington Ave New York NY 01003 Office Phone: 212-305-4565. Office Fax: 212-305-0999.

BIGNAN, GILLES, principal scientist, patent agent; b. Madagascar, July 5, 1968; PhD, Joseph Fourier U., 1994. Prin. scientist Johnson & Johnson, 2006—. Office: Johnson & Johnson Welsh & McKean Roads Spring House PA 19477 Business E-Mail: gbignan@its.jnj.com.

BIGNON, YVES-JEAN, oncologist, geneticist; b. Paris, Aug. 5, 1955; s. Michel and Marcelle (Guillaumin) B.; m. Edith Amiot, Mar. 21, 1999; children: Anne, Jean-Luc, Alice, Odelia. MD, U. Clermont-Ferrand, 1984, PhD, 1991. From intern in medicine to asst. U. Auvergne, France, 1980-89; INSERM fellow U. Calif., San Diego, 1989-90; conf. master U. Auvergne, 1991-92; prof. U. Blaise Pascal, France, 1992—; prof. oncology, biology U. Auvergne, Clermont-Ferrand, France, 1997—. Pres. Genetics and Cancer Group, France, 1993—; scientific bd. Nat. League Against Cancer, 1994—, Nat. Fedn. Cancer Ctrs., 1994—, founding mem. INSERM genetics com., 1995—, co-founder Diagnogene S.A.; sci. dir. Ctr. Jean Perrin, 2004, Canceropole Clara, 2005. Recipient Gold medal, Internat. Jour. Medicine, 1994, Ruban Rose prize. Mem. European Soc. Human Genetics, Am. Assn. Cancer Rsch., French Soc. Genetic Counseling, Am. Soc. Human Genetics, French Soc. Human Genetics (v.p.). Roman Catholic. Avocations: theology, running, wine, music. Office: Ctr J Perrin BP392 Oncol 58 Rue Montalembert 63011 Clermont Ferrand France Office Phone: 33 473 278050. Business E-Mail: yves-jean.bignon@cjp.fr.

BIGOT, JEAN-MICHEL ROGER, radiologist, educator; b. Paris, July 26, 1935; s. Alfred Georges and Simone (Cornevin) B.; m. Anne Le Guennec, Mar. 5, 1965; children: Christophe, Alexandra. Student, Le Havre, Janson de Sailly, France, 1950-52; MD, U. Paris, 1968. Externe Hosp. Paris., 1956-62, intern, 1964-68, chief clinic, 1968-74; radiologist Hosp. St. Antoine, Paris, 1974-76; chief radiology service Hosp. Tenon, Paris, 1976—; prof. U. Paris, 1974—, hon. prof., 2005. Contbr. over 280 artices to French and fgn. med. jours. Mem. various French and European med. socs., Radiol. Soc. N.Am., Am. Roentgen Ray Soc., European Congress Radiology (sci. sec. 1983), Internat. Congress Radiology (sec. gen. 1989). Avocations: modern art, painting, music. Home: 16 Rue Fosses Saint Jacques 75005 Paris France Office: Hopital Tenon 4 rue de la Chine 75020 Paris France Business E-Mail: jean-michel.bigot@tnn.aphp.fr.

BIHLDORFF, JOHN PEARSON, hospital director; b. Boston, Aug. 3, 1945; s. Carl Birger and Martha Bowling (McCandless) B.; m. Jane Sargent Lyman, Mar. 30, 1968; children: Jennifer, Nathan, David. AB, Harvard U., 1969; MPH, Yale U., 1971. With McMaster U. Med. Ctr., Hamilton, Ont., Canada, 1971-77, assoc. exec. dir., 1975-77; dir. program planning, asst. prof. divsn. med. adminstrn. Vanderbilt U. Med. Ctr. & Sch. Medicine, 1977-78; assoc. hosp. dir., COO U. Conn. Health Ctr.-John Dempsey Hosp., Farmington, 1978-81; asst. exec. dir. U. Conn. Health Ctr., 1981-82, hosp. dir., 1982-86; pres., CEO St. Luke's Health Found. and Hosp., New Bedford, Mass., 1986-91, Newton-Wellesley Hosp., Newton, Mass., 1991-2001. Chmn. bd. dirs. VHA of Mass., Inc., 1995-97; chmn. bd. dirs. VHA Healthfront, 1995-97; bd. dirs. Tufts Assocs. Health Plan, 1994-96; adj. faculty Mt. Olive Coll., 2006—. Home: 107 Elm St Canton MA 02021-1255

BIJLANI, RAMESH, retired medical educator, writer; b. Sukkur, Sind, Pakistan, Oct. 16, 1947; m. Lovleen Sethi, Jan. 16, 1974; 1 child, Arpita Lal. MBBS, All India Inst. Med. Scis., New Delhi, 1970, MD in Physiology, 1973; SM, MIT, Cambridge, 1979; DSc in Yoga (hon.), SVYASA, Bangalore, India; FAMS (hon.), NAMS, New Delhi, India. Prof. and head dept. physiology All India Inst. Med. Scis., New Delhi, 1996—2005; hon. mem. Sri Aurobindo Ashram, New Delhi, 2006—. Author: (book) Understanding Medical Physiology, Fundamentals of Physiology, Nutrition: a practical approach, The Return of Ram, The Human Machine, Our Body: a wonderful machine; editor: Teaching Physiology: Trends and Tools; author: Eating Scientifically, Back to Health through Yoga. Recipient Maj. Gen. SL Bhatia award, Assn. Physiologists and Pharmacologists India, 2004, Dr. ML Gupta prize, APPI, 2001, Internal Oration award, BP Koirala Inst. Health Scis., 1996, Dev Raj Bajaj prize, APPI, 1979; UNU fellowship, 1978—79, Nat. Acad. Med. Scis. fellowship, India, 2005. Achievements include research in nutrition in relation to cardiovascular disease and diabetes. Office: Sri Aurobindo Ashram Delhi Br Sri Aurobindo Marg 110 016 New Delhi India Office Fax: 91-11-2685-7449. Personal E-mail: rambij@gmail.com. E-mail: aurobindo@vsnl.com.

BIKMAZ, VEYSEL KEREM, neurosurgeon; b. Bandirma, Turkey, Aug. 17, 1970; MD, Trakya U., 1994. Neurosurgeon Okmeydani Ednl. and Rsch. Hosp., 2003—05; skull base rsch. fellow UAMS, 2005—07; neurosurgeon Istanbul Surgery Hosp., 2007—08; neorosurgeon Istanbul Neurosurgery and Pain Ctr., 2008—. Office: Hakki Yeten Caddesi Ascioglu Plaza N Istanbul 34349 Turkey Office Phone: 902122193535. Office Fax: 902122190606. Business E-Mail: info@kerembikmaz.com.

BILBAO, ITXARONE, surgeon; b. Bilbao, Aug. 28, 1958; Degree in Medicine and Surgery, U. Pais Vasco, 1981. Gen. practitioner Osakidetza Euskalerria, 1981—83, Medicus Mundi and Internat. Med. Cooperation Cameroun, 1984—90; resident, gen. surgery dept. Hosp. Vall d'Hebron, 1991—95, fellowship, gen. surgery, 1996—2001, cons. surgeon, hepatobiliary and liver transplant surgery, 2002—. Adj. prof. U. Autonoma Barcelona, 2002. Recipient award, Soc. Andaluza Trasplante Organo y Tejidos, Marzo, 2006, Sociedad Catalana Trasplante, 2007, Congreso Soc. Catalana Trasplantes; grant, Soc. Española Trasplante, Ciberehd and Novartis, 2010. Mem.: Commn. Asesora Trasplante Hepatico Cataluña, Soc. Española Trasplante, Soc. Española Trasplante Hepático. Avocation: mountain climbing. Office: Paseo Vall dHebron n° 119-129 Barcelona 08025 Spain Office Fax: 93 2746112. Business E-Mail: ibilbao@vhebron.net.

BILEZIKIAN, JOHN P., endocrinologist, educator; BA in Biochemistry magna cum laude, Harvard U., Cambridge, MA, 1965; MD, Columbia U., 1969. Fellow Am. Coll. of Physicians, Am. Coll. of Medicine, NY Acad. of Medicine; attending physician Presbyn. Hosp., NY, NY, 1985—; prof. dept. of medicine & pharmacology Columbia Univ., NY, NY, 1985—, chief divsn. of endocrinology, 1987—, dir. dept. of medicine, 1990—96, assoc. chair dept. fo medicine, 1996—. Pres. coll. of physicians & surgeons Alumni Assn., 1987—89; vis. prof. endocrinology dept. of medicine Univ. Md., 1995; vis. prof. Hong Kong Univ., 1996, Long Island Coll Hosp., 1997; vis. prof. bone & mineral metabolism Harvard Med. Sch., 1997. Recipient L. J. Henderson prize, Harvard Coll., 1965, Alpha Omega Alpha, Columbia Univ., 1968, J. Murray Steele award, NY Heart Assn., 1976, Steven Triennial prize, Coll. of Physicians & Surgeons, 1977, Rsch. Career Devel. award, Nat. Insts. of Health, 1977—82, Silver Medal, Alumni Assn., 1991, Alumni Medal, Alumni Fed. of Columbia Univ., 1993, Doody award: The Parathyroids, 1994—95, Vis. Lectureship award, Endocrine Fellows Found., 1996, Doody award: Priciples of Bone Biology, 1996—97, ASBMR Abstract Presentation award, 1997, Disting. Physician award, Endocrine Soc., 1998; named Neil Auerbach Meml. Lectr., Norwalk Hosp., 1998, Boy Frame Disting. Lectr., Henry Ford Hosp., 1998. Mem.: Assn. of Osteobiology, Assn. of programs Dirs. in Endocrinology & Metabolism, Internat. Soc. for Clin. Densitometry, Am. Assn. of Clin. Endocrinologists, Assn. of Am. Physicians, Assn. of program Dirs. in Internal Medicine, Internat. Bone & Mineral Soc., Am. Heart Assn., Am. Soc. for Clin. Investigation, Am. Soc. for Pharmacology & Exptl. Therapeutics, Am. Soc. for Bone and Mineral Rsch. (pres. 1995—96), Endocrine Soc., Am. Fed. for Clin. Rsch. Office: NewYork Presbyterian Columbia University Medical Center 622 West 168th St New York NY 10032 Office Phone: 212-305-2500.

BILFINGER, THOMAS VICTOR, surgeon, educator; b. Ridgewood, NJ, May 4, 1952; s. Victor Wilhelm and Heidi Erika (Muser) B.; m. Celia Betty Dameron; children: Elizabeth, Christine, Michael. MD, U. Zurich, Switzerland, 1978, ScD, 1979. Intern U. Chgo., 1980-81, rsch. fellow, 1981-82; resident in surgery U. Tex. Med. Br., Galveston, 1982-86, resident in cardiovascular surgery, 1986-88, instr. in surgery, 1988-89; asst. prof. surgery SUNY, Stony Brook, 1989-92, assoc. prof. surgery, 1992-99, prof. surgery, chief thoracic surgery, 1999—. Bd. dirs. cardiovascular intensive care unit SUNY, Stony Brook; rsch. assoc. Neurosci. Inst., SUNY, Old Westbury; sr. rsch. scientist Mind/Body Med. Inst., Harvard med. Sch., Mass.; mem. spl. populations rsch. dept. faculty NIDA, 1994—. Co-author: Evaluation of the Cardiac Surgical Candidate, 1992; mem. editl. bd. Advances in Neuroimmunology, Acta Pharmacologica Sinica, 1999—, Modern Aspects of Immunobiology, 2000—, Placebo, 2001—; guest editor: Internat. Jour. Cardiology, 1996, 98; editor in chief. Am. jour. case reports, 2008- Recipient Rsch. grant U. Chgo., 1981, Rsch. grant Eli Lilly, 1989, Rsch. grant NIH, 1991, Career Opportunity Rsch. Tng. award NIMH. Fellow ACS, Am. Coll. Cardiology, Am. Coll. Chest Physicians; mem. Am. Assn. Thoracic Surgery, Assn. for Acad. Surgery, Soc. Critical Care Medicine, Swiss Soc. Thoracic and Cardiovasc. Surgery, Soc. Thoracic Surgery. Office: SUNY Stony Brook Health Sc Ctr T19 Rm 080 Stony Brook NY 11794-0001 Office Phone: 631-444-1820. Business E-Mail: tbilfinger@notes.cc.sunysb.edu. *

BILGIN, MEHMET DINÇER, medical educator; b. Tarsus, June 13, 1964; MD, Ankara U. Med. Faculty, Turkey, 1988; PhD, Ill. Inst. Tech., Chgo., 1999. Rsch. assoc. Ravenswood Hosp., Wenske Laser Ctr., 1996—99; postdoc. rschr. Northwestern U., Med. Faculty, 1999—2000; asst. prof. Adnan Menderes U., Med. Faculty, 2000—06, assoc. prof., 2006—, prof., 2011—. Mem.: Aydin Med. Chamber, Am. Soc. Photobiology, Turkish Biophys. Assn. Avocations: photography, archaeology, sports. Office: Adnan Menderes University Med Faculty Aydin Ege 09010 Turkey Office Fax: 90-2562123166. Personal E-mail: mdbilgin@yahoo.com.

BILLER, BEVERLY M.K., endocrinologist, educator; b. NYC; BA, Brown U., 1979; MD, U. Okla., 1983. Lic. Mass., 1983, diplomate Am. Bd. Internal Medicine, 1986, Am. Bd. Internal Medicine-endocrinology, diabetes and metabolism, 1989. Intern Beth Israel Hosp., Boston, 1983—84, resident medicine, 1984—86; clin. fellow medicine Harvard Med. Sch., 1983—86, clin. and rsch. fellow endocrinology, 1986—89, instr. medicine, 1989—92, asst. prof. medicine, 1992—99, assoc. prof. medicine, 2000—; assoc. physician medicine Brigham and Women's Hosp., 1997—; clin. and rsch. fellow endocrinology Mass. Gen. Hosp., 1986—89, clin. asst. medicine, 1989—91, asst. physician medicine, 1992—97, 1997—99, attending physician, neuroendocrine clin. ctr., 1989—, attending physician, endocrinology consultation svc., 1990—, assoc. physician medicine, 2000—. Editl bd. mem. Jour. of Clin. Endocrinology and Metabolism, 1993—96, Pituitary, 1997—, assoc. editor Jour. of Clin. Endocrinology and Metabolism, 1999—2004. Recipient Mark R. Everett award, Univ. Okla. Coll. of Medicine, 1981, Coyne E. Campbell award, 1982, Divsn. of Endocrinology Ann. award, 1983, L.J. Moormon award, 1983, Janet M. Glasgow award, Am. Women's Med. Assn., 1983, Nat. Rsch. Svc. award, NIH, 1989, Clin. Assoc. Physician award, 1991, 18th Ann. Henry H. Turner Lectureship award, Univ. Okla. Coll. of Medicine, 1997. Mem.: The Growth Hormone Rsch. Soc., Assn. of Program Dirs. in Endocrinology and Metabolism, Am. Assn. of Clin. Endocrinologists, The Endocrine Soc., The Pituitary Assn. (clin. affairs. com. 1993—, clin. rsch. com. 1993—), Alpha Omega Alpha. Office: Massachusetts General Hospital EOO - 112 Ste 112 Zero Emerson Pl Boston MA 02114 Office Phone: 617-726-7948. Office Fax: 617-726-1241.

BILLER, JOSE, neurologist, educator; b. Montevideo, Uruguay, Jan. 18, 1948; B in Medicine, A.V. Acevedo Inst., Montevideo, Uruguay, 1965; MD, U. de la Republica, Montevideo, Uruguay, 1974. Diplomate Am. Bd. Neurology and Vascular Neurology. Intern Maciel Hosp., Montevideo, Uruguay, 1974—76, Columbus Hosp., Chgo.,

1976-77; resident in neurology Henry Ford Hosp., Detroit, 1977-78; Loyola U. Hosp., Hines VA Hosp., Ill., 1978-80, chief resident neurology Ill., 1979—80; fellow cerebral vascular diseases Bowman Gray Sch. Med., Winston Salem, NC, 1980-81, instr. neurology, 1981; asst. prof. neurology Loyola U., Chgo., 1982-84, prof., assoc. chmn. dept. neurology Stritch Sch. Med., 2003—, dir. neurology residency training program, 2003—05, acting chmn. dept. neurology, 2004—05, prof., chmn. dept. neurology, 2005—; asst. prof. neurology U. Iowa Coll. Medicine, Iowa City, 1984-87, assoc. prof. neurology, 1987-90, prof. neurology, 1990-91; prof. Northwestern Sch. Medicine, Chgo., 1991-94; dir. stroke program, dir. acute stroke care unit Northwestern Meml. Hosp., Chgo., 1991-94; prof., chmn. dept. neurology Ind. U., 1994—2003. Prof. ad-hororem U. of the Republic Sch. Medicine, Uruguay, 1997—; cons. physician neurology svc. VA Hosp., Iowa City, 1984—91; staff physician Northwestern Meml. Hosp., Chgo., 1991—94; neurology cons. Rehab. Inst. Chgo., 1991—94; active med. staff Ind. U. Hosps., 1994—2003, Loyola U. Hosp., 2003—; cons. Roudebush VA Med. Ctr., 1994—2003. Mem. editl. bd. Stroke, Stroke-Clin. Update, Neurol. Rsch., internat. bd. editors CNS Drugs; editor: Seminars in Cerebrovascular Diseases and Stroke, Jour. Stroke and Cerebrovascular Diseases; contbr. articles to profl. jours., chapters to books. Fellow: ACP, Am. Heart Assn., Am. Acad. Neurology; mem.: AMA, Am. Neurol. Assn., Inter-Am. Coll. Physicians and Surgeons, Uruguayan Internal Medicine Soc. (hon.), Argentinian Neurol. Assn. (hon.), Uruguayan Neurol. Soc. (hon.), Internat. Stroke Soc., Am. Soc. Neurology Investigation, N.Y. Acad. Sci. Office: Maguire Bldg 105/2700 2160 S First Ave Maywood IL 60153 Office Phone: 708-216-2438. Business E-Mail: jbiller@lumc.edu.

BILLMAN, GEORGE EDWARD, physiologist, educator; b. Ft. Worth, July 23, 1954; s. George Everett and Genevieve Smith (Summerson) B.; m. Rosemary Cecelia Gieske, Aug. 16, 1975; children: George Thaddeus, Elyse Therese. BS, Xavier U., Cin., 1975; PhD, U. Ky., 1980. Rsch. assoc. dept. physiology and biophysics U. Okla., Oklahoma City, 1980-82, asst. prof. dept. physiology & biophysics Okla. City, 1982—84; asst. prof. dept. physiology Ohio State U., Columbus, 1984-90, assoc. prof., 1990—96, prof., 1996—. Cons. Glaxo, Inc., Research Triangle Park, N.C., 1989-91, Eli Lilly Rsch. Lab., Indpls., 1987-88, Proctor & Gamble, 1995-97, Sanofi-Aventis, 1995-, CV Therapeutics, 2008, editor in chief, Frontiers Physiology, 2009-. Mem. editl. bd. Jour. Cardiovasc. Pharmacology, 2001—, Am. Jour. Physiology, 2004—07, Current Cardiovasc. Revs., 2004—, Jour. Applied Physiology, 2007—, Experimental Physiology, 2007—11, assoc. editor Pharmacology & Therapeutics, 1999—; editor: (book) Novel Therapeutic Targets for Antiarrhythmic Drugs, 2010; contbr. articles to profl. jours. Grantee Am. Heart Assn., 1982-84, NIH, 1986-89, 99—, Nat. Inst. on Drug Abuse, 1990-95; recipient New Investigator award NIH, 1983-86. Fellow Am. Heart Assn., Hearth Rhythm Soc.; mem. Am. Physiol. Soc., Sigma Xi. Roman Catholic. Avocations: camping, hiking, stamp collecting/philately, reading. Home: 2250 Sawbury Blvd Columbus OH 43235-1860 Office: Ohio State U Dept Physiology 302 Hamilton Hall 1645 Neil Ave Columbus OH 43210-1218 Business E-Mail: billman.1@osu.edu.

BILLMANN, FRANCK GEORGES, surgeon; b. Haguenau, France, Aug. 7, 1977; MD in Medicine, surgery, U. Freiburg, Germany, 2008; PhD, U. Strasbourg, France, 2008. Oberarzt St. Vincentius Kliniken - Chirurgie, 2002—10. Author alsacian poetry. Recipient Prix O'Excellence, De La Societe Anatomique De Paris, 2008, Prix des Sciences Académie des Marches de l'Est, Académie des Marches de l'Est, Strasbourg, France, 2009. Mem.: ACS, EACA, AAPA, SAGES, EAES, Ministere De La Culture France, Chevalier de L'orore Des Arts Et Des Letters, Assn. pour la Rsch. en Physiologie de l'Environ., Anatomische Gesellschaft, Deutsche Gesellschaft für Viszeralchirurgie, Deutsche Gesellschaft für Chirurgie. Office: St Vincentius Kliniken Allgemeinchirurgie-Südendstrasse 32 Sekretariat Prof Kiffner Karlsruhe Baden Wü D-76137 Germany Office Phone: + 4972181088111. Business E-Mail: franck.billmann@wanadoo.fr.

BILSKI, BARTOSZ, preventive and occupational medicine physician, researcher; b. Poznan, Poland, Jan. 26, 1973; s. Wlodzimierz and Stefania Bilski. MD, U. Med. Scis., Poznan, 1998; PhD, Nofer Inst. Occupl. Medicine, Lodz, Poland, 2000. Elctr., rschr. U. Med. Sci., Poznan, 2000—. Dir. Ctr. Labor Securus Occupl. Medicine and Hygiene, Poznan, 1999—. Author: Work Hygiene for Nurses, 2004, Work Hygiene for Physiotherapists, 2005, Work Hygiene in Nursing, 2009; contbr. articles to profl. jours. Grantee, Ministry of Health, Warsaw, 1998. Achievements include research in ototoxicity of organic solvents in work environment; standards of preventive medicine; occupational musculoskeletal complaints and diseases; occupational infectious diseases and other occupational diseases among medical staff and influence of might and shift work on worker's health. Avocations: mountain climbing, astronomy, coin collecting/numismatics. Office: Univ Med Sci Dept Preventive Medicine Smoluchowskiego 11 60 179 Poznan Poland Home: Ul. Lwa Tolstoja 25 60-461 Poznan Poland Business E-Mail: bilski@ump.edu.pl.

BIN, YU, ophthalmologist, educator; b. Qingdao, Shandong, China, July 21, 1967; Degree, Shandong Med. U., 1991; MS, Qingdao U., 2004. Assoc. prof. Shandong Eye Inst., Qingdao Eye Hosp., 1991—. Mem.: Chinese Ophthal. Soc. Avocations: swimming, singing. Office: 5 Yanerdao Rd Qingdao Shandong 266071 China Business E-Mail: maryyu721@sina.com.

BINA, WILLIAM F., III, dean, medical educator; BS in Nuc. Sci., US Naval Acad., Annapolis; MD, U. Nebr.; MPH in Internat. Health, Johns Hopkins U., Balt. Family practice residency Naval Regional Med. Ctr., Camp Pendelton, Calif., 1975—78; gen. preventive medicine residency Johns Hopkins U., 1982—84; joined Mercer U. Sch. Medicine, Macon, Ga., 1991, various positions in the family medicine dept. including prof., practicing physician and program dir. family residence program, assoc. dean, 2007—08, dean, 2008—. Dir. family practice residency program Med. Ctr. of Ctrl. Ga., 1992—97; bd. dirs. Ctrl. Ga. Health Network, 1996—99, Secure Health Plans Ga., 1996—; pres., chmn. bd. dirs. Ga. Acad. Family Physicians, 1998—2000. Project and med. dir. Ctrl Ga. Cancer Coalition, 2002—08; mem. steering com. to establish a primary health care facility in Macon and Bibb counties Ga., 2004—07. Served with USN. Office: Mercer University Sch Medicine Office of Dean 1550 College St Macon GA 31207 *

BIN ABDULRAHMAN, KHALID ABDULGHAFAR, physician, educator; b. Makkah, Saudi Arabia, Nov. 18, 1963; s. Abdulghafar Abdullah Bin Abdulrahman and Mezna Rutaiman Al-Johany; m. Afaf Hassan Magraby, Apr. 1, 1991; children: Waleed Khalid children: Talha Khalid, Maan Khalid, Amro Khalid, Yasser Khalid. MBBS, King Abdulaziz U., Jeddah, 1989; diploma in primary health care, King Saud U., Riyadh, Saudi Arabia, 1992; M in Health Sci., Med. Edn., U. Toronto, Can., 1999. Cert. family medicine Arab Bd. for Med. Specialization, 1993. Fellow family medicine U. Toronto, 1997—98; supr. Saudi Soc. Family & Cmty. Medicine, Riyadh; gen. supr. specialized acad. med. tng. SAMT, Riyadh, 2000—; dir. med. edn. ctr. King Saud U., Riyadh, 2001—, assoc. prof. family medicine, 2002, vice dean postgrad. and continuing med. edn., 2005. Mem. editl. bd.: Saudi Med. Jour., JFCM (Man of the yr. 2002). Named Man of Yr., Am. Biog. Instn., 2002. Mem.: Saudi Soc. Med. Edn. (v.p., supr. Riyadh office), Saudi Soc. Family & Cmty. Medicine. Office: King Saud U Coll Med PO Box 2925 Riyadh Saudi Arabia Office Fax: +966 1 4671840. Business E-Mail: dr_khalid_ksu@yahoo.com

BIN DAYNA, KHALIFA MUBARAK, surgeon; b. Bahrain, Dec. 21, 1955; married. MBChB, U. Alexandria, Egypt, 1980. Intern Univ. of Alexandria, Egypt, 1981; chief resident surgery dept. Univ. of Erlangen, Germany, 1989—93, cons. surgeon, 1993—94; rotating resident Salmaniya Med. Complex, Bahrain, 1982, jr. resident surgery dept., 1982—86, sr. resident sugery dept., 1986—88, chief resident surgery dept., 1995, cons. surgeon surgery dept., 1995—2000, sr. cons. surgeon surgery dept., 2000—. Author: (various articles) Minimally Invasive Surgery Jours., (book) Operative Surgery Book - Minimally Invasive Surgery page 386-389. Recipient Kingdom of Bahrain Golden Medal in Competency, King of Bahrain, 2008; named Best Surgeon, Amir of Bahrain, 1997, Prime Min., 2001. Mem.: 15 Pan Arab Surgeons Conf., Soc. of Surgery in Arabian Gulf (pres. 2005), Pan Arab Minimally Invasive Assn. (pres. 2005), Bahrain Surgeon Assn. (pres. 2004—05), Pan Arab Surgeon Assn. Bd., Bahrain Cancer Soc., European Assn. for Endoscopic Surgery and Other Conventional Techniques, European Soc. of Surg. Oncology, Exptl. & Rsch. of Surg. Soc., German Surg. Soc., German Soc. of Surg. Oncology. Office: Salmaniya Medical Complex PO Box 12 Bahrain *

BINDER, JEFFREY R., medical products executive; BA, Yale U.; M in Pub. Policy, Princeton U. Cons. Boston Consulting Group, Inc.; sr. mgmt. positions Howmedica Orthopedics; pres. DePuy Orthopedics, 1998—2000; CEO, pres. Spinal Concepts, 2000—03; pres., Abbott Spine Abbott Laboratory, Inc., 2003—06, v.p., 2004—05, sr. v.p., diagnostic ops., 2006—07; pres., CEO & bd. dirs. Biomet, Inc., Warsaw, Ind., 2007—; pres., CEO Interpore Spine Ltd., 2007—. Office: Biomet Inc 56 E Bell Dr Warsaw IN 46582-0587 Mailing: Biomet Inc PO Box 587 Warsaw IN 46581-0587 Office Phone: 574-267-6639. Office Fax: 574-267-8137. Business E-Mail: jeffrey.binder@biomet.com. *

BINDER, LEAH FRIEDA, health services organization executive; d. Henry J. and Dauna W. Binder; m. Sam Lyons Elowitch; 2 children. BA in Politics, Women's Studies, Brandeis U., 1984; Master's Degree and Master of Govt. Adminstrn., U. Pa. (Annenberg Sch. Communications and Fels Inst. of Govt.), 1994. Pub. policy dir. Nat. League for Nursing; sr. policy advisor to NYC Mayor Rudolph W. Giuliani; exec. dir. Healthy Cmty. Coalition, Franklin Health Access; v.p. Franklin Cmty. Health Network, Farmington, Maine, 1999—2008; CEO The Leapfrog Group, 2008—. Chair Maine Pub. Health Inst., Maine Ctr. for Pub. Health. Campaign co-chair United Way of Tri-Valley. Mem.: Maine Pub. Health Assn. (pres.). Office: The Leapfrog Group c/o Academy Health 1150 17th St NW Ste 600 Washington DC 20036 Office Phone: 202-292-6713. Business E-Mail: lbinder@leapfroggroup.org.

BINI, ROBERTO, physician, director; b. Napoli, Nov. 28, 1971; MD, Med. U. Torino, 1997, degree in Gen. Surgery, 2004. Med. dir. dept. emergency & gen. surgery SG Bosco Hosp., Torino, Italy, 2004—. Mem.: Italian Assn. Surgeon. Home: Corso Duca degli Abruzzi 86 Torino 10129 Italy Home Phone: 393473592421. Business E-Mail: re.bini@libero.it.

BIN-JALIAH, ISMAEEL MOHAMMED, physiologist, biomedical researcher, medical educator, neuroscientist, dean; b. Abha, Saudi Arabia, Mar. 11, 1974; s. Mohammed Abdullah Bin-Jaliah and Hadba Ali Al-Jobran; m. Najwa Lahiq Asiri, July 23, 2001; children: Lujain Ismaeel, Lubna Ismaeel children: Mohammed Ismaeel. MBBS in Medicine and Surgery, King Saud U., Abha, 1997; CBiol, MSB (hon.), Inst. Biology, Eng., 2004; PhD in Physiology, U. Birmingham, Eng., 2006—. Health Profession Practice Licensure Saudi Commn. for Health Specialties, 1998. Ho. officer Asir Ctrl. Hosp. Ministry of Health, Abha, Saudi Arabia, 1998—99; tchg. asst. Coll. Medicine King Khalid U., 1999—2006; post-graduate physiologist Med. Sch. U. Birmingham, England, 2001—06; asst. prof. physiology King Khalid U., Abha, Saudi Arabia, 2006—, dir. Medical Edn. Ctr., 2006—; sec. gen. Saudi Soc. Med. Edn., 2007—, vice dean coll. medical sci., 2008—. Asst. mem. admissions com. King Khalid U. Coll. Medicine, Abha, Saudi Arabia, 2000, mem. orgnl. com. second book fair, 00, mem. dept. physiology coun., 2007—, mem. quality assurance com., 2007—, mem. tchg. assistants selection com., 2007—, chmn. curriculum evaluation com., 2007—, mem. purchase com., 2007—; mem. Ctr. for Rsch. in Med. and Dental Edn. U. Birmingham, 2004—, mem. Ctr. Cardiovascular Scis., 2005—; chmn. establishing com. Nat. Rsch. Ctr. for Devel. of Health Scis. Edn. Saudi Arabia; mem. orgnl. com. Brain Awareness Week Internat. Brain Rsch. Orgn. Ad hoc reviewer Jour. Physiology, 2007—, Jour. Med. Edn., 2007—, Jour. Diabetes and its Complications, 2007—. Recipient ABHA prize in higher edn., Aseer Emirate, ABHA, Saudi Arabia; doctorate scholarship, King Khalid U., Saudi Arabia, 2000—06. Mem.: AAAS, Assn. Rschrs. Medicine and Scis., Internat. Soc. Arterial Chemoreception, Saudi Soc. Med. Edn., Inst. Biology, Islamic Med. Assn. of Kingdom of Saudi Arabia, Am. Physiol. Soc., Physiol. Soc. UK, Brit. Neuroscience Assn., Assn. Med. Edn. in Europe, Internat. Brain Rsch. Orgn., Internat. Soc. Autonomic Neuroscience, Am. Coll. Clin. Pharmacology (assoc.). Moslem. Avocations: reading, travel. Office: Dept Physiology Coll of Medicine King Khalid U PO Box 641 Abha Aseer Saudi Arabia Home: PO Box 2194 Abha Aseer Saudi Arabia Office Fax: +96672247570; Home Fax: +96672281168. Personal E-Mail: isbinjaliah@yahoo.com.

BINNIE, NANCY CATHERINE, retired nurse, educator; b. Sioux Falls, SD, Jan. 28, 1937; d. Edward Grant and Jessie May (Martini) Larkin; m. Charles H. Binnie. Diploma, St. Joseph's Hosp. Sch. Nursing, Phoenix, 1965; BS in Nursing, Ariz. State U., 1970, MA, 1974. Intensive care charge nurse Scottsdale (Ariz.) Meml. Hosp., 1968-70, coordinator critical care, 1970-71, John C. Lincoln Hosp., Phoenix, 1971-73; prof. nursing GateWay Community Coll., Phoenix, 1974-96; ret., 1996. Developer, coord. part-time evening nursing programs Gateway Community Coll., 1984-97, interim dir. nursing, 1989, 91. Mem. Orgn. Advancement of Assoc. Degree Nursing, Practical and Assoc. Coun. Nursing Educators, Ariz. Coun. Nurse Educators. Avocations: gardening, golf, sewing. Personal E-Mail: nbinnie@msn.com.

BINNIG, GERD KARL, physicist, educator; b. Frankfurt am Main, Germany, July 20, 1947; m. Lore Wagler, 1969 (div.); 2 children; m. Renate Binnig, 2003. BS in Physics, Johann Wolfgang Goethe U., Frankfurt, 1973; PhD, U. Frankfurt, 1978. Staff physics rsch. group, Zurich Rsch. Lab., IBM, 1978—2005, group leader Zurich Rsch. Lab., 1984—2005, assignment to Almaden Rsch. Ctr. San Jose, Calif., 1985—86. Hon. prof. physics U. Munich, 1986—; vis. prof. Stanford U., Calif., 1987—88; bd. dirs. Mercedes Automobile Holding AG, 1989—93, Daimler-Benz AG, 1990—; co-founder, cons., mem. adv. bd. Definiens AG (formerly Definiens Enterprise Image Intelligence Co.), 1994—. Author: Out of Nothing, 1989; mem. editl. bd.: Rev. Sci. Instruments, 1990—92. Recipient German Phys. Soc. prize, 1982, King Faisal Internat. prize for physics, 1984, Otto-Klung-Weberbank prize, Germany, 1984, Hewlett Packard Europhysics prize, 1984, Nobel prize in physics, 1986, Elliot Cresson medal, Franklin Inst., 1987, Minnie Rosen award, Ross U., NY, 1988, Bayerischer Verdienstorden, 1992; named to Nat. Inventors Hall of Fame, 1994; IBM Fellow, 1987. Fellow: World Tech. Network (World Tech. award-IT Hardware 2006), Royal Microscopical Soc. (hon.), Acad. Scis. (assoc.). Achievements include invention of a Scanning Tunneling Microscope; development of powerful microscopy technique, which can form an image of individual atoms on a metal or semiconductor surface by scanning the tip of a needle overthe surface at a height of only a few atomic diameters. Avocations: music, tennis, soccer, golf, reading. Office: Definiens AG Trappentreustrasse 1 80339 Munich Germany

BIOCIC, JOSIP STANKO, oral surgeon; b. Pakrac, July 30, 1979; DMD, Sch. Dental Medicine, U. Zagreb, 2004, postgrad. Oral surgeon U. Hosp. Dubrava, U. Zagreb, 2006—09. Office: Gojko Susak Av 6 Zagreb 10000 Croatia E-mail: biocicjosip@yahoo.com.

BIOLATTI, BARTOLOMEO, veterinarian, pathologist; b. Marene, Cuneo, Italy, Oct. 16, 1952; s. Luigi Biolatti and Maddalena Gandolfo; m. Maria Assunta Bellonio, Aug. 13, 1955; children: Cristina, Marco. D in Vet. Medicine, U. Turin, 1976. Diplomate European Coll. Vet. Pathologists, 1996. Asst. prof. vet. pathology U. Turin, Piemonte, Italy, 1980—83, assoc. prof. vet. pathology, 1983—93; ordinary prof. U. Padua, Veneto, 1993—98; prof. vet. pathology U. Turin, 1998—. Dean Vet. Coll. U. Turin, 2005—, U. Padua, 1995—98; head post grad. specialization Sch. Animal Health and Prodn. U. Turin, 2000—, head dept. animal pathology, 2003—05; mem. bioethical com. Italian NRC, Rome, 1992—2002, Calabria Regional Govt., Cosenza, 2000, Consortium Organ Transplant Rsch.; assoc. editor-in-chief European Soc. Vet. Pathology, Zurich, 2000—02; charter mem. European Coll. Vet. Pathology, Hannover, Germany, 1995—. Editor: (book) The Eldorado of New Biology: Clonation, Transgenic Animals and Stem Cells, 2003. Coun. mem. Town All, Marene, Italy, 1985—2005. Master: Italian Soc. Vet. Scis.; mem.: Italian Assn. Vet. Pathologists (assoc.), European Soc. Vet. Pathology (assoc.), Vet. Rsch. Club (assoc.). Avocation: tennis. Home: Colonnello Gay 7 Cuneo Marene 12030 Italy Office: U Turin Leonardo da Vinci 44 Torino Grugliasco 10095 Italy Office Fax: (39) 011 6709031. Business E-Mail: bartolomeo.biolatti@unito.it.

BIRCAN, CIGDEM, physiatrist; b. Izmir, Turkey, Sept. 15, 1966; d. Hikmet and Sukran Bircan. MD, Dokuz Eylul U., İzmir, Turkey, 1991. Resident EGE U. Sch. of Medicine, Izmir, Turkey, 1991—96; specialist Dokuz Eylul U. Sch. Medicine, Izmir, Turkey, 1996—2001, asst. prof., 2001—07, assoc. prof., 2007—. Mem.: Turkish Soc. Phys. Medicine and Rehab. Specialists. Office: Dokuz Eylul U Sch Med Dep Phys Med and Rehab Izmir 35340 Turkey Home Phone: +90(232) 381 86 22; Office Phone: +90(232) 4123960.

BIRCH, LEANN L., health sciences professor; AB in Psychology, Calif. State U., Long Beach, 1971; MA in Psychology, U. Mich., Ann Arbor, 1973, PhD in Psychology, 1975. Asst. prof. dept. psychology Ill. State U., Urbana-Champaign, 1975—76, asst. prof. human devel., 1976—81, nutritional scis. faculty, 1978—81, assoc. prof. human devel., 1981—86, chair divsn. human devel. & family ecology, 1984—88, 1991—92, prof. human devel. & nutritional scis., 1986—92; prof. head, human devel. & family studies Pa. State U., 1992—, disting. prof. human devel., 2003—, dir. Ctr. Childhood Obesity Rsch. Contbr. articles to profl. jours. Recipient Paul A. Funk Recognition award, U. Ill. Coll. Agr., 1992, Malcolm Trout Scholar award, Mich. State U., 1995, Pauline Schmitt Russell Disting. Rsch. Career award, Pa. State U. Coll.Health & Human Devel., 2000, Faculty Scholar medal, 2003. Achievements include research in factors that influence the developing controls of food intake from infancy through adolescence; predictors and consequences of eating behavior, including a focus on the development of food preferences, and on problems of energy balance, particularly obesity, dieting, and disordered eating. Office: Penn State U DEpt Human Devel & Family Studies 129 Noll Bldg University Park PA 16802 Office Phone: 814-863-0053. Office Fax: 814-863-7963. Business E-Mail: llb15@psu.edu. *

BIRCHER, ANDREA URSULA, retired psychiatric mental health clinical nurse specialist; b. Bern, Switzerland, Mar. 6, 1928; arrived in US, 1947; d. Franklin E. Bircher and Hedy E. Bircher-Rey. Diploma, Knapp Coll. Nursing, Santa Barbara, Calif., 1957; BS, U. Calif. San Francisco, 1961, MS, 1962; PhD, U. Calif., Berkeley, 1966. RN. Staff nurse, head nurse Cottage Hosp., Santa Barbara, 1957—58; psychiat. nurse, jr., sr. Langley-Porter Neuropsychiatric Inst., San Francisco, 1958—66; asst. prof. U. Ill. Coll. Nursing, Chgo., 1966-72; prof. U. Okla. Coll. Nursing, Oklahoma City, 1972-93, prof. emeritus, 1993—. Contbr. articles to profl. jours. Recipient Lifetime Achievement award, Internat. Biog. Ctr., Cambridge, England, Silver Bullet award, Internat. Thriller Writers/Reading Is Fundamental, 2007. Fellow: Am. Psychotherapy Assn., Ventura County Writers Club; mem.: ANA,

AAUP, N.Am. Nursing Diagnosis Assn., Internat. Soc. Psychiat.-Mental Health Nursing, Phi Kappa Phi, Sigma Theta Tau. Republican. Avocations: indoor gardening, reading, writing.

BIRD, ADRIAN, geneticist, educator; PhD in Genetics, U. Edinburgh, Scotland, 1972. With dept. biology Yale U., 1972—74; with Inst. Molecular Biology, Zurich, Switzerland, 1974—75, MRC Mammalian Genome Unit, Edinburgh, 1975—86, Inst. for Molecular Pathology, Vienna, 1987—90; joined U. Edinburgh, 1990—; prof. U. Edinburgh, Inst. Cell and Molecular Biology, 1990—; Buchanan chair genetics U. Edinburgh, 1990—; dir. Wellcome Trust Ctr. for Cell Biology, 1999—. Mem. bd. govs. The Wellcome Trust Ltd., 2000—10; mem. sci. adv. bd. Rett Syndrome Rsch. Found.; trustee Cancer Rsch. UK. Mem. editl. bd.: Molecular and Cellular Biology, Molecular Cell. Recipient Louis-Jeantet prize for medicine, Louis-Jeantet Found., 1999, Gabor medal, Royal Soc. London, 1999, Charles-Léopold Mayer prize, French Acad. Sciences, 2008, Gairdner Internat. award, Gairdner Found., Can., 2011. Achievements include research in structure and function of the mammalian genome, and in particular the role of DNA methylation. Office: U Edinburgh Wellcome Trust Ctr for Cell Biology M Swann Bldg Mayfield Rd Edinburgh EH9 3JR Scotland *

BIRD, FORREST M., retired medical inventor; b. Stoughton, Mass., June 9, 1921; MD, PhD, ScD. Technical air tng. officer Army Air Corps; founder Bird Corp., Bird Space Tech. Corp., Sandpoint, Idaho. Trustee emeritus Am. Respiratory Care Found. Inventor Bird Universal Medical Respirator for acute or chronic cardiopulmonary care, 1958, "Babybird" respirator, 1970. Inductee Nat. Inventors Hall of Fame, 1995; recipient Nat. Medal Technology, 2009. Avocation: collector & pilot of 18 vintage flying aircraft. Office: Bird Space Tech Corp PO Box 817 Sandpoint ID 83864-0817

BIRD, HECTOR RAMÓN, child psychiatrist, psychoanalyst, educator; b. San Juan, P.R., Feb. 5, 1939; s. Hector F. and Yvette (Baker) B.; m. Sandra Lopez, May 23, 1970; 1 child, Alejandra Y. BA, U. Mich., 1960; MD, Yale U., 1965; cert. in psychiatry and child psychiatry, Columbia U., 1972; cert. in psychoanalysis, W.A. White Inst., NYC. Diplomate Am. Bd. Psychiatry and Neurology. Asst. dir. child psychiatry St. Luke's Hosp., NYC, 1972-78; dir. tng. in child psychiatry Columbia U., NYC, 1978-80, prof. emeritus clin. psychiatry, 2006—; dir. child psychiatry U. P.R. Med. Sch., San Juan, 1980-86; dep. dir. child psychiatry N.Y. State Psychiat. Inst., NYC, 1986—2006. Contbr. articles to profl. jours. Founding dir., pres. bd. dirs. Teatro de la Opera, San Juan, 1982-86; dir. Pro-Arte Musical, San Juan, 1982-86, 2007-. Lt. USN, 1966-68. Recipient Profl. Achievement award Boricua Coll., N.Y.C., 1987, Wilfred C. Hulse Meml. award N.Y. Coun. on Child and Adolescent Psychiatry, 2001. Fellow Am. Acad. Child and Adolescent Psychiatry (Riger award 2007), Am. Acad. Psychoanalysis (trustee); mem. Am. Psychopathological Assn., Soc. Rsch. in Child and Adolescent Psychopathology, William A. White Psychoanalytic Soc. Roman Catholic. Office: 424 West End Ave 2H New York NY 10024 also: 1452 Ashford Ave 403 B San Juan PR 00907 Office Phone: 212-874-5311. Personal E-mail: hecbird@aol.com.

BIRD, SHARLENE, clinical psychologist; d. Rubin and Dina Bird. BA in Psychology & Hispanic Studies, Vassar Coll., 1979; MA in Applied Psychology, Adelphi U., 1986; MA in Human Resources Mgmt., New Sch. for Social Rsch., NYC, 1987; PsyD in Clin. Psychology, Yeshiva U., 1992. Lic. psychologist, N.Y. Clin. extern St. Mary's Children and Family Svcs., Syosset, N.Y., 1980-81; behavior modifier Flower Hosp./Terence Cardinal Cooke, NYC, 1981-82; clin. psychology extern Met. Ctr. for Mental Health, 1986-87; clin. psychology intern NYU Med. Ctr./Bellevue Hosp., NYC, 1989-90; postdoctoral fellow in human sexuality N.Y. Hosp./Cornell Med. Ctr., 1990-92; family therapist Roberto Clemente Family Guidance Ctr., NYC, 1991-93, 96-98; healthcare planning analyst Inst. for Family and Community Care, NYC, 1993-96; pvt. practice NYC, 1994—. Supr. NYU Med. Ctr./Bellevue Hosp., NYC, 1992—; part-time clin. instr. dept. psychiatry NYU Med. Ctr., 1995—; tng. cons. Inst. for Family and Cmty. Care, NYC, 1993; weekly permanent radio talk show co-host Siempre a Tu Lado, Sta. WADO 1280 AM, 1992—95. Chair bd. dirs. Mothers of Childrens with AIDS, N.Y.C., 1991-93. Mem.: APA, Assn. for Advancement of Behavior Therapy (chair pub. edn. and media dissemination com. 1996—99), Am. Group Psychotherapy Assn., Counselors and Therapists, Am. Assn. Sex Educators, Assn. Hispanic Mental Health Profls. (bd. dirs., mem.-at-large 1995—97, v.p. 1999—2001), Am. Orthopsychiat. Assn., N.Y. State Psychol. Assn., Sigma Delta Phi. Office: 112 W 56th St Rm C Ste 15 S New York NY 10019-3841

BIRD, YELENA AMELIA HAZEL, healthcare educator; b. London, Jan. 29, 1965; MD, PhD, NMSU, MPH, 2007. Asst. prof. environ. health Sch. Pub. Health, U. Sask., 2010—, academician, investigator. Cmty. Based Participatory Rschr. grant, Paso del Norte, Minority Rsch. fellow, Nat. Cancer Inst. Mem.: APHA. Avocations: jogging, reading, music. Office: 107 Wiggins Rd Saskatoon Saskatchewan S7N 5E5 Canada Office Phone: 306-966-8432. Business E-Mail: yelena.bird@usask.ca.

BIRGANDER, MATS, cardiologist; b. Helsingborg, Feb. 12, 1972; MD, Lund U., 2004. Physician Skånes Universitetssjukhus SUS, 2005—. Mem.: European Soc. Cardiology. Office: SFörstadsgatan 101 Malmö Skane 20502 Sweden Personal E-mail: mbirgander@yahoo.se.

BIRKENFELDT, REINHOLD, rheumatologist; b. Tallinn, June 16, 1934; MD, U. Tartu, 1960, PhD, 1968; DSc, Inst. Rheumatology, Moscow, 1988. Prof., head, dept. internal medicine Med. Faculty U. Tartu, 1988—92, prof., head, divsn. rheumatology, 1992—99, prof. emeritus, 1999. Mem.: Estonian Soc. Rheumatology. Office: Tallinna 29 Kuressaare Saaremaa 93811 Estonia Business E-Mail: reinhold.birkenfedt@kliinikum.ee.

BIRKETVEDT, GRETHE STØA, medical scientist, writer, musician; b. Sarpsborg, Norway, Sept. 17, 1942; d. Arne and Aase (Oscarsdatter) Støa; 1 child, Camilla Støa. Student, Tchrs. Tng. Coll., Stord, Norway, 1964; M of Phys. Edn., U. of Sport, Oslo, 1972; MD, Oslo U., 1983; MD, PhD, U. Tromsø, Norway, 1995. Diplomate, lic. med. NY; cert. tchr. phys. edn., music diplomate. Fulbright scholar, U.S., 1968-69; musician, composer Norwegian Composers Assn., Oslo, 1969-83; gen. practitioner Med. Assn. Oslo, 1983-92; med. scientist Gen. Practice Orgn., Oslo, 1992-93; asst. prof. Tromső Hosp., 1993-95; vis. prof. U. Pa., Phila., 1995-99. Asst. rsch. prof. Mt. Sinai Sch. Medicine, NYC, 2000—; hon. prof. Albert Schweitzer Internat. U. Geneva, Geneva, 2000—05; rschr. U. Tromsö, Norway, 2005—08; obesity dep. Aker U. Hosp., Oslo. Author: (book) At a Distance, 1976, (poems) 2d edit., 1977, These are the Days, 1978, Hildelin, A Symphonic Poem, 1980, In the Light of the Planet, 1994, The Body in the Brain, 2008; composer: (musical plays) Musikklek, 1980, (plays) Laughing Street No. 2, 1986, Circus in Town, 1994, Vriompeisen, 1997, Treatment of Overweight and Obesity in General Practice, 2000; contbr. articles to profl. jours., chapters to books. Recipient Writer's award, U. Altertumskunde, Munich, 1980, Golden Acad. award, Lifelong Achievement, Am. Bio Inst., 1999, Peace and Sci. Commemorative medal, Albert Schweitzer Internat. U., 2002; Norwegian Coun. Med. Rsch. grantee, 1996. Mem.: AAAS, Norwegian Assn. Journalism, Norwegian Assn. Music Composition, Norwegian Assn. Medicine, TONO Assn. Protection Musical Original Work, Soc. Study Ingestive Behavior, Norwegian Writers Ctr., Fulbright Alumni Assn. Avocations: music, writing, riding, painting, reading. Home: 74 Oak Knoll Dr Berwyn PA 19312 Office: Aker Univ Hosp Oslo Norway Personal E-mail: gsb42nor@aol.com.

BIRKHAHN, ROBERT H., emergency physician; b. Madison, Ind., Dec. 12, 1971; MD, U. Cin., 1997; MS, Weill Cornell Grad. Sch., 2003. Rsch. dir. NY Meth. Hosp., 2000. Exec. dir. Integrated Med. Rsch., LLC, 2007; assoc. prof. Weill Grad. Sch. Med. Scis., 2007. Empire Clin. Rsch. Investigator fellowship, NY State Dept. Health, grant, MediciNova, Alere. Fellow: Am. Coll. Emergency Physicians; mem.: Soc. Academic Emergency Medicine (Outstanding Reviewer award, Leadership award). Office: 54 Firwood Rd Port Washington NY 11050 Business E-Mail: birkhahn@doctoris.org.

BIRKHEAD, GUTHRIE S., medical educator; AB cum laude, Princeton U., NJ, 1975; MD cum laude, Yale U. Sch. Medicine, New Haven, Conn., 1979; MPH, John Hopkins U. Sch. Hygiene and Pub. Health, 1985. Intern, resident, internal medicine Univ. Hosp., Boston Univ. Med. Ctr., 1979—82; preventive medicine resident John Hopkins Univ. Sch. Hygiene and Pub. Health, Balt., 1984—85, Ctr. for Disease Control, Divsn. Surveillance and Epidemiologic Studies, Epidemiology Program Office, Atlanta, 1987—88; assoc. prof., epidemiology Sch. Pub. Health, U. Albany, SUNY; dir. Ctr. for Cmty. Health, AIDS Inst.; joined Office Pub. Health, NY State Dept. Health, 1988, dep. commr., 2007—, chief pub. health physician; founding dir. NY State Dept. Health Preventive Medicine Residency Program. Instr., epidemiology course U. Vt. Coll. Medicine, 1985—86; mem. and incoming chair Nat. Vaccine Adv. Com., US Dept. HHS, 2008—. Contbr. several articles to profl. jours. Recipient Nathan Davis award for Outstanding Govt. Svc., AMA, 2008. Fellow: NY Acad. Medicine; mem.: Soc. Scholars. Office: Sch Pub Health Univ Albany SUNY ESP Corning Tower Rm 1417 One University Pl Rensselaer NY 12144 also: NY State Dept Health Corning Tower Empire State Plz Albany NY 12237 Office Phone: 518-402-5382. Office Fax: 518-486-1415. Business E-Mail: gsb02@health.state.ny.us.

BIRKS, EMMA JANE, cardiologist; b. Hythe, Kent, Apr. 11, 1967; MD, Royal Free Hosp. Sch. Medicine, U. London, 1992; PhD, Imperial Coll. London, 2003. Spl. registrar cardiology & transplant medicine Harefield Hosp., 1999—2004, Chelsea & Westminster Hosp., Royal Brompton Hosp., Hammersmith Hosp., Hillingdon Hosp.; consult cardiologist transplantation & mech. circulatory support, sr. lectr. Royal Brompton & Harefield Hosp. NHS Trust, Imperial Coll. London, 2004—09; dir. advanced heart failure, transplant & mech. support U. Louisville Sch. Medicine, Jewish Hosp., 2009—. Investigator Brit. Heart Found. Project Grant, 1996—99; vice chair Gordon Rsch. Conf., 2011. Grant, Thoratec Corp., Cardiovasc. Biomed. Rsch. Unit, Nat. Inst. Health Rsch., Dept. Health, LVAD Rsch. grant, Royal Brompton & Harefield Charitable Trustees, Project grant, Brit. Heart Found. Mem.: Internat. Soc. Heart & Lung Transplantation, Am. Heart Assn., Brit. Transplantation Soc., Sci. Coun. Clin. Heart Failure & Transplant Medicine, Internat. Soc. Heart & Lung Transplantation, Sci. Coun. Mech. Circulatory Support. Avocation: travel. Office: 201 Abraham Flexner Way Ste 1001 Louisville KY 40202 Office Phone: 502-587-4384. Office Fax: 502-587-4184. Business E-Mail: e.birks@imperial.ac.uk, emma.birks@louisville.edu.

BIRMAHER, BORIS, psychiatrist; b. Cali, Colombia, Mar. 8, 1952; MD, Valle Coll. Medicine, 1975. Clin. instr. Haddassah Coll. Medicine, Hebrew U., 1981—83; asst. clin. prof. psychiatry Columbia U., 1983—88; asst. prof. U. Pitts., 1988—92, assoc. prof., 1992—2001, prof. psychiatry, 2001—, endowed chair early onset bipolar disorder, 2007—11. Office: 3811 O'Hara St 100 N Bellefield Pittsburgh PA 15213 Office Fax: 412-246-5230. Business E-Mail: shableskym@upmc.edu.

BIRNBAUM, ELISA HOPE, colon and rectal surgeon, director, educator; MD, U. Ill., Peoria, 1985. Lic. Mo., 1991, diplomate Am. Bd. Colon and Rectal Surgery, 2003, Am. Bd. Surgery, 2009. Resident in surgery LI Jewish Med. Ctr., New Hyde Pk., 1990; fellow in colon and rectal surgery Barnes-Jewish Hosp., St. Louis, 1991, program dir. colon and rectal surgery sect.; hosp. affiliations include Barnes-Jewish West County Hosp., St. Louis VA Med. Ctr., Progress West Health-Care Ctr.; prof. surgery sch. medicine Wash. Univ., St. Louis. Author: What's new in colon and rectal surgery, 2002, 2006, Work-up of the constipated patient, 2008; co-author: Stage IV rectal cancer with liver metastases: is there a benefit to resection of the primary tumor?, 2010, Laparoscopic colectomy using cancer principles is appropriate for colonoscopically unresectable adenomas of the colon, 2010, Laparoscopic versus open 2-stage ileal pouch: laparoscopic approach allows for faster restoration of intestinal continuity, 2010, various others. Named one of Best Doctors in America, 2010. Fellow: ACS; mem.: Am. Soc. Colon and Rectal Surgeons. Office: Washington University School Medicine Department of Surgery Campus Box 8109 660 S Euclid Ave Ste 14102 Queeny Tower Saint Louis MO 63110 Office Phone: 314-454-7177.

BIRNBAUM, HOWARD G., economist; b. NYC, Jan. 3, 1947; PhD, Harvard U., 1974. Prin. Analysis Group, Inc., 1997—. Mem.: Internat. Soc. Pharmacoeconomics and Outcomes Rsch. Avocations: bicycling, birdwatching, gardening. Office: 111 Huntington Ave Boston MA 02199 Business E-Mail: hbirnbaum@analysisgroup.com.

BIRNBAUM, LINDA S., federal agency administrator, toxicologist; b. Passaic, NJ, Dec. 21, 1946; BA in Biology, U. Rochester, NY, 1967; MS in Microbiology, U. Ill., Urbana, 1969, PhD in Microbiology, 1972. Diplomate Am. Bd. Toxicology. Vis. asst. prof. microbiology U. Ill., 1972; postdoc. fellow biochemistry U. Mass., Amherst, 1973—74; asst. prof. sci. Kirkland Coll., Clinton, NY, 1974—75; rsch. assoc., rsvh. fellow Masonic Med. Rsch. Lab., Utica, NY, 1975—79; sr. staff fellow nat. toxicology program Nat. Cancer Inst., Research Triangle Park, NC, 1979—80; rsch. microbiologist Nat. Inst. Environ. Health Svcs. (NIEHS) NIH, Research Triangle Park, NC, 1980—89, dir. NIEHS, 2009—, dir. Nat. Toxicology Program, 2009—, sr. investigator, Nat. Cancer Insi., 2009—; dir. exptl. toxicology divsn., Nat. Health & Environ. Effects Rsch. Lab., EPA, Research Triangle Park, NC, 1989—2008, acting dir. human studies divsn. Chapel Hill, NC, 2001—02, sr. toxicologist, 2008—09. Adj. prof. genetics SUNY Inst. Tech., Utica, 1976; adj. asst. prof., dept. environ. sci. U. NC Sch. Pub. Health, Chapel Hill, 1980—82, adj. assoc. prof., 1982—88, adj. prof., 1988—; adj. faculty Duke U., Durham, NC, 1995—. Mem. editl. bd. AGE, 1985—, Environ. Health Perspectives, 1988—, Human & Exptl. Toxicology, 1993—, Toxicology & Applied Pharmacology, 1989—, Chemosphere, 1999—; contbr. numerous articles to profl. jours., chapters to books. Mem. exec. bd. Am. Aging Assn., 1979—83, v.p., 1980—81; ofcl. avvisor Endometriosis Assn., 2007—. Recipient Conservation Achievement award, Nat. Wildlife Fedn., 1996, Ahlborg Memorial award, Karolinska Inst., Sweden, 1996; grantee, NIH, 1967—72, Mellon Found., 1974—75; fellow, Damon Runyon Found., 1973—74. Fellow: Acad. Toxicological Scis.; mem.: AAAS, Soc. Risk Analysis, Inst. Medicine, Women in Toxicology (Elsevier Mentoring award 2008), Internat. Union Toxicology (pres. 2010—), Gerontol. Soc., Internat. Soc. Study Xenobiotics, Am. Aging Assn. (former v.p.), Soc. Toxicology (pres. 2004—05, Pub. Comm. award 2006, Amb. award 2006), Am. Soc. Pharmacology & Exptl. Therapeutics (former chairperson, divsn. toxicology), Sigma Xi, Phi Kappa Phi, Phi Beta Kappa. Office: NIEHS Bldg 101 Rall Bldg B242 111 T Alexander Dr Research Triangle Park NC 27709 Office Phone: 919-541-3201. Office Fax: 919-541-2260. Business E-Mail: linda.birnbaum@nih.gov. *

BIRNS, MARK THEODORE, physician; b. Bklyn., Sept. 24, 1949; s. Leon and Naomi B.; m. Ann Krieger, Aug. 15, 1976; children: Samantha Lynn, Michael Eric, Kevin Douglas. BA, Case Western Res. U., 1971; MD, Albert Einstein Coll. Medicine, 1974. Diplomate: Am. Bd. Internal Medicine, Am. Bd. Gastroenterology. Intern Bronx Mcpl. Hosp. Ctr. Albert Einstein Hosps., 1974-75, resident in medicine, 1975-77; fellow in gastroenterology U. Oreg. Health Scis. Ctr., 1977-79; asst. chief gastroenterology Walter Reed Army Med. Ctr., 1979-83; asst. prof. medicine U. Health Scis., 1980-83; emergency physician Shady Grove Adventist Hosp., part time, 1980-83, Frederick Meml. Hosp., Washington, 1980-83; practice medicine specializing in gastroenterology and endoscopic biliary surgery Rockville, Md., 1983—; active staff Shady Grove Adventist Hosp., sec. med. staff, 1986-87, chief gastroenterology sect., vice chmn. dept. medicine, 1988, 89, mem. exec. com., 1990-92, mem. laser com., 1992, 93, 94, 95, mem. OR com., 1996-97; assoc. clin. prof. medicine dept. gastroenterology Georgetown U., Washington, 1988—; courtesy staff Suburban Hosp. Vice chmn. Health Delivery Orgn., Mid Atlantic Med. Svcs. Health Plan, 1997-2004, peer review com., 2005-09; treas., contract coord. Gastrointestinal Endoscopy Assocs., LLC, 1995—, Gastrointestinal Rsch. Assocs., LLC, 1999—. Major contbg. author: Radiology of the Liver, Biliary Tract, Pancreas and Spleen, 1987. Synagogue chair Israel Bonds Congregation B'nai Tzedek, 1994—, synagogue divsn. chair Washington, 2003—; alumni rep., mem. admissions com. Case Western Res. U., 1998—; healthcare adv. com. Eagle Bank, Md., 2000—09, Capital Digestive Care, Managed Care Contracting Com., 2008—, Fin. Com., 2009—. Served to maj. USAR. Named one of Top Doctors, Wash. Mag., 1993, 1994, 1995, 1999, 2004, 2005, 2008, 2010, Washington Consumer's Checkbook, 2011—. Fellow ACP, Am. Coll. Gastroenterology, Am. Gastroent. Assn.; mem. AMA (Physician Recognition award 1978, 81, 84, 87, 90, 93), Am. Gastroent. Assn., Am. Soc. Gastrointestinal Endoscopy (postgrad. edn. com. 1991-92), Md. Soc. Gastrointestinal Endoscopy (exec. bd.), Montgomery County Med. Soc. Home: 11413 Twining Ln Rockville MD 20854-1860 Office: 9711 Medical Center Dr Ste 308 Rockville MD 20850-3388 Office Phone: 301-251-1244.

BIRO, LASZLO, dermatologist; b. Czechoslovakia, May 31, 1929; came to U.S., 1956; s. Sandor and Margaret (Klein) B.; m. Dolores Macchiaroli, July 9, 1961; children: David, Lisa, Deborah, Michele. MD, Univ. Med. Sch., Debrecen, Hungary, 1953. Diplomate Am. Bd. Dermatology. Intern Kings County Hosp., Bklyn., 1957-58; resident Bellevue Hosp., NYC, 1958-60; pvt. practice medicine specializing in dermatology NYC, 1960-61, Bklyn., 1960—; emeritus dept. dermatology Bklyn. Hosp., Luth. Med. Ctr.; clin. prof. dermatology SUNY, Downstate Med. Ctr., 1971—. Contbr. articles on skin tumors to profl. jours. Fellow ACP, Am. Acad. Dermatology, N.Y. Acad. Medicine; mem. AMA, Kings County Med. Assn., Bay Ridge Med. Soc. (pres. 1987-88), N.Y. State Dermatol. Soc., Bklyn Dermatol. Soc., Internat. Soc. Tropical Dermatology, N.Y. Acad. Scis., Am. Coll. Cryosurgery (v.p. 1996), Semmelweis Sci. Soc. (pres. 1985). Office: 9921 4th Ave Brooklyn NY 11209-8347 Office Phone: 718-833-7616.

BIRON, CHRISTINE ANNE, medical science educator, researcher; d. R. Bernard and Theresa Priscilla (Sauvageau) B. BS, U. Mass., 1973; PhD, U. N.C., 1980. Rsch. technician U. Mass., Amherst, 1973—75; grad. rschr. U. N.C., Chapel Hill, 1975—80; postdoctoral fellow Scripps Clinic and Rsch., La Jolla, Calif., 1980; fellow U. Mass. Med. Sch., Worcester, 1981—82, instr., 1983, asst. prof., 1984—87; vis. scientist Karolinska Inst., Stockholm, 1984; asst. prof. med. svcs. Brown U., Providence, 1988—90, assoc. prof., 1990—96, prof., 1996—, Esther Elizabeth Brintzenhoff prof., 1996—, chair Dept. Molecular Microbiology & Immunology, 1999—2009, dir. grad. program in pathobiology, 1995—99; sci. adv. bd. Trudeau Inst., 2004—. Mem. AIDS and related rsch. study sect. 3 NIH, 1991-93; mem. exptl. immunology study sect. NIH, 1993-97, immunology working group sci. rev.; co-organizer Keystone Symposium on Innate Immunity to Pathogens, 2005; bd. sci. counselors subcom. basic scis. Nat. Cancer Inst., 2005—2010, bd. sci. counselors Nat. Inst. Allergy & Infectious Diseases, 2010-, chair, US Japan Immunology Bd., 2009-11, vis. prof., Trinity Coll. Dublin, 2010. Assoc. editor: Jour. Immunology, 1990—94, 2000, bd. editors: Procs. of Soc. for Exptl. Biology and Medicine, 1993—99, sect. editor: Jour. Immunology, 1995—99; editor: Jour. Nat. Immunity, 1994—98, Jour. Leukocyte Biology, 1999—2000; mem. editl. bd.: Virology, 2001—03; contbr. articles, revs. to sci. jours.; mem. adv. bd. editors: Jour. Exptl. Medicine, 2002—, mem. editl. bd.: Immunity, 2005—; editor: mBio, 2010—. Leukemia Soc. Am. fellow, 1981, Spl. fellow, 1983, scholar, 1987; grantee NIH, 1985—; rsch. grantee MacArthur Found., 1991-96. Fellow AAAS (scholar 2002-, chair com. med. csis., 2009-10, chair elect 2008-09, ret. chair coun. 2010-11); mem. Am. Assn. Immunologists (co-chmn. symposium 1990, 94, 95, 96, 98, 99, 2009, 10), Am. Soc. Virology, Am. Assn. Immunology (block co-chair nat. meetings 1996-99, program com. 1998-2000, awards com., 2008-10, chair 09-10), Am. Soc. Microbiology, Am. Acad. Microbiology, Am. Assn. of Microbiology, Soc. Natural Immunity (co-chair program for 2001 meeting), Sigma Xi. Office: Brown U PO Box G-B618 Providence RI 02912-0001

BIRREN, JAMES EMMETT, research and development company executive; b. Chgo., Apr. 4, 1918; m. Elizabeth S., 1942; children: Barbara Ann, Jeffrey Emmett, Bruce William. Student, Wright Jr. Coll., 1938; BEd, Chgo. State U., 1941; MA, Northwestern U., 1942, PhD, 1947, ScD (hon.), 1985; postgrad., U. Chgo., 1950—51; PhD (hon.), U. Gothenberg, Sweden, 1983; LLD (hon.), St. Thomas U., Can., 1990. Tutorial fellow Northwestern U., 1941—42; rsch. asst. project for study of fatigue Office Sci. Rsch. and Devel., 1942; rsch. fellow NIH, USPHS, 1946—47; rsch. psychologist gerontology unit NIH, 1947—51; rsch. psychologist NIMH, 1951—53, chief sect. on aging, 1953—64; dir. aging program Nat. Inst. Child Health and Human Devel., Bethesda, Md., 1964—65; dir. Gerontology Ctr.; prof. psychology U. So. Calif., 1965—89, Disting. prof. emeritus, 1992—, dean Davis Sch. Gerontology, 1975—86, Brookdale Disting. scholar, 1986—90, dir. Inst. Advanced Study in Gerontology and Geriat., 1981—89; dir. Borun Ctr. Gerontol. Rsch. UCLA, 1989—93, assoc. dir. Ctr. on Aging, 1990—; emeritus prof. and dean gerantology U. Southern Calif., LA. Fellow Ctr. for Advanced Study in Behavioral Scis., Stanford, Calif., 1978-79; Green vis. prof. U. B.C., 1979; vis. scientist Cambridge (Eng.) U., 1960-61; Harold E. Jones meml. lectr. U. Calif., Berkeley, 1965; mem. LA County Bd. Suprs.' Com. on Aging, 1967-69; sr. fellow U. So. Calif. Urban Ecology Inst., 1968-70; mem. Dean's Coun., U. So. Calif., 1970-86; chmn. aging rev. com. Nat. Inst. Aging, 1974-75; program dir. Integration of Info. on Aging: Handbook Project, 1973-76; mem. steering com. Care of Elderly, Inst. of Medicine, 1976-77; bd. dirs. Sears Roebuck Found., 1977-80; chmn. life course prevention rsch. rev. com. NIMH, 1985-87; cons. Roche Seminars on Aging Series, 1980-82. Author: Psychology of Aging, 1964; editor: Handbook of Aging and the Individual, 1959, (with K.W. Schaie) Handbook of the Psychology of Aging, 1996, Encyclopedia of Gerontology, 1996, (with R.B. Sloane) Handbook of Mental Health and Aging, 1992; contbr. articles to books, profl. publs.; bd. collaborators: Gerontologia, 1956-89; asst. editor: Jour. Gerontology, 1956-61, assoc. editor 1961-63, editor-in-chief 1968-74, chmn. publs. com., 1975-78, adv. editl. bd., 1956-69; bd. adv. editors: Devel. Psychobiology, 1967-69; adv. editor: Jour. Human Devel., 1957-58. Mem. adv. com. and del. White House Conf. on Aging, 1995. With USNR, 1943-46; to scientist dir. USPHS Scientist Corps, 1947-65. Recipient award for rsch. on problems of aging CIBA Found., 1956, Stratton award Am. Psychopath. Assn., 1960, Sr. 65er award Dist. 65 Retail Workers and Dept. Store Union, Sr. 65er award AFL-CIO, 1962, medal for meritorious svc. USPHS, 1965, citation Am. Assn. Ret. Persons, 1970, Am. Pioneers in Aging award U. Mich., 1972, commendation for disting. contbns. to field of gerontology Mayor of LA, 1968, 74, Merit award Northwestern U. Alumni Assn., 1976, Creative Scholarship and Rsch. award U. So. Calif., 1979, Disting. Educator award Assn. Gerontology in Higher Edn., 1983, Eminent Svc. award Stovall Found., 1984, award of Distinction Am. Fedn. for Aging Rsch., 1986, Sandoz prize for rsch. on aging, 1989, Can. Assn. Gerontology award, 1990, Disting. Emeritus award U. So. Calif., 1992, Pres.'s award Am. Soc. on Aging, 1996, Disting. Career Contbn. to Gerontology award Gerontol. Soc. Am., 2002, Ollie Randall award Nat. Coun. on Aging, 2004, Hall of Fame award Am. Soc. on Aging, 2004; USPHS rsch. fellow, 1946-47. Fellow AAAS, Am. Geriat. Soc. (founding fellow Western divsn.), Am. Psychol. Assn. (Disting. Sci. Contbn. award 1968, chmn. membership com. 1969, Disting. Contbn. award Divsn. Adult Devel. and Aging 1978, pres. divsn. 1955-56, editor newsletter 1951-55), Gerontol. Soc. (pres. 1961-62, chmn. publs. com. 1974-77, award for meritorious rsch. 1966, Brookdale award 1980); mem. Am. Physiol. Soc., Internat. Assn. Gerontology (chmn. exec. com. 1966-69, chmn. program com. 1968-69), Psychonomic Soc., Western Gerontol. Soc. (dir. 1965-, pres. 1968-69), Golden Key Club, Skull and Dagger Club, Sigma Xi, Phi Kappa Phi. Office: 3640 Dragonfly Dr #208 Thousand Oaks CA 91360

BIS, KOSTAKI G., medical educator; b. Detroit, Aug. 27, 1960; BS in Chemistry, Wayne State U., 1982, MD, 1986. Prof. Oakland U. William Beaumont Sch. Medicine William Beaumont Hosp., 1991—. Recipient Silver medal, Am. Roentgen Ray Soc., Radiol. Soc. N.Am.; named one of Best Drs. of America, 2003—, Americas Top Radiologists, Consumers Rsch. Coun. America, 2007. Fellow: Am. Coll. Radiology. Avocations: travel, clarinet. Office: 3601 W 13 Mile Rd Dept Radiology Royal Oak MI 48073 Office Fax: 248-551-3521. Business E-Mail: kbis@beaumont.edu.

BISARO, PAUL M., pharmaceutical executive, lawyer; B in Gen. Studies, U. Mich., 1983; JD, Catholic Univ., Washington, 1989. Assoc. Bishop, Cook, Purcell & Reynolds, Winston & Strawn, 1989—92; sr. cons. Arthur Andersen & Co.; gen. counsel Barr Pharmaceuticals, Inc., 1992—99, sr. v.p., strategic bus. devel., 1997—99, pres., COO, 1999—2007; pres., CEO Watson Pharmaceuticals, Inc., 2007—. Bd. dirs. Watson Pharmaceuticals, Inc., 2007—. Office: Watson Pharmaceuticals Inc Morris Corp Ctr III 400 Interpace Pky Parsippany NJ 07054 Office Phone: 862-261-7000. Business E-Mail: paul.bisaro@watsonpharm.com. *

BISCHEL, MARGARET DEMERITT, physician, consultant; b. Moorhead, Minn., Nov. 8, 1933; d. Connie Magnus Nystrom and Harriett Grace (Petersen) Zorner; m. Raymon DeMeritt, 1953 (div. 1958); 1 child, Gregory Raymon; m. John Bischel, 1961 (div. 1964); m. Kenneth Dean Serkes, June 7, 1974. BS, U. Oreg., Eugene, 1962; MD, U. Oreg., Portland, 1965. Diplomate Am. Bd. Internal Medicine, Nat. Bd. Med. Examiners. Resident, straight med. intern Los Angeles County/U. So. Calif. Med. Ctr., 1965-68, NIH fellow nephrology, 1968-70, asst. prof. renal medicine, 1970-74; asst. prof., instr. medicine U. So. Calif., 1968-74; instr. nephrology East L.A. City Coll., 1971-74; dir. med. edn. Luth. Gen. Hosp., Park Ridge, Ill., 1974-78, dir. nephrology sect., 1977-80, pres. med. staff, 1974-88; founding mem., med. dir., dir. med. svcs. Luth. Health Plan, Park Ridge, 1983-87; clin. assoc. prof. medicine Abraham Lincoln Sch. Medicine U. Ill., 1975-80; sr. cons. Parkside Assocs., Inc., Park Ridge, 1986-88; pvt. practice Chgo., 1974-88; physician Buenaventura Med. Clinic, Ventura, Calif., 1989-94, med. dir., 1992-94; prin. Apollo Managed Care Cons., Santa Barbara, Calif., 1988—. Trustee Luth. Health Care System, Park Ridge, 1986-90, Unified Med. Group Assn., Seal Beach, Calif., 1993-94; hon. lifetime staff mem. Luth. Gen. Hosp., Park Ridge; mem. formulary com. HealthNet, 1992-94, med. adv. com. TakeCare, 1993-94, quality assurance com. PacifiCare, 1993-94; mem. doctor's adv. network AMA, 1994-96; JCAHO advisor for behavioral health care providers, 2000—2006. Author: 40 books including Managing Behavioral Healthcare, 2d edit., 2006, 3rd edit., 2007, 2010, The Credentialing and Privileges Manual, 2d edit., 2005, 3rd edit., 2007, 11, Medical Review Criteria Guidelines for Managed Care, 9th edit., 2010, 10 th edit., 2011, Mng. Phys., Occupl., Speech Therapy and Rehab., 6th edit. 2008, 7th edit. 2009, 8th Edit., 2011; editor: Med. Mgmt. Manual, Managed Care Bull., managing Roadmissions, 2011; Mem. editl. bd. Capitation Mgmt. Report, 1998-2006; contbr. chpts. to books and articles to profl. jours. Fellow: ACP (Calif. Gov.'s advisor 1993—95); mem.: Am. Coll. Physician Execs. Avocations: real estate, gardening. Office: Apollo Managed Care Cons 860 Ladera Ln Santa Barbara CA 93108-1626 Office Phone: 805-969-2606. Personal E-mail: mbischel@cox.net. Business E-Mail: apollomanagedcare@cox.net.

BISH, LAWRENCE THOMAS, physician; b. Doylestown, Pa., June 20, 1980; BA, U. Pa., 2002, MD, PhD, 2011. Intern, dept. medicine U. Pa., 2011—. Peer reviewer Cardiovasc. Rsch., 2010—11, Internat. Jour. Biochemistry and Cell Biology, 2010—11, Jour. Pharmacy and Pharmacological Rsch., 2010—11; editl. bd. mem. World Jour. Methodology, 2011. Recipient Howard S. Silverman Meml. Scholar award, Am. Heart Assn., George W. Householder, III Meml. prize, U. Pa.; named Nat. Dean's List. Mem.: Am. Med. Student Assn. (mem. Med. Student Nat. Honor Soc.), Pi Gamma Mu Nat. Honor Soc., Golden Key Nat. Honor Soc., Phi Beta Kappa, Alpha Omega Alpha. Achievements include patents pending for methods of delivering heterologous molecules to the heart. Avocations: motorcycling, winemaking, cooking. Office: B400 Richards Bldg 3700 Hamilton Wa Philadelphia PA 19104 Office Fax: 215-746-3684. Personal E-mail: bogartbish@gmail.com.

BISHARA, JIHAD, epidemiologist; b. Israel, Nov. 20, 1961; MD, 1st Med. Sch. Medicine in Leningrad, Russia, 1987. Head infectious diseases unit Rabin Med. Ctr., 2005—. Prof. medicine Sackler Faculty Medicine, Tel-Aviv U., Israel; vis. prof. Cleve. Clinic Found. Office: Jabotinsky Petah-Tiqva 49100 Israel Office Fax: 972-3-923-9118. Business E-Mail: bishara@netvision.net.il.

BISHARA, SAMIR EDWARD, orthodontist; b. Cairo, Oct. 31, 1935; children: Dina Marie, Dorine Gabrielle, Cherine Noelle. B. Dental Surgery, Alexandria U., Egypt, 1957; diploma in orthodontics, 1967; MS, U. Iowa, 1970, cert. in orthodontics, 1970, D.D.S., 1972. Diplomate Am. Bd. Orthodontics (pres. Coll. Diplomates 1992). Practice gen. dentistry, Alexandria, 1957-68; specializing in orthodontics Iowa City, 1970—; fellow in clin. pedontics Guggenheim Dental Clinic, NYC, 1959-60; resident in oral surgery Moassat Hosp., Alexandria, 1960-61, mem. staff, 1961-68; asst. prof. dentistry U. Iowa, 1970-73, assoc. prof., 1973-76, prof., 1976—. Vis. prof. Alexandria U., 1974. Contbr. articles profl. jours., chpts. in books. Fellow Am. Coll. Dentists, Internat. Coll. Dentists; mem. ADA, AAAS, World Fedn. Orthodontists (hon.), Am. Assn. Orthodontics, Internat. Dental Fedn., Internat. Assn. Dental Research, Am. Cleft Palate Assn., Assn. Egyptian Am. Scholars, Egyptian Orthodontic Soc. (hon.), Columbian Orthodontic Soc. (hon.), Greek Orthodontic Soc. (hon.), Mexican Bd. Orthodontists (hon.), Brit. Orthodontic Conf. (hon.), Omicron Kappa Upsilon, Sigma Xi Office: U Iowa Coll Dentistry Orthodontic Dept Iowa City IA 52242 Home: 1521 McKinley Pl Iowa City IA 52246-4135 *

BISHNOI, ANIL KUMAR, chemistry professor; b. Haryana, Mar. 5, 1976; MSc, K.U.K, 1998; PhD, CCS U., Meerut, 2008. Asst. prof. G.N.K. Coll., Yamuna Nagar, 1998—. Mem.: Indian Chem. Soc. Avocations: reading, music. Office: G N K Coll Near Fountain Chowk Yamuna Nagar Haryana 135001 India E-mail: akumar@rediffmail.com.

BISHOP, ANNE HUGHES, retired nursing educator; b. Charlottesville, Va., June 27, 1935; d. Aubrey Scott and Virginia May (Flint) Hughes; m. Bobby Nelson Bishop, June 15, 1957; children: Kathryn B. Bartholf, Barry S. Bishop (Dec.). BSN, U. Va., 1958; MEd, Lynchburg Coll., Va., 1968; MSN, U. Va., 1986, EdD, 1980. Staff nurse Va. Bapt. Hosp., Lynchburg, 1958-59, instr., 1959-63, asst. dir., 1963-72, dir. Sch. Nursing, 1972-79; prof. and dept. chmn. nursing Lynchburg Coll., 1979-85, prof. nursing, 1979—97; DON Ctr. for Health Promotion, 1992—97; ret., 1997. Presenter in field. Co-author: The Practical, Moral and Personal Sense of Nursing, 1990, Nursing: The Practice of Caring, 1991, Nursing Ethics: Therapeutic Caring Presence, 1995, Nursing Ethics: Holistic Nursing Practice, 2001, Japanese translation, 2005, Beyond Friendship & Eros: Unrecognized Relationships Between Men & Women, 2001, Voice of Hope & Despair, 2004; co-editor: Caring, Curing, Coping, 1985; contbr. articles to profl. jours. Sec., dir. Free Clinic of Ctrl. Va., Lynchburg, 1987-96. Named Outstanding Scholar Lynchburg Coll., 1992, named to YWCA Acad. Women in Health/Sci., 1996; recipient Humanitarian award Nat. Conf. for Cmty. & Justice, 2003. Mem.: Soc. for Phenomenology and Human Sci. Democrat. Christian Ch. Avocations: genealogy, biking, reading, travel. Personal E-mail: abbishop107@comcast.net. *

BISHOP, ELIZABETH SHREVE, psychologist; b. Ann Arbor, Mich., Nov. 18, 1951; d. William Warner Jr. and Mary Fairfax (Shreve) B. AB, U. Mich., 1972; MA, Ohio State U., 1973, PhD, 1976. Lic. psychologist Mich. Psychologist Franklin County Program for the Mentally Retarded, Columbus, Ohio, 1974, WC Mental Health, Willmar, Minn., 1977-83; chief psychologist Battle Creek Child Guidance Ctr., Mich., 1981; dir. psychometrics Meridian Profl. Psychol. Cons., East Lansing, Mich., 1983-92; pres. Arbor Psychol. Cons., Ann Arbor, 1991—. Trainer Girl Scouts USA, 1993—, troop leader, 1968—69, 1971—72, 1973—74, 1980—82, 1984—86; deacon 1st Congl. Ch., 1996—2000, 2002—09, historian, 2010—. Assoc. Univ. London Inst. Edn., 1976. Mem. APA, AAUW (Ann Arbor pres. 2011-), LWV (Willmar v.p. 1979-81), Mich. Psychol. Assn., Mich. Women Psychologists (treas. 2002-06,2008-, pres.-elect 2005-06, pres. 2006-07, past pres. 2007-08), Coun. Exceptional Children (local pres. 1977-78), Internat. Coun. Psychologists (bd. dir. 1999-2002). Avocations: reading, travel, birdwatching, photography, music. Home: 1612 Morton Ave Ann Arbor MI 48104-4441 Office: Arbor Psychol Cons 1565 Eastover Pl Ann Arbor MI 48104-6316 Office Phone: 734-741-8844. Personal E-mail: arborpsych@sbcglobal.net.

BISHOP, KIM IRENE, pharmaceutical consultant, cognitive psychopharmacologist; arrived in Switzerland, 1996; d. Harold Dane and Irene (Pelletier) B. BA, Franklin and Marshall Coll., Lancaster, Pa., 1982; MS, Villanova U., Pa., 1986; PhD, U. London, 1995; DipPM, U. Basel, 2001. Coord. clin. rsch. Scheie Eye Inst. U. Pa., Phila., 1984-88; sr. clin. rsch. assoc. Allergan Pharms., Irvine, Calif., 1988-90; cons. Clin. Trials Rsch. Ltd., Maidenhead, Eng., 1994; sr. drug safety scientist Ciba Geigy, Basel, Switzerland, 1996-97; global projects liaison mgr. Novartis, Basel, Switzerland, 1997-99; founder, owner, prin. cons. Global Pharma Cons. LLC, Basel, 1999, Pa., 2005, clin. devel. and psychopharm. svcs. and cognitive assessment and rater tng. solutions Basel; authorized distbr. Tng. Campus, Cloud Based Edn. Mgmt. Network. Contbr. articles to profl. jours. Alumni regional amb. Villanova U. Overseas rsch. scholar Brit. com. for Vice Chancellors and Prins., London, 1991-94; European Behavioral Pharmacology Soc. scholar, 1994; scholar Brit. Assn. Psychopharmacology Bursary, Eng., 1993, 94. Mem. APA, INS, ISCTM, ECNP, Assn. Clin. Rsch. Profls., Am. Acad. Neurology, Drug Info. Assn., Drug Info. Assn., CWS Summit, Global Leaders, Internat. Soc. to Advance Alzheimer Rsch. and Treatment, Royal Soc. Medicine, Toastmasters (edn. v.p. 2009), 30 GPC Expert Assocs. Avocations: skiing, scuba diving, dance, horseback riding, bicycling. Office Phone: 570-546-7833. Business E-Mail: kib@globalpharmaconsultancy.com.

BISHOP, MALCOLM GRAHAM HAMILTON, medical essayist, retired dental surgeon; b. Montgomery, U.K., Aug. 10, 1944; s. Stanley Graham and Irene (Doughty) B.; m. Polly Ann Badman Bishop, Nov. 27, 1971; children: Auriol Caroline Ann, Olivia Frances Mary. BDS, U. London, 1968; LDS, Royal Coll. Surgeons, 1968; MSc, U. London, 1983; DGDP, Royal Coll. Surgeons, 1993. Dental surgeon in gen. practice, Hertford, Eng.; lectr. in dental radiology Kings Coll. Hosp., London, 1968-99. Pres. British Soc. Dental and Maxillo-Facial Radiology, 1993-94; lectr. ethics applied dentist Kings Coll. Hosp., London, 1998-99. Contbr. articles to profl. jours. Mem. Royal Soc. Medicine London, Athenaeum Club London. Personal E-mail: malcolmbishop57@btinternet.com.

BISHOP, RUTH FRANCES, microbiologist, research scientist, educator; b. Melbourne, Victoria, Australia, May 12, 1933; d. Percival Charles William and Una Frances Armitage (Wilson) Langford; m. Geoffrey James Bishop, Dec. 8, 1956; children: Thomas Geoffrey, Anne Frances, Michael William. BSc, U. Melbourne, 1954, MSc, 1958, PhD, 1961, DSc, 1978; FRACP (hon.), 2008, DMedSci (hon.), 2009. Rsch. fellow U. Liverpool, Eng., 1962-65, Royal Children's Hosp. Rsch. Found., Melbourne, 1968-74, CEO, 1990-91; rsch. fellow Nat. Health and Med. Rsch. Coun., Australlia, 1975-79, prin. rsch. fellow, 1980-91, sr. prin. rsch. fellow Australia, 1992-98, Murdoch Childrens Rsch. Inst., Melbourne, 1999—2009; profl. assoc. U. Melbourne, 1990-94, prof. Parkville, Victoria, Australia, 1995—; hon. res. fell, 2010—. Dir. Australian Med. Rsch. and Devel. Co., Melbourne, 1991-92; mem. regional grants interview com. Nat. Health and Med. Rsch. Coun., Australia, 1991-98; cons. WHO, Geneva, 1983—. Editorial bd. Revs. Infectious Diseases, 1989-99; contbr. articles to profl. jours., chpts. to books. Chmn. assocs. spl. activities 8th Asian Conf. ObGyn, Melbourne, 1979-81. Decorated officer Order of Australia. Fellow Australian Soc. Microbiology, Royal Australasian Coll. Physicians (hon.); mem. Am. Soc. Microbiology, Am. Soc. Virology, Pediat. Rsch. Soc. Australia (pres. 1972), Australian Soc. Med. Rsch., Australian Soc. Infectious Diseases, Nat. Assn. Rsch. Fellows Nat. Health and Med. Rsch. Coun. (sec. 1991-93). Avocations: reading, opera, tennis, gardening. Office: Royal Childrens Hosp/Murdoch Children Rsch Inst Enteric Virus Group Flemington Rd 3052 Melbourne VIC Australia Business E-Mail: r.bishop@mcri.edu.au.

BISI-JOHNSON, MARY ADEJUMOKE, microbiologist, educator; b. Ibadan, Nigeria, Mar. 5, 1971; BSc, Obafemi Awolowo U., 1994; PhD, Walter Sisulu U., 2011. Asst. lectr. Obafemi Awolowo U., 2003—05, lectr. II, 2005—. Postgrad. fellowship, Fed. Ministry of Edn. Nigeria, Travel grant, GlaxoSmithKline & Novartis, UK, Rsch. grant, Walter Sisulu U. Mem.: Nigerian Soc. Microbiology, Fedn. Infectious Diseases Socs. South Africa, Am. Soc. Microbiology. Avocations: reading, singing. Office: Walter Sisulu University Dept Med Microbiology Mthatha Eastern Cape 5117 South Africa Office Fax: 0867503739. E-mail: jumokade@yahoo.co.uk.

BISOGNANO, MAUREEN A., medical association administrator; BSN, MSN. RN. Staff nurse Quincy Med. Ctr., Mass., 1973, v.p. nursing, dir. nursing, 1981—82, dir. patient svcs., 1982—86, COO, 1986—87; sr. v.p. Juran Inst.; CEO Mass. Respiratory Hosp.; exec. v.p., COO Inst. Healthcare Improvement, Boston, pres., CEO, 2010—. Mem. Commn. on a High Performance Health System Commonwealth Fund; instr. Harvard Med. Sch.; rsch. assoc. divsn. social medicine and health inequalities Brigham and Women's Hosp.; bd. mem. ThedaCare Ctr. for Healthcare Value, Mayo Clinic Health Sys.-Eau Claire; spkr. at major confs. Named one of Top 25 Women Healthcare, Modern Healthcare mag., 2011. Mem.: Nat. Acad. of Sciences (Inst. Medicine). Office: Inst Healthcare Improvement 7th Fl 20 University Rd Cambridge MA 02138 Office Phone: 617-301-4800. Office Fax: 617-301-4848. *

BISSADA, NABIL KADDIS, urologist, educator, researcher, author; s. Kaddis B. and Negma Bissada; m. Samia; children: Sally, Nancy, Mary, Amy, Andrew. MD, Cairo U., 1963. Diplomate Am. Bd. Urology. Intern Cairo Univ. Hosp., 1964-65; resident in surgery Babelsharia Gen. Hosp., 1965-69; resident in urology U. N.C. Hosp., 1970-72, chief resident, 1972-73; asst. prof. urology U. Ark. for Med. Scis., 1973-77, assoc. prof., 1977-79; cons. urologist King Faisal Specialist Hosp. and Rsch. Ctr., Riyadh, Saudi Arabia, 1979-87; prof., chief urologic oncology Med. U. S.C., 1987—2003; chief urologic surgery Ralph H. Johnson Med. Ctr., 1987—2003; vice-chmn. dept. urology Med. U. S.C., 1999—2003; interim chmn. U. Ark. Med. Scis., 2006—08, prof. urology, 2003—, exec. vice chmn. dept. urology, 2003—. Spkr. in field. Author: Lower Urinary Tract Function and Dysfunction: Diagnosis and Management, 1978; Pharmacology of the Urinary Tract and the Male Reproductive System, 1982; cons. Prostate Biopsy, 2011, guest editor several med. jours. and periodicals; mem. editl. bd. Archives of Andrology; assoc. editor Arab J. Urol., Jour. Urology Nephrology; contbr. articles to profl. jours.; chpts. to books; pioneered several significant surgical and med. urologic treatment methods, developed the Charleston Pouch Technique for continent urinary diversion; rsch. in urologic reconstructive techniques. Recipient Silver award, Am. Urol. Assn. Fellow ACS, Internat. Coll. Surgeons (co-chmn. divsn. urology U.S. sect. 1989-91, chmn. 1991-93), Soc. Pediat. Urology; mem. Am. Urol. Assn., Ark. Urol. Soc. (pres., 2010-11), Carolina Urol. Assn. (pres., 1997-99), Egyptian-Am. Urol. Assn. (pres. 1990-92), Arab-Am. Urol. Assn. (pres. 1993-96), Arab Am. Medical Assn. (pres. Ark. chpt., 2006-08), Soc. Internat. D'Urologie, Soc. Urologic Oncology, Urodynamic Soc., Soc. Urology and Engring., Sigma Xi. Office: UAMS 4301W Markham St #540 Little Rock AR 72205 Office Phone: 501-686-5241. Business E-Mail: bissadanabilk@uams.edu.

BISSELL, MINA J., cancer biologist, researcher; b. Tehran, Iran, May 14, 1940; Student, Bryn Mawr Coll., 1959-61; AB in Chemistry cum laude, Radcliffe Coll., Cambridge, Mass., 1963; MA in Bacteriology and Biochemistry, Harvard U., Cambridge, Mass., 1965, PhD in Microbiology-Molecular Genetics, 1969; PhD (hon.), Pierre & Marie Curie U., Paris, 2001, U. Copenhagen, 2004. Milton rsch. fellow, 1969-70; Am. Cancer Soc. rsch. fellow, 1970-72; staff biochemist Lawrence Berkeley Nat. Lab. U. Calif., Berkeley, 1972-76, mem. sr. staff, 1976, co-dir. div. biology and medicine Lab. Cell Biology, 1980—, dir. cell and molecular biology divsn., 1988-92, coord. life scis., 1989-91, assoc. lab. dir. bioscience, 1989, dir. life scis. divsn. Lawrence Berkeley Nat. Lab., 1992—2002, mem. faculty dept. comparative biochemistry, 1979—, assoc. dir. biosciences, Lawrence Berkeley Nat. Lab., 1995—2002, disting. scientist, sr. advisor to the lab. dir. on biology Lawrence Berkeley Nat. Lab., 2002—, OBER/DOE Disting. Scientist Fellow in Life Sciences Lawrence Berkeley Nat. Lab., 2005—10. Vis. prof. Kettering Inst., U. Cin. Med. Schs., 1986-88; disting. vis. scientist Queensland Inst. Med. Rsch., Brisbane, Australia, 1982; mem. coun. Gordon Rsch. Conf., 1991-94; George P. Peacock lectr. pathology U. Tex., Dallas, 1992; Dean's lectr. Mt. Sinai Med. Sch., N.Y.C., 1993; presenter numerous lectures, condr. symposia; keynote spkr. Gordon Conf. on Proteoglycans, 1994, others. Mem. editl. bd. and sect. editor In Vitro Cell and Devel. Biology Rapid Comm., 1986—; mem. editl. bd. Jour. Cellular Biochemistry, 1990-92; assoc. editor In Vitro Cellular and Devel. Biology, 1990—, Molecular and Cellular Differentiation, 1992—, Molecular Carcinogensis, 1993-97, Devel. Biology, 1993—, Cancer Rsch., 1994—, Breast Jour., 1994—; contbr. numerous articles to sci. jours. Recipient 1st Joseph Sadusk award for breast cancer rsch., 1985, Ernest Orlando Lawrence award Dept. Energy, 1996, Mellon award, U. Pitts., 1998, Eli Lilly/Clowes award, American Assn. for Cancer Rsch., 1999, Krakower award in Pathology, 2003, Brinker award, Komen Found., 2003, Discovery Health Channel Med. Honors and Medal, 2004, Ann. Internat. award, French Nat. Inst. for Health and Med. Rsch. (INSERM), 2007, Pezcoller Found.-American Assn. Cancer Rsch. Internat. award for Cancer Rsch., 2007, American Cancer Soc. Medal of Honor, 2008, Federation of American Societies for Exptl. Biology, 2008, Mina J. Bissell award, U. Porto, 2008, Innovator award US Dept. Def. for breast cancer rsch., Excellence in Sci. award; Fogarty sr. fellow NIH, Imperial Can. Rsch. Fund Labs., London, 1983-84, Guggenheim fellow, 1992-93,, honored by Susan G. Komen Breast Cancer Found. Fellow AAAS, Inst. of Medicine, Am. Acad. Arts and Sciences, Am. Philos. Soc.; mem. NAS, Am. Soc. Cell Biology (mem. coun. 1989-91, Women in Cell Biology Career Recognition award 1993, pres. 1997), Internat. Soc. Differentiation (bd. dirs. 1990-96, pres.), Am. Assn. Cancer Rsch. (bd. dirs. 1999 2001). The pioneer in postulating, and then proving that the extracellular matrix (ECM), the mass of fibrous and globular proteins that surrounds cells performs a critical role in dictating a tissue's organization and function. In 1981, Dr. Bissell formulated the concept of a "dynamic reciprocity" This communication scheme between the nucleus, the cells and their microenvironment suggests that signals are sent into the cell through ECM receptors which attach to the cell's outer skeleton and convey important information to the nucleus and the chromosomes. Office: Lawrence Berkeley Nat Lab Div Life Scis U Calif 1 Cyclotron Rd Ms 83 101 Berkeley CA 94720-8260 Business E-Mail: mjbissell@lbl.gov.

BISTRIAN, BRUCE RYAN, internist, educator; b. Southampton, NY, Oct. 22, 1939; s. Peter and Mary Laura (Ryan) B.; m. Eleanor Alice Dix, Sept. 3, 1964; children: Tennille Ryan, Jordan Brooke, Britton Perry. BA, NYU, 1961; MD, Cornell U., 1965; MPH, Johns Hopkins U., 1971; PhD, MIT, 1975; AM (hon.), Harvard U., 1990. Diplomate in internal medicine, 1972, critical care medicine,1987-2007, Am. Bd. Internal Medicine. Intern Cornell U., NYC, 1965-66; metabolism fellow U. Vt., Burlington, 1968-69, resident in medicine, 1969-70; from asst. clin. prof. to assoc. prof. Harvard U. Sch. Medicine, Boston, 1975-90, prof. medicine, 1990—. Clin. assoc. physician rsch. resources divsn. NIH, 1975-78; lectr. MIT, 1981-84. Mem. editl. bd. Jour. Parenteral and Enteral Nutrition, 1985-2007, Harvard Health Letter, Women's Health Watch, Critical Care Medicine, European Jour. Clin. Nutrition, 2007-09; contbr. more than 400 sci. articles to profl. publs. Capt. U.S. Army, 1966-68. Recipient Goldberger award in clin. nutrition AMA, 2004; grantee Nat. Inst. Gen. Med. Scis., 1977-80, Nat. Inst. Arthritis, Metabolism and Digestive Disease, 1979-83, Nat. Inst. Arthritis, Diabetes, Digestive and Kidney Diseases, 1985-95, Nat. Cancer Inst., 1984-87. Fellow: ACP, Am. Soc. Nutritional Scis.; mem.: AMA, Inst. Medicine (com. on military nutrition rsch. 2001—), Mass. Med. Soc., Soc. Critical Care Medicine, Am. Soc. Parenteral and Enteral Nutrition (pres. 1989—90), Am. Soc. Clin. Nutrition (sec. 1993—96, v.p.-elect 1998, v.p. 1999, pres. 2000), Fedn. Am. Soc. Exptl. Biologists (bd. dirs. 2001—07, pres. 2005—06), Mass. Soc Mayflower Descs. (bd. assts. 2007—, surgeon 2008—). Presbyterian. Achievements include more than 40 patents in field. Subspecialties: Nutrition (medicine); Biochemistry (medicine). Current work: protein calorie malnutrition; total parenteral nutrition; nutrition and infection. Home: 229 Argilla Rd Ipswich MA 01938 Office: Beth Israel Deaconness Med Ctr 1 Deaconess Rd Boston MA 02215-5321 Business E-Mail: bbistria@bidmc.harvard.edu.

BISWAS, RAKA, engineering educator; b. Raghunathganj, Feb. 2, 1977; BSc, LAD Coll., 1997; MSc, LIT, 1999. Project asst. NEERI, 2002—07; lectr. Priyadarshini Coll. Engring. and Tech., 2007—10. Healthcare profl., med. transcription. Avocations: painting, music. Home: 30/2 Vithoba Apt LIT Layout Swa Nagpur Maharashtra 440021 India Personal E-mail: rakabiswasneeri@gmail.com.

BISWAS, SHARMISTHA, medical educator; b. India, Mar. 10, 1967; MBBS, Calcutta Nat. Med. Coll., 1991; MS, Mahatma Gandhi Inst. Med. Sci., Sevagram, India, 2006. Asst. prof. BSMC, West Bengal, India, 2006; assoc. prof. NRS Med. Coll., Kolkata, India, 2011—. Mem.: Indian Med. Assn., Anat. Soc. India. Avocations: reading, music. Home: BJ 145 Sector II Salt Lake Kolkata West Bengal 700091 India Personal E-mail: drsharmisthabiswas@rediffmail.com.

BISWAS MONDAL, RIMA, environmental scientist; b. India, May 10, 1978; MSc, Nagpur U., India, 1998, PhD, 2009. Rsch. scientist, cons. Nat. Environ. Engring. Rsch. Inst., Nagpur, 2005—. Mem.: IAEM. Avocations: painting, singing, reading. Office: Nehru Marg Nagpur Maharashtra 440020 India Office Fax: 7122249900. Business E-Mail: ra_biswas@neeri.res.in.

BITAR, WADIH EMILIO, orthopaedic surgeon, researcher; b. Guadalajara, Jalisco, Mexico, Sept. 18, 1951; s. Wadih Emilio Bitar and Estela Alatorre; m. Kathryn Elva DeFan de Bitar, Jan. 18, 1975; children: Michel Emilio Bitar DeFan, Gina Bitar DeFan. MD, U. Nat. Autonoma Mex., 1976; degree in orthopaedics and trauma surgery, Inst. Mex. Seguro Social, 1986; postgrad., Karolinska Hosp., Stockholm, 1986—88, U. Berne, Switzerland, 1993; MS, U. Colima, Mexico, 1999, PhD in Med. Sci., 2002, MD, 2002. Orthopaedics and traumatology surgeon Hosp. Angeles del Carmen, Guadalajara, Mexico, 1986—2007; cert. in spine surgery Inst. Mex. Seguro Social, Guadalajara, 1986, chief outpatient dept. splty., Ctr. Medico Occidente, 1986—97, prof. bone tumors, 1987—97, cert. orthopedics and traumatology, 1986; chief orthopaedics and traumatology dept. Hosp. Angeles del Carmen, Guadalajara, 1993—95; state del. Orthopaedic Coll. Jalisco, Guadalajara, 1998—. Coord. western zone Mexican Assn. Knee Surgery and Arthroscopy Mex. Assn. Orthopaedics and Traumatology, Guadalajara, 1993—95; mem. honor and justice com. Med. Coll. Orthopaedics, Guadalajara, 2005; regional coord. nat. bd. exam in orthopaedics and traumatology Mex. Bd. Orthopaedics and Traumatology, Guadalajara, 2000, gen. coord. bd. certification exam in orthopaedics and traumatology, Mexico City, 2000—01; pres. masters degree in med. sci. orientation surgery for degree exam., U. Guadalajara Inst. Mex. Seguro Social, Guadalajara, 2002, spine surgeon in spinal cord injury in animal models, 1986—2007, mem. trauma dept. emergency unit, 2002—07; pres. jury certification bd. exam orthopaedics and traumatology, 1997; v.p. orthopaedics Med. Coll. Jalisco, Guadalajara, 1999—2001, pres. orthopaedics, 2001—02; chief neuro mascular skeletal divsn. Hosp. Especialidades del Ctr. Med. Nat. Occidente, UMAE, IMSS, 2009. Contbr. articles to profl. publs. Recipient Nat. First Pl. award, Mex. Inst. Social Security, 1993, First Pl. award, Latin Am. Soc. Orthopaedics and Traumatology, 1995, U. Colima, 1998, First Pl. neurosci. award, Pedro Sarquis Merrewe Found., Jalisco, 2007; scholar, Karolinska Hosp., Stockholm, Sweden, 1988, Universitatsklinik fur Orthopaedie, Vienna, 1994; scholar in vascular microsurgery, 1996. Mem.: NY Acad. Sci., Mex. Assn. Exptl. Surgery, Internat. Soc. Orthopaedic Surgery and Traumatology (assoc.), Mex. Assn. Hip Surgery (assoc.; founding mem. 2000—07), European Soc. Sports Traumatology, Knee Surgery and Arthroscopy (assoc.), Mex. Assn. Orthopaedics and Traumatology (assoc. Nat. First Pl. award 1987), Mex. Assn. Knee Surgery and Arthroscopy (assoc.), Hosp. Angeles del Carmen (assoc.). Achievements include research and publications of advances in spinal cord traumatic injuries at the level of C5 and C6, targeting advances in the importance of the vascular process and it's repair during critical ischemia time, an accompanying phenomenon in the neurological spinal injury. Office: Hosp Angeles del Carmen Tarascos 3469 Suite 104 Guadalajara 45040 Mexico Office Fax: 52 33 38134444. Personal E-mail: dremiliobitar@prodigy.net.mx.

BITRAN, JACOB DAVID, internist; b. Thessaloniki, Greece, Sept. 23, 1947; arrived in U.S., 1952; s. David Jacob and Martha (Faratzl) Bitran; m. Linda Sue Androw, Dec. 26, 1970; children: Lauren, Dina. BS, U. Ill., Chgo., 1968, MD, 1971. Diplomate Am. Bd. Internal Medicine, Am. Bd. Med. Oncology, Am. Bd. Hematology. Intern in medicine Michael Reese Med. Ctr., Chgo., 1971 72, resident in internal medicine, 1973-75, clin. asst. prof. medicine, 1977-81, clin. assoc. prof., 1981-84; resident in pathology Rush Presbyn. St. Luke's Med. Ctr., Chgo., 1972-73; fellow in hematology/oncology U. Chgo., 1975-77, assoc. prof., 1984-88, prof., 1988-91; dir. divsn. hematology/oncology Luth. Gen. Hosp., Park Ridge, Ill., 1991—; prof. medicine U. Ill., Chgo., 1996-98. Mem. sci. adv. bd. Lederle Labs., Wayne, NJ, 1986—89. Editor: Lung Cancer, 1988. Fellow: ACP, Am. Coll. Chest Physicians; mem.: Am. Soc. Clin. Oncology (program chmn. 1990—91), Am. Assn. Cancer Rsch. (program chmn. 1988—89). Democrat. Achievements include development of usable chemotherapy regimen for non small cell lung cancer that has been in clinical use since 1976; research in dose intensive chemotherapy in breast cancer. Avocations: tennis, rowing. Office: Luth Gen Hosp 1700 Luther Ln Park Ridge IL 60068-1270 Office Phone: 847-268-8200.

BITTING, KEVIN NOEL, pediatric craniofacial orthotist, researcher; b. Kenmore, NY, Dec. 18, 1957; s. Harry Lincoln Jr. and Shirley Ann (Smith) B. BA, Villanova U., 1980; Degree in Prosthetics, Northwestern U., 1989. Cert. orthotist, Md. Rsch. asst. Villanova (Pa.) U., 1979; orthotist-prosthetist S.W. Lab., Burbank, Calif., 1988-99; chief pediatric craniofacial orthotist Cranial Therapies, Inc., Burbank, 1991—. Avocations: alpine skiing, physical fitness/swimming, computers.

BITTNER, VERA, cardiologist; b. Mainz, Germany, July 31, 1957; d. Friedrich and Lieselotte Bittner. MD, U. South Ala., Mobile, 1981; MSPH, U. Ala., 1995. Asst. prof. medicine U. Ala., Birmingham, 1987—93, assoc. prof. medicine, 1993—2000, dir. cardiovasc. disease residency program, 1998—, prof. medicine, 2000—, sect. head preventive cardiology, 2005—. Contbr. articles to profl. jours. Fellow, CDC and Am. Heart Assn., 1995. Fellow: ACP, Am. Heart Assn. (clin. exercise com. 2005—, chair clin. exec. prevention com. effective 2009, fellow 1991), Am. Coll. Cardiology (cardiovasc. disease prevention com. 2004—, chair prevention com. effective 2009—, edit. bd. mem. circulations); mem.: ULA (past pres.), Birmingham Cardiovasc. Soc. (pres. 2004—05), SE Lipid Assn. (pres. 2003—04), Nat. Lipid Assn. (bd. dirs. 2005—, pres. 2009—), Am. Assn. Cardiovasc. and Pulmonary Rehab. (bd. dirs. 2001—03), Delta Omega, Alpha Omega Alpha. Office: U Ala 701 19th St S - LHRB 310 Birmingham AL 35294

BIZIOS, DIMITRIOS, ophthalmologist; b. Kozani, Greece, May 2, 1977; Degree in Medicine, Lund U., 2004. Physician dept. clin. scis., ophthalmology Skåne U. Hosp., Lund U., 2004—. Office: Ophthalmology Clinic Skåne University Hosp Malmö Skåne 20502 Sweden Business E-Mail: dimitrios.bizios@med.lu.se.

BIZZI, EMILIO, neurophysiologist, educator; b. Rome, Feb. 22, 1933; arrived in U.S., 1963, naturalized, 1982; s. Vittorio and Anna (Galeazzi) Bizzi. MD summa cum laude with highest honors, U. Rome, 1958. Postdoctoral trainee Inst. Med. Pathology, U. Siena, Italy, 1958-60; postdoctoral trainee Inst. Physiology, U. Pisa, Italy, 1960-63; rsch. assoc. neurophysiol. lab., dept. zoology Washington U., St. Louis, 1963-64; vis. assoc. sect. physiology, lab. clin. sci. NIMH, Bethesda, Md., 1964-66; rsch. assoc. dept. psychology MIT, Cambridge, 1966-67, lectr. dept. psychology, 1967-68, assoc. prof. neurophysiology, 1969-72, prof., 1972-80, Eugene McDermott prof. brain scis. and human behavior, 1980—2002, inst. prof., 2002—, dir. Whitaker Coll., 1983-88, chmn. dept. Brain and Cognitive Scis., 1986-97. Mem. editl. bd.: Brain Theory Newsletter, 1980—, Jour. Motor Behavior, 1981—, Jour. Neurobiology, 1981—; contbr. articles to profl. jours., chapters to books. Recipient Alden Spencer award, Columbia U. Coll. Physicians and Surgeons, 1978, Hermann von Hlmholtz award, 1992; fellow Found. Rsch. Psychiatry, 1978—. Mem.: NAS, Inst. Medicine, Am. Acad. Clin. Neurophysiol., Acad. dei Lincei, Am. Acad. Arts and Scis. (pres. 2006—), Internat. Brain Rsch. Orgn. Office: MIT Dept Brain & Cognitive Scis Cambridge MA 02139-4307 Office Phone: 617-253-5769. Office Fax: 617-258-5342. Business E-Mail: ebizzi@mit.edu.

BIZZINI, MARIO, physical therapist, researcher; b. Corzoneso TI, Switzerland, June 2, 1963; s. Rosa and Franco Bizzini; m. Cinzia Cavadini, Sept. 1, 1997; 1 child, Luca. MS, U. Pitts., 2001. Cert. physiotherapist Swiss Red Cross, Geneva, 1988. Vis. fellow, sports medicine, phys. therapy U. Pitts., 2000—01; physiotherapist Schulthess Klinik, Zürich, Switzerland, 1989—2000, rsch. assoc., orthopaedics, sports medicine, neuromuscular rsch. lab., FIFA Med. Assessment and Rsch. Ctr., 2002—. Rehab. cons. Kloten Flyers, Zurich, 1998—. Author: (book) Sensomotorische Rehabilitation nach Beinverletzungen, 2000. Recipient Rsch. award, Swiss Sports Medicine Soc., 1998. Mem.: N.Am. Jour. Sports Phys. Therapy (mem. editl. bd.), Internat. Cartilage Repair Soc., Internat. Fedn. Sports Physiotherapy (expert group mem. 2003—), Swiss Sports Physiotherapy Assn. (com. mem. 2002—), European Soc. Sports Traumatology, Knee Surgery and Arthroscopy, Swiss Sports Medicine Soc., Swiss Physiotherapy Assn. Office: Schulthess Klinik Lengghalde 2 Zurich 8008 Switzerland Office Fax: 41443857590. Business E-Mail: mario.bizzini@kws.ch.

BIZZO, SOLANGE MARIA DINIZ, oncologist; b. Rio de Janeiro, Oct. 12, 1956; Degree, U. Fed. Rio de Janeiro, Sch. Medicine, 1980; PhD, U. Estadual Rio de Janeiro, 2010. Staff Inst. Nat. Câncer, 1984—. Master: Brazilian Coll. Surgeons. Home: Nicanor Nunes 169 Piratininga Niterói Rio de Janeiro 24350460 Brazil Personal E-mail: solbizzo@hotmail.com.

BJERKE, H. SCOTT, surgeon; b. Mpls., Dec. 26, 1956; s. Robert and Darline B.; m. Janet Anne Sikora, Sept. 1995; 1 child, Duncan BS honors, U. Mich., 1979; MD, U. Hawaii, 1983. Resident New Eng. Med. Ctr., Boston, 1983—88; chief divsn. surg. critical care U. Nev., Las Vegas, 1991—99; med. dir. trauma svcs. Clarian Health, Indpls., 1999—2009; med. dir. Trauma Svcs. Rsch. Med. Ctr., 2009—; clin. assoc. prof. surgery UMKC Sch. Med.; clin. prof. surgery Kans. City U. Medicine & Bioscis., 2010—. Bd. trustees Univ. Surgery Profls., Las Vegas, 1992 99 Co-author: (chpt.) Trauma, 6th edit., 1999 Med. dir. tactical medics Indpls. Police SWAT Team, 1999—; med. dir. Clark County Fire Dept., Las Vegas, 1992-99; IST physician FEMA Urban Search & Rescue, Oklahoma City, 1995; med. dir. Nye County Vol. Ambulance, Amargosa Spring, Nev., 1995-99 Recipient Congrl. Recognition Svc., Senator Bryan, 1995; Rsch. fellow UCLA Med. Ctr., L.A., 1988-90, Trauma fellow Cedars Sinai Med. Ctr., L.A., 1990-91, Clarian Med. Ethics fellow, 2006-2007 Fellow ACS, Assn. Surgery Trauma, Ea. Assn. Surgery Trauma; mem. Internat. Assn. Police Surgeons (life) Avocations: sports cars, scuba diving. Office: Midwest Trauma 6420 Prospect Room T207 Kansas City MO 64132 Home: 11716 Brookwood Leawood KS 66211 Office Phone: 816-276-9100. Personal E-mail: scottbjerke@mac.com.

BJERREGAARD, PREBEN, cardiologist, educator; b. Hansted, Denmark, Feb. 6, 1942; arrived in U.S., 1989; s. Emil Robin and Karen Bjerregaard; m. Ria Skovholm Knudsen, June 4, 1965; children: Torsten, Dorte, Jens. MD, U. Aarhus, 1969, DMSc, 1983. Diplomate in Cardiology Denmark, 1978. Cardiology fellow U. Okla., Oklahoma City, 1972—74; rsch. fellow U. Aarhus, Denmark, 1977—81, lectr., 1981—83, Aarhus Amtssygehus, 1983—84; asst. prof. medicine Aarhus Kommune Hosp., 1984—88; cons. cardiologist Ibn Al Bitar Hosp., Baghdad, Iraq, 1988—89; prof. medicine St. Louis U. Hosp., 1989—2006, St. Louis VA Med. Ctr., 2006—, Wash. U., St. Louis, 2010—. Bd. mem. IRB, St. Louis U., 1990—2003. Author: Electrocardiographic Atlas, 1981; co-editor: Cardiac Repolarization, 2003. 2d lt. Denmark Navy, 1970—71, Frederikshavn, Denmark. Achievements include discovery of a new disease called Short QT-Syndrome in 1999. Avocations: jazz, boating, Iraq history. Office: VA Med Ctr 915 N Grand Saint Louis MO 63106 Home: 8 Portland Ct Saint Louis MO 63108 Office Phone: 314-289-6329. Business E-Mail: preben.bjerregaard@va.gov. *

BJERVE, KRISTIAN S., physician, researcher; s. Sigvart Kristian and Olaug Margrete Bjerve; m. Eva Alice Olsen, Apr. 10, 1965; children: Yngvil, Torunn. MD, U. Oslo, Norway, 1969, PhD, 1974. Cert. med. dr. Norwegian Ministry Health, 1969, in clin. pathology Norwegian Ministry Health, 1979, in med. biochemistry Norwegian Ministry Health, 1979, in nuc. medicine Norwegian Ministry Health, 1998. Rschr. Norwegian State Hosp. & Norwegian Coun. Sci. and Humanities, Oslo, 1967—69, Norwegian State Hosp. & Norwegian Cancer Soc., Oslo, 1970—74; registered med. physician Lovisenberg Hosp., Oslo, 1974—75, Norwegian State Hosp., Oslo, 1975—83; editl. sec. Scandinavian Jour. Clin. and Lab. Investigations, Oslo, 1978—80; bd. mem., chmn. Nordic Soc. Clin. Chemistry and Clin. Physiology, Oslo, 1979—83; coun. mem. European Com. Clin. Lab. Standards, Oslo, 1982—89; nordkem expert group mem. NORDKEM, Oslo, 1982—91; profmed. biochemistry Med. Faculty, Norwegian U. Sci. and Tech., Trondheim, Norway, 1983—; head dept. Dept. Med. Biochemistry, St. Olavs Hosp., Trondheim, 1983—; vis. prof. Bowman Gray Sch. Medicine, Winston Salem, 1987; edn. com. mem. Faculty Medicine, Trondheim, 1989—90; head planning com.biochemistry and cell biology The Med. Faculty, Trondheim, 1991—93; bd. mem. Trondelag Med. Soc. Rsch. Fund, Trondheim, 1988—92, Norwegian Med. Physiol. Assn.'s Pub. Co., Oslo, 1992—2008, Nordic Soc. Clin. Chemistry, Norway, 2000—08; chmn. Cancer Rsch. Found. at St. Olavs Hosp., Trondheim U. Hosp., 1997—2008; mem.

bd. dirs. ISSFAL, 1999—2000; editor Scandinavian Jour. Clin. and Lab. Investigations, Trondheim, 2002—03; chmn. Norwegian Soc. Clin. Chemistry and Clin. Physiology, Trondheim, 2005—08; capt. Air Force, Norway, 1965—94. Contbr. scientific papers to profl. publs. Recipient Rsch. award, Trondelag Med. Soc., 1986. Mem.: Norwegian Med. Soc. Office: St Olavs Trondheim University Hosp Olav Kyrres gt 17 Trondheim N-7006 Norway Business E-Mail: kristian.s.bjerve@ntnu.no.

BJÖRKLUND, TOMAS, research scientist; b. Lund, Sweden, Feb. 3, 1979; MSc in Medicine, Biomedicine, Lund U., 2005, PhD in Neurosci., 2009. Postdoc. fellow, B.R.A.I.N.S Unit Lund U., 2009—10, postdoc. fellow, Neuronal Plasticity and Repair Unit, 2010—, asst. prof., neurosci., 2011, jr. group leader, Molecular Neuromodulation Unit, 2011—. Bd. dirs. Genepod Therapeutics AB, 2010, COO, 10. Mem.: Soc. Neurosci. Office: Molecular Neuromodulation Unit BMC A10 Lund 22184 Sweden Business E-Mail: tomas.bjorklund@med.lu.se.

BJORKMAN, DAVID JESS, dean, gastroenterologist, educator; b. Salt Lake City, Oct. 28, 1952; s. Jesse Harold and Violet Maureen (Neese) B.; m. Kaye Hansen, Aug. 20, 1975; children: D. James, Michael. BA, U. Utah, 1976, MD, 1980. Diplomate Am. Bd. Internal Medicine, Am. Bd. Gastroenterology. Intern Brigham and Womens Hosp., Harvard U. Med. Sch., 1980-81, resident in internal medicine, 1981-83; clin. fellow, rsch. fellow Harvard U. Med. Sch., Boston, 1983-85; instr. medicine U. Utah Sch. Medicine, Salt Lake City, 1985-88, asst. prof. medicine, 1988-92, assoc. prof. medicine, 1992, prof., assoc. dean, 2004, interim dean, 2004, dean, 2006—; dir. endoscopy U. Utah Med. Ctr., 1992-95, assoc. divsn. chief, 1995; exec. med. dir. U. Utah Med. Group, 2000—. Sce. rev. com. Nat. Cancer Inst., Bethesda, Md., 1991. Contbr. articles to profl. jours.; author over 100 reviews, books, book chpts., and abstracts. Fellow ACP, Am. Coll. Gastroenterology (chair publs. com. 1994—); mem. Utah State Med. Assn. (legis. com. 1990—), Am. Soc. Laser Medicine and Surgery, Am. Soc. Gastrointestinal Endoscopy (mem. governing bd. 1999-), Phi Beta Kappa, Alpha Omega Alpha (bd. dirs. 1979-82). Achievements include laser identification of colonic cancer using photoactive agent; research on therapeutic endoscopy, changes in intestinal membrane composition and fluidity. Office: Univ Utah Sch Med 30 N 1900 E Rom 1C109 50 N Medical Dr Salt Lake City UT 84132-0001 Home Phone: 801-943-9317; Office Phone: 801-581-6436. Business E-Mail: david.bjorkman@hsc.utah.edu. *

BJORNSSON, SIGURDUR, medical oncologist, department chairman; b. Princeton, NJ, June 5, 1942; s. Bjorn Sigurdsson and Una (Johannesdottir) S.; children: Kristin, Björn, Signy Sif. MD, U. Iceland, 1968. Diplomate Am. Bd. Internal Medicine. Intern U. Iceland Hosp., Reykjavik, 1969; resident New Britain Gen. Hosp., Conn., 1970-72; fellow Roswell Park Meml. Inst., Buffalo, 1974-78; rsch. asst. prof. medicine SUNY, Buffalo, 1977-78; cons. med. oncologist City Hosp., Reykjavik, 1978-96; attending physician internal medicine and oncology St. Joseph's Hosp., Reykjavik, 1978-96, chief dept. internal medicine, 1989-96; chief dept. hematology and med. oncology Reykjavik Hosp., 1996—2001; chief dept. med. oncology Landspitali U. Hosp., Reykjavik, 2001—08. Cons. med. oncologist U. Hosp., Reykjavik, 1978-96; lectr. medicine and oncology U. Iceland, Reykjavik, 1978—. Bd. dirs. Icelandic Cancer Soc., Reykjavik, 1980, pres., 1998-2008; bd. dirs. Icelandic Physicians for the Prevention Nuc. War. Mem. Am. Soc. Clin. Oncology, Am. Assn. Cancer Rsch., European Soc. for Med. Oncology, Icelandic Med. Assn. (bd. dirs. 1996-2002), Icelandic Assn. Med. Specialists (chmn.), Icelandic Soc. Internal Medicine, World Med. Assn. Home: Bergstadastraeti 78 101 Reykjavik Iceland

BLABER, MICHAEL, biomedical sciences professor; b. Biloxi, Miss., June 30, 1958; s. Keith and Jean Blaber; m. Sachiko I. Blaber, Apr. 14, 1987; 2 children. BA in Biochemistry, Molecular Biology, UC Santa Barbara, 1980; PhD, U. Calif., Irvine, 1990. Assoc. prof. chemistry Fla. State U., Tallahassee, 2000—05, assoc. prof. biomedical scis., 2005—. Editl. bd. mem. Molecular and Cellular Proteomics, 2001—06, Protein Sci., 2003—08, Archives Biochemistry and Biophysics, 2010—. Recipient Tchg. award, Fla. State U., 1999, Outstanding Sr. Faculty Rschr. award, Established Investigator award, Am. Heart Assn., 2000—03, E.K. Frey — E. Werle Commemorative Gold medal; Postdoc. fellowship, NIH, 1990—93. Mem.: AAAS. Achievements include patents for Protease Resistant Urokinase. Office: Fla State University 1115 W Call St Tallahassee FL 32306-4300 Office Fax: 850-644-5781; Home Fax: 850-644-5781. Business E-Mail: michael.blaber@med.fsu.edu.

BLACK, HENRY RICHARD, physician; b. NYC, June 1, 1942; s. David Robert and Beatrice (Morris) Black; m. Benita L. Daniels, Apr. 19, 2002; children: Matthew, Dana. AB, Columbia U., NYC, 1963; MD, NYU, 1967. Diplomate Am. Bd. Internal Medicine, cert. hypertension specialist Am. Soc. Hypertension, 2001. Intern Johns Hopkins Hosp., Balt., 1967—68, resident in internal medicine, 1970—71; resident Yale-New Haven Hosp., 1971—72, chief resident internal medicine, 1974—75; fellow Yale U., New Haven, 1972—74, practice medicine specializing in preventive cardiology and hypertension, 1975—92; asst. prof. Yale U. Med. Sch., New Haven, 1975—79, assoc. prof., 1979—88, prof., 1988—92, dir. hypertension svcs., 1975—92; Charles J. and Margaret Roberts prof. preventive medicine Rush U. Med. Ctr., Chgo., 1992—2006, chmn. dept. preventive medicine, 1992—2005; assoc. v.p. rsch., assoc. dean rsch. NYU Sch. Medicine, 2000—05, clin. prof. internal medicine, 2007—. Bd. dirs. Am. Heart Assn., Conn., 1985—87; fellow Coun. on Hypertension. Contbr. articles to profl. jours. With USPHS, 1968—70. Master: ACP; fellow: Am. Soc. Hypertension (exec. com. 1991—96, exec. coun. 2002—, pres. 2008—10, immediate past pres. 2010—), Am. Heart Assn. (coun. epidemiology & prevention, fellow coun. on nutrition), Internat. Soc. Hypertension; mem.: Am. Soc. Preventive Cardiology (pres. 1994—95), Columbia Coll. Alumni Assn. (bd. dirs. 1983—87, v.p., acad. affairs 1986—87), Am. Fedn. Clin. Rsch. Jewish. Office: NYU Sch Medicine 530 First Ave Skirball 9U 2V New York NY 10016 Home: 15 W 81st St New York NY 10024 E-mail: hrbmd63@gmail.com.

BLACK, JACINTH BAUBLITZ, clinical social worker; b. Corpus Christi, Tex., Feb. 17, 1944; m. Donald James Baublitz, Oct. 26, 1968 (div. June 1979); children: Jessica Ruth, Stefanie Elizabeth; m. Robert Drummond Black, Mar. 14, 1987. BA, Sam Houston U., 1965; MSW, Boston Coll., 1972; postgrad., Am. Assn. Sex Educators, Counselors and Therapists, Washington, 1976-77; advanced studies with Maxie Maultsby Jr., U. Ky., 1980. Cert., Acad. Cert. Social Workers, 1976; lic. social worker and marriage and family therapist, Mich.; diplomate Acad. Social Workers, 1988; nat. bd. cert. clin. hypnotherapist, 1995. Tchr. English and Spanish Brazosport Schs., Freeport, Tex., 1965-67; caseworker Harris County Child Welfare Unit, Houston, 1967-69; vocat. counselor Mass. Employment Security, Lowell, 1969-70; family therapist Cath. Family Service, Saginaw, Mich., 1973-75; contractual clin. social worker Midland-Gladwin Community Mental Health Ctr., 1975-80; pvt. practice clin. social work Midland, Mich., 1975—2005. Adj. prof. psychology Northwood Inst., 1982-85; cons., lectr., speaker various profl. and lay orgns. Author: Relationshift, 1983, A Singles Guide to Tight Spots and Tricky Situations, 1986; newspaper advice columnist Bay Area Rev., 1985-89. Bd. dirs. Big Sisters Am., Inc., Midland, 1978-80; mem. bd. mgrs. Midland County Hist. Soc., 1996—; commr. West Main Historic Dist. Commn., 2006—. Mem. NASW, Chem. City Garden Club, Women's Study Club, Midland County Hist. Soc. Episcopalian. Home: 4553 S Saginaw Rd Midland MI 48640-8554 Office: PO Box 2227 Midland MI 48641-2227 Office Phone: 989-496-2627.

BLACK, PAUL HENRY, medical educator, researcher; b. Boston, Mar. 11, 1930; s. Samuel Louis and May (Goldberg) B.; m. Sandra Merkin, June 2, 1962; children: Scott, Marc, Jeffrey. AB, Dartmouth Coll., 1952; MD, Columbia U., 1956. Diplomate Am. Bd. Internal Medicine. Intern Mass. Gen. Hosp., Boston, 1956-57, asst. resident in medicine, 1957-58, clin. and rsch. fellow, 1958-60, resident in medicine, 1960-61; sr. asst. surgeon Lab. Infectious Diseases USPHS Nat. Inst. Allergy and Infectious Diseases, NIH, Bethesda, Md., 1961-63; sr. surgeon Lab. Infectious Diseases USPHS Nat. Inst. Allergy and Infectious Diseases, U. Glasgow Inst. Virology, Scotland, 1963-64; sr. surgeon, comdr. Lab. Infectious Diseases USPHS Nat. Inst. Allergy and Infectious Diseases, NIH, Bethesda, Md., 1964-67; asst. prof. medicine Harvard U. Med. Sch., Boston, 1967-70, assoc. prof. medicine, 1970-80; asst. physician Mass. Gen. Hosp., Boston, 1967-70, assoc. physician, 1970-80, hon. physician, 1980—; dir. Hubert H. Humphrey Cancer Rsch. Ctr. Boston U., 1979-83; chmn., prof. microbiology, research prof. surgery, prof. medicine Boston U. Sch. Medicine, 1979-96, prof. emeritus, 1996—. Cons. Roswell Park Meml. Inst., Buffalo, 1976-80, Monsanto Chem. Corp., St. Louis, 1976-82, Collaborative Rsch., Inc. (Oscient Pharm.), Waltham, Mass., 1984-90; mem. subcom. on evaluation cancer ctrs. Nat. Cancer Adv. Bd., Bethesda, 1975-80; sci. cons. U.S.-Israel Binat. Sci. Found., Jerusalem, Israel, 1974—; mem. NIH Study Sect. Virology, 1968-72, Tumor Virus Detection Segment, Spl. Virus Cancer Program, Bethesda, 1972-76; mem. subcom. on environ. carcinogens, Am. Cancer Soc. Task Force on Cancer Prevention, 1975-82, sci. adv. bd. Worcester Found. for Exptl. Biology, Mass., 1976-78, sci. adv. bd. Dartmouth-Hitchcock Med. Ctr., Hanover, N.H., 1976-80, Gov.'s Task Force on AIDS, Commonwealth of Mass., Boston, 1983-94; chmn. spl. virus cancer program contract rev. com., Nat. Cancer Inst., 1977-79 Author monograph; contbr. 226 articles to profl. jours., chpts. to books Nat. Cancer Inst. grantee, 1967-87. Fellow AAAS; mem. Am. Soc. Clin. Investigation, Infectious Diseases Soc., Am. Soc. Microbiology, Am. Soc. Virology, Am. Assn. Med. Sch. Microbiology Chmn., Soc. Gen. Microbiology, Sigma Xi. Democrat. Jewish. Office: Boston U Sch Medicine 715 Albany St Boston MA 02118-2307 Home: 9 Commonwealth Ave Apt 6 Boston MA 02116-2111 Office Phone: 617-414-5881. Business E-Mail: pblack@bu.edu.

BLACK, PETER, neurosurgeon, educator; naturalized, USA; s. Thomas Herbert and Harriet Elizabeth (Peterson) B.; m. Katharine C. Black, June 15, 1967; children: Winifred, Libby, Katy, Peter Thomas, Christopher. AB, Harvard U., 1966; MD, CM, McGill U., 1970; PhD, Georgetown U., 1978; degree (hon.), Aristoteles U., Thessaloniki, Greece, 2010. Diplomate Am. Bd. Neurosurgery. Staff neurosurgeon Mass. Gen. Hosp., Boston, 1980—87; neurosurgeon-in-chief Brigham and Women's Hosp., Boston, 1987—2007, chmn. dept. neurosurgery, 2000—07; neurosurgeon-in-chief Children's Hosp., Boston, 1987—2004, chmn. dept. neurosurgery, 1987—2005; chief neurosurg. oncology Dana Farber Cancer Inst., Boston, 1987—2007; Franc D. Ingraham prof. neurosurgery Harvard Med. Sch., Boston, 1987—. Author The Surgical Art of Harvey Cushing, 1992, Harvey Cushing at the Brigham, 1993, Astrocytomas: Diagnosis, Management and Biology, 1993, Surgical Treatment of Epilepsy in Children, Neurosurgery Clinics of North America, 1995, Cancer of the Nervous System, 1997, 2d edit., 2004, Operative Neurosurgery, 1999, Brain Tumors in Adults. Neurological Clinics, Angiogenesis in Brain Tumors, 2004, Minimally Invasive Neurosurgery, 2005, Living with a Brain Tumor, 2006, Meningioma: A Comprehensive Text, 2009; contbr. more than 500 articles. Episcopalian. Avocations: piano, art. Office: Brigham and Women's Hosp 75 Francis St Boston MA 02115-6106 Office Phone: 617-525-7796. Business E-Mail: peterblackwfns@gmail.com.

BLACK, ROBERT LINCOLN, pediatrician, educator; b. LA, Aug. 25, 1930; s. Harold Alfred and Kathryn (Stone) Black; m. Jean Wilmott McGuire, June 27, 1953; children: Donald J., Douglas L., Margaret S. AB, Stanford U., Calif., 1952, MD, 1955. Diplomate Am. Bd. Pediat. Intern Kings County Hosp., Bklyn., 1955—56; resident and fellow Stanford U. Hosp., 1958—62; practice medicine specializing in pediat. Monterey, Calif., 1962—. Clin. prof. Stanford U., 1962—; cons. Calif. Dept. Health, Sacramento, 1962—; mem. Calif. State Maternal, Child, Adolescent Health Bd., 1984—93. Author (with others): California Health Plan for Children, 1979. Mem. Monterey Peninsula Unified Sch. Bd., 1965—73, pres., 1968—70; mem. Mid-Coast Health Sys. Agy., Salinas, Calif., 1975—80, pres., 1979—80; bd. dirs. Lucile Packard Found. for Child Health, 2000—, Lyceum of Monterey Peninsula, 1963—, Carmel Bach Festival, Calif., 1972—81. With USAF, 1956—58. Fellow: Am. Acad. Pediat. (Child Advocacy award sr. sect. 2002); mem.: Physicians for Social Responsibility, Monterey County Med. Soc., Calif. Med. Assn., Inst. Medicine of NAS. Democrat. Home: 976 Mesa Rd Monterey CA 93940-4612 Office: Ste 110 1900 Garden Rd Monterey CA 93940 Office Phone: 831-372-5841.

BLACK, TANYA WARD, counselor; b. St. Louis, Jan. 11, 1946; d. Herbert Ward, Sr. and Margaret Ward; m. Hollis M. Black III, Mar. 7, 1970; 1 child, Aubretia. BA in Fgn. Langs., Wheaton Coll., 1968; MA in Behavioral Sci., So. Ill. U., 1976; MEd in Counseling, Ala. A&M U., 1990. Lic. profl. counselor, nat. cert. counselor, cert. clin. mental health counselor, supr. of LPC interns. Multicultural tchr. Chgo., St. Louis, 1966—70; asst. dept. psychology So. Ill. U., 1971—76; tchr. Spanish and counselor Westminster Acad., Huntsville, Ala., 1980—84; tchr., advisor young adults, 1985—; lic. profl. counselor Trinity Counseling Ctr., Huntsville, 1992—2001, pvt. practice, Huntsville, 2001—. Presenter in field. Divorce recovery workshops for adults and children, 1991—; cons. infertility and pregnancy loss Huntsville, 1995—. Mem.: Am. Assn. Christian Counselors, Am. Counseling Assn. Avocations: backpacking, swimming, music.

BLACK, WILLIAM C., diagnostic radiologist, educator; MD, Med. Coll. of Va., Richmond, 1979. Diplomate Am. Bd. Radiology-diagnostic radiology, 1983. Resident diagnostic radiology Univ. of Va. Med. Ctr., Charlottesville, 1979—83, fellow cross sectional imaging, 1983—84; prof. radiology Dartmouth Med. Sch.; hosp. affiliations include lung/thoracic cancer program Lebanon radiology Dartmouth-Hitchcock Med. Ctr. Office: Dartmouth Hitchcock Medical Center Department Radiology 1 Med Ctr Dr Lebanon NH 03756 Office Phone: 603-650-7443. Office Fax: 603-650-5455.

BLACKBURN, ELIZABETH HELEN, molecular biologist; b. Hobart, Tasmania, Australia, Nov. 26, 1948; d. Harold and Marcia; m. John W. Sedat; 1 child. BSc in Biochemistry, U. Melbourne, Australia, 1970, MSc in Biochemistry, 1972; PhD in Molecular Biology, U. Cambridge, Eng., 1975; PhD in Molecular and Cellular Biology, Yale U., New Haven, 1977. Rschr. Med. Rsch. Coun. Lab. Molecular Biology, Cambridge, England, 1971—74; postdoc. fellow dept. biology Yale U., 1975-77; postdoc. fellow biochemistry U. Calif., San Francisco, 1977-78; asst. prof. dept. molecular biology U. Calif., Berkeley, 1978—83, assoc. prof., 1983—86, prof., 1986—90, prof. dept. microbiology and immunology, dept. biochemistry and biophysics San Francisco, 1990—, also Morris Herzstein endowed chair biology and physiology, chair dept. microbiology and immunology, 1993-99. Mem. adv. panel on cell biology NSF, 1982—85; mem. sci. adv. bd. Walter & Eliza Hall Inst. Med. Rsch., 1998—, Fred Hutchinson Cancer Rsch. Ctr., 2001—, Huntsman Cancer Rsch. Inst., U. Utah, 2003—; non-resident fellow Salk Inst. Biol. Studies, La Jolla, Calif., 2001—; mem. Presdl. Coun. Bioethics, 2002—04, NIH Nat. Adv. Coun. on Aging, 2003—06. Mem. editl. bd. Jour. Cell Biology, 1985—88, Sci., 1985—88, Molecular & Cellular Biology, 1988—, Jour. Eukaryotic Microbiology, 1992—98, Nucleic Acids Rsch., 2003—05, assoc. editor Jour. Protozoology, 1988—91, Molecular Biology of the Cell, 1992—2004; contbr. articles to profl. jours. Recipient Eli Lilly Rsch. award, 1988, Gairdner Found. Internat. award, 1998, Australia prize, 1998, Keio U. Med. Sci. Fund prize, 1999, Harvey prize, Technion-Israel Inst. Tech., 1999, Baxter award, Assn. Am. Med. Colleges, 1999, Passano Found. award, 1999, Novartis-Drew award for biomed. sci., 1999, Rosenstiel award, Brandeis U., 1999, Feodor Lynen award, 2000, Dickson prize for medicine, 2000, Am. Cancer Soc. medal of honor, 2000, G.H.A. Clowes Meml. award, Am. Assn. Cancer Rsch., 2000, Internat. award for cancer rsch., Pezcoller Found./Am. Assn. Cancer Rsch., 2001, Alfred P. Sloan Jr. prize, GM Cancer Rsch. Found., 2001, Bristol-Myers Squibb award for disting. achievement in cancer rsch., 2003, Robert J. & Claire Pasarow Found. Med. Rsch. award, 2003, Dr A.H. Heineken prize for medicine, 2004, Benjamin Franklin medal for life scis., Franklin Inst., 2005, Genetics prize, Peter Gruber Found., 2006, Albert Lasker award for basic med. rsch., 2006, Vanderbilt prize in biomedical sci., 2007, Louisa Gross Horwitz prize, Columbia U., 2007, Women & Sci. award, Weizmann Inst. Sci., 2008, L'Oréal-UNESCO award for women in sci., 2008, Medicine & Biomed. Rsch. prize, Albany Med. Ctr., 2008, Nobel prize in physiology/medicine, 2009, Pearl Meister Greengard prize, 2009, Paul Ehrlich & Ludwig Darmstaedler prize, Germany, 2009; named Calif. Scientist of Yr., 1999; named one of The 100 Most Influential People in the World, TIME mag., 2007. Fellow: AAAS, Am. Acad. Arts & Scis., Royal Soc. London; mem.: NAS (fgn. assoc.) (Molecular Biology award 1990), Inst. Medicine, Am. Acad. Microbiology, Genetic Soc. of America (bd. dirs. 2000—02), Am. Soc. Cell Biology (pres. 1998, E.B. Wilson medal 2001), Harvey Soc. NY. Achievements include discovery of structures called telomeres on the tips of chromosomes which hold them together; an enzyme called telomerase, the enzyme that restores the ends of chromosomes by replenishing telomeres, which are the protective caps that seal off these chromosome ends. Office: U Calif Dept Biochemistry & Biophysics Genentech Hall Mission Bay Campus 600 16th St MC 2200 San Francisco CA 94158-2517 Office Fax: 415-514-2913. E-mail: elizabeth.blackburn@ucsf.edu. *

BLACKBURN, HENRY WEBSTER, JR., retired epidemiologist; b. Miami, Fla., Mar. 22, 1925; s. Henry Webster and Mary Frances (Smith) B.; m. Nelly Paula Trocme, Jan. 10, 1951 (div. 1984); children: John Keith, Katia Trocme, Heidi Elizabeth; m. Stacy Richardson, Sept. 1, 1991. Student, Fla. So. Coll., Lakeland, 1942—43; BS, U. Miami, 1947; MD, Tulane U., 1948, DSc (hon.), 1999; MS, U. Minn., 1957; DSc (hon.), U. Kuopio, Finland, 1982. Intern Chgo. Wesley Meml. Hosp., 1948-49; physician Methodist Clinic, 1949; resident in medicine Am. Hosp. Paris, 1949-50; med. officer in charge USPHS, Austria, Fed. Republic Germany, 1950-53; med. fellow U. Minn., Mpls., 1953-56; ret. Divsn. Epidemiology, 1996; med. dir. Mut. Svc. Ins. Co., St. Paul, 1956; asst. prof. physiol. hygiene U. Minn., 1958-61, assoc. prof., 1961-68, prof., 1968—, lectr. medicine, 1956—, dir. lab. physiol. hygiene Sch. Pub. Health, 1972—, prof. medicine, 1972—, chmn. divsn. epidemiology, 1983-90, Mayo prof. pub. health, 1990-96. Vis. prof. U. Geneva, 1970; mem. adv. coun. Nat. Heart, Lung and Blood Inst., 1989-93; mem. com. on diet and health NRC, 1986-89; Ancel Keys lectr., 1991; mem. food adv. com. FDA, 1995-2000; Mayo chair in pub. health, 1988. Author: Cardiovascular Survey Methods, 1968, On the Trail of Heart Attacks in Seven Countries, 1995, "P.K." Irreverent Memoirs of a Preacher's Kid, 1999, If It Isn't Fun...Memoir of a Different Sort of Medical Life, Vol. I, 2001, Vol. 2, 2004; mem. editl. bd. numerous jours.; contbr. articles to profl. jours. Lt. (j.g.) USNR, 1942-50, capt. USPHS inactive res. Recipient Thomas Francis award in epidemiology, 1975, Naylor Dana award in preventive medicine, 1976, Louis Bishop award in cardiology, 1979, Gold Heart award Am. Heart Assn., 1990, Rsch. Achievement award Am. Heart Assn., 1992. Fellow APHA, Am. Coll. Cardiology, Am. Epidemiol. Soc.; mem. AAAS (chmn. med. sect.), Belgian Royal Acad. Medicine, Am. Heart Assn. (dir. 1971-74), Internat. Soc. Cardiology (coun. epidemiology 1971-74, chmn. 1986-91), Internat. Epidemiol. Soc., Alpha Omega Alpha, Phi Kappa Phi, Delta Omega. Office: U Minn Divsn Epidemiology 1300 S 2d St Minneapolis MN 55454-1075 Office Phone: 612-626-9396. Business E-Mail: black002@umn.edu.

BLACKBURN, RONALD, psychologist; b. Stockton, Durham, Eng., Oct. 20, 1938; s. Herbert and Constance (Heath) B.; m. Celia Bannister, Feb. 29, 1964; children: Mark, Andrew, Helen. MA, U. Cambridge, Eng., 1961; MSc, U. Birmingham, Eng., 1966; PhD, U.

Southampton, Eng., 1973. Clin. psychologist Leicester (Eng.) Area Service, 1962-65; sr. psychologist Broadmoor Hosp., Berks, Eng., 1966-71; prin. psychologist Rampton Hosp., Notts, Eng., 1971-74; sr. lectr. U. Aberdeen, Scotland, 1974-81; chief psychologist Park Lane Hosp., Liverpool, Eng., 1981-90; dir. rsch. Ashworth Hosp., Liverpool, 1990-93, prof. clin. and forensic psychology, 1993-99, emeritus prof., 1999—. Author: The Psychology of Criminal Conduct, 1993; editor Legal and Criminological Psychology, 2000—05; assoc. editor Brit. Jour. Clin. Psychology, 1982-91, Legal and Criminological Psychology, 1993-99; contbr. articles to profl. jours. Fellow Brit. Psychol. Soc., Internat. Orgn. of Psychophysiology(sr. award Divsn. Forensic Pychology, 2003, sr. scientist award British and Irish Group for the Study personality Disorder, 2007) Avocations: music, history, food, travel. Office: U Liverpool Dept Clin Psychology Liverpool L69 3GB England Personal E-mail: ronb@liv.ac.uk.

BLACKETOR, PAUL GARBER, minister; b. Birmingham, Ala., Feb. 10, 1927; s. Everly B. and Marie (Scokel) B.; m. Susan Blacketor (dec.); children: A. Wade, Paula. Christopher, Racheal. BS, Samford U., Birmingham, Ala., 1953; MS, Auburn U., 1954, MA, 1955, EdD, 1956. Ordained to ministry, Bapt. Ch., 1952. Pastor Heidrick (Ky.) Bapt. Ch., 1962-63, Clarks Summit (Pa.) Bapt. Ch., 1963-64, Dalton (Pa.) Bapt. Ch., 1963-65, Wilmington (Vt.) Bapt. Ch., 1969-88, Fitzwilliam (N.H.) Bapt. Ch., 1990—. Prof. Keene State Coll., N.H., 1966-97. Mem. N.H. Gen. Ct., 1984-90. Capt. U.S. Army, 1987, ret., officer chair Army Retiree Coun., Ft. Drum, NY, New Eng. Army Retiree Coun., Devens, Mass., Fort Drum Army Retiree Coun., NY. Mem.: Internat. Conf. Police Chaplains, Assn U.S. Army, Ret. Officers Orgn., Assn. Mil. Surgeons U.S., Am. Legion, VFW. Democrat. Home and Office: Ft Drum Army Retiree Coun New Eng Army Retiree Coun 104 Chimney Hill Dr Colchester VT 05446-7364 Personal E-mail: blacketor1@yahoo.com.

BLACKLER, ANTONIE WILLIAM CHARLES, retired biologist; b. Portsmouth, Eng., Oct. 19, 1931; came to U.S., 1964; s. Leslie Guy and Florence (Harris) B.; m. Rochelle Lois Melkin, Mar. 12, 1970; children— Mia Samantha, Joshua Harris. BS in Zoology, U. Coll., London, 1953, PhD, 1956. Professeur extraordinaire U. Geneva, Switzerland, 1961-64; prof. zoology Cornell U., Ithaca, NY, 1964—2009. Achievements include research on origins of sex. Home: 1005 Giles St Ithaca NY 14850

BLACKLOW, ROBERT STANLEY, internist, educator; b. Cambridge, Mass., June 24, 1934; s. Leo Alfred and Clara Edna (Cumenes) Blacklow; m. Winifred Young, Dec. 7, 1958; children: Stephen Charles, Kenneth Lawrence, David Alan. AB summa cum laude, Harvard U., 1955, MD cum laude, 1959; DSc (hon.), Kent State U., 1998; DMed. (hon.), U. Pecs, Hungary, 2001. Intern Peter Bent Brigham Hosp., Boston, 1959-60, resident, 1960-61, 63-64, 67-68; instr. Harvard U., 1967-70, asst. prof. medicine, 1970-76, assoc. prof., 1976-78, asst. to dean faculty of medicine, 1969-73, assoc. dean, 1973-78; prof. internal medicine Rush Med. Coll., 1978-85, dean, 1978-81; v.p. for med. affairs Rush-Presbyn.-St. Luke's Med. Center, Chgo., 1978-81, prof. medicine Jefferson Med. Coll., Phila., 1985-92, sr. assoc. dean, 1985-92; pres., dean Northeastern Ohio Univs. Coll. Medicine, Rootstown, 1992—2002, prof. cmty. medicine, prof. medicine, 1992—2002, prof. emeritus cmty. medicine, 2002—, 2002—; sr. scholar health policy Assn. Acad. Health Ctrs., Washington, 2002—05; vis. prof. social medicine Harvard Med. Sch., Boston, 2005—07, sr. lectr. global health and social medicine, 2007—. Mem. sci. adv. com. Nat. Fund Med. Edn., 1981—84, Nat. Cancer Inst., 1986—95; bd. dir. Nat. Resident Matching Program, 1993—2003, pres.-elect, 1994—95, pres., 1995—96, treas., 1998—99, 2001—03, pres.-elect, 1999—2000, pres., 2000—01; spl. cons. to dir. Nat. Inst. Alcohol Abuse and Alcoholism, 2003—06. Editor: (book) Signs and Symptoms, 1971, Signs and Symptoms, 6th edit., 1983; mem. editl. bd. Jour. Med. Humanities, 1997—2007. Trustee Chestnut Hill Sch., Newton, Mass., 1970—79, Belmont (Mass.) Hill Sch., 1973—79, Chgo. chpt. ARC, 1979, Greater Akron (Ohio) Musical Assn., 1993—2002, Phillips Brooks House Assn., Howard U., 2008—; mem. exec. com. Greater Akron (Ohio) Musical Assn., 1998—2002; dir. Akron Regional Devel. Bd., 1998—2003; mem. Ill. health svc. corps task force Ill. Dept. Pub. Health, 1980; corporator Belmont Hill Sch., 1978—. With USPHS, 1961—63. Sr. scholar, Assn. Acad. Health Ctrs., 2002—05. Fellow: ACP, Chgo. Soc. Internal Medicine, Inst. Medicine Chgo.; mem.: AAAS, Assn. Acad. Health Ctrs., Assn. Am. Med. Colls., N.Y. Acad. Sci., St. Botolph Club (Boston), Badminton & Tennis Club (Boston), Harvard Musical Assn., Longwood Cricket Club (Boston), Literary Club (Chgo.), Rowfant Club, Alpha Omega Alpha, Sigma Xi, Phi Beta Kappa. Home: 16 Birchwood Ln Lincoln MA 01773 Office: Dept Global Health and Social Medicine Harvard Med Sch 641 Huntington Ave Boston MA 02115 Business E-Mail: robert_blacklow@bms.harvard.edu.

BLACKMON, RONALD H., biologist, science educator; s. Henry L. and Lillian Blackmon. BS, Del. State U., 1980; MS, Howard U., 1985, PhD, 1988. Postdoctoral rsch. assoc. USDA-Insect Attractants, Behavior/Basic Biology Rsch. Lab., Gainesville, Fla., 1988-89; asst. prof. Elizabeth City State U., 1989-94, assoc. prof., 1994-96, prof., 1996—2008, chmn., 1995—2002, dean sch. math sci. tech., 2002—05, sr. res. prof., 2008—. Mem. acad. ops. com. Program for Minority Advancement in Biomolecular Scis., Chapel Hill, NC, 1991-2002; mem. Historically Minority Univs. program adv. bd. NC Biotech. Ctr., Research Triangle Park, NC, 1997-2003. Mem. adv. bd. State Employees' Credit Union, Elizabeth City, 1999. Recipient Biotech. Leadership award N.C. Inst. for Minority Econ. Devel., Durham, N.C., 1993. Mem. AAAS, Soc. for In Vitro Biology, N.C. Acad. Sci., Port Discover Hands on Sci. Ctr. (chmn., bd. dirs.)Sigma Xi. Avocations: reading science fiction, piano. Office: Elizabeth City State U ECSU Campus Box 930 Elizabeth City NC 27909 Office Phone: 252-335-3240. Office Fax: 252-335-3697. Business E-Mail: rhblackmon2@mail.ecsu.edu.

BLACKWELL, JOHN, science educator; b. Oughtibridge, Sheffield, Eng., Jan. 15, 1942; came to U.S., 1967; s. Leonard and Vera (Brook) B.; m. Susan Margaret Crawshaw, Aug. 5, 1965; children: Martin Jonathan, Helen Elizabeth. BSc in Chemistry, U. Leeds, Eng., 1963, PhD in Biophysics, 1967. Postdoctoral fellow SUNY-Syracuse Coll. Forestry, 1967-69; vis. asst. prof. Case Western Res. U., Cleve., 1969-70, asst. prof., 1970-74, assoc. prof., 1974-77, prof. macromolecular sci., 1977—, chmn. dept., 1985-95, F. Alex Nason prof., 1991-2000, Leonard Case Jr. prof., 2001—, assoc. dean rsch. and grad. studies Case Sch. Engring., 2005—07. Vis. prof. Kennedy Inst. Rheumatology, London, 1975, Centre National de Recherche Scientifique, Grenoble, France, 1977, U. Frieburg, Fed. Republic Germany, 1982; chmn. Gordon Conf. on Liquid Crystalline Polymers, 1992; cons. in field. Author: (with A.G. Walton) Biopolymers, 1973; mem. editorial bd. Macromolecules, 1989-92; adv. bd. Jour. Macromolecular Sci.-Physics, 1986—; internat. adv. bd. Acta Polymerica, 1992—; contbr. articles to profl. jours. Recipient award for disting. achievement Fiber Soc., 1981, Sr. Scientist award Alexander von Humboldt Found., Max Planck Inst. for Polymer Rsch., Mainz, Fed. Republic Germany, 1991, Rsch. Career Devel. award, 1973-77. Fellow Am. Phys. Soc. (exec. com. divsn. high polymer physics 1986-90, vice chmn. 1987-88, chmn. 1988-89); mem. Am. Chem. Soc. (chmn. cellulose divsn. 1999, Anselm Payen award 1999, divsn. councillor 2000-03), Am. Crystallography Soc. (chmn. fiber diffraction spl. interest group 1993-94), Biophys. Soc. (chmn. biopolymer subgroup 1975-76), Fiber Soc. Episcopalian. Home: 12614 Cedar Rd Cleveland Heights OH 44106-3220 Office: Case Western Res U Case Sch Engring Cleveland OH 44106-7220 Office Phone: 216-368-6370. Business E-Mail: john.blackwell@case.edu.

BLACKY, ALEXANDER, industrial hygienist, consultant; b. Vienna, Dec. 27, 1964; MD, Med. U. Vienna, 2002. Cons., hygiene and microbiology Med. U. Vienna, Dept. Hosp. Hygiene, 2002—. Office: Waehringer Guertel 18-20 Vienna 1090 Austria Office Fax: 0043 1 40400 1907. Business E-Mail: alexander.blacky@meduniwien.ac.at.

BLAGOSKLONOV, OLEG, nuclear medicine physician; b. Moscow, Feb. 8, 1973; arrived in France, 1999; s. Valery Blagosklonov and Galina (Koroleva) Blagosklonova; m. Oxana Podoprigora, Feb. 5, 1994; children: Alexandra Blagosklonova children: Zoe Blagosklonova. MD, Russian State Med. U., Moscow, 1998; MSc, U. Val-de-Marne, Creteil, France, 1999; PhD, U. Franche-Comte, Besancon, France, 2002. Cert. in nuc. medicine Institut Nat. des Sciences et Techniques Nucleaires, France, 2003. Physician trainee Russian State Med. U., Moscow, 1996—98; nuc. medicine and biophysics asst. U. Fzanche Comte Jean Minjoz U. Hosp., Besancon, France, 1999—2005; assoc. prof. med. imaging and biophysics, 2006—. Contbr. articles to profl. jours. Scholar, French Govt., 1998. Mem.: IEEE, French Soc. Biophysics and Nuc. Medicine. Office: Jean Minjoz U Hosp bv Fleming 25030 Besancon France Home: Szue de EArdoiriere Morre 25660 France Office Fax: +33-3-81669693. E-mail: oleg.blagosklonov@univ-fcomte.fr.

BLAHD, WILLIAM HENRY, nuclear medicine physician, director; b. Cleve., May 11, 1921; s. Moses and Rae (Lichtenstader) B.; m. Miriam Weiss, Jan. 29, 1971; children— Andrea Margery, William Henry, Karen Ruth. Student, Western Res. U., 1939-40, U. Ariz., 1940-42; MD, Tulane U., 1945. Diplomate Am. Bd. Nuclear Medicine (chmn. 1982, v.p. 1986-97, exec. dir. 1998-2003), Am. Bd. Internal Medicine (bd. govs. 1981). Resident in pathology and internal medicine VA Wadsworth Med. Ctr., 1948-52, ward officer metabolic rsch. ward, 1951-52, asst. chief radioisotope svc., 1952-56, chief nuclear medicine dept. LA, 1956-97, dir. nuclear medicine tng. program, 1997—, nuc. medicine residency program dir. Am. Bd. Nuc. Medicine, LA. Prof. dept. medicine U. Calif., Los Angeles; mem. ACGME residency rev. com. for nuclear medicine, 1979-97, chmn., 1991-97; mem. Joint Rev. Com. on Ednl. Programs in Nuclear Medicine Tech., 1986-93; mem. subcom. on naturally occurring and accelerator produced radioactive materials Com. on Interagency Radiation Rsch. and Policy Coordination, 1988-92; cons. nuclear medicine; mem. adv. com. on human uses radioisotopes Calif. Dept. Health Svcs.; mem. HEW Interagy. Task Force on Ionizing Radiation, 1978, dir. nuclear medicine Mt. Sinai Hosp., L.A., 1955-76, Valley Presbyn. Med. Ctr., Van Nuys, Calif., 1959-85, St. Joseph Hosp. Med. Ctr., Burbank, Calif., 1958-83. Author 3 textbooks on nuclear medicine. Contbr. numerous articles to med. jours. Served with U.S. Army, 1946-48. Grantee Muscular Dystrophy Assn. Am., 1965-69, Nat. Cancer Inst., 1973-76; recipient Lifetime Achievement award Wadsworth Physicians and Surgeons Alumni Assn., 2000, William H. Oldendorl Lifetime Achievement award West L.A. Med. Ctr., 2000. Fellow ACP, Am. Coll. Nuclear Physicians (bd. regents 1974-80); mem. AMA, Soc. Nuc. Medicine (trustee 1966-74, pres. 1977-78, Disting. Scientist award No./So. Calif. chpts. 1975, Disting. Sci. award We. Regional chpts. 1995, Disting. Pub. Svc. Career award Fed. Exec. Bd. L.A. 1998, Presdl. Disting. Svc. award 2000, 02), Health Physics Soc. (pres. So. Calif. chpt. 1964-66), Calif. Med. Assn. (sci. bd. 1975-81, chmn. adv. bd. nuclear medicine 1976-84), Am. Bd. Med. Spltys., COCERT, Soc. Exptl. Biology and Medicine, Los Angeles County, Calif. Med. Assns., We. Assn. Physicians, Am. Fedn. Clin. Rsch., Nat. Assn. VA Chiefs Nuclear Medicine (pres. 1985-87), We. Soc. Clin. Rsch., Alpha Omega Alpha. Office: Nuclear Med Dept VA Greater LA Healthcare 691/W115 11301 Wilshire Blvd Los Angeles CA 90073

BLAIN, CHARLOTTE MARIE, internist, educator; b. Meadeville, Pa., July 18, 1941; d. Frank Andrew and Valerie Marie (Serafin) Blain; m. John G. Hamby, June 12, 1971 (dec. May 1976); 1 child, Charles J. Hamby. Student, Coll. of St. Francis, 1958—60, DePaul U., 1960—61; MD, U. Ill., Chgo., 1965. CLU; diplomate Am. Bd. Family Practice, Am. Bd. Internal Medicine. Intern, resident U. Ill. Hosps., 1967—70; fellow in infectious diseases U. Ill., 1968—69; pvt. practice specializing in internal medicine and family practice Elmhurst, Ill., 1969—. Instr. U. Ill. Hosp., 1969—70; asst. prof. Loyola U., 1970—71; mem. staff Elmhurst Meml. Hosp., 1970—; clin. asst. prof. Chgo. Med. Sch., 1978—95, U. Ill. Med. Sch., 1995—, Rush Med. Coll., 1997—. Contbr. articles to profl. jours., chapters to books. Bd. dirs., v.p. Elmhurst Art Mus. Fellow: ACP, Am. Acad. Family Practice; mem.: AMA, DuPage Med. Soc., Am. Profl. Practice Assn., Am. Soc. Internal Medicine, Univ. Club (Chgo.). Roman Catholic. Avocations: Hapki Do (Black Belt), Tae-Kwan-Do (Black Belt), skiing. Home: 320 Cottage Hill Ave Elmhurst IL 60126-3302 Office: 135 Cottage Hill Ave Elmhurst IL 60126-3330 Office Phone: 630-832-6633. Personal E-mail: cblain@comcast.net. Business E-Mail: cblain@cmbyclinic.com.

BLAIR, CHARLES LEE, physician, educator; b. Stamford, Conn., May 1, 1954; s. Charles Francis Jr. and Mae E. (Gallmoyer) B.; m. Ellen Jill Weiss; children: Eric Charles, Melanie Alison, Hayley Grace. BA, U. Vt., 1976; MD, U. Conn., 1981. Diplomate in psychiatry and geriatric psychiatry Am. Bd. Psychiatry and Neurology. Resident in psychiatry U. Conn. Sch. Medicine, Farmington, 1981-85, asst. clin. prof. psychiatry, 1985-93, assoc. clin. prof. psychiatry, 1993—; John C. Leonard fellow Hartford (Conn.) Hosp., 1985-86, dir. psychiat. edn., 1988-90; pvt. practice Hartford, 1985—; clin. supr. Hartford Hosp./Inst. of Living Tng. Program, 2003—. Mem. psychiatry residency tng. com. U. Conn. Sch. Medicine, Farmington, 1983-84, 88-90. Named of one Top Psychiatric Doctors in Conn., Conn. Mag., 2008, 2009, 10, 11; Rock Sleyster Meml. scholar AMA, 1980-81. Mem. APA, Conn. Psychiat. Soc., Hartford County Med. Assn., Hartford Psychiat. Soc. (treas. 1991-92, sec. 1992-93, program chair 1993-94, pres. 1994-95), Soarig Soc. Am./Fedn. Aeronautique Internationale (Silver Badge, Gold Badge, Diamond Badge 2010, Vt. State 300 Kilometer Out of Return Speed Record award 2010), Phi Beta Kappa. Avocation: aviation. Home: 149 Steele Rd West Hartford CT 06119-1047 Office: 836 Farmington Ave Ste 221C West Hartford CT 06119 Personal E-mail: cleeblair@gmail.com.

BLAIR, MAUDINE, psychotherapist, communications executive, management consultant; d. Eugene Goode and Della Wright Blair. MA, U. Ga., Athens, 1964; PhD, Fla. State U., Tallahassee, 1969. Cert. group psychotherapist Nat. Registry Cert. Group Psychotherapists, transactional analyst, lic. psychotherapist Fla., cert. relationship specialist. Assoc. dir. counseling and pers. svcs. Fla. State U., Tallahassee, 1964—67; dir. and founder Blair's Counseling Svc., Tallahassee, 1970—, Blair's Counseling Satellite Ctr., Tifton, Ga., 1971—92, Tenn. Comm. and Mgmt. Inst., Townsend, Tenn., 1980—89, Blair's Lodge, Townsend, 1981—89; founder, pres. Fla. Comm. and Mgmt. Inst., Tallahassee, 1972—; co-founder, co-dir. CE Studies LLC, Tallahassee, 2005—. Co-editor: Transactional Analysis Rsch. Index vol. I, 1976, Transactional Analysis Rsch. Index vol. II, 1979; contbr. articles to profl. jours. Fellow: Am. Psychotherapy Assn., Am. Orthopsychiatric Assn.; mem.: APA (life), Fla. Assn. Marriage and Family Therapy (clin. mem.), Am. Assn. Marriage and Family Therapy (life; clin. mem.), Internat. Transactional Analysis (clin. mem.), Am. Group Psychotherapy Assn. (clin. mem.). Avocations: reading, travel, writing. Office: Blair's Counseling Svc PO Box 12697 Tallahassee FL 32317 also: CE Studies LLC PO Box 12337 Tallahassee FL 32317 Office Phone: 850-297-2190, 850-580-2600. Business E-Mail: BlairCare@att.net, CEStudies@att.net.

BLAIR, MITCH ELIOT, pediatrician, educator; b. London, Eng., Dec. 6, 1957; s. Andrew John and Jocelyn Blair; m. Susan Maxine Ashton Goodwin, Oct. 11, 1987; children: Nathan, Alecia. BSc, U. Coll., London, 1982, MBBS, 1983; MSc, U. London, 1989. Cert. pediatrician Royal Coll. Physicians, London, 1986, Royal Coll. Pediat. & Child Health, London, 1987, Royal Inst. Pub. Health, London, 1990. Ho. officer Stoke Mandeville Hosp., Aylesbury, England, 1983, Walsgrave Hosp., Coventry, England, 1983; sr. ho. officer, pediat. Charing Cross Hosp., London, 1984—85, clin. med. officer, pediat., 1985—86, registrar, neonatology, 1986—87, registrar, pediat., 1987—88, Northwick Park Hosp., London, 1988; clin. tng. fellow Med. Rsch. Coun., London, 1988—89; lectr., cmty. pediat. Nottingham U., England, 1989—90, sr. lectr., cmty. pediat., 1990—98; cons., reader Imperial Coll., London, 1998—; fellow faculty pub. health FFPH. Hon. prof. Tharves Valle U., 2007. Author: (book) Manual of Community Pediatrics, 2000, Child Public Health, 2003. Nat. trustee Musicspace U.K., Nottingham, England, 1997—98; chair Child Pub. Health Interest Group U.K., 2004—. Grantee, Dept. Health, 1992, European Union, 2000—02, London Nat. Health Svc., 2001. Avocations: jazz clarinet, swimming, pipe collection. Office: Mandala Ctr for Pediat & Child Pub Health Rsch Northwick Park Hosp Middlesex Harrow HA1 3UJ England Office Phone: 0044 208 869 3330. Business E-Mail: m.blair@imperial.ac.uk.

BLAIR, SARAH L., surgeon, educator; b. Buffalo, Sept. 8, 1966; MD, SUNY HSC Syracuse, 1992. Asst. prof., surgery U. Calif. San Diego, 2001—06, assoc. prof., surgery, 2007. Recipient Dept. Def. IDEA award; Terrell McElligott Surg. Oncology fellowship, City of Hope Nat. Med. Ctr., Breast Cancer Prevention grant, Keep a Breast. Fellow: ACS; mem.: Am. Assn. Cancer Rsch., Assn. Academic Surgeons, Assn. Breast Surgeons, Soc. Surg. Oncology, Alpha Omega Alpha. Avocation: hiking. Office: 3855 Health Sci Dr La Jolla CA 92093-0987 Office Fax: 858-822-6366. Business E-Mail: slblair@ucsd.edu.

BLAIS, MICHAEL ROLAND, retired urologist; b. Montreal, Can., Oct. 24, 1920; arrived in U.S., 1923; s. Joseph R. and Dehlia Marie (Tetreault) Blais; m. Evelyn Nena Blais, Apr. 5, 2004; children: Micheline, Michel, Lorraine, Roland. Home: 1632 Kaula Way Deland FL 32720 Home Phone: 386-736-6472; Office Phone: 386-747-0008. Personal E-mail: fishsician@bellsouth.net.

BLAIVAS, JERRY G., urologist, educator; MD, Tufts U., 1968. Diplomate Am. Bd. Urology. Resident surgery Boston Med. Ctr., Boston, 1969—71; resident urology New England Med. Ctr., 1973—76; chief Urogynecology Lenox Hill Hosp.; med. dir. Uro-Center, NY. Clin. prof. urology Cornell Univ.-Weill Med. Coll. Author: (books) Conquering Bladder and Prostate Problems: an Authoritative Guide for Men and Women; editor: (jours.) Neurourology and Urodynamics, Contemporary Urology. Mem.: Internat. Continence Soc., Societe Internationale d'Urologie, Soc. of Univ. Urologists, Soc. for Urodynamics and Female Urology, Am. Coll. of Surgeons, Am. Urological Assn., Soc. of Pelvic Surgeons, Am. Urogynecologic Soc., Am. Assn. of Genitourinary Surgeons. Office: NewYork-Presbyterian Hospital Weill Cornell 525 E 68th St New York NY 10021 Office Phone: 212-746-5454.

BLAKE, DIANE, pediatrician, educator; b. Lynn, Mass., Feb. 8, 1964; MD, Johns Hopkins Sch. Medicine, 1990. Assoc. prof. pediat. U. Mass. Med. Sch., 1997—. Fellow: Am. Acad. Pediat.; mem.: AMA, Soc. Adolescent Health and Medicine. Office: 55 Lake Ave N Worcester MA 01655 Business E-Mail: diane.blake@umassmed.edu.

BLAKE, RANDOLPH, psychology professor; b. Dallas, Tex., Dec. 22, 1945; BA with highest honors, U. Tex., Arlington, 1967; MA, Vanderbilt U., 1969, PhD, 1972. Nat. Inst. Mental Health postdoctoral fellow Baylor Coll. Medicine & U. Tex. Sensory Sciences Ctr., 1972—74; dir. undergrad. studies Dept. Psychology Northwestern U., 1976—77, asst. prof. psychology, 1974—77, assoc. prof. psychology, 1977—81, prof. psychology and neurobiology/physiology, 1981—88; investigator Vanderbilt Vision Ctr. Vanderbilt U., 1989—, Kennedy Ctr. investigator, 1988—, chmn. Dept. Psychology, 1988—96, 2002, 2004—05, prof. psychology, 1988—2000, Centennial prof. psychology, 2000—. Fellow Kennedy Ctr. for Human Develop. Recipient Early Career award, APA, 1977, Career Devel. award, NIH, 1978—83. Fellow: Am. Acad. Arts and Sciences, Japan Soc. Promotion Sci., Am. Assn. Advancement Sci., Am. Psychological Soc.; mem.: Visual Sciences Soc., Psychonomic Soc., Assn. Rsch. Vision and Ophthalmology (program com. 1983—85, chmn. program com. 1985), Sigma Xi. Office: Dept Psychology Vanderbilt Univ 512 Wilson Hall Nashville TN 37203 Office Phone: 615-343-7010. Office Fax: 615-343-8449. E-mail: randolph.blake@vanderbilt.edu.

BLAKELEY, LINDA, psychologist, producer, mediator, writer; b. Bklyn., July 26, 1941; children: Stacey, Scott. BA, UCLA, 1964; MA, Calif. State U., Northridge, 1977; PhD, Calif. Grad. Inst., 1985. Founder, dir. Parents Sharing Custody, Beverly Hills, Calif., 1984—87; pvt. practice self esteem, eating disorders, leadership stress mgmt., divorce mediation, conflict resolution Positive Self Images, Beverly Hills, 1984—95; CEO, founder, mem. The Magic Dress, 2010—. Prodr., host interview/talk show. Author: ABC's of Stress Management, 1989, Do It with Love: Positive Parenting After Divorce, 1988, (audio tape) Success Strategies, 1992; one-woman show The Magic Dress, 1998. Mem. adv. bd. Nat. Coun. Alcoholism and Drug Abuse, 1991-92. Mem.: Nat. Eating Disorder Assn., Calif. Psychol. Assn. (state bd. dirs. media com. 1989—92, chair-elect media divsn.), Mumbai Sister City (bd. dirs. 2007—08), Nat. Assn. Anorexia, Beverly Hills C. of C. (chmn. health care com. 1989, pres. women's network 1989—90). Office: 420 S Beverly Dr Ste 100 Beverly Hills CA 90212-4410 Office Fax: 310-578-2434. Business E-Mail: askdrlinda@drlindablakeley.com.

BLAKENEY, BARBARA A., public health service officer; BS, MS, U. Mass.; diploma, Worcester City Hosp. Sch. of Nursing. Primary care nurse practitioner Amherst Med. Assoc., Amherst, Mass., Boston City Hosp., Boston; prin. pub. health nurse for homeless svcs., addiction svcs. Dept. Health and Hosp., Divsn. Pub. Health, Boston; currently dir. health svcs. for homeless Boston Pub. Health Comm.; leave of absence. Recipient Pearl McIver Pub. Health Nurse award, Am. Nurses Assn., Theta Alpha chpt. Ann Kibirck Nursing Leadership award, Sigma Theta Tau; named one of 100 Most Powerful People in Healthcare, Modern Healthcare mag., 2002, 2003, 2004, 2006. Mem.: ANA (pres. 2002—06).

BLAKENEY-GRANADO, KAREN ELIZABETH, social service and community health program executive, consultant; b. Evanston, Ill., June 27, 1953; d. Elwood Francis and Irene Loretta (Filloon) Garlick; m. Ydalia Granado; children: Jesse Alan, Aaron Paul. Cert. in Christian edn., Angeles Bible Coll., LA, 1972; BA in Anthropology, Calif. State U., Long Beach, 1978; MS in Counseling Psychology, Mt. St. Mary's Coll., LA., 1992; cert. in non-profit mgmt., U. So. Calif., 1998. Commd. pastor Hosanna Ministries, 1994. Archaeologist VTM Corp., Vandenburg AFB, Calif., 1979-81; archaeologist, Arroyo Grande, Calif., 1981-82; acct. Airport Datsun/Volvo, Santa Maria, Calif., 1982-83; adminstrn. mgr. Concord Sys., Reseda, Calif., 1983-86; ins. broker Prudential Ins. Co., Torrance, Calif., 1986-87; mgr. legal compliance dept. G.J. Sullivan Cos., LA, 1987-92; psychotherapy intern Hosanna Ministries, Santa Monica, Calif., 1990-95; children's social worker Dept. Children and Family Svcs., LA, 1994-96; dir. social work Internat. Foster Family Agy., Carson, Calif., 1996-97; dir. youth svcs. L.A. Gay and Lesbian Ctr., Hollywood, Calif., 1997-99; dir. programs Chinatown Svc. Ctr., LA, 1999—2002; exec. dir. Schutrum-Piteo Found., Burbank, Calif., 2002—03; CEO, pres. Blackwolf, LLC Consulting, 2001—07; exec. dir. Grace Ctr., Pasadena, 2003—04, Blackwolf Gallery, 2003—; program officer First 5, LA, 2005—07, sr. program officer, 2007—08, mgr., dept. grant mgmt. & legal compliance, 2008—10, SPO Boot Start Cmtys. Dept., 2010—. Lectr. Calif. Poly. Inst. Archaeol. Field Sch., Mission San Antonio de Padua, 1978-81; co-founder, exec. dir. Inst. for trauma Intervention, L.A., 1993-96. Author: (poetry) Sacred Journey, 1995, Ydalia's Song, 1998. Bd. dirs. Art To Grow On, San Pedro, Calif., 1992-94, Desert Stream Ministries/AIDS Resource Ministry, L.A., 1985-91; mem. parent-tchr. adv. bd. Park Western Elem. Sch., San Pedro, 1993-94; dir. mem. Consortium for Homeless Youth Svcs., Hollywood, 1997-99; rep. L.A. County Svc. Planning Area Dist. 4 Coun., 1999-2002; mem. Asian-Pacific Islander police adv. com. L.A. Police Dept., 2000; mem. Nat. Network of Youth, 1997-2002; mem. Calif. Child, Youth and Family Coalition, 1998-2003; bd. dir. Coalition Against Slave Trafficking, 1999-2002, Coalition for Cmty. Health, 2001-03, Schutrum-Piteo Found., 2003-; mem. Dept. Pub. Social Svcs. long-term self sufficiency steering com. L.A. County, 2000-02. Mem. NAFE, Calif. Assn. Marriage and Family Therapists, Calif. Assn. Against Domestic Violence, Calif. Stat U.-Long Beach Anthropology Alumni Assn. (alumni bd. 1984-85), Calif. State Breast Feeding Roundtable. Avocations: poetry, art. Office Phone: 213-482-9488. E-mail: kblakeney90039@sbcglobal.net.

BLALOCK, CAROL DOUGLASS, psychologist, educator; d. Allan Martin and Mary Louise Douglass; m. Harvey Anthony Blalock, Aug. 27, 1976; children: Jeanne, Patricia, Elizabeth. BEd, U. S.D., 1968; MEd in Edn., U. Fla., 1976, EdS in Counseling, 1976, PhD in Curriculum and Instrn., 1980; postgrad., U. Md., 1980—81. Nat. cert. sch. psychologist Fla., 1990, lic. sch. psychologist Fla., 1990. Tchr. Metcalf Elem., Gainesville, Fla., 1968, Gainesville (Fla.) H.S., 1969; coord. environ. edn. Sante Fe C.C., Gainesville, 1974—78, adj. faculty, 1974—78; grad. rsch. fellow U. Fla., rsch. assoc., 1979; chmn. sci. dept. Oak Hall Prep. Sch., Gainesville, Fla., 1981—84; guidance counselor Trenton (Fla.) HS, 1984—87; psychologist Marion County Schs., Ocala, Fla., 1987—; adj. faculty U. South Fla., Tampa, 1990. Author: (chpt.) A Futures Perspective on Instructional Design, 1980; co-author: (conf. summary) Computer Conf. on the Future, 1979, (chpt.) Learning Networks: The Next Step, 1981. Aux. officer Gainesville (Fla.) Police Dept., 1985—95; mem. Holy Faith Cath. Ch., Gainesville, Fla., 1976. Mem.: Fla. Assn. Sch. Psychologists, Nat. Assn. Sch. Psychologists, APA, Phi Delta Kappa. Republican. Roman Catholic. Avocations: travel, music, art.

BLANCH, PETER D., physical therapist, researcher; b. Mt Morgan, May 20, 1962; B in Physiotherapy, U. Queensland, 1984; M in Applied Physiology, U. Sydney, 2001. Clin. rsch. mgr. Australian Inst. Sport, 1990—. Adviser Australian Swimming Sports Sci. and Medicine Adv. Bd., 1991—2004; rep. Australian Cricket Sports Sci. and Medicine Rsch. Adv. Panel, 2004—08; adj. prof. Canberra U., 2010; cons. Comcare Clin. Panel, 2011. Recipient Australian Sports medal, Australian Govt. Mem.: Australian Physiotherapist Assn. Avocations: running, bicycling. Office: Australian Inst Sport Leverrier Bruce ACT 2617 Australia

BLANCO, LILIAN DELOS REYES, biologist; b. Manila, Nov. 21, 1953; arrived in Australia, 1988; d. Delmar Vitancor and Gloria (delos Reyes) B. BS cum laude, U. of the East, Manila, 1975; M in Biology, U. of the Philippines, Quezon City, 1979; PhD, Macquarie U., Sydney, Australia, 1995. Cert. sci. specialist in biology Presdl. Decree Philippines. Sci. rsch. specialist I Philippine Atomic Energy Commn., Quezon City, 1978-81, sci. rsch. specialist II, 1982-84, sci. rsch. specialist III, 1985-87, sr. sci. rsch. specialist, 1988; profl. officer Macquarie U., Sydney, 1989, Australian postgrad. rsch. staff, 1990-93; interpreter various orgns., Australia, 1995; rschr. Macquarie U., 1995; rschr. Biol. and Chem. Rsch. Inst. NSW Dept. Agriculture, Rydalmere, 1995; rsch. officer Inst. Respiratory Medicine U. Sydney, 1996; rsch. officer U. Tech., Sydney, 1997-2000, external cons., Insearch Ltd. Pty., 1997—; co-propr. Interwoven Expressions, 1998. Health care interpreter Westmead Hosp. and Cmty. Health Svcs., 1993—; translator pvt. agys., 1999—. Author: String of Words and Solitude, Love Across the Sky. Founder CARE fellowship, Granville, New South Wales, Australia, 1991. Grad. scholar Nat. Sci. Devel. Bd., U. of the Philippines, 1975-77, Fgn. Lang. scholar Fgn. Svc. Inst. Ministry of Fgn. Affairs, Philippines, 1985-86, scholar Japan Internat. Coop. Agy., Tsukuba Science City, Japan, 1987, Postgrad. scholar Australian Govt., Sydney, 1990-93; fellow Internat. Atomic Energy Agy., U. Fla., Gainesville, 1984. Mem. Order of Internat. Fellowship. Adventist. Avocations: singing gospel music, listening to classical music, foreign language studies. Home: 1 Torres Cres Whalen 2770 Australia Office Phone: 612-88073601. Personal E-mail: l.blanco53@yahoo.com, lilian53@bigpond.com.

BLANCO BLANCO, IGNACIO, retired pulmonologist, researcher; b. Grado, Principality of Asturias, Spain, May 23, 1944; MD, U. Valladolid, Spain, 1967. Specialist in internal medicine, pneumology Gen. Hosp. Asturias and Silicosis Nat. Inst., Spain, 1975. Head, unit pneumology, med. officer Silicosis Nat. Inst., Spain, 1971—76; head, unit pneumology Virgen de la Arrixaca Hosp., Murcia, Spain, 1976—77, Valle del Nalón Hosp., Principality of Asturias, 1977—2009. Assoc. prof. med. pathology U. Murcia, Spain, 1976—77; clin. medicine, tng. officer U. Oviedo, Principality of Asturias, 1982—88. Contbr. articles to profl. jours. Biomed. Rsch. grant, Spain's Nat. Health Inst. Carlos III, Ministry of Health, Rsch. grant, Asturias's Soc. Respiratory Diseases. Fellow: Spain's Nat. Health Inst. Carlos III, Ministry of Health (mem., programme for specialised clin. rsch.); mem.: Spanish Soc. Pneumology and Thoracic Surgery (Rsch. grant), Spanish Registry of Patients with Alpha-1 Antitrypsin Deficiency (past coord., adv. com. mem.), European Respiratory Soc., Spain's Nat. Agy. Assessment and Prospective, Ministry of Sci. and Innovation. Achievements include patents for use of alpha-1 antitrypsin for the treatment of fibromyalgia severe bronchial asthma. Avocations: football, classical music, tennis, opera. Home: Comandante Caballero 10 Oviedo Principality of Asturias 33005 Spain Personal E-mail: ignablanco@yahoo.com.

BLAND, DEBORAH SHAFFER, nurse; b. Tampa, Fla., Jan. 20, 1954; d. Frank Solomon and Mary Louise (Swann) Shaffer; children: Danny, Dionne. LPN, Suwanee-Hamilton Nursing Sch., Live Oak, Fla., 1984; student, Ashworth Coll., 2006. LPN, Fla. Author: Skippy Goes to Ybor Square, 1998, Danny's Journey, 2004, (poetry chapbook) A Voice from Salt Springs, 2005. Chaplain Ladies Auxillary Post #10208, 2004-06, founder The Children's Book Depository, 2004; active Vet. of Fgn. Wars of U.S., Salt Springs, Fla.; mem. First Bapt. Ch., Salt Springs Christian Ch., Salt Springs; founder of A Journey in Poetry, 2003, Ocala Nat. Forest- Salt Springs newsletter, 2003, Salt Springs Country Poets, 2004; vol. Am. Red Cross Disaster, 2003-06; cmty. svc. activist, 2001-06. Mem.: Brick City Ctr. for the Arts, Fla. State Poets Assn. Achievements include development of PAVRSTB guitar learning method, 2004. Avocations: writing, painting, photography, gardening, guitar.

BLANK, EUGENE, pediatrician, radiologist, educator; b. Balt., May 8, 1924; s. Maurice Blank and Fannie Edith Jacob; m. Esther Honikberg, June 22, 1958; children: Lisa, Anne, Linda. BA, Johns Hopkins U., 1948, MD, 1954. Diplomate Am. Bd. Pediat., Am. Bd. Radiology. Prof. emeritus in pediats. and radiology Oreg. Health Scis. U., Portland, 1991—. Author: Pediatric Images Casebook of Differential Diagnosis, 1997, USMC 457703, 2010. 2d lt. USMC, 1942—45, South Pacific. Democrat. Avocation: writing. Home: 4940 SW Humphrey Park Rd Portland OR 97221 Home Phone: 503-292-0505. Personal E-mail: geneblank1@gmail.com.

BLANK, MARION SUE, psychologist, educator; b. NYC, Dec. 20, 1933; d. Morris David and Tillie Jean (Sherman) Hersch; m. Martin Blank, July 3, 1955; children: Donna, Jonathan, Ari. BA, CCNY, 1955, MS in Edn, 1956; PhD, Cambridge U., Eng., 1961. Asst. prof. Albert Einstein Coll. Medicine, 1965-70, assoc. prof., 1970-73; prof. dept. psychiatry Rutgers Med. Sch., Piscataway, NJ, 1973-83; mem. adj. faculty dept. psychiatry Columbia Coll. Physicians and Surgeons, NYC, 1980—83; pres. Darj on Learning, Inc., 2001—; co-dir. Devel. Neuropsychiatry Program, Columbia U., NYC, 2004—; dir. A Light on Literacy, 2005—, The Reading Kingdom, 2010. Dir. reading disabilities rsch. inst., pvt. practice, cons., 1983—; Nat. Tour lectr. Speech Pathology Assn. Australia, 1996. Author: Teaching Learning in the Preschool - A Dialogue Approach, Preschool Language Assessment Instrument, 1978, (with Rose and Berlin) The Language of Learning, 1978, Sentence Master, 1990-96, (with Berlin) A Parent's Guide to Educational Software, 1991, (with Marquis and Klimovitch) Directing School Discourse, 1994, Directing Early Discourse with Marquis and Klimovitch, 1995, The Reading Remedy, 2006, Reading Kingdom, 2010. Pinsent-Darwin fellow, 1960; recipient award of commendation N.J. Speech and Hearing Assn., 1979, Spl. Edn. award Software Pubs. Am., 1990, N.J., USPHS Career Devel. award, 1965-73; named N.J. nominee Kleffner Lifetime Svc. award Am. Speech Lang. Hearing Assn., 1994, 95, Upton Sinetair award, 2010. Fellow APA; mem. Assn. for Children with Learning Disabilities (profl. adv. bd., instr., adv. N.J. chpt.) Home: 802-66 Songhees Rd Victoria BC V9A 0A2 Canada Office Phone: 551-226-4149. Personal E-mail: dimarionblank@gmail.com. Business E-Mail: msb5@columbia.edu.

BLANK, STEPHANIE V., oncologist; b. New Haven, Aug. 15, 1966; BA, Yale U., 1988; MD, U. Calif., San Diego, 1994. Gynecologic oncologist NYU Sch. Medicine, 2001—. Office: 160 E 34th St New York NY 10016 Business E-Mail: stephanie.blank@med.nyu.edu.

BLANKENSHIP, JAMES COLEGROVE, cardiologist; s. John Harnly and Marian (Colegrove) Blankenship; m. Mary Stark, June 9, 1984; children: Leah Shikany, Bart James, Peter Stark. MD, Cornell U., 1980. Diplomate in internal medicine and interventional cardiology Am. Bd. Internal Medicine, cert. physician, investigator Assn. Clin. Rsch. Profl., 2008. With Marshfield (Wis.) Clinic, 1987—89; prof. medicine Temple U. Sch. Medicine, Phila., 1989—; dir. Catheterization Lab. Geisinger Med. Ctr., Danville, Pa., 1997—, chief cardiology, 2009—. Office: Geisinger Med Ctr 100 N Academy Dr Danville PA 17822 *

BLANKFEIN, ROBERT JEROME, retired neurologist; b. Nov. 5, 1931; s. Jules and Freda S. Blankfein; m. Leslie Wald Blankfein, June 27, 1998; 1 child, David. Grad., Hotchkiss Sch., 1950; BA, Yale U., New Haven, Conn., 1954; MD, NY Med. Coll., 1958. Diplomate in neurology Am. Bd. of Neurology and Psychiatry, 1971. Intern San Francisco Gen. Hosp. (Stanford U. Svc.), 1958—59; resident in internal medicine Bx VA Hosp., 1959—60, resident in neurology, 1960—63; vis. fellow neurology and myasthenia Clinic Columbia Presbyn. Hosp., 1962—63; neurophysiology fellow EEG Hosp. U. Penn., 1963—65; clin. asst. prof. neurology NY Med. Coll., 1971-74, clin. assoc. prof. neurology, 1975—2002; attending neurologist Met. Hosp. NY, NYC, 1986—2002, NY Hosp. Med. Ctr. Queens, 1979-95; fed. examiner neurology US Dept. Labor, 1992—2002; ret., 2002. Dir. neurology, Physicians Hosp., 1967-90, pres. med. bd., 1971-81; coord. Jour. Club Neurology Residents, NY Med. Coll., 1971-89; disting. lectr. dementia and aging, Sandoz-Dorsey Pharms., 1973-74; lectr. delirium, McNeil Pharms., 1984; presenter in field. Mem. editl. bd., consulting editor in neurology, Jour. Hosp. Physician, 1977-95; contbr. articles to profl. jours. Class agt. Hotchkiss Sch. 55th Reunion, Hotchkiss Sch. 60th Reunion; vice-chmn. Hotchkiss Fund, 2005—06. Fellow ACP, Am. Acad. Neurology, NY Acad. Medicine, Royal Soc. Medicine, Stroke Coun. of Am. Heart Assn., Yale Sci. and Engring. Soc.; mem. Assn. Rsch. Nervous and Mental Disease, NY Neurol. Soc., Am. Epilepsy Soc., Am. EEG Soc., Assoc. Alumni Neurol. Inst. NY Columbia Presbyn. Med. Ctr., Queens Acad. Medicine (mem. continuing edn. com. 1980-85), Yale Crew Assn., Yale Club NYC. Personal E-mail: robertblankfein@verizon.net.

BLANTON, PATRICIA LOUISE, periodontal surgeon; b. Clarksville, Tex., July 9, 1941; d. Ben E. and Mildred L. (Russell) B. MS, Baylor U., 1964, PhD, 1967, DDS, 1974, cert., 1975. Diplomate Am. Bd. Oral Medicine. Tchg. asst. Baylor Coll. of Dentistry, Dallas, 1963-67, asst. prof., 1967-70, spl. instr., 1970-73, assoc. prof., 1974-76; resident periodontics VA Hosp., Dallas, 1975; prof. Baylor Coll. of Dentistry, Dallas, 1976-85, Baylor U. Grad. Sch., Dallas, 1976—; prof., chmn. Baylor Coll. of Dentistry, Dallas, 1983-85, prof. emeritus, 1994—, disting. alumni, 2005. Disting. alumna Bd. Grad. Residency Program, 2008; cons. VA Hosp., Dallas, 1979-82; adj. prof. Baylor Coll. of Dentistry, Dallas, 1985—; cons. Commn. on Dental Accreditation and Coun. of Dental Edn., 1981—; v.p. State Anatomical Bd., Tex., 1983-85, Am. Coll. Dentists; mem. ADA-AADS Liaison Com., 1983—; chmn. Nat. Insts. Health, Oral Biology and Medicine Study Sect. II, 1985-86. Author: Periodontics for the G.P., 1977, Current Therapy in Dentistry, 1980, An Atlas of the Human Skull, 1980 (1st place honors 1981). Invited participant Am. Coun. on Edn., Austin, 1984; mem. liaison com. Dallas County Dental Soc.-Am. Cancer Soc., Dallas, 1976-78; bd. dirs. Dallas Dental Health Programs, 1992-93, S.W. Med. Found., 1992-93; bd. devel. Hardin-Simmons U., 1995—. Recipient Comdrs. award Europe Regional Dental Command, 2002; named one of Outstanding Young Women in Am., 1976; named Disting. Alumna, Baylor Coll. Dentistry, 2005. Fellow Internat. Coll. Dentists, Am. Coll. Dentists (pres. elect); mem. ADA (del., v.p.), Am. Dental Assoc. (v.p. 2010-), Tex. Dental Assn. (bd. dirs. 1995-97, v.p. 2002, pres. 2003—), Am. Assn. Anatomists, Am. Acad. Periodontology, Am. Acad. Oral Medicine, Am. Acad. Osseointegration, Am. Assn. Woman Dentists (Lucy Hobbs Taylor Woman Dentists of Yr., 2008), Tex. Soc. Periodontists (pres. 1998-99), S.W. Soc. Periodontology (pres. 1999-00), Dallas County Dental Soc. (pres. 1992-93, Lifetime Achievement award, 2008), Xi Psi Phi, Omicron Kappa Upsilon (pres. 1992-93). Avocations: reading, travel. Office: 4514 Cole Ave Ste 902 Dallas TX 75205-4172 Office Phone: 214-559-4670. Personal E-mail: pblantondds@att.net.

BLANTZ, ROLAND C., nephrologist, educator; b. Portland, Oreg. BA in Humanities and Chem. Engring., Johns Hopkins U., Balt., 1961, MD, 1965. Diplomate Am. Bd. Internal Medicine, Am. Bd. Nephrology. Resident U. Colo. Med. Ctr., 1965—67; fellow U. Tex. Southwestern Med. Sch., 1969—72; chief nephrology VA San Diego Healthcare Sys., 1972—90; prof. nephrology U. Calif., San Diego, 1980—, head nephrology, hypertension, 1988—. Contbr. articles to profl. jours. Capt. USAF, 1967—69. Recipient William S. Middleton award, Dept. Vets. Affairs, 2006, John Petess award, Am. Soc. Metrology. Mem.: Coun. Am. Kidney Socs. (chair 2001—02), Josiah Macy Found., Nat. Kidney Found. (Seldin award 2005), AAP, AFCR, ASCI, Am. Soc. Nephrology (pres. 2001—02). Office: Dept Medicine U Calif San Diego 9500 Gilman Dr #9111H La Jolla CA 92093 Office Phone: 858-552-7528. E-mail: rblantz@ucsd.edu.

BLASCHKE, TERRENCE FRANCIS, medicine and molecular pharmacology educator; b. Rochester, Minn., Oct. 4, 1942; s. Robert and Carmella Ann Blaschke; m. Jeannette F. Martin, June 8, 1968; children: Anne, John. BS in Math. cum laude, U. Denver, 1964; MD, Columbia U., 1968. Diplomate Am. Bd. Internal Medicine, Nat. Bd. Med. Examiners. Intern in medicine UCLA Ctr. for Health Scis., 1968-69, asst. resident, 1969-70; clin. assoc. metabolism br. Nat. Cancer Inst., NIH, Bethesda, Md., 1970-72; clin. rsch fellow div. clin. pharmacology dept. medicine U. Calif. Med. Ctr., San Francisco, 1972-74; asst. prof. medicine (clin. pharmacology) Stanford (Calif.) U. Sch. Medicine, 1974-81, asst. prof. pharmacology, 1978-81, assoc. prof. medicine (clin. pharmacology) and pharmacology, 1981-91, prof. medicine (clin. pharmacology)-molecular pharmacology, 1991—2006, prof. medicine and molecular pharmacology emeritus, 2006—, asst. dean for med. student advising, 2002—06; v.p. Pharsight Corp., Calif., 2000—02; adj. prof. Ind. U. Sch. Med., 2005—. Bd. govs. Am. Bd. Clin. Pharmacology, 1990-92; vis. worker div. molecular pharmacology Nat. Inst. for Med. Rsch., London, 1980-81, Ctr. for Biopharm. Scis., U. Leiden and dept. med. info. scis. Erasmus U., The Netherlands, 1990; mem. Medi-Cal drug use rev. bd. Calif. Dept. Health Svcs., 1993-96; chmn. generic drugs adv. com. FDA, 1990-94, mem. nonprescription drugs adv. com., 2003-; mem. bd. sci. advisors Merck Sharp and Dohme Rsch. Labs., Rahway, N.J., 1986-90; mem. pharmacology study sect. NIH, 1979-83; faculty of medicine Moi U., El Doret, Kenya; vis. prof. Ctr. Drug Devel. Sci., Georgetown U., 1997-98; spl. govt. employee FDA, 1997-. Mem. editl. bd. Drug Therapeutics: Concepts for Physicians, 1978-81, Rational Drug Therapy, 1984-85, Clin. Pharmacology and Therapeutics, 1981—, Drug Interaction Facts, 1983-87, Drug Metabolism and Disposition, 1994-2000; assoc. editor Ann. Rev. Pharmacology and

Toxicology, 1989—. Officer USPHS, 1970-72. Recipient faculty devel. award in clin. pharmacology Pharm. Mfrs. Assn. Found.; Burroughs-Wellcome scholar. Mem.: AAAS, ACP, Western Pharmacology Soc., Western Assn. Physicians, Western Soc. Clin. Investigation, Am. Fedn. Clin. Rsch., Am. Soc. Pharmacology and Exptl. Therapeutics (exec. com. clin. pharmacology divsn. 1986—89, chair clin. pharmacology divsn. 2002—03), Am. Soc. for Clin. Pharmacology and Therapeutics (chmn. liaison com. clin. pharmacology 1985—89, sci. program com. 1986—87, pres. 1988—89, assoc. sec.-treas. 1990—92, chmn. long range planning com. 1992—94, Rawls-Palmer award, Henry W. Elliott award, OSCAR B Hunter award), Phi Beta Kappa, Alpha Omega Alpha. Office: Stanford U Med Ctr Div Clin Pharmacology S-009 300 Pasteur Dr Stanford CA 94305-5130 E-mail: blaschke@stanford.edu.

BLASEY, CHRISTINE, psychologist, director; b. Silver Spring, Md., Nov. 28, 1966; BA, U. NC, 1984; PhD, U So. Calif.; MS, Stanford U., 1996. Vis. prof. Pepperdine U., 1995—97; rsch. psychologist Stanford U., 1998—2011; dir. Corcept Therapeutics, 2003—. Avocation: surfing. Office: 149 Commonwealth Dr Menlo Park CA 94025 Business E-Mail: cblasey@corcept.com.

BLASS, JOHN PAUL, retired physician, biochemist; b. Vienna, Feb. 21, 1937; arrived in U.S., 1938; s. Gustaf and Jolan (Wirth) B.; m. Birgit Annelise Knudsen, Dec. 20, 1960; children: Charles, Lisa. AB summa cum laude, Harvard U., 1958; PhD, U. London, 1960; MD, Columbia U., 1965. Postdoctoral fellow Am. Cancer Soc., Columbia U., 1962-63; intern Mass. Gen. Hosp., Boston, 1965-66, resident in medicine, 1966-67; research assoc. Nat. Heart and Lung Inst., Bethesda, Md., 1967-70; asst. prof. psychiatry and biol. chemistry UCLA, 1970-76, assoc. prof., 1976-78; mem. staff UCLA Hosps. Clinics, 1970-78; Winifred Masterson Burke prof. neurology, prof. medicine Cornell U. Med. Center, 1978—2005, prof. emeritus, 2005—11; sci. dir. CNS Pharms., 2009—11. Attending neurologist N.Y. Hosp.; mem. NBS-1 rev. com. NIH, 1981-84; councilor Nat. Inst. Aging, 1986-89; chmn. Nat. Adv. Panel on Alzheimers's Disease U.S. Congress, 1987-91, mem., 1993-96. Jour. Neurochemistry, 1981—86, Neurochem. Rsch., 1984—86, Neurochem. Pathology, Neurobiol. Aging, Jour. Neurol. Sci., 1990—2000, Jour. Molecular Neurosci., 1999—, assoc. editor Jour. Am. Geriatric Soc., 1982—87, Age, 1993—95, Yearbook of Neurology and Neurosurgery, 1992—; co-editor: Caring for Alzheimer's Patients, 1990—, Femilial Alzheimer's Disease, 1989—, Treatment of Alzheimer's Disease, 1989—, Principles of Geriatrics and Gerontology, 2d edit., 1990—, Principles of Geriatrics and Gerontology, 3d edit., 1994—, Principles of Geriatrics and Gerontology, 4th edit., 1998—, Concise Clinical Pharmacology: CNS Therapeautics, 2006; contbr. articles to profl. jours. Mem. sci. adv. bd. Will Rogers Inst., 1981-97, Allied Signal Aging Award Com., 1993-95. Served as asst. surgeon USPHS, 1967-70. Marshall scholar, 1958-60. Mem. Soc. Neurosci. (chmn. social issues com.), Biochem. Soc., Am. Soc. Biol. Chemists, Am. Soc. Neurochemistry (council, chmn. public policy com.), Internat. Soc. Neurochemistry (council, chmn. clin. com.), Am. Soc. Clin. Investigation, Am. Geriatrics Soc., Am. Fedn. Aging Rsch. (v.p., chmn. research com. 1982-87, pres. 1994-96), Assn. Alzheimers and Related Disease (sci. adv. bd. 1982-86), Am. Chem. Soc., Phi Beta Kappa, Sigma Xi, Alpha Omega Alpha. Jewish. Home: 93 Mercer St Apt 3E New York NY 10012 Personal E-mail: jpblass@yahoo.com.

BLASZYK, MICHAEL D., insurance company executive; Studied life sciences, Wayne State Univ., Detroit, Michigan; M in Health Services Adminstrn., Univ. Colo., Denver. Mng. ptnr William M. Mercer Consulting; CFO Univ. Hospitals Healthcare System, Cleveland, Ohio; sr. v.p. Cmty. Hospitals and Home Care; sr. exec. v.p., chief corp. officer, CFO Catholic Healthcare West. Taught health care finance and economics Boston Univ.; lectr. Case Western Reserve Univ. Office: Catholic Healthcare West 185 Berry St Ste 300 San Francisco CA 94107 *

BLATT, JULIE, hematologist, oncologist, medical educator; b. Miami, Oct. 22, 1951; MD, Johns Hopkins U., 1976. Resident Babies & Children's Hosp. of NY, Columbia U., 1976—78; fellow pediatric hematology/oncology NIH, Bethesda, 1978—81; chief pediatric hematology/oncology U. NC, Chapel Hill, prof., 1998—. Office: University of North Carolina 170 Manning Dr Chapel Hill NC 27599-7236 Office Phone: 919-966-1178. Business E-Mail: jblat@med.unc.edu.

BLATT, SIDNEY JULES, psychology professor, psychoanalyst, investigator; b. Phila., Oct. 15, 1928; s. Harry and Fannie (Feld) Blatt; m. Ethel Shames, Feb. 1, 1951; children: Susan, Judith, David. BS, Pa. State U., 1950, MS, 1952; PhD, U. Chgo., 1957; postgrad., Western New Eng. Inst. for Psychoanalysis, 1972. Postdoctoral fellow Neuropsychiat. Inst. of U. Ill. Med. Ctr., Psychiat. and Psychosomatic Inst. of Michael Reese Hosp., 1957—59; instr. Univ. Coll. U. Chgo., 1959-60; mem. faculty Yale U., New Haven, 1960—, prof. psychiatry and psychology, 1974—; mem. faculty Western New Eng. Inst. for Psychoanalysis, 1975—; Sigmund Freud prof. psychoanalysis Hebrew U., 1988—89. Ayala and Sam Zacks prof. art history Hebrew U., 1988—89; Fulbright sr. rsch. fellow, 1988—89; mem. Rsch. Fellowship Rev. Panel NIMH, 1966—69, mem. Psychology Tng. Rev. Panel, 1969—74; vis. prof. Ben Gurion U., 1992, 96, Univ. Coll., London, 1999—2003, Cath. U. Leuven, 2003, George Washington U., 2006, Bar Ilan U., 2006; Fulbright sr. specialist, 2006—. Author: Experiences of Depression: Theoretical, Research and Clinical Perspectives, 2004, Polarities of Experience: Reletedness and Self-Defination in Personality Development, Psychopathology and Therapentic process.; co-author (with J. Allison and C. Zimet): Interpretation of Psychological Tests, 1968, 2d edit., 1988; co-author: (with C.M. Wild) Schizophrenia: A Developmental Analysis, 1976; co-author: (with E.S. Blatt) Continuity and Change in Art: The Development of Modes of Representation, 1984; co-author: (with R.Q. Ford) Therapeutic Change: An Object Relations Perspective, 1994; co-editor (with D. Diamond): Attachment Research and Psychoanalysis, vols. I-III, 1999—2003; co-editor: (with Z.V. Segal) The Self in Emotional Distress, 1993; co-editor: (with J. Corveleyn, P. Luyten) The Theory and Treatment of Depression: Towards a Dynamic Interaction Model.; co-editor: (with D. Diamond & J. Lichtenberg) Attachment and Sexuality. Recipient Disting. Contbns. to Rsch. award, Assn. Med. Sch. Profs. Psychology, 1995, APA Divsn. Psychoanalysis, 2000, Founders' Disting. Tchg. prize, We. New Eng. Psychoanalytic Soc., 2001, Hans H. Strupp Disting. Contbns. to Psychoanalysis award, 2000, Bruno Klopfer and Marguerite R. Hertz awards for dist. contbns. to psychol. assessment, Soc. for Personality Assessment, 1989, 1994, Disting. Sci. Contbns. award, APA Divsn. Clin. Psychology, 2004, Otto Weininger award, Can. Psychol. Assn., 2006; named Disting. Practitioner of Psychology, Nat. Acad. Practice, 1983; fellow Found. Fund Rsch. in Psychiatry, 1961—64. Mem.: AAUP, AAAS, APA, Soc. Personality Assessment (pres. 1984—86), Am. Psychoanalytic Assn. (Outstanding Sci. Paper prize 2005, Mary S. Sigourney award 2006). Office: Yale Univ 300 George St Ste 901 New Haven CT 06511 Home Phone: 203-397-0167; Office Phone: 203-785-2090. Business E-Mail: sidney.blatt@yale.edu.

BLAU, HANNAH, pulmonologist, director; b. Tel Aviv, July 9, 1951; d. Drora and Israel Korman; m. Alexander Blau, Aug. 10, 1975; children: Daniella, Tamara, David, Naomi. MBBS, Melbourne U., 1974. Cert. pediatrics Israel, 1982, pulmonologist 1988. Dir., pulmonary and cystic fibrosis inst. Schneider Children's Med. Ctr. Israel, Petah Tikva, 1993—. Contbr. scientific papers. Achievements include research in pediatric pulmonology, cystic fibrosis, lung cell biology, induced sputum bacteriology and inflammatory markers. Home: 2 Hamaayan St Raanana Israel Office: Schneider Children's Med Ctr 14, Kaplan St 49202 Petah Tikva Israel Office Fax: 972-3-9253308. Business E-Mail: hblau@post.tau.ac.il, hblau@clalit.org.il.

BLAU, HELEN MARGARET, pharmacology educator; b. London, May 8, 1948; (parents Am. citizens); d. George E. and Gertrude Blau; m. David Spiegel, July 25, 1976; children: Daniel Spiegel, Julia Spiegel. BA in Biology, York U., Eng., 1969; MA in Biology, Harvard U., 1970, PhD in Biology, 1975; Doctorate (hon.), U. Nijmegen, Netherlands, 2003. Predoctoral fellow dept. biology Harvard U., Cambridge, Mass., 1969-75; postdoctoral fellow div. med. genetics, dept. biochemistry and biophysics U. Calif., San Francisco, 1975-78, asst. prof. dept. pharmacology Stanford (Calif.) U., 1978-86, assoc. prof. dept. pharmacology, 1986-91, prof. dept. molecular pharmacology, 1991—99, prof. dept. microbiology and immunology, 2002—, chair dept. molecular pharmacology, 1997—2001, dir. gene therapy tech., 1997—, Donald E. and Delia B. Baxter prof., 1999—, dir. Baxter Lab. in Genetic Pharmacology, 2002—. Rolf-Sammet-Fonds vis. prof., U. Frankfurt, 2003; plenary talk on stem cells, Academic des Sci. della France at Pontifical Acad., the Vatican, Modern Biotech. Symposium, 2003; co-chmn. various profl. meetings; spkr. in field. Mem. editorial bd. 14 jours. including Jour. Cell Biology, Somatic Cell Molecular Genetics and Exptl. Cell Rsch., Molecular and Cellular Biology, Genes to Cells, Molecular Therapy; contbr. articles to profl. jours. Mem. ad hoc molecular cytology study sect. NIH, 1987-88; mem. five-yr. planning com genetics and teratology br. NICHHD/NIH, 1989. Recipient Rsch. Career Devel. award NIH, 1984-89, SmithKline & Beecham award, 1989-91, Women in Cell Biology Career Recognition award, 1992, Excellence in Sci. award FASEB, 1999, McKnight Endowment Fund for Neurosci. award, 2001; Mellon Found. faculty fellow, 1979-80, William H. Hume faculty scholar, 1981-84; grantee NIH, NSF, Ellison Med. Found., Muscular Dystrophy Assn., March of Dimes, 1978—; Yvette Mayent-Rothschild fellow for vis. profs. Inst. Curie, Paris, 1995. Fellow AAAS, Havard Overseers; mem. NAS (del. to China 1991), Internat. Soc. Differentiation (pres. 2002-04), Am. Soc. for Cell Biology (nominating com. 1985-86, program com. 1990), Soc. for Devel. Biology (pres. 1994-95), Inst. Medicine (coun. mem.), Nat. Acad. Scis., Am. Soc. Gene Therapy (bd. dirs. 1999-2002). Avocations: skiing, swimming, hiking, music, theater. Office: Stanford U Sch Medicine 269 Campus Dr CCSR Rm 4215 Stanford CA 94305-5175 Fax: 650-736-0080. E-mail: hblau@stanford.edu.

BLAU, MONTE, retired radiology educator; b. NYC, June 17, 1926; s. Samuel and Rose (Cohen) B., m. Guitta Drimer, June 30, 1946; children: Saul, Hannah. BS in Chemistry, Poly. Inst. Bklyn., 1948; PhD in Phys. Chemistry, U. Wis., 1952. Rsch. chemist Geochronometric Lab., Yale U., 1952-53; with div. neoplastic diseases Montefiore Hosp., NYC, 1953-54; cancer rsch. scientist Roswell Park Meml. Inst., Buffalo, 1954-75; prof., chmn. dept. nuclear medicine SUNY, Buffalo, 1975-83; vis. prof. radiology Harvard Med. Sch., Boston, 1983-90. Mem. USP adv. panel on radiopharms.; chmn. med. adv. com. N.Y. State bur. Radiol. Health; chmn. med. isotopes adv. com. Los Alamos Nat. Lab. Mem. editorial bd. Jour. Nuclear Medicine. With USN, 1944-46. Mem. Soc. Nuclear Medicine (v.p. 1964, pres. 1972), Am. Chem. Soc., Am. Assn. Physicists in Medicine. Home: PO Box 605 South Wellfleet MA 02663-0605 Personal E-mail: mgblau@comcast.net.

BLAUFOX, ANDREW D., medical educator; b. Bronx, NY, Jan. 13, 1967; s. Donald M. Blaufox, and Paulette Blaufox; m. SauFung Yeung, June 12, 1994; children: Aaron Charles, Claire Breann. BA in Sociology, Bucknell U., Lewisburg, Pa, 1989; MD in Medicine, Albert Einstein Coll. Medicine, Bronx, NY, 1993. Diplomate Am. Bd. Pediat., 1996, in cardiology Am. Bd. Pediat., 2000, NY State, 2005. Asst. prof. pediat. Med. U. SC., Charleston, 2001—05, dir., pediatric pacing and device therapy, 2001—05, dir., non-invasive pediat. electrophysiology, 2001—05, dir., pediatric cardiology outpatient svcs., 2002—05; asst. prof. pediat. Albert Einstein Coll. Medicine, 2005—07, assoc. prof. clin. pediat., 2007—; dir., pediatric cardiac electrophysiology Cohens Children's Med. Ctr., New Hyde Park, NY, 2005—; pediatric cardiology fellowship rsch. supr. Schneider Children's Hosp., 2006—. Reviewer Jour. Cardiovasc. Electrophysiology, 2002—, Jour. Am. Coll. Cardiology, 2002—, 2002—, Circulation, 2004—, Am. Heart Jour., 2005—, Pacing and Clin. Electrophysiology, 2005. Founding bd. mem. East Cooper Montessori Charter Elem. Sch., Mount Pleasant, SC, 2002—05. Named, Best Doctors, 2003—08. Fellow: Am. Coll. Cardiology; mem.: Soc. Pediatric Rsch., Am. Heart Assn., Cardiology Young, NASPE, Heart Rhythm Soc., Pediatric and Congenital Electrophysiology Soc. Jewish. Office: Cohens Childrens med Ctr 269 01 76th Ave New Hyde Park NY 11040

BLAUFOX, MORTON DONALD, hypertension specialist, nuclear medicine physician, educator; b. NYC, July 19, 1934; s. Emanuel and Elizabeth (Rosenblum) B.; m. Paulette Goldberg, Dec. 20, 1958; children: Laurie Beth, Ellen Ruth, Andrew David. Degree, Harvard U., 1952-55; MD, SUNY, 1959; PhD, U. Minn., 1964. Diplomate Am. Bd. Internal Medicine, Am. Bd. Nuc. Medicine (bd. dirs. 1985-91). Intern Jewish Hosp. of Bklyn., NYC, 1959-60; fellow in medicine Mayo Found. Med. Edn. and Rsch., Rochester, Minn., 1960-64; advanced rsch. fellow Am. Heart Assn., 1964-66; rsch. fellow in medicine Harvard Med. Sch., Boston, 1964-66; asst. in medicine and radiology Peter Bent Brigham Hosp., Boston, 1964-66; asst. prof. radiology, also assoc. in medicine Albert Einstein Coll. Medicine, Bronx, NY, 1966-71, dir. sect. nuc. medicine, 1966-76, dir. unified dept., 1976-82, chmn. unified dept., 1982—, assoc. dir. clin. rsch. ctr., 1968-72, assoc. prof. radiology, 1971-76, prof. radiology, 1976—, assoc. prof. medicine, 1972-78, prof. medicine, 1978—; asst. attending physician Bronx Mcpl. Hosp. Ctr., 1966-71, assoc. attending, 1972, attending physician, 1972—; dir. divsn. nuc. medicine Montefiore Med. Ctr., 1976-82, chmn. dept. nuc. medicine, 1982—. Cons. kidney disease control program USPHS, 1967-72; mem. adminstrv. coun. nuc. medicine VA, 1972-73; mem. panel on radiopharms. U.S. Pharmacopeia, 1970-76; mem. hypertension adv. com. NYC Dept. Health, 1975-76; mem. Am. Bd. Nuc. Medicine, 1984-90; treas. exec. com., 1987-89, chmn., 1990; mem. clin. trials rev. com. Nat. Heart, Lung and Blood Inst., 1988-92, reviewer ready rsch., 1992—; mem. subcom. on non-pharmacologic therapy of Joint Nat. Com. on Detection Evaluation and Treatment of High Blood Pressure, 1991-92; mem. Brookhaven Linac Isotope Producer Users' adv. com. Brookhaven Nat. Lab., 1992-96; mem. internat. liaison com. World Fedn. Nuc. Medicine and Biology, 1992-94; active Coun. Cardiovasc. Radiology, hon. lifetime prof. medicine Shanxi U. Med. Sch., China, 1997; mem. adv. bd. Mobile Med. Mus., curator Mus. Hist. Med. Artifacts. Author: An Ear to the Chest: An Illustrated History of the Evaluation of the Stethoscope, 2002; co-author: Blood Pressure Measurement: An Illustrated History, 1998; editor (with others): Seminars in Nuclear Medicine, 1970—; editor: Evaluation of Renal Function and Disease with Radionuclides, 1972—, 2d edit., 1989—, Procs. Internat. Symposium, 1972—, 1975—, 1980—, 1987—, 1990—, PDR for Nuclear Medicine and Radiology, 1971—80, Unilateral Renal Function Studies, 1978; editor: (with others) Secondary Hypertension: Current Diagnosis and Management, 1981; editor: Non-Pharmacologic Therapy of Hypertension, 1987, Newer Diagnostic Methods in Nephrology and Urology, 1986; editl. bd.: Radionuclides in Nephrology, 1980, Jour. Nuclear Medicine, 1973—81, Nephron, Uroradiology, 1978—, Nuclear Medicine Comm., 1979—, Jour. Nuclear Medicine and Allied Sci., 1982, Renal Failure, 1985—89, Am. Jour. Hypertension, 1987—, Current Hypertension Reviews, 2004—; editl. bd. Current Med. Imaging Reviews, 2004, editor-in-chief, 2005; assoc. editor: Garnet's Pediatrics, 1972—, sect. editor for diagnostics and techniques: Current Opinions in Nephrology and Hypertension, 1992—96, contbr.: The Merck Manual, 14th, 15th and 16th edits., 1982—91, Merck Manual Medical Information Home Edit., 1997; contbr. articles to profl. jours. Recipient Edward Nobel Found. award, 1963, Albert Lasker pub. health svc. award, 1980, Lifetime Achievement award Internat. Soc. Radionuclides in Nephro Urology, 2001, Internat. Sci. Com. Radionuclides Nephrology (ISCORN), 1968-. Fellow ACP, Am. Nephrology Soc., Am. Coll. Nuc. Physicians, Coun. on High Blood Pressure Rsch., Coun. Cardiovasc. Radiology, Internat. Sci. Com. Radionuclides in Nephrourology, NY Acad. Medicine (libr. com. 1985—, chmn. sect. on nuc. medicine 1993-95, chmn. ad hoc com. artifact collection, chmn. history of medicine adv. com. 1995—); mem. AMA, Am. Heart Assn., Am. Physiol. Soc., Am. Fedn. Clin. Rsch., Am. Soc. Hypertension (membership com.), Soc. Nuc. Medicine (pres. Greater NY chpt. 1975-76, chmn. acad. coun. 1976-77, exec. and sci. coms., chmn. publ. com. 1979-82, trustee, Berson-Yalow award 1989), Ind. Soc. Nuc. Medicine, Internat. Soc. Nephrology, Internat. Hypertension Soc., Coun. on High Blood Pressure Rsch. (med. adv. bd.), NY Med. Soc., Am. Nephrology Soc., Med. Collectors Assn. (pres. 1983-2004), Swiss Soc. Nuc. Medicine (hon., corr.), Nat. Atomic Mus. (life), Sigma Xi. Achievements include research in hypertension, renal function and evaluation of renal function with radioisotopes, renal blood flow and renin secretion. Home: 101 Drake Smith Woods Ln Rye NY 10580-4316 Office: Montefiore Med Park 1695A Eastchester Rd Bronx NY 10461-2374 Office Phone: 718-405-8454. Business E-Mail: mdonald.blaufox@einstein.yu.edu.

BLAUVELT, BARBARA LOUISE, nutritionist; d. Starr Chester and Dorothy (Schofield) Blauvelt. BS, Brigham Young U., Provo, Utah, 1960; MS in Nutrition, Columbia U., 1964; PhD, U. Mass., 1969. Dietetic internship Yale New Haven Med. Ctr., 1961; nutrition program supr. divsn. pub. health nutrition Va. Dept. Health, Roanoke, 1970-95. Pvt. cons., 2002—. Author: Home Sweet Home, 2003; co-author: Kitchen Memories, 1998.

BLAZER, DAN GERMAN, II, psychiatrist, epidemiologist; b. Nashville, Feb. 23, 1944; s. Dan German and Mary Elizabeth (Owsley) Blazer; m. Sherrill Walls, Aug. 19, 1966; children: Dan German III, Natasha Leigh. BA, Vanderbilt U., 1965; MD, U. Tenn., 1969; MPH, U. N.C., 1979, PhD, 1980. Diplomate Am. Bd. Psychiatry and Neurology, cert. geriatric psychiatry. Fellow Montefiore Hosp. and Med. Ctr., NYC, 1975—76; asst. prof., assoc. prof., then prof. psychiatry Duke U. Med. Ctr., Durham, NC, 1976—, J.P. Gibbons prof. psychiatry, 1990—, interim chair of psychiatry, 1990—93, prof. cmty. and family medicine, 1986—; dean of med. edn. Duke U., 1992—99. Chair, bd. dirs. Am. Geriat. Soc., NY, 1983; bd. dirs. ret. persons svcs. Am. Assn. Ret. Persons, Alexandria, Va., 1987—92; pres. Psychiat. Rsch. Soc., Salt Lake City, 1988; chmn. epidemiology and disease control study sect. NIH, Bethesda, Md., 1988—. Author: Life is Worth Living, 1987, Depression in Late Life, 1993, Freud vs. God, 1998, Introduction to Clinical Research in Psychiatry, 1998, The Age of Melancholy, 2005. Recipient Rsch. Career Devel. award, NIMH, 1977, Alex Haley award, East Tenn. Bapt. Hosp., Knoxville, 1986, Disting. Svc. award, U. N.C. Sch. Pub. Health, Chapel Hill, 1989, Milo Leavitt award, Am. Geriat. Soc., 1997, Rema LaPouse award, APHA, 2001, Disting. Faculty award, Duke U. Med. Ctr., 2005; named Outstanding Alumnus, U. Tenn. Coll. Medicine, 2003. Fellow: Am. Assn. Geriatric Psychiatry (disting. life) (pres. 2005—06), Am. Psychopathol. Assn., Gerontol. Soc. Am. (Kleemeier award 2005), Am. Psychiat. Assn. (Oscar Pfister award 2008), Am. Coll. Psychiatrists (Geriatric Psychiatry Rsch. award 2003); mem.: Inst. Medicine NAS, 1995. Democrat. Avocations: hiking, reading. Office: Duke U Med Ctr PO Box 3003 Durham NC 27715-3003 Office Phone: 919-684-4128. Business E-Mail: blaze001@mc.duke.edu.

BLAZINA, JANICE FAY, pathologist; d. Joseph and Cordelia Evelyn B. BS, Youngstown State U., 1975; MD, Ohio State U., 1978. Diplomate Am. Bd. Pathology. Resident in anat. and clin. pathology U. Ala. Med. Ctr., Birmingham, 1978-82; assoc. pathologist various hosps., Bryan, Tex., 1982-83, High Plains Bapt. Hosp., Amarillo, Tex., 1983-84; fellow in blood banking Baylor U. Med. Ctr., Dallas, 1984-85; asst. prof. dept. pathology Ohio State U., Columbus, 1985-93, asst. prof. Sch. Allied Med. Professions, 1987-93. Asst. dir. transfusion svc. Ohio State U. Hosp., 1985-89, assoc. dir., 1989-90, dir., 1990-93, med. dir. histocompatibility, paternity, apheresis and phlebotomy svcs., 1987-93, divsn. med. tech., 1987-93; asst. med. dir. Carter Blood Ctr., Ft. Worth, 1993-95, med. dir., 1995-96. Contbr.

articles to profl. publs. Bremer Found. grantee, 1987. Mem. AMA, Am. Soc. Apheresis, Am. Soc. Histocompatibility and Immunogenetics, Am. Assn. Blood Banks (insp. 1987—), Ohio Assn. Blood Banks (trustee 1990-93, sec. 1992-93), Assn. Women Sci. Cen. Ohio (v.p. 1989-90, pres. 1990-91), Nat. Alliance Mentally Ill Tarrant County (sec. 2003-05, treas, 2006-07). Mem. Church of Christ. Avocation: gardening. Personal E-mail: bbpathd1@yahoo.com.

BLECHMAN, WILBUR JORDAN, medical educator; b. Washington, May 7, 1932; s. Charles and Florence (Goodman) B.; m. Sidell Ray Cohen, June 26, 1955 (dec. Mar. 1983); children: Michele, Michael, Ivy; m. Rachel Simonhoff Rudin, May 26, 1985. BS, Yale U., 1954; MD, Med. Coll. of Va., 1957. Diplomate Am. Bd. Internal Medicine and Rheumatology. Pvt. practice, North Miami Beach, Fla., 1961-94; clin. prof. of medicine U. Miami Sch. Medicine, 1980-95; dir. Resources for Children, Inc., Miami, 1994-95; state health officer Fla., 1995-96; courtesy prof. pub. health U. South Fla., 1996—2000; sr. cons. Fla. Dept. Health, Dept. Children and Families, 1996-98; program officer Lawton & Rhea Chiles Ctr. for Healthy Mothers & Babies, 1997-98, cons., 1998; adv. com. mem. Numerous Programs. Co-dir. Miami Arthritis Ctr., 1985-93; cons. Bertha Abess Children's Ctr., Miami, 1999-2007; co-chair child health and well-being task force Miami-Dade County Early Childhood Initiative, 1999-2001; sec. Youth Ethics Initiative, Inc., 2005-09; dir. Docs for Tots, Fla., 2007-10; cons. in field. Contbr. articles to profl. jours. Chmn. Fla. Kids Count Adv. Coun., 1992-94; mem. U.S. Kids Count Adv. Group, 1991-94; vice-chmn. Children's Trust, Miami-Dade County, 2003-09; v.p. Fla. Children's Forum, 2009-, vice chair, 2009-, bd. dirs. 1991-, Lawton Chiles Found., 2008—; sec. Youth Ethics Initiative, Inc., 2003—09, adv. bd. mem. Partnership America's Econ. Success, 2009-, Comm. Nemours Bright Start, 2009-. Recipient Disting. Svc. award The Arthritis Found., 1971, Physician's award for Outstanding Cmty. Svc. Fla. Med. Assn., Wyeth-Ayerst Labs., 1990, Hannah G. Solomon award Nat. Coun. Jewish Women, 1992, State Health Office Cmty. Friend award, 1993, Help and Hope award for Excellence in Rheumatology Arthritis Found. S.E. Fla., 1994, Recognition letter Sec. U.S. Dept. Health and Human Svcs., 1995, 5th Annual Lawton Chiles Advocacy award Fla. Chpt. March Dimes, 2005, Nancy D. Thomas Collaboration award, 2008; named 1993 Champion for Children Miami-Dade C.C., Friend of Coop. Extension, 1993. Mem. ACP, Am. Coll. Rheumatology, Fla. Soc. of Rheumatology (pres. 1970-71), Internat. Coun. for Control of Iodine Deficiency Disorders (bd. dirs. 1994-96), Kiwanis (pres. Internat. 1990-91, Citizen of Yr. Biscayne club 1992), Fla. Assn. Infant Mental Health (charter pres. 2001-03, pres. 2006-07). Home and Office: 5250 SW 84th St Miami FL 33143-8434 Personal E-mail: wilblechman@aol.com.

BLECHNER, MARK JACOB, psychologist, educator; b. NYC, Nov. 6, 1950; BA, U. Chgo., 1972; MS, Yale U., 1975, PhD, 1977; cert. in psychoanalysis, William Alanson White Inst., 1983. Trainee in clin. psychology NIMH, 1973-76; rsch. assoc. Haskins Lab., New Haven, 1974-77; pvt. practice clin. psychology, NYC, 1977—. Asst. clin. prof. psychology dept. psychiatry Columbia Coll. Physicians and Surgeons, 1981-94; dir., HIV-Clini. Svcs., tng. analyst, supr., William Alanson White Inst., 1984—, Manhattan Inst. for Psychoanalysis, 1985-90; asst. clin. prof. psychology postdoctoral program in psychoanalysis NYU, 1995—. Author: The Dream Frontier, Sex Changes; editor Hope and Mortality; editor-in-chief: Contemporary Psychoanalysis, 2007—; contbr. articles to profl. jours. Mem. AAAS, N.Y. Acad. Scis., Sigma Xi. Address: 145 Central Park W New York NY 10023-2004 Office Phone: 212-595-4648. E-mail: mark@markblechner.com.

BLECK, PHYLLIS CLAIRE, surgeon; b. Oak Park, Ill., Mar. 10, 1936; d. William Fred and Mildred A. (Jones) B. BS, U. Ill., 1958; MM, Northwestern U., 1968; DMA, U. So. Calif., 1970; postgrad., Autonoma U., Guadalajara, Mex., 1973-76; MD, Rush Med. Coll., 1979; MS in Surgery, U. Ill., 1983. Diplomate Am. Bd. Surgery, Am. Bd. Thoracic Surgery. Prin. trumpet Fla. Symphony Orch., 1960—66, Orch. Sinfonica Nat. de Peru, 1965; instr. Thornton Jr. Coll., 1966—68; lectr. U. So. Calif., 1969—73; asst. prof. Whittier Coll., 1971—73; intern Rush Presbyn. St. Luke's Med. Ctr., Chgo., 1979—80, resident, asst. in gen. surgery, 1980—82, instr. gen. surgery, 1982—84; resident in cardiothoracic surgery U. Medicine and Dentistry N.J., 1984—87; pvt. practice medicine specializing cardiothoracic surgery Aurora, Ill., 1987—; asst. prof. Rush U., 1996—. Editor: Mozart Divertimento for Winds; rsch. on vascular ischemia. Fellow ACS, Am. Coll. Chest Physicians, Ill. Thoracic Surg. Soc., Ill. Surg. Soc.; mem. AAAS, Soc. Thoracic Surgeons, Internat. Coll. Surgeons (pres. U.S. sect. 2004-2005, mem. internat. exec. coun. 2004-2008), Chgo. Surg. Soc., Kappa Delta Pi, Pi Kappa Lambda, Sigma Alpha Iota. Personal E-mail: p.bleck2@att.net.

BLECKER, DAVID L., nephrologist; MD, Tufts U. Diplomate Am. Bd. of Internal Medicine-nephrology. Resident Hahnemann Sch. of Medicine/ Med. Coll. of Pa.; fellow divsn. of nephrology and hypertension Hahnemann Med. Ctr.; hosp. affiliations include AtlantiCare Regional Med. Ctr. Mainland Campus, Kessler Meml. Hosp. Named Top Dr., Phila. Mag., 2006, 2008, 2009, 2010. Office: AtlantiCare Regional Medical Center - City Campus 1925 Pacific Ave Atlantic City NJ 08401 Office Phone: 609-345-4000.

BLEDAY, RONALD, colon and rectal surgeon, educator; MD, McGill U., 1977. Lic. Mass., 1984, diplomate Am. Bd. Surgery, 1990, Am. Bd. Colon and Rectal Surgery, 1993. Resident in surgery Brown Univ., 1984; fellow in surgical oncology Brigham and Women's Hosp., 1986, Dana-Farber Cancer Inst., 1986, Harvard Univ., 1986; resident in surgery and trauma Brown Univ.-RI Hosp., 1989; rsch. fellow in surgical oncology New England Deaconess Hosp., 1989; fellow in surgical endoscopy Mass. Gen. Hosp., 1990; fellow in colon and rectal surgery Univ. Minn., 1991; assoc. prof. med. sch. Harvard Univ.; hosp. affiliations include Brigham and Women's/Mass Gen. Health Care Ctr., Foxborough, Brigham and Women's Hosp., Mass.; sect. chief colorectal surgery divsn. Co-author: (articles) Risk factors for perineal wound complications following abdominoperineal resection, 2005, Local excision of distal rectal cancer: an update of cancer and leukemia group B 8984, 2008, Does gum chewing ameliorate postoperative ileus? Results of a prospective, randomized, placebo-controlled trial, 2006, Rectal carcinoid tumors: review of results after endoscopic and surgical therapy, 2008, The Better Colectomy Project: Association of Evidence-Based Best-Practice Adherence Rates to Outcomes in Colorectal Surgery, 2009, various others. Named one of Top Doctors, Boston Mag., 2009. Fellow: ACS; mem.: Soc. Surgical Oncology, New England Surgical Soc., Am. Soc. Colon and Rectal Surgeons. Office: Brigham and Womens Hospital 75 Francis St Boston MA 02115 Office Phone: 617-732-8460. Office Fax: 617-734-0336.

BLEIBERG, LEON WILLIAM, surgeon, podiatrist; b. Bklyn., June 9, 1932; s. Paul Pincus and Helen (Epstein) B.; m. Beth Daigle, June 7, 1970; children: Kristina Noel, Kelley Lynn, Kimberly Ann, Paul Joseph. Student, L.A. City Coll., 1950-51, U. So. Calif., 1951, Case Western Res. U., 1951-53; DSc with honors, Temple U., 1955; D in Podiatric Medicine, Pa. Sch. Podiatric Medicine, 1965; PhD, U. Beverly Hills, 1970. Intern various hosps., Phila., 1954—55; resident Bella Vista Hosp., Montebello, Calif., 1956—58; surg. podiatrist So. Calif. Podiatry Group, Westchester, Calif., 1956—75; health care economist, rschr. Drs. Home Health Care Svcs., 1976—; chmn. bd. Unltd. Healthcare, Metro Manila, Philippines; v.p. pub. rels. Bilbao Wellness Found., Upland, Calif.; CEO Med. Trianon, Newbury Park, Calif.; dir. biomechanics dept. Anti-Aging and Rejuvenation Clinic, Torrance, Calif.; CFO mktg. and devel. Immigration Ctr. for Law and Justice. Podiatric cons. U. So. Calif. Athletic Dept., Morningside and Inglewood (Calif.) High Schs., Royal Naval Assn., Long Beach (Calif.) Naval Sta.; exec. cons. Thomas Med. Group, Pomona, Calif., 1995, Cardiotel, Van Nuys, Calif., 1995; lectr. in field; healthcare affiliate Internat. divsn. CARE/ASIA, 1987; pres. Medica, Totalcare, Cine-Medics Corp., Strategic World-Wide Health Care Svcs.; exec. dir. Internat. Health Trust; developer Health Banking Program; adminstr. Orthotic Concepts, 1993; prof. health care econs. and med. rehab. Global U., Ontario, Calif., chmn. dept. health care econs., chmn. dept. biomechanics and phys. rehab.; CEO Integrated Wellness Ctrs., The Med. Trianon Found.; exec. dir. Med. Trianon; exec. dir. wellness divsn. Crown Golden Eagles; mem. nat. leadership Temple U., Phila.; CEO Global Health Share 2000. Prodr. (films) The Gun Hawk, 1963, Terrified, Day of the Nightmare; contbr. articles to profl. jours. Hon. Sheriff Westchester 1962-64; commd. mem. Rep. Senatorial Inner Circle, 1984-86; lt. comdr. med. svcs. corps Brit.-Am. Sea Cadet Corps, 1984—; co-chmn. health reform com. United We Stand Am., Thousand Oaks, Calif., exec. coun. State of Calif.; active 1st Security and Safety, Westlake Village, Calif., 1993—; track coach Westlake HS, Westlake Village; exec. sec. Nat. Coalition Parents Anti-Drug/Violence Corp., Inc. LA World Affairs Coun.; active Agoura C. of C., Oak Park C. of C., Las Virgenes C. of C.; ops. dir. healthcare dept. H. Martin Found.; county inspector U.S. Election Com., Calif.; bd. dirs. Power Search Unltd. Ministries, Philippines and U.S.; U.S. coord. Luntiang Pilipinas (Philippine Ecology Program); chmn., bd. dirs. Philippine Vets. Found.; ops. dir. healthcare dept. H. Martin Found. With USN, 1955-56 Recipient Medal of Merit, U.S. Presdl. Task Force, Grand award Top Personalities mag., 1999, Lifetime Achievement award Remington Registry, 2011. Mem. Filipino Vets. Found. (chmn., bd. dirs.), Philippine Pvt. Hosp. Assn. (Cert. of Appreciation 1979, Outstanding Svc. trophy 1979), Calif. Podiatric Med. Assn. (hon.), Am. Podiatric Med. Assn. (hon.), Acad. TV Arts and Scis., Royal Soc. Health (Eng.), We. Foot Surgery Assn., Am. Coll. Foot Surgeons, Am. Coll. Podiatric Sports Medicine, Internat. Coll. Preventive Medicine, Hollywood Comedy Club, Sts. and Sinners Club, Westchester C. of C. (hon. sheriff), Hals Und Beinbruch Ski Club, Beach Cities Ski Club, Orange County Stamp Club(coach), Las Virgenes Track Club, Am. Legion, Masons, Shriners, Scottish Rite. Home and Office: 55 N Wendy Dr Newbury Park CA 91320-4351 Office Phone: 805-499-6900. Personal E-mail: healthshare@verizon.net. Business E-Mail: healthshaw@ving.net.

BLEICH, MICHAEL ROBERT, dean, nursing educator; b. Columbus, Wis., Mar. 8, 1952; s. David Arthur and Lorraine Mary (Hanson) B.; children: Kirsten, Kara, Kaitlin. Diploma, St. Luke's Hosp. Sch. Nursing, Racine, Wis., 1976; BSN, Milton Coll., Wis., 1979; MPH, U. Minn., 1987; PhD, U. Nebr., 1998. RN, Wis., Nebr.; cert. advanced nursing adminstr. V.p. patient svcs. St. Mary's Med. Ctr., Racine, 1979-88; assoc. prof. Mt. Senario Coll., Ladysmith, Wis., 1982-90; cons. on nursing and healthcare Quality Healthcare Resources, Inc., Chgo., 1989-94; v.p. patient care svcs. Bryan Meml. Hosp., Lincoln, Nebr., 1990-96; cons. healthcare systems and leadership pvt. practice, Lincoln, 1996-98; internal cons. clin. sys. and performance improvement Health Midwest Johnson County, Overland Pakr, Kans., 1998-99; assoc. dean clin. and cmty. affairs, assoc. prof. U. Kans. Med. Ctr., Kansas City, 1999—2008; exec. dir., COO KU Health Ptnrs., Inc.; chmn., dept. health policy and mgmt. U. Kans. Sch. Medicine, 2006—08; dean and Carol A. Lindeman disting. prof Oreg. Health & Sci. Sch. Nursing, Portland, 2008—. Cons. healthcare systems and leadership, 1996—. Editor: (with M. Bratton) Information Management and Computers, 1990; contbg. author: Documenting Care, 1991, Encyclopedia of Nursing Quality Assurance, 1991, Commitment to Excellence: Developing a Professional Nursing Staff, 1987; contbg. author: Leading and Managing, 1995, Quality Management in Nursing and Health Care, 1996; mem. editl. bd. Jour. Nursing Care Quality, Jour. Nursing Edn., 2000—; contbr. articles to profl. jours. Named Nebr. Nurse of Yr., Nebr. Nurses Assn., 1993; W.K. Kellogg fellow;; Robert Wood Johnson nurse exec. fellow; recipient Johnson & Johnson-Wharton Fellowship for Nurse Execs., 1997. Mem. ANA, Am. Orgn. Nurse Execs., Sigma Theta Tau. Office: Oreg Health & Sci Univ Sch Nursing 3455 SW US Veterans Hospital Rd SN ADM Portland OR 97239-2941 Office Phone: 503-494-7444. Business E-Mail: bleichm@ohsu.edu.

BLEIWEISS, IRA JAY, pathologist, educator; b. Bklyn., Apr. 24, 1958; MD, St. George's U. Sch. Medicine, 1984. Prof., dir. surg. pathology Mt. Sinai Med. Ctr., 2002, prof., dir. anatomic pathology, 2011—. Office: Mount Sinai Med Ctr Pathology Dept New York NY 10029 Business E-Mail: i.bleiweiss@mountsinai.org.

BLENDON, ROBERT JAY, health policy educator; b. Dec. 19, 1942; s. Edward and Theresa Blendon; m. Marie C. McCormick, Dec. 31, 1977. BA, Marietta Coll., Ohio, 1964; MBA, U. Chgo., 1966; MPH, Johns Hopkins U., 1967, DSc, 1969. Fellow Ind. U. Med. Ctr., Indpls., 1965—66; instr. dept. med. care and hosps. Johns Hopkins U. Sch. Hygiene and Pub. Health, Balt., 1969—70, asst. to assoc. dean for health care programs Sch. Medicine, 1969—70, asst. prof. dept. med. care and hosps., 1970—71; asst. dir. planning and devel. Office of Health Care Programs, Johns Hopkins Med. Instns., Balt., 1970—71; spl. asst. for health affairs to dep. undersec. for policy coordination HEW, Washington, 1971—72, spl. asst. for policy devel. to asst. sec. to health and sci. affairs, 1971—72; sr. v.p. Robert Wood Johnson Found., Princeton, NJ, 1987; prof. health policy and polit. analysis, Kennedy Sch. of Govt. Harvard U. Sch. Pub. Health, Boston, 1987—, dep. dir. health policy, sr. assoc. dean, policy translation & leadership devel., 2010—. Vis. lectr. Princeton U., 1972—87; sr. policy analyst com. on health svcs. industry Cost of Living Coun., Washington, 1971. Mem. editl. bd.: Jour. of Am. Med. Assn., 1992—. Mem.: Inst. Medicine NAS, Council Fgn. Rels. Home: 478 Quinobequin Rd Newton MA 02468-2127 Office: Harvard U Sch Pub Health 677 Huntington Ave Boston MA 02115-6028 Office Phone: 617-432-4502. Business E-Mail: rblendon@hsph.harvard.edu.

BLENK, HOLGER, microbiologist, director; b. Hamburg, Germany, Oct. 23, 1942; s. Eberhard Wilhelm (E.) and Irma Maria Blenk; m. Birgit Johanna C. Blenk, June 6, 1975. Lt., Sch. ABC-Def., Sonthofen, Bavaria, 1964; MD, U. Hamburg, 1969; assoc. prof., U. Oradea, Romania, 2003. Cons. lab. medicine and microbiology U. German Army, Hamburg, 1970—75; head hygiene lab. German Army, Hamburg, 1976—82, head hygiene Ctrl. Inst. Koblenz, 1982—86, head pvt. lab. Nuernberg, 1986—2000; head microbiology lab. Euromed. Clinic, Fuerth, Germany, 2001—06, med. dir., 2006—. Lectr. infectiology Urology Clinic Ludwig-Maximillan U., Munich, 1988—2008; chmn. Synlab Acad. Further Med. Edn., 2005—08; prof. med. microbiology U. Oradea, Romania, 2003—. Editor: (book) Microbiology in Urology, 1998, Sexually Transmitted Diseases, 1987; contbr. articles to books. Col. M.D. German Med. Svcs., 1970—86. Mem.: German Assn. Med. Microbiologists (chmn. 1998—2004). Lutheran. Avocations: classical music, art, hunting, shooting, golf. Office: EuromedClinic Europa-Allee 1 Fuerth 90763 Germany Office Phone: 49 911 9714435. Business E-Mail: hblenk@labor-blenk.de.

BLEOTU, CORALIA GH, biologist; b. Dragasani, Nov. 3, 1972; PhD, Romanian Acad., 2008. Sr. rschr. Stefan S Nicolau Inst. Virology, Romanian Acad., 1998—, Faculty Biology, U. Bucharest, 2009. Recipient Outstanding Abstract award, 2nd World Congress, 2008. Mem.: Cytometry Assn. Romania, Romanian Soc. Immunology, Romanian Soc. Biochemistry & Molecular Biology, European Soc. Clin. Microbiology & Infectious Diseases. Office: 285 Mihai Bravu Ave Bucharest 030304 Romania Office Fax: 40213242590. Personal E-mail: cbleotu@yahoo.com.

BLESSING-MOORE, JOANN CATHERINE, allergist, pulmonologist; b. Tacoma, Sept. 21, 1946; d. Harold R. and Mildred (Benson) Blessing; m. Robert Chester Moore; 1 child, Ahna. BA in Chemistry, Syracuse U., 1968; MD, SUNY, Syracuse, 1972. Diplomate Am. Bd. Pediatrics, Am. Bd. Allergy Immunology, Am. Bd. Pediatric Pulmonology. Pediatric intern, then resident Stanford U. Sch. Medicine, Palo Alto, Calif., 1972-75, allergy pulmonology fellow, 1975-77; co-dir. pediatric allergy pulmonology dept. Stanford U. Children's Hosp., Palo Alto, Calif., 1977-84; clin. asst. prof. dept. Allergy Immunology Respiratory Disease (AIR) Stanford U. Sch. Medicine, Palo Alto, Calif., 1977-84, co-dir. pediatric pulmonology lab., 1977-84; clin. asst. prof. dept. immunology Stanford U. Hosp., 1984—; allergist Palo Alto Med. Clinic, 1984-90; pvt. practice allergy immunology-pediatric-pulmonary Palo Alto, San Mateo, Calif., 1990—. Dir. ednl. program for children with asthma Camp Wheeze, Palo Alto, 1975-90; cons. FDA, Allergy Pulmonary Adv. Bd., 1992-97; cons. in field. Author handbooks, camp program manuals; co-editor jour. supplements; mem. edit. bd. Allergy jours.; contbr. articles to sci. publs. Fellow Am. Acad. Allery, Asthma, Immunology (various offices 1980—, Joint Task Force Parameters of Care Asthma and Allergy, editl. bd. mem. 1989—, Outstanding fellow 1998, Women in Allergy award 2000), Am. Coll. Chest Physicians (com. mem. 1980—), Am. Coll. Asthma, Allergy and Immunology (mem. regent com. 1995-98); mem. Am. Thoracic Soc., Am. Lung Assn., No. Calif. Allergy Found. (bd. dirs., pres.), Peninsula Women's Assn., Santa Clara and San Mateo County Med. Soc. (bd. dirs. 1999-2004), Chi Omega. Republican. Presbyterian. Avocations: music, sailing, skiing, horseback riding, scuba diving. Office: 780 Welch Rd Ste 204 Palo Alto CA 94304-1518 also: Stanford Univ Hosp Dept Immunology Palo Alto CA 94304 Office Phone: 650-696-8236.

BLEVINS, MARYELLEN I., physician assistant; b. New Brunswick, NJ, Oct. 21, 1963; d. Joseph Saverio and Naomi Yolanda (Alvarado) Iacovacci; m. Olaf Rune Fredriksen, May 13, 1990 (div. 1996); m. Randall Dean Blevins, Nov. 5, 2003. BA in Chemistry, Boston U., 1986; BS in Health Science, CUNY/Columbia U., 1996; M Physican Asst. Studies, U. Nebr., 1999. Reg. physician assistant, N.Y.; cert. in basic life support, advanced cardiac life support, neonatal advanced life support, pediatric advanced life support, advanced trauma life support; cert. HIV/AIDS counselor. Biochem. rsch. tech. Boston U., 1984-86; biochem. rsch. tech. Sch. Medicine Harvard U., Boston, 1986-87; rsch. tech. Cold Spring Harbor (N.Y.) Lab., 1987-90, buyer, 1990-94; physician asst., house staff officer dept. surgery and medicine Samaritan Med. Ctr., Watertown, N.Y., 1997-2000, mem. staff emergency dept., 2000—10; orthop. 1st asst. Carthage Area Hosp., 2009—. House staff officer Benedictine Hosp., Kingston, N.Y., 2000-01; mem. staff emer. dept. EJ Noble Hosp., Alexandria Bay, N.Y., 2001-05, River Hosp. With Students Teaching AIDS to Students, 1995-96; vol. physician asst. student N.Y.C. Marathon, 1995, 96; participant Teddy Bear Clin., 1997; organizer Hurricane Georges Relief for St. Kitts, 1998, Women's Jour. Club, 1999—. N.Y. State Soc. Physician Assts. scholar, 1996. Fellow Am. Acad. Physician Assts. (treas. Student Soc. Student Acad. 1994-96); mem. N.Y. State Soc. Physician Assts. (cert., student treas. local chpt. 1994-96, rep. Project Access program 1995-96). Democrat. Avocations: archery, skiing, travel, reading. Home: 719 Washington St Watertown NY 13601-3902 Office: Tri Country Orthop 3 Bridge St Carthage NY 13619

BLEVINS, NIKOLAS, surgeon, educator; b. LA, Feb. 5, 1962; BS, Stanford U., 1984; MD, Harvard U., 1988. Assoc. prof. Stanford U., 2003—. Office: 801 Welch Ave Stanford CA 94305 Office Fax: 650-725-8502. Business E-Mail: nblevins@stanford.edu.

BLIM, RICHARD DON, retired pediatrician, health facility administrator; b. Kansas City, Mo., Nov. 8, 1927; s. Miles G. and Latha Mae (Daniels) Blim; m. Myrle Rae Blim, Apr. 12, 1952; children: Richard David, Carol Rae, John Miles. BA, U. Kans., 1949, MD, 1953. Diplomate Am. Bd. Pediat. Intern U. Kans., 1953—54, resident in pediat., 1954—56; practice medicine specializing in pediat.; pres. Pediatric Assocs., Kansas City, Mo., 1956—89; dir. med. affairs St. Lukes Hosp., Kansas City, 1989—99. Peter T. Bohan lectr. U. Kans., Kansas City, 1978; Max Seham lectr. U. Minn., Mpls., 1982; mem. editl. bd. Mo. Medicine, 1978—92, Pediatric Annals, 1982—92, Pediatric News, 1983—92. Bd. dirs. Cmty. Blood Ctr., Crittenton Children's Hosp.; mem. advancement bd. Kans. U. Med. Ctr. Served to sgt. US Army, 1946—48, PTO. Recipient Clifford G. Grulee award,

1984, Katherine Berry Richard MD award, Children Mercy Hosp., 1997; named Outstanding Med. Alumnus, U. Kans. Sch. Medicine, 1978. Fellow: Am. Acad. Pediat. (chmn. Mo. chpt. 1964—67, exec. bd. 1973—80, pres. 1980—81); mem.: AMA, Coun. Med. Spltys. Soc. (rep., exec. bd. 1974—80), Met. Med. Soc. (merit award 1996), Mo. Med. Assn., S.W. Pediatric Assn. (pres. Kansas City 1963), Jackson County Med. Soc. (pres. 1973), Inst. Medicine NAS, Kans. U. Med. Alumni (pres. 1973), Alpha Omega Alpha. Presbyterian. Home: 13820 Metcalf Ave #11120 Overland Park KS 66223 Home Phone: 913-851-0622. Personal E-mail: rdonblimmd@earthlink.net, rdonblimmd@gmail.com.

BLISSITT, PATRICIA ANN, neuroscience critical care nurse; b. Knoxville, Tenn., Sept. 23, 1953; d. Dewitt Talmadge and Imogene (Bailey) Blissitt. BSN with high honors, U. Tenn., 1976, MSN, 1985; PhD in Nursing, U. Wash., 2002; postgrad., U. Pa., 2003—05; postgrad. in Nursing Edn., Duke U., 2008. RN, cert. case mgmt., trauma nurse course, ACLS, in neurosci. nursing, CNRN, in critical care nursing, critical care clin. nurse specialist, RN advanced practice, adult health clin. nurse specialist. Staff nurse neurosci. unit City Memphis Hosp., 1976-78, head nurse neurosci. unit, 1978-79; physician's asst. Dr. John D. Wilson, Columbus, Miss., 1979-81; staff nurse med.-surg.-trauma ICU U. Tenn. Meml. Hosp., Knoxville, 1982-83; staff nurse neurosci. ICU Bapt. Meml. Hosp., Memphis, 1985-86, clin. nurse specialist neurosci., 1986-94, trauma coord., 1991-93, neuro case mgr., 1993-94; staff nurse neurosurg. ICU Harborview Med. Ctr., Seattle, 1994—2000, 2001—02, neurosci. clin. nurse specialist, 2007—; NIH postdoctoral fellow neuro critical care U. Pa., Phila., 2003—05; neurotrauma staff nurse surg. ICU Hosp. U. Pa., 2003—05; staff nurse neurosci. ICU Duke U. Med. Ctr., Durham, NC, 2005—07; neurosci. clin. specialist Harborview Med. Ctr., 2007—; asst. prof. U. Washington Sch. Nursing, Seattle, clin. faculty, 2007—; TNCC instr., 2009—. Nurse cons. neurosci. VA Hosp., Memphis, 1986—2011; mem. adv. com. Tenn. Bd. Nursing Practice; mem. test devel. com. Am. Bd. Neurosci. Nursing, 1996—2001, trustee, 2000—03, treas., 2002—03, chair test devel. com., 2003—06; editl. bd. AANN Clin. Practice Guidelines, 2007; lectr. in field; reviewer Am. J. of Critical Care, 2009—, Heart & Lung, 2009, AACN Am. Burnol Critical Care, 2009—, AACN Item Writer CCNS Exam, 2011; assoc. editor to editor Am. Assn. Neurosci. Nurses Clin. Practice Guidelines, 2011—. Author: AACN Advanced Critical Care, 2006, Anesthesia and Analgesia, 2007, AACN Advanced Critical Care Nursing, 2008; author: (with others) Critical Care Nursing in Clinics in North America, 1990, 2006, Guidelines for Critical Care Nursing, Care Management, 2001; mem. editl. bd. Focus on Critical Care, 1990—92, abstractor Nursing SCAN in Critical Care, 1995—99; author, reviewer, editor with others: Core Curriculum for Neuroscience Nursing, 5th edit., 2010; contbr. chapters to books, articles to profl. jours. Mem. rev. com. Neurosci. Nursing Found./AANN Scholarship com., 2001. Named CNRN of Yr. 2008; grantee, NIH/NINR/U. Wash., 1999—2002; scholar, Wash. State Nurses Found., 1990, Am. Assn. Neurosci. Nurses, 1999, AANN Scholar Com., 2001. Mem.: ANA (mem. coun. med.-surg. nurses), AACN (life; pres.-elect Greater Memphis area chpt. 1989—90, CCRN corp. exam. devel. com. 1989—92, pres. 1990—91, editl. cons. bd. 1990—92, chair program com. 1996—97, program com. 1997—2003, newsletter editor Puget Sound chpt. 1998—99, pres. 2002—03, chpt. edn. com. 2003—05, publs. chair, newsletter editor 2003—05, AACN Procedure Manual for Critical Care, 5th edit. 2005, cert. med.-surg. clin. nurse specialist), Am. Assn. Neurosci. Nurses Northwest Chpt. (edn. chair 2008—, pres. 2009—), AACN Mountain to Sound Chpt. (membership chair 2007—09, lifetime chpt. mem. 2008—, scholarship chair 2009—), Wash. State Nurse Assn., Soc. Critical Care Medicine, Neurocritical Care Soc. (charter), Tenn. Nursing Congress (pres. 1990—94), Western Inst. Nursing, Tenn. Nurses Assn. (com. practice 1992—93), NC Nurses Assn., Am. Assn. Neurosci. Nurses (pres. local chpt. 1989—90, chair nat. resource devel. com. 1992—94, pres. Memphis chpt. 1995—98, editor newsletter 1998—2000, 2001—02, chair test devel. com. 2003—07, pres.-elect Triangle chpt., edn. chair 2005—07, pres. Triangle chpt. 2006—07, chmn. resource devel. com., nurse practice com.), Am. Assn. Neurol. Surgeons (assoc.), Sigma Theta Tau. Methodist. Avocation: music. Home: 809 Olive Way Apt 809 Seattle WA 98101 Business E-Mail: pbliss@u.washington.edu.

BLITSHTEYN, SVETLANA, neurologist, researcher; b. Moldova, Mar. 25, 1976; MD, SUNY at Buffalo Sch. Medicine, 2002; degree in Neurology, Mayo Clinic, 2007. Neurology resident Mayo Clinic, 2003—07; CEO, neurologist Amherst Neurology, 2009—. Clin. asst. prof. neurology SUNY at Buffalo Sch. Medicine and Biomed. Scis., 2008—; cons. neurologist Brain and Spine Ctr., 2009—10. Recipient First Pl. Rsch. award, Fla. Soc. Neurology; grant, Mayo Clinic. Mem.: Am. Headache Soc. (US Human Health award), Am. Autonomic Soc., Am. Acad. Neurology. Office: 835 Hopkins Rd Williamsville NY 14221 Office Fax: 716-478-6917.

BLITZER, ANDREW, otolaryngologist, educator, research scientist, writer; b. Apr. 25, 1946; s. Martin Hollander and Lyrene Iris (Lave) Blitzer; children: Peter Morgen, Polly Volk. BA, Adelphi U., 1967; DDS, Columbia U. Sch. of Dental and Oral Surgery, 1970; MD, Mt. Sinai Sch. Medicine, 1973. Diplomate Am. Bd. Otolaryngology. Resident in gen. surgery Beth Israel Hosp., NYC, 1973—74; resident in otolaryngology Mt. Sinai Hosp., NYC, 1974—77; asst. prof. otolaryngology Coll. Phys. & Surg. Columbia U., NYC, 1977—82, assoc. prof. otolaryngology and oral surgery, 1982—84, prof. clin. otolaryngology and oral surgery, 1984—, prof. clin. otolaryngology in neurology, 1993—95; prof. clin. otolaryngology Coll. Physicians and Surgeons, Columbia U., acting chmn. dept. otolaryngology NYC, 1991—94; vice chmn. dept. otolaryngology Columbia U., NYC, 1983—91; dir. divsn. head and neck surgery Columbia-Presbyn. Med. Ctr., NYC, 1980—94, dir. multidiscipline head and neck tumor bd., dir. residency edn., 1978—94; acting dir. Otolaryngology Svc. Presbyterian Hosp.; lectr. dept. otolaryngology Mt. Sinai Sch. Medicine, NYC, 1977—; sr. attending otolaryngologist and dir. NY Ctr. for Voice and Swallowing Disorders St. Luke's/Roosevelt Med. Ctr., 1994—. Dir. NY Ctr. for Clin. Rsch.; cons., mem. spl. senses and lang. study sect. NIH. Co-author several books, author several textbooks; mem. editl. bd.: Otolaryngology-Head and Neck Surgery, The Laryngoscope, Jour. Otolaryngology, Jour. Rhinology; contbr. chapters to books, articles to profl. jours. Recipient award for excellence, Am. Assn. Orthodontists, 1970, Tchr.-Investigator award, Nat. Inst. Neurol. Communicative Disorders and Strokes, 1978—83, Maxwell Abramson Meml. award, Excellence in Resident Teaching, 1993. Fellow: ACS, Am. Broncho-esophagological Assn. (pres. 2009, Chevalier Jackson award 2006), Am. Acad. Otolaryngology-Head and Neck Surgery (bd. dirs. 2002—, Disting. Svc. award 1996, Honor award), Am. Laryngol., Rhinol., and Otol. Soc., Am. Laryngol. Assn. (James A. Newcomb award 1998, de Roaldes award 2009), Am. Acad. Facial Plastic and Reconstructive Surgery, Am. Soc. Head and Neck Surgery, NY Acad. Medicine. Achievements include being a pioneer and leading authority in the use of Botox for conditions with excessive muscle function, muscle pain, tremor & muscle spasm, including spasmodic dysphonia and facial lines & wrinkles; a pioneer in the field of neurolaryngology and has one of the ten fellowship programs in the country; developed new surgical techniques for the rehabilitation the paralyzed vocal cord; world leader in the management of voice and swallowing disorders, nasal and sinus surgery, laser surgery, management of facial lines and wrinkles and head and neck surgery. Avocations: running, skiing, photography, fly fishing. Office: 425 W 59th St 10th Fl New York NY 10019-1104 Office Phone: 212-262-9500. Office Fax: 212-523-6364.

BLITZER, MIRIAM G., medical geneticist, educator, medical association administrator; BA in Chemistry, U. Calif., Irvine; PhD in Human Genetics, U. Pitts. Cert. in clin. biomed. genetics and PhD med. genetics American Bd. Med. Genetics, 1984. Postdoctoral fellow in clin. biochem. genetics and med. genetics Tulane U. Sch. Medicine, New Orleans, asst. prof.; faculty mem. U. Md. Sch. Medicine, 1986—, prof., head divsn. human genetics, dept. pediat., co-dir. biochem. genetics lab., dir. maternal serum prenatal screening lab., faculty appointments in the departments of ob-gyn. & reproductive medicine and biochemistry & molecular biology. Mem.: Assn. Professors Human and Med. Genetics (pres. 2011—), American Bd. Genetic Consulting, American Bd. Med. Specialties (bd. dirs. 2011—), American Soc. Human Genetics (bd. dirs. 2006—09), American Bd. Med. Genetics (bd. dirs. 1996—2001, exec. dir. 2009—), American Coll. Med. Genetics, American Soc. Med. Genetics, Nat. Coalition Health Profl. Edn. in Genetics (bd. dirs. 2002—06). Office: University Md Sch Medicine BRB 11-037 655 W Baltimore St Baltimore MD 21201 also: American Bd Med Genetics 9650 Rockville Pike Bethesda MD 20814 Office Phone: 410-706-4065. Office Fax: 410-706-6105. Business E-Mail: mblitzer@peds.umaryland.edu, mblitzer@abmg.org. *

BLIZIOTIS, IOANNIS, physician; b. Athens, Attiki, Greece, May 22, 1975; s. Aristeidis Ioannis Bliziotis and Eleni Ioannis Hatzoglou; m. Antonia Kontadaki, Sept. 29, 2007; 1 child, Aristeidis Ioannis. MD, Charles U., 2nd Med. Faculty, Prague, Czech Republic, 1999; attending, U. London & London Sch. Hygiene & Tropical Medicine, 2006—; PhD student in Infectious Diseases, U. Crete, Sch. Medicine, Heraklion, Greece, 2006—. Lic. Panhellenic Med. Assn., 2000. Primary care physician Nat. Med. Svc., Akrata Health Ctr., Akrata, 2002—03; internal medicine resident,3rd Dept. Medicine, U. Athens, 2006—11. Sr. rschr. Alfa Inst. Biomedical Sciences, Athens, 2006—; mem. rsch. com. Alfa Inst. Biomed. Scis., 2008—. Contbr. 50 Scientific Papers to profl. jours. Infectious Diseases grant, Amfiaraion Found. Study Chemotherapeutic Agts., 2003, Travel & attendance grant, Clinical Microbiolody Infectious Diseases Nice,France, 2006, Travel grant, European Soc. Clin. Microbiology & Infectious Diseases, 2006. Office: Alfa Inst Biomed Scis Neapoleos 9 Athens Attiki 15123 Greece Home: Analipseos 28 152 35 Athens Greece Personal E-mail: janisbliz@yahoo.com. Business E-Mail: j.bliziotis@aibs.gr.

BLOBEL, GÜNTER, cell biologist, educator; b. Waltersdorf, Silesia, Germany, May 21, 1936; MD, U. Tübingen, Germany, 1960; PhD in Oncology, U. Wis., Madison, 1967. Fellow lab. cellular biology Rockefeller U., NYC, 1967-69, asst. prof. cell biology, 1969-73, assoc. prof., 1973-76, prof., 1976—, John D Rockefeller, Jr. prof., 1992—. Investigator Howard Hughes Med. Inst., Chevy Chase, Md., 1986—. Contbr. articles to profl. jours., chapters to books. Recipient Gairdner Found. Internat. award, 1982, Warburg medal, German Biochem. Soc., 1983, VD Mattia award, Roche Inst. Molecular Biology, 1986, Louisa Gross Horwitz prize, Columbia U., 1987, Waterford Bio-Med. Sci. award, 1989, Max-Planck Rsch. award, Alexander von Humboldt-Found., 1992, Albert Lasker award for basic med. rsch., 1993, Ciba Drew award in biomed. rsch., 1995, King Faisal Internat. prize for sci., 1996, Nobel prize in physiology/medicine, 1999, Ellis Island Medal of Honor, 2000. Mem.: NAS (US Steel award in molecular biology 1978, Richard Lounsbery award 1983), Am. Philos. Soc., Am. Soc. Cell Biology (pres. 1990, Wilson medal 1986), Am. Acad. Arts & Scis., German Soc. Cell Biology (hon.), Japan Biochem. Soc. (hon.), European Molecular Biol. Orgn. (assoc.). Office: Rockefeller U Lab Cell Biology 1230 York Ave New York NY 10065-6339 E-mail: Gunter.Blobel@rockefeller.edu. *

BLOCH, ANTOINE, cardiologist; b. Lausanne, Switzerland, Aug. 9, 1938; s. Paul and Herta (Sonnenfeld) B.; m. Josee Sánchez, Aug. 25, 1973. MD, U. Lausanne, 1963. Intern U. Lausanne Hosp., 1964-66; resident in medicine St. Antonius Hosp., Utrecht, The Netherlands, 1966-67, Lausanne and Geneva U. Hosps., 1967-70; chief resident U. Cardiac Ctr. Geneva, 1970-73, physician, 1975-80; cardiac fellow Mass. Gen. Hosp., Boston, 1973-75; privat-docent Geneva Med. Sch., 1975-80, charge de cours, 1980—2003. Chief cardiac unit Hosp. de la Tour, Geneva, 1981—2004, chief cardiovasc. medico-surg. dept., 1997—2001, med. dir., 2002—; prof. Golden Heart. Contbr. articles to profl. jours. Swiss Nat. Fund grant, 1977-79. Fellow Am. Coll. Cardiology, European Soc. Cardiology; mem. Am. Stroke Assn., Swiss Med. Assn.(emeritus mem.), Swiss Soc. Cardiology, French Soc. Cardiology Home: Rte du Crêt-de-Choully 33 CH-1242 Choully Switzerland Office: Hosp de la Tour General Direction Geneva CH-1217 Switzerland Office Phone: 41227197500. Business E-Mail: antoine.bloch@latour.ch.

BLOCH, ERICH, retired electrical engineer, science foundation director; b. Sulzburg, Germany, Jan. 9, 1925; arrived in U.S., 1948, naturalized, 1952; s. Joseph and Tony Bloch; m. Renee Stern, Mar. 4, 1948; 1 child, Rebecca Bloch Rosen. Student, Fed. Poly. Inst., Zurich, Switzerland, 1945—48; BSEE, U. Buffalo, 1952; degrees (hon.), U. Mass., George Washington U., Colo. Sch. Mines, SUNY Buffalo, U. Rochester, Oberlin Coll., U. Notre Dame, Ohio State U.; degree (hon.), Rensselaer Poly. Inst., 1989, Washington Coll., 1989, CUNY, NYC, 1991, Poly. U., Bklyn., 1993, St. Thomas Aquinas Coll. With IBM, 1952—75, v.p. gen. mgr. East Fishkill, NY, 1975—80, v.p. tech. personnel devel. Armonk, NY, 1980—84; mem. com. computers in automated mfg. NRC, 1980—84; dir. NSF, Washington, 1984—90; fellow Coun. on Competitiveness, 1990—; prin. Adv. Group Herou Consult Group, 1998—; mem. Pres.'s Coun. of Advisors for Sci. and Tech., 2001—. Past vis. disting. prof. George Mason U. Patentee in field. Recipient U.S. medal of tech., 1985, Computer World/Smithsonian award for innovation, 1991, Swedish Royal Order of the Polar Star, Robert Noyce award, Semiconductor Industry Assn., 1999, Eugene Merchant Mfg. medal, ASME and Soc. Mfg. Engrs., Vanevar Bush award, Nat. Sci. Bd., 2002, Fellow award, Computer History Mus., 2004. Fellow: AAAS, IEEE (Founder's award 1990, Computer Pioneer award 1993, 1994), Am. Acad. Arts & Sciences; mem.: NAE (Arthur M. Bueche award 1997), Japan Acad. Engring., Royal Swedish Acad. Engring. Scis., Am. Soc. Mfg. Engrs. (hon.), Am. Soc. Engring. Edn. Office Phone: 202-682-0164, 2025856836. Business E-Mail: ebloch@theadvisorygroup.com.

BLOCH, STEVEN, plastic surgeon; Studied, SUNY. Diplomate Am. Bd. Plastic Surgery. Intern Northwestern Meml. Hosp.; resident surgery and plastic surgery Univ. Wis., chief resident plastic surgery; plastic surgeon Bodybloch. Pres. Chgo. Soc. of Plastic Surgery. Office: Bodybloch Ste 2E 11660 Park Ave W Highland Park IL 60035 Office Phone: 847-432-0840.

BLOCK, BARTLEY CAVANOUGH, biologist, educator; b. Chgo., Apr. 12, 1933; s. David and Anne (Been) B.; m. Janet Jacobs, May 26, 1963; children: Kenneth, Deborah, Steven. BS, Northwestern U., 1954, MS, 1955; student, Pa. State U., 1955-58. Entomologist USDA, Beltsville, Md., 1959; asst. prof. Lycoming Coll., Williamsport, Pa., 1959-63, Drexel Inst. Tech., Phila., 1964-65, So. Conn. State Coll., New Haven, 1965-67, U. Bridgeport, Conn., 1967-74, assoc. prof. biology, 1974-92; chief med. writer Pharmedica Comm., New Haven, 1992-96; sr. sci. editor Pharos Healthcare Comm., Inc., Greenwich, Conn., 1996-97. Freelance med. writer, 1998—; adj. faculty., biology dept. RI Coll., 2010-; cons. in field. Author: Man, Microbes and Matter, 1974; inventor in field. Chmn. Milford Conservation Commn., 1982-86; mem. Inland Wetland Agy., 1988-90. Grantee U.S. AEC, 1960, USDA, 1960-62, NSF, 1962-63, Mellon Found., 1980; vis. fellow Yale U., 1988-89. Mem. AAAS, Am. Med. Writers Assn., Am. Inst. Biol. Sci., Am. Soc. Zool., Entomol. Soc. Am., Ecol. Soc. Am., Animal Behavior Soc. Democrat. Jewish. Avocation: photography. Home: 355 Blackstone Blvd Apt 349 Providence RI 02906-4951 Personal E-mail: jbblock2@cox.net.

BLOCK, NORMAN LOUIS, oncologist, educator; b. NYC, Aug. 31, 1938; s. Abraham Harold and Rose (Bodatsky) B.; m. Carolyn Lee Peck, May 12, 1967; children: Joseph, David, Adam, Nathaniel, Jessica. BA, NYU, 1959, MD, 1963. Diplomate Am. Bd. Urology. Intern Baylor U. Med. Ctr., Dallas, 1963-64, resident in surgery, 1966—67; resident in urology NYU Med. Ctr., NYC, 1967—71; fellow in urologic oncology Meml. Sloan Kettering Cancer Ctr., NYC, 1971-72; attending physician Miami VA Med. Ctr., 1972-96, Jackson Meml. Hosp., Fla., 1972—; chief urology VA Med. Ctr., 1975—85; assoc. prof. urology U. Miami, 1976-82, prof. urology, 1982—, prof. biomed. engring., 1982—, L. Austin Weeks prof., 1982—, prof. oncology, 1985—, prof. pathology, 2009—. Editl. reviewer 6 jours. Contbr. numerous articles to profl. jours., including Cancer Jour. Urology, Jour. Urology, Jour. Surg. Oncology. Capt. U.S. Army, 1964-66. Recipient numerous awards, fellowships, lectureships; named Best Doctor in Am. Super Doctors, South Fla., Best Oncologist. Mem. AMA, ACS, AAAS, Internat. Urology Soc., Internat. Soc. for Artificial Organs, Am. Fertility Soc., Am. Urol. Assn. (Southeastern sect.), Am. Soc. for Artificial Internal Organs, Am. Assn. Lab. Animal Sci. (Fla. divsn.), Southeastern Cancer Rsch. Assn., Soc. Surg. Oncology, Soc. Univ. Urologists, Southeastern Coop. Oncology Group, Soc. Govt. Svc. Urologists, So. Med. Assn., Confedn. Am. Urologists, Soc. Urologic Oncology, Colombian Urol. Soc., Fla. Med. Assn., Fla. Urologic Assn., Greater Miami Urologic Soc., Dade County Med. Soc., Bellevue Urologic Alumni Assn. Republican. Jewish. Achievements include holder six patents; research in new treatment for prostate cancer; development of new diagnostic test for bladder cancer; applied a new model for prostate cancer in animals; development of an artificial bladder, ureter, urethra sphincter. Avocation: wildlife photography. Office: U Miami Sch Medicine Dept Pathology R-5 PO Box 16960 Miami FL 33101-6960 Business E-Mail: nblock@med.miami.edu. *

BLOCK, ROBERT I., psychologist, researcher, educator, psychologist, researcher, educator; b. Newark, Jan. 30, 1951; s. Milton and Harriet (Safier) Block. BA with honors, Shimer Coll., 1969; MS, Harvard U., 1972, Rutgers U., 1977, PhD, 1981. Teaching asst. psychology dept. Rutgers U., New Brunswick, NJ, 1975-76; psychologist Lafayette Clinic, Detroit, 1982-84; rsch. assoc. psychiatry dept. Wayne State U., Detroit, 1982, instr., 1982-84; assoc. rsch. scientist dept. anesthesia U. Iowa, Iowa City, 1984-88, asst. prof. dept. anesthesia, 1988-94, assoc. prof. dept. anesthesia, 1994—. Cons. State of Mich., Lafayette Clinic, Detroit, Hoffmann La-Roche, Inc.; reviewer Psychopharmacology and Anesthesiology, NIH; mem. faculty senate Sch. of Medicine, Wayne State U., Detroit, 1982-84. Contbr. articles to Anesthesiology, Brit. Jour. Anaesthesia, Psychopharmacology, Pharmacol. Biochem. Behavior, Neuro Report. Grantee, Nat. Inst. on Drug Abuse, 1987—91, 1993—2000, 2004—10; fellow, Rutgers U. Mem. AAAS, Collegium Internat. Neuro-Psychopharmacologicum, Am. Psychol. Assn., Soc. Neurosci. Achievements include research on effects of nitrous oxide, benzodiazepines, marijuana, and other drugs on human associative processes, memory, cognition, brain structure and function. Home: 2029 Waterford Dr Coralville IA 52241-2734 Office: U Iowa Dept Anesthesia Westlawn Bldg Iowa City IA 52242

BLOCK, ROBERT W., medical association administrator, pediatrician; m. Sharon Block; children: Erika Mays, Andrea Wooldridge. MD, U. Pa., Phila., 1972. Diplomate American Bd. Pediat. Residency in pediat. Children's Hosp. Phila.; faculty mem., clin. physician U. Okla. Sch. Cmty. Medicine, Tulsa, 1975—2011, prof. and Daniel C. Plunket chmn. dept. pediat., sub-specialist in clin. and forensic child abuse pediat., adminstr. hospitalist practice & gen. pediatric clinic and normal newborn oversight, part-time faculty mem., 2011—. Author: Handbook of Behavioral Pediatrics, 1981; contbr. articles to profl. jours., chapters to books. Mem internat. adv. bd. Nat. Ctr. on Shaken Baby Syndrome; mem. adv. bd. Crosstown Learning Ctr.; founding mem., bd. dirs. Child Abuse Network; bd. dirs. American Red Cross Blood Services, Tulsa; vice chmn. Tulsa County Juvenile Justice Trust Authority; chmn. Tulsa County Med. Soc. Coun. on Med. Edn.; mem. of bd. and exec. com. Fit Kids Coalition Okla.; founding mem. Child Death Rev. Bd., 1992—; mem. Okla. Adv. Bd. on Child Abuse, Okla. Bd. Child Abuse Examination; former adv. bd. mem. Jr. League Tulsa, Okla. L.D. Assn.; former bd. mem. Margaret Hudson Program Teen Parents, Town and County Sch. Children with Learning Disabilities.

Physician US Army, 1972—75, Ft. Leavenworth, Kans. Recipient Parker J. Palmer Courage to Teach award, ACGME, 2001. Fellow: American Acad. Pediat. (v.p. & pres.-elect Okla. chpt. 1990—93, mem. Okla. chpt. exec. com. 1990—, pres. Okla. chpt. 1993—96, mem. com. on child abuse and neglect 1996—2002, mem. US adv. commn. on childhood vaccines 1999—2002, chmn. com. on child abuse and neglect 2002—06, mem. steering com. for family violence and prevention fund 2005—, v.p., pres.-elect 2010—11, pres. 2011—, SOCAN Outstanding Svc. to Maltreated Children award 2007, Spl. Achievement award 2009); mem.: Acad. on Violence and Abuse (pres.), Ray E. Helfer Hon. Soc. (Svc. in the Field of child Abuse award 2006). Avocation: woodcarving. Office: American Acad Pediat 141 Northwest Point Blvd Elk Grove Village IL 60007 Office Phone: 847-434-4000. Business E-Mail: executivecommittee@aap.org. *

BLODGETT, ANDREW D., physician; b. Detroit, Dec. 31, 1968; MS, Appalachian State U., 1998; DO, Kans. City U. Med. and Bioscis., 2004. Family physician Novant, 2007—. Cmty. clin. preceptor Wake Forest U. Sch. Medicine, 2008. Mem.: Am. Acad. Family Physicians. Office: 8420 University Executive Park Dr Charlotte NC 28262 Personal E-mail: ablodgett@hotmail.com.

BLOEMER, GARY FRED, orthopedic surgeon, educator; b. Cin., Aug. 18, 1954; s. Raymond Charles and Mildred (Hudephol) B.; children: David Edward, Klye Raymond, Elizabeth Rose. BS, U. Louisville, 1976, MD, 1982. Diplomate Am. Bd. Orthopedic Surgeons. Intern gen. surgery U. Lousiville, 1982-83, asst. clin. prof. orthopedics, 1988—; orthopedic surgery resident Med. Coll. of Ga., Augusta, 1984-87; sports medicine fellow Hughston Sports Medicine Clinic, Columbus, Ga., 1987; pvt. practice, Louisville, 1988—. Med. advisor St. Anthony Sports Medicine Ctr., Louisville, 1989-95; orthopedic cons. Campbellsville (Ky.) Coll., 1990—; exec. com. Frazier Rehab. Ctr., Louisville, 1992; vice chmn. emergency rm. com. Jewish Hosp., Louisville, 1994-96. Contbr. articles to profl. jours. Med. cons. Ky. Commn. for Handicapped Children, Louisville, 1988—2002; team physician Moore H.S., Louisville, 1988—2000. Fellow Am. Acad. of Orthopedic Surgeons; mem. AMA, Ky. Orthopedic Assn., Hughston Soc., Floyd E. Bliven Soc., Nat. Athletic Trainers Assn., Alpha Omega Alpha. Roman Catholic. Avocations: skiing, bicycling, boating, racquetball. Office: 3 Audubon Plaza Dr Ste 430 Louisville KY 40217-1319

BLOMGREN, BO, pathologist, researcher; b. Stockholm, July 14, 1960; s. Tor and Barbro Blomgren; m. Elena Ivanova, Aug. 12, 1995 (div. Mar. 1, 2007); 1 child, Anna. MD, Karolinska Inst., Stockholm, 1991; PhD in Medicine, Uppsala U., Sweden, 2004. Jr. lectr. Karolinska Inst., 1986—91, assoc. scientist, 1986—88; pathologist Danderyds Hosp., Stockholm, 1991—94, S:t Görans Hosp., Stockholm, 1994—95; assoc. prin. pathologist, cons. lectr. AstraZeneca, Södertälje, Sweden, 1995—. Capt. inf. Swedish Army, 1984. Decorated Defence of Country medal Swedish Armed Forces, Medal of Honor Swedish Fedn. Vol. Defence Edn. Tng.; recipient Stella suprema medicorum, Med. Assn., Karolinska Inst., 1993. Fellow: Swedish Med. Assn. (corr.); mem.: Internat. Soc. Stereology (corr.), Scandinavian Electron Microscopy Soc. (corr.). Avocation: amateur radio. Home: Hägerstensvägen 173 Hägersten Stockholm SE-126 53 Sweden Office: AstraZeneca R&D Safety assessment Bgn 681 Gärtuna Södertälje SE-151 85 Sweden Office Fax: 46855258823. Personal E-mail: bo.blomgren@comhem.se. Business E-Mail: bo.blomgren@astrazeneca.com.

BLOMQUIST, PRESTON HOWARD, ophthalmologist; b. Austin, Tex., Aug. 13, 1960; s. Gilbert Victor and Betty Jean Blomquist; m. Mary Denise Dobias, Mar. 31, 1960; children: Brooke Amanda, Kara Elyse. BSc in Engring., U. Tex., 1982; MD, U. Tex. Southwestern Med. Sch., Dallas, 1986. Diplomate Am. Bd. of Ophthalmology. Chief eye svcs. Permanente Med. Assn. of Tex., Dallas, 1993—94, assoc. med. dir. quality resource mgmt., 1996—97, physician dir. orgnl. performance and improvement, 1995—96; asst. prof. U. Tex. Southwestern Med. Ctr., Dallas, 1998—2004, assoc. prof., 2004—. Ophthalmology residency program dir. U. of Tex. Southwestern Med. Ctr., Dallas, 2002—; vice chair edn. dept. ophthalmology U. Tex. Southwestern Med., Dallas, 2011—. Recipient Ho Din, Southwestern Med. Found., 1986. Fellow: Am. Acad. Ophthalmology; mem.: Am. Ophthalmologic Soc., Assn. for Rsch. in Vision and Ophthalmology, Assn. Univ. Profs. Ophthalmology (assoc.), Am. Soc. Cataract and Refractive Surgeons. Office: Univ Tex Southwestern Med 5323 Harry Hines Blvd Dallas TX 75390-9057

BLONDIN, JOAN, nephrologist educator; b. Beaumont, Tex., Nov. 28, 1936; d. Joseph Albert and Ona Mae (Williamson) B. BS, La. Tech U., 1959; MNS, Cornell U., 1961; MD, La. State U., 1969. Diplomate Am. Bd. Internal Medicine. Instr. U. Ala., Tuscaloosa, 1961-62; rsch. assoc. Cornell U., Ithaca, NY, 1962-63; asst. specialist La. State U., Baton Rouge, 1963-65; intern Barnes Hosp., St. Louis, 1969-70, resident, 1970-72; fellow Washington U., St. Louis, 1972-74, asst. prof., 1974-78; ptnr. Nephrology Cons., Monroe, La., 1978-2000. Assoc. prof. La. State U. Sch. Medicine, Shreveport, 1978-98; adj. prof. human ecology La. Tech. U., 1988; prof. medicine La. State U. Health Scis. Ctr., 2000—; active staff St. Francis Med. Ctr., 1978-2001, North Monroe Cmty. Hosp., 1984-2000; adj. prof. Coll. Pharmacy, Northeast La. U., 1996—, med. staff LSU Hosp., 2001-. Contbr. articles to profl. jours. Bd. dirs. Central Bank; mem. adv. bd. Bank One; bd. trustees Nat. Kidney Found. of La., 1988-97; mem. La. Bd. Regents, 1989-94, chmn., 1992; med. dir. North La. Dialysis Ctr., 1992-97, Ruston Kidney Ctr. Fellow La. Cancer Society, 1966, NIH, 1968; recipient Disting. Svc. award La. Dietetic Assn., 1998, Outstanding Medicine Attending award LSU HSC, 2007. Mem. AAAS, ACP, End Stage Renal Disease (chmn. quality consensus com. 1994-96), Internat. Soc. Nephrology, Am. Soc. Nephrology (bd. advisors 2003—), Am. Diabetes Assn., Am. Soc. Nephrology (bd. adv. 2003—), Am. Soc. Tropical Medicine and Hygiene, Am. Soc. Parenteral and Enteral Nutrition, Am. Heart Assn. (coun. on hypertension), Renal Physicians Assn. (bd. dirs., fin. com. 1991-94, chmn. quality care com.), NY Acad. Scis., La. Med. Soc. (del. 1988-2001), Ouachita Med. Soc. (pres.-elect 1998-99, pres. 1999-2000, immediate past pres., exec. com. 2000), Sigma Xi, Alpha Omega Alpha, Phi Kappa Phi, Omicron Nu. Republican. Episcopalian. Avocations: music, needlepoint, reading. Office: LSU HSC Shreveport LA Business E-Mail: jblond@lsuhsc.edu.

BLONSHINE, SUSAN, medical association administrator; b. Corvallis, Oreg., Dec. 24, 1951; BS, Thomas Edison State Coll., 1993, grad. in Clin. Trial Adminstrn., 2010. Tech. ditector, cons. pulmonary function lab. Mich. State U., 1997—2011; pres., CEO TechEd Consultants, Inc., 1997—. Bd. trustees Nat. Bd. Respiratory Care, 1999—2011; bd. dir. Clin. and Lab. Standards Inst., 1999—2008, Nat. Asthma Educator Certification Bd., 2000—05. Recipient Excellence Mentoring award, Clin. and Lab. Standards Inst. Fellow: Am. Assn. Respiratory Care (life Sepracor Achievement award); mem.: European Respiratory Soc., Am. Thoracic Soc. Avocations: boating, quilting, reading. Office: 1012 Pelican Place Mason MI 48854 Office Fax: 517-753-5999. Business E-Mail: pblonshine@techedconsultants.com.

BLOOM, BARRY MALCOLM, research and development company executive, consultant; b. Roxbury, Mass., Aug. 12, 1928; s. Morris and Ann (Levine) B.; m. Joan Martha Ensign, June 27, 1956; children: Catherine, Brian, Joanna. SB, MIT, 1948, PhD, 1951, postgrad., 1967; LHD (hon.), Conn. Coll., 1992. Rsch. chemist Pfizer, Inc., Groton, Conn., 1952-63, dir. medicinal chems. and rsch., 1963-71, pres. ctrl. rsch. divsn., 1971-90, v.p. rsch., 1971-90, bd. dirs., 1973—93, corp. mgmt. com., 1984-93, sr. v.p. R & D, 1990-92, exec. v.p. R & D, 1992-93; cons. pvt. practice, 1993—2004. Bd. dirs. Congl. Commn. on Fed. Drug Approval Process, PMA Commn. on Drugs for Rare Diseases; cons. U.S. Congress Office Tech. Assessment, 1976-77; mem. Conn. Tech. Adv. Bd., 1985-90. Mem. editl. bd. Ann. Reports in Medicinal Chemistry, 1968-70; patentee in field. NRC postdoctoral fellow U. Wis., 1952; Poly. Inst. Tech. fellow N.Y.C., 1980; recipient Spl. Achievement award CT Innovations, Inc., 1997. Mem. Am. Chem. Soc. (chmn. divsn. medicinal chemistry 1967), Conn. Acad. Sci. and Engring., Pharm. Mfrs. Assn. (chmn. R & D sect. 1976). Home and Office: Mackintosh Rd Lyme CT 06371

BLOOM, BARRY THEIL, pediatrician, researcher; s. Lewis Theil and Olive Zoe Bloom; m. Alice Russell; children: Kristen Melissa, Jennifer Lynn Ray, Timothy Allen, Megan Ann Bystrek, Matthew Russell. BES in Human Biology, Kans. U., 1978, MD, 1981. Diplomate Am. Bd. Pediatrics, Am. Bd. Neonatal - Perinatal Medicine. Clin. neonatologist Wesley Med. Ctr., Wichita, 1986—, neonatal ICU med. dir., 1999—; from asst. prof. to assoc. prof. pediat. Kans. U. Sch. Medicine, Wichita, 1986—94, prof., 1994—, intern chmn., dept. pediat., 2008—. Dir. clin. improvement Pediatrix Med. Group, Inc, Ft. Lauderdale, Fla., 2000—05. Office: Pediatrix Medical Group 550 N Hillside Wichita KS 67214

BLOOM, DAVID ALAN, pediatric urology educator, department chairman; b. Buffalo, July 26, 1945; m. Martha Lichty, June 8, 1980. BS, Rensselaer Poly. Inst., 1967; MD, SUNY, Buffalo, 1971. Diplomate Am. Bd. Surgery, Am. Bd. Urology (exam. com. 1992-1996, Trustee, 2003-09), Am. Bd. Med. Spl. dir., 2007-. Intern UCLA, 1971-72, resident in surgery, 1972-75, chief resident, 1975-76, resident in urology, 1976-77, sr. resident, 1978-79, chief resident, lectr., 1979-80; vis. fellow, registrar Inst. Urology and St. Peter's Hosp., U. London, 1977-78; asst. prof. surgery U. Mich., Ann Arbor, 1984-86, assoc. prof., 1986-93, prof., 1993—, chief pediatric urology, 1984—2000, assoc. dean faculty affairs Sch. Medicine, 2000—07, chair dept. urology, 2007—. Cons. urology surgery br. Nat. Cancer Inst., NIH, Bethesda, Md., 1982, Naval Regional Med. Ctr., Portsmouth, Va., 1983, Walter Reed Army Med. Ctr., Washington, 1985, VA Hosp., Ann Arbor, 1985; locum in urology Gt. Ormond Street Hosp. for Sick Children and Inst. Urology, Shaftesbury Hosp., London, 1986; from asst. prof. surgery to clin. assoc. prof. Uniformed Svcs. U. Health Scis. Sch. Medicine, Bethesda, 1980-1985; presenter and cons. in field. Author: (with McGuire, Catalona and Lipshultz) Advances in Urology, 1995-97; mem. editl. bd. Urology, 1992-2007, Jour. Endourology, 1997-2003, Contemporary Urology, 1997-2007, British Jour. Urology, 1999-2002. Lt. col. M.C., U.S. Army, 1980-84. Mem. USAR 1984-1986, Fellow ACS (motion picture com. 1996-2002); mem. AMA, Am. Acad. Pediat. (exec. com. sect. on urology 1989-93, historian 1993-2000, chmn. 2001-02), Am. Assn. Clin. Urologists, Halsted Soc. (photographer, dir. 1999-2001), Longmire Surg. Soc., Am. Surg. Assn., Reed M. Nesbit Soc., Soc. for Pediatric Urology, Soc. Genitourinary Reconstructive Surgeons, Soc. Univ. Urologists, Am. Assn. Genito-urinary Surgeons (sec.-treas. 2007-), Uniformed Svcs. U. Surg. Assocs., Nat. Urologic Forum (sec.-treas. 1995-2002), European Assn. Urology, Soc. Internat. Urology. Office: U Mich 1500 E Med Ctr Dr Ann Arbor MI 48109-5330 Office Phone: 734-232-4943.

BLOOM, ERIC J., nephrologist, educator; MD, Temple U. Diplomate Am. Bd. of Internal Medicine, Am. Bd. of Internal Medicine-nephrology. Intern Med. Coll. of Pa., resident; fellow Temple Univ. Sch. of Medicine; tchr. Thomas Jefferson Univ. Hosp. Named Top Doc, Phila. Mag. Office: Albert Einstein Medical Center 5501 Old York Rd Philadelphia PA 19141 Office Phone: 215-456-7890.

BLOOM, FLOYD ELLIOTT, internist, neuroscientist; b. Mpls., Oct. 8, 1936; s. Jack Aaron and Frieda (Shochman) B.; m. D'Nell Bingham, Aug. 30, 1956 (dec. May 1973); children: Fl'Nell, Evan Russell; m. Jody Patricia Corey, Aug. 9, 1980. AB cum laude, So. Meth. U., Dallas, 1956; MD cum laude, Washington U., St. Louis, 1960; DSc (hon.), So. Meth. U., 1983, Hahnemann U., 1985, U. Rochester, 1985, Mt. Sinai U. Med. Sch., 1996, Thomas Jefferson U., 1997, Washington U., 1998, The Scripps Rsch. Inst., 2005. Intern Barnes Hosp., St. Louis, 1960—61, resident internal medicine, 1961—62; rsch. assoc. NIMH, Washington, 1962—64; fellow depts. pharmacology, psychiatry and anatomy Yale Sch. Medicine, 1964—66, asst. prof., 1966—67, assoc. prof., 1968; chief lab. neuropharmacology NIMH, Washington, 1968—75, acting dir. divsn. spl. mental health, 1973—75; commd. officer USPHS, 1974—75; dir. Arthur Vining Davis Ctr. for Behavorial Neurobiology; prof. Salk Inst., La Jolla, Calif., 1975—83; dir. divsn. preclin. neurosci. and endocrinology Scripps Rsch. Inst., La Jolla, 1983—89, chmn. dept. neuropharmacology, 1989—2005, prof. emeritus molecular, neurosci. dept., 2005—; editor in chief Sci. Mag., 1995—2000; founding CEO Neurome, Inc., LaJolla, Calif., 2000—06, chmn. bd., 2000—06, chief scientific officer, 2000—06. Mem. Pres. Commn. on Alcoholism, 1980—81, Nat. Adv. Mental Health Coun., 1976—80; chmn. sci. adv. bd. Pharmavene, Inc., 1994—98, Advancis Corp., 2000—07, Middlebrook Pharms., 2007—09; mem. Rsch. Adv. Com. Gulf War Vets. Illnesses, 2005—, President's Coun. Bioethics, 2006—09, Independent Citizens Oversight Com., 2007—, Calif. Inst. Regenerative Medicine; bd. dirs. Alkermes, Inc., Elan Pharms., 2007—09. Author: (with Cooper and Roth) Biochemical Basis of Neuropharmacology, 1971, 8th edit., 2002, (with Lazerson and Hofstadter) Brain, Mind and Behavior, 1984, (with Lazerson) 2d edit., 1988, (with C.A. Nelson) 3d edit., 2000, (with W. Young and Y. Kim) Brain browser, 1989; editor: Peptides: Integrators of Cell and Tissue Function, 1980, Progress in Brain Research, vol. 199, 1994, vol. 100, 1997, (with D.J. Kupfer) Neuro-Psychopharmacology: The Fourth Generation of Progress, 1994, Handbook of Chemical Neuroanatomy, 1997, The Primate Nervous System, 1997, vol. II, 1998, vol. III, 1999, (with Beal and Kupfer) The Dana Guide to Brain Health, 2003; co-editor: Regulatory Peptides, 1979-90, (with M. Randolph) Funding Health Sciences Research, 1990, The Best of the Brain from Scientific American, 2007; assoc. editor: Biological Psychiatry, 1993-95, (with Iversen, Iversen, Roth) Introduction to Neuropsychopharmacology, 2008; editor-in-chief Science, 1995-2000, Brain Rsch., 2000-10. Trustee Washington U., St. Louis, 1998—, chmn. nat. med. coun., 2000—. Disting. fellow Am. Psychiat. Assn., 1986; recipient A. Cressy Morrison award NY Acad. Scis., 1971, A.E. Bennett award for basic rsch. Soc. Biol. Psychiatry, 1971, Arthur A. Fleming award Science mag., 1973, Mathilde Solowey award, 1973, Biol. Sci. award Washington Acad. Scis., 1975, Alumni Achievement citation Washington U., 1980, McAlpin Rsch. Achievement award Mental Health Assn., 1980, Lectr.'s medal College de France, 1979, Steven Beering medal, 1985, Janssen award World Psychiat. Assn., 1989, Passerow Found. award, 1990, Herman von Helmholtz award, 1991, Pythagora award, 1994, Presdl. award Soc. for Neurosci., 1995, Golgi prize U. Brescia, 1996, Meritorious Achievement award Coun. Biology Editors, 1999, Gold medal Soc. Biol. Psychiatry, 1997, Disting. Svc. award Am. Psychiat. Assn., 2000, Thomas William Salmon medal, NY Acad. Medicine for Psychiatry and Mental Hygiene, 2004, Dedman Coll. Disting. Grad. award, So. Meth. U., 2005, Rhoda and Bernard Sarnat Internat. prize in Mental Health, Inst. of Medicine of the Nat. Academies, 2005; Disting. Fellow Am. Psychiat. Assn., 1986; named Sci. of Yr. Achievement Rewards for Coll. Scientists, 1996. Fellow AAAS (bd. dirs. 1986-90, pres.-elect 2001, pres. 2002, chmn. bd. dirs. 2003), Am. Coll. Neuropsychopharmacology (coun. 1976-78, chmn. program com. 1987, pres. 1988-89, Hoch award 1998); mem. NAS (chmn. sect. neurobiology 1979-83, co-chair reports rev. com. 2004-08, chair com. publs. 2007—), Inst. Medicine (coun. 1986-89, 93-95, Walsh McDermott medal 2004, Rhoda and Bernard Sarnat award in Mental Health 2005), Am. Philos. Soc. (chmn. Lashley award com. 2001—08), Am. Acad. Arts and Scis., Soc. Neurosci. (sec. 1973-74, pres. 1976, chmn. publs. com. 1999-2002), Am. Soc. Pharmacology and Exptl. Therapeutics, Am. Soc. Cell Biology, Am. Physiol. Soc., Am. Assn. Anatomists, Am. Neurol. Assn. (hon.), Rsch. Soc. Alcoholism (chmn. program com. 1985-87, pres.-elect 1989-91, pres. 1991-93), Swedish Acad. Sci. (fgn. assoc. 1989). Home: 628 Pacific View Dr San Diego CA 92109-1768 Office Phone: 858-784-9730. Business E-Mail: fbloom@scripps.edu. E-mail: fbloom@bloomsciassocs.net.

BLOOM, JANE MAGINNIS, emergency physician; b. Ithaca, NY, June 22, 1924; d. Ernest Victor and Miriam Rebecca (Mansfield) M.; m. William Lee Bloom, Mar. 31, 1944; children: David Lee, Jan Christopher, Carolyn Wells, Eric Paul, Joseph William, Robert Carl, Mary Catherine, Thomas Mark, Patrick Martin (dec.), Arthur Emerson. BS, U. Mich., 1968, MD, 1974. Diplomate Am. Bd. Internal Medicine, cert. in emergency medicine 2004. Rotating intern Wayne County Gen. Hosp., Eloise, Mich., 1974—75; resident in internal medicine St. Mary's Hosp., Rochester, NY, 1975-77; emergency physician Emergency Physicians Med. Group, Ann Arbor, 1986—2003. Fellow: Am. Coll. Emergency Physicians (life); mem.: AMA, Mich. State Med. Soc., Am. Coll. Physicians, Am. Med. Womens Assn., Am. Assn. Women Emergency Physicians, Washtenaw County Med. Soc. Avocations: walking, birdwatching. Home and Office: 537 Elm St Ann Arbor MI 48104-2515 Office Phone: 734-761-2435.

BLOOM, PATRICIA A., geriatrician, educator; MD, U. Minn. Diplomate Am. Bd. Internal Medicine. Internship Montefiore Med. Ctr.; assoc. prof. geriat. and palliative medicine Mt. Sinai Sch. of Medicine, assoc. prof. Dir. Integrative Health for the Martha Stewart Ctr. for Living / Coffey Geriat. Practice. Named one of Best Doctors, NY Mag., 1998—2010, Top Doctors: NY, Castle Connolly Med. Ctr., 1999—2011, America's Top Doctors, 2000—11. Office: Mount Sinai Medical Center One Gustave L Levy Place New York NY 10029-6574 Office Phone: 212-241-6500.

BLOOM, SHERMAN, retired pathology educator, photographer; b. Bklyn., Jan. 26, 1934; s. Philip and Sadie (Kaplan) B.; m. Miriam Fishman, Feb. 11, 1960; children: Naomi, Stephanie. BA, NYU, 1955, MD, 1960. Diplomate Am. Bd. Anat. Pathology. Intern in medicine Kings County Hosp., Bklyn., 1960-61; fellow in exptl. pathology, resident in anatomic and clin. pathology NYU Med. Ctr. and Bellevue Hosp., NYC, 1961-65; instr. pathology NYU Sch. Medicine, 1965-66; asst. prof. U. Utah Coll. Medicine, Salt Lake City, 1966-70, assoc. prof., 1970-72, U. South Fla. Coll. Medicine, Tampa, 1973-76, prof. pathology, 1976-77, George Washington U. Coll. Medicine, Washington, 1977-88; prof., chmn. dept. pathology U. Miss. Med. Ctr., Jackson, 1988-2000, prof. emeritus, 2000—, ret., 1999; pres. Photo-Tov Fine Arts, 2004. Cons. Sci. Rev., NIH; mem. cardiovascular study sect. NSF, FDA; dir. coun. on cardiovascular and geriatric health Amer Coll. Nutrition, 1998-01; bd. dirs. Scientists Ctr. Animal Welfare, pres. elect, 1987, pres., 1988. Mem. editl. bd. Jour. Am. Coll. Nutrition, 1982, Am. Jour. Cardiovascular Pathology, 1985; assoc. editor Cardiovascular Pathology, 1990; fine art photo pub. Jour. Miss. State Med. Assn.; contbr. numerous articles to profl. publs. Del. Utah State Dem. Party, 1968. NIH fellow, 1962; Dilthey Found. fellow, 1982. Fellow Am. Coll. Nutrition; mem. Internat. Acad. Pathologists, Am. Physiol. Soc., Am. Assn. Pathologists, Internat. Soc. Heart Research, Soc. Cardiovascular Pathology (pres. 1986-87), Photograph Soc. Am.(pres.). Jewish. Home and Office: 2584 Elizabeth St #5 Salt Lake City UT 84106 Personal E-mail: shermanbloom@mac.com.

BLOOMBERG, MIKE (MICHAEL RUBENS BLOOMBERG), mayor, New York City; b. Medford, Mass., Feb. 14, 1942; s. William and Charlotte Bloomberg; m. Susan Brown, 1975 (div. 1993); children: Emma, Georgina. BEE, Johns Hopkins U., 1964; MBA, Harvard U., 1966; D in Pub. Svc. (hon.), Tufts U., 2007; LHD (hon.), Bard Coll., 2007; LLD (hon.), U. Pa., Phila., 2008; D (hon.), Fordham U., 2009. Processing clerk Salomon Brothers, 1966—72, gen. ptnr. NYC, 1972—81; founder Bloomberg L.P., NYC, 1981, pres., CEO, 1981—2001; mayor NYC, 2002—. Chmn. World Trade Ctr. Meml. Found., 2006—. Co-author (with Matthew Winkler): Bloomberg by Bloomberg, 1997; appeared in (films) The Adjustment Bureau, 2011. Chmn., bd. trustees Johns Hopkins U., 1966—72; trustee Big Apple Circus, Ctrl. Park Conservancy, Met. Mus. Art, HS Econs. and Fin. Inst. Advanced Study, Lincoln Ctr. Performing Arts, Jewish Mus., NY Police/Fire Widows' and Childrens' Fund., Spence Sch., Prep for

Prep, S.L.E. Found., US Ski Team Ednl. Found., Serpentine Gallery, London. Recipient Golden Plate award, Acad. Achievement, 2004, Barnard Medal of Distinction, 2008, Bd. Dirs. award, Coun. Fashion Designers America, 2008, Mary Woodward Lasker award for Pub. Svc., Lasker Found., 2009; named New Yorker of Yr., Daily News, 2006; named one of Forbes 400: Richest Americans, Forbes mag., 1999—, The World's Richest People, 2001—, The 50 Most Generous Philanthropists, Fortune mag., 2005, The 100 Most Influential People in the World, TIME mag., 2007, 2008, The Global Elite, Newsweek mag., 2008. Fellow: American Acad. Arts & Sciences; mem.: US Chamber of Commerce (trustee). Independent. Jewish. Office: City Hall 52 Chambers St New York NY 10007-1222 *

BLOOMENSTEIN, RICHARD B., plastic surgeon; b. NYC, Oct. 29, 1934; s. Nelson S. Bloomenstein and Lucille A. Biermann; m. Susan J. Bloomenstein, Apr. 2, 1961; children: Laura, Ellen. BA, Columbia U., 1955; MD, SUNY Coll. Medicine, Bklyn., 1959. Diplomate Am. Bd. Plastic Surgery. Pvt. practice, Englewood, NJ, 1967—; plastic surgery resident Montefiore Hosp. and Med Ctr., 1967. Sr. attending staff Englewood Hosp. and Med. Ctr., chief plastic surgery dept., 1970—78, surg. dir. wound healing ctr., 2003—; attending physician Valley Hosp., Ridgewood, NJ, 1980—2008. Author: One Day Plastic Surgery, 1984; contbr. articles to profl. jours. Vol. surgeon Heal the Children, Englewood Hosp. and Med. Ctr., 1980—85. Capt. USAF, 1962—64. Fellow, SUNY and Kings County Hosp., 1961. Fellow: ACS; mem.: NJ Soc. Plastic Surgeons, Am. Soc. Plastic Surgeons (resident prize award 1970). Office: 245 Engle St Englewood NJ 07631 Office Phone: 201-569-2241.

BLOOMER, WILLIAM DAVID, radiologist, oncologist, educator; b. Aug. 19, 1944; s. Ward LaVern and Vera Catherine (Rochefort) B.; m. Lauren S. Taslitz, Aug. 10, 1986; children: Whitney Dana, Brian Andrew, Gregory Stewart. AB, U. Pa., 1966; MD, Jefferson Med. Coll., Phila., 1970. Diplomate Am. Bd. Radiology, Am. Bd. Nuclear Medicine. Intern Univ. Hosps., Cleve., 1970-71; clin. fellow in radiation therapy Harvard U. Med. Sch., Boston, 1971-74, instr., 1974-76, asst. prof., 1976-80, assoc. prof., 1980-83; rsch. mem. Harvard MIT Divsn. Health Scis. and Tech., Boston, 1978-83; mem. sr. common room Lowell House Harvard Coll., Boston, 1983-87; dir. radiotherapy, radiotherapist-in-chief Mt. Sinai Hosp., NYC, 1983-87; prof., chmn. dept. radiation oncology U. Pitts. Sch. Medicine, 1987-92; dir. Joint Radiation Oncology Ctr., 1987-92; dir. radiation oncology Presbyn. U. Hosp., Magee-Women's Hosp., Shadyside Hosp., 1987-92; assoc. dir. Pitts. Cancer Inst., 1987-92; pres. U. Radiotherapy Assocs., Inc., 1989-92; sr. lectr. engring. in medicine Carnegie Mellon U., 1989-92; chmn. radiation medicine North Shore U. Healthcare, 1992—2009. Prof. radiology Northwestern U. Med. Sch., 1992—09, pres. Radiation Medicine Inst., 1992—; dir. radiation oncology svcs. Condell Med. Ctr., 2004—; clin. prof., radiation & cellular oncology U. Chgo., Pritzker Sch. Medicine, 2009-. Contbr. articles to profl. jours. Mem. AAAS, Am. Coll. Radiology, Am. Soc. Therapeutic Radiologists, Soc. Nuclear Medicine, Am. Assn. Cancer Rsch., Am. Soc. Clin. Oncology, Am. Coll. Radiation Oncology (Gold medal 1998). Office: Radiation Medicine Inst 2650 Ridge Ave Evanston IL 60201-1718

BLOOMFIELD, CLARA DERBER, oncologist, educator, medical institute administrator; b. Flushing, L.I., NY, May 15, 1942; d. Milton and Zelda (Treuner) Derber; m. Victor A. Bloomfield, June 11, 1962 (div. 1983); m. Albert de la Chapelle, Jan. 1, 1984. Student, U. Wis., 1959-62; BA, San Diego State U., 1963; MD, U. Chgo., 1968. Diplomate Am. Bd. Internal Medicine, Nat. Bd. Med. Examiners. Intern in medicine U. Chgo. Hosps. and Clinics, 1968-69, resident internal medicine, 1969-70, U. Minn., Mpls., 1970-71, med. oncology fellow, 1971-73, chief resident in medicine, Jan.-June, 1972, instr., 1972-73, asst. prof. medicine, 1973-76, assoc. prof., 1976-80, prof. medicine div. oncology, 1980-89, dir. fellowship program med. concology, 1987—89, mem. univ. senate, 1986-89, mem. all univ. Commn. on Women, 1988-89; prof. medicine, chief div. oncology SUNY, Buffalo, 1989—97; head dept. medicine Roswell Pk. Cancer Inst., Buffalo, 1989—97; William G. Pace III prof. cancer research Ohio State U. Coll. Med. & Pub. Health, 1997—, dir., div. hematology & oncology, dept. Internal Medicine, 1997—. Mem. Kettering selection com. GM Cancer Rsch. Found., 1986-87; cons. Office Tech. Assessment, U.S. Congress, 1988; participant, chair various coms. Internat. Human Gene Mapping Workshops, Helsinki, Finland, 1985, France, 1987, Internat. Workshops Chromosomes in Leukemia, Lund, Sweden, 1980, Chgo., 1982, Tokyo, 1984, London, 1987, Buffalo, 1991; mem. nat. and sci. adv. bds. NIH, 1977—, mem. bd. sci. counselors divsn. cancer treatment, 1991—, organizer Internat. Hodgkins Disease Symposium, 1981; bd. dirs. cancer and leukemia group B, 1982—, mem. other coms., 1973— sponsored clin. trial groups, Nat. Cancer Inst., cons. S.W. oncology group; mem. nat. and sci. adv. bd. Don and Sybil Harrington Cancer Ctr., Amarillo, Tex., 1979—, Med. Coll. Pa., 1988—; bd. trustees Berlex Oncology Found., 1992—; vis. prof. dept. medicine W.Va. U., 1973, U. Ariz., Tucson, 1979, U. Fla., Gainesville, 1979, Emory U., Atlanta, 1980, U. Chgo., 1982, George Washington U., Washington, 1982, U. Tex., San Antonio, 1982, Brown U., Providence, 1982, Mayo Clinic, Rochester, Minn., 1982, U. Zurich, Switzerland, 1983, U. P.R., 1984, U. Witwatersand, S. Africa, 1984, Nihon U., Tokyo, 1984, Leukemia Soc. Mass., 1991; frequent invited speaker, guest lectr. symposia, workshops, continuing edn. courses, seminars, med. congresses, univs. in U.S., Europe, S. Am., Scandinavia, Eng., Japan, Republic of South Africa, New Zealand. Author: (with others) Recent Advances in Bone Marrow Transplantation, Vol. VII, 1983, New Prespectives in Human Lymphoma, 1984, Neoplastic Diseases of the Blood, 1985, Current Therapy in Hematology/Oncology 1984-85, 1985, Medical Genetics: Past, Present, Future, 1985, Directions in Oncology, Vol. 1, 1985, Medical Oncology, Basic Principles and Clinical Management of Cancer, 1985, Tumor Aneuploidy, 1985, Malignant Lymphomas and Hodgkins Disease: Experimental and Therapeutic Advances, 1985, Current Therapy in Internal Medicine, 1987, Genetic Maps, Vol. 4, 1987; contbr. over 250 articles, abstracts to profl. jours.; editor ann. Adult Leukemia series in Cancer Treatment and Rsch., 1979-85; cons. editor Leukemia and Lymphoma Yearbook of Cancer, 1980—; assoc. editor Cancer Rsch., 1981-88, editor, 91, Leukemia Rsch., 1984-87, Leukemia, 1987-89; mem. editorial bd. Jour. Clin. Oncology, 1983-88, Cancer Genetics and Cytogenetics, 1983-87, Directions in Oncology, 1984-86, Cancer Rsch. Bull., 1984-85, Med. and Pediatric Oncology, 1987—, Blood, 1988—, Annals of Medicine, 1989—, Seminars in Oncology, 1989—; editorial bd. Am. Jour. Hematology, 1985, assoc. editor, 1988—; reviewer 23 med. jours. Recipient Nat. Bd. award Med. Coll. Pa., 1981, Past State Pres.' Bus. and Profl. Women award U. Tex. System Cancer Ctr., M.D. Anderson Hosp. and Tumor Clinic, Houston, 1987, Joseph H. Burchenal Clinical Rsch. award, Am. Assn. Cancer Rsch., 2004; prin. or co-prin. investigator 8 grants, NIH, 1975—, also ACS, 1980-84, Minn. State Spl. Coleman Leukemia Rsch. Fund, 1981-89, Coleman Leukemia Rsch. Fund Endowment, 1981—, Baltzar W.A. von Platen Found., 1984-85, Genentech/Hoffman -LaRoche, 1988—. Mem. ACP, AAAS, Am. Assn. Cancer Rsch., Am. Soc. Hematology, Am. Soc. Clin. Oncology (bd. dirs. 1991—), Am. Fedn. Clin. Rsch., Cen. Soc. Clin. Rsch., N.Y. Acad. Scis., Inst. Medicine, Internat. Assn. Comparative Rsch. Leukemia and Related Diseases, Med. Soc. Finland (external mem.), Phi Beta Kappa, Alpha Omega Alpha, Sigma Delta Epsilon. Office: Comprehensive Cancer Ctr 320 W 10th Ave Columbus OH 43210

BLOOMGARDEN, GARY MICHAEL, neurosurgeon; b. NYC, Apr. 12, 1954; s. Leonard J. and Annette B.; m. Jennifer Anne Frenzilli, Mar. 16, 1957; children: Jessica Ellen, Kara Elizabeth. BA summa cum laude, SUNY, Buffalo, 1976; MD, NYU, 1980; MBA, U. NH, 1997. Diplomate Am. Bd. Neurosurgery, 1988. Surg. intern Parkland Meml. Hosp., Dallas, 1980-81; resident in neurosurgery Yale-New Haven Hosp., 1981-86, courtesy neurosurgeon, 1986—, Milford Hosp., Conn., 1986—2011, St. Mary's Hosp., Waterbury, Conn., 1995—, Hosp. St. Raphael, New Haven, 1986—, chief, spine sect., 2009—. Clin. asst. prof. neurosurgery Yale Sch. Medicine, 1987-2008. Fellow ACS, Internat. Coll. Surgeons; mem. AMA, Am. Assn. Neurologic Surgeons, Congress of Neurologic Surgeons, Conn. State Med. Soc., Conn. State Neurol. Soc., New Eng. Neurolosurgical Soc. Republican. Jewish. Office: Ste 316 330 Orchard St New Haven CT 06511-4430 Office Phone: 203-781-3400. Personal E-mail: gbloomgarden@gmail.com. E-mail: gmbloom@aol.com.

BLOOS, FRANK, critical care physician; b. Berlin, Feb. 20, 1964; s. Marlene and Dietrich Bloos; m. Petra Mueller, Sept. 3, 2004. MD, Free U., Berlin, 1989; PhD, U. Western Ont., 1998. Cert. anesthesiology Soc. Physicians Thuringia, Germany, 2000, intensive Care Medicine Soc. Physicians Thuringia, Germany, 2002. Rschr. A.C. Burton Vascular Biology Lab., London, Ontario, 1990—93; resident in anesthesiology U. Hosp. Jena, Germany, 1994—2001, cons. intensive care medicine, 2002—; med. coord. German Competence Network Sepsis, 2002—; sr. rschr. Ctr. Sepsis Control & Care, 2010—. Recipient Young Investigator award, Am. Coll. Chest Physicians, 1993, Upjohn Achievement award, Can. Soc. Critical Care Medicine, 1993; grantee, German Rsch. Soc., 1994—95, Fed. Ministry Edn. and Rsch., Germany, 2009—. Mem.: European Soc. Intensive Care Medicine, German Sepsis Soc. Office: Univ Hosp Jena Dept Anesthesiology Erlanger Allee 101 Jena 07747 Germany Office Fax: 4936419323102. E-mail: frank.bloos@med.uni-jena.de.

BLOUCH, GERALD B., medical products executive; BA, Bowling Green U.; MBA, Ohio State U. CFO Invacare Corp., 1990—93, treas., 1991—93; sr. v.p., Homecare divsn. Invacare International, 1992—94, chmn., 1993—, pres., Homecare divsn., 1994; COO Invacare Corp., 1994—96, pres., COO, 1996—2010, interim CEO, 2010, pres., CEO, 2011—. Bd. dirs. Invacare Corp., 1996—. Office: Invacare Corp One Invacare Way Elyria OH 44036 Office Phone: 440-329-6000. Office Fax: 440-366-9008. *

BLOUIN, ROBERT A., dean, pharmacy educator; BS, Mass. Coll. Pharmacy, Boston, 1975; PharmD, U. Ky., Lexington, 1978. Resident U. Ky. Med. Ctr., 1975—78, faculty U. Ky. Coll. Pharmacy, 1978—2003, prof., assoc. dean rsch./grad. edn., 1997—2003, exec. dir. Office Econ. Devel. & Innovations Mgmt., Vaughn & Nancy Bryson disting. prof., dean U. NC Sch. Pharmacy, Chapel Hill, 2003—. Achievements include research in the effects of infectious disease and trauma on altered physiologic states such as aging and obesity, and the expression and regulation of drug metabolizing enzymes. Office: U NC Sch Pharmacy CB #7360 Beard Hall Rm 100C Chapel Hill NC 27599-7360 Office Phone: 919-996-1122. Office Fax: 919-996-6919. E-mail: bob_blouin@unc.edu.

BLOUNT, BENROE WAYNE, physician, department chairman; b. Augusta, Ga., Feb. 8, 1950; s. Benroe and Loreen Moellering B.; m. Merry Teresa Van Dam, Feb. 14, 1974 Dec. May 8, 1974); m. Young Hui Cho, Nov. 23, 1976; children: Teresa Jana, Daniel Paul. BS, US Mil. Acad., 1972; MA, U. Calif., Berkeley, 1975; MD, U. Miami, 1983; MPH, U. Wash., Seattle, 1990. Commd. 2d lt. U.S. Army, 1972, advanced through grades to lt. col., 1990, ret., 1994; intern, resident DeWitt Army Hosp., Alexandria, Va., 1983-86; divsn. chief, dept. vice-chair Emory Sch. Medicine, Atlanta, 1994-99, 2004—; chair dept. family medicine U. Tenn., Memphis, 1999—2002; prof. Emory U., 2002—; chief family practice Kaiser, S.E., 2002—04. Contbr. articles to profl. jours., chpts. to books. Recipient Chmn. of Joint Chief of Staff award for Excellence in Mil. Medicine, 1993; named one of Outstanding Young Men of Am., Nat. Jaycees, Top Family Physicians in US, 2007—10, Best Dr. in Am., 2000, 2001, 2002. Independent. Office Phone: 404-778-6920, 404-778-6905. Business E-Mail: bwbloun@emory.edu.

BLOWER, PETER ROBIN, pharmacologist, educator; b. Romford, Essex, England, June 1, 1948; s. Ernest and Hilda Florence (Dowsett) B.; m. Margaret Alison Holden, Aug. 5, 1972; children: James Rupert, Michael Edward. MS in Biology, Inst. Biology, London, 1972; PhD, Aston U., Birmingham, Eng., 1977; DSc (hon.), U. East London, 1997. Chartered biologist Inst. Biology. Rsch. biologist Beecham Rsch. Labs, Harlow, Eng., 1969-73; sr. rsch. scientist Beecham Pharmaceuticals, Harlow, Eng., 1973-79, rsch. mgr., 1979-87; scientific advisor Smithkline Beecham, Harlow, Eng., 1987-92, dir. scientific support programs, 1992-96, dir. neurosci. product devel., 1996-2000; ind. pharm. cons., 2000—; chmn. Biophar Consulting Ltd., 2005—; exec. dir. Minster Pharmaceuticals Ltd., 2005—10. Mng. dir. Blower & Cook Ltd., London, 1978-93; non-exec. dir. Phytopharm plc, 2006—; external examiner U. London, 1981-87, U. Marseille, France, 1994. Contbr. more than 70 articles to sci. jours., chpts. to books; patentee in field. Chmn. govs. U. East London, 1994-97, dep. chmn. govs. 1993-94, gov., 1988-93; sci. advisor Hertford Regional Coll., Turnford, Eng., 1983-93. Inst. Biology fellow, London, 1994, Royal Soc. Medicine fellow, London, 1993. Mem. Brit. Pharmacological Soc., Brit. Soc. Gastroenterology, East India Club London (social). Methodist. Avocations: english mediaeval history, cartography, hill walking, gardening. Home: Poole House Poole Street CO9 4HP Halstead England E-mail: peter@rblower.freeserve.co.uk.

BLUESTEIN, PAUL A., physician, insurance company executive; BA, MD, Temple U., Phila. Diplomate American Bd. Ob-Gyn. Resident ob-gyn. Univ. Hosps., Cleve., 1972—77; past nat. med. dir., nat. dir. quality improvement MetLife Managed Care Svc. Group; v.p. managed care NYH Care Network Inc.; sr. v.p., chief med. officer ConnectiCare Inc., 1994—. Office: ConnectiCare Inc 175 Scott Swamp Rd PO Box 4050 Farmington CT 06034 *

BLUESTEIN, VENUS WELLER, retired psychologist, educator; b. Milw., July 16, 1933; d. Richard T. and Hazel (Beard) Weller; m. Marvin Bluestein, Mar. 7, 1954. BS, U. Cin., 1956, MEd, 1959, EdD, 1966. Diplomate Am. Bd. Profl. Psychology. Psychologist-in-tng. Longview State Hosp., Cin., 1956-58; sch. psychologist Cin. Pub. Schs., 1958-65; asst. prof. psychology U. Cin., 1965-70, assoc. prof., 1970-79, prof., 1979-93, prof. emerita, 1993—, dir. sch. psychology program, 1965-70, co-dir. sch. psychology program, 1970-75, dir. undergrad. studies, 1976-91, dir. undergrad. advising, 1991-93. Cons. child psychologist. Sec., U.S. exec. com. rsch. Children's Internat. Summer Villages, 1964—68; chmn. Ohio Interuniv. Coun. Sch. Psychology, 1967. Editor Ohio Psychologist, 1961-68, co-editor, 1972-79; contbr. articles to profl. publs. Vol. Hamilton County Parks, 1982—, vol. naturalist, 1995—; vol. educator Cin. Zoo, 1982—. Recipient George B. Barbour award, 1985; 20 Yrs. of Svc. award Cin. Zoo, 2002, Hamilton County Parks Dist., 25 Yrs. of Svc. award, 2007; named to Disting. Alumni Hall of Fame Norwood City Schs. Alumni Assn., 2007. Mem. AAUP, APA, Nat. Assn. School Psychologists, Ohio Psychol. Assn. (citation 1972, Disting. Svc. award 1968), Southwestern Ohio Sch. Psychol. Assn., Cin. Psychol. Assn. (sec. 1961-62), Sch. Psychologists Ohio, Forum for Death Edn. and Counseling, Kappa Delta Pi, Sigma Delta Pi, Psi Chi (award for outstanding mentor 1985, award for outstanding contbns. to undergrad. psychology students 1994). Avocations: horseback riding, photography. Office: U Cin Dept Psychology Ml 376 Cincinnati OH 45221-0001

BLUESTONE, CHARLES D., otolaryngologist; b. Pitts., Apr. 4, 1932; MD, U. Pitts., 1958. Cert. Am. Bd. Otolaryngology. Intern Montefiore Hosp. Pitts., 1958—58; resident U. Ill. Rsch. and Edn. Hosp., Ill. Eye and Ear Infirmary, Chgo., 1959—62; founder, dir. pediatric otolaryngology dept. Children's Hosp. Pitts., 1975, founder Otitis Media Rsch. Ctr., 1980, Eberly prof. pediatric otolaryngology, chief otolaryngology; prof. pediatric otolaryngology U. Pitts. Sch. Medicine. Named to Top Docs, Castle Connolly Med. Ltd., 2005, Pitts. Mag., 2005; finalist Health Care Hero, Lifetime Achievement, Pitts. Bus. Times, 2005. Mem.: Am. Soc. Pediatric Otolaryngology, Am. Acad. Pediat., Sect. Pediatric Otolaryngology and Bronchoesophagology (founding chmn. 1977—78), Am. Otol. Soc., Soc. Ear, Nose and Throat Advances in Children, Am. Acad. Otolaryngology - Head and Neck Surgery, Inc., Soc. U. Otolaryngologists. Office: Otolaryngology Childrens Hosp Pitts 45th St & Penn Ave 3d Fl Pittsburgh PA 15201 Office Phone: 412-692-5460. Business E-Mail: charles.bluestone@chp.edu.

BLUM, CONRAD B., endocrinologist, educator, MD, Northwestern U., 1971. Diplomate Am. Bd. Internal Medicine, 1976, Am. Bd. Internal Medicine-endocrinology, diabetes and metabolism, 1977. Resident internal medicine Brigham Women and Children's Hosp., Boston, 1975—76; fellow endocrinology, diabetes and metabolism Northwestern Univ. Med. Sch., Chgo., 1976—77; clin. prof. medicine Columbia Univ. Coll. of Physicians and Surgeons; hosp. affiliation includes NY-Presbyn. Univ. Hosp. of Columbia and Cornell. Office: NY-Presbyterian University Hospital of Columbia and Cornell 16 E 60th St New York NY 10022 Office Phone: 212-326-8421. Office Fax: 212-326-8782.

BLUM, HANS-CHRISTIAN, physician; b. Berlin, Oct. 9, 1954; MD, Coll. Francais de Berlin, 1974, U. Essen, 1985. Cert. in internal medicine, pulmonary medicine 1991, in allergology 1992, in environ. medicine 1994, in sleep medicine 2005. With Found. Pvt. Practice Pulmonary Medicine, Allergology & Sleep Medicine, Dortmund, 1992—, Founda. Sleep Lab., Dortmund, 1995—, Found. Somonolab-Ctrs. Sleep Medicine Essen & Dortmund with Ptnr. Dr.Riccardo Stoohs, 2000—05; pvt. practice pulmonary medicine, allergology & sleep medicine Dortmund, 2000—, 2008—. Former pres. Berufsverband der Pneumologen, Nordrhein-Westfalen, former v.p.; pres. NAV-Virchowbund, Westfalen-Lippe; bd. mem. Quality Mgmt. Kassenärztliche Vereinigung Westfalen-Lippe. Mem.: Deutsche Gesellschaft für Allergologie und Immunologie, Deutsche Gesellschaft für Schlafmedizin und Schlafforschung, Am Thoracic Soc., European Respiratory Soc., Deutsche Gesellschaft für Pneumologie. Avocations: golf, literature, art, theater. Office: Hermannstrasse 48-52 Dortmund North-Rhine-Westfalia 44263 Germany Office Phone: 0049-231-94117511. Personal E-mail: hcblum@t-online.de.

BLUM, JACOB JOSEPH, physiologist, educator; b. Bklyn., Oct. 3, 1926; s. Paul and Anna (Brown) B.; m. Ruth Marsey, June 3, 1960; children: Mark, Douglas, Lisa, Laura. BA, NYU, 1947; MS, U. Chgo., 1950, PhD, 1952. Mem. staff Naval Med. Rsch. Inst., Bethesda, Md., 1953-56; chief biophysics sect. gerontology br. NIH, Balt., 1958-62; prof. physiology Duke U., Durham, NC, 1962—, James B. Duke prof., 1980-97, James B. Duke prof. emeritus, 1997—. With AUS, 1945-46. Merck postdoctoral fellow, 1952, Guggenheim fellow, 1969, Fogarty sr. internat. fellow, 1992. Mem. Am. Physiol. Soc., Soc. Protozoologists (pres. 1991). Home: 16 Stoneridge Cir Durham NC 27705 Office Phone: 919-684-6937. Business E-Mail: j.blum@cellbio.duke.edu.

BLUM, RICHARD HOSMER ADAMS, foundation administrator, educator, writer; b. Ft. Wayne, Ind., Oct. 7, 1927; s. Hosmer and Imogene (Heino) B. AB with honors magna cum laude, San Jose State Coll., 1948; PhD, Stanford U., 1951. Rsch. dir. Calif. Med. Assn., San Francisco, 1956-58, San Mateo County (Calif.) Mental Health Service, San Mateo, 1958-60; lectr. Sch. Criminology, U. Calif., Berkeley, 1960-62, mem. faculty Stanford (Calif.) U., 1962-78, prof. dept. psychology, 1970-75, prof. dept. gynecology and obstetrics, 1982-97; mem. faculty Stanford (Calif.) U. Law Sch., 1975-78; chmn. bd. Am. Lives Endowment, Portola Valley, Calif., 1979—. Chmn. Internat. Rsch. Group on Drug Legis. and Programs, Geneva, 1969—78; pres. Bio-Behavioral Rsch. Group, Inc., Palo Alto, 1964—87; owner, operator Shingle Mill Ranch, 1964—; vis. fellow Wolfson Coll. U. Cambridge, 1984; vis. prof. social and polit. sci. U. Cambridge, 1997—98; dir. ethics program World Jurist Assn./World Peace Through Law Ctr., Washington, 2000—; dep. chmn. Commn. for the World Equity Ct.; prof. St. Josephs of Arimanthea Theol. Sem.,

Berkeley, Calif., China U. Polit. Sci. and Law, Beijing; officer Superior Ctr. Conservator for Health Care; guest prof. Northeastern U., Changchun; disting. vis. prof. Dalian U., China; pres. Knightsbridge Castle Found. Author: 30 books. Trustee Palace Mus. of the Last Emperor Puye, Manchuria, China. With U.S. Army, 1951-53, Korea. Decorated Bronze Star; recipient APA Presdl. citation. Fellow APHA (coun. sr. advisors), AAAS, Am. Psychol. Soc., Soc. Advanced Legal Studies (hon., life); mem. Archaeol. Inst. Am., Sigma Xi, Cosmos Club, Athenaeum Club, San Francisco Univ. Club. Unitarian. Home: PO Box 620482 Woodside CA 94062-0482

BLUM, SAMUEL, retired research scientist; b. Aug. 1920; BS Chemistry, Rutgers U., 1942, PhD Phys. Chemistry, 1950; cert. meterology, weather forecasting, UCLA. Ret. rsch. scientist IBM Watson Rsch. Ctr., 1990. Active alumni work Rutgers U. Mem. US Navy. Recipient Nat. Inventors Hall of Fame, 2002. Achievements include invention of Far Ultraviolet Surgical and Dental Procedures. Avocations: travel, gardening.

BLUMBERG, JOEL MYRON, cardiologist; b. NYC, Oct. 17, 1940; s. Howard Godfrey and Lily Ruth (Goldberg) Blumberg; m. Judith Ellen Green, Aug. 23, 1964; children: Amy, Hillary, Michelle. BA, DePauw U., 1962; MD, NYU, 1966. Diplomate Am. Bd. Internal Medicine. Intern NYU-Bellevue Med. Ctr., NYC, 1966—67, resident internal medicine, 1969—71; fellow cardiology Cornell U.-NY Hosp., 1971—73; pvt. practice internal medicine and cardiology Greenwich, Conn., 1973—; attending staff Greenwich Hosp., 1973—, coronary care cons., 1973—; physician to out-patients NY Hosp., 1973—77. Clin. instr. Cornell U. Med. Coll., 1971—77; clin. asst. prof. Yale Sch. Medicine, 1975—; lectr. preventive cardiology civic groups; bd. visitors DePauw U.; bd. incorporators Greenwich Hosp. Contbr. articles to profl. jours. Recipient Excellence tchg. award, 2002; named to Best Doctors America, 2005, Best Doctors NY, 2005, Best Doctors Conn., 2006. Fellow: Am. Heart Assn., Am. Coll. Cardiology, ACP; mem.: B'nai B'rith (Stamford, Conn.), Conn. State med. socs., Fairfield County, Greenwich, NY Heart Assn., Am. Soc. Internal Medicine. Home: 59 Old Stone Bridge Rd Cos Cob CT 06807-1511 Office: 55 Holly Hill Ln Ste #210 Greenwich CT 06830 Home Phone: 203-869-9055; Office Phone: 203-661-4242.

BLUMBERG, MARK STUART, health service researcher, scientist, director; b. NYC, Nov. 16, 1924; s. Sydney N. and Mollie (Leshrowitz) B.; m. Luba Monasevitch, 1952; children: Bart David, Eve Luise; m. 2d Elizabeth R. Conner, 1974. Student, Johns Hopkins U., 1942-43, Harvard U., 1943-44, student Sch. Pub. Health, 1955, DMD, 1948, MD, 1950. Intern, children's med. service Bellevue Hosp., NYC, 1950-51; ops. analyst Johns Hopkins U. Ops. Research Office, Chevy Chase, Md., 1951-54; exchange analyst Army Ops. Research Group (U.K.), West Byfleet, Eng., 1953-54; staff Occupational Health Program, USPHS, Washington, 1954-56; assoc. ops. analyst to dir. health econs. program Stanford (Calif.) Research Inst., 1956-66; asst. to v.p. adminstrn. to dir. health planning, office of the pres. U. Calif., Berkeley, 1966-70; corp. planning advisor to dir. spl. studies Kaiser Found. Health Plan, Inc., Oakland, Calif., 1970-94; dir. Kaiser Found. Health Plan of Conn., Hartford, 1982-94, Kaiser Found. Health Plan Mass., 1987-94; cons. risk adjusted measures Oakland, 1994—; founding ptnr. TruRisk LLC, 1998—. Various times cons. Pan Am. Health Orgn., Calif. State Dept. Mental Hygiene, Carnegie Commn. on Higher Edn., various agys. HHS. Contbr. writings to profl. publs. Vol. Grenfell Med. Mission, Harrington Harbour, Que., Can., summer 1948; mem. tech. adv. com. AB 524 State of Calif., 1992—97. Served with USNR, 1943-45; with USPHS, 1954-56. Mem. Ops. Research Soc. Am. (past mem. council, Health Applications sect.), Hosp. Mgmt. Systems Soc. (charter), Inst. of Medicine of Nat. Acad. Scis. Achievements include 5 recent US patents for computerized underwriting of group life and disability using medical claims data. Office Phone: 510-601-9536. Business E-Mail: msbmd@lycos.com.

BLUMBERG, MICHAEL ZANGWILL, allergist; b. Phila., July 29, 1945; s. Jerome Blumberg and Vivian Rose (Liebman) Steiger; m. Barbara Sue Gurman, June 9, 1973; children: Jessica Lynn, Jason Mark. AB, Brandeis U., 1967; MD, Jefferson Med. Coll., 1971; MSHA., Va. Commonwealty U., 1998. Diplomate Am Bd Pediatrics, Am Bd Allergy and Immunology. Intern, resident N.Y. Hosp., Cornell U. Med. Ctr., 1971-73; fellow in allergy and immunology Nat. Jewish Hosp.-U. Colo. Med. Ctr., 1973-75; chief allergy sect. major Scott Air Force Base, Ill., 1975-77; physician-ptnr. Va. Adult and Pediat. Allergy and Asthma, Richmond, 1977—, mng. ptnr., 1998—; assoc. clin. prof. pediatrics Med. Coll. Va., Richmond, 1977—2002, 2000—; chief of allergy Children's Hosp. of Richmond, 1987-2000; ptnr. Clin. Rsch., Richmond, 1998—. Med advisor Sanofi-Aventis, Astra Zeneca, Glaxo SmithKline, Merck; mem. editl. bd. Annals Allergy, Asthma and Immunology, 2010—. Contbr. articles and abstracts to profl jours; contbg. editor: Review in Allergy, 1978; mem ed bd: Jour Asthma, 1996—. Mem exec comt, pres, bd dirs, chmn Beth Shalom Home Va, Richmond, 1987—95; bd. dirs. Allergy Ptnrs., 1977—2010; vice chmn. Common Wealth Va. Adv. Bd. Respitatory Care Team, 2010—11; bd. dirs Jewish Community Ctr, Richmond, 1984—87, Va. Endowment Jewish Aged, 2009; bd dirs endowment fund, mem budget comt Jewish Fedn; pres. Richmond Jewish Found., 2002. Recipient Maimonides award, Jewish Fedn. Richmond, 2006, Chased award, Rudlin Torah Acad. Co. Svc., 2009; named one of Best Drs. in America, 2007—10, 2011—. Fellow: Am Acad Pediatrics, Col Chest Physicians, Am Col Allergy, Asthma and Immunology (pub. rels.com.); mem.: Allergy Ptnrs., Allergy and Asthma Soc. Va. (pres. 2002—04), Am Thoracic Soc, Am Acad Allergy, Asthma and Immunology (managed care com.), Am Col Allergy Sports Med (practice standards com. 1994—95), Friends of Brandeis Athletics, Masons, Phi Kappa Phi. Jewish. Avocations: exercise, history. Office: Allergy Partners-Richmond Hub 7605 Forest Ave Ste 103 Richmond VA 23229-4936 Home: 149 W Square Court Richmond VA 23238 Office Phone: 804-288-0055, 804-285-8465. Personal E-mail: mshadoc@comcast.net. Business E-Mail: mblumberg@allergypartners.com.

BLUME, RALPH S., rheumatologist, educator; Studied, Columbia U., 1964. Diplomate Am. Bd. Internal Medicine, Am. Bd. Internal Medicine-rheumatology. Intern Columbia-Presbyn. Med Ctr., resident, 1965—68, fellow, 1968—70; clin. prof. of clin. medicine Columbia Univ. Office: Columbia University 630 W 168th St Rm 2-463 New York NY 10032 Office Phone: 212-305-1181. Office Fax: 212-305-0485.

BLUMENBERG, ROBERT MURRAY, retired surgeon, educator; b. Rochester, NY, Jan. 5, 1934; s. Theodore Peter and Esther Frances (Sablowsky) B.; m. Linda Dibble, Dec. 13, 1962 (div. 1984); children: Andrew C., Dara R., Laura A.; m. Gayle Eastwood, Nov. 9, 1986; step child: David Hobbs. AB cum laude, Amherst Coll., Mass., 1955; MD, Albany Med. Coll., NY, 1959. Diplomate Am. Bd. Surgery. Surg. intern Strong Meml. Hosp., Rochester, 1959—60; asst. resident surgery Albany Med. Ctr. Hosps., NY, 1960—64, chief resident, 1964—65; instr. surgery Albany Med. Coll., 1967—68, asst. clin. prof., 1968—2000, prof. emeritus, 2000—; pvt. practice Schenectady, 1968—2003; attending surgeon, chief divsn. vascular surgery Ellis Hosp., Schenectady, 1968—2003; attending surgeon St. Clare's Hosp., Schenectady, 1968—2003, ret., 2003; vascular surgeon Vascular Inst., Albany Med. Coll., 2000—03. Cons. surgeon VA Hosp., Albany, Sunnyview Rehab. Hosp., Bellevue Maternity Hosp., Schenectady. Contbr. articles to med. jours., also chpts. to books. Capt. Med.Corps, US Army, 1965-67 USPHS grantee, 1963-65 Fellow ACS; mem. Soc. for Clin. Vascular Surgery (exec. com. 1978—, pres. 1981-82), Soc. for Vascular Surgery (sr.), Ea. Vascular Soc. (founding), Upstate NY Vascular Surg. Soc. (founding, pres. 1985-86), Am. Trauma Soc., Schenectady County Med. Soc., Vietnam Vascular Surg. Registry. Jewish. Avocations: golf, skiing, platform tennis, jazz. Home (Winter): 5050 Yacht Harbor Cir #101 Naples FL 34112 Home (Summer): PO Box 519 Siasconset MA 02564 Personal E-mail: robertblu@comcast.net.

BLUMENCRANZ, PETER WILLIAM, surgeon; b. NYC, Mar. 8, 1946; s. Bernard and Evelyn (Guttman) B.; m. Ann Frances Garfes, June 6, 1970; children: Brett, Lisa, Jennifer, Deborah, Todd. BA, U. Pa., 1966; MD, Cornell U., 1970. Diplomate Am. Bd. Surgery. Resident in surgery N.Y. Hosp.-Cornell U. Med. Ctr., NYC, 1970-76; fellow in surg. oncology Meml. Hosp.-Sloan Kettering Cancer Ctr., NYC, 1976-77; surgeon Diagnostic Clinic, Largo, Fla., 1977-79, Fla. Surg. Assocs., Clearwater, Fla., 1980-95; pres. Surg. Assocs. West Fla., Clearwater, 1995—2009; med. dir. Comprehensive Breast Care Ctr. Tampa Bay, 2009—. Bd. dirs. Morton Plant Mease Health Care; trustee Morton Plant Hosp., Clearwater, Fla., 1992—98, 2005—11; med. dir. Moffitt Morton Plant Cancer Care, Tampa, Fla., 2001—. Trustee Shorecrest Prep. Sch., St. Petersburg, Fla., 1982-88; bd. dirs. Pinellas unit Am. Cancer Soc., 2006-09. Lt. comdr. USN, 1972-74. Fellow Soc. Surg. Oncology, Am. Coll. Surgeons, Southeastern Surg. Congress; mem. Am. Soc. Breast Diseases, Fla. Soc. Clinical Oncology, Am. Soc. Clin. Oncology, Am. Soc. Breast Surgeons, State Fla. Cancer Coun., Fla. Soc. Gen. Surgeons. (bd. dirs. 1998—). Avocations: tennis, running. Office Phone: 727-462-2131.

BLUMENTHAL, DANIEL SENDER, medical educator; b. St. Louis, May 26, 1942; s. Herman T. and Eleonore G. B.; m. Janet M. Berstein, June 7, 1968 (dec. Jan. 1994); children: Rebecca, Jeffrey; m. Maojorie Speers, Jan. 1, 1998. BA, Oberlin Coll., 1964; MD, U. Chgo., 1968; MPH, Emory U., 1986. Diplomate Am. Bd. Pediat., Am. Bd. Preventive Medicine. Intern Charity Hosp., New Orleans, 1968—69, resident, 1970—72; med. epidemiologist Ctrs. for Disease Control, 1972—75; asst. prof. Emory U. Sch. Medicine, 1975—80; assoc. prof. dept. cmty. medicine and family practice Morehouse Sch. Medicine, 1980—85, prof., chmn. dept. community health and preventative medicine, 1985—, acting chmn. dept., 1982—85; health officer Fulton County, 1996. Mem. Nat. Adv. Coun. Maternal, Fetal and Infant Nutriton, USDA, 1979-82; med. cons. Job Corps, U.S. Dept. Labor, 1975-82; contbr. articles to profl. jours Bd. dirs. ACLU, 1983-87. With USPHS, 1972-75. Mem. APHA (mem. governing coun.), Am. Acad. Pediat., Am. Soc. Tropical Medicine and Hygiene, Assn. Tchrs. Preventive Medicine (pres. 1992-93), others. Office: Sch Medicine 720 Westview Dr SW Atlanta GA 30310-1458 Home: 1057 Washita Ave Atlanta GA 30307

BLUMENTHAL, DAVID, medical educator, former federal official; b. NYC, Aug. 31, 1948; s. Martin and Jane (Rosenstock) Blumenthal; m. Ellen G. Blumenthal, Aug. 9, 1970; children: Daniel, Karen. BA, Harvard Coll., 1970; MD, Harvard Med. Sch., 1975; MA of Pub. Policy, John F. Kennedy Sch. Govt., Harvard U., 1975; LHD (hon.), Rush U., Chgo., 2008. Diplomate American Bd. Internal Medicine. Intern, resident Mass. Gen Hosp., Boston, 1975—76, resident in medicine, 1979—80; profl. staff mem. US Senate Subcommittee on Health, Washington, 1977-79; clin. instr. medicine Harvard Med. Sch., Boston, 1980—87, instr. health policy, 1980—88, asst. prof. medicine, 1987—93, assoc. prof., 1993—99, prof. medicine, prof. health care policy, 1999—2009, Samuel O. Thier prof. medicine, 2004—09, prof. medicine, 2011—; nat. coord. for health info. tech. US Dept. Health & Human Services, Washington, 2009—11. Josiah Macy fellow health policy John F. Kennedy Sch. Govt., 1980—81, exec. dir. Ctr. Health Policy, 1981—87; asst. in medicine Mass. Gen. Hosp., 1983—87, assoc. physician, 1991—97, chief Health Policy Rsch. & Devel. unit, 1991—2009, physician, 1997—2009; assoc. physician, sr. v.p. Brigham & Women's Hosp., Boston, 1987—91; exec. dir. Task Force Future of Academic Health Centers, Commonwealth Fund, 1996—2002; dir. Inst. Health Policy, Mass. Gen. Hosp./Partners HealthCare Sys., Boston, 1998—2009. Co-author (with James A. Morone): Health Care and the American Presidency, 2002; contbr. articles to profl. jours., chapters to books. Mem. nat. adv. bd. Ctr. Nat. Policy, 1982—90; chair Mass. Commn. Future of Pub. Health, 1993—95; bd. trustees Alpha Ctr., Washington, 1992—, vice chmn. bd. trustees, 1995—98; chmn. bd. dirs. Mass. Peer Rev. Orgn., 1996—2002. Recipient Shannon award, NIH, 1992, Investigator award in health policy, Robert Wood Johnson Found., 2003; Jacob Wendell Scholar, 1968. Fellow: Assn. Health Services Rsch.; mem.: NAS (assoc.), Inst. Medicine, Soc. Gen. Internal Medicine, Nat. Acad. Social Ins., Mass. Pub. Health Assn., American Coll. Preventive Medicine, Alpha Omega Alpha, Phi Beta Kappa. Democrat. Mailing: Harvard Medical School 25 Shattuck St Boston MA 02115 *

BLUMENTHAL, DAVID S., cardiologist, educator; Attended, Weill Cornell Med. Coll., 1975. Resident internal medicine NY-Presbyn. Hosp., 1980—81, affiliation; fellow cardiovasc. disease Johns Hopkins Hosp., 1978—80; clin. prof. medicine Weill Cornell Med. Coll.; sr. v.p. Boston's Brigham and Women's Hosp.; exec. dir. ctr. for health policy mgmt. Kennedy Sch. of Govt., lectr.; founding chmn. Acad. Health; bd. mem. Univ. of Chgo. Health System, Univ. of Pa. Health System; physician Mass. Gen. Hosp., dir. inst. for health policy; nat. coord. Health Info. Tech., 2010—. Former bd. mem. New England Jour. of Medicine, nat. corr. Author: Heart of Power: Health and Politics in the Oval Office. Mem. Inst. of Medicine. Recipient Distinguished Investigator award, Acad. Health; grantee Dr. of Humane Letters, Rush Univ. Office: NewYork-Presbyterian Hospital Fl 1 407 E 70th St New York NY 10021 Office Phone: 212-861-3222.

BLUMENTHAL, MARK, organization administrator; b. Toledo, Sept. 4, 1946; s. Alfred and Frances (Schwartz) B.; m. Susan Ervin, 1971 (div. 1973); 1 child, Eva; m. Jacquelyn S. Small, 1978. BA in Govt. with honors, U. Tex., 1968. Editor/pub. HerbalGram, Austin, Tex., 1983—; exec. dir. Am. Bot. Coun., Austin, 1988—. Sci. clin. advisor U. Tex. Ctr. for Alternative Medicine, Austin, 1996—. Editor: Commission E Monographs, 1996; editor HerbalGram, 1983; editl. adv. bd. Vegetarian Times, 1994—. Bd. dirs. Useful Wild Plants/Tex. Inc., Austin, 1992—, Amazon Ctr. for Environ. Edn. and Rsch. Found., Helena, Ala., 1995—. With USAR, 1970. Recipient Cliff Adler Heart and Bus. award, 1992, Industry Achievement award Tex. Herb Growers and Marketers Assn., 1994. Office: American Botanical Council PO Box 144345 Austin TX 78714-4345

BLUMENTHAL, ROBERT P., medical researcher; MSc, U. Leiden, The Netherlands; PhD, Weizmann Inst., Israel. Postdoctoral work Inst. Pasteur, Columbia U., NYC; head membrane structure and function sect. Ctr. Cancer Rsch., Nat. Cancer Inst., NIH, Frederick, Md., 1980—, dir. Nanobiology Program, 2005—. Office: Ctr Cancer Rsch Nanobiology Program NCI Frederick Bldg 469 Rm 152 PO Box B Frederick MD 21702-1201 Office Phone: 301-846-5532. Office Fax: 301-846-5598. E-mail: BlumenthalR@mail.nih.gov. *

BLUMENTHAL, ROGER SCOTT, cardiologist; b. Washington, Jan. 17, 1960; s. Stanley and Anita B.; m. Wendy Post, Apr. 12, 1997. MD, Cornell U., 1985. Diplomate Am. Bd. Internal Med. Intern Johns Hopkins Hosp., Balt., 1985-86, resident in internal medicine, 1986-88, fellow in cardiology, 1988-92, mem. staff, 1992—; assoc. prof. Johns Hopkins U., dir. Ciccarone Preventive Cardiology Ctr.; prof. medicine Nat. Lipid Edn. Coun., 2007—. Editl. bd. Cardiology Rev., Cardiology Today, Jour. Women's Health. Mem. AMA, Am. Col. Physicians, Am. Col. Cardiologists, Md. chpt. Am. Heart Assn. (past pres.), Balt. divsn. Am. Heart Assn. (bd. dir.), SE Lipid Assn. (pres. 2004), Nat. Lipid Edn. Coun. Avocation: golf. Office: Johns Hopkins Hosp Divsn Cardiology-Blalock 524C 600 N Wolfe St Baltimore MD 21287 Address: Johns Hopkins at Timonium 110 W Timonium Rd Ste 2C Timonium MD 21093 Business E-Mail: rblument@jhmi.edu.

BLUMENTHAL, SUSAN JANE, physician, psychiatrist, educator, public health leader; m. Edward John Markey. BA, Reed Coll., Portland, Oreg., 1971; MD, U. Tenn., 1976; MPA, Harvard U., Cambridge, Mass., 1982; PhD (hon.), Trinity Coll., Washington, 1996, Ben Gurion U., Israel, 2005, Pine Manor Coll., Chestnut Hill, Mass. Diplomate Am. Bd. Psychiatry and Neurology. Intern. Stanford U. Sch. Medicine, 1976-77, residency and fellowship, 1977-80; fellow NIMH, 1980-81, assoc. dir. Psychiatry Tng. Rev., head suicide rsch. unit and coord. of project depression, 1982-85, chief behavioral medicine program, 1985-93, chief behavioral and basic prevention rsch. br., 1991-93; clin. asst. prof. Tufts Med. Ctr., 1981-82; clin. asst. prof. psychiatry George Washington Sch. Medicine, 1982-86; clin. assoc. prof. psychiatry Georgetown Sch. Medicine, Washingtown, 1986-91, clin. prof. psychiatry, 1991—; first dep. asst. sec. women's health US Dept. HHS, Washington, 1993—97, asst. surgeon gen., 1996—2005, sr. med. and e-health advisor, 2002—05, sr. sci. advisor, 2002—05, sr. global health advisor, 2003—05; clin. prof. psychiatry Tufts Sch. Medicine, 1995—; assoc. v.p. for health affairs George Washington U. Med. Ctr., 1998; dir., health and medicine program Ctr. Study of the Presidency & Congress, Washington, 2006—; sr. policy and med. advisor amfAR, Found. AIDS Rsch., 2007—; chair Global Health Program, Meridian Internat. Ctr., 2008—; pub. health editor Huffington Post, 2010—. Vis. prof. ob-gyn. George Washington U. Med. Ctr., 1998-99; disting. prof. women's studies Brandeis U., 1999—2007; vis. prof. Stanford U., 2004-05, Mayo Clinic, 2005; hon. prof. Ben Gurion U. Sch. Medicine, 2004-, med. dir. Discovery Channel/AFI global health series, 2006; chief med. advisor PBS Health Initiative, 2006; chair NIH Coord. Com. on Health and Behavior, 1991-94; co-chair NIH Reunion Task Force, 1992-94; chair Fed. Coord. Com. Breast Cancer, fed. coord. com. women's health and the environ., co-chair nat. breast cancer action plan; coord. Com. Women's Health Issues and Domestic Violence, 1994-98; mem. Pres.'s Interagy. Coun. on Women; sr. health advisor, White House Coun. on Youth Violence, 2000-02, sr. med. advisor to the sec., USDA, 2000-02; vis. fellow Harvard U. Sch. Govt., 2004-05; chair Save the Children, Nat. Adv. Coun. on Obesity Prevention, 2007—. Editor: Suicide Over the Life Cycle, 1989, Premenstrual Syndrome, 1985; mem. editl. bds.: Jour. Women's Health, Depression, health columnist: Elle Mag., Ladies Home Jour., U.S. News and World Report; pub. health editor and health columnist Huffington Post; med. dir.: Discovery/AFI global health film series; chief med. advisor: PBS Health Initiative; contbr. articles to sci. jours. Mem. Nat. Commn. on Sleep Disorders Rsch., workgroup on mental health Pres. Task Force on Health Care Reform; U.S. rep. global commn. on Women's Health WHO, chair, Global Health Program; trustee Meridian Internat. Ctr., 2005—, Save the Children, Capt. USPHS, 1992-94, rear adm., 1994—, co-chair Commn. Future Directions in Health & Future CSPC, 2008- Recipient Outstanding Svc. medal, 1989, Commendation medal, 1990, Meritorious Svc. medal, USPHS, 1992, Sec.'s Honor award for Domestic Violence, 1996, Asst. Sec. for Health's award for Breast Cancer, 1996, Am. Med. Writers award, 1996, Gretchen Poston award, The Nat. Race for the Cure, 1996, Founder's award, 1996, Pub. Svc. award, Nat. Alliance for the Mentally Ill, 1996, Surgeon Gen.'s Exemplary Svc. medal, 1997, Gracie award, Assn. Women Radio and TV Profls., 1997, Inspiration Leader award, Pa. Diabetes Assn., 1997, Spl. Assignment Svc. medal, USPHS, 1998, 2002, Women of Distinction award, Nat. Assn. Women in Higher Edn., 1998, Woman of Valor award, United Jewish Fedn., 1999, Mosaic award, Komen Found., 1999—2000, Founder's award, 2000, Feminist First award for Health, Feminist Majority, 2000, Congl. award, 2001, Congl. citation, 2002, Achievement medal, USPHS, 2002, Women's Ctr. Leadership award, 2003, Leadership award, Save the Children, 2004, Nat. Breast Cancer Awareness Pub. Svcs. Leadership award, 2004, Disting. Svc. medal, Spirit of Life Found., 2004, USPHS, 2006, Presdl. Sacher Medallion, Brandeis U., 2005, Internat. Health award, Embassy Italy, 2010; named Rockstar of Sci., 2010, Health Leader of Yr., Commd. Officer Assn., 2009; fellow, Harvard U. Sch. Govt., 2004. Fellow AMA (disting.); mem. Am. Psychiat. Assn. (cons. Joint Coun. on Pub. Affairs, Francis Braceland award for pub. svc. 1998), Am. Coll. Psychiatrists, Am. Med. Women's Assn. (past chair com. on publicity and pub. rels., Pres.'s citation, 1996), Congl. Club, Nat. Assn. Bus. and Profl. Women (Magnificent Seven award

1996), Internat. Club, Internat. Women's Forum, Am. Suicide Found. (past bd. dirs. Washington divsn., pres.), Starlight Found. (past chmn. sci. adv. bd.). Office Phone: 202-872-9800. Personal E-mail: healthinstitutes@gmail.com.

BLUMSTEIN, JAMES FRANKLIN, lawyer, educator, consultant; b. Bklyn., Apr. 24, 1945; s. David and Rita (Sondheim) B.; m. Andree Kahn, June 25, 1971 BA in Econs., Yale U., 1966, MA in Econs., LLB, 1970. Bar: Tenn. 1970, U.S. Ct. Appeals (6th cir.) 1970, U.S. Dist. Ct. (mid. dist.) Tenn. 1971, U.S. Supreme Ct. 1974, N.Y. 1985. Instr. econs. New Haven Coll., 1967-68; pre-law adviser office of dean Yale U., New Haven, 1968-69, sr. pre-law adviser office of dean, 1969-70, asst. in instrn. law shc., 1969-70; asst. prof. law Vanderbilt U., Nashville, 1970-73, assoc. prof., 1973-76, prof., 1976-99, spl. advisor to chancellor for acad. affairs, 1984-85, Centennial prof., 1999—2003, Univ. prof. constl. law and health law and policy, 2003—, chair faculty senate, 2001—02, univ. prof., 2003—. Assoc. dir. Vanderbilt Urban and Regional Devel. Ctr., 1970-72, dir. ctr., 1972-74; sr. rsch. assoc. Vanderbilt Inst. for Pub. Policy Studies, 1976-85, sr. fellow, 1985—, dir. health policy ctr., 1995—; Commonwealth Fund fellow, vis. assoc. prof. law and policy scis. law sch. Duke U. and Inst. of Policy Scis. and Pub. Affairs, 1974-75; adj. prof. health law med. sch. Dartmouth U., scholar-in-residence intermittently, 1976-78; John M. Olin vis. prof. Sch. Law, U. Pa., 1989; elected mem. Inst. Medicine NAS, 1990—; bd. dirs. St. Thomas Health Scis. Found., Alive Hospice, Nashville; cons. law, health policy, civil and voting rights, land use, state taxation, torts; scholar-in-residence Robert Wood Johnson Found. Ctr. in Health Policy, Meharry Med. Coll., 2010-11; lectr. in field. Editor: (with Eddie J. Martin) The Urban Scene in the Seventies, 1974, (with Benjamin Walter) Growing Metropolis: Aspects of Development in Nashville, 1975, (with Lester Salamon) Growth Policy in the Eighties (Law and Contemporary Problems Symposium), 1979; (with Frank A. Sloan and James M. Perrin) Uncompensated Hospital Care: Rights and Responsibilities, 1986, (with Frank A. Sloan and James M. Perrin) Cost, Quality, and Access in Health Care: New Roles for Health Planning in a Competitive Environment, 1988; (with Frank A. Sloan) Organ Transplantation Policy: Issues and Prospects, 1989, (with Frank A. Sloan) Antitrust and Health Care Policy (Law and Contemporary Problems Symposium), 1989, (with Clark C. Havighurst and Troyen A. Brennan) Health Care Law and Policy, 1998, supplement, 2007, bd. Jour. Health Politics, Policy and Law, 1981-01; mem. adv. bd. Nat. Fedn. Ind. Bus. Legal Found., 2003-; mem. pub.'s adv. bd. Nashville Banner, 1982-98; contbr. articles to profl. jours., op-ed articles to newspapers. Mem. Health Econs. Task Force, Middle Tenn. Health Sys. Agy., 1979; mem. Nashville Mayor's Commn. on Crime, 1981; chmn. Yale Alumni Schs. Com. Middle Tenn., 1983—; sec. Martin Luther King Jr. Holiday Com., State of Tenn., 1985—87; mem. Tenn. Gov.'s Task Force Medicaid, 1992—94; active Inst. Medicine Com. on Adequacy of Nursing Staffing, 1994—96; chmn. Tenn. adv. com. U.S. Commn. on Civil Rights, 1985—91, mem., 1991—97; bd. dirs. Alive Hosp., 2005—11, St. Thomas Health Svcs. Found.; mem. adv. bd. LWV, 1979—80; bd. dirs. Jewish Fedn. Nashville and Middle Tenn., 1981—90, mem. exec. com., 1988—90, chmn. cmty. rels. com., 1980—82, chmn. campus com., 1987—89; chmn. task force cost containment and med. malpractice Rand Corp., 1991—92, mem. adv. panel Office Tech. Assessment study of defensive medicine and use of med. tech., 1991—94; mem. adv. com. on The Records of Congress, 1997—99; cons. Leadership Nashville, 1977—, Tenn. Motor Vehicle Commn., 1986—87, Leadership Music, 1989—2002, Tenncare Reform Project, Office Gov. Phil Bredesen, 2004—, Acad. Country Music, 2005; panelist Am. Arbitration Assn., 1977—2002. Bates Jr. fellow, 1968-69; grantee Ford Found./Rockefeller Found. Population Program, 1970-73, Health Policy grantee HCA Found., 1986-90; grantee State Justice Inst., 1991—2000, Robert Wood Johnson Found., 1994—2000; named One of Outstanding Young Men in Am., 1971; recipient award Univ. Rsch. Coun., 1971-72, 73-74, 79-80, 94-95, Earl Sutherland prize achievement in rsch. Vanderbilt U., 1992, Paul J. Hartman award Outstanding Prof., 1982. Mem. ABA (sec. sect. legal edn. and admissions to bar 1982-83, chmn. subcom. on state and local taxation com. on corp. law and taxation sect. on corp., banking and bus. law 1983—, mem. accreditation com. sect. legal edn. and admissions to bar 1983-89, mem. com. on state and local taxation sect. on taxation 1983—), NAS (inst. of medicine), Assn. Am. Law Schs. (chmn. law, medicine and health care sect. 1987-88, mem. exec. com. 1988-92, 2d vice chmn. sect. local govt. law 1976-78, mem. sect. coun. 1980-86), Tenn. Bar Assn. (Pres.'s award 2004), N.Y. State Bar Assn., Nashville Bar Assn. (Liberty Bell award 1987), Assn. Yale Alumni (del.), Yale U. Law Sch. Alumni Assn. (exec. com. 1985-88), Univ. Club (Nashville). Home: 2113 Hampton Ave Nashville TN 37215-1401 Office: Vanderbilt U Sch Law 21st Ave S Nashville TN 37240-0001 Office Phone: 615-322-2615.

BLYTHE, MARGARET J., pediatrician, educator; MD, Ind. U., Indpls., 1972. Diplomate Am. Bd. Pediatrics, 1977, Am. Bd. Pediatrics-adolescent medicine, 2009. Intern Riley Hosp., Indpls., resident pediat., 1973—75, fellow adolescent medicine, 1984—85; hosp. affiliations includes Riley Hosp. for Children, Ind. Univ. (IU) Medical Group, IU Meth., IU Health Noth; physician IU Health; prof. pediat. Ind. Univ. Office: Indiana University Health 401 W 10th St Rm 1001 Indianapolis IN 46202 Office Phone: 317-278-7130, 317-247-8812.

BOADLE-BIBER, MARGARET CLARE, physiologist, educator; b. Melbourne, Australia, Jan. 18, 1943; arrived in U.S., 1967; d. Campbell Dean and Constance Ellen (Browne) Boadle; m. Thomas Ulrich Leonard Biber, Oct. 8, 1969; 1 child, Eric Gustav Nicholas Biber. BS, U. Coll. London, 1964; DPhil, Oxford U., Eng., 1967. Rsch. assoc. pharm. dept. Yale U. Sch. Medicine, New Haven, 1968-69, instr. pharm. dept., 1969-71, asst. prof. pharm. dept., 1971-75; assoc. prof. physiology dept. Va. Commonwealth U., Richmond, 1975-87, prof., 1987—, interim chair, 1991-93, chair, 1993—2007. Contbr. articles to profl. jours. Mem.: Soc. Neuroscience, Am. Soc. Pharm. and Exptl. Therapeutics, Am. Soc. Neurochemistry. Office: Va Commonwealth U 1101 E Marshall St Richmond VA 23298-0551 Office Phone: 804-628-3325. Business E-Mail: mbiber@vcu.edu.

BOAL, BERNARD HARVEY, cardiologist, educator, author; b. Winnipeg, Man., Can., May 14, 1937; arrived in US, 1964. s. Charles and Bessie (Carr) B.; m. Pamela Sures Brownstone, Oct. 28, 1962; children: Steven, Jeremy, Hilary. BS in Medicine, U. Man., 1962, MD, 1962. Licentiate Med. Coun. Can.; diplomate Nat. Bd. Med. Examiners, Am. Bd. Internal Medicine in medicine and cardiology. Intern Winnipeg Gen. Hosp., 1962-63, resident in medicine, 1963-64, U. Utah Hosps., Salt Lake City, 1964-66; USPHS trainee in cardiology NYU Med. Ctr., NYC, 1966-68; chief sect. cardiology Booth Meml. Med. Ctr., 1969-87; chief cardiology Cath. Med. Ctr. Bklyn. and Queens, 1987—2002; cons. L.I. Jewish Hosp.; mem. staff NYU Hosp., Bellevue Hosp., 1968-81; clin. assoc. prof. medicine N.Y. Med. Coll., 1981-89, Cornell U. Med. Coll., 1989-95; assoc. prof. medicine Albert Einstein Coll. Medicine, 1995-2000, N.Y. Med. Coll., 2000—03; chief cardiology Bklyn.-Queens region St. Vincents Cath. Med. Ctrs. N.Y., Jamaica, 2000—02; physician, electrophysiology sect. North Shore Univ. Hosp., Manhasset, NY, 2003—; clin. assoc. prof. medicine Hofstra Med. Sch. Lectr. in field. Guest editor several major cardiology jours.; asst. editor: HeartNet; contbr. chpts. to books, articles to med. jours. Co-inventor Kolker-Boal Cardiac Pacemaker Electrode. Chmn. physicians divsn. Queens County Cabinet United Jewish Appeals of Greater N.Y., 1978-80; charter mem., founding treas. B'nai B'rith UN unit, 1984—; U.S. physician rep. pacemaker working group of the Internat. Standards Orgn., Geneva, 1988-2004, chmn., 1990-2004. With US Army, 1966—68. Master Am. Coll. Cardiology (chmn. med. devices com., Heart House campaign 1976-78, chmn. bequests and endowments com. 1980-85, pacemaker com. 1987-95, trustee 1985-90, electrocardiology com. 1995-2001, budget/fin./investment com. 1996-2002, devel. com. 1997-2003); fellow ACP (treas. Queens chpt. 1976-78, sec. 1978-79, v.p. 1979-81, pres. 1981-85; govs. adv. coun. NY State 1982-85); fellow NY Cardiol. Soc., Am. Heart Assn., Heart Rhythm Soc. (founding mem., nat. adv. coun. 1984-85, exec. com. 1985-88, chmn. fin. com. 1985-88, trustee 1987-91); mem. AMA, Assn. Advancement Med. Instrumentation (pacemaker com. 1976-2004, chmn. pacemaker com. 1988-2004, bd. dirs. 1983-86, co-chmn. strategic planning com. 1983-85), Am. Heart Assn. (fellow coun. clin. cardiology), NY Heart Assn., Am. Soc. Internal Medicine, Queens Soc. Internal Medicine, US divsn. Israeli Med. Assn. (founding mem.). Office: North Shore Univ Hosp Manhasset NY Office Phone: 516-562-2300. Business E-Mail: bboal@boal.com. *

BOAT, THOMAS FREDERICK, pediatrician, pulmonologist, researcher, educator, dean; b. Pella, Iowa, Sept. 7, 1939; s. Bert Reuben and Anne Marie (Schoenbohm) B.; m. Barbara Mary Walling, June. 9, 1962; children: Sarah Elizabeth, Mary Barbara, Anne Christine. BA, Cen. Coll., Pella, 1961; MS, U. Iowa, 1965, MD, 1966. Diplomate Am. Bd. Pediat., Am. Bd. Pediat. Pulmonology. Resident in pediat. U. Minn., Mpls., 1966-68; clin. assoc. NIH, Bethesda, Md., 1968-70; fellow in pediat. pulmonology Case Western Res. U., Cleve., 1970-72, instr. pediat., 1972-73, asst. prof., 1973-76, assoc. prof., 1976-81, prof., 1981-82; prof., chmn. dept. pediat. U. NC, Chapel Hill, 1982-93; prof. pediat. U. Cin. Coll. Medicine, 1993—, chmn. dept. pediat., 1993—2007, exec. assoc. dean, 2007—11, dean, v.p. health affairs, 2011—; physician-in-chief Cin. Children's Hosp. Med. Ctr.; dir. Cin. Children's Hosp. Rsch. Found., 1993—2007; CEO U. Cin. Physicians, 2008—11. Prin. investigator Pediat. Pulmonary Specialized Ctr. Rsch., NIH, 1991-93; chmn. Am. Bd. Pediat., 1994. Mem. editl. bd. Lung Rsch. Jour. Bd. dirs. Ronald McDonald House, Chapel Hill, 1985-88, Cystic Fibrosis Found., chmn. rsch. devel. program, 1983—. Lt. comdr. USPHS, 1968-70. Fellow: Am. Acad. Pediat.; mem.: Assn. Accreditation Human Rsch. Programs (v.p. 2007—), Inst. of Medicine, Assn. Med. Sch. Dept. Chairs (pres.-elect 1994—97, pres. 1997—99), Am. Thoracic Soc. (chmn. pediat. assembly 1983—84), Am. Pediat. Soc. (pres. 2000—01). Office: Office of Dean University Cin Coll Medicine CARE/Crawley Bldg Ste E-870 PO Box 670555 Cincinnati OH 45267 Office Phone: 513-558-7333. Office Fax: 513-558-3512. Business E-Mail: thomas.boat@uc.edu. *

BOBICH, ZELJKO, psychologist, psychotherapist; b. Karlovac, Croatia, July 7, 1954; arrived in Eng., 1992; s. Vladimir and Katarina (Mavrovich) B.; 1 child, Gordan. Prof. Psychology, Zagreb U., Croatia, 1979, Diploma in Social Psychiatry, 1980, MSc in Med. Sci., 1981, MSc in Spl. Clin. Psychology, 1985, DSc in Med. Sci., 1989. Chartered clin. psychologist. Psychologist Jugoturbina, Karlovac, 1980; clin. psychologist Med. Ctr., Karlovac, 1980-84, cons. in psychodiagnostics, 1984-91; clin. psychologist Univ. Clinic, Belgrade, Yugoslavia, 1991, Oxfordshire Health Authority, Oxford, Eng., 1992-93; head psychology svc. for elderly Heathlands MH NHS Trust, Camberley, Surrey, Eng., 1993-98; clin. dir. brain injury rehab. unit Huntercombe Manor Hosp., Maidenhead, Berkshire, Eng., 1998, cons. clin. psychologist ICU, 1998-2000; pvt. practice, 1998—; establisher, dir. Psychology Consultants Ltd., 2001—; cons. clin. psychologist, England. Founder, dir. Janus Clinic, 2008. Author: Multiphasic Personality Inventory Karlovac, 1990, Anxiety--Patient's Manual, 1996, Recognise Your Enemy, 2000, The General Theory of Psychopathy, 2006, Risk Assesment R-72; author several psychometric tests and questionnaires; contbr. numerous articles to profl. jours. Mem. Brit. Psychol. Soc. Home: 45 Bloomsbury Way Blackwater, Camberley Surrey GU17 9LY England Office Phone: +44 (0) 1276-34822. E-mail: feedback@psychologyconsultants.com.

BOBROVA, LARISSA, medical researcher; b. Russia, May 7, 1977; PhD, I. M. Sechenov First Moscow State Med. U., 2000. Sr. rschr. I. M. Sechenov First Moscow State Med. U., 2010—. Mem.: European Dialysis and Transplant Assn., European Renal Assn. Home: Dorogobuzskaya 3-73 Moscow 121354 Russia Personal E-mail: mrlee2005@yandex.ru.

BOCALINI, DANILO SALES, medical researcher; b. São Paulo, Brazil, July 19, 1980; PhD, Fed. U. São Paulo, 2011. Rsch. scientist Fed. U. São Paulo, 2004—. Home: General Chagas Santos 392 São Paulo Saúde 04146-050 Brazil Personal E-mail: bocalini@fcr.epm.br.

BOCCARA, GILLES, anesthesiologist; b. Paris, Apr. 10, 1966; s. Isaac and Claudine Boccara; m. Murielle Benhamou, Mar. 10, 1991; children: Ethel, Gabriel, Lior. Degree, Yavne, Paris, 1983; MD, France, 1995, PhD, 2001. Clin. asst. Montpellier Med. U., France, 1995—99; practitioner Pitié-Salpétriere Hosp., Paris, 1999—2002; clin. physician Am. Hosp. Paris, Neuilly Sur Seine, 2002—. Contbr. articles to profl. jours. Mem. Nat. Pain Com., France, 2006—. With French Army, 1993—94. Mem.: French Note and Soc. Anstheiology, European Soc. Anaesthesiology, French Soc. Anesthesiology & Intensive Care Medicine, Soc. Cardiovasc. Anesthesia. Office: Am Hosp Paris 63 Blvd Victor Hugo Neuilly Sur Seine 92200 France Office Fax: 33 1 46 41 27 49. Business E-Mail: gilles.boccara@ahparis.org.

BOCCIERI, ARMANDO, maxillo-facial surgeon, consultant; b. Avellino, Italy, Nov. 4, 1953; s. Vincenzo Boccieri and Viittoria Rotondi; m. Roberta Fontana, May 2, 1995; children: Paola, Claudia. MD, U. of Rome, 1977, specialization in otorhinolaringology, 1979—81, specialization in plastic surgery, 1982—87. Registrar otorhinolaringology Hosp., Avellino, Italy, 1979—81, sr. registrar otorhinolaringology, 1981—87; registrar maxillo-facial surgery S. Camillo Hosp., Rome, 1988—94, sr. registrar maxillo-facial surgery, 1994—. Prof. Hosp. Sch. of Medicine of Rome, 1990—; cons. in nasal surgery, Rome, 1999—2003. Contbr. articles to profl. jours. Recipient Best Sci. Work, G.B. Grassi Hosp. Ostia - Rome, 2002. Achievements include invention of original technique for correction of the crooked nose. Home: Viale Umberto Tupini 133 Rome 00144 Italy Office: Casa di Cura Villa Europa Via Eufrate 27 Rome 00144 Italy Home Fax: 00390654220252. Personal E-mail: armando.boccieri@libero.it.

BOCCONE, LOREDANA, geneticist; b. Cagliari, Italy, Apr. 12, 1954; MD, Sch. Medicine, 1978. Cons., clin. genetics Ospedale Regionale Delle Microcitemie, 1982—. Office: Via Jenner S/N Cagliari Sardegna 09121 Italy Office Fax: 390706095532. Personal E-mail: dana.boccone2@hotmail.it.

BOCHKOVA, ANNA GEORGIEVNA, rheumatologist; b. Moscow Region, Nov. 13, 1955; PhD, Third Med. Inst., 1982. Sr. rsch. scientist, dept. spondyloarthritis Rsch. Inst. Rheumatology Russia RAMS, Moscow, 2004—. Mem.: ASAS. Office: Kashirskoe Shosse Moscow Capital 115522 Russia Business E-Mail: botchkova@inbox.ru.

BOCK, KLAUS DIETRICH, internist, educator; b. Leipzig, Sachsen, Germany, Dec. 11, 1922; s. Hans Wilhelm and Johanna Ilse (Oeser) Bock; m. Martha Agnes Birnbaum, June 21, 1972; 1 child, Hans-Andreas. MD, U. Heidelberg, 1950. Asst. Univ. Hosp., Heidelberg, Germany, 1950—57; rsch. fellow rsch. dept. CIBA AG, Basel, Switzerland, 1957—61; sr. resident Univ. Hosp., Essen, Germany, 1961—65, prof. and head. renal divsn., 1965—89, prof. internal medicine, docent internal medicine. Pres. European Medicum Collegium, 1982—84; hon. prof. U. Lima, Peru, 1975. Author: Angiotensin, 1966, Hochdruck- ein Leitf fuer die Praxis, 1969, 3rd edit., 1981, Wissenschaftliche und Alternative Medizin, 1993, editor 16 books; contbr. over 360 articles to profl. jours. 1st lt. German Army, 1940—45. Recipient F Gross Wissenschaft prize, Dtsch. Hochdruck-Liga, 1985. Avocation: horseback riding. Home: Schoenetweg 17 Kreuth Bavaria D-83708 Germany

BOCK, PETER, physician; b. Vienna, Oct. 2, 1971; MD, U. Vienna, 1998. Physician Donauspital Wien, 2006—. Travelling fellowship, EFORT. Mem.: Am. Foot and ankle Soc., Austrian Foot and Ankle Soc. (gen. sec. 2008—), European Foot and Ankle Soc. (mem. ednl. com. 2006—, Travelling fellowship). Office: Untere Viaduktgasse 57 / 6 Vienna 1030 Austria E-mail: bock_p@yahoo.com.

BOCK, WILLIAM C., cardiac electrophysiologist; MD, Med. U. SC. Diplomate Am. Bd. Internal Medicine, 1988, Am. Bd. Internal Medicine-cardiovasc. disease, 2001, Am. Bd. Internal Medicine-clin cardiac electrophysiology, 2004, cert. Nat. Com. for Quality Assurance Heart/Stroke Recognition. Resident internal medicine Carolinas Med. Ctr., 1986—88, hosp. affiliations include, Presbyn. Hosp.; fellow cardiovasc. disease Emory Univ., 1988—91. Office: Sanger Heart and Vascular Institute-Mercy 2001 Vail Ave Ste 340 Charlotte NC 28207 Office Phone: 704-304-1110. Office Fax: 704-304-1159.

BOCKERIA, LEO ANTONOVICH, cardiac surgeon; b. Ochamchira, Abkhasia, USSR, Dec. 22, 1939; s. Anton Ivanovich and Olga Ivanovna Bockeria; m. Olga Alexandrovna Soldatova Oct. 10, 1964; children: Ekaterina Leonidovna, Olga Leonidovna. Postgrad., Sechenov 1st Moscow Med. Inst., 1965—68, cand. of Med. Sci., 1968, D of Med. Scis., 1973. Sr. sci. worker Bakoulev Ctr. Cardiovasc. Surgery Russian Acad. Med. Scis., Moscow, 1968-74, chief lab. for hyperbaric oxygenation, 1973-77, dep. dir., 1977-93, prof. surgery, 1978; chief dept. of Surgery of Arrhytmias, 1979—94; academician Russian Acad. Med. Scis., Moscow, 1991, head, chmn. Inst. Cardiac Surgery, 1993—; head, chmn. Bakoulev Ctr. Cardiovasc. Surgery, Moscow, 1994—; chief cardiac surgeon Ministry of Pub. Health, 1996—2004, 2008—; head, chmn. dept. cardiovasc. surgery Sechenov Moscow Med. Acad., 1996—. Dir. Ctr. Surg. and Interventional Arrhythmology Ministry of Pub. Health, 1998—. Author: Textbook of Cardiovascular Surgery, 1989, 1996, Tachyarrhytmais, 1989, History of Cardiovascular Surgery, 1997, Cardiomyoplasty, 1997, History of Cardiovascular Surgery, 1998, Endovascular and Minimally Invasive Surgery of the Heart and Vessels in Children, 1999, Surgery in Patients with Simultaneous Pathology of Coronary and Carotid Arteries, 1999, Systems for Assisting and Substitution Circulation, 1999, Lectures on Cardiovascular Surgery, 1999, 2002, Lectures on Cardiology, 2001, Transmyocardial Laser Revascularisation, 2001, Minimally Invasive Myocardium Revascularisation, 2001, Coronary Heart Disease in Patients with Law Contractility of the Left Ventricle, 2001, Functional Diagnostics in Cardiology, 2002, Essays on History of Coronary Surgery, 2002, New Biological Materials and Treatments in Cardiac Surgery, 2002, Manual of Handicraft in Cardiac Surgery, 2002, History of Cardiovascular Surgery, 2003, Cardiooncology, 2003, Surgical Anatomy of the Coronary Arteries, 2003, Tranmyocardial Laser Revascularisation: Perfusion, Function and Metabolism of Mycocardium, 2004, Postinfarction Ventricular Septal Defect, 2005, The Health of Russia, Atlas, 2005—08, Socially Significant Diseases in Russia, 2006, Surgical Anatomy of the Heart, vol. 3, 2006, Infection in Cardiac Surgery, 2007; co-author (with V.I. Bourakovsky): Hyperbaric Oxygenation, 1974, 2nd. edit., 1981; editor: Children Diseases of the Heart and Vessels, 2004—, Annals of Surgery, 1996—, Bull. of Bakoulev Sci. CCVS, 2000—, Annals of Arrmythmology, 2004—, Clinical Physiology of Circulation, 2005—; co-editor: Jour. Jhorac a Cardiovascular Surgery, 1994—. Recipient Lenin's prize, 1976, State prize USSR, 1986, State prize RF, 2002 ; named Honored Sci Worker, 1994. Mem.: ACS (hon.), Pub. Palace Russia (com. head 2006—), All Russian Pub. League of Nation Health (pres. 2003—), All-Russian Found. Assisting Sick Children with Congenital Heart Diseases (pres. 1994—), European Assn. Cardiothoracic Surgery (coun. 2001—04), Am. Assn. Thoracic Surgery, Russian Soc. Cardiovasc. Surgeons (pres. 1995—). Office: Bakoulev Ctr Cardiovasc Sur 135 Roublevskoye Shosse 121552 Moscow Russia Home: App 64 Leninsky Pr 11 117041 Moscow Moskva Russia Fax: 7 (495) 4147867. Business E-Mail: leoan@heart-house.ru.

BOCKIUS, RUTH BEAR, nursing educator; b. Groffdale, Pa., Dec. 19, 1925; d. Weidler Romaine and Ruth Mary (Jacoby) Bear; m. Thomas B. Bockius Jr., Dec. 15 1945; children: Donna Ruth, Dawn Eileen. AA, Phoenix Coll., 1970; BSN, Ariz. State U., 1973, MEd, 1978. Instr. nursing Glendale (Ariz.) Community Coll.; coord. health edn. Samaritan Health Svcs., Phoenix; dir. patient/community edn. Maryvale Samaritan Hosp., Phoenix, edn. dir., ret., 1994. Grantee Fed. Nursing; AMA scholar, 1st Nat. Bank scholar. Mem. Am. Soc. Hosp. Edn. and Tng., Am. Hosp. Assn., Phi Theta Kappa, Phi Kappa Phi.

BOCKMAN, RICHARD, endocrinologist, educator; MD, Yale U., 1967; PhD in Physical Biochemistry, Rockefeller U., 1971; postgrad. in Medicine & Endocrinology, Cornell U.; attended, Johns Hopkins U. Diplomate Am. Bd. of Internal Medicine, lic. NY. Chief endocrine svc. Joan and Sanford Weill Cornell Med. Coll., prof. medicine; resident NY Univ. Bellevue Hosp.; fellow Am. Coll. of Physicians, Am. Soc. for Clin. Investigation. Cons. Strang Cancer Prevention Clinic, Meml. Sloan kettering Cancer Ctr.; co-dir. metabolic bone svc. Hosp. for Spl. Surgery, 1993—96; vis. prof. MD Anderson Cancer Ctr., Houston; co-organizer Internat. Conf. on Prostaglandins and Cancer, Rome, 1986, 1st Internat. Conf. on Prostaglandins & Cancer, Wash., DC. Dir. bd. The Paget Found. Recipient Busch Symposium, Waksman Inst. of Microbiology, 1984; named one of Best Doctors in NY, NY Mag., 2002—06, 2009—11, Americas Top Doctors list, 2003—08. Mem.: Harvey Soc., Clin. Translational Sci. Ctr. (WMC), Scientific Adv. Com. (TRAC), Am. Fed. for Clin. Rsch., NY Acad. of Sci., Orthopedic Rsch. Soc., Internat. Soc. of Clin. Densitometry, The Endocrine Soc., Am. Soc. for Bone & Mineral Rsch. Office: Hospital for Special Surgery 535 East 70th St New York NY 10021 Office Phone: 212-606-1000.

BOCKS, MARTIN LINDSEY, physician, educator; b. Cadillac, Mich., Mar. 7, 1972; BS, U. Mich., 1994; MD, Wayne State U. Sch. Medicine, 2000. Asst. prof. U. Mich., 2007—. Fellow: ACC; mem.: AHA, AOA. Office: 1500 E Med Ctr Dr Women's L1242 Ann Arbor MI 48109-5204 Business E-Mail: mbocks@umich.edu.

BOCKSERMAN, ROBERT JULIAN, chemist; b. St. Louis, Dec. 20, 1929; s. Max Louis and Bertha Anna (Kremen) B.; m. Clarice K. Kreisman, June 9, 1957; children: Michael Jay, Joyce Ellen, Carol Beth. BSc, U. Mo., 1952, MSc, 1955; postgrad., Far East Intelligence Sch, Tokyo, 1954. Chemist Sealtest Corp., Peoria, Ill., 1955-56; prodn. mgr. Allan Drug Co., St. Louis, 1957-59; rsch. chemist Monsanto Co., St. Louis, 1960-65, purchasing agt. Sauget, Ill., 1966-67; founder, pres. Pharma-Tech Industries, Inc., Union, Mo., 1967-84; tech. dir. Overlock-Howe Consulting Group, St. Louis, 1984-85; founder, pres. Conatech Consulting Group, Creve Coeur, Mo., 1985—. Sec., mem. industry packaging adv. com. Sch. of Engring. U. Mo., Rolla, 1979—, adj. prof. dept. food sci./nutrition, Columbia, adj. prof. dept. engring. mgmt., Rolla, vis. lectr., Clayton, Northwestern U., Evanston, Ill.; vol. tutor Ladue Sch. Dist.; tutor Parkway Sch. Dist., St. Louis, Clayton (Mo.) Sch. Dist.; tech. cons. Creve Coeur Fire Protection Dist.; cons. HAZMAT Team St. Louis County; mentor U. Mo. Dept. Food Sci. and Nutrition; tech. cons. hazardous products EPA, CPSC; mem. safety panel Info. Resources, Inc. Tech. reviewer Jour. Inst. of Packaging Profls., Jour. Packaging Tech., Mo. Waste Control Scholarship Grants and Research, Medical Device and Diagnostic Industry Jour., Medical Plastics and Biomaterials Publication.; mem. editl. adv. bd. The Forensic Examiner, Processing Mag.; panelist (Help Desk column) Medical Device and Diagnostic Industry mag., The Forensic Examiner; contbg. author: Packaging Forensics - Package Failure in the Courts. Mem. Mo. Waste Control Coalition; mem. stormwater engring. com. City of Creve Coeur, Mo., also mem. recycling and environ. com.; tech. cons. Hazmat Team, St. Louis County, Mo.; mem. St. Louis Emergency Response Team; nat. mem. Libr. Congress, Mo. Hist. Soc. With U.S. Army, 1952-54, Korea. Grantee Small Bus. Innovation, Clear Seas Rsch. Found. Mem. ASTM, Am. Coll. Forensic Examiners, Cons. Packaging Engring. Coun., Inst. Packaging Profls. (cert. packaging profl.), Am. Technion Soc., Inst. Food Technologists Arrangements (St. Louis), Nat. Forensic Ctr., Teltech Resource Network, Am. Chem. Soc., Am. Plastics Coun., Mo. Acad. Scis., N.Y. Acad. Sci., Acad. Sci. St. Louis, Assn. Cons. Chemists and Chem. Engrs., Am. Nutraceutical Assn., Nat. Dir. Expert Witnessess, Rotary Internat., Wash. U. Century Club, Juvenile Diabetes Rsch. Found., Sigma Xi. Achievements include research on toxicological effects of additives from packaging materials upon foodstuffs, on biological and photo degradation of polymers, on technology of form/fill/seal packaging engineering, new sterilization technologies for medical devices and pharmaceuticals, barrier properties of polymer films, toxicology of chemical dusts and fumes, and food irradiation effects on humans, neurotoxicity of organic solvents. Home: 54 Morwood Ln Creve Coeur MO 63141-7621 Office: Conatech Cons Group Inc 501 N Lindbergh Blvd Ste 105 Creve Coeur MO 63141-7844 Office Phone: 314-995-9767. Business E-Mail: rjbockserman@conatech.com.

BOCZKO, JUDD, urologist, educator; married. MD, Albert Einstein Coll. Medicine, Bronx, NY, 1999. Instr. urology U. Rochester Med. Ctr., NY, 2005—06; asst. prof. urology Westchester Med. Group's Ctr. Robotics Laparoscopy Advanced Urology, White Plains, 2006—11. Endourology Fellowship, 2005. Office: Westchester Med Group 210 Westchester Ave West Harrison NY 10604 Office Phone: 914-682-6470. Office Fax: 914-681-5264.

BODA, ZOLTAN, internist; b. Miskolc, Hungary, Oct. 5, 1947; s. Jenó and Ilona (Schön) B.; m. Emese Ujvarosi, July 5, 1975; 1 child, Judit. MD, U. Med. Sch., Debrecen, 1972, PhD, 1987; DSc, Hungarian Acad. Scis., 1996. Staff physician U. Med. Sch., Debrecen, 1972-77, resident 2d dept. medicine, 1972-75, asst. prof., 1977-83, sr. asst. prof., 1983-92, docent, 1993-98, prof., 2000—, dept. head, 1999—, dir., 2001—; intern Rikshospitalet, Oslo, 1978. Cons. Reanal Fine Chemist Factory, Budapest, Hungary, 1989—; chmn. hemostasis com. Hungarian Acad. of Sci., Debrecen, 1992-96. Author, editor: Clinical Hemostaseology, 1999 (Springer award 2000); author: (with others) Diagnosis of Arterial and Venous Thrombosis, 1987; patent Ristomycin as Platelet Aggregating Agent (award 1985); contbr. articles to profl. jours. Sub-lt. Hungarian Army. Mem. Internat. Soc. of Thrombosis and Hemostasis, Mediterranean League Against Thrombosis and Hemostasis, Danubian League Against Thrombosis and Hemostasis, Hungarian Soc. of Thrombosis and Hemostasis (gen. sec. 1994-97), Hemostasis Club of Debrecen (chmn. 1985-96). Avocations: tennis, fishing, collecting old hungarian paintings. Office: U Med Sch 2 Dept Med Nagyerdei krt 98 4012 Debrecen Hungary Home: Sestakert Utca 1 4032 Debrecen Hungary Office Phone: 3652255057. Business E-Mail: zboda@dote.hu.

BODEN, GUENTHER, endocrinologist; b. Ludwigshafen, Germany, Jan. 8, 1935; came to U.S., 1965; s. Alwin and Irma (Godelman) B.; m. Irene Ulrike Dingeldein, Dec. 12, 1970; children: Karin, Stephanie, Eric, Dirk. MS, Heidelberg U., Germany, 1956; MD, Munich U., 1959. Intern City Hosp. Hamburg, Germany, 1960-62; rsch. fellow in biochemistry U. Tübingen, Germany, 1963-65; rsch. fellow in medicine P.B. Brigham Hosp., Boston, 1965-67; resident physician Rochester (N.Y.) Gen. Hosp., 1967-70; rsch. prof. biochemistry Temple U. Sch. Medicine, Phila., 1986—, prof. medicine, 1977—2000, Laura H. Carnell prof. of medicine, 2000—. Chief div. endocrinology/metab. Temple U. Sch. Medicine, Phila., 1987—2009, dir. gen. clin. rsch. ctr., 1989—2003. Mem. editl. bd. Jour. Clin. Endocrine Metabolism, 1985-88, Clin. Diabetes, 1995—, Am. Jour. Physiology, 1998—; assoc. editor, Diabetes, 2001-06; contbr. articles to profl. jours. Rsch. grantee NIH, 1973—, Am. Diabetes Assn., 1985—; recipient Rochester N.Y. Diabetes award Rochester Acad. Medicine, 1970, Novartis Long Standing Achievement award in Diabetes, 2005. Fellow ACP; mem. Am. Diabetes Assn., Am. Soc. Clin. Investigation, Am. Endocrin Soc. Office: Temple Univ Hosp 3401 N Broad St Philadelphia PA 19140-5189 E-mail: bodengh@tuhs.temple.edu.

BODEN, SCOTT DAVID, orthopedic surgeon, spine surgeon, educator; b. Bklyn., Sept. 15, 1960; MD, U. Pa. Sch. Medicine, 1986. Cert. Am. Bd. Orthopedic Surgery. Intern George Washington U. Hosp., 1986—87, resident, 1987—91; spine fellowship Case Western Reserve U. Hosp., Cleve., 1991—92; clin. dir. Whitesides Orthop. Rsch. Lab.; assoc. prof. orthop. Emory U. Sch. Medicine, 1995, prof. orthop.; dir. Emory Spine Ctr., Atlanta, 1994—2004, Emory Orthop., Spine Ctr. & Sports Medicine Ctr., Atlanta, 2004—; staff mem. Emory U. Hosp., Crawford Long Hosp., Atlanta. Founder, chmn. Nat. Spine Network, Marietta, 1994—. Articles published on Spine-health.com When is back pain a fracture?, Bone graft substitutes for lumbar spine fusion surgery, 4 proven steps to prevent osteoporosis fractures. Fellow: Am. Acad. Orthop. Surgeons; mem.: Orthop. Rsch. Soc., Internat. Soc. for the Study of the Lumbar Spine, N.Am. Spine Soc. Achievements include being founder of the National Spine Network, a group of physicians, hospitals and institutions who specialize in the diagnosis and treatment of all problems of the spine. Office: Emory Orthop, Spine Ctr & Sports Medicine Ctr 59 Executive Park S Ste 3000 Atlanta GA 30329 Address: Nat Spine Network 3020 Roswell Rd NE Marietta GA 30062 Office Phone: 404-778-7143. Office Fax: 404-778-7117.

BODENHAUSEN, GALEN V., psychology professor; Prof. psychology Northwestern U., chmn. dept. psychology, prof. mktg., Kellogg Sch. Mgmt. Editor: Personality and Social Psychology Rev., 2006—09; contbr. articles to profl. jours. Office: Dept Psychology Northwestern Univ 2029 Sheridan Rd Evanston IL 60208-2710 Office Phone: 847-467-3887. Office Fax: 847-491-7859. E-mail: galen@northwestern.edu.

BODENHEIMER, THOMAS SIEGMUND, physician, educator; b. Seattle, June 13, 1939; MD, Harvard Med. Sch., 1965; MPh, U. Calif., Berkeley, 1969. Cert. Internal Medicine, 1995. Intern in family medicine Boston City Hosp., 1965—66; resident in internal medicine U. Calif. San Francisco Sch. Medicine, 1969—70, fellow in cmty. medicine, adj. prof. family and cmty. medicine, dir. Ctr. for Excellence in Primary Care. Mem.: Inst. Medicine. Office: Dept Family and Cmty Medicine San Francisco Gen Hosp Box SFGH-B80 WD83 San Francisco CA 94110 Office Phone: 415-206-6348. E-mail: tbodenheimer@fcm.ucsf.edu.

BODEY, GERALD PAUL, retired medical educator; b. Hazelton, Pa., May 22, 1934; s. Allen Zartman and Marie Frances (Smith) B.; m. Nancy Louise Wiegner, Aug. 25, 1956; children: Robin Gayle Sparwasser, Gerald Paul Jr., Sharon Dawn Brantley. AB magna cum laude, Lafayette Coll., 1956; MD, Johns Hopkins U., 1960. Diplomate Nat. Bd. Med. Examiners, Am. Bd. Internal Medicine, Am. Bd. Infectious Diseases, Am. Bd. Oncology. Intern Johns Hopkins U., Balt., 1960-61, resident, 1961-62; clin. assoc. Nat. Cancer Inst., Bethesda, Md., 1962-65; resident U. Wash., Seattle, 1965-66; internist to prof. medicine U. Tex./M.D. Anderson Cancer Ctr., Houston, 1975—95, emeritus prof. medicine, 1995—, ret., 2004. Mem. Am.-Soviet Meetings on Cancer Chemotherapy, 1974—78; adj. prof. microbiology, immunology and medicine Baylor Coll. of Medicine, Houston, 1975—99; active collaborative cancer treatment rsch. program Pan Am. Health Orgn., 1976—84; prof. internal medicine and pharmacology Med. Sch. U. Tex. Health Sci. Ctr., Houston, 1976—2004, clin. prof. Dental Sch., 1977—95; mem. orphan products devel. initial rev. group FDA, 1984—95; mem. lunar quartine ops. team Apollo 11-14, Manned Spacecraft Ctr., NASA, Houston, 1987—89; mem. joint commn. accreditation healthcare orgns. Hospitalwide Indicators Task Force; hon. prof. U. Peruana Cayetano Heradia, Lima, 2007—. European Jour. Clin. Microbiol. Infectious Diseases; former mem. editl. bd.: Cancer Rsch., Antimicrobial Agts. and Chemotherapy, Brazilian Jour. Infectious Disease; contbr. over 1100 articles to profl. jours. Past trustee Nat. AIDS Prevention Inst.; past bd. dir. Christian Coalition Reconciliation, Houston. Recipient Am. Chem. Soc. prize, 1956, Merck award, 1956, Robert B. Youngman Greek prize Lafayette Coll., 1956, Eugene Yourassowsky award U. Libre de Bruxelles, Belgium, 1995, Gran Ofcl. de Orden, Hipolito Unanue, Peru, 2007; scholar Leukemia Soc. Am., 1969-74; Henry Strong Denison fellow Johns Hopkins Sch. Medicine, Balt., 1958-60, Great Ofcl. of Order Hipolito Unanue award, Peru, named one of 300 Most Cited Authors award. Fellow ACP, Am. Coll. Chest Physicians, Infectious Diseases Soc. Am., Am. Coll. Clin. Pharmacology, Royal Coll. Medicine, Royal Soc. Promotion Health; mem. AMA, Nat. Acad. Medicine Peru (hon.), Am. Soc. Clin. Oncology, Infectious Diseases Soc. Am., Am. Soc. Clin. Pharmacology and Therapeutics, Am. Soc. Hematology, Am. Soc. Microbiol., Am. Sci. Affiliation, Internat. Soc. Complexity, Info. and Design, Christian Med. Soc., Tex. Med. Assn., Academia Peruana de Cirugia (hon.), Academia Nacional Medicina (hon.), Mediterranean Med. Soc. (hon.), Le Soc. Peruana Cancerologia (hon.), La Costarricensa Oncologie (hon.), Soc. Brasileira Cancerologia (hon.), Phi Beta Kappa, Sigma Xi. Methodist. Achievements include named awards to others from University of Texas MD Anderson Cancer Center: Gerald Paul Bodey Senior Immunocompromised Host Fellowship Training Award; Gerald Paul Bodey Senior Distinguished Professorship in Infectious Diseases, Gerald Paul Bodey Award for excellence in education, division of medical oncology. Office: U Tex MDACC Box 402 1515 Holcombe Blvd Houston TX 77030-4009 Office Phone: 713-792-6830. Business E-Mail: gbodey@mdanderson.org.

BODINE, PETER VAN NEST, biochemist, researcher; b. Syracuse, NY, Mar. 14, 1958; s. George Edward Bodine and Mary Rachel Goeble; m. Judith M. LaLonde, Dec. 27, 1986; children: Adam, Daniel, Benjamin. BS in Biology, Syracuse U., 1980; PhD in Biochemistry, Temple U., 1988. Rsch. asst. Syracuse U., NY, 1980-82; postdoctoral fellow Fels Rsch. Inst., Phila., 1988-91; asst. prof. pharmacology Thomas Jefferson U., Phila., 1991-92; Kendall-Mayo fellow Mayo Clinic & Found., Rochester, Minn., 1992-94; sr. rsch. scientist Wyeth Rsch., Radnor, Pa., 1994—99, prin. rsch. scientist, 1999—2003, assoc. dir. osteoporosis, Women's Health Inst. Collegeville, 2003—08, dir., project mgr., 2008—10; sr. dir. med. ops. speciality care bus. unit. Pfizer, 2010—. Adj. faculty Phila. Coll. Osteo. Medicine, Phila., 1991; mem. devel. com. Am. Soc. Bone and Mineral Rsch., Washington, 2003—07. Contbr. chapters to books, scientific papers, articles to profl. jours. Coach Syracuse Chargers Track Club, 1977—80; vol. Paris; deacon Park Central Presbyn. Ch., Syracuse, 1980-82. Park Ctrl. Presbyn. Ch., 1980—82; catechist Our Mother of Good Counsel Ch., Bryn Mawr, Pa., 2002—, mem. parish coun., 2002—07. Recipient Disting. Grad. Rsch., N.Y. Acad. Scis., 1988. Mem.: Project Mgmt. Inst., The Endocrine Soc., Am. Soc. Bone and Mineral Rsch. (Most Outstanding Abstract 2002), Internat. Bone and Mineral Soc. Democrat. Roman Catholic. Achievements include discovery of novel regulator of steroid hormone receptors; new regulator of mammalian bone formation; development of new collection of human bone cell lines. Avocation: running. Office: MDG SCBU Pfizer Collegeville PA 19426 Office Phone: 484-865-2717. Business E-Mail: pefer.bodine@pfizer.com.

BODIS, STEPHAN B., radiologist, oncologist, educator; b. Basel, Switzerland, Feb. 16, 1958; s. Istvan and Ruth (Kipfer) B.; m. Mirjam Christeler, Sept. 30, 1989; 4 children. BS, U. Baden, Switzerland, 1978; MD, U. Basel, 1985. Lic. cert. profl. physician, Switzerland; diplomate Am. Bd. Radiation Oncology, Swiss Bd. Radiation Oncology. Resident physician Dist. Hosp., Baden, 1985—87, U. Hosp., Zurich, 1987—89; clin. fellow, rsch. fellow Inst. Gustave Roussy, Villejuif/Paris, 1989—91; resident, rsch. fellow Joint Ctr. Radiation Therapy Harvard Med. Sch., Boston, 1991—95; attending physician Joint Ctr. for Radiation Therapy, Boston, 1995; head rsch. lab., dept. radiation oncology U. Zurich, 1995—99, assoc. physician, 2000—, asst. prof., 1999—2001, assoc. prof., 2001—03, prof., 2004—; chmn. Inst. for Radiation Oncology, Aargau Canton Hosp, Switzerland, 2004—. Contbr. articles to profl. jours. including Jour. Clin. Oncology, Blood, Cancer, Cancer Rsch. Sci. Grantee, Swiss NIH, 1997, Swiss Cancer League, 1995, 1999, 2001, 2006. Mem.: RTOG (affiliated mem., prin. investigator 2009—), European Soc. Hyperthermia (bd. mem.), EORTC (mem. protocol review com. 2004—, mem. radiotherapy group 2004—), Swiss Cancer League (mem. exec. com. 2008—), European Soc. Med. Oncology, European Soc. Therapeutic Radiation Oncology (radiobiology com. 1999—2005, bd. dirs. 2001—04, clinical com. 2008—), Am. Soc. Therapeutic Radiation Oncology, Swiss Soc. Radiation Oncology (v.p. 2008—). Avocations: classical music, travel. Office: Dept Radiation Oncology Kantonsspital Aarau Ag Aarau 5001 Switzerland Business E-Mail: stephan.bodis@ksa.ch.

BODKIN, CYNTHIA, medical educator; b. Feb. 12, 1975; MD, Upstate Med. U., 2002. Resident Mayo Clinic Coll. Medicine, fellow clin. neurophysiology; fellow sleep medicine Hennepin County Med. Ctr., Minn. Regional Sleep Ctr.; physician Ind. U. Health, 2008. Office: Indiana University School of Medicine Department of Neurology 714 N Senate Ave Ste 120 Indianapolis IN 46202 Office Phone: 317-948-5450. Office Fax: 317-944-6973. Personal E-mail: cindy_bodkin@yahoo.com.

BODMER, SIR WALTER FRED, cancer research administrator; b. Frankfurt-am-Main, Germany, Jan. 10, 1936; s. Ernest Julius and Sylvia Emily B.; m. Julia Gwynaeth Pilkington, Aug. 11, 1956 (dec. 2001); children: Mark William, Helen Clare, Charles Walter. BA, U. Cambridge, Eng., 1956, PhD, 1959; laurea (hon.), U. Bologna, Italy, 1987; DSc (hon.), U. Oxford, 1988, U. Bath, Eng., 1988, U. Edinburgh, 1990, U. Surrey, 1990, U. Hull, 1990, U. Bristol, 1991, U. Leuven, 1992, U. Loughborough, 1993, U. Lancaster, 1994, U. Aberdeen, 1994, Masaryk U., Brno., 1994, U. London, 1996, U. Salford, 1996, U. UMIST, 1997, U. Haifa, 1998, U. Witwatersrand, Johannesburg, 1998; LLD (hon.), U. Dundee, 1993. Rsch. fellow Clare Coll., U. Cambridge, Eng., 1958-60, fellow, 1961; demonstrator dept. genetics U. Cambridge, 1960-61; from vis. asst. prof. to prof. dept. genetics Stanford U. Sch. Medicine, Palo Alto, Calif., 1961-70; prof. dept. genetics U. Oxford, Eng., 1970-79; dir. rsch. Imperial Cancer Rsch. Fund, London, 1979-91, dir. gen., 1991-96; prin. Hertford Coll., Oxford, 1996—2005; head cancer & immunogenetics lab. IMM, Oxford, 1996—; head cancer and immunogenetics lab., Cancer Rsch. UK Weatherall Inst. Molecular Medicine, John Radcliffe Hosp. Headington, Oxford, England, 2005—. Hon. fellow Keble Coll., Oxford, 1981, Clare Coll., Cambridge, 1989; pres. Orgn. European Cancer Insts., 1990-93, v.p. the Parliamentary and Sci. Com., 1990-93; hon. v.p. Rsch. Defence Soc., 1990—; 1st pres. Internat. Fedn. of Assns. for Advancement of Sci. and Tech., 1992-94; pres. European Assn. for Cancer Rsch., 1994-96; chancellor U. Salford, 1995-2005; vis. prof. UMDS, 1996—; chmn. Nat. Radiol. Protection Bd., 1998-2003; chmn. bd. dirs. Laban Ctr., London, 1999-2005. Co-author (with others): The Genetics of Human Populations, 1971, Our Future Inheritance - Choice or Chance?, 1974, Genetics Evolution and Man, 1976, reprinted, 1999, The Book of Man, 1994; contbr. articles to profl. jours. Recipient the William Allen Meml. award, Am. Soc. Human Genetics, 1980, The Conway Evans prize Royal Coll. of Physicians, 1982, Rabbi Shai Shacknai Meml. lectureship in immunology and cancer rsch., 1983; John Alexander Meml. prize and lectureship, U. Pa. Med. Sch., 1984, Rose Payne Disting. Scientist lectureship, Am. Soc. for Histocompatability and Immunogenetics, 1985, Ellison Cliffe lecture and medal, Royal Soc. Medicine, 1987, The Michael Faraday award, 1994; named Knight Batchelor, 1986, hon. fellow Green Coll., Oxford U., 1993, Fellow Royal Soc., Royal Coll. of Pathologists, Royal Coll. of Surgeons (hon.), Royal Coll. Physicians (hon.), Royal Soc. Medicine (hon.), Internat. Inst. Biotech.; mem. Acad. Europea, Assn. for Sci. Edn. (pres. 1989-90), Brit. Assn. for the Advancement of Sci. (pres. 1987-88, v.p. 1989—2001, chmn. coun. 1996-2001), Brit Soc. for Histocompatibility and Immunogenetics (pres. 1990-91), Am. Acad. Arts and Scis. (fgn. hon. mem.), US Nat. Acad. Sci. (assoc.), Am.

Assn. Immunologists., Am. Philos. Soc. (fgn. mem.), Human Genome Orgn. (v.p. 1988-1990,pres. 1990-92), Brit. Assn. Cancer Rsch. (pres. 1998-2002). Office: John Radcliffe Hosp/Cancer & Immunogenetics Lab Weatherall Inst Molecular Medicine OX3 9DS Oxford England Home Phone: +44 1865 279405; Office Phone: +44 1865 222356, 44 (0)1865-222422. Office Fax: 44 (0)1865-222431. Business E-Mail: walter.bodmer@hertford.ox.ac.uk.

BODNER, DONALD ROGER, urologist, medical educator; b. Indpls., Aug. 31, 1953; s. Robert Stewart and Elizabeth (Wolf) B.; m. Linda Joy Abrams, Oct. 5, 1985; children: Robert, Daniel, Richard. BS, Trinity Coll., Hartford, Conn., 1975; MD, Ind. U., Indpls., 1979. Cert. Am. Bd. Urology. Resident in urology Case Western Res. U., Cleve., 1979-84, instr. urology, 1984-85, asst. prof., 1985-92, assoc. prof., 1992—99, prof., 1999—. Editor (urology sect.) Jour. Spinal Cord Medicine, 1994-2006; guest editor: Urologic Clin. Procedures-Spinal Cord Injury, 1993; editor-in-chief Jour. Spinal Cord Medicine, 2006—. Mem. Am. Urologic Soc., Internat. Spinal Cord Soc., Am. Paraplegia Soc. (pres. 1993-95). Office: UH Case Med Ctr Dept Urology 11100 Euclid Ave Cleveland OH 44106-1736 Office Phone: 216-844-3009. E-mail: donald.bodner@uhhospitals.org. *

BOEHLER, NIKOLAUS LORENZ, orthopaedic surgeon; b. Vienna, 1948; s. Jörg and Susi Boehler; m. Trixi Katharina Boehler; children: Caroline, Nathalie, Christoph. MD. Cert. specialist on orthop. surgery Austria, 1979. Prof. U., Vienna, 1966—79; head orthop. clinic Gen. Hosp. Linz, Austria, 1986—; pres., excom mem. European Fedn. Orthop. and Traumatology, Zuerich, Switzerland, 1991—; pres. European Arthroplasty Register, Linz Zuerich, Austria, 2003—. Contbr. scientific papers. Mem.: FRCS Eng. (hon.), European Fedn. Orthop., Traumatology (hon. Hon. membership 2007), CSOT Czech Orthop. Assn. (hon. Hon. membership 1994), AAOT AsociacionArgentina de Ortopedia y traumatologia (hon. Miembro Honorario Extranjero 2000), DGOOC German Orthop. Soc. (hon. Hon. membership 2003). Office: Orthop Clinic AKH Linz Krankenhausstrasse 9 Linz A 4020 Austria Office Phone: 43-73278063199. Office Fax: 43-73278063160. Business E-Mail: nikolaus.boehler@akh.linz.at.

BOEHM, GÜNTHER, pediatrician; b. Gerstungen, Germany, Oct. 24, 1946; s. Heinz Werner and Ingeborg (Fräbel) B.; m. Margaret Kessner, Apr. 7, 1968 (div. 1980); children: Andreas, Steffen; m. Heidi Dippe, July 2, 1981; 1 child, Alexander. MD, U. Leipzig, Fed. Republic of Germany, 1972, Habil., 1986. Pediatrician U. Leipzig, Fed. Republic of Germany, 1972-86, sr. physician dept. neonatology, 1986-92, docent of pediat. Germany, 1989-92; mem. rsch. dept. internat., head pediat. rsch. Milupa GmbH & Co. KG, Friedrichsdorf, 1994-99; permanent cons. Centre for Infant Nutrition, Milan, Italy, group mgr. Milupa Rsch., 1999; dir. infant nutrition rsch. Numico Rsch., 1999—2007, group mgr. Germany, 1999—2007; dir. infant nutrition rsch. Numico Wageningen, 2000—07; chief scientist officer Danone Rsch. Ctr. Spl. Nutrition, 2008—. Guest prof. Gondar (Ethiopia) Coll. Med. Scis., 1981-82; vis. prof. Nat. Rsch. Coun. Italy Inst. for Infant Nutrition, Milan, 1992-93; cons., chmn. working group postnatal devel. gastrointestinal tract Inst. Infant Nutrition, Milan, 1994—, guest prof. pediat. U. Pecs, Hungary, 2003—; prof., chair nutrition in growth and devel. Erasmus U. Rotterdam, 2005—. Patentee in field; contbr. numerous articles to profl. jours. Recipient prize European Assn. Perinatal Medicine, 1986, Virchow prize, 1989; neonatology fellow U. Milan, 1987, 90, 91, 92; pediat. fellow U. Lund, Sweden, 1984, 86-92; WHO fellow. Mem. Pediatric Soc. Germany, Soc. Perinatal Medicine of Germany, European Soc. Pediatric Gastroenterological Nutrition, German Soc. Pediatric Gastroenterological Nutrition, European Assn. Perinatal Medicine, N.Y. Acad. Scis., Am. Soc. Enteral and Parenteral Nutrition, Am. Acad. Pediatrics. Office: Danone Rsch Bahnstr 14-30 D-61381 Friedrichsdorf Germany Home Phone: 49 341 99 58 324; Office Phone: 49-6172-99-1320. Business E-Mail: guenther.boehm@danone.com.

BOEHM, STEPHAN K., gastroenterologist; b. Nuremberg, Bavaria, Germany, Oct. 7, 1963; s. Franz J. and Brigitta R. Böhm; m. Barbara Bona, Aug. 12, 1989; children: Cathrin A. Böhm, Christian A. Böhm. MD, Med. Sch. Julius-Maximilians-U. Würzburg, Germany, 1990, PhD, 1991. Cert. internal medicine specialist Physicians Orgn. Hesse, Germany, 2001, gastroenterologist 2004. Resident, dept. internal medicine U. Würzburg, 1990—92; postdoc. fellow GI Rsch. Lab., Vets. Adminstrn. Med. Ctr., San Francisco, 1992—94, GI Rsch. Lab., Dept. Surgery and Physiology, UCSF, San Francisco, 1994—96, asst. rsch. molecular biologist, 1996—97; fellow Dept. Internal Medicine and Gastroenterology, Marburg, Germany, 1997—2005; attending physician Evangelisches Krankenhaus Kalk, Cologne, Germany, 2005—08; head, dept. internal medicine and gastroenterology Katholische Kliniken Ruhrhalbinsel, Essen, Germany, 2008—. Contbr. scientific papers to profl. jours. Mem.: German Assn. Endoscopy and Imaging, German Assn. Digestive and Metabolic Diseases, German Assn. Internal Medicine, Am. Gastroent. Assn. Lutheran. Avocations: music (piano, choir), concerts, opera, theatre, comedy, sports (jogging, tennis), reading, travel. Office: Katholische Kliniken Ruhrhalbinsel Heidbergweg 22-24 Essen Northrhine-Westfalia 45257 Germany Office Fax: 49-201-455-2959. Business E-Mail: innere.medizin@kkrh.de.

BOFF, KENNETH RICHARD, engineering research psychologist; b. NYC, Aug. 17, 1947; s. Victor and Ann (Yunko) B.; m. Judith Marion Schoer, Aug. 2, 1969 (dec. Apr. 1997); children: Cory Asher, Kyra Melissa; m. Jacque Aelanda Coppler, Aug. 20, 1999. BA, CUNY, 1969, MA, 1972; MPhil, Columbia U., 1975, PhD, 1978. Research scientist Human Resources Lab., Wright Patterson AFB, Ohio, 1977-80; sr. scientist Armstrong Aerospace Med. Rsch. Lab. (now Airforce Rsch. Lab.), Wright Patterson AFB, Ohio, 1980—, dir. design tech., 1980-91, dir. human engring. div., 1991—97; chief scientist, human effectiveness directorate Air Force Rsch. Lab., 1997—2007; Edenfield Exec.-in-Residence Sch. Ind. & Sys. Engring. Georgia Inst. Tech., 2002—04; prin. scientist Tennebaum Inst. Ga. Inst. Tech., Atlanta, 2007—; chief scientist Socio Tech. Scis., Sarasota, Fla. Project custodian Internat. Air. Standard Coordination Com., Washington, 1984; chmn. com. Tri-Service Human Factors Tech. Adv. Group, Washington, 1984—; chair human factors com. NATO Adv. Group Aerospace R&D, Paris, 1992—; chair human sys. tech. panel Dept. Def., 1994-97; U.S. coord. NATO Rsch. and Tech. Orgn. Human Factors, 1997—. Editor: Handbook of Perception and Human Performance, 1986, Human Engineering Data Compendium, 1988, System Design: Behavioral Perspectives on designers, Tools and Organizations, 1987, Organizational Simulation, 2005; contbr. articles to profl. jours. Travel grantee Rank Prize Found., Cambridge, Eng., 1984; named Air Force Scientist of the Quarter, 1989; recipient Patent award for rap-com display tech., 1989, Human Factors Soc. award for best publ., 1989. Fellow Internat. Ergonomics Assn., Human Factors and Ergonomics Soc.; mem. IEEE (sr.), Human Factors Soc., Am. Psychol. Assn. (div. 21 engring. psychology). Avocations: computers, photography. Business E-Mail: ken.boff@ti.qatch.edu.

BOGA, AYPER, research scientist; b. Adana, Turkey, Nov. 17, 1969; MS, U. Cukurova Medicine Faculty, 1996, PhD, 2004. Lic. U. Cukurova Sci. Faculty, 1988. Rsch. scientist U. Cukurova Medicine Faculty, 2007. Mem.: Turkish Soc. Physiol. Sci. Avocation: reading. Office: University Cukurova Medicine Faculty Adana Balcali 01330 Turkey

BOGAN, RICHARD KEITH, medical educator, director; s. Jesse Cleveland Bogan and Edna Louise Putman Bogan; m. Shannon Marie Thornton; children: Martin Keith, Richard Larkin, Stephanie Ann, Laura Alyson Bogan Herpel, Ross Thornton. BS, Wofford Coll., 1996; MD, MUSC, Charleston, 1970. Diplomate Med. U. SC, 1970. Asst. prof. medicine U. Ala. Hosps., Birmingham, 1976—78; pulmonologist Pulmonary Assocs. SC, Columbia, 1978—94; med. dir. respiratory therapy Palmetto Bapt. Med. Ctr., Columbia, 1978—98; asst. clin. prof. U. SC Sch. Medicine, Columbia, 1978—; pres., med. dir. Sleep Disorder Ctrs.Am., Columbia, 1994—99; pres. Bogan Consulting, Columbia, 1994—; chmn., CMO SleepMed, Inc., Columbia, 1999—; dir., co-founder First Cmty. Bank, Lexington, SC, 1996—; intern. Internal U. Ala. Medicine Hosps., Birmingham, Ala., 1970—91; resident internal medicine Internal U. Ala. Hosps., 1971—72, 1974—75, chief med. resident, 1975—76; CMO R Bogan@sleepmed.md; assoc. clin. prof. USC, 2009—. Lt. comdr. USN, 1972—74, US Naval Base, Albany, Ga. Fellow: Am. Acad. Sleep Medicine, Am. Coll. Chest Physicians. Avocations: golf, skiing, scuba diving. Office: SleepMed Inc 1333 Taylor St Columbia SC 29201 Office Fax: 803-376-1876. Business E-Mail: rbogan@sleepmed.md. *

BOGARDUS, CARL ROBERT, JR., radiologist, educator; b. Hyden, Ky., June 26, 1933; s. Carl Robert and Jeannette Wanda (Eversole) B.; m. Norma Gail Shields, June 24, 1956; children: Carl Robert III, Cynthia Gail. BA, Hanover Coll., 1955; MD, U. Louisville, 1959. Diplomate: Am. Bd. Radiology, Am. Bd. Nuc. Medicine. Intern Penrose Cancer Hosp., Colorado Springs, Colo., 1959-60, resident, 1960-63; prof. U. Okla. Med. Ctr., 1963—, mem. staff, 1963—. Cons. Okla. hosps.; pres. Bogardus Med. Sys. Inc. Author: Practical Applied Physics of Radiology and Nuclear Medicine, 1969; contbg. author: Benign and Malignant Tumors of the Bladder, 1971, Radiation Biology for the Physician, 1973; contbr. articles to profl. jours. Fellow Am. Coll. Radiology (bd. chancellors, sec.-treas. 1987-91, pres. 1991-92); mem. Okla. Soc. Nuc. Medicine (charter pres. 1966), Am. Soc. Therapeutic Radiology (nat. sec. 1968-70, treas. 1987 88, pres. 1989-90), S.W. Regions Soc. Nuc. Medicine, Okla. Radiol. Soc. (treas. 1970, pres. 1974-75, counselor to Am. Coll. Radiology 1976-85), Okla. County Radiol. Soc. (pres. 1974). Office: U Okla Med Ctr 825 NE 101st Oklahoma City OK 73104 Home: 15021 Dourdan Ct Oklahoma City OK 73142-1807 Office Phone: 405-271-3577. Business E-Mail: carl-bogardus@ouohsc.edu.

BOGDAN, DONNA, sonographer; b. Ellenville, NY, Nov. 27, 1963; d. William Joseph and Catherine Ann Lewis; 1 child, Zachary Tyler. BS, Downstate Med. Ctr., Bklyn., 1986—88. Registered Diagnostic Medical Sonographer Am. Registry Diagnostic Med. Sonographers, 1988. Sonographer EVMS, Norfolk, Va., 1992—, Yale-New Haven Hosp., 1991—92; chief pediatric echocardiographer Mt. Sinai Hosp., New York, 1988—91. Contbr. scienitfic journals multiple scientific journals. Mem.: Soc. Diagnostic Med. Sonographers (advanced practice sonographer 2001—03). Office: Eastern Virginia Med Sch 825 Fairfax Ave Ste 310 Norfolk VA 23507 E-mail: bogdand@evmsmail.evms.edu.

BOGDAN, MICHAEL ANDREW, plastic surgeon; b. Washington, Apr. 12, 1971; s. Victor Michael and Ulla Eva-Maria Bogdan; m. Isidra Veve, Mar. 13, 1999; children: Alexander Michael, Andrew Edwin. BS in Zoology, BS in Chemistry, U. of Md., College Park, 1993; MD, Stanford U., Calif., 1998. Lic. Med. Bd. Calif., Bd. Med. Examiners, Colo., Edn. Dept., NY, Tex. Med. Bd., 2007, diplomate Am. Bd. Plastic Surgery, 2006. Intern in gen. surgery U. Calif.-San Francisco, Stanford Health Care, 1998—99; resident in plastic surgery Stanford U. Med. Ctr., 1999—2003, chief resident in plastic surgery, 2003—04; fellow in aesthetic surgey Manhattan Eye, Ear and Throat Hosp., NYC, 2004—05; cosmetic surgeon Napa Valley Plastic Surgery, Inc., Napa, Calif., 2005—07, Southlake Plastic Surgery, Tex., 2007—08; pvt. practice, 2008—11. Presenter in field. Author: (book chpt.) Advances in Plastic and Reconstructive Surgery; contbr. articles to profl. jours. and presentations (Tiffany award Am. Soc. of Aesthetic Plastic Surgery, 2004). Mem.: AMA, Rhinoplasty Soc., Dallas Soc. Plastic Surgery, Tex. Soc. Plastic Surgeons, Am. Soc. Aesthetic Plastic Surgery, Internat. Soc. Aesthetic Plastic Surgery, Am. Soc. Plastic Surgeons, ZedPlast, Alpha Lambda Delta, Phi Kappa Phi. Office: 410 N Carroll AVe Ste 170 Southlake TX 76092 Office Fax: 817-488-2490. Business E-Mail: info@drmichaelbogdan.com.

BOGDANOV, ALEXEI A., radiologist, educator; b. Moscow, Nov. 8, 1960; MS, M. V. Lomonosov Moscow State U., 1983; PhD, Inst. Exptl. Cardiology, Russian Med. Scis. Acad., 1989. Asst. prof. Harvard Med. Sch., 1996—99, assoc. prof., radiology, 1999—2005; asst., radiology and chemistry Mass. Gen. Hosp., 1996—99, assoc., radiology and chemistry, 1999—2005; prof. U. Mass. Med. Sch., 2005—. Postdoc. fellow Webster Ctr. Biol. Sci., Amherst Coll., 1990—91; vis. prof. German Cancer Rsch. Ctr., DKFZ, 2009; disting. vis. prof., lectr. Emory U., Atlanta. Fuji Film Seed grant, RSNA. Mem.: Soc. Molecular Imaging, Soc. Nuc. Medicine and Molecular Imaging, ISMRM (Young Investigators Rabi award), AACR, Am. Chem. Soc. Office: S6-434 University Mass Med Sch 55 Lake Ave N Worcester MA 01655 Business E-Mail: alexei.bogdanov@umassmed.edu.

BOGDONOFF, MORTON DAVID, internist, educator; b. NYC, Dec. 8, 1925; s. M. Myron and Minnie (Alpher) B.; m. Jano Segal, July 1, 1951 (div. 1971); children— Reid, Ladd, Jesse, Drue; m. Mary Patton Welt, May 9, 1975. MD, Cornell U., 1948. Diplomate: Nat. Bd. Med. Examiners, Am. Bd. Internal Medicine. Intern, jr. asst. resident, sr. asst. resident dept. medicine N.Y. Hosp., NYC, 1948-50; sr. asst. surgeon USPHS, Nat. Heart Inst., Johns Hopkins U., Balt., 1950-52; sr. asst. resident dept. medicine Duke Hosp., 1952-53, Eli Lilly Research fellow div. endocrinology and metabolism, 1953-54, chief resident dept. medicine, 1954-55; attending physician, chief metabolic div. Durham VA Hosp., 1955-56, cons., 1959-62; asso. prof. clin. medicine Med. Sch. U. Miami, 1956-57; assoc. dept. medicine Duke U., 1955-56, asst. prof. medicine, 1957-59, asso. prof., 1959-62, prof. med., 1962-69, asst. dean grad. med. edn., 1967-69; prof., chmn. dept. internal medicine U. Ill., Chgo., 1970-75; prof. medicine to prof. emeritus Med. Coll. Cornell U., 1975-95, 95—. Cons. Ft. Bragg Hosp., 1959-62, VA Hosps., Fayetteville, Durham, West-Side, Chgo.; mem. study sect. health svcs. rsch. NIH, 1966-70, Commonwealth Fund, 1985-94, Cath. Med. Ctr., 1990-94, Nat. Med. Fellowships, 1987-2002. Editor: Clin. Rsch., 1959—64; chief editor Archives of Internal Medicine, 1967—77, New Developments in Medicine, 1986—90; sci. editor: Drug Therapy, 1978—94; contbr. articles to profl. jours. Fellow Center Advanced Study Behavioral Scis., Stanford, 1977-78 Fellow A.C.P.; mem. Am. Fedn. Clin. Research (past pres.), Am., So., Central socs. clin. investigation, Assn. Am. Physicians, AAAS (chmn. Sect. N 1981-82), Endocrine Soc., Psychosomatic Soc. (past nat. councillor), Soc. Exptl. Biology and Medicine, AMA, Harvey Soc., Alpha Omega Alpha. Office: NY Hosp/Cornell Med Ctr 525 E 68th St New York NY 10021-4885

BOGEN, BJARNE, immunologist, educator; b. Oslo, Jan. 18, 1951; s. Victor and Birgit (Nesheim) B.; m. Gunn Irene Andersen, May 30, 1980 (div. May 1990); 1 child, Runar; m. Ida Elisabeth Dypvik, May 3, 1991; children: Ellen, Erik. MD, U Oslo, 1977; D Medicine, U. Tromsø, Norway, 1984. Cert. specialist in immunology and blood transfusion. Rsch. fellow U. Tromsø, 1979-84; sci. investigator Basel (Switzerland) Inst. for Immunology, 1985-86, assoc. prof. immunol ogy U. Oslo, 1986-92, prof., 1993—. Assoc. prof. Norwegian Coll. Vet. Medicine, Oslo, 1989—2004; chief attending physician Nat. Hosp., Oslo, 1995—; vis. prof. Stanford (Calif.) U., 1996-97, Harvard Med. Sch., Boston, 2004-05, mem. COE Ctr. Immune Regulation, 2007-; cons. Norwegian Cancer Soc., Oslo, 1996-98. Author: Immunology, 2000; contbr. articles on recognition of antibodies by T lympocytes to mem. jours., including Procs. NAS (U.S.), Cell, EMBO Jour.; editl. bd. Scandinavian Jour. Immunol., 1999—. Recipient Sr. Rsch. award Multiple Myeloma Rsch. Found., 1999. Mem. Norwegian Soc. for Immunology (pres. 1993-94), Scandinavian Soc. for Immunology (coun. 1995—), Henry Kunkel Soc., Norwegian Acad. Sci. and Letters (pres. 40th SSI meeting 2011). Avocations: tennis, sailing, skiing. Home: Pelvikveien 28 1335 Snarøya Norway Office: Ctr Immune Regulation Inst for Immunology Oslo University Hosp Rikshospitalet PO Box 4950 Oslo Nydalen 0424 Norway

BOGER, WILLIAM PIERCE, III, ophthalmologist; b. Phila., Oct. 16, 1945; s. William Pierce Jr. and Mae Elizabeth (Shelton) B.; m. Barbara Crawford, Aug. 10, 1968; children: Matthew, Andrew, John. AB in Biophysics magna cum laude honors, Amherst Coll., 1967; MD, Harvard U., 1971. Diplomate Am. Bd. Ophthalmology. Intern in medicine and pediat. U. Va. Hosp., Charlottesville, 1971-72; resident in ophthalmology Mass. Eye and Ear Infirmary, Boston, 1972-75; clin. fellow in ophthalmology Harvard U., Boston, 1975—76; fellow in pediatric ophthalmology and strabismus Children's Hosp. Med. Ctr., Boston, 1976, assoc. in ophthalmology, mem. full-time staff, 1976-80; pvt. practice specializing in pediatric ophthalmology, Concord, Mass., 1980—. Mem. staff Boston Children's Hosp. Med. Ctr., Boston, Emerson Hosp., Concord, Mass., Winchester Hosp., Mass., Mt. Auburn Hosp., Cambridge, Mass.; instr. Harvard U., 1976—; lectr. in field. Contbr. articles to med. jours., chpts. to book. Capt. M.C., USAR, 1971-81. Pathology grantee Mass. Gen. Hosp., Boston, 1969. Mem. AAAS, Am. Acad. Ophthalmology, Mass. Soc. Eye Physicians and Surgeons, New Eng. Ophthalmol. Soc., Am. Assn. for Pediatric Ophthalmology and Strabismus, Mass. Med. Soc. Office: Lexington Eye Assocs John Cuming Bldg 3d Fl Concord MA 01742 Home: 29 Irving St Cambridge MA 02138 Office Phone: 978-369-0713.

BOGGS, CHARLES HARMON, JR., retired surgeon; b. Washington, July 4, 1923; MD, Northwestern U., Evanston, Ill., 1950. Diplomate Am. Bd. Surgery. Intern Emergency Hosp., Washington, 1951, resident, 1952—53; intern Passavant Meml., Chgo., 1952; resident Northwestern U., Chgo., 1953—56; with VA Hosp., Roanoke, Va., 1956—57; pvt. practice Morgantown, W.Va., 1957—58, VAMC, Salem, Va., 1958—91; clin. instr. U. Va. Sch. Medicine, 1971—79, asst. prof. surgery, 1979—91; ret., 1991. *

BOGGS, JOSEPH DODRIDGE, pediatric pathologist, educator; b. Bellefontaine, Ohio, Dec. 31, 1921; s. Walter C. and Birdella Z. (Coons) B.; m. Donna Lee Shoemaker, June 12, 1964; 1 son, Joseph Dodridge. AB, Ohio U., 1941, Litt.D., 1966; MD, Jefferson Med. Coll., 1945. Intern Jefferson Med. Coll. Hosp., Phila., 1945-46; resident Peter Bent Brigham Hosp., Boston, 1946-48, asso. pathologist, 1947-51; instr. pathology Harvard Med. Sch., Boston, 1948-51; with Children's Meml. Hosp., Chgo., 1951—, dir. labs., 1951—; prof. pathology Northwestern U., Chgo., 1952-92, prof. emeritus, 1992—; dir. BSP Ins. Co., Phoenix. Contbr. articles to profl. jours. Mem. med. adv. bd. Ill. Dept. Corrections, Springfield, 1971-77; bd. dirs. Blood Systems Inc., Phoenix, 1972-94, Community Hosp., Evanston, Ill., 1958-61, Lorretto Hosp., Chgo., 1971-72; chmn. Chgo. Regional Blood Program, 1978-80; bd. dirs. Ben Venue Labs., 1985—. Capt. M.C., U.S. Army, 1948-51. Mem. Am. Soc. Study of Liver Disease, N.Y. Acad. Scis., Midwest Soc. Pediatric Research, Inst. Medicine, Ill. Soc. Pathologists (pres. 1965), Ill. Assn. Blood Banks (pres. 1969-70) Home and Office: 1448 N Lake Shore Dr Chicago IL 60610-6655

BOGH, MORTEN KARSTEN BENTZEN, dermatologist, trainee; b. Copenhagen, Nov. 22, 1977; MD, U. Copenhagen, 2006, PhD in Medicine, Dermatology, 2011. Physician, surgery Sønderborg Hosp., 2004—05; physician, medicine Amager Hosp., 2005, physician, surgery, 2006—07; physician medicine Kalundborg Hosp., 2006; physician, gen. medicine Copenhagen, 2007; physician, dept. dermatology Bispebjerg Hosp., 2007—, Malmo U. Hosp., Sweden, 2011—. Rschr. Newspaper Dagens Medicin, 2001—05; tchr., aviation medicine Roskilde Airport, 2007—08. Recipient award, Niels A Lassens Competition, Danish Med. Assn. Rsch. Fund, Danish Dermatol. Soc., Bispebjerg Hosp. Rsch. Fund; grant, Danish Med. Assn. Rsch. Coun. Mem.: Danish Wound Healing Soc., Danish Dermatol. Soc. Young Dr., European Soc. Dermatol. Rsch. Avocations: aviation, sailing. Office: Bispebjerg Hospital Dept Dermatology Bispebjerg Bakke 23 2400 Copenhagen Denmark Office Phone: (45) 35 31 60 04. Office Fax: (45) 35 31 60 10. Personal E-mail: bogh@dadlnet.dk.

BOGIE, KATH, biomedical engineer; b. England, Jan. 2, 1962; DPhil, Oxford U., 1998. Assoc. clin. scientist Queen Mary and Westfield Coll., U. London, London, 1989—94; rsch. bioengr. Nat. Spinal Injuries Centre, Stoke Mandeville Hosp., Aylesbury, 1989—92; cons. bioenginr. Tissue Viability Clinic, Nat. Spinal Injuries Centre, 1992—94; rsch. assoc. Case Western Res. U., Cleve., 1997—2001, sr. rsch. assoc. dept. orthops., 2001—09; sr. rsch. scientist Cleve. Veterans Affairs Med. Ctr., 2004—; adj. asst. prof. Depts. Orthops. & Biomed. Engring., Case Western Res. U., 2009—. Organ. faculty Women Sci. and Engring. Roundtable, Case Western Res. U., Cleve., 2002—. Mem.: Internat. Soc. Biomedianics, European Soc. of Biomechanics, Wound Healing Soc., RESNA. Office: Case Western U BRB 336 2109 Adelbert Rd Cleveland OH 44106 Office Fax: 216-778-4259. Business E-Mail: kmb3@case.edu.

BOGOSSIAN, GAIL, lawyer, insurance company executive; b. 1955; BA, Trinity Coll., Hartford, Conn.; JD, U. Conn. Past assoc. atty. Murtha, Cullina, Richter & Pinney; counsel Travelers Ins. Co.; spl. counsel LeBoeuf, Lamb, Greene & MacRae LLP; now v.p., gen. counsel ConnectiCare, 1996—2007; mng. dir. Corp. Counsel LLC, 2007—; sr. v.p., gen. counsel Averde Health, 2009—. Office: Averde Health Inc Firehouse Sq 21 Brace Rd West Hartford CT 06107

BOGREN, HUGO GUNNAR, radiology educator; b. Jönköping, Sweden, Jan. 9, 1933; came to U.S., 1970; s. Gunnar Hugo and Signe Victoria (Holmström) B.; m. Elisabeth Faxén, Nov. 1, 1956 (div. 1976); children: Cecilia, Niclas, Joakim; m. Gunilla Lady Whitmore, July 2, 1988. MD, U. Göteborg, Sweden, 1958, PhD, 1964. Diplomate Swedish Bd. Radiology. Resident, fellow U. Göteborg, 1958-64, asst. to assoc. prof. radiology, 1964-69; from assoc. prof. to prof. radiology and internal medicine U. Calif. Davis, Sacramento, 1972—. Vis. assoc. prof. U. San Francisco, 1970-71; vis. prof. U. Kiel, Fed. Republic Germany, 1980, cardiac magnetic resonance unit Royal Brompton Hosp. and Imperial Coll., London, 1986-87, 93-94, 2002-03; participant in med. aid fact finding mission, Bangladesh, 1992. Contbr. numerous articles to profl. jours., chpts. to books. Sr. Internat. Fogarty fellow NIH, London, 1986-87. Fellow Am. Heart Assn., Radiol. Soc., N.Am. Soc. Cardiac Imaging, Soc. Thoracic Radiology, Internat. Soc. Magnetic Resonance in Medicine, Soc. Cardiovasc. Magnetic Resonance, Soc. Cardiovasc. Computed Tomography, Swedish Assn. Med. Radiology, Swedish Cruising Club, Rotary; mem. Royal Gothenburg Sailing Club Sweden (hon.). Lutheran. Avocations: ocean sailing, skiing, classical music. Office: U Calif Davis Med Ctr Div Diagnostic Radiology 4860 Y St Ste 3100 Sacramento CA 95817-2307 Office Phone: 916-734-6535. Personal E-mail: hugobogren@aol.com. Business E-Mail: hugo.bogren@ucdmc.ucdavis.edu.

BOHANNON, NANCY JEAN, endocrinologist; b. Cherry Point, NC, Nov. 25, 1947; BS with Honors, U. Ill., Champaign-Urbana, 1968; MD, U. Calif., Davis, 1972. Pres. Med. Corp., 1974—. Dir. clin. rsch. cardiovasc. risk reduction program St. Luke's Hosp., 2007. Fellow: ACP, Am. Assn. Clin. Endocrinologists; mem.: Am. Fedn. Clin. Rsch., Am. Diabetes Assn. (Dorothy Frank fellowship), AMA. Avocations: horseback riding, skiing, scuba diving. Office: 1580 Valencia St Ste 504 San Francisco CA 94110 Office Fax: 415-648-6805. Business E-Mail: sugarnancy@pol.net.

BOHANON, KATHLEEN SUE, neonatologist; b. Mpls., 1951; BA summa cum laude, U. Minn., 1973, MD, 1977. Diplomate Am. Bd. Pediat., Am. Bd. Neonatal-Perinatal Medicine. Commd. 2d lt. USAF, 1973, advanced through grades to col., 1995; resident in pediats. Case Western Res. U., Cleve., 1977-80; gen. pediatrician USAF, 1980-85; fellow in neonatology Wilford Hall Med. Ctr., San Antonio, 1985-87; neonatologist, dir. neonatal ICU USAF Med. Ctr., Wright-Patterson AFB, Ohio, 1987-95, chmn. dept. pediat., 1995-98, chief med. staff, 1998-2000; ret., 2000; locum tenens neonatologist, 2001—03; staff neonatologist St. Mary's Hosp. and Med. Ctr., Grand Junction, Colo., 2004—06; ret., 2006. Asst. clin. prof. pediat. U. N.D. Sch. Medicine, Grand Forks, 1981-82; assoc. Wright State U. Sch. Medicine, Dayton, Ohio, 1987-2000, Uniformed Svc. U. Health Scis., Washington, 1988-2000; mem. com. Infant Bio-Ethics Com., Dayton, 1990-2000. Fellow Am. Acad. Pediat.

BOHMAN, BRYAN, anesthesiologist, hospital administrator; Grad., U. Calif., Davis, 1977; MD, U. Chgo., 1981. Resident internal medicine Stanford U. Hosp., 1981—82, resident anesthesia, 1984—86; anesthesiologist Associated Anesthesiologists Med. Group, Palo Alto, 1991—; dep. chief anesthesia service Stanford U. Hosp. and Clinics, 1994—98, chmn. med. exec. com., med. staff pres., 2007—08, assoc. chief med. officer, 2011—; chief of staff Stanford U. Sch. Medicine, 2008—11. Adj. clin. asst. prof. anesthesiology Stanford U. Sch. Medicine; mem. hosp. bd. Stanford U. Med. Ctr. Mem.: Calif. Soc. of Anesthesiology (delegate). Office: Associated Anesthesiologists 701 Welch Rd Ste 216B Palo Alto CA 94304 Office Phone: 650-323-0617. Office Fax: 650-323-4229. *

BOHN, MICHAEL J., psychiatrist; b. Milw., Oct. 1954; s. Robert James and Marian Carroll Bohn; m. Mary Pat Skelly Bohn; Sept. 28, 2001; children: Alexander Soltvedt, Patrick Soltvedt, John Michael, Catherine Mary. BS with honors, U. Wis. Madison, 1977; MD with honors, U. Wis. Med. Sch., Madison, 1985. Cert. physician Wis. Bd. Licensing, 1986. NIH grad. student fellow MIT Dept. Biology, Cambridge, Mass., 1977—80; rsch. fellow infectious diseases, dept. internal medicine U. Wis., 1985—86, psychiat. resident, hosp. & clinics, 1986—90, chief psychiat. resident, hosp. & clinics, 1989—90; niaaa postdoc., alcohol rsch. ctr. U. Conn., Farmington, 1990—92, psychiat. instr., health ctr., 1990—92; asst. psychiat. prof. U. Wis. Med. Sch., 1992—97, clin. asst. psychiat. prof., 2003—04; med. dir. W.S. Middleton VAMC Outpatient Substance Abuse Treatment Program, Madison, 1992—97, Gateway Recovery, Madison, 1997—2004; cons. Wis. Bur. Mental Health & Substance Abuse Svc., Madison, 2000—07; med. dir. Manning Counseling Ctr., Madison, 2003—04, Horizons House, Milwaukee, Wis., 2004—11; med. dir., adolescent substance abuse treatment program Aurora Psychiat. Hosp., Wauwatosa, Wis., 2005—11; pres. Wis. Soc. Addiction Medicine, 2005—07; med. dir. Benedict Ctr. Women's Harm Reduction Program, Milw., 2006—. Physician dir. Wis. Assn. Alcohol and Other Drug Abuse, Madison, 2004—08. Recipient Vincent Russo award, U. Wis. Med. Sch., 1984, Election award, Alpha Omega Alpha Med. Honor Frat., 1984, Exemplary Psychiatrist award, Nat. Alliance Mentally Ill, 1995, Outstanding Profl. Svc. award, Wis. Assn. Alcohol and Other Drug Abuse, 2001, Best Dr. award, Consumers Rsch. Coun. America, 2005—11. Mem.: State Med. Soc. Wis., Am. Psychiat. Assn. Office: Aurora Psychiat Hosp 1220 Dewey Ave Milwaukee WI 53213-2504 Office Fax: 414-454-6747. Business E-Mail: michael.bohn@aurora.org.

BOHN, PAUL BRADLEY, psychiatrist, psychoanalyst; b. Santa Monica, Calif., Apr. 11, 1957; m. Pamela Summit, Nov. 17, 1990. BA in Pharmacology, U. Calif., Santa Barbara, 1980; MD, U. Calif., Irvine, 1984; postgrad. in Psychoanalysis, L.A. Psychoanalytic Inst., 1988-93; PsyD, Grad. Inst. Contemporary Psychoanalysis, 1995. Diplomate Am. Bd. Psychiatry and Neurology, added qualifications in addiction psychiatry and forensic psychiatry. Psychiat. resident UCLA, 1984-88, assoc. dir. anxiety disorders clinic, 1989-95, clin. prof. psychiatry, 1989—, dir. social anxiety clinic, 1993-95; fellow U. So. Calif., LA, 1988-89; v.p. Pacific Psychopharmacology Rsch. Inst., Santa Monica, 1990—; pvt. practice psychiatry Santa Monica, 1988—. Expert reviewer, Med. Bd. Calif., U. (Berkeley) Calif. Pharma, 2003, Am. Jour. Psychiatry; editor, Psychiatric Clin. Faculty Assn. UCLA, Newsletter. Grantee Ciba-Geigy, Santa Monica, 1992, 92, Novartis, 1998. Mem. Am. Psychiat. Assn. (expert rivewer jour.; Disting. fellow), So. Calif. Psychiat. Assn. (past pres.), Anxiety Disorders Assn. of Am., Obsessive Compulsive Found. Office: 12300 Wilshire Blvd Ste 330 West Los Angeles CA 90025 Office Phone: 310-829-1924.

BOHR, VILHELM ALFRED, laboratory chief; b. Copenhagen, Dec. 3, 1950; arrived in U.S., 1982; s. Aage Niels and Marietta Bettina Bohr; m. Diane S. Okumoto, July 17, 1987; children: Christina, Eliot, Kenneth. MD, U. Copenhagen, 1978, PhD, DSc, 1987. Resident in medicine U. Copenhagen, 1978-80, postdoctoral fellow, 1980-82; rsch. scholar Stanford (Calif.) U., 1982-86; sr. staff fellow Nat. Cancer Inst., Bethesda, Md., 1986-88, med. officer, 1988-92; chief lab. molecular genetics Nat. Insts. Aging., NIH, Balt., 1992—. Office: NIH Nat Inst Aging Biomed Rsch Ctr Lab Molecular Gerontology 251 Bayview Blvd Ste 100 Rm 6B133 Baltimore MD 21224 Office Phone: 410-558-8162. Business E-Mail: vbohr@nih.gov.

BOICE, CHARLES, gynecologist, educator; MD, Loma Linda U., 1973. Diplomate Am. Bd. Ob-Gyn-gynecologic oncology. Asst. prof. gynecologic oncology dept. Univ. of Md. Hosp., Balt.; assoc. fellow program Cancer Inst. Washington Hosp. Ctr.; hosp. affiliations include Shady Grove Adventist Hosp., Capital Splty. Ctr., Holy Cross Hosp., Calvert Meml. Hosp., Georgetown Univ. Hosp., Southern Md. Hosp., Washington Adventist Hosp., Sibley Meml. Hosp. Office: Capital Women's Care Ste 205 10301 Georgia Ave Silver Spring MD 20902 Office Phone: 301-592-1600. Office Fax: 301-592-1602.

BOISAUBIN, EUGENE V., internist; b. St. Louis, Jan. 25, 1945; s. Eugene V. and Margaret T. (Titzler) B.; m. Jean Thorpe, Sept. 20, 1986; 1 child, Vincent. AB, Washington U., St. Louis, 1966; MD, U. Mo., 1971. Diplomate Am. Bd. Internal Medicine. Dir. gen. internal medicine Ben Taub Hosp., Houston, 1976-84, Meth. Hosp., Houston, 1984-93; clin. ethicist Robert Wood Johnson Found./U. Tex. Med. Br., Galveston, 1993—; intern and resident Baylor Coll. Medicine Hosps., Houston, 1971-75. Mem. educating healthcare ethics nat. project U.S. Dept. Edn., 1992-95; cons. for ethics and med. care Tex. Bd. Med. Examiners, 1994—. Contbr. over 100 articles to profl. jours., chpts. to books. Mem. AMA, Soc. Gen. Internal Medicine (regional chair 1982-86), Alpha Omega Alpha. Home: 2346 Gramercy St Houston TX 77030-3214 Office: University of Texas Medical Branch 301 University Blvd Galveston TX 77555-5302

BOISSERIE, JEAN-MARIE, researcher; b. Paris, July 8, 1932; s. Andre and Nicole (Bonnamy) B.; m. Violaine Jardin, June 9, 1965; children: Etienne, Anne-Laure. Diploma in engring., Ecole Nat. Ponts et Chaussees, 1956. Rschr. Elec. France Inst. Rsch., Paris., 1956-92; asst. Ecole Nat. Ponts et Chaussées, Paris, 1971-77; cons. Inst. Nat. Rsch. Info., Le Chesnay, France, 1971-97. Referee Internat. Jour. Numerical Methods, 1971-88. Author: The Finite Element Method in Thin Shell Theory, 1982; contbr. articles to profl. jours. With French Mil. Val., 1961-63. Roman Catholic. Home: 2B Rue Claude Debussy 78100 Saint Germain en Laye France Personal E-mail: jboisser@mac.com.

BOISSONNEAULT, ROGER M., pharmaceutical executive; BA in Biology, U. Conn.; MBA, Rutgers U. Various positions including v.p., female healthcare, dir., corp. strategic planning & dir., obstetrics, gynecology mktg. Warner-Lambert, 1976—96; pres., COO Warner Chilcott PLC (formerly Galen Holdings PLC), 1996—2000, bd. dirs., 1998—, pres., CEO Rockaway, NJ, 2000—. Office: Warner Chilcott PLC 100 Enterprise Dr Rockaway NJ 07866 Office Phone: 973-442-3200. Office Fax: 973-442-3283.

BOIVIN, GEORGES YVES PAUL, research scientist; b. Choisy-le-Roi, France, Nov. 3, 1948; s. Claude and Elise (Caillié) Boivin; m. Françoise Valverde, Apr. 19, 1975; children: Céline, Valérie. BS, U. Paris, 1966, MS, 1970, postgrad., 1974, PhD, 1982. Rsch. asst. U. Geneva, 1972-74, master asst., 1974-76, chargé rsch., 1976-82, INSERM, Lyon, France, 1982-90, dir. rsch., 1990—; team leader U. Lyon. Co-author: Industrial Fluorosis, 1975-77 (F. Tissot prize 1978). Councillor 4th dist. City of Lyon, 1989-2001, 2d vice mayor, 1995-2001. Decorated Acad. Palms French Ministry of Edn., 1998. Mem. Am. Soc. for Bone and Mineral Rsch., Internat. Assn. for Dental Rsch., European Calcified Tissue Soc., Internat. Soc. for Bone Morphometry (bd. dirs.). Roman Catholic. Office: INSERM Unité 1033 University Lyon 69372 Lyon France Home Phone: 33 4 78 30 16 85; Office Phone: 33 4 78 77 86 72. Business E-Mail: georges.boivin@univ-lyon1.fr.

BOJAN, ALICJA JOANNA, physician; b. Cracow, Poland, May 1, 1980; MD, Christian-Albrechts U. zu Kiel, 2006. Physician Sahlgrenska U. Hosp., Gothenburg, Sweden, 2006—. Office: Göteborgsvägen 31 Mölndal Västra Götaland 431 30 Sweden Business E-Mail: alicja.bojan@vgregion.se.

BOKAL, INNA IVANOVNA, physician; b. Artsizskiy, Odessa, Ukraine, Sept. 29, 1983; Student in Biol. Scis., Mechnikov Odessa Nat. U., 2006—. Physician dept. def. South Region Mil. Med. Clin. Ctr., Clinics Lab. Diagnostics, 2001. Home: Pirogovskaya 2 Odessa 65044 Ukraine Business E-Mail: bokali@list.ru.

BOKARICA, PERO, urologist; b. Dubrovnik, Croatia, June 29, 1971; s. Luka and Nada Bokarica; m. Dubravka Zupetic, Sept. 6, 1997; children: Luka, Stipe. MD, Zagreb U., Croatia, 1996. Cert. urologist Croatian Ministry Health. Phisician in tng. Clin. Hosp. Sestre Milosrdnice, Zagreb, 1996—97; family physician Home of Health Novi Zagreb, Zagreb, 1997—99; urologist in tng. Gen. Hosp. Sveti Duh, Zagreb, 2000—05, urologist, 2005—. Nat. communication officer Europen Soc. Residents in Urology, Zagreb, 2001—05. Mem.: European Assn. Urology (licentiate). Achievements include research in surgical treatment of Peyronie's disease. Avocations: tennis, science fiction, travel. Office: Gen Hosp Sveti Duh Sveti Duh 64 Zagreb 10000 Croatia Office Fax: +38513712026. Personal E-mail: pero.bokarica@zg.t-com.hr.

BOKERIA, LEO ANTONOVICH, surgeon; b. Ochamchira Abkhazian, Dec. 22, 1939; Grad., 1st Moscow Inst., 1965, Academician of AMS USSR, 1968. Dir. NTSSSH, 1994—; dir. ctr. surg. and interventional aritmologi Health Ministry, 1998—; surgeon Inst. Surgery and Organ Transplantation. Sr. rschr. cardiovascular surgery named Bakuleva; supr. Hyperbaric Oxygen Lab., 1974—77; dep. dir. sci. and head surg. treatment of arrhythmia dept., 1977—93; mem. editl. bds. jours., United States; chmn. com. Helth Ministry and Med. Sciences, Russia, 1993—98; founded Annals of Surgery for surgeons in various fields and the journal "Doctor"; mem. Pub. Chamber, Russia, 2005, chmn., Russia, 06. Editor (chief editor): (jours.) Thoracic and Cardiovascular Surgery, "Bulletin NTSSSH them. Bakuleva RAMS ", "Children's heart and blood vessels", "Clinical physiology of the circulatory system". Fellow: Am. Coll. Surgeons (hon. fellow); mem.: ALL-Russia Pub. Orgn. (pres. league of Nation's health 2003), Rossiyskogo Sci. Soc. (pres. cardio-vascular surgeons), Serbian Acad. Sciences (mem. 1997), Cardiothoracic Internat. Ctr. Monaco (mem. 1992), European Soc. Thoracic and Cardiovascular Surgeons (mem. 1992), Am. Assn. Thoracic Surgeons (mem. 1991). Office: Institute of Surgery and Organ Transplantation Bishkek Togolok-MOLD 3 / 1 720040 Russia Office Phone: 7663017, 7662668. *

BOKHARI, FARHAT, surgeon; MD. Cert. Am. Bd. Plastic Surgery. Tng. NYU Med. Ctr., Columbia Univ., State Univ., NY, Downstate med. Ctr., Mt. Sinai Med. Ctr., Clevland, Ohio; tng. with dr. Joseph McCarthy, dr. Sherrill Aston, dr. Daniel baker, dr. Barry Zide and dr. Bahman Guyuron; founder Dubai Cosmetic Surgery, United Arab Emirates, 2002, special cosmetic plastic surgeon, hair transplant surgeon. Mem.: Pakistani Physicians North America, Am. Soc. Maxillofacial Surgeons, Am. Soc. Laser Medicine, Am. Soc. Plastic Surgeons. Office: Dubai Cosmetic Surgery PO Box 57394 Al Wasl Rd Umm Seqiem Al Manara Area Dubai United Arab Emirates Office Phone: 97143485575. Office Fax: 97143486292. *

BOKOV, ANDREY, neurosurgeon; b. Bryansk, Russia, Sept. 19, 1976; PhD, Med. Acad. Nizhniy Novgorod, 2000. Sci. officer Sci. Rsch. Inst. Traumatology & Orthopedics, 2010—. Neurosurgeon Interregional Neurosurgical Ctr. Nizhniy Novgorod, 2001—. Mem.: World Spine Column Soc., AO Spine. Avocations: languages, travel. Home: Poltavskaya St Nizhniy Novgorod 603024 Russia Home Fax: 7-831-2787901. Personal E-mail: andrei_bokov@mail.ru.

BOLAND, GERALD LEE, health facility administrator; b. Harrisburg, Pa., Apr. 2, 1946; s. Vincent Harry and Alice Jane (Geiste) Boland; 1 child, Peter Alexander. BS, Lebanon Valley Coll., 1968. Acctg. trainee Armstrong Cork Co., Millville, NJ, 1968, payroll supr., plant ops. acct., 1969—70; sr. fin. acct. Lancaster Gen. Hosp., Pa., 1970—71, mgr. gen. acctg., 1972; mgr. corp. acctg. HMW Industries Inc., Lancaster, 1972; corp. contr. Fleck-Marshall Co. subs. Gable Industries, Lancaster, 1973—74, sec.-treas., 1974—75; contr. Dominion Psychiat. Treatment Ctr., Falls Church, Va., 1975—76; contr., dir. fin. Miller & Byrne Inc., Rockville, Md., 1976—79; v.p. internal auditing Medlantic Healthcare Group, Washington, 1979—88; v.p. ops. Kapner, Wolfberg & Assocs., Van Nuys, Calif., 1988—89; dir. acctg. Providence Hosp., 1989—95, asst. contr., 1995—2001, contr., 2001—11, ret. Mem.: Inst. Internal Auditors, Fin. Mgmt. Assn., Healthcare Fin. Mgmt. Assn., Inst. Mgmt. Accts., Am. Acctg. Assn. Home: 246 Grimaldi Way Hedgesville WV 25427-6797 Home Phone: 304-229-4106. Personal E-mail: jerryiam@frontier.com.

BOLAND, JAMES PIUS, surgeon, educator; b. Phila., Mar. 6, 1931; s. John Patrick and Beatrice Christine (Murphy) B.; m. Kathryn Ann Watts, May 18, 1963; children: Beatrice, James, Kathryn, Sara, Angela, Genevieve. BS, St. Joseph's Coll., Phila., 1948-52; MD, Jefferson Med. Coll., Phila., 1952-56; MPH, U. South Fla., 1998. Diplomate Am. Bd. Surgery, Am. Bd. Thoracic Surgery, Am. Bd. Surg. Critical Care. Asst. prof. to prof. Med. Coll. Pa., Phila., 1964-76; prof. surgery W.Va. U., Charleston, 1976—, chmn. dept. surgery, 1976—. Capt. USNR, ret. Decorated Navy Commendation medal. Fellow ACS. Roman Catholic. Office: W Va U/CAMC 3110 Maccorkle Ave SE Charleston WV 25304-1210 Home: 1108 Kanawha Blvd Charleston WV 25301

BOLDYREV, SERGEY YUREVICH, cardiologist; b. Kurganinsk, Krasnodar Region, Oct. 5, 1972; MD, Kuban Med. U., 1996. Heart surgeon Regional Klinik Hosp. # 1, 2002—. Office: Rossiyskaya 140 Krasnodar Krasnodar Region 350000 Russia Office Fax: 7 861 252 62 90. Business E-Mail: bolsy@rambler.ru.

BOLES, RICHARD GREGORY, clinical geneticist, researcher; b. Pasadena, Calif., Apr. 8, 1961; s. Richard Eugene and Dorothy Mae (Martolio) B.; children: Scott, Philip, Henry, Caroline. BS in Biochemistry magna cum laude, U. Ariz., 1983; MD, UCLA, 1987. Diplomate Am. Bd. Pediatrics, Am. Bd. Med. Genetics. Pediatric intern, resident Harbor-UCLA Med. Ctr., Torrance, Calif., 1987-90; fellow in genetics Yale U., New Haven, 1991-93; asst. prof. pediatrics Sch. Medicine U. So. Calif., LA, 1993—2004, assoc. prof. pediats. Sch. Medicine, 2004—; attending physician Children's Hosp. of L.A., 1993—, dir. prenatal diagnosis ctr., 1997-99. Mem. sci. adv. bd. United Mitochondria Disease Found., 1996—2006; mem. profl. adv. bd. Cyclic Vomiting Syndrome Assn. U.S.A./Can., 1998—. English lang. editor Micro Structure Bull., Uppsala, Sweden, 1994-99; contbr. more than 50 articles to sci. jours. Grantee United Mitochondrial Disease Found., 1997, NIH, 2000-03, Nat. Alliance on Rsch. in Schizophrenia and Depression, 2005-06. Mem. Soc. Inherited Metabolic Disease, Am. Soc. Human Genetics, Phi Beta Kappa, Reflex Sympathetic Dystrophy Syndrome Assn., American RSDHope, 2007-08. Achievements include ongoing research projects in mitochondrial genetics, especially regarding testing modalities; research in mitochondrial disease and cycling vomiting syndrome. Office: Children's Hosp LA Box 90 4650 W Sunset Blvd Los Angeles CA 90027-6062 Office Phone: 323-361-2178. Business E-Mail: rboles@chla.usc.edu.

BOLIE, VICTOR WAYNE, molecular biologist, researcher; b. Silverton, Oreg., July 23, 1924; BS in Physics, Iowa State U., 1949,

MS in Math., 1950, PhD in Math., Physics, Elec. Engring., 1952; BA in Chemistry, Coe Coll., 1957; MA in Physiology, Stanford U., 1959. Registered profl. engr., Okla., N.Mex. Rsch. adminstr. Collins Radio Co., 1952-57; assoc. prof. Iowa State U., 1957-58, prof., chmn. biomed. engring., 1959-63; rsch. adminstr. Rockwell Internat. Corp., 1963-66; prof. elec. engring. U. Ariz., 1966-67; chaired prof. Okla. State U., 1967-71; chmn. dept. elec. and computer engring. U. N.Mex., Albuquerque, 1971-76, prof. elec. and computer engring., 1976-95, prof. emeritus, 1995—. Team mem. Engring. Coll. Accred. Bd. Engring. & Tech., 1969-76 Author over 90 publs. in field; mem. editorial bd. Biomed. Engring. Trans. IEEE, 1967-70; dir. 33 MS and PhD theses; 38 patents, 2 copyrights. 1st lt., multi-engine pilot, instr., USAF, 1942-47. NSF sr. postdoctoral fellow, 1958-59; recipient Gold Ring Highest Acad. Achievement award USAF, 1944, Rsch. Dir. award Morris Animal Found., 1961, Disting Rsch. Svc. award U. N.Mex., 1988, Cert. Recognition Los Alamos Nat. Lab., 1988. Fellow: IEEE (nat. chmn. joint com. engring. in medicine and biology 1964—65); mem.: Am. Chem. Soc., Air Force Assn. Res. Officers Assn., Fed. Am. Soc. Exptl. Biology, Am. Soc. Microbiology, Am. Physiol. Soc., Am. Assn. Advancement Sci., Nat. Soc. Profl. Engrs., Portland City Club, Scottish Rite Freemasons, Phi Kappa Phi, Sigma Xi.

BOLLAG, UELI WERNER, physician, educator; b. Zurich, Switzerland, Jan. 15, 1941; m. Elisabeth Albrecht, Mar. 3, 1984. MD, U. Zurich, 1968; DTM&H, Sch. Tropical Medicine and Hygiene, Liverpool, 1972; MSEd, U. So. Calif., LA, 1981. Cert. FMH pediat. Swiss Soc. Pediat., 1976. Sr. registrar Regional Hosp., Montego Bay, Jamaica, 1975—76; reader Med. Faculty, Ilorin, Nigeria, 1978—79; asst. prof. Faculty of Health Scis., Maastricht, Netherlands; prof. Kathmandu U. Med. Sch., Dhulikel, Nepal. Cons. WHO, Papua New Guinea, 1985. Contbr. scientific papers. Achievements include research in otitis media, asthma, primary health care. Avocation: winemaking. Home: Waldheimstrasse 51 Bern 3012 Switzerland Personal E-mail: u.bollag@bluewin.ch.

BOLLERO, DANIELE, plastic surgeon; b. Ivrea, Sept. 12, 1971; Degree in medicine, U. Torino, 1997, degree in plastic surgery, 2002. Cons., dept plastic surgery Burn Unit, CTO Hosp., 2003—, Torino Football Club, 2010. Med. com. mem. Interplast Italy, 2002. Mem.: Società Italiana Ustioni, Società Italiana Chirurgia Plastica, Mediterranean Club Burns & Fire Disasters. Office: Via Ormea 93 Turin 10126 Italy Office Phone: 39 3479069444. Personal E-mail: dbollero@hotmail.com. Business E-Mail: info@danielebollero.it.

BOLLIGER, EUGENE FREDERICK, former surgeon; b. Detroit, Sept. 19, 1923; s. Eugene Hans and Julia Frederick (Larson) B.; m. Lois Ann Doan, Dec. 16, 1946; children: Mark, Glen, Cynthia. MD, U. Mich., 1946. Diplomate Am. Bd. Surgery. Intern, then surg. resident Grace Hosp., Detroit, 1947-52; ward surgeon Madigan Army Hosp., Ft. Lewis, Wash., 1952-54; asst. chief surgery 2d Gen. Hosp., Munchweiler, Germany, 1954-55; chief surgery U.S. Army Hosp., Pirmasson, then Wurzburg, Germany, 1955-57; attending surgeon Northwestern Hosp., Mpls., 1957-58; chief of surgery Dickey County Meml. Hosp., Ellendale, ND, 1958-82; surgeon SHARE HMO, Mpls., 1982-87; chief of surgery Mid-Dakota Hosp., Chamberlain, SD, 1988-91, Gregory (S.D.) Community Hosp., 1991-94, retired, 1994. Surg. cons. West Holt Hosp., Atkinson, Nebr., 1992-94, St. Anthony's Hosp., O.Neill, Nebr., 1992-94; real estate cons. Westin-Reid, Mpls., 1987-88. Major U.S. Army, M.C., 1949-57. Fellow ACS; mem. AMA. Republican. Lutheran. Avocations: piano, singing, woodworking, former pilot. Personal E-mail: bolligereugene@comcast.net.

BOLLING, STEVEN FREDRIC, cardiac surgeon, educator; b. Toronto, July 26, 1955; came to the US, 1958; s. Gustaf Fredric and Joan Elizabeth (Small) B.; m. Cheryl Lynn Huey, May 19, 1979; children: Michael Huey, Kathrine Huey. BS, U. Mich., Ann Arbor, 1976, MD, 1979. Diplomate Am. Bd. Surgery, 1988, Am. Bd. Thoracic Surgery, 1989. Surgical intern John Hopkins Hosp., Balt., 1979—80, surgical resident, 1980—84, cardiac surgery rsch. resident, 1981—82, cardiothoracic surgery resident, 1984—86; asst. prof. thoracic surgery U. Mich., Ann Arbor, 1986-91, assoc. prof. thoracic surgery, 1991—97, prof. thoracic surgery, 1997—99, prof. cardiac surgery, 1999—, Gayle Halperin Kahn Prof. Intergrative Medicine, 2003—, dir., multidisciplinary mitral valve clinic. Adj. staff St. Joseph's Mercy Hosp., Ann Arbor, 1988—; cons. Baxter Healthcare, Inc., 1994—, Medtronic, Inc., 1994—. Contbr. articles to profl. jours. and chpts. to books; patentee in field; mem. editl. bd. Jour. Surg. Rsch. Rsch. grantee NIH, 1987—, Am. Heart Assn., 1990—; recipient Resident Rsch. award, Am. Assn. for Academic Surgery, 1983, George D. Zuidema Rsch. award, 1984, Balt. Acad. Surgery Rsch. award, 1985, Young Investigator award Japan Surg. Soc., 1995; named Disting. Prof. South African Cardiac Soc., 1996, Korean Assn. for Thoracic Surgery, 1997, Japanese Assn. for Thoracic Surgery, 1997. Fellow ACS; mem. Soc. Univ. Surgeons, Am. Assn. for Thoracic Surgery, Soc. Thoracic Surgeons, Internat. Soc. for Heart and Lung Transplantation, Am. Soc. Transplant Surgeons, So. Thoracic Surgical Assn., Cardiothoracic Surgery Network. Co-inventor of heart valve ring, GeoForm ring. Office: Sect Cardiac Surgery Univ Mich Med Ctr 1500 E Med Ctr Dr Fl 3 2120 Taubman Ctr Box 0348 Ann Arbor MI 48109-0348 Office Phone: 734-936-4981. Office Fax: 734-764-2255. Business E-Mail: sbolling@umich.edu.

BOLLINGER, RALPH RANDAL, surgeon, researcher; b. Dearborn, Mich., Oct. 3, 1944; s. Ralph Perry and Edith Delores (Algren) B.; m. Monika Irmgard Koch, May 1, 1965; children: Christine Laura, Mark Randal. BS in Biology, Tulane U., 1966, MD, 1970, MS in Biochemistry, 1970, PhD in Immunology, Duke U., 1977, MBA with cert. in Health Svc. Mgmt., 1997. Diplomate Am. Bd. Surgery. Stress physiology rsch. physician USAF Sch. of Aerospace Medicine, Brooks AFB, Tex., 1972-74; postdoctoral fellow, instr. in surgery, dept. immunology Duke U., Durham, NC, 1974-76; resident in surgery Duke U. Med. Ctr., 1970—72, 1977—79, chief resident in surgery, 1979—80, asst. prof. surgery, 1980—86, asst. prof. immunology, 1981—86, chief of surg. transplantation, 1983—99, assoc. prof. immunology, 1986—95, assoc. prof. surgery, 1986—91, prof. surgery, 1991—2008, prof. emeritus, 2008—, prof. immunology, 1995—2008, chief gen. surgery, 1994—2003, vice chair surgery, 2004—06, sr. ednl. advisor, 2006—07. Vice councillor United Network for Organ Sharing, Richmond, Va., 1986-88, councillor, 1989-91, v.p., 1991-92, pres., 1992-93; sec. Southeastern Organ Procurement Found., Richmond, 1988-89, v.p., 1989-90, pres., 1990-91; v.p. Carolina Organ Procurement Agy., Greenville, N.C., 1985-87, pres., 1987-89; trustee N.C. Kidney Found., Chapel Hill, 1983-90; pres. elect Durham-Orange County Med. Soc. 2004, pres. 2005. Contbr. numerous articles to profl. jours.; editor: Transplant Management, 1988; mem. editl. bd. Am. Surgeon, 1988, Jour. Surg. Rsch., 1993—96, Jour. ACS, 1996, Graft, 1998, Jour. Investigative Surgery, 2001. Com. chmn. Troop 408, Boy Scouts Am., Durham, N.C., 1982-89; mem. staff/parish rels. com. Duke Meml. Meth. Ch., Durham, 1985-87, 2009-, chmn., 2003-2004, admin. bd., 2004-06, coun. on ministries, 1983-85, 2009-. Maj. USAF, 1972—74. Recipient La. Pathology Soc. award Tulane U., 1979, Golden Apple award Duke U., 1984, 89. Fellow ACS; mem. Aerospace Med. Assn. (environ. sci. award 1978), Am. Soc. Transplant Surgeons (membership com. 1988, councillor 1989-93), Transplantation Soc., Soc. Univ. Surgeons, Am. Surg. Assn., So. Surg. Assn., N.C. Assn. Biomed. Rsch. (sec. 2001-03, vice chmn. 2003-05, chmn. 2005-07). Republican. Avocations: scuba diving, gardening, white water canoeing. Home: 1120 Infinity Rd Durham NC 27712-9765 Office: Duke U Med Ctr PO Box 2910 Durham NC 27710-2910

BOLLINGER, SHARON MOORE, psychotherapist; b. Cape Girardeau, Mo., May 27, 1949; d. Raymond V. and Lucille (Broshuis) Moore; m. Skip Bollinger, Aug. 30, 1968; children: Kristell, Amber. AA, St. Louis C.C., 1988; BA in Psychology, Lindenwood Coll., St. Charles, Mo., 1990, MA in Profl. Counseling, 1992; postgrad., St. Louis U., 1996—2001; PhD in Counseling Psychology, EarthNet Inst., 2004. Lic. profl. counselor; nat. cert. counselor. Computer operator Clothworld/Brown Group, St. Louis, 1986-88; grad. asst. Lindenwood Coll., St. Charles, 1990-92, St. Louis. U., 1999—2000; dir. social svcs. Wentzville (Mo.) Park Care Ctr., 1993-98; pvt. practice psychotherapy St. Peters, Mo., 1998—; clin. therapist Provident Counseling, 2000—02; outpatient clinician Crider Ctr. for Mental Health, 2002—. Presenter in field. Newsletter editor Long Term Care Social Svcs. Mo., Social Svcs. Assn. Mo. Vol. counselor St. Joseph's Health Ctr.-Hospice, St. Charles, 1991, All Saints Ch., St. Peters, Mo., 1992. Mem.: ACA, Mo. Counseling Assn., Alpha Sigma Tau, Phi Theta Kappa. Avocations: languages, reading, crafts, dance, scuba diving.

BOLMAN, R. MORTON, III, (CHIP BOLMAN), surgeon, educator; b. Ft. Wayne, Ind., Dec. 6, 1946; s. Ralph Morton Bolman, II and Jean Bonham Bolman; m. Cecilia Patton, Oct. 10, 1975; children: Paige Roberts, Melissa Jean. MD, St. Louis U., 1973. Diplomate Am. Bd. Thoracic Surgery, 1984. Internship & residency in gen. surgery Duke U. Med. Ctr., NC; fellowship in thoracic surgery U. Minn. Hospitals; prof. surgery Harvard Med. Sch., Boston, 2005—; chief cardiac surgery Brigham and Women's Hosp., Boston, 2005—. Contbr. articles to profl. jours. Heavy hitter fund raiser PanMass Challenge, Boston, Albania, 2006—07. Recipient C. Walton and Richard C. Lillehei Prof. of Cardiovasc. and Thoracic Surgery award, U. Minn. Sch. Medicine, 1989—2005. Mem.: Am. Assn. Thoracic Surgery (chair edn. com. 2007—) Democrat-Npl. Protestant. Avocations: hiking, reading, bicycling, fly fishing. Office: Brigham and Women's Hosp Divsn Cardiac Surgery 15 Francis St Boston MA 02115 Office Fax: 617-264-6319. Business E-Mail: rbolman@partners.org.

BOLOGNESE, PAOLO A., neurosurgeon; MD cum laude, U. Turin, Italy, 1985. Lic. NY, 2009. Neurosurgical tng. Univ. Turin, 1990; intern SUNY Health Sci. Ctr., Bklyn., 1992, resident gen. surgery, 1994, fellow neurosurgery, 2001; tng. Chiari Inst., assoc. dir., 2001—; physician LI Jewish Med. Ctr., 2001—, North Shore Univ. Hosp., 2001—. Achievements include as a leading worldwide expert in the field of laser Doppler flowmetry applied to neurosurgery; top European figure in the field of neurosurgical intraoperative ultrasound. Office: North Shore University Hospital 865 Northern Blvd Great Neck NY 11021 Office Phone: 516-570-4400. Office Fax: 516-570-4444.

BOLOGNIA, JEAN LYNN, academic dermatologist; b. Hammond, Ind., July 1, 1954; d. John Paul and Jo Ann (Dill) B.; m. Dennis Lawrence Cooper, Aug. 25, 1985. BA summa cum laude, Rutgers U., 1976; MD cum laude, Yale U., 1980. Intern, resident in internal medicine Yale-New Haven Hosp., 1980-82, resident in dermatology, 1982-85; rsch. fellow dermatology Yale U. Sch. Medicine, New Haven, 1985-87, asst. prof. dermatology, 1987-93, assoc. prof. dermatology, 1993-97, prof. dermatology, 1997—, dir. residency tng. program, 1994-2000. Bd. dirs. Am. Bd. Dermatology, 2004—; lectr. in field. Author: Harrison's Principles of Internal Medicine, 2011, 17th edit., Textbook of Medicine, 2011. Mem.: Am. Bd. Dermatology (bd. dirs. 2004—), Med. Dermatology Soc. (pres. 2000), Dermatology Found. (bd. trustees 2003—10), Soc. for Investigative Dermatology (v.p. 2003—04, bd. dirs. 2004—06), Women's Dermatol. Soc. (bd. dirs. 1999—2003, v.p. 2004—05, pres. 2005—06), Am. Dermatol. Assn. (bd. dirs. 2003—08, v.p. 2009—10), Am. Acad. Dermatology (bd. dirs. 2004—08). Achievements include patent for enhancing depigmentation therapy; characteristics of nevi and melanoma, disorders of pigmentation. Office Phone: 203-789-1249. Business E-Mail: jean.bolognia@yale.edu.

BOLTON, LINDA BURNES, medical center administrator, educator; BSN, Ariz. State U., 1970; MSN, UCLA, 1972, MPH, 1976, DrPH in Population Health and Behavioral Sci., 1988. RN. Staff nurse Good Samaritan Hosp., Phoenix, 1970-71; instr. LA Southwest Coll., 1976-81, LA Cmty. Coll. System, 1976—; staff and charge nurse Cedars of Lebanon, LA, 1971-72; clin. nurse specialist Cedars-Sinai Med. Ctr., LA, 1972-81, asst. prof. nursing edn., 1981-82, dir. nursing rsch. dept., 1982-84, dir. nursing rsch. and devel. dept., 1984—, v.p. nursing, founder Geri and Richard Brawerman Nursing Inst.; clin. prof. assoc. Calif. State U., LA, 1988—; assoc. clin. prof., Sch. Nursing Univ. of Calif., San Francisco, UCLA. Mem. adv. bd. nursing program LA Trade Tech., 1978—, L.A.U.C., 1986—, S.M.C.C., 1989—, HCOP, 1983—, NIH, 1987—, Calif. State U. Sch. Nursing, LA, Calif. State U., Northridge, 1987—, nursing program LA Valley Coll., nursing program Santa Monica City Coll., health careers opportunity program Calif. Post Secondary Edn. Commn., maternal child health tech. rev. NIH, Nat. Cholesterol Edn. Program for Nurses, 1989—, health div. LA Commn. of the Status of Women, 1986, LA Southwest Coll., Nat. Heart, Lung, Blood Inst.; vice chair Inst. of Medicine Commn. on the Future of Nursing, 2009; prin. investigator, Cedars-Sinai Burns and Allen Rsch. Inst., American Acad. of Nursing Tech. Drill Down. Editl. bd. mem. American Journal of Nursing, NurseWeek; contbr. articles to profl. jours., books, book chpts., videos and audiotapes. Founder tutorial program for jr. high sch. students, Phoenix, 1965-66, adolescent mothers groups Maricopa County Health Dept., Phoenix, 1969-70; asst. to program participants in Job Corps programs, 1968-70, asst. in devising and implementing satellite obstetrical and neonatal clinics for Native Ams. and transcient farm workers, Phoenix, 1969-70; participant WICHE program to recruit and train ethnic students of color into schs. of nursing, 1971-75; chair nat. adv. com. Transform Care at the Bedside (TCAB) Robert Wood Johnson Found.; mem. Children's Def. Fund, Coun. for the Advancement of Nursing Sci., Nat. League for Nursing, Coalition for the Homeless LA, LA Regional Family Planning Coun.; pres. LA chpt., chair recruitment and action com., Coun. Black Nurses Inc. El Paso Natural Gas Honor scholar, 1966-69; recipient Cert. of Merit human rels. commn. City of LA, 1977, 79, 81-85, Cert. of Merit Am. Heart Assn., 1975-84, Coun. Black Nurses Inc., 1974-78, Morris Press Humanism award CSMC, 1986-87, CARE award NBA Pro-Am. Basketball of LA, 1988, United Way Silver award cmty. campaign; named one of Top 25 Women in Healthcare, Modern Healthcare mag., 2011. Fellow American Acad. of Nursing (past pres.); mem. American Coll. Obstetricians and Gynecologists Nurses Assn., ANA, American Pub. Health Assn., Assn. Univ. Women, Assn. Maternal Child Health, Black Congress on Health, Law and Econs., American Orgn. for Nurse Execs. (Lifetime Achievement award 2007), Assn. of Calif. Nurse Leaders, Nat. Black Nurses' Assn. (co-developer Cmty. Collaboration Model), Soc. Rsch. Adminstrs., UCLA Sch. Nursing and Sch. Pub. Health Alumni, Nat. Black Nurses Assn. (past pres.), Calif. Nurses Assn., Sigma Theta Tau., Chi Eta Phi. Office: Cedars Sinai Medical Center 2435 N Grand Ave Santa Ana CA 92705-8703 also: Cedars-Sinai Medical Center 8700 Beverly Blvd Los Angeles CA 90048 Office Phone: 310-423-3277. *

BOMBACK, ANDREW S., medical educator; b. NYC, Sept. 12, 1976; MD, Columbia U., 2003; MPH, U. NC, 2009. Asst. prof. Columbia U., 2009. Office: 622 W 168th St PH 4-124 New York NY 10032 Office Fax: 212-342-1814. Business E-Mail: asb68@columbia.edu.

BOMBARDIERI, GABRIELE, surgeon, educator; b. Ischia di Castro, Vitertbo, Italy, May 22, 1949; Grad., U. Rome, Sapienza, 1973, degree in Gen. surgery; degree in Cardiac Surgery, U. Bologna, 1979. Surgeon Cath. U. Rome, 1977—, adj. prof., 2000. Avocation: bicycling. Office: Largo Agostino Gemelli 8 Rome 00168 Italy Office Fax: 390630155881. Business E-Mail: gabombardieri@rm.unicatt.it.

BOMBLIES, KIRSTEN, molecular biologist, educator; m. Levi Yant. BA in Biochemistry and Biology, U. Pa., 1996; PhD in Genetics, U. Wis., Madison, 2004. Technician Salk Inst., La Jolla, Calif.; sr. postdoctoral rsch. assoc. Dept. Molecular Biology Max Planck Institute for Devel. Biology, Tubingen, Germany; asst. prof. organismic and evolutionary biology Harvard U., 2009—. Contbr. articles to profl. jours. Named a MacArthur Fellow, The John D. and Catherine T. MacArthur Found., 2008. Office: Harvard U HU Herbarium 22 Divinity Ave Cambridge MA 02138 E-mail: Kirsten.bomblies@tuebingen.mpg.de.

BOMER, KELLY VANDERBILT, facial plastic surgeon; Grad. in Chemistry and Math with honors, U. Calif.; MD with honors, Tulane U. Cert. otolaryngology head and neck sugery. Intern surgery Univ. of Chgo., resident otolaryngology head and neck surgery, surg. fellow facial plastic and cosmetic surgery, North Shore Ctr. Contbr. publs. in various med. jours. Mem.: AMA, Am. Acad. of Otolaryngology-Head and Neck Surgery, Am. Acad. of Facial Plastic and Reconstructive Surgery. Office: Rejuvent Medical Spa & Surgery 9155 East Bell Rd Scottsdale AZ 85260 Office Phone: 480-889-8880.

BONADONNA, GIANNI, oncologist; b. July 28, 1934; MD in Medicine and Surgery, Milan U., 1959; degree in Haematology, Ferrara U., 1973; degree in Oncology, Pavia U., 1973; laurea in Medicine (hon.), Turin U., 2004. Resident divsn. pathology Santa Cabrini Hosp., Montreal, 1960-61; postdoctoral rsch. fellow divsn. chemotherapy Sloan-Kettering Cancer Ctr., NYC, 1963-64; rsch. fellow diagnostics divsn. Nat. Inst. Cancer, Milan, 1964-69, asst., 1969-76, v.p., 1974-78; pres, Italian Assn. Med. Oncology, 1976—99; researcher, head dept. cancer medicine Istituto Nazionale Tumori, Milan, 1998, chair prospective clin. trial, 1999—; pres. Michelangelo Found. Cancer Rschs., 1999—. Recipient ACS Medal of Honor Am. Cancer Soc., 1991; grantee Bristol-Myers Squibb, 1993; award Internat. Soc. Chemotheraphy, David A. Karnorsky Meml. award Am. Soc. Clinical Onocology, Josef Steiner Cancer Rsch. prize U. Bern Switzerland, award Bristol-Meyers Squibb, Cancer Rsch. award Gen. Motors, 1995, Clin. Rsch. award Fedn. European Cancer Socs.; Paul Harris fellow Rotary. Fellow Royal Coll. Physicians London. Achievements include the first protocol with adjuvant CMF combination chemotherapy, demonstrating its efficacy in a variety of breast cancers and as primary chemotherapy for operable breast cancer; For Hodgkin's disease developed the ABVD combination therapy showing it to be non-cross resistant and superior to the traditional drug regimen. Office: c/o Michelangelo Found Via Giacomo Venezian 1 20133 Milan MI Italy Business E-Mail: gianni.bonadonna@istitutotumori.mi.it.

BONAGURA, VINCENT R., pediatrician, educator, researcher; b. NYC, Mar. 30, 1949; s. Vincent P. and Vivian M. Bonagura; m. Barbara Ann Liskin, June 3, 1962 (dec. Apr. 1994); children: Elizabeth, Vivi, Rebecca, Amy. BA, Columbia U., 1971, MD, 1975. Diplomate Am. Bd. Pediatrics, Am. Bd. Allergy and Immunology (bd. dir. 1999—), Bd. Diagnostic Lab. Immunology. Intern Babies Hosp.-Columbia-Presbyn. Med. Ctr., NYC, 1975-76, resident in pediat., 1976 78; asst. prof. pediatrics Columbia U., NYC, 1981-82, asst. prof. pediatrics and microbiology, 1982-85; chief divsn. allergy, immunology, rheumatology Schneider Children's Hosp./L.I. Jewish Med. Ctr., 1985-99; assoc. prof. pediatrics Albert Einstein Coll. Medicine, Bronx, N.Y., 1989-94, assoc. prof. pediatrics, microbiology and immunology, 1991-94, prof., 1994—; dir. divsn. allergy/immunology North Shore/L.I. Jewish Health Care Sys., 1999—. Adj. asst. prof. microbiology Columbia U.; dir. Am. Bd. Allergy and Immunology, 2000—; appointee allergy and immunology RRC ACGME, 2001—. Contbr. articles to profl. jours. Fellow Am. Acad. Allergy and Immunology (tng. dirs. exec. com., residency rev. com., 2002-); mem. Am. Assn. Immunology, Soc. for Pediatric Rsch., Am. Coll. Rheumatology, Am. Acad. Pediatrics, Alpha Omega Alpha. Avocations: tennis, music, gardening. Office: LI Jewish Med Ctr Dept Pediatrics Schneider Children's Hosp New Hyde Park NY 11040 Office Phone: 516-465-5359. E-mail: bonagura@lij.edu.

BONALDI-MOORE, LORRAINE KAY, nursing educator; d. William Leon and Betty Ann Larsen; m. Louis Anthony Bonaldi (div.); m. Richard Whittier Moore, Dec. 15, 2003; children: Nicholas, Andrew, Anthony. BSN, Pacific Luth. U., 1979; MBA, HCM, U. Phoenix, 2004, MSN, 2005. Nurse U. Calif. San Diego Med. Ctr., 1979—81, Children's Hosp., San Diego, 1981—89, Ctr. for Plastic Surgery, Reno, 1989—2000, Health Insight, Reno, 2001—03, Aesthetic Plastic Surgery, Eugene, Oreg., 2004—05, U. Nev., Reno, 2005—, Washoe Med. Ctr., Reno, 2005—. PALS instr. Mem.: AACN. Avocations: marathon running, volunteer work. Office: Univ Nev Reno NV 89557

BONANNI, FERNANDO B., JR., surgeon; BS, So. Ill. U., 1980—84; attended, U. Pa., 1984—86; MD, MCP Hahnemann U., 1986—90, The Reading Hosp. and Med. Ctr, 1995—2006. Diplomate Am. Bd. Surgery. Surg. resident Lehigh Valley Hosp, 1990—95; fellow Am. Coll. of Surgeons, Am. Soc. for Metabolic and Bariatric Surgery (ASMBS); med. dir. obesity treatment program The Reading Hosp. and Med. Ctr., 1995—2006; dir. inst. for metabolic bariatric surgery Ablington Meml. Hosp., 2006—. V.p. Soc. for Metabolic and Bariatric Surgery. Recipient 4th Pl. award, Am. Coll. of Surgeon, Paul R. Bosanac, M.D., Rsch. award, 1995. Mem.: Soc. of Am. Gastrointestinal Endoscopic Surgeons (SAGES), Soc. for Laparoendoscopic Surgeons. Office: Abington Memorial Health Center Main Bldg 2nd Fl 225 Newton Rd Warminster PA 18974 Office Phone: 215-441-6800.

BONANNI, GUGLIELMO, endocrinologist, educator; b. La Spezia, Mar. 5, 1946; Assoc. prof. U. Padua, Italy, 1971, 1985—. Mem.: Italian Soc. Andrology. Avocations: reading, diving. Office: Via Ospedale 105 Padua Veneto 35100 Italy Office Fax: 39049657391. Business E-Mail: guglielmo.bonanni@unipd.it.

BONANNO, BRUCE BRIAN, emergency physician; b. Irvington, NJ, June 29, 1955; s. Anthony Samuel and Jean Teresa Bonanno; children: Bryan Todd, Danielle Alexandra. BS, Union Coll., Schenectady, NY, 1977; MD, St. George's U., Grenada, 1983. Attending emer. rm. physician Misericordia Hosp., Phila., 1986—87, Monmouth Med. Ctr., Long Branch, NJ, 1987—92, Brick Hosp., NJ, 1992—93, Atlantic City Med. Ctr., 1992—93; attending emergency room physician St. Agnes Med. Ctr., Phila., 1992—93, Helene Fuld Med. Ctr., Trenton, NJ, 1993—95, CentraState Med. Ctr., Freehold, NJ, 1994—97, Bayonne Hosp., NJ, 1997—2000, Wilkes-Barre Gen. Hosp., Pa., 1999, Berwick Hosp., Pa., 1999—2000, Bayshore Cmty. Hosp., Holmdel, NJ, 2000—, Belmond Med. Ctr., Iowa, 2006—, Cmty. Gen. Hosp., Syracuse, 2006—08, Catskills Regional Med. Ctr., Harris, NY, 2006—08, Oswego Hosp., NY, 2008, Carthage Hosp., NY, 2008, Rosebud Reservation Hosp., Rosebud, SD, 2008, Meadowlands Hosp., Secoucos, NJ, 2008—10, Ottowa RHC, 2010—11. Tchr. Hahneman Sch. Medicine, 1987—92, Robert Wood Johnson Sch. Medicine, 1993, St. George's U. Sch. Medicine, 1993—; med. cons. Sta. News 12 NJ, 1996—2006. Host: (TV show) To Your Health, 1996—2006. Mem.: Nat. Assn. Med. Comm. (bd. dirs.), Am. Coll. Emergency Physicians (chairperson pub. rels. com., bd.dirs.).

BOND, ANNETTE, maternal and fetal medicine specialist; MD, Harvard Med. Sch., 1983. Resident obstetrics and gynecology NY Hosp.-Cornell Med. Ctr., 1983—87, fellow perinatal medicine, 1987—89; med. staff Greenwich Hosp. Office: Greenwich Hospital 5 Perryridge Rd Rm 1-251 Greenwich CT 06830 Office Phone: 203-863-3674.

BOND, DALE S., psychology professor, researcher; BA, Western Oreg. State U., Monmouth, 1995; MS, Purdue U., West Lafayette, Ind., 1998; PhD in Health Promotion, U. Utah, Salt Lake City, 2002. Residential counselor/caregiver King St. Mental Health Facility, Can. Mental Health Assn., Kamloops, Brit. Columbia, 1992—93; rsch. asst. dept. psychology Western Oreg. State U., 1994; intern divsn. children's mental health Marion County Health Dept., Salem, Oreg., 1995; tchg. asst. Purdue U., 1996—98; tchg. asst. dept. health promotion & edn. U. Utah, 1998—2002; asst. prof. cmty. health edn., dept. exercise sci. Va. Commonwealth U., Richmond, 2002—07, faculty dept. tchr. edn., dept. psychology, 2003—07; postdoc. rsch. fellow Miriam Hosp./Brown U. Warren Alpert Med. Sch., Providence, 2008, asst. prof. rsch., dept. psychiatry & human behavior, 2009—. Reviewer Am. Jour. Health Behavior, 2002—; contbr. articles to profl. jours. Mem.: APHA, Am. Soc. Bariatric Surgery, Am. Acad. Health Behavior, Soc. Pub. Health Edn., Am. Headache Soc. Office: Brown U Dept of Psychiatry & Human Behavior Box G BH Providence RI 02912 Office Phone: 401-793-8970. Business E-Mail: Dale_Bond@brown.edu. *

BOND, LINDA, relief organization administrator; b. Glace Bay, Nova Scotia, Can., June 22, 1946; Corps appointment The Salvation Army, Can. and Bermuda Territory, 1969—78, 1987—89, tng. appointment, 1978—82, 1989—91, territorial hdqs. appointment, 1982—87, divsn. hdqs. appointment, 1991—93, divisional comdr., 1993—95, chief sec., 1999—2002; undersec. pers. The Salvation Army, Internat. Hdqs., 1995—98, sec. spiritual life devel. and internat. ext. rels., 2005—08, gen., 2011—; divsn. comdr. The Salvation Army, UK Territory with the Republic Ireland, 1998—99; territorial comdr. and territorial pres. women's ministries The Salvation Army, USA Western Territory, 2002—05, The Salvation Army, Australia Eastern Territory, 2008—11. Office: The Salvation Army 101 Queen Victoria St London EC4P 4EP England *

BOND, MALCOLM JAMES, medical educator; b. Clare, Australia, Jan. 11, 1959; s. Leslie Edgar and Ruth Elaine (Maynard) B.; m. Carolyn Ann Warren, Apr. 30, 1994; children: Cameron James, Verity Elise. BA, Flinders U., Adelaide, Australia, 1981, BA with honors, 1982, PhD, 1990. Sr. tutor Flinders U., Adelaide, 1987—90, lectr., 1991—97, sr. lectr., 1998—2002, assoc. prof., 2003—. Cons. Paradigm Cons., Adelaide, 1987-99. Contbr. articles to profl. jours. Mem. Australian Psychol. Soc., Australian Coll. Edn., N.Y. Acad. Scis. Avocations: gardening, music, sports. Office: Flinders U Sch Medicine Gpo Box 2100 5001 Adelaide SA Australia Home Phone: 61 8 8278 9830; Office Phone: 61 8 7221 8503. Business E-Mail: malcolm.bond@flinders.edu.au.

BOND, RICHARD RANDOLPH, retired foundation administrator; b. Lost Creek, W.Va., Dec. 1, 1927; s. Harley Donovan and Marcella Randolph B.; m. Reva Stearns, Apr. 20, 1946; children: David, Philip, Josette, Michael. BS, Salem Coll., 1948, LHD (hon.), 1979, U. No. Colo.; MS, W.Va. U., 1949; PhD, U. Wis., 1955; postdoctoral studies, U. Mich., 1958—59. Various tchg. and fellowship positions, 1949—59; dean of faculty Elmira Coll., NY, 1959—63; dean Coll. Liberal Arts U. Liberia, Monrovia, 1963—64; chief of party Cornell U. Project in Liberia, Monrovia, 1964—66; v.p. acad. affairs Ill. State U., Normal, 1966—71; pres. U. No. Colo., Greeley, 1971—81, pres. emeritus, prof. zoology, 1981—89; state rep. Colo. Gen. Assembly, Denver, 1984—90; interim pres. Front Range C.C., Westminster, Colo., 1991; pres. Morgan C.C., Ft. Morgan, Colo., 1991—96, Cmty. Found., Greeley and Weld County, 1996—2000, Bond Family Found., 1995—. Founder Nat. Student Exch., 1st No. Savs. and Loan; cons., examiner North Ctrl. Accrediting Assn., 1969-82. Author: Colorado Postsecondary Options Act., 1988; contbr. articles to profl. jours. Bd. dirs., chmn. Sunrise Cmty. Health Ctr.; founding mem. Dream Team on Dropout Prevention; Dem. candidate for Col. 4th Congl. Dist., 1990; founder Colo. chpt. Dem. Leadership Coun., 1991—; co-chmn. Clinton Campaign, Colo., 1992; bd. dirs. Colo. chpt. Nat. Multiple Sclerosis Soc., Greeley Habitat for Humanity; chmn. bd. dirs. Univ. Schs. Found.; bd. govs. Univ. Schs., 2003—; bd. of trustee Aims CC, 2001—09. With US Army, 1945-47. Recipient Legislator of Yr. award DAV, 1988, Colo. Acad. Pediat., 1989; Mental Health award, 1990, Polit. Educator of Yr. award, Colo. Edn. Assn., 1991; fellow NSF, 1953-54, Am. Physiol. Soc., 1958, Carnegie Found., 1958-59. Mem. Am. Ornithologists Union, Am. Assn. Colls. and Univs. (bd. dirs. 1979-81), Colo. Assn. Colls. and Univs. (chmn. 1979-81), Rotary, Habitat for Humanity (bd. dirs. Greeley chpt.), U. Charter Sch. (bd. dirs.), Realizing Our Cmty. (bd. dirs.), Sigma Xi. Independent. Mem. United Ch. Of Christ. Avocations: gardening, stamp collecting/philately, camping, genealogy. Home and Office: 5601 18th St 51 Greeley CO 80634-2925 Home Phone: 970-330-6494. Personal E-mail: rrbond@comcast.net.

BONDAGJI, NABEEL SALEM, obstetrician, gynecologist, consultant; b. Makkah, Saudi Arabia, Dec. 31, 1959; s. Salem Husein Bondagji and Fatima Abdullghani; m. Layla Saleh Same, Apr. 2, 1987; children: Ahmed, Ola, Haneen, Maram, Ammar. MD, King Abulaziz U., Saudi Arabia, 1985. Intern KAUH, 1985—86; resident ob.-gyn. King Abdullaziz U., 1986—90; resident Dahousie U., Halifax, Canada, 1990—94; fellow in perinatology U. Man., Wennipeg, Canada, 1994—96; cons. ob.-gyn. KAUH, 1996—98; asst. prof. King Abdullaziz U., Jeddah, Saudi Arabia, 1998—; chmn. dept. ob-gyn. King Faisal Specielist Hosp. & RC, Jeddah, Saudi Arabia, 2002—. Cons. perinatologist King Abdulaziz U. Hosp., Jeddah, Saudi Arabia, 1996—. Fellow: Royal Coll. Phsicians and Surgeons Can.; mem.: Saudi Soc. Ob.-Gyn. (life Presentation award 2003). Achievements include research in fetal biometery and Cerebral Palsy. Avocation: reading.

BONDINELL, STEPHANIE, counselor, academic administrator; d. Peter Jr. and Gloria Lucille (Burden) Honcharuk; m. Paul Swanstrom Bondinell, July 31, 1971; 1 child, Paul Emil. BA, William Paterson U., 1970; MEd, Stetson U., 1983. Cert. elem. educator Fla., guidance counselor grades K-12 Fla. Tchr. Bloomingdale Bd. Edn., NJ, 1971-80; edn. dir. Fla. United Meth. Children's Home, Enterprise, 1982-89; guidance counselor Volusia County Sch. Bd., Deltona, Fla., 1988—. Coord. sch. improvement svcs., Deltona Lakes, 1996—98, Deltona Lakes, 2002—05. Sec. adv. com. Deltona Jr. HS, 1996—98, sec. PTA, 1982; vice-chmn. adv. com. Deltona Mid. Sch., 1988, chmn., 1991—92, 1991—92; mem. adv. com. Deltona HS, 1995—96; secondary sch. task force Volusia County Sch. Bd., 1986—; team leader Volusia County Sch. Accreditation Quality Assurance Team, 2003—11; mem. exec. com. Volusia County Reps.; mem. Rep. Presdl. Task Force; bd. dir. Deltona Arts Hist. Ctr., 2008—; mem. state adv. bd. Fla. Future Educators Am., 1990—92, 2003—09. Recipient Outstanding Ednl. Partnership award, S.W. Volusia C. of C., 1998, Sunshine State Medallion award, Fla. Pub. Rels. Assn., 1998, award, Volusia/Flagler Alcohol & Drug Abuse Prevention Coun., 1998—2010, Fla. Lottery Creative Tchg. award, 2002; named Deltona Lakes Tchr. of Yr., Volusia County Sch., 1991, 1996, Volusia County Sch. Dist. Accreditation Steering Com. Team Leaders, 2003—10, Volusia County Guidance Counselor of Yr., Volusia/Flagler Counseling Assn., 2006; Acad. scholar, Becton, Dickinson & Co., 1966, NJ State scholar, 1966—70. Mem.: AAUW, Am. Counseling Assn., Fla. Edn. Assn., Internat. Platform Assn., Volusia Tchrs. Orgn., NJ Edn. Assn., Fla. Assn. Counseling and Devel., Disvn. Learning Disabilities, Coun. Exceptional Children, Stetson U. Alumni Assn., Deltona Civic Assn., 4 Townes Federated Rep. Women's Club (sec., v.p.), Deltona Rep. Club (v.p. 1991—93). Avocations: painting, dance, writing. Home: 1810 W Cooper Dr Deltona FL 32725-3623 Office: Volusia County Sch Bd 2022 Adelia Blvd Deltona FL 32725-3976 E-mail: sbondine@mail.volusia.k12.fl.us. *

BONDY, PHILIP KRAMER, retired internist; b. NYC, Dec. 15, 1917; s. Eugene Lyons and Irene (Kramer) B.; m. Sarah B. Ernst, Mar. 18, 1949; children: Jonathan L., Jessica, Steven M. AB, Columbia U., 1938; MD, Harvard U., 1942; MA (hon.), Yale U., 1961. Intern Peter Bent Brigham Hosp., Boston, 1942-43; mem. staff Grady Meml. Hosp., Atlanta, 1943, 46-48, chief resident in medicine, 1947-48; mem. faculty Emory U., 1947-48, 49-52, asst. prof. medicine, 1951-52; Alexander Browne Coxe fellow physiol. chemistry Yale U., New Haven, 1948-49, mem. faculty, 1948-49, 52-74, 77-88, prof. medicine, 1961, 77-88, prof. emeritus, 1988—, C.N.H. Long prof. medicine, 1965-74, chmn. dept. internal medicine, 1965-72, assoc. dean for vets. affairs, 1983-89, chmn. com. outpatient svcs., 1960-62; chmn. med. divsn. Royal Marsden Hosp., 1972-77; Cancer Rsch. Campaign prof. Inst. Cancer Rsch., London; cons. Ludwig Inst. Cancer Rsch., Zurich, Switzerland, 1972-77; assoc. chief of staff for rsch. West Haven VA Med. Ctr., 1977-83, chief of staff, 1983-89. Mem. med. vis. com. Brookhaven Nat. Labs., 1969-73, chmn., 1973; mem. program project com. NIH-Nat. Inst. Arthritis and Metabolic Disease, 1964-68, chmn., 1966-68; mem. exptl. biol. sect. breast cancer task force NIH-Nat. Cancer Inst., 1973-76; mem. adv. coun. NIDDK, 1990-94; mem. planning com. Med. Rsch. Svc. VA, 1985-88, chmn., 1986-88; mem. N.E. region planning com. VA. Editor-in-chief Jour. Clin. Investigation, 1957-62, Yale Jour. Biology and Medicine, 1978-92; editor: Diseases of Metabolism, 6th, 7th, 8th edits, Yearbook of Endocrinology and Metabolism, 1963-64; editorial bd. Conn. Medicine, 1959-61, Yearbook of Medicine, 1954-84, Medicine, 1963-85, Merck Manual, 1969-00, Clinics in Endocrinology and Metabolism, 1973-84, Cancer Topics, 1975-79. Sec. libr. bd. City of Woodbridge, Conn., 1960-67; sec. bd. dirs. Southbury Tng. Sch. Found.; sec., bd. trustees Southbury Tng. Sch.; mem. Coun. on Mental Retardation, Conn., 1997-03; cellist Hamden Symphony Orch., 1994-2006, prin. cellist, 1996-2004. Capt. M.C., AUS, 1943-46, chair Evergreen Woods Concert Com., 2006-10. Recipient Edward Sutliffe Brainard prize Columbia U., 1938, Sigma Xi prize Emory U., 1949, Rsch. Career award NIH, 1962, 66. Fellow AAAS (chmn. sect. N on med. sci. 1979), Royal Coll. Physicians, Royal Soc. Medicine (v.p. sect. oncology 1975-77); mem. ACP (master), Endocrine Soc. (councillor 1964-67, mem. publs. com. 1965-72, chmn. 1968-72), Assn. Am. Physicians, Assn. Physicians Gt. Britain and Ireland, Am. Soc. Clin. Investigation, Am. Fedn. Clin. Rsch., Nat. Assn. VA Chiefs of Staff (mem. exec. com. 1986-88), Soc. Exptl. Biology and Medicine, Interurban Clin. Club, Inst. Cancer Rsch. (London, hon.). Home: 88 Notch Hill Rd Apt 265 North Branford CT 06471

BONFIGLIO, GIOVANNI, microbiologist, director; b. Catania, Mar. 18, 1963; Degree in Medicine, U. Catania, 1987, degree in Med. Microbiology, 1999; PhD, U. Milan, 1991. Rschr. asst. London Hosp. Med. Coll., 1991—93; sr. rschr. U. Catania, 1993—2006; dir. CCD GB Morgagni - Clin. & Functional Rsch. Lab., 2006—. Mem.: European Soc. Microbiology and Infectious Diseases, Italian Assn. Clin. Microbiology, Am. Soc. Microbiology. Avocations: tennis, reading. Office: via Del Bosco 105 Catania 95125 Italy Business E-Mail: bonfigio@unict.it.

BONILLA RODRIGUEZ, GUSTAVO ORLANDO, research scientist; b. Uruguay, Aug. 10, 1959; Degree in Pharmacy and Biochemistry, Fed. U. Santa Maria, Brazil, 1984; PhD in Genetics, State U. Campinas, Brazil, 1992. Asst. prof. State U. Sao Paulo, 1996—2007, assoc. prof., 2007. Mem.: Brazilian Soc. Biochemistry and Molecular Biology. Office: Rua Cristovao Colombo 2265 DQCA IBILCE Sao Jose do Rio Preto Sao Paulo 15054-000 Brazil Office Fax: (5517) 32212356. Business E-Mail: bonilla@ibilce.unesp.br.

BONINGER, MICHAEL LEE, physiatrist; BS in Mechanical Engring., Ohio State U., 1985, MD, 1989. Resident U. Mich. Hospitals, Ann Arbor, Mich.; asst. prof., Depts. Physical Medicine and Rehab. and Rehab. Sci. and Tech. U. Pitts., 1994—2000, medical dir., Ctr. for Assistive Tech., 1994—, medical dir., Human Engineering Research Laboratories, Dept. of Physical Medicine and Rehab., 1994—, research dir., Dept. Physical Medicine and Rehab., 1997—; medical dir. VA Ctr. Excellence for Wheelchairs and Related Technology VA Pittsburgh Healthcare System, 1999—2004, medical dir. VA Ctr. Excellence for Wheelchairs and and Associated Rehab. Engineering, 2004—07; assoc. prof., Dept. Physical Medicine and Rehab., Bioengineering and Rehab. Sci. and Tech. U. Pitts., 2000—03, prof., vice chair Dept. Physical Medicine and Rehab., Bioengineering and Rehab. Sci. and Tech., 2004—07, asst. dean, Medical Student Rsch., 2005—06, assoc. dean, Medical Student Rsch., 2006—, prof., interim chair, Depts. Physical Medicine and Rehab. Bioengineering Rehab. Sci. and Tech., 2007—. Editorial bd. mem. Archives of Physical Medicine and Rehab., 1999—, Jour. Rehab. Rsch. and Devel., 1999—. Named to Spinal Cord Injury Hall of Fame, Nat. Spinal Cord Injury Assn., 2006. Mem.: American Academy of Physical Medicine & Rehab., Assn. Academic Physiatrists. Office: Rehab Medicine Ctr 3471 Fifth Ave Ste 1103 Pittsburgh PA 15213

BONIS, LASZLO JOSEPH, consultant, executive, chemist; b. Budapest, Hungary, May 31, 1931; came to U.S., 1957; s. Joseph and Ilona (Hunvald) B.; m. Eva Markovich, July 31, 1955 (div. 1981); children: Andrea Christine, Peter Anthony Laszlo; m. Cheryl E. Olsen, Dec. 28, 1985. DM Ing. Mech. Enging., U. Tech. Sci., Budapest, 1953; MSc in Metallurgy, MIT, 1959, postgrad., 1959-60. Registered profl. engr., Calif., Mass.; cert. chemist Nat. Cert. Commn. Assoc. dir. material rsch. Electronics, Inc., Budapest, 1953-56; prof. U. Tech. Sci., 1953-56; rsch. asst. MIT, Cambridge, 1957-60; exec. v.p., tech. dir. Ilikon Corp., Natick, Mass., 1960-62, pres., tech. dir., 1962-74; mgmt. cons. Tech. Fin. and Mktg., Inc., Natick, Mass., 1974—; pres., chmn., tech. dir. Composite Container Corp., Medford, Mass., 1977-88; pres. T.F.M. Cons., Dover, Mass., 1988—. Editor: (4 vols.) Fundamental Phenomena in the Material Science; contbr. articles to profl. jours.; patentee in field. Bd. dirs. The Opera Co., Boston, 1962-85, pres., 1966-85; pres. Boston Opera House, 1991-94. Recipient Muse award Pub. Action for the Arts, 1984, George Washington award Am. Hungarian Found., 1984, Golden Door award Internat. Inst., 1980, Golden Diploma award Tech. U. Sci., Budapest, 2003; named One of Outstanding Young Men of Greater Boston C. of C., 1966. Fellow Am. Inst. Chemists; mem. N.Y. Acad. Scis., MIT Club. Office: TFM Cons 52 Haven St Dover MA 02030-2131 Business E-Mail: dr.bonis@tfmconsultants.com.

BONN, JOSEPH, intervention radioloist; MD, U. Va., 1979. Diplomate Am. Bd. Radiology-vascular and interventional radiology, Am. Bd. Radiology-radiology, lic. Pa., 1986. Intern gen. surgery Caritas Carney Hosp. Inc., 1980; resident gen. surgey St. Luke's Roosevelt Hosp., 1982; resident diagnostic radiology NY Presbyn. Hosp., 1986; fellow vascular-interventional radiology Pa. Hosp., 1987; hosp. affiliations include Bryn Mawr Hosp., Paoli Hosp., Lankenau Med. Ctr., dir. of interventional radiology. With Radiology Assocs.; dir. med. alumni Assn. Univ. Va.; exec. coun. Soc. of Interventional Radiology; chmn. Soc. of Interventional Radiology Found.; assoc. editor Jour. of Vascular and Interventional Radiology; pres. Phila. Angiography and Interventional Radiology Soc. Recipient Tchr. of the Year award, Thomas Jefferson Univ. Hosp., Disting. Reviewer award, Journal of Vascular and Interventional Radiology; named one of the Top Doctors, Phila. Mag., 2002, 2005, 2010—11. Mem.: Cardiovasc. and Interventional Radiology Soc., Soc. of Interventional Radiology, Pa. Radiol. Soc., Am. Coll. of Radiology. Office: Lankenau Medical Center 100 Lancaster Ave Wynnewood PA 19096 Office Phone: 484-476-2826. Office Fax: 484-476-6820.

BONNAR, JOHN, obstetrics and gynecology educator, consultant; b. Wishaw, Scotland, July 12, 1934; arrived in Ireland, 1975; s. John and Mary (Breen) B.; m. Elizabeth Murray, Sept. 17, 1960; children: John Paul, Christopher Matthew, Clare Elizabeth, James Peter. MB, BCh, U. Glasgow, Scotland, 1958, MD with honors, 1971; fellow, Trinity Coll., Ireland, 1976. Cert. ob-gyn. Sr. registrar ob-gyn. Royal Maternity Hosp. and Victoria Infirmary, Glasgow, Scotland, 1963-69; reader ob-gyn. U. Oxford, Eng., 1969-75; prof., head ob-gyn. Trinity Coll., Dublin, 1975-99, dean, faculty health scis.; v.p. Med. Protection Soc., London, 1998—; coun. mem. Royal Coll. Ob-Gyn., London, 1991-97. Cons. ob-gyn. Coombe Women's Hosp., Dublin, Ireland, St. James Hosp., Dublin, 1987-99; chmn. Nat. Haemophilia Coun. Ireland, 2004-2011. Author: Hemostatic Disorders of the Pregnant Woman and Newborn Infant, 1987; editor: Recent Advances in Obstetrics and Gynecology, 1996, 98, 2000, 03, 05. Fellow: Am. Gynecol. and Obstet. Soc., Royal Coll. Physicians (Ireland) (chmn. Inst. Obstetricians and Gynecologists 1999—2002), Royal Coll. Ob-Gyn (London); mem.: Soc. Pelvic Surgeons USA, Gynecol. Vis. Soc. Great Britain and Ireland. Avocations: fishing, hill walking, golf. Home: 58

Deerpark Rd Castleknock Dublin Ireland Office: Charlemont Clinic Charlemont Mall Ste 26 Dublin 2 Ireland Personal E-mail: johnbonnar@gamil.com. E-mail: jbonnar@indigo.ie.

BONNELL, BRUCE WILLIAM, surgeon; b. Bay City, Mich., Aug. 8, 1948; MD, U. Mich., 1974. Surg. intensivist Spectrum Health, 1979—. Fellow: ACS, Am. Coll. Critical Care Medicine. Home: 3056 Woodridge Cir NE Grand Rapids MI 49525 Personal E-mail: bruce.bonnell@spectrumhealth.org.

BONNEMA, STEEN JOOP, endocrinologist; b. Esbjerg, Denmark, Nov. 5, 1959; MD, Århus U., Denmark, 1986, PhD, 2002. Cons. dept. endocrinology Odense U. Hosp., 2000—. Office: Odense University Hosp Sdr Blvd 29 Odense 5000 Denmark Business E-Mail: steen.bonnema@dadlnet.dk.

BONNER, JACK WILBUR, III, psychiatrist, educator, administrator; b. Corpus Christi, Tex., July 30, 1940; s. Jack Wilbur and Irldene (Turner) B.; m. Myra Lynn Taylor; children: Jack Wilbur, IV, Katherine Lynn, Shelley Bliss AA, Del Mar Coll., Corpus Christi, 1960; BA with honors, U. Tex., Austin, 1961; MD, S.W. Med. Sch., U. Tex., Dallas, 1965. Diplomate Am. Bd. Psychiatry and Neurology. Intern U. Ark. Med. Center, 1965-66; resident Duke U. Med. Center, 1966-69; assoc. in psychiatry Highland Hosp. divsn. Duke U. Med. Center, Asheville, NC, 1971, asst. prof. psychiatry, 1972-80, dir. outpatient services, 1972-75, med. dir., 1975-81; chmn. bd. dirs., CEO, med. dir. Highland Hosp., Asheville, NC, 1981-92; med. dir. The Oaks Psychiat. Health Sys., Austin, Tex., 1992-93, exec. med. dir., 1993-94, med. dir. Behavioral Health Svcs. Greenville (S.C.) Hosp. Sys. Univ. Med. Ctr., 1994—2009, adminstr. Behavioral Health Svcs., 1996—2000, acad. chair, 1994—2009. Asst. clin. prof. Duke U. Med. Ctr., Durham, NC, 1982—87, asst. cons. prof. psychiatry, 1987—; clin. assoc. prof. U. NC Sch. Medicine, Chapel Hill, 1986—92, Quillen-Dishner Coll. Medicine, Johnson City, Tenn., 1989—92, U. Tex. Health Sci. Ctr., San Antonio, 1993—94, U. SC Sch. Medicine, Columbia, 1995—2004, GHS prof. clin. neuropsychiatry and behavioral sci., 2004—. Author: (with others) The Psychology of Discipline, 1983, Unmasking the Psychopath: Antisocial Personality and Related Syndromes, 1986; contbr. articles to profl. jours. Chmn. bd. dirs. The Highland Found., 1980-93; bd. dirs. Western N.C. Med. Peer Rev. Found., 1975-78; trustee La Amistad Found., Maitland, Fla., 1985-95, N.C. Symphony, 1987-92, Cooper Riis Found., Mill Spring, N.C., 2000- (exec. com. 2007-). Recipient Disting. Mentor award, 2009. Fellow: APA (trustee 1999—2005, chair fin. and budget com. 2002—09, Disting. Life Fellow, Warren Williams award 2002, Nancy C.A. Roeske cert. of recognition for excellence in med. student edn. 2005, Spl. Presdl. Commendation 2011), Am. Coll. Psychiatrists (treas. 1992—95, 2d v.p. 1999—2000, 1st v.p. 2000—01, pres.-elect 2001—02, pres. 2002—03, sec.-gen. 2006—, E.B. Bowls award 2000), So. Psychiat. Assn. (v.p. 1984—85, chmn. bd. regents 1988—89, pres. 1992—93); mem.: AMA, Found. Excellence Mental Health Care (sci. adv. bd. 2011—), Group Advancement Psychiatry (treas. 1991—99, pres.-elect 1999—2001, pres. 2001—03), Ctrl. Neuropsychiat. Hosp. Assn. (councillor 1981—85, pres. 1983—84), So. Med. Assn. (sec. sect. on neurology, neurosurgery and psychiatry 1977—80, chmn.-elect 1980—81, chmn. 1981—82), Nat. Anorexic Aid Soc. (nat. anorexia adv. coun. 1979—86), NC Psychiat. Assn. (pres. 1982—83), Buncombe County (NC) Med. Soc. (pres. 1983), Nat. Acads. Practice, Am. Group Psychotherapy Assn., Nat. Alliance on Mental Illness Greenville (bd. dirs. 2005—, v.p. 2006—08, pres. 2008—10), Nat. Assn. Psychiat. Health Sys. (trustee 1989—94, 1st v.p. 1990—91, pres.-elect 1991—92, pres. 1992—93), Benjamin Rush Soc. (exec. coun. 2006—, sec.-treas. 2008—10, v.p. 2010—), U. Tex. Southwestern Med. Sch. Alumni Assn. (bd. dirs. 1988—95, pres. 1989—91), Phi Theta Kappa. Home: Four Brookside Way Greenville SC 29605-1212 Office: Greenville Hosp Sys U Med Ctr Academic Svcs 701 Grove Rd Greenville SC 29605-5601 Office Phone: 864-455-7834. Business E-Mail: jbonner@ghs.org.

BONNER, JAMES RYAN, allergist, immunologist, educator; MD, U. Mich., 1971. Diplomate Am. Bd. Internal Medicine, 1974, Am. Bd. Internal Medicine-infectious disease, 1976, Am. Bd. Allergy and Immunology, 1979. Resident internal medicine Univ. Ala. Med. Ctr., 1972—74, fellow allergy & immunology, 1974—77; prof. pulmonary, allergy and critical care medicine divsn. Univ. Ala. Sch. of Medicine; staff Veterans Adminstrn. Hosp.; hosp. affiliations include Univ. of Ala. Hosp., Ala. Allergy and Asthma Ctr. Fellow: ACP (mem. ala. chpt.), Am. Coll. of Allergy, Asthma and Immunology; mem.: Med. Assn. of the State of Ala. Office: Veterans Affairs Medical Center 700 S 19th St Birmingham AL 35233-1927 Office Phone: 205-933-8101.

BONNER, JOHN TYLER, biology professor; b. NYC, May 12, 1920; s. Paul Hyde and Lilly Marguerite (Stehli) Bonner; m. Ruth Anna Graham, July 11, 1942 (dec. 2003); children: Rebecca, Jonathan Graham, Jeremy Tyndall, Andrew Duncan. Grad., Phillips Exeter Acad., 1937; BSc, Harvard U., 1941, MA, 1942, PhD (Jr. fellow 1942, 46-47), 1947; DSc, Middlebury Coll., 1970, Princeton U., 2006; LLD, Concordia U., 2003; DLitt, U. Coll. Cape Breton, 2005. Asst. to assoc. prof. Princeton U., 1947-58, prof., 1958-90, emeritus prof., 1990—, chmn. dept. biology, 1965-77, 83-84, 87-88. Lectr. embryology Marine Biol. Lab, Woods Hole, Mass., 1951—52; spl. lectr. U. London, 1957, Bklyn. Coll., 1966; trustee Biol. Abstracts, 1958—63; Arnold Bernhard vis. prof. Williams Coll., 1989; Raman prof. Indian Acad. Scis., 1990. Author: Morphogenesis, 1952, Cells and Societies, 1955, The Evolution of Development, 1958, The Cellular Slime Molds, 1959, The Cellular Slime Molds, rev. edit., 1967, The Ideas of Biology, 1962, Size and Cycle, 1965, The Scale of Nature, 1969, On Development, 1974, The Evolution of Culture in Animals, 1980; author: (with T.A. McMahon) On Life and Size, 1983; author: The Evolution of Complexity, 1988, Researches on Cellular Slime Molds, 1991, Life Cycles, 1993, Sixty Years of Biology, 1996, First Signals, 2000, Lives of a Biologist, 2002, Why Size Matters, 2006, The Social Amoebae, 2009; editor: Growth and Form, 1961, Evolution and Development, 1981; assoc. editor: Am. Scientist, 1961—69, mem. editl. bd.: Am. Naturalist, 1958—60, 1966—68, Jour. Gen. Physiology, 1962—69, Growth, 1955—89, Differentiation, 1976—90, Oxford Surveys in Evolutionary Biology, 1982—93; mem. bd. editors Princeton U. Press, 1965—68, 1971, trustee, 1976—82. Staff aero. med. lab. Wright Field, Wright Field, Ohio. Served to 1st lt. USAC, 1942—46. Recipient Selman A. Waksman award for Contbns. to Microbiology, Theobold Smith Soc.; Rockefeller Travelling fellow, France, 1953, Guggenheim fellow, Scotland, 1958, 1971—72, NSF Sr. Postdoctoral fellow, 1963. Fellow: Am. Acad. Arts. and Scis., Indian Acad. Scis. (hon.); mem.: NAS, Am. Philos. Soc., Soc. Growth and Devel., Am. Soc. Naturalists, Sigma Xi, Phi Beta Kappa. Business E-Mail: jtbonner@princeton.edu.

BONNER, STEPHEN BARNES, health facility administrator; b. Mpls., Sept. 13, 1946; s. John Farrington and Jane (Stinchfield) Bonner; children: Stephen, Ann, Leslie. BA, Amherst Coll., 1968; JD, William Mitchell Coll. Law, 1972. Bar: Minn., Ky., Ill. V.p., counsel Prudential Ins. Co. of America, 1980—82; exec. v.p., gen. counsel Capital Holding Corp., Lousiville, 1982—86, gen. counsel, COO Nat. Liberty Corp. Valley Forge, Pa., 1987; pres. Construction Info. Group McGraw-Hill Companies; exec. v.p. Keyport Ins. Co.; bd. mem. Cancer Treatment Centers of America (CTCA), 1996—, pres., CEO, 1999—. Chmn. govt. rels. com. Met. United Way Ky., Louisville, 1983; bd. mem. William Mitchell Coll. Law; trustee American Archtl. Found. Named one of 100 Most Influential People in Healthcare, Modern Healthcare mag., 2011. Master: Chgo. Bar Assn.; mem.: ABA, Hennepin County Bar Assn., Assn. Life Ins. Counsel, Ky. Bar Assn., Minn. Bar Assn. Office: Cancer Treatment Centers of America 1336 Basswood Rd Schaumburg IL 60173 Office Phone: 847-342-7458. *

BONNESS, MICHELLE R., plastic surgeon; Med. degree, U. Wis., Madison. Diplomate Am. Bd. Plastic Surgery, 2001, Am. Bd. Surgeons, 1995-2005. Resident in gen. surgery Univ. Ill., Chgo.; resident in plastic and reconstructive surgery Univ. Louisville, fellow in oculoplastic surgery, fellow in cosmetic surgery; fellowship in breast reconstruction Atlanta Plastic Surgery; chief plastic surgery divsn. St. Luke's Med. Ctr., Milw.; hosp. affiliations include Oconomowoc Meml. Hosp., Wis., Kindred Hosp., Greenfield, Wis., Elmbrook Meml. Hosp., Brookfield, Wis., St. Luke's med. Ctr., Milw.; plastic surgeon Bonness Cosmetic Surgery and Spa Vita. Recipient Best Plastic Surgeon, Shepherd Express 10th Ann. Readers' Choice awards, 2001; named one of the Top Drs., Milw. Mag., 2004. Master: Wis. State Med. Soc.; mem.: Am. Assn. Physicians and Surgeons, Wis. Soc. Plastic Surgeons (pres. 2008—10), Med. Soc. Waukesha County, Med. Soc. Milw. County, Am. Soc. Plastic Surgeons. Office: Bonness Cosmetic Surgery and Spa Vita 20320 W Greenfield Ave Brookfield WI 53045 Office Phone: 262-782-7021. Office Fax: 262-782-8738.

BONNE-TAMIR, BATSHEVA, retired medical educator; b. Tel Aviv, July 27, 1932; d. Alfred Bonne; 1 child, Eldad Tamir. Asst. prof. Tel Aviv U., Sch. Medicine, 1965—79, assoc. prof., 1979—87, prof., 1987—2003; head Nat. Lab., 1994—2004, Shalom and Varda Ypran Inst. HUman Genome Rsch., 1997—2004. Contbr. articles to profl. sci. jours. Home Phone: 972-9-7405755. Business E-Mail: bonne@post.tau.ac.il.

BONNETERRE, JACQUES M., health facility administrator, oncologist, educator; b. Aubenton, Aisne, France, July 21, 1930; s. Maurice and Simonne (Claude) B.; m. Marie Edith A. Couteaux, Sept. 30, 1995; children: Vincent, Loic, Capucine. MD, Lille U., France, 1976, PhD, 1986; M in Med. Mgmt., Ecole Superieure Commerce, Paris, 1992. Diplomate French Bd. Oncology. Resident U. Hosp., Lille, 1973-78; cons. med. oncology Ctr. Oscar Lambret, Lille, 1978-84, head med. dept., 1985—; prof. med. oncology Lille U., 1993; head breast cancer dept. Oscar Lambret Ctr., Lille, 2001—. Expert French Drug Agy., 1990—, European Drug Agy., 1995—, Nat. Fedn. Cancer Ctrs., Inserm, others, dir. Ctr. Oscar Lambret, Lille, 1996—2001. Author: Human Plasmocytoma, 1981, Professional Cancer, 1982. Mem. French Cancer Soc. (pres. 1998-99), Am. Soc. Clin. Oncology, Am. Assn. Cancer Rsch., European Soc. Med. Oncology, European Assn. Cancer Rsch. Office: Ctr Oscar Lambret 3 rue Frederic Combemale F-59020 Lille France Business E-Mail: j-bonneterre@o_lambret.fr.

BONNIE, RICHARD JEFFREY, lawyer, educator, consultant; b. Richmond, Va., Aug. 22, 1945; s. Herbert Herman and Helene Selma (Berz) B.; m. Kathleen Ford, June 15, 1967; children: Joshua Ford, Zachary Andrew, Jessica Katherine. BA, Johns Hopkins U., 1966; LLB, U. Va., 1969. Var: Va. 1969, U.S. Dist. Ct. (ea. dist.) Va. 1969; U.S. Ct. Appeals (4th cir.) 1969, U.S. Supreme Ct. 1986. Asst. prof. law U. Va., Charlottesville, 1969—70, assoc. prof., 1973—77, prof., 1977—87, John S. Battle prof., 1987—2007, Harrison found. prof. medicine and law, 2007; dir. Inst. Law, Psychiatry, and Pub. Policy, 1979—, prof. psychiatry, 2001—, prof. pub. policy, 2009—. Vis. fellow Inst. Criminology, Cambridge U., 1977; vis. prof. Cornell Law Sch., 1993-94, Parsons visitor Sydney Law Sch., 2005; assoc. dir. nat. Commn. Marijuana and Drug Abuse, 1971-73; reporter Nat. Conf. Commrs. on Uniform State Laws, 1972-74; cons. Spl. Action Office for Drug Abuse Prevention Exec. Office of the Pres., 1973-75; spl. asst. to US Atty. Gen., 1975; sec. Nat. Adv. Coun. on Drug Abuse, 1975-80; mem. Com. on Problem of Drug Dependence, Inc., 1979-84; charter fellow Coll. Problems of Drug Dependence, 1992—; cons. Am. Psychiat. Assn., Coun. Psychiatry and Law, 1979—, Am. Acad. Neurology, Com. Law, Ethics and Humanities, 2007-; mem. U.S. State Dept. Del. to investigate psychiat. practices in the Soviet Union, 1989; mem. World Psychiat. Assn. rev. team to investigate Soviet psychiatry, 1991; adv. bd. permanent coordination office Reforms in psychiatry in Ctrl. and Ea. Europe, former Soviet Union, 1993—; bd. dirs. Geneva Initiative on Psychiatry, 1996-2005, Global Initiative on Psychiatry, 2005-2007; pres. Am. Friends of Geneva Initiative on Psychiatry, 1997—, mem. MacArthur Found. Network on Mental Health and the Law, 1988-96; bd. dirs. Va. Capital Representation Resource Ctr., 1994-97, 2002—; mem. MacArthur Found. Network on Mandated Treatment, 2000-10, MacArthur Found. Network on Neurosci. and Law, 2007—; mem. Max Plank Network on Aging, 2005—; co-chair, bd. dirs. Physicians and Lawyers for Nat. Drug Policy, 2004—; steering com. underage drinking Nat. Inst. Alcohol Abuse and Alcoholism, 2004—; nat. commn. diversion and abuse of prescription Ctr. Addiction and Substance Abuse, 2003-04; chair commn. on mental health law reform Va. Supreme Ct., 2006—; cons. in field Author: The Marijuana Conviction: The History of Marijuana Prohibition in the United States, 1974, 2d edit. 1999, Legal Aspects of Drug Dependence, 1975, Psychiatrists and the Legal Process: Diagnosis and Debate, 1977, Marijuana Use and Criminal Sanctions: Essays in the Theory and Practice of Decriminalization, 1980, Criminal Law: Cases and Materials, 1982, 2d edit., 1986, The Trial of John W. Hinckley, Jr.: A Case Study in the Insanity Defense, 1986, rev. edit., 2000, 2008, Criminal Law, 1997, 2d edit., 2004, 3rd edit., 2010, Growing Up Tobacco Free, 1994, Mental Disorder, Work Disability and the Law, 1997, Reducing the Burden of Injury, 1999, The Evolution of Mental Health Law, 2001, Elder Mistreatment, 2002, Adjudicative Competence, 2002, Reducing Underage Drinking, 2003, Ending the Tobacco Problem, 2007, Law Touched Our Hearts, 2009. Chmn. Va. Human Rights Com., Dept. Mental Health and Mental Retardation, 1979-85; chair Commn. on Mental Health Law Reform, Va. Supreme Ct., 2006—; bd. dirs. Coll. on Problem of Drug Dependence, 1996-2000; mem. Steering Com. Underage Drinking, Nat. Inst. Alcohol Abuse and Alcoholism, 2005-, Comm. Increasing Rates of Organ Donation, 2005-07. Jefferson award, 2007; Inst. Criminology fellow Cambridge U., 1977. Fellow: Va. Law Found.; mem.: APA (hon. disting. mem. 2007), NAS (nat. assoc.), ABA (criminal justice-mental health stds. project adv. bd. 1981—87, task force on mental illness and the death penalty 2003—05), Nat. Inst. on Alcohol Abuse and Alcoholism (mem. steering com. on underage drinking 2005—), Inst. Medicine (Yarmolinsky medal 2002), Am. Acad. Psychiat. Law (Amicus award 1994), World Psychiat. Assn. (rev. team to investigate Soviet psychiatry 1991), Va. Bar Assn. (chmn. com. mentally disabled 1981—90, criminal law sect. coun. 1992—96), Am. Psychiat. Assn. (Isaac Ray award 1998, Spl. Presdl. Commendation 2003), Nat. Rsch. Coun. (com. on data and rsch. for policy on illicit drugs 1998—2000, chair com. elder abuse and neglect 2001—02, com. on law and justice 2002—, chair com. underage drinking 2002—, exec. com. divsn. com. behavioral & social scis. & edn. 2003—08, bd. behavioral, cogmitive & sensory sci. 2009—, mem., com. informing juvenile justice 2010—), Inst. Medicine of NAS (bd. neurosci. and behavioral health 1992—2001, vice chair com. preventing nicotine dependence in children and youth 1993—94, chair com. on opportunities in drug abuse rsch. 1995—96, membership com. 1995—98, chair com. injury prevention control 1997—98, com. to assess sci. base for tobacco harm reduction 1999—2001, com. to assess sys. for protection of human rsch. subjects 2000—02, chair com. to propose strategy to prevent/reduce underage drinking 2002—03, chair com. on reducing tobacco use 2004—07, com. on increasing rates of organ donation 2005—07). Office: U Va Sch Law 580 Massie Rd Charlottesville VA 22903 Business E-Mail: rjb6f@virginia.edu.

BONNIN, ALAIN PIERRE, physician, parasitologist, mycologist, professor of medicine; b. Dijon, France, June 10, 1959; s. André François and Paulette Marie Bonnin; m. Catherine Binet, Apr. 20, 1981; children: Marie Martine, Mathilde Françoise. MD, U. Burgondy, 1985, PhD, 1991. Resident U. Hosp. Dijon, 1983—87; asst. prof. U. Hosp. Dijon Sch. Medicine, 1987—91; asst. prof. staff physician U. Hosp., Dijon, 1991—96; prof. staff physician, chief parasitology mycology lab. U. Hosp. Sch. Medicine, Dijon, 1996—; dir. Biol. Resource Ctr., Ferdinand Cabanne, Dijon, 2002—; dir., lab. interactions mucosa-microorganisms U. Burgundy, Dijon, 2007—11, v.p., bd. trustee, 2007—; dir. Pole Environ. Microbiology and Health Risks Mixt Rsch. Unit Agroecology INRA, U. Burgundy and Agrosup, Dijon. Exec. v.p. U. Burgondy, Dijon, 2007—. Office: CHU Dijon Plateau Tech Biology 2 Rue Angélique Ducoudray Dijon 21070 France

BONORA, ENZO, medical educator, researcher, consultant; b. Mantua, Italy, Mar. 18, 1953; s. Gianfranco and Elisabetta (Iannoni) B.; m. Cristina Pancera, June 11, 1981; children: Giovanni, Benedetta, Federica, Alessandra. MD, U. Pavia, Italy, 1979; PhD, U. Florence, Italy, 1987. Cert. bd. internal medicine, bd. metabolic diseases, bd. endocrinology. Postdoctoral fellow U. Parma, Italy, 1979-83; rsch. fellow U. Verona, Italy, 1983-86, asst. prof., 1986-92, assoc. prof., 1992—2001, prof., 2001—, head sect. endocrinology, diabetes and metabolism, dept. medicine, 2009—. Vis. asst. prof. U. Tex., San Antonio, 1989-90; cons. Hosp. of Verona, 1983-89, sr. cons., 1989—2009, chief divsn. endocrinology & metabolism, 2009-. Recipient Sci. Achievement award Italian Diabetes Soc., 1992. Mem. European Assn. for Study of Diabetes, Am. Diabetes Assn. (Michaela Modan Meml. award 1997). Office: Endocrinologia e Malattie del Metabolismo Ospedale Maggiore 37126 Verona Italy Home: Galleria Enrico Ferri 6 46100 Mantova MN Italy Home Phone: 39 0376 322758; Office Phone: 39 045 8123110. Business E-Mail: enzo.bonora@univr.it.

BONOW, ROBERT OGDEN, cardiologist, educator; b. Camden, NJ, Mar. 11, 1947; m. Patricia Jeanne Hitchens, Sept. 12, 1982; children: Robert Hitchens, Samuel Crawford. BS in Chem. Engring. (magna cum laude), Lehigh U., Bethelehem, Pa., 1969; MD, U. Pa. Sch. Medicine, Phila., 1973. Diplomate in internal medicine Am. Bd. Internal Medicine, 1976, in cardiovasc. disease Am. Bd. Internal Medicine, 1981. Intern in medicine Hosp. U. Pa., Phila., 1973-74, resident, 1974-76; clin. assoc. cardiology br. Nat. Heart, Lung and Blood Inst., Bethesda, Md., 1976-79, sr. investigator, attending physician cardiology br., 1979-92, chief nuclear cardiology sect., 1980-92, dep. chief, 1989-92; Goldberg disting. prof. medicine, Feinberg Sch. Medicine Northwestern U. Med. Sch., Chgo., 1992—; chief divsn. cardiology Northwestern Meml. Hosp., Chgo., 1992—; attending physician dept. medicine VA Lakeside Med. Ctr., Chgo., 1993—2003, Evanston Hosp., Ill., 1994—2009. Pfizer vis. prof. cardiovasc. medicine Yale U., 1992, U. Mass., 1998; AHA/ACC Task Force on Practice Guidelines Com. on Cardiac Radionuclide Imaging, 1993-95; chair com. on mgmt. of patents with valvular heart disease, 1996—2008; vis. prof. various univs., 1982-99; mem. bd. extramural adivsors NHLBI, NIH, 2000—2006; mem. clin. rsch. roundtable Inst. of Medicine, Nat. Acad. Sci., 2003-05; co-dir. Bluhm Cardiovascular Inst., 2004-; mem. Northwestern Med. Faculty Found.; invited presenter at sci. sessions, symposia and acad. med. ctrs.; co-editor Braunwald's Heart Diseases. Mem. editl. bd. Am. Jour. Cardiology, 1983—, Jour. Am. Coll. Cardiology, 1983-87, 91-95, Circulation, 1986—, Cardiovascular Imaging, 1988—, Am. Jour. Cardiac Imaging, 1990-95, Internat. Jour. Cardiac Imaging, 1990-95, Jour. Heart Valve Disease, 1992-, Jour. Nuclear Cardiology, 1993—, Jour. Nuclear Medicine, 1994-2000, Cardiologia, 1995—, Am. Heart Jour., 1998—, JACC Imaging, 2007-, Jour. Thoracic and Cardiovasc. Surgery, 2008-; contbr. more than 380 publs. in med. jours. and 88 textbook chapters. Recipient NIH Director's award, 1986, USPHS Commendation medal, 1990, USPHS outstanding svc. medal, 1991, John Philips Meml. award, 2009; named to The Country's Best Doctor List, Good Housekeeping, America's Top Doctors, Best Doctors in America. Master Am. Coll. Cardiology (exhibits com. 1986-92, 1999-2000, program com. 1991-92, chair extramural edn. com., 1998—, trustee 1999-2004, Disting Fellowship award, 2000, Disting. Svc. award, 2006); fellow ACP (John Phillips Meml. award 2009), Am. Heart Assn. (chmn. sci. session program com. 1998-2000, bd. dirs. 1999-2004, chmn. Coun. on Clin. Cardiology, 1999-2001, chmn. Clin. Sci. Com. 2001-2002, pres. 2002-03, bd. dir. greater midwest affiliate,

2000-2006, Nat. Leadership award, 2003, Disting. Achievement award 2005, Gold Heart award, 2007); mem. AAAS, Am. Bd. Internal Medicine (subsplty. bd. cardiovasc. disease 1996-2001), Am. Soc. Clin. Investigation, Assn. Am. Physicians, Am. Heart Assn. Met. Chgo. (bd. govs. 1992-98, rsch. coun. 1992-98, pres. 2001-02), Am. Soc. Nuclear Cardiology (bd. dirs. 1994-98, chmn. edn. com. 1994-2000, nominating com. 1994-96), Assn. Profs. Cardiology (nominating com. 1993—, councillor 1994—, sec., treas. 1996-99, v.p. 1999-2000, pres. 2000-01), Chgo. Cardiology Group (pres. 1994-96),, Am. Fedn. Clin. Rsch., Assn. Am. Physicians, Assn. Univ. Cardiologists, Ctrl. Soc. Clin. Rsch., Alpha Omega Alpha. Office: Northwestern Univ Med Sch Cardiology Divsn 676 N St Clair Ste 600 Chicago IL 60611 Office Phone: 312-695-1105. Office Fax: 312-695-1434.

BONSU, BEMA K., pediatrician, educator; b. Accra, Ghana, May 15, 1964; MBChB, U. Ghana, 1990. Postdoc. fellow, pediat. emergency medicine Boston Children's Hosp., Harvard Med. Sch., 1995—98; assoc. prof., pediat. Nationwide Children's Hosp., Ohio State U., 1998—. Recipient Grant Morrow III award, Nationwide Children's Hosp., award, Ohio State U.; named Emergency Svcs. Employee of Yr., Nationwide Children's Hosp., Outstanding Reviewer of Yr., Soc. Academic Emergency Medicine. Mem.: Soc. Pediat. Rsch. Avocations: cartooning, reading. Office: 700 Childrens Dr Columbus OH 43205 E-mail: bonsub@gmail.com.

BONTE, FREDERICK JAMES, radiologist, educator, physician; b. Bethlehem, Pa., Jan. 18, 1922; s. Frederick R. and Harriett (Stoudt) B.; m. Cecile Poetzel; children: Frederick W., Stephen J., John A., Therese A., Suzanne M., Ann E. BS, Western Res. U., 1942, MD, 1945. Diplomate: Am. Bd. Radiology, Am. Bd. Nuclear Medicine. Intern Huntington Meml. Hosp., Pasadena, Calif., 1945-46; resident Univ. Hosp., Cleve., 1948-52; practice medicine, specializing in radiology and nuclear medicine Dallas, 1956—; mem. faculty Western Res. U. Sch. Medicine, 1952-56, asst. prof., 1952-56, chief radiotherapy and nuclear medicine, 1954-56; prof. U. Tex. Southwestern Med. Sch., Dallas, 1956—, chmn. dept. radiology, 1956-73, dean, 1973-80; dir. Nuclear Medicine Research Center, 1980—, Effie and Wofford Cain disting. chair in diagnostic imaging; Dr. Jack Krohmer prof. in radiation physics. Mem. bd. Nat. Coun. Radiation Protection and Measurements, 1966-71; radiology tng. com. Nat. Insts. Gen. Med. Scis., USPHS, 1966-70, Ad Hoc Study Sects., 1970-96, life mem., 1971-, residency rev. com. radiology AMA, 1966-69, adv. and rev. coms. VA, 1972—; trustee Am. Bd. Radiology, 1969-75; founding trustee Am. Bd. Nuclear Medicine, 1971-73, chmn., 1977-80; internat. cons. on med. edn. Contbr. articles to profl. jours. Capt. M.C., USAAC, 1946-48. Recipient Lifetime award, 2009, Am. Bd. Radiology, 2010. Fellow Am. Coll. Radiology, Am. Coll. Nuclear Physicians (Pres.'s award 1997), Am. Coll. Nuc. Medicine; mem. AMA (del., chmn. grad. med. edn. com., Roentgen Centennial Hartman medal 1995), Soc. Nuclear Medicine (De Hevesy Nuclear Pioneer award 1995), Am. Roentgen Ray Soc. (exec. com.), Radiol. Soc. N.Am., Sigma Xi, Alpha Omega Alpha. Achievements include research on experimental nuclear medicine and radiology, international consultant medical education. Home: 11138 Wonderland Trl Dallas TX 75229-3943 Office: 5323 Harry Hines Blvd Dallas TX 75390-9061 Home Phone: 214-352-4781; Office Phone: 214-648-2025. Business E-Mail: frederick.bonte@utsouthwestern.edu.

BOOKER, J. GARY, physician, researcher; b. Center, Tex., Jan. 22, 1953; s. James Julian and Sadie Rae Booker; m. Ruth Anne Martin, June 8, 1985; children: Anne, Emily. BS, La. State Univ., Shreveport, La., 1979; MD, La. State Univ. Med. Sch., Shreveport, La., 1984. Cert. psychaitry and Neurology Am. Bd. Acting chief psychiatry VA Med. Ctr., Pineville, La., 1989; asst. prof. La. State Univ. Med. Ctr., Shreveport, La., 1993—97; asst. dir. LSU Med. Ctr. Psychiatry Impatient Unit, Shreveport, La., 1995—97, med. dir., 1997; dep. corner psychiatry Corner's Office, Shreveport, La., 1998—; med. dir. Promise Hosp., Shreveport, La., 1998—; pvt. practice Shreveport, La., 1997—. Bd. mem. La. Alzheimer's Assn., 1998—2003. Petty officer 1st class USN, 1972—78. Mem.: APA, AMA, La. Psychaitric Assn., So. Med. Assn., Alpha Sigma Omicron. Presbyn. Achievements include research in prin. investagator drug rsch. clin. drug trials, 1997—. Avocations: carpentry, tree farming.

BOOM, MARC L., hospital administrator; m. Julie Boom; 3 children. BS in Biology with high honors, U. Tex., Austin; MD with high honors, Baylor U. Coll. Medicine, Waco, Tex.; MBA, The Wharton Sch. of U. Pa., Phila. Cert. in internal medicine and geriatric medicine. Resident in internal medicine Mass. Gen. Hosp., Harvard Med. Sch.; fellow in geriatric medicine and gen. medicine Hosp. of U. Pa.; asst. prof. clin. medicine Weill Cornell Med. Coll., NY; part-time practice in preventive medicine, lipid disorders and hypertension; pres., CEO, med. dir. Baylor-Meth. Primary Care Associates, Tex.; pres., CEO The Meth. Diagnostic Hosp., Tex.; sr. v.p., COO The Meth Hosp., Houston, exec. v.p., CEO, 2012—. Bd. dirs. Univ. Health Sys. Consortium; adj. prof. mgmt. Rice U., Tex. Bd. mem. Houston Ballet. Named a Modern Healthcare Up & Comer, 1999. Fellow: American Coll. Physicians, American Coll. Healthcare Executives; mem.: American Coll. Physician Executives, American Heart Assn. (past pres. Houston office, Disting. Svc. award 2007), Leadership Inst. Office: The Methodist Hosp 6565 Fannin Dunn Tower 200 Houston TX 77030 Office Phone: 713-441-2671. Office Fax: 713-441-1995. Business E-Mail: mboom@tmhs.org. *

BOON, MAURITS, otolaryngologist, educator; MD, SUNY, 1991—95. Diplomate Am. Bd. Otolaryngology. Intern Thomas Jefferson Univ. Hosp., resident, physician, 2000—; asst. prof. otolaryngology-head and neck dept. Thomas Jefferson Univ. Named one of the Top Docs, Phila. Mag., 2011. Office: Thomas Jefferson University Jefferson Medical College 925 Chestnut St 7th Fl Philadelphia PA 19107 Office Phone: 215-955-6760. Business E-Mail: Maurits.Boon@jefferson.edu.

BOONE, CHARLES W., physician, pathologist; b. Berkeley, Calif., Dec. 21, 1925; s. Harmon Dunscomb and Florence Celia (Chandler) B.; m. Alexandra Weekes, Dec. 21, 1992. MD, U. Calif., San Francisco, 1951; PhD, U. Calif., LA, 1964. Fellow Coll. Am. Pathologists. Intern gen. practice UCLA, 1954-56, resident pathology, 1956-60, PhD tng. Dept. Biochemistry, 1960-64; post doctoral tng. in Cell Biology Albert Einstein Coll. Medicine, Bronx, NY, 1964-65; chief cell biology sect. Nat. Cancer Inst., NIH, Bethesda, Md., 1965-80; chief pathology Al Hada Hosp., Taif, Saudi Arabia, 1980-84, program dir. chemoprevention branch, Divsn. of Cancer Prevention, 1984-90; divsn. chemoprevention NIH, NCI, Bethesda, 1991—. Author: (book) Cancer Prevention, 1992; contbr. over 140 articles to sci. jours. Ensign USN, 1943-45. Avocations: scuba diving, tennis, history. *

BOONE, DONNA CLAUSEN, physical therapist, statistician, researcher; b. Nebraska City, Nebr., Dec. 12, 1932; d. Otto Ralph and Hallie Rae Clausen; m. Robert William Boone, Apr. 3, 1965. BA in Zoology, U. Wyo., 1954; MS in Phys. Therapy, U. So. Calif., 1980, MS in Biometry, 1983. Lic. phys. therapist, Calif. Phys. therapist Ill. Hosp. Sch., Chgo., 1955—59, Calif. Hosp., LA, 1959—63; hemophilia specialist in phys. therapy Orthop. Hosp., LA, 1963—78, rschr., project dir. Hemophilia Ctr., 1967—78; instr. rsch. methods U. So. Calif., LA, 1982—83, Calif. State U., Long Beach, 1982—83; biostatistician immunulogy U. So. Calif., LA, 0983—1987, coord., statistician Nat. Clin. Trial, Silicone Study, 1987—93; phys. therapist Huntington Meml. Hosp., Pasadena, Calif., 1993—98; cons. Hemophilia Continuous Quality Improvement, Lompoc, Calif., 1998—. Internat. lectr., cons. World Fedn. Hemophilia, Montreal, Can., 1970-78; cons. biostatis. dentistry and pharmacology U. So. Calif., L.A., 1982-83, cons. orthop., U. Buffalo, 1982-83; continuous quality improvement coach Doheny Eye Inst., L.A., 1990-92, Huntington Meml. Hosp., Pasadena, Calif., 1993-97; cons. phys. therapy working group Nat. Hemophilia Found., 2000—. Editor: Comprehensive Management of Hemophilia, 1976, (internat. newsletter) World Hemophilia AIDS Ctr., 1984-93; contbr. articles to profl. jours. Co-chair United Way Campaign Orthopaedic Hosp., LA, chair, 1975—75; mem. Lompoc Rep. Women, 1998—, legis. chair, 2000—; vol. Rep. Campaign for Ho. of Reps., Glendale, Calif., 1996; recording sec. Santa Barbara County Rep. Women, 2000—01; lay leader St. Mary's Episcopal Ch., 1998—; bd. dirs. World Hemophilia Alliance, sec., 1996—; mem. alumni com. U. Wyo., 1999—; mem. med. adv. bd. Hemophilia Found. So. Calif., LA, 1974—78. Grantee Fed. Govt. Agys., 1967, 73; recipient Dr. Murray Thelin award Nat. Hemophilia Found., 1976, Disting. Alumna award U. Wyo., 1979, Achievement award Alpha Chi Omega, 1980, Spl. Achievement award for treatment advances 50th Anniversary of Nat. Hemophilia Found., 1998, Donna Clausen Boone ann. award Nat. Hemophilia Found. to Phys. Therapist, 1999—. Mem. Antique Automobile Club. Republican. Episcopalian. Avocations: gardening, antique autos, travel, reading, jazz music clubs.

BOONE, STEPHEN CHRISTOPHER, retired neurosurgeon; b. Navasota, Tex., Mar. 18, 1938; s. Berrill Harrison and Joyce (Taylor) Boone; m. Elizabeth Thompson, Apr. 9, 1960 (div. June 1979); children: Stephen, Michael, Laura; m. Susan Pate, Nov. 3, 1979; children: Christopher, Emily. BS, Duke U., 1960, MD, PhD, Duke U., 1965. Diplomate Am. Bd. Neurological Surgery. Surg. intern Duke Hosp., Durham, NC, 1965, resident in neurosurgery, 1967-72; chief neurosurgeon Brooke Army Med. Ctr., 1973-75; asst. chief neurosurgery Walter Reed Army Med. Ctr., Washington, 1975-77; from assoc. prof. to prof. neurosurgery U. NC, 1977-82; neurosurgeon Raleigh Neurosurgery Clinic, NC, 1982—2002; cons. Eastern Neurosurg. & Spine Assocs., Greenville, 2005—07. Brig. gen. USAR, 1962—89. Republican. Episcopalian. Business E-Mail: scboone38@nc.rr.com.

BOONSTRA, EELCO, retired physician, health studies educator; b. Pematang Siantar, Indonesia, Mar. 15, 1941; s. Gosse Boonstra and Harmina Boonstra-Holwerda; m. Nelly Margrete Sandvik; children: Birgitte Boonstra-Booij, Nils-Erik. MD, State U. Groningen, Netherlands, 1968; MPH, Nordic Sch. Pub. Health, Gothenburg, Sweden, 1990; PhD, U. Oslo, 2005. Cert. specialist gen. medicine Norwegian Med. Assn., 1980, specialist cmty. medicine 1991. Dist. med. officer Askvoll Municipality, Norway, 1971—77; regional med. officer Norwegian Agy. Internat. Devel., Molepolole, Botswana, 1978—80, leader, epidemiol. survey Botswana, 1984, sr. dist. med. officer Maun, Ngamiland, Botswana, 1995—98; mcpl. med. officer Health Authority Askvoll Municipality, 1980—94, 2002—08; med. officer in charge Nordic Clinic, InDevelop, Dar es Salaam, Tanzania, 1999—2001. Lectr., faculty health studies, quality assurance primary healthcare & diabetes Sogn og Fjordane U. Coll., 2009—. Pub. on malnutrition and quality of diagnosing and prescribing in primary health care Health Promotion Fishing Cmty. Botswana Askvoll. Mem.: Norwegian Med. Assn. (Hygiene prize 1993). Achievements include development of national trachoma control programme in Botswana and project on local health promotion in Askvoll, Norway. Avocations: travel, flute, painting. Home: Doktorbakke Askvoll 6980 Norway Home Phone: 4757734272. Business E-Mail: eelco.boonstra@enivest.net.

BOOTMAN, J. LYLE, dean, pharmacy educator; BS, U. Ariz. Coll.Pharmacy, 1974; MS in Pharmacy Adminstrn., U. Minn., 1976, PhD in Pharmacy Adminstrn., 1978; ScD, U. of Scis., Phila., 2006. Clin. resident NIH; faculty U. Ariz. Coll. Pharmacy, 1978—, acting dean, 1987—90, dean, 1990—, founding exec. dir. Ctr. Health Outcomes & Pharmacoeconomic Rsch. Bd. dirs. CMR Inst., Roanoke, Va., HTI, Phoenix. Named one of 50 Most Influential Pharmacists in America, Am. Druggist, 1997. Fellow: Am. Coll. Apothecaries, Am. Pharm. Assn. (trustee, pres. 1999—2000), Am. Assn. Pharm. Scientists, Am. Found. Pharm. Edn.; mem.: Inst. Medicine. Office: Coll Pharmacy 1295 N Martin PO Box 210202 Tucson AZ 85721 Office Phone: 520-626-1657. Office Fax: 520-626-0546. Business E-Mail: bootman@pharmacy.arizona.edu.

BOQUET-JIMENEZ, ERNEST, clinical microbiologist, educator, pharmacist; b. Ripollet, Barcelona, Spain, Jan. 12, 1946; s. Alfonso Boquet Busoms and Maria Reyes Jimenez Bigas; m. Maria Dolors Figueras, June 30, 1970; children: Meritxell, Ernest. Grad. in pharmacy, U. Barcelona, 1971, diploma in pub. health, 1972, D in Pharmacy, 1974. Prof. microbiology U. Barcelona, 1978—82; prof. U. Nursery Sch., Manresa, 1990-95; adj. prof. U. Barcelona, 1974-75, aggregate prof., 1975-77, specialist in clin. biology, 1999, specialist in microbiology and parasitology, 1986, European clin. chemist, 2001; dir. microbiology lab. Hospitalary Ctr., Manresa, 1974-83, Gen. Hosp. of Catalonia, Sant Cugat, 1985-89; dir. Echevarne Lab., Manresa, 1991-96; hon. prof. Albert Schweitzer Internat. U. Adviser San Juan de Dios Hosp., Manresa, 1978-89, San Andres Hosp., Manresa, 1980-89, Clinica Sagrada Familia, Barcelona, 1990-96, Clinica Platon, Barcelona, 1990-96, Clinica Teknon, Barcelona, 1992-96, Ministry of Health, Spain, PAHO, Washington, Ind. Aulabor Spain. Author: Manual de Tecnicas en Microbiologia, 1990, Microbiology EQAs in European Countries, 1992; author, co-editor: Garantia de Calidad en el lab, 1993, Curso de Microbiologia Clinica, 1993, Continous Quality Improvements in Clinical Labs, 1994, Diccionario Ingles-Espanol de Ciencias del Lab Clinico, 1997, Filariasis Etiologia y Diagnostico de Lab, 2000, El paludismo Etiologia, diagnostico y Tratamiento, 2001, Atlas of Clinical Parasitology, 2008, and 13 more books, editor, dir. electronic jour: Diagnostico in vitro; contbr. more than 125 articles to sci. jours. Mem. Am. Soc. Microbiology, Asociacion Espanola Farmaceuticos Analistas (v.p. 1987-91), Microbiology Quality Assurance of Spain (dir. 1978-97), N.Y. Acad. Sci. (life), European Conf. External Quality Assessment Organizers (v.p. 1992-95), European Ligand-Assay Soc. (bd. dirs. 1992-96), Fedn. Specialists of Colombia (hon.), Royal Acad. Pharmacy of Catalonia (hon.), Biochem. Fedn. of Argentina (hon.), Cuban Soc. Clin. Pathology (hon.), others. Home: Avda Pla de Bages 15 Sant Fruitos de Bages 08272 Catalonia Spain Office: F Boquet La Lluna 6 08291 Ripollet Spain E-mail: e.boquet.000@recol.es.

BORAAS, MARCIA, surgeon; MD, U. Pa., 1977. Diplomate Am. Bd. Surgery. Resident in surgery Hosp. of the Univ. of Pa., chief resident in gen. surgery; fellow Am. Cancer Soc.; fellow in surg. rsch. Harrison dept. of surg. rsch. Univ. Pa. Sch. of Medicine. Recipient I.S. Ravdin prize, Univ. Pa. Sch. of Medicine, 1977, The First Tickled Pink award, 2009; named Best Doctors in America, Best Doctors Inc., 2007, 2009—10, Top Docs, Phila. Mag., 2010. Office: Fox Chase Cancer Center 333 Cottman Ave Philadelphia PA 19111-2497 Office Phone: 215-728-6900.

BORADE, ATUL B., engineering educator; b. Amravati, India, Feb. 24, 1976; PhD in Engring. & Tech., Amravati U., Maharashtra, India, 1996. Prof. Jawaharlal Darda Inst. Engring. and Tech., Yavatmal, India, 2010—, head mech. engring. Editor in chief Internat. Jour. Mfg. Sys.; editl. & rev. bd. mem. Various Jours. Mem.: IIIE, ISTE, IFSCM, ISM. Avocation: reading. Home: Rajendra Saw Mill Nehru Timber Market Amravati Maharashtra 444606 India Home Phone: 919763702566. Personal E-mail: atulborade@rediffmail.com.

BORASI, GIOVANNI, medical educator; b. Morgex (AO), Feb. 19, 1944; Degree, U. Pavia, 1967; PhD, U. Milan, 1973. Prof. U. Milano Bicocca, 2010—. Mem.: AAPM. Home: Via Passo Buole 25/1 Reggio Emilia Emilia Romagna 42123 Italy Personal E-mail: giovanni.borasi@unimib.it.

BORCHGREVINK, HANS MELCHIOR, research administrator, research scientist; b. Oslo, Aug. 27, 1949; s. Henrik and Bjoerg (Roennenberg) Borchgrevink; m. Hanne Kristensen, Aug. 30, 1974; children: Hild, Henrik, Julie. BA, MD, U. Oslo, 1975, MHA, 1999. Research scientist Nat. Hosp. Inst. Audiology, Oslo, 1975-80; cons. audiology, asst. prof. Joint Med. Svc. Hdqs. Def. Command, Oslo, 1980-82; head dept. R&D Ministry of Environment, Oslo, 1982-83; cons. audiology, assoc. prof. Joint Med. Svc. Hdqs. Def. Command, Oslo, 1983-93; project mgr. to the dir. Nat. Hosp., Oslo, 1993—2001; exec. dir. medicine and health Rsch. Coun. Norway, Oslo, 2002—03, sr. cons. divsn. sci., 2003—05, spl. advisor internat. unit, 2005—. Cons. neuropsychology dept. neurosurgery Nat. Hosp., Oslo, 1978-2002; from asst. to assoc. prof. Norway State Acad. Music, Oslo, 1979—; internat. conf. organizer in field of hearing and neuropsychology, Oslo, Italy, Sweden, Australia; guest lectr. various univs., Europe, US, Asia, Australia, 1978—; founder Hearing Prophylaxis Program of Norwegian Armed Forces, 1980—; mem./invited expert rsch. study groups and coms. NATO, Internat. Orgn. Standardization, European Com. Standardization, Am. Conf. Govtl. Indsl. Hygienists's Threshold Limit Values for Phys. Agts. Com., Internat. Commn. Biol. Effects Noise, 1980—; project mgr. for the establishment of interventional ctr. Nat. Hosp., Oslo, 1994-96, audiological expert in NIH audiometry screening program HUNT, 1996—, clin. coord. yr. 2000 initiatives, 1999; ptnr. EU FP5 rsch. program on noise and hearing NOPHER 2000-03; coord. EU FP6 EU FP7 Researchers Night, 2005-09, mem. steering group EU FP7 Euraxess T.O.P., 2010-, Norwegian rep. European Commn. Steering Group Human Resources and Mobility, 2003—, European Commn. Programme Com. for Human Resources and Mobility, 2005-06, European Commn. Working Group on Career Appraisal Intersectorial Mobility, 2005; European Commn. Mem. State Group for JTI Innovative Medicine, 2006—; European Commn. Working Group for Labelling Charter/Code, 2006-08, EU Charter Code Promoters Network, 2008, EU Human Resources Strategy Group, 2009-; chmn. EU Working Group on Monitoring and Indicators, 2009-; invited spkr. EU Presidency Confs., Vienna, 2006, Copenhagen, 2006, Stuttgart, 2007, Lisbon, 2007, Praha, 2009, Budapest, 2011; chmn. Rennes, 2008; evaluator European Commn. Framework Program, 2008, German Ministry for Edn. & Rsch., 2008, Rsch. Coun. Norway 1995, Helse Rehabilitering Norway, 2007-; invited liturgical choir St. Peter's, Vatican, Rome, Italy, 2007; invited concert and liturgical choir Santa Maria in Aracoeli, Capital, Rome, 2010. Author: Voice and Song, 1982, 2009, (book chpts.) Music, Mind and Brain, 1982, Noise Induced Hearing Loss-Basic and Applied Aspects, 1986, Attention Deficit Disorder, 1989, Music, Language, Speech and Brain, 1991, NPM-X neuropsychol. test battery for children, 1991—, Man and Environmental Noise-International Advanced Research Workshop, 1995, The Workplace-Fundamentals of Health, Safety and Welfare, 1997, Noise Induced Hearing Loss: Basic Mechanisms, Prevention and Control, 2001, Brain, Hearing and Learning, 2004; editor, author: Hearing and Hearing Prophylaxis, 1982, Effects of Noise and Blasts, 1991, Scientific Basis of Noise-Induced Hearing Loss, 1996, Regional Health Programme for Health Region 2, 1996, Strategic Programs for the National Hospital, General Strategy, 1998, Activity Profile, 1999, Research Strategy, 1999, Regional Health Programme for Health Region South, 2001, Strategy for Medicine and Health, Rsch. Coun. Norway, 2002-03 Co-founder Nature and Youth, Oslo, 1967; choir condr. Consortium Vocale Oslo Cathedral, 1995—., Expo 2000 Hanover, CD Laudes, 1995, CD Laus mea Dominus, 2001, CD Exaudiam eum, 2007, CD Vultum Tuum, 2008; Lt. Joint Med. Svc. Hdqs. Def. Command, 1978; chmn. Norwegian Poly. Soc. Health, 2010-. Recipient Gutzmann medal Humboldt U., 1980, Norwegian Grammy award "Spellemannsprisen", 1975, Invited Liturgical Choir award Gregorian Chant 1st prize, Arezzo, Italy, 2004, Gregorian Chant All Time High Concert, Arezzo Hall, Italy, 2008; Student/Rsch. grantee Norwegian Rsch. Coun., 1971-79. Mem. Internat. Brain Rsch. Orgn., European Neurosci. Assn., European Brain and Behaviour Soc., NY Acad. Scis. Avocations: music, history of art, skiing, mountain tracking, sailing. Home: Sofies Gt 74 N-0454 Oslo Norway Office: Rsch Coun Norway Postboks 2700 St.Hanshaugen 131 Oslo Norway Office Phone: +47 2203 7160. Office Fax: 47 22037001. Business E-Mail: hmb@rcn.no.

BORDE, MICHEL GABRIEL, pediatrician; s. Pierre Amede and Isabella Charlotta Borde; m. Irene Madeleine Chartagnol (dec. Oct. 26, 2002); children: Armelle, Laurent. Med. studies, Rouen, France, 1958; MD in pediats., Rene Descartes, Paris, 1973. Clinic head pediat. dept. head Hosp. Provins, Paris, 1974—, med. care pres. France, 1978—79, also bd. dirs. Contbr. articles to profl. jours. Named Chevalier of Legion of Honor, 2003. Avocations: chess, archaeology, reading. Office: 6 rue Farabeuf 77160 Provins France Office Fax: 0033 164604033. E-mail: docteur.borde@ouline.fr.

BORDLEY, JAMES, IV, surgeon; b. Balt., Nov. 24, 1942; s. James III and Julia (Ross) B.; m. Dianne Redmond; children: Jessica, James V. BA, Yale U., 1965; MD, Columbia U. Physicians/Surgeon, 1970. Surg. intern Bassett Hosp., Cooperstown, NY, 1970-71, surg. resident, 1971-75, att. surgeon, 1978—; staff surgeon Naval Regl. Med. Ctr., Newport, RI, 1975-77; fellow biliary and pancreatic surgery U. Wash., Seattle, 1977; instr. surgery Columbia U., NYC, 1978-80, asst. prof. clin. surg., 1980—. Contbr. articles to profl. jours./publs. Lt. cmdr. USN, 1975-77. Fellow Am. Coll. Surgeons; mem. Soc. Surgery of the Alimentary Tract, Soc. Am. Gastrointestinal Endoscopic Surgeons. Office: Bassett Hosp 1 Atwell Rd Cooperstown NY 13326-1301

BORDLEY, ROBERT FRANCIS, automotive company researcher; b. Columbus, Ohio, Aug. 15, 1955; s. Robert Guy and Ann Mary Bordley. BS in Physics, Mich. State U., 1975, BA in Pub. Policy, 1976, MS in Systems Sci., 1976; MS in Ops. Rsch., U. Calif., Berkeley, 1977; MBA, U. Calif., 1979, PhD in Ops. Rsch., 1979. Intern Coop. League, Washington, 1975; assoc. sr. rsch. Gen. Motors Rsch. Labs., Warren, Mich., 1978-80, sr. rschr., 1980-82, staff rschr., 1982-86, sr. staff rschr., 1986—; supr. mission analysis group GM trilby design project, 1985—. Supr. decision support systems group, 1986—, mgr. decision support sect., 1987—, mem. decision analysis council, 1987—; dir. decision, risk and mgmt. sci. program NSF, 1990-91; mgr. mgmt., mktg. and science sect., GM, mgr. R&D portfolio planning, 1993—; adj. prof. U. Mich., Dearborn, 1980, Ann Arbor. Contbr. articles to profl. publs. Recipient Wildlife Conservation award Va. Game Commn. Assn., 1974, spkg. awards Am. Legion, 1971, 73, Best Publ. award, Gen. Motors Chmn.'s awards, award Gen. Motors Presdl. Coun.; Nat. Merit scholar, 1973-76, Mich. State U. alumni disting. scholar, 1973-76; NSF fellow, 1976-79, Elected fellow Am. State Assn., Inst. Ops. Rsch. & Mgmt. Sci. Mem. Ops. Rsch. Soc. Am., Am. Inst. Indsl. Engrs., Pub. Choice Soc., Inst. Mgmt. Scis., Am. Econ. Assn., Soc. for Promotion Econ. Theory, Soc. Risk Analysis, AAAS, James Madison Coll. Alumni Assn. (dir. 1982-84, pres. 1984—), Cosmos Soc., Phi Beta Kappa, Sigma Xi, Phi Kappa Phi. Home: 525 Choice Ct Troy MI 48085-4767 Office: Dept Operating Scis Gen Motors Research La Warren MI 48090

BORDLEY, WILLIAM CLAYTON (CLAY), pediatrician, educator; b. Washington, Dec. 14, 1959; Grad., U. NC, Chapel Hill, 1982; MD, John Hopkins Sch. Medicine, 1986, MPH, U. NC, Chapel Hill, 1993. Cert. in pediat. Intern, pediat. Children's Hosp. Phila., Pa., 1986—87, resident, pediat. Pa., 1990; fellow Robert Wood Johnson Clin. Scholars Program, Duke U. Med. Ctr., NC, 1993; chief, divsn. hosp. and emergency medicine, dept. pediat. Duke U. Med. Ctr., NC, med. dir., pediat. emergency dept.; chief, hospitalist svc. Duke Children's Hosp., 2002—; assoc. prof. pediat. Duke U., Durham, NC, assoc. prof., surgery. Recipient Samuel L. Katz Tchg. award, 2004; named a Health Care Hero-Category-Hospitalist, Triangle Bus. Jour., 2008. Avocation: soccer. Office: Duke Med Ctr Divsn Pediatrics and Emergency Medicine DUMC 3096 Durham NC 27710 Office Phone: 919 681 1850. Office Fax: 919-681-8521.

BOREL, JAMES DAVID, anesthesiologist; b. Chgo., Nov. 15, 1951; s. James Albert and Nancy Ann (Sieverson) B BS, U. Wis., 1973; MD, Med. Coll. Wis., 1977. Diplomate Am. Bd. Anesthesiology, Nat. Bd. Med. Examiners, Am. Coll. Anesthesiologists. Rsch. asst. McArdle Lab. for Cancer Rsch., Madison, Wis., 1972—73, Stanford U. and VA Hosp., Palo Alto, 1976—77; intern Cambridge Hosp., Mass., 1977—78; resident anesthesiology Peter Bent Brigham Hosp., Boston, 1978—80; fellow anesthesiology Ariz. Health Scis. Ctr., Tucson, 1980—81; assoc. anesthesiology U. Ariz. Coll. Medicine, Tucson, 1981—. Vis. anaesthetist St. Joseph's Hosp., Kingston, Jamaica, 1980; clin. fellow medicine Harvard Med. Sch., Boston, 1977-78; clin. fellow anesthesia Harvard Med. Sch., 1978-80; anesthesiologist Mt. Auburn Hosp., Boston, 1978-80; rsch. assoc. U. Ariz. Coll. Medicine, Tucson, 1980-81; rsch. assoc., 1980-81; active staff Mesa (Ariz.) Luth. Hosp., 1981—; courtesy staff Scottsdale (Ariz.) Meml. Hosp., 1982— Contbr. numerous articles to profl. jours Mem. AMA, AAAS, Ariz. Anesthesia Alumni Assn., Ariz. Soc. Anesthesiologists, Am. Soc. Regional Anesthesia, Can. Anesthetists' Soc., Internat. Anesthesia Rsch. Soc., Am. Soc. Anesthesiologists Office: Valley Anesthesia Consultant 1850 N Central Ave Ste 1600 Phoenix AZ 85004-4633 Office Phone: 602-262-8900.

BOREN, CLARK HENRY, JR., general and vascular surgeon; b. Marinette, Wis., Nov. 23, 1947; s. Clark Henry and Maryon Lillian (Peterson) Boren; children: Jenna Marie, Matthew William, Nathan Clark. BMS, Northwestern U., 1971, MD with distinction, 1973. Diplomate Am. Bd. Surgery. Resident in gen. surgery U. Calif.-H.C. Moffitt Hosp., San Francisco, 1973-79; rsch. fellow in vascular surgery Ft. Miley VA Hosp., 1976-77; vascular fellow Med. Coll. Wis./Milwaukee County Med. Complex, Milw., 1979-80; mem. staff Fox Valley Surg. Assocs., Ltd., Appleton, Wis., 1980—, pres., 1997—. Chmn. bd. United Health Wis., 1995—99. Contbr. articles to profl. jours. Mem.: AMA, ACS, Am. Assn. Vascular Surgery, Wis. Surg. Soc., Midwest Vascular Soc., Peripheral Vascular Surgery Soc., Wis. State Med. Soc., Phi Kappa Psi, Phi Eta Sigma, Phi Beta Pi, Alpha Omega Alpha. Democrat. Home: 330 W River Rd Appleton WI 54915 Office: Fox Valley Surg Assocs 1818 N Meade St Appleton WI 54911-3454 Home Phone: 920-996-0189; Office Phone: 920-731-8131. Business E-Mail: clark.boren@thedacare.org. *

BOREN, KENNETH RAY, endocrinologist, nephrologist; b. Evansville, Ind., Dec. 31, 1945; s. Doyle Clifford and Jeannette (Koerner) B.; m. Rebecca Lane Wallace, Aug. 25, 1967; children: Jennifer, James, Michael, Peter, Nicklas, Benjamin. BS, Ariz. State U., 1967; MD, Ind. U., Indpls., 1972; MA, Ind. U., Bloomington, 1974. Diplomate Am. Bd. Endocrinology, Am. Bd. Nephrology, Am. Bd. Internal Medicine, Hypertension Soc. Intern in pathology Ind. U. Sch. Medicine, Indpls., 1972, intern in medicine, 1972-73, resident in medicine, 1975-77, fellow in endocrinology, 1977-79, fellow nephrology, 1979-80, instr., 1980; physician East Valley Nephrology, Mesa, Ariz., 1980—. Chief of medicine Mesa Luth. Hosp., 1987—89, chief of staff, 1990—91; med. dir. RenalWest, 1996—, regional med. dir., 1996—99. Bd. dirs. Ariz. Kidney Found., Phoenix, 1984—, pres. 1993-94. Lt. USN, 1973-75. Fellow: ACP, Am. Soc. Nephrology, Am. Coll. Clin. Endocrinology; mem.: AMA, Am. Diabetes Assn., Am. Endocrine Soc., Internat. Soc. Nephrology, Ariz. Med. Assn., Maricopa County Med. Assn. Republican. Mem. Lds Ch. Home: 4222 E Mclellan Rd Ste 10 Mesa AZ 85205-3119 Office: SW Kidney Inst PLC 2141 E Warner Ste 101 Tempe AZ 85284 Office Phone: 480-969-8714. Personal E-mail: kenboren@cox.net. Business E-Mail: kboren@swkidney.com.

BORENSTEIN, DANIEL BERNARD, psychiatrist, educator; b. Silver City, N.Mex., Mar. 31, 1935; s. Jack and Marjorie Elizabeth (Kerr) B.; m. Bonnie Denice Ulland, June 11, 1967; 1 child, Jay Brian. BSChemE, MIT, 1957; MD, U. Colo., 1962. Diplomate Am. Bd. Psychiatry and Neurology. Intern U. Hosp. U. Ky., 1962-63; resident in psychiatry U. Colo. Med. Ctr., 1963-66; chief resident, psychiatry instr. U. Colo. Sch. Medicine, 1965-66; psychiatry instr. U. So. Calif. Sch. Medicine, 1966-67; asst. clin. prof. psychiatry UCLA Sch. Medicine, 1972-84, assoc. clin. prof., 1984-96, clin. prof., 1996—2008, hon. clin. prof., 2008—. Founder, dir. UCLA Mental Health Program for Physicians in Tng., 1980—84; clin. assoc. L.A. Psychoanalytic Soc. and Inst., 1967—71, pres. clin. assocs., 1970—71, faculty, 1973—83, sr. faculty, 1983—2005; pvt. practice medicine specializing in psychoanalysis and psychiatry, West L.A., 1966—; assoc. vis. psychiatrist UCLA Ctr. Health Scis., 1973—90; cons. Medicare Program, 1995—2005; examiner Am. Bd. Psychiatry and Neurology; reviewer various med. and psychiat. jours., 1991—. Author: Manual of Psychiatric Peer Review, 1985, Psychiatric Peer Review: Prelude and Promise, 1985; contbr. articles to profl. jours. Bd. dirs. L.A. Child Devel. Ctr., 1981—85, Found. Advancement Psychiat. Edn. and Rsch., 1991—2005, Coop. Am. Physicians/Mutual Protective Trust, 1994—2011. Lt. AUS, 1957—58. Recipient Disting. Clin. Prof. award, UCLA Sch. Medicine, 2006. Fellow: Am. Coll. Psychiatrists (com. on hon. fellowship 2002—05), Am. Psychiat. Assn. (life; mem. coun. area VI 1977—79, com. to rev. psychiat. news 1979—81, coun. area VI, dep. rep. assembly dist. brs. 1981—82, work group on competition and legis. 1981—83, nominating com. 1982—83, assembly liaison to peer rev. com. 1982—86, assembly rep. dist. brs. 1982—89, assemly liaison to fin. and mktg. com. 1986—87, assembly corr. group on subspecialization 1986—89, assembly liaison to coun. on econ. affairs 1987—89, med. student edn. com. 1987—90, bd. liaison jud. action commn. 1989—91, bd. trustees 1989—, com. managed care 1990—92, com. mem., bd. liaison to managed care com. 1992—99, bd. liaison econ. affairs coun. 1992—99, chmn. bd. ethics appeals, sec. 1995—97, v.p. 1997—99, pres.-elect 1999—2000, pres. 2000—01, chair med. dir. contract negotiating com. 2001, cons. bus. rels. com., chair nominating com. 2001—02, past pres. 2001—, bus. rels. com. 2002—05, fin. and budget com. 2003—06, elections com. mem. 2008—11, Disting. fellow); mem.: AMA (ho. dels., alt. 1998—2002, del. 2003—07), Am. Psychoanalytic Assn. (com. on confidentiality 1983—96, com. on govt. rels. and ins. 1983—2000), L.A. Psychoanalytic Soc. and Inst. (co-chmn. ext. divsn. 1973—74, chmn. peer rev. com. 1975—78, curriculum com. 1980—84), Calif. Psychiat. Assn. (exec. coun. 1977—79, 1981—95, chmn. jud. com. 1986—88, bd. trustees 1989—95, Spl. Recognition award 1995), Calif. Med. Assn. (ho. of dels. psychiat. splty. rep. 1979—84, com. on mental health and mental disabilities 1979—85, alt. del. ho. del. 1984—86, del. 1986—88, com. on mental health and mental disabilities 1987—88, bd. trustees 1992—2001, chmn. physicians benevolence oper. com. 1996—2001, chmn. bldg. com. 1999—2001), L.A. County Med. Assn. (chmn. mental health com. Bay dist. 1980—85, com. on substance abuse 1981—86, Bay Dist. bd. dirs. 1981—, Bay Dist. v.p. 1985—86, pres.-elect 1986—87, com. on well-being 1986—89, pres. 1987—88, exec. coun. 1988—91), So. Calif. Psychiat. Soc. (chmn. peer rev. com. 1974—77, exec. coun. 1976—89, ethics com. 1977—85, pres. 1978—79, chmn. fellowship and awards com. 1979—85, chmn. Commn. on Psychiatry and the Law 1980—81, Appreciation award 1979, 1st recipient Disting. Svc. award 1984, Outstanding Achievement award 1993, Outstanding Svc. citation 1975). Office: 151 N Canyon View Dr Los Angeles CA 90049-2721 Office Phone: 310-472-7386.

BORENSTEIN, DAVID GILBERT, internist, writer, rheumatologist; b. Bklyn. s. Murray and Mollie (Koren) B.; m. Dorothy Regina Fait, Aug. 6, 1972; children: Sylvia, Elizabeth, Rebecca. AB, Columbia U., 1969; MD, Johns Hopkins U., 1973. Diplomate Am. Bd. Internal Medicine, Am. Bd. Rheumatology. Intern in medicine Johns Hopkins Hosp., 1973-74, resident in medicine, 1974-76; fellow in rheumatology Johns Hopkins U., 1976-78; asst. prof. medicine George Washington U., Washington, 1978-83, assoc. prof. medicine, 1983-89, prof. medicine, 1989-96, prof. neurosurgery, 1991-96, clin. prof. neurosurgery, 1997-98, clin. prof. medicine, 1997—. Cons. Vaccine Injury Compensation Program, Dept. HHS, Washington, 1993-02, Sulzer Medica, Austin, Tex., 1997-02, Searle, Skokie, Ill., 1997-02, Merck-Medco, Rahway, NJ, 1997-99, OSHA, Dept. Labor, 1998-99, Merck, 1999-04, Pfizer, 2003-04, Epicept, 2004-2008, Pfizer, 2006-, Biovail, 2006-, Medtronic, 2009, Cephalon, 2009 Author: Low Back Pain: Medical Diagnosis, 1995, Neck Pain: Medical Diagnosis, 1996, Back in Control! A Conventional and Complementary Prescription for Eliminating Back Pain, 2001, Low Back and Neck Pain: Comprehensive Diagnosis and Management, 3d edit., 2007; contbg. author: Low Back Pain in Rheumatology, 1997; contbg. author Low Back Pain in Rheumatology, 2d edit., 2003, 4th edit., 2008, Inflammatory Arthridities and Psoriatic Arthritis in the Lumbar Spine 3d edit., 2004, Approach To Patient with Neck Pain in Current Rheumatology, 2004, 2nd edit., 2007, Arthritis in Orthopaedic Knowledge Update, 9th edit., 2008; author: Arthritic Disorders in The Spine, 2011, Heal Your Back: Your Complete Prescription for Preventing, Treating and Eliminating Back Pain, 2011, Spine Pain in Conns Current Therapy, 2011. Mem. Appellate Jud. Nominating Commn., State of Md., 1986-94; med. adv. bd. Arthritis Found. D.C., 1986-88, bd. dirs., 1999-2007, exec. bd. dirs., 2006-2007, v.p., 2006-08; med. adv. bd. Lupus Found. Greater Washington, 1992-2004. Fellow: ACP, Am. Coll Rheumatology (govt. affairs com. 1998—2004, chmn. govt. affairs com. 2001—04, bd. dirs. 2005—07, treas., Rsch. & Edn. Found. 2007—09, Exec. Com. 2007—09, pres. elect, 2009—10, pres. 2010—11); mem.: Pain Mgmt. Task Force (chmn. 2009—10), Acad. Medicine Washington, Rheumatism Soc. D.C. (pres. 1992—93), Internat. Soc. Study Lumbar Spine (membership com. 1999, chmn. 2002, Marriott LIfetime Achievement award 2011), Cosmos Club. Jewish. Avocations: skiing, squash. Office: Arthritis and Rheum Assocs 2021 K St NW Washington DC 20006-1003 Home Phone: 301-983-2340; Office Phone: 202-293-1470, 202-293-9415. Personal E-mail: dborenstein715@aol.com.

BORENSTEIN, PETER ANTERO, rabbi, neurologist, lecturer, researcher; b. Göteborg, Sweden, May 25, 1948; s. Ezra and Aini (Kokkonen) B.; m. Lena Strimling, Dec. 26, 1972 (div. 1985); 1 child, Henny; m. Eva Susanne Hedberg, Mar. 5, 1987; children: Joseph, Elias, Dinah. MD, Sahlgrenska U. Hosp., 1975, specialist in neurology, 1979. Resident in neurology Sahlgren's Univ. Hosp., Göteborg, 1975-79; asst. head dept. neurology East Hosp., Göteborg, 1979-81; pvt. practice in neurology Göteborg, 1976-95; cons. neurologist dept. neurology Lundby Hosp., Göteborg, 1983—91, 2010—; head Scandinavian Brain Ctr., Göteborg, 1991-95, 2000—; cons. neurologist, head stroke unit and stroke rehab. unit Skene (Sweden) Hosp., 1992—99, 2001—08; head stroke unit and stroke rehab. program Dept. Neurology U. Hosp., Linköping, Sweden, 1999-2000, cons. neurologist. Cons. neurologist Nat. Inst. for Mentally Retarded People, Göteborg, 1975-81, Stroke Unit, Sahlgrenska U. Hosp., Göteborg, 2008-2011; cons. neurologist Dept. Neurology, Lundby Hosp., Göteborg; pres. Second Internat. Aphasia Rehab. Congress, Göteborg, 1986; lectr. in aphasiology and other aspects of behavioral neurology. Author: Aphasia-Diagnostics and Rehabilitation, 1988, Aphasia and Other Disturbances of Speech and Language Function, 1989, Aphasia and Speech Disorders, 1988, 3d rev. edit., 2001. Rabbi Jewish Cmty., Göteborg, 2002—10. Mem. Acad. of Aphasia, World Fedn. of Neurology Rsch. Group on Aphasia and Cognitive Disorders, Royal Soc. Medicine (U.K.). Office: Scandinavian Brain Ctr Ingatorpsgatan 2 Gothenburg S-41262 Sweden Office Phone: 46-31-209303. Personal E-mail: peter.borenstein@yahoo.com. Business E-Mail: rabbi.peter.borenstein@gmail.com.

BORER, JEFFREY STEPHEN, cardiologist; b. Deland, Fla., Feb. 22, 1945; s. Lee Norton and Rita Doris (Feldt) B.; m. Brondi Beth Topchik, Sept. 16, 1978; children: Justine Isolde, Jon Andrew. BA in Govt., Harvard U., 1965; MD, Cornell U., 1969. Diplomate Am. Bd. Internal Medicine, Am. Bd. Cardiovascular Disease; cert. Bd. Nuclear Cardiology. Intern, then resident in medicine Mass. Gen. Hosp., Boston, 1969—71; clin. fellow in medicine Harvard U. Sch. Medicine, Boston, 1969—71; clin. assoc. in cardiology Nat. Heart, Lung and Blood Inst., NIH, Bethesda, Md., 1971—74, chief resident physician, 1973—74, sr. investigator, cardiology br., 1975—79; sr. Fulbright-Hays scholar, Glorney-Raisbeck fellow med. scis Guy's Hosp., U. London, 1974—75; assoc. prof. medicine Weill Cornell Med. Coll., Cornell U., NYC, 1979—82, prof., 1982—2008, Gladys and Roland Harriman prof. cardiovascular medicine, 1983—2008, prof. cardiovascular medicine in radiology, 1990—2008, prof cardiovascular medicine in cardiothoracic surgery, 1996—2008, dir., Howard Gilman Inst., 2000—08; chief cardiovasc. pathophysiology NY Presbyn. Hosp.-NY Weill Cornell Med. Ctr., 1996—2008; prof., chief divsn. cardiovasc. medicine SUNY Downstate Med. Ctr. and Med. Coll., Bklyn., NYC, 2008—, prof. cell biology, radiology, surgery, chmn. dept. medicine, 2009—; chmn., Howard Gilman Inst. Heart Valve Disease SUNY Downstate Med. Ctr., 2008—, 2008—, chmn., Inst. Cardiovasc. Translational Rsch., 2008. Chmn. cardiac and renal adv. com. FDA, Washington, 1981—82, 1983—87, 2001—04, cons., 1989—2000, 2004—, mem., 1977—87, 1999—2004, chmn. Circulatory Devices Adv. Com., 2008—09; mem. life scis. adv. com. NASA, Washington, 1984—92, mem. aero. med. adv. com., 1992—96, life and microgravity scis. and application adv. com., 1996—2001, biol. and phys. rsch. adv. com., 2001—05; chmn. NASA/Mir Peer Rev. adv. com., 1993—95, NASA-NIH Biomed. and Behavioral Rsch. adv. com., 1995—2003; mem. NASA Adv. Coun., 1995—99, US Valve Experts Com., AAMI, 2007—; vis. prof. Chinese Acad. Med. Scis., Beijing, 1993; adj. prof. medicine and cardiothoracic surgery Weill Cornell Med. Coll., 2008—09, adj. prof. cardiothoracic surgery, 2009—. Author 4 books; editor-in-chief Advances in Cardiology, 2001—, Cardiology, 2005-; mem. editl. bds. 11 med. jours.; contbr. more than 400 sci. articles on cardiovasc. disease to med. jours.; patentee in field. Sr. surgeon USPHS, 1971—79; trustee NYC Historic Properties Fund, 1984—90; mem. steering com. Assocs. of the Jewish Bd. of Family and Children Svcs., 1989—91; pres. Am. Friends of Israel Nat. Heart to Heart Assn., 1991—2004; adv. com. The NY Pub. Library Dance Collection, 1999—; bd. trustees Glorney Found., 2001—; pres. Corlette Glorney Found., 2004—. Recipient Investigator's award prize, European Cardiol. Soc., 1978, spl. award contbns. to cardiology, Assn. Thoracic and Cardiovascular Surgeons of India, 1985, Wiliam A. Johnston award, Internat. Soc. Heart Rsch., 1986, spl. citation contbn. to Mir program, NASA, 1997, Pub. Svc. medal, 1999, Hans-Peter Krayenbeuhl Meml. award, Internat. Acad. Cardiology, 2002, Transforming Lives through Rsch. award, SUNY Downstate Med. Ctr., 2009; named Thomas W. Smith Meml. lectr., 7th World Cong. on Heart Failure, 2000; travelling fellow, Am. Physicians Fellowship, 1981, Disting. fellow, Internat. Acad. Cardiol., 2005. Fellow: Internat. Acad. Cardiovascular Scis., NY Cardiol. Soc. (pres. 1990—91), Am. Coll. Chest Physicians (chmn. cardiology forum 1985—86, exec. com. clin. cardiology sect. 1991—95), Am. Soc. Clin. Investigation, Am. Coll. Cardiology (governing coun. NY chpt. 1991—93, pres. NY State chpt. 1997—98, gov. 1997—2000, bd. govs. 1998—2000, bd. govs. task force on cardiovasc. econs. 1999—2000, steering com., chmn.), Am. Heart Assn. (established investigator 1979—84, coun. clin. cardiology and circulation), Argentine Heart Assn. (hon.); mem.: Heart Valve Soc. Am. (pres. 2004—), Cert. Bd. Nuc. Cardiology (bd. trustees 1996—2002, chmn. com. due process and appeals 2002—04), Am. Soc. Nuc. Cardiology (fin. com. 1995—95), Soc. Cardiac Angiography and Interventions (gov. 1995—2000), Soc. Nuc. Medicine (trustee cardiovasc. coun. 1991—94), Harvard Club NYC. Avocations: sports, theater, opera, calligraphy, history. Office: State Univ NY Downstate Med Ctr 635 Madison Ave New York NY 10022 also: 445 Lenox Rd Brooklyn NY 11228 Office Phone: 212-289-7777.

BORG, RUTH I., home nursing care provider; d. Axel Gunner and Charlotte (Benston) B. Diploma, West Suburban Sch. Nursing, 1956; tchr.'s degree, Chgo. Conservatory, 1958; BSN, Alverno Coll., 1981. Staff nurse Bethany Meml. Hosp., Chgo.; head nurse psychiatry, head nurse long-term medicine VA North Chgo. Med. Ctr.; staff nurse, night supr. intermediate care VA Clement Zabiocki Med. Ctr., Milw.; pool nurse, in-home nursing care provider Milw. County Mental Health Complex; home nurse care provider Dr. Ghonsham Sooknandan, Kenosha, Wis., 1994—99. In-home nursing care provider. Contbr. articles to profl. jours. Recipient Mary D. Bradford Disting. Alumni award, 1998. Mem.: Wis. Nurses Assn. (nominations com.). Avocation: teaching and performing music. Home Phone: 262-652-3281.

BORGE, ANNE I.H., psychologist, educator; b. Oslo, Dec. 22, 1949; married; children: Taran, Mads I.H. PhD, MSc, U. Oslo. MNPF U. Oslo. Prof. U. Oslo, 1997—. Office: Univ Oslo Forskningsveien 3 373 Oslo Norway Business E-Mail: a.i.h.borge@psykologi.uio.no.

BORGES, EDSON, JR., medical association administrator; b. Sao Paulo, Brazil, May 6, 1960; MD, UNICAMP U. Estadual de Campinas, 1984; PhD, UNIFESP, UNESP, 2005. Med. dir. Fertility Ctr. de Fertilizaçào Assistida, 1998—. Office: Ave Brig Luis Antonio 4545 Sao Paulo 0401-002 Brazil Office Fax: 11-30188182.

BORIE, FRÉDÉRIC, medical educator, surgeon; b. Sarlat, France, Dec. 7, 1966; BACD, St. Joseph, Sarlat, 1984. Cert. Prof. digestive surgery CNU France, 2006. Chef clinique CH U. Montpellier, France, 1999—2003, particien, 2003—06. Prof. surgery U. Montpellier, France, 2006. Author: (med. manuscripts & books) Biliary Lithiasis. Mem.: Société Francaise De Chirurgie Digestive (licentiate; sfcd). Achievements include research in epidemiology digestive cancer and health economy. Office: Chirurgie Digestive CHU Caremecu Place du P Behre Nimes 30029 France Office Phone: 0466683141. Office Fax: 0467337424. Personal E-mail: fborie@yahoo.com. Business E-Mail: frederic.borie@chu-nimes.fr.

BÖRJESSON, LARS GUSTAV, colon and rectal surgeon, educator; b. Björketorp, Sweden, Jan. 6, 1963; s. Gustav Adolf and Karin Börjesson; m. Ann Eleonor Sandén, June 20, 1994; children: Fredrik Lars Börjesson-Sandén, Gustav Carl Börjesson-Sandén. MD, Uppsala U., 1988, Linköping U., 1988; PhD, Göteborg U., Sweden, 2000. Specialist in gen. surgery Swedish Social Dept., 1996, cert. assoc. prof. in surgery Sahlgrenska Acad., 2007. Intern Norra Älvsborgs Länssjukhus, Trollhättan, Sweden, 1988—91, resident, gen. surgery, 1991—96; staff colorectal surgeon Sahlgrenska U. Hosp., Gothenburg, 1997—2007, cons. colorectal surgeon, 2007—, residency program dir., dept. surgery, 2003—07; rsch. fellow Cleve. Clinic, Weston, Fla., 2003; assoc. prof. surgery Sahlgrenska Acad., 2007—. Superior residency program dir. gen. surgery Western County Sweden, Gothenburg, 2003—07; bd. mem. Swedish Internship Com., Stockholm, 2007—, Swedish Surg. Soc., Program Com., Stockholm, 2008—09; sec. Swedish Soc. Colon and Rectal Surgeons, 2009—. Contbr. scientific papers to med. publs. Mem.: Swedish Soc. Gastroenterology (Stockholm) (treas. 2003—07), Swedish Soc. Colon and Rectum Surgeons (Stockholm), Swedish Surg. Soc. (Stockholm), Råda Sport Fishing Club (Mölnlycke). Office: Sahlgrenska Univ Hosp Dept of Surgery Gothenburg 416 85 Sweden Office Fax: 46 31 25 14 63.

BORKAN, WILLIAM NOAH, electronics executive, biomedical engineer, entrepreneur; b. Miami Beach, Fla., Apr. 29, 1956; s. Martin Solomon and Annabelle (Hoffman) Borkan; m. Vivienne Eliane; children: Martin, Kenneth. Student, Carnegie Mellon U., 1977. Tech. Dominicks' Radio & TV Co., Miami Beach, 1971-74; computer programmer Mt. Sinai Hosp., Miami Beach, 1973-74; chief studio engr. Sta. WGMA, Hollywood, Fla., 1973-74; disc jockey Sta. WBUS-FM, Miami Beach, 1974; chief rec. engr. Dukoff Recording Studios, Miami, Fla., 1974-75; rec. studio design and constrn. TSI, Hollywood, 1975-77; chief design engr. Lumonics Co., Miami, 1974; svc. mgr. 21st Century Electronics Co., Miami, 1975; lab. tech., mem. curriculum com. elec. engring. dept. Carnegie-Mellon U.; mgr. Tech. Electronics Co., Pitts., 1976; pres. Borktronics Co., Miami, 1974-84; consulting specialist in neurobiometrics St. Barnabas Hosp., NYC, 1978-83; pres., CEO NeuroMed, Inc., 1980-85, Nice Tech., Inc., 1989-96; pres. Master Angler, Inc., 1990—2010. Pres. Electrovest Inc., 1995—; dir. Saints Venutres Ltd, 1999—; mng. mem. Aloha Investment Group, 2003—, Real Estate Investment & Mgmt.; cons. specialist in home automation, home theater and audio. Prodr.: Ho'olina: The Legacy, 2006, Shark Eyes and Restless Nights, 2007, Ho'dina: Hawallan Goddess, 2008; contbr. articles to profl. jours. Named Entrepreneur of Yr., Fla. Inc. Mag., 1992; grantee, Carnegie Corp., Carnegie Mellon U. Mem.: AAAS, NY Acad. Scis., Audio Engring. Soc., Assn. Advancement Med. Instrumentation, Refrigeration and Air Conditioning Engrs., Am. Soc. Heating. Achievements include numerous US and foreign patents in field; patents pending in field; development of great 4D movie ride dringing theme park grade rides to small shopping centers. Home: 3142 NE 166th St Miami FL 33160-3840 Office: Electrovest 12000 Biscayne Blvd Ste 502 Miami FL 33181-2725 Personal E-mail: bbbillfish@aol.com.

BORNHORST, JOSHUA, chemist; b. Minn., Jan. 1, 1974; Ph.D., Colo., 2003. Dir. chemistry, point care and immunology lab. sects. U. Ark., 2006—. Office: 4301 W Markham St #502 Little Rock AR 72205-7199 Business E-Mail: jabornhorst@uams.edu.

BORNSTEIN, HAROLD NELSON, physician; b. NYC, Mar. 26, 1947; s. Jacob and Maida (Seltzer) B.; m. Melissa Beth Brown; children: Robyn, Joseph, Alix, Jeremee. AB, Tufts U., 1968, MD, 1975. Resident in internal medicine Lenox Hill Hosp., NYC, 1975-78; fellow in gastroenterology Bridgeport (Conn.) Hosp., 1978-80; physician pvt. practice, NYC, 1980—. Adj. physician Lenox Hill Hosp., N.Y.C., 1980—. With USAR, 1969-74. Mem. ACP, Am. Soc. Gastrointestinal Endoscopy, Am. Gastroenterologic Assn. Office: 101 E 78th St New York NY 10021-0301 *

BORNSTEIN, LESTER MILTON, retired health facility administrator; b. Boston, Feb. 19, 1925; s. Harry and Celia B.; m. Marilyn Goldstein, Aug. 22, 1948; children: Aura Lynne, Michael Scott, Karen Jane. BS, Boston U., 1948; M.P.H. in Hosp. Adminstrn, Yale U., 1955. Adminstrv. resident Charles S. Wilson Meml. Hosp., Johnson City, NY, 1953-54; asst. dir. Barnert Meml. Hosp., Paterson, NJ, 1954-57, Newark Beth Israel Hosp., 1957-68; pres. Newark Beth Israel Med. Center, Newark, 1968-96. Served with AUS, 1943-45, ETO; to maj., Korean War 1950-53. Decorated Bronze Stars. Fellow Am. Coll. Hosp. Adminstrs., NJ Hosp. Assn. (chmn. bd. trustees 1978-79) Home: 6 Aherne Way West Orange NJ 07052-2102 Personal E-mail: lestb@aol.com.

BORNSTEIN, PAUL, medical educator, biochemist; b. Antwerp, Belgium, July 10, 1934; arrived in US, 1947, naturalized, 1952; s. Abraham and Mina (Ginsburg) B. BA, Cornell U., 1954; MD, NYU, 1958. Intern in surgery Yale-New Haven Hosp., 1958-59, intern in medicine, 1959-60, asst. resident in medicine, 1960-62; sr. fellow Arthritis Found. Pasteur Inst., Paris, 1962-63; rsch. assoc. NIH, Bethesda, Md., 1963-65, rsch. investigator, 1965-67; asst. prof. biochemistry and medicine U. Wash., 1967-69, assoc. prof., 1969-73, prof., 1973—2008, prof. emeritus Wash., 2008—, attending physician, 1968—. Mem. editl. bd. Jour. Biol. Chemistry, 1972-78, 80-85, Jour. Cell Biology, 1988-91, 94-97, Matrix Biology, 1993—2008; assoc. editor Arteriosclerosis, 1980-90, Collagen Related Rsch., 1981-88; contbr. articles to profl. jours. Served to sr. surgeon USPHS, 1963-67. Recipient Lederle Med. Faculty award USPHS, 1968, Rsch. Career Devel. award NIH, 1969, Macy Faculty Scholar award, 1975, Merit award NIH, 1989, Solomon Berson Alumni Achievement award NYU, 2004, Springer award ICCNS, 2008; Guggenheim fellow, 1985. Mem.: Internat. Soc. Matrix Biology (pres. 2001—03), Am. Soc. Matrix Biology (v.p. 2001—02, pres. 2002—03), Assn. Am. Physicians, Western Soc. Clin. Rsch., Am. Soc. Biol. Chemistry, Am. Soc. Clin. Investigation. Home: PO Box 219 Tesuque NM 87574 E-mail: bornsten@u.washington.edu.

BOROTA, LJUBISA, radiologist; b. Sabac, Serbia-Montenegro, June 25, 1958; s. Ilija and Ruza Borota; m. Olivera Casar, Oct. 7, 1989; children: Jana, Aleksa. MD, Med. Faculty, Beograd, Serbia-Montenegro, PhD, 1983. House officer, intern Med. Faculty, Beograd, 1983—84; rsch. fellow Inst. Oncology and Radiology, Beograd, 1984—85, specialist radiology, 1990—92, resident, 1987—90, Mil. Med. Acad., Beograd, 1985—86; trainee U. Hosp. Northern Norway, Tromsö, 1999—2003; specialist radiology Diakonhjemmets Hosp., Oslo, 2005—07, Clin. Ctr. Serbia, Beograd, 1992—97, U. Children Hosp., Beograd, 1997—99, Sect. Neuroradiology, Dept. Radiology, U. Hosp. Northern Sweden, Umeå, 2003—05. Mem.: Swedish Neuroradiol. Assn., Swedish Med. Assn., Norwegian Med. Assn. Office: Univ Hosp Northern Sweden Umeå 90185 Sweden Personal E-mail: pdetlic@gmail.com. Business E-Mail: ljubisa.borota@vll.se.

BOROVANSKY, JILL ALLISON, physician; b. Belvidere, Ill., Feb. 26, 1970; BS in Biology, N.Mex State U., 1992; MD, Tex. Tech Health Scis. Ctr., 1996. Internal medicine resident Mayo Clinic Ariz., 1996—2000, staff physician, 2000—, cons., 2004. Mem.: ACP (Ariz. chpt), Alpha Omega Alpha Honor Soc. Office: 13400 E Shea Blvd Scottsdale AZ 85259 Office Fax: 480-301-4070. Business E-Mail: borovansky.jill@mayo.edu.

BOROW, MALKE, law educator; b. NYC, June 22, 1965; JD, Columbia U., 1990. Dir., divsn. law and policy Israeli Med. Assn., 1997—. Lectr., med. ethics, law and medicine Max Stern Coll. Emek Yizrael, 2010. Office: Israeli Med Assn 35 Jabotins Ramat Gan 52136 Israel Office Fax: 97236100506. Business E-Mail: malkeb@ima.org.il.

BOROWICZ, KINGA KATARZYNA, physician, educator; b. Cracow, Mar. 20, 1969; MD, Med. U. Lublin, 1992. Prof. medicine Med. U. Lublin, 2004—. Mem. European Medicines Agy., 2010—. Recipient Sci. award, Ministry of Health and Social Care. Mem.: Polish Soc. Internal Medicine, Polish Soc. Pharmacology. Avocations: literature, hiking, aviation. Office: Jaczewskiego 8 Lublin Lubelskie 20-090 Poland Office Fax: 48 81 7187328. Business E-Mail: kinga.borowicz@umlub.pl.

BOROWITZ, JOSEPH LEO, pharmacologist, educator; b. Columbus, Ohio, Dec. 19, 1932; s. Joseph Peter and Anna Louise (Grundei) B.; children: Jon Joseph, Peter Joseph, Lynn Anne. BS in Pharmacy, Ohio State U., 1955; MS in Pharmacology, Purdue U., 1957; PhD in Pharmacology (NIH fellow), Northwestern U., 1960. Lt. then capt. Med. Svc. Corp US Army, 1955—65; chief biokinetics br. Sch. Aerospace Medicine, San Antonio, 1960—62; postdoctoral fellow dept. pharmacology Harvard U. Med. Sch., Boston, 1963—64; instr., then asst. prof. pharmacology Wake Forest U. Sch. Medicine, 1964—69; assoc. prof. pharmacology and toxicology Purdue U., 1969—74, prof., 1974—; sabbatical leave to Basel, Switzerland, 1984; vis. prof. sch. pharmacy U. P.R., 2001; sabbatical leave to Cambridge, England, 1976. Adj. prof. pharmacology Ind. Sch. Medicine, 1973—. Contbr. articles to profl. jours. Treas. Tippecanoe County (Ind.) Comprehensive Health Planning Coun., 1971-76. Recipient award for excellence in teaching Bowman Gray Sch. Medicine, 1969, Henry Heine award for excellence in teaching Purdue U. Coll. Pharmacy, 1983, Excellence Tchg. award Ind. Sch. Med. Lafayette Ctr., 2010, Excellence Faculty Advisor award Purdue U. Coll. Pharmacy, 2010; named NIH postdoctoral fellow, 1962-64; grantee NSF, 1965-68, NIH, 1971-74, 86-89, 89-94, 94-98, 1999-2004, 2004—, U.S. Army Med. Rsch., 1989-96, 97-2000. Mem.: Am. Soc. Pharmacology and Exptl. Therapeutics, Rho Chi. Roman Catholic. Office: Purdue U Dept Med Chem and Molec Pharmacology West Lafayette IN 47907 Home Phone: 765-463-3001. Business E-Mail: borowitz@purdue.edu.

BOROWSKY, IRIS WAGMAN, pediatrician, medical educator; b. Frederick, Md., Aug. 20, 1962; AB, Duke U., Durham, NC; MD, PhD in Neurosci., Washington U. Sch. Medicine, St. Louis, 1990. Diplomate Am. Bd. Pediat. Intern, resident pediat. Harbor-UCLA Med. Ctr., Torrance, Calif., 1990—93, gen. academic pediat. fellowship, 1993—94; asst., then assoc. prof. pediat. U. Minn., Mpls., 1994—, dir. gen. pediat., divsn. Gen. Pediat. & Adolescent Health. Staff physician U. Minn. Amplatz Children's Hosp., 1994—. Contbr. articles to profl. jours. Recipient Generalist Physician Faculty Scholars award, Robert Wood Johnson Found., 1999. Mem.: Soc. Adolescent Medicine, Ambulatory Pediat. Assn., Am. Acad. Pediat., Alpha Omega Alpha, Phi Beta Kappa. Office: U Minn Amplatz Childrens Hosp Phillips Wangensteen Bldg 4th Fl Rm 4 100 516 Delaware St SE Minneapolis MN 55455-2002 Office Phone: 612-626-2398. Office Fax: 612-626-2134. Business E-Mail: borow004@umn.edu. *

BORRIS, LARS CARL, surgeon; married. MD, Århus U., Denmark, 1981. Cert. specialist in orthop. surgery Danish Bd. Health, 1993. Registrar Aalborg Hosp., Denmark, 1982—88, rsch. fellow, 1989—94; sr. registrar Holstebro Ctrl. Hosp., Denmark, 1988—89, Århus U. Hosp., 1994—97, cons. surgeon, 1997—. Mem.: Danish Soc. Orthop. Surgery. Achievements include patents pending for urine test. Office: Århus Univ Hosp Nørrebrogade 44 Århus DK 8000 Denmark Office Phone: 4589494513. Office Fax: 4589494513. Business E-Mail: lborr@as.aaa.dk, larsborr@rm.dk.

BORSINI, FRANCO, pharmacologist, researcher; b. Prato, Italy, Dec. 6, 1951; s. Bruno Borsini and Osanna Magni; married; children: Valentina, Silvia. PhD, Mario Negri Inst., Milan, Italy, 1977—80. Rschr. Mario Negri Inst., Milan, 1984—89; head of lab. Menarini Pharmaceuticals, Florence, Italy, 1984—89; head of biology Boehringer Ingelheim Italia SpA, Milan, 1989—99; head of preclinic psychiatric rsch. Boehringer Ingelheim Pharma KG, Biberach an der Riss, Germany, 2000—. Recipient Best marks in the Faculty of Sci., Bank of Italy Bd., 1976. Mem.: European Behavioral Pharmacology Soc. (treas. 2001). Home: Panoramaweg 23 Bad Waldsee 88339 Germany Office: Boehringer Ingelheim Pharma KG Birkendorfer Strasse 65 Biberach an der Riss 88397 Germany Home Phone: 49 172 610 58 40; Office Phone: 49 7351 54 72 297. Business E-Mail: franco.Borsini@bc.boehringer-ingelheim.com.

BORZABADI-FARAHANI, ALI, orthodontist; b. Southampton, Eng. s. Ebrahim Borzabadi-Farahani and Sedigheh Barahimi. MSc in Orthodontics, Cardiff U., Eng., 2005. Rschr. Isfahan U. Med. Scis., Iran, 2007—, U. Birmingham, Shahid Beheshti U. Med. Scis., Tehran, Iran, U. Southern Calif.; hon. clin. lectr. dept. orthodontics Sch. Dentistry U. Birmingham, England. Reviewer World Jours. Orthodontics. Mem.: RCS (Edinburgh). Office: Orthoworld Leamington Spa Birmingham England also: Dept Orthodentsits Sch Dentistry University Birmingham Birmingham England Personal E-mail: faraortho@yahoo.com.

BOS, GARY D., orthopedist; b. Grand Rapids, Mich., Apr. 8, 1947; s. George and Clara Bos; m. Marcia L Battjes, June 4, 1969; children: Jeffrey A, Jana L, Joel E, Jori A. MD, U. Chgo., 1978. Diplomate Am. Bd. Orthop. Surgery. Prof. orthop. surgery U. N.C., Chapel Hill, 1993—2002, Ohio State U., Columbus, 2002—06. Cons. Zimmer Orthopedics, Warsaw, 1999—. Contbr. articles to profl. jours. Capt. USAF, 1969—74. Office Phone: 509-573-3989.

BOSCAMP, JEFFREY R., epidemiologist, educator; BA, Williams Coll., Williamstown, MA; MD, NY Med. Coll., New York, NY. Cert. pediatric infectious diseases. Rsch. assoc. Harvard Med. Sch., Boston; resident pediatrician Babies Hosp., Columbia Presbyterian Med. Ctr., New York, NY; resident internal medicine Yale Univ. Sch. of Medicine, Greenwich Hosp., Conn.; fellow in adult and pediatric infectious diseases Albert Einstein Coll. of Medicine, Bronx, NY; joined med. staff. Hackensack Univ. Med. Ctr., 1987, chief pediatric infectious diseases sect., 1990; cons. Toys "R" Us/Kids "R" Us, Morristown Meml. Hosp., Morristown, NJ, Holy Name Hosp., Teaneck, NJ, Univ. Hosp., Newark; assoc. prof. UMDNJ-NJ Med. Sch.; founder Sect. of Pediatric Infectious Diseases, Steven Bader Immunologic Inst.; chmn. pediat. Joseph M. Sanzari Children's Hosp., physician-in-chief. Mem. Catastrophic Illness in Children Relief Fund Commn. Recipient Lawrence B. Slobody prize in Pediat., NY Med. Coll., Outstanding Teacher award in Pediat., Morristown Meml. Hosp., 1993, Attending of the Year award, UMDNJ-NJ Med. Sch., 1998. Fellow: Pediatric Infectious Diseases Soc.; mem.: Am. Soc. for Microbiology, Infectious Diseases Soc. of NJ, Infectious Diseases Soc. of America, NJ Pediatric Leadership Coun., Am. Acad. of Pediat. (chmn. NJ chpt., mem. exec. com.), Alpha Omega Alpha. Office: Hackensack University Medical Center Don Imus Pediatric Bldg 30 Prospect Ave Hackensack NJ 07601 Office Phone: 201-996-5308.

BOSCIA, JON ANDREW, insurance company executive; b. Pitts., Apr. 15, 1952; s. Louis C. and Stella (Weryha) B.; m. Donna M. Lowar, Aug. 18, 1973; children: Nicole Marie, Brandon Jon. BA, Point Park Coll., 1973; MBA, Duquesne U., 1979. Corp. planner Consolidated Nat. Gas, Pitts., 1974-79; fin. sales rep. Westinghouse, Pitts., 1979-80; asst. v.p. Mellon Bank, Pitts., 1980-83; sr. v.p. Lincoln Nat. Pension, Ft. Wayne, Ind., 1983—98; pres. Lincoln Nat. Life Insurance Co., 1999—2004, Lincoln Financial Group, Phila., 1998—2001, chmn., CEO, 2001—07; pres. Sun Life Fin. Inc., 2008—. Bd. dirs. Georgia-Pacific Corp., Southern Co., Hershey Co., Sun Life Fin. Inc., 2011—. Contbr. articles to profl. jours. Mem. coms. Pitts. Bd. Edn., 1974-79; chmn. coms. Arlington Park, Ft. Wayne, 1983-86; mem. START program Ft. Wayne Community Schs., 1985; bd. dirs. The Phila. Orchestra Assn., Am. Coun. Life Insurers PPC Found. scholar, 1973. Mem. Nat. Assn. Bus. Economists, Planning Forum. Democrat. Methodist. Avocations: jogging, racquetball, playing drums, swimming, reading. Office: Sun Life Financial Inc 150 King St W M5H 1J9 Toronto Canada Office Phone: 0114169794800. Office Fax: 0114169793209. Business E-Mail: jon.boscia@sunlife.com. *

BOSCO, JOSEPH, orthopedist, surgeon, educator; Attended, U. Vt., 1982—86. Diplomate Am. Bd. of Orthopaedic Surgery. Intern Univ. Of NC Hosp., 1986—87, resident orthopaedic surgery, 1987—91; clin. fellow reconstructive surgery Univ. of Ariz., 1991—92; assoc. prof. NY Univ. Sch. of Medicine; with Jamaica Hosp. Med. Ctr., NY Univ. Hosp. for Joint Diseases; vice chair clin. affairs depts. NY Univ. Langone Med. Ctr., chair orthopaedic surgery dept. Co-author: (publs.) Survivorship analysis of cemented high modulus total hip arthroplasty, 1993, Loosening of a femoral stem associated with the use of an extended-lip acetabular cup liner. A case report, 1993, Long-term outcome of Volz total wrist arthroplasties, 1994, Sagittal and coronal biomechanics of the knee: a rationale for corrective measure, 2007, and numerous other publications. Office: New York University Langone Medical Center Skirball Institute 8 Unit 530 1st Ave New York NY 10016 Office Phone: 212-263-2192. Office Fax: 212-263-0231.

BOSE, KAUSHIK, medical educator; b. Kolkata, India, Nov. 24, 1962; PhD, U. Cambridge, 1995. Assoc. prof. Vidyasagar U., 2002—. Grant, Ruggles Gates Found., Royal Anthrop. Inst., Brit. Diabetes Assn. Fellow: Royal Soc. Promotion Health, Unit Biolocultural Variation and Obesity U. Oxford. Office: Dept Anthropology Vidyasagar University Midnapore West Bengal 721 102 India Personal E-mail: kaushikbose@cantab.net.

BOSELLI, JOSEPH, internist, educator; b. 1957; Studied, Hahnemann U. Diplomate Am. Bd. Internal Medicine, 1985. Intern Hahnemann Univ., resident. Assoc. prof. medicine dept. Drexel Univ. Named one of the Best Doctors, 2009—10, 2011—12, the Top Doctors, Phila. Mag., 2011. Office: Hahnemann University Hospital Broad and Vine Philadelphia PA 19102 Office Phone: 215-762-7000. Office Fax: 215-762-8109.

BOSHIER, MAUREEN LOUISE, health facilities administrator; b. Elizabeth, NJ, Oct. 1, 1946; d. John Henry and Mary Hanora (McGarry) B.; m. Robert Hall Rea, May 23, 1987. BSN, Coll. Misericordia, Dallas, Pa., 1968; MS in Psychiat. Nursing, U. Colo., 1973; MBA, U. Phoenix, 1987; LLD in Law & Policy, Northwestern U., Boston, 2010. Cert. healthcare exec. Clin. specialist psychiat. nursing Denver Gen. Hosp., 1973-74; dir. rehab. svcs. N.Mex. Cancer Control, Albuquerque, 1976-80; exec. dir. N.Mex. State Bd. Nursing, Albuquerque, 1980-84; exec. v.p. N.Mex. Hosp. Assn., Albuquerque, 1984-88; adminstr. surg. svcs., sr. nursing adminstr. U. N.Mex. Hosp., Albuquerque, 1988-94; CEO, pres. N.Mex. Hosps. and Health Sys. Assn., Albuquerque, 1994—2004; v.p. for ops. Eastern Va. Med. Sch., Norfolk, 2006—08, asst. prof., 2011—. Dir. Profl. Seminar Cons., Inc., Albuquerque, 1982—; v.p. exec. bd. N.Mex. Health Resources,

Albuquerque, 1981—, pres., 1989; vice chmn., bd. dirs. Hosp. Home Health Care, Albuquerque, 1978—; dir. Acad. Seminars, Inc., 1982—; mem. governing coun. for small and rural hosps. Am. Hosp. Assn., 1996—, women's dir. devel. program Kellogg Sch. Mgmt. Ctr. for Exec. Devel., 2003. Mem. adv. bd. N.Mex. Bus. Jour., 1995—; contbr. articles to profl. jours. Sec. N.Mex. Ballet Co., Albuquerque, 1982-87; vice chmn. Gov.'s Task Force on Nursing Issues, Albuquerque, 1982-88; adv. bd. Sub-area Coun. Health Sys., Albuquerque, 1980-84; mem. Leadership N.Mex. Class of 2000, alumni com. 2001—. Capt. U.S. Army, 1967-71, vice chair PAC & Appeals Com. Access Bd., 2007- chair Commn. Care Mgmt Cert., 2007-; commr. Case Mgr. Certification Commn., 2007-. Recipient Woman on the Move award YWCA, 1992, Wharton Sch. of Bus. fellowship for health care execs., 1993, Gov.'s award for Outstanding N.Mex. Woman, 1997, Frank Gabriel award for outstanding achievement N.Mex. Hosps. and Health Sys., 2004, Mary Catherene McGANN award, 2008; named Nurse of Yr., March of Dimes, 2002; fellow Johnson & Johnson, 1993. Mem. Am. Orgn. Nurse Execs. (vice chmn. legis. advocacy com. 1992-94, chmn. 1993-94), Am. Coll. Healthcare Execs. (diplomate, Regent's award 2000), N.Mex. Orgn. Nurse Execs. (treas. 1988-89, pres. 1990), N.Mex. League for Nursing, N.Mex. Nurses Assn. (Nurse Adminstr. award 1984), The N.Mex. Hosps. and Health Systems Assn. (Frank Gabriel award 2004), Rotary (Albuquerque bd. dirs. 2001—), Albuquerque C. of C. (mem. quality of life com. 1994—), Sigma Theta Tau (pres.-elect 1994, pres. 1995—, Mentor award Gamma Sigma chpt. 1994). Democrat. Avocations: music, dance, travel. Home: 375 Middle St Portsmouth VA 23704

BOSIO, ANGELO, pharmacologist, neuropsychiatrist, scientific advisor; b. Brescia, Italy, Jan. 18, 1955; s. Giulio and Teresa (Macetti) B.; m. Barbara Casa, July 1, 2000. MD, Milan U., 1980, degree in pharmacology, 1982, degree in psychiatry, 1988. Intern Milan U. Med. Sch., 1984-88, cons. psychiatrist, 1988—; dir. pharmacological dept. St. Anne Clinic, Brescia, 1987—, dir. neurol. dept., 1996—; hon. justice Ct. Appeals, Brescia, 2002—. Cons. Internat. Pharm. Cos., 1983—, WHO, 1988, others; dir. A.A.N. Drug Monitoring Svc., N.Y.C., 1994—. Author: Handbook of Reaction Time Evaluation, 1991; editor Jour. Percorsi Sanitari, 1986—, Neuroscis. Collection, 1988, H & W in Medicine, 1992—; editor videotapes Neurotransmission, 1988, Anxiolytic Drugs: An Up to Date, 1989, The Metamorphosis, 1991, Mioclonus and Piracetam, 1991, The Living Proof, 1991, Video Minds Series, 1995, Depression, 1995, Epilepsy, 1996; journalist Sci. and Med. Press, 1982—, mng. dir. A.A.N., 1992-2000; mng. dir. Drug Monitoring Svc., NY, 2000—. Recipient Nutrition Found. award, Italy, 1982. Fellow AAAS, N.Y. Acad. Scis., Internat. Psychogeriatric Assn., Italian Psychiat. Soc.; mem. Assn. Advancement Neurosci. (pres. Brescia chpt. 1987-92, Internat. chpt. 1990—). Roman Catholic. also: AAN Drug Monitoring Svc 575 Madison Ave Ste 1006 New York NY 10022-2511 Office: Assn Advancement Neurosci Via Ildebrando Vivanti 9 25133 Brescia BS Italy E-mail: bosio@pharmac.net.

BOSL, GEORGE JOSEPH, physician, oncologist; b. Cleve., Oct. 19, 1948; BS in Biology, John Carroll U., 1969; MD, Creighton U., 1973. Diplomate Am. Bd. Medicine, Am. Bd. Oncology. Intern N.Y. Hosp., 1973-74, resident in medicine, 1974-75, Sloan-Kettering Cancer Ctr., 1974-77; fellow in med. oncology U. Minn. Hosp., 1977-79; oncologist Meml. Sloan Kettering Cancer Ctr., NYC, 1979—, dir. oncology, hematology fellow program, 1986-94, head divsn. solid tumor oncology, 1989-97, assoc. physician-in-chief, 1994-97, chmn. dept. medicine, 1997—; prof. medicine Cornell U., NYC, 1991—, Patrick M. Byrne chair clinical oncology. Recipient Award for Excellence in Medicine, Soc. Meml. Sloan-Kettering, 2005. Mem. AMA, Am. Assn. Cancer Rsch., Am. Soc. Clin. Oncology, Alpha Omega Alpha. Office: Meml Sloan Kettering Ctr New York NY 10021 *

BOSNAR, ALAN, medical university administrator, physician; b. Rijeka, Croatia, May 25, 1961; s. Bozo and Kitty Bosnar; m. Laura Bosnar, July 16, 1994; 1 child, Petra. MD, Med. Sch., Rijeka, 1988, MSc, 1994; specialist exam in Forensic Medicine, Med. Sch., Zagreb, 1994; PhD, Med. Sch., Rijeka, 1999. Resident Clin. Hosp., Rijeka, 1988—89; jr. rschr. Med. Sch., Rijeka, 1989—94, asst., 1994—99, sr. asst., 1999—2002, asst. prof., 2003—; head Dept. Forensic Medicine U. Rijeka, 2004—. Rep. Croatian Profl. Assn. of Forensic Experts, Zagerb, 1998—2002. Mem. Croatian Commn. UNESCO, 2004—; pres. Ind. Trade Union of Sci. and High Edn. Republic of Croatia, U. Rijeka, 1991—93. Fellow: Am. Acad. Forensic Sci.; mem.: Am. Coll. Forensic Examiners. Roman Catholic. Achievements include performing forensic autopsies and indentification of war victims during the war ops. Avocations: swimming, bicycling, skiing. Home: Laginjina 7 Rijeka 51000 Croatia Office: Med Sch Dept Forensic B Branchetta 20 Rijeka 51000 Croatia Office Phone: 385 51213853. E-mail: alanbosnar@yahoo.com.

BOSNJAK, MARIJAN, retired biotechnologist; b. Lovrec, Imotski, Croatia, Dec. 2, 1934; s. Jakov and Andja (Petricevic) B.; m. Nada Kovacic, Mar. 10, 1962; children: Kresimir, Zeljana. BChemE, Zagreb U., 1959, MSc in Biotech., 1961, PhD in Biotech., 1973. Rschr. Pliva Co. Rsch. Inst., Zagreb, 1960-61; fermentation plant mgr. Pliva-Antibiotics, Zagreb, 1962-68; sr. rschr. Pliva-Rsch. Inst., Zagreb, 1969-2000; ret., 2000. Governing bd. Rudjer Boskovic Inst., Zagreb, 1995-2000; prof. math. model. biochem. engring. Faculty Biotechnol., Zagreb, 1984—; assoc. instr. org. chem. exercises Faculty of Technol., Zagreb, 1964-67. Author: (book) Introduction to Kinetics of Microbial Processes; contbr. articles to profl. jours.; patentee in field. Mem. Croatian Cultural Soc.-Matrix Croatica. Recipient Sci. award, Ministry Sci. of Croatia, 1988, Croatian Acad. Engring., 2004. Mem.: Am. Chem. Soc., Croatian Acad. Engring., Croatian Soc. Chem. Engring. (chmn. 1988), Croatian Soc. Biotech. (chmn. 1990—96). Roman Catholic. Avocations: occasional charitable activities, writing, ethics promotion. Home: Slovenska Ulica 19 10-000 Zagreb Croatia Personal E-mail: marijan.bosnjak@hatz.hr.

BOSSARD, ROBERT LEE, biologist, educator; b. Denver, July 22, 1961; s. Randall K. and Dorothy L. Bossard. BS in Biology, U. Utah, Salt Lake City, 1983; MS in Zoology, U. Okla., Norman, 1986; PhD in Entomology, Kans. State U., Manhattan, 1997. Adj. faculty St. Petersburg Coll. Contbr. articles to profl. jours. Vol. 4-H, Manhattan, 1995—96, Future Farmers Am., Manhattan, 1995—96, Samaritan's Purse, Salt Lake City, 2001—07, Nature Conservancy, Salt Lake City, 1992—93. Methodist. Office: Saint Petersburg Coll PO Box 13489 Saint Petersburg FL 33733

BOSSI, BRUNO, cytologist, biologist; b. Boves, Italy, Apr. 9, 1954; s. Sergio Bossi and Carla Giraudo; m. Ivana Occelli, Aug. 19, 1978; 1 child, Francesca. Biology, U. of Turin, 1973—77. Lab. technician Demonte Hosp., Demonte, Italy, 1977—78; asst. biologist Pathology Dept. - S. Croce Hosp., Cuneo, Italy, 1980—93; biologist Cytogenetic Lab. - S.Croce Hosp., Cuneo, Italy, 1994—97; head biologist of genetics Cytogegetic Lab. - S. Croce Hosp., Cuneo, 1998—2001; head biologist of cytogenetics Cytogenetic Lab. - S.Croce Hosp., Cuneo, Italy, 2002—. Tchr. of nutrition Nursing Sch., Cuneo, 1982—96, tchr. of human genetics, 1983—84; org. of genetics and pathology courses for drs. biologists and technicians S. Croce Hosp., Cuneo, 2002—03; lectr. cellular biology U. Turin, Cuneo, 2001—02, lectr. histology, 2002—05, lectr. vaginal cytology, 2002—05, lectr. med. genetics, 2003—05. Contbr. articles to profl. jours. Master: Archery Cuneo; mem.: Italian Cytology Soc., PA of Italian Biologists, Italian Pathology and Cytology Soc., Italian Human Genetics Soc., Panathlon Internat. (assoc.), Nat. Archery Coach (life). Catholic. Achievements include research in simple technique of codenaturation and fluorescence in situ hybridization with probes in a microcamera. Avocations: archery, information technology, photography, reading, travel. Office: Cytogenetic Laboratory S Croce Hospital Via M Coppino 26 12100 Cuneo Italy Office Fax: +39-0171-641484. Business E-Mail: anapat@ospedale.cuneo.it.

BOST, JANE MORGAN, psychologist; b. Corpus, Christi, Aug. 20, 1953; d. Clayton Aquilla and Eleanor (Hoving) Morgan; m. David Edward Bost, June 16, 1984; children: Christopher David, Morgan Jane. BS, Okla. State U., 1976, MS, 1980, PhD, 1984. English tchr. Perry High Sch., Okla., 1976—78; acad. advisor Okla. State U., Stillwater, 1980—82, staff therapist, 1982—83; counseling psychology intern Tex. A&M U., Coll. Statio, 1983—84; dir. counseling svcs. Southwestern U., Georgetown, Tex., 1984—92; asst. dir. counseling & mental health ctr. U Tex., Austin, 1992—98, assoc. dir. counseling & mental health ctr, 1998—. Contbr. articles to profl. jours. Collegue status faculty Creative Problem Solving Inst., Buffalo, 1985—86, 1988, 1991—94. Recipient Outstanding Young Women of Am, 1988, 1991, Merit Outstanding Staff award, U. Tex. Parents Assn., 2003—04; grantee Combat Violence against Woman Campus, US Dept. Justice, 2000, 2002, 2005. Mem.: APA, Nat. Register Health Svc. Providers Psychology, Tex. Psychol. Assn., Am. Coll. Pers. Assn. Methodist. Avocations: hiking, photography, reading, art, gardening. Office: U Tex Counseling & Mental Health Ctr Austin TX 78712

BOSTACA, IOAN VIRGIL, cardiologist, educator; b. Barlad, Moldova, Romania, Oct. 19, 1949; s. Virgil and Elena Bostaca; m. Tamara; 1 child Stefan. MD, U. Medicine, Iasi, Romania, 1973. Physician Gen. Hosp., Iasi, 1973—, resident, 1975-79; specialist physician Med. Clinic, Iasi, 1979-90, sr. physician, 1990—; cardiologist Med. & Cardiol. Clinic, Iasi, 1998—. Assoc. prof. internal medicine and cardiology, U. Medicine, Iasi. Author: Cardiac Failure, 1993, Osmolarity and Electrolytes, 1994, Diabetes Mellitus, 1994, 96, 98, 4th edit., 2001, Infective Endocarditis, 1995, Dictionary of Medicines in Cardiology, 1996, 2d edit., 2000, The Clues of Diagnosis in Medical Clinic, 1999, Guidebook in Clinical Practice, 2005; co-author: (with V. Dobrovici) English in Medicine: A Textbook for Doctors, Students and Nurses, 1999, Dictionary of Medicines in Cardiology 2000-2001, 2000, (with C. Marcu) Textbook of Electrocardiography, 2002, Challenges in Electrocardiography, 2005, Handbook of Therapeutics in Clinical Medicine, 2008, Cardiology Practitioners' Formulary, 2011. Fellow Med. and Surg. Soc.; mem. European Soc. Cardiology, Romanian Soc. Cardiology. Avocations: photography, computers, travel. Office: Hosp S F Spiridon Independentei No 1 700444 Iasi Romania E-mail: ibostaca@mail.dntis.ro.

BOSTIN, MARVIN JAY, hospital and health services consultant; came to U.S., 1956; 1 child, Shepard Craig. BS in Pharmacy, U. Toronto, 1955; MS in Hosp. Adminstrn., Columbia U., 1958; PhD in Pub. Adminstrn., NYU, 1972. Pharmacist New Mt. Sinai Hosp., Toronto, 1953-56; asst. adminstr. L.I. Jewish Hosp., New Hyde Park, NY, 1958-62; assoc. dir. Mt. Sinai Med. Ctr., Miami Beach, Fla., 1962-65; exec. v.p. E.D. Rosenfeld Assocs. Inc., hosp. and health svcs. cons., White Plains, NY, 1965-78; pres. M. Bostin Assocs., Inc., Stamford, Conn., 1979—. Guest scholar Brookings Instn., Washington, 1965; lectr. Sch. Pub. Health and Adminstrv. Medicine, Columbia U., N.Y.C., 1965-78, Grad. Sch. Pub. Adminstrn., 1967; lectr. Grad. Sch. Architecture and Planning, Columbia U., 1975-78; cons. to Bur. of Hearings and Appeals, Social Security Adminstrn., HEW, 1967-68; cons. task force on guidelines for constrn. and equipment of hosp. and med. facilities, USPHS, DHHS, 1987; mem. implementation work group on improving health Nat. Commn. on Children, 1992; spl. cons. to Office of Equal Health Opportunity, Office of Surgeon Gen., USPHS, 1966-67; project dir., Study Quantify Uniqueness Children's Hosps., Nat. Assn. Children's Hosps. Related Instns., 1978. Mem. Dade County (Fla.) Welfare Planning Coun., Miami, 1962-65; bd. dirs. South Fla. Hosp. Coun., Miami, 1963-65; cons. Nelson Mandela Children's Fund, Johannesburg, 2007-09. Fellow APHA, Royal Soc. Health (London), Am. Assn. Healthcare Cons. (chmn. monograph series com. 1970-71, exec. com. 1972-75, profl. standards com. 1974-76); mem. Am. Hosp. Assn. (life), Forum for Health Care Planning (dir. 1982-95), Am. Coll. Healthcare Execs., Internat. Hosp. Fedn. Office: M Bostin Assoc Inc 237 Strawberry Hill Ave Apt 25 Stamford CT 06902-2567 Office Phone: 203-961-0511. Business E-Mail: marvin@bostin.com.

BOSWELL, C.B., plastic surgeon; b. Ames, Iowa; m. Jill Yamauchi; 1 child, Avery. BS, So. Meth. U., Dallas, 1991; student, Oxford U., Eng., 1989; MD, U. Wis. Med. Sch., Madison, 1995. Cert. Am. Bd. Plastic Surgery, 2003. Resident in gen. surgery Barnes-Jewish Hosp., Washington U., St. Louis, 1995—99, rsch. fellow, 1997—98, resident in plastic surgery, 1999—2001; plastic surgery fellow San Francisco, 2001; plastic surgery and oculoplastic fellow Paces Plastic Surgery, Atlanta, 2002; founding ptnr. Body Aesthetic Plastic Surgery and Skin Care Ctr., St. Louis, 2002—. Contbr. articles to profl. jours. Recipient Physician's Recognition award, AMA, 1999; named one of America's Top Surgeons, Consumer's Rsch. Coun. America, 2006, 2007. Fellow: Am. Coll. Surgeons; mem.: St. Louis Area Soc. Plastic Surgeons, Mo. State Med. Soc., Am. Soc. Plastic Surgeons, Am. Bd. Plastic Surgery, Alpha Omega Alpha, Phi Beta Kappa, Alpha Lambda Delta. Avocation: fly fishing. Office: Body Aesthetic Plastic Surgery and Skincare Ctr Ste 170 969 N Mason Rd Saint Louis MO 63141 Office Phone: 314-628-8200. Office Fax: 314-628-9504.

BOSWORTH, WILLIAM POSEY, physician, physical education educator; b. Valdosta, Ga., Mar. 23, 1935; s. Paul Brooks and Myra Mae (Posey) B.; m. Wanda Marie Grimm; 1 child, Lynne Marie. BS, U. Tampa, 1957; MEd, Springfield Coll., Mass., 1961; postgrad., Orlando Jr. Coll., Fla., 1968; DO, U. Health Scis., Kansas City, Mo., 1972. Phys. edn. tchr., jr. high sch. tchr. Duval County Sch. Bd., Jacksonville, Fla., 1959—62; intern U.S. Naval Hosp., Phila., 1972—73; gen. practice medicine Jacksonville, 1974—. Physician athletic team, 1975—. Mem. Jacksonville Sports Com., 1981—86, chmn., 1986; mem. Duval County Hosp. Authority, 1982—86, chmn., 1986; mem. Fla. Gov.'s Coun. on Phys. Fitness and Sports, 1985—93, Duval County Sch. Bd., Jacksonville, 1986—90, Fla. Sunshine State Games Found., 1990—99, Sports in Fla. Found., 2000—. With USMCR, 1953—58, with USNR, 1969—99, capt. M.C., 1988—. Decorated Navy Commendation medals (2), Meritorious Svc. medal; recipient Physician's Recognition award, AMA, 1988, 1991, 1994, 1997, 1999, 2002, 2005, 2008; named Gen. Practitioner of Yr., Fla. Soc. Am. Coll. Family Physicians, 1982, Health Educator of the Yr., Duval County Coalition Against Tobacco, 1991. Mem.: AAU (pres. Fla. chpt. 1983—87, Life award 1967, Vol. Svc. 35 Yr. Gold Pin award 1988, named Outstanding Vol. 1992), PTA (hon. life-Fla. 2000, Nat. 2001), Freedoms Found. at Valley Forge (pres. Jacksonville chpt. 1995—97, Heart of Gold award 2005, Patriot Spirit of '76 award 2006), Assn. Mil. Surgeons U.S., Duval County Acad. Family Physicians (pres. 1984), Duval County Med. Soc., Fla. Soc. Sons of Am. Revolution (pres. 1980, 2000, Meritorious Svc. medal 1986, Disting. Svc. medal 2001), Fla. Med. Assn., Mandarin Mus. and Hist. Soc. (charter mem. 1992, life mem. 2001), Rotary Club of Mandarin (charter mem. 1975, pres. 1985—86), Rotary Club of San Jose (charter mem. 2003, Outstanding Svc. award 2005), Mandarin Cmty. Club (life; pres. 2002), Am. Legion 40/8 Honor Soc. (life; nat. med. officer 1989—91, Voyageur of Yr. 1990). Office: 9765 San Jose Blvd Jacksonville FL 32257-4402 Office Phone: 904-268-2227.

BOTCHAN, MICHAEL R., molecular biologist, biochemist; b. Bklyn., July 13, 1945; BA in Biology, NYU, 1967; PhD in Biophysics, U. Calif., Berkeley, 1972. Postdoctoral rsch. Cold Spring Harbor Lab., NY, 1972—74, sr. scientist, 1974—80; assoc. prof. dept. molecular biology U. Calif., Berkeley, 1980—94, prof. dept. molecular and cell biology, 1984—. Adj. assoc. prof. dept. microbiol. SUNY, Stony Brook, 1977—79; mem. adv. com. cell biology and microbiol. Am. Cancer Soc., 1978—81, mem. adv. com. nucleic acids and proteins, 1986—90, postdoctoral fellowship com. Calif. divsn., 1986—89; mem. virology study sect. NIH, 1986—91; mem. sci. adv. com. Damon Runyon-Walter Winchell Cancer Rsch. Fund, 1989—92, chmn. sci. adv. com., 1992; mem. sci. rev. bd. Howard Hughes Med. Inst. Contbr. articles to sci. jours.; mem. editl. bd.: Jour. Virology, 1984—90, Molecular and Cellular Biology, 1985—91, Oncogene, 1987—91; editor: Plasmid, 1986. Recipient NIH Merit award, 1987, 2004. Fellow: AAAS, Am. Acad. Arts & Scis.; mem.: NAS. Achievements include research in DNA virus transformation; eukaryotic DNA replication and transcription; recombination in somatic cells. Office: Dept Molecular and Cell Biology U Calif 401 Barker Hall Number 3204 Berkeley CA 94720-3204 Business E-Mail: mbotchan@berkeley.edu.

BOTCHKAREV, VLADIMIR A., dermatologist, research scientist, director, medical educator; s. Zoya G. Botchkareva and Arnold Z. Botchkarev; m. Natalia V. Botchkareva, 1987; 1 child, Vladimir V. MD, Med. Faculty Chuvash State U., Cheboksary, Russia, 1982. Physician Hosp. Urgent Med., 1982—84; asst. prof. Chuvash State U., 1984—89, assoc. prof., 1990—95; rsch. scientist Humboldt U. Berlin, 1995—99; rsch. asst. prof. Boston U. Sch. Med., 2000—04, assoc. prof., 2004—. Bd. dirs. North Am. Hair Rsch. Soc., 2003—. Mem. program com. North-American Hair Rsch. Soc. Recipient Career Devel. Award, The Dermatology Found., 2000, Ind. Scientist Award, NIH, 2002; grantee Rsch. Grants, Nat. Alopecia Arcata Found., 1999, 2001, Rsch. Grant, Nat. Cancer Inst., 2003; fellow Rsch. Fellowship, German Academic Exch. Svc., 1994. Mem.: Soc. Investigative Dermatology, USA. Achievements include research in molecular signaling mechanisms controlling skin and hair follicle biology in health and disease. Office: Boston U 609 Albany St Boston MA 02118 E-mail: vladbotc@bu.edu.

BOTHALE, KALPANA ANIL, medical educator; b. Warora, Maharashtra, India, Oct. 2, 1962; MBBS, GMC Nagpur, 1986, MD in Pathology, 1990. Lectr. NKP Salve Inst. Med. Scis. & Rsch. Ctr., Nagpur, 1992—2002, assoc. prof., 2002—. Mem.: IAC, VAPM. Avocation: cooking. Home: 28 Shastri Layout Khamla Nagpur Maharashtra 440025 India Personal E-mail: kalpana_bothale@yahoo.co.in.

BOTKIN, DANIEL BENJAMIN, biologist, environmental scientist, writer; b. Oklahoma City, Aug. 19, 1937; s. Benjamin Albert and Gertrude (Fritz) B.; m. Ellen Chase, Dec. 22, 1962 (div. 1976); children: Nancy, Jonathan; m. Erene Victoria Youngberg, Apr. 7, 1978 (dec. Mar. 1994); m. Jane M. O'Brien (dec. Feb. 2002); m. Diana G. Perez. BA, U. Rochester, 1959; MA, U. Wis., 1962; PhD, Rutgers U., 1968. From asst. to assoc. prof. Yale U., New Haven, 1968-76; assoc. scientist Marine Biol. Lab., Woods Hole, Mass., 1976-78; prof. biology U. Calif., Santa Barbara, 1978-92, chmn. environ. studies program, 1978-85; dir. program on global change biology dept. George Mason U., Fairfax, Va., 1993-97, prof. biology, 1993-99; pres. The Ctr. for the Study of the Environment, 1992—; rsch. prof. biology U. Calif., Santa Barbara, 1999—2004, emeritus, 2004—. Vis. prof. U. Notre Dame, 2003; disting vis. prof. Mich. State U., 2004; Astor lectr. Oxford U., 2007; disting. vis. scientist Long Beach Aquarium, Calif., 2008; disting. vis. scholar Green Mountain Coll., Vt., 2008. Author: Discordant Harmonies: A New Ecology for the 21st Century, 1990, paperback edit., 1992, Forest Dynamics: An Ecological Model, 1993, Our Natural History: The Lessons of Lewis and Clark, 1995, reprinted 2004, Passage of Discovery: The American Rivers Guide to the Missouri River of Lewis and Clark, 1999, No Man's Garden: Thoreau and a New Vision for Civilization and Nature, 2001, Strange Encounters: Adventures of a Renegade Naturalist, 2003, Beyond The Stony Mountains: Nature in the American West from Lewis and Clark to Today, 2004; (software) JABOWA, 1970, Timber: model of forest growth, 1983, 87, JABOWA-II, 1992, JABOWA-3 for Windows, 1999 JABOWA-4, 2004; co-author: Forest Succession, 1981, Environmental Studies, 1982, 87, Changing the Global Environment, 1989, Environmental Science: Earth as a Living Planet, 1995, 8th edit., 2011, The Blue Planet, 1999, Essential Environ. Sci., 2007, Powering the Future: A Scientist's Guide to Energy Independence, 2010; contbr. articles to profl. jours., popular mags. and newspapers. Trustee Santa

Barbara Bot. Garden, 1987-93; bd. dirs. Environ. Literacy Coun., Washington, 2003-06; trustee Am. Folklife Ctr., Libr. Congress, 2004-09; commr. US State Dept. to UNESCO; mem. nat. adv. bd. Stetson Kennedy Found., Jacksonville, Fla., 2006—. Recipient 1st Prize, Mitchell Internat. Prize for Sustainable Devel., 1991, Fernow prize for Internat. Forestry, 1995, Texty award, Textbook and Acad. Authors Assn., 2004; Astor Lectureship award Oxford U., 2007, named to Environ. Hall Fame, Calif. Polytechnic U., 1995; grantee EPA, NSF, NASA, NOAA, Mellon Found., New Bedford Whaling Mus., Pew Charitable Trusts, W. Alton Jones Found., World Wildlife Fund, SOHIO Alaska Corp.; fellow Woodrow Wilson Internat. Ctr. for Scholars, Washington, 1977-78, Rockefeller Bellagio Inst., Italy, 1985, East-West Ctr., Honolulu, 1985-87. Fellow AAAS; Cosmos Club, Explorers Club, Sigma Xi (lectr. 1981-83). Avocations: photography, hiking, music. Office: 245 8th Ave #270 New York NY 10011 Home Phone: 212-243-7937; Office Phone: 917-747-3068. E-mail: danielbotkin@rcn.com.

BOTSFORD, MARY HENRICH, retired ophthalmologist; b. Buffalo, Aug. 22, 1915; d. John William and Margarethe Ingeborg (Kähler) Henrich; m. Daniel Ray Botsford, Feb. 11, 1943 (dec. Dec. 1970); children: Daniel Jr., Janet B. Thrush, William H., Thomas H. BA, Mount Holyoke Coll., 1937; MD, U. Buffalo, 1941. Diplomate Am. Bd. Ophthalmology. Assoc. Ivan J. Koenig M.D., Buffalo, 1943-46, 56-60; pvt. practice Buffalo, 1960-84; retired, 1984. Staff St. Francis Hosp., Buffalo, 1962-72, Vets. Hosp., Buffalo, 1962-72, Gowanda State Hosp., Helmuth, N.Y., 1962-80, Buffalo Children's Hosp., 1943-96, Buffalo Gen. Hosp., 1943-96. Founding bd. dirs., vol. Habitat for Humanity, Buffalo, 1985-2005; vol. Meals on Wheels, Buffalo, 1985-96, Am. Cancer Soc., Buffalo, 1985-96. Recipient Outstanding Achievement in Medicine citation, SUNY, Buffalo, 1984. Mem. Am. Acad. Ophthalmology, Buffalo Ophthal. Club, N.Y. State Ophthal. Soc., Common Cause. Democrat. Lutheran. Avocations: bridge, classical music, travel, theater, reading. Home Phone: 716-929-5511.

BOTSTEIN, DAVID, geneticist, educator; b. Zurich, Switzerland, Sept. 8, 1942; naturalized, 1954; AB in Biochem. Scis. cum laude, Harvard U., 1963; PhD in Human Genetics, U. Mich., 1967. Woodrow Wilson fellow, 1963; instr. dept. biology MIT, Cambridge, Mass., 1967-69, asst. prof. genetics, 1969-73, assoc. prof. genetics dept. biology, 1973-78, prof., 1978-88; v.p. sci. Genentech, Inc., 1988-90; Stanford W. Ascherman prof. Stanford U. Sch. Medicine, Palo Alto, Calif., 1997—2003; dir., Lewis-Sigler Inst. for Integrative Genomics Princeton U., 2003—, Anthony B. Evnin Prof. Genomics, 2003—. Sci. adv. bd. Collaborative Research, Inc., 1978-87. Editor in chief Molecular Biology of Cell, 1992—2001; contbr. over 320 articles to profl. jours. Recipient Career Devel. award NIH, 1972-77; Eli Lilly and Co. award in microbiology and immunology, 1978, Genetics Soc. of Am. Medal, 1988, Rosenstiel award Brandeis U., 1992, Allen award Am. Soc. of Human Genetics, 1989, Inst. of Medicine, 1993, award Gruber Found. 2003; co-recipient Albany Med. Ctr. prize in Medicine, 2010. Mem. NAS, Genetics Soc. Am. (bd. dirs. 1984), Inst. Medicine. Achievements include proposing, with three colleagues, a method for mapping genes, leading to Human Genome Project, 1980. Office: 140 Carl Icahn Lab Lewis-Sigler Inst Integrative Genomics Princeton Univ Washington Rd Princeton NJ 08544

BOTT, JAY CORDELL, oncologist, hematologist; b. Salt Lake City, 1947; s. Leroy J. and Blanche T. Bott; m. Julie Christiansen, 1992. BA in Chemistry, U. Utah, 1971, BA in Med. Biology, 1974, MD hons. program in internal medicine, 1975. Cert. internal medicine, hematology, oncology. Intern Naval Regional Med. Ctr., San Diego, 1975—76, resident, 1976—78, fellow in oncology, hematology, 1979—80, 1981—82; fellow in oncology U. Utah Med. Ctr., Salt Lake City, 1980—81; with Utah Valley Regional Med. Ctr., Provo, 1983—, Mountain View Hosp., Payson, Utah, 1983—, Castleview Hosp., Price, Utah, 1984—, Timpanogos Regional Hosp., Orem, Utah, 1998—; founder Oxbow Ranch, Hanna, Utah; med. dir. Ctrl. Utah Clinic, 2011—. Former v.p. Ctrl. Utah Clinic; prior prin. investigator Nat. Surg. Adjuvant Breast Bowel Project, 1995-2004; est. one of the largest found. Quarter Horse breeding programs in U.S.; chmn. dept. hematology & oncology, Utah Valley Reg. Med. Ctr., Provo, 2006-; med. dir. Ctrl. Utah Clinic, 2011-. Mem. Nat. Rep. Com.; missionary LDS Ch., 1967—69; with High Coun. and Bishopric; organist LDS Ch., tchr. Sunday Sch. Cmdr. USNR, 1973—84. Named Utah Rep. Businessman of Yr., 2000, 2001. Fellow: ACP; mem.: Am. Guild Organists, Soc. Utah Med. Oncologists (treas. 2007—08, v.p. 2008—09, pres. 2009—), Am. Cancer Soc. (past. pres. Utah Vly. chpt.), Utah County Med. Assn. (past pres.), S.W. Oncology Group, Am. Soc. Hematology, Am. Soc. Clin. Oncology, Phi Kappa Phi, Phi Beta Kappa. Avocations: ranching, hunting, outdoorsports, classical piano, organ. Office: Ctrl Utah Clinic 1055 N 500 W Provo UT 84604-3305 also: Oxbow Ranch HC 63 Box 324 Hanna UT 84031-0024 Office Phone: 801-374-2367.

BOTTA, LUCA, surgeon; b. Naples, Sept. 18, 1978; MD, U. Napoli Federico II, 2003, PhD. Resident cardiac surgery, U. Bologna, 2008; cardiac surgeon Ospedale Niguarda Cà Granda, Milano, 2008—. Recipient Alessandro Pellegrini award, Italian Soc. Cardiac Surgery and De Gasperis Found., 2008; Clin. and Rsch. fellowship, St. Antonius Hosp., Nieuwegein, Netherlands. Avocations: travel, soccer, art. Office: Piazza dell'Ospedale Maggiore 3 Milano Lombardia 20162 Italy Business E-Mail: luca.botta@ospedaleniguarda.it.

BOTTAZZO, GIAN FRANCO, physician; b. Venice, Italy, Aug. 1, 1946; s. Alfredo Bottazzo and Luigia Calderan; m. Lamya Al-Saqqaf, Aug. 2, 1980; 1 child, Dana. MD with hons., U. Padua, Italy, 1971; Specialist Diploma, U. Padua, Italy, 1979, U. Florence, 1974; Commendatore (hon.), Italian Rep. for Scientific Merits, Rome, 1986; Laurea Honoris Causa in Medicine (hon.), U. Nantes, France, 1990. Cert. FRCP London, 1990, FRCPath London, 1992. Welcome Rsch. Fellow Middlesex Hosp., London, 1975—77, lectr. in clin. immunology, 1977—80, sr. lectr. in clin. immunology, 1980—83, reader in clin. immunology, 1984—89; prof., head dept. of immunology The London Med. Coll., 1991—98; scientific dir. Osp. Pediatrico Bambino Gesù, Rome, 1998—. Hon. cons. phys. Middlesex Hosp. Med. Sch., 1980—91, The Royal Hosp., London, 1991—98; med. and scientific dir. The Autoimmune Diseases Charitable Trust, London, 1992—2002. Contbr. articles more than 500 articles to profl. jours. and publs. Recipient Oskar Minkowski award, European Assn. for Study of Diabetes, Budapest, 1985, Diaz Cristobal Internat. prize, Internat. Diabetic Fedn., Madrid, 1985, Banting Meml. medal, Am. Diabetes Assn., San Antonio, Tex., 1992. Mem.: Italian Soc. Diabetes, Chilean Soc. of Endocrinology and Metabolism, Italian Pediat. Soc., Argentine Soc. Endocrinology and Metabolism. Achievements include discovery of of islet cell autoantibodies in type 1 diabetes, several new autoantibodies in endocrine autoimmunity, aberrant HLA class II molecule expression on autoimmune thyrocytes. Avocation: reading, listening to music. Office: Ospedale Pediatrico Bambino Gesù Piazza S Onofrio 4 00165 Rome Italy Office Phone: 00 3906 68592277. E-mail: bottazzo@opbg.net.

BOTTCHER, LOUISE, psychology professor; b. Roskilde, Mar. 6, 1973; MSc in Psychology, U. Copenhagen, 2003, PhD in Psychology, 2009. Asst. prof. Danish Sch. Edn., Aarhus U., 2010—. Recipient Textbook award, Samfundslitteratur, 2008, Rschr. award, Danish Assn. Children & Adults, 2009. Office: Tuborgvej 164Sealand Copenhagen NV 2400 Denmark Business E-Mail: boettcher@dpu.dk.

BOTTINI, EGIDIO, medical educator; b. Civitella Casanova, Pescara, Italy, Mar. 10, 1931; s. Nunzio Bottini and Margherita Sablone; m. Fulvia Gloria, Oct. 16, 1971; children: Nunzio, Massimo. MD, U. Rome, 1956. Medical diplomate. Asst. prof. U. Italy, 1959-70, prof. genetics, 1976-83, dept. dir., 1976-83, 85, dir. PhD Sch. of Pediats., 1986-2000, prof. peds., 1983—2006; ret., 2006; prof. under contract U. Italy, 2007—; chief of rsch. Nat. Rsch. Coun., Italy, 1962-76. Italian rep. Coun. of Europe Commn. for the Study of Metabolic Diseases, Strasbourg, 1970-72; Lincei prof. genetics Accademia Nazionale dei Lincei, Interdisciplinary Ctr. for Applied Maths., 1979-85; fellow U. Coll. Hosp. Medical Sch., London, 1960-61; invited rschr. Yale U., 1968-71. Contbr. articles to profl. jours. Grantee, NATO, 1972. Mem. European Soc. Pediat. Rsch., Assn. Genetics Italiana. Avocation: gardening. Office: Univ di Roma Tor Vergata Via Ricerca Scientifica 00133 Rome Italy Home Phone: 39-6-30889514; Office Phone: 39-6-72596030. Business E-Mail: bottini@med.uniroma2.it.

BOTTINO, MARCELA, medical researcher; b. Rio de Janeiro, Apr. 17, 1978; MD, Fundacao Tecnico Ednl. Souza Marques, 2001. Neonatal fellow McMaster U., 2006—08. Home: Rua Oscar Valdetaro 94/1401 Rio de Janeiro 22793670 Brazil Personal E-mail: marbottino@gmail.com.

BOTTONE, EDWARD JOSEPH, microbiologist, educator; b. Feb. 18, 1934; BS in Biology, CUNY, 1965; MS, Wagner Coll., 1968; PhD in Microbiology, St. John's U., 1973. Diplomate Am. Bd. Med. Microbiology. Med. technologist 34th Gen. Hosp. U.S. Army, Orleans, France, 1957-59; bacteriology tech. Mt. Sinai Hosp., NYC, 1959-60, assoc. dir. microbiology, 1969—74, dir. microbiology dept., 1975; bacteriology tech. Mt. Vernon (N.Y.) Hosp., 1962; supr. bacteriologist Greenpoint Hosp., Elmhurst Hosp., 1962—69; from assoc. prof. to prof. microbiology, 1975—81; prof. medicine Mt. Sinai Sch. Medicine, NYC, 1994—2008, prof. emeritus in medicine-infectious disease, 2008—. From adj. instr. to prof. med. microbiology/pathology Mt. Sinai Sch. Medicine, N.Y.C., 1970—. Mem. editl. bd. Jour. Clin. Microbiology, 1978-89, Manual Clin. Microbiology, 1990-91. Fellow Am. Acad. Microbiology (Sonnenwirth Meml. award 1996, Profl. Recognition award 2002); mem. Am. Soc. Microbiology (Disting. Achievements in Clin. Microbiology award NYC Br. 1995), AOA (Jacobi medal 1991), Soc. Infectious Diseases, NY Acad. Scis., Jacobi Medallion Mt. Sinai Alumni Assn. Personal E-mail: ebottnoe@optonline.net.

BOTVINICK, ELIAS H., nuclear medicine physician, researcher, medical educator; b. Bklyn., Aug. 11, 1942; s. Jacob Botvinick and Mollie Shabansky; m. Carroll L. Lavine, June 28, 1964; children: Matthew M., Jori L. Botvinick-Gnagy. MD, NYU, NYC, 1967. Diplomate Am. Bd. Nuclear Medicine. Fellow in cardiovasc. diseases U. Calif., San Francisco, 1973—75, resident in nuc. medicine, 1975—77, prof. medicine and radiology cardiovasc. divsn. and sect. nuc. medicine, 1975—, co-dir. adult cardiology noninvasive lab., dir. nuc. cardiology, 1990—. Lectr. in field. Contbr. articles to profl. jours. Maj. MC US Army, 1971—73, Vietnam. Decorated Bronze Star; recipient Established Investigator award, AHA, 1981. Master: Am. Soc Nuc. Cardiology (life; bd. dirs. 1995—98). Independent. Achievements include research in medical imaging. Avocations: painting, reading, swimming, music. Office: U Calif San francisco 500 Parnassus Ave San Francisco CA 94143 Office Phone: 415-353-1905. Office Fax: 415-353-8687. Business E-Mail: botvinicke@medicine.ucsf.edu.

BOUCHER, BRADLEY ALBERT, pharmacist, educator; b. Mpls., Dec. 21, 1955; s. Dwaine Edmund and Betty Jean Boucher; m. Barbara Sue Opitz, Oct. 27, 1979; children: Alexander Albert, Andrew Bradley, Adam Nicholas. BS in Pharmacy, U. of Minn., 1979, PharmD, 1983. Registered pharmacotherapy specialist Bd. of Pharm. Specialties, 1992. Fellow U. Ky., Lexington, 1983—84; prof. of pharmacy U. Tenn., Memphis, 1996—, assoc. prof. neurosurgery, 1997—. Mem. editl. bd.: Am. Jour. Pharm. Edn., 2006—09; contbr. articles to profl. jours., chapters to books. Treas. Houston HS Football Booster Club, Germantown, Tenn., 1999—2008. Recipient Merck award, U. Minn. Coll. Pharmacy, 1979. Fellow: Am. Coll. Clin. Pharmacy (hon.; treas. 1992—97, pres. 2001—02, Svc. award 2004), Am. Coll. Critical Care Medicine (hon.); mem.: Am. Soc. Health-Systems Pharmacists (fellow 1983—84), Soc. Critical Care Medicine, Am. Assn. Colls. of Pharmacy, Soc. Infectious Diseases Pharmacists, Nat. Acad. Practitioners (hon.), The Rho Chi Soc. (hon.; exec. coun. mem. 2011—), Phi Lambda Sigma Leadership Soc. (hon.). Episcopalian. Avocation: golf. Office: University Tenn 881 Madison Ave Rm 345 Memphis TN 38163 Business E-Mail: bboucher@uthsc.edu.

BOUDET, MARIE-JEANNE, surgeon, educator; b. Nogent-le-Rotrou, France, Apr. 1, 1963; d. André and Odette (Pauvert) Boudet. M in Biol. and Med. Scis., Faculty of Medicine Lariboisière, Paris, 1993; degree in specialized studies, Faculty of Medicine St. Antoine, Paris, 1993, MD, 1993; degree in in-depth studies (DEA), Faculty of Medicine Lariboisière-St. Louis, Paris, 1994. Extern Hosps. Tours, France, 1984—87; intern Hosps. Paris, 1987—92; clin. rschr. Louis Mourier Hosp., Colombes, France, 1992—93; clin. chief-asst. Hosps. Paris, Henri Mondor Hosp., Creteil, France, 1993—95; digestive surgeon, medico-surg. Dept. Digestive Pathology IMM, Paris, 1995—2004; digestive surgeon Dept. Surgery Policemen Hosp., Paris, 1998—2001; digestive surgeon Orsay Hosp., 2001—03, Clinique Alleray-Labrouste, Paris, 2001—. Tchr., med. students and nurses various hosps. and univs., 1990—. Contbr. articles and reports to numerous med. jours. and conf. procs. Mem.: Clin. Rsch. in Oncology and Radiotherapy Study Group (adminstrv. com. 1997—2002), French Nat. Soc. Gastroenterology, Internat. Assn. Surgery of Trauma and Surg. Intensive Care, Internat. Soc. Surgery, French Soc. Digestive Surgery (moderator various sessions), Assn. Surgeons of Pub. Assistance for Med. Evaluation, Univ. Assn. Surg. Rsch., Assn. Surg. Rsch. (asst. treas. 1993—2001, tchr. practical seminar clin. rsch. 1988, 1999). Roman Catholic. Avocations: movies, safaris, cooking. Home: 23 Rue Victor Hugo 92130 Issy-les-Moulineaux France Office: Clinic Alleray-Labrouste 64 Rue Labrouste 75015 Paris France Office Phone: 00-33-144-19-51-30, 00-33-144-19-50-00, 00-33-608-97-69-57, 0033145145250. Office Fax: 00-33-144-19-51-88. E-mail: aboutal@free.fr.

BOUDOT, JEAN-PIERRE LOUIS, biologist, researcher; b. Paris, July 31, 1948; s. André Boudot and Denise Verez. PhD, U. Nancy, France, 1982. Jr. rschr. Ctr. Pédologie Biologique CNRS, Vandoeuvre-lès-Nancy, France, 1977-82, sr. rschr., head program, 1982—. Contbr. articles to profl. jours. Office: Univ de Nancy I Fac des Sciences BP70239 7137 Limos UMR 54506 Vandoeuvre-les-Nancy France Fax: 33-3-83-68-42-84. E-mail: jean-pierre.boudot@limos.uhp-nancy.fr.

BOUDOULAS, HARISIOS, cardiologist, researcher, medical educator; b. Velvendo-Kozani, Greece, Nov. 3, 1935; married; 2 children. MD, U. Thessaloniki, Greece, 1959; D (hon.), U. Thessaloniki; numerous hon. Dr. degrees. Resident in internal medicine Red Cross Hosp., Athens, Greece, 1960-61, U. Salonica First Med. Clinic, 1962-66, resident in internal medicine and cardiology, 1962-66, lectr., 1969-70; postgrad. fellow, instr. div. cardiology Ohio State U. Coll. Medicine, Columbus, 1970-73, asst. prof. medicine, 1975-78, assoc. prof., 1978-80, dir. cardiac non-invasive lab., 1978-80, prof. medicine div. cardiology, 1980—2002, prof. pharmacy, 1984—2002, dir. cardiovascular rsch. div., 1983-86, dir. cardiovascular teaching and rsch. lab., 1992—2002; prof. medicine div. cardiology Wayne State U., Detroit, 1980-82, chief clin. cardiovascular rsch., 1980-82; chief cardiovascular diagnostic and tng. center VA Med. Ctr., Allen Park, Mich., 1980-82; chief sect. cardiology Harper-Grace Hosps., Detroit, 1982; hon. prof. U. Thesseloniki; hon. pres. Sci. Coun. Biomech. Car Rsch. Found. Acad. Ajhens, 2009—. Mem. Antepistelon Athens Acad., 1998—; dir. Ctr. for Clin. Rsch., pres. sci. coun. Biomed. Rsch. Found., Acad. Athens, 2002—08, hon. pres., Sci. Coun. Biomed. Rsch. Found. Acad. Affairs, 2009-. Editor in chief Hellenic Jour. Cardiology, 1990-2000; mem. editl. rev. bd. jours. cardiology; contbr. numerous articles to med. jours. Named Disting. Research Investigator, Cen. Ohio chpt. Am. Heart Assn., Columbus, 1983. Fellow ACP, Am. Coll. Cardiology (trustee Ohio chpt. 1993-97), Am. Heart Assn. (coun. clin. cardiology 1989-93, coun. exec. com. 1991-93, sci. com. 1991-93), European Soc. Cardiology (sci. com. 1991-93, valvular heart disease working group 1993—), Greek Heart Assn., Am. Fedn. Clin. Rsch., Laeneck Soc. (chmn. 1991-93), Hellenic Cardiol. Soc. (pres. 2005-07).

BOUDREAUX, GAIL KOZIARA, insurance company executive; B in Psychology with honors, Dartmouth Coll., Hanover, NH; MBA in Fin. and Health Care Adminstrn., Columbia U. Bus. Sch., NYC. Cert. employee benefit specialist. Various positions of increasing responsibility Aetna, Inc., 1982—2002, including regional mgr., capitol region, gen. mgr., Pacific Northwest market, v.p. customer svc., sr. v.p., pres. group ins.; pres. Blue Cross Blue Shield Ill., 2002—05; pres. Ill. divsn. Health Care Svcs. Corp., 2002, exec. v.p. external ops., 2006—08; exec. v.p. UnitedHealth Group, Inc., 2008—, pres. UnitedHealthcare, 2008—11, CEO UnitedHealthcare, 2011—. Ind. dir. Genzyme Corp., 2004—; bd. dirs. Dental Network America, America's Health Ins. Plans. Mem. Chgo. Network, YWCA Pres.'s Adv. Coun. Recipient Silver Anniversary award, NCAA, 2007; named one of The 50 Most Powerful Women in Bus., Fortune mag., 2008—10, The World's 100 Most Powerful Women, Forbes mag., 2009, Top 25 Women in Healthcare, Modern Healthcare mag., 2011; named to Ivy League 25-Yr. Anniversary Basketball Team, 1999, Dartmouth Coll. 25-Yr. Anniversary Basketball and Track & Field Teams, 1999, New Eng. Basketball Hall of Fame, 2003. Office: UnitedHealth Group Inc 9900 Bren Rd East Minnetonka MN 55343 also: UnitedHealth Group Inc PO Box 1459 Minneapolis MN 55440-1459 *

BOUFFORD, JO IVEY, health science association administrator, educator; b. Durham, NC, July 2, 1945; BA in Psychology magna cum laude, U. Mich., 1967, MD with distinction, 1971; DSc (hon.), SUNY, Bklyn., 1992. Diplomate Nat. Bd. Med. Examiners, Am. Bd. Pediats. Resident in social pediats. medicine Montefiore Hosp. and Med. Ctr., Bronx, N.Y., 1971-74, asst. attending physician, 1975-97, co-dir. Inst. for Health Team Devel., 1975-82, dir. residency program in social medicine, 1975-82; adminstrv. dir. Valentine Lane Family Practice, Yonkers, N.Y., 1975-82; v.p. med. ops. N.Y.C. Health and Hosps. Corp., 1982-83, v.p. med. and profl. affairs, 1983-85, exec. v.p., 1985, acting pres., 1985, pres., 1985-89; internat. fellow in comparative health sys. mgmt. King's Fund Coll., London, 1989-91, dir., 1991-93; prin. dep. asst. sec. for health US Dept. Health & Human Services, Washington, 1993-97, acting asst. sec. for health, 1997; dean, Robert F. Wagner Grad. Sch. Pub. Svc. NYU, 1997—2002, clin. prof. peds., 1997—, prof. pub. svc. health policy & mgmt., 2003—; pres. The NY Acad. Medicine, NYC, 2007—. Mem. Nat. Adv. Coun. for Health Professions Edn. US-DHHS, 1976-80; mem. tech. panel on the ednl. environ. Grad. Med. Edn. Nat. Adv. Coun., 1979-80; cons. on manpower programs divsn. medicine bur. Health Professions Edn. HRSA-DHHS, 1980-88; mem. N.Y. State Coun. on Grad. med. Edn., 1987-89, N.Y. State Commn. on Grad. Med. Edn., 1985-86; rep. of U.S. on exec. bd. WHO, 1994-97; U.S. staff dir. Gore-Chernomyrdin Commn. Health Com., 1994-97; various consulting positions. Mem. editl. bd. Jour. Med. Edn., 1980-86; mem. editl. adv. bd. The New Physician, 1979-89; contbr. articles to profl. jours.; presenter in field. Mem. Nat. Adv. Coun. of Agy. for Healthcare Quality and Rsch., 2000—04; bd. dirs. United Hosp. Fund, 1999—; chair sub-bd. on pub. health, Open Soc. Inst., 1998-2004; mem. N.Y. State Coun. on Grad. Med. Edn., 1987-89. Named one of The 100 Most Influential Women in NYC Bus., Crain's NY Bus., 2007. Fellow Am. Acad. Pediats.; mem. APHA, NAS Inst. Med. (coun. mem., fgn. sec.; Robert Wood Johnson health policy fellow 1979-80), Soc. Med. Adminstrs., Med. Adminstrs. Conf. Office: The NY Acad Medicine 1216 Fifth Ave New York NY 10029 Office Phone: 212-822-7201. Business E-Mail: jboufford@nyam.org. E-mail: jo.boufford@nyu.edu.

BOUGAS, JAMES ANDREW, physician, surgeon, educator; b. Bismarck, ND, Jan. 25, 1924; s. Andrew James and Mary (Psaltiras) B.; m. Tiina Parlin, June 27, 1953; children: Karen Louise, Tiina Maria. MD, Harvard U., 1948. Diplomate Am. Bd. Surgery, Am. Bd. Thoracic Surgery. Intern Columbia U. Svc., Bellevue Hosp., NYC,

1948-50, chief resident in surgery, 1952-53; resident Presbyn. Hosp., NYC, 1950-52, chief resident surgery, 1953; fellow Overholt Clinic, Boston, 1953-55, assoc., 1955-65; chief thoracic surgery U. Hosp., Boston, 1965-70; assoc. prof. surgery Boston U. Sch. Medicine, 1965—; dir. cardiopulmonary lab New Eng. Deaconess Hosp., 1955—65. Lectr. Tufts U. Sch. Medicine, Boston, 1965-70; chmn. Gordon Rsch. Confs., 1967-68. Contbr. articles to profl. jours. Pres. Heart Assn., Boston, 1967-69; chmn. Mass. Rehab. Commn. Adv. Com.; trustee Boston Tb Assn.; mem. Cardiac Adv. Group, Regional Med. Programs, NH, Mass., RI, 1969; cons. Numerous Boston & NE Hosp. With U.S. Army, 1942-44. Fellow AAAS; mem. ACS, Am. Coll. Cardiology, Am. Assn. Thoracic Surgeons, Soc. Thoracic Surgeons, Am. Coll. Cardiology, Am. Heart Assn., Mass. Med. Soc. (legis. com., coun.), Norfolk Dist. Med. Soc. (pres. 1989-90, Tri-State regional planning com.). Achievements include development of combined cardiac catheterization; porous metal prostheses fabrication and cardio-pulmonary physiology. Business E-Mail: jbougas@caregroup.harvard.edu.

BOUGHAMOURA, MOHAMED HUSSIN, neurosurgeon, educator; b. Monastir, May 1, 1969; MD, Coll. Medicine, 1999. Asst. prof. neurosurgery King Faisal U. Al-hasa, 2007—, cons. neurosurgery, 2007—. Mem.: Saoudi Assn. Neurol. Surgery. Avocation: football. Home: Sidi Messaoud Habib Thameur Khniss Monastir 5011 Tunisia Personal E-mail: mohamed.boughamoura@yahoo.fr.

BOUILLET, LAURENCE, physician, researcher; b. Grenobl, France, Aug. 28, 1968; MD, Grenoble U., 1999, PhD, 2006. Rsch. scientist JEA Lab.; rschr. Grenoble U. Hosp., 1999—, adj. prof., 2008. Office: Grenoble University Internal Medicine Dept France Grenoble 38043 France Office Fax: 33476765816. Business E-Mail: lbouillet@chu-grenoble.fr.

BOULLERNE, ANNE ISABELLE, medical educator; b. France, Mar. 19, 1966; PhD in Neuroscis., U. Bordeaux, France, 1996. Postdoc. fellow Wayne State U., Mich., 1996—98; instr. U. Chgo., 1998—2004; asst. prof. U. Ill., Chgo., 2005—. Recipient Travel award, Internat. Soc. Neuroimmunology; fellowship, Nat. Multiple Sclerosis Soc., Human Oligodendrocytes fellowship. Mem.: Soc. Neurosci., Internat. Soc. History Neuroscis., Internat. Soc. Neurochemistry, Am. Soc. Neurochemistry. Avocations: history, philosophy. Home: 1746 N Saint Michaels Ct Chicago IL 60614-5616 E-mail: aboulle@uic.edu.

BOULOUGOURIS, VASILEIOS, neuroscientist, researcher, psychologist; b. Athens, Greece, July 19, 1982; BA, Panteion U. Polit. and Social Scis., Athens, Greece, 2004; MPhil, U. Cambridge, 2006, PhD, 2009. Contbr. scientific papers to profl. jours. Recipient award, Pegasus Pub. Co. SA., 2005—06, Greek Ministry of Edn. Award for "Academic Excellence", 1999—2000, Socrates Comenius Student Travel award, Ministry Edn., 1998—99. Mem.: U. Athens Med. Sch. and NY Coll. Achievements include research in animal models of obsessive compulsive disorder and schizophrenia. Office: Eginition Hosp University Athens Med Sch Athens Greece Office Phone: 00302130057029. Personal E-mail: vboulougouris@googlemail.com. Business E-Mail: vasilis@vboulougouris.gr.

BOULTON, MATTHEW LESTER, epidemiologist, educator, physician; b. Indpls., Oct. 4, 1957; s. Kenneth Merlin Boulton and Barbara Ann Reeves; m. Chitra Stokes Stokes, Feb. 25, 2006; children: Ravinath Stokes, Nikhil Stokes; m. Linda Susan Blakey, June 20, 1981 (div. Jan. 12, 2002); children: Kathryn Elizabeth, Sarah Whitney. BS in Zoology, U. Nev., Las Vegas, 1980, BS in Plant Biology, 1980, MD, 1987; MPH in Epidemiology/Internat. Health, U. Mich., Ann Arbor, 1991. Regional med. dir. Livingston, Jackson, and Washtenaw County Health Depts., Ann Arbor, 1995—97; state epidemiologist & dir. bur. epidemiology Mich. Dept. Health, Lansing, 1997—2004, chief med. exec., 1998—2005; assoc. dean,assoc. prof. epidemiology, preventive medicine, and health mgmt. & policy U. Mich. Sch. Pub. Health, Ann Arbor, 2005—; assoc. prof. Internal Medicne/Infectious Disease Divsn., U. Michigan Med. Sch., 2005—11. Editl. bd. mem. Jour. Public Health Mgmt. and Practice, Bioterrorism and Biodefense. Contbr. articles to numerous jours. Bd. sci. counselors US Ctr. Disease Control & Prevention, Nat. Coordinating Ctr. for Infectious Diseases, Atlanta, 2008—09. Recipient Excellence in Tchg. award, U. Mich. Sch. Pub. Health, 2002, Disting. Alumnus of Yr., 2009, Pub. Health Practice, Chinese Govt., 2009, Disting. Svc. award, Mich. Pub. Health Assn., 2005, Romani award, U. Michigan Sch. Public Health, 2011, Outstanding Public Health Practitioner award, Chinese Govt., 2008; named Assn. Prevention Tchg. and Rsch.'s F. Marian Bishop Outstanding Educator Yr., 2005. Fellow: Am. Coll. Preventive Medicine (Outstanding Educator of Yr. 2005); mem.: APHA, Assn. Prevention Tchg. and Rsch., Assn. Tropical Medicine and Hygiene, Am. Med. Assn, Coun. State and Territorial Epidemiologists (exec. bd. 2002—04). Liberal. Methodist. Avocations: classical music, reading, gardening, piano, languages. Office: University Mich 1415 Washington Heights Ann Arbor MI 48109-2029 Office Fax: 734-764-9293.

BOUMA, MENNO JAN, epidemiologist, researcher; b. Willemstad, Curacao, Nov. 3, 1955; arrived in England, 1986; s. Jan Gerlof Bouma and Elisabeth Jantina (Hendrika) Smidt; m. Catherine Mary Lidwill, May 28, 1989; children: Sam, Christopher. BA in Psychology, U. Amsterdam, 1981; MD, U. Groningen, The Netherlands, 1984; MSC in Parasitology, U. London, 1987; PhD in Epidemiology, U. Leiden, The Netherlands, 1995. Trained gen. practitioner. Sr. house officer surgery and obstetrics St. Elisabeth Hosp., Willemstad, Curacao, Netherlands Antilles, 1985—86; sr. house officer tropical medicine Hosp. Tropical Diseases, London, 1988; project mgr. malaria Medecins Sans Frontieres, Pakistan, 1988—91, desk officer rsch. Amsterdam, 1991—92; gen. practitioner Montrose, Grampian Healthbd., Montrose, Scotland, 1992—94; rsch. fellow, lectr. Sch. Hygiene and Tropical Medicine U. London, 1995—2004, hon. sr. lectr. Cons. WHO, World Bank, Dept. for Internat. Devel., India, Pakistan, Nepal, 1996—2001. Grantee, European Union, Pakistan, 1989, Peel Found. and Brit. Coun., 1988, 1989, EPRI and Nat. Oceanic and Atmospheric Adminstrn. (NOAA), 1998, U. Mich. Howard Hughes Med. Inst., 2009—11; grant, U. Mich. & Howard Hughes Med. Inst., 2009—11. Fellow: Royal Soc. Tropical Medicine and Hygiene. Achievements include research in effects of climate change and climate variability (El Niño) on vector borne diseases (e.g. malaria, cholera) and natural disasters and applications for epidemic forecasting. Avocations: travel, natural history. Office: Lodge Puckaun Nenagh Co Tipperary Tipperary Ireland Personal E-mail: menno.bouma@lshtm.ac.uk.

BOUNTIOUKOS, MANOLIS, cardiologist; b. Thessaloniki, Greece, Aug. 17, 1968; s. Athanasios and Theodora Bountioukos; m. Teresa Spinaris, June 28, 1997; children: Vasiliki Bountioukos-Spinaris, Athanasios Bountioukos-Spinaris, Nikolaos Bountioukos-Spinaris, Hector Bountioukos-Spinaris. Diplomate cum laude, Aristotle U., 1993; PhD in Echocardiography, Erasmus U., Rotterdam, Netherlands, 2004. Diplomate Aristoteleio U., Thessaloniki, Greece, 1993. Rural physician Rural Med. Office, Perfecture Kozani, Alonakia, Greece, 1993—94; med. trainee internal medicine Mpodosakeio gen. Hosp., Ptolemaida, 1994—95; med. trainee cardiology George Papanikolaou gen. Hosp., Thessaloniki, 1998—2001; med. trainee emer. medicine Nat. Ctr. Emer. Medicine, 2000—01; cardiologist pvt. practice, Kozani, 2003—, Nat. Co. Elec., 2003—; cons. Psychiat. Clinic Agios Nikolaos, Kozani, 2003—. Lt. Mil. Dr., 1996—97, Military recruitment center, Maurodentri, Greece. Fellow, Erasmus U., Rotterdam, Netherlands, 2001—03, Erasmus Med. Ctr., 2001—. Fellow: European Soc. Cardiology; mem.: Cardiologic Soc. No. Greece, Hellenic Cardiologic Soc. (mem. working group in echocardiography, Sci. Abstract Presentation award, 24th Panhellenic Cardiologic Congress 2003, 1st Sci. award, 25th Panhellenic Cardiologic Congress 2004). Achievements include research in dobutamine stress echocardiography and myocardial tissue Doppler imaging. Home: Plateia Eleutherias 4 Kozani 501 00 Greece Office: Eleutheriou Venizelou 2 Kozani 501 00 Greece Home Fax: 302461040077. Personal E-mail: bountioukos@yahoo.com.

BOUQUOT, JERRY ELMER, dentist, educator; b. St. Paul, Minn., June 23, 1945; BA, St. Olaf Coll., 1967; DDS, U. Minn., 1971, MSD. Asst. prof. U. Minn., Sch. Dentistry, 1974—75; adj. prof. W.Va. U., Sch. Dentistry, 2002—11, prof., chair, 1975—94, U. Tex., Sch. Dentistry, Houston, 2004—; rsch. dir. Maxillofacial Ctr. Edn. & Rsch., 1994—2011. Pres. Eastern Soc. Tchrs. Oral Pathology, 1979—80, Western Soc. Tchrs. Oral Patholgy, 2009—; mem. bd. dirs. Am. Bd. Oral & Maxillofacial Pathology, 1991—99, Am. Cancer Soc., 1991—96; mem. bd. trustees Am. Acad. Oral Medicine, 2008—. Recipient Disting. Alumnus award, U. Minn., Heebink award, W.Va. U., Outstanding Educator award, St. George award, Am. Cancer Soc., President's Svc. award, Am. Acad. Oral Medicine; Postdoc. Mayo Clinic fellowship, Royal Dental Coll. Copenhagen. Fellow: Internat. Coll. Dentists, Am. Coll. Dentists, Academie Dentaire Internat., Am. Acad. Oral & Maxillofacial Pathology; mem.: Omicron Kappa Upsilon Hon. Dental Soc. Achievements include research in oral precancers and jawbone disorders. Avocation: reading. Office: University Tex Health Sci Ctr Dental Br Dept Diagnostic Scis 6516 M Houston TX 77030 Office Fax: 713-500-4416. Business E-Mail: bouquot@aol.com.

BOURGUET, PATRICK, nuclear medicine physician; b. Rennes, France, Apr. 12, 1950; PhD, U. Rennes, 1979, MD, 1985. Head nuc. medicine dpt Regional Cancer Inst. and U. Rennes, 1990—2000, dir. inst., head nuc. medicine dpt, 2000—10; treas. European Assn. Nuc. Medicine, 2006—09, v.p., 2009—10, pres., 2011. Mem.: European Acad. Scis., French Soc. Nuc. Medicine (pres. 1998—2004), Soc. Nuc. Medicine. Avocations: music, golf, travel. Office: rue de Bataille des Flandres-Dunkerque Rennes 35042 France Business E-Mail: p.bourguet@rennes.fnclcc.fr.

BOURKE, ANTHONY THOMAS CONAL, retired medical researcher, microbiologist; b. Blantyre, Malawi, Central Africa, Dec. 1, 1932; BA, Trinity Coll, U. Dublin, 1954, MA, MD, Trinity Coll, U. Dublin, 1962, MB,BCh, BAO, 1956; student, Daughters of Wisdom Sch. (formerly called La Sagesse Convent Sch.), Limbe, Malawi (formerly Nyasaland Protectorate), Central Africa, 1939—41, St. Aidan's Prep. Sch., Grahamstown, Cape Province, Union (now Republic of South Africa), 1942—45, St. Aidan's Coll., 1946, Mount St. Mary's Coll., Spinkhill via Sheffield, Eng., 1947—50; MPH, Johns Hopkins U., 1958; Diploma tropical medicine and hygiene, Conjoint Examing Bd. R.C.P. and R.C.S., London, Eng., 1959; ECFMG, Edn. Coun. Fgn. Med. Grads., 1960; DPH, Yale U., 1961; MSc, U. Liverpool, 1967. Capt. med. corps. U.S. Army Reserve, Washington; capt. med. corps, malaria cons. to surgeon U.S. Army Reserve (active), Thailand, Vietnam; sr. surgeon USPHS Reserve Atlanta, Francophone West Africa, 1969—70; resident in microbiology and immunology Royal Victoria Hosp., Montreal, Quebec, Canada, 1971—73; med. microbiologist microbiology divsn. State Health Lab. Svs., Perth, Western Australia, 1973—74; med. microbiologist State Health Dept., Queensland, Australia, 1974—78; clin. tchr. microbiology dept. microbiology U. Queensland, St. Lucia, Queensland, Australia, 1974—79; sr, med. officer health and med. svs. State Health Dept., Queensland, Australia, 1978—84, epidemiologist divsn. environ. and occupl. health, 1984—88, ret., 1985; rep. health dept. Stds. Assn. Australia Com., 1976—85, 1978—79; ad hoc lectr. Queensland U., Brisbane, Queensland, Australia, 1980—88; deputising mem. Water Quality Coun. Queensland, 1980—88; Commonwealth Quarantine officer dept. health Queensland, 1982—88; mem. Queensland Dept. Health Epidemiological Resource Group, 1982—88; lectr. food-borne and water-borne diseases Sch. Nursing Royal Brisbane Hosp., Queensland, Australia, 1984—88; mem. food tech. course assessment com. Queensland Agr. Coll. (now called Agr. Coll. U. Queensland), Lawes, Australia, 1984—89; mem. working group clin. epidemiology arboviral diseases Nat. Disease Control Program, Commonwealth Dept. Health, Canberra, ACT, Australia, 1986—88; examiner tropical microbiology Royal Coll. Pathologists Australasia, 1986—89; mem. tech. com. disinfection effluents Water Quality Coun. Queensland, 1988; cons. to various authorities Expo 88, Queensland State Govt. Dept. Family Svs., 1988—90; malaria cons. surgeon US Army Vietnam. Mem. Interdepartmental Adv. Com. Food Stds., 1976—88, Queensland Inst. Tech.'s Adv. Com. Health Surveying, 1979—83; chmn. Queensland Salmonella Liaison Com., 1982—88. Contbr. articles and pubs. to various jour. articles. Recipient Combat Med. Badge, Republic of Vietnam Gallantry Cross Unit Citation, Meritorious Unit Commendation, Cert. and Symbol of informal Order of the Bifurcated Needle, recognition for participation in Smallpox Target Zero, World Health Orgn., 1976, Cert. of Appreciation for svc. in Nigerian Relief Action, Internat. Com. of the Red Cross, 1968—69, Freedom from Smallpox badge, World Health Orgn., 1980, cert. of appreciation, served as Epidemiology cons. to Food and Beverage Divsn. of Expo, World Expo 88, 1988. Fellow: Australasian Faculty Pub. Health Medicine, Royal Australasian Coll. Physicians, Royal Coll. Pathologists Australasia, Am. Coll. Preventive Medicine.

BOURLA, DAN HAIM, ophthalmologist; b. Jerusalem, Jan. 19, 1969; MD, Joice and Irving Goldman Med. Sch., 1997. Attending retina specialist Rabin Med. Ctr., 2007—. Rsch. fellowship, Israel Med. Assn. Mem.: Am. Acad. Ophthalmology. Avocations: sports, filmmaking. Home: Hakatlav 265 Beit Arie 71947 Israel Business E-Mail: danb2@clalit.org.il.

BOURNE, FREDERICK JOHN, veterinary medicine educator, researcher; b. Evesham, Eng., Jan. 3, 1937; s. Sydney John and Florence Beatrice (Craven) B.; m. Mary Angela Minter, Sept. 12, 1959; children: Stephen John, Nigel William. B Vet. Medicine, Royal Vet. Coll., London, 1961; PhD, U. Bristol, Eng., 1972. Pvt. practice, Gloucestershire, Eng., 1961-66; lectr. animal husbandry U. Bristol Vet. Sch., 1966-74, reader, 1974-80, prof. vet. medicine, 1980-88, prof. animal health, 1988—, U. Reading, Eng., 1988-97. Dir. rsch. Agrl. and Food Rsch. Coun. Inst. for Animal Health, Compton, Eng., 1988-97, Biotech. and Biol. Scis. Rsch. Coun., 1994-97; chmn. ind. sci. group advising UK govt. in control of bovine tuberculosis, 1998—2007; hon. rsch. fellow Edward Jenner Inst. for Vaccine Rsch., 2001-. Contbr. over 250 articles to sci. jours. Decorated comdr. Brit. Empire. Mem. Royal Coll. Vet. Surgeons, Polis Acad. Scis. (fgn. mem.). Avocations: gardening, fishing, golf, music. Home Phone: 01934-852464. Personal E-mail: john@bourne26.wanadoo.co.uk.

BOURNE, LYLE EUGENE, JR., psychology professor; b. Boston, Apr. 12, 1932; s. Lyle E. and Blanche (White) H. BA, Brown U., 1953. Asst. prof. psychology U. Utah, 1956-61, assoc. prof., 1961-63; vis. assoc. prof. U. Calif., Berkeley, 1961—62, vis. prof., 1968—69; assoc. prof. psychology U. Colo., Boulder, 1963—65, prof., 1965—2001, prof. emeritus, 2002—, dir. Inst. Cognitive Sci., 1979—83, chmn. dept. psychology, 1983—91; clin. prof. psychiatry U. Kans. Med. Ctr., 1967—90. Vis. prof. U. Wis., 1966, U. Mont., 1967, U. Hawaii, 1969; cons. in exptl. psychology, VA, 1965-93. Author: Human Conceptual Behavior, 1966, Psychology of Thinking, 1971, Psychology: Its Principles and Meanings, rev. edits., 1976, 79 82, 85, Cognitive Processes, 1979, rev. edit., 1986, Psychology: A Concise Introduction, 1988, Psychology: Behavior in Context, 1998; acad. editor: Basic Concept Series, Learning-Cognition Series, Scott, Foresman Pub. Co., 1970-76, Charles Merill Co., 1980-84, Advanced Psychological Texts Series, Sage Publications, 1992—; editor Jour. Exptl. Psychology: Human Learning and Memory, 1975-80; cons. editor Jour. Clin. Psychology 1975-97, Jour. Exptl. Psychology: Learning, Memory and Cognition, 1984-92, Memory and Cognition, 1984-89. Recipient Rsch. Scientist award NIHM, 1969-74. Mem.: APA (coun. editors 1975—80, coun. reps. 1976—79, chmn. early awards com. 1978—79, bd. sci. affairs 1978—81, coun. reps. 1986—89, bd. sci. affairs 1989—92, pres. divsn. 3 1992, publ. and commn. bd. 1995—), Coun. Grad. Depts. Psychology (exec. bd. 1985—89), Soc. Gen. Psychology (pres. 2001), Rocky Mountain Psychol. Assn. (pres. 1987—88), Fedn. Behavioral Psychol. and Cognitive Scis. (v.p. 1994—95, pres. 1995—97), Soc. Exptl. Psychologists (chmn. 1987—88), Psychonomic Soc. (governing bd. 1976—81, chmn. 1980—81), Sigma Xi. Home: 783 Nordistal Ct Boulder CO 80304-1088 Home Phone: 303-776-7511; Office Phone: 303-492-4210. Business E-Mail: lyle.bourne@colorado.edu. E-mail: lbourne@psych.colorado.edu.

BOURNE, MICHELLE LYNN, physician assistant; b. Norman, Okla., July 10, 1976; d. Mike L. Trumble and Bobbie L. Ward, m. Brandon Lawson Bourne, May 4, 2002. BS in Biology with honors, East Ctrl. Univ., Ada, Okla., 1999; MS with distinction, Univ. Okla. Health Sci. Ctr., 2001. Cert. PA-C Nat. Commn. on Cert. of Physician Asst., lic. Okla. State Bd., cert. ACLS, BLS. Optician Eyemasters, Norman, 1993—94, Okla. Optical, Ada, 1994—98; orthop. med. asst. Orthop. Jack B. Howard Ctr., Ada, 1998—99, physician asst. Emergency Medicine-Okla. U. Med. Ctr., Oklahoma City, 2001—02, Family Practice Family Health South, Oklahoma City, 2002—03, Urgent Care Am Pm Clinic, Shawnee, Okla., 2003—, Integers Marshall County Family Medicine, Madill, Okla., 2004—. Mem. 7th Ann. Ronald E. McNair Rsch. Conf., Ada, 1998—99, 7th Ann. Ronald E. McNair Summer Rsch. Internship, 1998. Fellow: Fellowship of Christian Physician Asst., Okla. Acad. of Physician Asst., Am. Acad. Physician Asst.; mem.: Christian Med. and Dental Assn., Alpha Chi. Avocations: travel, movies, pets, church. Office: Intergers Marshall County Family Medicine Two Hospital Dr Madill OK 73446

BOURNE, PETER GEOFFREY, physician, educator, writer; b. Oxford, Eng., Aug. 6, 1939; s. Geoffrey Howard and Gwen (Jones) B.; m. Mary Elizabeth King, Nov. 9, 1974. MD, Emory U., 1962; MA in Anthropology, Stanford U., 1969. Fellow dept. psychiatry Med. Sch.; co-dir. Alcoholism Project, Emory U., 1962-63; intern King County Hosp., Seattle, 1963-64; rsch. psychiatrist Walter Reed Army Inst.; rschr. Washington, 1964-67; chief neuropsychiat. br. U.S. Army Med. Research Team, Vietnam, 1965-66; cons. S.E. Asia Health Br. (AID), Dept. State, 1966-67; resident dept. psychiatry, Stanford U. Med. Center, Palo Alto, Calif., 1967-69; dir. mental health unit Southside Comprehensive Health Center, Atlanta, 1969-71; founder, dir. Atlanta S Ctrl. Cmty. Mental Health Ctr., 1970-71; dir. Ga. Office Drug Abuse, 1971-72; spl. adviser for health affairs to Gov. Jimmy Carter of Ga., 1971-73; asst. dir. White House Spl. Action Office for Drug Abuse Prevention, 1972-74; cons. Drug Abuse Coun., Washington, 1974-76; pres. Found. for Internat. Resources, 1975-76; Mid-Atlantic coord., dep. campaign dir. Jimmy Carter Presdl. Campaign, 1975-76; spl. asst. for health issues to U.S. Pres., Washington, 1976-78; mem. U.S. del. to Exec. Coun. UNICEF, 1977; asst. sec. gen. UN, NYC, 1979-81; pres. Global Water, 1981-98; exec. v.p., pub. Devel. Internat., 1986-90; mem. U.S. Pres. Commn. on White House Fellows; head U.S. del. UN Devel. Program Governing Coun., 1978; emergency rm. physician Casualty Hosp., Washington, 1966-67; emergency room physician Kaiser Permanente Hosp., Santa Clara, Calif., 1967-69; psychiat. cons. Santa Clara County Hosp., 1968-69, San Mateo County Hosp., 1969; cons. WHO, Geneva, 1972, UN Divsn. on Narcotic Drugs, 1976; asst. prof. dept. psychiatry Emory U. Med. Sch., 1969-72, asst. prof. dept. preventive medicine and cmty. health, 1969-72; lectr. dept. psychiatry Harvard U. Med. Sch., 1974; v.p. Nat. Coordinating Coun. on Drug Abuse Edn., 1971-72; prof. psychiatry, chmn. dept. St. Georges Med. Sch., Grenada, 1979-98; pres. Peter Bourne Assocs., Washington, 1985-98. Mem. of jury The Lasker Awards, 1978—79; vice chancellor St. Georges U., Grenada, 1998—2001, vice chancellor emeritus, Grenada, 2001—; chmn. Med. Edn. Coop. with Cuba, 2000—; vis. fellow Green Templeton Coll., Oxford U., England, 2001—; bd. dir. Inst. Human Virology, Balt., Nat. Grad. U., Wash., Student Partnerships Worldwide, London. Author: Men, Stress and Viet Nam, 1970; editor: Psychology and Physiology of Stress, 1969, (with R. Fox) Alcoholism: Progress in Research and Treatment, 1973, Addiction, 1974, Acute Drug Abuse Emergencies, 1976, Water Resources: Social and Economic Aspects, 1983, Fidel, A Biography of Fidel Castro, 1986, Jimmy Carter: A Comprehensive Biography from Plains to the Post-Presidency, 1997; mem. editorial bd. Psychiatry, 1968—, Am. Jour. Drug Alcohol Abuse, 1973—; contbr. articles to profl. jours. and chpts. to books. Bd. dirs. Save the Children Fedn., Inst. for So. Studies; chmn. global bd. dirs. Hunger Project; chmn., bd. trustees Council on Hemispheric Affairs, 1986—; chmn. bd. dirs. Am. Assn. World Health, 1982-98, Health and Devel. Internat., 1997—, Youth Advocate Program, 1998—, Med. Edn. Collaboration with Cuba, 1998—, Inst. Caribbean and Internat. Studies, Windward Islands Rsch. and Edn. Found. Served to capt. U.S. Army, 1964-67. Decorated Bronze Star medal, Air medal, Combat Medics badge; recipient William C. Menninger award Central Neuropsychiat. Assn., 1967, Pub. Svc. award Nat. Assn. State Drug Abuse Program Coordinators, 1974, Pub. Svc. award Assn. Chinese Ams., 1978; named one of Five Outstanding Young Men, Atlanta Jaycees, 1971, one of Five Outstanding Young Men in Ga., Ga. Jaycees, 1972. Fellow Am. Psychiat. Assn. (disting. life, chmn. task force on drugs and drug abuse edn. 1969-73); mem. AAAS, Ga. Psychiat. Assn., Washington Psychiat. Soc., Royal Soc. Medicine, Med. Assn. Ga., Soc. for Internat. Health (pres. 1988-92), Am. Med. Soc. on Alcoholism, Am. Anthrop. Assn., World Fedn. for Mental Health. Democrat. Home and Office: 10500 Kings Ln Spotsylvania VA 22553 Business E-Mail: pbourne@igc.org.

BOURNE, ROBERT GEORGE, retired radiation oncologist; b. Brisbane, Australia, Jan. 28, 1932; MBBS, U. Queensland, 1955. Dep. dir. Queensland Radium Inst., 1986—94. Examiner, radiation oncology Royal Coll. Radiologists, 1972; examiner Royal Australian and New Zealand Coll. Radiologists, 1970—85, sr. examiner, radiation oncology, 1985—90, fed. councillor, 1991—94, pres., 1992—93. Avocations: tennis, reading. Home: 41 Violet St Yeronga Queensland 4104 Australia Business E-Mail: rgmrb@optusnet.com.au.

BOUSAMRA, MICHAEL, II, cardiothoracic surgeon; b. Highland Park, Mich., Aug. 12, 1959; married; 3 children. BS in Biochemistry, summa cum laude, U. Mich., Dearborn, 1981; MD, U. Mich., Ann Arbor, 1985. Diplomate Am. Bd. Thoracic Surgery. Intern gen. surgery Med. Coll. Va. Hosp., Richmond, 1985-86, resident gen. surgery, 1986-87, 88-91, cardiovasc. surgery rsch. fellow, 1987-88; resident cardiothoracic vascular surgery Washington U. Med. Ctr./Barnes Jewish Hosp., St. Louis, 1991-93; asst. prof. dept. cardiothoracic surgery Med. Coll. Wis., Milw., 1993—99; assoc. prof. dept. surgery U. Louisville, 1999—, dir. thoracic surgery, James Graham Brown Cancer Ctr., 2005—; pres. (non-profit) Drive Cancer Out, Louisville, 2006—. Attending staff Milw. County Med. Complex, 1993—95, Zablocki Vets. Adminstrn. Med. Ctr., Milw., 1993—99; assoc. attending staff Froedtert Meml. Luth. Hosp., Milw., 1993—99; dir. lung transplant prog. Jewish Hosp., Louisville, 1999—. Mem. editl. bd. Annals of Thoracic Surgery, Jour. Thoracic & Cardiovasc. Surgery; contbr. articles to profl. jours. Office: Univ Cardiothoracic Surgical Assoc 201 Abraham Flexner Way Ste 1200 Louisville KY 40202-3841 Business E-Mail: mbousamra@louisvilleheartsurgery.com. *

BOUSSAOUD, DRISS, neuroscientist, director; b. Morocco, Sept. 1, 1958; BC, U. Mohamed V Rabat, 1980; PhD, U. Claude Bernard Lyon, 1983. Dir. CNRS, 2004—. Pres. Mediterranean Neurosci. Soc., 2009—; founder & coord. French-Morocco Neurosci. Rsch. Consortium, 2008—, Euro-Mediterranean Neurosci. Consortium, 2010—. Fogaty Internat. grant, NIH. Mem.: Soc. Neurosci. Avocation: music. Office: 31 Chemin J Aiguier Marseille Bouches du Rhones 13402 France Office Fax: 04 91 16 89 48. Business E-Mail: driss.boussaoud@gmail.com.

BOUTINAUD, MARION, research scientist; b. Paris, Jan. 26, 1975; Ingenior, PhD, ENSAR U. Rennes 1, 2002. Rsch. scientist class 1 INRA, 2003—. Office: INRA UMRPL Saint Gilles Bretagne 35 590 France Office Fax: 00 33 2 23 48 51 01. Business E-Mail: marion.boutinaud@rennes.inra.fr.

BOUTROS, LINDA NELENE WILEY, retired medical/surgical nurse; b. New Orleans, Aug. 31, 1951; d. Robert Vernon and Marye Dell (Adcock) Wiley; m. Eddy Boutros, Dec. 23, 1972; children: Scott, Mark, Natalie. BS in Nursing, U. S.W. La., 1973. Cert. health care risk mgr. RN, relief charge, charge nurse, med./surgical flr. Bap. Hosp., Beaumont, Tex., 1973—76; RN, coord./supr. of nursing Kelsey Seybold Clinic, Missouri City, Tex., 1982-86; RN, head nurse S.W. Pediatric Ctr., Sugarland, Tex., 1986-87; RN, nursing supr. Westshore Hosp., Tampa, Fla., 1988-89; med.-surg. nurse Centurion Hosp., Carrollwood and Tampa, 1989-90, asst. head nurse med., 1990-91, relief supr., 1991, dir. surg. nursing svcs., 1992-93; nurse mgr. surg. floor, relief house supr. Univ. Cmty. Hosp. Carrollwood, Tampa, Fla., 1993-99, RN adminstrv. supr., 1999—2005, relief supr., 2005—08. Adj. faculty U. So. Fla. Coll. Nursing; clin. instr. for RN nursing students U. Cmty. Hosp. Carrollwood. Personal E-mail: lwboutros@mac.com.

BOUTWELL, ROSWELL KNIGHT, oncology educator; b. Madison, Wis., Nov. 24, 1917; s. Paul Winslow and Clara Gertrude (Brinkhoff) B.; m. Luella Mae Fairchild, Sept. 25, 1943; children—Paul F., Philip H., David K. BS in Chemistry, Beloit Coll., 1939; MS in Biochemistry, U. Wis., 1941, PhD, 1944; DSc, Beloit Coll., 1980. Instr. U. Wis., 1945-49, asst. prof., 1949-54, assoc. prof., 1954-67, prof. oncology med. ctr. Madison, 1967—. Vis. lectr. Inst. for Environ. Medicine, NYU, summer 1966; mem. cancer study group Wis. Regional Med. Program, 1967-70; mem. adv. com. on inst. research grants Am. Cancer Soc., 1967-74, chmn., 1972-74; mem. food protection com. NRC, 1971-75; mem. lung cancer segment Nat. Cancer Inst., 1971-75; mem. adv. com. on pathogenesis of cancer Am. Cancer Soc., 1960-63; mem. Nat. Cancer Adv. Bd., 1983-90; chief research Radiation Effects Research Found., Hiroshima, Japan, 1984-86; prof. emeritus, 1988—. Mem. editorial adv. bd. Cancer Research, 1959-64, assoc. editor, 1973-83; mem. editorial bd. Jpn. J. Cancer Res., 1985—; assoc. editor: Nutrition and Cancer, 1988—; mem. sci. adv. bd. Internat. Coun. for Coordinating Cancer Rsch., 1989-92, Dermigen, 1990—. Mem. Monona Grove Sch. Bd., 1952-54; bd. dirs. Madison Gen. Hosp. Found. Recipient Kenneth P. DuBois award Soc. Toxicology, 1998, medal of honor Am. Cancer Soc., 1998. Fellow AAAS, Am. Assn. Cancer Research (dir.), Am. Soc. Biol. Chemists (Clowes award). Office: U Wis Dept Oncology McArdle Lab 1400 University Ave Rm 1125 Madison WI 53706-1526 Office Phone: 608-262-5182. E-mail: rboutwell@msn.com.

BOVÉ, JEAN-CLAUDE GÉRARD, orthopedist; b. Versailles, France, Jan. 22, 1956; s. Raffaele and Maria Bové; m. Huguette Vermersch, Oct. 23, 1981 (div. Apr. 15, 1995); m. Odile Dutilleul, Sept. 23, 1995; children: Aurélie, Guillaume, Cécile, Marie. Grad., Lycée Albert Schweitzer, Mulhouse, 1973; MD, Strasbourg, France, 1986. Pvt. practice Clinique du Parc, Maubeuge, France, 1988—2001, Clinique du Val de Sambre, Maubeuge, 2001—. Contbr. to sci. publs. Capt. Svc. Santé Armées, 2004—08, Arras. Mem.: SOFCOT. Achievements include invention of orthopaedic implant. Home: 20 Rue l'Ermitage Maubeuge 59600 France Office: Clinique du Val Sambre 162 Rt Mons Maubeuge 59600 France Personal E-mail: bovejc@wanadoo.fr.

BOVILL, EDWIN GLADSTONE, pathologist, educator; b. Detroit; MD, U. Calif. San Francisco, 1972. Prof., pathology U. Vt. Coll. Medicine, 1982—, chmn., dept. pathology, 1993—. Fellow: Acad. Clin. Lab. Physicians and Scientists, Coll. Am. Pathologists; mem.: Internat. Soc. Haemostasis and Thrombosis, Am. Soc. Hematology, Am. Soc. Clin. Pathology, Alpha Omega Alpha. Avocations: skiing, sailing, board games. Office: 89 Beaumont Dr Burlington VT 05405 Office Fax: 802-656-8892. Business E-Mail: edwin.bovill@uvm.edu.

BOVORNKITTI, SOMCHAI, internist; b. Chantaburi, Thailand, Feb. 26, 1929; s. Kij Ng and Tonglao (Watanawongse) B.; m. Pratarnporn Chiamvichit (div.); m. Supanee Chanklad (div.); 1 child, Morakot; m. Vilawan Nantabhiwat, (div.); 1 child; Ubol Saensook; 2 children. B.Med., U. Med. Scis., Bangkok, 1952, MD, 1963. Lic. physician, Thailand. House officer Ormskirk County Hosp., England, 1953; chest resident Bellevue Hosp., NYC, 1955-56; lectr. U. Med. Scis., Bangkok, 1956-71; asst. prof. Mahidol U., Bangkok, 1971-75, assoc. prof., 1975-76, prof. medicine, 1976—90; chief chest svc. Siriraj Hosp., Bangkok, 1983-90. External examiner for diploma in tuberculosis and chest diseases Postgrad. Inst. of Medicine, U. Colombo, Sri Lanka, 1994. Editor-in-chief: Jour. Med. Assn. Thailand, 1968—72, editor in chief: Siriraj Hosp. Gaz, 1969—71, editor-in-chief: Asian Pacific Jour. Allergy and Immunology, 1983—85, Jour. Environ. Medicine, 1998—2000, Internal Medicine Jour. Thailand, 2000—, Jour. Royal Inst. Thailand, 2002—06, Jour. Traditional Thai and Alternative Medicine, 2007—, Jour. Health Sys. Rsch., 2007—11; editor: 30 textbooks in Chest and Environmental Medicine, 1954—2011; contbr., chapters to books, 1300 articles to med. jours. Advisor to minister Ministry of U. Affairs of Thailand, Bangkok, 1985-86; chmn. expert com. on non-communicable lung disease Ministry of Pub. Health, Bangkok, 1995. Decorated Knight Grand Cordon of the Most Noble Order of the Crown of Thailand, His Majesty the King of Thailand, 1986, of the Most Exalted Order of the White Elephant, 1990; recipient Albert Einstein Medal for Peace 3d class Albert Einstein Internat. Acad. Found., 1990. Fellow ACP (hon.), Royal Coll. Physicians London, Royal Inst. Thailand, Royal Australasian Coll. Physicians; mem. Edinburgh Chest Physicians and Surgeons (pres. Thailand chpt. 1983-84). Home: 5/159 Karuchard Tayat Pakkred Nontaburi 11120 Thailand Office: Royal Inst Sanam Suepa Bangkok 10300 Thailand Office Phone: 02 356 0470. Personal E-mail: s_bovornkitti@hotmail.com.

BOWDLER, ANTHONY JOHN, internist, anatomist, hematologist, educator; b. London, Oct. 16, 1928; came to U.S., 1967; s. Edward Thomas and Clara (Anthony) B.; m. Eleanor Madeleine Sladen, July 30, 1955; children: Noelle Clare, Jonathan Francis. BSc, U. Coll., London, 1949, MB, BS with honors, 1952, MD (Bilton Pollard fellow), 1962, PhD, 1967; postgrad. (Buswell Sr. fellow), U. Rochester, 1962-64. Intern Univ. Coll. Hosp., London, 1952, casualty med. officer, 1956, registrar and rsch. fellow, 1958-62; intern Dorking Hosp., Surrey, England, 1957, Hammersmith Hosp., London, 1953, Brompton Hosp., London, 1956; sr. instr. U. Rochester, NY, 1962-64; sr. lectr. U. Coll. Hosp. Med. Sch., London, 1964-67; assoc. prof. medicine Mich. State U. Coll. Human Medicine, East Lansing, 1967-70, prof. medicine, 1971-80, Marshall U. Sch. Medicine, Huntington, W.Va., 1980-97, prof. medicine emeritus, 1997—. Hon. cons. Univ. Coll. Hosp., London, 1967. Served as surgeon lt. Royal Navy, 1953-55. Fellow ACP, Royal Coll. Physicians, Royal Coll. Pathologists; mem. AMA, Am. Fedn. Clin. Rsch., Ctrl. Soc. Clin. Rsch. (emeritus), Am. Soc. Hematology (emeritus), Am. Soc. Clin. Oncology (emeritus), Brit. Med. Assn. (life). Researcher in internal medicine. Home: 4609 Sawgrass Dr E Ann Arbor MI 48108-8644

BOWEN, DAVID, legislative staff member; b. Summit, NJ; BS, Brown U., Providence, 1986; PhD, U. Calif., San Francisco, 1995. Postdoctoral appointment Regeneron Pharm.; sr. staff scientist, startup biotech. co; staff. mem. to Senator Edward Kennedy US Senate, Washington, 1999—2002; minority dep. staff. dir. US Senate Health, Edn., Labor & Pensions Com., 2002—05, minority staff dir., 2005—06, staff. dir., 2006—. Congl. fellow, AAAS, 1999, Vis. fellow, Harvard Med. Sch. Dept. Health Care Policy, 2000—02. Office: US Senate Health Edn Labor & Pensions Com 428 Dirksen Senate Office Bldg Washington DC 20515 Office Phone: 202-224-5375. Office Fax: 202-228-5044.

BOWEN, GLEN M., dermatologist, educator, oncologist; MD, U. Utah, 1990. Diplomate Am. Bd. Dermatology, 2005. Resident dermatology Univ. Mich. Med. Ctr., Ann Arbor, Mich., 1991—93, fellow immunological dermatology, 1993—95; fellow mohs surgery Univ. UT, Salt Lake City, 2000—01, assoc. prof. dermatology dept., hosp. affiliation includes, Intermountain Medical Center; co-dir. Multidisciplinary Melanoma Clinic Huntsman Cancer Inst.; dir. Melanoma Patient Care Svcs. Office: Huntsman Cancer Institute 2000 Circle of Hope Salt Lake City UT 84112 Office Phone: 801-585-0100.

BOWEN, JOHN METCALF, pharmacologist, toxicologist, educator; b. Quincy, Mass., Mar. 23, 1933; s. Loy J. and Marjorie (Metcalf) B.; m. Jean Alma Schmidt, Dec. 26, 1956; children: Mark John, Richard Kelley. DVM, U. Ga., 1957; PhD, Cornell U., 1960. Asst., then assoc. prof. Kans. State U., Manhattan, 1960-63; assoc., then prof. U. Ga., Athens, 1963-98, assoc. dean, dir. veterinary med. expt. sta., 1976-98. Cons. vet. medicine, 1998—. Mem. Am. Vet. Med. Assn., Soc. Neuroscis., Soc. for In Vitro Biology. Office: U Ga Coll Vet Medicine Athens GA 30602-7371

BOWEN, PATRICIA LEDERER, dental educator; b. Evanston, Ill., July 5, 1943; d. John Arthur and Edna Virginia Lederer; m. Clarence Henry Metzner, Jr., June 1, 1963 (div. Feb. 1972); children: Alan Reighard, Donald Fredrick Metzner, John Henry Metzner; m. Steven Casto Bowen, Mar. 31, 1973. Dental Hygienist, U. Louisville, Ky., 1972; B in Health Edn., U. Ky., Ft. Knox, 1982; MPA, We. Ky. U., Bowling Green, 1985. Pvt. practice dental hygienist, various locations, 1972-75; pub. health dental hygienist U.S. Army, Berlin, 1975-78; cmty. health dental hygienist U.S. Army Dental Activity, Ft. Knox, Ky., 1978-95, U.S. Army Health Svcs. Command, Ft. Knox, Ky., 1981-95; pub. health dental hygienist Meade County (Ky.) Sch. Sys., 1995-96, LaRue County (Ky.) Sch. Sys., 1995-96; instr. pub. dental health Elizabethtown (Ky.) C.C., 1996-97; asst. dir. Meade County Tourism, 1996-97, dir., 1997—2004. Reporter Meade County Messenger, 1998, news editor, 1999—2003; lectr. in field. Contbr. articles to profl. jours. Pub. health dental hygienist Lebanon Sch. Sys., Ohio, 1974—75; pub. health dental program presenter Grand Junction, Colo., 1973—74; CPR instr./instr.-trainer Am. Heart Assn., Ft. Knox, 1985—98, ARC, Ft. Knox, 1978—87; vol. libr. and literacy West Point Ind. Sch., 2004—; PR, edn. chmn. Pets In Need Soc., 2005—, bd. dirs., 2005—07, sec., 2009—10; instr. AARP Safe Driver, 2009—. Decorated Order of Mil. Med. Merit U.S. Army Health Svcs. Command; recipient Patriotic Civilian Svc. award, Dept. of Army, 1986, award for Excellence, Delta Dental Ins. Co., 1991, 1994. Mem.: Al-Anon GR (group rep. 2006—, dist. treas. 2008—), Ky. Oral Health Consortium (exec. sec.-treas. 1991—96, chair 1995—96), Ky. Dental Hygiene Assn. (chair pub. health dental hygiene 1980—84), Louisville Dental Hygiene Assn. (chair legislation 1982), Am. Assn. Pub. Health Dentistry, Am. Dental Hygiene Assn. (pub. health cons. Ky. 1979—80), Meade County C. of C. (dir. 1998, Vol. of the Yr. 1998), Assn. U.S. Army (v.p. publicity 1994—2004). Avocations: photography, travel, snorkeling, hiking, reading. Home: 67 Greenbriar Ct Brandenburg KY 40108 E-mail: pbowen@bbtel.com.

BOWEN, ROBERT E., surgeon; b. Boone, Iowa, May 6, 1952; BS, U. Ill., 1974, MD, 1978. Owner Robert Bowen M.D. Ltd., 1984—; dir. Ctr. Positive Aging, 2004—. Clin. assoc. medicine W.Va. U., 1982—. Named Best Cosmetic Surgeon, Jour. Newspaper. Fellow: Am. Acad. Anti Aging Medicine, Am. Soc. Laser Medicine & Surgery, Am. Coll. Chest Physicians; mem.: Am. Cosmetic Cellular Medicine Assn., Am. Acad. Cosmetic Surgeons. Office: 2000 Found Way 2400 Martinsburg WV 25401 Office Fax: 304-264-9082. Business E-Mail: rbowen3710@msn.com.

BOWEN, WILLIAM HENRY, dental researcher, educator; b. Enniscorthy, Ireland, Dec. 11, 1933; came to U.S., 1956, naturalized; s. William H. and Pauline (McGrath) B.; m. Carole Barnes, Aug. 9, 1958 children: William, Deirdre, Kevin, David, Katherine BDS, Nat. U. Ireland, Dublin, 1955; MSc, U. Rochester, NYC, 1959; PhD, U. London, 1965; DSc, U. Ireland, Dublin, 1974; D Odontologiae (hon.), U. Goteborg, Sweden, 1995, U. Oslo, Norway, 1991; D Odontologiae (honoris causa), U. Umeå, Sweden, 1993; MD (honoris causa), Nat. U. Irleland, 1995, Trinity Coll., Dublin, 1999. Diplomate Am. Bd. Dentistry, Inst. Medicine-NAS. Assoc. pvt. dental practice private dental practice, London, 1955-56; Quinten Hogg fellow Royal Coll. Surgeons, London, 1956-59, Nuffield Found. fellow, 1962-65, sr. research fellow, 1965-69, Sir Wilfred Fish fellow, 1969-73; acting chief caries prevention br. Nat. Inst. Dental Research, NIH, Bethesda, Md., 1973-79, chief, 1979-82; chmn. dental research U. Rochester, N.Y., 1982-95. Dir. Cariology Ctr., Rochester, 1984-95. Fellow AAAS (sect. R-Dentistry, chair elect 1989, chair 1990); mem. ADA (Gold medal 2000), European Orgn. Caries Rsch., Internat. Assn. Dental Rsch. (treas. 1982-88, v.p. 1988, pres. elect 1989, pres. 1990), Fedn. Dentaire Internationale, Inst. Medicine, Lab. Animal Sci. Assn., Zool. Soc. Roman Catholic. Home: 315 County Road 9 Victor NY 14564-9710 Office: U Rochester Ctr for Oral Biology 601 Elmwood Ave Rochester NY 14642-0001 Office Phone: 585-275-0772.

BOWER, ROGER HARRISON, endocrinologist, director; b. Rosebud, Mont., June 7, 1942; s. Paul Edgar and Elizabeth Dorothea Bower; m. Rose Ann Grady, Apr. 20, 1963; children: Jeffrey Harrison, Susan Elizabeth Cellini. BS, U. Nebr., Lincoln, 1966; MS, U. Nebr., Omaha, 1968, MD with high distinction, 1970. Cert. Am. Bd. Internal Medicine, 1974, endocrinology and metabolism Am. Bd. Internal Medicine, 1975, fellow Am. Coll. Physicians, 1978. Med. group comdr. 43rd Med. Group, Malmstrom AFB, Mont., 314th Med. Group, Little Rock AFB, Ark., 1993—95, 6th Med. Group, MacDill AFB, Fla., 1995—97, 77th Med. Group, McClellan AFB, Calif., 1997—99; dep. command surgeon USAF Air Materiel Command, Wright Patterson, Ohio, 1999—2001; chief med. officer Vets. Adminstrn. Med. Clinic, Daytona Beach, Fla., 2001—. Contbr. articles to profl. med. jours. Bd. mem. local chpt. ARC, Great Falls, Mont.; chmn. leadership com. Combined Fed. Campaign, Daytona Beach, 2003—06. Col. USAF, 1969—2001. Decorated Legion of Merit USAF, 6 Meritorious Svc. awards; recipient Pfizer Prize, U. Nebr., 1967, Lange award, 1967. Mem.: DAV (life), Am. Legion, Air Force Assn., Mil. Officers Assn., Assn. Mil. Surgeons U.S., Am. Coll. Physician Execs. Independent. Roman Catholic. Achievements include discovery and synthesis of four novel amino acids. Avocations: running, exercise, reading, travel. Office: Vets Administration Outpatient Clini 551 Nat Health Care Dr Daytona Beach FL 32114 Office Phone: 386-323-7541. Office Fax: 386-323-7570. Business E-Mail: roger.bower@va.gov.

BOWERFIND, EDGAR SIHLER, JR., retired medical association administrator, internist, educator; b. Cleve., May 7, 1924; s. Edgar Sihler and Edna (Strong) B.; m. Maria Washington Tucker, Apr. 28, 1956; children— Edgar Sihler III, Ellis Tucker, Jane Strong, William Minor Lile Student, Creighton U. Med. Sch., 1945-47; MD, Western Res. U., 1949. Diplomate Am. Bd. Internal Medicine. Intern Univ. Hosps. of Cleve., 1950-51, resident in medicine, 1954-56; practice medicine specializing in internal medicine Cleve., 1957-92; mem. faculty Case Western Res. U. Sch. Medicine, Cleve., 1956-92, asst. prof. medicine, 1965-92, dir. health clinics, utilization rev., 1965-92, asst. prof. emeritus, 1992—; chief med. services Horizon Ctr. Hosp., Cleve., 1981-83. Sec. Citizens Commn. on Grad. Med. Edn., 1964-66 Sub-deacon Episcopal Diocese Ohio, 1970-2008; trustee The Sihler Mental Health Found. Served with AUS, 1943-46, to capt. USAF, 1951-53. Decorated Bronze Star; Ogelbay fellow in medicine U. Hosps. Cleve., 1955-56 Home: Ste 806 2181 Ambleside Dr Cleveland OH 44106

BOWERS, RONALD E., critical care specialist; MD, U. Va., 1972. Diplomate Am. Bd. Internal Medicine, 1976, Am. Bd. Internal Medicine- pulmonary disease, 1978, Am. Bd. Internal Medicine-critical care medicine, 2005. Resident in internal medicine Vand Univ. Med. Ctr., Nashville, Tex., 1973—75, fellow in pulmonary critical care medicine, 1975—78; critical care specialist Morton Plant Hosp., Largo Med. Ctr., Fla. Office: Largo Medical Center 1301 2nd Ave SW Largo FL 33770 Office Phone: 727-581-8767. Office Fax: 727-581-2739.

BOWLER, JOHN V., neurologist; b. Durham, England, Mar. 22, 1959; BS, U. London, 1981, MB BS, 1984, MD, 1993. Ho. officer St. Helier Hosp., Carshalton, England, 1984—85; lectr. neurology Imperial Coll., London, 1995—98; cons. neurologist Royal Free Hosp., 1998—; ho. officer St.Thomas Hosp., 1985—85, sr. ho. officer intensive therapy, 1985—86; sr. ho. officer neurology Hammersmith Hosp., 1986—86; sr. ho. officer cardiology Nat. Heart Hosp., 1986—87; registrar Queen Mary's Hosp., Sidcup, 1987—87; registrar neurology Atkinson Morleys Hosp., London, 1987—88, Charing Cross Hosp., 1991—92. Editor: Vascular Cognitive Impairment - Preventable Dementia; contbr. articles to profl. jours. Fellow, Charing Cross Hosp., London, 1988—90, U. Western Ont., London, 1992—95, Stroke Coun., Am. Stroke Assn., Dallas, 2004. Fellow: Royal Coll. Physicians; mem.: Internat. Soc. Vascular Behavioural and Cognitive Disorders (founder), Am. Acad. Neurology (assoc.), Assn. Brit. Neurologists. Office: Royal Free Hospital Dept of Neurology Royal Free Hospital Pond Street NW3 2QG London England Office Fax: +44 (020) 74726829. Personal E-mail: j.v.bowler@blueyonder.co.uk. E-mail: j.bowler@ucl.ac.uk.

BOWLER, MICHAEL DERMOT, oral and maxillofacial surgeon; b. Palmerston North, New Zealand, Feb. 7, 1954; arrived in Australia, 1983, permanent resident, 1983; m. Libby Struck, Jan. 4, 1986; children; Emily, Katherine. DDS, Otago U., New Zealand, 1976. Pvt. practice, 1983—; sr. VMO oral & maxillofacial surgeon VMO Hunter New Eng. Area Health Svc., 1983—. Lt. col. Royal Australian Army Reserve. Recipient Travelling scholarship, Otago U., New Zealand. Fellow: Royal Coll. Surgeons Edinburgh & Ireland; mem.: ADA, RACDS, ASTMJS, IAOMS, AAOMS, BAOMS, ANZAOMS. Conservative. Roman Catholic. Avocations: gardening, photography, travel. Office: 9 Canberra St Charlestown 2290 Newcastle NSW Australia Office Phone: 61 2 4942 1211. Office Fax: 61 2 4942 3560. Personal E-mail: mdb@bowleroms.com.au.

BOWMAN, C. MICHAEL, physician; married; two children. BS in Chemistry with honors, U. Ill., 1968; PhD in Genetics, U. Wis., 1972, MD, 1975. Diplomate Am. Bd. Pediatrics, Am. Bd. Pediatric Pulmonology. Pediat. resident Vanderbilt U., 1975-78, chief resident, 1978-79; dir. comprehensive cystic fibrosis ctr. Med. U. S.C.; divsn. head Divsn. Pediat. Pulmonolgy; prof. pediats. Med. U. S.C., Charleston, 2000—. Fellow Am. Acad. of Pediat., mem. Am. Bd. of Pediat., Am. Thoracic Soc. Achievements include research in lung disorders in children. Office: Med U S C Ste 281 MSC 561 135 Rutledge Ave Charleston SC 29425-5610 Office Phone: 843-876 1555. Office Fax: 843-876-1583. Business E-Mail: bowmanm@musc.edu.

BOWMAN, JAMES EDWARD, pathologist, educator, b. Washington, Feb. 5, 1923; s. James Edward and Dorothy (Peterson) B.; m. Barbara Taylor, June 17, 1950, 1 child, Valerie June. BS, Howard U., 1943, MD, 1946. Intern Freedmen's Hosp., Washington, 1946-47, resident pathology St. Lukes Hosp., Chgo., 1947-50; chmn. dept. pathology Provident Hosp., 1950-53, Shiraz (Iran) Med. Ctr. Nemazee Hosp., 1955-61; vis. prof., chmn. dept. pathology faculty of medicine U. Shiraz, 1959-61; dir. labs. U. Chgo., 1971-80, prof. dept. pathology, medicine, com. on genetics, biol. scis., collegiate div., 1972-93, dir., 1973-93, prof. emeritus, 1993—. Cons. pathology, div. hosp. and med. facilities HEW, USPHS, 1968; mem. Health and Hosps. Governing Commn., Cook County, 1969-72; mem. exec. com. hemalytic anemia study group NHLI, NIH, Bethesda, Md., 1973-75, Sabbatical fellow Ctr. for Advanced Study in Behavioral Scis., Stanford U., 1981-82, Ethical, Legal & Social Issues, Nat. Human Genome Program NIH/DOE. Contbr. to books and articles to profl. jours. Capt. M.C., AUS, 1953-55. Spl. rsch. fellow NIH Galton Lab., Univ. Coll., London, 1961-62. Mem. Coll. Am. Pathologists, Am. Soc. Clin. Pathologists, Am. Soc. Human Genetics, Cen. Soc. Clin. Rsch., Am. Soc. Hematology, Am. Assn. Phys. Anthropologists, Acad. Clin. Lab. Physicians and Scientists. Home: 4929 S Greenwood Ave Chicago IL 60615-2815 Office: U Chgo Dept Pathology 5841 S Maryland Ave Chicago IL 60637-1463 Business E-Mail: jbowman@uchicago.edu.

BOWMAN, JEFFREY NEIL, podiatrist; b. Detroit, Apr. 25, 1957; s. Harry and Helen (London) B.; m. Carol Jane Bartlett, Apr. 12, 1986; 1 child, Dana. BS in Biology/Zoology, U. Mich., 1979; DPM, Ill. Coll. Podiatric Medicine, Chgo., 1983. Diplomate Am. Coun. Cert. Podiatric Physicians and Surgeons, Am. Acad. Pain Mgmt., Am. Bd. Podiatric Orthopedics. Resident Harris County Podiatric Surg. Found., Houston, 1983-84; physician Houston Foot Specialists, 1983-86, pres., CEO, 1986—. Bd. dirs. West Houston Surgicare, 1994—, dept. chmn. surgery, 1995—; mem. residency selection com. Houston Podiatric Residency Found., 1990—. Mem. adv. bd. KTRH Radio Sta., Houston, 1994—; physician Houston Marathon, 1984—; health care advisor Houston Ind. Sch. Dist., 1992-94. Recipient Cert. of Excellence, Disting. Physicians Am., 1994—. Fellow Internat. Soc. Podiatric Laser Surgery, Acad. Ambulatory Foot Surgery; mem. Am. Podiatric Med. Assn., Tex. Podiatric Med. Assn. (bd. dirs. 2001—), Harris county Podiatric Med. Assn. Republican. Jewish. Avocations: reading, golf, computers, investments. Office: 8945 Long Point Rd Ste 209 Houston TX 77055-3009 Home Phone: 713-666-9913; Office Phone: 713-467-8886. Personal E-mail: drbowman@swbell.net.

BOWMAN, MARJORIE ANN, physician, educator; b. Grove City, Pa., Aug. 18, 1953; d. Ross David and Freda Louise (Smith) Williamson; m. Robert Choplin. BS, Pa. State U., 1974; MD, Jefferson Med. Coll., 1976; MPA, U. So. Calif., LA, 1983. Intern, then resident in family practice Duke U., Durham, NC, 1976-79; med. officer USPHS, Hyattsville, Md., 1979-82; clin. instr. uniformed svcs. U. Health Scis., Bethesda, Md., 1980-83; dir. family practice residency, prof. Georgetown U. Sch. Medicine, Washington, 1983-86; chmn. dept. family practice, prof. Wake Forest U., Winston-Salem, NC, 1986—96; prof., chmn. dept. family medicine & cmty. health, dir. Ctr. Pub. Health Initiatives U. Pa., Phila, 1996—. Author: (Book) Stress and Women Physicians, 1985, 1990, Women in Medicine: Life and Career, 2002; editor: Archives Family Medicine, 1992—2000, Jour. Women's Health, 2001—05, Jour. Am. Bd. Family Medicine, 2003—; contbr. articles to profl. jours. Fellow Am. Acad. Family Physicians; mem. AMA, Soc. Tchrs. Family Medicine (bd. dirs. 1984-88, bd. dirs. Found. 1984-99, v.p. 1988-91, pres. 1991-92), Am. Pub. Health Assn. Republican. Unitarian Universalist. Office: Univ Pa 2 Gates 3400 Spruce St Philadelphia PA 19104-4283 Business E-Mail: bowmanm@uphs.upenn.edu.

BOWMAN, NED DAVID, medical administrator; b. Chattanooga, July 15, 1948; s. Ned Turner and Ernie June (White) B.; m. Linda Carol Eggers, Sep. 18, 1970; children: Robert, Jean, Elizabeth, Scott, Benjamin. BS, U. Tenn., 1971; MBA, Vanderbilt U., 1982. Adminstr. Oak Ridge Ortho. Ctr., Tenn., 1971—90; pres., CEO Ancillary Physicians Svcs., Inc., 1976—85; adminstr. Charlotte Eye, Ear, Nose and Throat Assn., NC, 1991—96; chief adminstrv. officer Bond Clinic, Winter Haven, Fla., 1996—99; CEO Image Care Radiology, LLC, 1999—2007; pres. Radiology Assembly Med. Group Mgmt. Assn., 2006; COO & adminstr. Legacy Heart Ctr., Plano, Tex., 2007—, COO, 2007—. Pres. Anderson County Health Coun., Clinton, Tenn., 1980-81, 94, 88; v.p. Knoxville Soc. for Advancement of Mgmt., Knoxville, 1974; bd. dirs. Tng. and Tech. Ctr., Oak Ridge, 1976-78; pres., CEO Ctrl. Fla. Physician's Network, Inc., 1998—; founding pres. Polk County Health Improvement Coun., 1997-99. Bd. dirs. C. of C., Oak Ridge, 1972-76, Boys Club Am., Oak Ridge, 1982-86, DRI, Knoxville, 1982, Great Smoky Mtn. coun. Boy Scouts Am., Knoxville, 1984-86, Piedmont Health Care Preferred Provider Orgn., 1992-94, Citrus Boys Club, Winter Haven, Fla., 1996—, Boys and Girls Club, Winter Haven, Fla., 1997-99; mem. gov. bd. dirs. Am. Soc. Ophth. Adminstrs., 1995-98; treas. UN com., Oak Ridge, 1980-86; trustee health plan Mechlenburg County Med. Soc., 1992-96; exec. bd. Indian Waters coun. Boy Scouts Am., 2002-03, Columbia. Recipient Certs. of Appreciation Vocat. Edn. Dept., Oak Ridge H.S., 1978, Anderson County Health Coun., Oak Ridge, 1980, Soc. for Advancement of Mgmt., Knoxville, 1976, Oak Ridge Human Resource Bd., 1975, Rotary Found. Dist. Svc. award. Mem. Am. Coll. Healthcare Execs., Am. Soc. Ophthalmic Adminstrs. (Outstanding Contbn. award 1995-97), Am. Coll. Med. Practice Execs., Med. Group Mgmt. Assn. (pres. Radiology Assembly 2006), Tenn. Med. Group Mgmt. Assn., Radiology Bus. Mgrs. Assn., Rotary Internat. (Paul Harris fellow), Winter Haven C. of C. (bd. dirs. 1998), Colin County Tex. Healthcare Com. Avocations: river rafting, hiking, travel.

BOWYER, SUZANNE LOUISE, pediatrician, educator; b. Toledo, Dec. 8, 1954; MD, U. Mich., 1979. Cert. Am. Bd. Pediat. Intern U. Mich., Ann Arbor, 1979-80, resident, 1980-82; fellow in pediatric rheumatology Nat. Jewish Hosp., Denver, 1982—84; pediatrician James Whitcomb Riley Hosp., Indpls.; assoc. prof. ped-rheumatology Ind. U. Med. Ctr. Fellow Nat. Jewish Hosp., Denver, 1982-84. Mem. Am. Assn. Physicians, Am. Acad. Allergy & Immunology, Am. Rheumatism Assn. Office: Ind U 702 Barnhill Dr Rm 5865 Indianapolis IN 46202-5128 Office Phone: 317-274-2172. Office Fax: 317-278-3031. Business E-Mail: sbowyer@iupui.edu.

BOYER, LAURENCE ALAN, physician, research educator; b. Denver, May 17, 1940; s. Sam G. and Tillie (Belstock) B.; m. M. Grace Jordison, Aug. 23, 1969; 1 child, David. BA, U. Colo., 1961; MD, Stanford U., 1966. Intern, resident pediatrics Yale U., New Haven, 1966-68, resident pediatrics Stanford Hosp., Palo Alto, Calif., 1968-69; fellow hematology Children's Hosp., Harvard U., Boston, 1972-74; instr. pediatrics Harvard Med. Sch., Boston, 1973-75; asst. prof. to prof. Ind. U. Sch. Medicine, Indpls., 1975-82; prof., dir. pediatric hematology/oncology U. Mich., Ann Arbor, 1982—, assoc. chair pediat., 1996—. Mem. study sect. NIH, Bethesda, Md., 1981—, cons. Amgen, Thousand Oak, Calif., 1988-2005, Genzyme; established investigator Am. Heart Assn., Dallas, 1978-83; internat. adv. bd. U. Malaysia, Sarawak. Assoc. editor Blood, 1993-98, Jour. Clin. Investigation, 1997-2002; contbr. articles to profl. jours, chpts. to books. Maj. U.S. Army, 1969-72. NIH grantee, Bethesda, 1976—; recipient Disting. Lifetime Career award, Am. Soc. Pediat. Hematology-Oncology, 2008, Outstanding award Alum Stanford Med. Sch., 2008, Disting. Lifetime Alumnus award, U. Colo., Boulder, 2010. Fellow ACP, Am. Acad. Pediatrics (E. Mead Johnson rsch. award 1983); mem. Soc. Pediatric Rsch. (pres. 1986), Am. Soc. Hematology (councillor 1988-92), Am. Soc. Clin. Investigation, Am. Soc. Cell Biology, Am. Assn. Pathologists, Am. Assn. Physicians, Am. Clin. Climate Assn. Republican. Jewish. Achievements include first to professorial chair named after him at University of Michigan in 2010. Avocation: swimming. Office: U Mich D3251 MPB 1500 E Medical Center Dr Ann Arbor MI 48109-5718 Office Phone: 734-764-7126. Business E-Mail: laboxer@med.umich.edu.

BOYAJIAN, TIMOTHY EDWARD, public health officer, educator, consultant; b. Fresno, Calif., Feb. 22, 1949; s. Ernest Adam and Marge (Medzian) B.; m. Tassanee Bootdeesri, Apr. 23, 1987 (div. June 2007), m. T. Viengmone Thavisay, Sept. 14, 2010. BS in Biology, U. Calif., Irvine, 1975; M of Pub. Health, UCLA, 1978. Registered environ. health specialist, Calif. Rsch. asst. UCLA, 1978-81; lectr. Chapman U., 29 Palms, Calif., 1982-84, 88-89; refugee relief vol. Cath. Relief Svcs., Surin, Thailand, 1985-86; lectr. Nat. Univ., LA, 1989-91; environ. health specialist Riverside County Health Svcs. Agy., Palm Springs, Calif., 1991-96; sci. tchr. South Gate (Calif.) HS, 1999—2004, Desert Hot Springs HS, 2004—05; sci. tchr. Centennial H.S. Compton Unified Sch. Dist., Calif., 2006—07; biology tchr. La Quinta HS Desert Sands Unified Sch. Dist., Calif., 2007—09; biology & chemistry tchr. Kiettisack Internat. Sch., Laos, 2009—. Mem. adj. faculty U. Phoenix, 1998—; cons. parasitologist S. Pacific Commn., L.A., 1979; pub. health cons. several vets. groups, L.A., 1981-84, 97—; cons. Assn. S.E. Asian Nations, Bangkok, Thailand, 1988. Veterans rights advocate, Vietnam Vet. Groups, L.A., 1981-84. With USMC, Vietnam, 1969-71. Recipient U.S. Pub. Health Traineeship, U.S. Govt., L.A., 1977-81. Mem. VFW Avocation: writing. Home: PO Box 515381 PMB 11497 Los Angeles CA 90051 Personal E-mail: timothy300@aol.com.

BOYARSKY, ANDREW HAROLD, surgeon, educator; b. Burlington, Vt., Feb. 18, 1952; BA, Rutgers U., 1974, MD, 1980. Diplomate Am. Bd. Surgery, Am. Bd. Surg. Critical Care. Intern U. Medicine and Dentistry N.J.-Rutgers Med. Sch., Piscataway, 1980-81, resident, 1981-85; fellow in vascular surgery Maimonides Med. Ctr., Bklyn., 1985-86; mem. staff Robert Wood Johnson Hosp., New Brunswick, NJ; assoc. prof. surgery U. Medicine and Dentistry N.J.-Robert Wood Johnson, 1986—. Office: UMDNJ-RW Johnson Med Sch Dept Surgery New Brunswick NJ 08903 Office Phone: 732-235-7920. *

BOYCE, H. WORTH, gastroenterologist, educator; b. Clinton, NC, Sept. 21, 1930; s. Henry Worth and Lena Craft Boyce; m. Jean Murphy Boyce, June 21, 1952; children: Henry, Steve, Cindy, Gregory, Mary. BS, MD, Wake Forest U., 1955; MS, Baylor U., 1961. Intern Tripler Army Med. Ctr., Honolulu, 1955—56; resident in internal medicine Brooke Army Med. Ctr., Ft. Sam Houston, Tex., 1957—59, resident in gastroenterology, 1960; chief gastroenterology svc. Walter Reed Army Med. Ctr., Washington, 1966—75; prof. medicine U. South Fla., Tampa, 1975—. Dir. gastroenterology U. South Fla., Tampa, 1975—90, dir. Swallowing Ctr., 1987—. Author: Techniques of Clinical Gastroenterology, 1975; contbr. chapters to books, articles to profl. jours. Col. US Army, 1955—75. Decorated Legion of Merit. Mem.: Am. Gastroent. Assn., Am. Soc. Gastrointestinal Endoscopy (pres. 1973—74, gov. 1985—88, Disting. Svc. award 1989, Rudolph Schindler award 1982). Republican. Methodist. Avocations: photography, gardening, golf. Office: Univ S Fla Coll Medicine Box 72 12901 Bruce B Downs Blvd Tampa FL 33612 Office Phone: 813-974-3374. Office Fax: 813-974-7031.

BOYCE, STEVEN W., cardiothoracic surgeon; BA, Johns Hopkins U., Balt., Md., 1977; MD, U. Md., Balt., Md., 1981. Cert. Nat. Bd. Medical Examiners, diplomate Am. Bd. Surgery, Am. Bd. Thoracic Surgery. Resident surgery Univ. Calif., San Francisco, 1982—86, fellow cardiothoracic surgery LA, 1987—89; physician cons. FDA/PMA PAnel Reviews; staff surgeon New Eng. Deaconess Hosp.; instr. cardiothoracic surgery Harvard Med. Sch.; surgical dir. Hear Failure and Transpant Program Wash. Hosp. Ctr. Named one of The Best Doctors in America, The Washingtonians Top Doctors. Fellow: ACS, Am. Coll. of Cardiology; mem.: 21st Century Cardiac Surgery Soc. (pres. 2009—10), Internat. Soc. for Minimally Invasive Cardiac Surgery, Heart Failure Soc. of America, Southern Thoracic Surgical Assn., Soc. of Thoracic Surgeons, Internat. Soc. for Heart and Lung Transplantation, Howard C. Naffziger Surgical Soc. Office: Washington Hospital Center 110 Irving St NW Washington DC 20010 Office Phone: 202-877-7000.

BOYD, ARTHUR BERNETTE, JR., surgeon, clergyman, beverage company executive; b. Durham, NC, June 29, 1947; s. Arthur Bernette and Mammie Lee (Chalmers) B.; m. Delphine Victoria Huffman, Mar. 14, 1981; children: Arthur III, Vicki BA, Fla. A&M U., 1969; postgrad., NYU, 1970; MD, Meharry Med. Coll., 1978; postgrad., U. N.C., Chapel Hill, 1998. Cert. ATLS instr., PALS. Intern surgery Howard U. Hosp., Washington, 1978—80; resident and chief resident surgery St. Luke's Hosp., Cleve., 1981—84; fellow liver transplant U. Pitts., 1984—85; chief surgeon, pres. Phoenix Med. Surg. Svc., Inc., Caribbean, Cleve., 1988—. Adj. prof. anatomy and physiology Cuyhoga C.C., Cleve., 1988—; cons. surgeon other hosps. and physicians, Cleve., 1988—; continuing med. educator dept. surgery Case We. Res. U. Sch. Medicine, Cleve., 1997-98; faculty med. bd. profl. preparation course U. Mo., Kansas City, 1997; chief adminstrv. fellow trauma, surg. critical care R.A. Cowley Shock Trauma Ctr., U. Md. Med. Sys., 1993-94, clin. instr. surgery, sr. trauma fellow, 1994-96; clin. instr. surgery, sr. fellow, traumatologist, Baltimore County, 1994—; co-traumatologist Prince George Cmty. Hosp., Cheverly, Md., 1994-95; pres., CEO Motown Beverage Co. Ohio, Cleve., 1998—, Towne Club Internat. Ohio, Inc., Cleve., 1998—, Nat. Fin. Group, Inc., Cleve., 1997—; pres., CEO, chmn. Star Beverage Corp., Shaker Heights, Ohio, 1997 Inventor: wheelchair with mechanism to raise or lower left or right buttocks of person, hemostat that carries two sutures, synthetic covering with zipper to cover bowel when abdomen unable to be closed after surgery Vol. Cleve. Cmty. Action Against Addiction, 1987-88, mentor Case We. U. Inner City Program, Cleve., 1988—; judge honors sci. projects Shaker Heights Mid. Sch., 1998; mem. Shaker Heights Cmty. Leaders Meetings Fellow ACS (assoc.), Internat. Coll. Surgeons; mem. AAAS, AMA, N.Y. Acad. Scis., Nat. Med. Assn. (mentor 1990—), Assn. Black Cardiologists, Ohio State Med. Soc., Cleve. Surg. Soc., Nat. Assn. Small Bus. Owners, Internat. Assn. Small Bus. Owners, Greater Cleve. Ministers Alliance, Masons, Omega Psi Phi, Alpha Phi Omega Democrat. Methodist. Avocations: reading, sports, golf. Office: Star Beverage 3277 Lee Rd Cleveland OH 44120-3451 Home and Office: Motown Beverage Co 3277 Lee Rd Cleveland OH 44120-3451 Office Phone: 216-991-4799. Personal E-mail: aboydstar@aol.com.

BOYD, BENJAMIN FRANKLIN, ophthalmologist; b. Panama, Oct. 1, 1924; s. Alfredo 01iverio Boyd and Silvia Diaz de Boyd; m. Vylma Cordovez de Boyd, Apr. 17, 1997. MD, Northwestern U., Chgo., 1949; degree in Ophthalmology, Gorgus Hosp., Republic of Panama, 1953; D with honoris causa, U. Santo Domingo, Republic of Dominicana, 1988, Fundacion Oftalmologica, Buenos Aries, Argentina, 1998, U. Panama, 1994. Diplomate Am. Bd. Ophthalmology, 1955. Founder sec. Sch. Medicine, U. Panama, 1954—68, dean, 1969—70; pres. Panama Acad. Medicine & Surgery, 1969—70; exec. dir. Pan-Am. Assn. Ophthalmology, Panama, 1960—85, pres., 1985—87, Acad. Ophthalmologia Internat., 1994—98; founder & editor in chief Highlights Ophthalmology, City of Knowledge, Panama, 1950—2005, emeritus counselor, 2006—08. Founder & prof. emiritus Panamanian Soc. Ophthalmogy. Contbr. articles to profl. jours. Recipient Sr. Achivement award, Bd. Trustees Am. Acad. Opthalmology, 2004, Gold medal, St. Louis Soc., 1992, Jorge Malbran Found., 1998, Singapore Nat. Eye Ctr., 2000, Colombian Nat. Found.Bogota, Colombia, 2001. Fellow: Am. Coll. Surgeons (Restorer of Sight 1993); mem.: Am. Acad. Ophthalmology (life), Internat. Coun. Ophthalmology (life). Roman Catholic. Avocation: reading. Home: Balboa Ave & Anastasio Ruiz St Los Delfines Bldg Tower1 Apt 28B Panama Panama Office: Highlights Ophthalmology PO Box 0819-06890 Panama Panama Office Phone: (507) 214-1561. Office Fax: (507) 214-1531. Business E-Mail: benboyd@thehighlights.net.

BOYD, DAVID M., physician; b. Fla., May 25, 1977; BSc, Fla. Internat. U., 2000; MD, Ross U. Sch. Medicine, 2006. Physician Family Practice Specialists Richmond, 2009—. Assoc. prof., family medicine Va. Commonwealth U. Sch. Medicine, 2010. Recipient Chief Resident award, St. Francis Family Medicine Residency. Mem.: Richmond Acad. Medicine, Am. Soc. Laser Medicine and Surgery, Va. Acad. Family Physicians, Am. Acad. Family Physicians. Avocations: golf, gourmet cooking, travel. Home: 13710 Arrowood Ct Midlothian VA 23112 Personal E-mail: davidboydmd@gmail.com.

BOYD, DEBORAH ANN, pediatrician; b. Urbana, Ohio, Jan. 30, 1955; d. John A. Sr. and Juanita Jean (Routt) B. BA cum laude, Wittenberg U., 1977; MD, U. Cin., 1982. Diplomate Am. Bd. Pediatrics, Nat. Bd. Med. Examiners. Intern Children's Hosp. Med. Ctr., Cin., 1982—83, pediat. resident, 1982—85; pediatrician Nat. Health Svc. Corps, Springfield, Ohio, 1985—89, Cmty. Hosp. Health Care Ctr., Springfield, 1989—97; staff pediat. primary care ctr., clin. faculty Children's Hosp. Med. Ctr., Cin., 1998—. Mem. Continuing med. edn. com. Mercy Med. Ctr., Springfield, 1989—, infection control com., 1987—. Adv. com. Miami Valley Child Devl. Ctr., Springfield, 1985—, New Parents as Tchrs., 1986—. Mem. Assn. of Clinicians for the Underserved, Am. Acad. Pediats., Ambulatory Pediat. Assn. Democratic. Avocations: bicycling, photography, basketball, music, church activities. Home: 12132 S Pine Dr Apt 240 Cincinnati OH 45241-1743 Office: Dept Gen Com Pediatrics Children's Hosp Med Ctr 3333 Burnet Ave Fl 4 Cincinnati OH 45229-3026 Office Phone: 513-636-7594.

BOYD, JEANEAN B., hospital administrator; b. Richmond, Va., Apr. 25, 1949; d. James Skinker and Jean (Mason) Brooks; 1 child, Amy Jeanean Boyd. Diploma in nursing, John Peter Smith Hosp., 1969; BSN, U. Tex., 1977, MSN, 1984. CNAA. Edn. coord. Tarrant County Hosp. Dist., Fort Worth, 1972-75; nurse mgr. Fort Worth Children's Hosp., 1975-77; asst. dir. nursing HCA Med. Plaza, Fort Worth, 1977-83, asst. adminstr. patient svcs. Plano, Tex., 1984-89; v.p. patient svcs. All Saints Hosps., Fort Worth, 1989—. Cons. Mgmt. 21, Nashville, 1988—; field cons. Hosp. Corp. Am., Nashville, 1980-89; adj. faculty mem. U. Tex., Arlington, 1980—. Mem. Am. Orgn. Nurse Execs., Tex. Orgn. Nurse Execs. (bd. dirs. 1984-86, nominating com. 1984, membership com. 1985-86), Am. Hosp. Assn., Tex. Hosp. Assn., NAFE, Businesswomen's Club. Office: All Saints Hosps 1400 8th Ave Fort Worth TX 76104-4110 *

BOYER, ALBERT BRUCE, optometrist, educator; b. St. George, Utah, Feb. 9, 1954; s. Albert Cleo and Venice Vay Boyer. AS, Dixie Coll., 1977; OD, So. Calif. Coll. Optometry, 1985, BS, 1995; PhD, MS, LaSalle U., 1996. Lic. optometrist Utah, Nev., Calif., Va., Alaska, Tex., Ariz., contact lens certification Nat. Eye Rsch. Found. Staff dr., surg. asst. Ophthalmologist Kern & Assoc., Huntington Beach, Calif., 1986—87; staff dr. Lenscrafters 2000, Bakersfield, Calif., 1987—88; pvt. practice Reno, 1988—90; staff dr. Keller & Assocs., Las Vegas, 1990—99; prof. LaSalle U., Las Vegas, 1997—2002; CEO, pres. Vision Care 20/20, Las Vegas, 1999—. Contbr. articles to profl. jours. With US Army, 1972—83. Recipient Top Optometrist award, Am.'s Top Optometrists Guide, 2002, Nat. Leadership award, Nat. Rep. Congress, 2003. Fellow: Am. Acad. Optometry; mem.: Am. Optometric Assn. (Optometric Recognition awards 1988—), Omicron Psi, Golden Key. Republican. Mem. Lds Ch. Achievements include new objective glaucoma testing with electro-oculagram; research in electro-oculography. Avocations: mountain hiking, restoring classic cars. Personal E-mail: albertbboyer@hotmail.com.

BOYER, DAVID STUART, ophthalmologist, educator; b. Chgo., Mar. 1, 1947; MD, Chgo. Med. Sch., 1972. Sr. ptnr. Retina Vitreous Assoc. Med. Group, 1977—. Clin. prof. ophthalmology U. So. Calif Sch. Medicine, 2008—; bd. mem., past pres. LA chpt. Am. Diabetes Assoc. Recipient Outstanding Alumnus award, U. SC Dept. Ophthalmology, David Shaw award, Hosp. Good Samaritan, Jules Stein Living Tribute award, Retinitis Pigmentosa Internat. Mem.: Alumni Assn. U. SC Ophthalmology Program (bd. dirs.), Discovery Fund Eye Rsch. (bd. dirs.), Am. Soc. Retinal Surgeons, Macula Soc., Retina Soc. Avocation: travel. Home: 13715 Magnolia Blvd Sherman Oaks CA 91423 Home Fax: 818-783-9196. Personal E-mail: vitdoc@aol.com.

BOYER, HERBERT WAYNE, biotechnology company executive, retired biochemist; b. Pitts., July 10, 1936; m. Grace Boyer, 1959. BS in Biology and Chemistry, St. Vincent Coll., Latrobe, Pa., 1958, DSc (hon.) (hon.), 1981; MS, U. Pitts., 1960, PhD, 1963. Post-grad. study Yale U., 1963—66; mem. faculty University of California, San Francisco, 1966—, prof. microbiology, 1966—75, prof. biochemistry and biophysics, 1975—91, prof. biochemistry and biophysics emeritus, 1991—; co-founder, dir. Genentech, Inc., San Francisco, 1976—2009, v.p., 1976—90. Investigator Howard Hughes Med. Inst., 1976—83; bd. dir. Allergan, Inc., Irvine, Calif., 1994—, chmn. bd. dirs., 1998—2001, vice-chmn. bd. dirs., 2001—. Mem. several editl. bds.; contbr. articles to profl. jours. Former trustee Scripps Rsch. Inst. Recipient V.D. Mattai award, Roche Inst., 1977, Albert and Mary Lasker award for basic med. research, 1980, Golden Plate award, Am. Acad. Achievement, 1981, Indsl. Rsch. Inst. Achievement award, 1982, Moet Hennessy-Louis Vuitton prize, 1988, Jerome H. Lemelson-MIT prize for excellence in invention and innovation, 1996, Nat. Tech. medal, 1989, Nat. Sci. medal, 1990, Perkin medal, Soc. Chem. Industry, 2007; co-recipient Swiss Helmut Horten Rsch. award, 1993, Shaw prize in Sci. & Medicine, Shaw Found., Hong Kong, 2004; named to Calif. Inventor's Hall of Fame, 1985, Nat. Inventor Hall of Fame, 2001. Fellow: AAAS, Am. Acad. Arts and Scis.; mem.: NAS, Am. Soc. Biol. Chemists. Achievements include obtaining, with Stanley N. Cohen, first patent in the field of recombinant deoxyribonucleic acid (DNA), 1980. Office: c/o Allergan Inc 2525 Dupnt Dr Irvine CA 92612

BOYER, JAMES LORENZEN, internist, educator; b. NYC, Aug. 28, 1936; s. Ralph R. and Alice M. B.; m. Phoebe Bennet, Feb. 23, 1963; children: Phoebe Christine, Anna Birch. AB, Haverford Coll., Pa., 1958; MD, Johns Hopkins U., 1962. Diplomate: Am. Bd. Internal Medicine. Med. intern N.Y. Hosp., NYC, 1962-63, resident in medicine, 1963-64, Yale-New Haven Hosp., 1966; postdoctoral fellow liver study unit Yale U., 1966-68; mem. faculty U. Chgo. Pritzker Sch. Medicine, 1972-78, prof. medicine, 1976-78, dir. liver study unit, 1972-78; prof. medicine, dir. liver study unit, chief divsn. digestive diseases Yale U. Med. Sch., 1978-96; dir. Yale Liver Ctr., 1984—2009, Ensign prof. of medicine, 1996—. Treas., bd. dirs. Am. Liver Found., 1976-85, chair Sci. Adv. Com., 2003-04, chmn. bd. dirs., 2004-08; dep. chmn. Nat. Digestive Disease Adv. Bd., 1981-84; coun. mem. NIDDK, 1985-90. Contbr. articles to profl. jours. Chmn. bd. trustees Mt. Desert Island Biol. Lab., Salsbury Cove, Maine, 1995-2003, 2011-, mem. bd. dirs., Haverford Coll., 2009-. Lt. comdr. USPHS, 1964-66. Josiah Macey faculty scholar, 1976 Mem. Am. Assn. Study Liver Disease (pres. 1980), Am. Fedn. Clin. Rsch., ACP, Am. Gastroenterol. Assn. (councillor 1983-86), Internat. Assn. Study Liver Diseases (v.p. 1982-84, pres.-elect 1986-88, pres. 1988-90), Am. Soc. Clin. Investigation, Assn. Am. Physicians, Soc. Clin. Rsch., Am. Clin. and Climatolgic Assn. Office: Yale U Sch of Medicine 333 Cedar St New Haven CT 06520-8014

BOYKO, EDWARD JOHN, internist, medical researcher; b. Bethlehem, Pa., Feb. 19, 1953; s. Edward and Mary (Levan) B.; m. Beth Welcome Alderman, Sept. 27, 1980; children: Eva Jane, Bryan Martin. BA, Columbia U., 1975; MD, U. Pitts., 1979; MPH, U. Wash., 1984. Intern, internal medicine U. Chgo. Hospitals and Clinics, Ill., 1979—80, resident, internal medicine Ill., 1980—82; fellow Robert Wood Johnson Scholars Program, U. Wash., Seattle, 1982-84; attending physician U. Colo., Denver, 1984—, asst. prof. medicine and preventive medicine, 1984—; asst. prof. dept. medicine U. Wash, 1989-92, assoc. prof, 1992—97, prof. medicine, 1997—; dir. Seattle Epidemiologic Rsch. and Info. Ctr. (ERIC); chief, gen. internal medicine sect. VA Puget Sound Health Care Sys. Spl. mem. NIH study sect., Washington, 1988; mem. Nat. Diabetes Data Group, NIDDK, 1992; adj. prof. dept. epidemiology, U. Wash. Contbr. articles to med. jours. Recipient Career Develop. award, Nat. Found. for Heitis and Colitis, 1986—89, U. Wash. Medicine/Ctr. of Excellence in Women's Health award for Outstanding Mentorship, 2004. Mem. Soc. Epidemiologic Rsch., Am. Diabetes Assn., Alpha Omega Alpha. Avocations: skiing, hiking. Home: 4551 NE 41st St Seattle WA 98105-5109 Office: VA Puget Sound Health Care Sys 111 M 1660 S Columbian Way Campus Box 358280 Seattle WA 98108 also: U Wash 1100 Olive Way Ste 1400 Seattle WA 98101 Office Phone: 206-764-2830. Office Fax: 206-764-2563. Personal E-mail: eboyko@u.washington.edu.

BOYLE, COLEEN A., public health service officer; MS in Biostatistics, U. Pitts., PhD in Epidemiology. Post. doc. tng. in epidemiol. methods Yale U., New Haven; faculty mem. in epidemiology U. Mass. Program in Pub. Health; joined Centers Disease Control and Prevention, Atlanta, 1984, joined divsn. birth defects and devel. disabilities, 1988, assoc. dir. Nat. Ctr. Birth Defects and Devel. Disabilities, 2001—10, dir. Nat. Ctr. Birth Defects and Devel. Disabilities, 2010—. Recipient Charles C. Shepard award, CDC, 1997. Office: Centers Disease Control and Prevention NCBDDD 1600 Clifton Rd Atlanta GA 30333 *

BOYLE, MARCIA, medical association administrator; BA, Skidmore Coll.; MS, Columbia Univ. Co-founder Immune Deficiency Found., 1980, pres., CEO, 1980—95, chair, 1980—2001, chair, pres., CEO, 2005—; dir. devel., Neurology and Brain Sci. Johns Hopkins Medicine; dir., dept. programs, capital projects, dir. prin. gifts Fund for Johns Hopkins Medicine; dir. devel. Wilmer Eye Inst. Co-founder Internat. Patient Orgn. Primary Immune Deficiency Diseases. Office: Immune Deficiency Found Ste 308 40 W Chesapeake Ave Towson MD 21204 Office Phone: 410-321-6647. *

BOYLE, PETER, epidemiologist, health science association administrator; b. Glasgow, Scotland, June 8, 1951; s. Brigid Boyle; m. Helena Mary McNicol; children: Helen, Kathleen, Eileen. BSc, U. Glasgow, 1974, PhD, 1984. Rsch. asst. dept. medicine U. Glasgow, 1974—77; sr. statistician West of Scotland Cancer Surveillance Unit, 1977—84; instr., asst. prof. Harvard Sch. Pub. Health, Boston, 1984—86; sr. scientist WHO Internat. Agy. Rsch. on Cancer, Lyon, Rhone, France, 1986—91, dir., 2004—; dir. divsn. epidemiology and biostats. European Inst. Oncology, Milan, 1991—2004. Prof. postgrad. sch. pathology U. Milan, 1996—; hon. prof. cancer epidemiology U. Birmingham, 1997—; vis. prof. U. Glasgow, 1999—; chmn. prevention and control Imperial Cancer Rsch. Fund, London, 1999—; hon. lectr. U. Coll., Dublin; hon. prof. cancer prevention/control Oxford U., England; hon. prof. Nat. Sch. Pub. Health, Madrid. Contbr. articles to profl. jours. Recipient Knight's Cross of Order of Merit, Republic of Poland, 2001. Fellow: Royal Soc. Edinburgh; mem.: Internat. Acad. Oral Oncology, European Soc. Therapeutic Radiology & Oncology (hon.). Achievements include research in disease prevention and the application of research findings to reduce population disease risk, particularly in the associations between tobacco, nutrition, hormones and cancer risk and how this risk is affected by genetic susceptibility.

BOYLE, ROBERT J., medical educator; b. Scranton, Pa., Aug. 4, 1947; s. John Joseph and Mary Jean Boyle; m. Karen Korade; children: Sarah Ann, Daniel Robert, John Brendan. BSc, Boston Coll., 1969; MD, Johns Hopkins U., 1973. Diplomate in pediatrics and in neonatal-perinatal medicine Am. Bd. Pediatrics. Pediatric resident Rainbow Babies and Children's Hosp., Cleve., 1973—76; neonatology fellow Women and Infants Hosp., 1976—78; asst. prof. pediat. Sch. Medicine, Wake Forest U., Winston-Salem, NC, 1978—83, Sch. Medicine, U. Va., Charlottesville, 1983—85, assoc. prof. pediat., 1985—2000, prof. pediat., 2000—. Dir., ethics consultation svc. U. Va. Health Sys., Charlottesville, 1989—2005, chair, ethics com., 2005—. Named Americas Top Doctors, Best Doctors in America, Guide to America's Top Pediatricians. Fellow: Am. Acad. Pediat.; mem.: Am. Soc. Bioethics and Humanities, Am. Pediatric Soc. Roman Catholic. Home: 1710 King Mountain Rd Charlottesville VA 22901 Office: Univ Virginia Sch Medicine PO Box 800386 Charlottesville VA 22908-0386 Office Fax: 434-924-2816. Business E-Mail: rjb6j@virginia.edu.

BOYTSOV, SERGEY, medical association administrator; b. Leningradskaya, Russia, Jan. 23, 1957; MD, S.M. Kirov Army Med. Acad., 1980. Sr. physician State Med. Ctr. Ministry of Pub. Health Russian Fedn., 2002—03; exec. dir. N.I. Pirogov Ctrl. Clinico-diagnostic Complex, 2003—06; dep. dir. Russian Cardiology Rsch. Complex, 2006—11; dir. Nat. Rsch. Ctr. Preventive Medicine, 2011—. Mem.: Am. Heart Assn., European Soc. Cardiology, European Soc. Arterial Hypertension, Russian Soc. Arterial Hypertension, Russian Sci. Assn. Cardiologists. Office: Petroverigsky Pereulok Moscow 101990 Russia Office Fax: 495-621-01-22. E-mail: prof-boytsov@mail.ru.

BOZALIS, JOHN RUSSELL, physician; b. St. Louis, Sept. 19, 1939; s. George Sauter and Ruth (Russell) B.; m. Sharon Louise Sabo, June 21, 1963; children: John Jr., David L., Diana. BA, U. Okla., 1961, MD, 1965; MS, U. Mich., 1971. Diplomate Am. Bd. Internal Medicine, Am. Bd. Allergy and Immunology. Intern Henry Ford Hosp., Detroit, 1965-66, resident, 1966-68, chief resident, 1968-69; fellow in allergy-immunology U. Mich., Ann Arbor, 1969-71, instr., 1969-71; clin. asst. prof. U. Tex., San Antonio, 1972-73; pvt. practice Okla. Allergy Clinic, Oklahoma City, 1973—. Clin. instr. Coll. Medicine, U. Okla., 1973, clin. asst. prof., 1977-83, clin. assoc. prof., 1983-89, clin. prof., 1989—; mem. courtesy staff Mercy Hosp., Bapt. Hosp., Deaconess Hosp., St. Anthony Hosp., Presbyn. Hosp., Children's Hosp., Okla. Tchg. Hosp., S.W. Med. Ctr. Trustee Casady Sch., 1977-85, United Way Okla. City, chmn. profl. divsn. 1983, Okla. Health Scis. Found.; bd. dirs. Infant Ctr., 1983-86, Allied Arts Okla. City, 1984-86, 92, Hosp. Hospitality House, 1983-86, United Way Greater Okla. City, 2006; vice chmn. health scis. ctr. U. Okla. Centennial Commn.; bd. trustees McGee Eye Inst., search com. for chmn. dept. ophthalmology and dir., 1991, Okla. City Mus. Art., 2003—, U. Okla. Found., 2003—; active Com. of 100, 1991; bd. trustees Okla. City Pub. Schs. Found., 1989—, Okla. Orthopedic and Arthritis Found., Inc., Bone and Joint Hosp., 1993; trustee Oklahoma City Mus. Arts, 2003—, U. Okla. Found., 2003; chmn. legis. task force for promotion of children's health State of Okla., 2002-06; pres. bd. Schs. Healthy Lifestyles, 1997—. Maj. USAF, 1971-73. Recipient Regents' Alumni award U. Okla., 1992; named Physician of Yr.-Pvt. Practice, U. Okla. Coll. of Medicine Alumni Assn., 1993, recipient dean's award, 1998. Fellow ACP, Am. Coll. Chest Physicians, Am. Acad. Allergy; mem. AMA, Am. Thoracic Soc., Okla. State Med. Assn. (del. 1993—, vice spkr. ho. dels. 1997, trustee 1993—), Okla. Lung Assn., Okla. Thoracic Soc. (pres. 1979), John M. Sheldon Soc., Okla. County Med. Soc. (editor Bull. 1978-83, chmn. orientation com. 1989—, pres. 1996, bd. trustees 1996—), Osler Soc. (pres. 1984), Okla. City Acad. Medicine, Robert M. Bird Soc., U. Okla. Coll. Medicine Alumni Assn. (chmn. rsch. com., pres. 1983-85), Okla. City C. of C. (bd. dirs. 1988-90). Republican. Episcopal. Avocations: hunting, golf, fly fishing, travel, gardening. Office: Okla Allergy and Asthma Clinic PO Box 26827 Oklahoma City OK 73126-0827 also: Okla Allergy and Asthma Clinic 750 NE 13th St Oklahoma City OK 73104 Home Phone: 405-843-7115; Office Phone: 405-235-0040. Business E-Mail: jbozalis@oklahomaallergy.com. *

BOZDECH, MAREK JIRI, physician, educator; b. Wildflecken, Bavaria, Federal Republic Germany, Oct. 12, 1946; s. Jiri Josef and Zofia Jadwiga (Swiatecka) B.; m. Frances Barclay Craig, Dec. 22, 1967; children: Elizabeth, Andrew, Matthew. AB, U. Mich., 1967; MD, Wayne State U., 1972. Diplomate Am. Bd. Internal Medicine, Am. Bd. Med. Oncology, Am. Bd. Hematology. Intern and resident in internal medicine U. Wis. Hosps., Madison, 1972-75, dir. clin. hematology lab., 1978-82, dir. bone marrow transplantation, 1984-85; asst. prof. medicine U. Wis., Madison, 1978-84, assoc. prof. medicine, 1984-85; clin. fellow in hematology Moffitt Hosp. U. Calif., San Francisco, 1975-76, postdoctoral fellow in hematology Cancer Research Inst., 1976-78, research assoc. Cancer Research Inst., 1977-78, assoc. prof., 1985-89; dir. adult bone marrow transplantation U. Calif. Med. Ctr., San Francisco, 1985-89; chief oncology Kaiser Permanente Med. Ctr., Santa Rosa, Calif., 1989-91; pvt. practice specializing in oncology Hematology Redwood Regional Oncology Ct., Santa Rosa, 1991—. Contbr. articles to profl. jours. Scout leader Boy Scouts Am., Novato, Calif., 1985; bd. trustees Pacific Found. Med. Care, 1995—. Recipient Nat. Research Service award NIH, 1977-78; Wayne State U. scholar, 1971. Mem. ACP, Am. Soc. Hematology, Am. Soc. Clin. Oncology, Assn. No. Calif. Oncologists (bd. dirs. 1994-97), Sonoma County Med. Assn. (bd. dirs. 1994-96). Avocations: skiing, gardening, music, films, theater. Home: 50 La Placita Ct Novato CA 94945-1244 Office: Redwood Regional Oncology 121 Sotoyome St Ste 203 Santa Rosa CA 95405-4822 Personal E-mail: mbozdech@mindspring.com, mbozdech@yahoo.com. *

BOZKAYA, SULEYMAN, oral surgeon; b. Bolvadin, Afyon, Turkey, Dec. 15, 1976; s. Arif and Selvi Bozkaya; m. Zeynep Ruveyde Topaloglu, May 17, 2003; 1 child, Zeynep Ece. PhD, Gazi U. Inst. Health Scis., Ankara, 2005. Rsch. asst. Gazi U. Faculty Dentistry, Ankara, 1997—2005, sr. resident, 2005—. Mem.: Assn. Turkish Oral Maxillofacial Surgeons. Office: Gazi Univ Faculty Dentistry Ankara 06510 Turkey Personal E-mail: sbozkaya@superonline.com. Business E-Mail: sbozkaya@gazi.edu.tr.

BOZKURT, SULEYMAN, medical researcher; b. Istanbul, Turkey, Jan. 25, 1965; MD, Hacettepe U. Sch. Medicine, 1991. Rsch. specialist, dept. surgery Bezmialem Vakif U. Sch. Medicine, 2010—. Office: Adnan Menderes Bulvari Vatan Caddes Istanbul Marmara 34093 Turkey E-mail: suleyman.bozkurt@isbank.net.tr.

BRAASCH, JOHN WILLIAM, retired surgeon, consultant; b. Rochester, Minn., Dec. 11, 1922; s. William Frederick and Nellie (Stinchfield) B.; m. Nancy Wheeler King, Mar. 21, 1946; children: William Frederick, Elizabeth King, Nancy Kathryn, Peggy Stinchfield. BS, Yale U., 1944; MD, Harvard U., 1946; MS in Physiology, U. Ill., 1948; PhD in Surgery, U. Minn., 1955. Diplomate Am. Bd. Surgery (bd. dirs. 1979-85). Intern St. Luke's Hosp., Chgo., 1946-47; resident in gen. surgery Mayo Clinic, Rochester, Minn., 1950-55; mem. attending staff Mpls. Gen. Hosp., 1955-57, Northwestern Hosp., Mpls., 1955-57; surg. staff New England Bapt. Hosp., Boston, 1957-80, New England Deaconess Hosp., Boston, 1957-80, Lahey Clinic Found., Boston, 1957-96, chmn. dept. surgery, 1971—83; sr. cons. dept. surgery Lahey Clinic, Burlington, Mass., 1983-96, ret., 1996. Asst. clin. prof. surgery Harvard Med. Sch., Boston, 1975—. Author 3 books, several book chpts.; also numerous articles. Capt. U.S. Army, 1948-50. Recipient Balfour award for rsch. Mayo Clinic Found., Rochester, 1955, Mayo Clinic Disting. Alumnus, 2007. Mem. Am. Surg. Assn., Soc. for Surgery Alimentary Tract (v.p. 1987-88), Internat. Soc. Surgery, So. Surg. Soc., New England. Surg. Soc. (pres. 1984-85), Boston Sur. Soc. (pres. 1982), Internat. Hepato-Pancreato-Biliary Surgery Assn. (hon.), Surgeons Travel Club. Republican. Avocations: tennis, gardening.

BRACKEN, RICHARD M., hospital administrator; b. Richmond, Va., 1977; m. Judith Bracken; 4 children. B, 1974; M, Med. Coll. Va., 1977. CEO Centennial Med. Ctr., Green Hosp. of Scripps Clinic & Rsch. Found.; various exec. positions HCA, Inc., 1981—95, pres. Pacific divsn., 1995—97, pres. Western Group, 1997—2001, COO, 2001—09, pres., 2002—09, chmn., CEO, 2009—. Bd. dirs. United Way of Met. Nashville; mem. Am. Soc. of Corp. Execs., Bus. Coun., Nashville Healthcare Coun., Cmty. Found. of Middle Tenn. Bd.; fellow Am. Coll. of Healthcare Exec. Mem.: Fedn. Am. Hosps. (bd. dirs.), Calif. Hosp. Assn. (bd. dirs.). Office: HCA Inc 1 Park Plz Nashville TN 37203 Office Phone: 615-344-9551. Business E-Mail: richard.bracken@hcahealthcare.com. *

BRACKETT, BENJAMIN GAYLORD, retired physiology and pharmacology educator; b. Athens, Ga., Nov. 18, 1938; s. Ernest Marshall and Julia Claire (Cook) B.; m. Ann Thornton Crawford, Aug. 22, 1959; children: Laura Ellen, Jeffrey Crawford, David Gregory Hill. DVM cum laude, U. Ga., 1962, BSA cum laude, MS in Chemistry, 1964, PhD in Biochemistry, 1966; MA (hon.), U. Pa., 1971. Diplomate Am. Coll. Theriogenologists. Postdoctoral fellow dept. biochemistry U. Ga., Athens, 1962-66, prof. Coll. Vet. Med., 1983—2002, prof. emeritus, 2003—, head dept. physiology/pharmacology, 1983-95; from assoc. to prof. dept. ob.-gyn. Sch. Medicine, U. Pa., Phila., 1966-74, prof. rsch. ob-gyn. and animal reprodn., Sch. Vet. Medicine, 1974—83. Cons. NIH, WHO, USDA and other orgns., 1969-2002, Office Tech. Assessment, US Congress; cons. on impacts of applied genetics, 1979-80; infertility prevention and treatment, 1986-87; contraceptive rsch. and devel. program cons. Ea. Va. Sch. Medicine, Norfolk, 1986-91; pres., chmn. bd. dirs. Reproductive Biol. Assocs., Inc., Atlanta, 1983-88; mem.

external sci. advisory bd., Wis., 1987-89, Calif., 1999-2000, Regional Primate Rsch. Ctrs.; presenter in field, vis. prof. ob-gyn. Monash U.and Queen Victoria Med. Ctr., Melbourne, Australia, 1983, U. Degli Studi Di Milano, 1985, Jiangsu Acad. Agrl. Scis., Nanjing, Kyoto U. 1986, U. Guelph, Ont., 1988, U. Bari, 1990, U. Bologna, 1991, U. Barcelona, 1993, Swedish U. Agrl. Scis., Uppsala, 1993, U. Sao Paulo, 1998, U. Zulia, Maracaibo, 2000. Co-editor: New Technologies in Animal Breeding, 1981; contbr. over 275 articles to profl. publs.; referee numerous jours.; editl. bd. mem. to numerous jours., 1966-. Grantee, NIH, USDA, others; recipient Rsch. Career Devel. award USPHS/NIH, 1971-76, Pres. award Korean Soc. Animal Reproduction, 1985, Four Chaplains Legion of Honor, 1985; Disting. Alumnus award Coll. Vet. Medicine, U. Ga., 1998, Internat. award in Animal Reprodn., Lazzaro Spallanzani, 1999. Fellow Japan Soc. Promotion Sci. Rsch.; mem. Internat. Embryo Transfer Soc. (pres. 1984-85, Pioneer award 2004), Am. Soc. Andrology, Soc. Reproduction and Fertility, Soc. Study Reproduction (sec. 1982-86), Am. Vet. Med. Assn., Ga. Vet. Med. Assn. Methodist. Achievements include development of repeatable procedure for in-vitro fertilization; research in enzyme-dependent sperm penetration of eggs; filming of the fertilization process; first showed that sperm cells can take up foreign DNA and transfer it into eggs at fertilization; research in nation's first human in-vitro fertilization; production of the first in-vitro fertilization calf; nation's first test-tube goat kids; the first babies in Georgia from clinical in-vitro fertilization to overcome human infertility; the definition of physical and chemical conditions for gametes, fertilization and development of viable cow blastocysts; large-scale application of in-vitro fertilization technology for production of genetically desirable cattle in tropical Venezuela. Home: 1701 Spartan Ln Athens GA 30606 E-mail: bgb@uga.edu.

BRACKMANN, DERALD E., otolaryngologist; b. Buckley, Ill., Feb. 13, 1937; s. Otto Henry Brackmann and Anna Mina Abraham; m. Charlotte Joyce Boyden, June 21, 1959; children: David, Douglas, Mark, Steven. Student, U. Ill., 1958, MD, 1962. Diplomate Am. Bd. Otolaryngology. Intern Ill. Ctrl. Hosp., Chgo., 1962—63; resident ob-gyn. Ill. Rsch. Hosp., Chgo., 1963—64; resident Otolaryngology Los Angeles County/U. So. Calif. Med. Ctr., 1966—70, chief otology, 1981—98; staff physician House Ear Clinic, LA, 1970—85, pres., 1985—. Chief ENT svc. St. Vincent Med. Ctr., 1971—98; clin. prof. otolaryngology U. So. Calif., clin. prof. neurologic surgery; clin. instr. House Ear Inst. Editor: Otologic Surgery, Neurotology, Neurological Surgery of the Ear & Skull Base; editl. bd.: jour. Advances in Otolaryngology-Head and Neck Surgery, Laryngoscoope, Neurotology; co-author (chpt.): Electrocochleography, 1976, Hearing Disorders, 1976, Acoustic Tumors: Diagnosis and Management, 1979, Acoustic Tumors Vol. 1 Diagnosis, 1979, Otolaryngology, 1980, Controversy in Otolaryngology, 1980, Butterworth International Medical Reviews; Otology, 1982, Disorders of the Facial Nerve, 1982, Essential Otolaryngology Head & Neck Surgery, 3d edit., 1983; author: Surgery of the Skull Base, 1983, Meniere's Disease: A Comprehensive Appraisal, 1983; contbg. editor: Neurological Surgery of the Ear and Skull Base, 1982; co-author: Gerald M. English Otolaryngology, Sensory Evoked Potentials, 1984, Cochlear Implants, 1985; author: The Facial Nerve, 1986; co-author: Ear and Skull Base, 1986, Conn's Current Therapy, 1988, Otologic Medicine and Surgery, 1988, Advances in Otolaryngology-Head and Neck Surgery, 1989, author: Operative Challenges in Otolaryngology Head and Neck Surgery, 1990, Neurosurgery Update 1: Diagnosis, Operative Technique and Neuro-Otology, 1990, Operative Techniques in Otolaryngology-Head and Neck Surgery, 1991, Surgery of Cranial Base Tumors, 1993; author: Handbook of Intraoperative Monitoring, 1994; co-author: Essential Otolaryngology, 1995, Otolaryngology, 1996; author: Atlas of Head & Neck Surgry-Otolaryngology, 1996, Disorders of the Vestibular System, 1996, Head and Neck Surgery Volume 2: Ear, 1996; co-author: Acoustic Tumors Diagnosis and Management, 2d edit., 1997, Diseases of the Ear. 6th edit., 1998, Essential Otolaryngology, 1998, Head and Neck Surgery-Otolaryngology, Vol. 2, 1998, Surgery of the Skull Base, 1998, Textbook of Clinical Neurology, 1998, Cranial Base Surgery, 1999; author: The Facial Nerve, 2000; co-author: Operative Techniques in Neurosurgery, 2001, Controversies in Otolaryngology, 2001, Surgery of the Ear, 5th edit., 2002, Essential Otolaryngology, 2003; editor: Neurologic Surgery of the Ear and Skull Base, 1982; contbg. editor: Otologic Surgery, 1994, 3d edit., 2001; co-editor: Neurotology, 1994; contbr. over 200 articles to profl. jours. Capt. USAF, 1964—66. Recipient Alumni Achievement award, U. Ill., 1997, Gold medal, Prosper Meniere's Soc., 2000; fellow, House Ear Inst. and Clinic, 1970—71. Fellow: AMA, Am. Laryngol. Rhinol. Otol. Soc., Am. Acad. Olotaryngology Head and Neck Surgery (pres. 1988, com. facial nerve disorders, pres. 1987—88); mem.: ACS, Asian Conf. Neurol. Surgeons, N.Am. Skull Base Soc. (pres. 1995—96), Rsch. Study Club, LA Soc. Otolaryngology (pres. 1986—87), Otolaryngology Soc. Australia (hon.), Royal Soc. Medicine (hon.), LA County Med. Assn., Calif. Med. Assn., Am. Otol. Soc. (task force subcertification, pres. 1995—96), Am. Neurotology Soc. (exec. coun., pres. 1984—85), Centurion Club, Alpha Omega Alpha. Republican. Achievements include research in neurotology; cochlear implant; auditory brainstem implant. Avocations: fishing, hunting. Office: House Ear Clinic 2100 W 3rd St Los Angeles CA 90057 Office Phone: 213-483-9930. Business E-Mail: dbrackmann@hei.org.

BRADARIC, NIKOLA, epidemiologist; b. Kotlenice, Dalmatia, Croatia, Dec. 19, 1947; s. Jozo and Anda Bradaric; m. Maja Salinovic, Aug. 16, 1962; children: Ivica, Dora, Domagoj. MD, Med. Sch. Zagreb, Croatia, 1971, MSc, 1987, PhD, 1994. Head dept. infection disease U. Hosp. Split, Croatia, 2000—; prof. Med. Faculty Split, 2000—, head nursery sch., 2002—, head infectology, 2006. Chief Dept. Infectious Diseases, U. Hosp. Split, 1989—92, 2000—08. Pres. Bowling Club Postar Split, 2007—. Mem.: Bowling Club Poštar. Home: Luciceva 13 Split 21000 Croatia Office: Univ Hosp Split Spinciceva 1 21-000 Split Croatia Office Fax: 0038521557207. Business E-Mail: nikola.bradaric@st.htnet.hr.

BRADBURY, MICHAEL WAYNE, molecular biologist; b. Famington, Maine, Nov. 13, 1953; s. Richard Douglas and Olive (Donahue) B. BS in Biology, Rochester Inst. Tech., 1976; MPh in Biology, Yale U., 1979, PhD in Biology, 1982. Postdoctoral fellow U. Calif., Davis, 1982-84; scientist Biosyne Corp., Houston, 1984-87; instr. Mt. Sinai Med. Sch., NYC, 1988-91, rsch. asst. prof., 1991-92, molecular biologist, 1993—. Assoc. editor: Jour. Exptl. Zoology, 1991—; contbr. articles to profl. jours. Mem. AAAS, Am. Genetic Assn., Am. Soc. of Zoologists, Soc. for Devel. Biology, Sigma Xi. Democrat. Avocations: naturism, photography, desktop pub. Office: Mt Sinai Med Sch Box 1039 1 Gustave L Levy Pl New York NY 10029-6500

BRADDOM, RANDALL LEE, physiatrist, educator; b. Monarch, Va., Oct. 29, 1942; s. Audy Lee and Ruth Janet Braddom; m. Diana Verdun, 2001; children from previous marriage: Eric C., Steven R., Karen L. BA, DePauw U., 1964; MD, Ohio State U., 1968, MS, 1971. Diplomate Am. Bd. Electrodiagnostic Medicine, Am. Bd. Phys. Medicine and Rehab. Rotating intern Mt. Carmel Hosp., Columbus, Ohio, 1968-69; resident in phys. medicine and rehab. Ohio State Univ. Hosps., Columbus, 1969-72; physiatrist, electromyographer Rancocas Valley Hosp., Willingboro, NJ, 1972-74, Phila. Naval Med. Ctr., 1972-74; asst. prof. phys. medicine and rehab. U. Cin., 1974-75, assoc. prof., dir. phys. medicine and rehab., 1975-81; med. dir. phys. med. and rehab. St. Francis-St. George Hosp., Cin., 1987-89, Providence Hosp., Cin., 1982-89; assoc. prof., dep. chmn. rehab. medicine Temple U., Phila., 1989-91; chmn. rehab. medicine Albert Einstein Hosp., Phila., 1989-91; v.p. med. affairs Moss Rehab. Hosp., Phila., 1989-91; practitioner Rehab. Assocs., Indpls., 1991-96; med. dir. Hook Rehab. Ctr., Indpls., 1991-98; prof., chmn. phys. medicine and rehab. Ind. U. Sch. Medicine, Indpls., 1991-98. Dir. Wishard Health Svcs., Indpls., Ind.; physiatrist Albert Einstein Med. Ctr. N., Phila., 1973; clin. instr. rehab. medicine Thomas Jefferson Coll. Med., Phila., 1972-74; assoc. in medicine Jewish Hosp., Cin., 1974-89; cons. phys. medicine and rehab. VA Hosp., Cin., 1975-81; dir. phys. med. and rehab. U. Hosps., U. Cin., 1975-81; assoc. clin. prof. phys. med. Ohio State U., Columbus, 1984-90; clin. assoc. prof. phys. medicine and rehab. U. Cin., Coll. Medicine, 1982-89; cons. St. Francis Hosp., Indpls., 1991-97; phys. med. and rehab. svc. chief Wishard Meml. Hosp., Indpls., 1991-2000; dir. phys. medicine and rehab. svc. Richard Roudebush VA Hosp., Indpls., 1991-97; vis. prof. Dept. Phys. Medicine and Rehab. U. Ark., 1992, U. Ky. Dept Phys. Medicine and Rehab., 1992, Dept. Internal Medicine Divsn. Phys. Medicine & Rehab. La. State U. Sch. Medicine, New Orleans, La., 1994, Baylor Coll. Medicine Dept. Phys. Medicine & Rehab., 1994, N.J. Sch. Medicine and Dentistry Dept. P.M. & R.; presenter in field; lectr. in field. Author: (with others) Physical Medicine & Rehabilitation Review, 1980; editor: Sports Medicine and Rehabilitation: A Sport-Scientific Approach, 1994, Physical Medicine and rehabilitation, 1996; contbr. articles to profl. jours. Founder, med. dir. ECCO Family Health Ctr., Inc., Columbus, 1970-72; bd. dirs. Nat. Paraplegia Found., 1975-80; med. adviser Easter Seals Soc. Southwestern Ohio, 1980-82; asst. scoutmaster Troop 291, Boy Scouts Am., 1982-84; chmn. Citizens for Our Schs. Tax Levy Campaign, Forest Hills Sch. Dist., Cin., 1985; trustee Total Living Concepts, Inc., Cin., 1977-85, Disability Svcs. Group, Inc., Cin., 1985-89; bd. examiners The Henry B. Betts award, 1991-94. Lt. comdr. USNR, 1972—74. Recipient Kiwanis Club Citizenship award, Dayton, 1960, Rsch. award Am. Paralyzed Vets. Assn., 1968, Am. Therapeutic Soc., 1968, Landacre Soc. award Ohio State U., 1978, Sidney Licht Lectureship Ohio State U., 1985, Alumni Achievement award Ohio State U., 1993, Sidney Licht Lectureship U. Minn., 1993, Randy Braddom award U. Cin. Coll. Medicine, 1989, Landwerlen award, Muscular Dystrophy Found. Ind., 1994, Lifetime Achievement award, AANEM, 2004; named Man of Yr. Columbus Citizen-Jour., 1970. Mem. Am. Acad. Phys. Med. and Rehab. (med. edn. com. 1983-86, membership recruitment group 1987, career brochure devel. group 1987, joint ann. meeting planning subcom. 1987-88, chairperson continuing med. edn. subcom. 1982-86, sci. program com. 1982-86, mktg. and comm. com. 1987-89, chairperson med. edn. com. 1986-88, sec. bd. govs. 1988-90, third-mem.-at-large 1990-91, 2nd mem.-at-large 1991-92, 1st mem.-at-large 1992-93, chair awards com. 1992-93, v.p. 1994-95, fin. com. 1994-95, chair annual meeting task force 1994-95, pres. elect 1994-95, pres. 1995-96, past pres. 1996-97, Disting. Clinician award 1997), Am. Assn. Electrodiagnostic Medicine (com. on edn. 1974-76, exam. com. 1975-76, liaision to assn. of acad. physiatrists 1988, chairperson courses com. 1986-89, pres.-elect 1989-90, bd. dirs. 1989-92, pres. 1990-91, immediate past pres.-chairperson long-range planning com. 1991-92, chmn. long range planning com. 1991-92, alt. del. AMA House of Dels. 1993-95, nominating com. 1993-94, chmn. 1994-95), Am. Assn. Electrodiagnostic Medicine, Assn. Acad. Physiatrists, Ohio State Med. Alumni Assn., AMA, Am. Bd. Electrodiagnostic Medicine (bd. dirs. 1994, long-range planning com. 1994, treas. 1995-98), Cin. Soc. of Phys. Medicine and Rehab. (pres., founder 1987-88), Internat. Med. Med. Assn. (U.S. counselor 1986-95). Presbyterian. Avocations: bicycling, writing, tennis. Office: 80 Oak Hill Rd Red Bank NJ 07701 Home Phone: 215-699-5035; Office Phone: 732-741-2313. Personal E-mail: rbraddom@earthlink.net.

BRADFORD, CAROL R., otolaryngologist, educator; MD, U. of Mich., 1986. Diplomate Am. Bd. Otolaryngology, 1993. Resident Univ. Of Mich., Ann Arbor, Mich., 1987—92; prof. and chair otolaryngology, co-dir. head and neck oncology program Univ. of Mich. Health System. Office: University of Michigan Health System 1500 E Medical Center Dr Ann Arbor MI 48109 Office Phone: 734-936-4000.

BRADFORD, WILLIAM DALTON, pathologist, educator; b. Rochester, NY, Nov. 2, 1931; s. William Leslie and Lenora Dee (Dalton) B.; m. Anne Bevington Harden, July 8, 1961; children—Scott Harden, Lisa B. Lee BA, Amherst Coll., 1954; MD, Western Res. U., 1958. Diplomate Am. Bd. Pediatrics, Am. Bd. Anatomic Pathology. Intern in pathology Boston Children's Med. Ctr., 1958-59, resident in pediatrics, 1959-61; teaching fellow in pathology Harvard Med. Sch., 1963-64, fellow Mead Johnson, 1963—64; asst. prof. pathology Duke U., Durham, NC, 1966-70, assoc. prof., 1970-81, prof., 1981—, assoc. dean, 1970-71, 74-78, 84-87, asst. to chancellor for health affairs, 1987-89, dir. pediatric pathology, 1966—, dir. pathology tng. program, 1974-2001. Pres. Durham YMCA, 1978, bd. dirs., 1976-83, 90-95; mem. bd. visitors YMCA Camps Sea Gull/Seafarer, chair, 2002-07; faculty chmn. athletics Duke U., 1979-85. Lt. comdr. USN, 1961-63. Recipient Golden Apple award Student Med. Assn., 1969, 93, 95, 98, Layman of Yr. award YMCA, 1974, 78, Disting. Tchr. award Duke Med. Alumni Assn., 1989, Life Time Achievement award, YMCA The Triangle, 2008. Mem. Internat. Acad. Pathology, Am. Assn. Pathologists, Soc. Pediatric Research, Group for Rsch. in Pathology Edn., Soc. for Pediatric Pathology (pres. 1987-88), Nat. Collegiate Athletic Assn. Council, Nat. Faculty Athletics Reps. Forum (chmn. 1985), Atlantic Coast Conf. (pres. 1982-83), Duke Med. Alumni Coun. (pres. 2000-01, exec. com. med. sch. admissions, vice-chmn. 2007—), Sigma Xi, Alpha Omega Alpha, YMCA Triangle (trustee). Office: Duke U Med Ctr PO Box 3712 Durham NC 27710-0001 Office Phone: 919-684-5112. Business E-Mail: bradf001@mc.duke.edu.

BRADLEY, CAROL ANN, nursing executive, editor; b. Genoa, Nebr., July 7, 1953; d. John Martin and Marguerite (Leonard) Brower; m. Jonathan R. Bradley, Nov. 30, 1985; children: Amanda, Emma. Assoc. Nursing, U. Nebr., Omaha, 1974, BSN, 1977; MSN, U. Ariz., 1978. Staff charge nurse U. Nebr., Omaha, 1974—77; mem. faculty, staff nurse U. Ariz., Tucson, 1977—78; clin. nurse specialist VA, San Diego, 1978—80; dir. nursing med. Good Samaritan Med. Ctr., Phoenix, 1980—85; v.p. patient care United Western Med. Ctr., Santa Ana, Calif., 1986—87; chief nursing officer Rancho Los Amigos Med. Ctr., Downey, Calif., 1987—92; v.p. patient care svcs. Huntington Meml. Hosp., Pasadena, Calif., 1992—99; regional v.p./editor Nurseweek Pub. Co., Sunnyvale, Calif., 2000—03; prin., owner Careforce Consulting Group, S. Pasadena, Calif., 1999—; faculty The Governance Inst., LaJolla, Calif.; regional CNO Tenet Healthcare, Inc., Santa Ana, Calif., 2003—09; sr. v.p., sys. CNO Legacy Health Sys., Portland, Oreg. Contbr. articles to profl. jours. Wharton/J & J fellow, 1991. Mem. Am. Orgn. Nurse Execs. (bd. dirs. 1994-97, chmn. edn. commn., pres. elect 1998, pres. 1999), Assn. Calif. Nurse Leaders (bd. dirs. 1988-90, sec. 1990-92, pres. 1992), CGFNS (pres. 2010-11). Democrat. E-mail: cabradley7753@msn.com.

BRADLEY, HARRISON KEITH, physician; b. Plattsburgh, NY, July 23, 1978; BA, Ctrl. Meth. Coll., 2001; MD, U. Mo., Columbia Sch. Medicine, 2005. Physician US Army, 2008—. Decorated Bronze Star medal US Army. Fellow: Am. Acad. Family Physicians. Home: 4112 Taneil Dr Manhattan KS 66502-8800 Personal E-mail: bradley.k.harrison@amedd.army.mil.

BRADLEY, JOHN ANDREW, surgeon; b. Huddersfield, Yorkshire, Eng., Oct. 24, 1950; s. Colin Bradley and Christine; m. Eleanor Mary Bolton; children: James, Michael. MB, BChir, U. Leeds, Eng., 1975; PhD, U. Glasgow, Scotland, 1982. Cons. surgeon Western Infirmary, Glasgow, 1984—93; prof. surgery and immunology U. Glasgow, 1993—97; prof. surgery U. Cambridge, England, 1997—. Pres. Brit. Transplantation Soc., 1999—2002. Editor: (jour.) Transplantation, 2002—; contbr. articles to profl. jours. Fellow: Royal Coll. Surgeons Glasgow. Office: Univ Cambridge Dept Surgery Cambridge CB2 2QQ England Business E-Mail: jab52@cam.ac.uk.

BRADLEY, KATHLEEN, obstetrician, perinatologist; b. LA, Dec. 24, 1959; d. Yvonne Bradley; m. David Pacic. BA, Occidental Coll., 1981; MD, St. George's Sch. Medicine, Bayshore, NY, 1988. Diplomate Am. Bd. Ob-Gyn. Intern, resident Bklyn. Hosp., 1988-92; pvt. practice; attending physician Cedars-Sinai Med. Ctr., LA, 1992—. Fellow Harbor-UCLA & Cedars Sinao Med. Ctr. Mem.: ACOG, L.A. Am. Med. Women's Assn. (pres. 2002), L.A. Radiologic Soc., L.A. Ob-Gyn. Soc., Maternal-Fetal Medicine Soc., Am. Inst. Ultrasound in Medicine. Office: 18399 Ventura Blvd Ste 249 Tarzana CA 91356-6402 Home: 32365 Lake Pleasant Dr Westlake Village CA 91361-3916

BRADLEY, LAURENCE ALAN, psychologist; b. Cleve., Sept. 13, 1949; s. Irving and Jeanne (Weil) B.; m. Gifford Weary, Dec. 28, 1974 (div. 1979); m. Elizabeth Wrenn, Oct. 3, 1981 (div. 1991), Virginia Wadley, March 26, 2007. BA cum laude in Psychology with honors, Vanderbilt U., Nashville, 1971, PhD in Psychology, 1975. Clin. intern Duke U. Med. Ctr., Durham, NC, 1975-76; asst. prof. U. Tenn., Chattanooga, 1976-77, Fordham U., Bronx, NY, 1977-80, Bowman Gray Sch. Med., Winston-Salem, NC, 1980-82, assoc. prof., 1982-89, adminstrv. head sect. med. psychology, 1981-89; assoc. prof., dir. epidemiology, edn. & health svcs. rsch. Multipurpose Arthritis & Musculoskeletal Disease Ctr U. Ala., Birmingham, 1989-92, prof., dir. epidemiology, edn. & health svcs. rsch., 1992-99; prof., dir. neurobehavioral medicine rsch. Multidisciplinary Clin. Rsch. Ctr., Birmingham, 1999—. Adj. assoc. prof. U. NC, Greensboro, 1983-89; vis. behavioral scientist Orebro Med. Ctr. Hosp., Sweden, 1986-92. Co-author: Health Psychology: Clinical Methods and Research, 1991; co-editor: Medical Psychology: Contributions to Behavioral Medicine, 1981, Coping with Chronic Disease: Research and Applications, 1983; assoc. editor: Clin. Psychology, Pain, 1995—2000, editl. bd.: Health Psychology, 1999—2001, Arthritis Care and Rsch., 1995—2004, Jour. Back and Musculoskeletal Rehab., 1999—. Rsch. grantee Robert Wood Johnson Found., 1983-86, Am.-Scandinavian Found., 1986, Am. Fibromyalgia Syndrome Assoc., 1996, Fetzer Inst., 2000-05, NIH, 1989— Fellow APA, Soc. Personality Assessment; mem. Internat. Assn. Study of Pain, Am. Pain Soc., Soc. Behavioral Medicine, Am Coll. Rheumatology, Arthritis Health Professions Assoc. (Disting. scholar, 1992), Sigma Xi, Phi Beta Kappa. Democrat. Achievements include research to determine that relaxation training and psychological therapy reduces pain behavior and number of painful joints among patients with rheumatoid arthritis, functional brain activity abnormalities are associated with chronic pain, ethnic differences in endogenous opioid regulation of pain in patients with knee osteoarthritis. Office: Univ Ala Divsn Clin Immunol and Rheumatol 177A Shelby Rsch Bldg 1825 Univ Blvd Birmingham AL 35294-0001 Office Phone: 205-934-8550. Business E-Mail: braddog@uab.edu.

BRADLEY, LINDA DARLENE, gynecologist; b. Cleve., June 25, 1955; MD, U. Cin. Coll. Medicine, 1981. Vice chair ob-gyn., Women's Health Inst. Cleve. Clinic, 1991—, bd. govs., 2006—10. Mem.: Am. Coll. Ob-gyn., Nat. Med. Assn., Am. Assn. Gynecologic Laparoscopists (pres.). Avocations: cooking, bicycling, walking. Office: 9500 Euclid Ave Desk A 81 Cleveland OH 44195 Office Fax: 216-636-5129. Business E-Mail: bradlel@ccf.org.

BRADLEY, PATRICK JAMES, otolaryngologist; b. Thurles, Ireland, May 10, 1949; s. Gerard and Nan (O'Leary) B.; m. Sheena Josephine Kelly, May 19, 1973; children: Paula, Darragh, Cormac, Eoin, Caitriona. MB, BChir, U. Coll. Dublin, 1973, Diploma in Child Health, 1975; MBA, Notingham U., 2002. Cert. surgeon in diseases of the ear, nose and throat. Intern St. Vincents Hosp., Dublin, 1973-74; registrar, sr. house officer Royal Coll. Surgeons, Dublin, 1974-77; S.H.O. Royal Victoria Eye/Ear Hosp., Dublin, 1977; registrar Royal Liverpool Hosp., 1977—82; cons. surgeon U. Hosp., Nottingham, England, 1982—2009; prof. head, neck, oncologic surgery Nottingham U., 2007—. Faculty mem. Internat. Sisson's Head and Neck Oncology Workshop, 1989—, Second World Meeting Laryncol. Cancer, Sydney, 1994; vice chmn. ENT Adv. Group, Trent Regional

Health Authority, 1990-96; clin. dir. dept. otolaryngology/audiology U. Hosp. Nottingham, 1991-96, clin. dir. audit and risk, 1996-2000; nat. lead clinician head and neck cancer, 2003-08, forensic archeologist, Nottingham Trent U., 2009, ret. cons., 2009 Contbr. chpts. to books and articles to profl. jours. Fellow Royal Coll. Surgeons Dublin (examiner), Royal Coll. Surgeons Edinburgh (examiner); mem. Otorhinolaryngological Rsch. Soc. (coun. 1993-96), Royal Soc. Medicine (coun. sect. laryngology/rhinology 1990-2000, pres. sect. laryngology/rhinology 1998-99), Brit. Assn. Otorhinology/Head and Neck Surgery (chmn. edn. & tng. com. 1999-2001, chmn. head and neck group 2000—08), British Assn. Head and Neck Oncologists (pres. 2003—05), European Larnygol. Soc. (pres. 2004-06), European Head and Neck Soc. (founding bd. mem. 2004), Midlands Inst. Otology (pres. 2005-07), European Salivary Gland Soc. (pres. 2007-09). Roman Catholic. Avocations: golf, skiing, travel, scuba.

BRADLEY, REBEKAH, healthcare educator, lab administrator; Adj. asst. prof. Emory U. Dept. Psychology, 2002—, assoc. dir. personality & psychopathology lab. Office: Deptartment of Psychology 532 Kilgo Cir Atlanta GA 30322 Office Phone: 404-727-7440, 404-727-7438. Office Fax: 404-727-7476, 404-727-0372. E-mail: psychlab@emory.edu, rbradl2@emory.edu.

BRADLEY, RICHARD EDWIN, retired academic administrator; b. Omaha, Mar. 9, 1926; s. Louis J. and Betsy (Winterton) B.; m. Doris I. McGowan, June 8, 1946; children— Diane, Karen, David. Student, Creighton U., 1946-48; BSD., U. Nebr., 1950, D.D.S., 1952; MS, State U. Iowa, 1958. Instr. State U. Iowa, 1957-58; asst. prof. Creighton U., 1958-59; asst. prof., chmn. dept. periodontics U. Nebr., 1959-62, assoc. prof., 1962-65, prof., 1965-67; assoc. dean Coll. Dentistry, 1967-68, dean, 1968-80; pres., dean Baylor Coll. Dentistry, 1980-90, pres., dean emeritus, 1990—; clin. prof. Coll. Dentistry U. Nebr. Med. Coll., Lincoln, 1990—; cons. dental edn., 199-93. Mem. Commn. A, Coun. on Dental Edn., 1986-93; pres. Am. Assn. Dental Schs., 1977-78; mem. nat. adv. com. on health professions edn. Dept. Health and Human Resources, 1982-86; pres. Am. Fund for Dental Health, 1986-87; mem. bd. of vis. Temple Univ. Sch. of Dentistry, 2001—. Editor: The New Dentist, 1992-94; contbg. editor Orban's Textbook of Periodontics, 1963; contbr. Clark's Clin., 1980. Mem. bd. visitors Temple U. Sch. Dentistry, 2003-. With USNR, 1944—46. Established Dr. Richard and Doris Endowed Fund periodontics U. Nebr. Found., 2006. Fellow AAAS, Internat. Coll. Dentists; mem. ADA, Am. Acad. Peridontology Found. (bd. dirs., pres. 1994-96), Am. Coll. Dentists (regent 1992-96, v.p. 1997-98, pres. Found. 2001-02), Sigma Xi, Omicron Kappa Upsilon. Office: U Nebraska Coll Dentistry Lincoln NE 68583-0740

BRADLEY, STERLING GAYLEN, microbiology and pharmacology researcher; b. Springfield, Mo., Apr. 2, 1932; s. Benn and Lora (Brown) B.; m. Lois Evelyn Lee, May 13, 1951; children: Don, Evelyn, John, Phillip; m. Judith Bond, July 24, 1974; 1 son, Kevin. BA, BS, Mo. State U., 1950; MS, Northwestern U., 1952, PhD (NSF fellow), 1954; PhD certificate med. mycology, Duke U., 1957. Grad. teaching asst. Northwestern U., Evanston, Ill., 1950-51, Abbott research asst., 1951-52, instr. biology, 1954; instr. dept. bacteriology and immunology U. Minn., 1956-57, asst. prof. dept. bacteriology, 1957-59, assoc. prof. dept. microbiology, 1959-63, grad. faculty genetics, 1961-68, prof., 1963-68, chmn. genetics faculty group, 1964; chmn. dept. microbiology Va. Commonwealth U., Richmond, 1968-82, prof. depts. pharmacology and microbiology, 1979-96, dean basic health scis., 1982-93; v.p. acad. affairs U. Md. Biotech Inst., Balt., 1996-99, Pa. State Hershey Med. Ctr., sr. assoc. dir. rsch. affairs, 1999—2005, vis. prof., humanities, 1999—2002, vis. prof., pharmcalogy, 2001—07, vis. prof., biochemical molecular biology, pharm., 2005—, interim dir. technol. devel., 2010—11, BB BioCritique Inc., 2008—, prin., 2009—. Vis. worker in pharmacology Cambridge (Eng.) U., 1978; mem. bd. sci. counselors NIH, 1968-72, chmn., 1970-72; mem. Internat. Com. Bacteriol. Systematics, 1966-74, exec. bd., 1970-74; mem. U.S. Pharmacopeial Com. of Revision, 1980-85; coord. Project 3 U.S.-USSR Joint Working Group on Microbiology, 1979-82; v.p. Found. Immunotoxicology, 1985-91, pres., 1991-97. Mem. editl. bd. Proc. Soc. Exptl. Biol. Medicine, 1966-72, Conf. on Anti-microbial Agts., 1960, Jour. Indsl. Microbiology, 1985-95; editor Jour. Bacteriology, 1970-78; contbr. articles to profl. jours. Trustee Southeastern U. Rsch. Assn., Inc., 1990-93; bd. dirs. Sci. Mus. Va. Found., 1993-98. Recipient Charles Porter award, 1983; named Mo. State U. Outstanding Alumnus, 1991, Life Achievement award Sci. Mus. Va., 1996; Eli Lilly postdoctoral fellow U. Wis., 1954-55; NSF postdoctoral fellow dept. genetics, 1955-56; NIH Sr. Fogarty internat. fellow, 1978. Fellow AAAS (life), Va. Acad. Sci. (life, past mem. council, sec. 1976-77); mem. Assn. Practical Profl. Ethics, Am. Acad. Microbiology, Am. Chem. Soc., Am. Soc. Microbiology (past mem. council, treas. 1985-91, ethics com. 1997-99, centennial com. chair 1994-99), Soc. Protozoologists, Soc. Indsl. Microbiology (past pres.), Am. Inst. Biol. Sci. (past dir., gen. chmn. 41st Meeting, 1989-90, bd. dirs. 1996-99), Soc. Toxicology, U.S. Fedn. Culture Collections (pres. 1984-86), Internat. Union Microbiol. Socs. (treas. 1994-99), Mycol. Soc. Am. (life), Torrey Bot. Club (life), N.Y. Acad. Scis. (life), Am. Soc. Pharm. and Exptl. Therapeutics, Am. Assn. Immunologists, Sigma Xi (life, pres. chpt. 1975-76, fin. com. 1991-99, audit com., 2010-), Am. Soc. Biochem. Molecular Biol. Achievements include research in the field of immunotoxicology, interactions between drugs and toxins, role of the protease 'meprin'. Home: 5300 Longwood Dr Durham NC 27713 Personal E-mail: sgbradley1932@yahoo.com.

BRADSHAW, MAJOR WILLIAM, dean, medical educator; b. Marlin, Tex., Feb. 2, 1940; m. Susan Robertson, 1964; children: Heather, Jennifer, Major. BA in Zoology with highest honors, U. Tex., 1962; MS in Anatomy with honors, Baylor Coll. of Medicine, 1966, MD with highest honors, 1967. Diplomate Am. Bd. Internal Medicine, Am. Bd. Infectious Diseases. Intern Osler Med. Svc., Johns Hopkins Hosp., 1968, med. resident, 1969; clin. fellow infectious diseases The Meth. Hosp., Houston, 1971-72; clin. assoc. NIH, 1969-71; asst. prof. medicine and microbiology and immunology Baylor Coll. of Medicine, 1972-76, assoc. prof. medicine, 1976-84, assoc. prof. microbiology-immunology, 1976—, assoc. dean, 1976-93, sr. assoc. dean, 1993-95, prof. medicine, 1984—, prof. molecular virology & microbiology, 2001, John S. Dunn prof. medicine, sr. v.p., dean of med. edn., 2004—06; founding dean U. Botswana Sch. Medicine, 2006—09; dir. Global Health Programs, Baylor Coll. Medicine, 2010—. Adv. coun. U. Tex. Marine Sci. Inst. Contbr. articles to profl. jours. Fellow ACP (past dir. S.E. dist. Tex.), Infectious Diseases Soc. Am.; mem. AMA, AAUP, Tex. Med. Assn., Harris County Med. Soc., Houston Soc. of Internal Medicine, Am. Soc. Microbiology, Assn. of Am. Med. Colls., Found. for Advanced Edn. in the Scis., Inc., S.W. Assn. of Student Pers. Adminstrs., Tex. Acad. of Physicians, Johns Hopkins U. Alumni Assn., Johns Hopkins Med. and Surg. Soc., Michael E. DeBakey Cardiovascular Soc., Infectious Diseases Soc. of Tex., Alpha Omega Alpha, Sigma Xi, Phi Beta Kappa, Phi Eta Sigma. Avocations: reading, fly fishing, fishing, scuba diving, travel. Office: U Botswana Sch Medicine Private Bag 0022 Gaborone Botswana also: Baylor Coll Medicine One Baylor Plaza Houston TX 77030 Home Phone: 713-528-6304; Office Phone: 713-798-8878. Office Fax: 713-798-3096. Business E-Mail: majorb@bcm.edu.

BRADWAY, ROBERT, medical products executive; BA in Biology, Amherst Coll., Mass.; MBA, Harvard U. Positions through mng. dir. healthcare practice Europe Morgan Stanley, NYC & London, 1988—2006; v.p. ops. strategy Amgen, Inc., Thousand Oaks, Calif., 2006—07, exec. v.p., CFO, 2007—10, pres., COO, 2010—. Office: Amgen Inc 1 Amgen Ctr Dr Thousand Oaks CA 91320-1799 Office Phone: 805-447-1000. Office Fax: 805-447-1010. *

BRADY, AARON JOHN, pharmacist; b. Belfast, Nov. 25, 1973; BSc with honors, Queen's U. Belfast Pharmacy, 1995, PhD, 2008. Clin. pharmacist, renal, King's Coll. Hosp. NHS, 1999—2002, clin. pharmacist, ICU, Belfast City Hosp., 2009—. Tchg. fellow Queen's U. Belfast, 2008—09. Fellow: Higher Edn. Acad.; mem.: Guild Healthcare Pharmacists, Soc. Gen. Microbiology, Pharm. Soc. Northern Ireland. Avocations: tennis, piano, guitar. Home: 74 Priory Pk Belfast Antrim BT10 0AG Northern Ireland Personal E-mail: aaron.brady@qub.ac.uk.

BRADY, KATHLEEN T., psychiatrist, educator; PhD in Pharmacology; MD, Med. U. SC, 1985. Diplomate Am. Bd. Psychiatry and Neurology-psychiatry, 1992, Am. Bd. Psychiatry and Neurology-addiction psychiatry, 2002. Resident psychiatry Med. Univ. SC, 1986—89, fellow addiction psychiatry, 1986—89, asst. dean for clin. rsch., 2005, dir. gen. clin. rsch. ctr., 2005, assoc. dean clin. and translational rsch., dir. clin. and translational rsch. ctr., prof. psychiatry; dir. Addiction Psychiatry Fellowship Program, 1994—2004. Pres. Am. Assn. of Edn. and Rsch. in Substance Abuse, 1994—96. Recipient Betty Ford award, 2001, Women of Achievement award, Gov. Jim Hodges, 2010; grantee First Mid-career Devel. Grant (K-24), Med. Univ. SC, 1999. Mem.: Am. Acad. of Addiction Psychiatry (pres.). Office: Medical University of South Carolina Department of Psychiatry 67 President St Box 250861 Charleston SC 29425 Office Phone: 843-792-5205. Office Fax: 843-792-4817. E-mail: bradyk@musc.edu.

BRADY, LUTHER W., JR., radiation oncologist, educator; b. Rocky Mount, NC, Oct. 20, 1925; s. Luther W. and Gladys B. AA, George Washington U., 1944, AB, 1946, MD, 1948, DFA (hon.), 2003, Colgate U., 1988, Pa. Acad. Fine Arts, 2009; DSc (hon.), Lehigh U., 1990; MD (hon.), Toyama U., Japan, 1996; D (hon.), U. Heidelberg, Germany, 1997. Diplomate Am. Bd. Radiology (treas. 1980-82, v.p. 1982-84, pres. 1984-86). Intern Jefferson Med. Coll. Hosp., Phila., 1948-50, resident in radiology, 1954-55; resident radiology Hosp. U. Pa., Phila., 1955-56; fellow Nat. Cancer Inst., 1954-57; practice medicine, specializing in radiation oncology Phila. Asst. instr. radiology Jefferson Med. Coll. Hosp., 1954-55, U. Pa., Phila., 1955, instr., 1956-57, assoc. radiology, 1957-59; asst. prof. radiology Coll. of Physicians and Surgeons, Columbia U., NYC, summer, 1959; assoc. prof. radiology Hahnemann Med. Coll. and Hosp., Phila., 1959-62, prof., 1963—97, Disting. Univ. prof., 1997-, chmn. dept. radiation oncology, 1970—97; asst. prof. radiology Harvard Med. Sch., Boston, 1962-63; Hylda/Cohn Am. Cancer Soc. prof. clin. oncology Drexel U. Coll. Medicine, 1967-; mem. med. radiation adv. com. Bur. Radiation Health, HEW, 1971-74; cons. radiation therapy various hosp.; mem. US del. to Interam. Congress Radiology, 1975, Internat. Congress of Radiology, 1981; sec. gen. Internat. Congress Radiology, 1985; med. adv. radiation therapy, med. affairs com., 1984-97; dir. Pa. Blue Shield, Camp Hill; chair Pa. Cancer Control Bd., 1989-97. Author: Tumors of the Nervous System, 1975, Cancer of the Lung, Clinical Applications of the Electron Beam; editor Cancer Clin. Trials (Am. Jour. Clin. Oncology), (with C. Perez) Principles and Practice of Radiation Oncology; editorial bd. Cancer; assoc. editor: Gynecologic Oncology, Am. Jour. Roentgenology, Cancer Research; sr. editor: Internat. Jour. Radiol. Oncology; contbr. articles on radiation therapy to profl. jour. Bd. dirs. Assn. Artists Equity of Phila., Welcome House, 1974-94, Settlement Music Sch., 1973—, Phila. Art Alliance, 1977-84; mem. oriental art com., trustee Phila. Mus. Art, 1974—, chmn. friends exec. com., 1968-72, mem. print, contemporary art and Indian art coms., 1974—; trustee Fleisher Art Meml., 1997-, Founders Award, 2003; trustee Curtis Inst. Music, 1997-, The Phillips Collection, 2003-05. Served to lt. M.C. USN, 1950-54. Recipient Grubbe award Chgo. Radiol. Soc., 1977, Gold medal Gilbert Fletcher Soc., 1984, Albert Soiland Gold medal U. So. Calif., 1985, del Regato Gold medal, 1986, Disting. Alumni award George Washington U., 1991, Padro Pio medal, 1993, James Logan award Colonial Dames of America, 2008. Fellow Am. Coll. Radiology (Gold medal 1983); mem. AMA (Gold medal Disting. Svc. award 1999, Am. Roentgen Ray Soc., Am. Radium Soc. (Gold medal 1981), Am. Cancer Soc. (Disting. award 2008), Am. Fedn. Clin. Rsch., Am. Bd. Radiology, Am. Soc. Clin. Oncology, Am. Coll. Radiation Oncology (Gold medal 1996), Am. Soc. for Therapeutic Radiology and Oncology (pres. 1971-72, Gold medal 1987), Am. Assn. for Cancer Rsch., Soc. Chmn. Acad. Radiation Oncology Program (pres.), Soc. Chmn. Acad. Radiology Dept. (pres.), Assn. Pendergrass Fellows, Internat. Soc. for Radiation Oncology, Internat. Skeletal Soc., Internat. Club Radiotherapists, James Ewing Soc., Radiation Rsch. Soc., Soc. Surg. Oncology, Assn. Univ. Radiologists, Radiation Rsch. Soc., Radiol. Soc. N.Am. (pres., Gold medal 1989), Del. Med. Soc., Med. Soc. State Pa., Pa. Radiol. Soc., Phila. County Med. Soc.(Strittmater award 1999), Phila. Roentgen Ray Soc. Clubs: Merion Cricket; Racquet, Union League (Phila.), Phila., Peale. Office: 230 N Broad St Philadelphia PA 19102-1121 also: Hahnemann U Hosp Broad & Vine MS-200 Philadelphia PA 19102 Office Phone: 215-762-1998. Business E-Mail: Lbrady@drexelmed.edu.

BRADY, PATRICIA MARIE, retired nurse; b. Taylor, Pa., Feb. 6, 1946; d. Herman John and Regina Theresa (Yonushka) Kovalan; m. Edward Joseph Brady, June 22, 1968 (dec. Mar. 1996); children: Maureen C., Edward M. RN, St. Joseph's Hosp., Carbondale, Pa., 1966. Cert. emergency nurse. Staff nurse med.-surg. Wilkes-Barre (Pa.) Gen. Hosp., 1966; staff nurse med. Dept. VA Med. Ctr., Wilkes-Barre, 1966—72, staff nurse ambulatory care, emergency rm. and primary care, 1977—2008; advisor with Lia Sophia, 2009. Mem. diabetes adv. com. Dept. VA Med. Ctr., 1993—. Assisted in formation diabetes edn. program VA, 1994; established and facilitated VA Med. Ctr. Pain Clinic, 1996-2008. Mem. Pittston (Pa.) Area Taxpayers Assn., 1995—; parishner Sacred Heart of Jesus Ch., Dupont, Pa., 1968—. Mem.: Emergency Nurses Assn., Am. Assn. Diabetes Educators (by-laws com. 1995—), W.Va. Ballroom Dance Soc., Humane Soc. U.S., Gotham Swing Club. Democrat. Roman Catholic. Avocations: crafts, golf, dance. Home: 1289 Suscon Rd Pittston PA 18640-9596

BRADY, PAUL SCOTT, diagnostic radiologist; Grad., Royal Coll. of Surgeons, Ireland. Diplomate Am. Bd. of Radiology-diagnostic radiology. Intern Cleve. Clinic Found., resident; fellow vascular and interventional radiology Northwestern Meml. Hosp., Chgo. Office: 101 E Olney Ave Ste 505 Philadelphia PA 19120 Office Phone: 215-456-7000. Office Fax: 215-254-2599.

BRADY, PETER A., cardiologist, consultant; b. Coventry, Eng., Sept. 13, 1961; MBChB, Liverpool U., 1987, MD, 2000. Cons., divsn. cardiovasc. diseases Mayo Clinic, 2000, cons., dir. Electrocardiography and Ambulatory Monitoring Lab., 2000—. Fellow: RCP (London), Heart Rhythm Soc., Am. Coll. Cardiology. Office: 200 1st St SW Rochester MN 55905 Business E-Mail: brady.peter@mayo.edu.

BRADY, ROSCOE OWEN, neurogeneticist, educator; b. Phila., Oct. 11, 1923; s. Roscoe O. and Martha (Roberts) Brady; m. Bennet Carden Manning, 1972; 2 children. Student, Pa. State U., 1941-43; MD, Harvard Med. Sch., 1947; postgrad., U. Pa., 1948-49. Intern Hosp. U. Pa., 1947-48; NRC fellow U. Pa., 1948-50, USPHS spl. fellow, 1950-52; sect. chief Nat. Inst. Neurol. Diseases and Blindness, NIH, 1954-67, asst. lab. chief neurochemistry Bethesda, Md., 1967-72; chief developmental and metabolic neurology br. Nat. Inst. Neurol. Disorders and Stroke, NIH, 1972—; pres., CEO Targeted Techs., Inc., Rockville, Md., 2006—. Professorial lectr. George Washington U. Sch. of Medicine, 1963—73; mem. faculty Georgetown U. Sch. of Medicine, 1965—; mem. med. staff Children's Hosp., Washington, 1992—; chmn. sci. adv. bd. Therascope, A.G., Heidelberg, Germany. Author (with Donald B. Tower): Neurochemistry of Nucleotides and Animo Acids, 1960; author: Basic Neurosciences, 1975; author: (with John A. Barranger) Molecular Basis of Lysosomal Storage Disorders, 1984; author: numerous articles. With US Naval Med. Corps. Recipient award, Gairdner Found., 1973, Lasker Found., 1982, Passano Found., 1982, Warren Alpert Found. award, 1992, Myrtle Wreath award, Hadassah, 1993, Exec. Excellence award, Sr. Execs. Assn., 1993, 2007 Nat. Medal Technology and Innovation. Mem.: NAS (J.S. Kolvenko medal 1991), Inst. of Medicine, Am. Soc. Human Genetics, Am. Soc. Clin. Investigation, Am. Acad. Mental Retardation, Am. Acad. Neurology (Cotzias award 1980), Am. Soc. Biol. Chemists. Achievements include development of biosynthesis of myelin sheath lipids, nature of metabolic defects in Gaucher's disease, Neimann-Pick disease, Fabry's diseases and Tay-Sachs disease; enzyme replacement and gene therapy for lipid storage diseases; discovery of aberrant metabolism of sphingolipids in neoplastic diseases; role of antigenic sphingolipids in neurological diseases. Office: Developmental and Metabolic Neurology Br NINDS Bldg 10 Rm 3D04 10 Center Dr MSC 1260 Bethesda MD 20892-1260 Office Phone: 301-496-3285. Office Fax: 301-496-9480. Business E-Mail: bradyr@ninds.nih.gov.

BRADY, STEPHEN R. P. K., physician; b. New London, Conn., Oct. 13, 1955; s. Richard Harris and Jeanne Margaret (Halpin) Brady; m. Marsha Anne Erickson, June 18, 1978 (div. Jan. 1993); 1 child, Ericka Anuhea; m. Elizabeth Ada Rewick, Dec. 27, 1994 (div. Nov. 2006). AB cum laude, Harvard U., Cambridge, Mass., 1977; MPH, U. Hawaii, 1978, postgrad., 1979; MD, U. Pa., Phila., 1982. Diplomate Am. Bd. Internal Medicine. Intern U. Hawaii, 1982-83, resident in internal medicine, 1983-85, clin. instr. Sch. Medicine, 1986-99, clin. asst. prof. Sch. Medicine, 1999—2003, assoc. prof. Sch. Medicine, 2003—, vice-chair Dept. Native Hawaiian Health, Sch. Medicine, 2003—06; physician Kaiser Clinics, Honolulu, 1985-86; physician, med. dir. Kokua Kalihi Valley, Honolulu, 1986-89; physician Waianae (Hawaii) Coast Health Svc., 1989-94; asst. med. dir., physician Am. Hawaii Cruises, Honolulu, 1989-95; physician Straub Clinic and Hosp., Honolulu, 1984—; interim chair dept. Native Hawaiian Health, 2009—11. Founding chair Hawaii Consortium Continuing Med. Edn. U. Hawaii Sch. Medicine, 1993—; mem. com. rev. and recognition Accreditation Coun. Continuing Med. Edn., 2004—10, bd. dirs., 2007—09, mem. cem. rev. recognition, 2004—10. Co-host: (khon morning news) Ask the Doctor, 1996—; host (TV series) Health in Paradise, 2001—03, UH on Call, 2005—06; editor: Hawaii Med. Jour., 2005—. Cubmaster Boy Scouts Am., Kailua, Hawaii, 1995—2000; trustee St. Louis Sch., 2006—. Comdr. US Mcht. Marine, 1989—. Recipient Po'okela award, 1991, 1993, 1995, 1999, Guy Milnor award, 1999, 2010, Cub Scouter award, Aloha coun. Boy Scouts Am., 1999, Cubmaster award, 2000, Disting. Eagle Scout award, Boy Scouts Am., 2008; named Scot of the Yr., State of Hawaii, 1999, Physician of the Yr., Honolulu County Med. Soc., 2002; named one of Best Drs. in America, 2001—; Rsch. grantee, Kuakini Med. Rsch. Inst., Honolulu, 1971, Pacific Health Rsch. Inst., Honolulu, 1972—78, Children's Hosp., Phila., 1979, Paul Harris fellow, 1995, Grand Marshall, Prince Kuhio Parade, Honolulu, 2008. Fellow: ACP-Am. Soc. Internal Medicine; mem.: APHA, ACP (gov. Hawaii chpt. 2009—), AMA, Ahahui O Na Kauka (pres. 2004—06), Soc. Epidemiologic Rsch., Hawaii Med. Assn. (chair cont. med. edn. com. 1987—, councillor, named Physician of Yr. 2007), Plaza Club, Soroptimist (pres. 1998—99), Rotary, Elks, Delta Omega. Congregationalist. Avocations: singing, scuba diving, music. Office: Dept Native Hawaiian Health 677 Ala Moana Blvd # 1016B Honolulu HI 96813 Office Phone: 808-587-8559. Business E-Mail: skbrady@hawaii.edu.

BRAGA, LÚCIA WILLADINO, neuroscientist, researcher, dean; d. Gildo and Nelida Gomes Willadino; m. Pedro Braga, Apr. 12, 1975; children: Raquel Willadino, Rafael Willadino, Filipe Willadino. DSc in Neuropsychology, U. Brazil, 1994; DSc with hons., U. Reims Champagne-Ardenne, 1998; degree, La Salpêtrière, 1998. Head rschr. neuroscis. SARAH Network Rehab. Hosps., Brasilia, Brazil, 1984—94, exec. dir., dir. Dept. Neuropsychology, 1994—; prof. neuroscis. SARAH U. Rehab. Scis., 1997—, dean Dept. Neurosciences, 1997—; bd. dirs. SARAH Network Rehab. Hosps. Mem. editl. bd. Jour. Applied Neuropsychology, 2001—, Jour. Pediatric Rehab., 2003—, Jour. Disability and Rehab., 2005—. Recipient Nat. Merit award, Fernando Henrique Cardoso Pres. Brazil, 2000; named

Hon. Citizen, Ho. of Reps., City Brasilia, 2002. Mem.: World Fedn. NeuroRehabilitation (v.p. region 2002—), Internat. Brain Injury Assn. (bd. govs. 2000—), Soc. Brasileira Lesão Cerebral (pres. 1998—), Acad. Multidisciplinary Neurotrama, Internat. Neuropsychol. Soc. (assoc.; bd. dirs. 2001—04). Avocations: music, scuba diving, movies, theater, reading. Office: SARAH Network Rehab Hosps Smhs Bloco a 70335-901 Brasilia DF Brazil Office Fax: 55 61 3226-5280. Personal E-mail: luciabraga@sarah.br.

BRAGA, MOISES HELENO, physician; b. Brasil, Mar. 18, 1978; Degree, Promove U., 1995, 2003. Physician Vila da Serra Hosp., 2010—. Mem.: Peripheral Nerves Soc. Avocation: running. Home: Av Augusto de Lima 385/1404 Centro 385 Belo Horizonte Minas Gerais 30190-001 Brazil Personal E-mail: moizeusss@yahoo.com.br.

BRAGANÇA, MAURA JULIA, research scientist; b. Natal, Brazil, July 6, 1958; Degree in Chem. Engring., UFRN, 1982; PhD in Chemistry, Pontifícia U. Católica, Rio de Janeiro, 1999. Rschr. CNEN/IRD, 1999—. Cons. Pontifícia U. Católica, 1992—97. Master: IRD. Office: Voluntários da Pátria 41/501 B1A Rio de Janeiro 22270000 Brazil Business E-Mail: maura@ird.gov.br.

BRAHME, JOHAN E., plastic surgeon; b. Malmo, Sweden, Nov. 1, 1954; m. Sevil K. Brahme. Attended, U. Mich., 1977—79, U. Calif., 1973—77, MD, 1979—81. Diplomate Am. Bd. Surgery, 1990, Am. Bd. Plastic Surgery, 1994, licensed to practice Calif. (lic. number G49912), 1983. Intern surgery dept. Univ. of Calif., San Diego, 1981—82; resident gen. surgery Univ. of Calif. Med. Ctr., San Diego, 1982—87, resident plastic surgery divsn., 1990—91, chief resident plastic surgery divsn., 1991—92, clin. instr. plastic surgery divsn., 1992, clin. instr., fellow surg. oncology, 1987—89; assoc. clin. prof. surgery Univ. of Calif. Sch. of Medicine, San Diego, 1999; fellow Orthopedic Hosp., Los Angeles, Calif., 1989—90; flight physician Lite Flight Emergency Aero Med. Svc., 1984—85; sr. staff Sharp Meml. Hosp.; clin. staff Thornton Hosp. Univ. of Calif. Med. Ctr., San Diego; active staff Scripps Meml. Hosp., La Jolla, Calif.; pvt. practice La Jolla Cosmetic Surgery Ctr. Contbr. numerous pub. works. Mem.: San Diego Med. Soc., Calif. Med. Assn., San Diego Soc. of Plastic Surgery (pres.), Am. Soc. for Plastic Surgery. Office: La Jolla Cosmetic Surgery Center 9850 Genesee Ave Ste 130 La Jolla CA 92037 Office Phone: 858-452-1981. Office Fax: 858-452-9910. Business E-Mail: johanbrahme@yahoo.com.

BRAINARD, DAVID HOYT, psychology professor, department chairman; AB in Physics, magna cum laude, Harvard U., 1982; MEE, Stanford U., 1989, PhD in Psychology, 1989. Systems programmer Aox Inc., Hopkinton, Mass., 1982—83; postdoctoral fellow Ctr. for Visual Sci. U. Rochester, 1990—91; asst. prof. psychology U. Calif., Santa Barbara, 1991—95, assoc. prof. psychology, 1995—99, prof. psychology, 1999—2001, U. Pa., 2001—, chmn. dept. psychology, 2005—, co-dir., Vision Rsch. Ctr., 2005—08, dir., Vision Rsch. Ctr., 2009—; cons. Hewlett-Packard Laboratories, 1991—97, Enroute, Inc., 1998—99. Appearance (films) Fat Man and Little Boy, 1989; contbr. articles to profl. jours. Fellow: Optical Soc. Am. Achievements include patents for method and apparatus for estimating true color values for saturated color values in digitally captured image data, 2004 (with X. Zhang). Office: Dept Psychology Univ Pa Ste 302C 3401 Walnut St Philadelphia PA 19104 Office Phone: 215-573-7579. Office Fax: 215-746-6848. E-mail: brainard@psych.upenn.edu.

BRAINERD, MARY KEITH, health insurance company executive; b. St. Paul, Minn., Sept. 28, 1953; d. Keith K. and Mary F. (Fitzgibbon) Knopp; m. Richard Charles Brainerd, Mar. 31, 1984, children: Andrew D., Mary Angela. BA, U. Minn., 1975; MBA, St. Thomas Coll., St. Paul, 1979. Health educator Teenage Med. Service, Mpls., 1976-78; tng. devel. St. Mary's Hosp., Mpls., 1978-79; research analyst Blue Cross & Blue Shield, Eagan, Minn., 1979-81, mgr. mkt. research, 1981-84; v.p. Health Maintenance Orgn. Minn., Eagan, 1984-85, COO; exec. v.p., COO HealthPartners, Inc., Mpls., 1994—2002, pres., CEO, 2002—. Instr. faculty Metro State U. St. Paul, 1984-86; bd. dirs. SurModics, Inc., 2009- Mem. sch. bd. Mounds Park Acad., St. Paul, 1986—; bd. dirs. Minn. Life/Securian, The St. Paul Found., Capital City Partnership, Minn. Coun. Health Plans, Alliance Cmty. Plans, Fed. Res. Bank Mpls. Recipient Medal of Distinction, Coll. St. Catherine, 1998, Award for Ethical Leadership, U. St. Thomas, 2002; named Exec. of Yr., Mpls./St. Paul Bus. Jour., 2007; named one of The Most Influential People in Bus., Bus. Jour., 1999, 2002, The Top 25 Women in Healthcare, Modern Healthcare mag. Mem. Women's Health Leadership Trust, Minn. Council Health Maintenance Orgns., Audobon Soc., Nature Conservancy. Clubs: Nature Conservancy. Avocations: hiking, cross country skiing, aerobics, birdwatching, reading. Office: HealthPartners Inc 8100 34th Ave S Minneapolis MN 55425

BRALIC, MARINA, neurologist; b. Rijeka, Croatia, Jan. 8, 1971; MD, Sch. Medicine, U. Rijeka, 1996, MSc, 2004. Neurologist, neurol. intensive care unit U. Hosp. Rijeka, 2006—. Soros Supplementary grant, Open Soc. Found. Mem.: Internat. Brain Rsch. Orgn. Avocation: travel. Office: Kresimirova 42 Rijeka 51 000 Croatia Office Fax: 385 51 334 606. Personal E-mail: bralic_marina@yahoo.com.

BRALY, ANGELA FICK, insurance company executive, lawyer; b. Dallas, July 2, 1961; married; 3 children. BBA, Tex. Tech. U., 1983; JD, So. Meth. U., 1985. Bar: Mo. 1985. Ptnr. Lewis Rice & Fingersh LC, St. Louis, 1987—99; interim gen. counsel RightCHOICE Managed Care Inc., St. Louis, 1997—98, exec. v.p., gen. counsel., corp. sec., 1999—2003; pres., CEO Anthem Blue Cross Blue Shield, St. Louis, 2003—05; exec. v.p., gen. counsel, chief pub. affairs officer WellPoint, Inc. (formerly Anthem, Inc.), Indpls., 2005—07, pres., CEO, 2007—, chair, 2010—. Bd. dirs. WellPoint, Inc., 2007—, The Procter & Gamble Co., 2009—, Blue Cross Blue Shield Assn., Nat. Inst. Health Care Mgmt., America's Health Ins. Plans, Nat. and Ctrl. Indiana Corp. Partnership, Inc.; mem. Bus. Roundtable, Bus. Coun. Named one of The 25 Most Influential Women in Bus., St. Louis Bus. Jour., 2000, The Top 25 Women in Healthcare, Modern Healthcare mag., 2007, 2009, 2011, The World's 100 Most Powerful Women, Forbes mag., 2007—09, The 50 Most Powerful Women in Bus., Fortune mag., 2007—10, 50 Women to Watch, The Wall St. Jour., 2008. Mem.: ABA, American Health Lawyers Assn., State Bar Mo., Bar Assn. Met. St. Louis, St. Louis Health Lawyers Network. Office: WellPoint Inc 120 Monument Cir Indianapolis IN 46204 Office Phone: 317-488-6000. *

BRAMMER, LAWRENCE MARTIN, psychologist, educator; b. Crookston, Minn., Aug. 20, 1922; s. Martin G. and Edna L. (Thiesen) B.; m. Marian S. Sjolin, Feb. 11, 1945; children: Karin Marie, Kristen Lenore. BS, St. Cloud State U., 1943; MA, Stanford U., 1948, PhD, 1950. Diplomate: Am. Bd. Prof. Psychology. Psychologist Stanford U. Counseling and Testing Ctr., 1948-50; assoc. dean students Sacramento State Coll., 1950-64; prof. ednl. psychology U. Wash., Seattle, 1964-88, prof. emeritus, 1988—. Author: Therapeutic Psychology, 6th edit., 1993, Helping Relationships, 8th edit., 2002, Outplacement and Inplacement Counseling, 1984, How to Cope with Life Transitions, 1991, Caring for Yourself While Caring for Others: A Caregiver's Survival and Renewal Guide, 1999. Lt. M.S.C. AUS, 1944-46. Fulbright fellow, 1961-62 Fellow APA; mem. ACA, Queen City Yacht Club, Elks. Democrat. Lutheran. Home: 8005 Sandpoint Way NE A23 Seattle WA 98115

BRAMSON, JAMES B., dentist, former dental association administrator; m. Joanne Bramson; children: Adam, Matt, Lauren. BS, U. Iowa, 1976; DDS, U. Iowa Coll. Dentistry, 1979. Pvt. practice, Parkersburg and Ackley, Iowa, 1979—86; assoc. dir. Coun. Dental Practice, ADA, 1987—90, dir. Coun. Dental Practice, dir. Commn. Relief Fund Activities, sec.-treas. Endowment & Assistance Fund Inc./Emergency Fund Inc., 1990—97, exec. dir. ADA Chgo., 2001—08; exec. dir. Mass. Dental Soc., 1997—2001; owner pvt. consulting firm, 2008—. Bd. mem. elect Nat. Found. Dentistry for Handicapped. Grantee Hillenbrand Fellowship, ADA/Am. Fund Dental Health, 1986—87. Mailing: c/o NFDH 1800 15th St Ste 100 Denver CO 80202

BRANCH, WILLIAM TERRELL, urologist, educator; b. Paragould, Ark., Dec. 7, 1937; s. William Owen and Mary Rose (Dempsey) B.; m. Lauinia McClure; children: Ashley Tucker, William T., Steven K. BS, Ark. State U., 1964, MD, 1971. Diplomate Am. Bd. Urology. Adminstrv. asst. mental retardation planning project State of Ark., Little Rock, 1964-66; intern U. South Fla. Sch. Medicine Affiliated Hosps., Tampa, 1971-72, resident in surgery, 1972-73, resident in urology, 1973-75, chief resident in urology, 1975-76; practice medicine specializing in urology Tampa, 1976—; mem. staff, sec. urology Tampa Gen. Hosp., 1976-78, vice chief urology, 1978-80, chief urology, 1980-82; mem. staff, co-chief surgery Meml. Hosp., Tampa, 1978-80, vice chief med. staff, 1980-82, chief med. staff, 1982-84, trustee, 1983-88, bd. dirs.; clin. prof. urology U. South Fla. Coll. Medicine, Tampa, 1994—. Mem. adv. bd. Suncoast Ednl. Telecommunications Systems, 1982; vice chmn., bd. dirs. Meml. Hosp., 1987-88; cons. in urology James A. Haley VA Hosp., Tampa, 1978—; mem. staff St. Joseph's Hosp., Tampa, 1976—, Tampa Gen. Hosp.; cons. staff Women's Hosp., Tampa; adv. bd. Glendale Fed. Savs., 1983-85, Beneficial Harbour Island Savs. Bank, 1985-87, South Trust Bank, 1988-2000, also bd. dirs., exec. com., chair audit com.; chief urology, bd. mem. Tampa Outpatient Surgery Facility, 2000—; chmn. vol. faculty com. Dept. Surgery U. South Fla. Coll. Medicine; chmn. bd. dirs. Shriners Hosp. for Children, Tampa. Author: (with others) Mental Retardation in Arkansas, 1964-66; A Demographic Study, 1966; cons. editor Jour. Fla. Med. Assn., 1978-93. Bd. dirs. Tampa Ballet, 1980, Tampa Charity Horse Show Bd. Dirs. Assn., 1985-87, Shriners Hosp. for Children, Tampa, 2000, Tampa Outpatient Surg. Facility,United Way, Tampa, 1983-90, mem. exec. com., 1984-88; mem. med. adv. bd. Nat. Kidney Found. of Fla., Inc., 1983-90; mem. Tampa Bay Super Bowl XXV Task Force, Super Bowl XXXV Task Force; mem. adv. bd. dirs. Salvation Army; founding chmn. Kettle com., vice chmn. adv. bd. dirs., chmn., 1998-2000. Recipient Disting. Alumnus award Ark. State U., 1986, named to Dunklin County Hall Honor, 2006. Fellow ACS (credit com. region IV, Fla. chpt. 1982-98, exec. com. Fla. chpt. 1985-92, sec., treas. 1987-88, pres.-elect 1989-90, pres. 1990-92, gov. 1990-96, bd. gov. chpt. activities com. 1991-96, alt. 1993, chmn. nomination com. 1995, chmn. applications com. region IV); mem. Am. Urol. Assn., Royal Soc. Medicine (affiliate), Fla. Med. Assn. (del. 1983, 88-96), Fla. Urol. Soc. (Milton Copeland award 1976, exec. com. 1978-82), Hillsborough County Med. Assn. (exec. com. 1978-81, treas. 1981-82, sec. 1983-84), Fla. Quality Med. Assurance, Inc. (bd. dirs., treas., chmn. exec. com. 1995, chmn. bd. govs.), Southeastern Surg. Congress, Greater Tampa C. of C. (dir. 1982-86, 87-90, chmn. med. meetings task force 1983-84, Super Star award 1983), Tampa Bay Surg. Soc. (founding mem., sec., bd. dirs. 1998, pres. 1999-2001), Tampa Hist. Soc., Hillsborough County Med. Soc. (pres. polit. action com. 1986-87, 88-89), Tampa Yacht and Country Club (gov. 1984-87), Centre of Tampa Club (founding mem. 1988-93, bd. dirs., chmn. mem. com., leading man ROJ Count #89), Univ. Club (treas. 1998-99, sec. 1999-2000, bd. dirs. 1998-99), Ye Mystic Krewe of Gasparilla (bd. dirs. 1991-2000, 1st lt. 1988-89, lord chamberlain 1994-95, chmn. exec. com. 1995-96, capt. 1996-98), King Gasparilla LXXXVI. Office: 2919 W Swann Ave Ste 303 Tampa FL 33609-4051 Office Phone: 813-877-0463.

BRANCHE, CHRISTINE M., federal agency administrator, epidemiologist; BA in Biology, U. Rochester; MSPH, PhD, UNC Chapel Hill. Epidemiology rsch. assoc. Burroughs Wellcome Co. (now GlaxoSmithKline); epidemic intelligence service officer, divsn. Injury Epidemiology and Control, US Public Health Service Ctr. Disease Control and Prevention, dir. divsn. unintentional injury prevention, Nat. Ctr. Injury Prevention and Control, 1996—2007; prin. assoc. dir. Nat. Inst. Occupl. Safety and Health, 2007—, acting dir., 2008—09, acting dir. Office Constrn. Safety and Health, 2009—. Technical consultation American Red Cross, US Dept. Defense, Nat. Football League, Internat. Consumer Product Health and Safety Org. Office: Nat Inst Occupational Health Ste 9200 Patriots Plaza Bldg 395 E St SW Washington DC 20201 *

BRANCHINI, FRANK J., insurance company executive; LHD (hon.), NY Coll. of Podiatric Medicine. Pres., COO EmblemHealth, Inc. (parent co. of HIP Health Plan (HIP) and Group Health, Inc. (GHI)); pres., CEO, vice-chmn. Group Health Inc. (GHI); chmn., CEO GHI HMO (subs. of Group Health Inc. (GHI)). Mem. NYC Governor's Medicaid Redesign Team. Bd. dirs. Battery Park Authority, Starlight Children's Found., American Arbitration Assn., NYC Partnership, NY Junior Tennis League; bd. trustee Cabrini Med. Ctr., chair bd. trustee, 2000. Recipient United Hosp. Fund's Disting. Trustee award, Ellis Island Medal of Honor, Jewish Nat. Fund's Tree of Life award, Arthritis Found. John E. Lawe award, Mental Illness Found. Person of the Yr. award, Catholic Health Care Found. Oanis Vitae Humanitarian award, Boy Scout of America Good Scout and Health Care Leadership award. Office: Group Health Inc (GHI) 441 Ninth Ave New York NY 10001-1681 also: GHI HMO 789 Grant Ave Lake Katrine NY 12449 *

BRAND, DONALD ALBERT, medical researcher, educator; b. New Rochelle, NY, Dec. 3, 1945; s. Charles Salmon and Norma Ruth Brand; m. Catherine L. Learned, Apr. 10, 1993; m. Gabriella Maresca, Sept. 12, 1964 (div.); children: Jeffrey Charles Brand-Ballard, Thomas Russell. BS, Antioch Coll., Yellow Springs, Ohio, 1968; MA, U. Wis., Madison, 1970; MPhil, Yale U., New Haven, Conn., 1975, PhD, 1976. Asst. prof., pub. health Yale U., New Haven, 1976—83, rsch. scientist, 1983—87, sr. rsch. scientist, 1987—89; sr. rschr. United Healthcare Corp., Minnetonka, Minn., 1990—95; assoc. prof., medicine N.Y. Med. Coll., Valhalla, 1996—2004, prof., medicine, 2004—07; adj. prof. medicine and pediatrics NY Med. Coll., Valhalla, 2007—. Mem., extremity radiography panel FDA, U.S. Pub. Health Svc., Rockville, Md., 1984—85; mem., site visit and spl. rev. com., trauma and burn program, nat. inst. gen. med. scis. NIH, U.S. Pub. Health Svc., Bethesda, Md., 1985; dir., primary care rsch. N.Y. Med. Coll., Valhalla, 1995—2007; dir. health outcomes rsch. Winthrop U. Hosp., Mineola, NY, 2007—; mem. rev. com. divsn. ind. rev. health resources and svcs. adminstrn. US Dept. Health and Human Svcs., 2005; cons. in field; prof. rsch. preventive medicine Stony Brook Med. Sch., 2008—. Contbr. articles to profl. jours. Grantee, Nat. Ctr. for Health Svcs. Rsch., U.S. Pub. Health Svc., 1979—80, Nat. Fund for Med. Edn., 1979—80, The John A. Hartford Found., 1983—87, Mar. of Dimes Birth Defects Found., 1989—90, Am. Coll. Gastroenterology, 1999—2000, Health Resources and Services Adminstrn., USPHS, 2000—07. Mem.: Soc. for Med. Decision Making. Achievements include development of several diagnostic decision aids for physicians in pediatrics, internal medicine, and trauma. Avocation: photography. Office: Winthrop U Hosp Office Health Outcomes Rsch 222 Station Plz N Mineola NY 11501 Business E-Mail: dbrand@winthrop.org.

BRANDEIS, STEVEN, colon and rectal surgeon, educator; MD, NYU, 1971—75. Diplomate Am. Bd. Colon and Rectal Surgery, 1982, Am. Bd. Surgery, 2001. Clin. asst. prof. surgery NYU Sch. Medicine; fellow colon & rectal surgery Robert Wood Johnson Univ. Hosp., New Brunswick, NJ, 1980—81; clin. fellow colorectal surgery Muhlenberg Regional Med. Ctr., 1980—81; colon & rectal surgeon NY Downtown Hosp.; resident surgery NYU Langone Med. Ctr.-Bellvue Hosp., NYC, 1975—80, colon & rectal surgeon. Co-author: (articles) Rectal perforation during barium enema. Report of a case, 1988. Office: New York University Medical Center 251 E 33 St 2nd Fl New York NY 10016 Office Phone: 212-695-5411. Office Fax: 212-696-5906.

BRANDENBURG, DAVID SAUL, gastroenterologist, educator; b. Linz, Austria, Apr. 12, 1948; arrived in US, 1948; s. Mayer and Syda Brandenburg; m. Bette Ellen Hirschberg, Aug. 8, 1971; children: Stacey, Mark, Marci. BA, Rutgers U., 1968; MD, Georgetown U., 1972. Bd. cert. internal medicine; bd. cert. GI. Intern, resident R.I. Hosp.-Brown U. Affiliated, Providence, 1972-75; gastroenterology fellow Emory U., Atlanta, 1975-77; pvt. practice Atlanta Digestive Diseases and Internal Medicine, 1977-82, Brandenburg and Kramer M.D., P.C., Atlanta, 1983-97; clin. asst. prof. medicine Emory U. Sch. Medicine, Atlanta, 1977—2008; with Atlanta Gastroenterology Assocs., 1997—. Med. dir. North Atlanta Endoscopy Ctr., Atlanta, 1986-2002; sec., v.p., pres. Ga. Soc. GI Endoscopy, Atlanta, 1980-86; chmn., med. adv. com. Ga. chpt. Crohn's and Colitis Found., Atlanta, 1995-97. Bd. trustees Temple Emmanuel, Dunwoody, Ga., 1985-91, 95-96, treas., 1988-89, v.p., 1990-91. Fellow Am. Coll. Gastroenterology (gov. 1991-95); mem. Am. Gastroenterol. Assn., Am. Soc. Gastrointestinal Endoscopy. Office: 5671 Peachtree Dunwoody Rd Ste 600 Atlanta GA 30342-2311 Office Phone: 404-257-9000.

BRANDENBURG, MARK ANDREW, emergency physician, educator; b. Tulsa, Okla., Feb. 25, 1966; BA, W.Va. U., Morgantown, 1988; MD, U. Okla., Oklahoma City, 1992. Diplomate Am. Bd. Emergency Medicine, 1998. Intern in internal medicine U. Okla., Oklahoma City, 1992—93, intern then resident in emergency medicine, 1993—97; emergency physician St. Francis Hosp., Tulsa, 1997—; clin. assoc. prof. U. Okla. Coll. Medicine. Clin. rschr. Trauma Emergency Ctr., Tulsa, 1997—; instr. Advanced Trauma Life Support, Tulsa, 1997—, Pediat. Advanced Life Support, Tulsa, 2000—; spkr. Child Safe, Tulsa, 2000—, child injury cons., 2000—. Author: CHILD SAFE: A Practical Guide for Preventing Childhood Injuries, 2000; contbr. articles. Med. advisor Safe Kids Campaign, Tulsa, 2000—03. Fellow: Am. Coll. Emergency Medicine (life), Am. Acad. Emergency Medicine (life); mem.: Assn. Advancement Automotive Medicine (assoc.). Personal E-mail: mbrand2435@aol.com.

BRANDON, KATHRYN ELIZABETH BECK, pediatrician; b. Sept. 10, 1916; d. Clarence M. and Hazel A. (Cutler) Beck; children: John William, Kathleen Brandon McEnulty, Karen (dec.). MD, U. Chgo., 1941; BA, U. Utah, 1937; MPH, U. Calif., Berkeley, 1957. Diplomate Am. Bd. Pediats. Intern Grace Hosp., Detroit, 1941-42; resident Children's Hosp. Med. Ctr. No. Calif., Oakland, 1953-55, Children's Hosp., LA, 1951-53; pvt. practice La Crescentia, Calif., 1946-51, Salt Lake City, 1960-65, 86—. Med. dir. Salt Lake City public schs., 1957-60; dir. Ogden City-Weber County (Utah) Health Dept., 1965-67; pediatrician Fitzsimmons Army Hosp., 1967-68; coll. health physician U. Colo., Boulder, 1968-71; student health physician U. Utah, Salt Lake City, 1971-81; occupational health physician Hill AFB, Utah, 1981-85; child health physician Salt Lake City-County Health Dept., 1971-82; cons. in field; clin. asst. U. Utah Coll. Medicine, Salt Lake City, 1958-64; clin. asst. pediatrics U. Colo. Coll. Medicine, Denver, 1958-72; active staff emeritus Primary Children's Hosp., LDS Hosp., and Cottonwood Hosp., 1960-67. Fellow APHA, Am. Pediat. Acad., Am. Sch. Health Assn.; mem. AMA, Utah Coll. Health Assn. (pres. 1978-80), Pacific Coast Coll. Health Assn., Utah Med. Assn., Salt Lake County Med. Soc., Utah Pub. Health Assn. (sec.-treas. 1960-66), Intermountain Pediat. Soc. Office: PO 171186 Salt Lake City UT 84117

BRANDSTRUP, BIRGITTE, surgeon, consultant; d. Poul and Grethe Laurvig Brandstrup; m. Peter Starup, June 10, 1993; children: Christian Brandstrup Starup, Camilla Louise Brandstrup Starup. PhD, U. Copenhagen, 2003. Cert. med. doctor Denmark, 1992. Jr. resident Grindsted Hosp., 1992—94; surg. resident Hvidovre U. Hosp., 1994—95, head endoscopic unit, intensive survaliance unit surg. gastroent. dept., 2010—; surg. resident Rigshospitalet, 1996, Glostrup U. Hosp., 1996—98; rsch. fellow Bispebjerg U. Hosp., 1999—2002; sr. resident Glostrup U. Hosp., 2003—04, Slagelse U. Hosp., 2005—06, Bispebjerg U. Hosp., 2006—08; cons. Glostrup U. Hosp., 2008—, chief. endoscopic. dept.; clin. assoc. prof. U. Copenhagen. Author: Restricted Intravenous Fluid Therapy in Colorectal Surgery, 2003, Rational Fluid and Electrolyte Therapy and Nutrition, 2004; contbr. chapters to books, articles to profl. jours. in perioperative fluid mgmt.; referee periodicals. Recipient 1st prize for best rsch. and presentation, Danish Gastroent. Soc. and Danish Surg. Soc., 2001, 2002, 2003. Achievements include research in changing principles for perioperative intravenous fluid therapy of surgical patients. Home: Farumgaards alle 14 Farum DK-3520 Denmark Office: Glostrup Univ Hosp Surg Dept Ndr Ringvej DK-2600 Glostrup Denmark Office Phone: +4543232300. Personal E-mail: bbrandstrup@hotmail.com.

BRANDT, CARL DAVID, research virologist; b. Bridgeport, Conn., Jan. 19, 1928; s. Carl August and Hildur (Wedberg) B.; m. Elsa Lund Erickson, Apr. 25, 1964; dec. Jan. 15, 2009; children: Karen, Erik. BS, U. Conn., 1949; MS, U. Mass., 1951; PhD, Harvard U., 1958. Rsch. instr. dept. vet. sci. U. Mass., Amherst, 1949-52, 54; rsch. virologist Charles Pfizer & Co., Inc., Ind. and Conn., 1958—62; assoc., dept. epidemiology Pub. Health Rsch. Inst., NYC, 1962—66; rsch. assoc. virology rsch. Children's Nat. Med. Ctr., Washington, 1966-79, sr. rsch. assoc., 1979-86, sr. scientist, 1986-94; ret., 1994. Instr. Georgetown U. Med. Sch., Washington, 1966-69; asst. prof. pediat. George Washington U. Med. Sch., Washington, 1969-74, assoc. prof., 1974-94, emeritus prof., 1994. Contbr. over 125 articles to profl. jours. 1st lt. USAF, 1952-54. Fellow Am. Acad. Microbiology, Infectious Diseases Soc. Am., Am. Coll. Epidemiology; mem. N.Y. Color Slide Club (bd. dirs. 1965-66), Silver Spring Camera Club (pres. 1970-71, 2009-10, bd. dirs. 2011-), Rock Creek Amateur Radio Assn. (pres. 1985-89), Widowed Persons Svc. of Montgomery County (Md.) (bd. dirs. 2011-, pres. 2011-). Avocations: photography, amateur radio, chess. Home: 819 E Franklin Ave Silver Spring MD 20901-4709

BRANDT, CARLOS TEIXEIRA, pediatric surgeon, educator; b. Teresina, Pernambuco, Brazil, Aug. 14, 1943; s. Frederico Brandt and Edith Teixeira da SILVA; m. Francesca Galeão Brandt, May 18, 1945; children: Karla Galeão, Katia Galeão, Karina Galeão, Carlos Brandt Filho. MSc in Surgery, Fed. U. of Pernambuco, Brazil, 1978; PhD in Med. Scis., The U. of Liverpool, England, 1983. Registrar in pediatric surgery Nat. Health Svc. Eng., 1977, registered specialist in pediatric surgery Brazilian Assn. for Pediatric Surgery, Brazil, 1975. Residency Fed. U. Pernambuco, Brazil, 1968—75, lectr., 1975—83, sr. lectr., 1983—95, assoc. prof., 1995, prof. of pediatric surgery, 1995—. Coord. of post grad. studies in surgery Fed. U. of Pernambuco, 1990—; brazilian rschr. Nat. Brazilian Rsch. Coun., Brasilia, Brazil, 2000—; scientifc dir. Altino Ventura Found., Recife, 2002—; vis. prof. Colo. U., Denver, 1989. Author: Introdução à Cirurgia Geral da Criança; editor: Anais da Facudade de Medicina do Centro de Ciências da Saúde da U. Federal de Pernambuco, 1990—; mem. editl. bd.: Acta Cirúrgica Brasileira, 1992—; contbr. articles to profl. jours. (Salomão Kelner prize, 2001). Mem.: Brazilian Assn. of Pediatric Surgeons (cipe São Paulo chpt. 1977—2003), Brazilian Coll. of Surgeons, Brazilian Assn. for the Developpment of Rsch. in Surgery, Brazilian Assn. for the Devel. of Pediatric Surgery (pres. sobradpec São Paulo chpt. 1990—2003). Achievements include research in auto implantation of splenic tissue into the major omentum in patients with hepatosplenic schistosomiasis mansoni. Home: Av Boa Viagem 5090 Apto 1201 Pernambuco Recife 51011 000 Brazil Office: Hospital das Clínicas UFPE Av Moraes Rêgo s/n Pernambuco Recife 50670 420 Brazil Office Fax: 55 81 3271-8519; Home Fax: 55 81 33420830. E-mail: carlosbrandt@bol.com.br.

BRANDT, CHRISTIAN, epidemiologist; b. Bremen, Germany, Jan. 17, 1966; s. Karl_Heinz and Irmtrud Brandt; m. Tatiana Borisova, 1999; children: Sebastian, Alexander. MD, Georg August U., Göttingen, 1994. Cert. specialist pediatrics Freistaat Sachsen, 2001, specialist hygiene, infection control Berlin, 2006. Head infection control unit Goethe U., Frankfurt am Main, Germany, 2006—. Mem.: Soc. Healthcare Epidemiology America. Office: Inst Med Microbiology Paul-Ehrlich-Str 40 Frankfurt 60596 Germany Office Fax: 49-69-63017713. Business E-Mail: christian.brandt@kgu.de.

BRANDT, FREDERIC SHELDON, dermatologist; b. June 26, 1949; BA, Rutgers U., 1971; MD, Hahnemann Med. Coll., 1975. Diplomate Am. Bd. Internal Medicine, Am. Bd. Dermatology, lic. physician N.Y., 1979, Fla., 1982, Calif., 1982. Intern NYU, NYC, 1975—76, resident in internal medicine, 1976—78; resident in dermatology U. Miami, Fla., 1978—81; pvt. practice dermatology Coral Gables, Fla. Clin. assoc. prof. dept. dermatology U. Miami, Fla.; clin. rsch. investigator Collagen Corp., 2003—; lectr. in field; mfr. Dr. Brandt Skin Care Products. Contbr. articles to profl. jours. Mem.: AMA, Miami Soc. for Dermatology and Cutaneous Surgery, Internat. Soc. Cosmetic Laser Surgeons, Internat. Soc. for Dermatologic Surgery, Fla. Soc. Dermatology, Fla. Med. Assn., Dermatology Found. Leaders Soc., Dade County Med. Assn., Am. Soc. Dermatologic Surgeons, Am. Acad. Dermatology, Phi Beta Kappa. Office: 4425 Ponce De Leon Blvd Ste 200 Coral Gables FL 33146 also: 317 E 34th St Sixth Fl New York NY 10016 Office Phone: 305-443-6606, 212-889-7096. Office Fax: 305-443-4890.

BRANDT, FREDRIC S., dermatologist; Attended, Drexel U., Phila., 1975. Diplomate Am. Bd. Internal Medicine, Am. Bd. Dermatology. Cancer rschr. Sloan-Kettering; cons. and prin. investigator Medicis Aesthetics, Mentor Biologics, Dermik, ColBar, Contura, Revance, Isolagen, Merz, Lumenis, Cutera, Palomar, Johnson & Johnson, Stiefel-GSK, Allergan. Author: (profl. manuscripts) 10 Minutes 10 Years, Age-Less, (profl. publs.) Brunner's gland adenoma associated with high output congestive heart failure, 1976, Guttate psoriasis following sterptococal throat infection, 1979, Topical nitrogen musard therapy in multicentric reticulohistiocytosis, 1982, and numerous others. Office: Advanced Cosmetic Dermatology Ste 200 4425 Ponce de Leon Blvd Miami FL 33146 Mailing: Advanced Cosmetic Dermatology 2nd Fl 323 East 34th St New York NY 10016 Office Phone: 305-443-6606, 212-889-7096. Office Fax: 305-443-4890, 212-686-7305.

BRANDT, JOHN HENRY, physician; b. Cleve., July 30, 1940; s. Harold Paul and Dorothy Helen (Kern) B.; m. Jon Ellison, July 30, 1963 (div. 1971); children: Sylvia Ann, Laura Ann; m. Marilyn Ruth Brandt, July 25, 1980. BA, Yale U., 1962; postgrad., Cambridge U., Eng., 1962—64; MD, Harvard U., 1970. Asst. to dir. Harvard Ctr. for Cmty. Health, Boston, 1968—69; clin. fellow Med. Sch. Harvard U., Boston, 1970—73, instr. psychiatry Med. Sch., 1973—74, 1974—99; resident psychiatrist McLean Hosp., Belmont, Mass., 1970—73, dir. Waverley House, 1973—74, attending psychiatrist, 1974—90, Mass. Mental Health Ctr., 1991—99; staff psychiatrist med. dept. MIT, Cambridge, 1979—99. Active Mass. Hist. Soc., New Eng. Hist. Geneal. Soc.; mem. Trinity Ch., Boston, 1988—. Fellow: Royal Soc. Medicine (London); mem.: Internat. Inst., N.Y. Acad. Medicine, Mass. Med. Soc., World Boston, Nichols House Mus., Colonial Soc., Russell Trust Assn., Harvard Musical Assn. (dir. 1990—93), English Speaking Union, Clare Assn., Am. Friends Cambridge U., Guild St. Luke, Yale Mory's Assn., Bostonian Soc., Gore Pl., Lincoln Land Conservation Trust, Soc. for Preservation New Eng. Antiquities, Trustees Reservations, Chief Execs. Club Boston, Harvard Club Boston (chmn. Ho. com. 1989—91, v.p. 1991—93), Boston Athenaeum, Harvard Faculty Club, Yale Club Boston (sec. 1988—90, dir. 1990—93), Cosmos Club, Thursday Evening Club, Yale Elizabethan Club, Phi Beta Kappa. Republican. Episcopalian. Avocation: music. Home and Office: PO Box 530 Lincoln MA 01773-0530

BRANDT, KEITH E., plastic surgeon, educator; b. San Antonio; s. Melroy and Bernice Brandt; m. Tina Lynn Brandt. BS, Tex. A&M U., College Station, 1979; MD, U. Tex., Houston, 1983. Cert. Am. Bd. Surgeons, 1990, Am. Bd. Plastic Surgeons, 1995, added qualification in surgery of hand 1995. Instr. surgery Washington U., St. Louis, 1991—92, assoc. prof., 1999—2005, William G. Hamm prof. surgery, 2006—; asst. prof. U. Tex., Houston, 1993—95, assoc. prof., 1996—99. Unit commr. Boy Scouts Am., Manchester, Mo., 2006. Named one of Am.'s Top Doctors, Castle Connolly Med., Inc., 2006—10, Am.'s Top Doctors Cancer, 2006—10. Mem.: Am. Assn. Surgery of Hand, Am. Soc. Reconstructive Microsurgery, Am. Bd. Plastic Surgery, Am. Soc. Plastic Surgeons. Avocation: running. Office: Washington U Divsn Plastic Surgery 660 S Euclid Campus Box 8238 Saint Louis MO 63110

BRANDT, STEPHEN J., hematologist, educator; b. Atlanta, Nov. 16, 1954; BS, Duke U., 1976; MD, Emory U., 1981. Prof., medicine, cell and devel. biology, cancer biology Vanderbilt U. Med. Ctr., 1990—; tenured prof., med. dir., stem cell transplant processing lab. Vanderbilt U., 1990—. Biomed. fellowship, Lucille P. Markey Charitable Trust. Mem.: AAAS, Am. Soc. Clin. Investigation, Am. Soc. Microbiology, Am. Soc. Hematology, Phi Beta Kappa, Alpha Omega Alpha. Avocations: photography, hiking. Office: Vanderbilt University Med Ctr Rm 777 Preston Research Bldg Nashville TN 37232 Office Fax: 615-936-2929. Business E-Mail: stephen.brandt@vanderbilt.edu.

BRANDWEIN-GENSLER, MARGARET, pathologist, educator; b. Bklyn., Feb. 16, 1958; BA, Barnard Coll., 1979; MD, Upstate Med. Coll., 1983. Assoc. prof., divsn. chief, head and neck pathology Mt. Sinai Sch. Medicine, 1990—2004; clin. prof. pathology and otolaryngology Montefiore Med. Ctr., Albert Einstein Coll. Medicine, 2004; prof. pathology and surgery, sect. head surg. pathology U. Ala., Birmingham, 2009—. Fellow: US & Can. Acad. Pathology, Coll. Am. Pathologists; mem.: Assn. Dirs. Anatomic & Surg. Pathology, Am. Acad. Otolaryngology Head & Neck Surgery, N.Am. Soc. Head & Neck Pathology (charter mem. 1997, pres. 2006—08). Office: 619 19th St S NP 3545 Birmingham AL 35249-7331 Office Fax: 205-975-5242.

BRANHAM, GREGORY HARRIS, facial plastic surgeon; b. Columbia, SC, Mar. 28, 1957; s. Clarence Stevenson and Theodocia (Hearon) B.; m. Cynthia Lynn Nowell, June 7, 1986; children: Allison, Matthew, Grace. BS in Biology, U. S.C., 1979, MD in Medicine, 1983. Asst. prof. St. Louis U., 1990-96, assoc. prof., 1996—2004, assoc. dean, 1995—2004; instr. Washington U., St. Louis, 1989-90, prof., chief facial plastic surgery & reconstructive surgery, sch. of medicine, 2010—, assoc. prof. otolaryngology-head & neck surgery, chief, divsn. plastic reconstructive surgery. Exec. com. mem. St. Louis U. Governing Coun., 1995—2004. Fellow Am. Coll. Surgeons, Am. Acad. Facial Plastic & Reconstructive Surgery (bd. examiner 1994—), Am. Acad. Otolarngology (award of honor, 1998). Office: Washington Univ Sch Medicine Dept Otolaryngology Box 8115 660 S Euclid Ave Saint Louis MO 63110 Office Phone: 314-432-7760. Business E-Mail: branhamg@ent.wush.edu.

BRANHAM, JOSEPH MORHART, biologist, educator; b. Washington, Jan. 31, 1932; s. Joseph Russell and Augusta Emma (Morhart) B.; m. Margaret Ann Taylor, Sept. 1, 1956; children: Russell, Charles. BS, Fla. State U., 1956, MS, 1958, PhD, 1963. Cert. biology/chemistry tchr., Fla. Rsch. asst. U. Del. Marine Lab., Lewes, summers 1950-56; rsch. asst. dept. biol. sci. Fla. State U., Tallahassee, 1956-58, tchg. asst. dept. biol. sci., 1958-62; assoc. prof. biology Oglethorpe U., Atlanta, 1962-65; NIH postdoctoral rsch. assoc. U. Edinburgh, Scotland, 1965-67; asst. prof. biology U. Hawaii, Honolulu, 1967-72; rsch. assoc. U. Utah, Salt Lake City, 1972-73; tchr. biology and chemistry Lake County Pub. Schs., Leesburg, Fla., 1973-89. Mem. land acquistion selection com. Lake County Water Authority, Tavares, Fla., 1986—, chmn. conservation com., 1990—; mem. pub. lands aquisitions com., Lake Co., Fla., 2005—; mem., bd. mem. Lake County Conservation Coun., 1990—; vol., trainer Lakewatch, Leesburg, 1990— Lalor fellow Lalor Found., Woods Hole, Mass., 1964; recipient Rsch. award NIH, Edinburgh, 1965-67, Bob Owen award St. Johns River Water Mgmt. Dist., 2010, Conservationist of Yr., St. Johns River Water Mgmt. Lake County, Ctrl. Fla., 2010. Fellow Sigma Xi; mem. AAAS, Am. Inst. Biol. Scis., N.Y. Acad. Sci., Civitan Internat., Nature Conservancy, Cousteau Soc. (charter), Civitan's Club (Leesburg, Fla.) (pres. 2010-). Republican. Episcopalian. Home: PO Box 38 Okahumpka FL 34762-0038 Personal E-mail: jmbranham@aol.com.

BRANNON, GUY EMILIO, psychiatrist; b. Bossier City, La., June 19, 1968; s. Guy Winfred and Ruby Rangel Brannon; m. Shelley Marie Lawson, Apr. 20, 1996; children: Dechlin Adair children: Grayson Alarich. BS, La. State U., Shreveport, 1991; MD, La. State U., Health Sci. Ctr., Shreveport, 1995. Diplomate La. State Bd. Med. Examiners, 1996. Intern La. State U. Med. Ctr., Shreveport, 1995—96, resident, 1996—99, chief resident, 1998—99; dir. adult psychiatric unit Brentwood-A Behavioral Health Co., Shreveport, 1999—. Asst. clin. prof. psychiatry La. State U. Health Scis. Ctr., Shreveport, 1999—; adj. prof. psychology La. State U., Shreveport, 2002—; pres., CEO PharmaComm., LLC, LaPharma, LLC, 2005. Contbr. chapters to books, articles to profl. jours. Fellow: Am. Assn. Integrated Medicine; mem.: AMA, Am. Assn. Psychiat. Medicine (diplomate), Assn. Clin. Rsch. Profls., Am. Soc. Clin. Pharmacology, La. Group Psychotherapy Soc., Am. Group Psychotherapy Assn., Am. Soc. Addiction Medicine, Am. Med. Polit. Action Com., La. Psychiat. Med. Assn. (N.W. La. chpt. v.p. 2000—01, N.W. La. chpt. pres. 2002—04, Dr. John M Bick award 1995), Am. Psychiat. Assn., So. Med. Assn., Am. Psychotherapy Assn., Am. Acad. Pain Mgmt., Mental Health Assn. Caddo - Bossier (bd. mem. 2000—05). Achievements include research in clinical drug trials. Office: Brentwood - A Behavioral Health Company 1002 Highland Ave Shreveport LA 71101 Personal E-mail: docbrannon@aol.com. E-mail: brentwoodoffice@aol.com.

BRANSCOMB, LEWIS MCADORY, physicist, researcher; b. Asheville, NC, Aug. 17, 1926; s. Bennett Harvie and Margaret (Vaughan) B.; m. Margaret Anne Wells, Oct. 13, 1951 (dec. Oct. 1997); children: Harvie Hammond, Katharine C. Branscomb Kelley; m. Constance Mullin, July 3, 2005. AB summa cum laude, Duke U., 1945, DSc (hon.); MS, Harvard U., 1947, PhD, 1949; DSc (hon.), Poly. Inst. N.Y., Clarkson Coll., Rochester U., U. Colo., Western Mich. U., Lycoming Coll., U. Ala., Pratt Inst., Rutgers U., Lehigh U., U. Notre Dame; DEng (hon.), Colo. Sch. Mines, 1999; D Pub. Politics, Carnegie Mellon U., 2000; DSc (hon.), SUNY, Binghamton; LHD (hon.), Pace U. Instr. physics Harvard U., 1950-51; lectr. physics U. Md., 1952-54; vis. staff mem. Univ. Coll., London, 1957-58; chief atomic physics sect. Nat. Bur. Standards, Washington, 1954-60, chief atomic physics div., 1960-62; chmn. Joint Inst. Lab. Astrophysics, U. Colo., 1962-65, 68-69; chief lab. astrophysics div. Nat. Bur. Standards, Boulder, Colo., 1962-69; prof. physics U. Colo., 1962-69; dir. Nat. Bur. Standards, 1969-72; chief scientist, v.p. IBM, Armonk, NY, 1972-86, mem. corporate mgmt. bd., 1983-86; dir. sci. and tech. policy program Kennedy Sch. Govt., Harvard U., Cambridge, Mass., 1986-96, Albert Pratt pub. service prof., 1988-94; Aetna prof. pub. policy and corp. mgmt. Harvard U., Cambridge, Mass., 1994-96, prof. emeritus, 1996—; dir. Belfer Ctr. for Sci. and Internat. Affairs, 2001—; adj. prof. Sch. Internat. Rels. and Pacific Studies, U. Calif., San Diego, 2005—, disting. rsch. fellow, Inst. for Global Conflict and Cooperation, 2007—. Mem.-at-large Def. Sci. Bd., 1969-72; mem. high level policy group sci. and tech. info. Orgn. Econ. Coop. and Devel., 1968-70; mem. Pres.'s Sci. Adv. Com., 1965-68, chmn. panel space sci. and tech., 1967-68; mem. Nat. Sci. Bd., 1978-84, chmn., 1980-84; mem. Pres.'s Nat. Productivity Adv. Com., 1981-82; mem. standing com. controlled thermonuclear rsch. AEC, 1966-68; mem. adv. com. on sci. and fgn. affairs Dept. State, 1973-74; mem. U.S.-USSR Joint Commn. on Sci. and Tech., 1977-80; chmn. Com. on Scholarly Communications with the People's Republic of China, 1977-80; mem. tech. assessment adv. coun. Office of Tech. Assessment, U.S. Congress, 1990-95; chmn. Carnegie Forum Task Force on Teaching as a Profession, 1985-86; dir. Lord Corp., 1987-; mem. pres.'s bd. visitors U. Okla., 1968-70; mem. astronomy and applied physics vis. coms. Harvard U. 1969-83, bd. overseers, 1984-86; mem. physics vis. com. M.I.T., 1974-79; mem. Pres.'s Com. Nat. Medal Scis., 1970-72; bd. dir. Am. Nat. Standards Inst., 1969-72; trustee Carnegie Instn., 1973-90, mem. Carnegie Commn. on Sci., Tech. and Govt., 1988-93; trustee Poly. Inst. N.Y., 1974-78, Vanderbilt U., 1980-2003, Nat. Geog. Soc., 1984-01, Woods Hole Oceanographic Instn., 1985-92, 93-98, LASPAU, 2002-2003; chmn. Nat. Info. Infrastructure-2000 steering com. NRC, 1994-95; Harvie Branscomb disting. vis. prof. Vanderbilt U., 1999-2000; rsch. assoc. Scripps Instn. Oceanography U. Calif., San Diego, 2005—. Author: Empowering Technology, 1993, Confessions of a Technophile, 1995, Korea at the Turning Point, 1996, Investing in Innovation, 1998, Industrializing Knowledge, 1999, Taking Technical Risks, 2001, Making America Safer, 2002, Seeds of Disaster, Roots of Response, 2006; editor Rev. Modern Physics, 1968-73. Trustee Telluride Inst., 1996-97; mem. Commn. on Global Info. Infrastructure, 1995—. USPHS fellow, 1948-49; Jr. fellow Harvard Soc. Fellows, 1949-51; recipient Rockefeller Pub. Service award, 1957-58, Gold medal exceptional service Dept. Commerce, 1961, Arthur Flemming award D.C. Jr. C. of C., 1962, Samuel Wesley Stratton award Dept. Commerce, 1966, Career Service award Nat. Civil Service League, 1968, Vannevar Bush award, nat. Sci. Bd., 2001, Proctor prize Rsch. Soc. Am., 1972, Okawa prize in Info. and Telecomm., 1998, prize for Info. and Telecomms. Ohkawa Found., 1998, Centennial medal, Harvard U., 2002. Fellow Am. Phys. Soc. (chmn. divsn. electron physics 1961-68, pres. 1979), AAAS (dir. 1969-73, 1999-2003, William Carey lectr. medal 2008), Am Acad. Arts and Scis.; mem. NAS (coun. 1972-75, 98-2001), Nat. Acad. Engring. (Arthur Bueche award), Engring. Acad. Japan (fgn. assoc.), Russian Acad. Sci., Washington Acad. Scis. (Outstanding Sci. Achievement award 1959), Nat. Acad. Pub. Adminstrn., Am. Philos. Soc., Phi Beta Kappa, Sigma Xi (pres. 1985-86). Office: U Calif San Diego Grad Sch Internat Rels Pac Studies 9500 Gilman Dr #0519 La Jolla CA 92093-0519 Office Phone: 858-454-6871. Business E-Mail: ibranscomb@branscomb.org.

BRANSFIELD, JAMES JOSEPH, retired surgeon; b. Chgo., Nov. 8, 1932; s. James Joseph and Beatrice Catherine (Greene) B.; m. Virginia Kaye Paully, Dec. 17, 1967; 1 child, Helena Theresa. BS, Loyola U., 1955, MD, 1957. Diplomate Am. Bd. Emergency Medicine, Am. Bd. Surgery. Pvt. practice specializing in surgery, Chgo., 1968—. Chief surgeon Chgo. Police Dept., 1983-94. Lt. comdr. USNR, 1960-63. Avocations: swimming, sailing. Home: 6200 N Knox Ave Chicago IL 60646-5030

BRANSOME, EDWIN DAGOBERT, JR., internal medicine educator; b. NYC, Oct. 27, 1933; s. Edwin Dagobert and Margaretta De Witt (Homans) B.; m. Janet Grace Williams, June 27, 1959; children: Edwin D. III, April Grace. AB, Yale U., 1954; MD, Columbia U., 1958. Intern, resident, rsch. fellow Peter Bent Brigham Hosp., Harvard Med. Sch., Boston, 1958-62; rsch. assoc. Columbia U. Coll. Physicians and Surgeons, NYC, 1962-64; assoc. Scripps Clinic and Rsch. Found., LaJolla, Calif., 1964-66; from asst. prof. to assoc. prof. MIT, Cambridge, Mass., 1966-70; prof. medicine, endocrinology and physiology Med. Coll. Ga., Augusta, 1970—2000, chief sect. endocrinology and metabolism, 1970—80, Augusta, 1999—2000, prof. emeritus, 2000—. Com. mem. US Pharmacopeia, Rockville, Md., 1976-90, trustee, 1990-2008, pres., 1999-2000, hon. mem. US Pharmacological Convention, 2009-, past pres., 2000-05; cons. Accelerated Pharm., Inc., 1999—2006, med. dir., 2006-; cons. in endocrinology and metabolism, 2000—, sci. advisor., with Quality mgmt. Com. Mem. editl. bd. Endocrinology, 1965-75, Diabetes Care, 2003-06; contbr. articles to profl. jours. Bd. dirs. TriDevel. Commn., Aiken, SC, 1987-91, treas., 1989-90; bd. dirs. Am. Diabetes Assn., Alexandria, Va., 1986-88; mem. bd. dirs. Alteon Inc., 1996-2006, Med. Quality Mgmt. Activity with Humana Mil. HS, trustee Patient Safety Peer Review Com., 2003-, Credentialling Com., 2005-, Aiken Opera Soc., 2009-. Postdoctoral rsch. fellow NIH, 1959-61, Am. Cancer Soc., 1962-64; recipient Pub. Policy award Ga. affiliate Am. Diabetes Assn., 1990. Fellow Am. Coll. Endocrinology(editl. bd. mem. 1965-71); mem. Am. Cancer Soc. (faculty rsch. assoc. 1976-70), Endocrine Soc., others. Achievements include patent (with others) in method of predicting biological activity of compounds by DNA models. Home and Office: 621 Magnolia St SE Aiken SC 29801-4903 Office Phone: 803-649-5150. Personal E-mail: bransomejr33@yahoo.com.

BRANSTETTER, BARTON F., radiologist, educator; grad., MD, U. Calif. Diplomate Am. Bd. Radiology-diagnostic radiology, Am. Bd. Radiology-neuroradiology. Resident Western Pa. Hosp., Univ. Pitts. Med. Sch., fellow neuroradiology, ENT radiology, and radiology informatics; dir., head and neck imaging Univ. Pitts. Med. Ctr. Presbyterian, clin. dir., neuroradiology, fellowship dir., neuroradiology; assoc. prof. radiology, otolaryngology and biomedical informatics Univ. Pitts.; hosp. affiliations include Magee-Womens Hospital of UPMC, UPMC McKeesport, UPMC Passavant, UPMC Shadyside, UPMC Mercy, UPMC St. Margaret. Recipient Stauffer award, Assn. of Univ. Radiologists (AUR). Office: Univeristry Pittsburgh Medical Center Presbyterian Radiology Department 200 Lothrop St Pittsburgh PA 15213 Office Phone: 412-647-9729. E-mail: branstetterbf@upmc.edu.

BRANTLEY, JEFFREY GARLAND, health science association administrator; b. Rocky Mount, NC, Nov. 4, 1949; s. Roy Garland and Irene (Cockrell) B.; m. Mary Mathews, Nov. 21, 1981. BA in History, Davidson Coll., 1971; MD, U. N.C., 1977. Diplomate Am. Bd. Psychiatry. Resident in psychiatry U. Calif., Irvine, 1981; pvt. practice psychiatry Laguna Niguel, 1981-82, Durham, NC, 1985-87; med. dir. Hospice Orange County, Laguna Niguel, Calif., 1982; clin. dir. Durham County Mental Health Ctr., NC, 1982-89; freelance cons., educator, 1990—; dir. mindfulness-based stress reduction program Duke Ctr. for Integrative Medicine, 1998—. Clin. assoc. dept. psychiatry U. Calif., Irvine, 1981-82; consulting assoc. Dept. Psychiatry Duke U., 1983—. Author: Calming Your Anxious Mind, 2003, 2nd edit., 2007, Five Good Minutes in the Evening, 2006, Five Good Minutes at Work, 2007; co-author: Five Good Minutes: 100 Morning Practices to Help You Stay Calm and Relaxed All Day Long, 2005. Mem.: N.C. Psychiat. Assn., Am. Psychiat. Assn. (disting. fellow 2008). Democrat. Buddhist. Avocations: sports, golf, jogging, music. Home and Office: 1109 Huntsman Dr Durham NC 27713-2370 Office Phone: 919-660-6741. Business E-Mail: brant006@mc.duke.edu.

BRASHER, GEORGE WALTER, physician, consultant; b. Jackson, Tenn., Dec. 7, 1936; s. George W. and Verla S. Brasher; m. Martha S. Brasher, Dec. 23, 1960; children: Suzanne Cheshier, George Brasher, John Brasher, David Brasher. BA, Lambuth U., 1959; MD, U. Tenn., 1961. Diplomate Am. Bd. Allergy and Immunology, Am. Bd. Pediatrics. Cons. Scott & White Clinic & Hosp., Temple, Tex., 1966—2007; emeritus prof. medicine Tex. A & M Coll. Medicine, 2008—. Dir. Allergy and Immunology Scott and White Clinic and Hosp., Temple, Tex., 1976-2006; prof. Medicine and Pediatrics Tex. A&M U. Coll. of Medicine, Temple, Tex., 1977-08. Contbr. articles to profl. jours. Fellow Am. Acad. Allergy and Immunology, Am. Acad. Pediatrics, Am. Coll. Allergy and Immunology; mem. AMA, Tex. Med. Assn., Bell County Med. Soc., Tex. Allergy Soc. Avocations: civil war history, amateur radio. Personal E-mail: gbrasher@excite.com.

BRASIER, MARTIN DAVID, palaeobiologist, geologist; b. Wimbledon, Eng., Apr. 12, 1947; s. Tom and Violette Brasier; m. Cecilia Joyce Clement, July 7, 1975; children: Matthew, Alexander, Zoë. BS in Geology with honors, London U., 1969, PhD, 1973; MA, Oxford U., 1988. Micropalaeontologist Brit. Geol. Survey, Leeds, England, 1972—73; lectr. geology Reading U., Berkshire, England, 1973—74; from. lectr. geology to reader in paleobiology Hull U., England, 1974—88; lectr., fellow Oxford U., England, 1988—96, reader in geology, 1996—2002, prof. paleobiology, 2002—. Chmn. Cambrian subcommn. UNESCO, Paris, 1990—94, project leader, 1988—92; chmn. earth scis. subfaculty Oxford U., 2002—04. Author: Microfossils, 1980, 2004, Darwin's Lost Worlds: the hidden history of animal life, 2009; editor: Precambrian-Cambrian Boundary, 1989; contbr. several articles to profl. journals. With Royal Navy, 1970. Fellow: St. Edmund Hall Oxford, Geol. Soc. London. Achievements include scientific and philosophical approaches needed for research into the origins of life, earliest cells, origins of plants and animals and the Cambrian explosion; definition of the Ediacaran system and of the Precambrian-Cambrian boundary; co-led a team that claims to have found new microfossils in the sandstone at the base of the Strelley Pool rock formation in Western Australia in 2011. Avocations: painting, early keyboards, numismatics, cryptography, sigillography. Office: Department of Earth Sciences South Parks Rd Oxford OX1 3AN England Office Phone: 0044 1865 272074. Office Fax: 0044 1865 272072. Business E-Mail: martinb@earth.ox.ac.uk. *

BRASIL, ISABELLA MONTENEGRO, biology professor; b. Fortaleza, May 3, 1964; B, Fed. U. Ceara, 1986, PhD, 2002. Assoc. prof. Fed. U. Ceara, 1994—. Home: 509 Rui Barbosa Ave Apt 01 Fortaleza Bairro Ceara 115-220 Brazil Home Fax: 55 33669752. Personal E-mail: isabella@ufc.br.

BRASLOW, NELSON M., insurance company executive; BS in Biology, Albright Coll., 1971; MD, Harvard Med. Sch., 1975; MPH, U. Conn., 1998; MBA, Wilkes U., 2000. Cert. in Internal Medicine and Pulmonary Disease. Resident and fellow, internal medicine and pulmonary diseases Mass. Gen. Hosp.; practiced internal and critical care medicine NY; med. dir. NY State Empire Plan Met. Healthcare Mgmt. Co.; v.p. sci. medicine MetraHealth Corp.; nat. med. dir. tech. assement United Healthcare Corp., 1996—98; regional med. dir. PacifiCare Health Sys., 2001—03; v.p. med. affairs Coventry Health Care, 2003—05, v.p. medical informatics, 2004—06; sr. med. dir. med. mgmt. Blue Cross Northeastern Pa.; exec. v.p., chief med. officer MVP Health Care, 2007—09; sr. med. dir. Dean Health Plan, 2010—. Fellow: American Coll. of Physician Executives; mem.: American Coll. of Chest Physicians, MENSA. Office: Dean Health Plan PO Box 56099 Madison WI 53705 Office Phone: 800-777-4793. *

BRASS, ERIC PAUL, internal medicine and pharmacology educator; b. Bklyn., Sept. 3, 1952; s. Edward A. and Barbara B.; m. Kathy E. Sietsema, Sept. 3, 1994; children: Carl, Courtney, Alexander. BSChemE, Case Western Res. U., 1974, MSChemE, 1975, PhD in Pharmacology, 1979, MD, 1980. Diplomate Am. Bd. Internal Medicine. Resident in internal medicine U. Wash., Seattle, 1980-82, fellow in clin. pharmacology, 1982-83; asst. prof. medicine and pharmacology U. Colo., Denver, 1983-89; assoc. prof. medicine and pharmacology Case Western Res. U., Cleve., 1989-93; asst. dir. Calif. Clin Trials, 1993-94; prof., chair dept. medicine Harbor-UCLA Med. Ctr., 1994—2000; dir. Harbor-UCLA Ctr. Clin. Pharm., 2000—; prof. medicine David Geffen Sch. Medicine, UCLA, 1994—. Mem., chair FDA Nonprescription Drug Adv. Com., 1995—2001. Contbr. more than 150 articles to sci. jours. Recipient Faculty Devel. award Pharm. Mfrs. Assn. Found., 1985; NIH rsch. grantee, 1985, 88, 93. Mem. Am. Soc. Clin. Pharmacology and Therapeutics (Young Investigator award 1987), Am. Soc. Clin. Investigation. Office: Harbor-UCLA Med Ctr 1124 W Carson St Torrance CA 90502-2004 Office Phone: 310-222-4050. Business E-Mail: ebrass@ucla.edu.

BRASSAI, ZOLTÀN BÈLA, internist, educator; b. Targu-Mures, Romania, Mar. 27, 1935; s. Miklos and Maria Brassai; m. Erzsebet Julianna Daroczi Brassai, Sept. 16, 1960; children: Attila, Zoltan, Erzsebet. MD, U. Med. and Pharm., Targu-Mures, 1958, DSc, 1970. From asst. to assoc. prof. U. Med. and Pharm., Targu-Mures, 1966—88, full prof., 1988—, vice-dean dept. gen. medicine, 1996—2000, head dept. internal medicine, 1996—. Inventor artheriography equipment. Mem. cultural dept. Contry Consie, Targu-Mures, 1990—94; bd. dirs. Transilvanian Mus. Soc., Targu-Mures, 1990, Sapientia Found., Targu-Mures, 2000. Mem.: N.Y. Acad. Scis., Hungarian Acad. Scis. Calvinist. Home: str Ghiocelului/9 4300 Targu Mures Romania Office: Spital Clinic Judetean Mures Gh Marinescu/50 4300 Targu Mures Romania

BRASZKO, JAN JOZEF, pharmacologist, educator; b. Latyczyn, Poland, Feb. 15, 1947; s. Jan and Genowefa (Wylupek) B. MD, Med. Acad. Bialystok, Poland, 1970, PhD in Pharmacology, 1975, PhD in Neurosci., 1989. Asst. Med. Acad. Bialystok, 1970-72, sr. asst., 1973-78, asst. prof., 1979-90, assoc. prof., 1991-96, prof., 1997—. Prorector for sci., Med. Acad. Bialystok, 1993-99, head dept. clin. pharmacology, 1994—, pres. senate R & D commn. 2002 . Contbr. articles to profl. jours. and books. Local sec. Solidarnosc Trade Union, 1981-89. Recipient Ann. Prize Polish Acad. of Scis., 1987, Ministry of Health, 1989, 91, 96, 2004, 2008 Mem. N.Y. Acad. Sci., European Behavioural Pharmacology Soc., Polish Pharmacological Soc., Polish Neurosci. Soc., Polish Acad. Sci. (com. therapy and drug scis. 2003-06), Sci. Coun. Inst. Pharmacology. Avocations: fine arts, swimming, jogging, futurology. Office: Med Univ Bialystok Waszyngtona 15A 15274 Bialystok Poland Business E-Mail: braszko@umwb.edu.pl.

BRAT, RADIM, cardiologist, surgeon, consultant; b. Ostrava, Czech Republic, Nov. 13, 1962; s. Adolf Brat and Jirina Bratova; m. Dagmar Gorgolova, Sept. 7, 1985; children: Martin, Zuzana Bratova. MD, Charles U., Faculty of Medicine, Hradec Kralove, 1987, PhD, 2001. Mem. of vascular team U. Hosp., Dept. of Surgery, Ostrava, Czech Republic, 1987—93; surgeon U. Hosp., Dept. of Cardiac Surgery, Ostrava, Czech Republic, 1993—98, vice head of dept., 1998—2003, head of dept., 2003—. Mem.: Czech Soc. of Cardiovasc. Surgeons, European Assn. for Cardio-Thoracic Surgery. Achievements include research in Methods of peroperative myocardial protection; Aortic Surgery. Office: U Hosp 17 Listopadu 1790 Ostrava 70852 Czech Republic

BRATER, DONALD CRAIG, medical educator, dean; b. Oak Ridge, Tenn., 1945; m. Stephanie Brater; 1 child, Aimee. BA in chemistry, Duke U., 1967; MD in pharmacy, Duke U. Med. Sch., 1971. Intern Duke U., 1970—71; resident in medicine U. Calif., San Francisco, 1971—73, fellow in clin. pharmacology, 1973—76; mem. faculty Southwestern Med. Sch.; joined faculty Ind. U. Sch. Medicine, Indpls., 1986, chmn. dept. medicine, John B. Hickam prof. medicine, prof. pharmacology and toxicology, 1990—2000, Walter J. Daly prof., 2000—, dean, 2000—, v.p. univ. clin. affairs, 2010—. Pres. U.S. Pharmacopoeia; bd. mgrs. Inproteo, Indpls.; adj. faculty mem. Purdue U. Sch. Pharmacy, active with Indpls. U. Sch. Medicine program in Kenya. Recipient Duke Med. Alumni Award, 2000, Friends of Pharmacy Award, Purdue U. Sch. Pharmacy, 2003. Mem.: Assn. Profs. Medicine, Am. Soc. Clin. Pharmacology and Therapeutics, Assn. Am. Physicians, Am. Soc. Clin. Investigation. Office: Ind U Sch Medicine 1120 W South Dr Fesler Hall Indianapolis IN 46202-5114 Office Phone: 317-274-8416. *

BRATINCSAK, ANDRAS, pediatrician; b. Hungary, Mar. 10, 1974; MD, Semmelweis U., 1999, PhD, 2005. Postdoc. rsch. fellow NIH, 2001—05; pediat. resident U. Hawaii, 2005—08; pediat. cardiology fellow U. Calif., San Diego, 2008—. Mem.: Am. Acad. Pediat., Am. Coll. Cardiology. Office: 3020 Children's Way MC5004 San Diego CA 92123 E-mail: bratiandris@yahoo.com.

BRATTON, TERESA SUE, pediatrician; b. Nashville, Oct. 14, 1948; m. Gustav Blomquist; children: Gus, Kerstin, Michael. BS, Vanderbilt U., Nashville, 1970, MD, 1974. Cert. master gardener Guilford County Agrl. Extension Agy. Asst. prof. U. Miss., 1979—81; pvt. practice pediatric allergist, 1982—2006; adj. clin. asst. prof., dept. pediat. U. NC, Chapel Hill, 1987—; physician, allergy & asthma clinic Guilford Child Health, 1985—. Chmn. Greensboro Med. Symposium, 1993, Blue Cross Blue Shield NC Physician Adv. Group, 1997—2004, Cmty. Health Improvement Fund, Moses Cone-Wesley Long Cmty. Health Found., 2000—04, Guilford County Asthma Coalition, 2004—. Co-chair Sawbones-Jawbones Charity Fund Raiser, 1994; pres. Greater Greensboro Soc. Medicine, 1994, Am. Lung Assn., Piedmont Br., 1994—95, bd. mem., 1992—98. Democrat. Avocations: tennis, hiking, bicycling, gardening. Office: Guilford Child Health 1046 E Wendover Ave Greensboro NC 27408 *

BRAUDE, ROBERT MICHAEL, retired medical librarian; b. LA, Sept. 27, 1939; m. Maxine Marie Moser, Nov. 24, 2007. BA, UCLA, 1962, MLS, MA, 1964; PhD, U. Nebr., 1987. Reference librarian Biomed Library Ctr. for Health Scis., UCLA, Los Angeles, 1964-65, head Medlars search sta., 1965-68; assoc. dir. U. Colo. Med. Library, Denver, 1968-75, dir., 1975-77, U. Nebr. Med. Library, Omaha, 1978-86; asst. dean for info. resources, Frances and John Loeb librarian Weill Med. Coll./Cornell U., 1986—; ret., 2001. Adj. faculty U. Denver, 1972-78; vis. assoc. prof. Sch. Libr. Sci., Pratt Inst., 1988—; del. White House Conf. on Libraries and Info. Services, 1979; mem. biomed. library rev. com. Nat. Library Medicine, Bethesda, Md., 1980-84, mem. panel on med. informatics long range planning project, 1985-86, mem. planning panel on outreach programs, 1988-89. Author: (continuing edn. syllabus) Planning: Strategic and Tactical, 1983, also articles and book chpts.; mem. editorial adv. bd. Bibliography of Bioethics; mem. editorial bd. ann. Statis. of Med. Sch. Librs. and U.S. and Can., 19887-93; mem. editorial bd. Jour. Am. Med. Informatics Assn. Sec.-treas. Children's Chorale, Denver, 1974-75, trustee, 1975-77 Fellow N.Y. Acad. Medicine, Med. Libr. Assn. (sec., bd. dirs. 1972-75, Janet Doe lectr. 1996, chmn. numerous coms. N.Y.-N.J. chpts., Outstanding Achievement award Midcontinental chpt. 1986, Noyes award 2002), Am. Coll. Med. Informatics; mem. ALA, Acad. Health Info. Profls. (disting.), Health Scis. Libr. Dirs. (stds. and practices com. 1980-83), Assn. Western Hosps. (chmn. hosp. librs. sect. 1976-77, membership com. 1976-77), Am. Med. Informatics Assn. (mem. editl. bd.). Personal E-mail: bobbraude@sbcglobal.net.

BRAUER, KEITH E., pharmaceutical executive; b. Palatine, Ill. BS, Ind. U., 1970; MBA, U. Mich., 1973. Mem. Air Nat. Guard; fin. analyst Ford Motor Co.; CFO NanoInk, Inc., bd. dirs., 2006—; v.p., fin., CFO Guidant Compass Group; assoc. fin. analyst, internat. oper. Eli Lilly & Co., 1974—76, staff fin. analyst, Pharm. Divsn., 1976—77, mktg. analyst, 1977—78, adminstr., coord., bus. planning, Med. Devices & Diagnostics Divsn., 1978—81; contr. Elizabeth Arden, Inc. (subs. Eli Lilly & Co.), 1981—84; v.p., fin., treas. Physio-Control Corp. (subs. Eli Lilly & Co.), Redmond, Wash., 1984—86; dir., corp. affairs Eli Lilly & Co., 1986—88, exec. dir., internat. fin., 1988, exec. dir., fin., chief acctg. officer, 1992—94; v.p., CFO Guidant Corp. (acquired by Boston Sci. Corp.), 1994—2006. Former bd. dirs. Cmty. Hosps. of Ind. Inc., Suros Surg. Sys., Inc.; bd. dirs. Nico Corp., Endocyte, Inc., 2006—. Mem. adv. bd. U. Mich. Bus. Sch. Corp.; chmn. bd. dirs. and fin. com. Cmty. Hosp. Ind., Inc.; bd. trustee Ind. Mus. Art. Mem.: Fin. Exec. Inst., Beta Gamma Sigma. Office: Endocyte Inc Bd Directors 3000 Kent Ave Ste A1 100 West Lafayette IN 47906 Office Phone: 765-463-7175. Office Fax: 765-463-9271. Business E-Mail: kbrauer@endocyte.com.

BRAULT, ROSE, healthcare administrator, educator; b. Gadsden, Ala., Apr. 20, 1944; d. Clement Edmond and Elizabeth Mary (McGuinn) B.; m. Stephen G. Gerzof, May 10, 1974 (div. June 1979); 1 child, David N.; m. Robert E. Lawrence, Dec. 25, 1992 (dec. Nov. 2001). BS, Boston Coll., 1966; MS, Boston U., 1977, EdD, 1985; adult nurse practitioner, U. Fla., 1996. Nurse Boston City Hosp., 1964-66, Boston Floating Hosp., 1967-68; nursing instr. Whidden Meml. Hosp., Everett, Mass., 1968-71, Univ. Hosp., Boston, 1971-72, staffing coordinator, 1972-73, med. clin. coordinator, 1973-74; dir. quality assurance St. Elizabeth's Hosp., Boston, 1979-81; dir. profl. services rev. Mass. Eye and Ear Infirmary, Boston, 1981-88; cons. quality assurance HCA Grant Ctr. and Charter Springs Hosp., Ocala, Fla., 1991, instr. pediatric nursing, med.-surg. nursing Cen. Fla. C.C., Ocala, 1990-94; instr. U. Ctrl. Fla., 1994-95; quality improvement practitioner Volusia County Pub. Health Dept., Daytona Beach, Fla., 1995-96; dir. health edn. svcs. Fla. Inst. for Neurologic Rehab., 1996-97; nurse practitioner Dept. Vets. Affairs, Bay Pines, Fla., 1997-98, Fla. Physicians Med. Group, Sebring, 1998—2000, Heartland Internal Medicine Assn., 2000—02, Health Essentials Inc., 2002—04, Good Shephard Hospice, 2002—04; asst. prof. Fla. So. Coll., 2004—07; assoc. prof. South U. Adj. faculty Boston Coll., Curry Coll., U. Mass., Simmons Coll., Northeastern U., 1979-88; chmn. ann. fund raising Mass. Eye and Ear Infirmary, Boston, 1987. Mem. ANA, APHA, Am. Acad. Nurse Practitioners (cert.), Fellow: Am. Acad. Nurse Practioners Avocations: boxer kennel, ornithology. Office: South Univ Tampa FL 33614 Office Phone: 863-680-3861. Personal E-mail: rosecws@earthink.net, rbrault@southuniversity.edu.

BRAUN, BARRY, kinesiologist; Asst. prof. pub. health U. Mass., Amherst, dir. Energy Metabolism Lab. Recipient Disting. Teaching award, U. Mass. Sch. Pub. Health & Sciences, 2007. Office: Energy Metabolism Lab 30 Eastman Ln Rm 3 Amherst MA 01003 also: 106 Totman Amherst MA 01003 Office Phone: 413-545-0331, 413-557-0146. E-mail: ebbraun@kin.umass.edu.

BRAUN, MARTIN, III, dermatologist, educator; BA, U. Md., College Park, Md., 1963—66; MD, U. Md., Balt., 1966—70. Diplomate Am. Bd. Dermatology, 1977, Am. Bd. Dermatology-dermatopathology, 1982, Am. Bd. Pathology, 1983, cert. Am. Bd. of Mohs Micrographic Surgery, 1991. Fellow mohs surgery precept with Dr Frederic Mohs, 1975; med. intern Washington Hosp. Ctr., 1970—71, dir. surgery; flight surgeon Travis Air Force Base, Calif., 1971—73; resident dermatology Univ. Mich. Med. Ctr., Ann Arbor, 1973—76; clin. prof. dermatology and medicine George Washington Univ.; hosp. affiliation include/s George Washington Univ. Hosp., Washinton Hosp. Ctr. Mem.: Internat. Soc. of Dermatol. Surgery, Am. Soc. for Dermatol. Surgery (mem. task force on CPT coding), Am. Coll. of Chemosurgery (chmn. ins. com.), Am. Coll. of Mohs Micrographic Surgery and Cutaneous Oncology (past pres.), Wash. DC Dermatol. Soc., Am. Acad. of Dermatology, Am. Coll. of Mohs Surgery. Office: Braun Dermatology Associates Ste 701 2112 F St Washington DC 20037 Mailing: Washington Hospital Center 110 Irving St Washington DC 20010 Office Phone: 202-293-7618, 202-877-7000.

BRAUN, MARY LUCILE DEKLE (LUCY BRAUN), psychotherapist, counseling administrator, educator; b. Tampa, Fla. d. Guthrie "Gus" J. and Lucile (Culpepper) Dekle; children: John Ryan, Matthew Joseph, Jeffrey William, Douglas Edwin. AB, Brenau Coll.; MA, U. Cen. Fla.; EdD, U. Fla. Cert. disability mgmt. specialist, rehab. counselor, victim advocate; lic. mental health counselor; lic. marriage and family therapist; nationally cert. counselor. Coord. Orange County Child Abuse Prevention, Orlando, Fla., 1983-88; cons. Displaced Homemaker Program, Orlando, 1989-94, DCS, Oviedo, Fla., 1983—99. Adj. prof. U. Ctrl. Fla., Orlando, Troy State U., 2002—; mem. adv. bd. Fla. Hosp. Women's Ctr., Orlando, 1989—95; bd. dirs. Children With Attention Deficit Disorders, Orlando, 1989—91, Parent Resource Ctr., Orlando; clin. dir. Response Sexual Abuse Treatment Program, 1993—95; cons. program devel. for children and adolescent treatment svcs., 1997—98; dir. clin. svcs. Rehab. and Indsl. Counseling, 1997—2002; cons., counselor contractor VA; counselor Share the Care Program; cons. Sr. Resources Alliance. Author: Someone Heard, 1987, Humor Us Soup, 1989, Child Abuse and Neglect: Resource Guide for Orange County Schools, 1985, 2d edit., 1987; contbg. author: Death from Child Abuse, 1986, Personality Types of Abusive Parents, 1993, Why Children Fight, 1992. Sustaining mem. Jr. League of Greater Orlando. Recipient Cmty. Svc. award Walt Disney World, 1987, Outstanding Alumna award Brenau U., 2006. Mem. ACA, Am. Acad. Marriage and Family Therapists, Fla. Counseling Assn., Nat. Bd. Cert. Counselors, Phi Kappa Phi, Kappa Delta Pi, Chi Sigma Iota, Alpha Delta Pi. Avocations: scuba diving, sailing, puzzles, travel.

BRAUN, STANLEY, orthodontist, educator; s. Max and Sarah Braun; m. Constance Ann Belle, June 25, 1955; children: Lory Susan Wasserman, Stephen Mitchell, Mark Charles. B of Mech. Engring., NYU, 1951, MME, 1952; DDS summa cum laude, Ohio State U., 1963. Cert. in orthodontics Ind. U. Sch. Dentistry, 1965, lic. Bd.

Dentistry Ohio, Ind., Ill., Ky. Asst. chief engr. Master Vibrator Co., Dayton, Ohio, 1956—58; assoc. prof. of orthodontics Ind. U., Indpls., 1965—69; pvt. practice in splty. orthodontics Indpls., 1965—96; clin. prof. of orthodontics U. of Louisville, 1976—95, Vanderbilt U. Med. Ctr., Nashville, 1994—2004, U. of Ill., Chgo., 1995—98, Marquette U., Milw., 1998, St. Louis U., 1999—2001. Rsch. fellow NIH, Washington, 1963—65; cons. in orthodontics to the surgeon gen. Dept. of Health, Washington, 1965—67; editl. bd. Jour., Angle Orthodontic Soc., Edina, Minn., 1995—; guest editor seminars in orthodontics. Mem. editl. bd.: Am. Jour. Orthodontics and Dentofacial Orthopedics, 1995—, Jour. Angle Orthodontic Soc., 1995—2005, Med. Sci. Monitor, 2004—; contbr. articles to profl. jours., chapters to books. 1st lt. USAF, 1952—54. Recipient Don Shusterman Meml. award, Ohio State U., 1963, Cert. of Recognition, NYU Orthodontic Soc., 1970, Disting. award, Am. Soc. of Dentistry for Children, 1963, Cert. of Recognition, Chgo. Dental Soc., 1965, Award of Recognition, Am. Acad. of Dental Medicine, 1975, Callahan Meml. Commn. award, Ohio State U., 1963. Mem.: Tau Beta Pi, Omicron Kappa Epsilon, Pi Tau Sigma. Achievements include Member of Engineering Team that Developed Fusing System for the First U.S. Intercontinental Ballistics Missile; design of Concrete Automatic Troweling Machine. Avocations: travel, stained glass creations, painting.

BRAUN, TODD I., infectious disease physician; Grad., Lehigh U., Hahnemann U. Diplomate Am. Bd. Internal Medicine, Am. Bd. Internal Medicine-infectious disease. Chief infectious diseases divsn. Abington Meml. Hosp. Named one of Top Docs, Phila. Mag., 2010, 2011. Mem.: Abington Health Physicians. Office: Abington Memorial Hospital Associates in Infectious Diseases Levy Med Plaza 1235 Old York Rd Ste 220 Abington PA 19001 Office Phone: 215-481-6350. Office Fax: 215-481-6359.

BRAUNER, DANIEL, geriatrician, educator, rheumatologist; MD, SUNY, Syracuse. Resident & fellow U. Ill. Cook County Hosp.; assoc. prof. med. U. Chgo. Med. Ctr., dir. geriatrics fellowship program; med. dir. Montgomery Place Health Care Pavilion. Mailing: 5841 S Maryland Ave MC 6098 Chicago IL 60637 Office: Outpatient Senior Health Center at South Shore 7101 S Exchange Ave Chicago IL 60649 E-mail: dbrauner@medicine.bsd.uchicago.edu.

BRAUNER, GARY JULES, dermatologist, cosmetic laser surgeon; b. Bridgeport, Conn., Sept. 14, 1941; s. Charles and Frances (Rabitz) B.; m. Judith Susan Schlosser, Aug. 29, 1965; children: Lisa Michelle, Wendy Ellen. BA magna cum laude, Yale Coll., 1963; MD, Harvard U., 1967. Diplomate Am. Bd. Dermatology and Am. Bd. Pathology in Dermatopathology. Intern Jewish Hosp. of St. Louis, 1967-68; resident in dermatology Mass. Gen. Hosp., Boston, 1968-70, chief resident dermatology, 1970-71; asst. to assoc. clin. prof. dermatology Albert Einstein Coll. of Medicine, Bronx, NY, 1971-87; assoc. clin. prof. dermatology NY Med. Coll., Valhalla, 1987-93, Mount Sinai Sch. of Medicine, NYC, 1993—. Chief dermatology Morrisania Hosp., Bronx, 1975-76, North Ctrl. Bronx Hosp., 1976-82; chief dermatology svc. Rikers Island Health Ctr., East Elmhurst, NY, 1975-79; provisional attending physician Englewood Hosp., NJ, 1975-78, assoc. attending physician, 1978-81, attending physician, dermatology, 1981—, chief dept. dermatology, 1992-03; attending physician Hackensack U. Med. Ctr., 1982—; asst. attending Westchester County Med. Ctr., 1987-91, Met. Hosp., NYC, 1987-93; attending physician, dermatology Pascack Valley Hosp., Westwood, NJ, 1992-2007, provisional attending dept. dermatology 1993-95, asst. attending, 1995-97; attending Mt. Sinai Med. Ctr., 1997-; lectr. in field. Contbg. editor Hosp. Physician, 1978—, Health Practitioner and Physician's Asst., 1978—; assoc. editor Dialogues in Dermatology, 1978-92, 95—, Jour. of the Am. Acad. of Dermatology, 1988-93, Laser Medicine and Surgery News and Advances, 1988-96; editor The Schoch Letter, 2003—; contbr. numerous articles to profl. jours. Maj. U.S. Army, 1971-74. Fellow Am. Acad. Dermatology (dir. 1992-97), Am. Soc. Dermatol. Soc.; mem. Am. Soc. of Laser Medicine and Surgery, Dermatol. Soc. Greater NY (pres. 1990-91), NY State Dermatol. Soc. (dir.), NJ State Med. Soc., Assn. for Mil. Dermatologists, Internat. Soc. Tropical Dermatology, Bergen County Med. Soc., NJ Dermatol. Soc., Soc. for Pediatric Dermatology, Internat. Soc. for Dermatol. Surgery (dir. 1997-99, treas. 2000-04, sec. 2004-06, pres. 2008-10), Internat. Soc. for Pediatric Dermatology, Med. Coun. Skin Cancer Found., NY State Med. Soc., NY County Med. Soc. Avocations: gardening, travel, photography. Office: 125 E 63rd St New York NY 10065-7310 Office Phone: 212-421-5080. Personal E-mail: dermlaser@aol.com.

BRAUN-FALCO, OTTO, retired dermatologist; b. Saarbruecken, Apr. 25, 1922; s. Andreas and Rosa (Falco) Braun; m. Sissy Golling, 1951; 1 child, Markus. Postgrad., Westphalia Wilhelms U., Münster, 1940—48; MD magna cum laude, Johannes Gutenberg U., Mainz, 1948; D (hon.), Rijksuniversiteit Gent, Belgium, 1980, Philipps U., Marburg, Germany, 1987, Humboldt U., Berlin, 1991, U. Liège, Belgium, 1991, Comenius U., Bratislava, Slovakia, 2007. Resident in dermatology and venereology U. Mainz, 1948, sr. physician dermatology clinic, 1954, assoc. prof., 1960; prof., chmn. dept. dermatology and venereology Phlipps U., Marburg, 1961, dean med. faculty, 1965-66; prof., chmn. dept. dermatology and venereology Ludwig Maximilian U., Munich, 1967, emeritus prof., 1991—; ret., 1991. Guest prof. dept. dermatology NYU Med. Ctr., NYC, 1965, NYC, 92; lectr. Dohi Meml., Sendai, Japan, 1968, Kung Sun Oh Meml., Seoul, Republic of Korea, 1978; vis. prof. Yonsei U., Seoul, 1979. Editor: Der Hautarzt, 1968—83, Archiv fur Dermatologische Forschung. Recipient Alfred-Marchionini Gold medal, Tokyo, 1982, Alvin J. Cox award, Psoriasis, Stanford, 1985, Stephen Rothman Gold medal, Soc. Investigative Dermatology, 1986, Herxheimer medal, Deutsch Dermatol Ges., 1990, Excellence award, European Soc. Dermatol. Rsch., Amsterdam, 1996, European Acad. Dermatology and Venerology, London, 1991, Clin. Care award, 2005, Cothenius Gold medal, Deutsche Acad. Naturforscher Leopoldina, zu Halle, 1997. Mem.: Internat. League Dermatol. Socs. (pres. 1977—82), Royal Soc. Medicine, Soc. Française de Dermatologie et de Syphiliyraphie, Nederlands Vereinigung van Dermatologen, Finnische Gesellschaft fur Dermatologie, Belgische Dermatologische Gesellschaft, Sudwestdeutsche Dermatologenvereinigung, Muenchener Dermatologische Gesellschaft, Deutsche Dermatologische Gesellschaft, Deutsche Akademie der Naturforscher Leopoldina zu Halle, Nat. Dermatol. Soc. (hon.), Australasian Coll. Dermatologists (hon.). Home: Faistenberger Str 4 D-81545 Munich Germany Home Phone: 0049-89-646588. Personal E-mail: prof.obf@t-online.de.

BRAUNSTEIN, GLENN DAVID, physician, educator; b. Greenville, Tex., Feb. 29, 1944; s. Mervin and Helen (Friedman) B.; m. Jacquelyn D. Moose, July 5, 1965; children: Scott M. Braunstein, Jeffrey T. Braunstein. BS summa cum laude, U. Calif., San Francisco, 1965, MD, 1968. Diplomate Am. Bd. Internal Medicine, subsplty. endocrinology, diabetes, metabolism. Intern, resident Peter Bent Brigham Hosp., Boston, 1968-70; clin. fellow in medicine Harvard U. Med. Sch., Boston, 1969-70; clin. assoc., reproduction rsch. br. NIH, Bethesda, Md., 1970-72; chief resident in endocrinology Harbor Gen. Hosp. UCLA, 1972-73; dir. endocrinology Cedars-Sinai Med. Ctr., LA, 1973-86, chmn. dept. medicine, 1986—; asst. prof. medicine UCLA Sch. Medicine, 1973-77, assoc. prof., 1977-81, prof., 1981—, vice chair dept. medicine, 1986—. Cons. AMA drug evaluations, 1990-1994; mem. internat. adv. com. Second World Conf. on Implantation and Early Pregnancy in Human, 1994; mem. endocrinologic and metabolic drugs adv. com. FDA, 1991-95, chmn., 1994-95, spl. advisor, 1995-2001, 04-, chmn., 2001-04; bd. mem. Am. Bd. Internal Medicine Endocrinology, Diabetes, Metabolism Subsplty., 1991-99, chmn., 1995-99, bd. dirs., 1995-99; bd. dirs. Am. Bd. Emergency Medicine 2002-06. Mem. editl. bd. Mt. Sinai Jour. Medicine, 1984-88, Early Pregnancy: Biology and Medicine, 1998, Am. Family Physician, 1995—, The Am. Jour. Medicine, 1996—, Clin. Endocrinology & Metabolism, 1978-80, 2008-; assoc. editor Integrative Medicine: Integrating Allopathic, Alternative and Complementary Medicine, 1997-2000, Endocrine Practice, 2010-, Maturas, 2010-. Bd. dirs. Israel Cancer Rsch. Fund, 1991-94, Cedars-Sinai Med. Ctr., 1997-2003; mem. Jonsson Comprehensive Cancer Ctr., 1991—. With USPHS, 1970—72. Recipient Gold Headed Cane Soc. award U. Calif. San Francisco Med. Ctr., 1968, outstanding achievement and cmty. svc. award Anti-Defamation League, 1997, James R. Klinenberg Chair in Medicine, 2000—, Sherman M. Mellinkoff Faculty award UCLA Sch. Medicine, 2002; Merck scholar, 1968, Mosby scholar, 1968. Fellow ACP (mem. adv. com. to gov., So. Calif. region 1989—, credentials com. So. Calif. region 1993); mem. AAAS, Cross Town Endocrine Club (chmn. 1982-83), Endocrine Soc. (publs. com. 1983-89, long range planning com. 1986-87, recent progress hormone rsch. com. 1993-98, ann. meeting steering com. 1993-98, spl. programs com. 1998—, media adv. com. 1999-2005, chmn. 2002-05, Disting. Physician award 2006), Pacific Coast Fertility Soc. (pres. 1988), Western Soc. for Clin. Rsch., Am. Fedn. for Clin. Rsch., Am. Thyroid Assn., Am. Fertility Soc., Western Assn. Physicians (pres. 1998-99), North Am. Menopause Assn., Assn. Am. Physicians, Am. Soc. Clin. Investigations (mem. nominating com. 1989), Univ. Calif. San Francisco Sch. Medicine Alumni Faculty Assn. (regional v.p. so. Calif., mem. bd. dirs. Israel Cancer Rsch. Fund 1991-94), Phi Delta Epsilon, Alpha Omega Alpha. Office: Cedars Sinai Med Ctr Dept Med Pla Level Rm 2119 8700 Beverly Blvd Los Angeles CA 90048-1865 Office Phone: 310-423-5140. Business E-Mail: braunstein@cshs.org.

BRAUNSTEIN, SETH, internist, educator; Attended, NYU; MD, PhD. Diplomate Am. Bd. Internal Medicine, 1975. Intern Univ. of Pa. Hosp., resident, fellow; physician; hosp. affiliation include Perelman Ctr. for Advanced Medicine, Penn Medicine Radnor; clin. dir. diabetes sect. Assoc. prof. medicine dept. Named one of the Top Doctors, Phila. Mag., 2004—11, the Am.'s Top Doctors, 2007, 2008, 2010. Office: Perelman Center for Advanced Medicine W Pavilion 4th Fl 3400 Civic Ctr Blvd Philadelphia PA 19104 Office Phone: 800-789-7366.

BRAUNTUCH, GLENN, pulmonologist; Attended, Columbia U. Coll. Physicians & Surgeons, 1978. Diplomate Am. Bd. Internal Medicine, Am. Bd. Internal Medicine-pulmonary disease. Intern St. Lukes-Roosevelt Hosp., NY, resident in internal medicine, 1979—81; fellow in pulmonary disease NYU Med. Ctr., 1981—84; with Holy Name Med. Ctr.; pulmonologist Englewood Hos. & Med. Ctr. Office: Englewood Hospital & Medical Center Bergen Medical Alliance 180 Engle St Englewood NJ 07631 Office Phone: 201-567-2050. Office Fax: 201-568-8936.

BRAUNWALD, EUGENE, physician, educator; b. Aug. 15, 1929; m. Nina H. Starr (dec.); m. Elaine R. Smith, 1993; children: Karen G., Allison, Jill. AB, NYU, 1949, MD, 1952; AM (hon.), Harvard U., 1972; MD (hon.), U. Lisbon, 1984; ScD (hon.), Mt. Sinai Med. Ctr., 1991; MD (hon.), U. Rome, 1991, U. Portg, 1992, U. Vienna, 1995, U. La Plata, Argentina, 1995, U. Rio de Janeiro, 1998, Carol Davila U., 2002, U. Athens, 2003, U. Padua, 2003, Bates Coll., 2003, Comenius U., Bratislava, 2004, U. Modena, 2005, U. Montreal, 2009. Diplomate Am. Bd. Internal Medicine, Am. Bd. Cardiovascular Disease. Intern, fellow Mt. Sinai Hosp., NYC, 1952—54; research fellow Columbia U. Coll. Physicians and Surgeons, NYC, 1954—55; clin. assoc. cardiovascular physiology lab. Nat. Heart Inst., Bethesda, Md., 1955—57; asst. resident Osler Med. Service, Johns Hopkins Hosp., Balt., 1957—58; chief cardiology sect., chief cardiology br., clin. dir. Nat. Heart and Lung Inst., Bethesda, 1958—68; prof., chmn. dept. medicine U. Calif.-San Diego, 1968—72; Hersey prof. of theory and practice of medicine Harvard U. Med. Sch., Boston, 1972—96, Herrman Blumgart prof. Medicine, 1980—89, chmn. study group, 1984—, Disting. Hersey prof., 1996—; faculty dean for acad. programs Harvard U., Boston, 1996—2003. Chmn. dept. medicine Brigham and Women's Hosp., 1972—96, Beth Israel Hosp., 1980—89; lectr. physiology George Washington U., 1959—62; from asst. clin. prof. to clin. prof. Georgetown U. Sch. Medicine, 1960—68; lectr. medicine Johns Hopkins U., 1960—68; trustee McLear Ptnrs., 1993—96; vis. prof. numerous U.S. and fgn. univs.; lectr. in field. Co-editor: Year Book of Cardiovascular and Renal Diseases, 1965—72, Year Book of Medicine, 1973—93, Harrison's Principles of Internal Medicine, 1967—; editor: Heart Disease, 1980—; mem. editl. bds.: Ciculation, Jour. Clin. Investigation, 1964—71, Jour. Cardiovascular Pharmacology, Am. Jour. Medicine, Am. Jour. Cardiology, New Eng. Jour. Medicine, numerous others. Bd. visitors Rockefeller U., 1978—82; mem. vis. com. MIT, 1979—85, Technion U., 1979. Recipient Arthur S. Fleming award, 1965, Superior Svc. award, HEW, 1967, Disting. Achievement award, Modern Medicine, 1968, Gustav Nylin award, Swedish Med. Soc., 1970, Williams award Outstanding Chmn. and Medicine, 1987, Bristol Myers Squibb Excellence in Cardiovascular Rsch. award, 1993, J. Allyn Taylor Internat. prize, Robarts Rsch. Inst., 1993, Gold medal, European Cardiac Soc., 2004. Master: Am. Coll. Cardiology (v.p. 1967, trustee 1967, 1970—75, Disting. Scientist award 1987); fellow: ACP (Phillips award 1991), Am. Acad. Arts and Scis.; mem.: NAS, Internat. Soc. Cardiology, Royal Soc. Medicine, Harvey Soc., Am. Heart Assn. (bd. dirs. 1966—75, v.p. 1966—70, Rsch. Achievement award 1972, Herrick award 1981), Am. Soc. Pharmacology and Exptl. Therapeutics (John Jacob Abel award 1965), Am. Physiol. Soc., New Eng. Cardiovascular Soc. (pres. 1987—88), Assn. Univ. Cardiologists, Western Soc. for Clin. Rsch. (pres. 1971—72), Am. Fedn. Clin. Rsch. (pres. 1969—70), Am. Soc. Clin. Investigation (pres. 1974—75), Western Assn. Physicians, Assn. Am. Physicians (Kober medal 1998), Assn. Profs. Medicine (pres. 1974—75), Johns Hopkins Soc. Scholars, Alpha Omega Alpha. Office: TIMI Study Group 350 Longwood Ave 1st Fl Boston MA 02115 Office Phone: 617-732-8989. E-mail: ebraunwald@partners.org.

BRAUT, BOUCHER FRANÇOISE, biomedical researcher; b. Alencon, France, Apr. 6, 1947; d. Marcel Boucher and Jacqueline Landais; m. Jean-Louis Braut, 1977; 1 child, Helene. Degree, Faculty Pharm., Angers, France, 1971, Faculty Pharm., Paris, 1978. Biomed. rschr. Faculty Medicine, Paris, 1974—. Roman Catholic. Office: Xavier Bichat Faculty Medicine 16 Rue Henri Huchard 75018 Paris France Office Phone: 33 (1) 44856211. Business E-Mail: braut@bichat.inserm.fr.

BRÄUTIGAM, PETER, physician; b. Achern, Germany, Sept. 18, 1958; s. Hans and Inge (Peters) B. Staatsexamen I, II, Freiburg U., Germany, 1981-85; Subintern, U. Vienna, 1983-84, U. Wash., 1985-86; Staatsexamen III, Tech. U., Munich, 1986; postgrad., 1986—. Cert. Bd. Nuclear Medicine. Resident dept. neurology U. Ulm., Germany, 1987-88; fellow, resident dept. nuc. medicine U. Freiburg, Germany, 1988-96; head dept. nuc. medicine Paracelsus Klinik Osnabrück, Germany, 1996-98, Clinique Ste Therese, Luxembourg, 1998—. V.p. Nat. PET Ctr. of Luxembourg, 2002—. Contbr. articles to med. jours. Recipient award Deutsche Krebshilfe, 1992; UGM grantee U. Pa., 1999. Mem. Soc. German Speaking Lymphologists (bd. dirs. 1992—, treas. 1997—), Soc. Nuclear Medicine, Internat. Soc. Lymphology (Presdl. award 1995), European Assn. Nuclear Medicine (award 2000). Avocations: sailing, bicycling, outdoor activities, flying. Office: Clinique Ste Therese 36 Rue Ste Zithe 2763 Luxembourg Luxembourg

BRAVENDER, TERRILL (TERRY) D., pediatrician; b. Feb. 7, 1966; MD, U. Mich. Med. Sch., 1992; MPH, Harvard Sch. Pub. Health, 1999. Cert. Am. Bd. Pediatrics, Adolescent Medicine. Intern, adolescent medicine Duke U. Med. Ctr., Durham, NC, 1992—96, staff, 1999—; fellow, internal medicine Children's Hosp. Boston, 1996—98, physician, pediat., 1998—99; instr., pediat. Harvard Med. Sch., Boston, 1998—99; assoc. prof. Duke U. Med. Sch., dir., adolescent medicine; private practice Duke Children's Primary Care, NC. Course dir., adolescent medicine rotation in the pediat. residency program Duke U. Sch. Medicine; co-founder, med. dir. Duke Eating Disorders Program (DEDP). Contbr. several articles to profl. jours. Office: Duke Childrens Primary Care 4020 N Roxboro Rd Durham NC 27704 Office Phone: 919-620-5374. Office Fax: 919-471-3820.

BRAVERMAN, IRWIN MERTON, dermatologist, educator; b. Boston, Apr. 17, 1929; s. Morris and Molly (Singer) B.; m. Muriel Stella Freedman, June 5, 1955; children: Paula, David, Michael. AB in Biology summa cum laude, Harvard U., 1951; MD, Yale U., 1955. Diplomate: Am. Bd. Med. Examiners, Am. Bd. Dermatology, Am. Bd. Pathology. Practice medicine specializing in dermatology New Haven; asst. prof. dermatology Yale U., New Haven, 1962-68, assoc. prof., 1968-73, prof., 1973—. Author: Skin Signs of Systemic Disease, 1970, 3d edit., 1997; contbr. articles to profl. jours. Served to capt. U.S. Army, 1956-58. Recipient Mr. and Mrs. J.N. Taub Internat. Meml. award for research in psoriasis Baylor Med. Coll., 1980, Lifetime Edn. award, Dermatology Found. 2008 Mem. AMA, New Eng. Dermatol. Soc. (v.p. 1990-91, pres. 1991-92), Am. Dermatol. Assn., Am. Acad. Dermatology (dir. 1980-83, Sulzberger Internat. lectr. 1989, Master of Dermatology 1993, Everett C. Fox Meml. lectr. 2001), Soc. Investigative Dermatology (bd. dirs. 1982-87, pres. elect 1991-92, pres. 1992-93, David M. Carter award for mentorship 1999), Am. Fedn. Clin. Rsch., Am. Assn. Physicians. Office: Yale U Med Sch 333 Cedar St New Haven CT 06510-3289 Home Phone: 203-795-9301; Office Phone: 203-785-4092. Business E-Mail: irwin.braverman@yale.edu.

BRAVERMAN, LEWIS E., endocrinologist, educator; Grad. in Biology, Harvard Coll.; MD, Johns Hopkins U., 1955; hon. doc. in Medicine, U. Parma, Italy. Diplomate Am. Bd. Internal Medicine, 1963, Am. Bd. Nuc. Medicine, 1972. Resident internal medicine Boston City Hosp., 1957—60; fellow endocrinology Thorndike Meml. Lab-Harvard, Boston, 1960—62; prof. medicine Boston Univ.; hosp. affiliation includes Boston Med. Ctr., Caritas St. Elizabeth's Med. Ctr. Co-author: (publs.) Iodide concentrations in matched maternal serum, cord serum, and amniotic fluid from preterm and term human pregnancies, 2008, Free T4 immunoassays are flawed during pregnancy, 2009, Colostrum iodine and perchlorate concentrations in Boston-area women: a cross-sectional study., 2009, Neonatal thyroxine, maternal thyroid function, and child cognition, 2009, Iodine content of prenatal multivitamins in the United States, 2009, and numerous other publs. Recipient award, Am. Thyroid Assn., The Endocrine Soc., The German Endocrine Soc., The Technion Univ. Sch. of Medicine (Haifa, Israel), Thai Am. Physicians Found., H. Jack Baskin, MD, Endocrine Tchg. award, Am. Assn. of Clin. Endocrinologists (AACE). Office: Boston University Department of Medicine E-113 715 Albany St Boston MA 02118 Office Phone: 617-638-7211. Office Fax: 617-638-7221. E-mail: lewis.braverman@bmc.org.

BRAWLEY, OTIS WEBB, oncologist, educator; b. Detroit, July 4, 1959; MD, U. Chgo.-Pritzker Sch. Medicine, 1985. Cert. Am. Bd. Internal Medicine, Am. Bd. Med. Oncology. Resident, internal medicine U. Hospitals Cleve., Case Western Reserve U., Cleve., 1985—88; fellow, oncology Nat. Cancer Inst., Bethesda, Md., 1988—90, asst. dir., Spl. Populations Rsch., 1995—2001, chief, Intramural Prostate Cancer Clinic, 1993—95, sr., divsn. cancer prevention and control; attending physician NIC Clin. Ctr., 1990, Nat. Naval Med. Ctr., Bethesda, Md., 1990; prof., hematology, oncology & epidemiology Ga. Ctr. for Excellence, Grady Meml. Hosp.; prof., hematology, oncology and medicine Emory U. Sch. Medicine; prof., epidemiology Emory Rollins Sch. Pub. Health; assoc. dir. to dep. dir., Winship Cancer Inst. Emory U.; chief, hematology and oncology svcs., med. dir., Ga. Cancer Coalition Ctr. of Excellence Grady Meml. Hosp.; chief med. officer Am. Cancer Soc., 2007—. Sr. investigator NIH, mem. adv. com. on women's health; mem. adv. com. NIH Office of Disease Prevention; chair NIH Consensus Panel on the Treatment of Sickle Cell Anemia; mem. oncologic drug adv. com. FDA; mem. Uniformed Svcs. U, Health Sci. Bd. Regents, Dept. Def., 2004, CDC; mem. adv. com. Prevention Breast and Cervical Cancer Early Detection and Control; co-chair Surgeon General's Task Force in Cancer

Health Disparities; bd. dirs. Theragenics Corp., 1995; invited lectr. in field. Contbr. articles to profl. jours.; editl. roles Contemporary Oncology, Prostate Cancer and Prostatic Diseases, Cancer Epidemiology Biomarkers and Prevention, & British Jour. Urology and Cure. Vol. Am. Cancer Soc. Prostate Cancer Com. Recipient Nat. Cancer Inst. and the Equal Employment Opportunity Officer's Commendation, 1991, 1993, US Pub. Health Svc. Crisis Response Svc. award, 2006, US Pub. Health Svc. Disting. Svc. Commendation, Key to St. Bernard Parish for work in New Orleans with Hurricane Katrina; Ga. Cancer Coalition Eminent Scholar. Mem.: Am. Assn. for Clin. Rsch., Am. Soc. Clin. Oncology, Nat. Med. Assn., ACP. Office: American Cancer Society 1599 Clifton Rd Atlanta GA 30329

BRAYDEN, DAVID JAMES, pharmacologist, educator, consultant; b. Dublin, Jan. 8, 1963; s. Kenneth Brayden and Alma Quinn; m. Anne P. O'Loughlin, Apr. 22, 1989; children: Kate children: Eleanor. PhD, U. Cambridge, 1989, MPhil, 1986; MSc, U. Coll. Dublin, 1985, BSc with honors, 1984. Rsch. fellow Stanford U., Stanford, Calif., 1989—91; sr. scientist Elan Biotech. Rsch., Dublin, 1991—2001; lectr. U. Coll. Dublin, Dublin, 2001—, sr. lectr., 2005, assoc. prof., 2006, dir. rsch. Sch. Agrl. Food Sci., 2007—; dir. Irish Drug Delivery Network, Sci. Found., Ireland, 2008—; cons. biotech. industry Ind. Novo-Nordisk Ltd. Rsch. fellow Conway Inst., U. Coll., Dublin, 2008—. Editor: European Jour. Pharm. Sci., 1999—2001; asst. editor Therapeutic Delivery, 2010, mem. editl. bd. Drug Discovery Today, London, 2001—, Jour. Pharmacy & Pharm., 2002—05, Adv. Drug Del. Rev., 2004—, Jour. Vet. Pharm. Ther., 2005— (Best Paper award, 2005), Open Drug Delivery Jour., 2009; contbr. articles to profl. jours. Fellow: Royal Acad. Medicine in Ireland; mem.: N.Y. Acad. Sci., Brit. Pharm. Soc., Am. Assn. Pharm. Sci., U.K.-Ireland Controlled Release Soc. (chmn. 2003—06, bd. sci. advisors 2007—10). Office: Sch Vet Medicine University Coll Dublin Dublin 4 Ireland Office Phone: 353 (1) 7166013. Business E-Mail: david.brayden@ucd.ie.

BRAŽDŽIUVIENĖ, EDITA, physician, aviation medical expert; b. Biržai, Lithuania, June 6, 1966; d. Romualdas Kukys and Elena Vida Kukiene; m. Rimgaudas Braždžius, July 22, 1992; children: Žygimantas Braždžius, Ričardas Braždžius. Gen. practitioner degree, Vilnius U., Lithuania, 1992. Nurse Ctrl. Hosp., Biržai, 1984—86; trained nurse Santariškiu Hosp. Vilnius U., 1990—91; resident for being a gen. practitioner/family dr. Vilnius U., 1992—95; gen practitioner/family dr., head dispensary N. Radviliškis Dispensary, Biržai, 1995—2005; gen. practitioner/family dr. Biržai Milk Factory, 1997—2001, AB Biržai Family Drs. Centre, 2005—; pediatrician on call Biržai Hosp., 2001—; pres. Biazai Aeroclub, 2010—. Aviation med. expert Civil Aviation, Biržai, 1999—; consulting dr. Lithuanian Arthritis Club, Biržai, 1996—2007. Mem.: Lithuania Aviation Med. Assn., Lithuania Hypertension League, World Hypertension League, Aerospace Med. Assn., Biržai Aviation Club (assoc.). Roman Catholic. Avocations: flying, painting, singing, piano, guitar. Home: P. Kalpoko G. 31 41180 Biržai Lithuania Office Phone: 370 68757696.

BRAZEAL, DONNA SMITH, psychologist; b. Greenville, SC, Feb. 10, 1947; d. G.W. Hovey and Ollie Occena (Crane) Smith; m. Charles Lee Brazeal, June 27, 1970 (div. May 1980). BA, Clemson U., 1971, MEd, 1975; postgrad., Western Carolina U., 1974, Furman U., Greenville, 1977, U. NC, Greensboro, 1982; PhD, Columbia Pacific U., 1994. Lic. sch. psychologist, SC, NC. Instr., head med. record dept. Greenville Tech. Coll., 1971-73; N.E. area chief psychologist Greenville County Schs., 1975-80; coord. psychol. svcs. Union County Schs., Monroe, NC, 1980-97; ret., 1997; pvt. practice psychology Monroe and Charlotte, NC, 1986—; mem., human rights com. RHA, Howell Care Ctrs., Clear Creek, 2010—. Mem. learning disabilities com. Greenville County Schs., 1978-79; co-founder, bd. dirs. Ctr. for Spiritual Awareness of NC, Monroe, 1982—. Co-author, co-editor: School Psychologist, 1980. Child find program coord. Union County, 1980-85; mem. various coms. Assn. for Retarded Citizens, Monroe; mem. Union County Assn. for Retarded Citizens; mem. interagy. coun. Piedmont Mental Health, Monroe, 1983-97; mem. adult edn. com. River Hills Cmty. Ch., 1985-86. Catawba Bus. Women scholar, 1965; NC Dept. Pub. Instrn. Pre-Sch. Incentive grantee, 1984. Mem. Nat. Assn. Sch. Psychologists, NC Assn. Sch. Psychologist (mem. pub. rels. com. 1984-85), Greenpeace, Humane Soc. U.S., Am. Mensa, Delta. Democrat. Interdenominational Christian. Home: PO Box 5432 Lake Wylie SC 29710 Personal E-mail: donny210@aol.com.

BREAUX, JOHN BERLINGER, lobbyist, former United States Senator from Louisiana; b. Crowley, La., Mar. 1, 1944; s. Ezra H., Jr. and Katherine (Berlinger) B.; m. Lois Gail Daigle, Aug. 1, 1964; children: John B., William Lloyd, Elizabeth Andre, Julia Agnes. BA in Polit. Sci, U. Southwestern La., 1964; JD, La. State U., 1967. Bar: La. 1967. Ptnr. Brown, McKernan, Ingram & Breaux, 1967-68; legis. asst. to Rep. Edwin W. Edwards, US House of Reps., 1968-69, dist. asst. to, 1969-72; mem. US Congress from 7th Dist. La., 1972—87; US Senator from La. Washington, 1987—2005; chief dep. whip, 1993—2005; mem. US Senate Finance Com., 1990—2005; chmn. US Senate Aging Com., 2001—03; sr. counsel Patton Boggs LLP, Washington, 2005—07, spl. sr. counsel, 2010—; Disting prof. comm. Manship Sch. Mass Comm. La State U., Baton Rouge, 2005—, sr. fellow Reilly Ctr. Media & Pub. Affairs, 2005—; ptnr. Breaux-Lott Leadership Group, Washington, 2008—10. Chmn. Nat. Water Alliance, 1987-88, Nat. Dem. Senatorial Campaign Com., 1989-90, founder, past chair, Dem. Leadership Coun., 1991-93; co-chmn. Nat. Bipartisan Commn. on Future of Medicare, 1998-99; co-chmn. Nat. Commn. on Retirement Policy, 1997-98; bd. dirs, CSX Corp., 2005-Recipient American Legion award; Moot Ct. finalist La. State U., 1966; Neptune award American Oceanic Orgn., 1980; named one of The 50 Top Lobbyists, Washingtonian mag., 2007. Mem. La. Bar Assn., Crowley Jr. C. of C., La. Jr. C. of C., Pi Lambda Beta, Phi Alpha Delta, Lambda Chi Alpha. Democrat. Office: Patton Boggs LLP 2550 M St NW Washington DC 20037 Office Phone: 202-457-6000. Office Fax: 202-457-6315.

BRECHER, MARK ELLIOTT, health facility administrator; b. Balt., June 13, 1956; s. Maxwell Isaac and Beatrice (Canter) B.; m. Maria Paoletti, July 25, 1987; children: Danielle, Juliana. BA in Chemistry, Emory U., 1978; MD, U. Chgo., 1982. Diplomate Nat. Bd. Med. Examiners, 1983, Am. Bd. Pathology, in anatomic & clin. pathology, 1987, in blood banking, transfusion medicine, 1989; lic. Ill., Minn., Fla., Arz., NC. Basic surgery resident University of Chicago, 1982-83, anatomic pathology resident, 1983—85, clin. pathology resident, 1985—87, chief resident, 1986—87; transfusion medicine fellow Mayo Clinic, Rochester, Minn., 1987-88, assoc. cons., 1988-89, sr. assoc. cons., 1989-92, instr., Lab. Medicine, 1989—91; asst. prof., Lab. Medicine Mayo Med. Sch., 1989—91; assoc. prof., Pathology University of North Carolina, Chapel Hill, 1992-98, dir., Stem Cell-HPC Lab., 1992—2009, prof., Pathology & Lab. Medicine Chapel Hill, 1998—, assoc. dir., Transfusion Medicine, 1992—95, dir., Transfusion Medicine, 1995—2009, dir., McLendon Clin. Labs., 2002, acting dir., Lab. Info. Sys., dir., Clin. Pathology Chapel Hill, 2003—06, vice chmn., dept. Pathology & Lab. Medicine, McLendon Clin. Lab., 2006—09, adj. prof., Dept. Pathology & Lab. Medicine, 2009—; sr. v.p., chief med. officer Laboratory Corp. of America Holdings, 2009—. Co-editor: Obstetrical Transfusion Practice, 1993, Massive Transfusion, 1994, Orthopedic Transfusion Practice, 1995, Hematopoletic Progenitor Cells: Processing, Standards and Practice, 1995, Research Design and Analysis, 1998, AABB Technical Manual, 1999, 14th edit., 2002; chief editor AABB Tech. Manual, 2005, Bacterial and Parasitic Contamination of Blood Components, 2003; reviewer Mayor Clinic Procs., Am. Jour. Clin. Pathology, Archives of Pathology and Lab., Medicine, Jour. Clin. Apheresis (also assoc. editor), 1997-, Clin. Microbiology Revs., Jour. Clin. Apheresis, Jour. Hematother, Transfusions; contbr. articles to profl. publs., chapter to book; author abstracts in field.; mem. editl. bd. Transfusion, 2003-, Blood Therapies in Medicine, 2005-. Chmn. US Dept. Health & Human Svcs., 2001—05; pres. Am. Soc. Apheresis, 2004—05; chmn., Adv. Com. on Blood Safety & Availability Dept. HHS. Grantee Mayo Found., 1988-89, 90-92, Am. Bionetics, 1990, Abbott Labs., 1990-91, Cutter Biol., 1990-91, Gen-Probe, 1992-93, USN, 1993—97, Nat. Heart Lung and Blood Inst., 1994-2009, Baxter, 1995, Bayer, 1995, Amgen, 1995, Biometric Imaging, 1998, Organonteknika, 1999-2001, Biomerieux, 2002—08. Fellow Coll. Am. Pathologists (life); mem. Am. Assn. Blood Bank (tech. & sci. workshop com. 1990-96, standards com. 1993-96), Am. Soc. Apheresis (bd. dirs., pres.-elect 2004, past pres.), N.C. Assn. Blood Bankers, Internat. Soc. for Hematotherapy and Graft Engring., Internat. Soc. Cellular Therapy, Am. Soc. Hematology, Minn. Assn. Blood Bank (v.p. 1990-91, program chair 1991, pres.-elect 1992) Achievements include research in mathematical analysis of transfusion strategies, bacteria contamination of blood products, the interactions of drugs and plasma exchange; stem cell processing. Office: Laboratory Corp of America Holdings 531 S Spring St Burlington NC 27215 Office Phone: 336-436-5274. Office Fax: 336-436-1569. E-mail: mark_brecher@labcorp.com. *

BREDA, JOHN ALEXANDER, physician, musician; b. Boston, Sept. 9, 1954; s. Alexander John and Eda (Feroli) B.; m. Karen Schultz, Aug. 14, 1988; 1 child, Joseph Samuel. MusB, MusM, New England Conservatory Music, Boston, 1972-78; postgrad., Harvard U., Cambridge, Mass., 1990; MD, U. Mass., Worcester, 1996. Diplomate Am. Bd. Internal Medicine, 2010; cert. instrument rated pilot. Symphonic musician Oreg. Symphony, Portland, 1982-89; med. rschr. Harvard Sch. Pub. Health, Boston, 1989-90, Harvard Med. Sch., Boston, 1990—; intern, resident Metro West Med. Ctr., Framingham, Mass., 1996-97; resident Miriam Hosp., R.I. Hosp., Brown U. Program, Providence, 1997-99; physician internal medicine Harvard Vanguard Med. Assocs., Medford, Mass., 1999—2001; physician internal medicine primary, urgent care Harvard U. Health Svcs., Cambridge, Mass., 2001—04, Fed. Aviation Administrn. Med. Examiner, 2005—; internat. med. examiner Bridgewater Goddard Pk. Med. Assocs., 2006—08; med. examiner Lead Nightime Hospitalist Whitter Rehab. Hosp., 2006—10. Instr. medicine Harvard Med. Sch., 2001—; woodwind instrument builder, cons. clarinet design, Boston, 1978—; guest lectr. New Eng. Conservatory Music, Boston, 1981. Performed with numerous musical orgns. including San Francisco Opera, 1980, Santa Fe (N.Mex.) Opera, 1980, Boston Symphony, 1978-81. Betty Lea Stone fellow Am. Cancer Soc., 1992, Tanglewood fellow Berkshire Music Ctr., 1982, Symphony Orch. Inst. fellow, 1996. Mem. AMA, Mass. Med. Soc. (Charles River dist. scholar 1992), Worcester Med. Soc. Avocations: flying, skiing, bicycling. Business E-Mail: jbreda@massmed.org.

BREDA, WAYNE JOSEPH, medical scientist inventor, entrepreneur; s. Joseph F. and Mary V. (Day) Breda; children: Susan, Jennifer, Jonathan. BS in Human Biology, Nat. U. Health Sci., Lombard, Ill., 1967, DC in Chiropractic Medicine; MD, Ross U., Sch. Medicine, North Brunswick, NJ, 1981. Dir. Patient And Rsch. Ctr. Nat. U. Health Sci., Lombard, 1982—84; exec. v.p. Analytical Labs. Environ. Excellence, Burr Ridge, Ill., 1984—88; pres. Am. Environ. Sci. & Tech., Geneva, Ill., 1988—98; prin. cons. Richard Oliver Internat., Chgo., 1999—2002, mem., 1999—2000; chief sci. officer Health Sci. Tech. LLC, Clarendon Hills, Ill., 2002—. Govs. sci. adv. com. contbr. Joliet Arsenal Redevel. Commn., Ill., 1993—95; joliet arsenal strategic devel. plan and reuse strategy State Ill. IDNR, Springfield. Mem.: AAAS (mem.), NY Acad. Sci., Am. Soc. Health Risk Mgrs., Am. Biol. Safety Assn. Home: 5 Tuttle Ave Clarendon Hills IL 60514-1153 Office: Health Sci Techs LLC Ill Oak Brook IL 60523 Home Phone: 630-915-1052. Personal E-mail: bbmd-bds.01@comcast.net.

BREDEL, MARKUS, neurologist, educator; MD, U. Vienna, 2000; PhD, Free U. Berlin, 2001. Vis. rsch. fellow experimental neuro-oncology U. Pitts. Cancer Inst. & Brain Tumor Ctr., 1996—97; neuro-oncology rschr. U. Vienna Inst. Neurology, 1998—2001; resident neurosurgery U. Freiburg, Germany, 2000—03; rsch. fellow divsn. oncology Ctr. Clin. Scis. Rsch., Stanford U. Sch. Medicine, Calif., 2003—05, vis. asst. prof. dept. neurosurgery, 2005—06; asst. prof. dept. neurol. surgery and Ctr. Genetic Medicine, Northwestern U. Feinberg Sch. Medicine, Chgo., 2006—, dir. Northwestern Brain Tumor Inst. Rsch. Program, Robert H. Lurie Comprehensive Cancer Ctr., 2006—. Vis. asst. prof. experimental neuro-oncology U. Freiburg, 2003—; mem. rev. panel Ariz. Biomedical Rsch. Commn., 2005—; consulting asst. prof. dept. neurosurgery Stanford U. Sch. Medicine, 2007—. Mem. editl. bd. Lancet Oncology, 2003—; contbr. articles to profl. jours. Recipient Preuss Rsch. award, Am. Assn. Neurol. Surgeons, 2003, German Pfizer Rsch. award for medicine, U. Freiburg, 2006; grantee Hölderlin Fgn. Exch. scholarship, Alfried Krupp von Bohlen & Halbach-Found./German Nat. Merit Found., 1999—2000; scholar Emmy-Noether Excellence Program, German Rsch. Found., 2003—05. Mem.: AAAS, European Orgn. Rsch. & Treatment of Cancer, Soc. Neuro-Oncology, European Assn. Neuro-Oncology, European Assn. Cancer Rsch., Am. Soc. Clin. Oncology (mem. edn. com. 2006—07, translational rsch. chair 2006—07, chair sci. program com. 2006—07, Merit award 2000), German Cancer Soc., German Med. Assn., Am. Assn. Cancer Rsch. (assoc. Rhone-Poulenc-Rorer Young Investigator award 1997). Achievements include patents in field. Office: Bredel Lab Northwestern University 303 E Superior St Lurie 6 250 Chicago IL 60611 Office Phone: 312-503-1822. Office Fax: 312-503-5607. Business E-Mail: m-bredel@northwestern.edu. *

BREDEMEIER, MARY ELIZABETH, counselor, educator; b. Eden, NC, Sept. 4, 1924; d. William Thomas and Cora May (Lewis) Robertson; m. Harry C. Bredemeier, Nov. 16, 1953; 1 child, Suzanne Leaphart. BS, James Madison U., 1944; MA, Columbia U., 1946; EdD, Rutgers U., 1972. Instr. Finch Coll., NYC, 1945-46; tchr. Ben Franklin Jr. H.S., Yonkers, N.Y., 1949-53; instr. Douglass Coll., New Brunswick, N.J., 1953-54; tchr., counselor Middlesex County Vocat. and Tech. H.S., Woodbridge, N.J., 1955-67; prof. edn. Montclair State Coll., Upper Montclair, N.J., 1967-88, prof. emeritus, 1988—. Cons. Miami (Fla.)-Dade Pub. Schs., 1989—2005. Author: Labor Problems in America, 1970, Social Forces in Education, 1980, Urban Classroom Portraits, 1988; contbr. numerous articles to profl. jours. Democrat. Avocations: tennis, swimming, reading, jewelry-making. Office: 7441 Wayne Ave Apt 15C Miami Beach FL 33141-2566 Home (Summer): Box 741 North Truro MA 02652 *

BREDENBERG, CARL E., surgeon; b. San Maeo, Calif., Mar. 18, 1940; s. Carl E. and Emma J. (Jeager) B.; m. Patricia Ann Vreeland; children: Carl E. III, Linnea J. Student, Princeton U., 1957-59; AB, Johns Hopkins U., 1962, MD, 1964. Diplomate Am. Bd. Surgery, Am. Bd. Thoracic Surgery; cert. special qualifications vascular surgery, added qualifications critical care; lic. physician Md., N.Y., Maine. Resident in surgery Johns Hopkins Hosp., Balt., 1964-72; asst. prof. dept. surgery SUNY, Syracuse, 1972-76, assoc. prof., 1976-80, prof. surgery, 1980-90, surgeon-in-charge vascular surgery svc., 1978-90, vice chmn., 1984-88, interim chmn., 1988-90; chief sect. of thoracic surgery Syracuse VA Med. Ctr., 1973-90; surgeon-in-chief Maine Med. Ctr., Portland, 1990—2009, prof. Surgery, 1990—2011, Tufts U. Sch. Med., 2011—. Prof surgery U. Vt.; staff U. Hosp. SUNY, Syracuse, 1972-90, VA Hosp., Syracuse, 1972-90, Crouse-Irving Meml. Hosp., Syracuse, 1972-90, Maine Med. Ctr., Portland, 1990—; courtesy staff Mercy Hosp., Portland, 1990—, edtl. bd. mem. Archives of Surgery, 2003- Contbr. numerous articles to profl. jours. Bd. dirs. Syracuse Rowing Assn., 1975-76; mem. vestry St. David's Episcopal Ch., 1979-82, chmn. fin. com. 1979-83, ch. sch. instr., 1981-90; mem. Bishop's com. St. Nicholas Episcopal Ch., 1992—. Capt. U.S. Army, 1965-67. Mem. AMA, ACS (past pres. Maine chpt., bd. govs., 1997-2003), Soc. for Vascular Surgery, Am. Assn. for Thoracic Surgery, Soc. U. Surgeons, Am. Surg. Assn., New Eng. Surg. Soc., Am. Physiol. Soc., N.Y. Acad. Sci., Internat. Soc. for Cardiovascular Surgery, New Eng. Soc. for Vascular Surgery (exec. com. 1993—, pres., 1998-99), Ea. Vascular Soc. (exec. coun. 1987-91, 95—), Soc. Internat. Chirugie, Assn. Acad. Surgery, Upstate N.Y. Vascular Soc. (pres. 1989-90), Maine Vascular Soc. (sec.-treas. 1991-93, pres. 1993—), others. Office: Maine Med Ctr Dept Surg 22 Bramhall St Portland ME 04102-3134

BREDENKAMP, JUERGEN, psychologist; b. Hamburg, Germany, Mar. 29, 1939; s. Hans and Anne Liese (Behrmann) B.; m. Karin Spies, Aug. 9, 1968; children: Silke, Birthe. Diploma in Psychology, U. Hamburg, 1963, PhD, 1964. Asst. prof. U. Heidelberg, Germany, 1964-72; prof. U. Bonn, Germany, 1972, 1984—2004, U. Goettingen, Germany, 1972-80, U. Trier, Germany, 1980-84. Author: The Test of Significance in Psychological Research, 1972, Psychology of Learning and Memory, 1977, Imagery and Learning, 1979, Theory and Design of Psychological Experiments, 1980, Imagery and Metacognition, 1992, Learning, Remembering and Forgetting, 1998; co-editor 4 vols. German Ency. Psychology, 1983; co-editor (jour.) Methodika. Mem. German Psychol. Assn. (pres. 1990-92), German Rsch. Coun. (elected surveyor 1988-92). Avocation: music. Office: Inst Psychlogy Kaiser Karl Ring 9 Bonn D-53111 Germany Office Phone: 0049 228 734329. Business E-Mail: juergen.bredenkamp@uni-bonn.de.

BREEN, KATHERINE ANNE, speech and language pathologist; b. Chgo., Oct. 31, 1948; d. Robert Stephen and Gertrude Catherine (Bader) Breen. BS, Northwstern U., 1970; MA, U. Mo., Columbia, 1971. Cert. speech pathologist. Speech/lang. pathologist Fulton (Mo.) Pub. Schs., 1971-73; co-dir. Easter Seal Speech Clinic, Jefferson City, Mo., summer 1972, 73; speech/lang. pathologist Shawnee Mission (Kans.) Pub. Schs., 1973-96; staff St. Joseph's Hosp., Kansas City, Mo., 1978-81, Midwest Rehab. Ctr., Kansas City, 1985; pvt. practice speech therapy Deborah A. King & Assocs., 2003—. Cons. East Ctrl. Mo. Mental Health Center; guest lectr. Fontbonne Coll., St. Louis. Vol., Mid Am. Rehab. Hosp, Bloch Cancer Hotline. Mem. NEA, Am. Speech and Hearing Assn., Kans. Speech and Hearing Assn., Kansas City Alumni Assn. of Northwestern U. (dir. alumni admissions coun., Outstanding Leadership award 1981, Svc. award 1991), Friends of Art Nelson/Atkins Art Gallery and Mus. (vol.), Nat. Trust Historic Preservation, Kansas City Hist. Found., Kans. City Sheltie Rescue, Oreg. Calif. Trails Assn., Zeta Phi Eta. Methodist. Home: 8318 Mackey St Shawnee Mission KS 66212-2728 Personal E-mail: kelly.breen@yahoo.com.

BREEN, KERRY JOHN, gastroenterologist; MB BChir, U. Melbourne, Australia, 1964, MD, 1979. Resident med. officer St Vincent's Hosp., Fitzroy, Victoria, Australia, 1965—68, dir. dept gastroenterology, 1978—93, exec. chmn. divsn. medicine, 1992—94, vis. gastroenterologist, 1995—; registrar Royal Prince Alfred Hosp., Sydney, NSW, Australia, 1969—70; fellow in gastroenterology Vanderbilt Med. Sch., Nashville, 1970—72. Pres. Med. Practitoners Bd. Victoria, Melbourne, 1994—2000, Australian Med. Coun., Canberra, ACT, Australia, 1997—2000; chmn. Australian Health Ethics Com., Canberra, 2000—06. Co-author: (text book) Ethics Law and Medical Practice, 1997. Fellow: Royal Australasian Coll. Physicians. Office: Level 6 55 Victoria Pde Fitzroy VIC 3065 Australia

BREGA, KERRY ELIZABETH, physician, researcher; b. Denver, Sept. 8, 1961; d. Charles Franklin and Betty Jean Brega. BA, U. Colo., 1983, MD, 1989. Diplomate Am. Bd. Spine Surgery, Am. Bd. Neurol. Surgery. Resident in neurosurgery U. Colo., Denver, 1990-95, asst. prof. neurosurgery, 1995—; dir. neurosurgery Littleton Adventist Hosp., Denver, 1998—; asst. prof. neurosurgery U. Colo., Denver, 1995—2005, assoc. prof. neurosurgery, med. dir. Stroke Ctr., 2006—, assoc. dir. neurosurg. residency tng. program, 2006—. Bd. dirs. Donor Alliance, Denver, 1994—. Mem. Am. Coll. Spine Surgery, Am. Assn. Neurol. Surgeons, Congress Neurol. Surgeons, Colo. Neurol. Soc., Alpha Omega Alpha. Office Phone: 303-315-1429.

BREGER STANTON, DONNA EVA, occupational therapist educator; b. San Francisco, Mar. 29, 1942; BS in Occupl. Therapy, San Jose State U, 1965; MA in Occupl. Therapy, U. Southern Calif., 1979. Dep. chief, clin. dir. hand & occupl. therapy US Pub. Health Commn. Corps, 1985—90; supr., hand therapy U. Calif., Davis Med. Ctr., 1991—97; assoc. prof., academic fieldwork coord. Samuel Merritt U., Oakland, Calif., 1998—; clin. doctoral rschr. Jefferson U., Phila, Phila. Pres., faculty orgn. Samuel Merritt U., 2006—08. Grant, Samuel Merritt U. Fellow: Am. Occupl. Therapy Assn.; mem.: Am. Soc. Surgery Hand, Am. Assn. Hand Surgery, Am. Occupl. Therapy Assn., Am. Soc. Hand Therapists (pres. 2005, pres.-elect 2004, v.p. 2003, Nathalie Barr Lectureship award). Avocations: walking, reading. Office: Samuel Merritt University 450 30th St Oakland CA 94609 Office Phone: 510-869-6743. Office Fax: 510-869-6951. Business E-Mail: dbreger@samuelmerritt.edu.

BREGMAN, ARTHUR, child and adolescent psychiatrist; MD, NY Med. Coll., Valhalla, NY, 1974. Resident psychiatry Univ. Miami Jackson Meml. Hosp.; asst. chief psychiatry Miami Children's Hosp., chief psychiatry; founder PsychSolutions, Inc., 1993. Office: PsychSolutions Incorporated 701 SW 27th Ave Ste 500 Miami FL 33135 Office Phone: 305-668-9000. Office Fax: 305-662-1788.

BREHM, ROBERT, rehabilitation hospital executive; V.p. Kessler Inst. for Rehabilitation, West Orange, NJ, chief adminstrv. office, pres. Spkr. in field. Named Healthcare Hero (accepted on behalf of Kessler Inst.), NJ Biz, 2008. Mem.: NJ Hosp. Assn. Office: Kessler Inst for Rehabilitation 1199 Pleasant Valley Way West Orange NJ 07052 Office Phone: 973-731-3600. Office Fax: 973-731-1237.

BREHM, SHARON STEPHENS, psychology professor, former academic administrator; b. Roanoke, Va., Apr. 18, 1945; d. John Wallis and Jane Chappel (Phenix) Stephens; m. Jack W. Brehm, Oct. 25, 1968 (div. Dec. 1979) BA, Duke U., 1967, PhD, 1973; MA, Harvard U., 1968. Clin. psychology intern U. Wash. Med. Ctr., Seattle, 1973-74; asst. prof. Va. Poly. Inst. and State U., Blacksburg, 1974-75, U. Kans., Lawrence, 1975-78, assoc. prof., 1978-83, prof. psychology, 1983-90, assoc. dean Coll. Liberal Arts and Scis., 1987-90; prof. psychology, dean Harpur Coll. of Arts and Scis. SUNY, Binghamton, 1990-96; prof. psychology and interpersonal comm., provost Ohio U., Athens, 1996—2001; v.p. acad. affairs Ind. U., 2001—03, sr. advisor to pres., 2004—05; chancellor Ind. U. Bloomington, 2001—03, prof. dept. psychology, 2001—. Vis. prof. U. Mannheim, 1978, Istituto di Psicologia, Rome, 1989; Fulbright sr. rsch. scholar Ecole des Hautes Etudes en Sciences Sociales, Paris, 1981-82; Soc. for Personality and Social Psychology rep. APA's Coun. of Reps., 1995-2000; chair governing bd. Ohio Learning Network, 1998-99 Author: The Application of Social Psychology to Clinical Practice, 1976, (with others) Psychological Reactance: A Theory of Freedom and Control, 1981, Intimate Relationships, 1985, 2d edit., 1992, (with others) Social Psychology, 1990, 4th edit., 1999, also numerous articles, and chpts. Mem. APA (fin. com. 1999-2001, 2002-04, pres. elect, 2005-06, pres., 2006-07). Office: Ind U 1101 E 10th St Bloomington IN 47405-7000 Personal E-mail: sbrehm@indiana.edu.

BREIDENBACH, WARREN CONRAD, III, plastic surgeon, hand surgeon; b. June 21, 1946; Grad., U. Calgary, Can.; MD, Harvard Med. Sch., 1975. Cert. Plastic Surgery, Hand Surgery. Postgraduate tng. in plastic surgery McGill U., Montreal; microsurgery fellow Eastern Vir. Med. Sch., Norfolk; Christine M. Kleinert hand fellow; ptnr. Kleinert, Kutz and Associates Hand Care Ctr., PLLC; asst. clin. prof. surgery (plastic and reconstructive) U. Louisville. Author of several articles. Recipient Clin. Rsch. Scholarship award, Am. Soc. Plastic Surgery and Reconstructive Surgery, Senior award. Mem.: Am. Soc. for Peripheral Nerve (sec.), Am. Soc. for Surgery of the Hand. Achievements include being appointed the first hand scholar with the Louisville Institute for Hand and Microsurgery; being the lead surgeon in all three successful hand transplant surgeries that took place in the US in 1999, 2001 and 2006. Office: Kleinert Kutz and Associates Hand Care Ctr PLLC Ste 700 225 Abraham Flxner Way Louisville KY 40202 Office Phone: 502-561-4263.

BREIER, ALAN, psychiatry professor, retired pharmaceutical executive; b. Toledo, May 22, 1953; m. Diane Rooney, May 30, 1981; children: Michael, Matthew. BA summa cum laude, U. Toledo, 1975; MD, U. Cin., 1980. Diplomate Am. Bd. Psychiatry and Neurology. Resident in psychiatry Yale U. Sch. Med., 1980—84; chief outpatient dept. Md. Psychiat. Ctr., Balt., 1987-93; chief pathophysiology and treatment unit NIH, Bethesda, Md., 1993-95, chief sect. clin. studies, 1995-97; chief med. officer, v.p. med. Eli Lilly & Co., Indpls., 1998—2008; prof. psychiatry Ind. U. Sch. Med., 2008—. Adj. prof. psychiatry U. Md., Balt., 1994—, Ind. U. Sch. Med., Indpls., 1997—2008. Mem. editl. bd. Schizophrenia Rsch., 1994—, Biol. Psychiatry, 1999—; editor: The New Pharmacotherapy of Schizophrenia, Olanzapine (Zyprexa): A Novel Antipsychotic, Current Issues in the Psychopharmacology of Schizophrenia. Recipient Lustman Rsch. award, Yale U. Sch. Medicine, 1982—84, Young Investigator award, Schizophrenia Rsch., 1987, A. E. Bennett award, Soc. Biol. Psychiatry, 1988, Joel Elkes Internat. award, ACNP, 1997. Office: Ind U Sch Med 1111 W 10th St PB 313 Indianapolis IN 46202 E-mail: abreier@iupui.edu. *

BREININ, GOODWIN M., physician; b. NYC, Dec. 10, 1918; s. Louis and Mary (Mirsky) B.; m. Rose-Helen Kopelman, June 22, 1947; children: Bartley James, Constance. BS, U. Fla., 1939; A.M., Emory U., 1940, MD, 1943. Diplomate Am. Bd. Ophthalmology (dir., vice chmn., cons.). Intern U.S. Marine Hosp., Stapleton, NY, 1944; resident ophthalmology N.Y. U.-Bellevue Med. Ctr., 1947-51, sr. Heed fellow ophthalmology, 1954, Daniel B. Kirby prof. research ophthalmology, 1957; Daniel B. Kirby prof. ophthalmology Bellevue and U. Hosps., 1959—2007, prof. emeritus ophthalmology, 2007—; chmn. dept. ophthalmology N.Y. U.-Bellevue Med. Ctr., 1959—2000; dir. eye svc. Bellevue and U. Hosps., NYC, 1959—2000; chmn. med. bd. N.Y. U.-Bellevue Med. Ctr., 1975-77. Mem. vision commn. NRC, 1960-65; hon. rsch. assoc. with Sir Andrew Huxley, U. Coll., London, 1966-67; chmn. vision rsch. tng. com. Nat. Insts. Neurol. Diseases and Blindness, 1963-64; chief cons. Manhattan VA Hosp.; cons. Manhattan Eye, Ear and Throat, St. Vincent's, Beth Israel hosps., Lenox Hills Hosp.; surg. gen. USPHS; chmn. Nat. Res. Rev. Com., 1976-77; vis. prof., cons. Hailie Selassie I Univ. Found., Ethiopia, 1972; lectr. Mem. various adv. coms. relating to field, mem. med. adv. bd. Nat. Coun. to Combat Blindness; pres. Council for U.S./USSR Health Exch., 1977; mem. Am. com. Internat. Agy. for Prevention of Blindness, 1980—; pres. 2d Internat. Symposium in Visual Optics, Tucson, 1982; lectr. in field, emeritus prof. ophthal. Author: The Electrophysiology of Extraocular Muscle, 1962; co-editor: Advances in Diagnostic Visual Optics, 1983; mem. editorial bd. Investigative Ophthalmology, Archives of Ophthalmology; Contbr. articles to profl. jours. Mem. bd. advisors for medicine Emory U., Atlanta; mem. coun. visitors Marine Biol. Labs., Woods Hole, Mass.; mem. vis. com. for drawings and prints Met. Mus. Art, N.Y.C., 2005— Capt. US Army, 1944—46. Recipient Knapp medal for contbn. ophthalmology, AMA, 1957, Edward Lorenzo Holmes lectr. citation and award for contbns. to med. sci., Inst. Medicine Chgo., 1959, Gifford lectr. and award, Chgo. Ophthal. Soc., 1970, Heed Ophthalmmic Found. award, 1968, Emory U. medal, 1993, Disting. Svc. award, NYU Sch. Medicine, 2003; named Wright lectr., U. Toronto, 1972, Lloyd lectr., Bklyn. Ophthal. Soc., 1971, May lectr., NY Acad. Medicine, 1974, guest of honor, Australian Coll. Ophthalmologists, 1974, Japanese Congress Neuro-Ophthalmology, 1979, Scobee lectr., 1977. Fellow Am. Acad. Ophthalmology and Otolaryngology (v.p. 1979, Sr. Honor award 1984), ACS, N.Y. Acad. Medicine (sec. sect. ophthalmology 1962-63, chmn. sect. 1967-68); mem. AAAS, AMA (sec. sect. on ophthalmology 1966-69, chmn. 1970-71), Rsch. Ophthalmology, Am. Ophthal. Soc., N.Y. Ophthal. Soc. (pres. 1980), Harvey Soc., Am. Commn. for Optics and Visual Physiology (chmn. 1970—), Am. Orthoptic Coun., Assn. Univ. Profs. Ophthalmology, Pan. Am. Assn. Ophthalmology, Century Assn., Practitioners Club, Charaka Club (N.Y.C.), Sigma Xi, Alpha Omega Alpha. Home: 912 Fifth Ave New York NY 10021-4159 Business E-Mail: gb7@nyu.edu.

BREITENBACH, MARY LOUISE MCGRAW, psychologist, chemical dependency counselor; b. Pitts., Sept. 26, 1936; d. David Evans McGraw and Louise (Schoch) Neel; m. John Edgar Breitenbach, Apr. 15, 1960 (dec. 1963); m. Joseph George Piccoli III, Aug. 15, 1987; children: Cary Plumer Frye and Douglas Plumer (twins), Kirstin Amethyst Gretchen Leticia Piccoli. Postgrad., Oreg. State Coll., 1960-61; BA, Russell Sage Coll., Troy, NY, 1958; MEd, Harvard U., Cambridge, Mass., 1983. Lic. profl. counselor, chem. dependency specialist, Wyo.; cert. addiction specialist, level III; cert. addiction counselor II, master addiction counselor. Paraprofl. psychologist St. John's Episc. Ch., Jackson, Wyo., 1963—94; pvt. practice Wilson, Wyo., 1983—. Counselor Curran/Seeley Found. Addiction Svcs., Jackson, 1989-91, Van Vleck House/Tri-County Group Home, Jackson, 1986-89, others; provider multiple employee assistance programs local and nat. cos.; adv. com. Learning Ctr., 1997—. Trustee Teton Sci. Sch., Kelly, Wyo, 1960-76; pres. bd. govs. Teton County Mus., 1989-91, Jackson; vestry mem. St. John's Ch., Jackson. Mem.: APA, LWV, Wyo. Psychol. Assn., Wyo. Assn. Counseling and Devel., Wyo. Assn. Addiction Specialists, Nat. Assn. Alcohol and Drug Addiction Counselors. Democrat. Episcopalian. Avocations: horseback riding, reading, gardening. Home and Office: 3625 N Cheney Ln Wilson WY 83014 Office Phone: 307-733-0310.

BREITFELD, PHILIP PAUL, pharmaceutical executive, oncologist; b. Geneva, NY, Mar. 4, 1953; m. Susan Gail Kreissman. AB in Chemistry, Princeton U.; MD, U. Rochester, 1979. Cert. Pediat., 1984, Pediat. Hematology-Oncology, 1998. Intern pediatrics U. Rochester, NY, 1979—80, resident pediatric hematological oncology NY, 1980—82; fellowship Children's Hosp.-Harvard, Boston, 1982—85; staff mem. Dana-Farber/Children's Hosp. Cancer Inst., Boston, 1985—88, U. Mass. Med. Ctr., Worcester, 1988—91, Riley Hosp. for Children, Ind. U., 1991—2000; staff mem. pediat. Duke U. Med. Ctr., Durham, NC, 2000—; assoc. cons. prof. pediat. Duke U., Durham, NC; med. dir. oncology EMD Pharm., Inc.; exec. dir. oncology devel., assoc. chief med. officer BioCryst Pharmaceuticals, Inc., Birmingham, 2007—. Vice chair Soft Tissue Sarcoma Com. Children's Oncology Group. Contbr. articles to med. jours. Office: BioCryst Pharmaceuticals Inc 2190 Parkway Lake Dr Birmingham AL 35244 Office Phone: 205-444-4600. Office Fax: 205-444-4640.

BRELAND-NOBLE, ALFIEE MATIESE, psychologist, researcher; b. Annapolis, Md., Mar. 14, 1969; d. Allen Eugene and Mattie McLeod Breland; m. Richard Noble, III, Aug. 17, 2002. BA, Howard U., 1991; MA, NYU, 1993; PhD, U. of Wis., 1997; M of Health Scis., Duke U., 2003—. Counselor U. Settlement, NYC, 1991—93, Young Adult Learning Acad., NYC, 1992—93; cultural diversity specialist Madison Inner City Coun. on Substance Abuse, Inc., Madison, Wis., 1994—96; asst. prof. Mich. State U., East Lansing, 1997—2002; staff psychologist Meridian Profl. Psychol. Cons., East Lansing, 2000—02; nat. rsch. svc. award postdoctoral fellow Duke U. Med. Ctr., Durham, NC, 2002—03, Nat. Rsch. Svc. postdoctoral rsch. fellow dept. psychiatry, 2003—. Cons. Okemos (Mich.) Pub. Schs., 2001, Flint (Mich.) Pub. Schs., 2001, Iowa City (Iowa) Pub. Schs., 2001; editl. bd. mem. Jour. of Black Psychology, 2002—, Dimensions of Counseling: Rsch., Theory and Practice, Kalamazoo, 1998—2002, Jour. of Multicultural Counseling and Devel., 1998, assoc. editor, 1997—98. Co-author: (book chpt.) Elementary School Counseling in the New Millennium, Violence in American Schools: Practical Guidelines for Counselors; contbr. articles to profl. jours. Recipient Outstanding Undergraduate Student scholarship, Delta Sigma Theta, 1987, dissertation fellowship, U. of Wis., 1996; named one of Young Leaders Under 30, Ebony Mag., 1999; fellow R25 Mentoring and Edn. for Mental Health Svcs. Rsch., NIMH, Yale U. and UCLA, 2001—02, Leopold Scheep Found., 1993. Mem.: ACA (clin. rsch. network com. 2002—), APA, Soc. for Rsch. on Adolescence, Soc. for Rsch. on Child Devel., Kappa Delta Pi, Alpha Kappa Alpha (Kappa Psi Omega chpt. pres. 1993—94). Democrat. Roman Catholic. Achievements include Created model that addresses mental health disparities of African American adolescents with depressive disorders under-utilization of mental health services; research in color consciousness. Avocations: step aerobics, reading, weightlifting, travel. Office: Duke U Med Ctr Box 3527 Durham NC 27710 Home: 1728 Ravenwing Dr Fuquay Varina NC 27526-5314 Personal E-mail: alfieeb@hotmail.com. E-mail: abreland@psych.mc.duke.edu.

BREM, HENRY, neurosurgeon, educator, researcher; b. Paterson, NJ, Aug. 14, 1952; s. Jacob and Adele (Machabanski) B.; m. Rachel Frydman, Jan. 28, 1978; children: Andrea, Alisa, Sarah. BA, NYU, 1973; student, Harvard U., 1973-74, MD, 1978. Diplomate Am. Bd. Neurosurgery. Intern in surgery Peter Bent Brigham Hosp., Boston, 1978-79; fellow in neurosurgery Johns Hopkins Hosp., Balt., 1979-80; resident in neurosurgery Neurol. Inst. N.Y. Columbia Presbyn. Med. Ctr., NYC, 1980-84; neurosurgeon Johns Hopkins U. Sch. Medicine, Balt., 1984—, prof. neurosurgery, ophthalmology and oncology, 1991—, dir. Hunterian Neurosurg. Lab., 1995—, assoc. dir. dept. neurosurgery, 1995—, Harvey Cushing profl, chmn. dept. neurosurgery, 2000. Office: Johns Hopkins Hosp Meyer 7-113 600 N Wolfe St Baltimore MD 21287-0005 Office Phone: 410-955-2252.

BREMNER, JAMES DOUGLAS, psychiatrist, researcher, education educator; b. Topeka, Kans., June 5, 1961; s. James Douglas and Linnea Bremner; m. Laura Viola Vaccarino, Aug. 1, 1991; children: Sabina Francesca, Dylan Vittorio. BS, U. Puget Sound, 1983; MD, Duke U. Sch. Medicine, 1987. Cert. Am. Bd. of Psychiatry and Neurology, 1996, Am. Bd. of Nuc. Medicine, 2001. Prof. psychiatry and radiology Emory U. Sch. Medicine, 2000—; dir. Emory Ctr. for Positron Emission Tomography, 2000—06. Asst. and assoc. prof. of psychiatry Yale U. Sch. of Medicine, 1992—2000. Author: (books) Does Stress Damage the Brain?, Before You Take That Pill Why The Drug Industry May Be Bad for Your Health. Achievements include research in brain imaging and neurobiology of mood and anxiety disorders. Home: 2125 Ponce de Leon Ave NE Atlanta GA 30307 Office: Emory Univ 306 E Mailstop 1256/001/AT 1256 Briarcliff Rd NE Atlanta GA 30306 Business E-Mail: jdbremn@emory.edu.

BRENAN, JOHN ANDREW, dermatologist, consultant; s. Andrew Brenan and Muriel Bridge; m. Marianne McNamara, July 27, 1956; children: Andrew, Jennifer, Joanne, Carolyn, David, Anthony. MBBS with honors, U. Melbourne, Australia, 1951. With R.M.O. St. Vincent's Hosp., Melbourne, Australia, 1952, 1954—55; clin. asst. dermatology dept St. Mary's Hosp., London, 1956—57; dermatologist St. Vincent's Hosp., Melbourne, Australia, 1960—90, cons. dermatologist, 1990, Mercy Hosp. Women, 1972—93, Dermagynaecology Clinic Mercy Hosp. Women, 1989—95. Pres. Victoria Br. Brit. Assn. Dermatologists, Melbourne, Australia, 1965, sec., 1970—73. Author: Textbook of Clinical Medicine, 1984, Vulva and Vaginal Manual, 2005. Flight lt. Royal Australian Air Force1951. Named hon. pres., World Congress Dermatology, 1997. Fellow: Am. Acad. Dermatology (non-resident), Royal Australasian Coll. Physicians, Australasian Coll. Dermatologists (mem. coun. 1969—71, mem. bd. censors 1971—78, chmn. Victoria faculty 1974—76, pres. 1983—85, Silver medal 1999); mem.: Internat. Soc. Dermatology (v.p. 1984—87), Australian Soc. Dermopathy Found. (treas. 1979—82), German Dermatology Soc. (corr.). Avocations: rowing, sailing. Office: 143 Victoria Parade Fitzroy 3065 Australia Home: 27 Holroyd St 3101 Kew VIC Australia Office Phone: 613 9419 4833. Office Fax: 613 9419 5590.

BRENDER, JEAN DIANE, epidemiologist, educator, nurse, university administrator; b. Bellingham, Wash., Nov. 23, 1951; d. Otto and Jennie Wilma Tolsma; m. Dennis Ray Brender, Aug. 30, 1975; 1 child, Valerie. BSN summa cum laude, Whitworth Coll., 1974; M of Nursing, U. Wash., 1979, PhD of Epidemiology, 1983. RN Tex. Staff nurse, infection control Sacred Heart Med. Ctr., Spokane, Wash., 1974-80; instr. nursing Intercollegiate Ctr. for Nursing Edn., Spokane, 1979-80, asst. prof. nursing, 1982-84; teaching asst. epidemiology U. Wash., Seattle, 1981-82; rsch. health scientist Audie L. Murphy Vets. Hosp., San Antonio, 1984-85; staff epidemiologist bur. epidemiology Tex. Dept. Health, Austin, 1986-87, acting program dir. environ. epidemiology program, 1987, dir. environ. epidemiology program, 1987-93, dir. noncommunicable disease epidemiology and toxicology, 1993-97; infectious disease epidemiologist Bur. Disease Control, 1997-99; also state environ. epidemiologist Tex. Dept. Health, Austin, 1993-97; assoc. prof. health svcs. rsch. Tex. State U., 1999—2005; assoc. prof. epidemiology Sch. Rural Pub. Health Tex. A&M Health Sci. Ctr., College Station, Tex., 2005—08; prof. epidemiology Tex. A&M Health Sci. Ctr., Sch. Rural Pub. Health, Tex., 2008—, assoc. dean rsch., 2009—. Bd. dirs. Agr. Resources Protection Authority; adj. instr. allied health scis. and health adminstrn. Tex. State U., 1988-90; adj. asst. prof. epidemiology U. Tex. Health Sci. Ctr.-Houston Sch. Pub. Health, 1985-93, adj. assoc. prof., 1993-2010. Contbr. articles to profl. jours. Recipient H.E.A.L.T.H. award, 1994; grantee in field. Mem. Internat. Soc. Environ. Epidemiology, Soc. Epidemiologic Rsch., Am. Coll. Epidemiology, Tex. Pub. Health Assn. (editl. bd.). Avocations: reading, church activities, skiing. Office: Tex A&M Health Sci Ctr Sch Rural Pub Health University and Adriance Lab Rd College Station TX 77843-1266 Business E-Mail: jdbrender@srph.tamhsc.edu. E-mail: jdbrender@aol.com.

BRENDLER, CHARLES BURGESS, urologist, educator; b. Charlottesville, Va., June 20, 1944; s. Herbert and Virginia Burgess B.; m. Lucretia Cattley Rock, June 18, 1966; children: Christopher, Amy, Emily, Peter. AB, Harvard Coll., 1966; MD, U. Va., 1974. Instr. urology Johns Hopkins U., Balt., 1980-81, asst. prof. urology, 1981-85, assoc. prof. urology, 1985-93; chief urology Balt. City Hosps., 1981-84; prof., chief urology U. Chgo., 1994—2006; prof. urology Northwestern U./Feinberg Sch. Medicine, 2007—09; vice-chmn. surgery NorthShore U. Health Sys., Ill., 2006, surg. exec. com., 2007—; clin. prof. urology U. Chgo., 2009—. Surg. exec. com. U. Chgo. Med. Ctr., 1994-2006, Sch. medicine, 2006-09, Health Sys. Ill., 2006-, surgery edn. com., 1994-2006. Assoc. editor: Glenn's Urologic Surgery, 1998; co-author: Campbell's Urology, 1985, 5th edit., 2007; co-author Operative Urology 1990, 3rd edit., 2002; contbr. articles to profl. jour. Capt. USAF, 1967-71. Mem. Am. Urol. Assn. (2d prize clin. rsch. 1983, 1st prize clin. rsch. Mid-Atlantic sect. 1991, 92), Am. Assn. Genito-Urinary Surgeons, Nat. Urol. Forum, Soc. Basic Urol. Rsch., Soc. Urol. Oncology, Am. Joint Commn. on Cancer (advisor task force on urol. cancer 1997), Alpha Omega Alpha. Democrat. Unitarian Universalist. Avocations: skiing, hiking, jogging, travel. Home: 434 W Arlington Pl Chicago IL 60614 Office: Evanston Hosp 2650 Ridge Ave Walgreen Bldg Ste 2507 Evanston IL 60201 Home Phone: 773-248-5138; Office Phone: 847-570-1090. Business E-Mail: cbrendler@northshore.org.

BRENES, JEREMY, homeopath, researcher; b. Oklahoma City, Dec. 18, 1973; s. Alvaro and June Brenes; m. Wenling Yu, Oct. 16, 2009. BS in Math., U. Okla., Norman, 1996; D in Homeopathy, British Inst. Homeopathy, London, 2003. Processing geophysicist Western Geophys., Houston, 1997—2001; pres., treas., cons., founder Homeopathic Village, Inc., Houston, 2003—. Author: (website) homeopathicvillage.com, 2002; author, pub. (books) Homeopathic Repertory of Heavy Elements, 2006; author: (books) Dice Roll Probability Tables, 2007, (newsletter) Homeopathic Village Electronic Newsletter, 2003—. Mem.: History Channel Club, Folio Soc. Avocations: reading, gardening, computers, arms and armor collecting.

BRENNAN, DAVID R., pharmaceutical executive; BBA, Gettysburg Coll. From sales rep. (US Divsn.) to gen. mgr. Merck and Co., Inc. and Chibret Internat. (subs. of Merck and Co., Inc.), 1975—92; joined

Astra Merck Inc., 1992; v.p. mktg. and bus. planning and develop. Astra Merck Inc. and Astra Pharma. LP, 1992—99; sr. v.p., commercialization and portfolio mgmt. AstraZeneca Pharma. LP, 1999—2001; pres., CEO AstraZeneca LP, Wilmington, Del., 2001—06; exec. dir. AstraZeneca PLC, 2005—, CEO London, 2006—. Mem. exec. bd. Pharma. Rsch. and Manufactures Am. Chmn. bd. dirs. Am. Heart Assn. (Southeastern Pa.); bd. dir. CEO Roundtable on Cancer. Office: AstraZeneca PLC 15 Stanhope Gate W1K 1AR London England Office Phone: 302-886-3000, 800-456-3669. *

BRENNAN, MARK JOSEPH, physiatrist; b. Detroit, June 25, 1958; s. Patrick John and Nanette Marie Brennan; m. Daniela Ariane Kollar, June 18, 1983 (dec. Dec. 11, 1991); m. Paula Elaine Brennan, Dec. 30, 1993; children: Luke, Dane, Ciara. BS in Biology summa cum laude, Mich. State U., 1980; MD, Wayne State U., 1984. Diplomate Am. Bd. Phys. Medicine and Rehab., Am. Bd. Electrodiagnostic Medicine. Intern internal medicine William Beaumont Hosp., Royal Oak, Mich., 1984—85, resident in phys. medicine and rehab., 1985—87, chief resident, 1988; dir. Wellness Phys. Medicine Ctr., Sterling Heights, Mich., 1988—. Cons., Detroit, 1990—; mem. adv. bd. Medview, Farmington, Mich., 1995—96, Blue Cross/Blue Shield, Detroit, 1997—. Sponsor Spl. Olympics, Detroit, 1988—, DAV, Detroit, 1988—, VFW, Detroit, 1988—. Fellow: Am. Acad. Phys. Medicine and Rehab., Am. Acad. Electrodiagnostic MEdicine; mem.: AMA, Macomb County Med. Soc., Macomb County Med. Soc., Mich. State Med. Soc., Am. Sports Medicine Soc., Am. Running Soc., Phi Kappa Phi. Republican. Roman Catholic. Avocations: sculpting, painting, travel, keyboards. Office Phone: 586-263-0820.

BRENNAN, MICHAEL D., endocrinologist, educator; MD, Royal Coll. Surgeons of Ireland, 1969. Diplomate Am. Bd. Internal Medicine, 1975, Am. Bd. Internal Medicine-endocrinology, diabetes and metabolism, 1977. Resident internal medicine Henry Ford Hosp., Detroit, 1971—72, Mayo Clinic, Rochester, Minn., 1972—75, fellow endocrinology, diabetes and metabolism, 1975—77, hosp. affiliation includes; assoc. prof. medicine Mayo Med. Sch., Rochester, Minn. Office: Mayo Clinic 200 First St SW Rochester MN 55905 Office Phone: 507-284-2511. Office Fax: 507-284-0161.

BRENNAN, MICHAEL W., ophthalmologist; b. Stanley, Wis., Nov. 15, 1943; m. Helen Brennan; 4 children. Master's in aeronautics, Stanford U.; MD, U. Tex., San Antonio, 1978. Intern in ophthalmology Brooke Army Med. Ctr., San Antonio, 1978—79, resident in ophthalmology, 1979—82; chief of surgery Womack Army Hosp., Fort Bragg, NC, 1982—86; staff Alamance Regional Med. Ctr., Burlington, NC, 1986; pvt. practice Alamance Eye Ctr., Burlington, NC; dir., chmn. Med. Alliance for Iraq. Aviator US Army, Vietnam. Mem.: Alamance Physicians' Assn., Alamance/Caswell Med. Soc., NC Med. Soc., Pan Am. Assn. Ophthalmology (exec. com.), Am. Acad. Ophthalmology (sec. state affairs 1997—2004, internat. envoy 2004—07, pres. 2009—10), NC Soc. Eye Physicians and Surgeons (pres. 2007—). Office: Alamance Eye Ctr 1016 Kirkpatrick Rd Burlington NC 27215 *

BRENNAN, MURRAY FREDERICK, surgeon, oncologist; b. Auckland, New Zealand, Apr. 2, 1940; came to U.S., 1970; m. Susan Chambers, May 26, 1973; children: Sean, Ryan, Meghan, Patrick. BSc, U. New Zealand, 1961; B Medicine B Surgery, U. Otago, New Zealand, 1964, ChM, MD, U. Otago, New Zealand, 1980, DSc (hon.), 1997; MD (hon.), U. Goteborg, Sweden, 1991. Surg. intern and resident U. Otago, 1965-69; clin. rsch. fellow Harvard Medical School, Boston, 1970-72, sr. resident, clin., rsch. fellow Peter Bent Brigham Hosp., Boston, 1972—75; sr. investigator, vis. scientist Nat. Cancer Inst., Bethesda, Md., 1975-81; prof. surgery, attending surgeon N.Y. Hosp./Cornell Med. Ctr., NYC, 1981—; vis. physician Rockefeller University, NYC, 1981-93; attending surgeon Meml. Sloan-Kettering Cancer Ctr., NYC, 1981—, chmn. dept. surgery, 1985—2006; pvt. practice NY. Dir. Am. Bd. Surgery; lectr. in field; bd. dirs. Ziopharm Oncology, Inc., Quality Sys., Inc., 2008—. Contbr. scientific papers, chapters to books. Fellow ACS (chmn. commn. on cancer, v.p., Disting. Svc. award, 2000), Royal Australian Coll. Surgeons, Brazilian Coll. Surgeons (hon.), Royal Coll. Surgeons in Ireland (hon.); mem. Inst. Medicine NAS, Royal Coll. Surgeons Edinburgh (hon.), Royal Coll. Physicians and Surgeons Glasgow (hon.), Asian Surg. Soc. (hon.), Assn. Surgeons of Gt. Britain and Ireland (hon.), Royal Coll. Surgeons Eng. (hon.), Royal Australasian Coll. Surgeons (hon.), Royal Coll. Physicians and Surgeons in Can. (hon), Soc. Surgical Oncology (former pres.), Am. Surgical Assn. (former pres.). Office: Meml Sloan-Kettering Cancer Ctr 1275 York Ave New York NY 10065 Office Phone: 212-639-6586. *

BRENNAN, TROYEN A., physician, retail pharmacy company executive; m. Wendy Warring; 2 children. MA philosophy & politics, Oxford U.; MD, JD, MPH, Yale U., 1984. Intern, resident Mass. Gen. Hosp.; internist Brigham & Womens Hosp., Boston, 1987—2006; pres., CEO Brigham & Women's Physicians Org., Boston, 1997—2005; prof. law & pub. health Harvard U. Sch. Pub. Health, 1992—2006; prof. medicine Harvard U. Med. Sch., 1995—2006; sr. v.p., chief medical officer Aetna, Inc., Hartford, Conn., 2006—08; exec. v.p., chief medical officer CVS Caremark Corp., Woonsocket, RI, 2008—. Trustee Am. Bd. Internal Medicine Found., Philadelphia; bd. govs. ACP. Contbr. chapters to books, articles to scholarly & scientific journals; author: (books) Just Doctoring: Medical Ethics in the Liberal State, 1991; co-author: A Measure of Malpractice: Medical Injury, Malpractice Litigation, & Patient Compensation, 1993, New Rules: Regulation, Markets, & the Quality of American Health Care, 1995, Health Care & Policy: Readings, Notes, & Questions, 1998. Mem.: Inst. Medicine. Office: CVS Caremark Corp 1 CVS Dr Woonsocket RI 02895 *

BRENNER, BARRY MORTON, physician; b. Bklyn., Oct. 4, 1937; s. Louis and Sally (Lamm) B.; m. Jane P. Deutsch, June 12, 1960; children: Robert, Jennifer. BS, L.I. U., 1958; MD, U. Pitts., 1962; MA (hon.), Harvard U.; DSc (hon.), Long Island U.; D.M.Sc. (hon.), U. Paris, (Pierre et Marie Curie); diploma (hon.), Charles U., Prague; fellow (hon.), Royal Coll. of Physicians, London; MD (hon.), U. Complutense, Madrid. Asst. prof. medicine U. Calif.-San Francisco, 1969-72, asso. prof. medicine and physiology, 1972-75; prof. medicine and physiology U. Calif., San Francisco, 1975-76; Samuel A. Levine prof. medicine Harvard Med. Sch., Boston; with Peter Bent Brigham Hosp., Boston, 1976—; dir. renal div. Brigham and Women's Hosp., Boston, 1979-2001, dir. emeritus, 2001—. Dir. physician-scientist program, Harvard Med. Sch., 1984-90, Harvard Ctr. for Study of Kidney Diseases, 1987-2000; cons. NIH. Editor: The Kidney, 2 vols., 1976, 8th edit., 2008, Renal Pathology, 2 vols., 1989, 2d edit., 1994, Textbook of Hypertension, 2 vols., 1990, 2d edit., 1995; Acute Renal Failure, 1985, 3d edit., 1994; co-editor Contemporary Issues in Nephrology, 1978-90; founding editor Current Opinion in Nephrology and Hypertension, 1992—; contbr. numerous articles to profl. jours. Recipient Homer W. Smith award N.Y. Heart Assn., 1984, George E. Brown award Am. Heart Assn., 1983, Merit award NIH, 1984, SKF Disting. Scientist award 1985, Donald W. Seldin and David Hume awards Nat. Kidney Found., 2003, Am. Acad. Arts and Scis., 1995, U. Pitt., Philip S. Hench Disting. Alumnus award, 1995, Legacy Laureate, 2008, Novartis award Coun. High Blood Pressure Rsch. Am. Heart Assn., 2005, rsch. grantee NIH, 1969-2000. Fellow AAAS, Molecular Med. Soc.; mem. Am. Soc. Cell Biology, Am. Physiol. Soc., Assn. Am. Physicians (councillor), Am. Soc. Clin. Investigation (councillor, v.p.), Am. Soc. Nephrology (councillor, pres., John P. Peters award, Robert G. Marins award), Am. Soc. Hypertension (exec. com., pres., Richard Bright award), Internat. Soc. Nephrology (councillor, Jean Hamburger award, Amgen Internat. prize), Western Assn. Physicians, Salt and Water Club, Interurban Clin. Club, Alpha Omega Alpha, Phi Sigma. Office: 75 Francis St Boston MA 02115-6110 Business E-Mail: bbrenner@partners.org.

BRENNER, DAVID ALLEN, academic administrator, medical educator; MD, Yale U. Resident Yale-New Haven Med. Ctr.; rsch. assoc. genetics and biochemistry branch Nat. Inst. of Arthritis, Diabetes, Digestive and Kidney Diseases, NIH; gastroenterology fellow U. Calif., San Diego, 1985; physician Veterans Affairs San Diego Healthcare Sys.; prof., chief Divsn. Digestive Diseases and Nutrition U. NC, Chapel Hill, 1993; vice chancellor health scis., dean Sch. Medicine U. Calif., San Diego, 2007—. Bd. dirs. AlphaOne Found., Alcoholic Beverage Med. Rsch. Found. Mem.: Am. Clin. and Climatological Assn., Am. Gastroenterological Assn. (chair Rsch. Policy Com.), Am. Coll. Physicians, Assn. Am. Physicians (sec.), Am. Soc. Clin. Investigation. Office: U Calif San Diego Sch Medicine 9500 Gilman Dr # 0602 La Jolla CA 92093-0602 Office Phone: 858-534-1501. E-mail: dbrenner@ucsd.edu. *

BRENNER, DAVID JONATHAN, radiation oncology and public health professor; b. Liverpool, Eng., June 9, 1953; BA in Physics Philosophy, Oxford U., 1974, MA in Physics Philosophy, 1979, DSc (hon.), 1996; MSc in Radiation Physics, St. Bartholomew's Hosp., U. London, 1976; PhD in Physics, U. Surrey, Guildford, 1980. Postdoctoral fellow Los Alamos Scientific Lab., 1979—81, staff mem., 1981—83; assoc. rsch. scientist, Radiological Rsch. Lab. Coll. Physicians & Surgeons, Columbia U., 1983—86, asst. prof., radiation oncology, 1986—92, assoc. prof., radiation oncology, Ctr. for Radiological Rsch., 1992—93, tenured assoc. prof., radiation oncology and pub. health, Ctr. for Radiological Rsch., 1993—94; prof., radiation oncology and pub. health, dir. radiological rsch. accelerator facility, Ctr. for Radiological Rsch. Columbia U. Med. Ctr., 1994—. Private investigator for several grants; mem. Columbia U. Senate, 1985—87, EPA Sci. Adv. Sub Com. on Radon Rsch., 1993—96; chairperson Columbia U. Radiation Safety Com., 1992—. Author: Radon, Risk, and Remedy, 1989; co-author (with Eric J. Hall): Making the Radiation Therapy Decision, 1996; contbr. several articles to peer-reviewed scientific lit.; assoc. editor Internat. Jour. Radiation Biology, 1991—96, mem. editl. bd. Radiation and Environ. Biophysics, 2002—. Recipient Oxford U. Carter Physics prize, 1974, Radiation Rsch. Soc. Annual Rsch. award, 1991; named Miller Prof., U. Calif. Berkeley, 2002. Mem.: Radiation Rsch. Soc. Exec. Coun. (physics councilor 1993—96), NAS (mem., BEIR VI Com. 1994—98), Nat. Coun. on Radiation Protection and Measurement (com. on 1-6 on linearity of dose response 1995—99, Robert D. Moseley award for Radiation Protection in Medicine 1992). Achievements include patents for Substance Detection with Monoenergetic Neutrons (with G. Randers-Pehrson). Office: Ctr for Radiological Rsch Columbia U 630 W 168th St VC 11-234 New York NY 10032 Office Fax: 212-305-9930, 212-305-3229. Business E Mail: djb3@columbia.edu.

BRENNER, JOEL I., cardiologist, educator; b. Feb. 8, 1946; BA, U. Pa., Phila., 1966; MD, N.Y. Med. Coll., NYC, 1970. Cert. Pediatrics, 1975. Intern pediat. NY Hosp.-Cornell U. Med. Ctr., NYC, 1970—71, resident pediatric cardiology, 1971—72; fellowship Yale-New Haven Hosp., 1972—74; asst. prof. pediatrics U. Va., Charlottesville, 1976-77; asst. prof. to prof. pediatrics U. Md., Balt., 1977-99; assoc. prof. Johns Hopkins U., Balt., 1999—; dir. pediatric cardiology Johns Hopkins Hosp. Co-dir. Fetal Cardiology Internat. Symposia, 1986—97. Mem.: Am. Heart Assn. (coun. cardiovascular disease in the young, past pres. Md. affiliate). Office: Johns Hopkins Hosp Brady 5 - Pediat Cardiology 600 N Wolfe St Baltimore MD 21287-0001 Office Phone: 410-614-6747, 410-955-5987. Office Fax: 410-955-0897. E-mail: jbrenne@jhmi.edu.

BRENNER, SYDNEY, molecular biologist, researcher; b. Germiston, South Africa, Jan. 13, 1927; naturalized, British citizen; s. Morris and Lena (Blacher) Brenner; m. May Woolf Balkind, 1952. MSc, U. Witwatersrand, Johannesburg, 1947, MB, BCh, 1951; DPhil, Oxford U., 1954. Postdoc. fellow U. Calif., Berkeley; sci. staff mem. Med. Rsch. Coun., Cambridge, England, 1957-92, dir. Lab. Molecular Biology, 1979-86, dir. molecular genetics unit, 1986-91; rsch. scientist dept. medicine U. Cambridge Sch. Clin. Medicine, 1992-96; founding pres., dir. Molecular Scis. Inst., Berkeley, Calif., 1996—2001; disting. rsch. prof. Salk Inst. Biol. Studies, La Jolla, Calif., 2000—. Carter-Wallace lectr. Princeton U., NJ, 1966, 77; Gifford lectr. U. Glasgow, Scotland, 1978—79; Dunham lectr. Harvard U., 1984; hon. fellow Exeter Coll., Oxford U., 1985; hon. prof. genetic medicine U. Cambridge Clin. Sch., 1989—96; mem. bd. sci. governors Scripps Rsch. Inst., La Jolla. Author: (column for Current Biology) Loose Ends, 1994—2000, (nonfiction) My Life in Science, 2001. Recipient Warren Triennial prize, Mass. Gen. Hosp., 1968, William Bate Hardy prize, Cambridge Philos. Soc., 1969, Albert Lasker Basic Med. Rsch. award, Lasker Found., 1971, Lasker-Koshland Spl. Achievement award, 2000, Charles-Leopold Mayer prize, French Acad. Scis., 1975, Gairdner Found. Internat. award, 1978, 1991, Krebs medal, Fedn. European Biochem. Societies, 1980, Ciba Medal, Biochem. Soc., 1981, Feldberg Found. prize, 1983, Rosenstiel award, Brandeis U., 1986, Louis Jeantet prize for medicine, Louis-Jeantet Found., Switzerland, 1987, Harvey prize, Technion-Israel Inst. Tech., 1987, Waterford Bio-Med. Sci. award, Rsch. Inst., Scripps Clinic, 1988, Kyoto prize, Inamori Found., Japan, 1990, King Faisal Internat. prize for sci., 1992, Novartis Drew award in biomed. rsch., 2001, Nobel prize in physiology/medicine, 2002, March of Dimes prize in devel. biology, 2002, Dan David prize, Tel Aviv U., 2002, Nat. Sci. & Tech. medal, Agy. for Sci., Tech. & Rsch (A*STAR), Singapore, 2006. Fellow: Royal Coll. Physicians (Neil Hamilton Fairley medal 1985), Royal Soc. London (Royal medal 1974, Copley medal 1991), Royal Coll. Pathologists (hon.); mem.: NAS (fgn. assoc.), Royal Soc. South Africa (fgn. assoc.), Am. Acad. Arts & Scis. (fgn. hon.), Chinese Soc. Genetics (hon.), Am. Philos. Soc. (fgn.), German Acad. Natural Scientists Leopoldina (Gregor Mendel medal 1970). Office: Salk Inst Biol Studies 10010 N Torrey Pines Rd La Jolla CA 92037-0346 E-mail: sbrenner@salk.edu. *

BRENT, GREGORY, endocrinologist, educator; Lic. Calif., 1982. Clinical fellow Brigham & Women's Hosp.; rsch. fellow Mass. Gen. Hosp. Dept. Molecular Biology; prof. med. & physiology UCLA David Geffen Sch. Med.; chief VA Greater LA Healthcare Sys. Endocrinology & Diabetes Div. Chmn. Nat. Inst. Health, Molecular & Cellular Endocrinology Study Section; former editorial bd. mem. Thyroid, Molecular Endocrinology & Endocrinology. Recipient Knoll Mentor award, The Endocrine Soc., Excellence in Edn. award, UCLA Sch. Med. Mem.: ATA (sec., Van Meter prize). Mailing: UCLA Department of Physiology VA Bldg Rm 111D Los Angeles CA 90095-1751 Office: David Geffen School of Medicine 650 Charles Young Dr S Box 915751 Rm 53-231 CHS Los Angeles CA 90095-1751 Office Phone: 310-825-5882. Office Fax: 310-206-5661. E-mail: gbrent@ucla.edu.

BRENT, LAWRENCE H., rheumatologist, educator; MD, Jefferson Med. Coll., 1979. Diplomate Am. Bd. Internal Medicine-internal medicine, rheumatology. Resident internal medicine Jefferson Med. Coll., 1982, fellow rheumatology, tchg. appointment; divsn. chmn. Albert Einstein Med. Ctr., program dir., rheumatology; intern W.Va. Univ. Med. Ctr., 1980; rsch. fellow immunology and pediatric rheumatology Ala. Med. Ctr., Birmingham. Recipient Arthritis Found. Postdoc. Rsch. Fellowship award; named Top Doc, Phila. Mag., 2007, 2010. Mem.: AAAS, ACP, Am. Coll. Rheumatology. Office: Albert Einstein Medical Center 5501 Old York Rd Korman Bldg Ste 103 Philadelphia PA 19141 Office Phone: 215-456-7380, 215-456-7890. Office Fax: 215-456-3898.

BRENT, ROBERT LEONARD, medical educator; b. Rochester, NY, Oct. 6, 1927; s. Charles and Rose (Katz) Brent; m. Lillian H. Hoffman, Aug. 21, 1949; children: David A., James R., Lawrence H., Deborah A. AB, U. Rochester, 1948, MD with honors, 1953, PhD, 1955, DSc (hon.), 1988; degree (hon.), Thomas jefferson U., 2008. Fellow Nat. Found., Strong Meml. Hosp., 1953-54; intern pediatrics Mass. Gen. Hosp., Boston, 1954-55; chief radiation biology Walter Reed Army Inst. Rsch., 1955-57; mem. faculty Jefferson Med. Coll., 1955—, prof. radiology, 1962—, also prof. pediatrics, Louis and Bess Stein prof. pediatrics, 1985—, emeritus chmn. pediats., 1999—; apptd. Disting. prof. Thomas Jefferson U., 1989. Mem. human embryology study sect. NIH, 1970—74; hon. prof. Norman Bethume U. Med. Sci., China, 1992, W. China U. Med. Scis., Chengdu, 1992; chmn. med. adv. bd. Nat. Found.; mem. fertility and maternal health com. FDA; trustee Health and Environ. Sci. Inst., 1991—94, pres. First Internat. Congress Birth Defects, China, 1994; Taylor lectr. Nat. Coun. Radiation Protection and Measurements, 2006. Editor in chief: Teratology, 1976—93. Apptd. mem. bd. trustee Fetus as a Patient Internat. Soc., 2006, World Assn. on Perinatal Medicine, 2006. With US Army, 1955—57. Recipient Med. Sch. award, Alpha Omega Alpha, 1952, Richie Meml. prize, U. Rochester Med. Sch., 1953, Lindback Found. award for Disting. Tchg., 1968, Burlington Internat. award, 1990, Landauer award, Health Physics Soc., 1995, Robley D. Evans Commemorative medal, 2001, Dean's medal, Thomas Jefferson U., 2007, Disting. Alumnus award, U. Rochester, 2008, Alfred I. duPont award, 2008, Doerenkamp Zbinden award, Rome, 2009, Recognition award, Ctr. Alternatives Animal Testing, Castle-Connelly award, 2011, William Liley medal, Internat. Soc. Meeting Taomina Sicily, 2011; fellow, Royal Soc. Medicine, 1971—72, FitzWilliam Coll., Cambridge, 1971—72; Lady Davis scholar, Hadassah Med. Ctr., Jerusalem, 1983—84. Mem.: AAAS, Ambulatory Pediat. Assn., European Teratology Soc., Japan Teratology Soc., Nat. Acad. Sci. (elected Inst. Medicine 1996), Nat. Coun. Radiation Protection, Soc. Devel. Biology, Am. Assn. Immunology (emeritus), Phila. Pediat. Soc., Phila. Coll. Physicians, Soc. Exptl. Biology and Medicine, Am. Acad. Pediat. (Merit citation 2001), Am. Pediat. Soc., Soc. Pediat. Rsch., Am. Soc. Exptl. Pathology, Radiation Rsch. Soc., Internat. Life Sci. Inst., Teratology Soc. (pres. 1967—68), Inst. Medicine NAS, Sigma Xi. Home Phone: 610-719-1996; Office Phone: 302-651-6880. E-mail: rbrent@nemours.org.

BRENT, THOMAS PETER, retired molecular pharmacologist; b. Leipzig, Germany, Nov. 7, 1937; came to U.S., 1972; s. Walter Manfred and Ruth Brent; m. Joanne Roblett, Mar. 31, 1966 (div. Mar. 1976); children: Timothy J., Matthew D.; m. Alva Wright, July 30, 1976. BA, Cambridge U., Eng., 1962, MA, 1966; PhD, London U., 1966. Rsch. fellow Chester Beatty Inst. for Cancer Rsch., London, 1966-68; asst. prof. McGill U., Montreal, 1968-72; asst. mem. St. Jude Children's Rsch. Hosp., Memphis, 1972-77, assoc. mem., 1977-85, mem., 1985—2003; assoc. prof. biochemistry U. Tenn. Coll. Medicine, Memphis, 1980-89, prof. pharmacology, 1990—2003. Mem. radiation study sect. NIH, 1981-85. Mem. editl. acad. Internat. Jour. Oncology, 1996—; contbr. more than 100 articles to profl. jours. With RAF, 1957-59. Recipient Damon-Runyan-Walter Winchell rsch. award, 1973-75; NIH grantee, 1973—2003. Mem. AAAS, Am. Assn. for Cancer Rsch., Biochem. Soc. U.K., DNA Methylation Soc. (bd. dirs. 1996), Radiation Rsch. Soc., Biophys. Soc., Short Wing Piper Club (pres. Tenn. chpt. 2003-). Avocations: aviation, running. Personal E-mail: tomalvabrent@hughes.net.

BRENTJENS, TRICIA EISENSTEIN, anesthesiologist, educator; b. NYC, Mar. 14, 1967; BSE, Duke U., 1989; MD, SUNY, 1993. Assoc. clin. prof. Columbia U., NY Presbyn. Hosp., 1998—. Recipient Physician of Yr. award, NYC Dept. Nursing. Mem.: ILTS, SCCM, ASA. Avocations: sailing, scuba diving, yoga. Office: Dept Anesthesiology 630 W 168th St PH 5 New York NY 10032 Office Fax: 212-305-3024. Business E-Mail: 164@columbia.edu.

BRENTNALL, TERESA A., gastroenterologist, educator; MD, U. Washington, Seattle, 1987. Resident UCLA, 1988—90; fellow U. Washington Dept. Gastroenterology, 1991—94, prof. Office: University of Washington School of Medicine 1959 N E Pacific St Box 356424 Seattle WA 98195-6424 Office Fax: 206-685-9478. E-mail: teribr@u.washington.edu.

BRESALIER, ROBERT SCOTT, gastroenterologist, educator; BS in Biol. Sci. with honors, SUNY, 1973; MD, U. of Chgo., 1978. Diplomate Am. Bd. Internal Medicine, 1981, Am. Bd. Internal Medicine-gastroenterology, 1983. Resident internal medicine Barnes-Jewish Hosp., 1978—81; fellow gastroenterolgy Univ. of Calif., San Francisco, 1981—84. Prof. gastrointerology, hepatology and nutrition internal medicine divsn. The Univ. of Tex. MD Anderson Cancer Ctr., 2003—. Author: (articles) Management of Barrett's Esophagus. Cases and Questions, 2005, Chemoprevention of colorectal neoplasia: advances and controversies (the COX-2 story), 2007, Neutrophil Gelatinase-Associated Lipocalin: A Novel Suppressor of Invasion and Angiogenesis in Pancreatic Cancer, 2008, Chemoprevention of colorectal cancer: why all the confusion?, 2008, Plasma glycoprotein profiling for colorectal cancer biomarker identification by lectin glycoarray and lectin blot, 2008, Barrett's esophagus and esophageal adenocarcinoma, 2008, Colorectal Adenomas in a Randomized Folate Trial: The Role of Baseline Dietary and Circulating Folate Levels, 2008, Cardiovascular events associated with rofecoxib: Final Analysis of the APPROVe Trial, 2008, Polyphenon E inhibits the growth of human Barrett's and aerodigestive adenocarcinoma cells by suppressing cyclin D1 expression, 2009, Nonsteroidal anti-inflammatory drug use after 3 years of aspirin use and colorectal adenoma risk: observational follow-up of a randomized study, 2009, Folic acid and risk of prostate cancer: results from a randomized clinical trial, 2009; editor: (books) Current Opinion in Gastroenterology. In: Large Intestine, 2008. Office: The University of Texas MD Anderson Cancer Center Unit 1466 Rm FCT13 6008 1400 Pressler Houston TX 77030-4009 Office Phone: 713-745-4340. Office Fax: 713-745-9295.

BRESLAWSKI, JAMES P., health products executive; CPA. CPA BDO Seidman; controller, v.p. fin., CFO Henry Schein, Inc., Melville, NY, 1980—90, pres. Sullivan Schein Dental subs., 1990—2005, exec. v.p., 1992—2005, pres., COO, 2005—. Past chmn. Dental Trade Alliance. Trustee Long Island Univ.; mem. bd. fellows Harvard Sch. Dental Med.; bd. dir. Nat. Found. of Dentistry for the Handicapped; past chmn. Am.Dental Trade Assn.; past pres. Dental Dealers of America. Mem.: Am.Inst. CPAs, NY State Soc. CPAs. Office: Henry Schein Inc 135 Duryea Rd Melville NY 11747

BRESLOW, ESTHER MAY GREENBERG, biochemistry professor, researcher; b. NYC, Dec. 23, 1931; d. Harry Daniel and Lillian (Solomon) Greenberg; m. Ronald Charles David Breslow, Sept. 4, 1955; children: Stephanie Ruth, Karen Ann. BS with distinction, Cornell U., Ithaca, NY, 1953; MS in Biochemistry, NYU, NYC, 1955, PhD in Biochemistry, 1959; postgrad., Radcliffe Coll., Cambridge, Mass., 1954-55. Postdoctoral fellow Cornell U. Med. Coll., NYC, 1959-61, rsch. assoc., 1961-64, asst. prof., 1964-72, assoc. prof., 1972-78, prof. biochemistry, 1978—2006, prof. emeritus, 2007—, acting chmn. dept. biochemistry, 1992-95. Mem. rev. panels NIH, Bethesda, Md., 1973—77, Bethesda, 1994—97, NSF, Bethesda, 1981—84. Mem. editl. bd. Jour. Biol. Chemistry, 1982-87, Internat. Jour. Peptide and Protein Rsch., 1956-; contbr. articles to profl. jours. Mem. Englewood Bd. Health, NJ, 1986-94; mem. Dem. Mcpl. Com., Englewood, 1985-91. Grantee, NIH, 1961—2007; fellow, Eli Lilly, 1954—55, USPHS, 1959—61. Fellow AAAS; mem. Am. Soc. for Biochemistry and Molecular Biology, Am. Chem. Soc. (sec. divsn. biol. chemistry 1972-76), Harvey Soc., Sigma Xi. Home: 44 W 77th St New York NY 10024 Office: Joan and Sanford I Weill Med Coll Cornell U 1300 York Ave New York NY 10021-4805 Office Phone: 212-746-6428. Business E-Mail: ebreslow@med.cornell.edu.

BRESLOW, LESTER, public health physician, educator; b. Bismarck, ND, Mar. 17, 1915; s. Joseph and Mayme (Danziger) Breslow; m. Devra J.R. Miller, 1967; children: Norman, Jack, Stephen. BA, U. Minn., 1935, MD, 1938, MPH, 1941, DSc (hon.), 1988. Diplomate Am. Bd. Preventive Medicine and Public Health. Intern USPHS Hosp., Stapleton, NY, 1938—40; dist. health officer Minn. Dept. Health, 1941—43; preventive medicine officer U.S. Army, 1943—45; chief bur. chronic diseases Calif. Dept. Pub. Health, Berkeley, 1946—60, chief divsn. preventive medicine, 1960—65, dir. dept., 1965—68; lectr. U. Calif. Sch. Pub. Health, Berkeley, 1950—68; prof. pub. health UCLA Sch. Pub. Health, 1968—, chmn. dept. preventive medicine and social medicine, 1969—72, dean, 1972—80, mem. divsn. cancer control, 1980—, dir. health promotion ctr., 1988—91, dean, prof. emeritus, 1980—; dir. study Pres.'s Commn. Health Needs of Nation, 1952. Cons. Office of Technology Assessment, Nat. Heart, Lung, Blood Inst., 1977, Nat. Cancer Inst., 1981—, chmn. bd. sci. counsellors divsn. cancer prevention and control, 1982—84; chmn. Nat. Com. on Vital and Health Stats., 1979—81; mem. US- China health scis. com. US Dept. HHS, 1982; bd. dirs., chmn. Calif. Ctr. Health Improvement, 1998—. Editor: Ann. Rev. Pub. Health, 1979—90, Encyclopedia Pub. Health, 2002; editorial cons. in field:. Active LA County Pub. Health Commn., 1996—, chmn., 1997—98, 2007. Capt. US Army, 1943—45. Decorated Bronze Star; recipient Lasker award, Mary Lasker Found., 1960, Porter prize, 1998, Outstanding Achievement award, U. Minn., 1970, Thomas Francis, Jr. Meml. award, U. Mich. Fellow: AAAS, ACP, Am. Coll. Preventive Medicine (Disting. Svc. award 1976); mem.: APHA (past pres., Sedgwick medal 1977, Dana award, Charles A. Dana Found. 1988, Healthtrac Found. Prize 1995, 1997), NY Acad. Medicine (Stephen Smith Achievement in Public Health award 2005), Inst. Medicine NAS (council 1978—80, chmn. bd. health promotion and disease prevention 1980—82, Lienhard award 1997), Assn. Schs. Public Health (pres. 1973—74), Am. Cancer Soc. (nat. dir., Calif. dir., chmn. adv. com. on rsch. etiology), Internat. Epidemiol. Assn. (past pres.), Am. Epidemiol. Soc., Public Health Cancer Assn. (past pres.), Am. Heart Assn. (fellow epidemiology sect.). Home: 10926 Verano Rd Los Angeles CA 90077-2224 Office Phone: 310-825-1388. Business E-Mail: breslow@ph.ucla.edu.

BRESLOW, NORMAN EDWARD, biostatistics educator, researcher; b. Mpls., Feb. 21, 1941; s. Lester and Alice Jane (Philp) Breslow; m. Gayle Marguerite Bramwell, Sept. 7, 1963; children: Lauren Louise, Sara Jo. BA, Reed Coll., 1962; PhD, Stanford U., 1967; Doctorates (honoris causa), U. Bordeaux II, 2001; Doctorates, U. Hasselt Katholiche U., Leuen, 2008. Trainee Stanford U., 1965—67; vis. research worker London Sch. Hygiene, 1967—68; instr. U. Wash., Seattle, 1968—69, asst. prof., 1969—72, assoc. prof., 1972—76, prof., 1976—, chmn. dept. biostats., 1983—93; statistician Internat. Agy. Research Cancer, Lyon, France, 1972—74. Mem. Hutchinson Cancer Ctr., Seattle, 1982—; statistician Nat. Wilms' Tumor Study, 1969—2003; cons. Internat. Agy. Rsch. Cancer, Lyon, 1978—79; assoc. prof. U. Geneva, 1994—2006. Co-author: (Scientific publ. nos. 32 and 82 on statistics in cancer rsch.) IARC, ISI (most highly cited publication in mathematical sciences for 1993-2003). Recipient Spiegelman Gold medal, APHA, 1978, Preventive Oncology Acad. award, NIH, 1978—83, Snedecor award, Com. of Pres.'s on Statis. Socs., 1995, R.A. Fisher lectr. award, 1995; named sr. U.S. Scientist, Alexander Humboldt Found., Fed. Republic of Germany, 1982; grantee rsch., NIH, 1984—; fellow sr. Internat., Fogarty Ctr., 1990. Fellow: AAAS, Royal Statis. Soc., Am. Statis. Assn. (com. on fellows 1996—2000, N. Mantel award 2002); mem.: Internat. Biometric Soc. (regional com. 1975—78, coun. 1994—2000, v.p. 2001, 2004, pres. 2002—03), Inst. Medicine-Nat. Acad. Scis., Internat. Statis. Inst. Avocations: ski mountaineering, hiking, bicycling. Office: Univ Wash Dept Biostatistics Seattle WA 98195-7232 Business E-Mail: norm@u.washington.edu.

BREUER, JOHANNES, physician, researcher; b. Issum, North-Rhine Westphalia, Germany, Apr. 14, 1960; s. Heinz and Maria (Lemmen) B.; m. Petra Reuschel, Oct. 18, 1987; children: Juliane, Svenja, Katinka, Nils. MD, Dusseldorf U., Germany, 1986. Post doctoral fellow U. Calif., San Diego, 1986-87; resident Children's Hosp. U. Tuebingen, Germany, 1988-94, sr. resident divsn. pediatric cardiology, 1994—2001, dir. pediatric cardiology rsch. lab., 1995—2001, dir. pediatric cardiology catheterization lab., 1999—2001; head divsn. of pediat. cardiology U. Bonn, 2001—, prof., 2009—. Contbr. articles to profl. jours., chpts. to books. Recipient Rsch. award German Heart Found., 1995, Arthur-Schlossmann award Saxonian Soc. Pediats., 1997. Mem. German Soc. Pediatric Cardiology (cert.), German Soc. Cardiology, German Soc. Pediatrics (cert.). Roman Catholic. Avocations: swimming, biking, walking, reading, classical music. Office: U Bonn Divsn Pediat Cardiology Adenauerallee 119 D-53113 Bonn Germany Office Phone: 49 228-28733350. E-mail: johannes.breuer@ukb.uni-bonn.de.

BREUR, HANS, pediatric cardiologist; b. Arnhem, Netherlands, May 17, 1977; MD, Utrecht U., 2003, PhD in Fetal Heart Block, 2003. Pediatrician, fellow pediat. cardiology Children's Heart Ctr., Wilhelmina's Children's Hosp., U. Med. Ctr. Utrecht, 2008—10, pediatric cardiologist, 2011. Recipient Hippocrates Study prize, Hippocrates Study Found., 2002. Office: Lundlaan 6 Utrecht 3584 EA Netherlands Office Phone: 0031887555555. Business E-Mail: h.breur@umcutrecht.nl.

BREUS, MICHAEL J., psychologist; BA in Psychology, Skidmore Coll.; MA, PhD, U. Ga. Cert. clinical psychology, clinical sleep disorders, diplomate Am. Bd. Sleep Medicine. Intern U. Miss. Med. Ctr., Jackson; fellow in psychiatry Western Psychiatric Inst. & Clinic, Pitts.; co-founder SoundSleep Solutions, Sleep Doctors On Call; co-founder & sr. ptnr. The Sleep Ctr. Mgmt. Inst.; sleep health expert WebMD; faculty Atlanta Sch. Sleep Medicine; sr. v.p. Arete Sleep Health. Chmn. clinical adv. bd. Sleep Holdings, LLC; editorial adv. bd. & columnist Sleep Rev. Mag. Author: Good Night: The Sleep Doctor's 4-Week Program to Better Sleep & Better Health, 2006. Office: 9989 N 95th St Scottsdale AZ 85258 Office Phone: 480-860-8998. E-mail: mbreus@SoundSleepSolutions.com.

BREWER, BARBARA BAGDASARIAN, nursing administrator; b. Providence, Apr. 18, 1950; d. Bagdasar and Grace (Sarkisian) Bagdasarian; m. Timothy F. Brewer III, May 28, 1983. BSN, U. R.I., 1972; MA in Liberal Studies, Conn. Wesleyan U., 1986; MSN, Yale U., 1988; MBA, Columbia U., 1992; PhD, U. Ariz., 2002. RN, Ariz., Conn., R.I. Staff nurse Miriam Hosp., Providence, 1972; head nurse orthopeds. unit Frisbie Meml. Hosp., Rochester, NH, 1973-76; staff nurse St. Francis Hosp. and Med. Ctr., Hartford, Conn., 1976; clin. coord. continuing care unit Middlesex Meml. Hosp., Middletown, Conn., 1976-86; dir. cardiology svcs. Lawrence and Meml. Hosp., New London, Conn., 1988-92, v.p. ambulatory svcs., 1992-95; adminstrv. leader emergency svcs. Tucson Med. Ctr., 1996-97; rsch. assoc. U. Ariz., Coll. of Nursing, 1998—2001; predoctoral fellow NIH, 1999—2002; project dir. U. Ariz., 2001—03; v.p. quality Clarian Health Ptnrs., 2003—05; dir. profl. practice John C. Lincoln North Mountain Hosp., 2005—10; clin. asst. prof. U. Ariz. Coll. Nursing, 2010—. Rschr. in field. Co-author: Improving Your Skills in 12-Lead ECG Interpretation, 1990. Mem.: ANA, Coun. Advancement Nursing Sci., Ariz. Org. Nurse Execs., Ariz. Nurses Assn., Am. Orgn. Nurse Execs., Sigma Theta Tau (treas. chpt. 2001—03). Business E-Mail: bbrewer@nursing.arizona.edu. *

BREWER, EILEEN D. (L. EILEEN DOYLE BREWER), nephrologist, educator; b. Houston, Oct. 27, 1944; MD, Washington U., St. Louis, 1971. Cert. Am. Bd. Pediat., Am. Bd. Pediat. Sub-Bd. in Pediatric Nephrology. Intern pediat. Children's Hosp., Washington U., St. Louis, 1971—72; resident pediat. nephrology U. Calif. San Francisco, 1972—74, fellow, 1974—77; chief renal sect. Tex Children's Hosp.-Baylor Coll. Medicine, Houston, 1994—, dir. Pediat. Nephrology Fellowship Program, prof. pediat. Mem.: So. Soc. Pediat. Rsch., Soc. Pediat. Rsch., Nat. Kidney Found., Women in Nephrology, Renal Physicians Assn. (bd. mem.), Internat. Soc. Peritoneal Dialysis, Internat. Soc. Nephrology, Internat. Pediat. Nephrology Assn., Am. Soc. Transplant Physicians, Am. Soc. Pediat. Nephrology, Am. Soc. Nephrology, Am. Pediat. Soc., Am. Fedn. Clin. Rsch. Office: Baylor Coll Medicine 6621 Fannin St, MC 3-2482 Houston TX 77030-2399 Office Phone: 832-824-3800. Office Fax: 832-825-3889. E-mail: ebrewer@bcm.tmc.edu.

BREWER, JEFFREY, foundation administrator, former Internet company executive; m. Deborah Brewer; children: Katherine, Sean. Degree in economics, So. Meth. U., Dallas. Co-founder, dir., chief tech. officer, v.p. devel. CitySearch, 2001; co-founder, CEO Overture Services, Inc. (formerly GoTo.com); mem. bd. dirs. Juvenile Diabetes Rsch. Found. Internat., NYC, 2004—10, pres., CEO, 2010—. Office: Juvenile Diabetes Found Internat 26 Broadway 14th Fl New York NY 10004 Office Phone: 212-785-9595. *

BREWER, JERRY DEWAYNE, dermatologic surgeon, researcher; s. Ashton Philip Brewer and Janet Sue Howe, Steven Gregory Howe (Stepfather); m. Jennifer Eileen Petersen, Dec. 18, 1999; children: Seth Ashton Brweer, Sarah Eileen, Jerry Benjamin, Joshua Steven Ray. BS, Brigham Young U., Provo, UT, 2000; MD, Wayne State U. Sch. Medicine, Detroit, 2004. Diplomate Am. Bd. Dermatology, 2008. Exec. bd. pres., student senate Wayne State U. Sch. Medicine, Detroit, 2003—04; intern Yale U. Sch. Medicine, New Haven, 2004—05; treas. sec. Mayo Fellows Assn., 2006—08; resident dermatology Mayo Clinic, 2005—08, chief resident dermatology, 2007—08, dermatologic surgery fellow Rochester, Minn., 2008—. Contbr. poster presentation, to numerous profl. jours. Vol. Rape Crisis Organisation, Provo, Utah, 1998—99, Code Blue (Wayne State U. Sch. Medicine), Detroit, 2000—03; troop com. chmn. Boy Scouts Am., Detroit, 2002—04; vol. Mayo Outreach Students and Tchrs., Rochester, Minn., 2006—07; missionary Ch. Jesus Christ Later Day Saints, Curitiba, Parana, Brazil, 1993—95, Sunday sch. tchr. Rochester, 2007—08, vol. Provo, 1996—97. Recipient Disting. Svc. award, Wayne State U. Sch. Medicine, 2004, Penfel award, 2004, Travel award, Mayo Clinic Grad. Sch. Med. Edn., 2006, Richard K Winkelman award, award, Dermatology Found. Cancer Devel., 2009. Mem.: AMA, AMA Polit. Action Com., Am. Med. Student Assn., Am. Acad. Dermatology, Alpha Omega Alpha. Conservative. Mem. Christian Ch. Avocations: cooking, woodworking, soccer, weightlifting, travel. Office: Mayo Clinic 200 1st St SW Rochester MN 55905 Office Phone: 507-284-3579. Office Fax: 507-284-2072. Business E-Mail: brewer.jerry@mayo.edu.

BREWER, ROBERT ALLEN, physician; b. Inpls., Jan. 29, 1927; s. Robert Dewayne and Viola Mae (Grant) Brewer; m. Mildred Noreen Barnett, Jan. 1, 1950 (dec. May 1997); children: Robert A. Jr., Raymond, Richard, Brian, Andrew. AA, St. Petersburg Jr. Coll., Fla., 1949; AB, Ind. U., 1952; MD, Ind U., Inpls., 1955. Emergency dept. staff physician Mound Park Hosp., St. Petersburg, Fla., 1960; staff physician Pinellas Hosp., Largo, Fla., 1961-68; pvt. practice Logansport, Ind., 1969—. Mem. Cass County Rep. Com., Logansport, Ind.; candidate for city coun., 1995. Capt. US Army, 1957—59. Mem.: AMA, Cass County Med. Assn., Ind. Med. Assn., Am. Acad. Family Practitioners (bd. cert. diplomate). Republican. Avocations: stamp collecting/philately, coin collecting/numismatics. Office: PO Box 119 803 E Broadway Logansport IN 46947-0119 *

BRIAN, GRANDE C., financial analyst; b. Freeport, Ill., Nov. 19, 1956; Degree in Acctg., Western Ill. U., 1978; MBA, Northern Ill. U., 1996. Supr. payroll, accts. payable, staff acct. Swedish Am. Hosp., 1978—86, cfo - highland hosp., 1986—90; contr. U. Ill. Coll. Medicine, Rockford, 1990—98, dir. adminstrv. ops., 1998—2005; sr. fin. analyst Rockford Health Sys., 2005—. Mem. Healthcare Fin. Mgmt. Assn., 1986—90, Med. Group Mgmt. Assn., 1998—2006; cert. med. practice exec. Am. Coll. Med. Practice Execs., 2005. Avocation: golf. Home: 507 Fairview St Durand IL 61024 Business E-Mail: bgrande@rhsnet.org.

BRIANZONI, ERNESTO, nuclear medicine physician, director; b. Matelica, Nov. 2, 1949; D, 1975, degree in Nuc. Medicine & Endocrinology, 1978. Dir. Unit Nuc. Medicine, 1999—2011; dir. dept. oncology Hosp. Macerata, 2003—. Mem.: EAMN, SNM, AIMN. Office: via santa Lucia n 1 Macerata 62100 Italy Office Fax: 3907332572466. Business E-Mail: ernesto.brianzoni@sanita.marche.it.

BRICCETTI, ALBERT B., physician, consultant; b. Mt. Kisco, NY, Sept. 22, 1940; s. Thomas Bernard and Joan Theresa Briccetti; m. Mary K. Campbell, June 2, 1984; children: Mark Thomas, Christine Elaine. AB, Johns Hopkins U., Balt., 1962; MD, Georgetown U., Washington, 1966. Diplomate Am. Bd. Internal Medicine, 1971, in rheumatology Am. Bd. Internal Medicine, 1972, Am. Bd. Med. Mgmt. Am. Coll. Physician Execs., 1992. Intern 2nd Med. (Cornell) Divsn., Bellvue Hosp., NYC, 1966—68; resident 2nd Med. Divsn. and Beth Israel Hosp., Boston, 1968—69; fellow Boston U. and Boston City Hosp., 1969—71; commd. maj. USAF, 1971, advanced through grades to col., 1978; chmn. dept. medicine Malcolm Grow USAF Med. Ctr., Washington, 1971—81; command surgeon USAF Acad., Colorado Springs, Colo., 1981—84; comdr. USAF Hosp. Torrejon Air Base, Spain, 1984—85; dep. command surgeon USAF Europe, Ramstein Air Base, Germany, 1985—87; dir. med. plans and resources Hdqrs. USAF, Bolling AFB, Washington, 1987—92; med. dir. Beaver Med. Group and EPIC Mgmt., Redlands, Calif., 1992—97; CEO, med. dir. Corona Regional Med. Group, Calif., 1997—99; prin. cons. Med. Directions LLC, Colorado Springs, 1999—. Dir. Air Force Village West, Riverside, Calif., 2006—10. Decorated Merritorious Svc. medal USAF, Legion of Merit; Jimmie Doolittle fellow, Aerospace Edn. Found., 1979. Master: ACP (gov. 1988—92, Laureate award 1992); fellow: Am. Coll. Rheumatology, Aerospace Med. Assn.; mem.: Flying Physicians Assn. (dir. 2003—). Avocation: flying.

BRICHTOVA, EVA, neurosurgeon, consultant; b. Prostejov, Moravia, Czech Republic, Sept. 15, 1970; d. Milos Zboril and Sophia Zborilova; m. Jaroslav Brichta, Sept. 9, 2004; m. Michal Dufek (div.). PhD, Masaryk U., Brno, Czech Republic, 1994, post grad, 2007—. Lic. med. doctor Czech Republic, 1st degree neurosurgery Czech Republic, 2d degree neurosurgery Czech Republic, cert. European Assn. Neurosurgery. Intern Dept. Neurosurgery St. Anne U. Hosp., Brno, Czech Republic, 1994—97, resident, 1997—2002; sr. resident specialist Dept. Pediat. Surg. Orthop. Faculty Hosp., Brno, 2002—. Cons. Pediat. Traumatology Ctr., Brno, Czech Republic, 2002—; lectr. in field. Contbr. articles to profl. jours. Lector Yoga in Daily Life, Brno, Czech Republic, 1996—2005. Recipient U. Sport award, Masaryk U., 1994, Honorary award, Czech Vegetarian Soc., 2001. Mem.: Ctrl. European Neurosurgery Soc., Czech Neurosurgery Soc., Czech Med. Coun. Achievements include mem. first league Czech national women's football team. Avocations: yoga, Tai-ji, football, horseback riding, painting. Office: Dept Pediat Surg Orthop Faculty Hosp Cernopolni 9 62500 Brno Czech Republic Home: Vranov 262 66432 Vranov Czech Republic Business E-Mail: brichtovae@seznam.cz.

BRICKER, NEAL S., physician, educator; b. Denver, Apr. 18, 1927; s. Eli D. and Rose (Quiat) B.; m. Miriam Thalenberg, June 24, 1951 (dec. 1974); children: Dusty, Cary, Susan, Daniel Baker; m. Ruth T. Baker, Dec. 28, 1980. BA, U. Colo., 1946, MD, 1949. Diplomate Am. Bd. Internal Medicine (bd. govs. 1972-79, chmn. nephrology test com. 1973-76). Intern, resident Bellevue Hosp., NYC, 1949-52; sr. asst. resident Peter Bent Brigham Hosp., Boston, 1954-55, asso. dir. cardio-renal lab., 1955-56; instr. Harvard, 1955-56; fellow Howard Hughes Med. Inst., 1955-56; from asst. prof. to prof. Washington U., 1956-72, dir. renal div., 1956-72; Mem. sci. adv. bd. Nat. Kidney Found., 1962-69, chmn. research and fellowship grants com., 1964-65, mem. exec. com., 1968-71; prof. medicine, chmn. dept. Albert Einstein Coll. Medicine, 1972-76; prof. medicine U. Miami, Fla., 1976-78, vice chmn. dept., 1976-78; Disting. prof. medicine UCLA, 1978-86; disting. prof. medicine, dir. sci. and tech. planning Loma Linda (Calif.) U., 1986-92; exec. v.p. Naturon Pharm., Riverside, Calif., 1992; clin. prof. medicine UCR/UCLA Program in Biomed. Scis., UCR, 1996—. Cons. NIH, 1964-68, chmn. gen. medicine study sect., 1966-68, chmn. renal disease and urology tng. grants com., 1969-71; vis. investigator Inst. Biol. Chemistry, Copenhagen, 1960-61; investigator Mt. Desert Island Biol. Labs.; advisor on behalf Inst. Medicine to Sen. Lowell Weicker. Assoc. editor: Jour. Lab. and Clin. Medicine, 1961-67, Kidney Internat, 1972; editorial com.: Jour. Clin. Investigation, 1964-68, Physiol. Revs, 1970-76, Am. Heart Assn. Publs. Com., 1974-79, Calcified Tissue Internat., 1978-86, Proc. Soc. Exptl. Biology and Medicine, 1978-86; editor: Supplements, Circulation and Circulation Research, 1974-79; contbr. articles to profl. jours., chpts. to books. Served with USNR, 1944-45; Served with U.S. Army, 1952-54. Recipient Gold-Headed Cane award U. Colo., 1949, Silver and Gold Alumni award, 1975; USPHS Research Career award, 1964-72; Skylab Achievement award NASA, 1974; Pub. Service award, 1975; George Norlin Silver medal award U. Colo. 1982, citation Kidney Found. So. Calif., 1984; honoree 50th Ann. Wash. U. Med. Sch. Renal Divsn., 2004. Fellow A.C.P.; mem. Am. Fedn. for Clin. Research, Central Soc. Clin. Research (council 1970-73), Assn. Am. Physicians, Am. Soc. for Clin. Investigation (pres. 1972-73, chmn. com. nat. med. policy 1973-77, Disting. Service award 1969), Internat. Soc. Nephrology (exec. com. 1966-81, v.p. 1966-69, treas. 1969-81, history honoree, video legacy honoree 2004), Internat. Congress Nephrology (pres. 1981-84), Am. Soc. Nephrology (1st pres., John Peters medal 1991), Am. Physiol. Soc., Soc. for Exptl. Biology and Medicine, Western Soc. Clin. Research, So. Soc. Clin. Investigation, Nat. Acad. Scis. (com. on space biology and medicine, ad hoc panel on renal and metabolic effects space flight 1971-72, mem. drug efficacy com. 1966-68, com. space biology, chmn. medicine in space sci. bd. 1972-81, com. chmn. 1978-81, chmn. com. renal and metabloic effects space flight 1972-74, chmn. study com. on life scis. 1976-81, mem. space sci. bd. 1977-81), Internat. Soc. nephrology, (hon.), Inst. Medicine of NAS, Internat. Soc. Nephrology, Sigma Xi, Alpha Omega Alpha. Home: 4240 Piedmont Mesa Claremont CA 91711-2332 Office: UCR/UCLA Riverside CA 92521-0121

BRICKMAN, JEFFREY L., hospital administrator; married; 3 children. BS in Biology, U. of Connecticut, 1973—78; BA in Bus. Adminstrn., U. of Connecticut, Storrs, Conn., 1978—80; MBA, Temple U., Phila., Pa., 1980—82. Adminstrv. resident State of Conn. Bur. of Health Planning, Hartford, Conn., 1980, Germantown Hosp. and Med. Ctr., Phila., 1981—82; asst. to the pres. Baystate Med. Ctr., Inc., Springfield, Mass., 1982—84, asst. v.p. med. affairs, 1984—86, v.p. med. support svcs., 1986—92, sr. v.p., 1992—99, COO, 1996—99; bd. dirs. Ronald McDonald House of Greater Springfield, 1993—99, Health New Eng., 1995—97, mem. fin. com., 1996—99; bd. dirs. Baystate Health Sys. Ins. Co. Ltd., 1996—99; chmn. Baystate Radiology and Imaging, 1996—99; bd. dirs., exec. com. Springfield Sch Volunteers, 1997—99; bd. dirs. The Nat. Conf., 1998—99; exec. v.p., COO, pres. Meridian Health System, Wall, NJ, 1999—2004; bd. dirs. VHA East Coast, 2000—04; chmn. Shore Rehab. Inst., 2000—04, bd. dirs., asst. treas. Monmouth Family and Children's Svcs., 2003—04, pres., CEO Provena St. Joseph Med. Ctr., Joliet, Ill., 2004—; bd. dirs. Alverno Clin. Labs., 2005—; vice chmn. Surg. Ctr. of Joliet, 2005—; hon. chairperson United Cerebral Palsy of Joliet, 2005. Chmn. program com., exec. com. mem. Health Care Mgmt. Assn. of Mass., 1985—86, sec., exec. com. mem., 1986—88; presenter Assn. of Infection Control Practitioners Nat. Meeting, Reno, 1989, Pride in Medicine Symposium, Springfield, 1990, Soc. for Health Sys., Wash., 1992, Mecon Nat. Client Conf., Dallas, 1996, Mecon Client Conf. Exec. Strategy Program, Phila., 1996, Assn. of Am. Med. Colleges Coun. of Tchg. Hosps. and Health Sys. Spring Meeting, New orleans, 2002; mem. The Healthcare Forum, 1990—99; mem. bd. of trustees Monmounth Ocean Hosp. Corp., 2000—04; pres., mem. bd. of trustees Meridian Hosps. Corp., 2000—04; policy devel. com. mem. NJ Hosp. Assn., 2003—04; mem. Will County Ctr. for Econ. Devel., 2004—. Co-author: (publs.) Surviving and Flourishing in Tough Times, 1992 (Hon. Mention award), Improving Clinical Engineering Services Through Consolidation, Innovative Strategies for Quality Improvement Using a Pharmacy Model, 1992, BHS Medical Physics and Radiation Safety Program Based on Work Redesign and Work-load Analysis (Regional Svc. award, 1997), Straight Talk: New Approaches in Healthcare, 2005. Chmn. edn. partnership com. Greater Springfield C. of C. Inc., 1995—96, mem chamber sub-com. on edn., 1996, chmn. mktg. sub-com., 1996—97, chmn. edn. works com., 1998—99. Finalist V.H.A. Leadership, 2004. Mem.: Am. Coll. of Healthcare Execs., Ill. Hosp. Assn. Avocations: active sports, travel. Office: Provena St Joseph Medical Center 333 N Madison Joliet IL 60435 Office Phone: 815-725-7133. E-mail: jlbrick@comcast.net.

BRIDGES, JAMES DONALD, radiation oncologist; MD, Uniformed Svcs. U. Health Sciences, 1987. Diplomate Am. Bd. Radiology-radiation oncology. Intern Nat. Naval Med. Ctr., 1988; resident Nat. Cancer Inst., 1991; hosp. affiliations include Md. Regional Cancer Care, Shady Grove Adventist Hosp., Md. Office: Shady Grove Adventist Hospital 9901 Medical Center Dr Rockville MD 20850 Office Phone: 800-642-0101.

BRIDWELL, KEITH HAPP, orthopedic surgeon; b. St. Louis, May 4, 1953; s. James Robert and Shirley (Happ) B.; m. Mala Gusman, Dec. 21, 1978 (dec. Jan., 2001); 1 child, Grace Marie. AB in Biology and Psychology, Washington U., St. Louis, 1973, MD, 1977. Diplomate Am. Bd. Orthopaedic Surgery, Am. Acad. Orthopaedic Surgeons. Clin. asst. prof. orthopedic surgery U. Ky., Lexington, 1983-84; asst. prof. orthopedic surgery, dir. spine surgery U. Cin. Med. Ctr., 1983-84; asst. prof. orthopedic surgery Washington U., St. Louis, 1984-90, assoc. prof. orthopedic surgery, 1990-95, prof., 1995-97, Asa C. and Dorothy W. Jones prof. orthopedic surgery, 1997—; chief, adult, pediatric spinal surgery Washington Univ. Sch. Medicine, St. Louis. Staff mem. Barnes-Jewish Hosp., fellow, 1993—, St. Louis Children's Hosp., transfusion com., 1985—, children's adv. com., 1986-92, Shriners Hosp. for Children, VA Hosp Associate editl. bd. Spine, 1989-95, dep. editor, 1995—; editl. bd. Jour. Spinal Disorders, SpineUniverse; co-editor in chief The Textbook of Spinal Surgery, 1991, 2d. edit., 1997; reviewer Jour. Bone and Joint Surgery, 1996—; section editor Principles of Orthopaedic Practice, 2d edit., 1997; contbr. articles to profl. jours. Grantee NIH, 1999—. Mem. Acad. Orthopaedic Soc., Am. Acad. Orthopaedic Surgeons, Clin. Orthopaedic Socl, Mid-Am. Orthopaedic Assn., Mo. State Orthopaedic Assn., N.Am. Spine Soc. (subcom. resident core curriculum 1995—, Outstanding Paper award 1999), St. Louis Orthopaedic Soc., Scoliosis Assn., Scoliosis Rsch. Soc. (Russell L. Hibbs award 1987, 91, Walter P. Blount award 1987, John H. Moe award 1995, bd. dirs. 1995-97, 2000—, grantee 1998—, 1st v.p. 2000—, pres. elect 2001, pres. 2002—), Am. Orthopaedic Assn. (internat. travelling fellowships subcom. 1998—, chmn. 1999-2000, editl. bd. AOA News 1999—), Fedn. Spine Assns. (chmn. program com. 1999, sec.-treas. 2000—), Eliot Soc. Washington U. Office: Washington U Sch Med Dept Orthop Surgery Box 8233 660 S Euclid Ave Saint Louis MO 63110 E-mail: bridwellk@wudosis.wustl.edu.

BRIEN, LOIS ANN, psychologist, educator; b. Cleve., Sept. 24, 1928; d. Alexander and Anne Lois (Katz) B.; m. Melvin Lintz, June 1961 (div. June 1964). BFA, Ohio U., 1950; MA, U. Ala., 1953; PhD, U. Iowa, 1959. Instr. Auburn (Ala.) U., 1953-55; clin. instr. Baylor Coll. Medicine, Houston, 1959-64; diagnostician Houston Speech and Hearing Ctr., 1959-64; faculty, speech com. Case Western Reserve U., Cleve., 1965-69; faculty, psychology San Francisco State U., 1970-72; pvt. practice San Francisco, 1969-79; faculty Calif. Sch. Profl. Psychology, Berkeley, 1971-79; pvt. practice Palm Springs, 1981-82; faculty, women's studies San Diego State U., 1983-86; pvt. practice Encinitas, Calif., 1982—; prof. psychology Nat. U., San Diego, 1984-87, dean Sch. Psychology, 1987-91, dean emeritus, assoc. faculty, 1991—. Contbr. articles to profl. jours. and textbooks. Commr. Marin County Commn. on the Status of Women, 1974-77. U.S. Office Edn. grantee, 1970-71. Mem. NOW, Am. Psychol. Assn., Calif. Assn. Marriage, Family Therapy, Am. Assn. Marriage, Family Therapy, Am. Acad. Psychotherapists. Democrat. Jewish. Avocations: tennis, gardening, hiking, bicycling, skiing. also: Nat U Dept Psychology University Park San Diego CA 92108 *

BRIER, PAMELA SARA, hospital administrator; b. LA, Sept. 5, 1945; d. Harry M. and Patricia (Weisberger); m. Stephen B. Brier, Sept. 11, 1966; 1 child, Jennifer. BA with honors, U. Calif., Berkeley, 1967; MPH, UCLA, 1972. Dir. reimbursement NYC Health & Hosps. Corp., 1981-83, sr. asst. v.p. fin., 1983-84, v.p. fin., 1984-88, sr. v.p. administrn., 1986-88, exec. v.p., 1988-89; exec. dir. Bronx Mcpl. Hosp. Ctr., 1989, Jacobi Hosp., Bronx, 1989—92, Bellevue Hosp. Ctr., NYC, 1992—95; exec. v.p., COO Maimonides Med Ctr., Bklyn., 1995—2003, pres., CEO, 2003—. Mem. NY State Hosp. Review and Planning Coun., 1991—96, NYC Cmty. Svc. Bd., 1995—2000, NYC Bd. Health, 2003, NYC Bd. Corrections, 2008; adj. faculty NYU Wagner Grad. Sch. Pub. Svc. Mem. NY State Hosp. Rev. and Planning Coun., 1991; chair bd. dirs. Housing Works, Inc., 1996—2003. Named one of The 100 Most Influential Women in NYC Bus., Crain's NY Bus., 2007, The 50 Most Powerful Women in NY, 2009. Office: Maimonides Med Ctr 4802 Tenth Ave Brooklyn NY 11219-2844 E-mail: pbrier@maimonidesmed.org.

BRIGGS, DICK DOWLING, JR., physician, educator; b. Electric Mills, Miss., Jan. 28, 1934; s. Dick Dowling and Anita (Carnathan) B.; m. Susan Hunt Davis, June 20, 1959 (dec. 2006); children: Adrienne Davis, Dick Dowling, III, Daniel Roth. BS, U. of South, 1956; MD, Washington U., 1960. Resident, fellow, chief resident U. Ala. Hosp., Birmingham, 1960-62, 64-68; prof. medicine U. Ala., Birmingham, 1964-95, prof., 1971-92, dir. divsn. pulmonary critical care, 1971-92, vice chmn. dept. medicine, 1981-95, eminent scholar chair in pulmonary diseases, 1989-95, emeritus eminent scholar chair, 1995—; pres., CEO, med. dir. U. Ala. Health Svc. Found., P.C., Birmingham, 1988-92, corp. med. dir. Complete Health, 1985—88, Triton Health Sys., Birmingham, 1995-97; chief med. officer Best Drs. Worldwide Health Svcs., Boston, 1997—2005. Cons. VA Med. Ctr., Birmingham, 1966-2003; trustee AmSouth Funds, Birmingham, 1992-2005. Assoc. editor (CDROM) UpToDate, 1994—; sr. editl. bd. Archives Internal Medicine, 1985-97; contbr. articles to profl. publs. Bd. dir. Am. Bd. Emergency Medicine, 1994—2002. Recipient Pulmonary Acad. award NIH, 1972-77, Breath of Life award Cystic Fibrosis Found., 1994; named to Ala. Tennis Hall Fame, 2003. Master: ACP (Laureate award 1995), Am. Coll. Chest Physicians (pres. 1984—85, master fellow 2002); mem.: Am. Bd. Pulmonary Disease (chmn. 1988—90), So. Med. Assn. (chmn. sect. medicine 1973—74), Am. Thoracic Soc. (pres. Ala. chpt. 1978—79), Assn. Pulmonary and Critical Care Medicine Program Dirs. (founding mem. 1984, pres. 1986—87), Newcomen Soc., US Tennis Assn. (Ala. Tennis Hall of Fame 2003), Rotary Club. Episcopalian. Avocations: tennis, music, travel, wine. Home: 2925 Southwood Rd Birmingham AL 35223-1232 Office: Univ Ala Birmingham Sch Medicine 1808 7th Ave S Birmingham AL 35294-0012 Personal E-mail: dickbriggsjr@gmail.com.

BRIGGS, JOSEPHINE PASHLER, federal agency administrator; b. Toronto, Ont., Can., Dec. 14, 1944; d. Peter E. and Marianne (Moreland) Pashler; m. Jurgen Schnermann, Oct. 14, 1980; children: Martin, Nikolaus. BA, Radcliffe Coll., Cambridge, Mass., 1966; MD, Harvard U., Boston, 1970. Diplomate Am. Bd. Internat. Medicine; lic. physician, N.Y., Mich. Intern and resident dept. internal medicine Mt. Sinai Sch. Medicine, NYC, 1970-74, fellow in clin. nephrology, 1973-75, assoc. in internal medicine, 1974-76, asst. dean students for the clin. yrs., 1975-76; rsch. assoc. Physiology Inst., U. Munich, 1979-85; asst. prof. divsn. nephrology Dept. Internal Medicine, U. Mich., Ann Arbor, 1985-88, assoc. prof., 1988-93, prof. and assoc. chair for rsch. programs, 1993—97, assoc. prof. physiology, 1990-93, prof., 1993—97; dir., divsn. kidney, urologic, and hematologic diseases NIH, 1997—2006; sr. sci. officer Howard Hughes Med. Inst., Chevy Chase, Md., 2006—08; dir. NIH Nat. Ctr. Complementary and Alt. Medicine, 2008—. Vis. asst. prof. dept. internal medicine U. Tex. Health Sci. Ctr., Dallas, 1983-84; rsch. fellow dept. physiology Yale U. Sch. Medicine, New Haven, 1976-79; sci. adv. bd. Nat. Kidney Found. of Mich., 1988-93, budget com., 1993-95, rsch. and fellowship grants rev. com., 1992-95; lectr. in field. Editl. bd. Am. Jour. Physiology, 1989-92, Jour. Lab. and Clin. Medicine, 1990—, Seminars in Nephrology, 1993—, Internat. Yearbook of Nephrology Dialysis Transplantation, 1993—, Kidney Internat., 1995-2000; contbr. numerous articles to profl. jours. including Am. Jour. Physiology, Pfluegers Arch., Kidney Internat.; contbr. chpts. to books; author abstracts. Recipient Vollhard prize German Nephrol. Soc., 1988, Alexander von Humboldt Sci. Exch. award, 1979-81; NIH grantee, NIHRO1 grantee, Am. Heart Assn., 1985-88; Kidney Found. fellow, 1976-77, NIH Rsch. fellow, 1978-79. Fellow Coun. for High Blood Pressure Rsch.; mem. Am. Soc. Nephrology (program com. 1994, sec.-treas. elect 1994), Am. Heart Assn. (council exec. com. 1993-95, program com. 1994, coun. on kidney in cardiovascular disease, coun. on high blood pressure), Am. Soc. Clin. Investigation (councilor 1989-92, nominating com. 1994), Mich. Soc. for Med. Rsch., Am. Physiol. Soc., Accreditation Coun. for Grad. Med. Edn. Office: NIH Nat Ctr Complementary and Alt Medicine Claude D Pepper Bldg 2B11 31 Center Dr Bethesda MD 20892 Office Phone: 301-435-6826. Office Fax: 301-435-6549. Business E-Mail: josephine.briggs@nih.gov. *

BRIGHAM, CRAIG D., surgeon; b. Portland, Oreg., May 6, 1954; BS, U. Oreg., 1976; MD, Northwestern U., 1982. Surgeon Ortho Carolina, 1988—, exec. com. mem., clin. quality, 2005—10. Chief, spine edn. orthop. surgery residency Carolinas Med. Ctr., 1989—2011. Named Tchr. of Yr., Carolinas Med. Ctr. Orthop. Residency, 1997, 2005, Physician of Yr., Ortho Carolina, 2010; NCAA Ednl. grant, Rsch. grant, Orthop. Rsch. & Edn. Fund, NSF. Mem.: Am. Orthop. Soc., Nat. Football Team Physician's Soc., Cervical Spine Rsch. Soc., Scoliosis Rsch. Soc. Avocations: guitar, exercise. Office: 2001 Randolph Rd Charlotte NC 28207 Business E-Mail: craig.brigham@orthocarolina.com.

BRIGHT, CEDRIC M., academic administrator, educator, physician; m. Maria Moore Bright; 1 child, Andrew Weldon. BA in Semiotics, Brown U., Providence; MD, U. NC, Chapel Hill. Residency tng. RI Hosp./Brown U, Providence; staff physician VA Med. Ctr., Durham, NC; assoc. clin. prof. internal medicine and cmty. family medicine Duke U. Med. Ctr., Durham; asst. dean admissions, dir. office spl. programs U. NC Sch Medicine, Chapel Hill, 2011—, assoc. prof. divsn. gen. medicine, dept. medicine, 2011—. Bd. dirs. Durham County Hosp. Corp., vice chmn. patient safety & quality com. and fin. com.; past chmn. of bd. Lincoln Cmty. Health Ctr. Mem. Governor's Quality Initiative, NC, NC State Genomics Taskforce; mem. patient safety taskforce NC Med. Soc. Fellow: American Coll. Physicians; mem.: Nat. Med. Assn. (pres. 2011—), Durham Acad. Medicine, Dentistry and Pharmacy (pres. 2010—11), Old North State Med. Soc. (pres. 2010—11). Office: University NC Sch Medicine Spl Programs CB # 7530 322 MacNider Bldg Chapel Hill NC 27599-7530 Office Phone: 919-966-7530. Office Fax: 919-966-7734. *

BRILL, AARON BERTRAND, nuclear medicine educator; b. NYC, Dec. 19, 1928; s. Louis And Cecile (Sroge) B.; m. Joan Booth Morrison, Sept. 1, 1950; children: Paul, David, Laurie. AB, Grinnell Coll., 1949; MD, U. Utah, 1956; PhD in Biophysics, U. Calif., Berkeley, 1961. Statistician Contra Costa County Health Dept., Martinez, Calif., 1949—50; res. asst. U. Calif., Donner Lab, 1950—52; biophysicist U. Utah Pediatrics Dept., Salt Lake City, 1952-56; intern Salt Lake City Gen. Hosp., 1956-57; USPHS officer Div. of Radiol. Health, Rockville, Md., 1957-64; asst. prof. radiology dept. radiology scis. Johns Hopkins Hosp. and Sch. of Hygiene, 1961-64; assoc. prof. radiol. Vanderbilt U. Sch. Medicine, Nashville, 1964-72; assoc. prof. medicine, biomed. engring. and physics, 1964-79; prof. radiology Vanderbilt U. Sch. Medicine, Nashville, 1972-79, SUNY, Stony Brook, 1979-87; sr. scientist, nuc. medicine coord. Brookhaven (N.Y.) Nat. Lab., 1979-87; prof. nuclear medicine U. Mass. Sch. Medicine, Worcester, 1987—97. Rsch. affiliate HST MIT, Cambridge, 1993-2005; affil. prof. Worcester Poly. Inst., Worcester, 1995-97; rsch. prof. radiol. sci. Vanderbilt U. Sch. Medicine, Nashville, 1997—, rsch. prof. physics, adj. prof. biomed. engring. Editor: Low Level Radiation Fact Book, 1st edit. 1982, 2d edit., 1985; editor: IEEE Trans Med. Imaging, 1986-92. Med. dir. USPHS, 1957-64, U. Calif. at Berkeley fellow, 1959-61. Fellow IEEE, Am. Coll. Nuclear Physicians, Am. Inst. Med. and Biol. Engring.; mem. NAS (com. on atomic casualties 1964-70, com. on biol. effects of ionizing radiation 1978-80; com.to assess sci. info. for radiation exposure and edn. program 2004-06, com. on assessment of CDC and prevention radiation studies from DOE contractor sites 2002-04, nat. coun. on radiation protection and measurement 1972-82, 92-97). Avocation: sailing. Office: Vanderbilt U Med Sch Dept Radiol Sci Mcn S1314 Nashville TN 37232-2675 Office Phone: 615-322-3190. Business E-Mail: aaron.brill@vanderbilt.edu.

BRILL, DAVID MORRIS, cardiologist, educator; MD, Harvard U., 1980. Diplomate Am. Bd. Internal Medicine, Am. Bd. Internal Medicine-cardiovasc. disease, Am. Bd. Internal Medicine-interventional cardiology. Intern Michael Reese Hosp. & Med. Ctr., 1981, resident internal medicine, 1983—84, fellow cardiology, 1984—87; fellow interventional cardiology Tufts-New Eng. Med. Ctr., 1987—88; asst. prof. cardiology dept. Uniformed Svcs. Univ. of the Health Sciences; prof. medicine George Wash. Univ.; hosp. affiliations include Shady Grove Adventist Hosp., Suburban Hosp., Frederick Meml. Hosp., Calvert Meml. Hosp., Cardiovasc. Consultants; dir. cardiac catheterization lab. Wash. Adventist Hosp. Named one of Top Doctors, Washingtonian Mag., 2011. Office: Cardiovascular Consultants 7901 Maple Ave Takoma Park MD 20912 Office Phone: 301-990-0040. Office Fax: 301-891-7009.

BRILL, DAVID R., radiologist; b. Chattanooga, Tenn., Dec. 13, 1941; s. Kenneth Grey and Prisculla (Ritchie) Brill; m. Elizabeth Allen, Aug. 23, 2003. BA, Wesleyan U., 1963; MD, U. Mo., 1967. Diplomate Am. Bd. Radiology, Am. Bd. Nuc. Medicine. Intern Marion County Gen. Hosp., Indpls., 1967—68; resident Vanderbilt U., Nashville, 1968—71; instr. U. Tex. S.W. Med. Ctr., Dallas, 1971—72; chief nuc. medicine Geisinger Med. Ctr., Danville, Pa., 1972—2000; radiologist Chambersburg Imaging Assoc., Pa., 1998—. Advisor in nuc. medicine Pa. Blue Shield, Camp Hill, 1989—. Contbr. articles to profl. jours., chpts. to books, exhibits. Clk. of session Grove Presbyn. Ch., Danville, 1988—93. Fellow: Am. Coll. Nuc. Medicine, Am. Coll. Nuc. Physicians (pres. 1996), Am. Coll. Radiology (chmn. com. on nuc. medicine stds. 1993—98); mem.: Pa. Radiol. Soc. (pres. 1997—98), Soc. Nuc. Medicine (ho. dels. 2000—04). Presbyterian. Avocation: birdwatching. Office: Chambersburg Imaging Assocs 25 Penncraft Ave Chambersburg PA 17202 Home: 828 Southern Fifth St Chambersburg PA 17201

BRILL, JANET BOND, nutritionist, educator; b. NYC, Sept. 15, 1957; d. Alma Halbert and Rudolph Richard Bond; m. Samuel Brill, June 10, 1984; children: Rachel Alana, Mia Alexandra, Jason Louis. MS in Edn., U. Miami, Fla., 1986; MS in Dietetics, Nutrition, Fla. Internat. U., 1992; PhD in Exercise Phisiology, U. Miami, Fla., 2000. Cert. Exercise Test Technologist Am. Coll. Sports Medicine, 1986, registered Dietitian Am. Dietetic Assn., 1994, cert. personal trainer Nat. Strength and Conditioning Assn., 2003; specialist in sports dietetics. Nutritionist, pvt. practice, Coral Springs, Fla., 1992—2009; adj. prof. U. Miami, Coral Gables, Fla., 2000—; dir. Nutrition for Fitness Together Franchise Corp. Freelance nutrition cons., 1994—. Author: (books) Cholesterol Down, Blood Pressure Down, Prevent A Second Heart Attack; contbr. articles to profl. jours. Mem.: Weight Mgmt. Practice Group (founding mem.), Sports and Cardiovasc. Nutritionists Practice Group, N.Am. Assn. for the Study of Obesity, Am. Dietetic Assn., Am. Coll. Sports Medicine, Alpha Epsilon Delta Honor Soc., Golden Key Honor Soc., Phi Kappa Phi Honor Soc. Avocations: marathon running, weight training, pesco-vegetarianism. Office Phone: 484-924-8696. Personal E-mail: janet@drjanet.com.

BRILL, KRISTIN L., surgeon; MD, MCP Hahnemann U. Diplomate Am. Bd. Surgery. Intern NY Methodist Hosp., resident; fellow Columbia Presbyn. Med. Ctr., Am. Coll. of Surgeons, Soc. of Surg. Oncology, Am. Coll. of Surg. Oncology Group, Am. Soc. of Clin. Oncology; program dir. the Janet Knowles breast cancer ctr. Cooper Univ. Hosp; dir. sect. of breast surgery dept. of surgery Cooper Univ. Hosp. Named Top Doc, SJ Mag., 2010, 2011, Phila. Mag., 2011, Readers Pick, S. Jersey Mags., Top Physicians for Women. Office: Cooper University Hospital One Cooper Plaza Camden NJ 08103 Office Phone: 856-342-2000.

BRILL, PAULA WOLFE, radiologist, educator; b. NYC, May 12, 1938; MD, Cornell U., 1962. Cert. Am. Bd. Pediat., 1970, Am. Bd. Radiology, 1971. Intern pediat. Bronx Mcpl. Hosp. Ctr., NY, 1962—63; resident radiology NY Hosp., 1966—68, resident pediat., 1968—71, attending radiologist, 1989; fellowship Cornell U., 1970—71; prof. radiology Cornell U. Med. Coll., 1989; sect. chief pediat. radiology, chair Radiology Quality Assurance Com. Weill Cornell Med. Coll., prof. radiology; attending radiologist NY-Presbyn. Hosp.-Weill Cornell Ctr., prof. radiology in pediat. Mem. med. adv. bd. Kathryn and Alan C. Greenberg Ctr. for Skeletal Dysplasias, Hosp. for Special Surgery. Co-author: Bone Dysplasias: An Atlas of Genetic Disorders of Skeletal Development; contbr. articles to med. jours. Recipient Prize in Diagnostic Radiology, Radiol. and Med. Physics Soc. of NY, 1971. Fellow: Am. Coll. Radiology, Am. Acad. Pediat. Office: NY Hosp-Cornell Med Ctr 525 E 68th St New York NY 10021 Office Phone: 212-746-2554. Office Fax: 212-746-0138. E-mail: brill@med.cornell.edu.

BRILLIANT, LARRY (LAWRENCE BRENT BRILLIANT), preventive medicine physician, entrepreneur; b. May 5, 1944; m. Girija Brilliant; children: Joe, Jon, Iris. Student, U. Mich.; MD, Wayne State U., 1969; MPH, U. Mich., 1977; DSc (hon.), Knox Coll., 2004. Cert. Preventive Medicine and Pub. Health. Med. officer, smallpox eradication and epidemiol. adv. Inter Country Team WHO (regional office-South East Asia, New Delhi), 1973—77; asst. prof., Internat. Health and Epidemiology, Sch. Pub. Health U. Mich., 1977—80, assoc. prof., dept. epidemiology, Sch. Pub. Health, 1981—88; co-founder, CEO The WELL (Whole Earth 'Lectronic Link), 1985—; co-founder, chair Seva Found., Berkeley, 1979, bd. dir., 1979—; mem. GBN network; exec. dir., chief philanthropy evangelist Google.org, 2006—09, advisor, 2009—; pres. Skoll Global Threats Fund, 2009—. Co-founder, CEO of a series of tech.-based companies Network Technologies Inc. and SoftNet Systems; co-founder, CEO Cometa Networks (joint venture with AT&T, IBM and Intel), 2004; epidemiologist, survey mgr. WHO Prevention of Blindness Prog., Katmandu, Nepal, 1980—81; staff mem. global commn. to certify smallpox eradicated in Burma, India, Nepal and Iran WHO, last med. officer to visit Iran in search of hidden smallpox; vol. first responder for smallpox bioterrorism response effort Ctrs. for Disease Control; bd. dirs. The Skoll Fund, 2009—; spkr. in field. Contbr. articles to profl. jours.; co-author: The Management of Smallpox Eradication in India, 1985; co-author: (with R.P. Pokhrel, N. Grasset, G. Brilliant) The Epidemiology of Blindness in Nepal, 1988; author: Boffa Newsletters. Bd. dir. Wavy Gravy Camp Winnarainbow; volunteered in Sri Lanka for tsunami relief, 2005; worked in India with WHO polio eradication program; established Pandefense; mem. Dean's adv. bd. Berkeley Sch. Pub. Health; mem. adv. bd. Grateful Dead-created Rex Found., Presidio World Coll. MBA program in sustainable bus., Future in Review (FiRe). Recipient Best Online Pub. award for WELL, Computer Press Assn., 1990, several awards from WHO and Govt. India for work in smallpox eradication, Peacemaker prize, Ctr. for Peace and Conflict Resolution, Wayne State U., Detroit, 2005, Ted prize (awards-a wish to change the world), 2006; named Internat. Pub. Health Hero, U. Calif., Berkeley Sch. Pub. Health; named one of the 100 Most Influential People in the World, TIME mag., 2008. Achievements include helping manage the WHO smallpox eradication program in South Asia; served as physician to members of the Grateful Dead. Office: Skoll Global Threats Fund c/o Skoll Found 250 University Ave Ste 200 Palo Alto CA 94301 Office Phone: 650-331-1031. Office Fax: 650-331-1033.

BRILLON, DAVID J., endocrinologist; MD, Brown U. Diplomate endocrinology, diabetes and metabolism, Am. Bd. of Internal Medicine. Intern Rochester Gen. Hosp., resident; fellow Univ. Calif. San Diego Med. Ctr.; prof. clin. medicine Weill Cornell Med. Coll.; attending physician NY Presbyn. Hosp. Office: NewYork-Presbyterian Columbia University Medical Center 622 West 168th St New York NY 10032 Office Phone: 212-305-2500.

BRIM, ORVILLE GILBERT, JR., former foundation administrator, writer; b. Elmira, NY, Apr. 7, 1923; s. Orville G(ilbert) and Helen (Whittier) B.; m. Kathleen J. Vigneron, May 30, 1944; children: John G., Scott W., Margaret L., Sarah M. BA, Yale U., 1947, MA, 1949, PhD in Sociology, 1951. Instr. sociology U. Wis., 1952-53, asst. prof., 1953-55; sociologist Russell Sage Found., NYC, 1955-64, asst. sec., 1959-64, pres., 1964-72, trustee, 1964-72, cons., 1972-74; pres. Found. for Child Devel., 1974-85; mem. core study group MacArthur Found. Rsch. Program Successful Aging, 1985-89; dir. MacArthur Found. Rsch. Network on Successful Mid Life Devel., 1989—2002; pres. Life Trends, Inc., 1991—2002; vis. scholar Russell Sage Found., 1985-86; interim pres. Social Sci. Rsch. Coun., 1998-99. Vice chmn. Am. Inst. for Rsch., 1971-88, chmn. 1988-91; chmn. bd. dirs. Automation Engring. Lab., 1959-67; dir. Consumer Behavior, Inc., 1957-61; chmn. environ. panel U.S. Office Edn., 1962-64; mem. drug rsch. bd. NAS., 1964-66, adv. com. on child devel., 1971-76; mem. mental health tng. com. NIMH, 1959-62; chmn. commn. social scis. NSF, 1968-69; nat. adv. food and drug coun. HEW, 1967-69; chmn. com. on work and personality in mid. years Social Sci. Rsch. Coun., 1972-79; trustee Found. for Child Devel., 1972-85, Ctr. for Creative Leadership, 1972-78, Mental Health Law Project, 1973-77, William T. Grant Found., 1975-84, Greenwich Hosp., 1972-77 Author: Sociology and the Field of Education, 1958, Education for Child Rearing, 1959, Personality and Decision Processes, 1962, Intelligence: Perspectives 1965, 1966, Socialization after Childhood: Two Essays, 1966, American Beliefs and Attitudes Toward Intelligence, 1969, The Dying Patient, 1970, Learning to Be Parents, 1980, Ambition: How We Manage Success and Failure Throughout Our Lives, 1992; editor: Lifespan Development and Behavior, Vol. 2-6, 1979-83, Constancy and Change in Human Development, 1980, How Healthy Are We? A Nat. Study of Well-Being at Midlife, 2004, Look At Me: The Fame Motive From Childhood to Death, 2009; cons. editor Child Devel., 1958-61, Sociology of Edn., 1963-69, Sociometry, 1959-62; mem. publ. com. The Public Interest, 1967-75. Served as 1st lt. USAAF, 1943-46. Recipient Wilbur Lucius Cross medal Yale Grad. Sch. Assn., 1975; Kurt Lewin Meml. award Soc. Psychol. Study Social Issues, 1979, Disting. Career Contbns. to the Sci. Study of Life Span Devel., Soc. for the Study of Human Devel., 2005. Fellow APA, AAAS, Am. Sociol. Assn., Am. Acad. Arts and Scis., Am. Orthopsychiat. Assn. (pres. 1974-75), Ea. Sociol. Soc. (pres. 1971-72); mem. Inst. Medicine of NAS, Soc. Rsch. Child Devel. (Disting. Sci. Contbns. award, 1985).

BRINDHABAN, AJIT, medical physicist, educator; b. Jaffna, Sri Lanka, Apr. 5, 1963; s. Selvadurai and Sivam Selvaratnam; m. Tracey Anne Horscroft, Jan. 26, 2001; 1 child, Abhishek Selvaratnam. BSc with honors, U. Jaffna, 1986; PhD, U. Auckland, 1992. Asst. lectr. U. Jaffna, 1987—88; rsch. & tchg. fellow U. Auckland, New Zealand, 1988—93; physicist Palmerston North Hosp., New Zealand, 1993—95; lectr. Universal Coll. Learning, Palmerston North, 1995—2001; assoc. prof. Kuwait U., 2001—. Chmn. Bloomfield Cricket Club, Palmerston North, 1995—2001. Mem.: European Congress Radiology (corr.), Am. Assn. Physics in Med. (corr.), Australasian Coll. Phys. and Engring. Sci. in Medicine (assoc.). Hindu. Achievements include research in Medical Imaging & Radiation Dose. Avocations: cricket, rugby, travel. Office: Kuwait University Dept Radiologic Scis PO Box 31470 Sulaibikhat Kuwait 90805 Kuwait

BRINDIS, RALPH, cardiologist, consultant, medical educator; b. New Brunswick, NJ, May 20, 1949; s. Bernard and Lenore Brindis; m. Claire Brindis, Dec. 17, 1972; children: Seth, Daniel. BS, MIT, Cambridge, Mass., 1971; MPH, UCLA, 1972; MD, Emory U., Atlanta, 1977. Cert. internal medicine Am. Bd. Internal Medicine, 1980, cardiovascular disease Am. Bd. Internal Medicine, 1983, interventional cardiology Am. Bd. Internal Medicine, 1999. Med. resident U. Calif., San Francisco, 1977—80, chief med. resident, 1980—81, cardiology fellow, 1981—83; staff cardiologist San Francisco Kaiser, 1983—2004; sr. advisor cardiovasc. disease No. Calif. Kaiser Permanente, Oakland, 2003—. Pres. and gov. Calif. chpt. Am. Coll. Cardiology, 1997—2000; clin. prof. medicine U. Calif., San Francisco, 1998—; chief cardiac svc. line and asst. physician in chief San Francisco Kaiser, 1999—2003; bd. trustees Am. Coll. Cardiology, Bethesda, Md., 2001—, chair strategic quality directions com., 2001—; chair Nat. Cardiovasc. Data Registry Am. Coll. Cardiology, 2003—, chief med. officer, 2004. Contbr. scientific papers. Pres. San Francisco chpt. Am. Heart Assn., 1991—92. Recipient Henry J. Kaiser award, U. Calif. San Francisco Sch. Medicine, 1989, Vol. of Yr. award (Calif. chpt.), Am. Coll. Cardiology, 1999, Prof. Medicine Tchr. of Yr. award, Assn. Clin. Faculty U. Calif. San Francisco, 1999; named John J. Sampson Exemplary Vol. of Yr., Am. Heart Assn. (San Francisco chpt.), 1993; named one of Am. Top Doctors Cardiovasc. Disease, 2001—06. Mem.: Alpha Omega Alpha, Delta Omega. Achievements include development of national cardiovascular data registry. Office: Oakland Kaiser Permanente Medical Center Hospital Bldg 2nd fl 280 West MacArthur Blvd Oakland CA 94611 Office Fax: 510-752-7456. Business E-Mail: ralph.brindis@kp.org.

BRINEY, ALLAN KING, retired radiologist; b. Wilkinsburg, Pa., Nov. 17, 1921; s. Alonzo Tripp and Helen Marie (Hardman) B.; m. Gayle Diane Briney, July 4, 1986; children: Ronald A., Nancy E., Barbara A., Douglas C. BS summa cum laude, U. Pitts., 1943, MD, 1945. Diplomate Am. Bd. Radiology; lic. real estate salesperson Ariz. Intern Pitts. Hosp., 1945-46; fellow in radiology Hosp. U. Pa., Phila., 1948-51; radiologist Topeka Med. Ctr., 1951-53, Murphy Meml. Hosp., Whittier, Calif., 1953-62, Whittier Radiology Med. Group, 1953-94, Memrad Med. Group, Whittier, 1995-97; chief of staff Presbyn. Intercommunity Hosp., Whittier, 1979, radiologist, 1959-97; ret., 1997. Capt. USAF, 1946-48. Fellow Am. Coll. Radiology. Libertarian. Deist. Avocations: skiing, bicycling, hiking, swimming, sailing. Home: 220 Cayuse Trl Sedona AZ 86336-9797 Personal E-mail: allanbriney@yahoo.com.

BRINKER, ALEXANDER, biologist, researcher; b. Vechta, Germany, Jan. 22, 1973; s. Reinhard and Hedwig Brinker; m. Anne Kuhlmann; 1 child, lilith Josefine. Degree in Biology, Albert Ludwigs U., Freiburg, 2000; Dr. rer. nat. summa cum laude, U. Constance, Konstanz, Germany, 2005. Rsch. assoc. Limnological Inst., Konstanz, 2001; rschr. Fishery Rsch. Sta., Langenargen, Germany, 2001—03, project leader aquaculture rsch., 2004—. Contbr. articles to profl. jours. Recipient Förderpreis, Verband Deutscher Fischereiverwaltungsbeamter und Fischereiwissenschaftler e.V., 2005, Environment Philosophy prize, Landesbausparkasse, 2006. Mem.: European Aquaculture Soc., European Assn. Fish Pathologists, Aquacultural Engring. Soc. (bd. dirs.), Am. Fisheries Soc. (Best Paper award 2006). Achievements include patents pending for method and feed for reduction of the content of undesired nutrients in the water discharged from a fish farm. Avocation: fly fishing. Office: Fishery Research Station Argenweg 50-1 88085 Langenargen Baden-Württemberg Germany Office Fax: 0049 7543 9308 20. Business E-Mail: alexander.brinker@lhzbw.bwl.de.

BRINKER, NANCY GOODMAN, foundation administrator, former ambassador; b. Peoria, Ill., Dec. 6, 1946; d. Marvin L. & Eleanor (Newman) Goodman; m. Robert Leitstein (div. 1978); 1 child, Eric Blake; m. Norman E. Brinker, Feb. 14, 1981 (div. 2001) B in Sociology, U. Ill., 1968; PhD (hon.), Southern Meth. U. Founder, CEO Susan G. Komen Breast Cancer Found., 1982—; founder edn. and fundraising event Susan G. Komen Race for the Cure, 1983—; founder, chair, CEO In Your Corner, Inc., 1994—98; US amb. to Hungary US Dept. State, Budapest, 2001—03, chief of protocol Washington, 2007—09. Spkr. in field; advocate for women's health issues in Congress; collaborating ptnr., Nat. Dialogue on Cancer; bd. dirs. LHC Group, Inc., 2006- Co-author: (with Catherine McEvily Harris) The Race Is Run One Step at a Time: Every Woman's Guide to Taking Charge of Breast Cancer and My Personal Struggle, 1995, (with Chriss Anne Winstone) Winning the Race: Taking Charge of Breast Cancer, 2001, (with Joni Rodgers) Promise Me: How A Sister's Love Launched the Global Movement to End Breast Cancer, 2010; articles published in nat. and internat. media. Bd. dirs. Physicians Reliance Network, Harvard Sch. Pub. Health, NYU Med. Sch. Found., Nat. Surg. Adjuvant Breast Project, Susan Komen Breast Cancer Found., Palm Beach Fellowship of Christians and Jews, Manpower, Inc., 2004-, US Oncology, Inc., Netmarket, Inc., Meditrust Corp.; mem. Nat. Cancer Adv. Bd.; bd. govs. Nat. Jewish Coalition.; mem. adv. bd. Harvard Ctr. for Cancer Prevention, Women's Health Initiative, Nat. Coalition of Cancer Suvivorship, Nat. Cancer Inst. Recipient Jefferson award for Hero award Coping Mag., 1996, Pub. Svc. award Oncology Nursing Soc., 1996, Greatest Pub. Svc. by a Pvt. Citizen, American Inst. Pub. Svc., 1997, Lifetime Achievement award Nat. Breast Cancer Awareness Month, 1997, Albert Einstein's Sarnoff Vol. award, Humanitarian of Yr. award Mt. Sinai, James Ewing Layman's award, Soc. Surg. Oncology, Humanitarian of Yr. award Rep. Women's Leadership Forum, Healthcare Humanitarian award, Global Conf. Inst., Tex. Gov. award, outstanding nat. svc., the first Salomon Smith Barney Extraordingary Achievement award, Champion of Prevention award, Nat. Found. for Ctrs. for Disease Control, internat. achievements in support of breast cancer rsch., Sword of Ignatius Loyola award, St. Louis Univ., Spl. Recognition award, Am. Soc. Clin. Oncology, Caring award, 1999, Cino del Duca award, 2000, Toastmasters Internat. Top Five Speakers award, 2001, Lifetime Achievement award, Sisters Network, 2001, Mary Woodward Lasker Pub. Svc. award in Support of Med. Rsch. & the Health Sciences, Lasker Found., 2005, Global Pathfinder award, Am. Soc. Breast Disease, 2006; named EVIE Profl. of the Yr., Profl. & Bus. Forum, 2005, Centennial Medal for Disting. Pub. Svc., American Assn. Cancer Rsch., 2007, Presdl. Medal of Freedom, The White House, 2009; named one of The 100 Most Important Women of 20th Century, Ladies Home Jour., 25 Most Powerful Women in America, Biography Mag., Top 10 Champions of Women's Health, Ladies Home Jour., 100 Most Influential People in the World, TIME mag., 2008; named to Cancer Rsch. and Treatment Fund, Inc. Cancer Survivors Hall of Fame. Office: Susan G Komen Breast Cancer Foundation PO Box 650309 Dallas TX 75265-0309 *

BRINKMAN, MICHAEL OWEN, health care consultant, educator; b. Chgo., May 15, 1936; s. Adam John and Alice Corrine (Davies) B.; m. Mary Judith Zeitz, Jan. 18, 1958; children: Stephen, Daniel, Julie, Amy, Carl, Mary Alice. BEE magna cum laude, Marquette U., 1958. Instr. Marquette U., Milw., 1957-59; engr. Wis. Electric Power, Milw., 1958-59, A.C. Electronics, Oak Creek, Wis., 1959-62; svc. engr. Nuclear-Chgo. Corp., Des Plaines, Ill., 1962-63, dir. of svc., 1963-66, plant mgr., 1966-67; gen. mgr. Electrovac, Melrose Park, Ill., 1968; mktg. analyst A.C. Electronics, Oak Creek, Wis., 1969-70; pres. On-Call Nat., Barrington, Ill., 1970-72, Hosp. Maintenance Cons., Columbus, Wis., 1972—. Co-author: (books) Clinical Engineering, 1975, Managing Your Medical Equipment, 1978, 82; contbr. numerous articles to profl. jours. Dep. committeeman Schaumburg Twp. Rep., Hoffman Estates, Ill., 1964-67; supt. Country Christian Schs., Nashotah, Wis., 1978-90, bd. dirs., 1990-95; bd. dirs. Victory Christian H.S., Neosho, Wis., 1991-2003, vol. tchr., 1991-2005; mem. Oconomowoc Bible Fellowship, elder, 1996—. Mem. Med. Equipment Repair Assocs. (exec. dir. 1973—), Triangle Fraternity, Eta Kappa Nu, Pi Mu Epsilon, Tau Beta Pi, Alpha Sigma Nu. Avocations: bible teaching, golf, stamp collecting/philately, antique glassware. Home: 443 W Prairie St Columbus WI 53925-1349 Office: Hosp Maintenance Cons Inc PO Box 309 Columbus WI 53925-0309 Office Phone: 920-623-4481. Personal E-mail: mobrinkman@sbcglobal.net. Business E-Mail: mbrinkman@meraserv.net.

BRINSON, MONICA EVETTE, mental health specialist, pharmaceutical sales representative; b. Hackensack, NJ, Feb. 19, 1971; d. Attichous and Gladys Brinson. BA, Rowan U., 1994; MBA student, Centenary Coll. Lic. health and life ins. Acct. exec. Total Media, Hackensack, NJ, 1994—98; ins. sales rep. Aetna U.S. Health Care, Fairfield, NJ, 1998—99; profl. sales rep. Solvay Pharms., mental health specialist. Contbr. articles to profl. publs. Mem.: NJ Assn. Women Bus. Owners, Women in Careers, Delta Zeta. Avocations: travel, golf, running, writing. Office: Sanofi-Synthelabo Pharms 90 Park Ave New York NY 10016 Home: Unit 1H 3050 Edwin Ave Fort Lee NJ 07024-3628 Personal E-mail: monbri201@aol.com.

BRINSTER, RALPH LAWRENCE, biologist, educator; BS, Rutgers U., New Brunswick, NJ, 1953; VMD, U. Pa., 1960, PhD in Physiology, 1964; MD (hon.), U. Basque Country, Spain, 1994; DSc (hon.), Rutgers U., 2000. Postdoc. fellow Jackson Lab., Bar Harbor, Maine, 1960; tchg. fellow dept. physiology U. Pa. Sch. Medicine, Phila., 1961-64, instr., 1964-65; asst. to assoc. prof. physiology U. Pa. Sch. Vet. Medicine, 1965-70, dir. Reproductive Physiology Training Prog., 1968—83, dir. Vet. Med. Scientist Training Prog., 1969—84, prof. physiology Sch. Vet. Medicine, 1970—, Richard King Mellon prof. reproductive physiology, 1975—; co-dir. Inst. Regenerative Medicine U. Pa., 2007—08. Lectr. Harvey Soc., NYC, 1984, Juan March Found., Madrid, 1992. Contbr. articles to profl. jours. Recipient Disting. Svc. award, USDA, 1989, Pioneer award, Internat. Embryo Transfer Soc., 1992, Charles-Leopold Mayer prize, French Acad. Scis., 1994, March of Dimes prize in devel. biology, 1996, Bower prize for achievement in sci., Franklin Inst., 1997, John Scott award for sci. achievement, City Trusts Phila., 1997, Pioneer in Reproduction Rsch. award, Nat. Inst. Child Health & Human Devel., 1998, George Hammel Cook Disting. Alumni award, Rutgers U., 1999, Ernst W. Bertner award, U. Tex. M.D. Anderson Cancer Ctr., 2001, Wolf Found. prize in medicine, Israel, 2003, Gairdner Found. Internat. award, 2006. Fellow: AAAS, Am. Acad. Microbiology, Am. Acad. Arts. & Scis.; mem.: AVMA, NAS, Great Britain Soc. Study Fertility, Am. Psychol. Soc., Am. Soc. Cell Biology, Soc. Study Reproduction (Carl Hartman award 1997), Inst. Medicine, Sigma Xi, Phi Zeta. Office: U Pa Sch Vet Medicine 3850 Baltimore Ave Philadelphia PA 19104 Office Phone: 215-898-8805. Office Fax: 215-898-0667.

BRINT, STEPHEN, ophthalmologist; b. Shreveport, La., Sept. 17, 1946; MD, Tulane U. Sch. Medicine, 1972. Physician Singer Brint Custom Vision, 1977—. Assoc. clin. prof. dept. ophthalmology Tulane U. Sch. Medicine, 1990—. Named one of Am.'s Best Drs., Castle Connolly. Fellow: Am. Coll. Ophthalmic Surgery, Am. Acad. Ophthalmology; mem.: Am. Soc. Cataract and Refractive Surgery. Avocations: classical music, travel. Home: 625 St Charles Ave Apt 10D New Orleans LA 70130 Personal E-mail: brintmd@aol.com.

BRIONES, DANIEL, dentist, surgeon; b. Santiago, Chile, June 28, 1977; s. Luis Briones and Gerda Sindermann. DDS, U. Mayor, Santiago, 2002, student in Oral and Maxillofacial Surgery, 2005—. Lic. in odontolog. scis. U. Major, 2002. Asst. U. Mayor, 2002—04, asst. prof., 2005—07, faculty, 2007—. Contbr. articles to profl. jours. Prayer group leader Cath. Ch., Santiago, 2002—07. Named Best Mountaneer, U. Mayor, 2002. Mem.: German Mountaneering Club (assoc.). Roman Catholic. Avocations: mountain climbing, skiing, ice climbing, soccer. Office: Univ Mayor Faculty Dentistry Av Libertador Bernardo O'Higgins 2013 Santiago Chile Home: La Gloria 115 LC, Dpto 803 7560936 Sauhajo Chile Office Phone: 5622336805. Office Fax: 3281000. Personal E-mail: dla.briones@gmail.com.

BRISCO, ELISE, optometrist; BA in Econs., U. Of So. Calif., LA, 1984; BS in Visual Sci., So. Calif. Coll. Of Optometry, LA, 1986, O.D. with distinction, 1988. Pvt. practice Hollywood Vision Ctr., West Hollywood, Calif., 1988—; clin. instr. So. Calif. Coll. Of Optometry, LA, Calif., 1995—2000; med. staff Cedars Sinai Med. Ctr., LA, 1995—; optometrist Moore White Med. Ctr., LA, 1991—92; team optometrist Mighty Ducks of Anaheim, Anaheim, Calif., 1993—96, Long Beach Ice Dogs, Calif., 1995—2002, LA Galaxy, LA, 1997—99; low vision cons. Ctr. for Partially Blind, Santa Monica, Calif., 1988—92. State dir. of comm. Calif. Optometric Assn., LA, 2000—. Contbr. articles to profl. jours. Recipient Optometric Recognition, Am. Optometric Assn., 1993; named Young Optometrist of Yr., 1996, 1992. Home: 955 Carrillo Dr Ste 105 Los Angeles CA 90048-5400 E-mail: hollywood_vision@yahoo.com.

BRISSETT, ANTHONY, plastic surgeon; b. Ont., Can., Nov. 6, 1967; BSc, Wayne State U., 1992, MD, 1996. Dir. facial plastic and reconstructive surgery Baylor Coll. Medicine, 2003—. Fellow: ACS. Office: 6500 Fannin St Ste 1701 Houston TX 77030 Business E-Mail: brisett@bcm.edu.

BRISTOW, CYNTHIA LYNN, immunologist; b. Altus, Okla., Aug. 19, 1951; d. Robert O'Neil Bristow and Gaylon Eva Walker; children: Charlie, Bo, Rachel, Mary Ann, Rudy. BA, Winthrop U., 1972; MS, Med. U. SC, Charleston, 1979, PhD, 1986. Postdoctoral assoc. biochemistry Med. U. SC, Charleston, 1986-88; postdoctoral assoc. dental rsch. ctr. U. NC, Chapel Hill, 1988-94, rsch. asst. prof., 1994-98; clin. immunologist pathology and lab. medicine U. NC Hosp., Chapel Hill, 1999-2001; faculty cellular physiology and immunology Rockefeller U., NYC, 2001—03; asst. prof. dept medicine Mount Sinai Sch. Medicine, NYC, 2003—08, dir. rsch. Inst Human Genetics and Biochemistry, 2003—; asst. prof. dept immunology and medicine Weill Cornell Med. Coll. Contbr. articles to profl. jours., chapters to books. Recipient Elsa Pardee Found. award, 1990; grantee, NIH, 1994. Mem.: NY Acad. Sci., Assn. Med. Lab. Immunologists, Am. Diabetes Assn., Am. Chem. Soc., Am. Assn. Immunologists, Am. Soc. Microbiology, Sigma Xi. Achievements include patents for biotechnology. Avocations: running, music, poetry, art, tennis. Office: 310 E 67 th St New York NY 10021 Home: 27 Vanderbilt Pkwy Dix Hills NY 11746 Home Phone: 917-301-3292; Office Phone: 646-962-2929. Business E-Mail: cyb2005@med.cornell.edu.

BRITTAIN, JAMES EDWARD, science and technology educator, researcher; b. Mills River, NC, May 20, 1931; s. Randall Francis and Velma Hassie (Gillespie) B.; m. Louise Mary Lambert, March 29, 1969 (dec. Mar. 27, 1972); m. Jo Ann Layne, Apr. 14, 1973. BS, Clemson U., 1957; MS, U. Tenn., 1959; MA, Case Western Res. U., 1969, PhD, 1970. Jr. rsch. engr. U. Tenn., Knoxville, 1958-59; asst. prof. elec. engring. Clemson (S.C.) U., 1959-66; asst. prof. history of sci. and tech. Ga. Inst. Tech., Atlanta, 1969-71, assoc. prof., 1972-91, prof., 1992-94, prof. emeritus, 1994—. Author: Engineering the New South, 1985, Alexanderson: Pioneer in American Electrical Engineering, 1992, Scanning The Past: A History of Electrical Engineering and Its Pioneers, 1999, Gun Fights, Dam Sites and Water Rights, 2001; editor: Turning Points in American Electrical History, 1977. With USAF, 1950-54. Smithsonian Instn. rsch. fellow, 1972-73; recipient rsch. contract Nat. Park Svc., 1974-75; grantee NSF, 1979. Fellow IEEE (chmn. history com. 1970-79, 88-89, assoc. editor proceedings 1990-, Centennial medal 1984), Royal Soc. Arts, Radio Club Am. (Batcher Meml. prize 1989); mem. Soc. History of Tech. (mem. exec. coun. 1978-80, 89-91, Usher prize 1971). Home: 600 Carolina Village Rd # 2509 Hendersonville NC 28792

BRITTON, CAROLYN B., neurologist, educator; MD, NYU, 1975. Resident in internal medicine Harlem Hosp., NYC, 1976—77; fellow in neurology Columbia- Presbyn. Hosp., 1981-83; assoc. prof. neurology Columbia Univ.; attendibng physician NY- Presbyn. Hosp. Office: New York- Presbyterian Hospital Room 232 710 W 168th St New York NY 10032 Office Phone: 212-305-5220. Office Fax: 212-305-4578.

BRITTON, MARK GORDON, respiratory medicine physician; b. Southampton, UK, Nov. 23, 1946; s. Gordon and Vera B.; m. Gillian Vaughan Davies, June 17, 1972; children: James, Edward, Christopher. MBBS, U. London, 1970, MSc, 1980, MD, 1983. Cons. physician St. Peter's Hosp., Chertsey, UK, 1983—. Sr. lectr. St. George's Hosp., London, 1983—, Imperial Coll., London, 2001—; hon. cons. King Edward VII Hosp., London, 1983—; chmn. Br. Lung Found., 1999—2005, council, 2005—, v.p., 2006—; mem. adv. coun. Indsl. Injuries, 2003; trustee Nat. Confidential Enquiry into Patient Outcome and Death, 2005—; vis. prof. U. Surrey, 2006—; chmn. adv. coun. PGMS, 2008—11. Fellow Royal Coll. of Physicians; mem. Am. Thoracic Soc., Br. Thoracic Soc., European Respiratory Soc. Home: Woodham House 92 Ashley Rd Walton-on-Thames Surrey KT12 1HP England Office Phone: 01932 877824. Personal E-mail: markbritton@btinternet.com. Business E-Mail: mark.britton@asph.nhs.uk.

BRITTON, SVEN FREDRIK, epidemiologist, educator; b. Dalarö, June 14, 1938; MD, Karolinska Inst., 1965, PhD, 1969. Prof. Karolinska Hosp., 1985—. Avocation: politics. Office: Karolinska Hosp Dept Infectious Diseases Solna Stockholm 17176 Sweden E-mail: sven.britton@ki.se.

BRKIC, AMILA, oral surgeon, educator; b. Livno, Bosnia-Herzegovina, Oct. 24, 1977; d. Arif and Sabira Brkic. PhD, Istanbul U., Turkey, 2009. Cert. specialist oral surgery Istanbul U., 2009. Rsch. asst., dept. oral and maxillofacial surgery Istanbul U., Turkey, 2005—09; asst. prof., oral surgery and dental implantology Sarajevo U., Bosnia-Herzegovina, 2009—. Home: Fra Andjela Zvizdovica 8 Sarajevo 71000 Bosnia-Herzegovina Office: Sarajevo University Faculty Dentistry Bolnicka Sarajevo 71000 Bosnia-Herzegovina Personal E-mail: amilabrkic@hotmail.com.

BRO, WILLIAM PRICE, medical association administrator; b. Evanston, Ill., Apr. 7, 1946; s. Kenneth Arthur and Patricia (Welch) B.; m. Johanna Ellen Hintze, Apr. 9, 1986; children: Ellen Price, John Kenneth. BS in Bus. Mgmt. with honors, U. Phoenix, 1998. Licensed 1st class radiotelephone, FCC. Meteorologist WISN-TV, Milw., 1968-69; ops. mgr. WXCL Radio, Peoria, Ill., 1969-80; pres. Broadcast Assoc., Inc., Springfield, Ill., 1980-82, PSR Corp., Peoria, 1982-94; news anchor WHOI-TV, Peoria, 1984; pres. High Point Group, Inc., Peoria, 1994—2002; pres., CEO Kidney Cancer Found., Evanston, Ill., 2002—. Advisor minority-owned radio, Peoria, 1993-96. Co-author (radio play) Peoria's War of the Worlds, 1972; author (text) How to Become an Announcer, 1973. Mem. Rep. Nat. Com., 1995-96; treas. pack 4 Cub Scouts Am., Peoria, 1996; mem. bd. Peoria Civic Opera, 1983-84; chmn. Nat. Kidney Cancer Assn., 1998—; exec. com. Ill. Valley Power Squadron, 1998—. Recipient Past Pres.'s award Peoria Heights C. of C., 1991. Mem. Peoria Radio Orgn. (founding mem.), Exptl. Aircraft Assn., Aircraft Owners and Pilots Assn., Cherokee Pilots' Assn., Rotary Club Peoria-North (sec. 1991-92), Willow Knolls Country Club (bd. dirs. 1998), Phi Theta Kappa. Republican. Unitarian Universalist. Avocations: flying, camping, boating. Office: Kidney Cancer Found Ste 203 1234 Sherman Ave Evanston IL 60202 *

BROADBERRY, RICHARD EDWARD, training services executive, biomedical scientist; b. Dublin, May 18, 1953; s. Noel Edward and Mabel Doreen Broadberry; m. Margaret Anne Hayward, Dec. 15, 1990; children: Amy Grace, Isobel Grace, Cornelia Grace. Sr. biomed. scientist Wessex Regional Transfusion Ctr., Southampton, England, 1973—78, 1991—93, Royal Bournemouth Hosp., England, 1998—2000, Southampton U. Hosps. NHS Trust, 2000—05; chief technologist Mennonite Christian Hosp., Hualien, Taiwan, 1979—83; assoc. rsch. fellow Mackay Meml. Hosp., Taipei, Taiwan, 1983—90, 1993—97; tech. advisor Tianjin Blood Ctr., China, 1997—98; dir. tng. Safe Blood China Found., Beijing, 2005—06; biomed. scientist Royal Hampshire County Hosp., 2006—. Assoc. prof. Yang Ming Med. Coll., Taipei, 1993—97. Author: God's Promise to the Chinese, The Beginning of Chinese Characters. Inst. Med. Lab. Scis. fellow, Portsmouth Polytech., 1973—77. Avocations: sports, music, films, travel, church activities. Home Phone: 441794389255. E-mail: broadiesrus@yahoo.co.uk.

BROADNAX, WALTER DOYCE, former academic administrator, educator; b. Starcity, Ark., Oct. 21, 1944; s. Walter and Mary Lee (Cotton) B.; m. Angel LaVerne Wheelock; 1 child, Andrea Alyce. BA, Washburn U., 1967; MPA, Kans. U., 1969; PhD, Syracuse U., 1975; Hon. Degrees, Washburn U., Topeka; Hon. Degree, Ctrl. State U. Ohio; degree (hon.), Kans. Wesleyan U., 2008. Dir. Svc. Children, Youth and Adults, Kans., 1979-80; prin. dep. asst. sec. US Dept. HHS, Washington, 1980-81, dep. sec., 1993-96; lectr. pub. mgmt. and pub. policy John F. Kennedy sch. govt. Harvard U., 1981-87, dir. innovations state and local govt., 1985-87; pres. NY State Civil Svc. Commn., 1987-90; commr. NY State Dept. Civil Svc., 1987-90; pres. Ctr. Govtl. Rsch., Inc., Rochester, NY, 1990-93; prof. school of pub affairs Univ of Md, Coll. Pk., Md., 1996-99; dean Coll. Pub. Affairs Am. U., 1999—2002; pres. Clark Atlanta U., 2002—08; disting. prof. Syracuse U., 2008—. Bd. dirs. Keycorp, Medecision, Inc., CNA Corp. Contbr. articles to profl. jours. Trustee Syracuse U., Coun. Ind. Colls., Ga. Found. Ind. Colls., Atlanta Regional Coun. Higher Edn., also vice chair bd. Recipient Maxwell Sch. of Citizenship and Pub. Affairs Spirit of Pub. Svc. award. Whiting scholar Washburn U., Pioneer award, Syracuse U. Fellow Nat. Acad. Pub. Adminstrn.; pres. ASPA (Outstanding Pub. Svc. award Nat. Capital Area chpt.), Nat. Acad. Pub. Adminstrn. (Nat. Pub. Svc. award), Nat. Assn. Ind. Colls. and Univs. (trustee). Avocations: reading, jogging, music. Home: 137 Avriel Dr Fayetteville NY 13066-9250 Office: Maxwell Sch Syracuse Univ Syracuse NY 13244-1020 Office Phone: 404-880-8502. Office Fax: 404-880-8500. Business E-Mail: wbroadnax@cau.edu.

BROADWAY, JESSICA, psychiatrist, educator; b. NC, Oct. 16, 1975; MD, Med. Coll. Ohio, 2001. Asst. prof. psychiatry Med. U. SC, 2005—. Office: 67 President St Charleston SC 29425 Business E-Mail: reynol@musc.edu.

BROCHIER, MIREILLE L., cardiologist, educator; b. Algiers, Algeria, Mar. 23, 1924; arrived in France, 1962; d. Emile B. MD, U. Algiers, Algeria, 1953, U. Hosp. Tours, France, 1962. Prof. cardiology U. Hosp. Tours, 1962—92; prof. emeritus U. Tours, 1993—. Pres. French Found. Cardiology, 1981—87, French Soc. Cardiology, 1989—91. Decorated Legion d'honneur Chevalier, 1976, 2000,2008, Officer, 1987—, Ordre Nat. merit Commandeur, 1998; recipient Laennec prize French Soc. Cardiology, 2005, decorated Légion d'honneur Commandeur, 2008. Home: 2 allée François Millet Tours 37000 France Personal E-mail: mireille.brochier@wanadoo.fr.

BROCK, HELEN RACHEL MCCOY, retired mental health and community health nurse; b. Cromwell, Okla., Dec. 10, 1924; d. Samuel Robert Lee and Ire Etta (Pounds) McCoy; m. Clois Lee Brock, Sept. 29, 1963; children: Dwayne, Joyce, Peggy, Ricki, Stacey. AS, Southwestern Union Coll., Keene, Tex., 1968; BS in Nursing, Union Coll., Lincoln, Nebr., 1970; postgrad., Vernon Regional Jr. Coll., Tex., 1972—76; MPH, Loma Linda U., Calif., 1983. Cert. ARC nurse. Dir. nursing Chillicothe (Tex.) Clinic-Hosp., 1970-77, Pike County Hosp., Waverly, Ohio, 1977-79, Marion County Hosp., Jefferson, Tex., 1979-81; nurse III, nursing unit supr, patient health educator Vernon State Hosp., Maximum Security for Criminally Insane, 1981-96; retired, 1996; nurse, admissions and assessments Texhoma Community Health Svcs., 1987-94. Mem. Rep. Party. Mem.: ACLJ, ASPCA, Humane Soc, Tex. Nurses Assn. Home: PO Box 238 Chillicothe TX 79225-0238

BROCK, JOHN WILLIAM, III, surgeon, urologist, educator; b. Louisville, Apr. 13, 1952; s. John W. and Sara (Fisher) Brock; m. Lisa Ann Trusler; children: Elizabeth Draper, Grace Ann, Anna Fisher. BS, Vanderbilt U., Nashville, 1974; MD, Med. Coll. Ga., Augusta, 1978. Diplomate Am. Bd. Urology. Resident urology Vanderbilt U., Nashville, 1979—82, chief resident, 1982—83; clin. asst. prof. Vanderbilt U. Sch. Medicine, 1983—91, assoc. prof. urology, pediat., 1992—99, prof. urology, pediat., 1999—; assoc. program dir. urology residents Bapt. Hosp., Nashville, 1989—91; dir. pediat. urology Vanderbilt U. Med. Ctr., 1992—, vice-chair surg. sciences sect., 2002—; surgeon-in-chief Vanderbilt Children's Hosp., 2002—. Sr. investigator Vanderbilt Cancer Group; invited vis. prof. Baylor U., Brown U., Boston Children's, U. Calif. San Francisco, U. Colo., Germany, Egypt, Bolivia, Argentina, Columbia, Guatemala; presenter in field. Mem. editl. bd.: Internat. Pediatric Surgery, Jour. Urology, Pediatric Urology Sect., mem. exec. com.: Jour. Pediatric Urology; contbr. articles to profl. jours., chapters to books. Mem. C. of C., Nashville. Recipient Eliot V. Newman award, Vanderbilt U., 1994, 2006, Best Rsch. Trainee award, Radiology Soc. N.Am., 1994, First prize, Resident Rsch. award, Soc. Pediat. Rsch., 1997, First prize, Fellow Rsch. award, 1997; named Best Doctor in Nashville, Nashville Life, 1996; named one of Best Doctors in Nashville, 1998; grantee, NIH Ctr. Excellence in Pediatric Nephrology and Urology, 1996—, Am. Found. Urol. Disease, 1998—99; scholar, 1993, 1995. Fellow: ACS, Soc. Pediat. Urology (ex-officio bd. mem., pres.-elect 2008), Am. Acad. Pediat.; mem.: AMA, Pediatric Urology Fellowship Dirs. (pres. 2007—08), Vanderbilt Urology Soc., Urodynamics Soc., Tenn. Urol. Assn., Spina Bifida Assn., Soc. Genitourinary Reconstructive Surgery, Soc. Fetal Urology, Nashville Surg. Soc., Nashville Acad. Medicine, Mid. Tenn. Urology Soc., Davidson County Pediat. Assn., Cumberland Pediat. Found., Am. Urol. Assn. (bd. mem. southeastern sect. 2003, Frank Hinman award 2002), Am. Fertility Soc., Rotary Club, Sigma Chi. Avocations: gardening, golf, outdoor activities. Office: Vanderbilt Children's Hosp 4102 Doctors Office Tower 2200 Childrens Way Nashville TN 37232-9820 Office Phone: 615-936-1060. Office Fax: 615-936-1061. E-mail: john.brock@Vanderbilt.edu.

BROCK, JOHN WILLIAM, III, surgeon; b. Louisville, Apr. 13, 1951; BS, Vanderbilt U., 1974; MD, Med. Coll. Ga., 1978. Dir. pediat. urology Vanderbilt U. Med. Ctr., 1992, assoc. prof. urologic surgery, pediat., 1992—99, prof. pediat., 1999, prof. urologic surgery, 1999, vice-chair sect. surg. scis., 2002; surgeon-in-chief Vanderbilt Children's Hosp., 2002—. Recipient Monroe Carell Jr. Prof. award, Jr. Family & Vanderbilt U. Med. Ctr., 2010. Fellow: ACS, Soc. Pediat. Urology (pres. 2009—10), Am. Acad. Pediat.; mem.: Alpha Omega Alpha. Avocation: golf. Office: 4102 DOT Vanderbilt Children's Hosp Nashville TN 37232 Office Fax: 615-936-1590. Business E-Mail: john.brock@vanderbilt.edu.

BROCK, NORBERT, retired pharmacologist; b. Dorsten, Westfalen, Germany, May 26, 1912; s. Johannes and Franziska (Hunecke) Brock; m. Edith Hilia Priske, Dec. 22, 1944; children: Barbara-Annette, Gabriela, Jürgen, Ulrich, Stephan. Degree in medicine, U. Düsseldorf, Germany, 1935, specialist internal medicine, 1947, specialist pharmacology and toxicology, 1960; D (hon.), Tech. U. Munich, 1978. Lectr. pharmacology and toxicology U. Berlin, 1943-45; head dept. pharmacology and toxicology Asta Werke AG, Bielefeld, Germany, 1949-79, head dept. exptl. cancer rsch., 1979-82; ret., 1982. Lectr. pharmacology and biometrics U. Münster, Germany, 1951, hon. prof. pharmacology, 54. Contbr. articles to profl. jours. Recipient Johann Georg Zimmermann award, Med. Acad. Hanover, 1977, Gerhard Domagk award, U. Münster, 1977, Deutsche Therapiewoche award, 1982, Deutscher Krebspreis, 1987, Cain award, Am. Assn. Cancer Rsch., 1988, Schmiedeberg-Plakette award, German Soc. Exptl. and Clin. Pharmacology and Toxicology, 1995, Charles F. Kettering prize, GM Cancer Rsch. Found., 1995, Plaque of Honor, U. Padua, Italy, 2003, Region of Veneto, 2003; named to, Order Fed. Republic Germany, 1988. Mem.: German Cancer Soc. (hon.), German Pharmacol. Soc. (hon.). Roman Catholic. Home: Am Rehhagen 10 33619 Bielefeld Germany

BROCK, THOMAS DALE, retired microbiology professor; b. Cleve., Sept. 10, 1926; s. Thomas Carter and Helen Sophia (Ringwald) B.; m. Mary Louise Louden, Sept. 13, 1952 (div. Feb. 1971); m. Katherine [illegible] Middleton, Feb. 20, [illegible]; children: Emily Katherine, Brian Thomas. BS, Ohio State U., 1949, MS, 1950, PhD, 1952. Research microbiologist Upjohn Co., Kalamazoo, 1952-57; asst. prof. Western Res. U., Cleve., 1957-59, Ind. U., Bloomington, 1960-61, assoc. prof., 1962-64, prof., 1964-71; E.B. Fred prof. natural scis. U. Wis., Madison, 1971-90, prof. emeritus, 1990—, chmn. dept. bacteriology, 1979-82; pres. Sci. Tech. Pubs., Madison, 1990-94, Savanna Oak Found., 2000—; mgr. Pleasant Valley Conservancy State Natural Area, 2007—. Found. for Microbiology lectr., 1971-72, 78-79 Author: Milestones in Microbiology, 1961, Principles of Microbial Ecology, 1966, Thermophilic Microorganisms, 1978, Biology of Microorganism, 7th edit., 1994, Basic Microbiology with Applications, 3d edit., 1986, A Eutrophic Lake, 1985, Thermophiles: General, Molecular and Applied Microbiology, 1986, Robert Koch: A Life in Medicine and Bacteriology, 1988, The Emergence of Bacterial Genetics, 1990, Shorewood Hills: An Illustrated History, 1999. Recipient Rsch. Career Devel. award NIH, 1962-68, Waksman award Soc. Indsl. Microbiology, 2003, Aldo Leopold award in Restoration Ecology, 2006, Invader Crusader award State of Wis., 2007, Cliff German award, 2009 Fellow AAAS; mem. Am. Soc. for Microbiology (hon. mem., chmn. gen. div. 1970-71, Fisher award 1984, Carski award 1988) Home and Office: 1227 Dartmouth Rd Madison WI 53705-2213

BROCK, WILLIAM ALTON, pediatric urologist; b. Bklyn., Mar. 29, 1946; s. Charles Henry and Mary (Campisi) Brock. BS, Fordham U., 1967; MMM, USC; MD, Emory U., 1971. Diplomate Am. Bd. Urology. Intern surgery N.Y. Hosp., NYC, 1971-72, resident surgery, 1972-73; resident urology U. Calif., San Diego, 1975-79; fellow pediatric urology U. Liverpool, Eng., 1979; chmn. dept. pediatric urology Children's Hosp., San Diego, 1984-85; clin. prof. urology Albert Einstein Coll. Medicine, Bronx, N.Y., 1989—; ptnr. Pediatric Urologic Assocs., San Diego, 1979-85, Pediatric Urology Assn., N.Y., 1993—; chief pediatric urology L.I. Jewish Med. Ctr., New Hyde Park, N.Y., 1985-98. Assoc. prof. urology U. Calif., San Diego, 1980-85, SUNY, Stony Brook, 1985-89; sci. advisor Nat. Kidney Found., San Diego, 1981-85; chmn. quality assurance dept. urology L.I. Jewish Med. Ctr., New Hyde Park, N.Y., 1989-92; vis. prof. Wake Forest Sch. Medicine, Winston-Salem, N.C., 1988, Ohio State U. Sch. of Medicine, 1992; clin. adj. prof. urology Cornell U. Med. Coll., 1995-98. Reviewer Jour. Urology, 1990-96; author med. textbooks; contbr. articles to profl. jours. Maj. USAF, 1973-75. Fellow ACS, Am. Acad. Pediatrics, N.Y. Acad. Medicine; mem. Soc. Pediatric Urology, Am. Urologic Assn., Pediatrics Soc. Dominican Republic (hon.). Roman Catholic. Avocations: computers, gardening, sailing, fly fishing. Office: 1999 Marcus Ave New Hyde Park NY 11042 Home: 23 Saddle Ridge Rd Gardiner MT 59030-9336 E-mail: docbrock@optonline.net.

BROCKENBROUGH, EDWIN CHAMBERLAYNE, surgeon; b. Balt., July 24, 1930; s. Edwin Chamberlayne Sr. and Martha Davis (Coale) B.; m. Jean McClure, May 4, 1968; children: John, Martha, Andrew, Ann, Susan. BA, Coll. William & Mary, 1952; MD, Johns Hopkins U., 1956. Intern Johns Hopkins Hosp., Balt., 1956-57, resident, 1957-59; sr. asst. surgeon Nat. Heart Inst., Bethesda, Md., 1959-61; chief resident surgery U. Wash., Seattle, 1961-64, faculty mem. dept. surgery, 1964-75; pvt. practice Seattle, 1975-98. Clin. prof. surgery U. Wash., 1984—; pres. King County Med. Soc., Seattle, 1992; trustee Health Resources N.W., Seattle; med. dir. Pacific Vasc. Inst., 1996—. Contbr. chpt. to book and articles to profl. jours. Sr. asst. surgeon USPHS, 1959-61. Fellow ACS (pres. Wash. State chpt. 1985), Seattle Surg. Soc. (sec. 1972); mem. North Pacific Surg. Assn. (pres.

1995-96), Pacific Coast Surg. Assn., Am. Rhododendron Soc. (pres. 1977-79, Silver medal 1985). Republican. Episcopalian. Avocations: gardening, photography, fishing. Home and Office: 3630 Hunts Point Rd Bellevue WA 98004-1114 *

BROCKMAN, LESLIE RICHARD, social worker; b. St. Paul, Aug. 10, 1940; s. Leslie Blair Brockman and Mary Emma (Miller) Hemenway; m. Rosemarie Lemus, Aug, 18, 1962; 1 child, Christopher Scott. BA, Loyola U. of L.A., 1963; MS, Troy State U., Ala., 1977; MS in Social Work, U. Tex., Arlington, 1984. Lic. profl. counselor; lic. chem. dependency counselor, marriage and family therapist; lic. clin. practitioner ACSW; diplomate clin. social work; cert. criminal justice specialist. Exec. dir. Family Assessment Consultation Therapy Svc., Ft. Worth, 1984—; commd. 2d lt. USAF, 1963, advanced through grades to maj., retired, 1983. Fellow NASW (diplomate); mem. ACA, Am. Assn. Marriage and Family Therapists, Am. Mental Health Counselors Assn., Am. Assn. Behavioral Therapists. Home: 6400 Trail Lake Dr Fort Worth TX 76133-4810 Home Phone: 817-294-1729; Office Phone: 817-913-0039. Personal E-mail: facts@sbcglobal.net. Business E-Mail: facts1@swbell.net.

BROCKMANN, HOLGER, nuclear medicine physician, researcher; b. Cologne, North Rhine-Westphalia, Germany, Apr. 2, 1973; s. Juergen and Dorit Brockmann. MD, U. Cologne, 2000. Clerkship Livingstone Hosp., Port Elisabeth, South Africa, 1999; resident Dept. Cardiology, U. Duesseldorf, Germany, 2000—04; resident, rschr. Dept. Nuc. Medicine, U. Bonn, Germany, 2004—. Contbr. scientific papers to profl. jours. Mem. Marburger Bund, Germany, 1998, Hartmann Bund, Germany, 2002. Mem.: German Soc. Nuc. Medicine. Avocations: running, golf, diving.

BROCKS, ERIC, ophthalmologist, surgeon; b. NYC, Apr. 24, 1946; s. William Benjamin and Muriel (Welk) B.; m. Irene Loretta Kraut, Dec. 19, 1970; children: Jason Matthew, Daniel Charles. BA with high honors, U. Rochester, 1968, MD, 1972. Diplomate Am. Bd. Ophthalmology, Nat. Bd. Med. Examiners. Intern medicine NYU Sch. Medicine, NYC, 1973, resident, chief resident ophthalmology, 1973-76; chief resident ophthalmology Bellevue Hosp., NYU Hosp., Manhattan VA Hosp., NYC, 1975-76; attending physician St. Francis Hosp., Beacon, NY, 1976-89; asst./assoc. attending physician Vassar Bros. Med. Ctr., Poughkeepsie, NY, 1976-80, attending physician, 1980—; clin. asst. ophthalmology Tisch (NYU) Hosp., NYC, 1976—2005; clin. asst. attending physician Bellevue Hosp. Ctr., NYC, 1976—2005; eye physician and surgeon Hudson Valley Eye Surgeons, P.C., Fishkill, NY, 1976—, pres., 2000—; med. dir. laser vision correction LCA Vision Laser Assocs., Mt. Kisco, NY, 1996—98; bd. dirs. Fishkill Ambulatory Surgical Ctr., NY, 2001—; med. dir. The Eye Inst., Vassar Brothers Med. Ctr., Fishkill, NY, 2005—; affiliate physician NY Eye Infimacy NYC, 2010—. Cons. ophthalmology Julia Butterfield Hosp., Cold Spring, NY, 1981—94, West Point Mil. Acad., Keller Army Hosp., West Point, NY, 1989—96; chief surgery St. Francis Hosp., Beacon, 1988—89, dir. ophthalmology sect., 1981—88, chief of staff, 1979—81; dir. dept. ophthalmology, mem. med exec. com. Vassar Bros. Med. Ctr., 1992—2000, 2009—, mem. peer rev. com., 1994—; clin. asst. prof. ophthalmology NYU Sch. Medicine, NYC, 1983—2005, course dir. ophthalmology elective, 1976—91; so. NY coord. Nat. Eye Care Project, San Francisco, 1985—96; adj. clin. asst. prof. ophthalmology Mt. Sinai Sch. Medicine, NYC, 1993—; mem. adv. bd. Fishkill Ambulatory Surgery Ctr., 2000—. Contbr. articles to profl. jours. Vol. admissions network U. Rochester, 1986-2000, co-chmn. 25th reunion com., 1993. Recipient 25 Yr. faculty svc. citation, NYU Sch. Medicine, 2001, Practice of Excellence, Laser Vision Ctr., 2001, 30 Yr. Svc. award, Vassar Bros. Med. Ctr., 2006, Physician honoree, 2006. Fellow ACS, Am. Acad. Ophthalmology (media coord. N.Y. state Nat. Eye Care projects 1978—, mem. pub. info. coun. 1985—, mem. refractive surgery interest group 1996—); mem. AMA, Am. Soc. Cataract and Refractive Surgery, Med. Soc. State NY (mem. ho. dels. 1984-89, 93-96, mem. subcom. officers and adminstrv. matters 1994, mem. govt. affairs subcom. 1987, mem. fed. legis. com. 1993-96), Dutchess County Med. Soc. (mem. exec. com. 1992-96, chmn. legis. liaison com. 1990-92, pres. 1990-91), Internat. Soc. Refractive Surgery, Boca West Club. Avocations: tennis, golf, reading. Office: Hudson Valley Eye Surgeons Vassar Bros Med Mall 200 Westage Bus Ctr Dr Fishkill NY 12524 Office Phone: 845-896-9280. E-mail: eyes@hves.com.

BROCKSTEIN, BRUCE, physician, educator; b. Chgo., May 16, 1964; BS, U. Ill., Urbana, 1986; MD, U. Chgo., 1990. Asst. prof. medicine U. Chgo., Hosps. and Clinics, 1996—99; divsn. head, hematology, oncology, med. dir., Evanston Kellogg Cancer Ctr. North Shore U. Health Sys., clin. assoc. prof. medicine U. Chgo., 1999—. Recipient Stephen B Weisman MD Humanitarian award, Cancer Wellness Ctr., Northbrook, Ill.; named one of Top Drs., Chgo. Mag., 2008, 2010. Mem.: Connective Tissue Oncology Soc., Am. Soc. Clin. Oncology. Avocations: running, hiking, baseball, soccer. Office: 2650 Ridge Ave # 4816 Evanston IL 60201 Office Fax: 847-570-2336. Business E-Mail: bbrockstein@northshore.org.

BROD, ROY DAVID, ophthalmologist, educator; b. Phila., Oct. 8, 1957; s. Kenneth Lester and Carlene Marcy (Chalick) B.; m. Janice Hope Prossack, May 7, 1983; children: Jamie, Rebecca. BS in Biochemistry magna cum laude, Tulane U., 1979; MD with honors, Temple U., 1983. Diplomate Am. Bd. Ophthalmology. Intern Presbyn. U. Pa. Med. Ctr., Phila., 1983-84; resident in ophtholmology La. State U. Eye Ctr., New Orleans, 1984-87; fellow in vitreoretinal Bascom Palmer Eye Inst., Miami, Fla., 1987-88; assoc. vitreoretinal surgeon Geisinger Med. Ctr., Danville, Pa., 1988-91; pvt. practice Lancaster, Pa., 1991—. Asst. prof. Thomas Jefferson U. Sch. Medicine, Phila., 1991-92; clin. asst. prof. Pa. State U. Sch. Medicine-Hershey Med. Ctr., 1992-95, clin. assoc. prof., 1995—; presenter in field. Contbr. articles to med. jours., chpts. to books. Recipient Outstanding Tchr. award Geisinger Med. Ctr., 1990, 91; Tulane scholar, 1976, E.J. and Sarah Evans scholar, 1979, scholar Measy Found., 1982; named among Best Doctors in Am., 2000. Fellow Am. Acad. Ophthlmology (Honor award 1998); mem. AMA, Assn. for Rsch. in Vision and Ophthalmology, Vitreous Soc. (exec. com.), Retina Soc., Rsch. To Prevent Blindness, Soc. for Contemplation Fascinating Fluorescein Angiograms, Atlantic Coast Vitreoretinal Study Group, Atlantic Coast Fluorescein Angiography Club, Pa. Med. Soc., Pa. Acad. Ophthalmology, Phi Beta Kappa, Alpha Omega Alpha, Phi Eta Sigma, Alpha Epsilon Delta, Omicron Delta Kappa. Avocations: sailing, tennis, bicycling. Office: PO Box 3200 Ste 310 2108 Medical Offices Lancaster PA 17604-3200 Office Phone: 717-399-8790. E-mail: RYJN@aol.com.

BRODATY, HENRY, psychogeriatrician, researcher, educator; b. Kirchseeon, Munich, Germany, July 4, 1947; arrived in Australia, 1948; s. Jacob and Sarah Brodaty; m. Karoline Mangel, Sept. 13, 1970; children: Nina Esther, David Jacob. MB BS, U. Sydney, Australia, 1970; MD, U. NSW, Sydney, 1985, DSc, 2006. Dir., med. supt. psychiatry unit Prince Henry Hosp., Sydney, 1980-90; dir. acad. dept. for old age psychiatry Prince Henry and Prince of Wales Hosps., Sydney, 1990—; clin. dir. program of aged care svcs. Eastern Sydney Area Health Svc., Sydney, 1990-96; prof. psychogeriatrics U. New South Wales, Sydney, 1990—, dir. Primary Dementia Collaborative Rsch. Ctr., 2006—; coord. psychogeriatric svcs. South-Eastern Sydney Area Health Svc., 1988—2002. Profl. mem. NSW Guardianship Bd., Sydney, 1989-2001; chmn. mem. several state and commonwealth coms. on aging and dementia. Author: Managing Alzheimer's Disease in Primary Care, 1999; mem. editl. bd. Alzheimer Disease and Associated Disorders, Alzheimer's and Demertic, Aging and Mental Health, Internat. Psychogeriats., CNS Drugs and Aging, Internat. Jour. Psychiatry in Medicine, Psychogeriat., Managing Alzheimer's Disease in Primary Care, 1998, rev. edit., 1999; co-editor: Evidence Based Demertic Practice, 2003, Psychogeriatic Svc. Delivery; contbr. more than 300 articles to profl. jours. Rotary Paul Harris internat. fellow, 1995; recipient Alumni Award U. NSW, 1994, Novartis Oration, Austrlasian Soc. Psychiatric Rsch., 2002; named officer Order of Australia, 2000. Fellow Royal Coll. Physicians, Royal Australian and New Zealand Coll. Psychiatrists (coll. medallion 1977, Organon jr. rsch. award 1978, Ian Simpson award 1987, Organor Sr. Rsch. award 2003), Australian Assn. Gerontology (exec. bd. mem. internat. coll geriat. psychoneuropharmacology; Rotary Vocat. Svcs. award, 2002); mem. Alzheimer's Disease Internat. (mem. exec. com. 1984—, chmn. med. and sci. adv. com. 1994—2002, vice-chmn. 1998-2002, chmn. 2002-05, hon. v.p. 2005—), Internat. Psychogeriatric Assn. (bd. dirs. 1994-2002, pres.-elect., 2011-, Bayer-AG Rsch. award 1989, Disting. Svc. to Field award, 2009). Avocations: theater, bicycling, reading. Office: Acad Dept for Old Age Psych Prince of Wales Hosp Randwick NSW 2031 Australia Fax: 61-2-9382 3762.

BRODELL, ANNE RAYNE, psychotherapist, consultant; b. Burlington, Vt., Aug. 29, 1956; d. Daniel J. and Virginia (Rayne) Brodell; married; children: David Brodell-Lake, Daniel Brodell-Lake. BA with honors in Religious Studies and Humanities, Stanford U., 1978; MA in Marriage, Family-Child Counseling, Santa Clara U., 1987, MBSR. Lic. marriage and family therapist, Calif. Supr. adapted aquatics Cmty. Assn. for Rehab., Palo Alto, Calif., 1978—85; family therapist Peninsula Children's Ctr., 1986-90, clin. supr., 1990—96, St. Elizabeth Seton Sch., Palo Alto, 1996—. Asst. coach men's and women's swim teams Stanford (Calif.) U., 1979; adj. prof. Dept. Counseling Psychology and Edn. Santa Clara U., 1996-98. Recipient athletic scholarship Stanford U., 1975, 76, 77; holder Am. record in 800 meter freestyle short course, 1973. Mem. Stanford U. Alumni Assn. Avocation: 3rd Degree Black Belt. Office: 1810 Birch St Palo Alto CA 94306-1103 Office Phone: 650-299-8585. Business E-Mail: annebrodellmft@sbcglobal.net.

BRODIE, ANGELA M., biomedical researcher, educator; b. Manchester, Lancashire, Eng., Sept. 28, 1934; d. Herbert Kent and Ann (Hargreaves) Hartley; m. Harry Joseph Brodie, Apr. 25, 1928; children: Mark, John. BS in Biochemistry with honors, Sheffield U., Eng., 1956, MS in Biochemistry, 1958; PhD in Chem. Pathology, Manchester U., Eng., 1961. Jr. scientific officer Nat. Blood Transfusion Svc., Manchester, 1956-57; rsch. asst. dept. hormone rsch. Christie Hosp. and Holt Radium Inst., Manchester, 1957-59; predoct. fellow Med. Rsch. Coun., Eng., 1959-61; postdoctorate tng. program in steroid biochemistry Clark U./Worcester Found. Exptl. Biology, Shrewsbury, Mass., 1961—62; staff scientist Worcester Found. for Expt. Biology, Shrewsbury, 1962—78, sr. scientist, 1978-79; res. assoc. prof. dept. pharmacology and exptl. therapeutics U. Md. Sch. Medicine, Balt., 1979-83, assoc. prof. dept. pharmacology and exptl. therapeutics, 1983-86, prof., 1986—; prof. divsn. reproductive endocrinology dept. physiology U. Md., 1985—. Invited presenter Am. Assn. Cancer Rsch., 1987; program leader prostate cancer divsn. oncology dept. medicine The Marlene and Steart Greenebaum Cancer Ctr. U. Md., 1988—; mem. ad-hoc biochem. endorcrinology study sect. NIH, 1982, 83, 85, spl. cons. social scis. and population dynamics, 1982, 84-88, 91, reproductive endocrinology, 1998—; mem. selection com. Roussel Prize, 1985-92; mem. nominating com. Women in Endocrinology, 1991-94, 97-99; chmn. liaison com. Am. Soc. Andrology, 1988-91; site visitor Cancer Rsch. Campaign Program Projects, Eng., 1993, 94, 95; reviewer Nat. Action Plan on Breast Cancer, 1995; mem. integration panel breast cancer program U.S. Army, 1998; chmn. numerous symposia; cons. in field. Editor, contbr. Jour. Enzyme Inhibition, 1990, proceedings 3rd Internat. Aromatase Conf., 1992, Breast Cancer Rsch. and Treatment, 1994; co-editor: Clin. and Biol. Rsch., 1986; rev. Endocrinology, Sci. Steroids, Biology of Reproduction, Cancer Rsch., Jour. Clin. Endocrinology and Metabolism, numerous others; mem. editl. bd. Steroids, 1964-66, 95—, Jour. Steroid Biochemistry, 1985—, Jour. Enzyme Inhibition, 1992—2006; abstractor Biol. Abstracts, 1968-70; assoc. editor Cancer Rsch., 2005—. Recipient Pharmacia Upjohn Internat. award for excellence in clin. rsch., 1998, Brinker Internat. award for breast cancer rsch. The Susan Co. Komen Breast Cancer Found., 2000, Kettering prize Gen. Motors, 2005, Regent's Gold medal U. Md., 2006, Sloan-Kettering C.C. Stock award, 2006, Dean's medal for rsch. U. Med. Sch., 2006, Landon award Am. Assn. Cancer Rsch., 2006, Gregory Pincus Lectr. award, 2007, Martin Abeloff award, 2008, Prin. Investigator Rsch. award NIH, 1975-; named Rsch. Lectr. of Yr., U. Md., Balt., 2006. Mem. AAAS (mem. program com. 1988-89, membership com. 1997—98, program com. 2007), Internat. Soc. Comparative Oncology, Soc. Study Reproduction (mem. pubs. com. 1985, membership com. 1987, nominations com. 1990, awards com. 1995-97), Endocrine Soc., Soc. Andrology, Soc. for Basic Urologic Rsch. (Coffey Lecture 2007). Achievements include 4 patents; research, development of formestane aromatase inhibitor, first selective aromatase inhibitor specifically designed for treatment of breast cancer; research in new treatments for prostate cancer, steroid biochemistry, endocrinology of breast and prostate cancer and other estrogen mediated diseases, reproductive endocrinology. Office: U Md Sch Medicine 655 W Baltimore St Baltimore MD 21201 Office Phone: 410-706-3137. Business E-Mail: abrodie@umaryland.edu.

BRODIE, HARLOW KEITH HAMMOND, psychiatrist, educator; b. Stamford, Conn., Aug. 24, 1939; s. Lawrence Sheldon and Elizabeth White (Hammond) B.; m. Brenda Ann Barrowclough, Jan. 26, 1967; children: Melissa Verduin, Cameron Keith, Tyler Hammond, Bryson Barrowclough. AB, Princeton U., 1961; MD, Columbia U., 1965; LLD hon., U. Richmond, 1987; LHD (hon.), High Point U., 1992. Diplomate Am. Bd. Psychiatry and Neurology. Intern Ochsner Found. Hosp., New Orleans, 1965-66; resident in psychiatry Columbia-Presbyn. Med. Center, NYC, 1966-68; clin. assoc. intramural research program NIMH, 1968-70; asst. prof. psychiatry, dir. gen. clin. research center Stanford U. Med. Sch., 1970-74; prof. psychiatry, chmn. dept. Duke U. Med. Sch., 1974-82, James B. Duke prof. psychiatry and behavioral scis., 1981—, prof. dept. psychology, prof. law, 1980—; psychiatrist-in-chief Duke U. Med. Center, 1974-82; chancellor Duke U., 1982-85, pres., 1985-93, pres. emeritus, 1993—. Mem. Pres. Biomed. Rsch. Panel, 1975; mem. Carnegie Coun. on Adolescent Devel., 1986-97; trustee Com. for Econ. Devel., 1986-93, subcom. on edn. and child devel., 1990; trustee Nat. Humanities Ctr., 1988-93; nat. rev. and adv. panel for improving campus race rels. Ford Found., 1990-94; bd. dirs. Mental Health and Behavioral Medicine, 1981-83, chmn., 1981-82; chmn. Com. on Substance Abuse and Mental Health Issues in AIDS Rsch., 1992-95; mem. Com. on Leadership Devel., Am. Coun. on Edn., 1990-93. Co-author: The Importance of Mental Health Services to General Health Care, 1979, Modern Clinical Psychiatry, 1982; co-editor: American Handbook of Psychiatry, vols. 6, 7 and 8, 1975, 81, 86, Controversy in Psychiatry, 1978, Psychiatry at the Crossroads, 1980, Critical Problems in Psychiatry, 1982, Signs and Symptoms in Psychiatry, 1983, Consultation-Liaison Psychiatry and Behavioral Medicine, 1986, AIDS and Behavior: An Integrated Approach, 1994, Keeping an Open Door: Passages in a University Presidency, 1996, The Research University Presidency in the Late Twentieth Century, 2005; assoc. editor Am. Jour. Psychiatry, 1973-81. Recipient A.E. Bennet Rsch. award, 1970, Soc. Biol. Psychiatry, Strecker award Inst., Pa. Hosp., 1980, Disting. Alumnus award Ochsner Found. Hosp., 1984, Disting. Med. Alumni award Columbia U., 1985, N.C. award for sci., 1990, William C. Menninger Meml. award ACP, 1994. Fellow: Royal Soc. Medicine; mem.: NAS, Soc. Biol. Psychiatry, Inst. Medicine, Internat. Soc. Sport Psychiatry, Royal Coll. Psychiatrists, Am. Psychiat. Assn. (sec. 1977—81, pres. 1982—83). Home: 63 Beverly Dr Durham NC 27707-2223 Office: Devonwood Co 3211 Shannon Rd Ste 603 Durham NC 27707

BRODINE, CHARLES EDWARD, physician; b. Sioux City, Iowa, May 10, 1925; s. Ivar and Dorothy B.; m. Lois Bliss, June 26, 1949; children: Stephanie Kay, Jennifer Leah, Charles Edward. BS, Iowa State U., Ames, 1948, research fellow malaria project, 1948-49; MD, Washington U., St. Louis, 1953. Intern St. Louis County Hosp., 1953-54, resident in internal medicine, 1954-55, U.S. Naval Hosp., Oakland, Calif., 1957-59; fellow in hematology, clin. instr. medicine U. Cin. and Cin. Gen. Hosp., 1955-57; head hematology svc. U.S. Naval Hosp., Oakland, 1959-61, Bethesda, Md., 1961-62, cons. in hematology, 1962-73; head divsn. rsch. hematology Naval Med. Rsch. Inst., Bethesda, 1962-66, chmn. dept. clin. investigation, 1966-70, exec. officer, 1970-73; program mgr. Navy frozen blood and trauma rsch. program research div. Bur. Medicine and Surgery U.S. Dept. Navy, Washington, 1962-71, dir. rsch. divsn., 1973-74; spl. asst. med. rsch. and devel. to Surgeon Gen. U.S. Navy, 1974-77; career mem. Sr. Foreign Svcs. U.S. Class of Minister Counselor; comdg. officer Naval Med. Rsch. and Devel. Command, Nat. Naval Med. Center, Bethesda, 1974-77; asst. med. dir. environ. health and preventive medicine Office Med. Svcs. Dept. State, Washington, 1977-90; mem. Agt. Orange Working Group, 1982-90; exec. com. Nat. Council Internat. Health, 1982-90. Bd. dirs. Gorgas Meml. Inst. Tropical and Preventive Medicine, 1973-89; mem. Bur. Medicine and Surgery Policy Council, 1974-77; med. adviser ARC, 1975-79; adv. com. Nat. Sickle Cell Disease, NIH, 1974-77; mem. com. on biomed. rsch. U.S.-Egypt Joint Working Group, 1975-77; mem. White House Working Group on Internat. Health, 1977; clin. asso. prof. dept. medicine Georgetown U., Washington, 1971—; Dept. State mem. Nat. Council for Internat. Health, 1978-89, amb., World Form Fedn., U. Cambridge, 2010, St. Johns Coll. US Cultural Attache World Forum, San Francisco, 2011. Contbr. articles to profl. jours. Mem. exec. com. Gorgas Meml. Inst., 1978-88, amb. knowledge World Form Fedn., 2011 Decorated Legion of Merit for blood rsch. project, 1968, 2nd Legion Merit Naval Med. Rsch. and Devel. Command, 1977; recipient NAVY Meritorious Service medal for work at Naval Med. Rsch. Inst., 1972, US Dept. Navy, 1973; Robert Dexter Conrad award for outstanding sci. achievement Sec. of Navy, 1977 Mem. AMA, Assn. Mil. Surgeons (sustaining membership award 1967), Acad. Medicine of Washington (bd. dirs. 1992—), Soc. for Cryobiology (editorial bd. 1964-66), Soc. Fed. Med. Agys., Western Soc. Clin. Investigation, Soc. Med. Cons. Armed Forces. Home: 211 Russell Ave Apt 57 Gaithersburg MD 20877 Personal E-mail: cebrodinemd@gmail.com.

BRODKIN, ADELE RUTH MEYER, psychologist; b. NYC, July 8, 1934; d. Abraham J. and Helen (Honig) Meyer; m. Roger Harrison Brodkin, Jan. 26, 1957; children: Elizabeth Anne Brodkin Brauer, Edward Stuart. Degree, Cornell U., 1954—56; BA, Sarah Lawrence Coll., 1956; MA, Columbia U., 1959; PhD, Rutgers U., 1977. Lic. psychologist N.J. Sch. psychologist pub. schs., 1961—73; assoc. dir. Infant Child Devel. Ctr. St. Barnabas Med. Ctr., Livingston, NJ, 1977-79; clin. asst. prof. dept. psychiatry U. Medicine and Dentistry N.J., Newark, 1979-90, clin. assoc. prof., 1990-2001. Vis. scholar Hasting Ctr. for Life Scis., NY, 1979; sr. child devel. cons.; cons. Scholastic, Inc., 1988—2009; consulting editor NAEYC, 2008—. Author: Between Teacher and Parent, Supporting Young Children As They Grow, 1994, The Lonely Only Dog, 1998, Fresh Approaches to Working with Problematic Behavior, 2001, Raising Happy and Successful Kids, 2006; co-author (with A.T. Jersild and E.A. Lazar): The Meaning of Psychotherapy in the Teacher's Life and Work, 1962; author, prodr.: (documentaries) Competing Commitments, 1984 (Best Ednl. Videotape award N.J. Cable); co-author, prodr.: (ednl. videos) Passage to Physicianhood, 1985; The Insidious Epidemic, 1986; columnist Between Tchr. and Parent, Pre-K Today mag., 1988—93, Early Childhood Today Mag., 1993—2007, Scholastic Parent and Child mag., 1990—2009, You and Today's Child, Instr. mag., 1992—93, Kids in Crisis, 1993—96, Ask Dr. Brodkin, Scholastic.com, 1997—2007, Ask a Psychologist, 2006—, E-Scholastic, 1995—2008, Instr. Mag., 1990—2011, Grandma, 2007—09; contbr. articles to profl. jours.; cons. editor NAEYC, 2009—. Fellow, NIMH, 1962; Adelaide M. Ayer fellow, Columbia U., 1962—63, Louis Bevier fellow, Rutgers U., 1976—77. Mem.: APA, SRCD, NAEYC, Am. Sociol. Assn., N.J. Psychol. Assn. Home and Office: 84 Pine St Chatham NJ 07928 Office Phone: 973-301-9188. Personal E-mail: brodkina@earthlink.net.

BRODKIN, ROGER HARRISON, dermatologist, educator; b. Newark, July 31, 1932; AB, Lafayette Coll., Easton, Pa., 1954; MD, Jefferson Med. Coll., 1958; MMS in Dermatology, NYU, 1967. Diplomate Am. Bd. Dermatology, Am. Bd. Med. Examiners. Intern Lenox Hill Hosp., NYC, 1958—59; resident dermatology, Bellevue Hosp. NYU, 1959—62, tchg. asst., 1962—64, instr. dermatology, 1964—66; clin. asst. prof. U. NJ Med. and Dental Sch., Newark, 1966—69, clin. assoc prof., 1969—79, clin. prof., 1979—; pres. Ctr. Dermatology, West Orange, NJ. Fellow: ACP, NY Acad. Medicine; mem.: Soc. Investigative Dermatology, Royal Soc. Medicine, Internat. Soc. Tropical Dermatology, NY Acad. Sci., Am. Soc. Dermatologic Surgery, Am. Acad. Dermatology, Sigma Psi. Office: Ctr Dermatology 101 Old Short Hills Rd West Orange NJ 07052-1000 Office Phone: 973-736-9535.

BRODY, BERNARD B., internist, educator; b. NYC, June 24, 1922; s. Abraham and Sarah (Berman) B.; m. Ruth M. Miller, Jan. 15, 1954; children: Sarah, Rachel. BS, U. Wis., 1943; MD, U. Rochester, 1951. Diplomate Am. Bd. Internal Medicine, Nat. Bd. Med. Examiners. Rsch. chemist U. Chgo. and Monsanto, Dayton, Ohio, 1943-47; resident U. Rochester, NY, 1951-53, clin. prof. pathology and medicine NY, 1981-90, prof. emeritus NY, 1990—; resident Genesee Hosp., Rochester, 1955-56, dir. clin. labs., 1967-81, sr. v.p. med. affairs, 1975-87; pvt. practice internal medicine Rochester, 1956-67. Cons. Eastman Kodak Co., 1971-92, Robert Wood Johnson Found., 1975-80, EDMAC Assocs., Inc., 1976-83; trustee Freedom Forum, 1980-98, 2006-09, emeritus trustee, 2009-; mem. adv. bd. Freedom Forum Media Studies Ctr., N.Y.C., 1985-98, adv. trustee Freedom Forum, 1998—2006. Bd. dirs. Rochester Mus. and Sci. Ctr., 1994-2003, hon. bd. dirs., 2003—; bd. dirs. Genesee Valley Med. Care, Rochester, 1962-68, Crestwood Children's Ctr., 1985-97, hon. bd., 1998—; chmn. med. adv. bd. St. Ann's Home, 1964-67; corp. mem. United Way, Rochester, 1980-87; mem. Citizens Com. Human Rels., 1980-85; v.p., mem. exec. bd. Otetiana coun. Boy Scouts Am., 1981-91; bd. dirs. Via Health Rochester Gen. Hosp., 2001-05; chmn. stewardship cabinet Lifespan, 2003—. 1st lt. U.S. Army, 1953-55. Mem. AMA, ACP, Am. Soc. Internal Medicine, Acad. Clin. Lab. Physicians and Scientists, Am. Assn. Clin. Chemistry, Sigma Xi, Alpha Omega Alpha Home and Office: 12 Huntington Brk Rochester NY 14625-1811 Home Phone: 585-381-6786; Office Phone: 585-381-6786. E-mail: Bbrody@rochester.rr.com.

BRODY, HAROLD JOSEPH, dermatologist; b. Sumter, SC, Jan. 11, 1949; s. Abram and Sara B. BA in Chemistry, Duke U., 1970; MD, Med. U. S.C., 1974. Intern U. Tex. Med. Ctr., 1974-75; resident Emory U. Med. Ctr., 1977-78. Author: Chemical Peeling, 1992, Chemical Peeling and Resurfacing, 1997; sr. editor Jour. Dermatologic Surgery & Oncology, 1991. Bd. dirs. Theatre in the Square, Atlanta, 1986-89, Onstage Atlanta, 1987-90, Calibre Prodns., Atlanta, 1994; mem. Duke U. Nat. Drama Adv. Bd., Durham, N.C., 1994-96. Mem.: Atlanta Dermatol. Assn. (pres. 1989), Ga. Dermatologic Assn. (pres. 2001), Am. Soc. Dermatologic Surgery (bd. dirs. 1989—91, sec. 1995—, v.p. 1998—, pres. 2000). Avocations: theater, reading, marathons. Office: Hailey & Brody 1218 W Paces Ferry Rd 200 Atlanta GA 30327 Office Phone: 404-525-7409.

BRODY, JANE ELLEN, journalist, researcher; b. Bklyn., May 19, 1941; d. Sidney and Lillian (Kellner) B.; m. Richard Engquist, Oct. 2, 1966; children: Lee Erik and Lorin Michael Engquist (twins). BS, N.Y. State Coll. Agr., Cornell U., 1962; MS in Journalism, U. Wis., 1963; HHD (hon.), Princeton U., 1987; LHD (hon.), Hamline U., 1993, SUNY Hlth. Sci. Ctr., 1999; LHD U. Minn. (hon.), 2000. Reporter Mpls. Tribune, 1963-65; sci. writer, personal health columnist New York Times, NYC, 1965—; mem. adv. council NY State Coll. Agr., Cornell U., 1971-77. Author: (with Richard Engquist) Secrets of Good Health, 1970; (with Arthur Holleb) You Can Fight Cancer and Win, 1977, Jane Brody's Nutrition Book, 1981, Jane Brody's The New York Times Guide to Personal Health, 1982, Jane Brody's Good Food Book, 1985, Jane Brody's Good Food Gourmet, 1990; (with Richard Flaste) Jane Brody's Good Seafood Book, 1994, Jane Brody's Cold and Flu Fighter, 1995, Jane Brody's Allergy Fighter, 1997, The New York Times Book of Health, 1997, The New York Times Book of Women's Health, 2000, The New York Times Guide to Alternative Health, 2001. Recipient numerous writing awards including Howard Blakeslee award Am. Heart Assn., 1971, Sci. Writers' award ADA, 1978, J.C. Penney-U. Mo. Journalism award, 1978, Lifeline award Am. Health Found., 1978 Jewish. Office: New York Times 620 8th Ave New York NY 10018-1405

BRODY, ROBERT, dermatologist, educator; b. Cleve., June 15, 1948; s. Melvin and Nancy Elizabeth Brody; m. Mary Ann Conn, July 23, 1988; children: Ian Hamilton Conn, Hartley Messing Conn, Matthew Grant Hutchinson. BA with distinction, Stanford U., 1970; MD, U. Mich., 1974. Diplomate Am. Bd. Dermatology. Intern internal medicine Cleve. Clinic, 1974—75, resident dermatology, 1975—78; pvt. practice Cleve., 1978—, 1982—; staff physician Kaiser-Permanente Med. Ctr., 1978—82, mem. prof. edn. com, 1978—82, chmn., 1980—82, sec. exec. com., 1980; asst. clin. prof. Case Western Res. U. Med. Sch., 1978—80, clin. instr., 1980—83, dermatology dept. rep. to gen. faculty, 1980—82; asst. physician U. Hosps. Cleve., 1979—; chief dermatology divsn. St. Luke's Hosp., Cleve., 1999. Contbr. articles to med. jours. Sec. Cleve. Play House Men's Com., 1979—82; mem. ann. fund com. Stanford U., 1978—, regional co-chmn., 1981—82. Mem.: Cleve. Acad. Medicine, Am. Acad. Dermatology. Home: 2870 Glengary Rd Cleveland OH 44120-1731 Office: 3461 Warrensville Ctr Rd Cleveland OH 44122-5227

BRODY, WILLIAM RALPH, academic administrator, radiologist, educator; b. Stockton, Calif., Jan. 4, 1944; m. Wendy Brody; 2 children. BSEE, MIT, 1965, MSEE, 1966; MD, Stanford U., 1970, PhD in Elec. Engring., 1975. Intern to resident and fellow dept. cardiovasc. surgery Stanford U. Sch. Medicine, Calif., 1970—73, tng. med. fellow cardiovasc. surgery, resident diagnostic radiology, 1975—77, assoc. prof. to prof. dept. radiology, dir. rsch. labs., 1977—86; with USPHS Nat. Heart, Lung, and Blood Inst., Balt., 1973—75; prof. Stanford U., 1982—84; founder, pres., CEO Resonex, Inc., 1984—87, chmn. bd. dirs., 1987—89; radiologist-in-chief Johns Hopkins Hosp., Balt., 1987—94; mem. staff depts. elec., computer engring., biomedical engring. Johns Hopkins U. Sch. Medicine, 1987—94, Martin Donner prof., dir. dept. radiology, 1987—94; prof. radiology, provost U. Minn. Acad. Health Ctr., 1994—96, spl. asst. to pres., 1996; pres. Johns Hopkins U., 1996—2008, Salk Inst. for Biological Studies, La Jolla, 2009—. Bd. dir. Medtronic Inc., Merc. Bankshares; mem. Pres.'s Fgn. Intelligence adv. bd. Contbr. articles to profl. jours. Mem. sci. adv. com. Whitaker Found., 1992—97, governing com., 1997—; fellow coun. cardiovasc. radiology Am. Heart Assn.; mem. internat. adv. bd. Nat. U. Singapore Inst. Sys. Sci., 1994—97; trustee Goldseker Found., 1996; mem. internat. acad. adv. panel, 1997; bd. dirs. Greater Balt. Com., 1997; trustee Balt. Mus. Art, 1997. Recipient Established Investigator award, Am. Heart Assn., 1980—84. Fellow: NAS (Inst. Medicine), IEEE, Am. Acad. Arts & Scis., Am. Inst. Med. and Biomedical Engring., Am. Coll. Cardiology, Am. Coll. Radiology; mem.: NAE, Internat. Soc. Magnetic Resonance in Medicine. Achievements include patents in field. Office: Salk Inst for Biological Studies Office of Pres PO Box 85800 San Diego CA 92186-5800 Office Phone: 858-453-4100 1261. E-mail: wrbrody@salk.edu.

BROGAN, GERARD, emergency physician; b. Queens, NY, June 13, 1959; MD, SUNY, Buffalo, 1985. Med. dir. North Shore LIJ Health Sys., 2009—. Immediate past pres. NY Am. Coll. Emergency Physicians, 2009. Fellow: Am. Coll. Emergency Physicians. Office: 102-01 66th Rd Forest Hills NY 11375 Business E-Mail: gbrogan@nshs.edu.

BROGAN, MICHAEL DALE, gastroenterologist, educator; b. Columbus, Ohio, Aug. 2, 1951; s. Virgil Dale Brogan and Joan Elizabeth Pesola; m. Martha Ann Brogan, Apr. 15, 1981 (div. Oct. 1994); children: Katherine, Ryan; m. Karen Deering Brogan, Aug. 1, 1998. BA cum laude, Ohio State U., 1973, MD, 1978. Bd. cert. internal medicine, gastroenterology, Md. Intern in internal medicine Mt. Sinai Hosp., NYC, 1978-79, resident in internal medicine, 1979-81; emergency rm. physician Holzer Med. Ctr., Gallipolis, Ohio, 1981-82; fellow in gastroenterology UCLA Med. Ctr., 1982-85, asst. prof., 1985-86; practicing physician Columbus Med. Gastroenterology, 1986—; clin. asst. prof. Ohio State U., Columbus, 1986—. Head endoscopy unit Mt. Carmel Hosp., Columbus, 1992-96; sect. head divsn. gastroenterology Riverside Hosp., Columbus, 1992-94. Contbr. numerous articles and abstracts to profl. jours. Mem. AMA, Am. Gastroenterol. Assn., Columbus Med. Assn., Alpha Omega Alpha. Avocations: personal fitness, computers, cinema. Office: Michael D PO Box 2097 Westerville OH 43086-2097 Home: 5923 Heritage Lakes Dr Hilliard OH 43026-7627 Office Phone: 614-486-5207. E-mail: mbrogan@columbus.rr.com.

BROGDON, BYRON GILLIAM, radiologist, educator; b. Ft. Smith, Ark., Jan. 22, 1929; s. Paul Preston and Lela Florence (Gilliam) B.; m. Barbara Walkow Schreiber, June 23, 1978; 1 child, David Pope; stepchildren: William and Diane Schreiber. BS, U. Ark., 1951, BS in Medicine, 1951, MD, 1952. Intern Univ. Hosp., Little Rock, 1952-53, resident, 1953-55, resident in radiology N.C. Bapt. Hosp., Winston-Salem, 1955-56; asst. prof. radiology U. Fla., 1960-63; assoc. prof. radiology and radiol. scis., radiologist-in-charge diagnostic radiology div. Johns Hopkins U. and Hosp., 1963-67; prof., chmn. dept. radiology U. N.Mex., 1967-77; from prof. chmn. radiology to disting. prof. emeritus U. South Ala., Mobile, 1978—96, disting. prof. emeritus, 1996—. Sabbatical leave Univ. Coll., Galway, Ireland, 1988; cons. in forensic radiology Office Med. Exam. State Ala., 1989—; coord. internat. diagnostic course in Davos, 1984-96; trustee Forensic Sci. Found., 2001-09, vice-chair, 2003-04; mem. adv. bd. The Virtopsy Found., Bern, Switzerland, 2006-; expert cons. Ministry of Health, Singapore, 2010-. Author: Opinions, Comments and Reflections on Radiology, 1983, Forensic Radiology, 1998, a Radiologic Atlas of Abuse and Torture, Terrorism, and Inflicted Trauma (winner Highly Commended Med. Book Competition award 2003), Brogdon's Forensic Radiology, 2nd Ed., 2010; contbr. articles to med. jours, 65 chapters in books, 1966-. Maj. USAF, 1953—60. Finalist Ann. Telly awards, 2004; recipient Disting. Alumnus award U. Ark., 1978, Ark. Travelers Commn. award Gov. of Ark., 1985, Disting. Achievement award Wake Forest U. Med. Alumni Assn., 1990, medal from city of Brescia, Italy, 1991, Joint Resolution of Commendation for outstanding profl. achievement Ala. Legis., 1994, Medal of Honor Leopold-Franzens U., Innsbruck, Austria, 1997, Republic of Austria Cross of Honor for Sci. and Arts 1st class, 2002, Highly Commended award, Brit. Med. Assn., 2003. Fellow Am. Coll. Radiology (pres. 1978-79, gold medal 1987), Am. Acad. Forensic Scis. (John B. Hunt award 1995, Disting. Fellow award 2001), Internat. Assn. Forensic Radiographers Gt. Britian (patron); mem. AMA (ho. of dels. 1988-95, Physician-Spkr. award 1979), Am. Roentgen Ray Soc. (life, exec. coun. 1974-75, 77-80, 84-90, 2d v.p. 1979-80, memb. bd. sr. radiologist sect., 2005-, gold medal 1996, lectr. sr. radiology sect., 2009), Southern Radiol. Conf. (life hon., pres. 1967-68, sec. 1984-96, Eskridge lectr. 1994), Radiol. Soc. N.Am., Am. Assn. Acad. Chief Residents in Radiology (faculty advisor 1979-2002, nat. sponsor 1983-93, Malcolm Jones orator 1996), Soc. Pediat. Radiology, Assn. U. Radiologists (pres. 1973-74, gold medal 1985), Soc. Chmn. Acad. Radiol. Depts. (sec.-treas. 1969-70), Swiss Soc. Med. Radiology (hon., Schinz medal 1992), Internat. Skeletal Soc. (Silver medal 2001), Med. assn. State Ala. (50 yrs. med. parctices distinction award 2002), Country Club Mobile, Sigma Xi, Alpha Omega Alpha, Sigma Chi (Significant Sig 1999). Office: Dept Radiology Univ S Ala Med Ctr 2451 Fillingim St Mobile AL 36617-2238 Home: 149 Batre Ln Mobile AL 36608 Office Phone: 251-471-7868. Business E-Mail: gbrogdon@usouthal.edu.

BROGI, EDI, pathologist; b. Italy, Mar. 20, 1962; MD, U. Florence, Italy, 1988, PhD, 1995. Assoc. attending pathologist Meml. Sloan-Kettering, 2000—. Office: Memorial Sloan-Kettering 300 E 66th St New York NY 10065 Business E-Mail: brogie@mskcc.org.

BROITMAN, SELWYN ARTHUR, microbiologist, educator, assistant dean; b. Boston, Aug. 30, 1931; s. Julius Z. and Sara (Sallus) B.; m. Barbara Merle Shwartz, June 13, 1953; children: Caryn Beth, Jeffrey Z. BS, U. Mass., 1952, MS, 1953; PhD, Mich. State U., 1956. Fellow Am. Coll. Gastroentology, 1989; dir. Biotech. Assocs., 1959—62; rsch. instr. dept. pathology Boston U. Sch. Medicine, 1963—64, asst. prof. dept. microbiology, 1965—69, assoc. prof. dept. microbiology, 1969—75, prof., 1975—, prof. pathology and lab. medicine, 1983—, asst. dean med. sch. admissions, 1983—, asst. dean divsn. grad. med. sci., 2007—, emeritus, 2011; assoc. prof. nutritional scis. Henry Goldman Sch. Grad. Dentistry Boston U., 1974—. Assoc. medicine dept. medicine Harvard Med. Sch., 1969-74; spl. sci. staff pathology Boston Med. Ctr., 2000-; rsch. assoc. Mallory Inst. Pathology, Boston City Hosp., Gastro Intestinal Rsch. Lab., 1956-71; assoc. in medicine Thorndike Meml. Lab., 1969-74; chair, co-chair of various admission programs Boston U. Sch. Medicine; adv.-at-large Acad. of Advisors, 2003 Contbr. articles to profl. jours. Founding mem. Digestive Disease Found. Served with USAR 373d Gen. Hosp., 1952-66 Recipient Outstanding Teaching award Boston U. Sch. Medicine 1st Yr. Class, 1976 Fellow Am. Coll. Gastroenterology; mem. AAAS, NAS (com. diet, nutrition and cancer 1980-83), Am. Soc. Investigative Pathology, Am. Soc. Nutritional Scis., Am. Assn. Cancer Rsch., Am. Fedn. Med. Rsch., Am. Soc. Microbiology, Soc. Exptl. Biology and Medicine, Nutrition Today Soc. (founding), Am. Gastroent. Assn., Boston Gastroent. Soc., N.Y. Acad. Scis., Boston Bug Club (pres. 1976), Sigma Xi. Achievements include development of post grad program, MA in med. scis. in preparation of a predicted shortage of physicians in the next decade, leading to MD, DMD or PhD degree 1986; research in adverse effects of prophylactic antibiotics on human gut flora; role of gut endotoxin in development of liver cirrhosis; rare variant of systemic mastocytosis in a female patient; lactase deficiency following Salmonella infection; protocol for the management of massive small bowel resection; relationship of intestinal absorption of dietary disaccharides to gut enzyme disaccharidase levels; first conclusive demonstration of the pathogenicity of parasitic disease Giardiasis; toxin mediated Clindamycin Colitis in experimental animals; the role of the intestinal flora in vitamin B12 deficiency in The Blind loop syndrome. Office: Boston U Sch Medicine Divsn Grad Med Scis L 317 715 Albany St Boston MA 02118 Office Phone: 617-638-5342, 617-638-5342, 617-638-5740. Personal E-mail: sabroitma@hotmail.com.

BROLIN, ROBERT EDWARD, physician, surgeon; b. Holland, Mich., Apr. 12, 1948; s. Edward Magnusson Brolin and Louise A. Mann; children: Lucinda, Brian. BA, DePauw U., Greencastle, Ind., 1970; MD, U. Mich., Ann Arbor, 1974. Diplomate Am. Bd. Surgery. Asst. prof. surgery U. Medicine & Dentistry N.J.-Robert Wood Johnson Med. Sch., New Brunswick, 1980-84, assoc. prof. surgery, 1984-89, prof. surgery, 1989-2000, U. Pitts. Med. Sch., 2001—. Mem. Am. Coll. Surgeons, Am. Soc. Bariatric Surgery (pres. 2000-01), Am. Soc. Clin. Nutrition, Obesity Soc., Soc. Univ. Surgeons, Soc. Surgery of Alimentary Tract. Avocations: jogging, stamp collecting/philately, duplicate bridge. Office: 666 Plainsboro Rd Ste 640 Plainsboro NJ 08536 Office Phone: 609-785-5870. Business E-Mail: rbrolin@njbariatricspc.com.

BROMAGE, TIMOTHY G., biological anthropologist, science educator; BA in Anthropology, Biology, Geology, Calif. State U., Sonoma, 1978; MA in Biological Anthropology, U. Toronto, 1980, PhD in Biological Anthropology, 1986. Prof. NYU Dept. Biomaterials & Biomimetics; dir. NYU Hard Tissue Research Unit. Office: 345 E 24 St 817B Schwartz New York NY 10010 Office Phone: 212-998-9597. Office Fax: 212-995-4445. E-mail: tim.bromage@nyu.edu.

BRON, DENIS, neurologist, researcher; b. Wettingen, Switzerland, May 30, 1971; s. Bernard Bron and Jutta Goebel; m. Andrea Bron, Aug. 15, 1996; children: Thery, David, Aline. MD, U. Basel. Doctor Inst. Physiology U. Basel, Switzerland, 1998; doctor dept. surgery, 1999; doctor internal med. dept., 1999, doctor dept. neurology Kantonsspital Aarau, Switzerland, 1999—2002, U. Hosp. Basel, Switzerland, 2002—. CEO Basel Myovcc AG, 2002. Author: Neuromuscular Disorders, 2002. V.p. Social Commn., Rheinfelden, 1998—99. Mem.: Swiss Med. Doctors. Achievements include patents pending in field. Avocations: hiking, literature, music.

BRONER, MARCELA VIVIANA, psychologist, consultant; d. Julio Broner and Dolly Rubinstein; m. Gabriel Hernando Taraciuk; children: Tamara Paula Taraciuk Broner, Luciano Alan Taraciuk, Leandro Ryan Taraciuk. Degree in Clin. Psychology, Medicine Sch. U. Buenos Aires, 1986. Lic. psicologia U. Andres Bello, Can., 1982. Cons. fertility Hosp. de Clinicas U. Buenos Aires, 1988—2006, cons. menopause, 1990—, cons. laparoscopy surgery, 1992—98, cons. gynecol. oncology, 1998—; psychology chief, dept. mental health Medicine Sch. U. Buenos Aires, 1990—, supr. psychotherapy, 1990—, psychodiagnostic, 1990—, postgrad. studies prof., 1995—. Contbr. scientific papers, chapters to books. Achievements include research in female psychosexuality. Office: Calle Costa Rica 6073 C1414BTM Buenos Aires Argentina

BRONIN, ANDREW, dermatologist; Studied, NY Coll. of Medicine. Diplomate Am. Bd. Dermatology. Internship NY sch. of medicine State Univ.; resident NY Hosp., Cornell Med. Ctr.; affiliate med. staff Greenwich Hosp.; with Yale-New Haven Hosp. Named one of Best Doctors, NY mag., 2008. Office: Greenwich Hospital 4 Rye Ridge Plz Rye Brook Port Chester NY 10573 Office Phone: 914-253-8080. Office Fax: 914-253-9303.

BRONNER, FELIX, physiologist, biophysicist, educator, painter; b. Vienna, Nov. 7, 1921; arrived in U.S., 1937, naturalized, 1943; s. Maurice and Lotte (Vogler) B.; m. Leah Horowitz, Oct. 12, 1947; children: Deborah Rachel, Ethan Samuel. BS, U. Calif., Berkeley and Davis, 1941; PhD (Quaker Oats fellow 1950-52), MIT, 1952; student, Kans. State Coll., 1938; postgrad., U. Minn., 1943, U. Va., 1946; D (hon.), Ecole Pratique des Hautes Etud, Paris, 1996. Rsch. assoc. MIT, 1952-54; Helen Hay Whitney fellow, Arthritis and Rheumatism fellow, Rockefeller Inst. Med. Rsch., NYC, 1954-56, asst., 1956; dir. lab. mineral metabolism Hosp. for Spl. Surgery, NYC, 1957-63; asst. prof. Cornell U. Med. Coll., 1961-63; assoc. prof. physiology U. Louisville Sch. Medicine, 1963-69; prof. oral biology U. Conn., 1969-86, prof. nutritional scis., 1976-89, prof. biostructure and function, 1986-89, prof. emeritus, 1989—. Vis. scientist Weizmann Inst., Israel, 1965, 76, Varon vis. prof., 1988; vis. scientist Pasteur Inst., Paris, 1977, U. Cape Town Med. Sch., 1984, 88, MRC disting. vis. scientist, 1991; guest scientist INSERM, Paris, 1972, Lyon, France, 1988; cons. USPHS, 1965-68, 70-71, USDA, 1978-79, 2001—08; vis. prof. Tel Aviv U. Sch. Medicine, 1976. Editor: (with C.L. Comar) Mineral Metabolism: An Advanced Treatise, 1960-69; (with A. Kleinzeller) Current Topics in Membranes and Transport, 1970-90; (with J. Coburn) Disorders of Mineral Metabolism, 1981-82; (with M. Peterlik) Calcium and Phosphate Transport Across Biomembranes, 1981; Epithelial Calcium and Phosphate Transport: Molecular and Cellular Aspects, 1984; Cellular Calcium and Phosphate Transport in Health and Disease, 1988; (with W.D. Stein) Cell Shape Determinants, Regulation, and Regulatory Role, 1989; (with D. Pansu) Calcium Transport and Intracellular Calcium Homeostasis, 1990; Intracellular Calcium Regulation, 1991; (with R V. Worrell) A Basic Science Primer in Orthopaedics, 1991; (with M. Peterlik) Extra-

and Intracellular Calcium and Phosphate Regulation: From Basic Research to Clinical Medicine, 1992; Nutrition and Health-Topics and Controversies, 1996; Nutrition Policy in Public Health, 1997; (with R.V. Worrell) Orthopaedics: Principles of Basic and Clinical Science, 1999; Nutritional Aspects and Clinical Management of Chronic Disorders and Diseases, 2003, Nutritional and Clinical Management of Chronic Conditions and Diseases, 2005; (with Mary C. Farach-Carson) Topics in Bone Biology, Bone Formation, vol. 1, 2003, Bone Resorption, vol. 2, 2005, Functional Engineering of Skeletal Tissues, vol. 3, 2006, Bone and Osteoarthritis, vol. 4, 2007, Bone and Cancer, vol. 5, 2009, Bone and Development vol. 6, 2010; mem. editl. bd. Am. Jour. Clin. Nutrition, 1968-76, Am. Jour. Physiology, 1985-97, Jour. Nutrition, 1986-95; contbr. articles to profl. jours.; exhibited in one-man shows, numerous juried shows, reviewed in July, 2003 ARTnews. Pres. Bur. Jewish Edn., Louisville, 1968-69. Served with AUS, 1942-46. Recipient André Lichtwitz prize, Nat. Inst. Health and Med. Rsch., France, 1974. Fellow AAAS, Am. Soc. Nutrition; mem. Am. Physiol. Soc., Biophys. Soc., Harvey Soc., Soc. Exptl. Biology and Medicine, Orthop. Rsch. Soc., Am. Soc. Bone and Mineral Rsch., Austrian Bone Soc. (hon.). Home: 33 Ferncliff Dr West Hartford CT 06117-1013 Office: U Conn Health Ctr Farmington CT 06030-6125 Office Phone: 860-679-2136. Business E-Mail: bronner@neuron.uchc.edu.

BRONNER, ULF ERIK, physician, researcher; b. Stockholm, July 4, 1956; s. Nils Erik and Gerd Birgitta Bronner; m. Anna Lena Bergh; children: Erik Gustaf, Emelie Victoria. MD, Karolinska Inst., Stockholm, 1981, PhD, 1994. Specialist in infectious diseases Nat. Bd. Health and Welfare, 1990. Sr. cons., dept. infectious diseases Karolinska U. Hosp., Stockholm, 1999—; dir. studies, dept. infectious diseases Karolinska Inst., 2002—05. Chmn. Nat. Swedish Expert Com. Clin. Parasitology, Stockholm, 2002—10; pres. Swedish Soc. Tropical Medicine and Internat. Health, Stockholm, 2009—10. Contbr. articles to profl. jours. Min., Lord's supper Swedish Missionary Ch., Stockholm, 2007. Named one of Best Clin. Tutor, Karolinska Inst., 1994. Fellow: Timmermansorden Lodge (Stockholm). Achievements include research in new dosage schedule for pentamidine treatment of sleeping sickness and malaria. Avocation: skiing. Office: Karolinska University Hosp Solna Dept Infectious Diseases Stockholm S-17176 Sweden Office Fax: 46-8-517 718 06. Business E-Mail: ulf.bronner@karolinska.se.

BRONSON, RICHARD ADAM, reproductive endocrinologist, educator; b. NYC, Feb. 22, 1941; s. William and Florence Bronson; m. Susan Kay Bronson, July 31, 1965; children: Andrew, Brian, Emily D'Agostino. BS, MIT, Cambridge, 1962; MD, NYU, 1966. Fellow Am. Coll. of Obstetrics & Gynecology, 1977, Certification in Reproductive Endocrinology Am. Coll. of Obstetrics & Gynecology, 1980. Internship Bellevue Hosp., NYC, 1966—67; resident in surgery NYU Med. Ctr., NYC, 1967—71; NIH extramural tng. fellowship U. Edinburgh, 1968—69; resident in obstetrics and gynecology U. Pa. Hosp., Phila., 1971—74; fellowship in reproductive endocrinology Pa. Hosp., 1974—76; asst. prof. obstetrics and gynecology Cornell U. Med. Ctr., NYC, 1978—84, assoc. prof. obstetrics and gynecology, 1984—88, SUNY, Stony Brook, 1988—2003, prof. obstetrics and gynecology, 2003—, prof. pathology, 2008—. Dir., lab. of human reproduction North Shore U. Hosp., Manhasset, NY, 1978—88; dir. reproductive endocrinology Stony Brook U. Med. Ctr., NY, 1988—90, acting dir. reproductive endocrinology, 1993—95, dir. reproductive endocrinology, 2003—, dir., andrology lab., 1988—. Editor: (textbook) Reproductive Immunology; assoc. editor Human Reproduction, 2003—06, mem. editl. bd. literary mag. (a collection of poetry) Xanadu, publisher (collection of poems) Search for Oz; author: Silent Music, 2009. Mem. Planned Parenthood NY, Planned Parenthood Nassau County. Lt. col. US Army M.C., 1976—78, Tripler Army Med. Ctr., Honolulu. Recipient NYU Founders' Day award, 1966, Poetry award, ACP, 2003, Poetry prize, Inst. Medicine in Contemporary Soc., 2005. Mem.: Soc. for Gynecologic Investigation, Soc. for the Study of Reproduction, Com. on Biotechnology & the Law - NY Bar Assn., Am. Soc. for the Immunology of Reproduction, Am. Soc. Reproductive Medicine (postgraduate course dir. 1992—92, reproductive immunology spl. interest group 1992—93, postgraduate course dir. 2000—00), European Soc. for Reproduction and Embryology, Endocrine Soc., Soc. Reproductive Endocrinologists, Internat. Soc. Reproductive Immunology, Am. Soc. Andrology, Am. Soc. for the Immunology of Reproduction (pres.), NY Obstet. Soc., Am. Coll. Obstetrics & Gynecology. Achievements include patents for a method of screening for infertility of sperm; development of immunobead binding assay to detect antisperm antibodies. Office: Stony Brook Univ Med Ctr Health Sciences Ctr T9-080 Stony Brook NY 11794-8091 Office Phone: 631-444-2731. Business E-Mail: richard.bronson@stonybrook.edu.

BROOK, DAVID WILLIAM, psychiatrist, researcher; b. NYC, Sept. 19, 1936; s. Michael Marysson and Hilda Jeanette (Ascher) B.; m. Judith Suzanne Muser, Dec. 15, 1962; children: Adam Michael, Jonathan Edward. BA, U. Rochester, 1958; MD, Yale U., 1961. Diplomate Am. Bd. Psychiatry and Neurology, Am. Bd. Addiction Psychiatry; cert. addiction psychiatry; cert. in addiction medicine Am. Soc. Addiction Medicine; cert. med. rev. officer; cert. group psychotherapist Nat. Registry Group Psychotherapists. Intern U. Chgo. Hosps., 1961-62; resident Mt. Sinai Hosp., 1962-65, asst. attending psychiatrist, 1973-80, assoc. attending psychiatrist, 1980-90, attending psychiatrist (cmty. medicine), 1994—; practice medicine specializing in psychiatry NYC, 1965—; clin. asst. in psychiatry Hillside Hosp., 1965-67; sch. psychiatrist N.Y.C. Bur. Child Guidance, 1967-69; asst. clin. prof. psychiatry Mt. Sinai Sch. Medicine, 1977-88, assoc. clin. prof., 1988-90, adj. assoc. prof., 1990-92, prof. cmty. and preventive medicine, 1994—2003, adj. prof. cmty. and preventive medicine, 2004—; assoc. prof. psychiatry N.Y. Med. Coll., Valhalla, 1990-92, prof. clin. psychiatry, 1992-94; prof. psychiatry NYU Sch. Medicine, 2004—. Adj. asst. prof. psychiatry Fordham U. Sch. Social Work, 1970-73; med. dir. Washington Sq. Inst. Psychotherapy and Mental Health, 1977-82; attending psychiatrist, acting dir. dept. psychiatry Mt. Sinai Svcs., Elmhurst Hosp. Ctr., 1989-90; attending psychiatrist Westchester County Med. Ctr., 1990-94; dir. divsn. drug abuse rsch., prevention and treatment N.Y. Med. Coll., Valhalla, 1990-94, adj. prof. clin. psychiatry, 1994-2001; prin. investigator, co-prin. investigator rsch. grants Nat. Inst. Drug Abuse; bd. examiner Am. Bd. Psychiatry and Neurology; attending psychiatrist, NYU Hosps., 2004—. Co-author, co-editor 6 books including Psychology of Adolescence, 1978, Group Therapy of Substance Abuse, 2002, Group Psychotherapy Approaches to addiction and Substance Abuse, 2011; contbr. over 150 articles to profl. jours., chpts. to books on group psychotherapy, adolescence, alcoholism, drug abuse and behavioral medicine; mem. editl. bd. Internat. Jour. Group Psychotherapy, Social Work in Health Care, Jour. Addictive Diseases, Jour. of Groups in Addiction and Recovery. Fellow Am. Group Psychotherapy Assn. (bd. dirs. 1992-95, 98-01), Am. Psychiat. Assn. (disting. life, exec. coun. NY County dist. br. 1988-91, mem. Assembly 1999—), NY Acad. Medicine, Am. Soc. Addiction Medicine, Am. Psychopathol. Assn.; mem., Group Psychotherapy Found. (bd. dirs. 1992-98), Am. Acad. Addiction Psychiatrists. Office: NYU School of Medicine 215 Lexington Ave New York NY 10016 Office Phone: 212-263-4661. Fax: 212-263-4660.

BROOK, MICHAEL MORRIS, cardiologist, educator; b. Burlington, Wis., Oct. 2, 1960; BS, Marquette U.; MD, U. Wis., 1986. Cert. in pediat. 1989, in pediat. cardiology 1992. Intern pediat. Children's Hosp. of Wis., Milw., 1986—87, resident pediatric cardiology, 1987—89; fellowship pediatric cardiology U. Calif. San Francisco Children's Hosp., 1989—92; attending med. staff pediat. Moffett Long Hosp. U. Calif. San Francisco, 1992, asst. prof. pediat., 1992—99, assoc. prof. to prof., 1999—, pediat. cardiologist, dir. Pediat. Echocardiography Lab. Office: U Calif San Francisco Box 0214 505 Parnassus Ave, Moffitt M3 San Francisco CA 94143-0214 Office Phone: 415-353-1689. Office Fax: 415-473-1689, 415-353-8675. E-mail: michael.brook@ucsf.edu.

BROOK, RICHARD A., pharmaceutical executive; b. NY, Dec. 2, 1964; BS, Rensselaer Poly. Inst., 1986, MS, MBA, 1987. V.p., bus. devel., head retrospective rsch. JestaRx Group, 2001—; ptnr. Edjudicate, 2005—11; v.p. Pharmacy Group, 2005—11, Nat. Managed Care Roundtable, 2005—11, TPG-Nat. Payor Roundtable, 2011. Mem.: Internat. Soc. Pharmacoeconomics and Outcomes Rsch. Office: 18 Hirth Dr Newfoundland NJ 07435-1710 Business E-Mail: rbrook@jestarx.com.

BROOKE, RALPH IAN, dental educator; b. Leeds, Eng., Apr. 25, 1934; s. Michael and Jeanette (Cohen) B.; m. Lorna Ruth Shields; children: Michael Jeremy Richard, Andrew Timothy. Baccalaureus Chirurgiae Dentium, Licentiate in Dental Surgery, Leeds U., England, 1957. Licentiate Royal Coll. Physicians, 1963. Sr. lectr. Leeds U., 1970-72; prof., chmn. dept. oral medicine U. Western Ont., London, Can., 1972-82, dean dentistry faculty, 1982-97, vice provost health scis., 1987-97. Chief dentistry Univ. Hosp., London, 1973-92. Contbr. articles to profl. jours.; mem. editl. bd. Can. Pain Jour., 1990. Recipient Barnabus Day award, 2011; named Hon. Alumnus Distinction, U. Western Ontario, 2006. Fellow Acad. Dentistry Internat. (hon.), Royal Coll. Dentists Can., Royal Coll. Surgeons; mem. Nat. Dental Exam Bd. (past chmn. Can. commn. on dental accreditation), Can. Faculties Dentistry (past pres.), Can. Acad. Oral Medicine (past pres.), Can. Dental Assn. (hon.), Can. Acad. Oral and Maxillofacial Pathology and Oral Medicine (hon.), Ont. Dental Assn. (bd. dirs.). Avocations: music, hiking. Office Phone: 519-661-3327. Business E-Mail: rbrooke@uwo.ca.

BROOKER, JEFF ZEIGLER, retired cardiologist; b. Columbia, SC, Nov. 1, 1941; s. Jefferson Zeigler and Virginia (Ligon) B.; m. Rhoda Arrowsmith, June 12, 1966; children: Jeff III, John, Rhoda. BS, U. S.C., Columbia, 1962; MD, Med. U. S.C., 1966. Cert. in interventional cardiology, clin. cardiac electrophysiology, cardiovasc. disease and internal medicine Am. Bd. Internal Medicine. Intern, resident Hosp. U. Pa., Phila., 1966-68; resident internal medicine Stanford U. Med. Ctr., Palo Alto, Calif., 1970-71, rsch. fellow cardiology, 1971-73; staff cardiologist Tex. Heart Inst., Houston, 1973-74; assoc. dir. cardiology Providence Hosp., Columbia, S.C., 1974-81; pvt. practice cardiology Columbia, 1981—2006; ret., 2006. Cons. peer rev. Jour. AMA, Chgo., 1976-77; local and regional rsch. com. Am. Heart Assn., Dallas, 1977-86. Mem. editl. bd. Jour. SC Med. Assn., Columbia, 1991—2006; editl. reviewer: Essentials of Echocardiography, 1977. Legis. liaison S.C. Med. Assn., Columbia, 1991-92. Lt. comdr. USN, 1968-70. Recipient Best Sci. Article award Roe Found., Columbia, 1991. Achievements include improved method for oral dipyridamole testing for ischemic heart disease; devising a percutaneous method for inserting pacing lead into the internal jugular vein yet still implant and pulse generator on the anterior chest wall; solving for mortality rate in terms of survival rate and disease prevalence. Office: 1625 Bernardin Ave Columbia SC 29204-2003

BROOKMEYER, RONALD, medical educator; b. NYC, Sept. 4, 1954; BS summa cum laude, Cooper Union Coll., NYC, 1975; MS, U. Wis., 1977, PhD, 1980. Lectr. statistics U. Wis., Madison, 1980—81; asst. prof. biostatistics Johns Hopkins U. Sch. Pub. Health, Balt., 1981—85; vis. biostatistician Nat. Cancer Inst., Bethesda, Md., 1986; assoc. prof. biostatistics Johns Hopkins U. Bloomberg Sch. Pub. Health, Balt., 1985—90, prof. biostatistics, 1990—, chair, dir. MPH prog., 2002—08. Chmn. internat. adv. com. UNAIDS, Geneva, 2008; nat. biosurveillance adv. com. CDC, 2008—. Contbr. articles to profl. jours. Recipient Golden Apple Tchg. award, Johns Hopkins U., 1985, 1999, 2004; vis. scholar Woodrow Wilson Sch. Pub. and Internat. Affairs, Princeton U., 2008—09. Fellow: AAAS (chmn. statistics sect. 2007), Am. Statistical Assn. (chmn. biometrics sect. 1996, chair-elect statistics in epidemiology sect. 2009); mem.: Soc. for Epidemiologic Rsch., Am. Pub. Health Assn. (Mortimer Speigelman gold medal in Health Statistics), Inst. Medicine, Biometrics Soc. (coun. mem. 2004). Achievements include research on the development of statistical methods in epidemiology. Office: Johns Hopkins Bloomberg Sch Pub Health E3142 7420 N Honeysuckle Ct Brimfield IL 61517-8901 Office Phone: 410-955-3519. Office Fax: 410-955-0958. E-mail: rbrook@jhsph.edu.

BROOKS, ARI, surgeon, educator; MD, Drexel U. Diplomate Am. Bd. Surgery-oncology surgery, Am. Bd. Surgery-general surgery. Intern NY State Univ. Sch. of Medicine, resident; assoc. prof. surgery Drexel Univ. Coll. of Medicine; afilliate faculty sch. of biomed. engring. Drexel Univ.; hosp. affiliations include Hahnemann Univ. Hosp., Cancer Treatment Centers of America, S. Jersey Regional Hosp. Adjunct faculty Ctr. for Women's Health; adjunct faculty molecular pathbiology Drexel Univ. Coll. of Medicine. Named Top Doctor, Phila. Mag., 2011, Best Doctors, 2009—11. Achievements include research in "Portable breast Cancer Sreener"; "Quantum Dots for Tumor Margin Detection"; "Surgical Site Infections Research Initiative"; "Portable Plasma Sterilizer"; "Magnetizable bone cement for local drug delivery"; "Development of the Drug Delivery Surgical Staple"; "Development and Testing of a Nano Scale Ultrasound Contrast Agent For Detection of Ovarian Cancer"; "Non-Thermal Atmospheric Pressure Electrical Discharge Plasma for Non-Surgical Treatment of Skin Diseases"; "Drexel/Tenet Women's Health Project"; "Translation Research, Development of the Drug Delivery Surgical Staple"; "Isolated single lung perfusion for directed gene therapy". Office: Hahnemann University Hospital Broad and Vine Philadelphia PA 19102 Office Phone: 215-762-7000. Office Fax: 215-762-8109.

BROOKS, DARRELL, surgeon; b. Lawrence, Kans., June 27, 1962; BS, Stanford U., 1985; MD, Stanford U. Sch. Medicine, 1993. Staff surgeon Buncke Clinic, 1999—. Asst. clin. prof. dept. plastic surgery Stanford U. Hosp., 2002—, U. Calif. San Francisco, 2005—, U. Calif. Davis, 2005—; mem. editl. bd. Microsurgery. Mem.: Calif. Soc. Plastic, Am. Soc. Peripheral Nerve, Am. Soc. Reconstructive Microsurgery, Am. Soc. Plastic Surgery. Office: 45 Castro St Ste 121 San Francisco CA 94114 Business E-Mail: darrellbrooks@usa.net.

BROOKS, DEBRA L., healthcare executive, neuromuscular therapist, artist; b. Cedar Rapids, Iowa, Dec. 10, 1950; children: Brei, Benjamin, Bryan. BA, Coe Coll., 1973; MS, Clayton Coll., 1999, PhD, 2000. Cert. neuromuscular therapy Fla., natural therapeutics specialist N.Mex. Tchr. Cedar Rapids Cmty. Sch. Dist., Iowa, 1973—92; COO NeuroMuscular Therapy Ctr., Walford, Iowa, 1994—. Educator Helping Hands Seminars, Cedar Rapids, 1992—2000, Debra Brooks' Seminars, Walford, 1993—; bus. and ednl. cons. Brooks Consults, Cedar Rapids, 1990—; mem. Iowa Bd. Examiners, 2001—03, Am. Assn. Homes & Aging, 2008—10, Obnova Citizens Advocacy Bd., 2008—10; chair adv. bd. ABLE, 2001—02; mem., chair Nat. Alliance State Bds., 2001—09; editl. bd. Momentum Media, 2000—; v.p. New Bohemia, 2009, bd. dirs., 2008—10, Spanda Inc. Cedar Rapids Vision Motion, 2008—, Old Creamery Theater, 2010—; editl. reviewer W W Norton Pub., 2007—. Pianist Cedar Rapids Symphony Discovery Chorus, 1985—91, Orchestra Iowa Discovery Chorus, 2008—; contbr. articles to profl jours and newsletters. Fundraiser, performer in musicals St Luke's Hosp, Cedar Rapids, 1978—91; fundraiser, performer in Follies Cedar Rapids Symphony, 1981—99; fundraiser, performer in telethons Variety Clubs Am, Cedar Rapids, 1989—91; mem Walford Cmty. Devel., 1994—98; editl. bd. Tng. and Conditioning Mag.; bd. dirs. Cedar Rapids Concert Chorale, 2005—09, chmn. fundraising, 2006—07. Recipient First in Nation Edn. Award, State of Iowa, 1991, Tribute Women of Achievement award, YWCA, 2001; named Outstanding Mentor of Yr., 2001. Mem.: Iowa Neuro-Muscular Therapy Ctr., Am. Coll. Healthcare Execs., Am. Massage Therapy Assn. (state v.p., edn. dir. 1992—94, nat. trustee Found. 1994—98, nat. bd. dirs. 1994—2002, nat. edn. slection com. 2002—), Profl. Women's Network (chmn. 2002—03). Avocations: singing, painting, pianist, power walking, philosophy. Office: Iowa NeuroMuscular Therapy Ctr PO Box 277 Walford IA 52351-0277

BROOKS, DENNIS ALBERT, pediatrician; b. Providence, Mar. 19, 1957; BA, U. Pa., 1979; MD, U. Cin. Coll. Medicine, 1984. Asst. prof. pediat. Johns Hopkins Med. Instns., 1988—2005; sr. dir. med. affairs, policy Merck, 2005—08; sr. med. dir. global med. affairs Wyeth Inc, 2009—10; attending physician, dept. pediat. Einstein Med. Ctr., Phila., 2009—; vaccine med. lead asia pacific med. affairs Pfizer Inc, 2010—. Mem.: Ambulatory Pediats. Assn., Am. Acad. Pediat., Nat. Med. Assn. (Grace James award). Avocations: reading, jogging, weightlifting. Home: 4177 Ironbridge Dr Collegeville PA 19426 Business E-Mail: dbrook16@jhmi.edu.

BROOKS, DURADO, health science association administrator, oncologist; MD, Wright State U. Sch. Med, 1982; MPH Harvard Sch. Pub. Health, 1999. Chief resident Wright State U. Affiliated Hosp.; fellow Harvard Sch. Pub. Health; med. dir. Cmty. Health Ctr., Dayton; asst. med. dir. Parkland Meml. Hosp. Cmty Oriented Primary Care Program, Dallas; dir. prostate & colorectal cancers Am. Cancer Soc., mem. internal editorial rev. bd. Office: American Cancer Society Center 250 Williams St Atlanta GA 30303 Office Phone: 404-315-1123. Office Fax: 404-315-9348.

BROOKS, ELIZABETH B., rheumatologist, educator; MD, Case Western Reserve U., 1993; PhD, Yale U., 1988. Cert. Am. Bd. Internal Medicine, 1996, in rheumatology 1998, 2008. Intern internal medicine Brigham & Women's Hosp., Boston, 1993—94, resident, 1994—96, clin. fellow rheumatology, 1996—99; asst. prof. Case Western. Reserve U., Cleve.; adult and pediat. rheumatologist Univ. Hosp., Case Med. Ctr., Rainbow Babies & Children's Hosp., Cleve. Contbr. articles to med. jours. Office: Divsn Pediat Rheumatology Rainbow Babies & Children's Hosp 11100 Euclid Ave Cleveland OH 44106 Office Phone: 216-844-3645, 216-844-8026. Office Fax: 216-844-7587. E-mail: Elizabeth.Brooks2@UHhospitals.org, elizabeth.brooks@case.edu.

BROOKS, FRANKLIN RAMON, psychologist, military officer; b. Margarita, CZ, Panama, Dec. 2, 1945; s. Sherman C. and Astrea (Bertonini) B.; m. Lenalee Bunch, July 6, 1950; children: Franklin Bryson, Marcus Ramon, Jennifer Jean; m. May 29, 1970. BS, Tex. A&M U., 1967; MS in Clin. Psychology, U. North Tex., 1971, PhD in Clin. Psychology, 1975. Cert. psychologist, Tex. 2d lt. U.S. Army, 1967, advanced through grades to col.; chief psychology svc. Frankfurt (Germany) Army Regional Med. Ctr., 1984-88, Eisenhower Army Med. Ctr., Ft. Gordon, Ga., 1988-89, chief dept. psychology, 1989-93; chief psychology svc. Brooke Army Med. Ctr., Ft. Sam Houston, Tex., 1993-95, chief dept. psychology, 1995-98, chief dept. behavioral medicine, 1998—2001; chief ops. officer Brown Sch., Laurel Ridge, 2001—02; pvt. practice San Antonio, 2002—. Clin. psychology cons. US Army Health Svc. Command, Ft. Sam Houston, 1993-95, Gt. Plains Regional Command, Ft. Sam Houston, 1995-2001; clin. dir. San Antonio Chronic Pain Inst., 2003—05. Fellow Am. Coll. Forensic Examiners (diplomate); mem. APA, Am. Psychol. Soc., Assn. Mil. Surgeons US, Am. Soc. Clin. Hypnosis. Roman Catholic. Avocations: movies, racquetball. Home: 2615 Oak Leigh San Antonio TX 78232 Personal E-mail: drfrbrooks@aol.com.

BROOKS, JOHN SAMUEL JOSEPH, pathologist, researcher; b. Phila., Feb. 2, 1948; BS in Biology, St. Joseph's Coll., Phila., 1970; MD, Thomas Jefferson U., 1974. Diplomate Am. Bd. Pathology. Resident in pathology U. Pa., Phila., 1974-78, chief resident, 1978, asst. prof., 1979-84, assoc. prof., 1984-88, prof., 1988-93, prof. pathology, 2002—, vice-chmn. pathology, 2004—; chmn. dept. pathology Roswell Pk. Cancer Inst., Buffalo, 1993—2002, chmn. dept. lab. medicine, 1997—2002, pres. med. staff, 1997-98; prof., vice chmn. pathology Med. Sch. SUNY, Buffalo, 1993—2002; chmn. dept. pathology Pa. Hosp., 2004—. Vis. prof. Royal Marsden Hosp./Inst.

Cancer Rsch., London, 1987; expert in immunohistochemistry. Author: Pathology, 1989; contbr. articles to New Eng. Jour. Medicine, Jour. of AMA, Jour. Urology, Internat. Jour. Ob.-Gyn. Pathology, Am. Jour. Pathology; editor Internat. Jour. Surg. Pathology, 1993-99; mem. bd. editors: Jour. Modern Pathology, Am. Jour. Surg. Pathology, and reviewer; contbr. over 140 articles to profl. jours. Fellow Royal Coll. Pathology; mem. AAAS, Am. Assn. Cancer Rsch., Pathology Soc. Phila. (pres. 1988-90), Ea. Coop. Oncology Group (chmn. sarcoma pathology com. Madison chpt. 1988-95), Internat. Acad. Pathology (edn. com. Atlanta chpt. 1989—), U.S.-Can. Acad. Pathology (coun. mem. 1993-96), Am. Soc. Clin. Pathologists (chair anat. pathology coun. 1995-97, dep. commr. 1997—, bd. dir. 2000—, v.p. 2004-2005, pres.-elect, 2005-2006, pres., 2006-07), Arthur Purdy Stout Soc. Surg. Pathologists (coun. mem. 1994), Internat. Soc. Bone and Soft Tissue Pathology (sec. 2008-), Am. Assn. Clin. Rsch., Fedn. Am. Soc. Exptl. Biology, Medicine Coverage Adv. Com. Lab. Diagnostics Panel, Internat. Soc. Bone and Soft Tissue Pathology (sec. 2008-) Nat. Internat. Reputation in Diagnostic Surg. Pathology Democrat. Roman Catholic. Achievements include research in significance of double phenotypes in sarcomas, growth factors in sarcomas, in immunohistochemistry; posthumous diagnosis of Pres. Cleveland's tumor. Office: Dept Pathology 6 Preston Bldg Pa Hosp 800 Spruce St Philadelphia PA 19107 Business E-Mail: john.brooks@uphs.upenn.edu.

BROOKS, PETER MICHAEL, physician, educator; b. Manchester, Eng., June 11, 1944; MBBS, Monash U., 1967; MD (hon.), U. Lund; MS, Am. Coll. Rheumatology. Diplomate Australian Rheumatology Assn. Prof. rheumatology U. Sydney, 1983—92; prof. medicine U. NSW, 1992—98; exec. dean faculty health scis. U. Queensland, 1998—2009; prof., dir. Australian Health Workforce Inst. U. Melbourne, 2010—. Bd. mem. Epworth Health, 2008, Primed Health, 2009; chair academic bd. Australian Coll. Health, 2011; cons. advisor JoFisherExec Search, 2011. Recipient Heberden Orator, Brit. Soc. Rheumatology. Fellow: RCP (Edinburgh), RCP (Glasgow), AFPHM, AFARM, RACP. Avocations: reading, walking. Office: Level 3 766 Elizabeth St Melbourne Victoria 3010 Australia Business E-Mail: brooksp@unimelb.edu.au.

BROOKS, PHILIP J., neurobiologist; BA in physiological psychology, Boston Coll.; MA in psychology, U. Toronto; PhD in neurobiology, U. NC, Chapel Hill. Postdoctoral fellow, lab. of neurogenetics NIH Nat. Inst. Alcohol Abuse and Alcoholism, Bethesda, 1993—2001, sci., lab. of neurogenetics, 2001—, acting chief molecular neurobiology sect. Office: Nat Inst Alcohol Abuse and Alcoholism MSC 8110 12420 Parklawn Dr Rm 451 Bethesda MD 20892-8110 E-mail: pjbrooks@mail.nih.gov.

BROOME, MARION E., dean, nursing educator; BSN, Med. Coll. Ga., 1973; MN in Family Health Nursing, U. SC, 1977; PhD in Child and Family Devel., U. Ga., 1984; post-doctoral studies, U. Ala., 1986—88. Instr. to assoc. prof. Med. Coll. Ga., 1978—88; nursing educator Rush U., Chgo., 1988—94; Children's Hosp. Wis. rsch. chair U. Wis., Milw., 1994—99; assoc. dean rsch. U. Ala., Birmingham, 1999—2004; dean Ind. U. Sch. Nursing, Indpls., 2004—, disting. prof., 2006—. Mem. nursing sci. study sect. NIH, 1997—2001; pres. Soc. Pediatric Nurses; bd. dirs. Assn. Care Children's Health, Midwest Nursing Rsch. Soc. Contbr. articles to profl. jours., chapters to books. Named Outstanding Alumnus of Yr., Med. Coll. Ga., 1988, Disting. Alumnus, U. SC, 2006; fellow Nurse Exec. Leadership Program, Assn. Colleges of Nursing, 2002—03. Fellow: Am. Acad. Nursing (editor-in-chief, Nursing Outlook 2003—). Office: Ind U Sch Nursing Office Ednl Svcs 1111 Middle Dr NU 117 Indianapolis IN 46202-5107 Office Phone: 317-274-1486. Office Fax: 317-278-1842. Business E-Mail: mbroome@iupui.edu.

BROOME, PATRICK J., dentist; BS in Biol. Sci. and Mktg., Clemson U., SC; MBA, Wingate U., NC; grad., Med. U. SC. Served as an adviser and cons. for many dental equipment and product mfrs.; clin. instr. Southeast Regional Tng. Ctr.; dentist Charlotte Ctr. for Cosmetic Dentistry. Named one of TopDentists, 2007—. Master: World Clin. Laser Inst.; fellow: Acad. of Gen. Dentistry; mem.: ADA, SC Dental Assn., NC Dental Assn., Am. Acad. Cosmetic Dentistry. Office: Charlotte Center for Cosmetic Dentistry 6849 Fairview Rd Ste 200 Charlotte NC 28210 Office Phone: 704-364-4711. Office Fax: 704-364-1963.

BROPHY, PATRICK DAVID, pediatrician, researcher; b. Calgary, Alta., Can., Aug. 21, 1965; s. David John and Deirdre Brophy; m. Jodi Lynn Yeo, Nov. 17, 1990; children: Michael Cormac, Joseph Caelan. BA with honors, U. Sask., Saskatoon, Can., 1992, MD, 1994; BSc, U. Regina, Sask., Can., 1988. Lectr. dept. pediat. U. Mich., Ann Arbor, 2001—02, asst. prof., 2002—, co-dir. pediatric lupus program, 2001—, assoc. dir. pediatric dialysis, 2005—; asst. prof. U. Iowa, 2007—. Contbr. articles to profl. jours. Recipient Basic Sci. Fellows award, Soc. Pediatric Rsch., 2001; grantee, Polycystic Kidney Found., 2000—03, NIH, 2005—; Carl W Gottschalk grantee, Am. Soc. Nephrology, 2002—04. Fellow: Am. Acad. Pediat., Royal Coll. Physicians Can. (corr.), Am. Soc. Nephrology (assoc.); mem.: Internat. Pediat. Nephrology Assn. (corr.), Am. Soc. Pediat. Nephrology (corr.). Roman Catholic. Achievements include research in Renal development. Avocations: golf, scuba diving, hockey. Office: Peds Dept 2612 J C P 200 Hawkins Dr Iowa City IA 52242-1089 Personal E-mail: pbrophy@umich.ed. Business E-Mail: pbrophy@umich.edu, patrick-brophy@viour.edu.

BROSCO, JEFFREY P., pediatrician, educator; b. Providence; married. BA, U. Pa., Phila., 1985, MD, PhD, U. Pa., Phila., 1992. Cert. pediat. 1996, developmental behavioral pedia. 2002. Resident pediat. Jackson Mem. Hosp., Miami, Fla., 1992—95; asst. prof. U. Miami, 1996—2001, assoc. prof., 2002—08, prof., 2009—. Scholar Generalist Faculty, Robert Wood Johnson Found., 1998—2003. Office: Univ Miami PO Box 016820 Miami FL 33101 Office Phone: 305-243-3371. Business E-Mail: jbrosco@miami.edu.

BROSE, JOHN ADOLPH, medical educator, dean; b. Teaneck, NJ, Oct. 6, 1950; s. Adolph Dahlke and Mary Wilhelmina (Quattlebaum) B.; m. Linda Diane Way, Aug. 20, 1972; children: Steven William, Christine Marie. DO, U. North Tex. Health Sci. Ctr., 1976; postdoc. fellow, Ohio State U., 1985-86. Cert. Am. Bd. Family Practice, 1979, Am. Osteopathic Bd. Family Practice, 1983. Resident Scott (AFB Ill.) Med. Ctr., 1979, resident faculty, 1979-82; prof. Ohio U., Athens, 1982—, asst. chmn. dept. family medicine, 1991—92, head academic tng. program, dir. family medicine fellowship program, 1983—2001; clin. assoc. prof. Ohio State U. Coll. Medicine, Athens, 1985—92, assoc. prof., 1992—2000; asst. prof. Ohio U. Coll. Osteo. Medicine, Athens, 1982—87, assoc. prof., 1987—93, prof., 1993—, dir. predoctoral family medicine fellowship program, 1983—2001, asst. dean ednl. devel. and rsch., 1992—94, asst. dean clin. rsch., 1994—2001, dean, 2001—. Mem. expert panel USP Family Medicine, 1990—. Served to maj. USAF, 1976—82. Named Outstanding Instr., Ohio State U., 13 times, recipient Std. Excellence award, 1995. Fellow Am. Acad. Family Physicians; mem. Am. Osteo. Assn., Am. Coll. Gen. Practice (undergrad. com. 1982—), Ohio Acad. Family Physicians (pres. Hocking Valley chpt., Ohio Family Practice Educator of Ur. 2001), Ohio Coun. Med. Sch. Deans (chmn. 2005-06). Office: Ohio Univ Coll Osteopathic Medicine 204 Grosvenor Hall Athens OH 45701 Office Phone: 740-593-2178. E-mail: brose@ohio.edu. *

BROSSNER, CLEMENS, urologist; b. Oberwart, Austria, Oct. 19, 1959; s. Otto and Margarete (Zettl) B. MD, U. Vienna, 1988. Tng. gen. practitioner Oberwart Hosp., Austria, 1989, resident in urology, 1993-95, 96-98, urologist, 1998—; resident in urology U. Vienna, Austria, 1995-96; prof. urology, 2006—. Contbr. articles to profl. jours. Recipient Theodor Körner prize Theodor Körner Fonds, 1997. Fellow: European Bd. Urology; mem.: Austrian Soc. Urology (past chmn. prostate study group 2000—03), European Assn. of Urology (reviewer European Urology, head urological dept. 2009). Avocations: tennis, mountainbiking. Home: Hahngasse 20/10 1090 Vienna Austria Office Phone: 0043400883940. E-mail: broessner@yahoo.de.

BROTHERS, JOYCE DIANE, television personality, psychologist; b. NYC; d. Morris K. and Estelle (Rapoport) Bauer; m. Milton Brothers, July 4, 1949; 1 child, Lisa Robin. BS, Cornell U., 1947; MA, Columbia U., 1950, PhD, 1953; LHD (hon.), Franklin Pierce Coll., Gettysburg Coll., Lehigh U., 1994, Mt. St. Mary Coll., 1998. Asst. in psychology Columbia U., NYC, 1948-52; instr. psychology Hunter Coll., NYC, 1948-52; ind. psychologist, writer, 1952—. Co-host: TV program Sports Showcase, 1956; appearances: TV program Dr. Joyce Brothers, 1958-63, Consult Dr. Brothers, 1960-66, Ask Dr. Brothers, 1965-75; hostess (TV syndication) Living Easy with Dr. Joyce Brothers, 1972-75; columnist TV syndication, N.Am. Newspaper Alliance, 1961-71, Bell-McClure Syndicate, 1963-71, King Features Syndicate, 1972—, Good Housekeeping mag., 1962—; appearances Sta. WNBC, 1966-70; radio program Emphasis, 1966-75, Monitor, 1967-75, Sta. WMCA, 1970-73, ABC Reports, 1966-67, NBC Radio Network Newsline, 1975—; news analyst radio program, Metro Media-TV, 1975-76, news corr., TVN, Inc., 1975 76, Sta. KABC-TV, 1977-82, Sta. WABC-TV, 1980-82,, 86-88, Sta. WLS-TV, 1980-82, NIWS Syndicated News Service, 1982-84, The Dr. Joyce Brothers Program, The Disney Channel, 1985, Sta. KCBS-TV News, 1987—; contbr. CBS News, 2003—, MSNBC, 2003—; spl. feature writer Hearst papers, UPI; current affairs spl. corr. Fox TV Syndication, 1990-97; featured on A&E's Biography 1999; author: Ten Days to a Successful Memory, 1959, Woman, 1961, The Brothers System for Liberated Love and Marriage, 1975, How to Get Whatever You Want Out of Life, 1978, What Every Woman Should Know About Men, 1982, What Every Woman Ought to Know About Love and Marriage, 1988, The Successful Woman, 1989, Widowed, 1990, Positive Plus: The Practical Plan to Liking Yourself Better, 1994. Co-chmn. sports com. Lighthouse for Blind; door-to-door chmn. Fedn. Jewish Philanthropies, N.Y.C., mem. fund raising com. Olympic Fund; mem. People-to-People Program. Winner $64,000 Question TV Program, 1956, $64,000 Challenge, 1957; recipient Mennen Baby Found. award, 1959, Newhouse Newspaper award, 1959, Am. Acad. Achievement award, Am. Parkinson Disease Assn. award, 1971, Deadline award Sigma Delta Chi, 1971, Pres.'s Cabinet award U. Detroit, 1975, Woman of Achievement award Women's City Club Cleve., 1981, award Calif. Home Econs. Assn., 1981, award Distrubutive Edn. Clubs Am., 1981, Golden Gavel Excellence in Comm. award Toastmasters, 1982, Pub. Svc. award Ridgewood Women's Club, 1987, Women Who Make a Difference award Sen. Bill Bradley, 1990, Gt. Am. award Bards of Bohemia, 1993, Diamond award, 1994, George M. and Mary Jane Leader Healthcare Achievement award, 1995, Nat. Cmty. Svc. award McQuade Children Svcs., 1998, Presdl. citation Am. Psychol. Assn., 2002. Mem. Sigma Xi. Office: NBC Westwood One Radio Network 1700 Broadway New York NY 10019-5905

BROTMAN, MARTIN, health care services executive, gastroenterologist; b. Winnipeg, Manitoba, Canada, June 26, 1939; MD, U. Manitoba, 1962. Diplomate Am. Bd. Internal Medicine, cert. in gastroenterology. Intern Winnipeg Gen. Hosp., 1962—63; resident internal medicine Mayo Grad. Med. Sch., Rochester, Minn., 1963—65, fellow gastroenterology, 1965—67; pvt. practice San Francisco; chmn. med. dept. Calif. Pacific Med. Ctr., San Francisco, 1992—95, pres., CEO, 1995—2009, interim CEO St. Luke's Hosp., 2005; pres. West Bay region Sutter Health, Sacramento, 2009—. Clin. prof. med. U. Calif. San Francisco, 1982—. Mem.: ACP, AMA, Am. Soc. Gastrointestinal Endoscopy, Am. Assn. Study Liver Diseases, Am. Soc. Internal Medicine, Am. Gastroentrol. Assn. (pres.-elect 2001—02, pres. 2002—03). Office: Sutter Health West Bay Region 345 California St San Francisco CA 94104 Office Phone: 916-733-8800.

BROTMAN, RICHARD DENNIS, counselor; b. Detroit, Nov. 2, 1952; s. Alfred David and Dorothy G. (Mansfield) B.; m. Debra Louise Hobold, Sept. 9, 1979. AA, East L.A. Jr. Coll., 1972; AB, U. So. Calif., 1974, MS, 1976. Lic. marriage, family and child counselor, Calif.; cert. counselor, Calif. Instructional media coord. Audiovisual divsn. Pub. Libr., City of Alhambra, Calif., 1971 78; clin. supr. Hollywood-Sunset Cmty. Clinic, LA, 1976—2008; client program coord. North Los Angeles County Regional Ctr. for Devel. Disabled, 1978-81; sr. counselor Eastern L.A. Regional Ctr. for Devel. Disabled, 1981-85; dir. cmty. svcs. Almansor Edn. Ctr., 1985-87; tng. and resource devel. Children's Home Soc. Calif., 1987-90; program supr. Pacific Clinics-East, 1990-94; assoc. dir. clin. svcs., dir. clin. svcs. Alma Family Svcs., 1994—2002; probable cause hearing officer Orange County (Calif.) Healthcare Agy., 1986—. Corp. dir. San Gabriel Mission Players, 1973-75. Mem. Am. Assn. for Marriage and Family Therapy (approved supr.), Calif. Pers. and Guidance Assn., Calif. Rehab. Counselors Assn. (officer), San Fernando Valley Consortium of Agys. Serving Devel. Disabled Citizens (chmn. recreation subcom), L.A. Aquarium Soc. Democrat. Home: PO Box 70070 Pasadena CA 91117-7070 Office Phone: 626-577-9728. Personal E-mail: brieftherapy@sbcglobal.net. *

BROTT, WALTER HOWARD, retired cardiac surgeon, educator, military officer; b. Alamosa, Colo., Sept. 5, 1933; s. Walter Hugo and Viola Helen (Roscher) B.; m. Marie Helen Kuzniewski; children: Cheryl Marie, Michelle Marie, Kevin Walter. BA, Yale U., 1955; MD, U. Kans., 1959. Diplomate Am. Bd. Surgery, Am. Bd. Thoracic Surgery. Commd. 1st. lt. U.S. Army, 1959, advanced through grades to col., 1974; intern Walter Reed Army Med. Ctr., Washington, 1959; resident in gen. surgery William Beaumont Gen. Hosp., El Paso, Tex., 1960-64; resident in thoracic surgery Fitzsimmons Army Med. Ctr., Denver, 1967-69; comdr. 3d Surg. Hosp., Vietnam, 1969, 18th Surg. Hosp., 1970; asst. chief thoracic and cardiovascular surgery Walter Reed Army Med. Ctr., 1971-76, chief cardiothoracic surgery, 1977-84; ret. U.S. Army, 1982. Chief surg. cons. Surgeon Gen. Army, Washington, 1976-77; prof. surgery and subsequent adjuvant prof. surgery Uniformed Svcs. U. Health Scis., 1976—; assoc. clin. prof. surgery U. Tenn., Knoxville, 1984-94, hon. clinical prof., 1994—; mem. joint rev. com. Coun. for Perfusion Edn. and Accreditation, 1981-87, 1st chief cardiothorasic surgery uniformed svc. U. Health Sci., Herbert Sch. Medicine. Contbr. articles to profl. jours.; chmn.: NATO editorial bd., sr. editor Emergency War Surgery Handbook, 1977-82. Mem. physicians' panel Heritage Found., 1991—. Decorated Legion of Merit with oak leaf cluster; decorated Bronze Star (U.S.), Cross of Gallantry (Vietnam), 1st class Action medal Vietnam; recipient Cert. of Achievement Surgeon Gen. U.S., 1973 Fellow ACS (grad. edn. com. 1977-78); mem. AMA (cons. panel coun. allied health edn. accreditation 1981-87), Walter Reed Assn., Soc. Thoracic Surgeons, Washington Med. Soc., Thoracic and Cardiovascular Surgeons, Thoracic Surgery Program Dirs. Assn., Am. Assn. for Thoracic Surgery, Assn. Med. Cons. to Armed Forces, Assn. Mil. Surgeons, Heritage Found. (Physicians Coun.), Internat. Platform Assn., Alpha Omega Alpha. Clubs: Yale (Washington); Marine Meml., Univ. Faculty Club (U. Tenn.). Lutheran.

BROUGHTON, MARGARET MARTHA (HAMIDA BROUGHTON), mental health nurse; b. London, Ky., Feb. 1, 1926; d. Edward Broughton and Stella Alice Johnson; m. Louis Kurt Henkel, May 17, 1947 (div. Nov. 1957); children: Gretchen Maria Henkel Clark, Suzanne Henkel Guthrie, Elizabeth Henkel Stark, David Lawrence Henkel, John Arthur Henkel. RN, Christ Hosp. Sch. Nursing, Cin., 1947; BA in Religious Studies, U. Calif., Santa Barbara, 2003; student, U. Spiritual Healing Sufism, 2007—; grad., 2010; MDiv, USHS, 2011; MDiv in Spiritual Ministry, Sufi Studies, 2011. Staff nurse, psychiatric nurse to asst. supt. psychiatric nurse and instr. Camarillo (Calif.) State Hosp., 1958—70; mental health nurse I and II, insvc. instr. Ventura County Mental Health, Calif., 1973—88; part-time spiritual group facilitator Hillmont Psychiatric Ctr., Ventura, Calif., 1995—. Democrat. Universalist Unitarian. Avocations: singing, reading, walking. Home: 980 Terracina Dr Santa Paula CA 93060 Personal E-mail: phoenixrise3@verizon.net.

BROUHARD, BEN HERMAN, hospital administrator, nephrologist; b. Indpls., Oct. 30, 1946; s. Edgar Elton and Emma Jean (Pevler) B.; m. Julia Ranney, June 12, 1970; 1 child, Katherine Jean. BA, Wabash Coll., 1968; MD, Ind. U., Indpls., 1972. Diplomate Am. Bd. Pediatrics, Am. Bd. Pediatric Nephrology. Resident Duke U., Durham, NC, 1972-74; fellow U. Tex., Galveston, 1974-76, asst. prof., 1976-79, assoc. prof., 1979-83, prof., 1983-88; dir. rsch., dept. pediatrics Cleve. Clinic Found., 1988-97; prof. pediat. Case Western Res. U., 1997—; chmn. dept. pediat. MetroHealth Med. Ctr., Cleve., 1997, exec. v.p. med. affairs, chief med. officer, 2000—. Bd. mem. Am. Jour. Disorders of Children, Chgo., 1981-91, Diabetes Care, Richmond, Va., 1989-92, Kidney Found. Ohio, Cleve., 1988—; mem. NIH site visit, Bethesda, Md., 1988; bd. dirs. MetroHealth Found., Inc. Author: Diabetes Mellitus in Childhood and Adolescence; editor Clin. Pediatrics, 1990—2001; contbr. articles to profl. jours. Grantee NIH, Am. Heart Assn., Kidney Found., Juvenile Diabetes Found. Mem. Soc. Pediatric Rsch., Am. Pediatric Soc., So. Soc. Clin. Investigation, Midwest Soc. Pediatric Rsch., Phi Beta Kappa, Sigma Xi, Alpha Omega Alpha. Office: MetroHealth Sys 2500 Metrohealth Dr Cleveland OH 44109-1900 Office Phone: 216-778-3474, 216-778-4900. E-mail: ben.brouhard@case.edu.

BROUMAND, STAFFORD R., plastic surgeon; b. 1959; m. Laura Tisch. BA Biology, Chemistry, Indianna U., 1981; MD, Yale U., 1985; grad. gen. surgery, Mount Sinai Medical Ctr., 1985—89. Cert. American Soc. of Plastic Surgeons. Clinical fellowship Mass. Gen. Hosp., Harvard Med. Sch.; intern College des Medicines de Paris, Paris, 1993; staff, burn victims Massachusetts Gen. Hosp. Shiners Burns Inst.; faculty, assoc. prof. of plastic surgery Mount Sinai Hosp., 1993—; dir. Plastic and Cosmetic Surgery Ctr., New York City. Mem.: Plastic Surgery Edn. Foun., The New York Regional Soc. of Plastic Surgery. Office: 740 Park Ave New York NY 10021 Office Phone: 212-879-7900. Office Fax: 212-879-3387. Personal E-mail: drbroumand@aol.com.

BROUSSARD, BRUCE D., health care company executive; b. 1962; MBA, U. Houston, 1989. CFO, bd. dirs. Sun Healthcare Group, Inc., 1993—96; exec. v.p., CFO Regency Health Svcs., Inc., 1996—97; CEO Harbor Dental Inc., 1997—2000; CFO US Oncology, Inc., Houston, 2000—06, pres., 2006—08, exec. v.p., pharm. svcs., 2003—06, pres., CEO, 2008—10, chmn., 2009—10; CEO US Oncology (divsn. McKesson Corp.), 2010—. Bd. dir. U.S. Physical Therapy Inc. Office: US Oncology Inc 10101 Woodloch Forest The Woodlands TX 77380 Office Phone: 281-863-1000. Business E-Mail: Bruce.Broussard@usoncology.com. *

BROWN, ALBERTA MAE, nurse; b. Columbus, Ohio, Nov. 11, 1932; d. Sylvester Clarence and Malinda (Mason) Angel; m. Norman Brown, Dec. 19, 1967 (dec. Jan. 1989); children: Charon, Charles, Stevan, Carole. Grad., Antelope Valley Coll., 1961; AA, L.A. Valley Coll., 1975; BS, Calif. State U., 1981. Nurses aid, vocat. nurse, respiratory therapist St. Bernardines Hosp., 1965-69, Good Samaritan Hosp., LA, 1969-70, Midway Hosp., LA, 1973-81; allergy nurse, instr. respiratory therapy VA Hosp., LA, 1970-93; also acting dept. head; nurse, respiratory splty. unit Jerry L. Pettis Meml. Hosp., Loma Linda, Calif., 1984-93; with Wadley Regional Med. Ctr., Texarkana, Tex., 1993-94; rehab. nurse Robert H. Ballard Rehab. Hosp., San Bernardino, Calif., 1994-98; nurse Ballard Rehab Hosp., San Bernardino, 1998—. Instr. L.A. Valley Med. Technoogists Sch., Compton Coll., 1979, Summit Career Coll., Colton, Calif., 2004—. Patentee disposible/replaceable tubing for stethoscope. Mem. Am. Assn. Respiratory Therapy, Nat. Honor Soc., Social-Lites, Inc. of San Bernardino Club, Order Ea. Star, Eta Phi Beta. Democrat. Baptist.

BROWN, ARTHUR EDWARD, physician; b. Trenton, NJ, June 7, 1945; s. Milton Charles and Jeanne Ruth (Swern) B.; m. Jo Frances Meltzer, Nov. 24, 1985. BS, Bucknell U., 1967; MD, Jefferson Med. Coll., 1971. Intern, resident Roosevelt Hosp., NYC, 1971-72, 74-76; trainee Nat. Cancer Inst., 1976-77; fellow infectious diseases Meml. Sloan-Kettering Cancer Ctr., NYC, 1976-78; clin. asst. physician Cornell U., Weill Med. Coll., NYC, 1978-82, asst. prof. medicine and pediat., 1979-85, assoc. prof. clin. medicine and pediat., 1985—94, prof. clin. medicine and pediat., 1994—; asst. attending physician Meml. Hosp. for Cancer and Allied Diseases, NYC, 1982—89, assoc. attending physician, 1989—93, attending physician, 1993—; asst. attending pediatrician NY Presbyn. Hosp., NYC, 1979—85, assoc. attending pediatrician, 1985-94, attending pediatrician, 1994—2004. Vis. assoc. physician The Rockefeller U. Hosp., NYC, 1995—96; cons. Anti-Infective Drugs adv. com FDA, USPHS, DHHS, 1997—; med. dir. Employee Health and Wellness Svc. Meml. Sloan-Kettering Cancer Ctr., NYC, 2002—, chief, 2003—. Editor: Infectious Complications of Neoplastic Diseases Controversies in Management, 1985, Infections in Oncology, 1993-2000; consulting editor Am. Jour. Medicine, 1984-86; mem. editl. bd. Antimicrobial Agts. and Chemotherapy, 1985-87, European Jour. Clin. Microbiology and Infectious Diseases, 1993-2005, Infections in Medicine, 1995-2008, Microbial Drug Resistance, 1996-2009; contbr. numerous articles to profl. jours. Trustee Peddie Sch., Hightstown, NJ, 1999—. Surgeon, USPHS, 1972-74. Recipient 2d pl. HeSCA Print Festival, 1985, Bronze Plaque award Film Coun. Columbus, 1985, Bronze medal Internat. Film & TV Festival, NYC, 1985, Semi-Finalist Am. Jour. Nursing Media Festival, 1986. Fellow ACP (councillor NY chpt. 2000-02, 2005-2008, NY chpt. pub. health com. 2000—, NY chpt. nominating com. 2004, 2008, Laureate award, 2009), Soc. Healthcare Epidemiology Am., Infectious Diseases Soc. Am. (state and regional bd. dirs. 1995-98); mem. NY County Soc. Internal Medicine (pres. 1994-96), NY State Soc. Internal Medicine (dir. 1995-2000), NY Soc. Infectious Diseases (sec., treas. 1993-97; v.p. 1997-98, pres.-elect 1998-99, pres. 1999-2000), Am. Soc. Microbiology, NY Acad. Scis., Internat. Immunocompromised Host Soc., NY Soc. Tropical Medicine Achievements include research on AIDS, management of infectious complications of neoplastic diseases. Office: Meml Sloan-Kettering Cancer Ctr 222 E 70th St New York NY 10021 Home: 20 Sutton Pl S Apt 15A New York NY 10022 Office Phone: 646-888-4001. Business E-Mail: brown2@mskcc.org.

BROWN, BARBARA JUNE, hospital and nursing administrator; b. Milw., Aug. 17, 1933; d. Carl W. and Nora Anne (Damrow) Rydberg; children: Deborah, Robert, Andrea, Michael, Steven, Jeffrey. BSN, Marquette U., Milw., 1955, MSN, 1960, EdD, 1970. RN, Wis.; cert. nurse adminstr. advanced. Adminstr. patient care Family Hosp., Milw., 1973-78; assoc. clin. prof. U. Wash., Seattle, 1980-87; assoc. adminstr. nursing Virginia Mason Hosp., Seattle, 1980-87; assoc. exec. dir. King Faisal Specialist Hosp., Riyadh, Saudi Arabia, 1987-91; adj. prof. Univ. Ariz., 2001—. Project dir. NIH, Sexual Assault Treatment Ctr., Milw., 1975-78; lectr., cons., 1974—. Founder, editor-in-chief: Nursing Adminstrn. Quar., 1976—; editor-in-chief, regional v.p. Nurse Week, Mountain West, 2000—04; editor-in-chief: Modern Nurse, 2005—06. Vol. ski instr. for disabled, Winter Park, Colo. Fellow: Nat. Acad. Practice, Am. Acad. Nursing (governing coun.); mem.: ANA, Grand County Pub. Health and Emergency Svcs. (chmn. health adv. com. 1994—96), Nat. League Nursing (bd. govs. 2002—05, bd. dirs.), Am. Orgn. Nurse Execs., Sigma Theta Tau. Office Phone: 520-825-5629. Personal E-mail: naqbb@aol.com.

BROWN, BARRY STEPHEN, research psychologist; b. Bklyn., Sept. 26, 1937; s. Isidore Brook and Barbara (Drazin) B.; m. Ann J. Foley, Feb. 25, 1961; children: Rebecca, David, Mariam. AB, Bklyn. Coll., 1958; MS, Western Res. U., Cleve., 1959, PhD, 1963. Chief divsn. rsch. and stats. D.C. Dept. Human Resources, 1974-75; chief svcs. rsch. br. Nat. Inst. on Drug Abuse, Rockville, Md., 1975-82, dir. divsn. clin. rsch., 1982-85, dir. divsn. prevention and comms., 1985-86, chief treatment and early intervention rsch. br. Balt., 1986-88, chief cmty. rsch. br. Rockville, 1989-92; collaborating scientist Tex. Christian U., Ft. Worth, 1993—; adj. prof. U. N.C., Wilmington, 1993—; sr. investigator Friends Rsch. Inst., Balt., 1995—. Adv. bd. Ctr. for Therapeutic Cmty. Rsch., N.Y.C., 1993—; cons. Nat. Devel. and Rsch. Insts., N.Y.C., 1993—. Editor: Handbook on Risk of AIDS, 1993; assoc. exec. editor: Jour. Substance Abuse Treatment, 1991-; mem. editl. bd. Substance Use and Misuse, 1989—, Jour. Behavioral Health and Rsch., 1989—, Jour. of Drug Issues, 1997—; contbr. over 125 articles to sci. jours., chpts. to books. Recipient award Nat. Assn. State Alcohol and Drug Abuse Dirs., 1986, USPHS, 1979; grantee Nat. Inst. on Drug Abuse, 1994, 96, 99, 2001, others. Mem. Soc. Psychologists in Addictive Behaviors. Achievements include development of national research program to assess efficacy of outreach strategies designed to reduce risk of HIV infection to drug users and sexual partners; organizer technical assistance program to share successful outreach models leading to federal legislation institutionalizing and funding outreach. Home: PO Box 1695 Carolina Beach NC 28428-1695 Business E-Mail: brownb@uncw.edu.

BROWN, CHRISTOPHER PATRICK, retired health care administrator, educator; b. Phoenix, June 7, 1951; s. Charles Francis and R. Patricia (Quinn) B.; m. Tracey Ann Wallenberg, May 23, 1987; 1 child, Ryan Matthew. AA in Biol. Scis., Shasta Coll., Redding, Calif., 1976; AS in Liberal Arts, SUNY, Albany, 1977; grad. Primary Care Assoc. Program, Stanford U., 1978; BA in Community Svcs. Adminstrn., Calif. State U., Chico, 1982; M. in Health Svcs., U. Calif., Davis, 1984. Cert. ordained minister 2010, ordained chaplain 2010. Gen. mgr. Pacific Ambulance Svc., El Cajon, Calif., 1974; primary care assoc. Family Practice, Oregon-Calif., 1978-82; cons. Calif. Health Profls., Chico, 1982-84; bus. ops. mgr. Nature's Arts, Inc., Seattle, 1985-86; instr. North Seattle C.C., 1984-89, program dir., 1986-89; asst. dir. Pacific Med. Clinic North, Seattle, 1990-92; dir. Pacific Med. Clinic Renton (Wash.), Pacific Med. Ctr., 1992-95; dir. ops./physician svcs. St. Luke's Regional Med. Ctr., Boise, Idaho, 1995-97, adminstr. ambulatory care, 1997-98; adminstr. St. Luke's Meridian (Idaho) Med. Ctr., 1997-98; COO, sr. v.p. Medford (Oreg.) Clinic, 1998-2000; pres./cons. Integra Healthcare Solutions, 2000—10. Mem. Butte County Adult Day Care Health Coun., Chico, 1982-84; bd. dirs., pres. Innovative Health Care Svcs., Chico, 1982-84; bd. dirs. Highline W. Seattle Mental Health Ctr., 1985-90, v.p. 1988-90; tech. adv. com. North Seattle C.C., 1992-93; bd. dirs. ARC, 1997-98; commr. planning commn. City of Central Point, Oreg., 2004-05. Mem. Internat. Platform Assn., Soc. Ambulatory Care Profls., Med. Group Mgmt. Assn., Multispecialty Group Exec. Soc., Accreditation Assn. for Ambulatory Health Care (accreditation surveyor 1996-97), Am. Legion. Avocations: gardening, woodworking, church activities. Home: Po Box 58433 Salt Lake City UT 84158 Business E-Mail: 1058brown@comcast.net.

BROWN, CHRISTOPHER REID, critical care specialist; MD, Northwestern U., 1982. Diplomate Am. Bd. Internal Medicine-pulmonary disease, Am. Bd. Internal Medicine, 1985, Am. Bd. Internal Medicine- critical care medicine, 1993. Intern Highland Gen. Hosp., Oakland, Calif., resident in internal medicine, 1982—85; fellow in pharmacology Univ. Calif., San Francisco, 1985—87; fellow in pulmoanry critical care medicine Calif. Pacific Med. Ctr., 1988—90; hosp. affiliation include Novato Cmmty. Hosp., Sutter Delta Med. Ctr., Calif. Pacific Med. Ctr., St. Luke's Campus, Calif. Pacific Med. Ctr. Office: California Pacific Medical Center 2351 Clay St Ste 501 San Francisco CA 94115 Office Phone: 415-923-3421. Office Fax: 415-600-1414.

BROWN, CINDY LYNN, family practice nurse practitioner, critical care nurse; b. Washington, July 11, 1956; d. Harry Carl and Betty (Gable) Sampson; m. Wayne Brown, 1998; children: Justin, Jesse. BSN, George Mason U., 1991; MSN, Marymount U., 1995. RN, Va.; CCRN; cert. family nurse practitioner; cert. clin. nurse specialist in critical care; cert. prescriptive authority; cert. ACLS, CPR instr./trainer, EMT; cert. chemotherapy adminstr. Coord. ARC, Honesdale, Pa., 1985-88; instr. CPR Fair Oaks Hosp., Fairfax, Va., 1988-97, extern critical care, 1990-91, trainer CPR instrn., 1991—; nurse critical care Washington Hosp. Ctr., 1991-94; flight nurse World Access Inc., 1993-94; emergency dept. nurse Mt. Vernon Hosp., Alexandria, Va., 1994-96; emergency nurse practitioner Potomac Hosp., Woodbridge, Va., 1996-97; family practice nurse practitioner Advanced Med. Ctr., Naples, Fla., 1997—. Lectr. in field; instr. sign lang. Fairfax County Schs., 1989-90; tissue and organ donation educator Nat. Student Nurses Assn., George Mason U., 1990-91, pres., 1990-91; 1st aid corps mem. ARC, Fairfax, 1988—92; mem. Nurse Practitioner Coun. Collier County, 1998—. Active nat. disaster relief health svc. team for Hurricane Andrew, ARC, Homestead, Fla., 1992, Miss. River Flood, 1993, Hurricane Marilyn, St. Thomas, V.I., 1995, Tropical Storm Jerry, Bonita Springs, Fla., 1995, Hurricane Fran, N.C., 1996, Hurricane George, Naples, Fla., 1998, Hurricane Charley, Naples, Fla., 2004. Named Nursing Student of Yr. Nursing Student Assn. Va., 1991, Student Leader of Yr. George Mason U., 1991. Mem. AACN (Essay award 1991), Am. Acad. Nurse Practitioners, Golden Key Honor Soc., Sigma Theta Tau (Leadership award Epsilon Zeta chpt. 1991), Alpha Chi, Delta Epsilon Sigma. Avocations: country western dancing, water sports. Home: 3231 60th St SW Naples FL 34116

BROWN, DANIEL B., intervention radiologist; MD, Hahnemann U., Phila., 1993. Diplomate Am. Bd. Radiology-radiology, Am. Bd. Radiology-vascular and interventional radiology. Resident diagnostic radiology Main Line Hosp. Bryn Mawr Campus, 1997; fellow vascular-interventional radiology Milton S Hershey Med. Ctr.; hosp. affiliations include Methodist Hosp., Thomas Jefferson Univ. Hosp., chief interventional radiology and interventional oncology. Author: (publ.) Percutaneous Ureteral Interventions, 2009, One Year survival with poorly differentiated metastatic pancreatic carcinoma following chemoembolization with gemcitavine and cisplatin, 2010, (jour.) Rsch. Reporting Standards for Image-guided Ablation of Bone and Soft Tissue Tumors, 2009, Thermal ablation of renal cell carcinoma, 2010, Thermal ablation, 2010. Named one of the Best Doctors in America, St. Louis, 2004—08, the Top Doctors, Phila. Mag., 2009—11. Office: Thomas Jefferson University Hospital Ste 5360 Gibbon Bldg 111 S 11th St Philadelphia PA 19107 Office Phone: 215-955-6440. Office Fax: 215-923-6754.

BROWN, DAVID L., cardiologist, educator; b. Phila., Oct. 6, 1955; s. Stanley and Barbara Ruth Brown; m. Nancy Budorick, May 26, 1996; children: Noah Daniel, Erin Lindsey. Med. degree, Baylor Coll. Medicine, 1982. Diplomate Am. Bd. Cardiology-cardiovascular disease, Am. Bd. Cardiology-interventional cardiology, Am. Bd. Internal Medicine. Resident in internal medicine Baylor Coll. Medicine, Houston, 1983—86; fellow in hermatology Univ. Calif. San Francisco Med. Ctr., 1986—88, resident in cardiovascular disease, 1988—90; fellow in interventional cardiology Cleve. Clinic, Ohio, 1992—93; prof. SUNY Stony Brook; with Stony Brook Univ. Med. Ctr. Editor in chief Heart Internat.; editl. bd. mem. Am. Jour. Cardiology, 2009. Contbr. scientific papers; editor: medical textbooks. Named to NY Mag.'s Best Doctors, 2010. Fellow: Soc. Cardiovasc. Angiography Intervention, Am. Heart Assn., Am. Coll. Cardiology. Democrat. Jewish. Achievements include research in Outcomes research in cardiovascular disease; Diagnosis and treatment of the vulnerable plaque; Volume-Outcome Relationship An Evaluation of the Oral Inflammatory Burden of Accute Coronary Syndrome Patients; African American Cardiac Patient Navigators To Improve Care Transition. Avocation: tennis. Office: Stony Brook University Medical Center Internal Medicine 3001 Expressway Dr N Ste 200 B Islandia NY 11749-5301 Office Phone: 631-444-9600. Office Fax: 631-444-9621.

BROWN, DAVID STANLEY, dental educator, researcher; b. UK, Dec. 11, 1947; s. Herbert Stanley and Mary Elizabeth Brown; m. Angela Kathleen Swonnell, June 12, 1971; children: Edward Q. F., A. Georgiana F. BSc in Zoology with 1st Class honors, Westfield Coll., U. London, 1969; PhD in Vertebrate Palaeoherpetology, U. Newcastle, Newcastle upon Tyne, Tyne & Wear, Eng., 1974. Sir James Knott rsch. fellow Newcastle U., 1973—74, Wilfred Hall rsch. fellow, 1974—75, lectr. oral anatomy, Sch. Dental Scis., 1979—, sr. tutor for BDS admissions, Sch. Dental Scis., 2004—; lectr. anatomy U. Aberdeen, Grampian, Scotland, 1975—79. Hon. treas. North Eng. Odontological Soc., Newcastle upon Tyne, 1991—, pres., 1999—2000. Contbr. articles to profl. jours. Mem.: MunroMagic. Avocations: photography, painting, music. Office: Sch Dental Sci Framlington Pl Newcastle upon Tyne Tyne & Wear NE2 4BW England Business E-Mail: d.s.brown@ncl.ac.uk.

BROWN, DIANE ROBINSON, sociology educator; b. Newark, Aug. 11, 1944; d. Eugene Jasper and Mary Rochelle (Davis) Robinson; m. Lafayette Brown, Jr., July 29, 1972 (div. 1979); m. Arthur D. Rogers, Nov. 25, 1987. AB in Sociology, Ind. U., 1966; MA in Sociology, U. Mass., 1968; PhD in Med. Sociology, U. Md., 1984. Programmer Prudential Ins. Co., Newark, 1967; system engr. IBM, Cambridge, Mass., 1968-70; info. coord. Community Devel. Adminstrs., Newark, 1970-72; staff assoc. Mass. State Coll. System, Boston, 1972-75; rsch. assoc. Inst. for Urban Affairs and Rsch., Washington, 1975-79, sr. rsch. assoc., 1979-86, acting dir., 1986-87, dir. rsch., 1987-90; assoc. prof. Howard U., Washington, 1990-93; assoc. dir. to dir. Ctr. for Urban Studies/Wayne State U., Detroit, 1993—2002; exec. dir. Inst. for the Elimination of Health Disparities, Sch. Pub. Health Univ. Medicine and Dentistry NJ, Newark, 2002—; prof., health edn. and behavioral sci. Sch. Pub. Health Univ. Medicine and Dentistry NJ, Newark. Grants assoc. NIH, 1991-93. Assoc. editor Humanity and Society, 1988—, Jour. Health and Social Behavior, 1989-; co-editor In and Out of Our Right Minds: The Mental Health of African American Women; contbr. articles to profl. jours. HUD grantee, 1986—, U.S. Dept. Edn. grantee, 1987-88; postdoctoral fellow, psychiatric epidemiology, John Hopkins Sch. Pub. Health, 1984-86; Ford Found. fellow, 1985-86. Mem. Assn. Social and Behavioral Scientists (exec. com. 1987—), Am. Pub. Health Assn. (coun. mental health sect. 1987—), D.C. Sociol. Soc. (exec. com. 1987—). African Methodist Episcopalian. Avocations: tennis, gardening. Office: Inst for the Elimination of Health Disparities Sch Pub Health U Medicine Dentistry NJ 65 Bergen St Bldg SSB Rm 742 Newark NJ 07107 Office Phone: 973-972-4382. Office Fax: 973-972-4403. Business E-Mail: browndi@umdnj.edu.

BROWN, DONALD CLYDE, surgeon; b. Pitts., May 17, 1936; MD, Case Western Res. U., 1961. Diplomate Am. Bd. Surgery. From intern to resident Allegheny Gen. Hosp., Pitts., 1961-64; resident Western Pa. Hosp., Pitts., 1964-67; med. staff Jeannette Hosp., Pa., 1969—2005; pvt. practice Irwin, Pa. With U.S. Army Med. Corps, 1967-69. Fellow ACS, Internat. Coll. Surgeons; mem. AMA. Office: Irwin Profl Ctr 100 Penna Ave Irwin PA 15642-3364 Office Phone: 724-864-5759. *

BROWN, DONALD ROBERT, psychology professor; b. Albany, NY, Mar. 5, 1925; s. J. Edward and Natalie (Rosenberg) B.; m. June Gole, Aug. 14, 1945; children: Peter Douglas, Thomas Matthew, Jacob Noah. AB, Harvard U., Cambridge, Mass., 1948; MA, PhD, U. Calif., Berkeley, 1951. Mem. faculty Bryn Mawr Coll., 1951-64, prof. psychology, 1963—. Sr. rsch. cons. Mellon Found., Vassar Coll., 1953-63; part-time vis. prof. Swarthmore Coll., U. Pa., also U. Calif.-Berkeley, 1953-61; fellow Ctr. Advanced Study Behavioral Scis., 1960-61; prof. psychology, sr. rsch. scientist, dir. Ctr. Rsch. Learning and Teaching, U. Mich., 1964—; cons. Peace Corps, 1965-71; hon. rsch. fellow Univ. Coll., London, 1970-71; Fulbright sr. rsch. fellow Max Planck Inst., Berlin, 1982; Netherlands Basic Sci. fellow, Leyden, 1983. Author: articles, chpts. in books; editor: Changing Role and Status of Soviet Women, 1967, Frontiers of Motivational Psychology, 1986; co-editor: Frontiers of Mathematical Psychology, 1990. Served with AUS, 1943-46, ETO. Fellow Am. Psychol. Assn., Chinese Acad. Sci.; mem. Soc. Psychol. Study of Social Issues, AAAS, AAUP, Sigma Xi, Psi Chi. Home: 2511 Hawthorne Rd Ann Arbor MI 48104-4031 Office: Dept Psychology Univ Michigan 3002 East Hall Ann Arbor MI 48109 Office Phone: 734-743-1097. Business E-Mail: donrobro@umich.edu.

BROWN, DUDLEY EARL, JR., retired health science association and federal agency administrator, retired military officer; b. Berryville, Va., Apr. 10, 1928; s. Dudley Earl and Rosa Lee (Costello) B.; m. Lelia Adrienne Motley, June 22, 1953; children: Lelia Brown Farr, David, Kevin. BA, Washington and Lee U., 1949; MD, Med. Coll. Va., 1953. Diplomate Am. Bd. Psychiatry and Neurology. Commd. lt. (j.g.) M.C. USN, 1953, advanced through grades to rear adm., 1974; intern Naval Hosp., Portsmouth, Va., 1953-54, resident in neuropsychiatry Bethesda, Md., 1957-60; svc. in Vietnam; commdg. officer Nat. Naval Med. Ctr., Bethesda, 1975-76, Naval Regional Med. Ctr., San Diego, 1976-78; fleet surgeon U.S. Pacific Fleet and staff surgeon, comdr.-in-chief U.S. Forces, Pacific, Pearl Harbor, Hawaii, 1978-80; dep. asst. chief med. dir. for profl. svcs. VA Ctrl. Office, Washington, 1980-82; assoc. dep. chief med. dir. VA, Washington, 1982-87; asst. prof. clin. psychiatry U. Pa. Med. Sch., 1967-70; prof. clin. psychiatry Uniformed Svcs. U. Health Scis., Bethesda, 1981—, Med. Coll. Va., Va. Commonwealth U., Richmond, 1987—2004; dir. health policy studies, dir. Washington office Abt Assocs. Inc., 1987-93, v.p., 1992—, mng. v.p., 1993—2001; ret., 2003. Sci. adv. bd. Ctr. Prisoner of War Studies, 1998-2003. Contbr. to med. jours. Decorated Legion of Merit; recipient Meritorious Svc. medal, Navy Commendation medal, VA Disting. Svc. medal, Disting. Alumnus Med. Coll. Va., 1993. Fellow ACP, Am. Psychiat. Assn., Am. Coll. Psychiatrists; mem. Washington Psychiat. Soc., Nat. Health Coun. (bd. dirs. 1989-94), Assn. Mil. Surgeons U.S., Soc. Med. Cons. to Armed Forces (v.p. 1988-89, pres. 1989-90), Phi Gamma Delta, Alpha Epsilon Delta. Presbyterian. Home: 2415 Black Cap Ln Reston VA 20191-3027 Personal E-mail: dearlbown@aol.com.

BROWN, EDWARD MEIGS, endocrinologist, educator; MD, Harvard Coll., 1972. Diplomate Am. Bd. Internal Medicine, 1975, Am. Bd. Internal Medicine-endocrinology, diabetes and metabolism, 1977. Resident internal medicine Peter Bent Brigham Hosp., Boston, 1973—74; fellow endocrinology NIH, Bethseda, Md., 1974—76; sr. physician Brigham and Women's Hosp.; prof. medicine Harvard Med. Sch. Co-author: (publs.) Mapping of human autoantibody binding sites on the calcium-sensing receptor, 2010, Alterations in phosphorus, calcium and PTHrP contribute to defects in dental and dental alveolar bone formation in calcium-sensing receptor-deficient mice, 2010, Calcium-corrected intact PTH: a clinically useful parameter for quantifying parathyroid function in patients undergoing hemodialysis, 2010, Pilot case-control investigation of risk factors for hip fractures in the urban Indian population, 2010, Clinical utility of calcimimetics targeting the extracellular calcium-sensing receptor (CaSR), 2010; author: and numerous other publs. Office: Brigham and Women's Hospital Department of Medicine- Endocrinology 75 Francis St Boston MA 02115 Office Phone: 617-732-5666. E-mail: embrown@rics.bwh.harvard.edu.

BROWN, EDWIN WILSON, JR., preventive medicine physician, educator; b. Youngstown, Ohio, Mar. 6, 1926; s. Edwin Wilson and Doris (McClellan) B.; m. Patricia Ann Currier, Aug. 9, 1952; children: Edwin Wilson, John Currier, Wende Patricia. Student, Carnegie Inst. Tech., 1943, Amherst Coll., 1943—44, Houghton Coll., 1946—47; MD, Harvard U., 1953, MPH (Nat. Found. fellow), 1957. Rsch. fellow U. Buffalo, 1953-54; intern E.J. Meyer Meml. Hosp., Buffalo, 1954-55; resident pub. health Va. Dept. Health, 1955-56; tchr. medicine specializing in preventive medicine Boston, 1958-61, Hyderabad, India, 1961-63; assoc. med. dir. People-to-People Health Found., Washington, 1965-66; assoc. prof. medicine Ind. U.-Purdue U., Indpls., 1966-85, dir. divsn. internat. affairs, 1966-74, assoc. dean student svcs., dir. internat. svcs., 1979-85; pres. Internat. Med.

Assistance, Inc., Indpls., 1986—. Med. dir. Ind. Dept. Correction, 1974-76; sr. med. edn. advisor King Faisal U., Dammam, Saudi Arabia, 1977-78; field dir. Harvard Epidemiol. Project, Egedesminde, Greenland, 1956-57; asst. prof. preventive medicine Sch. Medicine Tufts U., 1958-61; dep. chief staff Boston Dispensary, 1961; vis. prof. preventive medicine Osmania Med. Coll., Hyderabad, India, 1961-63; asst. dir. divsn. internat. med. edn., dir. AAMC-AID project internat. med. edn. Assn. Am. Med. Colls., Evanston, 1963-65; exec. sec. Study Group on Childhood Accidents, Boston, 1959-61; rsch. assoc. Sch. Pub. Health, Harvard U., 1959-60; dir. Curtis Pub. Co., Inc.; cons. Boston City Health Dept., 1959-60, WHO, 1973-74; chmn. bd. dirs. Med. Assistance Programs, Inc. Contbr. articles to profl. jours. Bd. dirs. Paul Carlson Found., Campus Teams, Iran Found., CARE/MEDICO, Internat. Students Inc. Served with AUS, 1944-46, ETO. Recipient Pub. Svc. award Vets. Day Coun. Indpls., 1996, Patriarch of Antioch's award Knight Comdr. of Order of St. Mark, 1998. Fellow Am. Pub. Health Assn.; mem. Assn. Tchrs. Preventive Medicine, Indian Assn. Advancement Med. Edn., Mass. Med. Soc., Internat. Policy Forum (bd. govs.), Nat. Policy Coun., Rotary Internat., Sigma Xi. Home and Office: 8153 Oakland Rd Indianapolis IN 46240-2747 Home Phone: 317-257-7454; Office Phone: 317-257-7454. Personal E-mail: edwinwbrownmd@gmail.com.

BROWN, ELLEN LESLIE, adult health and geriatrics nurse; b. Rahway, NJ, June 9, 1962; d. Howard M. and Marilyn (Rosner) Reiss; m. John C. Brown, Sept. 18, 1988; children: Gregg, Andy. BSN, U. R.I., 1984; MS, Columbia U., 1991, postgrad., 1993—. RN, N.Y.; cert. nurse practitioner in adult health; cert. adult nurse practitioner, gerontol. nures practitioner; cert. BLS. Ambulatory care nurse Columbia U. Health Svc., NYC, 1987-90; adult nurse practitioner VA, NYC, 1991-93; instr. clin. nursing Columbia U. Sch. Nursing, NYC, 1992-94, asst. prof. clin. nursing, 1994-95. Editor: (travel handbook) Columbia University Health Service, 1991. Mem. Am. Acad. Nurse Practitioners, Nat. Orgn. Nurse Practitioner Faculties, Soc. for Pub. Health Edn.

BROWN, EMERY N., neuroscientist, educator, statistician, anesthesiologist; BA, Harvard Coll., 1978; AM in statistics, Harvard U., 1984, MD, 1987, PhD in statistics, 1988. Prof. health sciences and tech. MIT, Cambridge, Mass., prof. computational neuroscience; Warren M. Zapol prof. anaesthesia Harvard Med. Sch./Mass. Gen. Hosp., Boston. Recipient NIH Dir.'s Pioneer award, 2007. Fellow: IEEE, AAAS, Am. Statistical Assn., Am. Inst. Med. and Biol. Engring.; mem.: Inst. Medicine, Assn. U. Anesthesiologists. Office Phone: 617-726-7487, 617-324-1879. E-mail: enbrown1@mit.edu, brown@neurostat.mgh.harvard.edu.

BROWN, FLORENCE M., endocrinologist, educator; MS, Princeton U., 1978; MD, Columbia U., 1982. Cert. Am. Bd. Internal Med., endocrinology & metabolism. Intern to resident St. Lukes Hosp. Ctr., 1982—85; fellow Joslin Diabetes Ctr., 1986—89, Brigham & Women's Hosp., 1986—89; instr. Harvard Med. Sch.; dir. Joslin-Beth Israel Deaconess Pregnancy Program. Office: Joslin Diabetes Center and Joslin Clinic One Joslin Pl Boston MA 02215 Office Phone: 617-732-2496.

BROWN, FREDERICK LEE, health facility administrator; b. Clarksburg, W.Va., Oct. 22, 1940; s. Claude Raymond and Anne Elizabeth (Kiddy) B.; m. Shirley Fiille Brown; children: Gregory Lee, Michael Owen-Price, Kyle Stephen, Kathryn Alonia. BA in Psychology, Northwestern U., Evanston, Ill., 1962; MBA in Health Care Adminstrn., George Washington U., Washington, 1966; LHD (hon.), U. Mo., 1995. Vocat. counselor Cook County Dept. Pub. Aid, Chgo., 1962-64; from adminstrv. resident to v.p. ops. Meth. Hosp. Ind., Inc., Indpls., 1965—72, v.p. ops., 1972-74; exec. v.p., COO Meml. Hosp. DuPage County, Elmhurst, Ill., 1974-82, Meml. Health Svcs., Elmhurst, 1980-82; pres., CEO CH Health Techs., Inc., St. Louis, 1983-93, Christian Health Svcs., St. Louis, 1986-93, CH Allied Svcs., Inc., St. Louis, 1988-93, BJC Health Sys., St. Louis, 1993—98, vice-chmn., 1999—2000; pres., CEO Christian Hosp. NE-NW, 1982—88, No. Ariz. Healthcare, Flagstaff, 2003—04. Adj. instr. Washington U. Sch. Medicine, St. Louis, 1982—2001; mem. chancellor's coun. U. Mo., 1990—94; mem. exec. com. HealthLink, Inc., 1986—92; pres., CEO Village North, Inc., 1986—93; chmn. shareholder comm. com. Am. Healthcare Systems, Inc., 1985—86, vice chmn., 1992; bd. dirs. Commerce Bank St. Louis, Am. Excess Inc. Ltd.; mem. corp. assembly Blue Cross Blue Shield Mo., 1991—95; vis. scholar, exec. in residence The George Washington U., 2001—02. Contbr. articles to profl. jours. Co-chmn. hosp. divsn. United Way Greater St. Louis, 1983, chmn., 1984, chmn. health svcs. divsn., 1985—86, vice chmn. region, 1988, bd. dirs., 1986—2001, exec. com., 1991—, chmn. audit com., 1992—2001; active Kammergild Chamber Orch., 1984—88, v.p., 1985—88, bd. dirs., 1987—91; active Mo. Heart Inst., 1988—92, Alton Meml. Hosp., 1987—91, bd. dirs., 1987—91; mem. exec. bd. St. Louis Area coun. Boy Scouts Am., 1989—2000, activities coun. chmn., 1993—95; chmn. Friends of Scouting Campaign, 1991—92; mem. medicaid budget task force Mo. Dept. Social Svcs., 1990; mem. emergency rm. svcs. task force St. Louis Regional Med. Ctr., 1985; mem. corp. assembly Blue Cross Blue Shield of Mo., 1991; bd. dirs. Sold on St. Louis, 1991—93, St. Louis Reg. Commerce & Growth Assn., 1993—98; bd. trustees Webster Hills Math. Ch., 1990—92, communion steward, 1987. Fellow Am. Coll. Healthcare Execs. (chmn. credentials com. 1978, chmn. task force governance and constituencies 1986-88; mem. Gold Medal award com. 1985, com. on ethics 1989-91, chmn. awards and testimonials com., 1992-93, bd. regents 1991-93, gov. dist. V, 1993-98); mem. Am. Acad. Med. Adminstrs. (life, state dir. 1988—, Health Care Exec. of Yr. 1990, Statesman in Healthcare, 1992), Hosp. Pres.'s Assn., Advt. Club Greater St. Louis, Am. Hosp. Assn. (coun. on mgmt. 1987, alt. del. for healthcare systems 1988-90, del. to ho. of dels. for health care systems 1991, fin. com. chair 1995, chair-elect 1998, chmn. 1999), APHA, George Washington U. Alumni Assn. for Health Svcs. Adminstrn. (preceptor 1975-93, Alumnus of Yr. award 1981, Frederick Gibbs award, 1993), Hosp. Assn. Met. St. Louis (bd. dirs. 1984-94, chmn. bd. 1988-89, sec. 1985-86, treas. 1987, chmn. coun. on pub. affairs and comm. 1985, vice chmn. 1987, various coms.), Greater St. Louis Health Care Alliance (co-chair 1992-96), Mo. Hosp. Assn. (mem. coun. on rsch. and policy devel. 1983-88, chmn. coun. on multi-instnl. hosps. 1986-88, mem. dist. coun. pres.'s 1986-89, bd. dirs. 1988-92, chmn. bd. trustees 1990), Ctrl. Ea. Profl. Rev. Orgn. (bd. dirs. 1982-85, various coms.), St. Louis Met. Med. Soc. (lay advisor 1990-92), Healthcare Execs. Study Soc., Internat. Health Policy and Mgmt. Inst. (bd. dirs. 1988—), Am. Protestant Health Assn. (bd. dirs. 1988-93, chmn. 1992-93), Pinnacle Peak Country Club, Forest Highlands Country Club. Republican. Home: 8409 E La Junta Rd Scottsdale AZ 85255-2859 Office Phone: 928-607-3069. Personal E-mail: fredlbrown@cox.net.

BROWN, GERALDINE, nurse, freelance writer; b. Clemson, SC; d. Isaac and Gladys (Patterson) B. AS in Nursing, U. D.C., 1973; real estate cert., Long and Foster Inst., 1984; cert. in TV broadcasting, Columbia Sch., 1987; BSN, Bowie State U., Md., 1989, MA in Comm., 1991, MSN, 2000; PhD, Howard U., DC, 1994. RN, D.C., FCC Third Class License. Supr. staff nurse Walter Reed Hosp., Washington, 1970—76; supr. clin. nurse Dept. Human Svcs., Washington, 1976—78, cmty. health nurse, 1978—84; nursing instr. Phillips Bus. Sch., Alexandria, Va., 1984—85; pvt. nurse Washington, 1973—; faculty Howard U. Coll. Nursing, 1994—2001. Dir. pub. affairs Bible Way Chs. Worldwide, Inc., Washington, 1978-91; soc. columnist As It Happens, Charlotte (N.C.) Post, 1964-66; soc. editor Washington Cafe Soc. mag, 1971; contbr. feature stories Capital Spotlight newspaper, 1978—; mem. faculty Coll. Nursing, Howard U., 1994—. Asst. organizer DC Mayor's United Nations Day, 1980; vol. Met. Boys and Girls Clubs, Washington, 1980—; vol. Nursing Instr., The Washington Saturday Coll., 1982-84; Co. ARC, 1973—, Big Sisters of the Washington Met. Area, 1988—. Recipient certs. of excellence Govt. of D.C., 1978-84; cert. of appreciation Mayor of D.C., 1980, Meritorious Pub. Svc. award, 1980; svc. trophy Washington Saturday Coll., 1984. Mem. ANA, NAACP, Nat. Coun. Negro Women, Smithsonian Inst. (assoc.), Nat. Black Nurses Assn., Washington Urban League, Chi Eta Phi, Sigma Theta Tau. Democrat. Avocations: stamp collecting/philately, travel, poetry. Office Phone: 202-244-0313. Personal E-mail: gerrib4@verizon.net.

BROWN, JASON WALTER, neurologist, educator, researcher; b. NYC, Apr. 14, 1938; s. Samuel Robert and Sylvia (Brown) B.; children: Jonathan Schilder, Jovana Millay; m. Carine Hoeusler; 1 child, Ilya. BA, U. Calif.-Berkeley, 1959; MD, U.S.C., 1963. Intern St. Elizabeth's Hosp., Washington, 1963-64; resident in neurology UCLA, 1964-67; practice medicine specializing in neurology NYC, 1970—; instr. Boston U. Med. Sch., 1969-70; asst. clin. prof. Columbia-Presbyn. Hosp., NYC, 1970-75; vis. asst. prof. neurology Albert Einstein Coll. Medicine, NYC, 1972-75; vis. assoc. prof. Rockefeller U., NYC, 1978-79; clin. assoc. prof. neurology NYU, 1975-79, clin. prof., 1979—; pres. Inst. Research in Behavioral Neurosci. Vis. scholar N.Y. Psychoanalytic Inst., 1993—. Author: Aphasia, Apraxia and Agnosia, 1972, Mind, Brain and Consciousness, 1977, Life of the Mind, 1988; editor: Jargonaphasia, 1982; English Translation of Aphasie by Arnold Pick (Aphasia), 1973, Neuropsychology of Visual Perception, 1989, Classics in Neuropsychology: Apraxia and Agnosia, Self and Process, 1991, Time, Will and Mental Process, 1996, Mind and Nature, 2000, The Self Embodying Mind, 2002, Process and The Authentic Self, 2005; contbr. numerous articles on neurology to med. jours.; mem. editl. bd. Jour. Nervous and Mental Disease, Aphasiology, Advances in Neurolinguistics. Grantee NIH; fellow Alexander von Humboldt Found., 1979—, World Rehab. Fund, 1982, Founds. Fund for Research in Psychiatry, 1974-75. Jewish. Home and Office: 66 E 79th St New York NY 10021-0244 Personal E-mail: drjbrown@hotmail.com

BROWN, JAY ALBERT, occupational medicine consultant; b. Ind., Aug. 18, 1948; MD, Ind. U., 1978; MPH, U. Wash., 1996. Cons., Haz-Map US Dept. Labor, 2006—. Author Haz-Map, Nat. Libr. Medicine, Toxicology and Environ. Health Info., 2000—, IDdx: Infectious Disease Queries, USBMIS iPhone Application, 2005—. Mem.: Am. Coll. Govtl. Indsl. Hygienists, Am. Coll. Occupl. & Environ. Medicine. Avocation: tennis. Home: 5426 Orca Pl NE Tacoma WA 98422 Personal E-mail: brownjay@haz-map.com.

BROWN, JEFFREY, pediatrician, educator; Attended, U. Md. Sch. Medicine, 1965. Diplomate Am. Bd. Pediatrics. Intern Hartford Hosp.; resident in pediat. Mt. Sinai Hosp., NYC, 1968—70; fellow neonatal-perinatal medicine NY Hosp. Cornell Med. Ctr., NY, 1970—71; clin. prof. pediat. NY Med. Coll.; with Westchester Med. Ctr.; pediatrician Greenwich Hosp. Office: Greenwich Hosp. Pediatrics Associates - NE Medical Group 26 Rye Ridge Plz Rye Brook NY 10573 Office Phone: 914-251-1100. Office Fax: 914-251-1109.

BROWN, JERRY MILFORD, health products executive; b. Anderson, SC, Apr. 30, 1938; s. James Milford and Jane Elizabeth (McCord) B.; m. Alice Alberta Thompson, July 30, 1960 (div. Nov. 2, 2007; children: John Milford, Allen Thompson; m. Janice Roleke Polites, Jan. 2008; 1 child: James Milford II. BS, Furman U., 1960; MA in Biology, Wake Forest U., 1963, Temple U., 1967; PhD in Physiology, Dental Sch., U. Md., 1972. Commd. lt. U.S. Army, 1960, advanced through grades to lt. col., 1980; rsch. instr. Hahanemann Med. Coll., Phila., 1967-68; sect. leader, exptl. medicine divsn. Biomed. Lab., Edgewood Arsenal, Md., 1967-68; instr. anatomy Med. Sch., U. Md., Balt., 1970-77; sect. leader exptl. medicine divsn. U.S. Army Rsch. Inst. Environ. Medicine, Natick, Mass., 1973-76; dep. dir. U.S. Army Med. Intelligence and Info. Agy., Ft. Detrick, Md., 1976-80; dir. internat. health affairs Dept. Def., Washington, 1980-84; chief plans ops. security 2d Gen. Hosp., Germany, 1984-87; med. coord. Fed. Emer. Mgmt. Agy., Washington, 1987-90; nat. disaster med. system staff, bd. govs. Nat. Coun. Internat. Health, 1980-90; cons. and spl. asst. to the pres. Bio Tech. Gen. Corp., Iselin, NJ, 1991-99; pres., chief oper. officer NeuroSurg. Internat., 1995—; v.p., chief oper. officer M/D Frontiers, Springfield, Va., 1990—; pres. Automated Med. Products, Inc., Springfield, Va., 1990—; CEO Automated Med. Products Corp., 1997—; mgr. Precision Med. Manufacturing L.L.C., Wheeling, Ill., 2002—. Vp. Automated Systems, 1991—; assoc. dir. rsch. nat. study ctr. trauma and emer. medicine U. Md.; U.S. mem. Internat. Com. Mil. Medicine and Pharmacy, 1981-87, U.S. mil. mem. Joint Civil/Mil. Med. Working Group U.S., NATO, 1981—; mem. program planning com. Internat. Assembly Emer. Med. Svcs., Balt., 1984; congress lobbyist; cons. in field. Contbr. articles to med. jours.; pub. books in field of philately. Commr. Explorer Scouts, Natick, Mass., 1975-76; trustee Cardinal Spellman Philatlic Mus., Weston, Mass., 1980-97. Decorated Meritorious Svc. medal with oak leaf clusters, Legion of Merit; recipient gold medal, Res. Officers Assn., 1960. Mem. Electron Microscopy Soc. Am., Am. Stamp Dealers Assn., Ctrl. Atlantic Stamp Dealers Assn. (pres. 1977-81), Rsch. and Engring. Soc. Am., Balt. Philatelic Soc., Sigma Alpha Epsilon, Sigma Xi. Republican. Baptist. Office Phone: 732-602-7717. Personal E-mail: jbrown@ironintern.com, btgc@mindspring.com.

BROWN, JOHN WILFORD, retired medical products executive, board member; b. Tenn., Sept. 15, 1934; s. Albert and Treva (Moody) Brown; m. Rosemary Kopel, June 7, 1967; children: Sarah Beth, Janine. BSChemE, Auburn U., Montgomery, Ala., 1957. Process engr. Ormet Corp., Hannibal, Ohio, 1958—62; sr. engr. Thiokol Chem. Corp., Marshall, Tex., 1962—65; with Squibb Corp., Princeton, NJ, 1965—72, asst. to pres., 1970—72; pres. Edward Weck & Co. (divsn. Squibb Corp.), 1972—77; pres., CEO Stryker Corp., 1977—2003, chmn., 1981—2009. Mem. exec. com. Mich. Econ. Devel. Corp., 2001—; bd. dirs. Gen-Probe Inc., 2005—, St. Jude Med., Inc., 2005—; chmn. bd. dirs. Inst. Health Tech. Studies (InHealth). Named one of Forbes 400: Richest Americans, 2006—. Mailing: St Jude Medical Inc Bd Directors 1 St Jude Medical Dr Saint Paul MN 55117 also: InHealth 1319 F St NW Ste 400 Washington DC 20004 Office Phone: 651-756-2000. Office Fax: 651-756-3301. Business E-Mail: jbrown@sjm.com. *

BROWN, JUNE GIBBS, retired government official; b. Cleve., Oct. 5, 1933; d. Thomas D. and Lorna M. Gibbs; children: Ellen Rosenthal, Linda Windsor, Victor Janezic, Carol Janezic. BBA summa cum laude, Cleve. State U., 1971, MBA, 1972; postgrad., Cleve. Marshall Law Sch., 1973-74; JD, U. Denver, 1978; postgrad. Advanced Mgmt. Program, Harvard U., 1983. Cert. govt. fin. mgr., 1995; CPA, Ohio. Real estate broker, officer mgr. N.E. Realty, Cleve., 1963-68; staff acct. Frank T. Cicirelli, C.P.A., Cleve., 1970-71; asst. to comptr. S.M. Hexter Co., Cleve., 1971; grad. tchg. fellow Cleve. State U., 1971-72; dir. internal audit Navy Fin. Ctr., Cleve., 1972-75; dir. fin. sys. design Bur. of Land Mgmt., Denver, 1975-76; project mgr. Bur. of Reclamation, 1976-79; insp. gen. Dept. Interior, Washington, 1979-81, NASA, Washington, 1981-85; v.p. fin. and adminstrn. Sys. Devel. Corp., a Burroughs Co., 1985-86; assoc. adminstr. for mgmt. NASA, 1986-87; insp. gen. U.S. Dept. Def., Arlington, Va., 1987-90; dep. insp. gen. USN-CINCPACFLT, 1990; insp. gen. USN Pacific Fleet, Pearl Harbor, Hawaii, 1991-93, HHS, Washington, 1993-2001; inspector gen. HHS, SSA, Washington, 1995-96; ret., 2001. Bd. dirs. Fed. Law Enforcement Tng. Ctr., 1984-85, Interagy. Auditor Tng. program Dept. Agr. Grad. Sch., 1983-85; chmn. interagy. com. on Info. Resource Mgmt., 1984-85; mem. bd. advisors Nat. Contract Mgmt. Assn., 1987-89, NSF, 2002-05; mem. Pres.'s Coun. on Integrity and Efficiency, 1993-2001, vice chair, 1994-97, 1998-2001, rep. Nat. Intergovtl. Audit Forum, 1994-98; bd. dirs. Insps. Gen. Auditor Tng. Inst. Mem. bd. advisors Howard U. Sch. Bus., 1987-89. Recipient award Am. Soc. Women Accts., 1969, 70, 71, Raulston award Cleve. State U., 1971, Pres.'s award Cleve. State U., 1971, Outstanding Achievement award U.S. Navy, 1973, Career Svc. award Chgo. region Fed. Exec. Bd., 1974, Outstanding Contbn. to Fin. Mgmt. award Denver region Fed. Exec. Bd., 1977, Donald L. Scantlebury award Joint Fin. Mgmt. Improvement Program, 1980, Outstanding Svc. award Nat. Assn. Minority CPA Firms, 1980, NASA Exceptional Svc. medal, 1985, Outstanding Achievement in Aerospace award, 1987, Woman of Yr. award, YWCA 1988, Bur. Land Mgmt., Dept. Interior, 1975, Disting. Pub. Svc. award Dept. Def., 1989, Meritorious Civilian Svc. award U.S. Navy, 1993, Nat. Capital Area chpt./Govt. Exec. Mag. award for leadership, 1994, George Washington U. Pi Alpha Alpha Pub. Svc. award, 1996; named Disting. Alumni Cleve. State U., 1990, named Outstanding Fellow of Coun. for Ethical Org. for Creating the Standards for Healthcare Compliance, 2001 Fellow Nat. Acad. Pub. Adminstrn. (standing panel exec. orgn. and mgmt., pub. svc. panel); mem. AICPA (mem. govt. auditing stds. 1996-99), Assn. Govt. Accts. (nat. pres. 1985-86, nat. exec. com. 1977-87, vice chmn. nat. ethics com. 1978-80, 90, chmn. fin. mgmt. standards bd. 1981-82, service award 1973, 76, 93, outstanding achievement award 1979, Robert W. King Meml. award 1988, dir. Hawaii chpt. 1991-93, Nat. Pres.'s award 1999, Disting. Fed. Leadership award 1998), Hawaii Soc. CPAs (bd. dirs. 1991-93), Am. Accts. Assn., Nat. Contract Mgmt. Assn. (bd. advisors 1988-90), NASA Alumni Assn., Women in Aerospace, ASPA (at-large mem. nat. coun. 1994-98, Profl. Responsibility Exemplary Practice award 1990, pres.-nat. capital area chpt. 1989), Exec. Women in Govt., Nat. Sci. Found. (adv. panel 2003-05), Beta Alpha Psi. Personal E-mail: igjgb@yahoo.com.

BROWN, KAREN T., vascular and interventional radiologist; Grad., U. Mich., 1973; MD, Boston U., 1979. Diplomate Am. Bd. Radiology-diagnostic radiology, Am. Bd. Radiology-vascular and interventional radiology. Intern Fulton-DeKalb Hosp. Authority, Atlanta, Grady Meml. Hosp., Atlanta; resident diagnostic radiology Mass. Gen. Hosp., 1981—84, fellow vascular and interventional radiology, 1984—85; prof. radiology Weill Cornell Med. Coll., NY, 1992—; hosp. affiliation includes Meml. Sloan-Kettering Cancer Ctr., NY. Author: (articles) Rates and patterns of recurrence for percutaneous radiofrequency ablation and open wedge resection for solitary colorectal liver metastasis, 2007, Radiofrequency ablation in the management of liver metastases from breast cancer, 2007, Combined portal vein embolization and neoadjuvant chemotherapy as a treatment strategy for resectable hepatic colorectal metastases, 2008. Named one of America's Top Doctors, Castle Connolly, 2004—10. Fellow: Am. Heart Assn.; mem.: Radiol. Soc. of N.Am., Am. Roentgen Ray Soc. Office: Memorial Sloan- Ketteing Cancer Center 1275 York Ave New York NY 10065 Office Phone: 212-639-2000.

BROWN, KATHE, recreational therapist, counselor; d. Stanley Joseph Kazmierczyk and Anna Baran; m. Robert Arthur Brown, Nov. 9, 1969; children: David Asher, Ariel Claire. BSc, Penn State U., University Park, 1966. Owner Integrated Touch Therapy, Princeton, NJ, 1998—. Vol. Princeton Hospice, 2000—. Avocations: tennis, travel. Home: 2110 N Ocean Blvd Apt 1402 Fort Lauderdale FL 33305-1952 Home Phone: 609-799-3396; Office Phone: 609-799-4118. Personal E-mail: tchspirit@aol.com.

BROWN, KIMBERLY ANN, gastroenterologist; MD, Wayne State U. Sch. of Medicine, 1985. Diplomate Am. Bd. Internal Medicine, 1988, Am. Bd. Internal Medicine-gastroenterology, 2002, Am. Bd. Internal Medicine-transplant hepatology, 2006. Resident internal medicine Univ. of Mich. Med. Ctr., 1985—89, fellow gastroenterology, 1989—92; hosp. affiliation include/s Henry Ford Macomb Hosps., Henry Ford Macomb Hosps.-Warren Campus, Henry Ford West Bloomfield Hosp.; physician Henry Ford Hosp. Author: (articles) The role of parental control practices in explaining children's diet and BMI, 2008, Incidence and prognostic implication of unrecognized myocardial scar characterized by cardiac magnetic resonance in diabetic patients without clinical evidence of myocardial infarction, 2008, Serum concentrations of lidocaine and its metabolites after prolonged infusion in healthy horses, 2008, and several others. Named one of Castle Connolly America's Top Doctors, 2002—10, 2011,

Castle Connolly America's Top Doctors for Cancer, 2005—07, 2009—10, 2011. Office: Henry Ford Hospital K 747 Bldg 7th Fl 2799 W Grand Blvd Detroit MI 48202-2608 Office Phone: 313-916-8865.

BROWN, LAUREN EVANS, zoologist, researcher, educator; b. Waukesha, Wis., Sept. 4, 1939; s. Winston Dever and Julianne Evelyn (Klatt) Brown; m. Jill Rae Hollingshead, Feb. 21, 1968; children: Lara Nell, Kara Anne Nash, Evan Saxon. BS in Biology, Carroll Coll., 1961; MS in Zoology, So. Ill. U., Carbondale, 1963; PhD in Zoology, U. Tex., Austin, 1967; postgrad. in Zoology, U. Melbourne, Australia, 1968. Lab asst., zoology Carroll Coll., Waukesha, Wis., 1957—61; rsch. asst. biochem. Dairyland Food Lab., Waukesha, 1960; tchg. asst. genetics Mark Twain Inst., St. Louis, 1961; tchg. & rsch. asst. zoology So. Ill. U., Carbondale, 1961—63, rsch. asst. plant ecology Pine Hills Field Sta. Pine Hills Swamp, Ill., 1963; tchg. & rsch. asst. zoology U. Tex., Austin, 1963—67; asst. prof. vertebrate zoology Ill. State U., Normal, 1967—71, assoc. prof., 1971—77, prof., 1977—2002, prof. emeritus, 2002—, curator amphibians and reptiles, 1990—, chair sect. ecology, evolution, ethology and systematic biology, 1978—79, interdisciplinary studies, 1996—, adj. prof., 2002—; maj. prof. numerous MS and PhD students. Endangered species and environ. cons., 1966—; mem. athletic coun. Ill. State U., 1992—95, mem. faculty svcs. com. Libr., 1999—2000, hon. libr., 2002—, grad. degree program maj. prof., 1967—; mem. Houston Toad Recovery Team US Fish and Wildlife Svc., 1978—84, 1998—2008; affiliate profl. scientist Ill. Natural History Survey, Champaign, Ill., 1997—; reviewer profl. jours.; presenter in field; hon. assoc. zoology Field Mus., Chgo., 2009—. Co-author: Recovery Plan for the Houston Toad, 1984; mng. editor Herpetologica, 1978—81, corr. editor Alytes, 2000—; mem. publs. bd.: Ill. Natural History Survey, 1999—; contbr. chapters to books, numerous articles to profl. jours., scientific papers. Grantee in field, 1962—. Mem.: YMCA, Baronial Order of Magna Charta, Clan Scott Soc., AARP, Nat. Audubon Soc. (John Wesley Powell Chpt. founding mem.), Mass. Soc. Geneologists, Rhode Island Genealogical Soc., Mo. Herpetological Assn., Chgo. Herpetological Soc., Md. Herpetological Soc., Internat. Soc. for the History and Bibliography of Herpetology, N.Am. Native Fishes Assn., Ill. Ornithol. Soc., Coleopterists Soc., Coun. Biology Editors, Internat. Soc. Study and Conservation Amphibians (mem. editl. bd. 2000—, mem. bd. councillors 2003—), Am. Soc. Ichthyologists and Herpetologists, Declining Amphibian Populations Task Force, Soc. Study Amphibians and Reptiles (conservation com. 1977), Herpetologists' League (bd. trustees 1979—80), Am. Rabbit Breeders Assn. (chair libr. com. 2001—02), SAR (bd. mgr. Gen. Joseph Bartholomew Chpt. 2008—, dir. 2010—), Soc. Colonial Wars, Soc. War of 1812. Achievements include rediscovery of the near extinct Houston Toad in Lost Pines. Avocations: hiking, breeding and rearing animals, genealogy, swimming. Home: 15958 E 2550 North Rd Hudson IL 61748-9391 Office: Ill State Univ Sch Biological Sci Campus Box 4120 Normal IL 61790-4120 Office Phone: 309-438-5990.

BROWN, LAURENCE G., former federal agency administrator, physician; BA, Earlham Coll., 1970; MD, Ohio State Univ., 1973. Cert. Family Practice, Advanced Trauma Life Support, Advanced Cardiac Life Support, Chem-Bio Preparedness. Residency in family practice, Lansing, Mich., 1973—76; private family practice Albany, Oreg., 1976—82; joined Fgn. Svc. US State Dept., 1982, Fgn. Svc. regional med. officer in Islamabad, Jakarta, London & Vienna, chief of med. clearances, chief fgn. programs, dep. med. dir. Washington, dir. office med. services, 2003—08. Fellow: Am. Acad. Family Physicians.

BROWN, LEE KELVIN, pulmonary, critical care and sleep medicine physician, researcher; b. Bklyn., Apr. 25, 1950; s. Bernard and Rosalind Schneider Brown; m. Carol Jean Yormack, Aug. 27, 1972; children: Matthew Ian, Douglas Elliot. BEE, MIT, 1972; MD, Mt. Sinai Sch. Medicine, 1976. Diplomate in internal medicine, pulmonary disease and critical care medicine Am. Bd. Internal Medicine, sleep medicine Am. Bd. Sleep Medicine. Resident medicine Mt. Sinai Hosp., NYC, 1976—79; fellow pulmonary disease Mt. Sinai Med. Ctr., Miami, Fla., 1979—81; assoc. prof. medicine Mt. Sinai Sch. Medicine, NYC, 1981—93; assoc. program dir. St. Joseph's Hosp. Med. Ctr., Phoenix, 1993—97; prof. clin. medicine U. Ariz., Tucson, 1994—97; chair divsn. sleep medicine Lovelace Health Sys., Albuquerque, 1997—2003; exec. dir. program sleep medicine Health Sci. Ctr. U. N.Mex., Albuquerque, 2003—, assoc. chief outpatient svcs., divsn. pulmonary, critical care medicine Sch. Medicine, 2003—, prof. medicine and pediats., 2003—, vice chair dept. internal medicine, 2004—. Mem. editl. bd. CHEST, —; contbr. chapters to books, articles to profl. jours. Asst. scoutmaster Boy Scout Troop 40, 1994—97; physician vol. Phoenix Open Golf Tournament, 1995—96; v.p. Rosalee Ranch Homeowners Assoc., Scottsdale, Ariz., 1996—97. Grantee, Grumman Aerospace Inc., 1968—72; Pulmonary Winter Course fellow, Fla. Lung Assn., 1980—81. Fellow: ACP, Am. Coll. Chest Physicians (chmn. sleep network 2004—06, Alfred Soffer Award for Editorial Excellence 2003), NY Acad. Medicine, Am. Acad. Sleep Medicine (bd. dirs. 2006—09, assoc. editor jour.), Am. Coll. Critical Care Medicine; mem.: Greater Albuquerque Med. Assn. (pres.-elect 2007, pres. 2008), Eta Kappa Nu, Tau Beta Pi. Achievements include research in respiration and neurological disease; pulmonary physiology; sleep disorders. Avocations: hiking, amateur radio, computer science. Office: Univ NMex Bldg #2 1101 Medical Arts Ave NE Albuquerque NM 87102 Office Phone: 505-272-6110. E-mail: lkbrown@alum.mit.edu, lkbrown@salud.unm.edu.

BROWN, LILLIAN ERIKSEN, retired nursing administrator, consultant; b. Seattle, Feb. 7, 1921; d. Peter Louis and Lena (Lien) Eriksen; m. Jan. 21, 1942 (div. Nov. 1963); children: Patricia Lee, Michael Gregory, Kevin William. Student, U. Calif., Berkeley, 1939-40; diploma, St. Luke's Hosp. Sch. Nursing, San Francisco, 1943; AB, Calif. State U., San Francisco, 1952; MPA, U. So. Calif., 1975. RN, Calif. Pub. health nurse San Francisco Dept. Health, 1946-50; asst. dir. nursing San Francisco Gen. Hosp., 1950-56; dir. nursing Weimar (Calif.) Med. Ctr., 1956-62, Orange County Med. Ctr., Orange, Calif., 1962-76; assoc. dir. hosp. and clins., dir. nursing, lectr. U. Calif. Med. Ctr., Irvine, 1976-82; assoc. hosp. adminstr. King Khalid Eye Specialist Hosp., Riyadh, Saudi Arabia, 1982-86; cons. AMI-Saudi Arabia Ltd., Jeddah, 1986-90. Chmn. Western Teaching Hosp. Coun. Dirs. Nursing, 1972-75, 80-81; mem. planning project com. Calif. Dept. Rehab., 1967-69, mem. adv. com., 1970-73; mem. ad hoc president's com. on hosp. governance U. Calif., 1981-82; pres. dirs. nursing coun. Hosp. Coun. So. Calif., 1972-74, mem. pers. practices com., 1976-78, 80-83, area rep., 1975-82; mem. dept. nursing adv. com. to establish baccalaureate program U. So. Calif., 1980-82; mem. adv. bd. various coll. nursing programs. Contbr. articles to profl. jours. Sec. Olive (Calif.) Little League, 1967-72; mem. com. on emergency med. svcs. Orange County Health Planning Coun., 1977-78, mem. health promotion task force, 1978-79. 2d lt. Nurse Corps, U.S. Army, 1944-45. Recipient Lauds and Laurels award U. Calif., Irvine, 1981 Fellow Am. Acad. Nurses; mem. ANA (cert. nurse adminstr. advanced), Nat. League for Nursing, APHA, Am. Orgn. Nurse Execs., Nat. Critical Care Inst. Edn., Calif. Nurses Assn. (Lillian E. Brown award named in her honor 1989), Calif. Orgn. for Nurse Execs. (hon.), Calif. Soc. for Nursing Svc. Adminstr., NOW. Democrat. Avocations: travel, stamp collecting/philately. Home: 1806 N Nordic Pl Orange CA 92865-4637 Personal E-mail: lebrown919@gmail.com.

BROWN, MICHAEL ROBERT, healthcare corporation executive; b. Joliet, Ill., Aug. 9, 1960; s. Robert Raymond and Virginia A. (Bianchi) B. AAS, Joliet Jr. Coll., 1980; BS, No. Ill. U., 1983, MBA, 1996. Cert. in mgmt. acctg., CPA in internal audit. Acctg. supr. northern region DeKalb (Ill.) Genetics, 1982-85; fin. analyst Baxter Healthcare Corp., Deerfield, Ill., 1985, sr. fin. analyst, 1985-87, sr. consols. analyst, 1987-88, mgr. acctg. svcs., 1988-89, mgr. corp. acctg., 1989-93, dir. fin. planning McGaw Park, Ill., 1993-95, asst. contr. renal divsn., 1995-99, v.p. fin. renal divsn., 1999—2003, dir. fin., medication delivery, 2003—05, dir. fin. compliance, 2005—. Vol. Jr. Achievement, United Way; bd. exec. advisors No. Ill. U; athletic adv. bd. Recipient Accounting Alumni of Yr., No. Ill. U., 2006. Mem. Inst. Mgmt. Accts., Chgo. Coun. Fgn. Rels., Fin. Exec. Internat., Inst. Internal Auditors, No. Ill. U. Alumni Assn., No. Ill. U. Exec. Club, Beta Gamma Sigma Honor Soc. Avocations: music, tennis. Personal E-mail: mrbrown9@aol.com.

BROWN, MICHAEL STUART, geneticist, educator; b. Bklyn., Apr. 13, 1941; s. Harvey and Evelyn (Katz) Brown; m. Alice Lapin, June 21, 1964; children: Jane Elizabeth, Ellen Sara. BA in Chemistry, U. Pa., 1962; MD, U. Pa. Sch. Medicine, 1966; DSc (hon.), Rensselaer Poly. Inst., 1982, U. Chgo., 1982, U. Pa., 1986, U. Buenos Aires, 1988, U. Paris, 1988, So. Meth. U., 1993, U. Miami, 1996, Rockefeller U., 2001, Duke U., 2009. Diplomate Am. Bd. Internal Medicine. Intern, resident in medicine Mass. Gen. Hosp., Boston, 1966-68; fellow digestive & hereditary disease, Nat. Inst. Arthritis & Metabolic Diseases NIH, 1968-70, fellow biochemistry, Nat. Heart Inst., 1970—71; asst. prof. U. Tex. Southwestern Med. Ctr., Dallas, 1971-74, prof., 1976—, Paul J. Thomas chair in medicine, dir. Jonsson Ctr. Molecular Genetics, 1977—, W. A. Moncrief disting. chair in cholesterol & arteriosclerosis rsch., 1989—. Bd. dirs. Pfizer Inc., 1996—. Co-editor: The Metabolic Basis of Inherited Disease, 1983. Recipient Pfizer award, Am. Chem. Soc., 1976, Passano Found. award, 1978, Lena Annenberg Hazen award, 1982, Louisa Gross Horwitz prize, Columbia U., 1984, Albert D. Lasker award for basic med. rsch., 1985, Nobel prize in physiology/medicine, 1985, Nat. Med. Sci., 1988, Warren Alpert Found. prize, 2000, Albany Med. Ctr. prize in medicine & biomed. rsch., 2003. Mem.: NAS (Lounsbery award 1979), Inst. Medicine, Royal Soc. London (fgn.), Assn. Am. Physicians, Am. Soc. Clin. Investigation. Office: UT Southwestern Med Ctr Dept Molecular Genetics 5323 Harry Hines Blvd Dallas TX 75390-9046 E-mail: mike.brown@utsouthwestern.edu. *

BROWN, NAN MARIE, retired minister; b. Winton, NC, Jan. 2, 1931; d. Richard and Aberdeen Elizebeth (Clanton) Watford; m. Joseph Linwood Blunt, June 9, 1947 (dec. Sept. 1970); children: Linette, Joseph Linwood Jr., Alvin; m. Frank Coolige Brown, Oct. 2, 1972; stepchildren: Ameedah Ali, Sami Nuridden. BS, D.C. Tchrs. Coll., 1972; MDiv magna cum laude, Va. Union U., 1982, D Ministry in Ch. Adminstrn., 1993; PhD in Pastoral Leadership (hon.), Va. U., Lynchburg, Va., 2003. Ordained to ministry Bapt. Ch., 1980. Clk., sec., adminstr. Dept. Commerce and AEC, Suitland, Germantown, Md., 1960-65; program analyst Job Corps, U.S. Office Econs., Washington, 1965-67; licensing asst. U.S. Nuclear Regulatory Commn., Bethesda, Md., 1967-72, pers. mgmt. analyst, 1972-74; mgr. nat. fed. women's program U.S. Dept. Energy, Germantown, 1974-76; nat. dir. fed. women's program U.S. Dept. Interior, Washington, 1979; asst. pastor Pleasant Grove Bapt. Ch., Columbia, Va., 1975-83; pastor Mt. Level Bapt. Ch., Dinwiddie, Va., 1983-87, New Hope Bapt Ch., Esmont, Va., 1987-89; founder, pastor The Way of Cross Bapt. Ch., Palmyra, Va., 1989—2003; vice moderator, moderator Albemarle Bapt. Assn., 1996-98; moderator Slate River Bapt. Assn., 1997-99; ret., 2003. Bd. dir. AIDS Svcs. Group, 1989-99, Women's Health, Va.; cons. Nan M. Brown Assocs., bus. cons.; vol. cons., reviewer AIDS proposals for funding Va. Health Dept., Richmond, 1979-89; founder, dir. Children's Saturday Enrichment Program, Palmyra, 1990—; gen. bd. Bapt. Gen. Conv. Va., social concerns com., 1990; vice moderator Slate River Bapt. Assn., 1995—; cert. AIDS trainer; adj. professor, Va. Union U., Samuel Dewitt Sch. Theology, Evans-Smith Leadership Inst. 1982—; founder, CEO The Way of the Cross Comm. Devel. Corp., Inc., 1998—2011; com. mem. Va. State Health Dept., 1995-97; exec. dir. aids edn., prevention US Dept. Health, Richmond, Va. Author: (devotionals) The Word in Season, 1986, The Patience To Wait, Vol. I, 1988, Vol. II, 1992; contbg. author: Wise Women Bearing Gifts, 1988, Those Preachin' Women, 1988, Sister to Sister, 1995, My Soul Explodes, 2005. Founder, pres. Black Women in Sisterhood for Action, Washington, 1979-82; vol. chaplain Martha Jefferson Hosp., Charlottesville, Va., 1993—; bd. dirs. AIDS Support Group, Charlottesville, 1990; active Fluvanna County Minority Health Coalition, 1993—, Fluvanna County Commn. on Youth, 1999—; U.S. del. to Internat. Women's Yr. Conf. on Women, Mexico City, 1975; participant First All-Africa Theol. Conf./Bapt. World Alliance, Zimbabwe; selected by Women's Internat. Dem. Fedn. to represent U.S. as del. to World Congress on Women, Moscow, 1987, others. Named Disting. Black Woman, Black Women in Sisterhood for Action, 1982; recipient recognition for cmty. svc. Interfrat. Coun., Charlottesville, 1993, award for excellence Sister Care Internat., 1995, spl. achievement and cmty. svc. award Charlottesville Tribune, 1996, Disting. Svc. award for pastoral leadership and care U. Va. Health Scis. Ctr., 2003, award, YVA Hosp. Mem. NAACP (pres. Fluvanna County chpt. 1979-81, cert. of appreciation 1994), Va. Women in Ministry (founder, pres. 1983-88, chaplain, Founder's award 1986, 90, 95), Hoop Health Desparities HIV/AIDS Work (award 2007), Emeritus The Way of Cross Bapt. Ch. (founder, pastor, award, 2008). Avocations: reading, music, sewing, travel, playing piano. Home Phone: 434-589-3641.

BROWN, NANCY A., health science association administrator; Grad., Ctrl. Mich. U., Mt. Pleasant, 1985. Spl. events dir. Mt. Carmel Mercy Hosp., Detroit; dir. devel./dep. dir. endowment campaign Mich. Cancer Found.; joined as metro Detroit dir. American Heart Assn., 1986, exec. v.p. Mass. to exec. v.p. New Eng. affiliate, nat. exec. v.p. sci. ops., COO, 2001—08, CEO, 2009—. Achievements include being the first female to be elected CEO of the the American Heart Association, 2008. Office: American Heart Association Nat Ctr 7272 Greenville Ave Dallas TX 75231 Office Phone: 214-706-1158. Business E-Mail: nancy.brown@heart.org. *

BROWN, POWEL H., oncologist, educator; BS, UNC, Chapel Hill; MD, PhD, NYU. Lic. Tex., cert. Nat. Bd. Parts 1, 2 & 3, diplomate Medical Oncology Am. Bd. Internal Med., Nat. Bd. Medical Examiners. Fellow Nat. Cancer Inst.; prof. Baylor Coll. Med.; assoc. dir. breast cancer rsch. Lester & Sue Smith Breast Ctr.; dir. Dan L. Duncan Cancer Ctr. Cancer Prevention & Population Sci. Program. Mem.: AAAS, AACR, Am. Soc. for Clinical Oncology, Alpha Omega Alpha Nat. Med. Honorary Soc. Office: 6620 Main St Ste 1350 Houston TX 77030 Office Phone: 713-798-1609. Office Fax: 713-798-1642. E-mail: pbrown@breastcenter.tmc.edu.

BROWN, ROBERT DALE, wildlife science educator, dean; b. Red Bluff, Calif., July 31, 1945; s. Charles Arthur and Carol Joyce (Dale) Brown; m. Regan Mensch, June 30, 1981; children: Alex, Jason, Adam. Student, U. Calif., Davis, 1963—65; BS, Colo. State U., Ft. Collins, 1968; PhD, Pa. State U., State Coll., 1975. From asst. prof. to assoc. prof. Tex. A&I U., Kingsville, 1975-81; from assoc. rsch. scientist to rsch. scientist C. Kleberg Wildlife Rsch. Inst., Kingsville, 1981-87; dept. head Miss. State U., Starkville, 1987-93, Tex. A&M U., College Station, 1993—2006, coord. Gulf Coast Coop. Ecosys. Studies Unit, 2002—06; dean Coll. Natural Resources N.C. State U., Raleigh, 2006—. Editor: Antler Development in Cervidae, 1983, Translocation of Wild Animals, The Biology of Deer, 1991. Lt. col. USMCR, 1968—93. Fellow Am. Inst. Nutrition, Wildlife Soc. (past pres.), mem. NC Forestry Coun., Nat. Assn. Univ. Fish and Wildlife Programs (past pres.). Episcopalian. Avocations: hunting, fishing, kayaking. Office: Dean Coll Natural Resources NC State Univ 2028 Biltmore Hall Campus Box 8001 Raleigh NC 27695-8001 Office Phone: 919-515-2883. Business E-Mail: bob_brown@ncsu.edu.

BROWN, ROBERT STEPHEN, JR., physician; b. NY, NY, Sept. 14, 1963; s. Robert Stephen and Judith (Kaufman) B.; children: Jacqueline Rachel Wilson Brown, Robert Dylan, and Jake Thomas. AB, Harvard Univ., 1985; MD, NYU, 1989; MPH, Univ. Calif. Berkeley, 1996. Attending physician Univ. Calif., San Francisco, 1995-96; med. dir. liver transplant Univ. NC, Chapel Hill, 1996-98; med. dir. for liver disease Columbia Univ., N.Y. Presbyterian, NY, 1998, attending physician, 2000—, chief, Ctr. for Liver Disease and Transplantation, 2005—, chief, divison Hepatobiliary and Abdominal Transplant Surgery, 2005; Frank Cardile prof. medicine and pediatrics in surgery Columbia U. Coll. Physicians and Surgeons, 2000—. Contbr. articles to profl. jour. Recipient Young Investigator award Am. Soc. Transplantation, 1996. Fellow Am. Coll. Physicians, Am. Coll. Gastroenterology, Am. Assn. Study Liver Disease, Am. Gastroenterological Assn.; mem. Am. Soc. Transplantation. Office: Ctr for Liver Disease NY Presbyterian 622 W 168th St Fl 14 New York NY 10032-3720 Office Phone: 212-305-0914. Business E-Mail: rb464@columbia.edu.

BROWN, RONALD DELANO, endocrinologist; b. Grosse Pointe, Mich., Dec. 28, 1936; s. Carroll Bradley and Alice Ruth (Chapper) B.; m. Marylee Ethel Lucas, July 27, 1957; children: Linda Diane, Kent William, Mark Steven. BS with distinction, U. Mich., 1959, MD with distinction, 1963. Diplomate Am. Bd. Internal Medicine, subspecialty in endocrinology and metabolism; lic. physician Mich. Intern Detroit Gen. Hosp., 1963-64; asst. resident in medicine U. Calif. Med. Ctr., San Francisco, 1966-68; chief resident in medicine San Francisco Gen. Hosp., 1968-69; fellow in endocrinology Vanderbilt U., Nashville, 1969-71, instr. medicine, 1969-71, asst. prof. medicine, 1971-73; assoc. prof. medicine Baylor Coll. Medicine, Houston, 1973-74, Mayo Med. Sch., Rochester, Minn., 1975-80; prof. medicine Health Scis. Ctr., U. Okla., Oklahoma city, 1980-93; clin. staff St. Joseph's Mercy Hosp., Clintown Twp., Mich., 1993—. Dir. U. Okla. Hypertension Ctr., 1986-93; chief clin. hypertension Health Scis. Ctr., U. Okla., 1980-93; chief hypertension VA Hosp., Oklahoma City, 1980-86; dir. multidisciplinary hypertension rsch. tng. program (NIH), Mayo Clinic, Rochester, 1977-80; chief endocrinology Ben Taub Hosp., Houston, 1973-74, assoc. dir. clin. rsch. ctr., 1973-74; coord. Tenn. Mid-South Regional Hyper-Control Program, Vanderbilt U., 1971-73; lectr. in field. Editl. bd. Jour. Clin. Endocrinology and Metabolism, 1987-91; reviewer for Life Scis., Annals of Internal Medicine, Jour. Lab. Clin. Medicine, Am. Jour. Medicine, Endocrinology, Mayo Clinic Proceedings, Steroids; contbr. 58 articles to profl. jours. Capt. USAF, 1964-66. Fellow ACP. Am. Coll. Endocrinologists; mem. Am. Soc. Hypertension, Am. Assn. Clin. Endocrinologists, Phi Kappa Phi, Phi Lambda Upsilon, Alpha Omega Alpha. *

BROWN, STEPHEN F., health facility administrator; BS, U. Ala. Joined Am. Med. Internat., 1976; CIO Am. Med. Internat. (now Tenet Healthcare Corp.), 1990—95; sr. exec. v.p., CIO Tenet Healthcare Corp., Dallas, 1995—99, exec. v.p., CIO, 1999—. Active The Wharton Sch., Info. Week mag., CEO mag., The Healthcare Collaboration Group, Sheldon I. Dorenfest and Assocs. Consulting; mem. adv. bd. Nat. Health Founds. Ctr. for Health Info. Tech. Contbg. author: Financial Information Systems Manual, 1992. Office: Tenet Healthcare Corp 13737 Noel Rd Ste 100 Dallas TX 75240 *

BROWN, SUSAN H., medical educator; b. Windsor, Nova Scotia, Can., Dec. 30, 1953; BSc, Acadia U., 1976; PhD, U. Western Ont., 1986. Arthur thurnau prof. kinesiology U. Mich., 1992—. Recipient Vis. Chair Professorship, St. Thomas U., NB, Can.; Alexander von Humboldt fellowship, German Govt. Avocations: travel, creative writing. Office: 1402 Washington Heights Sch Kines Ann Arbor MI 48109 Office Phone: 734-763-6755. Business E-Mail: shcb@umich.edu.

BROWN, VALERIE ANNE, psychotherapist, social worker, educator; b. Elizabeth, NJ, Feb. 28, 1951; d. William John and Adelaide Elizabeth (Krasa) B. BA summa cum laude (fellow), C.W. Post Coll., 1972; MSW (Silberman scholar), Hunter Coll., NYC, 1975; PhD, Am. Internat. U., 1996. Diplomate Am. Bd. Examiners, Am. Bd. Clin. Social Work, Nat. Assn. Social Work; cert. addictions specialist; cert. master hypnotherapist; cert. psychophilogic integration therapist. Social work intern Greenwich House Counseling Ctr., NYC, 1973-74, Metro Cons. Ctr., NYC, 1974-75; sr. psychiat. social worker, coadminstr. Essex County Guidance Ctr., East Orange, NJ, 1975-80; pvt. practice psychiat. social work, psychotherapy, 1979—. Sr. psychiat. social worker John E. Runnells Hosp., Berkeley Heights, NJ, 1980-86;

dir. social work Northfield Manor, West Orange, NJ, 1987; clin. coord. Project Portals East Orange Gen. Hosp., 1987-88; asst. dir. ARS/Century House Riverview Med. Ctr., Red Bank, NJ, 1988-93; sr. clin. case mgmt. specialist Prudential Ins. Co., Woodbridge, NJ, 1993; clin. dir. Greenhouse-KMC, Lakewood, NJ, 1994-2000, Shoreline-KBH, Toms River, NJ, 1996-2000; tech. advisor Nat. Comm. Network, 1988—; mental health clinician III UMDNJ-UBHC, Edison, NJ, 2000—; instr. Brookdale Coll., 1991—; co-founder Women's Growth Ctr., Cedar Grove, NJ, 1979; counselor Passaic Drug Clinic, 1978-80; field instr. Fairleigh Dickinson U., Madison, NJ, 1981-86, Brookdale Coll., 1989-92; field supr. Union Coll., Cranford, NJ, 1986; instr. Sch. Social Work, NYU, NYC, 1980-83, asst. prof., 1983-85; evaluator Intoxicated Driver Resource Ctr., Essex County, NJ, 1987-88. Alt. Monmouth County profl. adv. bd.; founding mem. Nat. Campaign Tolerance of So. Poverty Law Project, 2004. Recipient Congl. Order of Merit, Nat. Rep. Congl. Com., 2005; named Dist. Alumnae Mother Seton Regional H.S., Clark, N.J., 1997. Mem. NASW (Whittman Lifetime Achievement nominee 1997-98), Psi Chi, Pi Gamma Mu, Sigma Tau Delta. Avocations: reading, swimming, travel. Home and Office: 20 Ellsworth Ct Red Bank NJ 07701-5403

BROWN, VISEETA, health science association administrator; b. Houston, Oct. 9, 1965; d. Johnnye Crummedyo; m. Eric Brown. BS in Med. Records Adminisrn., Tex. So. U., Houston, 1987, MS in Health, 1996; PhD student in Human Svc. Registered health info. adminstr. Am. Health Info. Mgmt. Assn., 1999. Med. records supr. CIty Houston Health & Human Svcs., 1990—94, adminstrv. supr., 1994—2000; adj. instr. health info. tech. & profl. med. office program. Lone Star Coll. North Harris, 2000—07, asst. prof. Houston, 2007—08, assoc. prof. to program dir. health info. tech., 2007—; adj. prof. med. office mgmt./health care adminstrn. Kaplan U., 2009—. With Michael E. DeBakey VA Med. Ctr., Houston, 2000—07. Recipient Deans award, Texas Southern U. Coll. Pharmacy and Health Scis., 1986, Special Recognition award, Houston Department of Health and Human Svc. Divsn. Cmy. & Personal Health Svc., 1999, Special contribution award, Dept. Vets. Affairs Michael E. DeBakey VA Med. Ctr., Houston, 2002—05. Mem.: Am. Health Info. Mgmt. Assn.

BROWN, WARREN JOSEPH, physician; b. Bklyn., July 17, 1924; s. Benjamin Oscar and Angela Marie (Cahill) B.; m. Greet Roos, July 3, 1970; children: Warren James, Robert E., Suzanne J., Annemarie, Eric Jan. Student, Ursinus Coll., 1942-43; BS, Bethany Coll., 1945; MD, Ohio State U., 1949. Diplomate Am. Bd. Family Practice. Intern U.S. Naval Hosp., Long Beach and Oceanside, Calif.; resident Pottstown Hosp., Pa., 1950-51; assoc. Roos Loos Med. Group, Alhambra, Calif., 1951; practice medicine specializing in family practice Largo, Fla., 1953—2004. Sr. civilian flight surgeon FAA, 1964-2004; pres. Aero-Med. Consultants, Inc., Largo, 1969-. Author: Florida's Aviation History, 1980, 2d edit., 1993, Child Yank Over the Rainbow, 1977, Patients' Guide to Medicine, 10th edit., 1987, The World's First Airline: The St. Petersburg-Tampa Airboat Line, 1914, 1981, 2d edit., 1984. Historian Fla. Aviation Hist. Soc., 1978—, pres., 2004-05; chmn. Fla. Aviation Hall of Fame, 2002—: historian St. Petersburg-Clearwater-Tampa Hangar Order of Quiet Birdmen, 1969 . With USN, 1943-45, 49-50, 51-53. Fellow Am. Acad. Family Physicians; mem. Pinellas County Med. Assn., Fla. Med. Assn., Aircraft Owners and Pilots Assn., Am. Radio Relay League, Med. Amateur Radio Coun. (Southeastern, USA dir.). Home: 14607 Brewster Dr Largo FL 33774-4822 Home Phone: 727-595-2773; Office Phone: 727-542-4158. Personal E-mail: warenbrown@aol.com.

BROWN, WENDY WEINSTOCK, nephrologist, educator; b. NYC, Dec. 9, 1944; d. Irving and Pearl (Levack) Weinstock; m. Barry David Brown, May 2, 1971 (div. Sept. 1995); children: Jennifer Faye, Joshua Reuben, Julie Aviva, Rachel Ann. BA, U. Mass., 1966; MD, Med. Coll. of Pa., 1970; MPH, St. Louis U., 1999. Diplomate Am. Bd. Internal Medicine. Intern U. Ill. Affiliated Hosps., Chgo., 1970-71; resident in internal medicine The Med. Coll. Wis. Affiliated Hosps., Milw., 1971-74; gen. practitioner Vogelweh (W. Germany) Health Clinics, 1975-76; fellow in nephrology Med. Coll. of Wis. Milw. County Med. Complex, Milw., 1976-78; staff physician St. Louis VA Med Ctr., 1978—2003, acting chief, hemodialysis sect., 1983-85, chief dialysis/renal sect., 1985-90, dir. clin. nephrology, 1990—2003; staff physician St. Louis U. Hosps., 1978—2003, St. Louis City Hosp., 1982-85, St Mary's Health Ctr., St. Louis, 1994—2003; chief of staff VA Tenn. Valley Healthcare Sys., Nashville, 2003—06, Jesse Brown VA Med. Ctr., 2006—. Assoc. prof. internal medicine St. Louis U. Health Sci. Ctr., 1985—98, prof. internal medicine, 1998—2003; prof. medicine Meharry Med. Coll. Vanderbult Univ., 2003—. Reviewer Clin. Nephrology, Nephrology, Dialysis and Transplantation, Am. Jour. Nephrology, Am. Jour. Kidney Disease, Jour Am. Geriatric Soc., Jour. Am. Soc. Nephrology, Geriatric Nephrology and Urology, Kidney Internat.; med. editor NKF Family Focus; mem. editl. bd. Clin. Nephrology, Geriatric Nephrology, Internat. Urology and Nephrology, Advances in Renal Replacement Therapy; editor-in-chief: Advances in Chronic Kidney Disease, 2004-; contbr. articles to profl. jours. Mem. adv. coun. Mo. Kidney Program, 1985-91, chmn., 1988-89; numerous positions Nat. Kidney Found., 1984—, nat. chmn., 1995-97; bd. dirs. United Way, St. Louis, 1994-2003, Nat. Kidney Found. Ea. Mo. and Metro East, Inc., 1980-94; bd. dirs. Combined Health Appeal Greater St. Louis, Inc., 1988, pres., 1989-92; bd. dirs. Combined Health Appeal Am., 1991-98, sec., 1992-96, vice chmn., 1996-98. Recipient Upjohn Achievement award, Med. Coll. Wis. Affiliated Hosps., 1972, Cert. of Leadership, St. Louis YWCA, 1989, Chmn.'s award, Nat. Kidney Found. of Ea. Mo. and Metro East, 1990, award of excellence, 2002, Chmn.'s award, Nat. Kidney Found., Washington, 1990, Martin Wagner award, Nat. Kidney Found., 1999, award of excellence, Nat. Kidney Found. Ea. Mo. and Metro East, 2002; named Casual Corner Career Woman of Yr., 1986, Combine Health Appeal of Am. Vol. of Yr., 1991, Olympic Torch Bearer, 1996, St. Louis Health Profl. of Yr., 1997. Fellow ACP, AHA; mem. Am. Soc. Nephrology, Internat. Soc. Nephrology, Coun. on Kidney in Cardiovascular Disease, Am. Heart Assn., St. Louis Soc. Am. Med. Women's Assn., St. Louis Internists (v.p. 1983-84, pres. 1984-85), Women in Nephrology (pres. 2000-02), Internat. Soc. for Peritoneal Dialysis, Am. Geriatrics Soc., Soc. for Exec. Leadership in Acad. Medicine (bd. dirs., program chair 1999—), Alpha Omega Alpha. Jewish. Home: 416 W Grant Pl Apt G Chicago IL 60614-9319 Home Phone: 615-279-0388; Office Phone: 615-327-5330. Business E-Mail: wendy.brown@va.gov.

BROWN, WILLIAM VIRGIL, internal medicine educator; b. Royston, Ga., Sept. 25, 1938; m. Alice Brown; 2 children. BA in Physics and Chemistry, Emory U., 1960; MD, Yale U., 1964. Diplomate Am. Bd. Internal Medicine, Am. Bd. Endocrinology. Intern, asst. resident Osler Med. Svc. Johns Hopkins Hosp., Balt., 1964—66; clin. assoc. Nat. Heart and Lung Inst., Bethesda, Md., 1966—69; fellow in endocrinology and metabolism Yale-New Haven Hosp., 1969—70; asst. prof. medicine U. Calif. Dept. Medicine, San Diego, 1970—74, assoc. prof. medicine, 1974—78; dir. lipid rsch. clinic U. Calif., San Diego, 1972—78; prof. medicine Mt. Sinai Sch. Medicine, NYC, 1978—87, dir. divsn. arteriosclerosis and metabolism, 1978—87; pres., CEO Medlantic Rsch. Found., Washington, 1987—91; Charles Howard Candler prof. internal medicine, dir. divsn. arteriosclerosis and lipid metabolism Emory U., Atlanta, 1991—2009, pres. faculty coun. and univ. senate, 1998—99, prof. medicine emeritus Sch. Medicine, 2009—; chief of medicine Atlanta VA Hosp., 1998—2009. Chmn. Gordon Conf. on Lipid Metabolism, 1984; metabolism study sect. NIH, 1985; pres. Am. Bd. Clin. Lipidology, 2004—. Editor: Jour. Clinical Lipidology, 2007—. Fellow, Alexander von Humboldt. Master: ACP; mem.: Internat. Atherosclerosis Soc. (pres. 2009—), Nat. Lipid Assn. (pres. 2002—03), Am. Bd. Bioanalysis (high-complexity clin. lab. dir.), Am. Soc. Exptl. Biology, Am. Soc. Clin. Investigation, Am. Fedn. Clin. Rsch., Am. Heart Assn. (mem. physiology study sect. 1978—80, mem. credentials com. ateriosclerosis coun. 1978—80, chmn. credentials com. arteriosclerosis coun. 1979—82, mem. nutrition com. 1981—86, mem. several rsch. con., chmn. nutrition com. 1982—86, bd. dirs. 1983, vice chmn. edn. and cmty. program com., nat. pres. 1991—92, gold heart award 1996, R. Bruce Logue award 2000, fellow arteriosclerosis coun., fellow epidemiology and preventive cardiology coun., numerous others), Alpha Omega Alpha, Phi Beta Kappa. Achievements include research in structure and metabolism of lipoproteins; lipolytic enzymes, including their molecular and kinetic characteristics, diagnosis and treatment of the hyperlipoproteinemias; the relationship of lipoprotein metabolism to atheromatous vascular disorders. Office: 3208 Habersham Rd Atlanta GA 30305 Office Phone: 404-909-2095, 404-909-0227. Office Fax: 404-841-5623. Business E-Mail: wbrow925@bellsouth.net.

BROWNE, BARBARA J., internist, physiatrist; BA in Biology, Oberlin Coll., Ohio, 1982; MD, Medical Coll. of Pa., 1986. Diplomate Am. Bd. Physical Medicine and Rehab., Am. Bd. Internal Medicine. Med. dir. stroke and geriatrics program Magee Rehab. Hosp., rehab. specialists. Author: (jour.) Paraplegia, The Archives of Phys. Medicine and Rehab. Mem.: Am. Assn. of Electrodiagnostic Medicine, AMA, ACP, Am.Acad. of Phys. Medicine and Rehab. Office: Magee Rehabilitation Hospital 1513 Race St Philadelphia PA 19102-1177 Office Phone: 215-578-3000. Office Fax: 215-568-3736.

BROWNE, FREDERICK DOUGLAS, physiologist, educator; b. Springfield, Ohio, June 3, 1929; s. Charles David and Ruth Noami Browne; m. Joyce Louise Burton, June 11, 1955; children: Fred, Sharon, Michael, Regina, Stephan, Monica. BS, U. Dayton, Ohio, 1956; MS, Miami U., Oxford, Ohio, 1958; postgrad., Case Western Res. U., Cleve., 1963-66; postgrad. in Instrn. Anatomy, Coll. Medicine Case Western U., 1966; EdD, Nova U., Fort Lauderdale, Fla., 1981. Ordained permanent deacon Maronite Cath. Ch., 1992. Rschr. artificial organs and exptl. heart surgery Cleve. Clinic, 1958-63; predoctoral fellow Coll. Medicine Case Western Res. U., Cleve., 1963-66; instr. sci. Cleve. Bd. Edn., 1966-69; asst. prof. St. John's Coll., Cleve., 1969-73; instr. Sch. Anesthesia Cleve. Clinic, 1973-74; prof. anatomy and physiology Cuyahoga C.C., Warrensville, Ohio, 1973-92; chair/CEO Rameso, Inc., Copley, Ohio, 1993—. Contbr. articles to profl. jours. Pres., Bd. Cath. Edn., Diocese of Cleve., 1972-73; chmn. Civil Svc. Commn. Warrensville Heights, Ohio, 1970-72; councilman Warrensville Heights, 1982-85; bd. dirs. Summit County Cath. Social Svc.; parish rep. Boy Scouts Am., Cuyahoga County, 1958-63; mem. precinct com., AMA minority affairs com., Rep. Nat. Conv., 2004; pres. Holy Name Soc., St. Cecilia Cath. Ch., 1958-63. 2d lt. U.S. Army, 1952-54. NIH fellow, 1963-66, nominee Dr. of Yr. Summit County, 2007. Mem. AAUP, AMA, NRC, Nat. Assn. Advancement Sci., N.Y. Acad. Scis., Ohio Coll. Biology Tchrs. Assn., Secular Franciscan, Am. Legion, Knights of Columbus, Alpha Phi Alpha. Republican. Personal E-mail: hrtdr02@roadrunner.com.

BROWNE, JAMES DALE, otolaryngologist, educator; BS, Mercer U., 1978; MD, Med. Coll. Of Ga., 1982. Diplomate Am. Bd. Otolaryngology. Intern surgery NC Bapt. Hosp., 1983, resident otolaryngology, 1987; fellow otolaryngology Univ. Zurich Med. Fac-Switzerland, 1991; James A. Harrill prof. and chmn. dept. of otolaryngology-head and neck surgery Wake Forest Sch. of Medicine. Fellow: ACS; mem.: AMA, Ga. Med. Assn., Forsyth-Davie-Stokes Med. Soc., Am. Neurotological Soc., Am. Broncho-Esophagological Assn., Am. Acad. of Otolaryngology-Head and Neck Surgery. Office: Wake Forest Baptist Medical Center Medical Center Blvd Winston Salem NC 27157 Office Phone: 336-716-2011.

BROWNE, JOY, psychologist, radio personality; b. New Orleans, Oct. 24, 1950; d. Nelson and Ruth (Strauss) B.; Carter Thweatt, June 9, 1966 (div. 1979); 1 child, Patience. BA, Rice U.; PhD, Northeastern U.; postgrad., Tufts U. Registered psychologist, Mass. With rsch./optics dept. Sperry Rand, Boston, 1966-68; engr. space program Itek, Boston, 1968-70; head social svcs. dept. Boston Redevel. Authority, 1970-71; staff psychologist South Shore Counselling Assocs., Boston, 1971-82; on-the-air psychologist Sta. WITS, Boston, 1978-82, Sta. KGO, San Francisco, 1982-84; host, news Sta. KCBS, San Francisco, 1984-85; on-air psychologist Sta. WABC, NYC, 1985-87, ABC Talkradio, NYC, 1987-92, WOR Radio Network, NYC, 1992—, Sta. WABC-TV, 1995-97, Dr. Joy Browne Show, Syndicated Eyemark Entertainment, 1999—. On-air psychologist WCBS-TV Five O'Clock News, 1999; dir. Town of Hull Adolescent Outreach Program; cons. human sexuality PBS, 1994—. Author: The Used Car Game, 1971, The Research Experience, 1976, Nobody's Perfect, 1988, Why They Don't Call When They Say They Will and Other Mixed Signals, 1989, Dating for Dummies, 1998, 2d edit., 2006, 9 Fantasies That Will Ruin Your Life, 1998, It's a Jungle out There Jane! Understanding the Male Animal, 1999, Getting Unstuck: 8 Simple Steps To Solving Any Problem, 2002, Dating Disasters and How to Avoid Them, 2005, The Dr. Joy Browne Show Live on Discovery Health Network, 2006. Named One of 25 Outstanding Broadcasters USA Today, 1995-96, 100 Most Influential Talkers, Legend La., 1996, Best Female Talk Show Host, Nartash, 1996, 97, Female Talk Show Host of Yr., Vanity Fair Hall of Fame, 1996. Mem. APA (bd. dirs. 1994-97), Phi Kappa Phi (Communicator of Yr. award 1992). Office: care WOR Radio 111 Broadway 3d Fl New York NY 10006 Personal E-mail: drjoybrowne@hotmail.com. E-mail: drjoybrowne@compuserve.net.

BROWNE, ROGER MICHAEL, oral pathology educator, consultant; b. Birmingham, U.K., June 19, 1934; s. Arthur Leslie and Phyllis Maud (Baker) B.; m. Lilah Hilda Manning, May 31, 1958; children: Nicola Jane, Andrew Manning. BS, U. Birmingham, 1954, B of Dental Sci., 1957, PhD, 1960, DDS, 1974. Rsch. fellow U. Birmingham, 1958-60, lectr. in conservative dentistry, 1961-64, lectr. in dental pathology, 1964-67, sr. lectr. in oral pathology, 1967-77, prof. oral pathology, 1977-96, prof. emeritus, 1997—. Vis. prof. U. Lagos, Nigeria, 1969; postgrad. advisor in dentistry U. Birmingham, 1977-82, dir. Sch. Dentistry, 1986-89. Author: Colour Atlas of Oral Histopathology, 1975, Radiological Atlas of Diseases of the Teeth and Jaws, 1983, Atlas of Dental and Maxillofacial Radiology and Imaging, 1995; editor: The Investigative Pathology of Odontogenic Cysts, 1991, Self-assessment Picture Tests - Oral Radiology, 1997. Fellow Royal Coll. Pathologists, Dental Surgery Royal Coll. Surgeons (Charles Tomes medal 1995); mem. Internat. Assn. for Dental Rsch. (Disting. Scientist award in pulp biology 1991), Brit. Soc. Oral Pathology (pres. 1985-86, 91-94), Brit. Dental Assn. (pres. hosps. group 1986-87). Avocations: rugby football, tennis, walking. Office: Dental School St Chads Queensway B4 6NN Birmingham England

BROWNELL, KELLY DAVID, psychologist, educator; b. Evansville, Ind., Oct. 31, 1951; s. Arnold Buffum and Margaret Elizabeth (Egly) Brownell; m. Mary Jo Gabriele, Aug. 20, 1977; children: Matthew Joseph, Kevin David, Kristy Elizabeth. BA, Purdue U., 1973; PhD, Rutgers U., 1977. Postdoctoral fellow Brown U., Providence, 1977; from asst. prof. to assoc. prof. U. Pa., Phila., 1977—87, prof., 1987-90; prof. psychology Yale U., New Haven, 1991—, dir. Yale Ctr. Eating and Weight Disorders, 1994-2000, prof. epidemiology and pub. health, 2003—06, chair dept. psychology, 2003—06, dir. Rudd Ctr. for Food Policy and Obesity, 2005—08, master, Silliman Coll. Dir. Rudd Ctr. Food Policy and Obesity. Author: (books) Handbook of Eating Disorders, 1986, Handbook of Behavioral Medicine, 1988, Eating Disorders in Athletes, 1991, Eating Disorders and Obesity, 1995, vol. 2, 2002, Behavioral Medicine and Women, 1998, Food Fight, 2004; contbr. articles to profl. jours. Recipient Cattell award, N.Y. Acad. Scis., 1978, Choice award, ALA, 1989, Disting. Alumni award, Purdue U., 2001; named one of World's 100 Most Influential People, Time Mag., 2006. Fellow: APA (pres. divsn. health psychology 1989—90), Acad. Behavioral Medicine Rsch., Soc. Behavioral Medicine (pres. 1988—89); mem.: Inst. of Medicine, Assn. Advancement Behavior Therapy (pres. 1988—89). Office: Yale Univ Rudd Ctr 309 Edwards St Box 208369 New Haven CT 06520-8369 Office Phone: 203-432-7790. E-mail: kelly.brownell@yale.edu.

BROWNER, WARREN SETH, hospital administrator, internist, educator; s. David and Marian Browner; m. Robin L. Duryee, Dec. 1, 1979; children: Elise M. Duryee-Browner, Michael K. Duryee-Browner. AB, Harvard Coll., Cambridge, Mass., 1975; MD, U. Calif., San Francisco, 1979; MPH in Epidemiology, U. Calif., Berkeley, 1984. Diplomate Am. Bd. Internal Medicine. Prof. medicine, prof. epidemiology & biostatistics U. Calif., San Francisco, 1985—2000, adj. prof., 2000—; v.p. academic affairs Calif. Pacific Med. Ctr., San Francisco, 2000—09, sci. dir. CPMC Rsch. Inst., 2000—, CEO, 2009—. Gen. internist, chief gen. internal medicine, acting chief med. svc. San Francisco VA Med. Ctr. Author: Epidemiology and Public Health: Pretest Self-Assessment and Review, 1987, Designing Clinical Research: An Epidemiologic Approach, 2000, Publishing and Presenting Clinical Research, 1999; contbr. articles to profl. jours., chapters to books. Office: Calif Pacific Med Ctr PO Box 7999 San Francisco CA 94120 Office Phone: 415-600-6000. Business E-Mail: warren@cpmcri.org. *

BROWNER-ELHANAN, KAREN J., pediatrician; MD, Tel Aviv U., 1988. Registered NY, 1988, diplomate Am. Bd. Pediatrics. Pediat. resident Maimonides Med. Ctr., 1994—96; fellowship adolescent medicine Montefiore Med. Ctr., 2001—03; chief adolescent medicine NY Meth. Hosp. Office: New York Methodist Hospital 506 Sixth St Brooklyn NY 11215 Office Phone: 718-780-3000.

BROWNFIELD, ELISHA, physician, educator; b. Lawton, Aug. 12, 1965; MD, MCV, 1990. Asst. prof., internal medicine UTMB, 1993—97; assoc. prof., internal medicine Med. U. SC, 1997—. Named one of Best Drs. America. Fellow: ACP; mem.: SGIM. Office: Med University SC Dept Medicine 171 Ashley Ave Charleston SC 29425 Business E-Mail: brownfe@musc.edu.

BROWNING, FRANK SACHEVEREL, plastic surgeon; b. Oxford, Eng., Oct. 28, 1941; s. Frank Sacheverel and Ivy Mary Browning; m. Carol Angela Seed (div.); m. Mary Boyd Hiley, Aug. 23, 1996; children: Benjamin, Georgina, Rebecca. MB, BChir, St. Andrews U., Scotland, 1966. Sr. registrar plastic surgery NHS, Leeds, England, 1971—80, cons. surgeon, 1980—99; cons. Nuffield Hosps., Leeds, 1980—; microsurgery rsch. fellow St. Vincent's Hosp., Melbourne, Australia, 1975—76. Dir. med. svcs. Bramham (Eng.) Three Day Event, 1988—; hon. surgeon Leeds Rugby Union, 1992—. Contbr. chapters to books. Pres. Leeds Rugby Club, 1994—99. Recipient Spl. Horse Trial award, Brit. Horse Trials Assn., 1998. Fellow: Royal Coll. Surgeons London; mem.: Med. Equestrian Assn., Brit. Assn. Plastic Reconstructive and Aesthetic Surgeons. Anglican. Office: Leeds Nuffield Hosp 2 Leighton St Leeds LS1 3EB England Home: Terry Lug Farmhouse Bramham Prk Wetherby LS23 6LT England Office Phone: 01133882129.

BROWNING, GEORGE GORDON, otolaryngologist, researcher; b. Glasgow, Scotland, Jan. 10, 1941; s. George Gordon and Janet Smith (Money) B.; m. Annette Campbell Mallinson, June 12, 1971; children: Gillian Gordon, Jennifer Gordon, Grigor Gordon. MB ChB, U. Glasgow, 1964, MD, 1974. Resident house surgeon Western Infirmary, Glasgow, 1964-65; surg. trainee West of Scotland Tng. Scheme, Glasgow, 1965-72; sr. registrar Glasgow Tng. Scheme, Otolaryngology, 1972-78; sr. lectr. otolaryngology U. Glasgow, 1978-90; cons. otologist MRC Inst. Hearing Rsch., Glasgow, 1978—2003; hon. cons. otolaryngology Glasgow Royal Infirmary, 1978—; Titular prof. otolaryngology U. Glasgow, 1990-99, emeritus prof., 1999—; cons. adminstrv. charge dept. otolaryngology Head and Neck Surgery & The Scottish Sch. Audiology, Glasgow, 1991-98. Author: Updated ENT, 1982, 3d edit., 1994, Clinical Otology and Audiology, 1987, 2d edit., 1998; co-author: Otology, a structured approach, 1996, Picture Test in ENT; editor Clin. Otoloryngology, 2004—; co-editor: Scott-Brown's otolaryngology: Head and Neck Surgery, 2008; contbr. more than 100 articles to profl. jours. Founder, chmn. Glasgow West Conservation Soc., 1970-75. Fellow Royal Coll. Surgeons, Royal Coll. Physicians and Surgeons; mem. Brit. Soc. Academics in Otolaryngology (pres. 1994-99), Otorhinolaryngological Rsch. Soc. (pres. 1992-94), Royal Soc. Medicine (chmn. acad. bd. 2001-03, pres. sect. otology 1999-2000, v.p. 2005-07). Avocations: silversmithing, skiing, bicycling, glass fusing. Office: MRC Inst Hearing Rsch 8-16 Alexandra Parade Glasgow G31 2ER Scotland Office Phone: 0141 211 4695. E-mail: ggb@ihr.gla.ac.uk.

BROWNING, SUSAN L., hospital administrator; b. NY, Aug. 9, 1968; BA, MPH, Columbia U., 1990. V.p. adminstrn. NY Meth. Hosp., 1991—98; v.p. North Shore-LIJ Health Sys., 1998—2004, dep. exec. dir. Forest Hills Hosp., 2004—05, v.p. adminstrn., chief staff SI U. Hosp., 2005—10, sr. v.p. bus. devel. and practice mgmt. SI U. Hosp., 2010—. Pres., bd. dirs. Met. Health Administrators' Assn., 2000—01; chmn. Columbia U. Dept. Health Policy and Mgmt. Adv. Coun., 2005; treas., founding bd. mem. SI Camp Good Grief, 2010; vice chmn., chmn. elect. SI C. of C., 2011; examiner Malcolm Baldrige Nat. Quality Award Program, Nat. Inst. Stds. and Tech., US Dept. Commerce. Fellow: Am. Coll. Healthcare Execs. (nat. early careerists' com. chmn. 2004—06, Young Healthcare Exec. of Yr. award); mem.: Healthcare Leaders NY, Med. Group Mgmt. Assn. Avocations: cooking, gardening, hiking. Office: Staten Island University Hosp Staten Island NY 10305 Business E-Mail: sbrowning@siuh.edu.

BROWNING, WILLIAM DAVID, medical researcher; s. William Earl Browning and Evelyn Farmer; m. Judith Ellen Smallwood; children: Lizbeth Ellen, J. Collin. BS, Western Mich. U., Kalamazoo, 1970; MS, U. Mich., Ann Arbor, 1991, DDS, 1974. Dentist Browning & Szczesny, DDS, Grand Ledge, Mich., 1974—93; asst. prof. U. Tenn., Coll. Dentistry, Memphis, 1993—97; prof., prin. investigator Med. Coll. Ga., Sch. Dentistry, Augusta, 1997—2008, dir. clin. rsch.; endowed chair Ind. U., Sch. Dentistry, Indpls., 2008—, prin. investigator. Mem. editl. bd. Jour. Operative Dentistry, Indpls., 2000—, Jour. Esthetic & Restorative Dentistry, Chapel Hill, NC. Contbr. articles to sci. publs. Fellow: Am. Coll. Dentists; mem.: ADA (cons. 2006—), Soc. Color & Appearance Dentistry (sec. 2008). Avocations: travel, golf, tennis, cooking. Office: Ind University Sch Dentistry 1121 W Michigan St Indianapolis IN 46202 Office Fax: 317-278-2818. Business E-Mail: wbrownin@iupui.edu.

BROWNLEE, ROBERT CALVIN, pediatrician, educator; b. Due West, S.C., Mar. 13, 1922; s. Robert Calvin and Eleanor Louise (Pressly) B.; m. Judith Frances Irby; children: Eleanor Koets, Susan, Katherine Chambers, Jonathan, Robert Calvin. AB, Erskine Coll., 1943; MD, Vanderbilt U., 1945. Diplomate Am. Bd. Pediat. (pres. 1975), Am. Bd. Family Practice. Intern Vanderbilt U. Hosp., Nashville, 1945-46, resident, 1948-49, U. Va., Charlottesville, 1949-50; chief resident Vanderbilt U., Nashville, 1950-51; practice medicine, specializing in pediat. Christie Pediatric Group, Greenville, SC, 1951-70; dir. pediat. Greenville Hosp. Sys., 1970-75; assoc. exec. sec. Am. Bd. Pediat., Chapel Hill, NC, 1976, exec. sec., 1977-87, pres., 1987-92. Clin. prof. pediat. U. Pa., 1976-78; prof. pediat. U. S.C., 1971-75; clin. prof. U. N.C., 1978-96. Contbr. articles to med. jours. With AUS, 1943-45; with M.C. USAF, 1946-48, 53. Mem. Am. Acad. Pediat., Ambulatory Pediat. Assn. Presbyterian.

BROWNSTEIN, ALAN P., health foundation executive, consultant; b. NYC, Sept. 20, 1944; s. Charles S. and Thelma S. (Blauweiss) B.; m. Patricia Marie Rosenberg, June 15, 1968; children: Joshua B., Jeremy S. BS, SUNY-Buffalo, 1967, MSW, 1969; MPH, U. Mich., 1973. Dir. health policy and legisl. research Local 1199, Drug and Hosp. Union/Nat. Union Hosp. and Nursing Home Employees, RWDSU, AFL-CIO, NYC, 1970-72; dep. dir. Office Comprehensive Health Planning, Exec. Office Human Services Mass., Boston, 1973-75; dir. office grants mgmt. and devel. NYC Health and Hosps. Corp., 1975-77; asst. dir. dept. for the cmty. Cmty. Svc. Soc. NY, NYC, 1977-80; dir. Coun. Home Health Agys. and Cmty. Health Services, Nat. League Nursing, NYC, 1980-81; exec. dir. Nat. Hemophilia Found., NYC, 1981-94; pres., CEO Am. Liver Found., Cedar Grove, NJ, 1994—2004; pres. Nat. Down Syndrome Soc., NYC, 2005—07; exec. dir. Nat. Alliance Thrombosis and Thrombophilia, Tarrytown, NY, 2007—. Expert witness US Congress, 1971-95; cons. Citizens' Com. for Children, NYC, 1979-81, Blue Cross Mass., Boston, 1981, Office Maternal and Child Health, USPHS, Rockville, Md., 1983; mem. adj. faculty in health econs., hosp. and healthcare mgmt. program Sch. Bus. Adminstrn., Adelphi U., Garden City, NY, 1979-81, mem. profl. adv. bd., 1977-81; mem. adj. faculty in health svcs. mgmt. New Sch. for Social Rsch., NYC, 1979; mem. nat. adv. com. Nat. Pediatric HIV Resource Ctr. Co-author monographs: Consumers Guide to Health Insurance, 1974; Consumers Guide to Nursing Homes, 1975. Contbr. chpts. to books, articles to profl. jours. V.p. Health Systems Agy. Bd. G., Queens, NY, 1979-81, Jamaica Estates Assn., NY, 1980-92, Friends of Cunningham Pk., Queens, 1983-85; bd. dirs. Cmty. Health Charities, 2002—. Recipient Faculty Fund for Social Work Students award SUNY-Buffalo Sch. Social Welfare, 1969, Disting. Alumni award SUNY Buffalo, 1993; fellow NIMH, 1967-69, USPHS, 1972-73 Mem. APHA, Pub. Health Assn. N.Y.C. (bd. dirs. 1979-82), World Fedn. Hemophilia, Nat. Health Coun. (bd. dirs. 1988—), Digestive Disease Nat. Coalition (bd. dirs. 1994—), Am. Soc. of Assn. Execs., Nat. Ctr. for Non-Profit Bds., Health Care Quality Alliance (bd. dirs. 1996-2001). Office: Nat Alliance Thrombosis & Thrombophilia 120 White Plains Rd Ste 100 Tarrytown NY 10591 Office Phone: 914-220-5040.

BROWNSTEIN, CINDY, medical association administrator; B, Temple U., Phila., 1974. Exec. v.p. Epilepsy Found., 1995—2000; CEO Spina Bifida Assn., Washington, 2000—. Office: Spina Bifida Assn 4590 MacArthur Blvd NW Ste 250 Washington DC 20007 Office Phone: 800-621-3141 ext. 14. Office Fax: 202-944-3295. Business E-Mail: cbrownstein@sbaa.org. *

BROXMEYER, HAL EDWARD, medical educator, research scientist; b. Bklyn., Nov. 27, 1944; s. David and Anna (Gurman) B.; m. C. Beth Biller, 1969; children: Eric Jay, Jeffrey Daniel. BS, Bklyn. Coll., 1966; MS, L.I. U., 1969; PhD, NYU, 1973. Postdoctoral student Queens U., Kingston, Ont., Canada, 1973-75; assoc. rschr., rsch. assoc. Meml. Sloan Kettering Cancer Ctr., NYC, 1975-78, assoc., 1978-83, assoc. mem., 1983; asst. prof. Cornell U. Grad. Sch., NYC, 1980-83; assoc. prof. Ind. U. Sch. Medicine, Indpls., 1983-86, prof. medicine, microbiology and immunology, 1986—; sci. dir. Walther Oncology Ctr., Indpls., 1988—2009, chmn. microbiology and immunology, 1997—2010, Disting. prof., 2004—, Mary Margaret Walther prof. emeritus, 2009—. Mem. hematology II study sect. NIH, Bethesda, Md., 1981—86, 1995—2000, chair, 1997—2000; adv. com. NHLBI, NIH, Bethesda, 1991—94; chmn. bd. sci. counselors Nat. Space Biomed. Rsch. Inst., 1997—2006, mem. coun., 1999—2006; bd. dirs. Nat. Disease Rsch. Interchange, 1998—, chmn., 2007—09, chmn. emeritus, 2009—; co-chmn. sec. hematopoiesis Faculty of 1000 Medicine; adv. bd. mem. Jour. Clin. Invest, 2009—. Assoc. editor Exptl. Hematology, 1981—90, Jour. Immunology, 1987—92, Stem Cells, 1996—97, Brit. Jour. Haematology, 1998—, editor Jour. Leukocyte Biology, 1995—, sr. editor Stem Cells and Devel. (formerly Jour. Hematotherapy and Stem Cell Rsch.), 2000—, mem. editl. bd. Blood, 1983—87, Biotech. Therapeutics, 1988—95, Internat. Jour. Hematology, 1991—, Jour. Lab. Clin. Medicine, 1992—2006, Jour. Exptl. Medicine, 1992—, Annals Hematology, 1993—, Cell Transplantation, 1994—, Critical Rev. Oncology/Hematology, 1995—, Stem Cells, 1998—, Jour. Blood and Marrow Transplantations, 1998—, Cytokines, Cellular and Molecular Therapy, 1998—, Current Trends Immunology, 2004—, Internat. Jour. Biol. Scis., 2006—; contbg. editor: Blood Cells, Molecules and Diseases; contbr. chapters to books, over 680 articles to profl. sci. jours. Ednl. com. Leukemia Soc. Am., Indpls., 1983—86; nat. career devel. study sect. Leukemia and Lymphoma Soc., NY, 1991—95, 2000—04, 2010—. Recipient Founder's Day award NYU, 1973, Merit award Nat. Cancer Inst.; Leukemia Soc. Am. award, 1987-95, Spl. Fellow award, 1976-78, Scholar award, 1978-83, Gold medal City of Paris, 1993, World of Difference award Ind. Health Industry Forum, 1997, Landsteiner award Am. Assn. Blood Banks, 2002, Health Care Heroes award Indpls. Bus. Jour., 2002, Prestigious External Recognition award Ind. U. Purdue U. Indpls., 2003, Disting. Alumni award L.I. U., Bklyn. Ctr., 2005, Dr. Joseph T. Taylor Excellence in Diversity award Ind. U. Purdue U. Indpls., 2006, Dirk van Bekkum award Autologous Blood and Bone Marrow Soc., 2006, E. Donnall Thomas prize Am. Soc. Hematol, 2007, McCulloch and Till award, Can. Bone Marrow and Blood Transplant Group, 2009, Donald Metcalf award, Internat. Soc. Exptl. Hematol and Stem Cells, 2011. Mem.: AAAS, Internat. Cord Blood Transplantation Symposium (Cord Blood award 2008), Leukemia Lymphora Soc. (Mission Advancement award 2008, Glen W. Irwin Jr. MD Distinguished Faculty award 2008), Am. Soc. Blood and Marrow Transplantation, Am. Fedn. Clin. Rsch., Am. Soc. Hematology (coun. 2000—05, v.p. 2008, pres. 2010), Internat. Soc. Stem Cell Rsch., Internat. Soc. Exptl. Hematology (pres. 1990—91), Am. Assn. Immunologists, Am. Assn. Cancer Rsch., Soc. Leukocyte Biology, NY Acad. Scis. Achievements include 13 patents in field. Avocations: weightlifting, reading, art. Home: 1210 Chessington Rd Indianapolis IN 46260-1630 Office: Ind U Sch Medicine 950 W Walnut St Rm 302 Indianapolis IN 46202-5181 Office Phone: 317-274-7510. Office Fax: 317-274-7592. Business E-Mail: hbroxmey@iupui.edu.

BROZENA, SUSAN C., cardiologist; d. Vincent and Blanche Kaporch. RN, Wilkes-Barre Gen. Hosp. Sch. Nursing, 1972; BSN, Wilkes Coll., 1976; MD, Temple U., 1981. Diplomate in internal medicine and cardiovasc. medicine Am. Bd. Internal Medicine. Assoc. prof. medicine Hahnemann U., Phila., 1992—98; assoc. prof. medicine, Heart Failure and Transplant Ambulatory Care Program U. Pa., 1998—. Contbr. articles to profl. jours. Recipient Tchg. award, Temple U, 1990, U Pa., 2000. Fellow: Am. Coll. Cardiology, Am. Heart Assn.; mem.: Heart Failure Soc. Am., Internat. Soc. Heart and Lung Transplantation. Office: Penn Medicine at Radnor 250 King of Prussia Rd Wayne PA 19087 also: Cardiovas Medicine Divsn Univ Pa Hosp Heart & Vascular Ctr E Pavilion 2nd Fl 3400 Civic Center Blvd Philadelphia PA 19104

BROZOSKI, THOMAS J., otolaryngologist, researcher; PhD in Experimental Psychology, U. Va., 1969. Post-doctoral rschr. Dept. Pharmacology, U. Mich., 1975—76, Lab. Neuropsychology, Nat. Inst. Mental Health, 1976—78; tinnitus rschr. Dept. Surgery Southern Ill. U. Sch. Med. Contbr. articles to med. jours. Office: Southern Illinois University School of Medicine 801 N Rutledge Rm 3205 Springfield IL 62794-9620 Office Phone: 217-545-6583. E-mail: tbrozoski@siumed.edu.

BRTKO, MIROSLAV, cardiologist, educator; b. Liberec, Czech Republic, Dec. 17, 1963; s. Miroslav and Juliana Brtko; m. Jindra Rondiak, 1987; 1 child, Claire. MD, Charles U., Prague, 1988, PhD, 2005. Lic. in internal medicine Ministry of Health, Czech Republic, 1991, cardiology Ministry of Health, Czech Republic, 1996. Cardiology registrar U. Hosp.,Dept. of Cardiac Surgery Charles U., Hradec Kralove, Czech Republic, 1989—96, cons. of cardiology U. Hosp. Dept. of Cardiac Surgery, 1996—. Cons. interventional cardiology U. Hosp. Ist Internal Medicine Dept. Charles U., 2000—. Co-author: (CD ROM) Interactive Cardiac Surgery, 2003. Mem.: European Assn. Echocardiography, The European Soc. Cardiology (mem. working group on interventional cardiology), The Czech Soc. Internal Medicine, The Czech Soc. Cardiology. Achievements include research in postperfusion syndrom after operation in extracorporeal circulation; parenteral and enteral nutrition after cardiac operations; low-molecular weight heparins during coronary interventions; the long-term patency and flow pattern of mammarocoronary grafts; percutaneous coronary interventions after coronary artery bypass grafting. Office: Charles University Hosp Sokolska St 500 05 Hradec Králové Czech Republic Office Phone: 420495833678. Office Fax: 420495833026. Business E-Mail: brtkom@seznam.cz.

BRUBAKER, LINDA, gynecologist; b. Oak Park, Ill., Oct. 30, 1955; d. George Albert and Marian Constance Tetzlaff; m. Warren Earl Brubaker, June 25, 1983; children: Aleah, Anita, Keene. BA with honors, U. Ill., Chgo., 1977; post grad., U. Chgo., 1978; MD, Rush U. Rush Med. Coll., Chgo., 1984. Cert. Am. Bd. Ob-Gyn., lic. physician and surgeon Ill. Post sophomore fellow dept. pathology Rush U. Rush Med. Coll., Chgo., 1982—83; resident ob-gyn. Rush Presbyn. St. Luke's Med. Ctr., 1984—88, chief resident ob-gyn., 1987—88, adjunctive attending and fellow urogyne, 1988—90; instr. Rush Med. Coll., 1988—90, asst. prof. urogynecology, 1990—95, asst. prof. gen. surgery, 1993—95, assoc. prof. dept. ob-gyn. conjoint dept. surgery, 1995—99, prof. dept. ob-gyn. conjoint dept. surgery, 1999—2000; consulting provisional MacNeal Hosp., Berwyn, 1991—93; provisional Vencor Hosp., Chgo. and Northlake, 1992—95; gen. Ill. Masonic Med. Ctr., Chgo., 1995—2000; asst. attending Rush Presbyn. St. Luke's Med. Ctr., 1990—98, sr. attending, 1998—2000, Loyola U. Med. Ctr., Maywood, 2000, prof. departments ob-gyn. and urology, 2000—, dir. divsn. female pelvic medicine and reconstructive surgery, sr. assoc. dean clin. and translational rsch., 2010—, interim dean Strict Sch. Medicine, 2011—. Dir. Divsn. of Female Pelvic Medicine and Reconstructive Surgery Loyola U. Med. Ctr., Maywood, Ill., 2000—; vis. prof. Dept. Ob-Gyn. Karolinska Inst. Danderyd Hosp., Stockholm, 1999, Dartmouth-Hitchcock Med. Ctr., Lebanon, NH, 2002; presenter to profl. seminars and confs. Contbr. scientific papers, articles to profl. jours. Recipient Faculty Tchg. award, 1992, Ortho Pharmaceutical/CREOG, 1998; named Urogynecologist of Yr., Nat. Assn. Continence, 2002; grantee, NIH/NICHD, 2001—06, NIH/NIDDK, 2001—06, Eli Lilly & Co., 2002—. Fellow: ACS, ACOG (Outstanding Svc. on Edn. Commn. 1998). Avocations: sports, reading, orchids. Office: Loyola Univ Med Ctr 2160 S First Ave Maywood IL 60153 *

BRUCE, BUCKINGHAM, endocrinologist, educator; b. Pasadena, Calif., Feb. 10, 1946; MD, U. Calif., San Diego, 1972. Prof. pediatric endocrinology Stanford U., 1998—. Rsch. grant, NIH, JDRF. Mem.: ADA. Home: 761 Matadero Ave Palo Alto CA 94306 Business E-Mail: buckingham@stanford.edu.

BRUCE, DEB (DEBRA FULGHUM BRUCE), editorial consultant, medical writer, health communications specialist; PhD in Health Comm., U. South Fla., 2001. CEO Deb Bruce Consulting, Atlanta, 1989—. Has published several thousand feature articles for Women's Day, Prevention, Parenting, Baby Talk, Reader's Digest & Success, features & excerpts from health trade books have appeared in Men's Health, McCall's, US News and World Report, Glamour, Vogue, Cosmopolitan, Shape's Cook, Women's Day, Elan, USA Today, and Women's World Weekly, Esquire, Forbes, GQ, Prevention, Walking, Cooking Light, Redbook, Martha Stewart's Living, Reader's Digest, radio and TV guest appearances with co-authors include CNN News, CNN Medical Moments, ABC News, CBS News, CBS Early Show, NBC News, & Today Show, editor-in-chief Living Well, 1994—97, regular contbr. MightyWords.com (own collection page Debra Fulghum Bruce Health Collections), 1996—2000, writing projects with Parenting.com and Question & Answer titles with Little/Brown (NY), editl. cons. for ThirdAge.com, WebMD.com, 2006—09, med. writer Reader's Digest Medical Breakthroughs, 2000—02, Life Extension, 2002—06, writer, editor: Spotlight on Health Oprah.com, 2007—09; author: The Unofficial Guide to Alternative Medicine, 1998, The Unofficial Guide to Conquering Impotence, 1998, The Sinus Cure: 7 Simple Steps to Relieve Sinusitis and Other Ear, Nose and Throat Conditions, 2001, Miracle Touch: A Complete Guide to Hands On Therapies That Have the Amazing Ability to Heal, 2003; co-author (with Kimberly Thompson): Over Kill: How Our Nation's Abuse of Antibiotics and Other Germ-Killers is Hurting Your Health and What You Can Do About It; co-author: (with Harris H. McIlwain) Stop Osteoarthritis Now!, The Super Aspirin Cure for Arthritis, Diet for a Pain-Free Life-A Revolutionary Plan to Lose Weight, Stop Pain, Sleep Better, and Feel Great in 21 Days; co-author: (with Laurence Smolley) The Snoring Cure, Breathe Right Now; co-author: (with Jay Williams) The 24-Hour Turnaround; co-author: Making a Baby: Everything You Need to Know to Get Pregnant, 2000, The Fibromyalgia Handbook: A 7-Step Program to Halt and Even Reverse Fibromyalgia, Reversing Osteopenia: The Definitive Guide to Recognizing and Treating Early Bone Loss in Women of All Ages, Pain-Free Back-6 Simple Steps to End Pain and Reclaim Your Active Life, Pain-Free Arthritis-A 7 Step Plan for Feeling Better Again, Stop Osteoarthritis Now-A Step-by-Step Program for Ending the Pain and Stiffness of Osteoarthritis; writer with Ronald R. Fieve Bipolar II: Enhance Your Highs, Boost Your Creativity, and Escape the Cycles of Recurrent Depression-The Essential Guide to Recognize and Treat the Mood Swings of this Increasingly Common Illness, proposal writer/ghostwriter I'd Kill for a Cookie: A Simple Six Week Plan to Conquer Stress Eating, 1998, proposal and writer/collaborator with Vincent Fortanasce The Anti-Alzheimer's Prescription: The Science-Proven Plan to Start at Any Age, 2008, ghostwriter (health trade book on diet and fitness) Dr. Sears L.E.A.N. Kids Program, author (health trade books) Super Calcium Counter, Bone Boosters; co-author (with Cathy Cristie and Susan Mitchell): (health trade books) Smart Cookies Don't Get Stale; co-author: (with Harris H. McIlwain) The Osteoporosis Cure, 2000—03; co-author: (with Howard Smith) The Women's Guide to Ending Pain: An 8-Step Program, 2003; co-author: Winning with Arthritis, Winning with Back Pain, Winning with Heart Attack, Winning with Osteoporosis, Winning with Chronic Pain, Osteoporosis: Prevention, Management, Treatment & The 50+ Wellness Program, 1989—2003; ghostwriter for a Series of Parenting Books, Little, Brown and Co., 1999—2006, ghostwriter with John Chappatear The Daily Six: Simple Steps to Prosperity and Purpose. Named Alumnus of Yr., U. South Fla., 1998. Mem.: Assn. Health Care Journalists, Am. Med. Writers Assn. Avocations: travel, home renovation, investing. Office Phone: 770-457-8036. Office Fax: 770-454-9979. Business E-Mail: dfbruce@aol.com.

BRUCE, EUNICE ADJOA, public health service officer; b. Accra, Ghana, Apr. 22, 1964; PhD, U. Melbourne, Victoria, Australia, 2010; MPH, Deakin U., 2000. Clin./pub. health officer Dept. Health, Northern Ter., Australia, 2002—03; HIV/AIDS advisor World Vision Internat., 2003—05; rsch. asst. U. Melbourne, Melbourne Sexual Health Ctr., 2008—10; data entry -STIs archives Melbourne Sexual Health Ctr., 2008—10; area supr. Australian Bur. Stats., 2011—. Bd. mem. Dianella Cmty. Health Svcs., 1998—99; mem. Ctrl. Australia Lifestyle Support Team, 2002—03, HIV/AIDS/STI Country Coordinating Mechanism, 2003—05; peer reviewer - sci. paper Internat. Jour. Pub. Health, 2010. Recipient Moresby Best Practice Model award, UNFPA, 2005. Mem.: Sci. Adv. Bd., iAMscientist, GLG Healthcare Coun., Pub. Health Assn. Avocations: reading, writing. Home: 502/591 Elizabeth St Melbourne Victoria 3000 Australia Business E-Mail: ebruce@mshc.org.au.

BRUCE, JEFFREY NEIL, neurosurgeon; b. Plainfield, NJ, July 18, 1956; s. Thomas Edward and Olga Mildred (Kmosko) B.; m. Rebecca Jo Hulshizer, Aug. 8, 1981; children: Zachary Thomas, Samuel Stanford, Rachel Anne, Eliza Mille. BA, U. Va., 1978; MD, Robert Wood Johnson Med. Sch., 1983. Diplomate Am. Bd. Neurol. Surgery. Resident in neurosurgery Columbia Presbyn. Med. Ctr., NYC, 1985-90; med. staff fellow NIH, Bethesda, Md., 1984-85; asst. prof. Columbia U., NYC, 1990-96, assoc. prof. neurosurgery, 1996—2002, prof. neurol. surgery, 2002—, Edgar M. Housepian prof. neurol. surgery rsch., 2005—, vice chmn. dept. neurosurgery, 2009—; dir. Am. Bd. Neurol. Surgeons. Dir. Bartoli Brain Tumor Lab., Columbia U., NYC, 1990—; co-dir. neuro-oncology Columbia Presbyn. Cancer

Ctr., NYC, 1992—; pres. N.Y. Soc. for Neurosurgery, 1998—2001; co-dir. Brain Tumor Ctr. Mem. editl. bd.: Neurosurgery, 1997, Jour. Neuro-oncology, 2006—, Jour. Surg. Edn., 2000—. Brain Tumor Rsch. fellowship Assn. of Brain Tumor Rsch., 1990-92; recipient Nat. Brain Tumor Found. Rsch. award Nat. Brain Tumor Found., 1996. Fellow: ACS; mem.: Am. Acad. Neurol. Surgeons, Soc. Neurol. Surgeons, Congress of Neurol. Surgeons, Am. Assn. Neurol. Surgeons (exec. bd. joint sect. on tumors 2000—), Am. Brain Tumor Assn. (sci. adv. coun. 2000—), The Pituitary Soc., N.Am. Skull Base Soc., Am. Soc. for Clin. Oncology, N.Am. Soc. for Neuro-oncology. Avocation: music. Office: Neurol Inst Columbia U Rm 434 710 W 168th St New York NY 10032-2603 Office Phone: 212-305-7346. Business E-Mail: jnb2@columbia.edu.

BRUCE, SANDRA, health facility administrator; B, Western Mich. U.; MS in Health Adminstrn., U. Notre Dame. CEO Berrien Gen. Hosp.; former pres., CEO Mercy Gen. Health Ptnrs., Muskegon, Mich.; pres., CEO St. Alphonsus Health Sys., Boise, Idaho; bd. dirs. Resurrection Health Care Corp., pres., CEO, 2008—. Recipient Pastoral Assistance to Health Care Workers award, Pontifical Coun. Rome, 2011; named one of Top 25 Women in Healthcare, Modern Healthcare mag., 2011. Fellow: American Coll. of Health Care Execs.; mem.: American Soc. for Aging, American Coll. of Health Care Administrs., American Hosp. Assn., Idaho Hosp. Assn. (chmn.), Mich. Health and Hosp. Assn. (past chair), Cath. Health Assn. (immediate past chair bd. trustees). Office: Resurrection Medical Center 7435 W Talcott Ave Chicago IL 60631 Office Phone: 773-774-8000. *

BRUCE, STEPHANIE ROBIN, geriatrician; b. Ft. Myers, Fla., Dec. 7, 1966; Attended, Georgetown U., Columbia U.; MD, Duke U. Sch. Medicine, 2000. Cert. internal medicine, geriatric medicine. Intern & resident, geriatrics Duke U. Hosp., 2000—03; fellow Johns Hopkins U., Bayview Med. Ctr., Baltimore, 2003—04; geriatrician Washington Hosp. Ctr., 2004—, med. dir. Home Hospice Program, med. dir. inpatient geriatrics unit. Office: Washington Hospital Ctr 1340 Old Chain Bridge Rd Ste 202 Mc Lean VA 22101-3943 Office Phone: 202-877-7000.

BRUCE, THOMAS ALLEN, physician, educator; b. Mountain Home, Ark., 1930; s. Rex Floyd and Dora Madeline (Fee) B.; m. Dolores Fay Montgomery; children: T.K. Montgomery, Dana Fee Thomas. BSM, MD, U. Ark., 1955, DSc (hon.), 1995. Intern Duke Hosp., 1956-57; resident medicine Bellevue Hosp., NYC, 1957, Meml. Ctr. Cancer and Allied Diseases, NYC, 1958, Parkland Meml. Hosp., Dallas, 1958—59; cardiopulmonary trainee Southwestern Med. Sch. of U. Tex., 1959—60; cardiac rsch. fellow Hammersmith Hosp. and U. London Postgrad. Med. Sch., London, 1960—61, Harvard Bus. Sch., 1974. From instr. to prof. medicine Wayne State U., 1961—68, also asst. dean Sch. Medicine; prof. medicine, head cardiovascular sect. U. Okla. Med. Ctr., 1968—74; prof. medicine, dean Coll. Medicine U. Ark. Med. Scis., 1974—85, emeritus prof., 1997—; dean pro tem Coll. Pub. Health, 2001—, prof. health policy and mgmt., 2001—; prof. U. Ark. Clinton Sch. Pub. Svc., 2002—07, dean pro tem, 2003—04, assoc. dean, 2004—07, prof. emeritus, 2007—; med. dir. Barton Rsch. Inst., 1974—85; coord. Sino-am. Med. Exch. Program, 1979—85; rsch. support rev. com. NIH, 1983—85; program dir. W.K. Kellogg Found., 1985—97; co-chair session 312 Salzburg Seminar, Austria; mem. History of Medicine Assocs.; chair nat. adv. bd. cmty. health leadership program Robert Wood Johnson Found., 2004—06; policy adv. bd. Ark. Ctr. for Health Improvement, 1995—2009; chmn. bd. trustees Watershed Found.; adj. staff Ark. Cmty. Found.; bd. dirs. Heifer Internat., 1996—2006, chair, 2003—04. Master gardener, chmn. garden docents Wildwood Park Arts; pres. Taiwan-US Sister Rels. Alliance; bd. dirs. Garvan Woodland Gardens, 2000—06. Named Profl. of Yr., U. Ark. at Little Rock, 2003; named to U. Ark. Med. Scis. Coll. Medicine Hall of Fame, 2004; recipient Ark. Gov. Meritorious Achievement award, 1974, Lugene Chilcote award, 1999, Double Helix award U. Ark. Med. Sci., 2001, Lucy Lockett Cabe award Wildwood Park Arts, 2001, Giving Tree Soc. award, 2003, Ctrl. High Mus. Appreciation award, 2001, Ark. Ctr. Health Improvement award, 2002, Sen. David Pryor Carelink award, 2004, Bruce Commons Dedication award U. Ark. Med. Scis. Coll. Publ Health, 2004, Martin Luther King Salute to Greatness award, 2005, Humanitarian of Yr. award Just Communities Ark., 2007, Lifetime Achievement award Ark. Med. Soc., 2009; named Philanthropist of the Yr., Ark. Assn. Fundraising Profls., Merit award, Kaohsiung Med. U., 2009, Resolution Appreciation award, U. Ark. Bd. Trustees, 2009, Disting. Cmty. Svc. award Ark. Med. Dental Pharm. Assn., 2009, Visionary Pub. Health award, Ark. Minority Health Commn., 2011. Fellow: ACP, Am. Coll. Cardiology; mem.: AMA, APHA, Leila Arboretum Soc. (pres. 1989—92), Am. Rhododendron Soc., Ark. Caduceus Club, Alpha Omega Alpha, Sigma Xi. Rsch. and publs. on cardiovascular disease including left ventricular function in cardiac denervation, coronary heart disease, myocardial metabolism relating to phospholipids in graded cardiac ischmia, med. edn. with particular reference to rural health care, health promotion and disease prevention, primary health care, community-based pub. health. Home: 6 Spy Glass Ln Little Rock AR 72212-4418

BRUCK, LANCE, obstetrician, gynecologist, educator; Attended, NY Med. Coll., 1992. Diplomate Am. Bd. Ob-Gyn. Resident Montefiore Med. Ctr., 1993—97, Albert Einstein Coll. of Medicine, assoc. clin. prof. ob-gyn.; with ob-gyn. Stamford Hosp. Office: Stampord Hospital Obstetrics & Gynecology Department 30 Shelburne Rd Stamford CT 06902 Office Phone: 203-276-7853.

BRUCKSTEIN, ALEX HARRY, internist, gastroenterologist, geriatrician; b. Germany, Dec. 2, 1949; came to U.S., 1950; s. Jacob and Rose B., m. Dorothy Krausman, Mar. 23, 1973; children: Tammy, Sharon, Sarah, Michael. BS in Chemistry, CCNY, 1971; MD, Albert Einstein Coll. Medicine, 1975. Diplomate Am. Bd. Internal Medicine, Am. Bd. Gastroenterology, Am. Bd. Internal Medicine- Geriatrics. Intern in internal medicine Roosvelt Hosp., NYC; resident in internal medicine St. Luke's Hosp., NYC; resident in gastroenterology VA Hosp., N.Y.U., NYC; pvt. practice internal medicine, gastroenterology Staten Island, NY. Hosp. affiliations: Doctors' Hosp. Staten Island, N.Y., Staten Island U. Hosp. N., Staten Island U. Hosp. S., St. Vincent's Hosp., Staten Island; vis. clin. fellow Columbia U. Dept. Medicine, 1975-78, NYU Dept. Medicine, 1978-80; clin. asst. prof. medicine N.Y. Med. Coll., 1983-90, SUNY Health Sci. Ctr. at Bklyn., 1990—. Fellow ACP, Am. Coll. Gastroenterology; mem. AMA, Med. Soc. State N.Y., Richmond County Med. Soc., Am. Gastroent. Assn., N.Y. Soc. Gastrointestinal Endoscopy, N.Y. Acad. Gastroenterology, Am. Geriatrics Assn. Office: 2627 Hylan Blvd Staten Island NY 10306-4339 Home Phone: 516-239-9780; Office Phone: 718-667-3200. Personal E-mail: abrucksteinmd@gmail.com.

BRUEGGEMEIER, ROBERT W., dean, medical educator; BA in Chemistry, Mich. State U., East Lansing, 1972; MS in Medicinal Chemistry, U. Mich., Ann Arbor, 1975, PhD in Medicinal Chemistry, 1977. Postdoc. rsch. fellow biol. chemistry Harvard Med. Sch., Boston, 1977—79; asst. prof. divsn. medicinal chemistry & pharmacognosy Ohio State U. Coll. Pharmacy, Columbus, 1979—85, assoc. prof., 1985—90, prof., 1990—, chmn. divsn. medicinal chemistry & pharmacognosy, 1992—2003, dean Coll. Pharmacy, 2003—. Dir. radiochemistry/instrumentation support labs. Ohio State U. Comprehensive Cancer Ctr., 1979—, dir. hormones & cancer prog., 1985—; dir. Ohio State Biochemistry Prog.; bd. dirs. Ohio State U. Rsch. Found. Contbr. articles to profl. jours., chapters to books. Fellow: AAAS, Am. Assn. Pharm. Scientists. Achievements include research in medicinal chemistry, steroid chemistry and biochemistry; hormones and breast cancer, with an interdisciplinary focus on understanding the molecular role of estrogens in hormone-dependent cancers and in the development of new agents such as aromatase inhibitors for the treatment of hormone-dependent cancers. Office: OSU Coll Pharmacy 217 Parks Hall 500 W 12th Ave Columbus OH 43210 Office Phone: 614-292-5711. Office Fax: 614-292-3113. Business E-Mail: brueggemeier.1@osu.edu.

BRUERA, EDUARDO, oncologist, medical educator; b. Rosario, Argentina; MD, U. De Rosario, 1979. Oncologist U. Alberta and Cross Cancer Inst., Edmonton, Canada, 1984, prof. oncology, Alberta Cancer Found. chair palliative care; prof. medicine, F.T. McGraw chair in treatment of cancer U. Tex. MD Anderson Cancer Ctr., 1999—. Office: University of Texas MD Anderson Cancer Center 1515 Holcombe Houston TX 77030 Office Phone: 713-792-6084. Business E-Mail: ebruera@mdanderson.org.

BRUESCHKE, ERICH EDWARD, physician, researcher, educator; b. nr. Eagle Butte, SD, July 17, 1933; s. Erich Herman and Eva Johanna (Joens) B.; m. Frances Marie Bryan, Mar. 25, 1967; children: Erich Raymond, Jason Douglas, Tina Marie, Patricia Frances, Susan Eva. BS in Elec. Engring, S.D. Sch. Mines and Tech., 1956; postgrad., U. So. Calif., 1960-61; MD, Temple U., 1965. Diplomate Am. Bd. Family Practice, also cert. in geriatrics. Intern Germantown Dispensary and Hosp., Phila., 1965-66; mem. tech. staff Hughes Research and Devel. Labs., Culver City, Calif., 1956-61; practiced gen. medicine Fullerton, Calif., 1968-69; dir. research Ill. Inst. Tech. Research Inst., Chgo., 1970-76; research asst. prof. Temple U. Sch. Medicine, 1965-69; mem. staff Mercy Hosp. and Med. Center, Chgo., 1970-76; vis. prof. Rush Med. Coll., Chgo., 1974-76, prof., chmn. dept. family practice, 1976—95, program dir. Rush. Christ family practice residency, 1978-93, vice dean, 1992—93, acting dean, 1993-94, dean, 1994-2000, v.p. univ. affairs, 2000—02; trustee Anchor HMO, 1976-81, v.p. med. and acad. affairs, 1981—2000; trustee Synergon Health Systems, 1993—96, vice chmn., bd. dirs. Rush Presbyn. St. Lukes Health Assocs., disting. prof. medicine, 2002—, Rush Med. Coll. of Rush U., 2002—. Bd. dirs. Comprehensive Health Planning Met. Chgo., 1971—74, Fedn. of Ind. Ill. Colls. and Univs., West Suburban Higher Edn. Consortium; adv. com. Edn. to Careers, Health and Medicine/Chg. Bd. Edn.; med. dir. Chgo. Bd. of Health West Side Hypertension Ctr., 1974—78; sr. attending Presbyn.-St. Luke's Hosp., Chgo., 1976—2003; vis. attending Rush U. Hosp., Chgo., 2000—, assoc. editor Am. Wireless Assn. Review. Editor-in-chief Disease-a-Month, 1998-2003, assoc. editor Primary Cardiology, 1979-85; cons. editor for family practice Hosp. Medicine, 1986-2003; med. editor World Book/Rush Presbyn. St. Lukes/Med. Ency., 1987-2003, contbr. articles to profl. jours. Served with M.C., USAF, 1966-68. Named Physician Tchr. of Yr. Ill. Acad. Family Physicians, 1988, alumni of yr. Temple U. Sch. Medicine, 1996. Master Mason; fellow Am. Acad. Family Physicians, Inst. of Medicine of Chgo.; mem. IEEE (chmn. Chgo. sect. Engring. in Medicine and Biology group 1974-75), Internat. Soc. for Artificial Internal Organs, Am. Fertility Soc., Am. Occupational Med. Assn. (recipient Physician's recognition award 1969, 72, 75), Am. Wireless Assn., Chgo. Med. Soc., Am. Heart Assn., Am. Wireless Assn., Assn. for Advancement Med. Instrumentation, N.Y. Acad. Scis., Sigma Xi, Phi Rho Sigma, Eta Kappa Nu, Alpha Omega Alpha, Am. Rocket Soc., Inst. of Radio Engrs., Am. Med. Assn., Nat. Assn. Watch & Clock Collectors, Radio Club America. Home: 319 N Lincoln St Hinsdale IL 60521-3442

BRUGOS, BOGLARKA, physician, immunologist; b. Szatmarnemeti, Romania, May 5, 1975; d. Gyula Brugos and Berta Brugosne Bodor; m. Zoltan Vincze, May 2, 2003; children: Szabolcs Vincze, Reka Vincze. Diploma, U. Debrecen, Hungary, 1999. Cert. in spl. exam. 2005. Rsch. fellow U. Fla., Gainesville, 2002—03; physician 3rd Dept. Internal Medicine, Debrecen, 1999—. Personal E-mail: brugosb@gmail.com.

BRUIJN, LUCIE I., science association administrator; BS in Pharmacy, Rhodes U., South Africa; MS in Neurosci., U. London, PhD in Biochemistry. Postdoc. fellow Johns Hopkins U., Balt., U. San Diego; rsch. investigator dept. neurosci. Bristol Myers Squibb; v.p., sci. dir. Amyotrophic Lateral Sclerosis (ALS) Assn., Calabasas, Calif., 2001—09, sr. v.p. rsch. & devel., 2009—. Mem. adv. coun. Nat. Inst. Neurol. Disorders & Stroke. Mem.: Assn. Women in Sci., Soc. Neurosci. Office: ALS Assn 27001 Agoura Rd Ste 250 Agoura Hills CA 91301 Office Phone: 818-880-9007. E-mail: lucie@alsanational.org. *

BRUKARDT, GARY A., health facility administrator; Undergrad., Univ. Wisc.; grad., Am. Grad. Sch. Internat. Mgmt. With St. Luke's Med. Ctr., Phoenix, Presbyterian St. Luke's Med. Ctr., Denver; found., sr. officer Partners Nat. Health Plans; with VHA; chmn., pres. Healthnet, 1991—96; exec. vice-pres. Baptist Healthcare Affiliates, Nashville, 1991—96; pres., COO Renal Care Group, Nashville, 1996—2003, pres., CEO, 2003—06; chmn., CEO Specialty Care Services Group, Nashville, 2006—. Office: Specialty Care Services Corp One American Ctr 3100 West End Ave Ste 150 Nashville TN 37203 Office Phone: 615-345-5510. Office Fax: 615-345-5565. *

BRUMBACK, CLARENCE LANDEN, physician; b. Denver, Apr. 19, 1914; s. Carl Alvin and Hildur Athelia (Landen) B.; m. Lucile Leslie Gillie, June 17, 1943; children— Richard, Carl. AB, U. Kans., 1936, MD, 1943; MPH, U. Mich., 1948. Diplomate Am. Bd. Preventive Medicine. Intern U.S. Marine Hosp., San Francisco, 1943-44; dir. pub. health Laclede County, Mo., 1947, AEC, Oak Ridge, 1948-50; dir. Palm Beach County (Fla.) Health Dept., 1950-86; coord. grad. edn. Palm Beach County Health Dept., 1986-2000. Clin. prof. U. Miami; adj. prof. Fla. Atlantic U., Boca Raton, Fla.; trustee Am. Bd. Preventive Medicine, 1969-78. Mem. editl. bd. Jour. Public Health Policy, 1981-88; contbr. articles to profl. jours. Bd. dirs. Palm Beach County chpt. A.R.C., Am. Lung Assn. S.E. Fla., Heart Assn. Palm Beach County, Community Mental Health Center Palm Beach County, Palm Beach County unit Am. Cancer Soc., Palm Beach County Mental Health Assn., Palm Beach County Health Dept., 1950-86; pres. YMCA of Palm Beaches, 1970. With AUS, 1944-47. Recipient Meritorious Svc. award Fla. Public Health Assn., 1968; Merit award State of Fla., 1972; Physician of Yr. award Am. Assn. Public Health Physicians, 1975, Lifetime Achievement award, 2000. Fellow APHA (Sedgwick Meml. medal 1989, mem. exec. bd. 1964-70), Am. Coll. Preventive Medicine, Royal Soc. Health; mem. AMA (Dr. Nathan Davis award 1993), Fla. Med. Assn. (cert. of Merit award 1995), Palm Beach County Med. Soc., Rotary, Elks. Democrat. Lutheran. Home: 1242 Devonshire Way Palm Beach Gardens FL 33418-6864 Office: 800 Clemetis West Palm Beach FL 33401-5708

BRUN, DANIÈLE, psychoanalyst, emeritus professor; b. Paris, July 6, 1938; d. Max Brun and Renée Rottembourg; m. Conrad Stein, Aug. 29, 1987 (dec. Aug. 2010); m. Fred Ullmo, Apr. 20, 1958 (div. Mar. 11, 1981); children: Pierre-Antoine Ullmo, Pascale Ullmo(dec.), Edouard Ullmo. PhD, U. Paris VII, 1989. V.p. SIUEERPP - Séminaire Interuniversitaire d'enseignement en Psychopathologie et Psychanalyse, Paris, 2000—; pres. Société Médecine et Psychanalyse, Paris, 2001—, Groupement d'intérêt Scientifique: Nouvelles Approches de la Maladie et du Hndicap, Paris; mem. Espace Analytique, Paris; prof. emeritus U. Paris. Fondateur Centre de Recherches Psychanalyse et Médecine à l'Université Paris Diderot; cherakies de la legion d hon., 2011. Author: La Maternité et le Féminin, 1990, Mikael un Enfant en Analyse, Calmann Lévy, 1997, L'enfant Donné Pour Mort, La Passion Dans l'amitié, 2005, Les Enfants Perturbateurs, 2007, Mères Majuscutes Ed Odile Jacob, 2011, Chevalier de la Legion d'honneur, 2011. Bur. dir. Assn. Handicap, Solidarité, Equité, Paris, 2007. Home: 66 boulevard Saint Michel 75006 Paris France Home Phone: 0146345376. Personal E-mail: dbrun@noos.fr.

BRUNDAGE, GERTRUDE BARNES, pediatrician; b. Neptune, NJ, May 13, 1941; d. John Holt and Mary Downey (Chatham) B. BS in Chemistry, Marietta Coll., 1964; MD, Jefferson Med. Coll., 1971. Diplomate Am. Bd. Pediatrics. Chemist Lederle Labs., Pearl River, NY, 1964-67; intern pediatrics Harrisburg Polyclinic Hosp., Pa., 1971-72; resident pediatrics Wilmington Med. Ctr., Del., 1972-74; pediatrician St. Barnabas Med. Ctr., Livingston, NJ, 1974—2006, Coastal Family Health Svc., Biloxi, Miss., 2008—09. Chief dept. pediat. Hosp. Ctr. At Orange, 1990—98. Moderator Presbytery of Newark, 1996; active 1st Presbyn. Ch., elder, trustee, 1982—87, 1989—92, 2004—07. Mem. Am. Med. Women's Assn., Alpha Gamma Delta. Republican. Presbyterian. Avocations: choral singing, needlecrafts, gardening. Home: 3911 Baywood Ln Ocean Springs MS 39564 Home Phone: 228-447-3254. Personal E-mail: trudyb18@yahoo.com.

BRUNDTLAND, GRO HARLEM, international organization official, former prime minister of Norway; b. Oslo, Apr. 20, 1939; d. Gudmund and Inga (Brynolf) Harlem; m. Arne Olav Brundtland, 1960; children: Knut, Kaja, Ivar, Jorgen. MD, Oslo U., 1963; M.P.H., Harvard Sch. Pub. Health, 1965. Med. officer Nat. Directorate of Pub. Health, Oslo, 1965-67; asst. med. dir. Sch. Health Services, Oslo, 1968-74; minister of environment Norwegian Govt., 1974-79, M.P. from Oslo, 1977-79, mem. standing com. on fin., chmn. standing com. on fgn. and constitutional affairs, 1979-81, dep. leader Labour Party's parliamentary group, 1979-81, leader Labour Party and parliamentary group, 1981-92, standing com. on fgn. and constl. affairs, 1981-86, chmn. standing com. on fgn. and constl. affairs; prime min. Kingdom of Norway, 1981, 86-89, 90-96; dir.-gen. WHO, Geneva, 1998—2003; health policy fellow Harvard U., Cambridge, Mass.; mem. high level panel on threats, challenges and change UN, NYC, sec. gen. spl. envoy on climate change, 2007—. Contbr. scientific work in child growth and devel. Mem. Ind. Commn. on Disarmament and Security Issues, UN, 1980; chmn. World Commn. on Environment and Devel., 1983; bd. dirs. Better World Soc., 1985; founding mem. The Elders, 2007—. Recipient Third World prize Third World Found., 1989, Indira Gandhi prize, 1990, Onassis Found. award, 1992, World Ecology award, Internat. Ctr. for Tropical Ecology, 2001. Office: Special Envoy on Climate Change c/o UN Hdqs First Ave at 46th St New York NY 10017 *

BRUNEL, PATRICK CYRIL, cardiologist; b. Paris, Sept. 7, 1955; s. Guy Brunel and Sabine Marguerite Dubois de Hoves de Fosseux; m. Veronique Yolande Gorgeu, Oct. 14, 1982; children: Marie-Astrid Nathalie, Servane Dominique, Evrard Ludovic, Vianney Xavier. MD, Necker Enfants Malades Faculty, Paris, 1980; U. diploma in Vascular Pathology, U. Of Picardie, Amiens, 1986; M in Stats., Pierre Et Marie Curie, Paris, 1987; M in Pharmacology, Claude Bernard, Lyon, 1988. Board Certified Physician Ministry Of Edn., 1987, Board Certified In Cardiology Ministry Of Edn., 1987, Board Certified In Sport Medicine Ministry Of Edn., 1985, Board Certified In Vascular Pathology Acad. Of Picardie. Registrar U. Hospitals, Amiens, France, 1980—86; rschr. Arterial Hypertension Rsch. Ctr., Paris, 1986—87; cons. Internat. Rsch. Inst. Servier, France, 1985—86; human pharmacology project leader Ciba-Geigy Ltd., Basle, Switzerland, 1987—89, med. affairs group leader, 1989—95, head med. affairs, 1995—96; clin. rsch. group leader Novartis, Basle, Basle City, 1996—2002, global clin. rsch. liaison Tokyo, 2003; head sci. ops. Novartis Pharma SAS, Rueil-Malmaison, France, 2005—. Tchr. in pharmacology Louis Pasteur U., Strasbourg, Bas Rhin, 1999—2002. Author: (genealogy) La Famille du Bois de Hoves de Fosseux, 2003, Ascendance Des Enfants Brunel, 2005, (novel) La Fin Tragique De Madame De Mirmand Durant La Guerre Des Camisards, 2006. Bd. mem. AMIPS, Boulogne Billancourt. Capt. Dominique Larrey Mil. Hosp., 1982—83, Versailles. Recipient Silver medal, Necker Enfants Malades Faculty, 1987, Gold medal, U. Of Picardie, 1986. Mem.: French Industry Physicians' Assn., Ordre Nat. Des Medecins, Rotary Internat. Cath. Avocations: writing, skiing, travel, tennis, bridge. Office: Novartis Pharma SAS 2 4 Rue Lionel Terray Hauts De Seine Rueil-Malmaison 92506 France Office Fax: 33 01 55 47 65 93; Home Fax: 33 01 43 80 46 17. Personal E-mail: brunelve@wanadoo.fr. E-mail: patrick.brunel@novartis.com.

BRUNELL, PHILIP ALFRED, physician, educator; b. NYC, Feb. 1, 1931; s. Irving and Rose Brunell; children: Wayne, Robert, Rhonda. BS, CCNY, 1950; postgrad., N.Y. U., 1950-51; MS in Physiology, U. Ill., 1952; MD, U. Buffalo, 1957. Diplomate in pediatrics and pediatric infectious diseases Am. Bd. Pediatrics. Research asst. physiology U. Ill., 1951-52, teaching asst., 1952-53; intern E.J. Meyer Meml. Hosp., Buffalo, 1957-58; resident in pediatrics Children's Hosp., Buffalo, 1958-60; asst. in pediatrics Cornell U., 1960-61; instr. pediatrics Emory U., 1961-64; asst. prof. pediatrics N.Y. U. Sch. Medicine, 1964-71, assoc. prof., 1971-75; prof., chmn. dept. pediatrics U. Tex. Health Sci. Center, San Antonio, 1975-81, prof., head div. infectious diseases dept. pediatrics, 1981-87; attending physician Santa Rosa Children's Hosp., San Antonio, 1975-81; prof. pediatrics UCLA; chief pediatrics Bexar County Hosp. Dist. Teaching Hosps., San Antonio, 1975-81; vice chmn. Cedars Sinai Med. Ctr., LA, 1987-96, cons. in pediat., 1997-98, chief marked editor Infectious Disease Children, 1988—2009. Cons. Brooke Army Med. Ctr., Wilford Hall USAF Med. Ctr., 1977-81; mem. cons. group on vaccine devel., 1991-94; cons. FDA, 1994-96; vis. rschr. Nat. Inst. Allergy and Infectious Diseases, 1995; spl. expert Lab. Clin. Investigation Nat. Inst. Allergy and Infectious Dis., NIH, 1997-99, adj. investigator, 2007-, Gt. Ormund St. Childrens Hosp, London, 2000. Chief med. editor Infectious Diseases of Children, 1987—2009; contbr. chpts. to books; contbr. articles to med. jours. Chmn. Internat. Year of Child, San Antonio, 1979-80; bd. dirs. Santa Rosa Children's Hosp. Found. Served with USPHS, 1961-64. USPHS fellow, 1971-72, Lifetime Achievement award, U. Buffalo Sch. Medicine, 2002. Fellow Infectious Diseases Soc. Am. (awards com. 1979, chmn. 1982); mem. Am. Acad. Pediatrics (chmn. com. pediatric research 1977-78, chmn. com. infectious diseases 1978-85), Am. Soc. Microbiology, Am. Acad. Microbiology, Am. Pediatric Soc., Soc. Pediatric Infectious Diseases (council 1984, pres. 1987-89), World Pediatric Infectious Diseases Soc. (sec. 1996-2003, pres. 2d internat. conf.), Soc. Pediatric Research, San Antonio Pediatric Soc., Tex. Pediatrics Soc. (awards com.), Coun. Tex. Pediatric Dept. Chmn. (chmn. 1978-81), Tex. Med. Assn. (sec. treas. pediatric sect. 1979-80, pres. 1980-81), Bexar County Med. Soc., Tex. Infectious Disease Soc., Western Soc. Pediatric Rsch., LA Pediatric Soc. Home: 7111 Woodmont Ave Apt 713 Bethesda MD 20815-6235 Office: NIAID NIH Lab Clin Infectious Diseases Rm 11n229 Bldg 10 Bethesda MD 20892-0001 Business E-Mail: pbrunell@niaid.nih.gov.

BRUNER, WILLIAM EVANS, II, ophthalmologist, educator, researcher; b. Cleve., Oct. 10, 1949; s. Clark Evans and Pauline (Schrenk) B.; m. Susan Lee Fraser, June 7, 1975; children: Amanda Lee, Andrew Evans. BA, Wesleyan U., 1971; MD, Case Western Res. U., 1975. Diplomate Am. Bd. Ophthalmology. Intern in surgery Univ. Hosps., Cleve., 1975-76, resident in ophthalmology, 1976-79; fellow in cornea and anterior segment surgery Johns Hopkins Hosp., Balt., 1979-81; asst. prof. ophthalmology Case Western Res. U., Cleve., 1981-89, assoc., 1989-93, assoc. clin. prof., 1993-96, clin. prof., 1996—. Sr. editor; manual of Corneal Surgery, 1987; contbr. chpts. to med. textbooks and articles to profl. jours. Trustee Case Western Res. U, Cleve. Recipient Alfred S. Maschke award Case Western Res. U. Sch. Medicine, 1975, Clinical Tchg. award, Case Western Reserve U., 2003, 2006. Fellow Am. Acad. Ophthalmology; mem. Wilmer Residents Assn., cleve. Acad. Medicine, Alpha Omega Alpha, Tavern Club, Cleve. Skating club, The Kirtland Club. Avocations: boating, golf, music. Office: 1611 S Green Rd Cleveland OH 44121-4128 Home: 13515 Shaker Blvd #8A Cleveland OH 44120 Personal E-mail: bruner2020@aol.com.

BRUNETTO, ALGEMIR LUNARDI, oncologist, educator, pediatrician; b. Paim Filho, Brazil, July 10, 1950; s. Angelo and Santina Lunardi Brunetto; life ptnr. Anna Paula Morena Fontoura; children: Andre Tesainer, Leticia Tesainer. MD, Fed. U. RGS, Porto Alegre, Brazil, 1976; PhD, U. Newcastle, Tyne, Eng., 1990. Head pediatric oncology Hosp. Clinicas Porto Alegre, 1983—; dir. Inst. Oncologia Kaplan, Porto Alegre, 1996—2008. Prof. pediatric oncology Fed. U. RGS, 1981—2008; dir. fundraising Instituto Cancer Infantil RS. Pres. Childrens Cancer Found., Porto Alegre, 1992—2008. With Brazilian Artilary Army Livramento, 1971—72. Recipient Overseas Rsch. award, Com. Vice Chancellors & Principals U. UK, 1987, Hon. Citizen Porto Alegre, Instituto Cancer Infantil RS, 2002. Mem.: Childrens Oncology Group (corr.). Home: Santo Inacio 431 opto 701 Porto Allegro 593-1601 Brazil Office: Hosp Clinicas Porto Alegre Rua Ramiro Barcelos 2350 90035-903 Porto Alegre RS Brazil Office Fax: 55 51 3330 8087. Business E-Mail: abrunetto@hcpa.ufrgs.br.

BRUNGER, AXEL THOMAS, biophysicist, researcher, educator; b. Leipzig, Germany, Nov. 25, 1956; came to U.S., 1982; s. Hans and Hildegard (Müller) B. Diploma, Hamburg U., Germany, 1980; PhD, Tech. U. Munich, 1982. Postdoctoral fellow Max-Planck Inst., Martinsried, Germany, 1984; rsch. assoc. Harvard U., Cambridge, Mass., 1982-83, 85-87; asst. investigator Howard Hughes Med. Inst., New Haven, 1987-92, assoc. investigator, 1992-95, investigator, 1995—; asst. prof. Yale U., New Haven, 1987-91, assoc. prof., 1991-93, prof., 1993-2000, Stanford U., Calif., 2000—. Recipient Röntgen prize for bioscis. Würzburg U., 1995, Gregori Aminoff prize Royal Swedish Acad. Scis., 2003, Nat. Acad. of Sci., 2005; NATO postdoctoral fellow Deutscher Akademischer Austauschdienst, Bonn, Germany, 1982-83 Mem. AAAS, NAS, Am. Crystallographic Assn., Am. Chem. Soc., Protein Soc. Achievements include studies of protein structure and function, developments in macromolecular x-ray crystallography and solution NMR spectroscopy. Office: Stanford U J H Clark Ctr Rm E300-C 318 Campus Dr Stanford CA 94305-5432

BRUNI, GIOVANNA, research scientist; b. Pavia, Mar. 14, 1965; Degree in Pharm. Chemistry and Tech., U. Pavia, 1989, PhD, 1993. Rschr. U. Pavia, 1994—. Achievements include research in physico-chemical characterization of pharmaceutical compounds; resolution of problems related to the preformulation phase of active principle. Avocations: cooking, gardening. Office: Via Taramelli 16 Pavia 27100 Italy Business E-Mail: giovanna.bruni@unipv.it.

BRUNK, SAMUEL FREDERICK, oncologist; b. Harrisonburg, Va., Dec. 21, 1932; s. Harry Anthony and Lena Gertrude (Burkholder) B.; m. Mary Priscilla Bauman, June 24, 1976; children: Samuel, Jill, Geoffrey, Heather, Kirsten, Peter, Christopher, Andrew, Paul, Barbara BS, Ea. Mennonite Coll., 1955; MD, U. Va., 1959; MS in Pharmacology, U. Iowa, 1967. Diplomate Am. Bd. Internal Medicine, Am. Bd. Internal Medicine in Med. Oncology. Straight med. intern U. Va., Charlottesville, 1959-60; resident in chest diseases Blue Ridge Sanatorium, Charlottesville, 1960-61; resident in internal medicine U. Iowa, Iowa City, 1962-64, fellow in clin. pharmacology (oncology), 1964-65, 66-67, asst. prof. internal medicine, 1967-72; assoc. prof. internal medicine, 1972-76; fellow in medicine (oncology) Johns Hopkins U., Balt., 1965-66; clin. assoc. prof. med. Okla. State U. Coll. Osteo; vis. physician bone marrow transplantation unit Fred Hutchinson Cancer Treatment Ctr., U. Wash., Seattle, 1975; practice medicine specializing in med. oncology Des Moines, 1976-94; attending physician Iowa Luth. Hosp., 1976-94, Iowa Meth. Med. Ctr., 1976-94, Charter Hosp., 1976-94, Mercy Hosp. Med. Ctr., 1976-94; dir. med. oncology Hahne Regional Cancer Ctr., DuBois, Pa., 1994; attending physician DuBois Regional Med. Ctr., 1994; dir. Pa. Cmty. Cancer Care, 1995; attending physician St. Mary's Regional Med. Ctr., 1994; med. oncologist Cancer Treatment Ctrs. Am., Southwestern Regional Med. Ctr., Tulsa, Okla., 1995—2001, chief med. oncology Cancer Treatment Ctrs. Am., 2002—06; attending physician Meml. Med. Ctr., Tulsa, Okla., 1995—2005; med. oncologist Cancer Treatment Ctrs. Am., Eastern Regional Med. Ctr., Phila., 2006—09, Western Regional Med. Ctr., 2009—. Chief of staff Iowa Luth. Hosp., 1990, chmn. dept. internal medicine, 1988; cons. physician Des Moines Gen. Osteo. Hosp., 1976-94; prin. investigator Iowa Oncology Rsch. Assn. in assn. with N. Cen. Cancer Treatment Group and Ea. Coop. Oncology Group, 1978-83; prin. investigator Iowa Oncology Rsch. Assn. Cmty. Clin. Oncology Program, 1983-84; mem. cancer care com. St, Mary's, Pa., 1995. Contbr. articles to profl. jours. Bd. dirs. Iowa div. Am. Cancer Soc., 1971-89, Johnson County chpt., 1968-72. Mosby scholar, U. Va., 1959 Fellow ACP, Am. Coll. Clin. Pharmacology; mem. AMA, Okla. Medical Soc., Tulsa County Medical Soc., Am. Soc. Clin. Oncology, Raven Soc., Alpha Omega Alpha. Roman Catholic. Home: 11557 22nd Cir NE St Saint Michael MN 55376 Office: Cancer Treatment Ctrs America Western Regional Med Ctr 14200 W Filmore St Goodyear AZ 85338

BRUNNER, HANS RUDOLF, medical educator; b. Cin., June 18, 1937; s. Albert Brunnner and Gertrud Brunner; m. Dorette Barbara Schepp, Dec. 3, 1963; children: Barbara Franziska Brunner Neuenschwander, Stephan Hans Rudolf. MD, Basel U., 1963. Intern and resident U. Hosp., Geneva, 1964—69; rsch. assoc. and asst. prof. Columbia Presbyn. Med. Ctr., NYC, 1969—74; assoc. prof., prof. Lausanne U., Canton de Vaud, Switzerland, 1974—2003; prof. emeritus, 2003—. Cons. Several Pharm. Companies. Recipient Novartis award, Coun. High Blood Pressure Rsch. Am. Heart Assn., Main award, Internat. Soc. Hypertension, Benoist Prize, Swiss Fed. Govt. Home: Bahnhofstrasse 50 Riehen CH-4125 Switzerland Home Fax: 41-61-641 25 10.

BRUNNER, KIRSTIN ELLEN, pediatrician, psychiatrist; b. Allentown, Pa., July 26, 1959; d. John Wilson and Ulla Brita (Arvide) Brunner; m. Fred F. Martinez. BS, Muhlenberg Coll., Allentown, Pa., 1981; DO, Phila. Coll. Osteo. Medicine, 1986. Diplomate Am. Bd. Pediatrics, Am. Bd. Psychiatry and Neurology in child and adolescent psychiatry and adult psychiatry. Resident U. Ky., 1992; dept. dir. Integra Health Family Devel. Ctr., Cedar Rapids, Iowa, 1993-98; with Hamot Inst. for Behavioral Health, Erie, Pa., 1998-2001; med. dir. Hamot Child and Adolescent Psychiat. Unit, Erie, 1999-2001, Sarah Reed Children's Ctr., Erie, 2001—. Fellow Am. Acad. Pediatrics; mem. AMA, Am. Acad. Child and Adolescent Psychiatry, Am. Psychiat. Assn. Avocations: cross country skiing, soccer (outdoor and indoor). Office: Sarah Reed Children's Ctr 2445 W 34th St Erie PA 16506 Business E-Mail: kbrunner@sarahreed.org.

BRUNNER, THOMAS M., medical association administrator; BSEE, Lehigh U., Bethlehem, Pa.; MBA, U. Del., Newark. Exec. v.p. Lumenis, Inc. (formerly Coherent Med.); v.p. mktg., sales Cooper LaserSonics; pres., CEO Laserscope, Glaucoma Rsch. Found., San Francisco, 2003—. Bd. dir. OptiMedia, Am. Soc. Laser Medicine & Surgery, Abilities United, San Francisco Rotary Club. Office: Glaucoma Rsch Found Ste 600 251Post St San Francisco CA 94108 Office Fax: 415-986-3162. Business E-Mail: tbrunner@glaucoma.org. *

BRUNNQUELL, STEPHEN B. (S BRUNNQUELL), internist; BA in Economics, Lafayette Coll., 1973—77; MDiv., Seton Hall U., NJ, 1977—82, MA in Scripture, 1977—82; MD, U. of Medicine and Dentistry, NJ, 1985—89. Lic. NJ, 1992, diplomate Am. Bd. Medical Examiners, 1990, Am. Bd. Internal Medicine, 2002. Tng. internal medicine Yeshiva Univ.; med. dir. The Heritage, Norwood, 1988—; intern dept. medicine Montefiore Med. Ctr., Bronx, 1989—90, resident dept. medicine primary care track, 1990—91, chief resident, 1991—92; sr. ptnr. Harrington Park and Tenafly Park Med. Group, 1992—; pvt. practice specializing in internal medicine harrington Park and Tenafly, 1992—; mem. Bd. of Health, Harrington Park, 1994—, pres., 2009—; mem. adv. coun. dept. medicine Englewood Hosp. and Med. Ctr., NJ, 2004—, sect. chief dept. medicine, 2006—, sec. and treas., 2009—, med. staff, 2009—. Parish priest St. Luke's Church, Ho- Ho- Kus, NJ, 1980—83, St. Charles Church, Newark, 1983—85; bd. dirs. The Meland Found., Englewood, NJ, 2001—. Recipient Barge Oratorical prize, 1977, John J. Allen prize in Pub. Fin., 1977, Am. Bible Soc. award, 1982; named Primum Non Nocere, 1989, Top Dr., NJ Life Mag. Office: Englewood Hospital and Medical Center 350 Engle St Englewood NJ 07631 Office Phone: 201-894-3000.

BRUNO, BARBARA ALTMAN, social worker; b. NYC, May 26, 1947; m. Joseph Peter Bruno, Oct. 2, 1977. AB in English, Cornell U., 1969; MSW in Psychiat. Social Work, Calif. State U., Sacramento, 1974; PhD in Psychology, Columbia Pacific U., 1987. Diplomate clin. social work; lic. clin. social worker. Group facilitator San Francisco DWI Sch., 1975-76; social svc. coord. Kosher Nutrition Project, San Francisco, 1975-76; counselor SUNY, Purchase, 1980-81, Pace U. Counseling Ctr., NYC, 1981-84; group leader No. Westchester YMHA/YWHA, Pleasantville, N.Y., 1981-91; pvt. practice psychotherapy Pleasantville, 1984—2006. Adj. faculty Westchester Community Coll., Valhalla, N.Y., 1990—2010, COED program, Pleasantville, 1988-92; founder Weight Release Svcs., Pleasantville, 1989—, Thinside Out, Pleasantville, 1985-90. Author: Quakers, 1985, Worth Your Weight, 1996, (with Curtis Jones) From Segregation to Sobriety, 2000; editor Roundup, 1990-98; well being columnist Dimensions mag.; contbr. articles to profl. jours., chpt. to book. Fellow Soc. Clin. Social Work Psychotherapists (cert.), Nat. Assn. to Advance Fat Acceptance (chair Westchester-Rockland chpt. 1989-91, nat. bd. dirs. 1991-97, mental health advisor, nat. adv. bd.); mem. Acad. Cert. Social Workers, Assn. Size Diversity and Health (edn. co-chair).

BRUNO, JAMES ROBERT, plastic surgeon; b. Wilkes-Barre, Pa., Feb. 23, 1967; Undergraduate degree, Wilkes Coll.; DMD, Tufts U., Boston, 1992; MD, U. Pa., 1996. Cert. Am. Bd. Plastic Surgery, Am. Bd. Oral and Maxillofacial Surgery. Intern, plastic surgery Hosp. of U. Pa., Phila., 1996—97; resident, plastic reconstructive surgery U. Pa. Oral and Maxillofacial Surgery, Hosp. of U. Pa., 1993—99; fellow Cleveland Clinic Found., Ohio, 2000—02. Clin. asst. prof. Ohio State U., Columbus, 2002—03; staff mem. Children's Hosp., Columbus, 2002—03; staff physician Sibley Meml. Hosp., Washington, 2003, Inova Fairfax Hosp., Va., 2003, Suburban Hosp., Bethesda, Md., 2003; active mem. North Arundel Hosp., Glenn Burnie, Md., 2005. Volunteers surgical knowledge and skills with Catholic Charities of the Archdiocese of Washington. Named one of America's Top Plastic Surgeons, Consumers' Research Coun. America, 2006. Mem.: Am. Soc. Plastic Surgeons, Nat. Capital Soc. Plastic Surgeons, Am. Acad. Oral and Maxillofacial Pathology. Office: The Barlow Bldg 5454 Wisconsin Ave Ste 1250 Chevy Chase MD 20815 Office Phone: 301-215-5955. Office Fax: 301-215-5944.

BRUNO, JUDYTH ANN, chiropractor; b. Eureka, Calif., 1944; d. Harold O. and Shirley A. Nelson; m. Thomas G. Bruno, June 1, 1968; 1 child, Christina Elizabeth. AS, Sierra Coll., 1982; D of Chiropractic, Palmer Coll. of Chiropractic West, Sunnyvale, Calif., 1986. Diplomate Nat. Bd. Chiropractic Examiners. Sec. Bank Am., San Jose, Calif., 1965-67; marketer Memorex, Santa Clara, Calif., 1967-74; order entry clk. John Deere, Milan, Ill., 1977; system analyst Four Phase, Cupertino, Calif., 1977-78; chiropractic asst. Dr. Thomas Bruno, Nevada City, Calif., 1978-81; chiropractor Chiropractic Health Care Ctr., Nevada City, 1987-90; pvt. practice Cedar Ridge, Calif., 1991-99; allied health profl. Aspirus Ontonagon Hosp., Mich., 2000—; pvt. practice Trout Creek, Mich., 2008—, Ontonagon. Area dir. Cultural Awareness Coun., Grass Valley, Calif., 1977-99; vol. Nevada County Libr., Nevada City, 1987-88, Decide Team III, Nevada County, 1987-92, Active Parenting of Teen Facilitator Nev. Union H.S., 1989-93, judge sr. projects, 1992-99; mem. Hazel Sliger Libr., 1992-2003; mem. Interior Twp. Econ. Devel. Com., 2001-04; mem. Interior Twp. Visual Enhancement Com., 2004-08; vol. Trout Creek Libr., 2003-, sec., 2010-; chair publicity Trout Creek Art Show. Recipient Woman of Yr. award No. Mines Bus. and Profl. Women, 1997. Mem. Women Health Practitioners of Nevada County (founder 1993-99), Nevada County C. of C. (vol. task force health care 1993), Toastmasters (sec. 1988, pres. 1989, 98, edn. v.p. 1990, Early Risers Toastmaster of Yr. 1998). Democrat. Avocation: creativity development. Office: 142 Division St Trout Creek MI 49967 also: 910 River St Ontonagon MI 49953

BRUNS, DAVID EUGENE, medical educator, researcher; b. St. Louis, Dec. 12, 1941; s. Eugene H. and Ellen E. (Johnson) B.; m. M. Elizabeth Hirst; children: Elizabeth, David. BSChemE, Washington U., 1963, AB, 1965; MD, St. Louis U., 1973. Diplomate Nat. Bd. Med. Examiners, lic. Va. State Bd. Medicine. Instr. pathology Sch. Medicine Washington U., St. Louis, 1973—77, vis. prof. pathology, 1985—86; asst. prof. U. Va., Charlottesville, 1977—81, assoc. prof. dept. pathology, 1981—90, prof. pathology Sch. Medicine, 1990—, assoc. dir. clin. chem. and toxicology, 1977—2003, assoc. dir. molecular diagnostics, 1986—, dir. clin. chemistry, 2003—. Lectr. in field. Author, editor, with Lo and Wittwer: Molecular Testing in Laboratory Medicine, 2002; editor: Clin. Chemistry, 1990—; co-editor: Yearbook of Pathology and Laboratory Medicine, 1995—97; editor: Fundamentals of Molecular Diagnostics, 2007; contbr. articles to profl. jours.; author, editor (with Burtis and Ashwood): Tietz Textbook of Clinical Chemistry and Molecular Diagnostics, 4th edit., 2005, Tietz Fundamentals of Clinical Chemistry, 2008. Bd. dirs. Little League Baseball, Charlottesville. Recipient St. Louis-San Francisco RR Scholarship, Washington U., 1959—63, Disting. Scientist award, Nat. Acad. Clin. Biochem., 2007; Rsch. Grant award, NIH, Am. Cancer Soc., Am. Dairy Coun. Mem.: Am. Assn. Clin. Chemistry (bd. dirs. 2009—, Outstanding Contbns. to Rsch. award 1987, Outstanding Contbns. to Clin. Chemistry award 1998, Norman Kubasik award 2001, Bernard Gerulat award 2001, Presdl. Citation 2001, Miriam Reiner award 2003, Speaker Award 2003, Presdl. Citation 2005), Acad. Clin. Lab. Physicians and Scientists (mem. exec. coun. 1990—93, pres. 2003—04, Gerald T. Evans award 2007), Assn. Clin. Scientists (pres. 1985—86, Sunderman award 1987). Achievements include patents for immunochemical assays for human amylase isoenzymes and related monoclonal antibodies, 1993; identification of toxicity of polyethylene glycol. Avocations: travel, reading, theater. Office: Dept Pathology University Virginia Sch Medicine and He PO Box 800168 Charlottesville VA 22908 Office Phone: 434-924-9432. Business E-Mail: dbruns@virginia.edu. *

BRUNSON, CHERYL KAYE, medical association administrator; b. Madisonville, Ky., Feb. 6, 1971; Cert. ophthalmic technician Joint Commn. Allied Health Personnel Ophthalmology, 1997. Ophthalmic asst. San Gabriel Eye Ctr., 1994—96; lead technician Tex. Tech U., 1996—2004; office mgr. Dietlein Eye Ctr., 2004—. Ladies ministry leader Apostolic Lighthouse Ch. Avocations: golf, interior decorating, photography. Office: 311 Riverbend Dr Georgetown TX 78628 Personal E-mail: brunson.cheryl@yahoo.com.

BRUNSON, KENNETH WAYNE, cancer biologist; b. Chico, Tex., Sept. 18, 1936; s. George Starr and Gwendolyn Laverne (Mount) B.; m. Myrna Marquerite Lapré, Jan. 26, 1963; children: Gregory Sean, Geoffrey Gordon. BA in Biology and Chemistry, U. North Tex., 1964, MA in Biology and Chemistry, 1966; PhD in Microbiology and Biochemistry, U. Minn., 1973. Lectr. U. Calif., Riverside, 1974—75; postdoctoral fellow tumor biology, rsch. assoc. The Salk Inst. Biol. Studies, San Diego, 1974—77; asst. specialist U. Calif., Irvine, 1977—79; asst. prof. Sch. Medicine Ind. U., Indpls., Gary, 1979—84, assoc. mem. grad. sch. Bloomington, 1979—84; sr. rsch scientist Pfizer, Inc, Groton, Conn., 1984—91; dir. in vivo preclin. rsch. for health scis. U. Pitts., 1996—99, assoc. prof. Sch. Medicine, 1991—99, affiliate mem. Cancer Inst., 1991—94, sect. head cancer metastasis biology program, 1991—95, mem. Cancer Inst., 1994—99, dir. Tumor Model Lab. Cancer Inst., 1995—99; dep. dir. Inst. for Cancer Rsch. U. North Tex. Health Sci. Ctr., Ft. Worth, 1999—2002, dir., 2002—03, adj. prof. dept. molecular biology and immunology, 2000—01, 2003—04, mem. grad. faculty microbiology and immunology program, 2001—03, rsch. prof. dept. molecular biology and immunology, 2001—03; sr. dir. translational biology Sopherion Therapeutics, Inc., New Haven, 2003—06, pvt. cons., 2007—. Mem. expert panel workshop Exptl. Metastasis: Designing New Strategies, 1988; founding mem. sci. edn. com. Pfizer, Inc., Groton, 1987—91. Mem. editl. bd.: In Vivo, 2002—08, sci. advisor, editor vol. 7 of series: 10-vol. treatise Cancer Growth and Progression, 1986—89; contbr. articles to profl. jours. including Cancer Rsch., Nature, In Vivo, Jour. Nat. Cancer Inst. Mem. planning com. Regional Health

Adminstrn. Conf., Ind., 1984; mem. exec. bd. Shadyside Action Coalition, Pitts., 1993—96, chmn. parking and transp. com., 1993—95; mem. Lake Country Place Assn., 2001—04; bd. dirs. Tarrant County unit Am. Cancer Soc., 2002—03, bd. dirs.Lake County unit Merrillville, Ind., 1981—84; bd. dirs. Pa. Soc. Biomed. Rsch., 1997—99. With US Army, 1958—61. Recipient XVI Internat. Cancer Congress award Internat. Union Against Cancer, New Delhi, 1994. Mem. Am. Assn. for Cancer Rsch., Am. Assn. Immunologists, Am. Soc. Cell Biology, Am. Soc. for Microbiology, Am. Inst. Biol. Scis. Achievements include pioneering research in cancer metastasis models, some of which has been described in Sci. Am., Mar., 1979, Procs. of NAS, 1980, Cancer Growth and Progression, 1989, and Biologic Therapy of Cancer, 1995. Home and Office: 903 Skimmer Cove Hampstead NC 28443 Personal E-mail: nobletx@yahoo.com.

BRUNTON, PAUL ANTHONY, dentist; s. Roy Edward and Ann Brunton. BChD, U. Leeds, 1984; MSc, U. Manchester, 1992, PhD, 1996. Lectr. restorative dentistry U. Manchester, 1997—2002, sr. lectr. restorative dentistry, 2002—04; prof. restorative dentistry U. Leeds, 2004—; fellow Faculty Dental Surgery, Coll. Surgeons of Edinburgh, 1995, Faculty Gen. Dental Practice, 2006, Faculty Dental Surgery, Coll. Surgeons, England, 2009. Cons. Leeds Tchg. Hosp. NHS Trust, 2004—. Mem.: Brit. Endodontic Soc., Brit. Soc. Prosthetic Dentistry, Acad. Operative Dentistry (rsch. com. 2005—08), Brit. Dental Assn., Brit. Soc. Restorative Dentistry (sec. 2005—08). Conservative. Roman Catholic. Avocations: travel, gardening. Office: Univ Leeds Clarendon Way LS2 9LU Leeds England Office Fax: 00441133436165. Business E-Mail: p.a.brunton@leeds.ac.uk.

BRUSCA, RICHARD CHARLES, biologist, researcher, educator, administrator; b. LA, Jan. 25, 1945; s. Finny John and Ellenora C. (McDonald) B.; m. Caren Irene Spencer, 1964 (div. 1971); children: Alec Matthew, Carlene Anne; m. Anna Mary Mackey, 1980 (div. 1987); m. Wendy Moore, 1998. BS, Calif. Poly. State U., 1967; MSc, Calif. State U., LA, 1970; PhD, U. Ariz., 1975. Curator, rschr. Aquatic Insects Lab., Calif. State U., LA, 1969—70; resident dir. U. Ariz. and U. Sonora (Mex.) Coop. Marine Lab., Sonora, 1970—71; prof. biology U. So. Calif., LA, 1975—86; head Invertebrate Zoology sect. Los Angeles County Mus. Natural Hist., 1984—87; Joshua L. Baily curator, chmn. dept. invertebrate zoology San Diego Natural History Mus., 1987—93; prof., dir grad program in marine biology U. Charleston, SC, 1993—98, assoc. dir. Grice Marine Lab. SC, 1993—98; sr. rsch. scientist Columbia U., 1998—2001; rsch. scientist, dept. ecology and evolutionary biology U. Ariz., 1998—; exec. dir. Ariz.-Sonora Desert Mus., Tucson, 2003—09. Dir. acad. programs Catalina Marine Sci. Ctr., U. Southern Calif., 1980—83; adj. prof. Centro de Investigación en Alimentación y Desarrollo, 1999—; field rschr. No., Ctrl. and So. Ams., Galapagos Island, Polynesia, Australia, New Zealand, Antarctica, Saharan & Sub-Saharan Africa, Madagaskar, Europe, Caribbean; bd. dirs. Orgn. for Tropical Studies, Slocum-Lunz Found., Intercultural Ctr. for the Study of Deserts and Oceans, Sonoran Sea Aquarium, Tucson, Discover Life in Am., Southern Ariz. Buffelgrass Coordination Ctr., Comunidad y Biodiversidad, Mexico; mem. panels NAS/NSF; chairperson adv. com. Smithsonian Instn.; adv. com. Systematics Agenda 2000, chairperson adv. com., inland waters crustacea specialist Internat. Union for Conservation of Nature Species Survival Commn.; mem. adv. bd. All Species Found., 2001; mem. adv. bd. Sch. Natural Resources U. Ariz., 2003—; mem. Govs. Inhesive Species Adv. Coun., Ariz.; mem. sci. and tech. adv. team Sonoran Desert Conservation Plan, Pima County, Ariz., 2005—09; expert panel mem. Friends of Saguaro Nat. Pk. Author: Common Intertidal Invertebrates of the Gulf of California, 1980; co-author: A Naturalist's Seashore Guide, 1978, Invertebrates, 1990, 2d edit., 2003, English, Spanish, Portuguese, Italian transls., Isopod Systematics and Evolution, 2001, Seashore Guide to Northern Gulf of California, 2004, Conserving Migratory Pollinators and Nectar Corridors in Western North America, 2004, Distributional Checklist of the Macrofauna of the Gulf of California, 2005, The Gulf of California-:Biodiversity & Conservation, 2009; contbr. over 150 articles to sci. jours. Recipient U.S. Antarctic Svc. medal, 1965, numerous rsch. awards; granteee NSF, Nat. Geog. Soc., Charles Lindberg Found, David & Lucile Packard Found., NOAA, Nat. Park Svc., Dept. Def., Am. Philos. Assn., others. Fellow: AAAS, Linnean Soc. London; mem.: Soc. for Systematic Biology, Assn. Sea Cortez Rschrs. (hon.; life), Crustacean Soc. (pres.), Sigma Xi. Avocations: Mexican and Mesoamerican indigenous art and culture, Latin American politics. Office: Ariz-Sonora Desert Mus 2021 N Kinney Rd Tucson AZ 85743 Office Phone: 520-883-3007. Business E-Mail: rbrusca@desertmuseum.org.

BRUSCH, JOHN LYNCH, physician, educator, hospital administrator; b. Boston, Nov. 3, 1943; s. Charles and Margaret Agnes (Lynch) Brusch; m. Patricia Gahan, May 12, 1973; children: Amy Claire, Meaghan, Patrick. BS, Tufts U., 1965, MD, 1969. Diplomate Am. Bd. Internal Medicine, Am. Bd. Infectious Disease, Am. Bd. Geriatrics. Intern New Eng. Med. Ctr., Boston, 1969-70, resident in medicine, 1970-71, resident in infectious disease, 1971-74; asst. chief medicine Brighton Pub. Health Svc. Hosp., Boston, 1974-76; pvt. practice physician Cambridge, Mass., 1976—; chief medicine Youville Hosp., Cambridge, 1991—2007, dir. cmty. medicine, 1995—2007, sr. cons., 2007—; clin. assoc. medicine Mass. Gen. Hosp., Boston, 1996—2009; chief medicine Somerville Hosp., 1999—2009, med. dir., 2001—. Assoc. chief medicine Cambridge Health Alliance, 1999—, dir. hosp. bd., 2003—; asst. prof. medicine Harvard Med. Sch., 2001—; bd. dirs. North Cambridge Coop Bank. Co-author, editor: Infective Endocarditis: Management in the Era of Intravascular Devices, 2007; editor: Endocarditis Essentials, 2011; mng. editor: Emedicine, 2001—; contbr. articles to profl. jours.; co-author: Infective Endocarditis, 1996. Bd. dirs. Coun. on Aging, Belmont, 2000—09. With USPHS, 1974—76. Recipient Nancy Kahn award, 2010. Fellow: ACP; mem.: Infectious Disease Soc. Am., Equestrian Order of Holy Sepulchre, Am. Soc. Microbiology. Home: 52 Radcliffe Rd Belmont MA 02478-3340 Office: Cambridge Hosp 1493 Cambridge St Cambridge MA 02139-1099 Home Phone: 617-489-1424; Office Phone: 617-661-1800. Personal E-mail: jbruschmd@aol.com.

BRUSH, FLORENCE CLAPHAM, kinesiologist, exercise physiologist, physical education educator; b. Little Rock, May 16, 1928; d. Thomas Wilson and Clara Sumpter Clapham; children: Robert Charles, Elizabeth Wrenne. BS, BA, Tex. Women's U., 1950, MA, 1951; PhD, U. Md., 1966. Instr. U. Ark., Fayetteville, 1950—53; assoc. prof., aquatics dr. Northwestern State Coll., Natchitoches, La., 1953—54; asst. prof. U. Md., 1954—59, Temple U., 1963—64; rsch. assoc. divsn. rsch. Lankenau Hosp., Phila., 1962, 1963; assoc. prof. Direct Execise Physiology Lab. Portland State U., Oreg., 1965—69; assoc. prof. SUNY Coll. Cortland, 1971—92, assoc. prof. emeritus. Vis. scholar Inst. Growth and Devel., U. London, 1970—71, Emory U., 1976; tutor math. Editor: Jour. Phys. Edn., Oreg. Assn. Health Phys. Edn. Recreation, 1969—70; contbr. articles to profl. jours. Tchr. swimming, bd. dirs. YWCA; vol. ARC Aquatics and Blood Drives. Mem.: ACLU, United U. Professions (del. NY State assembly, state relag com., state com. elder abuse), Environ. Orgn., Am. Coll. Sports Medicine. Democrat. Presbyterian. Achievements include research in anthropometric, physiological, neurological and electromyographic correlates of motor performance. Avocations: piano, kayaking, birdwatching. Home: 773 Blue Creek Rd Cortland NY 13045 Personal E-mail: brushf@tyler.cortland.edu.

BRUSIUS, CARLOS, neurosurgeon; b. Sapiranga, Brazil, Jan. 20, 1961; Degree, U. PUCRS, 1988; postgrad. in Neurosurgery, Sociedade Brasileira De Neurocirurgia, 1994. Neurosurgery Hosp. Luterana, U. Brasil, 2010—. Office: Rua Padre Chagas 185/908 Porto Alegre 90570-080 Brazil Business E-Mail: cbrusius@uol.com.br.

BRUSOV, PAVEL GEORGIEVICH, surgeon, researcher, educator; b. Nygniy Tagil, Sverdlovsk, Russia, Jan. 23, 1938; s. Georgiy Sergeevich and Nina Gavrilovna (Garkunova) B.; m. Irina-Christina Boguslavovna Levitskaya, Mar. 4, 1961; children: Gleb, Georgiy, Ludmila. Physician, Med. Instn., Lvov, Russia, 1961; MD, U. Moscow, 1986; PhD, U. Moscow, St. Petersburg, 1974. Intern Khabarovsk Mil. Hosp., 1961; resident in surgery Mil. Med. Acad., St. Petersburg, Russia, 1968-70; thoracic surgeon Main Mil. Clin. Hosp., Moscow, 1971-78, surgeon, cons., 1978—84, main oncologist, 1984-86, chief surgery, 1987—89, head hosp., 1986—87; chmn. dept. surgery Mil. Inst. Postgrad. Med. Edn., 1990—98; surgeon gen. Russian Army, 1989-98; chmn. dept. oncology St. Med. Postgrad. Inst. Def. Min., 2001—09, chmn. dept. surgery, 2010—. Author, editor: Organization of Medical Care to the Injured with Mechanical Traumas, 1994, Forecasting in Disaster Medicina, 1995, Plasma Energy in Surgery, 1995, Course of Lections for Military-Field Surgery, 1996, Military-Field Surgery, 1996, Trauma of the Extremities in Combat, 1996, Gunshot Wounds of the Hand, 1999, (with G.R. McLatchie) Oxford Handbook of Clinical Surgery (translations into Russian), 1999, (with R.D. Rosin) Minimal Access General Surgery, 1998, Complex and infrequent forms of the malignant neoplasm different body sites, 2005, Clinical Oncology, 2008. With Russian mil., 1961-67, gen. maj., 1989-1998, ret., 1999. Recipient Laureate of State award of USSR, 1989, Laureate of State award of Russia, 1997, Laureate of Military Surgery, M. De Bakey award, 2002. Mem. Internat. Surg. Soc., European Thoracic Surg. Soc., Soc. Surgeons Moscow (chmn. sect. mil.-field surgery 1990-00), Assn. Surgeons N.A. Pirogov, Moscow Surgeons Soc. (pres. 2002-04), Moscow Oncology Soc. Office: Main Mil Hosp 3 Hospitalnaya Ploshad 105229 Moscow Russia Office Phone: 7 (499)-263-5513. Personal E-mail: brusovpg@hotmail.com. Business E-Mail: brusovpg@list.ru.

BRUST, JOHN CALVIN MORRISON, neurologist, educator; b. Syracuse, NY, Aug. 20, 1936; s. John C. M. and Constance (Cook) Brust; m. Mary Duncan, Oct. 23, 1965; children: Mary Duncan, Frederick Eliot Noyes, James Charles Morrison. AB, Harvard U., 1958; MD, Columbia U., 1962. Diplomate Am. Bd. Psychiatry and Neurology. Intern Presbyn. Hosp., NYC, 1962-63, resident in neurology, 1966-69, attending neurologist, 1969—; prof. clin. neurology Columbia U., NYC, 1975—. Author: Neurological Aspects of Substance Science, 1999, 2d edit., 2004, The Practice of Neural Science, 2000; contbr. articles to profl. jours. Lt. USNR, 1962—65. Fellow: Am. Acad. Neurology; mem.: N.Y. Practitioners Soc., Century Assn., Am. Clin. and Climatological Assn., Am. Neurol. Assn., Alpha Omega Alpha. Office: NY Neurol Inst Columbia University Med Ctr 710 W 168th St New York NY 10032 Business E-Mail: jcb2@columbia.edu.

BRUSTMAN, LOIS E., obstetrician, gynecologist, educator; BS, Union Coll., 1971; MD, NY Med. Coll., 1975. Diplomate Am. Bd. Ob-Gyn-maternal-fetal medicine, Am. Bd. Ob Gyn. Intern St. Vincent Hosp., 1979—80; resident ob-gyn. Albert Einstein Coll. of Medicine, 1980—84, fellow maternal-fetal medicine, 1985—88; assoc. prof. ob-gyn. NY Med. Coll.; bd. mem. Nat. Coun. of Women in Medicine, 1986—92; assoc. dir. ob-gyn. dept. Our Lady of Mercy Med. Ctr., dir. maternal-fetal medicine, 1998—2000, dir. maternal-fetal assessment ctr., 1998—2000; joined divsn. obstetrics and maternal-fetal medicine St. Luke's Roosevelt Hosp., 2000, dir. ob-gyn. dept. residency program, 2000—; chair Am. Coll. of Obstetricians and Gynecologists, 2001. Named one of The Best Doctors in NY, 1999, 2000, 2001. Mem.: Soc. for Maternal-Fetal Medicine, Am. Inst. of Ultrasound in Medicine, NY Obstet. Soc. Office: St. Luke's Roosevelt Hospital Department of Obstetrics and Gynecology 1000 Tenth Ave New York NY 10019 Office Phone: 212-523-7579.

BRUZA, JOHN M., internist, educator; MD, U. Okla., Norman. Diplomate Am. Bd. Internal Medicine-geriatric medicine. Intern Johns Hopkins Bayview Med. Ctr., resident; med. dir. geriatric medicine Ralston Penn Ctr.; asst. prof. medicine Hosp. of the Univ. of Pa. Named one of the Top Doctors, Phila. Mag., 2011. Mem.: Am. Geriatric Soc., ACP. Office: Hospital of the University of Pennsylvania Penn Medicine Radnor 250 King of Prussia Rd Wayne PA 19087 also: Ralston Penn Center 3615 Chestnut St Philadelphia PA 19104 Office Phone: 610-902-5600, 215-662-2746.

BRUZZESE, JEAN-MARIE, psychology professor; b. Bklyn., Aug. 25, 1968; PhD, Fordham U., 1997. Assoc. rsch. assoc. Columbia U. Coll. Physicians and Surgeons, 1997—2002; asst. prof. child & adolescent psychiatry NYU. Sch. Medicine, 2002—. Recipient AEC Rsch. Incentive award, NYU Sch. Medicine. Mem.: APA, Am. Thoracic Soc. (Early Career Achievement award). Office: 215 Lexington Ave 13 FL New York NY 10016 Business E-Mail: jean-marie.bruzzese@nyumc.org.

BRYAN, CHARLES STONE, internist, educator; b. Columbia, SC, Columbia, South Carolina, Jan. 15, 1942; s. Leon Stone and Mary Morrill (Leadbeater) Bryan; m. Donna Hennesee, Oct. 30, 1982; children: Eleanor Chandlee, Emily Singleton. Student, Harvard U., Cambridge, Mass., 1960-62; BA, Johns Hopkins U., Balt., 1964, MD, 1967. Diplomate Am. Bd. Internal Medicine, Am. Bd. Infectious Diseases. Intern in pathology Johns Hopkins Hosp., Balt., 1967-68; intern in medicine Vanderbilt U. Hosp., Nashville, 1968-69, resident, fellow, 1971-74; pvt. practice Columbia, SC, 1974-77; dir. infectious diseases U. SC Sch. Medicine, Columbia, 1977-93, Heyward Gibbes disting. prof. medicine, chmn. dept., 1992-2000; dir. Ctr. Bioethics and Med. Humanities, 2000—. Pres. Am. Osler Soc., 2010—11, Columbia Med. Soc., 1992—93; editor Jour. of the SC. Med. Assn., 1977; dir. Midlands Care Consortium, 1993—2004. Author: A Most Satisfactory Man, 1996, Osler: Inspirations from a Great Physician, 1997, Infectious Diseases in Primary Care, 2002, For Goodness Sake: The Seven Basic Virtues, 2006, A Hound Dog in Anderson: Essays on Medicine and Life, 2008; editor: Jour. S.C. Med. Assn., 1977—; author: A Oliver Wnedakk Homes: Physician And Man of Letters, 2009; contbr. articles to profl. jours. Chmn. Midlands Care Consortium, Columbia, 1993—2006. Surgeon USPHS, 1969—71. Recipient William Osler Medal, Am. Assn. for the History of Medicine, Theodore E. Woodward Award, Am. Clin. and Climatol. Assn., Laureate, ACP, Nicholas E. Davies Meml. Scholar Award, Lifetime Achievement Award, Am. Osler Soc. Master: ACP (Laureate award 1993, Nicholas E. Davies award 2007); fellow: Infectious Diseases Soc. Am., Royal Coll. Physicians (Edinburgh); mem.: Columbia Med. Soc. (pres. 1992), S.C. Infectious Diseases Soc. (pres. 1994), Am. Osler Soc. (sec.-treas. 2000—, pres. 2010), Am. Assn. History Medicine (William Osler medal 1967), Am. Clin. and Climatological Assn., Waring Libr. Soc. (pres. 1988). Avocations: medical history, golf. Office: U SC Sch Medicine 2 Richland Medical Park Dr Columbia SC 29203-6864 Office Phone: 803-540-1000. Personal E-mail: cboslerian@gmail.com. Business E-Mail: cbryan@gw.mp.sc.edu.

BRYAN, KATHERINE BYRAM, healthcare executive; b. Kans. d. John Charles and Jane Ballew (Price) Byram; 1 child by previous marriage, George Gurley III; children: Austin, Jack. BA, U. Mo., 1969, PhD in Counseling Psychology, 1979. With Corp. Health Examiners, NYC, 1978—, v.p. mktg., 1980—84; assoc. broker Sotheby's Internat. Realty, 2007—. Contbr. articles to profl. jours. Mem. adv. bd. John F. Kennedy Ctr., Washington, 1998—2001; jr. bd. dirs. Nelson Gallery, Kansas City, Mo., 1973—76; bd. dirs. Family Dynamics, NY, 1987—92, NYC Ballet, New Yale Hosp. Mem. APA, DAR, Colonial Dames Am., Biofeedback Soc. Am., Maidstone Club (East Hampton, NY), River Club (NYC), Everglades Club (Palm Beach, Fla.). Home: 150 East 72nd St New York NY 10021

BRYANT, BERTHA ESTELLE, retired medical/surgical nurse; b. Va., Jan. 11, 1927; d. E.F. and Julia B. Diploma, Sibley Meml. Hosp., Washington, 1947; BS, Am. U., 1948; MA, Tchrs. Coll., Columbia U., 1962. Staff nurse, head nurse NIH, Bethesda, Md., 1954-59; asst. dir. nursing USPHS Alaska Native Hosp., Mt. Edgecumbe, 1959-61; instr. Sch. Nursing, U. Mich., 1962-64; chief div. clin. nursing Bur. Nursing, D.C. Dept. Public Health, Washington, 1964-65; commd. Nurse Corps, USPHS, 1965, nurse dir., capt., 1974—. Nurse cons., hosp. facilities services br., div. hosps. and med. facilities Bur. Health Services, HEW, Silver Spring; nurse cons., social analysis br., div. health services research and analysis Nat. Center Health Services Research, Health Resources Adminstrn., HEW, Rockville, Md.; nurse cons. div. extramural research Nat. Center Health Services Research, Office Asst. Sec. Health, HHS, Hyattsville, Md., 1977-81 Contbr. articles to profl. jours. Mem. AAUW, Assn. Mil. Surgeons U.S., Commd. Officers Assn. USPHS

BRYANT, ETTA COLISH, child and adolescent psychiatrist; MD, U. Tex., Galveston, 1957. Diplomate Am. Bd. Psychiatry and Neurology, 1979, Am. Bd. Psychiatry and Neurology-child & adolescent psychiatry, 1980. Resident child & adolescent psychiatry Mt Zion Hosp. Med. Ctr., San Francisco, resident psychiatry, 1970—74; fellow public health and gen. preventive medicine Harvard Univ., Boston, 1959—60; hosp. affiliation Mills-Peninsula Health Svcs. Office: 448 N San Mateo Dr Ste 2 San Mateo CA 94401 Office Phone: 650-579-5781.

BRYANT, THOMAS EDWARD, physician, lawyer; b. Bellamy, Ala., Jan. 17, 1936; s. Howard Edward and Alibel (Nettles) B.; m. Lucie Elizabeth Thrasher, July 9, 1961; children: Thomas Edward, Evelyn Thaxton. AB, Emory U., 1958, MD, 1962, JD, 1967. Bar: Ga. 1967. Intern Grady Meml. Hosp., Atlanta, 1962-63; dir. health affairs OEO, Washington, 1969-71; pres. Nat. Drug Abuse Council, 1971-79; chmn., dir. Pres.'s Commn. Mental Health, 1977-79; chmn. Aspirin Found. of Am., 1987—, Nonprofit Mgmt. Assocs., Inc., 1989—. Pres. Friends of Nat. Library of Medicine, 1985—; exec. dir. County Behavioral Health Inst., 1997—. Served with USAF, 1963-65. Recipient Exceptional Service award OEO, 1971 Mem. Ga. Bar Assn., D.C. Bar Assn., Nat. Acad. Scis., Inst. Medicine. Clubs: Cosmos (Washington); Century Assn. (N.Y.C.). Democrat. Office: Non Profit Mgmt Assocs Inc 1555 Connecticut Ave NW Ste 200 Washington DC 20036-1126

BRYANT-GREENWOOD, PETER K., pathologist; b. Honolulu, Mar. 6, 1970; BSFS, Georgetown U., 1992; MD, John A. Burns Sch. Medicine, 1997; MBA, Johns Hopkins U., 2004. Dir., pathology svcs. Queen's Med. Ctr., 2009—; assoc. mng. ptnr. Hawaii Pathologists Lab.; CMO Risk Assessment Labs. LLC; pres., CEO Hawaii Health & Sci. LLC, Integrated BioSource LLC. Vice chair, dept. pathology JABSOM, 2008. Recipient award, Papanicolau Soc. Cytopathology, Stowell-Orbison award, US-Canadian Acad. Pathology, Inc., Po'okela Noi'i award, John A. Burns Sch. Medicine; named one of Best Drs. Pathology. Fellow: Coll. Am. Pathology. Home: 3488 Alani Dr Honolulu HI 96822 Personal E-mail: pgreenwood@queens.org.

BRYCE, THOMAS N., physiatrist, educator; Attended, Johns Hopkins U.; MD, Albany State U., 1993. Diplomate Am. Bd. Physical Medicine and Rehab., 2008, Am. Bd. Physical Medicine and Rehab.-spinal cord injury medicine, Am. Bd. Physical Medicine and Rehab.-pain medicine. Resident internal medicine Albany Med. Ctr., NY; resident rehab. med. Thomas Jefferson Univ. Hosp., Phila., 1994—97; med. dir. Spinal Core Injury Program Mt. Sinai Med. Ctr., NYC, 2001, med. dir. rehab. ambulatory svcs., 2008, assoc. prof. rehab. medicine, co-investigator Model Sys. for Spinal Cord Injury. Steering com. Consortium for Spinal Cord Medicine; rsch. grant reviewer European Sci. Found., The Craig H. Neilsen Found. Author several chpts. and sci. articles on pain and spinal cord injury. Office: Mount Sinai Medical Center Rehabilitation Medicine Associates 5 E 98th St 6th Fl New York NY 10029 Office Phone: 212-241-6321. Office Fax: 212-369-6389.

BRYLA, JADWIGA ANNA, biochemistry professor; b. Warsaw, July 9, 1943; MS, U. Warsaw, 1965, PhD, 1969. Asst. prof. U. Warsaw, 1969—76, assoc. prof., 1976—83, full prof., 1983—. Recipient Sci. Achievements award, Ministry of Sci. and Higher Edn., Polish Acad. Scis., Chancellor U. Warsaw. Mem.: Polish Biochem.

Soc., Polish Acad. Arts and Scis. Avocations: classical music, singing. Office: I Miecznikowa 1 Warsaw Mazovia 02-096 Poland Office Fax: 48 (22) 55-43221. Business E-Mail: bryla@biol.uw.edu.pl.

BUBRICK, MELVIN PHILLIP, surgeon; b. Chgo., June 2, 1944; m. Barbara Lynn Jacobs, Jan. 26, 1969; children: Jerome Bradley, Ellen Jeanne, Dena Beth. BA with honors, U. Ill., 1964, MD, 1968. Diplomate Am. Bd. Surgery, Am. Bd. Colon and Rectal Surgery; lic. Minn. Intern in surgery Univ. Hosps., Madison, Wis., 1968-69; resident in gen. surgery Hennepin County Gen. Hosp., Mpls., 1969-74; postdoctoral fellow colon and rectal surgery U. Minn. Health Scis. Ctr., Mpls., 1974-75; clin. instr. div. colon and rectal surgery U. Minn., Mpls., 1975-77, clin. asst. prof., 1977-78, clin. asst. prof. dept. surgery, 1978-80, asst. prof., 1980-87, assoc. prof., 1987—; chief surgery, program dir. surg. residency Hennepin County Med. Ctr., 1988-94; pres. Hennepin Facility Assocs., 1995—2000, chmn. bd. dirs., 1991—2001. V.p. Mpls. Med. Rsch. Found., 1991-2000; chmn. bd. dirs. Hennepin Faculty Assocs., 1991-2000, CEO, 1991-2001. Author: (with others) Conn's Therapy, 1985, The Pancreas. Principles of Medical and Surgical Practice, 1985, Applied Therapeutics: The clinical use of drugs, 4th rev. edit., 1988; contbr. over 90 articles to Minn. Med. jour., Am. Surg. jour., Diseases of Colon and Rectum, Surgery, others. Bd. dirs. Mpls. Med. Rsch. Found., Inc., 1981-89. Mem. AMA, ACS, Am. Assn. Surgery of Trauma, Am. Soc. Colon and Rectal Surgeons (co-chair Self Assessment Exam. Com. 1984-85), Am. Soc. Microbiology, Assn. Program Dirs. of Surgery, Cen. Surg. Assn., Collegium Internat. Chirurgiae Digestivae, Soc. Surgery of Alimentary Tract, Minn. Assn. Pub. Teaching Hosps., Minn. Surg. Soc., Minn. Med. Assn., Mpls. Surg. Soc., Hennepin County Med. Soc. (mem. and chair various coms. 1975—, Hennepin faculty assoc. 1983—). Achievements include research in assessment of bursting strength and healing of intestinal anastomoses, predictive value of surface oximetry in assessing healing in irradiated bowel, use of antibiotic microspheres for infected vascular grafts and peritonitis, clinical and anatomic assessment of first rib-clavicular decompression on subclavian catheters and pacemaker leads, influence of nutritional deficits in intestinal anastomotic strength, iron chelation with a Deferoxamine (DFO) conjugate in hemorrhagic shock. Personal E-mail: mbubrick@comcast.net. *

BUCAY, VIVIAN W., dermatologist; m. Moises Bucay; 3 children. Grad., John Hopkins U., Baylor Coll. of Medicine. Asst. prof. physician asst. studies Univ. of Texas Health Sci. Ctr., San Antonio; dermatology tng. Univ. of Miami, Baylor Coll. of Medicine, Houston. Author many publications. Named Texas Super Doctor, Texas Monthly Mag., 2004, 2005, 2006. Fellow: Am. Acad. of Dermatology; mem.: Am. Soc. for Laser Medicine and Surgery, Soc. for Pediatric Dermatology, Internat. Soc. of Dermatology, Am. Soc. of Dermatologic Surgery. Office: Vivian W Bucay 326 W Craig Pl San Antonio TX 78212 Office Phone: 210-692-3000. Office Fax: 210-692-3056.

BUCCINO, DANIEL L., psychotherapist, consultant; BA, MA, Johns Hopkins U., 1987; MSW, Smith Coll., 1989. Diplomate NASW, Am. Bd. Examiners in Clin. Social Work, lic. Clinical Social Worker. Clin. supr./student coord. cmty. psychiatry, psychotherapist Johns Hopkins Bayview Med. Ctr., Balt., 1989—; pvt. practice psychotherapy Balt., 1992—; founder, dir. Balt. Psychotherapy Inst., 1994—. Asst. prof. psychiatry Johns Hopkins U. Sch. Medicine, Balt., 2000—; clin. assoc. prof. U. Md. Sch. Social Work, Balt., 1996—; clin. assoc. prof., faculty field instr. Smith Coll. Sch. Social Work, Northampton, Mass., 1998—; chair Md. Bd. Social Work Examiners, 2010-; presenter and cons. in field. Editor: Maryland Social Work Legal Handbook, Vol. 1, 1994, Vol. 2, 1996; contbr. articles to profl. jours., books, and newspapers. Mem. Internat. Forum Psychoanalytic Edn., Johns Hopkins Civility Initiative, Md. Soc. Clin. Social Work, Clin. Social Work Assn., Internat. Ctr. Clin. Excellence. Avocations: music, films, running, reading. Office: 711 W 40th St Ste 456 Baltimore MD 21211-2199

BUCH, JAN, retired medical research administrator, director; b. Copenhagen, Feb. 2, 1943; s. Holger and Inger Buch; m. Jette Simonsen, Apr. 30, 1988. MD, Copenhagen U., 1969. With dept. cardiology and aviation medicine Rigs Hosp., 1969—75, with dept. cardiology invasive lab., 1977—83; med. and surg. resident Diakonissestiftelsen, 1975—77; with med. and cardiology dept. Amtsygehuset Glostrup, 1983—86; specialist internal medicine Copenhagen U., 1984, specialist cardiology, 1984; physician, cardiologist Copenhagen U. Hosp., Copenhagen, 1969—87; med. dir. Pfizer, Copenhagen, 1987—91; med. dir., world wide team leader, global team leader, cardiovas. metabolic endocrine obesity Pfizer Hdqs., NYC, 1992—2009, cons. cardiology, 2009—. Contbr. articles to profl. jours. Mem.: Danish Soc. History, Lit. and Arts, Danish Soc. Internal Medicine, Danish Cadiol. Soc. (Numerous grants 1969—87), Danish Bibliophile Club. Avocations: history, art, classical music. Home: Ceresvej 10 1863 Frederiksberg Denmark Personal E-mail: jbuch.cardio@gmail.com.

BUCH, SHAMA C., research scientist, educator; d. Chandrakant H. and Leela C. Buch. PhD, Cancer Rsch. Inst., Mumbai, 2001. Vis. rsch. assoc. Ctr. for Clin. Pharmacology, Pitts., 2001—03, rsch. instr., 2003—. Contbr. articles to profl. jours. Mem.: Am. Assn. Cancer Rsch. (assoc.). Office: Center Clin Pharmacology Ste 450 100 Technology Dr Pittsburgh PA 15219 Business E-Mail: buchs@dom.pitt.edu, scb30@pitt.edu.

BUCHANAN, GEORGE R., oncologist, hematologist, educator; b. Bloomington, Ill., Apr. 21, 1944; m. Chris Buchanan. BA with honors, Drake U., 1966; MD, U. Chgo., 1970. Cert. Am. Bd. Pediat., Am. Bd. Pediat. Sub-Bd. Hematology-Oncology. Intern pediatrics Children's Meml. Hosp., Chgo., 1970—71, resident hematologic oncology, 1971—73; fellowship hematology Children's Hosp., Boston, 1973—75; fellowship pediatric oncology Dana-Farber Cancer Inst., Boston, 1974—75; instr. Harvard U.; med. dir. Ctr. Cancer and Blood Disorders Children's Med. Ctr., Dallas; asst. prof. to. prof. pediat. U. Tex. Southwestern Med. Ctr., Children's Cancer Fund disting. chair pediat. oncology and hematology Dallas, dir. Barrett Family Ctr. for Pediat. Oncology; dir. pediat. hematology / oncology Southwestern Comprehensive Sickle Ctr. & North Tex. Hemophilia Ctr. Co-chair working group of strategic planning com. Nat. Heart, Lung and Blood Inst. (NHLBI); chair protocol review com. Sickle Cell Disease Clin. Rsch. Network. Contbr. articles to med. jours. Mem.: Soc. Pediat. Rsch., Hemophilia Thrombosis Rsch. Soc., Am. Soc. Pediat. Hematology-Oncology (pres. 1999—2002, Disting. Career award 2007), Am. Soc. Hematology (exec. com. 2001—05), Am. Pediat. Soc., Alpha Omega Alpha, Phi Beta Kappa. Office: Children's Med Ctr - Dallas 1935 Motor St Dallas TX 75235 also: UT Southwestern Med Ctr at Dallas 5323 Harry Hines Blvd Dallas TX 75390-9063 Office Phone: 214-648-8594, 877-445-1234. Office Fax: 877-445-1234. E-mail: george.buchanan@utsouthwestern.edu.

BUCHANAN, JOHN DONALD, retired nuclear scientist; b. Mesa, Ariz., Oct. 1, 1927; s. John Freeborn and Marguerite (Brimhall) B.; m. Donna Marie Smith, Aug. 27, 1955 (dec. June 24, 2010); children—Margaret MacNeil, John Michael, Andrew Tierney, David Brimhall. BS in Chemistry, U. Ariz., 1949. Diplomate Am. Bd. Health Physics. Sr. chemist Tracerlab, Inc., Richmond, Calif., 1950-59; staff assoc. Gen. Atomic divsn. Gen. Dynamics Corp., San Diego, 1959-62; mgr. nuc. applications and measurements Teledyne-Isotopes Inc., Palo Alto, Calif., 1962-71; mgr. applied rsch. Internat. Nutronics Inc., Palo Alto, 1971-73; supr. radiol. monitoring programs NUS Corp., Rockville, Md., 1973-75; sr. health physicist, radiochemist U.S. Nuc. Regulatory Commn., Washington, 1975-94. Author papers on radiation protection, radioanalytical chemistry, radioactivity measurements, radioisotope applications. Served with USNR, 1945-46. Fellow AAAS, Am. Inst. Chemists, Health Physics Soc.; mem. Am. Nuc. Soc., Am. Chem. Soc., Am. Acad. Health Physics, Phi Lambda Upsilon, Phi Delta Theta. Home: 7508 Dew Wood Dr Rockville MD 20855-1007

BUCHHOLZ, NOOR NIELS-PETER, urologist, surgeon, consultant; b. Muenster, Germany, Aug. 26, 1957; s. Erich Buchholz and Ingeborg Steinmann; m. Saima Salahuddin. MD, MB, BChir, Wilhelm U., Muenster, Germany, 1987. Rsch. fellow urology Flinders Med. Centre, Adelaide, Australia, 1994—97; lectr. urology Aga Khan U., Karachi, Pakistan, 1997—98; cons. urol. surgeon Erasmus U., Rotterdam, Netherlands, 1998—2000, Lincoln County Hosp., Lincoln, England, 2000—02, St. Bartholomew's Hosp., London, 2002—; urology specialist Dubai City Hosp., United Arab Emirates, 2010—. Dir. lithotryspi & stone svcs. St. Bartholomew's Hosp., London, 2002—; spkr., presenter in field. Contbr. articles to profl. jours. Grantee numerous rsch. grants. Fellow: Royal Dutch Soc. Medicine, Swiss Soc. Urology. Office: St Bartholomew's Hosp Smithfield London EC1A 7BE England Office Fax: 0044 203 465 5413. Personal E-mail: nb@lordoncologyconsultant.com.

BUCHI, J. KEVIN (JOHN KEVIN BUCHI), pharmaceutical executive; b. 1955; BA in Chemistry, Cornell U., Ithaca, NY, 1976; MBA, Northwestern U. J.L. Kellogg Grad. Sch. Mgmt., Evanston, Ill., 1982. CPA. Formerly with Eastman Kodak Co.; various fin. positions E.I. duPont de Nemours & Co., 1983—91; contr. Cephalon, Inc., 1991—96, sr. v.p., CFO, 1996—2006, head bus. devel., 2004—10, exec. v.p., CFO, 2006—09, exec. v.p., COO, 2010, CEO, 2010—. Bd. dirs. Encysive Pharmaceuticals Inc., 2004—08, Celator Pharmaceuticals, Inc., 2006—, Arana Therapeutics Ltd., 2009—. Office: Cephalon Inc 41 Moores Rd Frazer PA 19355 Office Phone: 610-344-0200. Business E-Mail: jbuchi@cephalon.com. *

BUCHIN, JACQUELINE CHASE, psychologist; b. Providence, Nov. 27, 1935; d. Leslie Thurber and Mary Hillyer (Lyon) Chase; m. Stanley Ira Buchin, Sept. 14, 1957; children: Linda Chase Sullivan, David Lyon, Gordon Tomlinson. BA, Wellesley Coll., 1957; MEd in Counseling Psychology, Antioch U., 1979; PsyD, Mass. Sch. Profl. Psychology, Boston, 1990. Lic. clin. psychologist Mass. Dir., coord. emergency housing program Multi-Svc. Ctr., Newton, Mass., 1978-81; family therapy intern Newtom Guidance Clinic, 1981-82, Framingham Youth Guidance, Mass., 1982-84; psychology intern The Arbour Hosp., Boston, 1984-85, Solomon Carter Fuller Hosp., Boston, 1985-86, Behavior Assocs., Boston, 1986-90; staff psychologist Biobehavioral Treatment Ctr., Brookline, Mass., 1990—; fellow in clin. cognitive therapy program Mass. Gen. Hosp., Boston, 1993-95, clin. assoc., 1995—, rsch. clinician, 1995—; clin. assoc. dept. psychology Ctr. for Anxiety and Related Disorders, Boston U., 2005—08; asst. prof. dept. psychiatry Tufts Sch. Medicine, Boston, 2007—11. Clin. instr. Psychology Dept. Harvard Med. Sch., Boston, 1995—; faculty mem. Inst. Cognitive Therapy Mass. Gen. Hosp., Boston, 1996—99; founding mem. Acad. Cognitive Therapy, 2000. Pres. Wellesley Jr. Svc. League, 1972—73; mem., bd. dirs. Jr. League of Boston, 1975—77; bd. dirs. Wellesley Cmty. Chest and Coun., 1972—73, Wellesley Friendly Assoc., 1972—73, Family Counseling Region W, 1969; bd. dirs. Wellesley chpt. ARC; bd. dirs. Wellesley Cmty. Child Care, 1976, Human Rels. Svc.; trustee Mass. Sch. Profl. Psychology, 1991—2007. Mem.: Assn. Advancement Cognitive Behavior Therapy. Episcopalian. Home: Union Wharf #304 Boston MA 02109-1206 Office: Biobehavioral Treatment Ctr 1051 Beacon St Brookline MA 02446-3282 Personal E-mail: jbuchin@att.net.

BUCHMAN, ARON S., neurologist, researcher; BS cum laude, Loyola U., Chgo., 1977; MD, Chgo. Med. Sch., 1982. Diplomate Am. Bd. Neurology, Am. Bd. Electrodiagnostic Medicine, cert. in clin. neurophysiology. Intern internal medicine Brookdale Hosp., Bklyn.; resident neurology Rush U. Med Ctr., Chgo., fellow in movement disorders & clin. neuropharmacology; fellow in clin. electrophysiology & neuromuscular diseases U. Brit. Columbia/Vancouver Gen. Hosp., Canada, 1987—88; assoc. prof. dept. neurol. scis. Rush U. Med Ctr., 1988—, dir. Electromyography (EMG) Lab., 1988—96. Research fellow NeuroMuscular Rsch. Ctr., Boston U., 1992—95; vis. scientist, dept. applied math. Weizmann Inst. Sci., Rehovot, Israel, 1995—97. Contbr. articles to profl. jours. Recipient Career Devel. award, Nat. Inst. Neurol. Disorders & Stroke/NIH, 1994—99; Patinkin Fellow, Regensberg Inst., Israel, 1979—80. Achievements include research in Alzheimer's disease and identifying the structural basis of clinical frailty in older persons; exploring the pathologic indices linking risk factors to the development of frailty so as to provide a conceptual basis for the development and testing of interventions to reduce the burden of this common syndrome in older adults. Office: Rush Memory Ctr Armour Academic Ctr 600 S Paulina StSte 1038 Chicago IL 60612 Office Phone: 312-942-3333. *

BUCHMAN, ELWOOD, internist, former pharmaceutical executive, director; b. Ottumwa, Iowa, June 10, 1918; s. Abe and Sarah (Redman) B.; m. Kathleen Field, June 8, 1945 (deceased); children: Elizabeth Anne, Bernard Kip; m. Eloise Marolf Schooley Buchman, June 30, 1989. BA, U. Iowa, 1940, MD, 1943. diplomate Am. Bd. Internal Medicine. Intern DC Gen. Hosp.; resident in internal medicine Wayne State U., VA Hosp., Detroit; fellow U. Pa., 1956; mem. staff Wayne State U. Med. Sch., VA Hosp., Detroit, 1946-52; assoc. prof. U. Iowa, Iowa City, from 1952; chief med. svc. VA Hosp., Des Moines, 1969-73; med. dir. Cintest Inc., Cin., 1980-86; former assoc. dir. Norwich Eaton Pharm. Co.; div. dir. Merrell Pharm. Rsch. Ctr., Cin. Sr. examiner numerous ins. cos. Contbr. numerous articles to med. jours. Served to capt. M.C., US Army; lt. col. USAR. Fellow ACP, Am. Coll. Gastroenterology, Am. Soc. Clin. Pharmacology Therapeutics; mem. Am. Profl. Practice Assn., Acad. Medicine Cin., Sigma Xi, Alpha Omega Alpha. Home and Office: 15456 N Boswell Blvd Sun City AZ 85351 Office Phone: 623-933-5936. Personal E-mail: buckeloise@aol.com.

BUCHSIEB, WALTER CHARLES, orthodontist, director; b. Columbus, Ohio, Aug. 30, 1929; s. Walter William and Emma Marie (Held) b.; m. Betty Lou Risch, June 19, 1955; children: Walter Charles II, Christine Ann. BA, Ohio State U., 1951, DDS, 1955, MS, 1960. Pvt. practice dentistry specializing in orthodontics, Dayton, Ohio, 1959-93; chmn. Ohio State U. Endowed Chair Orthodontics Fund Comm., 2004—08. Cons. orthodontist Miami Valley Hosp., Children's Med. Ctr., Dayton; orthodontic cons. Columbus Children's Hosp.; emeritus assoc. prof. dept. orthodontics Ohio State U. Coll. Dentistry, 1984—2004, clinic dir., 1993—98, mem. dean's adv. com.; mem. fin. and program com. United Health Found., 1971—73; com. chmn. Vig Williams endowed chair orthodontocs Ohio State U. Bd. dirs. Hearing and Speech Ctr., 1968-82, 2d v.p., 1976-78, pres., 1978-79; orthodontic advisor State of Ohio Dept. Health, Bur. Crippled Children's Svcs., 1983-84; elder Luth. ch., 1965-68, v.p. 1974. Capt. AUS, 1955-58. Named Alumnus of Yr., Ohio State U. Dental Alumni Coll. Dentistry, 2009, Dentist of Yr., Ohio State U. Dental Alumni Assn., 2009. Fellow Am. Coll. Dentists (pres. Ohio sect. 1988); mem. ADA (alt. del. 1968, del. 1991, coun. on ann. sessions and internat. rels. 1984-88), Am. Assn. Dental Schs., Am. Cleft Palate Assn., Am. Assn. Dental Schs., Internat. Assn. Dental Rsch., Ohio Dental Assn. (sec. coun. legis. 1969-78, v.p. 1978-79, pres.-elect 1979-80, pres. 1980-81, polit. action com. 1987-95, Coun. on constn. and By- Laws 1988-92, Achievement award 1989), Dayton Dental Soc. (pres. 1970-71), Am. Bd. Orthodontics, Gt. Lakes Assn. Orthodontists (sec.-treas. 1972-75, pres. 1977-78, Disting. Svc. award 2005), Internat. Coll. Dentists, Am. Assn. Orthodontists (chmn. coun. legis. 1976, speaker of house 1982-85, ad hoc com. to revise by-laws, coun. on govtl. affairs 1988-96, recipient James E. Brophy Dist. Svc. award 1992, Disting. Svc. award, 2005, bd. mem. polit. action com.), Pierre Fauchard Acad. (chmn. cen. Ohio), Coll. Diplomats Am. Bd. Orthodontics (pres. 1990-91, Parliamentarian 2008-10, hon. chmn. ann. session, hon. chmn. summer meeting, 2009), Ohio State U. Alumni Assn. (advs. group, Alumnus of Yr. award, 2009), Delta Upsilon (pres. Ohio State U. alumni chpt. 1997-99, alumni advisor 2000—), Psi Omega, Masons, Rotary (pres. 1973-74, Paul Harris fellow), Columbus Torch Club, Coll. Dentistry Alumni Revision (chmn. 2010). Republican. Lutheran. Home: 1212 Harrison Pond Dr New Albany OH 43054-9553 Office: Ohio State U Orthodontics Dept 305 W 12th Ave Columbus OH 43210-1267 Business E-Mail: walt1520@aol.com.

BUCHTA, RICHARD MICHAEL, pediatrician; b. Binghamton, NY, Feb. 8, 1941; s. Martin Joseph and Pauline (Perchinsky) Buchta; m. Diane Zirilli; children: Richard Jr., Daniel, Kymberley Rusch. BS, Le Moyne Coll., Syracuse, NY, 1963; MD cum-laude, Stritch-Loyola, Chgo., 1967. Lic. G16721, Calif., cert. Am. Bd. of Pediat., 1973, Am. Bd. of Pediat., sub-bd. Adolescent medicine, 2001, pediat. adv. life support 1996. Internship U.S. Naval Hosp., San Diego, 1967—68, pediat. residency, 1968—70; fellowship Children's Hosp. of L.A., 1973—74; asst. chief to pediat. U.S. Naval Hosp., Camp Pendleton, Calif., 1970—73; clin. instr. pediat. Univ. Calif., San Diego, 1972—74; pvt. practice LaJolla, Calif., 1974—83; attending physician Univ. Calif., San Diego, 1978—81, 1996—99; head divsn. Pediat. Scripps Clin., 1985—. Dir. med. edn. pediat. U.S. Naval Hosp., Camp Pendleton, Calif., 1970—73, dir. adolescent clin., 1970—73; asst. clin. prof. pediat. Univ. Calif., San Diego, 1975—79; supr. pediat. svc. Hillcrest Receiving Home, San Diego, 1975—83; clin. prof. Univ. Calif., San Diego, 1985—; physician U.S. Triathlon Team, 1985—87; cons. in field; lectr. in field; bd. dir. Eugene Booke Leadership, UCSD, 2007—. Contbr. articles publ. to profl. jour., chapters to books, scientific papers. Mem. Nat. Dem. Com., Washington, 1993—2004, Amnesty Internat. USA, 1987—2004; med. adv. bd. Medwell Group, 2002—04; mem. Carter Ctr., Atlanta, 1995—2007; mem. Scripps Office for the Protection Rsch. Subjects Com. Scripps Clin. Academic Affairs, 1999—; scientific adv. bd. Physicians Nutraceutical Lab., Calif., 2000—05. Ensign USN, 1966, lt. USN, 1967—71, lt. comdr. USN, 1971—77, hon. discharge USN, 1973, with USNR, 1973—87, comdr. USNR, 1977—83, capt. USN, 1983—87, ret. USNR, 1987. Named Best Dr. in Am., 1996—2007, Am. Top. Pediatratians, 2004—07. Mem.: N. Am. Soc. for Pediat Gyn., Physicians for Social Responsibility, Soc. for Adolescent Medicine, Am. Acad. of Pediat., Jesuit Cmty. Office: Scripps Clin Dept Pediat and Adolescent Medicine 3811 Valley Ctr Dr San Diego CA 92130 Home: 13403 Caminito Carmel Del Mar CA 92014 Office Phone: 858-764-3040.

BUCHWALD, HENRY, surgeon, educator, researcher; b. Vienna, June 21, 1932; arrived in U.S., 1939, naturalized; s. Andor and Renee (Franzos) B.; m. Emilie D. Bix, June 6, 1954; children: Jane Nicole, Amy Elizabeth, Claire Gretchen, Dana Alexandra. BA summa cum laude, Columbia U., 1954, MD, 1957; MS in Biochemistry, PhD in Surgery, U. Minn., 1967. Diplomate Am. Bd. Surgery. Intern Columbia/Presbyn. Med. Ctr., NYC, 1957-58; resident fellow in surgery U. Minn., Mpls., 1960-67; asst. prof. surgery U. Minn. Med. Sch., Mpls., 1967-70, assoc. prof., 1970-77, prof. surgery, prof. biomed. engring., 1977—, dir. grad. surg. tng., resident tng. program, in-tng. exam., chmn. credentials com.; chair Owen and Sarah Davidson Wangensteen Chair in Exptl. Surgery, 2001—. Pres. Minn. Inventors Hall of Fame, 1989-92, chmn. bd. dirs. 1992-94; vis. prof., lectr. McLaren Gen. Hosp., Flint., Mich., 1979, Buffalo Surg. Soc., Mpls., 1980, G.P. Wratten Surg. Symposium, Washington, 1980, Frontiers of Medicine Series, Chgo., 1980, Minn. Endocrine Club, Mpls., 1980, Symposium on Surgery, Tokyo, 1980, Northwestern Med. Assn., Sun Valley, Idaho, 1981, Mayo Clinic, Rochester, Minn., 1981, BSG/Glaxo Internat. Tchg. Day, Norwich, Eng., 1982, Mass. Gen. Hosp., Boston, 1983, SUNY, Stony Brook, 1984, DC Gen. Hosp., Washington, 1984, LA Surg. Soc., 1987, Sch. Dentistry, Dept. Continuing Edn., U. Minn., 1988, others; Alfred Strauss vis. lectr., Chgo., 1989; dir. postgrad. course Bariatric Surgery Primer, ACS; spkr., presenter, cons. in field. Author: (with others) Hepatic, Biliary and Pancreatic Surgery, 1980, Lipoproteins and Coronary Atherosclerosis, 1982, Atherosclerosis: Clinical Evaluation and Therapy, 1982, Nutrition and Heart Disease, 1982, Advances in Vascular Surgery, 1983, Advances in Surgery, 1984, others; contbr. Gibbon's Surgery of the Chest, 4th edit., 1983, Hardy's Textbook of Surgery, 1983, Implantable Pumps: ASAIO Primers in Artificial Organs, 1987, editor, author (textbook) Surgical Management of Obesity, 2006, (book) Pioneer of Gastrointestional Surgery, 2006; contbr. over 300 articles to profl. jours., trans.; mem. editorial bd. Chirurgia Generale, Jour. Clin. Surgery, Infu-Systems Internat., Diabetes, Nutrition and Metabolism, Obesity Surgery Jour. Am. Soc. Artificial Int. Orgn., Jour. Bacteriol. Surgery, Online Jour. Current Clin. Trials, also guest editor other jours. Capt. SAC, USAF, 1958-60. Recipient Inventor of Yr. award Minn. Inventors Hall of Fame, 1988, 90, Clin. Scholar award U. Minn., 1991, Diehl award U. Minn.; recipient numerous rsch. grants univs., Nat. Heart and Lung Inst., Nat. Cancer Inst., Nat. Inst. Arthritis, Metabolism and Digestive Diseases, NIH, med. founds., pharm. cos., corps., 1956—. Fellow ACS (gov. 1999—, Samuel D. Gross award 1969), Am. Surg. Assn., Soc. Univ. Surgeons, Ctrl. Surg. Assn. (program com. 1982-85, chmn. 1984-85, treas. 1992-94, pres. 1997-98), Assn. Acad. Surgery (Disting. Svc. award 1976), Epidemiology Coun. and Cardiovasc. Coun. Am. Heart Assn. (established investigator), Am. Coll. Cardiology, Soc. Surgery Alimentary Tract, Soc. Clin. Trials (program com. 1984-85); mem. AAAS, Minn. Surg. Assn. (First Clin. Rsch. award 1965), Mpls. Surg. Assn., Minn. Heart Assn., Am. Assn. History Medicine, Am. Soc. Artificial Internal Organs (program com. 1984-87, sect. editor Trans.), Internat. Study Group Diabetes Treatment with Implantable Insulin Delivery Devices (sec.-gen. 1984-88, chmn. 1989-94), St. Paul Surg. Soc. (hon.), Am. Coll. Nutrition (mem. editorial bd.), Am. Soc. Bariatric Soc. (pres. 1998-99), Internat. Soc. Obesity Surgery (pres. 2003-04), Owen H. Wangeensteen Soc. (pres. 2007), Paleopathology Club, Alpha Omega Alpha. Avocations: running, riding, tennis, reading, chess. Office: 420 Delaware St SE Minneapolis MN 55455 Office Phone: 612-625-8413. Business E-Mail: buchw001@umn.edu.

BUCK, HENRY WILLIAM, JR., obstetrician, gynecologist; b. Kansas City, June 4, 1934; s. Henry William Sr. and Nina Irene (Krebs) B.; m. Barbara Laviece Mallory, Sept. 6, 1963; children: Mallory Renee, Andrew William. BA, U. Kans., 1956, MD, 1960. Cert. Am. Bd. Ob.-Gyn. Gynecologist Student Health Svc. U. Kans., Lawrence, head gynecology dept. Student Health Svc., 1987—2005; clin. assoc. prof. Ob-gyn. U., Kans. Sch. Medicine, Kansas City; pvt. practice Lawrence, 1967—87; resident gen. surgery U. Okla., Okla. City, 1961—62; resident ob-gyn U. Kans., Kans. City, 1962—65. Pres. bd. dirs. Douglas County Citizens' Com. on Alcoholism, Lawrence, 1983-2005; chmn. task force HPV disease Am. Coll. Health Assn., 1988-02. Capt. USAF, 1965—67. Recipient Edward Hitchcock award, Am. Coll. Health Assn. Fellow ACS, Am. Coll. Ob-Gyns.; mem. AMA, Kans. Med. Soc., Kans. Ob-Gyn. Soc. (pres. 1980-81), Kappa Sigma, Omicron Delta Kappa. Republican. Lutheran. Avocations: photography, music, writing, travel. Home and Office: 306 Homestead Dr Lawrence KS 66049-2000 Office Phone: 785-843-5610. Business E-Mail: hbuck@ku.edu.

BUCK, JANE LOUISE, retired psychology professor; d. C. Robert and Viola Louise (Berger) B.; m. Leo Laskaris, Oct. 7, 1954 (div. Aug. 1978); 1 child, Julie. BA, U. Del., 1953, MA, 1959, MEd, 1966, PhD, 1971. Instr. U. Del., Newark, 1964-66; rsch. assoc. Rsch. for Better Schs., Phila., 1967-68; asst. prof. Del. State U., Dover, 1969-73, assoc. prof., 1973-77, prof. psychology, 1977-98; ret., 1998; pvt. cons. Cons. in stats. E.I. duPont de Nemours, Wilmington, Del., 1983-93; vis. prof. Ctr. for Sci. and Culture, U. Del., 1986. Author: Specifying the Risk, 1985; contbr. articles to profl. jours. Speaker, evaluator Del. Humanities Forum, 1980-88; pres. Del. Gerontol. Soc., Newark, 1987-88; mem. town coun. Chesapeake City, Md., 1998-2000; commr. parks and recreation, Chesapeake City, Md., 1998-99; bd. dirs. Friends of Cecil County Libr., 2000. Mem. AAAS (mem. sr. scientists and engrs.), AAUP (nat. coun. 1987-90, 93-99, 2010-, pres. Del. State U. chpt. 1976-80, 95-98, chief negotiator 1982-98, mem. nat. com. on historically Black instns. and scholars of color 1988-91, 98 2000, interim sec. Del. Conf 1991-92, pres. Del. conf. 1993-2000, mem. nat. com. govt. rels. 1994-97, Sternberg award for collective bargaining 1994, nat. pres. 2000-2006, mem. exec. com. nat. coun. 2006-09, 2010-11), Assn. for Psychol. Sci., Coun. Tchrs. Undergrad. Psychology, Am. Statis. Assn. (v.p. Del. chpt. 1999-2000), Danforth Assocs., Kappa Delta Pi, Psi Chi. Avocations: reading, gardening, sewing.

BUCK, LINDA B., biologist, educator; b. Seattle, Jan. 29, 1947; BS in Psychology, U. Wash., Seattle, 1975, BS in Microbiology, 1975; PhD in Immunology, U. Tex. Southwestern Med. Ctr., Dallas, 1980. Postdoc. fellow Columbia University, NYC, 1980—84; asst. prof. neurobiology Harvard University, Boston, 1991—96, assoc. prof., 1996—2001, prof., 2001—02; staff mem. divsn. basic scis. Fred Hutchinson Cancer Research Center, Seattle, 2002—; affiliate prof. dept. physiology & biophysics University of Washington School Medicine, Seattle, 2003—. Assoc. Howard Hughes Medical Inst., 1984—91, asst. investigator, 1994—97, assoc. investigator, Sweden, 1997—2000, investigator, 2001—; bd. dirs. DeCode Genetics Inc., 2005—09, Internat. Flavors & Fragrances Inc., 2007—. Contbr. articles to profl. jours. Recipient Scholar award, McKnight Endowment Fund for Neurosci., 1992, Takasago award for rsch. in olfaction, 1992, Disting. Alumnus award, U. Tex. Southwestern Med. Ctr., 1995, Unilever Sci. award, 1996, R.H. Wright award in olfactory rsch., 1996, Lewis S. Rosenstiel award, Brandeis U., 1997, Gairdner Found. Internat. award, 2003; co-recipient Nobel Prize in Physiology/Medicine, The Nobel Found., 2004. Fellow: AAAS, Am. Acad. Arts & Scis.; mem.: NAS, Inst. Medicine. Achievements include discovery of odorant receptors and the organization of the olfactory system. Office: Basic Scis Divsn Fred Hutchinson Cancer Rsch Ctr A3-020 1100 Fairview Ave N PO Box 19024 Seattle WA 98109-1024 Office Phone: 206-667-6316. Office Fax: 206-667-1031. E-mail: lbuck@fhcrc.org. *

BUCKLEY, CLIFFORD JAMES, surgeon, educator; b. Rahway, NJ, Nov. 24, 1936; BS in Chemistry, U. Pa., 1958; MD, Hahnemann U., 1962. Vascular surgeon USAF, 1963—78, Vascular Surg. Assocs., 1978—93; dir., divsn. vascular surgery, exec. com. mem., dept. surgery Scott & White Meml. Healthcare Sys., 1993—, exec. vice-chair. dept. surgery, 2008—; assoc. chief staff for surg. svc. Ctrl. Tex. Vets. Health Care Sys., 2007—. Clin. prof. surgery Uniformed Svcs. U. Health Scis., 1986—; prof. surgery Tex. A&M U. Health Sci. Ctr. Coll. Medicine, 1998—; cons. Endologix, Inc., 2006—; bd. mem. Internat. Soc. Endovascular Specialists, 2009—. Recipient Physicians Recognition award, AMA, Excellence in Health Care Delivery and Svc. award, Tex. A&M U. Health Sci. Ctr., Malcolm C. Grow award, USAF, Sys. Command Mederi award, Cert. of Merit; named Flight Surgeon of Yr., Mil. Airlift Command Flight Surgeon of Yr. Fellow: ACS, Royal Soc. Medicine, Southwestern Surg. Congress, Soc. Vascular Surgery; mem.: Tex. Surg. Soc. Avocations: travel, reading, snorkeling. Office: 2401 S 31st St Temple TX 76504-7115 Office Fax: 254-724-3173. Business E-Mail: cbuckley@swmail.sw.org.

BUCKLEY, JOHN JOSEPH, JR., healthcare executive; b. Evanston, Ill., Oct. 5, 1944; s. John Joseph and Mary Ruth (Smith) B.; m. Sarah Amelia Puceloski, May 16, 1970; children: Ruth Mary, Patricia Kimberly, John Joseph III. AB, Kenyon Coll., 1966; MBA, George Washington U., 1969. Asst. adminstr. Maricopa County Gen. Hosp., Phoenix, 1969-71, St. Joseph's Hosp. and Med. Ctr., Phoenix, 1971-74, assoc. adminstr., 1974-76, v.p., 1976-79, pres., 1984-88, St. Anthony's Hosp., Amarillo, Tex., 1979-84, St. Anthony's Devel. Corp., Amarillo, 1982-84; chief operating officer Harrington Cancer Ctr., Amarillo, 1982-84; sr. v.p. Mercy Health System, Cin., 1988-91; pres. So. Ill. Healthcare Enterprises, Carbondale, Ill., 1992—2001, Jack Buckley & Assocs., College Station, Tex., 2001—; interim pres., CEO St. Mary's Hosp. of East St. Louis, Ill., 2002; interim COO, St. Joseph Campus of Via Christi Med. Ctr., Wichita, Kans., 2003; interim CEO St. Joseph Regional Health Ctr., Bryan, Tex., 2003—04, CEO, 2004—08; pres., CEO, St. Joseph Health Sys., Bryan, Tex., 2005—09. Pres. So. Ill. Hosp. Svcs., Health Svcs. So. Ill., Regional Health Plan, 1992-2001,external adv. bd. mem, 2004- TAMU Health Sci. Ctr. Sch. Rural Pub. Health, chmn., 2004-11; exec.-in-residence TAMU Health Sci. Ctr. Sch. Rural Pub. Health, HPM Dept. MHA Program, 2009-; mem. external adv. bd. Coll. Bus. and Adminstrn., So. Ill. U., 2000-. Active Amarillo Alliance of Cmty. Svc. Execs., Amarillo Area Acad. Health Ctr. Corp., Amarillo Area Hosp. Home Care, Amarillo Found. Health and Sci., Panhandle chpt. Tex. Soc. to Prevent Blindness, Amarillo Jr. League, Children's Oncology Svcs. Tex. Panhandle; Amarillo diocesan coord. health affairs; adminstrv. com. Amarillo; pres. Mercy Svcs. Corp., 1984-88; bd. dirs. Greater Phoenix Affordable Health Care Found., 1984-88; trustee Kenyon Coll., Gambier, Ohio, 1991-95, alumni coun., 1998-2003, pres., 2001-02; active SI Edge, 1995-2003. Fellow: Am. Coll. Healthcare Execs. (regent Ariz. 1984—88, regent So. Ill. 1998—2002); mem.: St. Mary's Cath. Ch. (chair. leadership coun. 2009—), Tex. Assn. Voluntary Hosp. (sec. treas. 2008—09, bd. mem. and chair membership com.), HOSPAC (polit. action com. Tex. Hosp. Assn. 2006—09), Ariz. Hosp. Assn., Ariz. Kidney Found., Cath. Health Assn. U.S. (trustee 1985—91, chair Govt. rels. com. 1986—91), Ill. Hosp. Assn. (trustee 1995—2001, chmn. 2000), Tex. Hosp. Assn. (trustee 1983—84), The George Washington U. Alumni Assn. for Health Svcs., Mgmt. and Leadership (pres. 1995—97, Tex. Health bd. advisors 2010—, parliamentarian, bd. trustee, dir. ACHE-Southeast Tex. Chpt 2011—), Delta Phi (pres. alumni assn. 1988—2000). Republican. Roman Catholic. Office Phone: 979-731-8235. Business E-Mail: jackbuckleyjr@earthlink.net.

BUCKLEY, PETER FRANCIS, dean, psychiatrist; b. Dublin, June 19, 1962; came to U.S., 1992, s. John F. and Nóssin M. Buckley; m. Leonie Mary Buckley, Sept. 3, 1987, children: John, Brian. MB BChir, BAO, Univ. Coll. Dublin, 1986, MD, 1997. Asst. prof. psychiatry Case Western Res. U., Cleve., 1992-96, assoc. prof., 1996—2000; med. dir. Western Res. Psychiat. Hosp., Cleve., 1994-95, N.W. Behavioral, Cleve., 1995—2000; prof. psychiatric behavior, radiology, pharmacology & toxicology and grad. studies Ga. Health Sciences U., 2000—, chmn. dept. psychiatry and assoc. then sr. assoc. dean leadership devel., 2000—10, interim dean Med. Coll., 2010—11, dean Med. Coll., 2011—. V.p. for clin. affairs Healthcare Sys., Cleve., 1995-2010; med. advisor Nat. Alliance for Mentally Ill, Cleve., 1995-2010; mem. adv. bd. pharm. cos., 1995 2010. Author: (book) Examination Notes in Psychiatry, 1995, editor: (books) The Neurodevelopmental Basis of Schizophrenia, 1996, Schizophrenia, 1998, Sexuality and Serious Mental Illness, 1999; mem. editl. bd.: Am. Jour. Managed Care, 1998—. Participant Presdl. Forum on Mental Illness, 1999, mediation participant Ohio Dept. Mental Health, 1998. Recipient Mead Johnson award Am. Coll. Neuropsychopharmacology, 1995, Sr. Resident Rsch. award Royal Acad. Medicine, 1997, Lilly Schizophrenia Reintegration award Eli Lilly, 1999, Psychiatrist of Yr. award Ga. Psychiatric Physicians Assn., 2007, Exemplary Psychiatrist award Nat. Alliance on Mental Illness. Mem. Am. Psychiat. Assn., Biol. Psychiatry, Royal Coll. Psychiatrists, Assn. for Assertive Cmty. Treatment, Assn. Cmty. Psychiatrists, Ohio Psychiat. Assn. Roman Catholic. Avocations: golf, reading, soccer, hill walking, skiing. Office: Med Coll Ga AA 1006 997 St Sebastian Way Augusta GA 30912 Office Phone: 706-721-2231. Business E-Mail: pbuckley@georgiahealth.edu. *

BUCKLEY, REBECCA HATCHER, allergist, immunologist, pediatrician, educator; b. Hamlet, NC, Apr. 1, 1933; d. Martin Armstead and Nora (Langston) Hatcher; m. Charles Edward Buckley, III, July 9, 1955; children: Charles Edward IV, Elizabeth Ann, Rebecca Kathryn, Sarah Margaret. BA, Duke U., 1954; MD, U. NC, 1958. Intern Duke U. Med. Ctr., Durham, NC, 1958-59, resident, 1959-61, pediat. allergist and immunologist, 1961—. Dir., chair exam. com. Am. Bd. Allergy and Immunology, Phila., 1971—73, co-chair bd. dirs., 1982—84; chair Diagnostic Lab. Immunology, 1984—88; mem. staff Duke U. Med. Ctr., asst. prof. pediat. and immunology, 1968—72, assoc. prof. pediat., 1972—79, prof. pediat., 1976—79, prof. immunology, J. Buren Sidbury prof. pediat., 1979—. Contbr. articles to profl. jours. Fellow: AAAS (chair med. scis. sect. 2001—03); mem.: NAS (elected mem. 2011), Inst. Medicine of NAS, Am. Pediat. Soc. (coun. mem. 1991—, pres. 1999—2000, chmn. immune deficiency found. med. adv. com. 2003—), Southeastern Allergy Assn. (pres. 1978—79), Am. Acad. Pediat. (Bret Ratner award 1992), Soc. Pediat. Rsch., Am. Assn. Immunologists, Am. Acad. Allergy and Immunology (exec. com. 1975—82, pres. 1979—80, hon. fellow award 1999), Republican. Episcopalian. Home: 3621 Westover Rd Durham NC 27707-5032 Office: Duke U Med Ctr PO Box 2898 Durham NC 27710 Office Phone: 919-684-2922. Business E-Mail: buckl003@mc.duke.edu.

BUCKNALL, CLIFFORD ADRIAN, cardiologist; b. Sale, Eng., Feb. 25, 1956; s. Eric and Elsie Constance (Whittaker) Bucknall; m. Sarah Anne Topp, July 30, 1983 (div. 1996); children: Samuel Clifford, Thomas Adrian; m. Clare Collis, Nov. 22, 1997; children: Sophie Charlotte, Phoebe Holly. Degree, Leamington Coll., Eng., 1967-74; MB BS, Westminster Med. Sch., London, 1979; MD, London U., 1987. House surgeon Warwick (Eng.) Hosp. Nat. Health Svc., 1979-80, house physician Westminster Hosp. London, 1980, sr. house physician Nottingham (Eng.) Hosp., 1980-82; rsch. fellow in cardiology Guys Hosp., London, 1982-84; sr. registrar Guy's Hosp., London, 1987-89, dir. cardiology, 1992-93; registrar Brighton Hosp., England, 1984-85, King's Coll. Hosp., London, 1985-86, sr. registrar, 1986-87, cons. cardiologist, 1989-92; dir. cardiology and cardiothoracic Guys & St. Thomas' Hosp. (NHS) Trust, 1996-97, dir. cardiac svc. and thoracic surgery, 1996-97. Cons. cardiologist King's Coll., Dulwich Hosp., London Bridge Hosp., Sloane Hosp., London, 1989—, Guys and St. Thomas Hosp.; chief med. officer Royal and Sun Alliance, 1997-2000; dir. cardiac svcs. Guys and St. Thomas Hosp., 2002-05 Contbr. papers, chpts. to med. publs. Fellow Royal Soc. Medicine, Royal Coll. Physicians, European Soc. Cardiology; mem. Royal Coll. Surgeons, Brit. Cardiac Soc., Brit. Med. Assn. Anglican. Avocations: hockey, tennis, swimming. Office: London Bridge Hosp St Olaf House 27 Tooley Street SE1 2PR London England

BUCKNER, JOYCE, psychologist, educator; b. Benton, Ark., Sept. 25, 1937; d. Waymond Floyd Pannell and Willie Evelyn (Wright) Whitley; m. John W. Buckner, Aug. 29, 1958 (div. 1970); children: Cheryl, John, Chris. BA, Ouachita Bapt. Coll., 1959; MS in Edn., Henderson State U., 1964; PhD, North Tex. State U., 1970. Lic. psychologist, Tex., marriage and family therapist; cert. Nat. Registry Health Svc. Providers in Psychology; master trainer in imago relationship therapy. Assoc. prof. U. Tex., Arlington, 1970-80, chmn. dept. edn., 1976-78; pvt. practice Arlington, 1974—. Dir., chief profl. officer Southwest Inst. Relationship Devel.; appeard on tv shows including Oprah; spkr. in field. Author: Making Real Love Happen: The New Era of Intimacy. Mem. APA, Nat. Assn. for Imago Relationship Therapy (pres.), Nat. Speakers Assn., Am. Assn. Marital and Family Therapy. Avocations: dance, travel, art. Home: 6014 English Oak Dr Arlington TX 76016 Home Phone: 817-451-8588; Office Phone: 817-451-8009. Personal E-mail: joybuckner@aol.com.

BUCKNER-BROWN, JOYCE, allied health instructor; b. Greenwood, Miss. BS, Tougaloo Coll., 1977; M in Health Sci., Miss. Coll., 1991; PhD, Miss. State U., 1995. Registered respiratory therapist. Asst. prof. U. So. Miss., Hattiesburg, 1995-97; interim chair Jackson (Miss.) State U., 1997-98, asst. prof., 1998—2003, assoc. prof., 2003—. Cons. Joyce Buckner-Brown & Assocs., Ridgeland, Miss., 1999—. Seminar leader on health and wellness comm. chs., 1998-99. Grantee Ctrs. Disease Control, 1998, Miss. Tobacco Pilot Program, 1998-2000. Mem. APHA, ASPA, Nat. Assn. African Am. Studies (bd. dirs. 1997, leadership award 1999, 2000), Miss. Soc. Respiratory Care, Nat. Rural Health Assn., Nat. Minority Health Assn. Avocations: reading, travel. Office: Jackson State U Sch Allied Health Scis 350 W Woodrow Wilson Ave Jackson MS 39213-7681 E-mail: joyce.buckner-brown@jsums.edu.

BUCKSPAN, RANDY JAY, plastic surgeon; b. Nurnberg, Germany, Oct. 9, 1954; (parents Am. citizens); s. Harold and Betty Jane (Marker) B.; m. Amy Denise Boynton, May 2, 1981; children: Elizabeth Anne, Caitlin Elaine, Andrew David. BS in Chemistry, U. Tex., Austin, 1976; MD, U. Tex., Galveston, 1980. Diplomate Am. Bd. Plastic Surgery. Resident in gen. surgery Vanderbilt U. Hosp., Nashville, 1980-85; fellow in plastic surgery U. Ky., Lexington, 1985-87. Contbr. articles to med. jours. Mem. ACS, Am. Soc. Plastic Surgeons, Southeastern Soc. Plastic and Reconstructive Surgeons, Tampa Bay Soc. Plastic Surgeons. Avocations: bicycling, running, fishing, golf, swimming. Office: Apt 15008 6500 Champion Grandview Way Austin TX 78750-8365 Office Phone: 727-822-6531. Business E-Mail: drbuckspan@tampabayplasticsurgery.net.

BUCKWALTER, JOSEPH ADDISON, orthopedic surgeon, educator; b. Ottumwa, Iowa, June 21, 1947; s. Joseph Addison and Carole Ann (Kelly) B.; m. Kathleen Coen, May 31, 1975; children: Jody, Andrea, Abigail. BS with high distinction, U. Iowa, 1969, MS, 1972, MD, 1974. Diplomate Am. Bd. Orthopaedic Surgery (recert., oral examiner 1988—, dir. 1990—, mem. examinations com. 1992—, chmn. examinations com. 1992-93, chmn. cert. renewal com. 1992—); lic. surgeon Iowa. Intern in internal medicine U. Iowa, Iowa City, 1974-75, resident in orthopaedics, 1975-77, 78-79, Nat. Rsch. Svc. Award rsch. fellow, 1977-78, from asst. prof. to assoc. prof. orthopaedic surgery, 1979-85, prof. orthopaedic surgery, 1985—. Mem. R&D devel. com. VA Med. Ctr. Com., 1985-88; mem. orthopaedic tumor therapy group U. Iowa Cancer Ctr., 1981—, cancer edn. subcom., 1982-90; mem. grants and fellowships adv. com. Iowa City Vets. Med. Ctr., 1983-86, chief orthopaedic surgery, 1987-91; mem. Arthritis Found. Rsch. Com., 1985-86; mem. panel NIH Consensus Devel. Confs., Bethesda, Md., 1984, 88; mem. rheumatology rsch. adv. bd. Syntex Corp., 1987-94; mem. adv. bd. WHO Multinational Collaborative Study on Predictors of Osteoarthritis, 1992; mem. sci. adv. com. Specialised Ctr. Rsch. on Osteoarthritis Rush-Presbyn.-St. Luke's Med. Ctr., Chgo., 1993—; mem. Nat. Arthritis and Musculoskeletal and Skin Diseases Adv. Coun., NIH, 1993—; disting. lectr. Hosp. Spl. Surgery, N.Y.C., 1982, Coll. Physicians and Surgeons-N.Y. Orthopaedic Hosp., 1988, U. N.Mex., 1989; guest lectr. Wilford Hall Med. Ctr., San Antonio, 1983, vis. prof., 1984; vis. prof. U. Miami, Fla., 1986, Cath. Med. Colls., Seoul, Republic of Korea, 1989, U. Pitts., 1993, Ohio State U., Columbus, 1994; vis. orthopaedic prof. U. So. Calif., L.A., 1990; Am. Orthopaedic Assn. 1991 Internat. vis. prof. Nuffield Orthopaedic Ctr., Oxford (Eng.) U., 1991, vis. prof. orthopaedics, 1991; vis. prof. orthopaedics, U. N.C., 1991; OREF Hark lectr. and vis. prof. U. Wash., Seattle, 1992; Watson Jones lectr. Royal Coll. Surgeons (Gt. Britain), 1992; A.M. Rechtman lectr. Phila. Orthopaedic Soc., 1993; Predl. guest spkr. 1993 Japanese Orthopaedic Assn. Rsch. Meeting, Matsumoto, Japan, 1993; Kelly Rsch. Award vis. prof. Mayo Clinic, Rochester, Minn., 1993; participant numerous workshops and confs. Cons. reviewer: Jour. Bone and Joint Surgery, 1979—, cons. editor for rsch., 1989—; bd. assoc. editors: Jour. Orthopaedic Rsch., 1982-85, mem. editl. adv. bd., 1985-88, co-editor-in-chief, 1993—; mem. editl. adv. bd. Orthopaedics, 1986-90; reviewer: The Lancet, 1993—; contbr. articles to profl. jours. Student rsch. fellow U. Iowa Coll. Medicine, 1970. Fellow Am. Inst. Med. and Biol. Engring. (founding), Am. Acad. Orthopaedic Surgeons (mem. com. basic scis. 1983-85, chmn. com. evaluation 1985-90, mem. at large, bd. dirs. 1988-89, mem. steering com. for devel. Musculoskeletal Conditions in U.S. 1990-92, chmn. coun. for rsch. and sci. affairs 1990-93, 94—, sec. 1993-94); mem. AAAS, Inst. Medicine, Internat. Soc. Limb Salvage, Brit. Orthopaedic Assn. (companion mem.), Orthopaedic Rsch. Soc. (sec.-treas. 1985-88, bd. dirs. 1985-91, pres. 1989-90), Am. Orthopaedic Assn. (exch. fellowship com. 1989-90, chmn. internat. vis. prof. com. 1993—), Am. Orthopaedic Soc. for Sports Medicine (chmn. rsch. awards com. 1988-90, rsch. com. 1989-91), Internat. Skeletal Soc., Iowa Orthopaedic Soc., Johnson County Med. Soc.,

Musculoskeletal Tumor Soc., 20th Century Orthopaedic Assn., Girdlestone Orthopaedic Soc., Phi Beta Kappa, Alpha Omega Alpha. Office: U Iowa Hosps Dept Orthopaedics 200 Hawkins Dr Iowa City IA 52242-1009 Office Phone: 319-356-2595.

BUCKY, LOUIS P., plastic surgeon, educator; b. Highland Park, Ill., Feb. 21, 1960; MD, Harvard Med. Sch., 1986. Cert. Am. Bd. Surgery, 1993, Am. Bd. Plastic Surgery, 1997, lic. Pa., 1995, NJ, 1996. Intern in gen. surgery Mass. Gen. Hosp., Boston, 1986—87, resident in gen. surgery, 1987—92, resident in plastic surgery, 1992—94; fellow in craniofacial surgery Meml. Sloan-Kettering Cancer Ctr., NYC, 1994—95, Miami Children's Hosp., 1995; attending physician Children's Hosp. Phila., 1995—; asst. prof. U. Pa. Sch. Medicine, Phila., 1995—2004, assoc. prof. surgery, 2004—; attending surgeon, divsn. plastic & reconstructive surgery Hosp. of the U. Pa., Phila., 1995—, assoc. surgeon, divsn. plastic & reconstructive surgery, 1995—, co-dir., microsurgery rsch. lab., 1996—, chief, plastic & reconstructive surgery sect., 2007—; chief plastic surgery Presbyn. Med. Ctr. Divsn. Plastic & Reconstructive Surgery, 1996—2001; private practice plastic surgeon Phila., Ardmore, Pa. Chmn. Perspective and Advancements of Plastic Surgery Symposium; TV appearances Good Morning America, CNN, others. Co-author: Aesthetic Breast Surgery, 2009; contbr. articles to med. jours., chapters to books. Named Top Doc, Phila. Mag., 2001—07. Fellow: Am. Coll. Surgeons; mem.: Am. Assn. Plastic Surgeons, Northeastern Soc. Plastic Surgeons (pres. 2007), Am. Soc. Aesthetic Plastic Surgery, Am. Soc. Plastic Surgeons. Achievements include patents in field. Office: Pa Hosp Farm Journal Bldg Ste 101 230 W Washington Sq Philadelphia PA 19106 also: Hosp U Pa 10 Penn Tower 3400 Spruce St Philadelphia PA 19104 Office Phone: 215-829-6325. Office Fax: 215-829-8588. E-mail: lou.bucky@uphs.upenn.edu.

BUCOLO, GAIL ANN, biotechnologist; b. Port Chester, NY, July 27, 1954; d. Joseph Anthony and Jennie (Tomassetti) Bucolo. BS in French, Oneonta State Coll., 1976; MA in French, Middlebury Coll., 1977; postgrad., Columbia U., 1981—82; MS in Biotech., Manhattan Coll., 1995. Technician N.Y. Hosp., NYC, 1983-86; rsch. technician NYU Hosp., NYC, 1986; sr. rsch. technician Meml. Sloan Kettering, NYC, 1986-88, Columbia U., NYC, 1988-2001; tchr. Cathedral HS, NYC, 2001—04; rsch. tech. NY Meth. Hosp., Bklyn., 2004—08; substitute lectr. Kingsborough CC, Bklyn., 2009—. Corr. Scienceport, Rye, NY, 1994—96; adj. prof. Mercy Coll., Dobbs Ferry, NY, 1996—2004; summer rsch. intern Rockefeller U., 2003. With NY Meth. Hosp., 2004—08, Kingsborough CC, 2009—. Mem.: AAAS, N.Y. Acad. Scis., Sigma Xi. Roman Catholic. Achievements include research in factor VIII inhibitor and discovery that it inhibited reverse transciptase of HIV; spinal cord injury and neuronal regeneration. Home: 1025 Louise Ave Basement Apt Mamaroneck NY 10543 Office: Kingsborough CC Brooklyn NY 11235-2398 Personal E-mail: gailbucolo@aol.com.

BUCUR, ALEXANDRU, dental association administrator; b. Bucharest, Romania, Jan. 27, 1955; Degree in Maxillofacial Surgery; degree in Dentistry, Bucharest, 1983. Head, oral and maxillofacial chair Faculty Dental Medicine U. Medicine and Pharmacy Carol Davila, Bucharest, 2002—. Recipient Ordinance San. Virtue Comdt. award, Pres. of Romania. Fellow: European Assn. Cranio-Maxillofacial Surgery; mem.: Soc. Latina Capitis et Colli, Internat. Acad. Oral Oncology. Office: Calea Plevnei Bucharest 010221 Romania Personal E-mail: crystalvladan@gmail.com.

BUCZYNSKI, ANA KARLA DA COSTA, dentist; b. Cabo Frio, Rio de Janeiro, Feb. 27, 1981; Degree in Dentistry, U. Fed. do Rio de Janeiro, 2003. Dentist Brazilian Air Force, 2007—. Home: Rua Ângeli Neves 121 Apt104 Moneró Rio de Janeiro 21920-270 Brazil

BUDD, MAGGI A., psychologist, educator; b. Erie, Pa., June 6, 1968; PhD, U. North Tex., 2007; MPH, U. North Tex., Health Sci. Ctr., 2004. Diplomate in rehab. psychology Am. Bd. Profl. Psychology. Postdoc. fellow Johns Hopkins, 2007—09; instr. Harvard Med. Sch., 2009—; rehab. neuropsychologist VA Boston Healthcare, 2009—. Mem.: Am. Acad. Spinal Cord Injury Profls. (chairperson for rsch. com.). Achievements include research in sexuality and SCI, neuropsychological correlates and aging brain with SCI/D, and capacity to refuse medical treatment. Office: 940 Belmont St Bldg 8 SCI Brockton MA 02301 Personal E-mail: magbudd@yahoo.com.

BUDDE, THOMAS, cardiologist, educator; b. Essen, Germany, Feb. 11, 1957; s. Heinz and Renate (Herold) B.; m. Ute Stoermer; children: Sebastian, Adrian. MD, U. Düsseldorf, Germany, 1961; Habil., U. Münster, 1994. Lic. physician in internal medicine, cardiology and intensive care medicine, Germany. Resident U. Düsseldorf, 1981-88; jr./sr. attending physician U. Münster, 1988-95, sr. lectr., 1994—; head rsch. group Interventional Studies Inst. for Rsch. in Arteriosclerosis, Münster, 1991-95; head dept. internal medicine/cardiology Alfried Krupp Krankenhaus, Essen, 1995—, vice med. dir., 1998—; prof. U. Münster, 2000—. Author, editor: Experimental Studies on the Function of Subcutaneous-transvenous Defibrillators, 1995; co-author: Clinician's Manual on Management of Patients with Coronary Heart Disease, 1998; contbr. articles to profl. jours. Fellow: European Soc. Cardiology; mem.: European Cardiologist, German Soc. Cardiology, Rotary. Avocations: sailing, skiing. Home: Vossbergring 37 D-45259 Essen Germany Office: Alfried Krupp Hosp Alfried-Krupp-Strasse 21 D-45117 Essen Germany Office Phone: 49-201-434-2525. E-mail: budde.thomas@krupp-krankenhaus.de, budde.thomas@t.online.de.

BUDHIRAJA, ROHIT, physician; b. New Delhi, Apr. 19, 1974; MBBS, All India Inst. Med. Scis., 1995; MD, Upstate Med. U., 2000. Clin. instr. medicine Tufts U. Sch. Medicine, Boston, 2000—03; staff physician New Eng. Rehab. Hosp., Stoughton, Mass., 2000—03; pulmonary, critical care & sleep physician Southern Ariz. Veterans Affairs Hosp., Tucson, 2005—. Asst. prof. medicine U. Ariz., Tucson, 2006—11; assoc. editor Jour. Clin. Sleep Medicine, 2011. Recipient Young Investigator Respiratory Disease Forum award, U. NC, 2007; Young Investigator VISN 18 grant, Veterans Affairs. Fellow: Am. Coll. Chest Physicians, Am. Acad. Sleep Medicine (Young Investigator award 2009). Avocation: music. Office: Southern Arizona Va Health Care Sys Tucson AZ 85723 E-mail: budhi3@gmail.com.

BUDIMIROVIC, DEJAN B., academic child psychiatrist; b. Sabac, Serbia, July 19, 1962; arrived in US, 1994, naturalized; s. Borisav and Milijana Budimirovic; m. Tatjana Bojanic, May 23, 1992; children: Miliana, Andrei Budimirovich, Nicholas Budimirovich. MD magna cum laude, Belgrade Sch. Medicine, 1982—87. Diplomate Am. Bd. Psychiatry & Neurology, 1999, in child & adolescent psychiatry Am. Bd. Psychiatry & Neurology, 2000. Intern Belgrade Sch. Medicine, Serbia, 1987—89; family practitioner Zagreb, Croatia, 1990, Belgrade Sch. Medicine, Serbia, 1991—93; adult psychiatry residentcy tng. Harvard Med. Sch., Boston, 1984—97; child and adolescent psychiatry resident NYU, Bellevue Hosp, NYC, 1997—99; asst. prof. psychiatry Yale U. Sch. Medicine, New Haven, 1999—2003, Johns Hopkins Sch. Medicine, Balt., 2004—. Co-dir. adolescent svc. Yale-New Haven Psychiat. Hosp. Yale U. Sch. Medicine, 2000—01; med. dir. Children's Psychiat. Inpatient Unit Stony Brook U. Hosp., NY, 2004. Recipient Clin. Excellence award, Faculty & Dir. Child & Adolescent Psychiatry, NYU Child Study Ctr., 1999. Mem.: AMA, Am. Psychiat. Assn., Am. Acad. Child & Adolescent Psychiatry. Office: Johns Hopkins University Sch Medicine Clin Rsch Ctr 716 N Broadway 2nd Fl Baltimore MD 21205 Office Phone: 443-923-2634. Office Fax: 443-923-7628. Business E-Mail: budimirovic@kennedykrieger.org.

BUDINGER, THOMAS FRANCIS, biomedical scientist, educator; b. Evanston, Ill., Oct. 25, 1932; married, 1965; 3 children. BS in Chemistry magna cum laude, Regis Coll., 1954; MS in Phys. Oceanography, U. Wash., Seattle, 1957; MD, U. Colo., Denver, 1964; PhD in Med. Physics, U. Calif. Berkeley, 1971. Cert. in nuc. medicine 1973, lic. Calif., Pa. Asst. chemist Regis Coll., Colo., 1953—54; analytical chemist Indsl. Labs., 1954; sr. oceanographer U. Wash., 1960—66, Peter Bent Brigham Hosp., 1964; physicist Lawrence Livermore Lab., U. Calif., 1966—67; resident physician Donner Lab. and Lawrence Berkeley Nat. Lab., 1967—76; H. Miller Prof. med. rsch. and group leader rsch. medicine Donner lab., prof. elec. engring. and computer sci. Donner Lab., U. Calif. Berkeley, 1976—2008; founding chmn. bioengr. U. Calif., 1998—2004; prof. grad. sch. U. Calif. Berkley, 2008—; home sec. Nat. Acad. Engring., 2008—. Dir. med. svc. Lawrence Berkeley Lab., 1968—76; prof. elec. engring., computer sci. U. Calif. Berkeley, 1974—2008, founding chair bioengring., 1998, prof. bioengring., 1998—2008; sr. staff scientist Lawrence Berkeley Lab., 1980—2008; chmn. study sect. NIH, 1981—84; prof. radiology U. Calif. San Francisco, 1984—2008; founding chair, prof. bioengring., prof. elec. engring. and computer sci. Grad. Sch., U. Calif. Berkeley, 2008—. Contbr. 400 sci. papers to profl. publs. Recipient NASA Group Achievement award, 1976, Spl. Achievement award in nuc. tech. for med. diagnostics, Am. Nuc. Soc., 1984, Alumni Achievement award, Regis Coll., 1987, Ernst Jung-Preis, 1989, Merit award for Alzheimer's rsch., NIH, 1990, George de Hevesy Pioneer award, 1996, Gold medal, Am. Roentger Ray Soc., 2009; named Eugene P. Pendergrass New Horizons lectr., Radiol. Soc. North America, 1993. Fellow: Soc. Magnetic Resonance, Am. Inst. Med. and Biol. Engring.; mem.: NAE (councillor 2006—08, home sec. 2008—), AAAS, Nat. Acad Engring., Inst. of Medicine, Soc. Magnetic Resonance in Medicine (pres. 1984—85, Disting. Svc. medal 1989), Soc. Nuc. Medicine (Hal Anger Meml. lectr. 2010, Hermann L. Blumgart Cardiovascular lectureship 1987, Paul C. Aebersold award for basic sci. 1989, Disting. Sci. award 1991). Achievements include research in imaging body functions, electrical, magnetic, sound and photon radiation fields, electron microscopy, polar oceanography; nuclear magnetic resonance, reconstruction tomography and instrument development, and cardiology. Avocations: crew, fly fishing. Office: Lawrence Berkeley Nat Lab Dept Radiotracer Devel and Imaging Tech 1 Cyclotron Rd Mail Stop 55-121 Berkeley CA 94720-0001 Home Phone: 510-527-5623; Office Phone: 510-486-5435, 510-847-2158. Office Fax: 510-486-4768. Business E-Mail: tfbudinger@lbl.gov.

BUDNIKOVA, YULIA H., lab administrator; b. Kazan, Russia, Oct. 10, 1965; DSc, 1982; PhD, Kazan State U., 1990. Head lab. Arbuzov Inst. Organic and Phys. Chemistry Kazan Sci. Ctr. RAS, 2008—. Dir. Olefin Ltd Co., 2008—. Recipient State prize, Sci. & Tech. Republic of Tatarstan. Mem.: Menseleev Chem. Soc., ISE. Avocation: painting. Office: Arbuzov 8 Kazan Tatarstan 420088 Russia Office Fax: 7 843 2725335. Business E-Mail: yulia@iopc.ru.

BUDOFF, MATTHEW JAY, cardiologist; m. Victoria Billit, Oct. 3, 1998; children: Daniel Oliver, Garrett Clark. BS in Biochemistry, U. Calif., Riverside, 1986; MD, George Wash. U., DC, 1990. Lic. physician DC, 1990, bd. cert. Internal Medicine 1994, bd. cert. Cardiology 1997. Internal medicine internship and residency Harbor UCLA Med. Ctr., Torrance, Calif., 1990—93, cardiology fellow, 1994—97; rschr. physician LA Biomedical Rsch., Torrance, 1997—; asst. prof. UCLA Sch. Medicine, 1997—2003, assoc. prof., 2003—10, prof., 2010—. Editor (author): Enhancing Heart Health, 2003, Cardiac CT Imaging, 2006, Atlas of Cardiac CT, 2007; editor: Cardiovascular CT, 2010; contbr. articles to profl. jours., chapters to books. Named one of Am. Top Doctors for Men, 2007; named to LA Superdoctors, 2007. Fellow: Am. Coll. Cardiology, Am. Heart Assn. (life; bd. dirs. 2000—06); mem.: Soc. Cardiovascular CT (pres. 2010—), Soc. Atherosclerosis and Prevention (pres. 2006—, founder), Soc. Cardiovascular CT (exec. bd. mem. 2004—, founding mem.). Achievements include patents for imaging. Office: Los Angeles Biomedical Research Institut 1124 West Carson Street Torrance CA 90502 Business E-Mail: mbudoff@labiomed.org.

BUDUNELI, NURCAN, dental educator; b. Isparta, Turkey, May 25, 1967; PhD, Ege U. Sch. Dentistry, 1996. Prof., dept. periodontology Ege U. Sch. Dentistry, 2007. Office: Ege University Sch Dentistry Dept Periodontology Izmir 35100 Turkey Office Fax: 90-232-3880325. Business E-Mail: nurcan.buduneli@ege.edu.tr.

BUDWAY, RAYE J., surgeon; MD, MCP Hahnemann U., 1988. Diplomate Am. Bd. of Surgery-surg. critical care, Am. Bd. of Surgery-gen. surgery. Intern Western Pa. Hosp., 1989, resident, 1993; fellow Univ. of Pitts. Med. Ctr., 1995; dir. site surg. clerkship program Temple Univ. Med. Sch.; site program dir. gen. surgery residency program Allegheny Gen. Hosp.; dir. surg. breast disease program Western Pa. Hosp., dir. surg. intensive care. Named a top dr., Pitts. Mag., 2011. Fellow: ACS. Office: St Clair Hospital 1050 Bower Hill Rd Ste 302 Pittsburgh PA 15243 Office Phone: 412-942-5600.

BUDZYNSKA, BARBARA, medical researcher; b. Lublin, July 17, 1978; PhD, Med. U. Lublin, 2002. Rschr. Med. U. Lublin, 2002—. Mem.: Polish Neurosci. Soc. Office: Chodzki 4A Lublin 20-093 Poland Business E-Mail: basia.budzynska@umlub.pl.

BUECHE, MATTHEW J., orthopedist; married; 2 children. BS, Univ. Mich., 1980, MD, 1984. Cert. Am. Bd. Orthopaedic Surgery. Internship Univ. Mich., 1984—85, residency, 1985—89; fellowship Texas Scottish Rite Hosp., Dallas, 1989—90; pediatric orthopaedist M&M Orthopaedics, Naperville, Ill. Fellow: Am. Acad. Orthopaedic Surgery; mem.: Am. Acad. Pediatrics, Scoliosis Rsch. Soc., Pediat. Orthop. Soc. North America (bd. dirs. 2006—), Phi Beta Kappa. Office: M&M Orthopaedics Ste 101 1259 Rickert Dr Naperville IL 60540 *

BUEHLER, KEVIN J., pharmaceutical executive; BS, Carroll U., Waukesha, Wis. Retail mgmt. position Snyder Drug Stores; sales positions The Gillette Co.; regional sales mgr. consumer products divsn Alcon Inc., 1984, nat. accounts mgr., dir. nat. accounts, dir. sales and mktg., dir. US Managed Care and Falcon Generic Pharm. groups, 1996—98, v.p. US Managed Care and Falcon Generic Pharm. groups, 1998, v.p., gen. mgr. US consumer products divsn., 1999, v.p., regional mgr. Latin America and Caribbean, 2002, area v.p. Latin America, Can., Australia and Far East, sr. v.p. global markets, chief mktg. officer, pres., CEO, 2009—11; divsn. head Alcon Novartis, 2011—. Mem. exec. com. Novartis, 2011—. Office: Alcon Inc B-sch 69 6331 Hunenberg Switzerland *

BUESSELER, JOHN AURE, ophthalmologist, management consultant; b. Madison, Wis., Sept. 30, 1919; s. John Xavier and Gerda Pernille (Aure) B.; m. Cathryn Anne Hansen, Dec. 26, 1959; 1 child, John McGlone. PhB, U. Wis., 1941, MD, 1944; MBA, U. Mo., 1965; DHL (hon.), Rawls Coll. Bus., Tex. Tech. U., Lubbock, 2005. Intern Cleve. City Hosp., 1944-45; resident U. Pa. Hosp., 1948-51; practice medicine specializing in ophthalmology Madison, 1953-59; prof., founding chief ophthalmology U. Mo., Columbia, 1959-66, chmn. dept. surgery, 1960-61; exec. officer Mo. Crippled Children's Service, 1967-70; exec. dir. Kansas City Gen. Hosp. and Med. Ctr., 1969-70; founding dean Tex. Tech U. Sch. Medicine, Lubbock, 1970-73, founding v.p. health affairs Univ. Complex, 1970-75, prof. dept. ophthalmology, prof. health orgn. mgmt., 1971-98, founding chmn. dept. health orgn. mgmt., 1971—75, prof. grad. sch. faculty, 1972-80, chmn. dept. ophthalmology, 1973-75; adj. prof. bus. adminstrn. Coll. Bus. Tex. Tech., Lubbock, 1992-98. Univ. prof. (disting. and multi-disciplinary) Univ. Complex, 1973-98; founding v.p., CEO Tex. Tech. Univ. Health Scis. Ctr., 1971-74; pres. Radiol. Testing Lab., Inc., Madison, 1956-59; dir. House of Vision, Inc., Chgo., 1973-82; v.p. Madison Radiation Ctr., Inc., 1956-59; cons. NASA, mem. space medicine adv. group on devel. Orbiting Space Lab., Washington, 1963-66; cons. AEC, mem. Assn. Midwestern Univs.-Argonne (Ill.) Nat. Lab. biology com., 1965-69; cons. to pres. Argonne Univs. Assn., Chgo., 1967-68; comdr. 94th Gen. Hosp., U.S. Army Res., Mesquite, Tex., 1973-75; co-founder, incorporator, bd. dirs., past pres. Joint Commn. on Allied Health Pers. in Ophthalmology, Inc.; mem. Residency Rev. Com. for Ophthalmology, 1974-80, chmn., 1978-80; sr. cons., CEO, founder Health Orgn. Mgmt. Sys. Internat., 1978—; co-founder, founding chmn., chmn. bd. dirs. Tex. Aviation Heritage Found., Inc., 1997-99; co-founder, founding chmn., chmn. bd. dirs. Silent Wings Mus. Found., Inc., 2003-06. Contbr. articles to profl. jours. Served to capt. AUS, World War II, ETO; to maj. USAF, Korea; to col. USAR, Vietnam. Decorated Air medal with cluster, Legion of Merit; recipient Gold Medallion award for disting. achievement in ophthalmology Mo. Ophthal. Soc., 1967, Tex. Tech. U. Bd. Regents Resolution of Congratulations, 1973, Cert. of Citation Tex. Ho. of Reps., 1973, 87, Disting. Alumnus citation U. Wis. Sch. Medicine, 1987, Statesmanship award Joint Commn. on Allied Health Personnel in Ophthalmology, Inc., 2005 Fellow ACS, Am. Acad. Ophthamology (Disting. Svc. in Edn. award 1969); mem. AMA, Tex. Med. Assn., Mo. Ophthal. Soc. (founder, past sec.-treas., pres., dir.), Alpha Omega Alpha. Home: 3305 59th St Lubbock TX 79413-5517 Office Phone: 806-792-2974. *

BUETOW, DENNIS EDWARD, physiologist, educator; b. Chgo., June 20, 1932; s. Earl Frank and Helen Anna (Roeske) Buetow; m. Mary Kathleen Carney, Oct. 29, 1960; children: Katherine, Thomas-(dec.), Michael, Ellen. BA, UCLA, 1954, MS, 1957, PhD, 1959. Biologist NIH, Bethesda, Md., 1959-65; biochemist Balt. City Hosps., 1959-65; assoc. prof. physiology U. Ill., Urbana, 1965-70, prof., 1970—2000, head dept. physiology and biophysics, 1983-88, prof. emeritus, 2000—. Cons. in field. Contbr. articles to profl. jours. Grantee, NIH, NSF, Life Ins. Med. Rsch. Fund, Am. Heart Assn., USDA. Fellow: AAAS, Gerontol. Soc.; mem.: Am. Soc. Plant Biology, Am. Fedn. Aging Rsch., Soc. Protozoologists, Am. Physiol. Soc., Am. Soc. Cell Biology. Home: 2 Eton Ct Champaign IL 61820-7602 Office: Univ Ill 524 Burrill Hall Urbana IL 61801

BUETOW, KENNETH H., medical geneticist; BA in biology, Indiana U., 1980; PhD in human genetics, U. Pitts., 1985. With Fox Chase Cancer Ctr., Phila., 1986—98; dir. Ctr. Bioinformatics and Info. Tech. Ctr. Cancer Rsch., Nat. Cancer Inst., NIH, chief Lab. Population Genetics. Office: Nat Cancer Inst Ste 6000 2115 E Jefferson St Bethesda MD 20892 Office Phone: 301-435-1520. Office Fax: 301-435-8963. E-mail: buetowke@mail.nih.gov. *

BUFALINO, VINCENT JOHN, cardiologist, medical administrator; b. Chgo., May 29, 1952; m. Joan Bufalino; 2 children. BS in Biology magna cum laude, Loyola U., 1974; MD, Loyola U. Stritch Sch. Medicine, 1977. Cert. internal medicine, cardiovasc. disease. Intern and resident, internal medicine and cardiology Loyola Stritch Sch. Medicine; fellow to chief fellow, cardiovascular disease Loyola U. Foster McGaw Hosp.; pres., CEO Midwest Heart Specialists, chmn. bd., Midwest Heart Found.; med. dir., cardiologist Edward Heart Hosp., Naperville, Ill. Mem. practicing physicians adv. coun. HHS, 2006—, chmn. practicing physicians adv. coun., 2008—. Named to Chgo. Area Entrepreneurship Hall of Fame, 2008. Mem.: Am. Coll. of Cardiology (fellow), Am. Heart Assn. (past pres. Greater Midwest Affiliate, mem. nat. bd. dirs., chmn. advocacy coord. com., chmn., reimbursement access and coverage task force, mem. expert panel on disease mgmt., mem. steering com., Get With the Guidelines, chmn. ambulatory adv. working group, Physician of the Year Award 1997, Chmn.'s Award for Excellence in Vol. Leadership 2005, Gold Heart Award 2008, Am. Heartsaver Long Havil award 2002), DuPage County Med. Soc. (bd. dirs.). Office: Midwest Heart Specialists Edward Heart Hosp 4th Fl 801 S Washington St Naperville IL 60566

BUFFALO, ELIZABETH A., medical educator, researcher; BA magna cum laude, Wellesley Coll., 1988—92; vis. student, U. Oxford, 1990—91; MA in Philosophy, U. Calif., San Diego, 1993—95, PhD in Neuroscience, 1996—98; postdoc. tng., NIH, 1998—2005, NIMH, 1998—2005. Undergraduate rsch. asst., dept. Exptl. Psychology Oxford Univ., England, 1990—91; undergraduate rsch. asst. Wellesley Coll., 1992; rsch. asst., dept. Univ. of Calif., San Diego, 1993—98; intramural rsch. fellow, lab. Neuropsychology NIMH, 1998—2004;

asst. prof. Neurology at Yerkes Nat. Primate Rsch. Ctr. Emory Univ. Sch. of Medicine. Recipient Nat. Insts. of Health Intramural Rsch. Tng. award, 1998—2005; co-recipient Troland Rsch. award, NAS, 2011; grantee Predoctoral Humanities Fellowship, Univ. of Calif., San Diego, 1993—97; fellow McDonnell-Pew Ctr. for Cognitive Neuroscience, San Diego, 1994—98. Achievements include innovative, multidisciplinary study of the hippocampus and the neural basis of memory. Office: Yerkes National Primate Research Center 954 Gatewood Rd NE Atlanta GA 30329 Office Phone: 404-727-9294, 404-712-9431. E-mail: Buffalo@emory.edu.

BUFFET, PIERRE, physician, researcher; b. Boulogne-Billancourt, France, Mar. 19, 1965; MD, Paris U., 1995, PhD, 2000. Head, med. ctr. Inst. Pasteur, 2001—04; asst. prof. Paris U., Assistance Publique Hôsp. Paris, 2007—. Adviser WHO, 2010; cons. Sanofi-Aventis, 2010. Recipient Jean Mérieux award, Fondation Mérieux, 1999, Bourse Lavoisier award, French Ministry Fgn. Affairs, SFP award, French Soc. Parasitology, 2001, award, US Army Med. Materiel Devel. Activity, 2004. Mem.: Am. Soc. Tropical Medicine & Hygiene, Société Française de Parasitologie. Home: 63 Ave de Saint Mandé Paris 75012 France Personal E-mail: pierre.buffet@psl.aphp.fr.

BUFFLER, PATRICIA ANN, education educator; b. Doylestown, Pa., Aug. 1, 1938; d. Edward M. and Evelyn G. (Axenroth) Happ; m. Richard T. Buffler, Jan. 20, 1962; children: Martyn R., Monique L. BSN, Cath. U. America, 1960; M in Health Adminstrn. & Epidemiology, U. Calif., Berkeley, 1965, PhD in Epidemiology, 1973. Prof. epidemiology sch. pub. health U. Tex. Health Sci. Ctr., Houston, 1979—91; dean emerita, Sch., Pub. Health University of California, Berkeley, 1991—98, prof., epidemiology, 1991—. Bd. dirs. FMC Corp.; advisor US Pub. Health Svc. Centers for Disease Control & Prevention, US Dept. of Def., US Environ. Protection Agy., Nat. Insts. of Health; chmn. Societal Inst. of Math. Scis.; mem. NAS, Nat. Coun. Radiation Protection; advisor, mem. expert adv. panel on occupl. health WHO, 1985—2002; bd. sci. counselors Nat. Inst. for Occupl. Safety and Health, 1991—93; mem. adv. panel on mng. nuc. materials from warheads U.S. Congress Office Tech. Assessment, 1992—93; advisor, mem., bd. on water sci. & tech. Nat. Rsch. Coun., 1992—94; mem. Nat. Commn. on Superfund, Keystone Ctr., 1992—94; advisor, mem. environment, safety & health adv. com. US Dept. Of Energy, 1992—95; chair, bd. dirs. Mickey Leland Nat. Urban Air Toxics Rsch. Ctr., 1994—97; mem. Nat. Adv. Coun. on Environ. Health Scis., 1995—98; mem. sci. adv. bd. radiation adv. com. subcom. on cancer risks associated with electric & magnetic fields US Environ. Protection Agy., 1990—93, mem. sci. adv. bd., 1996—98. Contbr. articles to profl. jours. Pres. Soc. for Epidemiological Rsch., 1986, Am. Coll. of Epidemiology, 1992, Internat. Soc. for Environ. Epidemiology, 1992—93, Inst. of Medicine, 1994, Nat. Acad. of Sciences, 1994; fellow Am. Assn. for the Advancement of Sci., 1992, officer, med. sciences sect., 1994—2000. Fellow: AAAS, Inst. Medicine of NAS, Am. Coll. Epidemiology (pres.-elect 1990—91, pres. 1991—92); mem.: APHA (epidemiology sect, 1964—), Internat. Soc. for Environ. Epidemiology (pres.-elect 1989—91, pres. 1992—94), Soc. of Toxicology, Internat. Commn. on Occupl. Health, Internat. Soc. for Exposure Assessment (charter, bd. internat. councillors 1993—98), Internat. Epidemiol. Assn. (treas. 2008—), Soc. for Occupl. and Environ. Health, Am. Epidemiol. Soc., Soc. for Epidemiol. Rsch. (pres.-elect, pres., past pres. 1984—88), Collegium Ramazzini (mem .Nat. Bd. Pub. Health Examiners 2005—). Office: University of California 200 California Hall 3c 1500 Berkeley CA 94720-1500 Office Phone: 510-642-6000. Business E-Mail: patricia.buffler@fmc.com. *

BUFFUM, ROCKY ALLEN, medical association administrator; s. David M. and Juanita L. Buffum. AS in Paramedic Sci., Ivy Tech. CC, Kokomo, Ind., 2006; BA in Psychology, Am. Pub. U., Charles Town, W.Va., 2008; MPA, Am. Pub. U., 2009. Cert. DSPMA, 2011. Emergency response instr. Kokomo Area Career Ctr., Ind., 2006—; instr., trainer ARC, Kokomo, 2007—; exec. dir. Cass County Chapter American Red Cross, 2009—. Dir., emergency med. svcs. Harrison Twp., Kokomo, 2003—06. Coun. com. mem. Boy Scouts America, Kokomo, 2007—; vol. Grissom Air Mus., Kokomo, 1995—2004; mem. Phi Theta Kappa, Kokomo, 2005—06, Golden Key Honour Soc., Charles Town, 2008—. Recipient Eagle Scout, Boy Scouts America, 2001, Leader's Tng. award, 2007—08, Most Improved award, Harrison Twp. Trustee, 2004; James E. West fellow, Boy Scouts America, 2007. Mem.: Internat. Assn. Emergency Mgr., Loyal Order Moose, Nat. Eagle Scout Assn. Avocations: camping, reading, travel, history. Office: American Red Cross Cass County Chapter 120 W Market St Logansport IN 46947-3339 Business E-Mail: rqbuffun@casswhite.redcross.org.

BUHAC, IVO, gastroenterologist; b. Dubrovnik, Croatia, Sept. 4, 1926; s. Ivan and Blazenka (Dulcic) B.; m. Susanne Rossband, Sept. 14, 1963; 1 child, John. MD, U. Med. Sch., Zagreb, Croatia, 1952, ScD, 1963; MD, U. Med. Sch., Erlangen, Germany, 1962. Staff physician Hosp. O. Novosel, Zagreb, 1957-68; resident in gastroenterology VA Hosp., Richmond, Va., 1968-70; asst. prof. medicine Albany (N.Y.) Med. Coll., 1970-74, assoc. prof. medicine, 1974-82, prof. medicine, 1982-88, chief of gastroenterology, 1970-88. Contbr. articles to Gastroenterology, Hepatology, N.Y. State Jour. Medicine, Deutsche Medizinische Wochenschrift. Mem. Am. Gastroenterology Assn., Am. Assn. for Study of Liver Diseases, N.Y. Acad. Scis. Achievements include research on the pathophysiology of ascites formation in liver cirrhosis, diagnosis of disease causing death of Herod the Great. Home: 82 Robinwood Dr Clifton Park NY 12065-2737 E-mail: ibuhac@nycap.rr.com.

BUHAIN, WILFRIDO JAVIER, medical educator; b. Bacoor, Cavite, Philippines, Oct. 12, 1940; m. Carlota Torres; children: Ronald, Edgar. AA, BS, U. Philippines, 1959, MD, 1964. Diplomate Am. Bd. Internal Medicine, Am. Bd. Pulmonary Diseases. Rsch. fellow in cardiology U. Philippines, Philippine Gen. Hosp., 1964-65; rotating intern Queens Hosp. Ctr., NYC, 1965-66, resident in internal medicine, 1965-68; clin. fellow in pulmonary diseases Hosp. of U. Pa., 1968-69, chief pulmonary function lab. dept. medicine, 1971-72; rsch. fellow in pulmonary diseases Hosp. of U. Pa., VA Hosp., Phila., 1969-71; assoc. in medicine, cardiovascular-pulmonary div. med. dept. U. Pa. Sch. Medicine, 1971-72; assoc. in medicine, dept. medicine Mt. Sinai Sch. Medicine, CUNY, 1972-74; clin. instr. medicine Georgetown U., 1976-95; ret. Chief pulmonary function lab. dept. medicine Mt. Sinai Hosp. Svcs./City Hosp. Ctr. at Elmhurst, 1973-74; med. dir. respiratory therapy dept. Mt. Vernon Hosp., 1978—2003, chmn. dept. medicine, 1987-88, pres. med. staff, 1996-98; mem. exec. com. Alexandria Hosp., 1983; trustee, chmn. med. affairs coun. Inova Health Sys., 1998-99. Contbr. articles to profl. jours. Grantee, Queensborough Soc., Pa. Thoracic Soc. Fellow ACP, Am. Coll. Chest Physicians; mem. Alexandria Med. Soc., Va. Med. Soc., Philippine Med. Assn. (exec. dir., past pres. Metro-Washington), Assn. Philippine Physicians in Am. (v.p.). Avocations: tennis, golf, ballroom dancing.

BUHL, KEVIN J., biologist; b. Milw., Dec. 17, 1952; BA, St. Mary's U., Winona, Minn., 1975; MA in Biology, U. SD, 1991. Rsch. fish biologist US Geol. Survey, 1995—. Grad. student com. St. Cloud State U., Minn., 2010. Recipient STAR award, US Geol. Survey. Mem.: Soc. Environ. Toxicology and Chemistry. Avocations: motorcycling, gardening. Office: USGS 31247 436th Ave Yankton SD 57078 Office Fax: 605-665-9335. Business E-Mail: kevin_buhl@usgs.gov.

BUHNER, BYRON BEVIS, health science facility administrator; b. Hammond, Ind., Feb. 19, 1950; s. John Colin and Betty (Bevis) B.; children: Zachery Aaron, Rebecca Bevis. AB in Comm., Ind. U., 1976, MS in Human Resource Devel., 1981. Adminstr. Ind. U., Indpls., 1976-77, instr. evaluator sch. nursing, 1981-82; tng. specialist Ayr-Way, Target Stores, Indpls., 1977-81; assoc. exec. dir. Cen. Ind. Regional Blood Ctr., Indpls., 1984-88, pres., chief exec. officer, 1988—; founding mem. Blood Ctrs. Ins. Exch., Risk Retention Group, 1993, chmn. bd. dirs., 1993-96, dir., 1996—2006; adminstr. Blood Rsch. and Edn. Foundn. of Ind., Inc., Indpls., 1985-89, bd. mem., 1989-94. Dean's adv. coun. Ind. U. Sch. Liberal Arts, 1999—2006; bd. dirs. Irwin Union Bank & Trust, Hamilton County. Producer: Multi-Image film, Focus on Transition, 1981, A Manager's Perspective, 1981; photographer: Sound, Slide program, Wearable - Arts '81. Trustee Coun. Cmty. Blood Ctrs., 1986-97, chmn. purchasing com., 1988-92, chmn. fin. com., treas., 1992-94, v.p., 1994-96, pres., 1997-99, chmn. exec. com., chmn. group svcs. com., chmn. long-range planning com. Mem. Am. Acad. Healthcare Execs. (diplomate), Ind. U. Alumni Assn. (bd. dirs. 1983-88), Am. Assn. Blood Banks, Ind. Assn. Blood Banks (bd. dirs. 1988-91). Avocations: sailing, jogging, hockey, photography, coaching youth sports. Home: 13002 Fairfax Ct Mc Cordsville IN 46055 Office: Indiana Blood Ctr 3450 N Meridian St Indianapolis IN 46208-4437 Office Phone: 317 916 5001. Business E-Mail: bbuhner@indianablood.org.

BUHR, JURGEN CARL PETER, internist; b. Butzow, Mecklenburg, Germany, Mar. 3, 1943; s. Herman Carl Peter and Elsa Auguste Marie Frieda Buhr; m. Marion Roswitha Muller, Oct. 1, 1971; children: Silvia, Herwig. MD, U. Rostock, Germany, 1969. Study physician U. Rostock, 1962—68, learning specialist internist Butzow, 1969—73; learning specialist diabetology Berlin Diabetic Officer, 1973—76; internist, diabetological specialist Med. Ctr., Butzow, 1976—84, leader, 1984—90; rschr. U. Dresden, 1984—90; physican cons. Kreispoliklinic, Butzow, 1984—90; pvt. practice Butzow, 1991—; examination physician Mecklenburg, 1992—. Lectr. in field. Author: 23 articles in med. periodicals. Leader commn. of diabetes Orgn. Physicians in Country Mecklenburg, Schwerin, 1998—. Mem.: German Diabetological Orgn. Avocations: philosophy, astronomy, nature, travel. Home and Office: Am Ausfall 43 18246 Butzow Germany Office Phone: 0049 38461 2422.

BUI, DUC, surgeon, educator; b. Vietnam, Jan. 25, 1970; MD, Cornell U., 1995. Assoc. prof. surgery Stony Brook U. Med. Ctr., 2004. Office: HSC T-19 Rm 060 Stony Brook NY 11794 Business E-Mail: duc.bui@stonybrook.edu.

BUIST, NEIL ROBERTSON MACKENZIE, pediatric educator, medical association administrator; b. Karachi, India, July 11, 1932; m. Sonia Chapman; children: Catriona, Alison, Diana. Degree with commendation, U. St. Andrews, Scotland, MB, ChB, 1956; Diploma of Child Health, London U., England, 1960. Diplomate Am. Bd. Med. Genetics, Am. Bd. Clinical Genetics. House physician internal medicine Arbroath Infirmary, 1956-57; house physician externe cardiopulmonary dept. Hosp. Marie Lannelongue, Paris, 1957; house surgeon Royal Hosp. Sick Children, Edinburgh, Scotland, 1957; commd. far east med. officer Regimental Military Svc., 1957-60; house physician Royal Infirmary, Dundee, Scotland, 1960; registrar internal medicine Maryfield Hosp., Dundee, Scotland, 1960-62; lectr. child health U. St. Andrews, Dundee, Scotland, 1962-64; rsch. fellow pediatric microchemistry, Sch. Health Sci. U. Colo., Denver, 1964-66; asst. prof. pediatrics, Sch. Medicine U. Oreg., Portland, 1966-70; dir. Pediatrics Metabolic Lab, Oreg. Health Sci. U., Portland, 1966-93, Metabolic Birth Defects Ctr., Oreg. Health Sci. U., Portland, 1966-98; assoc. prof. pediat. and med. genetics Oreg. Health Sci. U., Portland, 1970—76, prof. pediat. and med. genetics, 1976—98, prof. emeritus. Med. cons. Northwest Regional Newborn Screening Program, Portland, 1970—; vis. prof. WHO, China, 1988, U. Colo., 1990, Wesley Med. Ctr., Kans., 1991, Phoenix Children's Hosp., Ariz., 1991, Tucson Med. Ctr., Ariz., 1991, U. Ill., Chgo., 1991, Kapoiolani Med. Ctr., Hawaii, 1992, Shriners Hosp. for Crippled Children., Hawaii, 1992, Ark. Children's Hosp., 1993, Australasian Soc. for Human Genetics, New Zealand, 1994, LBJ Med. Ctr., Americas Samoa, 1994, Mahidol U., Bangkok, 1996, U. P.R., 1996, U. Auckland (New Zealand), 1997, Ctrl. Valley Children's Hosp., 1996-, U. Rochester, 2004, emergency disaster response physician, N.W. Med. Teams Internat., Afghanistan, 2002, Ethiopia, 2004, Sri Lanka, 2005. Author: (with others) Textbook of Pediatrics, 1973, Inherited Disorders of Amino Acid Metabolism, 1974, 1985, Clinics in Endocrinolog and Metabolism: Aspects of Neonatal Metabolism, 1976, Textbook of Pediatrics, 1978, Practice of Pediatrics, 1980, Management of High-Risk Pregnancy, 1980, Current Occular Therapy, 1980, Practice of Pediatrics, 1981, Clinics in Endocrinology and Metabolism: Aspects of Neonatal Metabolism, 1981, Textbook of Pediatrics, 1984, Disorders of Fatty Acid Metabolism in the Pediatric Practice, 1990, Birth Defects Encyclopedia, 1990, 1991, Treatment of Genetic Disease, 1991, Pediatric Clinics of North Americs Medical Genetics II, 1992, Forfar & Arneil's Textbook of Paediatrics, 1992, 97, 2007, Galactosemia New Frontiers in Research, 1993, New Horizons in Neonatal Screening, 1994, New Trends in Neonatal Screening, 1994, Alpha-1-Antitrypsin Deficiency, 1994, Diseases of the Fetus and Newborn, 1995, Inborn Metabolic Diseases: Diagnosis and Treatment, 1995; cons. editor: Inborn Metabolic Disease Text, 1995; editorial bd. mem.: Jour. of Inherited Metabolic Diseases, 1977—2005, Kelley Practice of Pediatrics, 1980-87, Screening, 1991-96; jour. reviewer: Am. Jour. of Human Genetics, Jour. of Pediatrics, Pediatric Rsch., Screening. Adv. com. Tri County March of Dimes, Portland, 1977—; physician Diabetic Children's Camp, 1967—, Muscle Biopsy Clinic Shriners Hosp., 1989—; bd. dirs. Mize Info. Enterprises, Dallas, 1987—. Fellow Royal Coll. Physicians Edinburgh, Fogarty Internat. Vis. Scientist, Royal Coll. Physicians Edinburgh; mem. Brit. Med. Assn., Western Soc. Pediatric Rsch. (coun. mem. 1966—69), Pacific North West Pediatric Soc., Am. Pediatric Soc., Soc. for the Study of Inborn Errors of Metabolism, Soc. for Inherited Metabolic Disorders (treas. 1977-2000, pres. 2000-02), Oreg. Pediatric Soc., Oreg. Diabetes Assn., Portland Acad. Pediatrics, Internat. Newborn Screening Soc. Coun. (founding mem. 1988—). Avocations: fishing, gardening, travel.

BUJA, L. MAXIMILIAN, pathologist, academic administrator, educator; b. New Orleans, Dec. 30, 1942; s. Louis Marcus and Fay Maxine (Kofler) B.; m. Donna Steele Kinney, Apr. 7, 1966; children: Maximilian Kinney, Evan Louis, Gregory James. BS in Biology magna cum laude, Loyola U., New Orleans, 1964; MD with honors, Tulane U., 1967, MS in Anatomy, 1968. Diplomate Am. Bd. Pathology. Resident in pathology Nat. Cancer Inst./NIH, Bethesda, Md., 1970—72; sr. investigator pathology Nat. Heart and Lung Inst./NIH, Bethesda, Md., 1972—74; asst. prof. pathology U. Tex. Health Sci. Ctr. at Dallas, 1974—77, assoc. prof. pathology, 1977—81; prof. pathology U. Tex. Southwestern Med. Ctr. at Dallas, 1981—89, acting chmn. dept. pathology, 1988—89; prof. pathology and lab. medicine U. Tex. Health Sci. Ctr. at Houston, 1989—, chmn. dept. pathology and lab. medicine, 1989—96; chmn. dept. clin. lab. scis. U. Tex.-Houston Health Sci. Ctr., 1993—96, disting. chair pathology and lab. med., 1995—, dean, 1996—2003, exec. v.p. acad. affairs, 2003—, H. Wayne Hightower disting. prof. in med. scis., 2000—03; chief of svc. clin. pathology lab. Hermann Hosp., Houston, 1989—96; pathologist-in-chief clin. pathology lab. Lyndon Baines Johnson Gen. Hosp., Houston, 1990—96; prof. lab. medicine U. Tex. Anderson Cancer Ctr., Houston, 1990—. Lectr. pathology; mem. autopsy svc.; mem. Tex. Heart Inst. St. Luke's Episcopal Hosp., Houston, 1989—, dir. Cardiovascular Pathology Rsch., 1989—95, chief cardiovasc. pathology, 2000—; 1st Chancellor's Health fellow in edn. U. Tex. System; cons. in field. Author (with Hillis and Willerson): Ischemic Heart Disease-Clinical and Pathophysiological Aspects, 1982; author: (with others) Calcium Antagonists and Cardiovascular Disease, 1984; author: Physiology and Pathophysiology of the Heart, 1984, Cardiovascular Imaging, 1991, Cardiovascular Medicine, 1995; co-author: Netter's Illustrated Human Pathology, 2005; contbg. editor: Clin. Nuc. Cardiology, 1979; mem. editl. bd. Am. Jour. Cardiovascular Pathology, 1985—95, Am. Jour. Cardiology, 1982—88, 1999—, Am. Jour. Pathology, 1980—92, Archives of Pathology and Lab. Medicine, 1985—96, assoc. editor, 2006—, mem. editl. bd. Cardiovascular Pathology, 1991—, Circulation, 1983—88, Circulation Rsch., 1990—99, Lab. Investigation, 1984—2005, Tex. Medicine, 1984—87, Exptl. Molecular Pathology, 1999—, Jour. Am. Coll. Cardiology, 2000—04, Jour. Burns, 2001; assoc. editor: Circulation, 1993—2004; contbr. articles to profl. jours. Surgeon with USPHS, 1968-74. Recipient Joseph Diaz award Loyola U., Order of the Gold-Tipped Stethoscope award Tulane U., John Herr Musser Meml. prize; Sabbatical fellow German Sci. Found., U. Cologne, West Germany, 1988; grantee NIH, 1979, 80, 81, 84, 86-87, 89-90, 93-98, U. Tex., 1993—. Fellow: AAAS, Internat. Soc. for Heart Rsch., Am. Heart Assn. (fellow coun. on basic sci. on clin. cardiology, on atherosclerosis, on circulation, inaugural fellow basic cardiovasc. scis.), Am. Coll. Cardiology; mem.: AMA, U.S. and Can. Acad. Pathology, Tex. Soc. Microscopy, So. Soc. for Clin. Investigation, Soc. Exec. Leadership in Acad. Medicine, Histochem. Soc., Assn. Am. Med. Colls. (coun. deans 1996—2003), Am. Soc. Clin. Pathologists, Am. Soc. Clin. Investigation, Tex. Soc. Pathologists (pres. 1998, George T. Caldwell, M.D. Disting. Svc. award 2005), Tex. Med. Assn., Soc. Cardiovasc. Pathology (Merit award 1998), Internat. Acad. Pathology, Houston Soc. Clin. Pathologists (pres. 1995—96, Harlan J. Spjut award 1997), Harris County Med. Soc. (bd. dirs. 1997—), Coll. Am. Patholigsts, Am. Soc. Cell Biology, Am. Fedn. Med. Rsch., Am. Coll. Healthcare Execs. (assoc.), ACP Execs., Am. Soc. Investigative Pathology, Houston Philos. Soc., Sigma Xi Sci., Beta Beta Beta, Alpha Omega Alpha. Achievements include rsch. on cardiovascular pathology; on mechanisms of cell injury, with emphasis on cell membrane integrity and intracellular electrolyte balance; on measurement of intracellular electrolytes, electron probe x-ray microanalysis and fluorescent probes; on the devel. and regenerative potential of cardiac muscle. Office: U Tex Health Sci Ctr 7000 Fannin St Ste 1715 Houston TX 77030-1501 Office Phone: 713-500-3062.

BUJAK, DENISE A., accountant, insurance company executive; BA in Acctg., St. Ambrose U., Davenport, Iowa. CPA. Auditor Ernst & Young; various positions with Health Care Svc. Corp., Chgo., 1976—, sr. v.p., CFO, 2002—. Mem.: Chgo. Fin. Exch., Am. Soc. Women CPAs, Ill. CPA Soc., AICPA. Office: Health Care Service Corporation 300 E Randolph St Chicago IL 60601 Office Phone: 312-653-6000. Office Fax: 312-938-4209. *

BUKEN, NUKET ORNEK, physician, educator; b. Ankara, Turkey, Jan. 30, 1967; d. Cemil and Saime Ornek; m. Nuket Ornek, May 4, 1991; children: Kivilcim Ceren, Alp Eren. MD, Ankara U., 1990, PhD in Deontology, 2000. Intern Ankara U. Avicenna Hosp.; gen. practitioner emergency svc. Gazi U. Med. Faculty Hosp., Ankara, 1990—92; physician Ministry of Law, Ankara, 1992—2000; lectr. dept. deontology, med. ethics and med. hist. Hacettepe U., Ankara, 2000—. Cons. Chamber Medicine Ankara, 1996—. Master: Turkish Soc. Bioethics (assoc.); mem.: Turkish Bioethics Assn. Independent Thinkers. Islam. Avocations: travel, swimming. Home: Koza St 114-57 Cankaya Ankara 06700 Turkey Office: Hacettepe Univ Faculty Medicine Sihhiye Ankara 06100 Turkey Office Fax: 903123100580; Home Fax: 903124471328. Personal E-mail: nuketbuken@hotmail.com. Business E-Mail: buken@hacettepe.edu.tr.

BUKHARI, IQBAL ABDULAZIZ, dermatologist, consultant, researcher, educator; d. Abdulaziz Ali and Fatma Muhammad (Kashgari) Bukhari; m. Mufareh O. AlZahrani, July 21, 1985; children: Othman Mufareh AlZahrani, Abdulaziz Mufareh AlZahrani, Muhannad Mufareh AlZahrani, Farah Mufareh AlZahrani, Marah Mufareh AlZahrani. MBBS, King Faisal U. Coll. Medicine, Saudi Arabia, 1989. Diplomate Am. Bd. Laser Surgery and Medicine, Boston, 2004. Demonstrator King Faisal U., Dammam, 1990—2001, asst. prof., 2002—05, assoc. prof., 2006—. Cons. dermatologist King Fahad Hosp. U., AlKhobar, 1999—.

BUKOWSKI, ELAINE LOUISE, physical therapist, educator; b. Phila., Feb. 18, 1949; d. Edward Eugene and Melanja Josephine (Przyborowski) B. BS in Phys. Therapy, St. Louis U., 1972; MS, U. Nebr., 1977; D in Phys. Therapy, Drexel U., 2006. Lic. phys. therapist, NJ; diplomate sr. analyst, profl. adv. coun., Am. Bd. Disabilities Analysts, 2010. Clk. City of Phila., 1967; staff phys. therapist St. Louis Chronic Hosp., 1973, Cardinal Ritter Inst., St. Louis, 1973-74; dir. campus ministry musicals Creighton U., Omaha, 1974-75; tchg. asst. U. Nebr. Med. Ctr., Omaha, 1975-76; lectr. in anatomy U. Sci. and Tech., Kumasi, Ghana, 1977-78; chief phys. therapist Holy Family Hosp., Berekum, Ghana, 1978-79; coord. info. & guidance The Am. Cancer Soc., Phila., 1979-81; staff phys. therapist Holy Redeemer Vis. Nurse Assn., Phila., 1981-83, rehab. supr. Swainton, NJ, 1983-87; asst. prof. phys. therapy Richard Stockton Coll. NJ, Pomona, 1987-96, assoc. prof., 1996—2002, prof., 2003—, assoc. dir. post-profl. D of Phys. Therapy program, 2006—10; adv. bd. mem. Sch. Health Scis., 2008—10; dir.profl. post profl. Phys. Therapy Program DPT Program, 2010—. Bd. dirs. The Bridge, Phila., 1979-80; vacation relief phys. therapist, NJ, 1988—; profl. adv. coun. Holy Redeemer VNA, Swainton, 1982-93, chmn., 1985-91, pers. com., cons. hospice program, 1985-87, rehab. cons., 1987-88; legis. adv. coun. subcom. on edn. and health care Cape May & Cumberland Counties, 1988-90; utilization rev. cons. rehab. svcs., 1990; fitness screening team NJ State Legislature, 1990; geriatric rehab. del. Citizen Amb. Program, China, 1992; mid. states accreditation team evaluator, 1997-98. Co-author slide study program, (video) Going My Way? The Low Back Syndrome, 1976; author: Muscular Analysis of Everyday Activities, 2000; contbr. chpts. to book. Vol. Am. Cancer Soc., Phila., 1979-82, Walk-a-Day-in-My Shoes prog. Girl Scouts Am., Cape May County, NJ, 1983-86; task force phys. therapy program Stockton State Coll., Pomona, 1985-88. Recipient Vol. Achievement award, Am. Cancer Soc., 1981, Emeritus Status award, 2010; U.S. Govt. trainee, 1971, 1972, Physical Therapy Fund grantee, 1975—76. Mem. Am. Phys. Therapy Assn. (edn. sect., orthop. sect., vice chmn. so. dist. 1993-96, 99-2001, chmn. 1996-98, bd. dirs., ho. of dels. 1994-97, key contact voting dist. 2, mem. NJ legis. network 1989-96, 1999-2002, mem. mentoring program 1998—, chair nominating com. 2002-04, ethics com. 2007-), Phys. Therapy Club (sec. 1971-72), NJ Phys. Therapy Assn. (rsch. com. 1995-97, ethics com. mem. 2007-, Outstanding Svc. award, 2004). Avocations: gardening, music, reading, poetry. Office: Richard Stockton Coll NJ Physical Therapy Program 101 Vera King Farris Dr Galloway NJ 08205 Office Phone: 609-652-4416. Business E-Mail: elaine.bukowski@stockton.edu.

BULGER, ROGER JAMES, academic administrator; b. Bklyn., May 18, 1933; s. William Joseph and Florence Dorothy (Poggi) B.; m. Ruth Ellen Grouse, June 8, 1960; children: Faith Anne, Grace Ellen. AB, Harvard U., 1955, MD, 1960; postgrad., Cambridge U., Eng., 1955—56; degree (hon.), Thomas Jefferson U., 1995, U. Md., Western U. Health Scis., 1998, Kirkesville U. Osteo. Medicine, 1999, Rush U., 2001. Intern, then resident in internal medicine U. Wash. Hosps., 1960—62; trainee in infectious disease and microbiology U. Wash., 1962—63; renal and metabolic diseases Boston U., 1963—64; from asst. prof. to assoc. prof. medicine U. Wash. Med. Sch., Seattle, 1966—70; med. dir. Univ. Hosp., Seattle, 1967—70; prof. cmty. health scis., dean allied health Duke U. Med. Ctr., 1970—72; exec. officer Inst. Medicine, Nat. Acad. Scis., 1972—76; prof. internal medicine George Washington U. Sch. Medicine, 1972—76; prof. internal medicine, family and community medicine, dean Med. Sch., chancellor Worcester campus U. Mass., 1976—78; pres. U. Tex. Health Sci. Ctr., Houston, 1978—88; pres., CEO Assn. Acad. Health Ctrs., 1988—2005; sr. advisor to Nat. Ctr. for Minority Health and Disparities, NIH, 2006—07. Author: Hippocrates Revisited, 1973, In Search of Modern Hippocrates, 1987, Technology, Bureaucracy and Healing, 1988, Mission Management, 1998, The Quest for Mercy, 1998, Edmund Pellegrino, Philosopher and Physician, 2001, The Honorable Paul G. Rogers, A Portrait of Leadership, 2005; also articles, chpts. in books; mem. editl. bd. various jours. Bd. dirs. Georgetown U., Rsch. Am., Am. Internat. Health Alliance, Medicine/Pub. Health Initiative; chair, bd. trustee Inst. Advancement Multicultured & Minority Medicine, 2008-. Lionel de Jersey Harvard fellow, 1955-56. Fellow ACP, Royal Soc. Medicine, Acad. for Health Svcs. Rsch. (disting.); mem. Inst. Medicine, Infectious Disease Soc. Am., Nat. Acad. Social Ins. Home: 12505 Grey Fox Ln Potomac MD 20854 Office Phone: 301-646-1279. Personal E-mail: rbulger@comcast.net.

BULIC-JAKUS, FLORIANA, medical educator; b. Split, Croatia, Nov. 27, 1955; d. Stjepan Bulic and Olga Wesiag-Bulic; children: Marta Terezija Jakus, Viktorija Kristina Jakus. MD, U. Zagreb, Croatia, 1980, MSc in Natural Scis., 1985, PhD in Medicine, 1990. Lic. physician Croatia, 1981. From rschr. to prof. sch. medicine dept. biology U. Zagreb, 1983—2009, head dept. biology, 1996—, prof. sch. medicine dept. biology, 2007—. Expert Ministry Sci., Edn. and Sports, Zagreb, 2004—09. Recipient 4 Spl. awards, 4th Internat. Exhbtn. Inovations, New Ideas, Products and Techs., Zagreb, 2006, Ljudevit Jurak award, Acad. Med. Scis. Croatia, 2007; grantee, Ministry Sci. and Tech., Croatia, 2002—06, Ministry Sci., Edn. and Sports, Croatia, 2007—; fellow, Karolinska Inst., Cancerfonden, Sweden, 1990—93. Mem.: Croatian Micros. Soc., Croatian Soc. Lab. Animals, Internat. Soc. Devel. Biologists. Achievements include research in serumless culture of postimplantation embryo; mammalian developmental biology; teratogenesis, transplantation, experimental teratoma; tumor suppressor proteins in development. Avocations: music, skiing. Home: K S Gjalskog 36 Zagreb 10 000 Croatia Office: Dept Biology Sch Medicine Salata 3 Zagreb 10 000 Croatia Office Phone: 385-1-4566-807. Business E-Mail: floriana@mef.hr.

BULL, BRIAN STANLEY, pathologist, educator; b. Watford, Hertfordshire, Sept. 14, 1937; arrived in U.S., 1954, naturalized, 1960; s. Stanley and Agnes Mary (Murdoch) B.; m. Maureen Hannah Huse, June 3, 1963; children: Beverly Velda, Beryl Heather. BS in Zoology, Walla Walla Coll., 1957; MD, Loma Linda U., Calif., 1961. Diplomate Am. Bd. Pathology. Intern Yale U., 1961-62, resident in anat. pathology New Haven, 1962-63; resident in clin. pathology NIH, Bethesda, Md., 1963-65, fellow in hematology and electron microscopy, 1965-66, staff hematologist, 1966-67; rsch. asst. dept. anatomy Loma Linda U., 1958, dept. microbiology, 1959, asst. prof. pathology, 1968-71, assoc. prof., 1971-73, prof., 1973—, chmn. dept. pathology, 1973—, chmn. dept. pathology and human anatomy, 1993—, assoc. dean for acad. affairs Sch. Medicine, 1993-94, dean Sch. Medicine, 1994—2003. Cons. mfrs. of med. testing devices; mem. Internat. Commn. Standardization in Hematology, pres., 1997-99; founding dir. CentriHealth, bd. dirs. Mem. bd. editors Blood Cells, Molecules and Diseases, 1985-, editor-in-chief, 1985-94; contbr. chpts. to books, articles to med. jours.; patentee in field; editor-in-chief Blood Cells NY Heidelberg, 1985-94. Editor Understanding Genesis: Contemporary Adventist Perspectives, 2006. Served with USPHS, 1963-67. Nat. Inst. Arthritis and Metabolic Diseases fellow, 1967-68; recipient Merck Manual award, 1961, Mosby Scholarship Book award, 1961; Ernest B. Cotlove Meml. lectr. Acad. Clin. Lab. Physicians and Scientists, 1972; named Alumnus of Yr., Walla Walla Coll., 1984, Loma Linda U. Sch. Medicine Alumni Assn., Honored Alumnus, Loma Linda U. Sch. Medicine, 1987, Humanitarian award, 1991; named Citizen of Yr., Loma Linda C. of C., 1997, President's award, Loma Linda U. Adventist Health Scis. Ctr., 2003, Disting. U. Svc. award Sch. Medicine Loma Linda U., 2003, Inaugural lectr. Houwen Meml. lectr. Internat. Soc. for Lab. Hematology, 2005, Alumnus of Yr. Loma Linda U. Sch. Medicine, 2009. Fellow Am. Soc. Clin. Pathologists, Am. Soc. Hematology, Coll. Am. Pathologists, FDA Panel on Hematology and Pathology Devices, Nat. Com. on Clin. Lab. Stds., NY Acad. Scis.; mem. AMA, Calif. Soc. Pathologists, San Bernadino County Med. Soc. (William C. Cover Outstanding Contbn. to Medicine award 1994), Acad. Clin. Lab. Physicians and Scientists, Am. Assn. Pathologists, Sigma Xi, Alpha Omega Alpha. Adventist. Achievements include patents in field of blood analysis instrumentation; development of quality control algorithms for blood analyzer calibration; origination of techniques and instrumentation for the measurement of thrombosis risk and for regulation of anti-coagulation during cardiopulmonary bypass and solid organ transplantation. Office: LLUMC Rm 2516 11234 Anderson St Loma Linda CA 92354-2871 Office Phone: 909-558-4094. Business E-Mail: bbull@llu.edu.

BULL, W. JOHN, JR., plastic surgeon; m. Monica Bull; children: Johnny, Joey, Alex. Attended in Gen. Studies, La.State U., Baton Rouge, 1987—91; MD, La. State U., New Orleans, 1991—95. Diplomate Am. Bd. of Plastic Surgery, 2002, Am. Bd. of Plastic Surgery, 2004, lic. State of Ga., 2001, State of Ill., 2000. Resident gen. surgery Med. Coll. of Ga., Augusta, 1995—2000; fellow plastic surgery Loyola Univ. Med. Ctr., 2000—03; hosp. affiliation includes Naperville Surg. Ctr., The Ctr. for Surgery, Midwest Day Surgery Ctr.; active staff Rush-Copley Meml. Hosp., Edward Hosp.; plastic surgeon John Bull Ctr. for Cosmetic Surgery and MediSpa. Co-author: (publ.) Typical Versus Atypical Presentation of Obturator Hernia, 2001, Full thickness Burn injury in Wheelchair Bound Patient Case Report and literature review, 2002; author: Reconstruction of Defects of the Cranial Base, Techniques in Neurosurgery, 2003, Preventable Wheelchair-related Thermal Injury, 2005. Vol. medicine clinic for the homeless New Orleans Mission, 1993—95; vol. plastic and reconstructive surgery team Med. Mission, Cusco, Peru, 2002; vol. tattoo removal program Edward hosp., 2003—. Mem.: AMA, Ill. State Med. Soc., DuPage County Med. Soc., Chgo. Soc. of Plastic Surgery, Am.Soc. of Plastic Surgeons, Am. Soc. for Aesthetic Plastic Surgery. Office: The John Bull Center for Cosmetic Surgery and MediSpa 1307 Macin Drive Naperville IL 60564 Office Phone: 630-717-6000.

BULLARBO, MARIA ELSA SUSANN, gynecologist; b. Vora, Finland, May 24, 1958; d. Karl-Erik and Aino Susanna Westerberg; m. Dan Bo Peter Bullarbo, Sept. 12, 1987; children: Daniel Henrik, Andreas Erik Alexander, Josefine Jenny Alexandra. Degree, Uppsala U., Sweden, 1986; MD in Obstetrics & Gynecology, PhD in Obstetrics & Gynecology. Specialist in ob-gyn. Socialstyrelsen, Sweden, 1998. Specialist ob-gyn. Women's Clinic, Ostra Hosp., Gothenburg, Sweden, 2000—. Office: Womens Clinic Boras Hosp 51203 Boras Sweden Office Phone: 46703512780. Business E-Mail: maria.bullarbo@vgregion.se.

BULLARD-BATES, PATRICIA CAROL, psychologist, neuropsychologist; b. Purcell, Okla., Dec. 19, 1949; d. Howard Benjamin and Patricia Gilpin Bullard; m. Harvey Bullard-Bates (dec.); 1 child, Daniel Martin; m. Kent Robert Beduhn, Sept. 22, 2001. BA in Philosophy, Wellesley Coll., Mass., 1971; PhD in Clin. Psychology, Washington U., St. Louis, 1976. Lic. psychologist Washington, Md. Postdoctoral fellow U. Fla., Gainesville, 1976—79; coord. neuropsychology Med. Ctr. Rehab. Hosp., Grand Forks, ND, 1979—81; staff psychologist Royal Ottawa Rehab. Ctr., Ont., Canada, 1981—84, Nat. Rehab. Hosp., Washington, 1987—; cons., staff psychologist St. Vincent Hosp., Ottawa, 1984—87. Pres. Bethany, Inc., Washington, 1993—; activist Ch. of Saviour, Washington, 2005—. Grantee, NIH, 1977—79; scholar, Wellesley Coll., 1967—71. Mem.: APA, Nat. Register Health Svc. Providers in Psychology, Nat. Acad. Neuropsychology, Internat. Neuropsychol. Soc. Democrat. Avocation: jewelry making. Home: 10702 Lombardy Rd Silver Spring MD 20901-1631 Office: Creative Charge Therapy Ctr LLP 10702 Lombardy Rd Silver Spring MD 20901 Office Phone: 202-877-1956.

BULLEN, BRUCE M., insurance company executive; Grad., Williams Coll.; MPA, Harvard U. Commissioner, medicaid program Mass. State Govt.; sr. v.p., COO Harvard Pilgrim Health Care, interim CEO, 2009—10, sr. mgmt. positions; COO Blue Cross Blue Shield of Massachusetts, Inc. Bd. dirs. Neighborhood Health Plan, Boston Healthcare for the Homeless Program, Mass. Found. for the Humanities, Mass. Medicaid Policy Inst., Hebrew Rehabilitation Ctr., Vanguard Med. Associates. Mem.: American Pub. Human Services Assn. (v.p.), Nat. Assn. of State Medicaid Directors (past chmn.). Office: Blue Cross Blue Shield of Massachusetts Inc Landmark Center 401 Park Dr Boston MA 02215 *

BULLENS, DOMINIQUE MA, pediatrician; b. Feb. 13, 1967; married. MD, U. Ghent, Belgium, 1992; PhD, K. U. Leuven, Belgium, 2000. Cons.-rschr. pediat. allergology K. U. Leuven, 2000—. Office: KULeuven Lab Exp Immunol Herestraat 49 3000 Leuven Belgium Office Fax: 32-16-346035. Business E-Mail: dominique.bullens@med.kuleuven.be.

BULLOCK, JOSEPH DANIEL, pediatrician, educator; b. Cin., Jan. 23, 1942; s. Joseph Craven and Emilie (Woide) B.; m. Martha Foss, June 20, 1964; children: Jennifer Zane, Sarah Harrison. BA, Wittenberg U., 1963; MD, Ohio State U., 1967, degree in pediatrics, 1969; degree in immunology, allergy, U. Calif., San Francisco, 1971. Diplomate Am. Bd. Pediat., Am. Bd. Allergy and Immunology. Clin. prof. pediatrics Ohio State U., Columbus, 1971—; pres. Midwest Allergy Assocs., Inc., Worthington, Ohio, 1971—. Contbr. articles to profl. jours. Active fund raising Wittenberg U., Springfield, Ohio, 1980-83, Columbus Sch. for Girls, 1977-86. Served to capt. USAF, 1967-71. Recipient Mead Johnson award, 1965. Fellow Am. Acad. Pediatrics, Am. Acad. Allergy, Am. Coll. Allergists (Bd. Regents 1979-82, Clemens von Pirquet award 1968, 69, 70, 71), Am. Thoracic Soc., Interasma, Ohio Soc. Allergy and Immunology (pres. 1985-87). Clubs: Columbus Country; The Golf (New Albany, Ohio); Indian Creek Country (Miami Beach, Fla.), The Surf (Surfside, Fla.). Republican. Lutheran. Home: 189 N Parkview Ave Columbus OH 43209-1435 Office: 8080 Ravines Edge Ct Columbus OH 43235-5424 Home Phone: 614-258-0404; Office Phone: 614-846-5944. *

BULOTIENE, GIEDRE, psychiatrist; b. Kaunas, Lithuania, Sept. 6, 1961; MD, Vilnius U., 1986; PhD, Inst. Oncology, Vilnius U., 2007. Internship Rep. Vilnius Psychiat. Hosp., 1986—87; psychiatrist Vilnius Ctr. Skin and Venereal Diseases, 1987—90, Vilnius Clin. Psychotherapeutic Ctr., 1990—2000; psyhiatrist Inst. Oncology, Vilnius U., 2000—. Pres. Assn. Psychosocial Oncology, 2007—11, Lithuanian Soc. C G Jung Analytical Psychology, 2000—04. Grant, Sci. Com. St. Gallen Breast Cancer Conf., 2009, 2011, Swiss Nat. Found., 2011, Internat. Psychol. Oncology Soc. Mem.: Lithuanian Soc. Psychoanalysis, Lithuanian Soc. Psychotherapy, Lithuanian Assn. Psychiatrists, Soc. Psychotherapy Rsch., Internat. Psycho-Oncology Soc. Avocations: opera, art. Home: Liepyno 10 - 46 Vilnius 08108 Lithuania Personal E-mail: giebul@yahoo.com.

BUMGARNER, ROBERT L., pathologist, retired military officer; b. Long Branch, Calif., Oct. 15, 1944; BS in Physics, Mich. State U., 1967, MD, 1974. Diplomate in anat. pathology and clin. pathology Am. Bd. Pathology. Commd. ensign USN, 1967, advanced through grades to capt., 1987; intern, resident Naval Med. Ctr., Portsmouth, Va., 1975-79; chief of lab. Naval Submarine Med. Ctr., Groton, 1979-83; dir. Navy Drug Screening Lab., Jacksonville, 1983; force med. officer, commdr. submarine force U.S. Pacific Fleet, 1984-86; dir. for undersea medicine and radiation health USN, Washington, 1986-91; dir., commdg. officer Armed Forces Radiobiology Rsch. Inst., Bethesda, Md., 1991-95; dir. ancillary svcs. Naval Med. Ctr., San Diego, 1995-99; fleet surgeon U.S. Pacific Fleet, 1999—2001; prin. scientist Springfield Rsch. Facility, Def. Threat Reduction Agy., Alexandria, Va., 2002—04; prin. physician chem., biol., radiol., nuc., and high explosives health effects and response Sci. Applications Internat. Corp., Merrifield, Va., 2004—. Expert in toxicology, radiobiology, biol. agts. Fellow Coll. Am. Pathologists (lead lab. accreditation insp. 1996-99). Office: PO Box 4077 Merrifield VA 22116-4077 Office Phone: 703-676-5468. Business E-Mail: bumgarnerr@saic.com.

BUNCHMAN, HERBERT HARRY, II, retired plastic surgeon; b. Washington, Feb. 23, 1942; s. Herbert H. and Mary (Halleran) B.; m. Marguerite Fransioli, Mar. 21, 1963 (div. Jan. 1987); children: Herbert H. III., Angela K., Christopher; m. Janet C. Quinlan, Oct. 4, 1998. BA, Vanderbilt U., 1964; MD, U. Tenn., 1967. Diplomate Am. Bd. Surgery, Am. bd. Plastic Surgery. Resident in surgery U. Tex., Galveston, 1967-72, resident in plastic surgery, 1972-75; practice medicine specializing in plastic surgery Mesa, Ariz., 1975—2011; chief surgery Desert Samaritan Hosp., 1978-80. Contbr. articles to profl. jours. Eaton Clin. fellow, 1975. Mem. AMA, Am. Soc. Plastic Surgery, Am. Soc. Aesthetic Plastic Surgery, Singleton Surgical Soc., Tex. Med. Assn., So. Med. Assn. (grantee 1974). Office Phone: 602-432-4854. Office Fax: 480-833-2967. Business E-Mail: office@bunchman.com.

BUNCKE, GREGORY M., plastic surgeon; b. NYC, Jan. 16, 1956; s. Harry J. Buncke. BS, U. Calif., Davis; MD, Georgetown U., 1981. Cert. Am. Bd. Plastic Surgery, 1989, added qualification in Surgery of the Hand, 1992. Intern in gen. surgery and plastic surgery Stanford U. Hosp., 1981—82, resident in plastic surgery, 1982—87; fellow in hand and microsurgery Davies Med. Ctr., San Francisco, 1985—86; dir. Buncke Clinic and Plastic Surgery Inst., San Francisco; asst. clin. prof. surgery U. Calif. San Francisco; chmn., dept. plastic surgery Calif. Pacific Med. Ctr., San Francisco, chmn., divsn. microsurgery. Fellow: Am. Coll. Surgeons; mem.: Am. Soc. Surgery of the Hand, Am. Soc. Reconstructive Microsurgery, Am. Soc. Plastic Surgeons. Office: Davies Med Ctr MOB Annex 45 45 Castro St Ste 140 San Francisco CA 94114 Office Phone: 415-565-6136. E-mail: gbuncke@buncke.org.

BUNDESEN, CLAUS MOGENS, psychologist, educator; b. Copenhagen, Jan. 26, 1948; s. Marius and Jytte (Kjaer) B.; m. Else Windfeld Jacobsen, Mar. 25, 1971; children: Rune, Jon, Hanna. PhD in Psychology, U. Copenhagen, 1972, Dr. Phil. in Psychology, 1986. Asst. prof. psychology U. Copenhagen, 1973-75, rsch. fellow, 1975-78; vis. scholar Stanford (Calif.) U., 1977-78; assoc. prof. psychology U. Copenhagen, 1978-88, docent prof. psychology, 1988-95, prof. cognitive psychology, 1995—; dir. Ctr. for Visual Cognition, Denmark, 1993—, Danish Grad. Sch. Psychology, Copenhagen, 2003—08. Mem. editl. bd. European Jour. Cognitive Psychology, 1988—2005, assoc. editor, 1996—2001, editor-in-chief, 2002—05, mem. editl. bd. Psychol. Rsch., 1988—, Visual Cognition, 1993—2005, Psychol. Rev., 1996—2004, 2005—; contbr. articles to Jour. Exptl. Psychology, Perception & Psychophysics, Psychol. Rev. and other profl. jours. Recipient Aristotle prize, 2009; grantee Human Frontier Sci. Program, 1991-94; invited and keynote speaker in field. Mem. Internat. Assn. for Study Attention and Performance (coun. 1981-88, 92-2000, exec. com. 2002-10), European Soc. for Cognitive Psychology (organizer 6th conf. 1993, exec. com. 1990-98, 2001—, coun. 1999-2001, pres. 2007-08, v.p. 2009-10), Royal Danish Acad. Scis. & Letters, Knight of Order Dannebrog. Achievements include research in measurement of effects of visual size and orientation in pattern recognition and apparent movement; development of mathematical models of selective attention in vision. Home: Ulspilsager 66 2791 Dragør Denmark Office: U Copenhagen Dept Psychol Oster Farimagsgade 2A Copenhagen 1353 Denmark E-mail: Bundesen@psy.ku.dk.

BUNDY, ROBERT JOSEPH, critical care specialist; MD, Tufts U., 1981. Diplomate Am. Bd. Internal Medicine, 1984, Am. Bd. Internal Medicine- pulmonary disease, 1988, Am. Bd. Internal Medicine- critical care medicine, 2001, Am. Bd. Internal Medicine- Slep Medicine. Resident in internal medicine Univ. Hosp., Cleve., 1982—83, fellow in pulmonary disease, 1984—86; critical care specialist Windham Hosp., Conn. Mailing: Windham Hospital 112 Mansfield Ave Willimantic CT 06226 Office Phone: 860-456-7279.

BUNGO, MICHAEL WILLIAM, cardiologist, educator, administrator; b. Passaic, NJ, July 18, 1950; s. John C. and Mary Bungo; children: Elise Nicole, Jonathan Michael. BS in Chemistry, Rensselaer Poly. Inst., 1971; MD, N.J. Med. Sch., 1975. Diplomate Am. Bd.

Internal Medicine, Subsplty. Bd. Cardiovasc. Diseases, Am. Coll. Physician Execs., Bd. Cardiovas. Computed Tomography. Intern in internal medicine New England Deaconess Hosp., Boston, 1975-76, resident, 1976—78; asst. in medicine Peter Bent Brigham Hosp., 1976—77; cardiology fellow New England Deaconess Hosp., Harvard Med. Sch., 1978—80; head cardiovascular lab. NASA Johnson Space Ctr., Houston, 1980—85; mem. Aerospace Medicine Bd., 1980—91; dir. Space Biomed. Rsch. Inst. NASA Johnson Space Ctr., 1986—90; chief scientist med. scis. divsn. NASA, 1990—91; prof. medicine U. Tex., Galveston, med. dir. heart sta. divsn. cardiology, 1995—2002, vice chmn. dept. internal medicine, 1999—2002; assoc. dean U. Tex. Med. Sch., Houston, 2002—05, vice dean, 2005—07; chief of staff LBJ Gen. Hosp., 2002—06; pres. and CEO UT Physicians, 2005—07. Chmn. dept. medicine St. John Hosp., Houston, 1987—89; fellowship advisor NRC, Washington, 1984—89. Editor: Results of Life Sciences Aboard the Space Shuttle, 1987; contbr. abstracts and articles to jours., chpts. to books; tech. reviewer Circulation, Aviation, Space and Environ. Medicine, 1989—; mem. editl. bd. Aviation, Space and Environ. Medicine, 1997-2000. Recipient medal NASA, 1986. Fellow ACP, Am. Coll. Cardiology; mem. Am. Heart Assn., Aerospace Med. Assn. (Louis H. Bauer Founders award 1987), Tex. Med. Assn., Am. Coll. of Physician Exec., Phi Lambda Upsilon. Office: U Tex Houston Med Sch MSB Ste 1242 6431 Fannin St Houston TX 77030 Office Phone: 713-500-5532.

BUNKER, KIMBERLY LEANN, critical care nurse, emergency nurse practitioner; b. New Albany, Ind., Nov. 16, 1969; d. William Albert and Sherry Lee Taylor; m. Donald Edward Bunker, Sept. 23, 1995; children: Sara Ann, Taylor Matthew. AS in Nursing, Livingston C.C., 1991; BSN, Rutgers U., 2001. Staff nurse Scott County Hosp., Georgetown, Ky., 1991, Naples Cmty. Hosp., Fla., 1991—93; patient care coord. Naples Collier Home Health, 1993—94; staff nurse NY Downtown Hosp., NYC, 1995, Robert Wood Johnson Hosp., New Brunswick, NJ, 1995—2000; clin. rsch. coord. dept. surgery U. Medicine and Dentistry J, 2000—02. Owner, oper. Critical RN Cons. Svcs., Alpharetta, 2005. Head nurse Hunterdon County Red Cross, NJ, 2003, bd. mem., 2003. Mem.: Air and Surface Transport Nursing Assn., Emer. Nurses Assn., Alpharetta's Am. Legal Nurse Cons. Avocations: tennis, gardening. Home: 310 Galloway Ave Alpharetta GA 30004 Home Phone: 770-521-1063; Office Phone: 770-317-8244. Business E-Mail: info@criticalrnconsulting.com.

BUNKIS, JURIS, plastic surgeon; b. Lubeck, Germany, Aug. 27, 1949; came to the U.S., 1974; s. Janis and Jadviga (Buzinskis) B.; Tina Stensland Haworth, Oct. 8, 2005; children: Justin, Jessica. Degree, U. Toronto, 1970, MD, 1974. Intern gen. surgery Mary Imogene Bassett Hosp., Columbia U., Cooperstown, NY, 1974-75, jr. resident gen. surgery, 1975-76, Beth Israel Hosp., Mass. Gen. Hosp. & Shriner's Burn Inst., Harvard U., Boston, 1976-77; sr. resident gen. surgery Mary Imogene Bassett Hosp., Columbia U., Cooperstown, 1977-78, chief resident gen. surgery, 1978-79; sr. resident, chief resident plastic surgery Peter Bent Brigham & Children's Hosps., Harvard U., Boston, 1979-81; clin. instr. in surgery Harvard U., 1979-81; asst. prof. surgery divsn. plastic surgery U. Calif., San Francisco, 1981-83, asst. clin. prof. surgery, 1983-85; chmn., founder Orange County Plastic Surgery Medical Associations, Inc., 2002—. Asst. chief plastic surgery San Francisco Gen. Hosp. U. Calif., 1981-82, chief plastic surgery, 1983; chmn. bd. dirs., pres. Juris Bunkis M.D., Inc., Danville, Calif., 1983-95; chmn. bd. dirs., pres., med. dirs. Blackhawk Surgery Ctr., Inc., Danville, 1989-96, asst. med. dir., 1996-2001; chmn. bd. dirs., pres., sec. United Bridges, Inc., 1994-98, COO, bd. dirs., co-founder, OnlySports.com (now Captivision), Pleasonton, Calif., 1999-2001, sec., bd. dirs. 2001-02; chmn., co founder Orange County Plastic Surgery Medical Associations, Inc., 2002—; invited lectr. numerous confs. Film F-Stops (silver medal, Houston Film Festival 2001); contbr. chpts. to books and articles to med. jours. Vol. deputy San Bernardino County Sheriff's Dept. Recipient Angels Wings award, Angels Wings Found., Concord, Calif., 2000, Man of CharaAngel Winds award, Concord Actor award, Orange County Coun., Boy Scouts of Am.; Knight, Cavalieri di San Marco (Knights of San Marco), Venice, 1995. Mem. Am. Assn. Hand Surgery (mem. program com. 1983-84, socioecons. com. 84-85), Am. Soc. Plastic and Reconstructive Surgery (mem. Tel Med subcom. 1986-87), Am. Soc. Aesthetic Surgery, Calif. Med. Soc., Calif. Soc. Plastic Surgeons (mem. program com. 1984-85, mem. ethics com. 86-87, mem. newsletter com. 87-89, mem. B.M.Q.A. liaison com. 87-89), Alameda-Contra Costa Med. Assn., Lipoplasty Soc. N.Am., Internat. Soc. Aesthetic Plastic Surgery, Pan Pacific Surg. Assn., Latvian Med. and Dental Assn., Plastic Surgery Rsch. Coun., Assn. Medicorum Bohemoslovacorum J.E. Purkyne (hon.), Soc. Bohemoslovaca Chirurgiae Plasticae (hon., Prague). Avocations: flying, fly fishing, travel. Office: Orange County Plastic Surgery 30212 Tomas Rancho Santa Margarita CA 92688 *

BUNN, PAUL A., JR., oncologist, educator; b. NYC, Mar. 16, 1945; s. Paul A. Bunn; m. Camille Ruoff, Aug. 17, 1968; children: Rebecca, Kristen, Paul H. BA cum laude, Amherst Coll., 1967; MD, Cornell U., 1971. Diplomate Nat. Bd. Med. Examiners, Am. Bd. Internal Medicine, Am. Bd. Med. Oncology. Intern U. Calif., H.C. Moffitt Hosp., San Francisco, 1971-72, resident, 1972-73; clin. assoc. medicine br. Nat. Cancer Inst., NIH, Bethesda, Md., 1973-76; sr. investigator med. oncology br. Nat. Cancer Inst., Washington VA Hosp., 1976-81; asst. prof. medicine med. sch. Georgetown U., 1978-81; head cell kinetic sect., Navy med. oncology br. Nat. Cancer Inst., Bethesda, 1981-84; assoc. prof. medicine uniformed svcs. Univ. Health Scis., Bethesda, 1981-84; prof. medicine health scis. ctr. U. Colo., Denver, 1984—, head divsn. med. oncology, 1984-94, dir. cancer ctr., 1987—. Instl. rev. bd. NIH, Nat. Cancer Inst., 1982-84; intramural support contract rev. com. Nat. Cancer Inst., 1982-84; cancer com. U. Colo., 1984—, faculty senate health scis. ctr., 1985—, exec. com. sch. medicine, 1987—; med. bd. Univ. Hosp., 1987—; external sci. advisor cancer ctr. U. Miami, 1988-92, U. Ark., 1989-94, U. Va., 1991-94, others; oncology drug adv. com. FDA, 1992-96; sci. secretariat 7th World Conf. Lung Cancer, 1994; bd. dirs. Univ. Hosp. Resource Coun.; oncology drug adv. com. FDA, 1992-96. Author: Carboplatin (JM-8) Current Perspectives and Future Directions, 1990, Clinical Experiences With Platinum and Etoposide Therapy in Lung Cancer, 1992, (with M.E. Wood) Hematology/Oncology Secrets, 1994; assoc. editor Med. and Pediatric Oncology, 1984—, Jour. Clin. Oncology, 1991—, Cancer Rsch., 1992—, others; contbr. chpts. to books and articles to profl. jours. Bd. dirs. Colo. divsn. Am. Cancer Soc., 1989—, Leukemia Soc. Am., 1991—; bd. dirs. The Cancer Venture, 1993-94, Fair Share Colo., 1993-94; chmn. Solid Tumor Oncology Edn. Found., 1996—. With USPHS, 1973-84. Decorated Medal of Commendation; recipient Sci. of Yr. award Denver chpt. ARCS, 1992; named one of 400 Best Drs. in Am., Good Housekeeping Mag., 1991, 92; grantee Schering Plough, 1988-89, Burroughs Wellcome, 1991—, Bristol-Myers Squibb, 1993—, others. Fellow ACP; mem. AAAS, Am. Soc. Hematology (mem. sci. subcom. neoplasia 1989-92), Am. Assn. Cancer Rsch., Am. Soc. Clin. Oncology (chair program subcom. 1985-86, 90, pres.-elect 2001—), Am. Fedn. Clin. Rsch., Am. Assn. Cancer Insts. (bd. dirs. 1992—), Internat. Assn. Study Lung Cancer (bd. dirs. 1988—, pres. 1994-97, exec. dir.), Western Assn. Physicians, S.W. Oncology Group, Lung Cancer Study Group, Alpha Omega Alpha. Office: U Colo Cancer Ctr PO Box 6511 MS 8111 Aurora CO 80045 E-mail: paul.bunn@uchsc.edu.

BUNTIC, RUDY F., plastic surgeon; b. Can., Jan. 10, 1963; AB, Harvard U.; MD, McGill U., 1990. Cert. Am. Bd. Plastic Surgery, 1999, added qualification in Surgery of the Hand, 2000. Resident in gen. and plastic surgery Stanford U.; fellow in hand and microsurgery Davies Med. Ctr., San Francisco; chief microsurgery Calif. Pacific Med. Ctr., San Francisco; surgeon Buncke Clinic, San Francisco. Adj. clin. instr., plastic surgery Stanford U.; clin. faculty U. Calif. Contbr. articles to med. jours., chapters to books. Mem.: Am. Soc. Reconstructive Microsurgery, Am. Soc. Plastic Surgeons. Office: Buncke Clinic 45 Castro St Ste 121 San Francisco CA 94114 also: 101 N El Camino Real Ste A San Mateo CA 94401 Office Phone: 415-565-6136. Office Fax: 415-864-1654. E-mail: rbuntic@microsurgeon.org.

BURATYNSKI, THERESA JOAN, physician; b. Steubenville, Ohio, Apr. 21, 1964; d. Raymond Stanley and Anna Sue Buratynski; m. Peter Randall Daspit, Apr. 1, 2000. BSc, U. Akron, 1986; MPH, Johns Hopkins U., 1999; MD, Case We. Res. U., 1995. Student fellow pathology U. Hosps. Cleve., 1992—93; gen. med. officer Naval Hosp., Yokosuka, Japan, 1996—98; resident Navy Aerospace Medicine Inst., Pensacola, Fla., 1999—2000; head dept. aviation medicine Med. Clinic Kaneohe Bay, 2000—01; flight surgeon Marine Heavy Helicopter 363, Kaneohe, 2001—04; sr. med. officer Marine Aircraft Group 24, Kaneohe, 2004—05, 3rd Navy Constrn. Regiment, 2009—; med. officer Navy Health Clinic, Kaneohe, 2006—08; staff vets. Vet. Administrn. Hosp., Beckley, W.Va., 2009—. Contbr. articles to profl. jours. Activist Kailua Neighborhood, Hawaii, 2004—09; med. support and aid USN, 2000. Comdr. USN, 1996—. Decorated Navy Achievement medal, Navy Commendation medal; recipient Dr. Roger Keller, Jr. award for Genetics and Biotech., U. Akron, 1986, Daniel Lewis Raven, MD award, Case We. Res. U. Sch. Medicine, 1995, Physician Recognition award, AMA, 2003—06; Rsch. grantee, Am. Heart Assn., 1986, Armed Forces Health Scis. Edn. and Tng. scholar, USN, 1990—95, Betty Ford Ctr. Resident in Tng. scholar, 1991, March of Dimes rsch. scholar, 1991, fellow in pathology, U. Hosp. Cleve., 1992—93, Chattanooga Corp. grantee, 1985, Ohio Bd. Regents scholar, 1982—86. Mem.: APHA, Am. Coll. Occupl. and Environ. Medicine, Aerospace Med. Assn., Soroptomists Internat., Phi Sigma Alpha. Avocations: running, gardening, community service, reading. Office Phone: 304-255-2121. Personal E-mail: doctjb@hotmail.com *

BURBANK, KELTON, surgeon; b. Mass., Feb. 16, 1961; BA, WIlliams Coll., 1983; MD, U. Mass., 1991. Attending physician UMMHC-HealthAlliance, 2005—. Bd. dirs. New Eng. Orthop. Soc., 2002—. Mem.: NEOS, AANA, AOSSM, AAOS. Office: 100 Hosp Rd Ste 3C Leominster MA 01453 Office Fax: 978-840-0966. E-mail: kmbortho1@aol.com.

BURCHIEL, KIM JAMES, neurosurgeon; b. Holyoke, Mass., Apr. 23, 1950; m. Debra Burchiel; children: Jessica, Adrienne, Meridith, Cole. Attended undergraduate sch., U. Calif., San Diego; MD, U. San Diego, 1976. Cert. Am Bd. Neurol. Surgery, 1984, diplomate Am. Bd. Pain Medicine, Am. Bd. Med. Examiners. Intern, neurol. surgery Harbor Gen. Hosp., LA, 1976—77; resident, neurol. surgery U. Wash., Seattle, 1977—82, assoc. prof., 1982—88; head, divsn. neurosurgery Oreg. Health & Sci. U., Portland, 1988, John Raaf prof. chmn. dept. neurol. surgery, mem. exec. com., bd. dir., faculty and staff, Ctr. Health and Healing. Featured on Miracle Workers (ABC), 2006. Fellow: ACS; mem.: Western Neurological Soc. (pres.-elect), Am. Bd. Neurological Surgery (dir.), Soc. Univ. Surgeons (past pres.), Am. Bd. Pain Medicine (past pres.). Avocations: running marathons, fly fishing, skiing, moutaineering. Office: Oreg Health & Sci U Neurol Surgery Functional & Sterolactic Hatfield Rsch Ctr Mail Code L472 3181 SW Sam Jackson Park Rd Portland OR 97239 also: Ctr Health and Healing 3303 SW Bond Ave Portland OR 97329 Office Phone: 503-494-4314. Office Fax: 503-494-7161.

BURD, ROBERT MEYER, hematologist, oncologist, educator; b. NYC, Aug. 25, 1937; s. David and Anne (Popkin) B.; m. Alice Stoller, May 30, 1964; children: Russell J., Stephen J. AB, Columbia U., 1959, MD, 1963. Diplomate Am. Bd. Internal Medicine, Am. Bd. Hematology and Oncology. Intern Albert Einstein Med. Sch., NYC, 1963-64, resident in internal medicine, 1964-66; hematology fellow Montefiore Hosp., NYC, 1966-67; specializing in hematology and oncology pvt. practice medicne, Fairfield, Conn., 1969—; assoc. prof. medicine Yale U., New Haven, 1975, assoc. clin. prof. of medicine, 1975—; chief, hematology/oncology St. Vincent's Med. Ctr., 1980—2007; asst. prof. clin. medicine Columbia U. Coll. Physicians & Surgeons, 1998—. Chmn. hosp. com. on cancer, mng. ptnr. Med. Specialists of Fairfield, LLC, 1995—2007; attending physician Yale Hosp., New Haven; mem. staff Bridgeport (Conn.) Hosp.; adj. prof. medicine N.Y. Med. Coll.; med. cons. U.S. News and World Report, 1990; dir. oncology fellowship Yale-St. Vincent Hosp., 1991—96, N.Y. Med. Coll., St. Vincent's Med. Ctr., Bridgeport; adv. bd. rituxan Genentech; adv. bd. taxotere Aventis. Mem. editl. bd. (exhibitions), 1974—78. Active Leukemia Soc. Am., Hemophilia Found.; chmn. profl. edn. com. Am. Cancer Soc. Lt. comdr. USN, 1967-69. Ettinger Meml. fellow Am. Cancer Soc., 1982. Fellow ACP; mem. AMA, AAAS, Am. Soc. Hematology, Am. Soc. Internat. Medicine, Am. Soc. Clin. Oncology, N.Y. Acad. of Scis., Internat. Soc. Thrombosis and Hemostasis, Conn. Oncology Assn., Soc. Columbia Grads., Columbia U. Alumni Fedn. Coun., Columbia U. Alumni Club (pres. Fairfield Co. 1983-85, editor newsletter 1982-91), Bridgeport Med. Soc. (Physician of Yr. 1993). Office: 425 Post Rd Fairfield CT 06430-6232 Office Phone: 203-255-4545.

BURDI, ALPHONSE ROCCO, anatomist; b. Chgo., Aug. 28, 1935; s. Alphonse Rocco and Anna (Basilo) B.; m. Sandra Shaw, Mar. 22, 1968; children— Elizabeth Anne, Sarah Lynne. BS, No. Ill. U., DeKalb, 1957; MS, U. Ill., 1959, U. Mich., 1961, PhD, 1963; Doctorate (hon.), U. Athens, Greece, 2000. Predoctoral fellow physiology U. Ill., 1957-59; NSF summer fellow U. Mich., 1960, NIH trainee, 1960-61, NIH predoctoral research fellow, 1962, mem. faculty, 1962—, prof. emeritus cell and devel. biology, 2003—, emeritus prof. Coll. Lit., Sci., and Arts, 2009—. Rsch. scientist emeritus Ctr. Human Growth and Devel., 2003; dir. integrated pre-med.-med. program U. Mich. Mem. editorial bd.: Cleft Palate Jour. 1972-88, Am. Jour. Phys. Anthropology, 1971-75, C.C. Thomas Am. Lectr. Series in Anatomy, 1971-88, Jour. Dental Research, 1977-87. Grantee NIH. Mem. Internat. Assn. Dental Research, Am. Assn. Dental Research, Am. Cleft Palate Assn., Teratology Soc., Am. Assn. Anatomists, Am. Assn. Phys. Anthropology, Sigma Xi. Office: U Mich Dept Cell & Devel Biology Basic Science Research Bldg Ann Arbor MI 48109-0616 Home: 4731 Mulberry Woods Cir Ann Arbor MI 48105 Office Phone: 734-764-4358. Business E-Mail: alburdi@umich.edu.

BURES, JAN Z., physician, researcher; b. Hradec Kralove, Czech Republic, Jan. 1, 1954; s. Oldrich and Bozena (Pecholtova) B.; m. Eva Kosova, Aug. 26, 1978; children: Jan, Vojtech. MD, Charles U., Prague, Czech Republic, 1979, PhD, 1990. Physician Charles U. Hosp., Hradec Kralove, 1979—, prof. internal medicine, 2002—. Presenter in field. Author: Textbook of Internal Medicine, Atlas of Enteroscopy; contbr. articles to profl. jours. Recipient award Immunol. Soc. Czechoslovac Acad. Scis., 1988. Office: Charles U 2nd Dept Medicine 50005 Hradec Králové Czech Republic Business E-Mail: bures@lfhk.cuni.cz.

BURESLEY, SALWA MAJED, organ transplant surgeon; BS in Basic Med. Scis., Kuwait U., 1995, MBBCh in Medicine and Surgery, 1998. Cert. in basic laparoscopic surg. tng. course Kuwait Inst. Med. Specializations, 2000, in basic surg. skills course Kuwait, Royal Coll. Surgeons, England, 2001, in advanced laparoscopic surgery tng. course 2002, in advanced trauma life support Qatar, ACS, 2003, advanced trauma life support ATLS, Kuwait, 2009, in higher surg. tng. skills course Scotland, Edinburgh 2005; studied the German lang. Goethe Inst., Mannheim, Germany, 2006-08, studied the French lang Birlitz Inst., Kuwait, 2009, part 1 MRCS Edinburgh, 2007, part 2 MRCS Edinburgh, 2008. Intern in gen. surgery, medicine, pediat. Al-Amiri Hosp., Kuwait, 1998—99, gen. surgeon, 1999—2000, 2001—04, surgeon, Intensive Care Unit and critical care, 2002; intern in ob-gyn. Maternity Hosp., Sabah Med. Area, 1998—99; orthop. surgeon Al-Razi Orthop. Hosp., Kuwait, 2000; vascular surgeon Mubarak Hosp., Kuwait, 2000, urologist, 2000, surgeon, Intensive Care Unit and critical care, 2001, emergency and trauma surgeon, 2001, gen. surgeon, 2001; surgeon, Organ Transplant Ctr. Ibn Sina Hosp., Kuwait, 2004—06; fellow in organ transplantation Holweide Hosp., Cologne and Univ. Hosp., Essen, Germany, 2008—. Mem. organizing com. 10th Mid. East Soc. Organ Transplantation Congress, 2006. Contbr. articles to profl. jours., presentor at internat. meetings in field. Vol., post 2nd Gulf War Main Oper. Theatre, Ibn Sina Hosp., Kuwait, 1991. Mem.: German Med. Assn. Düsseldorf, Kuwait Med. Assn., Mid. East Soc. Orgn. Transplantation (life), Kuwait Soc. Transplantation (life). Achievements include attending a fellowship that will allow her to return to the Middle East as the first female transplant surgeon; speaks Arabic, English, and German. Personal E-mail: sburesley@yahoo.com.

BURGER, MAX MARCEL, biochemist; b. Zurich, Switzerland, July 8, 1933; s. Joseph and Olga (Humbel) B.; m. Monique Sautter, July 22, 1961 (div. 1984); children: Christina, Maya, Catherine, Elizabeth MD, U. Zurich, 1959; PhD in Biochemistry, Washington U., St. Louis, 1964. Intern hosps., Paris and Zurich, 1957-59; instr. biochemistry Washington U., 1964-65; mem. faculty Princeton U., 1965-72, prof. biochem. scis., 1971-72, chmn. adv. coun., 1972—2003; prof. biochemistry U. Basel, Switzerland, 1972—2004; chmn. Biocenter U. Basel, Switzerland, 1973-78; dir. Friedrich Miescher Inst., Basel, 1986—2000; vice chmn to chmn. Novartis Sci. Bd., Basel, 1999—. Corp. mem. Marine Biol. Lab., Woods Hole, Mass., 1966—; mem. study sects. NIH, 1968—72; mem. fellwship panels NSF, 1968—72; mem. Roche Rsch. Found., 1975—2001; mem., v.p. Swiss NRC, 1975—91; adv. Ger. Ministry Sci. & Israeli Nat. Res. Coun. R & D, 1978—2008; dir. CIBA-GEIGY, Inc., 1980—96; chmn. Nat. Med. and Nat. Biol. Rsch. Coun., 1981—84; mem. Gen Motors Cancer Rsch. Found., 1982—84; mem. exec. coun. European Med. Res. Coun., 1984—85; mem. sci. adv. bd. Inst. Pasteur, Paris, 1991—99; v.p. bd. dirs. Oxford Glyco Scis. (U.K.) Ltd., 1995—2003; chmn. bd. dirs. Novartis Agr. Discovery Inst., Inc., La Jolla, Calif., 1998—2000; bd. dirs. Genomics Inst. of Novartis Found., Inc., La Jolla, 1998—; bd. trustees Ger. Rheuma Res. Ctr., Berlin, 2005—; chmn. bd. dirs. 4Ab Inc. Basel and Jena, 2004—. Editor: BBA Cancer Revs., 1974—81; mng. editor: Cellular Biochemistry, 1981—; author: numerous books; contbr. articles to profl. jours. Hon. fgn. mem. Am. Acad. of Arts and Scis., 1988; founding mem. Senate Hermann von Helmholtz-Gemeinschaft Deutscher Forschungszentren, Berlin, 1995—2008; mem. sci. com. DKFZ, Heidelberg, 1993—2002. With Swiss Army, 1952—88. Decorated Order of Merit 1st Class, Fed. Republic Germany, 2005; recipient Waksman medal, 1971, Otto Naegeli prize, 1975, Cancer prize Swiss Cancer League, 1999; Helen Hay Whitney fellow, 1964-66 Mem.: Academia Europaea, Internat. Cancer Found. (chmn. 1998—2003), Internat. Union Against Cancer (coun. 1978—82, exec. coun. 1982—98), Internat. Union Biophysics (chmn. commn. membrane and cell biophysics 1975—80), Swiss Acad. Med. Sci. (hon.), Precolumbian Collectors Club, Swiss Acad. Ski Club. Address: 5 Pfaffenrainstrasse CH4103 Bottmingen Switzerland

BURGESS, JOHN HERBERT, cardiologist, educator; b. Montreal, Que., Can., May 24, 1933; s. John Frederick and Willa Reta (McGinness) B.; m. Andrea Clouston Rutherford, May 30, 1958; children: Willa, Cynthia, Lynn, John. BSc, McGill U., Montreal, 1954, MDCM, 1958. Med. resident Montreal Gen. Hosp., 1958-60, 62-64, dir. div. cardiology, 1973-94; Nuffield rsch. fellow U. Birmingham, England, 1960-62; McLaughlin rsch. fellow Cardiovas. Rsch. Inst., San Francisco, 1964—66; asst. prof. medicine McGill U., 1966-69, assoc. prof., 1969-75, prof., 1975—. Emeritus cardiologist McGill U. Health Ctr. Author: (autobiography) Doctor to the North: Thirty Years Treating Heart Disease Among the Inuit, 2008; contbr. articles to profl. jours. Decorated Order of Can.; hon. fellow Coll. Medicine, South Africa. Master ACP; fellow Am. Coll. Cardiology, Royal Coll. Physicians and Surgeons Can. (pres. 1990-92), Royal Coll. Physicians (Edinburgh), Royal Australasian Coll. Physicians (hon.), Royal Coll. Physicians (London); mem. Can. Soc. Clin. Investigation. Avocations:

cross country skiing, photography. Home: 639 Murray Hill West-mount PQ Canada H3Y 2W8 Office: Montreal Gen Hosp 1650 Cedar Ave Montreal PQ Canada H3G 1A4 Business E-Mail: john.burgess@muhc.mcgill.ca.

BURGESS, RICHARD RAY, biochemist, oncologist, biotechnologist, educator; b. Mt. Vernon, Wash., Sept. 8, 1942; s. Robert Carl and Irene Marjorie (Wegner) B.; m. Ann Baker, June 17, 1967; children—Kristin, Andreas BS in Chemistry, Calif. Inst. Tech., 1964; PhD in Biochemistry and Molecular Biology, Harvard U., 1969. Helen Hay Whitney fellow Inst. Molecular Biology, Geneva, 1969-71; asst. prof. oncology McArdle Lab. Cancer Research U. Wis., Madison, 1971-77, assoc. prof., 1977-82, prof., 1982—2008, dir. Biotech. Ctr., 1984-96, James D. Watson Prof. Oncology, 2001—, prof. emeritus, 2009—. Cons. in field; mem. NSF study sect. in biochemistry, 1979-84; chmn. bd. Consortium for Plant Biotech. Rsch., Inc., 1992-96. Series editor U. Wis. Biotech. Ctr. Resource Manuals; editor-in chief Jour. Protein Expression and Purification, 1990—; contbr. articles to profl. jours. Bd. dirs. Coun. Biotech. Ctrs., 1991-93; mem. Gov.'s Coun. on Biotech. Grantee NSF, 1978-80, 85-90, NIH, 1980—, Nat. Cancer Inst., 1971—; Guggenheim fellow, 1983-84; recipient medal Waksman Inst., 1999. Fellow AAAS, Am. Acad. Microbiology; mem. Am. Soc. Biochemistry and Molecular Biology, Am. Chem. Soc. (Pfizer award 1982), Am. Assn. Cancer Research, Am. Soc. Microbiology, Protein Soc. Home: 10 Knollwood Ct Madison WI 53713-3479 Office: U Wis McArdle Lab Cancer Rsch 1400 University Ave Madison WI 53706-1526 Office Phone: 608-263-2635. Business E-Mail: burgess@oncology.wisc.edu.

BURGET, DEAN EDWIN, JR., plastic surgeon; b. Toledo, June 29, 1936; s. Dean E. Sr. and Marie E. (Alwine) B.; m. A. Undine Ehrman, Mar. 16, 1957 (div. Mar. 1993); children: Mark A.E., Kevin Phillips, Undine Peeples; m. Gabriella Morocz, May 14, 1993. BS, U. Toledo, 1958; MD, Yale U., 1962. Diplomate Am. Bd. Plastic Surgery. Intern surgery U. Hosps., Cleve., 1962, resident in anesthesiology, 1963; resident in gen. surgery Hahnemann Med. Coll. and Hosp., Phila., 1966-68, asst. prof., dir. divsn. plastic surgery, 1972-75; resident in plastic surgery Temple U. Hosp., Phila., 1968-70, U.S. Govt. fellow in rehab. surgery, 1970-71, instr. plastic surgery, 1970-71, Med. Coll. Pa., Phila., 1970-71, assoc. clin. prof., 1979-81; staff surgeon, cons. surgeon various cmty. hosps., 1975—; pvt. practice Paoli, Pa., 1985—. Fellow ACS; mem. Am. Soc. Plastic and Reconstructive Surgeons, Pickering Hunt Club (Phila.), Ausable Club/Adirondack Mountain Res. (St. Huberts, NY), Yale Club (NYC), Rittenhouse Club (Phila.), Penn Club, St. Nicholas Soc. City of NY, Pa. Soc. Sons Revolution, Colonial Soc. Pa., Soc. Colonial Wars Pa., Nat. Huguenot Soc., Soc. War 1812, Phila. Soc. Promoting Agr. Office: 1410 Russell Rd Ste 205 Paoli PA 19301

BURGET, GARY CRITES, plastic surgeon; b. Toledo, Apr. 20, 1941; s. Marie and Dean Burget. BA, Yale Coll., New Haven, Conn., 1963; MD, Yale U., New Haven, Conn., 1967. Diplomate Am. Bd. of Plastic Surgery, 1980. Attending physician Children's Meml. Hosp., Chgo., 1985—, St. Joseph Hosp., Chgo., 1986—; attending physician, hosps. and clinics U. Chgo. Med. Ctr., clin. assoc. surgery, 1987—. Pres. The Rhinoplasty Soc., 2002—03. Author: (book) Aesthetic Reconstruction of the Nose (Mosby), Aesthetic and Reconstructive Rhinoplasty (Quality Medical); contbr. chapters to books, articles to profl. jours. Recipient Hon. Dieffenbach Medallion, Deutsche Soc. Plastic Chiurugie, 1990, Hon. award, Chgo. Soc. Plastic Surgeons, 2006, Northwestern U. Med. Sch. Divsn. Plastic Surgery, 2007; fellowship, Pediatric Plastic Surgery, The Children's Meml. Hosp., Ill., 1996. Fellow: ACS, Am. Acad. Facial Plastic and Reconstructive Surgeons; mem.: Am. Soc. Aesthetic Plastic Surgery, Am. Assn. Plastic Surgeons (Barret-Brown award 1991, Clinician of Yr. award 2006, Leonard R. Rubin award 2006), Can. Soc. Plastic Surgeons (hon.), Australian Soc. Plastic Surgeons (hon.), New Eng. Soc. Plastic Surgeons (hon.), Am. Soc. Plastic Surgeons, Inst. Medicine. Achievements include development of principles of facial aesthetics and artistic surgical techniques that have raised the standard of surgical reconstruction of the injured face to a new level. Office: 2913 N Commonwealth Ave Chicago IL 60657 Business E-Mail: adm@garyburgetmd.com.

BURGHER, LOUIS WILLIAM, physician, educator, academic administrator; b. Centerville, Iowa, Oct. 31, 1944; s. Wendell and Dorothy (Probasco) B.; m. Susan Stephens, May 20, 1979; children: Tanya Jo, Tara Lynn, Lucas William, Rachel Elizabeth. BS, U. Nebr., 1966, MD with honors, 1970, M in Med. Sci., 1972, PhD in Med. Sci., 1978. Diplomate Am. Bd. Internal Medicine, Am. Bd. Pulmonary Medicine. Intern U. Nebr. Coll. Medicine, 1970-71, resident in internal medicine, 1971-72; practice medicine specializing in pulmonary medicine Omaha, 1974-93; NIH fellow in pulmonary diseases Mayo Grad. Sch. of Medicine, Rochester, Minn., 1972-74, assoc. prof., 1981-97, chief sec. pulmonary medicine, 1980-84, prof., 1997—, vice chancellor, 1999—2001; pres. Clarkson Coll., Omaha, 2007—. Clin. rsch. assoc. in pulmonary disease U. Nebr. Coll. of Medicine, 1969-72; med. dir. pulmonary medicine Bishop Clarkson Meml. Hosp., Omaha, 1974-93, pres., CEO, 1993-97; pres., CEO Nebr. Health Sys., 1997-2001; mem. pulmonary-allergy drugs adv. FDA, 1984-86; Tb cons. to Nebr. Dept. Health, 1972-96; med. dir. Nebr. Opportunity for Vols. in ACTION, 1971-72; trustee Nebr. Found., 1982-94. Contbr. articles on pulmonary disease to profl. jours. Recipient Upjohn award Nebr. Coll. Medicine, 1970. Fellow Am. Coll. Chest Physicians; mem. AMA (coun. on med. edn. 1973-78, mem. liaison com. on med. edn. 1974-79), Nebr. Med. Assn., Zumbro Valley Med. Soc. (exec. com. 1973-74), Univ. Med. Ctr. Ho. Officers Assn. (pres. 1971-72), Nat. Assn. Med. Dirs. Respiratory Care (pres. 1985-87), Mayo Fellows Assn. (pres 1973-74), Nat. Acad. Scis. (mem. task force study Inst. Medicine), Nebr. Thoracic Soc. (pres. 1980-81), U. Nebr. Med. Ctr. Alumni Assn. (pres. 1986-88), Alpha Omega Alpha. Home and Office: 12229 N 179th Cir Bennington NE 68007 Office Phone: 402-689-2000. E-mail: lou@lburgher.net.

BURGIO, MICHAEL, medical researcher; b. Bklyn., Sept. 20, 1942; s. John Duffy and Diega Burgio; m. Roberta Somersetin, Aug. 28, 1966 (div. July 31, 1990); children: Todd, Andera Lyn. BS, CCNY, 1963; MS in Physics Electrophysiology Advanced Studies, NYU, 1971; degree in Advanced Studies Anatomy & Physiology. Med. rschr. Siemens Cardiac Pacemaker, Yardley, Pa., 1985—94, Home Infusion Therapy, Bklyn., 1994—97, Burgio Enterprises, Ltd., Bronx, 1995—. Lectr., EKG interpretation & electrophysiology; bd. dirs. United Medscan Corp., NJ; invited lectr. in numerous med. tchg. instns. US, S.Am., Europe. Author: (book) Manual for Rehabilitation

of Chronic Pulmonary Disease, 1989, Manual for Rehabilitation of Chronic Cardiac Disease, 1989, Training Manual for Cardiac and Pulmonary Rehabilitation, 1989, Nursing Manual of Policies and Procedures, (chpt.) Surgical Implant & Implantable Defibrilators of A/V Pacemaker and It's Functions; co-author: (pilot study) Disc Dessication in Low Impact Injury in Young Trauma Victims; author: Burgio's Consultation Agreement, Burgio's License Agreement; contbr. articles to profl. jours., chapters to books. Recipient Achievement Outstanding Contbr. award, Internat. Biog. Ctr. St. Thomas Pl. Eng., Diploma of Achievement Outstanding Contrib. to Cardiac Disease, IBC Cambridge, Eng.; named Outstanding Scientist, Internat. Biog. Ctr. St. Thomas Pl., Cambridge, Eng., 2010, Man of Yr., Am. Biog. Inst., World Forum, U. Cambridge, Eng., 2010, 2000 Outstanding Intellectuals of The 21st Century 6th Edit.; named one of 100 World Wide Scientist, IBC, Cambridge, Eng. Mem.: Internat. Biog. Ctr. (Cambridge) (mem. standing com., named outstanding scientist 2010). Roman Catholic. Achievements include development of new method to restart heart after surgery; 12 federal copyrights in field. Home: 918 Chace Ln NE Palm Bay FL 32905 Office Phone: 347-449-3489. Personal E-mail: michaelburgio09@gmail.com.

BÜRGLIN, THOMAS, research scientist; b. Switzerland, Aug. 5, 1959; PhD, U. Basel, 1987, Docent, 2001. Postdoc. fellow Harvard Med. Sch., 1988—. Asst. prof. U. Basel, 1994—2001; sr. rschr. Karolinska Inst., 2001. Mem.: Genetics Soc. America. Office: Hälsovägen 7 Novum Karolinska Inst Huddinge SE 141 83 Sweden Office Phone: 46 8 5858 3733. Business E-Mail: thomas.burglin@ki.se.

BURGOS, GILBERT, physician, insurance company executive; BS, Fordham U., NY; MD, Albert Einstein Coll. Med., Yeshiva U., NY; MPH, Harvard U. Past assoc. med. dir. Humana Health Plan, Washington; chmn. dept. adult medicine Humana/Mitchell-Trotman Med. Group, Washington; exec. dir. med. resource mgmt. Kaiser Permanente, Rockville, Md.; sr. v.p., med. dir. Vista Health Plan, Fla.; now chief med. officer Care Choices, Mich., 2003—07; chief med. officer, sr. v.p. health svcs. Mercy Meml. Hosp. System. Mem.: Am. Coll. Physician Exec. Office: Mercy Meml Hosp System 718 N Macomb St Monroe MI 48162

BURGUT, FADIME TUNA, psychiatrist, educator; b. Turkey, June 14, 1972; MD, Hacettepe U., 1995. Instr. Weill Cornell Med. Coll., 2003—05, asst. prof., 2005, 2005—09, Mt. Sinai Sch. Medicine, 2009—. Psychiatrist-analytic rsch. fellow Columbia U. Ctr. Psychoanalytic Rsch. and Tng., 2009—. Recipient Tchg. award, WCMC-Q Class Students, 2009. Mem.: Am. Acad. Psychoanalysis and Psychodynamic Psychotherapy, Am. Psychoanalytic Assn., Am. Psychiat. Assn. Avocations: travel, literature. Home: 392 Ctrl Pk W Apt 7H New York NY 10025 Personal E-mail: tunaburgut@gmail.com. Business E-Mail: ftb9002@med.cornell.edu.

BURK, RAYMOND FRANKLIN, JR., internist, educator, researcher; b. Kosciusko, Miss., Dec. 9, 1942; s. Raymond Franklin and Florence Annie (Davis) B.; m. Enikoe Vikor, June 17, 1967; children: Teresa Marie, Stephen Morrison. BA, U. Miss., 1963; MD, Vanderbilt U., 1968. Diplomate Am. Bd. Internal Medicine. Intern Vanderbilt Hosp., Nashville, 1968—69; resident in medicine Vanderbilt Hosp., Nashville, 1969—70; asst. prof. medicine and biochemistry U. Tex. S.W. Med. Sch., Dallas, 1975—78; assoc. prof. medicine and biochemistry La. State U. Sch. Medicine, Shreveport, 1978—80; assoc. prof. medicine U. Tex. Health Sci. Ctr., San Antonio, 1980—82, prof., 1982—87; prof. medicine Vanderbilt U., 1987—. Rschr. in field; mem. staff Vanderbilt U. Hosp., Nashville. Contbr. articles to med. jours. Maj. M.C., U.S. Army, 1970-73. Grantee NIH, 1974—. Mem. Am. Soc. Biol. Chemists, Am. Soc. Clin. Investigation, Am. Inst. Nutrition. Business E-Mail: raymond.burk@vanderbilt.edu.

BURKE, ANNE E., obstetrician, gynecologist, educator; b. Pa., Oct. 8, 1969; MD, U. Pitts., 1996; MPH, Johns Hopkins Bloomberg Sch. Pub. Health, 2002. Asst. prof. Johns Hopkins U. Sch. Medicine, 2003—. Sect. dir. Dept. Ob-Gyn., 2006—; adv. com. mem. Nat. Campaign to Prevent Teen and Unplanned Pregnancy, 2010—. Named one of Best Drs. in Balt.: Women Faculty grant, Johns Hopkins U. Sch. Medicine. Fellow: Soc. Family Planning, Am. Coll. Obstetricians and Gynecologists; mem.: Assn. Reproductive Health Profls., Delta Omega Pub. Health Honor Soc. Office: Johns Hopkins Bayview Med Ctr 4940 Eastern Ave A-101 Baltimore MD 21224 Business E-Mail: aburke@jhmi.edu.

BURKE, CHARLES J., orthopedist, educator; MD, U. Cin., 1981. Cert. Orthopaedic Surgery, 2009. Asst. prof. orthopedic surgery Univ. Pitts.; fellow Univ. Martin Luther Halle Wiltenberg; resident Univ. Pitts. Med. Sch.; hosp. affiliations include Univ. Pitts. Med. Ctr. St. Margaret, Univ. Pitts. Med. Ctr. Mercy, Univ. Pitts. Med. Ctr. Presbyn., Children's Hosp. of Pitts. of Univ. Pitts. Med. Ctr.; therapeutic radiology Univ. Mass. Med. Ctr., Worcester, 1982—83; orthopedic surgery Univ. Pitts. Med. Ctr., 1983—86. Office: University of Pittsburg Medical Center 200 Medical Arts Bldg 200 Delafield Rd Ste 4010 Pittsburgh PA 15215 Office Phone: 412-784-5770.

BURKE, DEBORAH M., psychology professor; BA, Barnard Coll.; PhD, Columbia U. With Pomona Coll., 1977, W M. Keck disting. svc. prof., psychology prof. Co-author: (publs.) Cherry Pit Primes Brad Pitt: Homophone Priming Effects on Young and Older Adults' Production of Proper Names, 2004, Aging and Language Production, 2004, Atrophy in insula predicts increased word-finding failures with aging, 2007, various publs. Office: Pomona College Cognition and Aging Lab 647 College Way Claremont CA 91711 Office Phone: 909-607-2578.

BURKE, JOHN PATRICK, internist, educator; b. Marshalltown, Iowa, Jan. 19, 1940; s. Raphael Eggleston and Marjorie N. (Busch) B.; m. Andrea Marie Keane, May 9, 1970; children: Paul, Matthew, Edward, Erin. BA, summa cum laude, U. Iowa, 1961, MD, 1964. Diplomate Am. Bd. Internal Medicine, Am. Bd. Infectious Disease. Intern Yale-New Haven Hosp., 1964-65, resident in medicine, 1965-67; rsch. fellow Harvard med. unit Boston City Hosp., 1968-70; chief infectious disease sect. LDS Hosp., Salt Lake City, 1970—; epidemic intelligence svc. officer Ctr. for Disease Control and Prevention, 1967—70; chief, dept. clin. epidemiology and infectious diseases Urban Ctrl. Region Intermountain Healthcare, Intermountain Med. Ctr., Salt Lake City, 2007—. Asst. prof. medicine U. Utah, Salt Lake City, 1970-75, assoc. prof., 1975-83, prof., 1983—, Mark Presdl. endowed chair in medicine, 1999—; spl. reviewer NIH, Bethesda, Md., 1978, 80; mem. tech. panel on infections within hosps. Am. Hosp. Assn., 1996; cons. Inst. Medicine, NAS, 1998—, Ctrs. for

Disease Control and Prevention, 1994, 99, 2005, Nat. Patient Safety Found., 1999, Lewin Group, 1999-2000; mem. sci. adv. coun. Heart and Lung Inst. LDS Hosp. Found., 1990—2005; co-founder Thera-Doc, Inc., 1999. Mem. editl. bd. Am. Jour. Infection Control, 1981-97, Infection Control and Hosp. Epidemiology, 1979-88, 2003-; contbr. numerous articles to med. jours., chpts. to books. Surgeon USPHS, 1967-70. NIH-Nat. Inst. Allergy and Infectious Disease grantee, 1974-79, 79-82, 83-85, 86-89, FDA, 1999. Fellow Infectious Disease Soc. Am., ACP, Soc. for Healthcare Epidemiology Am. (councillor 1981-82, treas. 1985-88, v.p. 1991, mem. bd. dirs. 1991-93, pres. 1992); mem. Utah Med. Assn. (del. 1975-77), Am. Epidemiol. Soc., Alpha Omega Alpha, Phi Beta Kappa. Mem. Christian Ch. Home: 1966 Yale Ave Salt Lake City UT 84108-1827 Office: LDS Hosp Med Office Bldg Ste 204 370 9th Ave Salt Lake City UT 84103 Office Phone: 801-408-1006. Business E-Mail: john.burke@hsc.utah.edu.

BURKE, MICHAEL J., psychiatrist, educator; b. Canton, Ohio, June 4, 1956; PhD, Med. Coll. Wis., 1985; MD, U. Kans. Sch. Medicine, 1989. Bd. cert. in gen., geriat., forensic psychiatry. Assoc. prof. psychiatry U. Kans. Sch. Medicine, 1993—. Chair Drug Utilization Rev. Bd., Kans. Health Policy Authority, 2003—; adv. bd. mem. Ctr. Environ. and Human Health, Wichita State U., 2006—; assoc. editor, psychiatry MedEdPORTAL, Multimedia Jour. Assn. Am. Med. Colls., 2008—; expertise in psychopharmacology and brain stimulation therapies. Recipient Kemper Tchg. Excellence fellowship, Office of Chancellor, U. Kans., Physician's Recognition award with commendation, AMA; named Outstanding Tchr., U. Kans. Sch. Medicine, Dept. Psychiatry. Master: APA, Assn. Dirs. Med. Student Edn. Psychiatry, Kans. Psychiat. Soc. Office: University Kans Sch Medicine Wichita KS 67214 Office Fax: 316-293-1874. Business E-Mail: mjburke@kumc.edu.

BURKE, REDMOND PAUL, cardiologist, surgeon; b. Honolulu, Hawaii, Nov. 4, 1958; married; 1 child. BA, Stanford U., Palo Alto, CA, 1980; MD, Harvard Med. Sch., Boston, MA, 1984. Lic. Mass., 1989, Fla., 1995, cert. Nat. Bd. Med. Examiners Diplomate, 1985, Advanced Trama and Life Support, 1986, Advanced CPR and Emergency Cardiac Care, 1989, Am. Bd. Surgery Diplomate, 1990, Am. Bd. Thoracic Surgery Diplomate, 1993, Am. Bd. Surgery Recertification, 2002. Rsch. asst., dept. immunology Stanford U. Children's Hosp., Palo Alto, Calif., 1977; rsch. asst., statistician, dept. radiology Palo Alto Veteran's Adminstrn. Hosp., Palo Alto, Calif., 1978; rsch. fellow, surgery Harvard Med. Sch., Boston, 1989—90, instructor, surgery, 1992—95; intern, surgery Brigham and Women's Hosp., Boston, 1984—85, resident, surgery, 1985—89, chief resident, cardiothoracic surgery, 1990—91, assoc., cardiac surgery, 1991—95, attending surgeon, 1992—95; clin. fellow, surgery Children's Hosp., Boston, 1984—89, assoc., cardiac surgery, 1991—95, attending surgeon, 1992—95, chief resident, cardiovascular surgery, 1992; chief, divsn. cardiovascular surgery Miami Children's Hosp., Fla., 1995—2002, mem. mortality review com. Fla., 1995—, divsn. chief, daily adminstrn. pediatric cardiovascular surgery program Fla., 1995—; apptd. cardiac surgeon, cardiac surgeon program Arnold Palmer Hosp., Orlando, Fla., 2002—. Vis. scientist MIT, Cambridge, Mass., 1989—92, mem. adv. com., spectroscopy lab., 1994—; vis. instr., dept. biomedical engring. U. Miami, Fla., 1995—; attending surgeon Boston Adult Congenital Heart Svc., Mass., 1992—95; mem. adv. com. Premier Cardiac Surgery Physician, 1999—; founder, co-dir. Congenital Heart Inst., Miami, Fla., 2002—; lectr. in field. Contbr. articles to profl. jours., chapters to books; reviewer Jour. Thoracic and Cardiovascular Surgery, 1995—, Annals of Thoracic Surgery, 1995—, mem. editl. bd. Heart Surgery Forum, 1999—, Jour. Laparoendoscopic & Advanced Surgical Techniques, 1999—, mem. med. team Miracle Workers, ABC, 2006—, guest appearance The View, 2006. Vice-chmn. American Heart Walk, Miami, Fla., 2000; mem. med. adv. bd. Children's Heart Found., 2004—; bd. dir. Island Dolphin Cove, Key Largo, Fla., 2000—. Recipient Best Doctor in Am. award, 2001—02, Fla. Med. Bus. Healthcare award, 2002, Valor award, Am. Diabetes Assn., 2004; named Best Doctors in South Fla., Miami Metro Mag., 1998—2000, Most Wired Physician, State Fla., 2002. Fellow: Am. Coll. Surgeons, Coun. on Cardiothoracic and Vascular Surgery, Am. Heart Assn.; mem.: Internat. Soc. for Heart and Lung Transplantation, Candidate Soc. Thoracic Surgeons, Mass. Med. Soc., Southern Thoracic Surgical Assn., Soc. Thoracic Surgeons (active mem. 1998—), Internat. Soc. for Minimally Invasive Cardiothoracic Surgery, Cardiothoracic Surgery Network, Harvard Med. Sch. Alumni Assn. (class rep. 1985—), Phi Beta Kappa. Achievements include performing the first pediatric heart lung transplant in New England in 1992; developing and refining of minimally invasive surgical techniques in pediatric cardiothoracic surgery; patents in field. Office: Miami Children's Hosp Dept Cardiovascular Surgery 3200 SW 60th Ct Ste 102 Miami FL 33155 Office Phone: 305-663-8401. Office Fax: 305-669-6574. Business E-Mail: redmond111@aol.com.

BURKE, RICHARD T., SR., healthcare company executive, former professional sports team executive; b. Raleigh, NC; m. Jude; children: Taylor, Ryan, Brendan, Ian, Shannon. Grad., Ga. State U., U. Va. Founder, chmn., CEO United HealthCare Corp., 1974—88; owner, CEO, gov. Phoenix Coyotes (formerly Winnipeg Jets) hockey club, 1995—2001; non-exec. chmn. UnitedHealth Group, Inc., Mpls., 2006—. Bd. dir. UnitedHealth Group, 1977—, First Cash Fin. Services, 1993—, Meritage Homes Corp., 2004—. Office: United-Health Group PO Box 1459 Minneapolis MN 55440-5979 *

BURKE, SHEILA P., federal agency administrator; b. San Francisco, Jan. 10, 1951; d. George Abbott and Mary Joan (Winfield) B.; m. David Chew, Jan. 1983; children: Daniel, Kathleen, Sarah. BSN, U. San Francisco, 1973; MA in Pub. Adminstrn., Harvard U., 1982. Staff nurse Alta Bates Hosp., Berkeley, Calif., 1973-74; dir. student affairs Nat. Student Nurses Assn., NY, 1974-75; dir. program and field svcs., 1975-77; legis. asst. Senator Bob Dole, 1977-78; profl. staff mem. Senate Com. Fin., U.S. Senate, 1979-82, dep. staff dir., 1982-85; dep. chief of staff Senate Majority Leader Bob Dole, U.S. Senate, 1985-86; chief of staff Senator Bob Dole, 1986-96; sec. U.S. Senate, Washington, 1995; undersec. Am. Mus. and nat. programs Smithsonian Instn., Washington, 2000—03, dep. sec., COO, 2004—07. Adj. nursing faculty Georgetown U.; rsch. asst. J.F. Kennedy Sch. Govt., Harvard U., 1980-81, advisor to dean, 1996, exec. dean, lectr. pub. policy, 1996-2000, adj. lectr., 2000—. Mem.: Inst. Medicine. Republican. Address: 1323 Merrie Ridge Rd Mc Lean VA 22101-1826 Office Phone: 571-257-9150. E-mail: sheila_burke@harvard.edu.

BURKE, WILLIAM J., geriatrician, psychiatrist, educator; MD, U. Nebr. Diplomate Am. Bd. Psychiatry and Neurology, 1986, Am. Bd. Psychiatry and Neurology-geriatric psychiatry, 2001. Resident in internal medicine Univ. Nebr. Med. Ctr., 1980—81; resident in psychiatry Wash. Univ. Barnes Hosp., 1981—84; prof. psychiatry Univ. Nebr. Med. Ctr., Omaha, vice chair rsch. dept. of psychiatry. Dir. psychopharmacology rsch. consortium UNMC. Named one of The Best Doctors in America. Fellow: Am. Psychiatric Assn., Am. Geriatric Soc. Office: The Nebraska Medical Center 42nd and Dewey Omaha NE 68198 Office Phone: 402-552-2000.

BURKE, WYLIE, medical geneticist; PhD, U. Wash., 1974, PhD, 1978. Assoc. dir. internal medicine residency prog. U. Wash., Seattle, 1988—94, founding dir. Women's Health Care Ctr., 1994, prof., chair med. history and ethics, 2000—, adj. prof. med. genetics and epidemiology. Vis. sci. CDC Nat. Ctr. Chronic Disease Prevention and Health Promotion, 1998; adv. coun. for human genome rsch. NIH, 1999—2003. Recipient Robert S. Evans award, U. Wash., 1978. Mem.: Inst. Medicine, Am. Pub. Health Assn., Am. Soc. Human Genetics, Assn. Prevention Tchg. and Rsch., Soc. Gen. Internal Medicine. Office: U Washington Box 357120 1959 NE Pacific Seattle WA 98195 Office Phone: 206-221-5482. Office Fax: 206-685-7515. E-mail: wburke@u.washington.edu.

BURKET, JOHN MCVEY, retired dermatologist; b. Des Moines, Oct. 4, 1935; s. George Austin and Elma (McVey) B.; m. Janice Lee Feilmeyer, Dec. 29, 1956; children: Denise, Bradley, Brent, Diana, Dawn, Brian. BA, U. Iowa, 1957, MD, 1960. Diplomate Am. Bd. Dermatology, Am. Bd. Dermopathology. Resident in dermatology U. Iowa Hosp., Iowa City, 1964; chief dermatology USAF, March AFB, 1964-66; pvt. practice dermatology Medford, Oreg., 1966—. Contbr. articles to profl. jours., chpts. to books. Avocations: hunting, fishing. *

BURKEY, BRIAN, otolaryngologist, educator; Attended, Johns Hopkins U., Balt. Md., 1981; MD, U. of Va. Sch. of Medicine, Charlottesville, Va., 1986. Diplomate Am. Bd. Otolaryngology. Intern gen. surgery St. Joseph Mercy Hosp., Ypsilanti, Mich., 1987; resident otolaryngology Univ. of Mich. Health System, Ann Arbor, Mich., 1991; fellow reconstructive and microvascular surgery The Ohio State Univ. Hosps., Columbus, 1991; adj. prof. dept. of otolaryngology Vanderbilt Univ. Med. Ctr.; hosp. appointment includes Cleve. Clinic. Mem. otolaryngology residency rev. com. Accreditation Coun. for Grad. Med. Edn., 2003—10, chair otolaryngology residency rev. com., 2008—10. Recipient Disting. Svc. award, Am. Acad. of Otolaryngology-Head and Neck Surgery, 2009; named one of the Best Doctors and America's Top Doctors, 2001—, the America's Top Doctors for Cancer, 2005—, the America's Top Surgeons, 2008—. Fellow: ACS; mem.: Am. Broncho-Esophagological Assn., Soc. of Univ. Otolaryngologists, Am. Head and Neck Soc., Am. Acad. of Otolaryngology-Head and Neck Surgery. Office: Cleveland Clinic Main Campus Mail Code A71 9500 Euclid Ave Cleveland OH 44195 Office Phone: 216-444-6601.

BURKHART, CRAIG GARRETT, dermatologist, researcher; b. Toledo, Apr. 15, 1951; s. Garrett Giles and Mary Katherine (Egarius) Burkhart; m. Anna Kristina Jutila, Apr. 12, 1975; children: Kristina Maria, Craig Nathaniel, Heidi Rebecca. BA, U. Pa., 1972; MD, Med. Coll. Ohio, 1975; MPH, U. Toledo, Ohio, 1983. Diplomate Am. Bd. Dermatology. Intern, resident, fellow U. Mich. Hosps., 1976-79; pvt. practice dermatologist, 1979—; pres. Gar-Nat Lab., Inc., 1997—. Clin. prof. medicine Med. U. Ohio; clin. asst. prof. dermatology Ohio U. Coll. Osteo. Medicine; editl. bd. Dermatology News, 1996—, Open Dermatology Jour., 2004—, Open Dermatology Letter, 2006—, Open Dermatology Review, 2006—, Dermatology Rsch. and Practice, 2006—; asst. editor Ohio Dermatologic State Jour., 2006—. Editor: Jour. Dermatology and Allergy, 1980—; mem. editl. bd. Jour. Current Adolescent Medicine, 1980—, mem. editl. adv. bd. Ohio State Med. Jour., 1982—, Cortlandt Forum, 1999—; contbr. chapters to books, articles to profl. jours. Mem. Toledo Zoo, Toledo Mus. Art. F. M. Douglass Found. Rsch. grantee, 1998, 2000, 2001. Mem.: AMA, Ohio Dermatologic Found. (bd. dirs. 2005—, v.p. 2006—), Toledo Acad. Medicine (bd. dirs. 2002—, v.p. 2005—), Mich. Dermatologic Assn., Ohio State Med. Assn., Ohio Dermatologic Assn. (bd. dirs. 2002—, pres. 2005—), Acad. Dermatology, U. Toledo Alumni Assn. (bd. dirs. 2006—), Med. U. Ohio Alumni Assn. (bd. dirs. 2000—03), Phi Beta Kappa (pres. N.W. Ohio 1984—86). Achievements include patents in field. Home: 4556 Crossfields Rd Toledo OH 43623-2628 Office: 5600 Monroe St Ste 106B Sylvania OH 43560-2728 Office Phone: 419-885-3403. Personal E-mail: cgbakb@aol.com.

BURKLE, FREDERICK MARTIN, JR., physician, educator; b. New Haven, Apr. 28, 1940; MD, U. Vt., Burlington, 1965; MPH, U. Calif., Berkeley, 1975; DTM, Royal Coll. Surgeons, Dublin, 2006. Capt. USN Res. MC, 1965—2000; sr. fellow Harvard Humanitarian Initiative, Cambridge, Mass., 2007—; internat. scholar Woodrow Wilson Internat. Ctr. Scholars, Washington, 2008—. Sr. scholar, vis. prof. Ctr. Refugee and Disaster Response Johns Hopkins Bloomberg Sch. Pub. Health, Balt., 2000—02. Fellow: Am. Acad. Pediat., Am. Colls. Emergency Medicine and Pediat.; mem.: Inst. Medicine. Home: 452 Iana St Kailua HI 96734 Office: Harvard Humanitarian Initiative 14 Story St Cambridge MA 02138 Business E-Mail: fburkle@hsph.harvard.com.

BURLAGE, DOROTHY DAWSON, clinical psychologist; b. San Antonio, Sept. 13, 1937; d. Joseph M. and Virginia (Hendrix) Dawson. BA, U. Tex., 1959; EdM, Harvard U., 1972, PhD, 1978. Lic. psychologist, Mass. Horace Lentz lectr. Harvard Coll., 1972-73; rsch. assoc. in psychiatry Harvard Med. Sch., Cambridge, Mass., 1976-78; rsch. assoc. Children's Hosp. Med. Ctr., Boston, 1978-79; clin. fellow psychology Harvard Med. Sch., 1978-80; staff psychologist Eliot Community Mental Health Ctr., Concord, Mass., 1980-85; instr. dept. psychiatry Harvard Med. Sch., 1984-88; mem. staff dept. psychiatry Newton Wellesley Hosp., 1986-92; cons. psychologist Harvard U. Health Svcs., 1991—2000; pvt. practice clin. psychologist Boston; clin. supr. Children's Hosp., Boston, 1994-96. Cons. in field. Co-author: Deep in Our Hearts, 2000; contbr. articles to profl. jours. Bd. dirs. Children's Mus., Boston, 1988-94, Families First, 1992-96, Profls. for Parents and Families, 1994; mem. scientist adv. bd. Mind Sci. Found., 1994. Grantee HEW, Bus. and Profl. Women's Found., 1976; fellow NIMH, 1972-73, 73-74, Zeta Tau Alpha, 1972-73; Woodrow Wilson fellow in Women's Studies, 1976-77. Mem. Am. Psychol. Assn., Mass. Psychol. Assn., AOA. Home: 166 Oakleigh Rd Newton MA 02458-2224

BURLINGAME, MARK WAYNE, cardiothoracic surgeon; b. St. Paul, Oct. 8, 1950; s. Charles Frank and Patricia Ann (Meyer) B.; m. Anine Marie Davidson, May 18, 1975; children: Patrick, Kathleen, Julia, Ross. BA in Biology, Northwestern U., 1971; MD cum laude, Creighton U., 1975. Diplomate Am. Bd. Surgery, Am. Bd. Thoracic Surgery; lic. surgeon, Ala., Wis., Mich., Pa. Quality control microbiologist Allergan Pharms., 1971; extern Tex. Heart Inst. Baylor U., 1974; intern U. Ala. Hosps., Birmingham, 1975-80; resident in cardiothoracic surgery Med. Coll. Wis. Hosps., Milw., 1980-82; pvt. practice Pontiac, Mich., 1982-83, Lancaster, Pa., 1983—; active staff Lancaster Gen. Hosp., 1983—. Dir. critical care Lancaster Gen. Hosp., 1993—, chmn. dept. surgery, 1997-2000, chief divsn. of cardiothacic surgery, 2000—; courtesy staff Lancaster Regional Med. Ctr., 1983—2001, Cmty. Hosp. Lancaster, 1983—2001. Contbr. articles to profl. jours. Rsch. fellow NSF, 1969, 70, Argonne Nat. Lab./U.S. Atomic Energy Commn., 1970; Summer fellow Creighton U., 1972. Fellow ACS, Am. Coll. Cardiology, Am. Coll. Chest Physicians, Soc. Thoracic Surgeons; mem. Pa. Med. Soc., Pa. Assn. Thoracic Surgery, Lancaster City and County Med. Soc., Beta Beta Beta, Alpha Omega Alpha. Avocations: piano, golf, gourmet food, wine. Office: Cardiothoracic Surgeons Lancaster 540 N Duke St Ste 110 Lancaster PA 17604-3555 Home: 39 Deer Ford Dr Lancaster PA 17601-5642 Home Phone: 717-295-9334; Office Phone: 717-544-4995. E-mail: CTSL@cardiacsurgeons.com.

BURM, JINPIL, pharmacologist, educator; b. Kwangju, Republic of Korea, Mar. 7, 1955; m. Sunhee Kim, Dec. 4, 1983; children: Chungwon, Yongwon. M of Biopharmaceutics, Chosun U., Korea, 1983, PhD, 1986. Pharmacist Min. of Drug and Health, Korea, 1981. Pharmacist Chosun U. Hosp., Kwangju, Republic of Korea, 1981—83; prof. pharmacology Dongsin U., 2003—04, Chosun Nursing Coll., Kwangju, Republic of Korea, 1983—2005, Christian Coll. of Nursing, 1987—90; vis. prof. U. of So. Calif., 1991—93; prof. of clin. pharmacy Chosun U., 1994—95; chair of student adminstrn. Chosun Nursing Coll., 1995—98; prof. of drug and health Chosun U., 1997—; chair of sch. adminstrn. Chosun Nursing Coll., 2000—02; prof. of pharmacology Kwangju Woman's U., 2003—. Dir. of dur Korean Coll. of Clin. Pharmacy, 1994—; vis. rschr. Chosun U. Pharm. Rsch. Inst., 1998—2000; editor Korean Coll. of Clin. Pharmacy, Seoul, Korea (South), 1998—2004; dir. Korean Soc. of Pharm. Sciences and Tech., 2000—02. Contbr. articles to profl. jours. Dir. Korean Food and Drug Adminstrn., Korean Assn. Against Drug Abuse, 1999—2006, Kwangju Winsurfing Assn., 1998—2006. Recipient award, Vice Prime Min., 2001, Fun Class Silver medal, Korean Winsurfing Assn., 2002, Korean Food and Drug Adminstrn., 2002. Avocations: windsurfing, skiing. Office: Chosun Nursing Coll 280 Seosuk-Dong Dong-Gu Kwangju 501-825 Republic of Korea Office Fax: 80-62-575-5900. Business E-Mail: jpburm@cnc.ac.kr.

BURMEISTER, LYNN A., endocrinologist, educator; BS with distinction, U. Minn., 1981, MD, 1985. Diplomate Am. Bd. Internal Medicine, 1988, Am. Bd. Internal Medicine-endocrinology, diabetes and metabolism, 2001, lic. Minn., 2002. Resident internal medicine Univ. Minn. Med. Ctr., 1986—88, fellow endocrinology and metabolism, 1988—89; instr. divsn. endocrinology, dept. medicine Univ. Minn. Hosps., 1990—91; assoc. prof. divsn. endocrinolog, dept. medicine Univ. Minn., 2002—; staff physician Univ. Minn. Med. Ctr., 2002—, med. dir. Univ. Minn. Physicians Medicine, 2002—; staff physician Oakland VA Hosp., Pitts., 1991—2001; asst. prof. divsn. endocrinolog, dept. medicine Univ. Pitts. Sch. of Medicine, 1991—96, 1997—2001; staff physician Pitts. Med. Ctr., Presbyn. Univ. Hosp., 1991—2001, Univ. Pitts. Med. Ctr, Montefiore Univ. Hosp., 1991—2001, Univ. Pitts. Med. Ctr., Horizon Hosp., 1997—99, Univ. Pitts. Med. Ctr., St. Margaret Hosp., 1999—2001. Named one of Best Doctors for Women, Minn. Monthly Mag., 2007, 2008. Mem.: Internat. Soc. of Clin. Densitometry, Am. Thyroid Assn., Am. Assn. of Clin. Endocrinologists, Endocrine Soc. Office: University of Minnesota Department of Medicine 420 Delaware St SE Minneapolis MN 55455 Office Phone: 612-626-1960. E-mail: Burme008@umn.edu.

BURN, IAN JOHN, retired surgeon, oncologist; b. London, Feb. 19, 1927; s. Cyril and Margaret (Cawthorne) B.; m. Fiona May Allan, Sept. 22, 1951; children: Alastair, Hilary, Lindsay, Jonathan. MB, BS, St. Bartholomew's Hosp., London, 1950; BA in Opera Studies, Manchester U., Eng., 2001. Surg. registrar St. Bartholomews and Hammersmith Hosps., 1955-65; travelling fellow Roswell Park Mem. Inst., Buffalo, 1961-62; cons. surgeon, asst. dir. surgical studies Royal Postgrad. Med. Sch. Hammersmith Hosp., London, 1965-73; cons. surgical oncologist Charing Cross Hosp., London, 1973-87; cons. surgeon King Edward VII Hosp., Midhurst, Eng., 1987-97, med. dir., 1993-95, cons. emeritus, 1997—. Author: Systematic Surgery, 1966, British Association of Surgical Oncology, The First Twenty Five Years, 1998, Journey of a Cancer Surgeon, 2007; editor: Notable Barber Surgeons, Farrand Press., 2008, The Company of Barbers and Surgeons, 2000; sr. editor European Jour. Surg. Oncology, 1986-94; co-editor: Understanding Cancer, 1977, European Handbook of Surgical Oncology, 1989, Breast Cancer, 1989, Operative Cancer Surgery, 1992. Med. adv. com. Women's Nat. Cancer Campaign; past chmn. current treatment com. Internat. Union Against Cancer; freeman City of London. Fellow Royal Coll. Surgeons (diplomate, Hunterian prof.), Royal Soc. Medicine (hon. sec. 1981-87, v.p. 1989-91; mem. U.I.C.C. Roll Honour, European Soc. Surg. Oncology (pres. 1987-91), World Fedn. Surg. Oncology Socs. (pres. 1992-95), Brit. Assn. Surg. Oncology (pres. 1980-83), Finnish Surg. Soc. (hon.), Belgian Assn. Surgeons (hon.), Barber-Surgeons Livery Co. Avocations: opera, writing, gardening. Home Phone: 01367-243551.

BURNEI, GHEORGHE, paediatric orthopaedics professor; b. Vulcana Pandele, Dambovita, Romania, Sept. 21, 1952; s. Gabriel and Lazarica Burnei; m. Doina Gabriela Burnei; children: Cristian, Anca. MD, UMF Carol Davila, Bucharest, PhD, 1978. Cert. prof. UMF Carol Davila, 2007. Resident dr. Grigore Alexandrescu Hosp., Bucharest, Romania, 1981—85; specialist registrar Mangalia Mcpl. Hosp., Constanta, Romania, 1985—91; assoc. prof. UMF Carol Davila, 1998—2007, prof., 2007—; head pediatric orthop. clinics Marie Sklodowska Curie Hosp., Bucharest, 2003. Author: (book) Osteosynthesis and Limb Lengthening in Pediatric Orthopedics, Pediatric and Orthopedic Surgery, Osteoporosis-Fundamental Facts, Electromagnetic Fields and their Biological Role, Malignant Bone Tumors and Electromagnetic Therapy. Recipient Nagrode-Naukowa prize, Children's Surgery Acad. Soc., Szczecin, Poland, 1993. Mem.: ARTOP (pres. 2008—). Achievements include development of original surgical techniques: continuous intraosseous lavage-drainage system, quadruple osteotomy, proximal radioulnar ligamentoplasty, arthroplastic hip reconstruction and limb lengthening. Home: Str Panselelor Nr 14 Bucharest 042065 Romania Office: Marie Sklodowska Curie Emerg Hosp Bd Constantin Brancoveanu Nr 20 Bucharest 041451 Romania Personal E-mail: mscburnei@yahoo.com.

BURNETT, LONNIE SHELDON, retired obstetrics and gynecology educator; b. Saratoga, Tex., Aug. 2, 1927; s. Lonnie and Lois (Swift) B.; m. Betty Pearle Scruggs, Dec. 22, 1950; children: Anne Julian, Michael Julian. BS, U. Tex., 1948; MD, U. Tex., Galveston, 1953. Diplomate Am. Coll. Ob-Gyn. (chmn. Tenn. sect. 1988-91, mem. com. on sci. program 1988-91). Intern Henry Ford Hosp., Detroit, 1953-54; resident in internal medicine Mayo Clinic, Rochester, Minn., 1954-55; resident in ob-gyn. Johns Hopkins Hosp., Balt., 1957-62, fellow in microbiology, 1962-64; asst. prof. microbiology Johns Hopkins U., Balt., 1964-67, asst. prof. ob-gyn., 1964-70, assoc. prof., 1970-76; chmn. dept. ob-gyn. Vanderbilt U., Nashville, 1976-95, prof. ob-gyn., 1976—2011, Frances and John C. Burch prof. ob-gyn., 1995—2011. Mem. ob-gyn. text com. Nat. Bd. Med. Examiners, 1988-91. Co-author: Novak's Textbook of Gynecology, 11th edit., 1988; contbr. articles to profl. jours. Capt. USAF, 1955-57. Macy scholar Josiah Macy Jr. Found., 1965-70. Mem.: Canby Robinson Soc. of Vanderbilt U. Med. Ctr. (pres. 2006—07), Nashville Acad. Medicine (pres. 1999—2000), Tenn. Ob-Gyn. Soc. (pres. 1988—90). Republican. Episcopalian. Avocation: photography. Home: 78 Concord Park W Nashville TN 37205-4707 Home Phone: 615-385-3048. Personal E-mail: lsburnett@comcast.net.

BURNS, C(HARLES) PATRICK, hematologist, oncologist; b. Kansas City, Mo., Oct. 8, 1937; s. Charles Edgar and Ruth (Eastham) B.; m. Janet Sue Walsh, June 15, 1968; children: Charles Geoffrey, Scott Patrick. BA, U. Kans., 1959, MD, 1963. Diplomate Am. Bd. Internal Medicine, subsplty. bds. hematology, med. oncology. Intern Cleve. Met. Gen. Hosp., 1963-64; asst. resident in internal medicine Univ. Hosps., Cleve., 1966-68, sr. resident in hematology, 1968-69; instr. medicine Case Western Res. U., Cleve., 1970-71; asst. chief hematology Cleve. VA Hosp., 1970-71; asst. prof. medicine U. Iowa Hosps., Iowa City, 1971-75, assoc. prof. medicine, 1975-80, prof., 1980—2006, prof. emeritus, 2006—, dir. sect. med. oncology, co-dir. divsn. hematatol./oncology, 1980-85, dir. div. hematology, oncology, blood marrow transplantation, 1985-99. Vis. scientist Imperial Cancer Rsch. Fund Labs., London, 1982-83; cons. U.S. VA Hosp.; mem. study sect. on exptl. therapeutics NIH, Cancer Ctr. Support Rev. Commn. Nat. Cancer Inst., NIH, NIH Cancer Clin. Investigation Rev. Com., Com. H Nat. Cancer Inst., VA Med. Rsch. Svc. Career Devel. Com.; mem. external adv. com. U. Oreg. Cancer Ctr., 1994-2000; mem. oncology group external adv. com., ACS, 2004-; cons. Irish Rsch. Bd., Dublin, 2000— Mem. bd. assoc. editors Cancer Rsch., 1988-2000, rsch. and publs. on hematologic malignancies, tumor lipid biochemistry, leukemia and oncology, role of oxidation in cancer treatment. Chair Med. Exec. Com.; mem., bd. dirs., vol. Medicine Clinic, Hilton Head, SC. Served to capt. USMC, 1964—66, Am. Cancer Soc. fellow in hematology oncology, 1968-69, USPHS fellow in medicine, 1969-70; USPHS career awardee, 1978; Outstanding Paper Presentation, Am. Oil Chemists Soc., 1992. Master ACP; mem. AAAS, Am. Bd. Internal Medicine (subsplty. bd. hematology test writing com. 1992-98, com. on recent advances in hematology, 2002—, chair 2006—), Am. Soc. Hematology (disting., emeritus), Am. Assn. Cancer Rsch., Internat. Soc. Hematology, Ctrl. Soc. Clin. Rsch., Am. Soc. Clin. Oncology, Soc. Exptl. Biology and Medicine, Oxygen Soc., Royal Soc. Medicine, Am. Fedn. Clin. Rsch., Internat. Soc. for the Study of Fatty Acids and Lipids, Phi Beta Pi, Lambda Chi Alpha, Alpha Omega Alpha. Home: 341 Greenwood Dr Hilton Head Island SC 29928 Home Phone: 843-671-2555. Business E-Mail: c-burns@uiowa.edu.

BURNS, SISTER ELIZABETH MARY, retired hospital administrator; b. Estherville, Iowa, Mar. 3, 1927; d. Bernard Aloysius and Viola Caroline (Brennan) B. Diploma in Nursing, St. Joseph Mercy Sch. Nursing, Sioux City, Iowa, 1952; BS in Nursing Edn, Mercy Coll., Detroit, 1957; M.Sc. in Nursing, Wayne State U., 1958; Ed.D., Columbia U., 1969. Joined Sisters of Mercy, Roman Cath. Ch., 1946; nursing supr. Mercy Med. Ctr., Dubuque, Iowa, 1952-55; supr. orthopedics and urology St. Joseph Mercy Hosp., Sioux City, 1955-56; dir. Sch. Nursing, 1958-63; chmn. dept. nursing Mercy Coll. of Detroit, 1963-73; dir. health svcs. Sisters of Mercy, 1973-77; pres., CEO Marian Health Ctr., Sioux City, 1977-87; sabbatical leave, 1988; ret., 2006. Coord. life planning Sisters of Mercy, 1989-90, mem. province adminstrv. team, 1990-98; cons. Trinity Health, 2001—. Bd. dirs. Mercy Sch. Nursing of Detroit, 1968-77, Mercy H.S., Farmington Hills, Mich., 2000-05; mem. exec. com. Greater Detroit Area Hosp. Coun., 1973-77; trustee St. Mary Coll., Omaha, 1981-82, Briar Cliff Coll., Sioux City, 1981-87, Battle Creek Health Sys., 1998-2000, 02-04, Mercy Med. Ctr., Sioux City, Iowa, 2001-05; chmn. Mercy Health Adv. Coun., 1978-80. Mem. Western Iowa League for Nursing (pres. 1960-62), Nat. League for Nursing, Sister Mercy Healthcare, Sisters of Mercy Shared Svcs. Coordinating Com., Cath. Hosp. Assn. (trustee 1977-80), Sisters of Mercy Health Corp. (trustee 1988-90, governance coord. 1998-2001), Mercy Health Svcs. (chair bd. 1990-95, membership bd. 1995-98, historian 1998-2004). Address: 28554 Eleven Mile Farmington MI 48336-1507

BURNS, JAMES, medical educator; b. Kenmore, NY, Aug. 15, 1965; MD, U. Va. Sch. Medicine, 1991. Assoc. prof., surgery Mass. Gen. Hosp., 2005—. Office: One Bowdoin Sq 11th Fl Boston MA 02114 Business E-Mail: burns.james@mgh.harvard.edu.

BURNS, PADRAIC, psychiatrist, educator; b. Des Moines, Aug. 31, 1929; s. Charles and Ethel P. (Bentz) B.; m. Ikuko Kawai, Oct. 19, 1959; children: Kenneth, Amelia, Margaret. BA, U. Chgo., 1948; postgrad., NYU, 1949-51; MD, Yale U., 1955. Diplomate Am. Bd. Psychiatry, 1965, Am. Bd. Child Psychiatry, 1967. Asst. prof. psychiatry Boston U., 1969-72, assoc. prof. psychiatry, 1972—. Capt. U.S. Army, 1957-59. Fellow Am. Acad. Child Psychiatry; mem. Am. Psychiat. Assn., Mass. Psychiat. Soc., Boston Psychoanalytic Soc. and Inst. Home: 9 Downing Rd Brookline MA 02445-2114 Office: 7 Orchard Rd Brookline MA 02445-2119 Office Phone: 617-414-5080.

BURNS, SANDRA N., nursing educator; b. Sacramento, Sept. 30, 1958; MSN, Kaplan U., 2010; PhD, Capella U. Asst. prof. & adj. faculty USN, 2010—. Reviewer Lippincott, 2011. Mem.: Alpha Beta Kappa Nat. Honor Soc. Avocations: Broadway shows, jazz, travel. Home: 20642 Iris Canyon Rd Riverside CA 92508 Home Fax: 951-867-3221. Personal E-mail: sandraburns58@gmail.com.

BURR, DAVID BENTLEY, anatomy educator; b. Findlay, Ohio, June 28, 1951; s. Willard Bentley and Dorothy Eleanor (Beiler) B.; m. Lisa Marie Pedigo; children: Kathryn Lise, Michael David, Erik Johan. BA, Beloit Coll., Wis., 1973; MA, U. Colo., Boulder, 1974, PhD, 1977. Instr. anatomy U. Kans. Med. Ctr., Kansas City, 1977-78, asst. prof. anatomy, 1978-80; asst. prof. anatomy and orthop. surgery W.Va. U., Morgantown, 1980-83, assoc. prof., 1983-86, prof., 1986-90; chmn. dept. anatomy and cell biology, prof. anatomy, bioengring. Ind. U., Indpls., 1990—, chmn., 1990—2011. Mem. adv. bd. dirs. Primate Found. Am., Tempe, Ariz., 1978-2008; cons. County Med. Examiner, Morgantown, 1983-89; mem. Adv. Group for the Treatment Human Remains, USDA, Monongahela Nat. Forest Svc., 1989; cons. NASA, 1990-91, Am. Inst. Biol. Sci., NAS, 1990—, U.S. Congress Office Tech. Assessment, 1990; mem. biochemistry study sect. Arthritis found., 1992-95; spl. grants rev. com. NIH, 1996-2000. Author: Structure, Function & Adaptation of Compact Bone, 1989, Skeletal Tissue Mechanics, 1998, Musculoskeletal Fatigue and Stress Fracture, 2001, Bridging the Gap Between Dental and Orthopaedic Implants, 2002; mem. editl. bd. Bone, 1993-2003, Jour. Bone and Mineral Metabolism, 1994-, Jour. Biomech., 1999-, Calcif. Tiss. Int., 2000-; assoc. editor Bone, 2004—, Jour. Musculoskeletal Neuronal Interactions, 2004—, Exptl. Biol. Medicine, 2006-09; contbr. articles to profl. jours. Pres. First Ward Sch. PTA, Morgantown, 1987—88; sec. Cub Scout Pack Com., 1989; chmn. troop com. Boy Scouts Am., 1993—95; linesman Morgantown Soccer League, 1988; sec. Classic Ragtime Soc., 1997—98; clk. witness and svc. First Friends Meeting, 1999—2001; mem. adminstrv. bd. Epworth United Meth. Ch., Indpls., 1992—93. Recipient Borelli award, Am. Soc. Biomechanics, 2008, Glenn W. Irwin Jr. Disting. Faculty award, IU Alumni Assn., 2010; Rsch. grantee NIH, 1988—, Orthopedic Rsch. and Edn. Found., 1985-86. Mem.: Internat. Soc. for Musculoskeletal and Neuronal Interactions (bd. dirs. 1999—2000, 2002—08), Assn. Anatomy, Cell Biology and Neurobiology Chairpersons (pres. 2001—02), Am. Anatomy Assn. (exec. com. 1998—2001, chmn. jour. trust fund com. 2002—04, sec.-treas. 2004—05, pres. 2007—09), Orthop. Rsch. Soc. (chmn. membership com. 2002—03, program chair 2005—06, pres. 2008—09), Internat. Soc. Bone Mineral Rsch., Am. Soc. Bone Mineral Rsch. (Gideon A. Rodan Excellence in Mentorship award 2010). Avocations: piano, racquetball, reading. Office: Ind U Sch Medicine Dept Anat & Cell Biology 635 Barnhill Dr Indianapolis IN 46202-5126 Office Phone: 317-274-7434. Business E-Mail: dburr@iupui.edu.

BURRIS, BOYD LEE, psychiatrist, psychoanalyst, physician, educator; b. Knoxville, Tenn., Jan. 28, 1930; s. Fred Roosevelt and Mildred Blanche Burris. BS, U. Tenn., Knoxville, 1951; MD, U. Tenn., Memphis, 1952. Diplomate in psychiatry Am. Bd. Psychiatry and Neurology; cert. in psychoanalysis. Tng. and supervising analyst Balt.-Washington Inst. for Psychoanalysis, Washington, 1974—, co-dir., 1980-86; clin. prof. psychiatry and behavioral scis. George Washington U. Sch. Medicine, Washington, 1983—; clin. prof. psychiatry Georgetown U. Sch. Medicine, Washington, 1990—; mem. bd. trustees Ctr. for Advanced Psychoanalytic Studies, Princeton, N.J., Aspen, Colo., 1982—, pres. bd. trustees and dir., 1994—2003; pvt. practice psychiatry and psychoanalysis Washington, 1960—. Active staff George Washington U. Hosp., 1963-96; cons. Potomac Found. for Mental Health, Bethesda, Md., 1969-78, St. Elizabeth's Hosp., Washington, 1969-88. Contbr. chpt. to book, articles to profl. jours. Lt. comdr. M.C., USN, 1954-56. Mem. Am. Psychiat. Assn. (chair tellers com. 1987-88), Am. Psychoanalytic Assn. (bd. on profl. standards 1982-86, 2000-2002), Balt./Washington Soc. for Psychoanalysis (pres. 1978-79). Home: 3100 Rolling Rd Chevy Chase MD 20815-4038 Office: 4545 42nd St NW Ste 310 Washington DC 20016-4623 Home Phone: 301-656-2564.

BURRIS, JAMES FREDERICK, federal healthcare administrator, educator; b. Mauston, Wis., Apr. 15, 1947; s. James Duane and Margaret Katherine (Jones) B.; m. Christine Tuve, July 3, 1971; 1 child, Cameron William Tuve. AB, ScB, Brown U., 1970; MD, Columbia U., 1974. Diplomate Am. Bd. Internal Medicine, Subspecialty Bd. Geriatrics, Am. Bd. Clin. Pharmacology; cert. physician exec. Certifying Commn. Med. Mgmt., 2011. Intern Roosevelt Hosp., NYC, 1974-75; resident in internal medicine Georgetown U. Med. Ctr., Washington, 1977-79; fellow in hypertension VA Med. Ctr., Washington, 1979-81; asst. prof. Sch. Medicine, Georgetown U., Washington, 1981-86, assoc. prof., 1986-91, coord. MD/PhD program, 1988-94, prof., 1991-97; clin. prof., 1997—; asst. dean Sch. Medicine, Georgetown U., Washington, 1987-90; assoc. dean Sch. Medicine Georgetown U., 1990-97, dir. continuing profl. edn., 1994-97; dep. chief R&D officer Vets. Health Adminstrn., U.S. Dept. Vets Affairs, Washington, 1997—2003; chief cons. Geriatrics and Extended Care, Vets. Health Adminstrn, US Dept. Vets. Affairs, Washington, 2003—; cons. Assn. Accreditation Human Rsch. Protection Programs, 2010—. Bd. dirs. Inst. for Clin. Rsch., Washington, 1989-92; bd. regents Am. Bd. Clin. Pharmacology, 1992-98, 2002-08; rsch. adminstr. cert. coun.; rsch. assoc. hypertension unit VA Med. Ctr., Washington, 1981-92; vis. investigator Centre Hospitalier, U. Vaudois, Lausanne, Switzerland, 1982-83; dir. clin. rsch. Cardiovasc. Ctr. No. Va., Falls Church, 1988-92; delegate White House Conf. Aging, 2005 Mem. editl. bd. Jour. Clin. Pharmacology, Jour. Am. Geriat. Soc., Clin. Pharmacology and Therapeutics; contbr. over 250 articles to profl. jours. Cubmaster Boy Scouts Am., 1995-98, asst. scoutmaster, 1998—, Nat. Capital Area Coun. High Adventure Com., 2009-, mem.; DC rep., 2010-. Lt. comdr. USPHS, 1975-77, reserves 1977—2010. Recipient svc. award ARC, 1970, outstanding svc. citation DAV, 1987, meritorious svc. award Am. Heart Assn., 1994, Cubmasters award Boy Scouts Am., 1998, James E. West award, 1997, Scouter's Tng. Key award, 2000, Vicennial medal Georgetown U., 2000; commd. officer student tng. and extern program scholar USPHS, 1973-74; rsch. fellow Found. for Rsch. of Cardiovascular Diseases, Lausanne, 1983; under-sec. health's exec. performance award U.S. Dept. of Vet. Affairs, 1999, 2000, commendation award, 2003 Fellow: ACP, Am. Coll. Cardiology, Am. Coll. Clin. Pharmacology (bd. regents 1990—95, 1998—2003, hon. regent 2003, sec. 2004—08, bd. regents 2008—, Disting. Svc. award 1992), Am. Coll. Preventive Medicine, Am. Geriatrics Soc.; mem.: AMA (physician's recognition award 1982, 1985, 1988, 1991, 1994, 1997, 2001), Am. Heart Assn. (chmn. rsch. peer rev. com. 1992—94, rsch. com. 1994—96, bd. dirs. Nation's Capital affiliate 1994—97, v.p. 1995—96, fellow couns. on high blood pressure rsch., circulation, epidemiology, coun. clin. cardiology), Sigma Xi. Achievements include education and research in hypertension, hyperlipidemia, preventive cardiology and clinical pharmacology; grants and contracts management and regulatory affairs and technology transfer administration; direction of continuing professional education programs; federal research and healthcare policy development and program implementation. Office: Vets Health Adminstrn (10P4G) Dept VA 810 Vermont Ave NW Washington DC 20420-0001 Business E-Mail: james.burris@va.gov.

BURRIS, JOHN EDWARD, academic administrator, biologist, educator; b. Feb. 1, 1949; s. Robert Harza and Katherine (Brusse) Burris; m. Sally Ann Sandermann, Dec. 21, 1974; children: Jennifer, Margaret, Mary. AB, Harvard U., 1971; postgrad., U. Wis., 1971—72; PhD, U. Calif., San Diego, 1976. Asst. prof. biology Pa. State U., University Park, 1976—83, assoc. prof. biology, 1983—85; dir. bd. biology NRC/NAS, Washington, 1984—89; exec. dir. Commn. Life Scis., 1988—92; dir., CEO Marine Biology Lab, Woods Hole, Mass., 1992—2000; pres. Beloit College, Beloit, Wis., 2000—08, Burroughs Wellcome Fund, Rsch. Triangle Pk., 2008—. Adj. assoc. prof. biology Pa. State U., University Park, 1985—89, adj. prof., 1989—2001; chmn. adv. com. student sci. enrichment program Burroughs Wellcome Fund, 1995—2002; life and microgravity scis. and applications adv. com. NASA, 1997—2001; trustee Krasnow Inst., 1999—2002. Bd. dirs. Radiation Effects Rsch. Found., Grass Found., 2001—07, Naples Stazione Zoological, Consiglio Sci., Morgridge Inst. Rsch., 2009—. Mem.: AAAS (bd. dirs. 2002—06), Am. Inst. Biol. Sci. (pres. elect 1995, pres. 1996), Phi Beta Kappa. Business E-Mail: jburris@bwfund.org.

BURROW, GERARD NOEL, internist, educator; b. Boston, Jan. 9, 1933; s. William and Noelle Elvira (Money) Burrow; m. Ann Huntington Rademacher, June 22, 1956; children: Peter Noel, Elisabeth Huntington, Sarah Rogers. BA, Brown U., 1954; MD, Yale U., 1958. From asst. prof. to prof. Yale U. Sch. Medicine, New Haven, 1966-76; prof. dept. medicine U. Toronto, Ont., Canada, 1976-81, Sir John and Lady Eaton prof. medicine, 1981-88, chmn. dept., 1981-88; vice-chancellor for health scis., dean U. Calif. Sch. Medicine, San Diego, 1988-92; dean Yale U. Sch. Medicine, New Haven, 1992-97; David Paige Smith prof. medicine Yale U., New Haven, 1997—2002; dean emeritus Yale U. Sch. Medicine, 2002—, David Paige Smith prof. emeritus medicine; CEO Sea Rsch. Found., Mystic, Conn., 2002—08. Chmn. Internat. Coun. Control Iodine Deficiency Disorders, 2006—. Author: The Thyroid Gland in Pregnancy, 1972, A History of Yale's School of Medicine: Passing Torches to Others, 2002; editor (with Ferris): Medical Complications During Pregnancy, 1975, 1982, 1988, 1994, 1999; editor: (with Duffy), 2004. Chmn., bd. dirs. U. Conn. Health Ctr., 2006—11; trustee U. Conn., 2006. Fellow: ACP, Royal Coll. Physicians (Can.). Office Phone: 860-625-3123. Business E-Mail: gerard.burrow@yale.edu.

BURROWES, JERRILYNN DENISE, nutritionist, educator; b. Bklyn. MS in Nutrition, NYU, 1985, PhD in Nutrition, 2002. Registered dietitian, cert. nutritionist. Assoc. prof., chair dept. nutrition NKR-CRN; prof. C.W. Post, LI U., 2003—. Office: CW Post LI University 720 Northern BLvd Brookville NY 11548 Office Fax: 516-299-3106. Business E-Mail: drjdb@optonline.net.

BURROWS, DESMOND DAVID, dermatologist, educator; b. Bangor, Ireland, July 11, 1930; s. Hugh and Maisie Burrows; m. Marie Louise Madden, Sept. 17, 1958; children: Colin, Nigel, Judith. MB, ChB, Queens U., 1953, MD, 1958. Cons. dermatologist Royal Victoria Hosp., Belfast, Northern Ireland, 1960-95; chmn. sci. com. Congress European Acad. Dermatology, Dublin, 1996—. Prof. Queens U., Belfast, 1990—. Contbr. scientific papers, chapters to books. Recipient Sir Archibald Gray medal, Brit. Assn. Dermatologists, 2009. Fellow Royal Coll. Physicians; mem. Brit. Assn. Dermatologists (hon.;, pres. 1991-92, Gray medal), European Soc. Contact Dermatitis (pres. 1992-93), Am. Dermatology Assn. (hon.), Dermatol. Soc. Norway (hon.), Dermatol. Soc. Spain (hon.), Dermatol. Soc. Finland, Dermatol. Soc. Sweden., Pacific Dermatol. Soc. (hon.). Avocations: golf, skiing, walking. Home and Office: Apts 66/67 Stritwillis Wharf Lockview Rd BT9 5JB Belfast Northern Ireland E-mail: desmond.burrows1@ntlworld.com.

BURROWS, ROBERT PAUL, optometrist; b. Chehalis, Wash. s. Fremont O. and Pauline A. (Kostick) B.; m. Marilyn Burrows. BS in Visual Sci., Pacific U., 1979, OD, 1981. Assoc. optometric physician L.E. Hedgen, O.D. & Assocs., Chehalis, 1981—86; ptnr. Lewis County Eye & Vision Assocs., Chehalis, 1986—. Active United Way, 1981—. Rsch. grant PTU, 1980. Mem.: Wash. Assn. Optometric Physicians, Am. Optometric Assn. (charter contact lens sect., Recognition awards 1984—2011), Twin City C. of C., Kiwanis (dir. 1984—85, 1989—90, 2000—03, 2010—), Omega Epsilon Phi. Methodist. Office: 1179 S Market Blvd Chehalis WA 98532-3427 Office Phone: 360-748-9228. Business E-Mail: lceye@localaccess.com.

BURROWS, SCOTT RENTON, lab administrator, researcher; b. Brisbane, Australia, Sept. 18, 1960; BSc, Griffith U., 1980; PhD, U. Queensland, 1997. Lab. head Queensland Inst. Med. Rsch., 2001—. Adj. assoc. prof. U. Queensland, 2002—. Contbr. scientific papers. Sr. Rsch. fellowship, Nat. Health and Med. Rsch. Coun., Australia. Avocation: travel. Home: 27 Oakmont Cres Albany Creek Queensland 4035 Australia

BURSTEIN, STEPHEN DAVID, neurosurgeon; b. Bklyn., Apr. 10, 1934; s. Moe and Anna (Bloch) B.; m. Ronnie Sue Deutsch, Oct. 8, 1972; 1 dau., Alissa Aimee. BA with distinction, U. Mich., 1954; MD, SUNY, Bklyn., 1958; MS in Neurosurgery, U. Minn., Rochester, 1965. Diplomate Am. Bd. Neurol. Surgery. Surg. intern Johns Hopkins Hosp., Balt., 1958-59; neurosurgery fellow Mayo Clinic, Rochester, 1961-65; chief dept. neurosurgery South Nassau Cmty. Hosp., Oceanside, NY, 1980—, pres. med. staff, 1980-82. Chief dept. neurosurgery Franklin Gen. Hosp., Valley Stream, N.Y., 1980—; prin. Neurol. Surgery & Neurology, P.C., Freeport, N.Y., 1965—. Contbr. articles to med. jours. Bd. dirs. South Nassau Cmty. Hosp., 1978—. Lt. USNR, 1959-61. Recipient Neurosurg. Travel award Mayo Found., 1966. Fellow ACS; mem. L.I. Hearing and Speech Soc. (bd. dirs.), N.Y. State Neurosurgeons Soc. (bd. dirs.), N.Y. State Neurosurg. Soc. (pres. 1981-82, exec. dir.), Sigma Xi, Alpha Omega Alpha. Jewish. Avocations: theater, travel. Office: Neurol Surg PC 100 Merick Rd Ste 128 Rockville Centre NY 11570 Home: 43 Chestnut Hill Roslyn NY 11576 Office Phone: 516-255-9031. Personal E-mail: sdburst@optonline.net.

BURSTEN, STUART LOWELL, physician, biochemist; b. LA, Jan. 19, 1953; s. Leo and Goldie (Zeff) B.; m. Colleen Sue Thompson, May 4, 1980; children: Elisa Michelle, Shawna Mariel, Tiana Marie; m. Lesley Domino, Mar. 26, 2000. BS in Biology, Stanford U., 1975, AB Psychology, 1975; MD, Yale U., 1980. Diplomate Am. Bd. Internal Medicine, Am. Bd. Nephrology. Intern Boston City Hosp., 1980-81; resident internal medicine U. Wash., Seattle, 1981-83, fellow nephrology, 1983-85, postdoctoral rsch. fellow, nephrology, 1985-86; acting instr. U. Wash. Sch. Medicine, 1986-88, asst. prof. medicine, 1988-92, clin. asst. prof. medicine, 1992-94, clin. assoc. prof. medicine, 1994-2001; co-dir., second messenger protein chemistry divsn. Cell Therapeutic, Inc., Seattle, 1992-95, prin. scientist, lipid biology and biochemistry, 1995-2000; prin. cons., rsch. dir. Inst. Lipid Studies, 2000—. Contbr. articles to profl. jours.; patentee. Rsch. dir. Friends of Snoqualmie Valley, Wash., 1986-89. Nat. Merit Found. scholar 1971, Nat. Grocers Assn. scholar, 1971, S&H Green Stamps Assn. scholar 1971; grantee NIH, 1975-78; recipient Northwest Kidney Found. Rsch. award, 1988-89, Nat. Inst. Arthritis, Diabetes, Digestive, and Kidney Diseases fellowship, 1985-86, others. Fellow: ACP; mem.: AAAS, Am. Stats. Assn., Am. Chem. Soc., Am. Soc. Nephrology, N.Y. Acad. Scis., Am. Fedn. Med. Rsch., Am. Heart Assn. Achievements include discovering that theobromine-based alkyl chains with patentable substitutions result in modulation of fatty acid and lipid peroxidative metabolism in mammalian cells, which in turn results in profound protection against acute inflammation and oxidant injury - this has introduced or is introducing an entire new class of compounds for treatment of a broad range of human diseases, incuding renal and liver disease, and protection against acute immune damage and the side effects of radiation; in addition, related compounds have been found to have potent anti-tumor activity based on interaction with lipid-directed enzymes. Home Phone: 707-255-0503; Office Phone: 707-252-8407. Business E-Mail: whitetreelucida@hotmail.com.

BURT, ALVIN MILLER, III, anatomist, cell biologist, writer, educator; b. Bridgeport, Conn., Aug. 14, 1935; s. Alvin Miller and Esther Louise (Carey) B.; m. Dorothy Hanlin, July 15, 1961 (div.); children: Constance Walker, Carolyn Marie; m. Judith Nath, July 13, 1991; 1 stepchild, Stephen Jacob Nath. BA, Amherst Coll., 1957; PhD (USPHS fellow 1960-61), U. Kans., 1962. Asst. prof. anatomy Med. Coll. Va., Richmond, 1962-63; instr. Yale U. Med. Sch., 1963-66; mem. faculty Vanderbilt U. Med. Sch., 1966—, prof. anatomy, 1974-85, prof. cell biology, 1985-2000, prof. cell biology emeritus, 2000—; prof. cell biology Nursing Sch. Vanderbilt U., Nashville, 1994-2000, prof. cell biology in nursing emeritus, 2000—; adj. prof. biology Vol. State Cmty. Coll. Gallatin, Tenn., 2008—; sole proprietor Old Hickory Design, Hendersonville. Vis. scientist Agrl. Rsch. Coun., Inst. Animal Physiology, Babraham, Cambridge, Eng., 1972-73. Author: Textbook of Neuroanatomy, 1993; contbr. articles to profl. jours. Vestryman Episcopal Ch. of Advent, Brentwood, Tenn., 1977-81, sr. warden, 1979-81, lay reader, chalice bearer, 1975-87, tchr. adult classes, mem. diocesan lay ministry com., 1981-85; lay reader, chalice bearer St. Philips Episcopal Ch., Donelson, Tenn., 1989-92, vestryman, 1991-92, mem. diocesan total ministry com., 1990-93; mem. Stephen Ministry Diocese of Tenn., 1991—95; dir. pastoral care St. Ann's Episcopal Ch., Nashville, 1993-96, lay reader, 1994—2010, chalice bearer, 1996—2010, vestryman, 2002-05; mem. steering com. Interfaith AIDS Ministry, 1994-96; vol. ombudsman rep. Mid Cumberland Human Resources Ctr., 2001—. Recipient Research Career Devel. award USPHS, 1968-73 Mem. Am. Assn. Anatomists, Am. Soc. Neurochemistry, Human Anatomy & Physiology Soc., Internat. Soc. Neurochemistry, Internat. Brain Rsch. Orgn., Soc. Neurosci., Tenn. Outdoor Writers Assn. (v.p. 1985-86, pres.-elect 1986-87, pres. 1987-88, chmn. bd. dirs. 1988-89), Southeastern Outdoor Press Assn. (Webmaster 2002-2005), Bass Anglers Sportsmens Soc., Tenn. Spoonplugging Club (bd. dirs. 1980-88, editor newsletter 1980-85), Sigma Xi. Home and Office: 149 Bay Dr Hendersonville TN 37075-4040

BURT, RANDALL WALTER, gastroenterologist, educator; BA in Med. Sci., U. Utah Hosp., 1965—71, MD, 1971—74. Diplomate Am. Bd. Internal Medicine, 1977, Am. Bd. Internal Medicine-gastroenterology, 1979. Intern Barnes Hosp., 1974—75, resident internal medicine, 1975—77; chief resident gastroenterolgy Univ. of UT Sch. of Medicine, 1977—79, sr. dir. prevention and outreach, interim dir.; hosp. affiliation include/s Univ. of UT Hosps. and Clinics, Univ. of UT Huntsman Cancer. Prof. medicine Univ. of UT Sch. of Medicine. Author: (articles) American founder mutation for attenuated familial adenomatous polyposis, 2008, Gonadal mosaicism and familial adenomatous polyposis, 2008, Colonic adenoma risk in familial colorectal cancer--a study of six extended kindreds, 2008, and several others. Named one of Castle Connolly America's Top Doctors, 2006—10, 2011, Castle Connolly America's Top Doctors for Cancer, 2005—07, 2009—10, 2011. Office: University of Utah 30 North 1900 East SOM 4R118 Salt Lake City UT 84132-2410 Office Phone: 801-585-3281. Office Fax: 801-581-3389.

BURT, RICHARD K., physician, educator; b. Billings, Mont., Oct. 20, 1956; m. Shalina Gupta; children: Michael, Rajan, Reena, Shantha. BS in Chemistry, U. Mo., 1980; MD cum laude, St. Louis U. Sch. Medicine, 1984. Diplomate Am. Bd. Internal Medicine, cert. in med. oncology. Resident Baylor Coll. Medicine, Houston, 1984—87, chief resident medicine, 1987; biotechnology tng. fellow, lab. exptl. carcinogenesis Nat. Cancer Inst., NIH, Bethesda, Md., 1987—90, clin. assoc., med. oncology br., 1990—91; vis. fellow, bone marrow transplantation Fred Hutchinson Cancer Ctr., Seattle, 1992, Johns Hopkins Hosp., Balt., 1992; clin. assoc., bone transplantation unit Nat. Heart, Lung & Blood Inst., NIH, 1993—94; asst. prof., dir. allogeneic bone marrow transplantation Northwestern U. Feinberg Sch. Medicine, Chgo., 1994—2000, assoc. prof., chief divsn. immunotherapy, 2000—. Mem. editl. bd. Bone Marrow Transplantation, 1998—, Regenerative Medicine, 2005—, Current Stem Cell Rsch. & Therapy, 2005—; contbr. articles to profl. jours., chapters to books. Lt. cmdr. USPHS, 1991—94. Recipient Compassionate Care Physician award, Robert J. Lurie Cancer Ctr., 1999, Fidelitas award, Lupus Found. America, 2000; grantee, Roderick Duncan Rsch. Fund, 1988, Nat. Multiple Sclerosis Soc., 1995, Am. Cancer Soc., 1996, Leukemia Soc. America, 1997—99, Nat. Inst. Allergy & Infectious Disease/NIH, 1999—, Cumming Found. Med. Rsch., 2002, Broad Found., 2002. Mem.: AAAS, AMA, Am. Soc. Blood & Marrow Transplantation. Avocations: flying, weightlifting, jogging. Office: Northwestern Feinberg Sch Health Scis Bldg Rm 8254 710 N Fairbanks Ct Chicago IL 60611 Office Phone: 312-908-0059. Fax: 312-908-0064. Business E-Mail: rburt@northwestern.edu. *

BURT, ROBERT AMSTERDAM, lawyer, educator; b. Phila., Feb. 3, 1939; s. Samuel Matthew and Esther (Amsterdam) B.; m. Linda Gordon Rose, June 14, 1964; children: Anne Elizabeth, Jessica Ellen.

AB, Princeton U., 1960; BA in Jurisprudence, Oxford U., 1962, MA, 1968; JD, Yale U., 1964, MA (hon.), 1976. Bar: D.C. 1966, Mich. 1973, U.S. Supreme Ct. 1971. Law clk. to chief judge U.S. Ct. Appeals D.C., 1964—65; asst. gen. counsel Office Pres.'s Spl. Rep. Trade Negotiations, 1965—66; senatorial legis. asst., 1966—68; assoc. prof. law U. Chgo. Law Sch., 1968—70; assoc. prof., then prof. law U. Mich. Law Sch., 1970—76; prof. law in psychiatry U. Mich. Med. Sch., 1973—76; Southmayd prof. Yale U. Law Sch., 1976—93, Alexander M. Bickel prof., 1993—. Spl. master U.S. Dist. Ct. Conn., 1987-92, 95. Author: Taking Care of Strangers, 1979, Two Jewish Justices: Outcasts in the Promised Land, 1988, Constitution in Conflict, 1992, Death Is That Man Taking Names: Intersections of American Medicine, Law and Culture, 2002. Bd. dirs. Benhaven Sch. Autistic Persons, New Haven, 1977—, chmn., 1983-96; bd. dirs. Judge David L. Bazelon Ctr. Mental Health Law, 1985—, chmn., 1990-00; bd. dirs. Slifka Ctr. Jewish Life at Yale, 1996—, pres. 2009-; mem. adv. bd. Project on Death in Am., Open Soc. Inst., 1994-04; mem. adv. bd. bioethics faculty scholars program Greenwall Found., 2003-. Rockefeller fellow, 1976, John Simon Guggenheim fellow, 1997—98. Mem.: NAS, Inst. Medicine. Democrat. Jewish. Home: 66 Dogwood Cir Woodbridge CT 06525-1254 Office: Yale U Sch Law PO Box 208215 127 Wall St New Haven CT 06511-6636 Office Phone: 203-432-4960. Business E-Mail: robert.burt@yale.edu.

BURTA, CALIN MARCEL, pharmaceutical executive; b. Vascau, Romania, July 13, 1970; Degree, U. Medicine and Pharmacy, Cluj-Napoca, Romania, 1996, PhD, 2006. First line sales mgr. Novartis Pharma Svcs., Romania, 2006—, with, sales field, 2011—. Mem.: Coll. Farmacistilor Romania, Romanian Pharm. Soc. Avocation: sports. Home: Amman 20 Sector 1 Bucuresti 011613 Romania Personal E-mail: calin.burta@gmail.com.

BURTON, BARBARA ABLE, psychotherapist; b. Columbia, SC; d. Eugene Walter Able and Mary Louise (Chadwick) Cantelou; 1 child, Stacia Louise. BA in Psychology, Ga. State U.; MSW, U. Ala., 1970. Diplomate Am. Bd. Examiners in Clin. Social Work, Internat. Acad. Behavioral Medicine, Counseling and Psychotherapy. Assoc. exec. dir. Positive Maturity, Inc., Birmingham, Ala., 1970—72; comm. orgn. planner Cmty. Svc. Coun., Inc., Birmingham, 1972—75; mem. adj. faculty U. Ala., Tuscaloosa, 1975—77; dir. Ensley Outpatient Drug Abuse Clinic, Birmingham, 1975—77; dir. Sch. Social Work, Miles Coll., Birmingham, 1977—78; program mgr. and clin. cons. Goodwill Industries Ala., Birmingham, 1977—81; pvt. practice New Orleans, 1983—. Cons. Omega Internat. Inst., New Orleans, 1988-94. Author: Love Me, Love Me Not, and Other Matters That Matter, 1990. Past chmn. policy and program com. Birmingham Urban League; mem. Ala. Adv. Com. on Social Svcs., Ala. Com. for Devel. Higher Ed., Ala. Conf. Social Work. NIMH fellow Inst. on Human Sexuality, U. Hawaii, 1976. Mem. NASW (diplomate in clin. social work), Am. Assn. Sex Educators, Counselors and Therapists, Pvt. Practitioners Unit of New Orleans, Acad. Cert. Social Workers, Internat. Platform Com., Psi Chi. Avocations: creative writing, reading, interior design. Office: 3480 Summit Trail Cumming GA 30041

BURTON, CHARLES VICTOR, neurosurgeon; b. NYC, Jan. 2, 1935; s. Norman Howard and Ruth Esther (Putziger) B.; m. Joy Burton; children— Matthew, Timothy, Andrew, Dawn, Stacy, Chad. Student, Johns Hopkins U., Balt., 1952-56; MD, N.Y. Med. Coll., 1960. Diplomate Am. Bd. Neurol. Surgery, Nat. Bd. Med. Examiners, Am. Bd. Forensic Medicine, Am Bd. Spinal Surgery. Intern surgery Yale U. Med. Ctr., 1961—62; asst. resident neurol. surgery Johns Hopkins Hosp., Balt., 1962—66, chief resident, 1966—67; assoc. chief surgery, chief neurosurgery USPHS Hosp., Seattle, 1967—69; vis. research affiliate Primate Ctr., U. Wash., 1967—69; asst. prof. neurosurgery Temple U. Health Scis. Ctr., Phila., 1970—73, assoc. prof., 1973—74, neurol. research coordinator, 1970—74; dir. dept. neuroaugmentive surgery Sister Kenny Inst., Mpls., 1974—81, med. dir. Low Back Clinic, 1978—81; med. dir. Inst. Low Back & Neck Care, Mpls., 1981—2004, Ctr. Restorative Spine Surgery, St. Paul, 2004—10, Pounceforte Techs. Ltd., 2006—, Sentinel Med. Assocs., 2010—. Biomed. Instrumentations Internat., Ltd., 1988-92; co-chmn. Joint Neurosurg. Com. on Devices and Drugs, 1973-77; chmn. adv. panel on neurologic devices FDA, 1974-77, Internat. Standards Orgn., 1974-76; mem. U.S. Biomed. Instrumentation Del. to Soviet Union, 1974; co-chmn. Am. Bd. Spine Surgery. Editor Neuroorthopedics jour., 1987-1998, editor The Burton Report; editor-in-chief www.burtonreport.com, 2000, 04, 06. Rsch. fellow, Nat. Polio Found., 1956, HEW, 1958, neurosurg. fellow, Johns Hopkins Hosp., 1960—61, 1962—67, 1969—70. Fellow ACS (exec. com. Minn. chpt. 1989-92); mem. Congress Neurol. Surgeons (chmn. com. materials and devices 1972-79), Am. Assn. Neurol. Surgeons, Minn. Neurosurg. Soc., AAAS, ASTM (chmn. com. materials 1973-78), Internat. Soc. Study of Lumbar Spine (exec. com. 1986-89), N.Am. Spine Soc. (exec. com. 1987-91, chmn. com. on profl. conduct 1991-92, dir. coun. mem. affairs 1992-94, bd. dirs. 1990-94), Am. Nat. Standards Inst. (med. device tech. adv. bd. 1973-78), Am. Bd. Spine Surgery (bd. dirs. 1997—, vice chair 2002—, chair ethics com. 1998—), Philadelphia County Med. Soc. (med.-legal com. 1970-74), Minn. Med. Assn. (Gold medal award, subcom. on med. testimony 1978—), Hennepin County Med. Soc. (med.-legal com. 1975—), Mpls. Acad. Medicine, Cor et Manus Soc., Profl. Assn. Diving Instrs. (underwater photography splty. diver), Am. Back Soc., Twin Cities Spine Soc. (pres. 1994-95), Back Pain Assn. Am. (hon. chmn. 1995—), Am. Bd. Spine Surgery (bd. dirs. 1997, chmn. ethics com., v.p. 2002—, chmn. med.-legal com., co-chmn. 2002—), Assn. Ethics Spine Surgery (v.p. 2006-, bd. dirs. 2007—), Assn. Med. Ethics (bd. mem. 2010-), Johns Hopkins U. Alumni Assn. (pres. Minn. chpt. 1988-92), Yale Surg. Soc., Alpha Epsilon Delta, Assn. Ethics Spine Surgery (co chmn. 2008-10). Achievements include patents for surgical devices, operating room fiberoptic headlights, clinical therapy systems and techniques. Home: The Lowry 901 350 St Peter St Ste 901 Saint Paul MN 55102 Office: Sentinel Med Associates Ste 220 Gallery Tower Office Bldg 514 St Peter St Saint Paul MN 55102 Office Phone: 651-287-8781. Business E-Mail: cburton@sentinel-med.org.

BURTON, CLAUDE S., III, dermatologist, educator; MD, Duke U., 1979. Diplomate Am. Bd. Internal Medicine, 1982. Resident internal medicine Duke Univ. Med. Ctr., Durham, NC, 1979—82, resident dermatology, 1982—84, hosp. affiliation include; prof. dermatology Duke Univ. Sch. of Medicine, Durham, NC. Office: Duke University Medical Center Department of Dermatology PO Box 3511 Durham NC 27710 Office Phone: 919-684-3432. Office Fax: 919-681-7991.

BURTON, KATHLEEN T., mental health services professional; b. Lynn, Mass., Jan. 29, 1962; d. Charles W. and Mary L. (Mayer) Burton. BA in Psychology/Comm., Notre Dame Coll., South Euclid, Ohio, 1985; MEd in Counseling, Cleve. State U., 1990, EdS in Counseling, 1991; PhD in Clin. Psychology, Saybrook Inst., San Francisco, 2006. Cert. rational marriage and family therapist, cognitive-behavioral therapy and sensory desensitization 2008. Human rels. & devel. coord. Kaiser Permanent, Cleveland Heights, Ohio, 1984—87; counselor Cleve. Treatment Ctr., 1989—90; tchg. asst., counselor intern Cleve. State U., 1989—91; cmty. trainer Woodland (Calif.) Cmty. Options, 1991—95; mental health profl., psychologist intern Davis, Calif., 1992—95; pvt. practice mental health profl. Woodland, Calif., 1995—2001; undergrad. psychology instr. Computer Quest Ltd., 2003, Life Course Navigation; personal growth coach and human rels. cons. Lakewood, Ohio, 2004—; co-dir. Kidz World and Career Svcs. Team, Cleve., 2008—09; group leader facilitator anxiety, phobias and panic St. Lukes, 2008—; group leader, facilitator, anxiety, phobias and panic St. Lukes Parish; group leader, facilitator HIV/AIDS St. Augustines Health Campus; parents leaders tng. cert., 2010—. Group facilitator human sexuality course dept. psychiatry Davis Med. Sch., 1994—2001; group leader, facilitator anxiety, phobias and panic Woodland Sr. Ctr., 1993—99; mental health cons., creator Mental Health Matters, Pub. TV, 1995; founder Sr./Youth Fair, Woodland, 1995; mental health writer Davis Enterprise; lectr. anxiety, phobias, panic, drug addictions, Moscow, Kiev, 1994. Author: (poetry) Hold on Tight; contbr. articles to profl. jours. Recipient 1st pl., Nat. Future Design Competition, 1984. Mem.: ACA, Nat. Assn. Cognitive Behaviorial Therapists. Roman Catholic. Avocations: gardening, dance, camping, hiking. Office Phone: 216-240-1215. Business E-Mail: ktburtonphd@yahoo.com.

BURTON, NOELLE M., clinical psychologist, psychoanalyst; b. Cinnaminson, NJ, Dec. 23, 1965; d. Robert Charles Burton and Patricia O'Brien Burton Loew; m. Michael F. Lachenmayer, June 9, 2001; children: Luke Burton Lachenmayer, Nathan Michael Lachenmayer. BA, Bucknell U., Lewisburg, Pa., 1988; MS in Clin. Psychology, Nova Southeastern U., Fort Lauderdale, Fla., 1993, PsyD in Clin. Psychology, 1997. Cert. in psychoanalysis and psychotherapy NYU, 2008. Clin. program specialist Cath. Charities, Wilmington, Del., 1996—97, clin. supr., coord., 1997—98; drug alcohol treatment specialist Help Counseling, Inc., Kennett Sq., 1997—98; therapist, clin. case mgr. Devereux Found., Malvern, Pa., 1998—2000, West Chester, Pa., 1998—2000; therapist Renfrew Ctr., 2000—01; clin. psychologist, pvt. practice Wayne, Pa., 2000—09; pvt. practice, psychoanalysis, psychotherapy Haverford, Pa., 2009—. Dir.-at-large Phila. Ctr. for Psychoanalytic Edn., 2003—; co-chair Divsn. 39 Spring Meeting 2006, Phila., 2003—; founding mem. and aupervising analyst Inst. Relational Psychoanalysis Phila.; asst. editor Psychoanalytic Dialogues, NYC, 2005—10, assoc. editor, 2010—; faculty Stephen A. Mitchell Ctr., NYC. Contbr. articles to profl. jours. Mem.: APA, Divsn. 39 APA, Phila. Soc. Psychoanalytic Psychology (dir.-at-large 2002—04), Internat. Assn. Rel. Psychoanalysis & Psychotherapy, Psi Chi, Delta Gamma (life). Avocations: running, reading, golf, hiking, camping, bicycling. Office: 355C W Lancaster Ave Haverford PA 19041 Home Phone: 640-664-1626; Office Phone: 484-557-7708. Business E-Mail: burtonnm@yahoo.com.

BURTON, RICHARD IRVING, orthopedist, educator; b. Providence, Sept. 18, 1936; s. Kenneth Gould and Edith Irving (Vayro) B.; m. Margaret Ann Leaman, Apr. 5, 1961; children: Thomas Kenneth, Douglas Leaman. BA, Amherst Coll., Mass., 1958; MD, Harvard U., Cambridge, Mass., 1962. Diplomate Am. Bd. Orthopaedic Surgery (examiner 1980—2002, bd. dirs. 1989-98). Intern U. Rochester, NY, 1962-63, resident in surgery NY, 1963-64; resident in orthopedic surgery Harvard U., 1966-70; fellow in hand surgery Roosevelt Hosp., NYC, 1970-71; asst. prof. Cleve. Clinic Found., 1971-72, head sect. surgery of hand, 1971-74, assoc. prof., 1973-74; mem. faculty U. Rochester Med. Sch., 1974—, head sect. surgery of hand, 1974—2003, prof. orthopedics, 1979—, Marjorie Strong Wehle prof. orthopedics, 1995-2000, dean's prof., 2000—02, assoc. chmn. dept. orthopedics, 1981-88, chmn., 1988—2000, acting chmn. dept. neurol. surgery, 2000—02, sr. assoc. dean for acad. affairs, 2002—; sr. assoc. orthopedist Strong Meml. Hosp., Rochester, 1974-79, orthopedist, 1979—; sr. assoc. dean for acad. affairs U. Rochester Med. Sch., 2002—. Chmn. cert. of added qualifications com. Am. Bd. Orthopaedic Surgery, 1994-98. Assoc. editor Jour. Hand Surgery, 1980-84; contbr. articles to profl. jours., chpts. to books. Mem. exec. com. Monroe County chpt. Am. Arthritis Found., 1983-86; elder Presbyn. Ch. Buswell Disting. Svc. fellow, U. Rochester, 1980-81. Recipient Exec. of Yr. award, Profl. Secs. Internat., Flower City chpt., 1981. Mem. ACS, Am. Acad. Orthopedic Surgeons (chmn. hand and wrist com. 1986-89, orthopedic resources com. 1989-91), Am. Bd. Orthop. Surgery (dir. 1988-98), Am. Bd. Med. Specialties (voting rep. 1995-98), Am. Soc. Surgery of the Hand (coord. divsn. edn. 1982-85, coun. 1985-89, chmn. membership com. 1991, v.p. 1990, pres.-elect 1991, pres. 1992), Am. Orthopedic Assn. (exec. com. 1986, resident rsch. conf. com. 1987-89, chair 1989, membership com. 1989-92, chmn. 1992, exec. com. 1992, forward planning com. 1996-99), Interurban Orthopedic Soc., Monroe County Med. Soc., NY State Med. Soc., Rochester Acad. Medicine, Rochester Orthopedic Soc., Soc. NY State Orthopedic Surgeons, Littler-Eaton Soc. Office: U Rochester Med Ctr Deans Office Box 706 601 Elmwood Ave Rochester NY 14642-0001

BURZIK, CATHERINE M., medical products executive; b. Nov. 11, 1950; m. Frank Burzik. BS in Math., Canisius Coll., 1972; MS in Math., U. Buffalo. Various mgmt. positions including software engr. Eastman Kodak; various mgmt. positions Critikon, Inc.; pres. Ortho-Clinical Diagnostics, Inc.; COO, exec. v.p. Applied Biosystems (subs. of Applera Corp.), Foster City, Calif., pres., 2004—06, sr. v.p. Applera Corp., Foster City, Calif., 2004—06; pres., CEO & bd. dirs. Kinetic Concepts, Inc., San Antonio, 2006—. Bd. dirs. Bausch & Lomb, 2007—, Fed. Res. Bank of Dallas, San Antonio, 2010—, Cordis Corp. Bd. trustees Keck Grad. Inst. Applied Life Sciences, Canisius Coll. Office: Kinetic Concepts Inc 8023 Vantage Dr San Antonio TX 78230 Office Phone: 210-255-6157. Office Fax: 650-638-5884. Business E-Mail: catherine.burzik@kci1.com. *

BURZYNSKA, BEATA, biology professor; b. Warsaw, Jan. 4, 1957; MSc, Warsaw Agr. U., PhD, 1982. Rsch. prof. Inst. Biochemistry and Biophysics, Polish Acad. Sci., 2009—. Rsch. grant, Nat. Ctr. R&D, Ministry Sci. and Higher Edn. Mem.: European Hematology Assn. Office: Pawinskiego 5A Warsaw Mazowieckie 02-106 Poland Business E-Mail: atka@ibb.waw.pl.

BURZYNSKI, STANISLAW RAJMUND, internist; b. Lublin, Poland, Jan. 23, 1943; came to U.S., 1970; s. Grzegorz and Zofia Miroslawa (Radzikowski) B. MD with distinction, Med. Acad., Lublin, 1967, PhD, 1968. Tchg. asst. Med. Acad., 1962-67, intern, resident, 1967-70; rsch. assoc. Baylor U., 1970-72, asst. prof., 1972-77; pvt. practice specializing in internal medicine Houston, 1977—; pres. Burzynski Clinic, 1979—. Dir. Burzynski Rsch. Lab., 1977-83; pres. Burzynski Rsch. Inst., Inc., 1983-. Contbr. articles to profl. jours. Nat. Cancer Inst. grantee, 1974, West Found. grantee, 1975. Mem. AMA, AAAS, Am. Assn. Cancer Rsch., Harris County Med. Soc., Polish Nat. Alliance (pres. Houston chpt. 1974-75), Soc. Neurosci., Soc. Neuro-oncology, Tex. Med. Assn., Sigma Xi. Roman Catholic. Achievements include discovery of antineoplastons components of biochem. def. system against cancer; described structure of Ameletin, 1st substance known to be responsible for remembering sound in animal's brain; invented new treatment for cancer, AIDS, viral infections, autoimmune diseases, neurofibromatosis, and Parkinson's disease; gene silencing theory of aging. Home: 20 W Rivercrest Dr Houston TX 77042-2127 Office: 9432 Katy Freeway Ste 200 Houston TX 77055-6330 Home Phone: 713-781-4782; Office Phone: 713-335-5697. Business E-Mail: info@burzynskiclinic.com.

BUS, JAMES STANLEY, toxicologist; b. Kalamazoo, June 27, 1949; s. Charles J. and Sena (Wolthuis) B.; m. Gerda W. Hekman, Apr. 20, 1974; children: Sara E., Timothy J., Brian M. BS in Medicinal Chemistry, U. Mich., 1971; PhD in Pharmacology, Mich. State U., 1975. Diplomate Am. Bd. Toxicology (v.p., pres. 1985-87). NIH predoctoral trainee Dept. Pharmacology, Mich. State U., East Lansing, 1971-75; asst. prof. environ. health U. Cin., 1975-76; scientist I (biochem. toxicologist) Chem. Industry Inst. Toxicology, Research Triangle Park, NC, 1977-84, scientist II (biochem. toxicologist), 1984-86; assoc. dir. pathology/toxicology, dir. drug metabolism rsch. The Upjohn Co., Kalamazoo, 1986-89; toxicology rsch. lab. Dow Chem. Co., Midland, Mich., 1989-91, project mgr., 1992-93, rsch. mgr., tech. dir., 1994—2001, dir. external tech., 2001—. Adj. assoc. prof. curriculum in toxicology U. N.C., Chapel Hill, 1984-88; adj. prof. pharmacology/toxicology Mich. State U., East Lansing, 1987—; safety assessment bd. advisors Merck, Sharp & Dohme Lab., West Point, Pa., 1985-86; mem. bd. sci. counselors EPA, 1996-2003, mem. sci. adv. bd., 2003-; mem. sci. adv. bd. NTP, 1997 2001, NCTR (FDA), 2006-. Co-editor: Patty's Industrial Hygiene and Toxicology, Vol. 3B, 1995; assoc. editor Toxicology and Applied Pharmacology, 1989-92, speciality editor, 2003—; editl. bd. Reproductive Toxicology, 1986-96; contbr. articles to profl. jours. Trustee Covenant Coll., Lookout Mountain. Ga., 1984-87. Recipient Robert A. Scala award, Environ. Occupl. Health Sci. Inst., Rutgers U., 1999, Disting. Alumni award, Mich. State U. Dept. Pharmacol. Toxicology, 2001. Fellow Acad. Toxicology Scis.; mem. Soc. Toxicology (pres. 1996-97, Achievement award 1987, Founders award 2010), Am. Soc. for Pharmacology and Exptl. Therapeutics, Teratology Soc., Am. Conf. Govt. Indsl. Hygiene (mem. chem. substances threshold limit value com. 1993-2002), Nat. Acad. Scis. (emerging issues and data on environ. contaminants com. 2002—2007, bd. on environ. scis. and toxicology 2005-). Republican. Achievements include research dealing with mechanisms of chemical toxicity, including oxidant and glutathione mediated toxicities. Office: Dow Chemical Co Toxicology Rsch Lab 1803 Bldg Midland MI 48674-0001 Office Phone: 989-636-4557. Business E-Mail: jbus@dow.com.

BUSARI, JAMIU, pediatrician, educator; b. London, June 28, 1968; s. Amope and Ishola Busari. MBChB, Ogun State U., Sagamu, Nigeria, 1985—91; MHPE, U. Maastricht, Netherlands, 1992—94, MD, 1994—96, PhD, 1999—2004. Registered Gen. Paediatrics Med. Specialist Registration Commn., Netherlands, 2003, cert. in bus. sec. health care delivery HBS, Boston, Ga., 2008, in exec. edn. program mng. healthcare delivery Harvard Bus. Sch., 2009. Specialist registrar, paediatrics Emma Children's Hosp., Academic Med. Ctr., Amsterdam, 1999—2003, St. Elisabeth Hosp., Willemstad, Curacao, 2000—02; chief attending physician, paediatrics St Lucas-Andreas Hosp., Amsterdam, 2004—05; cons. paediatrician Atrium Med. Ctr., Heerlen, Netherlands, 2005—, interim med. mgr., chair, dept. pediat., 2010; clin. coord., med. clerkship program Atrium Med. Ctr. & U. Maastricht, 2005—, dep. dir. pediat. residency tng. program, 2008, dir. pediat. residency tng. program, 2011; asst. prof. Ednl. Rsch. & Devel. Dept., 2008; dir. Pediat. Residency Tng. Program; assoc. prof. dept. ednl. r & d Faculty Healthy Medicine & Life Scis. U. Mass., 2011. Reviewer Advances in Health Sci. Edn., Med. Edn., Med. Edn. Online, BMC Med. Edn.; ednl. cons., project leader Quality Assurance Sys. for Med. Tng., Netherlands Antilles, 2001—; nat. adv. bd. Implementation of Rev. Postgrad. Tng. Curriculum, 2002—07, chmn. regional working com., 2007—; ednl. cons., postgrad. med. tng. program Elisabeth Hosp., 2005—; asst. prof. dept. ednl. R&D faculty health, medicine and life scis. U. Maastricht, 2007—; reviewer profl. jours. in field; med. tchr., ednl. cons. Paediat. HERMES Task Force, European Respiratory Soc., 2008. Contbr. chapters to books, papers to profl. jours. and pubs. Mentor Student Pugwash USA mentorship network, 1995—2000; co-founder, mem. Children4children Found., Willemstad, Curacao, 2001. Mem.: Pediatric Assn. Netherlands (licentiate), Dutch Med. Assn. (assoc.), Assn. Med. Edn. Europe (assoc.), European Soc. Paediatric Infectious Diseases (assoc.), Dutch Assn. Med. Edn. (assoc.; mem. com. on med. edn. and multiethnic communities 1999—2000). Avocations: soccer, reading, dance, travel, bicycling. Office: Atrium Med Ctr Dept Paed Henri Dunantstraat 5 6419 PC Heerlen 6401 CX Netherlands Personal E-mail: jobusar@hotmail.com. Business E-Mail: j.busari@atriummc.nl.

BÜSCH, ANNEMARIE, retired mental health nurse; b. Ger. d. Jurgen Julius and Anna (Stark) B. RN, Anschar Sch. Nursing, Kiel, Fed. Republic Germany, 1954; student, Traverse City State Hosp., Mich., 1959, Wayne State U., 1962, Colby-Sawyer Coll., New London, NH, 1981. Lic. nurse, N.H., Vt., Fed. Republic Germany. Asst. head nurse Univ. Eye Inst., Kiel, 1954-56; nurse aide, grad. nurse Ontario Hosp., London, Canada; staff nurse, charge nurse Grace Hosp., Receiving Hosp., Detroit, 1962-67; coll. health nurse Wayne St. U., Detroit, 1967-70; staff nurse Mary Hitchcock Meml. Hosp., Hanover, 1970-71, nurse mental health dept., 1978-82; charge nurse Dartmouth Coll. Health Svc., Hanover, NH, 1971-77; staff nurse, charge nurse Hanover Health Terrace; staff nurse Temporary Nurses, Inc., Hanover, Vis. Nurse Alliance of Vt. and N.H., White River Junction, Vt.; ret., 1997. Camp nurse Nat. Music Camp InterLochen, Mich.

BUSCH, DAVID FREDERICK, internist; b. Chgo., Apr. 12, 1943; s. Albert E. and Vera Ellman Busch; m. Cathy Lynne Anderson, Sept. 16, 1984; 1 child, Bailey Anderson. AB, Stanford U., 1964; MD, U. Chgo., 1968. Diplomate Am. Bd. Internal Medicine with subspecialty in infectious diseases, lic. physician Calif. Med. resident U. Cin. Hosp., 1968—70, 1972—73; infectious diseases fellow VA Hosp. Wadsworth, LA, 1973—75; staff physician, asst. prof. VA Hosp. Wadsworth/UCLA, 1975—77; infectious diseases cons. San Francisco, 1977—; internal medicine resident program dir., assoc. dir. Children's Hosp./Calif. Pacific Med. Ctr., San Francisco, 1982—2002; chief infectious diseases divsn. Calif. Pacific Med. Ctr., 1999—, chmn. instl. rev. bd., 2002—06. Mem. bd. dirs. Brown & Talent Med. Group, 2010—. Mem. editl. bd. Clin. Infectious Diseases, 1997—2000. Lt. comdr. Med. Corps USN, 1970—72. Fellow: Infectious Diseases Soc. Am. (chmn. bd. state/regional chpt. 1994—96, prin. investigator, bd. dirs. Emerging Infections Network 1996—), ACP; mem.: Am. Soc. Microbiology. Office: Infectious Diseases Assoc Med Group 2100 Webster St #400 San Francisco CA 94115 Office Phone: 415-923-3883.

BUSCHER, LEO F., JR., federal agency administrator; B in Bus. Adminstrn., U. Md. Pers. specialist US Dept. Treasury, Washington, 1962—63; adminstrv. asst. divsn. extramural activities Nat. Cancer Inst., NIH, 1963, grants mgmt. specialist, grants fin. officer, dep. grants mgmt. officer, and grants mgmt. officer, 1972—, dep. dir. adminstrn., 2007, dir. office grants adminstrn. Office: Nat Cancer Inst Office of Mgmt 31 Center Dr, Bldg 31 Bethesda MD 20892-0001 Office Phone: 301-496-7753. Office Fax: 301-402-3409. Business E-Mail: lb45u@nih.gov. *

BUSCHKE, HERMAN, neurologist; b. Berlin, Oct. 15, 1932; came to U.S., 1934, naturalized, 1945; s. Franz Julius and Ruth Helen (Minkowski) B.; children: Thomas, Katherine; m. Bertelle Selig, 1993. BA, Reed Coll., 1954; MD, Western Res. U., 1958. Diplomate: Am. Bd. Psychiatry and Neurology. Intern Bronx (N.Y.) Mcpl. Hosp. Center, 1958-59, resident in neurology, 1959-62; asst. instr. neurology Albert Einstein Coll. Medicine, Bronx, NY, 1961-62, asso. prof., 1969-74, prof., 1974—, prof. neurosci., 1974—; practice medicine specializing in neurology Bronx, NY, 1969—. Staff mem., attending neurologist Montefiore Med. Ctr.; instr. medicine Stanford U., 1962-63, asst. prof., 1963-69 Named Lena and Joseph Gluck Disting. Scholar in Neurology, 1973. Office Phone: 718-430-3846. Business E-Mail: herman.buschke@einstein.yu.edu.

BUSCHMANN, DIRK, neurosurgeon, consultant; b. Herpen, Germany, July 19, 1961; s. Kurt and Erika Buschmann; m. G. Freiwald Buschmann, Aug. 25, 1989; children: Fabian, Lenard. Studied physics and medicine, U. Munster, Essen, Berlin, 1983—89; studied pub. health, Frederic Inst. Tech., Cyprus, 2004, diploma in bus. adminstrn. summa cum laude, 2004; PhD, U. Essen, 1988; MD, U. Munster, 1989, Benjamin Franklin U., Berlin, 1997; MBA, FIT Inst., 2004. Cert. specialist in neurosurgery Arztekammer Westfalen, Lippe, Munster, 1997, specialist in spl. pain Arztekammer Westfalen, Lippe, Munster, 1999, specialist in neuroradiology Arztekammer Westfalen, Lippe, Munster, 1999, specialist in acupuncture Arztekammer Westfalen, Lippe, Munster, 2006. With Neuropsychol. Inst. U. Bielefeld, 1989—90; intern Bethel Hosp., Bielefeld, Germany, 1989—93, cons. dept. neurosurgery, 1993—99; asst. prof. Phys. Therapist Sch., Bad Rothendtelde, Germany, 1989—2001; neurosurg. intern Dept. Neurosurgery Gilead Hosp. Bethel, Bielefeld, 1990—91, neurosurg. resident Dept. Neurosurgery, 1991—93, neurosurg. pain cons. Dept. Neurosurgery and Anesthesiology, 1994—99; instr. in neurology Eva-Huser-Schule, Bad Rothenfelde, Germany, 1990—99; with Dept. Neurology Hospitation The Cleve. Clinic Found., 1992—93; sr. cons. Praxisklinik Herford, Germany, 1999—; neurosurg. cons. Klinikum Herford, 1999—; dir. German Pain Assn. Ctr. Herford, 2000—; instr. pub. health Frederic Inst. Tech., Cyprus, 2005—; chief MedConsult Consulting Inst., Herford, 2006—. Contbr. articles to profl. jours. Mem.: Spine Health, Pan Arab Union Neurol. Scis., Internat. Neuromodilation Soc., German Pain Assn., Neuromodulation Soc., Internat. Spinal Injection Soc., Bund German Neurosurgery, German Assn. Neurosurgery. Avocations: hunting, fishing. Office: Buschmann/von Glinski Hansastrasse 26 Herford 32049 Germany Office Phone: 49-5221-9983-15. Personal E-mail: buschmann.dirk@t-online.de. Business E-Mail: buschmann.dirk@mac.com.

BUSE, JOHN BERNARD, physician, educator; s. John Frederick and Maria Gordon Buse; m. Laura Lynn Raftery, Apr. 12, 1986; children: Katherine Elizabeth, Caroline Rose. BA, Dartmouth Coll., 1979; MD, PhD, Duke U., 1986. Cert. Nat. Cert. Bd. Diabetes Educators, 1998. Intern U. Chgo., 1986—87, resident, 1987—88, fellow, 1988—90, 1991—92, chief resident, 1990, asst. prof. medicine, 1992—94; assoc. prof. medicine U. N.C. Sch. Medicine, Chapel Hill, 1994—, dir. diabetes care ctr., 1994—, chief divsn. gen. medicine, 2001—. Mem.: Am. Diabetes Assn. (nat. bd. dirs. 2001—). Office: Univ NC Sch Medicine CB# 7110 Old Clinic 5039 Chapel Hill NC 27599-7110

BUSEMAN, SANDRA, physician; b. Sioux Falls, SD, Sept. 12, 1970; MD, U. SD, 1996; MSPH, U. Colo., 2002. Bd. cert. in phys. medicine & rehab., cert. in occupl. medicine, in preventive medicine & pub. health. Med. dir. City of Manchester Health Dept., 2003—05; occupl. medicine and med. dir., lifestyle medicine ThedaCare, 2007—08; physician Denver Health Ctr. Occupl. Safety and Health, 2009—10, Denver Vets. Adminstrn. Med. Ctr., 2010—. Bd. dirs. Am. Heart Assn. NH Affiliate, 2004—05; mem., cancer control adv. task force Am. Cancer Soc., NH, 2004—05; mem., adv. panel med. policy unit Colo. Divsn. Workers Compensation, 2006—08, chairperson, task force cumulative trauma med. treatment guidelines, 2009—10; affiliate asst. prof. U. Colo. Sch. Pub. Health, 2009—10. Fellow: Am. Bd. Preventive Medicine, Am. Bd. Phys. Medicine & Rehab. Avocations: hiking, art, movies. Personal E-mail: skbuseman@hotmail.com.

BUSER, BOYD RICHARD, dean, osteopath; b. Iowa City, Jan. 19, 1955; s. Charles L. and Ruth M. (Walker) B.; m. Pamela K. Lowe, Dec. 18, 1976; children: Michelle, Morgan, Charles. BA in Gen. Sci., U. Iowa, 1977; DO, Coll. Osteo. Medicine and Surgery, 1981. Diplomate Am. Bd. Gen. Practice, Am. Bd. Osteo. Manipulative Medicine. Intern Cranston Gen. Hosp., RI, 1981-82; asst. prof. family practice U. Osteo. Medicine and Health Scis., Des Moines, 1982-86; dir. Immediate Care Clinic South, Immediate Care Clinic West, Des Moines, 1982-86, Dietz Family Practice Clinic, Des Moines, 1982-84, West Des Moines Family Practice Clinic, 1984-86; prof. dept. osteo. manipulative medicine U. New Eng. Coll. Osteo. Medicine, Biddeford, Maine, chmn. dept. osteo. manipulative medicine, 1986—99, assoc. dean clin. affairs, 1999—2007, interim dean, 2005—07; v.p., dean U. Pikeville Ky. Coll. Osteopath. Medicine, 2007—. Mem. faculty-student forum U. Osteo. Medicine and Health Scis., clinic edn., scholarship, honors and awards, product standardization com., univ. self-study com., 1982-86; mem. curriculum U. New Eng. Coll. Osteo. Medicine, student promotion and evaluation, univ. self-appraisal, dean's steering com., faculty senate; presenter in field. Recipient Pre-doctoral fellowship Coll. Osteo. Medicine and Surgery, 1980. Mem. Am. Osteo. Assn. (editorial cons. 1989, osteo. manipulative medicine certifying bd. 1992, third v.p., trustee), Am. Acad. Osteopathy (program chmn. ann. convocation 1991, bd. govs. 1991—, bd. trustees, 1993—, coll. assistance com., chmn. membership com. 1989-91, edn. com. chmn. 1991—, component soc.'s com., undergrad. academies com., pres.-elect 1994), Ednl. Coun. Osteo. Prins., New Eng. Acad. Osteopathy (v.p. 1987-88, pres. 1988-89), Maine Osteo. Assn. (bd. dirs. 1989, pres. 1999-2001), Nat. Bd. Osteo. Med. Examiners (bd. dirs. 1993—, chmn. test constrn. com.), Am. Coll. Osteo. Family Physicians. Avocations: golf, racquetball. Office: University Pikeville Ky Coll Osteopath Medicine Office of Dean Armington 220 147 Sycamore St Pikeville KY 41501 Office Phone: 606-218-5411. Business E-Mail: boydbuser@upike.edu. *

BUSH, CHRISTINE GAY, dental hygienist; b. Toledo, Dec. 31, 1951; d. Jack G. and Virginia Aileen (Doyle) Tornga; m. John Howard Mosher, May 11, 1974 (div. July 1990); children: Heather Kristen, Andrew Jacob; m. Robert Milton Counts, July 5, 1991 (dec. Mar. 1993); m. Charles T. Bush II, June 16, 1998. BS in Dental Hygiene, U. Mich., 1974. Registered dental hygienist, Nat. Bd. Dental Examiners, Ind. State Bd. Dentistry, Fla. State Bd. Dentistry, Mich. State Bd. Dentistry. Asst. supr. dental hygiene Ind. U., South Bend, Ind., 1974-75; expanded functions hygienist South Bend Dental Ctr., 1975; periodontal hygienist Dr. John B. Lehman, South Bend, 1976-82, Dr. Cristene Maas, Longwood, Fla., 1983-84, Dr. Richard Altman, Orlando, Fla., 1984-85; dental hygienist Dr. H. Raymund Barcus, Winter Park, Fla., 1984—2000; periodontal hygienist Dr. Michael Abufaris, 2000—05. Adj. instr. So. Coll., Orlando, 1984. Med./dental mission Wekiva Presbyn. Ch., Honduras, 1987, 89, Diocese of Orlando, Dominican Republic, 1994, 95, Fla. Hosp. Found., Jamaica, 1997; deacon Presbyn. Ch., 1992; mem. Festival of Orchs. League. Mem.: Womans Club Winter Pk., Greater Orlando Dental Hygiene Assn., Messiah Soc., Shepherd's Hope (bd. dirs. 2006—08), U. Mich. Club Orlando (treas. 1998—2001), Alpha Chi Omega (Gamma Upsilon Gamma chpt. pres. 1995—97, lyre editor 1997—98, Gamma Upsilon Gamma chpt. pres. 1998—99, lyre editor 2000—01, Nat. Scholarship Commn. 2006, treas. 2007—08). Republican. Roman Catholic. Avocations: cross-stitch, playing piano, reading. Personal E-mail: ctbushx2@earthlink.net.

BUSH, DONNA, forensic toxicologist; BS in Chemistry, Loyola Coll., Balt., 1976; MS in Medicinal Chemistry, U. Md., Balt., 1980; MS in Environ. Toxicology, Johns Hopkins U., 1984; PhD in Forensic Toxicology, U. Md., Balt., 1988. Diplomate Am. Bd. Forensic Toxicology. Sr. technologist, clin. and forensic toxicology Md. Med. Lab., Inc., Balt., 1978-85; tech. dir. U.S. Army Forensic Toxicology Drug Testing Lab., Ft. Meade, Md., 1987-89; drug testing team leader, Divsn. Workplace Programs Ctr. for Substance Abuse Prevention, Rockville, Md., 1989—. Exec. sec. Drug Testing Adv. Bd., Substance Abuse and Mental Health Svcs. Adminstrn., Rockville, 1989—; faculty Am. Soc. Addiction Medicine, Bethesda, Md., 1992—, Fla. Sch. Addiction Studies, Tallahassee, 1991—, Southeastern Sch. Alcohol and Other Drug Studies, 1993—; invited lectr. internat. venues and confs.; dir. Nat. Lab. Certification Program. Contbr. chpts. to books, numerous articles to refereed profl. jours. and conf. procs., including Jour. Analytical Toxicology, Pharmacologist, Jour. Nat. Cancer Inst., Radiation Rsch., Sci., others. Recipient Nat. Rsch. Svc. awards, NIH, 1980-82. Fellow Am. Acad. Forensic Scis.; mem. Soc. Forensic Toxicologists (Ednl. Rsch. award 1986), Internat. Assn. Forensic Toxicologists, Am. Chem. Soc., Rho Chi. Avocations: gardening, yoga, meditation. Office: SAMHSA/CSAP Divsn Workplace Program 1 Choke Cherry Rd Rm 2 1033 Rockville MD 20857 Office Fax: 240-276-2610.

BUSH, EUGENE NYLE, retired pharmacologist, pharmacist; b. McKeesport, Pa., Apr. 14, 1952; s. Nyle E. and Rosalia M. (Merlino) B.; m. Janet Rosemary Ruscitto, May 7, 1977; children: Stephen Michael, Rebecca Renee, Timothy George. BS in Pharmacy, U. Pitts., 1977, PhD in Pharmacology, 1981. Registered pharmacist, Pa., Ill. Tchg. asst. U. Pitts., 1978—81; staff pharmacist We. Pa. Hosp., Pitts., 1977—81; pharmacologist Abbott Labs., 1981—87, sr. rsch. scientist Abbott Park, Ill., 1986—88, rsch. investigator, 1988—89, group leader, endocrine pharmacol., 1989—91, sr. group leader endocrine pharmacol., 1991—97, assoc. Volwiler rsch. fellow, 1996—2007; pharmacist Vista Med. Ctr., Waukegan, Ill., 2007—. Co-author numerous publs.; contbr. articles to profl. jours. Mem.: Am. Coll. Clin. Pharmacy, Am. Diabetes Assn., Am. Pharm. Assn., Endocrine Soc., Nat. Eagle Scout Assn., Sigma Xi. Republican. Roman Catholic. Avocations: gardening, photography, computers, bicycling. Home: 816 Bedford Ln Libertyville IL 60048-3002 Office Phone: 847-309-4135. Personal E-mail: genenbush@ameritech.net.

BUSH, MATTHEW LEE, otolaryngologist, educator; b. Charleston, W.Va., Mar. 22, 1977; MD, Marshall U. Joan C. Edwards Sch. Medicine, 2003. Asst. prof., dept. otolaryngology, head & neck surgery U. Ky., 2011—. Office: University Ky 800 Rose St Lexington KY 40536 Office Fax: 859-257-5096. Personal E-mail: mattkarynbush@yahoo.com.

BUSH-JOSEPH, CHARLES A., orthopedist; BS in Zoology and Physiology with honors, Univ. Mich., Ann Arbor, 1979; MD, Univ. Mich. Med. Sch., Ann Arbor, 1983. Lic. Ill., 1983, diplomate Nat. Bd. Med. Examiners, 1984, Am. Bd. Orthopaedic Surgery, 2000. Surg. intern Rush Presbyn. St. Luke's Med. Ctr., Chgo., 1983—84, resident, orthopaedic surgery, 1984—88, asst. prof., 1989—97, assoc. prof., dept. orthopaedic surgery, assoc. dir. sports medicine fellowship, 1998—2007, assoc. attending, 1998—, prof., dept. orthopaedic surgery, dir. sports medicine fellowship, 2007—; pediatric orthopaedic rotation The Children's Hosp., Denver, 1986; clin. and rsch. fellowship Cin. Sportsmedicine, 1988—89; attending physician MacNeal Meml. Hosp., Berwyn, Ill., 1989—99; head team physician Chgo. White Sox, 2003—; mng. ptnr. Midwest Orthopaedics at Rush, Chgo. Contbr. articles to numerous profl. jours. Mem.: Am. Orthopaedic Soc. Sports Med., Arthroscopy Assn. No. Am., Am. Acad. Orthopaedic Surgery, Orthopaedic Rsch. Soc., Ill. State Med. Soc., Chgo. Med. Soc., Herodicus Soc. Office: Midwest Orthopaedics at Rush 1725 W Harrison St Ste 1063 Chicago IL 60612 Office Phone: 312-432-2323. Business E-Mail: cbj@rushortho.com.

BUSHMA, MIKHAIL IVANOVICH, pharmacologist, educator; b. Novogrudok, Belarus, July 19, 1951; s. Ivan Ivanovich and Mariya Alexeyevna (Shunko) Bushma; m. Tatiana Vasilyevna Borisenko, Feb. 3, 1973; children: Vasill, Kizyl. PhD, Med. U., Tartu, Estonia, 1979; DSc, Med. U., Moscow, 1991. Jr. rsch. assoc. Inst. Biochemistry Acad. Scis., Grodno, 1977—82, sr. rsch. assoc., 1982—87, chief rsch. assoc., 1993—94; dep. mgr. rsch. Med. U., Grodno, 1994, mgr. rsch. lab., 1994—99, head dept. pharmacology, 1999—. Mem. specialized doctorate Inst. Biochemistry, Grodno, 2000—, Med. U., Minsk, Belarus, 2001—06. Capt. Med. Svc. Belarusian Army, 1968—74. Recipient award, Grodno Regional Adminstrn., 1992, Grodno City Adminstrn., 2004, 2007, Nat. Govt., 2006—08; grantee, Belarusian Republic Found. Fundamental Rsch., 1997—99, 1999—2001, 2002—04, 2005—07, 2009—11; NATO grantee, 2005—08. Office: Med U Gorkogo 80 230009 Grodno Belarus Office Phone: 375152 742487. Business E-Mail: pharma@grsmu.by.

BUSHNELL, DAVID LEWIS, physician; b. Madison, Dec. 2, 1952; BS, U. Ill., 1975, MD, 1979. Chief diagnostic imaging and radioisotope therapy Iowa City Vets. Hosp., 1992—. Mem.: Soc. Nuc. Medicine. Avocation: guitar. Office: University Iowa Hospital and Clinics Iowa City IA 52244 Business E-Mail: david-bushnell@uiowa.edu.

BUSKIRK, STEVEN, oncologist, educator; b. Nebr., Aug. 2, 1954; MD, U. Nebr., Coll. Medicine, 1979. Prof. radiation oncology Mayo Clinic Fla., 1985—, chair, dept. radiation oncology, 2009—. Mem.: Am. Soc. Clin. Oncology, Am. Soc. Therapeutic Radiology and Oncology, Am. Brachy Soc., Am. Coll. Radiology. Office: 4500 San Pablo Rd Jacksonville FL 32224 Business E-Mail: buskirk.steven@mayo.edu.

BUSSABARGER, MARY LOUISE, mental health services professional; b. Chgo., Sept. 16, 1923; d. Joseph and Nellie Wheelen Sterling; m. Robert Franklin Bussabarger, May 11, 1946; children: Wendi Newell, David. BA, U. Mo., 1960, MA English Lit., 1963. Instr. English U. Mo., Columbia, 1960—82; mental health commr. State of Mo., Jefferson City, 2001—07. Instr. English as a fgn. lang. Indo-Am. Soc., Calcutta, India, 1961—62, 1968—69, Seoul, South Korea, 1995—96; tchr. Yoga, 1969—2002; co-dir. Women's Place Agy., 1974—77; liaison officer Danforth Found., 1976—80. Mem. Mo. State Pres. Nat. Alliance for the Mentally Ill, 1985—88; commr. parks and recreation City of Columbia, 1975—77; mem. spkrs. bur. Internat. Women's Year, 1975—76; mem. Planning Coun. for Devel. Disabilities, 1990—97; trustee Mo. Special Needs Trust, 1989—2001, 2008—, 2010; mem. State Adv. Coun. for Psychiat. Svcs., 1985—90, 2007—, Mo. Protection and Advocacy, 1994—97; state mem. Mo. Chpt. Alliance for the Mentally Ill, 1991—; mem. nat. steering com. Nat. Women's Polit. Caucus, 1974—75; pres. Columbia Women's Polit. Caucus, 1975—76; del. State Dem. Convs., 1968, 1972, alt., 1976; mem. state steering com. Mo. Women's Polit. Caucus, 1972—76; chair Boone Co. Mental Health Bd. Mem.: MLA, AAUW, Delta Tau Kappa. Achievements include invitation and attendance to the John F. Kennedy School of Government at Harvard University for "Leadership for the 21st century", Oct. 2004.

BUSSE, WILLIAM WALTER, allergist, immunologist, educator; MD, U. Wis., 1966. Diplomate Am. Bd. Internal Medicine, 1972, Am. Bd. Allergy and Immunology, 1974. Resident internal medicine Cin. Gen. Hosp., 1967—68, 1970—71; fellow allergy and immunology Univ. of Wis., 1971—73, prof. medicine, head allergy and clin. immunology divsn., 1978—2004, George R. and Elaine Love prof., chair medicine; hosp. affiliations includes Univ. of Wis. Hosp. and Clinics. Dir. Am. Bd. of Allergy and Immunology, 1989—95; mem. expert panel Guidelines for the Diagnosis and Mgmt. of Asthma, 1989—2002, chair, 2002—; adv. coun. Nat. Inst. of Health, Nat. Heart, Lung and Blood Inst., 1996—2000; assoc. editor Am. Jour. of Respiratory and Critical Care Medicine, 1997—98, Jour. of Allergy and Clin. Immunology. Co-editor: Allergy: Principles and Practice and Asthma and Rhinitis. Recipient Folkert Belzer Life Achievement award, 2004, Am. Thoracic Soc. award, 2005, Citation award, Univ. of Wis. Sch. of Medicine and Pub. Health, 2008. Mem.: Assn. of Am. Physicians, Am. Acad. of Allergy, Asthma, and Immunology (bd. dirs. 1994—2004, pres. 2000—01). Office: University of Wisconsin Hospital and Clinics 600 Highland Ave Madison WI 53792-0002 Office Phone: 608-263-6400.

BUSSEL, JAMES BRUCE, pediatrician, obstetrician, gynecologist, educator; s. John David and Lili Renata Bussel; m. Charlotte Anne Cunningham-Rundles, Nov. 13, 1982; 1 child, Amy Christine Cunningham-Bussel. BS cum laude, Yale U., 1971; MD, Columbia Coll. Physicians and Surgeons, 1975. Diplomate in pediat. Am. Acad. Pediat., 1979, in pediat. hematology oncology Am. Acad. Pediat., 1981. Intern pediat. hematological oncology Cin. Children's Hosp., 1975—76, resident, 1976—78; fellowship pediat. hematology/oncology Meml. Sloan-Kettering Cancer Ctr.- NY Presbyn. Hosp., NYC, 1979—81; attending pediatrician NY-Presbyn. Hosp.-Weill Cornell Med. Ctr., NYC, prof. pediat. in ob-gyn., pediat., pediat. in medicine, 1999—. Lectr. in field. Contbr. articles to med. jours. Recipient Alpha Award for Contributions in Immunohematology, Am. Blood Resources Assn., 1998; named one of Top Doctors, Castle Connolly, Top Doctor NY, 2007. Mem.: Am. Soc. Hematology. Achievements include development of diagnosis and treatment of immune thrombocytopenias. Office: Weill Cornell Med NY Presbyn Hosp 525 East 68th St P695 New York NY 10021 Office Fax: 212-746-5121. Business E-Mail: jbussel@med.cornell.edu.

BUSSON, MARC, research scientist; b. Villejuif, France, Sept. 18, 1948; PhD, U. Paris VII, 1985. Biostatisticien, immunogenetic rschr. France Transplant, 1972—94, INSERM, 1978—2011. Mem.: Soc. Française Transplantation. Office: Saint Louis Hosp 1 Ave Claude Ve Paris Ile de France 75010 France Business E-Mail: marc.busson@univ-paris-diderot.fr.

BUSTAMANTE, JUAN, cardiologist; b. Valladolid, Spain, Dec. 31, 1977; MD, U. Valladolid, PhD, 2001, MS in Adminstrn. and Direction Health Sys., 2008. Resident, cardiovasc. surgery, Hosp. Clinico U. Valladolid, 2003—08, tchr., 2007—; asst. course dir. U. Autónoma Madrid; staff., cardiac surgery Hosp. U. La Princesa Madrid, 2008—. Grant, U. Valladolid, 1999—2002, Ministerio de Edn., Cultura y Deporte, 2000—01, U. Pompeu Fabra Barcelona, 2007—08. Mem.:

European Assn. Cardio-Thoracic Surgery, European Soc. Cardiovasc. Surgery, European Soc. Cardiology, Real Acad. Medicina Salamanca Spain, Real Acad. Medicina y Cirugía Valladolid (Accésit award 2007). Office: C/ Diego Leon 62 Madrid 28006 Spain Office Fax: 34 915202201. E-mail: bustamj@hotmail.com.

BUSTER, JOHN EDMOND, obstetrician, researcher; b. Oxnard, Calif., July 18, 1941; s. Edmound B. and Beatrice (Keller) B. Student, Stanford U., 1959-62; MD, UCLA, 1966. Diplomate Am. Bd. Obstetrics and Gynecology. Intern Harbor UCLA Med. Ctr., Torrance, Calif., 1966-67, resident, 1967-71, rsch. fellow, 1971-73, faculty, 1975—; prof. ob-gyn. UCLA Sch. Medicine, 1983, U. Tenn., Memphis, 1987-94; prof. ob-gyn., dir. divsn. reproductive endocrinology Baylor Coll. Medicine, Houston, 1994—; div. divsn. reproductive endocrinology UCLA Sch. Medicine. Examiner Am. Bd. Ob-Gyn. Contbr. articles to profl. jours. Served to lt. col. U.S. Army, 1973-75. Fellow: Am. Coll. Obstetricians and Gynecologists; mem.: Soc. Reproductive Endocrinologists, Am. Gynecol. and Obstet. Soc., Am. Soc. Reproductive Medicine, Soc. Gynecologic Investigation, Endocrine Soc. Presbyterian. Home: 1709 Dryden Rd Ste 1100 Houston TX 77030-2414 also: 3030 Post Oak Blvd Houston TX 77030

BUSTREO, FLAVIA, international organization administrator, epidemiologist; b. Padua, Italy, Aug. 17, 1961; d. Lino and Maria Bustreo. Grad. in Communicable Disease Epidemiology, London Sch. of Hygiene and Tropical Medicine, 1994; grad., CUAMM Coll., Padova, Italy, 1993; postgrad. in sports medicine & rehab., U. Padova, Italy, 1990, grad. in Medicine and Surgery with honors, 1987. Clinician Italian Assn. of Physicians, 1987. Clinician in internal medicine Inst. Gris, Treviso, Italy, 1990—91; sports medicine and rehab. physician Ctr. di Medicina Dello Sport, Venice, Italy, 1990—93; clinician rschr. Regional U. Ctr. of Sports Medicine, Padova, Italy, 1990—93; med. officer in the integrated program on communicable diseases WHO, Copenhagen, 1994—95, med. officer in the global tb program Geneva, 1995—97, med. officer in child health Khartoum, Sudan, 1997—99, dep. dir. and then dir. of partnership for maternal, newborn & child health, 2006—10, asst. dir.-gen. family women's and children's health, 2010—; sr. pub. health specialist World Bank Hdqs., Washington, 1999—2004; dep. dir. Child Survival Partnership, NYC, 2004—05. Presenter in field. Contbr. articles to profl. jours. Sec. of Venice sect. Interat. Physicians forPrevention of Nuc. War, Venice, 1990—2005; vol. Italian NGOs, Padova, 1992—93, Rijeka, Croatia, 1991—93; mem. of del. to Iraq to assess the situation of children in the country after the war and the sanctions Internat. Physicians for the Prevention of Nuc. War, Italy, 1992. Recipient Bank award for Capacity Bldg. for Sr. WHO and World Bank Staff, World Bank, 2000, Bank award for Senegal Cmty. Nutrition Project, 2002, Bank award for Preparation of the Healthy Start in Life Conf., 2002; scholar 3 Yr. Scholarship For Postgrad. Med. Studies, Italian Ministry of Universities and Sci. Rsch., 1988-1990. Avocation: languages. Office: WHO avenue Appia 20 1211 Geneva Switzerland *

BUSWELL, ARTHUR WILCOX, physician, surgeon; b. Oklahoma City, Jan. 6, 1926; s. Albert Currier and Enid May (Scott) Buswell; m. Loleta JoAnn Sherrill, June 11, 1950; children: Arthur Lee, Robert Joseph, Barbara JoAnn, Brian A., Gayla, Richard; m. Jane Marie Fuksa, Mar. 1, 1969. BS in Medicine, U. Okla., 1950, MD, 1952; AA in Med. Svcs., U.S. Army, 1963, student, 1963, Army Command and Gen. Staff Coll., 1966; postgrad., U. So. Calif., 1969. Intern Fitzsimons Army Hosp., Aurora, Colo., 1952—53; surg. resident Wesley Hosp., Oklahoma City, 1954—55; practice medicine and surgery Hennessey, Okla., 1955—63; dep. surgeon Ft. Wainwright and Yukon Command, 1963—65; chief staff Kingfisher Cmty. Hosp., 1956—57; supt. health Kingfisher County, 1960—61; chief profl. svc. Bassett Army Hosp., 1963—65; div. surgeon 1st Armored Div, Ft. Hood, Tex., 1965—67; 1st Inf. Div. Vietnam, 1967—68; med. project officer U.S. Army Combat Devels. Command Experimentation Command, Ft. Ord, Calif., 1968—72; also chief human factors div. and chief experimentation div. of experimentation command; chief profl. svcs. Reynolds Army Hosp., Ft. Sill, Okla., 1972—73; comdr. med. dept. activities Ft. Stewart, Ga., 1973—77; chief profl. svcs. Kenner Army Hosp., Ft. Lee, Va., 1977—78; comdr. med. dept. activities Alaska, 1979—83. Adj. asst. prof. med. scis. Baylor U., 1973—. Mem. Kingfisher Meml. Libr. Bd.; pres. Ft. Stewart Sch. Bd., 1977; bd. dirs. Ft. Stewart Fed. Credit Union, 1977, Chisholm Trail Mus., 1986—, Friends of Librs. in Okla., 1987—; pres. Friends of Libr. for Kingfisher County, 1984—88. With AUS, 1944—46, 1st lt. US Army, 1952—54, maj. to col. US Army, 1961—83. Decorated Legion of Merit with 2 oak leaf clusters, Soldier's medal, Bronze Star for Valor with oak leaf cluster, Meritorious Service medal, Air medal with 3 oak leaf clusters, Army Commendation medal, Gallantry cross with palm, Honor medal 1st class (both Vietnam); named Citizen of Yr., Kingfisher C. of C., 1988; named to Kingfisher H.S. Hall of Fame, 1987. Fellow: Royal Soc. Health; mem.: AMA, Garfield-Kingfisher County Med. Soc., Assn. Mil. Surgeons U.S., Army Aviation Med. Assn., Aerospace Med. Assn., Okla. State Med. Assn. Home: PO Box 703 Kingfisher OK 73750-0703

BUTCHER, LARRY L., neuroscientist, educator; b. Richmond, Ind., Feb. 21, 1940; s. Frederick L. Butcher and Ellen E. Jennings; m. Nancy J. Woolf, Dec. 24, 1983; children: Lawson, Ashley. BA, U. Mich., 1962, MS, 1964, PhD, 1967; postgrad., U. Goteborg, Sweden, 1967—69. Prof. UCLA, 1969—, dir., gerontology minor program, 1997—. Cons. Pilgrim Sch., LA, 2000—. Contbr. scientific papers to profl. jours. Mem.: Sigma Xi. Office: UCLA 405 Hilgard Ave Los Angeles CA 90095-1563 Business E-Mail: butcher@psych.ucla.edu.

BUTHIAU, DIDIER NICOLAS, physician; b. Dreux, France, Jan. 19, 1953; s. Albert Louis B. and Douceline Michele Colaneri; m. Sylvie Helene Beedham, June 30, 1984 (div. Dec. 2004); children: Norman, Candice. MD, Faculty Medecine, Paris, 1979. Intern Hosp. Paris, 1980-84, clin. chief, 1984-88; teaching dir. Edn. Offices, Paris, 1992—; cons. Clinic & Hosps., Paris, 1988—. Cons. in field; assoc. mem. Am. Hosp. Paris, 2007 Author: Clinical CT and MRI, 1991, CT and MRI in Oncology, 1995, Virtual Endoscopy, 2002, Meet the Professor-ASCO, 2005, 08; inventor in field. Expert Health Dept., France, 1998—. Recipient Nat. Acad. Medicine prize, Paris, 1994. Mem. AAAS, N.Y. Acad. Scis. Avocations: musician, diving, painting. Home: 3 Rue Casimir Pinel Neuilly-sur-Seine 92200 France Office: Am Hosp Paris 63 Bd Victor Hugo Navilly Sur Seine 92200 France Personal E-mail: didierbuthiau@hotmail.fr.

BUTKIEVICH, LAURA E., pharmacist; b. Feb. 15, 1980; PharmD, St. Louis Coll. Pharmacy, 2006. Clin. pharmacy specialist internal medicine U. Mo. Health Care, 2008. Mem.: Mo. Soc. Health-Sys. Pharmacists, Am. Coll. Clin. Pharmacy, Am. Soc. Health-Sys. Pharmacists. Office: One Hospital Dr Columbia MO 65212 E-mail: laurabutkievich@yahoo.com.

BUTLER, DAVID GEORGE, obstetrician, gynecologist; b. Bklyn., Dec. 27, 1939; s. Joseph I. and Margaret Frances (Kiley) B.; m. Mary Ann Casey, June 13, 1964; children: Mary, Jean, David, Kevin, Susan. BS in Biology, Coll. of the Holy Cross, 1961; MD, SUNY, Bklyn., 1965. Diplomate Am. Bd. Ob-Gyn. Intern St. Vincents-N.Y. Med. Ctr., NYC, 1965-66, resident in ob-gyn., 1966-70; attending physician Englewood Hosp., 1972—, Holy Name Hosp., 1972—; pvt. practice. Dir. ob-gyn. Holy Name Hosp., Teaneck, NJ, 1990—96, Teaneck, 1990—96. Mem. ACOG, Am. Assn. Gynecol. Laporoscopists. Home: 6 Ridge Rd Norwood NJ 07648-2416 Office: 420 Grand Ave Englewood NJ 07631-4141 Office Phone: 201-871-4040. Personal E-mail: drsbesf@yahoo.com.

BUTLER, DOUGLAS JOHN, physician; b. Greensboro, NC, Nov. 23, 1954; s. John C. and Jeannette Douglas. BA magna cum laude, Miami Univ., 1975; MD, Ohio State, 1978. Diplomate Am. Bd. Family Practice. Family medicine resident Moses Cone Hosp., Greensboro, 1978-81; attending physician, pvt. practice Ashe Meml. Hosp., Jefferson, NC, 1981-93, chief staff, 1982—83; emergency dept. physician Lake Norman Reg. Medical Ctr., Mooresville, NC, 1993; emergency dept. medical dir. Alexander Cmty. Hosp., Taylorsville, NC, 1993-2000, chief staff, 1999; locum tenens physician Indian Health Svc., 2000—; attending physician Old Fort Med. Clinic/McDowell Hosp., Marion, NC, 2001—02. Author: Ashe County Discovering the Lost Province, 1993, A Walk Atop America-50 State Summits and a Dream to Reach Them All, 2007; contbr. articles to profl. jours. Chmn. Ashe County EMS Coun., Jefferson, 1986—91. Mem.: Am. Heart Assn. (pres. Ashe County chpt. 1986—91), Jefferson Rotary. Avocations: photography, mountain climbing, travel.

BUTLER, GRACE CAROLINE, medical researcher; b. Lima, Peru, Dec. 19, 1937; (parents Am. citizens); d. Everett Lyle and Mary Isabella (Sloatman) Gage; m. William Langdon Butler, Dec. 28, 1961; children: Mary Dyer, William Langdon Jr. AA, Stephens Coll., 1957; BS in Nursing, Columbia U., 1960; postgrad., Union County Coll., 1984. Head nurse N.Y. State Psychiat. Inst., NYC, 1960-61; clin. instr. Columbia U., NYC, 1960-61; staff nurse, educator Vis. Nurse Service, Summit, N.J., 1962-63; health adminstr. Eagle Island Girl Scout Camp, Tupper Lake, N.Y., 1964; evening supr. Ashbrook Nursing Home, Scotch Plains, N.J., 1968-72; teaching asst. Scotch Plains-Fanwood (N.J.) Sch. System, 1975-78; staff nurse Westfield (N.J.) Med. Group, 1980-82, head nurse, 1982-83, supr., 1983-84; office adminstr. Harris S. Vernick, MD, PA, Westfield, 1984-86, corp. v.p., office adminstr., 1986-88. Assocs. in Medicine, Westfield, 1988-90; pvt. researcher, 1990—. Diabetes instr. Boehringer Manneheim Diagnostics, 1984—, Eli Lilly and Co., Indpls., 1984—; microbiologist tester Med. Technol. Corp., Somerset, NJ, 1984—; computer advisor Cordis Corp., Miami, 1985—. Asst. leader Girl Scouts U.S., Fanwood, 1970—73; bd. dirs. PTA, Scotch Plains, Fanwood, 1973—79; religious instr. All Sts. Episcopal Ch., Scotch Plains, 1967—82, 1995—, mem. altar guild, 1994—, mem. vestry, 1999—2005, lay eucharistic min., 2001—. Mem.: Am. Soc. Notarics, League Ednl. Advancement RNs, Columbia U./Presbyn. Hosp. Sch. Nursing Alumni Assn. Republican. Episcopalian. Avocations: sewing, water sports, gardening, wood refinishing. Home: 125 Russell Rd Fanwood NJ 07023-1063

BUTLER, JAY C., epidemiologist, former public health service officer; MD, U. NC, Chapel Hill, 1985. Med. epidemiologist Ctr. Disease Control and Prevention, Atlanta; dir. CDC Arctic Investigations Program, Alaska, 1998—2005; state epidemiologist Alaska Dept. Health and Social Services, 2005—07, dep. dir. sci. and medicine Divsn. Pub. Health, 2006—07, dir. Divsn. Pub. Health, 2007, chief med. officer, 2007—09; program dir. Divsn. Emerging Infections and Surveillance Services Nat. Ctr. for Preparedness, Detection and Control of Infectious Diseases, Centers for Disease Control and Prevention (CDC), Altanta, 2009—. Spkr. in field. Office: Centers for Disease Control and Prevention 1600 Clifton Rd Atlanta GA 30333 Office Phone: 907-465-3092. Office Fax: 907-586-1877. Business E-Mail: jay.butler@alaska.gov. *

BUTLER, KAREN MCBROOM, nurse; b. Durham, NC, Nov. 26, 1955; BSN, UNC, Chapel Hill, 1977; PhD, U. Ky., 2006. Staff nurse, clin. nurse mgr. U. Ky. Med. Ctr., 1979—82, nurse rschr., 1982—92; don U. Ky. Health Svc., 1992—2001; asst. prof. U. Ky. Coll. Nursing, 2001—. Faculty assoc., tobacco policy rsch. program U. Ky., 2006. Mem.: So. Nursing Rsch. Soc., Ky. Pub. Health Assn., APHA, Sigma Theta Tau Internat. Honor Soc. Avocations: cooking, reading, decorating. Office: University of Kentucky 423 College of Nursing Building Lexington KY 40536-0232 Office Phone: 859-323-5684. Office Fax: 859-323-1059. Business E-Mail: karen.butler@uky.edu.

BUTLER, LISA DEIRDRE, social studies educator; b. Toronto, Can., Mar. 7, 1959; BSc, U. Toronto, 1986; PhD, Stanford U., 1993. Rsch. psychologist, dept. psychiatry Stanford U. Sch. Medicine, 1994—2008; assoc. prof., social work Sch. Social Work U. Buffalo, 2009—. Office: Buffalo Ctr Social Rsch Buffalo NY 14214-8004 Business E-Mail: ldbutler@buffalo.edu.

BUTLER, MARIE GLADYS, nursing educator; b. Chester, Pa., June 12, 1951; d. Joseph Francis and Juanita Marie (Spear) B. Diploma, LPN, James Martin, 1983; AGS, C.C. of Phila., 1989; BSN, Thomas Jefferson U., 1991. LPN Care Pavillon of Walnut Park, Phila., 1983-84, Supior Care, Phila., 1984-85, Norrell, Jenkintown, Pa., 1986-87, Health Force, Jenkintown, 1987-91, Proto Call, Phila., 1990-91; staff nurse VA Med. Ctr., Phila., 1991-93; case mgr. Nursing Unlimited Homecare, 1993; RN staff nurse Brinton Manor Subacute Rehab., 1993-95, Nurse Power, 1993-97, Maxim Healthcare, 1995—; home care RN Absolute Nursing Care, Landsdown, Pa., 1995—96; PRN pool Taylor Hosp. Transitial Care Unit, 1995-96; RN Camp Sunshine, Thorton, Pa., 1995, 98; clin. nursing instr. James Martin Sch. of Practical Nursing, Phila., 1996; unit mgr. St. Ignatius Nursing Home, Phila., 1996-97; RN, unit mgr. CarePavillon, Phila., 1997; case mgr. Aspen Home Health Care, Phila., 1997—98; tele. svc. rep. TV Guide, Radnor, Pa., 1998—2001; CNA instr. Am. Trade Bus. Sch., Phila., 1999—2000; RN Ctrl. Health Svcs., Media, Pa., 2001—02, Pulmonary Care Inc., Havertown, Pa., 2002—03; instr. Harrison Career Inst., Phila., 2003—. Regional coord. Student Nurses Assn. Pa., Harrisburg, 1990-91; co-chair mentoring com. C.C. Phila. Alumni Assn., 1992; mem. mentor and shadowing program Thomas Jefferson U., Phila., 1992; RN Camp Sunshine, 1995. Mem. Ladies Aux. of VFW, Phi Theta Kappa (C.C. of Phila. chpt.), Sigma Theta Tau (membership com. Delta Rho chpt. 1992, 94, v.p. 1993-95, del. biannual conv. 1993, chmn. membership com. 1995—). Roman Catholic. Avocations: gardening, sewing, crocheting, walking, travel.

BUTLER, MERLIN GENE, physician, medical geneticist, educator; b. Atkinson, Nebr., Aug. 2, 1952; s. Garold Melvin and Berdena June (Sandall) B.; m. Ranae Ilene Kisker, Oct. 2, 1976; children: Michelle Ranae, Brian Gene. BA with very high distinction, Chadron State Coll., 1974, BS with very high distinction, 1975; MD, U. Nebr., Omaha, 1978; MS, U. Nebr., Lincoln, 1980; PhD, Ind. U., Indpls., 1984. Supervising physician Med. Info. Svcs., Omaha, 1978-80; rsch. assoc. dept. biology U. Notre Dame, South Bend, Ind., 1983-84; med. dir. North Ctrl. Ind. Regional Genetics Ctr., South Bend, 1983-84; dir. cytogenetics Meml. Hosp., South Bend, 1983-84; NIH postdoctoral fellow dept. med. genetics Sch. Medicine Ind. U., Indpls., 1980-83, adj. asst. prof. dept. med. genetics Sch. Medicine, 1984; asst. prof. dept. pediatrics Sch. Medicine Vanderbilt U., Nashville, 1984-90, dir. regional genetics program Sch. Medicine, 1984-98, dir. Cytogenetics Lab. dept. pediatrics Sch. Medicine, 1989-98, assoc. prof. dept. pediatrics, 1990-98, assoc. prof. dept. pathology, 1991-98, investigator John F. Kennedy Ctr. Rsch. on Edn. and Human Devel., Peabody Coll., 1987-98; assoc. dir. Inst. Behavior and Genetics; assoc. prof. dept. orthopedics Vanderbilt U., 1994-98. Adj. assoc. prof. dept. pediatrics Meharry Med. Coll., Nashville, 1988-98; genetics cons. Baptist Hosp., Nashville, 1985-98, Westside Hosp., Nashville, 1985-98, Nashville Gen. Hosp., 1985-98, chief, section of Med. Genetics and Molecular Medicine, Children's Mercy Hosp., Kansas City, Mo., 1998—, William R. Brown prof., chmn., 1998—, prof. dept. pediats., U. Mo.-Kansas City Sch. Medicine; prof. psychiatry behavioral scis. and pediat., dir., Div. Rsch. Dept. Psychiatry & Behavioral Scis. Kans. U. Med. Ctr., 2008-; mem. epidemiology genetic diseases subcom. Ind. State Bd. Health, 1983-84; faculty interviewer Vanderbilt U., 1987; peer reviewer Am. Jour. Human Genetics, Am. Jour. Med. Genetics, Clin. Genetics, Am. Jour. Diseases of Children, Dysmorphology and Clin. Genetics, Am. Jour. Mental Retardation, Jour. Pediatrics, So. Med. Jour., Human Mutations, Cancer Genetics and Cytogenetics, Pediatrics, Genomics, Prader-Willi Perspectives; mem. ad-hoc grant review com. NIH, 1990—, craniofacial assessment team Vanderbilt U., 1992-98; editl. bd. mem. Jour. Neurodevel. Disorders, 2008, Jour. Assited Reprodn. and Genetrics, 2009; lectr., presenter in field. Author: Fragile X Syndrome: A Major Cause of X-Linked Mental Retardation, 1988, 1989; author: (with others) Genetics for the Medically Oriented, 1983, Novak's Textbook of Gynecology, 11th edit., 1988, Birth Defects Encyclopedia, 1990, Prader-Willi Syndrome and Other Chromosome 15q Deletion Disorders, 1992, Human Genetics: New Perspectives, 1994, 1992 International Fragile X Conference Proceedings, 1992, Prader Willi and Angelman Syndromes Examples of Genetic Imprinting in Man, 1994, Prader-Willi Syndrome: A Guide for Parents and Physicians, 1995, Prader-Willi Syndrome: Clinical and Genetic Findings, 2000' editor: Genetics of Developmental Disabilities, 2005, Management of Prader-Willi Syndrome, 2006, Guide to America's Top Physicians, 2007-10, named the Best Doctors in America, 2007-2008, 2009 2010; mem. editl. bd. Prader-Willi Perspectives, 1992—, contbr. numerous articles to profl. jours. including Nature and New England Jour. Medicine. Grant reviewer March of Dimes Birth Defects Found., 1985—. Recipient Disting. Svc. award Chadron State Coll., 1986, Teaching award Osler Inst., 1989, Disting. Alumni award Ind. U., 2007, Lifetime Achievement award Prader-Willi Syndrome Assn., 2008, Distinguished Alumni Award, Indiana U. 2007; named one of America's Top Physicians Consumers Rsch. Coun., 2004-05, 2006-2007; grantee Univ. Rsch. Coun., 1985, 92-93, Tenn. Dept. Mental Health and Mental Retardation, 1986-91, Clin. Nutrition Rsch. Unit, 1986-88, Joseph P. Kennedy, Jr. Found., 1988, Clin. Rsch. Ctr. Meharry Med. Coll., 1989-98, Dept. Pathology, 1992-93, Orthopedic Rsch. Edn. Found., 1993-95, NIH, 1995—; Cancer Rsch. grantee Ind. U. Med. Ctr., 1980, Biomed. Rsch. Support grantee, 1985, 88, 89—, Clin. Rsch. grantee March of Dimes Birth Defects Found., 1987, 88, 90-92, Lyle V. Andrews Meml. scholar, 1974. Fellow Am. Coll. Med. Genetics (founder, diplomate, lab. practice subcom. 1993); mem. AMA (Physician Recognition award 1984, 87, 00), AAAS, Am. Bd. Med. Genetics (cert. clin. genetics and clin. cytogenetics), Am. Genetics Assn., Am. Soc. Human Genetics (cytogenetics resource com. 1992-97), Am. Fedn. Clin. Rsch., Coll. Am. Pathologists (cytogenetics resource com. 1992-97, molecular pathology resource com. 1993-97), So. Med. Assn., Davidson County Pediatric Soc., Metro. Med. Soc., Prader-Willi Syndrome Assn. (med. rsch. task force 1985—, diagnostic task force 1991—, sci. adv. bd. 1991—, chair 2000—), N.Y. Acad. Scis., Sigma Xi, Phi Chi. Avocations: gardening, camping, fishing, collecting sports memorabilia. Home: 6410 Hillside St Shawnee KS 66218-9070 Office: Kansas Univ Medical Ctr MS 4015 3901 Rainbow Blvd Kansas City KS 66160 Business E-Mail: mbutler4@kumc.edu.

BUTLER, PATRICIA, psychiatric and mental health nurse, educator, consultant; b. Galesburg, Ill., Aug. 31, 1943; d. Allen Dale and Mary Lacky; m. Glen William Butler, Mar. 14, 1964; children: Scott Lewis, Andrew William, Suzanne Elizabeth; m.Walter Sage Julio, April 8, 1980. AA in Nursing/Journalism, Sacramento City Coll., 1965; BS in Sociology/Psychology, SUNY, Albany, 1992. Cert. legal nurse cons., Nat. Alliance of Cert. Legal Nurse Cons., 2006. Clin. nurse Mercy Gen. Hosp., Sacramento, Sacramento Med. Ctr., Davis Cmty. Hosp., Calif., Woodland (Calif.) Meml. Hosp., 1965-74; dir. nurses Woodland Skilled Nursing, 1978-79; head nurse/psychiatry St. Croix Mental Health, Christiansted, 1974—78; clin. program mgr. Yolo County Mental Health, 1980—2005, legal nurse, cons., 2006—; cmty. program dir. Yolo County Conditional Release Program, Yolo County, 1986—2005; cons. State of Calif., Bd. Regd. Nursing, 2007—; hearing officer Superior Ct., Yolo County, 2008—. Instr. Yuba C.C., Marysville, Calif., 1988—. Author curriculum; mem. editl. adv. bd. Daily Democrat. Bd. dirs. Concilio of Yolo County, Woodland, 1984-87; mem. Red Cross Nat. Disaster Mental Health, 1996—. Recipient Bell award Mental Health Assn. Yolo County, 1993, Christine West award, 1999, Clara Barton award Yolo County Red Cross; NIMH grantee, 1989-90. Mem. LWV (recording sec. 1997, 98, co-pres. 1999—), Calif. Women Lead, Forensic Mental Health Assn. Calif. (sec. 1991-93, conf. planning 1990-91, dir. edn. and tng. 1996-98), Rotary Internat., Internat. Assn. Correctional & Forensic Psychology, Nat. Alliance Cert. Legal Nurse Cons., Calif. Assn. LPS

Hearing Officers. Independent. Roman Catholic. Avocations: diving, boating, travel, golf. Office: 1296 East Gibson Rd Box 271 Woodland CA 95776 Office Phone: 530-525-0641.

BUTLER, SHEILA WORD, retired occupational health nurse; b. Paducah, Ky., Sept. 12, 1944; d. Edwin Morris and Beatrice Aileen (Hobbs) Word; m. Benjamin Edward Butler, Dec. 4, 1976; 1 child, Michelle Renee. ADN, Paducah Jr. Coll., 1966. Cert. occupational health nurse, Am. Bd. Occupational Health, occupational hearing conservationist. Staff nurse Marshall County Hosp., Benton, Ky., 1966-67; shift nursing supr. Parkview Hosp., Dyersburg, Tenn., 1967-69, obstet. nursing supr., 1969-72; clin. nursing instr. State of Tenn. Dept. of Edn., Nashville, 1968-69; charge nurse Dravo-Groves-Newberg, Hamlettsburg, Ill., 1972-74; surg. nurse Western Bapt. Hosp., Paducah, Ky., 1974-76; ophthalmic asst. Dr. Harry Abell, Jr., Paducah, Ky., 1976-83; occupational health cons. self-employed, Paducah, Ky., 1983-86; plant nurse Air Products & Chemicals, Inc., Calvert City, Ky., 1986—2008. Bd. dirs. Nat. Nurses Soc. on Addiction, 1983-84; bd. dirs. Am. Bd. Occupational Health Nurses, 1994-2001, treas., 1997-99, chair Cohn adv. bd., 1999-2000; sec. Jackson Purchase Oper. Nurses, Paducah, 1975-76; cmty. asst. panel Agy. for Toxic Substance and Disease Registry of CDC, Atlanta, 1991-94; pres. Jackson Purchase Occupational Health Nurse, 1993-96. Mem. Nat. Arbor Day Found, Western Bapt. Hosp. Aux., KHELPS vol., Med. Corp. Unit State Ky., 2011. Named Student Nurse of Yr., Circle K-Paducah Jr. Coll., 1966, Ky. Col., Gov. Louie B. Nunn, 1971—; recipient Chem. Group Recognition award Air Products & Chems., 1990, 91. Mem. NAFE, Am. Assn. Occupational Health Nurses (pres. Jackson Purchase sect. 1993-95), Civil Def. of McCracken County, Order of Ea. Star, Esther # 5 Ruth, Daus. of the Nile Neith Temple, Chinese Shar-Pei Club of Am. Democrat. Methodist. Avocations: bicycling, swimming, gardening, needle work. Home: 248 Hayes St Benton KY 42025-6649 E-mail: swb912@mchsi.com.

BUTLER, VINCENT PAUL, JR., internist, educator; b. Jersey City, Feb. 16, 1929; s. Vincent Paul and Ruth Eilene (Lynch) B. AB, St. Peter's Coll., 1949; MD, Columbia U., 1954. Intern Presbyn. Hosp., NYC, 1954-55, resident, 1955-56, 58-59, asst. physician, 1963-68, asst. attending physician, 1968-71, asso. attending physician, 1971-74, attending physician, 1974—2004; trainee clin. immunology U. Rochester Med. Center, 1959-61; research fellow immunochemistry dept. microbiology Columbia U., 1961-63, asst. prof. medicine, 1963-70, assoc. prof., 1970-74, prof., 1974-98, prof. emeritus, 1999—, spl. lectr., 1999—. Asst. vis. physician 1st med. div. Bellevue Hosp., N.Y.C., 1963-68, Harlem Hosp., N.Y.C., 1968-88; mem. VA Merit Rev. Bd. in Immunology, 1974-77, chmn., 1976-77; mem. immunol. sci. study sect. NIH, 1979-83, chmn., 1980-83 Rsch. com. Arthritis Found., 1986-91, chmn., 1989-91; bd. trustees St. Peter's Prep. Sch., Jersey City, 1985-93, chmn., 1991-93. Lt. med. corps. USN, 1956—58. Recipient Rsch. Career Devel. award, NIH, 1968—73, Joseph Mather Smith prize, Columbia U. Coll. Physicians and Surgeons, 1973, P&S Disting. Svc. award, 2008; named Arthritis Found. investigator, 1963—68, Irma T. Hirschl Charitable Trust Career Scientist, 1973—78; fellow, Helen Hay Whitney Found., 1960—63; Josiah Macy, Jr. Found. scholar, Dept. Zoology, Univ. Coll., London, 1979—80. Fellow AAAS; mem. Assn. Am. Physicians, Am. Soc. Clin. Investigation, Am. Assn. Immunologists, Am. Soc. Pharmacology and Exptl. Therapeutics, Am. Heart Assn., N.Y. Heart Assn., Am. Fedn. Med. Research, Harvey Soc. Roman Catholic. Home: 66 Tulip St Summit NJ 07901 Office: 630 W 168th St New York NY 10032-3702 Personal E-mail: vpb2@comcast.net. Business E-Mail: vpb2@columbia.edu.

BUTLER, WILLIAM THOMAS, academic administrator, physician, educator; b. Boston, Aug. 10, 1932; s. Albert Quigg and Elizabeth West (Visknisski) B.; m. Marilou Beutel, Apr. 26, 1957; children: Marilyn West, Thomas Charles, Robin Eileen; m. Carol Ann Pike, Nov. 23, 1977. AB, Oberlin Coll., 1954; MD, Western Res. U., 1958; grad. program for health systems mgmt., Harvard U., 1974, A.M.P., 1979. Intern and asst. resident in internal medicine Mass. Gen. Hosp., Boston, 1958—61, clin. fellow in medicine, 1960—61, resident in internal medicine, 1964—65; rsch. fellow in bacteriology and immunology Harvard Med. Sch., 1960—61; clin. assoc. Lab. Clin. Investigations, Nat. Inst. Allergy and Infectious Diseases, NIH, Bethesda, Md., 1961—62, chief clin. assoc., 1962—63, clin. investigator, 1963—64, acting head clin. immunology sect., 1965—66; asst. prof. Baylor Coll. Medicine, Houston, 1966—68, assoc. prof., 1968—71, prof. microbiology and immunology, prof. internal medicine, 1971—2001, prof. immunology, 2001—, assoc. dean, 1973—74, dean admissions, 1974—77, acting exec. v.p., 1976—77, exec. v.p., dean, 1977—79, pres., 1979—96, chancellor, 1996—2004, chancellor emeritus, 2004—08, 2010—; interim pres. CEO Baylor Coll. Medicine, 2008—10, exec. dean, 2008—. Mem. spl. med. adv. group VA, 1981-91, chmn., 1984-91; bd. dirs. Lyondell Chem. Co., chmn. bd., 1997-2007; mem. Am. Quality and Productivity Ctr., 1991-2004, chmn. S.W. CEO Coun., 1997-98, mem., 1994—2004. Mem. forward planning com. Tex. Med. Ctr., 1981-96; bd. dirs. South Main Ctr. Assn., exec. com., 1980-94, chmn., 1989-91, coun. advisors, 1994—2004; past assoc. chmn. key group United Way Campaign, Flagship Divsn., group chmn., 1990; mem. Houston Econ. Summit Host Com., 1990; bd. dirs. Blvd. Oaks Civic Assn., 1982-85, Sci. Engring. Fair of Houston, 1985—2005, United Way Tex. Gulf Coast, trustee, 1993-99, exec. com. 1998-99; nat. bd. dirs. Points of Light Found., 1995-2004; mem. coordinating bd. Tex. Coll. and Univ. System, Health Professions Edn. Adv. Com., 1984-95, chmn., 1988-95, rsch. adv. com., 1987-90; mem. The Houston Forum, 1981—2004, bd. govs., 1983-92, 1996-2004; mem. Tex. Sesquicentennial Celebration Com., 1984-86; mem. bd. edn. blue ribbon com. Houston Ind. Sch. Dist., 1986; adv. bd. Covenant House Tex., 1987-90; HISD City-Wide Com., 1987; vice-chmn. health svcs., 1990 U.S. Savs. Bond Program. Mem. AMA, Am. Assn. Immunologists, Am. Soc. Clin. Investigation, N.Y. Acad. Scis., Infectious Diseases Soc. Am., Inst. Medicine, Nat. Acad. Scis. (membership com. 1992-96, sect. 12 1992—, vice chmn., 1992-94, chmn. 1994-96, com. on prevention and control of sexually transmitted diseases 1995-96, chmn. 1995-96), Assn. Acad. Health Ctrs., Assn. Am. Med. Colls. (chmn. coun. deans 1987-89, adminstrv. bd. 1983-90, exec. coun. 1984-92, mgmt. edn. programs planning com. 1986-96, chmn.-elect 1989-90, chmn. 1990-91, project 3000x2000 implementation com. chmn. 1991-2002, nominating com. chmn. 1982), Harris County Med. Soc., Houston Acad. Medicine, Tex. Med. Assn. (adv. coun. med. edn.), Houston C. of C. (bd. dirs. 1981-82, 83-89), Greater Houston Partnership, Inc. (bd. dirs. 1989, 92-99, co-chair healthcare task force 1994-97, bus. issues adv. com. 1994-99, govtl. rels. adv. com. 1995-97), Houston Mus. Nat. Sci. (ex officio 1989-94), River Oaks Country Club, Doctors' Club (bd. govs. 1980-84, pres. 1982), Harvard Bus. Sch. of Houston Club, Sigma Xi, Alpha Omega Alpha. Methodist. Achievements include research in numerous publs. on infectious disease and immunology. Office: Baylor Coll Medicine 1 Baylor Plz Ste 177A Houston TX 77030-3498

BUTNEV, VIKTOR YURIEVICH, research scientist; MD, N.I.Pirogov Moscow State Med. Sch., 1975—81; PhD, Inst. for Exptl. Endocrinology and Hormone Chemistry, 1981—86. Therapeutist State Exam. Bd. of N.I.Pirogov Moscow State Med. Sch., 1981. Jr. rsch. scientist Inst. for Exptl. Endocrinology and Hormone Chemistry, Moscow, 1981—88, sr. rsch. scientist, 1988—94; postdoctoral fellow dept. biol. scis. Wichita State U., Kans., 1994—98; protein hormone biochemist Nat. Hormone and Pituitary Program, Rsch. and Edn. Inst., Harbor-UCLA Med. Ctr., Torrance, Calif., 1998—99; postdoctoral fellow dept. physiology and biophysics U Iowa, Iowa City, 1999—2002; scientist Genzyme Glycobiology Rsch. Inst., Oklahoma City, 2002—. NIH grantee, 1999—2002. Mem.: AAAS, Soc. for Study of Reprodn., Endocrine Soc. Achievements include discovery, isolation, and characterization of glycosylated prolactin and its carbohydrate moiety. Office: Genzyme Glycobiology Rsch Inst 800 Research Pkwy Ste 200 Oklahoma City OK 73104 Personal E-mail: butnev@aol.com. Business E-Mail: viktor.butnev@genzyme.com.

BUTSCH, JOHN LORD, surgeon, educator; b. Rochester, Minn., Mar. 5, 1934; AB, Princeton U., 1956; MDCM, McGill U., 1960; MS in Surgery, U. Minn., 1967. Diplomate Am. Bd. Surgery. Intern U. Hosp., Ann Arbor, Mich., 1960-61; resident surgery Mayo Clinic, Rochester, 1961-65; clin. asst. dept. surgery Buffalo Gen. Hosp., 1968-70, clin. assoc. dept. surgery, 1970-72, asst. surgeon, 1972-78, assoc. surgeon, 1978-85, surgeon, 1985—; asst. attending surgeon Buffalo Children's Hosp., 1970-78, assoc. attending surgeon, 1978—; asst. attending surgeon Erie County Med. Ctr., 1983-96; from instr. in surgery to clin. prof. surgery SUNY, Buffalo, 1968—2002, clin. prof. surgery, 2002—06, emeritus clin. prof. surgery, 2006—; pub. health physician II N.Y. State Dept. of Health, Buffalo, 1980—. Chmn. com. ER Buffalo Gen. Hosp., 1970-72; mem. first year com. med. students SUNY Buffalo, 1982-89, ad hoc com. guidelines acad. promotions, 1985-86, med. faculty coun., 1987-93; team physician Buffalo Sabres Hockey Team, 1973-99; med. dir. Republic Steel Corp., 1973-82; med. cons. Niagara Mohawk Power Corp., 1974-2004; med. dir. Buffalo Forge, 1986-95, Clearing Niagara, 1994-98; rschr., lectr. in field. Contbr. articles to profl. jours. Bd. govs. Buffalo Tennis & Squash Club, 1987-89, pres., 2007, 2005-2008; mem. parents coun. St. Lawrence U., 1989-93; mem. Thursday Club Literary Soc., 1995—. Capt. U.S. Army, 1966-68. Fellow ACS (pres. western N.Y. chpt. 1982, exec. coun. 1983-85)); mem. Soc. Internat. de Chirugie, Collequim Interntat. Chirurgiae Digestivae, Ctrl. Surg. Assn. (membership com. 1994-97, chmn. audit com. 2002), Soc. for Surgery of the Alimentary Tract, Am. Trauma Soc., Univ. Assn. Emergency Med. Svcs., James Priestley Surg. Soc. (v.p. 1983-85), Surgeon's Travel Club (sec./treas. 1991-98, pres. 1986). Home: 174 Soldiers Pl Buffalo NY 14222-1259 Office: 4955 W Bailey Ave Amherst NY 14226 Office Phone: 716-886-1210. *

BUTT, MOHAMMAD ZAMAN, internist, geriatrician, researcher; b. Gujrat, Pakistan, Feb. 19, 1964; arrived in U.S.A., 1994; s. Anayat Ullah and Parveen Akhtar; m. Shumaila Zaman Butt, Oct. 22, 1993; children: Ummia, Ushnaa. BSc, Punjab U., 1984; MBBS, King Edward Med. Coll., 1989. Diplomate in internal medicine Am. Bd. Internal Medicine, 1998, in geriatric medicine Am. Bd. Internal Medicine, 2002, lic. physician N.Y., N.J., D.C. Surgeon Mayo Hosp., Lahore, Pakistan, 1990—91, physician, 1991; med. officer Omar Hosp., Lahore, 1992, Ittefaq Hosp., Lahore, 1993—94; resident internal medicine Brookdale U. Hosp., Bklyn., 1995—98; fellow geriatric medicine George Washington U. Hosp., Washington, 1999—2000; geriatrician Brookdale U. Hosp., 2001—03, Shorefront Jewish Geriatric Ctr., Bklyn., 2001—; hospice care specialist Met. Jewish Hospice, Bklyn., 2005—. Reviewer Geriatric Medicine Bd. Am. Bd. Internal Medicine, 2003; mem. staff Met. Jewish Health Sys., Bklyn., 2001—; healthcare provider Am. Heart Assn., Bklyn., 2002—. Host ednl. programs on TV:. Avocations: painting, travel, music, stamp collecting/philately, coin collecting/numismatics. Home: 2665 Homecrest Ave Apt 2S Brooklyn NY 11235 Office: Shorefront Jewish Geriatric Ctr 3015 West 29th St Brooklyn NY 11224 Office Phone: 718-266-5700. Personal E-mail: zamanbutt@hotmail.com.

BUTTS, HERBERT CLELL, retired dentist, educator; b. Dover, Tenn., Aug. 24, 1924; s. Sidney Lewis and Georgia (Sawyer) B.; m. Quay Coker; children: Marla Lyce, April Chyrese, Dawn Denise, Sidney Coker. Student, U. Tenn. Jr. Coll., 1942-43, Memphis State U., 1946-47; DDS, U. Tenn., 1950; MS, U. Iowa, 1966. Pvt. practice dentistry, Memphis, 1950-58; mem. faculty Coll. Dentistry, U. Tenn., Memphis, part-time 1950-58, 58-60, assoc. dean acad. affairs, 1978-81, spl. advisor to dean, 1986-2000; ret., 2000; fgn. svc. officer, dental edn. advisor State Dept. Fgn. Aid program, San Salvador, El Salvador, 1960-64; assoc. prof. St. Louis U. Sch. Dentistry, 1966-67; prof., chmn. dept. operative dentistry Coll. Dental Medicine, Med. U. S.C., Charleston, 1967-70, asst. dean for admissions and student affairs, 1970, 72-74, acting dean, 1971; editor-in-chief ADA, Chgo., 1974-77; dean Sch. Dental Medicine So. Ill. U., Alton, 1981-86. Editor U. Tenn. Coll. Dentistry Bull., 1990-2000. Active USNR, 1943-46. Recipient Outstanding Alumnus award U. Tenn. Coll. Dentistry, 1975. Mem. ADA, Tenn. Dental Assn. (fellowship award 1993), Memphis Dental Soc., Am. Coll. Dentists (pres. Tenn. sect. 1994, sec.-treas. Tenn. sect. 1995-98), Internat. Coll. Dentists, Am. Assn. Dental Schs., Ala. Dental Assn. (hon.), Am. Assn. Women Dentists (hon.), Omicron Kappa Upsilon. Home: 1360 Peabody Ave Memphis TN 38104-3636

BUTTS, HUGH FLORENZ, physician, psychiatrist, psychoanalyst; b. NYC, Dec. 2, 1926; s. Lucius Cornelius and Edith Eliza Butts; m. June Dobbs, June 9, 1953 (div. Dec. 1971); children: Lucia Irene, Florence, Eric Hugh; m. Clementine Riggsbee, Dec. 11, 1971; children: Sydney Clementine, Samantha Florenz, Heather Marguerita. BS, CCNY, 1949; MD, Meharry Med. Coll., Nashville, 1953. Diplomate Am. Bd. Psychiatry and Neurology. Intern Morrisania Hosp., 1956; resident Bronx VA Hosp., 1958; psychiatry instr. Columbia U., NYC, 1962-65, assoc. prof. psychiatry, 1965-67, asst. clin. prof. psychiatry, 1967-74; mem. faculty Columbia Psychoanalytic Clinic, NYC, 1962-87, supervising and tng. analyst, 1968-87; lectr. Columbia Coll., NYC, 1969-71; instr. Seek program CCNY, NYC, 1972-74. Prof. psychiatry Albert Einstein Coll. Medicine, Bronx, 1974-81; cons. Altanta U. Sch. Social Work, 1970-74; vis. prof. psychiatry Meharry Med. Coll., Nashville, 1980-82; dir. Bronx Psychiat. Ctr., 1974-79; 1st dept. commr. N.Y. State Office Mental Health, Albany, N.Y., 1975-76; chmn. adv. bd. The Med. Herald, 1991-02; presenter and lectr. in field; honoree, guest spkr. Vassar Coll. Program on African Studies, 2007. Pres., founder Clementine Pub. Co., 1989, Lit. Mind Assocs., 1989; author: The Blackness of Darkness, 1994; co-author: The Psychology of Black Language, 1973, 2d edit/, 1993; editor: Racism and Post Traumatic Stress Disorder, 2006; contbr. more than 300 articles to profl. jours. With USAAF, 1944-45; bd. mem., co-founder Health for Youths, 2011. Recipient Spl. Merit award Assn. for Psychoanalytic Medicine, 1967, Nat. Med. Assn. award, 2005, Annual Dr. Eugene F. Williams Sr. Scholar of Distinction award Nat. Med. Assn., 2006; Travel fellow Ford Found., 1972. Fellow: NY Acad. Scis., Am. Psychiat. Assn. (Disting. Life fellow 2003); mem.: Am. Psychoanalytic Assn. Achievements include completed the NYC marathon in 1991, 94 and 95. Avocations: gardening, fishing, antiques, violin, writing. Office: 350 Central Park W New York NY 10025-6547 Office Phone: 212-864-6191.

BUUREN, FRANK VAN, cardiologist; b. Iserlohn, Germany, Mar. 18, 1967; s. Arry Van and Doris Van Buuren; m. Jana Van Dobosch, Dec. 28, 2001; children: Marie Van, Marleen Van. PhD, Philipps U., Marburg, 1994; MBA, ULM, Germany, 2010. Lic. medicine practitioner U. Marburg, 1994, cert. hosp. mgr. U. Hannover, 2002, sportsmedicine specialist Med. Assn. Muenster, Germany, 1999, internal medicine specialist 2001, quality mgmt. specialist 2002, cardiology specialist 2003, intensive care medicine specialist 2005. Intern intensive care medicine U. Bonn Luedenscheid Hosp., Germany, 1997—2001; intern cardiology Heart Ctr. NRW, Germany, Bad Oeynhausen, 1994—97, 2001—04, sr. physician cardiology, 2005—, physician charge acctg., 2004—, physician charge quality mgmt., 2006—. Registrar cardiology Chelsea & Westminster Hosp., London, 1999; mem. inner cir. health care German Soc. Cardiology, Duesseldorf, 2005—, mem. inner cir. quality mgmt. medicine, 2005—; mem. sports cardiology European Assn. Cardiovasc. Prevention and Rehab., Sophie Antipolis, France, 2005—. Contbr. articles to profl. jours. Mem.: German Soc. Sportsmedicine, European Soc. Cardiology. Achievements include development of continuous refractometry as a new method to monitor the intravascular volume during hemodialysis. Office: Heart Ctr NRW Georgstraße 11 Bad Oeynhausen 32545 Germany

BUXBAUM, ROBERT COURTNEY, internist; b. Milw., Dec. 16, 1930; s. Edwin C. and Lillian (Tousman) B.; m. Ann S. Shocket, Dec. 26, 1955; children: Laura, Carl, Paula, Margaret. AB, Harvard U., 1952; MD, U. Pa., 1956. Diplomate Am. Bd. Internal Medicine, Am. Bd. Hospice and Palliative Medicine. Intern Henry Ford Hosp., Detroit, 1956-57; officer USPHS, San Carlos Apache Res., Ariz., 1957-59; resident, rsch. fellow U. Wis. Hosp., Madison, 1959-63; from rsch. assoc. to instr. Harvard Med. Sch., Boston, 1963-69, asst. prof. medicine, 1969—2004, clin. assoc. prof. medicine, 2004—. Internist Harvard Cmty. Health Plan (now Harvard Vanguard Med. Assocs.), Boston, 1969—; cons. health policy; founding mem. Mass. Compassionate Care Coalition, 1999-2010, v.p., 2000, 2003, pres., 2003—. Author: Sports for Life, 1979; contbr. articles to profl. jours. Chmn. Gov.'s Com. on Fitness, Mass., 1975—80. Fellow ACP. Fellow: Am. Acad. Hospice and Palliative Medicine. Avocations: playing oboe, swimming, skiing. Office: Harvard Vanguard Med Assocs Faulkner Hosp 1153 Centre St 6th Fl Boston MA 02130 Office Phone: 617-838-5437. Business E-Mail: robert_buxbaum@hms.harvard.edu.

BUXTON, DOUGLAS FRANCISCO, ophthalmologist, educator; b. NYC, Nov. 5, 1952; s. Jorge Norman and Amalia (Gonzalez) B. BA, Yale U., 1975; postgrad., Columbia U., 1977; MD, Cornell U., 1982. Diplomate Am. Bd. Ophthalmology, 1987, Nat. Bd. Med. Examiners; diplomate in cataract/implant surgery, 2002, penetrating keratoplasty, 2007, and laser in situ keratomileusis Am. Bd. Eye Surgery, 2002. Intern St. Vincent's Hosp. and Med. Ctr., NYC, 1982—83; resident NY Eye & Ear Infirmary, NYC, 1983—86, fellow cornea & external disease, 1986—88, attending surgeon, 1988—; asst. attending surgeon dept. ophthalmology Manhattan Eye, Ear and Throat Hosp., NYC, 1988—; clin. prof. ophthalmology N.Y. Med. Coll., 1991—. Contbr. articles to profl. jours. Fellow Am. Acad. Ophthalmology; mem. Am. Coll. Eye Surgeons, Am. Soc. Cataract and Refractive Surgeons, N.Y. Intra-Ocular Lens Implant Soc., N.Y. Keratorefractive Soc. Office: NY Eye and Ear Infirmary 310 E 14th St Ste 403 New York NY 10003-4201 Office Phone: 212-979-4410. Fax: 212-353-5772. Business E-Mail: dbuxton@nyee.edu.

BUXTON, JENNIFER ASKEW, pharmacist; b. Asheville, NC, Sept. 20, 1978; BS in Biology, U. NC, Chapel Hill, 2000, PharmD, 2003. Pharmacist Walgreens Optioncare, 2003—11, New Hanover Regional Med. Ctr., 2003—. Adj. faculty U. NC, Sch. Pharmacy, Campbell Sch. Pharmacy; bd. dirs. Tileston Health Clinic. Named Preceptor of Yr., U. NC Sch. Pharmacy. Mem.: APHA, FIP, NC Assn. Pharmacists (named Disting. Young Pharmacist), Am. Soc. Health Sys. Pharmacists (Disting. Svc. award), Am. Coll. Clin. Pharmacy. Business E-Mail: jbuxtonunc@gmail.com.

BUYSE, MARYLOU, pediatrician, geneticist, medical administrator; b. NYC, June 27, 1946; d. George J. and Barbara M. (Sauer) B.; m. Carl N. Edwards, Jan. 22, 1982. AB, Hunter Coll., 1966; MD, Med. Coll. Pa., 1970; MS in Prev. Health and Med. Adminstrn., U. Wis., Madison, 1993. Diplomate Am. Bd. Med. Genetics. Intern U. Mich., 1970-71; resident in pediatrics L.A. County-U. So. Calif. Med. Ctr., 1971-73, fellow, 1973-75, U. So. Calif. Sch. Medicine, 1975-84, asst. prof. pediatrics, 1973—75, 2004—, Tufts U., 1976-84; coord. Myelodysplasia Clinic Tufts-New Eng. Med. Ctr., Boston, 1976-79; dir. Cystic Fibrosis Clinic, staff pediatrician Ctr. for Genetic Counseling and Birth Defects Evaluation, 1975-82; med. dir. Ctr. for Birth Defects Info. Service, 1978-82, dir. center, 1982-94; pres. Medx Ltd., 1985-94, Ctr. for Birth Defects Info. Scis., Inc., 1985-94; dir. clin. genetics Children's Hosp., Boston, 1985-86; mem. med. adv. bd. Mass. Cystic Fibrosis Found., 1977-79; med. dir. Fernald State Sch., 1988—94; assoc. med. dir. MassPRO, 1993-95; mem. Mass. Bd. Registration in Medicine, 1994-95; assoc. med. dir. Care Advantage Health Sys., Inc., med. dir., 1996-97, United Health Care of New England, 1997-98, consulting physician advisor, 1998-99, v.p. health affairs, 1999-2001; pres., CEO Mass. Assn. Health Plans, 2001—09; chief med. officer Scott & White Health Plan, 2009—. Cons. in field. Assoc. editor Birth Defects Compendium, 2d edit., 1979; assoc. editor Syndrome Identification Jour., 1977-82, editor, 1982; editor Jour. Clin. Dysmortphology, 1982-86, Dysmorphology and Clinical Genetics, 1986-94;

editor-in-chief Birth Defects Encyclopedia, 1990. Chair RI Folic Acid Coun., RI March of Dimes, 1999-2001; dir. Mass. Health Consortium, 2001-, Martin's Pt. Healtch Care, 2006-; pres. Mass. Health Coun., 2007—; chair Jane Doe Inc., Gala, 2007. Recipient Physicians Recognition award AMA, 1975, Alumni Achievement award Med. Coll. Pa., 1987; named to Alumni Hall of Fame, Hunter Coll., 1998. Fellow: Mass. Med. Soc. (asst. sec.-treas. 1991—94, trustee 1991—2000, sec.-treas. 1994—96, v.p. 1996—97, pres.-elect 1997—98, pres. 1998—99), Am. Acad. Pediat.; mem.: AAAS, Mass. Health Coun. (v.p. 2005—, pres. 2007—), Teratology Soc., Am. Coll. Physicians Execs., Soc. Craniofacial Genetics (pres. 1986), Am. Med. Writers Assn., Am. Soc. Human Genetics, Am. Mgmt. Assn., Am. Med. Women's Assn. (pres. Mass. br. 39 1986—91), Charles River Dist. Med. Soc. (pres. 1993—95), Alpha Omega Alpha. Business E-Mail: mbuyse@swmail.sw.org.

BUYSSE, DANIEL J., psychiatrist, educator; B in English, U. Mich., B in Biomedical Sci., MD. Diplomate Am. Bd. Psychiatry and Neurology, Am. Bd. Psychiatry and Neurology-sleep medicine, lic. Pa., 1984. Resident Univ. of Pitts. Med. Sch., fellow; hospital affiliations include Univ. of Pitts. Med. Ctr., Western Psychiat. Inst. & Clin. Named one of Top Doctors, Pitts. Mag., 1996, 2002, 2011. Mem.: AMA, Am. Acad. of Sleep Medicine, Sleep Rsch. Soc., Soc. for Rsch. on Biol. Rhythms, Am. Psychiat. Assn., Pa. Psychiat. Assn. Office: Western Psychiatric Institute & Clinic 3811 O'Hara St Pittsburgh PA 15213 Office Phone: 412-624-1000.

BUZALAF, MARILIA AFONSO RABELO, research scientist, educator; b. Bauru, Brazil, Apr. 14, 1971; d. Américo Afonso and Sônia Aparecida Afonso Rabelo; m. Claudio Buzalaf, July 12, 1991; children: Nathalia Rabelo, Gabriel Rabelo, Rafael Rabelo. DDS, Bauru Dental Sch. U. South Pacific, Brazil, 1992, MS in Periodontology, 1995; PhD in Functional and Molecular Biology, Campinas State U., Brazil, 1999. Asst. prof. biochemistry Bauru Dental Sch., U. South Pacific, Bauru, Brazil, 1996—2002, assoc. prof. biochemistry, 2002—, pres. ethics comittee for animal rsch., 2003—, vice-head dept. biol. scis., 2004—. Cons. Found. Rsch., São Paulo, Brazil, 2002—, NRC, Brasília, Brazil, 2003—; adv. bd. Jour. Applied Oral Sci., Bauru, Brazil, 2002—. Mem.: Brazilian Soc. Dental Rsch. (assoc. Myiaki Issao award 2005), European Orgn. Caries Rsch. (assoc.), Internat. Assn. Dental Rsch. (assoc.). Catholic. Achievements include first to Biological rhythm for human plasma fluoride levels; Mechanism for fluoride incorporation into plaque after use of fluoride dentifrice; implementation of the quality control of public water fluoride levels; research in preventive methods for dental erosion. Avocations: running, bicycling, travel, reading, movies. Home: R Vivaldo Guimarães 10-10 Ap 18 Bauru 17014-510 Brazil Office: Bauru Dental Sch Univ S Pacific Al Octávio Pinheiro Brisolla 9-75 Bauru 17012-901 Brazil E-mail: mbuzalaf@fob.usp.br.

BUZARD, JAMES ALBERT, biomedical start-up consultant; b. Warren, Ohio, Nov. 2, 1927; s. Milton Vogan and Mary Cora (Matthews) B.; m. Caroline L. Jansen, July 28, 1951; children: Catherine A. Sazdanoff, James M. BS, Kent State U., Ohio, 1949; MA, U. Buffalo, 1951, PhD, 1954. Rsch. biochemist, then dir. R & D Norwich (N.Y.) Pharmacal Co., 1954—68; dir. devel., then exec. v.p. G.D. Searle & Co., Skokie, Ill., 1968—79, bd. dirs.; exec. v.p. Merrell Internat./Richardson Merrell Inc., Wilton, Conn., 1979—81, bd. dir.; exec. v.p. Merrell Dow Pharm., Inc., Cin., 1981—89, v.p. Marion Merrell Dow Inc., 1989—90; ret., 1990; mgmt.-health care cons., 1990—2011. Bd. dirs. Meridian Diagnostics Inc., Cin.; chmn. emeritus Biostart, Cin., Ohio. Contbr. 40 articles to profl. jours. With USNR, 1945-46, 51-55. Named Ohio Entrepreneur Yr., 1998. Republican. Roman Catholic. Avocations: woodworking, golf, gardening, painting. Office Phone: 847-283-0269. Business E-Mail: jabuzard@comcast.net. *

BUZARD, KURT ANDRE, ophthalmologist, b. Lakewood, Colo., Apr. 9, 1953; s. Donald Keith and Sonja Marie (Vik) B. BA in Math. and Physics, Northwestern U., 1975; MA in Applied Physics, Stanford, U., 1976; MD, Northwestern U., 1980. Diplomate Am. Bd. Ophthalmology, Nat. Bd. Med. Examiners. Intern medicine L.A. County-U. So. Calif. Med. Ctr., 1980-81; resident Jules Stein Eye Inst. UCLA, 1982-85; fellow cornea/refractive surgery Richard C. Troutman, MD, 1985-86; ophthalmologist, corneal specialist Las Vegas, Nev., 1986—. Staff physician Rancho Los Amigos Hosp., 1981-82; clin. asst. prof. div. ophthalmology dept. surgery U. Nev. Sch. Medicine, 1988—; clin. asst. prof. dept. ophthalmol. medicine Tulane U. Med. Ctr., New Orleans, 1991-2006; med. dir. S.W. Eye Procurement Ctr., Las Vegas, 1989-2004; affiliate Humana Hosp.-Sunrise, 1989-2006, Las Vegas Surg. Ctr., 1989—, Las Vegas Surg. Ctr., Med. Ctr. So. Nev., 1989-2006; assoc. staff Valley Hosp., Las Vegas, 1986-2006; mem. med. adv. bd. Donor Orgn. Referral Svc.; internat. hon. advisor Tung Wah Ea. Hosp., Hong Kong, 1999-. Author: (with Richard Troutman) Corneal Astigmatism: Etiology, Prevention and Management, 1992, (with Miles Friedlander and Jean Luc Febbraro) The Blue Line Incision and Refractive Phacoemulsification, 2000; mem. editorial bd. Refractive and Corneal Surgery, 1992-2000; contbr. articles to profl. jours. Mem. Las Vegas C. of C., 1989. Recipient Rsch. award Jules Stein Inst., L.A., 1985. Fellow Am. Acad. Ophthalmology (Honor award 1999), Am. Coll. Surgeons; mem. Am. Soc. Cataract and Refractive Surgery, AMA, Assn. for Rsch. in Vision and Ophthalmology, Castroviejo Soc., Colombian Soc. Ophthalmology (corr.), Eye Bank Assn. of Am.-Paton Soc., Internat. Soc. for Eye Rsch., Internat. Soc. Refractive Keratoplasty (long-range planning com., alternative rep. to Am. Acad. Ophthalmology, bd. dirs. 1992-94), Pan Am. Assn. Ophthalmology, Pan Am. Implant Assn., Phi Eta Sigma, Phi Beta Kappa. Avocations: computers, photography.

BUZZARD, JAMES A., paper, packaging and chemical company executive; BS in Pulp and Paper Tech., N.C. State U.; MBA in Fin., U. Pa. Joined WestVaco, 1978, purchasing mgr., Kraft Divsn., 1982—84, adminstrv. mgr., Container Divsn., 1984—86, area sales mgr., container plant Eaton, Ohio, 1986—88, corp. mktg. mgr., 1988—90, mgr., mktg. svcs., 1990—91, mgr., bus. planning, analysis, Envelope Divsn., 1991—92, mgr., Envelope Divsn., corp. v.p., 1992—94, interim mktg., sales mgr., Fine Papers Divsn., 1994—95, sales, mktg. mgr., 1995—98, asst. divsn. mgr., Fine Papers Divsn., 1998—99, sr. v.p., 1999—2000, mgr., Fine Papers Divsn., 1999—2000; exec. v.p. Westvaco Corp., 2000—02, MeadWestvaco Corp., Stamford, Conn., 2002—03, pres., 2003—. Mem.: Web Offset Assn. (mem. supplier adv. bd.). Office: MeadWestvaco 501 S 5th St Richmond VA 23219-0501 *

BYCZKOWSKI, JANUSZ ZBIGNIEW, toxicologist; b. Gdansk, Poland, May 29, 1947; came to U.S., 1979; s. Stanislaw and Halina (Osterczy) B.; m. Janina K. Slosarska, Aug. 6, 1977; children: Ian S., L. Peter. MSc in Toxicology, Acad. Medicine, Gdansk, 1970, PhD in Pharmacology, 1975, DSc in Biochem. Pharmacology, 1979. Diplomate Am. Bd. Toxicology. Cancer rsch. scientist dept. exptl. therapeutics Roswell Park Meml. Inst., Buffalo, 1979-80, 1985-87; adj. ast. prof. pharmacology Acad. Medicine Gdansk, 1980-83; pharmacologist and dir. of pharmacy Internat. Red Cross and Red Crescent, Tobruk, Libya, 1983-84; asst. prof. and rsch. scientist Coll. Pub. Health U. South Fla., Tampa, 1987-91; project scientist and study dir. ManTech. Environ. Tech., Inc., Dayton, Ohio, 1991-98; sr. toxicologist TN&A Inc., Cin., 1998-99, ind. cons., 1999—; health risk assessment specialist Ohio EPA, Columbus, 2000—. Editorial reviewer Bull. Environ. Contamination and Toxicology, Reno, Nev., 1989—, Free Radical Biology and Medicine, Baton Rouge, 1989—, Placenta, Manchester, Eng., 1991—; dean Polish Sect. N.Y. Coll. Advanced Studies, 2002-03; hon. prof. Albert Schweitzer Internat. U., 2000—. Contbr. articles to profl. publs., chpts. to books. Active mem. Solidarity, Poland, 1980-83. Recipient Rsch. award 1st degree Sci. Soc. Gdansk, 1975, Polish Pharmacol. Soc., 1977, Ministry Health and Social Welfare of Poland, 1977. Mem. AAAS, N.Y. Acad. Scis., Soc. Toxicology, Soc. for Risk Analysis (councilor Ohio chpt. 1994—). Achievements include finding mechanism of action of DDT on mitochondrial respiration; discovery of NAD-Dependent mode of action of vanadium, co-oxygenation of benzopyrene by lipoxygenase; developing physiologically-based pharmacokinetic model for lactational transfer of chemicals; consulting for U.S. Govt. Home: 212 N Central Ave Fairborn OH 45324-5006 Personal E-mail: jbyczkowski@netscape.net.

BYDLOWSKI, SÉRGIO PAULO, medical researcher, consultant; b. São Paulo, Brazil, Apr. 1, 1951; s. Abraham and Alta (Wajcman) B.; m. Cynthia Rachid, June 13, 1979; children: Daniel, Lyvia, Marcus. MD, Santa Casa Med. Sch., São Paulo, 1976; M of Molecular Biology, Escola Paulista Medicina, São Paulo, 1979, PhD in Molecular Biology, 1984. Postdoctoral fellow U. Cin. Sch. Medicine, 1984-86; vis. scientist Karolinska Hosp., Stockholm, 1989; from instr. to assoc. prof. pathophysiology Santa Casa Med. Sch., São Paulo, 1976-91; prof. physiology Santo Amaro Med. Sch., São Paulo, 1988-92; sci. dir. Blood Found., São Paulo, 1990, from asst. prof. to assoc. prof. hematology U. São Paulo Med. Sch., 1990—; dir. rsch. div. Pro-Sangue Hemocentro Found., São Paulo, 1990—. Advisor São Paulo Rsch. Supporting Found., 1992—; cons. Coord. for Improvement of Grad. Pers., Brasilia, Brazil, 1993—95. Contbr. articles to profl. and sci. jours. NIH fellow, U.S., 1984-86; Coun. of Europe scholar, Sweden, 1989; recipient Oswaldo Cruz award Brazilian Hematological Bd., 1991, Victorio Maspes award Blood Inst., São Paulo, 1992; elected mem. Nat. Acad. Medicine, 2003. Fellow Am. Heart Assn.; mem. AAAS, Am. Fedn. Med. Rsch., N.Y. Acad. Scis., Internat. Soc. for Heart Rsch., Nat. Acad. Medicine. Office: Fundacao Hemocentro Av Dr Eneias Carvalho Aguiar 5403-0000 São Paulo Brazil Home Phone: 5511 5573-3491; Office Phone: 5511 3082 2398. Personal E-mail: spbydlowski@globo.com. Business E-Mail: spbydlow@usp.br.

BYDON, ALI, neurosurgeon, educator; b. May 20, 1972; MD, U. Mich., Ann Arbor, 1999. Asst. prof., neurosurgery Johns Hopkins U., 2007—. Office: 600 N Wolfe St Meyer 7-109 Baltimore MD 21287 Office Fax: 410-502-3399. Business E-Mail: abydon1@jhmi.edu.

BYE, ERIK, occupational hygiene researcher; b. Oslo, Sept. 13, 1945; s. Martin Johansen and Nelly (Andersen) B., m. Kirsten Offenberg, Aug. 1, 1970; children: Tonje, Synne. MSc in Chemistry, U. Oslo, Norway, 1972, PhD, 1976. Rsch. asst. U. Oslo, Norway, 1972-78; sr. scientist Statens arbeidsmiljøinstitutt, Oslo, 1979-96, sci. advisor, 1997-2000, sr. scientist, 2001—. Postdoctoral fellow Eidgenössiche Technische Hochschule, Zürich, 1977; rsch. fellow Senter for Industriforskning, Oslo, 1987; surveillance occpl. environment & health, Norway. Mem. editl. bd. Scandinavian Jour. Work and Environ. Health, 1982-96; contbr. articles to profl. jours. Mem. Norsk Kjemisk Selskap, Norsk Yrkeshygienisk Forening, Norsk Forskerforbund. Avocations: trumpet playing, bicycling. Office: Nat Inst Occupl Health Postboks 8149 Dep 33 Oslo Norway Office Phone: 47 23 19 53 23. E-mail: erik.bye@stami.no.

BYEFF, PETER DAVID, hematologist, oncologist; b. Nov. 27, 1948; s. Herbert Isaac and Ruth Helen (Wolfe) B.; m. Gail Schneider, Apr. 2, 1982. BA, U. Pa., 1970; MD, Johns Hopkins U., 1974. Diplomate Am. Bd. Internal Medicine (subcert. in med. oncology and hematology), Nat. Bd. Med. Examiners. Intern Georgetown U. Hosp., Washington, 1974-75, resident in internal medicine, 1975-77; vis. fellow in hematology and oncology Columbia-Presbyn. Med. Ctr., NYC, 1977-81, Damon Runyon-Walter Winchell oncology fellow, 1977-81; dir. George Brag Cancer ctr.; exec. com. mem. Johns Hopkins U. Alumni Coun., John Hopkins Alumni Coun.; trustee New Britain Mus. Am. Art. Instr. Coll. Physicians and Surgeons, Columbia U., N.Y.C.; assoc. prof., attending physician U. Conn.; sr. attending physician Hosp. Ctrl. Conn., Southington, Conn., New Britain (Conn.) Gen. Hosp., med. dir. George Bray Cancer Ctr.; sr. investigator Gynecologic Oncology Group; prin. investigator Eastern Cooperative Oncology Group, Nat. Surg. Bowel and Breast project. Mem.: Am. Soc. Clin. Oncology, Am. Soc. Clin. Oncology Worforce Taskforce. Office: Bradley Med Bldg 55 Meriden Ave Ste 1-a Southington CT 06489-3237 also: 40 Hart St New Britain CT 06052-1743

BYEON, SUK HO, ophthalmologist, educator; b. Seoul, Republic of Korea, Oct. 18, 1971; s. Ho Bin Byeon and Ok Hee Kim; m. Hyung Joo Kim, May 29, 2002. MD, Yonsei U., Seoul, 1997. Diplomate Health & Welfare Dept., 1997. Instr. Yonsei U., 2006—, assoc. prof., 2010—. Mem.: Korean Ophthalmologist Soc. Office: Yonsei Univ Coll Medicine 134 Shincheon-dong Seodaemun-gu Seoul 120-752 Republic of Korea Office Fax: 82-2-312-0541. Business E-Mail: shbyeon@yuhs.ac.

BYGDEMAN, SOLGUN MARGARETA, clinical bacteriologist, retired medical educator; b. Sundsvall, Sweden, Dec. 12, 1934; d. Erik Gunnar and Ingrid Maria Margareta Garvin; m. Marc Allan Bygdeman (div.); 1 child, Lena. MD, Karolinska Inst., Stockholm, 1960, PhD, 1981, assoc. prof., 1983. Cert. Diploma in Tropical Medicine 1970. Cons. physician, oto-rhino-laryngology Sabbatsbergs Hosp., Stockholm, 1960—65; occupl. health physician County of Stockholm, Stockholm, 1966—69; physician, dept. clin. bacteriology Söder Hospital, Stockholm, 1970—79; cons. physician, rschr., clin. bacteriology Huddinge U. Hospital, Stockholm, 1980—99; Dean for student affairs for Karolinska Internat. Rsch. Tng. Program Karolinska Inst., Stockholm, 1988—90; splty. advisor (counsellor) in clin. bacteriology County of Stockholm, Stockholm, 1995—98; ret. Supr. (tutor) MS and PhD students Karolinska Inst., 1981—99; organizer of workshops in the USA, Canada, Pasteur Institute in Paris, New Zeeland, Australia and Sweden Huddinge U. Hosp. and Karolinska Inst.; Guest lectr. various internat. univs.; hon. mem. editl. bd. Internat. Jour. STD and AIDS and of Venereology; temporary advisor WHO, Geneva; mem. Organizing Com. Internat. Confs. Contbr. articles to internat. profl. jours. Grantee Rsch., Swedish Assn. Rsch. Cooperation with Developing countries, 1986—91, various sources, 1979—99. Mem.: Swedish Soc. Medicine. Avocations: square dancing, square dance instructor. Home: Björnhammarvägen 1 S 184 94 Åkersberga Sweden Home Phone: +46 854027009. Personal E-mail: solgun.bygdeman@swipnet.se.

BYRD, DAVID, physician, educator; b. Jacksonville, Fla., Aug. 17, 1954; BS, Tulane U., 1976; MD, Tulane Sch. Medicine, 1982. Prof. surgery U. Wash., 1992—. Mem.: Alpha Omega Alpha Honor Med. Soc. Office: University Washington Dept Surgery Box 356410 Seattle WA 98195 Office Fax: 206-543-8136. Business E-Mail: byrd@uw.edu.

BYRD, ELLEN STOESSER, school nurse practitioner; b. Dayton, Tex., Dec. 10, 1941; d. Edward Joseph and Nina Mae (Cannon) Stoesser; m. C. Robert Byrd, June 6, 1964; children: Byron, Preston, Aaron, Robyn. BSN, Baylor U., 1964. RN, Tex. Nurse Parkland Hosp., Dallas, 1964-65; nurse gyn. svcs. Baylor U. Med. Ctr., Dallas, 1965-66; charge nurse med./surg. Collin Meml. Hosp., McKinney, Tex., 1967-68; nurse newborn nursery St. Paul Hosp., Dallas, 1972; pvt. duty nurse Dist. 4 Tex. Nurse Assn., Dallas, 1976; sch. nurse Dallas Ind. Sch. Dist., 1989-90; home health nurse Rehab Home Care, DeSoto, Tex., 1994-98; dermatology nurse Dallas Bapt. U., 1999—2001, dir. health svcs., campus nurse, 2001—05, ret., 2005; sch. nurse Richardson (Tex.) Ind. Sch. Dist., 2001—. Mem. deans bd. Baylor U. Sch. Nursing, Dallas, 1994—, chmn. adv. bd. 1999—; advisor Baylor U. Woman's Coun., Dallas, 1995—, pres., mem. adv. coun., 1994-95. Author: History of Dallas CPA Wives, 1983, Biography of Mae Stoesser, 1988, Byrd Family 25 Years, 1990. Program chmn. Freedom Found. Valley Forge, Dallas, 1986—89; centennial cir. chmn. Dallas County Heritage Soc., Dallas; v.p. DeSoto Svc. League, 1990; pres. Dallas CPAs Wives Club, 1984—85; bd. visitors Wake Forest Divinity Sch., 2005—08; trustee Dallas Bapt. U., 2005—; deacon Cliff Temple Bapt. Ch., 1988. Recipient W.T. White Meritorious Svcs. award Baylor U. Alumni Assn., 1996, Ruth award, Dallas Bapt. U., 2005, 100 Legends in the Live. Mem. Richardson Jr. League, Presbyn. Presby Ptnrs. Repubican. Baptist. Avocations: basketball, gardening. Home: 304 Prince Albert Ct Richardson TX 75081-5059 Fax: 972-234-8448. Personal E-mail: ellenbyrd@aol.com.

BYRD, ISAAC BURLIN, retired biologist; b. Canoe, Ala., 1925; s. Isaac Britt and Mary Adline B.; m. Marjorie Fé Elmore, Sept. 24, 1949; children— Cathy Ann, Teresa Carol, Gary Curtis. BS, Auburn U., 1948, MS, 1950. Chief fisheries sect. Ala. Dept. Conservation, 1951-65; fed. aid coordinator fisheries research and devel. Bur. Comml. Fisheries, Dept. Interior, 1965-70; chief div. state-fed. relationships, fisheries research, devel. and mgmt. Nat. Marine Fisheries Service, St. Petersburg, Fla., 1970-85, asst. regional dir. S.E. Region, 1985-91, ret., 1991. Adminstr. Internat. Fisheries Agreement (for U.S. shrimp fishermen to fish Brazilian coastal waters), 1975-76; mem. adv. com. to organize 1st fishery mgmt. councils and to develop initial fed. policies under Fisheries Conservation and Mgmt. Act 1976 (for marine fisheries in fisheries conservation zone of U.S.); chmn. Gulf of Mexico State/Fed. Fisheries Mgmt. Bd., 1985-86, 88-89; chmn. South Atlantic State/Fed. Fisheries Mgmt. Bd., 1990-91 Contbg. author: McCanes Standard Fishing Ency., Internat. Angling Guide, 1965; contbr. articles to sci. jours. Served with USAAF, 1943-46. Recipient Gov. Ala. award outstanding tech. accomplishments conservation, 1964 Fellow Am. Inst. Fishery Research Biologists; mem. Am. Fisheries Soc. (pres. So. div. 1958, pres. 1965-66, asso. editor trans. 1955-58), World Mariculture Soc. (dir. 1972-73), Internat. Assn. Fish and Wildlife Agys., Gulf and Caribbean Fisheries Inst., Inland Comml. Fisheries Assn., Phi Kappa Phi, Omicron Delta Kappa, Gamma Sigma Delta, Alpha Zeta, Alpha Gamma Rho. Methodist. Achievements include initiating the 1st fisheries mgmt. and fisheries research program in state for Ala. Dept. Conservation.

BYRD, LARRY DONALD, behavioral pharmacologist; b. Salisbury, NC, July 14, 1936; s. Donald Thomas and Mildred (Gardner) B.; m. Corrinne Williams, Dec. 23, 1961; children: Kay, Lynn, Renee, Andrew. AB, E. Carolina U., Greenville, NC, 1962; MA, E. Carolina U., 1964; PhD, U. N.C., 1968; postgrad., Harvard U., 1967-70. Faculty E. Carolina U., 1962-64; tchg. and rsch. asst. exptl. psychology U. N.C., Chapel Hill, 1964-67; rsch. fellow pharmacology, instr. psychobiology Harvard Med. Sch., 1967-70; assoc. scientist Lab. Psychobiology New Eng. Reg. Primate Rsch. Ctr., 1969-74; psychobiologist, chmn. divsn. primate behavior Yerkes Primate Rsch. Ctr., Emory U., Atlanta, 1974-79, assoc. rsch. prof., chmn. divsn. primate behavior, 1979-80, lectr. dept. psychology, 1974-81, assoc. rsch. prof., chief divsn. behavioral biology, 1980-82, prof., chief divsn. behavioral biology, 1982-97, prof. dept. pharmacology, 1995-97; prof. emeritus, 1998. Adj. prof. dept. psychology Emory U., 1981-97; cons. Dept. Pharmacological and Physiol. Scis. U. Chgo., 1973, MIT Press, Cambridge, 1975, Nat. Ctr. for Toxicological Rsch. FDA, Jefferson, Ark., 1976-77, S.W. Found. for Rsch. and Edn., San Antonio, 1977, Naval Aerospace Med. Rsch. Lab. U.S. Naval Air Sta., Pensacola, Fla., 1977, G.D. Searle and Co., Skokie, Ill., 1986, Battelle Meml. Inst., Columbus, Ohio, 1989-94; mem. spl. rev. com. Contract Rev. Unit Nat. Inst. on Drug Abuse, Lexington, Ky., 1979-81, mem. spl. rev. com. biomed. rsch. rev. com., 1981-82, spl. rev. cons. clin., behavioral and psychosocial rsch. rev. com., 1981-82, mem., 1982-85, chmn., 1984-85, others; spl. rev. cons. dept. medicine and surgery VA, Washington, 1983, NSF, Washington, 1984, div. of rsch. resources NIH, Washington, 1983, mem. spl. study sect. div. rsch. grants, 1984, panel mem. Workshop on Implementation of Pub. Health Svc. Policy on Humane Care and Use of Lab. Animals, 1989, others; panel mem. USPHS Animal Welfare Forum Alcohol, Drug Abuse and Mental Health Adminstrn., 1985; active numerous other career related orgns. Editorial bd. Jour. Exptl. Analysis of Behavior, 1969-79, 87-91; assoc. editor Jour. Exptl. Analysis of Behavior, 1970-76; cons. editor Am. Jour. Primatology, 1980-83; editor Psychopharmacology Newsletter, 1976-82; editorial advisor Jour. Pharmacology and Exptl. Therapeutics, Jour. Exptl. Analysis of Behavior, others; contbr. numerous articles to profl. jours. Mem. sci. adv. com. Nat. Families in Action, 1991—95. Recipient Outstanding Alumnus award, E. Carolina U., 1977, Disting. Alumnus award, U. N.C., 1987. Fellow AAAS, Am. Psychol. Assn. (exec. com. psychopharmacology divsn. 1976-95, neurobehavioral toxicity test standards com. 1980-97, coord. Young Psychopharmacologist award 1985-95, bd. sci. affairs com. on animals in rsch. and ethics 1990-93); mem. Assn. for Assessment and Accreditation Lab. Animal Care (trustee 1990-98, exec. com. 1991-98, sec. 1993, vice chmn. 1994-96, chmn. 1996-98), Am. Soc. Pharmacology and Exptl. Therapeutics, Nat. Families in Action (sci. adv. com. 1991-95), Am. Soc. Primatologist, Behavioral Pharmacology Soc. (pres. 1984-86), Soc. Exptl. Analysis of Behavior (v.p. 1975-76, bd. dirs. 1970-78), European Behavioral Pharmacology Soc., Southeastern Pharmacology Soc., Am Pub. Health Assn., Behavioral Toxicology Soc., Southeastern Assn. for Behavior Analysis, Internat. Study Group Investigating Drugs as Reinforcers, Emory Neurosci. Group, Phi Sigma Pi. Home: 2730 Camp Branch Rd Buford GA 30519-4455 Business E-Mail: lbyrd@emory.edu.

BYRD, R. ANDREW, medical researcher; PhD, U. SC, 1977. Postdoctoral fellow then rsch. officer Molecular Biophysics Lab. Nat. Rsch. Coun. of Can.; sr. investigator Ctr. for Drugs and Biologics, FDA; founder, head macromolecular NMR sect. Ctr. Cancer Rsch., Nat. Cancer Inst., Frederick, Md., 1992—; chief Structural Biophysics Lab. Ctr. Cancer Rsch., Nat. Cancer Inst., NIH, 1999—, dir. molecular discovery program, 2009—. Chair Exptl. NMR Conf., 1992; co-chair Internat. Conf. on Magnetic Resonance in Biol. Systems, 1996. Office: Structural Biophysics Lab Nat Cancer Inst Bldg 538 Rm 120 PO Box B Frederick MD 21702-1201 Office Phone: 301-846-1407. Office Fax: 301-846-6231. E-mail: byrdra@mail.nih.gov. *

BYRD, STEVE (HENRY STEPHENSON BYRD), plastic surgeon, educator; BA with honors, North Tex. State U., 1968; MD with honors, U. Tex., Galveston, 1972. Diplomate Am. Bd. Surgery, 1978, Am. Bd. Plastic Surgery, 1980, lic. Tex., Utah. Surg. intern U. Tex. Southwestern Med. Ctr., Dallas, 1972—73, resident plastic surgery, 1977—79, prof., vice chair plastic surgery, 1979—2000, prof. clin. surgery, chief pediat. plastic surgery sect., 1979—; resident gen. surgery U. Utah Med. Ctr., Salt Lake City, 1973—77. Sec.-treas., bd. mem. Selected Readings in Plastic Surgery, 1980—; treas. Rhinoplasty Soc., pres., 1999—2001, Bd. Cert. Plastic and Cosmetic Surgeons Dallas, 1999—2001; chmn. Bd. Pediat. Surg. Alliance; bd. mem. Health Tex. Provider Network; sec. Preferred Surg. Specialist Tex.; attending staff Parkland Meml. Hosp., Dallas, U. Med. Ctr., Dallas; dir. plastic surgery svc., mem. cleft lip-craniofacial team Children's Med. Ctr., Dallas; dir. Dallas Day Surgery Baylor U. Med. Ctr., 1992—, chief plastic and reconstructive surgery svc., 1996—2002. Contbr. articles to med. jours. Mem. long-range planning task force Plastic Surgery Ednl. Found., 1991—, mem. mktg. com., 1991, bd. mem., 1993—95, mem. select com. on forward planning, 1996, bd. dirs., 1996—98, mem. internat. svc. com., 1997—99. Fellow: ACS; mem.: Dallas County Med. Soc., Dallas Soc. Plastic Surgeons (sec.-treas.), Tex. Soc. Plastic Surgeons, Tex. Med. Assn., Am. Cleft Palate Assn., Am. Soc. for Aesthetic Plastic Surgery (mem. edn. commn.), Am. Assn. Plastic Surgeons, Am. Soc. Plastic and Reconstructive Surgeons (mem. sci. program com. 1991, James Barrett Brown award 1984), Alpha Omega Alpha, Blue Key Honor Soc. Office: Dallas Plastic Surgery 9101 N Central Expy Ste 600 Dallas TX 75231-5956 Office Phone: 214-821-9662. Office Fax: 214-828-2609. Business E-Mail: info@drstevebyrd.com.

BYRD, WYATT, microbiologist, researcher; b. Panama City, Fla., June 23, 1958; s. Elizabeth and Isaac Byrd; m. Dagmar Beinenz, Sept. 18, 1962; children: Lewis, Fiona. PhD, U. of Ga., 1985—91. Rsch. assoc. Miami U., Oxford, Ohio, 1993—97; rsch. asst. Walter Reed Army Inst. Rsch., Silver Spring, Md., 1998—2004; rsch. assoc. New Mex. Vets. Adminstrn. Ctr., Albuquerque, 2007—. Mem.: Am. Soc. for Microbiology (assoc.). Office: 13701 Elena Gallegos Pl NE Albuquerque NM 87111 Personal E-mail: dagmarbyrd@comcast.net.

BYRNE, GEORGE MELVIN, physician; b. Aug. 1, 1933; s. Carlton and Esther (Smith) B.; m. Joan Stecher, July 14, 1956; children: Kathryne, Michael, David; m. Margaret C. Smith, Dec. 18, 1982; m. Barbara Barrett, May 19, 2001. BA, Occidental Coll., 1958; MD, U. So. Calif., 1962. Intern Huntington Meml. Hosp., Pasadena, Calif., 1962-63, resident, 1963-64; family practice So. Calif. Permanente Med. Group, 1964-81; physician-in-charge Pasadena Med. Office, 1966-81; asst. dir. family practice residency Kaiser Found. Hosp., LA, 1971-73; clin. instr. emergency medicine Sch. Medicine U. So. Calif., 1973-80; v.p. East Ridge Co., 1983-84, sec., 1984; dir. Alan Johnson Porsche Audi, Inc., 1974-82, sec., 1974-77, v.p., 1978-82. Bd. dirs. Kaiser-Permanente Mgmt. Assn., 1976-77; mem. regional mgmt. com. So. Calif. Lung Assn., 1976-77; mem. pres.'s cir. Occidental Coll., L.A. Drs. Symphony Orch., 1975-80; mem. profl. sect. Am. Diabetes Assn; Episcopal Diolese LA Program Group Disabilities. Fellow Am. Acad. Family Physicians (charter); mem. AMA, Calif. Med. Assn., L.A. County Med. Assn., Calif. Acad. Family Physicians, Internat. Horn Soc., Quarter Century Wireless Assn., Am. Radio Relay League (Pub. Svc. award), Sierra (life). Home: 528 Meadowview Dr La Canada Flintridge CA 91011-2816 Personal E-mail: GMByrne@aol.com.

BYRNE, JAMES, insurance company executive; BS, Aquinas Coll., Grand Rapids; MS in Adminstrv. Medicine, U. Wis.; MD, Med. Coll. Wis. Lic. surgeon and physician Mich., 1971, cert. American Bd. Family Practice, 1976. Intern Spectrum Health Butterworth Hosp., Grand Rapids; resident in family medicine Ventura County Med. Ctr.; owner family practice, Holland, Mich., 1977; med. dir. LakeShore HMO, Holland, 1986; med. dir. Alliance of Cmty. Health Plan (ACHP) Patient-Centered Med. Home Collaborative; med. dir. Priority Health, chief med. officer, 1997—. Recipient Ellis J. Bonner Outstanding Achievement award, Mich. Assn. of Health Plans, 2007. Mem.: Patient-Centered Primary Care Collaborative (exec. com. mem.), American Acad. Family Physicians. Office: Priority Health 1231 E Beltline NE Grand Rapids MI 49525 *

BYRNE, JOHN G., surgeon; BS in Biochemistry, U. Calif., Davis, 1982; MD, Boston U., 1987. Cert. Am. Bd. Surgery, 1996, Am. Bd. Thoracic Surgery, 1998. Intern and jr. resident U. Ill. Affiliated Hospitals, Chgo., 1987—89, sr. and chief resident in gen. surgery, 1992—95, adminstrv. chief resident in gen. surgery, 1994—95; rsch. fellow in cardiac surgery Harvard Med. Sch., Boston, 1989—92, assoc. prof. surgery; resident and chief resident in cardiothoracic surgery Brigham and Women's Hosp., Boston, 1995—97, assoc. chief and residency program dir., divsn. cardiac surgery; chair dept. cardiac surgery, William S. Stony prof. surgery Vanderbilt U. Med. Ctr., Heart and Vascular Inst., Nashville, 2004—. Contbr. articles to profl. jours. Fellow: ACS, Am. Coll. Cardiology. Office: Vanderbilt Heart and Vascular Inst 1215 21st Ave S MCE-N Tower Ste 5025 Nashville TN 37232-8802 also: Vanderbilt Med Ctr 1211 Med Ctr Dr Nashville TN 37232 Office Phone: 615-343-9195. Office Fax: 615-936-2815. Business E-Mail: john.byrne@vanderbilt.edu.

BYRNES, JOHN P., medical products executive; Joined Lincare Holdings, Inc., Clearwater, Fla., 1986, pres., 1996—2003, COO, 1996, CEO, 1997—, chmn., 2000—. Bd. dirs. Kinetic Concepts Inc., US Renal Care Inc. Office: Lincare Holdings inc 19387 US 19 N Clearwater FL 33764 Office Phone: 727-530-7700. Office Fax: 727-532-9692. Business E-Mail: jbyrnes@lincare.com. *

BYUN, JAE HO, medical educator; s. Dong Kuk Byun and Bun Seon Jeon. MD, Coll. Medicine, Kyungpook Nat. U., Daegu, 1993; PhD cum laude, Grad. Sch., Kyungpook Nat. U., Daegu, 2006. Lic. Ministry Health and Welfare, Republic Of Korea, 1993, cert. in radiology Korean Soc. of Radiology, 2001. Asst. prof. Asan Med. Ctr., U. Ulsan Coll. Medicine, Seoul, Republic of Korea, 2003—, assoc. prof., 2008—. Reviewer Am. Jour. of Roentgenology, Leesburg, Va., 2005—, Korean Jour. Radiology, Seoul, 2006—. Contbr. articles to sci. jours. Mem.: Korean Soc. Magnetic Resonance Medicine, Korean Soc. Abdominal Radiology, Korean Med. Assn., Korean Soc. Radiology. Avocations: golf, skiing. Office: Asan Med Center 388-1 Pungnap-2dong Songpa-gu Seoul 138-736 Republic of Korea Office Fax: 82-2-476-4719. Business E-Mail: jhbyun@amc.seoul.kr.

BYUN, JAE YONG, medical educator; b. Seoul, Republic of Korea, May 12, 1968; MD, Kyung Hee U., 1994, PhD, 2004. Bd. dir. Korean Balance Soc., 2006—; rsch. scholar Satnford U. Med. sch., 2010—. Mem.: Korean Otolaryn. Soc., AAO, ARO. Office: Coll Medicine Kyung Hee University Seoul 130-701 Republic of Korea Office Fax: 82-2-440-6521. Business E-Mail: otorhino512@naver.com.

BYUN, JONGHOE, medical researcher, educator; b. Cheongwongun, Choongchungbook-Do, Republic of Korea, Aug. 20, 1967; s. HongKyu Byun and JongDuk Lee; m. OkHan Kim, May 1, 1999; children: JoonSoo, HyunSoo. BS, Seoul Nat. U., Republic of Korea, 1990, MS, 1992, PhD, 1997. Rschr. Rsch. Ctr. Molecular Microbiology, Seoul Nat. U., 1992—97, Samsung Biomed. Rsch. Inst., Seoul, 1997—99; rsch. assoc. Duke U. Med. Ctr., Durham, NC, 1999—2002; asst. prof. Neurosci. Rsch. Inst., Gachon Med. Sch., Incheon, Republic of Korea, 2005—06, Dankook U., Yongin-si, Gyeonggi-do, Republic of Korea, 2006—. Sunday sch. tchr. NamSeoul Grace Ch., 2003—; chief planning officer Korean Soc. Gene Therapy, Seoul, 2008—, Korean RNA Soc.; academic bd. mem. Korean Peptide-Protein Soc. Fellowship, ChoongBook Assn., 1986, High Honor scholarship, Seoul Nat. U., 1989, fellowships, WooSan Assn., 1990—92. Achievements include development of novel potent hypoxia-inducible vector; novel angiogenesis assay for gene. Office: Dankook University Dept Molecular Biology 126 Jukjeon-dong Suji-gu Yongin Gyeonggi-do 448-701 Republic of Korea Office Fax: 82-31-8021-7201. Business E-Mail: jonghoe@dankook.ac.kr.

BYUN, JUNE-HO, oral and maxillofacial surgeon, educator; b. Busan, Republic of Korea, Aug. 6, 1970; s. Jung-Sook Kim; m. Hee-Kyeong An, Oct. 2, 2005; children: Dong-Hyun children: Ga-in. DDS, Pusan Nat. U., Korea, 1996, MS in Dentistry, 1999, PhD, 2005. Lic. dentist Ministry of Health and Welfare, Seoul, Korea, 1996. Intern, resident in oral and maxillofacial surgery Pusan Nat. U. Hosp., 1996—; army oral and maxillofacial surgeon Ministry Nat. Def., Republic of Korea, 2000—; fellow in oral and maxillofacial surgery Pusan Nat. U. Hosp., 2003—, Gyeongsang Nat. U. Hosp., Jinju, Republic of Korea, 2004—; instr. oral and maxillofacial surgery Gyeongsang Nat. U. Sch. Medicine, Jinju, 2004—, asst. prof. oral and maxillofacial surgery, 2007—. Capt. Republic of Korea Army, 2000—03. Mem.: Korean Rsch. Inst. Biosci. and Biotech., Korean Soc. Molecular and Cellular Biology, Korean Soc. Med. Biochemistry and Molecular Biology, Internat. Assn. Oral and Maxillofacial Surgeons, Korean Assn. Maxillofacial Plastic and Reconstructive Surgeons, Korean Assn. Oral and Maxillofacial Surgeons. Buddhist. Avocations: golf, baduk, travel. Home: Dongdaeshin-dong Seo-gu Busan 602-812 Republic of Korea Office: Gyeongsang Nat U Hosp Chilam-Dong 90 660-702 Jeonju Republic of Korea Office Fax: 82-55-761-7024. Business E-Mail: surbyun@nongae.gsnu.ac.kr.

BYUNG-RAE, JIN, biotechnologist, educator; b. Euryung, Kyungnam, South Korea, Oct. 23, 1962; m. Yoon Hyung-Joo, Oct. 8, 1989; children: Sil, Jin. BS, Dong A U., Busan, Republic of Korea, 1985; MS, Seoul Nat. U., 1987, PhD, 1994. Rschr. Genetic Engr. Res. Inst., Taejon, Republic of Korea, 1991—94; postdoctoral rschr. Seoul Nat. U., 1994—96; doctoral rsch. U. Calif., Davis, 1996—97; rschr. Sericulture & Entomology Rsch. Inst., Suwon, Republic of Korea, 1997—98; prof. Dong A U., Busan, 1998—. Chmn. dept. Biotechnology Dong A Univ., Busan, 2002—; mng. editor Internat. Jour. Indsl. Entomology, Seoul, 1999—2001, editor-in-chief, 2002—; editor Jour. Asia-Pacific Entomology, Seoul, 2002—. Achievements include patents in field. Office: Dong-A-Univ Dept Biotechnology 840 Hadangdong 604-714 Pusan Republic of Korea Home Phone: 82-31-244-3635; Office Phone: 82-51-200-7594. E-mail: brjin@daunet.donga.ac.kr.

BZOCH, KENNETH RUDOLPH, speech and language educator, department chairman; b. Chgo., Nov. 6, 1927; s. Rudolph and Mildred (Novotny) B.; m. Lorrayne M. Cali, Oct. 29, 1950; children: Kathleen Marie, Kevin Jude. BA, DePaul U., Chgo., 1951; MA, Northwestern U., 1952, PhD, 1956. Cert. clin. competence-speech pathology, CCC-audiology; lic. speech pathologist, Fla. Asst. prof. Loyola U., Chgo., 1953—57, Northwestern U., Chgo., 1957—59; assoc. prof. U. Fla., Gainesville, 1960—64, prof., chair, 1964—96, prof. emeritus. Program dir. Communicative Disorders and Craniofacial Ctr., Shands Hosp., U. Fla.; researcher in field. Author: Communicative Disorders Related to Cleft Lip and Palate, 5th edit., 2004, Receptive-Expressive Language Test: A Method of Assessing Language Skills in Infancy, 3d edit., 2004, How Babies Learn To Talk: A Book for New Parents and Grandparents, 2004. Cpl. USMC, 1946-47. Fellow Am. Cleft Palate Assn. (past pres.), Fla. Cleft Palate Assn. (hon., past pres.), Fla. Speech Lang. and Hearing Assn. (hon., past pres.). Home and Office: 640 NW 57th St Gainesville FL 32607-6103 Home Phone: 352-331-7171; Office Phone: 352-331-7171. Personal E-mail: bzoch@aol.com.

CABALLERO, FRANCISCO, surgeon; b. Guadalmez, Spain, Aug. 20, 1958; Degree in Medicine and Surgery, U. Barcelona, 1984; D in Medicine and Surgery, U. Autónoma de Barcelona, 2005. Transplant coord. Hosp. de la Santa Creu i Sant Pau, 1994—, chief, organ and tissue procurement transplantation, 2011. Recipient Societat Catalana de Trasplantaments award, Acadèmia de Ciències Mèdiques i de la Salut de Catalunya I Balears, Barcelona, 2006. Mem.: European Transplant Coordinators Orgn. Avocations: jogging, football, music. Office: Avd Sant Antoni M Claret 167 Barcelona 08025 Spain Office Fax: 0034935537655. Business E-Mail: fcaballero@hsp.santpau.es.

CABAY, ROBERT JOHN, physician, dentist, author, researcher, educator; s. John A. and Irene M. Cabay; m. Gina Grace Angela Bill, Aug. 8, 1993. BSGS, Northwestern U., Evanston, Ill., 1995; DDS, Loyola U. Chgo., Maywood, Ill., 1986; MPH, U. Ill., Chgo., 1991, MD, 2004. Diplomate Am. Bd. Quality Assurance and Utilization Rev. Physicians, Am. Bd. Pathology. Gen. dentist Charles J. Zasso, DDS, FAGD and Assocs., Ltd., Schaumburg, Ill., 1986—2009; resident physician dept. pathology Coll. Medicine, U. Ill., Chgo., 2004—08; Donald West King fellow oral & maxillofacial pathology Armed Forces Inst Pathology, Washington, 2007; cytopathology fellow dept. pathology Loyola U. Med. Ctr., Maywood, Ill., 2008—09; surgical patholgy fellow dept. pathology U. Ill., Chgo., 2009—10; vis. head & neck pathology fellow Mass. Gen. Hosp., 2010; asst. prof. clin. pathology Coll. Medicine, U. Ill., Chgo., 2010—, asst. prof., dept. oral medicine & diagnostic sciences, Coll. Dentistry, 2010—. Dental cons., 1999—. Children of Vets. scholar, U. Ill., 2000—04. Fellow: Am. Soc. Clin. Pathology, Coll. Am. Pathologists, Am. Inst. for Healthcare Quality, Acad. Gen. Dentistry; mem.: ADA, AMA, U.S. and Can. Acad. Pathology, Chgo. Dental Soc., Ill. State Dental Soc., Chgo. Med. Soc., Ill. State Med. Soc., Alpha Sigma Nu. Office: Univ Ill Chgo Dept Pathology 840 S Wood St Chicago IL 60612-4325

CABBABE, EDMOND BECHIR, plastic and hand surgeon; b. Aleppo, Syria, Feb. 21, 1947; Came to U.S., 1973; s. Bechir Wahid and Samia (Hamoui) C.; m. Rima Gorab, Apr. 22, 1973; children: Nabil, Samer, Monica. BS in Physics, Chemistry Biology, Damascus U. Sch. Scis., 1967, MD, 1972. Diplomate Am. Bd. Surgery, Am Bd. Plastic Surgery, cert hand surgery. Surg. intern St. Mary of Nazareth Hosp., Chgo., 1973-74; surg. resident U. Tenn., Chattanooga, 1974-78; resident in plastic surgery St. Louis U., 1978-80, asst. prof., 1980-86, asst. clin. prof., 1986-98, assoc. clin. prof., 1998—2003, clin. prof., 2003—; practice medicine specializing in plastic surgery Plastic Surgery Cons., St. Louis, 1986—2005, Advanced Plastic Surgery, Inc., St. Louis, 2005—; chief plastic surgery St. Anthony Med. Ctr., St. Louis, 1990-95, 2000—, De Paul Health Ctr., St. Louis, 1991—. Chief plastic surgery John Cochran VA Hosp., St. Louis, 1981-86; dir. cleft palate clinic Cardinal Glennon Children's Hosp., St. Louis, 1984-86; mem. adv. com. Healthlink CompMgmt., vice chmn., 1997-2001; mem. adv. bd. to Senator Christopher Bond, chmn. small bus. com. U.S. Senate, 1995-98 Editor: St. Louis Met. Medicine, 1991-93; mem. editl. bd.: Missouri Medicine, 1999—; contbr. articles to profl. jours. Mem. Arab Am. Anti Discrimination Com., Washington, 1982—, bd. dirs. Mo. Ctr. Patient Safety, 2005-. Recipient Excellence in Med. Leadership award, AMA, 2005. Fellow: AMA (mem. governing coun. Internat. Med. Grads. Mo. 2005—07, alt. del. 2005—10, Found. bd. mem. 2008—, del. 2010—), ACS; mem.: Syrian Am. Cult. Coun. (bd. mem.), Am. Soc. Aesthetic Plastic Surgery, St. Louis Area Soc. Plastic Surgeons (pres. 1993—95), St. Louis Soc. for Med. and Sci. Edn. (trustee 1991—93, pres. 1995), St. Louis Met. Med. Soc. (pres. 1995), Mo. Assn. Plastic Surgeons, Mo. State Med. Assn. (pres. Ins. Agy. 2009—, Citizenship and Cmty. award 1999), Nat. Arab Am. Med. Assn. Found. (chmn. 1999), Nat. Arab Am. Med. Assn. (pres. 1995), St. Louis Arab Am. Med. Assn. (pres. 1985—86), Am. Assn. Hand Surgery (sci. program com.), Am. Soc. Plastic and Reconstructive Surgeons (sci. program com). Roman Catholic. Avocations: writing, exercise, antiques, photography. Home Phone: 314-878-5362; Office Phone: 314-842-5885. E-mail: ebcsl@aol.com.

CABIN, HENRY SCOTT, cardiologist, educator; Attended, Yale U. Sch. Medicine, 1975. Diplomate Am. Bd. Cardiology-cardiovascular disease, Am. Bd. Cardiology-interventional cardiology, Am. Bd. Internal Medicine. Fellow in internal medicine Nat. Heart Lung and Blood Inst., Bethesda, 1978—81; prof. medicine Yale Univ.; with Yale Med. Group; resident in internal medicine Yale - New Haven Hosp., 1976—78, fellow in cardiovascular disease, 1981—82, cardiologist. Office: Yale - New Haven Hosp. 11 Harrison Ave Branford CT 06405 Office Phone: 203-483-8300. Office Fax: 203-483-8314.

CABRAL, ANTONIO CARLOS, medical educator; b. Belo horizonte, Apr. 10, 1955; Postdoc, U. Calif., San Francisco, 1990. Physician UFMG, 1979; prof. U. Fed. de Minas Gerais, 1984—. Recipient Zuspan award, Isshp London. Avocations: horseback riding, photography. Office: Alfredo Balena 909 Rm 1804 Belo horizonte Minas Gerais 30130-100 Brazil E-mail: accabral@hc.ufmg.br.

CABRERA-OTERO, SYLVIA, physician; b. San Juan, Jan. 15, 1945; d. Benigno Cabrera and Ana Otero; m. Antonio Nieves-Negron, Feb. 20, 1965; 1 child, Sylvianne. BS, U. PR, 1967, postgrad. in geriatrics, 1987-88, MPH, 1996; MD, U. Valencia, 1974. Diplomate Am. Bd. Sexology, 1995. Family medicine CDT Minillas, Bayamón, PR, 1978—2011, prin., owner, 1978—2011; active mem., staff Hosp. Hima San Pablo, Bayamón, 1985—; sex educator, therapist PR Coll. Physicians, 1987—2006. Sec. Found. Coll. Physicians, 2004—06; Sen. Pub. Health Coll. Physicians; pres. disciplines of pub. health Coll. of Physicians, 2006—. Fellow Am. Acad. Family Practice (past pres. PR chpt., postgrad. in fundamentals of mgmt.), Internat. Physicians; mem. AMA, Am. Acad. Sex Edn. (counselor and sex therapist), PR Med. Assn., World Assn. Sexology, Med. Found. P.R. Coll. Physicians (sec. 2004-06, pres. pub. health sect. 2006—), Bayamon P.R. Coll. Physicians (sec. 2006—). Avocations: writing, brewing, crocheting, guitar, teaching. Office: Z22 Ave Laurel Urb Lomas Verdes Bayamon PR 00956-3244 Office Phone: 787-798-5175, 787-798-5199. Personal E-mail: sylvia.c@onchurchpr.net. Business E-Mail: CDTminillas@yahoo.com.

CABRERA-TRIGO, JUAN, otolaryngologist; b. Asuncion, Paraguay, Dec. 27, 1928; arrived in Argentina, 56; s. Valentin Cabrera and Margarita Trigo; m. Maria Esther Bonaldo; 1 child, Patricia Beatriz; m. Josefina Farías-Queiróz (dec. 1963); children: Eduardo, Margarita. MD, Asunción U., 1953, Buenos Aires U., 1974. Chief otolaryngology dept. P. Piñero Hosp., Buenos Aires, 1976—80, C. Argerich Hosp.,

Buenos Aires, 1980—94; prof. otolaryngology Med. Sch. Buenos Aires U., 1989; prof. foniatrics clinic Med. Sch. U. del Salvador, 1990. Pres. Argentine Otolaryngol. Soc., Buenos Aires, 1982—84, Argentine Rhinological Soc., Buenos Aires, 1986—88; cons. in otolaryngology Med. Coll. Buenos Aires, 1975—94. Contbr. articles to profl. jours. Fellow Unión Cívica Radical, Buenos Aires, 1980. Mem.: Philosophy of Sci. Assn., Argentine Surgery Assn., Argentine Otolaryngology Fedn., Argentine Med. Assn. Union Civica Radical. Roman Catholic. Avocation: flying. Home: Calle Jose Barros Pazos 6474 C1439CJV Buenos Aires Argentina Office Phone: 01139680265. Personal E-mail: pbcabrera@gmail.com.

CABRIC, MILAN, biologist; b. Belgrad, Serbia, July 5, 1939; s. Dragoljub and Alica Čabrić; children: Kolja, Marko, Vesna, Boris, Nikola. MA, U. Belgrad, Serbia, 1965, MSc, 1983; PhD, Acad. Physical Edn., Warsaw, 1977. Rschr. Inst. Sport Sci., Belgrad, Serbia, 1966—73; docent, prof. assoc. U. Split, Croatia, 1973—86, 1987—; prof. U. Novi Sad, Serbia, 1986—92, Acad. Physics Edn., Warsaw, 1992—99, Faculty Medicine U. Torun, Poland, 1999—. Dept. head, human biology U. Torun. Contbr. articles various profl. jours. Recipient Scientific Rsch. award, Rector of U., 2005. Office: Coll Medicine Dept Antropology Univ Torun Str Swietojanska 20 Bydgoszcz 85 076 Poland Home: Kolonia Zacisze 13 21-500 Biala Podlaska Poland Office Phone: 48525851011. Business E-Mail: kizantrop@cm.nmk.pl.

CABROL, CHRISTIAN EMILE, cardiologist, surgeon; b. Chezy sur Marne, Aisne, France, Sept. 16, 1925; s. Roger and Lucienne (Gratiot) C. MD, Paris Sch. Medicine, 1954. Intern, resident, surgeon Parisian Hosp., 1948-67; chief outpatient surg. clinic Hosp. La Pitie, Paris, 1967-72, chief dept. cardiothoracic surgery, 1972-90. Prof. anatomy Med. Sch. Paris, 1955—94; dir. Sch. Surgery Paris, 1973—93; pres. France Transplant, 1988—94, Adicare Rsch. Ctr., 1988—. Editor: Mes 400 greffes, 1990, Don De Soi, 1996, Parole De Medecin, 1992, Manger Vrai, 1997, Bataille pour la Vie, 1994, Histoire de Coeur, 1999, De tout coeur, 2006, Les Peslicules Segmentaires du Poumon, 1953-55; contbr. articles to profl. jours. Pres. coun. Nat. Alimentation, 1996-99; mem. European Parliament, 1994-99; dep. mayor, Paris, 1989—2008. Recipient Gruntzig award European Soc. Cardiology, 1989, Claude Bernard award de La Ville de Paris, 1986, Grimbaum prize Inst. de France, 1956, Litteraire prize French Acad., 1996; named Comdr. de Legion of Honor, Officier de l'Ordre du Merite. Mem. Acad. Nat. Medicine, Acad. Nat. Surgery, Mediterranean Assn. Cardiology and CV Surgery (founder, pres.), Soc. Heart and Lung Transplantation (pres. 1986), Am. Assn. Thoracic and Cardiovascular Surgery, Acad. Nat. Medicine Brazil. Roman Catholic. Achievements include first cardiac transplantation in Europe, first heart-lung transplant in Europe. Office: Adicare Inst de Cardiologie 56 Bd Vincent Auriol 75013 Paris France Office Phone: 33-1-42164202. Business E-Mail: adicore@wanadoo.fr.

CACACE, ANTHONY T., audiologist, educator; BS in Speech Pathology & Audiology, SUNY, New Paltz; MS in Audiology, Syracuse U., PhD in Audiology & Neuroscience. Neurophysiology fellow NY State Health Dept. Wadsworth Labs; staff scientist Neurosciences Inst. & Advanced Imaging Rsch. Ctr.; staff audiologist Albany Med. Ctr. Hosp., former dir. Hearing Rehabilitation Ctr., former dir. audiology; dir. oto-neurological rsch. Albany Med. Coll. Div. Otolaryngology; audiologist Wayne State U., prof. comm. sci. & otolaryngology. Editor-in-chief Am. Jour. Audiology. Co-editor: Controversies in Central Auditory Processing Disorder, 2009. Fellow: Am. Acad. Audiology, Am. Speech, Language & Hearing Assn.; mem.: Am. Tinnitus Assn. (chmn. Scientific Adv. Com.). Office: Wayne State University Rackham Bldg Rm 202 31 Detroit MI 48202 Office Phone: 313-577-6753. E-mail: cacacea@wayne.edu.

CACIOPPO, JOHN TERRANCE, psychologist, educator, researcher; b. Marshall, Tex., June 12, 1951; s. Cyrus Joseph and Mary Katherine (Kazimour) Cacioppo; m. Barbara Lee Andersen, May 17, 1981 (div. 1998); children: Christina Elizabeth, Anthony Cyrus;. BS in Econs., U. Mo., Columbia, 1973; MA in Psychology, Ohio State U., 1975, PhD in Psychology, 1977. Asst. prof. psychology U. Notre Dame, Ind., 1977-79, U. Iowa, Iowa City, 1979-81, assoc. prof., 1981-85, prof. psychology, 1985-89, Ohio State U., 1989-98, Univ. chaired prof. psychology, 1998-99; Tiffany-Margaret Blake disting. svc. prof. U. Chgo., 1999—. Vis. faculty Yale U., 1986, U. Hawaii, 1990, U. Chgo., 1998—99; tng. grant dir. NIMH Social Psychology, 1993—98; co-dir. Inst. for Mind and Biology, 1999—2004, dir. social psychology program, 1999—2005, 2007—; dir. Ctr. Cognitive and Social Neurosci. U. Chgo., 2004—, dir., Arete Initiative, 2007—10. Editor: Psychophysiology, 1994—97; contbr. articles to profl. jours. Active John D. and Catherine T. MacArthur Found. Network 1995-98, 2007-; bd. dirs. Ohio State U. Rsch. Found., 1993-98 Recipient Early Career Contbn. award Psychophysiology, 1981, Troland Rsch. award NAS, 1989, Disting. Sci. Contbr. Psychophysiol., Soc. Psychophysiol. Rsch., 2000; NSF/NIH grantee, 1979—, Campbell award Soc. Personality and Social Psychology, 2000, Merit award NIH, 2010. Fellow: APA (past pres. 2 divsns., Disting. Sci. Contbn. award 2002, Presdl. Citation award 2008), Acad. Behavioral Medicine Rsch., Am. Psychol. Soc. (keynote spkr. ann. meeting 2002, bd. & dir. 2002—, pres. 2007—08); mem.: AAAS (chair elect psychology sect. 2009), Am. Acad. Arts and Scis., Soc. Exptl. Psychologists, Soc. Exptl. Social Psychology (Sci. Impact award 2009), Soc. Personality and Social Psychology (pres. 1995, Theoritical Innovation prize 2008, Disting. Svc. award 2008), Soc. Psychophysiol. Rsch. (bd. dirs. 1985—88, officer 1991—94, pres. 1992—93, bd. dirs. 1998—2000), Sigma Xi (nat. lectr. 1996—98). Office Phone: 773-702-1962. *

CADIEUX, ROGER JOSEPH, geriatrics services professional; b. Bay Shore, NY, Feb. 7, 1945; children: Kevin, Kristin BS, Northwestern State U., 1973; MD, La. State U., 1977. Cert. geriatric psychiatrist, RN anesthetist. Intern, then resident in psychiatry Coll. Medicine Pa. State U., Hershey, 1977-81, psychogeriatric fellow, instr. Coll. Medicine Milton S. Hershey Med. ctr., 1980-81, asst. prof. dept. psychiatry, 1981-93, assoc. prof. psychiatry, 1993-99; clin. prof. psychiatry, 1999—; dir. geriatric assessment program Pa. State U. Coll. Medicine, 1992-98; psychiat. cons. Jewish Home of Harrisburg, 1985—2010, Homeland Ctr. of Harrisburg, 1993—; program dir. Pa. Dept. Aging, 1986—, physician cons., 1987—; pres. Commonwealth Affiliates, P.C., 1992—. Contbr. articles to profl. jours. Fellow Am. Bd. Psychiatry and Neurology (disting. life, diplomate); mem. Am. Psychiat. Assn., Am. Geriatric Soc., Am. Assn. for Geriatric Psychiatry, Acad. Sleep Disorders Medicine, Alpha Omega Alpha. Office: 2215 Forest Hills Dr Ste38 Harrisburg PA 17112-1099 Home Phone: 717-566-0333; Office Phone: 717-540-5353. Personal E-mail: rjcpsy@aol.com.

CADY, BLAKE, surgical oncologist; b. Washington, Dec. 27, 1930; s. John Parmalee and Elizabeth (Blake) C.; children: Brian, Suzanne, Pamela. AB, Amherst Coll., 1953; MD, Cornell U., 1957. Diplomate Am. Bd. Surgery; lic. physician, Mass., NY, RI. Intern Tufts Surg. Svc. Boston City Hosp., 1957-58, resident Tufts Surg. Soc., 1958-59, resident Harvard Surg. Svc., 1961-65; USPHS clinic cancer trainee Meml. Hosp. for Cancer and Allied Diseases, NYC, 1965-67; fellow in surgery Cornell U. Med. Coll., 1965-67; fellow Sloan-Kettering Inst., 1965-67; staff surgeon Lahey Med. Clinic, Burlington, Mass., 1967-81; mem. surg. staff New Eng. Deaconess Hosp., Boston, 1967-97; chief surg. oncology New Eng. Deaconess, Boston, 1982-97; prof. surgery Brown U. Med. Sch., Providence, 1997—2007; emeritus prof., 2007—. Surg. liaison Dana Farber Cancer Ctr., Boston, 1982-1992; cons. surgery Uganda Cancer Inst., Kampala, Uganda, East Africa, 1971; assoc. clin. prof. surgery Harvard Med. Sch., 1975-82, assoc. prof., 1982-91, prof. 1991-97, emeritus prof., 1997—; dir. Breast Health Ctr., Women and Infants Hosp., Providence, 1997-2003; interum dir. Comprehensive Breast Ctr., RI Hosp., 2003-07. Editor emeritus: Surgical Oncology Clinic of North America; mem. editl. bd. several jours.; contbr. over 300 articles to profl. jours. Bd. dirs. Mass. div. Am. Cancer Soc., 1974, pres., 1991-93, nat. bd. dirs., 1993-99, chmn. tobacco policy com., 1991-93; chmn. bd. dirs. Tobacco Control Resource Ctr., 1994-2006, Planned Parenthood League Mass., 1984-85; chmn. Pub. Health Advocacy Inst.; chmn. Mass. Coalition for Healthy Future, 1991-93, Tobacco Control Oversight Coun. Mass.; pres. James Ewing Found., 1988. Lt. M.C., USN, 1959-61. Recipient Lemuel Shattuck medal Mass. Pub. Health Assn., 1983; ann. nat. divsn. award Mass. divsn. Am. Cancer Soc., 1984, Disting. Svc. award, 2000., Henry Chedwick Medal, Mass. Thoracic Soc., 1994 Mem. AMA, ACS (Mass. chpt., spl. rep. to regional cancer control com. subcom., regional cancer control com.), Am. Surg. Assn., Soc. Surg. Oncology (program chmn. nat. meetings 1980, 81, chmn. rsch. com. 1980-82, sec. 1984-86, v.p. 1986-87, pres.-elect 1987-88, pres. 1988, chmn. exec. com. 1989-90), Soc. Head and Neck Surgeons (program com. 1980, Hayes Martin lectr. 1998), Am. Assn. Endocrine Surgeons (v.p. 1982, local arrangements chmn. 1988, exec. coun. 1986-90, sec.-treas. 1991-94, pres. 1998), New Eng. Cancer Soc. (treas. 1976-83, sec. 1983-87, pres. 1991), New Eng. Surg. Soc. (recorder 1989, pres. 1995-96), Soc. for Surgery Alimentary Tract, Boston Surg. Soc. (pres. 1993), Halstead Soc. Avocations: sailing, travel. Home: 24 Walnut Pl Brookline MA 02445-6710 Office: Cambridge Hosp 1493 Cambridge St Cambridge MA 02139 Office Phone: 617-665-2001. Business E-Mail: bcady123@comcast.net.

CADY, DUANE MAYNARD, surgeon; b. Endicott, NY, 1934; m. Joyce Cady; 5 children. BS in Chem., Atlantic Union Coll., Mass.; MD, Loma Linda U., 1959. Diplomate Am. Bd. Surgery. Intern SUNY-Syracuse Med. Ctr., 1959-60, resident in surgery, 1960-64, clin. assoc. prof. surgery; pvt. practice NYC. Apptd. chair NY State Medicaid Managed Care Adv. Coun.; mem. NY State Pub. Health Couns. Task Force on Pain Mgmt.; mem. med. staff pres., chair dept. surgery, bd. trustees St. Joseph's Hosp., Syracuse. Captain & army surgeon Medical Corps US Army. Fellow Am. Coll. Surgeons; mem. AMA (coun. med. svc., bd. trustees, chair bd. trustees 2005-07, pres. AMA Found., 2004-06), Med. Soc. of the State of NY (past pres. & chmn.), Am. Soc. Gen. Surgeons. Mailing: PO Box 137 La Fayette NY 13084

CAEN, JACQUES PHILIPPE, physician; b. Metz, France, Mar. 11, 1927; s. Lucien and Renee (Levy) C.; m. Genevieve Francou, Feb. 2, 1951; children: Remi, Anne-Sophie. MD, U. Paris, 1951. Assoc. prof. medicine U. Paris VII, 1966-78, prof., 1978-95. Chief rsch. dept. hemostasis and thrombosis med. rsch. coun. U. Paris, 1971; mem. faculty Caius and Gonville Coll., Cambridge (Eng.) U., 1976-77; assoc. prof. U. Sydney, 1983. Author: Le sang d'une vie, 1994; contbr. articles to profl. jours. Decorated Legion of Honor Comdr. High Officer, Legion of Merit; recipient Honoris Causa, Suzhou, 1985, Maastricht, 1986, Shanghai, 1988, Fuzhou, 2001, Nanjing, 2004; named a Citizen of Honor, Suzhou, China, 2003. Fellow: Royal Coll. Pathologists London; mem.: French Found. on Sci. and it's Applications (pres. sci. coun.), Dutch Royal Acad. Arts and Scis., Chinese Acad. Sci. Engrs., French Acad. Tech., Am. Soc. Hematology (hon.), French Acad. Sci. (corr.), French Acad. Medicine, European Thrombosis Rsch. Orgn. (pres. 1972), Internat. Soc. Thrombosis and Hemostasis (sec.-gen. 1976, Robert S. Grant medal 1979). Home: 32 avenue Charles Floquet 75007 Paris France Office Phone: 33 01 53859227, 33153859225. Business E-Mail: ffcsa@academie-sciences.fr.

CAESAR, GODFREY WRENSFORD, biologist, educator; b. Georgetown, Guyana; Student, Queen's Coll., Georgetown; DSc, DePaul U., 1977. Pvt. practice, NYC. Presenter in field. Contbr. articles to profl. jours. Avocations: dance, jogging, cooking. Address: 209 W 137th St New York NY 10030-2406

CAETANO, RAUL, psychiatrist, educator; b. São Paulo, Brazil, May 5, 1945; came to U.S., 1978; s. Silvestre Vieira and Vera Vieira (Barbosa) C.; m. Patrice Vaeth, Sept. 30, 1995; children: Izabel, Lauren, Helena. MD, U. Rio de Janeiro, 1969, diploma in Psychiatry, 1971; MPH, U. Calif., Berkeley, 1979, PhD, 1983. Psychiatrist Pinel Hosp., Rio de Janeiro, 1969-73; asst. prof. State U., Rio de Janeiro, 1969-73; rsch. psychiatrist Inst. Psychiatry U. London, 1973-76; asst. prof. Inst. Psychiatry, Rio de Janeiro, 1976-78; vis. scholar Alcohol Rsch. Group, Berkeley, 1978-83, assoc. scientist to sr. scientist, 1983-94, dir., 1992—. Adj. prof. Sch. Pub. Health, U. Calif., Berkeley, 1991-98; assoc. dir. Calif. Pacific Med. Ctr. Rsch. Inst., San Francisco, 1992-93; prof., regional dean Sch. Pub. Health, U. Tex., 1998—, prof., dean Sch. Health Professions, U. Tex. Southwestern Med. Ctr., 2006-. Contbr. articles to profl. jours. WHO fellow, 1973-76; rsch. grantee Nat. Inst. Alcohol Abuse and Alcoholism, 1985—. Mem. APHA, Am. Coll. Epidemiology, Rsch. Soc. Alcoholism. Roman Catholic. Office: V8112 5323 Harry Hines Blvd Dallas TX 75390-9128 Office Phone: 214-648-1080. Business E-Mail: raul.caetano@utsouthwestern.edu.

CAFARO, DEBRA A., real estate company executive; b. Dec. 15, 1957; m. Terrence Livingston; 2 children. BA in Govt. magna cum laude, U. Notre Dame, 1979; JD, U. Chgo., 1982. Bar: Ill., Pa. Jud. clk. Hon. J. Dickson Phillips 4th cir. US Ct. of Appeals, 1982—83; founding mem. Barack Ferrazzano Kirschbaum Perlman & Nagelberg LLP, Chgo., 1986—97; pres. Ambassador Apartments, Inc., 1997—98; pres., CEO Ventas, Inc., Louisville, 1999—2003, chmn. bd., pres., CEO, 2003—. Adj. prof. law Northwestern U. Law Sch., 1988—92; bd. dirs. Ambassador Apartments, Inc., 1997—98, Weyerhaeuser Co., 2007—, chair fin. com., mem. compensation com.; bd. dirs. General Growth Properties, Inc., 2010—. Recipient Aiming High award, Legal Momentum, 2009; named Female Leader of the Yr., Comml. Property News, 2007, Outstanding Woman, Nat. Real Estate Investor Mag., 2008, Woman of Influence, Real Estate Forum, 2008, Best CEOs, Forbes, 2010; named one of Best of the Best, Real Estate Investment Trust (REIT) CEOs, 2003, 50 Women to Watch, Wall St. Journal, 2004, Top 25 Women in Healthcare, Modern Healthcare mag., 2011, Women to Watch, Crain's Chgo. Bus., 2011. Mem.: Nat. Assn. of Corp. Dirs., Nat. Assn. of Real Estate Investment Trusts (bd. dirs., immediate past chair). Office: Ventas Inc Ste 300 10350 Ormsby Park Pl Louisville KY 40223 *

CAFAROTTI, STEFANO, thoracic surgeon; b. Rome, May 4, 1980; MD in Gen. Thoracic Surgeon, Cath. U. Rome, 2011. Thoracic surgeon Dept. Surg. Scis., 2006—. Clin. fellows Dept. Cardiothoracic Surgery, Pulmonary Transplant and Esophageal Surgery Leuven, Belgium, 2011. Grant, Belgium. Mem.: Internat. Chest Wall Interest Group, Italian Thoracic Surgery Soc. Avocations: astronomy, jazz. Office: Largo F Vito 1 Rome 00168 Italy

CAGAYAN, MARIA STEPHANIE FAY SAMADAN, pharmacology professor; b. Makati, Philippines, Aug. 5, 1969; d. Buenaventura Mangundayao and Merle Sanchez Samadan; m. Allan Baga Cagayan, May 18, 1989; children: Bien Emile Samadan, Beatrice Anne Samadan, Basil Stephen Samadan. MD, UP Coll. Medicine, Manila, 1993. Cert. FPOGS Pune Ob-Gyn. Soc., 2002, in biochemistry UP Coll. Medicine, 2005, in Alternative Medicine UP Coll. Medicine, 2008. Assoc. prof. UP Coll. Medicine, 1999—. Dir. Rhythms Health and Wellness, Manila, 2007—; hon. editl. adv. bd. MIMS Philippines, Manila, 2008—. Author: (dance/exercise instruction) Sayuntis, (textbook) Essentials of Obstetric Nursing, Pharmacology for Beginners; poetry, Glimpses. Head Couples Christ Gawad Kalinga, Quezon City, Philippines, 2004—08. Recipient Internat. Publ. award, U. Philippines, 2006, Young Rschr. award, Pune Ob-Gyn. Soc., 2008. Home: 65 Yale St Cubao Quezon City 1109 Philippines Office: UP Coll Medicine 547 Pedro Gil St Ermita Manila 1000 Philippines Office Fax: 632- 5218251. Personal E-mail: faye_cagayan@hotmail.com. Business E-Mail: cagayanmsfs@druginfo.ph.

CAGGIULA, ANTHONY R., psychology professor; b. Phila., Mar. 3, 1941; m. Arlene Caggiula (dec. May 22, 2004). BA in Psychology, St. Joseph's Coll.; PhD, Princeton U. Rsch. asst., behavioral sciences dept. small crew effectiveness divsn. Naval Med. Rsch. Inst., Bethesda, Md., 1963—64; rsch. asst. in physiol. psychology Princeton U., NJ, 1964—65; lectr. dept. psychology U. Mich., 1967—68; asst. to full prof. psychology U. Pitts., 1968—, assoc. prof. behavioral neurosci., 1986—89, chmn. biopsychology tng. program, 1990—96, acting chmn. dept. psychology, 1997, chmn. dept. psychology, 1998; asst. prof. pharmacology U. Pitts. Sch. Medicine, 1968—73, assoc. to full prof. dept. psychiatry, 1994—. Rsch. fellow, U. Del., 1962—64, NIH Predoctoral fellow, Princeton U., 1965—66, NIH Postdoctoral fellow, U. Mich., 1966—68. Mem.: AAAS, Coll. on Problems of Drug Addiction, Soc. Rsch. on Nicotine and Tobacco, Soc. Neuroscience, Soc. Behavioral Medicine, NY Acad. Sciences, Internat. Soc. Neuroimmunomodulation, Internat. Soc. Psychoneuroendocrinology, Am. Psychol. Soc. Office: Dept Psychology 3131 Sennot Sq Univ Pitts Pittsburgh PA 15260 Office Phone: 412-624-4501. Office Fax: 412-624-4428. E-mail: tonypsy@pitt.edu.

ÇAGLARIRMAK, NECLA, biochemist, food engineer, educator, researcher; Diploma in Food Engring., Ege U., 1984, PhD in Food Chemistry, 1987; MS in Med. Microbiology, Dokuz Eylül U., 2007. With Saruhanli Coll. Celal Bayar U, Manisa, Turkey, food engr., 1980—84, prof. food and engring., 2003—11; mgr. Ctr. Environ. Studies. Contbr. articles to profl. jours. Grantee, NATO, 1992—99, Tubitak, UNICEF. Achievements include research in food biochemistry and engineering Rschs. Business E-Mail: necla.caglarimak@bayar.edu.tr.

CAGNEY, WILLIAM ROBERT, psychologist; b. Pitts., Oct. 7, 1937; s. Edward Patrick and Pearl Barbara (Sebastian) C.; m. Vivian Antoinette Tartaglia, June 26, 1965; children: Lori Anne, Julie Alissa, Melissa Beth. BS, Duquesne U., 1960, MA, 1965, PhD, 1968. Lic. psychologist, Pa.; cert. Nat. Register Health Svcs.; cert. profl. qualification in psychology Assn. State and Provincial Psychology Bds.; diplomate in clin. hypnotherapy NBCCH, Nat. Bd. cert. clin. Hypnotherapists. Psychology intern, staff psychologist Dixmont State Hosp., Glenfield, Pa., 1962-68; staff psychologist South Hills Child Guidance Ctr., Pitts., 1968-69; asst. dir., psychol. svcs. Woodville State Hosp., Carnegie, Pa., 1968-70; chief psychologist Counseling Ctr. of South Hills, Pitts., 1970-72; clin. dir. Chartiers MH/MR Ctr., Bridgeville, Pa., 1972-79; pvt. practice Pitts., 1971—. Cons. Outreach South, Mt. Lebanon, Pa., 1976-2004, South Hills Interfaith Ministries, Bethel Park, Pa., 1969-2003, Crisis Addiction Recovery Edn., Inc., Washington, Pa., 1984-88, YMCA South Hills, Pitts., 1977-78; field supr. dept. psychology U. Pitts., 1970-73, W.Va. U., Morgantown, 1973-78; resident psychologist Sta. KDKA-TV Pitts. Today, 1978-79; presenter seminars and workshops to profl. and cmty. groups, 1972—. Cons. Twp. Upper St. Clair Adminstrn., Police, Schs., Family Resource Program, Upper St. Clair, Pa., 1986-89. Fellow Pa. Psychol. Assn.; mem. APA, Greater Pitts. Psychol. Assn., Am. Group Therapy Assn. Avocations: exercise, art, music. Office: 1725 Washington Rd Ste 509 Pittsburgh PA 15241-1207 Home Phone: 412-833-6645; Office Phone: 412-833-9250. Business E-Mail: cagsfive@aol.com.

CAHILL, GEORGE FRANCIS, JR., physician, educator; b. NYC, July 7, 1927; s. George Francis and Eva Marion (Wagner) C.; m. Sarah Townsend duPont, Dec. 20, 1949 (dec. Jan. 24, 2010); children: Colleen Cahill Remley, Peter duPont, George Francis III, Sarah Rhett Cahill Zuckerman, Eva Wagner Cahill Georgakilis, Elizabeth Anglin Cahill. BS, Yale, 1949; MD, Columbia U., 1953; MA, Harvard U., 1966. Intern Peter Bent Brigham Hosp., Boston, 1953-54, resident, 1954-55, 57-58; rsch. fellow biol. chemistry Harvard U. Med. Sch., 1955-57; assoc. in medicine Peter Bent Brigham Hosp., 1962-65; practice medicine specializing in metabolism Boston, 1965-78; sr. physician Peter Bent Brigham Hosp., 1983—94; prof. medicine Harvard U., 1970-90, prof. emeritus, 1990—; prof. biol. scis. Dartmouth Coll., Hanover, NH, 1990—97. Prin. cons. endocrinology, metabolism VA, 1972-75; investigator Howard Hughes Med. Inst.,

1962-68, dir. rsch., 1978-85, v.p. sci. edn. and devel., 1985-89, sr. scientist, 1989-90, cons., 1991-1994; mem. rsch. tng. coms. NIH. Contbr. articles to profl. jours. Chmn. bd. dir. Greenwall Found., 1992-96; v.p. trustees Hotchkiss Sch., 1992-97; overseer Dartmouth Med. Sch. and the Everett C. Koop Inst., 1990-95. With USNR, 1945-47. Recipient Banting medal U.S., 1971, Banting medal Eng., 1974, J.P. Hoet award Belgium, 1973, Gairdner Internat. award Can., 1979. Fellow AAAS, Am. Acad. Arts and Scis.; mem. Am. Diabetes Assn. (pres. 1975, Lilly award 1965), Endocrine Soc. (Oppenheimer award 1963), Nat. Commn. on Diabetes, Am. Soc. Clin. Investigation, Assn. Am. Physicians, Am. Clin. Climatol. Assn., Am. Physiol. Soc. Home: 8 RiverMead Peterborough NH 03458

CAHILL, PATRICK JOHN, orthopedist; b. Oak Pk., Ill., Apr. 8, 1975; BS, Vanderbilt U., 1996; MD, U. Ill. Coll. Medicine, 2001. Staff physician Shriners Hosp. Children, 2007—. Office: Shriners Hosp for Children 3551 N Broad St Philadelphia PA 19140 Business E-Mail: pcahill@shrinenet.org.

CAHINHINAN, NELIA AGBADA, retired public health nurse, health facility administrator; b. Laguna, Philippines, Sept. 20, 1939; d. Manuel Navarro and Milagros Agbay (Adea) Agbada; m. Rodolfo DeGuia Cahinhinan, Jan. 29, 1967; children: Rodney Paul, Roel James, Renee Ann, Nelie Rose. Diploma, U. Philippines, 1961; BSN, U. Guam, 1985. RN; cert. in nursing adminstrn. Pub. health nurse Dept. Health, Laguna, 1962-67, Dept. Pub. Health and Social Svc., Agana, Guam, 1967-73; pub. health nurse supr., home care Dept. PHSS, Mangilao, Guam, 1974-82; cmty. health nurse supr. Regional Pub. Health Ctr., Dept. PHSS, Tamuning, Guam, 1982-86; nursing and program supr. maternal child health Family Planning Program, Dept. PHSS, Mangilao, 1986-89; asst. nursing adminstr. Bur. Family Health and Nursing Svcs., Dept. PHSS, Mangilao, 1990-94. Mem. adv. coun. Coll. Nursing, U. Guam, Mangilao, 1994-95; mem. nursing asst. program adv. coun. Guam C.C., Mangilao, 1995-96; mem. profl. adv. bd. Clarke Home Nursing Svc., Tamuhning, 1995-97. Bd. dirs. Am. Cancer Soc., Agana, 1976—78; mem., sec., chair nursing and health svcs. com. ARC, 1980—83. Recipient Centennial Leadership award Nat. League of Nursing, 1993, Outstanding Woman of Yr. award Govt. of Guam, 1996; named Guam Top Ten Suprs., Gov. of Guam, 1990. Mem.: Laguna Assn. Guam (pres. 2000—01, advisor 2002—11), Cath. Daus. of Ams. (treas. 1999—2001, 2011), Guam Meml. Hosp. Vol. Assn. (dir.-at-large 1999—2002, 2011), Guam Nurses Assn. (treas., dir. 1980, pres. 1994—95, comm. mems. 1999—2011, Svc. award 1983, Guam Nurse of Yr. 1985, Most Disting. Mem. award 1996), So. Tagalog Assn. (chmn. membership com. 1980—2011), U. Philippines Alumni Assn. (pres. 1991—93, advisor 1994—2011, treas., dir., Outstanding Svc. award 1993, Oblation award Outstanding Alumni and Cmty. Svc. 2005). Roman Catholic. Avocations: gardening, flower arranging. Home: PO Box 11234 Tamuning GU 96931-1234

CAI, GUANG-YAN, physician; b. China, Oct. 29, 1972; MD, PLA Postgrad. Med Sch., 2001. Chief physician PLA Gen. Hosp, 2009—. Office: 28 Fuxing Rd Beijing 100853 China Business E-Mail: caigy@301hospital.com.cn.

CAI, MINGJUN, neurosurgeon; b. China, Mar. 7, 1981; MD, Tongji Med. Coll., Huazhong U. Sci. and Tech., PhD, 2009. Attending neurosurgeon dept. neurosurgery Wuhan Gen. Hosp., 2009. Office: 627 Wuluo Ave Wuhan Hubei 430070 China Personal E-mail: mingjuncai@hotmail.com.

CAI, SUI XIONG, chemist; b. Shantou, Guangdong, China, Apr. 24, 1957; BS in Chemistry, U. Sci. and Tech. China, 1983; PhD in Organic Chemistry, U. Oreg., 1990. V.p., CTO Impact Therapeutics, Inc., 2010—. Bd. dirs. Sino-Am. Biotech. and Pharm. PA, 2002—10. Mem.: AAAS, Am. Assn. Cancer Rsch., Am. Chem. Soc., BayHelix. Office: 10 Xinghuo Rd High and New Tech Zone Nanjing Jiangsu 210061 China Business E-Mail: s.cai@impacttherapeutics.com.

CAICEDO, JUAN CARLOS, transplant surgeon, medical educator; MD, Nat. Univ. Colombia, 1993. Fellow Northwestern Meml. Hosp., 2006, solid organ transplant surgeon, dir. Hispanic Transplant Prog., asst. prof. surgery Divsn. Organ Transplantation. Named one of 40 Under 40, Crain's Chgo. Bus., 2009. Mem.: Bogota Transplant Network, Colombia Surgical Soc., Colombian Transplant Soc., Internat. Pediatric Transplant Assn., Am. Soc. Transplant Surgeons, Am. Coll. Surgeons. Office: 675 N St Clair Galter 17-200 Chicago IL 60611 Office Phone: 312-695-8900. *

CAIN, CHRISTOPHER MARDEN JOHN, orthopedic spinal surgeon; b. Adelaide, Australia, Sept. 24, 1961; s. David Marden and Janet Mary Cain; m. Sharon Patricia Lux-Cain, Apr. 17, 2009; children: Megan Elizabeth, Hayden James. MB BS, U. Adelaide, 1984, MD, 1991. Neurosurg. registrar Queen Elizabeth and Women's and Children's Hosps., Adelaide, 1987—88; trauma and spinal rsch. fellow Royal Adelaide Hosp., 1988—90, orthopaedic trainee, resident/registrar, 1990—93; clin. spinal fellow U. Hosp., Queens Med. Ctr., Nottingham, England, 1993—94; vis. med. specialist dept. orthopedics Flinders Med. Ctr., Adelaide, 1994—97, sr. vis. med. specialist dept. orthopedics, 1997—99; vis. med. specialist dept. orthopedics Royal Adelaide Hosp., 1994—98, sr. vis. med. specialist dept. orthopedics, 1998—, Women's and Children's Hosp., Adelaide, 1999—. Chair Orthop. Statewide Clin. Network, 2007—; specialist med. advisor to chief exec. dept. Health Govt. South Australia, 2007—. Recipient Rob Johnston award, Spine Soc. of Australia, 1990, Smith & Nephew Richards Acad. prize, Australian Orthopedic Assn., 1993, 3d prize Am. Orthopedic Residents Meeting, Am. Orthopedic Assn., 1993. Fellow: Australian Orthopedic Assn., Royal Australasian Coll. of Surgeons; mem.: AOSpine Asia Pacific (bd. dirs. 2003—05, ednl. coord. 2003—05), AOSpine Australia and New Zealand (chmn. 2003—05), Australian Med. Assn. (rep. surg. craft group South Australia br. 2001—03, fed. councilor 2002—07, v.p. South Australia br. 2003—05, mem. exec. coun. 2005, pres. South Australia br. 2005—07), Australian Soc. Orthopedic Surgeons (treas. 1996—99, chmn. South Australia br. 1998—2002). Achievements include design and development of standalone anterior interbody fusion cage; patents for design and method of fixation of the SynFix device - Cage with Screws and Intervertebral implant. Avocations: physical fitness, golf, tennis, carpentry. Office Fax: 61 8 8232 2780.

CAIN, HAROLD D., critical care specialist; MD, U. Tex. Southwestern Med. Ctr., Dallas, 1971. Diplomate Am. Bd. Internal Medicine, 1974, Am. Bd. Internal Medicine- pulmonary disease, 1978, Am. Bd. Internal Medicine- critical care medicine, 1999. Resident in internal medicine NC meml. Hosp., Chael Hill, 1972—74; fellow in pulmonary disease Baylor Univ. Med.Ctr., Houston, 1976—78; critical care specialist St. David North Austin Med. Ctr. Office: Saint David North Austin Medical Center 12201 renfert Wat Ste 260 Austin TX 78758 Office Phone: 512-977-0123. Office Fax: 512-977-0126.

CAIN, MARK P., medical educator; b. Frankfurt, Germany, Dec. 15, 1960; MD, Oreg. Health Scis. U., 1987. Prof. urology Ind. U. Healthcare, 1996—. Fellow: Am. Acad. Pediat. Office: Riley Hosp Children 705 Barnhill Indianapolis IN 46202 Office Fax: 317-274-7481. Business E-Mail: mpcain@iupui.edu.

CAIN, MICHAEL E., dean; married. BA cum laude, Gettysburg Coll., Pa., 1971; MD, George Wash. U., Washington, 1975. Diplomate Am. Bd. Internal Medicine, cert. in cardiovascular diseases and clin. cardiac electrophysiology and pacing. Tng. in internal medicine at Barnes Hosp. Wash. U. Sch. Medicine, St. Louis, rsch. fellow, clin. cardiology fellow and rsch. instr., asst. prof. medicine, 1981—87, dir. clin. cardiac electrophysiology lab. at Barnes Hosp., 1981—93, assoc. prof. medicine, 1987—93, prof. medicine, dir. cardiovascular divsn., 1993—2006, Tobias and Hortense Lewin prof. medicine, 1994—96, prof. biomed. engring., 1999—2006; clin. rsch. fellow clin. cardiac electrophysiology lab. U. Pa. Sch. Medicine, Phila.; prof. medicine and biomed. sciences, dean Sch. Medicine and Biomed. Sciences U. at Buffalo, 2006—, v.p. health sciences, 2011—. Former assoc. editor: Circulation, guest editor:, Circulation: Arrhythmias and Electrophysiology, mem. editl. bd.: Jour. American Coll. Cardiology, Jour. Cardiovascular Electrophysiology, Jour. Interventional Cardiac Electrophysiology, Nature Clin. Practice Cardiovascular Medicine; contbr. articles to profl. jours., chapters to books. Mem. ABIM Com. Clin. Cardiac Electrophysiology, 2000; cons. FDA Med. Devices Adv. Com., 2003; mem. sci. bd. The Sarnoff Endowment Cardiovascular Sci., former chmn. of bd.; mem. adv. com. Spanish Nat. Rsch. Ctr. Cardiovascular Diseases. Recipient Calvin Klopp award, William Beaumont Med. Rsch. Soc., 1975, Outstanding Rschr. of Yr. award, Missourian American Heart Assn., 2002, Hans-Peter Kragenbuehl Meml. award, Internat. Acad. Cardiology, 2005. Fellow: Heart Rhythm Soc. (past pres.), American Heart Assn. (Arthur E. Strauss award 2000), American Coll. Cardiology; mem.: Assn. Univ. Cardiologists, Assn. Subspecialty Professors, Assn. Professors of Cardiology (past pres.), Alpha Omega Alpha. Office: University at Buffalo 155 Biomedical Edn Bldg 3435 Main St Buffalo NY 14214 *

CAINE, VIRGINIA A., city health department administrator; BS, Gustavus Adolphus Coll., Minn., 1973; MD, N.Y. Upstate Med. Ctr., Syracuse. Resident U. Cin.; resident, infectious diseases U. Wash., Seattle; assoc. prof., medicine Ind. U. Sch. Medicine; dir. Marion Co. Health Dept., Indpls., 1993—. Mem., com. credentialing for pub. health workforce CDC, mem., bioterrorism and emergency preparedness com. Co-dir. Indpls. Campaign for Healthy Babies Initiative; bd. mem. Damien AIDS Ctr.; bd. mem., substance abuse Fairbanks Hosp.; bd. mem. Ind. AIDS Fund, Indpls. Alliance for Health Promotion, Ind. State Women's Health Com.; mem. Cmty. Drug Summit, Mayor's Commn. on Family Violence, City of Indpls. Mayor's Emergency Preparedness Task Force; mem. adv. bd. Women's Fund of Ctrl. Ind. Recipient Superstar award, Ind. AIDServe, 1998, Outstanding Svc. award, Indpls. Bus. Jour.; named one of Influential Women in Indpls., Indpls. Bus. Jour., The Ind. Lawyer. Mem.: Ind. Pub. Health Assn., Nat. Med. Assn. (chair, infectious diseases, co-chair, AIDS sect., Internist of Yr. 1999), Nat. Assn. of County and City Health Officials, Am. Pub. Health Assn. (pres. 2004—, New Leadership award). Office: Marion Co Health Dept 3838 N Rural St Indianapolis IN 46205-2930

CAKIRER, SINAN, radiologist, consultant, medical researcher; b. Sivas, Turkey, Feb. 17, 1969; s. Hidir and Gullu Cakirer; m. Derya Bora, Oct. 26, 1992; children: Kerem, Selin Ipek. MD, Hacettepe U. Faculty of Medicine, Ankara, Turkey, 1992; specialty in radiology, Istanbul U. Cerrahpasa Med. Faculty, Istanbul, Turkey, 1992—96. Diplomate radiology Turkish Ministry of Health, 1996, cert. radiology educator High Edn. Coun. of Turkey, 2003. Chief MRI unit Multimed Med. Imaging Ctr., Istanbul, Turkey, 1996—97; med. dir. Echomar Med. Imaging Ctr., Istanbul, 1997—98; chief radiology dept. Malatya Mil. Hosp., Malatya, Turkey, 1998—2000; cons. radiologist, MRI unit chief Istanbul Sisli Etfal Rsch. Hosp., 2000—03, neuroradiology sect. chief, MRI dir., 2003—. Assoc. prof. radiology Istanbul Sisli Etfal Rsch. Hosp, Turkey, 2003—; editor and reviewer Revista di Neuroradiologia; reviewer European Radiology, Med. Sci. Monitor. Contbr. articles to profl. jours. Recipient Best Contbr. to Eurorad, European Assn. of Radiology, 2002, Best Contbr. to head and neck radiology database, European Assn. of Head and Neck Radiology, 2002. Mem.: Turkish Assn. of Med. Doctors, Turkish Soc. of Radiology, Radiol. Soc. of N.Am., European Congress of Radiology. Avocations: travel, reading. Office: Istanbul Sisli Etfal Rsch Hosp Sisli Istanbul 80220 Turkey Home: Ada Kardelen 4/2 Daire 37 Atasehir 67 34758 Istanbul Istanbul Turkey E-mail: drcakirer@yahoo.com.

ÇAKIR KOÇAK, YELIZ, midwife; b. Çorum, Nov. 25, 1980; MS, Ege U., 2007. Rsch. asst. midwifery dept. Ege U. Izmir Atatürk Sch. Health, 2006—. Avocations: singing, swimming, theater. Office: Ege University Izmir Atatürk Sch Health Izmir Bornova 35100 Turkey Office Phone: 90232 3882851. Office Fax: 90232 3427975. Business E-Mail: yeliz.cakir@ege.edu.tr.

CAKMAK, MAHMUT, cardiologist, director; b. Adiyaman, Besni, Turkey, Dec. 27, 1969; m. Nazmiye Cakmak; 1 child, Ezgi. MD, Istanbul U., Turkey, 1993; degree in Cardiology, Siyami Ersek Hosp., Istanbul, 2006. Dir. Acibadem Hastanesi, Bursa, Turkey, 2006—08, Medicine Hosp., Istanbul, 2008—. Home: Sergul Sokak Saral Sitesi C Blok D5 34349 Istanbul Istanbul Turkey Home Phone: 902126304141; Office Phone: 905332360011. Personal E-mail: cakmakmn@yahoo.com.

CAKNIPE, CHRISTOPHER HOWARD, substance abuse services professional; b. Alexandria, Va., Dec. 12, 1970; s. John William Caknipe and Doreen Kay Lightner. B in Chemistry, U. South Fla., Tampa, 2002, grad. cert. in Hydrogeology, 2004; attending, Capella U. Registered environ. profl. Nat. Registry Environ. Profls. Substitute chemistry tchr. Polk County Schs., Fla., 1999—2000; molecular biologist U. of South Fla., Tampa, 2000—01, tchr.'s asst., 2002—04; hydrologic technician U.S. Geologic Survey, Tampa, 2003—04; geochemist U.S. Labs., Ft. Myers, Fla., 2004—05; environ. health specialist Va. Dept. of Health, 2005—07; substance abuse work, 2007—. Recipient Eager Beaver award, U.S. Geologic Survey, 2004. Mem.: Mensa (life), Phi Theta Kappa. Libertarian. Achievements include research in Using Hydrogen and Oxygen isotopes to discern baseflow and storm flow from total flow in low gradient streams. Avocations: basketball, collecting horror movies. Home and Office: 4010 Littlejohn Church Rd Lenoir NC 28645 Personal E-mail: ccaknipe@yahoo.com.

CALABRESI, PETER ARTHUR, neurologist, educator; b. New Haven, Oct. 13, 1962; BS, Yale Coll., 1984; MD, Brown U., 1988. Prof. neurology Johns Hopkins U., 2003—. Dir. Multiple Sclerosis Ctr., Johns Hopkins Hosp., 2003—. Office: Pathology Bldg 509 600 N Wolfe St Baltimore MD 21287

CALADO, ADRIANO ALMEIDA, urologist, educator; b. Jaboatão, Brazil, June 10, 1971; MD, Pernambuco State U. UPE, 1994; PhD, Fed. U. São Paulo UNIFESP, 2005. Prof., divsn. urology Pernambuco State U. UPE, 2006—. Rsch. scientist Inst. de Medicina Integral Prof. Fernando Figueira IMIP, 2010—11. Pediatric Urology fellowship, Fed. U. São Paulo. Mem.: Am. Urol. Assn., Brazilian Soc. Urology. Avocations: sports, swimming, travel. Home: Rua Afonso de Albuquerque Melo 420 Recife Pernambuco 52060-450 Brazil Home Fax: 81-34230700. Personal E-mail: caladourologia@yahoo.com.br.

CALAIS DA SILVA, FERNANDO, retired urologist; b. Lisbon, Aug. 20, 1937; MD, U. Lisbon, 1961. Chmn. Genito Urinary Portuguese Group, 1984—2011. Chmn., urol. dept. Lisbon Ctrl. Hosp., 1998—2007. Recipient Artur Ravara award, Portuguese Urol. Assn.

CALATAYUD, PAUL-ANDRE, biologist, entomologist, researcher; b. Tarbes, France, May 15, 1963; s. Andre and Andree Calatayud; m. Sabine Heitz, Dec. 18, 1993; children: Anais, Melanie. PhD in Biology and Entomology with honors, U. Lyon Inst. Applied Sci., Villeurbanne, France, 1990—93. Rsch. scientist IRD, Montpellier, France, 1993—97, IRD c/o CIAT, Cali, Colombia, 1997—2001, IRD c/o INRA, Versailles, France, 2001—02, IRD c/o ICIPE, Nairobi, Kenya, 2002—09, IRD c/o CNRS, Gif-sur-Yreth, France, 2009—11. Co-author: (books) Insect-Plant Interactions, 1996, Cassava-Mealybug Interactions, 2006, The Cereal Stem Borers of Sub-Saharan Africa and Their Antagonists, 2006; contbr. over 40 scientific papers to profl. jours., chapter to book. Music group mgr., Brazzaville, Congo, 1990—92. With French armed forces, 1987—88. Recipient Plant Protection and Environ. Orgn. award, 1994, Francisco Luis Gallego award, Columbian Entomol. Soc., 1999; scholar, French Ministry Rsch. and Edn., 1989. Mem.: French Entomol. Soc., French Assn. Forum of Respectful Reasoned Farming of the Environment (FARRE) (corr.). Achievements include research in feeding behavior of mealybugs; nutritional requirements of mealybugs (Pseudococcidae) using artificial diets; involvement of rutin and other related flavonoid glycosides in a defensive response of cassava plants towards mealybugs and bacteria; the role of O-caffeoylserine from the body surface of the cassava mealybug, Phenacoccus herreni, as a host-location stimulant to its parasitoids (Acerophagus coccois and Aenasius vexans); description of new entomophagous nematode species: Rhabditis colombiana n. sp. (Nematoda: Rhabditidae); description of sensory equipment of adults and larvae of Lepidoptera; description of host plants recognition, selection and acceptance; description of sensory equipment of larval endoparasitoid of Lepidoptera stem borers; identification of kairomone compounds from the larval body surface involved in host recognition for parasitism. Avocations: piano, travel, music, theater, astronomy. Home: 3 Residence des Vergognes Osmoy 78910 France Office: IRD c/o CNRS Ave de la Ter Bat 5 BP1 Gif-sur-Yvette 91198 France Business E-Mail: pcalatayud@icipe.org, calatayud@legs.cnrs.gif.fr.

CALDER, ROBERT AUSTIN, preventive medicine physician, administrator; b. Beloit, Wis., May 21, 1954; s. John T. and Rosemary A. (Austin) Calder; m. Daphne R. Calder, Aug. 17, 1979 (div. June 2007); children: Heather, Joseph; m. Debra Z. Calder, Feb. 7, 2009. BS, U. Wis., 1979; MD, Med. Coll. Wis., 1982; MS, U. Wis., Milw., 1984. Diplomate Am. Bd. Preventive Medicine. Chief, preventive medicine U.S. Army, Ft. Sill, Okla., 1985-87; epidemiologist Fla. Dept. Health, Tallahassee, 1987-90; assoc. dir. Merck & Co., Inc., West Point, Pa., 1990-91, dir., 1992-93, sr. dir., 1993-98, exec. dir., 1999—. Capt., U.S. Army, 1985-87. Eagle Scout, 1970. Fellow Am. Coll. Preventive Medicine. Roman Catholic. Avocations: sailing, bicycling. Home and Office: 137 E Wilson St Unit 512 Madison WI 53703 Office: Merck & Co Inc UG3AB-10 351 N Sumneytown Pk North Wales PA 19454 Office Phone: 608-354-9136. Business E-Mail: robert_calder@merck.com.

CALDERONI, ANTONELLO, internist, oncologist; b. Bodio, Ticino, Switzerland, Jan. 15, 1962; s. Carlo and Gina Calderoni; m. Jasenka Vogric; children: Margot, Senija. MD, U. Bern, Switzerland, 1987. Cert. Bd. Internal Medicine, Bd. Med. Oncology. Sr. registar Inst. Med. Oncology, Bern, 1995—2002; pvt. practice Lugano, Switzerland, 2002—. Mem.: Internat. Extranodal Lymphoma Study Group, European Soc. Med. Oncology, European Orgn. Rsch. and Treatment of Cancer, Am. Soc. Clin. Oncology. Home and Office: Oncology Varini/Calderoni via Fogazzaro 3 6900 Lugano Switzerland Home Phone: +41 91 922 6988; Office Phone: +41 91 922 6988. Office Fax: +41 91 922 74 75.

CALDWELL, JENNIFER ELIZABETH, occupational therapist, educator; b. Northern Ireland, Sept. 7, 1952; Diploma in Occupl. Therapy, Coll. Occupl. Therapists, 1974; PhD, Robert Gordon U., 1997. Lectr. Robert Gordon U., Aberdeen, 1987—. Mem.: Health Professions Coun., Brit. Assn. Occupl. Therapists. Home: 27 Cairngrassie Dr Portlethen Aberdeennshire Aberdeen AB12 4TY Scotland Personal E-mail: j.caldwell@rgu.ac.uk.

CALFEE, ROBERT CHILTON, psychologist, educator; b. Lexington, Ky., Jan. 26, 1933; s. Robert Klair and Nancy Bernice (Stipp) C. BA, UCLA, 1959, MA, 1960, PhD, 1963. Asst. prof. psychology U. Wis., 1964-66, assoc. prof., 1966-69; assoc. prof. edn. Stanford U., 1969-71, prof., 1971-98, prof. emeritus, 1998—; assoc. dean research and devel., dir. Ctr. for Ednl. Rsch., 1976-80; with Sch. Edn. U. Calif., Riverside, 1998—2005. Cons. and speaker in field; vice-chmn. State of Calif. Commn. for Establishment of Acad. Content and Performance Stds., 1996-2002; mem. com. on equivalancy and linkage of ednl. tests NRC/NAS, 1998-2000, Energy and Edn. Task Force, 2005-; mem. ednl. adv. bd., Leapfrog Edn., 1997-2005, edn. officer Moonshot. Author: Human Experimental Psychology, 1975, Cognitive Psychology and Educational Practice, 1982, Experimental Methods in Psychology, 1985, Handbook of Educational Psychology, Teach Our Children Well, 1995, (with Marilyn J. Chambliss) Textbooks for Learning, 1999; editor: Jour. Ednl. Psychology, 1984-90, Ednl. Assessment, 1992-2002. Trustee Palo Alto (Calif.) Sch. Dist., 1984-88; vice chair Calif. Commn. for Ednl. Stds.; chair ednl. adv. bd. Leapfrog Enterprises, ednl. officer, Moonshoot Served with USAF, 1953—57. Guggenheim Meml. fellow, 1972; fellow Center for Advanced Study in Behavioral Scis., 1981-82 Fellow AAAS, APA; mem. Am. Ednl. Rsch. Assn., Internat. Reading Assn. (named to Hall of Fame), Nat. Conf. Rsch. in English, Psychonomic Soc., Nat. Coun. Tchrs. English, Nat. Soc. Study of Edn. (bd. trustees), Sigma Xi, Monshoot (edn. officer). Office: U Calif Sch Edn 1207 Sproul Hall Riverside CA 92521-0001 Home: 995 Wing Pl Stanford CA 94305 Office Phone: 951-827-2774. Business E-Mail: robert.calfee@ucr.edu.

CALHOUN, NOAH ROBERT, retired oral maxillofacial surgeon, educator; b. Clarendon, Ark., Mar. 23, 1921; s. Noah and Della (Sherman) Calhoun; m. Cecelia Christopher, Oct. 19, 1950; children: Stephen Marc, Cecelia Noel. DDS, Dental Sch., Howard U., 1948; M.Dental Sci., Tufts Med. and Dental Sch., 1955. Oral surgeon VA Hosp., Tuskegee, Ala., 1950—52, Kessler AFB, Biloxi, Miss., 1952—53; chief dental service VA Hosp., Tuskegee, Ala., 1955—57, oral surgeon, asst. chief dental surgeon Washington DC, 1964—74; chief dental svc., oral surgeon VA Med. Center, 1974—; prof. oral surgery Dental Sch., Howard U., 1966—92, Georgetown U., 1975—93; prof. emeritus Dental Coll. Howard U., 1992—. Dir. Tuskegee Red Cross, Ala., 1962—64; chmn. Nat. Concerned VA Dentists, 1975, Inst. Medicine-NAS, 1975. Sect. editor Current Lit. in Internat. Oral/Maxillofacial Surgery, 1986, mem. editl. bd. Jour. Oral and Maxillo-facial Surveys, 1993; contbr. articles to profl. jours. Mem. fin. com. St. Michael Ch., Silver Spring, Md. Mem.: NAACP (trustee D.C. chpt.), ADA, Examine Bd. Oral Maxillo Surgery, Inst. Medicine Nat. Acad., Noah Calhoun Mem. Nat. Sci., Inst. Medicine of NAS, Am. Coll. Dentistry, Internat. Coll. Dentistry, Am. Soc. Oral and Maxillofacial Surgeons (Audio Visual award 1978), Bridge Masters Washington (pres.), Omicron Kappa Upsilon. Roman Catholic. Office: Dental Coll Howard U Washington DC 20001 Home Phone: 202 821 846. Personal E-mail: ncalh@comcast.net.

CALIFF, ROBERT MCKINNON, cardiologist, educator; b. Anderson, SC, Sept. 29, 1951; m. Lydia Carpenter, 1974; children: Sharon, Sam, Tom. Grad. summa cum laude, Duke U., 1973; MD, Duke U. Sch. Medicine, 1978. Cert. in internal medicine 1984, in cardiology 1986. Intern, cardiology U. Calif., San Francisco, 1978—79, resident, medicine, 1979—80; fellow, cardiology Duke U. Med. Ctr., Durham, NC, 1978, 1980—83, attending physician, 1983—, Donald F. Fortin Prof. Cardiology, prof. internal medicine, 1995—, dir., Clin. Rsch. Inst., 1995—2006, assoc. vice chancellor clin. rsch., 1995—2005, vice-chancellor, clin. rsch., 2005—, dir., Translational Medicine Inst., 2006—. Mem. cardiorenal adv. panel US FDA; mem. pharm. roundtable Inst. Medicine; dir., coord. ctr. Ctrs. for Edn. & Rsch. on Therapeutics. Cons. ABCNews.com OnCall+ Heart Disease Ctr.; editor: (textbook) Acute Coronary Care (1st and 2nd edits.); editor or co-editor (textbooks) Comprehensive Cardiovascular Medicine, Interventional Cardiovascular Medicine, and Atlas of Heart Diseases, sect. editor Textbook of Cardiovascular Medicine, editor-in-chief Am. Heart Jour.; contbr. several articles to peer-reviewed jours., contbg. editor (online resource) theheart.org, serves on numerous editl. bds. Recipient Clin. Rsch. prize, Am. Heart Assn., 2006; named one of 10 Most Cited Authors in the field of medicine, Inst. for Scientific Information. Fellow: Am. Coll. Cardiology; mem.: Alpha Omega Alpha, Phi Beta Kappa. Avocations: golf, basketball, listening to music. Office: Duke U Med Ctr PO Box 17969 DCRI 2400 Pratt St Rm 0311 Terrace Level Durham NC 27705 Office Phone: 919-668-8820. Office Fax: 919-668-7103

ÇALIS, MUSTAFA, physiatrist, educator; b. Kayseri, Turkey, Sept. 9, 1971; MD, Erciyes U. Med. Sch., 1994. Prof., rschr, physician Dept. Phys. Medicine and Rehab. and Algology, 2000—. Office: Talas Kayseri Melikgazi 38039 Turkey Business E-Mail. mcalis@erciyes.edu.tr.

CALKINS, CASEY MATTHEW, medical educator; b. Castro Valley, Calif., Jan. 22, 1969; BS, U. Calif., San Diego, 1992; MD, Med. Coll. Wis., 1996. Assoc. prof., pediat. surgery Med. Coll. Wis., 2005—. Office: Children's Corporate Ctr 999 North 92nd St Wauwatosa WI 53226 Office Fax: 414-266-6579. Business E-Mail: ccalkins@chw.org.

CALKINS, EVAN, physician, educator; b. Newton, Mass., July 15, 1920; s. Grosvenor and Patty (Phillips) C.; m. Virginia McC. Brady, Sept. 9, 1946; children: Sarah Calkins Oxnard, Stephen, Lucy McCormick, Joan, Benjamin, Hugh, Ellen Rountree, Geoffrey, Timothy. Grad., Milton Acad., 1939; AB, Harvard U., 1942, MD, 1945. Intern, asst. resident medicine Johns Hopkins, 1946-47, 48-50; chief resident physician Mass. Gen. Hosp., 1951-52, mem. arthritis unit, 1952-61; NRC fellow med. scis. Harvard, 1950-51, instr., asst. prof. medicine, 1952-61; practice medicine, specializing in rheumatology Boston, 1951-61, Buffalo, 1961—; prof. medicine SUNY, Buffalo, 1961—90, prof. emeritus, 1990—, chmn. dept. medicine, 1965-77; head dept. medicine Buffalo Gen. Hosp., 1961-68; dir. medicine E.J. Meyer Meml. Hosp., 1968-78; head gerontology sect. Buffalo VA Med. Ctr., 1978-90; head div. geriatrics/gerontology SUNY-Buffalo, 1978-90. Founder, pres. Network in Aging of Western NY, Inc., 1980-83; cons. Nat. Inst. Arthritis and Metabolic Diseases Tng. Grants Com., 1958-62, Program Project Com., 1964-68, Nat. Instn. Spl. Study Sect. for Health Manpower, 1969-77, for Behavioral Medicine, 1978-79; acad. awards com. Nat. Inst. on Aging, 1979-80, nat. adv. coun., 1985-88; dir. Western NY Geriat. Edn. Ctr., 1983-88, co-dir., 1988-90; dir. Multidisciplinary Ctr. on Aging SUNY, Buffalo, 1989-90, prof. family medicine, 1987-94; sr. physician and coord. geriat. programs Health Care Plan, 1990-97; ptnr. Promedicus Health Group, 1998-2001; pvt. practice rheumatology and geriatrics, 2001—; mem. adv. com. Dept. Family Medicine, 2009-. Editor: Yesterdays: Memoir from Six Generations of an American Family, 2006; editor: Handbook of Medical Emergencies, 1945, Geriatric Medicine, 1983, Practice of Geriatrics, 1986, 2d edit., 1991, New Ways to Care for Older People: Building Systems Based on Evidence, 1998, contbr. articles to profl. jours. Pres. Nat. Assn. Geriatric Edn. Ctrs., 1992-93. Capt. M.C. AUS, 1943-45, 46-48. Recipient Presdl. citation for Community Service, 1983, Lifetime Achievement award Network Agying WNY, 2010. Fellow ACP (master 1989, Laureate award N.Y. Upstate chpt. 1998), Am. Coll. Rheumatology (founder, pres. 1967-68, master 1986), Gerontol. Soc. Am. (chair clin. med. sect. 1989, Freeman award 1991), Am. Geriatrics Soc. (Milo D. Leavitt award 1986); mem. Am. Clin. and Climatological Assn. (v.p. 1987), Am. Soc. Clin. Investigation, Assn. Am. Physicians, Soc. Medicine Argentina (hon.), Argentine Soc. Gerontology and Geriatrics (hon.), Soc. Fellows John Hopkins U., Alpha Omega Alpha. Home: 3799 Windover Dr Hamburg NY 14075-6338 Office: Village Rheumatology 17 Long Ave Ste 110 Hamburg NY 14075-6388 Office Phone: 716-646-5188.

CALLAHAM, MICHAEL L., emergency physician, educator; MD, U. Calif., 1970. Resident emergency medicine U. So. Calif. L.A. County/U. So. Calif. Med. Ctr., 1974; prof. clin. medicine Med. Ctr. at U. Calif., San Francisco, 1990—, chief divsn. emergency medicine. Editor: Controversies in Trauma Management, 1984; author: Current Therapy in Emergency Medicine, 1987, Decision Making in Emergency Medicine, 1990, Current Practice of Emergency Medicine, 1991; dep. editor: Annals Emergency Medicine, editor in chief:, 2002—, peer reviewer: New Eng. Jour. Medicine, Jour. AMA, Jour. Am. Coll. Cardiology. Recipient Edn. award, Am. Coll. Emergency Physicians Calif. chpt., 2000. Mem.: Inst. Medicine, Coun. Sci. Editors (chmn. editl. policy com.), World Assn. Med. Editors (chmn. ethics com. 2002—). Office: Univ Calif San Francisco Med Ctr Emergency Medicine 505 Parnassus Ave San Francisco CA 94122

CALLAHAN, DANIEL JOHN, biomedical researcher; b. Washington, July 19, 1930; s. Vincent Francis and Anita (Hawkins) Callahan; m. Sidney Cornelia de Shazo, June 5, 1954; children: Mark Sidney, Stephen Daniel, John Vincent, Peter Thorn, Sarah Elisabeth, David Lee. BA, Yale U., 1952; MA, Georgetown U., 1957; PhD, Harvard U., 1965; DSc (hon.), U. Medicine and Dentistry of N.J., 1981; DHL (hon.), U. Colo., 1990, Williams Coll., 1992, Oreg. State U., 1997, SUNY, 2006, Charles U., Prague, 2008. Exec. editor The Commonweal, NYC, 1961—68; staff assoc. Population Council, 1969—70; co-founder, pres. The Hastings Ctr., 1969—96, sr. rsch. scholar, 1997—; resident scholar Aspen Inst. Humanistic Studies, 1975; co-dir. Yale-Hastings Program in Ethics and Health Policy, 2009—. Vis. asst. prof. religion Temple U., 1964; vis. asst. prof. religious studies Brown U., 1965; vis. prof. theology Marymount Coll., 1966; vis. prof. U. Pa., 1970; sr. fellow Harvard Ctr. for Population and Devel. Studies, 1996; cons. med. ethics, jud. coun. AMA, 1972—82, ACP, 1979—86; spl. cons. Commn. on Population Growth and Am. Future, 1970—71, NEH, 1979; hon. prof. Charles U. Med. Sch., Prague, 1997—; sr. lectr. Harvard Med. Sch., 1998—; sr. rsch. scholar Yale U., 2004—. Author: The Mind of the Catholic Layman, 1963, Honesty in the Church, 1965, The New Church, 1966, Abortion: Law, Choice and Morality, 1970, Ethics and Population Limitation, 1971, The Tyranny of Survival, 1973, The Teaching of Ethics in the Military, 1982, Setting Limits: Medical Goals in an Aging Society, 1987, What Kind of Life: The Limits of Medical Progress, 1990, The Troubled Dream of Life: Living with Morality, 1993, False Hopes: Why America's Quest for Perfect Health is a Recipe for Failure, 1998, What Price Better Health: Hazards of the Research Imperative, 2003, Medicine and the Market Equity v. Choice, 2006, Taming the Beloved Beast, 2009; also essays, articles:; co-editor: Christianity Divided: Protestant and Roman Catholic Theological Issues, 1961, Ethical Issues in Human Genetics, 1975, editor: Federal Aid and Catholic Schools, 1964, Secular City Debate, 1966, The Catholic Case for Contraception, 1969, The American Population Debate, 1971, Science, Ethics and Medicine, 1976, Knowledge, Value and Belief, 1977, Morals, Science and Sociality, 1978, Knowing and Valuing, 1979, Ethics Teaching in Higher Education, 1980, Ethical Issues in Population Aid, 1980, The Roots of Ethics, 1981, Ethics in Hard Times, 1981, Ethics, the Social Sciences and Policy Analysis, 1983, Abortion: Understanding Differences, 1984, Applying the Humanities, 1985, Representation and Responsibility, 1985, A World Growing Old, 1995, What Price Mental Health?, 1995, Promoting Healthy Behavior, 2000, The Role of Complementary and Alternative Medicine, 2002, Medicine and the Market, 2006; mem. editl. adv. bd.: Tech. in Soc., 1981—, mem. adv. bd.: Ency. of Life Scis., 1982, Sci., Tech. and Human Values, 1979—, Bus. and Profl. Ethics, 1981, Criminal Justice Ethics, 1982, Environ. Ethics, 1982, Jour. Bioethics, 1985—96. Mem. nat. adv. bd. Health Promotion Program, Henry J. Kaiser Family Found., 1987—91, N.Y. Panel and HIV Screening, 1987; adv. com. to dir. Ctr. for Disease Control, DHHS; mem. N.Y. Coun. for Humanities, 1975—79, Nat. Book Award Com., 1975, N.Y. State Health Adv. Coun., 1975—76; selection com. Ford-Rockefeller Program in Population Policy, 1975—78, Rockefeller Found. Program in Humanities, 1980; elector Nat. Medal for Lit., 1979—83; pub. mem. Am. Bd. Med. Specialties, 1982—87, N.Y. Sci. Policy Assn., 1985—91; mem. N.Y. Task Force on Life and Law, 1985—87; trustee U. Pa. Med. Ctr., 1987—91; mem. adv. com. on sci. integrity HHS, 1991—93. Recipient Thomas More medal, 1970, Daryl J. Mase Disting. Leadership award, 1987, Book of Yr. award, Am. Jour. Nursing, 1987, Henry Knowles Beecher award, The Hastings Ctr., 1989, James H. Hamilton Book award, Am. Coll. Health Care Execs., 1990, Pres. Cabinet award, U. Tex., 1995, Scientific Freedom and Responsibility award, AAAS, 1995, Joseph Leiter award, Nat. Libr. of Medicine, 1999, ARCHON award, Sigma Theta Tau Internat. Honor Soc. of Nursing, 1999, Washington Irving Book award for Fals Hopes, 1999, Career Achievement award, Soc. Bioethics and Med. Humanities, 2001, Morrison prize, MIT, 2002, Centennial medal, Harvard Grad. Sch. Arts and Scis., 2006, Bioethics Leadership award, Johns Hopkins U., 2006; named one of 200 Outstanding Young Men Leaders, Time mag., 1974; Tekolste scholar, Ind. Hosp. Assn., 1986, Bus. Enterprise Trust fellow, 1989—95. Fellow: AAAS (Sci. Freedom and Responsibility award 1996); mem.: Soc. for Study Social Biology (bd. dirs. 1987—95), Inst. Medicine of NAS, Am. Assn. for Advancement Humanities, Harvard Grad. Sch. Arts and Scis. (Centennial medal 2006), Harvard Grad. Soc. (coun. 1989—92, Sr. scholar 1994—2008). Office: The Hastings Ctr 21 Malcolm Gordon Rd Garrison NY 10524-5555 Home: 42 Whitman St Hastings On Hudson NY 10706 Business E-Mail: callahan@thehastingscenter.org.

CALLAHAN, EILEEN H., geriatrician, educator; MD, U. Medicine and Dentistry of NJ-Sch. Health Related Prof, 1991. Diplomate Am. Bd. Internal Medicine, 2004, Am. Bd. Anesthesiology-hospice and palliative medicine, 2005, Am. Bd. Internal Medicine-geriatric medicine, 2008. Resident internal medicine St. Vincent's Hosp Med. Ctr., 1992—94; fellow in geriatric medicine Mt. Sinai Med. Ctr., 1994—96, assoc. prof. medicine, assoc. prof. geriat. and palliative medicine. Office: Mount Sinai Medical Center One Gustave L Levi Place New York NY 10029-6574 Office Phone: 212-241-6500.

CALLAHAN, ELIZABETH F., dermatologist; BA, U. Vermont, 1988, MD, 1997. Diplomate Am. Bd. of Dermatology. Resident in dermatology Cleve. Clinic Found., chief resident in dermatology, 1997—2001; fellow in dermatologic surgery Mayo Clinic, fellow in MOHS surgery, 2001—02; founder SkinSmart Dermatology, dir. Mem.: Sarasota County Med. Soc., Am. Soc. for Dermatologic Surgery, Women's Dermatol. Assn., Am. Coll. of MOHS Surgery, Am. Acad. of Dermatology. Office: Skin Smart Dermatology Suite 214 5911 N Honore Ave Sarasota FL 34243 Office Phone: 941-308-7546. Office Fax: 941-308-7550.

CALLAHAN, LEIGH FLEMING, medical educator, researcher; b. Rutherfordton, NC, Feb. 24, 1957; d. George Arthur and Ruth Fleming Callahan; m. John Buckner Winfield. BS, U. N.C., Chapel Hill, 1979; PhD, Vanderbilt U., Nashville, 1992. Rsch. asst. Wistar Inst., Phila., 1979—81; rsch. assoc. Vanderbilt U., Nashville, 1981—93; epidemiologist Ctrs. Disease Control and Prevention, Atlanta, 1993—95; asst. prof. U. NC, Chapel Hill, 1995—99, assoc. prof., 1999—2010, prof., 2010—. Assoc. dir. Thurston Arthritis Rsch. Ctr., Chapel Hill, 1995—2000; rsch. fellow Cecil B. Sheps Ctr., Chapel Hill, NC, 1996—, UNC Ctr. Health Promotion & Disease Prevention, 2009—. Editor: Arthritis Care and Rsch.; contbr. articles to profl. jours. Trustee Arthritis Found., Atlanta, 1989—2006, sr. vice chair, 1999—2000, treas., 1997—98, vice chair, 1995—96, chair Tenn. chpt. Nashville, 1994, chair Carolinas chpt. Charlotte, NC, 2004—06, chair pub. health com., 2008—; chair Canadian Arthritis Network Sci. and Med. Adv. Com., 2008—; co-chair AF/COC OA Summit Intervention Working Group, 2008—09. Recipient Disting. Scholar award, Assn. Rheumatology Health Profls., 1995, Harding award, Arthritis Found., 2006, Addie Thomas Svc. award, Assn. Rheumatology Health Profls., 2010, Disting. Lectr. award, 2010. Mem.: APHA, Am. Coll. Rheumatology Rsch. & Edn. Found. (bd. dirs. 2009—), Assn. Health Svcs. Rsch., Soc. Epidemiologic Rsch., Am. Coll. Rheumatology. Avocations: scuba diving, reading, travel, bicycling, music. Home: 102 Greenwood Ln Chapel Hill NC 27514 Office: U NC 3300 Thurston Bldg CB 7280 Chapel Hill NC 27599 Office Fax: 919-966-1739. Business E-Mail: leigh_callahan@med.unc.edu.

CALLAHAN, LISA R., sports medicine physician; MD, East Carolina U. Diplomate Am. Bd. of Family Practice, Am. Bd. of Internal Medicine-sports medicine. Resident Stanford Univ. Sch. of Medicine, fellow; with Hosp. for Special Surgery, 1994—; co-dir. Women's Sports Medicine Ctr.; assoc. prof. dept. of medicine Weill Cornell Med. Coll., team physician WUSA NY Power, 2000—03; med. contbr. ABC News/Good Morning America, Lifetime's Speaking of Women's Health; contbg. editor Self Mag., columnist; editl. advisor Jour. of Women's Health, Women's Health Advisor, Food & Fitness Advisor. Bd. dirs. Am. Med. Soc. for Sports Medicine; dir. player care NY Knicks, Liberty Basketball Team. Host: (lifestyle show) Recipe for Health, 1996—98; author: (book) The Fitness Factor, 2002, (articles) 12th Annual Sports Medicine for the Young Athlete, A Musculoskeletal Profile of Elite Female Soccer Players. Named one of Best Doctors in New York, NY Mag., 2011. Office: Hospital for Special Surgery East River Professional Building 523 East 72nd St New York NY 10021 Office Phone: 212-606-1532. Office Fax: 212-327-1417.

CALLAN, CLAIR MARIE, physician, consultant; b. Sleaford, Lincolnshire, Eng., May 18, 1940; d. Joseph Edward and Murgaret Mary (Hart) Mills; m. John Patrick Callan, Apr. 4, 1964; children: Eoin, Grainne, Colm, Maeve. MB in B.Surgery; B in Art Obstetrics, U. Coll., Dublin, Ireland, 1963; MBA, U. Phoenix, 1993. Intern Mater Hosp., Dublin, 1963—64, resident anesthesia, 1964—65; staff physician Middletown, Conn., 1966—68; anesthesiologist St. Francis Hosp., Hartford, Conn., 1972—76; med. dir. Dept. Income Maintenance, Hartford, Conn., 1978—84, v.p. med. and regulatory affairs Abbott Labs., Abbott Pk., Ill., 1985—92, venture head, 1992—93, v.p. med. and regulatory affairs and advanced rsch. hosp. products divsn., 1993—; clin. asst. prof. med. Chgo. Med. Sch./U. Health Scis., 1987—; CEO Callan Consulting, 2004—. Sr. fellow Nat. Alliance Health Info. Tech. Contbr. articles to profl. jours. Pres. PTA, Wethersfield, Conn., 1974, Capitol Region Assn. Pvt. Swim Clubs, Hartford, 1978. Mem.: Am. Acad. Med. Dirs., AMA (pres. Conn. aux. 1979—81, v.p. sci. quality and pub. health 1999—2004, interim sr. v.p. profl. stds.), Am. Med. Women's Assn. (pres. 1984—85, councillor 1981—83). Republican. Roman Catholic. Avocations: tennis, golf, needlecrafts. Home: 1800 Amberley Ct Apt 208 Lake Forest IL 60045-1057

CALLAND, JAMES FORREST, surgeon, educator; b. Ind., Oct. 8, 1966; MD, Mt. Sinai Sch. Medicine, 1997. Asst. prof. surgery U. Va., 2007—11, assoc. chief med. officer-acute care, health sys., 2010—. Fellow: ACS; mem.: Am. Trauma Soc. (bd. dirs.). Avocation: guitar. Office: PO Box 800709 Charlottesville VA 22908 Office Fax: 434-982-4344. Business E-Mail: calland@virginia.edu.

CALLAR, DONNA HOWE, counseling administrator, educator; b. Moundsville, W.Va., June 29, 1940; d. Chester Ray and Freda Marie Howe; m. Donald Evan Callar, Nov. 19, 1972 (dec. Sept. 1996). BA, West Liberty State Coll., 1962; MEd, W.Va. U., 1965, MEd, 1968; PhD, Union Grad. Sch., 1987. Lic. profl. counselor Va., cert. clin. mental health counselor Nat. Bd. Cert. Counselors, Inc. Tchr. elem., prin., jr. high counselor Marshall County Schs., Moundsville, 1962—70; counselor elem. Berkeley County Schs., Martinsburg, W.Va., 1970—72; sch. social worker Fairfax County Schs., Va., 1973—90; counselor elem. Loudoun County Schs., Leesburg, Va., 1990—. Adj. prof. Bowie State U., Md., 1980—, U. Va., Fairfax, 1980—. Author: Those Dynamite Years--Teenagers, 1987; author: (pamphlet) Introducing Elementary Guidance, 1969. Recipient Excellence in Edn. award, Fairfax Cmty. Action, 1990; named Woman of Yr., Annandale chpt. Bus. and Profl. Women, 1980. Mem.: NEA, Va. Edn. Assn., Am. Sch. Counselors (W.Va. coord.), Alpha Delta Kappa. Avocations: flying, reading, sewing, antiques. Home: 1334 W Washington St Harpers Ferry WV 25425

CALLAWAY, CLIFFORD WAYNE, physician; b. Easton, Md., May 28, 1941; s. Charles Herschel and Anna Agnes C.; 1 child, David Wayne; m. Jackie Chalkley. BA, U. Del., Newark, 1963; MD, Northwestern U., Evanston, Ill., 1967. Diplomate Am. Bd. Internal Medicine, Am. Bd. Endocrinology, Diabetes and Metabolism, Am. Bd. Nutrition. Resident in internal medicine Northwestern U. Med. Ctr., Chgo., 1967—69, Mayo Grad. Sch. Medicine, Rochester, Minn., 1971—73, advanced clin. resident in endocrinology, 1973—75; assoc. cons. Mayo Clinic, 1975—78, cons. endocrinology, 1978—85, dir. nutrition and lipid clinics, 1980—85; rsch. assoc. Harvard Med. Sch., Boston, 1976—78; dir. ctr. clin. nutrition George Washington U., Washington, 1986—88; sr. sci. cons. Food & Nutrition Bd.,

NRC/NAS, Washington, 1987—88; pvt. practice Washington, 1988—. Contbr. articles to profl. jours.; co-author (with Catherine Whitney): The Callaway Diet: Successful Permanent Weight Control for Starvers, Stuffers, and Skippers, 1990, Surviving with AIDS: A Comprehensive Program of Nutritional Co-Therapy, 1991; co-author: (with Michael B. Alleert) Clinical Nutrition for the House Officer, 1992; co-author: (with Melanie Barnard, Brooke Dojny and Mindy Herman) Am. Med. Assn. Family Cookbook Good Food That's Good for You, 1997; co-author: (with Melanie Barnard and Brooke Dojny) Family Healthy Cookbook Good Food that's Good for You, 1997. Acting exec. sec. nutrition coordinating office HHS, Washington, 1980. Mayo Found. scholar, 1976-78. Mem. Am. Soc. Clin. Nutrition (treas. 1988), Am. Bd. Nutrition (bd. dirs. 1983-89, 95-98, sec.-treas. 1984-86, v.p. 1986-88), Am. Inst. Nutrition (chair and various coms.), Am. Dietetics Assn. (hon.), Am. Osler Soc. (bd. dirs.), Am. Assn. Clin. Endocrinologists (bd. dirs. 1992-95), Ctrl. European Ctr. for Health and Environment (bd. dirs.), Wash. Acad. Medicine. Achievements include development and writing of dietary guidelines for Americans (USDA/DHHS). Office: 2311 M St NW Ste 301 Washington DC 20037-1468 Office Phone: 202-331-3330. Personal E-mail: cwcallaway@aol.com. Business E-Mail: cwcallaway@doctorcallaway.com.

CALLAWAY, WARREN EUGENE, hospital administrator; b. Atlanta, Dec. 7, 1950; s. William Hubert and Juanita (Warren) C.; m. Martha Nell Clements, Dec. 28, 1973; children: Curtis William, Leigh Ann. BBA, Ga. State U., 1975, M of Health Adminstrn., 1977. Asst. adminstr. South Fulton Hosp., East Point, Ga., 1977-79, Redmond Pk. Hosp., Rome, Ga., 1979-82; adminstr. Parkway Med. Ctr., Decatur, Ala., 1982-85; pres. DFW Med. Ctr., Grand Prairie, Tex., 1985-86; adminstr. N.W. Regional Hosp., Margate, Fla., 1986-90; COO AMI Brookwood Med. Ctr., Birmingham, Ala., 1990-93; adminstr. Carraway Meth. Med. Ctr., Birmingham, 1993—. Mem. adj. faculty U. Ala., Birmingham, 1990—; bd. dirs. Ala. Diversified Svcs., Montgomery. Dist. chmn. Boy Scouts Am., Decatur, 1984-85; bd. dirs. YMCA, Birmingham, 1990-93. With U.S. Army, 1970-72. Fellow Am. Coll. Healthcare Execs.; mem. Ala. Hosp. Assn. (mem. legis. com. 1993—), Birmingham C. of C. (trustee 1990—), Newcomen Soc., Rotary Club. Baptist. Avocations: flying, skiing. Office: Carraway Methodist Med Ctr 1600 Carraway Blvd Birmingham AL 35234-1990 *

CALLEBERT, JACQUES, pharmacologist, educator; b. Coudekerque-Branche, June 3, 1956; Diploma in Pharmacy, Amiens U., 1980; PhD in Pharmacology, Paris Descartes U., 1989. Prof. pharmacology Facultés des Scis. Pharmaceutiques et Biologiques Paris V, 1996—. Biologist Med. Biochemistry and Molecular Biology Lab., Lariboisiere Hosp. Pariis, 1980. Office: 2 rue Ambroiuse PARE Hôpital Lariboisiè Paris 75010 France Office Fax: 33 1 49 95 84 77. Business E-Mail: jacques.callebert@lrb.aphp.fr.

CALLEN, JEFFREY PHILLIP, dermatologist, educator; b. May 30, 1947; s. Irwin R. and Rose P. (Cohen) C.; m. Susan B. Manis, Dec. 21, 1968; children: Amy, David. BS, U. Wis., 1969; MD, U. Mich., 1972. Diplomate Am. Bd. Internal Medicine, Am. Bd. Dermatology. Intern, resident in internal medicine U. Mich., Ann Arbor, 1972-75, resident in dermatology, 1975-77; from asst. clin. prof. to dir. residency tng. program U. Louisville Sch. Medicine, 1977-84, dir. residency tng. program, 1984-88; chief dermatology svc. Louisville VA Hosp., 1984-93, prof., chief dermatology divsn., 1988—. Author: Manual of Dermatology, 1980, Cutaneous Aspects of Internal Disease, 1981, Neurology Clinics North America, 1987, Dermatologic Signs of Systemic Disease, 1988, 3d edit., 2003, 4th edit., 2009, asst. editor Dermatology, 2nd edit., 2007, Color Atlas of Dermatology, 1993, 2d edit., 2000, Current Practice of Dermatology, 1995; editor: Clinics in Rheumatic Disease, 1982, Dermatologic Clinics, 1985, 89, 2002, Medical Clinics of North America, 1982, 84, 86, 89, Dermatologic Therapy, 2007; editor-in-chief Dermavision video program; mem. editl. bd. Internat. Jour. Dermatology, 1990-95, Jour. Watch Dermatology, 1999-, assoc. editor, 2005-, dep. editor 2005-; asst. editor Internat. Jour. Dermatology, 1993-95, Jour. Am. Acad. Dermatology, 1995-2003, Dermatology, 2nd edit., 2007; assoc. editor Archives Dermatology, 2003-; editor-in-chief Dermatology Up-to-Date, 2010-. Bd. dirs. Actor's Theater of Louisville, 1982-98, 2000-2009, sec., 1986-87, Ky. Arts and Crafts Found., 1991-97; bd. govs. JB Speed Art Mus., 1995-2003 Fellow ACP, Am. Acad. Dermatology (chmn. audio/visual edn. com., task force therapeutic agts., internal med. symposium 1978-83, chmn. sci. and tech. exhibits 1986-89, dir. various symposiums, mem. coun. sci. assembly 1993-98, chair 1997-98, chair com. to evaluate ann. meeting, 1999-2003, vice chair coun. on edn. 2002-2003, chair coun. on edn. 2003-07, v.p. elect 2003-04, v.p. 2004-05, bd. dirs. 1995-99, mem. exec. com. 1997-99, 2003-05, co-chair program for 21st century 1999-2000, chair psoriasis edn. conf. 2002, chair unity summit, chair task force on psoriasis edn. 2005, com. on maintenance cert. 2006—11), Am. Coll. Rheumatology (founder, chair skin disease study group 1996-98, 2000-02); mem. AMA, Am. Fedn. Clin. Rsch., Am. Dermatol. Assn. (bd. dirs. 2008-), Dermatology Found. (trustee 1984-90), Louisville Theatrical Assn. (bd. dirs. 1999-2002), Am. Bd. Dermatology (bd. mem. 2000-, v.p. elect, 10-11), Maintanance Cert. Com., (chair, 06-10). Achievements include research on condition in which systemic disease has cutaneous manifestations, lupus erythematosus, psoriasis, dermatomyositis. Office: U Louisville Dept Dermatology 310 E Broadway Ste 200 Louisville KY 40202-1745 Office Phone: 502-583-1749. Business E-Mail: jpcall01@louisville.edu.

CALLENDER, CLIVE ORVILLE, surgeon; b. NYC, Nov. 16, 1936; s. Joseph and Ida (Burke) C.; m. Fern Irene Marshall, May 25, 1968; children: Joseph, Ealena, Arianne. AB, Hunter Coll., 1959; MD, Meharry Med. Coll., 1963; DSc (hon.), Hunter Coll., 1998, Meharry Med. Coll., 2008. Diplomate Am. Bd. Surgery, 1970. Intern U. Cin., 1963-64; asst. resident Harlem Hosp., NYC, 1964-65, Howard U. and Freedmens Hosp., Washington, 1965-66, 67-68, chief resident, 1968-69, instr. dept. surgery, 1969-71; asst. resident Meml. Hosp. for Cancer and Allied Diseases, NYC, 1966-67; cons. surgery Port Harcourt Gen. Hosp., Nigeria, 1970, 71; med. officer D.C. Gen. Hosp., 1970-71; NIH postdoctoral rsch. and clin. transplant fellow U. Minn., 1971-73; asst. prof. surgery Howard U. Med. Coll., Washington, 1973-76, assoc. prof., 1976-81, prof. surgery, 1981—, vice-chmn. dept. surgery, 1980-95, chmn. dept. surgery, 1996—, LaSalle D. Leffall, Jr. prof. surgery, 1996—, dir. transplant ctr., 1973—. Transplantation cons., Bermuda, 1977, V.I., 1978, 82-86; cons. Ethiopian Surg., Amenity Med. Sch., 1984; G.P.A. Ford Meml. lectr., 1978; mem. task force on organ procurement and transplantation HEW, 1984; testifier com. on labor and human resources U.S. Senate, 1983; mem. end stage renal disease study com. Inst. of Medicine, 1989-90, mem. com. on xenograft transplantation: ethical issues and pub. policy, 1995-96, com. on non-heart-beating organ transplantation II, 1999, mem. com. to increase rates of organ donation, 2005-06; fellowship in liver transplantation Pitts. U., 1986-87; founder, prin. investigator Nat. Minority Organ and Tissue Transplant Edn. Program, 1991—; mem., increasing organ donation com. Inst. Medicine, 2005-06. Mem. editl. adv. bd. New Directions, 1974-91, Contemporary Dialysis and Nephrology Jour., 1993-95, Clin. Transplant Proceedings, 1998—, Am. Jour. Kidney Disease, 2001—); contbr. articles to med. jours. Testified for Ho. of Reps. Com. on Appropriation, U.S. Congress, 1992, others; councillor Soc. Organ Sharing, 1993, sec., 1995; chmn. tissue com. D.C. chpt. ARC, 1993-95; trustee Hunter Coll. Found., 2000. Recipient Hoffman LaRoche award, 1961, Charles Nelson Gold medal, 1963, Hudson Meadows award, 1963, Charles R. Drew Rsch. award, 1969, Daniel Hale Williams award, 1969, William Alonzo Warfield award, 1977, Howard U. Faculty Outstanding Unit award, 1982, 1st Humanitarian award Cmty. of Caring Ctr., 1990, Disting. Svc. award Surg. Sect. Nat. Med. Assn., 1990, Howard U. Health Affairs Disting. Svc. award, 1984, Outstanding Svc. award Dialysis and Transplant Support, Inc., 1993, Howard U. Legacy of Leadership in Health award, 1995, 11th ann. Minds in Motion award Sci. Skills Ctr., 1993, Edler Garnet Hawkins Humanitarian award Bronx Urban League, 1993; appreciation plaque for 1st renal transplant in V.I., Gov. St. Thomas, 1983, plaque for outstanding contbns. V.I. Legislature, 1984; named to Hunter Coll. Hall of Fame, 1989, Practitioner of Yr., Nat. Med. Assn., 1989, Scroll of Merit, Nat. Med. Assn., 1998, 1 of 10 Outstanding African Am. Male, WHMM-TV, Washington, 1994, 1 of 133 Gifts to the World Alumni Achievers, CUNY, 1995, Pearl Watson Meml. award for excellence in health care delivery Caribbean Am. Intercultural Orgn., Inc., 1995, Pioneer in Edn. award Inst. for Ind. Edn., 1995, Kidney Patients medal of Excellence 2nd Am. Assn., 1997, Leadership Edn. award Shiloh Bapt. Ch., 2002, Prof. Achievement award Hunter Coll. Hall Fame, 2002, Masons Pub. Svc. award, 2003, Humanitarian Svc. award Julia West Hamilton League, 2005, others. Fellow ACS (bd. govs. 1994-2000, LaSalle D. Leffall, Jr. award 1998, Mary McLeod Bethune Legacy award 2000)); mem. D.C. Med. Soc. (past vice chmn., chmn. surg. sect. 1994—, trustee 1995), Internat. Soc. Organ Sharing (sec. 1993—), Transplantation Soc., Am. Soc. Transplantation Surgeons (chmn. membership com. 1986, organ placement com. 1991, mem. ethics com. 1995-97), N.Y. Acad. Medicine, Am. Assn. Kidney Patients (bd. dirs. 1998), Nat. Assn. Former Foster Care Children Am. (bd. dirs. 1998-99), Nat. Kidney Found. (nat. bd. dirs. 1991-94, nat. capital area 1977-90), Am. Surg. Assn., Am. Coun. on Transplantation (bd. dirs.), Nat. Med. Assn., Soc. Surg. Assn., Inst. Cellular Therapeutics (adv. bd.), United Network of Organ Sharing (vice-chair 1996-98, chair 1998-00), Soc. Black Acad. Surgeons (pres. 2001—), Alpha Omega Alpha, Alpha Phi Omega, Alpha Phi Alpha. Office: 2041 Georgia Ave NW Washington DC 20060-0001 Office Phone: 202-865-1441. E-mail: ccallender@howard.edu.

CALLENDER, NORMA ANNE, counselor, public relations executive; b. Huntsville, Tex., May 10, 1933; d. C.W. Carswell and Nell Ruth (Collard) Hughes Bost; m. B.G. Callender, 1951 (div. 1964); remarried 1967 (div. 1973); children: Teresa Elizabeth, Leslie Gemey, Shannah Hughes, Kelly Mari; m. E Purfurst, June 1965 (div. Aug. 1965). BS, U. Houston, 1969; MA, U. Houston-Clear Lake, 1977; postgrad., Tex. So. U., Houston, 1971, Lamar U., Beaumont, Tex., 1972-73, U. Houston-Clear Lake, 1979, 87, 89-93, postgrad., 1998, St. Thomas U., 1985-86, Aerospace Inst., NASA, Johnson Space Ctr., 1986, San Jacinto Coll., Houston, 1988—99, postgrad., 2001—03; PhD, Cornerstone U., 1998. Cert. profl. reading specialist, Tex.; lic. profl. counselor. Tchr. Houston Ind. Schs., 1969-70; co-counselor, instr. Ellington AFB, Houston, 1971; tchr. Clear Creek Schs., League City, Tex., 1970-86; owner, dir. Bay Area Tutoring and Reading Clinic, Clear Lake City, Tex., 1970—, Bay Area Tng. Assocs., 1982-98, Bay Area Family Counseling, 1995—, Bay Area Speech and Lang., 2003—; cons., LPC intern Guidance Ctr., Pasadena Ind. Sch. Dist., Tex., 1993-95; prin., dir. pub. rels. Gateway Supply, Inc., 2005—10, Gateway Foods USA, 2005—10. Instr. San Jacinto Coll., Pasadena, 1980-81, 91-93; adj. instr. U. Houston, Clear Lake, 1986-91; founder, editor BATA Books Pub., 1997—. Author: numerous poems. State advisor U.S. Congl. Adv. Bd., 1985-87; vol., bd. dirs. Family Outreach Ctr., 1989-92; vol. Bay Area Coun. on Drugs and Alcohol, Nassau Bay, Tex., 1993-94; bd. dirs. Ballet San Jacinto, 1985-87; adv. bd. Cmty. Edn!. TV, 1990-92; charter mem. Nat. Women's History Mus., Washington, 2005. Recipient Franklin award U. Houston, 1965-67; Delta Kappa Gamma/Beta Omicron scholar, 1967-68, PTA scholar, 1973, Berwin scholar, 1976, Mary Gibbs Jones scholar, 1976-77, Found. Econ. Edn. scholar, 1976, Insts. Achievement Human Potential scholar, Phila., 1987. Master: Am. Contract Bridge League (life; master 2011); mem.: ACA, The NET: Bay Area Mental Health Providers Network, Clear Creek Educators Assn. (past, honorarium 1976, 1977, 1985), Sam Houston Chpt., Daughters of Am. Revolution, Leadership Clear Lake Alumni Assn. (edn. com. 1985, program and projects com. mem. 1986—87, charter), U. Houston Alumni Assn. (life), Phi Theta Kappa, Phi Delta Kappa, Kappa Delta Pi, Psi Chi (life), Phi Kappa Phi (life). Mem. Life Ch. Office: 16815 Royal Crest Ste 110 Houston TX 77058-2538

CALLIESS, IRIS TATJANA, psychiatrist, researcher; 2 children. BA in Slavic Languages, U. Heidelberg and Göttingen, Germany, 1988; MD, U. Göttingen, Germany, 1994; PhD, Med. Sch. Hanover, Germany, 2008. Diplomate in polish lang. and culture Jagiellonian U. Cracow, Poland, 1985, lic. in practice medicine State Chamber Physicians Lower Saxony, Germany, 1997. Psychiatrist, Littenheid, Switzerland, 1995—97; vis. rschr. Sigmund-Freud Inst., Frankfurt, Germany, 1998; psychiatrist tng. State Hosp. Mental Disorders, Berlin, 1999—2000; psychiatrist, rschr. Med. Sch. Hanover, 2001—08; project dir., rschr. Inst. Standardized and Applied Hosp. Mgmt., Med. Sch. Hanover, 2008—. Mem. core sci. com. European Psychiat. Assn., Strasbourg, France, chair young psychiatrists com., 2005—11; mem. sci. com. German Psychiat. Assn., Berlin, pres. german com. young psychiatrists and trainees, 2002—09. Fellowship, World Psychiat. Assn., 2005, 2008. Mem.: Friedrich-Naumann-Found., Berlin (selection com. mem., fellowship 1992—94). Achievements include initiator of a European network for young psychiatrists. Office: Med Sch Hanover Carl-Neuberg-Str. 1 30625 Hanover Germany Business E-Mail: calliess.iris@mh-hannover.de.

CALLISON, NANCY FOWLER, nurse administrator; b. Milw., July 16, 1931; d. George Fenwick and Irma Esther (Wenzel) Fowler; m. B.G. Callison, Sept. 25, 1954 (dec. Feb. 1964); children: Robert, Leslie, Linda. Diploma, Evanston Hosp. Sch. Nursing, 1952; BS, Northwestern U., 1954. RN, Calif.; cert. case mgr. Staff nurse, psychiat. dept. Downey VA Hosp., 1954-55; staff nurse Camp Lejeune Naval Hosp., 1955, 59-61; obstet. supr. Tri-City Hosp., Oceanside, Calif., 1961-62; pub. health nurse San Diego County, 1962-66; sch. nurse Rich-Mar Union Sch. Dist., San Marcos, Calif., 1966-68; head nurse San Diego County Community Mental Health, 1968-73; dir. patient care services Southwood Mental Health Ctr., Chula Vista, Calif., 1973-75; program cons. Comprehensive Care Corp., Newport Beach, Calif., 1975-79; dir. Manpower Health Care, Culver City, Calif., 1979-80; dir. nursing services Peninsula Rehab. Ctr., Lomita, Calif., 1980-81; clinic supr., coordinator utilization and authorizations, acting dir. provider relations Hawthorne (Calif.) Community Med. Group, 1981-86; mgr. Health Care Delivery Physicians of Greater Long Beach, Calif., 1986-87; cons. Quality Rev. Assocs., West L.A., 1988-93; case mgr. Mercy Physicians Med. Group, 1992-93; med. mgmt. specialist The Zenith Ins., 1993—99, Zurich Ins., 2001—04. Clin. coord., translator Flying Samaritans, 1965-, mem. internat. bd. dirs., 1975-77, 79-86, 89-95, 2005—, dir. San Quentin project, 1991-93, dir. univ. program, 1996-2000, pres. South Bay chpt., 1975-81, v.p., 1982-85, bd. dirs. San Diego chpt., 1987-90, pres. San Diego chpt. 1991-92, adminstr. Clinica Esperanza de Infantil Rosarito Beach 1990-93; dir. Playas Rosprito Clinic, 2004—.; dir. Playas Rsch. Clinic. Mem. Rehab. Nurse Coord. Network (bd. dirs., treas. 1997-98), U.S.-Mex. Border Health Assn., Cruz Roja Mexicana (Delegacion Rosarito 1986-92). Office Phone: 619-407-7815. Personal E-mail: nancycallison@hotmail.com.

CALLSEN, CHRISTIAN EDWARD, health products executive; b. 1938; married. AB, Miami U., 1959; MBA, Harvard U., 1966. With Cole Nat. Corp., Cleve., 1966-87, various mgmt. and v.p. positions, 1966-87, exec. v.p., 1983-87; pres. Hyatt Legal Svcs., Cleve., 1987-90, Profl. Vet. Hosps., Detroit, 1991, Profl. Med. Mgmt., Cleve., 1992—2000, Applied Med. Tech., Cleve., 1993-96; chmn., CEO Allen Med. Sys., Cleve., 1995-99; pres. Polymer Concepts, Inc., 1999; chmn. TAGA Med. Techs., Inc., 2000—05. Lt. USN, 1959-64. Office: 7555 Tyler Blvd Ste 1 Mentor OH 44060-4867 Home: 157 Hudson St Hudson OH 44236-2930 Office Phone: 440-953-9605. Personal E-mail: cec235@aol.com.

CALMENSON, MARVIN, retired surgeon; b. Aberdeen, SD, 1914; MD, Rush Med. Coll., 1938. Diplomate Am. Bd. Surgery. Intern Emanuel Hosp., Portland, Oreg., 1938-39; surg. fellow Mayo Fedn., Rochester, Minn., 1943-46; ret. Fellow ACS; mem. AMA. *

CALOBRACE, M. BRADLEY, plastic surgeon, educator; b. Marion, Ind., Dec. 15, 1962; BS in Biology-Chemistry summa cum laude, Manchester Coll., North Manchester, Ind., 1981—85; MD, Ind. U., Indpls., 1985—89. License to practice Ky. (lic. number 32666), diplomate Am. Bd. Medical Examiners, 1990, Am. Bd. Surgery-expired, 1995, Am. Bd. Plastic Surgery, 1999, cert. Ky. State Med. Bd., 1997. Clin. instr. surgery divsn. plastic and reconstructive surgery Univ. Louisville; hosp. affiliations include Calobrace Plastic Surgery Ctr., Jewish Hosp., Baptist East Hosp., Dupont Surgery Ctr., HealthSouth Surgery Ctr.; resident gen. surgery Univ. Southern Calif., LA, 1989—94, resident plastic and reconstructive surgery, 1994—96; fellow aesthetic surgery/reconstructive and aesthetic breast surgery Aesthetic and Reconstructive Inst. Baptist. Hosp., Nashville, 1996—97; owner Calobrace Plastic Surgery Ctr., CaloSpa, Cosmetic Breast Ctr. Speaker; mentor; luminary physician ptnr. Syneron; certified faculty speaker on injectables CME Scholar; nat. edn. faculty Allergan, roundtable cons. Juvederm, acad. faculty; with breast cancer task force Caritas Med. Ctr., 1998; cancer com. mem. Alliant Health System, 1998; emergency room com. mem. Jewish Hosp., 2000, surgical svcs. com. mem., 2001—04. Author: (articles) Cosmetic Surgery-Not Just for Women Anymore, 2001, Post-partum Rejuvenation-The Mommy Makeover, 2006, Men-On the Cutting Edge, 2006, The Medispa Makeover, 2007, numerous others; co-author: (book chpt.) Large Volume Ultrasound Assisted Lipoplasty, 1998. Recipient 1st place Sci. Exhibit for Rsch., Ind. Med. Assn., Summer Rsch. Stipend, 1986, Groves-Hardiman Scholarship for Rsch., 1986. Fellow: Am. Coll. Surgeons; mem.: LA County-Univ. Southern Calif. Soc. Grad. Surgeons, Botox Cosmetic Physicians Network, Ky. Soc. Plastic Surgeons, Greater Louisville Med. Soc., Ky. Med. Assn., AMA, Alpha Omega Alpha Honor Soc., Am. Soc. Plastic Surgeons, Am. Soc. Aesthetic Plastic Surgery, Patient Care Fund Com., Joint Coun. Interns and Residents, Univ. Southern Calif. House Officers' Assn., Am. Coll. Surgeons (southern Calif. chpt.). Office: Calobrace Plastic Surgery Center 2341 Lime Kiln Lane Louisville KY 40222 Office Phone: 502-899-9979. Office Fax: 502-899-9939.

CALOF, RACHEL PEARL, alcohol and drug counselor; b. Pocking, Germany, July 26, 1947; came to U.S., 1949; Children: Mark Jeffrey, Melissa Rose; m. Michael Philip Calof, Aug. 14, 1983. Degree in alcohol and drug counseling, Oxnard Coll., 1992. Cert. alcohol and drug therapist, addiction specialist, registered addiction treatment specialist. Program coord. alcohol and drug treatment program Simi Valley (Calif.) Hosp., 1992-2000, Vista Del Mar Hosp., Simi Valley, 2001—. Mem. Nat. Assn. Alcohol and Drug Counselors, Calif. Assn. Alcohol and Drug Counselors, Calif. Assn. Recovery Homes. Democrat. Avocations: counseling parents of handicapped children, research on dual diagnosis issues, research on physical handicaps and addiction. Home: 3052 Ferncrest Place Thousand Oaks CA 91362 E-mail: etohdr@yahoo.com.

CALONGE, BRUCE NEDROW (NED CALONGE), foundation administrator, former public health service officer; BA, Colo. Coll., 1987; MD, Univ. Colo., 1981; MPH, Univ. Wash., 1986. Cert. family & preventive med. Residency Oreg. Health Sci. U., 1981—84; fellowship Dept. Family Med. U. Wash., 1984—86, chief resident Dept. Preventive Med., 1985—86; chief preventive med. & rsch. Kaiser Permanente, Colo.; chief med. officer, state epidemiologist, exec. dir. state bioterrorism preparedness Colo. Dept. Public Health & Environment, Denver, 2002—10; pres., CEO The Colo. Trust, 2010—. Assoc. prof. epidemiology, biostatistics & rsch. methods Univ. Colo. Health Sci. Ctr., 1986—; pres. Colo. Bd. Med. Examiners; bd. dir. Colo. Acad. Family Practice, Colo. Found. for Med. Care, Colo. Prevention Ctr., Colo. Regional Health Info. Orgn. Contbr. articles to profl. jours. Recipient Pub. Health award, Am. Acad. Family Physicians, 2004, Robert Graham Physician Exec. award,

2004. Mem.: Colo. Med. Soc. (chmn. health affairs com.). Office: The Colorado Trust 1600 Sherman St Denver CO 80203-1604 Office Phone: 303-837-1200. E-mail: ned@coloradotrust.org. *

CĂLUGĂRU, MIHAI SEVER, ophthalmologist, educator; s. Ioan and Sabina Călugăru; m. Angela Viorica Baltes, Dec. 4, 1968; 1 child, Mihai Dan. MD, Inst. Medicine and Pharmacy, Cluj-Napoca, Romania, 1963, PhD, 1972. Cert. evaluating expert Nat. Coun. Sci. Rsch., U. Edn. Founder Deutscher Akademischer Austausch Dienst, U. Eye Clinic, Essen, Germany, 1972, 1996, Lübeck, Germany, 1993, Cologne, Germany, 1993; prof. ophthalmology U. Medicine and Pharmacy, Cluj-Napoca, 1994—. Head U. Eye Clinic U. State Hosp., Cluj-Napoca, 1996—2006. Contbr. articles to profl. jours.; author: Clinical Glaucoma Book, 1998, Clinical Book of Uveal Malignant Melanoma and Differential Diagnosis of Mass Lesions of the Ocular Globe, 2001, Ophthalmology, 2002, 2004. Recipient award, U. Medicine and Pharmacy, 1994, 1999. Mem.: Romanian Ophthal. Soc. Achievements include investigation on double blind placebo controlled study of doxium in the treatment of mild to moderate diabetic retinopathy; a randomized controlled study on the efficacy and safety of Sandostatin LAR in the therapy of patients with moderately or severe nonproliferative diabetic retinopathy (NPDR) or low risk proliferative diabetic retinopathy (PDR); a randomized multicentric, double-blind, placebo-controlled comparative phase III study in out patients with mild to moderate non proliferative diabetic retinopathy to assess the efficacy of treatment with a once daily administration of one 600 mg lipoic acid tablet for 24 months; diabetic retinopathy candesartan trial. Avocations: tennis, football. Office: Iuliu Hatieganu Univ Ophthalmology Faculty Medicine Strada Clinicilor 400006 Cluj-Napoca Romania Home Phone: 0040264442457; Office Phone: 0040264591468, 0741165094. Business E-Mail: mihai.calugaru@mail.dntej.ro.

CALUGI, ALBERTO, obstetrician; b. Latina, Italy, Dec. 16, 1938; s. Pietro Calugi and Bianca Micheli; m. Anna Maria Isabella, Sept. 11, 1978; children: Maurizio, Roberto, Graziella, Pietro, Matteo. MD, U. Rome La Sapienza, 1963. Diplomate Bd. Ob-Gyn, Bd. Anesthesiology, Bd. Surgery. Resident ob-gyn U. Rome La Sapienza, 1963—67; assoc. prof. ob-gyn U. Rome Tor Vergata, 1997—; rschr. ob-gyn U. Rome La Sapienza, 1970—87, U. Rome Tor Vergata, 1987—97. Chief obstetrics S. Eugenia Hosp. U. Tor Vergata, Rome, 1997—2002, dir. ob-gyn. S. Eugenio Hosp., 2003—. Author: (book) Ostetricia E Ginecologia, La Placenta; contbr. articles to profl. jours. Mem.: Italian Soc. Cytometry, Italian Soc. Ob-Gyn. Achievements include research in Best European Work From The European Society Of Hypertermia. Avocation: collecting old Roman coins. Office: Univ Tor Vergata S Eugenio Hosp Ple Umanesimo 10 00144 Rome Italy Office Fax: 0039.06.5919864. Business E-Mail: alberto.calugi@uniroma2.it.

CALVERT, JAY W., plastic surgeon, director; b. NJ, July 18, 1967; BA, Vanderbilt U., Nashville, 1990; MD, Cornell U., 1994. Dir. Rox Ctr., 2005—. Mem.: ACS, Calif. Soc. Plastic Surgeons, Rhinoplasty Soc., Am. Soc. Plastic Surgeons, Am. Soc. Aesthetic Plastic Surgery. Office: 465 N Roxbury Dr Ste 1001 Beverly Hills CA 90210 Office Fax: 310-248-6258. E-mail: jay@jaycalvertmd.com.

CALVERT, WILLIAM PRESTON, radiologist; b. Warrensburg, Mo., July 2, 1934; s. William Geery and Elizabeth (Spaulding) C.; m. Mary Kay Kersh, Apr. 4, 1976. BS, MIT, 1956; MD, U. Pa., 1960. Diplomate Am. Bd. Nuclear Medicine, Am. Bd. Radiology. Intern Pa. Hosp., Phila., 1960-61, resident in medicine, 1961-62, 64-66, chief med. resident, chief resident physician, 1965-66; resident in gastroenterology U. Miami, 1966-67, NIH fellow in gastroenterology, 1967-68, resident in radiology, 1968-71; radiologist Meml. Hosp., Hollywood, Fla., 1971-72; chief dept. radiology Larkin Gen. Hosp., South Miami, Fla., 1972-80, radiologist, 1980-89, Jackson Meml. Hosp., U. Miami, 1989-93, Univ. Hosp., Tammarac, Fla., 1993-95; part-time radiologist Northern Navajo Med. Ctr., Shiprock, N.Mex., 1995-2000; ret., 2000. Clin. instr. radiology U. Miami Sch. Medicine, 1971-76, clin. asst. prof. radiology, 1984-88, clin. assoc. prof. radiology, 1988-94. Bd. dirs. Wediko Farms Children's Svcs., Carbondale, Ill. Served with M.C., USAF, 1962-64. Mem. AMA, Fla. Med. Assn., Fla., Greater Miami radiol. socs., Soc. Nuclear Medicine, Radiol. Soc. N.Am., Explorers Club. Personal E-mail: calvertb12@aol.com, billcalvert100@gmail.com.

CALVI, LAURA M., endocrinologist, educator; MD, Harvard Coll., 1995; BA in Biol. Sci., Union Coll. Diplomate Am. Bd. Internal Medicine, Am. Bd. Internal Medicine-endocrinology, diabetes and metabolism, 2000. Intern internal medicine Mass. Gen. Hosp., 1995—96, resident internal medicine, 1996—98, fellow endocrinology and metabolism, 1998—2000; program dir., endocrinology fellowship Univ. of Rochester Med. Ctr.; assoc. prof. medicine Univ. of Rochester; hosp. affiliations include Highland Hosp., Strong Meml. Hosp. Office: University of Rochester School of Medicine and Dentistry 601 Elmwood Ave Box 693 Rochester NY 14642 Office Phone: 585-275-2901.

CALVIN, ALLEN DAVID, psychologist, educator; b. St. Paul, Feb. 17, 1928; s. Carl and Zelda (Engelson) C.; m. Dorothy VerStrate, Oct. 5, 1953; children: Jamie, Kris, David, Scott. BA in Psychology cum laude, U. Minn., 1950; MA in Psychology, U. Tex., 1951, PhD in Exptl. Psychology, 1953. Instr. Mich. State U., East Lansing, 1953-55; asst. prof. Hollins Coll., 1955-59, assoc. prof., 1959-61. Dir. Britannica Ctr. for Studies in Learning and Motivation, Menlo Park, Calif., 1961; prin. investigator grant for automated tchg. fgn. langs. Carnegie Found., 1960; USPHS grantee, 1960; pres. Behavioral Rsch. Labs., 1962-74; prof., dean Sch. Edn., U. San Francisco, 1974-78; Henry Clay Hall prof. orgn. and leadership, 1978—; prof. Pacific Grad. Sch. Psychology, 1984-2001, pres., 1984-. Author textbooks. Served with USNR, 1946-47. Mem. Am. Psychol. Assn., AAAS, Sigma Xi, Psi Chi. Home: 1645 15th Ave San Francisco CA 94122-3523 Office: 405 Broadway St Redwood City CA 94063 also: Pacific Grad School Of Psychology 1791 Arastradero Rd Palo Alto CA 94304-1337 Home Phone: 415-516-1338; Office Phone: 650-843-3402, 650-421-4802. Business E-Mail: a.calvin@pgsp.edu.

CALVIN, JAMES WILLARD, thoracic and vascular surgeon; b. Oakland, Calif., Dec. 7, 1929; s. George Fairchild and Mary Norris Calvin; m. Claudine Deprez (div. 1971); m. Carrie Carman, 1973; children: Carolyne, Frances, Sophie. BA, Stanford U., 1951; MD, MChir, McGill U., 1955. Diplomate Nat. Bd. Med. Examiners, Am. Bd. Surgery, Am. Bd. Thoracic Surgery, spl. qualifications gen. vascular surgery. Lectr. in astronomy Menlo Coll., Menlo Park, Calif., 1951; intern Stanford (Calif.) U., 1955-56, resident dept. surgery, 1959-63, chief resident dept. surgery, 1963-64; group practice Sansum Med. Clinic, Santa Barbara, Calif., 1964-66; pvt. practice Thoracic and Cardiovascular Med. Group, Inc., Ventura, Calif., 1966—95. Bd. dirs. Rehab. Inst. Santa Barbara, bd. trustees; scientific adv. coun. Ramus Med. Techns., Carpinteria, Calif., 1996-01; hosp. staff Cmty. Meml. Hosp., Ventura; chief staff Cmty. Meml. Hosp., Ventura, 1994; hosp. staff County Med. Ctr., Ventura Hosp., 1959-95. Contbr. articles to profl. jours. Quality of care reviewer Medicare, 1985—95; bd. dirs. Friends of the Libr., La Quinta, Calif., 1999—. With USAF, 1956—58. NIH rsch. fellow, 1960-61. Fellow ACS (rep. hosps. of Ventura County 1980-87), Am. Coll. of Chest Physicians; mem. AAAS, AMA, Am. Cancer Soc. (Ventura county chpt., bd. dirs. 1969-72), Am. Heart Assn. (coun. on cardiovascular diseases), Am. Lung Assn., Am. Thoracic Soc., Calif. Med. Assn., Internat. Cardiovascular Soc. (N.Am. chpt.), N.Am. Soc. for Pacing and Electrophysiology, Samson Thoracic Surg., Soc. for Clin. Vascular Surgery, Soc. for Thoracic Surgeons, Soc. Vascular Surgeons, So. Calif. Vascular Surg. Soc., Ventura County Heart Assn. (pres. 1965), Ventura County Med. Soc. (pres. 1979, bd. govs. 1975-81). Home: 47-515 Via Florence La Quinta CA 92253 Office Phone: 760-771-5117. Personal E-mail: jcalvin@dc.rr.com.

CAMACHO, ANTONINO GOMES, gastroenterologist; b. Funchal, Madeira Island, Portugal, Feb. 17, 1946; s. Delfino Gomes Camacho and Isabel Jesus; m. Maria João Barradas Pires Barradas Pires; children: Ana Paula Pires Camacho, Susana Pires Camacho. MD, Faculdade Medicina de Lisboa, Lisbon, Portugal, 1972. Resident Hosp. Santa Maria, Lisbon, 1972—74; head physician Naval Command of Cape Verde, Saint Vicent, 1974—75; resident in gatroenterology Civil Hosp. Lisbon, 1975—81; gastroenterologist Naval Hosp. Lisbon, 1981—93; head physican coloproctology Hosp. Santo António dos Capuchos, Lisbon, 1993—. Cons. Infirmary Sch. Lisbon, 1971—78; dir. dept. gastroenterology Naval Hosp., Lisbon, 1986—89; chmn. XI Coloproctology Nat. Congress, 1991—; gen. sec. Coloproctology Portuguese Soc., Lisbon, 1996—2002, v.p., 2002—06, pres., 2006—. Author: Gastroenterology Clinic 2000, 2000, (video) Proctology in the Ambulatory, 1990 (Portuguese proctology society, 1991). Commander Navy, 1974—93, Portugal, Comdr. Portuguese Navy, 1986. Mem.: AAAS, European Assn. Gastroenterology, Eurpean Consil of Coloproctology, Gastroenterology French Soc., Gastroenterology Portuguese Soc. Roman Catholic. Avocation: nautical events.

CAMAÑO-PUIG, RAMON, nursing educator; b. Barcelona, July 7, 1957; Degree in Nursing, U. Valencia, Spain, 1983; PhD, Leeds Met. U., Eng., 1997. Prof. titular U. Valencia, 2008—. Avocations: gardening, woodworking. Office: Faculty Nursing Jaime Roig Valencia 46010 Spain Office Fax: 34963864310. Business E-Mail: ramon.camano@uv.es.

CAMARGO, LUIS FERNANDO, physician; b. Sao Paulo, Brazil, June 5, 1962; MD, Fed. U. Sao Paulo, 1986; PhD, U. Sao Paulo, 1999. Head, transplant infectious diseases unit U. Fed. Sao Paulo, 1986—. Mem.: Internat. Transplantation Soc. Office: Avenida Albert Einstein 627 Cons 108 Sao Paulo 05651-901 Brazil Business E-Mail: luisfucamargo@uol.com.br.

CAMERON, ANGELA R., dentist; b. Morristown, Tenn. m. Jason Cunningham; children: Andrew, Alexis. BS in Biochemistry, Furman U., Greenville, SC, MS in Biophysical Chemistry, DDS with honors, U. Tenn. Cert. dentistry, diplomate Am. Bd. Surgery. Dentist Sophisticated Smiles, Johnson City, Tenn. Author: (publ.) Smile Line. Recipient Richard L. Sullivan Award for Excellence in Dental Rsch. (Oral Cancer), 2000, ACE Award, Tenn. Dental Assn., 2003—; named one of America's Top Dentists, Consumer's Rsch. Coun. of America, 2003—10, 40 Under 40, Bus. Journal, 2006. Fellow: Dental Orgn. for Conscious Sedation; mem.: First Dist. Dental Soc., Tenn. Dental Assn., Am. Assn. of Women Dentists, Am. Acad. of Dental Sleep Medicine, ADA, Acad. of Gen. Dentistry, Am. Acad. of Cosmetic Dentistry (sustaining mem.). Avocation: reading. Office: Sophisticated Smiles 189 Corporate Dr Ste 20 Johnson City TN 37601 Office Phone: 423-928-8359. Office Fax: 423-282-6018.

CAMERON, DANIEL, internist, medical researcher; Cert. primary care physician. Former head Nat. Task Force on Aging; former asst. prof. med. geriatrics NY Coll. Med.; founder Lyme Disease Practice & Rsch. Project. Mem.: Lyme Disease Assn., Internat. Lyme & Associated Diseases Soc. (pres.). Home: 657 E Main St Ste 2 Mount Kisco NY 10549-3424 Office Phone: 914-666-4665. Office Fax: 914-666-6271. E-mail: Cameron@LymeProject.com.

CAMINS, ANTONI, pharmacologist, educator; b. Barcelona, Aug. 10, 1963; Degree in Pharmacy, U. Barcelona, 1987, PhD in Pharmacology, 1992. Prof. pharmacology U. Barcelona, 1995—. Mem.: Spanish Pharmacology & Neurosci. Soc. Avocations: football, sports. Home: Pasatge Mulet Barcelona 08006 Spain Business E-Mail: camins@ub.edu.

CAMISA, CHARLES, dermatologist, educator; BS, Cornell U.; MD, Mt. Sinai Sch. of Medicine, 1977. Diplomate Am. Bd. Dermatology, 1981, cert. clin. & lab. dermatologic immunology. Resident dermatology NYU Med. Ctr., NYC, 1978—81, chief resident skin & cancer dept.; affiliate assoc. prof. dermatology Coll. of Medicine Univ. of South Fla.; dir. dermatology divsn. Ohio State Univ.; vice-chmn. dermatology dept. Cleve. Clinic Found., dir. residency program, 1987—2001; dir. phototherapy dept. Riverchase Dermatology. Editor: (jour.) Cutis, author 40 peer-reviewed articles and textbook chpts. on skin and oral disease, editor three textboooks on psoriasis. Named one of Best Doctors in America. Achievements include discovery of Camisa disease, a rare genetic variant of Vohwinkel's Syndrome. Office: Riverchase Dermatology and Cosmetic Surgery Naples Center 1015 Crosspointe Naples FL 34110 Mailing: Riverchase Dermatology and Cosmetic Surgery Fort Myers 7331 Gladiolus Fort Myers FL 33908 Office Phone: 239-596-9075, 239-437-8810. Office Fax: 239-596-9076, 239-437-8875.

CAMMARATA, ANGELO, surgical oncologist; b. Italy, 1936; s. Giuseppe and Giuseppina (Ruggiero) C.; m. Diane M. Donner, Apr. 25, 1965; children: Joseph, Marisa, Michael, Christina. BA, Upsala Coll., 1958; MD, N.Y. Med. Coll., 1962. Diplomate Am. Bd. Surgery. Intern N.Y. Polyclin. Hosp., NYC, 1962; resident, chief resident Met. Hosp. N.Y.C., 1963-67, asst. surgeon, 1968—; resident in surgery Meml. Hosp. Cancer and Allied Diseases, NYC, 1967-68; assoc. surgeon, attending surgeon, chief breast surgery Cabrini Med. Ctr., NYC; attending surgeon Beth Israel North Hosp., NYC; instr. surgery N.Y. Med. Coll., NYC, 1968-74, clin. asst. prof. surgery, 1974—. Vis. attending surgeon Met. Hosp. Ctr., N.Y.C. Contbr. articles to profl. jours. Fellow ACS, Internat. Coll. Surgeons; mem. AMA, N.Y. Cancer Soc., N.Y. Met. Breast Cancer Group, N.Y. Acad. Scis., Meml. Alumni Soc., Alpha Club. Office: 55 E 87th St New York NY 10128-1043 Office Phone: 212-427-2131.

CAMMAROTA, MARTÍN, molecular biologist, educator; b. Ciudad Autonoma de Buenos Aires, Jan. 6, 1969; PhD in Physiology, U. Buenos Aires, 1998. Molecular biologist Sch. Exact & Natural Scis., U. Buenos Aires, 1993. Assoc. prof. Pontifical Cath. U. Rio Grande do Sul, 2004—. Office: Av Ipiranga 6690 Fl 2 Porto Alegre Rio Grande do Sul 90610-000 Brazil Office Fax: 55 51 3320 3312. Business E-Mail: mcammaro@terra.com.br.

CAMMERMEYER, MARGARETHE, retired medical/surgical nurse; b. Oslo, Mar. 24, 1942; arrived in U.S., 1951; d. Jan and Margrethe (Grimsgaard) Cammermeyer; m. Harvey H. Hawken, Aug. 1965 (div. 1980); children: Matthew Hawken, David Hawken, Andrew Hawken, Thomas Hawken; m. Diane Divelbess, Mar. 2004. BS, U. Md., 1963; MA, U. Wash., 1976, PhD, 1991. RN Wash. Staff nurse VA Hosp., Seattle, 1970-73, clin. nurse specialist in neurology, epilepsy, 1976-81; clin. nurse specialist in neuro-oncology VA Med. Ctr., San Francisco, 1981-86, clin. nurse specialist in neuroscis., nurse rschr. Tacoma, 1986-96; ret., 1996; owner AdultCare, 2006—10; mem. DACOWITS. Co-author: Neurological Assessment for Nursing Practice, 1984 (named Book of Yr. ANA), Serving in Silence, 1994; co-editor, contbg. author: Core Curriculum for Neuroscience Nursing, 1990, 1993; contbr. articles to profl. jours.; host radio Internet talk show, 1999—2001. Mem. Def. Adv. Com. Women in Svcs.; hon. bd. Svc. Mem.'s Legal Def. Network; owner Adult Family Home, mgr.; commr. Whidbey Gen. Hosp. Served to capt. US Army, 1961—68, capt. to col. USAR, 1972—88, col. Wash. N.G. US Army, 1988—97. Decorated Bronze Star; recipient Presdl. cert. for Outstanding Cmty. Achievement Vietnam Era Vets., 1979, Woman of Power award, NOW, 1993, 1998, Human Rights award, ANA, 1994, Disting. Alumna award, U. Wash. Nursing, 1995; named Woman of the Yr., Woman's Army Corps Vets. Assn., 1984, Nurse of the Yr., VA, 1985. Home and Office: 4632 Tompkins Rd Langley WA 98260-9695 Office Phone: 360-221-5882. Business E-Mail: grethe@cammermeyer.com.

CAMP, SHARON L., reproductive health organization administrator; B. with honors, Pomona Coll.; MA, PhD, Johns Hopkins U. Sr. v.p. Population Action Internat., 1975—93; coord. Internat. Consortium for Emergency Contraception, 1993—98; pres., CEO Women's Capital Corp., 1998—2003, Guttmacher Inst., NYC, 2003—. Sr. lectr. Columbia U. Mailman Sch. Pub. Health; former chair Family Health Internat., Nat. Coun. Internat. Health, Internat. Ctr. Rsch. on Women; founding chair Reproductive Health Technologiess Project; former dir. Nat. Family Planning & Reproductive Health Assn., AVSC Internat. (name changed to EngenderHealth, 2001), Mgmt. Sciences for Health, Population Action Internat. Contbr. articles to profl. jours. Office: Guttmacher Institute Inc 125 Maiden Ln Frnt 7 New York NY 10038-4912 also: 1301 Connecticut Avenue NW, Ste 700 Washington DC 20036 Office Phone: 212-248-1111. Office Fax: 212-248-1951. *

CAMPAGNOLO, MARY FRANCES, physician; b. Teaneck, NJ, 1956; MD, George Washington U., 1982; MBA, Rutgers U., Camden, NJ, 2009. Diplomate with cert. added qualification in geriat. Am. Bd. Family Medicine. Intern Overlook Hosp., Summit, NJ, 1982—83, resident in family practice, 1983—85; staff physician Virtua-Meml. Hosp. of Burlington County, Mt. Holly, NJ, 1987—; chief dept. family medicine Virtua-Meml. Hosp. Burlington County, 1993—. Study commr. Gov. Corzine's NJ Disease Mgmt., 2008—10; with NJ Mandated State Health Benefits Commn., 2010—. Recipient Virtua Health Star award, 2006, named an Outstanding Woman of Burlington County, 2006; named one of Top Drs. 2003, N.J. Monthly Mag., Del. Valley Consumer, Top Drs. for Women, N.J. Living, Top Drs., Phila. Mag., 2004, South Jersey Mag., 2005, 2006, NJ Mag., 2010. Mem.: AMA, Am. Med. Women's Assn., Burlington County Med. Soc., Med. Soc. NJ (trustee 2003—, 2nd v.p. 2009—10, 1st v.p. 2010—), Am. Acad. Family Physicians (commn. quality 2003—07, alt. del. 2004—), NJ Acad. Family Physicians (past pres., chair. bd. 2000—01, Lifetime Achievement Chair award 2005). Office: Virtua-Lumberton Family Physicians Independence Plaza 1561 Rte 38 Ste 6 Lumberton NJ 08048 Office Phone: 609-267-2100. Business E-Mail: mcampagnolo@virtua.org.

CAMPANELLI, RICHARD M., former federal agency administrator; m. Shannon Campanelli; 3 children. BS in Economics, U. Va., JD. Trial atty. spl. litig. sect. of civil right divsn. US Dept. Justice, 1983—86; mem. S. Africa Working Group US Dept. State, 1986—87, sr. spl. asst. to atty. gen., 1987—89; atty. Gammon & Grange, PC, McLean, Va., 1989—2002; dir. Office for Civil Rights US Dept. Health and Human Services, Washington, 2002—05, counselor to the Sec., 2005—09. Past adj. prof. George Mason U.

CAMPANILE, GIUSEPPE, medical educator; b. Naples, Italy, Oct. 22, 1960; DVM, U. Naples, Federico, 1985, PhD in Animal Sci., 1990. Prof., dept. animal sci. U. Studies Naples, Federico, 2010—. Office: via F Delpino 1 Naples Campania 80137 Italy Business E-Mail: giucampa@unina.it.

CAMPAZZI, EARL JAMES, physician; b. NYC, Mar. 25, 1962; s. Earl James and Betty Elvira (Carlson) C. BA in Natural Sci., Johns Hopkins U., 1984, M of Health Sci., Immunology and Infectious Disease, 1986, M of Pub. Health, Health Care Fin. and Mgmt., 1991; MD, U. Pitts., 1989; postgrad. in MBA program, Duke U., 1999. Diplomate Am. Bd. Preventive Medicine. Resident physician in internal medicine Mercy Hosp. Pitts., 1989-90; resident in preventive medicine sch. hygiene and pub. health Johns Hopkins U., Balt., 1990-92, chief resident, 1992-93; pres. Campazzi & Assocs., Inc., Balt., 1993—. Cons. managed care planning sch. medicine Johns Hopkins U., 1992-93; cons. occupl. health Cons. Epidemiology and Occupl. Health, Washington, 1992-93; occupl. medicine physician Bethlehem Steel, Balt., 1992-95; treas. Md. Coll. Occupl. and Environ. Medicine; occupl. medicine physician CMC Occupl. Health, Balt., 1993-95; site med. dir. Worksite Ptnrs., Charleston, S.C., 1996-97. Scholar Mercyhurst Coll., scholar N.Y.C. Police Dept. Lt.'s Assn. Mem. AMA, APHA, Am. Coll. Physician Execs., Am. Coll.

Occupl. and Environ. Medicine, Johns Hopkins U. Alumni Coun. (exec. com.), Johns Hopkins U. Sch. Pub. Health Soc. Alumni (treas.), Am. Mensa, Ltd. Office: Campazzi & Assocs Inc 5973 SE Oakmont Pl Stuart FL 34997-8637 *

CAMPBELL, ALLAN MCCULLOCH, bacteriology educator; b. Berkeley, Calif., Apr. 27, 1929; s. Lindsay and Virginia Margaret (Henning) C.; m. Alice del Campillo, Sept. 5, 1958; children—Wendy, Joseph. BS in Chemistry, U. Calif., Berkeley, 1950; MS in Bacteriology, U. Ill., 1951; PhD, 1953; PhD (hon.), U. Chgo., 1978, U. Rochester, 1981. Instr. bacteriology U. Mich., 1953-57; research asso. Carnegie Inst., Cold Spring Harbor, NY, 1957-58; asst. prof. biology U. Rochester, NY, 1958-61, assoc. prof. NY, 1961-63, prof. NY, 1963-68; prof. biol. sci. Stanford U., Calif., 1968—2010, prof. biol. emeritus, 2010—, Barbara Kimball Browning prof. humanities and sciences Calif., 1992—. Author: Episomes, 1969; co-author: General Virology, 1978; editor Gene, 1980-90, mem. editl. bd., 1990—; assoc. editor Virology, 1963-69; assoc. editor Ann. Rev. Genetics, 1969-84, editor, 1984—; spl. editor Evolution, 1985-88; editl. bd. Jour. Bacteriology, 1966-72, Jour. Virology, 1967-75, New Biologist, 1989-92. Served with AUS, 1953-55. Recipient Research Career award USPHS, 1962-68 Mem. NAS, Am. Soc. Microbiology (Abbott-ASM Lifetime Achievement award 2004), Soc. Am. Naturalists, Genetics Soc. Am.; fellow AAAS, Am. Acad. Microbiology, Am. Acad. Arts and Scis. Democrat. Home: 947 Mears Ct Stanford CA 94305-1041 Office: Stanford University Herrin Labs RM 285B Mail Code 5020 Dept Biol Stanford CA 94305-5020 Home Phone: 650-493-6153. Business E-Mail: AMC@stanford.edu.

CAMPBELL, ANDREW C., facial plastic surgeon; m. Heidi Campbell; 4 children. MD, Indiana U. Diplomate Am. Bd. Facial Plastic Surgery, Am. Bd. Otolaryngology. Intern in gen. surgery Univ. Cin., resident in otolaryngology/head and neck surgery; med. dir. Quintessa Med. Spa, Sheboygan, Wis.; pvt. practice Campbell Facial Plastic Surgery. Author: various med. publs. and book chapters in the field of plastic surgery. Active Face to Face. Recipient Altar Peerless Meml. award, Best Med. Spa in Sheboygan County, Best of Sheboygan award, US Commerce Assn. Mem.: Sheboygan County Med. Soc. (pres.), Am. Acad. of Facial Plastic and Reconstructive Surgery. Avocations: fishing, wakeboarding, biking, auto racing, snowboarding, skiing, travel, fine dining, collecting wine. Office: Campbell Facial Plastic Surgery Prevea Health Center 1411 N Taylor Dr Sheboygan WI 53081 Office Phone: 888-409-3223.

CAMPBELL, ANDREW WILLIAM, immunotoxicology physician; b. Beirut, Apr. 3, 1948; s. William Alexander and Gisela (Landes) C.; children: Denia Giselle, Michelle Elise, Colin Alexander, Ian William. BA in Pre-med., Psychology, Franklin Piere Coll., Rindge, NH, 1970; MD, U. Autonoma de Guadalajara, Mex., 1974. Diplomate Am. Bd. Family Practice, Am. Bd. Forensic Examiners, Am. Bd. Forensic Medicine. Intern Pediat. Hosp. Infantil, Ob-gyn., Clin. Santa Monica, Guadalajara, Mex., 1974-75, Pub. Health Dept., Guadalajara, Mex., 1975-76; resident gen. surgery Orlando (Fla.) Regional Med. Ctr., 1977-78; resident family practice Med. Coll. Ga., Augusta, 1978-81; pvt. practice family physician Two Physician Practice, Sarasota, Fla., 1981, with former chief surgeon Eisenhower Med. Ctr., Augusta, Ga.; pvt. practice Augusta, Wrens and Louisvlle, Ga., 1983-84, Houston, 1985—; med. dir. Med. Ctr. for Immune and Toxic Disorders, Houston, 1993—. Staff mem. Meml. City Med. Ctr., Spring Branch Med. Ctr.; chmn. dept. family practice Sam Houston Meml. Hosp., Houston, 1987, chmn. credentials com., 88, exec. com., 1987—89; lectr. and spkr. at Artificial Implants and Toxic Exposure Symposia; faculty U. Tex. Sch. Medicine, 1993—98; cons., presenter in field; editor-in-chief Alternative Therapies in Health & Medicine; editl. bd. mem. Integrative Medicine: A Clinician's Jour. Author (with others): Health Effects of Toxic Chemicals, 1994, Textbook of Nephrology (2 vols.), 1995; co-editor: Internat. Jour. Occupl. Medicine and Toxicology, 1992—95; mem. editl. bd.: Toxicology and Indsl. Health, 1994—96; contbr. articles to profl. jours., chapters to books. Founder Clinic for the Indigent, St. John Vianney Ch., Houston, 1987; bd. trustees Sam Houston Meml. Hosp., 1987-93. Recipient Consumer's Choice award Am. Nurses in Bus. Assn., Houston, 1994. Fellow: Am. Acad. Family Physicians; mem.: Am. Bd. Forensic Examiners, Am. Assn. Physicians & Surgeons. Republican. Avocation: golf. Office: 9595 Six Pines Dr Ste 8210 The Woodlands TX 77380 Business E-Mail: answerwellness@gmail.com.

CAMPBELL, DAVID GRAHAM, orthopaedic surgeon; b. Adelaide, South Australia, Australia, Feb. 17, 1962; s. Graham Thomas Campbell and Merlene May Johnston; m. Melissa Elizabeth Nichols, May 19, 1990; children: Stephanie Charlotte, Madeleine Elizabeth, William Edward. B Medicine, BS, Flinders U., South Australia, 1986; PhD, U. Adelaide, 1996. Fracs Royal Australasian Coll. of Surgeons, 1996, Fellow Australian Orthopaedic Assn., 1999. Registrar St. Georges and SW Thames, London, 1989; fellow U. BC, Vancouver, Canada, 1997; sr. vis. med. officer, sr. lectr. Flinders Med. Ctr. and Flinders U., Adelaide, 1997—; cons. orthopaedic surgeon Wakefield Orthop. Clinic, Adelaide, 1997—. Dir. Bone and Soft Tissue Bank, Adelaide, 2000—; presenter in field. Contbr. articles to profl. jours. Mem. invection control com. Wakefield Hosp., Adelaide, 1990—; mem. adv. com. Glenelg Cmty. Hosp., Adelaide, 1990—. Recipient Clin. Rsch. award, Queen Elizabeth Hosp. Med. Staff Soc., 1992, Surg. Rsch. Soc. Inaugural prize, Australian Orthopaedic Registrars Assn., 1993, Best Presentation Fellowship Trainees award, Queen Elizabeth Hosp. Med. Staff Soc., 1994, Nimmo Rsch. prize, Royal Adelaide Hosp. Med. Staff Soc. Inc., 1994, Evelyn Hamilton award, Australian Orthop. Assn., 2005; named Best Trainee in Divsn. of Surgery, Queen Elizabeth Hosp., 2001; scholar, Australian Dept. Edn. and Rsch., 1992; Found. Cockburn Rsch. scholar, Royal Australasian Coll. Surgeons, 1992, travel grantee, Surg. Rsch. Soc. Australia, 1994, Mark Jolly scholarship, Royal Adelaide Hosp., 1997, rsch. grantee, Nat. Med. and Rsch. Coun., 2006. Fellow: Royal Australasian Coll. Surgeons (state dir. fellowship and tng., sci. sec. 2004—07); mem.: Australian Med. Assn., Arthroplasty Soc. Australia. Achievements include design of uni compartmental knee replacement designer. Office: Wakefield Orthopaedic Clinic 270 Wakefield St Adelaide 5000 Australia Home: 44 Pier St 5045 Glenelg SA Australia Home Phone: (08) 8376 5705; Office Phone: (08) 8236 4196. Office Fax: (08) 8236 4180. Personal E-mail: hipknee@tpg.com.au. Business E-Mail: dcampbell@woc.com.au.

CAMPBELL, DEBORAH E., obstetrician, medical educator; Grad., State U. of NY, 1978. Diplomate Am. Bd. Pediatrics, Am. Bd. Pediatrics-neonatal-perinatal medicine. Resident of pediat. Montefiore Med. Ctr., Bronx, 1979—81, fellow of nenatal-perinatal medicine, 1981—83; prof. clin. pediat. Albert Einstein Coll. of Medicine, chief sect. of neonatology dept of pediat., assoc. prof. of clin. obstetrics and gynecology and women's health; co-chair Albert Einstein Coll. of Medicine- Montefiore Med. Ctr. Rvw. Perinatal Ctr.; dir. divsn of neonatolgy Children's Hosp. at Montefiore; program dir. fellowship Neonatal Perinatal Medicine. Mem.: NYC and Bronx Infant Mortality Rvw. Coms., NICU Proj. Adv. Group, Am. Acad. of Pediat. Office: Jack D. Weiler Hospital 1825 Eastchester Rd Room 725 Bronx NY 10461 Office Phone: 718-904-4105. Office Fax: 718-904-2659.

CAMPBELL, EDWARD WALLACE, nutritionist; b. Elizabeth, NJ, June 29, 1939; s. Edward Wallace Sr. and Dorothy Mae (Fairchild) C.; m. Phyllis A. Vecere, Sept. 27, 1959 (div. 1985); children: Diane Theresa, Christina Marie. PhD, Am. Coll., 1988; DLitt, Wellington U., 1990; MD, Open Internat. U., 1991, DSc, 1992; diploma, Lyons Med. Lab. Sch. Diplomate Internat. Coll. Acupuncture, Am. Coll. Manipulation and Nutrition, Inst. for Human Biomechanics, Am. Bd. Nutrition and Clin. Nutrition; cert. wellness counselor; Australian postgrad. cert. in acupuncture. Pvt. practice, 1974-94; dean of students Nat. Nutrition Inst., Oak Park, Ill., 1988-92; exec. dir. Am. Bd. Nutritional and Naturopathic Cert., Toms River, NJ, 1989-92; dir. R & D Vitagenics Rsch., Brick, NJ, 1990-95; dir. rsch. World AIDS Rsch. Inc., 1995—2006; CEO www.Nutriprotocols.com, 2006—07; v.p. vitacroft.com, 2007—. Spkr. Nat. Health Fedn., 1987-93; prof. Open Internat. U. Author: Orthomolecular Protocol for Morbid Obesity with Adjunctive Congestive Heart Failure, 1987, Orthomolecular Protocols for the Physician, 1988, The Etiology of Hyperlipoproteinemia, 1990, Nutritional Management of Peripheral Vascular Diseases, 1991; contbg. editor: Am. Nutrition Cons. Assn. Jour., 1988-93. Assoc. mem. Am. Mus. Nat. History; mem. Nat. Arbor Day Found., Rep. Nat. Com., Washington, 1980—; del. Rep. Party Platform Planning Com., Washington 1991-92, Presdl. Trust, Washington, 1992; campaign trustee Rep. Presdl. Task Force, Washington, 1987, 93. Fellow Found. Complementary Medicine, Commonwealth (U.K.) Inst. Natural Medicine, Medicina Alternativa Sci. Soc., The Homeopathic Found.; mem. Internat. Assn. Holistic Health and Medicine, Am. Nutrition Cons. Assn., Nat. Health Fedn., Am. Assn. of Nutritional Cons., Wilson Ctr. Assocs., Homeopathy and Homotoxicology Symposium, Va. Sheriffs Inst., Law Enforcement Alliance Am., Am. Legion, Senators Club, Clan Campbell Soc. Methodist. Avocations: hunting, fishing, chess, numismatism. Personal E-mail: dr@vitacroft.com.

CAMPBELL, FRANCES ALEXANDER, psychologist; b. Greensboro, NC, Feb. 3, 1933; d. Norman and Nancy Miriam (Spoon) Alexander; m. Bobby Jack Campbell, Aug. 24, 1957; children: Carol Stuart, John William. BA, U. N.C., Womans Coll., 1955; MA, U. N.C., 1958, PhD, 1963. Lic. psychologist, N.C. Asst. prof. Rosary Hill Coll., Williamsville, NY, 1964—65; asst. prof., rsch. assoc. U. N.C. Sch. Medicine, Chapel Hill, 1968—71; rsch. assoc. Child Devel. Inst. U. N.C., Chapel Hill, 1972—78, investigator, 1975—80, coord. psychol. assessment, 1980—90, sr. investigator, 1990—93, fellow, 1994—99, sr. scientist, 2000—. Chmn. Acad. Affairs Internal Rev. Bd. on Human Subjects U. N.C., 1993—97; lectr. cons. rschr., China, India, Ireland, South Africa. Keynote spkr. Spearman Conf., Sydney, 2001; contbr. articles to profl. jours. Mem. bd. Brady Corp. Fedn. Recipient Alumni Disting. Svc. award, UNC-Greensboro, 2007. Fellow Am. Orthopsychiat. Assn.; mem. APA, Soc. Rsch. Child Devel., Soc. Rsch. Adolescence, Soc. Rsch. Adult Devel., Brady Corp. Found. (bd. mem.) Office: UNC Child Devel Inst Cb # 8180 Chapel Hill NC 27599-0001

CAMPBELL, GILBERT SADLER, surgeon, educator; b. Toronto, Ont., Can., Jan. 4, 1924; s. Gilbert S. and Ellen (Thorson) Campbell; m. Dorothy Jean Nugent, Sept. 18, 1947 (div. 1960); children: Kathryn Elln, Rebecca Sadler, Thomas Kim, William Riley; m. Joan Louise Hancock, Sept. 28, 1961; children: Susan Muffin, John Gilbert. Student, Hampden-Sydney Coll., Va., 1939-40; BA, U. Va., Charlottesville, 1943, MD, 1946; MS, U. Minn., Mpls., 1949, PhD, 1954. Intern U. Minn. Hosps., Mpls., 1946-47, tchg. asst., 1947-49, researcher Am. Cancer Soc., 1951-53, sr. surgery resident, 1953-54; instr. physiology U. Minn., Mpls., 1948-49, instr. surgery, 1954-55, asst. prof., 1955-58; prof. surgery U. Okla., Oklahoma City, 1958-65; prof. surgery and thoracic surgery U. Okla. Med. Ctr., Oklahoma City, 1958-65; prof. surgery, chief thoracic surgery U. Ark. for Med. Scis., Little Rock, 1965-90; cons. surgery Little Rock VA Hosp, 1965-90, Ark. Children's Hosp., Little Rock, 1973-90; mem. courtesy staff Ark. Bapt. Med. Ctr., Little Rock, 1972-90; prof. emeritus, 1990—. Contbr. articles in field to med. jours. Served to capt. US Army, 1949-51. Decorated Purple Heart, Bronze Star with oak leaf cluster, Silver Star with oak leaf cluster US Army; Mary R. Markle scholar, 1954-59; recipient Horsley prize U. Va., 1954; named Surgery Alumnus of Yr. U. Minn., 1983; named to U. Ark. Medicine Hall of Fame. Mem. Am. Assn. Thoracic Surgery, AMA (ho. of dels. 1976-82), Am. Physiol. Soc., Am. Surg. Assn., Halsted Soc. (pres. 1978), Internat. Cardiovascular Soc. (v.p. N. Am. Chpt. 1973), Societe Internationale de Chirurgie, Soc. Thoracic Surgeons, Soc. Univ. Surgeons, Soc. Vascular Surgery, So. Surg. Assn. (1st v.p. 1981), Western Surg. Assn., S.W. Surg. Congress (pres. 1980), Raven Soc., Alpha Omega Alpha Home: 66 River Ridge Rd Little Rock AR 72227-1526

CAMPBELL, JEFFREY WAKELING, neurosurgeon; b. Bryn Mawr, Pa., Apr. 8, 1965; s. Carl Merritt, Jr. and Janet Allen Campbell; m. Kathy Fisher Campbell, Apr. 5, 1997; children: Eleanor, Edmund. AB, Princeton U., NJ, 1987; MD, Jefferson Med. Coll., Phila., 1991. Intern gen. surgery U. Pitts., 1991—92, resident neurosurgery, 1992—98; fellow in pediatric neurosurgery Children's Hosp., Boston, 1998—99; dir. pediatric neurosurgery Strong Children's Hosp., Rochester, NY, 1999—2000, Med. U. S.C. Children's Hosp., Charleston, 2000—04; chief divsn. neurosurgery A.I. duPont Hosp. for Children, Wilmington, Del., 2004—. Office: A I duPont Hosp for Children 1600 Rockland Rd Wilmington DE 19803 Office Phone: 302-651-5993. Business E-Mail: jcampbel@nemours.org.

CAMPBELL, JOHN R., psychology professor; PhD, U. Minn., 1964. Prof. dept. psychology U. Minn., Mpls., chmn. dept. psychology. Contbr. articles to profl. jours. Office: Psychology Dept Univ Minn N478 Elliott Hall 75 East River Rd Minneapolis MN 55455-0344 Office Phone: 612-625-9351. Office Fax: 612-625-2079. E-mail: campb006@umn.edu.

CAMPBELL, JOHN RICHARD, pediatric surgeon; b. Pratt, Kans., Jan. 16, 1932; s. John Ross and Laura (Harkrader) C.; m. Susan Charlotte Baker, June 9, 1962; children: Kathryn, John Richard, George Ridgway. BA, U. Kans., 1954, MD, 1958. Diplomate Am. Bd. Surgery with cert. of spl. qualifications in pediatric surgery. Rotating intern Hosp. U. Pa., 1958-59; resident in gen. surgery U. Kans. Hosp., 1959-63; resident in pediatric surgery Children's Hosp. of Phila., 1965-67; asst. instr. U. Pa. Med. Sch., 1965-67; mem. faculty U. Oreg. Health Scis. Ctr., Portland, 1967—, prof. surgery emeritus, 2000, prof. surgery and pediatrics emeritus, 2000—, chief pediatric surgery, prof. emeritus surgery and pediats., 2000—; surgeon-in-chief Doernbecher Children's Hosp., Portland, 1967-99. Cons. VA, Shriners Crippled Children's hosps., Alaska Native Med. Ctr., Anchorage. Served to lt. comdr. M.C. USNR, 1963-65. Mem. A.C.S., Soc. Acad. Surgeons, Am. Acad. Pediatrics, Am. Pediatric Surg. Assn., Pacific Assn. Pediatric Surgeons, North Pacific Pediatric Soc., North Pacific Surg. Assn., Pacific Coast Surg. Assn., Portland Acad. Pediatrics, Portland Surg. Soc. Presbyterian. Office: Oreg Health Scis Univ 745 SW Gaines St # Cdw7 Portland OR 97239-2901 Office Phone: 503-494-7764. Business E-Mail: campbell@ohsu.edu.

CAMPBELL, JOHN ROY, animal science professor, academic administrator; b. Goodman, Mo., June 14, 1933; s. Carl J. and Helen (Nicoletti) C.; m. Eunice Vieten, Aug. 7, 1954; children: Karen L., Kathy L., Keith L. BS, U. Mo., 1955; MS, U. Mo., Columbia, 1956, PhD, 1960, DSc (hon.), 2005. Instr. dairy sci. U. Mo., Columbia, 1960-61, asst. prof., 1961-65, assoc. prof., 1965-68, prof., from 1968; assoc. dean, dir. resident instrn. Coll. Agr. U. Ill., Urbana-Champaign, 1977-83, dean Coll. Agr. Urbana, 1983-88; pres. Okla. State U., Stillwater, 1988-93. Author (with J.F. Lasley): The Science of Animals That Serve Mankind, 1969, The Science of Animals That Serve Humanity, 2nd edit., 1975, 3rd edit., 1985; author: In Touch with Students, 1972; author: (with R.T. Marshall) The Science of Providing Milk for Man, 1975; author: Reclaiming A Lost Heritage...Land-Grant and Other Higher Education Initiatives for the Twenty-First Century, 1998, Dry Rot in the Ivory Tower, 2000; author: (with M.D. Kenealy and K.L. Campbell) Animal Sciences...The Biology, Care and Production of Domestic Animals, 2004, rev. edit., 2010; author: (with K.L. Campbell) Companion Animals...Their Biology, Care, Health and Management, 2005, 2nd edit., 2009. Recipient Superior Tchg. award Gamma Sigma Delta, 1967, Internat. award for disting. svc. to agr., 1985, Disting. Svc. award Coll. Osteo. Medicine Okla. State U., 1992. Fellow Am. Dairy Sci. Assn. (dir. 1975-78, 80-86, pres. 1980-81, Ralston Purina Disting. Tchg. award 1973, Award of Honor 1987); mem. Nat. Assn. Coll. Tchrs. Agr. (Ensminger Interstate Disting. Tchr. award 1973, Teaching fellow 1973, Disting. Educator award 1990, Nat. Assn. State and Univ. and Land-Grant Colls. (commns. on home econs. and vet. medicine, com. on water resources, coun. of presidents), Okla. Futures, Nat. Coll. Naturopathic Med-.(mem. bd. dirs. 1997-), Gamma Sigma Delta. Office: Okla State U 201AS Stillwater OK 74078-0001 Personal E-mail: jrcampbell.educator@gmail.com. Business E-Mail: benita.bale@okstate.edu.

CAMPBELL, JUDY, medical/surgical nurse, educator; b. Kosciusko, Miss., Jan. 19, 1957; d. Wilbur Aaron and Linda Ann McGee; m. David Lee Campbell, Aug. 28, 1979; children: Jeremiah, Kari. AA, Holmes Jr. Coll., Goodman, Miss., 1977; BSN, U. So. Miss., Hattiesburg, 1979; MSN, U. Fla., Gainesville, 1995, PhD, 2008. RN, Fla., Nebr., cert. ARNP, Fla. Staff nurse Midlands Community Hosp., Papillion, Nebr., 1979-82; nurse supr., insvc., orientation coord. Titusville Nursing and Convalescent Ctr., Fla., 1983-85; staff nurse, ob-gyn unit Wuesthoff Meml. Hosp., Rockledge, Fla., 1985-88; asst. dir. nursing svc. Vista Manor Care Ctr., Titusville, 1988-90; staff nurse, orthopedic unit Wuesthoff Meml. Hosp., Rockledge, 1990-92; asst. prof. Brevard Cmty. Coll., Cocoa, Fla., 1990—2004. Assoc. degree nursing coord., 1999—2001; rsch. asst. U. Fla., 2004—08; asst. prof. Remington Coll. Nursing, Orlando, Fla., 2009—10. Vol. nurse sch. clinic. Recipient ROTC scholarship, Brevard Commty. Coll. Peer Awd., Brevard Commty. Coll. Svc. Learning Awd.,Brevard Cmty. Coll., 2000; Disting. Ed. Finalist, BCC Vol. Incentive Performance Award, 2001 (College-wide) and 2003 (Div.); Bcc Nursing Program recieved US Dept. of Ed. Career & Tech. Consortium designation as an Exemplary program, 2001; BCC Leadership Challenge Award & Extended Profl. Leave, 1993-1995; U. Fla. Alumni Fellowship; Hartford Bldg. Acad. Geriatric Nursing Capacity Scholarship, 2006-2008; Outstanding Grad. Rsch. award, UF Coll. Nursing, 2008, Lois Knowles Gerontol. Nursing award, 2009. Mem.: ANA, So. Nursing Rsch. Soc., Sigma Phi Omega (gerontology honor soc. 2005—09), Gerontol. Soc. Am., Fla. Nurses Assn. (Heather Scaglione Award 2001, Excellence in Tchg. award 2002), Nat. Scholars Honor Soc. Acad. Achievement, Sigma Theta Tau, Phi Theta Kappa. Personal E-mail: judy@marweb.com.

CAMPBELL, KEITH H. S., cell biologist, embryologist, educator; b. Eng., 1954; BS in Microbiology with honors, U. London; DPhil, U. Sussex. With Roslin Inst., 1991—97; head embryology PPL Therapeutics, 1997—99; prof. animal devel., Sch. Bioscis. U. Nottingham, 1999—. Mem. editl. bd.: Cloning and Stem Cells, Reproduction; reviewer papers in field; contbr. scientific papers to profl. publs. Co-recipient Shaw prize in life sci. and medicine, 2008. Achievements include with Ian Wilmut, the birth of Megan and Morag, two Welsh mountain sheep cloned from differentiated embryo cells in 1995; with Ian Wilmut, the production of a mammal cloned from adult cells, the lamb named Dolly in 1996; with Ian Wilmut, creating Polly, a sheep cloned from fetal skin cells that had been genetically altered to contain a human gene in 1997. Office: U Nottingham Sch Bioscis Rm 210 1st Fl South Lab Sutton LE12 5 England Office Phone: 44 (0) 115 951 6298. Office Fax: 44 (0) 115 951 6302. Business E-Mail: keith.campbell@nottingham.ac.uk.

CAMPBELL, LINZY LEON, molecular biology researcher, educator; b. Panhandle, Tex., Feb. 10, 1927; s. Linzy Leon and Eula Irene (McSpadden) C.; m. Alice P. Dauksa, Feb. 7, 1953. BA in Bacteriology and Chemistry, U. Tex., 1949, MA, 1950, PhD, 1952. Rsch. scientist U. Tex., 1947—51; predoctoral rsch. fellow NIH, 1951—52; postdoctoral rsch. fellow Nat. Microbiol. Inst., U. Calif. Berkeley, 1952—54; asst. prof., then assoc. prof. Wash. State U., 1954—59; assoc. prof. We. Res. U. Sch. Medicine, 1959—62; sr. rsch. fellow USPHS, 1959—62; prof. microbiology U. Ill. Urbana, 1962—72, head dept., 1963—71, dir. Sch. Life Scis., 1971—72; prof. microbiology, provost and v.p. acad. affairs U. Del., Newark, 1972—88, rsch. prof. molecular bioscis., 1988—89, Hugh M. Morris rsch. prof. molecular bioscis., 1989—. Editorial bd.: Jour. Bacteriology, 1961-65; editor, 1964-65, editor-in-chief, 1965-77; Contbr. articles to profl. jours. Served with USNR, 1944-46. Fellow AAAS; mem. Am. Soc. Microbiology (chmn. publ. bd. 1965-80, councilor at large 1962-64, v.p. 1972-73, pres. 1973-74), Am. Soc. Biochemistry and Molecular Biology. Office: U Delaware Dept Biology 400 Morris Library Newark DE 19717 Business E-Mail: campbell@udel.edu.

CAMPBELL, LYNDA JANE, cytogeneticist; b. Melbourne, Australia, Mar. 5, 1955; MBBS, U. Melbourne, 1977. Dir. Victorian Cancer Cytogenetics Svc. St. Vincent's Hosp. Melbourne, 1992—. Office: St Vincents Hosp Melbourne 41 Victoria Parade Fitzroy Victoria 3065 Australia Office Fax: 61392884155. Business E-Mail: lynda.campbell@svhm.org.au.

CAMPBELL, MAGDA, retired child psychiatrist, researcher, educator; b. Subotica, Yugoslavia, Jan. 22, 1928; arrived in U.S., 1957; d. Bela and Marija (Lipoženčic) Pijuković; m. Francis P. Campbell, July 2, 1961; children: Maria D., John F. MD, U. Belgrade, Yugoslavia, 1953. Diplomate in psychiatry and child psychiatry Am. Bd. Psychiatry and Neurology. From tchg. asst. to prof. psychiatry NYU, NYC, 1963-95, prof. emeritus, 1995—; dir. divsn. child adolescent psychiatry, 1987-91; dir. tng. edn., 1990—91; ret., 1995. Co-author: Child and Adolescent Psychopharmacology, 1985, Clinical Evaluation of Psychotropic Drugs for Psychiatric Disorders, 1993; contbr. over 225 articles to profl. jours., chpts. to books. Grantee NIMH, 1973-95. Fellow: Am. Coll. Neuropsychopharmacology (life; emeritus), Am. Acad. Child Adolescent Psychiatry (life), Am. Psychiatric Assn. (life). Office: NYU Med Ctr Dept Psychiatry 550 1st Ave New York NY 10016

CAMPBELL, MICHAEL C., medical researcher; b. Can., July 22, 1976; PhD, Columbia U., 2007. Postdoc. rschr. U. Pa., 2007—. Mem.: Am. Soc. Human Genetics. Office: 415 Curie Blvd Philadelphia PA 19104 Business E-Mail: mcam@mail.med.upenn.edu.

CAMPBELL, REGINNA GLADYS, medical/surgical nurse; b. Dover, NJ, Oct. 16, 1952; d. Reginal C. and Ruth E. Steele; m. Danny Kay Campbell, June 29, 1974 (div. Sept. 2004); children: Catherine, David. Diploma in nursing, St. Joseph Hosp. Sch. Nursing, 1977; BSN, Ind. Wesleyan U., 2006. Cert. post anesthesia nurse. Staff nurse, charge nurse ICU/critical care unit Cameron Hosp., Angola, Ind., 1977—84; staff nurse post anesthesia care unit Cmty. Health Ctr. Branch County, Coldwater, Mich., 1984—2005, dir. surg./pediat., 2005—09; travel nurse pediat. post anesthesia Fortus Group, 2009. 1st lt. Nurse Corp Res. US Army, 1991—2002, capt. Nurse Corp Res. US Army, 2003—04, Kuwait/Iraq, maj. Army Nurse Corp US Army, 2007. Decorated Army Achievement award, Army Accrediation medal. Mem.: Soc. Pediatric Nurse, Med. Surgical Assn., Ind. Soc. Perianesthesia Nurses (v.p 2000—01, pres.-elect 2001—02, maj. ICU head nurse 2007—), Am. Soc. Perianesthesia Nurses (membership com. 2001—02), Res. Officer Assn., Boy Scouts Am. (charter rep. 1995—2003), Angola Bus. and Profl. Women. Republican. Methodist. Home Fax: 908-673-1178. Personal E-mail: rcamp@dmei.net.

CAMPBELL, ROBBI ELIZABETH MARGARET, counselor, educator; b. Ballymoney, Northern Ireland, May 31, 1952; d. Robert and Joan Elizabeth (Rea) C.; m. Mostafa Kamel Ali El-Sayed, Mar. 17, 1980 (div. 1988); 1 child, Sara; m. Stuart Norman Kipling, Feb., 14, 2004. BA in Fine Arts with honors, Ulster Coll. Art & Design, Belfast, No. Ireland, 1975; diploma in teaching English fgn. lang., Chichester Coll., Eng., 1983; postgrad. diploma in counselling, Brighton U., Eng., 1990; MA in Counselling Psychology, Sussex U., Eng., 1993. Accredited counselor U.K. Register of Counselors; sr. accredited counsellor, Brit. Assn. Counselling and Psychotherapy. Graphic design asst., Saintfield, No. Ireland, 1973-76, mother's helper, nanny Pink Floyd, 1976-78, The King's Singers, Monty Python Films, 1979; tchr. English as fgn. lang. various locations, 1978-90; tchr. English and life skills to Vietnamese refugees, 1982-83; women's counselor Brighton Mosque, Eng., 1983-85; freelance counselor, cons. supr. Worthing, Eng., 1988—; dir. Arun Counselling Ctr., 2000—02. Counseling project mgr. Sussex Eye Hosp., Brighton, 1990—92; vis. lectr. various orgns., England, 1991—; lectr. in counseling Crawley (Eng.) Coll., 1992—93, sr. tutor, course dir. diploma in therapeutic counseling, 1993—99; external examiner Fareham Coll., 1997—2001; complaints mediator West Kent Coll., 1998—2002; assoc. counselor Ind. Counseling and Adv. Svcs., various locations, England, 1993—99; Corecare affiliate supr. and counsellor, 1994—; writer, checker Readers Digest, London, 1994—95; reader, reviewer Routledge Ltd., London, 1994—, Sage Publs., Ltd., 2000—; assoc. counselor ICAS, 1999—, Exec. Coach, 2003—; dir. Counselling-Cons.com, 2003—05, Coaching-consultants.com, company-consultants.com, 2004—05. Co-editor: European Jour. of Psychotherapy Counselling and Health, 1996—98; mem. editl. bd.: Psychotherapy, Counselling and Health, 1999—2003; contbr. articles to profl. jours. Fellow Brit. Assn. for Counselling and Psychotherapy (trustee 1994-98, dep. chair 1994-96, bus. com. 1999—, profl. accreditation 1991, 96, 2001—); mem. European Assn. Counseling, Westminster Pastoral Found., Nat. Counselling Network (exec. com. 2001-2002), Lead Body for Advice, Guidance Counselling and Psychotherapy (segment chair 1992-96), Counselling in Med. Settings Divsn. (chair 1991-94). Avocations: printmaking, poetry, fine art, painting, photography. Personal E-mail: robbicampbell@lycos.com, rc555@mac.com.

CAMPBELL, ROBERT MURRAY, JR., surgeon, researcher; b. Nashville, May 7, 1951; s. Robert Murray and Betty Ann (Kennedy) Campbell; m. Corey Le Campbell, Mar. 31, 2001; children: Abigail Le, Noah Robert. Studied, Vanderbilt U., Nashville, 1969—71; BA, Johns Hopkins U., Balt., 1973; MD, Georgetown U., 1977. Diplomate Nat. Bd. Med. Examiners, 1978, cert. in Orthopedics Am. Bd. Orthopedic Surgery, 1982. Resident in orthop. surgery Fitzsimmons Army Med. Ctr., Denver, 1978—81; orthopedist U.S. Army, Fort Meade, Md., 1981—85; fellow in pediatric orthops. A.I. Dupont Inst., Wilmington, Del., 1985—86; pvt. practice in pediatric orthops. San Antonio, 1986—92; from asst. prof. to assoc. prof. orthops. U. Tex. Health Sci. Ctr., San Antonio, 1992—2002, prof., 2003—08. Cons. U.S. Consumer Product and Safety Commn., 2000; mem., med. adv. com. Nat. Orgn. of Rare Disorders, 2000—; dir. Thoracic Inst., Christus Santa Rosa Children's Hosp., San Antonio, 2001—08, Ctr. Thoracic Insufficiency Syndrome, Children Hosp. Phila. Cons., reviewer Jour. of Bone and Joint Surgery, 1987—, Jour. Pediat. Orthop., —; contbr. articles to profl. jours. Participant Orthop. Edn. in Third World Countries, 1999—. Maj. US Army, 1983—85. Recipient Imagineer Award, Mind Sci. Found. of San Antonio, 1993, Miracle Maker Award, A.H. Robins/Wyeth Pediat., 1994, Therapeutic Achievement award, Nat. Org. Rare Diseases, 2005, Endowed Chair in Pediat. Orthopedics, Dielmann Pres. Coun., 2005, Hon. award, US House Reps. Resolution 1499, 2010, Disting. Alumni award, Johns Hopkins U., 2011; named to San Antonio (Tex.) Sci. and Tech. Hall Fame, 2005; grantee, Nat. Orgn. Rare Disorders, 1992—93, FDA Office Orphan Products Devel., 1994—2000. Fellow: Scoliosis Rsch. Soc. (chmn., growing spine com. 2002); mem.: Am. Acad. Pediat. (mem. task force pediatric device devel.), Pediatric Orthop. Soc. of N.Am. (edowed chair, pres. coun. 2004, Arthur H. Huene Excellence and Promise award 2006), Clin. Orthop. Soc. (pres. 2005). Achievements include invention of verticle expandable prosthetic titanium rib and the FDA approval of this device as a humanitarium use device; apparatus and method for effecting surgical incision through use of a fluid jet; co-invention of bioabsorbable intramedullary rod implant system; testified to the senate committee on health in support of the pediatric medical device safety and inmprovement act of 2007. Avocations: white-water rafting, bicycling, running. Office: Childrens Hosp Pa 3418 Civic Ctrl Blvd 2nd Fl Wood Philadelphia PA 19104 Office Phone: 215-590-1527. Business E-Mail: campbellrm@email.chop.edu.

CAMPBELL, TERRI GWEN GILL, epidemiology coordinator; b. Pampa, Tex., Dec. 26, 1962; d. Terry Lewis Gill and Sarah Ladon Gill-Northcutt; m. Mark G. Campbell, July 29, 1987. BSN, West Tex. State U., 1982—85. Cert. in Infection Control Certification Bd. for Infection Control, 2000; RN, Tex., 1986, Nat. Certification Corp., 1988. Staff devel. specialist NW Tex. Healthcare Sys., Amarillo, Tex., 1990—96, case mgr., 1996—98, epidemiology coord., 1998—. Mem. City Steering Com. for Weapons of Mass Destruction, Amarillo, 2000—; chmn., bioterrorism planning com., surveillance subcommittee City of Amarillo, 2000—02; chmn., bioterrorism planning com. City of Amarillo, Tex., 2002—. Chief of health and safety Potter County Fire Rescue, Amarillo, Tex., 2002—. Mem.: Assn. for Professionals in Infection Control and Epidemiology. Avocations: crafts, rappelling. Office: Northwest Texas Healthcare System 1501 S Coulter Amarillo TX 79106

CAMPBELL, THOMAS J., chiropractor, former state legislator; b. Bklyn., Oct. 27, 1954; s. Charles Marvin and Edna Mary (Sacer) C.; m. C. Lynn Hearn, July 2, 1983. AA in Social Scis., Fla. Tech. U., 1974; BA in Police Sci. and Adminstrn., Seattle U., 1977; DC, Life Chiropractic Coll., 1983; postgrad. in orthopedics, L.A. Chiropractic Coll., 1984-90. Diplomate Am. Acad. Pain Mgmt.; cert. chiropractic rehab. dr. Nat. Bd. Chiropractic Examiners-Physiotherapy; lic. chiropractor, Wash., Fla. Pvt. practice Chiropractic Spinal Care, Inc., 1984—; mem. Dist. 2 Wash. House of Reps., 1992—96, 1998—2011. Served to capt. Spl. Forces US Army, 1977—85. Recipient Appreciation for Svc. award Chiropractic Disciplinary Bd., 1989-93, Gov. Appreciation Certificate Wash. State Disciplinary Bd., Legislator of Yr. award Wash. State Labor Coun., 1999, Wash. State Trial Attys., 1999, Wash. State Vet. Assn., 1994, Wash. State Nurses Assn., 2000, others. Fellow Internat. Coll. Chiropractors; mem. Am. Chiropractic Assn. (alt. del. House of Dels. 1988-92), Wash. State Chiropractic Assn. (chmn. mem. com. 1984-85, dist. 4A 1985-86, dir. exec. bd. 1985-88, vice-chmn. disciplinary bd. 1990-93, legislative affairs com. 1986, Pres. award 1985, Dist. of the Yr. award 1985-86, Chiropractor of Yr. 1987, 89-91, 2001, Appreciation award 1994, Exceptional Svc. award 1994), Wash. State Chiropractic Assn., Pierce County Chiropractic Assn., Chiropractic Rehab. Assn. (bd. dirs.). Republican. Avocations: scuba diving, boating, fishing. Office: Campbell Chiropractic Clinic PO Box 70 Spanaway WA 98387-0070 *

CAMPBELL, TIMOTHY MICHAEL, physician; MD, West Va. U. Sch. of Medicine, 1982—86. Cert. internal medicine. Resident Mercy Hosp. of Pitts.; med. dir. Family Hospice and Palliative Care, 1989—2011; physician Campbell Philbin Med. Assocs. Office: Campbell Philbin Medical Associates Ste 5109 1400 Locust St Pittsburgh PA 15219 Office Phone: 412-281-2575.

CAMPBELL, WILLIAM EDWARD, mental hospital administrator, psychologist, psychotherapist; b. Kansas City, June 30, 1927; s. William Warren and Mary (Bickerman) C.; m. Joan Josselyn Larimer, July 26, 1952; children: William Gregory, Stephen James, Douglas Edward. Student, U. Nebr., 1944-45, MS, 1975; student, U. Mich., 1945, Drake U., 1948; BA, U. Iowa, 1949, MA, 1950; PhD in Psychology, U. Nebr., Lincoln, 1980. Psychologist Dept. Pub. Instrn., State of Iowa, 1951-52; hosp. adminstr. Mental Health Inst., Cherokee, Iowa, 1952-68; dir. planning and rsch. Dept. Social Svcs., State of Iowa, 1968-69; CEO Glenwood Resoucre Ctr. (formerly Glenwood State Hosp. Sch.), Iowa, 1969—; supt. Clarinda Mental Health Inst., Iowa, 1979—, founder and first warden, Clarinda Correctional Facility; assoc. prof. mental health adminstrn. Northwestern U., Chgo., 1982—; pres. River Bluffs Cmty. Mental Health Ctr., 1971—, also bd. dirs. Dir. Shared Mental Health Svcs., Clarinda/Glenwood; founder, chmn. Regional Drug Abuse Adv. Coun.; adj. prof. Sch. Pub. Health U. Minn., also preceptor grad. students in mental health adminstrn.; vis. faculty Avepane U., Caracas, Venezuela; adj. prof. Coll. Medicine and Health Adminstrn. Tulane U.; mem. vis. staff dept. psychiatry U. Nebr. Med. Ctr.-Creighton U. St. Joseph Med. Ctr.; apptd. State of Iowa Dept. Human Svcs. Exec. Mgmt. Team, 1997; doctoral advisor U. Neb., 2000—. Author works in field. UN spl. cons. to Venzuela for UNESCO; bd. dir. Polk County Mental Health; v.p., bd. dir. Mercy Hosp., Coun. Bluffs, Iowa; state pres. United Cerebral Palsy; charter mem., bd. dir. Pub. Broadcasting Sta. KIWR, Council Bluffs, Iowa, Glenwood-Mills County Econ. Devel. Found., Inc., 1985—; charter mem., bd. dir. Mills County Econ. Devel., 1987, Glenwood Resource Ctr., 1993—; bd. dir. On-With-Life, adminstr., 2005-; bd. dir., mem. human rels. and fin. coms. On-With-Life Found., bd. dir. Glenwood C. of C.; charter mem., organizer Loess Hills Alliance, 1998—, mem. land protection, econ. devel. and long range planning coms., 1999—; mem. Glenwood City Tree Bd.; vol. Creighton U. Med. Ctr., 1969-, U. Nebr. Med. Ctr., 1969-, also in mental health and substance abuse and long term care orgns. Served with AUS, 1944-46; col. Res.; vol. mem. Patient Advocacy Groups Health Care Facilities, Nebr., Kans., Iowa, Mo. Decorated Army Commendation medal; recipient Meritorious Service medal U.S. Army, 1982. Fellow Assn. Mental Health Adminstrs. (nat. com. chmn. 1970); mem. Assn. Med. Adminstrs., Am. Hosp. Assn. (nat. governing bd. psychiat. services sect., charter panelist nat. adv. panel on mental health services, mem. governing body psychiat. services sect.), Iowa Hosp. Assn., Health Planning Council of Midlands, Assn. Univ. Programs in Health Adminstrn. (mem. nat. task force on edn. of mental health adminstrs. 1969—), Am. Assn. on Mental Deficiency (chmn. adminstrn. sect. Region 8), Nat. Rehab. Assn., Assn. Retarded Children, Mental Health Assn., Phi Beta Kappa, Glenwwod Area C. of C. (mem. bd. dirs. 2004-), Iwoa Living Rd. Ways Task Force (mem. bd. dirs. 2008-). Home: 307 Louise Ave Glenwood IA 51534 *

CAMPBELL, WILLIAM O'NEAL, retired physician; b. McCaysville, Ga., May 22, 1928; s. Martin Hoyt Campbell and Pauline Kimsey; m. Reba Kathern Hughes, June 14, 1961; 1 child, Martin Lee. AA, Tenn. Wesylan Coll., 1948; MD, U. Tenn. Memphis, 1962. Diplomate Am. Acad. Family Physicians. Resident Carraway Meth. Hosp., Birmingham, Ala., 1965; family physician Copperhill, Tenn., 1965—77; staff physician Tenn. Valley Authority, Chattanooga, 1977—94; ret., 1994. Cons. U. So. Ala. Med. Mus., Mobile, Med. Mus., Foley, Ala. Mem.: AMA, WOC, Chattanooga and Hamilton County Med. Soc., Alpha Omega Alpha, Alpha Epsilon Delta. Home: 4900 Bal Harbor Dr Chattanooga TN 37416

CAMPBELL, WILLIAM WESLEY, medical educator, department chairman; b. Macon, Ga., Sept. 28, 1944; s. William Wesley Campbell, Sr. and Lessie Rose Campbell; m. Rhonda Marie Pridgeon, May 2, 1992; children: William Wesley III, Matthew Ryan, Shannon Leigh Ward. BA, Emory U., Atlanta, 1966; MD, Med. Coll. Ga., Augusta, 1970; MS in Health Adminstrn., Med. Coll. Va., Richmond, 1991. Lic. neurologist Am. Bd. Psychiatry and Neurology, 1978, in electrodiagnostic medicine Am. Bd. Electrodiagnostic Medicine, 1981, cert. added qualification Am. Bd. Psychiatry and Neurology, 1996, Am. Bd. Psychiatry and Neurology, 2009. Intern, straight medicine Med. Coll. Ga., 1970—71, neuromuscular fellow, 1979—80; air force gen. med. officer, 1971—73; resident in neurology Letterman Army Med. Ctr., 1973—76; staff neurologist Wilford Hall USAF Med. Ctr., 1976—79; pvt. practice Anderson, SC, 1980—81; asst. prof. neurology Med. Coll. Va., 1981—86, assoc. prof. neurology, 1986—90, prof. neurology, 1990—2000, Uniformed Svcs. U. Health Scis., Bethesda, Md., 2000—, prof., chmn. dept. neurology, 2004—. Author: (books) Essentials of Electrodiagnostic Medicine, 1999 (Hon. Mention award, Am. Med. Writer's Assn., 1999), Practical Primer of Clinical Neurology, 2002, DeJong's Neurologic Examination, 2005, Pocket Guide and Toolkit to DeJong's Neurologic Examination, 2008; contbr. articles to profl. jours. Mem. Am. Bd. Electrodiagnostic Medicine, Rochester, Minn. Active duty USAF, 1971—79, with USAR, 1983—2000, active duty col. US Army, 2000—, DC. Recipient Golseth Young Investigator award, Am. Assn. Electrodiagnostic Medicine, 1981; named Outstanding Tchr., Med. Coll. Va., 1988, 2002. Fellow: Am. Assn. Neuromuscular and Electrodiagnostic Medicine, Am. Acad. Neurology; mem.: Va. Watercolor Soc. (several awards for watercolor painting), Alpha Omega Alpha. Achievements include patents pending for analysis of movements in patients with seizures. Avocations: music, aviation, painting. Home: 11403 Hollowstone Dr North Bethesda MD 20852 Office: Uniformed Svcs U Health Scis Dept Neurology 4301 Jones Bridge Rd Bethesda MD 20814 Office Fax: 301-295-0620. Personal E-mail: wcampbellmd@gmail.com. Business E-Mail: wcampbell@usuhs.mil.

CAMPBELL-REARDON, CHRISTINE L., critical care specialist; MD, Boston U., 1988. Diplomate Am. Bd. Internal Medicine, 2001, Am. Bd. Internal Medicine- pulmonary disease, 2004, Am. Bd. Internal Medicine- critical care specialist, 2005. Resident in internal medicine Boston Med. Ctr., 1989—91, fellow in pulmonary and critical care medicine, 1995; liaison pulmonary thoracic oncology program Boston Univ, asst. prof. Sch. of Medicine; staff Boston Med. Ctr. Office: Boston Medical Center 725 Albany St 9th Fl Ste 9B Boston MA 02118 Office Phone: 617-638-7480. Office Fax: 617-638-7486.

CAMPHAUSEN, KEVIN A., oncologist, researcher; MD, Georgetown U., 1996. Intern Georgetown U., 1996—97; resident radiation oncology Joint Ctr. for Radiation Therapy, Harvard Med. Sch., 1997—2001; investigator Nat. Cancer Inst., NIH, Bethesda, Md., 2001—04; dep. chief Radiation Oncology Br. Ctr. Cancer Rsch., Nat. Cancer Inst., NIH, Bethesda, Md., 2004—07, chief Radiation Oncology Br., 2007—, head imaging and molecular therapeutics sect. Office: Nat Cancer Inst, NIH Bldg 10/CRC/Rm B2-3561 10 Center Dr, MSC 1682 Bethesda MD 20892 Office Phone: 301-496-5457. Office Fax: 301-480-5439. E-mail: camphauk@mail.nih.gov. *

CAMPION, EDMUND RONAN, orthopedist, educator; b. Hanover, NH, Feb. 17, 1954; BA, Harvard U.; MD, Dartmouth U., 1981. Cert. Am. Bd. Orthop. Surgery, 1993. Intern orthop. surgery St. Luke's Presbyn. Med. Ctr., Denver, 1981—82; resident U. NC, Chapel Hill, 1985—90; fellowship Alfred I. duPont Inst., Wilmington, Del., 1990—91; asst. prof. surgery U. NC Sch. Medicine, Chapel Hill, 1991—96, asst. prof. orthopaedics, 1996—98, dir., orthop. residency program, 1996—, assoc. prof., 1998—2005, prof. orthopaedics, 2006—; dir., dept. orthopaedics & orthop. residency program Wake Med. Ctr., Raleigh, 1991—96. Reviewer Jour. of Am. Acad. Orthopaedic Surgeons; contbr. articles to med. jours. Mem. Operation Smile, Panama, 1995, Colombia, 1996, Nicaragua, 1998, Mid. East, Asia, 1999. Office: Dept Orthopaedics CB #7055, Bioinformatics Bldg UNC Sch Medicine Chapel Hill NC 27599-7055 Office Phone: 919-966-9066, 919-968-3514. Office Fax: 919-843-5922. E-mail: ed_campion@med.unc.edu.

CAMPOLATTARO, BRIAN NICHOLAS, ophthalmologist, educator; b. Oct. 3, 1964; m. Wendy Campolattaro; 2 children. MD, U. Medicine and Dentistry NJ, 1990. Cert. Ophthalmology, 1995. Resident ophthalmology NY Eye & Ear Infirmary, NYC, 1991—94, now assoc. attending ophthalmology, assoc. prof. pediat. ophthalmology; fellowship pediatrics St. Louis Children's Hosp., Mo., 1994—95; pvt. practice Pediat. Ophthalmology of NY; clin. instr., dept. ophthalmology and visual sciences Yeshiva U. Albert Einstein Coll. Medicine, NYC. Contbr. articles to profl. jours. Named to Castle-Connelly's Best doctors in NY, 2001—07. Office: Pediat Ophthalmology of NY 30 E 40th St Ste 405 New York NY 10016 Office Phone: 212-684-3980. Office Fax: 212-684-0838.

CAMPOS, WUILKER KNONER, neurosurgeon; b. Campo Mourão, PR, July 14, 1977; M, Fed. U. Santa Catarina, 2004; postgrad., Sirio-Libanes Hosp., 2009. Residence neurosurgery Fed. Hosp. Bonsucesso, Rio de Janeiro; post grad. in neurointensive care Inst. Edn. and Rsch., Sirio-Libanes Hosp., Sao Paulo, Brazil; specializzazione chirurgia vertebrale ad indirizzo oncologico e degenerativo Inst. Ortopedico Rizzoli di Bologna, Italy; clin., rsch. fellow, dept. neurology sch. medicine Pain Ctr. and Divsn. Functional Neurosurgery, U. São Paulo; neurosurgeon, spine surgeon NEURON - Inst. Neurosurgery, Florianopolis, SC, Brazil, 2010—. Cons. Arquivos de

Neuro-Psiquiatria, Child's Nervous Sys. Mem.: AO Spine, Brazilian Soc. Neurosurgery. Avocations: soccer, walking, scuba diving. Office: 63 Menino Deus St Office 419 Florianopolis Santa Catarina 88020-210 Brazil Personal E-mail: wuilker@yahoo.com.br.

CANADY, ALEXA IRENE, pediatric neurosurgeon, educator; b. Lansing, Mich., Nov. 7, 1950; d. Clinton Jr. and Hortense (Golden) C.; m. George Davis, June 18, 1988. BS, U. Mich., 1971, MD cum laude, 1975; DHL (hon.), Marygrove Coll., 1994, U. Detroit, 1997; DSc (hon.), Ctrl. Mich. U., 1999, U. So. Conn., 1999, U. W. Fla., 2006. Diplomate Am. Bd. Neurol. Surgery. Intern in surgery Yale U., New Haven, 1975-76; resident in neurosurgery U. Minn., Mpls., 1976-81; fellow in pediatric neurosurgery Children's Hosp. Pa., Phila., 1981-82; instr. neurosurgery U. Pa., Phila., 1981-82; staff neurosurgeon, instr. neurosurgery Henry Ford Hosp., Detroit, 1982-83; asst. dir. neurosurgery Children's Hosp. Mich., Detroit, 1986-87, chief of neurosurgery, 1987-97; assoc. prof. neurosurgery Wayne State U., Detroit, 1988-91, vice chmn. neurosurgery, 1991—2001; prof. neurosurgery Sacred Heart Hosp., Pensacola, Fla., 1997—2001; prof. pediat. in neurosurgery Fla. State U., 2006—. Clin. instr. neurosurgery Wayne State U. Sch. Medicine, 1985, mem. internal rev. com. dept. anatomy, 1988, chmn. search com. dept. neurosurgery, 1989, internal rev. com. dept. neurology, 1991-92, 125th anniversary celebration com., 1992, internal rev. com. dept. pediat., 1993, chmn. search com. dept. ophthalmology, 1992-93, internal rev. com. dept. neurosurgery, 1994; chmn. neurobiol. devices panel, FDA, cons. neurol. devices panel Med. Devices Adv. Com., 1994—, chmn., 1998-2000, co-chair ctr. devices and regulatory health enhanced sci. rev., 2001; vis. prof. Med. Coll. S.C., 1990; clin. prof. dept. clin. scis., pediatric neurosurgery Fla. State Coll. Medicine, 2007-; mem. surg. com. Children's Hosp. Mich., chmn. operating room subcom. surg. com., intensive care unit com., med. record com., med. exec. com.; Detroit; presenter various profl confs. in U.S. and internat. Contbr. chpts. to books. Bd. dirs. Inst. Am. Bus., 1986-88. Recipient citation Women's Med. Assn., 1975, Candace award Nat. Coalition 100 Black Women, N.Y., 1986, Golden Heritage award, 1989, Leonard F. Sain Esteemed Alumni award U. Mich., 1990, Disting. Alumni award Everett H.S., Pres.'s award Am. Med. Women's Assn., 1993, Variety Heart award for Med., Sci. and Tech. Variety Club, 1994, Shining Star award Colgate-Palmolive Co./Starlight Found., 1994, Golden Apple award Roeper Sch., 1995, Athena award Alumni Assn. U. Mich., 1995, Golden Apple Faculty Tchg. award U. Fla. Pediat. Residents, 2004, Chmn. Recognition award Fla. Bd. Medicine, 2005; named Outstanding Young Woman in Am., 1977, Top 100 Bus. & Profl. Women of Am., 1985, Woman of Yr. Detroit Club Nat. Assn. Negro Bus. & Profl. Women's Club, Inc., 1986; named to Mich. Woman's Hall of Fame, 1989; grantee Am. Cancer Soc., 1979, Minn. Med. Found., 1979, Am. Cancer Soc., 1981-82, Widman Found. Early Intervention Treatment and Follow-Up of Infants with Post-hemorrhagic Hydrocephalus, 1984-85, Neuropsychol. Recovery and Family Adaptation to CHI Children's Hosp. Mich., 1987-88, Hydrocephalus Induced Endocrinopathies: Morphologic Correlates Children's Hosp. Mich., 1989, 91; finalist Inst. Medicine African Am. Portrait Gallery, 2006; poster placed in Nat. Acad. Medicine Gallery African Am. Physicians, 2006. Mem. AMA, ACS, Am. Assn. Neurol. Surgeons, Congress Neurol. Surgeons, Am. Soc. Pediatric Neurosurgery, Nat. Med. Assn. Detroit Med. Soc., Mich. Assn. Neurol. Surgeons (sec. 1992-93, v.p. 1994-95, pres. 1995-96), Transplantation Soc. Mich. (adv. bd. 1993-94), Mich. State Med. Soc. (child abuse and neglect divsn. 1986), Southeastern Mich. Surg. Soc. (sec. 1986-87), Soc. Crit. Care Medicine, Wayne County Med. Soc. (ethics com., pub. affairs com., law com.), U. Mich. Med. Ctr. Alumni Soc., Delta Sigma Theta. Office: 6064 Forest Green Rd Pensacola FL 32505 Office Phone: 850-416-7101. Personal E-mail: alexacanady@aol.com.

CANCRO, ROBERT, psychiatrist, educator; b. NYC, Feb. 23, 1932; s. Joseph and Marie E. (Cicchetti) C.; m. Gloria Costanzo, Dec. 8, 1956; children: Robert, Carol. Student, Fordham U., 1948-51; MD, SUNY, 1955. Intern Kings County Hosp., Bklyn., 1955-56, resident in psychiatry, 1956-59; attending staff Gracie Sq. Hosp., NYC, 1959-66; clin. instr. SUNY Downstate Med. Ctr., Bklyn., 1959-66; staff psychiatrist Menninger Found., Topeka, 1966-69; cons. Topeka State and VA Hosps., 1967-69; prof. dept. psychiatry U. Conn. Health Ctr., Farmington, 1970-76; prof., chmn. dept. psychiatry NYU Med. Ctr., 1976—2005; dir. N.S. Kline Inst. Psychiat. Rsch., 1982—2005. Cons. psychiat. edn. br. NIMH; biol. scis. sect. NIMH. Editor 10 books.; Contbr. articles on schizophrenia to profl. jours. Recipient Freida Fromm-Reichmann award, 1975, Strecker award, 1978, Dean award, 1981, Lehmann award, 1992. Fellow A.C.P., Am. Coll. Psychiatrists, Am. Psychiat. Assn.; mem. Am. Psychol. Assn., Assn. Am. Med. Colls., Am. Assn. Social Psychiatry (pres. 1984-86), N.Y. Acad. Scis., AAAS, AMA. Home: 118 Mclain Rd Mount Kisco NY 10549-4932 Office: NYU Med Ctr 550 1st Ave MHL-HN416 New York NY 10016-6402 Home Phone: 914-241-1131; Office Phone: 212-263-5744. Business E-Mail: robert.cancro@med.nyu.edu.

CANDIDO, KENNETH DAVID, anesthesiologist, educator; b. East Orange, NJ, Nov. 21, 1957; s. Albert Babbits and Rose Marie Candido; children: Rosemarie C., Albert J., Farrin, Jannah R. MD, U. del Noreste, Tampico, Mex., 1983. Diplomate Am. Bd. Anesthesiology, 1988. Assoc. mem., anesthesiology Lenox Hill Hosp., NYC, 1989—97; program dir., anesthesiology Cook County Hosp., Chgo., 1997—2001; dir., acute pain mgmt. Northwestern U. Med. Ctr., Chgo., 2001—05; dir., divsn. pain mgmt. Loyola U. Health Sys., Maywood, Ill., 2005—08; chmn. anesthesiology Adv. Ill. Masonic Med. Ctr., Chgo., 2007—. Contbr. articles to profl. publs. Recipient Educator of Yr., Northwestern U. Dept. Anesthesiology, 2003, Cook County Hosp., 2000—01, Rschr. of Year, U. Ill. Coll. Medicine, 1988—89, Award, Assn. U. Anesthesiologists, 2008—; Fellowship, Inst. Medicine Chgo., 2003—. Fellow: Inst. Medicine Chgo. (assoc.). Libertarian. Roman Catholic. Achievements include research in effect of buprenorphine on prolonging pain relief from local anesthetic injections. Avocations: sports, movies, theater, travel, weightlifting. Office: Advocate Ill Masonic Med Ctr 836 W Wellington Ave # 4815 Chicago IL 60601 Office Fax: 773-296-5088.

CANDOTTI, FABIO, pediatrician; MD summa cum laude, U. Brescia, Italy, 1987. Diplomate in pediats. and pediat. allergy and immunology; lic. physician, Italy. Med. staff fellow dept. pediatrics U. Brescia, Italy, 1988-89; enlisted Italian Army Sch. of Medicine, Florence, 1989; resident in pediatrics U. Brescia, 1989-92, staff mem. Bone Marrow Transplantation Unit Italy, 1990-91, postdoctoral fellow Lab. of Biotechnology, 1991-92; postdoctoral fellow Metabolism Br. NCI, NIH, Bethesda, Md., 1992-94; postdoctoral fellow Clin. Gene Therapy Br. NHGRI/NIH, Bethesda, 1994-96. Lectr. Italian Nat. Health Svc. Nursing Sch., Brescia, 1991-92; asst. prof. dept. pediatrics U. Brescia, 1996-97; tenure-track investigator NHGRI/NIH, Bethesda, 1998-2004, sr. investigator, 2004-; mem. animal care and use com. NHGRI, 1998-2002, vice chair animal care and use com., 2003-06, head NIH gene therapy interest group, 1998—, NHGRI liaison to NIH Office of Biotech. Activities, 1999—; mem. instnl. rev. bd. NHGRI, 2005-06, chmn. instnl. rev. bd., 2006—; attending physician dept. pediatrics Brescia City Hosp., Italy, 1996-97, Clin. Ctr., NIH, Bethesda, 1998—; investigator in field. Co-author: (book) The Child: Health and Disease, 1993; mem. editl. bd. Exptl. Hematology, 2003-05; contbr. articles to profl. jours., books, and publs. Physician, lt. Italian Army, 1988—. Recipient fellowship Italian Nat. Health Svc., 1988, Assn. for Child with Cancer, Brescia, 1990-91, Fondazione Golgi, Brescia, 1992-94; recipient awards nat. Ctr. for Human Genome Rsch. Scientific Retreat, Airlie, Va., 1995, 96, NIH Merit award, 1999, 05, others; grantee in field. Mem. Italian Soc. Pediatrics, Working Group on Human Genetics, Italian Soc. Pediatric Immunology and Allergy, Am. Soc. Gene Therapy (hematopoietic cell gene therapy com. 2004—07, chair gene therapy of genetic diseases com. 2007—), European Soc. Immunodeficiencies, Pan Am. Group for Immunodeficiency, Clin. Immunology Soc. (membership com. 2004-06, chmn. membership com. 2006—), Am. Soc. Clin. Investigation, Am. Soc. Hematology. Office: 49 Convent Dr 49/3A04 Bethesda MD 20892 Business E-Mail: fabio@nhgri.nih.gov.

CANDREIA, PEGGY JO, medical educator; b. Pawhuska, Okla., Aug. 23, 1944; d. Joseph Leonard and Wilma Jane (Brook) C. Student, U. Ozarks, 1965. Supr. credit and collections Credit Bur. Bartlesville, Okla., 1965-69; credit rep. Shell Oil Co., Tulsa, Okla., 1969-88; owner, mgr. Gorgeous Car Care, Tulsa, 1988-90; fin. analyst H.A. Chapman Inst., Children's Med. Ctr., Tulsa, 1990—2002, fin. coord. Children's Med. Network Telethon, 1994—2002; data coord. Hillcrest Healthcare Sys., Tulsa, 2002—03; asst. acctg. mgr. Preferred Pediat. Home Health Care, Tulsa, 2003—04; instr. med. office mgmt. Career Point Coll., 2005—. Founder local chpt. Parents and Friends of Lesbians and Gays, Tulsa, 1988-90; v.p. Tulsa Oklahomans for Human Rights, 1988-89; bd. dirs. Follies Rev., Tulsa, 1993-97, Broken Arrow Cmty. Playhouse, 1998-99; steering com., sec.-treas., Names Project, Tulsa, 1990—, co-chmn. ctrl. region logistics, Washington, 1996. Recipient Honor of Ky. Col., Presdl. Cmty. Svc. award, 2007. Mem.: Internat. Assn. Profl. Women. Republican. Roman Catholic. Avocations: designing homes, travel, skiing, fundraising, drawing. Home: 1525 N College Ave Tulsa OK 74110-2719

CANELLOS, GEORGE PETER, hematologist, oncologist, educator; b. Boston, Nov. 1, 1934; s. Peter and Pota C. (Coronios) C.; m. Jean H. Speare, July 27, 1958; children: Peter, George, Andrew Phillip. AB, Harvard U., 1956; MD, Columbia U., 1960; Doctor Honoris Causa, Nat. and Kapodestrian U. Athens, Greece, 1997. Diplomate Am. Bd. Internal Medicine, 1967, Am. Bd Internal Medicine, Hematology, 1972, Am. Bd. Internal Medicine, Medical Oncology, 1973; lic. Mass., 1962. Intern surgery Mass. Gen. Hosp., 1961—62, asst. resident medicine, 1962—63, sr. resident medicine, 1965—66, clin. rsch. fellow medicine, 1962, physician in medicine, 1966—, attending physician, hematology-oncology svc., 1997—; rsch. fellow Royal Postgraduate Med. Sch., London, 1966—67; active staff Children's Hosp. Med. Ctr., Boston, 1978—96, attending physician, 1977—78; clin assoc., medicine branch Nat. Cancer Inst., Bethesda, Md., 1963—65, sr. investigator, 1967-74, attending physician, medicine branch, 1967—75, clin. dir. Bethesda, Md., 1974-75; chief divsn. med. oncology Sidney Farber Cancer Inst./Dana-Farber Cancer Inst., Boston, 1975—95; med. dir. for network devel. Dana-Farber/Partners CancerCare, 1995—2004; attending physician Dana-Faber Cancer Inst., 1975—; cons. physician medicine Georgetown U. Hosp., Wash., 1971—75; sr. assoc. medicine Peter Bent Brigham Hosp., Boston, 1975—82; rsch. fellow medicine Harvard Med. Sch., 1962—63, assoc. prof. medicine Boston, 1975-83, prof., 1983-88, William Rosenberg prof. medicine, 1988—; physician Beth Israel Hosp., Boston, 1988—; attending physician, medical svc. Brigham and Women's Hosp., Boston, 1976—78, sr. physician, 1983—, physician, 1982—83, attending physician, hematology-oncology svc., 1997—. Asst. clin prof. med. Georgetown U. Sch. Medicine, Wash., 1971—74, assoc. clin. prof. medicine, 1974—75; assoc. prof. medicine Harvard Med. Sch., 1975—83, prof. medicine, 1983—88; sr. investigator and attending physician, medicine branch Nat. Cancer Inst., Bethesda, Md., 1967—73, head sect. on hematology investigations and asst. chief medicine branch, 1973—74, acting clin. dir., acting assoc. dir. for med. oncology, divsn. cancer treatment, 1974—75; oncologic drugs adv. com. Food and Drug Adminstrn., Wash., DC, 1984—88; vis. prof. U. Colo., 1976, Mayo Clinic, 1977, UCLA, 1978, Wadsworth VA Ctr., 1978, U. Fla., 1979, St. Bartholomew's Hosp., London, 1980, U. Rochester, 1981; McIllrath vis. prof. Sydney U., Australia, 1989; Ruitingavan Swieten Found. prof. Amsterdam Med. Ctr., 1989; Semler vis. prof. Boston U. Med. Ctr., 1992; Shenson vis, prof. Stanford U., 1992; vis. prof. McGill U., 1994; several other vis, prof. positions; prin. investigator Dana-Farber Cancer Inst., 1982—, mem. lymphoma com., 1982—, chair, lymphoma com., 1998—2003. Editor: Neoplastic Diseases of the Blood, 1985, 2d edit., 1991; editor in chief Jour. Clin. Oncology, 1988-2001, Oncology Up-to-Date, 2000-, The Lymphomas, 1998, 2nd edit., 2006, Lymphoma, the Oncologist, 2005-; editl. bd. European jour. of Cancer and Clin. Oncology, 1983-, Jour. Internal Medicine, 1989-, Current Opinion in Oncology, 1989-, Hematology/Oncology Clinics N.Am., 2004-. Am. Cancer Soc. Trust, Inc., 1986—; external review com. Wash. U. Cancer Ctr., St. Louis, 1996—; Med. Oncology Fellowship Selection Dana-Farber Cancer Inst./Dana-Farber Ptnrs. CancerCare, 1975—; Internat. Adv. Com. Specialty Care Exec. Com. Partners HealthCare Sys., 1997—; Clin. Rsch. Coordinating Com. Dana-Farber/Ptnrs. Cancer Care, 2001—. Recipient Achievement award, Nat. Conf. of Christians and Jews, 1984, Hippocratic award, AHEPA, 1985, Disting. Physician award, Hellenic Med. Soc. NY, 1988, Leonideion award, Pan-Laconian Fedn. US and Can., 1993, Disting. Svc. award for Sci. Achievement, Am. Soc. Clin. Oncology, 1996, Disting. Sci. award, HSCO, 1996, Lifetime Achievement award, Alpha Omega Coun., 1999, Key to the Cure award, Cure for Lymphoma Found., 1999, George Papanicolaou award, New England Hellenic Med. and Dental Soc., 2000, Perez-Santiago award lecture, Puerto Rican Soc. Hematology, 2003, Ellis Island Medal of Honor, NECO, 2004, San Salvatore award, Internat. Lymphoma Conf., 2005, Frank Moran award, U. Mich., 2006, Fishcher lecture, Yale, 2006. Fellow ACP, Royal Coll. Physicians London and Scotland; mem. Am. Soc. for Clin. Investigation, Assn. Am. Physicians, Am. Soc. Clin. Oncology (pres. 1993-94), Am. Assn. Cancer Rsch., Am. Fedn. for Clin. Rsch., Am. Soc. Hematology, Mass. Soc. Clin. Oncology. Office: Dana-Farber Cancer Inst 44 Binney St Boston MA 02115-6084 Home Phone: 781-237-1835; Office Phone: 617-632-3470.

CANGEMI, JOSEPH PETER, psychologist, consultant, educator; b. Syracuse, NY, June 26, 1936; m. Amelia Elena Santaló, Oct. 6, 1962; children: Michelle, Lisa Ann. BS, SUNY, Oswego, 1959; MS, Syracuse U., 1965; EdD, Ind. U., 1974; LLD (hon.), William Woods U., 1996; DHC (hon.), Moscow State U., 2001. Diplomate Am. Bd. Vocat. Experts, Am. Bd. Forensic Examiners, Am. Coll. Counselors, in Profl. Counseling Internat. Acad. Behavioral Medicine, Counseling and Psychotherapy, cognitive behavior therapist, life cert. sch. psychologist, counselor NY. Instr. Syracuse Pub. Schs., 1959-60, vocat. rehab. coord., rsch. assoc., 1961-65; instr., asst. dir. Carol Morgan Sch., Santo Domingo, Dominican Republic, 1960-61; asst. head basketball coach SUNY C.C., Syracuse, 1962-63, lectr., chmn. dept. psychology evening-extension divsn., 1962-65, vis. lectr., 1966; supr. edn. Orinoco Mining divsn. US Steel Corp., Ciudad Piar, Venezuela, 1965—66; supr. tng. and devel. Orinoco Mining divsn. U.S. Steel Corp., Puerto Ordaz and Ciudad Piar, Venezuela, 1966-68; asst. prof. psychology Western Ky. U., Bowling Green, 1968—76, assoc. prof., 1976, prof., 1979—2006, prof. emeritus, 2001—; scholar in residence, 2010—; dir. Creative Leadership and Change, Inc., 1970—. Project dir. U. Los Andes, Merida, Venezuela, Inter-Am. Devel. Bank, Washington, Western Ky. U., 1975—77; cons., advisor R. R. Donnelley & Sons, Coca Cola; cons. Gould Corp., Eaton Corp., Firestone Tire & Rubber Co.(US, South America, Asia), Uniroyal/Goodrich Tire and Rubber Co., Gen. Tire and Rubber Co., Jefferson Smurfit, Std. Products, Tyson Foods, others, Govt. & U. Lanzhou, China, US Army, Sealy Corp., Siemans Nuc. Power Co. Host conversation program Wester Ky. U. divsn. Radio, TV Film, 1968—71; author: Higher Education and the Development of Self-Actualizing Personalities, 1977, La Administracion Participativa, 1983, Higher Education in the United States and Latin America, 1983; author: (with Mario Noronha) Marketing Y Venda, Portuguese edit., 1992; author: (with Carl Kreisler) Raymond C. Gibson-Distinguished Kentuckian, Renowned Educator and Statesman: An Anthology, 1996; author: (with Mario Noronha, Casimir Kowalski, George Guttschalk) Falhas Organizaciones, Protuguese edit., 1996; editor (with George Guttschalk): Effective Management, 1980; editor: (with Casimir Kowalski) Perspectives in Higher Education, 1983, Andersonville Prison, Lessons in Organizational Failure, 1993; editor: (with Casimir Kowalski and Jeffrey Claypool) Participative Management: Employee Management Cooperation, 1985, Chinese edit., 1990; editor: (with Casimir Kowalski and Habib Khan) Leadership Behavior, 1998; editor: (with Tatiana Ushakova and Casimir Kowalski) Leadership for the 21st Century, Russian edit., Russian Academy of Sciences, 1997, Psychology of Contemporary Leadership, Russian Edit., Russian Acad. Scis., 2007; editor: (with R. Miller, C. Kowalski, T. Hollopeter) Developing Trust in Organizations, 2005; editor: (with Joel Snell and Casimir Kowalski) Social Essays on Chaos Theory, 2008; editor: Educator's Svc. Bull., 1971—72, Psychology and Edn.: An Interdisciplinary Jour., 1977—, Jour. Human Behavior and Learning, 1983—89, Orgn. Devel. Jour., 1983—89; mem. editl. bd. Archivos Panamenos de Psicologia, 1968—88, Coll. Student Jour., 1973—2004, Edn., 1976—, Faculty Rsch. Bull. Western Ky. U., 1981—86, Jour. Instrnl. Psychology, 1977—90, Counseling and Values, 1979—84, Technol. Horizons Edn. Jour., 1979—92, Jour. Fgn. Psychology, Russia, 1996—2003, Forensic Examiner, 1998—2004; contbr. 300 artcles to profl. jours., chapters to books; co-editor (with casimir Kowalsky & Henry Czaplicki): Heroes of Solidarity, 2010. Past mem. House of Goa, Lisbon, 1996—97; trustee William Woods U., 1988—. Recipient certs. and awards, US Army Armor Sch., 1974, Eaton Corp., 1974, 1976, ICETEX, Colombia, 1977, Colombian Nat. Assn. Indsl. Engrs., 1977, Decreto City of Bucaramanga, Colombia, 1983, Quality Control Assn., 1979, Decreto, State of Santander, Colombia, 1977, Excellence in Productive Tchg. award, Western Ky. U. Coll. Edn., 1979, 1991, 1999, Fireston Tire and Rubber Co. award, 1978, 1981, 1991, Profl.-Tech. Socs. award, 1983, Coll. Student Jour. and Models of Excellence award, 1983, Disting. Pub. Svc. award, Western Ky. U., 1983, Excellence in Pub. Svc. award, Coll. Edn., 1983, Disting. Alumnus award, SUNY, Oswego, 1983, award, Uniroyal-Goodrich Tire and Rubber Co., 1986, Excellence in Rsch. and Creativity award, Coll. Edn., Wester Ky. U., 1987, United Rubber Workers/Internat. Brotherhood Elec. Workers award, 1991, Jour. Edn. award, Project Innovation, 1992, Bridgestone-Firestone award, Valencia, Venezuela, 1994, Outstanding Contbn. award, Southeastern divsn. Redman Industries, 1996—97, Summit Excellence Svc. award, Western Ky. U., Coll. Ednl. Behavioral Scis., 2008; nominee Prof. of Yr. Nat. award, Carnegie Found., WKU, 1999—2000. Mem.: APA, ACA (past regional chmn. com. internat. edn.), Nat. Bd. Visitor Sch. Edn. Syracuse (exec. com. mem.), Nat. Bd. Visitors Sch. Edn. Ind. U., Mensa, Soc. Psychology Mgmt., InterAm. Soc. Psychology, Intenrat. Registry Ogn. Devel. Profls., Nat. Assn. Gifted (past mem., bd. dirs.), Internat. Assn. Edn. and Vocat. Guidance, Assn. Specialists Group Work (charter), Internat. Coun. Psychologists (past area chmn. Ky.), Nat. Vocat. Guidance Assn. Profl., Colombian Nat. Soc. Indsl. Engrs. (hon.), Panamanian Psychol. Assn. (hon.), Ky. Acad. Arts and Scis. (life), Alumni Assn. SUNY, Oswego, Capitol Arts Assn., Ind. U. Alumni Assn. (life), Olde Stone Country Club, Eta Sigma Gamma (health educator), Gold Key, Phi Delta Kappa, Sigma Tau Delta, Sigma Delta Psi, Psi Chi, Pi Kappa Delta. Home: 1409 Mt Ayr Cir Bowling Green KY 42103-4708 Office: Western Ky U Dept Psychology Bowling Green KY 42101 Office Phone: 270-842-3436. Fax: 270-842-0432. Personal E-mail: joseph.cangemi@wku.edu. Business E-Mail: joseph.cangemi@creativeleadershipandchange.com.

CANIZARES, CLAUDE ROGER, astrophysicist, educator; BA in Physics, Harvard U., 1967, MA in Physics, 1968, PhD in Physics, 1972. Postdoc. fellow MIT, 1971—74, prof., 1974—84, Bruno Rossi prof. exptl. physics, 1984—, dir. Ctr. Space Rsch., 1990—2002, v.p. rsch., assoc. provost, 2002—. Assoc. dir. Chandra X-Ray Obs. Ctr., Cambridge, Mass.; mem. adv. coun. NASA, 1992—2000, chair space sci. adv. com., 1993—94; chair space studied bd. NRC, 1994—2000; mem. sci. adv. bd. USAF, 1999—2003; bd. dir. L3 Comm. Inc., 2003—. Contbr. over 210 articles to profl. jours. Recipient Goddard medal, Am. Astronautical Soc., 1997, NASA Pub. Svc. medal, 2000; fellow Alfred P. Sloan Found., 1980—84. Fellow: Am. Acad. Arts & Scis., Am. Phys. Soc.; mem.: AAAS, NAS (coun. mem. 2005—08), Internat. Acad. Astronautics, Internat. Astron. Union, Am. Astron. Soc., Sigma Xi, Phi Beta Kappa. Office: MIT Rm 3 234 77 Massachusetts Ave Cambridge MA 02139-4309

CANNOM, DAVID S., cardiac electrophysiologist, educator; MD, U. Minn., 1967. Diplomate Am. Bd. Internal Medicine-cardiovasc. disease, 1975, Am. Bd. Internal Medicine, 1980. Resident internal medicine Yale-New Haven Hosp., Conn., 1968—69; fellow cardiovasc. disease Stanford Univ., Calif., 1971—73; founder LA Cardiology Assocs., 1985; clin. prof. medicine UCLA; dir. cardiology Good Samaritan Hosp. Mem.: North Am. Soc. for Pacing and Electrophysiology (immediate past pres.), Am. Coll. of Cardiology (past gov.), Am. Heart Assn. (past pres.). Office: Los Angeles Cardiology Associates Downtown Los Angeles Office 1245 Wilshire Blvd Ste 703 Los Angeles CA 90017 Office Phone: 213-977-0419.

CANNON, CAROLYN L., physician; b. Houston, Aug. 21, 1960; BS, Tex. A&M U., 1982; MD, U. Tex. Med Sch., Houston, 1993. Assoc. dir. divsn. respiratory medicine, dir. pediat. pulmonology fellowship tng. program U. Tex. Southwestern Med. Ctr., 2009—. Recipient NorTech Innovation award, NorTech and Crain's Cleve. Bus.; named one of Best Drs. in America; Rsch. grants, NIH. Mem.: Soc. Pediat. Rsch., Am. Thoracic Soc. Avocations: horseback riding, singing. Office: 5323 Harry Hines Blvd Dallas TX 75390-9063 Business E-Mail: carolyn.cannon@utsouthwestern.edu.

CANNON, STEPHEN ROBERT, surgeon, consultant; b. Feb. 8, 1950; MBBChir, Cambridge U., Eng., 1974, MA, 1975; MChOrth, Liverpool U., Eng., 1982. Sr. registrar Middlesex Hosp., London, 1981—88; cons. orthopaedic surgeon Royal Nat. Orthopaedic Hosp., 1988—. Contbr. articles to profl. jours., chapters to books. Fellow: Brit. Orthopaedic Assn. (pres. 2007—), Royal Coll. Surgeons; mem.: Internat. Limb Salvage Assn., European Musculoskeletal Oncology Soc., Brit. Assn. Surgery Knee. Office: Royal Nat Orthopaedic Hosp Brockley Hill Stanmore HA7 4LP England Home: St. Giles Lodge Amersham Road HP8 4RZ Chalfont St Giles England

CAN-PENG, LI, science educator; b. Eryuan, Yunnan, Dec. 25, 1974; PhD, Kagoshima U., 2005. Prof. Yunnan U., 2006. Avocation: running. Office: 2 N Cuihu Rd Kunming Yunnan 650091 China E-mail: lppp1974@yahoo.co.jp.

CANTAFORA, ALFREDO, biomedical researcher; b. Crotone, Italy, July 21, 1946; s. Michele and Teresa (Loria) C.; m. Ida Blotta, May 9, 1971; Maria Teresa, Chiara Enrico. Degree in chemistry, U. La Sapienza, Rome, 1970. Chemist Def. Adminstrn., Rome, 1972-73; rschr. Inst. Superiore di Sanita, Rome, 1973-79, sr. rschr., 1979-86, rsch. dir., 1986—. Prof. biochemistry U. Sci. M. Ficino, Treviso, Italy, 1984; nat. rep. Codex Alimentarius, The Hague, The Netherlands, 1978-83, Internat Union Pure Applied Chemistry, Oxford, Eng., 1979-83; project leader NRC Italy, 1988-94; mem. bd. advisors Am. Biographical Inst., 1992. Author: Methods of Analysis of Bile-CRC Press, 1994; contbr. articles to sci. jours. (award 1992). Mem. Soc. for Exptl. Biology and Medicine, N.Y. Acad. Scis. Avocations: stamp collecting/philately, oil books, wood carving. Home: Via Attilio Friggeri 75 00136 Rome Italy Office: Inst Superiore di Sanita Viale Regina Elena 299 00161 Rome Italy Office Phone: +39-06-49902766. Business E-Mail: cantafor@iss.it.

CANTO, MARCIA IRENE, gastroenterologist, educator; Grad., Johns Hopkins Sch. of Pub. Health; MD, U. Philippines, 1985. Diplomate Am. Bd. Internal Medicine, 1989, Am. Bd. Internal Medicine-gastroenterology, 2008. Resident internal medicine SUNY Health Sci. Ctr., Bklyn., 1989—91, fellow gastroenterology, 1993; dir. clin. rsch. gastroenterology divsn. Johns Hopkins Medicine. Assoc. prof. medicine and oncology Johns Hopkins Medicine. Named one of Castle Connolly America's Top Doctors, 2009—10, 2011, Castle Connolly America's Top Doctors for Cancer, 2009—10, 2011. Office: Johns Hopkins Medicine Rm 426 1830 E Monument St Baltimore MD 21205 Office Phone: 410-614-5388.

CANTOR, NANCY, academic administrator; b. NYC; m. Steven Brechin; children: Maddy, Archie. AB, Sarah Lawrence Coll., 1974, PhD in Psychology, Stanford U., 1978. Faculty, chair dept. psychology Princeton (NJ) U., 1991—96; dean Horace H. Rackham Sch. Grad. Studies, vice provost for acad. affairs U. Mich., Ann Arbor, 1996—97, provost, exec. v.p. acad. affairs, 1997—2001; chancellor U. Ill.-Urbana-Champaign, 2001—04; chancellor, pres. Syracuse U., NY, 2004—, disting. prof. psychology and women's studies. Mem. adv. bd. NSF; mem. com. on nat. needs in biomed. and behavioral sci. rsch. NRC, mem. com. on women in sci. and engrng. Co-author (or co-editor): 3 books; contbr. 50 articles to profl. jours., chpts. to books. Recipient Woman of Achievement award, Anti Defamation League, Academic Leadership Award, Carnegie Corp. of NY, 2008. Fellow: Soc. for Personality and Social Psychology, APA (Disting. Sci. award for early career contbn. in psychology), Am. Psychol. Soc.; mem.: Am. Assn. for Higher Edn. (vice chair bd. dirs.), Am. Acad. Arts and Sci., Inst. of Medicine of NAS. Office: Syracuse University Office of Chancellor 300 Tolley Adminstrn Bldg Syracuse NY 13244-1100 Office Phone: 315-443-2235. E-mail: cancellor@syr.edu. *

CANTOR, RICHARD IRA, physician, corporate health executive; b. NYC, Jan. 25, 1944; s. Jacob Alvin and Sarah Cantor; m. Patricia Ann Honeycutt, June 7, 1970. AB, NYU, 1965; MD, Med. Coll. Va., 1970; postgrad., Bellevue Hosp. Ctr., NYC, 1970-73. Diplomate Am. Bd. Internal Medicine. Intern Bellevue Hosp. Ctr., NYC, 1970-71, resident, 1971-73; internist N.Y. Med. Group, NYC, 1973-76; asst. med. dir. substance abuse programs Bellevue Hosp., 1973-76, med. dir. substance abuse programs, 1976-79; med. dir. Med Plan, NYC, 1979-84; employee health unit Equitable Life Assurance Soc. U.S., NYC, 1984-87; v.p., dir. health and med. svcs. Citibank, NYC, 1988-89, v.p., dir. health, med. and staff svcs., 1989-91; v.p., corp. med. dir. Citigroup, NYC, 1991—2008. Teaching asst. in medicine NYU Med. Ctr., NYC, 1970-73, asst. prof. clin. medicine, 1983—; attending physician Cabrini Med. Ctr., NYC, 1973-76, Bellevue Hosp. Ctr., 1973—; chmn. policy adv. bd. NYC Methadone Maintenance Treatment Programs, 1976-77; med. cons. Am. Fedn. State, County, and Mcpl. Employees, NYC, 1979-84. Columnist Ask Your Med Plan Doctor, Pub. Employee Press, 1980-84. NIH trainee in endocrinology Med. Coll. Va., 1968. Mem. ACP, AMA, Am. Coll. Occupl. and Environ. Medicine, Royal Soc. Medicine (London), Am. Coll. Physician Execs., NY Occupl. Med. Assn. (exec. com. 1997), Med. Execs., Med. Soc. County NY, Med. Soc. State NY, Nat. Corp. Med. Assocs., Internat. Soc. Travel Medicine, Med. Dirs. Forum, Phi Beta Kappa, Alpha Omega Alpha, Sigma Zeta. Office: 85 East End Ave New York NY 10022-4699 Office Phone: 917-848-0559.

CANTORE, ITALO, otolaryngologist; b. Potenza, PZ, Italy, July 16, 1976; s. Rocco Cantore and Rosa Capoluongo. Degree in Medicine and Surgery, Second U., Naples, Italy, 2002; PhD student, Cath. U. Sacred Heart, Rome, 2006—. Specialization and residency cert. in otolaryngology Cath. U., 2006; cert. in tchg. Q.O. Flacco Classical HS, 2004. Attending dept. gen. surgery Second U., 1999—2001, attending dept. internal medicine, 2001—02, attending dept. head and neck pathology, oral cavity diseases, audiology and and pitioniatry, 2002; attending emergency unit Loreto Mare Hosp., Naples, 2002; med. dr., otolaryngologist Cath. U. Sacred Heart, 2002—, rsch. mem. on various inner ear expts. on humans and exp. animals, 2002—, cooperator in inner ear rsch. protocol, 2006—07, mem. statal rsch. project, 2006—07, investigator mem. cochlear implant European Multictr., 2007—; mem. Italian Soc. Otolaryngology-Head Neck Surgery, Rome, 2005—; physician dept. otolaryngology head and neck surgery S Carlo Regional Hosp., Potenza, Italy, 2008—. Contbr. articles to profl. internat. sci. jours.; presenter (on numerous conf. and symposium). Recipient award, Oulu U.- Cath. U. Rome; named one of Best Italian Specialization Paper Work, Charles Holland Internat. Rsch. Audiology Ctr., 2007. Home: Via degli Oleandri 9 Potenza PZ 85100 Italy Home Fax: +39097136640. Personal E-mail: i.cantore@libero.it.

CANTRELL, ROBERT WENDELL, otolaryngologist, head and neck surgeon, educator; b. Neosho, Mo., Apr. 25, 1933; s. Lloyd L. and Ruby R. (Moffett) Cantrell; m. Young Hi Lee, Feb. 6, 1964; children: Mark L., Elizabeth L., Victoria L., Robert Wendell, Jr. Student, US Naval Acad., 1952—55; AB, George Wash. U., Washington, DC, 1956, MD, 1960. Diplomate Am. Bd. Otolaryngology 1969. Intern N.Y. Hosp-Cornell U., 1960—61; resident in otolaryngology Nat. Naval Med. Center, Bethesda, Md., 1965—69; chmn. dept. otolaryngology Naval Regional Med. Center, San Diego, 1969—76; chair dept. otolaryngology-head and neck surgery U. Va., Charlottesville, 1976—96; acting v.p., provost U. Va. Health Scis. Ctr., 1995—96, v.p., provost, 1996—2001; dir. Va. Health Policy Ctr., Charlottesville, 2001—04. Bd. dirs. Am. Bd. Otolaryngology, 1980—98, exec. v.p., 1990—98. Mem. editl. bd. Laryngoscope, 1976—88, Annals of Otology, Rhinology and Laryngology, 1977—88, Am. Jour. of Otolaryngology, 1978—82, Archives of Otolaryngology, 1979—88. Mayor City of Oakmont, Md., 1968—69. Capt. USN, 1961—76, capt. USNR, 1976—91. Recipient Huron W. Lawson prize, 1960; fellow, Am. Heart Assn., 1959. Mem.: Am. Otol. Soc., Am. Laryngol. Assn. (coun. 1988—90, treas. 1990—95, pres.-elect 1995, pres. 1996—97), Am. Broncho-Esophagological Assn. (pres. 1988—89), Soc. Univ. Otolaryngologists (pres. 1982), Am. Soc. Head and Neck Surgery (pres. 1985—86), Triological Soc. (v.p. So. sect. 1989—90, Mosher award 1974), Am. Acad. Facial Plastic and Reconstructive Surgery (v.p. So. sect. 1980—83), Am. Acad. Otolaryngology-Head and Neck Surgery (pres. 1987), AMA, Alpha Omega Alpha. Home: 1925 Owensville Rd Charlottesville VA 22901-8824

CANTU, ROBERT CLARK, neurosurgeon; b. Santa Rosa, Calif., Aug. 31, 1938; m. Tina Cantu; children: Rob, Elizabeth. BA, U. Calif., Berkley, 1960; MD, U. Calif., San Francisco, 1963. Cert. Neurological Surgery, 1970. Surgical intern Columbia-Presbyn. Hosp., NYC, 1963—64; resident Mass. Gen. Hosp., Boston, 1964—68; rsch. fellow physiology Harvard Med. Sch., Boston, neurosurgery staff; acting asst. dir. neurosurgery, dir. pediat. neurosurgery Boston City Hosp., Boston; chief neurosurgery svc., dir. sports medicine Emerson Hosp., Concord, Mass., co-dir. Neurologic Sports Injury Ctr., Brigham and Women's Hosp., Boston, clin. prof. Dept. Neurosurgery, co-dir. Ctr. for Study of Traumatic Encephalopathy Boston U. Sch. Medicine, Boston. Founding mem., chmn. med. adv. bd. Sports Legacy Inst., Waltham, Mass.; adj. prof. exercise and sport sci., med. dir. Nat. Ctr. Catastrophic Sports Injury Rsch. U. NC, Chapel Hill; neurosurgical cons. Boston Coll. Eagles, Boston Cannons; spkr. in field. Assoc. editor Medicine and Science in Sports and Exercise, Exercise and Sports Science Review; contbr. articles to med. jours. Mem.: Am. Coll. Sports Medicine (pres. 1992—93, treas. 1996—99). Avocation: running. Office: Emerson Hosp Ste 820 John Cuming Bldg 131 ORNAC Concord MA 01742 Office Phone: 978-369-1386. *

CANZIANI, MARCO, surgeon; b. Busto Arsizio, Italy, Mar. 14, 1975; Degree in Medicine, U. Insubria Varese, 2000, degree in Surgery, 2007. Staff med. officer Ospedale Di Circolo, Fondazione Macchi, Emergency Dept., 2005—06; gen. surgeon Multimedica S.p.a. Hosp. Castellanza, Operative Unit Gen. And Mini-invasive Surgery, 2007—. Contbr. articles to profl. med. jours. Mem.: Societa' Lombarda Di Chirurgia, Italian Soc. Surgery. Avocations: running, mountain climbing. Office: Ospedale Multimedica Viale Piemonte n70 Castellanza Varese 21053 Italy Business E-Mail: marcocanz@tiscali.it.

CANZONIER, WALTER JUDE, shellfish aquaculturist; b. New Brunswick, NJ, Feb. 6, 1936; s. Joseph V. and Mary M. (Patterson) C. BS, St. Peter's Coll., Jersey City, 1957; postgrad., Rutgers U., 1957-64. Teaching asst. dept. zoology Rutgers U., New Brunswick, NJ, 1958-59, rsch. asst. dept. oyster culture, 1960-67, rsch. assoc., 1968-71, 81-87; rsch. fellow Inst. Marine Biology, CNR, Venice, Italy, 1971-77; dir. Coastal Resources Applied Rsch. Lab., Venice, 1977-80; dir. R & D, Aquarius Assocs., Port Noris, NJ, 1987—. Mem. tech. coms. Italian Ministry Sanità and Ministry Merchant Marine, 1974-80, Interstate Shellfish Sanitation Conf., 1980—; cons. on marine sci. UNESCO, France, 1978—. Contbr. articles to profl. jours. Organizer, treas. Point Pleasant Beach Taxpayers Assn., NJ, 1963-70; bd. dirs. N.E. Regional Aquaculture Ctr., 1992-2005, mem. exec. com., 1993-96, 2001-05; mem. NJ Taskforce for Revitalization of Shellfish Industry, 1997, NJ Aquaculture Adv. Coun., 2000-04. Recipient numerous grants from pub. agys. in N.Am. and Europe, 1971—, NSA David Wallace award, 2009, Recognition Promotion Collaboration Rsch. Industry. Mem. Nat. Shellfisheries Assn., Soc. Invertebrate Pathology, World Aquaculture Soc. N.J. Aquaculture Assn. (trustee 1989—, pres. 1991-2006). Achievements include development of shellfish sanitation guidelines and regulations for state and national health agencies in North America and Europe; design of marine research and aquaculture facilities in Asia, Europe and North America; advocacy for legis. to promote comml. aquaculture devel. Home: 44 Cowart Ave Manasquan NJ 08736-3102 Office: Aquarius Assocs PO Box 662 Port Norris NJ 08349-0662 Home Phone: 732-223-5229; Office Phone: 856-785-0402. Personal E-mail: garugala@att.net.

CAO, CHUANBAO, biomedical researcher, educator; s. Chenying Cao and Manxiang Tian; m. Zhaohua Qiao, Sept. 10, 1989; 1 child, Tai. BS, Nanjing U., 1983; MS, U. Sci. and Tech. of China, 1989; PhD, U. Sci. and Tech. China, 1992. Cert. tchr. Ministry Edn., China, 2000. Assoc. prof. Beijing (China) Inst. Tech., 1994—98, prof., 1998—, dir. Rsch. Ctr. Materials Sci., 2000—. Contbr. articles to profl. jours. Mem.: Soc. Electronic China, Soc. Mech. Engring. China. Achievements include patents for preparation of non-soluble silk fibroin films and small tubes. Home: No5 Zhongguancun South Street Beijing 100081 China Office: Beijing Institute of Technology 5 No Zhongguancun South Street 100081 Beijing China Business E-Mail: cbcao@bit.edu.cn.

CAO, GUANGWEN, medical educator; b. Liaoning, China, Sept. 22, 1965; MD, Second Mil. Med. U., 1989, PhD, 1995. Prof., chmn. Second Mil. Med. U., 2002—. Contbr. articles to profl. med. jours. Office: Dept Epidemiology 800 Xiangyin Rd Shanghai 200433 China Business E-Mail: gcao@smmu.edu.cn.

CAO, JUN-LI, physician, educator; b. Xuzhou City, Jiangsu Province, Mar. 10, 1968; MD, Xuzhou Med. Coll., 1994; PhD, China U., 2006. Prof. dept. anesthesiology Affiliated Hosp. Xuzhou Med. Coll., 2006—. Recipient Jiangsu Sci. and Tech. Progress award, Govts. of Jiangsu Province. Mem.: Soc. Neurosci. Avocations: classical music, basketball. Office: Huaihai West Rd 84# Xuzhou Jiangsu 221002 China E-mail: caojl0310@yahoo.com.cn.

CAO, JUNRAN, research scientist; b. China, Sept. 20, 1978; PhD, U. Calif. Irvine, 2005. Rsch. fellow NIDA, 2005—07; rsch. scientist U. Va., 2007—. Mem.: SFN. Office: 1670 Discovery Dr Ste 110 Charlottesville VA 22901 Business E-Mail: jc4gm@virginia.edu.

CAO, SHOUSONG, medical researcher, educator; b. Longhai, Hunan, China, Dec. 20, 1957; s. Guanwen Cao and Baiyu Xiao; m. Joann Juan Liu, Sept. 27, 1987; children: Felicia, Joshua. MS, Peking Union Med. U., Beijing, 1987; MD, Xiangya Med. Coll., Changsha, China, 1983. Diplomate Shousong Cao Med. Diplomate Com., China, 1983. Vis. rsch. prof. Peking Union Med. U., Beijing, 2000—; vis. prof. Ctrl. South U., Changsha, Hunan, China, 2006—, Fourth Mil. Med. U., Xian, China, 2008—; sr. scientist Roswell Pk. Cancer Inst., Buffalo, 2003—. Bd. dir. PrimaNova BioSci., Inc, Medford, NY, 2006—; evaluator Current Drugs Ltd., London; reviewer Nat. Sci. Found., China, 2007—; evaluator Chang Jiang Scholar Prog., 2007—; edtl. bd. mem. The Open Colorectal Cancer Jour., 2008—. Reviewer Jour. Gastroenterology; contbr. numerous articles to profl. jours. Recipient Advanced and Technol. award, Chinese Academy Med. Scis., 1991, First prize, Ministry Public Health, 1995. Achievements include research in new anticancer drug discovery and development. Made major contribution to 5-fluorouracil/leucovorin and 5-fluorouracil/Irinotecan combinations, Xeloda, and selenium development; four US patents for method of reducing toxicity of anticancer agents and for method of augmenting the antitumor activity of anticancer agents; One UK patents. Home: 8771 Millcreek Dr East Amherst NY 14051 Office: Roswell Park Cancer Inst Elm & Carlton Sts Buffalo NY 14203 Office Fax: 716-846-8221. Personal E-mail: shousongc@yahoo.com. Business E-Mail: shousong.cao@roswellpark.org.

CAO, TONG, botanist, educator; b. Shanghai, Jan. 22, 1946; s. Youque Cao and Shizhao Lu; m. Chengying Yan, Apr. 1948; children: Hai, Yang. BS, Fudan U., 1968. Engr. Shenyang Biscuits Factory, China, 1968-78; rsch. assoc. Inst. Forestry & Soil Sci. Academia Sinica, Shenyang, China, 1978-84; vis. scholar dept. botany U. Alberta, Edmonton, Can., 1984-86; from assoc. prof. to prof. Inst. Applied Ecology Academia Sinica, Shenyang, 1986—2001; prof. Shanghai Normal U., 2001—. Author: Bryoflora of China, vol. 1, 1994, vol. 2, 1996, vol. 3, 2000, Bryoflora of Xizang, 1985; editor: Flora Bryoph. Shandong, 1998, Flora Yunnanica, vol. 17, 2000; contbr. articles to profl. jours. Mem. Chinese Acad. Scis. Office Phone: 86-21-64321008. Personal E-mail: ct1946@263.net.

CAPALDO, GUY, obstetrician, gynecologist; b. Bisaccia, Italy, Jan. 1, 1950; came to U.S., 1958; s. Arturo Nunziante and Maria Carmela (Ciani) C.; m. Kathy Nicita, Apr. 20, 1985. BSEE magna cum laude, U. Dayton, 1972; MS, Ohio State U., Columbus, 1973; MD, Med. Coll. Ohio, 1978. Diplomate Am. Bd. Ob-Gyn; cert. clin. densitometrist Internat. Soc. Clin. Densitometry. Research asst. Ohio State U., 1973-75; resident in ob-gyn Med. Coll. Ohio, Toledo, 1978-82; practice medicine specializing in ob-gyn Mansfield, Ohio, 1982—. Chief ob-gyn. dept. Mansfield Gen. Hosp., 1985—; lab. dir. Mansfield (Ohio) Ob-Gyn Assocs. Contbr. articles to profl. jours. Clinic physician Plan Parenthood, Mansfield, 1982—. Pres. scholar U. Dayton, 1968-72, Univ. fellow Ohio State U., 1972-75. Fellow Am. Coll. Ob-Gyn; mem. AMA, Ohio State Med. Assn., Richland County Med. Soc. Avocations: reading, fishing, travel, golf. Office: Mansfield Ob-Gyn Assocs 500 S Trimble Rd Mansfield OH 44906-3483 Office Phone: 419-756-6000.

CAPASSO, PATRIZIO, medical educator; b. Lima, Peru, Oct. 9, 1959; BSc, George Washington U., 1982, MD; DSc, U. Lausanne, 1986. Assoc. prof. radiology La. State U., 2000—02; prof. radiology and surgery U. Ill. Sch. Medicine, Rockford, 2002—08; prof. radiology and surgery, vice-chair dept. radiology U. Ky., 2008—. Cons. eV3, 2006—08, Cordis, 2006—09, Abbott Vascular, 2006—10; med. adv. bd. Bolton Med., 2006—09, GE Healthcare, 2007. Recipient Poster Presentation award, Swiss Soc. Radiology. Fellow: Cardiovasc. & Interventional Soc. Europe; mem.: SIR, SNIS, ACR, RSNA (Poster Presentation award). Avocation: golf. Home: 3621 Barrow Wood Ln Lexington KY 40502 Home Fax: 859-323-9849. Business E-Mail: pcapas777@uky.edu.

CAPECCHI, MARIO RENATO, geneticist, educator; b. Verona, Italy, Oct. 6, 1937; BS in Chemistry and Physics, Antioch Coll., Yellow Springs, Ohio, 1961; PhD in Biophysics, Harvard U., Cambridge, Mass., 1967; MD (hon.), U. Florence, Italy, 2004. Asst. prof. dept. biochemistry Harvard Med. Sch., 1969—71, assoc. prof., 1971—73; prof. biology U. Utah Sch. Medicine, Salt Lake City, 1973—, adj. prof. oncological scis., 1982—, prof. human genetics, 1989—, disting. prof. human genetics & biology, 1993—, co-chair dept. human genetics, 2002—. Investigator Am. Heart Assn., 1969—72, Howard Hughes Med. Inst., 1988—; chmn. Gordon Conf. Molecular Genetics, 1986, Banbury Conf. Devel. Genetics, Cold Spring Harbor, NY, 1989. Mem. editl. bd. Cell & Molecular Biology, 1982—, DNA, 1982—, Molecular & Cellular Biology, 1985—, Mechanisms of Devel., 1990—, Molecular Medicine, 1994—, Cell Structure & Function, 1994—, Neurobiology of Disease, 1994—2000, Devel. Biology, 1995—2001; contbr. articles to profl. jours. Recipient Am. Chem. Soc. Biochemistry award, 1969, Career Devel. award, NIH, 1972—74, Faculty Rsch. award, Am. Cancer

Soc., 1974—79, Bristol-Myers Squibb award for disting. achievement in neurosci. rsch., 1992, Gairdner Found. Inernat. award, 1993, Alfred P. Sloan Jr. prize, GM Cancer Rsch. Found., 1994, Molecular Bioanalytics prize, Germany, 1996, Kyoto prize, Inamori Found., Japan, 1996, Franklin medal for advancing knowledge of physical scis., 1997, Rosenblatt prize for excellence, U. Utah, 1998, Baxter award for disting. rsch. in biomed. scis., Assn. Am. Med. Colleges, 1998, Horace Mann Disting. Alumni award, Antioch Coll., 2000, Phoenix-Anni Verdi award for genetics rsch., Italy, 2000, Pioneers of Progress award, 2001, Jiménez-Diáz prize, Spain, 2001, Nat. Medal Sci., 2001, Albert Lasker award for basic med. rsch., 2001, John Scott Medal award, 2002, Massry prize, 2002, Gov.'s Sci. & Tech. award, Utah, 2002, Internat. Cancer Rsch. award, Pezcollar Found./Am. Assn. Cancer Rsch., 2003, Wolf prize in medicine, Israel, 2003, March of Dimes prize in devel. biology, 2005, Nobel prize in physiology/medicine, 2007, Jacob Heskel Gabbay award in biotech. & medicine, Brandeis U., 2007. Fellow: AAAS, Am. Acad. Microbiology, Molecular Med. Soc.; mem.: NAS, European Acad. Scis., Am. Soc. Hematology (hon. life), Am. Acad. Arts & Scis., European Acad. Scis., Genetics Soc. America, Internat. Genome Soc., Soc. Devel. Biology, Am. Soc. Biochemistry & Molecular Biology, Am. Soc. Microbiology, Am. Soc. Biol. Chemistry, Am. Biochem. Soc., Phi Kappa Phi. Achievements include pioneering work in gene targeting of the mouse embryo-derived stem cells. Office: U Utah Sch Medicine 15 N 2030 E Rm 5440 Salt Lake City UT 84112 also: U Utah Interdepartmental Prog Neurosci 401 MREB 20 N 1900 E Salt Lake City UT 84132-5331 Office Phone: 801-581-7096. Office Fax: 801-585-3425. E-mail: mario.capecchi@genetics.utah.edu. *

CAPEZZA, JOSEPH C., health insurance company executive; BS in Acctg., Fordham U. CPA. Gen. practice mgr., ins. industry specialist Coopers & Lybrand LLP, 1976—83; v.p., contr. Skandia America Reinsurance Co., 1983—85; v.p., CFO Willcox Inc. Reinsurance Intermediaries, 1985—90; sr. v.p., CFO Reliance Reinsurance Corp., Phila., 1990—2000, Group Health Inc., NY, 2000—01; CFO Harvard Pilgrim Health Care, Wellesley, Mass., 2002—07; exec. v.p., CFO Health Net, Inc., Woodland Hills, Calif., 2007—. Mem.: AICPA, Soc. Ins. Fin. Mgmt. (chmn. acctg. com. 1987—88, chmn. reinsurance com. 1992—93, pres. 1999—2001, exec. com., bd. dirs.). Office: Health Net Inc 21650 Oxnard St Woodland Hills CA 91367 Office Phone: 800-291-6911. Office Fax: 818-676-6000. *

CAPITANIO, UMBERTO, surgeon; b. Italy, July 27, 1981; MD, 2006. Physician Vita-salute San Raffaele Hosp., 2006—. Office: Via Olgettina 60 Milan 20132 Italy Personal E-mail: umbertocapitanio@gmail.com.

CAPKIN, MARK, internist, educator; MD, Temple U. Diplomate Am. Bd. Internal Medicine. Intern Albert Einstein Med. Ctr., resident. Tchg. appointment Sch. Medicine Temple. Univ. Named one of of the Top Doctor, Phila. Mag., 2011. Office: Albert Einstein Medical Center AEMC Klein Bldg Ste 331 5401 Old York Rd Philadelphia PA 19141 Office Phone: 215-456-8220. Office Fax: 215-456-8520.

CAPLAN, ARTHUR LEONARD, university program director, educator; b. Boston, Mar. 21, 1950; s. Sidney and Natalie (Fluke) C.; m. Margaret Brennan; 1 child, Zachary. BA in Philosophy, Brandeis U., 1971; MA in Philosophy, Columbia U., 1973, MPhil, 1975, PhD in History and Philosophy of Sci., 1979; seven degrees (hon.), colls. and med. schs. Tchr. U. Pitts., Columbia U.; staff assoc. in ethical issues in sci. and medicine The Hastings Ctr., 1975-76, assoc. for humanities, 1977-84, assoc. dir., 1984—87; instr. Sch. Pub. Health, Columbia U., NYC, 1977-78, assoc. for social medicine, 1978-81; prof. philosophy, surgery, dir. Ctr. for Biomedical Ethics U. Minn., Mpls., 1987-94; Emmanuel and Robert Hart prof. bioethics, chair dept. med. ethics, dir. Ctr. Bioethics U. Pa., Phila., 1994—. Vis. prof. U. Pitts., 1986; adv. bd. Poynter Inst., Nat. Marrow Donor Program, ARC; chair adv. com. UN on Human Cloning, Dept. Health and Human Svcs. on Blood Safety and Availability; mem. Presdnl. Adv. Com. on Gulf War Illnesses; mem. spl. adv. com. Internat. Olympic Com. on Genetics and Gene Therapy; mem. ethics com. Am. Soc. Gene Therapy; spl. adv. panel NIMH on Human Experimentation on Vulnerable Subjects; columnist MSNBC.com; frequent guest and commentator Nat. Pub. Radio, CNN, MSNBC, NY Times, Washington Post, Phila. Inquirer, and others; cons. in field many corps., non-profit orgns. and consumer orgns.; mem. nat. and internat. coms.; chair Nat. Cancer Inst. Biobanking Ethics Working Group; mem. bd. dirs. The Keystone Ctr., Tengion, The Nat. Ctr. Policy Rsch. on Women and Families, Octagon, Iron Disorders Found. and the Nat. Disease Rsch. Interchange. Author: Moral Matters, 1995, Prescribing Our Future: Ethical Challenges in Genetic Counseling, 1993, If I Were a Rich Man Could I Buy a Pancreas and Other Essays on Medical Ethics, 1992, When Medicine Went Mad: Bioethics and the Holocaust, 1992, Everyday Ethics: Resolving Dilemmas in Nursing Home Life, 1990, Beyond Baby M, 1990, Smart Mice, Not So Smart People, 2006, The Penn Center Guide to Bioethics, 2009; editor (with J. McCartney and D. Sisti) The Case of Terri Schiavo: Ethics at the End of Life, 2006; contbr. over 500 papers to profl. jours.; contbr. over 500 papers in refereed jours. medicine, sci., philosophy, bioethics and health policy; columnist bioethics MSNBC.com.; frequent guest, commentator Nat. Pub. Radio, CNN, MSNBC, The NY Times, Washington Post, Phila. Inquirer and many other media outlets. Mem. Clin. Health Care Task Force, Wash. (vice chmn. ethics working group 1993-94); cons. Office of Tech. Assessment U.S. Congress, Minn. Dept. Health, Am. Found. for AIDS Rsch., NIH, Dept. Health and Human Svcs., Nat. Marrow Donor Program, Lifesource-Organ Procurement Org., Nat. Acad. Scis.-Inst. Medicine, state legis. Pa., Minn., NY, NJ Recipient Commr.'s award Dept. Health and Human Svcs., 1993, McGovern medal Am. Med. Writers Assn.; named Person of Yr. USA Today, 2001; named One of the Fifty Most Influential People in Am. Health Care Modern Health Care mag., One of the Ten Most Influential People in Am. in Biotech. Nat. Jour., One of the Ten Most Influential People in Ethics of Biotech. Nature Biotech. Jour. Fellow: AAAS, Coll. Physicians Phila., NY Acad. Medicine, The Hastings Ctr.; mem.: Am. Assn. Bioethics (pres. 1993—95), Aspen Inst. (Mellon fellow), Am. Philos. Assn. (Centennial Prize), Ctrl. Soc. Clin. Rsch. Avocation: tennis. Office: U Pa 3401 Market St Philadelphia PA 19104-3318 Fax: 215-573-3036.

CAPLAN, LOUIS ROBERT, neurologist, educator; b. Balt., Dec. 31, 1936; s. Carl Clarence and Bess Pauline (Cohen) C.; m. F. Brenda Fields, Nov. 28, 1963; children: Laura, Daniel, Jonathan, David, Jeremy, Benjamin. BA cum laude, Williams Coll., 1958; MD summa cum laude, U. Md., 1962. Diplomate Am. Bd. Internal Medicine, Am. Bd. Psychiatry and Neurology. Intern to jr. asst. resident Boston City Hosp., 1962-64; resident Harvard Neurol. Unit, Boston, 1966-69; cerebrovascular fellow Mass. Gen. Hosp., Boston, 1969-70; neurologist Beth Israel Hosp., Boston, 1970-78; asst. prof. Harvard Med. Sch., Boston, 1970-78, prof. neurology, 1999; chief neurologist Michael Reese Hosp., Chgo., 1978-84; prof. neurology U. Chgo., 1980-84; chief neurologist New England Med. Ctr., Boston, 1984-97; prof., chmn. dept. neurology Tufts U., Boston, 1984-97, prof. medicine, 1989-97; neurologist Beth Israel Deaconess Med. Ctr., Boston, 1998—; prof. neurology Harvard Med. Sch., 1999—. Author: stroke: A Clinical Approach, 1986, 4th edit., 2009, Consultations in Neurology, 1987, The Effective Clinical Neurologist, 3rd edit., 2011, Vertebrobasilar Arterial Disease, 1993; author: (with others) Cerebral Small Artery Disease, 1993; author: Management of Persons with Stroke, 1993, Brainstem Localization and Function, 1993, Intercerebral Hemmorhage, 1994, Family Guide to Stroke, 1994, Brain Ischemia-Basic Concepts and Clinical Relevance, 1995, Stroke Syndromes, 2nd edit., 2001, Posterior Circulation Disease, 1996, Neurologic Disorders: Course and Treatment, 1996, 2d edit., 2003, Primer on Cerebrovascular Diseases, 1997; author: (with others) Clinical Neurocardiology, 1999; author: Uncommon Causes of Stroke, 2001, 2nd edit., 2008, Striking Back at Stroke--A Doctor-Patient Journal, 2003, Stroke, 2005, Brain Embolism, 2006, Stroke Essentials 2nd edit., 2010, What Do I Know? Stroke, 2011; co-editor (with Peter P. Urban): Brainstem Disorders, 2011; contbr. more than 600 articles to profl. jours. Bd. dirs. Solomon Schecter Day Sch., Boston, 1977-78, Chgo., 1983-85. Capt. U.S. Army, 1962-64. Recipient House Officer Tchg. prize Michael Reese Hosp., 1980. Fellow Am. Acad. Neurology, Am. Neurol. Assn., Stroke Coun. Am. Heart Assn. (chmn. 1987-89, sci. adv. com. 1990—), Royal Soc. of Medicine; mem. Coun. Med. Specialties Socs. (rep. 1982-90), Chgo. Neurol. Soc. (chmn. 1984-85), Boston Soc. Neurology and Psychiatry (pres. 1988-89), Chgo. Heart Assn. (chmn. stroke com. 1979-84), Australian Neurol. Soc. (hon.), German Neurol. Assn. (hon.), Phi Beta Kappa, Alpha Omega Alpha. Democrat. Jewish. Office: Beth Israel Deaconess MC Dept Neurology 330 Brookline Ave Palmer 127 Boston MA 02215-5400 Office Phone: 617-632-8911. Business E-Mail: lcaplan@bidmc.harvard.edu.

CAPLAN, RONALD MERVYN, obstetrician, gynecologist; b. Montreal, Dec. 12, 1937; came to U.S., 1971; s. Philip and Betty (Gamer) C.; m. Marilyn Gail Amdur, Dec. 23, 1962; children: Randy Sue, Gordon; m. Aliza Avital, Oct. 08, 2007. BSc, McGill U., Montreal, 1958, MD CM, 1962. Resident Royal Victorial Hosp., Montreal, 1963-67; instr. ob-gyn McGill U., 1968-71; practice medicine specializing in ob-gyn Montreal, 1968-71, NYC, 1971—; mem. attending staff Royal Victoria Hosp., Montreal, 1968-71; asst. attending physician in ob-gyn N.Y. Hosp., NYC, 1971, now assoc. attending physician. Clin. assoc. emeritus prof. ob-gyn NY Weill Cornell Med. Coll. Editor: (with William J. Sweeney, III) Advances in Obstetrics and Gynecology (Williams, Wilkins), 1978, Principles of Obstetrics, 1982. Fellow ACS, Am. Coll. Obstetricians and Gynecologists, Royal Coll. Surgeons (Can.); mem. AMA, N.Y. Med. Soc., Soc. Reproductive Surgeons, Griffis Faculty Club of Cornell U. Office: 955 Old Quaker Hill Rd Pawling NY 12564 Personal E-mail: rcaplanmd@gmail.com.

CAPLOVITZ, COLEMAN DAVID, retired physician; b. Liberty, Tex., Jan. 18, 1925; s. Harry and Rose Lillian (Friedenberg) C.; m. Marilyn Joy Grossberg, Aug. 12, 1950; children: Lori Rose Caplovitz Bohm, Karen Sue Caplovitz Barrett. BA, U. Tex., 1944; MD, U. Tex. Med. Br., Galveston, 1947. Diplomate Am. Bd. Internal Medicine. Intern St. Louis City Hosp., 1947-48, asst. resident medicine, 1948-49; resident medicine Jefferson Davis Hosp., Houston, 1949-51; clin. instr. medicine Baylor Coll. Medicine, Houston, 1953-54, clin. asst. prof. to clin. assoc. prof. medicine, 1954-73, clin. prof. medicine, 1973—2003, clin. prof. emeritus, 2003—. Sr. attending in medicine, Meth. Hosp., 1973-94, chief gen. med. sect., 1973-94. Capt. USAF, 1951-53, Japan. Recipient Kass Fellowship, 1947; hon. fellowship Technion U. Israel Inst. Tech., Israel, 2007. Fellow ACP; mem. AM. Coll. Cardiology (assoc.), Am. Soc. Internal Medicine, Am. Heart Assn., Houston Soc. Internal Medicine (pres. 1992), Willow Fork Country Club, Sigma Xi, Alpha Epsilon Delta, Alpha Omega Alpha, Phi Eta Sigma. Jewish. Avocations: golf, boating, photography, orchid culture. E-mail: cdcaplo@aol.com.

CAPOBIANCO, ANTHONY G., physician; b. Somerville, Mass., Feb. 19, 1928; MD, Georgetown U., 1952; degree in Sci. (hon.), Mass. Maritime Acad., 2005—. Diplomate Am. Bd. Surgery. Intern Boston City Hosp., 1952-53, resident in surgery, 1953-54, 56-59; mem. staff Met. West Med. Ctr., Natick, Mass.; med. cons. Mass. Maritime Acad. Fellow ACS; mem. Boston Soc. Surgery, Mass. Med. Soc. Office: 205 Newbury St Framingham MA 01701-4581 Office Phone: 508-626-0025. *

CAPODIFERRO, SAVERIO, dentist, researcher; b. Gioia del Colle, Bari, Italy, Oct. 6, 1976; s. Carmine Capodiferro and Rosa Regina. DDS, U. Bari, 2001. Oral pathologist U. Bari. Contbr. articles to profl. jours. Mem.: Italian Soc. Oral Pathology and Medicine (assoc.). Achievements include research in Oral pathology and medicine. Home: Noci Km 4 88 Gioia del Colle 70023 Italy Office: Dental Office Via Le Strettole n° 78 Gioia del Colle 70023 Italy Personal E-mail: saveriocapodiferro@libero.it.

CAPONE, ANTONIO FRANCESCO, orthopedist; b. Lecce, Lecce, Italy, Dec. 3, 1963; s. Vittorio Capone and Paolina Pugliese; m. Cecilia Costalunga, Oct. 8, 1995; children: Maria Alice, Carolina. MD, U. Florence, Italy, 1989; PhD, U. Florence, 1995. Rsch. resident dept. orthop. surgery U. Florence, Italy, 1989—94; resident dept. orthop. surgery U. Cagliari, Italy, 1995—99, assoc. prof. orthop. surgery, 2000—, chief orthop. dept., 2010. Author: (book) La Chirurgia Di Revisione Nelle Artroprotesi D'anca. Grantee Travelling fellow, Italian Soc. Orthop. and Traumatology, 1991. Mem.: Italian Soc. Of Ortho. and Traumatology. Avocations: volleyball, sailing, fishing, travel, windsurfing. Office Phone: 0706094373, 070372377. Office Fax: 070372377. E-mail: anto.capone@tiscali.it.

CAPOZZO, MARIA ANNA, psychologist, psychonologist; b. Cormons, Gorizia, Italy, May 6, 1974; d. Francesco Capozzo and Ladinea Pelesson. Diploma, Liceo Classico, Udine, 1993—98; degree in Psychology, U. Trieste, Italy, 2005. Cert. psychologist 2009. Tutor, M psychoncology U. Trieste, Trieste, 2006—08, rschr., 2006—, tchr., 2007. Contbr. articles to profl. jours. Psychologist Assn. Women Breast Cancer, Trieste, 2008—. Office: University Trieste via LGiorgieri 7 Trieste 34100 Italy Home: Via Capriva 18/C 34071 Cormons Gorizia Italy Office Phone: 0039-340-7816070. Personal E-mail: marpish@hotmail.com.

CAPPELLERI, JOSEPH C., statistician; b. Bklyn., Oct. 12, 1961; PhD, Cornell U., 1991; MPH, Harvard U., 1993. Sr. dir., biostats. Pfizer Inc., 1996—. Adj. prof., medicine Tufts Med. Ctr., 2007—; adj. prof., statistics UCONN, 2007—. Fellow: Am. Stats. Assn. Avocations: reading, exercise. Office: Pfizer Inc 445 Eastern Point Rd Groton CT 06340 Business E-Mail: joseph.c.cappelleri@pfizer.com.

CAPPELLUTI, ERIKA, critical care specialist; PhD, Va. Commonwealth U., 1992, MD, 1997. Diplomate Am. Bd. Internal Medicine, 2000, Am. Bd. Internal Medicine- pulmonary disease, 2003, Am. Bd. Internal Medicine- critical care medicine, 2006. Resident in internal medicine Univ. Mass. Meml. Med. Ctr., Worcester, 1997—2001, resident in pulmonary disease and critical care medicine, 2001—03, fellow pulmonary, critical care, 2003—04; critical care specialist Hartford Hosp. Mem.: AMA, ATS, ACP, ACCP. Office: Hartford Hospital 85 Seymour St ste 923 Hartford CT 06106 Office Phone: 860-547-1876. Office Fax: 860-520-1379.

CAPPETTA, PAMELA GUYLER, counselor; b. Huntington, Pa., May 16, 1949; d. Thomas Winslow and Lois Olene (Lukens) Guyler; m. Christopher John Boll, Aug. 16, 1969 (div. Aug. 1985); 1 child, Kirstin Boll Kochanek; m. Robert Christopher Cappetta, May 4, 1991 (div. Aug. 19, 2008). BS, Shippensburg U., 1971; MEd, Coll. William and Mary, 1980, EdD, 1990. Lic. profl. counselor, Va.; lic. marriage and family therapist, Va. Social worker York-Poquoson Social Svcs., Grafton, Va., 1981-84; coord. PACES family counseling ctr. Coll. William & Mary, Williamsburg, Va., 1984-87; family therapist TMJ rsch. ctr. Med. Coll. Va., Sch. Dentistry, 1984-88; clin. assoc., counselor Family Living Inst., Williamsburg, Va., 1985-88; clin. asst. prof. Med. Coll. Va., Sch. Dentistry, Richmond, Va., 1990-94; med. family therapist Norge Family Practice, Williamsburg, 1992-94; co-owner, counselor Family Living Inst., 1988-94; allied health prof. Williamsburg Place, 1993—; counselor pvt. practice, Williamsburg, 1995—. Dir. coord. Transitions, Williamsburg, 1992-94; holotropic breathwork practitioner, Williamsburg, 1996—; faculty Asheville (N.C.) Body-Mind Clinic, 1999-2003. Contbr. articles to profl. jours. Vol. Va. Breast Cancer Found., Williamsburg, 1995-2003; bd. dirs. Va. Cancer Pain Initiative, Richmond, 1996. Mem. ACA, Am. Acad. Pain Mgmt., Nat. Bd. of Cert. Counselors, Va. Counseling Assn., Assn. for Holotropic Breathwork Internat. (cert.), Eye Movement Desentization and Reprocessing Internat. Assn. Democrat. Avocations: travel, reading, walking dogs, bicycling. Office: Ste 2 362 McLaws Cir Williamsburg VA 23185 Office Phone: 757-253-5708. Business E-Mail: drpamm@cox.net.

CAPPS, LOIS RAGNHILD GRIMSRUD, United States Representative from California, former school nurse; b. Ladysmith, Wis., Jan. 10, 1938; d. Jurgen Milton and Solveig Magdalene (Gullixson) Grimsrud; m. Walter Holden Capps, Aug. 21, 1960 (dec.); children: Lisa Margaret, Todd Holden, Laura Karolina. BSN with honors, Pacific Luth. U., 1959; MA in Religion, Yale U., 1964; MA in Edn., U. Calif., Santa Barbara, 1990. RN Calif., cert. sch. nurse, Calif. Asst. instr. Emanuel Hosp. Sch. Nursing, Portland, Oreg., 1959-60; surgery fl. nurse Yale/New Haven Hosp., 1960-62, head nurse, out patient, 1962-63; staff nurse Vis. Nurse Assn., Hamden, Ct., 1963-64; sch. nurse Santa Barbara Sch. Dists., Calif., 1968-70, 77-98; dir. teenage pregnancy and parenting project Santa Barbara, 1985-86; mem. US Congress from 23rd Calif. dist., Washington, 1998—, mem. budget com., energy & commerce com., natural resources com. Mem. Addiction, Treatment, & Recovery Caucus, Bi-Partisan Pro-Choice Caucus, Aerospace Caucus, Art Caucus, Coalition Autism Rsch. & Edn., Bike Caucus, Congl. Brain Injury Task Force, Climate Change Caucus, Cmty. Coll. Caucus, Diabetes Caucus, Global Health Caucus, Goods Movement Caucus, Hearing Health Caucus, Congl. Heart & Stroke Coalition, Human Rights Caucus, Intelligent Transp. Sys. Caucus, Nat. Parks Caucus, Native Am. Caucus, Oceans Caucus, Organics Caucus, Passenger Rail Caucus, Port Security Caucus, Recycling Caucus, Renewable Energy & Energy Efficiency Caucus, Specialty Crop Caucus, Congl. Task Force Alzheimers Disease, Congl. Task Force Internat. HIV/AIDS, Tourism & Travel Caucus, Vision Caucus, Wine Caucus, Zoo & Aquarium Caucus, Congl. Working Grp. Parkinson's Disease, Dem. Homeland Security Task Force, Out of Iraq Caucus, Prescription Drug Task Force, New Dem. Coalition; co-chair Nat. Marine Sanctuary Caucus, Ho. Cancer Caucus, Coastal Caucus, Congl. Caucus Women's Issues, Biomed. Rsch. Caucus; founder, co-chair Nursing Caucus; founder Sch. Health & Safety Caucus; bd. dirs. Santa Barbara Women's Polit. Com. Active Grace Luth. Ch.; bd. dirs. Am. Red Cross, Am. Heart Assn., Santa Barbara, 1989—, Adoption Ctr., Santa Barbara, 1986—90, Family Svc. Agy., Santa Barbara, 1994—. Mem.: Goleta Valley C. of C., Santa Barbara C. of C., Am. Assn. Univ. Women. Democrat. Lutheran. Office: US House of Reps 1707 Longworth House Office Bldg Washington DC 20515-0523 Office Phone: 202-225-3601. Office Fax: 202-225-5632. Business E-Mail: lois.capps@mail.house.gov.

CAPRINO, DANIELA, pediatrician; b. Rome, Sept. 13, 1954; MD, Perugia, 1979, PhD, 1983. Fellow U. Perugia, 1979—83; med. dir. Gaslini Children's Hosp., 1983—, med. dir. coordinating psycho-oncology group, pediat. hematology oncology dept., 2000—. Master: AIEOP; mem.: CSD. Avocations: archery, hunting. Office: Largo Ggaslini 5 Genova 16148 Italy Office Fax: 39 0105636714. Business E-Mail: danielacaprino@ospedale-gaslini.ge.it.

CAPRIOGLIO, DAMASO, orthodontist; b. Rosignano Monferrato, Mar. 9, 1934; MD, Torino U., 1958; PhD in Dentistry, Rome U., 1964. Chmn. Dental Children Clinic Milano, 1959—; tchr. ethics Parma U., 2005—. Chmn., tchr. orthodontics U. Parma, 1990—2004; founder, editor orthodontic chain Martina Edit. Bologna, 1993—2011. Recipient Oscar of Success, Berlin U., 2004, Carrier award, Italian Acad. Orthodontics, 2010. Mem.: World Fedn. Orthodontics, European Orthodontic Soc. Avocation: golf. Office: Via Tadino 55 Milan 20124 Italy Office Fax: 0039 02 2043544. Business E-Mail: damaso.caprioglio@dentalchildren.net.

CAPRON, ALEXANDER MORGAN, lawyer, educator, bioethicist; b. Hartford, Conn., Aug. 16, 1944; s. Willaim Mosher and Margaret (Morgan) Capron; m. Barbara A. Brown, Nov. 9, 1969 (div. Dec. 1985); 1 child, Jared Capron-Brown; m. Kathleen West, Mar. 4, 1989; children: Charles Spencer West Capron, Christopher Gordon West

Capron, Andrew Morgan West Capron. BA, Swarthmore Coll., 1966; LLB, Yale U., 1969; MA (hon.), U. Pa., 1975. Bar: D.C. 1970, Pa. 1978. Law clk. to presiding judge U.S. Ct. Appeals, Washington, 1969—70; lectr., rsch. assoc. Yale U., 1970—72; asst. prof. law U. Pa., 1972—75, assoc. prof., 1975—78, vice dean, 1976, prof. law and human genetics, 1978—82; exec. dir. Pres.'s Commn. for Study of Ethical Problems in Med. and Biomedical and Behavioral Rsch., Washington, 1980—83; prof. law, ethics and pub. policy Law Ctr. Georgetown U., Washington, 1983—84, inst. fellow Kennedy Inst. Ethics, 1983—84; Topping prof. law, medicine and pub. policy U. So. Calif., LA, 1985—89, univ. prof., 1989—, prof. medicine and law, 1991—, Henry W. Bruce prof. equity, 1991—2006, Scott H. Bice chair in healthcare law, policy and ethics, 2006—; co-dir. Pacific Ctr. for Health Policy and Ethics, LA, 1990—; dir. ethics and health WHO, 2002—03, dir. ethics, trade, human rights and health law, 2003—06. Mem. bd. advisors Am. Bd. Internal Medicine, 1985—95, chmn., 1991—95; cons. NIH, mem. subcom. on human gene therapy, 1984—92, mem. recombinant DNA adv. com., 1990—95; chmn. Congrl. Biomedical Ethics Adv. Commn., 1987—91; mem. Joint Commn. on Accreditation of Healthcare Orgns., 1994—, mem. ethics adv. com., 1984—85; mem. Nat. Bioethics Adv. Commn., 1996—2001. Author (with Katz): Catastrophic Diseases: Who Decides What?, 1976; author: (with others) Genetic Counseling: Facts, Values and Norms, 1979, Law, Science and Medicine, 1984, supplements, 1987, 1989, 2d edit., Treatise on Health Care Law, 1991, Ethical Issues in Governing Biobanks. Global Perspectives, 2008; contbr. articles to profl. jours. Bd. mgrs. Swarthmore Coll., 1982—85; bd. trustees The Century Found. Fellow: AAAS, Hastings Ctr. (bd. dirs. 1975—98, Inst. Soc., Ethics and Life Scis.), Am. Coll. Legal Medicine (hon.); mem.: AAUP (exec. com. Pa. chpt.), Am. Law Inst., Internat. Assn. Bioethics (mem. bd. 1992—96, 2001—, v.p. 2003—05, pres. 2005—07), Am. Soc. Law, Medicine and Ethics (pres. 1988—89), Inst. Medicine of NAS (bd. dirs. 1985—90), Swarthmore Coll. Alumni Soc. (v.p. 1974—77). Office: U So Calif Gould Sch Law Los Angeles CA 90089-0071 Home Phone: 310-450-1815; Office Phone: 213-740-2557. Business E-Mail: acapron@law.usc.edu.

CAPUTO, ANTHONY, ophthalmologist; Attended, Univ Di Bologna, Italy, 1969. Diplomate Am. Bd. Ophthalmology. Resident UMDNJ-Univ. Hosp., 1971—74; fellow Wills Eye Hosp., 1974—75; prof. ophthalmology UMDNJ-NJ Med. Sch. Office: Clara Maass Medical Center 1 Clara Maass Drive Belleville NJ 07109 Office Phone: 973-450-2000.

CAPUTO, GREGORY MICHAEL, internist, educator; b. May 18, 1954; s. Joseph Vincent and Mary (Pisapia) C.; m. Leesa, June 10, 1978; children: Jennifer, Michael. BA in Biol. Sci., U. Del., Newark, 1976; MD, U. Md., 1980. Diplomate Am. Bd. Internal Medicine, Am. Bd. Infectious Disease. Intern Thomas Jefferson U. Hosp., Phila., 1980-81, clin. asst. prof. dept. medicine, 1987—90; from asst. prof. to prof. medicine Pa. State U., Hershey, 1990—98, prof., 1998—; resident Milton S. Hershey Med. Ctr., Pa. State U. Coll. Medicine, 1981—83, fellow divsn. infectious diseases, 1983—84; chief divsn. gen. internal medicine Milton S. Hershey Med. Ctr., 1996—2004, vice-chair dept. medicine, 2002—04, interim chair dept. emergency medicine, 2004—06, chief quality officer, 2006—, Robert Dye endowed prof. medicine, 2006—. Mem. staff Med. Ctr. Del., Wilmington, 1990—95, Alfred I. duPont Med. Ctr., 1990—, med. dir. diabetes amputation prevention program, 1993—99; dir. Cecil County Lyme Disease Clinic, Elkton, 1988—90; cons. Assn. Acad. Health Ctrs., Am. Lyme Disease Found., 1992—; vis. scholar Johns Hopkins Ctr. Preventive Cardiology, 2001—02; lectr. in field. Author: (chpt.) Comprehensive Textbook of Pulmonary Medicine, 1991, The Foot in Diabetes, 2d edit., 1994; co-author: (chpt.) Comprehensive Textbook Pulmonary Medicine Update, 1995, (computer program) The Prevention Guides for Clinicians and Patients, 1996; co-editor: Medical Consultation, 1997; reviewer New Eng. Jour. Medicine, Internal Medicine Jour., Clin. Infectious Diseases, Diabetes Care; contbr. articles to profl. jours. Recipient Fletcher Brown award, 1975, Disting. Physician award, Pa. State U. Coll. Medicine, 1995, Disting. Educator award, 2006; fellow, Harvard Med. Sch., 1984—85, C. Everett Koop Inst. Dartmouth Coll., 1996; vis. scholar, Johns Hopkins Med. Instns., 2001—02. Fellow ACP; mem. Am. Soc. Microbiology, Soc. Gen. Internal Medicine, Am. Diabetes Assn., Phi Beta Kappa, Phi Kappa Phi, Beta Beta Beta, Alpha Omega Alpha, Ctr. Quality Innovation (co-dir.). Avocations: music, tennis, hiking. Office: Milton S Hershey MC H1246A 500 University Dr Hershey PA 17033

CAPUTO, WAYNE JAMES, surgeon, podiatrist; b. Newark, Feb. 18, 1956; s. James Vincent and Jennie (DeMaio) C.; m. Phyllis A. Grillo, Nov. 20, 1984; children: Karla, Stefanie. BS in Biology, Syracuse U., 1978; D of Podiatric Medicine, NY Coll. Podiatric Medicine, 1982. Diplomate Am. Bd. Podiatric Surgery. Clin. asst. prof. NY Coll. Podiatic Medicine, NYC, 1984-89; chief dept. podiatric surgery Clara Maass Med. Ctr., Belleville, NJ, 1987—, Columbus Hosp., Newark, 1995—. Dir. residency in podiatric surgery Union (NJ) Hosp., 1990—. Contbr. articles to profl. jours. Fellow ACS, Am. Coll. Dermatologists. Office: Clara Maass Profl Med Ctr 5 Franklin Ave Belleville NJ 07109-3532 E-mail: w_j_caputo@juno.com.

CARABASI, MATTHEW H., oncologist, educator; MD, Thomas Jefferson U., 1980. Diplomate Am. Bd. Internal Medicine, Am. Bd. Internal Medicine-med. oncology, lic. Pa. Intern Hahnemann Univ. Hosp., Phila., resident; fellow Meml. Sloan Kettering Cancer Ctr., NY; assoc. prof., dept. med. oncology Thomas Jefferson Univ., 2005—; hosp. affiliations include Thomas Jefferson Univ. Hosp., Methodist Hosp. Divsn. of Thomas Jefferson Univ. Hosp. Named one of Top Docs, Phila. Mag., 2010. Office: Thomas Jefferson University Department of Medical Oncology 233 S10th St Philadelphia PA 19107 Office Phone: 215-503-8588. Office Fax: 215-503-9334. E-mail: matthew.carabasi@jefferson.edu.

CARAGINE, LOUIS PHILIP, JR., neurosurgeon; married; 3 children. BS in Biology, Georgetown U., Washington, DC, 1987, MS in Physiology and Biophysics, 1989, MD with honors, 1992; PhD in Physiology, Wayne State U., Detroit, 1998. Diplomate Am. Bd. Neurol. Surgery. Gen. surg. intern Detroit Med. Ctr., 1992—93; resident dept. neurol. surgery Sch. Medicine Wayne State U., Detroit, 2000; fellow U. Calif., San Francisco, 2000—02; assoc. Geisinger Med. Ctr., 2002—05, dir. Endovascular Neurosurg. Ste., 2002—05, dir. Vascular and Endovascular Neurosurgery and Interventional Neuroradiology, 2002—05; assoc. prof. Med. Ctr. The Ohio State U., 2005—09, dir. Endovascular Neurosurgery, 2005—, dir. Neurol. Surgery Intensive Care Unit, 2006; dir. cerebrovascular & endovascular neurosurgery St. Francis Med. Ctr., 2009—; primary investigator Patients Prone Recurrence Endovascular Treatment, 2010—. Mem. by-laws com. exec. com. cerebrovascular sect. Congress Neurol. Surgery, 2007—; primary investigator Wingspan HDE Stent Sys. for Intracranial Atherosclerotic Disease, 2007; sec. Ohio State Neurosurg. Soc.; presenter in field; lectr. in field. Reviewer: profl. jours.; contbr. articles to profl. jours. Recipient The Galbraith award, Cong. Neurol. Surgeons, 1998, Scholarly Activities Excellence award, Wayne State U. Sch. Medicine, 1998; fellow, NIH, 1989, Target, 2000—02; scholar, The Rhone-Poulenc Rorer Cong. Neurol. Surgeons, 1999. Fellow: Am. Assn. Neurol. Surgery (mem. young neurosurgeons com. 1999—, liaison 2005—, mem. coun. state neurosurgical socs. 2005—, maintenance cert. com. 2007—, exec. com. corresponding sect. CNS 2008—, exec. com. cerebrovascular sect. mem. 2007—); mem.: AMA, SNIS (exec. com. 2009—10), Bd. Neurointerventional Surgery (dir. 2009—10), Am. Surg. Assn., Am. Soc. Interventional Neuroradiology (sr.; exec. com. mem. 2009—), Am. Coll. Radiology, Neurocritical Care Soc., Am. Heart Assn. (stroke coun. 2003—05). Office: Saint Francis Med Ctr 150 S Mt Auburn Rd Ste 320 Cape Girardeau MO 63701 Office Phone: 573-331-5487. Business E-Mail: louispcaraginejr@hotmail.com.

CARAVATI, E. MARTIN, toxicologist; b. Richmond, Va., Oct. 18, 1954; MD, Med. Coll. Va., 1981; MPH, U. Utah, 1994. Med. dir. Utah Poison Control Ctr., 2000—. Prof. emergency medicine U. Utah Sch. Medicine, 1985; assoc. editor Clinical Toxicology. Fellow: Am. Coll. Med. Toxicology, Am. Acad. Clin. Toxicology. Home: 1138 Gilmer Dr Salt Lake City UT 84105 Business E-Mail: martin.caravati@hsc.utah.edu.

CARBON, ROMAN T, general, pediatric surgeon; b. Erlangen, Bavaria, Germany, Aug. 13, 1957; s. Ludwig Carbon and Maria Obermeier; m. Carolin von Frankenberg und Ludwigsdorff, Mar. 20, 1992; 1 child, Moritz. MD, Friedrich-Alexander U., Erlangen, 1985, Dr.med., 1986, Dr.med.habil., 2000. Bachelor Weizmann-Inst. of Sci., Rehovot, Israel, 1978-79; surg. asst. Friedrich-Alexander U., Germany, 1984-93, cons. surgeon, 1994-99, assoc. prof. pediatric surgery, 2000—; head dept. pediat. surgery U. Erlangen, 2010—; head Northern Bavarian U. Ctr. Pediat. Surgery, 2011—. Consult surgeon Weizmann Inst Soc, 1979—, German Soc. Surgery, 1987—, European Inst of Surgery, Hamburg, 1997—; consult docent Sch of Physiotherapy, Erlangen, 1985—. Author: (book) Pediatric Surgery, 1999, Tissue Management, 1999, Fibrin Sealing in Surgery, 2000, Biodegradables, 2001, Principles in Tissue Management, 2005; contbr. articles to profl. jours. Mem Freunde des Weizmann Inst, 1979. Mem.: Int Pediatric Endoscopic Group, Soc. Minimally Invasive Therapy, South German Soc. Pediat. Surgery (pres. 2011), Deutsche Gesellschaft fuer Chirurgie. Achievements include research in in carrier materials for tissue sealing, biodegradables, sealing concepts in MIS, tool implementation for MIS in pediatric surgery, scientific illustrations. Avocations: aquarell painting, skiing, art, architecture. Home: Rudelsweiherstr 31a 91054 Erlangen Bavaria Germany Office: Friedrich-Alexander U Maximiliansplatz 2 91054 Erlangen Bavaria Germany Office Fax: 0049-9131853-4432. Business E-Mail: roman.carbon@uk-erlangen.de.

CARBONELL, DAVID, psychologist; PhD in Clinical Psychology, DePaul U., 1985. Lic. clinical psychologist NY & Ill. Founder & dir. Anxiety Treatment Ctr., Chgo. Author: Panic Attacks Workbook: A Guided Program for Beating the Panic Trick, 2004. Mem.: Obsessive Compulsive Found., Ill. Psychological Assn., Internat. Assn. Cognitive Psychotherapy, Assn. Behavioral & Cognitive Therapies, Anxiety Disorders Assn. Am., Am. Psychological Assn. Office: 5105 Tollview Dr Ste 103 Rolling Meadows IL 60008 Office Phone: 847-481-5251. E-mail: director@anxietycoach.com.

CARBONELL, JOSEFINA G., healthcare company executive, former federal agency administrator; b. Cuba, 1950; 1 child, Alfredo. Grad., Fla. Internat. U., 1972. With Little Havana Activities and Nutrition Centers, Dade County, Fla., 1972—2001, pres., CEO, 1982—2001; asst. sec. for aging US Dept. Health & Human Services, Washington, 2001—09; sr. v.p. long term care Independent Living Systems, LLC, Miami, 2009—. Recipient Citizen of Yr. award, Miami, 1992, Charles Whited Spirit of Excellence award, Miami Herald, 1993, Cmty. Svc. award, Nat. Alliance for Hispanic Health, 1995, Monsignor Bryan Walsh Outstanding Human Svc. award, United Way, 1997, Commrs. Team award, Social Security Adminstrn., 1997, Claude Pepper Cmty. Svc. award, 2001; named one of The Most Influential Hispanic Women, Hispanic Bus., 2003; Kellogg Fellowship in Health Mgmt., John F. Kennedy Sch. Govt., Harvard U. Office: Independent Living Systems LLC 5201 Blue Lagoon Dr #270 Miami FL 33126

CARBONELL, TERESA, physiologist, educator; b. Barcelona, Mar. 29, 1963; Degree in Biology, U. Barcelona, 1986, PhD in Biochemistry and Physiology, 1992. Asst. prof. U. Barcelona, 1995. Grant, Ministry Edn., U. Calif., Davis. Mem.: NY Acad. Scis., Soc. Catalana de Biologia. Office: Avda Diagonal 645 Barcelona Catalonia 08028 Spain Office Fax: 934110358. Business E-Mail: tcarbonell@ub.edu.

CARDEN, ZACHARY FRANK, JR., retired dentist; b. Chattanooga, June 19, 1941; s. Zachary Frank and Mable (Torbett) C.; m. Anne Fowler, Jan. 28, 1967; children: Heather Anne, Zachary Frank III. BS, Carson-Newman Coll., 1963; med. technologist, Erlanger Hosp., Chattanooga, 1964; DDS, U. Tenn., 1974. Med. technologist Erlanger Hosp., Chattanooga, 1964-65, 68-70; pvt. practice Chattanooga, 1974—. Author: The Secret Files of Henry F. Sherwood, 2005, Tootie Greene, 2009. Pres. Civic Art League, Chattanooga, 1980. Capt. U.S. Army, 1965 68. With US Army, 1965—68. Decorated Commendation medal U.S. Army. Fellow: Internat. Coll. Dentists, Pierre Fauchard Acad., Am. Coll. Dentists; mem.: ADA (alt. del. 2008—), Am. Coll. of Dentists TN Section (chair), Chattanooga Craniomandibular Study Group (pres. 1985—86), Chattanooga Area Dental Soc. (treas. 1997—98, sec. 1998—99, pres.-elect 1999, pres. 2000—01), 3d Dist. Dental Soc. (chmn. peer rev. 1983—85, trustee for Hamilton County 1996, treas. 1997—98), Lookout Dental Study Group (pres. 1975), Tenn. Dental Assn. (del. 1983—85, chmn. coun. on ethics, by-laws and jud. affairs 1999—2003, v.p. 2000—, trustee 2006—08, pres. elect 2008—, pres. 2009—10, v.p. East Tenn., sci. editor Tenn. Dental Assn. Jour.), Am. Acad. Oral Medicine (Oral Medicine award 1974). Republican. Presbyn. Avocations: watercolor and oil painting, golf. Office Phone: 423-894-0052. Personal E-mail: zcarden@comcast.net.

CARDENAS, VICTOR JOSE, thoracic surgeon, educator; b. Iowa City, Mar. 24, 1958; BS in Biology, U. Houston, 1979; MD, U. Tex. Med. Br., 1983. Prof. medicine U. Tex. Med. Br., 1983—. Fellowship, U. Tex. Sys. Clin. Safety and Effectiveness Com. Fellow: Am. Coll. Chest Physicians; mem.: ACP, Soc. Critical Care Medicine, Am. Thoracic Soc., Phi Kappa Phi Honor Soc., Alpha Omega Alpha Honor Soc. Avocation: bicycling. Office: 122 Majuro Tiki Island TX 77554 Office Phone: 409-938-8966. Business E-Mail: vcardena@utmb.edu.

CARDENOSA, GILDA, diagnostic radiologist, educator; MD, Columbia U., 1984. Diplomate Am. Bd. Radiology-diagnostic radiology, 1984. Resident diagnostic radiology Mass. Gen. Hosp., Boston, 1985—89, fellow; prof. radiology Med. Coll. of Va.; dir. breast imaging Nelson Clinic; hosp. affiliations include Va. Commonwealth Univ. Med. Ctr. Office: Virginia Commonwealth University Medical Ctr Radiology Department 9000 Stony Point Pkwy Richmond VA 23235 Office Phone: 804-560-8906 ext. 7862. Office Fax: 804-237-6663. E-mail: gcardenosa@vcu.edu.

CARDIFF, ROBERT DARRELL, pathology educator; b. San Francisco, Dec. 5, 1935; s. George Darrell and Helen (Kohfield) C.; m. Sally Joan Bounds, June 23, 1962; children: Darrell, Todd, Shelley. BS, U. Calif., Berkeley, 1958, PhD, 1968; MD, U. Calif., San Francisco, 1962. Intern King's County Hosp., Bklyn., 1962-63; resident in pathology U. Oreg., Portland, 1963-66; NIH fellow U. Calif., Berkeley, 1966-68, mem. faculty med. sch. Davis, 1971—, prof. pathology Med. Sch., 1977—2005, disting. prof., 2005—, chair dept. pathology, 1990-96; dir. Ctr. for Med. Informatics U. Calif. Davis Healthcare Sys., 1996-98, faculty Ctr. for Comparative Medicine; chair Med. Informatics Grad. Group, 2002—04; dir. Ctr. Genomic Pathology, 2007—. Mem. sci. adv. bd. Contra Costa Cancer Fund, Walnut Creek, Calif., 1985-99; mem. Univ.-Wide AIDS Task Force, Berkeley, 1984-87; vis. prof. Sun-Yat Sen U. Med. Sci., Peoples Republic of China, 1985, 93, Harvard Med. Sch., 1990, U. Calif. San Diego, 1998-99. Mem. editl. bd. Human Pathology, 1992-2004, Tumor Markers, 1992—, Internat. Jour. Oncology, 1992—, Jour. Mamgland Biol. and Neoplasia, 1998—; contbr. articles to profl. jours Lt. col. US Army, 1968—71. Recipient Triton Rsch. award, Triton Bioscis., Inc., 1985, Sadusk award, Peralta Cancer Inst., 1986, Dist. Prof. award, 2005. Master: AAUP (exec. com. 1983—85); fellow: AAAS; mem.: Ctr. for Genomic Pathology (dir.), No. Calif. Pathology Soc. (pres. 1990—96), Sacramento Pathology Soc. (bd. dirs. 1985—96), Internat. Assn. Breast Cancer Rsch. (bd. dirs. 1984—96, pres. 2003—06, chair 2006—, chair, bd. govs. 2006—), Internat. Acad. Pathology, Pluto Soc., Sigma Xi. Avocations: basketball, skiing, jogging. Office: U Calif-Davis Ctr for Comparative Medicine 98 County Rd & Hutchison Dr Davis CA 95616 Office Phone: 530-752-2726.

CARDOSO, CLARECI SILVA, epidemiologist, educator; b. São Sebastião do Oeste, Minas Gerais, Brazil, Nov. 15, 1970; Degree in Psychology, U. Fed. de São João Del Rei, 1995; MD, U. Fed. de Minas Gerais, PhD, 2005. Epidemiologist Hosp. das Clínicas da U. Fed. de Minas Gerais, 2006—09; prof. U. Fed. de São João Del Rei., 2009—. Leader rsch. group Epidemiology & Evaluation New Techs. Health. Named Best Psychologist, Prominent Psychologist Minas Gerais, 2010. Fellow: Nações Unidas, CEPAL (cons.); mem.: Internat. Soc. Urban Health. Achievements include research in health technology, mental health and quality of life. Avocations: reading, exercise, travel. Office: Ave Sebastião Gonçalves Coelho 400 Divinópolis Minas Gerais 35501-296 Brazil E-mail: clarecicardoso@yahoo.com.br.

CARDOSO, ELIE PATRICK, physician, researcher, toxicologist; b. Beja, France, Apr. 24, 1949; s. Isaac Andre and Frida (Gozlan) C.; m. Simone Marie-Jeanne Beller; children: Ruth, Thomas. BS, Lycee Condorcet, Paris, 1968; MD, U. Paris, 1976; postgrad., U. Strasbourg, France, 1991. Vol. practitioner, Paris, 1976-79; occupl. health physician Somie, Paris, 1974-76, Interco. Occupation Health Assn., Strasbourg, France, 1979-81, 91—; vol. physician Paris and Strasbourg, 1982-91. Presenter 8th Internat. Symposium ISSA Rsch. Sect., Athens, 2003, XVII World Congress on Safety and Health at Work, Orlando, Fla., 2005, Increases in Reticulocyte Count and Carcinogenic Risk During Exposure to Benzene; presenter, spkr. XVIII World Congress on Health at Work, Seoul, Republic of Korea, 2008, Women Enzyme Inducing Solvents, Pregnancy, and Teratogenic Risks. Author: Cancer Prevention and Control, 2001, Cancer Screening Theory, 2001, 8th Internat. Symposium, 2003; inventor in field; contbr. articles on carcinogenic risk by solvents to profl. jours. Grantee Sci. Action in Rsch. and Occupation Health, 1993, Cisme_Sci. Action in Rsch., 1999. Avocations: music, sports. Office: AST 67 3 Rue de Sarrelouis 67080 Strasbourg France Personal E-mail: simoneeliecardoso@yahoo.fr. Business E-Mail: e.cardoso@ast67.org.

CARDOSO, LUCILENE, nursing educator, researcher; b. Santa Rita do Passa Quatro, São Paulo, Brazil, July 11, 1978; B, Ribeirão Preto Coll. Nursing, U. São Paulo, 2003, D, 2008. Rschr., prof. Ribeirão Preto Coll. Nursing, U. São Paulo, 2009—. Office: University Sao Paulo Ribeirao Preto Sch Nursing Ave Bandeirantes 3900 Ribeirão Preto São Paulo 14040-902 Brazil Business E-Mail: lucilene@eerp.usp.br.

CARDWELL, HAROLD DOUGLAS, SR., retired rehabilitation services professional; b. Varnell, Ga., July 17, 1926; s. Arlie Amber and Hettie Ellen (Eledge) C.; m. Priscilla Dean Rumley, July 3, 1954; children: Harold Douglas, Jr., Ruth Ellen Cardwell-Landau. AA, Daytona Beach C.C., 1972; student, U. Fla., 1970; BA, Fla. Tech. U., 1974; postgrad., Clemson U., 1975. Registered landscape architect Fla. Chem. operator Fercleve Chem. Corp., Oak Ridge, Tenn., 1945-46, draftsman C.M. Price Constrn. Co., Daytona Beach, Fla., 1947-48; bookkeeper, expediter W.A. Cardwell Constrn. Co., Gatlinburg, Tenn., 1948-49; office mgr., sales rep. J.H. Gordon Lumber Co., St. Augustine, Fla., 1949-51; asst. mgr. King Bros. Lumber Co., St. Augustine, 1951-56; pvt. practice landscape architect Port Orange, Fla., 1956-67; sr. rehab. specialist State of Fla. Divsn. of Blind Svcs., Daytona Beach, 1967-99, ret., 1999. Vice chmn. Daytona Beach Preservation Bd., 1987-98; adv. task force Daytona Beach City Govt., 1987; vice chmn. Volusia County Hist. Commn., Deland, Fla., 1989-92; mem. adv. bd. Volusia County Hist. Preservation Bd., Deland, 1992-94; adv. bd. mem. Flagler Centennial Com., Tallahassee, Fla., 1986; pres. Fla. Anthropol. Soc., Gainesville, 1988-89; chmn. Daytona Beach Preservation Bd., 1998-2006. Recipient Historian of Yr. award Volusia County Hist. Commn., 1988, Lazarus award for Preservation, Fla. Anthropol. Soc., 1988. Mem. Am. Hort. Therapy

Assn. (registered hort. therapist, nat. treas. 1978-80), Fla. Nurserymen and Growers Assn. (bd. dirs. 1963-64, 68-69), Halifax Hist. Soc. (bd. dirs. 1974—), Fla. Hist. Soc. (bd. mem., 2000—), Lions (Pres.' award in leadership Port Orange/South Halifax club 1988). Democrat. Methodist. Avocations: history, anthropology, historical tools, prehistoric tools, writing, research. Home: 1343 Woodbine St Daytona Beach FL 32114-5740

CAREK, DONALD J(OHN), child psychiatry educator; b. Sheboygan, Wis., Aug. 10, 1931; s. Peter and Rose (Gergisch) C.; m. Frances M. Schaefer, Jan. 28, 1956; children: Carla, Thomas, Therese, Peter, Mary Beth, Christopher MD, Marquette U., 1956. Diplomate Am. Bd. Psychiatry and Neurology (examiner in child psychiatry, psychiatry). Intern Walter Reed Army Hosp., 1956-57; resident U. Mich. Hosps., 1959-63; pediatrician Fort Meyer Dispensary, Arlington, Va., 1958-59; instr. psychiatry U. Mich., Ann Arbor, 1962-65, asst. prof., 1965-66; dir. day care Children's Psychiat. Hosp., Ann Arbor, 1965-66; assoc. prof. psychiatry and pediatrics Med. Coll. Wis., Milw., 1966-74, acting chmn. div. human behavior, 1970-73, prof. psychiatry, 1974-76; pres. med. staff Milw. Psychiat. Hosp., 1971-73; prof. psychiatry and pediatrics, chief youth divsn. Med. U. S.C., Charleston, 1976-96, emeritus prof. psychiatry, 1996—; staff psychiatrist Vols. in Medicine, Hilton Head, SC, 2004—. Co-author: Guide to Psychotherapy, 1966; author: Principles of Child Psychotherapy, 1972; mem. editorial bd. Am. Jour. Child & Adolscent Psychiatry, 1988-93; contbr. articles to profl. jours. Bd. dirs. Cedarcrest Girls Residential Treatment Ctr., 1969-71. Capt. USAR, 1956-59. Named Best Doctors in America Southeast Region, 1995. Fellow Am. Acad. Child Psychiatry (life, com. on adolscent psychiatry 1979-85, com. on psychotherapy 1986-90), Am. Psychiat. Assn., Am. Coll. Psychiatrists (membership com. 1991-98); mem. AMA, AAAS, Am. Orthopsychiatry Assn., Am. Psychosomatic Soc., Soc. Profs. Child Psychiatry, S.C. Med. Assn. (mental health com. 1992-93), S.C. Dist. Cr. Am. Psychiat. Assn., Charleston County Med. Soc., S.C. State Bd. Med. Examiners (med. disciplinary commn. 1992-95), Alpha Omega Alpha, Alpha Sigma Nu. Roman Catholic. Home: 97 Nightingale Ln Bluffton SC 29909 Office: Med Univ SC 171 Ashley Ave Charleston SC 29425-0001 Home Phone: 843-705-7343; Office Phone: 843-792-2436. Personal E-mail: dcarek@sc.rr.com.

CAREN, JEFFREY F., cardiologist, educator; MA in Philosophy, U. Calif., Berkeley; MD, U. Calif., San Francisco. Cert. internal med. 1974, cardiovascular disease 1979. Intern LA County Hosp., 1971—72, resident, 1972—74, fellow, 1976—78, UCLA-West LA Veteran's Medical Ctr., Am. Coll. Cardiology; chief med. & critical care LA Cmty. Hosp.; asst. clinical prof. med. U. Calif. David Geffen Sch. Med.; attending physician Cedars-Sinai Heart Inst. Div. Cardiology. Mem. Cardiology Performance Improvement Com. Major Medical Corp. US Army. Mem.: LA County Medical Assn Beverly Hills Chpt. (bd. mem.). Office: Cedars-Sinai Medical Center 8700 Beverly Blvd Los Angeles CA 90048 Mailing: 8635 W 3rd St #890-W Los Angeles CA 90048 Office Phone: 310-659-0714. Office Fax: 310-659-0664.

CAREW, LYNDON B., JR., nutritionist, educator; s. Lyndon Belmont and Myrtle L. (Woodworth) C.; children: Leslie, Audre. BS, U. Mass., Amherst, 1955; PhD, Cornell U., Ithaca, NY, 1961; diploma, Essex Agrl. Inst., Hathorne, Mass., 1950. Dir. Colombian nat. poultry program, animal nutrition lab. Rockefeller Found., Bogota, Colombia, 1961—65; rsch. assoc. Cornell U., 1965—66; dir. poultry rsch. Hess & Clark Div. Richardson Merrell, Ashland, Ohio, 1966—69; prof. animal sci. U. Vt., Burlington, 1969—, prof. nutrition food sci., 1969—. Lectr. in field; nutrition edn. cons. Vt. Info. System, Shelburne, 1982—. Contbr. articles to profl. jours. Vol. Mid-Atlantic Consortium W.K. Kellogg Found., Burlington, 2003—08, Open Spaces Com., Shelburne, Vt., 1970—75, Governor's Coun. Phys. Fitness, Montpelier, Vt., 1983—85, Vt. Health Policy Corp., Montpelier, 1985, Vt./Honduras Partners of the Americas, Burlington, 1985—2005. Numerous grants, 1970—2008. Mem. Vt. Nutrition Coun. (pres. 1975-77, 83-85), Animal Nutrition Rsch. Coun. (chmn. bd. trustees 1984-85), Endocrine Soc., Am. Inst. Nutrition, Poultry Sci. Assn., Nutrition Edn. Soc., Vt.-Honduras Ptnrs. Am. (bd. dirs. 1996—2006). Avocations: music, travel, journalism. Office: University Vt 570 Main St 107B Terrill Hall Burlington VT 05405 Home: 205 Collamer Cir Burlington VT 05405 Office Phone: 802-656-5893. Business E-Mail: lcarew@uvm.edu.

CAREW, THOMAS JAMES, neuroscientist, educator; b. Calif. m. Mary Jo Carew. BS in Psychology, Loyola U., Los Angeles; MS, Calif. State U., Los Angeles; PhD, U. Calif., Riverside, 1970. Prof. psychiatry Columbia U. Coll. of Physicians & Surgeons, 1970—76, NYU Sch. of Medicine, 1976—83; prof. Yale U., 1983—90, John M. Musser prof., chair dept. psychology, 1990—99; prof. neurobiology & behavior U. Calif., Irvine, Calif., 1999—2001, Donald Bren prof. & chair Ctr. for Neurobiology of Learning & Memory, 2001—. Author several articles published in various journals; co-author: (books) Perspectives in Neural Systems and Behavior, 1989, Mechanistic Relationships Between Development and Learning, 1998; author: Behavioral Neorobiology, 2000. Recipient Merit award, NIH, 1990, Dylan Hixon prize, 1990. Fellow: AAAS, Am. Acad. Arts & Sciences; mem.: Soc. Neuroscience (pres. 2007), Soc. Exptl. Psychology. Achievements include research in neural basis of behavior and animal behavior. Office: U Calif 2205 McGaugh Hall 301 Qureshey Research Lab Mail Code 4550 Irvine CA 92697-4550 Office Phone: 949-824-6114. Office Fax: 949-824-2447. Business E-Mail: tcarew@uci.edu.

CAREY, BENEDICT, science writer; b. 1962; BS in Math., U. Colo., 1983; studied journalism, Northwestern U., 1985. Staff writer Hippocrates mag., 1987—97; health and fitness reporter Los Angeles Times, 1997—2004; science and med. writer New York Times, 2004—. Author: The Unknowns. Recipient U. Mo. Lifestyle award, 2002. Office: New York TImes 620 8th Ave New York NY 10018 Business E-Mail: bencarey@nytimes.com. *

CAREY, JOHN CLAYTON, pediatrician, educator, medical geneticist; b. Balt., 1946; MD, Georgetown U., 1972; MPH, U. Calif., Berkeley, 1976. Diplomate Am. Bd. Med. Genetics, Am. Bd. Pediatrics. Prof. pediat. U. Utah Med. Ctr., Salt Lake City, vice chmn. Dept. Pediat. Co-author: Medical Genetics, 4th edit., 2004, Care of the Child with Trisomy 18/13, 1996, rev. edit. 2000, 2008. Softly Written, Softly Spoken, 2002; editor-in-chief Am. Jour. Med. Genetics; contbr. over 260 articles to profl. jours. Med. advisor Support Orgn. Trisomy 18, 13 and Related Disorders, Utah Birth Defects Network, Pregnancy Risk Line. Office: U Utah Med Ctr Pediatrics 2C412 SOM 50 Mario Capecchi Dr Salt Lake City UT 84132-0001 Office Phone: 801-581-8943.

CAREY, JOHN P., otolaryngologist, educator; MD, Wash. U., St. Louis, 1991. Diplomate Am. Bd. Otolaryngology. Resident gen. surgery Va. Mason Hosp., Seattle, 1991—93; resident otolaryngology - head and neck surgery Univ. of Wash, 1994—98, fellow otolaryngology, 1993—94; fellow neurotology The Johns Hopkins Univ., 1998—2000, assoc. prof. otolaryngology - head and neck surgery; hospital affiliation includes Johns Hopkins Hosp. Co-author: (publs.) Orientation of human semicircular canals measured by three-dimensional multiplanar CT reconstruction, 2005, Responses of irregularly discharging chinchilla semicircular canal vestibular-nerve afferents during high-frequency head rotations, 2005, Angular vestibulo-ocular reflex gains correlate with vertigo control after intratympanic gentamicin treatment for Meniere's disease, 2005, The effect of binocular eye position and head rotation plane on the human torsional vestibuloocular reflex, 2006, Axis of Eye Rotation Changes with Head-Pitch Orientation during Head Impulses about Earth-Vertical, 2006, and numerous others. Office: Johns Hopkins Hospital 600 N Wolfe St Baltimore MD 21287 Office Phone: 410-955-5000.

CAREY, MARTIN CONRAD, gastroenterologist, molecular biophysicist, educator, medical geneticist; b. Clonmel, Ireland, June 18, 1939; came to U.S., 1967; s. John Joseph and Alice (Broderick) C.; m. Antonieta Fernandez, July 1, 1972 (div. 1987); children: Julian Albert, Dermot Martin. MB, BCh BAO with 1st class honors, Nat. U. Ireland, 1962, MD, 1981, DSc, 1984, LLD (hon.), 1992, DSc (hon.), 2010; AM (hon.), Harvard U., 1989. Intern St. Vincent's Hosp., Dublin, 1962-63, resident, 1965-67, Nat. Maternity Hosp., Dublin, 1963, St. Luke's Hosp., Dublin, 1964, Queen Charlotte's Hosp., London, 1964; asst. prof. medicine Boston U. Sch. Medicine, 1973-75, Harvard U. Med. Sch., Boston, 1975-79, assoc. prof., 1979-88, Lawrence J. Henderson assoc. prof. health sci. & tech., 1979-88, 88-91, faculty mem. Grad. Sch. Arts & Scis., 1983—, assoc. mem. dept. cellular & molecular physiology, 1983—, prof. medicine, 1988—, prof. health sci. & tech., 1991—; external examiner Com. on Higher Doctorates, Hong Kong U., 2010. Mem. staff Brigham and Women's Hosp., Boston, 1975—; McIlrath guest prof. Royal Prince Alfred Hosp., U. Sydney, 1987; cons. Gipharmex S.A., Milan, 1984—87, Dow Chem. Co., Midland, Mich., 1984—87, Merix, Inc., Needham, 1986—96, Oculon, Cambridge, 1987—95, Ciba-Giegy, Summit, NJ, 1988—93, Labs. Fournier, Dijon-Diax, 1992—93, Aventis, Frankfurt, 1993—2002, Genzyme, 1993—2002, Merck & Co., 2001—03, Dublin Molecular Medicine Centre, 2001—08, Mpex Biosci., Inc., San Diego, 2002—03, Chrysalis Biotech., Inc., Galveston, Tex., 2003—04, Peptimmune, Inc., Cambridge, Mass., 2006—, Daiichi-Sankyo Inc., Parsippany, NJ, 2007—, Relypsa, Inc., Santa Clara, Calif., 2008—. Author: Bile Salts and Gallstones, 1974, Hepatic Excretory Function, 1975; assoc. editor: Jour. Lipid Rsch., 1978-81; mem. editl. bd. Am. Jour. Physiology, 1976-81, Hepatology, 1981-84, Gastroenterology, 1983-88; editor: Future Perspectives in Gastroenterology, Springer, 2008; contbr. articles to profl. jours Recipient Acad. Career Devel. award NIH, 1976, MERIT award, 1986, 2004, Adolf Windaus prize Falk Found., 1984, Huddinge Sikhuis medal Karolinska Inst., Stockholm, 1992, Fitzgerald medal U. Coll., 1993, Ismar Boas medal German Soc. for Digestive and Metabolic Diseases, 2002; hon. fellow med. faculty Nat. U. Ireland, Dublin, 2003; postdoctoral fellow Boston U. Sch. Medicine, 1968-73, Guggenheim Found. fellow, 1974, Fogarty Internat. fellow NIH, 1968, Fulbright fellow, 1967-68. Fellow AAAS, Royal Coll. Physicians Ireland; mem. Gastroenterology Rsch. Group (vice-chmn., steering com.), Am. Soc. Clin. Investigation, Am. Gastroent. Assn. (Disting. Achievement award 1990, William Beaumont prize 2000), Am. Oil Chemists Soc., Biophys. Soc., Interurban Clin. Club, Am. Assn. Physicians, Royal Irish Acad. (hon.), St. Botolph Club, The Club of Odd Volumes, Harvard Musical Assn., Boston Athenaeum. Roman Catholic. Achievements include patents in field. Office: Brigham and Womens Hosp Div Gastroenterology 75 Francis St Boston MA 02115-6106 Home Phone: 781-237-8581; Office Phone: 617-732-5822. Business E-Mail: mccarey@rics.bwh.harvard.edu.

CAREY, MARY G., cardiologist, educator; b. Rochester, NY, Mar. 8, 1967; PhD, U. Calif., San Francisco, 2001. Assoc. prof. U. at Buffalo, 2003—. Fellow: Am. Heart Assn. Office: 209 Wende Hall Buffalo NY 14212 Business E-Mail: mgcarey@buffalo.edu.

CAREY, ROBERT MUNSON, physician, educator; b. Lexington, Ky., Aug. 13, 1940; s. Henry Ames and Eleanor Day (Munson) C.; m. Theodora Vann Hereford, Aug. 24, 1963; children: Adonice Ames, Alicia Vann, Robert Josiah Hereford. BS, U. Ky., 1962; MD, Vanderbilt U., 1965; Doctor Honoris Causa, Fed. U. Ceara, Brazil, 1998. Diplomate Am. Bd. Internal Medicine, Am. Bd. Endocrinology and Metabolism, Nat. Bd. Med. Examiners. Intern in medicine U. Va. Hosp., Charlottesville, 1966; jr. asst. resident in medicine N.Y. Hosp.-Cornell Med. Ctr., NYC, 1968-69, sr. asst. resident, 1969-70; instr. endocrinology, dept. medicine Vanderbilt U. Sch. Medicine, Nashville, 1970-72; postdoctoral fellow in medicine St. Mary's Hosp. Med. Sch., London, 1972-73; asst. prof. internal medicine, endocrinology and metabolism U. Va. Sch. Medicine, Charlottesville, 1973-76, assoc. prof., 1976-80, prof., 1980—, James Carroll Flippin prof. medical sci. and dean, 1986—2002, prof. u., 2002—, David A. Harrison III disting. prof. medicine, 2002—, assoc. dir. Clin. Rsch. Ctr., 1975-86, prof., dean emeritus, 2002—, head. div. endocrinology and metabolism, dept. internal medicine, 1978-86, chmn. gen. faculty, chmn. med. adv. com., chmn. exec. com., 1986—. Attending staff U. Va. Hosp., Charlottesville, 1973—, pres. clin. staff, 1977-79, vice chmn. med. policy com., 1986—, adv. bd. 1986—; mem. study sect. on exptl. cardiovascular scis. NIH, 1982-85; mem. cardiovascular and renal adv. com. USDA, 1988—; vis. prof. div. nephrology, U. Miami Med. Sch., Fla., 1979, 83, 84, Hosp. das Clinicas da Univ., Fed. do Ceara, Forteleza, Brazil, 1981, hypertension div. Mt. Sinai Sch. Medicine, N.Y.C., 1981, div. pediatric endocrinology N.Y. Hosp.-Cornell Med. Ctr., 1981, dept. endocrinology St. Vincent's Hosp., Univ. Coll., Dublin, Ireland, 1982, depts. physiology and endocrinology Mayo Grad. Sch. Medicine, Rochester, Minn., 1984, div. rsch. Cleve. Clinic Found., 1984, Genentech, Inc., San Francisco, 1984, divs. endocrinology and metabolism U. Mass., U. Pa. Sch. Medicine, Boston U. Med. Sch., 1984, U. N.C. Sch. Medicine, 1985, Harvard Med. Sch., Boston, 1987, Jefferson Med. Coll., 1988; Bley Stein vis. prof. endocrinology U. So. Calif., 1987; Pfizer vis. prof. in pharmacology U. Chgo., 1988; co-organizer 3d Internat. Meeting on Peripheral Actions of Dopamine, Charlottesville, 1989; v.p. Va. Ambulatory Surgery, Inc., 1986—; speaker, presenter numerous nat. and internat. profl. meetings and congresses. Author: (with E.D. Vaughn) Adrenal Disorders, 1988; co-editor: Hypertension: An Endocrine Disease, 1985; mem. editorial bd. Jour. Clin. Endocronlogy and Metabolism, 1981-84, Hypertension jour., 1983-84, 2002-08, Am. Jour. Physiology: Heart and Circulatory Physiology, 1987-89, Am. Jour. Hypertension, 1987—; author over 300 articles, revs., papers for profl. jours., contbr. 19 chpts. to books. Mem. exec. com. and fin. com. U. Va. Health Services Found., 1986—; bd. dirs. Va. Kidney Stone Found., Inc., 1986—, The Harrison Found., Inc. U. Va., 1986—, Dyslexia Ctr., Charlottesville, 1986—. Surgeon (lt. comdr.) USPHS, 1966-68, res., 1968—. Recipient Attending Physician of Yr. awrd dept. internal medicine U. Va. Med. Ctr., 1983-84, Disting. Alumnus award and Founder's medal Vanderbilt U.; USPHS fellow Vanderbilt U., 1970-72; recipient numerous NIH grants as co-prin. and prin. investigator, 1972—, Thomas Jefferson award, U. Va., 2003; named to Hall Disting. Alumni, U. Ky., 2000. Master ACP (program com. regional meeting 1987); fellow Coun. for High Blood Pressure Rsch. AHA (program com. 1984-86, exec. and long rang planning coms. 1992—; chair-elect 2002-04, chair 2004-06, past chair 2004-08); mem. Inst. Medicine of NAS, Am. Heart Assn. (established investigator 1975-80, chair, coun. ops. com., 2006-08), Va. affiliate Am. Heart Assn. (bd. dirs. 1977-83, pres. 1979-80, Disting. Service award), The Endocrine Soc. (fin. com. 1988—, chair devel. com. 1991-92, pres. elect 2007-08, pres. 2008-), Am. Fedn. Clin. Rsch. (so. sect. councilor 1978-81, nominating com. 1982), So. Soc. Clin. Investigation (nominating com. 1982, sec.-treas. 1985-86), Inter-Am. Soc. for Hypertension, Am. Soc. Clin. Investigation, Am. Clin. and Climatol. Assn., Am. Soc. Hypertension (intersocietal affairs com. 1986—), Internat. Soc. Hypertension, Assn. Am. Physicians, AMA, Albemarle County Med. Soc., Med. Soc. Va., Assn. Am. Med. Coll.s Coun. of Deans, Inst. of Medicine, Nat. Acad. of Scis., The Raven Soc., Alpha Omega Alpha (Disting. Med. Alumnus award Vanderbilt U. 1994). Home: 2805 Magnolia Dr Charlottesville VA 22901 Office: U Va Sch Medicine PO Box 801414 Charlottesville VA 22908-1414

CAREY, WILLIAM BACON, pediatrician, educator; b. Phila., Dec. 6, 1926; s. Henry Reginald and Margaret (Bacon) Carey; m. Ann Lord McDougal, July 21, 1956; children: Katharine Blayney, Laura Bacon, Elizabeth McDougal. BA, Yale U., New Haven, Conn., 1950; MD, Harvard U., Boston, 1954. Diplomate Am. Bd. Pediatrics. Intern Phila. Gen. Hosp., 1954-55; resident in pediatrics Children's Hosp. Phila., 1955—57, 1959—60, dir. sect. on behavioral pediatrics, 1989—; practice medicine specializing in pediatrics Media, Pa., 1960-89. Instr. pediat. U. Pa. Sch. Medicine, Children's Hosp. Phila., 1961—73, assoc. in pediat., 1973—79, clin. asst. prof., 1979—82, clin. assoc. prof., 1982—90, clin. prof., 1990—. Co-editor books, Clinical and Educational Applications of Temperament Research, 1989, Prevention and Early Intervention: Individual Differences as Risk Factors for the Mental Health of Children, 1994; author (with S. C. McDevitt): Coping with Children's Temperament: A Guide for Professionals, 1995; author: (with M. Jablow) Understanding Your Child's Temperament, 1997, revised edit., 2005; contbr. articles to profl. jours.; developer Infant Temperament Questionnaire, 1970, co-developer Toddler Temperament Scale, 1978, Behavioral Style Questionnaire, 1976, Middle Childhood Temperament Questionnaire, 1980, Early Infancy Temperament Questionnaire, 1990, BASICS Behavioral Adjustment Scale, 2002; co-editor: (books) Developmental-Behavioral Pediatrics, 1st edit., 1983, 2nd Edit., 1992, 3rd Edit., 1999, 4th Edit., 2009. Pres. Friends of Wyck (House), Germantown, Phila., 1980—; bd. dirs. Benchmark Sch., Media, Pa., 1989—. Capt. M.C. US Army, 1957—59. Recipient Wistar-Haines award, 2001. Fellow: Am. Acad. Pediat. (Rsch. grantee 1975, 1980, 1985, Aldrich award 1991, Practitioner Rsch. award 1992); mem.: Coll. Physicians Phila., Phila. Pediatric Soc. (bd. dirs. 1969—71), Soc. Devel. and Behavioral Pediat. (exec. coun. 1983—85, pres-elect 1989—90, pres. 1990—91), Academic Pediatric Assn., Soc. Rsch. Child Devel., Am. Pediat. Soc., Inst. Medicine NAS, Franklin Inn Club, Phi Beta Kappa. Home: 511 Walnut Ln Swarthmore PA 19081-1140 Home Phone: 610-543-0818; Office Phone: 215-590-1467. Personal E-mail: wbcarey@att.net. Business E-Mail: carey@email.chop.edu.

CARGILL, PAULA MARIE, social worker, gerontologist; b. Henrietta, NC, Sept. 18, 1943; d. John Edwin and Mabel Anne (Bridges) C. BA in Sociology/French, Winthrop Coll., 1965; MSW, So. Bapt. Theo. Sem., 1973; MS in Social Work, U. Louisville, 1975; grad. in gerontology, U. Mich., 1983. Lic. clin. practice social worker, lic. nursing home adminstr. Social worker Connie Maxwell Children's Home, Greenwood, S.C., 1965, 70-71; tchr. French secondary pub. schs., N.C., S.C., 1965-70; instr. sociology and French North Greenville Coll., Tigerville, S.C., 1973-74, adj. assoc. instr., 1973-85; clin. social worker S.C. Dept. Mental Health, Simpsonville, 1975-77; social work supr. J Health Care Ctr., Inc., Simpsonville, 1977-84, S.C. Dept. Corrections, Greenville, 1984-89, 90-91; exec. dir. Grady H. Hipp Nursing Ctr., Greenville, S.C., 1989-90; access and in-home program dir. Sr. Action, Greenville, 1991-92; social worker S.C. Dept. Health and Environ. Control, 1992; social work cons. Interim Healthcare, 1992-96; dir. social work Richard Michael Campbell Vets. Nursing Home, Anderson, S.C., 1993; social worker, nursing home and rehab. agy. cons. Aging Cons. Svcs., Greenville, 1982—; ctr. dir. Choice Cmty. Mental Health, Greenville, 1996-97; social worker Bon Secours St. Francis Homecare, Greenville, 1997-2000; bereavement coord. Bon Secours St. Francis Hospice, 2001—10, SC Upstate Sr. Band Flutist; french instr. Sr. Action, Inc. Contbr. articles to religious mag. Bd. dirs. Greenville County Alcohol/Drug Abuse Commn., 1981-84, Ch. Cmty. Ministries, Greenville Bapt. Assn., 1982-2000, Grady H. Hipp Nursing Ctr., 1985-89, Rolling Green Village Retirement Ctr., 1990-91, 97-2000, Upstate Alzheimer's Assn., 1990-92, 94-2000, mem. edn. com., 2000—; bd. dirs. Greenville County Mental Health Assn., 1999-2000; mission action cons. So. Bapt. Conv., 1982-83; coun. mem. Bapt. Women, Greenville, 1979-81, 88-91. Mem. NASW (bd. dirs. S.C. chpt. 1976-77, 79-81, 83-85, 90-91, 2002—), S.C. Health Care Assn., Alumni Leadership Greenville. Avocations: languages, travel, walking, dollhouses. Home and Office: 1 Kenilworth Dr Greenville SC 29615-2320

CARHUAPOMA, JUAN RICARDO, critical care neurologist, researcher; b. Lima, Peru, Sept. 1, 1965; s. Cirilo Carhuapoma and Enedina Fernandez, m. Elizabeth Ann Sutherland, May 15, 1997; 1 child, Ethan. MD, Cayetano Heredia Peruvian U., 1991. Intern Henry Ford Hosp., Detroit, 1993-94, neurology resident, 1994-97; neuro ICU fellow Johns Hopkins U. Sch. Medicine, Balt., 1997-99, mem.

neurology faculty, 1999-2000, Columbia U. Coll. Physician and Surgeons, NYC, 2000—01; mem. faculty neurology and neurol. surgery Wayne State U., Detroit, 2001—. Cons. IC USA, Balt., 2000—. Contbr. articles to profl. jours., chpts. to books. Recipient Daland Fellowship Am. Philosophical Soc., 1999-2001. Mem. AAN, Am. Heart Assn., Soc. Critical Care Medicine. Home: 707 S President St Apt 1124 Baltimore MD 21202-4493 Fax: 212-305-2792. E-mail: jcarhuap@med.wayne.edu.

CARIOGGIA, ENZA, health science association administrator; b. Bari, Italy, Jan. 23, 1954; Degree in Physics, 1982, degree in Med. Physics, 1986. Health physics dept. collaborator Inst. Tumori G. Paolo Ii Inst. Cancer Rsch., 1985—2000, health physics dept. dir., 2000—. Mem.: ESTRO, Assn. Italiana Di Fisica Medica. Office: Via Oflacco 65 Bari 70124 Italy Office Fax: 39-080-5555459. Personal E-mail: enza.carioggia@poste.it.

CARL, ALLEN LAURENCE, surgery educator; b. Queens, NY, Apr. 14, 1953; s. O. Edward and Muriel (Lerner) C.; m. Susan A. Ross, Dec. 26, 1981; children: Alissa, Andrew, Scott, Danielle. BA with honors, SUNY, Binghamton, 1975; MD, SUNY, Buffalo, 1979. Diplomate Nat. Bd. Med. Examiners, Am. Bd. Orthopaedic Surgery; lic. surgeon, N.Y. Intern in gen. surgery Albert Einstein Hosp., Bronx, N.Y., 1979-80; resident in orthop. surgery, clin. instr. SUNY, Stony Brook, 1980-81; resident in orthop. surgery Bellevue Hosp., NYC, 1981-85; fellow in spinal surgery Toronto (Ont., Can.) Gen. Hosp., 1985-86; asst. prof. orthop. surgery Albany Med. Coll., 1986-91, assoc. prof. orthop. surgery, 1991-97, prof. orthopedic surgery, 1997—, vice chmn. orthop. surgery, 1993—, assoc. prof. pediat., 1994—. Cons. and presenter in field; mem. N.Y. State Spinal Cord Injury Rev. Bd. Contbr. articles to Head and Neck Surgery, Contemporary Orthops., Foot and Ankle, Spine, Jour. of Bone Joint Surgery Am., Jour. Trauma, Med. Outlook for Orthop. Surgeons, Jour. Orthop. Trauma, Current Opinions in Orthops., Jour. Orthop. Techniques. Fellow ACS, Am. Acad. Orthop. Surgeons, Acad. Pain Mgmt., The Spine Jour., Am. Orthop. Assn.; mem. Am. Spine Injury Assn., Am. Spinal Injury Soc., N.Am. Spine Soc. (mem. profl. and tech. liaison com., mem. subcom. materials and devices), New Eng. Spine Study Group, Ea. Orthop. Assn., Internat. Soc. Minimal Intervention in Spinal Surgery, Scoliosis Rsch. Soc. (mem. instrumentation com., internat. traveling fellow), Acad. Orthop. Soc., Group Internat. Cotrel-Dubousset, Cervical Spine Rsch. Soc Achievements include patents for Dynamized Anterior Vertebral Body Fixation Device (concept and structure), Shape Memory Scoliosis and Limb Implant; patents for virtual reality 3-D spinal imaging and implant placement, spinal care treatment. Office Phone: 518-262-5088. Personal E-mail: alcsar@nycap.rr.com.

CARLES, GABRIEL, gynecologist; b. St. Mandé, France, Oct. 23, 1952; s. Henri Carles and Marie-Madeleine De Preville; m. Elisabeth Bompart, July 24, 1993; children: Sébastien, Laura. MD, U. Toulouse, 1980. Physician Health Ctr., Djibouti, 1981—82. Physician, ob-gyn. Hosp. St. Laurent, 1982—2008. Recipient Ordre Nat. du Merite award, 2004. Master: Med. Commn. Achievements include research in tropical diseases and pregnancy. Office: Hosp Saint-Laurent Ave De Gaulle 97320 Saint-Laurent Du Maroni French Guiana France Home: 16 Allee de la Residence du Maroni 97320 Saint-Laurent Du Maroni French Guiana France Office Phone: 0594348753. Office Fax: 0594348740; Home Fax: 0594348760. Personal E-mail: gabriel.carles@wanadoo.fr. E-mail: g.carles@ch-ouestguyane.fr.

CARLOTTI, RONALD JOHN, food scientist; b. Martins Ferry, Ohio, Sept. 20, 1942; s. John Peter and Mary Rose (Pilla) C.; m. Eileen Theresa Dorsey, May 17, 1969; children: Lori Ann, Christina Maria, Jennifer Ann, Theresa Maria. Student, Wheeling Jesuit U., W.Va., 1960—63; BS, Ohio State U., 1964; MS, W.Va. U., 1966, PhD, 1970; MM, Aquinas Coll., 1996. Postdoctoral fellow dept. biochemistry U. Iowa, Iowa City, 1971—72, asst. rsch. scientist dept. pediats., 1973—74; corp. nutritionist Kellogg Co., Battle Creek, Mich., 1974—77; mgr. nutrition/basic rsch. Frito Lay divsn. Pepsico, Dallas, 1977—82, prin. scientist new products Frito Lay divsn., 1982—85; sr. rsch. scientist Amway Corp., Ada, Mich., 1985—89; dir. food sci. and tech. Country Home Bakers, Grand Rapids, Mich., 1990—93; pres. Carlotti and Assocs., Grand Rapids, 1994; pres., CEO Natura Inc., Lansing, Mich., 1995—2001; regulatory affairs and devel. specialist Ranir Corp., Grand Rapids, 2002—05. Tech. rep. Snack Food Assn., Crystal City, Va., 1978-82, Grocery Mfrs. Am., Washington, 1975-77; nutritionist Am. Frozen Food Assn., Washington, 1990-93; vis. asst. prof. chemistry Grand Valley State U., Allendale, Mich., 2002; adj. faculty Davenport U., 2004—, Baker Coll., Muskegon, Mich, 2005—, Allen Pk., Mich., 2006—, mem. sci. adv. bd. Aquinas Coll., Concord Rapida, Mich. Contbr. articles to profl. jours. Pres. Mary Immaculate Sch. Bd., Dallas, 1981-83. Recipient Lovable Spud award, Nat. Potato Promotion Bd., Denver, 1981. Mem. Am. Chem. Soc., Am. Assn. Cereal Chemists, Inst. Food Tech. Roman Catholic. Achievements include start-up of new biotechnology-based food and chemical ingredients company, development of patented taste-appealing shelf-stable blend of fruit juice and milk, development of patented antioxidant system protecting food, pharmaceuticals and plastics against air and/or photo-oxidation, development of nutritionally improved (low fat/low calorie) prototype of Tostitos Baked tortilla chips, of high potency dry dog food, of nutritionally improved fruit pies for diabetics, of specially formulated pumpkin pie which will not allow for the growth of pathogenic bacteria innoculated after baking in testing required to verify that the product can be stored at ambient temperature for up to five days; initiation of tech. and regulatory functions for corporate products. Home: 6921 Maplecrest Dr SE Grand Rapids MI 49546-9208

CARLSEN, MARYBAIRD, clinical psychologist; b. Salt Lake City, Utah, Aug. 31, 1928; d. Jesse Hays and Susannah Amanda (Bragstad) Baird; m. James C. Carlsen, May 1, 1949; children: Philip, Douglas, Susan, Kristine. Student, St. Olaf Coll., 1946-47; BA, Whitworth Coll., 1950; MA, U. Conn., 1967; PhD, U. Wash., 1973. Profl. organist, piano tchr., Wash., Oreg., Ill., Conn., 1949-68; staff counselor Presbyn. Counseling Svc., Seattle, 1976-79; pvt. practice clin. psychologist, marriage therapist, cognitive, devel. psychology, career devel. Seattle, 1978-95; cons. creative aging Walla Walla, 1996—. Chmn. sr. adult adv. coun. Seattle Parks Dept., 1975-76; adv. bd. Northwest Ctr. for Creative Aging, 1995-98; mem. steering com. Quest Learning Inst., Walla Walla, Wash., 1997-2001, mem. faculty, 1997—; mem. nat. adv. bd. Ctr. for Creative Retirement, Asheville, N.C., 1998-2001. Author: Meaning-Making: Therapeutic Processes in Adult Development, 1988, Creative Aging: A Meaning-Making Perspective, 1991, 2d edit., 1996, Transformational Meaning-Making and the Practices of Career Counseling, 1991; contbr. chpts. to books and articles to profl. jours. Grantee PEO Rsch., 1972, U. Wash. Women's Guidance Ctr., 1972. Mem. AAUW, APA, Am. Soc. Aging, Nat. Coun. on Aging.

CARLSON, BRUCE MARTIN, anatomist; b. Gary, Ind., July 11, 1938; s. Martin E. and Esther (Granquist) C.; m. Jean Ann Hyslop, Aug. 18, 1968; children: Martin, James. BA, Gustavus Adolphus Coll., 1959; MS, Cornell U., 1961; MD, PhD, U. Minn., 1986. Exchange scientist Inst. of Devel. Biology, Moscow, 1965-66; Fulbright fellow Hubrecht (Netherlands) Inst., 1973-74; Joshiah Macy scholar U. Helsinki, Finland, 1981-82; exchange scientist Inst. of Physiology, Prague, Czechoslovakia, 1971; asst. prof. of anatomy to prof. U. Mich., Ann Arbor, 1966—2006, prof. biology, 1979—2006, prof. emeritus, 2006—, chmn. dept. anatomy and cell biology, 1988-2000, rsch. scientist Inst. Gerontology, 1989—2006, dir. Inst. Gerontology, 2000—04, emeritus prof. Fellow Fetzer Inst., Kalamazoo, Mich., 1990-96, trustee, 1998—, John E. Fetzer Meml. Trust, Kalamazoo, 2011-; mem. study sects. NIH, 1986-90, Nat. Bd. Med. Examiners, 1994-96; NIH Fogerty fellow, U. Otago, Dunedin, New Zealand, 1999-00. Author: The Regeneration of Minced Muscles, 1972, Patten's Foundations of Embryology, 1974, 4th edit., 1981, 5th edit., 1988, 6th edit., 1996, Regeneration (in Russian), 1986, Human Embryology and Developmental Biology, 1994, 3d edit., 2004, 4th edit., 09, Principles of Regenerative Biology, 2007, Beneath the Surface, 2007; editor: From Message to Mind, 1988, Regeneration and Transplantation, 1990, Stem Cell Biology, 2010, others. Recipient Disting. Alumni award Gustavus Adolphus Coll., 1979, Newcomb-Cleveland prize AAAS, 1972, 650th Anniversary medal, Charles U., Prague, silver medal Russian Acad. Nat. Scis., 2004, Henry Gray award Am. Assn. Anatomists, 2004. Fellow: Russian Acad. Natural Scis., Am. Assn. Anatomists; mem.: Am. Fisheries Soc., Gerontol. Soc. Am., Internat. Soc. Devel. Biology, Soc. Devel. Biologists, Assn. of Anatomy, Cell Biology and Neurobiology Chairpersons (pres. 1995), Am. Soc. Ichthyologists and Herpetologists, Am. Soc. Zoologists (divsn. chmn. 1987—89), Am. Assn. Clin. Anatomists, Am. Assn. Anatomists (nominating com. 1991, exec. com. 1994, pres. 1997—99). Lutheran. Achievements include invention of techniques of free muscle transplantation. Home: 1345 Waterford Dr Minneapolis MN 55422-4283 Business E-Mail: brcarl@umich.edu.

CARLSON, CHAD, physician, educator; b. Duluth, Minn., Dec. 25, 1973; BA, U. Wis., Madison, 1997; MD, U. Wis., Madison Sch. Medicine, 2000. Asst. prof. neurology NYU Sch. Medicine, 2006—. Mem.: Am. Acad. Neurology, Am. Epilepsy Soc. Avocation: photography. Office: Rm 1201 HCC12 530 1st Ave New York NY 10021 Business E-Mail: chad.carlson@nyumc.org.

CARLSON, DORI M., optometrist; b. Hallock, Minn. m. Mark Helgeson; children: Seth, Ian. OD, Pacific U. Coll. Optometry, Forest Grove, Oreg., 1989. Residency in rehabilitative optometry American Lake and Seattle VA Hospitals; optometrist Heartland Eye Care, Park River, Grafton, ND, 1990—. Mem. adv. com. ND Blue Cross and Blue Shield, mem. ND legis. com.; cons. Accreditation Coun. on Optometric Edn. Named ND Young Optometrist of Yr., 1995, Optometrist of Yr., 2003. Fellow: American Acad. Optometry; mem.: American Pub. Health Assn., American Optometry Assn. (bd. trustees 2004—, pres.-elect 2010—11, pres. 2011—), ND Optometry Assn. (pres. 1998). Office: Heartland Eye Care 121 Briggs Ave N Park River ND 58270 Office Phone: 701 284 7330. *

CARLSON, JAMES C., healthcare services executive; Grad., Rider Univ. Mgmt. positions through pres. we. group ops. Prudential Ins. Co.; CEO Workscape Inc.; exec. v.p., pres. United Healthcare UnitedHealth Group, Inc.; pres., COO Amerigroup Corp., Virginia Beach, Va., 2003—07, pres., CEO, 2007—08, chmn., pres., CEO, 2008—. Bd. dir. Nat. Kidney Found.; bd. mem. Va. Aquarium & Marine Sci. Ctr., Va. Beach Neptune Festival; mem. health sector adv. bd. Fuqua Sch. Bus. Duke Univ. Office: Amerigroup Corp 4425 Corp Ln Virginia Beach VA 23462 *

CARLSON, JANET FRANCES, psychologist, educator; b. Newport, RI, Oct. 3, 1957; d. Robert Carl and Alice Marion (Orina) Carlson; m. Kurt Francis Geisinger, Sept. 22, 1984. BS summa cum laude, Union Coll., Schenectady, 1979; MA in Clin. Psychology, Fordham U., 1982, PhD in Clin. Psychology, 1987. Lic. psychologist NY and Tex., cert. sch. psychologist NY. Clin. psychology intern Conn. Valley Hosp., Middletown, Conn., 1983-84; rsch. fellow Schering-Plough Found., Bronx, NY, 1984-85; psychologist I Creedmoor Psychiat. Ctr., Queens Village, NY, 1985-86; psychologist Hallen Sch., Mamaroneck, NY, 1986-88; asst. prof. psychology Fordham U., Bronx, NY, 1988-89; asst. prof. sch. and applied psychology Fairfield (Conn.) U., 1989-93, dir. sch. and applied psychology programs, 1989-90; from asst. prof. counseling and psychol. svcs. to prof. SUNY, Oswego, 1993—2002, assoc. dean Sch. Edn., 1998-2001; prof. psychology, head dept. gen. academics Tex. A&M U., Galveston, 2002—08. Cons. N.Y.C. Bd. Edn. Office Rsch., Evaluation and Assessment, 1988—92; vis. asst. prof. psychol. LeMoyne Coll., Syracuse, NY, 1992—93; dir. Office Tchg. Resources in Psychol., 2001—06, vis. prof. ednl. psychology and psychology, 2006—09; rsch. prof. Buros Ctr. Testing U. Nebr., 2009—; assoc. dir. Buros Inst. Mental Measurements. Recipient Sugarfree scholarship, 1984—85; grantee Sigma Xi, 1984—85. Fellow: APA (pres. divsn. 2009), Am. Ednl. Rsch. Assn.; mem.: NASP, NY Assn. Sch. Psychologists, Northeastern Ednl. Rsch. Assn. (ed newsletter 1988—91, bd dirs. 1990—93, pres. 1995—96), Sigma Xi, Psi Chi, Phi Kappa Phi (pres. 1995—96).

CARLSON, JOHN, gynecologic oncologist, educator; MD, Georgetown U., 1974. Diplomate Am. Bd. Ob-Gyn., 1981, Am. Bd. Ob-Gyn.-gynecologic oncology, 1990. Resident ob-gyn. Hosp. Univ. Pa., Phila., 1975—78; fellow gynecologic oncology Anderson Cancer Ctr., Houston, 1978—80; gynecologic oncologist St. Peter's Univ. Hosp. Office: St. Peter's University Hospital 254 Easton Ave Cares Bldg New Brunswick NJ 08901 Office Phone: 732-745-8600.

CARLSON, NOEL G., biology professor; b. Provo, Utah, Nov. 28, 1956; PhD, U. Ariz., 1992. Postdoc. fellow Duke U., 1995; rsch. assoc. prof., dept. neurobiology & anatomy U. Utah, 1995—, adj. assoc. prof., dept. neurology, 2004. Recipient VA Merit award; Rsch. grant, NIH. Mem.: Gerontol. Soc. America, Soc. Neurosci. Avocations: bicycling, hiking. Home: 3515 Ceres Dr Salt Lake City UT 84124 Personal E-mail: ngcarlson@hotmail.com.

CARLSON, RENÉ A., veterinarian; m. Mark Carlson. DVM, U. Minn. Coll. Veterinary Medicine, 1978. Clin. internship in small animal medicine and surgery, Springfield, Mass., 1978—79; veterinarian Elm Valley Vet. Clinic, Elmwood, Wis., 1980—84, Spring Harbor Animal Hosp., Madison, Wis., 1984—90, Chetek Vet. Clinic, Wis., 1990—96, Animal Hosp. of Chetek, 1996—. Patron Chetek Hydroflites, Kinship; coun. mem. Chetek Luth. Ch., missionary Malawi, 2006; bd. dirs. American Vet. Med. Found., 1999—2002, Lakeview Med. Ctr., 2006—08. Mem.: American Vet. Med. Assn. (mem. house dels. 1996—2003, v.p. 2004—06, mem. coun. on edn. 2006—10, pres. 2011—), American Animal Hosp. Assn., Minn. Vet. Med. Assn., Wis. Vet. Med. Assn. (Wis. Veterinarian of Yr. 2001), Northwestern Vet. Assn. Office: Animal Hosp of Chetek 941 County Hwy M 941 24 1/2 St Chetek WI 54728-7925 Office Phone: 715-859-6650. Office Fax: 715-859-6657. *

CARLSON, ROBERT MARSHALL, health facility administrator; b. Jamestown, NY, Oct. 6, 1950; s. Marshall Lawrence and Alice (Christine) C.; m. Robin Shankey, May 29, 1987; children: Todd Marshall, Scott Thomas. BS, Bowling Green State U., Ohio, 1972; postgrad. in pub. health, U. Utah, 1972; ME in Health Edn., U. Toledo, 1977. Planning analyst, then found. dir. Riverside Hosp., Toledo, 1975-78; hosp. planning coord. Med. Coll. Ohio, Toledo, 1978-80, asst. hosp. dir. for ambulatory programs, 1980-81; cons. P.M.S. (Planning & Mgmt. Services) Inc., Bloomington, Minn., 1981-82; dir. health tech. mktg., sr. cons. Ellerbe Cons. Group, Bloomington, 1983-85; mktg. dir. Ellerbe Assocs. Inc., Mpls., 1986; v.p. Ellerbe Assocs., 1987-89, Export USA Publs., Mpls., 1989-91; dir. physician svcs. HealthEast, St. Paul, 1991-95; exec. adminstr. OSF Med. Group, OSF Healthcare Systems, Peoria, Ill., 1995-99; dir. clin. svcs. Phycor, Inc., Nashville, 1999-2000; sr. assoc. Progressive Healthcare, Inc., Nashville, 2000—02; adminstr. Medicine Patient Care Ctrs., Vanderbilt U. Med. Ctr., Nashville, 2003—06; v.p., exec. dir. ambulatory clinics Tulane U. Hosp. and Clinic, New Orleans, 2007—. Served to commdr., Med. Svc. Corps., USNR, 1972-98. Mem. Med. Group Mgmt. Assn., Am. Coll. Med. Practice Execs., Assn. Mil. Surgeons of U.S., Profl. Ski Instrs. Am., Res. Officers Assn., Phi Kappa Phi, Kappa Sigma. Lutheran. Office: Tulane U Hosp and Clinic 1415 Tulane Ave Ste 6122 New Orleans LA 70112 Business E-Mail: bob.carlson@unthsc.edu.

CARLSON, ROGER DAVID, psychologist, educator, minister; b. Berkeley, Calif., Nov. 19, 1946; s. George Clarence and Elizabeth (Norris) C.; m. Ema T. Paviolo, June 11, 1977 (div. 1994); children: Erik Andreas Paviolo, Lucas Sven Paviolo, Justin Nikolaus Paviolo. AB, Calif. State U., Sacramento, 1968, MA, 1969; PhD, U. Oreg., Eugene, 1972; cert. theol. studies, Pacific Sch. of Religion, Berkeley, Calif., 1994; MDiv, Pacific Sch. Religion, Berkeley, Calif., 1996. Ordained deacon, 1996, elder, 1998 United Meth. Ch., ecclesiastical endorsement pastoral counselor 2009; lic. psychologist Pa., 1977, Calif., 2001, Oreg., 2002, Wash., 2009, cert. sex therapist AASECT. Assoc. prof. psychology Lebanon Valley Coll., Annville, Pa., 1972-85; rsch. assoc. Eugene Pub. Schs., 1985-87; assoc. prof. edn. Williamette U., Salem, Oreg., 1987-88; vis. assoc. prof. psychology Whitman Coll., Walla Walla, 1988—89, 1990—91; assoc. prof. psychology Ea. Wash. U., 1991-92; adj. prof. Linfield Coll., 1993—; pastor Coburg (Oreg.) United Meth. Ch., 1992-94, Florence (Oreg.) United Meth. Ch., 1994—2001, Covenant United Meth. Ch., Reedsport, Oreg., 1995—99, 1st United Meth. Ch. of Stayton, Oreg., 2001—03, Dennett Chapel United Meth. Ch., Portland, Oreg., 2003—09; assoc. prof. psychology Pacific U., Forest Grove, 2005—07, Woodlawn United Meth. Ch., Portland, Oreg., 2009—. Vis. scholar dept. history and philosophy of sci., life mem. Cambridge (Eng.) U., 1979-80; life mem. Wolfson Coll., Cambridge U.; psychologist, pvt. practice, 1977-1985, 2001—, pastoral counselor, 2009-, Sr. Connections, 2009-. Author books, contbr. rsch. papers, jour. articles and book chpts. on numerous subjects in field. Mem. Friends Radio Sta. KPFA, v.p. 1969, pres. 1970; Wolfeboro Pioneer, Boy Scouts Am., 1959; co-founder, Pathways of Faith, Florence, Oreg., 1998; bd. dirs., Ecumenical Ministries Oreg., 2003-04; pres. Oreg. Soc. of Clin. Hypnosis, 2006-07; bd. mem. Oreg. State Bd. Psychologist Examiners, 2010-. Recipient Presdl. Sports award. Fellow Am. Coll. Heraldry; mem. APA, Oreg. Psychol. Assn., Oreg. Soc. Clin. Hypnosis (v.p. 2005-06, pres. 2006-07), Am. Psychol. Soc., Soc. for Clin. and Exptl. Hypnosis, Am. Coll. Psychology, Soc. for Philosophy and Psychology (mem. exec. com. 1975-76), Am. Assn. Sexuality Educators, Counselors, Therapists, SAR, Airplane Owners and Pilots Assn., Sons Union Vets. Civil War, Am. Radio Relay League, Vasa Lodge, Order of St. Luke, Psi Chi. Methodist. Office Phone: 503-245-2929. Business E-Mail: r.d.carlson.80@cantab.net.

CARLSSON, ARVID EMIL, pharmacologist, educator; b. Uppsala, Sweden, Jan. 25, 1923; s. Gottfrid and Lizzie (Steffenburg) Carlsson; m. Ulla-Lisa Christoffersson, Dec. 29, 1945; children: Bo, Lena, Hans, Maria, Magnus. MD, U. Lund, Sweden, 1951; MD (hon.), U. Cagliary, Italy, 1976; PharmD (hon.), U. Uppsala, 1977; PhD (hon.), U. Helsinki, Finland, 1990, U. Marburg, Germany, 1991. Asst. prof. U. Lund, 1951—56, assoc. prof. dept. pharmacology, 1956—59; prof. pharmacology U. Göteborg, Sweden, 1959—89, prof. emeritus, 1989—, chmn. dept. pharmacology, 1959—76. Vis. scientist lab. chem. pharmacology Nat. Heart Inst., NIH, Bethesda, Md., 1955—56. Recipient James Parkinson award, Parkinson's Disease Found. NY, 1970, Pehr Dubb's Gold medal, Med. Soc. Gothenburg, 1970, Anders Jahre's Med. prize, U. Olso, Norway, 1974, Stanley R. Dean award, Am. Coll. Psychiatrists, 1975, Wolf prize in medicine, Israel, 1979, Gardner Found. Internat. award, 1982, Paul Hoch prize, Am. Psychopathol. Assn., 1990, Fred Springer award, Am. Parkinson Disease Assn., 1990, William K. Warren Schizophrenia Rsch. award, 1991, Julius Axelrod medal, Cathecholamine Club, 1992, Japan prize in psychology/psychiatry, Japan Sci. & Tech. Found., 1994, Lieber prize, Nat. Alliance Rsch. Schizophrenia & Depression, 1994, Lundbeck Found. Rsch. prize, Denmark, 1995, Gold medal, Swedish Parkinson Assn., 1996, Soc. Biol. Psychiatry, Can., 1998, U. Bari, Italy, 1999, Antonio Feltrinelli Internat. award, Rome, 1999, Nobel prize in physiology/medicine, 2000; co-recipient Bristol-Myers award for disting. achievement in neurosci. rsch., 1989, Open Mind award in psychiatry, Janssen Rsch. Found., Paris, 1992. Fellow: Acad. Medicine & Psychiatry (hon.), Swedish So. Biol. Psychiatry (hon.), Med. Soc. Gothenburg (hon.); mem.: NAS, Royal Swedish Acad. Scis. (Hilda & Alfred Erikkson's prize 1985), German Pharmacological Soc., Am. Coll. Neuropsychopharmacology (fgn.), Japanese Pharmacological Soc. (fgn.), Royal Soc. Sci. & Arts, Scandinavian Soc. Psychopharmacology (hon.), German Soc. Biol. Psychiatry (hon.). Achievements include research of neurotransmitter dopamine and its effects in Parkinson's disease; development of a method for measuring the amount of dopamine in brain tissues. Office: Göteborg U Dept Pharm Medicinaregatan 7 Box 431 SE 405 30 Gothenburg Sweden Business E-Mail: arvid.carlsson@pharm.gu.se. *

CARLSSON WALLIN, MARIE, obstetrician; b. Falun, Sweden, July 6, 1959; MD, U. Linköping, Sweden, 1985; PhD student, U. Lund, 2007—. Cons. Hosp. Norrköping, Sweden, 1993—2001; sr. cons. Hosp. Ystad, 2001—. Mem.: Médecins Sans Frontières, Swedish Ob-Gyn. Orgn. Avocations: travel, music, literature. Home: Sankt Knuts Torg 4 Malmö 21157 Sweden Personal E-mail: marie.carlsson.wallin@gmail.com.

CARLTON, BARRY S., physician, educator; b. NYC, Jan. 16, 1947; MD, SUNY Downstate, 1972. Assoc. prof. John A. Burns Sch. Medicine U. Hawaii, 1991—. Office: 1356 Lusitana St Psychiatry Honolulu HI 96813 Business E-Mail: carltonb@dop.hawaii.edu.

CARLTON, PAMELA G., pediatrician, adolescent medicine; MD, U. So. Calif., 1996. Diplomate Am. Bd. Pediatrics, 1999. Resident pediat. Children's Hosp., LA, 1996—97, fellow adolescent medicine, 1999—2000; pediatrician Lucile Packard Children's Hosp., Stanford. Clin. sci. adv. coun. Nat. Eating Disorders Assn.; mem. adv. bd. Eating Disorders Recovery Support Inc. Author: (publ.) Take Charge of Your Child's Eating Disorder. Mem.: Assn. of Professionals Treating Eating Disorders, The Internat. Assn. for Eating Disorders Professionals, The Nat. Eating Disorders Assn., The Acad. for Eating Disorders. Office: Lucile Packard Children's Hospital Ste 205 2490 Hospital Dr Mountain View CA 94040 Office Phone: 650-962-4500. Office Fax: 866-769-8602.

CARLTON, PAUL KENDALL, JR., physician; b. Roswell, N.Mex., May 13, 1947; s. Paul Kendall and Helen C. (Sweat) C.; m. Dorothea Janice Prichard, July 5, 1969; children: Paul Kendall III, Christianne Joy, Stephanie Jill, Luke Jeffrey. BS, USAF Acad., 1969; MD, U. Colo., 1973, DSc (hon.), 2003. Diplomate Am. Bd. Surgery, 1980, 1990, 2000. Commd. 2d lt. USAF, 1969, advanced through grades to lt. gen., 1999; resident in surgery Wilford Hall Med. Ctr., San Antonio, 1973-78; comdr. USAF Hosp. Torrejon, Madrid, 1985-88, Scott Med. Ctr., Scott AFB, Ill., 1988-91; command surgeon Air Edn. and Tng. Command, San Antonio, 1991-94; comdr. Wilford Hall Med. Ctr., San Antonio, 1994-99, surgeon gen., 1999—2002; prof., dir. Homeland Security Health Sci. Ctr. Tex. A&M, 2002—. Decorated Air medal, Legion of Merit (2), Def. Disting. Svc. medal, Airman's medal; recipient Hoekton Silver award AMA, 1978, Nathan Davis award, AMA, 2001. Fellow ACS (gov. 1992-96). Avocations: hunting, flying. Office: Tex A&M U Health Sci Ctr Office of Innovation and Preparedness College Station TX 77845 also: 7th Fl 301 Tarrow St College Station TX 77840-7896

CARLUCCI, MARIE ANN, nursing administrator, consultant; b. NYC, Apr. 22, 1953; d. Clarence Hugh and Anna Rebecca (Mills) McNamee; m. Paul Pasquale Carlucci, Aug. 18, 1973; children: Christine, Patricia. Diploma in nursing, Mt. Vernon Hosp. Sch. Nursing, NYC, 1974; BS in Behavioral Sci. summa cum laude, Mercy Coll., 1991; MPH, N.Y. Med. Coll., 1997. Cert. emergency nurse; cert. nurse adminstr.; lic. healthcare risk mgr.; cert. legal cons. Staff nurse Mt. Vernon (N.Y.) Hosp., 1974-82, Lawrence Hosp., Bronxville, N.Y., 1982-84, No. Westchester Hosp., Mt. Kisco, N.Y., 1984-91, asst. dir. nursing, mem. nurse mgmt. and ethics coms., 1991-94; asst. DON svcs. Ferncliff Manor, Yonkers, N.Y., 1994-95, dir. nursing svcs., 1995-97; dep. dir. nursing svcs. Taylor Care Ctr., Westchester, N.Y., 1997-2000; dir. residential svcs. Hillsborough (Fla.) Assn. for Retarded Citizens, 2000; dir. nursing Am. Retirement Corp., Sun City Center, Fla., 2000—01; med.-legal nurse cons., 2001—. Religious edn. tchr. St. John and St. Mary's Ch., Chappagua, N.Y., 1984-99; campaign mgr. Com. to Elect Paul P. Carlucci, Chappagua, 1990; mem. Surrogate Decision Making Com., N.Y. Commn. Quality Care for Mentally Disabled; mem. bd. trustees Field Home-Holy Comforter, 1995-99; guardian ad litem 13th Judical Cir., Tampa, Fla., 2000—; bd. adv. Hillsborough County Children's Svcs., 2002-. Mem.: Phi Gamma Mu, Psi Chi. Roman Catholic. Home: 3916 Appletree Dr Valrico FL 33594-4315

CARMEL, PETER W., neurosurgeon; b. Bklyn. m. Jacqueline Bello; 3 children. BA, U. Chgo., 1956; MD, NYU Bellevue Coll. Medicine, 1960; DMS in Neuroanatomy, Columbia U. Coll. Physicians & Surgeons, NYC, 1970. Rsch. assoc. NIH; neurosurgery residency Neurol. Inst. NY; faculty Columbia U., 1967—98; attending neurosurgeon Columbia-Presbyn. Med. Ctr., 1967—94; prof. neurol. surgery, dir. pediat. neurol. surgery Columbia U. Coll. Physicians & Surgeons; prof., chair dept. neurol. surgery Univ. Med. & Dentistry NJ (UMDNJ), 1994—; co-med. dir. Neurol. Inst. NJ, Newark, 1999—; prof. surgery NJ Med. Sch. Founder Neuro-Endocrine Lab. Inst. Study of Human Reproduction, Columbia U. Coll. Physicians & Surgeons, 1969. Contbr. articles to profl. jours., chapters to books. Past chair Nat. Coalition Rsch. Neurol. Diseases & Stroke, Nat. Found. Brain Rsch.; mem. NJ Commn. Spinal Cord Rsch.; bd. dirs. Nat. Patient Safety Found., Nat. Health Mus. Recipient Outstanding Med. Educator award, Edward J. Ill Excellence in Medicine Awards, 2006; named a Top Doctor, NJ Monthly Mag., 2005; named one of Best Doctors in America, Am. Health Mag. Mem.: AMA (chair coun. long range planning 2000—01, bd. trustees 2002—, pres. AMA Found. 2006—07, pres.-elect 2010—11, pres. 2011—), American Assn. Neurol. Surgeons (Disting. Svc. award 2008), Congress Neurol. Surgeons. Office: Drs Office Ctr Neuro 90 Bergen St Newark NJ 07103-2425 Office Phone: 973-972-2905. Business E-Mail: carmel@umdnj.edu. *

CARMEN, HANGANU STELA, dental educator; b. Barlad, Romania, Dec. 2, 1957; Degree in Dentistry, Carol Davila U. Medicine and Pharmacy, Bucharest, Romania, 1984; MS in Dentistry, U. Bergen, Norway, 1999. Asst. prof. Gr. T. Popa U. Medicine and Pharmacy, Iasi, Romania, 1991—99, lectr., 1999—2003, assoc. prof., 2003—. Bd. of dean Faculty Med. Dentistry, 2008. Mem.: Romanian Assn. Oro-dental Pub. Health, Romanian Assn. Dental Edn., European Assn. Dental Pub. Health, Internat. Assn. Dental Rsch. Avocations: opera, travel. Office: Universitatii Nr 16 Iasi 700115 Romania Personal E-mail: carmenhanganu1957@yahoo.com.

CARMEN, ROBERT G., insurance company executive; m. Cindy Carmen; 2 children. BS in occupl. therapy, Loma Linda U., Calif.; MPA, U. Colo., Denver. V.p. Castle Med. Ctr. Adventist Health, Oahu, Hawaii, 1975, pres. Castle Med. Ctr., pres. Glendale Adventist Med. Ctr., pres. White Meml. Med. Ctr., sr. v.p. Roseville, 1983, pres. Southern Calif. region, 1992, COO Southern Calif. region, 1999, COO, exec. v.p., 1999—2007, dir., CEO, pres., 2007—. Chmn. Mission Hosp. Laguna Beach; chmn. bd. South Coast Med. Ctr.; trustee Loma Linda Univ. Med. Ctr. Mem.: American Coll. Healthcare Exec., Calif. Healthcare Assn. Office: Adventist Health 2100 Douglas Blvd Roseville CA 95661 Office Phone: 916-781-2000. *

CARMICHAEL, DAVID BURTON, physician; b. Santa Ana, Calif., Sept. 12, 1923; s. David Burton and Phyllis (Adams) Carmichael; m. Ava Louise Smith, Dec. 26, 1944; children: Catherine Ann, Heather Sue, Linda L., Ava L. Student, Graceland U., 1940-42; BA, MD, U. Iowa, 1946; postgrad., Harvard U., 1949-50; LL.D. (hon.), Graceland U., Iowa, 1985. Diplomate Am. Bd. Internal Medicine. Clin. and research fellow medicine Mass. Gen. Hosp., Boston, 1949-50; cons. cardiovascular diseases U.S. Naval Hosp., San Diego, Camp Pendleton, 1956-86, U.S. VA, 1960-82; chief dept. medicine Scripps Meml. Hosp., La Jolla, Calif., 1961-63, 65-67, chief staff, 1970-71. Clin. prof. medicine U. Calif. at San Diego, 1968—; pres. De Anza Lab. Corp., 1962-72, Carmichael-Carson Med.-Clin. Lab. Corp., 1962-75; sr. ptnr. Med. Clinic; founding med. dir. Cardiovascular Inst. Scripps Meml. Hosps., 1985-96; pres. Orange County Pioneer Coun., 1993-94; trustee GDE Systems, Inc., 1992-94. Contbr. articles to profl. jours. Trustee Millicent Rogers Mus., Taos, N.Mex., 1986—90, Graceland U., Iowa, 1987—2011, Rancho de las Golondrinas Mus., Santa Fe, 1989—2009. Rear adm. USNR. Decorated Legion of Merit; recipient Alumni Disting. Service award Graceland U., 1967. Master ACP (gov. So. Calif. region III 1972-76, Laureate award 1991); fellow Am. Coll. Cardiology (dir., sec. 1975, trustee 1979-85, Disting. Fellow award 1994, Mastership 2001), Am. Coll. Chest Physicians, Am. Heart Assn.; mem. AMA (chmn. specialty soc. and service delegation 1985-87, 93-96, mem. grad. med. edn. adv. com. 1983—89, chmn., 1985-87, chmn. sect. council on clin. cardiology, Disting. Svc. award 1997), San Diego County Heart Assn. (pres. 1959-60), San Diego Biomed. Rsch. Inst. (pres. 1958-59, 62-63, vice chmn. residency rev. com. internal medicine 1971-78), Soc. Med. Cons. to the Armed Forces, San Diego Soc. Internal Medicine (pres. 1959-61). Republican. Mem. Community Ch. of Christ. Home: 8333 Calle Del Cielo La Jolla CA 92037-3033 Office Phone: 858-459-4356. Personal E-mail: ascdbc@aol.com.

CARMICHAEL, LOUIS DAVID, internist, educator; BA, Harvard U., Cambridge, 1965—69; MD, Albert Einstein Sch. of Medicine, Bronx, 1973—76; MPH, Columbia U., NY, 1981—83. Diplomate Am. Bd. Internal Medicine. Intern Bronx Lebanon Hosp. Ctr., NY, 1976—77, resident; assoc. prof. clin. medicine coll. of physicians and surgeons Columbia Univ., 1991—; assoc. attending physician Presbyn. Hosp., 1991—; fellow NY-Presbyn. Hosp.-Columbia Univ. Med. Ctr. Co-author: The Epidemiology of peritonitis in acute peritoneal dialysis: a comparison between open-and closed-drainage systems, 1993. Office: Presbyterian Hospital 903 Park Ave New York NY 10021 Fax: 212-535-4796.

CARMICHAEL, WAYNE W., retired research scientist; b. Longview, Wash., Aug. 22, 1947; BSc, Oreg. State U., 1969; PhD, U. Alta., 1974. Prof. Wright State U., 1976—2007. Office: 42184 Tweedle Rd Seaside OR 97138 Business E-Mail: wayne.carmichael@wright.edu.

CARMODY, MARGARET JEAN, retired social worker; b. Wauwatosa, Wis., Aug. 5, 1924; d. Peter and Gertrude Francelia (Brown) Galijas; m. James Matthew Carmody, Apr. 3, 1971 (dec. May 2005). BA, Marquette U., 1945; MA, U. Chgo., 1949. Social worker Denver Gen. Hosp., 1950-51; Fulbright fellow France, 1951-52; med. social work cons. U. Ill., Chgo., 1954-60; health scientist, adminstr. USPHS, Washington, 1960-96; ret., 1996. Mem. Acad. Cert. Social Workers. Democrat. Roman Catholic. Home: 40 Riverside Ave Apt 9I Red Bank NJ 07701 Home Phone: 732-758-8327. Personal E-mail: gertrude8@verizon.net.

CARMONA, RICHARD HENRY, health facility administrator, former Surgeon General of the United States; b. NYC, Nov. 22, 1949; m. Diana Sanchez; 4 children. AA, Bronx Cmty. Coll., CUNY; BS in biology and chemistry, U. Calif., San Francisco, 1977, MD, 1979; MPH, U. Ariz., 1998. Surgical resident U. Calif., San Francisco; prof. surgery, pub. health and family and cmty. medicine U. Ariz., 1985—2002, disting. prof. pub. health, Mel & Enid Zuckerman Coll. Pub. Health Tucson, 2006—; dir., trauma services Tucson Med. Ctr., 1985—93; surgeon, dep. sheriff Pima County Sheriff's Dept., 1986—2002; CEO Kino County Cmty. Hosp., 1995—96, Pima Health Care System, 1997—99; chmn. State of Ariz. So. Regional Emergency Med. Sys., 1990—2002; surgeon gen. US Dept. Health & Human Services, Washington, 2002—06; vice chmn. Canyon Ranch, Tucson, 2006—, CEO health divsn., 2006—; pres. Canyon Ranch Inst., Tucson, 2006—. With US Army, 1967—70. Named one of Top 10 Latinos in Healthcare, LatinoLeaders mag., 2004. Fellow: Am. Coll. Surgeons. Office: Canyon Ranch Inst 8600 E Rockcliff Rd Tucson AZ 85750 Office Phone: 520-239-8561. Office Fax: 520-749-0662. *

CARNEIRO, JOÃO REGIS IVAR, medical educator, researcher; b. Eloi Mendes, Minas Gerais, Brazil, Feb. 19, 1967; s. Regis Ximenes and Helena Ivar Carneiro; m. Monica Toniato Borges, Sept. 22, 2001; 1 child, Arthur Borges. Degree in Medicine, Fed. U. Rio de Janeiro, 2001, PhD, 2008. Medicine prof. Souza Marques U., Rio de Janeiro, 2001—; rschr. Fed. U., Rio de Janeiro, 2001—, coord. morbid obesity unit, 2002—. Mem.: Brazilian Diabetes Soc. (Rio de Janeiro chpt.). Achievements include research in obesity, diabetes and metabolism. Office: Federal Univ Rua Rodolpho Paulo Rocco Rio de Janeiro 22471150 Brazil Office Phone: (55)(21) 22747545. Home Fax: (55)(21)22747545. Personal E-mail: endoregis@uol.com.br.

CARNEIRO, RONALDO DOS SANTOS, surgeon; b. Rio de Janeiro, Mar. 17, 1946; m. Mary Alice Schuch; 3 children. BS, Cath. U. Rio Grande do Sul, Porto Alegre, Brazil, 1964; MD, Fed. U. Rio Grande do Sul, Porto Alegre, 1970. Diplomate Am. Bd. Plastic Surgery, Am. Bd. Surgery of the Hand; lic. physician, Brazil; lic. physician, surgeon, Pa., Calif. Intern Emergency Hosp. of Porto Alegre, Fla., 1968-69; preceptor dept. thoracic surgery Cath. U., Rio de Janeiro, 1969; preceptor in hand surgery Santa Casa Hosp., Rio de Janeiro, 1969; intern, resident Union Meml. Hosp., Balt., 1971-75, preceptor in hand surgery, 1975; resident in plastic surgery Allentown (Pa.) and Sacred Heart Hosp. Ctr., 1975; fellow in hand surgery dept. orthop. Jackson Meml. Hosp. and U. Miami (Fla.) Affiliated Hosps., 1977; maytag fellow in plastic surgery, fellow in exptl. microsurg U. Miami Sch. Medicine, 1978, assoc. prof. dept. orthop. and rehab., 1987, assoc. prof. clin. surgery, 1989-92; instr. hand surgery dept. orthop. Med. Sch. of U. Rio Grande do Sul, 1979-85; chief of hand surgery Hosp. Independencia, Porto Alegre, 1979-85; pvt. practice Western Hand Ctr., Downey, Calif., 1985-87; chief sect. hand surgery dept. plastic surgery Cleveland Clinic Naples, Fla., chmn. divsn. surgery, 2000—02, chief dept. hand surgery. Tchg. asst. lab. classes and rsch. Physiology Exptl. Inst., Med. Sch. Fed. U. of Rio Grande do Sul, 1967-68; with microsurgery lab. Union Meml. Hosp., Balt., 1974-75, U. Miami, 1978; instr. orthop. residents and med. students in hand surgery svc. dept. orthop. and rehab., U. Miami Sch. Medicine, 1987-91; vis. prof. Louisville Inst. Hand and Microsurgery, 1986; illustrious vis. prof. Sindicato Dos Medicos de Santa Maria, Brazil, 1989; internat. invited prof. IX Bolivian Nat. Meeting Orthop. and Traumatology, 1990, XVI Ecuadorian Nat. Meeting Orthop. and Traumatology, 1990, Venezuelan Nat. Meeting Hand Surgery, 1990, 1st Nat. Panamanian Congress, 1991, XVII Nat. Meeting Colombian Soc. Surgery of the Hand, 1990, XXV Regional Meeting So. Br. Brazilian Soc. Surgery of the Hand, 1st Ann. Internat. Meeting of Orthop. in Panama, 1992; cons. Children's Med. Svcs., Fla., 1987; presenter in field. Contbr. numerous articles to profl. jours. Named 1 of Best Drs. in Am., S.E. Region, 1996-97, 1998; rsch. grantee Biomatrix, Inc., U. Miami, 1987-88. Mem. Am. Soc. Surgery of the Hand, Brazilian Hand Soc. (pres. so. br. 1985), Brazilian Plastic Surgery Soc., Brazilian Soc. for Surgery of the Hand, Brazilian Med. Soc., Colombian Soc. Hand Surgery, Ecuadorian Soc. Orthop., Internat. Fedn. Socs. for Surgery of the Hand (com on infections of the hand), Venezuelan Soc. Hand Surgery, Fla. Hand Soc., Soc. Orthop. Surgeons De Santa Cruz De La Sierra Bolivia, S.Am. Hand Soc. (hon.). Office: Carneiro Hand Surgery Inst 8340 Collir Blvd 303 Naples FL 34114 Office Phone: 239-348-4040.

CARNEVALE, FRANCISCO CESAR, radiologist; b. Sao Paulo, Jan. 13, 1966; MD, Faculdad Medicina U. Mogi Das Cruzes, Sao Paulo, PhD, 1990. Chief interventional radiology unit U. Sao Paulo Med. Sch., 2002—. Office: Rua Teodoro Sampaio 352/17 Sao Paulo 05406-000 Brazil Business E-Mail: fcarnevale@uol.com.br.

CARNEY, ANDREW SIMON, surgeon; b. South Shields, England, Aug. 17, 1965; arrived in Australia, 2001. s. Michael Carney and Margaret Storey. BSc with 1st class honors, U. Edinburgh, Scotland, 1983, MBBChir with distinction, 1988; MD, Flinders U., Australia, 2005. Sr. house officer Edinburgh Royal Infirmary, 1990-93; specialist registrar Queen's Med. Ctr., Nottingham, Eng., 1994-99; traveling fellow Mt. Sinai & N.Y. Hosps., NYC, 1998; vis. fellow in head and neck surgery Royal Adelaide Hosp., Australia, 1999-2001; sr. lectr. in otolaryngology Flinder Med. Ctr., Bedford Park, Australia, 2000—07, assoc. prof., 2007—10, prof., 2010—; dir. Flinders Voice Clinic, Australia, 2000—; lead clinician Head and Neck Clinic, 2001—, head of ENT unit, 2005—. Mem. editl. bd. Scalpel, editor. Austrailian Supplement Otolaryngology Head & Neck Surgery, 2009-; referee, contbr. articles to profl. jours. Trustee Brit. Med. Students Trust, London; chmn. Brit. Jr. Drs. Conf., 1996-97, Brit. Med. Assn. Student Com., London, 1987-88. Recipient Gold medal sect. laryngology Royal Soc. Medicine, 1998, Rhinology prize Midland Inst. Otology, 1998, 99; traveling scholar Jour. Laryngology and Otology, 1998. Fellow: Am. Acad. Otolaryngology - Head and Neck Surgery, Royal Coll. Surgeons Edinburgh, Royal Australian Coll. Surgeons; mem.: Am. Rhinological Soc., Australian Rhinological Soc. (sec. 2007—10, chair Flinders clin. rsch. ethics com. 2007—, v.p. 2010—). Avocation: sailing. Office: Flinders Pvt Hosp Bedford Park SA 5042 Australia Business E-Mail: scarney@ent-surgery.com.

CARNEY, JEAN KATHRYN, psychologist; b. Ft. Dodge, Iowa, Nov. 10, 1948; d. Eugene James and Lucy (Devlin) C.; m. Mark Krupnick, Jan. 1, 1977 (dec. Mar. 2003), m. Constantin Fasolt, July 12, 2008; 1 child, Joseph Carney Krupnick. BA, Marquette U., 1970; MA, U. Chgo., 1984, PhD, 1986. Registered clin. psychologist, Ill. Reporter Milw. Jour., 1971-76, editorial writer, 1976-79; asst. prof. psychology St. Xavier Coll., Chgo., 1985-86; dir. Lincoln Park Clinic, Chgo., 1986-87; pvt. practice psychotherapist Chgo., 1987—. Sci. staff Michael Reese Hosp. Med. Ctr., Chgo., 1987-2002; instr. Northwestern U. Med. Sch., 1991-95; clin. asst. prof. U. Ill. Coll. Medicine, 1993—. Editor: Self Regulation: Attention and Attachment, Psychoanalytic Inquiry, 2002, Jewish Writing and the Deep Places of the Imagination, 2005. Recipient Best Series Articles, 1975, Best Editorial, 1978, Milw. Press Club, William Allen White Nat. Award for Editorial Writing, 1978, Robert Kahn Meml. Award for Research on Aging, Univ. Chgo., 1985. Mem. APA, Ill. Psychol. Assn., Chgo. Assn. Psychoanalytic Psychology. Office: 111 North Wabash # 1221 Chicago IL 60602-2115 Personal E-mail: jkcarney@usa.net.

CARNEY, JOHN M., dermatologist; MD, Nothwestern U. Diplomate Am. Bd. Dermatology, 1984. Resident dermatology Univ. Hosp., Cleveland, Ohio, 1981—84; fellow physiology Harvard Med. Sch., Boston, 1984—85; fellow dermatologic surgery University Tenn. Med. Ctr., Memphis, 1985—86; hosp. affiliation include University of Ark. Med. Sciences. Office: SW Med Arts Bldg 11321 Interstate 30 Ste 201 Little Rock AR 72209 Office Phone: 501-455-4700.

CARNIOL, PAUL J., plastic and reconstructive surgeon, otolaryngologist; b. NYC, Sept. 26, 1951; s. David A. and Diane (Hadler) C.; m. Renie Rich, Jan. 3, 1976; children: Michael P., Alan R., Eric T. BA, NYU, 1972; MD, U. Pa. Sch. Medicine, 1976. Diplomate Am. Bd. Otolaryngology, Am Bd. Facial Plastic and Reconstructive Surgery, Am. Bd. Cosmetic Surgery, Am. Bd. Med. Examiners. Resident, surgery U. Pa., Phila., 1976-77, resident, plastic and reconstructive surgery, 1981-83; resident, surgery North Shore U. Hosp., Manhasset, NY, 1977-78; resident, surgery and otolaryngology, clin. tchg. fellow Mass. Eye and Ear Infirmary, Harvard Med. Sch., Boston, 1978-81; attending plastic surgery, head and neck surgery Overlook Hosp., Summit, NJ, 1983—; clin. prof. NJ Med. Sch., U. Medicine & Dentistry NJ, Newark, 1994—. Instr. courses on lasers in plastic surgery, facial rejuvenation; chief sect. otolaryngology Overlook Hosp., 1992-97; courtesy staff, St. Barnabus Hosp., 1996-; mem. Univ. Hosp. staff 1998-; police surgeon, Summit, NJ, 1997-, New Providence, NJ, 1997-; mem. bd. health New Providence, 2002-, emergency response team, 2003-; mem. Union County emergency response team, 2004; vis. prof. dept. otolaryngology U. Pa. Sch. Medicine, 2006; cons., lectr., presenter in field. Editor: Laser Skin Rejuvenation, 1998, Facial Rejuvenation, 2001; co-editor: Clinical Procedures In Laser Skin Rejuvention, 2007; co-editor: (with G. Monheit) Aesthetic Rejuvenation Challenges and Solutions: A World Perspective, 2010; spl. editor: Am. Jour. Cosmetic Surgery, mem. editl. bd.: Jour. Cosmetic and Laser Therapy, Facial Plastic Surgery

Times, Plastic Surgery Products, 1999, Jour. Aesthetic Dermatology and Cosmetic Dermatologic Surgery, 1992—94, Jour. Cutaneous Laser Surgery, 2000; contbr. articles to profl. jours., chapters to books. Interviewer for admissions com. U. Pa., Phila., 1987—. Recipient Cmty. Svc. award, Ciba-Geigy, Summit, 1978, Found. award, NYU, 1972, Alumni Gold Medal award, 1972, Silver Shield, PBA 55, 2003; named Top Cosmetic Surgeons, NJ Savvy Mag., 2006—09, Top Physician in NY Met. Area, Castle Connolly Ltd., 2006—10, Top Plastic Surgeons, Consumer's Rsch. Coun., 2006—08, 2010; named one of Top Cosmetic Surgeons in NJ, NJ Life Magazine and Castle Connelly Med., Ltd., 2004. Fellow: ACS (coun. mem. NJ chpt. 2004—, pres. NJ chpt. 2009—10), Am. Acad. Cosmetic Surgery (chmn. edn. com. 1995—97), Am. Acad. Facial Plastic and Reconstructive Surgery (dir. courses lasers, facial plastic surgery and cosmetic surgery 1996—98, care com., chmn. new tech. and surg. devices com. 1997—2000, v.p. R & D 2001—03), Am. Acad. Otolaryngology, Nead and Neck Surgery (bd. govs. 1991—); mem.: ACS, AMA, NJ Acad. Facial Plastic Surgery (pres. 2003—), Med. Soc. N.J. (trustee 2005—, bd. dirs.), Union County Med. Soc. (planning com. 1986—89, exec. com. 1995—97, chmn. program com. 1995—, exec. bd. 1997—, treas. 1999—2000, v.p. 2000—02, pres.-elect 2002—03, pres. 2003—04), NJ Acad. Otolaryngology (pres. 1993—96, 1997—), NJ Med. Soc. (mem. coun. comm. 1996—2002, coun. on med. svcs. 2002—, mem. coun. legislation 2004—, mem. bd. trustees 2005—08), Internat. Soc. Cosmetic Laser Surgery (bd. dir. 1998—2001, v.p. 2001—03, trustee 2005—07, pres. elect 2007—08), Phi Beta Kappa. Avocations: golf, fishing, bicycling, Tae Kwon Do. Office: 33 Overlook Rd Ste 401 Summit NJ 07901 Office Phone: 908-598-1400.

CARO, IVOR, dermatologist; b. Johannesburg, June 2, 1946; came to U.S., 1975; s. Herbert and Rachel (Eisenstein) C.; m. Sheryl Helaine Marsden, Dec. 14, 1969; children: Howard Seth, Glen. MB, BCh, U. Witwatersrand, 1969. Diplomate, Am. Bd. Dermatology. Resident U. Witwatersrand, Johannesburg, 1971—74; fellow St. John's Hosp., London, 1974—76; asst. prof. U. N.C., Chapel Hill, 1975—78; pvt. practice Seattle, 1978—99; clin. prof. U. Wash., Seattle, 1978—99; chief dermatology, attending dermatologist Va. Mason Med. Ctr., Seattle, 1978—99; asst. prof., dir. internat. program dermatology Harvard Med. Sch., Boston, 1999—2003; dir. dermatol. clin. investigation unit Mass. Gen. Hosp., Harvard Med. Sch., 2000—03; sr. med. dir. Genentech, South San Francisco, 2003—. Contbr. to profl. publs. and textbooks. Fellow: Am. Acad. Dermatology; mem.: Soc. Investigative Dermatology, Pacific Dermatol. Soc., Noah Worcester Dermatol. Soc. (sec., treas. 2000—04, pres. 2004—05). Office: Genentech 1 DNA Way MS 444 B South San Francisco CA 94080 Office Phone: 650-225-6370. Business E-Mail: icaro@gene.com.

CARO, WILLIAM ALLAN, physician, educator; b. Chgo., Aug. 16, 1934; s. Marcus Rayner and Adeline Beatrice (Cohen) Caro; m. Ruth Fruchtlander, June 15, 1959 (dec.); children: Mark Stephen, David Edward; m. Joan Peters, Oct. 18, 1997. Student, U. Mich., 1952-55; BS in Medicine, U. Ill., 1957, MD, 1959. Intern Cook County Hosp., Chgo., 1959-60; resident in internal medicine U. Ill. Rsch. and Ednl. Hosps., 1960-61; resident in dermatology Hosp. U. Pa., 1961-62, 64-66; Earl D. Osborne fellow dermal pathology Armed Forces Inst. Pathology, Washington, 1966-67; asst. in medicine U. Ill. Coll. Medicine, 1960-61; asst. instr. U. Pa. Med. Sch., 1961-62, 64-66; from asst. prof. to assoc. prof. dermatology Northwestern U. Med. Sch., 1967—81, prof., 1981—; pvt. practice specializing in dermatology Chgo., 1967—. Chief dermatology sect. MacDonald Army Hosp., Ft. Eustis, Va., 1962—64; attending physician Chgo. Wesley Meml. Hosp., 1969—72, Northwestern Meml. Hosp., 1972—, mem. med. exec. com., 1977—79; cons. Rehab. Inst. Chgo., Mcpl. Tb Sanitarium Chgo., 1968—74. Mem. editl. bd. Cutis, 1975—; assoc. editor: Year Book Pathology and Clin. Pathology, 1977—80. Mem. medicine adv. bd. U. Ill. Coll. Medicine, 1988—; trustee Northwestern Meml. Hosp. Chgo., 1986—87, bd. dirs., 1988—91, Northwestern Meml. Corp., 1987—2000, mem. exec. com., 1988—91. Served as capt. M.C. USAR, 1962—64. Recipient Gold medal, 2011. Mem.: AMA, Am. Bd. Dermatology (diplomate 1966, bd. dirs. 1981—91, v.p. 1989—90, pres. 1990—91), Dermatology Found. (Clark W. Finnerud award 2002), Pacific Dermatol. Assn., Internat. Soc. Dermatology, Am. Soc. Dermatopathology (pres.-elect 1995—96, bd. dirs. 1995—2000, pres. 1996—97), Am. Dermatol. Assn. (bd. dirs. 1993—98, v.p. 2004—05), Chgo. Dermatol. Soc. (editor trans. 1971—73, pres. 1983—84, Founders award 1992, Gold medal 2011), Am. Acad. Dermatology (Gold award sci. exhibit 1970), U. Ill. Med. Alumni Assn. (exec. bd. 1977—80), Phi Kappa Phi, Alpha Omega Alpha. Office: 676 N Saint Clair St Ste 1840 Chicago IL 60611-2927

CAROFF, PHYLLIS M., social work educator; b. Bklyn., Feb. 22, 1924; d. Harry and Irene (Lesser) Friedman; m. Joseph Caroff, May 16, 1943; children: Michael, Peter. BA, Douglass Coll., 1944; MSW, N.Y. Sch. Social Work, 1947; DSW, Columbia U., 1969; DHL (hon.), Hunter Coll, CUNY, 1995. Caseworker ARC, 1944-45; caseworker, student supr. Community Service Soc., NYC, 1956-61; from lectr. to assoc. prof. Hunter Coll. Sch. Social Work, NYC, 1961-76, prof., 1976-87; dir. Postmasters Program in Advanced Clin. Social Work, 1977-87; pvt. practice psychotherapy NYC, 1964—. Cons. VA Hosp., N.Y.C., 1977-85, USPHS Hosp., S.I., 1974—; mem. adv. bd. Found. Thanatology, 1976—; mem. profl. adv. com. Grad. Program in Social Work, Inst. Health Professions, Mass. Gen. Hosp., 1980-86. Author: (with others) Before Addiction, 1973; editorial bd. Clin. Social Work Jour., 1972-, Jour. Gerontol. Social Work, 1978-; editor: (with others) Social Work in Health Services: An Academic Practice Partnership, 1980, A New Model in Academic/Practice Partnership, 1985, Psychosocial Advances in Clinical Social Work, 1985. Mem. exec. com. of bd. Planned Parenthood N.Y.C., 1974-79, chmn. rsch. and evaluation com., 1974-77, bd. dirs., 1971-86. Named Disting. Practitioner, Nat. Acad. Practice in Social Work, 1983; NIMH fellow, 1964-65; various grants. Fellow Am. Orthopsychiat. Assn., N.Y. Acad. Medicine; mem. AAUP, Nat. Assn. Social Workers (chmn. clin. council 1981-84, mem. peer rev. adv. com. 1982-84), N.Y. State Soc. Clin. Social Work Psychotherapists, The Douglass Soc. Home: 15 W 81st St New York NY 10024-6022

CAROSELLA, CHRISTINE E., internist, educator; BA in Chemistry cum laude, U. Rochester, 1983—87; MD, NY Med. Coll., 1988—92. Diplomate Am. Bd. Internal Medicine. Intern Westchester Med. Ctr., resident, 1992—95; physician Med. Rsch. Assocs., 1995—; asst. prof. medicine NY Med. Coll., 1996—. Recipient Patient's Choice award, 2008—09; named Compassionate Dr., 2010; named one of Top Doctors, Castle Conolly, 2010—. Mem.: ACP, Univ. Rochester Alumni. Office: New York Medical College 40 Sunshine Cottage Rd Valhalla NY 10595 also: Medical Research Associates Physicians 19 Bradhurst Ave 3090 Hawthorne NY 10532-2190 Office Phone: 914-594-4000.

CAROSELLA, EDGARDO DELFINO, medical researcher, director; b. Buenos Aires, Apr. 9, 1951; s. Osvaldo Carosella and Amalia Blanco; m. Sylvelie Cronin, Dec. 1, 1984; children: Astrid, Ségolène. MD, U. Salvador, Buenos Aires. Dep. head med. rsch. divsn. Com. l'Energie Atomique, Paris, 1995—2007; rsch. dir. head hemato-immunology dept. CEA Hôsp. St. Louis, Paris, 1995—. V.p. Ctr. d'Etude Polymorphisme Humain, Paris, 1997—. Recipient Merit award, 13th Internat. Congress Histocompatibility and Immunogenetics, 2002, Blaise Pascal medal, European Acad. Scis., 2009. Mem.: European Acad. Scis., Acad. Sci. Inst. France (Grand prix 1996). Avocations: philosophy, painting, horseback riding. Home: 116 Rue de la Faisanderie Paris 75116 France Office: CEA SRHI Hôsp Saint Louis 1 Av Claude Vellefaux Paris 75010 France Office Fax: 33 1 57 27 67 80. Business E-Mail: edgardo.carosella@cea.fr.

CARP, NED Z., surgeon; Grad., U. Pa.; MD, Temple U. Intern Abington Meml. Hosp., resident; fellow Fox Chase Cancer Ctr., Am. Coll. of Surgeons; hosp. affiliations include Bryn Mawr Hosp., Paoli Hosp., Lankenau Med. Ctr., chief gen. surgery, dir. surg. oncology, chmn. tumor bd.; clin. asst. prof. Thomas Jefferson Univ. Mem.: Ea. Coop. Oncology Group, Soc. for Surg. Oncology, The Am. Radium Soc., Am. Soc. for Gastrointestinal Endoscopy, Am. Soc. of Clin. Oncology. Office: Lankenau Medical Center 100 Lancaster Ave Wynnewood PA 19096 Office Phone: 484-475-2000.

CARPENTER, BRIAN D., psychotherapist, educator; BA in Psychology & English cum laude, Williams Coll., 1986; PhD in Clin. Psychology, Case Western Reserve U., 1997. Lic. Mo. Clin. Psychologist. Psychology intern New Orleans Vet. Affairs Med. Ctr., 1996—97; postdoctoral fellow, psychology dept. Phila. Geriatric Ctr., 1997—98; NRSA postdoctoral fellow U. Pa., 1998—2000; adj. faculty mem. Pa. State U., 1998—2000; assoc. prof. Wash. U., St. Louis, 2000—, clin. supervisor for grad. student trainees, psychology dept., 2006—; psychotherapist, independent practice, 2000—. Intern (assessment), psychology dept. Cleve. Psychiatric Inst., 1992—93; clin. researcher, geriatric psychiatry U. Hosp. Cleve., 1992—93; psychotherapist (assessment & therapy), U. Counseling Svcs. Case Western Reserve U., 1993—95; psychotherapist (assessment & therapy), HIV Early Intervention Program Free Clinic Greater Cleve., 1993—96; psychotherapist (assessment & therapy), Geriatric Psychiatry & Geriatric Evaluation & Mgmt. Cleve. Vet. Affairs Med. Ctr., 1995—96; several adminstrv. positions Wash. U.; invited lectr. in field. Contbr. several articles to jours.; reviewer for several jours. Bd. mem. Band Together, St. Louis, 2005—07; vol. Visiting Nurse Assn. Hospice, Mo., 2003—05; vol. therapist Free Clinic Greater Cleve., Ohio, 1992—96; home visitor Little Brothers/Friends of the Elderly, Phila., 1998—99, CommuniCare Elder Svcs., Phila., 1999—2000; pres. Frontrunners, St. Louis, 2006; spkr. bureau Visiting Nurse Assn. Hospice, 2001—03. Recipient Grad. Dean's Instructional Excellence award, 1994, Marie Haug Student award of the U. Ctr. on Aging and Health, 1997, NIH Nat. Rsch. Svc. award, 1998—2000; Nat. Merit Corp. Scholarship Recipient, 1982—86, Wash. U. Kemper Grant for Tchg. Enhancement, 2001, Brookdale Nat. Fellowship, 2002—04, NIMH Advanced Rsch. Inst. in Geriatric Mental Health Scholar, 2004—06. Mem.: Psychologists in Long-Term Care, Nat. Coun. on Family Rels., Gerontological Soc. America, Am. Psychological Soc., APA (co-chair, continuing edn. com. divsn. 20 2007—, Divsn. 20/Retirement Rsch. Fund Grad. Rsch. Proposal award 1996, Divsn. 12/Sect. II Student Rsch. award 1997), John D. & Catherine T. Found. Rsch. Network on Successful Midlife Develop. Office: Dept Psychology Washington U Campus Box 1125 Saint Louis MO 63130 Office Phone: 314-935-8212. Office Fax: 314-935-7588. Business E-Mail: bcarpenter@wustl.edu.

CARPENTER, CHARLES COLCOCK JONES, internist, educator; b. Savannah, Ga., Jan. 5, 1931; s. Charles Colcock Jones and Alexandra (Morrison) C.; m. Sally R. Fisher, Nov. 29, 1958; children— Charles Morrison, Murray Douglas, Andrew Fisher. AB, Princeton, 1952; MD, Johns Hopkins, 1956. Diplomate: Am. Bd. Internal Medicine (mem. bd. 1976—, exec. com. 1980—, chmn. 1983-84). Intern Johns Hopkins Hosp., Balt., 1956-57, resident, 1957—59, 1961—62, practice medicine, specializing in infectious disease, 1962-73; asst. prof. medicine Johns Hopkins, 1962-67, assoc. prof., 1967-69, prof., 1969-73; physician-in-chief Balt. City Hosps., 1969-73; prof., chmn. dept. medicine Case Western Res. Sch. Medicine, 1973-86; physician-in-chief Case Western Res. Univ. Hosp., 1973-85; prof. medicine Brown U., 1986—, dir. Internat. Health Inst., 1993—98, dir. AIDS Ctr., 2006—. Dir. Cholera Research Program, Johns Hopkins Center Med. Research and Tng., Calcutta, India, 1962-64; chmn. cholera panel U.S.-Japan Coop. Med. Sci. Program, 1965-72; mem. U.S.-Japan Coop. Med. Sci. Program (U.S. del.), 1973—2000, chmn., 1990-2000; mem. adv. bd. Sch. Medicine Johns Hopkins U., 1982-97; mem. Nat. Adv. Coun. Allergy and Infectious Diseases, 1985-89; chmn. extramural cons. AIDS exec. com. NIH, 1986-87, nat. adv. com. for AIDS, NIH, 1992-93; chmn. adv. coun. AIDS Rsch., NIH, 1995-2000; dir. Lifespan/Tufts/Brown Ctr. for AIDS Rsch., 1998-. Trustee Internat. Ctr. for Infectious Disease Rsch., Bangladesh, 1979-83, Internat. Child Health Found., 1985-96, Miriam Hosp., 1992-97. Sr. asst. surgeon USPHS, 1959-61. Recipient John E. Fogarty Internat. Health Recognition Award, NIH, 2003, John H. Chafee Award for Leadership in Healthcare, Am. Heart Assn., 2004, Disting. Chair Medicine award, Assn. Profs. Medicine, 2007, Susan Colver Rosenberger medal, Brown U., 2009, Leopold medal, Lawrenceville Sch., 2011. Fellow ACP (master 1992, Disting. Physician award, 2003), AAAS (chmn. med. scis. sect. 1994-96); mem. Inst. Medicine NAS, Am. Soc. Clin. Investigation, Assn. Am. Physicians (sec. 1975-81, councillor 1981-86, v.p. 1986-87, pres. 1987-88), Infectious Diseases Soc. Am. (Smadel medal 1991), Johns Hopkins Soc. Scholars, Johns Hopkins Med. and Surg. Assn. (pres. 1995-97), Order of the Sacred Treasure (Japan). Home: 12 Half Mile Rd Barrington RI 02806-4104 Office Phone: 401-793-4025. Personal E-mail: ccjc@lifespan.org.

CARPENTER, PAUL LYNN, cardiologist; b. Fairmont, Minn., Jan. 14, 1946; s. Orlo Earnest and Mae Elizabeth (Poulson) C.; m. Rhoda Ann Jordeth, Mar. 15, 1969; children: Amy Elizabeth, Emily Anne, Abigail Lynn. BSChE, U. Minn., 1968, MD, 1974. Diplomate Am. Bd. Internal Medicine. Chem. engr. 3M Co., St. Paul, 1968-69, USPHS, Cin., 1970-71; extern So. Bapt. Hosp., Ailoun, Jordan, 1975; resident in internal medicine Northwestern Hosp. U. Minn., Mpls., 1975-78, fellow in cardiology, 1978-80; invasive cardiologist Ctrl. Plains Clinic, Sioux Falls, SD, 1980-81, North Ctrl. Heart, Ltd., Sioux Falls, 1981—; asst. clin. prof. dept. medicine U. S.D. Sch. Medicine, Sioux Falls, 1982-90, assoc. clin. prof. dept. medicine, 1990-98, clin. prof. medicine, 1998—; dir. cardiovascular tng. Avera Heart Hosp., Sioux Falls, 2006—. Chmn. cardiac care com. Mckennan Hosp., Sioux Falls, 1984-98, co-dir. cardiac catheterization lab., 1988—, dir. cardiac rehab., 1990—, dir. cardiology, 2003-; pres. North Ctrl. Heart, Ltd., 1984-85; dir. cardiovasc. tng. Avera Heart Hosp., 2006—. Girls basketball coach YMCA, Sioux Falls, 1987-96; girls coach Sioux Falls Soccer Assn., 1991-94; Sunday sch. tchr. Ctrl. Bapt. Ch., Sioux Falls, 1987-94. Fellow Am. Coll. Cardiology (gov. S.D. 1987-90), Am. Coll. Chest Physicians; mem. ACP, AMA, S.D. State Med. Assn., Christian Med. Soc. (life), Alpha Omega Alpha, Tau Beta Pi. Avocations: civil war and native american history, travel, sports, fishing. Office: No Ctrl Heart Ltd 4520 W 69th St Sioux Falls SD 57108 Home Phone: 605-339-3924; Office Phone: 605-977-5000. Business E-Mail: pcarpenter@ncheart.com.

CARPENTER, ROBERT JAMES, healthcare company executive; b. San Diego, Mar. 14, 1945; s. John A. and Carmen E. (Ewbank) C.; m. Alma Lee, July 22, 1967; children— Christine, Catherine. BS, U.S. Mil. Acad., 1967; MS in Computer Sci, Stanford U., 1969; MBA (J. Spencer Love fellow 1973), Harvard U., 1975. Co-founder VacTex Inc.; chmn. Hydra Biosciences; With Baxter Travenol Labs., Inc., 1975-81; dir. prodn. planning div. Fenwal Labs., Deerfield, Ill., 1976-78, pres., 1978-81; pres., CEO and chmn. Integrated Genetics Inc., Framingham, Mass., 1981-89; exec. v.p. Genzyme Corp., 1989-91; pres., chmn. and CEO Geltex Inc., 1991—93; exec. v.p., CEO and chmn. IG Labs. Inc., 1991; bd. chmn. Biosurface Technology, Inc., 1993—; pres. Boston Medical Investors, Inc., 1994—; pres, CEO Aquila Biopharmaceuticals Inc., 1995—98; pres. Peptimmune, Inc., 2002—04, bd. chmn., 2002—07. Bd. dirs. Genzyme Corp., 1994—. Served with capt. U.S. Army, 1967-73. Decorated Bronze Star, Army Commendation medal (2). Office: Genzyme Corp Bd Directors 500 Kendall St Cambridge MA 02142 Office Phone: 617-252-7500. Office Fax: 617-252-7600. Business E-Mail: robert.carpenter@genzyme.com. *

CARPENTER, WILLIAM F., III, hospital management company executive, lawyer; BA, JD, Vanderbilt Univ. Ptnr. Waller Lansden Dortch & Davis, Nashville, 1983—98; gen. counsel Am. group HCA, Inc., 1998—99; sr. v.p. to exec. v.p., gen. counsel, corp. sec. LifePoint Hospitals Inc., Brentwood, Tenn., 1999—2006, pres., CEO, 2006—. Bd. dir. Psychiatric Solutions Inc., 2004—, Fedn. Am. Hospitals. Office: Lifepoint Hospitals Inc Ste 200 103 Powell Ct Brentwood TN 37027 *

CARPENTER-MASON, BEVERLY NADINE, retired quality assurance professional; d. Frank Carpenter and Thelma Deresa (Williams) Carpenter Smith; m. Sherman Robert Robinson Jr., Dec. 26, 1953 (dec. 1986); 1 child, Keith Michael Robinson (dec.); m. David Solomon Mason Jr., Sept. 10, 1960; 1 child, Tamara Nadina Mason. Grad., Shadyside Hosp. Sch. Nursing, Pitts.; BS, St. Joseph Coll., North Windham, ME, 1979; MS, So. Ill. U., 1981; PhD, Columbia Pacific U., 1995. RN Pa., DC, Fla., cert. PNP, RN NY, Md.; cert. state ombusmon long term care North Pinellas Pasco County Long Term Care Ombudsman Coun., parish nurse 2004, lay spkr. 2008, lay del. Fla. Conf. United Meth. Ch., 1998, 2009. Staff nurse med. surgery, ob gyn neonatology and pediat. Pa., NY, Wyo., Colo. Wyo., Fla. and Washington, 1954—68; mgr. clinician dermatol. svcs. Malcolm Grow Med. Ctr., Camp Spring, Md., 1968—71; PNP Dept. Human Resources, Washington, 1971—73; asst. DON Glenn Dale Hosp., Md., 1973—81; nursing coord. medicaid divsn. Forest Haven Ctr., Laurel, Md., 1981—83, spl. asst. to supr. for med. svcs., 1983—84; spl. asst. to supt. for quality assurance Bur. Habilitation Svcs., Laurel, 1984—89; exec. asst. quality assurance coord. Mental Retardation Devel. Disabilities Adminstrn., Washington, 1989—91; bd. dirs., coord. quality assurance health svcs. divsn. UPARC, Clearwater, Fla., 1993—94; owner, prin. BCM Assocs., 1992—2005. Mem. exec. com. Am. Found. Edn. Healthcare Quality, 1995—97; cons. Dist. V, Fla. Dept. HHS, 1997—2002; cons., lectr. in field; mem. Parish Nurses United Meth. Ch. Fla. Conf.; mem. editl. bd., co-developer, case study editor Am. Jour. Quality Assurance, 1984—2005. Author: Quality Assurance: Toward a Paradigm of Universality, 1995; contbr. articles to profl. jours. Mem., star donor ARC Blood Dr., Washington, 1985—; mem. health and human svcs. bd. Fla. Dept. Children and Families, 1997—2000, cons. Dist. XI, 1998; bd. dirs. Pinellas County (Fla.) Coun., Pinellas County WAGES Coalition, 1999; mem. Parish Nurse Assn., 2004—; vol. chief cons. Am. Bd. Med. Quality 2005 Cert. Examination Devel., 2005—; vol. curriculum specialist cons. Accreditation Coun. for Edn. and Tng., 2001—; chief cons. Am. Coll. Med. Quality, 2005; lay del. United Meth. Ch. Fla. Conf., 1998—2009; bd. ordained ministry apptd. by the bishop of United Meth. Ch., 2004—09; bd. dirs. North Pinellas divsn. Am. Cancer Soc., 2002—04; bd. trustees, dir. Upper Pinellas Assn. Retarded Citizens Bd./Found., 2002—; chair nominations com. Prince Georges Nat. Coun. Negro Women, Md., 1984—85; exec. sec. Pipers Meadow Home Owners Assn., 1993—2001; mem. Long Term Care Fla. State Ombudsman Coun., 2000—05. Recipient awards, Dept. Air Force and DC Govt., 1966—92, Della Robbia Gold medallion, Am. Acad. Pediat., 1972, John P. Lamb Jr. Meml. Lectureship award, E. Tenn. State U., 1988, Outstanding Svc. award, U.S. Congress Adv. Bd. Svc., 1991, Internat. Hippocrates award, Internat. Biog. Inst., London, 2009; named Woman of the Yr., 1997; named to Hall of Fame, Am. Biog. Inst., 2011; grantee, North Pinellas Fla. Soroptimist. Fellow: Am. Coll. Med. Quality (mem. jour. editl. bd., contbg. editor 1985—2004, chmn. publs. com. 1987—2003, asst. treas. 1988—93, chief cons., case study editor, founding mem., Svc. award 1999, disting. fellow, named Disting. Fellow); mem.: NAFE, Internat. Platform Assn., Healthcare Quality Inst., Assn. Retarded Citizens, Am. Bd. Quality Assurance and Utilization Rev. Physicians (asst. treas. 1988—94, chair exam. com. 1990—93, chief proctor exam. com. 1995—97, Chmn. of the Yr. award 1993, Calvin R. Openshaw Svc. award 1992, presdl. citation), Internat. Assn. Mental Retardation (internat. conf. lectr. 1988), Top Ladies of Distinction (1st v.p. 1986—91), World Cir. Lang. Club (1st v.p. 2003—05, corr. sec. 2005—08), Soroptimists Internat. (sec. Pinellas chpt. 1999, Achievement in Healthcare award 1997), Order Ea. Star (Achievement award Deborah chpt. 1991). Democrat. Avocations: studying languages, travel, reading, writing, collecting antiques.

CARPENTIER, ALAIN FRÉDÉRIC, cardiac surgeon; b. Toulouse, France, Aug. 11, 1933; PhD, U. Paris. Prof. emeritus Pierre and Marie Currie U.; head, dept. cardiovascular surgery Georges Pompidou European Hosp., Paris. Vis. prof. Mt. Sinai Sch. Medicine, NYC. Publisher: The French Correction (about mitral valve repair). Bd. dir. World Heart Found. Recipient Prix mondial Cino Del Duca, 1996, Medallion for Scientific Achievement, Am. Assn. Thoracic Surgery, 2005; co-recipient (with Albert Starr) Lasker-DeBakey Clin. Med. Rsch. award, Lasker Found., 2007. Mem.: French Acad. Scis. Achievements adapting valves from pigs, to prevent people who have artificial heart valves from taking blood thinners the rest of their life; with another colleague performed the first successful replacement of a human valve with an animal valve in 1965; implanted an improved version of this valve in someone who survived 18 years in 1968; developed a valve repair surgery; involved with one of the world's first computer-assisted robotic surgeries in Paris, 1998; performed emergency mitral valve repair procedure on Charlie Rose (PBS TV inteviewer) in 2006. Mailing: Georges Pompidou European Hosp 20 Rue Leblanc CV Surgery 75015 Paris France Office Phone: 011 33 1 5609 3601. Office Fax: 011 33 1 5609 3604. Business E-Mail: alain.carpentier@egp.aphp.fr. *

CARPENTIERI, SARAH C., neuropsychologist, researcher, clinical psychologist; m. James F. Asbury; 2 children. BBA/BA, U. Notre Dame, 1989; MS, U. Memphis, 1991, PhD, 1994; postgrad., Northeastern U., Boston, 1999—2001, U. Houston, 2001—02. Lic. psychologist, neuropsychologist, healthcare provider Mass., 1997, Tex., 2003. Rschr. St. Jude Children's Hosp., Memphis, 1990—94; psychology intern Harvard Med. Sch. /Children's Hosp., Boston, 1994—95; neuropsychology post-doctoral fellow Harvard Med. Sch., 1995—97, instr., asst. psychology and neuropsychologist, 1997—2003; assoc. rsch. and neuropsychologist Children's Hosp., Boston, 1997—2003; asst. prof. Baylor Coll. Medicine, Houston, 2003—; pediat. neuropsychologist Tex. Children's Hosp., Houston, 2003—. Lead investigator pediatric brain tumor rsch. program Children's Hosp., Boston, 1998—; reviewer various med. jours., 1998—; cons. Dana Farber Cancer Inst., Boston, 2001—04; prin. investigator Pediat. Oncology Rsch. Studies, 2003—; neuropsychology and psychology cons., 2003—. Contbr. articles to profl. jours., chapters to books. Grantee Rsch., Pitino Found., 1999—2000, Murphy Child's Trust, 1999—2000, S&S Found., 1997—2003; fellow VanVleet, U. Memphis, 1993—94. Mem.: APA, Tex. Psychol. Assn., Mass. Psychol. Assn., Nat. Acad. Neuropsychology, Internat. Neuropsychology Soc. Achievements include research in area of neurocognitive functioning and polymorphisms. Business E-Mail: sarah.carpentieri@carpenburymed.com.

CARPER, BARBARA ANNE, nursing educator; BSN, Tex. Women's U., 1959; clin. cert. in anesthesia, U. Mich., 1962; MEd, Columbia U., 1966, EdD, 1975. Instr. U. N.Mex. Coll. Nursing, Alburquerque, 1966-69; assoc. prof. Tex. Women's U. Coll. Nursing, Denton, 1976-80, prof., coord. doctoral program, 1980-82; prof. grad. program U. So. Maine Sch. Nursing, Portland, 1982-84; prof., chairperson dept. nursing Colby-Sawyer Coll., New London, 1984—89; prof. Regents Coll., SUNY, Albany, 1985-89; assoc. prof., coord. undergrad. program U. N.C. Coll. Nursing, Charlotte, 1989-91, interim dean, 1991-92, prof., assoc. dean for acad. affairs, 1992—99, prof., 1994—99, prof. emeritus. Vis. scholar Harvard U., 1981-82; mem. Nursing Theory Think Tank, 1982; mem. exec. bd., chmn. project com. New Eng. Orgn. Nursing, 1986-88; vis. prof. Marion A. Buckley Sch. Nursing, Adelphi U., 1989-90; Green Chair honor prof. Harris Coll. Nursing, Tex. Christian U., 1980-81; Margaret D. McLean lectr. Meml. U. Nfld., Can., 1990; numerous consultations, workshops, lectures, seminars and speeches in field. Mem. editorial bd. Jour. Advances in Nursing Sci., 1978-99, Asian Jour. Nursing Studies, 1993-95; contbr. articles to profl. jours. Bd. dirs., mem. exec. com., mem. patient and cmty. svcs. com. Nat. Kidney Found. N.H., 1987-89; bd. dirs. Hospice at Charlotte, 1991-97, co-chairperson ethics adv. com., 1995-97, vice chair at large 1996-97; bd. dirs. Cmty. Health Svcs., 1991-94. Fellow Am. Acad. Nursing (co-chair ethics/legal adv. com. 1983-86, mem. planning com. 1988, Ann. Sci. Sessions of Acad., mem. expert panel on ethics 1991—); mem. ANA (coun. nurse rschrs.), N.C. State Nursing Assn., Sigma Theta Tau (Disting. lectr. 1994-95), Phi Kappa Phi.

CARR, DAVID B., geriatrician, educator; MD, U. Mo., 1985. Diplomate Am. Bd. Internal Medicine, 1989, Am. Bd. Internal Medicine-geriatric medicine, 2000. Intern Mich. State Univ. East Lansing; resident internal medicine Mich. State Assoc. Hosps., 1986—88; fellow in geriatric medicine Duke Univ., 1988—90; assoc. prof. medicine and neurology Wash. Univ. Sch. of Medicine, prof. medicine, clin. dir. divsn. of geriat. and nutritional sci., dir. geriatric fellowship program, med. dir. parc provence; med. dir. The Rehab. Inst. of St. Louis; hosp. affiliation includes Barnes Jewish Hosp. Recipient Excellence in Tchg. of Internal Medicine award, Mich. State Univ., 1987, Excellence in Tchg. of Med. Students award, 1987—88, AMA Alene and Meyer Koplow award, Wash. Univ., 1997, Health South Regional Med. Dir. Leadership award, 2007; named Best Doctors in America, Best Doctors Inc., 2002, 2009—10; named one of Top 44 Providers with the Highest Patient Satisfaction, Americas Top Doctors, Castle Connolly Med. Ltd., 2002—10. Office: Barnes-Jewish Hospital/Washington University 1 Barnes Jewish Hospital Plaza Saint Louis MO 63110-1003 Office Phone: 314-747-3000.

CARR, DAVID TURNER, physician; b. Richmond, Va., Mar. 12, 1914; s. John Ernest and Mary Lela (King) Carr; m. Rosemary Rudow, June 18, 1948 (div. 1953); 1 child, Jennifer Anne Carr Oderkirk; m. Christine Nadeau, Dec. 27, 1979. Student, U. Richmond, 1931-33; MD, Med. Coll. Va., 1937; MS in Medicine, Mayo Grad. Sch. Medicine, 1947. Intern, then asst. resident Grady Hosp., Atlanta, 1937-39; resident chest diseases Bellevue Hosp., NYC, 1940-41; fellow medicine Mayo Clinic, 1943-47, cons. medicine, 1947-79, chmn. dept. oncology, 1975; dir. Mayo Comprehensive Cancer Ctr., 1975; assoc. dir. Ctr. Cancer Control, 1976-79; prof. medicine Mayo Med. Sch., 1964-79, M.D. Anderson Hosp. and Tumor Inst., Tex. Med. Ctr., Houston, 1979-92; med.-legal cons., 1992—. Mem.-at-large bd. dirs. Am. Lung Assn., 1959—74, v.p., 1971—72; bd. dirs. Rochester Civic Theatre, 1951—70, pres., 1965—67; bd. dirs. at large Am. Cancer Soc., 1967—74, pres. Minn. divsn., 1974—75, mem. am. joint com. cancer, 1971—79, chmn. am. joint com. cancer, 1979—82. Fellow: AAAS, ACP; mem.: Am. Thoracic Soc. (v.p. 1963—64), Internat. Assn. Study Lung Cancer (v.p. 1974—76, pres. 1976, treas. 1976—82), Ctrl. Soc. Clin. Rsch., Peruvian Atni-Tb Assn. (hon.), Rochester C. of C. (pres. 1959—60). Achievements include research in pulmonary diseases. Home and Office: PO Box 9300 Rancho Santa Fe CA 92067 Office Phone: 858-759-1798.

CARR, MARCUS EUGENE, JR., internist; b. Greensboro, NC, Mar. 9, 1949; s. Marcus Eugene and Alsie May (Barham) C.; m. Sarah Martin, Oct. 17, 1975 (div. June 1992); children: Joseph, Jonathan, Ashley, Mary Katherine, Christian, Stephen; m. Sheryl L. Zekert, Nov. 1993. BS in Physics, Davidson Coll., 1971; PhD in Biomed. Engrng., U. N.C., 1975, MD, 1979; postgrad, U.S. Army War Coll., 1999. Diplomate Am. Bd. Internal Medicine, Am. Bd. Hematology. Commd. 2nd lt. USAR, 1971, advanced through grades to capt., 1978; ret., 1979; intern N.C. Meml. Hosp., Chapel Hill, 1980-81, jr. resident internal medicine, 1981-82, sr. asst. resident in internal medicine, 1982-83, chief resident, 1983-84; asst. prof. medicine Med. Coll. Va., Richmond, 1985-91, asst. prof. pathology, 1988-91, assoc. prof. pathology, internal medicine, 1991—98; founder, pres. Hemodyne, Inc., Richmond, Va., 1993—; comdr. U.S. Army Hosp., 1995—97, 2000—02; prof. medicine pathology VCU Sch. Medicine, 1998—2005, clin. prof. medicine, 2005—; prof. biomed. engrng. VCU Sch. Engrng., 2005—; clin. prof. medicine Robert Wood Johnson Sch. Med. UMDNJ, 2006—; exec. dir. clin. rsch. hemostasis Novo Nordisk, Inc., Princeton, NJ, 2005, v.p. U.S. rsch., 2005—; v.p. hemostasis rsch. Novo Nordisk Rsch. US, North Brunswick, NJ, 2006—08; hematology disease area lead Pfizer Inc., Collegeville, Pa. Tissue and transfusion com., rsch. and devel. com., McGuire V.A. Med. Ctr., M-III med. curriculum com., admissions com. Sch. of Medicine, promotions com. dept. of pathology, Med. Coll. Va.; presenter in field. Contbr. more than 130 sci. articles to profl. jours. Mem. Richmond Blood Club, Bon Air Bapt. Ch., Richmond. Recommd. maj. M.C., USAR, 1987, advanced to col., 1999, served in Desert Storm, Operation Enduring Freedom, also in Kosovo; with 28th Combat Support Hosp., Operation Iraqi Freedom, 2007. Recipient med. student rsch. fellowship, 1977; grantee: So. Med. Assn., 1983, Med. Coll. Va., 1985, A. D. Williams Faculty, 1985, VA Rsch. Adv. Group, 1985, '86. 88-91, Massey Ctr. Instl. grant 1987-88, Burroughs-Wellcome, 1989, 90-91, 92—. Fellow Am. Heart Assn., Am. Coll. Physicians, Am. Coll. Angiology, Internat. Coll. Angiology, Internat. Coll. Hematology; mem. Am. Coll. Physicians, Am. Soc. Hematology, Am. Fedn. Clin. Rsch. (coun. on thrombosis), Am. Heart Assn., Internat. Soc. Thrombosis and Haemostasis, Internat. Soc. Exptl. Hematology, Nat. Hemophelia Found., N.Y. Acad. Scis., Assn. Military Surgeons of U.S., So. Soc. Clin. Investigation, Am. Soc. Clin. Pathologists, Internat. Fibrinogen Rsch. Soc., Sigma Xi. Achievements include patents in field of hematology. Home: 12 Appaloosa Trl Holland PA 18966-2593 Office: 1100 Campus Rd Princeton NJ 08540 Personal E-mail: marcus.e.carr@pfizer.com. Business E-Mail: mcrr@novonordisk.com.

CARR, MICHAEL C., pediatric urologist; b. Cleve., Nov. 22, 1955; MD, U. Cin., 1985; PhD, Ohio State U., 1982. Assoc. dir., pediatric urology Children's Hosp. Phila., 1998—. Office: Children's Hosp Philadelphia 34th Civic Center Blvd Philadelphia PA 19104 Office Fax: 215-590-3985. Personal E-mail: carr@email.chop.edu.

CARR, MINDY LEA, healthcare educator; m. Barry Lee Farr, May 14, 2006; 1 child, Tara Lea Smith. BSN, Pa. Coll. Tech., Williamsport, 1999; MEd, Pa. State U., State Coll, 2008. Cert. in nursing mgmt. Penn State U., 1989. Staff nurse Sunbury Cmty. Hosp., 1975—76; psychiat. nurse Danville State Hosp., Pa., 1976—81; staff nurse icu, ccu Evang. Cmty. Hosp., Lewisburg, Pa., 1981—82; staff nurse psychiat. Geisinger Med. Ctr., Danville, Pa., 1982—84, staff nurse neonatal icu, 1984—88, nurse mgr. pediatric unit, 1988—2000; clin. dir. Pa. Coll. Tech., Williamsport, Pa., 2001—, adj. health sci. faculty, 2004—10, asst. prof., adj. faculty, 2004—10. Mem. Order Amaranth, Sunbury, 1999—, officer, 1999—. Mem.: Alpha Chi (charter mem.), Pi Lambda Theta, Alpha Sigma Lambda.

CARR, NORMAN JOHN, pathologist, researcher; b. Springs, South Africa, Jan. 11, 1960; s. Norman Richard and Anne (Marquis) C.; m. Nicola Taylor, July 9, 1983; children: Christopher John, Anne Elizabeth. MB, BS, St. George's U., London, 1983. MRCPath., 1991. Adj. asst. prof. Uniformed Svcs. U. Health Scis., Bethesda, Md., 1992-94; staff pathologist Armed Forces Inst. Pathology, Washington, 1992-94; cons. pathologist RAF Inst. Pathology, Eng., 1992-95; rsch. fellow St. Mark's Hosp., England, 1995—2002; head histopathology Royal Hosp. Haslar, Eng., 1995-2000; dir. dept. cellular pathology Southampton (Eng.) U. Hosps., 2000—05, cons. cellular pathology, 2009—; prof. pathology St. Matthew's U., Cayman Islands, 2005—06; cons. pathologist Southern IML Pathology, Wollongong, 2006—09; prof. anat. pathology U. Wollongong, Australia, 2006—. Cons. aviation pathologist Air Accidents Investigations Br., Eng., 1992-2000; reviewer sci. and med. jours., 1993—; splty. advisor in histopathology Def. Secondary Care Agy., U.K., 1997-2000; Hon. sr. clin. lectr., dep. dir. edn. Southhampton Univ., 2002-05 Contbr. more than 30 articles to med. and sci. jours., chpts. to books; presenter, creator posters and presentations to sci. confs. and meetings. Wing comdr. RAF, 1984-2000. Cert. disting. svc. U.S. Army, Washington, 1994. Fellow Royal Coll. Pathologists; mem. Assn. Clin. Pathologists (Thames Valley rep. 1988-92), Internat. Acad. Pathology. Mem. Anglican Ch. Avocations: piano, natural history, astronomy. Office: Cellular Pathology Southampton General Hospital Tremona Rd Southampton SO16 6YD England E-mail: n.j.carr@soton.ac.uk.

CARR, RONALD EDWARD, ophthalmologist, educator; b. Newark, Sept. 17, 1932; s. Frank Edward and Mildred (Sasso) C.; m. Nancy May Gould, June 8, 1957; children: Peter Richardson, Jacqueline Marie, Timothy Edward. AB, Princeton U., 1954; MD, Johns Hopkins U., 1958; M.Sc., NYU, 1963. Intern Bellevue Hosp., NYC, 1958-59; resident NYU Med. Ctr., NYC, 1959-63; clin. assoc. NIH, Bethesda, Md., 1963-64, assoc. ophthalmologist, 1964-65; asst. prof. ophthalmology NYU Med. Ctr., 1965-67, assoc. prof., 1967-71, prof., 1971—. Author: Visual Electrodiagnosis, 1981, Electrodiagnostic Testing of the Visual System, 1990. Served to lt. comdr. USPHS, 1963. Recipient Knapp award AMA, 1966 Fellow Am. Acad. Ophthalmology, ACS; mem. Am Ophthal. Soc., N.Y. Ophthal Soc., Assn. Research in Ophthalmology Clubs: Princeton, Stone Horse Yacht. Democrat. Episcopalian. Home: 130 E End Ave New York NY 10028-7553 Office Phone: 212-263-7360. E-mail: nancycarr2@aol.com. *

CARRADINI, LAWRENCE, retired comparative biologist, science administrator, researcher; b. Astoria, NY, Apr. 18, 1953; s. George John and Florence (Camuti) C.; m. Susan Marie Peterson, Sept. 23, 1972 (divorced), m Margaret Mary Smith, Sept. 24, 2010; 1 child, Daniel Lawrence. BS in Zoology, Columbia Pacific U., 1989, MS in Vertebrate Reproductive Physiology and Physiol. Ecology, 1992. From technician to lab. supr. Charles River Labs., Wilmington, Mass., 1978-91, rschr., 1991; sr. scientist, mgr. biol. labs. Mass. Health Rsch. Inst., Boston, 1992-96; chief labs. Mass. Biologic Labs., U. Mass. Med. Sch., Boston, 1996—2010; mgr. Bio-A Facility Biogen Idec Bio 6 Flexforce, Cambridge, Mass., 2011—. Chmn. Instnl. Animal Care and Use Com., State Lab. Inst./Orphan Biologics Inst./Mass. Dept. Pub. Health/Mass. Biologics Lab., 1995-96; apptd. to State DPGS task force on procurement practices; mem. Lake Survey, U. N.H., Salem, 1982-83; instr. Internat. Children's Vaccine Tng. Program; ex officio mem. instnl. animal care and use com. U. Mass. Med. Sch., 1997—2000. Mem. editl. bd. Internat. Jour. Advances in Contraceptive Delivery Systems; contbr. articles to Jour. Lab. Animal Sci., Jour. Am. Vet. Med. Assn.; author poetry: Burning Heads, 1996, Om I Am, 1999; contbr. poetry lit. mags. and Contemporary Foreign Literature, 2001; contbr. (anthology): Selected Poems by Twenty Post-Beat Poets, 2004. Officer, selectman apptd. mem. 208 Water Quality Study Com., Salem, N.H., 1981-82, chmn., selectman apptd. mem., 1982-83; mem. adv. bd. Internat. M.C. Chang Meml. Festschrift; pres., chmn. bd. dirs. Lowell Celebrates Kerouac, Inc.; local organizer for Lowell reading UN Dialogue Among Nations Through Poetry, 2001; online assoc. editor lit. jour. RedEft. N.Y. State Regents scholar, 1971; hon. mention Richard A. Seffron Meml. Poetry award 1994. Mem. Soc. for Cryobiology, Nat. Am. Assn. Lab. Animal Sci., Am. Assn. Lab. Animal Sci. (New Eng. chpt., cert. nat. lab. animal technologist, item writer technician cert. exam. program), Lab. Animal Mgmt. Assn., Internat. Platform Assn., N.Y. Acad. Scis., Trout Unlimited. Democrat. Achievements include development of reliable method to cycle estrus in syrian hamsters; co-development of commercially available cryopreserved 1-cell mouse embryos for use in media assays; co-application of 1-cell technology toward development of commercially available cryopreserved, fertilized, pronuclear-staged mouse oocytes for DNA microinjection; development of central technical services group Massachusetts Biologic Laboratories. Home: PO Box 8797 Lowell MA 01853-8797 E-mail: lawrence.carradini@umassmed.edu.

CARRANZA, DAFNIS CAROLINA, dermatologist; b. El Salvador, Oct. 31, 1974; MD, UCLA, 2003. Physician UCLA Dermatology, 2003—08, clin. instr., 2007—08; mohs surgeon Jackson Clinic, 2008—. Recipient Edith & Carl lanky Meml. award, UCLA Sch. Medicine, Chancellors Svc. award, UCLA. Fellow: Am. Acad. Dermatology (Members Making A Difference award, Vol. Leadership); mem.: Women's Dermatologic Soc., Nat. Hispanic Med. Assn., Am. Coll. Mohs Surgery. Avocations: hiking, reading, travel. Home: 232 Meadowlark Cove Medina TN 38355 Personal E-mail: dafniscarranza@yahoo.com.

CARRELL, ROBIN WAYNE, hematologist, educator; b. Christchurch, New Zealand, Apr. 5, 1936; s. Ruane George and Constance Gwendoline (Rowe) C.; m. Susan Wyatt Rogers, Jan. 27, 1962; children: Sarah, Rebecca, Thomas, Edward. MB ChB, U. Otago, New Zealand, 1959; BS, U. Canterbury, New Zealand, 1965; MA, PhD, U. Cambridge, Eng., 1968, ScD, 2002. House physician, pathology registrar Christchurch (New Zealand) Hosp., 1960-64, head dept. clin. biochemistry, assoc. prof., 1968-75; univ. lectr., hon. cons., dept. clin. biochemistry Addenbrooke's Hosp. U. Cambridge, Eng., 1976-78, prof., dir. hematology, 1986—2003, fellow Trinity Coll. Eng., 1987—; prof. pathology, dir. Molecular Pathology Lab. Christchurch Clin. Sch. Medicine, U. Otago, New Zealand, 1979-85. Contbr. articles to profl. jours. Fellow Royal Coll. Physicians (London), Royal Coll. Pathology, Royal Soc. (London), Royal Soc. New Zealand (Hector medal and prize 1986); mem. Brit. Soc. of Thrombosis and Haemostasis (pres. 1999). Avocations: walking, local history. Home: 19 Madingley Rd Cambridge CB3 0EG England Office: University Cambridge Trinity Coll Cambridge CB2 1TQ England Business E-Mail: rwc1000@cam.ac.uk.

CARREON, HIJINIO, physician; b. Princeton, Ill., Nov. 15, 1977; BA, Drake U., 1999; DO, Des Moines U.-Osteo. Med. Ctr., 2003. Attending physician Mercy Med. Ctr., 2007—. Office: 1111 6th Ave Des Moines IA 50314 Business E-Mail: hijinid.g.carreon@dmu.edu.

CARRICK, FREDERICK ROBERT, neurologist, researcher; b. Toronto, Ont., Can., Feb. 26, 1952; s. Donald Thomas and June Madeline Carrick; m. Eve Diminture, Dec. 29, 1973; children: Tricia A. Carrick-Merlin, James E. DC, Can. Meml., Toronto, 1979; PhD, Walden U., Mpls., 1996. Diplomate in chiropractic neurology Am. Chiropractic Assn., 1985, diplomate Am. Acad. Chiropractic Neurology, Va., 1989, Am. Chiropractic Neurology Bd., Va., 1995, Am. Acad. Pain Mgmt., Va., 2000, cert. in childhood devel. disorders ABCN, Tex., 2004, vestibular rehab. ACNB, Tex., 2005, in electrodiagnostics 2005. Clin. neurologist Epsom Clinic, NH, 1979—90; prof. neurology Carrick Inst. Grad. Studies, Cape Canaveral, Fla., 1984—; disting. post grad. prof. clin. neurology Logan Coll., St. Louis, 1990—99; prof. emeritus neurology Parker Coll., Dallas, 1997—2000. Contbr. sci. articles to profl. publs. Cpl. Can. Army Commando, 1970—73, Cyprus, Middle East. Decorated Medal UN-FICYP UN, Medal Svc. de la Paix Govt. Can. Fellow: ACA, Royal Coll. Physicians and Surgeons, Am. Coll. Clin. Neurology, European Acad. Chiropractic Neurology, Internat. Coll. Chiropractors. Avocations: aviation, boating, martial arts. Office: Carrick Inst Graduate Studies 203-8941 Lake Dr Cape Canaveral FL 32920 Office Fax: 321-868-6468. Business E-Mail: registrar@carrickinstitute.org.

CARRICO, VIRGIL NORMAN, physician; b. Cumberland, Md., Aug. 28, 1940; s. Virgil Norman and Lucille E. Carrico; m. Nina Lois Lemper, Aug. 17, 1963; children: Pamela Beth Carrico-Miller, Sandra Kelly (dec.). BA, Wabash Coll., 1962; MD, Ind. U., 1966. Diplomate Am. Bd. Family Practice. Intern Marion County Gen. Hosp., Indpls., 1966-67; resident in family practice Akron (Ohio) City Hosp., 1970-72, chief resident in family practice, 1972, assoc. dir. family practice residency, 1972; chief family practice Bryan Cmty. Hosp., chief of staff, 1977-78, preceptor Bryan Area Health Edn. Ctr.; past preceptor cmty. medicine Med. Coll. Ohio, Toledo, clin. asst. prof. family medicine, clin. prof. family medicine; past preceptor preventive medicine and family practice Ohio State U.; med. dir. Bryan Area Health Edn. Ctr. Past pres., bd. dirs. Bryan Med. Group, Inc. Contbr. articles to profl. jours. Trustee YWCA, Bryan, Ohio, v.p., 1990-92; bd. dirs. United Fund, pres., 1990-92; bd. dirs. Jr. Achievement, 1981-83, Bryan Area Found. Capt. USAF, 1967-70. Fellow Am. Acad. Family Physicians (bylaw coms. 1989, 90, 91, 92, nat. chmn. 1993, chmn.

patient care svcs. commn. 1988-89, chmn. mem. svcs. commn. 1989-90); mem. Soc. Tchrs. Family Medicine, Ohio Acad. Family Medicine, Am. Acad. Family Medicine, Williams County Med. Soc. (rpes. 1976-79, sec.-treas., v.p. 1980-83), Ohio Acad. Family Physicians (del. to ho. of dels. 1972-85; pres. Fulton County chpt. 1973-85, chmn. resident affairs subcom., nominating com., student awards, fin. com., ref. com. of the ho. of dels.; treas. 1985-87, v.p. 1987-89, bd. dirs. 1983-92, pres.-elect 1990-91), Rotary Internat. Avocations: golf, travel, reading. Office: Bryan Med Group 442 W High St Bryan OH 43506-1681 Office Phone: 419-636-4517. Personal E-mail: bmg@bright.net. *

CARRIER, FRANCE, medical educator; b. Beauport, Que., June 9, 1961; d. Philippe Carrier and Therese Pare; m. Steven I. Hirschfeld; 1 child, Joshua Samuel. PhD, U. Montreal, 1988. Postdoctoral fellow Biotechnology Rsch. Inst., Montreal, Que., 1988—89; vis. assoc. NIH, Bethesda, Md., 1989—91; vis. scientist Nat. Cancer Inst. NIH, Bethesda, 1991—98; prof. medicine U. Md., Balt., 1998—. Mem. Greenebaum Cancer Ctr., Balt. Contbr. articles to profl. jours., chapters to books. Grantee Rsch. grantee, NIH, 2007—; Internat. fellow, Human Frontier Sci. Program Orgn., 1990, Rsch. grantee, NIH, 1999—2003, Am. Cancer Soc., 2000—02, 2004—07, A-T Children's Project, 2003—06. Mem.: Am. Assn. for Cancer Rsch. (sponsor, Brigid Leventhal award 2002), N.Y. Acad. Scis., Cosmos Club (Elected mem. 1999). Achievements include patents for methods for determining the presence of functional p53 in mammalian cells and for inhibitors of the S100-p53 protein-protein interaction and methods of inhibiting cancer employing the same; research in genotoxic stress-response, cancer progression, chromatin remodeling. Office: Univ Md 655 W Baltimore St Rm 10-037 Baltimore MD 21201-1595 Office Phone: 410-706-5105. Business E-Mail: fcarr001@umaryland.edu.

CARRILLO, JULIO CESAR, auxological and medical educator; b. Bogota, Colombia, June 24, 1951; s. Cesar Carrillo and Angelica Fonseca; m. Martha Beatriz Rodriguez, Sept. 30, 1988; 1 child, Illa Carrillo Rodriguez. MD in Endocrinology and Rsch. Tng., Nat. U. Colombia, Bogota, 1984. Asst. prof. Nat. U. Colombia, Bogota, 1984—88, assoc. prof., 1988—99, prof., 1999—. Coord. auxology unit Nat. U. Colombia, Bogota, 1991—2000; mem. Colombian Interinstitutional Iodine Deficiency Disorders Com., Bogota, 1991—; cons. WHO/Panamerican Health Orgn., Washington, 1992, Panamerican Health Orgn., Bogota, 1995; mem. sci. com. Biometrie Humaine et Anthropologie, Paris, 1998—2004; assoc. investigator UMR No. 6578 anthropology unit CNRS/Mediterranean U., Marseille, France, 2003—04. Editor: Colección Cuadernos de Auxologia No. 3, 1995, Bataille y la Voluntad de Transgresión, 1995; author: (poetry) Lejana, 1987, Femme Fatale Blues, 1989; author: (with others) Congenital Hypothyroidism, 1988; author: (book) Iodine Deficiency Disorders - A Contemporary Vision, 1995; author: (with O. Sababria) Atención Integral a Colectivos Humanos en la Región Amazónica Colombiana - Proyecto de Saneamiento Ambiental en La Pedrera - Amazonas, 1995; author: Time's Equation, 1995, Iodine Deficiency Disorders Elimination, 1996; author: (with M. B. Rodriguez) Yosusi's Dream, 1996; author: (novels) Paititi 5128, 1990; contbr. articles to profl. jours. Mem. TEA Auxological Found., Bogota, 1995. Recipient Colombia Honors Sci. Contbn., Kiwanis, Sci. prize, French Biometrics Soc., 2000, 2001. Mem.: Pediat. Colombian Soc., European Anthropol. Assn., Assn. pour la Coop. Internationale, Soc. de Biometrie Humaine Latinamerica (corr.), Pediat. Colombian Soc. (assoc. Sci. prize 1986), Medicine History Colombian Soc. (assoc.). Avocations: literature, music, art, films, writing. Home: 7 Place Jules Verne 93380 Pierrefitte-sur-Seine France Office Phone: 5713165539. Office Fax: 00571 3165539; Home Fax: 00571 2681062. Personal E-mail: jcc1951@yahoo.com. Business E-Mail: jccarrillof@unal.edu.co.

CARRION, VIVIEN, hospital administrator; b. Manhattan, Feb. 19, 1953; MD, SUNY, Buffalo, 1980. Neonatal dir. regional perinatal outreach Regional Perinatal Ctr. Women and Children's Hosp. Buffalo, 1992, med. dir. neonatal transport team, 1992—. Neonatal fellowship, Women and Children's Hosp., 1992. Mem.: Am. Acad. Pediat. (mem. sect. transport medicine). Avocations: swimming, writing. Office: 219 Bryant St Buffalo NY 14222 Business E-Mail: vcarrion@upa.chob.edu.

CARRO, ERIC F., neurosurgeon; b. San Juan, P.R., Dec. 1, 1949; BS, U. P.R., 1970, MD, 1974. Diplomate Am. Bd. Neurol. Surgery. Assoc. prof. U. P.R., San Juan, 1982—; pvt. practice neurosurgery, 1981—. Mem.: Caribbean Assn. Neurol. Surgeons, Am. Assn. Neurol. Surgeons. Office: 73 Santa Cruz St Office 207 Bayamon PR 00961 Office Phone: 787-740-2166. Business E-Mail: eric.carro@upr.edu.

CARROL, EDWARD NICHOLAS, retired psychologist; b. Newark, June 22, 1943; s. Wilfred and Ruth (Gluck) C.; m. Anne Marie McDonald, May 27, 1973 (div. May 1989); 1 child, Abbe Galen; m. Virginia Paisley Herbruck, Oct. 6, 1996. BA, Columbia U., 1965; MA, NYU, 1970, U. Del., 1975, PhD, 1979. Diplomate Am. Acad. Pain Mgmt. Dir. Pain Clinic, VA Med. Ctr., Cleve., 1979—2003, dir. pain psychology sect. Pain Mgmt. Ctr., 2003—09. Mem. Internat. Assn. Study of Pain, Midwest Pain Soc. Republican. Jewish. Avocations: dogs, classical and country music. Home: 21490 Claythorne Rd Shaker Heights OH 44122-1964 Home Phone: 216-932-3460.

CARROLL, FRANK EDWARD, JR., radiologist, researcher; b. Phila., Oct. 25, 1941; s. Frank Edward Sr. and Marie Elizabeth (Mullin) C.; m. Saramae Dorothy Dever, Sept. 4, 1965; children: Frank Leonard, Mark Edward. BS in Biology, St. Joseph's Coll., 1963; MD, Hahnemann Med. Coll., 1967. Diplomate Am. Bd. Radiology. Rsch. asst. Hahnemann Med. Coll. and Hosp., Phila., 1965-66; rotating intern U.S. Naval Regional Med. Ctr., Oakland, Calif., 1967-68; submarine med. officer U.S. Submarine Med. Sch., U.S. Naval Submarine Base, Gorton, Conn., 1968, SSBN 659 Will Rogers Polaris Nuclear Submarine, 1968-69; staff physician Armed Forces Staff Coll., Norfolk, Va., 1969-70; diagnostic radiology resident St. Mary's Hosp. and Med. Ctr., San Francisco, 1970-72; resident, fellow, rschr. U. Calif. San Francisco Sch. Medicine, 1972-73; asst. prof. diagnostic radiology Yale U. Sch. Medicine, New Haven, 1973-74; staff radiologist Broadway Hosp., Vallejo, Calif., 1974-75, Franklin (Pa.) Regional Med. Ctr., 1975-83; asst. prof. diagnostic radiology Vanderbilt U. Med. Ctr., Nashville, 1983-87, chief sect. pulmonary imaging, 1983—2000, assoc. dir. divsn. diagnostic radiology, 1984, dir. lab. radiologic rsch., 1984-85, assoc. prof. diagnostic radiology, 1987-94, dir. diagnostic radiology, 1985-89, assoc. prof. physics and astronomy, 1993-99, prof. diagnostic radiology, 1994—2004, emeritus prof. diagnostic radiology, 2004—, prof. physics and astronomy, 1999—; founder Mxisystems, Inc., Nashville. Adj. asst. prof. diagnostic radiology Duke U. Med. Ctr., Durham, N.C., 1981-83; cons. in field; referee jours. in field, including Investigative Radiology, Acad. Radiology, Radiology, Chest, Jour. Applied Physiology, Archives of Internal Medicine, Am. Jour. Neuroradiology, others; grant reviewer NIH, Washington. Contbr. articles to profl. jours., chpts. to books. Bd. dirs. Nashville Opera, 1988-94, Franklin Emergency Ambulance Svc., 1975-83, St. Patrick's Sch. Bd., 1975-83; asst. scoutmaster Boy Scouts Am., Franklin, 1975-83, physician and merit badge counselor, Nashville, 1983—; pres. Am. Cancer Soc., Franklin, 1975-83; design prodn. vol. Cheekwood Fine Arts Mus., Nashville, 1995—. Lt. comdr. USNR, 1963—73, submarine med. officer USNR, 1968—71, base physician Armed Forces Staff Coll., 1970—71. Fellow Am. Coll. Radiology, Am. Coll. Chest Physicians; mem. Am. Soc. Laser Medicine and Surgery, Soc. Photo-Optical Instrumentation Engrs., Soc. for Magnetic Resonance Imaging, Assn. Univ. Radiologists, Radiol. Soc. N.Am., Soc. thoracic Radiology, Tenn. Radiologic Soc., Mid. Tenn. Radiologic Soc. Achievements include production of pulsed, tunable, monochromatic X-rays by the free electron laser; designed and commissioned dedicated tabletop laser tunable, synchrotron source for monochromatic 3-D mammography without breast compression, k-edge imaging, auger cascade radiotherapy, phase contrast imaging, time-of flight imaging and protein crystallography; evaluation of lung water by magnetic resonance imaging. Home: 1216 Vintage Pl Nashville TN 37215-4707 Office: Vanderbilt U Med Ctr Emeritus Office 211 Oxford House Nashville TN 37232-4245 Office Phone: 615-322-0860. Business E-Mail: frank.carroll@vanderbilt.edu.

CARROLL, JACK ADIEN, rehabilitation hospital administrator; b. Mar. 28, 1950; BA, Ohio State U., 1972; MD, U. Cin., 1975; M Health Adminstrn., U. Minn., 1991. Dir. communication disorders U. N.D. Med. Ctr. Rehab. Hosp., Grand Forks, 1975-89, assoc. exec. dir., 1986-90, exec. dir., 1990; COO United Hospital-Rehab, Grand Forks; adminstrv. dir. Altru Health System, Grand Forks, ND; pres., CEO Sheltering Arms Physical Rehab. Hosp. & Clinics, 1998—2006, Magee Rehab. Hosp., 2006—. Office: Magee Rehab 1513 Race St Philadelphia PA 19102-1177

CARROLL, JOHN DOUGLAS, mathematical and statistical psychologist, educator; b. Phila., Jan. 3, 1939; s. John Joseph and Nolie Fay (Godwin) C.; m. Sylvia Stevens Booma, Jan. 2, 1965; children: Gregory Alan, Steven Douglas BS honors, U. Fla., 1958; PhD, Princeton U., 1963. Rsch. asst. dept. psychology Yale U., 1961—63; math., statis. psychologist Bell Labs., Murray Hill, NJ, 1963—65, 1966—89; Bd. Govs., prof. mgmt. and psychology Rutgers Bus. Sch., Newark, 1990—. Asst. prof. indsl. engring. and ops. rsch. NYU, 1965-66, adj. assoc. prof. stats., 1968-70; acting prof. psychology U. Calif. San Diego, 1975-76; acting prof. social sci. U. Calif. Irvine, 1975-76, vis. rsch. prof. cognitive sci., 1993; adj. prof. stats. Baruch Coll., CUNY, 1971; adj. prof. mktg. U. Pa., 1978-79, Procter & Gamble adj. prof. mktg., 1987-89 Contbr. numerous articles and chpts. to profl. publs.; author computer programs for multidimensional analysis of behavioral sci. data; assoc. editor: Psychometrika, 1973—, Jour. Exptl. Psychology, 1978-88; mem. editl. bd. Jour. Classification, 1984—, Jour. Mktg. Rsch., 1994—; editor Methodika, 1987-93 Ednl. Testing Svc. psychometric fellow, 1958-61; NIMH fellow, 1959-61 Fellow AAAS, APA (active Divsn. 5, pres.-elect 1990-91, pres. 1991-92, Disting. Sci. Contbn. award 1989), Am. Psychol. Soc. (William James fellow 1989), Am. Statis. Assn. (program chair stats. in mktg. sect. 1992, chair stats. in mktg. sect. 1993-94, exec. com. 1991-95); mem. Psychometric Soc. (trustee 1971-77, 81-83, 84-87, 93-96, pres. 1975-76, editl. coun. 1975-81, Lifetime Achievement award 2010), Classification Soc. N.Am. (governing coun. 1974-77, pres. 1980-83, bd. dirs. 1984-96), Internat. Fedn. Classification Socs. (rep. to coun. 1984—, v.p./pres.-elect 1995, pres. 1996—), Soc. Multivariate Exptl. Psychology (editl. adv. bd. 1980-81, pres. 1982-83), Ea. Psychol. Assn., Psychonomic Soc., Soc. Math. Psychology, Am. Mktg. Assn., Assn. Consumer Rsch., Soc. Consumer Psychology, Inst. for Ops. Rsch. and Mgmt. Scis., Phi Beta Kappa, Sigma Xi, Beta Gamma Sigma Home: 14 Forest Dr Warren NJ 07059-5802 Office: Rutgers University Rutgers Bus Sch Mktg Dept 1 Washington Pk Newark NJ 07102-3027 Office Phone: 973-353-5814. Business E-Mail: dcarroll@rci.rutgers.edu.

CARROLL, KAREN COLLEEN, pathologist, infectious diseases specialist; b. Balt., Nov. 7, 1953; d. Charles Edward and Ida May (Simms) C.; m. Bruce Cameron Marshall, Feb. 13, 1982; children: Kevin Charles Marshall, Brian Thomas Marshall. BA, Coll. Notre Dame of Md., 1975; MD, U. Md., 1979. Diplomate Am. Bd. Internal Medicine, Am. Bd. Infectious Diseases, Am. Bd. Pathology. Intern U. Md., 1979-80, U. Rochester, AHP, 1980-82, chief med. resident in internal medicine, 1982-83; fellow infectious diseases U. Mass., 1984-86; fellow med. microbiology Health Scis. Ctr. U. Utah, 1989-90; asst. prof. pathology U. Utah Med. Ctr., Salt Lake City, 1990-97, adj. asst. prof. infectious diseases, 1990-97, assoc. prof. pathology, adj. assoc. prof. infectious disease, 1997—2002; dir. microbiology lab. Associated Regional and Univ. Pathologists, Inc., Salt Lake City, 1990—2002; assoc. prof. pathology and medicine John Hopkins Med. Instns., 2002—06, dir. med. microbiology divsn., 2002—, prof. pathology and medicine, 2006—. Dir. microbiology lab. Assoc. regional & U. Pathologists Inc., Salt Lake City, 1990—2002. Contbr. articles to profl. jours. Fellow Am. Acad. Microbiology, Coll. Am. Pathologists, Infectious Diseases Soc. Am.; mem. Am. Soc. for Microbiology. Avocations: skiing, hiking, reading. Office Phone: 410-955-5077. Personal E-mail: kcmicro@hotmail.com.

CARROLL, WILLIAM LUKE, physician, educator; MD, Jefferson Med. Coll., 1989. Diplomate Am. Bd. Family Medicine, 1998, lic. to practice Pa., 1992. Intern internal medicine Med. Ctr. Del., Wilmington, 1989, resident family medicine, 1992; staff Bryn Mawr Hosp., Paoli Hosp., 1992—; physician Marple-Newtown Sch.; med. dir. Devereux Whitlock Ctr.; clin. asst. prof. family medicine Thomas Jefferson Univ. Named Top Doc, Main Line Today Mag., 2006, 2007, Phila. Mag., 2010. Office: Bryn Mawr Hospital 5048 W Chester Pike Edgemont PA 19028 Office Phone: 610-325-9200. Office Fax: 610-325-9663.

CARRUTHERS, S. GEORGE, medical educator, physician; b. Londonderry, No. Ireland, Sept. 18, 1945; came to Can., 1977; s. Moses and Alice McKeague (Nicholl) C.; m. Gillian Margaret Devon, Oct. 4, 1969; children: Alison, David, Bruce, Michael. MB, BCh, Queen's U., Belfast, No. Ireland, 1969, MD, 1975. Diplomate Am. Bd. Internal Medicine, Am. Bd. Clin. Pharmacology (sec.-treas. 1996-98, chair 1998-2000). Intern Royal Victoria Hosp., Belfast, 1969-70; tchr. Belfast City Hosp./Queen's U. Belfast, 1970-75; Fogarty Internat. fellow NIH Kans. U. Med. Ctr., Kansas City, 1975-77; asst. prof. U. Hosp./U. Western Ont., London, Can., 1977-82, assoc. prof., 1982-87, prof. dept. medicine, 1987-88, 1995-2000, prof. dept. pharmacology and toxicology, 1987-88, 1995-2000; Carnegie and Rockefeller prof., head dept. medicine Dalhousie U., Halifax, N.S., Can., 1988-95; physician-in-chief Victoria Gen. Hosp., Halifax, 1988-91, pres. med. staff, 1992-93; chief medicine London Health Scis. Ctr., 1995—2000; dean faculty medicine and health scis. United Arab Emirates U., Al Ain, 2001—. Bd. commrs. Victoria Gen. Hosp., 1992-93; rep. Brit. Med. Assn., London, 1973-75; Richard Ivey prof., chmn. dept. medicine U. Western Ont., 1995-2000; pres. Foyle Coll. OBA, 1993-94; chmn. Cardio-Cerebrovascular Rsch. Adv. Coun.; bd. dirs. Heart and Stroke Found. Can., 1998-00 Co-author: Handbook of Clinical Pharmacology, 1978, 2d edit., 1983; co-editor: Melmon & Morelli's Textbook of Clinical Pharmacology, 4th edit., 2000. Fellow ACP (gov. Ont. 1998-2001, Laureate award Ont. chpt. 2005), Royal Coll. Physicians Can., Royal Coll. Physicians (London and Glasgow), Am. Coll. Clin. Pharmacology, Can. Acad. Health Scis.; mem. Am. Soc. Clin. Pharmacology and Therapeutics (nominating com. 1989, v.p. 1991-92, awards com. 1992-98, sci. program com. 1995-2000, bd. dirs. 1997-2001, vice chmn. sci. program com. 1998-99, chmn. 1999-00), Can. Soc. for Clin. Pharmacology (pres. 1984-86, Piafsky Young Investigator award 1982, Disting. Achievement award 1992), Can. Hypertension Soc. (pres. 1990-91, bd. dirs. 1988-92, 99-2000, Disting. Svc. award 1995), Can. Assn. Profs. Medicine (pres. 1994-95), Brit. Pharm. Soc., West Haven G&C Club. Presbyterian. Avocations: travel, reading. Home and Office: United Arab Emirates Univ PO Box 17666 Fac Medicine Al Ain United Arab Emirates N6A 4G5 Home Phone: +971-3-761-2625; Office Phone: +971-3-767-8686. Fax: +971 3 767 2008. Personal E-mail: carruthers@uaeu.ac.ae, carrutha@hotmail.com.

CARSON, BENJAMIN SOLOMON, neurosurgeon; b. Detroit, Sept. 18, 1951; s. Robert Solomon and Sonya (Copeland) Carson; m. Lacena Beatrice Rustin, July 6, 1975; children: Murray Nedlands, Benjamin Solomon Jr., Rhoeyce Harrington. BA, Yale U., New Haven, 1973; MD, U. Mich. Sch. Medicine, Ann Arbor, 1977; DSc (hon.), Gettysburg Coll., 1988, Andrews U., 1989, Sojourner-Douglas Coll., 1989, Shippenburg U., 1990, Jersey City State Coll., 1990, Southwestern Adventist Coll., 1992, U. Mass., Boston, 1992, Marygrove Coll., 1993, U. Detroit Mercy, 1994, Spalding U., 1994, Western Md. Coll., 1994, Morgan State U., 1994, LI U., 1994, NC State U., 1994, Tuskegee U., 1995, Yale U., 1996, Del. State U., 1996, Med. U. South Africa, 1997, U. Del., 1997, Coll. William & Mary, 1998; numerous other hon. degrees. Diplomate American Bd. Neurol. Surgery, American Bd. Pediat. Neurol. Surgery, Nat. Bd. Med. Examiners. Surg. intern Johns Hopkins Hospital, Balt., 1977-78, neurosurg. resident, 1978-82, chief resident, fellow neurol. surgery, 1982-83, dir. divsn. pediatric neurosurgery, 1984—; sr. registrar Sir Charles Gairdner Hosp., Perth, Western Australia, 1983-84; asst. prof. neurol. sugery, asst. prof. oncology Johns Hopkins School Medicine, 1984—91, asst. prof. pediat., 1987—96, assoc. prof. neurol. surgery, oncology, plastic surgery and pediat., 1991—99, prof. neurol. surgery, oncology, plastic surgery and pediat., 1999—. Sr. neurosurgical resident Loch Raven VA Hosp., Balt., 1980, Balt. City Hospitals, 1981; co-dir. Johns Hopkins Cleft & Craniofacial Ctr., 1991—; bd. dirs. Kellogg Co., 1997—, Costco Wholesale Corp., 1999—, America's Promise, 2000—. Author: Gifted Hands, 1989, Think Big, 1996, The Big Picture, 1999, Take the Risk: Learning to Identify, Choose, and Live with Acceptable Risk, 2008; contbr. articles to profl. jours., chapters to books. Hon. chair Md. Red Cross, 1987; mem. med. adv. bd. Children's Cancer Found., 1987—. Recipient Cum Laude award, Radiol. Soc. North America, 1982, Howard L. Cornish Humanitarian award, Omega Psi Phi, 1987, Meml. award for outstanding svc. to underprivileged children, Continental Societies, Inc., 1987, Achievement award, Detroit Med. Soc., 1987, Md. State Dept. Health & Mental Hygiene, 1989, Liberty Bell award, Phila., 1987, George Washington Carver award, 1993, Citation for Excellence, Detroit City Coun., 1987, Phila. City Coun., 1987, Mich. State Senate, 1987, Partner in Health award, Md. Health Convocation, 1988, Outstanding Achievements in Medicine award, Howard U., Balt., 1988, American Black Achievement award, Ebony mag., 1988, Dr. Daniel Hale Williams award, Jefferson Med. Coll., Phila., 1989, Outstanding Svc. & Excellence in Medicine award, Med. Soc. Eastern Pa., 1989, Andrew White Medal, Loyola Coll., Balt., 1989, Leonard F. Swain Esteemed Alumni award, U. Mich., 1989, Booker T. Washington award, Bus. League Balt., 1990, Benjamin E. Mays Meml. award, NC State U., 1991, Spl. Recognition award, Nat. Coun. Negro Women, 1991, Appreciation award, Nat. Assn. Equal Opportunity & Higher Edn., 1991, Essence award, 1993, Horatio Alger award, 1994, Martin Luther King, Jr. award for cmty. svc., Johns Hopkins Hosp., 1994, Golden Plate award, American Acad. Achievement, 1995, Outstanding Achievement award, Anheuser-Busch Co., 1996, Congress Racial Equality, 1996, Making A Difference award, NAACP Balt. chpt., 1998, Tree of Life award, Jewish Nat. Fund, 1998, Pub. Svc. award, American Inst. Pub. Svc., 2000, Disting. Svc. to Children award, Nat. Assn. Elem. Sch. Principals, 2002, Ralph Metcalfe award, Congl. Black Caucus, 2003, Medical award of excellence, Ronald McDonald House Charities, 2003, Spingarn award, NAACP, 2006, Ford's Theatre Lincoln Medal, The White House, 2008, Presdl. Medal of Freedom, 2008; named a Living Legend award, Libr. Congress, 2000; named one of Top 100 Black Physicians in America, Black Enterprise Mag., 2001, America's Top 20 Physicians & Scientists, CNN/TIME Mag., 2001, America's Best Leaders, US News & World Report, 2008; named to Soc. of World Changers, Ind. Wesleyan U., 2007; Paul Harris fellow, Rotary Internat., 1988, John Conley Scholar, American Acad. Otolaryngology Head & Neck Surgeons, 1993. Mem.: AMA, AAAS, Inst. Medicine, American Cleft Palate-Craniofacial Assn., Md. Neurol. Soc., Congress Neurol. Surgeons, American Assn. Neurol. Surgeons, Nat. Med. Assn. (Clin. Practitioner of Yr. award 1988, Living Legend award 1992, William E. Matory award 1992, Excellence in Medicine award 1994), Nat. Pediatric Oncology Group, Monumental Med. Soc., Md. Congress Parents & Teachers (hon. life), Alpha Omega Alpha. Achievements include first to successfully separate a pair of Siamese twins joined at the head in 1987, leading a 70-member surgical team working for 22 hours; conducted the first intrauterine procedure to relieve pressure on the brain of a hydrocephalic fetal twin, and a hemispherectomy, in which an infant suffering from uncontrollable seizures has half of its brain removed. Office: Johns Hopkins Hosp 600 N Wolfe St Harvey 811 Baltimore MD 21287-0005 Office Phone: 410-955-7888. Office Fax: 410-955-0626. *

CARSON, CULLEY CLYDE, III, urologist, educator; b. Westerly, RI, Feb. 25, 1945; s. Culley Clyde Jr. and Dorothy (Scarborough) C.; m. Mary Jo McDonald, Aug. 10, 1970; children: Culley Clyde IV, Hilary. BS, Trinity Coll., 1967; MD, George Washington U., 1971. Diplomate Am. Bd. Urology. Intern Dartmouth Med. Ctr., 1971-72, resident surgery, 1971-73; fellow urology Mayo Clinic, Rochester, Minn., 1975-78; instr. urology U. Minn. Mayo Med. Sch., Rochester, 1978; asst. prof. urology Duke U. Med. Ctr., Durham, NC, 1978-84, assoc. prof., 1984-88, prof., 1988-93, Rhodes Disting. chair, 1993—; prof., chmn. urology U. N.C., Chapel Hill, 1993—, Rhoads disting. prof., 2000—. Chief urology Durham VA Hosp.; mem. new drug panel U.S. FDA; mem. exec. com. U.S. Pharmacopea. Author: Endourology, 1985, Atlas of Urologic Endoscopy, 1986, Impotence, 1992, 98, Complications of Invasive Procedures, 1995, Textbook of Erectile Dysfunction, 2009, Textbook of Men's Health 2nd edit., 3rd edit.,2009; editor-in-chief Mediguide to Urology, 1994—, Contemporary Urology, 1997—; contbr. chpts. to urol. texts. Maj. M.C., USAF, 1973-75. Named Command Flight Surgeon of Yr., USAF, 1974, Healthcare Hero, Rsch. Triangle, 2007; recipient Calvin Klopp Rsch. award, 1971, Friedman rsch. prize, 1971, Cristol Mayo Alumni award, 1992, Jesse H. Neal award, 2001; rsch. fellow Am. Heart Assn., 1969, O'Dea travel fellow, 1978, Book award, Royal Coll. Medicine, 1999. Fellow ACS, Am. Surg. Assn.; mem. AMA, AAAS, Am. Assn. Genitourinary Surgeons, Am. Urol. Assn. (pres. SE sect. 2006, Disting. Contbn. award 2011, Outstanding Contbn. award 2011), Sexual Medicine Soc. (pres. 2003), Internat. Soc. Urology, Am. Fertility Soc., Soc. Urol. Pros Surgery (pres. 2006), NY Acad. Scis., Mayo Alumni Assn., Gov.'s Club, Carolina Club, Trinity Club (Hartford), Sigma Xi, Psi Chi, Alpha Omega Alpha. Home: 10387 Holt Chapel Hill NC 27517-8542 Office: UNC 2113 Physicians Office Bldg Chapel Hill NC 27517 Office Phone: 919-966-2574. Personal E-mail: culleyccarson3@hotmail.com. Business E-Mail: carson@med.unc.edu.

CARSON, DONALD GROVES, gynecologist; MD, U. Pitts. Sch. of Medicine, 1977. Resident Magee Womens Hosp., Pitts., 1981; intern Magee Womens Hosp. of Univ. of Pitts. Med. Ctr. (UPMC), 1978; hosp. affiliation includes Magee Womens Hosp. of UPMC Health Sys. Fellow: Am. Congress Obstetricians and Gynecologists. Office: Magee-Womens Hospital University of Pittsburgh Medical Center 300 Halket St Pittsburgh PA 15213 Office Phone: 412-641-1000.

CARSON, JAY WILMER, pathologist, educator; b. Ki-Jang, Korea, Oct. 6, 1933; came to U.S., 1960; s. Han Kyu and Jin Chan (Son) Cha; m. Jennifer C. White, June 28, 1968 (dec. Aug. 1990); m. Teresa M. Alberda, July 14, 1995. MD, Seoul Nat. U., 1958. Diplomate Am. Bd. Pathology. Intern Bellevue Hosp. Ctr., NYC, 1961-62; resident in pathology Albert Einstein Coll. Medicine, NYC, 1963-66; fellow U. Montreal, Que., Canada, 1967-68; chief anatomic pathology VA Hosp., Martinez, Calif., 1969-91; dir. cytopathology VA Med. Ctr., San Francisco, 1992-96; assoc. clin. prof. U. Calif. Med. Sch., San Francisco, 1992—. Aviation med. examiner FAA, Oklahoma City, 1987-96; assoc. clin. prof. U. Calif., Davis, 1985—; hosp. comdr. 347th Gen. Hosp., Sunnyvale, Calif., 1992-1993, 6253d Army Hosp., Santa Rosa, Calif., 1994-96. Patentee needle aspiration device. Mem. chmn.'s adv. bd. Nat. Rep. Com., Washington, 1995-96. Col. USAR, 1971-96. Decorated Order of Military Med. Merit, Meritorious Svc. Medal with one oakleaf cluster, Sr. Flight Surgeon Badge. Fellow Coll. Am. Pathologists; mem. Internat. Acad. Pathology, Assn. Mil. Surgeons U.S. (life), Res. Officers Assn. (life), U.S. Army War Coll. Alumni Assn. (life), Soc. U.S. Army Flight Surgeons (life). Avocations: fly fishing, violin making. Home: 1550 Sorrel Ct Walnut Creek CA 94598-4800 Personal E-mail: j.carson1@att.net.

CARSON, JEFFREY L., internist; b. Phila., Oct. 11, 1951; s. Albert Carson and Jackie Zeitz; m. Susan Carson, June 1977; children: Josh, Jennie, Rachael, Dylan. BA in Polit. Sci., U. R.I., 1973; MD, Hahnemann Med. Coll., 1977. Diplomate Am. Bd. Internal Medicine. Chief med. resident Hahnemann Med. Coll. and Hosp., Phila., 1979-80; Henry J. Kaiser fellow U. Pa./Hosp., Phila., 1981-82; asst. prof. medicine UMDNJ - Rutgers Med. Sch., Camden, NJ, 1982-87; assoc. prof. medicine UMDNJ - Robert Wood Johnson Med. Sch., New Brunswick, NJ, 1987-94, chief, Divsn. of GIM, 1987—, prof. of medicine, 1987—, Richard G. Reynolds chair, 1996—. Sr. internat. fellow U. Oxford, U.K., 1995-96; mem. epidemiology study sect. NIH, Bethesda, 1990-94, reviewers res., 1994-98; adhoc reviewer Agy. for Health Care Policy and Rsch., Bethesda, 1990—. Rsch. grantee Agy. for Health Care Policy and Rsch., 1993, Focus grant NIH, 1990-95, 2003-2009, Ortho-Biotech, Bridgewater, N.J., 1995. Fellow am. Coll. Physicians; mem. Soc. Gen. Internal Medicine (chair mid-atlantic sect. 1990-91, other offices)I. Avocations: sailing, coaching little league baseball. Office: UMDNJ-RWJ Med Sch 125 Paterson St New Brunswick NJ 08901-1962 Business E-Mail: carson@umdnj.edu.

CARSON, PHILLIP JAMES, surgeon; b. Adelaide, Australia, May 5, 1954; MBBS, U. Adelaide, 1978. Assoc. prof. surgery Royal Darwin Hosp., 1990—, Flinders U., 1996—; dir. divsn. surgery Royal Darwin Hosp., 1991—96, dir. gen. surgery, 1996—2006. Vis. scholar, ACS. Fellow: RCS Eng., RCS Edinburgh, Royal Australasian Coll. Surgeons. Avocations: bicycling, music, woodworking. Office: Royal Darwin Hosp Rocklands Dr Tiwi Darwin Northern Territory 0811 Australia Office Fax: 64 8 89228601.

CARSON, REGINA E., healthcare administrator, geriatric specialist; b. Washington; BS in Pharmacy, Howard U., Washington, DC; MBA in Mktg., Loyola Coll., Balt., MBA in Health Care Adminstrn. Asst. prof., asst. dir. pharmacy U. Md., Balt., 1986-88; asst. prof., coord. profl. practice Howard U., Washington, 1988-95; prin. Marrell Cons., Randallstown, Md., prin., mng. ptnr., 1993—. Drug utilization rev. cons. Md. Pharmacy Assn., Balt., 1986—90; cons. pharmacist Balt. County Adv. Coun. Drug Abuse, Towson, Md., 1984—86; edn. cons. Assn. Black Women in Higher Edn., Accra, Ghana, 2000; program evaluator Train Pharm., U. Medicine and Pharmacy Cluj, Romania, 1999—2002; master gardener U. Md., College Park, 2001—. Bd. dirs. N.W. Hosp. Ctr. Aux., Randallstown, Joshua Johnson Coun., Balt. Mus. Art, Alzheimers Assn. Ctrl. Md.; bd. trustees C.C. of Baltimore County, 1997—2010; extension adv. bd. U. Md., 2008—; v.p. Delicados Inc., Balt.; bd. mem. U. Md., 2008—; master gardener, 2007—. Recipient Grigore T. Popa medal, U. Medicine and Pharmacy, Iasi, Romania, 2000; named Outstanding Alumni, Howard U. Coll. Pharmacy, 1992. Fellow: Am. Soc. Cons. Pharmacists; mem.: Nat. Assn. Retail Druggists (adv. com., long-term care com.), Nat. Pharm. Assn. (life, Outstanding Women in Pharmacy 1984), Nat. Assn. Black MBA (life), Am. Assn. Colls. Pharmacy, Nat. Assn. Health Svc. Execs. Avocations: gardening, art. Home: 1400 Radical Rd Sumter SC 29153

CARSONS, STEVEN E., rheumatologist, immunologist, educator; Studied, NY Med. Coll., 1975. Diplomate Am. Bd. Internal Medicine, Am. Bd. Internal Medicine-rheumatology, Am. Bd. Allergy and Immunology, Am. Bd. Pediatrics. Resident Maimonides Med. Ctr., Bklyn., 1976—78; fellow SUNY, Bklyn., 1978—80; program dir. SUNY Health Sci. Ctr., assoc. prof. of medicine, prof. of medicine, rheumatology, allergy and immunology; chief divsn. of rheumatology allergy and immunology Winthrop Univ. Hosp. Office: Winthrop University Hospital 259 1st St Mineola NY 11501 Office Phone: 516-663-2097. Office Fax: 516-663-2946.

CARSTENSEN, EDWIN LORENZ, retired biomedical engineer, biophysicist; b. Oakdale, Nebr., Dec. 8, 1919; s. August Hans and Opal Lois (Norwood) C.; m. Pam McDonald, Aug. 1, 1947; children: Richard Lorenz, Allen Brent, Laura Lee, Loretta Dee, Christina Marie. BS, Nebr. State Tchrs. Coll., 1941; MS, Case Inst. Tech., 1947; PhD, U. Pa., 1955. Mem. sci. staff div. war rsch. Columbia U., 1942-45; head lab. sect. U.S. Navy Underwater Sound Reference Lab., Orlando, Fla., 1945-48; rsch. assoc. Moore Sch. Elec. Engring., U. Pa., 1948-55, asst. prof. elec. engring., 1955-56; prin. investigator U.S. Army Biol. Lab., Fort Detrick, Frederick, Md., 1956-61; assoc. prof. elec. engring. U. Rochester, 1961-73, prof., 1973-88, Arthur Gould Yates prof. engring., 1988-90, Arthur Gould Yates prof. engring. emeritus, 1990—, dir. biomed. engring., 1971-83, prof. biophysics, 1981-90, univ. mentor, 1982—, sr. scientist in elec. engring., 1990—. Dir. Rochester Ctr. for Biomed. Ultrasound, 1986-90. Author: Biological Effects of Transmission Line Fields, 1987; contbr. numerous articles to profl. publs. Fellow Acoustical Soc. Am., IEEE, Am. Inst. Ultrasound in Medicine; mem. Biophys. Soc., Biomed. Engring. Soc., Nat. Acad. Engring. Democrat. Home: 103 Eastland Ave Rochester NY 14618-1027 Office: U Rochester Dept Elec/Computer Engring Rochester NY 14627 Personal E-mail: ecarsten@rochester.rr.com.

CARSTENSEN, LAURA LEE, psychology professor; b. Phila., Nov. 2, 1953; d. Edwin Lorenz Carstensen and Pam. McDonald; m. Ian H. Gotlib, Aug. 27, 1995; 1 child, David Joseph Pagano. BS, U. Rochester, 1978; MA, W.Va. U., 1980, PhD, 1983. Asst. prof. Ind. U., Bloomington, 1983-87, Stanford U., Calif., 1987-94, assoc. prof., 1995, prof. psychology, Barbara D. Finberg dir. Inst. Rsch. on Women and Gender, 1997—2001, dir. Life-span Devel. Lab., Fairleigh S. Dickinson Jr. Prof. in Pub. Policy; founding dir. Stanford Ctr. on Longevity. Sci. cons. Max Planck Inst. Human Devel. & Edn., Berlin, 1992-, mem. bd. sci. advisors; assoc. dir. Terman gifted project Stanford U., 1994—; mem. MacArthur Found. Rsch. Network on an Aging Soc. Author book chpt.; co-author Psychology: The Study of Human Experience, 1991; co-editor: Handbook of Clinical Gerontology, 1987, Growing Old or Living Long: Take Your Pick, 2006, The Influence of a Sense of Time on Human Development, 2006; contributor of several articles to profl. jours. Recipient First Investigator award, Nat. Inst. Aging, 1987, MERIT award, 2005; Guggenheim Fellow, 2003—04. Fellow APA, Gerontol. Soc. Am. (mem.-at-large 1994—, Kalish Innovative Publication award 1993, Disting. Career award), Am. Psychol. Soc.; mem. Assn. for Psychological Sci. Office: Stanford U Dept Psychology Bldg 420 Jordan Hall RM 167 Stanford CA 94305-2130 Office Phone: 415-723-3102. Business E-Mail: laura.carstensen@stanford.edu. E-mail: LLC@psych.stanford.edu.

CARSWELL, JANE TRIPLETT, retired family physician; b. Raeford, NC, Feb. 26, 1932; d. Arthur Dula and Madeline Mapp (Warburton) C.; m. Kenmer A. Roberts, 2000. Student, Flora Macdonald Coll., 1950-52; AB in Chemistry, U. N.C., 1954; MD, Med. Coll. Va., 1958. Diplomate Am. Bd. Family Practice. Resident Med. Coll. Va., Richmond, 1958-61; practice medicine specializing in family medicine Harlan, Ky., 1961-62, Lenoir, NC, 1962—. Chmn. Lenoir Human Relations Com., N.C., 1962-64; vice-chmn. Caldwell County Council Status of Women, Lenoir, 1976-78 Mem. Caldwell County Med. Soc. (pres. 1965), N.C. Acad. Family Physicians (N.C. Family Physician of Yr. award 1983), N.C. Med. Soc., Am. Acad. Family Practice (Nat. Family Dr. of Yr. award 1984) Presbyterian. Avocations: hiking, backpacking, skiing, photography.

CARTA, PAOLO, nephrologist; b. Cagliari, Oct. 6, 1978; MD, U. Cagliari, 2003. Physician Renal Unit Careggi U. Hosp. Florence, 2009—. Office: Viale Pieraccini 17 Florence 50123 Italy Business E-Mail: cartapa@aou-careggi.toscana.it.

CARTER, BRUCE THOMAS, ophthalmologist; b. Front Royal, Va., Mar. 28, 1944; MD, U. Va., 1970. Cert. ophthalmology, 1977. Intern ophthalmology Ky. Med. Ctr., Lexington, 1970—71; resident pediat. ophthalmology U. Va. Hosp., Charlottesville, 1973—76; fellowship U. Pitts., 1976—77; staff mem. Martha Jefferson Hosp., Charlottesville, Va.; pediatric ophthalmologist U. Va. Health Sys.; pvt. practice. Clin. instr. ophthalmology U. Va. Sch. Med., 1977—78, clin. asst. prof., 1978—85, clin. assoc. prof., 1985—. Office: Albemarle Pediat Ophthalmology & Strabismus PC 1101 E Jefferson St Ste 3 Charlottesville VA 22902 also: U Va Health Sys Dept Ophthalmology PO Box 800715 Charlottesville VA 22908-0715 Office Phone: 434-295-5193. Office Fax: 804-977-0714. Business E-Mail: btcarter.md@gmail.com.

CARTER, CHARLENE ANN, psychologist; b. Marshall, Mich., Apr. 7, 1941; d. Charles V. F. and Eva L. (Hesling) Hampton.; m. Ross E. Carter, Jan. 15, 1966; children: Laura, Paul. BA in Psychology and Sociology, Albion Coll., Mich., 1962; MA in Clin. Psychology, Mich. State U., East Lansing, 1964, PhD in Clin. Psychology, 1968. Lic. psychologist, Wis. Clin. intern VA Hosp., Battle Creek, Mich., 1963-65, Psychol. Clinic Mich. State U., East Lansing, 1965—66, Counseling Ctr. Mich. State U., 1966—68, asst. prof., 1968—69; pvt. practice Bangor, Maine, 1971, Media, Pa., 1974-75; assoc. clin.prof. dept. psychiatry Med. Coll. Wis., Milw., 1983—2011; pvt. practice, 1988—; ret. Dir. clin. tng. Wis. Sch. for Girls, Oregon, Wis., 1969—70; staff psychologist The Counseling Ctr., Cmty. Mental Health Ctr., Bangor, Maine, 1971; mem. staff Aurora Psychiat. Hosp., 1992—, Rogers Hosp., 2001—; psychologist cons. Office of Hearing and Appeals, Social Security Adminstrn., Milw., 1986—91; lectr. in field. Contbr. articles to profl. jours. USPHS fellow, 1962, 65, 66. Mem. APA. Office: Maplewood Exec Ctr 250 N Sunnyslope Rd Ste 290 Brookfield WI 53005 Personal E-mail: charmomma@yahoo.com.

CARTER, CHARLES CONRAD, medical educator; b. Seattle, July 20, 1924; s. John Hempstead Carter and Thea Turner; m. Marylu Hopper, June 20, 1948; children: Charles Conrad Jr., Christopher Richard, John Hempstead II, Ronald Lynn. BA, Reed Coll., Portland, Oreg., 1946; MD, U. Oreg., Portland, 1948. Diplomate Am. Bd. Psychiatry and Neurology, 1957. Clin. instr. U. Oreg. Med. Sch., Portland, 1956—62, asst. prof. neurology, 1962—67, assoc. prof. neurology, 1967—70, prof. neurology, 1970—79; chief of neurology VA Hosp., Roseburg, Oreg., 1981—88; clin. prof. neurology Oreg. Health Scis. U., Portland, 1988—. Vis. assoc. prof. Washington U. Sch. Medicine, St. Louis, 1969—70. Bd. dirs. Western EEG Soc., 1972—79, Psychosurg. Bd., Salem, Oreg., 1973. Capt. med. corps USAF, 1951—53. Spl. NINDS fellow, NIH, 1969. Mem.: Am. Acad. Neurology, Alpha Omega Alpha. Home: 4884 NW Promenade Ter Unit 211 Portland OR 97229 Office: Oregon Health Scis U 3181 SW Sam Jackson Park Rd L226 Portland OR 97239 Office Phone: 503-629-9948. Office Fax: 503-494-7242. Business E-Mail: cccartermb@comcast.net.

CARTER, KIMBERLY FERREN, nursing director; b. Wheeling, W.Va., July 15, 1963; d. Donald Ray and Nan Shaw Ferren; m. Gregory Lawrence Carter; children: Leanna, Brandon. Diploma, Ohio Valley Gen. Hosp. Sch. Nursing, Wheeling, 1984; BSN, Radford U., 1986; MSN, U. Va., 1987, PhD, 1997. Cert. breast health facilitator Am. Cancer Soc.; RN; cert. 2nd Degree Reiki practitioner. Pub. health nurse educator Ctrl. Shenandoah Health Dist., Staunton, Va., 1987—88; nursing edn. specialist edn. and health promotion Kennestone Regional Health Care Sys., Marietta, Ga., 1988—90; asst. prof. nursing West Ga. Coll., Carrollton, Ga., 1990—92; from instr. to prof. Radford U., Va., 1992—; assoc. dir. Radford U., Sch. of Nursing, 2004—09, dir., 2009—. Bd. dirs. Salem Rsch. Inst.; bd. rev. Advances in Nursing Sci., Fredericksburg, 1999—, Jour. Advanced Nursing, 2004—; rsch. cons. VA Med. Ctr., Salem, 1997—2002; mem. adv. bd. Radford U. Environ. Health Ctr., 2004—10; mem. rsch. coun. Carilion Clinic, 2005—07, 2010—; rsch. coord. HCA Montgomery Lewis Gale Hosp., 2007—; workforce subcom. Va. Rural Health Assn., 2008—. Co-author: (profl. stds. document) Essentials of Baccalaureate Nursing Ed. for Entry Level Cmty./Pub. Health Nursing (C/PHN), 2000, Carter Skin Lesion Assessment Tree, 2003—04; author: (book) Documenting Health Assessment Findings: an Applications Module, 1995, Instructor's Guide and Test Bank for Sims, 1995; bd. rev. Jou. Advanced Nursing, 2004—. Mem. Roanoke Valley Allegheny Regional Adv. Coun. Homelessness, Roanoke, 1996—; mem. Radford U. IRB, 2002—07, chair, 2004—07. Recipient Am. Cancer Soc. award for Outstanding Svc. and Commitment to Breast Cancer Detection, 1999, Outstanding Alumnus award, St. Clairsville Schs., 2006, Ruth Spencer Dunfee Profl. Achievement award, Ohio Valley Gen. Hosp. Sch. Nursing Alumni Assn., 2007, Outstanding Professor award, Waldren Coll., Radford U., 2008, award, Million Dollar Cir. Radford U., 2011; grantee Quality Enhancement grant, Radford U., 2003, 2005; fellow in Acad. Leadership, Am. Acad. Colls. Nursing, 2004—05; Curriculum Devel. grantee, Helene Fuld Health Trust, 2001—03, Faculty Seed grantee, Radford U., 1999, Faculty Rsch. grantee, 1997, Tobacco Control grantee, Am. Cancer Soc., 2003, Faculty-Student Collaborative grantee, 2003, grant, Radford U. Curriculum Internationalization, 2004, Waldron Rsch. scholar, 2005, 2008, Tech. Devel. Grant, Verizon Found., 2010—, Spl. Appropriation grant, US Dept. Edn., 2009—10. Mem.: Phi Kappa Phi, Sigma Theta Tau (corr. sec. 1996—2000, 2002—04). Office: Radford U Box 6964 Radford VA 24142 Office Phone: 540-831-7700. Business E-Mail: kcarter@radford.edu.

CARTER, LINDA WHITEHEAD, oncological nurse, educator; b. Bluefield, W.Va., Dec. 20, 1941; d. Lee Joseph and Kathleen (Witherspoon) Whitehead; m. J. Stephen Carter, Mar. 11, 1961; children: Paul Scott, Kristin Hope. Student, Westmoreland Coll., Youngwood, Pa., 1980-83, St. Vincent Coll., Latrobe, Pa., 1984-85; BSN, Carlow Coll., Pitts., 1986; MSN, U. Pitts., 1992. RN Pa., cert. advanced oncology nurse, clin. nurse specialist. Oncology staff nurse Westmoreland Hosp., Greensburg, Pa., 1986-93, facilitator support group, 1988-93, oncology educator, 1990-93; clin. nurse specialist Magee Women's Hosp., Pitts., 1993-94; homecare nurse, 1996—; home care nurse U. Pitts. Med. Ctr. Home Care, 1996—2011, case mgr., 1998—2005. Faculty Carlow Coll. Divsn. Nursing, Pitts., 1993-97; grad. asst. Pitts. Cancer Inst., 1990; grad. clin. nurse specialist Allegheny Gen. Hosp., Pitts., 1991-92; nurse of hope Am. Cancer Soc., 1987, mem. pub. edn. com. Westmoreland Unit, 1987-88, mem. nursing edn. com., 1987-94, mem. profl. edn. com., 1990-93, bd. dirs., 1989-92. Mem. editl. rev. bd. Oncology Nursing Forum, 1994-98. Named Vol. of Yr., Am. Cancer Soc., 1988, Pa. Div. scholar, 1987, Nat. scholar, 1989-91. Mem. ANA, Pa. Nurses Assn., Nat. League for Nursing, Oncology Nursing Soc. (nominating com. Greater Pitts. chpt. 1990-91, newsletter com. 1992-93, chair awards com. 1997-2001, Found. liaison com. chair), Internat. Soc. Nurses in Cancer Care, Sigma Theta Tau. Home: 2922 Bryer Ridge Ct Export PA 15632-9393 Personal E-mail: lincarter101@comcast.net, lincarter101@yahoo.net.

CARTER, MELVA JEAN, retired medical technician; b. Pitts., Aug. 24, 1942; d. William Skinner and Gladys Gaines; m. Samuel Edward Carter, June 15, 1965; 1 child, Daphne Denise. Bus. cert., Detroit Inst. Comms., 1962; AS, Wayne County C.C., 1979; postgrad., Wayne State U., 1982. Cert. med. lab. technician bd. eligible. Teletype oper. N.Y. Telephone Co., NYC, 1963—65; credit cons. Creditors Svc., Detroit, 1965—68; med. lab. technician Profl. Labs., Detroit, 1977—80; exec. office mgr. ARC, Detroit, 1969—77, med. lab. technician II, 1980—2004. Taught first aid various pub. schs.; pvt. tchr. music and voice. Observer search and rescue CAP-Aux. USAF, Selfridge AFB, Mich.; vol. neighborhood watch Mayor's Anti-Arson Com., Detroit, 2001—; neighborhood canvasser Dept. Elections, Detroit, polling site assessor, citywide insp., 2006; manned several first aid stas.; poll challenger Mich. Dept. Elections, Detroit, 1983—2007; dir. bibl. plays at various chs. Recipient Name placed on Wall of Tolerance, Montgomery, Ala., Spirit of Detroit award, City Coun. Detroit, 1989, Comty. Svc. cert., Mayor's Com., 2004, Cert. Recognition, House of Miracles, 2004. Mem.: So. Poverty Law Ctr., Murray Hill Block Club (block patrol 2000—). Democrat. Pentacostal. Avocations: bowling, drawing, music, reading, coin collecting/numismatics.

CARTER, SARALEE LESSMAN, immunologist, microbiologist; b. Chgo, Feb. 19, 1951; d. Julius A. and Ida (Oiring) Lessman; m. John B. Carter, Oct. 7, 1979; children: Robert Oiring, Mollie. BA, Nat. Coll., 1971. Supr. lab. immunology Weiss Meml. Hosp., Chgo., 1973—80; lab. immunology supr. Henrotin Hosp., Chgo., 1980—84; tech. dir. Lexington Med. Labs., West Columbia, SC, 1984—; mem. nat. workshop faculty Am. Soc. Clin. Pathologists; clin. instr. faculty Med. U. SC. Rschr. Legionnaires Disease and mycoplasma pneumonia World Soc. Pathologists, Jerusalem, Israel, 1980; co-chmn. SC Young Profls. George Bush. Contbr. articles to profl. jours. Mem.: Rep. Senoritorial Inner Cir., Am. Soc. Clin. Pathologists (subspecialty cert. in microbiology and immunology, cert. med. technologist). Office: 1742 South Lake Dr Ste 90 # 303 Lexington SC 29073

CARTER, YVONNE MARIE, medical educator; b. LA, Aug. 15, 1969; BA, U. Calif., Berkeley, 1990; MD, Columbia U., 1995. Asst. prof. Georgetown U. Med. Ctr., 2006—. Contbr. scientific papers. Scholar Health Policy Leadership Scholarship, Soc. Thoracic Surgeons, Am. Coll. Surgeons. Fellow: ACS, Am. Bd. Thoracic Surgeons; mem.: U. Calif. Alumni Assn., Assn. Black Cardiovasc. and Thoracic Surgeons, Women Thoracic Surgery. Avocations: running, snowboarding. Office: 3800 Reservoir Rd NW 4 PHC Divsn Washington DC 20007 Business E-Mail: ymc01@gunet.georgetown.edu.

CARTIER, PHILIPPE EDMOND, orthopedist, surgeon, consultant; b. Paris, June 2, 1941; s. Daniel Claude and Juliette Savary Cartier; m. Aliette Sylvie Le Vasseur, Apr. 28, 2000; children: Pascale Heckets-weiler, Emmanuelle, Jean Philippe, Vincent, Geraldine. MD, U. René Descartes, Paris, 1970; D in Medicine and Surgery, Edn. and Culture Dept., Madrid, 1996. Resident pediatric orthopaedic surgery Inst. Calot, Berck-Plage, France, 1972—73; orthopaedic surgeon Clinique du Cèdre - Orthopaedic Dept., Rouen, France, 1974—82, Les Mauss-ins Knee Ctr., Paris, 1982—90; med. dir. Les Lilas Knee Ctr., France, 1991—2003, Hartmann Knee Inst., Neuilly-sur-Seine, France, 2004—. Cons. surgeon Smith & Nephew, Memphis, 1975—. Co-author: The Knee and the Cruciate Ligament, Knee Surgery Complications, Pitfalls and Salvage, 1992, Fifteen Years of Clinical Experience with Hydroxyapatite Coatings in Joint Arthroplasty, 2004, Total Knee Arthroplasty: a Guide to get Better Performance, 2005, Die Unikondylare Schlitten Prothese, 2005; editor: Unicompartmental Knee Arthroplasty, 1997. 1st lt. French Air Force, 1965—66. Mem.: Soc. Française Hanche Genou, European Fedn. of Nat. Assn. Orthop. and Traumatology, Am. Acad. Orthop. Surgeons, French Soc. Orthop. and Traumatology, Argentine Orthop. Assn., European Soc. Knee and Arthroscopy, Internat. Soc. Knee, Internat. Soc. Orthop. and Traumatology Surgery. Roman Catholic. Achievements include patents for Smith and Nephew genesis unicompartmental knee prosthesis. Avocations: tennis, fishing. Home: 7 bd Richard Wallace Neuilly-sur-Seine 92200 France Office: Clinique Hartmann 26 bd Victor Hugo Neuilly-sur-Seine 92200 France Office Fax: 33-1-47585713; Home Fax: 33-1-46241315. Business E-Mail: philippe-cartier@sfr.fr.

CARTSOS, VICKY M., orthodontist; b. Mich., Oct. 13, 1967; DMD, U. Athens, 1991; M in Orthodontics, Tufts Sch. Dental Medicine, 1995. Orthodontist Pvt. Practice Orthodontics, 1995—2004, asst. prof. Boston U., 2005—06; dir. Tufts U. Sch. Dental Medicine, 2006—. Cons. Ednl. Industry, 2004. Mem.: NESO, TAO, AADR, IADR, AAO. Avocations: tennis, travel, swimming. Office: 1 Kneeland St Boston MA 02155 Business E-Mail: vicky.cartsos@tufts.edu.

CARTY, ARTHUR JOHN, science policy advisor, research administrator; b. Hookergate, County Durham, Eng., Sept. 12, 1940; arrived in Can., 1965; naturalized, 1969. George M. and Evelyn Carty; m. Helene Cloutier, Sept. 3, 1967; children: Richard, Stephane, Roxanne. BSc, U. Nottingham, Eng., 1962, PhD, 1965; DSc honoris causa, U. Rennes, France, 1986, Carleton U., Ottawa, Can., 1997, U. Waterloo, Can., 1997; Prof. Honoris Causa, Nat. Chiao-Tung U., Taiwan, 1998; DSc honoris causa, Acadia U., NS, Can., 1999, McMaster U., Hamilton, Can., 2000, Queen's U., Kingston, Can., 2001, U. Ottawa, Can., 2002, St. John's Meml. U. Nfld., 2003, Okanagan U., 2004, U. Calgary, 2004, U. Nottingham, Eng., 2006. Asst. prof. chemistry Meml. U. Nfld., St. John's, Can., 1965-67, U. Waterloo, Ont., Canada, 1967-69, assoc. prof. chemistry Ont., 1969-75, prof. chemistry Ont., 1975-94, chmn. dept. chemistry Ont., 1983-89, dean rsch. Ont., 1989-94; pres. Nat. Rsch. Coun. Can., Ottawa, Ont., 1994—2004; mem. Sch. Grad. Studies and Rsch. U. Ottawa, 1995—; nat. sci. advisor to Govt. of Can., 2004—08; exec. dir. Waterloo Inst. Nano-tech., 2008—. Dir. Guelph-Waterloo Ctr. for Grad. Work in Chemistry, 1975—79; mem. internat. adv. bd. Asia Pacific Econ. Coop. Ctr. for Tech. Foresight, Thailand, 1998—, numerous others. Mem. Math. Info. Tech. and Complex Systems, 1999—, Can. Stroke Network, 2000-04, Genome Can., 2000-04, Communitech Assn. Inc., 2000-03; chmn. Can. Light Source Inc., 1999—; mem. Can. Space Agy. Adv. Coun., 2000-. Decorated officer Ordre Nat. du Mérite (France), officer Order of Can.; recipient Royal Soc. award Nuffield Found., 1974, Purvis award Soc. Chem. Industry, 1997, Queen Elizabeth II jubilee medal, 2002, Walter Hitschfeld award Can. Assn. Univ. Rsch. Adminstrs., 2006. Fellow Royal Soc. Can.; mem. Am. Chem. Soc., Can. Soc. for Chemistry (v.p. 1989-90, pres. 1990-91, Alcan award 1984, E.W.R. Steacie award 1995), Chem. Inst. Can. (Montreal medal 1996), Can. Inst. Chemistry (hon. fellow), Fields Inst. Rsch. in Math. Scis. (hon. fellow), Engring. Inst. Can. (hon.). Office: Nat Sci Adv to the Govt of Can Industry Canada 235 Queen St Ottawa ON K1A 0H5 Canada Business E-Mail: carty@awaterloo.ca.

CARUANA, SALVATORE M., otolaryngologist, educator; BS cum laude, Buffalo U.; MD, Mt. Sinai Sch. Medicine, 1989. Diplomate Am. Bd. Otolaryngology. Resident otolaryngology NY Eye and Ear Infirmary, 1991—95; fellow head and necksurgical oncology Meml. Sloan- Kettering Cancer Ctr., NYC, 1995—97; asst. prof. clin. otolaryngology Columbia Coll.; chief divsn. of head and neck surgery Columbia Univ. Med. Ctr.; otolaryngologist NY- Presbyn. Hosp. Office: New York Presbyterian Hospital 180 Ft Washington Ave 7th Fl New York NY 10032 Office Phone: 212-305-5335. Office Fax: 212-305-3975.

CARUBBI, FRANCESCA, medical educator; b. Reggio Emilia, Italy, Nov. 21, 1956; MD, Modena U., 1981; PhD in Hepatology, Italian Ministry U., 1990. Cons. dept. medicine U. Modena, 1992—, assoc. prof. nutrition and dietetics Grad. Med. Sch., 1993—. Mem.: Atherosclerosis Soc. Office: Dept Medicine Endocrinology & Metabolism Modena 41100 Italy Office Fax: 39 059 3961322. Business E-Mail: carubbi@unimore.it.

CARUCCI, JOHN A., physician; b. Lyndhurst, NJ, Dec. 17, 1963; s. John Joseph and Dorothy Ann Carucci; m. Ingrid Helena Olhoffer, Aug. 21, 1999; 1 child, Isabella Ann. BA, Columbia U., 1981—85; MS, New York U., 1985—87; MD, PhD, SUNY, 1994. Cert. dermatology Am. Bd. of Dermatology, 1998, Mohs Micrographic Surgery Am. Coll. of Mohs Micrographic Surgery and Cutaneous Oncology, 2000. Dir., mohs micrographic and dermatologic surgery Cornell-New York Presbyn. Hosp., New York, 2001—. Contbr. articles to profl. jours. including the Jour. Am. Acad. Dermatology, Archives of Dermatology, Dermatol. Surgery (Presdl. Citation from the Am. Acad. of Dermatology, 2001), chapters to books. Recipient career devel. award in dermatol. surgery, Dermatology Found., 2003; named one of Best Drs. in America, 2007—08; Dermatologist Investigator Rsch. fellows, Dermatology Found., 1998—99, Human Immunology Consortium grant, DANA Found., 2007. Mem.: Internat. Transplant Skin Cancer Collaborative (bd. of dirs. 2001—, chmn. rsch. com.). Roman Catholic. Avocations: guitar, musical composition, running, weight training. Office: Weill Cornell Med Coll 1305 York Ave 9th Fl New York NY 10021 Business E-Mail: jac2015@med.cornell.edu.

CARUSO, AILEEN SMITH, managed care consultant; b. Albany, NY, July 25, 1949; d. Robert Vincent and Mary (Prince) Smith; 1 child, Patrick Michael. AAS in nursing, Russell Sage Jr. Coll., Albany, 1970; BSBA cum laude, Coll. St. Rose, 1994. Cert. case mgr., adminstr. Physician Practice Mgmt. (CAPPM); RN N.Y. Staff nurse neuro and thoracic surgery units VA Hosp., 1970-71; staff nurse family practice Milton F. Gipstein, MD, Schenctady, N.Y., 1971-74; psychiat. nurse Peter F. Andrus, MD, Albany, 1977-81; coll. health nurse State U. N.Y., Albany, 1979-82; orthopedic staff nurse Rosa Road Orthopedics, Schenectady, 1980-82; coll. health nurse Union Coll., Schenectady, 1982-87; customer svc. rep. Empire Blue Cross, Albany, 1987-88; fin. planner N.Y. Life Ins., Albany, 1988-89; sr. mgr. Corp. Health Demensions, Troy, N.Y., 1989-94, dir. implementation and tng., 1994-96, dir. implementation and corp. case mgmt., 1996, v.p. implementation, 1997, v.p. ops., 1998-99; dir. clin. ops. U.S. Oncology Network, 1999—2004; dir. cancer care program St. Peters Hosp., Albany, NY, 2004—; med. program mgr. Take Care Health Sys., 2010—. Mem. adv. bd. Amgen, MGI Pharma, CTI Pharm., 2004; advisor Gen. Elec. Corp. R&D Safety Com., Schenectady, 1992-94; chmn. profl. devel. Northeast N.Y. Health Promotion, Albany, 1994-99; com. chair Schenectady Health Coalition, 1993-95; edn. and by laws com., com. chair govt. affairs Am. Occupational Health Nurses, Albany, 1994-99; cert. adminstr. physician practice mgmt.; chmn. N.Y. state sect. Patient Advocate Found., N.Y., 2000—; cons. in field. Co-author: Occupational Health Services Administrative/Patient Management Manual. Pres. Ch. Women, St. George's Episcopal Ch., 1994-97, mem. exec. bd. dir., 1989-97, sr. vestry, 2004—, mem. exec. search com., 1998-99, also lector, sr. vestry, 2004—10; chmn. worksite program N.E. N.Y. Tobacco-Free Coalition, 1993-94; co-mgr. The Bookshop at St. Georges, 1993-95; mem. Futures Charity Golf Tournament; mem. USON Exec. Leadership/Clin. Leadership Coun., mem. exec. bd., 2002—; co chair Cancer Survivors Day, 2001-02; mem. reimbursement com. U.S.O.N Clin. Leadership Coun.; mem. Nat. Patient Advocate Found., 2001-06, state policy liaison, 2006; co-chair N.Y. state task force Patient Advocate Found., 2005—, N.Y. State Policy Liaison; mem. Am. Cancer Soc. Making Strides Work; planning com. Health Info. Exch. NY, 2006—. Recipient Rector's Recognition award St. George's Ch., 1991, U.S. Oncology Excellence award, 2004, Outstanding Leadership and Advocacy award Nat. Patient Advocate Found., 2004, 05, 06. Mem. Am. Assn. Occupl. Health Nurses (chair govtl. affairs com., 1989-99), Schenectady County Health Promotion Consortium, Health Promotion Coun. of N.E. N.Y., Oncology Nurses Soc., Soc. Radiation Oncology Adminstrs., Am. Soc. Therapeutic Radiation Oncologist, Am. Soc. Radiation Oncology, Hospice and Palliative Care Assn. N.Y., Capital Dist. Case Mgmt. Assn. (nominating com.), Am. Acad. Physician Practice Mgmt., Health Info. Exch. N.Y. (planning com.), Schenectady County Bus. and Profl. Women, Alpha Sigma Lambda. Avocations: travel, reading, golf. Home: 1156 Spearhead Dr Scotia NY 12302-3122 Office: Saint Peters Hosp Ste 100 317 S Manning Blvd Albany NY 12208 also: Momentive Performanc Materials 360 Hudson River Rd Waterford NY 12188 Home Phone: 518-382-0350; Office Phone: 518-233-2209. Business E-Mail: asmithcaruso@nycap.rr.com.

CARUSO, LUCIANO GAETANO, retired physician; b. Lentini, Feb. 1, 1947; Degree in Medicine & Surgery, Catania U., 1971. Specialization in liver diseases and metabolism U. Messina, 1987. Hon. rsch. fellow Academic Dept. Royal Free Hosp. Sch. Medicine, U. London, 1984—85, hon. lectr., 1984—85; chief cons. an outpatients svc. liver and HIV diseases U. Catania, 1986—2007, component as prof. rep. adminstrv. coun., 1988—97, head Inst. Internal and Emergency Medicine, 1988—2001, head dept. internal medicine, 2001—07. Avocations: sailing, photography, astronomy, birdwatching. Home: via Nuovaluce 67/4 Tremestieri Etneo Catania 95030 Italy Home Fax: 39 95 221914. Personal E-mail: lgacaruso@tin.it.

CARUSO-NEVES, CELSO, medical educator; b. Rio de Janeiro, Dec. 26, 1967; PhD, Fed. U. Rio de Janeiro, 1996; postdoc., Johns Hopkins Sch. Medicine, 2006. Assoc. prof., head, biochemistry and cell signaling lab. Fed. U. Rio de Janeiro, 1994—. Recipient award, Jour. Club Kidney Internat., 2007, Michel Jamra Young Investigation award, Fedn. Exptl. Biology Socs., Brazil, 2008, Brazilian Soc. Clin. Investigation, Brazil, 2010; named one of Scientists of State, Found. Rsch. Rio de Janeiro, 2009. Mem.: NY Acad. Sci., Am. Physiol. Soc. Avocations: surfing, soccer, Ju Jitsu. Home: Ave Prefeito Dulcídio Cardoso 333 B2 102 Rio de Janeiro 22630-022 Brazil Home Fax: 55-21-22808193.

CARVALHO, ANA CECÍLIA BEZERRA, pharmacist; b. Várzea Alegre, Ceará, Brazil, Nov. 2, 1978; PhD, U. Brasilia, 2010. Rschr. Nat. Health Surveillance Agy., 2005—. Mem.: Câmara Técnica de Medicamentos Fitoterápicos. Avocations: writing, dance. Office: Sia Trecho 3 Área Especial 57 Bloco B Brasília 71.200-980 Brazil Personal E-mail: anacecijp@yahoo.com.br.

CARVALHO, ANDRÉ FÉRRER, psychiatrist, educator; b. Brazil, Apr. 6, 1977; MD, Fed. U. Ceara, 2000; PhD, Fed. U. Rio Grande do Sul, 2005. Assoc. prof. Fed. U. Ceara-Faculty Medicine, 2006—. Mem.: Brazilian Assn. Psychiatry. Office: Monsenhor Bruno 777 Fortaleza Ceara 60115190 Brazil Office Fax: 558532617227. Business E-Mail: andrefc7@terra.com.br.

CARVALHO, JULIE ANN, psychologist; b. Washington, Apr. 11, 1940; d. Daniel Henry and Elizabeth Cecilia (Gardiner) Schmidt; children: Alan R., Dennis M., Melanie D., Celeste A., Joshua E. BA with high honors, U. Md., 1962, postgrad., 1962-63, 68-73, Va. Poly. Inst., 1979-88, Argosy U., 2003—04; MA, George Washington U., 1966; PhD in Social Policy, Human Devel., Va. Tech. Walden U. Social sci. rsch. analyst Mental Health Study Ctr., NIMH, Adelphi, Md., 1963-67; edn. and tng. analyst Computer Applications, Inc., Silver Spring, Md., 1967-68; edn. program specialist, program analyst Nat. Ctr. for Ednl. R&D, U.S. Office of Edn., Washington, 1969-73; equal opportunity specialist Office of Sec., HEW, Washington, 1973-77; legis. program, civil rights analyst Office for Civil Rights Dept. Health and Human Svcs., Washington, 1977-85; ind. cons. Adj. lectr. No. Va. C.C., George Mason U., Montgomery Coll., Strayer U., Park U., Shepherd Coll., Germanna Coll., U. Md. U. Coll., Va. Internat. U., Prince William Hosp., Fairfax County Pub. Schs., Fairfax County Dept. Social Svcs., all Washington area, 1986—; proposal evaluator, edn. dept. HUD, HHS Ed. Dept., 1989—; presenter in field. Contbr. articles to profl. jours. Bd. dirs. Child Care Ctrs., 1970—76, HEW Employees Assn., 1973—78; steering com. Alliance for Child Care, 1975—80. Mem.: ASPA (condr. panels 1975, 1991), APA (panel condr. 1969, 1975, editor Bull. of Peace Psychology 1991—97, divsn. 48), Soc. Psychol. Study of Social Issues (presenter, congl. bd. ednl. reform 2010), Unitarian Universalists for Social Justice (bd. dirs. Balt.-Washington region 2003—07), Federally Employed Women (nat. editor 1975—79), Psychologists Soc. Responsibility (cons., chair action com. on status of women), Capitol Area Social Psychologists Assn. (conf. chmn. 1985, 1993), Fairfax County Assn. for the Gifted (pres. 1980), Phi Alpha Theta, Psi Chi, Alpha Sigma Lambda (hon.). Home and Office: Apt 428 13430 Coppermine Rd Herndon VA 20171-4488 Business E-Mail: jcarvalho@nvcc.edu.

CARVALHO, LUIS ALBERTO, physicist, consultant; b. Paraguacu Paulista, Sao Paulo, Brazil, Mar. 3, 1971; s. Luiz Antonio and Regina Célia Carvalho; m. Valeria Mellaci Barros, Apr. 18, 1998; 1 child, Luisa. PhD, U. Sao Paulo, 2000; postgrad., UNIFESP, Brazil, 2001—03. Cons. rsch. sr. Eyetec, Sao Carlos, Sao Paulo, 1997—2003; vis. scientist Physics Inst., Sao Carlos, 2000—03. Project dir. Fapesp - Pipe, Sao Carlos, 1996—2003; rsch. scholar U. Calif., Berkeley, 1998—99. Author: (chapter in book) Wave Front Measurements of the HumanEeye Using the Hartmann-Shack Sensor and Current State-of-the-Art Technology for Excimer Laser Refractive Surgery, Histórico da Topografia de Córnea, Cultura Medica, Presbyopia & Accommodation: Anatomy, Physiology and Optics, Wavefront Analysis, Aberrometers and Corneal Topography, Highlights of Ophthalmology. Recipient Best tech. product of the yr. award, Finep, Brazil, 2001; grantee, Fapesp, Brazil, 1999, 2001. Achievements include development of the first surgical and computerized videokeratograph; patents pending for computerized surgical videkeratograph; cyllindrical based wave-front sensor; patents for an artificial intelligence algorithm using zernike pol. for detection of corneal patterns, a pupilometry system attatched to VKS instruements. Home: Rua das Hortencias 436 Sao Paulo Sao Carlos 13566-533 Brazil Office: Instituto de Física de São Carlos Rua Trabalhador Saocarlense 400 Sao Paulo Sao Carlos 13560-970 Brazil Office Fax: 55 16 274 3012; Home Fax: 55-16-274-3012. Business E-Mail: luisalberto@eyetec.com.br. E-mail: lavcf@ifsc.sc.usp.br.

CARVALHO, MÁRIO HENRIQUE BURLACCHINI, medical educator; b. Salvador, Bahia, Brazil, Apr. 1, 1969. D, U. Fed. da Bahia, 1992; PhD, U. de São Paulo, 2005. Prof. Med. Sch. U. São Paulo, 2000—. Cons. Fleury Medicine & Health, 1999—2011. Avocation: sports. Office: Avenida Doctor Eneas de Carvalho Aguiar 255 10 A São Paulo 05403000 Brazil E-mail: marioburlacchini@uol.com.br.

CARVALHO, VIVIANE FERNANDES, medical researcher; b. Sao Paulo, Brazil, July 6, 1974; Degree in Nursing, U. São Paulo, 2002, PhD in Health Sci., 2008. Sci. rsch. adviser Faculty Medicine U. São Paulo, 2005—; profl. edn. mgr. Systagenix, 2010. Asst. prof. U. Guarulhos, 2009. Mem.: Brazilian Enterostomal Therapists Assn., Brazilian Burns Assn. Avocations: gardening, travel. Home: Domingos José Sapienza 337 Apt 53 337 São Paulo 02618-000 Brazil Home Fax: 55 11 3062-0415. Personal E-mail: vivianefcarvalho@usp.br.

CARVALHO-SILVA, LUCIANO BRUNO DE, nutritionist, educator; b. Poços de Caldas, Minas Gerais, Brazil, Feb. 9, 1980; Grad., U. Alfenas, 2002; PhD, State U. Campinas, 2008. Rsch. scientist, prof., food and nutrition State U. Campinas, 2002—. Adj. prof. Fed. U. Alfenas, 2006. Avocations: reading, music, walking. Home: Dr João Sampaio n 1849 Apto 72 Alfenas Minas Gerais 37130000 Brazil Personal E-mail: lucianobrunocs@gmail.com.

CARVER, DAVID HAROLD, retired pediatrician; b. Boston, Apr. 18, 1930; s. Elias and Lottie (Jaffe) C.; m. Patricia Jo Nair, Aug. 2, 1963; children: Randolph Nair, Rebecca Lynn, Leslie Allison. AB magna cum laude, Harvard U., 1951; MD, Duke U., 1955. Intern Johns Hopkins Hosp., 1955-56; rsch. fellow pediatrics Cleve. Met. Hosp./Case We. Res. Med. Sch.), 1956-58; jr. asst. resident Children's Hosp. Med. Center, Boston, 1958-59, sr. asst. resident, 1959-60, chief resident, 1960-61, USPHS spl. rsch. fellow Harvard Med. Sch., 1961-63; asst. prof. pediatrics Albert Einstein Coll. Medicine, 1963-66; from assoc. prof. to prof. pediatrics Johns Hopkins U. Med. Sch., 1966-76; prof. pediatrics U. Toronto Med. Sch., 1976-88, chmn. dept. pediat., 1976—86; physician-in-chief Hosp. Sick Children, Toronto, 1976-86; chmn. dept. pediatrics U. Toronto, 1976-86; prof. pediat. Robert Wood Johnson Med. Sch., New Brunswick, NJ, 1988—2005, chmn. dept. pediatrics, 1988—2000, assoc. dean faculty affairs, 2000—04, spl. advisor to the dean, 2004—05; chief pediats. Robert Wood Johnson U. Hosp., 1988—2000; ret., 2005. Mem. study sect. USPHS Ctr. Disease Control, 1971-73; mem. provincial research grants rev. com. Ont. Ministry Health, 1977-83, chmn., 1981-83 Assoc. editor: Textbook of Pediatrics, 14th edit, 1968, 15th edit., 1972, 16th edit., 1977; mem. editl. bd. Pediatrics, 1973-79. With epidemic intelligence svc., USPHS, 1956-58. Recipient Schaffer award clin. teaching Johns Hopkins U. Med. Sch., 1973, Bain Clin. Tchg. award Hosp. Sick Children, 1978, Hon. award Robert Wood Johnson U. Hosp., 1997; Kennedy scholar, 1966-73 Mem. Am. Acad. Pediatrics (com. on infectious diseases 1973-79), Infectious Disease Soc. Am., Am. Soc. Virology, Internat. Soc. Interferon Rsch., Harvard Club Princeton, Soc. Pediat. Rsch., Am. Pediat. Soc. Home: 2416 Windrow Dr Princeton NJ 08540

CARVER, JOHN H., medical association administrator; b. Buffalo, Dec. 27, 1965; s. Robert L. Carver and Katherine E. Smith; stepfather, Gerald J. Smith; m. Paula D. Deinhart, Oct. 18, 1992; children: Madeline Haase, Charles John. BS in Bus./Mgmt. Econs., SUNY, Buffalo, 1988; C.M.R. in Sci. and Medicine, Bus. Healthcare, Cert. Med. Representative Inst., 1997; postgrad., St. Bonaventure U., 2001, MS in Exec. and Profl. Leadership, 2002; MBA in Internat. Bus.Adminstrn., Beijing Inst. Tech., 2001. Forms products broker Moore Bus. Products, Amherst, N.Y., 1990-92; med. liaison, ctrl. nervous sys. specialist Solvay Pharms., Inc., Marietta, Ga., 1992-97; founding mgr. Med. Sci. Liaison Programs, Forest Labs., Inc., NYC, 1997—2001, sr. ctrl. area mgr., 2001—. Adj. instr. in pharmacology Lake Erie Coll. Osteo. Medicine, Erie, Pa., 1996-98; bd. dirs. Westfield Devel. Corp., N.Y., 2001-2002. Mem.: Classical Ballet of We. NY (bd. dirs.), Lockport City Ballet (bd. dirs.). Avocations: yacht racing, flying sail planes, downhill skiing, mountain biking, photography, archery. Office: Forest Labs Inc 909 Third Ave New York NY 10022-4731 E-mail: John.Carver@FRX.com.

CARVER, JOSEPH R., cardiooncologist; b. Phila., Mar. 4, 1947; MD, Hahnemann U., 1972. Chief staff Abramson Cancer Ctr., 2005—. Office: 1600 Penn Tower 3400 Spruce St Philadelphia PA 19104 Office Fax: 215-662-4020. Business E-Mail: jrc@mail.med.upenn.edu.

CASAL, ROBERTO FERNANDO, medical educator; b. Buenos Aires, Feb. 19, 1974; MD, U. Buenos Aires, 1998. Asst. prof. medicine Baylor Coll. Medicine, 2009—. Dir., interventional pulmonology and bronchoscopy lab. Michael E. deBakey VA Med. Ctr., 2009—; adj. asst. prof. medicine U. Tex. MD Anderson Cancer Ctr., 2010—. Recipient award, U. Tex. Med. Sch., Houston. Mem.: Am. Coll. Chest Physicians, Am. Thoracic Soc., Am. Assn. Bronchology and Interventional Pulmonology. Avocation: soccer. Office: 2002 Holcombe Blvd Pulmonary Sect 1 Houston TX 77030 Business E-Mail: casal@bcm.edu.

CASALE, ALFRED STANLEY, thoracic and cardiovascular surgeon; b. Passaic, NJ, Nov. 28, 1955; s. Alfred Stanley and Regina Josephine (Cembor) C.; m. Mary Louise Cavell, Aug. 1, 1976; 1 child, Katherine. BA, Johns Hopkins U., 1976, MD, 1980. Diplomate Am. Bd. Surgery, Am. Bd. Thoracic Surgery; cert. Surg. Critical Care. Intern Johns Hopkins U., Balt., 1980-81, resident in surgery, 1981-85, resident in thoracic surgery, 1985-88, asst. prof., 1988-90; surgeon Mid Atlantic Surg. Assocs., Morristown, NJ, 1990-2000, ptnr., 1993—2000; chief cardiac surgery U. Hosp., UMD N.J., Newark, 2000—01; dir. cardiothoracic surgery Geisinger Wyoming Valley Med. Ctr., Wilkes-Barre, Pa., 2001—; surg. dir. Heart Inst., Geisinger Health Sys., Danville, Pa., 2002—, assoc. chief med. officer, 2008—. Assoc. chief cardiac surgery Atlantic Health Sys., Florham Park, NJ; chief cardiac surgery Gen. Hosp. Ctr., Passaic, NJ, 2000; mem. cardiovasc. health adv. panel N.J. Dept. Health, Trenton; assoc. prof. N.J. Med. Sch., UMD N.J., 2000—01. Contbr. articles to profl. jours. Dir. Madison YMCA, N.J., 1990-96, Am. Heart Assn., Morristown, 1990-2001, Luzerne County, 2002—, Kirby Child Care Ctr., Madison, 1992-96. Fellow Am. Coll. Surgeons, Am. Coll. Cardiology, Am. Coll. Chest Physicians; mem. Assn. Acad. Surgery (Resident Rsch. award 1984), Internat. Soc. Heart Transplantation, Soc. Thoracic Surgery. Avocations: skiing, tennis, fishing, shooting. Office: Geisinger Wyo Valley Med Ctr 1000 E Mountain Blvd Wilkes Barre PA 18711 Business E-Mail: ascasale@geisinger.edu. E-mail: al@casale.org.

CASALE, PASQUALE, urologist, consultant, researcher; MD, Albert Einstein Coll. Medicine, Bronx, NY, 1996. Diplomate Am. Bd. Urology, 2004. Attending pediat. urologist Children's Hosp. Phila., 2004—; attending surgeon U. Pa., Phila., 2004—. Achievements include specialization in robotic pediatric urologic surgery and laparoscopy. Office: Children's Hosp Phila 34th St and Civic Ctr Blvd Philadelphia PA 19104 Office Fax: 215-590-3985. Business E-Mail: casale@email.chop.edu.

CASALE, THOMAS BRUCE, medical educator; b. Chgo., Apr. 21, 1951; m. Jean M. Casale; 1 son, Jeffrey G. BS cum laude, U. Ill., 1973; MD, Chgo. Med. Sch., 1977. Diplomate Am. Bd. Internal Medicine, Am. Bd. Allergy and Immunology. Resident in internal medicine Baylor Coll. Medicine, Houston, 1977-80; med. staff fellow lab. clin. investigation NIAID, NIH, Bethesda, Md., 1980-84; from asst. prof. to prof. internal medicine U. Iowa, Iowa City, 1984-94, prof. internal medicine, 1994-96; dir. Nebr. Med. Rsch. Inst., 1996-99; adj. prof. pediatrics Coll. Medicine U. Nebr., 1996—; clin. prof. medicine Creighton U., Omaha, 1997-99, prof., assoc. chair dept. medicine, dir. clin. rsch., 1999—, chief allergy/immunology, 2001—. Chief med. staff fellow lab. clin. investigation, NIAID, NIH, Bethesda, 1982-83; attending physician VA Med. Ctr., Iowa City, 1984-96, staff physician, 1986-96, clin. investigator, 1991-96; asst. dir. tchg. allergy/immunology divsn. dept. internal medicine U. Iowa, Iowa City, 1989-92, acting dir., 1992, dir., 1993-96, faculty interdisciplinary immunology grad. degree program U. Iowa, 1993-96; bd. dirs. Am. Bd. Allergy and Immunology, Am. Acad. Allergy, Asthma and Immunology; reviewer over 15 profl. and sci. jours. Contbr. over 200 articles to profl. publs.; mem. editl. bd. Jour. Allergy Clin. Immunology, 1988-93, clin. asthma revs., 1996-99, Allergy & Clinical Immunology Internat., 1997-2002, Jour. World Allergy Org., 2003—; editor Respiratory Digest, 1999—, Ann. Allergy, Asthma & Immunology, 1999—. Mem. asthma technical adv. group Am. Lung Assn., 1989-96. Lt. commdr. USPHS, 1980-83, USPHS Res., 1983—. Recipient Dr. John J. Sheinin Rsch. award Chgo. Med. Sch., 1977, Clin. Investigator VA, 1991-96, Am. Soc. Clin. Investigation, 1992; grantee NIH, 1986-91, 87-90, 92-93, 93-94, VA Merit Rev., 1986-89, 89-92, 92-96, Environ. Health Sci. Core Ctr., 1990-96, Novartis Pharms., 1997—, Sepracor, Inc., 1997, Immune Tolerance Network, 2003—, others. Fellow ACP, Am. Acad. Allergy Immunology (cutaneous allergy com. 1985-90, postgrad. edn. com. 1988-91, chmn. 1989-90, program com. dermatologic diseases sect. 1988-93, sec. 1989-90, vice chmn. 1990-91, chmn. 1991-92, prof. edn. coun. 1998—, chair 1998—, sec. 1993-95, vice chair 1995—, chmn. bronchoalveolar lavage com. 1991-95, 98—, others), Am. Coll. Allergy Immunology (profl. allergy/immunology edn. com. 1989-94); mem. Am. Acad. Allergy Asthma Immunology (bd. dirs. 2001—, sec., treas. 2004—, pres.-elect 2006-07, pres. 2007-08, past pres. 2008-), Am. Fedn. Clin. Rsch., Am. Thoracic Soc. (sec. allergy immunology and inflammation scientific assembly 1990-91, chair-elect 1991-93, chair program com. 1992-93, chair 1993-95, long-range planning and policy com. sci. assembly on allergy immunology and inflammation 1991-96, sci. conf. com. 1991-93, bd. dirs. 1993-95, chair asthma adv. com. 1995-99), Am. Bd. Allergy and Immunology (bd. dirs. 1999—, co-chmn. 2003-04, chmn. 2005-), Iowa Soc. Allergy Immunology (pres. 1987-89), Am. Assn. Immunologists, Midwest Sect. Am. Fedn. Clin. Rsch., Ctrl. Soc. Clin. Rsch., Am. Soc. Clin. Invest., Am. Lung Assn. (mem. rsch. coordinating com. 1996-99), European Respiratory Soc. Office: Creighton U Dept Medicine 601 N 30th St Ste 5850 Omaha NE 68131-2137 Office Fax: 402-280-4115. Business E-Mail: tbcasale@creighton.edu.

CASALINO, LAWRENCE PETER, health sciences professor; BA in Philosophy, Boston Coll., 1970; MD, U. Calif., San Francisco, 1979; MPH, U. Calif., Berkeley, 1992, PhD, 1997. Co-founder, family physician Coastside Med. Clinic, Half Moon Bay, Calif., 1980—2000; clin. asst. prof., dept. medicine Stanford U. Med. Ctr., 1995—2000; asst. prof., dept. health studies U. Chgo., 2000—07, assoc. prof., dept. health studies, 2007—08; Livingston Farrand assoc. prof. pub. health Weill Cornell Med. Coll., NYC, 2008—, chief divsn. outcomes & effectiveness rsch., dept. pub. health, 2008—. Med. staff pres. Seton Med. Ctr., Coastside, Calif., 1984—86; bd. mem., v.p. Serra Med. Group IPA, 1985—92; bd. dirs. Integrated Bay Area Network, 1993—94; faculty, Robert Wood Johnson clin. scholars program U. Chgo., 2000—06, faculty grad. program in health adminstrn. & policy, 2001—08, faculty Ctr. Health & Social Scis., 2005—08; mem. nat. adv. com. Robert Wood Johnson Found., 2008—; bd. dirs. Am. Med. Group Assn. Found., 2008—. Mem. eidtl. bd. Med. Care Rsch. & Rev., 2002—, peer reviewer for numerous med. jours.; contbr. articles to profl. jours. Recipient Investigator award in Health Policy Research, Robert Wood Johnson Found., 2000—04; grantee Woodrow Wilson fellowship, 1966—70. Office: Weill Cornell Med Coll Dept Pub Health 402 E 67th St New York NY 10065 Office Phone: 646-962-8084. Office Fax: 646-962-0281. Business E-Mail: lac2021@med.cornell.edu. *

CASCIANO, DANIEL ANTHONY, biologist, educator; b. Buffalo, Mar. 1, 1941; s. Frederick James and Rose Ann C.; m. Gertrude Ann Tara, Aug. 22, 1964; children: Anne, Jonathan. BS, Canisius Coll., 1962; PhD in Cell Biology, Purdue U., 1971. Rsch. asst. Roswell Park Meml. Inst., Buffalo, 1963—64; rsch. asst. dept. biol. scis. Purdue U., West Lafayette, Ind., 1965—66, tchg. asst., 1969, rsch. trainee, 1966—71; trainee NIH, 1966—71; postdoctoral investigator U. Tenn., Oak Ridge Nat. Labs., 1971—73; assoc. prof. dept. biochemistry and molecular biology U. Ark. for Med. Scis., Little Rock, 1974—90, prof. dept. biochemistry and molecular biology, 1990—, prof. dept pharmacology and toxicology, 1990—; rsch. biologist Nat. Ctr. Toxicological Rsch., Jefferson, Ark., 1973, program dir. divsn. mutagenesis rsch., 1976—78, dir. divsn. genetic toxicology, 1979—97, dir. divsn. genetic and reproductive toxicology, 1997—99, dep. dir. for rsch., 1999—2000, acting dir., 1999—2000, dir., 2000—06; pres. Dan Casciano and Assocs., 2006—; sr. sci. advisor, applied sci. U. Ark., Little Rock, 2008—. Contbr. articles to profl. jours. Mem. Tissue Culture Assn., Environ. Mutagen Soc., AAAS, Beta Beta Beta. Home and Office: 47 Marcella Dr Margeux Pl Little Rock AR 72223-9172 Office Phone: 501-837-2401. Business E-Mail: dcasciano@sbcglobal.net.

CASCON, ALBERTO, medical researcher; b. Santander, Spain, May 8, 1970; PhD, U. Leon, 2000. Staff scientist Nat. Cancer Rsch. Ctr., 2001—. Office: Melchor Fernandez Almagro 4 Madrid 28029 Spain Business E-Mail: acascon@cnio.es.

CASDEN, ANDREW MICHAEL, orthopedist; b. Bklyn., June 13, 1957; s. Daniel D. and Hannah L. (Bernstein) C.; m. Jeri Casden, Aug. 3, 1981; children: Jared, Ryan, Michael BA, Cornell U., 1979; MD, Cornell U. Med. Coll., 1983. Bd. cert. Am. Bd. Orthop. Surgery; diplomate Nat. Bd. Med. Examiners; lic. NY. Intern gen. surgery The NY Hosp., Cornell Med. Ctr., NYC, 1983-84; Chgo. Spine Fellowship Rush Presbyn.-St. Luke's Med. Ctr., 1988—89; resident orthop. surgery Hosp. for Joint Diseases, Orthop. Inst., NYC, 1984-88; chief spine surgery., dept. orthop. Mount Sinai Med. Ctr., NYC, 1989—98; asst. prof. orthop. surgery Mount Sinai Sch. Medicine, NYC, 1989—98, asst. prof. neurosurgery, 1994—98; asst. prof. orthop. surgery Albert Einstein Coll. Medicine, Yeshiva Univ., NYC, 1999—; assoc. dir., spine surgery Spine Inst. NY, Beth Israel Med. Ctr., NYC, 1998—. Dir. (coarse) Pedicle Screw Fixation of the Thoracic Spine, 2002, 2003; presenter in field. Contbr. articles to profl. jours. Mem. Am. Acad. Orthop. Surgeons (com. on evaluations 1995), Am. Spinal Injury Assn., N.Am. Spine Soc., Scoliosis Rsch. Soc. Office: Beth Israel Med Ctr Spine Inst NY Phillips Ambulatory Care Ctr 10 Union Square E # 5P New York NY 10003 Office Phone: 212-844-8696, 212-844-8674, 914-934-0027. Business E-Mail: acasden@chpnet.org.

CASE, DAVID BARTLETT, internist, educator; b. Plainfield, NJ, Mar. 17, 1942; s. George and Caroline (Bartlett) C.; m. Jean Brookhart, Aug. 2, 1969; children: Thayer Stimson, Nelson Chipman. AB, Princeton U., 1964; MD, Columbia U., 1968. Intern, then asst. resident Johns Hopkins Hosp., Balt., 1968-70; fellow Columbia Presbyn. Hosp., NYC, 1972-75; asst., then assoc. prof. Cornell U. Med. Coll., NYC, 1975-84, clin. assoc. prof., 1984—. Mem. Council on High Blood Pressure Research, 1979—; vis. lectr. Columbia U. Coll. of Physicians and Surgeons, 1997—. Contbr. chapters to books, articles to profl. jours. Recipient Andrew Mellon Tchr. Scientist award Cornell U., 1978. Master ACP (gov. downstate I); fellow Am. Coll. Clin. Pharmacology, Am. Heart Assn. Achievements include research in hypertension. Office: 635 Madison Ave New York NY 10022-1009 Office Phone: 212-857-4660. Personal E-mail: dbmdny@aol.com, davidb.casemd@gmail.com.

CASE, GREGORY C., insurance company executive; b. 1962; m. Mamie Case. BA summa cum laude, Kans. State U., 1985; MBA, Harvard U., 1989. With Fed. Reserve Bank Kansas City; investment banker Piper, Jaffray and Hopwood; ptnr., head fin. svc. & global ins. practices McKinsey & Co., 1988—2005; pres., CEO AON Corp. (AON Brokerage Group), Chgo., 2005—. Bd. dir. Discover Fin. Services, 2007—. Mem.: Economic Club of Chgo., Fin. Services Roundtable, Internat. Ins. Society, Inc. Office: Aon Corporation 200 E Randolph St Chicago IL 60601 *

CASE, ROBERT BROWN, physician; b. Columbus, Ohio, July 19, 1920; s. William Lyman and Margaret (Brown) C.; m. Nan Barkin, Nov. 9, 1973; 1 child, Lisa Case. BA, Ohio Wesleyan, 1943; BS, MIT, 1943; MD, Columbia U., 1948. Diplomate Am. Bd. Internal Medicine. Intern and resident St. Luke's Hosp., NYC, 1948-52, chief lab. of exptl. cardiology, 1956-95, sr. attending physician, 1971-95; rsch. fellow Harvard Sch. of Pub. Health, Boston, 1952-54; rsch. assoc. Nat. Heart Inst., Bethesda, Md., 1954-56; prof. emeritus medicine Columbia U., NYC, 1991—. Chief cardiac consultation clinic N.Y.C. Dept. Health, 1962-70; mem. cardiovascular study sect. Nat. Heart Inst., 1970-74. Mem. editl. bd. Circulation Rsch., 1977-85; contbr. articles to profl. jours. & publs., co-author: (with Moss, Arthur J.)Recommendation for Revision of the Standard ECG Leads including Reversal of Lead A VR, It Is Time for A Change, Annals of Noninvasive Electrocardiology, 2010. With USPHS, 1954-56. Rsch. Career devel. grant NIH, 1962-72. Felow Am. Physiol. Soc., N.Y. County Med. Assn., N.Y. State Med. Assn., Am. Heart Assn., Am. Fedn. for Clin. Rsch. Home and Office: 130 E 75th St New York NY 10021-3241 Office Phone: 212-249-5613.

CASE, STEVE (STEPHEN MCCONNELL CASE), healthcare investment company executive, former media and entertainment company executive; b. Honolulu, Aug. 21, 1958; s. Daniel and Carol Case; m. Joanne Barker, 1985 (div. 1996); 3 children; m. Jean Villanueva, 1998. BA in Polit. Sci., Williams Coll., 1980. With mktg. dept. The Procter & Gamble Co., 1980—82; mng. new pizza devel. Pizza Hut divsn. PepsiCo, 1982—83; with Control Video, 1983—85, Quantum Computer Svcs., 1985—92; co-founder, CEO America Online LLC, 1992—2001, chmn., 1995—2001, AOL Time Warner, NYC, 2001—03, Exclusive Resorts LLC, Denver, 2004—; chmn., CEO Revolution LLC, Washington, 2005—. Bd. dirs. America Online, 1992—2001, Time Warner Inc. (previously AOL Time Warner), 2001—05; co-founder, chmn. Case Found., 1997—; founder Revolution Health.com, 2007—; investor RediClinic, 2006—; mem. President's Coun. on Jobs & Competitiveness, 2011—. Co-founder, chair Accelerate Brain Cancer Cure, 2001—. Named Named Entrepreneur of Yr., Inc. Mag., 1994. Office: The Case Foundation 1717 Rhode Island Ave NW 7th Fl Washington DC 20036 also: Exclusive Resorts LLC 1515 Arapahoe St Denver CO 80202-3150 Office Phone: 202-467-5788. Office Fax: 202-775-8513. *

CASELLA, ANTHONY JOHN, cardiologist; b. NYC, Mar. 8, 1945; s. Anthony Daniel and Benedetta Ann Casella; m. Kathleen Ann Barrs, Aug. 31, 1986; children: Daniel Edward, Eric Michael; 1 child from previous marriage, Joseph Anthony. BA, NYU, 1966; MD, N.Y. Med. Coll., 1970. Diplomate Am. Bd. Internal Medicine. Intern, resident N.Y. Hosp.-Meml. Hosp., 1970-73; fellow cardiology Columbia-Presbyn. Med. Ctr., NYC, 1975-77; cardiologist Diagnostic and Clin. Cardiology PA, West Orange, NJ, 1977—. Cardiologist St. Barnabas Med. Ctr., Livingston, NJ, 1977—, Clara Maass Med. Ctr., Belleville, NJ, 1977—; assoc. St. Michaels Med. Ctr., Newark, 1984—. Mem.: AMA, Essex County Med. Soc., Alpha Omega Alpha. Republican. Roman Catholic. Office: Diagnostic & Clinical Cardiology 375 Mount Pleasant West Orange NJ 07052-2724 Office Phone: 973-731-9442.

CASELLA, SAMUEL JOSEPH, pediatric endocrinologist; MD, SUNY, 1981. Diplomate Am. Bd. Pediatrics, 1985, Am. Bd. Pediatrics-pediatric endocrinology, 1986. Resdient pediatrics Upstate Med. Ctr., Syracuse, NY, 1982—84; fellow pediatric endocrinology NC Meml. Hosp.-Univ. NC, Chapel Hill, 1984—86; sect. chief, pediatric endocrinology Dartmouth-Hitchcock Med. Ctr., 2001—; assoc. prof. pediatrics Johns Hopkins Univ. Office: Dartmouth-Hitchcock Medical Center Pediatric Endocrinology, Diabetes and Me One Medical Ctr Dr Lebanon NH 03756 Office Phone: 603-653-9877. Office Fax: 603-650-0907.

CASERIO, REBECCA JOANN, dermatologist, educator; b. Pa., Aug. 2, 1949; d. James Joseph and Jolanda Marie (Denale) C.; m. Chris Max Allen, Apr. 15, 1978 (dec.). BS summa cum laude, U. Pitts., 1971, MD cum laude, 1975. Intern Montefiore Hosp., Pitts., 1975—76, resident in internal medicine, 1976—78, chief resident, 1978; staff internist Penn Group Health Plan, Pitts., 1978—80; resident in dermatology U. Pitts., 1981—83, chief resident in dermatology, 1983; dir. hair clinic Falk Clinic, Pitts., 1984—87, clin. asst. prof. dermatology, 1985—92, clin. assoc. prof. dermatology, 1992—2001. Mem. Pa. Med. Soc., Pitts. Acad. Dermatology, Pa. Acad. Dermatology, Am. Acad. Dermatology, Am. Soc. Dermatol. Surgeons, Allegheny County Med. Soc., Am. Contact Dermatitis Soc., Internat. Soc. Cosmetic & Laser Surgery, Am. Soc. Photodynamic Therapy, Phi Beta Kappa, Kappa Kappa Gamma, Alpha Omega Alpha, Beta Beta Beta, Alpha Epsilon Delta. Roman Catholic. Home: 4142 Bigelow Blvd Pittsburgh PA 15213-1408 Office Phone: 412-784-1606.

CASEY, KENNETH LYMAN, neurologist; b. Ogden, Utah, Apr. 16, 1935; s. Kenneth Lafayette and Lyzena (Payne) C.; m. Jean Louise Madsen, June 21, 1958; children— Tena Jeanette, Kenneth Lyman, Teresa Louise. BA, Whitman Coll., Walla Walla, Wash., 1957; MD with honors, U. Wash., Seattle, 1961. Diplomate Am. Bd. Neurology and Psychiatry. Intern in medicine Cornell U. Med. Center-N.Y. Hosp., 1961-62; USPHS officer lab. neurophysiology NIMH, 1962-64; fellow in psychology McGill U., Montreal, Que., Canada, 1964-66; mem. faculty U. Mich. Med. Sch., Ann Arbor, 1966—, prof. neurology and physiology, 1978—2005, prof. emeritus neurology, prof. emeritus molecular and integrative physiology, 2005—; resident in neurology U. Mich Hosp., 1971-74; chief neurology svc. VA Med. Center, Ann Arbor, 1979—2002, cons. in neurology, 2002—. Sci. adv. com. Santa Fe Neurol. Inst., 1984-; H.K. Beecher lectr. Harvard Med. Sch., 2006 Assoc. editor Clin. Jour. Pain, 1984—, Pain, 1991—; editor-in-chief Am. Pain Soc. Jour. Pain Forum, 1991-99; contbr. articles to profl. jours., chpts. to books. Grantee, NIH, 1966—; Spl. fellow, 1964—66, Bristol-Myers rsch. grantee, 1988—93. Fellow: Am. Acad. Neurology (Mitchell B. Max award 2011); mem.: Internat. Assn. Study Pain (hon. life mem.), Wayne County Med. Soc. (Rhoades lectr. and medalist 2002), Am. Pain Soc. (pres. 1984—85, F.W.L. Kerr Basic Sci. Rsch. award and lecture 1998, named hon. life mem. 2005), Soc. Neurosci., Am. Neurol. Assn., Am. Acad. Neurology, Am. Physiol. Soc., Alpha Omega Alpha (J.J. Bonica disting. lectr. and award 1991), Sigma Xi, Phi Beta Kappa. Unitarian Universalist. Achievements include named lectureship established in his honor by Pfizer Co. in 2002. Home: 2775 Heatherway Ann Arbor MI 48104-2852

CASEY, MURRAY JOSEPH, physician, educator; b. Armour, SD, May 1, 1936; s. Meryl Joseph and Gladice (Murray) C.; m. Virginia Anne Fletcher; children: Murray Joseph Jr., Theresa Marie, Anne Franklin, Francis Xavier, Peter Colum, Matthew Padraic. Student, Chanute Jr. Coll., 1954-55, Rockhurst Coll., 1955-56; AB, U. Kans., 1958; MD, Georgetown U., 1962; postgrad., Suffolk U. Law Sch., 1963-64, Howard U., 1965, U. Conn., 1977; MS in Mgmt., Cardinal Stritch Coll., 1984; MBA, Marquette U., 1988. Diplomate Nat. Bd.

Med. Examiners, Am. Bd. Ob-Gyn; cert. in theology Creighton U., 2003. Intern USPHS Hosp.-Univ. Hosp., Balt., 1962-63; staff physician USPHS Hosp., Boston, 1963-64; rsch. staff Lab Infectious Diseases, Nat. Inst. Allergy and Infectious Diseases, NIH, Bethesda, Md., 1964-66; virologist, resident physician Columbia-Presbyn. Med. Ctr. also Francis Delafield Hosp., NYC, 1966-69, USPHS sr. clin. trainee, 1969-70; fellow gynecol. oncology, resident dept. surgery Meml. Hosp. Cancer and Allied Diseases, Meml. Sloan-Kettering Cancer Ctr., NYC, 1969-71; Am. Cancer Soc. fellow, 1969-71; ofcl. observer in radiotherapy U. Tex. M.D. Anderson Hosp. and Tumor Inst., Houston, 1971; vis. scientist Radiumhemmet Karolinska Sjukhuset and Inst., Stockholm, 1971; asst. prof. ob-gyn U. Conn. Sch. Medicine, 1971-75, asso. prof., 1975-80, dir. gynecologic oncology, 1971-80, also mem. med. bd.; Linson fellow Am. Coll. Surgeons Commn. on Cancer, 1979—89, 1995—2006; prof., assoc. chmn. dept. ob-gyn U. Wis. Med. Sch., 1980-89; prof., chmn. dept. ob-gyn. Creighton U., Omaha, 1989-94; chief ob-gyn. and dir. gynecologic oncology St. Joseph Hosp., Creighton U. Med. Ctr., Omaha, 1989-94; dir. gynecologic oncology Creighton Cancer Ctr., 1996—. Faculty coun. Creighton U., 1992—, acad. coun., 1992—, mem. instl. rev. bd., 1994—2004, univ. rank and tenure com., 1998—2001, 2007—, cancer ctr. adv. bd., 1994—, prin. investigator Cancer Ctr., 2001—02, Sch. Medicine rank and tenure com., 2005—07, chair Sch. Medicine rank and tenure com., 2006—07, fin. adv. com., 2008—; acting bd. dirs. Mo. Valley Consortium, Cmty. Coop. Oncology Program; chief ob-gyn Mt. Sinai Med. Ctr., Milw., 1980—82, dir. gynecologic oncology, 1980—89, also mem. med. exec. com., prin. investigator, 2001—06; chmn. research adv. com., mem. council Conn. Cancer Epidemiology Unit. Editor, contbr. articles in sports medicine to profl. jours., chpts. to books; rsch. in oncogenesis and tumor immunology. Bd. dirs., mem. exec. com., chmn. profl. edn. com. Hartford unit Am. Cancer Soc., dir. Milw. divsn., exec. com. 1985-87, v.p., 1985-86, pres.-elect, 1986-87, 1st v.p. exec. com. Wis. divsn. 1987-89, bd. dirs., chmn. profl. edn. com., 1987-89, bd. dirs., 1989-96, exec. com. Nebr. divsn., 1989-93, pub. edn. and communications com., profl. edn. com. vice chair, 2nd v.p., 1990-91, 1st v.p., pres.-elect, 1991-92, pres., 1992-93, bd. dirs. Douglas County unit, 1993—; mem. mayor's adv. com. Cancer Survivors Park, City of Omaha, 1991-92; mem. Parks and Recreation Bd., City of Omaha, 1993-94; mem. med. svcs. 1980 Winter Olympic Games, Lake Placid, N.Y.; mem. med. supervisory team U.S. Nordic Ski Team. Lt. (j.g.) USPHS, 1962-64, lt. comdr., 1964-66; col. USAR, 1988-94. Fellow: ACS, Am. Coll. Ob-Gyn; mem.: AAAS, Omaha Ob-Gyn. Soc., Milwaukee Gynecologic Soc., Assn. Mil. Surgeons, Am. Urogynecol. Soc., Lake Placid Sports Medicine Soc. (v.p. 1981—84, pres. 1984—86), Soc. Meml. Gynecol. Oncologists (exec. bd. 1979—84, pres. 1982—83), Internat. Assn. for Advancement of Humanistic Studies in Medicine, N.Am. Menopause Soc., Internat. Menopause Soc., Am. Soc. Clin. Oncology, Am. Radium Soc., Internat. Gynecol. Cancer Soc., New Eng. Assn. Gynecol. Oncologists (pres. 1980—81), European Soc. Gynecol. Oncologists, Soc. Gynecol. Oncologists, Am. Fertility Soc., Am. Assn. Gynecologic Laparoscopists, Am. Soc. Colposcopy, N.Y. Acad. Scis., Am. Coll. Sports Medicine, Can. Assn. Ob Gyns., Soc. of Gynecol. Surgeons, St. George Soc., Cedarburg C. of C. (dir. 1983—85, Ambassadors com. 1983—89, chmn. bus. indsl. program com. 1985, 1987—89, hon. life mem., amb. emeritus), Beta Gamma Sigma. Office: Creighton U Sch Medicine Dept Ob-Gyn 601 N 30th St # 4700 Omaha NE 68131-2137

CASEY, ROSEMARY D., pediatrician, educator; Attended, Immaculata Coll.; MD, Harvard Med. Sch. Diplomate Am. Bd. Pediatrics, 1980. Intern Children's Hosp. Pa., resident, dir. gen. pediatric faculty practice, 1989—97; hosp. affiliations include Bryn Mawr Hosp., 1997—, Lankenau Med. Ctr., 1997, Paoli Hosp., 1997; Robert Wood Johnson Clin. scholar Univ. Pa.; assoc. prof. pediats. Jefferson Med. Coll. Office: Lankenau Medical Center 100 East Lancaster Ave Wynnewood PA 19096 Office Phone: 484-580-1000.

CASHER, MICHAEL I., psychiatrist, educator; b. New Haven, Mar. 22, 1951; BA, Johns Hopkins U., 1972; MD, U. Mich. Med Sch., 1976. Clin. asst. prof., dir. inpatient psychiatry U. Mich., 2007—. Recipient Irma Bland award, Am. Psychiat. Assn.; named Tchr. of Yr., Alpha Omega Alpha, U. Mich. Mem.: Mich. Psychiat. Soc., Assn. Academic Psychiatry, Am. Psychiat. Assn. Avocations: guitar, tennis. Office: VH 9C 9150 1500 E Medical Center Dr Ann Arbor MI 48103 Business E-Mail: mcasher@med.umich.edu.

CASHMAN, SUZANNE BOYER, health services administrator, educator; b. Phila., Apr. 14, 1947; d. Vincent Saul and Ethel (Wolf) Boyer; m. Daniel Cashman, Jan. 16, 1971; children: Adam, Rebecca, David. BA, Tufts U., 1969; MS, Cornell U., 1973; ScD, Harvard U., 1980. Sr. analyst Urban Sys. Rsch., Cambridge, Mass., 1979-82; cons. Mass. Dept. Pub. Health, Boston, 1982-83; spl. asst. to v.p. Brigham and Women's Hosp., Boston, 1983-85; assoc. dir. rsch. Boston U. Office Spl. Projects, 1985-89; asst. prof. Boston U. Sch. Pub. Health, 1985-96; evaluator Cmty. Oriented Primary Care, Boston, 1989-91; assoc. dir. Ctr. for Cmty. Responsive Care, Boston, 1991-97; pub. health cons. U. Mass. Med. Ctr., Worcester, 1998; prof. dept. family medicine, cmty. health, dir. cmty. health Med. Sch. U. Mass., Worcester, 1999—, faculty preventive medicine residency, 1999—; co-dir. Cmty. Engagement Core CTSI. Cons. Acad. Health Ctrs., Derby, Conn., Columbia, SC, Atlanta, Balt., 1995—97; conf. planner New. Eng. Rural Health Roundtable; city mgr. Pub. Health Jade Force, Worcester. Co-editor: Community Oriented Primary Care, 1998; contbr. articles to profl. jours. Mem. leadership tng. program., sec. alumni orgn. com. NCCJ, Boston, 1995—2008; sec. bd. exec. com., conf. planner Cmty.-Campus Partnerships for Health and New England Rural Health Roundtable; task force Healthy People 2010 Curriculum; leadership support team Common Pathways; bd. dirs. Cmty. Ptnrs., Inc., 2003—, Cmty-Campus Partnerships Health. Mem APHA, Assn. for Prevention Tchg. and Rsch. (conf. planner, bd. dirs., exec. com. 2002-10), Mass. Pub. Health Assn. Avocations: yoga, sewing, cooking, jogging, gardening. Home: 17 Calvin Rd Newtonville MA 02460-2104 Office: U Mass Med Ctr Dept Family Medicine 55 Lake Ave N Worcester MA 01655-0002 Office Phone: 774-442-2930. Business E-Mail: suzanne.cashman@umassmed.edu.

CASIDA, JOHN EDWARD, toxicology and entomology professor; b. Phoenix, Dec. 22, 1929; s. Lester Earl and Ruth (Barnes) Casida; m. Katherine Faustine Monson, June 16, 1956; children: Mark Earl, Eric Gerhard. BS, U. Wis., 1951, MS, 1952, PhD, 1954; D (hon.), U. Buenos Aires, 1997. Research asst. U. Wis., 1951-53, mem. faculty, 1954-63, prof. toxicology & entomology, 1959-63, U. Calif.-Berkeley, 1964—; scholar-in-residence Bellagio Study and Conf. Center, Rockefeller Found., Lake Como, Italy, 1978. Messenger lectr. Cornell U., 1985; Sterling B. Hendricks lectr. USDA and Am. Chem. Soc., 1992; dir. Environ. Chemistry and Toxicology Lab., U. Calif., Berkeley, 1964—; William Muriece Hoskins chair in chem. and molecular entomology U. Calif., Berkeley, 1996—, faculty rsch. lectr., 1998; lectr. in sci. Third World Acad. Scis., Buenos Aires, 1997. Author: rsch. publs. With USAF, 1953. Recipient medal, 7th Internat. Congress Plant Protection, Paris, 1970, Disting. Svc. award, USDA, 1988, Wolf prize in agr., Wolf Found., Isreal, 1993, Koro-Sho prize, Pesticide Sci. Soc. Japan, 1995; named Jeffery lectr., U. New South Wales, Australia, 1983; fellow Haight traveling fellow, 1958—59, Guggenheim fellow, 1970—71. Fellow: Entomol. Soc. (Bussart Meml. award 1989); mem.: NAS, European Acad. Scis., Soc. Environ. Toxicology and Chemistry (Founder's award 1994), Pesticide Sci. Soc. Japan (hon.), Soc. Toxicology (hon.), Am. Chem. Soc. (Internat. award rsch. pesticide chemistry 1970, Spencer award in agrl. and food chemistry 1978), Royal Soc. UK (fgn.). Home: 1570 La Vereda Rd Berkeley CA 94708-2036

CASILLAS, JACQUELINE NIETO, hematologist, oncologist, educator; b. Long Beach, Calif., June 25, 1966; 1 child. BS in Biology, Loyola Marymount U., LA, 1988; MD, UCLA, 1995, MS in Health Services, 2003. Cert. Pediat., 1998, Pediat. Hematology-Oncology, 2002. Intern pediat. Harbor-UCLA Med. Ctr., Torrance, Calif., 1995—96, resident, 1996—98; fellowship pediat.-hematology-oncology David Geffen Sch. Medicine, UCLA, 1998—2001, post doctoral fellowship in cancer prevention and control rsch., clin. instr., 1998—2001, asst. prof. hematology/oncology, dept. pediat., 2001—, physician pediat. hematology/oncology, mem. endocrine surg. unit. Mem., Patients and Survivors Program Area UCLA Jonsson Comprehensive Cancer Ctr. Contbr. articles to profl. jours. Office: Jonsson Comprehensive Cancer Ctr 10833 Le Conte Ave Los Angeles CA 90095 Office Phone: 310-825-6185, 310-206-8089. E-mail: jcasillas@mednet.ucla.edu.

CASINI, ALESSANDRO, gastroenterologist, educator; b. Florence, Mar. 30, 1952; MD, U. Florence, 1977, degree in Gastroenterology & Human Nutrition, 1981. Asst. prof. gastroenterology U. Florence, 1980—88, mem. faculty sch. medicine, 1981, asst. prof. gastroenterology, 1990—2000, chief alcohol rsch. and treatment ctr., U. Hosp. Florence, 1994—2000, chief Agy. Nutrition, U. Hosp. Florence, assoc. prof. gastroenterology & human nutrition, 2000—; vis. rsch. prof. gastroenterology and liver disease Mt. Sinai Sch. Medicine & Albert Einstein Coll. Medicine- CUNY, 1988—90. NIH grant, Pathophysiol. Mechanisms Non-Alcoholic Fatty Liver Disease. Mem.: European Assn. Study Liver Disease, Italian Soc. Human Nutrition, Italian Assn. Liver Disease, Italian Soc. Gastroenterology. Office: Largo Brambilla 3 Florence Tuscany 50134 Italy Business E-Mail: alessandro.casini@unifi.it.

CASINO, GONZALO, journalist; b. Vigo, Spain, Oct. 28, 1961; Degree in Medicine, Cantabria U., 1985. Med. journalist, editor El País, 1999—2009, author Escepticemia.com, 1999— Recipient Internat. Sci. Journalism prize, Higher Coun. Sci. Rsch., 1994. Mem.: Spanish Assn. Sci. Communication. Avocation: art. Office: Girona 54 Barcelona Cataluña 08009 Spain Business E-Mail: gcasino@escepticemia.com.

CASOLA, STEFANO, medical researcher; b. Naples, Italy, Nov. 16, 1968; MD, U. Federico, Naples, Italy, 1993, PhD, 1999. Group leader IFOM Foundation-FIRC Inst. Molecular Oncology, 2006—. Asst. prof. European Sch. Molecular Medicine, U. Milan, Italy, 2006. Recipient Career Devel. award, Gioavanni Armenise, Harvard Found. Mem.: Italian Soc. Immunology and Allergology. Office: IFOM-IEO Campus Via Adamello 16 Milano 20139 Italy Business E-Mail: stefano.casola@ifom-ieo-campus.it.

CASON, NICA VIRGINIA, retired nursing educator; b. Edna, Tex. 1 child, Cynthia Diane. Diploma, Lillie Jolly Sch. Nursing, 1965; BSN, U. Tex. Med. Br., Galveston, 1967; MSN, U. So. Miss., 1981. RN Miss. Pub. health nurse Miss. State Dept. Health, Pascagoula, 1978; nursing instr. Miss. Gulf Coast Community Coll.-Jackson County Campus, Gautier, 1981-84, chair ADN program, 1984—2004, ADN divsn. chair, 2004—08. Col. USAFR, ret. Mem. NOADN, Nat. League Nursing, Sigma Theta Tau, Phi Kappa Phi.

CASPER, MARC NOLAN, scientific instrument company executive; b. NYC, Mar. 10, 1968; s. Herman and Betty Casper. BA, Wesleyan U., 1990; MBA, Harvard U., 1995. Assoc. cons. Bain & Co., Inc., Boston, 1990-92, strategy cons., 1992—93; assoc. Bain Capital, Boston, 1995-96; pres., Americas Dade Behring Inc., Deerfield, Ill., 1997—2000; pres., CEO Kendro Lab. Products, Newton, Conn., 2000—01; pres., life & lab. sciences Thermo Electron Corp. (subs. of Thermo Fisher Scientific Inc.), 2001—05; sr. v.p. Thermo Electron Corp. (subs. of Thermo Fisher Scientific Inc.), 2003, exec. v.p., 2006—07; pres. Analytical Technologies Group (subs. of Thermo Fisher Scientific Inc.), 2007—09; exec. v.p. Thermo Fisher Scientific, Inc., Waltham, Mass., 2007—08, exec. v.p., COO, 2008—09, pres., CEO, 2009—. Bd. dirs. Zimmer, Inc., 2009—. Mem. Phi Beta Kappa. Office: Thermo Fisher Scientific 81 Wyman St Waltham MA 02454 *

CASPER, MONICA J., sociologist, educator; b. Chgo., Sept. 1, 1966; BA, U. Chgo., 1988; PhD, U. Calif., San Francisco, 1995. Asst. prof. sociology U. Calif., Santa Cruz, 1996—2000, assoc. prof., 2000—04; exec. dir. Intersex Soc. N.America, 2003; assoc. prof. sociology Vanderbilt U., 2004—08, dir. women, gender studies; prof. humanities, arts, cultural studies divsn. Ariz. State U., 2008—. Gen. editor NYU Press, Biopolitics Book Series, 2009; editl. collective Feminist Wire, 2011. Mem.: Soc. Study Social Problems (C. Wright Mills award), Am. Studies Assn., Am. Sociol. Assn. Avocations: creative writing, hiking. Office: PO Box 37100 Phoenix AZ 85069-7100 Office Fax: 602-543-3006. Business E-Mail: monica.casper@asu.edu.

CASSCELLS, SAMUEL WARD, III, cardiologist, educator, former federal agency administrator; b. Wilmington, Del., Mar. 18, 1952; s. Samuel Ward and Oleda (Dyson) C.; m. Roxanne Bell, Feb. 10, 1990; children: Sam, Henry, Lillian. BS cum laude, Yale U., 1974; MD magna cum laude, Harvard U., 1979. Intern then resident Beth Israel Hosp., Boston, 1979-82; cardiology fellow Mass. Gen. Hosp., Boston, 1982-85; Kaiser fellow clin. epidemiology Brigham and Women's Hosp. and Harvard Sch. Pub. Health, 1984-85; rsch. fellow Nat. Heart, Lung, and Blood Inst., Bethesda, Md., 1985-91; vis. scientist Scripps Inst. Medicine and Sci., LaJolla, Calif., 1991-92; chief cardiology, T.R. and M. O'Driscoll Levy prof. medicine U. Tex. Med. Sch., Houston, 1994-2000; John E. Tyson Disting. prof. medicine and public health U. Tex. Health Sciences Ctr., Houston, 2000—, v.p. biotech., 2000—02; asst. sec. for health affairs US Dept. Def., Washington, 2007—09. Chief cardiology Hermann Hosp., Houston, 1994-2001; dir. clin. rsch. Tex. Heart Inst., 2004—; co-founder Prizm Pharms., La Jolla, 1992—, Selective Genetics, La Jolla, Volcano Found., Sacramento, Calif., LifeSentry Inc., Houston, Claritas Capital, Nashville; founder Pres. Bush Ctr. Cardiovasc. Health, Houston, Alliance for Nano Health; bd. dirs. Lifeline Systems; adv. bd. U. Houston Law Ctr. Health Law and Policy Inst., 1999-2001; adv. Bio Houston; adv. bd. GE, Spectrocell, Lifeline Sys. Mem. editl. bd. Circulation, 1992—, Am. Jour. Cardiology, 1992—, Tex. Heart Inst. Jour., 1992—, Vascular Medicine, 1995-2001, U.T. Lifetime Newsletter, 1996—, Jour. Royal Soc. Medicine 1999—, Heart Watch, 2001--; contbr. articles to profl. jours. Mem. Bush-Cheney HHS Transition Adv. Com., 2001—; pres. George W. Bush Healthcare Adv. Com., 2001—; mayor's adv. com. to Med. Strike Force, 2001--; task force on bioterrorism Ctr. for Strategic and Internat. Studies, 2001--; bd. dirs. CapCURE; prostate cancer adv. bd. M.D. Anderson Cancer Ctr.; founder Alliance for Nano Health, Houston, 2004. Decorated Meritorious Svc. medal U.S. Army, Joint Svc. Commendation medal; recipient First Harvard/CIMIT award for med. innovation, 2001, Gen. Maxwell Thurman award, Am. Telemedicine Assn., 2004; named Hero of the Flood, Meml. Hermann Healthcare Sys., Houston, 2002. Mem.: Am. Clin. and Climatological Assn., Assn. Profs. Cardiology (bd. dirs.), Assn. Univ. Cardiologists, Am. Coll. Cardiology, Houston Cardiology Soc. (pres. 1995—96), Soc. Vascular Biol. Medicine (bd. dirs. 1997—2000), Am. Heart Assn. (Houston bd. dirs. 1992—2001), Met. Club, Met. Club (Washington), Sankaty Head Golf Club, The Siasconset Casino Assn., The Dancers, Tejas Breakfast Club, Bidermann Golf Club, Coronado Club, Houston Country Club, City Tavern Club, Farmington Country Club, Vicmead Hunt Club, Union Boat Club, Chevy Chase Club. Office: U Tex Med Sch Health Sci Ctr 7000 Fannin St Houston TX 77030

CASSEL, CHRISTINE KAREN, physician; b. Mpls., Sept. 14, 1945; d. Charles Moore and Virginia Julia (Anderson) Cassel. BA, U. Chgo., 1967; MD, U. Mass., 1979. Diplomate Am. Bd. Internal Medicine (chmn. 1998-99). Intern, resident in internal medicine Children's Hosp., San Francisco, 1976—78; fellow in bioethics Inst. Health Policy Studies, U. Calif., San Francisco, 1978—79; fellow geriatrics Portland VA Hosp., Oreg., 1979—81; asst. prof. medicine and public health U. Oreg. Health Scis. U., 1981—83; asst. prof. geriatrics and medicine Mt. Sinai Med. Ctr., NYC, 1983—84; prof. medicine, prof. pub. policy U. Chgo., 1989—95, chief gen. internal medicine, 1985—95; chmn. and prof. geriatrics and medicine Mt. Sinai, 1995—2002; dean Sch. Medicine Oreg. Heatlh and Sci. U., 2002—03; pres., CEO Am. Bd. Internal Medicine and ABIM Found., 2003—. Adj. prof. medicine U. Pa., 2004—; mem. Pres.'s Coun. Advisors on Sci. and Tech. (PCAST), 2009—. Author: Ethical Dimensions in the Health Professions, 1981, 2nd edit., 1993, Geriatric Medicine: Principles and Practice, 1984, 4th edit., 2003, Nuclear Weapons and Nuclear War: A Sourcebook for Health Professionals, 1984, Geriatric Medicine, A Practical Guide to Aging, 1997, Medicine Matters: What Geriatric Medicine Can Teach American Health Care, 2005. Bd. dirs. Greenwall Found., 1999—2004, chmn., 1999—2004. Henry J. Kaiser Family Found. faculty scholar, 1982—85, Hastings Ctr. fellow. Master ACP (regent 1989—98, pres. 1996—97); fellow: Am. Geriatrics Soc.; mem.: Am. Soc. Law and Medicine (bd. dirs. 1988—94), Soc. Health and Human Values (pres. 1986), Physicians for Social Responsibility (dir. 1983—86, pres. 1988—89), Inst. of Medicine (coun. 2002—). Office: American Board Internal Medicine Ste 1700 510 Walnut St Philadelphia PA 19106-3699 Business E-Mail: ccassel@abim.org. *

CASSELBRANT, MARGARETHA, otolaryngologist; MD, U. Lund, 1973. Diplomate Am. Bd. Otolaryngology. Resident Univ. of Lund, 1978, Malmo Gen. Hosp., Malmo, Sweden; fellow Univ. of Pitts., 1982; hosp. affiliation include/s UPMC Presbyterian South Surgery Ctr., Children's Hosp. of Pitts. of UPMC, UPMC Children's Surgery Ctrs.; chief divsn. pediatric otolaryngology Children's Hosp. of Pitts. of UPMC; prof. pediatric otolaryngology Univ. of Pitts. Mem. Am. Acad. of Otolaryngology-Head and Neck Surgery Found. (AAO-HNS). Named Best Doctor, 2003—04, 2005—06, 2007—08, 2009—10; named one of Top Doctors, Pitts. Mag., 2008, 2009, 2010. Mem.: European Soc. for Pediatric Otorhinolaryngology, Assn. for Rsch. in Otolaryngology, Am. Soc. of Pediatric Otolaryngology, Am. Laryngological, Rhinological and Otological Soc. Office: Childrens Hospital of Pittsburgh of UPMC 4401 Penn Ave Fl 3 Pittsburgh PA 15224 Office Phone: 412-692-5460. Office Fax: 412-692-5701. E-mail: margaretha.casselbrant@chp.edu.

CASSELL, CAROL ANNE, health facility administrator; b. Buffalo, Apr. 25, 1936; BA, U. N.Mex., 1970, PhD in Health Edn., 1980. Diplomate Am. Bd. Sexology. Project dir., teen pregnancy prevention Ctr. Disease Control and Prevention, 1996—2004; dir. Critical Pathways Consulting, 2005—. Bd. dirs. Nat. Campaign Prevent Teen and Unplanned Pregnancy, 1998—2003, Healthy Teen Network, 2001—03. Recipient Lifetime Achievements award, Nat. Orgn. Adolescent Pregnancy Prevention and Parenting; named one of Rschr. of Yr., Healthy Teen Network, 2009. Fellow: Am. Bd. Sexology; mem.: Soc. Sci. Study Sexuality (Pub. Svc. award 2010). Avocation: art. Home: 720-14 Tramway Ln Albuquerque NM 87122 Personal E-mail: carolmcassell@yahoo.com.

CASSELL, ERIC JONATHAN, physician; b. NYC, Aug. 29, 1928; s. Hyman William and Anne (Lake) Goldstein; m. Joan M. Fishman, Oct. 17, 1957 (div. 1987); children: Justine, Stephen; m. Patricia M. Owens, May 26, 1990. BA, Queens Coll., 1950; MA, Columbia U., 1950; MD, NYU, 1954; DIIL (hon.), Med. Coll. Pa., 1985. Intern 3rd med. divsn. Bellevue Hosp., NYC, 1954—55, asst. resident 3rd med. divsn., 1955—56, physician 3rd, 4th med. divsn., 1965—66; USPHS trainee in infectious diseases Weill Med. Coll., Cornell U., NYC, 1959—61; clin. prof. pub. health Cornell U., NYC, 1971—2007; attending physician French Hosp., NYC, 1961—74; assoc. attending physician Mt. Sinai (N.Y.) Hosp., 1966—71; assoc. dir. ambulatory care Cmty. Med., Mt. Sinai, 1966—68; attending physician N.Y. Presbyn. Hosp., 1984—; asst. resident 3d med. divsn. Bellevue Hosp., NYC, 1958—59; prof. Pub. Health Emeritus, 2007—; adj. prof. medicine McGill U., 2006. Clin. assoc. prof. medicine NYU, 1965—66, Mt. Sinai Hosp., 1966—71; bd. dirs. Hasting's Ctr., Garrison, NY, 1973—2006; commr. Nat. Bioethics Adv. Commn., 1997—2001; vis. investigator Meml. Sloan Kettering Cancer Ctr., 1999—2008; adj. prof. medicine McGill U., Montreal, Canada,

2005—. Author: Healer's Art, 1976, Place of Humanities in Medicine, 1984, Talking with Patients (2 vols.), 1985, The Nature of Suffering, 1991, 2d edit., 2004, Doctoring: The Nature of Primary Care Medicine, 1997; editor: Changing Values in Medicine, 1979. Capt. M.C. US Army, 1956—58. Master: ACP; fellow: N.Y. Acad. Medicine; mem.: Inst. of Medicine of NAS. Democrat. Jewish. Avocations: woodworking, metalworking. Personal E-mail: eric@ericcassell.com.

CASSELL, GAIL HOUSTON, microbiologist, researcher; b. Goodwater, Ala., Jan. 25, 1946; m. Ralph H. Cassell; 1 child, Cynthia. BS in Bacteriology, U. Ala., 1969, MS in Microbiology, 1971, PhD in Microbiology, 1973; DSc (hon.), Thomas Jefferson U., 1996. From asst. prof. to prof. U. Ala., Birmingham, 1975-87, prof., chmn. Dept. of Microbiology, 1987—, from asst. prof. to prof., Dept. Comparative Medicine, 1973-86, prof., 1986—, McCauley Endowed Professorship, 1994; v.p. sci. affairs Eli Lilly and Co., Indianapolis, disting. Lilly rsch. scholar infectious diseases. Sr. scientist Cystic Fibrosis Ctr., U. Ala. at Birmingham, 1981, Multipurpose Arthritis Ctr., 1977, Comprehensive Cancer Ctr., 1976-89; dir. Mycoplasma Diagnostic Lab., 1982; vis. prof. MIT, 1985, U. Bordeaux II, France, 1983; vis. scientist MRC Cellular Immunology Unit, Oxford U., Eng., 1983, Trudeau Inst., Saranac Lake, N.Y., 1975-77; basic scientist vis. prof. Dept. Ob-gyn., Duke U., 1989; mem. various study seats. Co-author numerous book chpts.; mem. editorial bd. European Jour. Epidemiology, 1989, Jour. Clin. Microbiology, 1987-90, Infection and Immunity, 1987; contbr. articles to Jour. Med. Sci. and other profl. jours. Bd. dirs. Rsch. Am. Recipient President's Achievement award, U. Ala., Birmingham, 1995, Nathan B. Brewer Sci. Achievement award in Comparative Medicine. Mem. NAS, NIH (chmn, adv. coun. to the dir., NIAID adv. coun.), Nat. Ctr. for Infectious Disease (bd. sci. councilors), Inst. Medicine (coun. mem.), Am. Soc. Microbiology (former pres.), US-Japan Coop. Med. Sci. Program (mem. 1996-). Achievements include research in areas of lung disease and microbiology. Office: Dept Microbiology Univ Ala Bbrb Rm 27611 Birmingham AL 35294-0001

CASSELL, JACKIE ANNE, epidemiologist, educator; BA in Med. Scis. and English Lit., U. Cambridge, 1985; BM BCh in Clin. Medicine, U. Oxford, 1988; BA in Philosophy, U. Sussex, 1992; diploma in Family Planning, Royal Coll. Obstetricians and Gynaecologists, 1992; MSc in Epidemiology, London Sch. Hygiene and Tropical Medicine, 1999; diploma in Genitourinary Medicine, Royal Soc. Apothecaries, 1994; MD, U. Cambridge, 2008. Lic. physician Faculty Pub. Health, 2004, physician in genitourinary medicine 2006. Intern Royal Free Hosp., London, 1992—96; resident Mortimer Market Ctr., U. Coll., London, 1996—2002, 2005—; with in epidemiology and pub. health U. Coll. London, 2002—06; sr. lectr. Brighton and Sussex Med. Sch., 2006—07; prof. primary care epidemiology, 2007—. Cons. in field. Contbr. articles to profl. jours. Mem., ind. sci. adv. com. Gen. Practice Rsch. Database, 2006—; mem. sci. com. ISSTDR Conf., 2009; adviser to nat. pilots of chlamydia screening Dept. of Health, Eng., United Kingdom, 2001—02, mem. of sexual health data group and bd. for common dataset for sexual health, 2003; oral evidence on sexual health, on behalf of brit. med. assn. Select Com. of the Ho. of Commons, London, United Kingdom, 2001—01. Grantee, Med. Rsch. Coun. U.K., 2003—, 2004, 2005, 2006, Wellcome Trust, 2008, Nat. Inst. Health Rsch., 2010; fellow, Wellcome Trust, 1998—2002, 2008. Fellow: Faculty Pub. Health, Royal Coll. Physicians, Brit. HIV Assn., Brit. Assn. Sexual Health and HIV (rep. BCCG 2004—). Achievements include research in the impact of health system factors on the transmission and care of HIV and sexually transmitted infections; methods for the use and potential of electronic patient records. Office: U Brighton Brighton and Sussex Med Sch Mayfield House BN1 9PH Falmer Brighton England Office Fax: 01273644440. Business E-Mail: j.cassell@bsms.ac.uk.

CASSIDY, JAMES PATRICK, priest, university chancellor, health care administrator; b. Mt. Vernon, NY, May 10, 1925; s. Patrick J. and Helen (Curran) C. BA, St. Joseph's Sem. & Coll., Yonkers, NY, 1950; PhD, Fordham U., 1963. Ordained priest Roman Cath. Ch., 1951; lic. psychologist, NY, Conn., NJ. Parish priest Archdiocese NY, NYC, 1951-64, marriage counselor family life bur., 1957-65, dir. Cana Confs., 1960-64, dir. family cons. svcs., 1965-72, exec. dir. dept. health and hosps., 1972—; guidance counselor St. Barnabas HS, Bronx, 1954-57; intern clin. psychology St. Vincent's Hosp., NYC, 1964-65, sr. clin. psychologist, 1965-72; chancellor NY Med. Coll., Valhalla, 1987-92; cons. Pontifical Coun. for Health Care, Vatican City, 1990—; pres. Internat. Assn. Cath. Health Care Instns., Vatican City, 1992—; staff psychologist Pontifical N.Am. Coll., 2000—03. Adj. prof. Fordham U., Bronx, 1965-66; assoc. prof. St. John's U., Jamaica, NY, 1965-75, dir. pastoral counseling, 1969-75. Mem. task force NYC Planning Commn., 1973; mem. adv. coun. on youth drug and alcohol problems NYC Dept. Mental Health, 1974; mem. steering com.on alcoholism Gov. of NY, NYC, 1976; mem. Assn. for a Better NY, 1985, Cath. Charities, USA; mem. adv. coun. health com. NY State Senate, 1985. Recipient Terence Cardinal Cooke award, NY Med. Coll., 1985, Gran Ofcl. award, Orden Heraldica Cristobal Colon, Dominical Republic, 1988; named to Knights of Malta, 1988. Fellow NY Acad. Medicine; mem. APHA, Am. Hosp. Assn., NY State Psychol. Assn., NY Athletic Club, Larchmont Shore Club. Avocations: photography, reading, boating. Home: PO Box 533 Ridgefield CT 06877 Office: St Patrick's Cathedral 460 Madison Ave New York NY 10022 Office Phone: 212-753-2261 ext. 256. Personal E-mail: monsjcassidy@juno.com.

CASSIMATIS, EMMANUEL G., educational association administrator, psychiatrist, educator; b. Athens, Greece, Oct. 10, 1944; came to U.S., 1963; s. George P. and Maria (Giannioti) C.; m. Patricia G. Cutler, Dec. 26, 1968; children: Dimitri, Maro. BA in Biology, U. Chgo., 1967; MD, Harvard U., 1971; diploma in psychoanalysis, Washington Psychoanalytic Inst, 1986. Diplomate Am. Bd. Psychiatry and Neurology. Commd. 2d lt. U.S. Army, 1972, advanced through grades to col., 1986; chief dept. psychiatry Kenner Army Hosp., Ft. Lee, Va., 1975-76; asst. chief in-patient psychiatry Walter Reed Army Med. Ctr., Washington, 1976-78, dir. psychiat. edn., 1978-83, chief outpatient psychiatry, 1982-86; chief dept. psychiatry U.S. Army Hosp., Berlin, 1986-88; dep. comdr. clin. svcs. Frankfurt (Fed. Republic of Germany) Army Regional Med. Ctr., 1988-91; psychiatry cons. Office Surgeon Gen., U.S. Army, Washington, 1991-92, chief grad. med. edn., 1992-93, chief med. edn. divsn., 1993-95; assoc. dean clin. affairs and prof. psychiatry F. Edward Hebert Sch. Medicine, Bethesda, Md., 1995—2009; v.p. internal affairs Uniformed Svcs. U. Health Scis., 1995—2009; pres., CEO Ednl. Commn. Fgn. Med. Graduates, Phila., 2009—. Chmn. Found. Advancement Internat. Med. Edn. and Rsch., 2009—. Mem. AMA (coun. on med. edn.), Am. Psychiat. Assn., Am. Acad. Psychoanalysis and Dynamic Psychiatry, Assn. Mil. Surgeon of U.S., Washington Psychoanalytic Soc., Soc. of Med. Cons. to the Armed Forces. Office: Uniformed Svcs U Health Sch Medicine Rm A1008 4301 Jones Bridge Rd Bethesda MD 20814-4712 also: ECFMG 3624 Market St Philadelphia PA 19104-2685 *

CASSINELLO, JAVIER GUILLERMO, oncologist, researcher; b. La Coruña, Spain, May 28, 1956; s. Guillermo Cassinello and Nachi Espinosa; children: Rodrigo Guillermo, Victoria. MD, Complutense U., Madrid, 1979. Lic. med. oncologist Ednl. Min., 1990. Attending physician Hosp. 12 de Octubre, Madrid, 1990—92, Hosp. Miguel Servet, Zaragoza, Spain, 1992—96; head dept. med. oncology Univ. Hosp., Guadalajara, Spain, 1996—. Contbr. articles to profl. jours. Scholar med. oncology scholar, 1992, 2002. Mem.: Med. Oncology Orgn. (madrid 1992—2003). Home: Calle General Moscardo 28 28020 Madrid Spain Personal E-mail: jacaes@sescam.jccm.es.

CASSIS, TAMI BUSS, dermatologist, educator; BS in Psychology, U. Wis., 1995; MD, U. Louisville, 2001. Diplomate Am. Bd. Dermatology. Cosmetic dermatology intern The Dermatology and Aesthetic Ctr., Boca Raton, Fla., 2004; intern internal medicine Univ. of Louisville, Ky., 2002, resident divsn. dermatology Ky., 2005, asst. clin. prof., dept. dermatology Ky., 2005—; vol. faculty, dept. dermatology Veterans Adminstrn. Hosp., 2005—; hosp. affiliations include Advanced Dermatology and Dermaesthetics of Louisville, Ky., 2005—, Cassis Dermatology and Aesthetics Ctr., Ky., 2008—. Named one of 40 Under 40, Bus. First, 2006, Top Doc, Louisville Mag., 2009; grantee Wilds Found. Rsch. Fellowship, 1994, Golden Key Honor Soc., 1994, Psi Chi Psychology Nat. Honor Soc., 1994, Order of Omega Nat. Honor Soc., 1995, Hilldale Found. Fellowship, 1994, Alpha Omega Alpha Honor Soc., 2001. Mem.: Women's Dermatologic Soc. (bd. dirs. 2007, bus. interest group task force 2009, young physicians task force 2009, membership com. 2011), Am. Soc. of Dermatologic Surgery, Ky. Med. Assn. (legis. com. 2007, cancer com. 2007), Med. Dermatologic Soc. (edn. work grou 2006), Am. Chem. Soc., Am. Soc. of Laser Medicine, Gamma Phi Beta Alumni Assn. Office: Cassis Dermatology and Aesthetics Center Ste 100 9301 Dayflower St Prospect KY 40059 Office Phone: 502-326-8588. Office Fax: 502-326-8589.

CASSMAN, MARVIN, biochemist; b. Chgo., Apr. 4, 1936; s. Harry and Anna (Singer) C.; m. Alice M. Baker, June 24, 1972. BA, U. Chgo., 1954, BS, 1957, MS, 1959; PhD, Albert Einstein Coll. Medicine, 1965. Postdoctoral fellow U. Calif., Berkeley, 1965-67, asst. prof. Santa Barbara, 1967-75; adminstr. Nat. Inst. Gen. Med. Sci. NIH, Bethesda, Md., 1975-78, sect. chief, 1978-84, program dir., 1984-89, dep. dir., 1989-93, acting dir., 1993-96, dir., 1996—2001; exec. dir. Inst. for Quantitative Biomedical Rsch., U. Calif., San Francisco, 2001—. Mem. staff subcom. in sci., rsch. and tech. U.S Ho. of Reps., Washington, 1982-83; sr. policy analyst Office Sci. and Tech. Policy The White House, Washington, 1985-86. Recipient Sr. Exec. Svc. award USPHS, 1987, Pres. Meritorious award, 1991. Jewish. Avocations: music, racquetball. Office: U Calif 513 Parnassus Ave Rm 5115 San Francisco CA 94143-0400 Home: 875 Haight St San Francisco CA 94117-3216

CASSO, RAMIRO RAUL, physician, academic administrator; b. Laredo, Tex., Aug. 4, 1922; s. Francisco Margarito and Josefa (Villarreal) C.; m. Emma Laurel, July 18, 1949; children: Thelma Casso Morales, Lydia Casso Tummel, Sylvia Casso, Daniel, David BSME, Tex. A&M U., College Station, 1943; BA in Chemistry, Baylor U., Waco, Tex., 1952; MD, U. Tex., Southwestern Med. Sch., Dallas, 1956. Diplomate Am. Bd. Family Practice. Hydraulic engr. Internat. Boundary and Water Commn., Laredo, 1948-50; tchr. math. Martin HS, Laredo, 1946—48; med. intern Robert B. Green Hosp., San Antonio, 1956-57; pvt. family med. practice McAllen, Tex., 1957—95; v.p. instnl. advancement South Tex. CC Hidalgo-Starr County CC Dist., McAllen, 1995—2002. Adj. prof. Tex. A&M U. Health Sci. Ctr., 1999-2004; bd. dirs. McAllen Med. Ctr. Hosp., 1975-85; founder, bd. dirs. Nuestra Clinica del Valle, 1975-85; mem. nat. adv. bd. health rsch. facilities NIH, Washington, 1964-67; participant White House Confs. on Food and Food Nutrition and Health, Washington, 1965-69; spkr. on pub. health and primary care issues pertaining to South Tex. and US-Mex. borderlands; presenter Hispanic health issues position Tex. Minority Health Conf., Houston, 1999 Author: Great Minds of the 21st Century, 2010. Mem. McAllen Ind. Sch. Dist. Sch. Bd., 1959-65; mem., v.p. Tex. Bd. Health, Austin, 1977-81, 91-97; mem. Texas Human (Employment) Rights Commn., Austin, 1983-87; established charity clinic for farm workers United Farmworkers, McAllen, 1968; founded Nuestra Clin. Hidalgo County, Tex., 1974; bd. dirs. Area Health Edn. Ctr., 1997-98; pres., bd. dirs. El Milagro Clinic Bd., 1998—; founder El Milagro Charity Primary Care Clinic, McAllen, Tex., 1995. Capt. anti-aircraft arty. US Army, 1943-46 Named McAllen Man of Yr., McAllen C. of C., 1996, Notable Rio Grande Valley Hispanic, U. Tex.-PanAm., Edinburg, 1999, 100 Outstanding Hispanic-Ams. in Tex. in 20th Century Latino Monthly Mag., 2000, Star Supporter of Edn., South Tex. Coll., 2006; recipient Bishop Medeiros Golden Deeds award Tex. AFL-CIO and United Farmworkers, 1970, yearly award Hidalgo County Women's Polit. Caucus, 1991, Disting. Citizen award League United L.Am. Citizens, 1997, Living Legend award South Tex. C.C., 2002, Golden Trowel Masonic award City of Rio Grande and McAllen Tex. Lodges, 2003; Dr. Ramiro R. Casso S.T.C.C. Nursing and Allied Health Ctr. bldg. named in his honor, 2001. Fellow Am. Acad. Family Physicians; mem. AMA (life), Tex. Med. Assn. (life). Democrat. Baptist. Avocations: travel, reading, hunting, fishing. Office: El Milagro Clinic 901 E Vermont St Mcallen TX 78501 Home: 3400 West Pecan Mcallen TX 78501 Home Phone: 956-686-8012. Home Fax: 956-686-5515.

CASSON, ALAN GRAHAM, thoracic surgeon, researcher; b. Birmingham, Eng., Apr. 22, 1958; arrived in Can., 1981; m. Sharon Margaret Coffey; 1 child, Angela. MB ChB, Manchester U., Eng., 1981; MSc, Meml. U., St. John's, Nfld., Can., 1986. Asst. prof. surgery and oncology U. Western Ont., Canada, 1991-93; asst. prof. surgery, program dir. thoracic surgery U. Toronto, Canada, 1994-97; prof. thoracic surgery U. of Warwick, England, 1997-98; cons. thoracic surgery Heartlands Hosp., Birmingham, England, 1997-98; prof. surgery, head divsn. thoracic surgery Dalhousie U., Halifax, N.S., Canada, 1998—2006; F. H. Wigmore prof. and head dept. surgery Royal U. Hosp., U. Sask., Saskatoon, Canada, 2006—. Author: Oncogene Activation in Esophageal Cancer, 1992, Key Topics in Thoracic Surgery, 1999, Molecular Biology of Cancer, 2004; asst. editor Cancer Detection and Prevention; mem. editl. bd. Jour. Surg. Oncology, Diseases of the Esophagus; contbr. chpts. to surg. textbooks and articles to profl. jours. Fellow ACS, Royal Coll. Surgeons Can., Am. Coll. Chest Physicians (Young Investigator award 1993); mem. Internat. Soc. for Diseases of the Esophagus, Am. Assn. for Thoracic Surgery, Am. Assn. Cancer Rsch., Soc. Thoracic Surgeons, World Ortn. Specialized Studies Diseases Esophagus (mem. permanent sci. com.). Avocations: fly fishing, squash, sailing. Office: Royal University Hosp Dept Surgery 103 Hosp Dr Rm 2646 Saskatoon S7N 0W8 Canada Home Phone: 902-479-7091; Office Phone: 306-966-8641.

CASTELE, THEODORE JOHN, radiologist; b. New Castle, Pa., Feb. 1, 1928; s. Theodore Robert and Anne Mercedes (McNavish) C.; m. Jean Marie Willse, Oct. 20, 1951; children: Robert, Ann Marie, Richard, Mary Kathryn, Thomas, Daniel, John. BS, Case Western Res. U., 1951, MD, 1957. Diplomate Am. Bd. Radiology, 1962. Intern then resident U. Hosps. Cleve., 1957-61, fellow, 1961-62; dir. of radiology Luth. Med. Ctr., Cleve., 1968-75, 77-89, chief of staff, 1975-81; pres. Med. Ctr. Radiologists, Inc., Cleve., 1978-95; v.p. med. and copr. devel. Health Cleve. Inc., 1989-91; chmn. Lakeshore Radiology Inc., Cleve., 1991-96, emeritus chmn., 1996—; chmn. Cmty. West Found(formerly Fairveiw Lutheran Hosp. Found.), 2002—09, chmn. emeritus, 2009—. Med. editor sta. WEWS-TV-ABC, Cleve., 1975-99; chmn. bd. Med. Cons. Imaging Co., Cleve., 1981-97; asst. clin. prof. radiology Case Western Res. U., chmn. dean's tech. coun. Sch. Medicine, 1996—, chmn. vis. com. Cleve. Health Scis. Libr., chmn. campaign for future of acad. medicine, 1998—. Exec. editor Prime mag., 2000—. Chmn. Southwestern dist. Greater Cleve. coun. Boy Scouts Am., 1969, 73; mem. bd. med. cons. Cleve. Police Dept., pres., 1988-90; trustee Comty. Dialysis Ctr., chmn. 1997-99, chmn. emeritus, 2000—; active Luth. Med. Ctr. Found., chmn. bd. trustees, 1969-75, pres., 1988-90; trustee Case Western Res. U., Blue Cross/Blue Shield Ohio, Greater Cleve. Hosp. Assn., Fairview Health, Luth. Med. Ctr., 1975-80, Fairview Hosp. Found.; bd. trustees Fairview Luth. Hosp. Found., 1999—, No. Ohio Lung Assn.; chmn. Health Mus. Cleve., 1996—, Humility of Mary Healthcare Sys., 1995-98; dir. Coun. Pub. Reps. for NIH, 1999-2001. With USN, 1946-47. Recipient Order of Merit award Boy Scouts Am., 1971, Silver Beaver award, 1972, Nat. Disting. Eagle Scout award, 1984, Frances Payne Bolton Sch. of Nursing Disting. Svc. award, 1990, Outstanding Philanthropist award Nat. Soc. of Fundraising Execs., 1991, Alumnus of the Yr. award Dept. Radiology of Case Western Res. U., 1996, LMC Found. Women's Bd. award, 1996, Luth. Hosp. award Fairview Health Sys. Bd., 1996, Midwest Nursing Rsch. Soc. Media award, 1998, Lamplighter Humanitarian award 2001; named Knight of the Equestrian, Order of the Holy Sepulchre of Jerusalem, 1993—; recipient Magis award St. Ignatius H.S.; named to Med. Hall of Fame, Case Western Res. U., Cleve. Mag., 1999, No. Ohio Italian-Am. Found., 1999, Art Caring award, Cmty. West Found., 2007, Mother Madelains award, 2009 Fellow Am. Coll. Radiology; mem. AMA (Physician Spkr. Gold award 1978, 80, Silver 1979, Bronze 1978, Benjamin Rush award 1989, Golden Achievement award Golden Age Ctrs., 1996, chmn. Ohio del. 1987-96), Ohio State Med. Assn. (5th dist. councilor 1977-79, Spl. award 1979, Disting. Svc. award 1997), Cleve. Radiol. Soc. (pres. 1969-70), Cleve. Med. Libr. Assn. (pres. 1996, 97-98), Case Western Res. U. Med. Alumni Assn. (pres. 1971-72, 91-92, Disting. Svc. award 1987, Spl. Trustees award 1997, Univ. medal 1998), Cleve. Acad. Medicine (pres. 1974-75, Disting. Mem. award 1990, Disting. Svc. award 1984, Spl. Honor award and portrait 1998), Ohio State Radiol. Soc. (Silver award 1990). Home: 18869 Canyon Rd Cleveland OH 44126-1703 Office: Case Western Reserve Univ Sch Medicine Cleveland OH 44106

CASTELL, DONALD OVERTON, gastroenterologist; b. Washington, Sept. 19, 1935; m. June Castell. MD, George Washington U., 1960. Diplomate Am. Bd. Internal Medicine. Intern U.S. Naval Hosp., Bethesda, Md., 1960—61, resident in medicine, 1962—65; fellow in gastroenterology Tufts U., 1967—69; gastroenterologist Allegheny Grad. Hosp., Phila.; prof. medicine Hahnemann U., Phila. Adj. prof. Temple U., Phila. Recipient Disting. Alumnus award, George Washington U., 1990. Mem.: ASCI, AFCR, ACP, Am. Gastroent. Assn. (pres. 1998—99, June and Donald O. Castell, MD, Esophageal Clin. Rsch. award named in his and his wife's honor 2000, Disting. Educator award 2001). Office: Medical University of South Carolina 25 Courtenay Dr ART 7100A Charleston SC 29425 Home: 187 Wentworth St Charleston SC 29401 Business E-Mail: castell@musc.edu. *

CASTELLANI, JOHN J., lobbyist; b. 1951; m. Terry Castellani. BS in Biology, Union Coll., Schenectady, NY, 1972. Environ. scientist, strategic planner Gen. Elec. Co.; v.p. resources and tech. Nat. Assn. Manufacturers, 1977—80; v.p. state, fed. and internat. govt. rels. TRW, Inc., 1980—92; exec. v.p. Tenneco, Inc., 1992—99; pres. Bus. Roundtable, 2001—10; pres., CEO Pharm. Rsch. & Manufacturers of America (PhRMA), Washington, 2010—. Roman Catholic. Office: PhRMA 950 F St NW Suite 300 Washington DC 20004 Office Phone: 202-835-3400. Office Fax: 202-835-3414. *

CASTELLANO, BARTOLOMEO V., otolaryngologist, educator; MD, Universidad Autonoma de Guadalajara, 1979. Diplomate Am. Bd. Otolaryngology. Resident in otolaryngology NYU Med. Ctr., 1981—84; fellow in plastic surgery Mt. Sinai Med. Ctr., 1984—85; asst. prof. otolaryngology NYU; otolaryngologist Mt. Sinai Med. Ctr. Office: Mount Sinai Medical Center 78 Todt Hill Rd Ste 204 Staten Island NY 10314-4528 Office Fax: 718-273-2626.

CASTELLANOS MALO, JUAN ARTURO, gastroenterology surgeon; b. Querétaro, Mex., Sept. 28, 1945; s. José Jesús Castellanos and Emma Malo Sautto; m. Maria Elena Hernández Muñoz, May 23, 1970; children: Maria Elena Castellanos, Juan Arturo Castellanos, Emma Castellanos. D in Surgery, Universidad Nacional Autonoma de México, 1976. Chief edn. Hosp. Gen. de Queretaro, Mexico, 1979—82, chief surgery, 1983—86, subdir., 1986—88; postgrad. chief med. faculty U. Autonoma de Queretaro, 1988—90; mem. state faculty com. trauma ACS, Chgo., 1998—. Cons. Com. Civil Protection, Secretaria de Salud del Edo. Queretaro, 1998—2004; med. dir. Enlace Medico Asistencia, Queretaro, 2005—. Author: (medical book) Intestinal Infections; co-author: Physiopathology Surgical of Digestive Apparatus, General Surgery, Test Review and Autorate Mexican Counsel of General Surgery; contbr. chapters to books. A.H. Robins grantee, Universidad de Guanajuato, 1970. Fellow: Internat. Coll. Surgerons (life), Asociacion Mexicana de Cirugia Endoscopica (life), Asociacion Mexicana de Gastroenterologia (life), Asociacion Mexicana de Cirugia Gen. (life), Am. Coll. Surgery (life). Roman Catholic. Avocation: travel. Home: Fuente de Trevi #602 Prados Campestre Querétaro 76190 Mexico Office: Juan A Castellanos Malo Bulevar Jardines de la Hacienda 76180 Queretaro QRO Mexico Office Fax: 442+1923038; Home Fax: 442+1923038. Personal E-mail: juancastellanos@hotmail.com.

CASTELLINO, RONALD AUGUSTUS DIETRICH, radiologist, educator; b. NYC, Feb. 18, 1938; s. Leonard Vincent and Henrietta Wilhelmina (Geffken) C.; m. Joyce Cuneo, Jan. 26, 1963; children: Jeffrey Charles, Robin Leonard, Anthony James. Student, Creighton U., Omaha, 1955-58, MD, 1962. Diplomate: Am. Bd. Radiology. Rotating intern Highland Alameda County Hosp., Oakland, Calif., 1962-63; USPHS/Peace Corps physician Brazil, 1963-65; resident in diagnostic radiology Stanford U. Hosp., 1965-68, chief resident, 1967-68; asst. prof. radiology Stanford U. Med. Sch., 1968-74, assoc. prof., 1974-81, prof., 1981-93, chief diagnostic oncologic radiology, 1970-89, chief CT body scanning, 1979-89, dir. div. diagnostic radiology and assoc. chmn. dept. radiology, 1981-86, acting chmn. dept. diagnostic radiology and nuclear medicine, 1986-89, prof. emeritus NYC, 1993—; chair dept. radiology, Carroll and Milton Petrie chair Meml. Sloan Kettering Cancer Ctr., NYC, 1990-98; prof. radiology Cornell Med. Sch., 1994-98, chief med. officer R-2 tech., 1998—2007, chief med. officer hologic, 2007—09. Mem. U.S. Cancer del., People's Republic China, 1977 Co-editor: Pediatric Oncologic Radiology, 1977; assoc. editor; Lymphology, 1973-97, Investigative Radiology, 1985-94, Academic Radiology, 1994-97, Radiology, 1986-94, Postgrad. Radiology, 1986-98; contbr. numerous rsch. papers to profl. jours., chpts. to books. Recipient T.F. Eckstrom Fund award, 1978, Guggenheim fellow, 1974-75 Mem.: N.Y. Acad. Medicine, N.Y. Roentgen Soc., Calif. Acad. Medicine, N.Am. Soc. Lymphology (charter), Soc. Cancer Imaging (charter), Soc. Thoracic Radiology (charter), Calif. Radiol. Soc., Calif. Med. Assn. (adv. panel sect. radiology 1972—89), Western Angiography Soc. (charter), Internat. Cancer Imaging Soc. (charter), Am. Roentgen Ray Soc., Soc. Cardiovascular and Interventional Radiology (charter), Radiol. Soc. N.Am., Assn. Univ. Radiologists (exec. com. 1981—85), Am. Coll. Radiology, Internat. Soc. Lymphology (exec. com. 1975—85), Am. Soc. Therapeutic Radiation Oncologists (hon.), Alpha Omega Alpha. Personal E-mail: rcastellino@sbcglobal.net

CASTELLINO, SHARON MARIE, pediatrician, educator; b. Ealing, Eng., Aug. 12, 1967; AB, Mt. Holyoke Coll., 1988; MD, Duke U., 1992. Assoc. prof. pediat. Wake Forest U. Sch. Medicine, 2004—. Recipient Young Investigator award, Lance Armstrong Found. Mem.: Am. Soc. Pediat. Oncology, Alpha Omega Alpha Med. Honor Soc. Avocations: painting, running. Office: Dept Pediat Medical Center Blvd Winston Salem NC 27157 Office Fax: 336-716-3010. Business E-Mail: scastell@wfubmc.edu.

CASTELLO, MANUEL ADOLFO, retired pediatrician, educator; b. Buenos Aires, Nov. 27, 1935; MD, Buenos Aires U., 1961; degree in Pediat., Neonatology and Child Health, Rome U., 1964. Dir. dept. pediat. Sapienza U. Rome, 1997—2008, prof., 1995—2008. Mem. sci. commn. ENI Found.; v.p. Commn. Regione Lazio; bd. mem. Sapienza Found., Nat. Inst. Migrants and Poverty. Recipient award, Nat. Acad. Medicine Rome, Ministry of Edn. Mem.: Internat. Acad. Pediat. (pres.). Avocation: swimming. Home: Via Antonio Pollaiolo 5 Rome I-00197 Italy Home Fax: 0039068070750. Business E-Mail: manuel.castello@uniroma1.it.

CASTER, ANDREW IAN, ophthalmologist; b. Coral Gables, Fla., Oct. 30, 1954; s. Milton and Carolyn (Teperson) C.; m. Jacqueline Jacobs, Oct. 15, 1989; children: Bryce, Jocelyn. AB, Harvard Coll., 1976; MD, Harvard Med. Sch., 1980. Diplomate Am. Bd. Ophthalmology; cert. Coun. Refractive Surgery Quality Assurance, 2000. Resident UCLA Jules Stein Eye Inst., LA, 1981-84; intern Wadsworth VA Hosp., Los Angeles, 1980-81; resident UCLA Jules Stein Eye Inst., Los Angeles, 1981-84; med. dir. Caster Eye Ctr., Beverly Hills, Calif., 1986—. Refractive surgery clin. adv. bd. Alcon Lab., 2003—07; clin. instr. ophthalmology UCLA Sch. Medicine; mem. med. staff Cedars-Sinai Med. Ctr. Author: Lasik: The Eye Laser Miracle; contbr. articles to profl. jour. Spl. advisor Everychild Found.; bd. dirs. Wonder or Reading. Recipient Alumni Rsch. award, Jules Stein Eye Inst. UCLA, 1994, Visx Star Surgeon award, 1998, 1999, 2000, 2001, Excellence Laser Vision Correction, Alcon Centurion, 2005; named Best Laser Eye Surgeon in LA, LA Mag., 1999; named one of Best Doctors in Am., 2005—06, 2007—, Castle Connolly Best Doctors, 2009—. Fellow ACS, Am. Acad. Ophthalmology, Calif. Assn. Ophthalmology (asst. v.p. 1992); mem. Am. Soc. Cataract and Refractive Surgeons, Internat. Soc Refractive Surgeons. Achievements include performing almost 30,000 vision correction treatments and participation in clinical trials in laser vision correction; patents for apparatus to induce relaxation and sleep in infants. Avocations: skiing, travel, photography, golf. Office: Caster Eye Ctr 9100 Wilshire Blvd Ste 265E Beverly Hills CA 90212-3482 Office Phone: 310-274-1221.

CASTIGLIA, PATRICIA ANNE THORSON, dean, nursing educator; b. Johnson City, NY; d. Theodore William and Isabelle Alice (Lane) Thorson; children: Karen, Patricia, Joseph. Diploma in Nursing, St. Vincent's Hosp., NYC, 1955; BSN, U. Buffalo, 1962; MSN, SUNY, Buffalo, 1965; PhD, SUNY, 1976. RN, N.Y.; cert. sch. nurse tchr., N.Y. Staff nurse Our Lady of Lourdes Hosp., Binghamton, NY, 1955-56; asst. head nurse Hosp. of the Good Shepherd, Syracuse, NY, 1956; sch. nurse tchr. North Collins Cen. Sch., North Collins, NY, 1956-62; clin. instr. SUNY, Buffalo, 1965-73; asst. prof. Niagara U., NY, 1976-77; from asst. prof. dir. ind. study to assoc. prof. SUNY, Buffalo, 1977-89, assoc. dean, 1983-89; acting dean, assoc. prof. SUNY at Buffalo Sch. Nursing, 1989; dean, prof. Coll. Nursing and Health Scis. U. Tex., El Paso, 1990—2002, asst. to pres. for health affairs, 2001—02, prof. emeritus, 2002—, SUNY, Buffalo, 1991—, cons. for higher edn. issues; interim assoc. dean U. Tex. Med. Br., Galveston, 2004—. Stockholder, treas. Profl. Nurse Consultants P.C., Buffalo; pediatric nurse practitioner Erie County Health Dept., Buffalo, 1982-89; vis. prof. SUNY Buffalo, 2003, 05, 06; dean emeritus Am. Assn. Colls. Nursing, 2003. Author chpts. to books; chair book of yr. awards Pediatric Nursing, 1986-88; manuscript reviewer Pediatric Nursing, Clin. Nurse Specialist, 1985—; editor: Jour. of Pediatric Health Care; co-editor: Child Health Care: Process and Practice, 1992; contbr. articles to MCN, Pediatric Nursing, Jour. Pediatric Health Care. Recipient Reach award YWCA, 1995, Charles and Shirley Leavell Endowed chair; named Nurse of Yr., Tex. Nurse Assn. 1996, Woman of the Yr. in Edn., El Paso Commn. for Women, 1996; grantee P.I. Kellogg Cmty. Partnership; SUNY Faculty Exch. scholar, Albany, 1985. Fellow Am. Acad. Nursing; mem. NAPNAP, N.Y. State Nurses Assn., Coalition of Nurse Practitioners, U. Buffalo Alumni Assn., St. Vincent's Alumni Assn., Rotary Internat., Sigma Theta Tau. Roman Catholic. Avocations: travel, piano, theater, reading, knitting. Personal E-mail: pcastiglia@adelphia.net.

CASTILLÓN, JUAN JOSÉ, psychiatrist, educator, psychologist; b. Lérida, Spain, June 2, 1945; s. Jesús Castillón and Maria Teresa Zazurca; m. Maribel Espezel, Oct. 13, 1973; children: Marcos, Maria Teresa. MBBCh, Spain U. Sys., 1968; grad., U. Barcelona, 1974; PhD in Medicine, Surgery, Autonomous U. Barcelona, 1986. Specialist in psychiatry Faculty Medicine, U. Barcelona, 1972. Internal med. resident, Psychiatry Svc. Hosp. Santa Cruz y San Pablo, Barcelona, 1970—72, prof. psychology, sch. nursing, 1970—72, asst. psychiatrist, 1972—83, psychiatrist head, outpatient psychiatry sect., 1983—; pvt. practice Barcelona, 1988—2010. Dir. doctoral thesis Dept. Psychiatry & Med. Psychology, Sch. Medicine, Autonomous U. Barcelona, practice asst. prof. psychology, 1972—75, assoc. prof., 1975—80, 1981—89, class asst. prof., 1980—81, lectr., coord. med. psychology, 1981—82, prof. psychiatry, 1986—2009, prof. psychiatry, doctoral course, 1989—93, assoc. prof., 1993—2009. Contbr. scientific papers to profl. jours. Mem. Ciutadans-Ciudadanos, Barcelona, 2005—10, Adv. Coun. Psychiat. Care and Mental Health Generalitat Catalunya, Barcelona, 1984—87, chmn. study group on liaison psychiatry, 1984—87, sec. study group psychiat. outpatient care, 1984—87. Avocation: tennis. Home: Rosellón 38 Alella 08328 Spain Office: Hosp Santa Cruz y San Pablo S Antonio Ma Claret 167 Barcelona 08019 Spain Office Fax: 932919186. Personal E-mail: 6059jcz@comb.cat. Business E-Mail: jcastillon@santpau.cat.

CASTLE, JOHN KROB, merchant banker; b. Cedar Rapids, Iowa, Dec. 22, 1940; s. Clyo F. and Emma (Krob) C.; m. Marianne Sherman, Sept. 20, 1969; children: William Sherman, John Sherman, James Sherman, David Alexander. SB, MIT, 1963; MBA with high distinction, Harvard U., 1965; LHD (hon.), NY Med. Coll., 1988, Canisius Coll., 2004. Assoc. Donaldson, Lufkin & Jenrette, Inc., NYC, 1965-68, v.p., 1968-71, exec. v.p., 1971-73, mng. dir., 1973-80, chief operating officer, 1979-84, pres., 1980-86, chief exec. officer, 1985-86; pres., chief exec. officer Branford Castle, Inc., NYC, 1986—; also founder, chmn., CEO Castle Harlan, Inc., NYC, 1987—, also founder, chmn., chief exec. officer, 1987; chmn., gen. ptnr. Castle Harlan Ptnrs. III, IV and V. Bd. dirs. Morton's Restaurant Group, Inc., Perkins & Marie Callender's; former dir. Equitable Life Assurance Soc. US, Sealed Air Corp. Author: Financial Executives Handbook: Dividend Policy and Equity Financing, 1970, The Strategy of Corporate Financing: Packaging a Merger of Acquisition, 1971, Acquisition and Merger Negotiation Strategy, 1971; co-pub. Castle Connolly Guides, 1991—, Parent's Helper, 1996. With NY Med. Coll., chmn. bd., 1979-90; life mem. corp. MIT, 1987-; mem. vis. com. dept. econs., dept. physics; trustee NY Presbyn. Hosp.; chmn. Rhodes Scholar Selection Com., NY State, 1986-90, Columbia-Presbyn. Health Sci. Adv. Coun.; endowed Castle Krob Fellowship for grad. study in econs. MIT, Castle Krob Fund for rsch. support at NY Med. Coll., Castle Krob Devel. Chair in econs. MIT, John K. Castle Publs. Fund on Ethics, Politics and Econs., Yale U. Mem. Links Club, Met. Club, Harvard Club, NY Yacht Club, Palm Beach Polo Club, Doubles Ltd., Club Collette, Sailfish Club, Sleepy Hollow Country Club. Home: 1095 N Ocean Blvd Palm Beach FL 33480-3230 Office: Castle Harlan Inc 150 E 58th St New York NY 10155-0002 Business E-Mail: jcastle@castleharlan.com.

CASTON, J(ESSE) DOUGLAS, retired medical educator; b. Ellenboro, NC, June 16, 1932, s. Lemuel Joseph and Myrtice Elizabeth (Vassey) C.; m. Mary Ann Keeter, June 1, 1958; children: John Andrew, Elizabeth Anne, Mary Susan. AB, Lenoir Rhyne Coll., 1954; MA, U. N.C., 1958; PhD, Brown U., 1961. Fellow Carnegie Instn., Washington, Balt., 1961-62; asst. prof. anatomy Case Western Res. U., Cleve., 1962-71, assoc. prof., 1971-76, prof., 1976-98, co-dir. Devel. Biology Ctr., 1971-77, prof. emeritus, 1999—. Cons. Diamond Shamrock Corp., Cleve., 1975-77; coordinator Core Acad. Program, Sch. Medicine, 1985-94. Patentee folate assay, methotrexate assay; contbr. numerous articles to sci. jours., 1962—. With AUS, 1954—56. Fellow H.W. Wilson, 1956; grantee USPHS, 1963—, Cancer Soc., 1963— Mem. Am. Chem. Soc., AAAS, Am. Soc. Zoologists and Developmental Biologists, Biophys. Soc., Soc. Cell Biology, Am. Assn. Anatomists Episcopalian. *

CASTRO, INÊS VIEIRA, pathologist; b. Belo Horizonte, Feb. 19, 1966; MD, UFMG, 1989; PhD, FMUSP, 2006. Head and neck pathologist Hospital das Clínicas FMUSP, 1993—2001; pathologist Ctr. Diagnóstico Campinas, 1999—. Mem.: Soc. Brasileira Patologia. Avocation: cooking. Office: Alameda dos Ibiscos 437 Campinas São Paulo 13101-644 Brazil Business E-Mail: i.v.castro@uol.com.br.

CASTRO, MARIA GRACIELA, medical educator, geneticist, researcher; b. Buenos Aires, Mar. 2, 1955; d. Nestor Antonio Castro and Maria Esther Rodriquez; m. Pedro Ricardo Lowenstein, Jan. 12, 1988; 1 child, Elijah David Lowenstein. BSc 1st class in Chemistry, Nat. U. La Plata, Argentina, 1979, MSc in Biochemistry, 1981, PhD in Biochemistry, 1986. Fogarty postdoctoral fellow Lab. Neurochemistry and Neuroimmunology Nat. Inst. Child Health and Human DEvel., NIH, Bethesda, Md., 1986—88; sr. rsch. fellow Lab. Molecular Endocrinology, dept. biochemistry and physiology U. Reading, England, 1988—90; lectr. neurosci., dept. physiology U. Wales Coll., Cardiff, 1991—95; sr. lectr. medicine Sch. Medicine U. Manchester, England, 1995—98, prof. molecular medicine, 1998—2001; prof. medicine UCLA, 2002—, prof. molecular pharmacology, 2004—. Lectr. dept. molecular and life scis. U. Abertay, Dundee, Scotland, 1991—92; dir. molecular medicine and gene therapy U. Manchester, England, 1996—; expert Women in Sci. Tech., Sheffield, 1996—; mem. neurosci. panel Wellcome Trust, 1999—; co-dir. dept. molecular medicine Cedars-Sinai Med. Ctr., 2001—, co-dir. bd. govs. Gene Therapeutics Rsch. Inst., 2001—; bd. govs. The Linda Tallen and David Paul Kane Found., 2003—; mem. Jonsson Comprehensive Cancer Ctr. UCLA, 2004—, mem. Brain Rsch. Inst., 2005—; chair in gene therapeutics Medallions Group, 2006—. Mem. editl. bd.: Jour. Endocrinology, Jour. Molecular Endocrinology, Current Gene Therapy, Gene Therapy, Pituitary, 2000, Neuro Molecular Medicine, 2001—; contbr. articles to profl. jours. Rsch. grantee, Brit. Heart Found., 1997, Med. Rsch. Coun., 1998, Biotech. and Biol. Rsch. Coun., 1999—2000, Wellcome Trust, 1999, NIH, Nat. Inst. Neurol. Disorders and Stroke, 2003—. Mem.: Am. Soc. Microbiology, Soc. Neuro-oncology, Am. Assn. Immunologists, Am. Assn. Cancer Rsch., Nat. Inst. Neurol. Disorders and Stroke, Internat. Soc. Nerovirology (founding mem.), Soc. Neurosci., Endocrine Soc., Am. Gene Therapy Assn. Achievements include patents in field; research in program in development of gene therapy for chronic neurological diseases and brain cancer; application to FDA to start a Phase I clinical trial for glioma in human patients. Office Phone: 310-423-7303. Business E-Mail: castromg@cshs.org.

CASTRO, MARIO, internist, critical care physician, medical professor; b. Mantanzas, Cuba, Sept. 14, 1964; US, 1975; s. Moises Angel and Julia Margot (Madruga) Castro; m. Marianne Castro, Oct. 1, 1988. BA in Biology, MD, U. Mo., Kansas City, 1988; MPH, St. Louis U., 1998. Diplomate Am. Bd. Internal Medicine, cert. in pulmonary diseases and critical care medicine, diplomate Nat. Bd. Med. Examiners, lic. Minn., Iowa. Resident internal medicine Grad. Sch. Medicine., Mayo Clinic, Rochester, Minn., 1988—91, pulmonary/critical care fellowship, instr. medicine, 1991—94; asst. prof. medicine Washington U. Sch. Medicine, St. Louis, 1994—2001, dir. pulmonary function lab., Asthma & Allergy Ctr., 1994—2005, assoc. prof. medicine & pediat., 2001—08, sr. fellow Ctr. Health Policy, 2006—, prof. medicine & pediat., 2008—. Attending physician med. scv. Barnes-Jewish Hosp., St. Louis, 1994—, chmn. asthma design team, 1997—99; adj. assoc. prof. cmty. health St. Louis U. Sch. Pub. Health, 2003—. Assoc. editor Yr. Book of Pulmonary Disease, 1998—2001; editor: Clin. Asthma, 2008; ad hoc reviewer Am. Jour. Respiratory Cell Molecular Biology, Am. Jour. Respiratory Critical Care Medicine, European Respiratory Jour., Jour. Allergy Clin. Immunology, CHEST, New Eng. Jour. Medicine, Jour. Rheumatology; contbr. articles to profl. jours., chapters to books. Recipient Humanitarian Recognition award, CHEST Found., 2005; grantee Burgher Family Endowed fellowship, 1993—94. Fellow: Am. Coll. Chest Physicians (mem. sci. com. 1997—98); mem.: Am. Lung. Assn. (Mo. chpt., chmn. asthma com. 1996—2000, bd. dirs. 1997—2006, pres.-elect 2001—03, pres. 2003—05, mem. sci. adv. com. 2003—, Vol. of Yr. award 1998, Disting. Svc. award 2001), St. Louis Regional Asthma Consortium (chmn. 1999—2003, founding bd. mem. 1999—, treas. 2004—), Internat. Med. Assistance Found. (bd. dirs. 2006—), Am. Thoracic Soc., Delta Omega, Alpha Omega Alpha. Roman Catholic. Office: Washington U Sch Medicine Divsn Pulmonary & Critical Care Medicine Box 8052 660 S Euclid Ave Saint Louis MO 63110-1010 Office Fax: 314-362-2307. Business E-Mail: castrom@wustl.edu. E-mail: mcastro@dom.wustl.edu. *

CASTRO, RENATA RODRIGUES TEIXEIRA, cardiologist; b. Rio de Janeiro, Sept. 13, 1977; MD, Fed. Fluminense U., 2000; DSc, Rio de Janeiro's State U., 2010. Cardiologist intensive care Brazilian Navy, 2004—. Assoc. rschr. Fed. Fluminense U., 2003. Avocations: music, sports, travel. Home: Rua Franz Weissman 410 / 1110 Rio de Janeiro 22775051 Brazil Personal E-mail: castrorrt@gmail.com.

CASTRO-GAGO, MANUEL, pediatrics educator; b. Barro, Pontevedra, Spain, Aug. 30, 1947; s. Manuel Castro Rey and Dolores Gago Rebon; m. Maria Ines Novo Rodriguez, Mar. 29, 1975; children: Adriana Maria, Maria Ines, Manuel Jose. MD cum laude, U. Santiago Compostela, 1971, PhD cum laude, 1978. Assoc. prof. pediat. Sch. Medicine U. Santiago de Compostela, Spain, 1971—76, titular prof. pediat. Sch. Medicine, 1979—93, prof. pediat. Sch. Medicine, 1993. Adj. clinician Hosp. Clinico Univ., Santiago de Compostela, 1974-79, chief divsn., 1979-82, chief svc. neuropediatrics, 1982-. Contbr. more than 500 rsch. papers to profl. jours. and books. 2d lt. Spanish armed forces, 1974-75. Recipient Pediatric Investigation award Galician Pediatric Assn., 1991, 95, 99. Mem.: AAAS, Pediat. Soc. Spain Gastroenterology, Hepatology and Nutrition (award 2001), Internat. Child Neurology Assn., European Pediatric Neurology Soc., NY Acad. Scis., Iberam. Soc. Neurourology, Groupe Latin Pediatrie, Iberam. Acad. Child Neurology, European Soc. Neuropediats, Japanese Soc. Child Neurology, Spanish Neuropediat. Assn. (pres. reunion 1985, pres. 1991—93, pres. V. Congress 1998), Galician Pediatric Assn. (hon.), Spanish Pediat. Assn. (hon. investigation award 1991, 2001, Outpatient Pediat. sect. award 1991), World Muscle Soc. Roman Catholic. Avocations: reading, travel, research. Office: Sch Medicine San Francisco S/No 15705 Santiago de Compostela Spain Office Phone: 34 981 951121. Business E-Mail: manuel.castro.gago@usc.es.

CASTRO JIMÉNEZ, MIGUEL ÁNGEL, epidemiologist; b. Bucaramanga, Colombia, May 25, 1973; Degree in Medicine, U. Indsl. Santander, Colombia, 1998, MS in Epidemiology, Pub. Health, 2007. Physician Salud Plena IPS Ltd., Bucaramanga, 1999—2003; prof., biostats. U. Indsl. Santander, Colombia, 2002—03, epidemiologist, Epidemiologic Rsch. Ctr., 2003—06; epidemiologist Nat. Cancer Inst., Colombia, 2003; cons. epidemiologist Nat. Network Labs., NIH, Colombia, 2007—, Ministry of Social Protection, Colombia, 2008. Physician, social svc. rural cmty. San Pedro Claver Hosp., Mogotes, Colombia, 1998—99; prof., clin. investigation and biostats. U. Militar Nueva Granada, Colombia, 2005—06; cons. Adminstrv. Dept. Sci., Tech., and Innovation Colciencias, Colombia, 2008; prof., clin. epidemiology U. El Bosque, Bogotá, Colombia, 2008—09. Contbr. articles to numerous sci. profl. jours. Recipient award, San Jorge U. Hosp., U. Tech. Pereira, 1998, Juan Jacobo Muñoz Internat. prize, Sanitas Internat. Orgn., 2010; named to Dean's List, Sch. Medicine, U. Indsl. Santander, 1996. Mem.: Colombian Alpha Level Study Group, Salud Poblacional, Estadística Aplicada y Scis. Aliadas, Grupo Colombiano Estudios Alfa en Epidemiología. Avocations: basketball, writing. Home: PO Box 358677 Bogotá Cundinamarca Colombia Personal E-mail: mcastro2505@yahoo.es.

CASTRONOVO, VINCENZA ELENA, psychologist, researcher; b. Milan, Oct. 27, 1968; d. Costantino Castronovo and Donatella Taroni Castronovo. PhD in Clin. Psychology, U. Parma, Italy, 2001; B in Neuropysiology, U. Milan, 1990. Registered polysomnographic technologist Assn. Polysomnographic Technologists, 1990, lic. clin. psychologist Italian State Orgn., 2002. Rsch. asst. sleep disorders ctr. Baylor Coll. Medicine, Houston, 1989—90; technologist sleep medicine and neurophysiology IRCCS H San Raffaele, Milan, 1990—96, sleep lab. coord., 1991—, rschr., 2000—, clin. psychologist, 2001—; rsch. asst. sleep disorder clinic Stanford (Calif.) U., 1991. Prof. electroencephalography U. Milan, 1997—2001. Contbr. articles to profl. jours. Mem.: European Soc. Sleep Technologists (hon.; pres. 2001—03). Avocations: tennis, travel, swimming. Office: Hosp San Raffaele Sleep Dis Ctr Via Stamira D Ancona 20 20127 Milan MI Italy

CATALANO, LOUIS WILLIAM, JR., neurologist; b. Bklyn., Apr. 20, 1942; s. Louis William and Aileen (Bobb) C.; m. Diana Catalano; children: Louis William III, Jamea Elizabeth, Adriana Louise. BS cum laude, U. Pitts., 1963, MD, 1967. Diplomate Am. Bd. Psychiatry and Neurology, Am. Bd. Electroencephalography, Am. Bd. Pain Medicine, Am. Bd. Med. Examiners. Intern Presbyn.-St. Luke's Hosp., Chgo., 1967-68; rsch. assoc. NIH, Bethesda, Md., 1968-70; fellow neurology The Neurol. Inst., NYC, 1970-73; clin. assoc., prof. neurology U. Pitts. Sch. Med., 1973—; pvt. practice Greensburg, Pa., 1973—. Staff Westmoreland Regional Hosp., Greensburg, 1973—; Frick Hosp., Mt. Pleasant, Pa., 1991—, Somerset Hosp., Torrance (Pa.) State Hosp., 2000—; lectr. in field. Contbr. articles to profl. jours. Pres. Neurol. Inst. Western Pa.; bd. dirs. Epilepsy Found. Western & Ctrl. Pa., Am. Red Cross Westmoreland & Chestnut Ridge Chpt., Pa., 2000-. Spl. fellow Columbia U., NIH, 1970-73, epilepsy minifellow, Bowman Gray Sch. Medicine, Winston-Salem, N.C., 1988. Fellow: Am. Acad. Neurology, Royal Soc. Medicine; mem.: AMA, Pa. Neurol. Soc. (pres. 2010—), European Fedn. Neurol. Socs., Pitts. Neurosci. Soc., Latrobe Acad. Medicine, World Fedn. Neurology, Pa. Med. Soc., Am. Sleep Disorders Assn., Am. Acad. Clin. Neurphysiology, Am. Soc. Neuroimaging, Am. Med. Electroencephalographic Assn., Am. Acad. Pain Mgmt., Alpha Omega Alpha, Sigma Xi. Avocations: sport fishing, scuba diving, skiing, travel. Office Phone: 724-537-0885.

CATALANO, ROBERT ANTHONY, ophthalmologist, hospital administrator, writer; b. Albany, NY, Nov. 24, 1956; s. Anthony Joseph and Ida Santa (Muscolino) C.; m. Madeline Faye Kalmer, Aug. 6, 1978; children: Christopher, Ruth, Thomas, Matthew. BS, Union Coll., Schenectady, 1978; MD, U. Va., 1982; MBA, Rensselaer Poly. Inst., 1992. Resident in ophthalmology Albany Med. Coll., 1983-86, vice-chmn. dept. ophthalmology, 1989-90, acting chmn., 1990-91; fellow in pediatric ophthalmology Wills Eye Hosp., Phila., 1986-87; v.p. med. affairs Olean (N.Y.) Gen. Hosp., 1991-93, COO, 1994-95, pres., CEO, 1995—2001; med. dir. Albany Med. Ctr. Hosp., 2001—08, interim chief med. officer, 2005—06, chief med. officer, 2006—08, St. Luke's - Roosevelt Med. Ctr., 2008—; chief clin. quality officer Continuum Healthcare Ptnrs., 2010—. Bd. dirs. Westlink Corp. Author: Atlas of Ocular Motility, 1989, Ocular Emergencies, 1992, Pediatric Ophthalmology: A Text/Atlas, 1994, When Autism Strikes, 1998; contbr. articles to profl. jours. Recipient Nat. Found. award March of Dimes Found., 1978, Robert D. Reinecke award Albany Med. Coll., 1985, Shannon award U. Va., 1982; Heed Found. fellow, 1986, Forty Under Forty award, 1993. Mem.: So. Tier Healthcare Network (bd. dirs. 1994—2001, chmn. 2001), Western N.Y. Hosp. Assn. (bd. dirs. 1992—95, 1999—2001, treas. 2001), Am. Coll. Physician Execs., Acad. Ophthalmology, Alpha Omega Alpha. Roman Catholic. Office: St Luke's Roosevelt Med Ctr 1000 10th St New York NY 10019 Office Phone: 212-523-4303.

CATALONA, WILLIAM J., surgeon, urologist, educator, researcher; b. Cleve., Nov. 14, 1942; s. William and Lucille Evelyn Catalona; m. Janet Pauline Flenner; 1 child, Alexander Paul. BS, Otterbein Coll., 1964; MD, Yale U., 1968. Diplomate Am. Bd. Urology. Intern in surgery Yale-New Haven Hosp., 1968-69; resident in surgery U. Calif., San Francisco, 1969-70; clin. assoc. surgery br. Nat. Cancer Inst., Bethesda, Md., 1970-72; resident in urology Johns Hopkins U. Hosp., Balt., 1972-76; assoc. prof. urology Washington U. Sch. Medicine, St. Louis, 1976-82, prof., 1982—, chief urology, 1984-99; prof. urology Northwestern U. Feinberg Sch. of Medicine. Dir. clin. prostate cancer program Robert H. Lurie Comperhensive Cancer Ctr.; cons. Am. Cancer Soc., Nat. Kidney Found. Contbr. numerous articles to med. jours., including New Eng. Jour. Medicine, Jour. AMA, Am. Jour. Human Genetics. Recipient Donald S. Coffey Physician-Scientist award, Prostate Cancer Found., 2005, General H. Norman Schwartzkopf Prostate Cancer Pioneer award, Fla. Prostate Cancer Network, 2005. Mem. Am. Urol. Assn. (Gold Cystoscope award 1986, Eugene Fuller medal 1998, Hugh Hampton Young award), Am. Assn. Genitourinary Surgeons (Barringer medal 1999, Keyes medal, 2003), Soc. Urologic Oncology (founding, pres. 1994-95, Charles Huggins medal 2005), Clin. Soc. Genitourinary Surgeons, Johns Hopkins Soc. Scholars, St. Louis Acad. Sci., 2003. Achievements include introduction of prostate specific antigen test for prostate cancer screening; developed free PSA blood test for increasing accuracy of PSA; identified chromosomal regions statistically linked to familial prostate cancer; a pioneer nerve-sparing radical prostatectomy for prostate cancer. Office: Northwestern U Feinberg Sch Medicine Dept Urology 675 N St Clair St Ste 20-150 Chicago IL 60611 Office Phone: 312-695-4471. Business E-Mail: wcatalona@nmff.org.

CATES, MARSHALL E., pharmacist, medical educator; b. Ripley, Tenn., Oct. 16, 1962; s. Franklin E. Cates and Geneva S Palmer; m. Deborah L. Bailey, Dec. 16, 1988; children: Dalton M., Bailey P. BS in Biology, Rhodes Coll., Memphis, 1984; PharmD, U. Tenn., Memphis, 1991. Registered pharmacist Tenn., 2011, Ala., 1996, cert. psychiat. pharmacist Bd. Pharm. Specialties, 1996. Psychiat. pharmacy practice resident U. Tenn., Memphis, 1991—92; clin. pharmacy specialist in psychiatry VA Med. Ctr., Salt Lake City, 1992—95; asst. prof. pharmacy practice Samford U. McWhorter Sch. of Pharmacy, Birmingham, Ala., 1995—2001, assoc. prof. pharmacy practice, 2001—06, prof., 2006—, asst. dean student affairs, 2007—11. Program dir. psychiat. pharmacy practice residency VA Med. Ctr., Tuscaloosa, Ala., 1997—2003. Assoc. editor Internat. Jour. Pharmacy Edn. and Practice, editl. bd. psychiatry panel (biomed. jour.) Annals of Pharmacotherapy, reviewer, Pharmacotherapy, American Journal of Health-System Pharmacy. Recipient Excellence in Pharmacy award, Mylan Pharms. Inc., 1991, Pharmacy Leadership award, Bristol-Myers Squibb, 2005. Fellow: Am. Soc. Health-Sys. Pharmacists; mem.: Ala. Pharmacy Assn., Am. Coll. Clin. Pharmacy, Am. Assn. Coll. Pharmacy (acad. leadership fellow 2004—05), Coll. Psychiat. and Neurologic Pharmacists, Ala. Soc. Health-Sys. Pharmacists (bd. dirs. 2002—04, pres. 2004—05, Health-Sys. Pharmacist of Yr. award 2006), Rho Chi Pharm. Honor Soc., Phi Lambda Sigma Pharmacy Leadership Soc. Office: Samford Univ Sch Pharmacy 800 Lakeshore Dr Birmingham AL 35229 Business E-Mail: mecates@samford.edu.

CATHEY, MICHAEL W., foundation administrator; b. Okla. Various positions including dir. major gifts and planned giving Boy Scouts America, Okla., Colo., Washington; dir. devel. Am. Med. Assn. Found., 2002; exec. dir. devel. Nat. Safety Coun., Chgo., 2002—08; dep. exec. dir. Nat. PTA; dir. Am. Veterinary Med. Found., Ill., 2008—. Mem.: Assn. Fundraising Professionals, Rotary Club. Office: Am Veterinary Med Found 1931 N Meacham Rd Ste 100 Schaumburg IL 60173-4360 *

CATIZONE, CARMEN A., health science association administrator, secretary; BS, U. Ill. Coll. Pharmacy, Chgo., 1983; MS, U. Ill. Grad. Coll., 1987. Test & measurement dir. Nat. Assn. Bds. of Pharmacy, Mt. Prospect, Ill., 1985—88, exec. dir., sec., 1988—. Named Alumnus of Yr., U. Ill. Coll. Pharmacy, 1997. Office: Nat Assn of Bds of Pharmacy 1600 Feehanville Dr Mount Prospect IL 60056-6014 Office Phone: 847-391-4502. Fax: 847-698-0124. E-mail: exec-office@nabp.net. *

CATLIN, FRANCIS IRVING, physician; b. Hartford, Conn., Dec. 6, 1925; s. Robert Irving and Frances Rose (Maleski) C.; m. Rebecca Vaughan Graham, June 11, 1948; children: Robert, Andrew, Martha. AA, Princeton U., 1949; MD, Johns Hopkins U., 1948, DSc, 1959. Diplomate: Am. Bd. Otolaryngology. Intern Union Meml. Hosp., Balt., 1948-49; resident in otolaryngology Johns Hopkins Hosp., Balt., 1950, 52-54; from instr. to assoc. prof. Johns Hopkins U. Med. Sch., Balt., 1956-72; prof. otorhinolaryngology and communicative scis. Baylor U. Med. Sch., Houston, 1972-91, prof. emeritus, 1991—. Chief otolaryngology svc. Tex. Children's Hosp., 1972-91, emeritus staff, 1991—, mem. credentials com., 1989—. Contbr. articles to med. jours. Capt. M.C. USAF, 1950-52. Fellow Am. Otol. Soc.; mem. AMA, ASTM (F29 com. on anesthesia and respiratory equipment 1989-2004), Tex. Med. Soc., Am. Acad. Otolaryngology, Am. Coun. Otolaryngology, Am. Laryngological, Rhinological and Otol. Soc., Am. Speech and Hearing Assn. (life), Houston Philos. Soc., Am. Soc. Pediat. Otolaryngology (charter mem. 1985—, v.p. 1985-86, pres. 1986-87, guest hon. 2000, 07). Episcopalian. Home: 8580 Woodway Dr #1124 Houston TX 77063

CATO, ROBERT K., internist, educator; MD, Cornell U. Diplomate Am. Bd. Internal Medicine, 1996. Intern Univ. of Pa. Hosp., resident; chief gen. medicine divsn. Penn Presbyterian Med. Ctr.; med. dir. Penn Ctr. for Primary Care; physician Penn Presbyterian Med. Ctr. Asst. prof. medicine dept. Penn Presbyterian Med. Ctr. Mem.: AMA, ACP (assoc.), Soc. of Gen. Internal Medicine, Alpha Omega Alpha Honor Soc. Office: Penn Presbyterian Medical Center Medical Arts Bldg Ste 102 51 N 39th St Philadelphia PA 19104 Office Phone: 215-662-9990.

CATOE, BETTE LORRINA, pediatrician, educator; b. Apr. 7, 1926; d. John Booker and Laura Beola (Adams) C.; m. Warren J. Strudwick, Sept. 17, 1949; children: Laura Christina, Warren J., William J. BS cum laude, Howard U., 1948, MD, 1951. Intern Freedmen's Hosp., Washington, 1951-52; pediat. resident Howard U./Freedman's Hosp., 1952-55, practice medicine specializing in pediatrics Washington, 1956—2003; instr. bacteriology Howard U., 1955-57; mem. staff Providence Hosp., Columbia Hosp., Howard U. Hosp., Wash., Hosp. Ctr.; sch. health officer Dept. Health, Washington, 1960-64; clin. instr. Howard U., 1956-58; pediat. cons., family devel. cons., rehab. cons, 2003—; cons. income maint. admin. Govt. DC, 2003—; with DC Medchi Soc. Mem. DC Health Planning Adv. Coun., 1967-77, chmn. 1973-77; chmn. DC Devel. Disabilities Adv. Coun., 1970-74; mem. DC Mayor's Commn. on Food and Nutrition, 1971-72, Mayor's Commn. on Maternal and Child Health, 1978-84, appt. vice chmn. Pub. Benefit Corp., 1997-2001; mem. DC Commn. Jud. Tenure and Disabilities, 1977-2001, chmn. Bd. Public Benefit Corp. of DC, 1998-2001; bd. govs. St. Alban's Sch., 1978-84; bd. dirs. DC Health and Welfare Coun., 1968-73, pres., 1973-74; del. Democratic Nat. Conv., 1976; bd. dirs. Met. Washington Health and Welfare Coun., 1970-72, Parent Coun. of Washington, 1974-75, Met. Med. Founds., Inc., Silver Spring YMCA, 1977-80, Kingsburg Ctr., 1997-99; mem., chair emergency med. com. Mayor's Health Policy Coun., 1998-2001; cons. income maintenance adminstrn. Govt. of DC Dept. Human Svcs., 2003—; v.p. Fort Stevens Recreation Ctr., 2010-, Ft. Stevens Sr. Citizens Coun., 2010-, officer North Portal Civic Assn. Washington, 2010-. Named D.C. Hall of Fame, 2006, History Maker, 2003. Mem.: NAACP, AMA, Women's Aux. Medico-Chirurg. Soc., Assn. Comprehensive Health Planners (dir. 1975—77), Urban League, Am. Med. Women's Assn., Nat. Med. Assn. (chmn. pediat. sect. 1981—83), D.C. Chirurg. Soc. (trustee 1996—99, nominating com. 2000—03, jud. legis. com. 2001—03), Women's Nat. Dem., Jack and Jill Am., Carrousels Club (nat. v.p. 1986—88, nat. pres. 1988—90), Links Club, Century Club of Nat. Assn. Negro Bus. and Profl. Women's Clubs (pres. 1985—89), Alpha Kappa Alpha. Home and Office: 1748 Sycamore St NW Washington DC 20012-1031 Office Phone: 202-882-2406. Personal E-mail: bcatoestrudwick@yahoo.com.

CATTAMANCHI, ADITHYA, thoracic surgeon, educator; b. Chgo., July 7, 1976; MD, U. Calif., San Francisco, 2003, MAS, 2010. Asst. prof. medicine U. Calif., 2009—. CFO World Alliance Lung and Intensive Care Medicine Uganda, 2010. Recipient Tchg. award, U. Calif., Dept. Epidemiology & Biostats.; fellow Clin. Rsch. fellowship, Doris Duke Charitable Found.; rsch. grants, NIH. Mem.: Internat. Union Against Tb and Lung Disease, Am. Thoracic Soc. Avocation: tennis. Office: San Francisco General Hosp Pulmonary Divsn Rm 5K1 1001 Potrero Ave San Francisco CA 94110 Personal E-mail: adithyac@hotmail.com.

CATTERALL, WILLIAM A., pharmacology educator; b. Providence, Oct. 12, 1946; s. William V. and Alice C. Catterall. BA in Chemistry, Brown U., Providence, 1968; PhD in Physiol. Chemistry, Johns Hopkins U. Sch. Medicine, Balt., 1972. Postdoc. rsch. fellow Lab. Biochem. Genetics, NIH, Bethesda, Md., 1972—74, staff scientist, 1974—77; assoc. prof. dept. pharmacology U. Wash. Sch. Medicine, Seattle, 1977—81, prof., 1981—, chmn. dept. pharmacology, 1984—; chmn. interdisciplinary com. on neurobiology U. Wash., Seattle, 1986—. Editor-in-chief Molecular Pharmacology, 1985—90, founding mem. editl. bd. Neuron, 1988; contbr. articles to profl. jours., chapters to books. Recipient Young Scientist award, Passano Found., 1981, Jacob Javits Neurosci. Investigator award, Nat. Inst. Neurol. and Communicative Disorders & Stroke, 1984, 1991, Basic Sci. prize, Am. Heart Assn., 1992, Mathilde Solowey award in neurosci., NIH, 1995, H.B. Van Dyke award in pharmacology, Columbia U., 1995, Sr. Neurosci. Investigator award, McKnight Found., 1998, Bristol-Myers Squibb award for disting. achievement in neurosci. rsch., 2003, Gairdner Found. Internat. award, Can., 2010. Mem.: NAS (chair sect. physiology & pharmacology 1998—2001), Soc. Neurosci., Am. Soc. Biol. Chemists, Am. Soc. Pharmacology & Exptl. Therapeutics, Am. Acad. Arts & Scis., Royal Soc. London (fgn.), Inst. Medicine. Achievements include discovery of voltage-gated sodium and calcium channel proteins, which are responsible for generation of electrical signals in the brain, heart, skeletal muscles, and other excitable cells. Avocations: sailing, skiing. Office: U Wash Dept Pharmacology Box 357280 HSC F427 Seattle WA 98195-7280 E-mail: wcatt@uw.edu. *

CATTERTON, MARIANNE ROSE, occupational therapist; b. St. Paul, Feb. 3, 1922; d. Melvin Joseph and Katherine Marion (Bole) Maas; m. Elmer John Wood, Jan. 16, 1943 (dec.); m. Robert Lee Catterton, Nov. 20, 1951 (div. 1981); children: Jenifer Ann Dawson, Cynthia Lea Uthus. Student, Carleton Coll., 1939—41, U. Md., 1941—42; BA in English, U. Wis., 1944; MA in Counseling Psychology, Bowie State Coll., 1980; postgrad., No. Ariz. U., 1987—91. Registered occupl. therapist, Occupl. Therapy Cert. Bd. Occupl. therapist VA, NYC, 1946—50; cons. occupl. therapist Fondo del Seguro del Estado, PR, 1950—51; dir. rehab. therapies Spring Grove State Hosp., Catonsville, Md., 1953—56; occupl. therapist Anne Arundel County Health Dept., Annapolis, Md., 1967—78; dir. occupl. therapy Ea. Shore Hosp. Ctr., Cambridge, Md., 1979—85; cons. occupl. therapist Kachina Point Health Ctr., Sedona, Ariz., 1986. Regional chmn. Conf. on revising Psychiat. Occupl. Therapy Edn., 1958-59; instr. report writing Anne Arundel C.C., Annapolis, 1974-78. Editor: Am. Jour. Occupl. Therapy, 1962—67. Active Md. Mental Health Assn., 1959—60; mem. task force on occupl. therapy edn. Md. Dept. Health, 1971—72; chmn. Anne Arundel Gov. Com. on Employment of Handicapped, 1959—63; gov.'s com. to study vocat. rehab. Md., 1960; com. mem. Annapolis Youth Ctr., 1976—78; curator Dorchester County Heritage Mus., Cambridge, 1982—83; citizen interviewer Sedona Acad. Forum, 1993, 1994; vol. Respite Care, 1994—98, Verde Valley Caregivers, 1993—; ministerial search com. Unitarian Ch. Anne Arundel County, 1962; v.p., officer Unitarian-Universalist Fellowship Flagstaff, 1988—93, v.p., 1993—97; co-moderator, founder Unitarian-Universalist Fellowship Sedona, 1994—96, pres., 1997—98, co-pres., 2001—03. Mem.: Dorchester County Mental Health Assn. (pres. 1981—84), Md. Occupl. Therapy Assn. (del. 1953—59), Am. Occupl. Therapy Assn. (chmn. history com. 1958—61), PR Occupl. Therapy Assn. (co-founder 1950), Sedona Muses, Population Connection, Ret. Officers Assn., Pathfinder Internat., Air Force Assn. (sec. Barry Goldwater chpt. 1991—92, 1994—2006), Toastmasters, Internat. Club (chmn. publicity Annapolis chpt. 1966), Severn Town Club (treas. 1965, sec. 1971—72, 1994—95), Delta Delta Delta. Republican.

CATUZZO, PAOLA, radiologist; b. Turin, Italy, July 29, 1974; Degree in Physics, U. Tourin, 2000, specialist in Med. Physics, 2006. Med. physics specialist AUSL Valle d'Aosta, 2007—. Office: Viale Ginevra 1 Aosta 11100 Italy Business E-Mail: pcatuzzo@ausl.vda.it.

CATZ, AMIRAM, physiatrist; b. Haifa, Israel, June 24, 1952; s. Iona and Klara (Graif) C.; m. Yehudit Rosenberg, June 19, 1975; children: Noa, Eyal, Neta. MD, Hebrew U., Jerusalem, 1981; diploma in Rehab. Medicine, Tel Aviv U., 1986, MS, 1990, PhD, 2005. Lic. MD, Israel. Resident in neurosurgery Tel Aviv Med. Ctr., 1982-83; resident in phys. medicine and rehab. Loewenstein Rehab. Hosp., Raanana, Israel, 1983-90, specialist in phys. medicine and rehab., 1990-93, med. dir. spinal dept., 1994—, head, Helsinki Ethics Com., 2008—11; med. dir., CEO Loewenstein Hosp., 2011—. Sr. house officer in spinal injuries Stoke (Eng.) Mandeveile Hosp., 1988; instr. faculty of medicine Tel Aviv U., 1989-94, lectr., 1994-01, sr. lectr., 2001-05, clin. assoc. prof, 2005-, head, Rehab. Dept. Faculty Medicine Tel Aviv U., 2008-. Author (chpts. in books) Introduction to Rehabilitation Medicine, 1990, Handbook of Neurology: Aging and the Autonomic Nervous System, 1999, Advances in Physical and Rehabilitation Medicine, 2005, Fundamental in Rehabilitation Medicine, 2011; author, rschr. numerous monographs; contbr. articles to profl. jours. in the fields of rehabilitation, spinal injuries, Autonomic Nervous System, and neurophysiology. Maj. Israeli Def. Force, 1978-94. Mem. Israel Med. Assn. (chmn. exam. com. phys. med. rehab. 1992-2005, adv. com. degree in phys. med. rehab. 1995—), Israel Assn. Phys. Medicine and Rehab., The Internat. Spinal Cord Soc. (sci. com. mem.), Internat. Soc. Rehab. Medicine (internat. SCI dataset liaison officer 2003-). Achievements include development of a disability scale specific for spinal cord injuries, a measure of ability realization and an aiding device for tetraplegia. Home: Rupin 23 44209 Kfar Sava Israel Office: Loewenstein Rehab Hosp 273 Ahuza St 43100 Ra'anana Israel E-mail: amcatz@post.tau.ac.il.

CATZ, BORIS, endocrinologist, educator; b. Troyanov, Russia, Feb. 15, 1923; came to U.S., 1950, naturalized, 1955; s. Jacobo and Esther (Galbmilion) C.; m. Rebecca Schechter; children: Judith, Dinah, Sarah Lea. BS, Nat. U. Mex., 1941, MD, 1947; MS in Medicine, U. So. Calif., 1951. Intern Gen. Hosp., Mexico City, Mex., 1945-46; prof. sch. medicine U. Mex., 1947-48; instr. medicine U. So. Calif., 1952-54, asst. clin. prof., 1954-59, 1959-83, clin. prof., 1983—; pvt. practice LA, 1951-55, Beverly Hills, Calif., 1957—. Chief Thyroid Clinic L.A. County Gen. Hosp., 1955-70; sr. cons. thyroid clin. U. So. Calif., L.A. Med. Ctr., 1970—; clin. chief endocrinology Cedars-Sinai Med. Ctr., 1985-87. Author: Thyroid Case Studies, 1975, 2d edit., 1981; contbr. numerous articles on thyroidology to med. jours. Capt. U.S. Army, 1955-57. Rsch. fellow medicine U. So. Calif., 1949-51; Boris Catz lectureship in his honor Thyroid Rsch. Endowment Fund, Cedars Sinai Med. Ctr., 1985. Fellow ACP, Am. Coll. Nuclear Medicine (pres. elect 1982), Royal Soc. Medicine, Am. Thyroid Assn. (Disting. Svc. award 2001); mem. AMA, AAAS, Cedars Sinai Med. Ctr. Soc. History of Medicine (chmn.), L.A. County Med. Assn., Calif. Med. Assn., Endocrine Soc., Am. Thyroid Assn., Soc. Exptl. Biology and Medicine, Western Soc. Clin. Rsch., Am. Fedn. Clin. Rsch., Soc. Nuclear Medicine, So. Calif. Soc. Nuclear Medicine, N.Y. Acad. Scis., L.A. Soc. Internal Medicine, Collegium Salerni, Cedar Sinai Soc. History Medicine, B'nai B'rith Club, The Profl. Man's Club (past pres.), Endocrine Soc., Phi Lambda Kappa. Office: 435 N Roxbury Dr Beverly Hills CA 90210-5027

CAUCE, ANA MARI, dean, psychology professor; b. Havana, Cuba, Jan. 11, 1956; came to U.S., 1959; d. Vicente and Ana (Vivanco) C. BA summa cum laude, U. Miami, Fla., 1979; MS in Psychology, Yale U., New Haven, 1979, MPhil, 1982, PhD in Psychology, 1984. Psychology lectr. U. Del., Newark, 1983—84, asst. prof. psychology, 1984—86, U. Washington, Seattle, 1986—90, assoc. prof. psychology dept., 1990—96, prof. psychology dept., 1990—97, dir. clin. tng., psychology dept., 1996—2000, prof. & chair, Am. ethnic studies, 1996—, dir. honors program, 2000—02, Earl R. Carlson prof. psychology, 2000—, chair psychology dept., 2002—05, exec. vice provost, 2005—08, dean coll. arts and sciences, 2008—. Bd. dirs. CONSEJO Counseling and Referral Svc. for Hispanics, Seattle; mem. minority initiatives com. Alliance for Children, Youth and Families, Seattle; mem com. on cons. and edn. Wash. Coun. for Prevention Child Abuse and Neglect; mem. system analysis adv. com. child and adolescent svc. system project dept. social and health svcs. State of Wash.; speaker and cons. in field; lectr. Quinnipiac Coll., North

Haven, Conn., 1979; clin. supr. psychol. svcs. tng. ctr. U. Wash., 1986—. Contbr. numerous chpts. to books and articles to profl. jours.; editorial bd. Am. Jour. Community Psychology; reviewer: Journal of Personality and Social Psychology, Journal of Child Clinical Psychology, Journal of Adolescent Research. The Grant Found. grantee, 1986-87, Grad. Sch. Rsch. Fund U. Wash. grantee, 1987-88, Nat. Inst. Child Health and Human Devel. grantee, 1988—; recipient Silver Knight award Miami Herald, 1974; Yale Bush Ctr. in Child Devel. and Social Policy fellow, 1983; Elizabeth Kay Donor scholar, 1976-77. Fellow (hon.) Am. Psychol. Assn. (clin. psychology div., community psychology div., psychology of women div., soc. for study ethnic minority issues div.); mem. Soc. for Rsch. in Child Devel., Soc. for Rsch. on Adolescence, Am. Psychol. Soc., Phi Kappa Phi, Sigma Xi. Office: Univ Washington 050 Comm Bldg Box 353765 Seattle WA 98195-3765 Office Phone: 206-543-5340. Office Fax: 206-543-5462. Business E-Mail: cauce@u.washington.edu.

CAUDLE, MICHAEL RAY, obstetrician, gynecologist, researcher; b. Charlotte, NC, Aug. 22, 1951; s. Bob Ray and Jacqueline (Butler) C.; children: Robert, Catherine, Joseph, Lori. BA, U. N.C., 1972; MD, Wake Forest U., 1977. Diplomate Am. Bd. Ob-Gyn. Resident dept. ob-gyn U. Va., 1977-81; instr. ob-gyn U. Utah, 1981-82; pvt. practice ob-gyn Harriman, Tenn., 1983-84; asst. prof. U. Tenn., 1984-86, assoc. prof., 1987-91, prof., 1991—, also chmn. dept., 1987; dean grad. sch. medicine U. Tenn. Med. Ctr., 1995—2005; vice chancellor Health Affairs, 2005—. Contbr. articles to profl. jours. Dir. State Utah Family Planning Program, 1981-82. Research fellow U. Utah, 1981-82. Fellow Am. Coll. Ob-Gyn (rsch. fellow 1981). Baptist. Avocation: cello. Office: U Tenn Med Ctr 1924 Alcoa Hwy Knoxville TN 37920-1511 Office Phone: 865-544-9290.

CAULFIELD, JAMES BENJAMIN, pathologist, educator; b. Mpls., Jan. 1, 1927; s. Linus Joseph and Olive Bell (Curtis) C.; m. Virginia Walsh, Jan. 28, 1950; children: Ann, John, Clare. BA, Miami U., Oxford, Ohio, 1947; BS, U. Ill., 1948, MD, 1950. Intern Henrotin Hosp., Chgo., 1950-51; resident U. N.C., Chapel Hill, 1951-52, U. Kans. Med. Ctr., Kansas City, 1954-55; vis. investigator Rockefeller Inst., NYC, 1955-56; instr. pathology Harvard U., 1959-64, asst. prof., 1964-70, assoc. prof., 1970-75; asst. pathologist Mass. Gen. Hosp., Boston, 1960-64, assoc. pathologist, 1964-75; prof., chmn. dept. pathology U. S.C., 1975-85; prof. pathology U. Ala., Birmingham, 1985—. Adj. prof. Med. U. S.C., Charleston, 1981-85; rsch. on collagen network of heart and changes associated with alterations in the network. Contbr. articles to profl. jours. Served with USN, 1944-46, 52-54. Mem. Am. Soc. Cell Biology, Am. Soc. Pathology, Internat. Acad. Pathology, Fedn. Exptl. Pathology, Electron Microscopy Soc., Internat. Study Group for Heart Research (treas. Am. sect. 1972-85), N.Y. Acad. Scis., Harvard Club, Boston Athenaeum Club, Sigma Xi, Phi Eta Sigma. Office: U Ala Dept Pathology 506 Kracke Bldg 619 19th St S Birmingham AL 35233-0001

CAUSHAJ, PHILIP, surgeon; b. NYC, Sept. 20, 1954; s. Sam A. and Virginia V. (Cakrane) C.; m. Angela S.H. Hodja, July 11, 1976; children: Katherine Emily, Samuel Robert. MD, Johns Hopkins U., Balt., 1979. Diplomate Am. Bd. Surgery, Am. Bd. Surg. Critical Care, Am. Bd. Colon and Rectal Surgery. Active staff Emerson Hosp., Concord, Mass., 1985—97; courtesy staff New Eng. Deaconess Hosp., Boston, 1987—89; chief surg. endoscopy U. Mass. Hosp., Worcester, 1989—91; chair surg. Med. Ctr. Ctrl. Mass., Worcester, 1990—97; chair Bridgeport Hosp., Yale New Haven Health, New Haven, 1997—98; surgeon in chief dept. surgery We. Pa. Hosp., Pitts., 1998—2008. Mem. ACS, Am. Coll. Gastroenterology, Am. Soc. Colon and Rectal Surgeons, New Eng. Soc. Colon and Rectal Surgeons, Soc. Am. Gastrointestinal Endoscopy, Soc. Am. Endoscopic Surgeons, Soc. for Surgery of the Alimentary Tract. Liberal. Office: We Pa Hosp 4800 Friendship Ave Pittsburgh PA 15224 Business E-Mail: pfc920@cs.com.

CAUSSY, DEORAJ HARRY, epidemiologist; b. Curepipe, Plaines Wilhems, Mauritius, Jan. 13, 1947; s. Ragoonanund Caussy; m. Debasri Caussy; children: Rick D. children: Pamela S., Roy S. BSc in Biology with honors, McMaster U., Hamilton, Ont., Can., 1982, MSc in Molecular Biology/Virology, 1984, PhD, 1988. Med. lab. scientist Regional Virus Lab., Birmingham, England, 1971—76; chief med. lab. technologist Regional Virology Lab., Hamilton, Ont., Canada, 1976—80; epidemiologist, modeler Familty Health Internat., Research Triangle Park, NC, 1991—92; rsch. epidemiologist divsn. reporductive health HIV sect. Ctrs. for Disease Control and Prevention, Atlanta, 1992—93; epidemiologist WHO, New Delhi, 1995—. Epidemiologist Family Health Internat., Durham, NC, 1991—92; Forgarty vis. fellow Nat. Cancer Inst., Bethesda, Md., 1988—91; presenter, cons. in field. Author: A Field Guide for Detection, Managment and Surveillance of Arsenicosis, 2005; contbr. articles to profl. jours. Fellow, Inst. Med. Lab. Scis., London, 1975; Terry Fox scholar, Cancer Soc. Can. Office: WHO Ring Rd IP Estate New Delhi 110 002 India Office Fax: +91-11-23379507; Home Fax: +91-11-23379507. Business E-Mail: caussyd@searo.who.int.

CAUTILLI, RICHARD, JR., orthopaedic surgeon; Grad., Bucknell U., Lewisburg; attended, Jefferson Med. Coll., 1985. Diplomate Am. Bd. Orthopaedic Surgery, Am. Bd. Orthopaedic Surgery-orthop. sports medicine. Resident orthop. Thomas Jefferson Univ. Hosp.; fellow sports medicine and arthroscopy Univ. Conn.; surgeon Cautilli Orthop. Surg. Specialist, St. Mary Med. Ctr. Named one of the Top Doctors, Phila. Mag., 2011. Achievements include first to first surgeons in the nation to earn a Subspecialty Certificate in Orthopaedic Sports Medicine. Office: Saint Mary Medical Center 115 Floral Vale Blvd Ste C Yardley PA 19067 Office Phone: 215-504-6101. Office Fax: 215-504-1910.

CAVALIERE, FRANCESCO, oncologist; b. Rome, July 8, 1963; s. Renato Cavaliere and Maria Clara Nasi; m. Monica Ara, Oct. 25, 1997; children: Camilla, Renato, Roberto. MD, La Sapienza U., Rome, 1988. Cert. gen. surgeon La Sapienza U., 1993. Attending surgeon Regina Elena Cancer Inst., Rome, 1993—2005, San Camillo, Forlanini, Rome, 2005—. Contbr. scientific papers. Recipient Ministero della Sanita, 1997—99. Mem.: E.S.Y.S. (counselor 2008), S.P.I.G.C. (counselor 2001—03), S.I.T.I.L.O. (counselor 2004). Office: San Camillo / Forlanini Viale Gianicolense Rome 00199 Italy Home: Via di Fiorenza Tor 13 199 Rome RM Italy Office Phone: 0039 6 58704719. Business E-Mail: francescocavaliere@fastwebnet.it.

CAVALIERE, LUDOVICO FRANK ROLAND, rheumatologist; s. Orlando Arturo Cavaliere and Marcella Daini; m. Rossella Bastianini, June 8, 1986; children: Alexander Roland, Matthew Peter. MD, U. Degli Studi Di Bologna, Italy, 1985. Diplomate Am. Bd. Rheumatology. Resident in internal medicine N.Y. Med. Coll., Valhalla, 1986—89, rheumatology fellow, 1989—91, instr. medicine, 1992—95, dir. rheumatology fellowship tng. program, 1998—2005, asst. prof. medicine, 1995—2003, assoc. prof. clin. medicine, 2003—05, acting dir. rheumatology fellowship program, 1997—98; attending physician rheumatology Lincoln Med. and Mental Health Ctr., Bronx, NY, 1991—97; chief Divsn. Rheumatology Albany (N.Y.) Med. Ctr., 2005—, dir. rheumatology fellowship tng. program, 2005—, assoc. prof. medicine, 2005—. Fellow: ACP, Am. Coll. Rheumatology; mem.: Arthritis Found. Office: Albany Med Coll Divsn Rheumatology 47 New Scotland Ave Albany NY 12208 also: 1367 Washington Ave Ste 101 Albany NY 12206 Office Fax: 518-489-4506.

CAVALIERE, ROSSELLA, neurologist; b. Tuscany, Italy, Nov. 24, 1957; arrived in U.S., 1987; d. Pietro Bastianini and Dora Landi; m. Ludovico Frank Cavaliere, June 8, 1986. MD summa cum laude, U. Bologna, Italy, 1984. Diplomate Am. Bd. Neurology. Neurology resident St. Vincent's Hosp. and Med. Ctr., NYC, 1991—94, neuroimaging fellow, 1994—95; neurology attending physician Health Ins. Plan, NYC, 1996; neurorehabilitation fellow Burke Rehab. Hosp., White Plains, NY, 1996—97, neurology attending physician, 1997—98; movement disorder fellow Beth Israel Med. Ctr., NYC, 1998—99; neurology attending physician Helen Hayes Hosp., West Haverstraw, NY, 1999—2005; neurology attending physician pvt. practice Capital Neurol. Assocs., Albany, NY, 2005—06; neurologist MS care ctr. Ctr. Disability Svcs., Albany, 2007—. Pvt. practice, 2005—06; neurologist Disability Svc. Health Care Ctr. Mem.: MS Consortium, Am. Acad. Neurology. Office: Ctr Disability Svcs Neurology Dept 314 S Manning Blvd Albany NY 12208 Office Phone: 518-437-5963.

CAVALIERI, THOMAS ANTHONY, dean, internist, educator; b. Phila., May 16, 1951; s. Anthony and Mary Cavalieri; m. Donna Marie, Dec. 1, 1979; children: Mary, Anthony, John Paul, Annamaria. Mt. St. Mary's Coll., Emmitsburg, Md., 1973; DO, Coll. Osteo. Med. and Surgery, Des Moines, 1976. Diplomate in internal medicine and geriatric medicine Am. Bd. Internal Medicine, Am. Osteo. Bd. Internal Medicine. Chief divsn. geriat. UMDNJ-Sch. Medicine, Stratford, 1987-96, dir., founder Ctr. for Aging, 1987-96; chair dept. medicine UMDNJ-Sch. Osteo. Medicine, Stratford, 1996—2008, exec. dir. NJ Geriatric Edn. Ctr., 1990-2000, prof. medicine, 1995—, endowed chmn. primary care rsch., interim dean, 2006—08, dean, 2008—; chief divsn. geriat. Our Lady of Lourdes Med. Ctr., Camden, NJ; chief medicine Kennedy Meml. Hosp.-Univ Med. Ctr., Stratford; med. dir. St. Mary's Cath. Home. Mem. adv. bd. Violence Inst. N.J., Newark, 1996—; cons. U.S. Dept. Health and Human Svcs., Trenton, N.J., 1998—, bd. dirs. Nat. Bd. of Osteo. Med. Examiners, 1999. Mem. Commn. on Aging, N.J., 1999—; mem. med. morals com. Diocese of Camden; mem. N.J. Drug Utilization Rev., 1999—. Grantee Nat. Inst. on Aging, 1999—, Dept. HHS, 1998—. Fellow Am. Coll. Physicians, Gerontol. Soc. Am., Am. Geriat. Soc.; mem. Am. Coll. Osteo. Internists (bd. dirs. 1996—, pres.-elect 2003), S. Jersey Cath. Med. Assn. (pres. 2003). Roman Catholic. Avocations: boating, fishing, music, theater. Office: UMDNJ Sch Osteo Medicine Office of Dean One Medical Center Dr Stratford NJ 08084 1501 Office Phone: 856-566-6764. *

CAVALLARO, JOSEPH JOHN, retired microbiologist; b. Lawrence, Mass., Mar. 18, 1932; s. John and Salvatrice (Zappala) C.; m. Margaret Hare, Aug. 24, 1964; children: Theresa Margaret, Sandra Marie; m. Kathleen Frances Kraus, Dec. 2, 1972; children: Elizabeth Camille, Danielle Kay, Gina Kathleen. BS, Tufts U., 1952; MS, U. Mass., 1954; PhD, U. Mich., 1966. Pub. health sanitarian Hartford (Conn.) Health Dept., 1954-55, 57-61; tchg. asssoc. dept. microbiology U. Mass., Amherst, 1961-62; rsch. virologist Med. Rsch. Labs. Charles Pfizer & Co., Groton, Conn., 1966-67; rsch. assoc. dept. epidemiology Sch. Pub. Health U. Mich., Ann Arbor, 1967-70; microbiologist, diagnostic immunology tng. br. Ctrs. for Disease Control, Atlanta, 1971-86, rsch. microbiologist anaerobic bacteria br., 1986-2000; ret., 2000. Lectr. resident pathologists Grady Meml. Hosp., Atlanta, 1975; asst. prof. pathology Morehouse Sch. Medicine, 1982-85, clin. assoc. prof., 1986-97; adj. asst. prof. pathology and lab. medicine Emory U. Sch. of Medicine, 1985-2000; cons. Pan Am. Health Orgn., Colombia and Brazil, 1976-77, WHO, 2003. Prin. author: lab. manuals; contbr. articles to profl. jours., chapters to books. Served with M.C., AUS, 1955-57. Registered specialist microbiologist Nat. Registry Microbiologist, Am. Acad. Microbiologist. Fellow Am. Acad. Microbiology; mem. Am. Soc. Microbiology, Sigma Xi. Democrat. Home: 1325 Balsam Dr Decatur GA 30033-2905 Personal E-mail: cavallaro@mindspring.com.

CAVALLI, VANESSA, research scientist; b. Limeira, Dec. 17, 1977; PhD, Piracicaba Dental Sch., Unicamp, 2000, degree in Restorative Dentistry, 2007. Postdoc. rsch. scientist U. Campinas, 2011—. Assoc. prof. U. Taubaté, 2007—. Grant, FAPESP, CNPq. Mem.: IADR. Avocations: reading, travel. Home: Angela Carolina Campari Pace St 241 Americana São Paulo 13468-810 Brazil Personal E-mail: vcavalli@yahoo.com.

CAVALLINI, CLAUDIO, cardiologist; b. Treviso, Italy, Jan. 26, 1954; MD, U. Bologna, 1979. Chief cardiologist U. Hosp. Perugia, 2005—. Bd. dirs. Regional Ethical Com. Mem.: FIC, GISE, ANMCO. Avocation: bicycling. Office: Azienda Ospedaliera di Perugia Perugia 06100 Italy Business E-Mail: claudio.cavallini@ospedale.perugia.it.

CAVALLI-SFORZA, LUIGI LUCA, geneticist, educator; b. Genoa, Italy, Jan. 25, 1922; arrived in U.S., 1970; s. Pio and Attilia (Manacorda) Cavalli-Sforza; m. Albamaria Ramazzotti, Jan. 12, 1946; children: Matteo, Francesco, Tommaso, Violetta. MD, U. Pavia, 1944; MA, Cambridge U., Eng., 1950, DSc (hon.), 1994, Columbia U., 1980. Asst. rsch. Istituto Sieroterapico Milanese, Milan, 1945—48, dir. rsch., 1950—57; asst. rschr. dept. genetics Cambridge U., 1948—50; prof. genetics U. Parma, Italy, 1951—62; prof. genetics, dir. Istituto di Genetica U. Pavia, Italy, 1962—70; prof. genetics Stanford U., Calif., 1970—92, chmn., 1986—90, prof. emeritus, 1992—, U. San Raffaele, Milan, 2005—, L'Istituto di Genetica Molecolare, Pavia, Italy, 2008—. V.p. Internat. Congress Genetics, Tokyo, 1968. Author: Genes Peoples and Languages, 2000, L' Evoluzione della Cultura, 2010; co-author (with W. Bodmer): The Genetics of Human Populations, 1971, Genetics, Evolution and Man, 1976; co-author: (with M. Feldman) Cultural Transmission and Evolution, 1981; co-author: (with A. Ammerman) The Neolithic Transition in Europe, 1984; co-author: (with P. Menozzi and A. Piazza) History and Geography of Human Genes, 1994; co-author: (with Francesco Cavalli-Sforza) The Great Human Diasporas, A History of Human Diversity, 1996; co-author: (with A. Moroni and G. Zei) Consanguinity, Inbreeding and Drift in Italy, 2004; editor: African Pygmies, 1986. Med. officer Italian Army, 1947—48. Recipient T.H. Huxley lecture in anthropology, 1972, Weldon award in biometry, 1975, Allen award, Human Genetics Premio Acad., Lincei, 1982, prize, Fyssen Found., 1992, Catalonia award, 1993, prize, Balzan Found., 1999, Kistler hon. prize, Found. for Future, 2004; hon. fellow, Gonville and Caius Coll. Cambrige U. Mem.: AAAS, French Acad. Scis., U.S. Nat. Acad. Sci., Royal Soc. London, Japanese Soc. Human Genetics, European Acad. Sci. Lincei, Am. Soc. Human Genetics (pres. 1989). Business E-Mail: cavallisforza@gmail.com.

CAVANAGH, HARRISON DWIGHT, ophthalmologist, educator; s. William Edwards and Marie Corrine (Logue) C.; m. Lynn Ayres Gantt, Dec. 27, 1964; 1 dau., Catherine DuVal. AB, Johns Hopkins U., 1962, MD (Joseph Collins scholar 1963-65), 1965; PhD in Biology, Harvard U., 1972. Life diplomate Am. Bd. Ophthalmology. Intern Johns Hopkins Hosp., 1965-66, resident in ophthalmology, 1969-73; fellow corneal surgery Mass. Eye and Ear Infirmary, Boston, 1973-75; instr. ophthalmology Johns Hopkins Med. Sch., 1969-73; asst. prof. Harvard U. Med. Sch., 1975-76; mem. faculty Emory U., 1976-87, F. Phinizy Calhoun prof. ophthalmology, chmn. dept., 1978-87; prof. Georgetown U., Washington, 1987-91; Disting. Univ. prof., vice chmn. dept. ophthalmology U. Tex. Southwestern Med. Ctr., Dallas, 1991-95, W. Maxwell Thomas chair prof., 1995—; med. dir., assoc. dean clin. svcs. Zale Lipsky U. Hosp./U. Tex. Southwestern Med. Ctr. Vis. prof. Georgetown U., 1986-87; cons., chmn. visual scis. study sect A NIH, 1980-84; Heed Found. scholar, 1973-74; sci. adv. panel Nat. Soc. Prevention Blindness, Knights Templar Found.; civilian cons. USAF, 1983-86, USN, Bethesda Naval Hosp., 1989-91; mem. neuroscis. behavior study sect. NIH, 1989-93; organizing com. 3rd-4th Internat. Conf. on Confocal Microscopy and 4th-5th Internat. Conf. on 3D Image Processing in Microscopy, 1991—. Editor-in-chief Jour. Cornea, 1989-96, Eye and Contact Lens Jour., 2002-2007; mem. editorial bd. Jour. Scanning, Bioimaging Jour.; contbr. articles to profl. jours. Recipient Heed Found. award, 1981, Gold medal for lifetime achievement, Brit. Contact Lens Assn., Sr. Sci. Investigators award, Rsch. to Prevent Blindness, Inc., 1996, 35th Castroviejo Gold medal, 2009; named 2d Joseph Koplowitz lectr., Georgetown U., 1983, 14th Waldert lectr., U. Rochester, 1987, 5th Morton B. Server lectr., U. Calif., Berkeley, 1991, George Nissal lectr., Brit. Contact Lens Assn., 1997, 21st James McDonald lectr, Loyola U. Chgo., 1998, 3d Maxwell Boschner lectr., U. Toronto, Top Ophthalmologists Consumer Res Coun. award, 2002; named one of Best Drs. in America, 1979, Best Drs. in Dallas, 2007, Tex. Super Drs., 2008, Castle Connolly Top Dr., 2008. Fellow: ACS, Internat. Coll. Surgeons, Royal Microscopy Soc., Am. Acad. Optometry (lectr. 2005, Max Shapiro award 2001, Hon. Fellowship award), Royal Soc. Medicine, Am. Acad. Ophthalmology (hon.; assoc. sect. govt. rels. and rsch. 1979—83, Honor Recognition award 1982, Whitney Sampson lectr. 1997, Sr. Achievement award 1999); mem.: Singapore Nat. Eye Ctr. (mem. sci. adv. bd. 2010—), Eye Bank Assn. Am. (bd. dirs. 1997—99, R. Townley Paton, M.D. award 2000, Bausch and Lomb Visionaries award 2005), South-Ctrl. Eyebank Assn. (pres. 1997), Assn. Rsch. in Vision and Opthalmology (exec. sec.-treas. 1981—86, Honor Recognition award 1987), New Eng. Ophthal. Soc., Internat. Soc. Contact Lens Rsch. (pres. 2009—11, Montague Ruben medal 2005, Brit. Contact Lens Assn. medal 2007), Internat. Eye Found. Eye Surgeons, Keratorefractive Soc. (bd. dirs.), Castroviejo Soc. Corneal Surgeons (pres. 1988—90, Honor Recognition award 1987, 1996), Contact Lens Assn. Ophthlamologists Am. (pres. 1987, Honor Recognition award 1988, 20th Conrad Behrens medal lectr. 1989, 7th Donald Korb award 2008, 31st World Ophthalmology Congress Hamano Gold medal 2008), Harvard Club (Dallas, N.Y.), Park Cities Club, Johns Hopkins Club (comdr.), Order of St. John (U.S., U.K.), Phi Beta Kappa. Republican. Episcopalian. Home: 27 Lakeside Park Dallas TX 75225-8110 Office: U Tex Southwestern Med Ctr Dept Ophthalmology 5323 Harry Hines Blvd Dallas TX 75390-9057 Office Phone: 214-648-8074, 214-645-2020. Business E-Mail: dwight.cavanagh@utsouthwestern.edu.

CAVANAGH, JAMES ELLSWORTH, JR., medical educator; b. Plattsburgh, NY, Jan. 31, 1930; s. James Ellsworth and Marjorie Carroll Cavanagh; m. Susan Caldwell Dodd, Oct. 9, 1976; stepchildren: Mary Harwood Dodd, Anna Walker Dodd, Robert Howe Dodd Jr.; m. Elizabeth Brady Cavanagh, Aug. 25, 1951 (div. 1975); children: Ralph Carroll, Robert Ellsworth, John Henry, Caitlin Cavanagh Wold. BA, Dartmouth Coll., Hanover, NH, 1951; MD, Harvard Med. Sch., Boston, 1954. Diplomate Am. Bd. Surgeons, Chgo., 1963, Am. Coll. Surgeons, Chgo., 1967. Surg. intern Boston U. Boston City Hosp., 1954—55, surg. resident, Harvard U., 1955—57; surg. resident Dartmouth Affiliated Hosps., Hanover, NH, 1959—61, chief surg. resident, 1961; with dept. surgery Charleston Naval Hosp. US Navy, SC, 1957—59; gen. surg. practice Portsmouth Hosp., NH, 1962—76, Tallahassee Meml. Hosp., 1976—97; faculty, clin. assoc. prof., dept. biomed. scis. Fla. State U. Coll. Medicine, Tallahassee, 2001—. Admissions com. mem. FSU Coll. Medicine, Tallahassee, 2001—. Contbr. articles to profl. surg. jours. Mem. Leon County Water Resource Com., Tallahassee, 1999—2009. Lt. USN, 1959—61, Charleston Naval Hosp. Recipient Eagle Scout award, Nat. Coun., Boy Scouts Am., 1947. Mem.: New Eng. Surg. Soc. (sr. mem. 1975—). Avocations: tennis, bird photography. Home: 3950 Bellac Rd Tallahassee FL 32303 Office: Fla State Univ Coll Medicine 1115 West Call St Tallahassee FL 32306 Business E-Mail: jim.cavanagh@med.fsu.edu.

CAVANAUGH, JAMES HENRY, health products executive, retired federal official; b. Orange, NJ, Mar. 3, 1937; s. James H. and Madeline Rachel (McFerren) C.; m. Esther Sally Musselman, Jan. 20, 1962; children: Elizabeth Anne, Michael Patrick. BS, Fairleigh Dickinson U., 1959; MA, U. Iowa, 1961, PhD, 1964. Asst. adminstr. Princeton Hosp., NJ, 1961-62; asst. prof. hosp. and health care adminstrn. U. Iowa, 1964-66; spl. asst. to surgeon gen. USPHS, 1966-67, dir. office comprehensive health planning, 1967-68; dep. asst. sec. health & sci. affairs US Dept. Health Edn. & Welfare, 1969-71; staff asst. for health affairs The White House, The White House, 1971-73, asst. dir. domestic council, 1973-74, dep. dir., 1974-75, dep. chief of staff, 1975-76; v.p. corp. devel. Allergan Pharms., Irvine, Calif., 1977-78, sr. v.p. sci. and planning, 1978-81; spl. cons. to Pres. The White House, 1981; pres. Allergan Internat., 1981-82, SmithKline BioSci. Labs., 1983-85, Smith Kline & French Labs. US, Phila., 1985-01; gen. ptnr. HealthCare Ventures, LLC. Founding bd. dirs. Marine Nat. Bank, Santa Ana Calif.; chmn. Shire Pharms. Group, PLC, 1999-2008, bd. dirs., Middlebrook Pharms., Verenium Corp., 1992-, chmn., 1998- Mem. Pres.'s Export Council, 1981-85; bd. dirs. Proprietary Assn., 1980-82; trustee Nat. Com. for Quality Health Care, nat. chmn. 1988; trustee emeritus Calif. Coll. Medicine; mem. nat. adv. com. Am. Refugee Com. Recipient Disting. Alumnus award U. Iowa Coll. Medicine, Disting. Alumni Achievement award U. Iowa. Mem. Am. Hosp. Assn. (hon.), Pharm. Mfrs. Assn. (bd. dirs. 1986-88), Union League Club (Phila.), Nassau Club. Episcopalian (vestryman). Office: HealthCare Ventures LLC 44 Nassau St Princeton NJ 08542-4506 Office Phone: 609-430-3930. *

CAVANAUGH, STEVEN M., healthcare company executive; BA magna cum laude, U. Toledo; MA in Fin., U. Mich. Joined Manor Care, Inc., Toledo, 1993, gen. mgr. impatient and outpatient rehab. ops., v.p., dir. corp. devel., 1999—2006, CFO, 2006—. Mem. Bus. Adv. Coun., U. Toledo. Office: Manor Care Inc 333 N Summit St Toledo OH 43604 Office Phone: 419-252-5554. *

CAVANNA, LUIGI, oncologist, consultant; b. Piacenza, Italy, Jan. 22, 1953; s. Giuseppe Cavanna and Elisabetta Bocciarelli; m. Marisella Gatti, June 30, 1990. Degree in Medicine and Surgery, U. Pavia, Italy, 1978. Cert. hematology specialist U. Pavia, 1981, internal medicine specialist 1986, oncology specialist 1990, gastroenterology specialist. Dir., dept. internal medicine Hosp. Piacenza, 1994—2001, dir., dept. oncology and hematology, 2001—. Author: (book) Ultrasound In Hematology, Ultrasound In Internal Medicine; contbr. articles to 130 sci. internat. publs. Recipient Hon. Citizen award, Gold's Heart award, Gold's Scalpel award. Mem.: European Group Blood and Marrow Transplantation, European Soc. Med. Oncology, Am. Soc. Med. Oncology. Office: Piacenza Gen Hosp ESMO Designated Ctr Integrated Oncology & Palliative Care Via Giuseppe Taverna 49 29121 Piacenza PC Italy Business E-Mail: l.cavanna@ausl.pc.it.

CAVAZZUTI, GIOVANNI BATTISTA, pediatrician, educator; b. Modena, Italy, Dec. 14, 1929; s. Filippo Cavazzuti and Wanda Simonini; m. Maria Teresa Camurri, June 16, 1963; children: Giovanna, Lucia. Medicine and Surgery, U. Modena, Italy, 1953; Specialization in Paediatrics, 1955; Habilitation in Clin. Paediatrics, Rome, 1960; Habilitation in Child Neuropsychiatry, 1967. Univ. asst. Inst. Clin. Paediatrics, Modena, Italy, 1954—71, assoc. prof. paediatrics, 1971—73, prof. neonatology, 1973—86, prof. paediatrics, 1986—99. Dir. div. neonatology Gen. Hosp. Modena, Italy, 1976—99; dir. Inst. Paediatric Clinic, Modena, Italy, 1986—96; dir. dept. of gynecol. obstetrics, pediatrics, Modena, 1994—2000; dir. Specialization Schs. Paediatrics, Child Neuropsychiatry, Modena, 1977—2001. Author: Principi e Pratica di Pediatria, 1985, 2005, Manuale di Neuropediatria, 1998, 4th edit., 2005; editor: Notiziario di Neuropediatria, 1980—95; mem. editl. bd.: Up-To-date Pediats., 1998—, Trends in Medicine, 2001—; contbr. articles to profl. jours. Mem. Mcpl. Coun., Modena, Italy, 1990—95, Fondazione Cassa di Risparmio, Modena, 2000—05. Named Knight Cmdr. of San Silvestro, Papa Catholic Ch., Rome, 1996. Mem.: Theatine Acad. Scis., Italian History Medicine Soc., Italian Soc. Bioethics (v.p. 2006—), Soc. Europenne de Neurologie Pediatrique Bruxelles (pres. 1982—84), Catholic Physicians Assn. (pres. 1990—99), NY Acad. Scis., Lions Dist. TB Italy (officer 1987—2007), Lions Club Modena Estense (pres. 1986—87, 2005—06). Avocations: history, travel, hunting. Home: 126 Via Buon Pastore 41100 Modena Italy Office: Hesperia Hosp Via Arqua 80 41125 Modena MO Italy Office Phone: 059 393101. Personal E-mail: g.cavazzuti@virgilio.it.

CAVENEE, WEBSTER K., director; b. Sept. 12, 1951; BS in Biology, Kansas State U., 1973. Vis. rsch. scientist Ctr. Cancer Rsch. MIT, 1979—81; assoc. Howard Hughes Med. Inst., U. Utah, 1981—83; assist. then assoc. prof. microbiology & molecular genetics U. Cincinnati, 1983—86; vis. prof. Karolinska Inst., Stockholm, 1985; dir. Ludwig Inst. Cancer Rsch., prof. medicine, neurology, pathology, & human genetics McGill U., 1986—91; Sokolow vis. prof. U. Calif., San Francisco, 1988, dir., prof. Ludwig Inst. for Cancer Rsch. LaJolla, 1991—. Mem. GM Adv. Council, Cancer Rsch. Found.; chair exec. com. World Alliance Cancer Rsch. Organizations, 2002; fellow Nat. Found. Cancer Rsch., 2003. Fellow: Am. Acad. Microbiology, Internat. Union Against Cancer, Am. Assn. Cancer Rsch.; mem.: NAS, Inst. Medicine, Am. Soc. Clinical Investigation (hon.), Am. Soc. Microbiology, Am. Assn. for Advancement of Sci., Am. Soc. Human Genetics. Office: Ludwig Inst 9500 Gilman Dr La Jolla CA 92093-0660 E-mail: wcavenee@ucsd.edu.

CAVEZZI, ATTILIO, surgeon, consultant; b. San Benedetto del Tronto, Italy, May 7, 1961; MD, Bologna U., Italy, 1988; specialization in Vascular Surgery, Modena U., Italy, 1993. Freelance cons. Vascular Unit Clinic Stella Maris and Poliambulatorio Hippocrates, San Benedetto del Tronto, 1990—. Achievements include research in angiology, phlebology, lymphology and venous surgery. Office: Poliambulatorio Hippocrates Via Giovanni Xxiii 7 63074 San Benedetto del Tronto AP Italy Office Fax: +39-0735-4431160. Personal E-mail: info@cavezzi.it.

CAVRIC, GORDANA, physician; b. Hrvatska, Aug. 19, 1968; MSc, Med. Sch. Zagreb, 1993. Physician U. Hosp. Merkur, 2008—. Home: Aleja Antuna Augustincica 18 Zagreb Hrvatska 10000 Croatia Personal E-mail: gcavric@yahoo.com.

CAWOOD, JENNY LIND, social worker, poet; b. Harlan, Ky., Aug. 15, 1940; d. James Abram and Lillian Greer Cawood; m. Hartwell Lynn Chenault, Mar. 1966 (div. 1986); children: James Cawood Chenault, Henry Brian Chenault. BA in Speech, Abilene Christian U., 1962; MSW, U. Louisville, 1966. LCSW Va. Dir. social work Battey State Hosp., Rome, Ga., 1967—68; clin. social worker Child and Family Svcs., Monroe, Mich., 1974—78; oncology social worker The Toledo Hosp., 1978—79; clin. social worker Ide Cmty. Mental Health, Toledo, 1979—80, Cmty. Mental Health Ctr. West, Toledo, 1980—84; unit social worker St. Albans Hosp., Radford, Va., 1984—85; clin. social worker Human Affairs Internat., Raleigh, NC, 1988. Mgr. rental properties. Avocations: poetry, doing poetry readings. Office Phone: 501-922-3436.

CAWVEY, CLARENCE EUGENE, retired physician; b. Du Quoin, Ill., May 16, 1929; s. Clarence Eli and Lois Jane (Matheny) C.; m. Paulina Isabel Hincke, Sept. 12, 1953 (dec. Apr. 1973); children: Janet Edna (dec.), William Clarence (dec.), Paulina Ann, Jean Hincke; 1 stepchild, Douglas Lance Hester; m. Linda Mae Rice, Jan. 26, 1974. BA, Yale U., 1951; MD, U. Chgo., 1955. Diplomate Am. Bd. Family Practice. Intern Cook County Hosp., 1955-56; resident in psychiatry Brook Army Hosp., 1956-57; ptnr. Pinckneyville (Ill.) Med. Group, 1958—98; ret., 1998. Clin. asst. prof. Med. Sch. So. Ill. U., Springfield, 1976-2000, adv. com. continuing med. edn., 1977-2000; exec. com. Ctrl. Ill. Profl. Rev. Orgn., Champaign, 1988-2002; bd. dirs., chmn. First Nat. Bank, Pinckneyville. Founding mem., pres. Perry County Health Dept., Pinckneyville, 1970. Capt. U.S. Army, 1956-58. Fellow Am. Acad. Family Physicians; mem. AMA, Ill. State Med. Soc. (del. 1960-70), Perry County Med. Soc. Republican. Methodist. Avocations: skiing, photography, travel, gardening. Home: 204 W Laurel St Pinckneyville IL 62274-1019

CEASOR, AUGUSTA CASEY, medical technician, microbiologist, clinical laboratory scientist; b. Birmingham, Ala., Feb. 22, 1943; d. Augustus and Willie Mae (Stubbs) C. AS, SUNY, 1981; BS, So. Ill. U., 1981. Cert. clin. lab. scientist Nat. Cert. Agy. Lab. asst. Mt. Sinai Hosp., Miami Beach, Fla., 1967—68; lab. technician Coordinated Lab. Svcs., Jamaica, NY, 1969—71; med. technician Andrew Radar U.S. Army Health Clinic, Ft. Myer, Va., 1972—76; med. technologist Armed Forces Inst. Pathology, Washington, 1976—91, Dept. Army, Mil. Dist. Wash., Ft. Myer, 1991—97; ret. Dept. of Army, 1997; cons. clin. lab. sci., 1997—. Dept. asst. Webster U., Ocala, Fla., 1999; sci. fair judge Am. Soc. Microbiology, Washington, 1988—97, emeritus judge, 2009; high sch. sci. mentor Minority Women in Sci., 1989—; spkr. to profl. groups; records mgr. Marion County Govt., 2000—01. Mem. editl. bd. Metroscope Newsletter, 1985-98, editor, 1989-98; tech. asst. Mycobacteriology Rsch., 1985-90. Active minority alumni scholarship com. So. Ill. U., Carbondale, 1981—; mem. Montgomery Knolls Cmty. Assn., Silver Spring, Md., 1983-96, v.p., chmn. safety and environ. com., 1984-85. Recipient Cert. of Meritorious Svc., 1991, Performance award, 1987, 89, 93, 95-97. Fellow: Alpha Mu Tau (scholarship com. 1995—97, program/social chair 2001—02, newsletter editor 2003—05, program/social chair 2004—05); mem.: DC Soc. (editl. bd. mem.), Fla. Soc. for Clin. Lab. Sci. (dir. Dist. II 2000—05, bd. dirs. 2000—, newsletters columnist 2001—, chair membership devel. com.), Capital Area Soc. for Clin. Lab. Sci. (pres.-elect 1995—96, pres. 1996—97, past pres. 1997—98), D.C. Soc. Med. Tech. (chair profl. and pub. rels. 1985—86, chair program com. 1986—87, pres. 1988, chair microbiology 1988—89, chair awards 1988—98, past pres. 1989, chair profl. and pub. rels. 1992—93, Past Pres. award 1988, Svc. award 1989, Mem. of Yr. 1989—90, Disting. Svc. award 1991, Profl. Achievement award in Microbiology 1994), Am. Bd. Bioanalysis, Internat. Soc. Clin. Lab. Tech. (cert. gen. supr.), Am. Soc. Med. Tech. (Region II Coun. 1986—93, Region II microbiology chair 1988—89, chair Region II 1990—93, coun. Region II 1996—97, mem. devel. com., Cert. of Recognition 1990), Am. Soc. Clin. Lab. Sci. (minority forum sec. 1994—96, forum scholarship com. 1996—2005, chair forum scholarship com. 1997—2004, editor The Forum newsletter 2002—10, forum for the concerns of minorities scholarship liaison 2004—, emeritus mem. 2009, Omicron Sigma award 1987—97, 2001, 2002, 2003, 2004, 2005). Roman Catholic. Achievements include research in unique toxin of mycobacterium ulcerans.

CEBI, AYSEGUL, chemistry professor; b. Samsun, Turkey, Jan. 1, 1977; MSc, Mayis U., 2002; PhD, Yuzuncu Yil U., 2007. Vice dean Giresun U., 2008—. Office: Yenimahalle Eren sok Piraziz Giresun Karadeniz 28000 Turkey Personal E-mail: cebiaysegul@hotmail.com.

CECCATTO, VANIA MARILANDE, medical educator; b. Rio Claro, Brazil, July 27, 1964; D, U. Fed. Ceará, 2001. Assoc. prof. U. Estadual do Ceará, 1998—. Office: Ave Paranjana 1700 Campus do Itaperi Fortaleza Ceará 60740-903 Brazil Office Fax: 085 3101 9796. Business E-Mail: ceccatto@uece.br.

CECCHI, GUILLERMO, research scientist; b. Argentina, Aug. 27, 1963; PhD, Rockefeller U., 1999. Rsch. staff mem. IBM Corp., 2001—. Postdoc. fellow Cornell U. Med. Sch., 2000—01. Mem.: Soc. Neurosci. Office: 1101 Kitchawan Rd Yorktown Heights NY 10598 Business E-Mail: gcecchi@us.ibm.com.

CECH, SVATOPLUK, embryologist, educator, research scientist; b. Josefov, S. Moravia, Czech Republic, Jan. 14, 1940; s. Antonin and Frantiska (Lysonkova) Cech; m. Jana Kleinwachterova, Mar. 17, 1962; children: Lenka, Barbora. MD, Masaryk U., Brno, Czech Republic, 1963, PhD, 1975; DSc, Charles U., Prague, Czech Republic, 1985. Fellow Masaryk U., 1963-77, sr. lectr., 1978-85, prof., 1986—. Rsch. fellow U. Copenhagen, 1975, Med. HS, Hannover, Germany, 1978, Univ. Clinic, Essen, Germany, 1981; vis. prof. Med. U. Luebeck, Germany, 1987; guest investigator U. Bonn, Germany, 1995; vice dean and acad. coun. med. faculty Masaryk U., Brno, Czech Republic, 2000—03. Author (with M. Dvorak, J. Stastna, P. Travnik and D. Horky): The Differentiation of Rat Ova during Cleavage, 1978 (Czech Med. Soc. prize, 1979), Stored Materials in the Course of Development of the Mammalian Ovum, 1983; author: (with M. Dvorak, J. Stastna, P. Travnik and J. Tesarik) The Differentiation of Preimplantation Mouse Embryos, 1985 (Czech Med. Soc. prize, 1987); mem. editl. bd. Scripta Medica, 2000—10; contbr. articles to profl. jours., chapters to books; editor: proceedings, texts, others. Recipient Silver medal, Med. Faculty J. E. Purkyne U., 1990, Bronze medal, Masaryk U., 1994, Hon. medal, Palacky U., 2000, Med. Faculty Masaryk U., 2000. Mem.: Soc. History Sci. Tech., N.Y. Acad. Scis., European Microscopy Soc., Czechoslovak Microscopy Soc., Czech Soc. Histochem. and Cytochem., European Cell Biology Orgn., Czech Anat. Soc., Anatomische Gesellschaft Germany, Czechoslovak Biol. Soc. (sci. sec., chmn. 1976—, J. E. Purkyne medal 1990, 2000). Roman Catholic. Avocations: music, history of medicine. Office: Masaryk U Dept Histology Kamenice 3 62500 Brno Czech Republic Home Phone: 420-549 240 854; Office Phone: 420-549493448. E-mail: scech@med.muni.cz.

CECH, THOMAS ROBERT, chemistry professor, former non-profit institute administrator; b. Chgo., Dec. 8, 1947; m. Carol Lynn Martinson; children: Allison E., Jennifer N. BA in Chemistry, Grinnell Coll., Iowa, 1970; PhD in Chem., U. Calif., Berkeley, 1975; DSc (hon.), Grinnell Coll., 1987, U. Chgo., 1991, Drury Coll., 1994, Colo. Coll., 1999, U. Md., Baltimore County, 2000, Williams Coll., 2000, Charles U., Prague, 2002, Ohio State U., 2003, Moscow State U., 2004, U. Vt., 2005, U. Buenos Aires, 2007, Dartmouth Coll., 2008, Rockefeller U., 2009. Postdoc. fellow dept. biology MIT, Cambridge, Mass., 1975—77; asst. prof. to assoc. prof. chemistry U. Colo., Boulder, 1978—83, prof. chemistry, biochemistry and molecular, cellular & devel. biology, 1983—90, disting. prof. dept. chemistry & biochemistry, 1990—; dir. Colo. Initiative Molecular Biotech., 2009—. Co-chmn. Nucleic Acids Gordon Conf., 1984; non-resident fellow Salk Inst., La Jolla, Calif., 1999; investigator Howard Hughes Med. Inst., Chevy Chase, Md., 1988—99, 2009—, pres., 2000—09. Assoc. editor Cell, 1986—87, RNA Jour.; contbg. editor: Sci. mag., 1999; contbr. articles to profl. jours. Trustee Grinnell Coll. Recipient Am. Inst. Chemists medal, 1970, Rsch. Career Devel. award, Nat. Cancer Inst., 1980—85, Young Sci. award, Passano Found., 1984, Harrison Howe award, 1984, Pfizer award, 1985, V.D. Mattia award, 1987, Louisa Gross Horowitz prize, Columbia U., 1988, Heineken prize, Royal Netherlands Acad. Arts & Scis., 1988, Gairdner Found. Internat. award, 1988, Lasker Basic Med. Rsch. award, 1988, Rosenstiel award, Brandeis U., 1989, Warren Triennial prize, 1989, Nobel prize in chemistry, 1989, Hopkins medal, Brit. Biochem. Soc., 1992, Feodor Lynen medal, 1995, Nat. Sci. medal, 1995, Mike Hogg award, M.D. Anderson Cancer Ctr., 1997, Wright prize, Harvey Mudd Coll., 1998, Gregor Mendel medal, Acad. Sci. Czech Republic, 2002; named Westerner of Yr., Denver Post, 1986; fellow, NSF, 1970—75; Nat. Cancer Inst. rsch. fellow, 1975—77, Guggenheim fellow, 1985—86. Mem.: NAS, AAAS (Newcombe-Cleve. award 1988), RNA Soc. (v.p. 1993—96), European Molecular Biology Orgn., Am. Philos. Soc., Am. Acad. Arts & Scis., Am. Soc. Biochem. Molecular Biology, Inst. Medicine. Office: U Colo Cristol Chemistry 334B Boulder CO 80309-0215 Office Phone: 303-492-4606. E-mail: Thomas.Cech@colorado.edu.

CEDAR, HOWARD, molecular biologist; b. NYC, Jan. 12, 1943; s. Morris and Tannie (Feitelson) Cedar; m. Zipora Kriger, Mar. 12, 1967; m. Joseph Cedar; m. Dahlia Cedar; m. Noa Cedar; m. Yoav Cedar; m. Yonaton Cedar; m. Daniel Cedar. BSc., MIT, 1964; MD, PhD, NYU, 1970. Intern NYU Med. Sch., 1970-71; rsch. assoc. NIH, Bethesda, Md., 1971-73; lectr. dept. cellular biochemistry & human genetics Hebrew U. Hadassah Med. Sch., Jerusalem, 1973-75, sr. lectr., 1975-78, assoc. prof., 1978-81, prof., 1981—, Harry & Helen L. Brenner chair molecular biology. Recipient Gairdner Internat. award, Gairdner Found., Can., 2011; co-recipient Wolf Found. prize in Medicine, Israel, 2008. Mem.: Human Genome Orgn., European Molecular Biology Orgn., Israel Acad. Scis. & Humanities. Jewish. Office: Hebrew U Med Sch Hadassah Medical Center Ein Karem 91999 Jerusalem Israel *

CEDAR, MERYL NEWMAN, pediatrician; m. Phil Cedar; 2 children. Attended, SUNY Downstate Med. Ctr., 1981. Diplomate Am. Bd. Pediatrics. Clin. instr. in pediat. Weill Cornell Med. Ctr.; resident Weill Cornell Med. Coll.; with Lenox Hill Hosp.; intern in pediat. NY Presbyn. Hosp. - Weill Cornell Med. Ctr., resident in pediat., 1982—84, fellow, 1984—87, pediatrician early intervention program, asst. attending pediatrician; pediatrician NY Presbyn. Hosp. - Weill Cornell. Mem. voluntary faculty com. Weill Cornell Med. Ctr.; preceptor Weill Cornell Med. Coll. Recipient Tchg. Excellence, 2009; named one of the Best Doctors in America Database, 2009—10; named to NY Mag., Castle Connolly, Guide To America's Top Pediatricians. Avocations: bicycling, travel. Office: New York Presbyterian Hospital 215 E 79th St New York NY 10075 Office Phone: 212-737-7800.

CEDERBAUM, STEPHEN D., clinical geneticist, educator; b. Bklyn. married; 2 children. BA in Chemistry with honors, Amherst Coll.; MD with honors, NYU, 1964. Lic. Calif., 1971, cert. Am. Bd. Clin. Genetics-Med. Genetics, 1982, Am. Bd. Clin. Biochemical Genetics-Med. Genetics, 1982. Intern Barnes-Jewish Hosp., 1965, resident, 1965—66; fellow Univ. Wash. Med. Ctr., 1968—70; prof. pediat. UCLA; hosp. affiliation includes UCLA Med. Ctr., Santa Monica, Stewart and Lynda Resnick Neuropsychiatric Hosp.; physician Ronald Raegan UCLA Med. Ctr., 1971—. Office: University California Los Angeles Children's Health Center 635 Charles E Young Dr S Rm 347 Los Angeles CA 90095-7332 Office Phone: 310-825-0402.

CEDERHOLM, JAN, medical educator; b. Uppsala, June 28, 1947; Cert. assoc. prof. Uppsala U., 1985. Assoc. prof. Dept. Pub. Health and Caring Scis., Family Medicine and Clin. Epidemiology, 1990—. Mem.: European Assn. Study Diabetes. Office: BMC Box 564 Uppsala S-75122 Sweden Business E-Mail: jan.cederholm@pubcare.uu.se.

CEDOLINI, ANTHONY JOHN, psychologist; b. Rochester, NY, Sept. 19, 1942; s. Peter Ross and Mary J. (Anthony) C.; m. Clare Marie De Rose, Aug. 16, 1964; children: Maria A., Antonio C., Peter E. Student, U. San Francisco, 1960-62; BA, San Jose State U., 1965, MS, 1968; PhD in Ednl. Pscyhology, Columbia Pacific U., 1983. Lic. ednl. psychologist, sch. adminstr., marriage, family, child counselor, sch psychologist, sch. counselor, social worker, real estate broker, Calif. Ptnr., founder Cienega Valley Vineyards and DeRose Winery (formerly Almaden Vineyards) and Comml. Shopping Ctrs., 1968—; coord. psychol. svcs. Oak Grove Sch. Dist., San Jose, Calif., 1968-81, asst. dir. pupil svcs., 1977-81, dir. pupil svcs., 1981-83; pvt. practice, ednl. psychologist Ednl. Assocs., San Jose, 1983—. Co-dir. Biofeedback Inst. of Santa Clara County, San Jose, 1976-83; ptnr. in Cypress Ctr.-Ednl. Psychologists and Consultancy, 1978-84; cons., program auditor for Calif. State Dept. Edn.; instr. U. Calif., Santa Cruz and LaVerne Coll. Ext. courses; guest spkr. San Jose State U.; lectr., workshop presenter in field; owner Grove Bldg. Author: Occupational Stress and Job Burnout, 1982, A Parents Guide to School Readiness, 1971, The Effect of Affect, 1975; contbr. articles to profl. jours. and newspapers. Co-founder, bd. dirs. Lyceum of Santa Clara County, 1971—, Graham Owners Club of Calif., founder, contbr. Nostalgia Vintage Car Mus., 1974-78. Avocations: coin collecting/numismatics, antiques, winemaking, classic cars, woodcarving. Home and Office: 1183 Nikulina Ct San Jose CA 95120-5441 Office Phone: 408-997-2700. Personal E-mail: tonyced@pacbell.net.

CEDZYNSKI, MACIEJ, microbiologist, research scientist, immunologist; b. Lodz, Poland, May 19, 1966; s. Andrzej Boguslaw and Urszula (Wieclawska) C.; m. Dorota Marta Prosniak, Aug. 13, 1988; 1 child, Marta. MS, U. Lodz, 1990; D in Biol. Scis., Polish Acad. Scis., Lodz, 1996; D of Habilitation in Med. Scis., Med. U. Lodz, 2005. Rsch. asst. Microbiology and Virology Ctr. Polish Acad. Scis., Lodz, 1990-91, sr. rsch. asst., 1992-96, mem. organizing com. internat. symposium, 1996, asst. prof., 1996—99, asst. prof., head dept., 1999—2003, Med. Biology, 2004—06, assoc. prof., head dept.,

2008—, Inst. Med. Biology, Polish Acad. Sci., Ctr. Med. Biology, 2006—08. Sci. guest Robert Koch-Inst., Wernigerode, Germany, 1992; vis. rschr. Inst. Organic Chemistry, Russian Acad. Scis., Moscow, 1997, Inst. Virology Slovak Acad. Scis., Bratislava, Slovak Rep., 2000., SNBTS, Nat. Sci. Lab., Edinburgh, 2005, 07. Co-author: Inflammation Patophysiology and Clinics, 1998. Fellow Found. Polish Sci., 1996; grantee Fedn. European Microbiol. Scis., 1994, Polish Com. Sci. Rsch., 1992, 2000, 06, IUIS, 2001, Polish Ministry Sci. & Higher Edn., 2010. Mem. Polish Microbiol. Soc. (v.p. Lodz regional com. 1996-2000). Office: Inst Med Biology PAS Ul. Lodowa 106 93-232 Lodz Poland E-mail: mcedzynski@cbm.pan.pl.

CEKIN, ENGIN IBRAHIM, otolaryngologist, educator; b. Merzifon, Turkey, Nov. 25, 1966; s. Mitat and Nurhan Cekin; m. Fugen Erdogan, June 7, 1991; 1 child, Irem. MD, Hacettepe U., Ankara, Turkey, 1990. Physician Zekai Tahir Burak Women's Hosp., Ankara, 1991—94, Turkish Navy Ship, Sancaktar Navy Ship, Mersin, Turkey, 1995—98; resident in otolaryngology Gulhane Military Medical Acad. Haydarpasa Tng. Hosp., Istanbul, Turkey, 1998—2001; specialist in otolaryngology Gulhane Mil. Med. Acad., Ankara, 2001—04; asst. prof. GATA Haydarpasa Tng. Hosp., Istanbul, 2004—10, assoc. prof., 2010—. Business E-Mail: iecekin@hotmail.com.

CELENTANO, CLAUDIO, obstetrician, researcher; b. Naples, Italy, May 11, 1970; s. Ciro Celentano and Olimpia Elefante; m. Giuseppina Gallo. MD, U. Chieti, Pescara, Italy, 1994. Bd. cert. in med. genetics. Sr. specialist dept. ob-gyn. San Massimo Hosp., Penne, Italy, 2000—; resident in med. genetics U. Chieti, 2001—05. Mem.: Am. Coll. Ob-Gyn. (assoc.). Office: Dept ObGyn San Massimo Hosp 1 Brigata alpini st 65017 Penne Italy Home: Via Caduti Per Servizio 4 65129 Pescara PE Italy Fax: +390854492395. E-mail: ccelen@tin.it.

CELESIA, GASTONE GUGLIELMO, neurologist; b. Genoa, Italy, Nov. 22, 1933; came to U.S., 1959, naturalized, 1970; s. Raffaele Amadeo and Ottavia (Tortrino) C.; m. Linda Irene Pike, Aug. 1, 1964; children: Gloria, Laura. MD, U. Genoa, 1959; MS, McGill U., Montreal, 1965. Diplomate Am. Bd. Psychiatry and Neurology in Neurology, Am. Bd. Psychiatry and Neurology in Clin. Neurophysiology. Intern Madison Gen. Hosp., Wis., 1960; resident in neurology Montreal Neurol. Inst./McGill U., Montreal, Que., Canada, 1962-66; fellow neurophysiology U. Wis., Madison, 1960-62, asst. prof. neurology, 1966-69, assoc. prof., 1970-73, prof., 1974-79, 1979-83; chief neurology svc. VA Hosp., Madison, 1979-83; prof. neurology Loyola U., Chgo., 1983—99, chmn. dept. neurology, 1983-99, prof. neurology, 2000—03; cons. Exec. Svc. Chgo., 2003—. Cons. Exec. Svc. Core of Chgo. Editor in chief: Electroenceph. Clin. Neurophysiol., 1988-99; contbr. articles to profl. jours. Fellow Am. Acad. Neurology; mem. AMA, Am. Acad. Clin. Neurophysiology (pres. 1993-95), Am. Neurol. Assn., Wis. Neurol. Soc. Wis. Med. Alumni Assn., Wis. Neurol. Soc. (pres. 1975-76), Soc. Neurosci., Am. Epilepsy Soc., AAAS, Am. Soc. Office: 25 E Washington St Ste 1500 Chicago IL 60602-1804 Personal E-mail: g.celesia@comcast.net.

CELI, FRANCESCO SAVERIO, geriatrician, endocrinologist; b. Italy; MD, U. Rome, 1987. Resident in geriat. U. Rome, 1987—91; spl. vol., divsn. geriat. Johns Hopkins U. Sch. Medicine, Balt., 1991—92, rsch. fellow, lab. clin. physiology-diabetes unit Nat. Inst. on Aging-Gerontology Rsch. Ctr., NIH, Balt., 1992—94; resident in internal medicine Greater Balt. Med. Ctr., 1994—97; clin. fellow in endocrinology U. Md., Balt., 2000—02; mem. clin. endocrinology br. Nat. Inst. Diabetes and Digestive and Kidney Diseases, NIH, Bethesda, Md. Office: NIDDK NIH Bldg 10-CRC Rm 6-3940 10 Center Dr Bethesda MD 20892 Office Phone: 301-435-9267. Office Fax: 301-480-4517. E-mail: fc93a@nih.gov.

CELI, LEO ANTHONY G., intensivist, infectious disease specialist, internist, informatician, researcher; s. Valentin Gale and Galicana Gutierrez Celi. MD, U. Philippines, Manila, 1990; MS, MIT, Cambridge, 2009; MPH, Harvard U., 2010. Cert. critical care medicine Am. Bd. Internal Medicine, 2009, infectious disease Am. Bd. Internal Medicine, 2006, diplomate Am. Bd. Internal Medicine, 2011. Med. resident Cleve. Clinic, 1991—94; clin. rsch. fellow and faculty Harvard Med. Sch., Boston, 1994—98; clin. fellow and faculty Stanford U. Sch. Medicine, Calif., 1998—2000; ICU cons. Visicu, Baltimore, 2000—02; rsch. fellow Harvard-MIT Health Scis. and Tech., Cambridge, 2007—10; ICU & infectious disease specialist Dunedin Hosp. & U. Otago, New Zealand, 2002—07; intensivist Beth Israel Deaconess Med. Ctr., 2010—; rsch. scientist MIT Divsn. Health Scis. & Tech., 2010—. Dir., founder Sana, Cambridge, Mass., 2008. Recipient Info. Tech. award, Mass. Med. Soc.; Rsch. Scholarship, Nat. Libr. Medicine, 2007—10. Roman Catholic. Home: 350 Third St Apt 1608 Cambridge MA 02142 Office: Harvard-MIT Health Scis and Tech Divsn 77 Massachusetts Ave E25-505 Cambridge MA 02139 Business E-Mail: lceli@mit.edu.

CELIK, ALPER, surgeon; b. Aksaray, Turkey, Feb. 26, 1975; s. Omar Seyfettin and Kezban Celik; m. Asli Duru, May 10, 2003. MD, Ankara U., Turkey, 1999. Surg. resident Dept. Gen. Surgery Ankara Oncology Hosp., Demetevler, Turkey, 2000, gen. surgery resident Dept. Gen. Surgery, 2000—04, cons. surgeon Dept. Gen. Surgery, 2004—05; consulting surgeon Faculty Medicine Dept. Gen. Surgery Gaziosmanpasa U., Tokat, Turkey, 2005—. Dir. various rsch. projects.; presenter in field; postgrad. fellow on laparoendoscopic surgery Toscana U., 2005; rschr. Dept. Gen. Surgery Tepecik Tng. and Rsch. Hosp., Izmir, Turkey, 2005. Reviewer: Internat. Jour. Gynecol. Cancer; contbr. rsch. papers to profl. publs. Mem.: Turkish Soc. Surg. Oncology (assoc.). Independent. Achievements include development of secretory breast carcinoma with extensive intraductal component; first to colonoscopic removal of inguinal hernia mesh; research in micrometastatic breast carcinoma in Turkish pPopulation; mammographic screening of women. Avocations: transcendental meditation, gardening, tai chi. Home: Batisitesi Mh 5 Cd 280 Sk No:6/3 6320 Mesa, Batikent Ankara Turkey Office Fax: 00-90-356-2133832. Personal E-mail: doktoralper@hotmail.com.

ÇELIK, SEVIM, nursing educator; b. Çaycuma, Turkey, Nov. 2, 1976; d. Ibrahim and Hayriye Akgül; m. Kadir Çelik, Oct. 28, 2000; 1 child, Boran. RN, Istanbul U., Turkey, 1997, MSc, 2000, PhD, 2004. Editor: Jour. Intensive Care Nursing, 2005. Mem.: Intensive Care Nursing Assn. (bd. mem. 2001—03, sec. 2003—05). Office: Zonguldak Karaelmas U Zonguldak Sch Nursing 67100 Site Zonguldak Turkey

CELIK, TURGAY, cardiologist, educator; b. Elazig, Mar. 18, 1970; MD, Gulhane Med. Faculty, 1993. Assoc. prof., cardiology, 2000, Gulhane Mil. Med. Acad., Sch. Medicine, 2006—. Mem.: Turkish Soc. Cardiology. Avocations: history, tennis. Office: Gulhane Tip Fakultesi Gen Tevfi Ankara 06018 Turkey Office Fax: 00903123044250. E-mail: benturgay@yahoo.com.

ÇELIKTEN, ALPER, thoracic surgeon; b. Giresun, June 1, 1980; MD, Gazi U., 2005. Thoracic surgeon Yedikule Tchg. Hosp. Chest Diseases and Thoracic Surgery, 2006—. Mem.: Turkish Soc. Thoracic Surgeons, Turkish Thoracic soc., ESTS. Office: Telsiz Mah G-2 sok 4 Daire 7 ZEY Istanbul 34020 Turkey E-mail: alceli@yahoo.com.

CELLENO, LEONARDO, dermatologist; b. Rome, July 10, 1951; Degree in Medicine and Surgery, Cath. U. Rome, 1980, Specialization in Dermatology and Venereology, 1983. Dermatologist Bus. Unit Dermatology Integrated Complex Cath. U. Rome, 2002—. Prof., sch. specialization dermatology Cath. U. Rome, 1985—2011, prof., coord., degree cosmetic sci. and tech., 2006; mem., sci. com. European Union, 1990—2000. Recipient Knight's award, Pres. Italian Republic. Mem.: Italian Assn. Dermatology and Cosmetology (pres.), Italian Soc. Dermatology. Avocations: photography, fishing. Office: Via Cesare Beccaria 98 Rome Lazio 00196 Italy Office Fax: 0039-0-636006633. Personal E-mail: lcelleno@libero.it.

CELLO, JOHN P., gastroenterologist, educator; MD, Harvard U., 1969. Diplomate Am. Bd. Internal Medicine, 1972, Am. Bd. Internal Medicine-gastroenterology, 1977. Resident internal medicine Peter Bent Brigham Hosp., 1970—72; fellow gastroenterology Univ. of Calif. San Francisco Med. Ctr., 1975—77, med. dir. bariatric surgery; dir. med. edn. in gastroenterology San Francisco Gen. Hosp. Prof. medicine and surgery Univ. of Calif. San Francisco. Recipient Distinguished Educator award, Am. Gastroenterology Assn., Am. Soc. for Gastrointestinal Endoscopy. Fellow: Am. Gastroent. Assn.; mem.: ACP, Western Soc. for Clin. Investigation, Am. Soc. of Gastrointestinal Endoscopy, Calif. Acad. of Medicine. Office: University of California San Francisco General Hospital Ste NH3D 1001 Potrero Ave San Francisco CA 94110 Office Phone: 415-206-4746.

CELMER, VIRGINIA, psychologist; b. Detroit, June 26, 1945; d. Charles and Stella (Kopicko) C. BA in English, Marygrove Coll., 1968; MA in Theol. Studies, St. Louis U., 1977; PhD in Counseling Psychology, Tex. Tech. U., 1986. Lic. psychologist; lic. chem. dependency counselor; cert. internat. cert. alcoholism and drug abuse counselor; cert. group psychotherapist; cert. sex addiction therapist level II, multiple sex addiction therapist. Chaplain Mercy Ctr. for Health Care Svcs., Aurora, Ill., 1977-81; grad. asst. counselor U. Counseling Ctr., Tex. Tech. U., Lubbock, 1982-86, pre-doctoral intern in counseling psychology, 1985-86; post-doctoral intern Consultation Ctr., San Antonio, 1986-89, staff psychologist, 1989-90; pvt. practice psychologist San Antonio, 1989—. Instr. dept. psychology Tex. Tech. U., Lubbock, 1981-85, Oblate Sch. Theology, San Antonio, 1989-90. Contbr. articles to profl. jours. Mem. APA, Tex. Psychol. Assn., Bexar County Psychol. Assn., Am. Group Psychotherapy Assn., San Antonio Group Psychotherapy Assn., Nat. Assn. Alcoholism and Drug Abuse Counselors, Tex. Assn. Alcoholism and Drug Abuse Counselors. Office: 5440 Babcock Rd Ste 110 San Antonio TX 78240-3946 Office Phone: 210-641-7400.

CENTAFONT, LUCY ANN ALEXANDER, occupational therapist, consultant; b. Anchorage, Alaska, Apr. 6, 1953; d. Robert C. and Lucy Ann (Morgan) Alexander; m. Richard A. Centafont, May 13, 1978; children: Ryan Alan, Jeffrey Richard, Lauren Ann. BS in Occupational Therapy, Temple U., 1977, MS, 1987; BS in Health Edn., Slippery Rock U., 1975. Occupational therapy cons. Bucks County Assn. for Retarded Citizens, Doylestown, Pa.; dir. occupational therapy Community Found. for Human Devel., Sellersville, Pa.; chief occupational therapy Rolling Hill Hosp., Elkins Park, Pa.; pvt. practice occupational therapy cons. Southampton, Pa. Mem. Am. Occupational Therapy Assn., Pa. Occupational Therapy Assn. (developmental disabilities spl. interest group, adminstrv. sch. sys. spl. interest group).

CENTENO, ROBERT FRANCIS, plastic surgeon; b. Frederiksted, St. Croix, Jan. 30, 1968; s. Juan Centeno and Lucrecia Monte-Elliott. BS, Dickinson Coll., Carlisle, Pa., 1989; MBA, U. Pa., Phila., 1995; MD, MCP Hahnemann Sch. Medicine, Phila., 1995. Cert. in plastic surgery Am. Bd. Plastic Surgery Inc., 2005. Resident Hahnemann U.; v.p., ptnr. BodyAesthetic Plastic Surgery, St. Louis, 2002—; assoc. med. dir. gov. Juan F. Luis Hosp. & Med. Ctr. Pres. St. Croix Plastic Surgery Inc., 2008—. Editor: Cosmetic Surgery Sect. ePlasty: Open Access Jour. and Reconstructive Surgery; editorial reviewer Plastic and Reconstructive Surgery Jour., Aesthetic Surgery Journal; contbr. articles to profl. jours. Ensign US Pub. Health Svc. Recipient Best Rsch. Paper award, Am. Soc. Aesthetic Plastic Surgery, 2004, Southeastern Pa. Med. Soc. award, Dickinson Coll. Multicultural Affairs award; named one of Am. Top Surgeons, Aesthetic Plastic Surgery Consumers Rsch. Coun. Am., 2006—08; fellow, Inst. Reconstructive Plastic Surgery, NYU Med. Ctr.; Judith Mausmer MD award Excellence in Cmty. Preventative Medicine Nat. Health Policy Fellowship. Fellow: ACS; mem.: Am. Soc. Plastic Surgeons. Independent. Roman Catholic. Avocation: travel. Office: St Croix Plastic Surgery Inc Beeston Hill Med Ctr Ste 12 Christiansted VI 00820 Office Phone: 340-719-2777. Personal E-mail: rfcenteno@gmail.com. Business E-Mail: drcenteno@stcroixplasticsurgery.com.

CEPHAS, MARCELLUS, psychiatrist; Grad., Universidad de Montemorelos Facultad de Medicina, 1987; completed additional psychiatry tng., New Eng. Med. Ctr. Hosps., Morehouse Sch. of Medicine. Diplomate Am. Bd. Psychiatry. Hosp. affiliations include Rome Meml. Hosp., Wash. Adventist Hosp. Named one of the Top Doctors, Washingtonian Mag., 2011. Office: Washington Adventist Hospital Ste 200 7610 Carroll Ave Takoma Park MD 20912 Office Phone: 301-891-2077. Office Fax: 301-891-2080.

CEREGHINO, JAMES JOSEPH, health facility administrator, neurologist; b. Portland, Oreg., Oct. 27, 1937; s. Joseph Thomas and Amelia E. (Arata) C. BS, Portland State Coll., 1959; MD, U. Oreg., 1964; MS in Neurophysiology, Linfield U., 1971. Intern Good Samaritan Hosp., Portland, 1964-65; resident Good Samaritan Hosp. and Med. Ctr., Portland, 1965-68; rotating resident in neuropathology Sch. of Medicine U. Wash., 1967; rotating resident in child neurology U. Calif. Med. Ctr., San Francisco, 1968; rotating resident in psychiatry Med. Sch. U. Oreg., 1968; neurol. cons. pub. health svc.-health svcs. and mental health adminstrn.-neurol. and sensory disease control program HEW, Rockville, Md., 1968-70, staff neuroglogist epilepsy br. NIH Bethesda, Md., 1970-85; chief epilepsy br. convulsive, devel. and neuromuscular disorders program Nat. Inst. Neurol. Disorders and Stroke, Bethesda, Md., 1985-93; dir. rsch. Epilepsy Ctr. Oreg. Health Scis. U., Portland, 1993—. Prof. dept. neurology Oreg. Health Scis. U., 1993—; attending neurologist VA Med. Ctr., Portland, 1993-2004, WOC physician, 2005-; devel. coun. Neurol. Sci. Inst., 1998—2000, brainet coun., 2000—; mem. Oreg. Health Scis. U. Instnl. Rev. Bd., 1994—; spkr. in field. Editor-in-chief Epilepsia, 1986-94, emeritus, 1994-97, supplements editor, 1994-97; editl. bd. CNS News, 1999-2008; contbr. articles to profl. jours. Capt. USPHS, ret. Recipient Ford Found. Scholar, 1953—55. Fellow: Am. Clin. Neurophysiology Soc. (pub. rels. com. 1980—81); mem.: Oreg. Partnership for Alzheimer's Rsch., Alzheimer's Assn. Oreg. (rsch. com. 2000—03), Alzheimer's Rsch. Alliance Oreg. (exec. coun. 1994—2000, chmn. rsch. awards com. 1995—2001), World Fedn. Neurology (epidemiology rsch. group 1978—), Epilepsy Found. Oreg. (sec. 1993—97, region 9 rep. to Epilepsy Found. Am. 1996—2004, pres. 1997—99, v.p. 2001—02), Uniformed Svcs. Orgn. Neurologists (chmn. awards com. 1984—85), Med. Soc. D.C. (sect. neurology and neurol. surgery 1971—94), Internat. League Against Epilepsy (edn. com., coun. mem. 1985—94), Epilepsy Internat. (libr. devel. com. 1981, chmn. 1981—85), Epilepsy Found. Am. (profl. adv. bd. Washington chpt. 1969—93, speaker's bur. 1972—93, v.p. 1973—75, region IX rep. to EFA profl. adv. bd. 1996—2004), Am. Neurologic Assn., Am. Epilepsy Soc. (membership com. 1970—74, chmn. 1975—77, chmn. edn. com. 1978—80, constn. com. 1980—81, dir. continuing med. edn. 1981—83, 1st v.p. 1982—82, pres. 1983—84, v.p. to ILAE 1985—86, coun. 1985—94), Am. Acad. Neurology, Oreg. Gardeners and Ranchers Assn. (bd. dirs. 2006—), U. Oreg. Med. Sch. Alumni Assn. Office: Oreg Health Scis Univ Epilepsy Ctr CR120 3181 SW Sam Jackson Park Rd Portland OR 97239-3011 Office Phone: 503-494-5682. Business E-Mail: cereghin@ohsu.edu.

CERESINI, GRAZIANO, endocrinologist; b. Parma, June 5, 1956; MD, U. Parma, Italy, PhD, 1983. Physician U. Parma, 1984—2011. Mem.: SIGG Italian Soc. Geriat., SIE Italian Soc. Endocrinology, AME Italian Assn. Clin. Endocrinologists, Am. Assn. Clin. Endocrinologists, Endocrine Soc. Avocation: bicycling. Home: Via Marconi 94 Felino-Parma 43035 Italy Personal E-mail: ceresini@unipr.it.

CERFOLIO, NINA ESTELLE, psychiatrist, educator; b. Paterson, NJ, Feb. 15, 1960; d. Robert David and LaVerne Estelle Cerfolio. BA, Grinnell Coll., 1986; MD, Chgo. Med. Sch./U. Health Scis., 1991. Cons., liaison fellow Meml. Sloan Kettering, NYC, 1991—94; human sexuality fellow Cornell U. Med. Ctr., NYC, 1992—93; cons. liaison attending psychiatrist NYU, NYC, 1993—94; chief psychiat. emergency room and walk-in clinic St. Vincent's Hosp., NYC, 1995—98; attending psychiatrist NYU Med. Ctr., NYC, 1998—, clin. asst. prof. psychiatry, 1999—; clin. asst. prof. ob/gyn. NYU Downtown Hosp., NYC, 1998—. Contbr. articles to profl. publs. Founding mem. Grief Relief Network, 2001; pregnancy expert F Pregnancy Mag., 2002; bd. advisors Achilles Track Club, Disabled Iraqi Vets., 2004—; bd. dirs. Tri-State Cmty. Adv. Bd. Edn. Broadcasting, 2003—. Oncology fellow, Am. Cancer Soc., 1992—93. Fellow: Am. Psychiat. Assn. (founding mem. early career psychiatry exec. coun. 1996—98, corr. mem. com. on women, coun. on nat. affairs 1998—99, chmn. com. on women NY County dist. br. 2002—03, mem. exec. coun. NY County dist. br. 2002—06, disting., Woman of Yr. 2006); mem.: Morgagni Med. Soc. (mem. exec. com. 1997—99). Avocations: ironman competitions, tennis, ultra-marathons, triathlons. Home: 20 E 9th St 4J New York NY 10003 Office: 2 Fifth Ave # 5 New York NY 10011 Office Phone: 212-414-0531. Office Fax: 212-414-0531. Business E-Mail: ninacerf@nyc.rr.com.

CERISE, FREDERICK P., academic administrator, former state agency administrator; BS, Univ. Notre Dame, 1984; MD, La.State Univ., 1988; MPH, Harvard Univ., 2001. Residency Univ. Ala. Med. Ctr., Birmingham, 1988—91; staff physician through medical dir. & CEO Earl K. Long Med. Ctr., Baton Rouge, 1991—2004; medical dir. La. State Univ. Health Care Svc. Divsn.; assoc. prof. clinical med. La. State Univ., v.p. health affairs and med. edn., 2007—; sec. La. Dept. Health & Hospitals, Baton Rouge, 2004—07. Bd. mem. Baton Rouge Area Found. Office: La State Univ Office Health Affairs and Med Edn 3810 W Lakeshore Dr Baton Rouge LA 70808 Office Phone: 225-578-6935. Office Fax: 225-578-5524. Business E-Mail: fcerise@lsu.edu.

CERNADAS, MANUELA, critical care specialist, educator; MD, U. Pa., 1993. Diplomate Am. Bd. Internal Medicine, 1996, Am. Bd. Internal Medicine- pulmonary disease, 1999, Am. Bd. Internal Medicine- critical care medicine, 2002. Resident in internal medicine Brigham and Women's Hosp., 1994—96, fellow in pulmonary critical care medicine, 1996—99; asst. prof. Med. Sch. Harvard Univ.; critical care specialist Brigham and Women's Hosp. Office: Brigham and Women's Hospital Department of Medicine 15 Francis St Boston MA 02115 Office Phone: 617-525-1035. Office Fax: 617-732-7421.

CERQUEIRA, MANUEL DECASTRO, nuclear medicine physician; b. Minho, Portugal, Nov. 25, 1948; AB, Franklin and Marshall Coll., Lancaster, Pa.; MD, NYU, 1976. Diplomate Am. Bd. Nuclear Medicine, Am. Bd. Internal Medicine, Am. Bd. Cardiovascular Diseases. Intern, resident Bellevue Hosp. Ctr., NYC, 1976-80; resident cardiology, fellow nuclear medicine Yale-New Haven Hosp., 1980-83; sr. staff Veteran's Affairs Med. Ctr., Seattle; prof. Georgetown U., Washington, 1983—; chmn., dept. nuc. medicine & staff cardiologist Cleve. Clin. Found., 2004—. Chmn. Nuc. Regulatory Commn. Adv. Com. on Med. Uses of Isotopes, 1999. Mem. ASNC, Am. Coll. Cardiology, Am. Heart Assn., Soc. Nuclear Medicine. Office: Cleve Clin Jb3 9500 Euclid Ave Cleveland OH 44195 Office Phone: 216-444-2665.

CERRONE, FEDERICO, pulmonologist, educator; Attended, Georgetown U., Wash. DC, 1986. Diplomate Am. Bd. Internal Medicine, Am. Bd. Internal Medicine-pulmonary disease, Am. Bd. Internal Medicine-critical care medicine, Am. Bd. Internal Medicine-sleep medicine, lic. NJ. Resident in internal medicine Bronx Mcpl. Hosp., NY, 1987—89; tng. in pulmonary disease Georgetown Univ. Hosp., Wash., DC, fellow in pulmonary critical care medicine, 1989—92; asst. clin. prof. medicine Univ. Medicine and Dentistry Med. Sch., Newark; with Morristown Med. Ctr.; pulmonologist Overlook Med. Ctr. Mailing: c/o Morristown Medical Center 100 Madison Ave Morristown NJ 07960

CERVANTES MONTEIL, FELIPE, general and vascular surgeon; b. Mexico City, Mex., June 26, 1962; s. S. Daniel Cervantes and Guillemette Monteil de Cervantes; m. Adriana Zorrilla, Oct. 18, 1986; children: Daniel, Ricardo, Alonso. MD, La Salle U., Mexico City, 1986. Diplomate Mexican Bd. Gen. Surgery, Mex., 1991, Mexican Bd. Vascular Surgery, Mex., 1994. Gen. surgeon Nat. U. Mex., Mexico City, 1988—91, prof. surgery, 1996—; vascular surgeon Paris U., 1991—93; mem. surg. staff Am. Brit. Cowdray Med. Ctr., Mexico City, 1992—, asst. dir. tchg. and rsch. divsn., 1999—2004, dir. oper. rm. svcs., 2004—. Counselor ABC Found., Mexico City, 2003. Recipient Pres. award, Med. Assn. Am. Brit. Cowdray Med. Ctr., 2003. Fellow: ACS (assoc.); mem.: French Assn. Digestive Surgery, French Assn. Surgery, Mexican Assn. Vascular Surgery (assoc.), Mexican Assn. Gen. Surgery (assoc.). Home: Sur 132 108 - 408 Mexico City 01120 Mexico Office: Am Brit Cowdray Med Ctr Sur 136 116 col Las Americas Mexico City 01120 Mexico Home Fax: (55) 52721508. Business E-Mail: fcervantes@abchospital.com.

CERVIA, JOSEPH STEVEN, medical educator; b. NYC, Apr. 10, 1959; s. Joseph T. and Margaret (Bleier) C.; m. Denise Laura Blumberg, Aug. 10, 1986; children: David Michael, Lisa Danielle, Michael Jason. BS in Biology summa cum laude, St. John's U., 1980; MD, N.Y. Med. Coll., 1984. Diplomate Nat. Bd. Med. Examiners, Am. Bd. Internal Medicine, Am. Bd. Pediatrics, Subspeciality Bd. Infectious Diseases Internal Medicine and Pediatric; cert. HIV specialist. Intern in medicine, pediat. Brookdale Hosp. Med. Ctr., Bklyn., 1984-85, resident in medicine, pediat., 1985-88; fellow in infectious diseases N.Y. Hosp. Cornell Med. Ctr., NYC, 1988-90; asst. prof. medicine, pediat. SUNY Health Sci. Ctr., Stony Brook, 1990-92; attending physician Nassau County Med. Ctr., East Meadow, NY, 1990-92, dir. pediatric-maternal HIV svc., 1990-92; asst. prof. pediat. and medicine Cornell U. Med. Coll., 1992—96, assoc. prof. pediat. and medicine, 1996—99, assoc. prof. medicine and pediat., 1999—2004; prof. clin. medicine and pediat. Albert Einstein Coll. Medicine, 2004—. Dir. program children with AIDS The NY Hosp. Cornell Med. Ctr., 1992—99; with Comprehensive HIV Care and Rsch. Ctr. LI Jewish Med. Ctr., 1999—2004; global med. dir., sr. v.p. Pall Corp., 2004—. Contbr. articles to profl. jours. Eagle scout Boy Scouts Am., NY, 1974, asst. scoutmaster, 1977-80. Recipient Bausch and Lomb Hon. Sci. award, 1977, competitive and scholastic excellence scholarships, St. John's U., 1977-80, Harrison Scholarship award N.Y. Med. Coll., 1984, Henry Christian Meml. award Am. Fedn. Clin. Rsch., 1990. Fellow ACP, Am. Acad. Pediatrics, Pediatric Infectious Disease Soc., Infectious Disease Soc. Am., Am. Acad. HIV Medicine (bd. dirs.); mem. AAAS, AMA (physician's recognition award 1993—), Am. Soc. Microbiology, Am. Fedn. Clinic Rsch., AIDS Clin. Trials Group. Roman Catholic. Achievements include findings in the importance of the monocyte in leishmania donovani infection; immuno modulatory effects of granulocyte macrophage colony-stimulating factor and their T-cell dependence, characterizing long-term survival in children with AIDS; protection against serious bacterial infection in children with AIDS; factors influencing quality of life in children with AIDS, therapeutics for adults and children with HIV, healthcare associated infections and other infectious diseases issues. Home: 9 Pine Dr N Roslyn NY 11576-2015 Office: 400 Community Dr Manhasset NY 11030 Home Phone: 516-625-9069; Office Phone: 516-562-4280. Personal E-mail: jcervia@hotmail.com. Business E-Mail: jcervia@nshs.edu.

CERVO, LUIGI, medical researcher; b. Naples, Italy, June 21, 1956; PhD, Open U., Milton Keynes, Eng., 2005. Head, exptl. psychopharmacology 'Mario Negri' Inst. Pharmacological Rsch., 1978—. Mem.: Italian Soc. Neuropsychopharmacology, Italian Soc. Neurosci., European Behavioural Pharmacological Soc., Soc. Neurosci. Office: Via La Masa 19 Milan 20156 Italy Office Fax: 39 0239001916. Business E-Mail: luigi.cervo@marionegri.it.

CERVONKA, DANIEL STEPHEN, medical educator; b. Phila., Sept. 1, 1963; s. Barbara Ann Cervonka. BS in Social and Health Svc., Roger Williams U., 1987; degree in Physician Assoc. Studies, Yale U., 1989; postgrad., Nova Southeastern U., 1998; M in Physician Assoc. Studies, U. Nebr., 2003; postgrad., Bond U. Lectr. surgery Yale U. Sch. Medicine, New Haven, 1990—93; chief physician assoc. Griffin Hosp., Derby, Conn., 1997—; pres., cofounder U. Physician Assocs., Fairifield, Conn., 1999—2003; v.p. mission devel. One World Medicine, Hamden, Conn., 2000—; asst. clin. prof. Quinnipiac U., Hamden, Conn., 2002—. Lectr. in surgery(emergency medicine) Yale U. Sch. of Medicine, New Haven, 1990—; assoc. dir. physician asst. dept. Cornell U. Med. Coll., NYC, 1992—95. Home: 39 AP Gates East Haddam CT 06423 Office: Griffin Hosp Emergency Medicine 130 Division St Derby CT 06418 E-mail: daniel.cervonka@yale.edu.

CESAR, REGINA GRIGOLLI, physician; b. Brazil, July 24, 1968; PhD, Santa Casa de Misericordia SP Sch. Medicine, 1992. Chief-pediat. intensive care Santa Casa de Misericordia de SP Sch. Medicine, 2008—. Mem.: Brazilian Pediat. Intensive Care Soc. Avocations: surfing, skateboarding, movies. Home: Marcilio Dias 104 Lapa Sao Paulo 05077120 Brazil Personal E-mail: reginautiped@uol.com.br.

CESARIO, THOMAS CHARLES, retired dean, medical educator; b. Kenosha, Wis., June 19, 1940; BS, U. Wis., 1961, MD, 1965. Resident in internal medicine Harvard U., 1965-67, fellow Irvine, U. Calif., Irvine, 1969—72; dean med. sch. U. Calif. Irvine Sch. Medicine, Irvine, 1994—2006. Home Phone: 949-640-6416; Office Phone: 949-824-5747. E-mail: tccesari@uci.edu.

CESCAU, PATRICK, retired consumer products company executive; b. Paris, 1948; Grad. with bus. degree, ESSEC; MBA, INSEAD. Org. officer Unilever, 1973, controller, dep. fin. dir., 1988—2000, fin. dir., 0199—2000, dir., internat. foods divsn., 2001—, chmn., 2004—08. Non-exec. dir. Pearson PLC; Conseiller du Commerce Exterieur de la France Holland. Recipient Legion d'Honneur, 2005. Office: Unilever PO Box 68 EC4P 4BQ London England

CETIN, CEM, physician; b. Zonguldak, Apr. 5, 1973; MD, Ankara U., 1997, specialist in Sports Medicine, 2001. Head sports medicine dept. Suleyman Demirel U., 2003—. Physician M.P. Antalyaspor, 2008—. Mem.: Turkish Sports Medicine Assn., Health Bd. Mem. Turkish Football Fedn. Avocations: travel, music. Office: Suleyman Demirel University Dept Isparta Faculty Medicine 21260 Turkey Business E-Mail: cem@med.sdu.edu.tr.

CETIN, MUSTAFA, physician, educator; b. Nigde, July 10, 1966; MD, Cukurova U., 1990; degree in Hematology, Erciye U., 1997. Prof. medicine Erciyes U. Med. Faculty, 2003—. Office: Erciyes University Med Faculty Kayseri 38039 Turkey Office Fax: 905323956392. Business E-Mail: mcetin@erciyes.edu.tr.

CEYLAN, ASLI FAHRIYE, healthcare educator; b. Ankara, Turkey, June 1, 1977; PhD, Ankara U., 2007. Asst. lectr. U. Wyo., Laramie, 2008—. Office: University Wyo 1000E University Laramie WY 82071 Personal E-mail: asliceylanisik@gmail.com.

CHA, BONG KUEN, orthodontist, educator; b. Seoul, Republic Of Korea, Aug. 26, 1958; m. Jung Mee Kim; children: Sang Muk, He Yin. BS, Kyunghee U., Seoul, 1984; MS, Seoul Nat. U., 1990; PhD, Berlin U., 1995. Dept. chief orthodontics Bundang CHA Hosp., SeongNam City, Kyeong-Ki, Republic of Korea, 1998; prof. dept. orthodontics Dental Hosp., Kangnung Nat. U., Kangwon, Republic of Korea, 1998—. Office: Dental Hosp Kangnung Nat Univ Kangunugdaehangno 120 Jibyeon Dong Kangnung City Kangwon 210702 Republic of Korea Home Phone: 33-640-3152; Office Phone: 82-33-640-3192. Business E-Mail: korth@kangnung.ac.kr. E-mail: korth@nukw.ac.kr.

CHA, JAE MYUNG, medical educator; b. Republic of Korea, May 9, 1971; MD, Kyung Hee U., PhD, 1996. Assoc. prof. Kyung Hee U. Hosp., Gang Dong, 2007—. Grant, United European Gastroenterology Assn., 2011. Office: 149 Sangil-Dong Gangdong-Gu Seoul 134-727 Republic of Korea Business E-Mail: dramc@hanmail.net.

CHA, JAEHO, microbiology professor, department chairman; b. Seoul, Republic of Korea, Nov. 18, 1963; PhD, Cornell U., 1994. Chair dept. microbiology Pusan Nat. U., 2009—. Named Best Tchr., Pusan Nat. U. Mem.: Americal Soc. Microbiology, Korean Soc. Microbiology and Biotech. Office: 30 Jangjeon-dong Geumjeong-gu Busan Kyungsangnam-do 609-735 Republic of Korea Office Fax: 82-51-514-1778. Business E-Mail: jhcha@pusan.ac.kr.

CHA, JENNIFER, periodontist; BS, U. Nevada, 1981—85; DMD, Washington U. Sch. of Dental Medicine, 1985—89; MS in Periodontics, Northwestern U. Dental Sch., 1991—93. Resident Jewish Hosp., 1989—90; preclinical instr. periodontics dept. Northwestern Univ. Dental Sch., 1991—92, clin. instr. periodontics dept., 1991—93; clin. instr. implant innovations dental implant surgical course Beijing Traditional Medicine Hosp., 1997; co-founder Dental Implant Inst. Worldwide, Las Vegas, Nev., 1998—. Asst. instr. Minnesota Dental Assn., 1993; co-founder The Nevada State Bd. of Periodontology, 2001. Co-author: (research publications) Innovations in Periodontics, Compendium, Dentistry Today, The Journal of Implant & Advanced Clinical Dentistry. Mem.: Am. Dental Implant Assn., ADA, Internat. Congress of Oral Implantologist, The Am. Acad. of Periodontology, The Am. Acad. of Laser Dentistry, The Am. Acad. of Oral and Maxillofacial Radiology, Clark County Dental Soc., Nevada Dental Assn., Chicago Dental Assn., Calif. Dental Assn. Office: Dental Implant Institute 59 Las Tunas Arcadia CA 91007 Office Phone: 626-446-0700.

CHA, SANG-HOON, radiologist, educator; b. Seoul, Republic of Korea, Feb. 25, 1963; MD, Seoul Nat. U. Coll. Medicine, 1987, PhD, 1995. Prof. Chung Buk Nat. U. Hosp., 1992—. Chief Sect. Diagnostic & Interventional Neuroradiology, 1992—; chmn. Dept. Radiology, 2008—. Mem.: World Fedn. Interventional Neuroradiology, Korean Radiol. Soc., Korean Soc. Neuroradiology, Head & Neck Radiology, Korean Soc. Interventional Neuroradiology. Office: 410 Seongbong-ro Heungduk-gu Cheongju Chung Buk 361-711 Republic of Korea E-mail: shcha@chungbuk.ac.kr.

CHA, SANG-WOO, gastroenterologist, director; b. Seoul, Republic of Korea, Feb. 26, 1966; MD, Soon Chun Hyang U., PhD, 1992. Divsn. chief, gastroenterology & hepatology, dir. Digestive Disease Ctr. Eulji U. Hosp., 2005—. Mem.: KSPB, KGA, KSGE, ASGE. Office: 1306 Dunsan-dong Seo-gu Eulji University Daejeon 302-799 Republic of Korea Business E-Mail: swcha@eulji.ac.kr.

CHA, SE DO, internist; b. Seoul, Korea, Dec. 17, 1942; came to U.S., 1966, naturalized, 1977; s. Young Sun and Hee Joo (Chang) C.; m. Elsa Jane Greene, Dec. 21, 1974; 1 child, Elizabeth. MD, Yon Sei U., 1966. Diplomate Am. Bd. Internal Medicine. Intern Presbyn.-U. Pa. Med. Ctr., Phila., 1966-67; resident in medicine Harrisburg (Pa.) Hosp., 1967-70; chief resident in medicine Roger Williams Gen. Hosp., Providence, 1970-71, cardiologist, 1973-75; fellow in cardiology Deborah Heart and Lung Center, Browns Mills, N.J., 1971-73, cardiologist, 1975—; from asst. dir. adult cardiac catheterization lab. to dir. Deborah Heart and Lung Ctr., Browns Mills, NJ, 1975—2003. Instr. Brown U., Providence, 1973-75. Contbr. articles to profl. jours. Fellow ACP, Soc. for Cardiac Angiography; mem. AMA, Fedn. Clin. Rsch., Am. Heart Assn. Office: Deborah Heart and Lung Ctr Trenton Rd Browns Mills NJ 08015 Office Phone: 609-893-6611. Personal E-mail: csedo1942@gmail.com. Business E-Mail: c.sedo@yahoo.com.

CHABNER, BRUCE A., oncologist, researcher; b. Shelbyville, Ill., June 3, 1940; married; 2 children. BA summa cum laude, Yale Coll., New Haven, 1961; MD cum laude, Harvard Med. Sch., Boston, 1965; DPhil (hon.), U. Nebr., 2001. Diplomate Am. Bd. Internal Medicine, cert. in med. oncology. Intern, jr. resident internal medicine Peter Bent Brigham Hosp., Boston, 1965-67; sr. resident Yale-New Haven Med. Ctr., 1969-70; sr. staff fellow, sr. investigator, lab. clin. pharmacology & med. oncology svc. Nat. Cancer Inst., NIH, Bethesda, Md., 1971-72, sr. surgeon, divsn. cancer treatment, 1972-75, head biochem. pharmacology sect., lab. clin. pharmacology, 1973-75, chief clin. pharmacology br., clin. oncology program, 1976-80, assoc. dir. clin. oncology program, divsn. cancer treatment, dep. clin. dir., 1980-82, dir. divsn. cancer treatment, 1982-95; prof. medicine Harvard Med. Sch., 1995—; clin. dir., chief hematology/oncology Mass. Gen. Hosp. Cancer Ctr., 1995—; assoc. dir. clin. sci. Dana-Farber/Harvard Cancer Ctr., 1999—. Chmn. subcom. on hematologic and neoplastic disease therapy US Pharmacopeia, 1974—79; mem. study sect. experimental therapeutics NIH, 1974—79; mem. molecular biology adv. bd. Nat. Cancer Inst., 1977; Pfizer lectr. in clin. pharmacology U. Vt., 1980, Yale U., 1981, Brown U., Providence, 1987; vis. prof. U. Capetown, South Africa, 1981; chmn. program on folate & antifolate polyglutamates Airlie Conf. Ctr., Warrenton, Va., 1981; assoc. mem. com. med. oncology Am. Bd. Internal Medicine, 1981—83, mem. parent bd., 1985—87; Terry Fox Meml. lectr. Princess Margaret Hosp., Toronto, Ont., Canada, 1982; William Dameschek meml. lectr. Tufts U., Medford, Mass., 1985; program chmn. conf. new biology NAS Inst. Medicine, 1988, mem. roundtable for devel. drugs & vaccines against AIDS, 1988—; Centennial vis. prof. medicine U. Toronto, 1989; William N. Creasy vis. prof. clin. pharmacology U. So. Calif., 1989; Gertrude Victorson Ratner Meml. lectr. Evanston Hosp., Ill., 1989; clin. advisor Peregrine Pharmameuticals, Tustin, Calif., 2009—; mem. Nat. Cancer Adv. Bd., Bethesda, acting chmn., 2010—11, chmn., 2011—. Co-author (with Dan Longo): Principles and Practices of Cancer Chemotherapy and Biological Response Modifiers; founding editor-in-chief The Oncologist, 1996—, editor-in-chief Cancer Treatment Reports, 1976—79, assoc. editor Blood, 1979—80, Cancer Rsch., 1982—84, 1990—, mem. editl. bd. Jour. Clin. Investigation, 1984—89, Internat. Medicine for the Specialist, 1990—; contbr. articles to profl. jours., chapters to books. Served with USPHS, flag rank Rear Adm., 1991. Recipient Melville Jacobs award, Am. Radium Soc., 1986, Steven Beering award for advancement of biomed. sci., Ind. U., 1993, Bob Pinedo prize for pioneering work in cancer rsch., Med. Knowledge Inst., The Netherlands, 2007. Mem.: ACP, Am. Assn. Physicians, Am. Soc. Hematology, Am. Soc. Clin. Investigation, Am. Soc. Clin. Oncology (program com. 1982, David A. Karnofsky Meml. award 1985), Am. Assn. Cancer Rsch. (program com. 1979—81, Bruce F. Kane award for drug devel. 1998), Alpha Omega Alpha, Phi Beta Kappa. Office: Mass Gen Hosp 55 Fruit St Lawrence House 214 Boston MA 02114-2696 Office Phone: 617-724-3200. Office Fax: 617-724-3166. Business E-Mail: bchabner@partners.org. *

CHABOT, JOHN ANTHONY, surgeon; b. Sanford, Maine, 1957; s. J. Richard and Delores E. Chabot. BS in Engring. Sci., Tufts U., 1979; MD, Dartmouth Med. Sch., 1983. Diplomate Am. Bd. Surgery. Fellow, pathology Mary Hitchcock Med. Ctr., Hanover, NH, 1980—82; intern, resident, fellow, transplantation Columbia-Presbyn. Med. Ctr., NYC, 1983-90; surgical chief, thyroid clinic NY-Presbyterian Hosp./Columbia U. Med. Ctr., NYC, 1991—96, asst. prof. surgery, 1991—98, assoc. dir., surgical residency program, 1992—96, dir., surgical intensive care, 1995—97, chief, hepatobiliary and pancreatic surgery, 1995—2002, vice-chmn., dept. surgery, 1996—2002, attending surgeon, 1998—, chief, divsn. gen. surgery, 2002—06, chief, divsn. GI/Endocrine surgery, 2006—; asst. attending surgeon Columbia U. Coll. Physicians and Surgeons, NY, 1991—98, assoc. prof., clin. surgery NY, 1998—2008, prof., clin surgery NY, 2008—, med. dir., operating rooms NY, 1999—2004, vice-chair, gen. surgery NY, 2008—. Contbr. several articles to profl. jours. Recipient Upjohn Young Scientist award, 1987, Blakemore prize for Surgical Rsch., 1987—88, Blakemore award for surgical rsch., 1990, Ortho Found. award, 1990, Thomas C. King Resident Tchg. award, 1998, Spl. Recognition award, NY-Presbyn. Hosp., 2004, Physician of Yr., Nursing Svc., NY-Presbyn. Hosp., 2008; named one of America's Top Doctors, Best Doctors, NY Mag.; Irvington House Inst. Fellowship, 1985—87, Habif Scholar, 1991. Fellow: ACS; mem.: NY Transplantation Soc., NY Surgical Soc., AMA, Am. Hepato-Pancreato-Biliary Assn., Am. Assn. Endocrine Surgeons, Alpha Omega Alpha, Sigma XI, Tau Beta Pi. Office: NY Presbyn Hosp Columbia U Med Ctr Irving Pavilion Rm 819 161 Fort Washington Ave New York NY 10032-3713 Office Phone: 212-305-9468, 212-305-9467. Office Fax: 212-305-5992.

CHADWICK, EDWARD G., hospital administrator; BA in Economics and minor in Math, U. Mich., 1980; MBA in Finance, U. Chgo., 1986. With U. Chgo. Hospitals, Western Suburban Med. Ctr., Trinity Health, Mich., 1988—2009, sr. v.p., CFO, 2005—09; owner Integrated Healthcare Fin. Strategies LLC, 2009; exec. v.p. fin., CFO Wake Forest Baptist Med. Ctr., 2009—. Office: Wake Forest Baptist Medical Center Medical Center Blvd Winston Salem NC 27157 Office Phone: 336-716-2011. *

CHAE, CHANHEE, veterinary pathologist, educator; b. Seoul, Republic of Korea, May 14, 1964; s. Jongku Chae and Chunja Son; m. Hyunjung Kim, May 14, 1994; children: Kijae, Junghyun. PhD, U. Nebr. Med. Ctr., Omaha, Nebraska, 1989—92. Assoc. prof. Seoul Nat. U., Seoul, Republic of Korea, 1994—. Recipient Hiill's Asian Vet. Young Scientist, 2002. Achievements include publishing more than 100 papers in an internationally recognized journal (SCI journal). Office: Seoul Nat U Coll Vet Med San 56-1 Shillim-Dong Seoul 151-742 Republic of Korea Office Fax: 82-2-871-5821. Business E-Mail: swine@plaza.snu.ac.kr.

CHAE, JONG-MOON, orthodontist, educator; b. Daegu, Republic Of Korea, Mar. 28, 1964; m. Jeong-Hwa Seo, Feb. 14, 1993; 1 child, Yu-Jeong. DDS, Kyungpook Nat. U., Daegu, 1988, MS, 1998, PhD, 2005. Diplomate Korean Dental Assn., 1988, orthodontic Korean Assn. Orthodontists, 1999. Dir. Kyung Pook Dental Clinic, Kimcheon, 1991—95, Fatima Hosp., Daegu, 2000—05; asst. prof. Eulji U., Daejeon, Republic of Korea, 2005—07, Wonkwang U., Sch. Dentistry, Daejeon Dental Hosp. Dir. Korean Orthodontic Rsch. Inst. Inc., Seoul, 1993—. Contbr. articles to profl. jours. Fellow: World Fedn. Orthodontists; mem.: Charles H. Tweed Internat. Found., Korean Orthodontic Rsch. Inst. Inc, Am. Assn. Orthodontists, Korean Assn. Orthodontists. Office: Wonkwang Univ Daejeon Dental Hosp Doonsan-Dong Seo-Gu 1268 302-120 Daejeon Daejeon Republic of Korea Business E-Mail: jongmoon@wonkwang.ac.kr.

CHAE, JOON-SEOK, veterinarian, educator; b. Iksan, Jeonbuk, Korea, Mar. 10, 1961; s. Kyu-tae Chae and Yeon-ryea Han; m. Mae-rim Cho, Feb. 22, 1987; children: Seong-woo, Seong-meen. PhD, Chonbuk Nat. U. Coll Vet. Medicine, 1994—94; MS, Chonbuk Nat. U. Coll. Vet. Medicine, 1990, DVM, 1987. Vet. Vet. Med. Tchg. Hosp. Chonbuk Nat. U., Jeonju, Jeonbuk, Republic of Korea, 1988—92, tchg. asst. Vet. Med. Tchg. Hosp., 1992—95; post-doctoral Coll. Vet. Medicine Tex. A&M U., College Station, 1995—97; post-doctoral Sch. Vet. Medicine U. Calif., Davis, 1998—2000; asst. prof. Coll. Vet. Medicine Chonbuk Nat. U., Jeonju, 2000—. Co-pres. Sci. Lab Ctr. Co., Ltd., Daejon, 2000—02; gen. sec. Inst. Molecular Biology and Genetics Chonbuk Nat. U., Jeonju, 2000—02, chip Biosafety Rsch. Inst., 2002—; dir. Vet. Med. Tchg. Hosp., Coll. Vet. Medicine Conbuk Nat. U., Jeonju, 2002—. Author: Manual of Clinical Procedures in Small Animal; contbr. numerous articles to profl. jours. Cons. Adv. Com. North Jeolla Province, Jeonju, 2003. Staff sgt. US Army, 1982—84, Gangwon. Grantee Rsch., Jinan-Gun, 2001—02, Ministry Maritime Affairs and Fisheries, 2002—04, U.S. Army, 2003—04, Korea Rsch. Found., 2003—, Korea NIH, 2000—03, Korea Rsch. Found., 2000, Ministry Sci. and Tech., 2001—02, Korea Sci. and Engring. Found., 2001—04, Korea Rsch. Found., 2001—02, U.S. Army, 2001—02; fellow Post-Doctoral, Korea Rsch. Found., 1995—96, NIH, 1998—99. Mem.: Am. Soc. Microbiology (corr.), Internat. Assn. Food Protection (corr.), Concerted Action Project on Integrated Control of Ticks and Tick-born

Diseases (assoc.), Am. Soc. Rickettsiology (life), The Korean Soc. Molecular and Cellular Biology (life), The Korean Soc. Vet. Clinics (life), The Korean Soc. Vet. Sci. (life). Achievements include research in Discovery of transmission vector and life cycle of Neorickettsia (Ehrlichia) risticii in horses. Avocations: travel, climbing. Home: 105-1103 Hyundae APT 1-418 Hyoja-dong Jeonju Jeonbuk 560-856 Republic of Korea Office: Chonbuk Nat Univ 664-14 1ga Duckjin-Dong Duckjin-Gu Jeonju Jeonbuk 561-756 Republic of Korea Office Fax: +82-270-3778. E-mail: jschae@chonbuk.ac.kr.

CHAE, SOOKWAN, dermatologist; b. Seoul, Republic of Korea, Apr. 3, 1968; MD, PhD, Seoul Nat. U., 2002. Physician Samsung Hosp., 1997—2001. Dermatologist Liposution and Laserlipolysis at Samsung Miso Clinic, 2009—11. Mem.: IBMS, ASLMS. Office: Dongku Samsung1dong 294-1 2nd Fl Sams Taejeon 300-812 Republic of Korea E-mail: drchaesk@gmail.com.

CHAGANTI, RAJU S., geneticist, educator, researcher; b. Samalkot, Andhra, India, Mar. 12, 1933; came to U.S., 1960. s. Sanyasi Raju and Seetasiromani (Vallury) C.; m. Seeta Ramam Kurada, Aug. 20, 1966; children: Seeta, Sara. BS with honors, Andhra U., 1954, MS, 1955; PhD, Harvard U., 1964. Diplomate Am. Bd. Med. Genetics. Mem. Med. Rsch. Coun. Radiobiology Unit, Harwell, Berkshire, England, 1967—71; rsch. assoc. N.Y. Blood Ctr., NYC, 1971—73, assoc. investigator, 1973—76; asst. prof. Meml. Sloan-Kettering Cancer Ctr., NYC, 1976—83, assoc. prof., 1983—87, prof., 1987—, William E. Snee chair NYC, 1995—. Profl. assoc. N.Y. Hosp., N.Y.C., 1979—; founder, bd. dirs. Cancer Genetics, Inc., Rutherford, NJ Editor: Genetics in Clinical Oncology, 1985; contbr. articles to profl. jours. Recipient research awards NIH, Nat. Cancer Inst., 1979—. Fellow AAAS, Am. Coll. Med. Genetics; Harvey Soc. Achievements include research in the genetic basis of cancer development. Home: 235 Pascack Rd Hillsdale NJ 07642 Office: Meml Sloan-Kettering Cancer Ctr 1275 York Ave New York NY 10021-6094 Office Phone: 212-639-8121. Business E-Mail: chagantr@mskcc.org.

CHAGAS, ANTONIO CARLOS PALANDRI, cardiologist, educator; b. Sao Caetano Do Sul, São Paulo, Brazil, Oct. 7, 1952; MD, Med. Sch. ABC Found., 1977; PhD, U. São Paulo, 1992. Assoc. prof. medicine, cardiology Heart Inst., U. São Paulo Med. Sch., 1996—. Fellow: European Soc. Cardiology, Am. Coll. Cardiology; mem.: Am. Heart Assn. Home: Rua Manoel Coelho 909 Sao Caetano Do Sul Sao Paulo 09510112 Brazil Home Fax: 55-11-42218533. Personal E-mail: antonio.chagas@incor.usp.br.

CHAGPAR, ANEES BAHADURALI, surgeon; b. Toronto, Ont., Can., Dec. 8, 1971; MS; MD, U. Alberta, 1996, MPH. Intern U. Saskatchewan, Saskatoon, Canada, 1996—97, resident, 1997—2002; fellow U. Tex. MD Anderson, Houston, 2002—03; surgeon U. Louisville Hosp., Louisville, Norton Health Care, Louisville, Jewish Hosp., Louisville; assoc. prof. surg. oncology U. Louisville, Louisville; dir. Multidisciplinary Breast Clin. James Graham Brown Cancer Ctr.; acad. adv. dean Med. Edn. Recipient Leadership award (Young Physician) AMA Found. 2006. Mem.: Surgeons Can., Royal Coll. Physicians, Soc. Surg. Oncology, Am. Soc. Breast Surgeons, Am. Soc. Clin. Oncology, Am. Assn. Cancer Rsch., Am. Coll. Surgeons (Oncology Group). Office: Smilow Cancer Hospital Breast Ctr 1 Fl Suite A 25 Park St New Haven CT 06520 Office Phone: 502-629-6950. Office Fax: 502-629-3183. E-mail: anees.chagpar@nortonhealthcare.org.

CHAHINIAN, A(RAM) PHILIPPE, oncologist; b. Paris, June 21, 1942; came to U.S., 1974; m. Marjorie Ellen; 1 child, Michael J. B., Buffon Coll., Paris, 1960; MD, Paris U., 1969. Diplomate Am. Bd. Internal Medicine, Am. Bd. Med. Oncology Intern, resident Paris Univ. Hosps., France, 1968-74; fellow noeplastic diseases Mt. Sinai Sch. Medicine, NYC, 1974-76, asst. prof., 1976-79, assoc. prof., 1980-88; prof. clin. medicine Coll. Physicians and Surgeons Columbia U., NYC, 1990-92; prof. dept. medicine Mt. Sinai Sch. Medicine, NYC, 1995—2007, prof., 1995—2007; med. dir. oncology PRA Internat., NYC, 2007—. Adj. prof. dept. neoplastic diseases Mt. Sinai Sch. Medicine, N.Y.C., 1992-95. Author: Lung Cancer, 1976; author (with others) of books; contbr. articles to profl. jours. Lt. Med. Corps, French Army, 1970. Rsch. grantee Nat. Cancer Inst., 1984. Fellow Am. Coll. Physicians; mem. Am. Soc. Clin. Oncology, Am. Assn. Cancer Rsch., Am. Fedn. Clin. Rsch., N.Y. Acad. Scis. Achievements include research in treatment of various cancers including lung cancer, asbestos related cancers, and mesothelioma by transplantation of human cancers into mice.

CHAI, FENG YIH, physician; b. Johor Baru, Aug. 16, 1979; MD, CM, McGill U., 2005; postgrad master student, U. Kebangsaan Malaysia, 2009. Med. officer Dept. Surgery, Faculty Medicine, U. Kebangsaan Malaysia, 2005—. Mem. editl. bd. Asian Pacific Jour. Tropical Biomedicine. Recipient Outstanding Svc. award, Ministry Health, Malaysia, 2009. Mem.: Malaysian Med. Assn. Avocation: reading. Office: Universiti Kebangsaan Malaysia Med Ctr Kuala Lumpur 56000 Malaysia E-mail: chaifengyih@gmail.com.

CHAI, TOBY C., urologic surgeon, research scientist; b. Taipei, Taiwan, Oct. 5, 1964; arrived in USA, 1970; BA, Johns Hopkins U., 1989; MD, Ind. U., Indpls., 1989. Lic. urology Am. Bd. of Urology. Asst. prof. U. of Md. Sch. of Medicine, Balt., 1997—2002, assoc. prof., 2002—07, prof., 2007—. Recipient Young Investigator award, Soc. for Basic Urologic Rsch., 2001, Basic Rsch. Essay Winner, Soc. for Urodynamics and Female Urology, 2001, Pfizer Internat. Cardura Competitive award, Pfizer Co., 2001, Dornier Rsch. scholarship, Am. Found. for Urologic Diseases, 1995—97; grantee, NIH, 2001, Mentored Clinician-Scientist Career Devel. award, 1996—2001, 2002. Fellow: ACS. Office: U MD Divsn Urology 29 S Greene St Ste 500 Baltimore MD 21201

CHAIDARUN, SUSHELA SONGTANIN, endocrinologist, researcher; b. Sawankaloke, Sukhothai, Thailand, Apr. 13, 1963; arrived in U.S., 1994; d. Kittisak and Kanitha Songtanin; m. Sumet Chaidarun; children: Arthur Nachapon, Leo Pirapon, Tricia Tanyawan. MD, Chulalongkorn U., 1988; PhD, U. Birmingham, Eng., 1994; postgrad., Harvard U., 1994—98. Bd. certified internal medicine Am. Bd. Internat. Medicine, bd. certified endocrinology & metabolism. Postdoctoral rsch. fellow Mass. Gen. Hosp./ Harvard Med. Sch., Boston, 1994—98; med. resident internal medicine St. Vincent Hosp./Worcester Med. Ctr., U Mass. Med. Sch., Worcester, 1998—2001; endocrine clin. fellow U. Va. Health Sys., Charlottesville, 2001—03. Rsch. fellow /assoc. Harvard Med. Sch., Boston, 1994—98. Contbr. articles to profl. jours. Grantee Travel grant, Am. Endocrine Soc./Women in Endocrinology, 1996. Mem.: AMA, ACP (Med. Jeopardy Championship award Mass. chpt. 2000), Am. Assn. Clin. Endocrinologists, Am. Diabetes Assn., Am. Endocrine Soc. Avocations: travel, cooking, music. Office: Endocrine Sec Dept Medicine Dartmouth Hitchcock Med Ctr Lebanon NH 03756-1000 Home Phone: 603-277-9307; Office Phone: 603-650-8630. Personal E-mail: schaidarun@hotmail.com. Business E-Mail: sushela.s.chaidarun@hitchcock.org.

CHAIKEN, BERNARD HENRY, internist, gastroenterologist; b. Bklyn., Oct. 14, 1927; s. Max and Esther (Golland) C.; m. Mildred Gilbert, Dec. 5, 1950; children: Barry Glenn, Caryl Joy Gordon. Student, NYU, 1944-45; MD, U. Tex., Dallas, 1949. Diplomate Am. Bd. Internal Medicine, subspecialty Bd. Gastroenterology. Intern Boston City Hosp., 1949-50; resident physician Cushing VA Hosp., Framingham, Mass., 1950-51, Phila. VA Hosp., 1953-54; staff physician VA Hosp. Dallas, 1954-55, VA Hosp., East Orange, NJ, 1955-56; attending physician Overlook Hosp., Summit, NJ, 1956—, St. Barnabas Med. Ctr., Livingston, NJ, 1956—2010. Vis. fellow Hosp. of U. Pa., Phila., 1954; clin. instr. Southwestern Med. Sch., U. Tex., Dallas, 1954-55; clin. asst. prof. medicine Seton Hall Coll. Medicine, Jersey City, 1956-58. Contbr. articles to med. jours. Capt. U.S. Army M.C., 1951-53. Fellow ACP, Am. Coll. Gastroenterology (Best Clin. Vignette Paper and Poster Presentation 1995); mem. Am. Soc. Internal Medicine, Am. Gastroenterol. Assn., Med. Soc. N.J., NJ Gastroenterol. Soc. (pres. 1964-65), Alpha Omega Alpha. Home: 12 Taylor Rd Short Hills NJ 07078-2226 Office: 58 Chatham Rd Short Hills NJ 07078-2321 Office Phone: 973-376-5750.

CHAIKIN, HARRY LOUIS, internist; MD, Thomas Jefferson U., 1978. Diplomate Am. Bd. Internal Medicine, Am. Bd. Geriat. Medicine. Intern Wilmington Gen. Hosp., 1979; resident Christiana Care Health Sys., 1981; hosp. affiliation includes Atlantic City Med. Ctr., Bacharach Inst. for Rehab. Named one of the Top Doctor, NJ Monthly, 2005, Phila Mag., 2007, 2009—11. Office: AtlantiCare Regional Medical Center City Campus 1925 Pacific Ave Frederiksted VI 00840 Office Phone: 609-345-4000.

CHAIT, MAXWELL MANI, physician; b. Linz, Austria, Nov. 7, 1947; came to the U.S., 1953; s. Morris and Eva (Lederman) C.; m. Lynne Robin Milstein C.; children: Alanna Rose, Daniel Lawrence, Michael Paul. BA magna cum laude, U. Utah, Salt Lake City, 1969; BS cum laude, U. Calif., San Francisco, 1969, MD, 1972. Diplomate Am. Bd. Internal Medicine, 1975, Am. Bd. Gastroenterology, 1977, Am. Bd. Geriatric Medicine; lic. N.Y., Utah. Med. intern U. So. Calif. Med. Ctr., L.A. County, 1972-73; resident in medicine Cornell Coop. Hosps., North Shore U. Hosp., Manhasset, NY, 1973-75; fellow GI Cornell Coop. Hosps., Meml. Sloan-Kettering Cancer Ctr., NYC, 1975-77; attending physician White Plains (NY) Hosp., 1977—. Trustee Crohn's & Colitis Found., 2000—02; lectr. in field. Pres. Westchester Assn. of Hebrew Schs., 1992-94; former mem. bd. trustees Temple Israel of White Plains; former coach baseball, softball, basketball Scarsdale Recreation Dept. Fellow Am. Coll. Gastroenterology, Am. Coll. Physicians, Am. Gastroenterological Assn., Am. Soc. Gastrointestinal Endoscopy, Am. Coll. Specialists Genatics (Disting. Master); mem. N.Y. Acad. Gastroenterology, N.Y. Soc. Gastrointestinal Endoscopy, Westchester Acad. Medicine, Crohn and Colitis Found. of Am. (CMAC com.), ACP Office: Hartsdale Med Group 180 E Hartsdale Ave Hartsdale NY 10530-3544 Office Phone: 914-725-2010. Personal E-mail: mdgi77@aol.com.

CHAK, AMITABH, gastroenterologist, researcher; b. Lucknow, India, June 11, 1959; arrived in U.S., 1966; s. Anand Mohan and Kusum Chak; m. Anjani Kaul, Dec. 18, 1988; children: Avinash, Ashwin. BS, Yale U., 1978, MS, 1979; MD, Columbia U., 1984. Asst. prof. Case Sch. Medicine, Cleve., 1991—99, assoc. prof., 1999—2005, prof. medicine and oncology, 2005—. Fellow: Am. Soc. Gastrointestinal Endoscopy, Am. Gastroenterological Assn., Am. Coll. Gastroent., Am. Coll. Physicians. Office: U Hosps Case Med Ctr 11100 Euclid Ave Cleveland OH 44106-5066 Office Phone: 216-844-5386, 216-844-6172. *

CHAKKERA, HARINI A., physician clinical scientist and researcher, educator; b. Bangalore, India; MD, Bangalore U., India, 1994; MPH, U. Calif., Berkeley, 2002. Fellowship, nephrology U. Calif., San Francisco, 2003, fellowship, transplant nephrology, 2005; cons., divsn. nephrology, hypertension & kidney transplantation Mayo Clinic, Phoenix, 2005—, asst. prof., Mayo Coll. Medicine, 2005—; asst. rsch. prof. Ctr. Metabolic Biology Ariz. State U., Tempe, 2009—. Contbr. numerous articles to profl. jours. Recipient Multidisciplinary Clin. Rsch. Career Devel. award, NIH, 2008; named one of America's Top Physicians, Consumers Rsch. Coun. America, 2007; grant, NIH, 2001, Ruth L. Kirschstein NRSA grant, 2003. Fellow: Am. Soc. Nephrology; mem.: Am. Diabetes Assn., Am. Coll. Physicians, Am. Soc. Transplantation (Fellowship grant clin. rsch. 2003). Office: Mayo Clinic Ariz 5777 East Mayo Blvd Phoenix AZ 85054 Business E-Mail: chakkera.harini@mayo.edu.

CHAKRABARTI, SUBHO, psychiatrist, educator; b. Kolkata, India, Sept. 6, 1963; MBBS, JIPMER, Pondicherry, India, 1987; MD, PGIMER; MAMS, Nat. Acad. Med. Scis., 1990. Asst. prof. PGIMER, Dept Psychiatry, 1997—2001, assoc. prof., 2001—06, additional prof., 2006—10, prof., 2010—. Recipient Academic and Rsch. awards, PGIMER, IPS & Others. Fellow: Indian Psychiat. Soc., Internat. Soc. Affective Disorders, Royal Coll. Psychiatrists; mem.: Nat. Acad. Med. Scis. (India). Avocation: reading. Office: PGIMER Dept Psychiatry Sector 12 Chandigarh 160012 India E-mail: subhochd@yahoo.com.

CHAKRABARTY, ANANDA MOHAN, microbiologist; b. Sainthia, India, Apr. 4, 1938; arrived in U.S., 1965; s. Satya Dos and Sasthi Bala (Mukherjee) Chakrabarty; m. Krishna Chakraverty, May 26, 1965; children: Kaberi, Asit. BSc, St. Xavier's Coll., 1958; MSc, U. Calcutta, India, 1960, PhD, 1965. Sr. rsch. officer U. Calcutta, 1964-65; rsch. assoc. biochemistry U. Ill., Urbana, 1965-71, prof. dept. microbiology Med. Ctr., 1979-89, disting. prof., 1989—; mem. staff GE R&D Ctr., Schenectady, NY, 1971-79. Editor: (book) Genetic Engineering, 1977, Biodegradation and Detoxification of Environmental Pollutants, 1982. Recipient Inventor of the Yr. award, Patent Lawyers' Assn., 1982, Pub. Affairs award, Am. Chem. Soc., 1984, Disting. Scientist award, EPA, 1985, Merit award, NIH, 1986, Pasteur award, 1991, Proctor & Gamble award, 1995; named Scientist of Yr., Indsl. Rsch. Mag., 1975; scholar, U. Ill., 1989. Mem.: Am. Soc. Biol. Chemists, Am. Soc. Microbiology. Home: 206 E Julia Dr Villa Park IL 60181-3340 Office: U Ill Med Ctr Dept Microbiology M/C 790 835 S Wolcott Ave Chicago IL 60612-7340 Office Phone: 312-996-4586. Business E-Mail: pseudomo@uic.edu.

CHAKRABORTY, JOANA, physiologist, educator, science administrator; b. Calcutta, India, June 1, 1934; arrived in U.S., 1962; d. Mohadev and Nilima Mukherjee; m. Ajit Chakraborty; 1 child, Mellary. BS, Sci. Coll., Calcutta, 1954, MS, 1956; PhD, Inst. of Nuclear Physics, Calcutta, 1962. Rsch. asst. Inst. Nuc. Physics, Calcutta, 1960-62, lectr., 1963—69; postdoctoral asst. Iowa State U., Ames, 1962-63; fellow Ford Found., Harbor UCLA Med. Ctr., 1969—70; dir. Electron Microscopy Lab. Med. Coll., Toledo, 1970-89; from asst. prof. to assoc. prof. Med. Coll. Ohio, Toledo, 1972—82, prof., 1982—, interim chmn., 1991-94. Spkr. in field. Author: Chemical Exposure and Toxic Responses, 1997; contbr. chapters to books, articles to profl. jours. Recipient World AIDS Found. award; Rsch. grantee, NIH, others. Mem.: AAAS, Am. Soc. Microbiology, Internat. AIDS Soc., N.Y. Acad. Scis., Am. Soc. Cell Biology. Office: Coll Medicine University Toledo 3035 Arlington Ave Toledo OH 43614-2598 Business E-Mail: joana.chakraborty@utoledo.edu.

CHAKRABORTY, NILANJAN, medical researcher; b. Kolkata, West Bengal, India, May 9, 1963; PhD, Kalyani U., 1985. Scientist d ICMR Virus Unit, 2009—. Office: ID & BG Hosp 57 Dr S C Banerjee Rd Beliaghata Kolkata West Bengal 700 010 India Personal E-mail: nilanjanchakraborty@ymail.com.

CHAKRAVARTI, ANITA, medical educator, director; b. Gujrat, India, Sept. 15, 1952; MBBS, Govt. Med. Coll., Aurangabad, Maharashtra, 1974; MD, Lady Harding Med. Coll., New Delhi, 1981. Lectr. U. Coll. Med. Scis., 1983—86; tchr., rschr., undergrad. and postgrad. med. students Maulana Azad Med. Coll., 1986, asst. prof., 1986—89, assoc. prof., 1989—94, prof., 1994—2008, incharge, diagnostic & advanced virology lab., 2006, dir., prof., 2008—. Nodal officer, dengue sero surveillance lab. Delhi Govt.; head, med. microbiology dept. Faculty Med. Scis. Delhi U., 2009; assessor Nat. Accrediation Bd. Testing & Calibration Labs., New Delhi, 2011. Recipient Rashtriya Ekta award, Asian Art and Culture Soc., J.B. Srivastava Nat. award, Indian Coun. Med. Rsch., Dr. S. Radhakrishnan Meml. Nat. Tchrs. award, Nat. Bd. Child and Women Devel. Charitable Trust; WHO fellowship, Indo Hungarian Cultural Exch. Programme fellow, U. Grants Commn. Fellow: Internat. Med. Scis. Acad.; mem.: Gastrointestinal Infection Soc. India, Indian Virological Soc., Am. Soc. Microbiology, Indian Assn. Med. Microbiologist. Avocations: reading, music, travel. Home: 79 South Pk Apt Kalkaji New Delhi Delhi 110019 India Personal E-mail: dochak@yahoo.com.

CHAKRAVARTI, ARAVINDA, geneticist; b. Calcutta, India; m. Shukti Chakravarti; children: Priya, Indira. BStat, Indian Statistical Inst., Calcutta, 1974; PhD, U. Tex., 1979; postdoctoral study, U. Wash., 1980. James Jewell prof. genetics Case Western Res. U., Cleve.; prof. medicine, pediatrics and molecular biology and genetics Johns Hopkins Sch. Medicine, Balt., 2000 , dir. McKusick-Nathans Inst. Genetic Medicine, 2000, dir. Ctr. for Complex Disease Genomics; prof. biostatistics Johns Hopkins U. Bloomberg Sch. Pub. Health, Balt. Nat. adv. coun. NIH Nat. Human Genome Rsch. Inst., 1997—2000; mouse genomics and genetics sci. panel NIH, 2000—. Mem.: Inst. Medicine, Am. Soc. Human Genetics (bd. dirs. 1996—98, nominations com. 2001, awards com. and chair 2001—04, pres. 2008). Office: Johns Hopkins U Sch Medicine Inst Genetic Medicine Broadway Rsch Bldg Ste 579 733 N Broadway Baltimore MD 21287 Office Phone: 410-502-7525. Office Fax: 410-502-7544. E-mail: aravinda@jhmi.edu.

CHAKRAVARTY, PRABIR, medical researcher; b. India, Jan. 18, 1960; PhD, SUNY, Buffalo, Calcutta U., 1989, diploma in Getman Lang., 1989. Rsch. assoc. Roswell Pk. Cancer Inst., Buffalo, 1989 93; vis. scientist Albert Einstein Coll. Medicine, NY, 1996, rsch. assoc., instr., 1997—2001, asst. prof., 2001—06; rsch. adviser Advanced Immunogenetics Lab., Bhadereshwar, India, 2006—. Vis. rschr. Calcutta U., 1991—2009. Contbr. articles to numerous sci. profl. publs. Recipient New Investigator award, US Army. Mem.: Indian Nat. Sci. Congress Assn. (Young Scientist award), Indian Assn. Cancer Rsch., Am. Assn. Cancer Rsch. Avocation: reading, listening to music, writing. Office: 1300 Morris Pk Ave Bronx NY 10461 E-mail: prabir9p@yahoo.com.

CHALAL, JOSEPH B., orthopedist, surgeon; b. Phila., Pa., Nov. 14, 1956; BA in Biology, Lafayette Coll., Easton, Pa., 1978; MD, U. Pa. Sch. Medicine, Phila., 1982. Cert. Am. Bd. Orthop. Surgery, diplomate Nat. Bd. Med. Examiners, lic. Fla., NY. Intern, gen. surgery Beth Israel Med. Ctr., NY, 1982—83, resident, gen. surgery NY, 1983—84; asst. resident, orthop. NY Orthop. Hosp. Columbia-Presbyn. Med. Ctr., NY, 1984—85, resident, orthop. surgery, 1985—86, chief resident, Jr. Annie C. Fellow, orthop. surgery, 1986—87; fellow North Sydney Orthop. and Sports Medicine Ctr., Australia, 1987; private practice Performance Orthopedics of the Palm Beaches, Fla.; chmn., surgical laser com. Palms West Hosp., 1990—; med. dir., physical theraphy JFK Med. Ctr., 1990—, Palms West Hosp., 1991—, Wellington Regional Med. Ctr., 1992. Hosp. appointments Wellington Regional Med. Ctr., Fla., 1988—, Palms West Hosp., Loxahatchee, Fla., 1988—, Palm Beach Regional Hosp., Lake Worth, Fla., 1988—95, Columbia/JFK Med. Ctr., Atlantis, Fla., 1988—, Delray Cmty. Hosp., Fla., 1991—, Pinecrest Rehabilitation Hosp., Delray Beach, Fla., 1992—, Bethesda Meml. Hosp., Boynton Beach, Fla., 1993—; chmn., com. for secondary athletics Palm Beach Med. Soc., 1991, mem., com. for secondary athletics, 1992—; presenter in field. Contbr. articles to profl. jours. Team physician Atlantic HS, 1988—89, Santaluces HS, 1988—, Wellington HS, 1988—, West Palm Beach Stingrays (US Basketball League), 1988—92, South Fla. Renegades Minor League Football Sys., 1988—90, Royal Palm HS, 1997—98; orthop. cons. Nat. Athletic League Boxing Championship, Pompano, Fla., 1988, 1989, Miami Heat, Pre-Season Camp Palm Beach CC, 1989—94, NBA Southern Rookie League (Miami Heat, Atlanta Hawks, Charlotte Hornets, & Orlando Magic), 1992, 1994, Wellington Aces Team Tennis, 1990, 1991, Palm Beach CC, 1989—, Miami Heat Rookie Camp Palm Beach CC, 1994, Miami Heat Pre-Season Camp Fla. Atlantic U., 1995—, Jimmy Connors' Corel Tennis Champions Palm Beach Polo Golf and Country Club, 1996, Fla. Beachdogs Continental Basketball League, 1996, Nuveen Seniors Tennis Tournament, Delray Beach, Fla., 1998. Fellow: Am. Acad. Orthop. Surgeons, ACS; mem.: Palm Beach County Med. Soc., Arthroscopy Assn. N.Am., Internat. Arthroscopy Assn., Fla. Orthop. Soc., Fla. Med. Soc., AMA, Alpha Omega Alpha, Phi Beta Kappa.

Office: Performance Orthopedics of the Palm Beaches 7593 Boynton Beach Blvd Ste 280 Boynton Beach FL 33437 Office Phone: 561-733-5888. Office Fax: 561-733-5851. Business E-Mail: jchalal@popb.md.

CHALAM, KAKARLA VENKATA, physician, educator; b. Pedamuttevi, India, Aug. 1, 1959; s. Kasturi C.; m. Aruna Potla, June 3, 1982; 1 child, Sandeep. IS, Loyola Coll., 1972; MD, Guntur Med. Coll., India, 1978; MS, Postgrad. Inst., Chandigarh, India, 1983; PhD, U. S.C., 2004; MBA, Webster U., 1999. Diplomate Am. Bd. Ophthalmology. Asst. instr. U. Tex. Southwestern Med. Sch., Dallas, 1992-94; asst. prof. U. S.C. Sch. Medicine, Columbia, 1994-97, assoc. prof., 1998—2000, program dir., 1994-2000; prof. U. Fla. Sch. Medicine, 2000—, chmn., 2000—, chmn. basic and clin., 2004—. Sect. editor Ocular Pharmacology, 1997-2000. Fellow Royal Coll. Surgeons Edinburgh. Republican. Avocations: photography, classical music, technical writing, ping pong/table tennis. Address: 580 W 8th St Jacksonville FL 32209-6511 Office Phone: 904-244-9361. Personal E-mail: kvchalam@aol.com.

CHALIAN, ARA A., otolaryngologist, educator; MD, Ind. U. Diplomate Am. Bd. Otolaryngology, 1994. Resident Ind. Univ. Sch. of Medicine; fellow Hosp. of the Univ. of Pa.; assoc. prof. otolaryngology: head and neck surgery Univ. of Pa.; dir. facial plastic reconstruction, patient safety officer, dir. microvacular lab. Penn Medicine. Named one of the Top Docs, Phila. Mag., 2005—11, Best Doctors in America, 2005—06, 2007—08, 2009—10, America's Top Doctors, 2007, 2008, 2010. Office: Hospital of the University of Pennsylvania 5 Silverstein 3400 Spruce St Philadelphia PA 19104 Office Phone: 215-662-2777.

CHALIF, RONNIE, medical association co-founder, artist; m. Seymour Chalif, June 13, 1954; children: John Lewis, Peter Adley. Grad. with honors, Parson Sch. Design, 1953; BS in Art Edn., NYU, 1954. Buyer I. Magnin & Co., NYC, 1954—59; artist, sculptor, painter, 1968—; co founder, dir., hon. pres. Neuropathy Assn., NYC, 1995—2009, pres., 2005—09, hon. pres., 2009—. One-woman shows include Guild Hall Mus., East Hampton, NY, Benson Gallery, Bridghampton, NY, 1972, 1975, Fed. Court House, NYC, 1984—85, Marymount Manhattan Coll. Gallery, 1986, Jackob K. Javits Fed. Bldg., 1986, Gayle Willson Gallery, 2000, 2003, Garrison Arts Ctr., NY, 1989, Benton Gallery, Southampton, NY, 1989, Arlene Bujese Gallery, 1996, 2006, exhibited in group shows at GE Co., Fairfield, Conn., 1983, Benson Gallery, 2000—02, Atelier 14, NYC, 2000, Ashwagh Hall, East Hampton, NY, 1987—2008, Guild Hall Mus., 1992—93, Arlene Bujese Gallery, 1995—2006, others, Represented in permanent collections Guild Hall Mus., Continental Telephone Co., Washington, McGraw-Hill, Inc., Cadillac-Fairview, Dallas, GE Internat. Hdqs., Fairfield, Grey Advt. Inc., NYC, US Home Corp., Houston, Zimmerli Art Mus., New Brunswick, NJ, World Trade Ctr.; author, illustrator: Exercising with Neuropathy, 2001; Represented in permanent collections Sculpture Garden of the Gus & Judy Leiber Mus., East Hampton, NY. Mem.: Women's Caucus for Art, Women in Arts Found., Nat. Assn. Women Artists, NY Soc. Women Artists. Business E-Mail: ronnie.chalif@yahoo.com.

CHALIKIAN, ALICE BEATRICE, chiropractor; b. Bucharest, Romania, Dec. 7, 1974; arrived in U.S., 1984; d. Nubar and Mary Anahid Chalikian. BA in Biology, Calif. State U., Northridge, 1997; DC, So. Calif. U. Health Scis., 2001. Mem.: Armenian Med. Assn., Am. Chiropractic Assn. (lobbyist student assn. 1998—), Calif. Chiropractic Assn. (lobbyist student assn. 1998—2002), Armenian Young Profl. Assn. So. Calif., Hyeties, Armenian Gen. Benevolent Union. Ea. Orthodox Gregorian. Avocations: painting, poetry, beach volleyball, skiing, dance. Office Phone: 188-837-2542. E-mail: chiroalice@yahoo.com.

CHALK, BARBARA ANN, surgical nurse; b. Watertown, NY, May 1, 1936; d. Herbert Graham Chalk and Julia Rosemead Donaldson. Diploma in nursing, House of Good Samaritan Hosp., Watertown, 1957. Staff nurse oper. rm. Ho. of Good Samaritan Hosp., 1957—59; head nurse neurosurgery oper. rm. U. Va. Hosp., Charlottesville, 1959—75; clin. coord. neurosurgery oper. rm. Sentara Norfolk Gen. Hosp., Va., 1975—2000; ret., 2000. Nat. treas. Am. Assn. Neuroscience Nurses, 1975—79; bd. dirs. AURN, Va., publicity commn. chmn., 1980—82, pres., 1982—83, v.p., 1984—85; chmn. admission commn. AANN, 1973—75, tres., 1974—79, fin. commn., 1975—79, pres. southeastern chpt. Va., 1979—80, publicity chmn. southeastern chpt. Va., 1978, 81, pres. elect, 1981—82, surg. core curriculum comm., 1980—84, clin. core curriculum comm., 1980—84. Co-editor: Core Curriculum for Operating Room Nurses-Neurosurgery; contbr. articles to profl. jours. Vol. Heart Hosp., Sentara Norfolk Gen. Hosp., 2000—, Parkinson Support Group, 2000—; bd. dirs. Parkinson Disease Assn., Virginia Beach, Va., 2003—. Recipient Cert. of Merit, Parkinsons Disease Assn., Va., 2001. Avocations: needlepoint, ceramics. Home: 944 Adelphi Rd Virginia Beach VA 23464 Home Phone: 757-424-5262.

CHALK, ROSEMARY ANNE, health science association administrator; b. Cin., May 25, 1948; d. John Henry and Virginia R. (Kamphaus) Chalk; m. Michael Anthony Stoto, June 28, 1986; children: Anna Murilius, Benjamin John. BA, U. Cin., 1970; postgrad., George Washington U., 1970-72. Policy analyst Libr. of Congress, Washington, 1972-75; rsch. fellow MIT, Cambridge, Mass., 1982-83; program dir. AAAS, Washington, 1976-86; cons. Harvard Sch. Pub. Health, Boston, 1986-87; study dir. Inst. of Medicine-Nat. Academies, Washington, 1987-89, dir., Children, Youth, and Families Bd., 2000—; study dir. NAS, Washington, 1989—. Cons. The Field Found., N.Y.C., 1986-87, The Acadia Inst., Bar Harbor, Maine, 1988-91; adv. com. on ethics and values studies NSF, 1984-87. Editor: Science, Technology and Society: Emerging Relationships, 1988; contbr. articles to profl. jours. Fellow AAAS (coun. and section officer 1987—), Fedn. Am. Scientists (coun. mem. 1982-90), Student Pugwash USA (bd. dirs. 1988—). Roman Catholic. Office: Institute of Medicine 500 Fifth Street NW Washington DC 20001 Office Phone: 202-334-1230. E-mail: rchalk@nas.edu.

CHAMBERLAIN, JOHN LOOMIS, III, retired pediatrician, educator; b. Balt., July 18, 1930; s. John Loomis Jr. and Marie (Brosius) C.; m. Eleanor Fulton, 1956 (div. Apr. 1976); m. Amelie Marie Chamberlain, Apr. 29, 1977; children: Carolyn, Allison, John Loomis IV. BA, Amherst Coll., Mass., 1953; MD, U. Va., Charlottesville, 1957. Pediatrician Lexington Clinic, Ky., 1962-66; asst. prof. pediat. U. Ky. Sch. Medicine, Lexington, 1962-66; clin. prof. child health and devel. George Washington Sch. Medicine, Washington, 1966—; pediatrician Office of Drs. Howard, Daisley and Ong, Washington, 1966-70; pvt. practice, 1970—89; ret., 1992. Chmn. med. staff Children's Hosp., 1976—79. Editor-in-chief Clin. Proceedings, 1979-84; mem. editl. rev. bd. Contemporary Pediat., 1984-87, Pediat. in Review, 1985-88. Col. U.S. Army, 1991-93. Decorated Army Commendation medal US Army, Meritorious Svc. medal; recipient Gilchrist Hollaman award, St. Albans Sch., 2011. Fellow Am. Acad. Pediat. (v.p. Washington chpt. 1985-88); mem. Vis. Nurse Assn. (med. adv. bd. 1972-89), D.C. Med. Soc. (exec. bd. 1988-89), U. Va. Med. Alumni Assn. (pres. 1992-93), Cosmos Club. Republican. Episcopalian. Avocation: self education. Home: 4321 Westover Pl NW Washington DC 20016-5553

CHAMBERLAIN, RONALD S., surgeon, educator; MD, George Wash. U., 1991. Diplomate Am. Bd Surgery. Resident in surgery George Wash. Univ. Med. Ctr., 1992—97; fellow in surgical oncology Nat. Cancer Inst., 1994—96; fellow in hepatobiliary surgery Meml. Sloan- Kettering Cancer Ctr., 1998—99; prof. surgery Univ. of Medicine and Dentistry NJ, Newark; chmn. St. Barnabas Med. Ctr., surgeon in chief. Office: Saint Barnabas Medical Center 94 Old Short Hills Rd Livingston NJ 07039 Office Phone: 973-322-5000. Office Fax: 973-322-4309.

CHAMBERS, CHRISTOPHER V., family and adolescent medicine physician, educator; MD, Duke U., Durham, NC, 1980; AB, Princeton U., NJ, 1976. Diplomate Am. Bd. Family Practice, Am. Bd. Family Practice-adolescent medicine. Fellow adolescent med. Univ. Calif. Sch. Med., San Francisco, 1985; intern Thomas Jefferson Univ. Hosp., resident family medicine, 1983, prof. dep. family medicine, clin. dir. vaccine ctr., chmn. office human rsch., dir. clin. trials. Co-author: A prospective, observational cohort study of nonsteroidal anti-inflammatory drug (NSAID) use and the management of NSAID-related gastrointestinal symptoms by primary care patients, 2003, Primary care physician beliefs regarding usefulness of self-monitoring of blood pressure, 2003, Development of a scale to measure adults perceptions of health: Preliminary findings, 2007, Hematuria: etiology and evaluation for the primary care physician, 2008, Immunologic non-inferiority of Fluarix versus Fluzone in US adults: A randomized, phase III study, 2008, various others. Named one of Top Docs, Phila. Mag., 2010. Office: Thomas Jefferson University 1015 Walnut St Room 401 Philadelphia PA 19107 Office Phone: 215-955-2357. Office Fax: 215-955-0640.

CHAMBERS, DENNIS GERARD, surgeon, consultant; b. York, Eng., Jan. 20, 1929; arrived in Australia, 1960; s. Percy and Lily Chambers; m. Jessie Dumphy, Apr. 25, 1957; children: Denise Amanda, Julie Anne, Lynne Michelle, Christina Helen. B in Medicine, B in Surgery, Edinburgh U., Scotland, 1952. Resident med. officer Royal Infirmary, Edinburgh, 1952-53; surg. registrar Kingston Gen. Hosp., Hull, Eng., 1953-54, Kidderminster Gen. Hosp., Eng., 1959-60; rural family physician, surgeon Clare, Australia, 1960-94; sr. cons. Pregnancy Adv. Ctr., Flinders Med. Ctr., Adelaide, Australia, 1994—. Contbr. articles to profl. jours. Capt. Royal Army Med. Corps, 1954-58. Fellow Royal Australian Coll. Gen. Practitioner's; licentiate Royal Coll. Physicians, Royal Coll. Surgeons. Avocations: music, gardening, squash, golf. Office: Pregnancy Advisory Ctr 21 Belmore Ter Woodville Park SA 5011 Australia Fax: 08-8243-3998. Business E-Mail: dennis.chambers@health.sa.gov.au.

CHAMBERS, JOSEPH, gynecologic oncologist, educator; MD, Georgetown U., Washington DC, 1977; PhD. Diplomate Am. Bd. Ob-Gyn, 2009, Am. Bd. Ob-Gyn-gynecologic oncology. Clin. prof. ob-gyn. SUNY Downstate Med. Ctr.; resident ob-gyn. Univ. Va. Hosp., Charlottesville, 1978—81; fellowgynecologic oncology Yale-New Haven Hosp., Conn., 1982—84; gynecologic oncologist Univ. Hosp. Brooklyn Long Island Coll. Hosp. Office: Long Island College Hospital 339 Hicks St Brooklyn NY 11201 Office Phone: 718-780-1000.

CHAMBLISS, LINDA R., obstetrician, consultant; b. Summit, NJ, Feb. 13, 1951; d. Robert E. and Alice (Dunne) C.; children: Alice, Kevin, Christopher, Daniel Patrick. BSN, Duke U., Durham, NC, 1973; MD, Mich. State U., East Lansing, 1980; MPH, Johns Hopkins U., Balt., 2004. Diplomate with spl. certification in maternal-fetal medicine Am. Bd. Ob-Gyn. Pediat. intern U. Chgo., 1980—81; resident in ob-gyn. Cook County Hosp., Chgo., 1981—85; fellow in maternal-fetal medicine U. So. Calif.-LA County Hosp., LA, 1988—90; chief obstetrics Indian Health Svcs., Tuba City, Ariz., 1985-88; clin. prof. ob-gyn. Coll. Medicine, U. Ariz., 2001—06; prof. ob-gyn. St. Louis U., 2006—07, med. dir. labor and delivery, 2006—07; chief obsterics, dir., maternal fetal medicine Dept. Ob-Gyn. St. Joseph Hosp. Med. Ctr., Phoenix, 2008—; clin. prof. ob-gyn. U. Ariz., Coll. Medicine, Creighorn U., Sch. Medicine. Clin. prof. ob-gyn. U. Ariz. Coll. Medicine, Creighton U. Sch. Medicine. Comdr. USPHS, 1985—. Recipient Nat. Edn. award, Coun. on Resident Edn. in Ob-Gyn., 1995, 2007, 2011, Nat. Faculty Excellence award, 1995, Alumna Excellence award, Mich. State U., 1996, Alumni award, 2001, Humanitarian of Yr., St. Joseph Hosp. Phoenixaz, 2009; named Tchr. of Yr., Dept. Ob-Gyn., Maricopa Med. Ctr., 1991, Alumni of Yr., Mich. State U., Coll. Human Medicine, 2000. Fellow ACOG; mem. AMA (cons.), AAUW, Soc. Maternal Fetal Medicine, Am. Women's Med. Assn., Am. Inst. Ultrasound Medicine. Democrat. Office: 500 W Thomas Rd Ste 800 Phoenix AZ 85013 Personal E-mail: lrchambliss@yahoo.com.

CHAMBON, PIERRE, molecular biologist; b. Mulhouse, France, Feb. 7, 1931; BS, MD, U. Strasbourg, France; D (hon.), U. Liège, Belgium, 1985, Autonomous U. of Nuevo León, Mex., 2002; PhD (hon.), Sapporo Med. U., Japan, 1999; DSc (hon.), U. Lausanne, Switzerland, 2001. Rsch. asst. Inst. Biol. Chemistry, Faculty Medicine, U. Strasbourg, 1956—61, assoc. prof., 1962—66, prof. biochemistry, 1968—91, emeritus prof., 2002—; prof. Faculty Medicine, U. Louis Pasteur, Strasbourg, 1992—93, Coll. de France, Paris, 1993—2002, hon. prof., 2002—. Dir. Lab. Molecular Genetics of Eukaryotes, Nat. Ctr. Sci. Rsch. (CNRS), Paris, 1977—2002; dir. molecular biology & genetics engring. unit Nat. Inst. Health & Med. Rsch. (INSERM), Paris, 1978—2002; founder, dir. Inst. Genetics and Cellular & Molecular Biology (IGBMC), Strasbourg, 1994—2002, dir. emeritus, 2002—; founder, dir. Mouse Clin. Inst. (ICS), Strasbourg, 2002—06. Mem. editl. bd. Cell, 1987—, Molecular Cell, 2004—, numerous others; contbr. articles to profl. jours. Recipient Richard Lounsbery prize, NAS/French Acad. Scis., 1982, Charles Oberling prize in cancer rsch., Paris, 1986, Harvey prize, Technion-Israel Inst. Tech., 1987, King Faisal Internat. prize in sci., 1988, Sir Hans Krebs medal, Fedn. European Biochem. Societies, 1990, Roussel prize, Paris, 1990, Louis Jeantet prize in medicine, Geneva, 1991, Robert A. Welch award in chemistry, Houston, 1998, Louisa Gross Horwitz prize, Columbia U., 1999, Alfred P. Sloan, Jr. prize, GM Cancer Rsch. Found., 2003, March of Dimes prize in devel. biology, 2003, Albert Lasker award for basic med. rsch., 2004, Gairdner Found. Internat. award, Can., 2010. Fellow: AAAS, NY Acad. Scis. (hon. life) (Louis & Bert Freeman Found. prize 1981); mem.: NAS (fgn. assoc.), Am. Acad. Arts & Scis. (fgn. hon.), European Molecular Biology Orgn., German Soc. Cell Biology (hon.), Chinese Soc. Genetics (hon.), Royal Swedish Acad. Scis. (fgn.), French Acad. Scis., Academia Europaea. Achievements include contributing to the understanding of the biology of nuclear hormone receptors, and characterizing the role of these receptors in development and disease. Office: IGBMC BP 10142 67404 Illkirch France Fax: 03 90 2450 01, 0033(0)3 88 65 3225. Business E-Mail: chambon@igbmc.fr.

CHAMPAGNE, RONALD OSCAR, academic administrator; b. Woonsocket, RI, Jan. 2, 1942; s. George Albert and Simone (Brodeur) Champagne; m. Ruth Inez DesRuisseux, Nov. 25, 1970. BA, Duquesne U., 1964; MA, Cath. U. Am., 1966, Fordham U., 1970, PhD, 1973. Instr. math. Sacred Heart U., Bridgeport, Conn., 1966-69; asst. prof. math. Manhattanville Coll., Purchase, NY, 1969-75, dir. advanced studies program, 1973-75; prof. math., v.p., dean of faculty Salem Coll., W.Va., 1975-82; prof. math., pres., trustee St. Xavier U., Chgo., 1982-94, pres. emeritus, 1994—; prof. philosophy, v.p. for devel. Roosevelt U., Chgo., 1996—2001; v.p. devel. Nat. Alzheimer's Disease and Related Disorders Assn., 2001—03, sr. v.p. devel., 2003—05; interim pres. Shimer Coll., Ill., 2007—08, Merrimack Coll., North Andover, Mass., 2008—10, Roger Williams U., 2010—. Author: LP Spaces of Complex Valued Functions, 1966, A Formalization of the Dialectical Development of Intelligence, 1974. Mem.: Philosophy of Sci. Assn., Math Assn. Am., Exec. Club Chgo., Econs. Club Chgo., Carlton Club. Roman Catholic. Office: Roger Williams University Office of President One Old Ferry Rd Bristol RI 02809 Office Phone: 401-253-1040.

CHAMPLIN, RICHARD EUGENE, hematologist, oncologist, medical educator; b. Milw., Feb. 13, 1949; BS in Engring. Scis., Purdue U., West Lafayette, Ind., 1971; MD, U. Chgo. Pritzker Sch. Medicine, 1975. Diplomate American Bd. Internal Medicine, cert. in hematology and med. oncology. Intern medicine LA County Harbor-UCLA Med. Ctr., 1975—76, resident hematologic oncology, 1976—78; fellowship UCLA Ctr. Health Scis., 1978—80, asst. prof. medicine, 1981—85, assoc. prof., 1985—90; prof. medicine U. Tex. MD Anderson Cancer Ctr., Houston, 1990—, chmn. dept. hematology, 1995—97, exec. com., divsn. cancer medicine, 1997—, Robert C. Hickey chair clin. cancer care, 1998, chmn. dept. stem cell transplantation & cellular therapy, 1998—. Exec. editor The Oncologist, 2005—, assoc. editor Biology of Blood & Marrow Transplantation, 1999—, Exptl. Hematology, 2002—, mem. editl. bd. Bone Marrow Transplantation, 2002—, Blood, 2002—; contbr. articles to profl. jours., chapters to books. Pres. Coun. Donor Collections & Transplant Centers, bd. dirs. Nat. Marrow Donor Program, Mpls., 1990—93; v.p. bd. dirs. Found. Accreditation Cellular Therapy, 1996—. Recipient New Investigator Rsch. award, Nat. Inst. Arthritis, Diabetes, Digestive & Kidney Diseases, 1982—84, Faculty Achievement award, U. Tex. MD Anderson Cancer Ctr., 2002, Waun Ki Hong award for Excellence in Team Sci., 2008; Giannini Found. fellowship, 1979—81. Fellow: ACP; mem.: Transplantation Soc. (Lifetime Achievement award 2011), Internat. Soc. Cell Therapy, American Soc. Clin. Oncology, American Assn. Cancer Rsch., Internat. Soc. Exptl. Hematology, American Soc. Hematology, American Soc. Blood & Marrow Transplantation (pres. 1992—94, Thomas Lecture award 2004), Alpha Omega Alpha. Office: Univ Tex MD Anderson Cancer Center 1515 Holcombe Blvd PO Box 301402 Unit 423 Houston TX 77030 *

CHAN, ALEXANDER, internist; arrived in U.S., 1983; 1 child. BS, U. Calif., Irvine, 1992; MS with honors, Am. U. Carribean, Plymouth, Monserrat, 1994, MD, 1996. Diplomate Am. Bd. Internal Medicine. Hospitalist The Permanente Med. Group, Modesto, Calif., 2000—07; team lead hospitalist Modesto Kaisler Permanente Med. Group, Calif., 2002—06, sub-chief pharmacy and therapeutic com., mem. utilization com., 2000—04, sub-chief utilization mgmt., 2004—07; med. dir. Primary Critical Care Med. Group, 2007—10; local site leader Primary Med. Care Med. Group, 2008—; chair medicine Emanual Med. Ctr, Turlock, Calif., 2009—. Mem quality control com. Permanente Med. Group, Modesto, Calif., 2000—07, mem. utilization mgmt., 2000—07. Recipient Butler Svc. award, Kaiser Permanente, 2002; scholar, Calif. Fedn., 1984—87. Fellow: ACP; mem.: AMA, Am. Soc. Internal Medicine. Avocations: ceramics, cooking, deep sea diving, deep sea fishing, travel. E-mail: alexahanmo@gmail.com.

CHAN, BERNARD WAN BUN, physician; b. Hong Kong, Oct. 31, 1935; s. Shing Chue and So Chun (Chung) C.; m. Dieneke Kroeze, Mar. 9, 1968; children: Robert, George, Marius. MB, BS, U. London, 1960, MD, 1970. Mem. sci. staff Med. Rsch. Coun., Eng., 1964-66; Elmore rsch. scholar Cambridge (Eng.) U., 1966-70. Chmn. med. affairs. Can. Cancer Soc., Ont., 1987. Fellow Royal Coll. Physicians (Can.), Royal Coll. Physicians (U.K.) Office: 6th Fl Crawford House 70 Queens Rd Central Hong Kong Office Phone: (852) 2849 4459. E-mail: hematology@netvigator.com.

CHAN, CHIU-PO JOSEPH, periodontist, health facility administrator, researcher, medical educator; b. Hong Kong, May 2, 1953; s. Yee-Hing C. and Wai-Yam Hung; m. Man-Ching Cheng, Aug. 5, 1979; children: Lin-I, Lin-Chieh. DDS, Nat. Taiwan U., Taipei, 1978; cert., La. State U., 1985. Periodontics of Dentistry. Resident, chief resident dental dept. Chang Gung Meml. Hosp., Taipei, 1978-82, assoc. prof., chmn. dept. periodontics, 1982—92, 1999—2005, chmn. dental dept., 1992-99. Fellow Internat. Coll. Dentistry, 2001—; dir. Acad. Periodontology, Taiwan, 1986—2001, pres., 2002—03; dir. Acad. Implant Dentistry, 2006—; investigator rsch. in dentistry, periodontology Chang Gung Med. Rsch. Com. and Nat. Sci. Coun., Taiwan, 1990—97. Author: Chinese Glossary of Periodontics, 1991; contbr. articles to profl. jours. Avocations: music, swimming, singing, poetry. Home: 131 4/F Section 1 Roosevelt Rd Taipei Taiwan Office: Chang Gung Meml Hosp Dental Dept 199 Tung Hwa N Rd Taipei Taiwan Office Phone: 886 02-27135211-3535. Business E-Mail: carol@adm.cgmh.org.tw.

CHAN, CLEMENT K., ophthalmologist; b. Hong Kong, June 7, 1955; MD, Loma Linda U. Sch. Medicine, 1980. Med. dir., pres. Southern Calif. Desert Retina Cons., 1989—. Assoc. clin. prof. dept. ophthalmology Loma Linda U., 1994—. Travel grant, Club Jules Gonin, 2010. Fellow: ACS, Am. Acad. Ophthalmology (award 2006); mem.: Calif. Acad. Eye Physicians and Surgeons, Am. Soc. Retina Specialists (Achievement award 2003, Sr. Achievement award 2007), Retina Soc., Alpha Omega Alpha. Avocations: theater, music, literature. Office: 36949 Cook St Ste 101 Palm Desert CA 92211 Office Fax: 760-340-2369. E-mail: pschan@aol.com.

CHAN, DANIEL SIU-KWONG, psychologist; b. Swatow, China, June 6, 1952; arrived in US, 1973; s. Hon-Kwong and Suet-Hing (Wong) C.; m. Rosario Arroyo, Dec. 14, 1985; children: Nathaniel Arroyo, Jennifer Arroyo. BA, Buena Vista Coll., 1977; MS, U. La Verne, 1980; PhD, U.S. Internat. U., 1984. Diplomate psychopharmacology; lic. psychologist, Calif. Dir. Indochinese outreach program Chinese Cmty. Ch., San Diego, 1980—81; exec. dir. Chinese Social Svc. Ctr., San Diego, 1981-82; rehab. counselor Asian Rehab. Svcs., Inc., LA, 1982-84; program dir. Hawthorne (Calif.) Cmty. Group Home, 1984-86; psychologist Pacific Clinics, Pasadena, Calif., 1986-89; attending psychologist Fairview Devel. Ctr., Costa Mesa, Calif., 1989—; pvt. practice San Gabriel Valley, Calif., 1989—. Cons. psychologist Ingleside Hosp., Rosemead, Calif., 1991—95, Garfield Med. Ctr., Monterey Park, 1993—99, Asian Youth Ctr., Rosemead, 1993—96, Rosemead, 2000—03, Allied Physicians Calif., San Gabriel, 1993—, Project SHINE, Inc., Downey, Calif., 1982—88. Mem.: APA, Neurosci. Edn. Inst., Am. Coll. Advanced Practice Psychologists, Internat. Coll. Prescribing Psychologists, Prescribing Psychologists Register. Republican. Presbyterian. Avocations: classical music, reading, travel. Home: 11107 Movino Ave Sunland CA 91040 2121 Office: Dr Daniel S Chan 3733 Rosemead Blvd Ste 201 Rosemead CA 91770-1981 Office Phone: 818-229-6121. Personal E-mail: drdschan@aol.com.

CHAN, GEORGETTE, surgeon; MBBS, postgrad., Nat. U., Singapore, Royal Coll. of Surgeons, Edinburgh. Fellowship gen. surgery Acad. Medicines, Singapore, 2005; Overseas fellowship tng. in advance surg. techniques in breast treatment with Umberto Veronesi European Inst. Oncology, Milan, 2006; pvt. practice Breast Surgery Centre, Mt. Elizabeth Med. Centre; cons. breast surg. oncology and gen. surgery Singapore Gen. Hosp.; breast specialist and gen. surgeon Breast Surgeon Singapore. Author scientific papers on breast surgery and oncology. Achievements include research in Cancer Prevention at the Cornell Med. Ctr. and Meml. Sloan-Kettering Cancer Centre, NY. Office: Singapore General Hospital Outram Rd Singapore 169608 Singapore Office Phone: 6562223322. Office Fax: 6562249221. *

CHAN, GERTRUDE PANGILINAN, medical researcher, consultant; b. Manila, Philippines, Mar. 13, 1944; d. Rafael Salonga and Dolores Maglalang Pangilinan; m. Edward Elvena Chan, May 21, 1967; children: Marz Peter P., Heidi P., Mark Philip P. MD, U. Santo Tomas, Manila, 1970. Diplomate Philippine Bd. Dermatology, 1992. Med. specialist Dermatology Rsch. and Tng. Svcs., Dept. Health, Manila, 1978—86; assoc. prof. sect. microbiology U. Santo Tomas, Faculty Medicine and Surgery, 1986—95; head, leprosy rsch. study group and residency tng. dermatology Rsch. Inst. Tropical Medicine, Dept. Health, Filinvest Corporate City, Alabang, 1987—. Cons. at Cook Island Western Pacific Region, WHO, Manila, 1992—92; accredited clin. trialist Bur. FDA, Dept. Health, 1987—. Author: (book) An Atlas and Handbook on the Diagnosis and Treatment of Common Skin Disorders and Leprosy; contbr. articles to profl. jours., chapters to books. Bd. dirs. Found. Assistance Hansenites, Manila, 1998—2001; parishioner St. Therese Child Jesus Parish, Antipolo, Rizal, 1996—2005; mem. RITM Coop. Orgn., Filinvest Corporate City, Alabang, Muntinlupa, 1995—2005. Grantee, NIH, Atlanta, 1990, WHO, Western Pacific Region, 1992; fellow, League Asian Dermatology Soc., Janssen Rsch. Coun., Manilla, 1997; Leprosy Rsch. grantee, Culion Found., Inc., 1990. Fellow: Philippine Leprosy Soc., Philippine Dermatol. Soc. (hon.; mem. bd. examiners 2003, coun. elders 2003—05), Philippine Soc. Cutaneous Medicine (hon.; pres. 1996—2000, chmn. bd. examiner 1996—2000, pres., bd. examiners 1996—2000); mem.: Philippine Med. Assn. (licentiate Outstanding Physician award 2003), Philippine Dermatol. Rsch. & Testing Found. (hon.; pres., chmn. bd. 1996—2005), Internat. Sci. Carbon Dioxide Therapy Group (assoc.; in charge dermatology application guidelines 2005—05). Roman Catholic. Avocations: swimming, cooking, needlecrafts, reading. Home: 11 Kent Filinvest Mayamot Antipolo 1820 Philippines Office: Rsch Inst Tropical Medicine Filinvest Corporate City Alabang Muntinlupa 1770 Philippines Office Fax: (632)8096334; Home Fax: (632)6811413. Personal E-mail: chanfamily@pacific.net.ph. Business E-Mail: gchan@ritm.gov.ph.

CHAN, HENG-LEONG, dermatologist; b. Oct. 1, 1952; m. Koon chu Cheung; children: Ka-Man, Ka-Po. MD, Nat. Taiwan U., 1979. Cert. Bd. Dermatology, Taipei, 1982. Vis. staff Chang Gung Meml. Hosp., Taipei, Taiwan, 1983—2001, chmn., 1990—2001; vice supt. Yin Shu-Tien Meml. Hosp., Taipei, 2001—; supt. Fu-Shin Skin Clinic, Taipei, 2005—. Editor: Jour. Clin. Dermatology. Bd. dir. Skin Rsch. and Developement Found., Taipei. Fellow: Internat. Soc. Cosmetic Dermatology (assoc.), Am. Acad. Dermatology (assoc.); mem.: Taipei Med. Assn. (mem. jud. panel 1999—2002), Med. Laser Soc. (bd. dirs. 1997—), Chinese Dermatology Soc. (pres. 1994—98, bd. dirs. 1994—2002, cons. 2003—), Intermat. Soc. Dermatopathology, Chang Gung Meml. Hosp. Physician Alumni Assn. (pres.). Achievements include research in aluminum oxide microdermabrasion in the treatment of acne scars. Office: Fu Shin Skin Clinic 3F No 50 Fu Xin North Rd Taipei 104 Taiwan Office Fax: +886287727516. Business E-Mail: drhlchan@yahoo.com.

CHAN, HSIANG SUI, surgeon; Grad., Nat. U., Singapore, 1986; M in Medicine (Surgery), Royal Coll. Surgeons, 1991. Fellow Royal Coll. Surgeons, Edinburgh, 1991; fellowship Acad. Medicine, Singapore, 1997; surgery tng. Lahey Clinic, Burlington, Mass., chief resident surgery dept., 1996; tng. Mass. Gen. Hosp., clin. fellow surgery dept.; surgeon surgery dept. Singapore Gen. Hosp. (SGH); surgeon surg. oncology Nat. Cancer Centre; gen. surgeon Gleneagles Med. Centre. Office: Gleneagles Medical Centre 6 Napier Rd Number 03-01 Singapore 258499 Singapore Office Phone: 6567334111. Office Fax: 6567334222. *

CHAN, KENNETH D., critical care specialist; MD, U. Calif., 1979. Diplomate Am. Bd. Internal Medicine, 1982, Am. Bd. Internal Medicine- pulmonary disease, 1988, Am. Bd. Internal Medicine-critical care medicine, 1989. Intern Alameda County Med. Ctr., Oakland, Calif., resident in internal medicine, 1979—83; fellow in pulmonary critical care medicine Univ. Calif. Davis Med. Ctr., Martinez, 1983—85; critical care specialist Calif. Pacific Med. Ctr. Office: California Pacific Medical Center 789 Vallejo St San Francisco CA 94133-3834 Office Phone: 415-982-6691.

CHAN, KENNY H., pediatric otolaryngologist; MD, Loma Linda U., Calif., 1977. Diplomate Am. Bd. Otolaryngology. Surgery intern Oreg. Health Scis. U., 1978—79, otolaryngology resident, 1979—83; pediat. fellow Children's Hosp. Pitts., 1983—85; prof. dept. otolaryngology U. Colo. Health Scis. Ctr.; chief pediat. otolaryngology Children's Hosp. Colo. Contbr. articles to profl. jours. Named one of Top Drs. in Denver, 5280 Mag. Fellow: ACS, Am. Acad. Pediat.; mem.: Am. Acad. Otolaryngology-Head & Neck Surgery. Achievements include conducting an 18 year study concluding with research linking rhinosinusitis to be a relatively common primary cause of toxic shock syndrome in children. Office: Childrens Hosp Colo Otolaryngology Dept 13123 E 16th Ave B455 Aurora CO 80045

CHAN, KIN MING, geriatrician, consultant; b. Singapore, Nov. 21, 1959; s. Sing Fook Chan and Foo Hoi Leong; m. Teo Lai Kheng, Sept. 5; children: Shona Chan Wai Kay, Trina Chan Wai Yan, Udella Chan Wai Peng. MB, Nat. Univ. Singapore, 1983; MD, Sch. Postgradute Med. Studies, Singapore, 1988; Diploma Geriatric Medicine, Royal Coll. Surgeons Physicians, Glasgow, UK, 1991. Dept. head Alexandra Hosp., Singapore, 1995—2000, Changi Gen. Hosp., Singapore, 1998—2000; cons. Chan KM Geriatric Med. Clin., Singapore, 2000—02; cons. and dir. Eldercare Medicine Pte Ltd, Singapore, 2002—. Adv. bd. mem. Moral Network of Older Persons, Singapore, 1999; expert Ministry of Health, Singapore, 2001; chmn. Ang Mo Kio Hosp. Pte Ltd, Singapore, 2002. Author, editor: Geriatric Medicine for Singapore, 1996, Common Problems of the Aged, 2001. Pioneer Boon Teck Cmty. Health Svc., Singapore, 1987—97; cmty. resource vol. Ministry of Cmty. Devel., Singapore, 1987—. Recipient pres. citation, Nat. Coun. Social Svc., 1992, Tributes award, NCSS, 1999; fellow, Royal Inst. Public Health, U.K., 1991, Acad. Medicine, Singapore, 1993. Mem.: Am. Geriatric Soc., Soc. Geriatric Medicine (v.p. 1996—2000). Presbyn. Achievements include first to the first geriatric ctr. in Singapore and involved in organising geriatric svc. for the western sector of Singapore. Avocations: photography, computers, gym workout. Office: Eldercare Medicine Pte Ltd Gleneagles Med Ctr #08-07, 6 Napier Rd Singapore Singapore 258499

CHAN, LAWRENCE SIU-YUNG, dermatologist, educator; b. Hong Kong, Dec. 10, 1949; came to U.S., 1975; s. Cheong-Yin Chan and Chun-Fun Wu. AA, Montgomery Coll., Takoma Park, Md., 1978; student, Messiah Coll., Grantham, Pa., 1978-79; BS, BS, MIT, 1981; MD, U. Pa., 1985. Diplomate Am. Bd. Dermatology, Nat. Bd. Med. Examiners. Intern Rutgers Med. Sch., Camden, NJ, 1986-87; resident U. Mich., Ann Arbor, 1987-91; asst. prof. Wayne State U., Detroit, 1991-93, Northwestern U., Chgo., 1993—2002, dir. immunodermatology divsn., 1993—2002; assoc. prof. U. Ill., 2002—05, dir. immunology rsch., 2002—, prof., 2005—, head dept. dermatology, 2005—. Adj. lectr. U. Mich., 1991-93. Author: (med. textbook) Blistering Skin Diseases, 2009; editor: (sci. textbook) Animal Models of Human Inflammatory Skin Disease, 2003. Recipient Clin. Investigator award, NIH, Bethesda, 1996; grantee Merit Rev., VA Rsch. Com., 1996; Small Project, High-risk Project and Rsch. Project grantee, NIH, 2001. Fellow Am. Acad. Dermatology; mem. Soc. Investigative Dermatology, Ctrl. Soc. Investigative Dermatology (chmn. 1995), Dermatology Found. (Career Devel. award 1993), Am. Assn. Immunologists, Am. Soc. Investigative Pathology, Microcirculatory Soc., Coun. Sci. editor, Alpha Omega Alpha, Am. Dermatol. Assn. Achievements include identification of a novel skin basement membrane component, generation of two animal model of atopic dermatitis, generation of an animal model of an autoimmune hairloss disorder alopecia areata. Office: U Ill Dept Dermatology 808 S Wood Chicago IL 60612-3010 Office Phone: 312-996-6966. Business E-Mail: larrycha@uic.edu.

CHAN, LEIGHTON, physiatrist, educator; BA in polit. sci., Dartmouth Coll., 1983; MD, UCLA, 1990; MS, U. Wash. Sch. Medicine, 1994; MPH, U. Wash. Sch. Pub. Health, 1996. Cert. Nat. Bd. Med. Examiners, 1991, Physical Medicine and Rehab., 1995, Electrodiagnostic Medicine, 1998. Internat. affairs intern to Senator Paul Tsongas US Senate, Washington; intern in medicine U. Wash., Seattle, 1990—91, resident in rehab. medicine, 1991—94, chief resident rehab. medicine, 1993—94, instr. rehab medicine, clin. scholar, Robert Wood Johnson fellow, 1994—96, asst. prof. rehab medicine, 1996—2002, assoc. prof. rehab medicine, 2002—06; sr. sci., chief rehab. medicine dept. NIH Clin. Rsch. Ctr., Bethesda, Md., 2006—. Congl. fellow to Rep. Jim McDermott US House of Reps., Washington, 1996. Recipient Outstanding Tchr. award, U. Wash. Sch. Medicine, 2002, Outstanding Continuing Med. Edn. Faculty award, 2004. Mem.: Inst. Medicine, Am. Congress Rehab. Medicine, Am. Assn. Neuromuscular and Electrodiagnostic Medicine, Assn. Academic Physiatrists (Yound Academician award 1999), Am. Acad. Physical Medicine and Rehab. (Presdl. Citation award 2004). Office: NIH Rehabilitation Medicine Dept Bldg 10 CRC Rm 1-1469 10 Ctr Dr MSC 1604 Bethesda MD 20892-1604 Office Phone: 301-496-4733. Office Fax: 301-402-0663. E-mail: chanle@cc.nih.gov.

CHAN, MARGARET, Director General of World Health Organization; b. Hong Kong, 1947; m. David Chan; 1 child. Attended, Northcote Coll. Edn., Hong Kong; BA, U. Western Ont., Can., 1973, MD, 1977, DSc (hon.), 1999; MSc in Pub. Health, Nat. U. Singapore, 1985. Rotating intern Victoria Hosp., London, Ont., Canada, 1977—78; med. officer maternal & child health svcs. Hong Kong Dept. Health, 1978—85, sr. med. officer family health svcs., 1985—87, prin. med. officer health adminstrn., 1987—89, asst. dir. personal health svcs., 1989—92, dep. dir., 1992—94, dir., 1994—2003; dir. Dept. Protection of Human Environment WHO, 2003—05, dir. Communicable Diseases Surveillance and Response, 2005, rep. of dir.-gen. for pandemic influenza, 2005—06, asst. dir.-gen. communicable diseases, 2005—06, dir.-gen., 2006—. Recipient Order of the British Empire, Her Majesty Queen Elizabeth II, UK, 1997, Prince Mahidol award, His Majesty King Bhumibol Adulyadej, Thailand, 1999; named one of 100 Most Powerful Women, Forbes mag., 2007—09, The Global Elite, Newsweek mag., 2008. Fellow: Royal Coll. Physicians. Achievements include effectively managing outbreaks of avian flu and SARS in Hong Kong. Office: Office of Director General WHO Hdqs Avenue Appia 20 1211 Geneva 27 Switzerland Office Phone: 41 22 791 2111. Office Fax: 41 22 791 3111. *

CHAN, MICHAEL W.Y., science educator; b. Hong Kong, Apr. 26, 1969; BS, Tunghai U., 1992; PhD, Chinese U. Hong Kong, 2003. Asst. prof. Nat. Chung Cheng U., 2007—. Mem.: Am. Assn. Cancer Rsch. Office: Nat Chung Cheng University Rm 452 Dept Life Sci Min Hsiung Chia Yi 621 Taiwan Business E-Mail: biowyc@ccu.edu.tw.

CHAN, NOR NORMAN, physician; b. Wuhan, China, May 27, 1967; MB, BChir, U. Liverpool, Eng., 1991; DCh, Royal Coll. Physicians, 1995; MD, U. London, 2002. Specialist registrar in diabetes and endocrinology Hemel Hempstead Gen. Hosp., Herts, England, 1995-96, Watford Gen. Hosp., Herts, England, 1996—97, Chelsea & Westminster, London, 1997-98, Charing Cross Hosp., London, 1998; rsch. fellow U. Coll., London, 1998-2000, Middlesex Hosp., London, 2000—03; asst. prof. dept. medicine and therapeutics The Prince of Wales Hosp., Hong Kong, 2003—06; clin. dir. Qualigenics Diabetes Ctr., Hong Kong Resort Internat., 2004—. Editor: Hong Kong Medical Diary; mem. editl. bd.: Primary Care Clinic CMP Medica; contbr. articles contbr. articles to profl. jours. Editl. bd. Primary Care Clinic, CMP Medicine. Rsch. grantee Astra Pharm., 1998, Brit. Heart Found., 1998; Brit. Heart Found. Rsch. fellow U. Coll., London, 1998-2000. Master Royal Coll. Physicians; mem. Brit. Diabetic Assn., Soc. Endocrinology, Hong Kong Atherosclerosis Soc. (hon. sec.) Office: Qualigenics Diabetes Ctr Upper Level Pier 3 11 Man Kwong St Ctrl Hong Kong China Home: 7C Birchwood Pl 96 MacDonnell Rd Mid-Level Hong Kong Office Phone: 852 3607 7800. Business E-Mail: norman.chan@qualigenics.com.

CHAN, PHILIP, retired dermatologist, military officer; b. Oceanside, NY, Oct. 14, 1946; s. Walter O. and Anna (Yee) C. BA, Harvard U., 1968; MD, Columbia U., 1972. Diplomate Am. Bd. Dermatology. Commd. capt. U.S. Army, 1973, advanced through grades to col., 1987; dermatologist Martin Army Cmty. Hosp., Ft. Benning, Ga., 1995-98; ret. U.S. Army, 1998; tchr. Tai Chi, Reiki, blues harmonica, ballroom dancing Columbus, Ga., 1999—. Adj. asst. prof. Uniformed Svcs. U. Health Scis., 1995—97; part-time instr. Rankin Arts Ctr., Columbus State U., 2002—08. Editor (govt. pub.) Procs. of Vesicant Workshop, 1987; contbr. articles to profl. jours. Fellow: Am. Acad. Dermatology; mem.: AMA, Assn. Mil. Dermatologists, Mensa. Home: 6300 Milgen Rd #1285 Columbus GA 31907-0962

CHAN, PHILIP J., medical educator; married; 3 children. BA cum laude in biology, Kalamazoo Coll., 1979; MS in Physiology, Mich. State U., 1981, PhD in Physiology, 1983. Diplomate Am. Bd. Bioanalysis. Dir. sperm processing & IVF and embryo transfer lab. Kennedy Meml. Hosps./U. Med. Ctr., Cherry Hill, NJ, 1983—87; dir. labs Hillcrest Fertility Ctr., Tulsa, 1987—89; dir. andrology/male reproduction and molecular biology labs. Loma Linda U. Health Care, Calif., 1989—. Mgr. info. sys. lab. computers and network Loma Linda U. Health Care, Inc., 1991—; from instr. to asst. prof. U. Medicine and Dentistry of N.J. Sch. Osteopathic Medicine, 1983-87; assoc. prof. Oral Roberts U. Sch. Medicine, 1987-89; from assoc. prof. to prof. Loma Linda U. Sch. Medicine, 1989—, mem. comparative medicine study sect. NIH, 1994-98, chmn. site visit Nat. Ctr. for Rsch. Resources, 1999; insp. Coll. Am. Pathologists, 1993—. Contbr. articles to profl. jours. Recipient Walter-MacPherson First Pl. Rsch. award The Walter E. Macpherson Soc., 1997, Outstanding Attending Staff Physician award WYETH, 2003, Nat. Faculty award Coun. on Resident Edn. in Ob Gyn., 2006. Mem. Am. Soc. Reproductive Medicine, Soc. Assisted Reproductive Tech., Am. Assn. Bioanalysts. Avocations: computers, stamp collecting/philately, coin collecting/numismatics, piano. Office: Loma Linda U Fac Med Office Dept Ob-Gyn Ste 3950 11370 Anderson St Loma Linda CA 92354-3450

CHAN, SIU-KI, pathologist; b. Hong Kong, Apr. 21, 1978; MBChB, Chinese U. Hong Kong, 2003. Assoc. cons. Kwong Wah Hosp., 2011—. Fellow: Hong Kong Acad. Medicine, Hong Kong Coll. Pathologists. Office: Dept Pathology Kwong Wah Hosp Yaumati Kowloon Hong Kong

CHAN, SIU-WAI, materials science educator; m. Cheung; children: L.Y., K.Y. BS, Columbia U., 1980; ScD, MIT, 1985. Mem. tech. staff Bellcore, Murray Hill, NJ, 1985-86, Red Bank, NJ, 1986-90; assoc. prof. materials sci. Columbia U., NYC, 1990—2002, prof., 2002—. Presdl. Faculty fellow, NSF, 1993, Guggenheim fellow, 2003—04. Office: Columbia U Sch Engring & Applied Sci 200 Mudd Bldg MC 4701 500 W 120th St New York NY 10027-8031 Business E-Mail: sc174@columbia.edu.

CHAN, WOON LING, biomedical researcher, educator; d. Ah Chan Chan and Suit Mui Lo; m. Foo Yew Liew, Jan. 4, 1974; 1 child, Tze Vun Liew. B.Sc with honors, U. Malaya, Kuala Lumpur, Malaysia, 1971, PhD, 1977; DSc, U. London, 2002. Post doctoral rsch. asst., fellow dept. zoology U. Coll. London, U. London, 1979—86; rsch. fellow dept. microbiology Guy's Campus King's Coll., U. London, 1986—89; mem. sci. staff, divsn. immunobiology Nat. Inst. for Biol. Stds. and Control, South Mimms, Hertfordshire, England, 1989—93; sr. lectr. dept. virology Med. Coll. St. Bartholomew's Hosp., U. London, 1993—97; reader dept. med. microbiology Bart's and London Sch. of Medicine, Queen Mary, U. ondon, 1997—2001; reader dept. biochem. pharmacology William Harvey Rsch. Inst., Queen Mary Sch. of Medicine, U. London, 2001—. Mem. coll. experts Med. Rsch. Coun., London, 2005—. Grantee, Med. Rsch. Coun., 1983—99, Sci. and Engring. Rsch. Coun., UK, 1984—87, 1985—88, Joint Rsch. Bd., St. Bartholomew's Hosp. Trust, UK, 1994—97, Scotia Pharm. Ltd, 1994—97, Wellcome Trust, Eng., 2001—03, 2002—06, Scottish Exec., Scottish Health Dept., 2001—04, Brit. Heart Found., 2002—06; recepient, Vacation Scholarship, Wellcome Trust, UK, 1995—98, 2001. Fellow: Royal Coll. Pathologists. Office: WHRI Queen Mary Univ London Charterhouse Sq London EC1M 6BQ England E-mail: w.l.chan@qmul.ac.uk.

CHAN, YEAN YEAN, medical educator, researcher; b. Malaysia, Aug. 17, 1977; PhD, U. Sains Malaysia, 2008. Lectr., rschr. U. Sains Malaysia, 2008—. Recipient Gold medal, Internat. Trade Fair Ideas-Inventions-New Products, Salon Internat. Des Inventions Geneva, Excellence Scientists award, Ministry High Edn., Malaysia, 2005; Young Women Life Scis. fellow, UNESCO-LOREAL, Travel grant,

ICAAC-IDSA. Mem.: Am. Soc. Microbiology, Am. Chem. Soc. Avocation: travel. Office: University Sains Malaysia Sch Med Scis Kota Bharu Kelantan 16150 Malaysia E-mail: yean@yahoo.com.

CHANCE, KENNETH BERNARD, SR., endodontist educator, academic administrator; b. NYC, Dec. 8, 1953; s. George E. and Janie L. (Bolles) Chance; m. Sharon Lee Lewis, July 11, 1981 (div.); children: Kenneth Bernard, Dana Marie, Christopher, Jacquelyn; m. Keli Green Chance, July 17, 2010. BS, Fordham U., Bronx, NY, 1975; DDS, Case Western Res. U., Cleve., 1979; Cert. in Endodontics, U. Medicine and Dentistry NJ, 1982; Cert. in Bus. Adminstrn., Internat Bus. & Mgmt. Ctr., U. Ky. Gatton Coll. Bus. and Econs., 2007. Asst. attending Jamaica Hosp., Queens, NY, 1981-87; chief endodontics Kings County Med. Ctr., Bklyn., 1982-91; assoc. prof. endodontics U. Medicine and Dentistry NJ, 1987; also dir. external affairs NJ Dental Sch.; asst. attending North Ctrl. Bronx Hosp., NY, 1983-91, Kingsbrook Jewish Med. Ctr., 1986-92; asst. dean external affairs and urban resource devel. NJ Dental Sch., 1989-97; cons. Harlem Hosp., NYC, 1982-90; health policy advisor to US Senator Frank Lautenberg of NJ, 1991—99; dir. health policy program The Joint Ctr. Polit. and Econ. Studies, 1993-94; acting chmn. dept. endodontics NJ Dental Sch., 1994-97; fed. rels. adv. com. U. Medicine and Dentistry NJ, 1994-97; dean, prof. endodontics Meharry Med. Coll. Sch. Dentistry, 1997-2000; prof., dir. divsn. endodontics U. Ky., Lexington, 2000—. Spkr., presdl. leadership lecture series Megar Evers Coll., 2006. Sci. reviewer Jour. of Dental Edn., 2004—. Mem. healthcare task force Congl. Black Caucus, 1994—2001; trustee Case Western Res. U., 2005—, mem. alumni and univ. rels. com., 2005—06, mem. presdl. search com., 2006, vice chmn. academic affairs and student life com., 2006, mem. audit com., 2006; mem. nat. adv. com. Robert Wood Johnson Summer Med. and Dental Edn. Program, 2006; min. music, sr. organist Sharon Bapt. Ch., Bronx, 1983—91, Greater Zion Hill Bapt. Ch., NYC, 1972—81. Recipient Dr. Paul P. Sherwood award for excellence in endodontics Case Western Res. U. Dental Sch., 1979, Cmty. Svc. award U. Medicine and Dentistry NJ, 1997, Tenn. Outstanding Achievement award, 1998, Outstanding Academician award U. Medicine and Dentistry NJ, 1999, Disting. Alumnus of Yr. award, Case Western Res. U., 2004, Found. grant award U. Medicine and Dentistry NJ, 1984, Exceptional Merit award, 1985, Excellence award, 1990, Disting. Practioner award Nat. Acad. Practice Dentistry, 2001, Faculty award U. Ky., Sch. Dentistry, 2005, award Megar Evers Coll., 2006; fellow Nat. Dental Leadership Devel. PEW, 1991, Robert Wood Johnson Health Policy, 1991, Pierre Fauchard Acad., 1996; named to The Best Dentists in America Woodward/White, Inc., 2004, Top Dentists, 2011, Faculty award U. Ky. Sch. Dentistry, 2008, Appreciation & Recognition award, Case Western Res. U. Dental Sch., 2011, Appreciation & Recognition Commitment award, case western Res. U., Sch. Dental Medicine, 2011. Fellow Am. Coll. Dentists, Internat. Coll. Dentists; mem. ADA, Internat. Assn. Dental Rsch., Am. Dental Edn. Assn. (chair minority affairs sect. 2003), Am. Assn. Dental Schs., Nat. Dental Assn., Am. Assn. Endodontists, Greater Met. Dental Soc. NY (pres.-elect 1986-87, v.p. 1984-86), Ky. Assn. Endodontists, Omicron Kappa Upsilon (pres.-elect 2006, pres. 2007). Home: 2140 Mangrove Dr Lexington KY 40513 Office Phone: 859-323-5891. Business E-Mail: kbchan2@uky.edu.

CHANDLER, ARTHUR BLEAKLEY, pathologist, educator; b. Augusta, Ga., Sept. 11, 1926; s. Clemmons Quillian and Mary Isabella (Bleakley) Chandler; m. Jane Stoughton Downing, Sept. 2, 1953; children: Arthur Bleakley, John Downing. Student, U. Ga., 1943-44; MD, Med. Coll. Ga., 1948. Diplomate Am. Bd. Pathology. Intern Baylor U. Hosp., Dallas, 1948-49; resident in pathology, NIH trainee in cancer dept. pathology Med. Coll. Ga., 1950-51, asst. in pathology, 1949-50, mem. faculty, 1949—, prof. pathology, 1962-2000, chmn. dept., 1975-2000, emeritus prof., emeritus chmn., 2001—. Com. mem. Nat. Heart, Lung and Blood Inst., 1969—93. Mem. editl. bd. Haemostasis, 1975—83, Pathology Rsch. and Practice, 1987—2001;, author papers in field; contbr. chapters to books. Trustee Young Mens Libr. Assn. Fund, 1962—72, Historic Augusta, Inc., 1966—69, Augusta-Richmond County Mus., 1965—87, Dan Printup Meml. Trust, 1985—2000, Acad. Richmond County, 1984—. Officer AUS Med. Corps, 1951—53. Fellow Commonwealth Fund, Thrombosis Rsch. Inst., Oslo, 1963—64. Mem.: AMA, Sch. Medicine Alumni Assn. Med. Coll. Ga. (pres. 1996—97), Richmond County Med. Soc. (trustee 1984—2002, sec. 1987, v.p. 1988), Med. Assn. Ga., Ga. Heart Assn., Ga. Assn. Pathologists (pres. 1984—85), Am. Heart Assn. (chmn. coun. on thrombosis 1978—80, chmn. com. on coronary lesions and myocardial infarctions 1980—82, fellow coun. arteriosclerosis), Am. Soc. Hematology, Am. Assn. Pathologists, Coll. Am. Pathologists, Am. Assn. History Medicine, Internat. Soc. for History of Medicine, Internat. Soc. Thrombosis and Haemostasis, Internat. Acad. Pathology, Alpha Omega Alpha. Episcopalian. Achievements include invention of the Chandler Loop method for producing a thrombus in vitro. Home: 803 Milledge Rd Augusta GA 30904-4351 Office: Med Coll Ga Dept Pathology Augusta GA 30912

CHANDLER, AUSTIN GRACE, psychologist; BA in Psychology with honors, Columbia U., 1978; PhD, Fordham U., 1982; postgrad. in Bus., U. N.C., Greensboro, 1990. Lic., clin. psychologist. Corp. cons. Farr Assocs., 1983-85; mem. adj. faculty, founder, dir. coll. counseling ctr. Greensboro Coll., 1985-92; founder, pres. Allied Counseling and Consulting Enterprises, 1992—; chief psychologist Evergreens Sr. Health Care Facilities, NC, 1997—2001; psychology cons. Therapeutic Alternatives, Inc., NC, 2002—03; dir. psychology Guilford Child Health, Inc., NC, 2003—09. Mem. adj. faculty U. N.C., Greensboro; bd. dirs. Ashley Industries. Author: (with Jack Bornstein) Food is Killing You, 1997; contbr. articles to profl. jours. Bd. dirs. N.C. Aging and Mental Health Coalition. Recipient Psychologist of Yr. award N.C. Chiropractic Assn. Mem. APA, N.C. Psychol. Assn., Prescription Privileges for Psychologists Register (charter), Sigma Xi. Avocations: painting, writing, following the stock market, skiing. Office: Allied Counseling & Consulting Enterprises 8200 Crows Nest Ln Greensboro NC 27455-9294 Office Phone: 336-272-1050. Office Fax: 336-643-6850.

CHANDLER, JAMES JOHN, surgeon, educator; b. Dayton, Ohio, Nov. 13, 1932; s. James Kapp and Margaret Bertha (Paulson) Chandler; m. Fleur Elizabeth Varney, July 23, 1955; 1 child, Jennifer Hauge. AB, Dartmouth Coll., 1954, diploma in medicine, 1955; MD cum laude, U. Mich., 1957. Diplomate Am. Bd. Surgery. Intern Harvard Surg. Svc., Boston City Hosp., 1957-58, jr. asst. resident, 1958; resident, chief resident in surgery, clin. fellow Am. Cancer Soc. U. Oreg. Hosps., Portland, 1961-64, instr. surgery, 1964; hon. staff, chmn. surgery Med. Ctr. at Princeton, NJ, 1972—92, pres. med. and dental staff, 1993-94; clin. prof. surgery U. Medicine and Dentistry N.J.-Robert Wood Johnson Med. Sch., Piscataway, 1976—; emeritus staff Robert Wood Johnson U. Hosp., New Brunswick, NJ; asst. track coach HUN Sch., Princeton, 2011—. Cons. in surgery Princeton U.; trustee Med. Ctr. Princeton, 1993—94. Contbr. chapters to books, articles to profl. jours. Bd. dirs. Trinity Counseling Svc., 1968—, chmn., 1968—72; pres. Princeton Day Sch. PTA, 1976—78, trustee, 1976—81; mem. alumni coun. Dartmouth Med. Sch., 1981—86, Dartmouth Coll., 1983—86; mem. Govs. Task Force on Cancer in NJ, 2000—08; active All Sts. Episcopal Ch., Princeton, 1965—. Lt. USN, 1958—60, served to lt. comdr. USNR, 1960—61. Fellow: ACS (pres. N.J. chpt. 1976—77, gov. 1981—87), Soc. Surg. Oncology; mem.: Soc. Surg. Alimentary Tract, Med. Soc. N.J. (sec., chmn. surgery sect. 1967—69), Am. Soc. Clin. Oncology, Gatineau Fish and Game Club, Nassau Gun Club (pres. 2001—02), Bedens Brook Club, Alpha Omega Alpha. E-mail: drjaychandler@aol.com.

CHANDLER, ROBERT CHARLES, healthcare consultant; b. Birmingham, Ala., Apr. 15, 1945; s. Coleman Duke and Myrtle (Cleveland) C.; m. Anne; children: Jason Charles, Jonathan Robert. BS in Pharmacy, Samford U., 1968; MS in Hosp. and Health Adminstrn., U. Ala.-Birmingham, 1972. Registered pharmacist. Pharmacy intern Carraway Meth. Hosp., Birmingham, 1968-69; chief pharmacist Holy Family Hosp., Birmingham, 1969-70; v.p. Ft. Sanders Med. Ctr., Knoxville, Tenn., 1971-78; sr. v.p. Bapt. Med. Ctrs., Birmingham, 1978-79; exec. v.p. Princeton, 1979-85; pres. E. Tenn. Bapt. Hosp., Knoxville, 1985-90, The Bapt. Health Sys. East Tenn., Knoxville, 1986-90; ptnr. Ward Howell Internat., Atlanta, 1991-98, TMP Worldwide, Atlanta, 1998-99; sr. v.p., global practice leader Healthcare and Pharms., Stratford Group, Atlanta, 2000—01; exec. v.p., nat. practice leader for healthcare and life scis. DHR Internat., Atlanta, 2002—. Bd. dirs. Am. Healthcare Sys. San Diego, 1988-90; chmn. bd. dirs. SunHealth Care Plans Tenn., 1986-88; bd. dirs. Ala. Quality Assurance Found., Birmingham, 1984-85, Ala. Med. Rev., Birmingham, 1980-84; mem. adv. bd. Blue Cross/Blue Shield, Birmingham, 1983-85; mem. liaison com. Jefferson County Med. Soc., Birmingham, 1984-85; various faculty appts. U. Ala., Birmingham, Emory U. Sch. Medicine, Atlanta; divsn. chmn. United Way, Birmingham, 1984; bd. dirs. United Way Greater Knoxville, 1987-88, Knoxville Opera Co., 1988; Sunday sch. tchr. Dawson Bapt. Ch., Birmingham; deacon chmn. 1st Bapt. Ch., Knoxville, 1988-90. Recipient Cert. Appreciation, Tenn. Gov. Ray Blanton, 1978, Disting. Svc. award Tenn. Com. on Employment of Handicapped, 1978, Award of Excellence Ala. Pub. Rels. Coun., 1979. Fellow Am. Coll. Hosp. Adminstrs.; mem. Birmingham Regional Hosp. Coun. (pres.-elect 1985), Hosp. Alliance Tenn. (pres. 1987-88), Ala. Hosp. Assn. (trustee 1984-85), Birmingham C. of C. (chmn. health svcs. com. 1980), The Club (Birmingham), Rotary (mem. group study exch. 1977). Office: DHR Internat 100 Galleria Pkwy Ste 1150 Atlanta GA 30339 Business E-Mail: rchandler@dhrinternational.com.

CHANDLER, ROBERT LESLIE, healthcare marketing & communication executive; b. Phila., Mar. 3, 1948; s. Joel Leslie and Evelyn Laney (DeLaney) C.; m. Pamela Lin Gemmel, Sept. 22, 2002; children: Jillian Delaney, Morgan Lindsey, Brooks Robert. AS, Atlantic C.C., 1969; BS, Bowling Green State U., 1971; MS, Ohio U., 1972; MBA in Hosp. Adminstrn., Wagner Coll., 1980. Dir. pub. rels. Athens Mental Health Ctr., Ohio, 1972; internal comms. editor, pub. affairs dept. Owens-Corning Fiberglas Corp., Toledo, 1972-74; dir. cmty. rels. Wyandotte Gen. Hosp., Mich., 1974-76; v.p. asst. adminstr. mktg., pub. affairs Meth. Hosp., Bklyn., 1976-82; exec. v.p. Burson-Marsteller Pub. Rels., NYC, 1982-95; pres. Chandler Chicco Co., 1995—; sr. v.p. mktg. & comm. inVentiv Health, 2011—. Spl. cons. Am. Soc. Hosp. Mktg. and Pub. Rels./Am. Hosp. Assn., 1989—90; spkr. at numerous comms. confs. Contbr. articles to profl. jours. Mem. budget com. United Way Mich., 1975—76; bd. dirs. NY chpt. Am. Heart Assn, 1990—91. Recipient EU Healthcare Consultancy of Yr. award, Holmes Report, 2008-09; Healthcare EU Consultancy of Yr. award, PR Week, 2008, Health Care Agency of Decade, 2010, Individual Lifetime Achievement SABRE award, 2010; Agy. of Yr. award Holmes Report, 2002-07; ranked a Best Agy. to Work For, Holmes Report, 2001-2008; numerous other awards; medal of Merit, Ohio U. Alumni, 2007; Am. Heart Assn. NJ/NY State scholar, 1969. Mem. Pub. Rels. Soc. Am. (Silver Anvil awards), Soc. Profl. Journalists, Am. Soc. Health Care Mktg. and Planning, Am. Coll. Healthcare Execs. (assoc.), Healthcare Comm. & Mktg. Assn.; Healthcare Mktg. & Comm. Council.; Sigma Delta Chi, Kappa Tau Alpha.

CHANDLER, VICKI L., biologist, educator; BS in Biochemistry, U. Calif., Berkeley; PhD in Biochemistry, U. Calif., San Francisco, 1983. NSF plant postdoc. fellow, dept. biol. scis. Stanford U., Calif.; faculty U. Oreg., 1985—97; Regents' prof. dept. plant scis. and molecular & cellular biology U. Ariz., Tucson, 1997—, dir. BIO5 Inst., 2004—09, also Carl E. & Patricia Weiler endowed chair for excellence in agriculture and life scis.; chief program officer for sci. Gordon & Betty Moore Found., Palo Alto, Calif., 2008—. Appt. biol. directorate adv. com. NSF, 2001—04; bd. dirs. Bioindustry Orgn. Southern Ariz. Mem. editl. bd.: Plant Physiology, Genetics; contbr. articles to profl. jours. Founding mem. bd. visitors Pima Cmty. Coll., Tucson; appt. commr. Ariz. Dept. Commerce & Econ. Devel. Recipient Rschr. of Yr. award, U. Ariz. Coll. Agrl. & Life Scis., 2001—02, NSF Faculty award for women scientists and engineers, NIH Director's Pioneer award, Presdl. Young Investigator award. Fellow: AAAS; mem.: NIH (Dir.'s Pioneer award 2005, Presdl. Young Investigator award, Searle Scholar award), NAS (coun. mem. 2007—10), Genetics Soc. America (bd. dirs.), Am. Soc. Biochemistry & Molecular Biology, Internat. Soc. Plant Molecular Biology (bd. dirs.), Am. Soc. Plant Biologists (past pres.), Rosalind Franklin Soc. Office: U Ariz Dept Plant Scis Keating Bldg Rm 102 303 1657 N Helen St Tucson AZ 85721 Office Phone: 520-626-4272. Business E-Mail: chandler@ag.arizona.edu.

CHANDLER, WILLIAM FREDERICK, neurosurgeon; b. Chgo., July 25, 1945; s. George Marshall and Maxine Searle Chandler; m. Susan Elizabeth Chandler, Jan. 3, 1970; children: Scott, Justin. BA, Northwestern U., 1967; MD, U. Mich., 1971. Fellow in neurosurg. rsch. Karolinska Inst., Stockholm, 1977; asst. prof. neurosurgery La. State U., New Orleans, 1977-79, U. Mich., Ann Arbor, 1979—83, assoc. prof. neurosurgery, 1983—89, prof. neurosurgery, 1989—, prof. internal medicine, 2003—. Author: Carotid Artery Injuries, 1982, Ultrasound in Neurosurgery, 1989. 1st lt. USAR, 1972-77. Recipient Nat. Pres.'s award Mich. State Med. Soc., 1982, Disting. Svc. award Neurosurgery Sect. on Tumors, 1997; named one of Best Doctors in America, 2003-2004 Mem. Congress Neurol. Surgeons (pres. 1992), Am. Assn. Neurol. Surgeons (bd. dirs. 1981-, current chmn.), Soc. Neurol. Surgeons, Am. Acad. Neurol. Surgery, Mich. Assn. Neurol. Surgeons (pres. 1986-88), ABMS (bd. dirs.), American Bd. Neurol. Surgery (chmn. 2005-08). Presbyterian. Avocations: tennis, skiing. Office: Univ Mich Med Ctr 1500 E Medical Center Dr Ann Arbor MI 48109-0005 E-mail: wchndlr@umich.edu.

CHANDNA, PREETIKA, dentist, educator; b. New Delhi, Aug. 29, 1980; BDS, Christian Dental Coll., 2003, MDS, 2007. Physician ITS-Ctr. Dental Studies & Rsch., Muradnagar, 2007, Subharti Dental Coll., Meerut, Uttar Pradesh, India, 2008—, lectr. Avocation: reading. Home: J-58 Shastri Nagar Meerut Uttar Pradesh 250004 India Personal E-mail: drpreetikachandna@gmail.com.

CHANDOLA, RAKESH MOHAN, physics professor; b. Dehradun, Uttarakhand, India, June 15, 1964; Postgrad., 1980—85. Asst. prof., med. physics Govt. of Chhattisgarh, Dept. Radiotherapy, Pt. J. N. M. Med. Coll., Raipur, India, 1987—2007, assoc. prof. med. physics, 2007—; dir. Chhattisgarh State Level Radiation Safety Cell, Govt. of Chhattisgarh, 2006—. Mem.: Assn. Med. Physicists India. Avocations: literature, writing, cricket. Home: House 27/273 New Shanti Nagar Raipur Chhattisgarh 492001 India Personal E-mail: rakemohachan@rediffmail.com.

CHANDOR, STEBBINS BRYANT, pathologist; b. Boston, Dec. 18, 1933; s. Kendall Stebbins Bryant and Dorothy (Burrage) C.; m. Mary Carolyn White, May 30, 1959; children: Stebbins Bryant Jr., Charlotte White. BA, Princeton U., 1955; MD, Cornell U., 1960. Diplomate Am. Bd. Pathology. Intern Bellevue Hosp., NYC, 1960-61, resident, 1965-66, Stanford U. Med. Ctr., Palo Alto, Calif., 1962-65; pathologist Tripler Army Med Ctr, Honolulu, 1966—69; instr. Cornell U., Ithaca, NY, 1966; asst. prof. U. So. Calif. Med. Ctr., LA, 1969-73, assoc. prof., 1974-76, SUNY, Stony Brook, 1976-80; dir. clin. lab. Univ. Hosp., Stony Brook, 1978-80; dir. JMMS Labs., Huntington, 1981-91; prof., chmn. dept. pathology Marshall U. Sch. Medicine, Huntington, W.Va., 1981—91, assoc. dean for clin. affairs, 1990-91; prof., vice chmn. Sch. Medicine U. So. Calif., 1991—2004, dir. labs. U. Hosp., 1991—2004, prof. emeritus, 2004—, mem. provost oversight com. athletic affairs, 2006—, mem. faculty senate, 2008—10; adv. bd. mem. Phoresus Pharm., Inc., 2011—; cons. Dako Na Inc., 2011—. Bd. dirs. Immunopathology Med. Ctr., 1969—76; mem. provosts oversight com. U. So. Calif., 2005—; pres. Ret. Faculty Assn., U. Southern Calif., 2007—08, mem. faculty senate, 2008—10. Contbr. articles to profl. jours. Pres. San Marino Tennis Found., 1975; governing bd. U. Path. Consortium, 1999-2004; mem., faculty senate, U. Southern Calif., 2008-10. Served to maj. USAR, 1966-69. Decorated Army Commendation medal; recipient Physicians Recognition award AMA, 1983, 86, 89, 93, 99, 04. Fellow Am. Assn. Med. Colls., Am. Soc. Clin. Pathologists (dep. commn. 1993-98, continuing edn. bd. dirs. 1990-96, chair by-law com., 1993-96, chmn. pathology group, 1993-98, v.p. 1997-98, pres. 1999-2000, awards com. 2001-), Coll. Am. Pathologists (state commr. I&A program 1987-91, dist. commr. 1991-99); mem. Calif. Soc. Pathologists (sec.-treas. 1974-75, pres.-elect 1975-76), Assn. Am. Pathologists, W.Va. Assn. Pathologists (pres. 1985-86), Assoc. Path. Chmn. Acad. Clin. Lab. Physicians and Scientists (rep. CAS 1991-2003, adminstrv. bd. 1997-2003), Am. Assn. Med. Colls. (exec. coun. 1998-2000), LA Acad. Medicine, Rt. Faculty Assn. (bd. dirs. 2005—), U. So. Calif. Ret. Faculty Assn. (bd. dirs. 2005—, v.p. 2006-07, pres.-elect 2006-07, pres. 2007—08), Princeton Club, Valley Club (v.p. 1975, bd. dirs. 1993), City Club (v.p. 1988-89, pres. 1989-90), Valley Hunt Club, The Valley Club Montecito (bd. dirs., 2007-09). Republican. Episcopalian. Home: 2170 East Valley Dr Santa Barbara CA 93108 Office Phone: 323-442-9611. Personal E-mail: sbchandor@verizon.net. Business E-Mail: chandor@usc.edu.

CHANDRA, PRAKASH, psychiatrist; b. Muzaffarpur, Bihar, India, Jan. 2, 1977; MD, Maulana Azad Med. Coll., 2002. Sr. house officer Oxford & Edinburgh Psychiatry Residency, 2003—06; neuroscience rschr. U. Oxford, 2006—07; resident physician SUNY Downstate Med. Ctr., 2007—, chief resident, 2010—. Mem.: APA, AMA, Soc. Neurosci. Office: SUNY Downstate Med Ctr 451 Clarkson Ave Brooklyn NY 11203 Personal E-mail: dr_pchandra@yahoo.com.

CHANDRA, PRANJAL, biotechnologist, educator; b. Gorakhpur, Uttar Pradesh, India, Jan. 1, 1984; MSc, MTech, Tech. U. Uttar Pradesh, PhD, 1980. Lectr., rschr. Med. Diagnostics Rsch. Group, Amity Inst. Biotechnology, Amity U., India, 2008—. Cons. Koshika LifeScis. Acad., 2008—11. Mem.: Korean Chem. Soc. Avocation: history. Home: Vishnupuram Basharatpur Gorakhpur Uttar Pradesh 273004 India Personal E-mail: pranjalmicro13@gmail.com.

CHANDRA, RANJIT KUMAR, research scientist, educator, physician; b. Mailsi, Punjab, India, Feb. 2, 1938; s. Hukam Chandra and Kaushalya Devi-Khurana; children: Sujata Chandra-Pike, Amrita, Tarang Chandra-Faeh, Rahul. MBBS, Panjab U., Amritsar, India, 1960; MD, All India Inst. Med. Scis., New Delhi, 1963; Doctorate (hon.), Pontificial Cath. U., Santiago, Chile, 1981; PhD (hon.), Beijing Med. U., 1987; DM (hon.), Universite di Chile, Santiago, 1993; DrMedChir (hon.), Universite di Napoli, Italy, 1994; DSc (hon.), Panjab U., Chandigarh, India, 2003. Lic. Med. Coun. of India, 1960, Med. Coun. of Can., 1977, diplomate Am. Acad. of Pediat., 1982. Lectr. Postgrad. Inst. Med. Edn. and Rsch., Chandigarh, India, 1964—65; asst. prof. All-India Inst. Med. Scis., New Delhi, 1966—74; rsch. prof. Meml. U. of Nfld., St. John's, Canada, 1975—2001; pres., vice-chancellor Université Internationale des Sciences de la Santé, Crans-sur-Sierre, Switzerland, 2002—04. Cons. WHO, Geneva, 1966—2000, Indian Coun. of Med. Rsch., New Delhi, 1966—75, NAS, Washington, 1979—94, Health Can., Ottawa, Ontario, 1979—99; editor-in-chief Nutrition Rsch., New York, 1980—2003; pres. Internat. Congress of Nutrition, Montreal, Quebec, Canada, 1993—97; editor Reviews of Biomed. Books and Jours., Toronto, Ontario, Canada, 2004—, Survey Nutritional Immunology, Toronto, Ontario, Canada, 2006—. Author: (book) Nutrition, Immunity and Infection, 1977; editor: Nutrition and Immunology, 1992; author: over 20 books. Pres. Friends of India Assn., St. John's, Newfoundland, Canada, 1996—97. Recipient Medal in Medicine, Royal Coll. of Physicians of Can., 1982, prize, Hermes GmbH, 1988, Queen's Jubilee medal, Queen Elizabeth II, 2002; named Officer of Order of Can., 1990. Master: Am. Coll. Physicians; fellow: Royal Coll. Pediatrics and Child Health, Royal Coll. Physicians Can.; mem.: NAS, Am. Acad. Allergy. Achievements include patents for nutritional supplement for the elderly; nutritional supplement for children; nutritional supplement for adolescents; patents pending for nutritional supplement for adults; nutritional supplement for infants, iron (III) hydroxide polymaltose; discovery of Chandra-Khetarpal syndrome; first to establish nutritional immunology; research in food allergy and allergic disease. Office: TSAR Health 3044 Bloor St W Ste 316 Toronto ON Canada M8X 2Y8 Home: PK 2 DLF Phase 4 Y-182 Regency 122 002 Gurgaon India Office Fax: 91-124-405-1832. Personal E-mail: rkchandra2004@yahoo.com.

CHANDRA, SATISH, psychologist; b. Dankaur, India, Dec. 22, 1944; arrived in U.S.A., 1966, permanent resident; s. Murari Lal and Yashoda Devi. BSc in Physics, Chemistry and Math., U. Allahabad, 1961; BSEE with hons., Indian Inst. Tech., 1966; MA in Psychology, SUNY, 1975; postgrad., U. Rochester, 1969—71; postgrad. in Clin. Psychology, SUNY, 1971—77. Engr. electronics divsn. Gen. Dynamics, 1968—69; rsch. Dept. Psychology Harvard U., Cambridge, Mass., 1977—78; rschr., tchr. & cons. Boston, 1978—. Contbr. articles to profl. jours. Fellow, U. Rochester, 1969—70. Mem.: APS, Am. Chem. Soc., Soc. Philosophy and Psychology, N.Y. Acad. Scis. Achievements include research in psychology leading to end of B.F. Skinner's school of psychology; economics: a new theory of money, multiplying finance resources available to government for research and development and other purposes; chemicals leading to more effective and economical treatments with fewer side effects for various medical conditions; medicine and physics, such as a new theory of relativity showing how observing organisms can drastically modify properties of the physical world relative to themselves at an everyday level; laboratory research with rats discovering a new effect drastically modifying biological clocks with theoretical and practical applications to biology. Home: 97 Madelaine Ave Toronto ON Canada M1L2X6 Personal E-mail: satchandrag@gmail.com.

CHANDRA, SURESH, agricultural studies educator; b. Bulandshahr, Uttar Pradesh, India, Feb. 1, 1977; BTech, GBPUAT, Pantnagar, 1998; MTech, AMU, Aligarh, 2002. Asst. prof. SVP U. Agr. and Tech. Meerut, 2005—, tchr., rschr., 2005—. Contbr. articles to profl. publs. Mem.: SRDA (Meerut), ISAE (New Delhi). Avocation: travel. Office: SVP University Dept Agrl Engineering and Food Tech Meerut Uttar Pradesh 250110 India Office Phone: 09457130397. Office Fax: 0121-2888505. Personal E-mail: chandra21778@yahoo.co.in.

CHANDRA, V SUBHASH, surgeon; MBBS, St. John's Med. Coll., Banglore, India, 1977. With Hover Gen. Hosp., Milford Chest Hosp., The Royal Surrey County Hosp., Kent and Canterbury Hosp., Kent and The Gen. Infirmary; registrar and rsch. fellow internal medicine Kent and Canterbury Hosp., 1983; surgeon Wockhardt Super Speciality Hosp., Banglore, India. Fellow: Royal Coll. of Physicians; mem.: Manipal Hosp. (founder Manipal Heart Found. 1991). Achievements include has performed more than 16000 Coronary and Non Coronay Interventions; conducts active Electrophysiology program and performs ablations regularly. Office: Wockhardt Super Speciality Hospital 1643 N Ambazari Rd Nagpur Uttar Phradesh 440033 India Office Phone: 917126624289. *

CHANDRAN, NATTERI VEERARAGHAVAN, psychotherapist, hypnotherapist, educator; b. Madras, India, Aug. 13, 1946; s. Natteri and Kamala Veeraraghavan; m. Chitra Ganapathy, Nov. 12, 1973; children: Aditi, Shiv. B of Medicine and Surgery, Madras U., 1969; diploma in clin. hypnosis, Melbourne U., Australia, 1975. Diplomate Am. Bd. Med. Psychotherapists; med. diplomate. Resident Madras Med. Coll., 1969—71; med. officer Mental Health Authority, Victoria, Australia, 1971-77; teaching assoc. dept. psychiatry U. Melbourne, 1973-78, clin. asst. dept. psychiatry, 1976-78; med. dir. health svcs. Royal Melbourne Inst. of Tech., 1978-83; pvt. practice Victoria, 1983—; mem. teaching faculty Australian Soc. Hypnosis, Victoria, 1986— Med. cons. Royal Melbourne Inst. Tech., 1979—83; bd. govs. Schizophrenia Rsch. Found., India, 1993—; Congress amb., mem. nat. adv. com. 27th World Fedn. Mental Health Biennial Congress at Melbourne, 2003; mem. Internat. Com. Bodhidharma Ctr., 2009, Devel. Bd. Royal Childrens Hosp. Bioethics Ctr., Melbourne, 2009. Reviewer: profl. publ. Stress and Health Jour. Internat. Soc., 2005—. Founder The East West Ctr., The East West Overseas Aid Found. Australia, Melbourne, 1992, The East West Found. India, Madras, India, 1993, The East West Found. Papua New Guinea, 1995; hon. patron Internat. Artists Mus. Melbourne Meet, 1998; gen. sec. Pondicherry Students' Assn. and Pondicherry Students' Welfare Soc., 1963—64; spkr. Student Assembly Pondicherry, 1966, 1967; founder, trustee The East West Found. US; bd. dirs. Tribal India Health Found., 2005—. Recipient Sir. C.P. Ramaswami Iyer trophy, 1964, cert. recognition cmty. svc., Prime Minister Australia, 2001, Hind Rattan award, New Delhi cmty. svc., 2004; named Hon. Patron, Internat. Artists' Mus., Melbourne Meet, 1998; Nat. Merit scholar, Govt. India, 1962—70. Fellow Am. Bd. Med. Psychotherapists; mem. Am. Psychiat. Assn. (internat. mem.), Australian Med. Assn., Internat. Soc. Hypnosis, Royal Australian Coll. G.P.s, Australian Soc. Hypnosis, Australian Coll. Psychol. Medicine, Indian Psychiat. Soc., World Fedn. Mental Health Biennial Congress (mem. nat. adv. com. 2003). Office: 407-409 Swanston St 6th Fl Melbourne 3000 Australia Office Phone: +61 3 96636271. Personal E-mail: chandran@chandran.com.au.

CHANDRASEKHAR, MASIYAPPA RAJASEK, health faculty administrator, researcher; b. Shimoga, India, Feb. 25, 1955; s. Rajasekhar Masiyappa and Jayamma Rajasekhar; m. Dhanalakshmi Chandrasekhar, May 1, 1987; children: Harshhavardhan Rajasek Chandrasekhar, Nandini Rajasek Chandrasekhar. MBBS, Bangalore Med. Coll., 1980, MD, 1985; postgrad., BOE Rajiv Gandhi U. Health Scis., Bangalore, 1997. Lectr. Ambedkar Med. Coll., Bangalore, 1985—87, asst. prof., 1987—89, assoc. prof., 1989—92, prof., 1992—97; prof., head Kaznataka Inst. Med. Scis., Hubli, 1997—2005; prin. Raichur Inst. Med. Sci., Raigwa, 2005—. Project coord. HIV/Aids RRTC-03, Karnataka, 2002—05. Reviewer Jour. Sci. and Indsl. Rsch., 2003; contbr. articles and publs. to profl. jours. Recipient Bharatiya Gold, Health and Edn., 2004, Med. award, Devel. Assn., 2005, Lifetime achievement award, 2005. Mem.: Indian Assn. Med. Microbiologists (life), Country Club (life). Avocations: literature, art, photography, music. Home: 1926 A 23 Cross Prasanthnagar Bangalore 560 079 India Office: Raichur Inst Med Scis Raichur India Office Phone: 918532235855. Personal E-mail: rchbvb81@yahoo.com.

CHANDRASEKHAR, SUJANA S., otologist, educator, neurotologist; 4 children. BS cum laude, CCNY, 1984; MD, Mt. Sinai Sch. Medicine, NYC, 1986. Intern, residency otolaryngology NYU Med. Ctr., 1986—92; fellow in otology/neurology House Ear Inst., LA, 1993; from asst. to assoc. prof. U. Medicine and Dentistry NJ-NJ Med. Sch., Newark, 1994—2001, dir. otology/neurotology, 1996—2001; assoc. prof. otolaryngology Mt. Sinai Sch. Medicine, NYC, 2001—04, clin. assoc. prof. otolaryngology, 2004—; dir. NY Otology, 2005—. Dir. otology/neurotology Mt. Sinai Med. Ctr., NYC, 2001—04, dir. cochlear implant program, 2001—04. Recipient Honor award, AMA, 2000, Am. Acad. Otolaryngology-Head and Neck Surgery, 2002, Rsch. Thesis Award, Trological Soc., 2004. Office: 1421 3rd Ave New York NY 10028-1802 Office Phone: 212-249-3232. Office Fax: 212-249-3287. Personal E-mail: newyorkotology@gmail.com.

CHANDRASEKHARAN, RAJASEKHARAN, medical educator; b. Chenganoor, Pathanamthitta Dist., May 29, 1959; MBBS, Med. Coll. Hosp., Thiruvananthapuram, 1981, MD, 1988. Lectr., medicine Med. Coll. Hosp., 1986—92, head, dept. infectious diseases, 2007—09, prof., medicine, 2007—; cons. physician Indian Space Rsch. Orgn., 1992—93; physician Ministry of Health, Oman, 1993—97. Resource persons Kerala State Aids Control Soc., 2005—. Author: Diagnostic Value of Microwoman in Neurological Disorders, 2010. Recipient Best Dr. award, Rotary Club Trivandrum, award, U. Kerala. Fellow: BMJ Case Reports Jour.; mem.: IEEE EMBS, Indian Med. Assn. Avocations: reading, chess, badminton. Home: TC15/1543-1 MP Appan Nagar Vazuthacaud Thiruvananthapuram Kerala 695014 India Personal E-mail: drcrajasekharan@yahoo.com.

CHANDRASHEKAR, SUDHA, healthcare educator, consultant; b. Chennai, Tamil Nadu, India, May 5, 1975; d. Vajapeyum Krishnamachar and Kamala Parthasarathy; m. Gangur Cheluve Gowda Chandrashekar, June 21, 1999; children: Amoolya, Akash. BS in Medicine and Surgery, Kempegowda Inst. Med. Scis., Bangalore, India, 1998, MS in Pub. Health, 2003; MS in Health Economics and Pharmacoeconomics, Pompeu Fabra U., Barcelona, 2008; PhD student in Health Economics, London Sch. Hygiene and Tropical Medicine, 2008—. Diploma in indsl. hygiene Annamalai U., 2005. Jr. sci. officer NIMH and Neuroscis., Bangalore, Karnataka, 2003—04; occupl. health cons. RIA Diagnostics, Bangalore, 2004—05; asst. prof. A.J. Inst. Med. Scis., Mangalore, Karnataka, India, 2004—; cons. economist London Sch. Hygiene and Tropical Medicine, 2005—; asst. prof. St. John's Rsch. Inst., Bangalore, Karnataka, 2007—. Contbr. articles to profl. rsch. jours. (P Ashwath award, 2000, Mohanmal award, 2001, Best Paper award, 2005). Ednl. cons. Capitol institutions, Bangalore, Karnataka, India, 2005. Recipient Young Scientist award, Karnataka Assn. Cmty. Health, 2003, Best Paper award, UNAIDS, 2006, 2008, Global Health Leadership award, Internat. Devel. and Rsch. Ctr., Can., 2008; HIV Rsch Trust scholarships, IDRC. Fellow: Indian Pub. Health Assn.; mem.: Internat. AIDS Economic Network, Internat. Pub. Health Assn., Internat. AIDS Soc., Karnataka Assn. Cmty. Health (sci. com. 2007—08, Young Scientist award 2004), Indian Acad. Allergy and Immunology (Best Paper award 2003), Indian Assn. Occupl. Health (exec. com. mem. 2007—08, Young Scientist award 2004). Avocations: swimming, travel, badminton, reading, chess, embroidery. Home: 206 15th B Cross West Chord Rd Mahalaxmipuram Bangalore Karnataka 560086 India Office: Saint John's Rsch Inst Sarjapur Rd Bangalore Karnataka 560034 India Office Fax: 91-80-25532037; Home Fax: 9180-400300. Personal E-mail: sudhashreec@yahoo.co.in. Business E-Mail: nrc@iphcr.res.in.

CHANDRAVANSHI, SHIVCHARAN L., ophthalmologist, educator; b. Gwalior, Madhya Pradesh, India, Apr. 6, 1975; MBBS, Gajara Raja Med. Coll. Gwalior, 1999, MS, 2004. Orbit & oculoplasty fellow Shankar Nethralay, Chennai, India, 2005—07, cons., oculoplasty Ahaliya Found. Eye Hosp., Palghat, Kerala, India, 2007; asst. prof. ophthalmology Ministry Health, Govt Madhya Pradesh, 2007—; cons. Shyam Shah Med. Coll., Rewa, Madhya Pradesh, 2007—11. Mem.: Madhya Pradesh State Ophthalmic Soc., Oculoplasty Assn. India, Delhi Ophthal. Soc., All India Ophthal. Soc. Avocation: music. Office: Shyam Shah Med Coll Dept Ophthalmology Rewa Madhya Pradesh 486001 India Personal E-mail: dr_scl@rediffmail.com.

CHANG, BARBARA KAREN, medical educator, director; b. Milltown, Ind., Jan. 6, 1946; m. M.F. Joseph Chang-Wai-Ling, Oct. 6, 1967; children: Carla Marie Yvonnette, Nolanne Arlette. BA, Ind. U., 1968; MA, Brandeis U., 1970; MD, Albert Einstein Coll. Medicine, 1973. Diplomate Am. Bd. Internal Medicine, Am. Bd. Med. Oncology, Am. Bd. Hematology. Resident in internal medicine Montefiore Med. Ctr., Bronx, NY, 1973-75; fellow in hematology/oncology Duke U. Med. Ctr., Durham, NC, 1975-78; staff physician VA Med. Ctr., Augusta, Ga., 1978-95, chief hematology/oncology, 1980-89, assoc. chief of staff edn., 1990-95, chief of staff, chief med. officer Albuquerque, 1995—2002; prof. medicine Med. Coll. Ga., Augusta, 1978-95; assoc. dean U. N.Mex. Sch. Medicine, Albuquerque, 1995—2002; cons. Capital Assets Realignment for Enhanced Svcs. Program VA Ctrl. Office, Washington, 2002—03, dir. program evaluation Office Academic Affiliations, 2003—07, acting dir. grad. med. edn., 2006—07; dir., Med. and Dental Edn., 2007—. Mem. Sci. Adv. Bd., Washington, 1983-88; mem. expert panels computer applications Dept. Vets. Affairs, Washington, 1988-95; Va. liasion to steering com. group on resident affairs Assn. Am. Med. Colls., 2000-06; Va. rep. Coun. Grad. Med. Edn., 2006-, Accreditation Coun. Grad. Med. Edn., 2006-; presenter in field. Contbr. numerous articles on cancer rsch. to profl. jours. Youth coord. Am. Hemerocallis Soc., Augusta, 1993-95, pres. local chpt. 1997, Albuquerque, garden judge 1997-03, region 6 youth liaison, 2000-01, exhbn. judge, 2001—, nat. youth liaison com., 2003-. Grantee Nat. Cancer Inst., Am. Cancer Soc., 1978-93; David M. Worthen award Acad. Excellence Dept. Vet. Affairs, 2000. Fellow ACP, Am. Soc. Clin. Oncology, Bioelectromagnetic Soc. (bd. dirs. 1983-86). Business E-Mail: barbara.chang@va.gov.

CHANG, BERNARD YI PING, ophthalmologist, consultant; b. Kuching, Sarawak, Malasia, Aug. 19, 1968; s. Chih Kang Chang and Janet Poh Lian Tan; m. Wendy Charmian Lum Hee, July 22, 1995; children: Peter, Jeanette. BSc, U. Bristol, Eng., 1990; MBChB, U. Bristol Med. Sch., 1993. Specialist registrar, ophthalmology West Yorkshire Rotation, Leeds, England, 1999—2003, fellow, oculoplastics, lacrimal & orbital surgery Dublin, 2001; cons. ophthalmologist Leeds Tchg. Hosps. NHS Trust, 2003—. Yorkshire rep. Brit. Med. Assn. OGC, England, 2004—; coll. rep. Nat. Ocular Oncology Group, England, 2005—. Contbr. scientific papers. Vis. surgeon Opportunities in Tng. Initiative, LTHT, Madagascar, 2008—. Fellow: RCS (Edinburgh), Royal Coll. Ophthalmologists (coun. mem. 2004—); mem.: Am. Acad. Ophthalmology, European Soc. Ophthalmic Plastic & Reconstructive Surgery, Brit. Oculoplastic Surgery Soc. Avocations: tennis, badminton, dance. Office: Saint James Univ Hosp Dept Ophthalmology Chacellors Wing LS9 7TF Leeds England Business E-Mail: bypchang@doctors.org.uk.

CHANG, CHANG, research scientist; b. Bayanhaote, Jan. 12, 1975; PhD, Osaka U., 2007. Rsch. assoc. U. Minn., 2007—. Home: 425 13th Ave SE 1206 Minneapolis MN 55414 Business E-Mail: chang497@umn.edu.

CHANG, CHAW-LIANG, pediatrician, director; b. Hsinchu, Taiwan, Feb. 6, 1971; s. Chang Sung-Wen and Chiu Lien-Chiao; m. Hong Ching-Hui, Dec. 16, 2001; children: Jimmy, Jenny. MD, Sch. Medicine, Chang Gung U., 1997. Cert. Bd. Pediatrician, Taiwan, 2001, Bd. Pediat Neurology, Taiwan, 2004. Fellowship pediatric neurology Mackay Memorial Hosp., Taipei, 2002—04; dir., dept. pediat. Sinwu Br., Taoyuan Gen. Hosp., Taoyuan, 2002—05, Cathay Gen. Hosp., Hsinchu, 2008—. Reviewer Jour. Pediat. Biochemistry, 2010—. Med. officer and instr. Army Armored Corps Sch., 1997—99, Taiwan. Mem.: Taiwan Child Neurology Soc., Taiwan Pediat. Assn. Achievements include new neonatal sonographic findings. Office: 678 Sect 2 Junghua Rd Hsinchu 30060 Taiwan Office Phone: 882-3-5278999 ext.8001. Personal E-mail: juliancsr@yahoo.com.tw.

CHANG, CHENG-SHYONG, hematologist; MD, China Med. U., 1983. Chief Divsn. Hematology Changhua (Taiwan) Christian Hosp., 1993—2003, vice-supt., 2003—. Office: Changhua Christian Hosp 135 Nanhsiao St Changhua 500 Taiwan Business E-Mail: 15120@cch.org.tw.

CHANG, CHIEN-CHENG, engineering educator, director; b. Taipei, Taiwan, June 14, 1958; BS, Nat. Taiwan U., 1980; PhD, U. Calif., Berkeley, 1985. Disting. prof., dir., inst. applied mechanics Nat. Taiwan U., 2009—. Joint rsch. fellow Acad. Sinica, 2009. Named Outstanding Scholar, Found. Advancement Outstanding Scholarship. Fellow: Electromagnetics Acad. Avocations: reading, walking, basketball. Office: 1 Roosevelt Rd Section 4 Taipei 10617 Taiwan Office Fax: 886 2 23625238. Business E-Mail: mechang@iam.ntu.edu.tw.

CHANG, CHIH-CHAO, medical educator; b. Taipei, Taiwan, Feb. 15, 1952; BVM, Nat. Taiwan U., 1976; PhD, NY Med. Coll., 1990. Rsch. assoc. Vet. Gen. Hosp., Taipei, Taiwan, 1981—83; postdoc. rschr. NY Med. Coll., 1990—91, cons., 2004—06; postdoc. rschr. Columbia U., 1991—94, asst. prof. clin. pathology, 1994—2003, clin. asst. prof., 2003—. Fellowship, Cancer Rsch. Found. America, Lymphoma Rsch. Found. America. Mem.: Am. Soc. Histocompatibility & Immunogenetics. Avocation: music. Office: VC15-204 630 W 168th St New York NY 10032

CHANG, CHIUNG-HSIN, obstetrician, gynecologist, educator; b. Taiwan, Nov. 29, 1961; MD, Chung-Shan Med. Coll., 1987. Chair, dept. ob-gyn., assoc. prof. Nat. Cheng Kung U. Hosp., 2010—. Mem.: Taiwan Assn. Ob-Gyn. Avocations: reading, exercise. Office: Sheng-Li Rd 138 Tainan Central-West 70428 Taiwan Office Fax: 886-6-276-6185. Business E-Mail: ahsin@mail.ncku.edu.tw.

CHANG, CHONG BUM, medical educator; b. Seoul, Republic of Korea, Oct. 13, 1969; MD, Seoul Nat. U. Coll. Medicine, 1995, PhD, 2006. Clin. fellow Seoul Nat. U. Coll. Medicine, 2003—04, rsch. fellow, 2004—05; asst. prof. Seoul Nat. U. Bundang Hosp., 2005—. Editl. bd. Sports Medicine, Arthroscopy, Rehab., Therapy and Tech. Jour., 2009, Korean Arthroscopy Soc., 2010, Korean Soc. Osteoporosis, 2011, Korean Knee Soc., 2011. Mem.: Korean Orthopaedic Assn., Korean Soc. Bone Metabolism, Korean Soc. Osteoporosis, Korean Arthroscopy Soc., Korean Knee Soc. Avocation: tennis. Office: 166 Gumiro Bundanggu Seongnamsi Gyinggido 463-707 Republic of Korea Office Fax: 82-31-787-4056. Personal E-mail: drchuc@chol.com.

CHANG, CHOONG HYUN, plastic surgeon, educator; b. Seoul, Korea, Sept. 23, 1949; s. Kwan Ik Chang and Gae Ja Lim; m. Yeon Soo Shin, May 18, 1976; children: Hosoon, Young. MD, Kyung Hee U., Seoul, 1975, M in Plastic Surgery, 1978; PhD, Joong Ang U., Seoul, 1991. Lic. plastic surgeon Korea. Intern Kyung Hee Med. Ctr., Seoul, Republic of Korea, 1975—76, resident, 1976—80; chief plastic surgery Dong Suwon Hosp., Suwon, Republic of Korea, 1983—84; assoc. prof. plastic surgery Kyung Hee U. Sch. of Medicine, Seoul, Republic of Korea, 1984—93; dir. Dr. Chang Plastic Clin., Seoul, Republic of Korea, 1993—2002; prof. Sung Kyun Kwan U., Seoul, 2002—. Spl. rschr. Kitasato U., Sangamihara, Japan, 1989—90. Author: Journey of Cultured Skin, 1993, Father, My Father, 1993, Japenese Beauty was in Sight of Chang's Eye, 1997, In My Life, 2005; co-dir.: Maj. Korean Army, 1980—83. Mem.: Korean Cleft Palate Craniosurgery Assn., Korean Soc. Aesthetic Plastic Surgery, Korean Soc. Plastic Reconstructive Surgery, Japanese Soc. Plastic and Reconstructive Surgery. Avocations: golf, writing, coin collecting/numismatics. Home: Mido Apt 106 701 Dae Chi Dong Kang Nam Gu Seoul 135 702 Republic of Korea Office: Kang buk samsung Hosp Plastic Surgery 108 Pyung Dong Jongro gu Seoul Republic of Korea 110 746 Office Phone: 82-2 2001 2180, 02 2001 2177. Business E-Mail: eppeen@hanmail.net.

CHANG, CHRIS C.N., pediatric surgeon; b. Taiwan, June 20, 1943; s. Shu-Ming and Yu-Bow (Chow) C.; m. Rose Lee Chang, Mar. 4, 1972; children: Lynda, Steven. MD, Nat. Taiwan U., 1969. Intern Nat. Taiwan Univ. Hosp., 1968-69, resident in surgery, 1970-72, Albert Einstein Med. Ctr., Phila., 1972-76; resident in pediat. surgery St. Christopher's Hosp. for Children, Phila., 1976-78; dir. pediat. surgery Lehigh Valley Hosp., Allentown, Pa., 1993—. Fellow ACS, Internat. Coll. Surgeons, Am. Acad. Pediats.; mem. Am. Pediat. Surg. Assn. Office: 1259 S Cedar Crest Blvd Ste 210 Allentown PA 18103 Office Phone: 610-402-7999. Business E-Mail: chris.chang@lvh.com. *

CHANG, D. S. JOHNSON, anti-aging physician; b. Changhua City, Taiwan, Jan. 28, 1960; s. John Chan Chang and A. Eun Sell; children: Apollo W., Austin W. BS, MD, PhD, Peking U., Beijing, 2004. Cert. pharmacist Taiwan Govt., physician Taiwan Govt., China, Canada. CEO Johnson Gen. Hosp. and Care Gr., Changhua, Taiwan, 1997—, Omegame Med. Genetic Anti-Aging Group, Beijing, 2004—. Genetic treatment dr. Genetic Inst., Peking U., Beijing, 2004—. Chmn. Changhua Acupuncture Assn., Changhua, Taiwan, 1989—95. Recipient Golden award, Peking U., 2003. Master: Rotary Internat. (life; chief 2005—07, grant servicer 2006, Great Svc. award 2007—08). American Heritage. Achievements include research in genetic antiaging. Avocations: travel, golf. Home: 99 Changtsau Rd Changhua 500 Taiwan Office: Johnson Gen Hosp Care Group 425 Changtsau Rd

Changhua 500 Taiwan Office Phone: 886-4-7638877 ext. 2822. Office Fax: +886-4-7639876 ext.2815; Home Fax: +886-4-7617607. Personal E-mail: johnsonchangmd@yahoo.com.tw. Business E-Mail: johnson.hospita@msa.hinet.net.

CHANG, DEBBIE I-JU, health programs and research executive, director; BS in Chem. Engring., MIT, 1984; MPH, U. Mich., 1987. Presdl. mgmt. intern Health Care Fin. Adminstrn. Office Legislation and Policy, 1987-89; sr. health policy advisor Senator Donald W. Riegle Jr., 1989-94; dir. office legis. and intergovt. affairs Health Care Fin. Adminstrn., Washington, 1994-98; dir. State Children's Health Ins. Program Health Care Fin. Adminstrn., Dept. HHS, 1997-99; dir. Medicaid coverage benefits and payments Health Care Fin. Adminstrn., Balt., 1998; dep. sec. health care financing Medicaid Md. Dept. Health and Mental Hygiene, Balt., 1999—2003; sr. v.p., exec. dir. Nemours Divsn. Child Health and Prevention Svcs., Del., 2004—. Contbr. articles to profl. jours. Office Phone: 302-444-9127. Personal E-mail: dchang@nemours.org.

CHANG, GENE, cardiologist, educator; MD, Tufts U., 1991. Diplomate Am. Bd. Internal Medicine-cardiovasc. disease, 2008, Am. Bd. Internal Medicine-interventional cardiology, 2009. Resident internal medicine New Eng. Deaconess Hosp., Boston, 1991—94; fellow cardiovasc. disease Hosp. of the Univ. of Pa., 1995—98, fellow interventional cardiology, 1998—99; asst. prof. clin. medicine Univ. of Pa., Phila.; dir. catheterization lab. Penn Presbyn. Med. Ctr., Phila. Office: Penn Presbyterian Medical Center Philadelphia Heart Institute 4th Fl Ste 400 51 N 39th St Philadelphia PA 19104 Office Phone: 215-662-9000.

CHANG, HANG-SEOK, endocrine surgeon, educator; b. Pusan, Oct. 11, 1963; PhD, Yonsei U., 1999. Bd. dir. Korean Thyroid Assn., 2009, dir., sci. coun., 2010; dir., Thyroid Cancer Ctr. Yonsei U. Coll. Medicine, 2010—, prof., dept. surgery, 2011. Named Best Prof. of Yr., Pochon CHA U., Gangnam Severance Hosp., Yonsei U. Fellow: ACS; mem.: Korean Soc. Head and Neck Oncology (bd. dirs. 2010), Korean Assn. Endocrine Surgeons (bd. dirs. 2005), Korean Surg. Soc., Asia-Oceania Thyroid Assn., Asian Assn. Endocrine Surgeons, Internat. Assn. Endocrine Surgeons. Avocations: painting, reading. Office: Gangnam PO Box 1217 Seoul 135-720 Republic of Korea Office Phone: 82-2-2019-3376. Office Fax: 82-2-3462-5994. Business E-Mail: surghsc@yuhs.de.

CHANG, HEEKYUNG, pathologist, researcher; b. Pusan, Republic of Korea, Mar. 28, 1957; d. Sooho Chang and Chaeyoung Chung (Stepmother). MD, Pusan U., 1981, PhD, 1989. Diplomate. Instr. Med. Coll. Kosin U., Pusan, 1987—90, from asst. prof. to assoc. prof., 1990—99, prof. Med. Coll., 2000—. Visiting associate professor Medical School, Harvard University, Cambridge, Boston; visting researcher Tsukuba University, Tsukuba, Ibarakiken, Japan, 1993—93; directorship of pathology Daewoo Okpo Hospital, Geje, Kyungsang Namdo, Republic of Korea, 1986—; corresponding(active) member AACR(Amercian association for cancer research), Phildelphia, Pa, —; regular member USCAP, Ga, —. Contbr. articles to profl. jours. V.p. Assn. Prevention of AIDS, Pusan, 2001—. Mem.: Korean Assn. Women Drs. (gen. mgr. 2000—02), New Eng. Soc. Pathologists, U.S. and Can. Assn. Pathologists, Am. Assn. Cancer Rsch. (corr.), Internat. Club Zonta (treas. Busan divsn. 2000—02). Office: Kosin U Med Coll 34 Amnam-Dong, Suh-Ku Pusan 602-702 Republic of Korea Home Phone: 82 51 744 5585; Office Phone: 82 51 990 6323. Office Fax: 82 51 24 7420. Business E-Mail: changhkg@ns.kosinmed.or.kr.

CHANG, HERNAN ROBERT, infectious disease consultant; s. Hector Chang and Julia Pinares. MD, San Marcos U., Lima, Peru, 1982, U. Geneva, Switzerland, 1988. Diplomate Am. Bd. Internal Medicine, 2010, Infectious Diseases Am. Bd. Infectious Diseases, 2002. Rsch. fellow Dept. Microbiology Inst. Tropical Medicine, Antwerp, Belgium, 1984—85; rsch. fellow Dept. Genetics and Microbiology U. Geneva Med. Sch., 1986—92; sr. lectr. Dept. Microbiology, Nat. U. Singapore, 1992—95; rsch. fellow Deaconess Hosp., Harvard Med. Sch., Boston, 1996—97; resident Salem Hosp., Mass., 1997—2000; fellow New Eng. Med. Ctr., Boston, 2000—01, Boston U. Med. Ctr., 2001—02; cons. Salem Hosp., Mass., 2002—04, Infectious Disease Cons., Jacksonville, Fla., 2004—. Chief resident Salem Hosp., Mass., 1999—2000, EPGC, 2011, Stanford Grad. Sch. Bus. Author: Elysium: A Collection of Haiku and Senryu, 2005, MRSA-Spider Bites: The Flesh-Eating Epidemic that Threatens America, 2006, MRSA and Staphylococcal Infections, 2006; contbr. articles to profl. jours.; edtl. bd. Open Gen. Internat. Medicine Jour. Recipient Maxwell Finland Award, Mass. Infectious Diseases Soc., 2002; grantee Rsch., Swiss NSF, 1993—95, Finanz-Pool 3R Found., Switzerland, 1988—91. Fellow: ACP, Am. Coll. Physicians; mem.: AMA, Med. Res. Corp., Dictionary Soc. N.Am., The Mind Soc., Epimetheus Soc., Sigma Xi Rsch. Soc., Mass. Med. Soc., Swiss Soc. for Cell Biology, Molecular Biology and Genetics, Swiss Soc. for Microbiology, European Soc. Clin. Microbiology and Infectious Diseases, Infectious Diseases Soc. Am., Am. Soc. for Microbiology, Mass. Med. Soc. (com. pubs. 2001—02), Am. Acad. HIV Medicine, Internat. Soc. Travel Medicine (cert. travel health 2003), Boston Med. Libr. (life; bd. trustees 2003—04), Rotary Club, Omega Soc., Genius Soc., Intertel, Cerebrals, Top-One-Percent Soc., One-in-a-Thousand Soc., Glia Soc., Internat. Soc. for Philos. Enquiry, Triple Nine Soc., Mensa, Shriners, York Rite, Scottish Rite, Grand Lodge of Mass. Office: Jacksonville Multisplty Group 3627 University Blvd S Ste 500 Jacksonville FL 32216

CHANG, HO GUEN, hospital administrator; MD, Choong-Ang U., 1975—81; grad., Chungang U., 1981; M, Choong-Ang U., 1982—85. Prof. orthop. surgery Hallym Univ. Sacred Heart Hosp., 1999—, dir. spine ctr., 2006—08; chief dept. of orthop. surgery Hallym Sacred Heart Hosp., 2007—; internship Hangang Sacred Heart Hosp., 1981—82, residency orthop. surgery, 1982—86, instr. orthop. surgery, 1989—91, asst. prof. orthop. surgery, 1991—94, assoc. prof. orthop. surgery, 1995—99, prof. orthop. surgery spine ctr., 2008—, dir., 2008—, pres., 2008—. Vis. prof. spine divsn. of orthop. dept. Johns Hopkins Hosp., 1994—95. Army Svc., 1986—89. Mem.: Korean Orthop. Assn. (Treas. 1992—93, Sec. 1992—93). Office: Hangang Sacred Heart Hospital Youngdeung Dong Youngdeung Gu Seoul Republic of Korea Office Phone: 0226395001. Personal E-mail: hgc2000@dreamwiz.com. Business E-Mail: hgchang@hallym.or.kr. *

CHANG, HYEJUNG, statistician, educator; b. Seoul, Republic of Korea, Feb. 23, 1963; PhD, U. Ill., Urbana-Champaign, 1993. Asst. biostatistician Meml. Sloan-Kettering Cancer Ctr., 1993—94; sr. rschr. Korea Health Industry Devel. Inst., 1995—2001; prof., assoc. sch. mgmt. Kyung Hee U., Seoul, Republic of Korea, 2001—. Mem. rev. com. pharmacy and therapeutics Korean Food and Drug Agy., 2002; co-editor Korean Soc. Med. Informatics, 2005; editor Health Svc. Mgmt. Rev., 2007—08; internat. scholar Saginaw Valley State U., 2007—08; adv. com. mem. Prime Core Consulting Co., 2009. Fellowship, Kyung Hee U. Fellow: Korean Soc. Med. Informatics; mem.: Korean Soc. Preventive Medicine. Avocations: calligraphy, Tae Kwon Do. Office: Kyung Hee University Dongdaemoon-gu Hoegi-dong 1 Seoul 130-701 Republic of Korea Office Fax: 822-961-0515. Business E-Mail: hjchang@khu.ac.kr.

CHANG, HYEUN WOOK, pharmacist, educator; b. Republic of Korea, Feb. 5, 1952; PhD, Grad. Sch. Pharm. Scis., 1987. Prof. Coll. Pharmacy, Yeungnam U., 1988—, dean, 2000—02. Editl. adv. bd. Benthan Sci. Pub., Inflammation & Allergy Drug Targets, 2008—09; v.p. Pharmaceutical Soc. Korea, 2009—10; chmn. Yuseong Ednl. Found., 2005—. Office: Daedong 214-1 Gyeongsan Gyeongbuk 712-749 Republic of Korea Office Fax: 82-53-810-4654. Business E-Mail: hwchang@yu.ac.kr.

CHANG, HYUN KYU, rheumatologist, educator; b. Hongseong, Chungcheongnamdo, Republic of Korea, Nov. 22, 1959; m. Mee Young Kim, Oct. 4, 1986; children: Eun Sun, Yoon Ho. MD, Hanyang U., Seoul, Republic of Korea, 1984, PhD, 1993. Diplomate in internal medicine, rheumatology Korean Assn. Internal Medicine. Resident internal medicine Hanyang U. Hosp., Korea, 1985—88; fellow allergy and immunology U. Tenn., 1993—94; fellow rheumatology Hosp. Rheumatic Diseases, Hanyang U., Korea, 1997—98; assoc. prof. Ulsan U., Asan-Kangnung Hosp., Kangnung, Kangwondo, Republic of Korea, 1996—2001; assoc. prof., chief divsn. rheumatology Dankook U., Cheonan, Chungcheongnamdo, Republic of Korea, 2001—. Contbr. articles to profl. jours. Achievements include research in rheumatology specializing in Behcet's disease. Office: Dankook U Hosp Dept Internal Medicine 16-5 Anseo-dong 330-715 Cheonan Chunghceongnamdo Republic of Korea Office Fax: +82-41-556-3256. Business E-Mail: hanks22@naver.com.

CHANG, IN HO, urologist, educator; b. Seoul, Republic of Korea, Sept. 30, 1972; MD, Chung-Ang U., 1997; PhD, Chung-Ang U. Grad. Sch., 2005. Fellow, dept. urology Chung-Ang U. Hosp., 2008—09, asst. prof., 2010—. Rsch. grant, Ministry of Edn., Sci. & Tech. Fellow: Korean Urinary Tract Infection Assn.; mem.: Korean Urol. Assn. Avocations: travel, reading, exercise. Office: Chung-Ang University Hosp 224-1 He Seoul 156-755 Republic of Korea Office Fax: 82 2 6294 1406. Business E-Mail: caucih@cau.ac.kr.

CHANG, JAE CHAN, physician, hematologist, oncologist, educator; b. Aug. 29, 1941; arrived in US, 1965; s. Tae Whan and Kap Hee (Lee) Chang; m. Sue Young Chung, Dec. 4, 1965; children: Sung-Jin, Sung-Ju, Sung-Hoon. MD, Seoul Nat. U., 1965. Diplomate Am. Bd. Internal Medicine, Hematology, Med. Oncology, Am. Bd. Pathology (Hematology). Intern Ellis Hosp., Schenectady, NY, 1965—66; resident Harrisburg Hosp., Pa., 1966—69, fellow in nuc. medicine, 1969—70; fellow in hematology and oncology, instr. U. Rochester, 1970—72; chief hematology sect. VA Hosp., Dayton, Ohio, 1972—75; hematopathologist, co-dir. hematology lab. Good Samaritan Hosp., Dayton, 1975—2002, dir. oncology unit, 1976—2001, chief hematology and oncology sect., 1976—2003; clin. prof. medicine U. Calif., Irvine, Calif., 2003—, dir. hematology and oncology fellowship program, 2003—05; mem. Chao Family Comprehensive Cancer Ctr., U. Calif., Irvine, 2003—. Asst. clin. prof. Ohio State U., Columbus, 1972—75; assoc. clin. prof. Wright State U., Dayton, 1975—80, clin. prof., 1980—99, prof., 1999—2003, co-dir. hematology and med. oncology fellowship program, 1993—98; cons. hematology VA Hosp.; adv. com. Greater Dayton Area chpt. Leukemia Soc. Am., 1977; trustee Montgomery County Soc. Cancer Control, Dayton, 1976—85, Dayton Area Cancer Assn., 1985—88, Cmty. Blood Ctr., 1982—86, Hipple Cancer Rsch. Crt., 1999—2003. Contbr. articles to profl. jours., columns in newspapers. Recipient Med. Econ. Essay Competition award, 1990, Wright State U. Acad. of Medicine award, 1985, Laureate award, ACP-ASIM Ohio Chpt., 2001, Spl. Commendation, Ohio Senate, 2002, Orange County Physician of Excellence award, Orange County Soc. Calif., Orange Coast Mag., 2007, 2009. Fellow: ACP; mem.: Montgomery Med. Soc. (dir. 1990—93), Dayton Soc. Internal Medicine (pres. 1989), Am. Soc. Clin. Oncologists, Am. Soc. Hematology. Office: UCI Med Ctr Div Hematology/ Oncology Chao Family Comp Cancer Ctr 101 The City Dr Orange CA 92868 Home: 33 Rose Trellis Irvine CA 92603 Office Phone: 714-456-6578. Business E-Mail: jaec@uci.edu.

CHANG, JOHN T., internist, researcher; s. Zui L. and Ruth Chang; m. Alice A. Kuo, Oct. 23, 2004. BA, Northwestern U., 1990; MPH, Yale U., 1995; MD, Northwestern U. Med. Sch., 1996; PhD, UCLA, 2006. Diplomate Am. Bd. Internal Medicine. Clin. instr. UCLA Sch. Medicine, LA, 1999—2005, vis. asst. prof., 2005—06, asst. clin. prof., 2007—. Adj. staff RAND Health, Santa Monica, Calif., 2005—09. Contbr. articles to profl. jours. Grantee Weinerman fellow, Yale U. Sch. Medicine, 1994; fellow, HRSA/UCLA, 1999—2002, UCLA Sch. Medicine, 2002—06. Mem.: Healthcare Info. & Mgmt. Sys. Soc., Am. Med. Informatics Assn., ACP, AcademyHealth, Soc. Gen. Internal Medicine. Office: Zynx Health 10880 Wilshire Blvd Ste 300 Los Angeles CA 90024 Business E-Mail: jchang@zynx.com.

CHANG, JONG-SOO, molecular biologist; b. Yechon-gun, Kyungpook, Republic of Korea, Sept. 27, 1962; s. Seok-Rae Chang and Jang-Yon Kwon; m. Sohn Young-Mi, May 15, 1964; children: Chang-Hyun, Heywon. PhD, Kyungpook Nat. U., Daegu, Republic of Korea, 1991. Rschr. Mitsubishi Kasei inst. of Life Scis., Machida-shi, Tokyo, 1992—94, POSTECH, Pohang, Republic of Korea, 1995—97; prof. Daejin U., Pochon-gun, Republic of Korea, 1997—, chmn. dept. life sci., 1999—2001, dir. Basic Sci. Inst., 2002—. Contbr. articles to profl. jours. 2d lt. inf. Korean armed forces, 1986—87. Mem.: Korean Soc. for Molecular and Cellular Biology, Am. Soc. for Biochemistry and Molecular Biology. Office: Daejin U Sundan-Ri 487-711 Pocheon Gyeonggi-do Republic of Korea Office Fax: 82-31-539-1850. E-mail: jchang@daejin.ac.kr.

CHANG, JOSEPH YOON, personal care products company executive; b. Ipoh, Perak, Malaysia, Oct. 22, 1952; s. Chee Kong and Philomena (Wong) Chang; m. Wan Ping Wong Chang, Oct. 16, 1974; children: Colin, Christopher. BS with honors, U. Portsmouth, Eng., 1974; PhD in Pharmacology, U. London, 1978. Postdoc. fellow Johns Hopkins U., Balt., 1978-80, rsch. assoc., 1980-81; sr. rsch. scientist Wyeth Labs., Radnor, Pa., 1981-85, assoc. dir., 1985-87; dir. Wyeth-Ayerst Rsch., Princeton, NJ, 1988-91; pres., chief sci. officer Osteoarthritis Scis. Inc., Boston, 1991-94, Binary Therapeutics, Inc., Boston, 1994—97; v.p. clinical studies & pharmacology Pharmanex LLC (divsn. Nu Skin Enterprises, Inc.), Provo, Utah, 1997—2000, pres., 2000—06; exec. v.p. product devel., chief sci. officer Nu Skin Enterprises, Inc., 2006—. Bd. dirs. Optimer Pharmaceuticals, Inc., 1998—. Author: The Aging Myth: Unlocking the Mysteries of Looking and Feeling Young, 2011 (NY Times Bestseller). Arthritis Found. fellow, Johns Hopkins U. Sch. Pub. Health. Mem.: AAAS, Arthritis Found. (Md. chpt.), Reticuloendothelial Soc., Inflammation Rsch. Assn., American Soc. Pharmacology & Exptl. Therapeutics. Achievements include patents in field. Avocations: fishing, tennis. Office: Nu Skin Enterprises 75 West Ctr Provo UT 84601 *

CHANG, JUN-DONG, orthopedic surgeon, educator; b. Seoul, Republic of Korea, July 9, 1955; s. Jung-Suk Chang and Won-Hee Park; m. Kyung-Ok Joo, Oct. 27, 1984; children: Hye-Sang, Yong-Sang. MD, Yonsei U., Seoul, 1979; PhD, Korea U., Seoul, 1992. Cert. ECFMG, USA, in orthop. surgery Min. of Health and Social Affairs, Republic of Korea. Intern Severance Hosp., Yonsei U., Seoul, 1982—83, resident in orthop. surgery, 1983—87; prof., chief dept. orthop. Hangang Sacred Heart Hosp., Hallym U., Seoul, 1988—; fellow in arthroplasty Hosp. for Spl. Surgery, Cornell U., NYC, 1993—94, Mass. Gen. Hosp., Harvard U., Boston, 1994—95. Supr. Mil. Med. Assn., Seoul, 2001. Editor: Jour. Arthroplasty, 1997—, Jour. Korean Hip Soc., 1997—2002, Jour. of the Korean Orthop. Assn., 1999—2005; author: (book) Revision of Total Hip Arthroplasty; contbr. articles to profl. jours. Capt. Med. Svc., 1979—82, South Korea. Recipient Acad. award, Hallym U., 1991, 1992; grantee, Health and Social Affairs, Republic of Korea, 1996, Hallym U., 2006. Mem.: Korean Musculoskeletal Transplantation Soc. (pres. 2005—), Korean Fracture Soc. (trustee 2004—), Korean Knee Soc., Korean Hip Soc. (pres. 2005—), Korean Orthop. Assn., Internat. Soc. Orthop. Surgery and Traumatology, Orthop. Rsch. Soc. Office: Hangang Sacred Heart Hosp 94-200 Youngdungpo-Dong Youngdungpo-Gu 150-020 Seoul Republic of Korea Office Phone: 82-19-310-1865. Office Fax: 82-2-2631-9337; Home Fax: 82-2-2631-9337. Personal E-mail: jdchangos@yahoo.com.

CHANG, KIHONG, otolaryngologist, educator; b. Incheon, Mar. 24, 1960; MD, Cath. U. Korea, PhD, 1988. Assoc. prof. Dept. Otolaryngology HNS, St. Marys Hosp., U. Korea, 2000—. Avocations: tennis, golf. Office: # 62 Youido-Dong Yeongdeungpo-Gu Seoul 150-713 Republic of Korea Office Fax: 82-2-786-1149. Business E-Mail: khchang@catholic.ac.kr.

CHANG, LIANG-CHIH, physical education educator; b. Kaohsiung, Oct. 23, 1976; PhD, Nat. Pingtung U. Sci. and Tech., 2008. Asst. prof. Ching Kuo Inst. Mgmt. and Health, 2008—10, Nat. Open U., 2010—. Office: 172 Zhongzheng Rd Luzhou New Taipei City 247 Taiwan Office Fax: 011-886-222897896. E-mail: lianchih@yahoo.com.tw.

CHANG, LI-CHIEN, pharmacist, educator; s. Chun-Ting Chang and Bi-Shan Lien; m. Hsiao-Feng Lee, Jan. 26, 1964; 1 child, Chi-Yun. BS, Nat. Def. Med. Ctr., Taipei, 1988, MS, 1992, U. Mich., 1998, PhD, 2001. Cert. pharmacist Dept. Health, Taiwan, 1988. Tchg. asst. Nat. Def. Med. Ctr., Taipei, 1988—90, instr., 1992—96, asst. prof., 2002—. Vis. rsch. scientist U. Mich., Ann Arbor, 2004—05. Sr. editor: Taiwan Pharm. Jour., 2005—; contbr. articles to profl. jours. Editl. bd. Open Chem. and Biomed. Methods Jour., 2008—. Recipient Rsch. award, Nat. Sci. Coun., Taiwan, 1993, 1994, Grad. Symposium award, Am. Assn. Pharm. Scientists, 2000, Excellent Mil. Med. Pers. award, Dept. Nat. Def., Taiwan, 2005; named one of Top Ten Selected Papers, Perfusion Line (Internat. Page on Extracorporeal Tech., 2005, Outstanding Scientists of 21st Century, Internat. Biog. Ctr., England, 2007; grantee, Nat. Sci. Coun., Taiwan, 2002—; Nat. Def. Dept. Advance Edn. scholar, Dept. Nat. Def., Taiwan. Mem.: Pharm. Soc. Taiwan, Am. Assn. Pharm. Scientists, Controlled Release Soc. Achievements include patents pending for non-toxic membrane-translocating peptides; research in synthesis of PEG-modified protamine for clinical heparin reversal; development of low molecular weight protamine (LMWP) as nontoxic heparin/low molecular weight heparin antidote I-III; research in application of polyion-sensitive electrodes to pharmaceutical domain. Office: National Defense Medical Center 161 MinChun E Rd Sect 6 Taipei 114 Taiwan Business E-Mail: lichien@mail.ndmctsgh.edu.tw.

CHANG, LIN, medical educator, researcher; MD, UCLA Med. Sch., 1986. Lic. med. Am. Bd. Internal Medicine, 1987. Asst. prof. medicine Harbor-UCLA Med. Ctr., Torrance, 1993—97; prof. medicine David Geffen Sch. Medicine- UCLA, 1997—. Co-dir. Ctr. for Neurobiology Stress- UCLA, 1997—; bd. mem. Rome Found., McLean, Va., 2005—; GI adv. panel mem. FDA, Rockville, Md., 2005—. Recipient Janssen award in Gastroenterology, Basic or Clin. Rsch., 2002; R01 rsch. grants, NIH, 1996—. Fellow: Am. Gastroent. Assn. (councilor 2005—); mem.: Functional Brain Gut Rsch. Group (councilor 2004—, sec., treas., pres. elect), Am. Coll. Gastroenterology. Achievements include research in irritable bowel syndrome. Office: David Geffen Sch Medicine at UCLA 10945 LeConte Ave Los Angeles CA 90095 Office Fax: 310-794-2864. Business E-Mail: linchang@ucla.edu.

CHANG, MEE SOO, pathologist; b. Seoul, Republic of Korea, Dec. 17, 1959; MD, Hanyang U., 1984, PhD, Seoul Nat. U., 1996. Chief Dept. Pathology, Seoul Nat. U. Boramae Hosp., 1991—. Office: 41 Baramae-gil Dongjak-gu Seoul 156-707 Republic of Korea Office Fax: 82-2-870-3866. Business E-Mail: meesooch@snu.ac.kr.

CHANG, NANCY T., investment company executive; b. Taiwan; PhD in Biological Chemistry, Harvard U. With Roche Inst. of Molecular Biology, 1980—81; dir., rsch., Molecular Biology Group Centocor Inc., 1981—86; co-founder Tanox Inc., 1986, chmn., 1986—2003, pres., 1986—2007, CEO, 1990—2007; mng. dir. OrbiMed Advisors, LLC, 2007, sr. mng. dir., chmn., Asia. Assoc. prof., molecular virology Baylor Coll. Medicine; bd. dirs. Biotechnology Industry Orgn., Houston Tech. Ctr., BioHouston, Greater Houston Partnership, Charles River Labs. Internat. Inc. Contbr. articles to profl. jour. Named Houston Entrepreneur of Yr.; named one of Top 20 Houston Women in Tech.; named to Tex. Sci. Hall of Fame, 2001.

Office: OrbiMed Advisors LLC 767 Third Ave 30th Fl New York NY 10017 Office Phone: 212-739-6400. Office Fax: 212-739-6444. Business E-Mail: changn@orbimed.com.

CHANG, PHILLIP J., plastic surgeon; Attended, U. Rochester 1992. Diplomate Am. Bd. Plastic Surgery, Am. Soc. of Plastic Surgeons. Resident Loma Linda Univ. Med. Ctr., 1996; fellow Univ. of Rochester, 2000; hosp. appointments include Inova Fair Oaks Hosp., Inova Loudoun Hosp.; tech. instr. Plastic Surgery Soc. Named Top Dr., Health and Beauty Mag., 2009—11. Office: c/o Aesthetica Cosmetic Surgery & Laser Center Ste 275 19450 Deerfield Ave Leesburg VA 20176 Office Phone: 703-729-5553.

CHANG, RICHARD S., thoracic surgeon; MD, Drexel U., Phila. Diplomate Am. Bd. Thoracic Surgery, Am. Bd. Surgery, lic. Pa., 2003. Resident surgery NY Med. Coll.; fellow cardiothoracic surgery Thomas Jefferson Univ. Hosp.; hosp. affliations includes Aria Health, Phila. Named one of Top Doctors, Phila. Mag., 2011. Office: Aria Health Ste 214 Knights and Red Lion Roads Philadelphia PA 19114 Office Phone: 215-612-5050. Office Fax: 215-612-5214.

CHANG, SAM S., urologist, surgeon, educator; b. Seoul, Republic of Korea, Feb. 19, 1966; m. Michelle Chang; children: Grace, Rachel, Julia. AB, Princeton U., NJ, 1988; MD, Vanderbilt U., Nashville, 1992. Asst. prof. urol. surgery Vanderbilt U. Med. Ctr., 2000—05, assoc. prof. urol. surgery, 2005—. Sec., treas. Rhamy-Shelley Vanderbilt Urology Soc., 2002—04; com. chair Am. Joint Com. Cancer, Chgo., 2003—; bd. Vanderbilt U. Med. Ctr. Alumni Assoc., 2004—; exec. com. Soc. Urol. Oncology, 2004; prostate bd. Am. Urol. Assn. Found., 2006—; exam com. ABU/Am. Urol. Assn., 2008—. Recipient CaPCURE Young Investigator award, Prostate Cancer Found., 2001—04, Disting. Svc. award, Soc. Urol. Oncology, 2005; named to Best Doctors in Am., 2006—; fellow, Meml. Sloan-Kettering Cancer Ctr., NYC, 1999—2000, Am. Urol. Assn./European Assn. Urology, 2006. Mem.: AMA (assoc.), Tenn. Med. Assn. (alt. ho. of dels. 2003—05), Am. Urol. Assn. (assoc.; guidelines panel-treatment superficial bladder cancer 2004—, mem. prostate adv. coun. 2004—). Office: Vanderbilt University Medical Center A-1302 Medical Center North Nashville TN 37232-2765 Office Fax: 615-322-8990. Business E-Mail: sam.chang@vanderbilt.edu.

CHANG, SE-HO, nephrologist; b. Sancheong, GyeongNam, Republic of Korea, Feb. 23, 1963; s. Jisuk Chang and Byungduk An; m. Miwon Lee; children: Jaehoon, Yoonhee. MD, Gyeongsang Nat. U., Jinju, Republic of Korea, 1987, PhD, 1998. Cert. bd. internal medicine Min. Ministry of Health and Welfare, Republic of Korea, 1991. Resident internal medicine Gyeongsang Nat. U. Hosp., Jinju, Republic of Korea, 1988—91; dir. internal medicine Mil. Masan Hosp., Republic of Korea, 1992—94; fellowship nephrology Samsung Seoul Hosp., Republic of Korea, 1995—96; instr. divsn. nephrology Gyeongsang Nat. U. Coll. Medicine, 1996—98, asst. prof. divsn. nephrology, 1998—2002, assoc. prof. divsn. nephrology, 2002—07, chmn. internal medicine Gyeongsang Nat. U. Hosp., Jinju, 2005—08, dir. office rsch., 2005—08, prof. divsn. nephrology, 2007—, dir. clin. depts., 2009—11; postdoctoral fellow U. Fla. Coll. Medicine, Gainesville, 2000—02. Capt. Korean Army, 1991—94. Home: 108-701 Dulmal Hanbo Apt, Jinju Gyeongnam 660-775 Republic of Korea Office: Gyeongsang Nat U Hosp Chilam-Dong 90 660-702 Jinju Gyeongsangnam-do Republic of Korea Office Phone: 51 750 8067. Office Fax: 55 758 9122. Business E-Mail: shchang@gnu.ac.kr.

CHANG, SEONG-HWAN, medical educator; b. Busan, Republic of Korea, Feb. 2, 1969; B, Seoul Nat. U., 1994, PhD, 2008. Instr. Konkuk U. Coll. Medicine, 2003—05; asst. prof. Konkuk U. Sch. Medicine, 2005—09, vice dir., gastroenterology, 2007, assoc. prof., 2009—. Dir., transplantation ctr. Konkuk U. Med. Ctr., 2011. Mem.: Korean Soc. Endoscopic & Laparoscopic Surgeons, Korean Soc. Transplantation, Korean Assn. HBP Surgery, Korean Surg. Soc., Korean Med. Assn. Avocations: reading, mountain climbing. Office: 4-12 Hwayang-dong Gwangjin-gu Seoul 143-729 Republic of Korea Office Fax: 82-2-2030-7749. Business E-Mail: csh@kuh.ac.kr.

CHANG, STANLEY, ophthalmologist; BEE, MIT, 1964—68; MS in Biomedical Electronic Engring., U. Pa., 1968—70; MD, Columbia U., 1970—74. Lic. NY, Conn., diplomate Nat. Bd. Med. Examiners, 1975, Am. Bd. Ophthalmology. Vis. clin. fellow med. Columbia U. Coll. Physicians and Surgeons, NYC, 1974—75; intern Dept. Medicine Columbia-Presbyterian Med. Ctr., NYC, 1974—75; resident in ophthalmology Mass. Eye and Ear Infirmary, Boston, 1976—78; clin. fellow ophthalmology Harvard Med. Sch., Boston, 1977—78; fellow vitreoretinal diseases Bascom Palmer Eye Inst. Univ. Miami, 1978—79; asst. prof. clin. ophthalmology Cornell U. Med. Coll., NYC, 1979—81, asst. prof. ophthalmology, 1981—84, assoc. prof. clin. ophthalmology, 1984—87, assoc. prof. clin. ophthalmology (with tenure), 1987—92, prof. ophthalmology, 1993—94; Edward S. Harkness prof. and chmn. ophthalmology Columbia U., NYC, 1995—; asst. attending in ophthalmology The NY Hosp., 1979—84, assoc. attending in ophthalmology, 1984—92, attending in ophthalmology, 1993—94; cons. in ophthalmology Meml. Sloan Kettering Cancer Ctr., NYC, 1991—94; sr. attending in ophthalmology St. Luke's Roosevelt Hosp. Ctr., NYC, 1994—; dir. and chief of svc. ophthalmology NY Presbyterian Hosp. - Columbia Campus, 1996—. Recipient John Milton McLean medal, Cornell U. Med. Coll., 1993, G.B. Bietti Internat. Found. award, Rome, 1993, Scientific Achievement award, Escalon, Inc., NJ, 1993, Alvin M. Behrens award ophthalmology, Columbia U., 1997; named one of Medical Marvels, New York Mag., 2006. Fellow: Am. Acad. Ophthalmology (Sr. Honor award 1998); mem.: The Macula Soc., The Vitreous Soc. (W.H. Helmerich III award 1998), Club Jules Gonin (Hermann Wacker prize 1992), The Retina Soc., Pan Am. Assn. Ophthalmology, Assn. Rsch. Vision and Ophthalmology, Rsch. to Prevent Blindness (assoc.), Am. Eye Study Club, Am. Soc. Ophthalmic Ultrasound, Chinese Am. Ophthalmology Soc., NY Soc. Clin. Ophthalmology, NY State Med. Soc., Chinese Am. Med. Soc. (Scientific Achievement award 1999), Bascom Palmer Alumni Assn., Mass. Eye & Ear Alumni Assn., Columbia P & S Alumni Assn., Alpha Omega Alpha. Achievements include patents for method and apparatus for treatment of complicated retinal detachments, patent number 5,037,384 issued 1991. Office: Dept Ophthalmology Edward S Harkness Eye Inst 635 West 165th St New York NY 10032 Office Phone: 212-305-2725. Office Fax: 212-305-5962.

CHANG, SUNG MAN, psychiatrist, educator; b. Kunsan, Republic of Korea, Jan. 30, 1973; MD, Seoul Nat. U., 1998, PhD, 2008. Resident Dept. Psychiatry, Seoul Nat. U. Hosp., 1999—2003, clin. instr., 2006—07; asst. prof. Dept. Psychiatry, Kyungpook Nat. U. Hosp., 2008—. Head Cmty. Mental Health Ctr., Jung-Gu, Daegu, Republic of the Congo, 2008. Mem.: Korean Soc. Depressive and Bipolar Disorders, Korean Assn. Geriatric Psychiatry, Korean Soc. Biol. Therapies Psychiatry, Korean Coll. Neuropsychopharmacology, Korean Neuropsychiatric Assn. Office: 200 Dongduk-ro Jung-Gu Daegu 700-721 Republic of Korea Office Fax: 82-53-426-5361. Business E-Mail: psyjang@knu.ac.kr.

CHANG, SUNG OK, nursing educator; b. Seoul, Republic Of Korea, Feb. 5, 1960; d. Chun Joon and Young Ja Chang; m. Jai Young Choi, Oct. 4, 1984; 1 child, Jin Ho Choi. BA, Korea U., Seoul, 1982, MA, 1986; PhD, Yonsei U., Seoul, 1996. RN Ministry of Health and Welfare, South Korea, 1982, GNP, 2008. Lectr. Dept. Nursing, Coll. Medicine, Korea U., 1984—94, rsch. fellow, 1994—97, dir., 2007—; chair academic affair com. Korean Psychiat. and Mental Health Nursing Academic Soc., Seoul, 1996—97; postdoc. fellow Coll. Nursing, U. RI, Kingston, 1997—98; chair hospice rsch. dept. Cancer Rsch. Inst., Korea U., 1998—2000; asst. prof. Korea U., Coll. Nursing, Seoul, 2000—04, assoc. prof., 2002—06, prof., 2006—. Editor in chief Jour. Korean Gerontol. Nursing, 2005—06, Jour. Korean Fundamental Nursing, Seoul, 2001—03, editor, 2004—, Jour. Korean Acad. Nursing, Seoul, 2001—02, reviewer, 2008—, Jour. Advanced Nursing, Osney Mead, Oxford, England, 2004—; editor Jour. Sigma Theta Tau Internat. Honor Soc. Nursing, Chpt. at Large, Seoul, 2002—04, Jour. Human Subjectivity, 2008—. Contbr. articles to profl. jours. Grant, Med. Sci. Rsch. Inst., Korea U., 1995, Med. Scis. Rsch. Inst., Korea U., 1997, 2000, Korean Rsch. Found., 1996, 2002, 2008, Korea U., 2003, 2005, Korea Health Promotion Found., 2005. Mem.: Korean Soc. Sci. Study Subjectivity, Korean Gerontol. Nursing Soc. (chair academic affair com. 2002—04), Korean Acad. Fundamentals Nursing (v.p. 2010—11, pres. 2012—), Korean Soc. Nursing Scis., Korea Nurses Assn. Office: College Nursing Korea University 126-1 5-ka Anam-dong Sungbuk-ku Seoul 136-705 Republic of Korea Office Phone: 82-2-3290-4918. Office Fax: 82-2-927-4676. Business E-Mail: sungok@korea.ac.kr.

CHANG, SUN-YRAN, hospital administrator; b. Taiwan, Apr. 29, 1949; Studied, Nat. Def. Med. Ctr., Taiwan; M in Health Adminstrn., Tulane U., New Orleans. Resident dept. of surgery Tri-Svc. Gen. Hosp., Taiwan, attending physician dept. of surgery, Chief dept. of Urology, lectr. dept. of surgery; assoc. prof. dept. of surgery Nat. Def. Med. Ctr., Taiwan, prof. dept. of surgery, supt., Taoyuan Armed Forced Gen. Hosp., Taiwan; dep. supt. Tri-Svc. Gen. Hosp., Taiwan, supt.; dir. med. affairs bur. Ministry of Nat. def., Taiwan; supt. Kang-Ning Gen. Hosp., Taiwan, Taipei City Hosp., Taiwan. Office: Taipei City Hospital 145 Zhengzhou Rd Datong Dist Taipei Taiwan Office Fax: 88625598379. *

CHANG, SYLVIA TAN, retired health facility administrator, educator; b. Bandung, Indonesia, Dec. 18, 1940; came to U.S., 1963. d. Philip Harry and Lydia Shui-Yu (Ou) Tan; m. Belden Shiu-Wah Chang, Aug. 30, 1964 (dec. Aug. 1997); children: Donald Steven, Janice May. Diploma in nursing, Rumah Sakit Advent Indonesia, 1960; BS, Philippine Union Coll., 1962; MS, Loma Linda U., 1967; PhD, Columbia Pacific U., 1987. Cert. RN, PHN, ACLS, BLS instr., cmty. first aid instr., IV, TPN, blood withdrawal. Head nurse Rumah Sakit Advent, Bandung, Indonesia, 1960—61; critical care, spl. duty and medicine nurse, team leader White Meml. Med. Ctr., LA, 1963—64; nursing coord. Loma Linda U. Med. Ctr., 1964—68; team leader, critical care nurse, relief head nurse Pomona Valley Hosp. Med. Ctr., Calif., 1966—67; evening supr. Loma Linda U. Med. Ctr., 1967—69, night supr., 1969—79, adminstrv. supr., 1979—94; sr. faculty Columbia Pacific U., San Rafael, Calif., 1986—94; dir. health svc. La Sierra U., Riverside, Calif., 1988—2010. Site coord. Health Fair Expo La Sierra U., 1988-89; adv. coun. Family Planning Clinic, Riverside, 1988-94; blood and bone marrow drive coord. La Sierra U., 1988—. Counselor Pathfinder Club Campus Hill Ch., Loma Linda, 1979-85, crafts instr., 1979-85, music dir., 1979-85; asst. organist U. Ch., 1982-88. Named one of Women of Achievement YWCA, Greater Riverside C. of C., The Press Enterprise, 1991, 2000, Safety Coord. of Yr. La Sierra U., 1995. Mem. Am. Coll. Health Assn., Pacific Coast Coll. Health Assn., Adventist Student Pers. Assn., Sigma Theta Tau. Republican. Seventh-day Adventist. Avocations: music, travel, collecting coins, shells and jade carvings. Home: 26393 Santa Andrea St Loma Linda CA 92354-4182

CHANG, TA-YUAN, medical educator, researcher; m. Hsiu-Mei Tang. PhD, Nat. Taiwan U., Taipei, 2004. Asst. prof. Dept. Occupl. Safety and Health, China Med. U., Taichung, Taiwan, 2004—09, assoc. prof., 2009—. Cpl. Airforce, 1996—98, Chiayi, Taiwan. Recipient 14th Outstanding Rsch. award, Taiwan Pub. Health Assn., 2008. Mem.: Internat. Soc. Environ. Epidemiology, Internat. Commn. Occupl. Health. Avocations: swimming, jogging, travel. Office: China Med University 91 Hsueh-Shih Rd Taichung 40402 Taiwan Office Fax: 886-4-22079225. Business E-Mail: tychang@mail.cmu.edu.tw.

CHANG, THOMAS MING SWI, research scientist, biotechnologist, physician, educator; arrived in Can., 1952; m. Lancy Yuk Lan Jin, June 21, 1958; children: Harvey, Victor, Christine, Sandra. BSc, McGill U., Montreal, Que., Can., 1957, MD, CM, 1961, PhD, 1965. Intern Montreal Gen. Hosp., 1961-62; rsch. fellow depts. physiology and chemistry McGill U., 1962-65, asst. prof. physiology, 1966-69, assoc. prof., 1969-72, prof. physiology, 1972—2007, prof. emeritus physiology, 2007—, dir. artificial organs rsch. unit, 1975-79, prof. medicine, 1975—2007, prof. emeritus medicine, 2007—, dir. Artificial Cells and Organs Rsch. Ctr., 1979—, assoc. Dept. Chem. Engring., 1985—2002, assoc. Dept. Chemistry, 1986—2001, prof. biomed. engring., 1990—2007, prof. emeritus biomed. engring., 2007—, dir. MSSS-FRSQ Rsch. Group (d'equipe) on Blood Sub. in Transfusion Medicine, 2002—09; lab. and clin. rschr. med. scis., biotech., biomed. engring. Montreal, 1962—; mem. Greatest Mc Gilliam McGill U., 2011. Mem. staff Royal Victoria Hosp.; hon. staff Montreal Chinese Hosp., 1990-, cons., 1970-90; fellow Med. Rsch. Coun., 1962-65, scholar, 1965-68, career investigator, 1968-99; hon. prof. Nankai U., 1983—, Peking Union Med. Coll., 2007-. Author: Artificial Cells, 1972, Biomedical Application of Immobilized Enzymes and Proteins, Vols. I and II, 1977, Artificial Kidney, Artificial Liver and Artificial Cells, 1978, Hemoperfusion-Kidney and Liver Supports and Detoxification, 1980, Hemoperfusion, 1981, Past, Present and Future of Artificial Organs, 1983, Microencapsulation and Artificial Cells, 1984, Hemoperfusion and Artificial Organs, 1985, Blood Substitutes, 1988, Blood Substitutes and Oxygen Carriers, 1993, Blood Substitutes: Principles, Methods, Products & Clinical Trials, Vol. I, 1997, II, 1998, Artificial Cells, Biotechnology, Nanomedicine Regenesatins Medicine, Bood Substitutes, Bioencap Solution Cell Stem Cell Therapy, 2007; editor-in-chief: Artificial Cells, Blood Substitutes and Biotechnology, 1985-; serial editor: Regenerative Medicine, Artificial Cells & Nanomedicine, 2006-; sect. editor: Internat. Jour. Artificial Organs, 1977—2009, Trans. Am. Soc. Artificial Organs, 1977-2001; assoc. editor: Biotechnology Ann. Rev., 1995—; mem. editl. bd. Jour. Biomaterial Med. Devel. and Orgn., 1972-87, Jour. Membrane Sci., 1975-92, Jour. Bioengring., 1975-79, Jour. Enzyme and Microbial Tech., 1978-86. Recipient Decorated officer, Order of Can., 1992—, Can. 125th Confereration medal, 1993, Queen Elizabeth Jubilee medal, 2002. Fellow Royal Coll. Physicians Can., Royal Soc. Can.; mem. Internat. Soc. Artificial Organs (trustee 1982-87, 89-92, congress pres. 1991, pres. 1994-96, immediate past pres. 1996-98), Can. Soc. Artificial Organs (pres. 1980-82), Internat. Soc. Artificial Cells, Blood Substitutes and Biotech. (hon. pres. 1990—, hon. congress pres. 1994, 97, 2001), Internat. Symposium Blood Substitutes (hon. pres. 2003—), Internat. Soc. Microencapsulations (hon.), Internat. Acad. Nanomedicine (pres. 2009-10, past pres., 2010-). Achievements include invention of artificial cells, nanomedicine and blood substitutes. Avocations: tennis, classical music, history, computers, weight training. Office: McGill U Artificial Cells and Organs Rsch Ctr 3655 Drummond St Rm 1004 Montreal PQ Canada H3G 1Y6 Business E-Mail: artcell.med@mcgill.ca.

CHANG, UNJAE, nutritionist, educator; b. Seoul, Republic of Korea, July 28, 1957; s. WonGil Chang and YunSoon Kim; m. YeonMin Ahn, May 28, 1984; children: JinBok, YeokBoo. PhD, U. RI, Eng., 1992. Rschr. Doo San Rsch. Lab, Seoul, 1982—88; asst. prof. KyonYang U., NonSan, Republic of Korea, 1992—93; prof. DongDuk Women's U., Seoul, rschr. Exhibitions include Diet Cartoon. Fellow: Korean Jour. Cmty. Nutrition. Home: 22-102 Walkerhill Apt Kwangjangdong Seoul 143-752 Republic of Korea Office: DongDuk Womens Univ 23-1 Walgokdong Sungbukku Seoul 136-714 Republic of Korea Office Fax: 82-2-940-4609. Business E-Mail: uj@dongduk.ac.kr.

CHANG, VICTOR TSU-SHIH, oncologist, researcher, educator; b. Queens, NY, Nov. 28, 1956; s. M.H. and C.H. (Chu) C. SB/SM in Chem. Engring., MIT, 1979; MD in Physiology with honors, NYU, 1983. Diplomate Nat. Bd. Med. Examiners, Am. Bd. Internal Medicine, Hematology, Med. Oncology, Palliative Medicine. Faculty scholar Project Death in Am.; intern Johns Hopkins Hosp., Balt., 1983—84; rsch. assoc. Howard Hughes Med. Inst., Balt., 1984—85; intern, resident Good Samaritan Hosp., Balt., 1985—87, chief resident, 1987—88; fellow hematology-oncology Cornell U. Med. Coll., NYC, 1988—91, fellow clin. pharmacology, 1991—92; fellow cancer pain Meml. Sloan Kettering Cancer Ctr., NYC, 1992—93, asst. profl. clin. medicine U. Medicine and Dentistry N.J., N.J. Med. Sch., Newark, 1993—2001, assoc. prof., 2001—; staff physician East Orange VA Med. Ctr., NJ, 1993—, faculty scholar Project Death in Am. Open Soc. Inst., 2000. Mem. Am. Soc. Clin. Oncology, Am. Pain Soc., Am. Soc. Hematology, Eastern Coop. Oncology Group (pain and symptom subcom. 1994—), Chinese Am. Med. Soc. (bd. dirs. 1992-96), Radiation Therapy Oncology Group, Chinese Alumni MIT (bd. dirs. 1989-91, newsletter contbr. 1990-92). Avocations: music, history.

CHANG, WEI-TIEN, preventive medicine physician, educator; s. Zhi-Chee Chang and Hsiu Ching Chen; m. Yi-Hui Chiu, Dec. 31, 1995; children: Yu-Chen, Hung-Jen. MD, Nat. Taiwan U., Taipei, 1994; PhD, Nat. Taiwan U., 2007. Cert. physician Dept. Health, Taiwan, 1994, internal medicine Soc. Internal Medicine, Taiwan, 1997, cardiology Soc. Cardiology, Taiwan, 1999, provider Soc. Traumatology, Taiwan, 1999, emergency physician Soc. Emergency Medicine, Taiwan, 2000, Soc. Critical Care Medicine, Taiwan, 2003, critical care instr. 2008. Internship Nat. Taiwan U. Hosp., 1993—94, resident internal medicine, 1994—97. Chief resident internal medicine Nat. Taiwan U. Hosp., 1997—98, fellow cardiology, 1997—99, chief resident emergency medicine, 1998—2000, fellow emergency medicine, 1998—2000, vis. staff emergency medicine, dept. chief, Douliu, Yunlin, Taiwan, 2007—08; lectr. emergency medicine Nat. Taiwan U. Coll. Medicine, Taipei, 2003—07, asst. prof., 2007—; rsch. assoc. U. Chgo., 2004—06; sec. gen. Soc. Emergency and Critical Care Medicine, Taiwan, 2010—. Author: (book) Textook of Complementary and Alternative Medicine; contbr. scientific papers to profl. jours. Com. edn. Soc. Emergency and Critical Care Medicine,Taiwan., 2008—. Attending, Nat. Sci. Com., Taiwan, 2007—. Mem.: Soc. Emergency and Critical Care Medicine, Taiwan (instr. 2008, sec. gen. 2010—), Am. Heart Assn. (instr. 1999). Achievements include patents for leverage-assisted active compression-decompression (ACD) CPR device; patents pending for wrapped temperature-regulating blanket for hypothermia therapy; ice cap for hypothermia therapy; first to translational physiology of hypercapnic resuscitation. Avocation: music. Office: Nat Taiwan Univ Hosp No 7 Chung-Shan S Rd Taipei 100 Taiwan Office Fax: 886-2-23223150. Personal E-mail: weitienchang@gmail.com. Business E-Mail: wtchang@ntu.edu.tw.

CHANG, WEN-KUI, software quality engineer; m. Yen-Hua Chen, Oct. 3, 1972; children: Christine Chi-Chen, I-Fan. PhD, Tamkang U., Taiwan, 1982. Certified ISO 15504 Course iNTACS/Germany, 2005, Certified European Project Manager Innovation Mgr. Consortium/Germany, 2005. Prof. Tunghai U., Taichung, Taiwan, 1989—; dean Coll. Info. Engring., Chang Jung Christian U., Taiwan, 2008; pres. Chinese Soc. Quality, 2007. Instr. SEI Authorized CMMI, 2006; lead appraiser SEI Authorized SCAMPI, 2008. Office: Tunghai Univ PO Box 5- 809 Taichung 40704 Taiwan Office Fax: 886-4-2359-1567. E-mail: wkc@thu.edu.tw.

CHANG, WOOHYOK, ophthalmologist, educator; b. Daegu, Republic of Korea, Aug. 17, 1970; m. Sujin Jeong, July 19, 1997; children: Jaewon, Sunwoo. MD, Yeungnam U., Daegu, 1996. Cert. Korean Ophthalmology Soc., 2001. Asst. prof. Yeungnam U. Coll. Medicine, Daegu, 2006—10, assoc. prof., 2010—. Reviewer Indian Jour. Ophthalmology. Capt. Korean Air force, 2001—04. Fellow, Chunma Med. Found., 1995. Mem.: European Vitreoretinal Soc., Am. Acad. Ophthalmology. Office: YUMC Dept Ophthalmology 317-1 Daemyung-Dong Nam-Gu 705-717 Daegu Daegu Republic of Korea Office Phone: 82-53-620-3443. Office Fax: 82-53-626-5936. Business E-Mail: changwh@ynu.ac.kr.

CHANG, YOUNG WOON, medical educator; b. Seoul, Republic of Korea, Aug. 22, 1954; s. So Sae Chang and Tae Hee Cheon; m. Eun Hee, Feb. 24, 1990; children: Eun Jee, Michael Myung. MD, Kyung Hee Med. Sch., Seoul, 1979, PhD, 1987. Intern Kyung Hee Med. Ctr., Seoul, 1982—83, resident, 1983—86, clin. fellow, 1986—89; asst. prof. Kyung Hee Med. Sch. Kyung Hee U., 1989—94, assoc. prof., 1994—99, prof. Dept. Gastroenterology, 1999—. Vis. rsch. fellow Southwestern Med. Sch., Dallas, 1992—94. Contbr. articles to profl. jours. Vol. Josep Charity Hosp., Seoul, 1996—. 1st lt. Korean Army, 1979—82. Mem.: Korean Soc. Gastrointestinal Endoscopy, Korean Soc. Gastroenterology, Korean Assn. Internal Medicine. Roman Catholic. Avocation: mountain climbing. Office: Kyung Hee Univ Dept Gastroenterology 1 Hoiki-Dong Dongdaemoon-gu Seoul 130-702 Republic of Korea Home Phone: 82-2-534-9550; Office Phone: 82-2-958-8150. Business E-Mail: cywgi@chollian.net.

CHANG, YU CHAO, dentist; b. Taichung, Taiwan, Sept. 9, 1966; s. Yaw Ying Chang and Chen Chau Yeh; m. Li Chen Huang; children: Ya-Rou, Ya-Sin. DDS, Chung Shan Med. and Dental Coll., Taiwan, 1991, MS, 1996; PhD, Chung Shan Med. U., Taiwan, 2002. Lectr. Chung Shan Med. and Dental Coll., Taiwan, 1996—99; assoc. prof. Chung Shan Med. U., Taiwan, 1999—2006, prof. Coll. Oral Medicine, 2006—, chmn. Inst. Stomatology, 2006—. Vis. staff Chung Shan Med. U. Hosp., Taiwan, 1996—. Recipient Exptl. Pathology Group Meeting award, Internat. Assn. for Dental Rsch., 1997, Rsch. award, Nat. Sci. Coun., 1998—2000, Divsn. Travel award, Internat. Assn. for Dental Rsch. S.E. Asia Divsn., 2000, Outstanding Alumnus award, Chung Shan Med. U., 2005. Office: Sch Dentistry Chung Shan Med Univ Taichung 402 Taiwan

CHANG, YUAN, neuropathologist, researcher, educator; m. Patrick S. Moore, 1989. MD, U. Utah. Neuropathologist, rschr. Columbia U., NY, 1992, prof. pathology, 1992; prof. dept. pathology U. Pitts. Sch. Medicine, 2002—. Mem. editl. bd.: Am. Jour. Pathology, Jour. Human Virology; contbr. articles and reviews in medical literature with Patrick S. Moore. Recipient Meyenburg Found. award Cancer Rsch., Robert Koch Prize, NYC Mayor's award for Excellence in Sci. and Tech., Paul A. Marks Prize, Meml. Sloan-Kettering Cancer Ctr., 2003, Charles S. Mott prize, GM Cancer Rsch. Found., 2003. Achievements include discovery of causative agent of Kaposi's Sarcoma-associated Herpes virus or human herpes virus 8; research in disorders that involve a compromised immune system. Office: Hillman Cancer Ctr Research Pavilion 5117 Centre Ave Ste 1.8 Pittsburgh PA 15213-1863 Office Phone: 412-623-7721. Office Fax: 412-623-7715. E-mail: yc70@pitt.edu.

CHANG, YU-LING, psychologist, educator; b. Taiwan, Jan. 2, 1976; PhD, U. Fla., Gainesville, 2008. Psychology intern dept. psychiatry U. Calif., San Diego, 2007—08, postdoc. fellow, 2008—10; asst. prof. Nat. Taiwan U., 2010—. Office: Nat Taiwan University Dept Psychology Taipei 10617 Taiwan Business E-Mail: ychang@ntu.edu.tw.

CHANGEUX, JEAN-PIERRE, neuroscientist, educator; b. Domont, France, Apr. 7, 1936; B, Ecole Normale Supérieure, Paris, 1957, M, 1958; D, Paris U., 1964; D (hon.), U. Torino, Italy, 1989, U. Dundee, Scotland, 1992, U. Stockholm, 1994, U. Lausanne, Switzerland, 1996, USC, 1997, Montréal U., 2000, Hebrew U. Jerusalem, 2004, Ohio State U., Columbus, 2007. Zoology instr. Ecole Normale Supérieure, 1958-60, asst. prof. faculty sci., 1960-66; dir. unit molecular neurobiology Pasteur Inst., Paris, 1972—2006; prof. Coll. de France, Paris, 1975—2006. Pres. Nat. Adv. Com. Bioethics, France, 1992—98. Author: (titles translated from French) Neuronal Man: The Biology of Mind, 1985, Conversations on Mind, Matter and Mathematics, 1995, What Makes Us Think. A Neuroscientist and a Philosopher Argue About Ethics, Human Nature, and the Brain, 2002, The Physiology of Truth, 2004, Nicotinic Acetylcholine Receptors: From Molecular Biology to Cognition, 2004, other titles in French; contbr. articles to profl. jours. Recipient Alexandre-Joannidès prize, French Acad. Scis., 1977, Gairdner Foundation Internat. award, 1978, Wolf Found. prize in medicine, Israel, 1982, Ciba-Geigy-Drew award in biomed. rsch., 1985, F.O. Schmitt prize, Neuroscis. Rsch. Inst., 1986, Rita-Levi-Montalcini prize, Fidia Found., 1988, Carl-Gustav-Bernhard medal, Swedish Acad. sci., 1991, Louis-Jeantet prize for medicine, 1993, Thudichum medal, Biochem. Soc., 1993, Camillo Golgi medal, Accademia Nazionale dei Lincei, 1994, Max-Delbrück Medal in molecular medicine, 1996, Jean-Louis Signoret prize in neuropsychology, Ipsen Found., 1997, Eli Lilly award in preclin. neurosci., European Coll. Neuropsychopharmacology, 1999, Langley award for basic rsch. on nicotine & tobacco, 2000, Karl Spencer Lashley award in neurosci., Am. Philos. Soc., 2002, Golden Eurydice award, Internat. Forum Biophilosophy, 2006, award, Nat. Acad. Scis. Wash., 2007, Neuronal Plasticity prize, IPSEN Found. Geneva, 2008, Pioneer award, Internat. Coll. Neuro Psychopharmacology, 2008, Passarow award, LA, 2010. Mem.: NAS, AAAS, European Molecular Biology Orgn., European Acad. Scis., Hungarian Acad. Scis., Romanian Acad. Med. Scis., Royal Acad. Scis., Am. Neurology Assn. (hon.), Japanese Biochem. Soc. (hon.). Mailing: Récepteurs et Cognition URA CNRS 2182 Institut Pasteur 28 rue du Dr Roux 757242 Paris France E-mail: changeux@pasteur.fr.

CHANGHYEOK, AN, surgeon; b. Chuncheon, Republic of Korea, Jan. 20, 1963; MD, Cath. U. Med. Coll., PhD, 1989. Chmn., dept. surgery Uijeongbu St' Mary Hosp., 2009—. Mem.: Korean Assn. Coloproctology. Office: Uijeongbu St' Mary Hosp 65-1 kumoh-dong Uijeongbu Kyeunggi-Do 480-717 Republic of Korea Office Phone: 82-31-820-3998. Office Fax: 82-31-847-2717. Business E-Mail: achcolo@catholic.ac.kr.

CHANTLER, CYRIL, pediatrician, educator; b. Bury, Lancs., Eng., May 12, 1939; s. Fred and Majorie (Clark) C.; m. Shireen Saleh, July 13, 1963; children: Paul, Jonathan, Nariane. BA, St. Catharine's Coll., Cambridge, Eng., 1960; MBBChir, Cambridge U., Eng., 1963; MD, Guys Hosp./Cambridge U., 1973. Jr. appointments Guys Hosp./Hosp. for Sick Children/Royal Postgrad. Med. Sch., 1963-71; travelling fellow Med. Rsch. Coun., U.K., San Francisco, 1971-72; cons., sr. lectr. Guy's Hosp., London, 1972-80, prof. pediatric nephrology, 1980—, chmn., gen. mgr. hosp. mgmt. com., 1985-88; prin. United Med. and Dental Schs. Guy's and St. Thomas Hosps., 1992-98; vice-prin. Kings Coll., 1998-2000; dean Guy's Kings and St. Thomas Med. and Dental Sch., 1998-2000; mem. policy bd. Nat. Health Svcs., 1989-95; mem. Gen. Med. Coun., 1994—2003; chmn. stds. com., 1996—2002; ret., 2003. Pro-vice chancellor U. London, 1997-2000; chmn. Coun. of Heads of U.K. Med. Schs., 1998-99; chmn. Great Ormond St. Children's Hosp., 2001—08; chmn. King's Fund, London, 2004—, chmn. Beit meml. fellowships med. rsch., 2003—09, chmn. U. Coll. London Ptnrs. AHS, 2009- Mem. coun. Southwark Cathedral. Fellow Acad. Med. Scis., Royal Coll. Physicians and Child Health, Royal Coll. Physicians; mem. AMA (mem. editl. bd.), European Soc. Pediat. Nephrology (hon.), Internal. Pediat. Nephrology Assn. (hon.), Brit. Assn. Med. Mgrs. (pres. 1991-97), Am. Pediat. Soc. (hon.), Inst. Medicine USA. Avocations: reading, opera. Personal E-mail: chantler@doctors.org.uk.

CHAN WAH HAK, CHARLES, cardiologist, educator; b. Port Louis, Mauritius, Feb. 27, 1957; s. Ting-Khin Chan Wah Hak and Kwee-Lan Chui Wan Cheong; m. Chan Paik Poh, July 2, 1986; children: Chan Wah Hak Yee Sen, Chan Wan Hak Charleen Min Li. MD with honors, Nat. U. Ireland, 1982. House physician City Gen. Hosp., Stoke-on-Trent, England, 1982—83; house surgeon N. Staffordshire Royal Infirmary, Stoke-on-Trent, 1983; sr. house officer Meml. Hosp., Darlington, England, 1983—84; registrar, clin. lectr. cardiology Aberdeen (Scotland) Royal Infirmary, 1984—86; registrar cardiology Green Ln. Hosp., Auckland, New Zealand, 1986—88, Singapore Gen. Hosp., 1988—89, sr. registrar, 1989—91, sr. registrar cardiology, 1992—93, cons. cardiologist, cons.-in-charge cardiac catheterization labs. Singapore Heart Ctr., 1993—98; sr. interventional fellow cardiac dept. Charles Nicolle Hosp., U. Rouen, France, 1991—92; sr. cons. cardiologist Nat. Heart Ctr., Singapore, 1998—, dir. adult diagnostic and interventional cardiac catherization labs., 1999—; clin. assoc. prof. medicine Nat. U. Singapore, 2001—. Advisor Chien Found., Singapore, 2000—. Contbr. numerous articles to profl. jours. Scholar, Govt. Singapore, 1991. Fellow: Acad. Medicine Singapore, Am. Coll. Cardiology, Royal Coll. Physicians (Edinburgh). Avocations: golf, teaching, trekking. Home: 12 Lucky Crescent Singapore 467734 Singapore Office: Nat Heart Ctr Mistri Laing 17 3d Hosp Ave Singapore 168752 Singapore

CHAO, DAVID M., medical researcher; BA, Harvard U., MA in Biology; PhD in Biology, MIT. Rschr. Novartis Insts. of Biomedical Rsch.; pres., CEO BioMed Valley Discoveries, 2007—09; exec. v.p. Stowers Inst. for Med. Rsch., Kansas City, Mo., 2008—09, pres., 2009—10, pres., CEO, 2010—. Pre-doctoral fellow, Howard Hughes Med. Inst. Office: Stowers Institute for Medical Research 100 E 50th St Kansas City MO 64110 Office Phone: 816-926-4000. Office Fax: 816-926-2000. *

CHAO, DAY-YU, medical educator; b. Taiwan, Dec. 22, 1969; PhD, Nat. Taiwan U., 2003. Prof. Nat. Chung-Hsing U., 2007—. Asst. rschr. Field Epidemiology Tng. Program, Taiwan, 1994—99; postdoc. rschr. DVBID/CDC, 2003—06, Academic Sinica, 2006—07. Grant, Cold Spring Harbor. Fellow: Am. Soc. Microbiology; mem.: Am. Soc. Virology. Avocations: jogging, hiking, movies, travel. Office: 250 Kwo-Guang Rd Taichung 401 Taiwan Business E-Mail: dychao@nchu.edu.tw.

CHAO, EDWARD C., internist, endocrinologist; b. La., June 13, 1972; s. Hung-Ju and Martha Chao; m. Sarah Poffenberger, Nov. 8, 2009. BS in Biology, UCLA, 1994; MA in Med. Scis., Boston U., 1996; Dr. of Osteo. Medicine, U. New Eng. Coll. Osteo. Medicine, Biddeford, Maine, 2002. Cert. Am. Bd. Internal Medicine. Rsch. coord. radiology Brigham and Women's Hosp., Boston, 1996—97, rsch. coord. thrombolysis in myocardial infarction study, 1997—98; resident internal medicine Loma Linda U. Med. Ctr., Calif., 2002—05; physician internal medicine Kaiser Permanente, San Diego, 2005—; fellow endocrinology U. Calif. San Diego Med. Ctr., 2007—09, chief fellow, endocrinology, 2008—09; aast. prof., clin. prof. medicine, fellow U. Calif. San Diego Sch. Medicine and Attending Physician, Internal Medicine, VA San Diego, 2009—; mem. UCSD Sch. Medicine Nat. Ctr. Leadership Academic Medicine Profl. Devel. Program, 2011. Columnist, mem. editl. bd. Endocrine Today; mem. Arthur Vining Davis group on Humanism in Medicine; reviewer Advances in Therapy, and Annals in Medicine Jour.; with Pharm. Design, Diabetes Therapy, Jour. Clin. Endocrinology & Metabolism; chair San DiegoStep Our Walk to Stop Diabetis, 2011. Author: (abstract) 72nd Annual Postgraduate Conf., Loma Linda University; author: (co-investigator) (sci. abstract) Annual Sci. Sessions, Am. Diabetes Assn.; author: (jour. article) Brain Research; contbr. scientific papers presented research at Clinical Investigators Workshop; author (co-investigator): Nature Reviews Drug Discovery. Vol. Make-A-Wish Found., San Diego, 2005—, team capt., 2008—; vol. Am. Diabetes Assn: Tour Cure, team capt., 2008—10; event chair Entertainment, Planning Com. Step Out: Walk to Fight Diabetes, 2011; vol. physician U. Calif., San Diego Student-Run Free Clinic, 2010—, San Diego Symphony, 2010—. Recipient Scholastic Rsch. award, Am. Diabetes Assn., 2003, Excellence Tchg. award, U. Calif., San Diego Sch. Medicine, 2010, scholarship, C.V. Starr Found., 1990—94; grant, Endocrine Fellows Found., 2008. Mem.: Am. Assn. Clin. Endocrinologists, Endocrine Soc., San Diego Osteo. Med. Assn. (assoc.), San Diego County Med. Soc. (assoc.), ACP (assoc.), Sigma Sigma Phi (life). Achievements include research in the effect of pioglitazone on peripheral edema in patients with Type II diabetes mellitus on insulin; the impact of rosiglitazone on the microvascular and macrovascular circulation; The role of fatty acid oxidation in insulin resistance in individuals with metabolic syndrome. Avocations: running, travel, dance, classical music. Office: VA Calif San Diego Healthcare System 3350 La Jolla Village Dr 111G San Diego CA 92161 Personal E-mail: edwardchao1@yahoo.com. Business E-Mail: edward.chao@va.gov.

CHAO, JOHANN YUNGFA, dermatology and disease consultant, educator, director; b. Tainan, Taiwan, Apr. 25, 1925; naturalized, US, 1991; s. Tu-sheng and Hsu-yeh Chao; m. Sarah Shu-hua Fan, Apr. 22, 1954; children: Phyllis, Elena, Peter, Arlene. MD, Nat. Taiwan U. Med. Coll., Taipei, 1950; grad. in leprosy and dermatology, U. Hong Kong, 1953; grad. in dermatology, U. Tokyo, 1962, Mayo Clinic, Rochester, Minn., 1979. Physician Hong Kong Leprosarium, Hong Kong U., China, 1952—53; instr. master course Pub. Health Sch. Taiwan U., 1953; chief dept. prevention Lo-shen Leprosarium, Sinchuang, Taipei, 1953—55; chief dept. dermatology Mackay Meml. Hosp., Taipei, 1956, sr. cons., 2005—; med. dir. Happy Mt. Leprosy Colony, Taipei County, 1956; leprosy cons. USN Med. Rsch. Unit II, Taipei, 1979—80, Taiwan Leprosy Relief Assn. and Found., Taiwan, Happy Mt. Colony Mentally Handicapped or Disabled, Taipei; clin. prof. dermatology and leprosy Taipei Med. U., 2005—; pvt. practice Edison, NJ. Author: Common Knowledge of Leprosy, 1996, 2d edit., 1998; contbr. scientific papers to various med. confs. and mag. Active in med. svcs. and social relief activities, Taiwan, 1950—; mem. Congress Com. sponsoring XII World Congress, Taipei; mem. bd. Taipei and Nat. Assns. YMCA, 1946—; pres. Happy Mt. Colony Leprosy in Disabled and Handicapped Child and Adult, 1954—, bd. chmn., 1954—. Lt. med. officer Air Force, 1964, Taiwan. Recipient Excellent Alumni award Tainan HS, 1995, Top Ten Med. Contbr. award in Taiwan, 1995, Appreciation award fifty five yr. med. svc., Nat. Physician Assn. Union, 2005; named Top Ten Med. Contbr. Taiwan promoter Tri-Nation, Japan, Korea and Taiwan Internat. Exch. Program Christian Med. Assn., 1995. Fellow: Taiwan Physician Assn., Taipei Physician Assn. (Appreciation award 2005); mem.: Happy Mount Colony Mentally Retarded and Disabled Child and Adult (supt. and chmn.), Internat. Christian Med. and Dental Assn. (exec. mem. 1997—2002), Taiwan Leprosy Relief Assn. (charter mem. 1958, ex-pres. 1998—2006), Chinese Dermatol. Soc. (charter mem., supr. 1974—76). Avocations: softball, tennis, golf, swimming. Home: 3d Fl 60 To-sheng W Rd Taipei 11158 Taiwan

CHAO, JULIE, medical educator; b. Taiwan, Jan. 7, 1940; PhD, Iowa State U., 1970. Prof. Med. U. SC, 1974—. Recipient Rsch. Career Devel. award, NIH, E. K. Frey-E. Werle Promotion prize, U. Munich, Appreciation award, Med. U. SC. Mem.: Coun. High Blood Pressure Rsch., Am. Heart Assn., Am. Soc. Hypertension, Biochem. Soc., Kinin Club. Office: 173 Ashley Ave Charleston SC 29425 Business E-Mail: chaoj@musc.edu.

CHAO, RONALD PHILIP, plastic surgeon; s. Thomas and Norma Louise Chao. MD, NY Med. Coll., 1996. Lic. physician Calif., Ind., Fla. Resident in surgery St. Mary's Hosp. Yale U. Sch. Medicine, Waterbury, Conn., 1996—2002; plastic surgery fellow U. Tex., San Antonio, 2002—03; cosmetic surgery fellow Am. Acad. Cosmetic Surgery, Munster, Ind., 2003—04; hair transplant fellow Med. Hair Restoration, Heathrow, Fla., 2004—05; pvt. practice Beverly Hills, Calif., 2005. Cons. in field. Contbr. chapters to books. Deacon Berkeley (Calif.) Bible Fellowship Ch., 1989—91. Recipient Med. Student Tchg. award, St. Mary's Hosp. Dept. Surgery, Waterbury, Conn., 2001; Trustee Merit scholar, NY Med. Coll., 1992. Mem.: AMA, Internat. Soc. Hair Restoration Surgery, Calif. Acad. Cosmetic Surgery, Am. Acad. Cosmetic Surgery. Achievements include research in postoperative care in cosmetic surgery and hair transplantation. Avocations: trumpet, shooting, fishing, aquariums, travel.

CHAO, RUTH, psychologist, educator; b. Keelung, Taiwan, Apr. 1, 1967; arrived in U.S., 1996; d. Shi-yi Chao and Chin Chang. BS, Nat. Taiwan U., 1989; PhD, U. Mo., 2005—. Clin. psychologist Samaritan Psychology Clinic, Chia-yi, Taiwan, 1994—96; rschr. U. Mo., Columbia, 2002—03, clin. supr., 2001—03; doctoral counselor Mich. State U., East Lansing, 2003—04; asst. prof. Tenn. State U., 2005—07, U. Denver, 2007—. Cons. Mich. State U., East Lansing, 2003—04, coord., 2003—04; founder Pals Across Cultures Program, U. Denver, 2008. Author: (exhbn.) Listening to Clients' Voices (Winter Roundtable Scholarship, 2004), (vistas) Non-traditional Students on Counseling Needs, 2004, Clients' Perceptions of Mental Health Services, 2005, (book chpt.) Going through Cultural Barriers in Counseling, 2004, Integrating Taoism and Western Therapeutic Approaches in the Treatment of Anxiety, 2005, Integrating Holland's Theory with Tao-te Ching for Career Counseling, 2005, (book) Multicultural Competence in Counseling: A Statistic Exploration, 2008, (encyclopedia entry) Cultural Psuchology; translator: (book) Abnormal Psychology, 1995, Social Psychology, 1995, Teaching and Learning, 1997; author: Historical Review of Multiculturalism, How Ethical is Contemporary Multicultural Training?, 2003, (exhbn.) Adult Students' Perspectives on Counseling and Education (ACCA Grant Award, 2004), Re-thinking Non-traditional College Students' Counseling Needs, 2004, Toward a Successful Experience at Graduate School, 2003, Gender and Smoking: A Qualitative Study, 2004, Minority Clients' Perspectives on Multicultural Competence, 2004, Counselors' Multicultural Self-awareness: A Way to Client Advocacy, 2004, A Qualitative Analysis of College Students' Smoking, 2003, (exhbn.) Creating a Hoslitic Environment for Clients (Rsch. and Profl. Devel. Award, 2003), College Smokers' Perspectives on Smoking (Rsch. Award, Sch. of Medicine, U. of Kans., 2003), Racial Identity Development in Minority Counselors (Winter Roundtable Scholoarship, Columbia U., 2002); contbr. articles to profl. jours.; author: (Encyclopedia) Cross-Cultural Psychology, Confucianism, (Book) Multicultural Competencies in Counseling: A Statistical Exploration, 2008, (Encyclopedia) Loss of Face, 2008; contbr. chapters to books, articles to profl. jours. Christian student leader, Taipei, 1988—89. Recipient Multicultural Rsch. award, 2002, Outstanding Acad. Achievements award, 2002, Walter Scott Monroe Rsch. fellowship, 2002—03, Superior Rsch. award, 2004, Rsch. scholarship, Profl. R&D Support award, 2004, faculty rsch. award, Tenn. State U., Am. Coll. Counseling Rsch. award, 2005, Am. Psychol. Assn. ProDigs award, 2006, Am. Psychol. Fund award Counseling Psychology, 2007, Apple award, U. Denver, 2008. Mem.: APA, Am. Counseling Assn., Internationalization Group (U. Denver), Psi Chi (life). Office Phone: 303-871-2556. Personal E-mail: ruth_chao2000@yahoo.com. Business E-Mail: cchao3@du.edu.

CHAO, TING-HSING, cardiologist, educator; s. Chung-Teh Chao and Chuen-Hsia Wang. MD in Medicine, Taipei Med. U., Taiwan, 1991. Registered physician Taiwan, diplomate Taiwan, Bd. Taiwan Soc. Internal Medicine, Bd. Taiwan Soc. Cardiology, Bd. Soc. Emergency and Critical Care Medicine, Taiwan. Rsch. assoc. dept. medicine and clin. sci. Kyoto U., Japan, 2004—05; resident internal medicine Nat. Cheng Kung U. Hosp., Tainan, Taiwan, 1993—96, chief resident internal medicine, 1996—97, fellow cardiology, 1997—98, attending physicina cardiology, 1998—, clin. lectr. internal medicine, 2000—06, asst. prof., 2006—09, 2009—, dir. cath lab. cardiology, 2007—08, chief cardiovasc. ward, 2006—08, clerkship dir., 2006—09, sec.-gen. med. affairs and head internal medicine, Dou-Liou br., Yun-Lin county, 2009—10, vice supt., 2010—. 2nd. lt. Navy Chinese Army, 1991—93. Rsch. grant, Nat. Sci. Coun., 2003—05, fellowship, Asian Pacific Soc. Cardiology, 2008, European Soc. Cardiology, 2009. Mem.: Soc. Emergency and Critical Care Medicine (Taiwan), Taiwan Soc Ultrasound Medicine, Taiwan Soc. Cardiology, Taiwan Soc. Internal Medicine, Formosan Med. Assn. (Taiwan). Buddhist. Achievements include breakthroughs in the genetic research of the occurrence of coronary artery disease; research in vascular regeneration. Avocations: basketball, badminton, singing, guitar. Office: Nat Cheng kung University Hosp Dept Medicine No 138 Sheng-Li Rd Tainan 704 Taiwan also: Nat Cheng kung University Hosp Dou-Liou Br Dept Medicine No 345 Chuang-Ching Rd Yun-Lin County 64 Dou-Liou City Taiwan Office Phone: 886-6-2353535 ext. 2392, 886-5-5332121 ext. 5101 or 6006. Office Fax: 886-6-2753834, 886-5-5334521. E-mail: chaotinghsing@yahoo.com.tw.

CHAOUAT, GERARD CHARLES PAUL, researcher; b. Alger, France, May 6, 1944; s. Yves David Chaouat and Jacqueline Balensi. BA, U. Paris, 1962; MD, Faculty Lariboisiére, Paris, 1968; PhD, U. Paris 6, 1979; Cert. in Immunology, Inst. Pasteur, 1969; PhD (hon.), Pecs U., Hungary, 1998. Intern Hosp. Region de Paris, 1968-72; chercheur benevole Inst. Nat. Santé et Rsch. Med., 1973-76; grantee Med. Rsch. Coun., Brit. Coun., Wellcome Rsch. Lab., 1974; attache rsch. Ctr. Nat. Rsch. Sci., 1974; vis. scientist NIH, Bethesda, Md., 1981-82; from charge de rsch. to dir. rsch., 1982-99; emeritus dir. rsch., 2011—. Contbr. articles to profl. jours. Treas. Syndicat Nat. des Chercheurs Sci., 1998—2010. Recipient Munskgaard award, USA, 1988. Mem.: Soc. Francaise Immunology, Internat. Soc. Immunology Reproduction (Pres. d'honneur). Avocations: model rocketry, space travel, plastic models. Home: A 442 11 17 rue de Chine Paris France Office: Hosp A Beclere INSERM 782 92141 Clamart Cedex France Office Phone: +33 145374450. Personal E-mail: gerard_chaouat@wanadoo.fr.

CHAPA, JEFFREY, obstetrician, gynecologist; Grad., Wash. U.; MD, St. Louis U. Sch. Medicine. Cert. maternal-fetal medicine, obstetrics & gynecology, clinical genetics. Intern U. Hosp. Cleveland, resident; fellow U. Chgo. Hosp.; head of maternal fetal medicine Cleveland Clinic. Mem.: Am. Coll. Med. Genetics, Soc. for Maternal-Fetal Medicine, Am. Coll. Obstetricians & Gynecologists. Office: 5001 Rockside Rd Mail Code HC-30 Independence OH 44131 Office Phone: 440-312-8888.

CHAPELON-ABRIC, CATHERINE, internal medicine cardiologist; d. Guy and Denise Chapelon; m. Catherine Chapelon, Oct. 7, 1989; children: Laurie Abric, Alexis Abric. Baccalauréat, Lycée Molière, Paris, 1973; MD in Medicine, Paris VI, 1983; degree in Internal Medicine, Paris, 1986. Cert. MD Paris, 1983, registered cardiologist France, 1989, praticien hospitalier Paris, 1990. Interne des hopitaux Assistance Publique, Paris, 1980—84; chef de clin. asst. Âssistance Publique de Paris, Paris, 1984—88, praticien hospitalier, 1990—. Head internal medecine dept. Hospital du Perpétuel Secours, Levallois Perret, Haut s de Seine, France, 1995—2000; editl. dir. Elsevier, Paris, 1990—; med. cons. Am. Hosp. Paris, Paris, 2005—. Contbr. articles to rsch. jours. Mem.: Soc. Méd. Hôsp. Paris, Coll. Médecine des Hôsp. Paris, Soc. Française Cardiologie, Soc. Nat. Française de Medecine Interne. Office: CHU Pitié Salpétrière 47-83 Boulevard 'Hôsp Paris 75013 France Office Phone: 0033142178042. Business E-Mail: catherine.chapelon@psl.aphp.fr.

CHAPLIN, HUGH, JR., preventive medicine physician, educator; b. NYC, Feb. 4, 1923; m. Alice Dougherty, June 16, 1945; 4 children; m. Lee Nelken Robins, Aug. 5, 1998. AB, Princeton U., 1943; MD, Columbia U., 1947. Diplomate Am. Bd. Internal Medicine, Nat. Bd. Med. Examiners. Intern Mass. Gen. Hosp., Boston, 1947-48, resident, 1948-50; fellow in hematology Brit. Postgrad. Med. Sch., London, 1951-53; physician in charge Clin. Center Blood Bank, NIH, Bethesda, Md., 1953-55, Commonwealth Fund fellow Wright Fleming Inst. Microbiology, London, 1962-63, Josiah Macy Faculty scholar, 1975-76. Instr. in medicine Washington U. Sch. Medicine, St. Louis, 1955-56, asst. prof. medicine and preventive medicine, 1956-62, asso. dean, chmn. admissions com., 1957-62, asso. prof., 1963-65, prof., 1965, William B. Kountz prof. preventive medicine, 1965-83; dir. IWJ Inst. of Rehab., St. Louis, 1964-72; prof. pathology, dir. Barnes Hosp. Blood Bank, St. Louis, 1983-91; emeritus prof. pathology and medicine, 1991—; mem. Am. Standards Com. for Blood Transfusion Equipment; mem. subcom. on transfusion problems NRC, 1959-62, mem. com. on blood and transfusion problems, 1963-67; chmn. ad hoc blood program research com. ARC, 1967-73, bd. govs., 1978-84 Assoc. editor Transfusion, 1960-98; contbg. editor Vox Sanguinis, 1960-79. Served with USNR, 1942—45. Mem. Am. Fedn. Clin. Research, Central Soc. Clin. Research, Am. Soc. Clin. Investigation, Assn. Am. Physicians, Am. Internat. socs. hematology, Brit. Med. Research Soc., Brit. Royal Soc. Medicine, Am. Assn. Blood Banks (sci. program com. 1959-60, Emily Cooley award 1968, Morton Grove-Rasmussen award 1985), Phi Beta Kappa, Alpha Omega Alpha, Sigma Xi. Office: Washington U Sch Medicine Box 8118 4949 Barnes Hospital Plz Saint Louis MO 63110-1003 E-mail: hughchaplin@yahoo.com.

CHAPMAN, BARRY LLOYD, retired cardiologist, educator, army officer; b. Werris Creek, NSW, Australia, June 6, 1936; s. Lloyd George and Winifred Cordell (O'Shea) C., m. 1961 (div. 1988); children: Sandra Jane, Ian David, Michael Andrew, Louise Anne. MB, BChir, U. Sydney, NSW, 1960. Resident med. officer Royal Newcastle Hosp., NSW, Australia, 1960—62, med. registrar, 1963—66, fellow medicine, 1967—70, found. dir. coronary care, 1968—70, staff specialist in medicine, 1973—91, cons. cardiologist, 1984—87, sr. cons. cardiologist, 1988—91; rsch. fellow, sr. registrar West Middlesex Hosp., Isleworth, 1971—73; with Hammersmith Hosp., London, 1971—73; sr. cons. cardiologist, found. dir. electrocardiography svcs. John Hunter Hosp., Newcastle, 1991—2001; from clin. to conjoint lectr. medicine faculty medicine and health scis. U. Newcastle, 1979—2001; ret., 2001. Mem. various coms. and bds. related to tchg. hosp. and univ. med. sch. matters; mem. Australian Soc. Med. Rsch., Gastroent. Soc. Australia; amb. to Australia, The World Forum St. John's Coll., U. Cambridge, England, 2010. Contbr. articles and papers to profl. jours. and confs. Emeritus mem. Internat. Coll. Angiology. Maj. Royal Australian Inf. Res. Forces, 1955—73. Recipient Bronze medallion and Instr.'s Cert., Royal Life Saving Soc. Australia, 1949—53, Efficiency Decoration, Australian Mil., 1970, Anniversary of Nat. Svc. 1951-1972 medal, 2003, Australian Def. medal, 2006, award, U. Newcastle, NSW, 2000, Bd. Hunter Postgrad. Med. Inst., Newcastle, NSW, 2008, medal, Am. Biog. Inst., Raleigh, NC, Da Vinci Diamond award, Internat. Biog. Ctr., Cambridge, Lifetime Achievement award, World Congress Arts, Scis. & Comm., Am. Medal of Honor; named Man of Yr., Am. Biog. Inst., Raleigh, NC, 2008; named one of 500 Great Leaders, 2010. Fellow: Cardiac Soc. Australia and New Zealand, Royal Australasian Coll. Physicians (life), Royal Soc. Medicine London (life); mem.: Internat. Coll. Angiology (emeritus fellow), Am. Chem. Soc., Australian and New Zealand Soc. History of Medicine, Am. Inst. Ultrasound in Medicine (emeritus fellow), NY Acad. Scis. (active mem.), AAAS (emeritus), Royal United Svcs. Inst. NSW (life), Returned and Svcs. League Australia, Nat. Servicemen's Assn. Australia, Royal NSW Regiment Assn. (1/19 bn.), Sydney U. Regiment Assn., Internat. Soc. for Heart Rsch., Diggers Newcastle Club, Club Macquarie, Imperial Svc. Club, Royal Automobile Club of Australia, Mayfield Ex-Services Club. Presbyterian. Avocations: history, classical music, genealogy, gardening, crossword puzzles, literature. Home: 31 Elbrook Dr Rankin Park NSW 2287 Australia

CHAPMAN, HOPE HORAN, psychologist; b. Chgo., Feb. 13, 1954; d. Theodore George and Idelle (Poll) H.; m. Stuart G. Chapman, Dec. 4, 1983. BS, U. Ill., Champaign-Urbana, 1976; MA, No. Ill. U., DeKalb, 1979; cert. lawyer's asst. program, Roosevelt U., Chgo., 1996-97; student, Ballet Russe Sch., 1999—2002. Lic. pharmacy technician, Ill.; notary public, Ill., 2002—; diplomate Am. Bd. Disability Analysts. Psychologist Glenwood State Hosp. Sch., Iowa, 1979-83, Gov. Samuel H. Shapiro Devel. Ctr., Kankakee, Ill., 1985-86, dir. staff tng. and devel. Glenkirk, 1988-90; clin. assoc. Bennett & Assocs., 1990-91; psychologist Singer Mental Health & Devel. Ctr., Rockford, Ill., 1992-93; forensic psychologist Elgin Mental Health Ctr., Ill., 1993-94. Contbr. articles to profl. jours., papers to confs. Active Omaha Symphonic Chorus, 1981-83; mem. Omaha Pub. Schs. Citizens Adv. Com., 1980-81; mem. edn. com. Anti-Defamation League, 1980-85, chmn. com. anti-Semitism and Jewish youth, 1983; commr. youth commn. Village of Hoffman Estates, Ill., 1988-94; vice chmn. oversight com. Vogelei Teen Ctr., 1988-94; commr. Environ. Commn., Village of Hoffman Estates, 1994-2000, chmn. Schaumburg Twp. Mental Health Bd., 1993-94; election judge Cook County, 1992—; judge's asst. Cook County Cir. Ct., 1996-2004, membership chmn. Chicagoland chpt. U.S. Amateur Ballroom Dancers Assn. 2003; mem. coun. Roosevelt U. Alumni Bd., Robin campus, 2004-05; counselor Life Span Crisis Line, 2005—09; mem. health care availability and access com. Gen. Assembly State of Ill. 44th Dist., 2007—08. State of Ill. scholar; recipient Nat. Fed. Paralegal Assns. award of Distinction, 2004, Hon. Mention, 2010. Fellow Am. Coll. Forensic Examiners; mem. APA, Am. Bd. Disability Analysts, Ill. Paralegal Assn. (Pro Bono Svc. award 2004, 05, 06, 07, 08, 09), Salt Creek Ballet Guild, Phi Kappa Phi, Psi Chi. Jewish. Personal E-mail: Hopehcmail@cs.com.

CHAPMAN, LOREN J., psychology professor; b. Muncie, Ind., Jan. 5, 1927; s. Herbert L. and Lurana Gertrude (Treff) C.; m. Jean Marilyn Paulsen, June 6, 1953; children: Nancy, Laurence. AB cum laude, Harvard U., Cambridge, Mass., 1948; MS, Northwestern U., Evanston, Ill., 1952, PhD, 1954. USPHS postdoctorate research fellow U. Chgo., 1954-56, instr., asst. prof., 1956-59; assoc. prof. U. Ky., Lexington, 1959-62; from assoc. prof. to prof. Southern Ill. U., Carbondale, 1962-67; prof. U. Wis., Madison, 1966-93, NIMH rsch. scientist, 1988-93; prof. emeritus, 1994—. Author: Disordered Thought in Schizophrenia, 1973; contbr. articles to profl. jours. Recipient Disting. Scientist award Soc. for Sci. Clin. Psychology, 1992; NIMH research grantee, 1952-97. Fellow AAAS, APA (Disting. Sci. award for application of psychology 1999); mem. Am. Psychopathol. Assn., Soc. Rsch. Psychopathology (pres. 1989, Joseph Zubin award 1992), Am. Psychol. Soc. (William James fellow 1995). Home: 129 Richland Ln Madison WI 53705-4834 Office: Univ Wis Dept Psychology 1202 W Johnson St Madison WI 53706-1611 Office Phone: 608-238-8426.

CHAPMAN, MICHAEL WILLIAM, orthopedist, educator; b. Newberry, Mich., Nov. 29, 1937; m. Elizabeth Casady; adopted sons: Mark, Craig. AA, Am. River Coll., Sacramento, Calif., 1957; BA, U. Calif., Davis, 1958; BS, U. Calif., San Francisco, 1959, MD, 1962. Diplomate Am. Bd. Orthopaedic Surgery (ad hoc appeal com. 1986, site visitor 1986, certification renewal com. 1985-88, certification renewal com. chmn. 1986-88). Intern San Francisco Gen. Hosp., 1962-63, asst. chief orthopaedic surgery svc., 1971-79, acting chief orthopaedic surgery svc., 1972-73; resident in orthopaedic surgery U. Calif., San Francisco, 1963-67, asst. prof. dept. orthopaedic surgery, Sch. Medicine, 1971-76, assoc. prof. dept. orthopaedic surgery, Sch. Medicine, 1976-79; resident in orthopaedic surgery U. Calif. Hosps., San Francisco, 1963-64, Samuel Merritt Hosp., Oakland, Calif., 1964, Highland-Alameda County Hosp., Oakland, 1965, Children's Hosp. of the East Bay, Oakland, 1966, Shriners Hosp., Honolulu, 1966-67; fellow Nat. Orthopaedic Hosp., London, 1967-68; chmn. dept. orthopaedic surgery U. Calif., Davis, Sacramento, 1979-99, prof. dept. orthopaedic surgery, 1981-2000, David Linn chair orthopaedic surgery, 1998-2001, prof. emeritus, 2000—. Panelist Calif. Crippled Children Svcs. Panel in Orthopaedic Surgery; cons. VA Hospital, Martinez, Calif.; co-chmn. Zimmer Trauma Panel, 1983-84; vis. prof. Fresno Valley Med. Ctr., 1975, Dept. Orthopaedics, U. Calif., Davis, 1976, U. Hawaii, Honolulu, 1977; vis. prof., cons. to Surgeon Gen. U.S. Army, Europe, 1978; vis. prof. U. Basel, Switzerland, 1979, Phoenix Orthopaedic Residency Program, 1979, Stanford U., 1981, U. Hawaii, 1982, U. So. Calif., L.A., 1984, SUNY, Buffalo, 1985, U. Utah, 1985, U. Iowa Coll. Medicine, 1987, Duke U. Sch. Medicine, 1988, U. Calif. Irvine, Div. Orthopaedics, 1990, U. S.C., 1990, Mass. Gen. Hosp., Harvard U., 1990, Boston U., 1994, Stanford U., 1995, Med. Coll. Pa., 1996, numerous others; also guest lectr. numerous instns.; insp. for residency rev. com. ad hoc appeal com. Accreditation coun. for Grad. Med. Specialist Site, 1983-86. Editor: (with M. Madison) Operative Orthopaedics, 1988 (Best New Book in Clin. Medicine Assn. Am. Pubs.); contbr. numerous articles and numerous abstracts to profl. jours.; presenter exhibits, audiovisual programs, some 500 other presentations; cons. editor Skiing Mag., 1973-77; mem. bd. assoc. editors Clin. Orthopaedics and Related Rsch., 1982-85, Internat. Med. Soc. Paraplegia, 1972-80; reviewer Jour. Bone and Joint Surgery, 1980-85, trustee, 1995-03, sec. to bd. trustees, 1999, chmn. bd. trustees, 2000; past reviewer New Eng. Jour. Medicine; patentee in field. With U.S. Army, 1968-70. Decorated Army Commendation medal; recipient Outstanding Tchg. award U. Calif., San Francisco, 1972, Outstanding Tchr. award U. Calif., Davis, 1984, 93; named One of Best 100 Doctors Am., Good Housekeeping Mag.; Fogarty Sr. Internat. fellow NIH, 1978-79, 80-81; grantee Johnson & Johnson, 1983-84, Zimmer Inc., 1983-85, 85-86, 87-90, Interpore Internat., 1985-86, 89-90, Collagen Inc., 1985-86, 88-89, Upjohn Inc., 1985-86, Orthopaedic Rsch. and Edn. Found., 1988-89. Mem. AMA (Physicians Recognition award 1989-96), ACS, Am. Acad. Orthopaedic Surgeons (bd. dirs. 1982-83, numerous coms., Zimmer award for Disting. Contbn. to Orthop. Surgery, 2002), Am. Orthopaedic Assn. (bd. dirs. 1985-86, pres. 1990-91, various coms.), Internat. Orthopaedic Assn., Assn. for Study of Internal Fixation (N.Am. chpt.), Internat. Soc. Orthopaedic Surgery and Traumatology, Internat. Soc. for Fracture Repair, Brit. Orthopaedic Assn., South African Orthopaedic Assn. (hon.), Am. Acad. Orthopaedic Surgeons, Am. Assn. for Surgery of Trauma, Am. Bd. Med. Spltys., Assn. Am. Med. Colls., Leroy C. Abbott Orthopaedic Soc., Austrian Trauma Assn., Paul R. Lipscomb Soc., Northwestern Med. Assn., Orthopaedic Rsch. Soc., Orthopaedic Trauma Assn., Sierra Club, U. Calif. San Francisco Alumni Assn., Western Orthopaedic Assn., Houston Orthopaedic Assn. (hon.), Calif. Med. Assn., Calif. Orthopaedic Assn., Sacramento-El Dorado Med. Soc., Wilson Interurban Orthopaedic Soc., Alpha Omega Alpha. Avocations: skiing, mountain climbing, backpacking, tennis, bicycling. Office: U Calif-Davis Sch Med Dept Orthopedics 4860 Y St Ste 3800 Sacramento CA 95817-2307

CHAPMAN, PAUL B., oncologist; b. Chgo., Dec. 14, 1955; BA, Cornell U., Ithaca, NY, 1977; MD, Cornell U. Med. Coll., 1981. Diplomate Am. Bd. Internal Medicine, Am. Bd. Med. Oncology. Intern medicine U. Chgo. Hosp., 1981—82, resident oncology, 1982—84; fellow Meml. Sloan-Kettering Cancer Ctr., NYC, 1982—88, clin. asst., 1988—91, asst. attending physician, 1991—97, assoc. attending physician, 1997—2005, attending physician, 2005—, head melanoma sect., Clin. Immunology Svc. Dept. Assoc. prof. medicine Cornell U. Weill Med. Coll., NYC, 2005—06, prof. medicine, 2006—. Named one of America's Top Doctors, Castle Connolly Med. Ltd., 2002—09, Top Doctors for Cancer, 2005—07. Mem.: Am. Soc. Clin. Oncology. Office: Meml Sloan-Kettering 1275 York Ave New York NY 10021-6007 *

CHAPMAN, ROBERT JAMES, psychiatrist, educator; b. Delaware, Ohio, July 10, 1936; s. Edward Samuel and Frances Mae (Stephenson) Chapman; m. Janice Holmes, June 18, 1960; children: Steven Holmes, Scott Edward, Erik Wellington. AB, Oberlin Coll., 1958; MD, Ohio State U., 1963. Diplomate Am. Bd. Psychiatry and Neurology. Instr., fellow, USPHS U. Rochester Sch. Med., NY, 1968—69; asst. prof. clin. psychiatry Dartmouth Med. Sch., Hanover, NH, 1869—1979, asst. prof. cmty. and family med., 1976—79, assoc. prof. clin. psychiatry, 1980—94, adj. assoc. prof. psychiatry, 1994—2002, adj. assoc. prof. psychiatry emeritus, 2003—10. Dir. comprehensive alcoholism svcs. program Dartmouth Med. Sch., Hanover, 1973—75, dir. Robert Wood Johnson Primary Care/Physician Mgr. residency program, 1977—79, dir. fellowship program rural cmty. psychiatry, 1979—81; dir. Mt. Ascutney Psychiat. Assocs., Windsor, Vt., 1984—94, Choate Psychiat. Assocs., New London, NH, 1995—99. Contbr. chapters to books, articles to profl. jours. Bd. dirs. Peace Corps Physician, Nigeria, 1964—66; mem. Area Planning Coun., NH, 1977—80; bd. dirs. Planned Parenthood Assn. Upper Valley, Lebanon, 1970—78; chmn. profl. adv. com. Hanover Vis. Nurse Svc., 1979—80; bd. dirs. Hanover Conservation Coun., 2003—; mem. Handel Soc. Dartmouth Coll., 1983—88; mem. steering com. Upper Valley Health Care Coalition, White River Junction, Vt., Lebanon, NH, 1984—86. Sr. asst. surgeon USPHS, 1964—66. Fellow: Am. Psychiat. Assn. (disting. life); mem.: AAAS, AMA, Global Health Coun., Physicians for Social Responsibility, N.H. Psychiat. Soc. (pres. 1983—84, chmn. ethics com. 1985—86), Union Concerned Scientists, Amnesty Internat., Human Rights Watch, Internat. Physicians for Prevention Nuc. War, Physicians for Human Rights. Avocations: camping, canoeing, photography, wilderness travel. Home: 33 Rip Rd Hanover NH 03755-1616

CHAPMAN, RONALD WILLIAM, public health service officer, state official; b. Sept. 17, 1961; MPH in Health Behavior & Health Edn., U. Mich.; MD, U. Souhtern Calif., 1989. Cert. Family Medicine. Resident North Colo. Med. Ctr.; fellow San Francisco Dept. Family Practice U. Calif., San Francisco, chief Integrating Medicine and Pub. Health Program, health administr. fellow Mercy Healthcare, Sacramento; chief Medicine and Pub. Health Sect. Calif. Dept. Health Services; pub. health officer, dept. dir. Solano County Health and Social Svcs., Calif., 1999; chief med. officer Partnership HealthPlan of Calif., dir. Calif. Dept. Pub. Health, 2011—. Trains family practice residents on the in-patient medicine svc. Mercy Gen. Hosp., Sacramento; asst. prof. U. Calif., Davis. Recipient Nathan Davis award for Outstanding Govt. Svc. (career pub. servant at the county level), AMA, 2008. Mem.: Solano County Med. Soc. Office: California Department of Public Health 1615 Capitol Ave Sacramento CA 95814-5015 Office Phone: 916-440-7600. *

CHAPPELL, LOUIS TERRY, physician; b. South Haven, Mich., Dec. 23, 1942; BA, DePauw U., 1965; MD, U. Mich., 1969. Med. dir. Celebration Health Assn., 1978—. Mem.: Am. Coll. Advancement in Medicine, Internat. Coll. Integrative Medicine (bd. dirs. 2000—11). Office: Box 248 122 Thurman St Bluffton OH 45817 Office Fax: 419-358-1855. Business E-Mail: terrychappell@healthcelebration.com.

CHAPPELL, RICHARD LEE, biology educator, neuroscientist; b. Buffalo, Mar. 9, 1938; s. G. Howard and Gertrude Lyth (Myers) C.; m. Alice Carol Merckens, Sept. 6, 1968; children: Carol, Dreux. BS in Engring., Princeton U., 1962; PhD, Johns Hopkins U., 1970. Asst. prof. biology Hunter Coll., CUNY, NYC, 1970-74, assoc. prof., 1975-79, prof., 1980—, chmn. dept., 1987-90; exec. officer PhD program in biology Grad. Ctr. CUNY, NYC, 1993—2008, chmn. coun. exec. officers, 2001—08; chair Antarctic Program Task Force, Nat. Coun. BSA, 2008—; adj. sr. scientist Marine Biol. Lab., Woods Hole, Mass., 2010—. Cons. Bell Lab., Murray Hill, N.J., 1982-83, chmn. Physiology and Neuroscience Subprogram CUNY, N.Y.C., 1986-88. Author: Antarctic Scout, 1959; contbr. articles to profl. jours. Chmn. Sci. Devel. Program, Inc., NYC, 1980-2007. Lt. USN, 1962-66. Recipient Antarctic medal U.S. Congress, 1959; Chappell Peak, Antarctica, named in his honor; grantee Nat. Eye Inst., NIH, 1971-2004, NSF, 2006—. Fellow The Explorers Club (bd. dirs. 1972-75); mem. Assn. for Rsch. in Vision and Opthalmology, Am. Polar Soc. (v.p. 1989-97, pres. 1997-2000), IEEE, Marine Biol. Lab. Corp., Sigma Xi. Office: Hunter Coll Dept Biol Scis 695 Park Ave New York NY 10065-5085 Home: 175 East 96th St Apt 26B New York NY 10128-6213 Office Phone: 212-772-5294. Business E-Mail: rchappell@gc.cuny.edu.

CHARABI, SAMIH AHMED, otolaryngologist; b. Cairo, Jan. 25, 1949; s. Ahmed Mohamed and Awatef Mohamed (El Shazly) C.; m. Birgitte Wittenborg Paulsen, Dec. 17, 1990; children: Salem, Salma, Sarah. MD, Copenhagen U., 1983, DMSc, 1997. Physician Nat. Hosp./Rigshospitalet, Copenhagen, 1983-85, 90, Bispebjerg Hosp., Copenhagen, 1986-88, Glostrup (Denmark) U. Hosp., 1987-88, Aalborg (Denmark) U. Hosp., 1989; physician, specialist in ENT/head and neck surgery Gentofte U. Hosp., Hellerup, Denmark, 1991—2002; assoc. prof. Copenhagen U., 2000—02; otolaryngologist ENT Clinic, Denmark, 2002—. Contbr. articles to profl. jours. Named Best Rschr., Scandinavian Soc. Otolaryngology, 1996. Mem. Barany Soc., European Acad. Otology/Neurotology, Coll. Oto-Rhino-

Laryngologicum Amicitiae Sacrum. Avocations: squash, tennis, swimming, chess. Home: Ahlmanns Alle 12 2900 Hellerup Denmark Office: ENT Clinic Gl Kongevej 120 1850 Frederiksberg Denmark E-mail: charabi@dadlnet.dk.

CHARAP, PETER JEFF, internist, educator; MD, NYU, 1984. Diplomate Am. Bd. of Internal Medicine. Fellow cmty. medicine Mt. Sinai Med. Ctr., NY, resident internal medicine; asst. clin. prof. medicine Mt. Sinai Sch. of Medicine. Recipient Patient's Choice award, Compassionate Dr. award; named Recognized Dr., Health-Grades; named one of the Top Doctors, Castle Conolly. Mem.: AMA, Soc. of Gen. Internal Medicine. Office: Mount Sinai Medical Center One Gustave L Levy Place New York NY 10029 Office Phone: 212-241-6500.

CHARASH, BRUCE D., cardiologist, educator; b. NYC, Apr. 8, 1956; BA in Chemistry, Cornell U., 1977, MD, 1981. Lic. NY State, 1982, cert. Am. Bd. Internal Medicine, 1984, Cardiovascular Disease subspecialty 1987. Intern internal medicine Mt. Sinai Med. Ctr., 1982, resident internal medicine, 1982—84; instr. Cornell Med. Sch., 1986—87, asst. prof. medicine, 1987—93; fellow, divsn. cardiology NY Hosp.-Cornell Med. Ctr., 1984—86, asst. attending physician, 1986—91; sr. attending physician Lenox Hill Hosp., 1991—2005, chief cardiac care unit, 1991—2005; clin. assoc. prof. medicine NYU Med. Sch., 1993—2005; vis. assoc. prof. medicine SUNY Health Ctr., Bklyn., 1998—2005; assoc. prof. clinical medicine Columbia U., 2005—; attending physician NY-Presbyn. Hosp. Founder, chmn. Doc to Dock, Inc., Bklyn.; investigator in field. Contbr. to profl. publs., jours., abstracts, and chap. in books; author: Heart Myths, 1991. Daniel and Elaine Sargent Cardiology Fellow, 1985. Fellow: Am. Coll. of Cardiology; mem.: AMA, ACP, Am. Red. Cross-NY Chap. (med. dir. AED program), Alpha Omega Alpha, Phi Kappa Phi, Phi Beta Kappa. Office: 16 E 60th St Ste 330 New York NY 10022 Address: Doc to Dock Inc 300 Douglass St Brooklyn NY 11217 Office Phone: 212-606-0006. Business E-Mail: bdc2104@gmail.com. E-mail: bruce.charash@doctodock.org.

CHARI, SURESH T., gastroenterologist, educator; MD, BJ Med. Coll. U. of Poona, India, 1982. Diplomate Am. Bd. of Internal Medicine-gastroenterology, 2009. Resident internal medicine Univ. of Ariz. Health Sci. Ctr., 1993—96; intern Univ. of Ariz. Med. Ctr., 1994; rsch. fellow Univ. Hosp. of Heidelberg, Mannheim; resident gen. medicine Postgraduate Inst. of Med. Edn. and Rsch., fellow hepatology; fellow gastroentrology G. B. Pant Hosp. Univ. of Delhi; fellow gastroenterology Mayo Clinic, 1997—99, cons. gastroenterology divsn., head pancreas interest group gastroenterology and hepatology divsn. Councilor Am. Pancreatic Assn., 2007, pres., 09; prof. medicine Mayo Med. Sch. Author: (articles) Diagnosis of IgG4-Related Tubulointerstitial Nephritis, 2011, Weight loss precedes cancer-specific symptoms in pancreatic cancer-associated diabetes mellitus, 2011, Clinical profile of autoimmune pancreatitis and its histological subtypes: an international multicenter survey, 2011, and several others. Mem.: Internat. Assn. of Pancreatology (councilor 2008—12). Office: Mayo Clinic Mayo Bldg 9th Fl 200 First St SW Rochester MN 55905 Office Phone: 507-284-2141.

CHARKES, N. DAVID, nuclear medicine physician, educator; b. NYC, Aug. 13, 1931; s. William Evans Charkes and Julia Boginsky; m. Nancy Ellen Amsterdam, Dec. 20, 1953; children: Susan, Evan, Alice. AB, Columbia U., 1952; MD, Washington U., St. Louis, 1955. Cert. Am. Bd. Internal Medicine, Am. Bd. Nuc. Medicine. Intern Mass. Meml. Hosp., Boston, 1955—56; physician Walter Reed Inst. Med. Rsch., Ft. Detrick, Md., 1956—58; resident in medicine Univ. Hosp., Balt., 1958—61, USPHS fellow in endocrinology, 1958—61; dir. nuc. medicine Albert Einstein Med. Ctr., Phila., 1962—66, Temple U. Hosp., Phila., 1966—80, rsch. prof. nuc. medicine, 1980—95, prof. emeritus, 1995—. Contbr. over 75 articles to profl. jours. Capt. US Army, 1956—61. Fogarty Sr. Internat. fellow, NIH, 1976. Mem.: Soc. Nuc. Medicine (pres. NY chpt. 1966, trustee 1970—72, Berson Yalow award NY chpt. 1985), Soc. Indsl. & Applied Math. Achievements include research in bone scanning, thyroidology, mathematical modeling and computer simulation of biomedical data. Avocation: woodworking. Office: Temple Univ Hosp Sect Nuc Medicine Philadelphia PA 19140 Home Phone: 610-642-1719. Office Fax: 215-707-2059. Business E-Mail: david.charkes@temple.edu.

CHARLES, HAL CECIL, lab administrator, educator; b. Jackson, Miss., July 16, 1949; BA, U. Miss., 1971; PhD, U. New Orleans, 1981. Assoc. prof. radiology, dir. Duke Image Analysis Lab., Duke U. Sch. Medicine, 1987—. Fellow: Internat. Soc. Magnetic Resonance Medicine; mem.: AAPM. Office: Ste 301 Hock Plz 2424 Erwin Rd Durham NC 27705 Business E-Mail: cecil.charles@duke.edu.

CHARLES, LUENDA E., public health service officer, researcher; arrived in US, 1981; d. Eric and Princess Charles. BSc in Clin. Lab. Sci., Union Coll., Lincoln, Nebr., 1984; MPH, Emory U., Atlanta, 1993; PhD, U. NC, Chapel Hill, 2000. Clin. lab. scientist out-patient clinic KennMed Shallowford, Marietta, Ga., 1991—95; rsch. epidemiologist Ctr. Disease Control, Morgantown, W.Va., 2003—. Mem.: Internat. Commn. Ocpl. Health, Internat. Epidemiol. Assn., Delta Omega. Avocations: reading, music, piano, travel.

CHARLES, ROBERT S., urologist, educator; married; 3 children. Undergrad., Emory U., Atlanta; MD, Temple U., Phila., 1980. Diplomate Am. Bd. Urology, 1986. Intern Pa. Hosp., Phila., 1981, resident, 1982, Univ. Pa., 1986; on staff Fox Chase Cancer Ctr.; clin. asst. prof. urology dept. Temple Univ.; surgeon-in-chief urology divsn. Abington Meml. Hosp.; urologist Urology Health Specialists Ltd. Liability Co. Named one of the Top Doctors, Phila. Mag., 2010—11. Fellow: ACS; mem.: Pa. Med. Soc., Montgomery County Med. Soc., Phila. Urol. Soc., Am. Assn. of Clin. Urologists, Am. Urol. Assn. Avocation: golf. Office: Abington Memorial Hospital 1200 Old York Rd Abington PA 19001 Office Phone: 215-481-2000.

CHARLOT, JOSEPH LEONCE, JR., preventive medicine physician; b. Bklyn., Oct. 19, 1967; s. Joseph Leonce and Marie Andree Charlot; m. Denise Michelle Johnson, July 11, 1967. BA, Rutgers U., 1986—90; MD, U. Medicine & Dentristry NJ, 1990—95, MPH, 1991—93. Med. Rev. Officer Med. Rev. Officer Certification Coun., Ill. State, 2001, Advanced Cardiac Life Support Am. Heart Assn., Ill. State, 2004, Basic Life Support Am. Heart Assn., Ill. State, 2004, Preventive Medicine Am. Bd. of Preventive Medicine, Ill. State, 2003, Am. Bd. of Preventive Medicine, Ill. State, 2004; Prison Religious Vol. Prison Fellowship, Va. State, 1999. Resident physician U. of Md. Med. Sys., Balt., 1995—97, Trover Clinic, Madisonville, Ky., 1997—98; locum tenens occupl. medicine physician Concentra Med. Centers, Richmond, Va., 1999—2000; resident physician Ft. Wayne Med. Found., Ft. Wayne, Ind., 2000—00; med. dir. Cmty. Occupl. Medicine, Elkhart, Ind., 2001—02; 2004plant occupl. medicine physician Daimler Chrysler Kokomo Transmission Plant, Kokomo, Ind., 2002; med. dir. US Health Works, Branford, Conn., 2004—. Prison religious vol. Prison Fellowship, Richmond, Va., 1999—2000; religious vol. Kokomo Rescue Mission, Kokomo, Ind., 2003—03; physician vol. Kokomo Cmty. Health Initative, 2002—03. Fellow Rsch. Fellowship, Robert Wood Johnson Med. Sch., 1991. Mem.: APHA (assoc.), AMA (assoc.), Am. Coll. of Preventive Medicine (assoc.), Christian Med. and Dental Associations (assoc.). Avocations: basketball, reading, computer programming, bicycling, weightlifting. Office: Naval Health Clinic Occupational Medicine Dept 47149 Base Rd Patuxent River MD 20670 Personal E-mail: jcharlot@md.metrocast.net.

CHARLTON, JOHN KIPP, pediatrician; b. Omaha, Jan. 26, 1937; s. George Paul and Mildred (Kipp) C.; m. Susan S. Young, Aug. 15, 1959 (dec. June, 2003); children: Paul, Cynthia, Daphne, Gregory. AB, Amherst Coll., 1958; MD, Cornell U., 1962. Intern Ohio State U. Hosp., Columbus, 1962-63; resident in pediatrics Children's Hosp., Dallas, 1966-68, chief resident in pediatrics, 1968-69; fellow in nephrology U. Tex. Southwestern Med. Sch., Dallas, 1969-70; pvt. practice medicine specializing in pediatrics, Phoenix, from 1970; chmn. dept. pediatrics Maricopa Med. Ctr., Phoenix, 1971-78, 84-93, pres. med. staff, 1991; med. dir., bd. dirs. Crisis Nursery, Inc., 1977—. Clin. assoc. prof. pediat. U. Ariz. Coll Medicine, asst. dean for student affairs, 2000-2007; dir. student coun, 2007-. Author articles and book revs. in field, author Reach Out & Real Arizona Honaree, 2010. Pres. Maricopa County Child Abuse Coun., 1977-81; bd. dirs. Florence Crittenton Svcs., 1980-83, Ariz. Children's Found., 1987-91; mem. Gov.'s Coun. on Children, Youth and Families, 1984-86. Officer M.C., USAF, 1963-65. Recipient Hon. Kachina award for volunteerism, 1980, Jefferson award for volunteerism, 1980, Horace Steel Child Advocacy award, 1993, Reach out Read, Ariz., 2010, Cmty. Quarterback award, 2003; named Clin. Sci. Educator of Yr., U. Ariz., 1997, 99, 2000, 2001, Best Doctor in Am., 1996-2010, MISS Found. Phoenix award, 2006; named a Health Care Hero Phoenix Bus. Jour., 2007, Lifetime Achievement award, Phoenix Bus. Jours., 2011. Mem. Am. Acad. Pediatrics, Ariz. Pediatric Soc., Maricopa County Pediatric Soc. (past pres.). Office: Maricopa Med Ctr 2601 E Roosevelt St Phoenix AZ 85008-4973 Home: 4040 N 58th St Phoenix AZ 85018 Office Phone: 602-344-5404. Business E-Mail: kipp_charlton@dmgaz.org.

CHARLTON, RANDAL, former medical products executive; Former pres., CEO University Genetics Co.; former pres. Am. diagnostic sls. Internat. Embryos; former chmn. Agrogene Plant Sciences; co-founder, CEO Asterand, 2000—07; entrepreneur in residence, spl. asst. to pres. econ. devel. Wayne State U., 2007—. Former consultant World Bank; bd. dirs. Genetics Squared, 2004—; chmn. of bd. MichBio, 2004—. Recipient Entrepreneur of the Yr. award, Mich. Venture Capital Assn., 2005, TechTown, 2005. Office: Wayne State U 5700 Cass Ave Detroit MI 48202

CHARNEY, DENNIS S., dean, psychiatrist, educator; b. NYC, Mar. 31, 1951; s. Joseph Louis and Charlotte Marilyn (Landman) C.; m. Andrea Robin Orson, May 28, 1972; children: Allison, Meredith, Lauren, Alexander, Danielle. BA, Rutgers U., 1973; MD, Pa. State U., 1977. Diplomate American Bd. Psychiatry and Neurology, 1988. Chief resident Clin. Neuroscience Res. Unit, New Haven, 1980-81, chief, 1983-88; assoc. chief biol. sci. Conn. mental Health Ctr., New Haven, 1981-82; asst. prof. Yale U. Sch. Medicine, New Haven, 1981-85, assoc. prof., 1985—2000; dir. Affective Disorders Clinic, New Haven, 1981-83; chief psychiatry svc. West Haven (Conn.) VA Med. Ctr., 1988—2000; chief, mood & anxiety disorders rsch. prog. NIMH, Bethesda, Md., 2000—04, chief, experimental therapeutics & pathophysiology, 2000—04; prof. Howard U., Washington, 2002—; dean rsch. Mt. Sinai Sch. Medicine, NYC, 2004—05, prof. psychiatry, neuroscience & pharmacology & biol. chemistry, 2004—, dean academic and sci. affairs, 2005—07, dean, 2007—08, Anne and Joel Ehrenkrantz dean, 2008—; sr. v.p. health svcs. Mt. Sinai Med. Ctr., NYC, 2005—07, exec. v.p. academic affairs, 2008—. Mem. exec. com. Conn. Mental Health Ctr., 1984-88, Yale Clin. Rsch. Ctr.; residency selection com. Yale U. Dept. Psychiatry, 1984-88; cons. in field; bd. dirs. Nat. Space Biomedical Rsch. Inst.; mem. adv. bd. OCD Found, Inc., 1988; mem. scientific adv. bd. Neurogen, Inc., 1988, Nat. Ed. Alliance for Borderline Personality Disorder, Anxiety Disorders Assn. Am. Editor-in-chief (jour.) Biological Psychiatry; mem. editorial bd. Jour. Affective Disorders, Jour. Anxiety Disorders; rev. numerous profl. jours. including Jour. Am. Med. Assn., Am. Jour. Psychiatry, Jour. Clin. Psychiatry; contbr. articles to profl. jours.; author: Molecular Neurobiology for the Clinician, 2003; co-author: The Peace of Mind Prescription, 2004; co-editor: Pediat. Psychopharmacology: Principles & Practice, 2003, Neurobiology of Mental Illness, 2nd ed., 2004. Mem. Am. Assn. for Advancement Sci., Am. Coll. Neuropsychopharmacology, Nat. Inst. Mental Health (mem. small grant rev. bd.), Am. Coll. Neuropsychopharmacology, Inst. Medicine, Soc. for Neuroscience, Am. Psychiatric Assn., Soc. Biol. Psychiatry, Conn. Psychiatry Soc. Democrat. Jewish. Office: Mt Sinai Sch Medicine Office of Dean 1 Gustave L Levy Pl New York NY 10029 Office Phone: 212-241-5674. E-mail: dennis.charney@mssm.edu. *

CHARNEY, NATALIE J., behavioral health services professional, researcher, educator, clinician, administrator; d. Frances E. and Leon A. Seidman; m. David Charney (dec.); 1 child, Melissa D Jonassen. BA in Psychology cum laude, U. Pa., 1988, MA in Social Gerontology, 1991, MSEd in Counseling Psychology, 1991; PhD in Health Care Adminstrn., Suffield U., 2005. Bd. cert. med. psychotherapist/psychodiagnostician, cert. cognitive behavioral therapist, diplomate in co-occurring disorders profl., internat. cert. co-occurring disorders profl.; cert. in problem gambling. Rsch. and adminstrv. assoc./acting dir. psychoendocrinology in psychiatry Hosp. U. Pa., Phila., 1972—82; pvt. practice Phila., 1991—; asst. adminstr. Phila. Mental Health Clinic, Phila., 1983—85; adminstr. sect. geriatric psychiatry Hosp. U. Pa., Phila., 1985—93; dir. family-based mental health svcs. Dr. Warren E. Smith CMH/MR/SA Ctrs., Phila., 1993—95, dir. mental health svcs. divsn., 1995—96; mgr. mental health svcs. divsn., vocat. rehab. programs Phila. OIC, 1998; dir. admissions, adult outpatient behavioral health svcs. and rsch. Cmty. Coun. for MH/MR, Inc., Phila., 1998—2004; clin. assoc. in psychiatry U. Pa. Med. Sch., Phila., 1992—, staff therapist Ctr. for Cognitive Therapy, 1992—; project dir. Sobriety Through Out Patient Inc., Phila., 2004—; exec. dir. Treatment and Recovery Partnership, Phila., 2006—. Mem. Am. Bd. Psychotherapists and Psychodiagnosticians; presenter in field. Mem. editl. bd. The Med. Psychotherapist; contbr. articles to profl. jours. Mem. Phila. Office of Addictions Svcs. Adv. Bd., Dept. Behavioral Health and Intellectual Disability Svcs., City of Phila., 2009—. Recipient Cert. of Gratitude, Sled Toys for Tots, 1994. Mem.: APA (assoc.), Nat. Assn. Cognitive-Behavioral Therapists, Gerontol. Soc. Am. (rsch. edn. and practice com., pvt. sector task force 1989—92), Phila. Coalition of Cmty. Care Providers (mental health dirs. com., children's mental health com.), Pa. Cmty. Providers Assn. (family-home based subcom., mental health com. 1993—96). Office: Med Tower 255 S 17th St Ste 1907 Philadelphia PA 19103 Office Phone: 215-725-6080. Personal E-mail: ncharney@verizon.net.

CHARROW, JOEL, pediatrician, geneticist, educator, director; b. NYC, May 24, 1951; s. Saul David and Doris Elaine (Yates) C.; m. Martha K. McClintock, Oct. 23, 1982; children: Benjamin Whitmore, Julia Rachel. BS in Chemistry and Psychology, Antioch Coll., 1972; MD, Mt. Sinai Sch. Medicine, 1976. Diplomate Nat. Bd. Med. Examiners, Am. Bd. Pediatrics; diplomate in clin. genetics and biocehem. genetics. Am. Bd. Med. Genetics. Pediatric intern Children's Meml. Hosp./Northwestern U. Med. Sch., Chgo., 1976-77, resident in pediatrics, 1977-79, fellow in clin. and biochem. genetics, 1979-81; attending physician Children's Meml. Hosp., Chgo., 1981; from asst. prof. to assoc. prof. pediatrics Northwestern U. Med. Ctr., Chgo., 1981-94, prof. pediatrics, 2002—; dir. Genetics Lab., head sect. clin. genetics Children's Meml. Hosp., Chgo., 1991—, head, divsn. genetics, birth defects, metabolism, 2006—. Mem. adv. bd. Fabry Disease Registry, 2001—. Contbr. chpts. to books, more than 60 articles to profl. jours. Regional coord. Internat. Collaborative Gaucher Group, 1994—; mem. health profl. adv. com. March of Dimes, Chgo., 1986-2004; mem. sci. adv. com. Nat. Tay-Sachs and Allied Diseases Assn., 1984—; mem. State of Ill. Genetic and Metabolic Diseases Adv. Com., 1989-97, 2007-, chmn, 2009; mem. Genetics Task Force of Ill., 1982—, v.p., 1990-91, pres., 1991-93. Recipient Bela Schick Pediatric Soc. award Mt. Sinai Sch. Medicine, 1976. Fellow Am. Coll. Med. Genetics (founding), Am. Acad. Pediatrics; mem. Midwest Soc. for Pediatric Rsch., Soc. for Inherited Metabolic Disorders, Bone Dysplasia Soc., Internat. Neurofibromatosis Assn., Alpha Omega Alpha. Office: Children's Meml Hosp Sect Clin Genetics 2300 N Childrens Plz Chicago IL 60614-3394 Office Phone: 773-880-4462.

CHARTCHAI, RATTANAMAHATTANA, surgeon; married; 3 children. Grad. in Medicine, Mahidol U., bangkok Thailand. Bd. cert. surgeon in plastic surgery Thai Bd. of Plastic Surgery Med. Coun. Thailand, diplomate Thai Bd. of Plastic Surgery, Thai Bd. of Gen. Surgery. Fellowship Tokyo Univ., Japan, Emory Univ. Hosp., Atlanta, Georgia; lead plastic surgeon Samitivej Hosp. Sukhumvit; surgeon DRCHARTCHAI Plastic Surgery, Thailand. Lectr. in cosmetic surgery and microsurgery Prince of Songkhla Univ. Mem.: Soc. of Plastic and Reconstructive Surgeons Thailand, Med. Coun. Thailand, Nat. Acad. of Medicine, Soc. Aesthetic Plastic Surgeons Thailand, Soc. Plastic and Reconstructive Surgeons Thailand, Royal Coll. Surgeons Thailand. *

CHARTOUMPEKIS, DIONYSIOS, physician; b. Chios, Greece, Nov. 11, 1981; MD, U. Patras, 2005, PhD, 2010. Postdoc. rschr. U. Patras, 2010—11. Recipient award, IDOF, 2010. Mem.: Patras Med. Assn. Office: Asklipiou St Patras Achaia 26504 Greece E-mail: dchartoumpekis@yahoo.com.

CHARYTAN, CHAIM, nephrologist; b. Poland, May 25, 1938; MD, Albert Einstein, 1964. Chief, renal divsn. NY Hosp. Med. Ctr. Queens, 1971—. Fellow: ACP; mem.: Am. Soc. Nephrology, Nat. Kidney Found., Renal Physicians Assn. Avocations: sailing, woodworking. Office: 56-45 Main St Flushing NY 11355 Business E-Mail: charytan@pol.net.

CHASE, MICHAEL DAVID, physician; b. Jan. 13, 1954; MD, U. Kans. Sch. Medicine, 1979. Diplomate Am. Bd. Internal Medicine, 1983. Resident internal medicine U. Kans. Med. Ctr.; joined Colo. Permanente Med. Group, subs. Kaiser Permanente, Denver, 1986, regional dept. chief Internal Medicine, 1999—2001, asst. to assoc. med. dir. quality, 2001—. Assoc. clin. prof. U. Colo. Health Scis. Ctr., 2002—. Office: Colorado Permanente Medical Group 10350 E Dakota Ave Denver CO 80247 Office Phone: 303-338-3362. Business E-Mail: michael.d.chase@kp.org. *

CHASE, ROBERT ARTHUR, surgeon, educator; b. Keene, NH, Jan. 6, 1923; s. Albert Henry and Georgia Beulah (Bump) Chase; m. Ann Crosby Parker, Feb. 3, 1946; children: Deborah Lee, Nancy Jo, Robert N. BS cum laude, U. N.H., 1945, DSc (hon.), 1993; MD, Yale, 1947. Diplomate Am. Bd. Surgery, Am. Bd. Plastic Surgery. Intern New Haven Hosp., 1947—48, asst. resident, 1949—50, sr. resident surgery, 1952—53, chief resident surgeon, 1953—54; mem. faculty Yale Sch. Medicine, 1948—54, 1959—62, asst. prof. surgery, 1959—62; mem. faculty U. Pitts., 1957—59, resident plastic surgeon, also teaching fellow, 1957—59; attending surgeon VA Hosp., W. Haven, Conn., 1959—62, Grace New Haven Community Hosp., 1959—63; prof., chmn. dept. surgery Stanford Sch. Medicine, 1963—74, Emile Holman prof. surgery, 1972—; prof. surgery U. Pa., 1974—77; attending surgeon Pa. Hosp., Hosp. U. Pa., Grad. Hosp., Phila., 1974—77; pres., dir. Nat. Bd. Med. Examiners, Phila., 1974—77; prof. anatomy Stanford (Calif.) U., 1977—. Cons. plastic surgery Christian Med. Coll. and Hosp., Vellore, India, 1962; cons. to surgeon gen. USAF, 1970—; Benjamin K. Rank prof. Australasian Coll. Surgeons, 1974. Author: Atlas of Hand Surgey; editor: Videosurgery, 1974—; mem. editl. bd.: Med. Alert Communication, —; contbr. articles to profl. jours. Mem. bd. overseers Dartmouth Med. Sch., 1998-; mem. found. bd. U. N.H., 1998-. Maj. M.C. AUS, 1949—57. Recipient Francis Gilman Blake award, Yale Sch. Medicine, 1962, Henry J. Kaiser award, Stanford U. Sch. Medicine, 1978, 1979, 1984, 1986, 1990, 1993, Calif. Golden Apple award, 1991, Albion William Hewlett award, 1992, Pettee award, U. N.H., 1998; named an Hand Ctr. in his name, Stanford U., 2004. Fellow: ACS, Australasian Coll. Surgeons (hon.); mem.: AMA, NAS, Halsted Soc., Am. Soc. Most Venerable Order Hosp., St. John of Jerusalem, Inst. Medicine (exec. com. 1976, coun. 1986—), Soc. Univ. Surgeons, Found. Am. Soc. Plastic and Reconstructive Surgery (dir.), Am. Cancer Soc. (clin. fellowship com.), James IV Assn. Surgeons, Pacific Coast Surg. Soc., Western Surg. Assn., Soc. Clin. Surgery, Plastic Surgery Rsch. Coun., Am. Assn. Surgery Trauma, Am. Soc. Cleft

Palate Rehab., Am. Soc. Surgery Hand (pres.), Conn. Med. Soc., Santa Clara County Med. Soc., Am. Surg. Assn., San Francisco Surg. Soc., Calif. Acad. Medicine (pres.), Am. Soc. Clin. Anatomists (hon.; pres.), South African Soc. Plastic and Reconstructive Surgery (hon.), South African Soc. Surgery Hand (hon.), Am. Assn. Plastic Surgery (hon.), Am. Assn. Clin. Anatomists (hon.; pres.), Am. Assn. Plastic Surgeons (hon.), Sigma Xi, Phi Beta Kappa. Home: 69 Pearce Mitchell Pl Stanford CA 94305 Office: Stanford U Div Anatomy 269 Campus Dr Stanford CA 94305-5102 Home Phone: 650-473-9049; Office Phone: 650-725-6618. E-mail: rchase6880@aol.com.

CHASE, SANDRA LEE, clinical pharmacist, consultant; b. Oak Park, Ill., July 31, 1959; d. William Warren and Charlene Lois (Johnson) Chase; children: Kyle Thaddeus Bloch, Matthew William Bloch. Student, Mich. State U., 1977-80; BS in Pharmacy, U. Mich., 1983, PharmD, 1984. Lic. pharmacist Mich.; cert. leader arthritis found. YMCA Aquatic Program. Rsch. asst. U. Mich., Ann Arbor, 1980-81; pharmacy intern Three Rivers (Mich.) Hosp., 1981, Cmty. Pharmacy, Ann Arbor, 1980-83; pharmacy intern, grad. intern St. Francis Hosp., Wilmington, Del., 1982-83; resident in hosp. pharmacy Thomas Jefferson U. Hosp., Phila., 1984-85, clin. pharmacist in cardiopulmonary medicine, 1985-89; sr. med. info. coord. ICI Pharms. Group, Wilmington, Del., 1989-92; clin. pharmacist Thomas Jefferson U. Hosp., Phila., 1989-93, clin. pharmacist drug use policy and clin. svcs., 1993-98; clin. pharmacy specialist Spectrum Health, Grand Rapids, Mich., 1999—2008; cardiopulmonary clin. specialist & pres. SL Chase Inc., 2007—10; med. sci. liaison Otsuka Pharms. America, 2010—. Adj. asst. prof. clin. pharmacy Temple U. Coll. Pharmacy, 1990—98, Ferris State U. Coll. Pharmacy, 1999—; clin. instr. in pharmacy practice Phila. Coll. Pharmacy and Sci., 1985—87, clin. asst. prof., 1987—88, clin. assoc. prof., 1988—98; instr. clin. care cardiopulmonary medicine in nursing Episcopal Hosp., Phila., 1986—88, Thomas Jefferson U. Hosp., Phila., 1985—91, Our Lady of Lourdes Med. Ctr., Camden, NJ, 1988—91; coord., prof. pharmacology and drug therapeutic for advanced nursing practice course Sch. Nursing Ctr. Profl. Devel., U. Pa., Phila., 1994—2001; mem. Pa. Osteoporosis Soc. Bd., 1996—98; presenter in field; co-chair Mich. Cardiovascular Alliance, 2008—. Mem. editl. bd.: RN, referee:; contbg. editor; mem. editl. bd.: Med. Econs., referee: AHFS Drug Info., Am. Druggist, Am. Jour. Hosp. Pharmacy, Nursing 96 Drug Handbook, Nursing 97 Drug Handbook, Pharmacotherapy, Annals of Pharmacotherapy, U. Hosp. Consortium Monographs; contbr. articles to profl. jours. Mem. adv. bd. Nursing Mothers Network; cert. leader aquatic program Arthritis Found. YMCA, 2000—; chmn. Coll. Pharmacy Alumni Soc., 2000—04; mem. women's heart advantage steering com. Spectrum Health, 2003—05; mem. alumni bd. govs. U. Mich. Coll. Pharmacy, 1991—97, 1998—2004, chair bd. govs., 2000—03; mem. Heartbeat Gala com. Am. Heart Assn., 2004—07; mem. State of Mich. Task Force for Cardiovasc. Health, 2002—03; bd. dirs. U. Mich Alumni Soc., 2004—; mem. bd. Mich. Pharmacy Found., 2007—09; bd. dirs. Corey Lake Assn., 2003—07. Recipient Alumni Svc. award, U. Mich. Coll. Pharmacy, 2006. Fellow: Mich. Pharmacists Assn. (mem. exec. bd. 2002—08, pres.elect 2005, pres. 2006, chair bd. 2007—08, Bowl of Hygeia 2011); mem.: Mich. PAC (bd. mem. 2009—), Mich. Pharm. Found. (mem. exec. bd. 2006—09), Pulmonary Hypertension Assn., Am. Heart Assn., Aerobics and Fitness Assn. Am., Western Mich. Soc. Health-Sys. Pharmacists (bd. dirs. 1998—2000), Mich. Soc. Health Sys. Pharmacists (chair edn. com. 2000—, Pharmacist of Yr. 2003, Pres. award for advocacy 2007), Del. Pharm. Soc. (conv. com. 1990—94, ACPE com. 1990—94), Am. Soc. Health Sys. Pharmacists, Am. Coll. Clin. Pharmacy, U. Mich. Alumni Assn. (bd. dirs. 2004—), Rho Chi. Republican. Lutheran. Avocations: aerobics, waterskiing, cross country skiing, gardening. Business E-Mail: schase731@aol.com.

CHASE, THOMAS NEWELL, neurologist, researcher, educator, entrepreneur; b. Westfield, NJ, May 23, 1932; s. Newell Adams and Gudrun Margarethe (Eskesen) C.; 1 child, Thomas Newell. BS, MIT, 1954; postgrad., Columbia U., 1957-58; MD, Yale U., 1962; postgrad., Harvard U., 1963-66. Engr. Singer Mfg. Co., Bridgeport, Conn., 1954-55; technician Columbia U. Coll. Phys. and Surgs., 1957-58; intern in internal medicine Yale-New Haven Med. Center, 1962-63; asst. resident in neurology Mass. Gen. Hosp., Boston, 1963-64, resident, 1965-66; fellow in neuropathology Harvard U. Med. Sch., 1964-65; guest worker NIMH, Bethesda, Md., 1966-68, chief unit on neurology, 1968-70, chief sect. exptl. therapeutics, 1970-74; chief lab. of neuropharmacology Nat. Inst. Neurol. and Communicative Disorders and Stroke, Bethesda, 1974-76, dir. intramural research, 1974-83, chief pharmacology sect., 1976—2005, chief exptl. therapeutics br., 1983—2005; CEO Hamilton Pharms., Inc., 2005—07, Chase Pharms. Corp., 2007—. Assoc. editor Jour. Psychiatry and Neurosci.; mem. editl. bd. Progress in Neuro-Psychopharmacology, Drug Devel. Rsch., Parkinsonian and Related Disorders, Contemporary Neurology, Neurotoxicology Rsch., Neurodegenerative Diseases; contbr. articles to med. jours. Served with Signal Corps U.S. Army, 1955-57. Recipient Winternitz prize in pathology, 1960, Ramsay prize for clin. medicine, 1961, diploma of recognition of merit for humanitarian svcs. Govt. of Bolivia, 1974, USPHS Meritorious Svc. medal, 1978, 96, USPHS Outstanding Svc. medal, 1991, Springer prize for Parkinson's disease rsch., 1994; summer fellow, 1960; USPHS summer fellow, 1961; Nat. Inst. Neurol. Diseases and Blindness spl. fellow, 1966-68. Fellow Am. Coll. Neuro-Psychopharmacology; mem. Am. Neurol. Assn., Am. Acad. Neurology, Am. Soc. Exptl. Neurotherapeutics (pres. 1997-2001), Soc. Neurosci., delegate US Pharmacopeia, Internat. Brain Rsch. Orgn., World Fedn. Neurology, Movement Disorder Soc. Office: Chase Pharm Corp Ste 520 1825 K St NW Washington DC 20006 Office Phone: 202-378-8564. Business E-Mail: tchase@chasepharmaceuticals.com.

CHASE, TIMOTHY, dentist; Grad., Boston U. Gen. practice residency Columbia Presbyterian Hosp., Veterans Adminstrn. Hosp.; clin. instr. NYU Dental Sch.; faculty mentor Spear Advanced Dental Edn. Ctr., Scottsdale, Ariz. Mem.: Acad. of Gen. Dentistry, Am. Acad. of Cosmetic Dentists, Am. Dental Soc. Office: SmilesNY Cosmetic & Implant Dentistry Lobby F 220 East 63rd St New York NY 10065 Office Phone: 888-757-7645. Office Fax: 212-421-0410. Business E-Mail: drchase@smilesny.com.

CHASSIN, ERIC, orthopedist; MD, Rush Med. Coll. Cert. Am. Bd. Orthopaedic Surgery Examiners. Staff physician Hinsdale Hosp., Good Samaritan Hosp., Hinsdale Surg. Ctr., Salt Creek Surgery Ctr.; ptnr. Hinsdale Orthopaedic Assoc. Intern Rush Presbyterian-St. Luke's Med. Ctr., resident, fell., total joint replacement. Mem.: Am. Acad. Orthopaedic Surgeons, AMA. Office: Hinsdale Orthopaedic Assoc 550 W Ogden Ave Hinsdale IL 60521

CHATARD, PETER RALPH NOEL, JR., retired plastic surgeon; b. New Orleans, June 25, 1936; s. Peter Ralph Sr. and Alberta Chatard; m. Patricia Myrl White, Jan. 31, 1963; children: Andrea Michelle, Faedra Noelle, Tahra Deonne. BS in Biology, Morehouse Coll., 1956; MD, U. Rochester, 1960. Diplomate Am. Bd. Plastic Surgery, Am. Bd. Otolaryngology. Intern Colo. Gen. Hosp., 1960-61; asst. resident in gen. surgery Highland Gen. Hosp., Rochester, NY, 1963-64; resident in otolaryngology Strong Meml. Hosp., Rochester, 1964-67; resident in plastic and reconstructive surgery U. Fla., 1980-82; staff otolaryngologist Group Health Corp. of Puget Sound, Seattle, 1967-68; practice medicine specializing in otolaryngology Seattle, 1968-80; practice medicine specializing in plastic surgery, 1982—; clin. asst. prof. otolaryngology, head and neck surgery U. Wash., Seattle, 1975—. Plastic surgery cons. western sec. Maxillofacial Rev. Bd. State of Wash., 1982-90, cons. Conservation of Hearing Program, 1968-80; trustee Physicians and Dentist Credit Bur., 1974-80, 84-87, pres. 1976-77, 84-85; active staff mem. Northwest Hosp., Seattle; courtesy staff Swedish Hosp., Overlake Hosp., Bellevue, Stevens Meml. Hosp., Edmond, Wash., Seattle, others. Capt. USAF, 1961-63. Fellow ACS, Am. Rhinologic Soc., Seattle Surg. Soc., Am. Acad. Facial Plastic and Reconstructive Surgery, Am. Acad. Otolaryngology-Head and Neck Surgery, Northwest Acad. Otolaryngology and Head and Neck Surgery, Soc. for Ear, Nose and Throat Advances in Children, Pacific Oto-Ophthalmological Soc.; mem. Am. Soc. Plastic Surgery, Am. Soc. for Aesthetic Plastic Surgery, Inc., Lipoplasty Soc. N. Am., Wash. Soc. Plastic Surgeons, Nat. Med. Assn., King County Med. Soc., Wash. State Med. Assn., N.W. Soc. of Plastic Surgeons. Avocations: photography, cynology, microcomputing, architecture. Home: 13211 Frazier Pl NW Seattle WA 98177-4132 Office: Peter Chatard 5002 Flagstone Dr Sarasota FL 34238-4439 Personal E-mail: chatard@aol.com. *

CHATCHAWAN, URAIWAN, medical educator; b. Loei, Thailand, Oct. 15, 1967; PhD, Khon Kaen U., 2005. Asst. prof., divsn. phys. therapy, faculty assoc. med. scis. Khon Kaen U., 1990—. Mem.: Phys. Therapy Assn. Thailand. Office: Faculty Assoc Medical Scis Maung Khon Kaen 40002 Thailand Office Fax: 006643202085. Business E-Mail: uraiwon@kku.ac.th.

CHATELIER, PAUL RICHARD, aviation psychologist; s. Paul and Mary Chatelier; m. Mary Lu Moss; children: Michael, Suzanne. BS in Biology, Chemistry, Psychology, U. Fla., 1960; MA in Psychology, U. Miss., 1962; postgrad., U. N.Mex., 1967-69. Joined USN, 1962, advanced through grades to capt., 1986; sr. v.p. strategic planning Perceptronics, Inc., Washington, 1986—93; with Office Sci. and Tech. Policy Exec. Office of Pres. U.S., Washington, 1993—96; dir. for edn. tech. edn. activity Dept. Def., Washington, 1996—. U.S. rep. on human factors NATO, Brussels, 1978—86; mem. task force tng. and wargaming Def. Sci. Bd., 1986—88, task force edn. and tng., 1999, U.S. rep. on tng. Tech. Coop. Panel, Washington, 1986—87; mem. indsl. adv. com. U. Ctrl. Fla. Inst. for Simulation and Tng.; edn. and tng. cons. Office Sci. and Tech. White Ho., 1993—96; workshop dir. internat. tng. and human factors; del. at large human factors and medicine panel NATO, 1999; dep. dir. Advanced Distributed Learning Co Lab., Alexandria, Va., 1999—2001; cons. Potomac Inst. for Policy Studies, 2002—, Naval Postgrad., 2009—. Co-author: (book) Psychology of Reality, 1985; editor: Manprint & System Integ, 1988, International Human Factors, 1991, Advanced Technology for Training Design, NATO, 1993, Opening the Classroom Doors...Distance Learning, 1995, Virtual Reality Trainings Future?, 1997. Career advisor Fairfax County Pub. Sch., 1982—88. Mem.: Nat. Security Indsl. Assn. (chmn. manpower pers. tng. 1986—89), Va. Human Factors Soc. (pres. 1982—83), Nat. Human Factors Soc. (mem. exec. coun. 1982—85). Avocations: tennis, community activities. Home: 8021 W Point Dr Springfield VA 22153-3023 Personal E-mail: pchat@mindspring.com.

CHATHA, DEEP SINGH, radiologist; b. London, Oct. 30, 1970; BSc, U. Toronto, MSc, 1994, MD, 1999. Diagnostic radiologist CML Healthcare, 2006—. Cons. radiologist and site quality control CML Healthcare, 2006—11; jour. reviewer Clin. Orthopedics and Related Rsch., 2008—11, Skeletal Radiology, 2010—11. Recipient Resident Rsch. award, RSNA, 2002; named Tchr. of Yr., McGill U. Dept. Radiology, 2006. Fellow: Royal Coll. Physicians and Surgeons Can.; mem.: BC Radiology Assn., Am. Roentgen Ray Soc., Can. Assn. Radiologists, Radiologic Soc. N.Am. Avocations: hiking, camping, running, bicycling. Office: 790 Bay St Ste 418 Toronto ON Canada M5G 1N8 Personal E-mail: dchatha@hotmail.com.

CHATOOR-KOCH, IRENE, child psychiatrist; b. Kassel, Hessen, Germany, Nov. 10, 1937; came to U.S., 1969; d.Hugo and Maria Koch; m. Ramcoomair Chatoor, Mar. 18, 1968. MD, Ruperto Carola U., Heidelberg, Fed. Republic of Germany, 1965. Diplomate Am. Bd. Pediatrics, Am. Bd. Psychiatry and Neurology in Psychiatry, Am. Bd. Psychiatry and Neurology in Child Psychiatry. Intern City Hosps. Kassel and Amberg, Fed. Republic of Germany, 1965-67; resident pediatrics City Hosp. Amberg, Fed. Republic of Germany, 1967-68; intern Providence Hosp., Washington, 1969-70; resident pediatrics Children's Hosp., Washington, 1970-72; resident adult psychiatry George Washington U. Med. Ctr., Washington, 1972-74; fellow child psychiatry Children's Hosp., Washington, 1974-76; part-time pvt. practice College Park, Md., 1976-86; part-time faculty Children's Hosp. Nat. Med. Ctr., Washington, 1978-86, full time faculty, 1986—; assoc. prof. psychiatry and child health and devel. George Washington U. Med. Sch., Washington, 1985-94, prof. psychiatry & behavioral scis. & pediat., 1994—; vice chair dept. psychiatry Children's Nat. Med. Ctr., Washington, 1996—. Fellow Am. Acad. Child and Adolescent Psychiatry, Am. Psychiat. Assn; World Assn. Infant Mental Health, Eating Disorders Rsch. Soc. Office: Children's Nat Med Ctr 111 Michigan Ave NW Washington DC 20010-2916

CHATRATH, HEMANT, medical educator; b. New Delhi, July 12, 1978; MD, U. Delhi, 2002. Asst. prof., clin. medicine Ind. U. Health Physicians, 2009—. Office: 550 University Blvd Indianapolis IN 46202 Personal E-mail: hemantchatrath@yahoo.com.

CHATT-ELLIS, ALLEN BARRETT, psychologist, neuroscientist; b. Phoenix, July 17, 1949; s. Arthur Beecher Ellis and Helen (Scheidt) Chatt; m. Gail Nancy Anguish, Aug. 21, 1971. BS in Psychology with honors, SUNY, Buffalo, 1971; MS in Psychology, Fla. State U., 1974, PhD in Psychology and Neuroscience, 1978. Rsch. asst. Fla. State U., Tallahassee, 1971-76; predoctoral fellow in neuroanatomy U. Tex. Med. Br., Galveston, 1977; postdoctoral fellow in neurology sch. medicine Yale U., New Haven, 1978-80, rsch. asst. prof. neurology Sch. Medicine, 1981-87, rsch. assoc. prof., 1988—91, retirement scholars chair, 1991; rsch. psychologist VA Med. Ctr., West Haven, Conn., 1978-84, sr. rsch. psychologist, 1985-90, sr. rsch. psychologist disability retirement pension, 1991—; founder, exec. dir., consulting psychologist Phoenix Fund for Neurologically Challenged, New Haven, Tallahassee, 1991—. Grant reviewer NSF, 1982—, NIH, 1982—, VA, 1982—; vis. prof. neuroscience Beijing Normal U., 1987, U. Glasgow, 1994—95; neuroscience reviewer Am. Psychol. Soc. Convs., 1991—97; psychol. cons., case mgr. neurologically impaired; pvt. funding neurol. rsch.; courtesy prof. movement scis. Fla. State U., 1999—2002, 2007—; courtesy eminent scholar, 2003—07. Contbr. chapters to books, articles to profl. jours.; mem. editl. rev. bd. Brain Rsch., 1983—86, Exptl. Neurology, 1982—86, Exptl. Brain Rsch., 1984—88, Quar. Jour. Exptl. Physiology, 1986. Sponsor Bobby Bowden Classic/Fellowship Christian Athletes golf tournament, 1992—2004, Bill Campbell Challenge/Children's Miracle Network golf tournament, 1996—99; mem. devel. bd. Sands Fund Excellence Coll. Human Scis., Fla. State U., 1999—; bd. dirs. Wal-Mart/Children's Miracle Network, No. Fla., 1996—99, Jennifer Harrison Fund, 1995—; judge Sam Walton Cmty. Leadership Scholarship Program, 1998—99, Allen Barrett and Gail Chatt-Ellis Fellowship Series in Neurosci. Fla. State U., 2003—; sponsor Jennifer Harrison Meml. Golf Tournament, 1991—2000, Freedom Scholarship Batavia HS Class 1965, 1992—; underwriter Camp Sunshine/ Jennifer Harrison Learning Ctr., 1992—; sponsor Goodspeed Opera Ho., 1995—, Fla. State U. Seminole Classic, 1998—2000, Boy's Town Invitational N. Fla., 1998—2000, Phoenix Fund Scholarship Applied Biomedical Undergraduate Study, 1999—; adopted US Army Vet. of Iraq Family Wounded Warriors Project, 2004—; mem. Rep. Senatorial Inner Cir., Washington, 1985, Eisenhower Commn., 1995; life mem. Rep. Nat. Com., 1993—; mem. adv. bd. Ellingsworth Press, 1998—. Recipient Most Sr. Benefactor award, Children's Miracle Network, 1996—99, Gold Miracle Maker award, 1998, Platinum Miracle Maker award, 1999; Regents scholar, NY State, 1965—69, VoReHab scholar, 1965—71, Nat. Merit Scholar commendation, 1965, Rsch. grantee, VA, 1978—91, NIH, 1982—87. Mem.: AAAS, Soc. Pain Practice Mgmt., Am. Epilepsy Soc., Soc. Neuroscience, Epilepsy Found. Am., Am. Psychol. Soc., Yale Neurology Alumni Assn. (charter), Fla. State U. Found.'s Doak S. Campbell Soc. (ann. cir. leader). Republican. Achievements include development of neurosurgical procedure increasing the effectiveness of stellate ganglion blocks for the treatment of relfex sympathetic dystrophy in humans; discovery of differential neuronal circuits involved in focal and secondarily generalized seizure activity in neocortical model of epilepsy; brain cells that become abnormal initially in focal and secondarily generalized seizure activity; mid brain neuronal circuits modulating pain; thermal evoked potential in humans and the localization of cortical cells responsive to pain. Home: 699 Goose Ln PO Box 1449 Guilford CT 06437-0549 also: 2349 Golden Eagle Dr E Tallahassee FL 32312-4008 Personal E-mail: abcephoenix@aol.com.

CHATTERJEE, DEBABRATA, retired surgeon; b. Chandernagore, India, Dec. 1, 1937; s. Debendranath and Nandarani (Mukherjee) C.; m. Adele Patricia Powell, Sept. 17, 1971 (dec. Mar. 1999); children: Crispin Dara, Justin Sanjay. MB BS, Calcutta U., India, 1960; ChM, Liverpool U., Eng., 1970. House surgeon medicine, surgery, gynae, ortho, urology N.R.S. Med. Coll. Hosp., Calcutta and Kent, Eng., 1960-64; univ. rsch. fellow U. Liverpool, Eng., 1965-67; surg. registrar London, Liverpool & Leeds, Eng., 1965-70; sr. surg. registrar, tutor, asst. gen. surgery Univ. Coll. Cork, Ireland, 1970-71; asst. gen. surgeon Ireland, 1971-74; lectr., cons. gen. surgeon Univ. Hosp. W.I., Jamaica, 1974-77; cons. surgeon N.W. Thames Regional Authority London & Plymouth Gen. & Royal Infirmary, Edinburgh, 1977-81; cons. gen. surgery BUPA Hosp., Harpenden, Eng., 1978-95; cons. gen. surgeon Daliburgh Hosp., South Uist, Scotland, 1982-95; med. practitioner South Uist, Scotland, 1982—; ret., 2002. Emeritus prof. surgery West Bengal Govt., Calcutta; disting. prof. BWW Soc., L.A.; tching, rsch. and svc. adminstr. London, Leeds, Liverpool, Cork, Jamaica and Edinburgh, 1965—, univ. undergrad. and postgrad. tchr., 1965-81; rschr. in field; examiner U. W.I., 1974-77. Author 8 books of verse; contbr. articles to profl. jours. Recipient Disting. Prof. award BWW Soc., 2003, Glory of India award India Internat. Friendship Soc., 2005; rsch. fellow/grantee Medica Rsch. Com., Liverpool U., 1966, 67, rsch. and publs. grantee U. W.I., Jamaica, 1974, 75, 76, grantee Med. Rsch. Coun. Eire, 1971, Med. Edn. and Rsch. Coun., Belfast, 1972, 73. Fellow Royal Coll. Surgeons England and Edinburgh, Royal Soc. Medicine, Internat. Coll. Surgeons (sr. fellow), Assn. Surgeons Gt. Britain; mem. AAAS, Brit. Assn. Advacement of Sci., Brit. Assn. Surg. Oncologists (founding mem.), Assn. Endoscopic Surgeons (founding mem.), Soc. Laparoscopic Surgeons U.S.A., N.Y. Acad. Scis. (Charles Darwin Assoc. 1999), Brit. Med. Assn., Hosp. Cons. Specialists Assn., European Assn. Endoscopic Surgery. Avocations: history of philosophy, playing indian classical musical instruments. Office Phone: 0044(0)7866516788. Personal E-mail: debuchatterjee1@yahoo.com.

CHATTERJEE, KANU, cardiologist, educator; b. Calcutta, India, Mar. 1, 1934; s. Gopal Lal and Basanti Chatterjee; m. Docey Edwards, May 9, 1975. MD, R.G. Kar Med. Coll., Calcutta, India, 1956. Cert. Internal Medicine Am. Bd. Internal Medicine, 1973, diplomate Cardiovascular Disease Am. Bd. Cardiology, 1975. Resident internal medicine Royal Coll. Physicians, Edinburgh, 1965, fellow cardiovascular disease London, 1965; Lucie Stern prof. medicine U. Calif., San Francisco, 1989—2002, Ernest Gallo disting. prof. medicine, 2002—. Contbr. several articles to profl. jours.; editl. bd. mem. Circulation, American Journal of Cardiology, and Journal of Critical Care. Recipient Gifted Teacher award, Am. Coll. Cardiology, 1990. Achievements include discovery of First to discover: post pacing t-wave changes; First to discover vasodilators in mitral regurgitation; First to discover relationship between endocardial potentials and ventricular volume. Office: Univ Calif San Francisco 505 Parnassus Ave Ste M-1182 San Francisco CA 94143-0124 Office Fax: 415-502-8627.

CHATTERTON, ROBERT TREAT, JR., reproductive endocrinology educator; b. Catskill, NY, Aug. 9, 1935; s. Robert Treat and Irene (Spoor) Chatterton; m. Patricia A. Holland, June 24, 1956 (div. 1965); children: Ruth Ellen, William Matthew, James Daniel; m. Astrida J. Vanags, June 4, 1966 (div. 1977); 1 child, Derek Scott; m. Carol J. Lewis, May 24, 1985. BS, Cornell U., 1958, PhD, 1963; MS, U.

Conn., 1959. Postdoctoral fellow Med. Sch. Harvard U., 1963-65; rsch. assoc. div. oncology Inst. Steroid Rsch. Montefiore Hosp. and Med. Ctr., NYC, 1965-70; asst. prof. Coll. Medicine U. Ill., 1970-72, assoc. prof. Coll. Medicine, 1972-79; prof. Med. Sch. Northwestern U., Chgo., 1979—. Mem. sci. adv. com. AID, chairperson Instnl. Rev. Bd. Northwestern U., 1982—83, mem. intellectual properties com., 1987—95, chairperson radiation safety com., 2000—02; dir. Immunoassay Facility, R. H. Lurie Cancer Ctr. Northwestern U. Med. Sch., 1997—; dir. clin. labs., dept. ob-gyn. Northwestern Med. Facutly Found., 1996—99, dir. shared clin. labs., 1999—. Contbr. articles to profl. jours. Grantee, NIH, 1972—90, 1995—2010, NSF, 1975, 1995—98, AID, 1971—86, Army Office Rsch., 1987—94. Mem.: AAAS, Am. Assn. Clin. Rsch., Am. Assn. Cancer Rsch., Chgo. Assn. Reproductive Endocrinologists (pres. 1987—88), Soc. Study Reproduction, Soc. Gynecologic Investigation, Endocrine Soc., Am. Chem. Soc., N.Y. Acad. Scis., Phi Kappa Phi, Sigma Xi. Presbyterian. Achievements include patents for method of totally suppressing ovarian follicular devel. and method of ovulation detection. Home: 6001 N Knox Ave Chicago IL 60646-5821 Office: Northwestern U Olson 8408 710 N Fairbanks Ct Chicago IL 60611-3015 Office Phone: 312-503-5272. Business E-Mail: chat@northwestern.edu.

CHATTOPADHYAY, BRAJADULAL, biology professor; b. Kolkata, Jan. 13, 1962; PhD in Biophysics & Molecular Biology, 1985. Assoc. prof. Jadavpur U., 1998—. DBT Overseas fellow, Dept. Biotech., Govt. of India, DBT Postdoc fellow, grant, Intellectual Ventures Asia Pvt. Ltd. Avocation: music. Office: Raja SC Mollick Rd Kolkata West Bengal 700032 India E-mail: bdc_physics@yahoo.co.in.

CHATTOPADHYAY, MUNMUN, medical researcher; b. Kolkata, India, Sept. 3, 1969; PhD, Jiwaji U., 1998. Rsch. investigator U. Mich., 2004—10, rsch. asst. prof., 2010—. Rsch. grant, Diabetes Action Rsch. and Edn. Found., Mich. Diabetes Rsch. and Tng. Ctr., travel grant, Peripheral Nerve Soc. Mem.: Gerontology Soc. India, Peripheral Nerve Soc., Am. Diabetes Assn., Am. Soc. Gene Therapy, Soc. Neuroscience. Avocations: music, sports, reading. Office: University Mich 5248 Biomedical Sci Rsch Bldg 109 Zina Pitcher Pl Ann Arbor MI 48109 Business E-Mail: munmunc@umich.edu.

CHATTOPADHYAY, SAURABH, medical educator; b. Kolkata, West Bengal, India, Nov. 11, 1974; MD in Forensic Medicine, Inst. Med. Scis., Banaras Hindu U., NRS Med. Coll., 1999. Asst. prof. Govt. West Bengal, 2007—11. Home: 23/12 Gariahat Rd 1st Fl Ballygung Kolkata West Bengal 700029 India Personal E-mail: chattopadhyaydrs@rediffmail.com.

CHATURVEDI, RAJNISH KUMAR, toxicologist, educator; b. India, Aug. 1, 1978; MS, Jiwaji U., Gwalior, 2000, PhD, 2006. Jr. rsch. fellow Indian Inst. Toxicology Rsch., Lucknow, Utter Pradesh, India, 2001—03, sr. rsch. fellow, 2003—06, scientist, asst. prof., 2008—; postdoc rschr. Weill Cornell Med. Coll., Cornell U., NYC, 2006—08. Recipient Young Scientist award, India Uttar Pradesh Coun. Sci. and Tech., 2005, Lucknow Youth Icons award, Social Environ. & Ednl. Devel. Soc. and iNext-India, 2009; Young Investigator Travel fellowship, Fedn. European Neuroscience Soc., 2006, travel fellowship, Internat. Soc. Neurochemistry, 2008, Young Investigator Travel grant, Fedn. Asian-Oceanic Neuroscience Socs. Mem.: Internat. Neurotoxicology Assn., Internat. Brain Rsch. Orgn., Internat. Soc. Neurochemistry, NY Acad. Scis., Soc. for Neuroscience. Achievements include research in Parkinson's and Huntington. Avocation: gardening. Home and Office: Industrial Toxicology Rsch Ctr Devel Toxicology Divsn 80 MG Marg Lucknow 226001 India Personal E-mail: rajnishitrc@rediffmail.com.

CHATURVEDI, SHAILESH, surgeon; b. Jaipur, Rajasthan, India, Sept. 10, 1950; s. Umesh and Shail Kumari Chaturvedi; m. Sujata Sharma, Feb. 18, 1980; children: Rahul, Rohit Shailesh, Shuchi. MBBS, SMS Med. Coll., 1974; MS in Surgery, U. Rajasthan, 1977; MD, U. Cambridge, 1983; PhD (hon.), Internat. Yorker U., NY, 2007. Cert. full specialist registration Gen. Medical Coun., 1977. Head svc. Surg. High Dependency Unit Aberdeen Royal Infirmary, Scotland, 2002—. Cons. surgeon Albyn Hosp., Aberdeen, 2001—; cons. breast and gen. surgery Aberdeen Royal Infirmary, 2001—; sr. lectr. Aberdeen U., 2001—, supr. edn., 2001—, regent Med. Sch., 2002—; sr. lectr. in field. Editor (referee): (medical website) Cyber Medical College; contbr. articles to profl. jours. Educator Internat. Med. Penal, Scotland, 2003. Officer commdg. surg. divison Royal Air Force, 1995—99, Wegberg, Germany. Recipient Meritorious Svc. award, World Org. Gastro-Enterology, 1991; scholar, Ministry Edn., India, 1968; Prof. Beterello scholarship, World Org. Gastro-Enterology, 1996. Fellow: Royal Coll. Surgeons Glasgow, Royal Coll. Surgeons Edinburgh, Internat. Coll. Surgeons, Royal Coll. Physicians and Surgeons, Assn. Surgeons Gt. Britain and Ireland, Royal Coll. Surgeons (hon.), Indian Assn. Surg. Oncology (hon.; guest lectr. 2003, Merit award 2004, 2005); mem.: Nat. Geographic and Royal Photographic Soc., Brit. Assn. Surg. Oncology, Brit. Med. Assn., Brit. Mensa. Independent. Hindu. Achievements include development of local flap for breast reconstruction in breast cancer patients; research in serum enzyme estimation for early diagnosis of Tetanus; first to computer aided diagnosis of acute abdominal pain and differential diagnosis; research in neo-adjuvent chemotherapy for breast cancers and patterns of metastatic; nipple reconstruction after breast reconstruction following mastectomy. Avocations: cricket, photography, martial arts, stamp collecting/philately, reading. Office: Aberdeen Royal Infirmary Foresterhill Aberdeen AB25 2ZN Scotland Home: 2 Broadstraik Drive AB32 6JG Westhill Scotland Office Phone: 441224554840.

CHATZIDARELLIS, ELEFTHERIOS, urologist, researcher; b. Athens, Greece, Mar. 4, 1976; Degree in Medicine, Aristotelion U. Thessaloniki, Greece, 2000; PhD in Medicine, Kapodistriakon U. Athens, 2010. Registrar dept. urology Sismanoglio Hosp., U. Athens, 2006—10; hon. clin. fellow dept. reconstructive & andrology U. Coll. Hosp. London, 2010; sr. clin. rsch. fellow dept. urology Robotic Ctr. Hertfordshire, Lister Hosp., 2010—. Rsch. fellow European Bd. Urology, 2009—10. Clin. fellowship, European Assn. Urology. Mem.: Gen. Med. Coun., Endourological Soc., European Assn. Urology. Avocations: basketball, water-skiing, soccer. Home: Rodopis 39b Athens Attiki 15234 Greece Personal E-mail: chatzid@yahoo.gr.

CHATZIMAVROUDIS, GRIGORIS, surgeon, senior registrar; b. Thessaloniki, Greece, Apr. 7, 1973; s. Panayiotis and Anastasia Chatzimavroudis; m. Panayiota Nalbanti, 1999; children: Panayiotis, Dimitris. MD, Aristotle U., Thessaloniki, 1999, MSc, 2004, PhD, 2007. Cert. gen. surgeon Ministry of Health, Greece, 2008. Gen. practitioner Gen. Hosp. Serres, Nigrita, Greece, 1999—2000, Greek Air Force, Larissa, Greece, 2001—02; resident gen. surgery 2nd surg. dept. Aristotle U., Thessaloniki, Greece, 2002—07, sr. registrar 2nd surg. dept., 2008—. Vis. dir. Surg. Clinic Heidelbeg U., Greece, 2005, vis. surgeon, 08. Contbr. articles to numerous sci. jours. Recipient First prize, Greece, 2005, 2007. Mem.: Greek Surg. Assn., European Assn. Endoscopic Surgery, European Hernia Soc., European Soc. Coloproctology, Greek Soc. Surg. Infections, Surg. Assn. Northern Greece. Greek Orthodox. Avocations: travel, basketball. Office: Aristotle Univ Ethnikis Aminis 41 Thessaloniki Greece Home: Kampouridou 19 552 36 Panorama Greece Office Fax: 302310210401. Personal E-mail: gchatzim@med.auth.gr.

CHATZIMELETIOU, KATERINA, molecular geneticist; b. Thessaloniki, Greece, Nov. 25, 1974; d. Kosmas and Valasia Chatzimeletiou. BSc in Biol. Scis. with honors, U. Essex, Eng., 1997; MSc in Human Reprodn. Biology with distinction, Imperial Coll., London, 1998; PhD in Preimplantation Genetics, Leeds U., Eng., 2003. Rsch. asst. St. Thomas Hosp., London, 1999; molecular cytogenetic lab mgr. The London Bridge Fertility Ctr., London, 2003—. Achievements include research in identification of spindle abnormalities in human embryos. Office: The London Bridge Fertility Centre 1 St Thomas St London SE19RY England Personal E-mail: katerinachatzime@hotmail.com.

CHATZOUDI, MARIA, dentist; b. Patra, Greece, Mar. 5, 1977; Diploma in Dentistry, Aristotle U., Thessaloniki, 2000; DDS in Dentistry, U. V, Paris, 2008. Dentist Personal Pvt. Dental Practice, 2001—07, 2010—, Alec Waugh Dental Practice, 2007—08, Stuart Cox Dental Practice, 2008—09, Alisson Brett Dental Practice, 2008—09. With, orthodontic splty. Aristotle U., 2009—. Recipient award, Instn. Nat. Scholarships Greece; scholarship, Denmark Govt. Avocation: dance. Office: 75 Komninon St Kalamaria Thessaloniki Macedonia 55132 Greece E-mail: mariachatzoudi@yahoo.gr.

CHAU, GAR-YANG, surgeon; b. Taipei, Taiwan, Sept. 8, 1958; s. Shieu-Nam Chau and Hwei-Fen Chen; m. Rhuei-Fen Warng, Dec. 21, 1985; children: Lori, Ken, Ivy. MD, Nat. Taiwan U., Taipei, 1984; MPH, Columbia U., NYC, 1989. Cert. gen. surgeon Dept. of Health/Taiwan, 1990. Chief resident in gen. surgery Taipei Veterans Gen. Hosp., Taiwan, 1989—90, attending surgeon, 1990—; rsch. assoc. Pitts. U., 1995—96; assoc. prof. Nat. Yang-Ming U., Taipei, Taiwan, 1998—. Cons. Nat. Health Inst., Taipei, Taiwan, 1999—. Author: (chapter in book) Surgery for gastrointestinal cancer- a multidisciplinary approach, Surgical Oncologic Clinic of North America; contbr. articles to profl. jours. Mem.: Taiwan Surg. Assn., Internat. Assn. of Surgeons and Gastroenterologists. Achievements include design of Intraportal chemotherapy for treatment of hepatocellular carcinoma; research in the results of hepatic resection for treatment of hepatocellular carcinoma; the mechanism of metastasis of hepatocellular carcinoma; experience in more than 800 liver resections with a particular reputation for dealing with tumors orginating from the cirrhotic liver. Currently heads program taking on 200 liver resections annually. Avocations: golf, fishing. Office: Taipei Veterans Gen Hosp/Surgery 201 Shih-pai Rd Sect 2 Taipei 112 Taiwan Office Fax: +886-2-28757537. E-mail: gychau@vghtpe.gov.tw.

CHAU, NEARKASEN, medical researcher; b. Cambodia, Cambodia, Oct. 27, 1948; s. On Chau and Kim-Chéng Sun; m. Marie-Jeanne Dieulin, Oct. 4, 1976; children: Kénora, Olivier. PhD, Faculty Scis. U. Henri Poincare, Nancy, France, 1976, U. Paris Descartes, U. Paris-Sud. Rschr. INSERM, 1978—93, rsch. dir., 1994—, dir., 1994—. Mem.: Lorhandicap Rsch. Group. Buddhism. Achievements include research in mathmatics, epidemiology and public health. Avocations: travel, sports, botany, music, reading. Home: 8 Rue du Breuil Heillecourt F-54180 France Office: INSERM Unit 669 97 Blvd Port Royal Paris F-75679 France Office Phone: 33383576146. Business E-Mail: nearkasen.chau@wanadoo.fr.

CHAU, WAI YIP, surgeon; b. Hong Kong, Aug. 19, 1970; m. Jessica Moncada, May 29, 1998; children: Jade Marie, Ariel Jessica. MD, St George's U. Sch. Medicine, Genada, West Indies, 1998. Cert. Am. Bd. Surgery, 2004. Bariatric fellow Hackensack U. Med. Ctr., NJ, 2003—04; bariatric surgeon U. Med. Ctr. Princeton, 2004—. Presenter in field. Contbr. articles to profl. jours. Recipient Glenn A Sanford Meml. award, North Oakland Med. Ctrs., 2003. Mem.: Am. Soc. Bariatric Surgeons. Home: 1 Eldridge Dr Robbinsville NJ 08691 Office: 666 Plainsboro RD STE 640 Plainsboro NJ 08536-3019 Office Fax: 732-274-3435.

CHAUDARY, MURID AHMED, surgeon; b. Nairobi, Africa, Nov. 5, 1944; s. Ibrahim Rahamtulla and Fatima Bibi; married, Aug. 14, 1976; children: Ambereen, Saadiya, Rehan. MBChB, U. Leeds, 1971, M in Surgery, 1983. Intern St. Luke's Hosp., Bradford, England, 1971—72; lectr. anatomy U. Birmingham, England, 1972—73; registrar surgery Westminster Hosp., London, 1973—76; registrar Southend-on-Sea, 1976—78; registrar surgery Hammersmith Hosp., London, 1978—79; rsch. assoc. Imperial Cancer Rsch. Fund, London, 1986—88; sr. lectr. Guy's Hosp., London, 1988—98; cons. surgeon Waterford (Eng.) Hosp., 1998—. Author: (chpt.) High Risk Breast Cancer, 1991, Breast Cancer-Controversies, 1994, Recent Developments in the Study of Benign Breast Disease, 1994. Clin. Rsch. Fellow, Imperial Cancer Rsch. Fund, 1979—86. Fellow: Assn. Surgeons Great Britain, Royal Coll. Surgeons; mem.: British Assn. Surg. Oncology, British Breast Group. Avocations: reading, walking, music, shooting. Home: 7 Manor House Dr Northwood Middlesex HA6 2UJ England Office: Watford Gen Hosp Vicarage Rd Watford WD18 5HB England Home Phone: 01923-842077. Personal E-mail: muridmail@yahoo.com.

CHAUDHRY, HUMAYUN JAVAID, physician, educator; b. Karachi, Pakistan, Nov. 17, 1965; arrived in US, 1971, naturalized, 1978; s. Hukam Dad and Riffat Sultana (Bhatti) C.; m. Nazli Tabasum Iqbal, June 7, 1992; children: Shaun Hatim, Haris Iqbal. BA, NYU, 1986, MS, 1989; DO, N.Y. Coll. Osteo. Medicine, 1991; SM, Harvard Sch. of Pub. Health, 2001. Diplomate Nat. Bd. Osteo. Med. Examiners, Am. Osteopathic Bd. Internal Medicine; lic. physician, surgeon, N.Y., Am. Bd. Internal Medicine, 1996. Intern St. Barnabas Hosp., Bronx, NY, 1991-92; resident in internal medicine Winthrop-U. Hosp., Mineola, NY, 1992-95, chief med. resident, 1995-96; asst. prof. medicine N.Y. Coll. Osteo. Medicine, Old Westbury, 1997—2003, chmn. dept. medicine, 2001—07, med. dir., 2003—05, clin. assoc. prof. medicine, 2003—, asst. dean for pre-clin. edn., 2003—05, asst. dean health policy, 2005—07; attending physician, dir. med. edn. Long Beach (N.Y.) Med. Ctr., 1996-2001; attending physician Island Park NY Med. Care, 1996-98, Family Care Ctr., Long Beach, NY, 1996-99, Acad. Health Care Ctr., N.Y. Coll. Osteopathic Medicine, 2001—07; mem. staff Winthrop U. Hosp., 2001—07; commr. Suffolk County Dept. Health Svcs., NY, 2007—09; pres., CEO Fed. State Med. Boards, 2009—. Reporter, news editor, TV anchorman Third World Broadcasting Network, N.Y.C., 1986-95. Author: Fundamentals of Clinical Medicine, 2004; mem. editl. bd.: New Physician, 1991—99; contbr. articles pub. to profl. jours. Bd. mem. Multifaith Forum of LI, 2000—07. Capt. USAF Res., 1999—2002, maj. USAF Res., 2002—07. Regents Coll. scholar State of N.Y., Albany, 1982; recipient Essay Competition award N.Y.C. Fire Dept., 1979. Fellow: ACP (Nassau West dist. pres. 2000—07, Laureate award 2005), Am. Coll. Osteo. Internists; mem.: AMA, Suffolk County Med. Soc., So. Poverty Law Ctr., Med. Soc. State of NY, Nassau Soc. Internal Medicine (bd. dirs. 1996—98, v.p. 1998—99, pres. 1999—2000), NY State Osteo. Med. Soc., Assn. Osteo. Dirs. Med. Educators (bd. dirs. 2001—03, treas. 2003—04, pres. 2007—09), Am. Coll. Osteo. Internists (bd. dirs. 1999—2006, sec.-treas. 2006—07, pres. 2008—09), NY State Soc. Internal Medicine (pres. resident physicians sect. 1995—96, bd. dirs. 1996—2000), Harvard Alumni Assn., Harvard Club NY, Islamic Ctr. LI, NY Coll. Osteo. Medicine Alumni Assn. (sec. bd. dirs. 1995—98, pres. 1998—2000, bd. dirs. 2000—02), Amnesty Internat. Muslim. Avocations: reading, cinema, travel. Office: Fedn State Med Bds 400 Fidler Wiser Rd Euless TX 76039 *

CHAUHAN, MAHESH, dentist, researcher, director; b. New Delhi; s. Dn Chauhan; m. Sejal Chauhan; 1 child, Pavitra; 1 child, Greeshma. BDS, Maulana Azad Dental Coll., New Delhi, 1990. Cert. advanced implant surg. and prosthetic techniques Ohio State U., 1994, complex restorative treatments Ohio State U. Adj. asst. prof. Ohio State U. Sch. Dentistry, Colombus, 1994—95; dir. Mother Dental Implant Clinic, New Delhi, 1995—. Cons. Ohio Dept. Health, Columbus, 1994—95; lectr. in field. Contbr. articles to profl. jours. Recipient Gold medal, Delhi Govt., 1990, Best Student award, Delhi U., 1990, Ofcl. Recognition for Outstanding Contbrn., Gov. Ohio, 1995. Mem.: Indian Acad. Osseointegration (chmn. No. com. 2005), Internat. Congress Oral Implantologist (corr.), Indian Soc. Oral Implantologist (life), Indian Dental Assn. (life). Hindu. Achievements include research in fiber reinforced composites; dental implants. Avocations: travel, photography, painting, philosophy. Home: 46-C Daryaganj New Delhi 110002 India Office: Mother Dental Implant Clinic 7 Ansari Rd 110 002 New Delhi India Personal E-mail: m_chauhan_in@yahoo.com, drmaheshchauhan@gmail.com.

CHAUHAN, RAJESH, physician, consultant; b. Mainpuri, India, June 25, 1961; s. Brij Pal Singh and Shashi Chauhan; m. Sandeepa Singh, June 22, 1986; children: Shruti, Shivendra Pratap Singh. MBBS, Armed Forces Med. Coll., 1983; diploma in Family Medicine, U. Colombo, 2003; cert. in Disaster Mgmt., Ignou, 2004; cert. in Computer Applications, CDAC, 2005. Lic. physician Med. Coun. India, 1985. Med. officer Organized Pub. Sector, India, 1983—2005; sr. med. officer to col. Botswana Def. Force, Gaborone, Botswana, 1993—96; CEO & med. dir. Family Healthcare Ctr., Agra, India. Peer reviewer in field; contbr. over 100 articles to profl. jours. Recipient Merit cert., Bostwana Def. Force, 1996. Fellow: All India Med. Soc., Indian Soc. Malaria and Other Communicable Diseases; mem.: Coll. Gen. Practioners. Achievements include new modality to treat paronychia by needle aspiration rather than by incising with a scalpel; research in circustantial hypertension a third category of hypertension that afflicts substantial population along with recommendations for different line of management; first to relate on malarial immunity and establishment of small spleen; research in earliest clinical manifestation of HIV infection in people of southern african region; world'S first report of coexisting varicose veins, varicocoele and haemorrhoids; world's first empirical treatment modality of malaria in p. falciparum endemic zone with chloroquine & doxycycline; invention of innovative cheap, sturdy and comfortable finger splint; proposing circumcision as a modality for HIV prevention, proposing compulsory educatiion with a free mid day meal for children of impoverished parents in addition to other population control measures. Home: Family Health Care Ctr 154 Sector 63 AV Colony Sikandra Agra 282007 India Personal E-mail: drchauhanrajesh@yahoo.com.

CHAUHAN, SHIVKUMAR, medical geneticist; b. Nagpur, India, Nov. 24, 1973; MS; PhD, HSSC, 1995. Dir. 'PreGen' Preventive Genetics Diagnostic Ctr., 1997. Recipient Indian Leadership award, All India Achievers Found. Office: 3rd Fl Daya Chambers Next to Haldirams Ajni Sq Wardha Rd Nagpur Maharashtra 440015 India Office Phone: 91 9325880818, 91 9422120459. Personal E-mail: shivkumar_chauhan@rediffmail.com.

CHAULET, PIERRE, chest disease physician, consultant; b. Algiers, Algeria, Mar. 27, 1930; s. Alexandre Edme and Suzanne Claire (Tamiatto) C.; m. Claudine Simone Guillot; children: Luc, Anne, Eve-Marie. MD, U. Paris, 1957; specialist in TB and chest diseases, U. Tunis, Tunisia, 1960. Med. specialist Ministry of Pub. Health, Tunis, 1957-62; asst. clinician Univ. Hosp. Ctr., Algiers, 1962-67, lectr., 1967-71; prof. Univ. Hosp., Algiers-West, 1971-94; med. officer WHO/GTB, Geneva, 1994-98. Chief physician Med. Svcs., Tunis, 1957—62, Algiers, 1962—94; rsch. program mgr. Nat. Orgn. Scientific Rsch., Algiers, 1971—2000; nat. expert Ministry of Health, Algiers, 1997—; internat. cons. Internat. Union Against Tb and Lung Disease and WHO, 1981—; sr. cons. WHO, 2002—; expert cons. Econ. and Social Nat. Coun., Algeria, 2006—. Co-author (WHO tech. documents): TB/HIV Clinical Manual, 1996, Guidelines for the Management of Drug Resistant Tuberculosis, 1996, Treatment of TB, Guidelines for National Programmes, 1997, 2d edit., 2003, Tuberculosis Handbook, 1998, rev. 2003, Practical Approach to Lung Health Manual on Initiating PAL Implementation, 2008; contbr. articles to profl. jours. Del. to Popular Communal Assembly of Algiers City, Algeria, 1967-71; mem. exec. bur. Algerian Med. Union, 1977-82; v.p. Nat. Human Rights Observatory, Algeria, 1992-96; health advisor to head of govt., Algeria, 1992-94; mem. Nat. Coun. Hosps. Reform, 2002. Capt.-physician, Nat. Liberation Army, Algeria, 1957-62. Recipient Ricaux Tuberculosis prize, Nat. Acad. Medicine, Paris, 1967, Algerian Resistance medal, Pres. Algerian Republic, 1984, Social Merit medal, Republic of Senegal, 1989, Internat. award Princess Chichibu Meml. Found., 1999. Mem. Am. Coll. Chest Physicians, Fedn. Maghrebine of Respiratory Diseases, Algerian Soc. Pneumophtisiology (exec. com. 1964-94), N.Y. Acad. Scis. Avocations: literature, history, politics. Home: Rue Du Hoggar 8 Hydra 16405 Algiers Algeria Personal E-mail: pierre_chaulet@yahoo.fr.

CHAUSSY, CHRISTIAN G., urologist, researcher, education educator; Diploma, U. Munich, 1970. Lic. MD German Govt., 1972, fellow Royal Coll. Surgeons, Eng., 1980, lic. Calif. Bd. Med. Quality Assurance, 1985. Dept. surgery transplantation unit U. Cambridge, 1975; active staff, co-dir., transplant unit U. Munich, 1975—76, cons. transplant unit, 1977—84; active staff Mcpl. Hosp. Munich Thalkirchner Strasse, 1975—78, Klinikum Grosshadern, U. Munich, 1978—79, sr. staff mem., 1980—84; faculty, dir. prof. urology dept. surgery divsn. urology UCLA Med. Ctr., 1985—86; chmn. dept. urology Mcpl. U. Assoc. Hosp., Munich, 1986—, mem. bd. dirs. laser ctr., 1997—, med. co-dir., 1998—; prof. urology U. Regensburg, Germany. Tchr. U. Munich, 1972—74, tchr. transplantation unit, 1975—84, instr. urology, 1975—79, asst. prof. urology, 1979—80, assoc. prof. urology, dir. dept. urology, 1980—84, dir. endourology tng. program dept. urology, 1982—84, examiner med. exams, 1987—; prof. surgery, urology UCLA Med. Ctr., 1985—86, dir. endourology tng. program, 1985—86; chmn. dept. urology, prof., mem. med. faculty Mcpl. U. Assoc. Hosp., Munich, 1986—; examiner bd. urology, Bavaria, 1987—; emeritus chmn. dept. urology Urankenh Muenchen Hariahing; prof. urology U. Regensburg; clin. prof. urology Ueck Sch. Medicine USC LA. Author (and co-author) over 500 med. articles and publs. Decorated Cross of the Order of Merit Germany; recipient Langenbeck award, German Surgical Soc., 1975, Motion Picture award, Am. Urological Assn., 1983, Heinrich-Spohr award, Soc. of Friends and Sponsors of Univ. of Duesseldorf, 1984, Gruene Rosette of European Sci. award, 1985, Anniversary award, German Surgical Soc., 1991, Internat. Lithotripsy award, Dornier Med. Sys., 1994, Lifetime Achievement award, Endourological Soc., 2007, Inventors Urology award, European Soc. Urology, 2011, Ritterv Frisch award, 2010. Mem.: Soc. of Friends and Sponsors of Ludwig-Maximilians U. Munich, Max-Planck Soc., LA County Urological Soc., Kuratorium fur Heimdialyse, European Intrarenal Surgery Soc., European Soc. for Organ Transplantation, German Urological Soc. (C.E. Alken award 1976, Maximilian-Nitze award 1981, Motion Picture award 1982, C.E. Alken award 1983). Achievements include worldwide first treatment of a patient with kidney stone with extracorporeal shock waves.

CHAVAKIS, TRIANTAFYLLOS, internist, researcher; b. Athens, Greece, Aug. 5, 1974; s. Nikolaos Chavakis and Ekaterini Chavaki. MD, Justus Liebig U Giessen, Germany, 2000, PhD, 2001. Medical lic. Landesprüfungsamt Hessen, Germany, 2002. Physician dept. of Internal Medicine U. Giessen, Germany, 2000—01, post-doctoral rsch. fellow Inst. Biochemistry, 2001—02; physician dept. medicine U. Heidelberg, Germany, 2002—. Rsch. group leader primary investigator in vascular biology and immunology Dept. of Medicine, U. Heidelberg, Heidelberg, Germany, 2002—. Contbr. scientific papers, articles to profl. jours. Recipient Second prize, Internat. Competition Thrombosis Arteriosclerosis and Vascular Biology, 1998, Young Investigator award, Am. Soc. for Hematology, 1997, European Arteriosclerosis Soc., 1999, Internat. Soc. for Thrombosis and Haemostasis, 2001, 2003, Otto Hahn medal, Max Planck Found., 2001, Gotthard Schettler prize, German Soc. for Angiology, 2003, Oskar Lapp Prize, German Found. for Cardiology, 2003; grantee Rsch., Novartis Found., 2001, German Rsch. Found., 2001, 2002, 2003; fellow, Max-Planck-Foundation, 2001. Mem.: German Soc. for Thrombosis and Haemostasis (Young Investigator award 1998, 2000, prize 2002), Am. Soc. for Biochemistry and Molecular Biology. Achievements include patents for anti-thrombotic action of high molecular weight kininogen; anti-inflammatory action of S. aureus extracellular adherence protein; first to describe the anti-inflammatory extracellular adherence protein of S. aureus, explain impaired wound healing in S. aureus infected wounds, develop novel therapy for autoimmune disease; describe anti-thrombotic and anti-inflammatory action of kininogen as a novel medicant against thrombotic disease; describe novel pathway for inflammatory cell recruitment in diabetes; identify novel family member junctional adhesion molecules; novel mechanisms of inflammation; research in role of urokinase receptor in inflammation; mechanisms of induction of immune tolerance. Office: Dept Medicine I Univ HD Im Neuenheimer Feld 410 Heidelberg 69120 Germany

CHAVERS, BLANCHE MARIE, pediatrician, educator, researcher; b. Clarksdale, Miss., Aug. 2, 1949; d. Andrew and Mildred Louise C.; m. Gubare Mpambara, May 21, 1982; 1 child, Kaita. BS in Zoology, U. Wash., 1971, MD, 1975. Diplomate Am. Bd. Pediats. Intern U. Wash., Seattle, 1975-76, resident in pediatrics, 1976-78; instr. U. Minn., Mpls., 1982, asst. prof. pediatrics, 1983-90, assoc. prof. pediatrics, 1990-99, prof. pediatrics, 1999—. Attending physician dept. pediatrics, U. Minn. Sch. Medicine, Mpls., 1982. Co-editor: Am. Jour. Kidney Diseases, 2001—; contbr. articles to profl. jours. Recipient Clin. Investigator award NIH, 1982; Pediatric Nephrology fellow U. Minn., 1978-81. Mem. Am. Soc. Nephrology, Am. Soc. Pediatric Nephrology, Internat. Soc. Nephrology, Internat. Soc. Pediatric Nephrology, Am. Soc. Transplantation, Internat. Pediatric Transplant Assn. Democrat. Methodist. Avocations: tennis, reading, collecting African artifacts, art. Office: Univ Minn MMC 491 420 Delaware St SE Minneapolis MN 55455-0348

CHAVES-CARBALLO, ENRIQUE, neuropediatrician; b. San Jose, Costa Rica, Dec. 2, 1936; arrived in U.S., 1955, arrived in Saudi Arabia, 1996; s. Enrique Chaves and Celina Carballo; m. Vilma Irene Peralta, Aug. 26, 1961; children: Antonio, Maria, Miguel, Karen. MD, U. Okla., 1963. Diplomate Am. Bd. Psychiatry and Neurology, Am. Bd. Pediatrics. Prof. pediatrics and neurology Ea. Va. Med. Sch., Norfolk, 1979-89, U. Kans., Kansas City, 1990-94; chief pediatric neurology King Faisal Specialist Hosp. and Rsch. Ctr., Riyadh, Saudi Arabia, 1996—2002; fellow pediatrics Mayo Clinic, 1964—67, fellow neurology, 1972—75; clin. prof. pediatrics U. of Kans., Kans. City, 2003; clin. prof. hist. medicine U. Kans., Kans. City, Kans., 2004. Author: The Tropical World of Samuel Taylor Darling, 2007, Memorias y Trabajos, 2008; contbr. articles to profl. jours., chapters to books; reviewer numerous jours. Recipient award Am. Neurol. Assn.; fgn. scholar Wesleyan U., 1955; grantee Rockefeller Archives, 1979. Fellow Am. Acad. Neurology; mem. Am. Assn. Hist. Medicine, Costa Rica Assn. Neuroscis. (hon.), Child Neurology Soc., Internat. Child Neurology Soc., Iberoam. Acad. Pediat. Neurology, Profs. Child Neurology, Soc. for Study of Inborn Errors of Metabolism, Soc. for Inherited Metabolic Disorders. Achievements include research in Reye syndrome, history of medicine and inborn errors of metabolism. Personal E-mail: echaves17@hotmail.com.

CHAVEZ-CROOKER, PAMELA, technologist; b. Antofagasta, May 8, 1968; PhD, Kyoto U., 1998. Postdoc. rschr. U. Hawaii, Manoa, 1999; assoc. prof. U. Antofagasta, 2000—07; CTO Aguamarina SA, 2007—. Bd. dir. ASEMBIO-Biotech. Cos. Assn. Chile, 2011—. Mem.: Endeavor Entrepreneur. Office: Esmeralda 1807 1 Antofagasta 1240000 Chile Business E-Mail: pchavez@aguamarina.cl.

CHÁVEZ VALENCIA, VENICE, physician; b. Apatzingán, Michoacán, Méx., Mar. 23, 1979; Degree in Internal Medicine, UNAM, 2010. Physician Inst. Mexicano del Seguro Social, 2005. Mem.: Colegio de Medina Interna de Méx. Avocations: reading, writing, music. Office: 22 October Av 14 Corregidora Av Apatzingán Michoacán 60600 Mexico Personal E-mail: drvenicechv@yahoo.com.

CHAVIN, WALTER, biological sciences educator, researcher; b. NYC, Dec. 6, 1925; s. Isidor and Fanny (Kesch) C. BS, CCNY, 1946; MS, NYU, 1949, PhD, 1954. Rsch. asst. N.Y. Aquarium, NYC, 1947-48; instr. dept. zoology U. Ariz., Tucson, 1949-51; rsch. specialist dept. fishes Am. Mus. Natural History, NYC, 1951-53; prof. biol. scis. Wayne State U., Detroit, 1953-90, prof. emeritus, 1990—; prof. radiology Wayne State U. Med. Sch., Detroit, 1975-80; dir. Radiation Biology Inst. Wayne State U., Detroit, 1959-71; pres. Chavin Design and Fine Arts, Inc., 2007—. Research assoc. Argonne (Ill.) Nat. Lab., 1955-58. Contbr. 225 articles to profl. jours. NSF Sr. Postdoctoral fellow, 1960-61; Rsch. grantee NSF, AEC, NIH. Fellow AAAS (sec. 1978-85), N.Y. Acad. Scis.; mem. Nat. Assn. Photoshop Profls., Am. Physiol. Soc., Am. Soc. Zoologists (treas., sec.), Soc. Exptl. Biology and Medicine (com. 1986-90), Endocrine Soc., Am. Orchid Soc., South Fla. Orchid Soc., Pan Am Orchid Soc., Am. Bonsai Soc., Gold Coast Bonsai Soc., Lighthouse Bonsai Soc., Palm Beach Bonsai Soc., Sigma Xi (chpt. pres. 1974), Palm Beach Digital Imaging Group, Boca Raton Mus. Art, Art League. Independent. Home: 16484 Bridlewood Cir Delray Beach FL 33445-6678 E-mail: raja25@bellsouth.net.

CHAWLA, INDER, physical medicine and rehabilitation physician; MD, Nagpur U. Diplomate Am. Bd. Physical Medicine and Rehab. Intern Nagpur Med. Coll., 1973; resident Univ. Rochester Med. Ctr., 1978, Clin Penn, 1980; hosp. affiliation includes Wash. Adventist Hosp., Md. Office: Washington Adventist Hospital 7600 Carroll Ave Takoma Pk Takoma Park MD 20912 Office Phone: 301-891-5393. Office Fax: 301-891-6184.

CHAYA, MAYASANDRA SUBRAMANYA, physical education educator; b. Bangalore, India, Feb. 15, 1953; MS, U. Mysore, 1974; PhD in Yoga Sci., Bangalore U., 2005. Officer Corp. Bank, 1977—97; assoc. prof. SVYASA Yoga U., 2005—. Cons., yoga therapy, academic coun. mem. SVYASA, 1998—2011; dir. Diet Clinic and Yoga Ctr. Bangalore, 1998—2011; rsch. cons., yoga and physiology St. John's Rsch. Ctr. Med. Coll. and Hosp., 2006—11. Avocations: yoga, reading. Office: 104 10th D Main Rd I Block Jayanagar Bangalore Karnataka 560011 India Office Fax: 26608645.

CHAYET, ARTURO S., ophthalmologist, surgeon, consultant; b. Monterrey, Mexico, Dec. 23, 1959; s. Jose and Dora Chayet; m. Silvia Chayet, Aug. 14, 1982; children: Daniel D., Leon R., Jose B. MD, U. La Salle, Mexico City, 1983. Cert. Mexican Bd. Ophthalmology, 1989. Dir. Codet Eye Inst., Tijuana, Mexico, 1988—; founder, dir. Banco De Ojos Del Noroeste, Tijuana, Mexico, 1988—92; pres. Colegio De Oftalmologos De Baja Calif., Tijuana, Mexico, 1994—95, Centro Mexicano De Cornea, Mexico City, 1997—98. Named Hon. Prof. Yr., U. Calif. San Diego Dept. Ophthalmology, 2001. Mem.: Sociedad Mexicana De Oftalmologia, Internat. Soc. Refractive Surgery (Lans award 2000, Caseebeer award 2005), Am. Soc. Cataract and Refractive Surgery, Am. Acad. Ophthalmology (Achievement award 2001). Achievements include development of Intralasik; invention of Bitoric Excimer Laser Treatments; design of Chayet Lasik Drain; development of Nidek Mk 2000 Microkeratome. Office: Codet Eye Institute Padre Kino 10159 Bc Tijuana 22320 Mexico Business E-Mail: arturo.chayet@arisvision.com.mx, arturo.chayet@codetvision.com.

CHECTON, JOHN BURT, cardiologist; b. Jersey City, Feb. 6, 1952; s. John Bert and Margaret Mary (Donahue) C.; m. Maria Geiger; children: Meghan Farrell, Stephanie Margaret, Tara Maria, John Geiger. BS in Biology, Rensselaer Poly. Inst., 1974; MD, UMDNJ-N.J. Med. Sch., 1978. Diplomate Am. Bd. Internal Medicine, Am. Bd. Cardiovasc. Disease, Am. Bd. Critical Care Medicine, Am. Coll. Nuclear Cardiology, Certification Coun. Nuclear Cardiology. Intern Monmouth Med. Ctr., Long Branch, NJ, 1978-79, resident, 1979-80, chief resident, 1980-81, attending physician, dir. cardiology, 1985—, dir. cardiac catheterization lab, 1997—; ptnr. Monmouth Cardiology Associates, LLC, Long Branch, NJ, 1984—. Mem. staff Jersey Shore Med. Ctr., Neptune, N.J. Cardiovascular disease fellow U. Louisville Sch. of Medicine, 1981-83, chief fellow, 1982-83. Fellow Am. Coll. Cardiology, Am. Heart Assn., Am. Coll. Chest Physicians; mem. ACP, AMA, Am. Soc. Internal Medicine, Am. Soc. Nuclear Cardiology, Am. Soc. Nuclear Medicine, Monmouth Beach Club, Skytop Club, Navesink Country Club, Am. Soc. of Enchocardiography, Monmouth County Med. Soc., N.J. Med. Soc. Republican. Roman Catholic. Avocations: tennis, jogging, hockey. Office: Monmouth Cardiology Associates LLC 215 Brighton Ave Long Branch NJ 07740-5219 Office Fax: 732-222-4862.

CHEDID, ANTONIO, pathologist, educator, researcher; b. Barranquilla, Colombia, May 5, 1936; came to U.S., 1966; s. Aziz Antonio and Maria (Turbay) C.; m. Hoda Abi-Rached; children: Anthony John, Marie-Claude, Erica Houda. BS, Coll. of Barranquilla, 1954; MD, U. Madrid, 1962. Diplomate Am. Bd. Pathology. Intern Columbus Hosp., Chgo., 1967-68; resident in pathology Michael Reese Hosp., Chgo., 1968-72; instr. pathology Pritzker Sch. Medicine U. Chgo., 1972-73; asst. prof. pathology U. Cin. Coll. Medicine, 1973-76; assoc. prof. pathology Chgo. Med. Sch., North Chicago, Ill., 1976-84, prof. pathology, 1985—, prof. microbiology and immunology, 1995—, prof. medicine, 1997—. Author: (pen name Anthony Strong) The Phoenicians in History and Legend, 2002, The Idea of God, 2007; current work: immunology of alcoholic liver disease; specialties include pathology, medicine, hepatology and immunology. Mem. Am. Assn. Pathology, Internat. Assn. for Study of the Liver, Am. Assn. for Study Liver Diseases, Am. Soc. for Cell Biology, Fedn. Am. Socs. Exptl. Biology, Internat. Acad. Pathology. Home: 650 Rockefeller Rd Lake Forest IL 60045-3142 Office: Rosalind Franklin U Chgo Med Sch 3333 Green Bay Rd North Chicago IL 60064-3037 Home Phone: 847-295-7429; Office Phone: 847-578-3409. Business E-Mail: antonio.chedid@rosalindfranklin.edu.

CHEE, CHEE PIN, neurosurgeon, consultant; b. Georgetown, Penang, Malaysia, June 19, 1953; s. Kim Seong Chee and Hup Inn Ooi; m. Irene Soh Gim Gan, Dec. 25, 1980; children: Oswin Chuan Yinn, Rowena. MB, BS, U. Malaya, Kuala Lumpur, Malaysia, 1979, MD, 1991. House officer Univ. Hosp., Kuala Lumpur, 1979-80, med. officer, 1980-83, lectr. neurosurgery, assoc. prof., 1986-91, head neurosurgery, 1988-91; neurosurg. registrar Inst. Neurol. Scis. Southern Gen. Hosp., Glasgow, Scotland, 1983-84; sr. neurosurg. registrar Royal Victoria Hosp., Belfast, Northern Ireland, 1984-86; cons. neurosurgeon Pantai Med. Ctr., Assunta Hosp., Tung Shin Hosp., Kuala Lumpur, 1991—; vis. cons. neurosurgeon Subang Jaya Med. Ctr., 1996—; cons. neurosurgeon Gleneagles Intan Med. Ctr., Kuala Lumpur, 1996—; staff neurosurgeon Group Health Coop. of Puget Sound, Seattle, 1990; chmn. 50 Med. Specialists Ctr., Kuala Lumpur, 1993-94. Convener neurosurgery 7th Congress Asian Surg. Assn., Penang, 1989; neurosurgery organizer 11th Asian Pacific Fedn. Congress, Internat. Coll. Surgeons, Kuala Lumpur, 1996; organizing com. Penang Internat. Tchg. Course in Neurology, 1996, internat. advisory bd. 10th Asian-Australian Congress of Neurological Surgery, Lahore, Pakistan, 1999. Contbr. over 30 articles to profl. jours. Recipient Penang Best Acad. Student award, 1973. Fellow Royal Coll. Surgeons (Edinburgh), Royal Coll. Physicians and Surgeons (Glasgow), Internat. Coll. Surgeons; mem. ACNS/AASNS/WFNS (exec. com. joint ednl. meeting 2004—), Royal Coll. Surgeons, Royal Coll. Physicians (licentiate), Congress Neurol. Surgeons, Asian Oceanian Skull Base Soc. (exec. com. 1997—), Malaysian Soc. Neuroscis. (coun. 1994-96), Asian Congress Neurol. Surgeons (exec. com. 1997—, pres. 2008-), Internat. Chinese Fedn. Neurosurg. Scis. (exec. com. 2004—), Neurosurg. Assn. Malayasia (pres. 2007-), Chung Ling Alumni Assn. (med. advisor 1995—), Kiwanis (dir. Kidney Found. Bangsar 1994—, v.p. 1991-95, pres. 1995-98, advisor Taman Tun 1997—), Internat. Assn. Neurorestoratology (co-chmn., invention cordination com). Avocations: philatelics, antiques, art collection, music, kois keeping. Office: Gleneagles Intan Med Ctr Ste 209 2d Fl/Med Ofc Block 282 50450 Kuala Lumpur 50450 Malaysia Home Phone: 603-22833446; Office Phone: 603-42578331, 603-22823494. Personal E-mail: drcpchee@yahoo.com. Business E-Mail: cnsc@pc.jaring.my.

CHEE, JOHN, engineering educator; b. Malacca, Malaysia, May 10, 1952; B Eng, Nat. U. Singapore, 1976. Prin. lectr. Electronic & Computer Engring., 1991—. Recipient Tech. Team Excellence award, Ngee Ann Poly. Mem.: IEEE, Instn. Engrs., Singapore, Biomed. Engring. Singapore. Avocation: guitar. Office: 535 Clementi Rd Biomed Engineering Singapore 599489 Singapore Office Fax: 654608697. Business E-Mail: chj@np.edu.sg.

CHEEMA, FAISAL HABIB, surgeon, researcher; b. Hafizabad, Punjab, Pakistan, Mar. 26, 1977; s. Habib Ullah and Safia Begum Cheema; m. Ayesha Faisal Shaukat, Aug. 11, 2001. MBBS, The Aga Khan U., Karachi, Pakistan, 2000. Extern in histopathology Shaukat Khanum Meml. Cancer Hosp. and Rsch. Ctr., Lahore, 1996; extern in gen. surgery and urology Mansoorah Hosp., Lahore, 1997; extern in gen. surgery King Edward Med. Coll. and Mayo Hosp., Lahore, 1997; extern in cardiac surgery Punjab Inst. Cardiology, Lahore, 1999; extern in cardiothoracic surgery St. Joseph Med. Ctr. and Loyola U., Chgo., 2000; extern in pediatric trauma surgery Johns Hopkins U. Hosp., Balt., 2000; rsch. assoc. in heart transplantation Dept. Thoracic and Cardiovasc. Surgery and Robert Van Kampen Heart Transplant Resource Ctr. Loyola U. Med. Ctr., Chgo., 2001; postdoctoral rsch. fellow in surgery Divsn. Cardiothoracic Surgery Dept. Surgery Coll. Physicians and Surgeons Columbia U. - NY Presbyn. Hosp., NYC, 2002—05, asst. surg. fellow Cardiopulmonary Procurement Team Heart and Lung Transplant Program, 2002—, preceptor gross anatomy Dept. Anatomy, 2004—, assoc. rsch. scientist Divsn. Cardiothoracic Surgery Dept. Surgery, 2005—. Reviewer Annals of Thoracic Surgery, Blackwell Synergy Pubs., Jour. Heart and Lung Transplantation; mem. organizing com. 14th Biennial Asian Congress on Cardiothoracic Surgery; founder Young Pakistani Physicians Resource Ctr., 2004. Contbr. articles to abstracts, book chpts. and manuscripts, scientific papers, articles to profl. jours. Coord. Sponsor A Child's Mind Project, Karachi, Pakistan, 1998—2000. Sci. fellow, Govt. Coll. Lahore, Pakistan, 1994—95, Start-up Rsch. grantee, Columbia U., 2002—05, 2003—04, 2004—05, 2005—06, Clin. Rsch. Indsl. grantee, Edwards Lifescis. Corp., 2004—05, NIH grantee, 2004—, New Era Cardiac Care scholar, 2006. Mem.: AMA, Islamic Med. Assn. N.Am., Assn. Physicians Pakistani Descent of N.Am. (taskforce visa and licensure issues 2003, young physicians task force 2004, mem. com. young physicians 2005, best sci. poster presentation 2005, disting. oral presentation 2005), Doctors Worldwide, Heart Net, Academic Rsch. Coun., Am. Soc. Artificial Internal Organs, Internat. Soc. Heart & Lung Transplantation, N.Y. Acad. Scis. (future entrepreneur 2005), Pakistan Med. & Dental Coun., Am. Heart Assn. (coun. on cardio-thoracic and vascular surgery 2003), Khwarzimic Sci. Soc. (life), Aga Khan U. Alumni Assn. Islam. Achievements include discovery of renal papilla as a niche for adult kidney stem cells; patents pending for Casein Hydrolysate as additive for Dialysate in Hemodialysis. Avocations: skydiving, travel, squash, horseback riding. Home: 106 Haven Ave Apt 20 New York NY 10032 Office: Coll Physicians and Surgeons Columbia U NY Presbyn Hosp MHB 7 GN 435 177 Fort Washington Ave New York NY 10032 Office Fax: 212-342-5309; Home Fax: 212-342-5309. Business E-Mail: fc2020@columbia.edu.

CHEHAB, NIZAR, plastic surgeon; Cert. plastic surgeon Lebanon. Chief aesthetic plastic surgery dept. Mid. East Hosp.; cons. plastic surgeon Lebanon-Canadian Hosp., Beirut; specialist aesthetic plastic surgery Beirut Med. Ctr., Lebanon, dir. cosmetic surgery. Prof. Lebanese Univ., Lebanon. Author articles about facelift, liposuction, tummy tuck, breast implant, laser treatment and many other. Office: Beirut Medical Center 6th Fl Sarolla Center Hamra St Beirut Lebanon Office Phone: 9611752575. Business E-Mail: info@drnizarchehab.com. *

CHE HON, WAN HAZMY, orthopedic surgeon, consultant, sports medicine surgeon; b. Seremban, N.Sembilan, Malaysia, Aug. 21, 1964; s. Che Hon Abdul Wahab and Sharifah Ainon Syed Mohd; m. Zainab Yahaya, July 31, 1988; children: Wan Dalila Wan Hazmy, Wan

Ahmad Hasif Wan Hazmy, Wan Ahmad Syafiq Wan Hazmy, Wan Aqilah Wan Hazmy, Wan Ahmad Ihsan Wan Hazmy. MD, State U. of Ghent, Belgium, 1984—91; M in surg. orthop., Nat. U. of Malaysia, Kuala Lumpur, Malaysia, 1994—98. Fellowship in traumatology AO Internat., Switzerland, 1999, AM (Malaysia) Acad. of Medicine, 2001, Fellowship in arthroscopy, arthroplasty and sports surgery Wakefield Orthop. Clinic and Royal Adelaide Hosp., Australia, 2002. Intern U. Hosp., Ghent, Belgium, 1990—91; med. officer Seremban Hosp., N.Sembilan, Malaysia, 1992—94; surg. registrar Kuala Lumpur Hosp., Kuala Lumpur, Fed. Ter., Malaysia, 1994—98; orthop. and trauma surgeon Seremban Hosp., N.Sembilan, Malaysia, 1998—2001, cons. orthopaedic, trauma, and sports surgeon, 2002—. Adj. lectr. Internat. Med. U., Seremban, N.Sembilan, Malaysia, 1998—. Editor: (book) Biography of Muslim Scholars and Scientists, Islamic Medicine and Code of Med. Ethics, Current Issues in Islamic Medicine: Cloning and Organ Transplantation; contbr. book Guideline of "Ibadah" for Patients. Med. vol. to Moloccan Islands Malaysian Med. Relief Soc., Ambon, Moloccan Islands, Indonesia, 2000; specialist in charge, games med. village XXI South East Asia Game, Kuala Lumpur, Fed. Ter., Malaysia, 2001; advisor Charity Clinic Project, Seremban, N.Sembilan, Malaysia, 2001—03. Recipient Excellent Work Performance Award, Ministry of Health, Malaysia, 1997, Prof. N. Subramaniam Award for Outstanding Performance in M. Surg. Orthop. Program, Malaysian Orthop. Assn., 1999, Trauma Fellowship, AO Internat., Switzerland, 1999, fellowship in arthroscopy, arthroplasty and sports surgery, Australian Orthop. Assn., 2002; scholar sub splty. Scholarship for Sports Surgery, Govt. of Malaysia, 2002. Fellow: Asia Pacific Orthop. Assn. (licentiate); mem.: Malaysian Orthop. Assn. (mem. 1996), Seremban Hosp. Islamic Soc. (life; pres. 1999—), Islamic Med. Assn. of Malaysia (life; state chmn. 1998—), Malaysia Med. Relief Soc. (life). Islam. Achievements include invention of KWH dynamic foot splint for patients with foot drop. Avocations: travel, soccer, stamp collecting/philately, astronomy. Office: Orthop Dept Seremban Hosp Jln Rasah N Sembilan Seremban 70300 Malaysia Office Fax: 606-7604515; Home Fax: 606-7604515. Personal E-mail: whazmy@tm.net.my.

CHEIFETZ, ADAM S., physician; b. Rochester, NY, Feb. 25, 1971; BA, Brown U., 1993; MD, Cornell U. Med. Sch., 1997. Dir. Ctr. Inflammatory Bowel Diseases Beth Israel Deaconess Med. Ctr., 2006—. Asst. prof. medicine Harvard Med. Sch., 2008. Recipient Best Dr., Boston Mag., 2007—10. Mem.: ACG, CCFA, AGA. Office: BIDMC 330 Brookline Ave Rabb 425 Boston MA 02215 Business E-Mail: acheifet@bidmc.harvard.edu.

CHEIKHROUHOU, IMENE, research scientist; b. Tunisia, Jan. 11, 1980; Degree in Engring., Nat. Engring. Sch. Sfax, Tunisia, 2003, M, 2004. Rsch. scientist, computer aided diagnosis sys. U. Evry Val d'Essonne France, 2007—. Asst. prof. Higher Inst. Indsl. Mgmt. Sfax, Higher Inst. Electronic and Communication Sfax, 2004—08. Grant, Conseil Regional d'Ile de France, scholarship, Ministry of Higher Edn. Tunisia. Avocations: swimming, reading. Home: 53 Blvd de l'Yerres Evry Paris 91000 France Personal E-mail: imene.kachouri@yahoo.fr.

CHELLY, JACQUES E., anesthesiologist; b. Paris; s. David and Mirielle; m. Lorelee Chelly; children: Marjorie, Brice, Thomas, David. BS, Monte-Rouge Coll., Paris, 1970; MD, Necker-Enfants Malades Med. Sch., Paris, 1976; MS in Pharm., Lariboistiere-St. Louis Med. Sch., Paris, 1979; PhD in Pharm., U. Houston, 1985, MBA, 1992. Resident Broussais Hosp., Paris, 1976—79; attache asst. dept. biochem. Necker-Enfants Malades Med. Sch., 1975—76; attache asst. dept. pharm. Broussais-Hotel-Dieu Med. Sch., 1976—77, asst. dept. pharm., 1977—80, chief dept. pharm., 1980—2001; lectr. dept. anesthesiology Baylor Coll. Medicine, Houston, 1981, rsch. instr. dept. anesthesiology, 1982, rsch. asst. prof. dept. anesthesiology, 1982—86, assoc. prof. dept. anesthesiology, 1986; prof., dir. divsn. clin. pharm. U. Tex. Health Sci. Ctr., 1989—92, prof., dir. clin. rsch. dept. anesthesiology, 1992—97; prof., dir. clin. rsch. orthopedic anesthesia U. Tex. Med. Sch., 1997—2002; prof., vice chmn. clin. rsch. U. Pitts. Sch. Medicine, 2002—, prof. orthopaedic surgery, 2002—. Vis. assoc. prof. dept. pharm. U. Houston, 1980—81; vis. prof. U. Pitts., 2002—03, dir. orthopaedic anesthesia, 2002; staff anesthesiologist Broussais Hosp., 1977—80; attending physician Hermann Hosp., Houston, 1992—2002, dir. dept. clin. rsch., 1991—93; dir. orthopaedic anesthesia Meml. Hermann Hosp., 1998—2002; attending anesthesiologist U. Pitts. Med. Ctr. South Side, U. Pitts. Med. Ctr. Presbyn., Magee Hosp.; dir. cardiovascular anesthesia rsch. lab. Baylor Coll. Medicine, 1980—87; dir. clin. rsch. U. Tex. Med. Sch., Houston, 1992—2002; vice chmn. clin. rsch. U. Pitts. Sch. Medicine, 2002—; presenter, lectr. in field. Editor: Peripheral Nerve Block Technique, 1999, Continious Peripheral Nerve Block Techniques: An Illustrated Guide, 2001, Peripheral Nerve Block Technique, 2d edit., 2003; contbr. articles to profl. jours., chapters to books. Recipient Flouthane prize, France, 1980, Outstanding Rsch. Facilitator award, U. Tex. Med. Sch., Houston, 1996, Excellence Surg. Pain Mgmt. award, 2000. Mem.: Am. Soc. Regional Anesthesia and Pain Medicine, Am. Soc. Pharm. and Exptl. Therapeutics, Western Pharm. Soc., Coun. High Blood Pressure, Coun. Basic Sci., Am. Heart Assn., Tex. Gulf Coast Anesthesia Soc., Soc. Cardiovascular Anesthesiologists, Tex. Soc. Anesthesiologists (alt. del. 2002), Internat. Anesthesia Rsch. Soc., Am. Soc. Anesthesiologists, French Soc. Pharm., French Soc. Anesthesiology. Office: UPMC Presbyn-Shadyside Hosp Dept Anesthesiology 5230 Centre Ave Ste M-104 Pittsburgh PA 15232

CHEMTOB, DANIEL, physician, public health service officer; s. Nessim Chemtob and Esther Guetta; m. Michele Dalvy; children: Boaz, Nathan, Raphael. Grad. in Med. Stats., Paris VI U., 1986; MD, U. Paris XIII, 1986; MPH, Hebrew U., Jerusalem, 1996; DEA in Advanced Studies in Anthropology and Sociology in Politics, Paris VIII U., France, 1992; DEA in Pub. Health in Developing Countries, Paris VI U., 1992. Diplomate France, 1984, Israel, 1989, lic. pub. health specialist Israel, 1996. Physician residency pub. health specialization Ministry Health, Jerusalem, 1992—96, first and founding dir. dept. TB and AIDS, 1996—. Nat. tb program mgr. Ministry Health, Jerusalem, 1997—; vis. rschr., vis. rsch. fellow Hebrew U., Jerusalem, 1987—92. Mem., bd. trustees Midreshet Beit Ham, Jerusalem, 1988—93; initiator bilingual sch. Jewish and Arab children Dou Leshoni Sch., Jerusalem, 1996—2001. Postdoctoral fellow, Johns Hopkins Sch. Pub. Health, Balt., 2004—06. Fellow: Soc. Pub. Health Physicians in Israel (licentiate). Avocations: travel, ping pong/table tennis, history. Office: Ministry Health Dept Tuberculosis & AIDS Pierre Koenig 33 Jerusalem 91010 Israel Office Fax: 972 2 5657751. Business E-Mail: daniel.chemtob@moh.health.gov.il.

CHEN, ALLEN YUNG-NIEN, neurologist; b. Tainan City, Taiwan, Mar. 21, 1971; MD, Kaohsiung Med. U., Taiwan, 1996; PhD, U. Warwick, Eng., 2009. Chief, neurology Fong-Shan Hosp., 2010—. Home: 1 Ln 37 Yuanshan Rd Niaosong Kaohsiung 83341 Taiwan Fax: 886-7-7317123 ext. 229*2; Home Fax: 886-7-7312292. Personal E-mail: epapers@ynchen.plus.com.

CHEN, ALVIN CHAO-YU, orthopaedic surgeon; b. Cha-I, Taiwan, Aug. 31, 1963; s. Pu-Sheng Chen and Mai-Hwa Wang; m. Tiffany Ing-Zuei Lo, Dec. 17, 1956; children: Anita, Alan, Alice. Med. Bachelor, China Med. Sch., Taichung, Taiwan, 1988. Chief Chang Gung Hyperbaric Oxygen Ctr., Taoyuan, Taiwan, 1997—2001; attending physician Chang Gung Med. Ctr., Taoyuan, 1995—2002; asst. prof. Chang Gung U., Taoyuan, 1999—. Rsch. fellow Harvard U., Cambridge, Mass., 2001—. Recipient Rsch. award, Chang Gung Med. Ctr., 1997, 1998, Type B Rsch. award, NSC, 1999. Mem.: Am. Assn. Orthop. Surgeon. Avocations: golf, fencing. Office: Chang Gung Med Ctr 5 Fu-Hsin St Kweishan Taoyuan 333 Taiwan Office Phone: 886-3-3281200 ext. 2420. Office Fax: 886-3-3278113. Personal E-mail: alvin_ortho@yahoo.com. Business E-Mail: alvinchen@adm.cgmh.org.tw.

CHEN, AMY Y. Y., dermatologist; b. Taipei, Taiwan, Nov. 18, 1977; BS, MIT, 2001; MD, Wayne State U. Sch. Medicine, 2007. Rsch. asst. Harvard-MIT Health Sci. and Tech., 1999—2001; post sophomore fellow, dept. pathology U. Pitts. Sch. Medicine, 2004—05; transitional internship Framingham Union Hosp., Metrowest Med. Ctr., Harvard Med. Sch. Affiliated Program, 2007—08; dermatology clin. rsch. fellow Boonshoft Sch. Medicine, Wright State U., Dept. Dermatology, 2008—09, dermatology resident, 2009—, chief adminstrv. resident, 2011. Resident mem. Volunteerism Com., Am. Acad. Dermatology, 2011; reviewer Jour. Am. Acad. Dermatology, 2010, Jour. Drugs Dermatology, 2009. Travel grant, Am. Acad. Dermatology. Mem.: Mass. Med. Soc., Women's Dermatologic Soc., Internat. Soc. Dermatology, Med. Dermatology Soc., Am. Acad. Dermatology. Avocation: travel. Office: 1 Elizabeth Pl Ste 200 Dayton OH 45408 Office Fax: 937-224-3356. Business E-Mail: ayyen@alum.mit.edu.

CHEN, ANDREW LAWRENCE, orthopedist, surgeon, sports medicine specialist; b. Alliance, Ohio, May 30, 1971; s. Pei-Ying and Diana Hung Chen; m. Colleen Theresa Gilmartin, Oct. 12, 2002; children: Haley Frances, Dillon Andrew. BA, Johns Hopkins U., Balt., 1993, MS, 1994, MD, 1997. Orthopaedic surgeon Hosp. for Joint Diseases, NYC, 1997—2003; fellow Steadman-Hawkins Sports Medicine Clinic, Vail, Colo., 2003—04; sports medicine and shoulder surgeon Littleton Orthopaedics, NH, 2004—06, attending orthpaedic surgeon, 2004—; sports medicine and shoulder surgeon Alpine Orthopaedics, Littleton, 2006—; faculty Summer Olympic Training Event, 2008. Mem. admissions com. Johns Hopkins Sch. Medicine, 1996—97; assisting physician Alvin Ailey Dance Co., NYC, 1997—2003, Denver Broncos (NFL), 2003—04, Colo. Rockies (Maj. League Baseball), Denver, 2003—04; team physician US Ski and Snowboard Assn., Park City, Utah, 2006—; head team physician US Ski Jumping, 2008—; stadium physician Madison Sq. Garden, NYC, 1998—2003; cons. Gerson-Lehrmann Group, NYC, 2003—, Depuy Mitek, Inc., Raynham, Mass., 2004—; pres. Hyperion, Inc., NYC, 2004—; presenter in field. Author: (book) Care of the Mature Athlete, 2010; dir.: (instructional video) The Encore RSP: Surgical Technique, Reverse Total Shoulder Arthroplasty; med. editor: Verimed, Inc., 1998—; contbr. chapters to books, articles to profl. jours. Supporter Littleton Hospice, 2004—06, Littleton Athletic Program, 2004—06; delegate Am. Orthop. Soc. Sports Medicine, 2009—; Physician team head US Ski Jumping, 2008—; contbr. Spl. Olympics, NH, 2004—06. Recipient Rsch. Internship award, US Dept. Def., 1988—89, Rsch. Tng. award, NIH, 1990; named Exec. Chief Resident, Hosp. for Joint Diseases, 2002—03, Tchr. of Yr., 2003; scholar, Balt. Med. Soc., 1994—97; Senatorial scholar, Md. State Senate, 1989—97, Md. Disting. scholar, Md. Dept. Edn., 1989—93, Rsch. fellow, NSF, 1991. Mem.: Am. Coll. Sports Medicine, NH Orthopaedic Soc., New Eng. Shoulder and Elbow Soc., Am. Orthop. Soc. Sports Medicine (del. state of NH), Am. Acad. Orthopaedic Surgeons, Tau Beta Pi (chpt. v.p. 1992), Phi Beta Kappa. Achievements include patents pending for transdermal drug delivery system for treatment of joint pain; transdermal glucosamine and chondroitin delivery system; novel suture and suture fixation device; invention of novel suture and locking device for arthroscopic surgery; device for arthroscopic meniscal repair; device for electronic medical record storage. Avocations: mountain biking, hiking, golf, skiing, snowboarding. Home: Po Box 437 Franconia NH 03580-0437 Office: Alpine Clinic Profile Rd Po Box 297 Franconia NH 03580 Business E-Mail: achenmd@yahoo.com.

CHEN, BO-CHING, agricultural studies educator; b. Tainan, Taiwan, Feb. 21, 1972; PhD, Nat. Taiwan U., 2004. Assoc. prof., dept. post-modern agr. MingDao U., 2004. Office: 369 Wenhua Rd Peetow Changhua 52345 Taiwan Business E-Mail: bcchen@mdu.edu.tw.

CHEN, CHEE DHANG, medical researcher; b. Kuala Lumpur, Malaysia, June 15, 1979; BS in Biotech., U. Malaysia Sabah, 2003; MS in Med. Entomology, U. Malaya, 2006. Rsch. officer Inst. Med. Rsch., Kuala Lumpur, 2004—08, U. Malaya, Kuala Lumpur, 2009—. Fellow: Royal Soc. Tropical Medicine and Hygiene; mem.: Malaysian Soc. Parasitology and Tropical Medicine. Office: Inst Biological Scis University Malaya Kuala Lumpur Wilayah Persekutuan 50603 Malaysia Personal E-mail: zidannchris@yahoo.com.

CHEN, CHERYL CHIA-HUI, nursing educator; b. Taiwan, Oct. 17, 1971; DNSc, Yale U. Sch. Nursing, 2003. Assoc. prof. Nat. Taiwan U. Coll. Medicine, 2008—. Office: 1 jen-Ai Rd Sect 1 Taipei 100 Taiwan Business E-Mail: cherylchen@ntu.edu.tw.

CHEN, CHICH FU, medical association administrator; b. Fu Jian, China, Nov. 20, 1940; BPharm, Nat. Defense Med. Ctr., Sch. Pharmacy, Taipei, Taiwan, 1965; MS, Nat. Defense Med. Ctr., Inst. Biophysics, 1969. Tchg. asst. to assoc. prof. Nat. Defense Med. Ctr., 1975; assoc. to prof. Nat. Yang Ming U., Taipei, 1975—88; dir. Nat. Rsch. Inst. Chinese Medicine, Taipei, 1988—2004. Contbr. scientific papers. Recipient Academic award, Lifu Med. Rsch. Found., Taipei, 2000. Mem.: Internat. Soc. Oriental Medicine (hon. pres. 2003—). Home: No 23 Kingman St Taipei 100 Taiwan Office Phone: 886-2-2369-0756. Fax: 02-2365-4243. Personal E-mail: chichfuchen@email.com.

CHEN, CHIEN-JEN, epidemiologist, Minister of Health, Minister of Science; b. Kaohsiung, Taiwan, June 6, 1951; s. Hsin-An Chen and Lien-Tze Wei; m. Fong-Ping Lo, Aug. 14, 1977; children: Yi-Ju, Yi-Wen. BS, Nat. Taiwan U., Taipei, 1973, MPH, 1977; ScD in Epidemiology, Johns Hopkins U., 1983. Assoc. prof. Nat. Taiwan U., 1983—86, prof. Grad. Inst. Pub. Health, 1986—94, dir., 1993—94, 1994—97, prof. Grad. Inst. Epidemiology, 1994—97, dean Coll. Pub. Health, 1999—2002; disting. rsch. fellow Genomics Rsch. Ctr., Academia Sinica, Taipei, 2006—. Rsch. fellow Columbia U., 1989-90, Inst. Biomed. Scis., Acad. Sinica, 1988-93.; sr. assoc. dept. epidemiology Johns Hopkins U., 1995-2006; adj. prof. dept. epidemiology and biostats. Tulane U., 1995-2006; dir. gen. divsn. life scis. Nat. Sci. Coun., Taipei, 1997-99, dep. min., 2002-03, Nat. Sci. Coun.; min. Dept. Health, Taipei, 2003-05, Nat. Sci. Coun., Taipei, 2006-08, cutter lectr., preventive medicine, Harvard U. Contbr. numerous articles to profl. jours. Recipient Outstanding Rsch. award, Nat. Sci. Coun., 1986—96, Outstanding Rsch. Fellow award, 2003, Med. Rsch. award, Ching-Hsing Med. Found., 1990, United Med. Found., 1992, Outstanding Tchg. award, Ministry Edn., 1992, Academic award, 1997, Health medal, second rank, Dept. Health, 1996, Health medal, first rank, 2005, Outstanding Anti-Cancer Rsch. award, Taiwan Cancer Found., 1999, Presdl. Sci. prize, Taiwan, 2005, Achievement medal, first rank, Exec. Yuan, Taiwan, 2005, Officier dans L'Ordre Des Palmes Academifues, Ministry Edn. France, Knight Equestrain Order of Holy Sepulehre Jerusalem; named an Outstanding Scholar, Found. Outstanding Scholarship, 1995—99; grantee Fogarty Internat. Rsch. fellowship, NIH, 1989. Fellow Am. Coll. Epidemiology; mem. Acad. Sinica (academician), Third World Acad. Scis.; hon. mem. Mongol. Acad. Sci., Delta Omega Hon. Soc. Pub. Health. Office: Genomics Rsch Ctr Academia Sinica 128 Academia Rd Sect 2 Taipei 11529 Taiwan Home: 107-10F Rooservelt Rd Taipei 100 Taiwan Office Phone: 886 2 2787 1270. Business E-Mail: cjchen@ntu.edu.tw, chencj@gate.sinica.edu.tw.

CHEN, CHIH-CHENG, biomedical researcher; b. Tainan, Taiwan, June 13, 1965; PhD, U. Coll. London, 1998. Asst. rsch. fellow Inst. Biomed. Sci., Acad. Sinica, 2003—, assoc. rsch. fellow, 2011—. Adj. asst. prof. Nat. Taiwan U., 2003—, Nat. Yang-Ming U., 2003—, Nat. Def. Med. Ctr., 2003—. Mem.: Chinese Physiol. Soc., Internat. Assn. Study Pain, Soc. Neurosci. Taiwan. Avocation: tai chi. Office: Inst Biomed Sci 128 Academia Rd Sect 2 Taipei 115 Taiwan Business E-Mail: chih@ibms.sinica.edu.tw.

CHEN, CHIN-EN, hospital administrator; b. Tainan, Taiwan, May 4, 1961; MD, Chung-Shan Med. Coll., 1986. Vice-supt. Golden Hosp., 2011—. Office: 12-2 Minsheng E Rd Pingtung 900 Taiwan Office Fax: 08-7216032. Business E-Mail: chinenmd@ms21.hinet.net.

CHEN, CHIUNG-TONG, pharmacologist, researcher; s. Jih-Tang Chen; m. Ling-Ling Hwang, Mar. 26, 1991; children: Jennifer, Ian. BS, China Med. U., Taichung, Taiwan, 1986; MS, Nat. Yang-Ming U., Taipei, Taiwan, 1988; PhD, Ohio State U., 1997. Rsch. assoc. East Tenn. State U., Johnson City, 1997—99; asst. investigator Nat. Health Rsch. Insts., Taipei, 1999—2003, assoc. investigator Zhunan, Taiwan, 2003—; adj. asst. prof. Taipei Med. U., 2003—05. Dir. lab. animal ctr. Nat. Health Rsch. Insts., Zhunan, 2005—. Contbr. articles to profl. jours. Mem.: Pharm. Soc. of Republic of China (corr.), Am. Assn. Lab. Animal Sci. (corr.), Chinese Soc. Lab. Animal Scis. (corr.), Pharmacol. Soc. Taiwan (corr.), Am. Assn. Cancer Rsch (corr.). Office: Nat Health Rsch Insts 35 Keyan Rd Zhunan Miaoli 35053 Taiwan Business E-Mail: ctchen@nhri.org.tw.

CHEN, CHRISTOPHER, gynecologist, obstetrician, health facility administrator; b. Singapore; s. Pow Loke Chen and Soon Hee Choong; 1 child, Adrian. MB BS, U. Singapore, 1964; MD (hon.), Ricardo Palma U., Lima, Peru, 2006; MD in Reproductive Medicine (hon.), Yorker Internat. U., 2006; MD, U. Queensland, Australia, 2009; MD (hon.), U. Newcastle, Australia. Assoc. prof. dept. ob-gyn. U. Singapore, 1969—78; sr. lectr. Flinders U., Adelaide, Australia, 1978—87; head dept. reproductive medicine, clin. prof. K. K. Hosp. Nat. U. Singapore, 1987—93; dir. Gleneagles IVF Ctr., Gleneagles Hosp., Singapore, 1993—; infertility specialist, sr. gynecologist and obstetrician, pvt. practice Singapore, 1993—; hon. prof. Sch. Medicine, U. Queensland, Australia. Examiner Nat. U. Singapore; lectr. Edith Cowan U., Perth, Australia, 2002—; hon. prof., sr. cons., ob/gyn. Sri Ramachandra Med. Coll. and Rsch. Inst., Sri Ramachandra U., Harvard Med. Internat., 2005—; prof. faculty health U. Newcastle, Australia, 2005—; hon. prof. Ricardo Palma U., Lima, Peru, 2005—, U. Queensland Sch. Medicine, Australia; editor-in-chief Internat. Surgery, Jour. Internat. Coll. Surgeons. Contbr. sci. articles to profl. jours. Congress pres. Internat. Coll. Surgeons, Singapore, 2006; conf. pres. Internat. Forum Minimally Invasive Surgery, Nanjing, China, 2010; Sponsor Silver Screen Awards Ball, Singapore, 2002. Recipient Vandemataran award, India, 2004, Key to the City of Manila, Philippines Pres., Benigno Aquino III; named Lord of Stokes, Eng., Baron of Warter; fellow, Viswa Jyotish Vidyapith, 2004. Fellow: ACS, Royal Australian and New Zealand Coll. Obstetricians and Gynecologists, Acad. Medicine Singapore, Internat. Coll. Surgeons (pres. Singapore sect. 1991—, congress pres. 32d world congress 2000, world treas. 2000—04, co-editor Internat. Surgery jour. 2002—, world corp. sec. 2005—06, Congress pres. 2006, world pres. 2007—, hon. fellow, pres. 2009, chmn. sci. orgn. com. 2009, Max Thorek prof., chair surgery), Internat. Coll. Surgeons (hon.; chmn. sci. organising com., Beijing Conf. 2009, pres., Beijing Conf. 2009), Royal Australian Coll. Obstetrician and Gynecologists, Royal Coll. Obstetricians and Gynecologists (William Blair-Bell Meml. lectr. 1987); mem.: Fertility Soc. Australia, Brit. Med. Assn., Am. Soc. Reproductive Medicine, N.Y. Acad. Scis., European Soc. Human Reproduction and Embryology (Spirit Enterprise award 2008). Roman Catholic. Achievements include discovery of world's first success in human egg freezing; world's first IVF triplet pregnancy; produced Asia's first IVF sextuplets in Singapore, 1998. Avocations: painting, balinese gardening, recorder. Office: Christopher Chen Ctr for Reproductive Medicine Annexe Block Gleneagles Hosp 04-38 6A Napier Rd Singapore 258500 Singapore Office Phone: 65 6474 3900. Business E-Mail: info@cccrm.com.

CHEN, CHUAN-YU, medical researcher, educator; d. Ching-Pao Chen and Shou-Lien Fu. PhD, Johns Hopkins U., Balt., 2003. Cons. Am. Samoa Mental Health Stats. Data Infrastructure Project, Pago Pago, Md., 2002; postdoc. Johns Hopkins U., 2003—04; assoc. investigator, divsn. mental health and addiction medicine Nat. Health Rsch. Insts., Miaoli, Taiwan, 2009—; adj. assoc prof., dept. social medicine Inst. Pub. Health Nat., Yang-Ming U., Taipei, Taiwan, 2010—. Contbr. scientific papers to profl. jours. Recipient Morton Kramer award, Johns Hopkins U., 2003, Devel. award, Ctr. Adolescent Health Promotion and Disease Prevention, 2004. Mem.: Coll. Problems Drug Dependence, Phi Beta Kappa. Office: Nat. Yang Ming University No 155 Sec 2 Linong St Beital Dist Taipei 112 Taiwan Business E-Mail: chuanychen@ym.edu.tw.

CHEN, CHUN-SIANG, neurologist, educator; MD, Universidade De Sao Paulo, 1978. Diplomate Am. Bd. Neurol. Surgery. Intern Mt. Sinai Hosp., resident, 1999—2005; fellow St. Lukes Roosevelt Hosp., 2006; dir. Microsurgical Dissection Lab.; asst. rsch. prof. microdissection lab. of the dept. of neurosurgery Mt. Sinai Med. Ctr., 1992—. Author: (publ.) Microsurgical Anatomy of the Cavernous Sinus, 1992, The anatomical basis for surgical approaches to the craniovertebral junction, 1995, Preauricular transpetrosal approaches to the clivus, odontoid process, and cervical spine, 2004. Named one of NY Best Doctors, Castle Connolly, 1994. Office: Mount Sinai Medical Center Neurosurgery Department 5 E 98th St 17th Fl New York NY 10029 Office Phone: 212-241-8480. Office Fax: 212-410-0603.

CHEN, DAOZHEN, medical educator; b. Xuyi, Jiangsu, Oct. 29, 1971; D, SE U., 2008. Prof. Wuxi Matemaland Child Health Care Hosp., Affiliated Med. Sch. Nanjin, 2010. Office: 48 Huaishu Rd Wuxi Jiangsu 214002 China Business E-Mail: chendaozhen@163.com.

CHEN, DAVID Y T., urologic oncologist; MD, Cornell U., NY, 1997. Diplomate Am. Bd. Urology. Resident urology NY-Presbyn. Hosp./Weill Cornell Med. Ctr., NY; fellow Howard Hughes Med. Inst.; fellow urologic oncology dept. NY-Presbyn. Hosp./Weill Cornell Med. Ctr., NY; attending surgeon Fox Chase Cancer Ctr. Named one of the Top Doctors, Phila. Mag., 2011; scholar Rsch. Sholar, NIH. Fellow: ACS; mem.: Phila. Urol. Soc., Eastern Coop. Oncology Group, Soc. of Urologic Oncology, Soc. of Laparoendoscopic Surgeons, Am. Urol. Assn. Office: Foc Chase Cancer Center 333 Cottman Ave Philadelphia PA 19111-2497 Office Phone: 215-214-3270.

CHEN, DING-SHINN, gastroenterologist, educator, dean; b. Taiwan, July 6, 1943; m. Hsu-Mei Hsu; 2 children. Bachelor in Medicine, Nat. Taiwan U. Coll. of Medicine, 1968; PhD (hon.), Kaohsiung Med. U., 2002. Mil. med. doctor of ROC Army Min. of Nat. Def. (Republic of China), 1968—69; resident dept. internal medicine Nat. Taiwan U. Hosp., 1969—72, chief resident dept. internal medicine, 1972—73, clin. tng. internal medicine and gasteroenterology, 1973, staff physician dept. internal medicine, 1978—96, chief divsn of gastroenterology/hepatology dept. internal medicine, 1996—2001; rsch. asst. Nat. Sci. Coun. of the Republic of China, 1973—75; vis. fellow Nat. Cancer Ctr. Rsch. Inst., Tokyo, 1975; vis. scientist, Nat. Inst. of Allergy and Infectious Disease NIH, Bethesda, Md., 1979—80; vis. staff mem. dept. internal medicine Nat. Taiwan U. Coll. of Medicine, 1973—75, instr. dept. internal medicine, 1975, staff physician, 1975—78, assoc. prof. dept. internal medicine, 1978—83, prof., 1983—, dir. Grad. Inst. of Clin. Medicine, 1985—88, dean, 2001—. Founding dir., Hepatitis Rsch. Ctr. Nat. Taiwan U. Hosp., Taipei, 1987—2001; mem. hepatitis control com. dept. of health Taiwan Govt., 1982—, chmn. hepatitis control com., 1997—; med. advisor Blood Donation Assn., 1991—; advisor Taipei Inst. of Pathology, 1991—; reg. adv. mem. Am. Gastroenterological Assn., 1996—; adj. prof. Grad. Inst. of Clin. Medicine Nat. Taiwan U. Coll. of Medicine, 1996—2001; nat. chair-prof. of medicine Ministry of Edn., 1997—2003; science and technology advisor to Premier Taiwanese Govt., 1998— Author various articles in publs.; assoc. editor Journal of Biomedical Science, 1994—, Journal of Internal Medicine, 1999—, Hepatology, 2001—06, Molecular Carcinogenesis, 2005—, mem. of several editl. bds., referee for manuscript of scientific journals. Recipient Abbott Laboratories Rsch. award, 1986, Outstanding Rsch. award in Biology and Medicine, Nat. Sci. Coun., 1987—93, Grand award, Soc. of Chinese Bioscientists in America, 1993, Hou Jin-Duei Outstanding Contribution award in Basic Sci., 1994, Outstanding Achievement award, Found. for the Advancement of Outstanding Scholarship, 2005, Trieste Sci. prize in Med. Sciences, Third World Acad. Scis., 2006. Fellow: Third World Acad. of Sciences; mem.: American Gastroenterological Assn., American Assn. for the Study of the Liver, Asian-Pacific Assn. for the Study of Liver, Asian-Pacific Assn. of Gastroenterology (chmn. program com. 1999—2006, coun. mem. 2004—06), Internat. Assn. for Study of Liver (v.p. 2000, pres. 2004—06), Gastroenterological Soc. Taiwan (pres. 1997—2003), Formosan Med. Assn. (pres. 2001—04), Taiwan Assn. for Study of Liver (pres. 1995—97), Academia Sinica (curator coun. mtg. 1993—, ctrl. adv. com. 1996—, adv. coun. Inst. of Biomedical Sciences 1996—), NAS (fgn. assoc. 2005—), Caring Physicians of the World, World Med. Assn. Office: National Taiwan University College of Medicine 1 Jen-Ai Road Section 1 Taipei 100 Taiwan Office Phone: 886-2-23123456 ext. 8000, 886-2-23562185. Office Fax: 886-2-23224793, 886-2-23317624.

CHEN, DONGBAO, medical educator, director; b. Shaanxi, China, May 26, 1965; PhD, Beijing Agrl. U., 1991. Assoc. prof. U. Calif. San Diego, 2004—08; assoc. prof., dir. U. Calif., Irvine, 2008—. Grant, NIH, NHLIBI. Mem.: Soc. Gynecologic Investigation, Am. Physiol. Soc., Perinatal Rsch. Soc., Endocrine Soc., Soc. for Study Reproduction. Avocation: Go. Office: University Calif Med Surgery 1 Bldg 810 Rm 140 Irvine CA 92697 Business E-Mail: dongbaoc@uci.edu.

CHEN, GUOXUN, medical educator; b. Wuhan, Hubei, China, Feb. 10, 1965; PhD, U. Tex. Southwestern Med. Ctr., Dallas, 2001. Asst. prof. U. Tenn., Knoxville, 2006—. Recipient New Investigator award, Am. Heart Assn. NPAM Coun. Mem.: Am. Soc. Nutrition, Am. Heart Assn. Office: Rm 229 Jessie Harris Bldg 1215 W Knoxville TN 37996 Office Fax: 865-974-3491. Business E-Mail: gchen6@utk.edu.

CHEN, HAIFENG, health science association administrator, researcher; s. Rensheng Chen and Minyu Xu; m. Min Chen, Jan. 28, 1994; children: Sharon Lucia, Raymond Louis. BS, Sun Yat-sen U., Guangzhou, Guangong Province, China, 1982; MS, Sichuan U., Chengdu, Sichuan Province, China, 1985; PhD, U. Saarlandes, Saarbrücken, Germany, 1992. Postdoc. fellow U. Kans. Med. Ctr., Kans. City, 1992—96; postdoc. scientist Cell Genesys, Inc., Foster City, Calif., 1996—97; rsch. scientist Genovo, Inc., Sharon Hill, Pa., 1997—2000, Avigen, Inc., Alameda, Calif., 2000—05; v.p. Asklepois Bio-Pharm., Inc., Chapel Hill, NC, 2005—06; CEO Virovek, Inc., Hayward, Calif., 2006—. Ch. deacon Chinese Christ Ch. Hayward, Calif., 2000—10. Postdoc. fellowship, Marion Merrell Dow Found., 1992. Mem.: Am. Soc. Gene and Cell Therapy. Achievements include patents for technologies for large-scale production of adeno-associated virus. Office: Virovek Inc 3521 Investment Blvd Ste 1 Hayward CA 94545 Office Fax: 510-887-7178. Personal E-mail: haifengchen05@yahoo.com. Business E-Mail: info@virovek.com.

CHEN, HARRY L., public health service officer, former state legislator; b. NYC, Aug. 7, 1952; m. Anne D. Lezak; 3 children. BA, U. Mich., 1973; MD, Oreg. Health Sciences U., 1979. Internship Boston U., Boston City Hosp., 1979—80; resident Oreg. Health Sciences U., 1981—83, chief resident, 1983; faculty mem. George Washington U. Med. Ctr. Dept. Emergency Medicine, 1983—88; emergency physician, emergency dept. Rutland Regional Medical Ctr., 1988—2011, medical dir., 1998—2004; mem. Dist. 1 Vt. House of Reps., Montpelier, 2004—08; vice chair. Vt. House Edn. & Health Care Com., 2007; commr. Vt. Dept. Health, 2011—. Interim exec. dir. Vt. Program on Quality in Health Care, 2010. Mem. Barstow Meml. Sch. Bd., 1995—2007; trustee U. Vt., 2007—. Recipient Legislative award, Vt. Children's Forum, 2004, Physician's Award for Cmty. Svc., Vt. State Medical Soc., 2008. Democrat. Office: Vermont Dept Health 108 Cherry St Burlington VT 05402 Office Phone: 802-863-7200. Office Fax: 802-865-7754. *

CHEN, HONG-DUO, dermatologist, immunologist; b. Shaoxing, Zhejiang, China, Feb. 18, 1933; s. Shunbin Chen and Chayi Hu; m. Ming Zhai, Sept. 18, 1966; 1 child, John Z.S. MD, China Med. U., 1956; student, U. of Pa, 1979—82. From resident to prof. No. 1 Hosp. of China Med. U., Shenyang, Liaoning, China, 1956—83, prof. dept. dermatology, 1983—. Rsch. assoc. sch. medicine U. Pa., Phila., 1979—80; vis. prof. U. Pa., 1980—82; chmn. dept. dermatology No. 1 Hosp. of China Med. U., 1985—2002, pres., 1988—94, the 9th Internat. Congress of Dermatology, Beijing, 1994—; mem. internat. adv. com. Archives of Dermatology, 1998—2001; pres. the 5th Asian Dermatol. Congress, Beijing, 1998; dir. rsch. lab. clin. immunology No. 1 Hosp. of China Med. U., 1999—. Editor: Chinese Jour. Dermatology, 1994—, The Chinese Jour. Dermatological Congress, 1998—; contbr. articles to profl. jours. V.chmn. Liaoning provincial com. Chinese People's Polit. Cons. Conf., Shenyang, Liaoning, China, 1986. Recipient First Class award, Ministry, 1984, Nat. Outstanding Specialist award, Ministry of Labour and Pers., 1986, Nat. Medal of May Day award, All-China Fedn. of Trade Union, 1987, Second Class award, Ministry, 1988, Nat. Model Worker award, All-China Fedn. of Trade Union, 1989, Third Class award, Ministry, 1993. Master: Chinese Soc. of Dermatology (pres. 1994); mem.: Chinese Med. Assn. (exec. coun. 2000), Chinese Acad. Engring. (academician 1999—), Internat. Soc. of Cosmetic Dermatology (adv. coun. 1998), Mem. of Chinese Med. Assn., Asian Dermatol. Assn. (coun. mem. 1998), Internat. Soc. of Dermatology (bd. dir. 2001). Avocations: volleyball, jogging.

CHEN, HUBIAO, medical educator; b. Hunan, China, Aug. 15, 1962; PhD, Beijing Med. U., 1988. Assoc. prof., dept. botany Sch. Pharm. Scis. Beijing Med. U., 1990—97; prof., dept. natural medicines Sch. Pharm. Scis. Peking U. Health Sci. Ctr., 1997—2006; asst. prof. Kanazawa U., Japan, 2000—02, Sch. Chinese Medicine Hong Kong Bapt. U., 2006—10, assoc. prof., 2010—. Recipient 2nd Class prize, Nat. Edn. Com., 3rd Class prize, Chinese Drug Adminstrn. Mem.: Jour. Chinese Pharm. Scis., China Jour. Chinese Materia Medica, China Wild Plant Conservation Assn. (medicinal plants conservation com.), Chinese Traditional Drugs Resources Ecology Assn., Medicinal Botany and Plant Medicine Chinese Bot. Assn. Avocations: photography, music. Office: 7 Baptist University Rd Kowloon Tong Hong Kong China

CHEN, HUNG YI, cardiologist; b. Taipei, Taiwan, Aug. 30, 1967; MS, Yang-Ming U., 2007. Chief cardiology Taipei City Hosp., Heping Br., 2004. Office: 33 Sec 2 Zhonghua Rd Taipei 10065 Taiwan Office Phone: 00-886-938666638. E-mail: anigi426@ms24.hinet.net.

CHEN, HUNG-CHI, academic administrator, plastic surgeon; b. Chung-hwa, Taiwan, Sept. 5, 1949; s. Kuo-hsiung Chen and Bih-tao Hsieh; m. Yueh-bih Tang Chen, Dec. 25, 1979; children: Shih-heng, Wei-yin. MD, Nat. Taiwan U., Taipei, 1974; MA in Health Adminstrn., Kaohsiung Med. U., Taiwan, 2006. Resident gen. surgery Nat. Taiwan U. Hosp., 1976—80; rsch. fellow St. Vincent's Hosp./U. Melbourne, Australia, 1982—83; attending surgeon dept. plastic surgery Chang Gung Meml. Hosp., Taipei, 1983—2000, chief dept. plastic surgery, 2000—03; supt. E-da Hosp., Kaohsiung, Taiwan, 2003—10, Internat. Med. Svc. Ctr., China Med. U. Hosp., Taichung, Taiwan, 2010—. Rschr. Louisville Hand Ctr., 1989; fellow Kleinert Inst. Hand Surgery, Louisville, 1991—92. Contbr. articles to profl. jours., chapters to books. Recipient Outstanding Rsch. award, Nat. Sci. Acad., Taiwan, 1993, Outstanding Physician award, Taipei Physicians' Assn., 1997. Fellow: ACS, Internat. Coll. Surgeons; mem.: Soc. Surgery of the Hand (pres. 2000—02), Soc. Plastic Surgery. Achievements include research in microvascular transfer of intestine for various reconstructive purposes including reconstruction of esophagus and voice, urethra, vagina and the prevention of surgical complications. Avocation: drawing. Office: Cosmetic Surgery Center China Medical Univ Hosp Bldg 11F 2 Yuh-Der Road Taichung City Taiwan 40447 *

CHEN, HUNG-CHUN, education educator; s. Tze-Zeng Chen and Liu-Yeh Chen Lu; m. Tsung-Fang Tsai, Apr. 13, 1956; children: Cheng-How, Tze-Ying. MD, PhD, Kaohsiung Med. U., 1992—2000. Prof. & chief, dept. of nephrology Kaohsiung Med. U. Hosp., Taiwan, 2000—; dir., faculty of renal care Kaohsiung Med. U., Taiwan. Chief editor Acta Nophrologica Taiwan Soc. Nephrology. Recipient Young Investigator award, 6th Internat. Congress on Nutrition and Metabolism in Renal Disease, 1991, Taiwan Soc. of Nephrology, 1995, Prof. Chen Wang-Yu award, 1998, Prof. Chen Fan-Wu Award, Taiwan Soc. of Endocrinology and Metabolism, 2002, award, Nat. Sci. Coun., Taiwan, 1991, 1993, 1994, 1998, 1999, 2000. Mem.: Taiwan Soc. of Nephrology (mem. exec. bd. 1998). Office: Kaohsiung Med Univ 100 Tzyou First Rd Kaohsiung 807 Taiwan Office Fax: +886-7-3228721; Home Fax: +886-7-3228721. E-mail: chenhc@kmu.edu.tw.

CHEN, IRVIN SHAO YU, microbiologist, educator; b. Toms River, NJ, Sept. 29, 1955; s. Tseh-An and Cheh-Chen (Chang) C.; m. Diven Sun, June 21, 1981; children: Katrina Nai Ching, Kevin Nai Hong. BA, Cornell U., 1977; PhD, U. Wis., 1981. Asst. prof. UCLA Sch. Medicine, 1984-86, assoc. prof., 1986-90, prof., 1990—. Dir. AIDS Inst. UCLA, 1991—, Core BSL3 SCID-hu Mouse Lab., 1989—, Core Human REtrovirus Lab., 1989—, AIDS Ctr. Virology Lab., 1986, UCLA Sch. of Medicine Core Human Retrovirus Facility, 1989; Wellcome vis. prof. microbiology East Carolina U., 1993; bd. dirs. Arthur Ashe Found. for the Defeat of AIDS. Mem. editl. adv. bd. Oncogene, 1986, Cancer Cells, 1989; mem. editl. bd. AIDS Rsch. and Human Retrovirus, 1990, Jour. of Virology, 1991; contbr. articles to Sci., Nature, Cell; contbr. chpt.: HTLV-1 and HTLV-II in Virology, 1990. Grantee NIH, 1982—, U. Calif. U. Task Force on AIDS, 1986—; recipient Jr. Faculty award Am. Cancer Soc., 1984, Scholar award Leukemia Soc. Am., 1989, Stohlman Scholar award, 1992, Jr. Faculty award Am. Cancer Soc., 1984, Richard F. Dwyer-Eleanor W. Dwyer Award for Exellence Jonsson Comprehensive Cancer Ctr., 1984, Merit award Nat. Cancer Inst. Mem. AAAS, Am. Soc. Microbiology, Jonsson Comprehensive Cancer Ctr. Achievements include patent for retroviral polypeptides associated with human transformation; first to achieve molecular cloning of human T-cell leukemia virus type II, discovery of trans-activation gene as essential gene for HTLV-II, molecular basis for HIV-1 tropism for macrophages. Office: UCLA Sch Medicine Dept Medicine and Immunology 11-934 Factor Los Angeles CA 90024-1678

CHEN, JAMES PAI-FUN, biology professor, researcher; b. Fungyuan, Taichung, Taiwan, May 1, 1929; came to U.S., 1952; s. Chuan and Su-wuo (Lin) C.; m. Metis Hsiu-chun Lin, Dec. 19, 1964; children: Mark Hsin-tzu, Eunice Hsin-yi, Jeremy Hsin-tao. BS, Houghton Coll., NY, 1955; MS, St. Lawrence U., 1957; PhD, Pa. State U., 1961. From instr. to assoc. prof. Houghton Coll., 1960-64; rsch. assoc. Coll. of Medicine U. Vt., Burlington, 1964-65; rsch. assoc. Sch. of Medicine SUNY, Buffalo, 1965-68; asst. prof. U. Tex. Med. Br., Galveston, 1968-75; sr. rsch. assoc. NASA/Johnson Space Ctr., Houston, 1975-76; rsch. assoc. prof. U. Tenn. Meml. Rsch. Ctr., Knoxville, 1976-78; assoc. prof. Coll. of Medicine U. Tenn., Knoxville, 1978-84, prof. Grad. Sch. of Medicine, 1984—2003, prof. emeritus Grad. Sch. of Medicine, 2005—. Rsch. rev. com. Tex. affiliate Am. Heart Assn., Austin, 1974-76; co-investigator Spacelab I project, Johnson Space Ctr., Houston, 1976-83; vis. prof. Trnovo Hosp. Internal Medicine, Ljubljana, Yugoslavia, 1985. Grantee Robert Welch Found., 1970-74, Ortho Rsch. Found., 1971-75, NIH, 1975-82, Am. Heart Assn. Tex. affiliate, 1969-72, 74-75, Am. Heart Assn. Tenn. affiliate, 1984-85, 89-90, U.S. Army Med. Rsch., 1988-91. Fellow Internat. Soc. Hematology; mem. Am. Assn. Immunologists, Am. Soc. Biochemistry and Molecular Biology, Internat. Soc. Thrombosis and Haemostasis, Internat. Fibrinogen Rsch. Soc., Internat. Soc. Fibrinolysis Proteolysis, Am. Bd. Bioanalysis (clin. lab. dir.). Achievements include research in thrombosis and hemostasis; discovery of additional proteolytic fragmentation in the high temperature trypsin cleavage of human IgM; development of a radioimmunoassay for fragment E-neoantigen and applied it to the clinical assay of hypercoagulable state; discovered evidence of the coagulopathy in Pichinde virus-infected guinea pigs; establishment of blood tests to monitor trauma patients for thromboembolism; recognized that hypercoagulability in preterm infants with intraventricular hemorrhage is associated with fibrinolytic shutdown; ascertained that complement and cytokines are responsible for antibody-mediated hypercoagulability in the anti-T-cell therapy of transplantation. Office: U Tenn Med Ctr Grad Sch Medicine Box 2 1924 Alcoa Hwy Knoxville TN 37920-1511 Home Phone: 865-690-7003. Business E-Mail: jchen@uthsc.edu.

CHEN, JAW-WEN, cardiologist, researcher; b. Taipei, Taiwan, Apr. 10, 1959; s. Jong-Peng Chen and Ju-Ying Neu. MD, Kaohsiung Med. U., Taiwan, 1984. Resident Vet. Gen. Hosp., Taipei, 1986-90, chief resident, 1990-91, fellow, 1991-93, vis. staff, 1993—; postdoctoral rschr. Stanford U., Calif., 1997-98; assoc. prof. Nat. Yang-Ming U. Sch. Medicine, Taipei, 2003—06, prof., 2006—. Sec. gen. Taiwan Soc. Lipids Athersclerosis, 2002-06, pres. 2006-. Author: When You Can Not Hide, 1984; contbr. articles to profl. jours. Mem. Am. Heart Assn., Internat. Soc. Lipids Arthersclerosis, NY Acad. Sci. Avocations: reading, writing, chess. Office: Vet Gen Hosp 201 Shih-Pai Rd Sect 2 Taipei Taiwan Business E-Mail: jwchen@vghtpe.gov.tw.

CHEN, JIH-JUNG, medical educator; s. Ming-Chuan Chen and Chen-Mei Cheng; m. Yu-Chen Liang, June 3, 2000; children: Zih-Rong, Rou-Chian. BaS in Med. Tech., China Med. U., Taichung, Taiwan, 1989; MS in Natural Products, Kaohsiung Med. U., Taiwan, 1994; PhD in Pharm. Scis., Kaohsiung Med. U., 1997. Lic. medical technologist in lab. medicine Exam. Yuan Republic China, 1989. Prof. Tajen U., Pingtung, Taiwan, 1997—, Nat. Pingtung Inst. Commerce, Taiwan, 2007—. Dir. natural products lab. Tajen U., 1997—. Contbr. articles to profl. jours. 2d lt. Taiwan Army, 1989—91. Mem.: Chinese Natural Products Soc. (life), Pharm. Soc. Taiwan (life). Achievements include research in bioactive natural products and new drug development. Avocation: music. Home: No5-4 Gueiren Rd Pingtung City Pingtung County 907 Taiwan Office: Tajen Univ No 20 Weishin Rd Yanpu Shiang Pingtung 907 Taiwan Office Fax: 886 8 7625308; Home Fax: 886 8 7625308. Business E-Mail: jjchen@mail.tajen.edu.tw.

CHEN, JIU-CHIUAN, medical educator, researcher; b. Taipei, Taiwan, Jan. 20, 1966; MD, Taipei Med. U., 1992; DSc, Harvard U., 2002. Rsch. fellow Harvard U., Sch. Pub. Health, 2002—03, rsch. assoc., 2003—08; asst. prof. U. NC, Chapel Hill, 2004—09, mem. admission com., dept. epidemiology, 2004—09, chair, doctoral qualifying exam. com., occupl. and environ. epidemiology, 2005—06, adv. com., environ. epidemiology tng. program, 2006—07; assoc. prof. U. So. Calif., Keck Sch. Medicine, 2009—. External adv. bd. NIEHS-UCLA Ctr. Gene-Environment Studies Parkinson's Disease, 2011; neurol., aging, and musculoskeletal epidemiology study sect. mem. Nat. Inst. Health, Ctr. Sci. Rev., 2011. Recipient Rosenblith award, Health Effects Inst., Jr. Faculty Devel. award, U. NC, Chapel Hill; grant, Nat. Inst. Aging, Nat. Heart, Lung, and Blood Inst. Innovative Rsch. Program. Mem.: Environ. and Occupl. Medicine Assn. (Taiwan), Internat. Soc. Advance Alzheimer Rsch. and Treatment, Sleep Rsch. Soc., Internat. Soc. Environ. Epidemiology, Soc. Epidemiologic Rsch. Avocations: hiking, rugby, movies. Office: Divsn Environ Health Dept Preventive Medicine 2001 N Soto St MC 9237 Los Angeles CA 90089 Office Phone: 323-442-2949. Business E-Mail: jcchen@usc.edu.

CHEN, JOHN CALVIN, retired psychiatrist; b. Augusta, Ga., Apr. 30, 1949; s. Calvin H. Chen and Lora L. Liu. BA in History, Pacific Union Coll., 1971; MD, Loma Linda U., 1974; PhD in Philosophy, Claremont Grad. U., 1984; JD, UCLA, 1987; MA in History, Calif. State U. LA, 2011. Bar: Calif. 1987, US Dist. Ct. (ctrl. dist.) Calif. 1988; diplomate Am. Bd. Psychiatry and Neurology, Child and Adolescent Psychiatry. Resident in psychiatry Loma Linda U. Med. Ctr., 1975-77; fellow in child and family psychiatry Cedars-Sinai Med. Ctr., LA, 1977-78; psychiat. cons. San Bernardino County Mental Health Dept., Calif., 1979-83; pvt. practice Claremont, Calif., 1980-84; fellow in child and adolescent psychiatry U. So. Calif., LA, 1983-84; law clk. to Hon. William P. Gray US Dist. Ct., LA, 1987-88; mental health psychiatrist LA County Dept. Mental Health, LA, 1988-94, Alameda County Health Care Svcs. Agy., Fremont, Calif., 1994-97; physician specialist LA County Dept. Health Svcs., 1997—99; sr. physician, 1999—2003; attending physician Martin Luther King Jr. Hosp., LA, 1997—2004; child and adolescent psychiatrist Augustus F. Hawkins Mental Health Ctr., LA, 1997—2004, chief child/adolescent svc., 1998—2003; staff Behavioral Neuroscience Rsch. Ctr., Charles Drew Univ., 2003—05; ret., 2005. Adj. instr. social scis., philosophy, Fullerton Coll., Calif., 1989-90; adj. asst. prof. psychiatry Charles Drew U., 1998-2004, asst. clin. prof., 2004-09; asst. clin. prof. psychiatry UCLA Sch. Medicine, 1998-2004; faculty Trinity Coll. Grad. Studies, 2004-2008. Contbr. chapters to books Calif. hist., articles to profl. jours. Univ. fellow, Claremont Grad. Sch., 1980—81. Mem.: Chinese Hist. Soc. Southern Calif., Chinese Hist. Soc. America, Am. Hist. Assn., Phi Kappa Phi, Phi Alpha Theta, Golden Key Internat. Honor Soc. Office: 745 E Valley Blvd PMB 120 San Gabriel CA 91776-3549

CHEN, JONATHAN M., thoracic surgeon, educator; b. Berkeley, Calif., Oct. 6, 1968; BS cum laude, Yale U., New Haven, 1990; MD, Columbia U. Coll. Physicians and Surgeons, NYC, 1994. Intern, resident gen. surgery NY Presbyn. Hosp./Columbia U. Med. Ctr., NYC, 1994—99, rsch. fellow, cardiac surgery, 1997—98, chief resident gen. surgery, 1999—2000, fellow cardiothoracic surgery, 2000—02, advanced fellow, mechanical cardiac assistance, 2002, advanced fellow in congenital cardiac surgery, 2003—04, attending surgeon, 2002—. Asst. prof. surgery Columbia U. Coll. Physicians and Surgeons, 2004—; site chief, pediatric surgery NY Weill Cornell Med. Ctr., 2004; asst. prof. Cardiothoracic Surgery, Weill Cornell Med. Coll., NYC, assoc. prof., 2007; dir. pediat. cardiovascular surgery Xly Presbyn. Hosp. NY Weill Cornell, 2007; surg. dir. pediat. heart transplantation Morgan Stanley Children Hosp., 2008. Contbr. articles to med. jours. Recipient Best Sr. Resident Tchg. award, Columbia U., dept. surgery, 2000, Blakemore Rsch. award, 2000; named Physician of Yr., NY Presbyn. Hosp., 2002; named one of 40 Under 40, Crain's NY Bus. Mag., 2006; named to, Best Drs. NY, 2007. Mem.: ACS, Am. Assn. Hearts Surgeons, Am. Acad. Pediatrics, Am. Coll. Cardiology, Soc. Thoracic Surgeons, Internat. Soc. Heart and Lung Transplantation, Soc. Alum. NY Presbyterian, Am. Soc. Transplantation, NY Soc. for Thoracic Surgery. Office: Morgan Stanley Childresn Hosp NY Presbyterian CHN Rm 270 3959 Broadway New York NY 10032 Office Phone: 212-305-5975. Office Fax: 212-305-4408. Business E-Mail: jmc23@columbia.edu.

CHEN, JUZA, urologist, educator; b. Kutaisi, Georgia, July 7, 1949; MD, Nalchik U., Russia, 1973. Assoc. prof. Tel Aviv Sourasky Med. Ctr., 1974—, dir., Sexual Health Clinic Dept. Urology, 1995—; rsch. fellow Med. Coll. Va., Richmond, 1992—94, U. Coll. London Midlesex Hosp., London, 1997, Elisabetinen Hosp., Linz, Austria, 2002. Recipient award, Israeli Urol. Assn., 2006; Pfizer Israeli Rsch. grant, 2001, Pfizer Internat. Rsch. grant, 2002. Mem.: ILSSM, ESSM, ISSM, EUA, AUA. Avocations: art, music, sports. Home: 8 Kosovsky Str Tel Aviv 62917 Israel Office Phone: 97236973475. Home Fax: 97235060859. Business E-Mail: juza@tasmc.health.gov.il.

CHEN, KOW-TONG, physician, researcher; b. Taipei, Taiwan, Aug. 2, 1947; s. Wun-Chi Chen and Yi-Pin Chen-Chang; m. Mu-Tan Fan, Dec. 15, 1949; 1 child, Yu-Lin. PhD, Nat. Def. Med. Ctr., Taipei, Taiwan, 1998. Physician of internal medicine Army Hosp., Taipei, Taiwan, 1972—84; dir. field epidemiology tng. program Dept. of Health, Taipei, 1984—2003; dir. Ctr. Disease Control, Taipei, Taiwan, 2003—04; prof. dept. pub. health Coll. Medicine Nat. Cheng-Kung U., 2004—; chmna. dept. pub. health Coll. Medicine Nat. Cheng-Kung U. Dir. Ctr. Disease Control, Taipei, 2003—04; dir. gen. Ctr. STD Control. Mem.: Family Physician Assn., Occupl. Physician Assn., Pub. Health Assn. Office Phone: 866-933890260. E-mail: ktchen@mail.ncku.edu.tw, kowton@ms81.hinet.net. *

CHEN, KUEN HAI, physician; b. Tachia, Taiwan, May 23, 1937; arrived in U.S., 1966, naturalized, 1976; s. John Bei and Yeh (Liang) Chen; m. Fu Mei Lai, Jan. 1, 1966; children: Richard, Humphrey, Christopher. BS, Nat. Taiwan U., Taipei, 1959, MD, 1964. Diplomate Am. Bd. Family Practice. Intern Ill. Ctrl. Hosp., Chgo., 1966—67; resident gen. surgery Sister's Hosp., Buffalo, 1967—69; resident gen. surgery C and O Hosp., Huntington, W.Va., 1970—71; fellow spinal cord injury svc. VA Hosp., East Orange, NJ, 1971—72; chief Veteran's Hosp., East Orange, NJ, 1972—76; staff mem. First Ave. Med. Ctr., NYC, 1976—. Adv. bd. Dupont, 1999—, Mc Neil Health Network, 1999—, Agouron, 2000—, Bristol Myers Roche, 2000—; cons. Schering/Key Glaxo Wellcome Inc. Nat. Irritable Bowel Syndrome Awareness Registry, 2000—; mem. physicians coun. Heritage Found., 1994—; dir. K.F.C. Corp.; analyst Am. Bd. Disability, 1999. Author: Am. Spoken English; founding prodr. GOP TV, 1994—. Mem. Presdl. Adv. Commn., 1992, Presdl. Commn. Am. Agenda, 1992; del. Presdl. Trust, 1992; pres. Parents' Assn., 1980—84; hon. chmn. Physician's Adv. Bd.; chmn. Nominating Com., 2008—; adv. mem. Rep. Nat. Commn. Am. Agenda, 1992—; chmn. adv. bd. Rep. Nat. Com., 1994—, hon. co-chmn. bus. adv. coun., 1998, mem. adv. coun., 1998, hon. co-chmn., 1999—; founding mem. Rep. Campaign Coun., 1994—, nat. campaign advisor, 1995—; founding mem. Eisenhower Commn., 1995—96; mem. Rep. Senator Adv. Coun., 1997—; chmn. adv. coun. Rep. Nat. Com., 1999; mem. Rep. Senator Inner Cir., 1998—; hon. co-chair inaugural com. 43d Pres. of US, 2001; del. NJ Rep. Presdl. Task Force, 1994—98; co-chmn. Election Adv. Bd., 2000—; chmn. joint session, bd. deaconess mtgs. Taiwan Union Presbyn. Ch., NY, 1983, active NY; elder Taiwan Presbyn. Ch. No. Jersey, 2007—; v.p. Nat. Taiwanese Presbyn. Coun., Nebr., 2006—09, pres., 2009—. With Taiwan Air Force, 1965. Recipient Disting. Svc. and Leadership award, Nat. Taiwan U., Patriotic award, US Pres., Congl. Medal of Distinction, 2001, Rep. of Yr. award, Presdl. Bus. Commn., 2002—03, Rep. Senatorial Medal of Freedom, 2002; named Mem. of Yr., Rep. Presdl. Task Force, 1996, Physician of Yr., 2001—03, Rep. of Yr., 2002, Bus. Man of Yr., 2004—07, Patriot of Yr., 2007. Fellow: Am. Geriat. Soc., Am. Acad. Family Physician; mem.: AMA (Physician Recognition award 1969, 1972, 1975, 1978, 1981, 1984, 1987, 1990, 1993), NAPCUSA (treas. 2009—11, vice chmn. 2011—), Nat. Taiwanese Presby. Ch. (NE chpt.) (chmn., treas. 2009—), Presdl. Bus. Commn., Nat. Irritable Syndrome Awareness Registry, N.Am. Taiwanese Med. Assn. (bd. dir. greater NY chpt. 1985—, pres. 1987—89, chmn. edn. com. 1989—95), W.Va. Med. Inst., Nat. Bd. Addiction Examiners (Dr. addiction counselor), Am. Spinal Injury Assn., Taita Jing-Fu Med. Found. (hon. dir.), Internat. Soc. Paraplegia, NY County Med. Soc. (mem. com. healthcare agency), Am. Coll. Emergency Physicians, NY Acad. Sci., Am. Bd. Disability Analysis, Nat. Taiwan U. Alumni Assn. (bd. dir. 1981—, chmn. edn. com. 1984—94, treas. 1991—94, chmn. by-law com. 1994—96, pres. 1999—2001), Heritage Found., Nat. Taiwan U. Med. Coll. Alumni Assn. (exec. dir. 1979—81, pres. 1981—83, permanent bd. dir. 1984, trustee 1985—88, chmn. edn. com. 1987—95, chmn. fund campaign com. 1988—94, N.Y. chpt. bd. dir. 1994, chmn. by-law com. 1994—), Alpha Omega Alpha. Presbyterian.

CHEN, LEO LI-TZONG, medical researcher; b. Hong Kong, Aug. 6, 1955; PhD, Kaohsiung Med. U., 2001. Chmn. Instn. Rev. Bd., Nat. Health Rsch. Inst., 2010—; dep. dir., investigator Nat. Inst. Cancer Rsch., Nat. Health Rsch. Inst., 2008—. Physician Kaohsiung Med. U. Hosp., 1988; adj. attending physician Veterans Gen. Hosp., 1995—2006, Nat. Taiwan U. Hosp., 1995—2009, Tri-svc. Gen. Hosp., 2006—07, Nat. Cheng-Kung U. Hosp., 2007. Recipient Rsch. award, Ann. Meeting Joint Taiwan Oncology Socs., 2003, Outstanding Rsch. award, Kaohsiung Med. U., 2005—06, Rsch. Achievement award, Nat. Health Rsch. Inst., 2010. Mem.: Soc. Gastroenterology Soc., Chinese Oncology Soc., Digestive Endoscopy Soc. Taiwan, Am. Soc. Clin. Oncology, European Soc. Med. Oncology. Avocations: golf, singing. Office: 367 Sheng-Li Rd Tainan 704 Taiwan Personal E-mail: chiang.blanca@gmail.com.

CHEN, LEON, periodontist; Grad., U. Mich., 1985—88; DMD, Harvard U. Sch. of Dental Medicine, 1988—93; attended Rsch. Program, Forsyth Dental Inst., 1992—93; MS in Periodontics, Northwestern U. Dental Sch., 1993—95. Resident Northwestern Univ., 1995. Hon. co-chmn. Bus. Adv. Coun., 2000; diplomate Internat. Congress of Oral Implantologist, 2003—; lectr. Am. Acad. of Periodontology, 2009; co-founder Asia region Am. Dental Implant Assn., 2010. Editor: (magazine) International Magazine of Oral Implantology, 2005. Recipient US Senatorial Certificate of Commendation, 2001, Asia Pacific Festival and Trade-show Professional Services award, 2002, Star of Taiwan award, 2003, Asian Pacific Professional Services award, 2005, Taiwan Government Model of Taiwan Entrepreneurs award, 2007, Taiwan National award, 2008; named Asian Chamber Business Person of the Year, 2000, 2001, Congressional District Business Person of the Year, 2001, Consumer Review Periodontists of the Year, 2001, Consumer Review Periodontist and Implantologist of the Year, 2003; named one of Las Vegas Life Top Dentist, 2002, Top Influential Person in Asia, 2009; nominee Summerlin's Best Dentist, Summerline Mag., 2005. Fellow: Internat. Congress of Oral Implantologists; mem.: Am. Acad. of Anti-Aging Medicine, Am. Coll. of Oral Implantology, Am. Acad. of Implant Dentistry, Implant Prosthodontics Sect. of the ICOI, Internat. Congress of Oral Implantologists, Am. Acad. of Periodontology. Office: Dental Implant Institute 59 Las Tunas Arcadia CA 91007 Office Phone: 626-446-0700.

CHEN, LIN-CHI, engineering educator; b. Yi-Lan County, Taiwan, June 24, 1975; PhD in Chem. Engring., Nat. Taiwan U., 2001. Postdoc. rsch. fellow, dept. chem. engring. Nat. Cheng-Kung U., 2002, Inst. Biomed. Scis., Acad. Sinica, 2002—05, Nat. Taiwan U., 2001—02, asst. prof., dept. bio-indsl. mechatronics engring., 2005—09, assoc. prof., 2009—, group leader, Bioenergy Rsch. Ctr., 2006. Editl. bd. mem. Smart Materials Rsch. Jour., Hindawi Pub. Co., 2010. Recipient Rsch. award, Nat. Taiwan U., Tchg. award, Collegiate Excellence Tchg. award. Mem.: Taiwan Biomechatronics Soc., Assn. Chem. Sensors Taiwan, Internat. Soc. Electrochemistry, Am. Chem. Soc. Avocations: music, reading, travel. Office: Dept Bio-Industrial Mechatronics Engineering Nat Taiwan University Taipei 10617 Taiwan Business E-Mail: chenlinchi@ntu.edu.tw.

CHEN, MING FONG, hospital administrator, cardiologist; b. Taiwan, Oct. 13, 1949; s. Jin-Tien Chen and Chau-Chi Tang; m. Mei-Yuh Tsai, Sept. 24, 1977; children: Natasha C.Y., William Y.L. MD, Nat. Taiwan U., Taipei, 1975, PhD, 1990, exec. MBA, 2002. Resident dept. internal medicine Nat. Taiwan U. Hosp., 1977—81, attending physician cardiology, 1981—, dir. critical care medicine, 1993—2006, sec. med. affairs, 1999—2002, dir. Fin. Mgmt. Ctr., vice supt., 2002—07, dir. Health Mgmt. Ctr., chief dept. internal medicine, 2003—07, supt., 2008—. Prof. internal medicine Nat. Taiwan U. Med. Coll., 1995—. Author: Coronary Artery and Heart Disease, 1997, Cardiovascular Disease, 2007, Coronary Artery Disease and Health Promotion, 2007. Ensign Taiwan Navy, 1975—77. Fellow: ACP, European Soc. Cardiology, American Coll. Cardiology; mem.: Taiwan Soc. Hypertension, Taiwan Soc. Therosclerosis & Cardiovasc. Diseases, Taiwan Soc. Internal Medicine (sec.-gen. 1993—2005, pres. 2005—). Office: Nat Taiwan Univ Hosp Dept Internal Medicine 7 Chung Shan S Rd Taipei 100 Taiwan Business E-Mail: mfchen@ntuh.gov.tw. *

CHEN, PANG-CHI, gastroenterologist, educator; b. Taichung, Taiwan, Sept. 8, 1947; m. Ying-Erl Lin, Dec. 24, 1976; children: Chang-Ming, Jeffrey P. MD, Kaohsiung Med. Coll., Taiwan, 1973. Attending physician Chang Gung Meml. Hosp., Taipei, Taiwan, 1979—, dir. digestive endoscopy, 1990—2002; assoc. prof. China Med. Coll., Taichung, 1979-94, Chang Gung U. Med. Coll., Taipei, 1988—; clin. prof. Chang Gung Meml. Hosp., 1999—, dir. gastroenterology, 2002—05. Editor-in-chief Gastroenterological Jour. Taiwan; editorial adv. Chang Gung Med. Jour.; author: Gastrointestinal Endoscopy. Recipient Dr. Takemitaro award, Taiwan Med. Assn., 1979, Cheng-Hsing Found. award, 1984; named disting. citizen, City of Taipei, 1996. Mem.: Am. Gastroenterol. Assn., Am. Soc. for Gastrointestinal Endoscopy, Formosan Med. Assn., European Assn. Gastroenterology and Endoscopy, Gastroenterol. Soc. Taiwan (exec. bd., pres. annual congress 1998, exec. bd., pres. autumn convention 2007), Digestive Endoscopy Soc. Taiwan (exec. bd., pres. 14th ann. congress), Internat. Assn. Surgeons and Gastroenterologists. Office: Chang Gung Meml Hosp 199 Dun Hua N Rd Taipei Taiwan 105 E-mail: pc0028@cgmh.org.tw.

CHEN, PAULINE W., surgeon, writer, medical educator; b. Boston, Sept. 6, 1964; married; 2 children. MD, Northwestern U. Feinberg Sch. Medicine, 1991. Intern, gen. surgery Yale-New Haven Hosp., Conn., 1991—92, resident, gen. surgery Conn., 1991—93, resident Conn., 1995—98; fellow Nat. Cancer Inst., NIH, Bethesda, Md., 1993—95, UCLA, 1998—2000, clin. instr., 1998—2000, asst. prof.; lectr. Yale U. Sch. Medicine, Conn., 1997—98. Invited lectr. in field. Author: Final Exams: A Surgeon's Reflections on Mortality, 2007 (on the NY Times bestseller list); published articles in NY Times, Washington Post, and Prevention Mag., writer Dead Enough? The Paradox of Brain Death, Virginia Quarterly, 2005 (finalist, Nat. Mag. award, 2006), Morbidity and Mortality: A Surgeon Under Exam, 2007, (weekly online column) NY Times-Doctor and Patient, 2008—. Recipient UCLA Outstanding Physician of Yr. award, 1999, George Longstreth Humaness award for most exemplifying empathy, kindness, and care in an age of advancing technology, Yale U.; co-recipient Staige D. Blackford prize for Nonfiction, 2005; finalist James Kirkwood prize in Creative Writing, 2002.

CHEN, PETER Y., radiation oncologist, educator; b. Detroit, June 19, 1952; BS, U Ill., Champaign-Urbana, 1974; MD, U Ill., 1978. Clin. assoc. prof. Oakland U. Wm Beaumont Sch. Medicine, Rochester, Mich., 2009—10, prof., 2010—; staff radiation oncologist, co-medical dir. Beaumont neurosci. ctr. Dept. Radiation Oncology, William Beaumont Hosp., Royal Oak, Mich., 1988—2011, assoc. dir. resident edn., 1991—2007, med. dir., Gamma Knife Ctr., 2006—11, prof., 2010—. Co-chair Head and Neck Tumor Bd., Wm Beaumont Hosp., Royal Oak, 1990—2011; bd. dirs., treas. Greater Mich. Gamma Knife, Royal Oak, 2005—11; sec. Premier Radiation Oncology Svcs., Royal Oak, 2005—11; clin. assoc. prof. Oalkand U. Willilam Beaumont Sch. Medicine, Rochester, 2009—10, prof., 2010—11. Named one of Top Drs., Detroit Hour Mag., 2009—11, Best Drs. in Am., Best Doctors, Inc. One Boston Pl., 2009—. Fellow: Am. Coll. Radiology; mem.: Mich. Soc. Therapeutic Radiology, Am. Soc. Clin. Oncology, Mich. Radiol. Soc., Am. Soc. Radiation Oncoloyg. Avocations: tennis, art, painting, writing, reading. Home: PO Box 202 Bloomfield Hills MI 48303-0202 Office Phone: 248-551-7038. Home Fax: 248-551-1199. Business E-Mail: pchen@beaumont.edu.

CHEN, PING, surgeon; b. Mishan City, HeiLongJiang Province, China, Oct. 5, 1957; BS, Haerbin Med. U., 1982. Chief Su Bei People's Hosp. JiangSu Province, 2001—. Prof. Yang Zhou U., 2001. Recipient Advanced Sci. and Tech. award, JiangSu Province. Mem.: Chinese Med. Assn. (Yangzhou br.), 333 Project of JiangSu Province. Avocations: reading, travel. Office: 98 NanTong West Rd Yangzhou JiangSu 225001 China Business E-Mail: 250537471@qq.com.

CHEN, RUN QIU, medical educator; b. Canton, China, 1964; PhD, U. Hong Kong, 2009; M in Reproductive Scis., Monash U., 2000. Lectr. RMIT U., 1996—2002; cm asst. prof., lectr., tchg. cons. U. Hong Kong, 2002—. Cons. Hong Kong Chinese Herbalists Assn., 2008. Grant, Australasian Menopause Soc., U. Hong Kong. Mem.: Hong Kong Registered Chinese Medicine Practitioners Assn., Hong Kong Assn. Integration Chinese-Western Medicine. Avocation: travel. Office: 10 Sassoon Rd Pokfulam Hong Kong 852 Hong Kong Business E-Mail: rqchen@hku.hk.

CHEN, SHENG-HWANG, medical educator; b. Taiwan, June 2, 1974; PhD, Lynn U., 2007. Asst. prof. Hsin Sheng Coll. Medicine Care and Mgmt., 2010—. Office: 418 Gaoping Sec Zhongfeng Rd Longtan Twp Taoyuan 325 Taiwan Personal E-mail: piper602@hotmail.com.

CHEN, SHIH-CHING, hospital administrator, educator; b. Taiwan, May 27, 1961; MD, Kao-Hsiung Med. U., 1986; PhD, Tohoku U., Japan, 2006. Prof. Taipei Med. U., 1993—. Bd. mem. Taiwan Acad. Phys. Medicine & Rehab., 1996—, Taiwan Rehab. Engring. & Assistive Tech. Soc., 2011—; vice supt. Taipei Med. U. Hosp., 2011—. Recipient Clin. Rsch. award, Taipei Med. U., Taiwan, 2006, Rsch. Guidance award, 2010. Avocation: music. Office: 252 Wuxing St Xinyi Dist Taipei 110 Taiwan Business E-Mail: csc@tmu.edu.tw.

CHEN, SHIU-JEN, pharmacologist, educator; b. Taiwan, Apr. 20, 1963; MS in Pharmacology, Nat. Def. Med. Ctr., 1992; PhD, Grad. Inst. Life Scis., Nat. Def. Med. Ctr., 2000. Dir., dept. nursing, Kang-Ning Jr. Coll. Med. Care & Mgmt., 2009—11. Vis. scientist William Harvey Rsch. Inst., St. Bartholomew's Hosp. Med. Coll., London, 1993—94, Dept. Physiology, U. Mich., 1999—2000; assoc. prof., dept. physiology Nat. Def. Med. Ctr., 2000—, postdoc., dept. pharmacology, 2000—01; vis. asst. prof., dept. physiology Med. Coll. Ga., 2005—06. Recipient Excellent Sci. Article award, Pharmacological Soc. Taiwan; named Excellent Tchr., Pvt. Sch. Assn., Taiwan, 2008—10, Kang-Ning Jr. Coll. Med. Care and Mgmt., Taiwan, 2008—10, Disting. Employee, Dept. Health, Exec. Yuan, Republic of China, Nat. Labs. Foods and Drugs. Mem.: Chinese Physiol. Soc., Pharmacological Soc. Taiwan. Avocations: swimming, badminton. Office: 137 Lane 75 Sec 3 Kangning Rd N Taipei 114 Taiwan Office Fax: (02)2633-7356. Business E-Mail: sjchen@knjc.edu.tw.

CHEN, SHUNLE, medical educator, director; Prof. medicine Renji Hosp., Shanghai Jiaotong U. Sch. Medicine, 1986—; dir. Shanghai Clin. Ctr. Rheumatology, 2002—. Pres. APLAR, 2000—02. Contbr. articles to profl. jours. Recipient Master award, ACR, 2004, APLAR, 2008. Office: Shanghai Renji Hosp 145 Shandongbeil 200001 Shanghai Shanghaish China Office Phone: 8621-63363475.

CHEN, SOPHIE SM, medical researcher; b. Taiwan, Dec. 20, 1942; PhD, Columbia U., 1973. Rsch. assoc. prof. NY Med. Coll., 1997—2006; rsch. dir. Ovarian and Prostate Cancer Rsch. Trust Lab., 2007—. Adj. asst. prof., biochemistry dept. NYU Sch. Dentistry, 1986—87; sec. Chinese Am. Chem. Soc., 1991—95. Recipient Miles Outstanding Sci. award, Bayer Inc USA, Miles Tech. Achievement award, Bayer Inc. USA. Mem.: NY Acad. Science, Brit. Sci. Assn., European Cancer Assn., Royal Soc. Medicine. Avocations: music, swimming, hiking. Office: 10 Nugent Rd Guildford Surrey GU2 7AF England Office Fax: 44-1483269031. Business E-Mail: s.chen@opcart-lab.org.

CHEN, STEPHEN SHI-HUA, pathologist, biochemist; b. Taipei, Taiwan, Republic of China, Dec. 25, 1939; came to U.S., 1965; s. Ah-wen and Shun (Pan) C.; m. Hsin-Hsin Yii, July 5, 1969; children: Peter T., Margaret T. MD, Nat. Taiwan U., 1964; PhD, U. Pitts, 1972. Diplomate Am. Bd. of Pathology. Asst. prof. pathology U. Pitts., 1972-76; staff pathologist Presbyn. Hosp., Pitts., 1973-76; asst. prof.

pathology dept. Stanford U., Palo Alto, Calif., 1976-80, clin. assoc. prof. pathology dept., 1980-96, clin. prof., 1996—2009; staff pathologist Veterans Affairs Med. Ctr., Palo Alto, 1976—. Contbr. articles to Jour. Cellular Physiology, Jour. Chromatography, Clinica Chimca Acta. Fellow Coll. Am. Pathologists; mem. Am. Soc. Investigative Pathology, U.S. and Can. Acad. Pathology Inc., Am. Soc. Clin. Pathologists, Am. Soc. Cytopathology. Achievements include chromatography of phospholipids. Office: Vets Affairs Med Ctr 113 3801 Miranda Ave Palo Alto CA 94304-1207

CHEN, TUNG-SHENG, medical researcher; b. Hsinchu, Taiwan, Jan. 25, 1973; PhD, Chung Yuan Christian U., 2009. Postdoc. rschr. China Med. U., 2009—. Bd. dirs. Formosan Blood Purification Found., 2006—. Mem.: Am. Chem. Soc. Avocation: baseball. Personal E-mail: raycelina@gmail.com.

CHEN, WEI-HSI, physician, consultant; b. Hong Kong, Jan. 12, 1961; MD, Kaohsiung Med. U., 1990, MSc; LLM, Nat. First U. Sci. & Tech., 2000. Cons. Kaohsiung Chang Gung Meml. Hosp., 2000—. Bd. dir. Kaohsiung County Physician Assn., 2002; coun. sci. expert Taiwan Consumer Found., 2004; coun. law Taiwan Med. Assn. Nation, 2008. Recipient Social Contbn. Prize, Republic of China Taiwan Br., Buddhas Light Internat. Assn., Nat. Against Drug prize, Govt. Republic China. Avocation: reading. Office: 123 Tai Pei Rd Kaohsiung City Kaohsiung 833 Taiwan Business E-Mail: e49130@ms14.hinet.net.

CHEN, WEI-JAO, medical educator, surgeon; b. Taichung, Taiwan, Nov. 15, 1939; s. Wen-Chiang and Pin (Wu) C.; m. Shiang-Yang Tang, Jan. 1, 1970; children: Yo-Shen, Yo-Yi. BM, Nat. Taiwan U., Taipei, 1965; D in Med. Scis., Tohoku U., Sendai, Japan, 1973; MPH, Johns Hopkins U., 1989. Resident dept. surgery Nat. Taiwan Univ. Hosp., Taipei, 1966-70, dep. dir., 1987-91; prof. surgery and pub. health Nat. Taiwan U. Coll. Medicine, Taipei, 1975—, dean, 1991-93; pres. Nat. Taiwan U., 1993—2005. Chair Assn. East Asian Rsch. Univs., 2002—03. Author: Story of Separation of Conjoined Twins, 1980; editor: Asia Pacific Jour. Clin. Nutrition, 1993—, Nutrition, 1994-; contbr. articles to profl. jours. Active Press Coun., Taiwan, 1994—. With Taiwanese Air Force, 1965-66. Recipient Ten Outstanding Young Person award JCA Club, 1979, Outstanding Sci. Achievement award Exec. Yuen, 1980. Mem. Surg. Soc. Taiwan, Taiwanese Assn. Pediatric Surgery (pres. 1990-92), Chinese Assn. Parenteral and Enteral Nutrition (pres. 1992-96), Formosa Med. Assn. (pres. 1995-98), Nutrition Soc. Taiwan (pres. 2003-06). Avocations: hiking, jog, golf. Office: Nat Taiwan U Hosp Dept Surg 7 Chung-Shan S Rd Taipei 100 Taiwan Home: 15 Hsin-Yi Rd Sec II Taipei 100 Taiwan Office Phone: 886-2-23123456 ext. 62122, 886-2-23123456 ext. 65281. Business E-Mail: chenwjh@ntu.edu.tw.

CHEN, WILLIAM T., plastic surgeon; b. Taipei, Taiwan, July 5, 1952; came to U.S., 1965; s. George and Ann Chen; m. Emma Chen, Jan. 16, 2000; children: Connor, Audrey. MD, U. Ill. Coll. Med., 1977. Diplomate Am. Bd. Otolaryngology. Gen. surg. resident U. Ill. Med. Ctr., Chgo., 1977—79; otolaryn. intern U. So. Calif.-LA County Med. Ctr., LA, 1979—80, otolaryn. resident, 1981—84; resident Harbor UCLA Med. Ctr., Torrance, Calif., 1980—81; pathology resident White Meml. Med. Ctr., LA, 1984—85; pvt. practice Calif., 1985—. Staff North Bay Med. Ctr., Fairfield, Calif., 1985, Vaca Valley Hosp., Vacaville, Calif., 1987, Calif. Pacific Med. Ctr., San Francisco, 1992—2005, El Camino Hosp., Mountain View, Calif., 1998. Mem. AMA, Am. Acad. Facial Plastic Reconstructive Surgeons, Am. Acad. Otolaryngology-Head and Neck Surgery, Calif. Med. Assn., Solano County Med. Assn. Office: Bay Med Ctr Ste 200 2801 Waterman Blvd Fairfield CA 94534 Office Phone: 707-428-3687. Office Fax: 707-428-4381.

CHEN, XIAOLI, medical researcher; b. China, Apr. 9, 1970; MD, Shanghai Med. U., MPH, 1997; PhD, Toyama Med. & Pharm. U., 2004. Asst. scientist Johns Hopkins Bloomberg Sch. Pub. Health, 2009—. Mem.: Am. Assn. Cancer Rsch., Am. Soc. Nutrition. Avocations: hiking, running, bicycling, yoga, travel. Office: 615 North Wolfe St Rm E2612 Baltimore MD 21205 Business E-Mail: xchen@jhsph.edu.

CHEN, XINGUANG, healthcare educator, researcher; b. Tianmen, China, Mar. 2, 1954; MD, Tongti Med. Coll., Wuhan, China, 1982; PhD, U. Hawaii, 1992. Assoc. prof., chair, dept. biostats. Tongji Med. U., 1994—97; rsch. assoc. U. Southern Calif., LA, 1996—97, asst. prof., 1998—2003; assoc. prof. Wayne State U., Detroit, 2003—09, prof. with tenure, 2010—. Pub. health advisor Wuhan Bur. Pub. Health, China, 1997—; guest prof. Hainan Med. Coll., China, 2001—10; advisor Nebr. Prevention Ctr. Alcohol and Drug Abuse, 2003—08; assoc. editor Jour. Child and Family Studies, 2007—; guest prof. Sun Yatsen U., 2010—. Mem.: APHA, Soc. Epidemiologic Rsch., Soc. Chaos Theory in Psychology and Life Sci., Assn. Psychol. Sci. Avocations: exercise, fishing, music. Office: 4707 St Antoine St Hutzel W534 Detroit MI 48201 Business E-Mail: jimchen@med.wayne.edu.

CHEN, XULIN, medical educator; b. Hubei, China, Apr. 27, 1964; PhD, Inst. Microbiology CAS, 1999. Prof. Wuhan Inst. Virology Chinese Acad. Scis., 2005—. Office: 44 Xiao Hong Shan Zhong Qu Wuchang Wuhan Hubei 430071 China Office Fax: 86-27-87198466. Business E-Mail: chenxl@wh.iov.cn.

CHEN, YAJUN, physiologist; b. Shandong, China, Jan. 26, 1974; EdB, Qufu Normal U., 1998; PhD, Chinese U. Hong Kong, 2006. Rsch. fellow, lectr. Dept. Sports Sci. and Phys. Edn., Chinese U. Hong Kong, 2006—. Lectr. Hong Kong Inst. Edn., 2008—. Mem.: Internat. Soc. Advancement Cytometry, Soc. Chinese Scholars Exercise Physiology and Fitness, Hong Kong Assn. Sports Medicine and Sports Sci., Am. Physiol. Soc., Am. Coll. Sports Medicine. Avocations: music, tennis, badminton. Office: Chinese University Hong Kong G02 Kwok Sports Bldg Hong Kong Shatin 00852 Hong Kong Office Fax: 2603 5781. E-mail: yjch2011@gmail.com.

CHEN, YANGCHAO, biomedical researcher, educator; b. Hunan, China, Feb. 28, 1976; PhD, Zhongshan U., 2003. Rsch. asst. prof. Chinese U. Hong Kong, 2007—09, asst. prof., 2009—. Grand Challenges Explorations grant, Bill & Melinda Gates Found., Gen. Rsch. grant, Rsch. Grants Coun., Hong Kong, Rsch. grant, Food and Health Bur., Hong Kong, Innovation and Tech. grant, Innovation and Tech. Commn., Hong Kong. Mem.: Am. Assn. Cancer Rsch. Avocation: swimming. Office: Chinese University Hong Kong Sch Biomed Scis Hong Kong 852 China Office Fax: 852-26961100. Business E-Mail: frankch@cuhk.edu.hk.

CHEN, YAN-HUA, medical educator; d. YueFu Chen; m. Qun Lu; children: Hope Lu, Wendy Lu. PhD, Emory U., Atlanta, 1993. Rsch. fellow Harvard Med. Sch., Boston, 1994—2000; asst. prof. East Carolina U. Sch. Medicine, Greenville, NC, 2000—. Grass Found. scholarship, Hopkins Marine Sta. of Stanford U., 1989. Mem.: Am. Soc. for Cell Biology. Achievements include research in Publish papers, presentations at national and international meetings. Office: Dept Anatomy and Cell Biology East Carolina Univ Sch Med Greenville NC 27858

CHEN, YIH-WEN EDWIN, dentist; b. Taipei, Taiwan, Jan. 18, 1959; s. Shien-Chang Chen and Pi-Yen Chen Hu; m. Jing-Ru Hsiung; children: Guan-Lin, Tzy-Ting Grace. DDS, Taipei Med. U., 1986. Diplomate Taiwan Bd. Orthodontists. Resident, tchg. asst. Taiwan Med. U. Hosp., Taipei, 1988—93, attending staff, 1993—98; pvt. practice Ta Fong Dental Clinic, Taipei, 1998—. Med. cons. Medipal Health Group, Taipei, 1994—98; tchg. staff Taipei Med. U., 2000—04. Author: Super Smile, 2004, Clinical Orthodontic Handbook, 2006, Atlas of Clinical Orthodontic, 2007. Lt. Taiwan Army, 1986—88. Recipient Army Plaque, Dept. of Def., 1988. Master: Taiwan Assn. Orthodontists. Buddhist. Avocations: travel, volleyball, baseball, swimming, reading. Office: 2F No 684 Sec 5 Chung Shan N Rd Taipei 111 Taiwan Office Fax: (02)2831-8553. Personal E-mail: ywc168@seed.net.tw.

CHEN, YUNG-CHUAN, engineering educator; b. Kaohsiung, Taiwan, Apr. 25, 1964; s. Jinn-Tsair Chen and Chin-Li Huang; m. Ying-Chin Chen. PhD, Nat. Sun Yat-Sen U., Taiwan, 1996. National Certificate of Mechanic, Ministry of Econ. Affairs, R.O.C., 1993. Mech. engr. Taiwan Machinery Mfg. Co., 1986—94; engr. MRT Bur., Kaohsiung City Govt., 1994—99; asst. prof. I-Shou U., Kaohsiung, 1999—2000; assoc. prof. Nat. Pingtung U. of Sci. and Tech., Pingtung, Taiwan, 2000—. Contbr. 78 papers and numerous articles to profl. jours. Mem.: Optical Soc. of Am. Office: Nat Pingtung U of Sci and Tech 1 Hseuh Fu Rd Neipu Hsiang Pingtung 91201 Taiwan Office Fax: 886-8-7740398. E-mail: chuan@mail.npust.edu.tw.

CHEN, ZHU, Chinese government official, hematologist; b. Shanghai, Aug. 17, 1953; Student, Shangrao Med. Sch., Jiangxi, China, 1975—77; M in Med. Sci., Shanghai Second Med. U., 1981; PhD, Inst. Hematology, St. Louis Hosp., U. Paris VII, 1989; postdoctoral study, St. Louis Hosp., U. Paris VII, 1989; D honoris causa (hon.), U. Genova, Italy, 1997; DSc honoris causa (hon.), U. Hong Kong, 2005; DSc honoris causa, U. Paris VII, 2005. Tchg. asst. Shangrao Med. Sch., 1977—78; intern dept. medicine Shanghai Rui-Jin Hosp., 1981—84; intern Ctrl. Lab. Hematology St. Louis Hosp., Paris, 1984—85; prof. Shanghai Rui Jin Hosp., 1990—, dir. Shanghai Inst. Hematology, 1995; dir. Chinese Human Genome Ctr., Shanghai, 1998, min. health Govt. of China, Beijing, 2007—. Vis. prof. divsn. med. oncology Mt. Sinai Med. Ctr., NYC, 1991; vis. prof. Inst. Hematology St. Louis Hosp., Paris, 1992—93; co-chair Interacademy Panel; coun. mem. Human Genome Orgn.; vice dir. Nat. Life Sci. Ctr., Shanghai. Recipient Sci. and Tech. award, Ho Leung Ho Lee Found., 1996, Qise prize, Nat. League against Cancer, France, 1997, Qui-Shi award for outstanding young scientists, China, 1998, Cheung Kong Scholars Achievement award, Nat. Ministry Edn., China, 1999; named Knight, Nat. Order of Legion of Honor, France, 2002. Mem.: Inst. Medicine (fgn. assoc.), European Acad. Arts, Sciences & Humanities (titular mem.), NAS (fgn. assoc.), French Acad. Sciences (fgn. assoc.), Chinese Acad. Sciences (v.p. 2000—07). Office: Shanghai Inst Hematology Rui-Jin Hosp 197 Rui-Jin Rd Shanghai 200025 China *

CHENAY, CHRISTIAN JEAN-MARIE, biomedical engineer; b. Angers, France, June 20, 1921; s. Amédée Jean Marie Chenay and Noémie Emilie Tardy; m. Marthe Catherine Jamet, Apr. 27, 1950; children: Christian, Jean Marie. Lic. in Natural Sci., U. Rennes, France, 1942; Lic. in Phys. Scis., U. Paris, 1944, MD, 1946, radiologsit, 1973. Cert. engring. in electronic and electrophysiology. Resident Red Cross Hosp., Paris, 1945-48; asst. prof. Faculty of Scis., Paris, 1948-69; dir. Lab. de Radiology, Chevilly-Larue, France, 1965—. Lt. French Res., 1944-60. Mem. Physiologists de Langue Francaise, Am. Heart Assn. Achievements include improvements in xray medical devices and ultrasonics. Home: 144 avenue du Pdt Franklin Roosevelt 94550 Chevilly Larue Larue France Office Phone: 330146879993. Office Fax: 33014687993. Personal E-mail: chenaypere.christian@neuf.fr.

CHENEY, ANNA MARIE JANGULA, retired medical/surgical clinical specialist; b. Wishek, ND, Nov. 27, 1935; d. Jacob Jangula and Eva Wald; m. Edwin J. Cheney, Feb. 6, 1965; children: Alan, Deborah, Darrell. Diploma, Sisters of St. Joseph Sch. Nursing, Grand Forks, ND, 1957; BSN, St. Louis U., 1960; MSN, UCLA, 1965. Oper. rm. instr. Sisters of St. Joseph, Grand Forks, 1957-58; staff nurse Cardinal Glennon Meml. Hosp., St. Louis, 1958-60, VA Med. Ctr., St. Louis and L.A., 1960-62, head nurse West L.A., 1963-64; staff nurse UCLA Med. Ctr., 1964-65; head nurse Meml. Hosp., Culver City and L.A., 1965-66; staff nurse West Pk. Hosp., Canoga Park, Calif., 1980-84, VA Med. Ctr., Sepulveda, Calif., 1984-89, clin. nurse specialist med./surg., 1989—94, clin. nurse specialist ambulatory care, 1994; charge nurse ambulatory care West L.A. Med. Ctr., Calif., 1996—97, ret. Calif., 1997. Instr. CPR Am. Heart Assn., L.A., 1991-94; facilitator stop smoking Am. Cancer Soc., L.A., 1991—, instr. breast self exams, 1991—. Contbr. articles to profl. jours. Vol. mem. spkr. bur. Am. Cancer Soc., 1997—; bereavement minister Archdiocese LA, 2003—. Recipient Outstanding Spkrs. award, 1998, Project Team Leadership award, 1999, 1st place age group, Am. Heart Assn. 5K Run, 1996, 1998, Mission Delivery Person Vol. of the Yr., Am. Cancer Soc., 2004—05; named Outstanding Pub. Spkr., 1993; grantee, UCLA, 1963—64. Mem. Toastmaster Internat. (v.p. edn. 1991-92, pres. 1992-93, Cert. of Appreciation 1992, competent toastmaster, Toastmaster Leadership Excellence award 1995, Bronze award 1998). Democrat. Roman Catholic. Avocations: horticulture, singing, tennis, jogging, reading. Home: 23741 Highlander Rd West Hills CA 91307-1825

CHENEY, BRIGHAM VERNON, physical chemist, consultant; b. Salt Lake City, June 11, 1936; s. Silas Lavell and Klara (Young) C.; m. Marsali McAllister, Aug. 20, 1964; children: Jill, Mark Vernon, Heather, Karin, Brigham McAllister, John David. BA, U. Utah, 1961, PhD, 1966. Rsch. asst. U. Utah, 1964-66; rsch. scientist Upjohn Co., Kalamazoo, 1966-71, scientist, 1971-75, sr. rsch. scientist, 1975-98; cons. Vis. scientist Oxford (Eng.) U., 1986-87. Contbr. articles to profl. jours. Missionary LDS Ch., Germany, 1956-59, high councilor, Lansing, Mich., 1969-75, Grand Rapids, Mich., 1975-78, bishop, Kalamazoo, 1978-84; leader Boy Scouts Am., 1972-98. With U.S. Army NG, 1959-67. Mem. Am. Chem. Soc., Sigma Xi, Phi Eta Sigma, Sigma Pi Sigma. Home: 1765 N 2000 W Provo UT 84604-1128 Personal E-mail: bvcheney@iprovo.net.

CHENG, DIANA, obstetrician gynecologist; b. NY, Mar. 11, 1951; BA, U. Pa., 1972; MD, Johns Hopkins Sch. Medicine, 1976. Resident, ob-gyn. Tufts U. Affiliated Hosps., 1976—80; fellow reproductive health UCLA Sch. Medicine, 1980—81; pvt. practice, 1981—95; med. dir. women's health Md. Dept. Health and Mental Hygiene, 1995—. Bd. dirs. Md. chpt. Mar. of Dimes, 1996—2008, chair cmty. grants rev. com. Md. and Nat. Capital Area chpt., 2006—; prin. investigator Md. Pregnancy Risk Assessment Monitoring Sys., 1999—; sr. assoc. faculty Population, Family and Reproductive Health, Johns Hopkins Bloomberg Sch. Pub. Health, 2007—; bd. dirs. Md. Healthcare Coalition Against Domestic Violence, 2010—. Contbr. articles to profl. jours. Recipient Vol. Recognition award, Mar. of Dimes; named one of Md. Top 100 Women, Md. Daily Record, America's Top Obstetricians and Gynecologists, Consumer Rsch. Coun. Fellow: ACOG (mem. healthcare underserved com.); mem.: Balt. City Domestic Violence Fatality Rev. Team, Maternal and Child Health Tng. Program (mem. nat. adv. com.), Md. Fetal Alcohol Spectrum Disorder Coalition (co-chair). Avocations: literature, travel, piano. Office: 201 W Preston St Rm 313 Baltimore MD 21201 Office Fax: 410-333-5233. Business E-Mail: chengd@dhmh.state.md.us.

CHENG, H. H., soil scientist, agronomic and environmental science educator emeritus; b. Shanghai, Aug. 13, 1932; arrived in U.S., 1951, naturalized, 1961; s. Chi-Pao and Anna (Lan) Cheng; m. Jo Yuan, Dec. 15, 1962; children: Edwin, Antony. BA, Berea Coll., 1956; MS, U. Ill., 1958, PhD, 1961; LLD (hon.), U. Minn., 2004. Lic. profl. soil scientist Minn. Rsch. assoc. Iowa State U., Ames, 1962-64, asst. prof. agronomy, 1964-65; asst. prof. dept. agronomy and soils Wash. State U., Pullman, 1965-71, assoc. prof., 1971-77, prof., 1977-89, interim chmn., 1986-87, chmn. program environ. sci. and regional planning, 1977-79, 88-89, assoc. dean Grad. Sch., 1982-86; prof., head dept. soil, water and climate U. Minn., St. Paul, 1989—2001, prof. emeritus, 2002—. Vis. scientist Juelich Nuc. Rsch. Ctr., Germany, 1971-73, 79-80, Academia Sinica, Taipei, China, 1978, Fed. Agrl. Rsch. Ctr., Braunschweig, Germany, 1980; mem. acad. adv. coun. Inst. Soil Sci., Academia Sinica, Nanjing, China, 1987-2000; mem. adv. bd. Inst. Botany, Academia Sinica, Taipei, 1991-2000; mem. first sci. adv. bd. Dept. Ecology State of Wash., 1988-89; chief tech. advisor project on water-saving agr. N.W. China, UNDP, 2001-04; mem. agr. and natural resources bd., Nat. Acad., 2003-09, mem. NRC Com. Miss. River and Clean Water Act, 2005-07. Editor: Pesticides in the Soil Environment: Processes, Impacts, and Modeling, 1990; assoc. editor Jour. Environ. Quality, 1983-89; mem. edit. bd. Bot. Studies (formerly Bot. Bull. Academia Sinica), 1988—, Jour. Environ. Sci. and Health, Part B-Pesticides, Food Contaminants, and Agrl. Wastes, 2000-03; cons. editor: Pedosphere, 1991—; contbr. articles to profl. jours. Tech. adv. Mekong-Miss. River Partnership, 2003—09; mem. US Grad. Sch. Deans; del. China's Ministry of Edn., US Sys. Grad. Edn., 1984; leader US People-to People Agronomy Del. to China, Amb. Programs, 1999, US People-to People Agronomy Del. to Cuba, 2001. Recipient U. Minn. Coll. Agrl., Food and Environ. Scis. Internat. Achievement award, 2004, Berea Coll. Disting. Alumnus award, 2006; Fulbright rsch. scholar State Agrl. U., Ghent, Belgium, 1963-64. Fellow AAAS (life), Am. Soc. Agronomy (life mem., bd. dir. 1990-2000, exec. com. 1994-2000, pres. 1998-99), Soil Sci. Soc. Am. (life mem., divsn. chair 1985-86, bd. dir. 1990-93, exec. com. 1994-97, pres. 1995-96, co-chair Smithsonian soils exhibit com. 2002—09); mem. Am. Chem. Soc., Soc. Environ. Toxicology and Chemistry, Internat. Soc. Chem. Ecology, Internat. Humic Substances Soc., Coun. Agrl. Sci. and Tech., Soil and Water Conservation Soc., Minn. Assn. Profl. Soil Scientists (Soil Scientist of Yr. 2003), Inst. Internat. Devel. in Edn. and Agrl. and Life Scis. (chair bd. dir. 2000—), Miss. River Basin Inst. Internat. Coop. (chair, bd. dir. 2004—), Sigma Xi (pres. U. Minn. chpt. 1995-96), Phi Kappa Phi, Gamma Sigma Delta (pres. Wash. State chpt. 1988-89, Award of Merit U. Minn. chpt. 2000). Methodist. Office: University Minn Dept Soil Water & Climate 1991 Upper Buford Cir Saint Paul MN 55108-0010 Office Phone: 612-625-1244. Business E-Mail: hcheng@umn.edu.

CHENG, JEN-KUN, anesthesiologist, educator; b. Kao Shong, Taiwan, Apr. 24, 1964; MD, Nat. Yang-Ming Med. Coll., 1990; PhD, Nat. Taiwan U., 2005. Operating rm. dir. Mackay Meml. Hosp., 2009—. Asst. prof. Taipei Med. U., 2006—. Grant, Internat. Assn. Study Pain. Mem.: Am. Soc. Anesthesiologists. Avocation: golf. Home: 7F-1 18 Alley 1 Ln 159 Roosevelt Taipei 116 Taiwan Personal E-mail: jkcheng@usa.net.

CHENG, JIANJUN, engineering educator; b. Ma Anshan, Anhui, China, Aug. 1, 1970; PhD, U. Calif., Santa Barbara, 2001. Assoc. prof. U. Ill. Urbana-Champaign, 2011—. Recipient Prostate Cancer Found. Competitive award, 2007, NSF CAREER award, 2008, NIH Dirs. New Innovator award, 2010, Xerox award, 2010. Home: 2304 Lynwood Dr Champaign IL 61821 Business E-Mail: jianjunc@illinois.edu.

CHENG, JONATHAN J., plastic surgeon, educator; b. Bradford, Pa., Mar. 27, 1974; BA, Rice U., 1996; MD, Baylor Coll. Medicine, 2000. Resident, plastic and reconstructive surgery Med. Coll. Wis., 2000—06, postdoc. rsch. fellow, 2003—04; hand, peripheral nerve, microvasc. surgery fellow Wash. U., 2006—07; Kroll meml. scholar, perforator microsurgery UZ Gent, 2007; asst. prof. UT Southwestern Med. Ctr., 2008—. Vice-chief, pediat. plastic surgery Children's Med. Ctr., Dallas, 2010—; dir., nerve biology lab. U. Tex. Southwestern Med. Ctr., 2010—, faculty senator, 2010—; sect. editor, hand and peripheral nerve Case Revs. Plastic Surgery, 2010—. Pilot grant, NIH. Fellow: Am. Bd. Plastic Surgery; mem.: Plastic Surgery Rsch. Coun., Am. Soc. Surgery Hand (Young Leaders Forum award). Avocations: skiing, bicycling, photography. Office: 1801 Inwood Rd 4th Fl Dallas TX 75390 Office Fax: 214-645-3148. Business E-Mail: jonathan.cheng@utsouthwestern.edu.

CHENG, JUEI-TANG, pharmacologist; b. Changhwa Shan, Taiwan, China, June 15, 1949; s. Fon-Yue and Chin (Lin) C.; m. Chun-Shin Chang; 1 child, Chun-Sheng. PhD, Shizuoka Coll. Pharm. Scis., 1978.

Registered pharmacologist. Editor: Chinese Pharm. Jour., 1993—, Jour. Chinese Medicine, 1993—. Fellow Am. Coll. Clin. Pharmacology; mem. Internat. Brain Rsch. Orgn., Basic Neuroscis. Soc. Avocations: golf, stamp collecting/philately. Office: Nat Cheng Kung U Coll Medicine Dept Pharmacology Tainan 70101 Taiwan Office Phone: 886-6-235-3535. Business E-Mail: jtcheng@mail.ncku.edu.tw.

CHENG, KENNETH P., ophthalmologist; MD, U. Pitts. Diplomate Am. Bd. Ophthalmology. Resident Univ. of Pitts.; fellow Childrens Hosp. of Pitts.; hosp. affliation include/s Children's Hosp. of Pitts. of UPMC, UPMC Children's Surgery Ctrs.; consulting physician pediatric ophthalmology Children's Hosp. of Pitts. of UPMC. Office: Childrens Hospital of Pittsburgh of UPMC 1000 Stonewood Drive Ste 310 Wexford PA 15090 Office Phone: 724-934-3333.

CHENG, KUNG-SHAN, medical researcher; b. Taipei, May 26, 1972; PhD, U. Utah, 2005. Rsch. assoc. Duke U. Med. Ctr., 2005—10; rschr., reviewer Ctr. Drug Evaluation, 2010—. Assoc. editor Med. Physics, 2005, editl. bd. mem., 11; reviewer Internat. Jour. Hyperthermia, 2005, Physics Medicine and Biology, 2009, Jour. Thermal Biology, 2009, FDA, Dept. Health, Exec. Yuan, 2011. Mem.: Soc. Thermal Medicine. Office: Ctr Drug Evaluation 12F 15-1 Taipei 100 Taiwan E-mail: acosine@yahoo.com.

CHENG, LIANG, pathologist; b. Zhejiang, China, Nov. 9, 1965; came to U.S., 1988; MD, Beijing Med. U., 1987; MS, U. Ill., 1990. Diplomate Am. Bd. Pathology. Resident Case We. Res. U., Cleve., 1993—97, instr. pathology, 1994—97; fellow Mayo Clinic, Rochester, Minn., 2007—; prof. pathology, urology Ind. U. Sch. Medicine, Indpls., 1999—, assoc. prof. pathology, 2008—. Spkr., cons. in field. Co-author: (chpts.) Therapeutics: Methods and Applications of Direct Gene Transfer, 1994, Immunotherapeutics Approaches for the Treatment of Cancer, 1995; editor: Essentials of Anatomic Pathology 2d edit., 2005; contbr. articles to profl. jours. Recipient Resident Competition award Cleve. Soc. Pathologists, 1997, Young Investigator Travel award, 1998, Eminent Scientist of Yr. Gold award, Internat. Rsch. Promotino Coun., 2000; Am. Cancer Inst. grantee, Clarian Value Fund grantee, Biomed. Rsch. Fund grantee, Dept. Def. grantee; Molecular Biology Lab. fellow U. Ill., 1990. Mem. AAAS, Am. Assn. Cancer Rsch., Am. Urologic Assn., U.S. and Can. Acad. Pathology (Stowell-Orbison award 1996), Coll. Am. Pathologists (cert. recognition), Am. Soc. Clin. Pathologists (cert. recognition), Internat. Soc. Urologic Pathology, Assn. Molecular Pathology. Office: Ind U Sch Medicine 350 W 11th St CPL 4010 Indianapolis IN 46202-5149 Office Phone: 317-491-6442. Personal E-mail: liang_cheng@yahoo.com. Business E-Mail: lcheng@iupui.edu.

CHENG, SHIH-PING, surgeon; b. Chang Hua, Taiwan, Sept. 13, 1972; s. Chiu-Fu Cheng and Yu-Ping Hsieh; m. Miao-Yu Wu, June 6, 2004; children: Yi-Hsin, Yi-Chen. MD, Nat. Taiwan U., Taipei, Taiwan, 1997; PhD, Inst. Pharmacology Nat. Yang Ming U., Taipei, Taiwan, 2011. Diplomate Dept. Health, Taiwan, 1997. Attending surgeon Mackay Meml. Hosp., Taipei, 2004—, resident surgery, 1999—2004. Second lt. med. officer US Army, 1997—99, Taiwan. Recipient Oral Presentation award, Taiwan Surg. Soc. Gastroenterology, 2004; vis. scholar, U. Mich., Ann Arbor, Mich., 2007—08. Achievements include research in endocrine surgery. Office: Mackay Meml Hosp No 92 Sec 2 Chung-Shan N Rd Taipei 10449 Taiwan Office Fax: 886-2-27233897.

CHENG, SHI-YANN, physician, director; b. Taiwan, Jan. 1, 1960; BS, Nat. Taiwan U., 1983; MD, Nat. Yang-Ming U., 1990. Resident physician, ob-gyn. Kaohsiung Vets. Gen. Hosp., 1990—95; obstetrician, gynecologist God's Help Hosp., 1995—99, Chinal Med. U. Beigang Hosp., 1999—2006, dir., dept. ob-gyn., 2006, dir., dept. med. edn. and rsch., 2009—. Lectr. Sch. Medicine China Med. U., 2009. Recipient Clin. Edn. Devotion award, China Med. U. Mem.: Taiwan Assn. Med. Edn., Taiwan Soc. Ultrasound in Medicine, Taiwan Assn. Ob-Gyn. Avocations: swimming, jogging. Office: 123 Shinder Rd Beigang Yunlin 65152 Taiwan Office Phone: 886-5-7837933. Office Fax: 886-5-7836439. Business E-Mail: shiyann.cheng@msa.hinet.net.

CHENG, THERESA, neurosurgeon; d. Wayne and Florence Cheng. Degree in Biomed. Engring., Marquette U., 1982; MD, PhD, Med. Coll. Wis., Milw., 1989. Diplomate Am. Bd. Neurol. Surgeons, cert. Advanced Trauma Life Support ACS, 1996, Advanced Cardiac Life Support Am. Heart Assn., 1989; Eucharistic Ministry Cath. Ch., 1980. Tchg. asst. engring. level math. and physics Marquette U., Milw., 1979—82; tchg. asst. med. gross anatomy dept. anatomy and cellular biology Med. Coll. Wis., Milw., 1983—84, rsch. asst. dept. medicine, endocrinology, 1984, rsch. asst. dept. neurology, 1984, tchg. asst. med. neuroanatomy dept. anatomy and cellular biology, 1984—87, adj. instr. med. neuroanatomy dept. anatomy and cellular biology, 1987—89; neurosurgery resident Mayo Clinic, Rochester, Minn., 1989—95, post-doctoral fellow molecular genetics, 1992—93, spl. fellow neurosurgery, 1998—99; cons. neurosurgery Luther Midelfort, Mayo Health Sys., Eau Claire, Wis., 1995—2002, chmn. dept. neurosurgery, 2000—02; chief neurosurgery Affinity Health Systems, Oshkosh, Wis., 2002—, dir. med. ops., 2007—. Contbr. articles to profl. jours. Med. dir. Think First Found., Eau Claire, Wis., 2000—02; co-director of neuro-peds-trauma icu Luther Midelfort, Mayo Health Sys., Eau Claire, Wis., 2001—02; eucharistic min. Cath. Ch., 1980—2003; bd. of directors Gold Cross Ambulance Svc., Fox Valley area, Wis., 2002—; elected to the med. exec. committe Luther Midelfort, Mayo Health Sys., Eau Claire, Wis., 2001—; pres. elect, bd. of directors, profl. adv. bd. Epilepsy Found. of Western Wis., Eau Claire, Wis., 1999—2002; bd. dirs. Dunn-Eau Claire-Pepin County Med. Soc., 1999—2002. Recipient 2nd Pl. award, Wis. State Fair, 1985; grantee, Mayo Clinic, 1992; scholar, Nicolet Clinic, 1979, 1980; Coll. scholar, AAUW, 1979, Med. Coll. of Wis. Summer Rsch. fellow, Med. Coll. Wis., 1983. Master: Epilepsy Found. Western Wis. (hon.); mem.: AAAS, Am. Assn. for Cancer RSch., Wis. State Med. Soc., Am. Assn. Neurol. Surgeons, Caduceus Soc., Samaritan Club, Alpha Epsilon Delta, Tau Beta Pi (life). Avocations: outdoor activities, sports and recreation, music, writing, community volunteering. Office: Affinity Health Systems Ste 203 2700 W Ninth Ave Oshkosh WI 54904 E-mail: tcheng@affinityhealth.org.

CHENG, TSUNG O., cardiologist, educator; b. Shanghai, Mar. 30, 1925; came to U.S., 1950, naturalized, 1960; s. Keith S. and Fanny (Wang) C.; m. Marie Ellen Roe, June 18, 1955; children: Mark Dudley, Yvonne Joyce. BS, St. John's U., China, 1945; MD, U. Pa., 1950, MS in Medicine, 1956. Diplomate Am. Bd. Internal Medicine (subsplty. cardiovasc. disease), Nat. Bd. Med. Examiners. Intern St. Barnabas Hosp., Newark, 1950-51; resident in medicine Cook County Hosp., Chgo., 1952-55; fellow in cardiovasc. disease George Washington U., Washington, 1955-56; instr. cardiology Harvard Med. Sch. Mass. Gen. Hosp., Boston, 1956-57; fellow in cardiorespiratory physiology Johns Hopkins U. Sch. Medicine and Hosp., 1957-59, staff cardiac cath. lab., 1957—59; asst. prof. medicine SUNY Downstate, 1959-70; practice medicine specializing in cardiology Washington, 1970—; assoc. prof. medicine George Washington U., 1970-72; chief cardiology D.C. Gen. Hosp., 1971-72; prof. George Washington U., 1972—. Dir. cardiac catheterization lab. George Washington U. Med. Ctr., 1972—78, assoc. dir. cardiology, 1972—75; asst. physician Cardiac Clinic Johns Hopkins Hosp., 1957—59; dir. cardiopulmonary lab. Bklyn. Hosp., 1959—66, co-chief Pediat. Cardiac Clinic, 1959—66, chief Adolescent Cardiac Clinic, 1961—66, attending physician Adult Cardiac Clinic, 1959—66; chief Pediat. Cardiac Clinic Cumberland Hosp., Bklyn., 1963—66; asst. chief cardiology VA Hosp., Bklyn., 1966—69, chief cardiovasc. lab., 1966—70, chief cardiology, 1969—70; asst. vis. physician Kings County Hosp. Med. Ctr., Bklyn., 1964—70; attending physician U. Hosp., SUNY, Bklyn., 1967—70; cons. Beth Isreal Med. Ctr., NYC, 1970—82; guest lectr. Chinese Med. Assn., 1972—73, 1975, 77, 79, 83, 86, 89, 92, Chinese Ministry Health, 1990; hon. prof. Shanghai 2nd Med. U., 1986—, Qingdao Med. Coll., 1989—, Binzhou Med. Coll., 1992—, Taishan Med. Coll., 1992—, Tongji Med. U., Wuhan, China, 1994—, U. Cape Town, South Africa, 1995—, U. Natal, Durban, South Africa, 1995—, U. Morón, Buenos Aires, 2003—, Beijing Hosp. and Med. Coll. Peking U., 2007—; hon. dir. Quingdao Cardiovascular Rsch. Inst., 1990—, Inst. Invasive Therapy PLA 150th Ctrl. Hosp., Luoyang, China, 1994—; hon. pres. Dandong 1st Hosp., Liaoning Province, China, 1988—, Shanghai St. Luke's Hosp., 1990—, Binzhou Med. Coll. Affil. Hosp., 1992—, Taishan Med. Coll. Affil. Hosp., 1992—, Jujiang Med. Coll. Affil. Hosp., Jiangxi, China, 1994—, 2nd People's Hosp., Jin De Zhen, Jiangxi, 1994—, China Heart Failure Assn., 2001—; vis. prof. Peking Union Med. Coll., 1986—, Sun Yatsen Med. U., Canton, 1992—, Cairo U., Egypt, 1994—, U. Oxford, 1995—, U. Witwatersrand Med. Sch., Johannesburg, 1995—, U. Paris Hosp., Tenon, France, 1995—, Cath. U. Inst. Cardiology, Rome, 1996—, Inst. Clin. Physiology, Nat. Rsch. Coun., U. Pisa, Italy, 1996—, Inst. Clin. Physiology, Nat. Rsch. Coun., U. Milan, Inst. Pathol. Anatomy, Med. Sch. U. Milan, 1996—, U. Dusseldorf, Germany, 1997—, U. Hamburg, Germany, 1997—, U. Hannover, Germany, 1997—, U. Melbourne, Australia, 1997—, U. NSW, Sydney, 1997—, U. Istanbul, Turkey, 1999—, U. Athens, Greece, 1999—, U. Córdoba, Spain, 2000—, U. Las Palmas, Spain, 2000—, U. Complutense, Madrid, 2000—; vis. prof. Med. Faculty Charite Humboldt U. Berlin, 2001—; vis. prof. Chinese U. Hong Kong, 2002—, Capital U. Med. Scis., Beijing, 2002—, U. Geneva, 2003—, U. Zurich, 2003—, U. Bern, Switzerland, 2003—, U. Tex., Houston, 2003—, McMaster U., Hamilton, Ont., Canada, 2004—; v.p. Am. Ctr. Chinese Med. Sci., 1982—91; pres. Friends of St. Luke's Hosp., Shanghai, 1991—, chmn. bd., 1992—; disting. sr. visitor Royal Brompton Hosp./Nat. Heart and Lung Inst. London, 1995—; hon. advisor Guangdong Soc. Interventional Cardiology, Guangzhou, China, 1996—; guest editor-in-chief CVD Prevention and Control, 2009; cons.-in-chief Internat. Jour. Cardiovasc. Medicine & Related Diseases, 2009—; hon. dir. Cardiovasc. Inst., Huazhong U. Sci. and Tech., Wuhan, China, 2010—. Sr. editor: Vascular Medicine, 1983—88, Angiology, 1986—97; editor: The International Textbook of Cardiology, 1986—87, Percutaneous Balloon Valvuloplasty, 1992; mem. editl. bd.: Catheterization and Cardiovasc. Diagnosis, 1991—99, Catheterization and Cardiovasc. Interventions, 1999—2003, Jour. Noninvasive Cardiology, 1997—, Chinese Jour. Misdiagnostics, 1999—; mem. editl. bd. Internat. Jour. Cardiology, 2006—; co-editor: Congestive Heart Failure, 1991, 2d edit., 1997, Modern Cardiology, 1994, 2d edit., 2002, Genetics of Cardiovasc. Diseases, 1995, Textbook of Congestive Heart Failure, 2003; editl. cons.-in-chief: Internat. Jour. Cardiovascular Medicine, 2003—, contbg. med. editor: Cortlandt Forum, 1997—98, roving amb. Chinese cardiovascular sci.: Internat. Jour. Cardiology, 2007—; contbr. articles to profl. jours. and textbooks, chapters to books. Recipient Lifetime Achievement Disting. Rschr award, George Washington U. Sch. Medicine, 2007. Fellow ACP, Am. Coll. Chest Physicians, Am. Coll. Cardiology (ofcl. rep. to stds. com. on catheters Assn. Advancement Med. Instrumentation 1971—), Am. Heart Assn., Coun. Clin. Cardiology, Soc. Cardiac Angiography and Interventions(founding), Internat. Coll. Angiology, Am. Coll. Angiology, Soc. Geriat. Cardiology (founding), Royal Soc. Medicine; mem. AAAS, Am. Fedn. Clin. Rsch., Am. Heart Assn., Washington Heart Assn. Home: 7508 Cayuga Ave Bethesda MD 20817-4822 Office: George Washington U Med Ctr 2150 Pennsylvania Ave NW Washington DC 20037-3201 Office Fax: 202-741-2324.

CHENG, WEN-NUAN KARA, psychology professor; b. Taipei, Taiwan, Mar. 3, 1966; MS in Health Sci., Johns Hopkins U., 1991; PhD, U. Wales, 2007. Assoc. prof. Taipei Phys. Edn. Coll., 1998—. Psychol. cons. Home: PO Box 81-851 Taipei 105 Taiwan Personal E-mail: kara_cheng@yahoo.com.

CHENG, YI-QIANG (ERIC CHENG), microbiologist, educator, biochemist; b. Suizhou City, Hubei Province, People's Republic of China, Feb. 1, 1968; PhD, Mich. State U., 1999. Assoc. prof. U. Wis., Milw., 2003—. Vis. prof. Wuhan U. Coll. Pharm. Scis., 2011. Recipient Idea award, US DoD Breast Cancer Rsch. Program. Mem.: Soc. Indsl. Microbiology and Biotech., Am. Soc. Microbiology, Am. Assn. Cancer Rsch., Am. Assn. Advancement Scis. Avocations: tennis, golf. Office: 3209 N Maryland Ave Dept Biol Sci Milwaukee WI 53211 Business E-Mail: ycheng@uwm.edu.

CHENG, YUAN-KAI, physician; s. Chong-Wu Cheng and Hsei Hsiao; m. Li-Hua Chang; children: Yurn-Jur, Chih-Wen, Chih-An. PhD, Tung-Hai U., Taichung, Taiwam, 2006. Diplomate Taiwan, 1992. Attending physician Nat. Taiwan U. Hosp., Taipei, 1996—98, China Med. U. Hosp., Taichung, 1998—2006; chief & attending physician Buddhist Tzu Chi Gen. Hosp., Taichung, 2006—07; pres. Dr. Cheng's OtoRhino Laryngol. Clinic, Taichung, 2010—. Contbr. articles to profl. jours. Grant, Nat. Sci. Constn., 2003. Mem.: Taiwan Otolaryn. Soc. Achievements include research in management of snoring and sleep apnea; role of oxidative stress in the pathogenesis of inflammatory diseases (nasal polyps & allergy) in the upper airway. Office: Dr Cheng's OtoRhinoLaryngological Clinic 376 Sec 4 Henan Rd Taichung Nantun 40874 Taiwan Office Phone: 886-4-22513502.

CHENG, YUE, molecular geneticist, educator, pathologist; arrived in U.S., 2003; s. Renbin Cheng and Benzhao Zhou; m. Yuxing Xiong, Mar. 16, 1988; 1 child, Jasmine S. Cheng MBBS in medicine, Anhui Med. Coll., Hefei, China, 1982; MS in oncology, Sun Yatsen U. Med. Sci., Guangzhou, China, 1987; PhD in biology, Hong Kong U. Sci. and Tech., 2002. Asst. prof. Sun Yatsen U. Med. Sci., Guangzhou, 1989—93; vis. asst. rschr. U. Calif., Irvine, 1993—95; vis. scholar Hong Kong U. Sci. and Tech., 1995—2002; vis. fellow Nat. Cancer Inst., Bethesda, Md., 2003—08; res. fellow City Hope Nat. Med. Ctr., 2008—10; res. asst. prof. Hong Kong U., 2010—. Dir. grad. course Sun Yatsen U. Med. Sci., Guangzhou, 1991-93. Editor: (book) Tumor Suppressor Genes, 2011; contbr. articles to profl. jours. Grantee Sun Yatsen U. Med. Sci., 1991, scholar Am. Chinese Med. Bd., NY, 1993; NIH fellow, 2003-08, grant Hong Kong U., 2010- Mem.: AAAS, Internat. Union Against Cancer, Am. Soc. Hematology, Am. Assn. Cancer Rsch., Chinese Med. Assn. Hong Kong. Achievements include first identification of tumor suppressor gene activities in nasopharyngeal carcinoma; detection of tumor suppressive region at chromosome 3p21.3 in human cells which has led to identification of critical genes associated with development of various sporadic cancers; establishment of a theoretical basis: multiple genes may be used in gene therapy for the treatment of nasopharyngeal carcinoma. Avocations: music, travel, swimming, hiking, photography. Personal E-mail: yuecheng@hotmail.com.

CHEON, YONG-PIL, medical educator; arrived in U.S., 1999; s. Chulgyu Cheon and Soonsuk Oh-Cheon; m. Hyun Sook Kim-Cheon, Apr. 16, 1994; children: Jimin, Soobin, James. PhD, Hanyang U., Seoul, 1996. Dir. of human in vitro fertilization lab. Asan Med. Ctr., Seoul, 1995—99; lectr. Hanyang U., Seoul, 1997—99; postdoctoral rsch. fellow Population Coun., NYC, 1999—2001; postdoctoral rsch. assoc. U. Ill., Urbana-Champaign, 2001—02, vis. rsch. asst. prof., 2002—; asst. prof. Sungshin Womens U., 2005—; assoc. prof. Sungshin Women's U., 2011. Employee asst. Magellan Behavioral Health, Chgo., 2001—. Mem.: Soc. for the Study of Reproduction (licentiate), Endocrine Soc. (licentiate travel grant 2002). Office: Sungshin Women's Univ 249-1 Dongseondong 3ga Seongbukgu Seoul 136-742 Republic of Korea E-mail: ypcheon@sungshin.ac.kr.

CHEON, YOUNG KOOG, medical educator; b. Seoul, Republic of Korea, Apr. 10, 1965; MD, Kunghee U., 1991; PhD, Soonchunhyang U., 2005. Assoc. prof. Konkun U. Med. Ctr., Digestive Disease Ctr., 1999—. Editor Korean Assn. Internal Medicine, 2009—11; reviewer Am. Coll. Gastroenterology, 2009—11. Recipient Universal award, Am. Biog. Inst.; named one of Leading Health Profl. of World, Internat. Biog. Ctr., Cambridge, Eng. Office: 4-12 Hwayang-dong Gwangin-gu Konkuk Seoul 143-729 Republic of Korea Office Fax: 82-22030-5029. Personal E-mail: ykskyOO1@hanmail.net.

CHEONG, SEON-WOO, biologist, educator; d. Moon-Ok Park; m. Chun-Sik Yoon, Dec. 31, 1989; children: Ho-Jung Yoon, Do-Hwan Yoon. PhD, Kyungpook Nat. U., Daegu, Republic of Korea, 1991. Vis. prof. Tokyo U., 1996—97; prof. Changwon Nat. U., Kyungnam, Republic of Korea, 1991—. Contbr. articles to profl. sci. jours. Mem. environ. com. Provincial Office, Changwon, Kyungnam, Republic of Korea, 2003—08. Grantee Rsch. Fund, Korea Rsch. Found., 1999—2006. Office: Changwon Nat Univ Sarim-Dong 9 641-773 Changwon Gyeongsangnam-do Republic of Korea Home Phone: 82 55 262 7733; Office Phone: 82 55 213 3454. Office Fax: 82 55 213 3459. Business E-Mail: swcheong@changwon.ac.kr.

CHERENKO, SERGIY MAKAROVITCH, endocrine surgeon, researcher; b. Kyiv, Ukraine, June 4, 1961; s. Makar Petrovitch and Elvina Sergiivna Cherenko; m. Svitlana Olexandrivna Danilova, Aug. 28, 1980; children: Maria Sergiivna, Sergiy Sergiyovitch. BM, Kiev Med. Inst., Ukraine, 1984, M Med. Sci. in Surgery, 1990; DMS in Surgery, Kiev Med. Acad. Postgraduate Edn., Ukraine, 2000. Cert. supreme category of surgical qualification Pub. Health Ministry Ukraine, 1998, sr. sci. worker in surgery Supreme Attestational Com. Ukraine, 2004, prof. surgery Ministry Edn. Ukraine, 2005. Gen. surgeon Kyiv Clin. Hosp. 15, Ukraine, 1985—89; prof. asst., chair hosp. surgery Nat. Med. U., Kyiv, 1990—2000; chief dept. endocrine surgery Ukrainian Sci. and Practical Ctr. Endocrine Surgery, Transplantation Endocrine Organs and Tissues, Kyiv, 2000—, vice dir. sci., 2001—. Sci. editor (med. jour.) Clin. Endocrinology and Endocrine Surgery; contbr. handbook of general surgery; translator: (handbook of medicine) Davidson's Principles & Practice of Medicine, 16th edit. Mem.: European Soc. Endocrine Surgery, European Soc. Surgery. Achievements include patents for in treatment and diagnostics of endocrine diseases. Office: Ukrainian Ctr Endocrine Surgery 121 Kharkivske shose Kyiv 02091 Ukraine Office Fax: 38044 5607546. Personal E-mail: scher@mail.i.com.ua. E-mail: endosurg@unet.net.ua.

CHEREPAHINA, NATALIE, physician; b. Moscow, Mar. 20, 1960; Degree, Moscow Med. Acad. IM Sechenova, 1987. Physician Moscow Med. Acad. IM Sechenova, 1987—2011. Home: Sovetskaya Vidnoe Moscow 142700 Russia

CHEREPAKHINA, NATALIE, immunologist; b. Moscow, Mar. 20, 1960; Degree, Moscow Med. Acad., 1987. Immunologist Moscow Med. Acad., 1990—. Asst. prof. Moscow Med. Acad. Avocations: literature, art. Home: Sovrtskaja Vidnoe Moscow 142700 Russia Personal E-mail: weg222@tandex.ru.

CHERIF, ABOUR HACHMI, biology and science educator; b. Sebha, Libya, Sept. 5, 1953; came to U.S., 1978; s. Hachmi Ahmed Cherif and Fatima (Milad) Ahmed; m. Farah Movahedzadeh, Apr. 11, 2004; children: David Tejeda, Nuria Cherif, Zaena Cherif. BS in Biology, Tripoli U., 1972-76; MS in Teaching Biology, Portland State U., 1980-82; PhD in Sci. Edn., Simon Fraser U., 1983-89. Cert. in biology, Libya; cert. leader in environ. issue forums trainers workshops. Biology instr. Sebha Tchr. Inst., Libya, 1976-77; biology lab. instr. Sebha U., Libya, 1976-78; sci. edn. instr. Simon Fraser U., Burnaby, Can., 1986-90; MAT developer in sci. Columbia Coll., Chgo., 1990-91, biology sci. edn. instr., 1990—; sci. instr. Aristotle Acad., Chgo., 1001—; environ. instr. Assn. for Promotion and Advancement of Sci. Edn., Vancouver, Can., 1989-90; biology & sci. prof. Columbia Coll. Chgo., 1990—2003; dir. faculty devel. DeVry U. Sys., 2003—04, dir. faculty acdemic leadership devel., 2004—05, dir. sci. & math. curriculum, 2005—06, assoc. dean curriculum sci., math. & clin. lab. sys., 2006—; pres. Am. Assn. U. Adminstrn., 2008—09. Curriculum evaluator The Commonwealth of Learning, Vancouver, Can., 1990; curriculum designer Columbia Coll., Chgo., 1990-91; curriculum developer, dir. rsch. devel. Aristotle Acad., Chgo., 1991—; sci. edn. spl. reviewer acad. stds. exams. numerous pub. schs. dists.; co-chair planning com. 3d Ann. Internat. Conf. of Human Factors in

Devel., Chgo., 1998; Ann. Conf. Assn. Coll. & U. Biology Educators, Chgo, 2002, bd. dirs., exec. com. Internat. Inst. for Human Factor Devel. Soc. Founder, mng. editor Forward to Excellence in Tchg. and Learning newsletter, sci. and math. dept. Columbia Coll., 1993; editor, mem. editl. bd. profl. jours. including Rev. for Human Factors Studies, Am. Biology Tchr., co-editor 5 textbooks; contbr. numerous articles to profl. jours. Developer MAT Grad. Program, 1991; sci. display, Simon Fraser U., 1988. Recipient Grad. Scholarship award The Ministry of Higher Edn., Tripoli, Libya, 1978-85, Pres'. PhD Rsch. award Simon Fraser U., Burnaby, Can., 1985, Teaching award Aristotle Acad., 1992, Teamwork award 1993; named Personality of Month Mawaheb: Multi-Cultural Mag., Ontario, 1991, 94, Rsch. award IIHFD Inst., 1998, Outstanding Departmental Svc. award ISTA, 1999, Columbia Coll., 2002. Democrat. Achievements include design of anumber of science programs & many of science & science education courses. Avocations: reading, writing, photography, soccer, fishing, poetry. Office: DeVry Univ Sys Dept Academic Affairs 1221 N Swift Rd Addison IL 60101-6106 Home: 200 N Jefferson St Apt 1401 Chicago IL 60661-1279 Office Phone: 630-953-3605, 630-353-7014. Fax: 630-574-1969. Personal E-mail: abourc8@comcast.net, abourcherif@att.net. Business E-Mail: acherif@devry.edu.

CHERMANN, JEAN CLAUDE, virologist, researcher; b. Paris, Mar. 23, 1939; s. Camille Andre and Benbeneda (Montoya) Chermann; m. Pearron Daniele Chermann, Dec. 22, 1962; children: Jean Francois, Olivier. B, Michelet, 1959; Maitrise Biochemistry, Paris U., 1963, PhD, 1967. Rsch. asst. Pasteur Inst., Paris, 1963—77, head lab., 1977—87, chief viral oncology lab.; rsch. dir. Inst. Nat. de le Recherche Medicale, Marseille, France, 1988—. Vis. scientist Nat. Cancer Inst., Bethesda, Md., 1971. Decorated Ordre Nat. du Merite Pres. de la Republique France, Ordre Nat. Legion d'Honneur France; recipient King Faisal Internat. prize, Medicine, 1993. Achievements include development of with Francoise Barre-Sinoussi and Luc Montagnier isolation of HIV-the causative agt. of AIDS. Office: URRMA R&D Z1 des Paluds BP 1055 Aubagne 13781 France Office Phone: 33442824211. Personal E-mail: jean.claude.chermann@hotmail.com. Business E-Mail: cherma@urrma.eu.

CHERNECKY, CYNTHIA, nursing educator; b. Dec. 24, 1955; MN, U. Pitts., 1980, PhD, Case Western Res. U., 1991. Prof. Ga. Health Scis. U., 1996—. Recipient Beverly Koerner Outstanding Alumni award, U. Conn., Mary Nowatny Excellence award, Oncology Nursing Soc., ONF Quality of Life award. Fellow: Am. Acad. Nursing. Achievements include research in vascular access and lung cancer. Avocations: walking, travel. Office: 987 St Sebastian Way Augusta GA 30912 Business E-Mail: cchernecky@georgiahealth.edu.

CHERNETSOVA, ELENA SERGEEVNA, chemist; b. Moscow, Mar. 9, 1980; d. Irina L'vovna Chernetsova and Sergey Fedorovich Idrisov; m. Alexander Borisovich Starostin, Nov. 23, 2002. MSc in Chemistry, Lomonosov Moscow State U., 2002, MSc in Pedagogics, 2002, PhD, 2005. Rsch. fellow Lomonosov Moscow State U., 2002—; engr. Inst. Elementoorganic Chemistry, Moscow, 2004—05. Contbr. articles to profl. jours. Recipient I.P. Alimarin award, Lomonosov Moscow State U., 2004; grantee, Soros Found., 2004—05; scholar, Govt. of Moscow, 2004. Mem.: All-Russian Mass Spectrometry Soc. (assoc.). Office: Lomonosov Moscow State Univ Leninskie Gory 1 Bldg 3 Moscow 119992 Russia Office Fax: +7 095 939 46 75. Personal E-mail: chern_es@rambler.ru. Business E-Mail: chernetsova@environment.chem.msu.ru.

CHERNEW, MICHAEL E., health economist, health care policy professor; b. Pitts. BS in Economics, Wharton Sch., U. Pa., 1986; PhD in Economics, Stanford U., Calif., 1993. Mgmt. cons. Strategic Planning Assocs., Washington, 1986—88; rsch. assoc. dept. economics Stanford U., 1990—91; intern RAND Corp., Santa Monica, Calif., 1991; lectr. prof. dept. health mgmt. and policy, dept. economics U. Mich., Ann Arbor, asst. prof., 1993—99, assoc. prof., 1999—2004, prof., 2004—06, asst. prof. dept. internal medicine, 1996—2000, assoc. prof., 2000—06; prof. dept. health care policy Harvard Med. Sch., Boston, 2006—. Mem. tech. adv. panel Ctr. Medicare & Medicaid Svcs. (CMS), 2000, 04, 10; co-dir. Robert Wood Johnson Scholars in Health Policy Rsch. Program, Mich., 2002—06; mem. Medicare Payment Adv. Commn. (MedPAC). Co-editor: American Jour.Managed Care, 2003—; sr. assoc. editor Health Svcs. Rsch., 2006—, mem. editl. bd. Med. Care Rsch. & Rev., 1999—, Health Svcs. Rsch., 1999—2006, Health Affairs, 2003—08; contbr. articles to profl. jours. Recipient John D. Thompson award, Assn. Univ. Programs in Health, 1998, Alice S. Hersh Young Investigator award, Assn. Health Svcs. Rsch., 1999, Health Care Rsch. award, Nat. Inst. Health Care Mgmt. Found., 2009; NSF fellowship, 1988—92. Mem.: Inst. Medicine. Office: Harvard Med Sch Dept Health Care Policy 180 Longwood Ave Boston MA 02115 Office Phone: 617-432-0174. E-mail: chernew@hcp.med.harvard.edu. *

CHERNG, CHEN-HWAN, anesthesiologist, researcher; b. Taipei, Taiwan, Oct. 18, 1959; s. Chun-Shi Cheng and Li-Hwa Ten; m. Huei-Chi Liu, Nov. 20, 1984; children: Chia-Shin Cheng, Chia-Dan Cheng. D of Med. Sci., Nat. Def. Med. Sch., Taipei, 1994. Dir. clin. anesthesia dept. anesthesiology Tri-Svc. Gen. Hosp., Taipei, 1998—.

CHERNICOFF, DAVID PAUL, osteopathic physician, educator; b. NYC, Aug. 3, 1947; s. Harry and Lillian (Dobkin) C. AB, U. Rochester, 1969; DO, Phila. Coll., 1973. Diplomate Nat. Bd. Osteo. Examiners, Am. Osteo. Bd. Internal Medicine, also in Hematology/Oncology. Rotating intern Rocky Mtn. Hosp., Denver, 1973-74; resident in internal medicine Cmty. Gen. Osteo. Hosp., Harrisburg, Pa., 1974-76; fellow in hematology and med. oncology Cleve. Clinic, 1976-78; asst. prof. medicine sect. hematology/oncology Chgo. Coll. Osteo. Medicine, 1978-82, assoc. prof., 1982-89; co-chmn. tumor task force Chgo. Osteo. Med. Ctr., 1978-89, dir. clin. cancer edn., 1978-89; asst. clin. prof. medicine Pa. State U. Coll. Medicine, Harrisburg, 1993—; pvt. practice, 1979. Med. dir. Keystone Peer Rev. Orgn., 1997-2000; chmn. tumor task force Olympia Fields (Ill.) Osteo. Med. Ctr. Trustee, mem. clin. exec. com. Ill. Cancer Coun., 1982-89; bd. dir. Chgo. unit Am. Cancer Soc., 1981-86, chief sec. of Hematology-Oncology Hosp. of Chgo. Coll. Osteo Medicine, 1981-89; carrier adv. com. Xact Medicare Svcs., 1997-2000; med. dir. Keystone Peer Rev. Orgn., 1997-2000. Contbr. articles to med. jours. Fellow Am. Coll. Osteo. Internists, Pa. Osteo. Med. Soc. Ea. Coop. Oncology Group (sr. investigator 1981-89), Am. Soc. Clin. Oncology; mem. Am. Osteo. Assn. Office: Carlisle Regional Cancer Ctr 25 Sprint Dr Carlisle PA 17015 Office Phone: 717-960-3750. Personal E-mail: yablood2000@yahoo.com.

CHERNOBELSKY, SEMYON ILYICH, otolaryngologist; b. Minusinsk, Russia, Mar. 6, 1952; s. Ilya Emmanuilovich Chernobelsky and Anna Evseevna Hazanova; m. Ludmila Grigorievna Kravchenko, Dec. 8, 1977; children: Polina, Victoria. MD with honors, Med. Inst., Krasnoyarsk, Russia, 1975. ENT-phoniatrician Opera House, Krasnoyarsk, 1978—; rschr., sr. lectr. Acad. Music, Krasnoyarsk, 1982—, prof., 2005—; cons. Regional Hosp., Krasnoyarsk, 1985—; sr. lectr. Med. Inst., Krasnoyarsk, 1990—. Contbr. articles to profl. jours. Mem.: Union Russian Phoniatricians. Avocations: piano, singing. Office: Opera House Perensona 2 660049 Krasnoyarsk Russia Home: ul. Dubrovinskogo 56-20 660049 Krasnoyarsk Krasnoyarskiy Kray Russia Office Phone: 7 3912 274463. Business E-Mail: semyon@ktk.ru.

CHERNOF, DAVID, internist; b. Chgo., Dec. 6, 1935; s. Joseph and Fannie (Cassata) C.; m. Lorna Jean Laff, Mar. 30, 1958 (dec. 2000); children: Bruce, Steven, Kenneth; m. Chris Provenzano, 2002. AB, Harvard U., 1957; MD, UCLA, 1961. Diplomate Am. Bd. Internal Medicine, Am. Bd. Hematology, Am. Bd. Med. Oncology, Am. Bd. Geriatrics. Staff physician City of Hope, Duarte, Calif., 1967-68; pvt. practice Northridge, Calif., 1968-91; pres. D.C. Healthcare Cons. Inc., 1995—. Pres. med. staff Northridge Hosp., 1980-81, trustee, 1991; assoc. prof. medicine UCLA, 1984—; bd. dirs. Blue Cross Calif., L.A., 1987-91, sr. v.p., corp. med. dir., 1991-95; chief med. officer Local Initiative Authority L.A. County (now LA Care), 1996-98; cons. Calif. Health Care Assn., Hotel Employees and Restaurant Employees Internat. Union., State Calif. Dept. Managed Care, 1993-2002; chmn. sci. adv. com. C. Everett Koop's Self Care Advisor, 1996; bd. mem. Santa Barbara Neighborhood Clinics, 2001-09, chmn. 2004-09, Healthcare Hero, 2008; bd. mem. Adventures in Caring, 2002-, bd. chair, 2004-; med. dir. Ventura County, State of Calif., 2003-05. Chmn. sci. adv. com. The Essential 1999 Women's Health Guide; contbr. articles to sci. jours.; contbr. introduction to From Residency to Reality (book). Bd. dirs. So. Calif. Health Policy Rsch. Consortium, 1990-93; mem. Los Angeles County Managed Care Planning Coun., 1993-94; chmn. freshman interview com. Harvard Radcliffe Alumni Assn., San Fernando Valley, Calif., 1996-2000; bd. dirs. Hosp. Coun. No. and Ctrl. Calif. Found., 1991-95; chair health svcs. adv. com. Sch. Pub. Adminstrn., U. So. Calif., 1993—2000; mem. Mayor's Commn. on Healthy Kids; chmn. bd. Calif. Kids Found., 1995-2003. Fellow ACP, Nat. Health Found.; mem. So. Calif. Ind. Practice Assn. (founding pres. 1985 87), Northridge Physicians Preferred Provider Assn. (founding pres. 1983-91), Calif. Med. Assn. (bd. dirs. polit. action com. 1989-94, chmn. Medi-Cal com. 1989-91, trustee 1991-94), L.A. County Med. Assn. (treas. 1987-88, pres.-elect 1988-90, pres. 1990-91, bd. dirs. polit. action com. 1987-91), LA County Healthcare Access Taskforce, 1987-92, Health Svcs. Rsch. Found. (bd. dirs. 1992), Santa Barbara Symphony Assn. (bd. dirs. 2010-, bd. sec. 2010-). Democrat. Jewish. Avocations: gardening, music, sports. Business E-Mail: chernof@usc.edu.

CHERNOFF, AMOZ IMMANUEL, hematologist, consultant; b. Malden, Mass., Mar. 17, 1923; s. Isaiah and Celia (Margolin) C.; m. Renate R. Fisher, Jan. 25, 1953; children: David F., Susan N., Judith A. BS in Chemistry with honors, Yale U., 1944, MD cum laude, 1947. Diplomate Am. Bd. Internal Medicine. Med. intern Mass. Gen. Hosp., Boston, 1947-48; asst. resident in medicine Barnes Hosp., St. Louis, 1948-49; fellow in hematology Michael Reese Hosp., Chgo., 1949-51, asst. dir. hematology research lab., 1950-51; A.C.P. fellow Washington U. Sch. Medicine, St. Louis, 1951-52; USPHS spl. research fellow, 1952-53; instr. in medicine, 1952-54; asst. prof., 1954-56; assoc. prof. medicine Duke U., 1956-58; chief sect. hematology VA Hosp., Durham, N.C., 1956-58. Rsch. prof. U. Tenn. Meml. Rsch. Ctr., Knoxville, 1958-79, dir., 1964-77; assoc. vice chancellor for acad. affairs Ctr. Health Scis., 1977-79; prof. medicine Coll. Medicine, Memphis, 1966-79; med. dir. Cystic Fibrosis Found., Atlanta, 1975-77; dir. div. blood diseases and resources Nat. Heart Lung and Blood Inst., NIH, Bethesda, Md., 1979-88; assoc. exec. dir. sci. affairs Am. Assn. Blood Banks, Arlington, Va., 1988-90; cons. transfusion medicine programs. Contbr. articles to profl. jours. Served with U.S. Army, 1943-45. Recipient Campbell award Yale U. Sch. Medicine, 1947, Research Career award USPHS, 1962-77 Fellow ACP; mem. Am. Soc. Clin. Investigation, Am. Soc. Hematology, Internat. Soc. Hematology, Cen. Soc. Clin. Rsch., So. Soc. Clin. Investigation, Soc. Exptl. Biology and Medicine, Am. Fedn. Clin. Rsch., Am. Assn. Blood Banks, Sigma Xi, Alpha Omega Alpha. Business E-Mail: Achernoff9785@comcast.net.

CHERNOFF, ARTHUR, endocrinologist, educator; MD, U. Pa. Intern Pa. Hosp.; resident internal medicine Columbia- Presbyn. Hosp., NY, fellow endocrinology and metabolism NY; clin. assoc. Nat. Inst. of Health; divsn. chair, program dir. Albert Einstein Med. Ctr. Named Topd Doc. Fellow: Am. Coll. of Endocrinology. Office: Albert Einstein Medical Center 5501 Old York Rd Philadelphia PA 19141 Office Phone: 215-456-7890.

CHERNOW, BART, retired medical administrator; b. NYC, June 26, 1947; BA, Queens Coll., 1968; MD, SUNY, NYC, 1976. Internal medicine intern Nat. Naval Med. Ctr., Bethesda, Md., 1976-77, internal medicine resident, 1977-79, endocrine fellow, 1979-81; dir. rsch. dept. critical care medicine Bethesda Naval Hosp., 1981-85, head acad. affairs, 1985-86; assoc. prof. anesthesia Harvard Med. Sch., Boston, 1986-90; assoc. dir. surg. ICU Mass. Gen. Hosp., 1986-90; prof. medicine, anesthesia and critical care Johns Hopkins U. Sch. Medicine, Balt., 1990-99; physician-in-chief Sinai Hosp., 1990-97; program dir. John Hopkins U./Sinai Hosp. Program in Internal Medicine, 1990-97; vice dean for rsch. and tech. Sch. Medicine Johns Hopkins U. Sch. Medicine, 1997-99; pres., CEO GMP Cos., Inc., Ft. Lauderdale, Fla., 1999—2004, chief tech. officer, 2004—06; prof. medicine U. Miami, Miami, Fla., v.p. spl. programs and resource strategy Miller sch. medicine, 2007—10, vice provost tech. advancement, 2007—10; ret. Adj. prof. medicine Johns Hopkins U. Sch. Medicine, 1999—2009. Editor: Pharmacologic Approach to the Critically Ill Patient, 1983, 88, 94; editor-in-chief: Critical Care Medicine, 1990-97. Comdr. med. corps USNR, 1969-86. Recipient Achievement award Am. Coll. Nutrition, 1995. Fellow ACP (master), Am. Coll. Critical Care Medicine; mem. Soc. Critical Care Medicine (Presdl. citation 1997), Am. Coll. Chest Physicians (regent 1990-98, pres. 1996-97, master fellow, chair, founder CHEST found.1996-2002). Home: Chernows L'Ambiance 4240 Galt Ocean Dr Apt 2303 Fort Lauderdale FL 33308

CHERRY, ANDREW LAWRENCE, JR., social work educator, researcher; b. Dothan, Ala., Nov. 11, 1943; s. Andrew L. Cherry and Wyalene Cain; m. Mary Elizabeth Dillon, July 16, 1988. MSW, U. Ala., Tuscaloosa, 1974; D Social Work, Columbia U., 1986. Child welfare worker Escambia County Dept. Pensions and Securities, Brewton, Ala., 1968-72; psychiat. social worker Bryce State Hosp., Tuscaloosa, 1974-79; instr. Salisbury (Md.) State Coll., 1981-85; asst. prof. Marywood Coll. Sch. Social Work, Scranton, Pa., 1986-87; prof. Barry U. Sch. Social Work, Miami, Fla., 1987—2003; prof. mental health Sch. Social Work U. Okla., Tulsa, 2003—, endowed prof. mental health sch. social work, 2003—. Cons. Informed Families Dade County, Miami, 1990—98, Miami Coalition for Care to Homeless, 1991—93, NAACP Minority Media and Telecomm. Coun., 1992—2000; with drug abuse prevention program Cath. Charities, Miami, 1991—2000, Broward Children's Svc., Ft. Lauderdale, 1992—94, The Biscayne Inst., 1994—2004, St. Luke's Addiction Recovery Ctr., 1995—2000; interim dir. child welfare divsn. Cath. Charities, 1998—2000; project evaluator Substance Abuse and Mental Health Svcs. Adminstrn., Okla., 2004—. Author: The Socializating Instinct: Individual, Family and Social Bonds, 1994, A Research Primer for the Helping Professions: Methods, Statistics, and Writing, 2000, Examining Global Social Welfare Issues Using MicroCase, 2002, 2d edit., 2004; co-author: Social Bonds and Teen Pregnancy, 1992; co-editor: Teenage Pregnancy: A Global View, 2001, Substance Abuse: A Global View, 2002; series advisor Greenwood Press World View of Social Issues, 1999, Cherry, A. & Dillon, M. E, 2010, Using The DSM-IV-TR in Social Work and The Helping Professions. Eddie Bowers Publishing Co., Inc.; contbr. articles to profl. jours. Bd. mem. Mental Health Assn. Tulsa, Okla. Scholar, NIMH, 1979. Fellow: Am. Orthopsychiat. Assn.; mem.: NASW, N.Y. Acad. Scis., Conf. Social Work Edn. Achievements include research in and devel. of the social bond theory; extensive work and rsch. among the mentally disabled, homeless, at-risk children and the addicted. Office: U Okla Tulsa Campus 4502 E 41st St Ste 3J08 Tulsa OK 74135-2512 Office Phone: 918-660-3363. Business E-Mail: alcherry@ou.edu.

CHERRY, JAMES DONALD, pediatrician; b. Summit, NJ, June 10, 1930; s. Robert Newton and Beatrice (Wheeler) C.; m. Jeanne M. Fischer, June 19, 1954; children: James S., Jeffrey D., Susan J., Kenneth C. BS, Springfield Coll., Mass., 1953; MD, U. Vt., 1957; MSc in Epidemiology, London Sch. Hygiene and Tropical Medicine, 1983. Diplomate Am. Bd. Pediat., Am. Bd. Pediat. Infectious Diseases. Intern, then resident in pediat. Boston City Hosp., 1957-59; resident in pediat. Kings County Hosp., Bklyn., 1959-60; rsch. fellow in medicine Harvard U. Med. Sch.-Thorndike Meml. Lab., Boston City Hosp., 1961-62; instr. pediatrics U. Vt. Coll. Medicine, also asst. attending physician Mary Fletcher DeGoesbriand Meml. hosps., Burlington, Vt., 1960-61; asst. prof., then assoc. prof. pediat. U. Wis. Med. Sch., Madison, 1963-66; assoc. attending physician Madison Gen., U. Wis. hosps., 1963-66; dir. John A. Hartford Rsch. Lab., Madison Gen. Hosp., 1963-66. Mem. faculty St. Louis U. Med. Sch., 1966-73, prof. pediatrics, 1969-73, vice chmn. dept., 1970-73; mem. staff Cardinal Glennon Meml. Hosp. Children, St. Louis U. Hosp., 1966-73; chief divsn. infectious diseases UCLA Med. Ctr. UCLA Sch. Medicine, 1973-2000, prof. pediat., 1973—; acting chmn. dept. pediatrics UCLA Med. Ctr., 1977-79; attending physician, chmn. infection control com. UCLA Med. Ctr., 1975-93; cons. Project Head Start; vis. worker dept. cmty. medicine Middlesex Hosp. and Med. Sch., London, 1982-83, vis. worker Common Cold Rsch. Unit, 1969-70; acad. visitor U. Cambridge, Eng., 2000-01. Co-editor: (Textbook) Pediatric Infectious Diseases, 1981, 6th edit., 2009; assoc. editor Clin. Infectious Diseases, 1990—99, Am. regional editor Vaccine, 1991—2000, cons. editor Pediatric Research, 2004—; contbr. scientific papers numerous in field; editl. reviewer (profl. jours). Bd. govs. Alexander Graham Bell Internat. Parents Orgn., 1967-69. With USAR, 1958-64. Recipient Disting. Academic Achievement award, U. Vt., 1984, Med. Sci. award, Med. Alumni UCLA, 2005; John and Mary R. Markle scholar acad. medicine, 1964. Mem. AAAS, APHA, Am. Acad. Pediat. (mem. exec. com. Calif. chpt. 2 1975-77, mem. com. infectious diseases 1977-83, assoc. editor 19th Red Book 1982), Am. Soc. Microbiology,Soc. Pediat. Rsch., Infectious Diseases Soc. Am., Am. Epidemiol. Soc., Am. Pediat. Soc., L.A. Pediat. Soc., Internat. Orgn. Mycoplasmologists, Am. Soc. Virology, Pediat. Infectious Diseases Soc. (pres. 1989-91, Disting. Physician award 2003), Alpha Omega Alpha. Office: UCLA David Geffen Sch Medicine and Mattel Children's Hosp Dept Pediatrics Rm 22-442 10833 Le Conte Ave Los Angeles CA 90095-1752 Office Phone: 310-825-5226. Business E-Mail: jcherry@mednet.ucla.edu.

CHERRY, KENNETH JEROME, JR., surgeon; b. Richmond, Va., Oct. 22, 1947; s. Kenneth Jerome and Alice (Cottingham) Cherry; m. Robin Wheeler, Sept. 10, 1983; children: Katherine, Sarah, Kenneth III. Undergrad., Duke U., Durham, NC, 1970; MD, U. Va., Charlottesville, 1974. Diplomate Am. Bd. Surgery, Gen. Vascular Surgery. Intern, resident surgery U. Va., Charlottesville, 1974-80; resident vascular surgery U. Calif. San Francisco, 1980-81; instr. surgery Mayo Med. Sch., Rochester, Minn., 1981—84, asst. prof. of surgery, 1988—95, assoc. prof. of surgery, 1995—, prof. of surgery, 1995—2004; prof. of surgery, head divsn. vascular surgery U. Va. Health Sys., 2004—. Surgeon Rochester Meth. Hosp., St. Mary's Hosps., Rochester. Contbr. articles to profl. jour. Mem. ACS, Am. Surg. Assn, Midwestern Vascular Surg. Soc., Soc. Vascular Surgery (Disting. Fellow), Peripheral Vascular Soc., Soc. for Vascular Surgeons. Avocations: reading, history, outdoor activites. Home: 1010 Tanglewood Rd Charlottesville VA 22901 Office: Divsn Vascular Surgery Univ Va Health System PO Box 800679 Charlottesville VA 22908-0679 Office Phone: 434-243-7052. Business E-Mail: kjc5kh@virginia.edu.

CHERRY, ROBERT A., surgeon; BA, Columbia U., NYC, 1987, MD, 1987—91. Lic. gen. surgery & surgical critical care ACS, 1997. Internship North Shore U. Hosp., NY, 1991—92, resident gen. surgery, 1992—96; fellowship trauma and critical care R. Adams Coulley Shock Trauma Ctr., U. Md., 1996—97; trauma program med. dir. Penn State Shock Trauma Ctr., Hershey, Pa., 2002—09; chief sect. trauma & critical care Penn State Milton S. Hershey Med. Ctr., 2004—08, assoc. chief quality officer, 2009—; program chair Intercoll. Master Profl. Studies Degree Homeland Security, 2010; chief mem. officer, v.p. clin. effectiveness Loyola U. Med. Ctr., 2010—, prof. surgery Stritch Sch. Medicine, 2011—. Program chair, master homeland security degree in pub. health preparedness Penn State Coll. Medicine, 2005. Office: Loyola University Med Ctr Ste 1739 Bldg 101 216 D 1st Ave Maywood IL 60153 *

CHERSICH, MATTHEW FRANCIS, epidemiologist, statistician; b. Johannesburg, Jan. 21, 1975; s. Robert and Ethel Chersich; life ptnr. Fiona Scorgie. MBBCh, U. Witwatersrand, South Africa, 1998, DTM & H, 2002; PhD, U. Gent, Belgium, 2007; MSc in Pub. Health, London Sch. Hygiene Tropical Medicine, 2003. Diplomate obstetrics Coll. Medicine, South Africa, 2000, child health Coll. Medicine, South Africa, 2001, Faculty Pub. Health, UK, 2007. Med. officer Coronation Hosp., Gauteng, South Africa, 2000—01; trial physician Perinatal HIV Rsch. Unit, Soweto, Gauteng, 2001—02; epidemiologist Internat. Centre Reproductive Health, Mombasa, Coast Province, Kenya, 2005—; tech. advisor Reproductive Health and HIV Rsch. Unit, U. Witwatersrand, Johannesburg, 2007—. Cons. World Health Organisation, Geneva, 2003—08. Contbr. articles to profl. jours. Vol. SJ Refugee Snc., Rome, 1997; lay min. cath. ch. Johannesburg. Recipient South African Jr. Chess Champion, 1995. Mem.: Kenya Med. Assn., Gen. Med. Coun. UK, Coll. Medicine South Africa. Mem. Catholic Ch. Achievements include World Chess Championship participant Halle Germany 1996. Business E-Mail: matthewf.chersich@icrhk.org.

CHERTOW, GLENN M., internist, nephrologist, researcher; b. Bklyn., May 25, 1963; s. Jerome and Sylvia Fay Chertow; m. Dara Beth Nachmanoff; children: Caleb, Elazar, Solana. BA, U. Pa., 1985; MD, Harvard U., 1989, MPH, 1995. Diplomate Am. Bd. Internal Medicine, Am. Bd. Nephrology. Resident, fellow, then chief resident Brigham's Women's Hosp., Boston, 1989-95, mem. faculty, asst. dir. of dialysis, 1995-98; asst. prof. medicine in residence U. Calif., San Francisco, 1998—2001, assoc. prof. medicine in residence, 2001—04, assoc. prof. epidemiology and biostatistics, 2004—05, prof. epidemiology and biostatistics, 2005—07, prof. medicine in residence, 2005—07; prof. medicine Stanford U. Sch. Medicine, 2007—, assoc., Ctr. Health Policy, Ctr. for Primary Care and Outcomes Rsch., 2008—. Contbr. more than 75 articles to sci. and profl. jours. Recipient President's award, Nat. Kidney Found., 1999, Nat. Torchbearer award, Am. Kidney Fund, 2007; named one of Top Doctors in Bay Area, San Francisco mag., 1999—2000, 2002—04. Mem.: Am. Society Clinical Investigation. Office: Stanford U A175 MC 5303 300 Pasteur Dr Stanford CA 94305

CHERVIN, RONALD DAVID, neurology educator; b. NYC, Dec. 1, 1961; s. André and Alma C.; m. Stephanie Marie Alt, July 13, 1997. BA, Harvard U., 1983; MD, Stanford U., 1988; MS in Clin. Rsch., U. Mich. Sch. Pub. Health, 1997. Diplomate Am. Bd. Psychiatry and Neurology, Am. Bd. Sleep Medicine. Intern in internal medicine Cornell U. Med. Ctr., NYC, 1988-89, resident in neurology, 1989-92; postdoctoral fellow, sleep medicine Stanford Sleep Ctr., Calif., 1992-94; assoc. prof. neurology U. Mich., Ann Arbor, Mich., 1994, prof. neurology; dir. U. Mich. Sleep Disorders Ctr., 2000—, Michael S. Aldrich Collegiate Prof. Sleep Medicine. Contbr. several articles to profl. jours.; assoc. editor Sleep, mem. editl. bd. Sleep Medicine, Jour. Clin. Sleep Medicine, ad hoc reviewer for several profl. jours. Recipient Ind. Scientist Career Devel. award NIH, 1997, Rsch. grantee, 1999, 2004. Mem. Am. Acad. Neurology (Sleep Sci. award, 2004), Am. Acad. Sleep Medicine, Sleep Rsch. Soc.(bd. dirs.), Internat. Pediat. Sleep Assn. (bd. dirs.). Office: Sleep Disorders Ctr Rm C728 1500 E Medical Center Dr Ann Arbor MI 48109-5845 Office Phone: 734-647-9064. Office Fax: 734-936-5377.

CHESNEY, RUSSELL WALLACE, pediatrician, educator; b. Knoxville, Tenn., Aug. 25, 1941; s. Jack and Helen Wallace (McColl) C.; m. Patricia Joan Cook, June 8, 1968; children: Karen, Christopher, Gillian. AB, Harvard U., Cambridge, Mass., 1963; MD, U. Rochester, NYC, 1968. Diplomate Am. Bd. Pediatrics. Intern then resident Johns Hopkins U. Hosp., Balt., 1968-70, 72-73; renal fellow NIH, Balt., 1970-72, Montreal Childrens Hosp., Montreal, Que., Canada, 1973-75; asst. then prof. U. Wis., Madison, 1975-85; prof., vice chmn. U. Calif., Davis, 1985-88; Le Bonheur prof., chair Dept. Pediat. U. Tenn. Health Sci. Ctr., Memphis, 1988—. Mem. Rsch. Study Sect. NIH, Washington, 1983—88, mem. Nat. Kidney and Urology Diseases Adv. Bd., 1988—91; sec.-treas., pediat. dept. chmn. Am. Med. Schs., 1993—99, pres., 2001—03; mem. coun. Am. Pediat. Soc., 1995—2004, v.p., 2001—02, pres., 2002—03; chmn. Fed. Pediat. Orgn., 1995—96; Birdsong lectr. U. Va., 1995; vice chair Task Force on Pediat. Edn., 1996—99; chair Am. Bd. Pediats., 2000—02; bd. trustees Assn. Children's Hosps., 2002—07. Contbr. articles to profl. jours., chpts. to text and med. books. Lt. comdr. USPHS, 1970-72, Balt. Recipient Founders award in Pediatric Rsch., So. Soc. Pediatric Rsch., 1993; Jour. Pediatrics lectr. U. Rochester, 1985, Paul Gaffney lectr. U. Pitts., 1988, Ira Greifer award, 2010 Mem. Am. Pediat. Soc. (mem. coun. 1995-, v.p. 2001-02, pres. 2002-03), Am. Acad. Pediats. (pres. Tenn. state chpt. 1995-98, E. Meade Johnson award 1985, Nutrition award 1996, St. Geme award 2001, Henry Barnett award 2004), Am. Soc. Pediat. Nephrology (Founders award 2005), Internat. Pediat. Nephrology Assoc. (Iragreifer award 2010), Soc. for Pediat. Rsch. (pres. 1986-87), Midwest Soc. for Pediat. Rsch. (pres. 1984-85), Am. Soc. for Pediat. Nephrology (pres. 1986-87), VA Merit Rev. Bd. (chmn. 1988-90). Office: U Tenn Dept Pediat Le Bonheur Childrens' Med Ctr 50 S Dunlap St, Rm 306 Memphis TN 38103-2893 Office Phone: 901-287-5036, 901-488-2070. Office Fax: 901-287-5036. Business E-Mail: rchesney@utmem.edu.

CHESS, LEONARD, medical educator, researcher; b. NYC, Apr. 9, 1943; BS, MIT, 1964; MD, SUNY, Downstate, 1968. Prof. medicine, pathology and cell biology, rschr. Columbia U., Coll. Physicians and Surgeons, 1977—. Recipient Merit award, NIH; Autoimmunity Ctr. Excellence. Mem.: Am. Assn. Immunologists, Assn. Am. Physicians, Am. Soc. Clin. Investigation, Interurban Clin. Club. Office: Columbia Presbyterian Medical Ctr 63 New York NY 10032 Business E-Mail: lc19@columbia.edu.

CHESSIN, DAVID BRIAN, medical educator; b. NJ, Jan. 27, 1974; BA, Lehigh U., 1996; MD, UMDNJ Robert Wood Johnson Med. Sch., 2000. Clin. asst. prof., surgery Mt. Sinai Med. Ctr., 2008—. Named one of Top Surgeon, Guide to America's Top Surgeons, 2010, Best Drs. in America, 2011. Fellow: ACS; mem.: NY Soc. Colon and Rectal Surgeons, Am. Soc. Colon and Rectal Surgeons. Office: 25 East 69th St New York NY 10021 Office Fax: 212-535-3717. Business E-Mail: david.chessin@mssm.edu.

CHESSLER, RICHARD KENNETH, gastroenterologist, endocrinologist; b. NYC, Apr. 6, 1944; BS, Fairleigh Dickinson U., Rutherford, NJ, 1965; MD, Chgo. Med. Sch., 1969. Diplomate Am. Bd. Internal Medicine and Gastroenterology. Asst. chief gastroenterology Englewood Hosp., NJ, 1982—, chief endoscopy NJ, 1992-99; asst. prof. medicine Mt. Sinai Hosp., NYC, 1994-97. Author: Chemical Technicians Ready Reference Book, 1996; mem. editl. bd. Practical Gastroenterology, 1977—. Fellow ACP, Am. Coll. Gastroenterology (bd. govs. 1989). Avocations: ski, racquetball, golf. Office: 1555 Center Ave Fort Lee NJ 07024-4612 Office Phone: 201-945-6564.

CHESSON, ANDREW LONG, JR., dean, neurology educator; b. Raleigh, NC, Nov. 29, 1948; s. Andrew L. C.; m. Linda Denise Illian, July 29, 1972; children: Andrew III, Lisa. BA, U. Tex., 1970; MD, U. Tex. Med. Sch., 1974. Lic. med. dr. Tex., La.; cert. Am. Bd. Psychiatry and Neurology, Am. Bd. Sleep Medicine; accredited Clin. Polysomnographer. Intern U. Tex. Med. Br., Galveston, 1974-75, resident in neurology, 1975-78; staff neurologist, dir. VA Hosp. neurology outpatient clinic VA Med. Ctr., Shreveport, 1978-85, cons., 1985—, clin. dir. dept. neurology Shreveport, 1993-95; instr. neurology La. State U. Med. Ctr., Shreveport, 1978-79, asst. prof. neurology, 1979-84, assoc. prof., 1984-93, dir. neurophysiology labs., 1988—2009, prof., 1993—, dean, 2009—. Assoc. dean for acad. affairs La. State U. Med. Ctr., Shreveport, 1994—, mem. various coms., 1978-94, acting chmn. dept. neurology, 1994-95; chief resident U. Tex. Med. Br. Dept. Neurology, 1977-78; reviewer in field; presenter in field. Contbr. chpts. to books and articles to profl. jours. Edward P. Stiles grantee, 1987. Fellow Am. Acad. Neurology (chmn. quality assurance subcom. sect. on sleep 1995—), Clin. Sleep Soc., Am. Sleep Disorders Assn. (chmn. stds. of practice com. 1995—); mem. AMA. Avocations: camping, backpacking, canoeing, wood working. Office: La State University Med Ctr Office of Dean 1501 Kings Hwy Shreveport LA 71130-3932 *

CHESTER, ALEXANDER CAMPBELL, III, physician; b. NYC, Dec. 21, 1947; s. Alexander C. II and Gladys (Edelhauser) C.; m. Kimberly Robinson Chester, Dec. 20, 1970; children: Kristin Elizabeth, Alexander C. IV. BS cum laude, Georgetown U., 1969; MD, Columbia U., 1973. Diplomate Am. Bd. Internal Medicine, Nat. Bd. Med. Examiners; advanced achievement in internal medicine; voluntary recert., 1998. Intern Georgetown U., Washington, 1973-74, resident in medicine, 1974-76, clin. fellow in nephrology, 1976-77, rsch. fellow in nephrology, 1977-78, clin. instr. medicine, 1978-80, clin. asst. prof. medicine, 1980-84, clin. assoc. prof. medicine, 1985-89, clin. prof. medicine, 1990—. Govs. com. for coll. affairs ACP, 1980-90; clin. prof. medicine Georgetown U. Med. Ctr.; reviewer Annals of Internal Medicine, Jour. Rheumatology, bd. dirs. Cardiovasc. Kidney Hypertension Ins., Georgetown U. Med. Ctr. Contbr. articles to profl. jours. and publs. Named one of Top Doctors, Washingtonian Mag., 1999, 2002, 05, 08, Area Outstanding Specialists, Checkbook mag., 1998, 2005, Area Outstanding Specialists Checkbook mag., 2002, 05, 09; featured in Consumers' Guide to Top Doctors, editors of Checkbook Mag., 2002, 03, 09, Best Drs. in America, 2011, Best Dirs. Inter Consolation Svc., 2011. Mem. AMA, ACP (gov.'s nominating com.), Am. Soc. Internal Medicine (alt. del. Nat. Meeting 1980), Hippocrates-Galen Med. Soc. (sec., treas. 1991-92, pres. 1993-94), Osler Soc. (sec., treas. 1986-88, pres. 1989-90), Nat. Kidney Found. (coun. clin. nephrology, dialysis and tranplantation, profl. adv. bd. 1983-86, program com. ann. kidney symposium 1983-86), Am. Heart Assn. (coun. kidney 1988-90), Clinico-Pathol. Soc. (pres. 2003-04), Am. Rhinologic Soc., Soc. for Study Human Behavior and Evolution, Am. Assn. Chronic Fatigue Syndrome, Myalgic Encephalomyelitis Assn. (U.K.), Cosmos Club, Phi Beta Kappa. Achievements include research in nasal reflexes, sick building syndrome and chronic fatigue syndrome. Home: 4618 Laverock Pl NW Washington DC 20007-2544 Office: 3301 New Mexico Ave NW Ste 348 Washington DC 20016-3622 Office Phone: 202-362-4467. Office Fax: 202-362-2303.

CHESTER, MARC A., pulmonologist; b. Balt., Mar. 23, 1974; MD, St. George's U. Sch. Medicine, 2003; MS, SUNY, Buffalo, 1999. Pediat. pulmonologist Pediat. Lung Ctr., 2009—. Avocations: soccer, scuba diving, mountain climbing, bicycling. Office: 2730-A Prosperity Ave Fairfax VA 22031 Office Fax: 703-289-1420. Personal E-mail: vududoc@aol.com.

CHET, ILAN, soil microbiologist; b. Haifa, Israel, Apr. 12, 1939; s. Aaron and Yaffa (Vlodowsky) C.; m. Ruth Geffen, Oct. 5, 1964; children: Gal, Guy, Dana, Tal, Tom. BSc with honors, Hebrew U., Rehovot, Israel, 1962, MSc with honors, 1964, PhD, 1968. R. Merton prof. Gottingen (Fed. Republic Germany) U., 1978; sr. lectr. Hebrew U., Rehovot, 1972-75, assoc. prof., 1975-78, prof., 1978—2001, v.p. R&D, 1992—2001; pres. Weizmann Inst. Sci., Rohovot, Israel, 2001—, prof. Dept. Biol. Chemistry. Vis. prof. Colo. State U., Ft. Collins, 1979-80, Harvard U., Cambridge, Mass., 1980, Rutgers U., N.J., 1994-95; dept. head Hebrew U., Rehovot, 1981-83, dean, 1986-89; vis. scientist Dupont de Nemours Co., Wilmington, Del., 1989-90, v.p. for R&D, 1991—. Contbr. articles to profl. jours.; patentee in field. Recipient Kadrma prize, Phytopath Soc., Israel, 1979, A. Z. Cohen prize, 1982, Burchardt medal Gottingen U., 1982, Olitzky prize, Microbiol. Soc. Israel, 1989, Rothchild prize for agr., 1990, Max-Planck-Forschungs-Preis, Alexander von Humboldt-Stiftung, 1994, Israel prize, 1996, Arima prize, 1996, Wolf prize for agr., Wolf Found., Israel, 1998. Fellow Am. Phytopath. Soc.; mem. Israel Soc. Microbiology, Israel Soc. Plant Pathology (com. chmn. 1989—), Israel Nat. Acad. Scis., Am. Soc. Microbiology, Internat. Orgn. Biotech. Office: Hebrew Univ PO Box 12 76100 Rehovot Israel Office Phone: 972 8 9489236. Office Fax: 972 8 9468785. Business E-Mail: chet@huzi.ac.il.

CHEUNG, CHI YUEN, physician; b. Hong Kong, Jan. 22, 1970; MBBS, U. Hong Kong, 1994; PhD, Maastricht, Netherlands, 2009. Med. officer Queen Elizabeth Hosp., Hong Kong, 1995—. Contbr. articles to profl. med. jour. Fellow: RCP (UK), Hong Kong Acad. Medicine, Hong Kong Coll. Physicians. Achievements include research in HIV renal medicine pharmacogenetics and renal transplantation. Office: Queen Elizabeth Hosp 30 Gascoigne Rd Kowloon Hong Kong Personal E-mail: simoncycheung@gmail.com.

CHEUNG, KWOK-LEUNG, surgeon; b. Hong Kong, Feb. 5, 1963; s. Shu-Hang C. and Yuk-Wa Wu; m. Po-Yin Loretta Fung, Dec. 22, 1991; children: Ian, Victoria. MB BS, U. Hong Kong, 1987; MD, U. Nottingham, 2001. Sr. med. officer surgery Queen Mary Hosp., Hong Kong, 1995-99; cons. breast surgeon Nottingham U. Hosps., 2001—, head, breast svcs., 2007—10, lead clinician, breast cancer, 2007—. Clin. sr. lectr. U. Nottingham, 2004—06, assoc. prof., 2006—; rschr. in field. Contbr. articles to profl. jours. Hon. clin. rsch. fellow Nottingham City Hosp., 1995, med. rsch. fellow U. Nottingham, 1999-2001. Fellow Royal Coll. Surgeons Edinburgh, Coll. Surgeons Hong Kong, Hong Kong Acad. Medicine, Am. Coll. Surgeons; mem. British Assn. Cancer Surgery, Assn. Breast Surgery, European Soc. Mastology, Am. Soc. Clin. Oncology. Office: Nottingham City Hosp Profl Unit Surg Hucknall Road NG5 1PB Nottingham England E-mail: kl.cheung@nottingham.ac.uk.

CHEUNG, MEI-CHUN, psychologist, educator; PhD, Chinese U. Hong Kong. Registered clin. psychologist Hong Kong Psychol. Assn., Pacifi Care, Tsim Sha Tsui, Hong Kong, 2005; registered social worker Social Workers Registration Bd. Asst. prof. Hong Kong Poly. U., 2006—; clin. psychologist Child Assessment Svc., Dept. Health, Hong Kong, 2002—03, Chinese U. Hong Kong, 2001—02, lectr., 2006—, registered clin. psychologist, 2001—02, 2003—06. Author: (book) Four Approaches to Improve Children's Cognitive Function (in Chinese). Bd. mem. Bd. Chinese Neuropsychologists; vice chairperson Hong Kong Neuropsychol. Assn.; v.p. Inst. Neuroplasticity, Hong Kong. Fellow: Hong Kong Psychol. Soc.; mem.: APA, Internat. Neuropsychol. Soc. Office: Inst Textiles & Clothing PolyU The Hong Kong Poly Univ Hung Hom 00000 Hong Kong Office Fax: 85227731432. Business E-Mail: tccmchun@inet.polyu.edu.hk.

CHEUNG, POLLY SUK-YEE, surgeon; MBBS, U. Hong Kong, 1977. Cons. surgeon Kwong Wah Hosp., Hong Kong, 1990; hon. cons. surgeon Hong Kong Sanatorium & Hosp., hon. cons. gen. surgery, founder breast care ctr. Hong Kong, 1999, hon. dir. breast care ctr.; surgeon Breast & Endocrine Surgery Ctr., Hong Kong; fellow Royal Coll. of Surgeons, England, Am. Coll. of Surgeons, Royal Australasian Coll. of Surgeons. Lectr. surgery dept. Queen Mary Hosp., Hong Kong, 1980—90; hon. assoc. prof. surgery dept. Univ. of Hong Kong. Recipient Outstanding Women Professionals award, Hong Kong Women Professionals & Entrepreneurs Assn., 1999, The Most Successful Women award, JESSICA Mag., 2003. Fellow: Hong Kong Acad. of Medicine; mem.: Hong Kong Med. Jour. (jour. reviewer), Asian Jour. of Surgery (jour. reviewer), World Jour. of Surgery (jour. reviewer), British Jour. Surgery (jour. reviewer), Breast Surgery Internat. (coun. mem.), Hong Kong Sanatorium & Hosp. (operation theatre adv. com.), Women's Commn., Consumer Coun., Hong Kong Breast Cancer Found. (founder). Achievements include setting up the first breast-screening program in Hong Kong at Kwong Wah Hosp. using low dose mammography. Office: Breast & Endocrine Surgery Centre Ste 802 Central Bldg 1-3 Pedder St Central Hong Kong Office Phone: 85225264775. Office Fax: 85225249372. Business E-Mail: polly@pca.hk. *

CHEUNG, WING-HOI LOUIS, medical educator; b. Hong Kong, Feb. 17, 1974; PhD, Chinese U. Hong Kong, 2000. Rsch. assoc. prof. Chinese U. Hong Kong, 2005—. Office: The Chinese University HongKong Dept Orthopaedics & Traumatology Shatin Hong Kong Business E-Mail: louis@ort.cuhk.edu.hk.

CHEUNG, YUN CHUNG, radiologist, educator; b. Hong Kong, Hong Kong, China, Sept. 7, 1962; s. Fong Cheung and Kuan Yung; m. Li Chin Chen, July 18, 1967; children: Benny, Felicia. B in Medicine, China Med. Coll., Taiwan, 1990. Lic. Radiologist Bd. Med. Examiners, Taiwan, 1995. Head of Radiological Department Ton Yen General Hospital, Chui Pei, Sun Chui, Taiwan, 1995—96; asst. prof. dept. diagnostic radiology Chang Gung Meml. Hosp. , Taoyuan, Taiwan, 1996—. Lectr. Chang Gung U., Taoyuan, 1999—. Office: Chang Gung Meml Hosp 5 Fu Hsing St Kwei Shan Taoyuan Taiwan Home Phone: 886-3-3344410; Office Phone: 886-3-3281200 ext 2575.

CHEVALIER, ROBERT LOUIS, nephrologist, educator, medical researcher; b. Chgo., Oct. 25, 1946; s. Frank Charles and Marion Helen (Jahnke) C.; m. Janis Julia Slezak, Dec. 23, 1970; 1 child, Juline Arianne. BS, U. Chgo., 1968, MD, 1972. Diplomate Am. Bd. Pediatrics, Bd. Pediatric Nephrology. Pediatric resident U. NC, Chapel Hill, 1972-75, postdoctoral fellow, 1975-77; nephrology fellow U. Colo., Denver, 1977-78; asst. prof. U. Va., Charlottesville, 1978-83, assoc. prof., 1983-88, prof., 1988—, chief pediatric nephrology, 1978-91, vice chmn. pediatrics, 1988-96, Genentech prof., 1993-97, acting chmn. pediat., 1996-97, chmn. pediat., 1997—; Shepherd prof., 1997—, dir. NIH Child Health Rsch. Ctr. Established investigator Am. Heart Assn., 1983-88. Mem. editl. bd. Renal Failure, 1988—, Pediatric Nephrology, 1995-97, Kidney Internat., 1998—; contbr. numerous articles to profl. jours., chpts. to books. Chmn. med. adv. bd. Nat. Kidney Found. Va., Richmond, 1986-89. Fellow Am. Acad. Pediatrics, Am. Heart Assn.; mem. Am. Pediatric Soc., Am. Physiol. Soc., Am. Soc. Nephrology, Am. Soc. Pediatric Nephrology (pres. 1991-92), Am. Bd. Pediatrics, Internat. Pediat. Nephrology Assn. (councillor 1999—), Soc. Pediatric Rsch., So. Soc. Pediatric Rsch. (pres. 1990-91, chair internat. workshop on devel. nephrology 2001). Office: U Va Dept Pediat / Divsn Nephrology PO Box 800386 Charlottesville VA 22908-0386 Office Phone: 434-924-5093. Office Fax: 434-982-3561. E-mail: rlc2m@virginia.edu.

CHEVRAY, PIERRE M., medical educator; s. René and Keiko Chevray; m. Keiko Yamaguchi, 1992; children: Kenji, Yukiko. BS, Mass. Inst. Tech., 1987; MD, PhD, Johns Hopkins U. Sch. Medicine, 1994. Cert. Am. Bd. Plastic Surgery, MD Tex., Md. Resident gen. surgery Johns Hopkins Hosp., 1994—98, resident plastic surgery, 1998—2000; asst. to assoc. prof. U. Tex. M.D. Anderson Cancer Ctr., Houston, 2000—08; clin. asst. to clin. assoc. prof. Baylor Coll. Medicine, Houston, 2000—; plastic surgeon Meth. Hosp., Inst. Reconstructive Surgery, Houston, 2008—. Mem.: Houston Soc. Plastic Surgeons (treas., sec., v.p., pres.), Am. Assn. Plastic Surgeons, Am. Soc. Reconstructive Microsurgery, Am. Soc. Plastic Surgeons. Office: Methodist Hosp 6560 Fannin St Ste 2200 Houston TX 77030 Office Phone: 713-441-0714. Office Fax: 713-793-1474. Business E-Mail: pmchevray@tmhs.org.

CHEW, CHIN HIN, physician, educator; b. Singapore, Oct. 23, 1931; s. Benjamin and Hock Neo Chew; m. Anna Hui, July 21; children: Elaine, Eileen, Eirene, Edward. B Medicine B Surgery, U. Hong Kong, 1955. Sr. physician dept. medicine Tan Tock Seng Hosp., Singapore, 1965—79, med. dir., 1979—81, emeritus cons., 1995—; dir. med. and hosp. svcs. Ministry Health, Singapore, 1991; hon. advisor postgrad. med. studies, adj. prof. Nat. U. Singapore, 1991—. Chmn. TB com. Ministry Health, 1981—91; mem. disciplinary complaints and audit com. Singapore Med. Coun., 2005—; head del.

World Health Assembly, Geneva, 1981, Geneva, 85. Contbr. articles to profl. publs. Mem. Singapore Med. Coun. and Specialists Accreditation Bd., 1973—; found. chmn. Nat. Med. Ethics Com., Singapore, 1994—2000. Recipient Pub. Adminstrn. Gold medal, Pres. of Singapore, 1982, Coll. medal, Royal Australasian Coll. Physicians, 1994, Gold medal emeritus advisor, Royal Coll. Physicians, 2000, Lifetime award, Nat. Arthritis Found. (Singapore), 2005; named Internat. Health Profl. of Yr., 2007. Master: ACP; fellow: Royal Australasian Coll. Physicians, Royal Coll. Physicians London, Edinburgh, Glasgow, Acad. Medicine Singapore (editlr annals 1971—73, master 1973—75, Gordon Ransome orator 2007, Coll. Physician's Lectr. 2008), Hong Kong Coll. Physicians (hon.), Coll. Physicians Singapore (hon.); mem.: Royal Coll. Physicians London, Edinburgh and Glasgow (mem. policy com. 1995—2001), Assn. Physicians Gt. Britain and Ireland (sr.). Office: Nat U Singapore Sch Medicine No 5 12 Medical Dr Singapore 117598 Singapore Home: 23 Balmoral Road #19-25 Balmoral Point 259806 Singapore Singapore Business E-Mail: mdccch@nus.edu.sg.

CHEW, KEITH ELVIN, health services administrator, consultant; b. Webb City, Mo., Jan. 1, 1957; s. David Elvin and Melinda Lou (Barker) C. BS in Physiology with distinction, U. Ill., 1979, MS in Biol. Sci., 1981, postgrad., 1981-83; MA in Health Svc. Adminstrn., Sangamon State U., Springfield, Ill., 1986. Cert. med. practicoe exec. Instr. Sangamon State U., 1985-86; program dir. So. Ill. U. Sch. Medicine, Springfield, 1984-86; dir. bus. and clin. affairs Tex. Tech Health Sci. Ctr., Lubbock, 1986-88; cons. Profl. Cons. Svcs., Long Grove, Ill., 1988-90; adminstr. Primary Care Family Ctr., Libertyville, Ill., 1988-90; instr. Coll. St. Francis, Joliet, Ill., 1991; adminstr. North Suburban Clinic, Skokie, Ill., 1990-91; cons. KEC Healthcare Mgmt. Cons., Forest Lake, Ill., 1991-92; dir. practice mgmt. Contemporary Mgmt. Assocs., Inc., Portsmouth, NH, 1992-95; exec. dir. Network, Health Mgmt. Ltd. Partnership-Drs. Hosp., Springfield, 1995-96, v.p., 1996-97; CEO Imaging Radiologists, MSO, Inc., Springfield and Chgo, 1998—2000, Imaging Radiologists, LLC, Springfield and Chgo., 2000—02; prin. Vinculum Cons., LLC, 1998—2006; sr. cons. McKesson Corp. (formerly Per-Se Technologies), 2006—. Author: reports and articles. Bd. mem. U. Ill.-Springfield Brookens Libr.; vol. WUIS Pub. Radio, WSEC Pub. TV. Mem. Am. Coll. Med. Practice Adminstrs. (cert. med. practice exec. 1994), Med. Group Mgmt. Assn., Leader's Bd. Med. Practice Execs., Radiology Bus. Mgmt. Assn. Avocations: music (aural and vocal), golf, fishing, aviation, gardening. Home: 18 Hawks Nest Chatham IL 62629-2016 Home Phone: 217-483-6467; Office Phone: 217-971-5293. Personal E-mail: kechew@springnet1.com. Business E-Mail: keith.chew@mckesson.com.

CHEY, WILLIAM D, physician, researcher; s. Fan and William Y Chey; m. Janine Zwiren, Nov. 26, 1960; children: Samuel William, Russell David, Josephine Julianna. MD, Emory U. Sch. Medicine, 1986. Intern and resident in internal medicine Emory U. Sch. Medicine, Atlanta, 1986—89, fellow in gastroenterology U. Mich., Ann Arbor, 1990—93, faculty mem., 1993—; dir. gi physiology lab. U. Mich. Health Sys., Ann Arbor, 1993—; prof. medicine, 2007—; co-dir. Mich. Bowel Control Progarm, 2008—; co-editor-in-chief Am. Jour. Gastroenterology, 2010—. Mem. Rome Found. Functional GI Disorders, 2004—, bd. trustees, 2010—. Named one of The Best Doctors in Am., 2001—. Fellow: Am. Gastroent. Assn. (chair clin. practice sect. 2006—08), Am. Coll. Gastroenterology (bd. trustees 2010), Am. Coll. Physicians; mem.: Am. Soc. Gastrointestinal Endoscopy (corr.), Internat. Found. Functional GI Disorders (corr.; adv. bd. mem. 2005—). Office: U Mich Health System 3912 Taubman Ctr Ann Arbor MI 48109-0362 Business E-Mail: wchey@umich.edu. *

CHEY, WILLIAM YOON, physician; b. Ki Jang, Korea, Jan. 21, 1930; s. Kee Bok and Myungkwon (Lee) C.; m. Fan K. Tang, May 21, 1959; children: William D., Donna C., Richard D., Laura C. MD, Seoul Nat. U., Korea, 1953; MSc, U. Pa., 1962, DSc, 1966. Intern NYC Hosp., 1954-55, resident, 1955-56; resident in pathology Mount Sinai Hosp., NYC, 1956-57; fellow in hepatology Seton Hall Med Coll., Jersey City, 1957-58; practice medicine specializing in gastroenterology Phila., 1967-71; attending physician Temple U. Med Center, Phila., 1963—; rsch. fellow in gastroenterology Samuel S. Fels Rsch. Inst., 1959-60; rsch. assoc. Samuel S. Fells Rsch. Inst., 1961, instr. medicine, 1961, assoc., 1963, asst. prof., 1965-68, assoc. prof., 1968-71; prof. medicine U. Rochester, NY, 1971-77, NY, 1988—2000, clin. prof. NY, 1977-88; sr. attending physician, founding dir. Isaac Gordon Ctr. for Digestive Diseases and Nutrition, The Genesee Hosp., 1971-91; dir. divsn. gastroenterology and hepatology U. Rochester Sch. Medicine and Dentistry, 1992-2000; physician Strong Meml. Hosp., Rochester, 1992-2000; founding dir. William B. and Sheila Konar Ctr. for Digestive Liver Disease, Rochester, 1995—2000. Dir. Rochester Inst. Digestive Diseases and Scis., NY, 2000—; cons. gastroenterologist Canadaigua VA Hosp., Canadagiua, 1977—; emeritus prof. Cath. U. Med. Coll., Seoul, Republic of Korea, 1983—86; clin. prof. medicine Yunsei U. Sch. Medicine, 1984—86; vis. prof. Peking Union Med. Coll., Chinese Acad. Med. Scis., Beijing, 1985—, Hallym U. Coll. Medicine, Choonchun, Republic of Korea, 1986—, Shanghai Med. U., 1987, Korea U. Coll. Medicine, Seoul, 1991—; mem. surgery and bioengring. study sect. Nat. Inst. Diaetes, Digestive and Kidney Diseases, NIH, Bethesda, Md., 1982—86. Contbr. articles to profl. and sci. jours and textbooks; mem. editorial bd. The Pancreas, Am. Jour. Physiology; editor in chief, Clin. Endoscopy. Fellow Am. Coll. Gastroent., Am. Gastroent. Assn. (Disting. Clinician award 2004, Mentors Rsch. award 2007, mem. AGA Legacy Soc.,2007); mem. AAAS, Am. Fedn. Clin. Rsch., Am. Physiol. Soc., Am. Assn. Study Liver Disease, Am. Pancreatic Assn. (pres. 1999-2000), Internat. Assn. Pancreatology, Am. Motility Soc., Am. Soc. Gastrointestinal Endoscopy, Am. Soc. Acupuncture, Am. Coll. Acupuncture, Korean Soc. Gastrointestinal Endoscopy, Sigma Xi. Home: 133 Crescent Hill Rd Pittsford NY 14534 Office: 222 Alexander St Ste 3100 Rochester NY 14607 Business E-Mail: williamchey@ridds.org.

CHHABRA, APJIT KAUR, ophthalmologist, educator; b. New Delhi, Dec. 21, 1961; MBBS, King George Med. Coll., Lucknow, 1985, MS in Ophthalmology, 1988. Prof., head, oculoplastics and orbit clinic, eye dept. King George Med. U., 1989. Recipient Mohan Lal Meml. Gold medal, State Ophthalmic Soc. Mem.: Uttar Pradesh State Ophthal. Soc., Oculoplastics Assn. India, All India Ophthal. Soc. Avocations: music, gardening, crafts. Home: 6B La Pl Bunglows Shah Najaf Rd Lucknow Uttar Pradesh 226001 India Personal E-mail: apjit@rediffmail.com.

CHI, CHING-CHI, dermatologist, researcher; b. Taichung, Taiwan, Mar. 12, 1969; s. Rong-Lin Chi and Miao Chan; m. Shu-Hui Wang, Sept. 11, 1967; children: Szu-Yu, Szu-Nien. MD, Taipei Med. U., 1994; MMS, Chung Shan Med. U., 2004. Lic. med. practitioner Taiwan, 1994, cert. dermatology specialist Taiwan, 2000; instr. Taiwan, 2004. Intern Chang Gung Meml. Hosp., Taipei, 1993—94, resident Dept. Dermatology, 1996—2000, attending physician Dept. Dermatology, 2000—01, Putz, Taiwan, 2001—, clin. instr., 2004—; mil. med. officer Taiwan Army, Taiwan, 1994—96. Reviewer Internat. Jour. Dermatology, 2005, Expert Rev. Dematol., 2006—; instr. health edn. beauticians and hairdressers Bur. Health Chiayi County Governemnt, 2002; instr. Chang Gung Inst. Tech., Putz, 2004—. Contbr. articles to profl. jours. Scholar, 18th World Cong. Dermatology, 2004. Mem.: Am. Acad. Dermatology, Formosan Med. Assn., Laser and Photonics Medicine Soc. Republic of China, Taiwanese Dermatol. Assn., Taiwan Med. Assn. Office: Chang Gung Memorial Hospital-Chiayi 6 Sec West Chia-Pu Rd Chiayi 61363 Taiwan Business E-Mail: chingchi@cgmh.org.tw.

CHI, JE GEUN, retired pathologist; b. Seoul, Republic of Korea, Feb. 25, 1938; Kyu Hyock and Chung Wha (Lee) C.; m. Mina Lee, May 8, 1965; children: Yong-suk, Yong-seung. MD, Seoul Nat. U., 1962, MS, 1964, PhD, 1968. Lic. physician, Korea, U.S.A.; anatomical pathology specialist diplomat, Korea, U.S.A., neuropathology specialist diplomat, U.S.A. Resident Seoul Nat. U. Hosp., 1962-67; instr. pathology Seoul Nat. U., 1969-70; resident Boston Children's Hosp., Boston, 1970-71, 73-75, Beth Israel Hosp., Boston, 1971-73; instr. pathology Seoul Nat. U., 1969-70; lectr. neuropathology Harvard Med. Sch., Boston, 1975-76; head pathology dept. Seoul Nat. U. Children's Hosp., 1985—2003; prof., chmn. dept. pathology Seoul Nat. U. Coll. Medicine, 1992-96; prof. emeritus, 2003—; v.p. Korean Acad. Sci. and Tech., 2000—04. Author: Diagnostic Ultrastructural Neuropathology, 1991, Sequential Atlas of Human Development, 1992, Diagnostic Ultrastructural Pathology, 1992, Color Atlas of Pathology, 1998, Atlas of Human Embryo and Fetus, 2001; editor Jour. Korean Med. Sci., 1987-93, Seoul Jour. Medicine, 1994-95. Recipient Best Paper award, Dongshin-Smith Kline, Seoul, 1985, Med. Achievement award, Nat. Acad. Scis., Korea, 1992. Fellow: Third World Acad. Sci.; mem.: Nat. Acad. Medicine Korea (pres. 2004—06), Korean Soc. Teratology (pres. 1998—), Korean Soc. Med. Genetics (pres. 1997—99), N.Y. Acad. Scis., Korean Acad. Med. Scis. (pres. 1999—2003), Korean Acad. Sci. and Tech. (v.p. 2001—04), Korean Soc. Pathologists (pres. 1996—97). Home: Hanyang Apt 22-203 Apkujong-dong Kangnam-gu Seoul 135 906 Republic of Korea Office: Seoul Nat U Coll Med 28 Yongon-dong Chongno-gu Seoul 110-744 Republic of Korea Personal E-mail: chi3802@hotmail.com. *

CHI, LOIS WANG, retired biology professor, research scientist; b. Fuchow, China, May 12, 1921; came to U.S., 1941; d. Leland and Ada (Pang) Wang; m. Henry Chi; children: Lanie, David, Joycelyn. BS, Wheaton Coll., 1945; MS, U. So. Calif., 1947, PhD, 1954. Rsch. fellow Loma Linda U., Calif., 1954-57; instr. to assoc. prof. biology Immaculate Heart Coll., LA, 1957-66; assoc. prof. to prof. biology Calif. State U., Dominguez Hills, 1966-91, rsch. dir., 1979-86, prof. emeritus, 1986—. Mem. NIH Nat. Adv. Allergy and Infectious Disease Coun., 1973-74; dir. Minority Biomed. Rsch. Program Calif. State U., Dominguez Hills, 1979-86, Minority Honor Program, 1982-86. Contbr. more than 30 articles to profl. jours. Co-founder, pres. and v.p. Chinese Am. Faculty Assocs. So. Calif., Chinese Am. Engrs. and Scientists Assocs. So. Calif. Home: 2839 El Oeste Hermosa Beach CA 90254-2234

CHIA, JEAN-SAN, medical educator; b. Taipei, Taiwan, July 18, 1956; s. Yue-Pou Chia and Yue-Min Shen; m. Jin-Pei Chen, Sept. 10, 1983; children: Chung-Tun, Yue-Jen. DDS, Nat. Taiwan U., Taipei, 1980, PhD, 1994. Attending physician dental dept. Nat. Taiwan U. Hosp., Taipei, 1986—; assoc. prof. Nat. U. Coll. Medicine, Taipei, 1994—2002, prof. dept. microbiology, 2002—. Contbr. articles to profl. jours. Dental surgeon Taiwan Mil., 1980—82. Mem.: Am. Soc. Microbiology. Office: Nat Taiwan Univ 1 Jen-Ai Rd Taipei Taiwan Home: 1st Sect # 214 104-1 Hou-Pin Zst Rd Taipei Taiwan Office Phone: 886 2 2312 3456 ext 8222. Business E-Mail: chiajs@ha.mc.ntu.edu.tw.

CHIA, JOHN KAI-SHENG, physician; b. Taipei, Taiwan, May 23, 1953; MD, UCLA Sch. Medicine, 1979. Physician ID Med., 1990—. Mem.: Infectious Disease Soc. America. Office: 23560 Crenshaw Blvd 101 Torrance CA 90505 Personal E-mail: chiasann@pol.net.

CHIA-MING, TUNG, engineer; b. Kaohsiung, Taiwan, July 24, 1976; MS, Nat. Kaohsiung First U. Sci. and Tech., 2007; PhD candidate, Nat. Cheng Kung U. Engr. Indsl. Tech. Rsch. Inst., 2007—. Home: 38 Bixin Ln Ziguan Dist Kaohsiung 82643 Taiwan Office: Bldg R1 31 Gongye 2nd Rd Annan Dist Tainan City 70955 Taiwan Office Phone: 886-6-3847064. Personal E-mail: frank.tung@gmail.com.

CHIANELLI, RUSSELL R., engineering educator, director; b. Newark, May 22, 1944; BS, Poly. Inst. Bklyn., 1970, PhD, 1974. Group head and sr. rsch. assoc. Exxon Rsch. and Engring. Corp. Rsch., 1974—98; prof. and dir. Materials Rsch. and Tech. Inst. U. Tex., El Paso, 1998—. Recipient Lifetime Achievement award, Academia Mexicana, 1997, Outstanding Rsch. award, UTEP, 2004, Chancellor's Entrepreneurship and Innovation award, Tex. U. Sys., 2006, Achievement award, SW Catalysis, 2009. Office: 500 W University Ave El Paso TX 79968-0685 Office Fax: 915-747-6007. Business E-Mail: chianell@utep.edu.

CHIANG, CHENG-WEN, internal medicine educator, physician; b. I-Lan, Taiwan, Oct. 24, 1943; s. Are-Jee (Yuh) C.; m. Yang Mei-Yu Chiang, Nov. 8, 1972; children: Chiang, Yih-Shien, Chiang, Yih-Tsung. MD, Nat. Taiwan U., Taipei, 1971. Intern Nat. Taiwan U. Hosp., 1970—71, resident dept. internal medicine, 1972—75; lectr. Chang Gung Meml. Hosp., Taiwan, 1979—82, assoc. prof., 1982—88, dir. CCU, 1987—92; prof. cardiovasc. medicine Chang Gung U., Taiwan, 1989—2000, dir. 1st cardiovasc. divsn., 1992—98; vice supt. Cathay Gen. Hosp., Taipei, 2001—03. Vis. physician Case Western Reserve U., Cleve., 1981. Editor Jour. of Ultrasound in Medicine of the Republic of China, 1987-92, Acta Cardiologica Sinica, 1987-93; chief editor Chang Gung Medical Jour., 1990-2000. Recipient Cheng-Hsing Med. award Med. Assn. Taiwan, 1979; Internat. scholar Cleve. Clinic, 1982; rsch. fellow Johns Hopkins Hosp., Balt., 1982. Fellow Soc. for Ultrasound in Medicine Taiwan (standing supr. 1992-94, chmn. med. consultation com. 1992-94, pres. 1994-96, hon. pres. 1996-98), Western Pacific Assn. Critical Cre Medicine Taiwan (bd. dirs., chmn. edn. com. 1992-94), Taiwan Soc. Cardiology (bd. dirs., chmn. preventive cardiology com. 1993-95, v.p. 1995-97, chmn. quality control com. 1997-99, chmn. sci. com. 1999-2001, v.p. 2001-03—, chmn. bd. supervision 2003-05, pres. 2005-07, Long Ting award 2001), Asian Fedn. Ultrasound in Medicine (councilor 1998-2001, treas. 2001-04, pres. elect 2004-2007, pres. 2007-10), World Fedn. Ultrasound Medicine (co-opted coun. 2003-06, coun. 2006-09, v.p. 2011-), World Heart Fedn. (bd. mem. 2009-11), Asian Pacific Soc. Cardiology (pres. elect 2005-2007, pres. 2009-11). Avocations: music, bicycling, boating. Office: Cathay Gen Hosp 280 Sect 4 Jen-Ai Rd Taipei 106 Taiwan E-mail: cwchiang@ms1.cgh.org.tw.

CHIANG, CHING WEN, otolaryngologist; b. Taiwan, Apr. 4, 1971; MD, Nat. Taiwan U., 1996. Attending physician Lotung Poh-Ai Hosp., 2002—10, dir., dept. otorhinolaryngology, 2010—. Resident physician Nat. Taiwan U. Hosp., 1998—2002. Mem.: Taiwan Otolaryn. Soc. Achievements include development of Laser-assisted submucosal septoplasty. Avocation: travel. Home: 23 Ln 135 Sec3 Fushin Rd Lo-Tung, I-Lan 26562 Taiwan

CHIANG, MICHAEL FRED, physician; b. Pitts., Aug. 6, 1970; BS, Stanford U., 1991; MD, Harvard U., 1996. Resident in ophthalmology Johns Hopkins Hosp., 1997—2000, fellow pediat. ophthalmology, 2000—01; assoc. prof., ophthalmology and biomed. informatics Columbia U., NYC, 2003—. *

CHIANG, WENCHANG, food scientist, educator; b. Taichung, Taiwan, May 18, 1949; s. Chin-ling Chiang and Pao-mei Lin; m. Chin-Yun Hsu, Mar. 28, 1974; 1 child, Pey-jen. PhD, U. Tokyo, 1978. Cert. agrl. chemitry, Exam. Yuan, 1972. Instr. Inst. Food Sci. & Tech., Nat. Taiwan U., Taipei, 1978—79, assoc. prof., 1979—84, dir., 1997—2000, prof., 1984—; head Ctr. Food and Biomolecules, Nat. Taiwan U., Taipei, 2005—. Gen. sec. Chinese Inst. Food Sci. and Tech. Soc., Taipei, 1988—89; pres. Health Food Soc. Taiwan, Taipei, 1999—2003. Contbr. articles to profl. sci. jours. With Army, 1973, Taipei. Recipient Rsch. award, Nat. Sci. Coun., 1985, Food Sci. and Tech. Achievement award, Chinese Inst. Food Sci. and Tech. Soc., 1988, Sci. Achievement award, Chinese Agrl. Chem. Soc., 1996, Health Food R & D Achievement award, Health Food Soc. Taiwan, 2005. Mem.: Health Food Soc. Taiwan. Achievements include research in anti-cancer, blood lipid and sugar-lowering, and immune and hormone-regulating activities of adlay; comparsion of regulation system on health food between Taiwan and foreign countries; development of application of food extruder to develop grain processing and texturized protein products; patents pending for isolation of lactam compound from adlay bran and its use on anti-proliferative cancer cells. Avocations: travel, singing, reading, jogging. Office: Inst Food Sci & Techno NTU 1 Sec4 Roosevelt Rd Taipei 10617 Taiwan Office Phone: 886-2-33664115. Office Fax: 886-2-23638673. Business E-Mail: chiang@ntu.edu.tw.

CHIARAMIDA, SALVATORE, cardiologist, educator, health facility administrator; b. NYC, Sept. 15, 1948; s. Joseph and Dina (DiBlasi) C.; m. Susan Postula, June 14, 1970; children: Todd, Tory. BS in Chemistry, Fordham Coll., 1970; MD, N.Y. Med. Coll., 1974. Diplomate Am. Bd. Internal Medicine, Am. Bd. Cardiovasc. Diseases. Intern North Shore U. Meml. Hosp., 1974-75, asst. resident in internal medicine, 1975-76, sr. resident in internal medicine, 1976-77, fellow in cardiology, 1977-79; fellow in medicine Cornell U. Med. Coll., 1975-77; chief cardiology Raritan Bay Med. Ctr., 1979-89, Our Lady of Mercy Med. Ctr., Bronx, NY, 1989—2000, assoc. dir. medicine, 1999—2000, COO, 1999, exec. v.p. clin. ops., 1999; dir. coronary care unit Med. Univ. S.C., Charleston, 2000—, prof. medicine, 2000—. Instr. cardiology North Shore U. Hosp., 1977-79; clin. instr. medicine U. Medicine and Dentistry N.J., 1981-83, clin. asst. prof., 1983; clin. assoc. prof. N.Y. Med. Coll., 1990—99, prof. clin. medicine, 1999-2002; cons. Woodbridge (N.J.) Devel. Ctr., 1989; v.p., trustee Mercy Care PHO, 1994-2000; bd. dirs. Cath. Health Care Network, Cath. Health Care Network Physicians Orgn., Servitas IPA, Cath. Healthcare Resources LLC, Benefice Health LLC, Cath. Health Care Sys.; prof. medicine Med. U. S.C., 2000—, dir. CCU, 2001—. Contbr. articles to profl. jours. Fellow: ACP, Am. Coll. Cardiology. Office: Heart & Vascular Ctr Ashley River Tower 7066 25 Courtenay Dr Charleston SC 29425-5920 Office Phone: 843-876-4761. Business E-Mail: chiara@musc.edu.

CHIARENZA, GIUSEPPE A., neurologist, pediatrician, educator; b. Milan, Apr. 21, 1947; Degree in medicine and surgery, cum laude, U. Catania, Italy, 1971; specialization in pediat., U. Milan, 1975, specialization in neurology, 1977. Internship U. Milan, 1971—74, sr. rschr., 1974—92; fellowship in pediat. Helsinki U. Ctrl. Hosp., 1972—73; dir. child and adolescent psychiatry Azienda Ospdaliera G. Salvani Hosp., 1993—; prof. child neuropsychiatry Cath. U. Milan, 2000—. Contbr. articles to profl. jours. Fellow: Internat. Acad. Rsch. in Learning, Internat. Orgn. Psychophysiology (v.p. internat. affairs 1996—, pres. 2010—); mem.: European Fedn. Societies Psychophysiology (sec. 1992—97, v.p. 1997—2000, pres. 2000—03), World Psychiatric Assn., Psychoneurobiology Sect. (sci. sec.-treas. 1986—96, chmn. 1996—), European Neurosci. Assn., Italian Soc. Pediat. (v.p. 2004—), Italian Soc. Psychiatry, Italian Soc. Electroencephalography and Clin. Neurophysiology, Italian Soc. Psychopharmacology, Italian Soc. Psychophysiology (sci. sec.-treas. 1990—93, pres.-elect 1994—96, pres. 1996—98). Office: Catholic University of Sacred Heart Institute Pediatrics Largo Fra Agostino Gemelli 1 20123 Milan Italy *

CHIAZZE, LEONARD, JR., biostatistician, epidemiologist, educator; b. Falconer, NY, June 19, 1934; s. Leonard and Jennie (Bondi) C.; m. Ellen Anne Bergman, June 12, 1954; children: Kathleen, Caroline, Michael, Ellen. AA, SUNY, Jamestown, 1953; BS, U. Buffalo, 1955, MBA, 1957; ScD, U. Pitts., 1964. Instr. stats. U. Buffalo, 1955—57; biostatistician Nat. Cancer Inst., Bethesda, Md., 1957—66, acting chief biometry br., 1975—76; asst. prof. Georgetown U. Sch. Medicine, Washington, 1966—69, assoc. prof., 1969—77, prof., 1977—2005, prof. emeritus, 2005—, founder, dir. grad. program in biostats., 1970—94, dir. biostats. and epidemiology divsn., 1966—94, dir. occupl. health studies divsn., 1994—2005. Mem. Com. Toxicology, NAS/NRC, 2000—04, Data and Safety Monitoring Bd., Nat. Inst. on Drug Abuse, 1995—2009, Georgetown U. Instl. Rev. Bd., Washington, 1998—2009. Contbr. articles to profl. jours. Served with USPHS, 1957-66. Recipient Disting. Svc. award, 2004—05. Fellow:

APHA, Am. Coll. Epidemiology; mem.: Soc. Occupl. and Environ. Health (past pres. governing coun.), Soc. Epidemiologic Rsch., Am. Statis. Assn., Sigma Xi, Beta Gamma Sigma. Home: 11237 Waycross Way Kensington MD 20895-1034 Home Phone: 301-946-4658. Personal E-mail: lchiazze@gmail.com.

CHIBA, TOMOKI, research scientist; s. Akihiro and Reiko Chiba; m. Maki Nomura, Oct. 10, 1992; children: Eri, Koyo. PhD, Tsukuba U., Ibaraki, Japan, 1994. Rschr. Tokyo Met. Inst. Med. Sci., 1997—. Avocations: travel, tennis, skiing. E-mail: tchiba@rinshoken.or.jp.

CHIDAMBARA MURTHY, KOTAMBALLI N., food scientist; b. Chamarajanagara, India, Apr. 27, 1976; PharM, Govt. Coll. Pharmacy, 2001; PhD, Ctrl. Food Technol. and Rsch. Inst., 2006. Postdoc. rsch. assoc. VFIC, Tex. A&M U., 2006—10. Rsch. mechanism cancer prevention dietary molecules Vegetable and Fruit Improvement Ctr., 2006. Recipient Disting. Alumni award, Govt. Coll. Pharmacy, India, Prathibha award, JSS Instn., Mysore, India, 1998. Mem.: Am. Chem. Soc. Avocations: reading, ping pong/table tennis, camping. Office: 1500 Research Pky Ste 120A Ctr College Station TX 77845 Office Fax: 979-862-4522. Personal E-mail: kncmurthy@gmail.com.

CHIEFFI, GIOVANNI, biology educator; b. Naples, Italy, July 19, 1927; s. Lorenzo and Matilde (Notarloberti) C.; m. Anna Maria Valentino; children: Matilde, Lorenzo, Gabriella, Sergio, Silvia, Paolo. MD, Faculty Medicine & Surgery, Italy, 1950. Asst. to prof. Univ. Naples, 1950-62; rsch. assoc. Wayne State Univ., 1954-55, State Univ. Iowa, 1955-56; prof. Univ. Messina, Italy, 1962-63, Univ. Camerino, Italy, 1963-68, Univ. Naples, 1968—. Bd. dirs. Genetica. Co-author: Biologia, 1995, Nature, London, 1958, 61, Internat. Review of Citology, 1996. Mem. Acad. Nazionale Dei Lincei, Acad. Pontaniana, Soc. Nazionale Sci. Office: Univ Naples VIa Costantinopoli 16 80138 Naples Italy Home: Via Pirro Ligorio 20 80129 Naples NA Italy E-mail: giovanni.chieffi@unina2.it.

CHIEN, CHIH-YEN, otolaryngologist; s. Chin-Fang Chien and Yu-Kue Tseng; m. Hui-Tzu Chen, July 11, 1968; children: Yi-Hsuan, Min-Ju. MD, Kaohsiung Med. U., 1990. Atending physician Kaohsiung Chang Gung Meml. Hosp., Taiwan, 1994—. Mem. AAO-HNSF, Alexandria, Va., 2002—. Reviewer Nat. Health Inst., Kaohsiung, 1998—2003. Mem.: Otolaryngology Soc.Taiwan. Office: Kaohsiung Chang Gung Memorial Hospital 123 Ta-Pei Road Niao-Sung Hsiang Kaohsiung 833 Taiwan

CHIEN, CHUNG-LIANG, medical educator; b. Taipei, Taiwan, Nov. 13, 1961; MS, Nat. Taiwan U., 1989; PhD, Columbia U., 1995. Lectr. Nat. Taiwan U., Coll. Medicine, 1995—96, assoc. prof., 1996—2006, prof., 2006—, assoc. dean internat. affairs, 2006—, assoc. dean student affairs, 2007—. Dep. dir. NTU Ctr. Genomic Medicine, 2007—; pres. Assn. Anatomists Republic China, 2010; editl. bd. Jour. Biomedicine and Biotechnology, 2010. Author variour articles in publs. Recipient Ching-Hsing Med. award, Ching-Hsing Found., 2005, Excellent Tchr. award, Nat. Taiwan U., 2007—09. Mem.: Taiwan Soc. Stem Cell Rsch., Assn. Anatomist China, Soc. Neurosci., Am. Soc. Cell Biology. Avocations: music, bicycling. Office: Nat Taiwan University Coll Medicine 1 Section 1 Jen-Ai Rd Taipei 100 Taiwan Office Fax: 886-2-23915292. Business E-Mail: chien@ntu.edu.tw.

CHIEN, KE-HUNG, ophthalmologist; b. Taichung, Taiwan, May 30, 1979; MD, Nat. Def. Med. Ctr., 2004. Physician dept. ophthalmology Tri-Svc. Gen. Hosp., 2006—. Mem.: Ophthalmology Soc. Taiwan. Avocation: travel. Office: 325 Sect 2 Cheng-Gong Rd Nei Taipei 886 Taiwan Home Phone: 886 226934665; Office Phone: 886 2-8792 3311. Personal E-mail: yred8530@gmail.com.

CHIEN, KENNETH R., biotechnologist, cardiovascular researcher; BA, Harvard Coll., Cambridge, Mass., 1973; MD, Temple U. Sch. Medicine, Phila., 1980, PhD, 1983. Intern medicine Parkland Meml. Hosp., Dallas, 1980—81, resident medicine, 1981—82; clin. rsch. fellowship cardiology U. Tex. Southwestern Med. Ctr., Dallas, 1982—84, asst. prof. medicine, divsn. cardiology, 1984—88; assoc. prof. medicine U. Calif., San Diego, 1988—92, prof. medicine, 1992—2005; prof., Charles Sanders endowed chair medicine Harvard Med. Sch., 2005—, prof. dept. cell biology, 2005—. Mem. Ctr. Molecular Genetics, U. Calif., San Diego, 1988—2005; adj. prof. Salk Inst., La Jolla, Calif., 2000—; sci. dir. Cardiovasc. Rsch. Ctr. Mass. Gen. Hosp., 2005—; dir. cardiovasc. disease program Harvard Stem Cell Inst., 2006—; founder Inst. Molecular Medicine China, Peking U. Contbr. articles to profl.jours. Recipient Lamport award, Am. Physiological Soc., 1985, Disting. Svc. award, Nat. Heart, Lung & Blood Inst., 1995; co-recipient Med. Rsch. award, Pasarow Found., 1996; grantee NSF Rsch. Fellowship, 1971. Achievements include discovery of progenitor cells (similar to stem cells) residing in the heart capable of generating functioning heart muscle cells, having significant implications both for the study of the heart's development and for the potential therapeutic application of cells to repair or replace damaged heart tissue. Office: Mass Gen Hosp Richard B Simches Rsch Ctr CPZN 185 Cambridge St Boston MA 02114 Office Phone: 617-643-3440. Office Fax: 617-643-3451. E-mail: kchien@partners.org. *

CHIEN, LI-CHIEN, emergency physician; b. Kaohsiung, Taiwan, Jan. 3, 1968; MD, Yang-Ming U., 1992; MBA, I-su U., 2005. Chief traumatology Nat. Yang-Ming U. Hosp., 2009—, asst. prof., 2010. Mem.: Formosa Assn. Surgeons Trauma. Office: 152 Shin-min Rd Yi-Lan 26402 Taiwan Personal E-mail: maxchien1114@yahoo.com.tw.

CHIEN, LI-YIN, community health nurse, educator, researcher; b. Taipei, Taiwan, July 22, 1968; d. Tseng-Der Chien and Suan-Hua Chen; m. Chen-Jei Tai, Dec. 12, 1995; children: Felicia I-Chen Tai, Eunice I-Chia Tai. BS, Nat. Taiwan U., Taipei, 1990; MPH, Johns Hopkins U., 1992; ScD, Johans Hopkins U., 1998. RN Dept. Health, Taiwan, 1990. Post-doctoral fellow U. B.C., Vancouver, Canada, 1998—99, rsch. assoc., 2000—01; asst. prof. Nat. Yang Ming U., Taipei, 2001—04, assoc. prof., 2004—07, cons. prof., 2007—. Assoc. editor Jour. Health Scis., 2011—; editor ISRN Nursing, 2011—; com. mem. Nursing Rsch. Com. Taiwan Nurses Assn.; expert Nursing Rsch. Internat. Coun. Nurses, 2010—. Rsch. grantee, Nat. Sci. Coun., Taiwan, 2002—. Mem.: Taiwan Cmty. Health Nursing Assn., Taiwan Nurses Assn. (licentiate), Sigma Theta Tau (hon.). Office: National Yang Ming Univ 155 Section 2 Li-Nong Street Taipei 11221 Taiwan Office Fax: 886-2-28238614. Business E-Mail: lychien@ym.edu.tw.

CHIEN, SUFAN, surgeon, educator; b. Zhejiang Province, China, July 20, 1938; came to U.S., 1982; s. Jiaxing and Julian (You) C.; m. Lorrain Wilson; children: Samson, Lynn. MD, Shanghai 1st Med. Coll., 1962. Resident dept. gen. surgery Zhongshan Hosp. Shanghai 1st Med. Coll., 1962—66, attending gen. surgeon, 1975—79; supr. cardiopulmonary bypass Shanghai Inst. Cardiovasc. Diseases, 1975—82, attending surgeon cardiovasc. surgery, 1979—82; vis. scientist cardiovasc. divsn. Mayo Clinic, Rochester, Minn., 1982—84; vis. scientist physiology and biophysics La. State U. Med. Ctr., Shreveport, 1984—85; vis. scientist surgery, physiology and biophysics U. Ky. Med. Ctr., Lexington, 1985—87, asst. prof. divsn. cardiothoracic surgery, 1987—93, assoc. prof., 1993—96; assoc. prof. surgery U. Louisville, 1996—2004, prof. surgery, 2004—; v.p. Novera LLC, 2002—. Invited lectr., presenter in field; mem. sci. rev. com. study sect. NIH. Author: Hibernation Induction Trigger for Organ Preservation, 1993; mem. editl. bd. Internat. Medicine Rev., 1979-84; contbr. articles and abstracts to med. jours., chpts. to books. Mem. grant rev. com NIH, AHA, VA, DOD. Grantee NIH, VA, U.S. Army, AHA, Univ. Fellow Am. Coll. Angiology; mem. AHA, N.Y. Acad. Scis., Chinese Med. Assn., Chinese Surg. Assn., Chinese Soc. Thoracic Surgeons, Shanghai Med. Soc., Internat. Soc. Heart and Lung Transplantation, Wound Healing Soc. Office: U Louisville Sch Medicine Rudd Heart-Lung Ctr 1200 201 Abraham Flexner Way Louisville KY 40202-3841 also: University Louisville 316 MDR Bldg S Floyd Louisville KY 40202 Office Phone: 502-852-4418. Personal E-mail: sufanc@netscape.net.

CHIH, YU-KUN, orthodontist; s. Yun-Fe Chih and Gen-Yu Shih; m. Kuo-Hsiang Lin, Jan. 16, 1988; children: Pin, Heng. DDS, Nat. Def. Med. Ctr., Taipei, 1986. Cert. Taiwan Assn. Orthodontists. Clin. dir. Hsinchu Armed Forced Hosp., Taiwan, 1996—2005, Tao-Yuan Armed Forced Gen. Hosp., Taiwan, 2005—. Home: 4F No39 Juguang Rd Hsinchu 300 Taiwan Office: Hsinchu Armed Forced Hosp No3 WuLing Rd Hsinchu 300 Taiwan

CHIHOTA, VIOLET, medical researcher; b. Mutare, Zimbabwe, Aug. 4, 1967; MSc, London Sch. Hygiene and Tropical Medicine, 1995; PhD, Stellenbosch U., 2011. Rsch. fellow Stellenbosch U., 2002—04; head epidemiology unit, dep. dir. Aurum Inst., 2010—. Rsch. Leave fellowship, Wellcome Trust, Rsch. Planning grant, Bill and Melinda Gates Found. Avocations: reading, hiking, gardening. Office: 29 Queens Rd Parktown Johannesburg 2193 South Africa Business E-Mail: vchihota@auruminstitute.org.

CHILA, ANTHONY GEORGE, osteopathic educator; b. Youngstown, Ohio, Dec. 14, 1937; s. Paul and Anne (Jurenko) C.; m. Helen Paulick, Oct. 9, 1965; 1 child, Anne Elizabeth. BA, Youngstown State U., 1960; DO, Kansas City Coll. Osteopathy and Surgery, 1965. Assoc. prof. family medicine Mich. State U. Coll. Medicine, East Lansing, 1977-78, Ohio U. Coll. Medicine, Athens, 1978-83, prof. family medicine, 1983, chief clin. research, 1982; chmn. instl. rev. bd. Ohio U., Athens, 1986-88. George C. Kozma Meml. lectr. Cleve. Acad. Osteo Medicine, 1979, Andrew Taylor Still Meml. lectr., Chgo., 1990, Sutherland Meml. Lectr., San Francisco, 1992. Contbr. numerous articles to profl. jours. Trustee Saint Vladimir's Orthodox Theol. Sem., Tuckahoe, N.Y., 1975-89; active Kootaga Area coun. Boy Scouts Am. Mem.: AAAS, Am. Assn. Orthopaedic Medicine, N.Y. Acad. Scis., Cranial Acad., Am. Acad. Osteopathy (pres. 1983—84, 1985—86, Scott Meml. lectr. Kirksville, Mo. 1984, Thomas L. Northup lectr. Las Vegas 1986, Gutensohn-Denslow award 1995, Andrew Taylor Still medallion of honor 1997), Am. Coll. Gen. Practitioners, Am. Osteo. Assn. (Louisa M. Burns lectr. Clearwater, Fla. 1987), Gen. Charles Grosvenor Civil War Round Table. Republican. Avocations: stamp collecting/philately, coin collecting/numismatics, chess, American Civil War history. Office: Ohio U Coll Osteo Medicine Grosvenor Hall Athens OH 45701 Home Phone: 740-593-8660. Business E-Mail: chila@ohio.edu.

CHILDRESS, JAMES FRANKLIN, theology and medical educator; b. Mt. Airy, NC, Oct. 4, 1940; s. Roscoe Franklin and Zella Bessie (Wagoner) C.; m. Georgia Monroe Harrell, Dec. 21, 1958 (dec. Aug. 1994); children: (twins) Albert Franklin, James Frederic; m. Marcia Day Finney, May 10, 1997. BA, Guilford Coll., NC, 1962; B.D. cum laude, Yale Div. Sch, New Haven, 1965; MA, Yale U., New Haven, 1967, PhD, 1968. Asst. prof. dept. religious studies U. Va.-Charlottesville, 1968-71, assoc. prof. dept. religious studies, 1971-75, chmn. dept. religious studies, 1972-75, 86-94, prof. religious studies and med. edn., 1979—, dir. Inst. Practical Ethics, 2000—, John Allen Hollingsworth prof. ethics; Joseph P. Kennedy, Sr. prof. Christian ethics Kennedy Inst. Ethics, Georgetown U., Washington, 1975—79. Vis. prof. U. Chgo. Divinity Sch., 1977, Princeton U., 1978, Coll. Physicians and Surgeons, Columbia U., 1978; cons. and lectr. in field. Author: Priorities in Biomedical Ethics, 1981, Moral Responsibility in Conflicts, 1982, Who Should Decide? Paternalism in Health Care, 1982, Practical Reasoning in Bioethics, 1997; co-author: Principles of Biomedical Ethics, 1979, 6th edit., 2009, co-editor: Westminster Dictionary of Christian Ethics, 1986, Belmont Revisited: Ethical Principles for Biomedical Research and Practise, 2005, Organ Donation: Opportunities for Action, 2006; contbr. articles to profl. jours., chpts. to books. Trustee Guilford Coll., Greensboro, N.C., 1983-85; mem. subcom. on human gene therapy NIH, Bethesda, Md., 1984-92, mem. NIH recombinant DNA adv. com., 1988-90, 2002-04; mem. Biomed. Ethics Adv. Com., 1988-89; mem. Nat. Bioethics Adv. Commn., 1996-2001; vice-chmn. Task Force on Organ Transplantation, HHS, 1985-86; bd. dirs. United Network for Organ Sharing, 1987-89. Recipient numerous awards and grants in field including Disting. Prof. award U. Va., 1984, Va. Prof. of Yr. award Coun. for Advancement and Support Edn., 1990; Am. Coun. Learned Socs. fellow, 1972-73, Wilson Ctr. fellow, 1984-85, Guggenheim fellow, 1984-85, Thomas Jefferson award, U. Va., 2002, Life Achievement award Am. Soc. Bioethics & Humanities, 2004 Fellow Inst. Social Ethics and Life Scis., Am. Acad. Arts and Scis., Inst. Medicine; mem. Soc. Christian Ethics (bd. dirs. 1973-76), Am. Acad. Religion, Am. Philos. Assn. Democrat. Mem. Soc. Of Friends. Avocations: tennis, reading, music. Office: U Va Dept Religious Studies PO Box 400126 Charlottesville VA 22904-4126 Office Phone: 434-924-6724. E-mail: Childress@virginia.edu.

CHILDS, ERIN THERESE, psychotherapist; b. Redlands, Calif., Apr. 2, 1958; d. C. Russell and Maryann (Carpenter) Childs. BA in Psychology cum laude, Loyola Marymount U., LA, 1979, MA magna cum laude in Counseling Psychology, 1980; postgrad. in behavioral medicine, Calif. Grad. Inst., 1982—. Lic. marriage, family & child therapist 2008, cert. profl. coach 1982, Calif. youth counselor II Chino Youth Svcs., Calif., 1980. Counselor chem. dependency Behavioral Health Svcs., Gardena, Calif., 1981—83, pvt. practice psychotherapy LA, 1986—. Vis., adjunct faculty Phillips Grad. Inst., Grad. Sch. Psychology, 1997—2000; instr. Human Svcs. Program U. Phoenix, 2000—06; psychotherapist, cons. Thomas Aquinas Psychotherapy Clinic, Encino, Calif., 1981—83; clin. dir. Emergency Crisis Counseling, West LA, 1983; counselor, unit supr. Southbay Outpatient Unit, Behavioral Health Svcs., Gardena, Calif., 1980—82; dir. driving under the influence program, 1984—86; clin. treatment coord. New Beginnings, Century City Hosp., LA, 1985—86; staff psychotherapist, cons. immune supressed unit, 1987—93; instr. cmty. svcs. Pierce Jr. Coll., Woodland Hills, Calif., 1983, Santa Monica City Coll., 1984, West LA CC., Culver City, 1984; mental health clinician Addiction Medicine Dept. Cedar Sinai Med. Ctr., LA, 1997—2000; facilitator Cancer Support Group H.O.P.E. Found., 2001—05; oral examiner Calif. State Bd. Behavioral Sci. Examiners for Marriage Family Therapists, 1996—2001. Pres. St. Matthews Luth. Ch., North Hollywood, Calif., 2002—03, coun. mem., 2003—, v.p., 2005—06, sec., 2007—08; participant Honolulu Marathon, 2001, Vancouver Marathon, 2003, San Francisco Marathon, 2005, LA Marathon, 2006—07, Big Sur Marathon, 2008; fundraiser Nat. AIDS Marathon. Mem.: Calif. Assn. Marriage & Family Therapists, Alpha Sigma Nu, Psi Chi. Democrat. Lutheran. Office: 11650 Riverside Dr Ste 7 Studio City CA 91602 Office Phone: 818-985-4200. E-mail: etchilds@sbcglobal.net.

CHILMONCZYK, ZDZISLAW, chemist, researcher; b. Szczecinek, Poland, Aug. 24, 1946; s. Michal and Eugenia (Norko) C.; m. Irena Bozenna Krawczyk, Dec. 14, 1968; children: Justyna, Rafal. MSc, Warsaw U., Poland, 1969, PhD, 1977. Rsch. assoc. Warsaw U., 1969-77, lectr., 1977-83; rsch. assoc. Bern (Switzerland) U., 1979-80; head divsn. Pharm. Rsch. Inst., Warsaw, 1983—; rsch. assoc. Zürich (Switzerland) U., 1985-86. Dep. dir. Pharm. Rsch. Inst., Warsawr, 1996—. Contbr. articles to profl. jours.; inventor in field. Mem. Polish Chem. Soc. Office: Pharm Research Inst Rydygieva 8 01-793 Warsaw Poland

CHILOW, BARBARA GAIL, social worker; b. Grand Forks, ND, June 7, 1936; d. Alfred Thomas and Florence (Micken) Seeley; m. Steven Chilow, Aug. 15, 1987; children: John Mark Doss, Timothy Stephen Doss, Elizabeth De La Cruz, David Chilow. BS, UCLA, 1957; MSW, U. So. Calif., 1970; MPA, Calif. State U., Long Beach, 1985. Lic. social worker, Calif., Utah, marriage, family and child counselor, Calif. Social worker Dept. Pub. Welfare, San Diego, 1957, Dep. Pub. Assistance, Whitman, Mass., 1966-68; psychiat. social worker State of Calif., Pomona, 1971-73; clin. social worker Orange County Dept. Mental Health, Santa Ana, Calif., 1973-74, sr. clin. social worker, 1974-79; dep. dir. mental health Orange County Human Svcs. Agy., Santa Ana, Calif., 1979-80, dep. regional mgr., 1980-82, adminstrv. mgr. II, 1982-93; clin. coord. Brightway at St. George, Utah, 1993-2000; pvt. practice Newport Beach, Calif., 1977—93; owner, mgr., pvt. practice Desert Hills Therapeutic Svcs., St. George, 1998—2005; clin. coord. Lighthouse Behavioral Health Svcs., Inc., St. George, 2005. Chmn. So. Calif. Case Mgmt. Coun., 1987-89, Orange County Bd. and Care Quality Com., Santa Ana, 1984-89. Pres. Winchester Hills Homeowners Assn., St. George, 1995-97; mem. Southwestern Spl. Svc. Dist. Bd., 1997-, chair bd., 2006—; mem. Leadership Dixie, 1998-99; trustee Music Hall Found.; gala bd. Cancer Soc., 2003-04 Mem. NASW, AAUW (v.p. 2002), DAR (Boston Tea Party chpt.), Alliance for Mentally Ill (pres. Orange County chpt. 1994-95), Phi Alpha Alpha, Gamma Phi Beta. Democrat. Presbyterian. Avocations: hiking, piano, reading, travel. Office: Turningleaf Wellness Ctr Bldg C Ste 7 1071 E 100 S Saint George UT 84770 Home: 2200 Beacon Ridge Dr Las Vegas NV 89134-5319 Office Phone: 435-652-1202. Personal E-mail: bchilow@yahoo.com.

CHILTON, LANCE ALIX, pediatrician; b. Akron, Ohio, Nov. 2, 1944; BA in Human Scis., Johns Hopkins U., 1966, MD, 1969. Diplomate American Board of Pediatrics. Intern U. Wash., Seattle, 1969—70; resident pediat. U. Pitts., 1972—74; faculty mem., dept. pediatrics U. N.Mex., 1975—82, assoc. prof. pediatrics, 2005—; former pediatrician Gallup Indian Med. Ctr.; pediatrician U. N.Mex. Hosp., N.Mex., 1975—82; former pediatrician Lovelace Pediat., Albuquerque, 1982—2005; pediatrician Lovelace Med. Ctr., N.Mex., 1982—2005, St. Vincent Regional Med. Ctr., Santa Fe, 1995—, Holy Cross Hosp., Taos, 2005—, U. N.Mex. Hosp., 2005—. Assoc. prof. pediatrics U. N.Mex., 1975—81, 2005—. Columnist: Albuquerque Jour. Mem., Adv. Com. Immunization Practices Ctr. Disease Control. Recipient Cmty. Svc. award, N.Mex. Med. Soc., 2006. Mem.: N.Mex. Med. Soc., N.Mex. Pub. Health Assn., N.Mex. Pediat. Soc., Am. Acad. Pediat. (mem. first Indian child project adv. com., former chmn. com. on Native Am. child health, former vice chair Dist. VIII, Native Am. Child Health Adv. award 2002, Sr. Child Advocacy award 2010). Office: 306A San Pablo SE Albuquerque NM 87108 Office Phone: 505-272-9242.

CHIMOSKEY, JOHN EDWARD, physiologist, medical educator; b. Traverse City, Mich., Apr. 15, 1937; s. Edward John and Jane Marie (Langworthy) C.; m. Dianne Marie Dailey, June 1962 (div. 1973), Marolyn Cecile Goodrich Walker, April 10, 2010; children: Stefan John, David Clifford. Student, U. N.Mex., 1955-56, Cen. Mich. U., 1956-58; MD, U. Mich., 1963. Rsch. fellow in physiology U. Mich., Ann Arbor, 1959-63; intern dept. medicine U. Calif., San Francisco, 1963-64; rsch. fellow in physiology Harvard Med. Sch., Boston, 1964-66; rsch. fellow in muscle rsch. Retina Found., Boston, 1966-67; assoc. prof. in physiology Hahnemann U., Phila., 1969-70; resident, rsch. fellow in dermatology Stanford U., Palo Alto, Calif., 1970-71; asst. prof. in bioengrng. U. Wash., Seattle, 1971-74; assoc. prof. in physiology and surgery Baylor Med. Coll., Houston, 1974-78; prof. Mich. State U., East Lansing, 1978-99, chmn. dept. physiology, 1989-93, prof. emeritus, 1999—. Guest scientist U.S. Naval Air Devel. Ctr., Johnsville, Pa., 1969-70; adj. assoc. prof. in bioengring. Rice U., Houston, 1974-78; dir. Taub Labs. for Mech. Circulatory Support, 1974-78; physiology cons. Stedman's Med. Dictionary, 1990-97; dir. grad. program Mich. State U., East Lansing, 1986-90, dir. cardiovascular tng. program, 1982-94; del. U.S.-USSR cooperation in artificial heart devel., 1976-77. Contbr. articles to profl. jours. Active Kauai Mus., Bishop Mus. Lt. comdr. USNR, 1967-69. Fulbright fellow, Brazil, 1990. Mem. Am. Physiol. Soc., Nat. Assn. Photoshop Profls., Kauai (Hawaii) Hist. Soc., Victor Vaughn Soc., Navy League, Kauai Soc. Artists, Alpha Omega Alpha. Home: 316A Makani Road Kapaa HI 96746-1249 Personal E-mail: palaoa@hawaii.rr.com.

CHIN, CHIH-HUI, physician; b. Taipei, Oct. 15, 1968; MD, China Med. U., 1994. Vis. staff Cathay Gen. Hosp., 2000—. Office: 280 Sect 4 Ren-Ai Rd Taipei 100 Taiwan Business E-Mail: chchin@cgh.org.tw.

CHIN, HONG WOO, oncologist, educator, researcher; b. Seoul, Korea, May 14, 1935; came to U.S., 1974; s. Jik H. and Woon K. (Park) C.; m. Soo J. Chung, Dec. 27, 1965; children: Richard Y., Helen H., KiSik. MD, Seoul Nat. U., 1962, PhD, 1974. Diplomate Am. Bd. Radiology; cert. Korean bd. internal medicine. Resident in radiation oncology Royal Victoria Hosp., Montreal (Que., Can.) Gen. Hosp., 1975-79; asst. prof. U. Ky., Lexington, 1979-86; assoc. dir. Radiarium Found., Overland Park, Kans., 1987-88; clin. prof. radiology U. Mo., Kansas City, 1987-91; chief radiation oncology Va. Med. Ctr., Shreveport, La., 1988; assoc. prof. La. State U., Shreveport, 1988; prof. and dir. radiation oncology Creighton U. Sch. Medicine, Omaha, 1988-90; dir. dept. radiation oncology Creighton U. Cancer Ctr., Omaha, 1988-90; chief radiation oncology Overton Brooks VA Med. Ctr., Shreveport, La., 1990—2003, Dayton (Ohio) VA Med. Ctr., 2003—. Prof. La. State U. Med. Ctr., Shreveport. Author monographs. Lt. comdr. USN, 1967-70. Mem. Pan Am. Med. Assn. (mem. coun. 1984—), AMA, Am. Coll. Radiology, Am. Soc. Therapeutic Radiology and Oncology, Radiation Rsch. Soc., Am. Biograph Assn. (rsch. bd. advisors 1988), Internat. Platform Assn. Roman Catholic. Home: 3860 Mesquite Dr Dayton OH 45440

CHIN, PHILIP LOU, surgeon; b. Chgo., Dec. 30, 1963; BA, Northwestern U., 1985, MD, 1989. Intern, resident Med. Coll. Wis., 1989—95; surg. oncology fellow City Hope, 1995—98; surgeon Smart Dimensions, Lite Dimensions Surg. Weight Loss, 1999—, Kaiser Permanente, 2011—. Vice chmn. dept. surgery Fountain Valley Regional Med. Ctr., 2004—06; chmn. Orange Coast Meml. Med. Ctr., 2006—. Fellow: ACS; mem.: Soc. Surg. Oncology, Am. Soc. Metabolic & Bariatric Surgery. Avocations: running, reading, art. Office: 9961 Sierra Ave Fontana CA 92335 Personal E-mail: pchinho@yahoo.com.

CHIN, TAIWAI, surgeon; b. Hong Kong, Sept. 4, 1952; MD, Nat. U. Taiwan, 1982. Chief pediatric surgery Taipei Eterans Gen. Hosp., 2003—. Office: 201 Shek Pai Rd Taipei 112 Taiwan Business E-Mail: twchin@vghtpe.gov.tw.

CHIN, WILLIAM WEI LIM, medical researcher; b. Kuala Lumpur, Apr. 7, 1979; PhD, Nat. U. Singapore, 2010. Med. technologist Singapore Gen. Hosp., 2002—05; rsch. officer Nat. Cancer Ctr. Singapore, 2005—09; sr. scientist Abbott Labs., 2009—. Recipient Frederick Urbach Travel award, Am. Soc. Photobiology, 2008; fellowship, European Soc. Photobiology, 2008, grant, Nat. Med. Rsch. Coun. Singapore. Avocations: reading, yoga, exercise. Home: 20A West Coast Rd #03-33 Singapore 126820 Singapore Personal E-mail: chin.will@gmail.com.

CHINARD, FRANCIS PIERRE, physiologist, consultant physician educator; b. Berkeley, Calif., June 30, 1918; s. Gilbert and Emma (Blanchard) C.; m. Josephine L. Wise, June 23, 1943; children: Suzanne F., Jeanne M., Marc F. AB, U. Calif., Berkeley, 1937; MD, Johns Hopkins U., 1941. Intern, jr. asst. resident in medicine Presbyn. Hosp., NYC, 1941-42; asst. physician Hosp. Rockefeller Inst., NYC, 1945-49; instr. to assoc. prof. medicine and physiol. chemistry Johns Hopkins Sch. Med., Balt., 1949-54; asst. prof. medicine U. Md., 1954-62, assoc. prof., 1962-63; physician Johns Hopkins Hosp., 1956-63; prof. exptl. medicine, dep. dir. med. clinic McGill U., Montreal Gen. Hosp., Canada, 1963—64; prof. medicine NYU, 1964-68, adj. prof., 1968-70, career scientist N.Y.C. Health Rsch. Coun., 1964-68; prof. medicine, chmn. dept. U. Medicine and Dentistry N.J., Newark, 1968-75, prof. exptl. medicine, 1975-77, prof. rsch. medicine, 1977—, prof. physiology, 1978—, Disting. prof., 1989—, emeritus, 1996; physician-in-chief Balt. City Hosp., 1962-63; acting physician-in-chief Goldwater Meml. Hosp., NYC, 1965-67; dir. med. svc. Martland Hosp., Newark, 1970-71; cons. physician VA Hosp., East Orange, NJ, 1971-79, 93-95. Mem. staff Balt. City Hosps., 1953-63; cons. in field; pres. Faculty Practice Svc. Corp., N.J. Med. Sch., 1986-88; vis. scientist Med. Rsch. Coun. Can., McGill U., Montreal, 1989-90; lectr. in field. Author: (With J.W. Bauman Jr.) Renal Function, 1975; editorial com.: Jour. Clin. Investigation, 1954-59, Jour. Applied Physiology, 1959-65, Am. Jour. Physiology, 1959-65, Circulation Research, 1967-72, Microvascular Research, 1981-89, Revue française des Maladies respiratoires, 1979-93, clin. and investigative medicine, 1985-96; contbr. articles on indicator-dilution techniques, membrane permeability and transport, pulmonary, renal function, free radicals and history of medicine, physiology, and med. ethical issues to med. jours. Mem. profl. adv. com. Martha's Vineyard Guidance Ctr., 1968-75; mem. pulmonary disease adv. com. Nat. Heart and Lung Inst., 1971-75, chmn., 1974-75, mem. bd. sci. counselors, 1976-80, chmn., 1978-80. Served to maj. M.C. USAAF, 1942-45. Decorated Legion of Merit; recipient Lucian award McGill U., 1989, Sir William Osler Humanitarian award N.J. Thoracic Soc., 1991, Laureate award N.J. chpt. Am. Coll. Physicians, 1993, Charles L. Brown & Disting. Prof. award Alumni Assn. N.J. Med. Sch. Fellow: ACP, AAAS, N.Y. Acad. Scis.; mem.: Osler Soc. NC (counselor), Am. Chem. Soc., Am. Soc. Biochemistry and Molecular Biology, Am., Can. Socs. Clin. Investigation, Soc. Exptl. Biology and Medicine, Assn. Am. Physicians, Am. Physiol. Soc., Peripatetic Soc., Acad. Medicine NJ (trustee 1972—78), Am. Heart Assn. (rsch. com. NJ affiliate 1975—81), Inst Français Washington (trustee 1994—2005, hon. trustee 2005—), Microcirculatory Soc. (Landis award), Am. Thoracic Soc., Soc. Scholars (Johns Hopkins), N.Y. Clin. Soc., Med. History Soc. NJ (pres. 1984—86), Am. Assn. History of Medicine (councilor), Harvey Soc., Interurban Clin. Club, Century Assn. Club (N.Y.C.), Charaka Club, Sigma Xi, Alpha Omega Alpha. Democrat. Achievements include research in pulmonary diseases, kidney and lung physiology; transcapillary water movement. Office: 40 Warren Pl Montclair NJ 07042-2534 Office Phone: 973-746-7847.

CHINET, THIERRY CHRISTIAN, pulmonologist; b. Paris, Dec. 4, 1959; s. Emile and Jacqueline (Bernard) C. MD, U. Paris, 1986, M in Stats., 1987. Resident Hosps. of Paris, 1982-86; asst. prof. Hosp. of Paris/U. Paris, 1986-88, 91-92, prof. in pulmonary medicine, 1993—; postdoctoral rsch. fellow U. N.C., Chapel Hill, 1988-91. Mem. sci. com. French Cystic Fibrosis Found., Paris, 1995—. Asst. editor jour. Revue des Maladies Respiratoires, 1993-96; contbr. articles to profl. jours. Recipient Prix Rose Lamarca Fond. pour Recherche Medicale, 1993. Mem. Am. Thoracic Soc., European Respiratory Soc., Soc. Pneumologie Langue Française. Avocations: saxophone, tennis, scuba diving, skiing. Business E-Mail: thierry.chinet@apr.aphp.fr.

CHING, HO, surgeon; b. Kaoshung, Taiwan, Feb. 20, 1950; arrived in U.S., 1970; d. Feng Chih and Ai Hua Yin Ho; m. Stephen Jay Keller; children: Lisa, Michele. BS, Nat. U. Taiwan, Taipei, 1970; PhD, U. Cin., 1975, MD, 1984. Rsch. fellow Roche Molecular Biol. Inst., Nutley, NJ, 1975—76; Fogarty fellow Nat. Cancer Inst., NIH, Bethesda, Md., 1976—78; rsch. assoc. U. Cin., 1978—80; chief surg. resident Jewish Hosp., Cin., 1989, surgeon, 1989—91, Donna Stahl Assocs., Cin., 1991—2000; pvt. practice surgery Cin., 2000—. Assoc. dir. surg. resident program Jewish Hosp., 1992, mem. exec. com., 2001—03; chmn. women in medicine Acad. Medicine, Cin., 1998; co-chair dept. surg. Bethesda North Hosp., Cin., 2005—07; lead surgeon coord. Bethesda Hosp. Breast Ctr., 2007—; co dir. Mary Jo Cropper Family Ctr. Breast Care, 2010—. Recipient Top Drs., Cin. Mag., 2008—11; named one of, 2001, 2003, 2007. Fellow: ACS; mem.: Am. Soc. Micriobiology, Cama Cinti (pres. 2005—06), Am. Soc. Cell Biology. Avocations: yoga, travel. Office: Mary Jo Cropper Family Ctr Bethesda North Hosp 10494 Montgomery Rd Cincinnati OH 45242 Office Phone: 513-891-1200. Business E-Mail: drho@fuse.net.

CHINGCHIH, HSIA, nephrologist; b. Taipei, Apr. 13, 1961; D, Nat. Yang-Ming Med. Sch., 1987. Chief Sect. Nephrology, Internal Medicine, 1996—. Master: Taiwan Soc. Nephrology. Avocation: music. Office: 5 Sec 4 Ren-Ai Rd Taipei 106 Taiwan Office Fax: 88627015999. Personal E-mail: nobodytiger@yahoo.com.tw.

CHINITZ, LARRY A., cardiac electrophysiologist; Grad., New York U. Sch. of Medicine, 1975—79. Diplomate Am. Bd. of Internal Medicine-cardiovasc. disease, 1985. Intern NYU Med. Ctr., 1979—80, resident tng., 1980—83; fellow NYU Med. Ctr. (Cardiology), 1983—85. Co-author: (journal articles) How to perform non-contact mapping, Results of catheter ablation of typical atrial flutter, BREATHE: base rest rate evaluation of apnea therary, Cardiac vein angioplasty for biventricular pacing, and numerous others. Office: Heart Rhythm Center 403 East 34Th St 4Th Fl New York NY 10016 Office Phone: 212-263-7149. Office Fax: 212-263-0625.

CHINNAIYAN, ARUL M., pathologist, researcher; BS in Cell & Molecular Biology, U. Mich.; PhD in Pathology, U. Mich. Med. Sch., MD. Investigator Howard Hughes Med. Inst.; prof. pathology & urology U. Mich., dir. pathology rsch. informatics, dir. cancer bioinformatics; dir. Mich. Ctr. for Translational Medicine. Recipient Competitive award, Prostate Cancer Found., 2005, 2006, Outstanding Achievement in Cancer Rsch. award, Am. Assn. Cancer Rsch., 2008. Mem.: Assn. Am. Physicians, Am. Soc. Clinical Investigation. Achievements include discovery of a chromosomal translocation that is unique to prostate cancer. Office: 1500 E Medical Center Dr Ann Arbor MI 48109-5940 Office Phone: 734-615-4062. Office Fax: 734-615-4498.

CHINO, FUMITOSHI, physician, researcher; b. Okaya, Nagano, Japan, May 30, 1934; s. Masayuki and Akiko Chino; m. Machiko Furuhata, Nov. 23, 1964; 1 child, Bun. MD, Shinshu U., Matsumoto, Japan, 1959, PhD, 1964. Cert. MD Minister of Health and Welfare. Rschr. NIH, Murayama, Tokyo, 1964—87, dir. Shinagawa, Tokyo, 1987—95. Head clinic, Chuo, Tokyo, 2002—. Grantee, Ministry of Health and Welfare, 1999. Mem.: Nat. Inst. Infectious Diseases (life), Tennis Club. Achievements include research in refinement of abnormal toxicity test for endotoxin. Avocations: writing, drawing, travel. Home: 4-15-26 Higashiohizumi Nerima 178 0063 Japan Office: 4-15-26 Higashiohizumi Nerima-ku Tokyo 178 0063 Japan E-mail: chinof@msh.biglobe.ne.jp.

CHINTALA, SREENIVASULU, medical educator, researcher; b. India, Nov. 10, 1964; PhD, Sri Krishnadevaraya U., 1995. Asst. prof. oncology Roswell Pk. Cancer Inst., 2009—. Sr. Rsch. fellowship, Coun. Sci. and Indsl. Rsch., India, Rsch. grant, NIH. Mem.: AAAS, PanAm. Soc. Pigment Cell Rsch. (Travel award), Assn. Microbiologists India, Am. Assn. Cancer Rsch. Office: Roswell Pk Cancer Inst Dept Cancer Biology Buffalo NY 14263 Business E-Mail: sreenivasulu.chintala@roswellpark.org.

CHINTHALAPALLY, VENKATESHWAR RAO, medical educator; b. Hyderabad, India, Feb. 1, 1961; PhD, Osmania U., 1987. Prof. U. Okla. Health Scis. Ctr., 2004—. Chief, nutritional carcinogenesis Am. Health Found. Cancer Ctr., 1998—2003. Recipient George Lynn Cross award, Bd. Regents U. Okla., Superior Rsch. and Creative Activity award, Outstanding Rschr. award, Am. Health Found. Cancer Ctr., Outstanding Young Rsch. Scientist award, Coun. Sci. and Indsl. Rsch. Mem.: AAAS, Am. Assn. Clin. Oncology, Am. Chem. Soc., Am. Assn. Cancer Rsch. Avocations: tennis, reading, water sports. Office: 975 NE 10th St BRC 1203 OUHSC Oklahoma City OK 73104 Office Fax: 405-271-3225. Business E-Mail: cv-rao@ouhsc.edu.

CHIOU, A. PORTIA, plastic surgeon; Grad., Bryn Mawr Coll.; MD, Med. Coll., Pa. Diplomate Am. Bd. Plastic Surgery. Resident gen. surgery and plastic surgery Lahey Clinic Med. Ctr., Burlington, Mass.; fellow microsurgery and breast reconstruction Meml. Sloan-Kettering Cancer Ctr., NYC; fellow craniofacial and aesthetic surgery Marchac Fellowship, Paris; physician The Boston Ctr. Office: The Boston Center 170 Commonwealth Ave Boston MA 02116 Office Phone: 617-267-0710. Office Fax: 617-726-2824.

CHIOU, JIN-CHERN, engineering educator, director; b. Kaohsiung, Nov. 9, 1957; PhD, U. Colo., 1990. Prof., dir., dept. elec. engring. Nat. Chiao Tung U., 1999—. Vice supt. China Med. U. Hosp., 2008. Recipient Disting. Rsch. Prof. award, Chinese Inst. Engrs. Mem.: IEEE. Avocations: golf, hiking. Office: 1001 Ta Hseuh Rd Hsinchu 30010 Taiwan Office Fax: 886-3571-5998. Business E-Mail: chiou@mail.nctu.edu.tw.

CHIOU, SHIH-HWA, ophthalmologist; b. Taipei, Taiwan, Nov. 30, 1968; MD, PhD, Nat. Yang-Ming U., Taipei, 2002. Cert. ophthalmologist Acad. Assn. Taiwan Ophthalmology, 1998. Attending ophthamologist Taipei Veterans Gen. Hosp., 2000—; dir. divsn. ophthalmology Taoyuan Vets. Hosp., Taiwan, 2003—04. Assoc. prof. Nat. Yang-Ming U., Taipei, 2004—. Recipient Young Investigator award molecular imaging, Molecular Imaging and Stem Cell Rsch., Soc. Molecular Imaging, 2005. Achievements include research in retinal stem cell and adult human stem cell. Office: Dept Ophthalmology No 201 Sec 2 Shih-Pai Rd Taipei 11217 Taiwan Office Fax: 886-2-28748647. Business E-Mail: shchiou@vghtpe.gov.tw.

CHIOU, TZEON-JYE, oncologist, hematologist, educator; b. Chia-Yi, Taiwan, Apr. 20, 1954; s. Wen-Bi and Chin-Lan (Lin) C.; m. Woan-Fang Tzeng, OCt. 25, 1981; children: Chi-Te, Chi-Yi. MD, Nat. Defense Med. Ctr., Taipei, Taiwan, 1979; specialist in oncology, Acad. Sinica, Taipei, Taiwan, 1990; specialist in hematology, Taiwan Hematology Soc., 1987. Diplomate Taiwan Bd. Internal Medicine, Family Physician Bd. Resident Vets. Gen. Hosp., Taipei, Taiwan, 1981-84, chief resident, 1984-85; attending physician Vets. Gen. Hosp., Taipei, Taiwan, 1985-86; assoc. prof. dept. medicine Yang Ming U., Taiwan, 1990—; med. cons., reviewer labor ins. Taiwan, 1988-93. Sr. faculty dept. medicine Vets. Gen. Hosp., Taipei, 1990—; med. cons. Nat. Health Ins. Co., Taiwan, 1995—. Sec. gen. Chinese BMT Transplant. Roc., Taipei, 1992-96. Major Taiwan Med. Corps, 1987-90. Recipient Faculty Devel. award Nat. Cancer Inst., Bethesda, Md., 1993. Mem. Am. Assn. Cancer Rsch., Am. Soc. Clin. Oncology, Internat. Soc. Exptl. Hematology, Chinese Bone Marrow Soc. (mem. exec. com.), Chinese Oncologist Soc. (mem issue bd. 1995—). Kow Ming Tarn, Taiwan. Buddhist. Avocations: mountain climbing, joke telling, reading. Home: No 53 F10 Sec2 Nan-Chang Rd 100 Taipei Taiwan Office: Vets Gen Hosp-Taipei No 201 Sec2 Shih-Pai Rd 11217 Taipei Taiwan

CHIOU-TAN, FAYE, physician, educator; b. Hsin-Chu, Taiwan, Mar. 27, 1964; d. George and Tricia Chiou; m. Filemon Tan, Jr.; children: Filemon III, Michelle. AB, Princeton U., NJ, 1985; MD, Baylor Coll. of Med., Houston, 1990. Diplomate Am. Bd. Electrodiagnostic Medicine, Am. Bd. Phys. Med. Rehab. Asst. prof. Baylor Coll. Medicine, Houston, 1995—2002, assoc. prof., 2003—09, residency program dir., 2007, prof., 2009—. Contbr. articles to profl. jours. Chief svc. phys. medicine and rehab. Harris County Hosp. Dist., Houston, 2000—, dir. electrodiagnosis, 1995—, dir. Ctr. for Trauma Rehab. Rsch., 2000—; med. Harris County Hospital; Best Doctors in Am., 2007-. Recipient Excellence in Rsch. Writing award Assn. Acad. Physiatrists/Am. Jour. Phys. Medicine and Rehab., 1999, 2000, 2003; named one of Am's Top Physicians, Consumer's Rsch. Coun. Am., 2003, 04, Fulbright and Jaworski Tchng. award, 2002,2007, Fulbright and Jaworski Enduring Ednl. Materials award, 2008, Top 100 Health Profls., Internat. Biographical Ctr., 2008, Outstanding Scientist, 2010, Outstanding Coun. Svc. award, Am. Acad. PMR, 2011. Mem.: AmJ PMR (edlt. bd. mem. 2004—09), PMR (assoc. editor), Am. Bd. Electrodiagnostic Medicine (examiner 2006—09), Assn. Acad. Physiatrists (chair rsch. 2006—07, program com. 2007—08), Am. Assn. Neuromuscular Electrodiagnostic Medicine (chmn. 2005—08, nominating com. mem. 2010—, mem. rsch. com., chair web cme ctr.). Avocations: cooking, hiking. Office: Baylor Coll Medicine Dept PM&R 3601 N MacGregor Way Ste 240 Houston TX 77004

CHIPMAN, DENNIS CLARENCE, JR., forensic psychiatrist, consultant; b. Seattle, Jan. 7, 1934; s. Dennis Clarence and Esther (Ränghild) Chipman; m. Karen Antoinette Ekern, Mar. 17, 1968 (div. Oct. 1982); children: Judith, Kimberly, Jason, Carolyn; m. Sandra Kay Woodell, Feb. 6, 1983. MD, U. Wash. Diplomate Am. Bd. Psychiatry and Neurology, subspecialty forensic psychiatry 2009, diplomate Am. Bd. Adolescent Psychiatry, 2003. Intern U. Nebr. Hosp., Omaha, 1959-60; resident U. Wash. Hosp. Sys., Seattle, 1960-63; pvt. practice Seattle, 1963-66; dir. Mental Health Ctr., Kingsport, Tenn., 1969-84; pvt. practice Kingsport, 1969-84, Hickory, NC, 1984-86; med. dir. Pinewood Hosp., Texarkana, Ark., 1986-89, Charter Hosp. Mobile, Ala., 1989-94; chief psychiatrist Patrick B. Harris Hosp., Anderson, SC, 1994—2001, sr. psychiatrist, 2001—; cons. forensic psychiatry, 1994—. Cons. Meth. Children's Home, Greenville, Tenn., 1969—75, Disability Determinations Divsn. Vocat. Rehab. Bd. dirs. Sheltered Workshop, Kingsport, 1973—80, Gateways Farm for Girls, New Boston, Tex., 1988—94, Home of Grace for Women, Mobile, 1990—94, New Haven Program, Mobile, 1990—94. Capt. US Army, 1966—68. Named to Guide to America's Top Psychiatrists, Consumer Rsch. Coun. Am., 2003—. Mem.: AMA, Internat. Soc. Philos. Enquiry, US Chess Fedn., Am. Psychiat. Assn., Am. Mensa Ltd., Civtan Club, Rotary, Kappa Sigma. Libertarian. Baptist. Avocations: music, chess, reading, travel. Home: PO Box 5587 Anderson SC 29623-5587 Office Phone: 864-231-6868. Personal E-mail: c1219d@aol.com.

CHIPMAN, KELLY DEANNE, pharmaceutical sales specialist, oncological nurse; b. Lynwood, Calif., Aug. 19, 1966; d. Otis Lee and Judy Cornelia Brewer. BSN, Brigham Young U., Provo, UT, 1987. RN. Staff nurse LDS Hosp., Salt Lake City, 1988; on call staff UT Valley Regional Med. Ctr., Provo, 1988, oncology nurse, 1993—2000; oncology sales specialist Alza Pharms., Calif., 2000—01, Ortho-Biotech, 2001, Novartis Pharmaceuticals Oncology Divsn., 2002—. ATAQ rep. Amgen, Calif.; presenter at meetings ONS Fall Conf., Dallas. Contbr. articles nursing publ. Treas. UT Water Ski Club. Recipient Frontier Performance Team of Yr. award, Novartis Pharms., 2006, Pres.'s Club award, 2006, MVP award, 2006, Team award, APEX. Mem.: Oncology Nursing Soc. (cert. oncology nurse 1994—, local mem. planning com. nat. mtg.). Avocations: water-skiing, bicycling, hiking, skiing, cooking. Home Fax: 801-766-4141. Personal E-mail: kellychipman19@yahoo.com.

CHIPURICI, MARIUS ADRIAN, pharmacologist, educator; b. Oradea, Romania, Apr. 2, 1969; s. Ion and Elisabeta Chipurici; m. Daniela Chipurici, May 25, 2000; 1 child, Raluca-Miruna. Degree in chemistry, U. Babes-Bolyai, Cluj, Romania, 1992, degree in physics, 1997; MD, U. Carol Davilla, Bucharest, Romania, 1998; M in Biophysics (hon.), U. Oradea, Romania, 2003. Tchr. h.s., Oradea, 1992—97; dir. Youth and Sport Dept., Oradea, 1997—2001; med. dr. Romanian Gymnastics Fedn., Bucharest, 2001—02; asst. to prof., lectr. U. Oradea, 2002—04, dir. youth dept., 2005—. Recipient diploma of honor, Internat. Fedn. Body Building, 1998. Home: Stefan Cel Mare Oradea Romania Office: Faculty Medicine and Pharmacy 1 December 10 Oradea Romania Office Phone: 0040 728728494. Office Fax: 0040 259412319. Personal E-mail: mchipurici@yahoo.com. Business E-Mail: mchipurici@uoradea.ro.

CHIRICOSTA, RICHARD ALAN (RICK CHIRICOSTA), insurance company executive; b. Springfield, Ohio, Feb. 23, 1956; s. Raymond Carl and Janice Marie (Trenner) C.; m. Sheila Ann Hart, Apr. 30, 1982; children: Matthew Alan, Christine Marie. BBA in Acctg., U. Toledo, 1978. CPA, Ohio. Audit supr. Ernst & Whinney, Toledo, 1978-84; corp. internal auditor Blade Communications, Inc., Toledo, 1984-86; asst. v.p., controller Blue Cross & Blue Shield of Ohio Western Div., Toledo, 1986-89; v.p. adminstrn., CFO Med. Life Ins. Co., Cleve., 1989—98; v.p., CFO Nat. Interstate Corp., 1998—99; v.p. fin., contr. Medical Mutual of Ohio, Cleve., 1999—2006, exec. v.p. mergers & acquisitions, 2006—09; pres. life group Consumers Life Ins. Co., 2006—09; pres., CEO Medical Mutual of Ohio, Cleve., 2009—. Instr. acctg. Owens Tech. Coll., Toledo, 1982-86, mem. acctg. adv. bd., 1984. Bd. mem. Kidney FOund. of Ohio, Broadway Sch. of Music & the Arts, Cleve. Mem. AICPA, Ohio Soc. CPA's, River Oaks Racquet Club (rocky River, Ohio). Clubs: Can. Friends of Mine (Detroit). Roman Catholic. Avocations: music, sports. Office: Med Mutual of Ohio 2060 E Ninth St Cleveland OH 44115 Office Phone: 216-687-7000. Office Fax: 216-687-6164. *

CHIRINOS, JULIO ALONSO, physician, researcher; s. Julio Chirinos and Josefina Medina de Chirinos; m. Melissa Ryan. MD, Santa Maria Cath. U., Arequipa, 2000. Diplomate Am. Bd. Internal Medicine, 2005. Internal medicine specialist Jackson Meml. Med. Ctr./U. Miami Sch. Medicine, 2001—04. Contbr. articles to profl. jours. Recipient Thrombosis Young Investigator award, European Soc. Cardiology, 2005, Population Sci. Young Investigators award, 2006, Clin. Rsch. Young Investigator award, Interam. Soc. Cardiology, 2007. Mem.: Am. Soc. Echocardiography, Am. Heart Assn., Am. Coll. Cardiology. Achievements include research in endothelial cell biology and cell-derived membrane microparticles in multiple conditions, including venous thrombosis, atrial fibrillation, sepsis and heart failure; assessing the important prognostic role of arterial stiffness and wave reflection in the prognosis of patients with coronary artery disease; large studies of cardiovascular disease in Hispanic populations in South America; the role of imaging in the evaluation of cardiovascular system. Avocations: scuba diving, travel. Home: 3166 Stillwood Ln Garnet Valley PA 19061-2051 Office Fax: 215-823-4440. Personal E-mail: jchirinos@prevencionperu.org.

CHIRON, HARLAN S., orthopedic surgeon, educator; b. NYC, Oct. 24, 1941; d. Albert Edward and Rose L. Chiron; m. Judy G. Chiron, Feb. 17, 1990; children: Stewart, Pamela, Diana. BA, Lafayette Coll., Easton, Pa., 1962; MD, Chg. Med. Sch., 1966. Intern Hosp. for Joint Disease, 1966—67, resident, 1967—68, 1970—72, fellow, 1972—73; ptnr. S. Fla. Orthopedic Assn., Miami, 1974—, pres., 1985—; prof. U. Miami, 1974—2006. Chief orthopedic surgery Victoria Hosp., Miami, 1978—80, S. Miami Hosp., 1993—96. Capt. USAF, 1970—72. Frauenthal fellowship, Hosp. for Joint Disease, NYC, 1972. Avocations: tennis, piano, reading, photography. Office: S Fla Orthopedic Assn Ste 203 4675 Ponce de Leon Blvd Miami FL 33146

CHIS, ADRIANA AURELIA, pharmacist; b. Pitesti, Jud Arges, Romania, Nov. 30, 1957; PhD candidate in Medicine and Pharmacy, U. Iuliu Hatieganu, Cluj Napoca, Romania, 2011. Sr. pharmacist, medicine and pharmacy U. Iuliu Hatieganu, 1982; adminstr. S.c. Egeria S.r.l., 1992—2009; head, drug warehouse S.c. Polisano S.r.l., 2009—10; mfg. mgr. S.c. Polipharma Industries S.r.l., 2010—. Home: St Siretului Nr 12 Sc B Ap 30 Sibiu 550395 Romania Personal E-mail: a.adriana.chis@gmail.com.

CHISHIMA, MAKOTO, occupational therapist, researcher; b. Furukawa, Japan, May 7, 1960; m. Mutsumi Maeda, June 7, 1987; children: Yoshihiko, Maya. Grad., Hirosaki U., Japan, 1983; MEng, Shinshu U., Japan, 2004, DEng, 2011. Lic. occupl. therapist Japan. Occupl. therapist U. Tokyo Hosp., Hongo, 1983—93; assoc. prof. Sch. Health Sci., Shinshu U., Matsumoto, Japan, 1993—. Mem.: IEEE, Engring. in Medicine & Biology Soc., Japan Assn. Occupl. Therapists (assoc.). Achievements include development of assistive technology; brain computer interface; research in biosignal processing. Office: Sch Health Scis Shinshu U Asahi3-1-1 Matsumoto 3908621 Japan Business E-Mail: mchishi@shinshu-u.ac.jp.

CHISIN, ROLAND GEORGES, physician, educator; b. Toulouse, France, Jan. 31, 1947; MD, U Paul Sabatie, 1973. Dept. head Hadassah Med. Ctr., 1997—. Full prof. Hadassah Sch. Medicine, Hebrew U., Jerusalem, 2007—. Recipient Gold medal, Faculty Medicine, Toulouse. Home: Habanai 14/4 Jerusalem 926424 Israel Personal E-mail: chisin@hadassah.org.il.

CHITAMBAR, CHRISTOPHER RAJIV, internist, oncologist, hematologist; b. Allahabad, India, Apr. 16, 1950; BS, Ewing Christian Coll., 1971; MD, Christian Med. Coll./Punjab U., Ludhiana, India, 1977. Diplomate Am. Bd. Internal Medicine with subspecialties in hematology and oncology. Intern Brackenridge Hosp., Austin, Tex., 1977-78, resident in internal medicine, 1978-80; fellow in hematology and oncology U. Colo. Health Scis. Ctr., Denver, 1980-83; active staff Froedtert Meml. Luth. Hosp., Milw.; prof. medicine, divsn. hematology/oncology Med. Coll. Wis., Milw. Mem. AAAS; mem. Am. Fedn. Clin. Rsch., Am. Soc. Clin. Oncology, Am. Soc. Hematology. Office: Med Coll Wis FMLH Clin Cancer Ctr Divsn Neoplastic Diseases 9200 W Wisconsin Ave Milwaukee WI 53226 Office Phone: 414-805-4600. Office Fax: 414-805-4604.

CHITHAMBARAN, SAMBHU, marine biologist, educator; b. Mayyanad, Kerala, India, Apr. 21, 1967; MSc, U. Kerala, 1989, PhD, 2006. Rsch. assoc. U. Kerala, 1997—2002; R & D project contr. Nat. Prawn Co., 2001—10; scientist's pool officer CSIR, Govt of India, 2003—05; sub insp. fisheries Dept. Fisheries, Govt of Kerala, 2005—07; assoc. prof. faculty marine scis., cons. King Abdulaziz U., 2010—. Recipient Gold medal, Sree Narayana Trusts, Kollam, Best Sci. Paper award, Soc. Fisheries Technologists, India; Jr. Rsch. fellowship, U. Kerala. Mem.: Indian Aquaculture Soc., Soc. Fisheries Technologists (India), Tropical Aquaculture Scientists. Avocations: aquariums, gardening. Office: Al Murjan Jeddah Obhur 21589 Saudi Arabia E-mail: csambhu@yahoo.com.

CHITWOOD, WALTER RANDOLPH, JR., surgeon, director; b. Va., Jan. 16, 1946; MD, U. Va., 1974. Dir. East Carolina Heart Inst., East Carolina U., 2003—. Office: 115 Heart Dr Ste 3100 Greenville NC 27834 Business E-Mail: chitwoodw@ecu.edu.

CHIU, DAVID TAK WAI, surgeon; b. Kwangtung, China, Oct. 23, 1945; s. Bud Yick and Lai Kwai (Lum) C.; m. Lilian Wah-Ying Shen, June 19, 1973; children: Vincent, Edmund, Jerome, Miranda. BA, U. Mo., St. Louis, 1969; MD, Columbia U., 1973. Diplomate Am. Bd. Plastic Surgery. Intern Barnes Hosp., St. Louis, 1973—74, resident in gen. surgery, 1974—77; resident in plastic surgery Columbia-Presbyn. Med. Ctr., 1977—79; fellow NYU Med. Ctr., NYC, 1980, instr. surgery, 1981, asst. prof., 1981—89, dir. NY Nerve Ctr., 2003—, dir. Hand Surgery Svc., 2006—; supervisory attending Bellevue Hosp. Hand Clinic, NYC, 1981—89; assoc. dir. plastic surgery, chief hand/microsurgery and replantation surgery divsn. plastic surgery Columbia Presbyn. Med. Ctr., NYC, 1989—94, dir. microsurgery ctr., 1993, chief plastic surgery divsn. dept. surgery, 1994—97, prof. clin. surgery anatomy and cell biology, 1990—2001, Thomas S. Zimmer prof., 1994—2000, Calvin F. Barber prof., 2000—01, dir. ctr. restorative surgery, 2000—; clin. prof. surgery NYU, 2001—06, prof. surgery (plastic), 2006—08, prof. surgery plastic & neurosurgery, 2008—; chief hand svcs. NYU Med. Ctr., 2006—. Adj. prof. anatomy and cell biology Coll. Physicians and Surgeons Columbia U., NYC, 2001—. Author: Introduction to Microsurgery: A Lab Manual, 1985; mem. editorial bd. Jour. Reconstructive Microsurgery, 1990—2008. Recipient Alumni Fedn. Columbia U. medal, 1995. Fellow: ACS; mem.: AMA, Fedn. Chinese Med. Soc. Found. (founding pres. 2002, founding trustee 2002—), World Soc. Reconstructive Microsurgery (founding mem.), Tissue Engring. Soc., Sunderland Soc. (pres. 2008—), Am. Acad. Pediat. (splty. fellow 1992), Internat. Soc. of Reconstructive Microsurgery, Northeast Soc. Plastic Surgery, Royal Soc. Medicine, Am. Soc. Peripheral Nerve Surgery (pres. 1999—2001, founding mem.), Am. Assn. Hand Surgery, Am. Soc. Plastic and Reconstructive Surgeons, Am. Soc. Surgery of Hand, Am. Soc. Reconstructive Microsurgery (pres. 1998—99), NY Regional Soc. Plastic and Reconstructive Plastic Surgery (pres. 1997—98), Coll. Physicians and Surgeons Alumni Assn. (dir. 1984, pres. 2001—02, Bronze medal 1973, Gold medal 1997), Plastic Surgery Rsch. Coun., NY Soc. Surgery of Hand (pres. 1996—97), NY State Med. Soc., NY County Med. Soc., Am. Assn. Plastic Surgeons, Chinese Am. Med. Soc. (dir. 1983—, pres. 1985—87, Presdl. medal 1987, Disting. Svc. award 1988, Scientific award 2001), Fedn. Chinese Am. and Chinese Can. Med. Socs. (founder 1994, founding pres. 1994—96, chmn. bd. dirs., Outstanding Achievement award 1996). Office: Ctr Restoration Surgery 900 Park Ave New York NY 10075 Office Phone: 212-879-8880. Business E-Mail: office@davidchiumd.com.

CHIU, HSIEN JANE, hospital administrator; b. Taipei, Taiwan, Aug. 28, 1961; married. MPH, Harvard U., 1996; PhD, Nat. Yang-Ming U., Taiwan, 2004; MBA, Nat. Taiwan U., 2007. Diplomate in pyschiat. Dept. Health, Taiwan. Supt., dept. health Yuli Hosp., Hualien, Taiwan, 2003—08; supt. Jianan Mental Hosp., Tainan, Taiwan, 2008—. Office Fax: 886-6-279-7659.

CHIU, JAMES SHING-PING, mediator, surgeon, educator; 2 children. MB, BS, U. Hong Kong, 1967; LLB with honors, U. London, 2007. Lic. Med. Coun. Can., 1976, Fed. Licensing Exam. Bd., 1976, cert. specialist in gen. surgery Med. Coun. Hong Kong, 1998. Registrar Newcastle Regional Hosp. Bd., Newcastle-on-Tyne, England, 1971—73, Northern Gen. Hosp., Sheffield, England, 1973—74; sr. resident to chief resident Ottawa U. Hosps., Ont., Canada, 1974—77; cons. in gen. surgery & vascular surgery Grace Hosp. & Seven Oaks Gen. Hosp., Winnipeg, Man., Canada, 1977—82; hon. clin. lectr. U. Hong Kong Med. Sch., 2000—; hon. cons. surgeon St. Paul's Hosp., 2003—09; adj. asst. prof. Chinese U. Hong Kong, 2010—. Assessor, gen. mediator Hong Kong Internat. Arbitration Ctr.; gen. meditation interest group vice chmn., commn. mem. Hong Kong Medition Coun.; assessor, instr., cmty. mediator Hong Kong Medition Ctr.; bldg. mgmt. mediator, lands tribunal, assessor, coach meditation Law Soc. Hong Kong. Contbr. articles to profl. med. jours. on attractive dispute resolutions. Divisional surgeon St. John Ambulance, Hong Kong, 1991—93; bd. rev. mem. Inland Revenue Dept., Hong Kong, 2004—07. Recipient 1st award, Hong Kong Soc. Gastroenterology, 1987. Fellow: ACS (Hong Kong chpt. coun. mem. 1995—98, 2001—10), Royal Coll. Surgeons (Eng.), Hong Kong Acad. Medicine, Surgeons Hong Kong Coll., Royal Coll. Surgeons (Can.), Royal Coll. Surgeons (Edinburgh); mem.: Med. Coun. Hong Kong (coun. mem. 2006—), Hong Kong Med. Assn. (coun. mem. 1991—95, 2003—10). Avocation: literature. Office: Rm 1202 Island Beverley 1 Great George St Causeway Bay Hong Kong Office Phone: 852-2810-9833. Personal E-mail: mediators.hk@gmail.com.

CHIU, JOHN TANG, physician; b. Macao, Jan. 8, 1938; s. Lan Cheong and Yau Hoon C.; m. Bonnie Doolan, Aug. 28, 1965 (div. Apr. 1986); children: Lisa, Mark, Heather; m. Karin Adams, Jan. 3, 2000. Student, U. Vt., BA, 1960, MD, 1964. Diplomate Am. Bd. Allergy & Immunology. Pres. Allergy Med. Group, Inc., Newport Beach, Calif., 1969-72, 1972—. Clin. prof. medicine U. Calif., Irvine, 1975—. Contbr. articles to profl. jours. Active Santa Ana Heights Adv. Commn., 1982-83; life mem. Orange County Sheriff's Adv. coun., 1987—. Recipient Freshman Chem. Achievement award Am. Chem. Soc., 1958. Fellow Am. Acad. Allergy Asthma and Immunology(emeritus mem.), Am. Coll. Allergy and Immunology(emeritus mem.), Am. Coll. Chest Physicians (sec. steering com. allergy 1977-81), Orange County Med. Assn. (chmn. comm. com. 1985-88, comm. com., mem. bull. editl. bd. 1995-2001). Avocations: skiing, golf, aerobics, travels. Office: Allergy Med Group Inc 400 Newport Center Dr Newport Beach CA 92660-7601 Office Phone: 949-644-1422. Personal E-mail: allergymed@yahoo.com.

CHIU, PAO CHIN, pediatrician; b. Taipei, Taiwan, May 6, 1956; MD, Nat. Yang Ming U., 1982. Attending physician Kaohsiung Vets. Gen. Hosp., 1989. Bd. mem. Taiwan Human Genetic Soc., 2005. Recipient Disting. award, Kaohsiung Vets. Gen. Hosp. Mem.: Taiwan Pediat. Assn. Avocations: reading, hiking, farming. Office: Dept Pediat 386 Ta Chung 1st Rd Kaohsiung 813 Taiwan Office Fax: 88673468207. E-mail: paochinped333@yahoo.com.tw.

CHIU, PETER YEE-CHEW, physician; came to U.S., 1965; naturalized, 1973; s. Man Chee and Yiu Ying Chiu; m. Elisa; children: Emma, Clara. BS, U. Calif., Berkeley, 1969, MPH, 1970, DrPH, 1975; MD, Stanford U., 1983. Diplomate Am. Bd. Family Practice, Am. Bd. Preventive Medicine; registered profl. engr., Calif.; registered environ. health specialist, Calif. Asst. civil engr. City of Oakland, Calif., 1970-72; assoc. water quality engr. Bay Area Sewage Services Agy., Berkeley, 1974-76; prin. environ. engr. Assn. Bay Area Govts., Berkeley, 1976-79; intern San Jose Hosp., Calif., 1983-84, resident to chief resident physician, 1984-86; ptnr. Chiu and Crawford, San Jose, 1986-89, Good Samaritan Med. Group, San Jose, 1989-90, The Permanente Med. Group, 1991—. Adj. prof. U. San Francisco, 1979-83; clin. asst. prof. Stanford U. Med. Sch., 1987-2009, adj. clin. prof., 2009-. Contbr. articles to profl. publs.; composer, pub. various popular songs Asia, US. Bd. mem. Calif. Regional Water Quality Control Bd.,Oakland, 1979-84, Bay Area Comprehensive Health Planning Coun., San Francisco, 1972-76; mem. Santa Clara County Ctrl. Dem. Com., 1987—; mem. exec. bd. Calif. State Dem. Ctrl. Com., 1989-; commr. U.S. Presdl. Commn. on Risk Assessment and Risk Mgmt., Washington, 1993-97; mem. U.S. Presdl. Rank Rev. Bd., Washington, 2000; hearing bd. mem. alt. Bay Area Air Quality Mgmt. Dist., San Francisco, 2002—. Recipient Resident Tchr. award Soc. Tchrs. Family Medicine, 1986, Resolution of Appreciation award Calif. Regional Water Quality Control Bd., 1985, Norman Mineta Lifetime Achievement award Silicon Valley Asian Pacific Am. Dem. Club, 2006. Mem. Chi Epsilon, Tau Beta Pi. Democrat. Achievements include co-authored one of the first comprehensive regional environmental management plans in US; pioneered a comprehensive framework for enviromental health risk management. Avocations: songwriting, recording. Office: The Permanente Med Group 770 E Calaveras Blvd Milpitas CA 95035-5491

CHIU, YI-CHEN (YULANDA CHIU), nursing educator, researcher; d. Chin-Chun Chiu and Pi-Chu Chiu Wu; m. Ting-Huang Chang, Apr. 12, 2004; 1 child, Tiffany Chang. PhD, Sch. Nursing U. Mich., Ann Arbor, 2002. Lic. nurse, Taiwan, 1990. Asst. prof. Sch. Nursing Chang-Gung U., Taoyuan, Taiwan, 2002—. Rschr. Sch. Nursing Chang-Gung U., 2002—. Practioner Ching-Hi Internat. Meditation Assn., Taiwan, 1990—. Grantee, Nat. Sci. Consul Taiwan, 2003, 2004—, Chang-Gung Meml. Hosp. CMRPD, 2005. Achievements include research in attention impairment and disoriented behavior in Taiwanese early dementia patients. Office: Sch Nursing Chang-Gung U 259 Wen-Hwa 1st Rd Taoyuan 333 Taiwan Personal E-mail: chiuyuhong@yahoo.com. E-mail: yulandac@mail.cgu.edu.tw.

CHIU, YI-WEN, nephrologist, educator; b. Kaohsiung, Taiwan, Apr. 4, 1967; MD, Kaohsiung Med. U., 1992. Asst. prof. Kaohsiung Med. U., 2007—. Editl. bd. mem. Clin. Nephrology, 2011. Named Best Intern, Kaohsiung Med. U. Hosp., Best Resident. Mem.: Taiwanese Assn. Diabetes Educator, Taiwan Soc. Internal Medicine, Taiwan Soc. Nephrology. Avocation: golf. Office: 100 Tzyou 1st Rd Kaohsiung 807 Taiwan Business E-Mail: chiuyiwen@kmu.edu.tw.

CHIURAZZI, PIETRO, medical educator; b. Rome, Aug. 25, 1967; MD, Cath. U., 1992; PhD, Erasmus U., 2001. Rsch. fellow Erasmus U., Rotterdam, Netherlands, 1998—2000; rsch. scientist U. Messina, Italy, 1999—2002, Cath. U., Rome, 2002—05, assoc. prof., 2005—. Avocations: reading, languages. Home: via G Donizetti 20 Roma 00168 Italy Business E-Mail: pietro.chiurazzi@rm.unicatt.it.

CHIVERTON, PATRICIA ANN, nursing educator; b. Rochester, NY, Nov. 21, 1947; d. Paul and Eleanor (Buyck) Gilmore; 1 child, Laura. BS, Ctrl. Mo. State U., 1970; MS, U. Rochester, 1980, EdD, 1990. Exec. dir. Alzheimer's Assn., Rochester, NY, 1987-89; clin. assoc. U. Rochester, 1987-89, clin. chief psychiat. mental health nursing, 1990-97, asst. prof. clin. nursing, 1994-95, interim chair health care sys. divsn., 1994-95, assoc. prof. clin. nursing, 1996—99, CEO cmty. nursing ctr., 1996—2005, assoc. dean clin. affairs. Sch. Nursing and Med. Ctr., 1998—99, interim dean, Sch. Nursing and Med. Ctr., 1999—2000, dean, Sch. Nursing and Med. Ctr., 2000—08, v.p. strong health nursing, Pamela York Klainer endowed chair in nursing entrepreneurship, 2007—. Judge Book of the Yr., Am. Jour. Nursing, 1999, reviewer, 1998—; cons. F.f. Thompson Continuing Care Facility, Canadaiguia, N.Y., 1997-99. Contbr. chpts. to books. in field. Rep. N.Y. State Alzheimer's Assn., 1985-88; bd. dirs. Health and Wellness Ctr., Livingston County, N.Y., Monroe County Long Term Care Agy., Rochester, 1997—. Mem. Am. Psychiat. Nurses Assn. (pres. Northwestern chpt. 1995-97, Excellence in Leadership award 1994), Ea. Nursing Rsch. Soc., Nat. Acads. Practice (Disting. Practitioner), Sigma Theta Tau. Office: U Rochester Sch Nursing 601 Elmwood Ave Rochester NY 14642-0001 E-mail: patricia_chiverton@urmc.rochester.edu.

CHIVIACOWSKY, SUZETE, physical education educator; b. Pelotas, Rio Grande do Sul, Brazil, Mar. 8, 1963; PhD, FMH, 2000. Assoc. prof. Fed. U. Pelotas, 1989. Office: Rua Luis Camões 625 Pelotas Rio Grande do Sul 960650-030 Brazil Business E-Mail: schivi@terra.com.br.

CHIVIAN, ERIC SETH, psychiatrist, environmental scientist, educator; b. Newark, June 10, 1942; children: Cybele, Dylan C., Judah B. AB, Harvard U., 1964, MD, 1968. Staff psychiatrist MIT, 1980—2000; asst. clin. prof. psychiatry Harvard Med. Sch., 1987—, dir. Ctr. for Health and the Global Environment, 1996—. Spkr. in field. Contbr. articles to profl. jours. Recipient Nobel Peace prize, 1985; named one of the 100 Most Influential People in the World, TIME mag., 2008. Mem.: AAAS, Internat. Physicians Prevent Nuc. War (co-founder, treas. 1980—85), Physicians for Social Responsibility. Achievements include research in first large scale scientific survey of American and Soviet teenagers' attitudes about the future; US-USSR relations and nuclear war; health implications of species extinction and loss of biodiversity. Home: 136 Carter Pond Rd Petersham MA 01366-9728 Office Phone: 617-384-8530. E-mail: eric_chivian@hms.harvard.edu.

CHIXIN, DU, ophthalmologist, educator; b. Hangzhou, China, Oct. 16, 1967; MS in Medicine, Zhejiang U., 1993. Prof. First Affiliated Hosp., Coll. Medicine, Zhejiang U., 2007—. Rsch. assoc. Bascom Palmer Eye Inst., 2010—. Recipient Sci. and Technol. Progress award, Zhejiang Province. Mem.: ARVO. Office: Dept Ophthalmology 79# Qingchun Rd Hangzhou Zhejiang 310003 China Office Fax: 86-571-87072577. Business E-Mail: duchixin@126.com.

CHIZNER, MICHAEL A., cardiologist, educator; MD, Cornell U. (Weill), 1974. Diplomate Am. Bd. Internal Medicine, 1977, Am. Bd. Internal Medicine-cardiovasc. disease, 1979. Resident internal medicine NY Hosp., NYC, 1974—77; fellow cardiovasc. disease Georgetown Affiliation Hosps., Washington, 1977—79; clin. prof. medicine Univ. of Fla. Coll. of Medicine, Univ. of Miami Sch. of Medicine, Nova Southeastern Univ., Barry Univ.; chief med. dir. The Heart Ctr. of Excellence Broward Health. Editl. adv. bd. The Am. Heart Hosp. Jour., Cardiovasc. Reviews and Reports. Author various articles and book chpts. Named one of Best Physicians in the US, Top Docs, Castle Connelly. Fellow: ACP, Am. Heart Assn., Am. Coll. of Cardiology. Office: Broward General Medical Center 1625 SE 3rd Ave Ste 300 Fort Lauderdale FL 33316 Office Phone: 954-355-5001. Business E-Mail: mchizner@browardhealth.org.

CHLEBOWSKI, ROWAN THOMAS, oncologist, educator; b. July 29, 1945; MD, PhD, Case Western Res. U., 1974. Cert. internal medicine 1980, med. oncology 1981. Resident Cleve. Met. Gen Hosp., 1974—76, intern, 1974—76; fellow med. oncology LA County/U. Southern Calif. Med. Ctr. and Sch. Medicine, 1976—79; prof. medicine David Geffen Sch. Medicine, UCLA; chief dept. internal medicine, med. oncology/hematology Harbor-UCLA Med. Ctr. Mem. healthy and at-risk populations program UCLA Jonsson

Comprehensive Cancer Ctr.; prin. investigator Women's Health Initiative, Bethesda, Md., 1991—. Contbr. articles to profl. jours. Achievements include research in women's health, breast cancer and prostate cancer, especially on hormonal mediation of cancer and cancer prevention. Office: 16 Crestwood Dr Rancho Palos Verdes CA 90275 also: UCLA Jonsson Comprehensive Cancer Ctr 8-684 Factor Bldg PO Box 951781 Los Angeles CA 90095-1781 Office Phone: 310-825-5268, 310-222-2217. Office Fax: 310-206-5553. Business E-Mail: rchlebow@whi.org.

CHLEWICKI, WOJCIECH, engineering educator, researcher; b. Szczecin, Poland, Mar. 23, 1974; PhD, Szczecin U. Tech., 2005; postgrad., U. Patras, Greece, 2003. Rschr. PET Ctr., Aarhus U. Hosp., Denmark, 2003—04; asst. prof. Faculty Elec. Engring., Szczecin U. Tech., Poland, 2005—, rsch. project mgr., 2009—. Rschr. Lab. EPR Tomography, Poznan U. Tech., Poland, 2009—. Avocation: travel. Office: Sikorskiego 37 Szczecin Zachodniopomorskie 70-313 Poland E-mail: wchlewi@yahoo.com.

CHLOUVERAKIS, CONSTANTINOS STEPHANOS, endocrinologist, researcher; b. Crete, Greece, Oct. 15, 1928; s. Stephanos and Eleni Chlouverakis; m. Ellen Nancy Merns, Aug. 2, 1975; children: Harry Charles Chlouverakis-Papas, Eleni. MD, U. Athens, 1953; MD cum laude, 1958. Tng. cert. in medicine U. Hosp. Athens, 1957. Brit. Coun. scholar U. Birmingham, England, 1958—60; sr. scientist, metabolic reactions rsch. unit Med. Rsch. Coun., London, 1965—70; prof. medicine SUNY, Buffalo, 1970—75; dir., dept. endocrinology and diabetes ctr. Nat. Gen. Hosp. Athens, Greece, 1979—97. Cons. physician Veterans Adminstrn. Hosp., Buffalo, 1970—78, G.J. Meyer Meml. Hosp., 1970—75; advisor Health Ministry Greece, Athens, 1977—79; cons. and vis. prof. Guys Hosp. Med. Sch., London, 1981—82; pres. Greek Assn. Endocrinology, Athens, 1990—91; rsch. fellow, part time lectr. U. London, Guys Hosp. Med. Sch., 1961—65. Author: (book) Doctors and Patients, The Age of Confusion; contbr. chapters to books, articles to profl. jours. Fullbright scholarship, Rsch. fellowship, U. Minn., Dept. Phys. Hygiene, 1960—61. Personal E-mail: ccostis@ymail.com.

CHMIELOWSKI, KAROL, retired neurologist; b. Ulanów, Poland, May 4, 1935; s. Jan Chmielowski and Aniela Chmielowska; m. Jolanta Grazyna Michalczuk, June 13, 1964; children: Joanna Ewa Chmielowska-Rumpel, Monika Galbarczyk. D, Mil. Med. Acad., 1963, M of Neurology, 1975, M of Nuc. Medicine, 1981. Physician Mil. Base, Warsaw, 1964—72; asst. neurologist Mil. Inst. of Higiene and Epidemiology, 1972—74; asst., sr. lectr. Ctrl. Clin. Hosp. of Mil. Med. Acad., 1975—2003, asst. prof., 1975—2003; asst., prof. Mil. Med. Inst., 2004—05. Col. Med. Svc., 1955—96, Poland. Recipient Emergency Force in the Svc. of Peace medal, UN, 1978. Mem.: Sci. Coun. of Radioisotope Ctr., Sci. Coun. in Ctrl. Clin. Hosp. of Mil. Med. Acad., Polish Assn. of Nuc. Medicine (bd. mem. 1982—2005). Roman Catholic. Avocations: opera, classical music, travel. Office: Mil Med Inst Szaserów 128 Warsaw 00-909 Poland Personal E-mail: kchmielowski@aster.pl.

CHO, ARTHUR KENJI, retired pharmacologist, educator; b. Oakland, Calif., Nov. 7, 1928; PhD, UCLA, 1958. Rsch. scientist Nat. Heart Inst., 1965—70, prof. Dept. Molecular and Med. Pharmacology UCLA, 1970—95, prof. emeritus, 1995—. Home: 3393 Colbert Ave Los Angeles CA 90066 E-mail: acho@mednet.ucla.edu.

CHO, BAIK HWAN, medical educator, director; s. Ju Sun Cho and Sun Yeop Kim; m. Young Kyung Chun, Feb. 22, 1976; children: Yong Hyun, Ik Hyun. PhD, Chonnam U., Kwangju, Republic of Korea, 1988. Med. dr. Ministry of Health, Republic of Korea, 1976. Prof. Chonbuk Nat. U., Jeonju, Republic of Korea, 1984—2008; dir. Jeonbuk Cancer Ctr., Jeonju, 2006—. Chmn. Korean Soc. Parenteral and Enteral Nutrition, Seoul, Republic of Korea, 2008—; cons. Nat. Cancer Ctr., Cancer Control Program, Seoul, 2008—. Capt. Korean Army, 1981—84. Rsch. grant, Ministry of Health, Republic of Korea, 2006. Home: Songchun Hyundai Apt 402-1102 Jeonbuk Jeonju Republic of Korea Office: Jeonbuk Univ Med Sch Keumam dong Jeonju Jeonbuk 561-180 Republic of Korea Business E-Mail: chobh@chonbuk.ac.kr.

CHO, BYOUNG SOO, pediatrician, director; b. Incheon, Republic of Korea, Oct. 12, 1951; s. Seung Yun Cho and Kee Ok Hyun; m. Koo Weon Cho; children: Kun Hee, Won Hee. MD, Kyung Hee U., Seoul, Korea Med. Assn., 1977; PhD, Korea U., Seoul, 1986. Dir., dept. pediat. Kyung Hee U. Hosp., Seoul, Republic of Korea, 1982—. Dir. Korea Sch. Health Assn., Seoul, Republic Of Korea, 1998—2008. Recipient Kowhang Med. award, Kyung Hee U., 2006. Home: 142-1902 LLL's Apt 19 Jamsidong Seoul Republic of Korea Office: Kyung Hee Univ Hosp 1 Hoeki-Dong Dongdaemun-Ku Seoul 130-702 Republic of Korea Office Phone: 82-2-958-8302. Office Fax: 82-2-958-9778; Home Fax: 82-2-923-8248. Business E-Mail: koreakidney@naver.com.

CHO, CHUL KOO, oncologist; b. Busan, Jan. 31, 1954; BS, Seoul Nat. U., 1980; PhD, SNUH, 1994. Dir. gen. Korea Cancer Ctr. Hosp., 2010—. Mem.: Korean Soc. Radiation Oncology (First prize). Avocations: stamp collecting/philately, reading, travel. Home: Songpa-Ku Ohkeum-Dong Seoul 139-706 Republic of Korea Home Fax: 970-2412. Personal E-mail: chcho@kirams.re.kr.

CHO, CHUN SUNG, neurosurgeon; b. Seoul, Republic Of Korea, Jan. 8, 1970; s. Kyung Ho Cho and Myung Sook Lee; m. Hyun Kyung Jeong; children: Yun Jae, Young Jae. Dr., Dankook U. Med. coll., Choenan, Chungnam, Republic Of Korea. Prof. Dankook U. Hosp., 2005—, surgeon, 2008—. Lt. Chungnam. Office: Dankook Univ Hosp Neurosurgery Anseodong Cheonan Chungnam 330 715 Republic of Korea Office Phone: 82 41 550 3965. Business E-Mail: babyface@dankook.ac.kr.

CHO, DAE HO, health facility administrator, educator; s. Jung Gak Cho and Il Bok Kim; m. Hyun Jeong Park, Nov. 9, 1997; 1 child, Won Chang. PhD, Chgo. Med. Sch., 1995. V.p. Rsch. Inst. Women's Health, Seoul, Republic of Korea, 2005—. Contbr. articles to profl. jours. Mem.: Am. Assn. Immunologists. Office: Sookmyung Womens Univ Chungpa-Dong 2-Ka Yongsan-Ku Seoul 140742 Republic of Korea Business E-Mail: cdhkor@sookmyung.ac.kr.

CHO, DER-YANG, hospital administrator; MD, Nat. Yang-Ming U., Taiwan; MHA, Asia U., Taiwan. Neurosurgery staff Taichung Veterans Gen. Hosp., Taiwan; cheif dept. of neurosurgery China Med. Coll. Hosp.; vice supt. Yen Hosp.; supt. Nanjing Benq Hosp., China; prof. China Med. Univ.; vice supt. dept. of stroke ctr. China Med. Univ. Hosp., vice supt. surgical dept., supt. Office: China Medical University Hospital 91 Yuh-Der Rd Taichung 40447 Taiwan Office Phone: 886422052121. E-mail: d5057@www.cmuh.org.tw. *

CHO, EUI-SIC, dental educator; b. Kimje, Jeonbuk, Republic Of Korea, Oct. 1, 1964; s. Young-Gil and Hwa-Kyung Cho; m. Mee-Kyung Jeong; children: Gun-Joon, Bo-Yoon. DDS, PhD, Chonbuk Nat. U., Jeonju, Republic of Korea, 1998. Cert. dentist Republic of Korea, 1989. Postdoc. fellow U. Rochester, NY, 2000—02; prof. Chonbuk Nat. U., Jeonbuk, 1996—. Capt. dentistry, 1992—95, Jeongju. Home: 107/401 I'Pk Hyoja Dong 3Ga Jeonju Jeonbuk 560-870 Republic of Korea Office: Chonbuk Nat Univ 664-14 Duckjin Dong Jeonju Jeonbuk 561-756 Republic of Korea Office Fax: 82-63-270-4004. Business E-Mail: oasis@chonbuk.ac.kr.

CHO, EUN KYUNG, medical oncologist, educator; d. Jung Jin Cho and Jin Lee; m. Choongki Lee, Jan. 16, 1994; children: Myungjin Lee, Hwayoung Lee. MD, Hanyang U., Seoul, Republic Of Korea, 1988; PhD, Hanyang U., Seoul, 1995. Cert. Bd. Med. Dr. Assn. Internal Medicine, 1995. Asst. prof. Gachon U., Inchon, Republic of Korea, 2001—05, assoc. prof., 2005—11, prof., 2011—. Postdoc. fellowship Harvard Med. Sch., Brighum Women's Hosp., Boston, 2005—07. Home: 12-1001 Sunkyung APT Dachi1dong Kangnam Seoul 135-836 Republic of Korea Office: Gachon Univ Gil Hosp 1198 Guwoldong Namdonggu Inchon 405-760 Republic of Korea Office Fax: 82324324355. Personal E-mail: ekcho7@hanmail.net. Business E-Mail: ekcho@gilhospital.com.

CHO, EUNYOUNG, epidemiologist; BS in Food Sci. and Nutrition, Seoul Nat. U., 1988, MS in Nutrition, 1991; DSc, Harvard Sch. Pub. Health, 1999. Rsch. fellow dept. nutrition Harvard Sch. Pub. Health, Boston, 1999—2002; instr. medicine Harvard Med. Sch., Boston, 2002—, asst. prof. medicine, 2005—. Office: Channing Lab 181 Longwood Ave Boston MA 02115

CHO, GEUM JOON, obstetrician, gynecologist; b. Seoul, Republic Of Korea, Sept. 5, 1975; s. Jaeyeol Cho and Yangnim Kee; m. Ji Hae Kim, Aug. 7, 1999. Degree, Korea U. & Postgrad. Sch., Seoul. Diplomate obstetrics & gynecology Korean Soc. Obstetrics and Gynecology, 2006. Intern Korea U. Med. Ctr., Seoul, 2001—06, resident Seoul; mil. dr. Armed Forces Seoul Hosp., 2006—09. Contbr. scientific papers to profl. jours. Capt. Army, 2006—09. Recipient Best Article award, Korean Soc. Obstetrics and Gynecology, 2007, Best Poster Presentation award, Korean Soc. Fetal Medicine, 2008, 1st Pl. Poster Presentation, XIX Asia Pacific Mil. Medicine Conf., 2009; grant, Korean Mil. Med. Assn., 2008, fellowship, Dept. Ob-Gyn., Guro Hosp., Coll. Medicine, Korea U., 2009—. Mem.: Korean Soc. Menopause, Korean Assoc. Obstetrics and Gynecology. Home: 101-1206 Yoowon apt Shinjung-dong Yangchun-gu Seoul 158-849 Republic of Korea Office: Guro Hosp Coll Medicine Korea Univ Dept Ob-Gyn 80 Guro-gu Guro-dong Seoul 152-703 Republic of Korea Office Phone: 82-2-2626-1833. Personal E-mail: md.gjcho@gmail.com. Business E-Mail: md_cho@hanmail.net.

CHO, GOO-YEONG, medical educator; b. Daegu, Replic of Korea, Nov. 5, 1966; s. Seok-Bong Cho and Dong-Heui Kim; m. Han-Gul Choi, Oct. 9, 1969; children: Su-Jeong, Yeon-Sik. MD, Ulsan U., Republic of Korea, 2000; PhD, Ulsan U., 2003. Cert. in cardiology Korea. Resident Asan Med. Ctr., Seoul, 1990—95; prof. Hallym U., Seoul, 1999 ; clin. fellow Asan Med. Ctr., Seoul, 1998—99; rsch. fellow U. Queensland, Brisbane, Australia. Editor Korean Soc. Echocardiography, 2004—. Contbr. articles various clin. rsch. Mem.: Korean Soc. Circulation. Office: Hallym U Sacred Heart Hosp Pyeonchon Dong 896 431-070 Gyeonggi Gyeonggi do Republic of Korea Business E-Mail: cardioch@medimail.co.kr.

CHO, HAN IK, retired pathologist; b. Chungyang, Republic of Korea, Apr. 26, 1943; MD, Seoul Nat. U., 1967, PhD, 1972. Physician, prof. Seoul Nat. U. Hosp., 1976—2008; pres. Korea Assn. Health Promotion, 2010—. Mem.: Internat. Soc. Lab. Hematology, World Assn. Pathology and Lab. Medicine (hon.). Avocation: golf. Home: 23-903 Woomyun-ro 198-8 Seocho-dong Seocho Seoul 137-779 Republic of Korea Personal E-mail: hanik@snu.ac.kr.

CHO, HYONG-HO, medical educator; b. Gwangju, Republic of Korea; m. Min-Kyung Song; 1 child, Da-Eun. MD, Chonnam Nat. U., Gwangju, PhD, 2006. Cert. otolaryngologist Republic of Korea, 2005. Clin. prof. Chonnam U. Hosp., Gwangju, 2005; assoc. prof. Chonnam Nat. U. Med. Sch., Gwangju, 2007—. Grant, Korean Rsch. Found. Mem.: Korean Soc. Otolaryngology Head and Neck Surgery. Achievements include research in hearing restoration using stem cell. Office: Chonnam Nat Univ Med Sch Hack Dong Dong Gu 8 501-746 Gwangju Republic of Korea Office Phone: 82-62-220-6772. Office Fax: 82-62-228-7743. E-mail: victocho@hanmail.net.

CHO, HYUNG LAE, surgeon; b. Chung Do, Oct. 12, 1969; MD, Pusan Nat. U., 1994. Chief, dept. orthop. surgery Good Samsun Hosp., 2002—. Mem.: Korean Knee Assn., Korean Orthop. Assn., Arthroscopic Assn. N.Am. Office: 193-5 Jurye Dong Sasang Ku Busan 617-718 Republic of Korea Personal E-mail: hljo88@hanmail.net.

CHO, IN RAE, urologist, educator; s. Te-Je Cho and Bun-Han Cho-Lee; m. Ji-Young Cho-Hwang; children: Jason Hyun-Kug, Claire Hyun-Ah. MD, Yonsei U., Seoul, Republic of Korea, 1985, MS, 1991; PhD, Korea U., Seoul, 1998. Cert. urologist Ministry Health, Republic of Korea, 1993. Intership Yonsei U. Severance Hosp., Seoul, 1985—86, residency, 1989—93, rsch. clin. fellow, 1993—95; instr. Inje U. Seoul Paik Hosp., Seoul, 1995—97, asst. prof., 1997—2001; sr. fellow Dept Urology, U. Wash., Seattle, 1997—99; assoc. prof. Inje U. Ilsan Paik Hosp., Koyang, Republic of Korea, 2001—06, prof., 2006—. Mil. med. officer Ist Co. Korean Army, 1986—89. Mem.: Korean Andrological Soc. (dir. 1989—), Korean Uro-Genital Infection Inflammation Soc. (dir. 2002—), Korean Prostate Soc. (dir. 1997—), Korean Urol. Assn. (editl. mem. 2005—), European Urol. Assn., Am. Urol. Assn. Office: Dept Urology Inje Univ Ilsan Paik Hosp 2240 Daehwadong Ilsanseogu Gyeonggi Koyang 411-706 Republic of Korea Office Phone: 82-31-910-7230. Office Fax: 82-31-910-7239. Business E-Mail: ircho@paik.ac.kr.

CHO, JAE HOON, surgeon; b. Seoul, Republic of Korea, Jan. 2, 1972; PhD, Korea U., MD, 1997. Mem. Korean Soc. Otorhinolaryngology, Head and Neck Surgery, 1997—. Avocation: saxophone. Office: 4-12 Hwayang-dong Gwangjin-gu Seoul 143-729 Republic of Korea Business E-Mail: jaehoon@kuh.ac.kr.

CHO, JEONG YEON, radiologist, educator; b. Seoul, Republic of Korea, Aug. 13, 1964; s. Nam Gyu Cho and Hee Soon Kwon; m. Sung Hee Park, Jan. 24, 1991; children: Sung Min, Sung Jae. MD, Seoul Nat. U., 1990, MS, 1997, PhD, 2000. Cert. physician Ministry Health and Welfare, Korea, 1990, diagnostic radiologist Ministry Health and Welfare, Korea, 1997. Resident Seoul Nat. U. Hosp., 1993—97, clin. fellow, 1997—98; radiologist Samsung Cheil Hosp., Seoul, 1998—, dir. Ultrasound Ctr., 2002—; prof. Sungkyunkwan U. Sch. Medicine, Seoul, 1999—. Vis. clin. prof. U. Toronto, Canada, 2003—04. Contbr. book. Recipient, Korean Soc. Med. Ultrasound, 1999, 2000, 2002, 2005, Am. Inst. Med. Ultrasound, 2000, Radiol. Soc. N.Am., 2000, World Fedn. Ultrasound in Medicine and Biology, 2000, 2003. Fellow: Korean Soc. Uroradiology; mem.: Korean Soc. Med. Ultrasound (grantee 1997), Korean Radiol. Soc., Soc. Uroradiology. Home: 77-1104 Hyundai-Apt Apgujeong-dong Seoul 135-110 Republic of Korea Office: Samsung Cheil Hospital Sunkynkwan Univ 1-19 Mookjeong-dong Jung-gu Seoul 100-380 Republic of Korea Office Fax: 82-2-2000-7369. Business E-Mail: radjycho@skku.edu.

CHO, JIN HEE, medical educator; b. Republic of Korea, Sept. 16, 1960; MD, Cath. U. Korea; PhD, Cath. U. orea, 1996. Vis. fellowship U. Calif., San Diego, Allergy and Immunology Lab., 2000—01; instr. Cath. U. Korea, Uijengbu St. Mary's Hosp., 1993—94, asst. prof., 1994—2003; assoc. prof. Cath. U. Korea, Kangnam St. Mary's Hosp., 2003—08, 2008—. Dir., pub. rels. Korean Rhinologic Soc., 2004—06, dir., med. ins., 2006—08, dir., allergy and immunology dept., 2008—11; dir., med. ins. com. Korean Soc. Otorhinolaryngology-Head and Neck Surgery, 2008—11. Mem.: Korean Rhinologic Soc. Avocations: golf, singing, hiking. Office: # 62 Yeouido-dong Yeoungdeungpo-gu Seoul 157-713 Republic of Korea Office Fax: 82-2-786-1149. Business E-Mail: entcho@catholic.ac.kr.

CHO, KWAN HO, radiation oncologist, director; b. Seoul, Republic Of Korea, Oct. 17, 1953; s. Hee Kyung Cho and Ok Soon Kim; m. Young Joo Same. MD, Yonsei U., Seoul, 1979. Diplomate Am. Bd. Radiology, 1994, cert. Ministry Health & Welfair, Korea, 1987. Rotating internship Yonsei U. Hosp., Seoul, 1979—80, residency, 1984—87; rschr. Med. U. SC., Charleston, 1987—88; residency ST. Agnes Hosp, Balt., 1988—89; rschr. U.Minn., Mpls., 1989—90; residency U. Minn Hosp and Clinics, 1990—93, asst. prof., 1993—2000, assoc. prof., 2000—01; dir. Proton Therapy Ctr., Nat. Cancer Ctr., Goyang, Republic of Korea, 2001—. Contbr. articles to numerous profl. jours. Rsch. com. Korean Soc. Therapeutic Radiology and Oncology, Seoul, 2006—08; internat. rels. Korean Soc. Head and Neck Oncology. Capt. ROKAF, 1981—84, Suwon. Recipient Best Rschr. of yr., Korean Soc. Therapeutic Radiology and Oncology, 2002;, Nat. Cancer Ctr., 2001—08. Mem.: ASTRO. Achievements include research in radiation oncology field. Office: Nat Cancer Ctr Madu-Dong Ilsan-Gu 809 410-769 Goyang Republic of Korea Office Phone: 82-31-920-1720. Business E-Mail: kwancho@ncc.re.kr.

CHO, KWANG REE, surgeon; b. Gangneung, Gangwon-Do, Republic of Korea, Aug. 23, 1969; s. Kyung-Ja Choi; married; 1 child, Yeon-Woo. PhD, Seoul Nat. U., 2006. Cert. in thoracic and cardiovasc. surgery Ministry Health and Social Affairs, Korea, 1999. Vis. scientist Mayo Clinic, Rochester, Miss., 2002—03; clin. instr. Seoul Nat. U. Hosp., Republic of Korea, 2003—04, clin. asst. prof., 2004—06; attending surgeon Cheju Halla Gen. Hosp., Jeju-City, Jeju-Do, Republic of Korea, 2006—. Reviewer European Jour. Cardiothoracic Surgery, 2008. Contbr. med. articles to jours. Capt., mil. surgeon, 1999—2003, Seoul. Recipient Medtronic Cardiac Surgery award, Korean Coronary Artery Surgery Forum, 2008. Mem.: Korean Soc. Critical Care Medicine, Assn. Thoracic and Cardiovasc. Surgeons Asia, Internat. Soc. Minimally Invasive Cardiac Surgery, Korean Soc. Thoracic & Cardiovasc. Surgery (internat. interchange com. 2006—, Woo-Cheon Pk. Young Kwan Rsch. award 2005). Office: Cheju Halla Gen Hosp 1963-2 Yeon-Dong 690-766 Jeju-City Jeju-do Republic of Korea Personal E-mail: ckrym@yahoo.co.kr.

CHO, KYUNGYUN, microbiologist, educator; b. Republic of Korea, Sept. 2, 1965; PhD, Cornell U., 1996. Prof. Hoseo U., 2001—, assoc. dean, 2008—10. Dir. Myxobacteria Bank, 2007—. Mem.: Korean Soc. Microbiology and Biotech., Microbiol. Soc. Korea. Office: Dept Biotech Hoseo University Asan Chungnam 336-795 Republic of Korea Office Fax: 82-41-548-6231. Business E-Mail: kycho@hoseo.edu.

CHO, MOON-JUNE, radiologist, oncologist; b. Kyungki Do, Republic of Korea, June 24, 1957; s. Ki-Young Cho and Kyung-Hee Kim; m. Eun-Ju Yu, Jan. 16, 1988; children: Shi-Jin, Shi-Young, Shi-Yun. MD, Seoul Nat. U., PhD, 1994. Lic. doctor Republic of Korea, 1983. Intern Seoul Nat. U. Hosp., 1983—84, resident, 1984—87, fellow, 1987—88; chairperson dept. therapeutic radiology Chungnam Nat. U. Hosp., Taejon, Republic of Korea, 1989—. Exch. scientist MD Anderson Cancer Ctr., Houston, 1995—96; dir. Korean Soc. for Therapeutic Radiology and Oncology, Seoul, Republic of Korea, 1984—2003. Contbr. articles to profl. jours. Grantee Devel. of Safety Control Reference, Korea Food and Drug Adminstrn., 2002. Mem.: Am. Soc. for Therapeutic Radiology and Oncology (corr.). Progressive. Office: Chungnam Nat U Hosp 640 Daesa-dong Jung-ku Daejeon 301-040 Republic of Korea Office Fax: 82-42-220-7899; Home Fax: 82-42-484-7687. Personal E-mail: mjcho@cnu.ac.kr.

CHO, MYEONG-CHAN, cardiologist, researcher; b. Kimhae, Republic of Korea, Feb. 19, 1958; s. In-Hwan Cho and Soon-Jeon Bae; m. Kwang-Joo Kim, Dec. 14, 1985; children: Kwan-Hyun, Seung-Yeon. Degree, Seoul Nat. U., 1979, MD, 1983, PhD, 1992—96. Cert. physician Ministry of Health and Welfare, 1983, Korean Soc. Internal Medicine, 1987, cardiologist Korean Soc. Internal Medicine, 1995. Chief in cardiology Capital Armed Forces Gen. Hosp., Seoul, Republic of Korea, 1987—90; intern Seoul Nat. U. Hosp., Republic of Korea, 1983—84, resident, 1984—87, clin. fellow, 1990—91; lectr. Coll. Medicine, Chungbuk Nat. U., Cheongju, Republic of Korea, 1991—93, asst. prof., 1993—98, assoc. prof., 1998—2003, prof., 2003—; dir. med. rsch. inst. Chungbuk Nat. U., 2007—09; vis. prof. dept. cardiology Royal Infirmary Glasgow U., Scotland, 1994; postdoctoral rsch. fellow dept. cardiology U. Calif., San Diego, 1996—97; rsch. scientist dept. cardiology U. NC, Chapel Hill, 1997—98; chief in cardiology, dir. of cardiovasc. lab. Chungbuk Nat. U. Hosp., Cheongju, Republic of Korea, 1998—, dir., dept. planning and adminstrn., 2003—04, chmn. dept. internal medicine, 2004—09, vp, 2009—. Cons. mem., planning com. Korean Soc. Lipidology and Atherosclerosis, Seoul, 2002—; cons. mem., sci. com. Korean Soc. Circulation, Seoul, 2002—05; adv. mem., stem cell therapy Korea FDA, Seoul, 2003—; v.p. Working Group on Cardiovascular Basic Rsch., Seoul, 2006—; rsch. dir. Korean Soc. Hypertension, Seoul, 2007—09, dir. sci. com., 2009—; sec. gen. Korean Soc. Heart Failure, Seoul, 2010—. Author: Textbook of Cardiovascular Medicine, 2001, Textbook of Internal Medicine, 2004, The Manual of Interventional Cardiology, 2004, Guidelines for Medical Management, 2004, Hypertension Window, 2006, The Manual of Heart Failure, 2007; contbr. articles to profl. jours. Mem. bd. dirs. Dept. Planning and Adminstrn., Nat. U. Hosp., Seoul, Republic of Korea, 2003—03. Capt. Med., 1987—91, Seoul. Grantee, Korean Soc. Circulation, 1999, 2002—, Ministry of Health and Welfare, 1999—2002, Korea Rsch. Found., 2000—02, 2002—03, Hankok Med. Rsch. Found., 2000, Korea Sci. and Engring. Found., 2001—03, Korean Soc. Internal Medicine, 2001, Rsch. Ctr. for the Bioresource and Health, 2001—, Ministry of Sci. & Tech., 2002—03, Stem Cell Rsch. Ctr., 2002—, Korean Soc. Hypertension, 2004—05, Korean Sci. and Engring. Found., 2005. Mem.: Asia Pacific Soc. Heart Failure, Asia Pacific Soc. Cardiology, Heart Failure Assn. European Soc. Cardiology, Am. Stroke Assn., Am. Heart Assn., Korean Soc. Tissue Engring. (assoc.), Korean Soc. Molecular Biochemistry and Molecular Biology (assoc.), Korean Soc. Hypertension (assoc.), Korean Soc. Echocardiography (assoc.), Korean Soc. Lipidology and Atherosclerosis (assoc.), Korean Soc. Circulation (assoc.; pres. Jungbu divsn. 2004—), Korean Soc. Internal Medicine (assoc. Cheongram Sci. Award 2001), Korean Med. Assn. (assoc.). Achievements include patents for the use of catechin for preventing or treating coronary restenosis; the method for preventing or treating coronary restenosis with catechin; the oral formulation of paclitaxel and its derivative containing p-glycoprotein inhibitor for the prevention of vascular restenosis; the method of antihypertensive screening with mammalian TCTP gene and its protein. Home: 104-304 Daelim Apt Yongdam-Dong Sangdang-Gu-Cheongju 360-190 Republic of Korea Office: Chungbuk Nat Univ Hosp 62 Gaeshin-Dong Heungduk-Gu Chungbuk Cheongju 361-711 Republic of Korea Office Fax: 82-43-273-3252. Business E-Mail: mccho@cbnu.ac.kr.

CHO, MYEONG-JE, plant biologist, researcher; b. Taegu, Republic of Korea, Feb. 28, 1959; s. Sang-Soo Cho and Byeong-Soon Lee; m. Hyeon-Ok Ham, June 4, 1960; children: Yu-Ree, Yu-Na. BS with honors, Seoul Nat. U., 1984, MS, 1986; PhD, U. Ill., Urbana-Champaign, 1991. Rsch. assoc. U. Calif., Berkeley, 1994—98, asst. rschr., 1998—99, assoc. specialist, 1999—2004, specialist, 2004—07. Hon. scientist Rural Devel. Adminstrn., Suwon, 1998—2006; cons. Ventria Biosci., Sacramento, 1999—99, Exelixis, Inc., San Francisco, 2000—01, Scigen Harvest, Seoul, 2000—01; v.p. Byotix, Inc., Richmond, Calif., 2001—04; sci. advisor Genomine, Inc., Pohang, 2002—05. Editor: In Vitro Application in Crop Improvement; contbr. articles to profl. jours. Mem. Gracepoint Fellowship Ch. Mem.: Amer. Soc. Plant Biol. Achievements include patents for plant transformation; gene expression systems; gene isolation and characterization. Home: 13 Ulster Pl Alameda CA 94502 Office: 4010 Pont Edenway Hayward CA 94545 Personal E-mail: myeongjecho@yahoo.com.

CHO, NAM HOON, pathologist, researcher; b. Seoul, Nov. 10, 1960; s. Hwan-gu Cho and Seung-kyo Rheu; m. Hee-jung An, Jan. 7, 1961; children: Jung-youn, In-sung. MSc, Yonsei U. Coll. Medicine, Seoul, 1986; MD, 1990, PhD, 1995. Cert. physician Severence Hosp., 1986, in pathology Korean Bd. Anatomic Pathology. Rsch. fellow Yonsei U. Sch. Medicine, Seoul, 1993—95, asst. prof., 1995—2000; visiting investigator Meml. Sloan-Kettering Cancer Ctr., NYC, 1980—2000; assoc. prof. Yonsei U. Coll. Medicine, Seoul, 2000—05, prof., 2005—, vice dean academic affairs, 2006—. Com. on planning Korean Soc. Pathologists, 2002—; inspection coun. chmn. Korea Inst. of Gen. Test Evaluation, 2006—; exec. Urogenital Rsch. Mtg. KEOP, 2002—; edn. com. Korean Ob-Gyn Pathology Assn., 2002—; cons. Korean Urol. Oncology Soc., 2002, Korean Medicine Healthcare Edn. Com., 2004—. Contbr. scientific papers to profl. jours. Capt. Republic of Korea Army, 1990—93. Recipient Excellent Abstract prize, Colposcopy Inst., 2002, Excellence award, Yonsei U., 2005, Grand prize Best Paper, Bumsuk Academic Grant, 2006, Yuhan Med. award, Yuhan Pharmacy & Korean Med. Assn., 2007. Mem.: European Assn. Cancer Rsch., U.S. and Can. Pathology, Am. Assn. Cancer Rsch. Avocations: Baduk, squash, reading. Home: Kannam-ku Daechi-dong Dongbu Ctr 16 Seoul Republic of Korea Office: Yonsei Univ Coll Medicine Sinchon-Dong 134 120-752 Seoul Seoul Republic of Korea Business E-Mail: cho/p88@yuhc.ac.kr.

CHO, NAM-JOON, research scientist, educator; b. Seoul, Oct. 10, 1972; BS, U. Calif. Berkeley, 1996; PhD, Stanford U., 2000. Postdoc. fellow Stanford U., 2007—11; assoc. prof. Nanyang Technol. U., 2011—. Postdoc. fellow, Roche Inc, Am. Liver Found., grant, Nat. Rsch. Found. Mem.: Am. Chem. Soc., Materials Rsch. Soc. Office: 381 NS Mall Stauffer III Palo Alto CA 94305 Business E-Mail: ncho@stanford.edu.

CHO, SEHYUN, medical educator; b. Seoul, Republic of Korea, Oct. 15, 1959; MD, Cath. U. Korea, 1986, PhD, 1998. Assoc. prof. Cath. U. Korea, Med. Coll., 1995—. Mem.: Korean Assn. Study Hepatocellular Carcinoma, Korean Soc. Gastroenterology, Korean Assn. Study Liver, Korean Soc. Internal Medicine, Korean Med. Assn. Office: Saint Marys Hosp 62 Yeouido-dong Yeongdeungpo-gu Seoul 150-713 Republic of Korea

CHO, SU-IN, medical educator; s. Gil-Nam Cho and Jeong-Hee Hur; m. Chi-yeon Lim; children: Youn-jin, Youn-young. MD, Dong-Eui U., Busan, Republic of Korea, PhD in Korean Medicine, 1994. Assoc. prof. Coll. Korean Medicine, Dongshin U., Naju, Jeonnam, Republic of Korea, 2000—07. Mem. herbal medicine sensory test Korea Food & Drug Adminstrn., Seoul, 2005—10. Office: Mulgeum-eup Pusan Nat University Sch Korean Medicine 626-770 Yangsan Republic of Korea Business E-Mail: sicho@pusan.ac.kr.

CHO, SUNG WON, gastroenterologist; b. Seoul, Republic of Korea, Mar. 10, 1953; s. Kwan Rae Cho and Jung Aee Joo; m. Dan Yee Won, Oct. 26, 1984; children: Jung Il, Sang Yong. MD, Yonsei U., 1974—80, M in medicine, 1982—86; PhD, Soon Chun Hyang U., 1990—94. Diplomate Bd. Cert. Korean Assn. of Internal Medicine, 1984, Korean Med. Assn., 1980. Internship and residency Soon Chun Hyang U. Hosp., Seoul, Korea (South), 1980—84, assoc. prof., 1994—95; prof. of medicine Dept. of Gastroenterology, Ajou U. Sch. of Medicine, Suwon, Korea (South), 1995—2003; rsch. fellow Academic Dept. of Medicine, Royal Free Hosp., London, 1987—89. Vice dir. Ajou U. Hosp., Suwon, Korea (South), 2001—03; directorships Dept. of Gastroenterology, Ajou U. Hosp., Suwon, Korea (South), 1997—2003. Author: (book) Korean Assn. of Gastroenterology, Korean Assn. of Family Medicine. Recipient Best Article Publ., Korean Jour., Korean Assn. for the Study of the Liver, 2002, Best Oral Presentation, 2003, Best Article Publ., Internat. Jour., 2001; Genomic Rsch. Ctr. for Liver and Digestive Disease, The Ministry of Health and Welfare, 2001. Mem.: European Assn. for the Study of the Liver (corr.), Korean Assn. for the Study of the Liver (corr.), Korean Assn. of Gastroenterology (corr.), Korean Study Group of Hepatocellular (corr.). Office: Ajou Univ Hosp San 5 Wonchon-Dong 442-721 Suwon Republic of Korea Office Fax: 82-31-219-5999. E-mail: sung_woncho@hotmail.com.

CHO, SUNG-IL, medical educator, internist; b. Seoul, Republic of Korea, July 18, 1961; m. Ockjoo Kim. MD, Seoul U., 1986; DSc, Harvard Sch. Pub. Health, Boston, 1999. Assoc. prof. Seoul Nat. U. Sch. Pub. Health, 2001—; post doctoral rsch. fellow Harvard Sch. Pub. Health. Contbr. scientific papers. Home: Nowongu Junggyedong Hyundai Apt 101-504 Seoul 139-934 Republic of Korea Office: Seoul Nat Univ 28 Jongno-gu Yeongun-dong Seoul 110-460 Republic of Korea Business E-Mail: scho@snu.ac.kr.

CHO, WILLIAM CHI-SHING, medical research scientist; s. Mangkeung Cho and Chung-hing Ng. BS in Chinese Medicine, U. Hong Kong, BSc with honors; MPhil, PhD, degree, Chinese U. Hong Kong. Registered Chinese med. practitioner Chinese Medicine Coun. Hong Kong. Sci. officer clin. oncology Queen Elizabeth Hosp., Kowloon, Hong Kong; hon. fellow oncology Hong Kong Poly. U., Kowloon. Contbr. more than 120 med. jours., book, & med. jour. editor-in-chief, jour. reviewer (Renowned grant). Fellow: Hong Kong Soc. Molecular Diagnostic Sci., Inst. Biomedical Sci. UK; mem.: Hong Kong Inst. Med. Lab. Sci. Achievements include research in cancer biomarkers, oncoproteomics, pharmacology, integrative & Chinese medicine; patents for serum biomarkers in lung cancer. Office: 13/F Block R Dept Clin Oncology Queen Elizabeth Hosp 30 Gascoigne Rd Kowloon Hong Kong Office Fax: 852 2958 5455. Business E-Mail: chocs@ha.org.hk.

CHO, WON-TAK, orthodontist; b. Republic of Korea, May 8, 1968; DDS, Wonkwang U., 1992, MSD, 1995. Chief orthodontist Ye Dental Clinic, 1998—. Dir. Daejeon Ice-Hockey Assn., Republic of Korea. Recipient Pierre Fauchard award, Am. Biog. Inst., 2010, Best Korean award, Hankook Ilbo, 2011; named New Korean of the yr., SiSa-Today and Herald Media, 2011. Fellow: WFO; mem.: Korean Assn. Orthodontists (dir. info. & communication 2008—10), Am. Assn. Orthodontists (Internat.). Office: Gounson B/D 3F Ye Dental Clinic Seogu Daejeon 302830 Republic of Korea Office Fax: 82424882834. Business E-Mail: yedentist@gmail.com.

CHO, YONG PIL, education educator; b. Seoul, Republic of Korea, Feb. 8, 1964; s. Sung Dong Cho and Jong Soon Kim; m. Jeong Won Kim, Apr. 23, 1994; children: Hee Jung, Hee Jae. MD, Yonsei U., 1988; MS in Medicine, Ulsan U., 1999, PhD, 2004. Assoc. prof. U. Ulsan Med. Coll., Seoul, 2002—. Fellow, rsch. scientist divsn. cardiovascular rsch. lab. Caritas St. Elizabeth's Med. Ctr., Boston, 2006—. Contbr. scientific papers. Mem.: Korean Surg. Soc. (assoc.), Korean Soc. for Vascular Surgery (assoc.), Internat. Soc. for Vascular Surgery (assoc.). Office: Seoul Asan Hosp Dept of Surgery 388-1 Poongnap-dong Songpa-gu Seoul 138-736 Republic of Korea Office Fax: 82-2-474-9027. Business E-Mail: vascho@medigate.net.

CHO, YONGRAE, psychologist, educator; s. Hosoon Lee; m. Sugjae Lee, May 2, 1992; children: Hyunwoo, Hyunjoon. BA, Seoul Nat. U., 1986, MA, 1988, PhD, 1998. Lic. clin. psychologist Republic of Korea. Clin. psychology resident Seoul Nat. U. Hosp., 1990—93; full-time lectr. Chosun U., Gwangju, Republic of Korea, 1994—97, asst. prof., 1997—2001, assoc. prof., 2001—03; vis. scholar U. Tex., Austin, 2001—02; dir. Student Counseling Ctr. Hallym U., Chuncheon, Gangwon-do, Republic of Korea, 2003—05, assoc. prof., 2003—08, chair, dept. psych., 2005—06, prof., 2008—, dir., Gangwon-do Psychol. Support Ctr. for Disaster Victim, 2008—. Peer reviewer Internat. Jour. Dermotology, 2011—. Contbr. articles to profl. jours. 2d lt. South Korean Army, 1988—89. Recipient Rsch. Paper award, Med. Sch. Chosun U., 1999, Best Tchr. award, Chosun U., 2001, Ilsong Rsch. Paper award, 2005, Outstanding Scholar Award, Korean Psychol. Assn., 2007. Mem.: Korean Assn. Cognitive-Behavior Therapy (mem. ed. bd. 2001—, editor 2005—07), Korean Clin. Psychology Assn. (program chmn. 2002—03, mem. editl. bd. 2003—07, program chmn. 2004—05, mem. editl. bd. 2009—), Assn. Advancement Behavior Therapy, Korean Psychol. Assn. Office: Hallym University 39 Hallymdaehak Gil Gangwon 200 702 Republic of Korea Home: Misozium Apt 106-801 Gangwon 200-780 Republic of Korea Office Fax: 82332563424. Business E-Mail: yrcho@hallym.ac.kr.

CHO, YOON H., medical educator; b. Republic of Korea, Aug. 26, 1958; PhD, U. Bordeaux 1, 1992. Assoc. prof. U. Bordeaux 1, 1999—. Fellowship, Human Frontier Sci. Program, grant, Alzheimer's Assn. Mem.: Soc. Neurosci. Office: INCIA University Bordeaux 1 Ave Talence Aquitaine 33405 France Office Fax: 33540008743. Business E-Mail: y.cho@cnic.u-bordeaux1.fr.

CHO, YOUNG KEOL, medical educator, researcher; b. Youngyang, Republic of Korea; s. Kyungseok and Bunhyang Lee Cho; m. Myung Hi Kwon, Apr. 16, 1989; children: Kanginn, Sunghwan. MD, Hanyang U., Seoul, 1987, PhD, 1993. Prof. U. Ulsan Coll. Med., Seoul, 1993—. Pub. health physician Divsn. AIDS Korean NIH, 1990—93; vis. asst. prof. Harvard Med. Sch., 1997—98. Contbr. articles to profl. journals. Cons. Korean Anti-AIDS Fedn., Seoul, 1993—2002. Mem.: Korean Soc. Virology, Korean Soc. Ginseng, Internat. AIDS Soc., American Soc. Microbiology. Achievements include research in Korean red ginseng intake attenuates HIV-1 genes, resolution on the cause of HIV-1 outbreak among Korean hemophiliacs; patents for method of deleting nef gene in HIV-1 using red ginseng Australia. Avocations: jogging, mountain climbing. Office: Univ Ulsan Coll Medicine Dept Microbiology 388-1 Pungnap-dong Songpa-ku Seoul 138-040 Republic of Korea Home: 109-1202 SSangyong Apt Sungsoo-dong Sungdong Republic of Korea Home Phone: 82-054-683-3022; Office Phone: 82-2-3010-4283. Personal E-mail: ykcho2@amc.seoul.kr.

CHO, YOUNG-WUK, medical educator; b. Seoul, Republic of Korea, June 15, 1963; s. Neung-Hyun Cho and In-Ae Choi; m. Yeon-Soo Kim; children: Hyun-Jin, Hyun-Ree. MD, Kyung Hee U., Seoul, Republic of Korea, PhD, 1994. Cert. physician Ministry Health & Welfare, 1987. Head biomed. sci. inst. Kyung Hee U. Sch. Medicine, Seoul, 2004—, head brain, 2006—. Office: Kyung Hee Univ Sch Medicine Hoigi-dong Dongdaemoon-gu Seoul 130-701 Republic of Korea Office Fax: (82) 2 967 0534. Business E-Mail: ywcho@khu.ac.kr.

CHOAY, PATRICK HENRI, pharmaceutical executive; Nat. pharmacist diploma, U. Paris, 1969, DSc, 1973, PharmD, 1977. Rsch. asst. Centre Nat. de la Recherche Scientifique, Paris, 1969-75; gen. mgr. Laboratoire Choay, Paris, 1982-83; dir. rsch. Inst. Choay, Paris, 1975-84; pres. Lab. CCD, Paris, 1986—, Lab. Bailly, 1995—, Prodimed S.A.S., 1992—, Lab. Creat, 2001—, Lab. Bioes, 2003—, Lab. Gomenol, 2004. Lectr. biochemist and biophysics U. San Francisco, 1977; lectr. organic chemistry Worcester Found., Shrewsbury, Mass., 1975. Col. French Army Med. Corps. Recipient chevalier de l'Ordre Nat. de la Legion d'Honneur, 2004. Mem. French Nat. Pharm. Acad. Office: Patrick Choay SA 48 Rue des Petites Ecuries 75010 Paris France Business E-Mail: patrick@choay.com.

CHOBANIAN, ARAM, medical educator, cardiologist, former academic administrator; b. Pawtucket, RI, Aug. 10, 1929; s. Van and Marina (Arsenian) C.; m. Jasmine Goorigian, June 5, 1955; children: Karin, Lisa, Aram. BA, Brown U., Providence, 1951; MD, Harvard U., Cambridge, Mass., 1955; LHD (hon.), Boston U., 2006. Intern, resident U. Hosp., Boston, 1955-59, cardiovasc. rsch. fellow, 1959-62; asst. prof. Boston U. Sch. Medicine, 1964—70, prof., 1964—70; dean Sch. Medicine Boston U., 1988—2003, provost Med. Campus, 1996—2003, pres., 2003—05, pres. emeritus, 2005—; prof. Boston U. Sch. Medicine. Dir. Nat. Rsch. and Demonstration Ctr. in Hypertension, 1985-90; chmn. FDA Cardiovasc. and Renal Adv. Com., 1978-80, NIH Hypertension and Arteriosclerosis adv. com., 1977-78; chmn. Cardiovasc. Study Sect. B. NIH, 1982-84; chmn. Joint Nat. Com. on Hypertension, NIH, 1988, 2003; Sandoz lectr. Royal Coll. Physicians and Surgeons Can., 1989; mem. NIH Nat. Heart, Lung and Blood Adv. Coun., 1993-96; mem. bd. extramural advisers Nat. Heart, Lung and Blood Inst., 1999-2002. Author: Heart Risk Book, 1982; mem. editl. bd. New England Jour. Medicine, Hypertension, Jour. Hypertension, Jour. Vascular Biology, Hypertension Rsch., Cardiovasc. Pharmacology Postgraduate Medicine. Pres. Am. Heart Assn., Boston, 1974-75; bd. dirs. Armenian Culture Soc.; chmn. bd. trustees Wolfson Found., Fund for Armenian Relief, Mass. Tech. Collaborative, New England Healthcare Inst.; fellow trustee Armenian Assembly of Am. Capt. USAF, 1956-57. Recipient Cmty. Edn. and Disting. Svc. award Am. Heart Assn., Boston, 1975, 78, Eastman Kodak award Nat. Acad. Clin. Biochemistry, 1987, Abbott Lectr. Am. Soc. Hypertension, Lifetime Achivements award Mass. Med. Soc., 2008, Shattuck Lectr., 2009. Fellow ACP, Am. Acad. Arts and Scis.; mem. Am. Heart Assn. (chmn. coun. high blood pressure rsch. 1984-86, Corcoran lectr. 1989, award merit 1990, Modern Medicine award 1990, Lifetime Achievement award in hypertension Bristol-Myers Squibb), Nat. Heart, Lung and Blood Inst. (Freis award 1997), Ellis Island Medal of Honor, 2007, Am. Soc. Clin. Investigation, Assn. Am. Physicians, Am. Physiol. Soc., New England Cardiovasc. Soc. (pres. 1985-86), Mass. Med. Soc. (chmn. pub. com. 2003—09), Phi Beta Kappa, Sigma Xi, Alpha Omega Alpha. Home: 5 Rathburn Rd Natick MA 01760-1011 Office: Boston U 650 Albany St Boston MA 02118 Office Phone: 617-638-0300. Business E-Mail: achob@bu.edu.

CHODOROW, NANCY JULIA, psychoanalyst, educator; b. NYC, Jan. 20, 1944; d. Marvin and Leah (Turitz) C.; children: Rachel Esther Chodorow-Reich, Gabriel Isaac Chodorow-Reich. BA, Radcliffe Coll., 1966; PhD, Brandeis U., 1975; grad., San Francisco Psychoanalytic, 1993. Cert. in adult psychoanalysis Am. Psychoanalytic Assn., 1993. From lectr. to assoc. prof. U. Calif., Santa Cruz, 1974-86, from assoc. prof. sociology to prof. Berkeley, 1986—2005, clin. faculty dept. psychology, 1999—, prof. emeritus, 2005; tng. and supervising analyst Boston Psychoanalytic Inst., 2007—. Faculty San Francisco Ctr. Psychoanalysis; vis. prof. psychiatry Harvard Med. Sch., 2005-06, lectr. Psychiat., 2006-, geographic rule tng. & supervising analyst Pitts. Psychoanalytic Inst., 2009-. Author: The Reproduction of Mothering, 1978 (Jessie Bernard award Sociologists for Women in Soc. 1979, named one of Ten Most Influential Books of Past 25 Years, Contemporary Sociology 1996), 2nd edit., 1999, Feminism and Psychoanalytic Theory, 1989, Femininities, Masculinities, Sexualities, 1994, The Power of Feelings: Personal Meaning in Psychoanalysis, Gender, and Culture, 1999 (L. Bryce Boyer prize Soc. for Psychol. Anthropology 2000); contbr. articles to profl. jours. Fellow Russell Sage Found., NEH, Ctr. Advanced Study Behavioral Scis., ACLS, Guggenheim Found., Radcliffe Inst. for Advanced Study; recipient Contbn. to Women and Psychoanalysis award APA, L. Bryce Boyer prize Soc. for Psychol. Anthropology, 2000. Mem. Internat. Psychoanalytic Assn., Am. Psychoanalytic Assn.(plenary spkr., 2010), San Francisco Ctr. Psychoanalysis, Boston Psychoanalytic Inst., Office Phone: 617-354-1200.

CHOE, BYUNG-HO, pediatrician, educator; Prof. dept. pediat., assoc. dean curriculum Sch. Medicine Kyungpook Nat. U., Daegu, Republic of Korea, 2006—07; mgr. med. svc. support Kyungpook Nat. U. Hosp. Editor in chief Korean Jour. Pediat. Gastroenterology & Nutrition, 2009—; chair nutrition com. Korean Pediat. Soc., 2009—. Author: (chpt.) Transplantation of the Liver, 2d edit., 2005; contbr. articles to profl. jours. Achievements include research in evaluation of biliary atresia with mangafodipir trisodium-enhanced MR cholangiography. Business E-Mail: bhchoi@knu.ac.kr.

CHOE, EUN SANG, neuroscientist; b. Pusan, Republic of Korea, Dec. 2, 1962; s. Kum Jah Yu; m. Jeom Yee Hur, Oct. 20, 1990; children: Jong Gook, Jong Min David. BS in Biology, Pusan Nat. U., 1985, MS in Biology, 1987; PhD in Anatomy and Cell Biology, East Carolina U. Sch. Medicine, Greenville, NC, 2000. Postdoctoral assoc. MIT, Cambridge, 2000; rsch. assoc. U. Mo., Kansas City, 2001—02; asst. prof. Chosun U. Coll. Dentistry, Kwangju, 2002, Pusan Nat. U., 2002—06, assoc. prof., 2006—. Recipient Sigma Xi grant-in-aid of rsch. award, Scientific Rsch. Soc., 1999, Travel award, Am. Soc. Pharmacology and Exptl. Therapeutics, 2002. Mem.: Korean Soc. for Drug Abuse, Korean Soc. Brain and Neural Sci., Internat. Brain Rsch. Orgn., Soc. for Neuroscience. Achievements include research in drug addiction. Office: Pusan Nat Univ Divsn Biol Sci 30 Jangjeon-dong Kumjeong-gu Pusan 609-735 Republic of Korea Office Fax: 82-51-581-2962. Business E-Mail: eschoe@pusan.ac.kr.

CHOE, GHEEYOUNG, pathologist, educator; b. Seoul, Republic of Korea, Jan. 19, 1963; MD, Seoul Nat. U., 1996, PhD. Chair, dept. pathology Seoul Nat. U. Bundang Hosp., 2003—. Mem.: Korean Soc. Pathologists. Office: 166 Gumi-ro Bundang-gu Seongnam Gyeonggi 463-707 Republic of Korea Office Fax: 82-31-787-4012. Business E-Mail: gychoe@snu.ac.kr.

CHOE, JIN, obstetrician, gynecologist, biomedical researcher; m. Su-Jee Park, Dec. 5, 1992; children: Jong-Wook, Gewon. MD, Seoul Nat. U., 1988, MS, 1997, PhD, 1999. Lic. Republic of Korea, 1988, Obstetrics and Gynecology Specialist Republic of Korea, 1993. Intern Seoul Nat. U. Hosp., Republic of Korea, 1988—89, resident dept. obs. and gynecology, 1989—93, fellow maternal fetal medicine, 1996—97, fellow disvn. human genetics, 1997—98; captain Seoul Dist. Milt. Hosp., 1993—96; instr. Seoul Boraeme Municipal Hosp., 1998—2001; asst. prof. dept. obs. and gynecology Seoul Nat. U., 2000—01; v.p. Hamchoon Inst. Infertility and Genetics, Seoul, 2001—; vice dir. dept. prenatal diagnosis Hamchoon Women's Clinic, Seoul, 2001—. Peer reviewer Med. Sci. Monitor, NYC, 2006—. Capt. Republic of Korea armed forces, 1993—96. Recipient poster award, Korean Soc. Med. Genetics, 2006. Mem.: Internat. Soc. Ultrasound in Obstetrics and Gynecology, Internat Soc. Prenatal Diagnosis, Fetal Therapy, Internat. Down's Syndrome Screening Group, Korean Med. Assn., Korean Soc. Med. Genetics (mem. prenatal diagnosis com 2003—, mem. molecular genetics com. 2003—). Avocations: photography, golf. Office: Hamchoon Women's Clinic 1621-7 Seocho-1-dong Seocho-gu Seoul 137-878 Republic of Korea Office Fax: 919-684-5584. Personal E-mail: jchoemd@gmail.com. Business E-Mail: jchoe@hamchoon.com.

CHOE, JUNG-YOON, medical educator, director; b. Daegu, Republic of Korea, Oct. 22, 1960; s. Hong-Doo Choe and Myung-Won Park; m. Joo-Hee Huh Choe, Feb. 15, 1987; children: Joon-Hyeok, Youngeun, Jae-Hyeok. MD, 1985; PhD, Keimyung U., Daegu, 1994. Cert. Bd. Internal Medicine, 1989, Sub-splty. Bd. Rheumatology, 1998. Prof. Cath. U. Daegu Sch. Medicine, 1994—; vis. scholar U. Calif. San Diego, 2002—03. Dir., pub. rels. Korean Rheumatism Assn., Seoul, Republic of Korea, 2006—. Named Best Clin. Scientist, Daegu Med. Assn., 2006. Office: Cath Univ Daegu 3056-6 Daemyung 4-Dong Namgu 705-718 Daegu Daegu Republic of Korea Office Phone: 82-53-650-4577. Business E-Mail: jychoe@cu.ac.kr.

CHOE, KYLE SEUNG, facial plastic surgeon; s. Jung B. and Sung W. Choe; m. Hee C. Yoo, Dec. 21, 1996; children: Caleb, Grace, Samuel. BA, Occidental Coll., 1994; MD, U. Rochester, 1998. Diplomate Am. Bd. Otolaryngology, 2004. Resident NY Eye & Ear Infirmary, NYC, 1999—2003; fellow facial plastic surgery U. Rochester, NY, 2003—04; pvt. practice Virginia Beach, 2004—. Contbr. articles to profl. jours. Mem.: AMA, Am. Acad. Otolaryngology (Humanitarian Efforts Travel award 2003), Am. Acad. Facial Plastic Surgery (Ben Shuster Meml. award 2004). Avocations: reading, tennis. Office: 4400 Corporation Ln 102 Virginia Beach VA 23462 Office Phone: 757-309-5050.

CHOE, YEON HYEON, medical educator; s. Dong Lim Choe and Ok Soon Ban; m. Mi Kyung Chun, May 13, 1983; children: Joo Young, Joo Ae. MD, Seoul Nat. U., Republic Of Korea, 1983, PhD. Chief radiologist Sejong Gen. Hosp., Pucheon, Kyunggi-do, Republic of Korea, 1990—93; prof. Sungkyunkwan U. Sch. Medicine, Seoul, 1994—, Dir. MRI Samsung Med. Ctr., Seoul, 2003—. Leader One Family Med. Svc., Seoul, 2003—06. Recipient Berlex Best Poster award, North Am. Soc. Cardiovasc. Imaging, 2003, 2007. Office: Samsung Med Ctr Sungkyunkwan Univ 50 Ilwon-dong Gangnam-gu Seoul 135-710 Republic of Korea Office Fax: 82-2-3410-2559. Business E-Mail: yhchoe@skku.edu.

CHOEN, SEOW, surgeon; Grad., Nat. U., Singapore, 1981. With St. Marks' Hosp., London, 1989; surgeon Seow-Choen Colorectal Centre Pte Ltd., Singapore. W Wallace green lectr. St. Luke's Hosp. Found., Kans., 1994; with editl. bd. Diseases of the Colon and Rectum, United States, Colorectal Disease (European), Brit. Jour. Surgery, England, Jour. Coloproctology (Indian), Digestive Surgery, Germany; co editor Techniques in Coloproctology; pres. Asian Fedn. Coloproctology, 2005—07, Soc. Colorectal Surgeons, Singapore, 2005—07. Contbr. chapters to books pub. 33 chpts. in surg. textbooks, more than 253 original articles in peer reviewed surg. jours. Recipient 1st Am. Soc. of Colon and Rectum Surgeons Internat. Travelling Fellowship, 1993, Excellence for Singapore award, 2000. Mem.: Eurasian (Europian-Asian) Colorectal Tech. Assn. (pres.), Israel Soc. of Colon and Rectal Surgeons (mem. of honor 2008), Royal Australasian Coll. of Surgeons (hon. mem. section colon and rectal surg. 1999), Colorectal Surg. Soc. Australia (hon. life mem. 1999). Achievements include establishing the first colorectal surgery department in Asia which offered patients the latest surgical techniques at the Singapore General Hospital; 1st Asian to be invited as the ESR Hughes Lecturer for the Royal Australian College of Surgeons, 1999; 1st Asian to be the Rupert B Turnbull Memorial Lecturer for the Cleveland Clinic, Ohio, USA, 2004; 1st Asian to be invited as the Philip Gordon lecturer for the Canadian Colorectal Society, 2005. Office: Seow-Choen Colorectal Centre Pte Limited Mt Elizabeth Medical Centre 3 Mt Elizabeth Number 03-09 228510 Singapore Office Phone: 6567386887. Office Fax: 6567383448. *

CHOI, BYUNG HYUNE, medical educator; b. Busan, Republic of Korea, Mar. 12, 1969; PhD in Molecular Biology, Seoul Nat. U., 1999. Rsch. fellow Harvard Med. Sch., 2000—01; asst. prof. Inha U. Coll. Medicine, 2008—. Editor Korean Tissue Engring. and Regenerative Medicine Soc., 2008. Office: 7-206 Sinheung-dong Jung-gu Incheon 400-712 Republic of Korea Personal E-mail: bhchoi0312@hanmail.net.

CHOI, BYUNG-WAN, surgeon, educator; b. Jeon-ju, Republic of Korea, Oct. 13, 1974; MD, Chonbuk Nat. U. Med. Sch., 1999, M in Med. Sci., 2003. Divsn. spine, dept. orthop. surgery Gwangju Veterans Hosp., 2008—10; asst. prof., dept. orthop. surgery Inje U., Haeundae Paik Hosp., 2011—. Adj. prof. Chosun U., 2008, Chonbuk Nat. U., 2009. Mem.: North Am. Spine Soc., Korean Soc. Spine Surgery. Avocation: reading. Office: 1435 Jwa-dong Haeundae-gu Busan 612-030 Republic of Korea Office Fax: 82-51-797-0249. Business E-Mail: alla1013@naver.com.

CHOI, CHANGJIN, medical educator; b. Seoul, Jan. 24, 1967; PhD, Cath. U. Korea, 2001. Adj. prof. med. edn. Cath. U. Korea, 2010—11, assoc. prof. family medicine, 2011—. Mem. edn. com. Korean Soc. Med. Edn., 2010—11. Mem.: Korean Acad. Family Medicine. Avocations: jogging, reading. Office: # 505 Banpo-dong Seocho-Gu Seoul 137-701 Republic of Korea Business E-Mail: fmchcj@catholic.ac.kr.

CHOI, EUNG HO, dermatologist, educator; b. Seoul, Republic of Korea, Mar. 23, 1963; MD, PhD, Yonsei U., 1988. Resident and intern, dept. dermatology Yonsei U. Wonju Coll. Medicine, 1988—92, assoc. prof., asst. prof., instr., dept. dermatology, 1995—2005, head prof., dept. dermatology, 2006—11, prof., dept. dermatology, 2007—; vis. scientist, dept. dermatology U. Calif. San Francisco, Calif., 2003—05. Bd. dirs. Korean Soc. Skin Barrier Rsch., 2006—08, v.p., 2010; gen. dir. Pan Asian Pacific Skin Barrier Rsch. Soc., 2010; chief Basic Med. Rsch. Inst. Yonsei U. Wonju Coll. Medicine, 2010—11. Recipient Inbong Rsch. award, Korean Dermatology Assn., 1998, Best Rsch. Prof. award, Yonsei U. Wonju Coll. Medicine, 2008, 2010. Mem.: Korean Soc. Skin Barrier Rsch., Soc. Investigative Dermatology, Korean Soc. Investigative Dermatology, Korean Atopic Dermatitis Assn., Korean Dermatologic Assn. Avocations: hiking, travel. Office: 162 Ilsan-dong Wonju Kangwon-do 220-701 Republic of Korea Office Fax: 82-33-7482650. Business E-Mail: choieh@yonsei.ac.kr.

CHOI, GUN, neurosurgeon; b. Seoul, Feb. 3, 1960; s. Dogi and Chunhak (Kim) Choi; m. Sunmee Kim, Oct. 6, 1990. BS in Medicine, Hanyang U., Seoul, 1993, MA, 1998, PhD in Neurosurgery, 2002. Dir. neurosurgery Yangpyung Ctrl. Hosp., Republic of Korea, 1993—95, Anyang Ctrl. Hosp., Republic of Korea, 1995—97, Jeju Ctrl. Hosp., Republic of Korea, 1997—99, Wooridul Spine Hosp., Seoul, 1999—2004, v.p. med. affairs, 2004—06, pres. med. affairs, 2006—. Invited asst. prof. Hanyang U., Seoul, 2007—; lectr. in field; pres. Wooridul Internat. Spine Hosp., pres., Non Invasive Spine Ctr.; program chair World Congress Minimally Invasive Spine Surgery & Tech., 2008, course dir., 08. Contbr. articles to profl. jours. With Korean Army, 1982—83. Recipient Most Valuable Presentation award, Wooridul Spine Found., Seoul, 2002, Best Innovative Med. Technique, 2003, Best Presentation award, 2006, Best Oral Presentation award, Internat. Intradiscal Therapy Soc., Albi, France, 2007; fellow, Bd. of Minimally Invasive Spinal Surgery, 2002. Mem.: Internat. Musculoskeletal Laser Soc., Royal Coll. Physicians and Surgeons, Internat. Soc. Minimally Invasive Spinal Surgery, Korean Soc. Minimally Invasive Spinal Surgery (exec. dir. 2007—). Achievements include development of a new surgical technique. Avocation: golf. Office: Wooridul Spine Hosp 47-4 Chungdam-dong Gangnam-gu Seoul 135-100 Republic of Korea Office Phone: 82 2-513-8000. Office Fax: 82 2-513-8146. Personal E-mail: spine.choi@gmail.com. Business E-Mail: choigun@wooridul.co.kr.

CHOI, GYU-SEOG, medical educator; b. Gumi, Gyeongsangbugdo, Republic of Korea, May 1, 1963; s. Jai Il Choi and Bong Dan Park; m. Youn Ju Jeong; children: Yun Young, Min Chang. PhD, Kyungpook Nat. U., Daegu, Republic of Korea, 2000. Cert. Bd. Surgery, Korean Surg. Soc., 1992. Surg. resident Dept. Surgery, Sch. Medicine, Kyungpook Nat. U., Daegu, 1988—92, asst. prof., 1998—2002, assoc. prof., 2002—07, prof., 2007—; vis. prof. Cancer Rsch. UK, Oxford, England, 2000—02. Dir. Knuh Robotic and Mis Tng. & Rsch. Ctr., Daegu, 2002—08. Contbr. articles to profl. surg. jours. Lt.-capt. Korean Army, 1992—95. Fellow: Korean Coloproctology Soc. Achievements include research in more than 1200 laparoscopic colorectal cancer surgery, a novel approach of colorectal cancer surgery by robotics. Office: Kyungpook Nat Univ Hosp Samduk 2ga Jung-Gu 50 700-721 Daegu Daegu Republic of Korea Office Fax: 82-421-0510. Business E-Mail: kyuschoi@mail.knu.ac.kr.

CHOI, HAN YONG, hospital administrator, urologist, educator; b. Seoul, South Korea, Aug. 21, 1952; s. Du Jin Choi and Bong Lim Lee; m. Hyun Sook Kim, Nov. 18, 1978; children: Jiwoong, Youngwoong. MD, Seoul Nat. U., 1977, PhD in Microbiology, 1991. Intern, resident urology Seoul Nat. U. Hosp., 1977—82; fellow urology Duke U. Med. Ctr., Durham, NC, 1992—94; urology staff Samsung Med. Ctr., Seoul, 1994—, chief urology, 1999—2005, exec. dir., 2003—04, v.p. clin. svc., 2004—08, pres., 2008—. Prof. urology Sungkyunkwan U. Sch. Medicine, Seoul, 1997—. Contbr. articles to profl. jours. Mem.: Korean Urol. Oncology Soc., Urol. Assn. Asia, European Assn. Urology, Korean Urol. Assn., American Urol. Assn. Office: Samsung Med Ctr Dept Urology 50 Il-Won Dong Kang-Nam Ku Seoul 135-710 Republic of Korea Office Phone: 82-2-3410-3551. Office Fax: 82-2-3410-3883. Business E-Mail: hychoi@smc.samsung.co.kr. *

CHOI, HO-SUN, medical educator; b. Gwangju, Republic of Korea, Nov. 3, 1949; s. Gaebang Choi and Yangsoon Shin; m. Heesook Shin, Nov. 13, 1977; children: Munyeong, Jaeyeong. MD, Chonnam Nat. U. Med. Sch., Gwangju, 1974; PhD, Chonnbuk Nat. U., Junju, Republic of Korea, 1985. Diplomate Ministry Health, 1974. Prof. Chonnam Nat. U. Med. Sch., Republic of Korea, 1982—, chmn., ob-gyn., 2001—04; dir. Clin. Rsch. Chonnam U. Hosp., 1999—2000. Author: significance of human papillomavirus genotyping with high-grade cervical intraepithelial neoplasia treated by a loop electrosurgical exicion procedure, 2010; contbr. articles to profl. jours. Maj. Mil., 1980—81, Gwangju. Recipient Best Poster awards, European Soc. Gynecologic Cancer, 2005. Mem.: Korean Soc. Ob-Gyn., Seoul (planning com. 2001—04), Am. Cervical Colposcopy and Cervical Pathology, Korean Soc. Gynecologic Oncology and Colposcopy (info. and comm. com. 2005—07, vice chmn. 2008), Korean Cancer Assn., Internat. Gynecologic Cancer Soc. Achievements include research in photodynamic therapy of choriocarcinoma transplanted to the hamster cheek pouch; detection of HPV genotypes in cervical lesions by the HPV DNA chip and sequencing; human papillomavirus genotyping by HPV DNA chip in cervical cancer and precancerous lesions; a comparison of modified Monoprep2 of liquid-based cytology with ThinPrep Pap test; transvaginal evisceration after radical abdominal hysterectomy; pelvic aspergillosis with tubo-ovarian abscess in a renal transplant recipient; postoperative pelvic lymphocele, treatment with simple percutaneous catheter drainage; survival rate and prognostic factors in patients with stage IB and IIA cervical cancer treated by radical hysterectomy and pelvic lymphnode dissection; significance of human papillomavirus genotyping with high grade cervical intraepithelial neoplastia treated by a loop electrosurgical excision procedure; human papillomavirus L1 capsid protein and human papillomavirus type 16 as prognostic markers in cervical intraepithelial neoplasia 1. Office: Chonnam University Hosp Dept Ob-Gyn 671 Jebong Ro Donggu Gwangju 501 757 Republic of Korea Business E-Mail: hschoi@jnu.ac.kr.

CHOI, HWANG, urologist, educator; b. Seoul, June 16, 1945; s. Jae Wee Choi and Keum Sun Kim; m. Jung Eun Kim, Aug. 13, 1948; children: Won Joon, Won Sik. MD, PhD, Seoul Nat. U., 1974. Chief dept. urology Seoul Nat. U. Hosp., 1996—2001; dir. Seoul Nat. U. Children's Hosp., 2001—05. Contbr. articles to profl. jours. Pres. Safe Kids Korea, Seoul, 2003—06. Mem.: Korean Urol. Assn. (pres. 2002—04). Office: Seoul Nat Univ Hosp 28 Yeongeon-dong Jongno-gu Seoul 110-744 Republic of Korea Office Fax: 82-2-742-4665. Business E-Mail: hchoi@snu.ac.kr.

CHOI, HYOUNG T, science educator; s. Dooshik Choi and Woonyong Yang; m. Moon Y. Kim, July 24, 1982; children: Yoonjae, Jongjae. PhD, U. Calif., Santa Barbara, 1987. Postdoc. fellow Scripps Clinic & Rsch. Found., San Diego, 1987—88; prof. Kangwon Nat. U., Chunchon, 1988—. Staff., rsch. & devel. Pacific Ctrl. Rsch. Inst., Suwon, Republic of Korea, 1976—81. Cons. Korea Forest Rsch. Inst., Seoul, 2005. Grantee, Korea Rsch. Found., Korea Scis. & Engring. Found., 1990—. Mem.: Microbiological Soc. Korea. Avocations: basketball, walking. Office: Kangwon Nat Univ Hyoja 2-dong Chunchon Gangwondo 200-701 Republic of Korea Office Fax: 82-33-242-0459. Business E-Mail: htchoi@kangwon.ac.kr.

CHOI, IHN-GEUN, psychiatrist, educator; b. Whaseong, Gyeonggido, Republic of Korea, June 16, 1954; s. Young Gu Choi and Myo Sik Hong; m. Mi Ok Kim, Feb. 22, 1981; children: Shou Ran, Kwang Who. MD, Seoul Nat. U. Coll. Medicine, 1981; MS, Seoul Nat. U. Grad. Sch., 1985, PhD, 1992. Instr. dept. neuropsychiatry Hallym U. Coll. Medicine, Seoul, 1989—91, asst. prof. dept. neuropsychiatry, 1991—95, assoc. prof. dept. neuropsychiatry, 1995—2000, prof. dept. neuropsychiatry, 2000—06. Editor-in-chief: Korean Jour. Biol. Psychiatry; contbr. articles to profl. jours. Capt. Korean Army, 1985—88. Fellow, Vanderbilt U. Med. Ctr., Nashville, 1995—96. Mem.: Korean Acad. Addiction Psychiatry (v.p.), Korean Soc. Biol. Psychiatry (v.p.), Korean Psychoanalytic Soc., Korean Neuropsychiatric Assn. (Whanin Psychiat. award 2005), Internat. Psychoanalytical Assn., World Fedn. Socs. Biol. Psychiatry, Internat. Soc. Biomedical Rsch. Alcoholism. Achievements include research in The genetic characteristics of alcohol metabolism in type I alcoholism fall between nonalcoholism and type II alcoholism. The genetic effects of ADH2B-C come from the ADH1B*47Arg/*47Arg genotype. Avocations: golf, skiing. Home: Acroriver 101-601 752-36 Bangbaebondong Seoul 137-826 Republic of Korea Office: Hangang Sacred Heart Hosp 94-200 Youndungpodong Youngdungpogu Seoul 150-719 Republic of Korea Office Fax: 82-2-2677-9095. Personal E-mail: ihngeun@nate.com. Business E-Mail: ihngeun@hallym.or.kr.

CHOI, IN-HO, life science educator; b. Daegu, Korea, Dec. 30, 1957; s. Jong-Rok Choi and Malcho Yoon; m. Kyoungsook Park; 1 child. BS, Yonsei U., Seoul, Korea, 1981; MA, Ind. State U., 1985, PhD, 1989. Postdoctoral rschr. U. Pa., Phila., 1989-91; asst. prof. Yonsei U., Wonju, Korea, 1991-94, assoc. prof., 1994-99, prof., 1999—. Vis. scientist Smithsonian Tropical Rsch. Inst., Panama City, Panama, 1997-98; cons. Daewoo Found., Seoul, 1992. Contbr. articles to profl. jours. Rsch. grantee Ind. Acad. Sci., Indpls., 1988, Korea Sci. and Engring. Found., Seoul, 1994-96, Internat. Rsch. Exch. Program, Korea Rsch. Found., 1996-98. Mem. Korean Assn. Biol. Sci., Soc. Comparative and Integrative Biology, Japanese Soc. Biol. Sci. in Space. Avocations: collecting shells, photography, poetry, movies, travel. Office: Yonsei U Dept Life Sci 234 Maeji Ri Heungup-Myon Wonju, Kangwon-Do 222-710 Republic of Korea

CHOI, IN HO, orthopaedic surgeon, educator; s. Cheol-Won Choi and Chan-Ok Heo; m. Hyeong-Seon Choi, Apr. 21, 1979; children: Yoon-Jung, Yoon-Hyeong, Yoon-Hyo. MD, Seoul Nat. U., 1976, PhD, 1986. Lectr. orthop. surgery Seoul Nat. U. Hosp., Republic of Korea, 1984—87, asst. prof. orthop. surgery, 1987—92, assoc. prof. orthop. surgery, 1992—98; fellow orthop. surgery Alfred I. DuPont Inst., Del., 1987—89; prof. Seoul Nat. U. Children's Hosp., 1984—; prof., chmn. orthop. surgery Seoul Nat. U. Hosp., 2000—04. Dir. Korean Human Tech. and Rsch. Found., Seoul, 1998—2000. Capt. Army, 1981—84, Seoul. Recipient Russell S. Hibbs award, Scoliosis Rsch. Soc., 1988. Mem.: Pediatric Orthopaedic Soc. N.Am. (corr. Sherman S. Coleman award 1994), Internat. Pediatric Orthopaedic Think Tank (life), Korean Orthopaedic Assn. (life; dir. bd. exam com. 2002—05). Achievements include patents for development of skeletal external fixator. Office: Seoul Nat Univ Hosp 28 Yongon-dong Chongno-gu Seoul 110-744 Republic of Korea Office Fax: 82-2-745-3367. E-mail: inhoc@snu.ac.kr.

CHOI, JAEWAN, ophthalmologist, educator; s. Soon Choi and Soon Sung Lee; m. Sun Young Park, Jan. 20, 1976. MD, Seoul Nat. U., 2000; MS, U. Ulsan, Republic of Korea, 2005. Diplomate Korean Bd. Ophthalmology 2005. Resident Asan Med. Ctr., Seoul, 2001—05, clin. instr., 2005—. Contbr. articles to profl. jours. Mem.: Korean Soc. Ophthalmology (licentiate Grand prize in film festival 2003, Grantee for overseas tng. 2006), Korean Glaucoma Soc. (life), Assn. Rsch. in Vision and Ophthalmology (life). Home: Megatrium102-1102 Hangangro Yongsan-gu Seoul 140-753 Republic of Korea Office: Asan Medical Center 388-1 Pungnap-2-dong Songpa-gu Seoul 138-736 Republic of Korea Office Fax: 82-2-470-6440; Home Fax: 82-2-470-6440. Business E-Mail: deskshot@naver.com.

CHOI, JIN YOUNG, dental educator; b. Daegu, Republic of Korea, Feb. 11, 1961; Dr.med., George August U. Goettingen, 1998. Prof., dept. oral & maxillofacial surgery Sch. Dentistry Seoul Nat. U., 1998—. Office: 275-1 Yeongeon-dong Seoul Jongno-gu 110-768 Republic of Korea Office Fax: 82-2-766-4948. Business E-Mail: jinychoi@snu.ac.kr.

CHOI, JINHO, oral and maxillofacial surgeon; b. Seoul, Republic of Korea, Nov. 30, 1964; s. Daesup Choi and Chan-Rye Chung; m. Soyoung Lee, Oct. 15, 1996; children: Wonjun, Jiwon. PhD, Yonsei U., Seoul, 1997. Lic. DDS Korea Health & Welfare Orgn., 1989. Asst. prof. Med. Coll., Inha U., Inchon, Republic of Korea, 1996—, chmn. dept. denistry, 2002—. Contbr. articles to profl. jours. Home: 264-246 Imun 2-Dong Dongdaemun-Gu Seoul 130-829 Republic of Korea Office Fax: 82-32-890-2475. Personal E-mail: jinochoi98@yahoo.com. E-mail: jinho98@inha.ac.kr.

CHOI, JIN-HUGH, dental educator; b. Hampyung, Jeonnam, Republic of Korea, Feb. 20, 1964; DDS, MS, Chonnam Nat. U., PhD, 1988. Lectr. Coll. Medicine, Soonchunhyang U., Chung, 1998—2000; asst. prof. Coll. Medicine, Pochon CHA U., 2000, Coll. Medicine, Chung-Ang U., 2006—10. Fellow: World Fedn. Othodontists; mem.: Korean Assn. Orthodontists, Am. Assn. Orthodontists. Avocations:

reading, movies. Office: # 936-31 Daechi-dong Gangnam-gu Seoul 135-998 Republic of Korea Business E-Mail: profchoi@cau.ac.kr.

CHOI, JIN-HYUK, oncologist, educator; s. Sil Ja Lee; m. Min Jeong Oh, May 4, 1992; children: June Ho, Hyo Sun. MD, Yonsei U., Seoul, Korea, 1988, MS in Medicine, 1991, PhD, 1996. Cert. dr. medicine Korean Govt., 1988, specialist Korean Assn. Internal Medicine, 1992, in hematology-oncology Korean Assn. Internal Medicine, 1996. Rotating intern Yonsei U. Med. Ctr., Seoul, 1988—89, resident internal medicine, 1989—92; rsch. instr. Yonsei Cancer Ctr., Seoul, 1992—93; instr. Ewha Womans U. Coll. Medicine, Seoul, 1993—96, asst. prof., 1993—96, Ajou U. Sch. Medicine, Suwon, Republic of Korea, 1996—2007, assoc. prof., 1996—2007, prof., 2007—, chmn., dept. hematology oncology, 2006—. Contbr. scientific papers. Recipient Roche Tumor award, 2002, SK award, 2003, ESMO Travel award, 2004. Mem.: European Soc. Med. Oncology, Am. Soc. Clin. Oncology, Am. Assn. Cancer Rsch. Office: Ajou Univ Sch Medicine San 5 Wonchon-dong Suwon Gyeonggi-do 443-721 Republic of Korea Office Fax: 82-31-219-5983. Business E-Mail: jhchoimd@ajou.ac.kr.

CHOI, JOHN U., periodontist, educator; b. Seoul, Korea (South), Apr. 1, 1962; s. Chin Hang and Young Ja Choi; m. Hijae Kim; children: Christine A, Ashley J. DDS, U. So. Calif., 1990, PhD, 2001. Periodontist U. of So. Calif., 1994. Rsch. instr. U. So. Calif., Los Angeles, 1990—96; post-doctoral fellow Nat. Institutes of Health U. So. Calif., 1990—96; peridontist Pvt. practice, Fullerton, Calif., 1996—. Recipient Periodontology Award, U. of So. Calif., 1990; grantee Rsch. Grant, NIH, 1991-1996; fellow Craniofacial Biology Grant, Nat. Institutes of Health U. So. Calif., 1990-1991; scholar Dentist Scientist Award, NIH, 1991-1996. Mem.: ADA, Orange County Dental Soc., Calif. Dental Assn., Am. Acad. Periodontology, Sigma Xi. Office: 301 W Bastanchury Rd Suite 255 Fullerton CA 92835 Office Fax: 714-449-8653. Business E-Mail: jcperio@aol.com.

CHOI, JOON HYUK, medical educator; b. Daegu, Republic Of Korea, Aug. 21, 1963; s. Doo Man Choi and Jeong Soon Gu; m. Jeong Ryae Jeon, June 10, 1989; children: Yeong A., Yeong Eun. MD, Yeungnam U., Daegu, 1987; MS, Yeungnam U., 1990, PhD in Medicine, 1993. Cert. Korean Soc. Pathologist, 1991. Internship Yeungnam U. Hosp., 1987—88, resident in pathology, 1988—91, Andong Sung So Hosp., 1991—92; rsch. fellow Yeungnam U. Coll. Medicine, Daegu, Republic of Korea, 1992—93, instr. pathology, 1996—98, asst. prof. pathology, 1998—2002, assoc. prof. pathology, 2002—07, prof. pathology, 2008—. Vis. clinician Mayo Clinic, Rochester, Minn., 2000—01; vis. asst. prof. Mt. Sinai Hosp., NYC, 2001; rsch. fellow Brigham and Women's Hosp., Boston, 2001. Co-author: Textbook of Pathology, 2007, Essential Pathology, 2008. Physician Korean Army, 1993—96. Home: Sang-dong Suseong-Gu Daegu 706-775 Republic of Korea also: 102-1602 Chung-wha Apt Sang-dong Daegu 706-775 Republic of Korea Office: Yeungnam Univ Coll Medicine 317-1 Daemyung-Dong Nam-Gu 705-717 Daegu Daegu Republic of Korea Home Phone: 82 53 219 1113; Office Phone: 82 53 620 3335. Office Fax: 82 53 656 1429. Business E-Mail: joonhyukchoi@ynu.ac.kr.

CHOI, JOON YONG, plastic surgeon; Grad., Seoul Nat. U. Med. Coll. Bd. cert. tng. plastic surgery dept. samsung med. ctr. Samsung Seoul Hosp.; adv. dr. plastic surgery dept. Samsung Med. Ctr.; chief dir. Dream Aesthetic Medicine Breast and Figure Rsch. Ctr.; chmn. plastic surgery dept. Cath. Med. Ctr.; dir. Dream Plastic Surgery Clinic. Mem.: Internat. Confederation Plastic reconstructive and Aesthetic Surgery, Korean Cleft-Palate-Craniofacial Assn., Korean Microsurgical Soc., Korean Soc. Reconstructive Hand Surgery, Korean Med. Assn., Korean Soc. Aesthetic Plastic Surgery, Korean Soc. Plastic and Reconstructive Surgeons. Office: Dream Plastic Surgery Clinic Apkujung Subway Sta Apkujung Subway Sta Seoul Republic of Korea Office Phone: 8225461616. Office Fax: 8225461614. *

CHOI, KEE-JOON, medical educator; b. Seoul, Republic of Korea, Oct. 4, 1962; s. Myung-Ja Han; m. La-Gyung Moon, Aug. 15, 1991; children: Yoon-Hee, Yoon-Sun. MD, Korean Med. Assn., 1987; PhD, Seoul Nat. U., Republic of Korea, 2000. Assoc. prof. Asan Med. Ctr., Ulsan U., Seoul, 2003—08, prof., 2008—. Contbr. articles to profl. publs. and jours. Capt. Capital Armed Forces Gen. Hosp., 1993—94, Seoul. Home: 127-404 Olympic Apt Oryun-dong Seoul Songpa-Gu 138-786 Republic of Korea Office: Ulsan Univ Asan Med Ctr 388-1 Poongnap-dong Songpa-gu Seoul 138-736 Republic of Korea Office Fax: 82-2-486-5918. Business E-Mail: kjchoi@amc.seoul.kr.

CHOI, KI CHOON, medical researcher, educator; b. Hwasoon, Chunlanamdo, Republic of Korea, Sept. 13, 1965; s. Won Duk Choi and Gwi Rae Jung; m. Choi Ki Choon, Dec. 10, 1994; children: Gee Woo, Woon Hyuck. PhD, Gifu U., Japan, 2004. Cert. animal inseminor Ministry Agr., 1991. Rsch. prof. Coll. Medicine, Seoul, Republic of Korea, 2005—; instr. Seojung Coll., Yang ju, Kyunggido, Republic of Korea, 2008—. Editl. staff Korean Soc. Grassland & Forage Sci., Cheonan, Kyunggi, 2000—. Pvt. first class Korean Army, 1990, Kwanhju. Grant, Ministry Agr., 2008. Mem.: Nat. Inst. Animal Sci. (seonghwan 2009—). Achievements include research in nanoparticle & cancer. Office: Nat Inst Animal Sci Seonghwan-Eup Cheonan Republic of Korea Home: Seonghwan-Eup 330-801 Cheonan Chungnam Republic of Korea Office Fax: 82-41-580-6779; Home Fax: 82-41-580-6779. Personal E-mail: choiwh@rda.go.kr. Business E-Mail: choiwh@korea.kr.

CHOI, KYOUNG HYO, medical educator; b. Taegu, Republic Of Korea, May 12, 1965; s. Yong Hak Choi and Soon Jo Shin; m. Jeong Hye Hwang, Sept. 12, 1996; children: Bum Joon, Do Yeon. MD, Seoul Nat. U., 1989, MS in Medicine, 1999; PhD, Korea U., Seoul, 2004. Diplomate Korea (South), 1989, Korean Bd. of Rehab. Medicine, 1997, Korean Soc. of Sports Medicine, 2007. Intern Seoul Nat. U. Hosp., 1992—93, resident, 1993—97; asst. prof. U. Ulsan Coll. Medicine, Seoul, 2001—05, assoc. prof., 2005—10, prof., 2010—. Vis. scholar U. NC Hosp., Chapel Hill, 2004—05. Author: (books) Swallowing Disorder: Rehabilitation Medicine, 2002, Pressure Ulcer: Rehabilitation Medicine, 2002, Swallowing and Nutrition: Pediatric Rehabilitation, 2006, Chronic Pain: Rehabilitation Medicine, 2008, Orthosis: Rehabilitation Medicine, 2008; translator: Myofascial Pain and Dysfunction, 2003, A System of Orthopedic Medicine, 2008, Easy Injections, 2009; contbr. chapters to books. Dir. Pub. Health Ctr., Ansung, 1989—92. Recipient Pres. Citation award, Am. Acad. Phys. Medicine and Rehab., 2002, Ernest W. Johnsond Excellence in Rsch. Writing award, Assn. Academic Physiatrists, 2005, Pres. Citation award, Asan Med. Ctr., 2006. Mem.: Korean Assn. Sports Medicine (licentiate), Korean Acad. Rehab. Medicine (licentiate), Korean Soc. Pediatric Rehab. Medicine (corr.), Internat. Soc. Phys. and Rehab. Medicine (corr.), Korean Assn. Pain Medicine (corr.), Korean Stroke Soc. (corr.), Korean Med. Assn. (life). Achievements include invention of treatment system for dysphagia; research in dysphagia and stem cells. Avocations: travel, golf. Home: 104-503 Samsung Apt Daechi-dong Kangnam Seoul 135-968 Republic of Korea Office: Asan Med Ctr 388-1 Poongnap-dong Songpa-gu Seoul 138-736 Republic of Korea Office Phone: 82 2 3010 3800. Office Fax: 82 2 3010 6853.

CHOI, KYUNG UN, pathologist; b. Busan, Republic of Korea, June 19, 1971; d. Soo Kyeung Kim; m. Sang Hwa Jin, Apr. 7, 2001; 1 child, Hee Choi Jin. MD, Pusan Nat. U., Korea, 2003. Cert. pathologist Korea, 2002. Intern, resident and fellow dept. pathology Pusan Nat. U., 1996—2002, instr., 2003—05, asst. prof., 2005—. Exhibitor European Congress of Pathology. Contbr. articles to profl. jours. Recipient Basic Medicine award, Korean Jour. Pathology. Mem.: Korean Soc. Pathologists (life). Office: Pusan Nat Univ Hosp 1-Ga Ami-dong Seo-gu Busan 602-739 Republic of Korea Office Fax: 82-52-242-7422. Business E-Mail: kuchoi@pusan.ac.kr.

CHOI, MOON SEOK, medical educator; b. Seoul, Republic Of Korea, Dec. 25, 1965; s. Seok Won Choi and Jae Soo Kim; m. Yeun Hong, Oct. 10, 1991; children: Jeong Woo, Yeun Jae. MB, Seoul Nat. U., 1990, MS in Medicine, 2002, PhD in Medicine, 2004. Lic. dr. Korean Med. Assn., 1990, in internal medicine Korean Med. Assn., 1995, in gastroenterology Korean Assn. Internal Medicine, 2000, in endoscopy Korean Assn. Gastrointestinal Endoscopy, 2000. Residency in internal medicine Seoul Nat. U. Hosp., 1991—95; fellowship in gastroenterology Samsung Med. Ctr., Seoul, 1998—2000; asst. prof. Samsung Med. Ctr., Sungkyunkwan U., Seoul, 2000—04, assoc. prof., 2004—. Vis. scholar U. Calif Med. Ctr., San Diego, 2003; vis. assoc. prof. U. Calif. Davis Med. Ctr., 2006—07; mem. sci. program com. Asia-Pacific Assn. Study of Liver 2008, Seoul, 2007—. Assoc. editor: Korean Jour. Gastroenterolgy, 2007; contbr. articles to profl. jours. Capt., med. officer Korean Army, 1995—98, South Korea. Mem.: Korean Assn. Study Liver (mem. sci. program com. 2007—, Rsch. grant 2006), Korean Assn. Internal Medicine, Korean Soc. Gastrointestinal Endoscopy, Korean Soc. Gastroenterology, Asia-Pacific Assn. Study Liver, Korean Liver Cancer Study Group, Am. Assn. Study Liver Disease. Office: Samsung Med Ctr 50 Irwon-Dong Gangnam-Gu Seoul 135-710 Republic of Korea Office Fax: 82 2 3410 6983. Personal E-mail: drmschoi@gmail.com. Business E-Mail: mschoi@skku.edu.

CHOI, SEONHYEONG, medical educator; b. Republic of Korea, Aug. 24, 1976; Degree in Medicine, Ewha Womans U., 2001. Asst. prof. Sungkyunkwan U. Kangbuk Samsung Hosp., 2010—. Mem.: Korean Soc. Radiology. Office: 108 Pyeong-dong Jongno-gu Seoul 110-746 Republic of Korea Personal E-mail: dr_philic@naver.com.

CHOI, SEUNG JAE, plastic surgeon, researcher; b. Seoul, Korea, Aug. 16, 1964; s. Il Choi and Chung He Kim; m. Chung Min Ha, Oct. 27, 1993. MD, Yonsei U., Seoul, Korea, 1990; PhD, U. Tokyo, 1996. Intern U. Tokyo, 1991-92, resident, 1992-96; fellow, clin. instr. dept. plastic and reconstructive surgery Korea U., Seoul, Republic of Korea, 1997—98; staff dept. plastic and reconstructive surgery Bundang Jesaeng Gen. Hosp., 1998—2001; asst. prof. dept. plastic and reconstructive surg. Hallym U. Hangang Sungshim Hosp., Seoul, Republic of Korea, 2001—02; attending prof. Hallym U., Seoul, Republic of Korea, 2002—, Korea U., Seoul, Republic of Korea, 2003—, Yonsei U., 2008—. Contbr. articles to profl. jours. Mem. Japan Soc. Plastic and Reconstructive Surgery, Korea Soc. Plastic and Reconstructive Surgery. Avocations: golf, tennis, swimming, boxing, baseball. Home: Hanshin Seorae Apt 3-805 Seocho-ku Seoul Republic of Korea Office Phone: 82-2-541-8811. Personal E-mail: tokyo@tokyodoc.com.

CHOI, SEUNG MIN, cardiologist; b. CheonNam, Republic of Korea, Jan. 25, 1974; MD, Kok-Kuk Med. Sch., 1999. Interventional cardiologist & cons. Nat. Med. Ctr., Seoul, Republic of Korea, 2008—. Mem.: Korean Med. Assn., Korean Assn. Internal Medicine, Korea Soc. Interventional Cardiology. Office: Euljiro 6-Ga Jung-Gu Seoul 100-799 Republic of Korea Personal E-mail: choichoism@gmail.com.

CHOI, SO YOUNG, nursing educator, researcher; b. Republic of Korea, Dec. 3, 1969; PhD, Pusan Nat. U., 2002. Assoc. prof. Coll. Nursing, Gyeongsang Nat. U., 2003. Mem.: Korean Soc. Nursing Sci. Office: Gyeongsang Nat University Coll Nursing 92 Chilam-Dong Jinju Gyeongsangnam 660-751 Republic of Korea Business E-Mail: csy4214@hanmail.net, css4214@gnu.ac.kr.

CHOI, SOO BONG, medical educator; b. Gangjin, Jeonranamdo, Republic of Korea, Mar. 15, 1951; MD, Seoul Nat. U., 1976, PhD, 1983. Prof. Sch. Medicine, Konkuk U., 1996—. Mem.: European Assn. Study Diabetes. Office: 620-5 Koyhyun-Dong Chun Ju Chungcheongbuk-do 380-704 Republic of Korea Office Fax: 82-43-845-2128. Business E-Mail: mellitus@empal.com.

CHOI, SUING-IL, education educator, researcher; b. Youngwol, Republic of Korea, July 18, 1954; s. Byungduk Choi and Hyesun Kim; m. Soonhee Sung, May 1, 1953; children: Soohoon, Yeon. PhD, Iowa State U., 1983—87. Registered profl. engr., The Indsl. Manpower Mgmt. Inst., 1991. Officer Korean Air Force, Seoul, 1976—80; sr. engr. PoongLim Constrn. Co., Seoul, Republic of Korea, 1980—81; rsch. asst. Iowa State U., Ames, Iowa, 1983—87; sr. rsch. fellow Korean Inst. of Constrn. Tech., Seoul, Republic of Korea, 1988—91, head, planning & coordination divsn., 1991—92; prof. Korea U., Jochiwon, Republic of Korea, 1992—. Evaluation com. mem. Ministry Constrn./Transp., Seoul, Republic of Korea, 2002—, Nat. Inst. Environ. Rsch., Seoul, 2002—; v.p. Korea Water & Wastewater Assn., Seoul, 2002—04; consulting com. mem. Ministry of Environment, Seoul, 2003—. Editor: (jour.) Jour. of Korean Soc. of Environ. Engineers, Jour. of Korean Soc. of Water and Wastewater; translator: (book) Integrated Design of Water Treatment Facilities, Drinking Water Microbiology; composer: Intro. of new Tech. in Water Treatment. Recipient Phi Kappa Phi, Iowa State U. Chpt., 1985, Sigma Xi, 1988, Presdl. Award, Govt. of Korea, 2000, Nat. award for contbn., 2006, Recognition of Contbn., Korean Soc. of Water and Wastewater, 2001, award, Ministry Environ., 2002. Mem.: Korean Soc. Water and Wastewater (pres. 2005—). Achievements include patents pending for direct filtration of recycled water; upflow declined plate settler. Avocations: travel, music. Office: Korea Univ 208 Sechang Youngi Jochiwon 339-700 Qatar Home: 203-501 Hyundai Vil 94-1 Jookjun 1dong 449-160 Yongin 449-160 Republic of Korea Office Fax: +82-2-928-7430, +82-41-867-5170. E-mail: eechoi@korea.ac.kr.

CHOI, SUNG IL, medical educator; b. Seoul, Republic of Korea, Sept. 5, 1970; MD, Kyung Hee U., PhD, 1996. Assoc. prof. Kyung Hee U. Hosp. Gangdong, 2006—. Office: #149 Sangil-dong Gangdong-gu Seoul 134727 Republic of Korea Business E-Mail: drchoi@khu.ac.kr.

CHOI, TAE-IN, physician, researcher; b. Yesan, Republic of Korea, Feb. 8, 1962; MD, Essen Med. Sch., Germany, 1998. Physican Essen U. Hosp., Germany, 1998—2000, Inje U. Sanggye Hosp., Republic of Korea, 2001—05; chief rschr., physician Radiation Health Rsch. Inst. & Clinic, 2005—. Adj. prof. Sch. Medicin, Sungkyunkwan U., 2009—. Mem.: Koearn Diabetes Assn., Korea Acad. Family Medicine. Office: 388-1 Ssangmoon-3 Dong Dobong-GU Seoul 132-703 Republic of Korea Office Fax: 82-2-3499-6622. Business E-Mail: choimd@khnp.co.kr.

CHOI, TAE-JIN, virologist, educator; b. Yesan, S. Korea, Apr. 22, 1964; PhD, U. Calif., Berkeley, 1993. Rsch. assoc. U. Wis., Madison, 1993—95; from full time lectr. to assoc. prof. Pukyong Nat. U., Busan, Republic of Korea, 1995—2006, prof., 2006—07. R&D dir. Chloland, Busan, 2004—. Mem.: Am. Soc. Virology. Achievements include patents pending for early gene promoter originated from Chlorella Virus SS-2 isolated in Korea; promoters originated from Chlorella Virus HS-1; novel DNA Adenine Methyltransferase gene from Feldmannia Species Virus(FsV). Office: Pukyong National University 599-1 Daeyeon 3-Dong Nam-Gu 608-737 Busan Busan Republic of Korea Office Fax: +82-51-629-5610. Business E-Mail: choitj@pknu.ac.kr.

CHOI, WON SUK, internist, researcher; b. Seoul, Republic Of Korea, Aug. 12, 1977; s. Young Ok Choi and Kyung Ae Yang; m. Sung Eun Song, Jan. 29, 2005; children: Hee Seung, Hee Joon. PhD, Korea U. Grad. Sch., Seoul, 2009. Cert. dr. Ministry of Health and Welfare, 2002, Korean Bd. Internal Medicine, 2007. Intern Korean U. Hosp., Seoul, 2002—03, resident internal medicine, 2003—07; sr. rschr. Korea Ctr. Disease Control and Prevention, Seoul, 2007—08; fellow Korea U. Ansan Hosp., 2008—, lectr. divsn. infections disease, dept. internal medicine, 2009—; adj. prof. Korea U. Coll. Medicine, 2009—. Contbr. articles to profl. med. jours. Presbyterian. Home: Yongdoo-Dong Dongdaemun-Gu Seoul Republic of Korea Office: Korea Univ Ansan Hosp Gojan 1-Dong Danwon-Gu 152-703 Ansan Republic of Korea Office Phone: (82)31-412-6555. Personal E-mail: cmcws@hanmail.net.

CHOI, YOUN SEOK, gynecologist, educator; b. Daegu, Republic Of Korea, Apr. 30, 1968; s. Doo Sung and Hwa Soo (Ye) Choi; m. Jeong Suk Kim, Nov. 11, 1970; children: Seokyung, Junhyeok. MD, Kyungpook Nat. U., Daegu, 1993; PhD, Keimyung U., Daegu, 2006. Diplomate Ministry of Health and Welfare, 1993. Med. specialist Fatima Hosp., Daegu, 2001—02; asst. prof. Cath. U., Daegu, 2003—. 1st lt. South Korean Army, 1994—97. Named Best Jour. of Yr., Korean Soc. Gynecologic Endoscopy, 2005. Home: Chunglim Town 102-1403 Daegu 706-767 Republic of Korea Office: Cath Univ Daemyung-4-Dong Namgu 706-718 Daegu Daegu Republic of Korea Office Fax: 82-53-650-4078. Business E-Mail: drcys@cu.ac.kr.

CHOI, YOUNG CHEOL, surgeon, educator; b. Seoul, Republic Of Korea, Jan. 7, 1965; s. Chang Ho Choi and Soon Cheol Kim; m. Young Kyung Ha, Oct. 12, 1991; children: Yoo Jin, Hyung Seok. MD, Chung-Ang U., Seoul, 1989, MS, 1994, PhD, 2000. Diplomate Korean Bd. Gen. Surgery, 1994. Instr. Sungkyunkwan U. Sch. Medicine, Masan, Gyeongsangnam-do, Republic of Korea, 1997—99, asst. prof., 1999—2003, assoc. prof., 2003—09, prof., 2009—. Achievements include research in trauma. Office: Masan Samsung Hosp Hapsung 2-Dong 50 630-522 Masan Gyeongsangnam-do Republic of Korea Office Fax: 82-55-290-6584. Business E-Mail: masancyc@hanmir.com.

CHOI, YOUNG DEUK, medical educator; b. Seoul, Republic of Korea, May 12, 1961; s. Man Jin Choi and Bok Soon Park; m. Kwang Hee Baek, Oct. 9, 1986; children: Hye Seung, Hye Jo, Young In. MD, Yonsei U., Seoul, 1986, MS, 1993, PhD, 1998. Med. diplomate. Intern Coll. Medicine Yonsei U., Seoul, 1986-87, resident Coll. Medicine, 1987-91, instr. Coll. Medicine, 1995-98, asst. prof. Coll. Medicine, 1998—2001, assoc. prof. Coll. Medicine, 2003—08, prof. Coll. Medicine, 2008—; chief Masan (Rep. Korea) Hosp., 1991-94; fellow Ewha Woman's U. Mokdong Hosp., Seoul, 1994-95, Harvard Med. Sch., 2001—02; dir. CTC Med. Devices, 2009—. With Severance Hosp., Seoul, 1998. Cons. Chungang mag. health care, 1999, Chosun mag. cancer cons., 1999; contbr. articles to profl. journals Cons. Befrienders, Seoul, 1998. Grantee Coll. Medicine Yonsei U., 1997-98, Ginseng grantee Korean Soc. Ginseng, 1999-2002; grantee Nat. Health Care, 2009-13, Nat. Ministry for Health, Welfare and Family Affairs. Mem. AAAS, Korean Urol. Assn., Korean Urol. Oncology Assn., Korean Andrology Assn., American Urol. Assn., Soc. Basic Urol. Rsch., Internat. Soc. Impotence Rsch. Avocations: golf, driving, antique collection. Home Phone: 82-2-518-0403; Office Phone: 82-2-2228-2317. Office Fax: 82-2-312-2538.

CHOI, YOUNG HEE, psychiatrist, educator; b. Seoul, South Korea, Feb. 8, 1957; s. Suck Sung Choi and Bok Rae Kim; children: Aran, Sang Yoo. MD, Korea U., Seoul, 1983; M.Medicine, Korea U., 1990; PhD, Inje U., Kimhae, South Korea, 2003. Cert. psychiatrist Korea, 1990, cognitive therapist ACT. Prof. of psychiatry Inje U., Seoul Paik Hosp., Seoul, Republic of Korea, 1996—. Vis. fellow UCLA/NPI, LA, 1994—96. Editor: CyberPsychology & Behavior. Home: #304-706 Family Apt 138-202 Moonjung-Dong Songpa-Ku Seoul Republic of Korea Office Phone: 310-301-6989. Office Fax: 82-2-2270-0344. Business E-Mail: lotha208@kornet.net.

CHOI, YOUNG WHAN, science educator; b. Sancheong-gun, Gyeongnam, Nov. 13, 1961; PhD, Gyeongsang Nat. U., 1992. Agrl. rschr. Nat. Inst. Hort. Herbal Sci. RDA, 1993; prof. Miryang Nat. U., 1993—2006, Pusan Nat. U., 2006—, vice-dean, 2006—07; vis. prof. Nat. Ctr. Natural Products Rsch., 2003—05. Recipient Prime Mins. award, Ministry of Food, Agr., Forestry and Fisheries, 2008, Premier Prof. award, Pusan Nat. U., 2009, award, 2010. Mem.: Korean Soc. Life Sci., Korean Soc. Hort. Sci. Tech. (bd. dir. 2003—). Office: 50 Chunghakri Samrangjineup Miryang Gyeongnam 627-706 Republic of Korea Office Fax: 82-55-350-5529. Business E-Mail: ywchoi@pusan.ac.kr.

CHOI, YOUNG-JUNE JUNE, environmental engineer, director; b. Seoul, Republic of Korea, Mar. 1, 1965; s. Kang-soo Choi and Kyung-ja Hyun; m. Sarah Seung-sil Lim, Dec. 7, 1991; 1 child, Yu-jin. BA in Earth & Environ. Sys. Sci., Seoul Nat. U., 1988, MSc in Earth & Environ. Sys. Sci., 1991; MEng. in Civil & Environ. Engring., Pa. State U., 1999, PhD in Civil & Environ. Engring., 2003. Tech. mktg. deputy mgr. Hitachi Data Sys., Seoul, Republic of Korea, 1991—96; MIS dep. mgr. Gen. Electric, Republic of Korea, 1996—97; asst. rschr., civil and environ. engring., Pa. State U., 1997—2003, assoc rschr. civil and environ. engring. Univ. Pk., 2003—05; dir., chief R & D officer Waterworks Rsch. Inst., Seoul Met. Govt. Seoul, 2005—. Dir. The Membrane Soc. Korea, 2005—, Korean Soc. Water and Wastewater, 2005—, Korean Soc. Environ. Engrs., 2005—, Korean Soc. for Life Cycle Assessment, 2005—. Organizing com. IWA T&O Symposium, 2007—08; project evaluation com. Swiss Nat. Sci. Found., 2009—; adv. com. mem. Korea Water and Wastewater Works Assn., 2009—; com. for the next generation water supply sys. project Ministry Land, Transportation, and Maritime Affairs, 2009—; mem. forum for Hazardous microorganisms in groundwater sys. Ministry Environments, 2009—; organizing com. Internat. Conf. Membranes for Green Growth, 2009—10; com. standards mem. Korea Water and Wastewater Works Assn., 2010—; adv. com. for advanced water treatment techns. Incheon City Govt., 2010—; adv. com. for techs. K-water, 2011—. Recipient New Technologies award, 5the Environ. Chemistry Symposium, U. Pk., 2002, Best Manuscript award, Korean Soc. on Water Quality, Korean Soc. Water and Wastewater, 2007, UN Pub. Svc. awards, 2009, Nat. Grand awards, 2010. Avocations: tennis, mountain climbing, painting. Office: 552-1 Cheonhodaero Gwangjin-Gu Seoul 143-820 Republic of Korea Office Fax: 82-2-3146-1811. Business E-Mail: membrano@korea.kr.

CHOI, YUN SUN, radiologist, educator; d. Eui Kyu and Tae Jin (Kim) Choi; m. Dae Joon Park, Dec. 21, 1996; 1 child, Geun Il Park. MD, Chung Ang U., Seoul, Republic of Korea, 1990, MS, 1993; PhD, Korea U., Seoul, 1998. Diplomate Korean Bd. Radiology, 1995. Clin. fellow radiology Seoul Nat. U. Hosp., 1995—96; vis. fellow radiology and imaging Hosp. for Spl. Surgery, Weill Medial Coll. Cornell, NYC, 2004—05; instr. radiology Eulji U. Sch. Medicine, Seoul, Republic of Korea, 1998—2000, asst. prof., 2000—04, assoc. prof. radiology, 2004—09, prof. radiology, 2009—; chief dept. radiology Eulji Hosp., 2008—. Contbr. articles to profl. jours. Recipient Cert. of Merit, Radiol. Soc. N.Am., 2006; grant, Korean Food and Drug Adminstrn., 2004. Mem.: Korean Soc. Musculoskeletal Radiology (sec. gen. 2009—10), Asian Musculoskeletal Soc. (sec. gen. 13th ann. meeting 2011), Korean Radiol. Soc. (jour. reviewer 2000—). Office: Eulji Hosp Dept Radiology 280-1 Hagye 1-dong Nowon-gu Seoul 139-711 Republic of Korea Home: Kumho Bestville 101-1702 58 Jamwon-dong Seoeho-gu Seoul 139-907 Republic of Korea Office Phone: 82-2-970-8375. Office Fax: 82-2-970-8346. Business E-Mail: cys0128@eulji.ac.kr.

CHOI, YUNG HYUN, biologist, educator; b. Geochang, Kyungsang-namdo, Republic of Korea, Feb. 16, 1964; s. Hyo Soon Choi and Eun Jo Kim; m. Yoo Young Shin; children: Su Yun, Kelly Choi, Soo Kyeong. PhD, Pusan Nat. U., Republic of Korea, 1995. Cert. tchr. Vis. fellow NIH, Bethesda, Md., 1995—99; rsch. assoc. Georgetown U. Med. Sch., Washington, 1999—2000; prof. Dong-Eui U., Pusan, 2000—. Author: (book) The Biology of AIDS, 1995; contbr. articles to profl. jours. With South Korean Army, 1989—91. Mem.: Radiation Rsch. Soc., Am. Soc. Cell Biology, Am. Assn. Cancer Rsch. (assoc. Young Investigator award 1997). Home: Usung Apt 103-607 Gaegeum 3 Dong Pusan Republic of Korea Office: Dong-Eui U Oriental Med Coll Dept Biochemistry Pusan 614-052 Republic of Korea Home Phone: 82-51-892 3578. Office Fax: +82 51 853 4036. Business E-Mail: choiyh@deu.ac.kr.

CHOJNACKI, KAREN A., surgeon, educator; MD, SUNY, 1995. Diplomate Am. Bd. Surgery. Intern Thomas Jefferson Univ. Hosp., resident; fellow Univ. So. Calif.; assoc. prof. dept. of surgery Thomas Jefferson Univ. Office: Thomas Jefferson University Hospital - Center City Campus 111 S 11th St Philadelphia PA 19107 Office Phone: 215-955-6000.

CHOLEWKA, PATRICIA ANNE, nursing educator; m. Michael A. Cholewka; children: Maureen, Kathleen. Diploma in Nursing, Bellevue Sch. Nursing, NYC, 1967; BSN magna cum laude, Castleton State Coll., Vt., 1979; MPA in Pub. and Nonprofit Mgmt. Policy, NYU, NYC, 1987, MA in Healthcare Informatics, 2005; EdD in internat. Edn. Devel., Columbia U., NYC, 1999. RN; cert. nursing adminstrn. ANA; cert. Nat. Assn. Healthcare Quality. Mgr. med.-surg. clin. svcs. in acute and managed care orgns., 1967-95; asst. prof. dept. nursing NY Coll. Tech., CUNY, NYC, 1995—; rschr. healthcare policy and econ. mgmt., 1993—; exch. officer Internat. Faculty Exch., NYCCT-Lithuanian U. Health Scis., Nursing Faculty Exch. Health-care orgn. devel. cons. Razgrad Hosp., Bulgaria, 1993, Lithuanian U. Health Scis., 1996-98, Lviv (Ukraine) Mcpl. Health Dept., 1998; reviewer curriculum med. quality mgmt., Am. Coll. Med. Quality, 2005, prin. investigator US Lead Instn. for US Dept. Edn., 2010-; project dir. US Dept. Edn. Author: Comparative Analysis of Two Post-Soviet Healthcare Organizations in Lithuania and Ukraine: Implications for Continuous Quality Improvement, 1999, Factors Affecting Sustainable Health Care Management Programs in Post-Soviet Transitional Economics, Health Capital and Sustainable Socioeconomic Development, 2008, (co-editor) Health Capital and Sustainable Socioeconomic Development, 2008; editor Jour. Healthcare Quality; guest editor Internat. Jour. Econ. Devel.; mem editl. bd Nursing Outlook, Jour. Nursing Scholarship, Jour. Transcultural Nursing. Mem. citizen emergency response team, Bay Ridge, 2004—; mem. cmty. coun., 2003—. Recipient Disting. Rsch. award, Columbia U., 1999, Fed. Nurse Traineeship award, NYU, 2003, Fulbright award, US Dept. State, 2007—10; named, 2009—10, Baldridge Examiner, US Dept. Commerce, 2009—10; grant, US-EU Atlantis Program Policy, 2010—. Mem. Am. Nursing Informatics Assn., Phi Delta Kappa, Sigma Theta Tau Internat. Republican. Roman Catholic. Office Phone: 718-260-5661. Personal E-mail: pacholewka@verizon.net. Business E-Mail: pcholewka@citytech.cuny.edu.

CHOLLET, PHILIPPE JEAN MARIE, oncologist, educator; b. Tulle, France, July 3, 1943; s. Jean René and Lucienne (Fleyssac) C.; m. Françoise S. Boschet, Dec. 26, 1967; children: Severine, Thomas. Baccalaureat, Coll. Lakanal, Treignac, France, 1960; MD, U. D'Auvergne, Clermont-Ferrand, France, 1969; MSc, U. Blaise Pascal, Clermont-Ferrand, 1967; D Human Biology, U. Paris-Sud, 1971. Intern in internal medicine Ctr. Hosp. Univ., Clermont-Ferrand, 1967-72, chief clinic, 1972-76, resident in endocrinology Sherbrooke, Que., Can., 1968-69; prof. oncology 2d class U. D'Auvergne, 1979-91, prof. oncology 1st class, 1991—2007; expert for BIOMED 2 European Econ. Cmty., Bruxelles, Belgium, 1995—; head hosp. de jour Ctr. Jean Perrin, Clermont-Ferrand, 1991—, head med. oncology dept. Clermont, 1999. Internat. trial coord. OERTC, Brussels, 1988—; expert in anti-cancer drugs Agence du Medicament, Paris, 1994—; v.p. EORTC Chronotherapy Study Group. Contbr. over 400 articles to profl. publs. Vice mayor Town of Treignac, 1989—. Recipient Chevalier de la Légion d'Honneur, 2007. Mem. AAAS, Am. Soc. Clin. Oncology, European Soc. Med. Oncology, French Soc. Immunology, NYAS, Lion's Club. Office Phone: 33473278005.

CHON, JOANNA K., urologist; Undergrad., U. Pa.; MD, George Wash. U. Diplomate Am. Bd. Urology. Resident Mercy Hosp. Med. Ctr., Univ. Md. Med Ctr.; fellow Female Urology, Urodynamics Cedars-Sinai Hosp.; urologist Abington Meml. Hosp. Named Recognized Dr., HealthGrades; named one of the Top Doctors, Phila. Mag., 2011. Office: Abington Meml. Hospital 1200 Old York Rd Abington PA 19001 Office Phone: 215-481-2000.

CHON, SOON-HO, medical educator; b. Marburg, Germany, May 10, 1967; s. Kwang Cha Chon; m. Sae Mi Yoo, May 10, 2001; 1 child, June Raphael. MD, PhD, Hanyang U. Coll. Medicine, Seoul, Republic Of Korea, 2000. Lic. medicine Korean Soc. Health, 1993, cert. Korean Soc. Thoracic and Cardiovasc. Surgery, 2000. Clin. fellow Puchon Sejong Hosp., Gyonggi Do, Republic of Korea, 2000—01; chief surgeon Anyang Metro Hosp., 2001—03; assoc. prof. Hanyang U. Guri Hosp., Gyonggi, 2003—. English editor Hanyang Med. Reviews, Seoul, 2004—08. Contbr. articles to profl. publs. (Hanyang U. Sci. Citation Index award, 2006). Mem.: Korean Soc. Intensivist, Internat. Bronchoesophageal logical Soc., Internat. Soc. Minimally Invasive Cardiac Surgery, Korean Soc. Thoracic and Cardiovasc. Surgery. Home: Gwangjang Dong Hyundai Seoul Gwangjin Gu 1007-201 Republic of Korea Office: Hanyang Univ Guri Hosp Gyomun Dong 249-1 Guri Gyonggi Do 471-701 Republic of Korea Office Phone: 82-31-560-2300. Office Fax: 82-31-568-9948. Business E-Mail: shchon@hanyang.ac.kr.

CHONE, CARLOS TAKAHIRO, head and neck surgeon; b. Japan, June 17, 1968; MD, U. Campinas, 1991, PhD, 2000. Prof. U. Campinas, 1996—. Adj. prof. U. Vampinas, 2006. Mem.: Internat. Sentinel Node Soc., Internat. Fedn. Head and Neck Oncologic Soc., Am. Acad. Otolaryngology Head and Neck Surgery, Brazilian Bd. Otorhinolaryngology, Brazilian Soc. Head and Neck Surgery. Avocations: reading, movies, travel. Office: Ave Dr Heitor Penteado 1541 Campinas Sao Paulo 13087-000 Brazil Business E-Mail: carloschone@uol.com.br.

CHONG, CHEE-FAH, emergency physician; b. Tawau, Sabah, Malaysia, Mar. 5, 1969; s. Fui-Hiong Chong and Chiew-Len Chung; m. Mei-Fang Li, Oct. 25, 1972; children: Yung-Xhiang Chang, Jia-Ming Chang. MD, Taipei Med. U., Taiwan, 1995, MS, 2003. Cert. emergency physician Taipei, 2000. Intern Nat. Taiwan U. Hospt; resident Shin-Kong Wu Ho-Su Meml. Hosp., Taipei, Taiwan, dir., emergency dept., 2006—. Chief sec. Soc. Resuscitation Medicine, Taipei, Taiwan, 2001—02. Mem.: Soc. Emergency Medicine (editor 2004—). Office: Shin-Kong Wu Ho-Su Memorial Hosp No95 Wen-Chang Road Shih-Lin Dist Taipei 111 Taiwan Office Fax: 886-2-28353547. Personal E-mail: jackchong@tmu.edu.tw. Business E-Mail: m002202@skh.org.tw, m002202@m8skh.org.tw

CHONG, VERNON, retired surgeon, military officer; b. Fresno, Calif., Nov. 13, 1933; s. Seu Ling and Ruth (Lee) C.; m. Ann Sumiko Kawana, Sept. 7, 1957; children: Christopher Lee, Gerald Scott, Douglas James. BA, Stanford U., 1955, MD, 1958. Diplomate Am. Bd. Surgery. Intern Gen. Hosp. of Fresno (Calif.) County, 1958-59, resident in gen. surgery, 1959-63; commd. capt. USAF, 1963, advanced through ranks to maj. gen., 1987; chief gen. surgery svc. USAF Hosp., Scott AFB, Ill., 1963-65, staff surgeon, dir. edn. Tachikawa AFB, Japan, 1965-68; staff surgeon, instr. surgery David Grant USAF Med. Ctr., Travis AFB, Calif., 1968-70, dep. comdr., dir. hosp. svcs., 1976—78, comdr., 1978—81; surgeon, chief surgery, dir. hosp. svcs. USAF Acad. Hosp., Colorado Springs, Colo., 1970-74; dep. comdr. USAF Regional Hosp., March AFB, Calif., 1974—76; comdr. Malcolm Grow USAF Med. Ctr., Andrews AFB, Md., 1981-85; command surgeon Hdqrs., Mil. Airlift Command, Scott AFB, 1985-87; comdr. Wilford Hall USAF Med. Ctr., Lackland AFB, Tex., 1987-90, Joint Mil. Med. Command, San Antonio; command surgeon Hdqrs. Air Tng. Command, Randolph AFB, Tex., 1990-91, Hdqrs. U.S. European Command, 1991-94; ret., 1994; network dir. Vets. Integrated Svc. Network VA, Grand Prairie, Tex., 1995-2000; spl. asst. to network dir. Vets. Integrated Svc. Network-21, McClellan Clinic, Sacramento, 2000—03, ret., 2003. Bd. dirs. Alamo chpt. ARC, San Antonio, 1987-88, No. Calif. Retired Officers Cmty. Law, 2004; trustee Air Force Village Found., 1987-90; bd. dirs. San Antonio chpt. ARC, 1995—, No. Calif. Ret. Officers Cmty., 2004—, Calif. Vets. Bd., 2004—. Decorated D.S.M., Legion of Merit with bronze oak leaf cluster; recipient Order of Sword award USAF, 1989. Fellow ACS (gov. 1985-90); mem. Assn. Mil. Surgeons U.S. (bd. mgrs. 1997—, chmn. 2002-04), Soc. Air Force Clin. Surgeons (bd. govs. 1971-73), Am. Coll. Physician Execs., Calif. Vets Bd. Methodist. Avocation: physical fitness. Home: 1820 Starview Ln Lincoln CA 95648

CHONG, YONG YEOW, rheumatologist; b. Malaysia, Dec. 4, 1970; MBBS, Nat. U. Singapore, 1995; grad diploma in Healthcare, SingHealth-SMU, 2008. Assoc. cons. physician Singapore Gen. Hosp., 2007—09, cons. physician, 2009—11; specialist rheumatology Raffles Hosp., Singapore, 2011—. Mem. Acad. Medicine, Singapore, 2008; mem. chpt. rheumatology Coll. Physician. Fellow, Singapore Health Svcs., 2006. Master: RCP; mem.: Singapore Med. Assn., Nat. Arthritis Found. (Singapore), Allergy and Clin. Immunology Soc. Singapore, Singapore Soc. Rheumatology. Avocations: reading, swimming, jogging. Home: 57 Lorong H Telok Kurau #01-02 Singapore 426065 Singapore Personal E-mail: yongyeow@hotmail.com.

CHONMAITREE, TASNEE, pediatrician, educator, epidemiologist; b. Bangkok, Dec. 9, 1949; came to U.S., 1975; d. Surajit and Arporn (Maitong) C.; m. Somkiat Laungthaleong Pong, June 27, 1981; children: Ann L. Pong, Dan L. Pong. BS, Mahidol U., 1971; MD, Siriraj Med. Sch., 1973. Diplomate Am. Bd. Pediat., Am. Bd. Pediat. Infectious Diseases. Rotating intern Siriraj Hosp., Bangkok, 1973—74, resident in pediat., 1974—75, Lloyd Noland Hosp., U. Ala., Birmingham, 1975—78; fellow infectious disease U. Rochester, NY, 1978—81; asst. prof. pediat. U. Tex. Med. Br., Galveston, 1981—87, asst. prof. pathology, 1985—87, assoc. prof. pediat. and pathology, 1987—94; prof. pediat. and pathology, 1994—. Assoc. dir. clin. virology lab. U. Tex. Med. Br., Galveston, 1985-92, dir. divsn. pediat. infectious disease, 1985-92. Contbr. 80 articles to profl. jours. Grantee NIH, 1993—. Fellow Am. Acad. Pediat., Pediat. Infectious Diseases Soc., Infectious Diseases Soc. Am.; mem. Soc. Pediat. Rsch., European Soc. for Pediat. Rsch., Tex. Infectious Disease Soc. Buddhist. Avocation: classical music. Home: 1906 Cherrytree Park Cir Houston TX 77062-2327 Office: U Tex Dept Pediat Med Br Ninth St & Market Galveston TX 77555-0001 Office Phone: 409-772-2798. Business E-Mail: tchonmai@utmb.edu.

CHOO, KENG EE, pediatrician, educator; b. Malaysia, Apr. 4, 1945; MBBS, U. Singapore, 1970. Prof., cons. pediatrician hosp. U. Sains Malaysia, 2006—10. Named Outstanding Pediatrician in Asia, Asia-pacific Pediatric Assn. Fellow: Royal Coll. Physicians (London, Edinburgh, Glasgow, Ireland). Avocations: reading, music, exercise. Office: Jalan Sultanah Raja Perempuan Zainab Kota Bharu Kelantan 16150 Malaysia Office Fax: 609 765 3370. Business E-Mail: kechoo@kb.usm.my.

CHOO, SUK JUNG, medical educator; b. Seoul, Republic Of Korea, Jan. 26, 1964; s. Inn Ki Choo and Yoon Ki Min; m. Jung Myeong Kim, Sept. 30, 1992; children: Hyun Young, Soe Young, Hyun Young, Soe Young, Do Young. MD, Yonsei U. Med. Sch., Seoul, 1988; M in Med. Sci., Korea U. Coll. Medicine, Seoul, 2001; PhD in Medicine, U. Ulsan Coll. Medicine, Seoul, 2004. Cert. ECFMG, 2004. Duran rsch. fellow Internat. Heart Inst. Mont. Found., Missoula, 1996—98; clin. fellow cardiac surgery Brigham and Women's Hosp., Boston, 2005—06, Asan Med. Ctr., U. Ulsan Coll. Medicine, Seoul, 1998—2000, faculty appointment, 2000—, assoc. prof., 2005—. Contbr. scientific papers. Capt. Army, 1993—96, Korea. Mem.: Korean Soc. Thoracic and Cardiovasc. Surgery, Korean Med. Assn. Office: Asan Med Ctr 388-1 Pungnap-2Dong Songpa-gu Seoul 138-736 Republic of Korea Office Phone: 82230103954. Business E-Mail: sjchoo@amc.seoul.kr.

CHOOKLIN, SERGE N., surgeon; b. Lviv, Ukraine, Sept. 17, 1958; s. Nikolaj I. and Alla A. (Karymova) C.; m. Natalja S. Dubchak, Sept. 17, 1988; children: Elena, Serge. MD, Med. Inst. Lviv, 1981. Asst. Med. Inst. Lviv, 1981-88, asst. prof., 1988-95, docent, 1995-97, prof., 1997—. Mem. Internat. Surg. Soc., European Assn. Study of Liver, European Acad. Allergology & Clin. Immunology, European Digestive Surgery, European Soc. Clin. Investigation, European Soc. Intensive Care Medicine. Home: Pasychna 38/10 290038 Lviv Ukraine Office: Med Univ Pekarska 69 79010 Lviv Ukraine

CHOONG HUN, LEE, engineering company executive, director; b. Seoul, Republic Of Korea, Mar. 15, 1957; m. Cho Mi Young, Mar. 26, 1962; children: Lee Sun Hong, Lee Sun Yook. PhD, KAIST, Seoul, 1991. Dir. Hyundai Electronics, Ichon, Republic of Korea, 1992—2001. Home: Dobong Chang5dong Dong A Green Apt Seoul Republic of Korea Office: Wonkwang Univ Shin Yong Dong 344-2 Iksan 570-749 Republic of Korea Office Fax: 82-63-850-7138. Business E-Mail: chlee@wonkwang.ac.kr.

CHOPPIN, PURNELL WHITTINGTON, science administrator; b. Baton Rouge, July 4, 1929; s. Arthur Richard and Eunice Dolores (Dolin) Choppin; m. Joan Harriet Macdonald, Oct. 17, 1959; 1 child, Kathleen Marie. MD, La. State U., 1953; DSc (hon.), Emory U., 1988, La. State U., 1988; MD (hon.), U. Cologne, 1988; DSc (hon.), Tulane U., 1989, Washington U., 1991, Med. U. S.C., 1995, U. Md., Baltimore County, 1995; DHL (hon.), Mt. Sinai Sch. Medicine, 1996; DSc (hon.), U. Mass., 1999, Northwestern U., 1999; LLD (hon.), St. Francis Xavier U., 2000; DSc (hon.), Rockefeller U., 2000, Johns Hopkins U., 2002, West Va. U., 2006. Diplomate Am. Bd. Internal Medicine. Intern Barnes Hosp., St. Louis, 1953—54, asst. resident, 1956—57; fellow, rsch. assoc. Rockefeller U., NYC, 1957—60, asst. prof., 1960—64, assoc. prof., 1957—60, prof., sr. physician, 1970—85, Leon Hess prof. virology, 1980—85, v.p. acad. programs, 1983—85, dean grad. studies, 1985; v.p., chief sci. officer Howard Hughes Med. Inst., Chevy Chase, Md., 1985—87, pres., 1987—99, pres. emeritus, 2000—; prin. Washington Adv. Group, 2000—10. Chmn. sect. 43 microbiology and immunology NAS, 1989—92, chmn. class IV med. scis., 1983—86, mem. com. on reorganization structure, 1985—86, coun., 2000—03, Inst. Medicine, 1987—92, exec. com., 1988—91; mem. virology study sect. NIH, 1968—72, chmn. virology study sect., 1975—78; bd. dirs. Royal Soc. Medicine Found. Inc., NYC, 1978—93; mem. adv. com. fundamental rsch. Nat. Multiple Sclerosis Soc., 1979—84, chmn. adv. com. fundamental rsch., 1983—84; mem. adv. coun. Nat. Inst. Allergy and Infectious Diseases, 1980—83; mem. bd. scis., cons. Meml. Sloan-Kettering Cancer Ctr., NYC, 1981—86, chmn. bd. scis., 1983—84; co-chair NRA Task Force Goals and Ops., 1999—2000; mem. commn. on life scis. NRC, Washington, 1982—87; mem. sci. rev. com. Scripps Clinic and Rsch. Found., La Jolla, Calif., 1983—85, chmn. sci. rev. com., 1984; mem. coun. for rsch. and clin. investigation Am. Cancer Soc., NYC, 1983—85; mem. com. priorities for vaccine devel. Inst. Medicine, Washington; mem. governing bd. NRC, 1990—92. Contbr. articles to profl. pubs., chapters to books on virology, cell biology, infectious diseases, 1958; editor: Procs. Soc. Exptl. Biology and Medicine, 1966—69; assoc. editor: Virology, 1969—72; editor, 1973—86; assoc. editor: Jour. Immunology, 1968—72, Jour. Supramolecular Structure, 1972—75, mem. editl. bd.: Jour. Virology, 1972—85, Comprehensive Virology, 1972, mem. overseas adv. panel: Biochem. Jour., 1973—77. Capt. USAF, 1954—56, Japan. Recipient Howard Taylor Ricketts award, U. Chgo., 1978, Waksman award for Excellence in Microbiology, NAS, 1984, Alumni Achievement award, Washington U. Sch. Medicine, 1990, Dean's medal, Harvard Med. Sch., 1992, Meml. Sloan-Kettering medal for outstanding contbns. to biomed. rsch., 1998, Spl. Recognition award, Assn. Am. Med. Colls., 1999, medal, U. Calif. San Francisco, 2000; named to alumni Hall of Distinction, La. State U., Baton Rouge, 1983. Fellow: AAAS; mem.: NAS, Am. Soc. Virology (pres. 1985—86), Am. Clin. and Climatological Assn., Practitioners Soc. N.Y., Infectious Diseases Soc. Am., Soc. Cell Biology, Am. Assn. Immunologists, Harvey Soc., Am. Soc. Microbiology (chmn. virology divsn. 1977—79, divsn. group council 1983—85), Am. Soc. Clin. Investigation, Assn. Am. Physicians,

Am. Philos. Soc. (coun. 1998—2002, v.p. 2000—06, coun. 2007—), Am. Acad. Arts and Scis., Alpha Omega Alpha, Sigma Xi (chpt. pres. 1980—81). Office: Howard Hughes Med Inst 4000 Jones Bridge Rd Chevy Chase MD 20815-6789

CHOPRA, DEEPAK, medical products executive; b. Oct. 22, 1946; s. Krishna Chopra; m. Rita Chopra; children: Mallika, Gotham. Grad., All India Inst. Med. Sci.; BS in Electronics, Punjab Engrng. Coll., Chandigarh, Punjab, India, MS in Semiconductor Electronics, U. Mass., Amherst. Various positions RCA Semiconductors, TRW Semiconductors, Intel Corp., ILC Tech., Inc., 1976—79, various positions, including pres., chmn., CEO & COO, United Detector Tech. Divsn., 1980—87; founder OSI Sys., Inc., 1987, pres., CEO, 1987—, chmn., 1992—. Author: Return of the Rishi, 1989, Quantum Healing, 1990, Perfect Health, 1990, Unconditional Life, 1991, Creating Health, 1991, Creating Affluence, 1993, Ageless Body, Timeless Mind, 1993, Restful Sleep, 1994, Perfect Weight, 1994, Journey Into Healing, 1994, The Seven Spiritual Laws of Success, 1995, Return of Merlin, 1995, Como Crear Abundancia/How to Create Wealth, 1999, Everyday Immorality: A Concise Course in Spiritual Transformation, 1999, How to Know God: The Soul's Journey into the Mystery of Mysteries, 2000, The Daughters of Joy: An Adventure of the Heart, 2002, Book of Secrets: Unlocking the Hidden Dimensions of Your Life, 2004, Peace Is the Way: Bringing War and Violence to an End in Our Time, 2005 (Quills award-religion/spirituality, 2005), Ask The Kabala: Oracle Cards/Kabala Guidebook, 2006, Power Freedom and Grace: Living from the Source of Lasting Happiness, 2006, Life After Death: The Burden of Proof, 2006, Kama Sutra: Including the Seven Spiritual Laws of Love, 2006, Buddha: A Story of Enlightenment, 2007, The Third Jesus: The Christ We Cannot Ignore, 2008; (with David Simons, Vicki Abrams) Magical Beginnings, Enchanted Lives, 2005; albums include A Gift of Love, 2001, Grow Younger, Live Longer, 2001, The Soul of Healing Meditations, 2001, The New Physics of Healing, 2002, Chakra Balancing, 2004, Body, Mind & Soul, vol. 2, 2007, Whispers of Spirit & Happiness, 2008, Rasa Living Wellness, vol. 1, 2008. Office: OSI Systems Inc 12525 Chadron Ave Hawthorne CA 90250 Office Phone: 310-978-0516. Office Fax: 310-644-7213. Business E-Mail: dchopra@spacelabshealthcare.com. *

CHOPRA, INDER JIT, endocrinologist; b. Gujranwala, India, Dec. 15, 1939; came to U.S., 1967; s. Kundan Lal and Labhwati (Bagga) C.; m. Usha Prakash, Oct. 16, 1966; children: Sangeeta, Rajesh, Madhu. B of Medicine and BS, All India Inst. Med. Scis., New Delhi, India, 1961, MD, 1965. Intern All India Inst. Med. Scis., New Delhi, 1961-62, clin. resident, 1962-65, registrar in medicine, 1966-67; resident Queens Med. Ctr., Honolulu, 1967-68; fellow in endocrinology Harbor Gen. Campus UCLA Sch. Medicine, 1968-71; asst. prof. of medicine UCLA, 1971-74, assoc. prof., 1974-78, prof., 1978—. Mem. VA Merit Rev. Bd. in Endocrinology, 1988-91. Contbr. more than 285 rsch. articles, revs. and book chpts. to profl. lit. Recipient Rsch. Career Devel. award, NIH, 1972. Master Am. Coll. Physicians; mem. Endocrine Soc. (Ernst Oppenheimer award 1980), Am. Thyroid Assn. (Van Meter-Armour award 1977, Parke-Davis award 1988, Disting. Svc. award 1995), Am. Soc. Clin. Investigation, Assn. of Am. Physicians, Western Assn. Physicians, Am. Fed. for Clin. Rsch. Achievements include patent for radioimmunoassay for measurement of thyroxine and triiodothyonine. Office: UCLA Sch Medicine Ctr for Health Scis 24-130 Warren Hall 900 Veteran Ave Los Angeles CA 90024-2703 Home Phone: 818-222-5683; Office Phone: 310-825-2346. Business E-Mail: ichopra@mednet.ucla.edu.

CHOPRA, JAGJIT SINGH, neurologist; b. Lahore, Pakistan, 1935; Degree in Medicine, Punjab U., 1959; PhD, Queen's U., Belfast, Northern Ireland, 1967. With Dept. Neurology, Royal Victoria Hosp., Belfast; asst. prof. Dept. Neurology, Postgrad. Inst. Med. Edn and Rsch., Chandigarh, India, 1968, prof., neurology, head, neurology; founder dir. prin. Govt. Med. Coll. and Hosp., Chandigarh, 1991—95, sec., 1991—95; prof. emeritus Postgrad. Inst. Med. Edn. and Rsch., Chandigarh, 1995—, Nat. Acad. Med. Scis., India; senator Baha Farid U. Med. Scis. Lectr. U. Grants Commn.; vis. prof. Various Instns., guest spkr.; editor in chief Neurology India, World Neurology, 1999—; chmn. special selection com. Govt. Punjab State; chief guest Convocation Dayanand Med. Coll., Ludhiana, 2010, Movement Disorders Asian & Oceanan Conf., 2010. Contbr. scientific papers, chapters to books, articles to sci. jour. publs.; editor: (book) Neurology in Tropics. Recipient Padma Bhushan, Pres., India, 2008, Dr. B. C. Roy Nat. award, 9th Amrut Modi Rsch. award, Merit award, Nat. Acad. Med. Scis., Disting. Alumenus award, Govt. Med. Coll., Patiala, Life Time Achievement award, Madras Neuro Trust & Sai Krishna Neurosci. Hosp., Hydrabad, New Con, Delhi, 2010, award, Indian Neurologists America, Indian Acad. Neurology, Govt. Med. Coll. Kota Rajasthan, 2010, Neurol. Soc. India, 2010, KMC Oration Dept. Neurology Kota, Bulden Sorigh Oration award, Nat. Acad. Med. Scis., Half Dozen other Oration award. Master: RCP, Edinburgh; fellow: RCP, Edinburgh, Indian Acad. Neurology (founder fellow), Fulton Soc., Nat. Acad. Med. Scis.; mem.: Ulster Med. Soc., Assn. Brit. Neurologists, London Med. Soc., Internat. Fedn. Clin. Neurophysiology (mem., exec. com.), World Fedn. Neurology (vice chmn. 1985—, co chmn., fin. com., mem., pub. rels., ethical, structure and functions, publ. and website, African Project, Stroke Liason Coms.), Am. Neurol. Assn. (hon.), Am. Acad. Neurology (hon.). Achievements include training of scores of superspecialists in Neurology most of whom are heading the departments of Neurology at various places in India and abroad. Home: House 1153 Sector 33C Chandigarh India Home Phone: 91 172 2661532; Office Phone: 91 172 2668532. Personal E-mail: jagjitscd_04@rediffmail.com.

CHOPRA, PREM KUMAR, psychiatrist, educator; b. Australia, Aug. 29, 1970; s. Hari Dass and Narinder Chopra; m. Rinku Chopra; 1 child, Vivek Kumar. MBBS, MSc, MPsych, U. Melbourne. Lic. Gen. Med. Coun. U.K., Med. Practitioners Bd. Victoria, Australia. Sr. lectr. U. Melbourne, Victoria, Australia, 2005—. Dir. postgraduate med. tng. St Vincent's Mental Health Svc., Melbourne, Australia; cons. in field. Fellow, RANZCP Lilly. Fellow: Royal Australian and New Zealand Coll. Psychiatrists; mem.: Royal Australasian Coll. Med. Administrs. Achievements include research in psychiatric rehabilitation. Office: St Vincent's Mental Health Service 41 Victoria Pde 3065 Victoria Fitzroy VIC Australia Office Fax: +61 3 92884147. Business E-Mail: pchopra@unimelb.edu.au.

CHOTI, MICHAEL ANDREW, surgical oncologist; b. Calif., June 15, 1957; MD, Yale U. Sch. Medicine, 1983. Active staff surgery The Johns Hopkins Hosp., 1992—; vice chair dept. surgery Johns Hopkins Sch. Medicine, 2008—. Office: 600 N Wolfe St Blalock 665 Baltimore MD 21287 Office Fax: 410-614-4667. Business E-Mail: mchoti@jhmi.edu.

CHOTIGEAT, URAIWAN, neonatologist; b. Suphanburi, Thailand, Dec. 31, 1954; arrived in US, 1996; adopted d. Thawat and d. Phayao Chotigeat. BS in Medicinal Sci., Mahidol U., Bangkok, 1977; MD, Siriraj Mahidol U., Bangkok, 1979; diploma in pediat., Children Hosp., Thai Bd. Pediat., Bangkok, 1985; cert. in neonatology, La. State U., 1996. Cert. Thai Med. Coun. (sub Thai bd. in neonatology). Gen. physician Ministry of Pub. Health, Songkla, Thailand, 1980—82; pediatric resident Children Hosp., Bangkok, 1982—85; gen. pediatrician Prachinburi Hosp., Thailand, 1985—94; neonatologist Children Hosp., Bangkok, 1994—96; fellow in clin. neonatology La. State U. Med. Ctr., New Orleans, 1996—97; neonatologist dept. pediat. Queen Sirikit Nat. Inst. Child Health, Bangkok, 1997—. Mem. med. com. Pediatric Soc. Thailand, Bangkok, 2005. Contbr. articles to profl. jours. Grantee, Dept. Pharmacy Hosp., Chulalongkorn U., 1997, 1998, Dept. Pediat., Tropical Medicine Hosp., Mahidol U., 2001, NIH, 2001—05, Nat. Rsch. Fund Ctr, 2002—04, Abbott Labs. Co., 2002—03, Nat. Rsch. Fund Ctr., 2004—. Mem.: Infectious Diseases Assn. Thailand, Soc. Pediat. Nutrition Thailand, Thai Med. Women's Assn., Neonatal Soc. Thailand (med. com.), Royal Coll. Thai Pediatricians (cert. in neonatology-perinatology 1999, sec. continuing med. edn. com. 2004—, mem. sub bd. neonatology-perinatology 2006). Avocations: jogging, badminton, stamp collecting/philately, internet searching. Home: 32/12 Soi Assumption 2 Petshakasem Rd Bangkok 10160 Thailand Office: Queen Sirikit Nat Inst Child Health Rajavithee Rd 10400 Bangkok Rajathevee, Bangkok Thailand

CHOU, CHI-CHUNG, medical educator; b. Yang Mei, Taiwan, May 9, 1966; s. Ting-Li Chou and Jin-Shih Liou; m. Kai-Lin Cheng, Nov. 26, 1994; 1 child, Deana Abby. BSc in Vet. Medicine, Nat. Chung-Hsing U., Taichung, Taiwan, 1990, MSc, 1992; PhD, U. Fla., Gainesville, 2001. Cert. civil svc. Ministry Exam., Taiwan, 1992, dr. vet. medicine Coun. Agr., Taiwan, 1993. Rsch. assoc. CCTRP, Coll. Vet. Medicine, NC State U., Raleigh, 2001—02; asst. prof., vet. medicine Nat. Chung-Hsing U., 2002—07, tech. specialist, vet. tchg., 2003—, lab. supr., pharmacology and toxicology, 2006—, assoc. prof., vet. medicine, 2007—, dir., fgn. student affairs, 2007—09, prof., vet. medicine, 2010—; dep. dean Office Internat. Affairs, 2010—. With vet. drug inspection and policy com. Coun. Agr., Taipei, Taiwan, 2004. Translator: (book) Veterinary laboratory Medicine, Interpretation and Diagnosis, Pharmacokinetics Made Easy; contbr. numerous articles to profl. jours. 2nd lt. Army, 1992—94, Chinmen, Taiwan. Recipient Caligraphy award, Various Orgns., Chin-O medal, Nat. Chung-Hsing U., 1990, Cert. Academic Excellence, Coll. Vet. Medicine, U. Fla., 1999, Tchg. and Svc. Excellence, Coll. Vet. Medicine, Nat. Chung-Hsing U., 2006, Spl. Report award, SeparationsNow-.Com, John Wiley & Sons Ltd., 2007, Excellence Rsch. & Industry Liaison, Nat. Chung-Hsing U., 2007, Best Mentor award, 2008; grantee, Nat. Sci. Com., Taiwan, 2003—05, Coun. Agr., Taiwan, 2004—11, Nat. Sci. Com., Taiwan, 2007—. Mem.: Taiwan Vet. Assn., Poultry Sci. Assn., Soc. Toxicology. Achievements include patents for high performance liquid chromatography method for differentiation of meat species and evaluation of meat freshness; research in microdialysis model for free-moving horses and avian; drug residue and food safety; patents pending for new combination of amphericol antibiotics and thereof. Avocations: reading, calligraphy, writing, softball, badminton. Office: Nat Chung-Hsing Univ 250-1 Kuo Kuang Rd Taichung 402 Taiwan Office Phone: 886-4-22840404 x 177. Office Fax: 886-4-22862073. Business E-Mail: ccchou@nchu.edu.tw.

CHOU, CHIU-FANG, medical researcher; b. Taipei, Taiwan, Dec. 24, 1968; PhD, U. Ill., Chgo., 2006. Postdoc. rschr. U. Minn., 2006—08; health svcs. rschr. Ctrs. Diseases and Prevention, 2008—. Adj. asst. prof. U. Ill., Chgo., 2009. Recipient Travel award, Minn. Population Ctr.; Seed grant. Mem.: APHA, Am. Health Info. Mgmt. Assn., Acad. Health. Avocation: photography. Office: 4770 Buford Hwy NE K-10 Atlanta GA 30341 Business E-Mail: cchou@cdc.gov.

CHOU, HSIANG-TAI TOM, cardiologist, educator; b. Taipei, Oct. 13, 1949; MD, Nat. Def. Med. Ctr. Sch. Medicine, Taiwan, 1974; PhD, Kobe U., Japan, 1990. Prof., medicine China Medial U. Hosp., Taichung, Taiwan, 1990—. Fellow: Am. Coll. Cardiology. Avocation: golf. Home: 4F-1 159 1st Sect Taichung Kang Rd Taichung 403 Taiwan Personal E-mail: chou.hsieh@msa.hinet.net.

CHOU, LIN-SHING, plastic surgeon; b. Taiwan, Jan. 5, 1956; MD, Nat. Def. Med. Sch., 1980. Chief, dept. plastic surgery Far Eastern Meml. Hosp., 2007—10; chief SinHoMei Plastic Surgery, 2010—. Home: GinYei 3rd Rd Ln 162 46 6F Taipei 104 Taiwan Personal E-mail: chouplasty119@yahoo.com.tw.

CHOU, PESUS, epidemiologist, educator, researcher; b. Tainan, Taiwan, Nov. 9, 1948; d. Ding-Yuej and Ming (Lu) C.; m. Gin-Kai Lin (dec. Sept. 1992). BS, Nat. Taiwan U., 1971, MS, 1973; DrPH, Tulane U., 1985. Sec., sec. gen. Cancer Soc. in Republic of China, Taipei, 1974-86; instr. Nat. Yang-Ming Med. Coll., Taipei, 1977-83, assoc. prof., 1983-92, prof. epidemiology, 1992—; dean student affairs Nat. Yang-Ming U., 1991-97, dir. Inst. Pub. Health, 1991-94, dir. Cmty. Medicine Rsch. Ctr., 1996—. Named one of Ten Outstanding Women in Republic of China, 1984; Hon. Citizen in Kinmen, 1992. Mem. Soc. Preventive Medicine of Republic of China (chmn. 1993-99), Human Rights Edn. Found. (exec. dir. 1996-2009, bd. dirs. chmn. bd. 2009), Delta Omega. Avocations: travel, art. Office: Nat Yang-Ming U Shih-Pai 11221 Taipei Taiwan Office Fax: 001 886 2 28201461. Business E-Mail: pschou@ym.edu.tw.

CHOU, TING-CHAO, inventor, educator; b. Taiwan, Sept. 9, 1938; arrived in U.S., 1965, naturalized, 1976; s. Chao-Yun and Sheng-Mei (Chen) C.; m. Dorothy Tsui-chin Tseng, June 26, 1965; children: Joseph Hsin-I, Julia Hsin-Ya. BS, Kaohsiung Med. Coll., Taiwan, 1961; MS, Nat. Taiwan U., 1965; PhD, Yale U., 1970. Tchg. asst. pharmacology Nat. Taiwan U., 1964-65; rsch. asst. pharmacology Yale U., 1969; postdoctoral fellow Johns Hopkins U., Balt., 1969-72; assoc. Sloan-Kettering Inst. Cancer Rsch., NYC, 1972-78, assoc. mem., 1978—88, acting chmn. dept. pharmacology, 1984—88, mem., 1988-95, head lab. biochmn. pharmacology, 1988-98, dir. preclin. pharmacology core lab., 1995—. Asst. prof. Grad. Sch. Med. Sci. Cornell U., 1972—78, assoc. prof., 1978—88, prof. pharmacology, 1988—2000; vis. prof. Chinese Second Mil. Med. U., Shanghai, 1992—, Tonji Med. U., 1993—, Nanjing Med. U., China, 1994—; hon. prof. Chinese Acad. Med. Scis., Beijing, 1993—, Chinese Acad. Mil. Med. Scis., Beijing, 1995—; cons. in field. Author (with J. Chou): Dose Effect Analysis with Microcomputers, 1986; author: (with M. Hayball) CalcuSyn for Windows, Biosoft, 1996; author: (with N. Martin) CompuSyn for Drug Combinations, ComboSyn Inc., 2004; co-editor (with D. Rideout): Synergism and Antogonism in Chemotherapy, 1991; mem. editl. adv. bd.: Cancer Biochemistry Biophysics, 1984—2004, Jour. of the Nat. Cancer Inst., 1988—92, Kaohisung Jour. Med. Scis., 1992—, chmn. pub. bd.: Bio/Pharma Quar., 1995—2002; contbr. scientific papers over 293 articles on cancer, and AIDS chemotherapy and theoretical biology to profl. jours.; cited in over 12000 sci. papers in bio-med. jours.based on 7th ISI Web of Science Search. Chmn. Lim-Wang Meml. Scholarship Fund, 1998—2003; mem. adv. bd. divsn. biotechnology and pharm. rsch. Nat. Health Rsch. Inst., Taiwan, 2001—02. Rsch. grantee Nat. Cancer Inst., Nat. Inst. of Allergy and Infectious Diseases, Elsa U. Pardee Found. and Am. Cancer Soc., 1975—. Mem. AAAS, Am. Assn. Cancer Rsch., Am. Soc. Pharmacology and Exptl. Therapeutics, Am. Soc. Preventive Oncology (founding mem.), Am. Soc. for Biochem. and Molecular Biol., Am. Bur. Med. Advancement in China (bd. dirs. 1991-2003, v.p. 1994-98), NY Acad. Sci., Kaohsiung Med. Coll. Alumni Assn. Am. (bd. dir. 1968-91, pres. 1972), Harvey Soc., Am. Philos. Assn., Sigma Xi, Am. Philosophical Assn. Achievements include 25 US patents ranked among the top 99 percentile based on the US Patent and Trademark Office records; inventions mainly in anticancer agents including desoxyepothilones, ardeemins, ningalins, and iso-oxazole-fludelone; creator of the unified theory of dose and effect, median-effect equation and plot, multiple drug effect equation, combination index theorem and plot, dose-reduction index and plot, and polygonogram; life-time theoretical work was published in a leading scientific journal, Pharmacological Reviews in 58:621-681 2006. Office: Sloan-Kettering Inst Cancer Rsch 1275 York Ave New York NY 10021-6007 Business E-Mail: chout@mskcc.org.

CHOU, YOU-LI, biomedical engineer, educator; b. Tainan, Taiwan, Oct. 19, 1936; s. Chao-Fu and Chen-Ho Chou; m. Yu-Yuen Huang, Jan. 29, 1964; children: Paul Pei-Hsi, Joyce Chia-Hsien, Jeff Cheng-Hong. BS, Nat. Cheng Kung U., Tainan, 1960, MS, 1963; PhD, U. Tenn., 1976. Prof. Nat. Cheng Kung U., Tainan, 1970—, prof. emeritus, 2002—, founding dir. Inst. Engrng. Sci. Tainan, 1979—85, founding dir. Inst. Biomed. Engrng., 1988—94; vis. prof. dept. orthop. U. Va., 1986—87; founding pres. Taiwanese Soc. Biomechanics, 1993—97; founding mem. adv. com. Nat. Health Rsch. Inst., Taiwan, 1996—; dist. chair prof. Nan Jeon Inst. Tech., Tainan, 2002—. Founding dir. Orthop. Biomechanics Rsch. Ctr. Nat. Cheng Kung U., Tainan, 2000—02; mem. adv. com. Nat. Sci. Coun., Taiwan, 1991—96, Nat. Bur. Stds., Taiwan, 1995—99; founding pres. United Pioneer Corp., Va., 1976—. Contbr. 160 articles to profl. jours. Bd. dirs. Nan-Long Inst. Tech., Tainan, 1980—; founding pres. Engrng. Sci. Ednl. Found., Tainan, 1994—96; pres. Nat. Cheng Kung U. Alumni Assn., 2000—02. Recipient Outstanding Achievement award, Exec. Yuan, Taiwan, 1995, Nat. Sci. Coun., Taiwan, 1999. Mem.: Taiwanese Soc. Biomechanics (bd. dirs. 1993—, named Father of Taiwanese Soc. Biomechanics 2001), Tainan Golf Club (bd. dirs. 1991—), Internat. Rotary (sr.; bd. dirs. 1976—). Achievements include patents for CAD/CAM custom made cushion for wheelchair-seated patients. Home: 99 Chieng Nien Rd 700 Tainan Taiwan Office: Nat Cheng Kung U 1 Univ Rd 701 Tainan Taiwan E-mail: ylchou@mail.ncku.edu.tw.

CHOUDHARY, ADIL MUSHTAQ, gastroenterologist; b. Dec. 19, 1964; MB, BChir, U. Karachi, Pakistan, 1989. Diplomate in internal medicine and gastroenterology Am. Bd. Internal Medicine, in Gastroenterology Am. Bd. Internal Medicine. Intern medicine/gen. surgery Civil Hosp. and Dow Med. Coll., Karachi, 1990, resident internal medicine, 1991—93, NYU VA/Bellevue Hosp. Ctr., Manhattan, 1993—96; tchg. asst. medicine NYU Sch. Medicine, Manhattan, 1994—96; fellow gastroenterology Yale U. Gastroenterology Program at Bridgeport (Conn.) Hosp., 1996—99; advanced fellow therapeutic gastrointestinal endoscopy Tulane U. Med. Ctr., New Orleans, 1999; pvt. practice gastroenterology and internal medicine Rio Pecos Med. Assocs., Roswell, N.Mex., 1999—2000, Digestive Disease Inst., So. N.Mex. Med. Assocs., Roswell, 2001—08; clin. asst. prof. medicine U. N. Mex. Sch. Medicine, 2003—; with Huguley Med. Assocs., Burleson, Tex., 2008—; founder Huguley Ctr. Digestive & Liver Disorders, 2009. Vol. tchg. faculty family practice residency Ea. N.Mex. Med. Ctr., Roswell, mem. pharmacy and therapeutics com.; vol. pharmacy practice faculty U. N.Mex. Coll. Pharmacy, Albuquerque, 2001—02; mem. grad. med. edn. com. Ea. N.Mex. Family Practice Residency Program, 2001—; bd. dirs. Southeastern N.Mex. Physicians IPA, Inc.; presenter in field. Contbr. articles to profl. jours. Recipient Man of Yr., Am. Biographical Inst., 2005; named Top Dr., Ft. Worth Tex. Mag., 2010; Janssen Pharmaceutica USA scholar, World Congress Gastroenterology, Vienna, 1998. Fellow: ACP, Royal Soc. Medicine, Royal Inst. Pub. Health, Royal Soc. for Promotion of Health, Am. Soc. Gastrointestinal Endoscopy, Am. Gastroent. Assn., Am. Coll. Gastroenterology (Cert. for outstanding contbn. to the field of gastroenterology and hepatology 1999, 1997); mem.: AMA (Physician's Recognition award in continuing med. edn. 1998—2001, 1999—2002), Crohn's and Colitis Found. Am., Inc., Am. Assn. for Study Liver Diseases. Home: PO Box 126469 Fort Worth TX 76126 Office Phone: 817-551-7332.

CHOUDHURY, MUHAMMAD, urologist, educator; MD, Bangladesh, 1972. Diplomate Am. Bd. Urology. Resident urology Columbia-Presbyn. Med. Ctr., NY, 1977—78, NY Med. Coll., 1978—80, prof. urology; fellow urologic oncology Roswell Pk. Cancer Inst., Buffalo, 1980—81; dir. urological svcs. Westchester Med. Ctr., chief urological oncology. Fellow: ACS; mem.: AMA, Soc. of Urology Chairpersons and Program Dirs., NY Acad. of Medicine, Westchester Acad. of Medicine, NY State Urological Soc., Am. Urological Assn. NY chpt., Am. Urological Assn., Am. Assn. of Clin. Urologists. Office: Westchester Medical Center 100 Woods Rd Valhalla NY 10595 Office Phone: 914-493-7000.

CHOUGH, CHUNGKEE, neurosurgeon, educator; b. Seoul, Republic of Korea, Nov. 5, 1965; s. Youngsun and Songja (Hwang) Chough; m. Youngah Choi, Aug. 27, 1992; children: Nahyeon, Junwon. MD, Cath. U. Korea, Seoul, 1990, PhD, 2002. Lic. Korean Med., cert. Korean Bd. Med. Examiners, 1990, Korean Bd. Neurol. Surgery, 1995. Internship & neurosurg. resident Seoul St. Mary's Hosp., Republic of Korea, 1990—95; instr. dept. neurosurgery Cath. U.

Korea, 1998—2001, asst. prof. dept. neurosurgery, 2002—09; vis. scholar dept. neurosurgery U. Pitts., 2005—07; assoc. prof. dept. neurosurgery Cath. U. Korea, 2010—; chief dept. neurosurgery Yeouido St. Mary's Hosp., 2009—. Expert adviser Auto Insurance Med. Fee Rev. Coun. Korea, 2009—; mem. judging panel Indsl. Accident Compensation Insurance Korea, 2010—; mem. sci. com. Korean Tissue Engring. and Regenerative Medicine Soc., 2011—; reviewer in fields; chief dept. neurosurgery Teouido St. Marys Hosp. Contbr. articles to profl. jours. Capt. Korean Army, 1995—98. Mem.: Korean Tissue Engring. and Regenerative Medicine Soc., Congress Neurol. Surgeons, Internat. Soc. Advancement Spine Surgery, Korean Spinal Neurosurg. Soc. (sci. com. mem.), Korean Neurosurg. Soc. Roman Catholic. Avocations: golf, history, painting, music, running. Office: Yeouido St Mary's Hosp Dept Neurosurgery #62 Yeouido-dong Yeongdeungpo-gu Seoul 150-713 Republic of Korea Office Phone: 82-2-3779-1042, 82-10-3696-6186. Office Fax: 82-2-786-5809. Business E-Mail: chough@catholic.ac.kr.

CHO-VEGA, JEONG HEE, dermatologist; b. Seoul, Republic of Korea, July 6, 1961; MD, Ewha Womans U., PhD, 1980. Pathology resident Meth. Hosp., 2006—08; vis. asst. prof. UT MD Anderson Cancer Ctr., 1999—2002; instr. UT MD Anderson Cancer, 2002—06; dermatopathology fellow UT MD Anderson Cancer Ctr., 2008—09; dermatopathologist St. Joseph Dermatopathology, 2009—. Fellow: Am. Assn. Cancer Rsch., Am. Soc. Dermatopathology, Am. Acad. Dermatology; mem.: Am. Soc. Clin. Pathology, Coll. Am. Pathologists. Avocations: photography, travel, sports. Office: 6909 Greenbriar St Houston TX 77030 Office Fax: 713-660-9466. Personal E-mail: vegaelena@ymail.com.

CHOW, RITA KATHLEEN, nursing consultant; b. San Francisco, Aug. 19, 1926; d. Peter and May (Chan) Chow. BS, Stanford U., 1950, nursing diploma, 1950; MS, Case Western Res. U., 1955; profl. diploma in nursing edn. adminstrn, Columbia U., 1961, EdD, 1968; B of Individualized Studies, George Mason U., 1983. Asst. in teaching Stanford U., Calif., 1951—52; instr., dir. student health Fresno Gen. Hosp. Sch. Nursing, Calif., 1952—54; instr. Wayne State U. Coll. Nursing, Detroit, 1957—58; rsch. assoc., project dir. cardiovasc. nursing rsch. Ohio State U., Columbus, 1965—68; commd. officer USPHS, 1968, advanced through grades to nurse dir. (capt.), 1974; spl. asst. to dep. dir. Nat. Ctr. Health Svcs. Rsch., Health Svcs. and Mental Health Adminstrn., HEW, Rockville, Md., 1969—73, dep. dir. manpower utilization br., 1970—73; dep. dir. Office Long Term Care; dep. chief nurse officer USPHS, Rockville, 1973—77; chief quality assurance br. div. long-term care Office Stds. and Certification, Health Standards and Quality Bur., Health Care Fin. Adminstrn., HHS, 1977—82; supervisory clin. nurse and spl. asst. to health systems adminstr. USPHS Indian Hosp., HRSA, HHS, Rosebud, SD, 1982—83; dir. patient edn., asst. dir. nursing G. W. Long Hansen's Disease Ctr., USPHS, Carville, La., 1984—89; dir. nursing Fed. Med. Ctr., Ft. Worth, 1989—95; pvt. cons., 1993—98, dir. Nat. Interfaith Coalition on Aging, Natl. Coun. on Aging, Washington, 1998—. Author: (book) Identifying Nursing Action with the Care of Cardiovascular Patients, 1967, Cardiosurgical Nursing Care: Understandings, Concepts and Principles for Practice, 1975; mem. editl. bd. Nursing and Health Care, 1983—95, contbr. articles to profl. jours. With Nurse Corps US Army, 1954—57, with USAR, 1954—68. Recipient Nursing Svc. award, Assn. Mil. Surgeons U.S., 1969, Commendation medal, USPHS, 1972, Meritorious Svc. medal, 1977, DSM, 1987, citation for outstanding contbn. to cardiovascular nursing, Am. Heart Assn., 1972—79, award for disting. achievement in nursing rsch., Nursing Edn. Alumni Assn., Columbia U. Tchrs. Coll., 1973, Disting. Alumnus award, Case Western Res. U. Sch. Nursing, 1979, Women's Honors in Pub. Svcs. award, ANA, 1988, USPHS Commendable Svc. medal, U.S. Dept. Justice, Bur. Prisons, 1995, Holistic Nurse of the Yr. award, Am. Holistic Nurses Assn., 2001, Artist of Life First prize, Internat. Womens Writing Guild, 1987, Chief Nurse Officer award, USPHS, 2003, Spirituality & Aging award, Nat. Interfaith Coalition Aging, Nat. Coun. Aging, 2009; grantee, Sigma Theta Tau, 1966. Fellow: Am. Assn. Advancement Sci., Am. Acad. Nursing, Gerontological Soc. Am., Nat. Gerontological Nursing Assn. (bd. dirs., Lifetime Achievement award 2010), Am. Assn. of Integrative Medicine (diplomate Coll. of Nursing 2003).

CHOW, STEPHEN HEUNG WING, physician; b. Hong Kong, Nov. 26, 1954; s. Hon Wing Chow and Kam Wah Choi; m. Clare Chau Fung Sin, Mar. 10, 1986; children: Tin Yee, Tin Yan, Chow Tin Bo, Tin Yau, Tin Sum. MBBS, Hong Kong U., 1979; diploma in child health, Royal Coll. Surgeons and Physicians, Ireland, 1992; diploma in practical dermatology, U. Wales, UK, 1994. House officer Queen Elizabeth Hosp., Hong Kong, 1979, Nethersole Hosp., Hong Kong, 1980; gen. practice medicine Hong Kong, 1981—; founder Human Bioenergy Devel. Ltd., Hong Kong, 1990—. U.S. Bicentennial Scholar, 1978. Fellow Hong Kong Coll. Gen. Practitioner, Royal Australian Coll. Gen. Practitioner; mem. Hong Kong Med. Assn. Home: B1 240 Prince Edward Rd Kowloon China Office: 235 Ground Fl Nam Cheong St Kowloon China

CHOW, VINCENT TAK-KWONG, biomedical scientist, educator; b. Georgetown, Penang, Malaysia, Sept. 3, 1958; arrived in Singapore, 1978; s. Michael and Maureen (Li) C.; m. Mei-Choo Loke, Dec. 16, 1984; children: Joel, Jerome, Clara-Anne. MB BS, Nat. U. Singapore, 1983, PhD, 1991, MD, 1996; MSc, U. London, 1986; diploma in microbiology, U. Coll. London, 1987, MRC in Pathology, 2000. Registered Singapore Med. Coun., Gen. Med. Coun. U.K. House officer Ministry of Health, Singapore, 1983-84, med. officer, 1984; sr. tutor Nat. U. Singapore, 1984-91, lectr., 1991-93, sr. lectr., 1994-98, assoc. prof., 1998—, head dept., 2002—05. Vis. scientist Japan Soc. for Promotion of Sci., 1991, 97, 2001. Contbr. over 150 articles to sci. publs. Overseas grad. scholar, 1985-87; acad. rsch. grantee Nat. U. Singapore, 1985—; Asian Molecular Biology Orgn. fellow, 1991; recipient Murex Virologist award Asia Pacific Soc., 1995. Fellow: Royal Coll. Pathologists; mem.: Asia Pacific Soc. Med. Virology (pres.), Internat. Soc. Infectious Diseases, N.Y. Acad. Scis. Roman Catholic. Achievements include British patent for detection of dengue and other flaviviruses using NS3 gene primers and probes; isolation of novel human genes HEP-COP, DENN, Huel, MLL3, MOST-1. Office: Nat University Singapore School Medicine Microbiology Dept Singapore 117597 Singapore

CHOW, YEN-HUNG, researcher; b. Taipei, Taiwan, Nov. 21, 1966; PhD, Nat. Def. Med. Ctr., Taiwan, 1997. Rsch. assoc. U. Ga., 2002—05; asst. investigator Nat. Health Rsch. Insts., 2006—. Adj. asst. prof. Nat. Chya-Yi U., Taiwan, 2007—10. Mem.: Molecular Cellular Biology Assn. (Taipei). Office: 35 Keyan Rd Zhunan Town Miaoli County 350 Taiwan Business E-Mail: choeyenh@nhri.org.tw.

CHOWCHUEN, BOWORNSILP, plastic surgeon, educator; b. Khon Kaen, Thailand, May 24, 1959; s. Bhadoonsilp and Wantee Chowchuen; m. Prathana Kittiwanwanit; children: Purich, Pachanok, Suphapit, Kritapas. BSc, Mahidol U., Bangkok, 1980, MD, 1982; MBA, Khon Kaen U., Khon Kaen, Thailand, 1996. Diplomate diploma Thai Bd. Gen. Surgery, Thai Bd. Plastic Surgery. Tchg. staff Khon Kaen U., 1986—; mgr. Khon Kaen U. Book Ctr., 1997—99; assoc. prof. plastic surgery Khon Kaen U., 1999—, asst. dean for adminstrn., 1999—2001, assoc. dean for quality improvement, 2001—, dir. Performance Mgmt. and Quality Assurance Office, 2004—. Project dir. project for multidisciplinary mgmt. of cleft lip palate Khon Kaen U., 2000—, project dir. Smile Train Cleft Care Project, 2000—. Contbr. articles to profl. jours. Mem.: Am. Cleft Palate and Craniofacial Assn., Assn. Plastic Surgeons Thailand, Royal Coll. Surgeons Thailand, Alumni Assn. Coll. Grad. Sch. Mgmt. Khon Kaen U. (pres. 1999—2000). Office: Fac Med Khon Kaen U Friendship Hwy Khon Kaen 40002 Thailand Home: 123/1122 Khon Kaen U 42000 Muang Loei Thailand Office Fax: 66 43348375. Business E-Mail: bowcho@kku.ac.th.

CHOWDHARY, ABHAY, microbiologist, director; b. Jalna, India, Mar. 5, 1954; MBBS, B. J. Med. Coll., Pune, 1975; MD, DHA, GMC, Aurangabad, DM in Virology, FIMSA, 1980. Prof. & head, dept. microbiology Grant Med. Coll. & Sir J. J. Hosp., Mumbai, 2002—08; dir. AIDS Rsch. & Control Ctr., 2005—09, Haffkine Inst., Mumbai, 2008—. Recipient Presdl. Oration award, Indian Assn. Med. Microbiologists, Rajiv Gandhi Vidya Shiromani award, Rashtriya Vidya Saraswati Puraskar; named one of Best Citizens of India, Internat. Pub. House; fellowship, Internat. Med. Scis. Acad., Fogarty fellowship. Office: Haffkine Inst Parel Mumbai Maharashtra 400012 India Office Phone: 912224150826. Office Fax: 912224161787. Personal E-mail: abhaychowdhary@yahoo.com.

CHOWDHURY, MAJEEDUL HASAN, medical educator; m. Soheli Akhter Chowdhury; children: Sumaiya Akhter, Samira Akhter, Sharika Akhter. BSc with honors, U. Dhaka, Bangladesh, 1976, MSc, 1977; PhD, U. Newcastle-upon-Tyne, Eng., 1987. Postdoc. rsch. affiliate dept. pathology Columbia U., NYC, 1988—91; asst. prof. medicine Albert Einstein Coll. Medicine, Yeshiva U., NYC, 1992—96; asst. prof. biochemistry, endocrinology Touro Coll., NYC, 2004—07; asst. prof. NYC Coll. Tech., CUNY, Bklyn., 2007—; summer vis. prof. North South U., Dhaka, 2008. Cons. ethnobot. rsch. U. Devel. Alternative, Dhaka, 2008. Contbr. articles to profl. publs. Office: NYC Coll Tech CUNY 300 Jay St Brooklyn NY 11201-2983 Office Phone: 718-260-4907. Office Fax: 718 254-8629. Business E-Mail: mchowdhury@citytech.cuny.edu.

CHOWDHURY, UJJWAL KUMAR, cardiac surgeon, educator; b. Kolkata, West Bengal, India, Oct. 2, 1955; s. Aloke Kumar and Narayani Chowdhury; m. Sanjukta Chowdhury, Dec. 10, 1982; children: Priyanka, Sreenita, Abhishek. MBBS in Anatomy, Armed Forces Med. Coll., Poona, Maharashtra, India, 1979; MS in Gen. Surgery with 1st class, Inst. Postgrad. Med. Edn. and Rsch., Kolkata, 1984; MCh, Christian Med. Coll., Vellore, Tamil Nadu, India, 1991. Diplomate Nat. Bd. Exams, New Delhi, 1990. Additional prof., dept. cardiac surgery All India Inst. Med. Scis., New Delhi, 1996—; sr. cardiac surg. fellow, active mem. allograft team, spl. tng. implantation left ventricular assist devices Prince Charles Hosp., Brisbane, Australia, 1991—93; sr. cardiac surg. fellow Royal Alexandra Hosp. Children, Sydney, 1993—94, Royal Prince Alfred Hosp. Sydney, 1994. Tng. robotic cardiac surgery Intuitive Sugr. Vinci Surg. Sys. Tng. Workshop, Synnyvale, Calif., 2003. Contbr. more than 120 articles to cardiac surg. jours. Fellow: Australasian Soc. Cardiac and Thoracic Surgeons (Sydney), Indian Assn. Cardiothoracic Surgeons (New Delhi), Indian Assn. Cardiovasc. and Thoracic Surgeons (life); mem.: Soc. Thoracic Surgeons. Achievements include development of a novel technique of septation of the aortopulmonary window using a fenestrated, unidirectional, valved fabric patch; new technique of tumor thrombetomy from inferior vena cava in patients with renal cell carcinoma with inferior vena caval extension without cardiopulmonary bypass. Avocations: photography, music, aquariums. Home: S-III/436 Hawa Singh Block Asiad Village Ansari Nagar New Delhi Delhi 110049 India Office: All India Inst Med Scis Dept Cardiothoracic and Vascular Surgery Ansari Nagar New Delhi Delhi 110029 India

CHOWHAN, NAVEED MAHFOOZ, oncologist; b. Pakistan, Oct. 19, 1960; came to U.S., 1979; Student, Mao and Forman Christian Coll., Pakistan, 1979; MD cum laude, U Cetec, Dominican Republic, 1982. Bd. cert. internal medicine, 1986, hematology, 1992, oncology, 1993. Resident internal medicine Georgetown U. Svc., D.C. Gen. Hosp., Washington, 1983-86; fellowship oncology-hematology SUNY, Stony Brook, 1988-91, clin. asst. prof. dept. medicine divsn. oncology, 1992-94; pvt. practice New Albany, Ind., 1994—; cert. physician investigator Acad. Pharm. Physicians and Investigators, 2007—. Pvt. practice, South Bend, Ind., 1986—88; attending physician Meml. Hosp. and St. Joseph Med. Ctr., South Bend, 1987—88, Floyd Meml. Hosp., New Albany, 1994—, chair cancer conf., 1995—97, 2001, 03, dir. stem cell transplant unit, 1997—2000, chair cancer com., 1997—2000, 2011—, sec. med. staff, 1998—2000, vice-chair staff, 2001, chair credentials com., 01, chmn. med. staff, 02; attending physician Clark Meml. Hosp., Jeffersonville, Ind., 1994—, mem. cancer com., 1995—2000, chair blood transfusion com., 1997, cancer liaison physician, 1999—2001; mem. Com. on Rsch. Involving Human Subjects, 1993—94; pioneer bone marrow transplant program SUNY, Stony Brook, 1994; investigator, rschr. and presenter in field. Contbr. articles to profl. jours. Recipient Leadership award, Nat. Rep. Congl. Com. Physician Adv. Bd., 2002; named Physician of Yr., 2003. Fellow ACP; mem. Am. Soc. Clin. Oncology, Am. Soc. Hematology, Cancer Ctr. Ind. (med. dir. 2010-). Office: 2210 Greenvalley Rd Ste 1 New Albany IN 47150-6809

CHOY, DANIEL SHU JEN, physician, research scientist; b. Shanghai, May 29, 1926; came to U.S., 1941; s. Jun Ke and Jessie (Wu) C.; m. Rhea Brown, Dec. 27, 1985; children: Martha, DAniel Jr. BA, Columbia Coll., 1944, MD, 1949. Intern Meadowbrook Hosp., 1949-50; resident Francis Delafield Hosp.-Columbia U., NYC, 1951-54; fellow Am. Cancer Soc., 1951-54; dir. laser lab. St. Luke's-Roosevelt Hosp. Ctr.-Columbia U., NYC; asst. clin. prof. med. Columbia U., NYC; chief tumor svc. French Hosp., NYC, 1962-74; attending physician Lenox Hosp., NYC; assoc. attending physician, rsch. scientist cardiology lab. St. Luke's Roosevelt Hosp., NYC, dir. laser lab. Inventor aeroplast, 1950, laser angioplasty, 1980, percutaneus laser disc decompression, 1986, left ventricular assist device—intraventricular balloon, 1987, myocardial angiogenesis, 1989. Fellow ACP, Explorers Club; mem. Am. Soc. Clin. Oncology (founding, Am. Bd. Laser Surgery (founding, bd. dirs. 1985—). Invented sequential sound wave phase shift for first non-surgical treatment of titanus 2000. Home: 300 E 74th St Apt 26F New York NY 10021-3716 Office: 66E 80 St New York NY 10075

CHOYKE, PETER L., radiologist, researcher; Degree, Pa. State U.; MD, Jefferson Med. Coll. Intern Waterbury Hosp., Conn.; resident in diagnostic radiology Yale-New Haven Hosp.; from asst. prof. to assoc. prof. radiology Georgetown U. Sch. Medicine; sr. staff investigator diagnostic radiology dept. NIH Clin. Ctr., 1987, chief magnetic resonance imaging, diagnostic radiology dept., 1992, chief rsch. activity diagnostic radiology dept.; chief, sr. clinician molecular imaging program, head imaging sect. Ctr. Cancer Rsch., Nat. Cancer Inst., NIH, 2004—. Office: Molecular Imaging Program Nat Cancer Inst Bldg 10 Rm 1B40 10 Center Dr Bethesda MD 20892 Office Phone: 301-451-4221. Office Fax: 301-402-3191. E-mail: pchoyke@nih.gov. *

CHRETIEN, PAUL BERNARD, oncologist, medical researcher; b. San Angelo, Tex., May 13, 1931; s. Joseph Rodney and Celeste Regina Chretien; m. Jane Susan Henkel, Apr. 11, 1970; children: Jean Paul, Yves Rene. BS, St. Louis U., Coll. Arts and Sci., 1953; MD, St. Louis U., Sch. Medicine, 1957. Diplomate Am. Bd. Surgery, lic. State of Md. From intern to chief resident, dept. surgery N.Y. U. Bellevue Hosp. Ctr., 1957—62; nat. cancer inst. fellow, oncology Mem. Sloan-Kettering Cancer Cent., 1962—66; sr. investigator, asst. chief surgery br. Nat. Cancer Inst., 1966—72, chief, tumor immunology sect., surgery br., founding mem. immunotherapy contracts prog., 1972—80, coord., head, neck cancer contracts prog., div. cancer treatment, 1974—80; prof., dir. rsch., dept. surgery U. Md. Sch. of Medicine, 1983—93. Mem., sr. exec. svc. U.S. Civil Svc., 1976—80; co-originator, co-chmn. First Head and Neck Cancer Rsch. Workshop, 1980; cons., immunotherapy prog. Hoffmann-LaRoche Inc., 1980—92; v.p., med. affairs Alpha 1 Biomedicals Inc., 1982—94; originator, chmn. First Internat. Conf. Head and Neck Cancer, 1984. Contbr. over 225 sci. abstract papers, articles, book chpts. Capt. Med. Corps. USAR, 1959—69. Mem.: Soc. Surg. Oncology, Clin. Immunology Soc., Am. Soc. Clin. Oncology, Am. Radium Soc., Am. Head Neck Soc., Am. Coll. Surgeons, Am. Fedn. Med. Rsch., Am. Assoc. Immunologists, Am. Assoc. Cancer Rsch., Am. Assoc. Advancement Sci. Achievements include assigned FDA IND 14,738 for first clinical trial of Thymosin alpa 1 (1978); designed successful NCI sponsored trial of Thymosin Alpa 1 for patients with small cell carcinoma of the lung in 1978 and patients with non small cell carcinoma of the lung in 1990. Office: 10201 Grosvenor Pl Rockville MD 20852-4645 Office Phone: 301-493-6160. Office Fax: 301 493 9581. Business E-Mail: chretien.paul@yahoo.com.

CHRIST, BODO E.A., anatomist; b. Greene, Germany, Feb. 4, 1941; s. Hermann and Ema Christ; m. Liliana Falla-Vilanueva Falla-Christ, May 9, 1994; children: Jana Maria, Anna Katharina; m. Gesine Eichhoff Christ (div.); children: Volko, Martin, Valentin, Jesko. MD, U. Goettingen, Germany, 1968; PhD, U. Bochum, Germany, 1975. Prof. U. Bochum, 1976—90, U. Freiburg, Germany, 1990—2001, dean faculty of medicine, 1997—99. Vis. prof. U. Leiden, 1988, U. Calif., San Francisco, 1994, Stanford U., Calif., 2000, U. Basel, Switzerland, 2006—07; pres. Anatomische Gesellschaft, 2004—06. Contbr. 500 articles to profl. jours. Mem.: German Acad. Scis., Am. Assn. Anatomists. Avocations: painting, book binding. Home: Obere Lachen 4 79110 Freiburg Germany Office: Inst Anatomy and Biology Albertstrasse 17 Freiburg Germany 79104 Business E-Mail: bodo.christ@anat.uni-freiburg.de.

CHRISTAKIS, NICHOLAS ALEXANDER, internist, social scientist, educator; BS in Biology, Yale U., New Haven, 1984; MPH, Harvard Sch. Pub. Health, Boston, 1988; MD, Harvard U., Mass., 1989; PhD in Sociology, U. Pa., Phila., 1995. Diplomate Nat. Bd. Med. Examiners, Am. Bd. Internal Medicine, lic. Mass. Rsch. asst. Marine Biol. Lab., Woods Hole, 1981—83, Institut de Recherches sur les Maladies du Sang, Département d'Oncologie Expérimentake, Hopital Saint-Louis, Paris, 1981—82; rsch. assoc. Nat. Inst. Neurological Communicative Disorders and Stroke, NIH, 1982—83; rsch. assoc., WHO Harvard U. Internat. Collaborating Ctr. for Health Legislation Harvard Sch. Pub. Health, 1987—88; rsch. assoc. Harvard U. Health Transition Project, 1988—89; tchg. fellow, dept. hsitory sci. Harvard U., Cambridge, 1987—88; resident, medicine U. Pa. Med. Ctr., Phila., 1989—91; clin. scholar Robert Wood Johnson Found., U. Pa., Phila., 1991—93; asst. instr., dept. medicine U. Pa., Phila., 1990—91, sr. fellow, Leonard Davis Inst. Health, 1991—95, fellow, dept. medicine, 1991—94, Nat. Rsch. Svc. Award Fellow, dept. sociology and divsn. gen. internal medicine, 1993—95, instr., dept. medicine, 1994—95; rsch. assoc., Population Rsch. Ctr. and Ctr. on Aging U. Chgo., 1995—2001, core faculty, Robert Wood Johnson Clin. Scholars Program, 1995—99, asst. prof. sociology, 1995—98, asst. prof. medicine, 1995—98, assoc. prof. sociology, 1999—2001, assoc. prof. medicine, 1999—2001, prof. sociology, 2001, prof. medicine, 2001; attending physician U. Chgo. Med. Ctr., 1995—2001; home hospice physician Horizon Hospice, Chgo., 1999—2001; attending physician, palliative medicine svc. Mass. Gen. Hosp., 2002—06; prof. sociology, faculty arts and sciences Harvard U., 2005—; prof. med. sociology, dept. health care policy Harvard U. Med. Sch., 2001—; attending physician, dept. medicine Mt. Auburn Hosp., Harvard Med. Sch., 2006—. Dir. Robert Wood Johnson Scholars in Health Policy Program, Harvard U., 2002—05, mem. exec. com., 2005—08; bd. dirs. Horizon Hospice, Chgo., 1998—2001; co-dir., Robert Wood Johnson Found. Clin. Scholars Program U. Chgo., 1999—2001; vis. prof., Sydney Inst. Palliative Medicine Royal Prince Alfred Hosp., Australia, 1999, Australia, 2000; vis. prof., Ctr. on Ethics and the Professions Harvard U., 2001—02; vis. fellow Edith Cowan U., Perth, Australia, 2000; invited presenter in the field. Author: Death Foretold: Prophecy and Prognosis in Medical Care, 1999; mem. editl. bd.: Brit. Med. Jour., Jour. Palliative Medicine, Palliative Medicine, Am. Jour. Sociology, and others; contbr. articles to profl. jours.; ad-hoc reviewer. Recipient Disting. Researcher award, Nat. Hospice and Palliative Care Organization, 2006; named one of The World's Most Influential People, TIME mag., 2009. Mem.: Inst. of Medicine. Achievements include research in social factors that affect health, health care, and longevity. Office:

Harvard Univ Med Sch Dept Health Care Policy 180 Longwood Ave Boston MA 02115-5899 Office Phone: 617-432-5890. Office Fax: 617-432-5891. Business E-Mail: christakis@hcp.med.harvard.edu.

CHRISTEN, ARDEN GALE, dental educator, researcher, consultant; b. Lemmon, SD, Jan. 25, 1932; s. Harold John Christen and Dorothy Elizabeth (Taylor) Deering; m. Joan Ardell Akre, Sept. 10, 1955; children: Barbara, Penny, Rebecca, Sarah. BS, U. Minn., 1954, DDS, 1956; MSD, Ind. U., 1965; MA, Ball State U., 1973. Lic. dentist, Ind. Commd. 1st lt. USAF, 1956, advanced through grades to col., 1972; base dental surgeon Zaragoza Air Base, Spain, 1970—73; dental surgeon, cons. preventive dentistry RAF Bentwaters, England, 1973—75; officer air force preventive dentistry Sch. Aerospace Medicine, Brooks AFB, Tex., 1978—80; prof., chmn. dept. preventive dentistry Ind. U., Indpls., 1981—93, dir. preventive/cmty. dentistry, 1993—2000, co-dir. nicotine dependence program, 1997—, acting chair oral biology, 2000—04, prof. emeritus oral biology, 2004—, dir., tobacco edn. program Fairbanks, 2004—. Sr. med. svc. cons. Surgeon Gen., U.S. Air Force, U.S. and Eng., 1974-80; spl. cons. to asst. surgeon gen. for dental svcs., Washington, 1975-80. Co-author: Primary Preventive Dentistry, 4th edit., 1995; contbr. over 300 articles to profl. jours. Bd. dirs. Bexar County chpt. Am. Cancer Soc., San Antonio, 1976-80, Marion County chpt., Indpls., 1980—; mem. Ind. divsn. Pub. Edn. Standing Com., Indpls., 1980. Decorated Service medal with 2 oak leaf clusters, Legion of Merit. Fellow Am. Coll. Dentists; mem. ADA, Am. Acad. Oral Pathology, Internat. Assn. Dental Rsch., Am. Acad. History of Dentistry (v.p. 1984-85, pres. 1986-87). Presbyterian. Avocations: photography, classical music, travel, writing. Home: 7112 Sylvan Ridge Rd Indianapolis IN 46240-3541 Office: Ind U Sch Dentistry 1121 W Michigan St Indianapolis IN 46202-5186 Office Phone: 317-284-1168. Business E-Mail: achriste@iupui.edu.

CHRISTEN, WILLIAM G., epidemiologist, educator; Assoc. prof. Harvard Medical Sch.; assoc. epidemiologist Brigham and Women's Hosp. Office: Brigham and Women's Hospital Division of Preventive Medicine 900 Commonwealth Ave E 3rd Fl Boston MA 02215 Office Phone: 617-278-0795. Office Fax: 617-734-1437. E-mail: wchristen@rics.bwh.harvard.edu.

CHRISTENSEN, ALAN J., psychology professor, department chairman; BS in Psychology, U. Utah, Salt Lake City, 1987, MS in Clin. Psychology, 1991, PhD in Clin. Psychology, 1993. Lic. psychologist Iowa, health svc. provider Iowa. Intern in clin. psychology Portland VA Med. Ctr./Oreg. Health Sciences U., 1992—93; asst. prof. psychology U. Iowa, Iowa City, 1993—97, assoc. prof. psychology, 1997—2001, dir. clin. tng., dept. psychology, 1998—2005, prof. psychology, 2002—, chmn. dept. psychology, 2006—; assoc. prof. internal medicine U. Iowa Coll. Medicine, 1999—2002, prof. internal medicine, 2002—; sr. scientist, dept. vet. affairs Iowa City VA Med. Ctr., 2004—. Contbr. articles to profl. jours. Fellow: Soc. Behavioral Medicine (Early Career award 2000); mem.: APA (mem. Divsn. 38, Disting. Sci. award 2000), Acad. Behavioral Medicine Rsch., Am. Psychosomatic Soc. (Early Career award 1999). Office: Dept Psychology Spence Laboratories Psychology Univ Iowa Iowa City IA 52242 Office Phone: 319-335-3396, 319-335-2405. Office Fax: 319-335-0191. Business E-Mail: alan-christensen@uiowa.edu.

CHRISTENSEN, JAMES R., medical educator; b. Nebr., May 2, 1950; BS, Nebr. Wesleyan U., 1972; MD, U. Nebr., 1975. Assoc. prof., phys. medicine, rehab., and pediat. Kennedy Krieger Inst. and Johns Hopkins U. Sch. Medicine, 1992—. Office: Kennedy Krieger Inst 707 North Broadway Baltimore MD 21205 Office Fax: 443-923-9445. Business E-Mail: christensenj@kennedykrieger.org.

CHRISTENSEN, JENS JØRGEN ELMER, clinical microbiologist; b. Nestved, Sealand, Denmark, Oct. 20, 1952; s. Aage Elmer and Inger (Madsen) C.; m. Birgitte Steen Hansen, (div. 2003); children: Martin, David. MD, U. Copenhagen, 1980; DSc, U. Aarhus, 1999. Med. diplomate. Physician dept. clin. microbiology Bispeboerg Hosp., Copenhagen, 1982-85; physician dept. medicine Kalundborg (Denmark) Hosp., 1985-88; physician dept. clin. microbiology Hillerød (Denmark) Hosp., 1990-92, Herlev (Denmark) Hosp., 1992-95; physician, co-head dept. clin. microbiology Århus (Denmark) U. Hosp., 1995-96; physician Statens Seruminst., Copenhagen, 1988-90, staff specialist dept. clin. microbiology, 1996-2000, head unit of clin. microbiology, 2000—. Mem. bd., chmn. Young Microbiologists, Copenhagen, 1987-90; guest rschr. Ctrs. for Disease Control and Prevention, Atlanta, 1995. Contbr. articles to profl. jours. Mem. Danish Soc. Clin. Microbiology (bd. sec. 1990-96), Danish Soc. Immunology, Orgn. Clin. Microbiologists (bd. dirs. 1996—), N.Y. Acad. Scis. Avocations: tennis, badminton, wind-surfing. Office: Statens Seruminst Dept Clin Microbiol Artilleri vej 5 2300 Copenhagen S Denmark Home Phone: 4550402483; Office Phone: 4532683572. Business E-Mail: jjc@ssi.dk.

CHRISTENSEN, LISE HANNE, pathologist, researcher; b. Copenhagen, Sept. 23, 1947; d. Helge Arne and Ruth Christensen; life ptnr. Hans Henrik Sand; children: Marie Christensen Begovich, Paula Christensen Begovich. MD, U. Copenhagen, 1977. Pathologist Rigshospitalet, Copenhagen, 1984—2005; sr. pathologist Bispebjerg Hosp., Univ. Hosp., Copenhagen, 2005—. Cons. rschr. Contura A/S, Soborg, Denmark, 1999—. Achievements include detection of how different bulking agents behave in human tissue. Office: Bispebjerg Hosp Pathology Bispebjerg Bakke 23 2400 Copenhagen Denmark Home Phone: 22880236; Office Phone: 4535312385. Office Fax: 4535313901. Business E-Mail: lc24@bbh.hosp.dk, lc24@bbh.regionh.dk.

CHRISTIAN, CORA L.E, health facility administrator, physician; b. St. Thomas, VI, Sept. 11, 1947; d. Alphonso Augustine and Ruth Christian; m. Simon B. Jones-Hendrickson, Oct. 23, 1976; children: Nesha Christian-Hendrickson, Marcus Christian-Hendrickson. BS in Biology, Marquette U., 1967; MPH, Johns Hopkins U., 1975; MD, Jefferson Med. Coll., Phila., 1971. Diplomate Am. Coll. Forensic Examiners, Am. Bd. Quality Assurance and Utilization Rev., Am. Acad. Family Practice. Pvt. family-based practice, Frederiksted, VI, 1975—; asst. commr. Dept. Health, St. Croix, VI, 1977—91; educator, CEO, now med. dir. VI Med. Inst., Inc, St. Croix, 1978—; dir., prin. investigator US VI Household Survey, St. Croix, VI, 1988; chief med. cons., med. dir. Hovensa, LLC, St. Croix, 1990—; cons. VI AIDS Edn. and Tng., NYC, 1992—2005. Pres. Caribbean Studies Assn., 2000—01; pres., exec. sec., treas. VI Med. Soc., St. Croix, 1995—. Contbr. articles to profl. jours., chapters to books. Bd. dirs. Am. Cancer Soc., St. Croix, 1991—2005. Named to Trail Blazers for Women's History, Women's Bus. Ctr., 2000; Paul Harris fellow, Rotary, 1997. Mem.: AARP (nat. bd. dirs. 2004—10, vice chair ins. trust 2006—10), SGI (area leader 2010—), Interfaith Coalition (pres. 2010), Am. Acad. Family Physicians (pres. VI chpt. 1976—, com. mem. 1996—2005). Buddhist. Avocation: dance. Home: PO Box 1338 Frederiksted VI 00841 Office: VI Med Inst Inc PO Box 5989 Christiansted VI 00823-5989 Office Fax: 340-712-2449. Personal E-mail: cchrisitian@hovensa.com, corachristian@gmail.com.

CHRISTIAN, JOE CLARK, medical genetics researcher, educator, medical genetics researcher, educator; b. Marshall, Okla., Sept. 12, 1934; s. Roy John and Katherine Elizabeth (Beeby) C.; m. Shirley Ann Yancey, June 5, 1960; children: Roy Clark, Charles David. BS, Okla. State U., 1956; MS, U. Ky., 1959, PhD, 1960, MD, 1964. Cert. clin. geneticist, Am. Bd. Med. Genetics. Resident internal medicine Vanderbilt U., Nashville, 1964-66; asst. prof. med. genetics Ind. U., Indpls., 1966-69, assoc. prof., 1969-74, prof., 1974-99, assoc. dean basic scis. and regional ctrs., 1996-98, prof. emeritus, assoc. dean emeritus, 1999—. Served with USAR, 1953-60. Mem.: AMA, Am. Soc. Human Genetics. Democrat. Methodist. Avocations: bicycling, farming. Office: Ind U Dept Med/Molecular Genetics 410 W 10th St Indianapolis IN 46202-4033 E-mail: jcristi@iupui.edu.

CHRISTIAN, JOHN EDWARD, health science association administrator, educator; b. Indpls., July 12, 1917; s. George Edward and Okel Kandus (Waltz) C.; m. Catherine Ellen Spooner, July 23, 1948; 1 dau., Linda Kay. BS, Purdue U., 1939, PhD, 1944. Control chemist Upjohn Co., 1939-40; faculty Purdue U., Lafayette, Ind., 1940—, prof. pharm. chemistry, 1950-59, head dept. radiol. control, 1956-59, prof. bionucleonics, head dept., 1959-82; chmn. adminstrv. com. Trace Level Research Inst., 1960-88; dir. Inst. for Environmental Health, 1965-88; head Sch. Health Scis., 1979-82, Hovde Disting. prof., 1979-88, Hovde Disting. prof. bionucleonics and health scis. emeritus, 1988—. Vis. prof. radiation therapy Ind. U. Sch. Medicine, 1970-88; Harvey Washington Meml. lectr. Purdue U., 1955; Edward-Kremers Meml. lectr. U. Wis., 1956; vis. lectr. U. Tex., 1959, Taylor U. Ann. Sci. Lecture Series, Upton, Ind., 1960; Julius A. Koch Meml. lectr. U. Pitts., 1961 Assoc. editor Radiochem. Letters. Mem. revision com. U.S. Pharmacopeia, 1950-60, mem. adv. panel on radioactive drugs, 1960-70; adv. com. isotope distbn. AEC, 1952-58, mem. med. adv. com., 1967-75; mem. radiation and chem. def. sect. Ind. Dept. Civil Def., 1954—; vice chmn. Radiation Control Adv. Commn., Ind., 1958—; mem. exec. com. Ind. Comprehensive Health Planning Council, 1972-76; mem. adv. com. radiopharms. FDA, 1970-75; mem. Ind. Gov.'s Pesticide Council, 1970-73; Alumni research councilor Purdue Research Found., 1964-88; mem. Ind. Environmental Mgmt. Bd., 1972-87, Nat. Energy Policy Task Force, Dept. Energy, 1981-83; mem. Bd. Grants Am. Found. for Pharm. Edn., 1989—. Recipient award Chilean Iodine Ednl. Bur., 1956, Julius Sturmer award Phila. Coll. Pharmacy and Sci., 1958, Leather medal Purdue U., 1971, Hovde Faculty Purdue U. fellow, 1988. Fellow AAAS (past sec. and chmn. pharm. sci. sect., mem. council), Ind. Acad. Sci.; mem. AMA (spl. affiliate), AAUP, Am. Inst. Architecture (bd. dirs. 1998—, Gibson award 1999), Am. Assn. Colls. Pharmacy (past mem. exec. com., chmn. conf. tchrs., chmn. conf. grad. study and grad. tchrs., chmn. com. study grad. edn. in pharmacy), Am. Chem. Soc. (past chmn. Purdue sect.), Am. Pharm. Assn. (Ebert medal 1957, Justin L. Powers Research Achievement award 1963, past chmn. sci. sect.), Acad. Pharm. Sci. (past v.p.), Ind. Pharm. Assn., Am. Pub. Health Assn., Am. Nuclear Soc., Am. Soc. Bacteriology, Health Phys. Soc., Historic Landmarks Found. of Ind. (bd. dirs., exec. com. 1997—), Frank Lloyd Wright Bldg. Conservancy (Wright Spirit award 1997), Sigma Xi (past pres. Purdue chpt., research award Purdue chpt. 1950), Rho Chi, Phi Lambda Upsilon, Sigma Pi Sigma., Eta Sigma Gamma, Gamma Sigma Delta. Home: 1301 Woodland Ave West Lafayette IN 47906-2371 Office: Purdue U Sch Health Scis Civil Engring Bldg West Lafayette IN 47907

CHRISTIAN, JOSEPH RALPH, physician; b. Chgo., June 15, 1920; s. Ralph F. and Anna M. (Across) Co; m. Marcia Pomeroy, Sept. 25, 1944; children— Patricia Ann, Joseph Ralph. AA, U. Chgo., 1941; MD, Loyola U., Chgo., 1944. Diplomate: Am. Bd. Pediatrics. Intern Cook County Hosp., Chgo., 1944-45, resident, 1945-46, 48-49; faculty Stritch Sch. Medicine, Loyola U., Chgo., 1948-61; prof. Stritch Sch. Medicine, Loyola U. (pediatrics), 1957-61, chmn. dept., 1960-61; attending pediatrician Loyola Service at La Rabida Sanitarium, 1948-61; chmn. dept. pediatrics Mercy Hosp., 1960-61; chief pediatrics Lewis Meml. Maternity Hosp., 1951-61; chmn. dept. pediatrics Rush Presbyn.-St. Luke's Med. Center, Chgo., 1961-85; prof. pediatrics U. Ill. Coll. Medicine, Chgo., 1961-70; prof. Rush Med. Coll., Chgo., 1970-85, prof. emeritus, 1985—, chmn. dept. pediatrics, 1970-85. Sr. attending pediatrician children's div. Cook County Hosp., 1959-65 Editor: Pediatrics Digest, 1962-78; Mem. editorial bd.: Childcraft, 1963-87; Contbr. articles to med. jours. Chmn. poison control com. Chgo. Bd. Health, 1961-69; chmn. med. com. Infant Welfare Soc., Chgo., 1958-61; chmn. 9th Ill. Congress Maternal and Infant Health, 1962; chmn. bd. trustees Holy Cross Chgo., 1970-75. Served to capt. M.C. AUS, 1946-47. Recipient Clin. Faculty award Stritch Sch. Medicine, 1954, 57 Fellow Am. Coll. Chest Physicians, Am. Acad. Pediatrics (chmn. film rev. com. 1963-73, chmn. com. residency fellowships 1964-67), Am. Pub. Health Assn., A.C.P.; mem. A.M.A., Am. Fedn. Clin. Research, Am. Pediatric Soc., Am. Heart Assn., Ambulatory Pediatric Assn., Am. Assn. Poison Control Centers, Am. Assn. Maternal and Infant Health, Ill. Assn. Maternal and Infant Health (pres. 1964), Am. Pediatric Soc., Chgo. Pediatric Soc. (pres. 1964-65), Midwest Soc. Pediatric Research, Assn. Med. Sch. Pediatric Dept. Chairmen. Home: 3 Oakbrook Club Dr Apt E107 Oak Brook IL 60523-1330 Office Phone: 630-832-7648.

CHRISTIANSEN, RICHARD LOUIS, orthodontist researcher and research administrator, educator, dean; b. Denison, Iowa, Apr. 1, 1935; s. John Cornelius and Rosa Katherine C.; m. Nancy Marie Norman, June 24, 1956; children: Mark Richard, David Norman, Laura Marie. DDS, U. Iowa, 1959; MSD, Ind. U., Indpls., 1964; PhD, U. Minn., 1970; PhD (hon.), Nippon Dental U., Tokyo, 2000. Prin. investigator Nat. Inst. Dental Research NIH, Bethesda, Md., 1970-73, chief craniofacial anomalies program br., 1973-81, dir. extramural Nat. Inst. Dental Research, 1981-82; prof. dept. orthodontics U. Mich., Ann Arbor, 1982—, dean, Sch. Dentistry and dir. W.K. Kellogg Found. Inst., 1982—2001, prof., dean emeritus, 2001—. Organizer state-of-the -art workshops in field of craniofacial anomalies and other aspects of oral health; founder Internat. Union Schs. Oral Health, 1985; organizer oral health conf. in Poland, 1989, Jordan, 1995. Contbr. chpts. to books and articles to profl. jours. Chmn. Region III United Way, U. Mich., Ann Arbor, 1984; chmn., v.p. Trinity Luth. Ch., Rockville, Md., 1975; v.p. and chmn. planning task force Trinity Luth. Ch., Ann Arbor, chmn. bd. Sequoia Sr. Housing; vice chmn., bd. dirs. Luth. Soc. Svcs. Mich., 1997—; with USPHS, 1959-82, mem. dental prof. adv. com., 2005-. Recipient Commendation medal USPHS, 1980, Cert. of Recognition NIH, 1982, Disting. Svc. award, 2007, others; named Dental Alumnus of Yr., U. Iowa, 2005, Southeast Mich. Philanthropy award, 2006, Disting. Svc. award, Univ. Mich., Sch. Dent. 2007. Fellow Internat. Coll. Dentists, Am. Coll. Dentists, Pierre Fauchard Acad.; mem. Am. Assn. Orthodontists, Am. Assn. Dental Sch., ADA (rsch. coun.), Mich. Dental Assn., Am. Assn. Dental Rsch. (dir. craniofacial biology group 1975-79, v.p. 1979-80, pres. 1981-82), Omicron Kappa Upsilon (com. mem.), USPHS(dental profl. adv. com. mem. 2005-) Achievements include research in craniofacial research and international oral health. Avocations: reading, jogging, tennis, sailing. Business E-Mail: vista@umich.edu.

CHRISTIANSEN-GÖZZER, JOSÉ MARIANO, psychiatrist; b. Chimbote, Ancash, Peru, Sept. 19, 1948; arrived in Belgium, 1984; s. Carlos Alfredo Christiansen-Gonzales, Ana Maria Gözzer-Pizarro; m. Christine Raspe; children: Elisa, Jeanne; m. Luz Eugenia Mostacero, Oct. 18, 1975 (div.); children: Anna-Liv, Carlos-Gustavo, Ilse-Fabiola. MD, Sch. Medicine Trujillo, Peru, 1976; MS, Sch. Medicine San Marcos, Lima, 1980, Sch. Medicine Louvain, Brussels, 1988; PhD, Sch. Medicine Louvain, 1998. Diplomate. Intern U. Trujillo, Regional Hosp. Trugillo, 1975—76; resident U. San Mareos, Lima, Peru, 1976—79, U. Louvain, Brussels, 1984—88; dir. Jicamarca Project H. Valdizan Hosp., 1980—84; physician Inst. of Rsch. Le Nidoux, Malonne, Belgium, 1989—, I.M.P. Reumonjoie, Malonne, 1989—; child psychiatrist cons. Ctr. Neurologie W. Lennox, Ottignies, Belgium, 2000—. Chief trauma practice Peruvian U. Cayetano Heredia, Lima, 1978—80; cons. prof. Cath. U. Lima, 1981—84; child psychiatrist cons. Ctr. Placet Louvain, 1989—93, Reine Fabiola Hosp., Auvelais, Belgium, 1992—2000. Contbr. numerous articles to profl. jours. Pres. Centre Placet, Louvain-La-Neuve, Belgium, 1988—89; Malonne Belgium, 1994—. Mem.: AAAS, Societe Royale de Medecine Mentale de Belgique, N.Y. Acad. Sci. Roman Catholic. Avocations: gardening, reading, jogging, movies. Mailing: Ctr Hospitalier Regional Val de Sambre 75 Rue Chere Voie 5060 Sambreville Belgium Office Phone: 071-265211. Personal E-mail: jose.christiansen@hotmail.com.

CHRISTIDIS, NIKOLAOS, dentist; b. Stockholm, Jan. 10, 1978; s. Ioannis and Rita Christidis. DDS, Karolinska Institutet, Stockholm, 2002; Attending, Karolinska Inst., Dept Dental Medicine Sect Orofacial Pain & Jaw Function, Stockholm, 2008; PhD in Med. Scis., 2010. Lic. in Dentist Socialstyrelsen, 2002. Dentist specialist clinic Cmty. dental care, Stockholm county coun., 2002—. Specialist stomatognathic physiology Eastman Inst., 2011; subject tchr. dept. dental medicine Karolinska Inst., 2006. Contbr. articles to profl. jours. Recipient Best sci. poster award, 2007; grantee, Karolinska Inst. Founding, 2007—08, Swedish Dental Soc., 2004—10. Mem.: Bd. Swedish Odontological Tchrs., Bd. Stockholm Dental Assn. Office: Karolinska Inst Dept Dental Medicine Sect Orofacial Pain & Jaw Function Box 4064 Huddinge 141 04 Sweden Office Fax: 468 6080 881. Personal E-mail: nikolaos.christidis@ftv.sll.se. Business E-Mail: nikolaos.christidis@ki.se.

CHRISTIE, AMIEL COLIN, pathologist, consultant; b. Sydney, NSW, Australia, Mar. 26, 1920; s. Colin and Helen Mary (Seton) C.; m. Betty Margaret Stewart, Oct. 5, 1955; children: Andrew, Jonathan, Rosemary, David. MBBS, Sydney U., 1942, MD, 1955; Diploma Clin. Pathology, London U., 1948. Med. diplomate. Pathology registrar Royal Prince Alfred Hosp., Sydney, 1942-44; dir. pathology Repatriation Hosp., Perth, 1946-47; asst. pathologist Royal Marsden Hosp., London, 1949-54; dir. pathology Royal Hosp. for Women, Sydney, 1955-61; cons. pathologist The Wollongong Hosp., Australia, 1962-84, emeritus cons., 1984—. Contbr. articles to profl. jours. Capt. Australian Army Med. Corps, 1944-46. Fellow Royal Coll. Pathologists of Australasia, Royal Coll. Pathologists (Eng.); mem. AAAS, Am. Soc. Clin. Pathologists, Assn. Clin. Pathologists (Gt. Britain), Internat. Soc. Dermatopathology, Internat. Soc. Haematology. Mem. Ch. of England. Avocations: tennis, reading. Home: 170 Edinburgh Rd Castlecrag Sydney NSW 2068 Australia Office: 39 Market St NSW 2500 Wollongong Australia

CHRISTIE, DENNIS L., gastroenterologist, educator; MD, Northwestern U., Feinberg, 1968. Diplomate Am. Bd. Pediatrics, 1992, Am. Bd. Pediatrics-pediatric gastroenterology, 2005. Fellow pediatric gastroenterology UCLA Ctr. Health Sci., 1974—76; resident pediatrics Univ. of Washington Med. Ctr., 1969—71, intern, 1969; chief gastroenterology, hepatology, and nutrition divsn. Seattle Children's Hosp.; mem. adv. bd. Children's Univ. Med. Group, chmn. contracting com. Prof. pediatrics Univ. of Washington Sch. of Medicine. Author: (articles) A child with Kabuki syndrome and primary sclerosign cholangitis successfully treated with usodiol and cholestryamine, 2006, Gastrointestinal Stromal Tumor, 2006, Serum Immune Responses Predict Rapid Disease Progression among children with Crohn's Disease: Immune Responses Predict Disease Progression, 2006, Family-based intervention for children with inflammatory bowel disease: A Pilot Study, 2007, Cognitive-behavioral therapy for children with functional abdominal pain and their parents decreases pain and other symptoms, 2010. Named top dr., Seattle Mag., 2004, 2005, 2006, 2008, 2009, 2010, Seattle Metropolitan Mag., 2006, 2007, 2008, 2009, 2010, 2011. Mem.: Am. Gastroent. Assn., N. Am. Soc. for Pediatric Gastroenterology. Office: Childrens Hospital Medical Center 4800 Sand Point Way NE MS 7830 Seattle WA 98105-3901 Office Phone: 206-987-2521.

CHRISTIE, DONALD MELVIN, JR., physician; b. Lewiston, Maine, May 5, 1942; s. Donald Melvin and Dorothy Carolyn (Doble) Christie. AB, U. Rochester, 1964, MD, 1968; Diplome de litt. francaise contemporaine, U. Paris, 1963. Diplomate Am. Bd. Internal Medicine, cert. added qualifications in sports medicine; strength and conditioning specialist Nat. Strength and Conditioning Assn., 2005. Med. intern U. Iowa Hosps. and Clinics, Iowa City, 1968—69, resident, 1969—70, U. Iowa Hosps. and Clinics, Iowa City, 1973; chief med. resident U. Iowa Hosps. and Clinics, Iowa City, 1973—74; asst. prof. preventive medicine and medicine U. Rochester (N.Y.) Sch. Medicine, 1974—77; physician, dir. clin. svcs. Princeton (N.J.) U. Health Svcs., 1977—83; clin. instr. family medicine U. Med. and Dentistry N.J., Rutgers U., 1978—83; internist Cmty. Health Plan, Poughkeepsie, NY, 1983—98; internist, dir. sports medicine St.

Mary's Regional Med. Ctr., Lewiston, Maine, 1999—2000; dir. sports medicine Med. Rehab. Assocs., Lewiston, 2001—02; pvt. practice sports medicine Lewiston, 2002—. Contract escort-interpreter (French) U.S. Dept. State, 1964—70; coord. Robert Wood Johnson Found. grant & primary care tng. evaluation U. Rochester, 1974—77; coord. internal medicine Hudson Valley Family Practice Residency, St. Francis Hosp., Poughkeepsie, NY, 1989—93, tchg. attending, 1990—98; dir. dept. internal medicine Vassar Bros. Hosp., Poughkeepsie, NY, 1992—98; cons. in field. Trustee Gould Acad., Bethel, Maine, 1984—; bd. dirs. Franco-Am. Heritage Ctr., Lewiston, Maine, 2007—, Maine Music Soc., 2008—. With US Army, 1970—72. Decorated Army Commendation medal. Fellow: ACP (chmn., coun. med. socs. 2001—03, ex officio mem. bd. regents 2001—03), Am. Coll. Sports Medicine; mem.: New Eng. Nordic Ski Assn. (chair sports sci. com. 2002—06), Am. Med. Soc. Sports Medicine (bd. dirs. 1999—2003). Democrat. Home: 7 Fairview Ave Gray ME 04039-9730 Office: The Gym 746 Main St Lewiston ME 04240 Home Phone: 207-657-8181; Office Phone: 207-754-0339. Personal E-mail: dchristie@roadrunner.com.

CHRISTIE, LAURENCE GLENN, JR., surgeon, educator; b. Houston, May 13, 1930; s. Laurence Glenn and Tommie Katherine (Myers) C.; m. Constance Graham Kelsey, Sept. 15, 1973; 1 child, Susan Eilzabeth. BS, Washington and Lee U., 1953; MD, Med. Coll. Va., 1957. Diplomate Am. Bd. Surgery. Intern Med. Coll. Va., Richmond, 1957-58, resident in surgery, 1957-62, clin. instr., 1963—2007; practice medicine specializing in gen. and vascular surgery, Ft. Smith, Ark., 1962-63; practice medicine specializing in gen. and vascular surgery Richmond, 1963—2008. Mem. active staff Henrico Doctors Hosp.; mem. courtesy staff Johnston-Willis Hosp., Stuart Circle Hosp., St. Mary's Hosp., Richmond Meml. Hosp., St. Luke's Hosp., Retreat Hosp.; chmn. dept. surgery, chmn. med. exec. com., med. dir. Henrico Doctors Hosp., also vice chmn. bd. trustees, 1981—2008, chief staff, 1974, 75, 82; pres., founding mem. Med. Planning Corp.; mem. bd. trustees Henrico Drs. Hosp., vice chmn. bd. trustee, 1981-2008, Organized & Established Henrico Drs. Hosp., 1974; mem. sci. adv. bd. Richmond chpt. Nat. Found. for Ileitis and Colitis. Contbr. articles to profl. jours. Fellow ACS; mem. AMA, Southeastern Surg. Congress, So. Med. Assn., Richmond Acad. Medicine, Richmond Surg. and Gynecol. Soc., Med. Soc. Va., Humera Soc., Bull and Bear Club, Irish Setter Club of Greater Richmond, Irish Setter Club Am. Episcopalian. Home Phone: 804-749-4318; Office Phone: 804-749-4319. Personal E-mail: killagay@earthlink.net.

CHRISTIE, NEIL ALEXANDER, thoracic surgeon, educator; b. Toronto, Can., June 12, 1963; MD, U. Toronto, 1987. Asst. prof. surgery U. Pitts., 1998—. Apptd. and attending physician Presbyn. & Shadyside Hosp., 1998—. Mem.: RSC (Can.), ACS, Am. Thoracic Soc., Am. Assn. Thoracic Surgeons. Avocations: skiing, sailing. Office: 5200 Centre Ave Ste 715 Pittsburgh PA 15232 Office Fax: 412-623-0329. Business E-Mail: christiena@upmc.edu.

CHRISTMAN, MICHAEL F., geneticist, biomedical researcher; BS in Chemistry, with honors, U. NC, Chapel Hill; D in Biochemistry, U. Calif., Berkeley, 1985. Jane Coffin Childs postdoc. fellow MIT; asst. prof. dept. radiation oncology U. Calif., San Francisco; assoc. prof. dept. microbiology U. Va.; prof., founding chair dept. genetics & genomics Boston U. Sch. Medicine, 2001—07; pres., CEO Coriell Inst. Med. Rsch., Camden, NJ, 2007—. Mem.: AAAS, Genetics Soc. of America. Office: Coriell Inst 403 Haddon Ave Camden NJ 08103 Business E-Mail: christman@coriell.org. *

CHRISTO, PAUL J., medical association administrator; b. Mt. Prospect, Ill., July 8, 1968; BS, U. Notre Dame, 1990; MD, U. Louisville Sch. Medicine, 1995. Cert. anesthesiologist, pain medicine specialist Hopkins U. Assoc. prof. Johns Hopkins Medicine, 2001, dir., Blaustein Pain Treatment Ctr., 2003—08, dir., Multidisciplinary Pain Fellowship Program, 2003—. Vis. prof. pain medicine Am. Academcy Pain Medicine/Pfize. Performer (host): (radio show) Gains on WBAL Radio. Named Super Dr., The Wash. Post Mag.; named one of 70 Best Pain Mgmt. Physicians in Am., Becker's ASC Rev., Top Doctors, Balt. Mag.; Mayday Pain and Soc. fellowship, Mayday Soc. Avocations: music, piano. Office: Divsn Pain Medicine Johns Hopkins Baltimore MD 21205 Office Fax: 410-502-6730. Business E-Mail: pchristo@jhmi.edu.

CHRISTOFFEL, KATHERINE KAUFER, pediatrician, epidemiologist, educator; b. NYC, June 28, 1948; d. George and Sonya (Firstenberg) Kaufer; children: Kevin, Kimberly. BA, Radcliffe Coll., 1969; MD, Tufts U., 1973; MPH, Northwestern U., 1981. Diplomate Am. Bd. Pediat., Nat. Bd. Med. Examiners. Intern Columbus (Ohio) Children' Hosp., 1972-73; resident then fellow Children's Meml. Hosp., Chgo., 1973-76; asst. prof. Sch. Medicine U. Chgo., 1976-79; asst. prof., then assoc. prof. Northwestern U. Med. Sch., Chgo., 1979-91, prof., 1991—; dir. Nutrition Evaluation Clinic Children's Meml. Hosp., Chgo., 1982-2000; med. dir. violent injury prevention ctr. Children's Meml. Med. Ctr., Chgo., 1993—2000, interim dir. Mary Ann and J. Milburn Smith Child Health Rsch. Program, 2000—03, interim co-dir. Children's Meml. Inst. for Edn. and Rsch., 2001—03, med. and rsch. dir. Consortium to Lower Obesity in Chgo. Children, 2003—, dir. Ctr. on Obesity Mgmt. and Prevention, 2004—. Dir. then assoc. dir. Pediatric Practice Rsch. Group, Chgo., 1984-97; dir. statis. scis. and epidemiology program Children's Meml. Inst. for Edn. and Rsch., 1994-2000; chmn. steering com. HELP Network, Chgo., 1993-99, pres. bd. dirs., 1999—2006. Contbr. numerous articles to med. jours. Recipient M. Fay Spencer Disting. Woman Physician Scientist award, Nat. Bd. Hahnemann Med. Sch., 1997; named one of 10 Most Powerful Women in Medicine in Chgo., Chgo. Sun Times, 2004. Fellow Am. Acad. Pediat. (spokesperson on firearms 1985—, injury com. 1985-93, coun. on pediatric rsch. 1996-2000, chair adolescent violence task force 1994, 1st Injury Control award 1992); mem. APHA (Disting. Career award 1991), Am. Coll. Epidemiology, Soc. for Pediatric Rsch., Am. Pediat. Soc., Ambulatory Pediatric Assn. (bd. dirs. 2000-2003, Rsch. award 2000). Avocations: hiking, walking, creative writing, photography. Office: Childrens Meml Hosp 2300 N Childrens Plz #157 Chicago IL 60614-3394 *

CHRISTOFFERSEN, HARDY, orthopedist; b. Frederiksberg, Denmark, Oct. 30, 1945; MD, Copenhagen U., 1975. Cons. Thy-Mors Hosp., 1995, leader orthop. dept., 2009—. Avocation: stamp collecting/philately. Office: Højtoftevej 2 Thisted Thy 7700 Denmark Business E-Mail: tskirhc@dadlnet.dk.

CHRISTOPHER, DEVASAHAYAM JESUDAS, pulmonologist, researcher; b. Neyyoor, Tamilnadu, India, Mar. 8, 1961; s. Devasahayam and Amy Yesudhas; m. Manju Michael; children: Shona Arlin, Johan Jesudas, Surina Amy. BSc, Am. Coll., Madurai, 1980; MBBS, Christian Med. Coll., Vellore, India, 1986. Lic. Nat. Bd. Examinations, New Delhi, 1992. Tutor Christian Med. Coll., Vellore, 1991—92, lectr., 1992—97; sr. registrar Middlesex Hosp., London, 1997—98; advanced trainee registrar Queen Elizabeth Hosp., Adelaide, Australia, 1998—99; fellow in respiratory medicine Queen Elizabeth Hosp. and U. Adelaide, Australia, 1999—2000; head dept. pulmonary medicine Christian Med. Coll., Vellore, 2000—; assoc. prof. pulmonary medicine Christian Med. Hosp., Vellore, 2000—01, prof., 2001—, dep. med. supt., 2006—, course dir. diploma allergy, 2006—; v.p. Indian Assn. Respiratory Care, 2006—. Ch. elder, lay preacher Penial Tabernacle, Vellore, 2000—07. Recipient Rising Stars award, Grand Challenges Can., 2011; fellow, Raj Nanda Found. & Brit. Thoracic Soc., 1997, Internat. travel fellowship, Am. Assn. Respiratory Care, 2005. Fellow: Am. Coll. Chest Physicians (hon.), Royal Coll. Physicians & Surgeons Glasgow; mem.: Assn. Respiratory Care India (v.p. 2006—), Royal Coll. Physicians, Nat. Acad. Allergy (life), Indian Chest Soc. (life Dr. O. A. Oration award 2009), European Respiratory Soc. (assoc.), Am. Assn. Respiratory care. Achievements include research in respiratory physiology, tuberculosis, pleural diseases, COPD, bronchial asthma. Office: Pulmonary Medicine CMC Ida Scudder Rd Tamilnadu Vellore 632004 India Office Fax: 91-4162211570. Business E-Mail: djchris@cmcvellore.ac.in.

CHRISTOPHER, ROBERT PAUL, retired physical medicine physician; b. Cleve., Apr. 27, 1932; s. Walter Matthews and Charity Marie (Roberts) C.; m. Doreen Mary O'Leary, Apr. 28, 1962; children: Robert Jr., Judith, Mark. BS, Northwestern U., 1954; MD, St. Louis U., 1959. Diplomate Am. Bd. Physical Medicine and Rehab. Chief rehab. medicine V.A. Hosp., Ann Arbor, Mich., 1963-67; asst. prof. rehab. medicine U. Mich., 1964-67; assoc. prof. rehab. medicine U. Tenn., Memphis, 1967-71, prof. rehab. medicine, 1971-2001, ret., 2001. Med. dirs. Les Passees Children's Rehab. Ctr., Memphis, 1976-98, Le Bonheur Hosp. Rehab. Svcs., Memphis, 1981-2001, Regional Med. Ctr. Rehab. Svcs., Memphis, 1967-2001, assoc. med. dir. St. Joseph Rehab. Ctr., Memphis, 1981-98. Contbg. author: Seating the Cerebral Palsey Child, 1983; author: sound/slide program Systems of Physical Therapy in Cerebral Palsy, 1971; contbr. articles to profl. jours. Pres. Mid-South Health Systems Agy., Memphis, 1980; mem. Mayor's Adv. Council for Disabled, Memphis, 1977-98. Recipient Disting. Svc. Commn. on Accredited Rehab. Facilities, 1982. Fellow Am. Acad. Phys. Medicine and Rehab. (sec. 1982-88, v.p. 1992—, pres. elect 1993, pres. 1994), Am. Acad. Cerebral Palsy (pres. 1987); mem. AMA, Am. Congress Rehab. Medicine, So. Soc. Phys. Medicine and Rehab. (sec. 1976-2000), Am. Bd. of Phys. Medicine and Rehab. (vice chmn. 1992-98), East Memphis Cath. Club (bd. dirs. 1969 80), K.C. (Grand Knight 1969-70). Avocations: travel, swimming. Home: 818 Island Club Sq Vero Beach FL 32963 5505 Personal E-mail: drbobchris1@bellsouth.net.

CHRISTOU, ALIKI, medical researcher; b. Darwin, Australia, Apr. 25, 1980; M in Internat. Health, Curtin U., 2009. Rsch. officer Curtin U., 2008. Office: Kent St Bentley Perth 6000 Australia Personal E-mail: alikichristou@yahoo.com.au.

CHRISTOV, IVAYLO IVANOV, biomedical engineer, researcher; b. Sofia, Bulgaria, Jan. 6, 1951; s. Ivan Dimitrov Christov and Travanka Georgieva Christova; m. Irena Georgieva Christova, Oct. 14, 1978; children: Iana Ivaylova Simova, Vera Ivaylova Christova. MSc in Electronic Engring., Tech. U., Sofia, 1978, PhD, 1989, DSc, 2006. Assoc. prof. Ctr. Biomed. Engring., Bulgarian Acad. Scis., Sofia, 1996—2007, head dept., 1999—, prof., 2007—. Contbr. articles to profl. jours. Recipient Gold medal Internat. Tech. Plovdiv Fair, Bulgarian C. of C. and Industry, 1984, 1986, Medal for Inventions, Bulgarian Ministry Health, 1988; NATO fellow, Consiglio Nazionale delle Ricerche, 2000—01, 2003—04. Achievements include patents for ECG amplifier; research in denoising of surface electrocardiogram signals for micropotentials recovery; pattern recognition in computerized electrocardiography and characterization of the repolarization phase; electrocardiogram arrhythmia analyses by automated heart beat classification. Avocations: travel, sports. Office: IBPhBME Bulgarian Academy Sciences Acad G Bonchev Blok 105 Sofia 1113 Bulgaria Home: Stresher Str 8A Sofia 1606 Bulgaria Business E-Mail: ivaylo.christov@clbme.bas.bg.

CHRISTY, NICHOLAS PIERSON, physician; b. Morristown, NJ, June 18, 1923; s. Leroy and Elizabeth (Baker) C.; m. Beverly Vairin Morris, June 21, 1947 (dec. Mar. 1997); children: Nicholas Pierson, Martha Vairin; m. Caroline P. Adams, June 26, 1999. AB, Yale, 1945; MD, Columbia, 1951. Diplomate: Am. Bd. Internal Medicine. Intern, asst. resident medicine, 1951—54; asst. vis. physician Delafield Hosp., NYC, 1955-66, vis. physician, 1966-75; asst. vis. physician 1st med. div. Bellevue Hosp., NYC, 1958-66; assoc. attending physician Presbyn. Hosp., NYC, 1962-78, attending physician, 1978-93. Dir. med. svc. Roosevelt Hosp., NYC, 1965-79; faculty Columbia Coll. Phys. and Surg., NYC, 1956—, assoc. prof. medicine, 1962-65, assoc. clin. prof., 1965-67, clin. prof. medicine, 1967-71, prof. medicine, 1971-79, lectr. in medicine, 1979-88, sr. lectr. medicine, 1988-93, spl. lectr. in medicine, 1993—; mem. Columbia U. Health Scis. adv. coun., 1993—; prof. medicine, assoc. dean vets. affairs Health Sci. Ctr. at Bklyn., SUNY, 1979-88, prof. emeritus, 1988—; chief staff Bklyn. VA Med. Ctr., 1979-88; writer-in-residence, alumni writer Coll. Physicians and Surgeons, Columbia U., 1988—; assoc. Nat. Humanities Ctr., Research Triangle Park, NC, 1979; cons. FDA, 1966, Bd. of Health, NYC, 1965—, NIH Nat. Inst. Diabetes, Digestive and Kidney Diseases tng. grants divsn., 1969-72, endocrinology study sect., 1975-79; cons., bd. dirs. Royal Soc. Medicine Found., 1984-93. Editor, co-author: The Human Adrenal Cortex, 1971; editor-in-chief: Jour. Clin. Endocrinology and Metabolism, 1963-67; assoc. editor: Beeson-McDermott Textbook of Medicine, 1968-75; cons. editor, 1975-79; cons. Med. Dictionary (Dorland), 1988; adv. editor and contbr. Internat. Dictionary of Medicine and Biology (Endocrinology), 1986; mem. adv. bd.: Am. Jour. Medicine, 1971-88; contbr. numerous papers to profl. publs. Served to lt. (j.g.) USNR, 1943-46, PTO. Recipient Borden award, Joseph Mather Smith prize Columbia; John and Mary R. Markle scholar; NIH tng. grantee, 1959-65, endocrinology study sect. grantee, 1958-69; honoree St. Luke's Roosevelt Hosp. Alumni Assn., 2000. Fellow Am. Med. Writers Assn. (hon., Swanberg award 1989); mem. Harvey Soc., AAAS, Soc. Exptl. Biology and Medicine, Am. Soc. Clin. Investigation, Assn. Am. Physicians, Am. Fedn. Clin. Rsch., A.C.P., NY Acad. Medicine, Laurentian Hormone Conf., Am. Physiol. Soc., NY State Med. Soc., NY County Med. Soc., Am. Clin. and Climatol. Assn. (recorder 1977-88, pres. 1990), Am. Assn. Study Liver Diseases, Endocrine Soc. (sec.-treas. 1978-89, Ayerst award 1986), NY Clin. Soc., NY Med. and Surg. Soc., Assn. Am. Physicians, Interurban Clin. Club, Hosp. Grads. Club, Peripatetic Soc., Practitioners Soc., Elizabethan (Yale), Colony (Yale), Century Assn. (pres. 1987-90, hon. 1995—).

CHRONISTER, VIRGINIA ANN, retired school nurse, educator; b. York, Pa, Sept. 25, 1940; d. Ernest B. and Mary L. (Anderson) Stokes; m. Burton F. Chronister, June 13, 1964; children: Scott E., Karen A. Student, York Jr. Coll., Millersville U., Pa.; diploma, Harrisburg Hosp., Pa., 1961; BS in Profl. Arts, St. Joseph's Coll., North Windham, Maine, 1985; M. (equivalency), Pa. State U., 1989; postgrad., St. Joseph's Coll., North windham, Maine. RN, Pa.; cert. sch. nurse (edn. specialist II), Pa. Charge nurse Harrisburg Hosp., 1961-64; instr., practical nurses York City Sch. Dist., 1964-68; instr., med. sec. Yorktowne Bus. Inst., York, 1983; sch. nurse West York Sch. Dist., York, 1983—2007. Substitute sch. nurse, 1972-83, 2007-10; health cons. for 2-day care ctr. ECELS. Recipient Cardiac Nursing award. Mem.: AAUW, NEA, York/Adams PSEA-R (co-chair mem. com. 2008—), West York Area Edn. Assn. (pres. 1990—2003, negotiator 1999—2001, pres. 2002—07, chief negotiator 2004—07), York County Coord Coun., United Ostomy Assn. (charter mem.), York County Sch. Nurse Assn. (pres. 1991—92, sec. 1998—), Harrisburg Hosp. Alumnae Assn., Nat. Assn. Sch. Nurses, Pa. Sch. Health Assn., Pa. State Edn. Assn. (sch. nurse sect. 2007—), Beta Sigma Phi (pres. Theta master chpt. 2000, pres. 2001—). Home: 2090 Loman Dr York PA 17408-4214

CHRYSOHOOU, CHRISTINA, cardiologist; b. Athens, July 14, 1967; MD, U. Patras, 1993; PhD, U. Athens, 2000. Postdoc. fellow Vets. Affairs Med. Ctr., Washington, 2004—05; rsch. assoc. U. Athens, Med. Sch., 2000—04, sr. registrar cardiologist, 2006—. Cons. Med. Sch. Athens, 2000—04. Contbr. articles to profl. sci. jours. Recipient Young Investigators award, European Soc. Hypertension; Postdoc. fellowship, Hellenic Cardiology Soc. Mem.: European Heart Failure Assn., European Atherosclerotic Soc., European Soc. Cardiology. Avocations: piano, classical music. Home: 46 Paleon Polemiston Str Glyfada Attica 16674 Greece Home Fax: 3012109600719. Personal E-mail: chrysohoou@usa.net.

CHU, BENJAMIN K., hospital administrator; BA in Psychology, Yale U., 1974; MD, NYU, 1978; MPH, Columbia U., 1985. Diplomate Am. Bd. Internal Medicine, 1982. Intern, resident Kings County Hosp., 1978; assoc. prof., clinical med., assoc. dean for clinical affairs NYU, 1994—2000; sr. assoc. dean Harlem Hospital Center, NYC, 2000—02; sr. v.p., med. affairs N.Y.C. Health and Hosp. Corp., 2001—02, pres., CEO, 2002—05; pres., southern california region Kaiser Foundation Health Plan, Inc. and Kaiser Foundation Hospitals, 2005—. Office: Kaiser Found Health Plan and Hospitals Corp 7th Fl 393 E Walnut St Pasadena CA 91188 Office Phone: 626-405-7983. Office Fax: 626-405-2583. Business E-Mail: benjamin.chu@kp.org.

CHU, CHIH-HSUN, veterinarian; b. Ping Tung, Taiwan, Dec. 11, 1964; s. Tien-Shun Chu and Li-Chao Yang; m. Meng-Rong Lee; children: Heng-Rui, Heng-Chi. MD, China Med. U., Taiwan, 1990. Diplomate Taiwan Soc. Internal Medicine, 1997. Vis. staff Kaohsiung Vets. Gen. Hosp., Taiwan, 1999—. Office: Kaohsiung Vets Gen Hosp 386 Tu chung 1st Rd Kaohsiung 813 Taiwan Office Fax: (886)-7-3468291. Business E-Mail: chchu@isca.vghks.gov.tw.

CHU, CHRISTINA S., gynecologic oncologist, educator; BA in Applied Math., Northwestern U., 1990, MD, U. Pa., 1995. Diplomate Am. Bd. Ob-Gyn-gynecology oncology. Intern Hosp. of the Univ. of Pa, resident, fellow, Am. Coll. of Ob-Gyn; asst. prof. ob-gyn Univ. Pa. Sch. of Medicine. Contbr. (publs.) Weight lifting in patients with lower extremity lymphedema secondary to cancer: a pilot and feasibility study., The immune adjuvant properties of front-line carboplatin-paxlitaxel: A randomized phase II study of alternative schedules of intravenous oregovomab-chemo-immunotherapy in advanced ovarian cancer., Low podoplanin expression in pretreatment biopsy material predicts poor prognosis in advanced-stage squamous cell carcinoma of the uterine cervix treated by primary radiation., and numerous others. Recipient AACR-Glaxo SmithKline Scholar in Tng. award, 2001; named one of Top Docs, Phila. Mags., 2010, 2011. Mem.: AMA, Soc. of Gynecologic Oncologist, Am. Coll. of Ob-Gyn, American Assn. for Cancer Rsch. (assoc.). Office: Hospital of the University of Pennsylvania 3400 Spruce St Philadelphia PA 19104 Office Phone: 215-662-4000.

CHU, EUGENE POH HWYE, surgeon; b. Asahan, Sumatra, Indonesia, Apr. 15, 1931; s. Sam Yak Chu and Siam Lim; m. Lee Soei Boan Lily; children: Galinia Ing Hoei, Arean Sheuh Hoei, Philip Wen Hoei. MBBS, U. Melbourne, Australia, 1956. Med. officer-in-charge Kwong Wah Hosp., Kowloon, Hong Kong, 1962-63, surg. specialist, 1963-67; cons. surgeon Bapt. Hosp., Kowloon, Hong Kong, 1967—, St. Theresa Hosp., Kowloon, Hong Kong, 1967—, St. Paul's Hosp., Kowloon, Hong Kong, 1967—. Chief surg. services Bapt. Hosp., Kowloon, 1969-80; hon. lectr. surgery, Hong Kong U., 1964-69. Fellow Royal Coll. Surgeons Edinburgh, Royal Coll. Surgeons Eng., Am. Coll. Surgeons, Hong Kong Surg. Soc., Internat. Soc. Surgeons; mem. Hong Kong Med. Assn. (mem. council 1967-70). Clubs: Royal Hong Kong Jockey, Royal Hong Kong Golf. Anglican. Avocations: golf, coin collecting/numismatics. Office: Ste 1401 Grand Centre 8 Humphreys Ave Tsim sha tsui Kowloon Hong Kong Office Phone: 852-23675445. Business E-Mail: echu1@netvigator.com.

CHU, IN TAK, medical educator; b. Republic of Korea, May 26, 1959; MD, Cath. U. Korea, 1984, PhD, 1995. Prof. The Cath. Orthop. Clinic, 1992—2011. Recipient 1st. prize, European Foot Ankle Soc. Office Fax: 8225547576. Business E-Mail: itchu@hanmail.net.

CHU, KANG-CHU, physician, educator; b. Yi Hsin, Kiang-Su, China, July 1, 1930; s. Ming Chu and Yang-Chu Hsu; m. She Cheng Lee, Sept. 12, 1958; children: George, Bryan. MD, Nat. Def. Med. Ctr., Taipei, Taiwan, 1955. Physician Tri-svc. Gen. Hosp., Taipei, 1955—66, 1969—79; asst. prof. Nat. Def. Med. Ctr., Taipei, 1955—66, assoc. prof., 1969—79; postdoctoral rsch. fellow Tulane U. Sch. Medicine, New Orleans, 1968; vis. prof. Tulane Med. Sch., New Orleans, 1979; physician Charity Hosp., New Orleans, 1979—84, China Med. U. Hosp., Taichung, Taiwan, 1984—. Prof. China Med. U., Taichung, 1984—, dean, 1986—90. Author: Textbook of Pathology, 1990, The A to Z of Pathology, 2002; contbr. articles to profl.

jours. Mem.: China Med. Assn., Taiwan Pathology Assn. Home: 1-49 Hsin Yi Rd Sec 4 Taipei 106 Taiwan Office: China Med Univ Hosp 2 Yuh Der Rd Taichung 404 Taiwan Personal E-mail: bryanchu@ms23.hinet.net. Business E-Mail: d0333@mail.cmuh.org.tw.

CHU, KENT-MAN, surgeon; b. Hong Kong, July 12, 1963; MB, BS, U. Hong Kong, 1987, MS, 2001. Intern medicine U. Hong Kong, Queen Mary Hosp., 1987, intern surgery, 1988, med. officer dept. surgery, 1988—95, sr. med. officer, 1995—98; assoc. prof. dept. surgery U. Hong Kong, 1998—2006, prof. surgery, 2006—, chief divsn. upper GI surgery, 1998—. Hon. clin. asst. prof. U. Hong Kong, 1998; dir. surg. endoscopy ctr. Queen Mary Hosp., 2003—; dir. Surg. Forum U. Hong Kong, 2005—; lectr. in field; cons. in field. Contbr. chpts. to books, articles to profl. publs. Fellow ACS (internat. guest scholar 1999), Royal Coll. Surgeons Edinburgh, Coll. Surgeons Hong Kong, Hong Kong Acad. Medicine; mem. Internat. Gastric Cancer Assn., Internat. Soc. Surgery, Japanese Gastric Cancer Assn., Hong Kong Med. Assn., Hong Kong Soc. Minimal Access Surgery, Asian Surg. Assn. (sec. gen. 2005—, assoc. editor jour. 2005—), Soc. Surgery Alimentary Tract, Endoscopic and Laparoscopic Surgeons Asia. Office: U Hong Kong Dept Surgery Queen Mary Hsp, Pokfulam Rd Hong Kong China

CHU, TSANN MING, immunochemist, educator; b. Kaohsiung, Taiwan, Apr. 18, 1938; came to U.S., 1963, naturalized, 1971; s. Tsi Fa and Su Lian (Sun) C.; m. Bonnie Diane Covert, Sept. 28, 1967; children: Nancy, Daniel. BS, Nat. Taiwan U., Taipei, 1961; MS, N.C. State U., Raleigh, 1965, DSc (hon.), 2001; PhD, Pa. State U., University Park, 1967. Fellow Med. Found. Buffalo, 1967-69, Buffalo Gen. Hosp., 1969-70; assoc. chief cancer rsch. scientist, dir. diagnostic immunology and clin. chemistry Roswell Park Meml. Inst., Buffalo, 1970-76, dir. cancer rsch. in diagnostic immunology research and biochemistry, 1976-98; asst. prof. exptl. pathology SUNY, Buffalo, 1970-74, assoc. prof., 1974-77, prof., 1977-98, prof. emeritus, 1999—. Cons. nat. prostatic cancer project Nat. Cancer Inst., NIH, 1973-84, mem. com. cancer immunodiagnosis, 1978-79, mem. tumor immunology com., 1979-81; mem. immunology and immunotherapy com. Am. Cancer Soc., 1979-81; rsch. cons. Nat. Sci. Coun., Taiwan, 1976-94, vis. prof., 1986; adv. coun. Internat. Soc. Oncodevel. Biology and Medicine, 1978-94; mem. sci. rev. panel N.J. Commn. on Cancer Rsch., 1983-85, 87-99; cons. Merit Rev. Bd., VA, 1980-85, 94-98; mem. cancer therapeutic program rev. com. Nat. Cancer Inst., 1985-88; reviewers reserve NIH, 1988-92, 94-98; mem. scientific adv. coun. Internat. Acad. Tumor Marker Oncology, 1986-1998; mem. sci. coun. Swedish Cancer Found., 1988-1998; adv. com. Nat. Def. Med. Ctr. Cancer Rsch. Group, 1993-97. Mem. editl. bd. Tumor Biology, 1983-92, Jour. Clin. Lab. Analysis, 1985—, Jour. Tumor Marker Oncology, 1988-2003, Cancer Investigation, 1989-2003; contbr. over 300 articles to profl. jours. Recipient Presdl. citation Am. Urol. Assn., 1993, Am. Found. for Urologic Disease, 1993, Dornier Innovative Rsch. award, 1993, Symposium award Roswell Park Cancer Inst. and Geritourinary Cancer, 1993, Disting. Alumni award Pa. State U., 1994, N.C. State U., 1995, Abbott award Internat. Soc. Oncodevel. Biology and Medicine, 1996, Achievement in Health Care award D'Youville Coll., 1998, Honors award Pres. U.S., 1999, Pioneers Sci. award Western N.Y., 2002, Humanitarian award Pa. State U., 2006, Clin. Rsch. Excellence award, 2007, In The Know award, Prostate Net, 2007; fellow United Health Found. Western N.Y., 1968-69, Pa. State U., 1997. Mem. Am. Chem. Soc. (Jacob F. Schoellkopf medal 1997), Am. Assn. Clin. Chemists (Van Slyke award 1997), Am. Assn. Cancer Rsch. (cancer rsch. cover legend 1998), Am. Assn. Immunologists, Am. Urol. Assn. (hon.), Am. Soc. Biochem. and Molecular Biology, Am. Assn. Investigative Pathology, Biochem. Soc. (London), Am. Urological Assn. (hon.), Buffalo Urol. Soc., Taiwan Urol. Assn. (hon.), Phi Lambda Upsilon. Achievements include discovery of the prostate specific antigen PSA; development of prostate specific antigen PSA test for early detection of prostate cancer. Office: Roswell Park Cancer Inst Elm And Carlton St Buffalo NY 14263-0001

CHU, TZONG-SHINN, physician scientist, medical educator; b. Kee-Lung, Taiwan, Sept. 1, 1957; m. Guey-Shiun Huang, Apr. 26, 1987; children: Fang-Ying, Jia-Ching. MD, Nat. Taiwan U., 1982, PhD, 1997. Cert. med. doctor Dept. Health, Taiwan, 1982, Taiwan Bd. Internal Medicine, 1987, Taiwan Bd. Nephrology, 1989. Resident Dept. Internal Medicine Nat. Taiwan U. Hosp., Taipei, 1984—87, fellow in nephrology, Divsn. Nephrology, Dept. Internal Medicine, 1987—89, attending physician Dept. Internal Medicine, 1989—, asst. prof. Dept. Primary Care Medicine, 1998—2001; assoc. prof. Dept. Primary Care Medicine Nat. Taiwan U. Coll. Medicine, 2001—; fellow in nephrology U. Tex. Southwestern Med. Sch., Dallas, 1993—95. Exec. sec. Prof. Wan-Yu Chen Found., Taipei, 1995—. Mem. editl. bd.: Acta Nephrologica, 2005—; contbr. articles to Biochemical and Biophysical Rsch. Comms., to Jour. Clin. Investigation, to Jour. Formosan Med. Assn. Sec. gen. Taita Jing-Fu Found., Taipei, 2003—05. Recipient Rsch. award, Nat. Sci. Coun. Taiwan, 2000. Mem.: Taiwan Soc. Nephrology (award 2001), Taiwan Assn. Med. Edn. (sec. gen. 2004—), Internat. Soc. Nephrology, Am. Soc. Nephrology (assoc.). Achievements include development of two-step medical education program in Taiwan; general internal medicine training and demonstration center in Taiwan. Office: Nat Taiwan Univ Hosp 7 Chung-Shan South Rd Taipei 100 Taiwan Office Fax: 886-2-23934176. Business E-Mail: tschu@ntu.edu.tw.

CHUA, BOON TIN, medical researcher; b. Singapore, July 26, 1974; PhD, Nat. U. Singapore, 2004. Jr. rsch. fellow Inst. Molecular and Cell Biology, 1998—2004; postdoc. fellow Cancer Rsch. UK, 2004—07; sr. rsch. fellow Inst. Med. Biology, 2007—09, project leader, 2009—. Joint grant, ASTAR-NKTH. Avocations: reading, travel, movies. Office: Inst Med Biology 8A Biomedical Grove #06-06 Immunos Singapore 138648 Singapore Business E-Mail: boontin.chua@imb.a-star.edu.sg.

CHUAH, GERARD, surgeon; Med. degree, Nat. U., Singapore, 1998; M of Medicine in Opthalmology, Postgrad. Sch. Medicine Nat. U., Singapore. Cert. advance splty. tng. 1997, accredited as a specialist in opthalmology Singapore, registered specialist UK(Gen. Med. Coun. Specialist Register), Hong Kong(Specialist Register of the Hong Kong Acad. of Medicine). Fellowship Royal Coll. Surgeons, Edinburgh, 1993, 1994; fellowship in vitreoretinal surgery Univ. Toronto, 1997—98; fellowship in med. retina NY Eye and Ear Infirmary, 1998; fellowship Acad. Medicine, Singapore, 1998; former clin. tutor nat. Univ., Singapore; former vis. cons. Eye Inst. Nat. Healthcare Group; former head Alexandra Hosp. Eye Svc., Bus. Devel. Eye Inst. Nat. Healthcare Group; cons. eye surgeon and med. dir. asian diabetic and retinal disease ctr. Camden Med. Ctr.; cons. eye surgeon Total EyeCare Ctr. With Gen. Med. Coun., England; vis. prof. Qingdao Hai Ci Group Hosps.; vis. lectr. Shanghai Ren Ji Hosp. Group; chmn. Nat. Kidney Found. Children's Med. Fund2001, 2001—05. Office: Total EyeCare Center Camden Medical Centre One Orchard Blvd Number 06-01 Singapore 248649 Singapore Office Phone: 6567386868. Office Fax: 6567389655. *

CHUANG, CHIA-CHANG, medical association administrator; b. Taipei, Taiwan, May 14, 1962; PhD, Nat. Cheng Kung U., MD, 2010. Dir., disaster medicine Nat. Cheng Kung U. Hosp., 2002—. Assoc. prof. Faculty Coll. Medicine Nat. Cheng Kung U., 2009. Recipient Humanitarian Med. Relief award, Dept. Health, Taiwan, 2010; grant, 2000—06. Master: Tainan Regional Emergency Operation Ctr. Dept. Health; mem.: Taiwan Soc. Emergency Medicine, Soc. Emergency and Critical Care Medicine (Taiwan). Avocations: mountain climbing, sports. Office: 138 Sheng-Li Rd Dept Emergency Medicine Tainan 80428 Taiwan Office Fax: 886-6-235-9562. Business E-Mail: chuanger@mail.ncku.edu.tw.

CHUANG, JIE-YU, physician; b. Taipei, Taiwan, June 21, 1982; MD, Taipei med. U., 2007. Chief resident Tri-Svc. Gen. Hosp., 2010—. Tchg. asst. Nat. Def. Med. Ctr., 2007—11. Contbr. articles to profl. publs. Recipient Presdl. award, Taipei Med. U. Mem.: Harvard Med. Sch. Postgrad. Assn. Avocations: dance, music, writing. Office: University Irvine Toxicology Dept Irvine CA 92620 Business E-Mail: simone@mail.ndmctsgh.edu.tw, anaulu@gmail.com.

CHUANG, TSU-YI, dermatologist, epidemiologist, educator; b. Amoy, China, May 21, 1946; arrived in U.S., 1976, naturalized, 1988; s. Hsi and Kia-Ling (Huang) C.; m. Lydia Ling-Chuan Lee, Dec. 22, 1973; children: Chester, Nancy. BM, Nat. Taiwan U., Taipei, 1971; MPH in Epidemiology, U. Wash., 1978. Diplomate Am. Bd. Dermatology, Am. Bd. Preventive Medicine. From asst. prof. to assoc. prof. dermatology U. Wis., Madison, 1984-92; chief dermatology svc. Middleton VA Med. Ctr., Madison, 1984-90; assoc. prof. dermatology Wright State U., Dayton, Ohio, 1990-95, dir. immunopathology lab., 1994-95; dir. dermatology clinic Frederick A. White Health Ctr., Dayton, 1995; prof. dermatology Ind. U., Indpls., 1995—2003, med. dir. melanoma program, 1996—2003, Arthur L. Norins prof., dir. dermatology clinic, 1999—2001; clin. prof. dermatology U. South Fla. Coll. Medicine, Tampa, 2004—06, U. So. Calif., LA, 2007—. Vis. prof. Wright State U., Dayton, 1990, Nat. Taiwan U., Taipei, 1991-97; vis. scientist Mayo Clinic, Rochester, 1986-92, Moss lectr. Meriter Found., 2002; mem. guidelines/outcomes com., 1996-2001, melanoma guidelines task force, 1997-2010, melanoma/skin cancer com., 2004-2008, adv. editor Dermalogica Sinica 2008-. Co-author: Conn's Current Therapy, 1992, The Challenge of Dermato-Epidemiology, 1997, Sleisenger & Fordtran's Gastrointestinal and Liver Disease, 2002; ad hoc reviewer Arch Dermatol., Chgo., 1990-99, Jour. Am. Acad. Dermatology, 1986-2004, Internat. Jour. Dermatology, 2001-; editor Dermatologica Sinica, Taipei, 1994-96; contbr. over 100 articles to profl. jours. Pres. Rochester (Minn.) Chinese Culture Assn., 1980-82; v.p. Orgn. of Chinese Ams., Madison, 1986-90; pres. Midwest Chinese Christian Assn., Dayton, 1993-94, Indpls., 1996-97, Indiana Chinese-Am. Profls. Assn., Indlps. 1998. Rsch. grantee U. Wis., 1985-89, Schering, Glaxo, Genentech, Amgen 1986-2004; VA merit rev. bd. grantee Dept. Vets. Affairs, 1986-88, 90-94; recipient Burdette-Kunkel award Mary Margaret Walther Program for Cancer Care Rsch., 1996-97, 21st Century Research & Technology Fund award, 2000-02, Fellow Am. Acad. Dermatology (editl. cons. Am. Acad. Dermatology jour. 1986-2004), Am. Soc. for Dermatol. Surgery; mem. Ind. Chinese Profls. Assn. (pres. 1998). Achievements include first historical cohort study of human papilloma virus infection in U.S. in a defined population, first study confirmen the link human papilloma virus and cervical cancer, first prospective cohort study establish the link between HPV and cervical cancer in 1981, first historical cohort study of genital herpes virus infection in U.S. in a defined population, first incidence study of polymyalgia rheumatica in the U.S. in a defined population, first population-based incidence study of skin cancer in US in two well-defined populations Rochester, Minn. and Kawai Island, Hawaii. Office: Desert Oasis Health Care 69-844 Hwy 111 Ste A Rancho Mirage CA 92270 Office Phone: 760-318-4869. Business E-Mail: chuang007@yahoo.com.

CHUBB, STEPHEN DARROW, health products executive; b. Newton, Mass., Mar. 16, 1944; s. Phillip Darrow and Clarissa Stoddard (Nye) C.; m. Kathleen Alice Zimmerman, 1973. BS, U.S. Naval Acad., 1965; MBA, Northwestern U., 1974. CPA, Ill. With Am. Can Co., 1970—73, Baxter Labs., Deerfield, Ill., 1974—81; pres. Hyland Diagnostics, 1978—81; pres., chief exec. officer, dir. Cytogen Corp., 1981—84, T Cell Scis., Inc., 1984—86, Matritech Inc., 1987—2007; dir. Charles River Labs., 1994—, Compucyte, Cambridge, Mass., 1992—2001, I-Stat, Princeton, NJ, 1999—2002, Care Group Healthcare Sys., 2007—. Alumni adv. bd. Northwestern U., 1998, dir. Allegrodx, Boston, 2008-, dir. Immunetics Inc., Boston, 2009- Bd. dir. Sherwood Cmty. Assn., 1978-79, v.p., 1979-80; trustee Huntington Theatre Co., Boston, 1991-95, treas., 1992-95; trustee Mt. Auburn Hosp., Cambridge, 1995—, vice chmn., 2001-06, chmn., 2007-. With USN, 1965-70; capt., USNR (ret.). Recipient Meritorious Svc. medal, Combat Action Ribbon, U.S. Navy. Mem. AICPA, John Evans Club Northwestern U., US Naval Acad. Alumni Assn., Naval War Coll. Found. Avocation: deep sea diving.

CHUDIK, STEVEN, orthopedist; BS, Univ. Chgo.; MD, Univ. Chgo. Pritzker Sch. Med. Staff physician Hinsdale Hosp., Good Samaritan Hosp., Hinsdale Surg. Ctr.; physician Hinsdale Orthopaedic Assoc. Intern, resident Univ. N.C., Chapel Hill; fell. Sports Medicine and Shoulder Surgery Hosp. Spl. Surgery, NYC. Mem.: Arthroscopy Assn. North America, Am. Coll. Sports Medicine, Am. Orthopaedic Soc. Sports Med., Am. Coll. Surgeons, Am. Acad. Orthopaedic Surgeons. Office: Hinsdale Orthopaedic Assoc 550 W Ogden Ave Hinsdale IL 60521

CHUI, CHAN HON, surgeon; MBBS, Nat. U., Singapore, 1990. Cert. Specialist Accreditation in paediatric Surgery Ministry of Health, Singapore. Basic surg. tng. and fellowship Royal Coll. Surgeons, Glasgow; advanced surg. tng. pardiatric surgery Acad. Medicine, Singapore; lead devel. paediatric surg. oncology KK Women's and Children's Rsch. Hosp., Tenn.; founder Children's Cancer Rsch. Lab., 2003; head. paediatric surgery dept. KKH, 2005—07; past pres. oncology group Coll Surgeons Singapore, com. mem. chpt. paediatric surgeons; pvt. practice Mt. elizabeth Med. Centre, East Med. Centre; paediatric surgeon East Shore Hosp., Singapore; vis. cons. Singapore Gen. Hosp.; sr. cons. paediatric surgery dept. KK Women's and Children's Hosp., Singapore; paediatric surgeon Surgery Centre for Children Pte Ltd. Clin. lectr. Yoo Loo Lin sch. medicine Nat. Univ. Singapore; instr. advanced trauma life support course. Author pub. in many peer-reviewed internat. and local jours. Recipient Health Manpower Devel. Programme (HMDP) Scholarship, St. Jude Rsch. Hosp., 1999, Best Clin. Tchr. award, KKH, 2003. Mem.: Soc. Internat. Paediatric Surg. Oncology, Paediatric Surgery Singapore. Achievements include as one of the pioneering surgeons who developed the Paediatric Minimally Invasive Surgery Programme at KKH; renowned in the region for his work in paediatric oncological surgery, especially in neuroblastoma and soft tissue sarcomas. Office: Surgery Centre for Children Pte Ltd. Mt Elizabeth Medical Centre 3 Mt Elizabeth Number 10-08 228510 Singapore Office Phone: 6567337381. Office Fax: 6567334939. *

CHUN, AUDREY K., geriatrician, educator; MD, Baylor Coll. of Medicine. Diplomate Am. bd. of Internal Medicine. Internship Baylor Coll. Medicine; fellow Mt. Sinai Hosp.; asst. prof. geriatrics and palliative medicine Mt. Sinai Sch. of Medicine, asst. prof. medicine. Office: Mount Sinai Medical Center One Gustave L Levy Place New York NY 10029-6574 Office Fax: 212-241-6500.

CHUN, CHURL HONG, medical educator, consultant; b. Kwangju, Chonnam, Republic of Korea, Sept. 22, 1955; s. Kang Hyun Chun and Mal Lyui Kim; m. Kwang Mee Kim, June 27, 1982; children: Ji Young, Keun Churl. MD, Chonnam Nat. U. Sch. Medicine, Kwangju, Republic of Korea, 1989, PhD, 1991. Lic. orthopedist Korea Orthopaedic Assn., 1989. Prof. orthop. surgery Wonkwang U. Sch. Medicine, Iksan, Republic of Korea, 1991—. Dir. Korea Soc. Knee Surgery, Seoul, 1991—, Korea Orthop. Soc. Sports Medicine, Seoul, 1995—, Korea Arthroscopy Soc., 1997—; vis. prof. UCLA Sch. Medicine Med. Ctr., 1993—94; faculty orthop. surgery Ind. U. Sch. Medicine, Indpls., 2002—04. Contbr. articles to profl. jours. Dir. Assn. Grads. Dept. Orthop. Surgery Chonnam Nat. U. Hosp., Kwangju, Republic of Korea, 2000—05. Recipient award, Korean Orthop. Assn., 1996, Korean Soc. Fractures, 1997, Korean Arthroscopy Soc., 2001, Korean Knee Soc., 2005, Korean Sports, 2007. Achievements include development of new anatomical Y-plate; new wedge shaped plate for high tinial osteotomy. Home: Apt 101 1006 GSXI Eoayang-dong Iksan City Chonbuk 570 300 Republic of Korea Office: Wonkwang Univ Hosp Dept Orthop Surgery Shinyong-Dong 570-711 Iksan Jeollabuk-do Republic of Korea Office Phone: 82-63-859-1363. Office Fax: 063-852-9329. Personal E-mail: cch@wonkwang.ac.kr.

CHUN, JIN K., physician, educator; b. Seoul, Republic of Korea, May 4, 1957; MD, U. Va. Med. Sch., 1983. Assoc. prof. Mt. Sinai Med. Ctr., 1990—. Office: 5 E 98th St New York NY 10029 Business E-Mail: jin.chun@mountsinai.org.

CHUN, MIN HO, physician; Student in Premedicine, Seoul Nat. U., Republic of Korea, 1980—82, MD, 1986, MSc, 1996. MD 1986. Intern Seoul (Republic of Korea) Nat. U. Hosp., 1989—90, resident phys. and medicine rehab., 1991—95; clin. fellow phys. and medicine rehab. Asan Med. Ctr., Seoul, 1995—96; instr. U. Ulsan Coll. of Medicine, Asan Med. Ctr., Seoul, Republic of Korea, 1997—99, asst. prof., 1999—2003, assoc. prof., 2003—. Contbr. articles pub. to profl. jour. Mem.: Korean Acad. of Rehab. Medicine (life). Avocation: travel. Office: Asan Med Ctr 388-1 Pungnap-2dong Songpa-gu Seoul 138-736 Republic of Korea

CHUN, YONGMIN, orthopedist; b. Seoul, Republic of Korea, Feb. 1, 1974; s. Chun Kwangkook and Seo Yoonsil; m. Cho Youngae; 1 child, Chun Junyoung. MD, Yonsei U. Coll. Medicine, Seoul, 1998, M, 2004, PhD, 2008. Cert. orthop. surgeon Ministry Health Welfare Republic of Korea, 2003. Fellow orthop. surgery Severance Hosp. Yonsei U. Coll. Medicine, Seoul, 2003—04, 2008—; capt. flight surgeon Aerospace Med. Ctr., Chung Joo, Republic of Korea, 2004—07; fellow orthop. surgery shoulder svc. Mass. Gen. Hosp., Boston, 2007—08. Clin. cons. Severance Hosp. Yonsei U. Coll. Medicine, 2008—. rschr., 2008—; asst. prof. Yonsei U. Arthroscopy Joint Rsch. Inst., 2009—. Contbr. articles to profl. jours. Office: Yonsei U Dept Orthop Surgery 134 Shinchondong CPO Box 8044 Seoul 120-752 Republic of Korea Office Fax: 82-2-363-6248. Business E-Mail: severanscopy@yuhs.ac.

CHUN, YOUNG-JIN, pharmacist, educator; b. Daegu City, Republic of Korea, Dec. 5, 1965; s. Jeongsook Park; m. Jeehyun Lee, May 14, 1994; children: Jinha, Jinha. BS, Seoul Nat. U., 1988; PhD, Korea Advanced Inst. Sci. and Tech., Daejeon, Republic of South Korea, 1994, MS, 2000. Lic. pharmacist. Vis. scientist Med. Coll. of Va., Richmond, 1991—92; postdoctoral fellow Vanderbilt U. Sch. Medicine, Nashville, 1994—96, vis. scholar, 2000—01; rsch. scientist Korea Rsch. Inst. Chem. Tech., Daejeon, Republic of Korea, 1996—97; asst. prof. Chung-Ang U. Coll. Pharmacy, Seoul, Republic of Korea, 1997—2002, assoc. prof., 2002—. Contbr. articles to profl. jours. Bd. dirs. Korea FDA, Seoul, 2000—03. Fellow: Korean Soc. Toxicology (assoc.); mem.: Korean Soc. Biochemistry (assoc.), Korean Soc. for Molecular Biology (assoc.), Pharm. Soc. Korea (assoc.), Am. Assn. for Cancer Rsch. (assoc.). Achievements include patents for specific cytochrome P450 1B1 inhibitors. Office: Coll Pharmacy Chung-Ang Univ 221 Huksuk-Dong Dongjak-Gu Seoul 156-756 Republic of Korea Office Fax: 82-2-825-5616. E-mail: yjchun@cau.ac.kr.

CHUNG, CHOON HEE, medical educator; b. Cheongju, Chungcheongbuk-Do, Republic Of Korea, Aug. 30, 1963; s. Chung and Kim; m. Eun Young Lee; children: Jiwon, Wookyung. MD, PhD, Yonsei U., Seoul, 1999. Diplomate Korean Med. Assn., 1987. Assoc. prof. Yonsei U., Wonju, Kangwon-Do, Republic of Korea, 2001—06, prof., 2006—. Sr. fellow U. Wash., 1999—2000; vis. scholar Northwestern U., 2007. Contbr. articles to profl. jours. Dir., com. camp Korean Diabetes Assn., Seoul, 2006. Capt. Korean Army, 1991—94, Kyunggi-Do. Scholar, Korean Rsch. Fund, 2007. Mem.: Am. Diabetes Assn. Home: 109-302 Wondong Apt Won-Dong Wonju Kangwon-Do 220 Republic of Korea Office: Yonsei Univ Wonju Coll Medicine Ilsan-Dong 162 220-701 Wonju Gangwon-do Republic of Korea

CHUNG, CRAWFORD K., critical care specialist; MD, U. Hongkong, 1971. Diplomate Am. Bd. Internal Medicine, 2007, Am. Bd. Internal Medicine- critical care medicine, 2007, Am. Bd. Internal Medicine-pulmonary disease, 2007. Intern Queen Mary Hosp., Hong Kong; resident in internal medicine St. Louis Univ. Group of Hosps., 1972—75; resident in pulmonary disease Wash. Univ. Barnes-Jewsih

Hosp., St. Louis, 1975—76; fellow in pulmonary critical care medicine Barnes Hosp., 1976—77; asst. clin. prof. in medicine Univ. Calif, San Francisco; hosp. affiliation include Brown and Toland Physicians, Calif. Pacific Med. Ctr. Office: California Pacific Medical Center 3838 California St Ste 508 San Francisco CA 94118 Office Phone: 415-831-9788. Office Fax: 415-751-6158.

CHUNG, ESTHER KYUNGHI, pediatrician; b. Washington, Aug. 20, 1965; MD, Columbia U. Coll. Physicians and Surgeons, NYC, 1991; MPH, Columbia Sch. Pub. Health, 1991. Cert. Am. Bd. Pediat. Intern pediat. Children's Hosp. & Rsch. Ctr., Oakland, Calif., 1991—92; resident pediat. St. Christopher's Hosp. for Children, Phila., 1992—94; fellow gen. academic pediat. Children's Hosp. Phila., 1994—96; med. staff mem. Hosp. U. Pa., Phila., 1996—99, U. Calif. San Francisco Med. Ctr., 1999—2001, Thomas Jefferson U. Hosp., Phila., 2002; hosp. appointment Jefferson Pediat. Nemours-Alfred I. duPont Hosp. for Children, Wilmington, Del., 2002—; clin. asst. prof. U. Pa., Phila., 1996—99; asst. clin. prof. U. Calif., San Francisco, 1999—2001; asst. prof. Thomas Jefferson U.-Jefferson Med. Coll., Phila., 2002—06, assoc. prof., 2006—. Med. cons. Phila. Dept. Pub. Health; faculty advisor Bridging the Gaps. Editor-in-chief Visual Diagnosis in Pediatrics 2 editions, assoc. editor The Five-Minute Pediatric Consult (all 5 edits.). Bd. dirs. Trinity Cooperative Day Nursery; regional edn. coord., immunization edn. program Pa. AAP Educating Physicians in their Communities (EPIC) Program. Mem.: Phila. Pediat. Soc. (treas.). Office: Jefferson Pediat duPont Childrens Health Program 833 Chestnut St Ste 300 Philadelphia PA 19107 Office Phone: 215-861-8800. Fax: 215-861-8815. Business E-Mail: echung@nemours.org.

CHUNG, HAE-YOUNG, science educator; b. Republic of Korea, Apr. 19, 1956; BS, Pusan Nat. U., Republic of Korea, 1980; PhD, Toyama Med. and Pharm. U., Japan, 1985—88. Prof. Pusan Nat. U., Busan, Republic of Korea, 1989—. Post-doctoral rschr. U. Tex. Health Sci. Ctr., San Antonio, 1994—95. Achievements include research in Aging. Office: Pusan Nat Univ Dept Pharmacy Jangjeon-Dong Geumjeong-Gu 30 609-735 Busan Busan Republic of Korea Office Fax: 82-51-518-2821. E-mail: hyjung@pusan.ac.kr.

CHUNG, HAI LEE, pediatrician, educator; b. Taegu, Republic of Korea, Feb. 13, 1959; d. Tai Ho Chung and Huyk Ja Kwon; m. Shung Chull Chae, Jan. 29, 1983; children: Min Ji Chae, Min hi Chae. MD, Kyungpook Nat. U., Taegu, Korea, 1983, MS, 1986, PhD, 1991. Intern Kyungpook Nat. U. Hosp., Taegu, Republic of Korea, 1983—84, resident Dept.of Pediat., 1984—87; asst. prof. Dept.of Pediat. Cath. U., Taegu, 1991—94; rsch. fellow Dept.of Pathology and Lab. Medicine Albany (N.Y.) Med. Coll., 1993—94; assoc. prof. Dept. of Pediat. Cath. U., 1995—2000, prof., 2001—. Mem. editl. bd.: Jour. of Korean Allergy, Asthma and Immunology, 2000—; contbr. articles to profl. jours. Mem.: Am. Acad. Allergy, Asthma and Immunology, Korean Soc. Pediatric Allergology and Rspiratory Disease, Korean Soc. Allergology, Korean Soc. Pediat., Korean Med. Assn. Office: Catholic Univ Taegu Dept Pediat Sch of Medicine Daemyung 4 Dong Nam-gu 3056-6 Taegu 705-034 Republic of Korea E-mail: hlchung@cu.ac.kr.

CHUNG, HWAN YUNG, neurosurgeon; b. June 16, 1927; s. Yoon Sik and Bok Hyun (Bak) C.; m. Jong Sun Kim; children: Hyo Min, Hyo Sook, Hyo Sun, Chun Kee, Hyo Gyung, Soon Gi. MD, Junnam U., 1949; PhD, Korea U., 1966. Diplomate Korean Neurosurgery Specialty, Korean Gen. Surgery Specialty Bd. Commd. lt. Republic of Korea Army, 1951, advanced through grades to col., 1965, discharged, 1965; intern Junnam Univ. Hosp., Gwangju, Korea, 1949-50; neurosurg. resident, neurosurgeon Korea Univ. Hosp., Seoul, 1956-60; neurosurgeon 121st Evacuation Hosp., U.S. Army in Korea, 1960-61, Letterman Gen. Hosp., San Francisco, 1961-62; chief neurosurgeon 1st Korean Army Hosp., Daegu, 1963-65; clin. asst. prof. Gyungbook U., Daegu, 1963-65; asst. prof. Korea U., 1965-66; from asst. prof. to assoc. prof. to prof. Yonsei U., Seoul, 1966-72; prof., chmn. neurosurgery Hanyang U., Seoul, 1972-92, prof. emeritus, 1992—. Hosp. dir. Joong-Ang Gen. Hosp., 1992-93, Hanyang U. Hosp., 1986-87; dir. Hyehwa Neurosurgical Hosp., 1999—. Decorated Bronze Star, 1952; Hwarang Medal of Honor, Korea, 1952; recipient Citation of Merit, Ministry Def., Republic of Korea, 1964, Citation of Merit, Ministry Health and Welfare, 1987, Presdl. Nat. decoration, 1992. Mem. Korean Neurosurg. Soc. (pres. 1978-79, adv. 1980-98, hon. pres. 1998—), Korean Microsurg. Soc. (pres. 1984-85), Korean Vascular Surg. Soc. (adviser 1984-92), Pan-Pacific Surg. Assn. (pres. Korean chpt. 1984-2000, v.p. hdqrs. 1984-2000), Korea Spinal Neurosurgery Soc. (pres. 1987-91, hon. pres. 1991—), Internat. Soc. for Minimal Intervention in Spinal Surgery (pres. 2002-05), Korea Soc. for Minimal Intervention in Spinal Surgery (hon. pres. 1997—), Korean Peripheral Nerve Soc. (hon. pres. 2009-). Office Phone: 822-766-3379. Business E-Mail: chungspine@hanmir.com.

CHUNG, IN SIK, biotechnologist, educator; s. Moondu Chung and Samsun Kim; m. Younghee Song, Jan. 15, 1965; children: Alex, Jay. PhD, Auburn U., 1986. Vis. scientist Cornell U., Ithaca, NY, 1991—92, Ohio State U., Columbus, 2001—02; dept. chair Hyung Hee U., Suwon, Republic of Korea, 2003—. Dept. chair Kyung Hee U., Suwon, 1989—93. Editor: (journal) Plant Cell Reports (Springer), 2000—. Fellow, Korean Ministry Edn., 1980—84. Mem.: Am. Soc. Virology, Soc. InVitro Biology, Internat. Soc. Plant Molecular Biology (assoc.). Achievements include research in Plant Edible Vaccine; Medical Biotechnology; Plant Biotechnology; Plant Metabolic Engineering. Office: Kyung Hee Univ 318-Ho Dept Genetic Engring Suwon 449-701 Republic of Korea Office Fax: 82-31-202-9885. E-mail: ischung@khu.ac.kr.

CHUNG, JIN WON, physician, educator; b. Seoul, Nov. 15, 1971; MD, Chung-Ang U., PhD, 1997. Assoc. prof. Chung Ang U. Coll. Medicine, 2007—. Office: 224-1 Heukseok-Dong Dongjak-Gu Seoul 156-755 Republic of Korea Office Fax: 82-2-825-7571. Business E-Mail: drjwchung@cau.ac.kr.

CHUNG, JUN CHUL, surgeon, educator; b. Seoul, Republic of Korea, Feb. 21, 1972; MD, Soonchunhyang U., 1997; PhD, Sungkyunkwan U., 2006. Clin. prof. Dept. Surgery, Divsn. Hepato-Biliary-Pancreatic Surgery, Sungkyunkwan U. Coll. Medicine, 2005—06; asst. prof. Soonchunhyang U. Coll. Medicine, 2007—. Mem.: Korean Soc. Endoscopic & Laparoscopic Surgeons (bd. dirs. 2005—06), Korean Assn. Hepato-Biliary-Pancreatic Surgery (bd. dirs. 2005—06). Avocations: swimming, tennis. Office: 1174 Jung-dong Wonmi-gu Bucheon Gyeonggi 420-767 Republic of Korea Office Fax: 82 32 621 5016. Personal E-mail: capcjc@hanmail.net.

CHUNG, KIAN FAN, thoracic physician, educator, researcher; b. Rose-Belle, Mauritius, Feb. 12, 1951; arrived in Eng., 1970; s. Young Cheong and Ah-Line (How) S.; m. Soop Chin Ng-Kee-Kwong, July 9, 1977; children: Joanne, Katie, Annabelle. MB, BChir, U. London, 1975, MD, 1983, DSc, 2001. Intern Addenbrookes Hosp., Cambridge, 1975-76; resident Middlesex Hosp., London, 1976, Radcliffe Infirmary, Oxford, 1977, Hammersmith Hosp., 1978; chef-de-clinique Geneva Med. Sch., 1978-79; lectr. medicine Med. Sch., Charing Cross Hosp., London, 1979-82; vis. scientist Cardiovasc. Rsch. Inst., U. Calif., San Francisco, 1983-85; sr. lectr., cons. physician Nat. Heart and Lung Inst. and Royal Brompton Hosp., London, 1986—; prof. respiratory medicine Imperial Coll. Sci., Tech. and Medicine U. London, 1994—. Mem. coll. experts Med. Rsch. Coun., England, 2006—. Author: Therapeutics of Respiratory Disease, 1994; editor: Pharmacology of Respiratory Tract, 1993, Asthma: Mechanisms and Protocols, 2000, Cough, 2005—; co-editor: Molecular Methods in Asthma, 2000, Cough: Causes, Mechanisms and Therapy, 2003, Pharmacology & Therapeutic of Airway Diseases, 2009; editor: Airway Smooth Muscle in Asthma and COPD, 2009; mem. editl. bd. Pulmonary Pharmacology, London, 1989-94, European Respiratory Jour., 1995—99, Am. Jour. Respiratory Critical Care Medicine, 1996-2005, European Jour. Allergy Clin. Immunology, 1999-2005, European Jour. Clin. Pharmacology, European Jour. Pharmacology, 2008-; contbr. articles to profl. jours. Dorothy Temple-Cross travelling fellow Med. Rsch. Coun. U.K., 1983-84, Wellcome Trust rsch. program grantee, 1992—, NIH grantee, 2001—, Med. Rsch. Coun., 2007-; Harold Boldero scholar Middlesex Hosp. Med. Sch., London, 1975. Fellow Royal Coll. Physicians (London); mem. Am. Thoracic Soc., Brit. Pharmacological Soc., Nat. Inst. Health Rsch.(sr. investigator 2009). Avocations: travel, history. Office: Nat Heart & Lung Inst Imperial Coll Dovehouse St London SW3 6LY England Personal E-mail: f.chung@imperial.ac.uk.

CHUNG, KING-THOM, microbiologist, toxicologist, educator; came to U.S., 1966; s. Aa-Yuan and Yi-Ing (Buu) C.; m. Lan-Seng Fang, Oct. 27, 1973; children: Theodore, Serena. MA, U. Calif., Santa Cruz, 1967; PhD, U. Calif., Davis, 1972. Scientist Frederick Cancer Rsch. Ctr., Md., 1973—77; vis. asst. prof. Food Sci. Inst. Purdue U., West Lafayette, Ind., 1977—78; assoc. prof. Tunghai U., Taichung, Taiwan, 1978—80; prof., chmn. dept. Soochow U., Taipei, Taiwan, 1980—87, dean, 1983—87; vis. scientist U.S. Meat Animal Rsch. Ctr., Clay Center, Nebr., 1987—88; assoc. prof. biology U. Memphis, 1988—93, prof., 1993—. Mem. adv. bd. Dept. Agr. and Forestry, Taiwan Provincial Govt., Taichung, 1982-87; exec. sec. Internat. Symposium on Biogas, Microalgae and Livestock Wastes, Taipei, 1980. Author: (in Chinese) Environment and Pollution, 1987, Intellectuals and Academic Education, 1987, Stories of 25 World Leading Microbiologists, 1996; contbr. articles to profl. jours. Grantee Am. Inst. Cancer Rsch., 1992. Fellow Am. Acad. Microbiology; mem. Am. Soc. Microbiology, Am. Acad. Microbiology, Inst. Food Technologists, Sigma Xi. Achievements include the illustration of the significance of azo reduction in the azo dye mutagenesis and carcinogenesis, quantitative structure activity relationships (QSAR) of aromatic amines, molecular mechanisms of aromatic amines induced bladder cancer, polyphenols and health, and history of microbiology. Office: U Memphis Dept Biology Memphis TN 38152-0001 Office Phone: 901-678-4458. Business E-Mail: kchung@memphis.edu.

CHUNG, KYUNG WON, medical educator, biomedical researcher; b. Seoul, Republic of Korea, Aug. 15, 1938; s. Jin Rok Chung and Yoon Hee Kim; m. Young Hee Min, Aug. 20, 1966; children: Harold Mooinn, John Moojohn. MS in Biology, Yonsei U., Seoul, Republic of Korea, 1966; MS in Anatomy, St. Louis U., 1969; PhD in Anatomy and Cell Biology, U. Okla. Coll. Medicine, Okla. City, 1971. Asst. prof. SUNY, Bklyn., 1972—77, U. Okla. Coll. Medicine, 1977—79, assoc. prof., 1979—86, prof., vice chmn., 1986—, dir. human anatomy, 1988—2007. Chmn. State of Okla. Anat. Bd., Okla. City, 1993—2008; vis. prof. Oxford U., 2005. Author: (textbook) Gross Anatomy, Board Review Series, Temas Clave Anatomia, 2008, Anatomie Humaine, 1995. Recipient Aesculapian award, U. Okla. Coll. Medicine, 1979—80, 1983—84, 1986, 1988, Edger W. Young Lifetime Achievement award, 1990, Stanton L. Young Master Tchr. award, 1992, Lifetime Achievement award, Korean Cultural Ctr. Orange County, Calif., 2007, 2003; named David Ross Boyd Disting. Prof., U. Okla. Coll. Medicine, 1993. Mem.: Am. Assn. Clin. Anatomists, Endocrine Soc., Am. Assn. Anatomists. Home: 809 Hollowdale Edmond OK 73003 Office: University Okla Coll Medicine 940 Stanton L Young Blvd Oklahoma City OK 73104 Office Phone: 405-271-2377. Office Fax: 405-271-3548. Business E-Mail: kyung-chung@ouhsc.edu.

CHUNG, MAN PYO, physician, educator; b. Seoul, Republic Of Korea, Aug. 4, 1961; s. Soon Jo Chung and Il Soon Song; m. Seoun Min Ahn, Apr. 19, 1986; children: Seung Hwan, You Seun. BS, Seoul Nat. U., 1985, M, 1990, PhD, 1995. Diplomate Nat. Health Adminstrn., Seoul, 1986. Intern Seoul Nat. U. Hosp., 1986—87, resident dept. medicine, 1987—90; physician Samsung Med. Ctr., Seoul, 1993—; rsch. scientist U. Iowa Med. Coll., Iowa City, 2000—02; prof. Sungkyunkwan U. Sch. Medicine, Seoul, 1997—. Capt. Seoul Dist. Mil. Hosp., 1990—93. Achievements include research in interstitial lung disease. Office: Samsung Med Ctr Dept Medicine 50 Ilwon-dong Kangnam-ku Seoul 135-710 Republic of Korea Business E-Mail: mpchung@skku.edu.

CHUNG, SAJUN, medical educator; b. Kangwondo-do, Republic of Korea, June 13, 1949; MD, Kyunghee U., Seoul, Republic of Korea, 1973, PhD, 1981. Prof. Kyunghee U. Coll. Medicine, Seoul, 1981—, vice dean, 1992—93; chmn., dir., dept. pediat. Coll. Medicine Kyunghee U. Hosp., Seoul, 1992—93; dir., rsch. sect. Kyunghee U. Hosp., Seoul, 1998—2002, dir., 2003—04. Vis. prof., divsn. child neurology Kurume U., Japan, 1985—87; rschr. Nat. Inst. Neurosci. NCNP, Tokyo, 1986; exec. bd. mem. Asia-oceanian Child Neurology Assn., 2001—04. Recipient Kohwang Med. award, Kyunghee U., Appreciation award, Japanese Pediat. Soc., 1995, 1999, Japanese Neurology Soc., 2004, Asia and Oceanian Child Neurology Soc., 2010. Master: Korean Child Neurology Soc. (pres. 2001—04); mem.: Korean Soc. Maternal & Child Health (editor-in-chief 2001—05), Child Neurology Soc., European Pediat. Neurology Soc., Korean Pediatric Soc. (editor-in-chief, exec. bd., publ. 1994—2000, Sukchun Academic Rsch. award 1998, Sukchun Academic award 1997), Am. Neurol. Assn. (corr.), Internat. Child Neurology Assn., ILAE, Nat. Acad. Medicine Korea. Avocation: golf. Office: Kyunghee University Hosp Dept Pediat #1 Hoeki-dong Dongdaemun-ku Seoul 130-702 Republic of Korea Home: #501-1202 Sambo Garden Apt Banpo-l-dong Seoul Seocho 135-280 Republic of Korea Business E-Mail: sajchung@khmc.or.kr.

CHUNG, SOCHUNG, medical educator; b. Seoul, Republic of Korea, Feb. 25, 1967; MD, Yonsei U., 1991, PhD, 2001. Prof. Sch. Medicine, Konkuk U., 2010—. Office: 4-12 Hwayang-dong Gwangjin-gu Seoul 143-729 Republic of Korea Office Fax: 82-2-2030-7748. Business E-Mail: scchung@kuh.ac.kr.

CHUNG, STEVE, physician; b. San Francisco, May 5, 1969; MD, Northwestern U., 1994. Intern Northwestern U. Sch. Medicine; resident neurology U. Calif. San Francisco, fellow epilepsy; neurologist, epileptologist, med. dir. Neurology Residency Program Barrow Neurol. Inst., 2002—. Recipient Nat. Epilepsy Rsch. Award, 1998, American Acad. Neurology Edn. & Rsch. Found. Award, 1999. Mem.: American Clin. Neurophysiology, American Epilepsy Soc., American Neurology Assn., American Acad. Neurology. Office: Barrow Neurological Institute 500 W Thomas Rd Phoenix AZ 85020 Business E-Mail: sschung@chw.edu.

CHUNG, SUNG PIL, medical educator; b. Chonju, Republic of Korea, Nov. 8, 1968; s. Hong Seok Chung and Chun Ja Kim; m. Soo Mee Park, May 12, 1968; children: Seokwon, Yesol. MD, Yonsei U., Seoul, Republic of Korea, 1992; PhD, Yonsei U., 2002. Cert. emergency physician Ministry Health, Republic of Korea, 1998. Asst. prof. Chungnam Nat. U. Hosp., Daejon, Republic of Korea, 2001—06; assoc. prof. Yonsei U., Seoul, 2006—; edn. mem. Korean Assn. Cardiopulmonary Resuscitation, Seoul, 2004—. Editl. mem. Korean Soc. Emergency Medicine, Seoul, Republic of Korea, 2002—; mem. Korean Soc. Clin. Toxicology, Seoul, Republic of Korea, 2006—, Korean Soc. Critical Care Medicine, Seoul, Republic of Korea, 2008—. Office: Gangnam Severance Hosp 712 Eonju-ro Gangnam-gu Seoul 135-720 Republic of Korea Home: Raemian Greater Yeoksam-dong Seoul Gangnam-gu 203 1203 Republic of Korea Business E-Mail: emstar@naver.com.

CHUNG, THOMAS, ophthalmologist; MBBS (hon.), Faculty Medicine, U. Hong Kong, 1997; Master Medicine in Ophthalmology, Nat. U. Hong Kong, 2004. Hon. clin. asst. prof. Dept. Ophthalmology and Visual Sciences, Chinese U., Hong Kong, 2005—08; hon. asst. prof. Eye Inst., U. Hong Kong, 2008—; assoc. cons. Hosp. Authority, Hong Kong, 2008—09; ind. ophthalmologist Canada, 2009—. Assoc. fellow Coll. Ophthalmologists, Hong Kong, 2000; reviewer jour. Asian Jour. Ophthalmology, 2006—, Am. Jour. Ophthalmology, 2006—. Contbr. articles to peer reviewed jours. Fellowship, Hong Kong Acad. Medicine, 2004, Coll. Ophthalmologists Hong Kong, 2005. Fellow: RCS Edinburgh, Royal Coll. Physicians and Surgeons Can.; mem.: Am. Assn. Aesthetic Medicine and Surgery, Med. Coun. Can. (licentiate). Personal E-mail: thomascthomasc@yahoo.com.

CHUNG, WEN-HUNG, geneticist, dermatologist; b. Nantou, Taiwan, May 26, 1971, s. Shin-Shon Chung and Sho-Shan Cho; m. Shuen-Iu Hung, Jan. 29, 2005. MD, Chung Shan Med. U., Taiwan, 1997. Cert. dermatologist Dept. of Health of the Exec. Yuan, Taiwan. Attending physician in dermatology Chang Gung Meml. Hosp., Taipei, Taiwan, 2003—. Lectr. in genetic counseling Dept. of Health of the Exec. Yuan, 2005—; mem. adv. com. Nat. Clin. Care for Genomic Medicine, Academia Sinica, Taipei, 2003—. Reviewer Jour. Dermatol. Sci., Japan, 2005—, Annals of Internal Medicine, 2005—. Recipient Highest Impact Factor Rsch. prize, Chang Gung Meml. Hosp., 2004, Super Rsch. award, 2004, Taipei Outstanding Young Man award, 2005, Young Scientist Rsch. award, Taiwan Med. Soc., 2005; named one of Top 10 Rising Stars in Taiwan, 2006. Fellow: Am. Soc. Dermatology (assoc.); mem.: Chinese Dermatol. Soc., Am. Soc. Human Genetics (assoc.). Achievements include discovery of strong genetic marker for Stevens-Johnson syndrome; genetic markers linked to adverse drug reaction induced by anti-epileptics (carbamazepine) and anti-hyperuricemia (allopurinol). Office: Dept Dermatology No199 Tung-Hwa N Rd Taipei 105 Taiwan Personal E-mail: wenhungchung@yahoo.com.

CHUNG, WOO CHUL, gastroenterologist, educator; b. Seoul, Republic of Korea, July 19, 1968; MD, Cath. U. Korea, 1993, PhD, 2010. Assoc. prof. dept. internal medicine St. Vincent Hosp., Suwon, Gyunggi, Republic of Korea, 2002—. Mem. academic com. Korean Coll. Study Helicobacter and Upper Gastrointestinal Rsch., 2011. Mem.: Korean Soc. Gastrointestinal Cancer, Korean Assn. Study Intestinal Diseases, Korean Soc. Gastroenterology, Korean Soc. Gastrointestinal Endoscopy. Office: 93 Jungbu-Daero Paldal-gu Suwon Gyunggi 442-723 Republic of Korea Office Fax: 82-31-253-8898.

CHUNG, WOO-YEONG, medical educator, director; b. Busan, Republic Of Korea, Feb. 14, 1956; m. Hae-Sun Park; children: Jae-Won, Yun-Seo. MD, Korean Med. Assn., 1980; PhD, Busan Nat. U., 1991. Postdoc. fellowship, dept. pediat. nephrology UCLA Med. Ctr., 1987—88; prof. dept. pediat. Busan Paik Hosp., 1985—, dean, internat. affairs, Coll. Medicine, Inje U., 2005—; vice chmn. Korean Soc. Pediat. Endocrinology, Seoul, 2007—; dir. Regional Rare Diseases Ctr. Korean Ctr. Disease Control, Seoul, 2007—. Office: Busan Paik Hosp Dept Pediat 633-165 Kaekum Dong Busanjin Ku Busan 614-735 Republic of Korea Office Fax: 82-51-895-7785. Business E-Mail: chungwy@korea.com.

CHUNG, YEUN-JUN, geneticist, educator; b. Seoul, Republic of Korea, Apr. 28, 1964; s. Jae-Hyung Chung and Hee-Kyun Shin; m. Seon-Hee Yim, Mar. 11, 2001; children: Woo-Chan, Mina. MD, Cath. Med. Coll., Seoul, 1989, PhD, 1998. Asst. prof. Cath. U. Med. Coll., Seoul, 1998—2003, assoc. prof., 2004—; prof. Pohang (Republic of Korea) U. Sci. and Tech., 2005—. Vis. scholar Japan Internat. Sci. and Tech. Exch. Ctr., Sukuba, Japan, 1999; project leader Sanger Inst., Cambridge, England, 2001—04; mem. adv. bd. Ministry Health and Welfare, 2005—. Author: Mouse Models of Cancer Oncogenomics: Molecular Approaches to Cancer, 2004; contbr. articles to profl. jours. With dept. Virology NIH of Korea, 1993—96, Seoul. Recipient Best Paper awards, Cath. U. Postgrad. Sch., 1996, 1997. Mem.: Korean Soc. Cancer Rsch., Korean Soc. Med. Biochemistry and Molecular Biology, Korean Med. Assn. (diplomate). Roman Catholic. Achievements include research in genome-wide screening of genomic alterations and their clinicopathological implications in non small cell lung cancers; complex haplotypes, copy number polymorphisms and coding variation in two recently divergent mouse strains; ArrayCyGHt: a web application for analysis and visualization of arrayCGH data; whole-genome mouse BAC microarray with 1-Mb resolution for analysis of DNA copy number changes by array comparative genomic hybridization; evidence of genetic progression in human gastric carcinomas with microsatellite instability; microsatellite instability-associated mutations associate preferentially with the intestinal type of primary gastric carcinomas in a high-risk population. Avocation: travel. Office Fax: +82-2-596-8969. Business E-Mail: yejun@catholic.ac.kr.

CHUNG, YOON-SOK, endocrinologist, educator; b. Seoul, Republic of Korea, Sept. 29, 1963; s. Kyong-Yong Chung and Young-Ock Lim-Chung; m. Eun-Ha Ryu, Nov. 13, 2003; 1 child, Engeneia. MD, Yonsei U., Seoul, Republic of Korea, 1988, PhD, 1997. Post-doctoral fellow Musculoskeletal Disease Ctr., VA Hosp., Loma Linda, Calif., 2001—02. Mem.: Endocrine Soc. Office: Dept Endocrinology Ajou Univ Hosp 5 Wonchon-Dong Youngtong-Gu Kyonggi-Do Suwon 443-721 Republic of Korea Office Fax: 82-31-219-4497. Business E-Mail: yschung@ajou.ac.kr.

CHUNG, YOUNG IN, psychiatrist, educator; b. Hadong Province, Republic of Korea, Sept. 19, 1956; s. Pan Jong and Soon Jo Chung; m. Hyun Ok Cho, June 20, 1982; 1 child, Jee Yoon. MD, Pusan Nat. U. Sch. Medicine, 1982; M of Med. Sci., Pusan Nat. U. Grad. Sch., 1985, PhD, 1992. Lic. Min. Health and Welfare, Republic of Korea, 1982. Prof. Pusan Nat. U. Sch. Medicine, Republic of Korea, 1989—; dir. Office Computer and PR, Pusan Nat. U. Hosp., 2000—01, Office Internat. Affairs, Pusan Nat. U., 2002—03; pres. Korean Assn. Fgn. Student Adminstrs., Seoul, 2002—03; chmn. Dept. Psychiatry, Pusan Nat. U. Hosp., 2002—; dir. Office Planning and Coordination, Pusan Nat. U. Hosp., 2003—03. Vis. scientist Lab. Neurobiology, Burke Med. Rsch. Inst., White Plains, NY, 1993—95; vis. psychiatrist Manly Hosp., Sydney, 1997—97, Janssen Rsch. Inst., Antwerp, 2000—00. Editor: (journal) Korean Jour. Psychopharmacology, Clinical Psychopharmarcology and Neurosci. Commr. External Cooperation Com., Korean Med. Assn., 2004—05; dir. Bd. Mental Health Rev., Pusan, 1997—2000, Pusan Cycling Corp., Pusan, 2004—05. Capt. Korean Mil., 1987—89. Grantee, Korean Psychiat. Rsch. Found., 2001. Mem.: Korean Acad. Schizophrenia, Korean Soc. Pschopharmacology, Korean Neuropsychiatric Assn., Collegium Internationale Neuro-Psychopharmacologicum, Am. Psychiat. Assn., Korean Med. Assn. Achievements include research in Biochemical and Clinical Schizophrenia and Mood Disorder. Home: #126-1902 Yongho-Dong Nam-Gu Pusan 608-091 Republic of Korea Office: Pusan Nat U Hosp 1-10 Ami-Dong Seo-Gu Pusan 602-739 Republic of Korea Office Fax: 82-51-248-3648. E-mail: yichung@pusan.ac.kr.

CHUNG, YOUNG-HWA, internist, educator; b. Pyeong-Taek, Gyeonggi-Do, Republic Of Korea, Feb. 15, 1957; m. Kyung-Ran Lee; children: Jie-Hoon, Jie-Sun. MD, Coll. Medicine, Seoul Nat. U., Republic Of Korea, 1981; MS, Grad. Sch. Med. Sci., Seoul Nat. U., Republic Of Korea, 1984; PhD, Grad. Sch. Med. Sci., Korea U. Lic. practical medicine & surgery KMA, 1981, diplomate Korean Bd. Internal Medicine, 1985, cert. gastroenterology KAGE, 1993. Intern Seoul Nat. U. Hosp., 1981—82, resident, dept. internal medicine, 1982—85; chief, dept. internal medicine Seoul Dist. Hosp., 1985—88; rschr. Inst. Liver Rsch., Seoul Nat. U., Republic of Korea, 1988—89; instr. Dept. Internal Medicine, Asan Med. Ctr., U. Ulsan Coll. Medicine, 1989—91, asst. prof., 1991—95, assoc. prof., 1995—2000, prof., 2000—. Vis. rschr. Klinik fur Viszeral-und Transplantationschirurgie, Medizinische Hochschule Hannover, Klinik fur Viszeral-und Transplantationschirurgie, Hannover, Germany, 1992; rsch. assoc. NIDDK, NIH; mem. sci. com. Korean Soc. Gastroenterology, Seoul, Republic of Korea, 1996—97; mem. intelligence com. Korean Acad. Med. Sci., Seoul, 1997—99; mem. exec. coun. Inst. Social Sci., U. Ulsan Coll. Medicine, Seoul, 1998—99; mem. publ. com. Korean Assn. Study Liver (KASL), Seoul, 1997—99, mem. sci. com., 1999—2001, sec. gen., 2006—07, Organizing Com. 3rd Seoul Internat. Liver Symposium, Seoul, Republic of Korea, 2006—07; organizer 4th Korea-Japan Liver Symposium, Seoul, 2007; mem. adv. bd. 18th Conf. Asian-Pacific Assn. Study Liver, Seoul, 2007—08; mem. organizing com. 6th Internat. Meeting Hepatocellular Carcinoma Ea. & Western Experiences, Seoul, 2008—; mem. Organizing Com. Korea-Japan Liver Symposium, Seoul, 2008—; assoc. editor Liver Internat., Calgary, Canada, 2008—; chmn., divsn. gastroenterology U. Ulsan Asan Med. Ctr., 2009—; editor New Horizons, Gastroenterology Focus, Liver Internat., World Jour. Gastroenterology, 2010—. Fellowship, Divsn. Gastroenterology, Seoul Nat. U. Hosp., 1988—89, grant, Ministry of Health and Welfare, 2000, 2002, 2008. Mem.: Internat. Assn. Study Liver, Asian-Pacific Assn. Study Liver, Korean Assn. Study Liver (sec. gen. 2006—07, Academic award 2002), Korean Soc. Gastroenterology (Dr. Paul Janssen award 2000), Korean Assn. Internal Medicine, Korean Acad. Med. Sci. Achievements include patents for hepatic fibrosis inducing method by repeated injection of allylalcohol; patents pending for diagnosis of hepatocellular carcinoma using TGF beta1 as a serologic marker; diagnosis of postoperative recurrence in patients with hepatocellular carcinoma; single nucleotide polymorphism for prognosis of hepatocellular carcinoma; single nucleotide polymorphism for recurrance of hepatocellular carcinoma. Home: D-206 Hanyang Apt Yeouido-Dong Youngd Seoul 150-010 Republic of Korea Office: University Ulsan Asan Med Ctr 86 Asanbyeongwon-gil Songpa-Gu Seoul 138 736 Republic of Korea Office Fax: 82-2-476-0824. Business E-Mail: yhchung@amc.seoul.kr.

CHUNG, YOUNG-YOOL, orthopedist; b. Gwangju, Republic of Korea, Sept. 8, 1963; s. Jong-harm Chung and Sang-rim Ko; m. Soon-Jin Kim; children: Hyung-seok, Young-seok, Ye-eun. MD, Chonnam Nat. U., Gwangju, 1988. Cert. orthop. surgeon Korean Med. Assn., 1993. Chief edn. dept. Gwangju Christian Hosp., 2007—. Editl. staff Korean Hip Soc., Seoul, Republic of Korea, 2006—. Deacon Gwangju Seo-nam Ch., 1990—2008. Capt. Korean Army, 1993—96. Home: Jinwall-Dong Gwangju Republic of the Congo Office: Kwangju Christian Gen Hosp Yangrim-Dong 503-715 Gwangju Republic of Korea Office Phone: 82-62-650-5063. Office Fax: 82-62-650-5066. Business E-Mail: paedic@chol.com.

CHUNG-WELCH, NANCY YUEN MING, biologist, director; b. NYC, July 28, 1960; d. Thomas Richard and Jennie Kan Fee (Lew) Semler; m. James Michael Welch, June 29, 1985. BS, Northeastern U., Boston, 1982; PhD, Boston U., 1990. Rsch. technician dept. biology Boston U., 1983-85, tchg. fellow dept. biology, 1987-89; rsch. fellow surgery Mass. Gen. Hosp., Harvard Med. Sch., Boston, 1989-94; instr. in surgery Harvard Med. Sci., 1994-95; rsch. assoc. prof. Boston U., 1996-97; product mgr. Oncogene Rsch. Products, Cambridge, Mass., 1997-99, BD Bioscis., Bedford, Mass., 1999—2002; mktg. mgr. Fisher Sci., Hampton, NH, 2002—05, dir. bus. devel., 2005—07, Thermo Fisher Scientific, Waltham, Mass., 2006—07, life scis. cons., 2008—. Contbr. articles to profl. jours. including Jour. Cellular Physiology, Differentiation, Analytical Biochemistry, Surg. Forum, Microvascular Rsch., Biotechniques, Jour. Electrophoresis. Recipient Grad. Rsch. award Boston U. Grad. Sch., 1987, Biology Dept. Grad. Travel award, 1988-89, Grega-Zacharkow Young Investigator award Microcirculatory Soc., 1988; named Outstanding Young Woman of Mass., 1988; Repligen Corp fellow, 1993-95 strategic planning and commercial business development of technologies and platforms for the life sciences products/tools industry, with domestic and international experience in needs analysis, technology assessment, licensing, distribution deals, partnerships, strategic alliances, strategic customer relationships, mergers/acquisitions hands-on marketing executive that has conceptualized, launched and managed products and services for the laboratory medical, biotech/pharma, academic and government markets. Personal E-mail: nchung@tiac.net.

CHUNG-YI, CHEN, dean, educator; b. Jhongli, Taoyuan, Taiwan, Feb. 11, 1972; PhD, Kaohsiung Med. U., 1999. Tchg. asst. Dept. Pharmacy, Kaohsiung Med. U., 1997—2000; asst. prof., dir., Basic Med. Sci. Edn. Ctr. Fooyin U., 2001—03, assoc. prof., dir., 2004—06, prof., dir., 2007, prof., dean, Sch. Med. and Health Scis., 2007—. Recipient award, Nat. Sci. Coun., 1997—2000, Outstanding Alumnus award, Jhongli Sr. HS, 2001, Rsch. Stipend award, Nat. Sci. Coun., 2002—. Office: 151 Ching-Hsueh Rd Kaohsiung Ta-Liao 831 Taiwan Office Fax: 886-7-7863667. Business E-Mail: xx377@mail.fy.edu.tw.

CHUNPRAPAPH, BOONMEE, physician, educator; b. Songkhla, Thailand, Nov. 23, 1938; came to U.S., 1966; s. Yen Hua Tseng; m. Kaysorn Suttajit, July 29, 1944; children: Benj, Kabin. MD, U. Med. Sci., Bangkok, 1964. Diplomate Am. Bd. Orthopedic Surgery. Rotating intern Samaritan Hosp., Troy, N.Y., 1966-67; pvt. practice gen. surgery Youngstown (Ohio) Hosp. Assn., 1967-68; pvt. practice specializing in orthopedic surgery Univ. Hosp., Mobile, Ala., 1968-71; assoc. prof. U. Ill., Chgo., 1980—. Contbr. articles to profl. jours. Fellow ACS, Internat. Coll. Surgeons; mem. AMA, Acad Orthopedic Surgeons, Am. Soc. Surgery of the Hand. Avocations: photography, gardening, tennis. Office: U Ill Coll Medicine 835 S Wolcott Ave M/C 844 Chicago IL 60612-7307 Office Phone: 312-996-7161.

CHUNTRASAKUL, CHOMCHARK, retired surgeon, writer, medical educator; b. Trang, Thailand, Jan. 22, 1937; s. Chaey and Chun Chuntrasakul; m. Patchaneepan Muangman, May 31, 1969 (div.). MD, Mahidol U., Bangkok, 1963; MD (hon.), Mahidol U., 2009. Diplomate Am. Bd. Surgery, 1972. Fellow in vascular surgery Albany (N.Y.) Med. Ctr., 1971; fellow in burns St. John's Mercy Med. Ctr., St. Louis, 1972; from asst. prof. to assoc. prof. dept. surgery Siriraj Hosp. Mahidol U., Bangkok, 1975—85, prof., 1985—98, prof. emeritus, 1998—, cons., instr., 1998—, dep. dir. hosp., chair Out Patient Dept., 1984—89, dep. dean Med. Sch., 1993—98; jt. pres. World Congress Surgery, 2002; hon. advisor IBC, med. adv. to gen. dir. Cambridge. Dep. gen. Am. Biog. Inst. Rsch. Assn., 2011. Hon. advisor Health Care Com. Senator, Thailand, 2001—; founder Thai Soc. Burn Injuries, 1989, Soc. Parenteral and Enteral Nutrition Thailand, 1989, PENA, 1938, Thai Soc. Wound Healing, 2005; pres. RCST, 2001—03; mem. com. Brain Bank Vol., Thailand, 2000—. Recipient Royal Academic medal, 1938, Golden prize, 1938, High Level of Royal medals, 1980, 1990, 1993, Med. Svc. Outstanding award, Mahidol U., 1986, Outstanding award, Trauma Assn., 1989, Excellent People award, Trang Province, 2002, Lifetime Achievement award, World Congress Arts Scis. and Comm., 2009, Achievement award, IBC, Cambridge, Eng., 2011, Great Leader award, Order of Silver Cross, Disting. Svc. Order, Am. Biog. Inst., 2011, Disting. Svc. Order & Cross, ABI, 2011; named Disting. Medicine Faculty, Siriraj Hosp., Mahidol U., 2009—10; named to Hall of fame, IBC. Mem.: ACS, Thai Soc. Wound Healing (pres. 2005—), Internat. Coll. Surgeons (Outstanding award, Thailand sect. 1990), Am. Burn Assn., Thai Med. Assn., Royal Coll. Surgeons Thailand (pres. 2001—03), Parenteral and Enteral Nutrition Soc. Asia (pres. 1995—). Avocations: walking, gardening, music, academic interest. Office: Mahidol U Siriraj Hosp Dept Surgery Pranok Rd 10700 Bangkok Thailand Home: 489/7 Rajvithi Rd 10400 Bangkok Bangkok Thailand Office Phone: (66)2-4197727-9. Office Fax: (66)2-4129841. Business E-Mail: sicct@mahidol.ac.th, chomchark@loxinfo.co.th.

CHUNXIA, CAO, research scientist; b. China, Mar. 8, 1975; PhD, Xi'an Jiaotong U., 2008. Postdoc. rschr. U. Fla., 2009—. Home: 2811 SW Archer Rd Apt V186 Gainesville FL 32608 Personal E-mail: chunxiacao@yahoo.com.cn.

CHUO, LIANG-JEN, psychiatrist, researcher; b. Taichung, Taiwan, June 25, 1946; s. King-Gua Chuo and Ling-poung Wang; m. Grace Tsai, July 1, 1948; children: Andrew, Peter, Timothy. MD, Nat. Def. Med. Ctr., Taipei, 1972. Cert. Nat. Bd. Psychiatry, Dept. Health, Taiwan, 1981, Nat. Bd. Geriatric Medicine, 2008, Nat. Bd. Geriatric Psychiatry, 2009. Attending psychiatrist Taipei (Taiwan) Vets. Gen. Hosp., 1979—84, Taichung (Taiwan) Vets. Gen. Hosp., 1984—, chief gero-psychiatry, 2006—. Bd. med. mission com. Chinese Christian Med. Mission. Chmn., bd. exec. com. Chinese Christian Med. Mission, Taipei, 1997. Maj. Med. Officer Army, 1974—78, Taipei, Tri-Svc. Psychiatry Hosp. Decorated Stander of Med. Officer of Army Chief of the Gen. Staff; named Excellent Physician, Vets. Affairs Commn., 2008. Mem.: Internat. Psychogeriatric Assn. (life), Taiwan Alzheimer's Disease Assn. (life). Avocations: music, ping pong/table tennis, sightseeing. Office: Taichung Vets Gen Hosp 160 Sect 3 Taichung Harbor Rd Taichung 40763 Taiwan Office Phone: 886-4-24613097. Office Fax: 886-4-24613097. Personal E-mail: ljchuo@gmail.com. Business E-Mail: ljchuo@vghtc.gov.tw.

CHURCH, GWYNNE D., pediatrician, educator; b. Apr. 23, 1969; MD, Med. Coll. Wis., 1999. Cert. Pediat., 2002. Intern pediat. pulmonology Rush Presbyn. St Luke's Med. Ctr., Chgo., 1999—2000; resident Children's Hosp., Oakland, Calif., 2000—02; fellowship U. Calif., San Francisco, 2002, asst. clin. prof. pediat. pulmonary. Office: U Calif San Francisco Box 0632 521 Parnassus Ave C344 San Francisco CA 94143-0632 Office Phone: 415-476-8629. Office Fax: 415-476-9278. E-mail: churchg@peds.ucsf.edu.

CHURCH, TIMOTHY ROBERT, medical educator, researcher; b. Cin., Nov. 4, 1950; s. Bill Grant and Elizabeth Ellen Church; life ptnr. Ann Louise Fredrickson; children: Ellen Rachel, Elizabeth Gene. PhD, U. Minn., Mpls., 1984. Biostatistician Medtronic, Inc, Mpls., 1980—82, mgr. biometry, 1982—87, dir., tachyarrhythmia clin. studies dept., 1993—96; rsch. fellow U. Minn., Mpls., 1975—80, sr. rsch. assoc., 1987—93, assoc. prof., 1996—2006, prof., 2006—. Prin. investigator Minn. PLCO, Mpls., 1999—. Contbr. numerous peer-reviewed jours articles to profl. jours. including: New England Jour. Medicine, Am. Jour. Epidemiology, Biometrics, Circulation and Statistician. Mem. Virginia Piper Cancer Inst. at Abbott Northwestern Hosp., Mpls., 1999—2002, Humphrey Cancer Ctr. at North Meml. Hosp., Mpls., 2003—. Mem.: Am. Assn. for Cancer Rsch., Soc. Epidemiologic Rsch., East North Am. Region Biometric Soc., Soc. Clin. Trials, Am. Statis. Assn., Delta Omega Honor Soc. Achievements include research in screening for colorectal cancer reduced deaths, led to nationwide recommendation for screening; efficacy of first rate-adjusting cardiac pacemaker; lowered energy requirements of steroid eluting cardiac pacing leads; lower defibrillation energy of implantable cardioverter/defibrillators using active can electrodes; lead-time biased ascertainment in epidemiology studies of chronic disease. Home: 1405 Osceola Ave Saint Paul MN 55105 Office: Univ Minn Environ Health Scis Ste 350 200 Oak St SE Minneapolis MN 55455-2008 Business E-Mail: trc@cccs.umn.edu.

CHURCHEY, RANDY L., real estate company executive; BS, U. Ala. Ptnr., Health Care Practice Coopers & Lybrand, LLP, chmn., Hospitality and Real Estate Practice; sr. v.p., CFO FelCor Lodging Trust, Inc.; pres., COO RFS Hotel Investors, Inc., 1999—2003, bd. dirs., 2000—03; pres. The Encore Companies, 2003—06; pres., CEO Beverly Enterprises, Inc. (BEI), 2006—07; interim CEO Great Wolf Resorts, Inc., 2008, bd. dirs.; founder, co-chmn. MCR Devel., LLC; pres., CEO & bd. dirs. Education Realty Trust, 2010—. Bd. dirs. Innkeepers USA Trust, 2004—. Office: Education Realty Trust 530 Oak Court Dr Ste 300 Memphis TN 38117 Office Phone: 901-259-2500. Office Fax: 901-259-2594. Business E-Mail: rchurchey@edrtrust.com. *

CHURCHILL, MAIR ELISA ANNABELLE, pharmacy professor; b. Liverpool, Eng., Nov. 28, 1959; BA in Chemistry, Swathmore Coll., Pa., 1981; PhD in Chemistry, Johns Hopkins U., 1987. Lab. asst. Swarthmore Coll., 1979-81; teaching asst. Johns Hopkins U., Balt., 1981-83; non-clin. sci. staff grade I MRC Lab. Molecular Biology, Cambridge, Eng., 1987-93; asst. prof. biophysics U. Ill., Urbana, 1993-98; assoc. prof. biophysics U. Colo., Denver, 1998—. Contbr. numerous articles to profl. jours. Am. Cancer Soc. fellow, 1987-89, Cambridge U. fellow, 1988-91. Mem. Am. Chem. Soc., Sigma Xi (assoc.). Office: U Colo Sch Medicine Dept Pharm PO Box 6511 MS8303 Aurora CO 80045

CHURCHILL, ROBERT JOSEPH, radiologist, educator, dean; b. Rockford, Ill., June 4, 1946; MD, Loyola U., 1972. Intern internal medicine U. Ind., Indpls.; resident diagnostic radiology Loyola U., Maywood, Ill., 1973—76, fellow, 1976—77, vice chair radiology; fellow, adviser GE; joined as chair, prof. radiology U. Mo. Sch. Medicine, Columbia, 1987, vice dean, 1995—98, interim dean, 1998, interim vice chancellor, CEO health sciences ctr., 1998—2000, Gwilym S. Lodwick, MD, and Maria Antonia Lodwick disting. prof. radiology, Hugh E. and Sarah D. Stephenson dean, 2009—. Founder Mo. Radiology Imaging Ctr. Office: University Mo Sch Medicine MA202 Medical Scis Bldg Columbia MO 65212 Office Phone: 573-884-9080. E-mail: ChurchillR@missouri.edu. *

CHUTKOW, LEE ROBINSON, retired physician; b. Denver, Feb. 10, 1927; s. Samuel and Yvette (Robinson) C.; m. Mary Lou Murdock, June 1957 (div.); 1 child, John; m. Betty Miller Hanish, June 3, 1973 (dec. Sept. 2001); children: Jennifer Hanish Chutkow Baldwin, Jonathan Hanish; m. Theodora Ladnya, Dec. 28, 2005. PhB, U. Chgo., 1948; MD, U. Colo., 1954. Diplomate Am. Bd. Psychiatry and Neurology. Intern Strong Meml. Hosp., Rochester, N.Y., 1954-56; resident in psychiatry U. Colo. Med. Ctr., Denver, 1956-59; pvt. practice psychiatry Newark, 1959-64, Los Alamos, N.Mex., 1964-68, Louisville, 1969—2001; staff psychiatrist River Region Mental Health, Mental Retardation Bd., Louisville, 1969—74; clin. dir. Ctrl. State Hosp., Louisville, 1974—77, 1982-89; staff psychiatrist Seven Counties Svcs., Inc., Louisville, 1980—85, 1990-95, River Valley Svcs., Owensboro, Ky., 1995—96; med. dir. Lincoln Trail Hosp., Radcliff, Ky., 1996—2001; clin. faculty dept. psychiatry U. Louisville; pvt. practice psychiatry Tucson, 2002—06; psychiatric cons. Pima Health Svcs., Tucson, 2003—05. Served with USN, 1945-46. Mem. AMA, Am. Psychiat. Assn. Democrat. Jewish. Home: Apt 10108 7500 N Calle Sin Envidia Tucson AZ 85718-7365 Home Phone: 520-219-1775. *

CHUTORIAN, ABE M., pediatric neurologist, educator; b. Winnipeg, Man., Can., Feb. 8, 1929; s. Morris and Rose (Cohen) C.; m. Helen Carol Olasker, Sept. 2, 1951; children: Leslie, Sandra, Tracy. MA, U. Man., 1952, MD, BSc, U. Man., 1957. Diplomate Am. Bd. Pediatrics, Neurology. Intern Winnipeg Gen. Hosp., 1957-58; resident L.A. Children's Hosp., 1958-60; from fellow of neurology to prof. pediatrics and neurology Columbia U., NYC, 1960-90, prof. clin. neurology Coll. Physicians and surgeons, 2009—; prof. pediats. and neurology Cornell U. NY Presbyn. Hosp., 1990—, chief dept. pediatric neurology, 1990—2004. Adv. bd. Riverdale Mental Health, NY, 1985—. Mem. editl. bd. Pediatric Neurology Jour., 1992—; assoc. editor ACTA Neuropediatrica, 1996—; contbr. chpts. in books, articles and abstracts to profl. jours. Fellow Am. Acad. Pediatrics, Am. Acad. Neurology; mem. AMA, Am. Neurol. Assn., Internat. Chile Neurol. Soc., Child Neurology Soc., NY State Med. Soc., NY County Med. Soc. Avocations: chess, opera, ballet, cinema, travel. Office: 6th Fl 55 Central Park W Apt 14D New York NY 10023-6077

CHUU, CHIH-PIN, biologist; b. Taipei, Taiwan, Apr. 9, 1976; s. Der-San Chuu and Li-Chu Lee; m. Pay-Shan Wu, Dec. 10, 2004; 1 child, Joanna Midori. PhD, U. Chgo., 2005. Postdoc. scholar U. Chgo., 2005—09; asst. investigator Nat. Health Rsch. Insts., Miaoli County, Taiwan, 2009—. Women Bd. fellowship, Nat. Inst. Health, 2000—02, Postdoc. fellowship, 2008—09, grant, Nat. Sci. Coun., Taiwan, 2008. Mem.: Am. Assn. Cancer Rsch. Home: 5F No41 Keyen Rd Zhunan Town Miaoli County 35053 Taiwan Office: Nat Health Rsch Insts R2-2021 35 Keyen Rd Zhunan Town Miaoli County 35053 Taiwan Office Fax: 886-37-587408. Business E-Mail: cpchuu@nhri.org.tw.

CHVETSOV, ALEXEI V., medical physicist, educator; b. Tashkent, Uzbekistan, Apr. 9, 1961; arrived in U.S., 2002; MSc, Moscow Engring. Physics Inst., 1985, PhD, 1992. Cert. radiation expert Ohio,

Am. Bd. Radiology. Assoc. med. physicist Tom Baker Cancer Ctr., Calgary, Alberta, Canada, 1998—2002; asst. prof. Case Western Res. U., Cleve, 2002—. Contbr. articles to profl. jours., chpts. to books. Fellow, German Acad. Exch. Svc., 1992—93. Mem.: Can. Orgn. Med. Physicists (cert.), Am. Assn. Physicists in Medicine. Achievements include research in adaptive numerical methods, stability of numerical algorithms; inverse problems in radiation therapy, inverse treatment planning. Office: Case Western Res U 11100 Euclid Ave Lerner Tower B-181 Cleveland OH 44106 Office Fax: 216-844-2005. Business E-Mail: alexei.chvetsov@case.edu.

CIANCIO, SEBASTIAN GENE, periodontist, educator; b. Jamestown, NY, June 21, 1937; m. Marilyn Bonfiglio; children: Michele Ann, Sebastian. DDS, SUNY, Buffalo, 1961. Diplomate Am. Bd. Periodontology; cert. periodontist, 1965. Postdoctoral fellow depts. pharmacology and periodontology SUNY, Buffalo, 1963-65, instr., 1964-65, asst. clin. prof. pharmacology, asst. prof. periodontology, 1966, acting co-chmn. dept. periodontology, 1967-68, acting chmn., 1968, chmn. dept. periodontology, 1969-72, prof., chmn. dept. periodontics-endodontics, 1972-80, chmn. dept. periodontics, 1980-99, clin. prof. dept. pharmacology, 1973—, dir. Ctr. for Dental Studies, 1988—, chair dept. periodontics and endodontics, 1999—, Disting. Svc. prof., 2001—. Mem. vis. faculty Sch. Dentistry, U. Zurich, Switzerland, 1976; dental chmn. com. on revision U.S. Pharmacopeia, 1981—, pres. Internat. Acad. Periodentology Author: Clinical Pharmacology for Dental Professionals, 1980, 3rd edit., 1989; editor Biological Therapies in Dentistry, ADA Guide to Dental Therapeutics, 1998-, Periodontal Insights; contbr. numerous articles to profl. jours., chpts. to books. Bd. dirs. Internat. Health Care Found., 1993—. Capt. U.S. Army Dental Corps, 1961-63. Recipient George B. Snow prize in Prosthetic dentistry, 1961, hon. citation U. Chile, 1980, Gies. Found. award in Periodontics, 1988, Sch. of Dental Medicine Dean's award, 1992, Disting. Scientist award in pharmacology Am. Assn./Internat. Assn. for Dental Rsch., 2003; named Alpha Omega Dental Educator of Yr., 1971, Buffalo Dental Man of Yr., 1987. Fellow: Am. Acad. Periodontology (exec. com. 1981—, v.p. 1989—90, pres. 1991—92, v.p. found. 1996—98, Spl. citation 1983, Clin. Rsch. award 1996, Presdl. award, Gold Medal award 2001), Internat. Coll. Dentists; mem.: ADA (chmn. cons. coun. on dental therapeutics 1976—78, cons. coun. ondental edn. 1982—95, coun. on sci. affairs 1995—), Internat. Acad. Periodontology (pres. 2009—11), Fedn. Dentaire Internationale, Erie County Dental Soc., 8th Dist. Dental Soc., Dental Soc. State of N.Y. (Jarvie-Burkhardt award 1997), Nat. Soc. Dental Rsch. (bd. dirs. 1981—84), Internat. Assn. Dental Rsch., Omicron Kappa Upsilon. Office: SUNY at Buffalo Dept of Periodontology Buffalo NY 14214 E-mail: ciancio@buffalo.edu.

CIARKA, AGNIESZKA, cardiologist; d. Maria and Andrzej Ciarka. MD, Med. U., Warsaw, 2001; PhD, Free U. Brussels, MPH, 2004. Rsch. fellow Erasme Hosp., Brussels, 2002—04; internal medicine, cardiology fellow Free U., 2004—. Pres. Assn. Med. Doctors of Polish Origin in Belgium, 2007. Contbr. articles to profl. jours. Recipient Young Cardiologist award, Belgian Soc. Cardiology, 2004, Best Poster award, French Soc. Arterial Hypertension, 2005, European Soc. Cardiology, 2006, Morlait Dapseus prize, 2005; nominee Young Pole of Yr., Belgium, 2007; grantee, Erasme Hosp., 2004, Rsch. fellow, Divsn. Cardiovasc. Disease, Mayo Clinic, Rochester, Minn., 2004; Travel grant, European Soc. Cardiology, 2008—, grant, Stefan Batory Found. and Found. Cardiac Surgery, Belgium. Office: Erasme Hosp 808 Route de Lennik Brussels 1070 Belgium Business E-Mail: aciarka@ulb.ac.be.

CICHOCKI, FRANK, JR., research and development company executive; b. East Chgo., Ind., Apr. 28, 1971; PhD, Purdue U., 2000. Advanced engr. Owens Corning, 2000—02; mgr. r & d Ethicon Inc., 2002—. Recipient Phillip B. Hofmann award, Johnson and Johnson. Office: Ethicon Inc US Hwy 22 W Somerville NJ 08876 Business E-Mail: fcichock@its.jnj.com.

CICIRELLI, VICTOR GEORGE, psychologist; b. Miami, Fla., Oct. 1, 1926; s. Felix and Rene (DeMaria) C.; m. Jean Alice Solveson, Aug. 9, 1953; children: Ann Victoria, Michael Felix, Gregory Sheldon. BS, Notre Dame U., 1947; MA, U. Ill., Urbana, 1950; M.Ed., U. Miami, 1956; PhD (Univ. fellow), U. Mich., 1964; PhD, Mich. State U., 1971. Asst. prof. ednl. psychology U. Mich., 1963-65; dir. student teaching for elem., secondary and M.A.T. programs U. Pa., 1965-67; assoc. prof. early childhood edn. Ohio U., 1967-68; dir. research Nat. Evaluation of Head Start Westinghouse Learning Corp. at Ohio U., 1968-69; Office Edn. postdoctoral fellow U. Wis. Inst. Cognitive Learning, 1969-70; prof. human devel. Purdue U., 1970-73, prof. devel./aging psychology, 1974—, dir. devel. psychology program, 1977-78, 80-81, 82-83, 92-93, 96, 99-2001. Vis. sci. fellow Max Planck Inst. for Human Devel. and Edn., Berlin, 1991; fellow Ctr. for Health Policy Rsch., J. Hillis Miller Health Sci. Ctr., Sch. Medicine, U. Fla., Gainesville, 1991; Petersen vis. scholar in gerontology and family studies Oreg. State U., 2004-05; rsch. adv. bd. Calif. Commn. for Tchr. Preparation and Licensing, 1973-78; scholar NSF Inst., Ohio U., 1956, Am. U., 1958, U. Fla., 1960; cons. in field. Author: Helping Elderly Parents: Role of Adult Children, 1981, Family Caregiving: Autonomous and Paternalistic Decision Making, 1992, Sibling Relationships Across the Life Span, 1995, Older Adults' Views on Death, 2002; mem. editl. bd.: Jour. Marriage and the Family, 1990—, Jour. Family Psychology, Jour. Youth Adolescence, 2007; mem. editl. bd. Health Psychology, 2011; contbr. articles to profl. publs. Bd. dirs. Nat. Com. on Prevention of Elder Abuse, 1988-91; mem. adv. com. Ind. Geriatric Edn. Ctr., U. Ind., 1991. Grantee OEO, 1968-69, 71-73, U.S. Office Edn., 1971-73; Nat. Inst. Edn., 1973-74, NIH, 1973-74, Office Child Devel., 1973-74, Nat. Ret. Tchrs. Assn./Am. Assn. Ret. Persons Andrus Found., 1978-82, 90-92, 95, Retirement Rsch. Found., 1984-85, 87-89; fellow Andrew Norman Inst. Advanced Study, Andrus Gerontology Ctr., U. So. Calif., 1984, Gerontology Soc., 1983-84. Fellow APA, Gerontol. Soc.; mem. Internat. Soc. Study Behavioral Deve., Am. Psychol. Soc., Am. Assn. Aging, Nat. Coun. on Family Rels., Soc. for Research Child Devel., Phi Kappa Phi. Roman Catholic. Home: 1221 N Salisbury St West Lafayette IN 47906-2415 Office: Purdue U Dept Psychol Sci West Lafayette IN 47907 Office Phone: 765-494-6925. Business E-Mail: vcicirel@psych.purdue.edu.

CID, MARIA OLÍMPIA, surgeon, educator; b. Évora, Portugal, July 22, 1960; married. MD, Coimbra U., Portugal, 1984. Cert. cons. gen. surgeon Portuguese Med. Assn., 2005. Resident gen. surgeon Ctrl. Hosp. Lisbon, Portugal, 1984—95; head and neck cons. surgeon Portuguese Inst. Oncology, Lisbon, 1996—, mem. clin. adminstrn., 2007—. Asst. prof. surgery Lisbon U., 2007—. Contbr. articles to profl. jours. Mem.: Portuguese Soc. Oncology, Lisbon Soc. Med. Sci., Portuguese Soc. Gen. Surgery, Portuguese Med. Assn. Office Phone: 00351219666244. Business E-Mail: olimpia.cid@sapo.pt.

CIECHANOVER, AARON JUDAH, biochemist, educator; b. Haifa, Israel, Oct. 1, 1947; MS summa cum laude, Hebrew U. Hadassah Sch. Medicine, Jerusalem, 1971, MD, 1974; PhD, Technion-Israel Inst. Tech., Haifa, 1981. Intern Technion-Israel Inst. Tech, Rambam Med. Ctr., 1973—74, clin. tng., 1974—79; rsch. fellow dept. biochemistry Technion-Israel Inst. Tech., 1977—79, lectr. dept. biochemistry, 1979—81, sr. lectr., 1974—87, assoc. prof., 1987—92, prof., 1992—, dir. Rappaport Family Inst. Med. Rsch., 1993—2000, disting. rsch. prof., 2002—. Vis. sci. Inst. Cancer Rsch., Fox Chase Cancer Ctr., Phila., 1978—81; postdoc. fellow dept. biology MIT/Whitehead Inst. Biomed. Rsch., Cambridge, Mass., 1981—84; vis. prof. Dana Farber Cancer Inst., Harvard Med. Sch., Boston, 1985—86, Washington U. Sch. Medicine, St. Louis, 1987—2001, Kyoto U. Sch. Medicine, Japan, 2000, Northwestern U. Sch. Medicine, Chgo., 2002—03, Karolinska Inst., Stockholm, 2003, Rockefeller U., NYC, 2004; disting. vis. rsch. prof. Nat. Cheng Kung U., Taiwan, 2007—. Mem. editl. bd. Israel Med. Assn. Jour., 1999—, Exptl. Biology & Medicine, 2006—, Cell Death & Differentiation, 2007—; contbr. numerous articles to profl. jours. With Israel Def. Forces, 1974—77. Recipient Rsch. Career Devel. award, Israel Cancer Rsch. Fund, 1983—84, Austria Ilse & Helmut Wachter prize, U. Innsbruck, Austria, 1999, Alkales award for disting. sci. achievements, Jewish Nat. Fund, 2000, Albert Lasker award for basic med. rsch., 2000, Israeli Prime Min. prize, Aman Found., 2002, Israel prize in biology, 2003, Eminent Scientist award, Japan Soc. Promotion of Sci., 2003—06, Nobel prize in chemistry, 2004, Golden Plate award, Acad. Achievement, 2005; grantee Fulbright Fellow, 1981—84; Eleanor Roosevelt Meml. Fellow, Am. Cancer Soc., 1988—89. Fellow: Fedn. Asian Chem. Societies, European Acad. Scis., Royal Soc. Chemistry (hon.), Am. Acad. Arts & Scis. (fgn. hon.); mem.: AAAS, NAS (fgn. assoc.) (fgn. assoc.), Ukrainian Acad. Scis. (fgn.), Nat. Acad. Sci. & Tech. South Korea, Albert Schweitzer World Acad. Medicine, Polish Acad. Medicine, Soc. Exptl. Biology & Medicine (hon.), Am. Chem. Soc. (hon.), Pontifical Acad. Scis., Am. Philos. Soc. (fgn.), Israeli Nat. Acad. Scis. & Humanities, European Acad. Scis. & Arts, Inst. Medicine (fgn. assoc.) (fgn. assoc.), European Molecular Biology Orgn. Office: Vascular & Cancer Bio Rsch Ctr/Technion Israel Inst Tech Rappaport Faculty Medicine & Rsch Inst 31999 Haifa Israel Office Phone: 972 4 829 5356. Office Fax: 972 4 852 1193. Business E-Mail: c_tzachy@netvision.net.il. E-mail: mdaaron@tx.technion.ac.il. *

CIEJKA, ELZBIETA BEATA, physical therapist, educator; b. Lodz, May 6, 1962; MS, U. Sch. Phys. Edn., 1997; PhD, Med. U., 2005. Physiotherapist Clinic Rehab., 1983—97, prof., 1997—2001, HS Physiotherapy, 1997—2005; lectr. Inst. Cosmetology & Health Care, 2007; head master Rehab Inst. Outpatient Clinic, 2001—. Fellow: Polish Soc. Physiotherapy, Lodz. Avocations: sports, mountain climbing. Home: Zamenhofa Lodz 90-510 Poland Personal E-mail: elzbieta.ciejka@gmail.com.

CIEPIELA, OLGA, medical researcher; b. Poland, Aug. 7, 1981; MSc, Med. U. Poznan, 2006; PhD, Med. U. Warsaw, 2011. Asst. Med. U. Warsaw, 2011—. Recipient Team Sci. award, Rector Med. U. Warsaw, scholarship, Mazovia Voivodeship, Polish Govt. Mem.: Polish Soc. Exptl. and Clin. Immunology, Polish Soc. Lab. Diagnostics, Polish Soc. Allergology. Avocations: skiing, travel, literature. Office: Marszalkowska 24 Warsaw Mazovia 00-576 Poland Business E-Mail: olga.ciepiela@wum.edu.pl.

CIERPKA, MANFRED, physician, psychoanalyst, researcher; b. Nuertingen, Germany, Apr. 13, 1950; s. Erich and Maria (Gehring) C.; m. Astrid Bruess, Feb. 14, 1952, children: Lukas, Arne. MD, U. Ulm, Germany, 1977; degree in psychiatry and psychotherapeutic medicine, U. Goettingen, Germany, 1991. Resident in psychosomatics U. Ulm, 1978; resident BKH Guenzburg, 1979-83, resident Outpatient Clinic of Psychotherapy, 1984-87, dir. Outpatient Clinic of Psychotherapy, 1987-91; prof. Ctr. Family Therapy, Goettingen, 1991-98, Heidelberg, 1998—. Dir. Lindau Psychotherapy Weeks, 1989—; cons. German Med. Assn., 1995—. Author: Assessment of Families with a Schizophrenic Offspring, 1990; editor: Family Diagnostics, 1988, Textbook of Family Diagnostics, 1996, 2d edit., 2003, Psychotherapy of Eating Disorders, 1997, 2d edit., 2003; editor: Psychotherapeut, 1994—, Praxis der Kinderpsychologie und Kinderpsychiatrie, 1994—. Fellow, Studienstiftung des Deutschen Volkes, 1973—77. Mem. Internat. Psychoanalytic Assn., Soc. for Psychotherapeutic Rsch. Office: U Heidelberg Ctr Fam Therap Bergheimerstr 54 69115 Heidelberg Germany Office Phone: 0049 6221 564700. Business E-Mail: manfred_cierpka@med.uni-heidelberg.de.

CIFREK, MARIO, electrical engineer, educator; b. Varazdin, Mar. 24, 1964; Dipl. Ing, in Elec. Engring. and Computing, U. Zagreb, 1987, PhD in Elec. Engring. and Computing, 1997—97. Rsch. asst. U. Zagreb, Faculty Elec. Engring. & Computing, 1987—97, sr. asst., 1997—98, asst. prof., 1998—2003, assoc. prof., 2003—08, vice dean edn., 2006—10, prof., 2008—. Recipient award, U. Zagreb. Mem.: EMBS, IEEE, IMS, SPS, Croatian Med. & Biol. Engring. Soc., Croatian Soc. Comm., Computing, Electronics, Measurement & Control, Croatian Standards Inst., Internat. Fedn. Med. & Biol. Engring. Avocations: bicycling, music, photography. Office: Unska 3 Zagreb HR-10000 Croatia Business E-Mail: mario.cifrek@fer.hr.

CIGARROA, FRANCISCO GONZALEZ, academic administrator, pediatric surgeon; b. Laredo, Tex., Dec. 1, 1957; s. Joaquin and Barbara Cigarroa; m. Graciela Alarcon; children: Maria Cristina, Barbara Carisa. BS, Yale U., 1979; MD, U. Tex. S.W., 1983. Diplomate Am. Bd. Surgery, Am. Bd. Pediat. Surgery. Dir. pediat. surgery U. Tex. Health Sci. Ctr., San Antonio, 1994—2000, dir. pediat. abdominal organ transplantation, 1994—2000, pres., 2000—09; chancellor U. Tex. Sys., 2009—. Assoc. prof. U. Tex., San Antonio, 1994—2000; mem. Gov.'s Coun. Sci. and Biotech., Tex., 2002, Pres.'s Com. on Nat. Medal of Sci., 2003—; dir. adv. coun. pub. health U.S. Sec. of Health and Human Svcs., 2002—. Contbr. chapters to books; co-author: Abnormal Surgery in Infancy and Childhood, 1993, Hepatobiliary and Pancreatic Disease: the Team Approach, 1994, Surgical Correction of Laryngotraceo Esophageal Cleft. Recipient Brotherhood/Sisterhood award, Nat. Conf. for Cmty. and Justice, 2005; named Mr. S.Tex., Washington Birthday Assn., Larado, Tex., 2003; named a Person of Vision, Prevent Blindness, Tex., 2005. Avocations: guitar, hunting. Office: U Tex Sys Office of Chancellor 601 Colorado St, 4th Fl Austin TX 78701 Office Phone: 512-499-4201. E-mail: chancellor@utsystem.edu.

CIGLER, PETR, chemist; b. Ceske Budejovice, Aug. 25, 1978; MSc, Charles U. Prague, 2001; PhD, Inst. Chem. Tech., Prague, 2008. Rsch. assoc. Scripps Rsch. Inst., La Jolla, 2008—09; rsch. scientist Inst. Organic Chemistry and Biochemistry, AS CR, v.v.i., 2009—. Recipient prize, Ministry of Edn., Youth and Sports Czech Republic, 1995, Sanofi-Aventis prize, 2006, Unipetrol prize, 2008, Alfred Bader prize, 2011. Mem.: Czech Chemistry Olympiad (presidium mem. 2007—), Czech Chem. Soc., Am. Chem. Soc. Avocations: music, hiking. Office: Inst Organic Chemistry and Biochemistry AS CR vvi Flemingovo nam 2 Prague 16610 Czech Republic Business E-Mail: ciglerp@centrum.cz.

CIGLIANO, BRUNO, surgeon, educator; b. Naples, Italy, July 7, 1952; Degree in Medicine, Naples, 1976, degree in Pediat. Surgery, 1985. Aggregate prof. U. Naples Federico II, Italy, 1977—. Home: via F Cilea 112 Napoli Campania 80127 Italy Home Phone: 390815793312; Office Phone: 39335493133. Personal E-mail: cigliano@unina.it.

CILENTO, BENJAMIN WEST, plastic surgeon; b. Pa., Jan. 16, 1967; MD, Albert Einstein Coll. Medicine, 1998. Ceo Tex. Facial Plastic Surgery & Rhinology, 2010—. Decorated Commendation award US Navy; recipient Postsic Furgusen award, AAO-HNS; Rsch. grant, Am. Heart Assn. Fellow: Am. Bd. Facial Plastic & Reconstructive Surgery, Am. Bd. Otolaryngology, Am. Acad. Otolaryngology; mem.: Am. Acad. Facial Plastic & Reconstructive Surgery (John Orlando Roe award). Office: 9301 Pinecroft Ste 100 The Woodlands TX 77380 Office Fax: 281-364-9095. E-mail: bencilento@mac.com.

CIMINI, ANNAMARIA, biology professor; b. Pescara, Dec. 30, 1960; M in Biol. Scis., U. L'Aquila, 1985. Prof. dept. basic & applied biology U. L'Aquila, 2006—. Adj. prof. Temple U. Phila., 2011. Office: via Vetoio n 10 L'Aquila Abruzzo 67100 Italy Office Fax: 390862433273. Business E-Mail: annamaria.cimini@univaq.it.

CIMPEAN, ANCA MARIA G., medical educator; b. Romania, July 2, 1972; MD, Victor Babes U. Medicine and Pharmacy Timisoara, PhD, 1997. Assoc. prof. histology UMFVBT, 2011—. Mem.: Romanian Soc. Morphology and Embryology. Office: Piata Eftimie Murgu 2 Timisoara Timis 300041 Romania Personal E-mail: ancacimpean1972@yahoo.com.

CIOANCA, OANA, pharmacist; b. Turda, Cluj, Nov. 13, 1978; Degree in Pharmacy, Gr. T. Popa U. Medicine and Pharmacy, Iasi, Romania, 2003, PhD, 2010. Hon. asst. Gr. T. Popa U. Medicine and Pharmacy, Faculty Pharmacy, Dept. Pharmacognosy-Phytotherapy, 2004—05, assist on probation, 2005—08, asst., 2008—. Mem.: GA, AMAPSEEC. Avocations: painting, music. Office: Universitatii 16 Iasi 700117 Romania E-mail: oana.cioanca@gmail.com.

CIOFFI, UGO, surgeon, educator; b. San Paolo, Brazil, Nov. 26, 1955; s. Gerardo Cioffi, Filomena Bello; m. Sara De Pascalis; children: Gerardo, Alfredo. MD, U. Naples, Italy, 1981; PhD in Cardiovasc. Pathophysiology, U. Milan, Italy, 1996. Resident dept. surgery U. Milan, 1983—88, fellow dept. surgery, 1988—92, rschr. dept. surgery, 1993—, prof., rschr., 2000—06, prof. surgery, 2006—. Reviewer Jour. Thoracic and Cardiovasc. Surgery, 2002; external clin. reviewer Lancet, 2006—; mem. editl. bd. Open Cardiovasc. and Thoracic Surgery Jour., ISRN Surgery, Hawaii, JOur. Med. Cases; reviewer Thorax, 2009, Ann Thorac Surg., 2009; editl. bd. mem. Open Thoracic Surg., Open Journ. Gastroenterol.; reviewer Thoracic Cancer Wiley. Reviewer: Medical Journal Internat. Surgery, 1990, European Jour. Cardiothoracic Surgery Index Copernicus Thorax, 2009, Annals of Thoracic Surgery, 2009—. Recipient award, Sheffield Academic Press, 1999, Year Book Diagnostic Radiology, 1999, Internat. Biog. Ctr. Cambridge, Eng., 2005—09, Internat. Hippocrates award, Internat. Biog. Ctr., 2009; named Outstanding Intellectuals 21st Century, 2000, 2008—10, Internat. Health Profl. of Yr., 2007, 2009, 2007, 2009, Foremost Internat. Scientists, Cambridge Blue Book, 2007; grantee Hosp. Maggiore Milan, Ministry of Pub. Health, Italy, 2003, 2005, Found. IRCCS Ospedale Maggiore Policlinico, 2006—07. Mem.: AAAS (award 2002), Am. Biog. Inst. (Great Muscles of 21st Century 2011, Albert Einstein award 2011, Leading Intellectual World award 2011), Cardio Thoracic Surgery Network. Office: Ospedale Maggiore Policlinico Beretta Est Via Francesco Sforza 35 20122 Milan MI Italy Home Phone: +39-3388804789; Office Phone: 39-02.55035568. Office Fax: 39-02.55034165. Business E-Mail: ugo.cioffi@unimi.it.

CIOLAC, EMMANUEL GOMES, physical education educator, researcher; b. São Paulo, Brazil, Mar. 7, 1977; DSc, U. São Paulo, 2010, PhD. Sci. rschr. Inst. Orthopedics & Traumatology, Sch. Medicine, U. São Paulo, 2003—10, head therapeutic exercise, phys. fitness divsn., 2010—. Adj. prof. U. Grande ABC, 2011. Rsch. grant, Sociedade de Cardiologia do Estado de São Paulo. Mem.: Am. Coll. Sports Medicine. Avocations: running, reading. Office: R Dr Ovidio Pires de Campos 333 LEM Sao Paulo 05403-010 Brazil Office Fax: 55-11-30696041. Business E-Mail: egciolac@hcnet.usp.br.

CIRAULO, DOMENIC ANTHONY, psychiatrist, educator; 3 children. BS, U. Hartford, Trinity Coll., 1971; MD, Georgetown U., 1975. Diplomate in psychiatry with added qualification in addiction psychiatry Am. Bd. Psychiatry and Neurology. Med. resident Inst. Living, Hartford, 1975—77; chief resident psychiatry Mass. Mental Health Ctr., Boston, 1977—78; clin. fellow psychiatry Harvard Med. Sch., Boston, 1977—78, clin. instr., 1978—79, lectr. psychiatry, 2002—; asst. prof. psychiatry U. Conn. Sch. Medicine, Farmington, 1979—84; from asst. prof. to assoc. prof. psychiatry Tufts U. Sch. Medicine, 1984—92, prof. psychiatry, 1992—96, lectr. pharmacology, 1993—; chief psychiatry svc. VA Med. Ctr./Outpatient Clinics, Boston, 1995—2001; psychiatrist in chief Boston Med. Ctr., 1996—; prof., chmn. divsn. psychiatry Boston U. Sch. Medicine, 1996—. Chair R&D com. VA Outpatient Clinic, Boston, 1987—94; mem. exec. com. dept. psychiatry Tufts U. Sch. Medicine, Boston, 1989—93, mem. addiction medicine com., 1989—96; sr. cons. Norcap Addictions Program, Norfolk, Mass., 1990—96; mem. dean's com. VA Med. Ctr., Boston, 1996—; mem. exec. com. Boston U. Sch. Medicine, 1996—, com. mem., 2001—02; gen. clin. rsch. ctr. adv. com. Boston U. Med. Ctr., 1997—; sci. adv. com. Boston U. Cmty. Tech. Fund, 1997—2000; chmn. steering com. NIAAA Clin. Investigators Group, 2009. Author: (book) Drug Interactions In Psychiatry, Clinical Manual of Chemical Dependence; contbr. chapters to books. Grantee, Nat. Inst. On Drug Abuse, 1995—, Nat. Inst. On Alcoholism and Alcohol Abuse, 1997—, Nat. Inst. On Drug Abuse, 2002—, 2002—, 2002—. Fellow: Am. Psychiat. Assn. (disting. fellow); mem.: AMA (ad hoc com. on physicians health 1996), FDA Adv. Bd., Am. Bd. Psychiatry and Neurology (examiner), Mass. Med. Soc., Mass. Psychiatry Soc. (com. on alcohol and addiction 1984—). Office: Boston Univ Sch Medicine Ste 914 720 Harrison Ave Boston MA 02118

CIRILLO, JEANNINE L., pharmacist; d. Willie Gedeon and Lottie Clara Vadenais; m. Francis E. Cirillo, June 29, 1957; children: Sharlene Jean, Leslie Frances, Alison Jane. BS Pharmacy, U. R.I., 1955; DPharm, U. Ill., Chgo., 1994. Cert. pharmacist R.I., Mass. With Gagne Pharmacy, Bellingham, Mass., 1955—76; staff pharmacist St. Elizabeth Cmty. Health Ctr., Lincoln, Nebr., 1977—82, Overlook Hosp., Summit, NJ, 1983—94, Owen Healthcare, Wareham, Mass., 1994—97, Oaks Bluff, Mass., 1997—. Mem. adv. coun. and edn. com. N.J. Drug Info. and Poison Control Ctr., 1989—94; various positions N.J. Soc. Health Sys. Pharmacists, 1990—93; del. People to People Internat., Germany, 1993, Hungary, 93; N.J. del. ann. meeting Am. Soc. Health Sys. Pharmacist. Bd. dirs. Hunterdon (N.J.) Mental Devel., 1988—94. Avocations: sailing, crafts, bicycling, bridge, knitting. Home: 14 Quamhasset Rd Buzzards Bay MA 02532-5608 Office Phone: 508-693-0410 x 214.

CIRPAR, MERIC, medical educator; b. Ankara, Turkey, Feb. 7, 1974; MD, Ankara U., 1999. Cert. orthop. and traumatology specialist Kirikkale U., 2004. Assoc. prof. dept. orthop. and traumatology Kirikkale U. Sch. Medicine, 2006—. Mem.: TOTBID. Avocations: fishing, history. Office: Saglik Caddesi Kirikkale 71100 Turkey E-mail: drmeric@yahoo.com.

CISKE, KAREN LYSBETH, retired medical/surgical nurse; b. Chgo., Dec. 28, 1937; d. Harry and Cleo Atkinson; m. Donald Albert Ciske, Mar. 21, 1959. BSN, Northwestern U., Chgo., 1960; MSN, U. Minn., Mpls., 1967. RN Ill., 1960, Minn., 1962. Staff nurse Wesley Meml. Hosp., Chgo., 1960—61; instr. nursing Ill. Masonic Sch., Chgo., 1961—62, Mounds-Midway Sch. Nursing, St. Paul, 1962—65; clinician, supr. U. Minn. Hosp., Mpls., 1967—74; cons. Primary Nursing Devel., Arden Hills, Minn., 1974—83; asst. prof. Bethel Coll. Sch. Nursing, St. Paul, 1983—2002; ret., 2002. Creator, dir. Advanced Primary Nursing Conf., Mpls., 1978; co-creator primary nursing professionalizing nursing U. Minn. Hosp., Mpls., 1968—74. Contbr. articles to profl. jours.; editor: Nursing Dimensions, 1979. Organist Presbyn. Ch. of the Way, Shoreview, Minn., 1974—98, facilitator youth music, chmn. fundraising. Faculty rsch. grantee, Bethel Coll., 1990. Mem.: Minn. Nurses' Assn., Am. Guild Organists, Sigma Theta Tau. Avocations: travel, gardening, music, reading. Home: 1708 Lake Valentine Rd Arden Hills MN 55112

CISNEROS, LAURA E., internist, hematologist, oncologist; BA, U. Ill., Chicago; MD, U. Autonomous of Tamaulipas, Mex. Cert. Internal Medicine, Med. Oncology, Hematology. Internal medicine and pediatrics residency U. Autonomous of Tamaulipas; hematology-oncology fellowship U. Kansas, Kansas City; hematologist and med. oncologist Hematology Oncology Assoc. of Ill., 2000—. Mem.: Am. Coll. of Physician Executives, Am. Soc. of Hematology, Am. Soc. of Clinical Oncology. Office: Hematology Oncology Assoc 188 Honey Bee Ln Brownsville TX 78520-9111

CITORES, LUCÍA, medical researcher; b. Cobos de Cerrato, Palencia, Spain, Sept. 7, 1968; d. Heraclio Citores and Silvina González; m. José María Bassols, 1999; children: Samuel Sjur Bassols, Iris Bassols. Degree in Chemistry, U. Valladolid, Spain, 1990, PhD in Biochemistry, 1996. Postdoc. rschr. Norwegian Radium Hosp., Oslo, 1997—2004; contratado del programa Ramón y Cajal U. Valladolid, 2004—, non-civil servant tenured lectr., 2004—. Achievements include patents for non-toxic ribosome inactivating proteins with two chains, process for the preparation thereof and applications. Office: Univ Valladolid Prado de la Magdalena s/n 47005 Valladolid Spain

CITRIN, JUDITH, counselor, artist, educator; b. Chgo., Ill., May 29, 1934; d. Harvey and Estelle (Lieberman) Goldfeder; m. Jeremy Levin, 1954 (div. 1963); 1 child, Jeffrey Scott Levin; m. Phillip Citrin, 1968 (div. 1984); m. Tom Wallace, 1997. Student, Art Inst. Chgo., 1943, student, 1947—48, U. Ill., 1951—53, Am. Acad. Art, 1953—54, Adler Inst., 1975, C.G. Jung, 1979—98, Esalen Inst., 1981. Asst. prodr., rschr. WTTW Channel 11, Chgo., 1963—68; pvt. practice, 1963—; freelancer, 1968—; Reiki healer & transformational counselor, 1978—; group facilitator, tchr. Oasis Ctr., 1981—99, Loyola U., 1984—85, Fatima Ctr., Notre Dame U., 1986; group facilitator Interface Watertown, Mass., 1987—; lectr. Internat. Assn. Near-Death Studies, 2003, Internat. Soc. Energy & Energy Medicine, 2003; dir. Transformational Travel, 1987—2007, Clearing House; facilitator Healing Cir., 1979—87; group facilitator Golden Sufi Meditation Group, 1995—; artist residency Cultural Ministry Morocco, Marrakech, Morocco, 1979—80; works exhibited Musee des Oudaias, Rabat, Morocco, 1980, Art Inst. Chgo., 1973—77, 1981, Nat. Mus. Am. Art Smithsonian Instn., 1982, Nat. Acad. Design, NYC, 1982, Chgo. Cultural Ctr., 1979, Mus. Art U. Okla., 1978, C.G. Jung Inst., 1983. Contbg. writer Under Sign Pisces, 1972; contbg. artist Black Maria, 1972, Corona Mag., 1986; contbg. editor New Art Examiner, 1978; contbg. author Anais Nin: A Book Mirrors, 1997. Ill. Arts Coun. grant, 1977, Royal Air Maroc funding grant, 1980—81. Mem.: Inst. Noetic Scis., ISSSEEM (founding mem.), Am. Reiki Assn., Spiritual Emergence Network, Arts Club Chgo., Assn. Holistic Health. Home and Office: 423 Greenleaf Ave Wilmette IL 60091-1911 Office Phone: 847-256-4483. Personal E-mail: judithcitrin@sbcglobal.net. *

CIUREA, STEFAN, medical physician; b. Romania, Aug. 22, 1971; MD, U. Medicine and Pharms. Iasi, Romania, 1996. Splty. in stemcell transplantation. Asst. prof. U. Tex. MD Anderson Cancer Ctr., 2007—. Chief med. resident Pinnacle Health Hosps., Harrisburg, Pa. Mem.: Am. Soc. Blood and Marrow Transplantation, Am. Soc. Clin. Oncology, Am. Soc. Hematology. Office: 1515 Holcombe Blvd Unit 423 Houston TX 77030 Business E-Mail: sciurea@mdanderson.org.

CIVANTOS, FRANCISCO J., otolaryngologist, plastic surgeon, educator; Attended, Harvard U.; MD, Columbia U. Coll. of Physicians and Surgeons. Diplomate Am. Bd. Otolaryngology. Resident Univ. of Ill. Coll. of Medicine, Chgo.; fellow Vanderbilt Univ. Med. Ctr., Nashville; assoc. prof. otolaryngology Univ. of Miami Miller Sch. of Medicine; co-dir. divsn. of head and neck surgery Univ. of Miami Health System. Named one of the Top Doctors, 2011, the Best Doctors in America, 1996—. Fellow: ACS. Office: University of Miami Hospital and Clinics Department of Otolaryngology ENT 1475 NW 12th Ave Miami FL 33136 Office Phone: 305-243-5214.

CIVELEK, A. CAHID, nuclear medicine physician, division director; b. Antakya, Hatay, Turkey, Feb. 23, 1953; arrived in US, 1981, naturalized, 1992; s. Mehmet Cevri and Necdet Civelek; m. Mary Lynn Patrick, July 19, 1979 (annulled 1995); children: Aylin Necdet-(dec.), Cevri Arif. MD, Istanbul U., 1976. Lic. Md., 1984, diplomate in nuclear medicine Am. Bd. Nuc. Medicine, 1986, lic. Mo., 2003. Resident nuc. medicine Johns Hopkins Med. Inst., Balt., 1982—84, nuclear medicine fellowship, 1984—85, dir. nuc. cardiology, 1991—2003, dir. nuc. medicine residency program, 1995—98, acting dir. clin. nuc. medicine, 1995—98; dir. divsn. nuc. medicine St. Louis U. Hosp., 2003—07; prof. radiology, dir. divsn. nuc. medicine, dept. radiology U. Louisville Hosp. Assoc. prof. radiology Johns Hopkins Med. Inst., 1995—2003; prof. St. Louis U., 2003—07, U. Louisville, 2007—. Contbr. articles to profl. jours.; referee, reviewer various med. jours., 1986—; contbr. to profl. publs. Recipient Best Sci. Paper award, Armed Forces Radiobiology Rsch. Inst., 1984, 1990; named to Ams. Top Physicians, Consumers' Rsch. Coun. Am., 2005—06; grantee Rsch. grants, Bristol-Myers Squibb, 2005—06. Fellow: Am. Soc. Clin.Oncologists, Am. Coll. Radiology, Soc. Cardiovasc.Computed Tomography, Am. Assn. Nuc. Cardiology, Am. Coll. Angiology (sci. coun. mem. 1991), Am. Heart Assn. (radiology coun. 1989—), Johns Hopkins Med. & Surg. Assn. (Founding Mem.), Soc. Nuc. Medicine (cardiovasc. coun 1991, brain imaging coun. 1991), Am. Coll. Nuc. Physicians (life), Am. Soc. Nuc. Cardiology (life; founding mem. 1993). Achievements include development of Nuclear cardiology in the division of nuclear medicine at Johns Hopkins Med. Inst. Home: APT 811 1 Riverpointe Plz Jeffersonville IN 47130-3212 Office: University Louisville 530 S Jackson St Louisville KY 40202 Business E-Mail: cahid.civelek@louisville.edu.

CLAES, DANIEL JOHN, physician; s. John and Claribel Claes; m. Gayla Christine Claes, Jan. 19, 1974. AB magna cum laude, Harvard U., 1953, MD cum laude, 1957. Intern UCLA, 1957-58; Bowyer Found. fellow rsch. in medicine LA, 1958-61; pvt. practice specializing in diabetes, 1962—. V.p. Am. Eye Bank Found., 1978—83, dir. rsch., 1980—, pres., 1983—, chmn., CEO, 1995—; pres. Heuristic Group of Orgns., 1981—, Cavendish Assocs., 2002—, CTO, 2007—, CEO, 2008—; biotech. cons. SIRA Techs., 1995—. Contbr. articles to profl. jours. Mem. LA Mus. Art, 1960—. Mem.: AAAS, AMA, Cell Transplantation Soc., Diabetes Tech. Soc., Am. Math. Soc., Internat. Pancreas and Islet Transplant Assn., Internat. Diabetes Fedn, Am. Diabetes Assn. (profl. coun. on immunology, immunogenetics and transplantation), LA County Med. Assn., Calif. Med. Assn., Royal Commonwealth Club (London), Harvard and Harvard Med. Sch. So. Calif. Club. Achievements include research in supercomputer bioinformatics in medicine, computational chemistry, molecular modeling, quantum chemistry, genomics, proteomics and preventive care; ongoing research in computational epigenetics and cardiovascular disease, brain function, molecular targeting and transgenerational, effects. Office: Am Eyebank Found 15237 W Sunset Blvd Ste 108 Pacific Palisades CA 90272-3690

CLAFLIN, JAMES ROBERT, pediatrician, allergist; b. Apr. 30, 1946; m. Marcee Claflin; children: James Sean (dec.), Brian Scott (dec.), Susan Nicole, Timothy Lynn. Student, Northwestern State Coll.; MD, U. Okla., 1971. Diplomate Am. Bd. Pediatrics, Am. Bd. Allergy Immunology. Intern U. Tex. Med. Br., Galveston, 1971-72; advanced through grades to lt. col. USAF, 1969-84, chief pediatric svcs. Goodfellow AFB, 1972-73, 75-77, chief pediatric svcs. and hosp. svcs. RAF Upper Heyford Eng., 1977-80, chief allergy and clin. immunology Carswell AFB, 1982-84; fellow allergy/immunology Willford Hall USAF Med. Ctr., Lackland AFB, Tex., 1980-82; ret. USAF, 1984. Clin. asst. prof. pediatrics, Oklahoma U.; presenter in field. Contbr. articles to profl. jours. Advisor child welfare com. Tom Green County, 1976-77; mem. child welfare com. RAF, Upper Heyford, Eng., 1978-80; mem. sch. and pub. health com. Tarrant County Med. Soc., 1984-85, chmn., 1986-87, publs. com., 1988-89, religion and meml. com., 1989; mem. quality assurance and infectious disease coms. Cook-Ft. Worth Children's Hosp., 1986-89; v.p. Brenham State Sch. Parent Assn., 1987-88; pres. Parents Assn. for the Retarded of Tex., 1987-88; chmn. cmty. conscience com. Wedgwood Bapt. Ch. Recipient Svc. award Am. Diabetes Assn., 1976. Fellow Am. Acad. Pediatrics, Am. Coll. Allergy (mem. com. on allergic rhinitis, mem. com. on adverse reactions to food 1991-96), Am. Acad. Allergy; mem. AMA (Am. Coll. Allergy, Asthma and Immunology (spkr. ho. of dels. 2001-03, bd.regent, 2005-08), Oklahoma County Med. Soc. (pres.-elect 2003-04, pres. 2004-05) Okla. State Med. Assn. (sec.-treas. 2003-05, v.p., 2005—06), Okla. Allergy and Asthma Soc. (pres. 1998-2000). Home: 750 NE 13th St Oklahoma City OK 73104-5051

CLAIN, MICHAEL R., orthopedist, surgeon, educator; Attended phi beta kappa and magna cum laude, Brown U., 1980—84; attended, Columbia U., 1984. Diplomate Am. Bd. of Orthopaedic Surgery, cert. Nat. Bd. of Med. Examiners. Intern gen. surgery Mt. Sinai Hosp., 1984—85; resident orthopaedic surgery Lenox Hill Hosp., 1986—90; fellow foot and ankle Univ. of Tex. and Baylor Coll. of Medicine, 1990—91; clin. instr. orthopaedics and rehab. Yale Univ.; clin. adj. assoc. prof. Quinnipiac Univ. Sch. of Health Sciences; with Greenwich Hosp., Orthopaedic & Neurosurgery Specialists. Recipient Gordon Dewart award; named one of Top Doctors, Conn. Mag., 2001—05, 2007—11, NY Mag., 2008—09, 2011, Best Doctors, 2008, Top Doctors, Castle Connolly NY Metro Area, 2008—11, Greenwich Mag., 2009—11, New Canaan Mag., 2009—11, Westport Mag., 2009—11, Stamford Mag., 2010—11, Wag Best Doctors, 2010. Mem.: Am. Orthopaedic Foot and Ankle Soc., Greenwich Med. Soc., Fairfield County Med. Assn., Conn. State Med. Soc., Am. Acad. of Orthopaedic Surgeons. Office: Orthopaedic and Neurosurgery Specialists 6 Greenwich Office Pk 10 Valley Dr Greenwich CT 06831 Office Phone: 203-869-1145.

CLAIRE, TEMPLEMAN, gynecologist, educator; MBBS, U. NSW, Sydney, 1989. Fellow pediatric and adolescent gynecology U. Louisville, 1998—2000; fellow in advanced laparoscopic surgery St Mary's Hosp., Milw., 2000—02; asst. prof. osterrics and gynecology U. Southern Calif., 2002—, chief gynecology, 2002—, Childrens Hosp. LA, 2002—. Named one of Best Drs. in America. Fellow: Royal Australian and New Zealand Coll. Ob-Gyn.; mem.: Am. Assn. Gynecologic Laparoscopists. Avocation: yoga. Office: Level 3 1500 San Pablo Ave Los Angeles CA 90033

CLAMAR, APHRODITE J., psychologist; b. Hartford, Conn. d. James John and Georgia (Panas) Clamar; m. Richard Cohen, June 24, 1973. BA, CCNY, 1953; MA, Columbia U., 1955; PhD, NYU, 1978; student, S. Adler Conservatory Acting, 1987-91. Mgmt. cons., psychologist Milla Alihan Assocs., NYC, 1957-62; rsch. psychologist coord. Inst. Devel. Studies N.Y. Med. Coll., NYC, 1964; intern psychologist Bellevue Psychiat. Hosp., NYC, 1964-66; assoc. prof. Fashion Inst. Tech., NYC, 1966-69; supervising psychologist Lifeline Ctr. Child Devel., NYC, 1966-67; chief psychologist I Spy Health Program Beth Israel Med. Ctr., NYC, 1967-70; dir. community-sch. mental health programs Soundview Community Svcs., Albert Einstein Coll. Medicine Yeshiva U., NYC, 1970-73; dir. treatment program court-related children, dept. child psychiatry Harlem Hosp.; mem. faculty dept. psychiatry Coll. Physicians and Surgeons Columbia U., NYC, 1973-76; pvt. practice psychotherapy, NYC, 1976—; co-founder, pres. Richard Cohen Assocs. Pub. Rels. Agy., NYC, 1979—99; prof. John Jay Coll., CUNY, 2000—06. Cons. to pub. health and mental health agys., N.Y.C., 1976-91; mem. faculty Lenox Hill Hosp. Psychoanalytic Psychotherapy Tng. Program, 1982-88; theater producer, artistic dir. Tom Cat Cohen Prodns., Inc., 1990—. Author: (with Budd Hopkins) Missing Time, 1981; contbr. articles to profl. jours. Fellow: AAAS; mem.: APA, Authors Guild. Democrat. Greek Orthodox. Home: 43 Crown St Kingston NY 12401 Office Phone: 845-339-4533.

CLANCY, CAROLYN M., federal agency administrator; b. Phila., July 19; m. Bill Clancy. BS in Math. and Chemistry, magna cum laude, Boston Coll., 1975; MD, U. Mass., 1979. Henry J. Kaiser Family Found. fellow U. Pa., 1982—84; asst. prof. medicine, dir. med. clinic Med. Coll. Va., 1984—90; with Agy. Healthcare Rsch. & Quality (AHRQ), US Dept. Health & Human Services, 1990—, dir. Ctr. Outcomes & Effectiveness Rsch., 1997—2002, acting dir. AHRQ, 2002—03, dir. AHRQ, 2003—. Clin. assoc. prof. dept. medicine George Washington U. Sr. assoc. editor Health Services Rsch., mem. editl. bd. Annals Internal Medicine, Annals Family Medicine, American Jour. Med. Quality, Med. Care Rsch. & Rev. Recipient William B. Graham prize for health svcs. rsch., Assn. Univ. Programs Health Adminstrn., 2009; named The Most Powerful Physician-Exec., Modern Healthcare/Modern Physician mags., 2009. Master: ACP; mem.: Inst. Medicine. Office: Agy Healthcare Rsch and Quality John M Eisenberg Bldg 540 Gaither Rd Rockville MD 20850 Office Phone: 301-427-1200. Office Fax: 301-427-1201. E-mail: cclancy@ahrq.gov, director@ahrq.hhs.gov. *

CLAPAUCH, RUTH, medical educator, researcher; b. Rio de Janeiro, Aug. 4, 1957; d. Luiz and Regina Lea Clapauch; m. Edward Izydorczyk, Sept. 26, 1981; 1 child, Bruna Izydorczyk. MS in Endocrinology, Fed. U. Rio de Janeiro, 1995; PhD in BioScis., State U. Ris de Janeira, 2009. Lic. Fed. U. Rio de Janeiro, 1980, endocrinologist Cath. U. Rio de Janeiro, 1982. Intern Clin. Medicine Fed. U., Rio de Janeiro, 1980; resident, endocrinology IEDE, 1981—82; med. adviser Roussel Uclaf, Brazil, 1987—90; endocrinology postgrad. instr. Carlos Chagas Inst. Med. Postgrad. Estácio De Sá U., Rio de Janeiro, 1988—; creator, coord. female endocrinology clinic Hosp. da Lagoa, Ministry Health, Rio de Janeiro, 1992—; creator, coord. Andrology Clinic Hosp. da Laboa, Minister Health, Rio de Janeiro, 2005—. Advisor Tech. Cammera Drugs-Nat. Agency San. Surveillance, Brasilia, Brazil, 2004—05; reviewer & mem. editl. com. Brazilian Archives Endocrinology & Metabolism, Sao Paulo, Brazil, 2004—; reviewer Sci. and Pub. Health, Rio de Janeiro, 2007, Ciência e Saúde Coletiva, Brazil, 2007—, Clinics, 2008—. Contbr. articles to profl. jours. Mem.: Brazilian Soc., Brazilian Soc. Endocrinology (assoc.; pres. female endocrinology and andrology dept. 2001—05, mem. continuing med. edn. commn. 2005—, pres. continuing med. edn. commn. 2005—09), Internat. Soc. Study Aging Male (assoc.), Endocrine Soc. (assoc.). Achievements include research in andropause diagnosis in osteoporotic and normal men; hormonal replacement therapy and vascular effects in healthy and unhealthy menopausal women. Avocation: travel. Office: AV das Américas 500 BC 16/228 Barra Da Tijuca Rio de Janeiro 22631000 Brazil also: 2 Av Ataulfs de Paiva 135/1716 Leblon Rio-de Jenerio 22431000 Brazil Office Phone: 55 21 24930963, 52141419800, 55214419800. Home Fax: 55 21 24930963. Personal E-mail: rclapauch@uol.com.br. Business E-Mail: draruthclapauch@cremerj.org.br.

CLAPTON, CHARLES M. (CHUCK CLAPTON), legislative staff member; b. Boston, May 22, 1968; BA in History, Boston Coll., 1990; JD, Cath. U. Columbus Sch. Law, Washington, 1995. Legis. aide to Senator Arlen Specter US Senate, 1995—96; counsel & sr. legis. asst., Rep. Harris Fawell US House of Reps., 1997—98; health counsel US House Energy & Commerce Com., 1999—2004, chief health counsel, 2004—05; health care policy advisor to Rep. Dennis Hastert US House of Reps., 2006—07; chief health counsel US House Ways & Means Com., 2007—08; Republican health policy dir. US Senate Health, Edn., Labor & Pensions Com., 2008—. Republican. Office: US Senate Health Edn Labor & Pension Com 428 Dirksen Senate Office Bldg Washington DC 20515 Office Phone: 202-225-4527. Office Fax: 202-226-1010.

CLARK, CRAIG BOYD, cardiologist; b. Des Moines, Feb. 18, 1966; m. Jane Ellen Clark. DO, Des Moines U., 1995. Diplomate Am. Bd. Internal Medicine, Am. Bd. Cardiovasc. Disease, Nat. Bd. Echocardiography, Am. Bd. Quality Assurance and Utilization Rev. Physicians. Resident in internal medicine U. Iowa, Des Moines, 1995—98; fellow in cardiovasc. diseases U. Iowa Hosps., Iowa City, 1998—2001, chief fellow, 2000—01; assoc. in medicine U. Iowa Coll. Medicine, Iowa City, 2001—02, clin. asst. prof. dept. medicine, 2004—08, clin. assoc. prof., 2008—; attending cardiologist Iowa Heart Ctr., P.C., Des Moines, 2002—08, Iowa Health Cardiology, 2008—; chair dept. medicine Iowa Luth. Hosp., Des Moines, 2006—09, VA Nat. Quality Scholar, 2001—02. Adv. bd. PDxMD-.com, 1999—2000; med. dir. coun. Iowa Heart Ctr. PC, 2007; adj. clin. assoc. prof. cardiology Des Moines U., 2007—. Reviewer EBSCO Pub., 2007; contbr. articles to profl. jours. Investigator Clinicals Trials in Cardiology. Recipient Outstanding Resident award, 1998; named one of Top Dr. in Cardiology, DSM Mag., 2008; named to Top Drs., Des Moines, 2008, Americas Top Physicians, Consumer Rsch. Coun. America. Fellow: Am. Soc. Echocardiography (fase selection & My Heart Tssk Force com. 2008—), Am. Coll. Cardiology (bd. govs., pres. Iowa chpt. 2007, credentials & membership com. 2008—, peer reviewer sci. statement 2008—, Bristol-Meyers Squibb award 2001); mem.: Am. Heart Assn. (invited author, expert consensus document 2010, fellow coun. clin. cardiology), Heart Failure Soc. Am. Office: Iowa Health Cardiology 1301 Pennsylvania Ave Ste 100 Des Moines IA 50316 Office Phone: 515-263-2400. Business E-Mail: clarkcb@ihs.org.

CLARK, DAVID EUGENE, surgeon; b. New Orleans, Jan. 21, 1950; s. Frank Eugene and Lucille Sommer C.; m. Susan Mann, June 10, 1972; children: Emily, Sarah, Susannah. AB, Dartmouth Coll., 1971; MD, George Washington U., 1975; MS, U. So. Maine, 1995; MPH, Harvard U., 1995. Surg. intern Dartmouth Affiliated Hosps., 1975-76; resident in surgery Maine Med. Ctr., 1976-80; fellow in traumatology U. Md., 1981-82; attending surgeon Maine Med. Ctr., Portland, 1983—; clin. asst. prof. U. Vt., 1983—2005, prof., 2005—. Mem. faculty Harvard Injury Control Rsch. Ctr., 1998—. Contbr. articles to profl. jours. Fellow: ACS (trauma com. mem. 2002—). Democrat. Office: Maine Med Ctr 22 Bramhall St Portland ME 04102-3134 Office Phone: 207-774-2381.

CLARK, GORDON HOSTETTER, JR., physician; b. New Haven, Aug. 5, 1947; s. Gordon Hostetter and Elizabeth Master (Mapes) C.; m. Gail Marie Theroux, July 23, 1988; children: Emily Blakeslee Clark Ehl, Christopher Robert, Heather Mays Richmond, Adam Arthur. BA, Yale U., 1970; MDiv, Pacific Sch. Religion, 1973; MD, George Washington U., 1977. Diplomate Am. Bd. Psychiatry and Neurology, Am. Bd. Med. Mgmt., Am. Coll. Physician Execs.; cert. in adminstrv. psychiatry, APA, 1992; cert. physician exec. Commn. in Med. Mgmt., 1998. Intern, then resident, then fellow Dartmouth-Hitchcock Med. Ctr., Hanover, N.H., 1977-81; staff psychiatrist Lakes Region Med. Health Ctr., Laconia, N.H., 1981-82, med. dir., 1982-86; dir. psychiat. unit Lakes Region Gen. Hosp., Laconia, 1986-89; med. dir. behavioral svcs. St. Vincent Health Ctr., Erie, Pa., 1990-93; dir. med./profl. adminstrn. Deerfield Mgmt. Group, Erie, Pa., 1991-94; pres. Deerfield Profl. Assocs., 1992-94; med. advisor Deerfield Behavioral Health Network, 1994-95; sr. psychiat. cons. Med. Groups Divsn. Maine Harvard Cmty. Health Plan, Portland, Maine, 1995-96; pres., med. dir. Integrated Behavioral Healthcare, Portland, Maine, 1995—2007; med. dir. Behavioral Health Network of Maine, 1995-99, Augusta (Maine) Mental Health Inst., 1995-96; assoc. med. dir. Maine Dept. Mental Health and Mental Retardation, Augusta, 1995-96; med. dir. med.-psychiat. program Westbrook (Maine) Cmty. Hosp., 1996-97; sr. physician advisor CMG Healthsource Maine, Maine, 1996-97; chief exec. and med. officer Integrated Behavioral Healthcare, Inc., Scarborough, Maine, 2007—. Adj. asst. prof. clin. psychiatry Dartmouth Med. Sch., Hanover, 1983-90; clin. asst. prof. psychiatry U. Pitts. Sch. Medicine, 1990 96; clin. assoc. prof. psychiatry U. Vt. Med. Sch., 1996-2004; chmn. com. psychiatrists in NH Cmty. Mental Health Ctrs., Concord, 1982-86; med. liaison to Pa. Office Mental Health and Mental Retardation and Erie County Office Mental Health and Mental Retardation, 1991-94; bd. dirs. Med. Network, Inc., credentials com. 1995-98, med. mgmt. com. 2002-07, med. dir. depression mgmt. program, 2002-07, mem. bylaws and nominating com., 2006, fin. com. 2007-, audit com., 2007, Continuing Med. Edn. Com., 2009-; New Eng. region adv. com. Cigna Behavioral Health Care, 2000-2001; New Eng. region pharmacy and therapeutics com. Cigna Health Care, 2000, nat. pharmacy and therapeutics com., 2001; depression work group MaineHealth, 2002-05; mem. provider adv. com., 2004-07, quality mgmt. improvement com. Anthem Behavioral Health, 2004 06, Behavioral Healthcare Program Quality Indicators Com., Maine Med. Ctr., 2009-. Exec. v.p. Erie Phiharm., 1991—92. Recipient Exemplary Psychiatrist award Nat. Alliance for Mentally Ill, 1992; recipient Benjamin Manchester award George Washington U., 1977. Fellow: Am. Coll. Physician Execs., Am. Assn. Social Psychiatry (mem. coun. 1993—99), Am. Coll. Mental Health Adminstrn., Am. Psychiat. Assn. (life; examiner oral part of exams. cert. adminstrn. psychiatry 1993—96, com. on stds. and survey procedures 1998—2001, APA/Bristol-Myers Squibb fellowship selection com. 1999—2002, task force develop guidlines psychiat. practice mental health ctrs., com. state and cmty. psychiatry sys., com. chronically mentally ill, Falk fellow 1979—81); mem.: Maine Psychiat. Assn. (chair program com. 1996—97), We. Pa. Psychiat. Soc. (pres. elect 1992—94), Psychiat. Physicians Pa. (fed. legis. rep. pbu. psychiatry com. 1993—94, treas. 1994, coun., govt. rels. com.), Nat. Psychiatric Alliance (chmn. med. staff com. 1992—94, exec. com. 1992—95), Am. Coll. Psychiatrists, Am. Assn. Psychiat. Adminstrs. (coun. 1996—97, pres.-elect 1997—99, pres. 1999—2001), Am. Assn. Cmty. Psychiatrists (founding pres. 1984—90, bd. dirs. 1984—92, com. psychiat. practice in cmty. mental health ctrs. guideline devel., Disting. Svc. award 1990). Avocations: skiing, biking, hiking, golf. Home: 10 Park St Yarmouth ME 04096-7757 Office: Integrated Behavioral Healthcare Inc 200 Professional Dr Scarborough ME 04074 Office Phone: 207-883-0711. *

CLARK, HARRY WESTLEY, federal agency administrator; b. 1946; BA in Chemistry, Wayne State U., Detroit, 1969; MD, U. Mich., Ann Arbor, 1973, MPH, 1974; JD, Harvard U., 1981. Diplomate American Bd. Psychiatry & Neurology. Psychiatry resident Neuropsychiatric Inst., U. Mich. Hosp., 1974—77; fellow in substance abuse VA Med. Ctr., San Francisco, 1984—86, chief associated substance abuse programs; assoc. clin. prof. dept. psychiatry U. Calif., San Francisco; dir. Ctr. Substance Abuse Treatment, Substance Abuse & Mental Health Services Adminstrn. (SAMHSA), US Dept. Health & Human Services, Rockville, Md., 1998—. Former sr. program cons. Substance Abuse Policy Rsch. Program, Robert Wood Johnson Found. Recipient Vernelle Fox Award for Excellence in Addiction Medicine, Edn., and Pub. Svc., Calif. Soc. Addiction Medicine, 2000, Leadership award, Nat. Treatment Accountability Safer Communities, 2001, Secretary's award for disting. svc., HHS, 2001, 2003, Clifford R. Gross award for fed. pub. svc., Md. chpt. ASPA, 2002, Presdl. Rank award of meritorious exec., US Govt., 2003, Presdl. Rank award of disting. exec., 2008. Fellow: American Soc. Addiction Medicine (John P. McGovern award 2008); mem.: DC Bar. Office: Ctr Substance Abuse Treatment 1 Choke Cherry Rd Rockville MD 20857 *

CLARK, IRA C., hospital administrator, educator; BA in Gen. Sci., U. Iowa, 1959, MA in Health and Hosp. Adminstrn. with honors, 1966; grad. Bus. Adminstrn., Rider Coll., 1963. Adminstrv. asst. divsn. Hosps. Iowa State Dept. Health, Des Moines, 1964; spl. asst. dir. planning and devel. Montefiore Hosp. and Med. Ctr., Bronx, N.Y., 1970, asst. dir., 1965-70; assoc. dir. Jersey City Med. Ctr., 1970-71, exec. dir., 1971-75; CEO Woodhull Hosp. and Mental Health Ctr., 1982-84; exec. dir. Bellevue Hosp. Ctr., 1984-85; CEO, regional adminstr. Kings County Hosp. Ctr., Bklyn., 1976-87; pres. & ceo Pub. Health Trust Jackson Meml. Hosp., 1987—. Bd. dirs. Fla. Hosp. Assn., So. Fla. Hosp. Assn.; panelist Robert Wood Johnson Found. Symposium, Princeton, N.J., 1986; chmn. Coun. Exec. dirs. N.Y.C. Health and Hosps. Corp., 1978-82; chmn. com. strategic planning Coun. Exec. dirs. Counterpart com. bd. dirs.; spl. adv. panel Emergency Svcs. Act, Advanced Para-medic Tng. N.J.; adj. faculty, lectr. various Univs.; spkr. in field. Author: The History and Development of Continuing Physical Education, 1966. Recipient Disting. Svc. award Commr. Mental Health, N.Y., 1981. Mem. Am. Hosp. Assn. (house dels., charter mem. pub. gen. hosps. sect., com. nominations bd. trustees pub.-gen. hosp. sect.), Assn. Am. Med. Colls. (gen. assembly coun. teaching hosps.), N.J. Hosp. Assn. (vice chmn., chmn. coun. govt. ops. of bd. trustees, spl. com. polit. strategy).

CLARK, JACK, retired health facility administrator; b. Munford, Ala., Feb. 23, 1932; s. Raymond E. and Ora (Camp) C.; m. Louise Omega Lackey, Jan. 30, 1951; 1 son, Terry Wayne. BS, Springhill Coll., Mobile, Ala., 1960. Staff acct. Max E. Miller, C.P.A., Mobile, 1960-62; comptr. Mobile Gen. Hosp., 1962-67; assoc. adminstr. fin. Univ. Med. Ctr., Mobile, 1967-74; regional mgr. Humana Inc., Mobile, 1974-75, v.p., 1975-80, sr. v.p., 1980-84, exec. v.p., 1984-93, Galen Health Care, Mobile, 1993-94; ret. Columbia-HCA Healthcare, 1994. Trustee Mid-South region Humana hosps., 1974-87, Southwestern region, 1987-89, region IV, 1989-91, region 2, 1991-93, Regional Hosps., Columbia/HCA, 1994—. Bd. dirs. Agape S. Ala., Mobile, 1983, Rainbow Omega, 2000—; trustee Faulkner U., Montgomery, Ala., 1993—. Served in USAF, 1952-56, Korea. Mem. Hosp. Fin. Mgmt. Assn. (assoc.), Am. Hosp. Assn., Ala. Hosp. Assn., Ala. Hosp. Assn. Accts. (pres. so. council, dir. 1967-68), Mobile C. of C. Democrat. Mem. Ch. of Christ. Home: 6449 Canebrake Rd Mobile AL 36695-3817

CLARK, K. REED, medical geneticist, pediatrician; b. Dec. 31, 1961; married; 2 children. BS in genetics, Ohio State U., PhD in molecular genetics. Grad. tchg. asst. in molecular genetics Ohio State U., Columbus, Ohio, 1986—92, lectr. genetics, 1992—97, postdoctoral fellow in molecular medicine, dept. pediat., 1992—97, asst. prof. molecular medicine, dept. pediat., 1997—2002, assoc. prof. molecular medicine, dept. pediat., 2002—; dir. Viral Vector Core Lab. Columbus Children's Rsch. Inst., 1998—, assoc. dir. Ctr. for Gene Therapy, 2005—. Mem.: AAAS, Am. Soc. Microbiology, Am. Soc. Gene Therapy, Soc. Pediatric Rsch. Office: Columbus Childrens Rsch Inst Ctr Gene Therapy 700 Childrens Cr Columbus OH 43205-2696 Office Phone: 614-722-2739. E-mail: clarkr@ccri.net.

CLARK, KEITH F., otolaryngologist; MD, U. of Mich., Ann Arbor, 1978; PhD in Laryngeal Physiology, U. of Okla., 1999. Intern surg. William Beaumont Hosp., Detroit, 1979; resident otorhinolaryngology Univ. of Iowa, Iowa City, 1983; hosp. affiliations include Univ. Hosp. and Children's Hosp., Okla., The Okla. City Ear, Nose and Throat Clinic. Fellow: ACS, Triologic Soc., Am. Acad. of Otolaryngology, Head and Neck Surgery; mem.: Okla. County Med. Soc., Okla. Acad. of Otolaryngology. Office: The Oklahoma City Ear, Nose and Throat Clinic 333 NW 9th St 300 Oklahoma City OK 73102 Office Phone: 405-272-6027. Office Fax: 405-272-8315.

CLARK, KENNETH EDWARD, physiologist, educator; b. Albany, NY, Apr. 16, 1945; s. Byron B. and Gladys L. Clark; m. Starla Rae Dagel, Feb. 27, 1977; children: Heather Michelle, Barbara Christina, Amy Elizabeth. BS, Purdue U., Lafayette, Ind., 1969, PhD, U. Iowa, Iowa City, 1975. Prof. dept. ob-gyn. U. Cin., 1977—2011. Reproductive physiologist dept. ob-gyn. U. Cin., 1977—. Contbr. articles to profl. jours. Grantee, NIH, 1978—. Mem.: Soc. Study Reprodn., Soc. Gynecol. Investigation, Perinatal Rsch. Soc., Endocrine Soc., Am. Physiology Soc. Home: 9179 Coachtrail Ln Cincinnati OH 45242 Office: U Cin Dept OB-gyn 231 Albert Sabin Way Cincinnati OH 45267 Office Phone: 513-558-6552. Personal E-mail: kclark61@cinci.rr.com. Business E-Mail: kenneth.clark@uc.edu.

CLARK, KEVIN D., medical products executive; Pres. ImmunoVision, Inc., Springdale, Ark., 1987—95, COO, 1987—, IVAX Diagnostics, Inc., Miami, Fla., 2007—, acting CEO, 2008, pres., CEO, 2010—. Mem. adv. bd. Ark. BioVentures, 2000—03; mem. exec. com. U. Ark. Tech. Devel. Found., 2003—. Mem.: Ark. Biotech Assn. (exec. v.p. 1995—2004, pres. 2002). Office: IVAX Diagnostics Inc 2140 N Miami Ave Miami FL 33127 Office Phone: 305-324-2300. Office Fax: 305-324-2585. *

CLARK, MICHAEL EARL, psychologist; b. Berea, Ohio, July 20, 1951; s. William Gray and Marguerite Jane (Charles) C.; m. Laura Lynn Putt, June 19, 1976 (div. Nov. 1987); 1 child, Brian Gray. BA, Kent State U., 1974, PhD, 1978. Asst. dir. chem. dependency unit N.D. State Hosp., Jamestown, N.D., 1978-79; staff psychologist VA Med. Ctr., Chillicothe, Ohio, 1979-84, Bay Pines, Fla., 1984-89; clin. dir., pain program James A. Haley Vets. Hosp., Tampa, Fla., 1989—. Assoc. prof. dept. psychology U. South Fla., Tampa, 1986—, clin. asst. prof. dept. neurology Sch. Medicine, Tampa, 1991—; adj. psychologist, counseling ctr. U. South Fla.; cons. to the correctional med. authority, State of Fla., 1993—2004; adv. bd. Pain Program Accreditation and Nat. Pain Data Bank, nat. pain mgmt. coordinating com.; mem. nat. pain edn. com., chmn. nat. outcomes com. Dept. Vets. Affairs; cons. Fla. State Bd. Psychology; expert examiner Fla. State Bd. Psychology, 2003—; cons. in field. Contbr. chpts. to Innovations in Clinical Practice, 1991, Social Psychology: A Sourcebooks, 1983, Pain Management: A Practical Guide for Clinicians, 2001, Weiner's Pain Management: A Practical Guide for Clinicians, 2005, articles to Biofeedback and Self-Regulation, Jour. Personality Assessment, Jour. Clin. Psychology, Brit. Jour. Clin. Psychology, Jour. Dental Rsch., The VA Practitioners, Psychol. Assessment, Pain Forum, Am. Jour. Pain Mgmt., Jour. Spinal Cord Medicine, Vets. Health Sys. Jour., Jour. Rehab. Rsch. & Devel., Clin. Jour. Pain. and Pain Medicine, scientific papers others; ad hoc reviewer and federal practitioner: Biofeedback and Self-Regulation, ad hoc reviewer: Psychol. Assessment, Clin. Jour. Pain, Jour. Rehab. R&D, Archives of Physical Medicine and Rehabilitation, Am. Pain Soc. Bulletin, Pain Jour. of Personality Assesment, Psychol. Bulletin; ad hoc reviewer JAMA, The Lancet, Jour. Gen. Internal Medicine, Jour. Brain Injury; editor: Am. Pain Soc. website; mem. editl. bd.: Jour. Opioid Mgmt. Pain Medicine; contbr. articles to profl. jours. Vice-chmn. Paint Valley Mental Health Bd., Chillicothe, 1980-84. Mem. Am. Pain Soc., Am. Acad. Pain Mgmt., Internat. Assn. for Study of Pain. Democrat. Home: 9645 Fox Hearst Rd Tampa FL 33647-1829 Office: Psychology Svc (116B) VAMC 13000 Bruce B Downs Blvd Tampa FL 33612-4745 Home Phone: 813-973-8116; Office Phone: 813-972-2000 x 7484. E-mail: michaeleclark2@msn.com.

CLARK, RACHAEL ANN, dermatologist, scientist, educator; b. Bellevue, Wash., Dec. 28, 1966; MD, Harvard Med. Sch., PhD, 1998. Asst. prof. dermatology Brigham and Women's Hosp. and Harvard Med. Sch., 2007—. Recipient Translational Rsch. award, Leukemia and Lymphoma Soc., Clin. Investigator award, Damon Runyon Cancer Rsch. Found.; US Presdl. scholarship, Wash. State Commn. Presdl. Scholars. Fellow: Am. Acad. Dermatology (Young Investigator award). Home: 11 Locust St Belmont MA 02478 Business E-Mail: rclark1@partners.org.

CLARK, RICHARD T., pharmaceutical company executive; b. Johnstown, Pa., Mar. 7, 1946; married; 2 children. BA in Liberal Arts, Washington & Jefferson Coll., 1968; MBA, Am. U., 1970. Quality control insp., indsl. engr., quality control analyst, lead supr. pharm. prodn. MSD, 1972—78, sr. new products planner, 1978—81, prodn. mgr. Elkton Pharm. Labs., 1981—83, mgr. indsl. engring., 1983—84; sr. mgr. indsl. engring. MPMD, 1984—85, dir. ops. improvement, 1985—86; sr. dir. mgmt. engring. Merck Sharp & Dohme/MPMD, 1986—89; exec. dir. mgmt. engring. Merck Pharm. Mfg. Divsn., 1989—91; v.p. materials mgmt. and mgmt. engring. MMD, 1991—93, v.p. procurement & materials mgmt., 1993—94, v.p. North American ops., 1994—96, sr. v.p. North American ops., 1996—97; exec. v.p., COO Merck-Medco Managed Care, 1997—2000; chmn., pres., CEO Merck Medco Health Solutions, Inc. (formerly Merck-Medco Managed Care, L.L.C.), 2000—02; chmn. Merck Medco Health Solutions, Inc., 2002—03; sr. v.p. quality comml. affairs Merck Mfg. Divsn., 1997, pres., 2003—05; pres., CEO Merck & Co., Inc. (formerly Schering-Plough Corp.), Whitehouse Sta., NJ, 2005—07, chmn., pres., CEO, 2007—10, chmn., CEO, 2010, chmn., 2011—. Bd. dirs. Merck & Co., Inc., 2005—. Lt. US Army, 1970—72. Mem.: Pharmaceutical Rsch. & Manufacturers of America (chmn. 2008—). Office: Merck & Co Inc One Merck Dr Whitehouse Station NJ 08889-0100 *

CLARK, ROBERT THOMAS, ophthalmologist; b. Detroit, Sept. 21, 1951; s. Robert Charles and Mary Jane Clark; m. Deborah Ann Burcz, June 13, 1975; children: Robert Matthew, Kirstin Sarah. BS, U. Notre Dame, South Bend, Ind., 1973; MD, Wayne State U., Detroit, 1978. Ptnr. Met. Eye Surgeons, Detroit, 1982—84; pres. Clark Eye Ctr., Brighton, 1990—; dir. refractive surgery William Beaumont Hosp., Royal Oak, 1995—2004; chief ophthalmology Huron Valley Hosp., Detroit, 1986—. Fellow: Am. Coll. Surgeons, Am. Acad. Ophthalmology. Office: Clark Eye Ctr 7575 W Grand Ave Brighton MI 48114

CLARK, SANDRA ANN, psychotherapist, writer, publisher; b. Long Branch, NJ, Dec. 4, 1942; d. Richard Marshall and Margaret (Novak) C.; children: Rebecca L., Benjamin C., Rachael A. BA, Valparaiso U., 1966; MSW, SUNY, Albany, 1968; ACSW, DCSW, BCD, CFCH. Lic. psychotherapist, critical incident stress mgr., trauma & debriefing specialist, independent clin. social worker, NH, clin. social worker, Maine; diplomate clin. social worker, NASW, 1999; bd. cert. diplomate in clin. social work ABE, 1999; cert. fellow in clin. hypnotherapy NBCCH, 2009, cert. fellow in clin. hypnosis. Pvt. practice psychotherapy, Kittery, Maine, 1982—; asst. exec. dir., coord. children's program N.H. Parents Anonymous, Portsmouth, 1985-86; mental health cons. Strafford County Head Start, Somersworth, N.H., 1985-88; interim exec. dir. N.H. Parents Anonymous, Portsmouth, 1986-87; home sch. coord. Portsmouth Sch. System, 1986-87; clin. social worker Rockingham Counseling Ctr., Exeter, NH, 1986—89, York County Counseling Svcs., Kittery, 1989-90; exec. dir. Growing Consciousness Assn., Saco, Maine, 1995-96. Faculty U. Conn., Concord, NH, 1987. Named Outstanding Intellectuals of 21st Century, 2000, A Woman Who Sets the Standard, Internat. Review Bd. Bus. and Profl. Women, 2009, Great Minds of 21st Century, 2010, 2000 Notable Am. Women. Mem. NASW, Acad. Clin. Social Workers, Am. Hypnosis Tng. Acad., Hypnosis Info. Network, Eye Movement Desensitization Reprocessing Internat. Assn., N.H. Mediators Assn., No. N.E. Soc. Clin. Hypnosis, Hypnosis Info. Network, Portsmouth Group Psychotherapy Soc., Co-Occuring Collaborative Serving Maine. Independent. Home: 25 Old Ferry Ln Kittery ME 03904-1305 Office: Merremac Mill 3rd Fl 44 Merrimac St Newburyport MA 01950 Home Phone: 207-439-5149; Office Phone: 978-462-4904. Personal E-mail: hausonhill@aol.com.

CLARK, SHERYL DIANE, physician; b. Cleve., May 8, 1952; d. Crandall and Martha Jayne (McNeilly) C.; children: Milan, Gabriel. BA, Beloit Coll., 1974; postgrad., Hampstead Clinic Child Analysis and U. London, 1976-77; MD, Case Western Res. U., 1982. Diplomate Am. Bd. Dermatology. Intern Mt. Sinai Med. Ctr., Cleve., 1982-83; rsch. fellow Case Western Res. U., Kenya, Kenya, Africa, 1983-84, Washington U., St. Louis, 1984-88; resident in dermatology Barnes Hosp., St. Louis, 1985-88; vis. assoc. physician Rockefeller U. Hosp., NYC, 1990—93; asst. attending physician N.Y. Presbyterian Hosp., NYC, 1988—; asst. clin. prof. medicine Cornell Med. Ctr., NYC, 1991—; pres. Sheryl Clark Enterprises, NYC, 1991—. Cons. Rodale Press, N.Y.C., 1995—; speaker in field. Co-editor: Jour. of Biomed. Engring. and Technology, 1977-78; contbr. articles to profl. jours. Rep. rape task force N.Y. Hosp., 1988-90; ofcl. spokesperson dermatology NY Presbyn. Hosp., 1989-1991. Recipient Pres. Vol. Source award, 2009. Fellow N.Y. Acad. Medicine, Am. Acad. Dermatology (leadership ctr. volenterism 2008-); mem. AMA (cons. scientific advisory coun. 1992), Am. Soc. Lasers Medicine and Surgery, Am. Med. Women's Assn., Caribbean Med. & Edn. Found. (bd. dirs.), Soc. Investigative Dermatology, Internat. Soc. for Androgenic Disorders, Med. Soc. State of N.Y., N.Y. County Med. Soc., Phi Beta Kappa, Alpha Omega Alpha. Avocations: painting, scuba, skiing, sailing. Office: 109 E 61st St New York NY 10065-8101 Office Phone: 212-750-2905.

CLARK, SUSAN, surgeon; b. London, Mar. 16, 1965; MA, Cambridge U., Eng., 1983, MB, BChir, 1989, MD, 1999. Cons. colorectal surgeon Royal London Hosp., 2003—06, St Mark's Hosp., Harrow, England, 2006—. Clin. Rsch. fellow, Imperial Cancer Rsch. Fund, 1995—97. Fellow: Royal Coll. Surgeons Eng., Royal Soc. Medicine. Home: 25 Kelso Pl London W8 5QG England Office: Polyposis Registry St Mark's Hosp HA1 3UJ Harrow HA1 3UJ England Office Fax: 442084001. Business E-Mail: s.clark8@uhs.net.

CLARKE, GARY NORMAN, reproductive biologist; b. Ouyen, Victoria, Australia, Sept. 10, 1951; s. Mervyn and Norma Clarke; m. Susan Biggs; children: Emily, Oliver. BSc, Monash U., 1971, BSc with honors, 1972, MSc, 1976; DSc, Melbourne U., 2005. Scientist Royal Women's Hosp., Melbourne, 1976-84, sr. scientist, 1985-95;

scientist-in-charge Melbourne U., 1995—, prof., 2005—. Vis. scientist U. Hawaii, 1977-78; cons. Hamad Hosp., Qatar, 1988; plenary lectr. 4th World In Vitro Fertilization Congress, 1985. Contbr. book chpt.: CRC Handbook of the Laboratory Diagnosis and Treatment of Infertility, 1990; contbr. sci. papers and rsch. articles to profl. jours. Rsch. grantee Royal Women's Hosp., 1988, traveling scholar, 1992; rsch. grantee Nat. Health and Med. Rsch. Coun., 1989; fellow Queensland Acad. Arts and Scis., 2005. Mem. Med. Scientists Assn. Victoria, Fertility Soc. Australia (founding mem., bd. dirs. 1991-96), Scientists Reproductive Tech. (founding mem., nat. coun. 1994-96). Avocations: bird watching, art appreciation, travel, reading. Office: The Royal Women's Hosp Andrology Unit Parkville 3052 Victoria Australia Business E-Mail: gary.clarke@thewomens.org.au.

CLARKE, MICHAEL F., oncologist, educator; BA, Ind. U., 1973; MD, Ind. U. Sch. Med., 1977. Intern U. Mo., 1978; resident Ind. U. Sch. Med., 1980; assoc. dir. Stanford Inst. Stem Cell & Regenerative Med.; prof. med. & oncology Stanford U. Sch. Med. Recipient Rackham award, U. Mich. Mem.: Am. Assn. Physicians, Am. Soc. Clinical Investigation. Office: 875 Blake Wilbur Dr MC 5826 Stanford CA 94305 Office Phone: 650-498-6000, 650-498-5852. E-mail: mfclarke@stanford.edu.

CLARKE, RICHARD LEWIS, health science association administrator; b. Indpls., Sept. 9, 1948; s. John Richard and Opal (Emmons) C.; m. Linda DeMattia, Aug. 12, 1972; children: John, Laura, R. Bradley. BS, Bradley U., 1971; MBA, U. Miami, 1972. Bus. mgr. Jackson Meml. Hosp., Miami, 1973-76; controller Palmetto Gen. Hosp., Hialeah, Fla., 1976-80; sr. v.p. fin. Swedish Med. Ctr., Englewood, Colo., 1980-86; pres. Healthcare Fin. Mgmt. Assn., Westchester, Ill., 1986—, CEO. Bd. dirs., treas. Colo. Hosp. Assn. Trust, Denver. Fellow Healthcare Fin. Mgmt. Assn.; mem. Am. Soc. Assn. Execs., Econ. Club of Chgo. Avocations: sailboat racing, skiing. Office: Healthcare Fin Mgmt Assn 2 Westbrook Corp Ctr Ste 700 Westchester IL 60154 *

CLARKIN, JOHN FRANCIS, health care management executive; b. Atlantic City, Dec. 30, 1936; s. John Francis and Agnes (Winterholer) C.; m. Dorothy Louise Piffath, 1 son, John F. BSBA, Rider Coll., 1959; postgrad., Temple U. Cert. mgmt. cons. Inst. Mgmt. Cons., 1968. Mktg. rep. Scott Paper Co., Indpls., 1960-62; systems and mktg. rep. Burroughs Corp., Phila., 1962-67; dir. Mid-Atlantic health care ops. mgmt. practice Coopers & Lybrand, Phila., 1967-92; v.p. corp. fin. svcs. Crozer-Keystone Health Sys., Upland, Pa., 1992-97; pres. Clarkin Group, West Chester, Pa., 1997—98, 2008—; v.p. bus. svcs. Thomas Jefferson U. Hosp., Phila., 1998—2008. Lead instr., spkr. numerous profl. meetings and seminars. Author: Topics in Health Care Financing, 1982; (with others) Handbook of Health Care Accounting and Finance, 1982, 89, Billing Systems, 2 vols., 1982, 89, Managing Accounts Receivable, 1990; contbr. articles to profl. jours. Mem. Grand Oak Run Civic Assn., 1970—. With U.S. Army, 1959. Grantee Rotary Club, 1955—59. Mem. Inst. Mgmt. Cons., Hosp. Mgmt. Systems Soc., Hosp. Fin. Mgmt. Assn., Med. Group Mgmt. Assn., Am. Hosp. Assn., Vesper Club, Pickering Racquet Club. Republican. Roman Catholic. Home: 1421 Grand Oak Ln West Chester PA 19380-5951 Office: Clarkin Group 1421 Grand Oak Ln West Chester PA 19380-5951 Office Phone: 215-588-2194.

CLARKSON, JOHN G., ophthalmologist, educator, medical association administrator; m. Diana Teasdale; children: Paige, David. BS, Princeton U.; MD, Miami Sch. Medicine, 1968. Intern U. Hosp., Boston; resident ophthalmology U. Miami/Jackson Meml. Med. Ctr., Fla.; ophthalmic pathology, retinal and vitreous surgery fellow Johns Hopkins U., Balt.; chmn. dept. ophthalmology, dir. Bascom Palmer Eye Inst., 1991—96; sr. v.p. med. affairs, dean Sch. Medicine U. Miami, 1995—2006, dean emeritus, prof. ophthalmology, 2006—; exec. dir. Am. Bd. Ophthalmology, 2006—. Mem.: Macula Soc., Retina Soc., Am. Ophthalmol. Soc., Am. Acad. Ophthalmology, Am. Bd. Ophthalmology (bd. dirs.), Club Jules Gonin. Office: American Bd Ophthalmology 111 Presidential Blvd Ste 241 Bala Cynwyd PA 19004-1075 also: University Miami Miller Sch Medicine Suite 1560 1120 NW 14th St Miami FL 33136 Office Phone: 305-243-7878. Business E-Mail: jclarkson@miami.edu. *

CLARREN, STERLING KEITH, pediatrician; b. Mpls., Mar. 12, 1947; s. David Bernard and Lila (Reifel) C.; m. Sandra Gayle Bernstein, June 8, 1970; children: Rebecca Pia, Jonathan Seth. BA, Yale U., 1969; MD, U. Minn., 1973. Pediatric intern U. Wash. Sch. Medicine, Seattle, 1973-74, resident in pediatrics, 1974-77, asst. prof. dept. pediatrics, 1979-83, assoc. prof., 1983-88, prof., 1988, Robert A. Aldrich chair in pediatrics, 1989—2005; clin. prof. pediatrics U. B.C. Faculty of Medicine, Vancouver, 2005—; CEO Can. N.W. FASD Rsch Network, Vancouver, 2005—; co-leader FASD sect. NeuroDevelopment Network Can. Head divsn. congenital defects U. Wash. Sch. Medicine, 1987-95, head divsn. hosp. medicine, 2002-04; dir. dept. congenital defects Children's Hosp. and Med. Ctr., Seattle, 1987-96, dir. fetal alcohol syndrome clinic Child Devel. and Mental Retardation Ctr. U. Wash., 1992-2001, dir. Fetal Alcohol Syndrome Network, 1995-2001; dir. inpatient svcs. Children's Hosp. and Med. Ctr., Seattle, 1996-2004. Contbr. articles to profl. jours.; patentee for orthosis to alter cranial shape. Cons. pediatrician Maxillofacial Rev. Bd., State of Wash., Seattle, 1984-90, chmn. Health-Birth Defects Adv. Com., Olympia, 1980-90; mem. gov.'s task force on FAS State of Wash., 1994-95; mem. fetal alcohol adv. com. Children's Trust Found., Seattle, 1988—; bd. dirs. Seattle Children's Home, 2003—; mem. adv. bd. Nat. Orgn. on Fetal Alcohol Syndrome; mem. fetal alcohol com. Inst. Medicine, NAS, 1994-95; bd.dirs. North Cascades Inst., 2010-. Rsch. grantee Nat. Inst. Alcohol Abuse & Alcoholism, 1982 , Ctrs. for Disease Control, 1992—. Fellow AAAS; mem. Soc. for Pediatric Rsch., Teratology Soc., Rsch. Soc. on Alcoholism (pres. fetal alcohol study group 1993), Am. Cleft Palate Assn., N.Y. Acad. Scis. Avocations: cross country skiing, fishing, hiking, sailing. Home: 8601 Paisley Dr NE Seattle WA 98115 Office: Devel Neurocsi Child Health 4480 Oak St Rm L408 Vancouver BC V6H 3V4 Canada Office Phone: 604-875-2996.

CLASSON, ROLF ALLAN, medical products executive; b. Nassjo, Sweden, Aug. 20, 1945; s. Allan K.E. and May Britt (Lagerquist) C.; m. Birgitta Larsson, Feb. 3, 1968; children: Peter, Karin, Erik. M in Bus. Econs., Gothenburg U., 1969. Personnel mgr. Pharmacia, Uppsala, Sweden, 1969-74; mgmt. cons. Asbjorn Habberstad, Stockholm, 1974-77; mktg. mgr. Pharmacia, Uppsala, 1977-80; div. gen. mgr. Tarkett, Ronneby, 1980; pres. Pharmacia Infusion, Uppsala, 1981-84, Pharmacia Devel. Co. Inc., Piscataway, NJ, 1984-90; pres., chief oper. officer Pharmacia Biosystems AB, 1990—91; exec. v.p. Bayer Corp., 1995—2002, exec. v.p., worldwide mktg., sales & services, group diagnostics, 1991—92, pres., group diagnostics, 1995—2002, sr. v.p., sales & services, group diagnostics, 1992—95, chmn. exec. comm., health care div., 2002—04; vice-chmn. Hillenbrand Industries, Batesville, Ind., 2004—05, interim pres., CEO, 2005—06; chmn. Hill-Rom Holdings, Inc. (formerly Hillenbrand Industries, Inc.), Batesville, Ind., 2006—. Mem. supv. bd. Bayer HealthCare AG; bd. dir. Enzon Pharmaceuticals, ISTA Pharmaceuticals, Millipore Corp., Auxilium Pharmaceuticals. Office: Hillenbrand Industries Mail Code K71 1069 State Route 46 E Batesville IN 47006-8835 *

CLAUDIO, MANUEL P.A., medical educator, health facility administrator; b. Manila, June 23, 1938; s. Eduardo L. and Gorgonia A. Claudio; m. Adelina C.B. Claudio, May 1, 1965; children: Basil, Kevin, Kenneth, Liesl. MD, U. E. Ramon Magsaysay Meml. Med. Ctr., Quezon City, The Philippines, 1962; MBA, Northwestern U., 1993. Cert. Am. Bd. Med. Mgmt., Am. Bd. Quality Assurance and Utilization Rev. Physicians. Chmn. dept. medicine Humana Hosp., Hoffman Estates, Ill., 1981—83; chief sect. pulmonary medicine Mercy Hosp. Med. Ctr., Chgo., 1981—2000, med. dir. respiratory care dept., 1988—2000, pres. med. and sci. staff faculty, 1989—91; clin. asst. prof. medicine U. Ill. Coll. Medicine, Chgo., 1983—98; program dir. pulmonary medicine Mercy Hosp. Med. Ctr., Chgo., 1979—98. Contbr. articles to profl. publs. Pres. Philippine Med. Assn. Chgo., 1968; exec. dir. Assn. Philippine Practicing Physician Am., Chgo., 1972; bd. advisors Cath. charities, Chgo., 1986—; bd. pres. Am. Lung Assn. Metro Chgo., 2004—06; bd. govs. Inst. Medicine, Chgo., 2006—10; bd. dirs. Respiratory Health Assn. Metro Chgo., 2006—. Recipient Leadership award, Philippine Med. Assn. Chgo., 1968, Disting. Physician award, Philippine Med. Assn., 1992, Herbert De Young medal, Am. Lung Assn., Metro Chgo., 2006, Helping Hands award, Cath. Charities Chgo., 2010, Leadership & Svc. award, Inst. Medicine Chgo., 2010; named to Chgo.'s Filipino-Am. Hall of Fame, 1997. Fellow: ACP, Inst. Medicine Chgo.; mem.: Am. Thoracic Soc. Roman Catholic. E-mail: mpac38@Comcast.net.

CLAUSEN, JERRY LEE, psychiatrist; b. Wausau, Wis., Nov. 5, 1939; s. Douglas William and Florence Jean (Amidon) Clausen; m. Nancy Eileen Longdon, Aug. 3, 1962; children: Keith Rusell, Pamela Dawn. BA, Wesleyan U., Middletown, Conn., 1961; MD, Albany Med. Coll., NYC, 1965. Diplomate in psychiatry and addiction psychiatry Am. Bd. Psychiatry and Neurology, cert. Am. Soc. Addiction Medicine. Psychiatry intern Upstate Med. Ctr., Syracuse, 1965-66, psychiat. resident, 1966-67, 69-71, asst. attending, 1971-72, attending, 1972-80; staff psychiatrist Onondaga Mental Health Clinic, Syracuse, 1971-72; courtesy staff Benjamin Rush Psychiatric Ctr., Syracuse, 1971-84, active staff, 1984—2004; pvt. practice psychiatry Syracuse, 1971—2004; clin. asst. prof. SUNY, 1972—. Staff psychiatrist Onondaga Pastoral Counseling Ctr., Syracuse, 1971—72, Syracuse, 1981—97, psychiat. dir., 1973—81; cons. psychiatrist Loretto Rest Geriatric Ctr., Syracuse, 1972—74. Tchr. 1st Universalist Ch., Syracuse, 1966—. Lt. comdr. USN, 1967—69. Fellow: Am. Psychiat. Assn. (chmn. ins. mktg. com. 1979—88, disting.); mem.: N.Y. State Med. Soc., Onondaga County Med. Soc. Avocations: walking, tennis, cross country skiing.

CLAUSMAN, GILBERT JOSEPH, retired medical librarian; b. Los Angeles, Nov. 8, 1921; s. Pete John and Lila (Mason) C. AB, Willamette U., 1947; BS, Columbia U., 1948, MS, 1952. Med. librarian N.Y. Acad. Medicine, NYC, 1948-55; med. librarian NYU Med. Ctr., NYC, 1955-86, librarian emeritus, 1987—. Cons. Milton Helpern Library Legal Medicine, 1963-88. Served with USN, 1942-45 Mem. Med. Libr. Assn. (pres. 1977-78), Archons of Colophon, N.Y. Acad. Medicine, Acad. Health Info. Profls. Home: 2150 Post Rd Fairfield CT 06824-5669

CLAUSS-EHLERS, CAROLINE S., psychologist, educator, journalist; b. Manhasset, NY, July 17, 1967; d. Harold Wilson and Carole (Page) Clauss; m. Julian Charles Edward Clauss-Ehlers; children: Isabel S., Sabrina S. BA with honors, Oberlin Coll., 1989; MA, Columbia U., 1992, EdM, 1993, PhD, 1999. Bilingual clinician Henry St. Settlement, Cmty. Consultation Ctr., NYC, 1992-96; clin. interviewer N.Y. State Psychiat. Inst., NYC, 1995-98; predoctoral intern in clin. psychology NYU Med. Ctr./Bellevue Hosp., NYC, 1996-97; columnist HOY, 2002—08; psychologist pvt. practice, 2000—. Adj. asst. prof. psychology and edn. Tchr. Coll., Columbia U., 1998—2001; asst. prof. counselling psychology Rutgers U. Grad. Sch. Edn., 2001—08, assoc. prof. counseling psychology, 2008—; guest correspondent Univision, 2002—; cons. in field; editor Jour. Multicultural Counseling & Devel., 2011—. Author: Diversity Training for Classroom Teaching: A Manual for Students and Educators, 2006; co-editor: Community Planning to Foster Resilience in Children, 2004; contbr. articles to profl. jours.; editor: Encylopedia of Cross-Cultural School Psychology, 2010, Jour. Multicultural Counseling & Devel., 2011—. Oberlin Alumni scholar, 1992; Tchrs. Coll. scholar, 1994-96; Leopold Schepp Found. fellow, 1994-97; Rosalynn Carter fellow for mental health journalism, 2004-05. Mem. APA (mem. leadership initiative woman in psychology), N.Y. State Psychol. Assn., Leadership Inst. Women Psychology. Office: Rutgers U 10 Seminary Pl New Brunswick NJ 08901 Office Phone: 732-932-7496 ext. 8312. Business E-Mail: cc@gse.rutgers.edu, caroline.clauss-ehlers@gse.rutgers.edu.

CLAVER, MARIA LENA, social sciences educator; b. LA, Mar. 2, 1975; MSW, UCLA, 1997, PhD, 2006. Asst. prof. Calif. State U., Long Beach, 2007—. Rschr. Vets. Affairs, 2006—. Recipient Most Inspirational Prof. award, Calif. State U. Mem.: Gerontol. Soc. America, Calif. Coun. Gerontology & Geriat. (Betty and James Lubben Emerging Leadership award), Am. Soc. Aging, Sigma Phi Omega. Office: Calif State University Long Beach Family & Consumer Scis GERO Long Beach CA 90840 Office Fax: 562-985-4414. Business E-Mail: mclaver@csulb.edu.

CLAWSON, DAVID KAY, orthopedic surgeon; b. Salt Lake City, Aug. 8, 1927; s. David J. and Elva (Gundry) C.; m. Janet Dorothy Smith, June 1, 1952; children: Kim Debra, David Roger. Student, U. Utah, 1944-45, 47-48; MD, Harvard U., 1952. Diplomate: Am. Bd. Orthopedic Surgery. Intern Stanford U. Hosp., 1952-53, resident gen. surgery, 1953-54; resident orthopedic surgery Stanford U. Hosp., also San Francisco City and County Hosp., 1954-57; fellow in orthopedics Nat. Found. Infantile Paralysis, 1955-58; hon. sr. registrar Royal Nat. Orthopedic Hosp., London, Eng., 1957-58; asst. prof. UCLA Med. Sch., 1958; asst. prof. surgery, head div. orthopedic surgery U. Wash. Med. Sch., 1958-61, assoc. prof. surgery, head div. orthopedic surgery, 1961-65, prof., 1964-83, chmn. dept. orthopedics, 1964-75; dean Coll. Medicine, U. Ky., 1975-83, vice chancellor for clin. profl. services, 1982-83; exec. vice chancellor U. Kans. Med. Ctr., Kansas City, 1983-94, cons. to chancellor, 1994; prof. orthopaedic surgery U. Ky., 1994—, cons. to dean, 1994—. Mem. Accreditation Coun. for Grad. Med. Edn., 1977-88; chmn. residency rev. com. on structure and functions, 1987-88; chmn. coun. of deans Assn. Am. Med. Coll., 1985-86, chmn. of the assembly, 1988-89, immediate past chmn., 1989-90, disting. svc. rep. to exec. coun., 1992-95; active Am. Orthopaedic Soc. for Sports Medicine, 1972-87, founder, 1972; active Assn. Orthopaedic Chmn., 1971-73, founder, 1971. Contbr. med. jours.; mem. editorial bd.: Clin. Orthopedics and Related Research, 1964—. Mem. Heart of Am. coun. Boy Scouts Am., 1989—, mem. adv. bd., 1989-92, Regional Task Force and Edn. Found., 1972—. With USNR, 1945-46. Exchange fellow Am. Orthopedic Assn., 1967 Mem. AMA (coun. for med. affairs 1988—), Am. Acad. Ortho. Surgeons (coun. on health policy 1990-95), Am. Orthopaedic Assn., Assn. Acad. Health Ctrs., Assn. Am. Univs., Assn. Bone and Joint Surgeons (pres. 1977), Harvard Med. Sch. Alumni Assn. (pres. 1984-85), Henry Clay Meml. Found. (pres. 2007-09). Home: 3785 Jamaica Ct Lexington KY 40509-9506 also: 10 E Roanoke St Seattle WA 98102-3257

CLAY, MARGARET LEONE, community psychologist, consultant, human ecologist; b. St. Joseph, Mo., Oct. 23, 1923; BS with honors, distinction, U. Mich., 1956, MS, 1958, PhD, 1962. Teaching fellow psychology dept. U. Mich., Ann Arbor, 1958-59, lectr., 1963-71, rsch. asst., 1956-60, asst. rsch. psychologist, 1960-62, assoc. rsch. psychologist Mental Health Rsch. Inst., 1962-82, asst. dir., 1965-68, asst. prof. psychiatry dept. Med. Sch., 1975-82, asst. prof. emeritus, 1982—; pvt. practice human svcs. cons. Hillman, Mich., 1982—. Mem. faculty extension svc. U. Mich. Sch. Pub. Health, Ann Arbor, 1969-72; mem. vis. faculty Rutgers U. Summer Sch. Alcohol Studies, New Brunswick, N.J., 1972-76; mem. bd. rsch. advisors Walden U., Naples, Fla., 1979-82; bd. dirs. Thunder Bay Cmty. Health Svcs., 1983-2006, chmn. bd., 1993-95. Author: Fundamentals of Alcohol and Other Drug Problems, 1996, Another Way to Live, 2003; co-author: Studies Guide for Accreditation of Counselors; contbr. articles to profl. jours. Mem. Gov.'s Sect. 20 Rev. Com., Lansing, Mich., 1976; mem. Gov.'s Task Force on Drinking Driver Problem, Lansing, 1970-74; bd. mem. Gov.'s Adv. Commn. on Substance Abuse, Lansing, 1976-83; coun. mem. Statewide Health Coord. Coun., Lansing, 1977-83; mem. Mich. Coun. on Crime and Delinquency, Lansing, 1979—, pres., 1981-83; bd. mem. Mich. Coalition on Substance Abuse, 1986-96, Shelter, Inc., 1989-92, No. Regional Acad./Cmty. Health System, 1993-97; co-founder N.E. Mich. Cmty. Partnership for Prevention, 1991—; bd. dirs. Northeast Mich. Comm. Mental Health Bd., 1993—, chmn., 1996-98. Recipient Disting. Svc. award Mich. Alcohol and Addiction Assn., 1977, Outstanding Svc. award Mich. Prevention Assn., 1993, Award for Outstanding Svc. in Prevention, 1993; named Vol. of Yr. Nat. Coun. on Alcoholism, Mich., 1985. Mem. APHA, APA (vis. psychologist 1976-78), Am. Assn. Correctional Psychologists (sec.-treas. 1975-77), N.Am. Assn. Alcohol Problems (program chmn. 1970-72), Alcohol and Drug Problems Assn. N.Am. (chmn. rsch. com. 1973-75, program chmn. 1976-78, bd. dirs. 1980-82, Outstanding Svc. award 1978), Mich. Pub. Health Assn. (hon. life, chmn. mental health div. 1969-70) Mich. Primary Care Assn. (Bd. Mem. of Yr. 2004). Avocations: music, theater, nature. Office: 9885 Farrier Rd Hillman MI 49746 Office Phone: 989-742-4262. Business E-Mail: mlclay@iserv.net.

CLAYCOMB, CECIL KEITH, biochemist, educator; b. Twin Falls, Idaho, Oct. 19, 1920; s. Cecil R. and Frilla E. (Reams) C.; m. Elizabeth Jane Gregg, Mar. 10, 1943; children: John K., Mary E. BS, U. Oreg., Eugene, 1947, MS, 1948, PhD, 1951. Prof., head dept. biochemistry Dental Sch. U. Oreg., Portland, 1951-82, dir. minority recruitment, 1971-74, asst. to pres./dir. minority student affairs, 1974-84, coordinator basic sci. curriculum, 1951-77, chmn. admissions com., 1959-69, emeritus, 1985—; emeritus prof. biochemistry Oreg. Health and Sci. U., 1986—. Contbr. articles to sci. jours. Served to 1st lt. AUS, 1943-46. Scholar dental bd. New South Wales, Sydney, Australia, 1970 Mem. Am. Chem. Soc., Internat. Assn. Dental Research, AAAS, Res. Officers Assn., Sigma Xi. Home: 1950 NW 192nd Ave Beaverton OR 97006

CLAYMAN, RALPH VICTOR, urologist, medical educator, dean; b. NYC, Nov. 3, 1947; m. Carol Heineman, 1974; children: Matthew Abe, Bradley Ulysses. BS cum laude, Grinnell Coll., 1969; MD, U. Calif., San Diego, 1973. Diplomate Am. Bd. Urology. From intern to resident dept. surgery U. Minn. Hosp., Mpls., 1973-75, clin. resident dept. urologic surgery, 1975-77, rsch. resident dept. urologic surgery, 1977-78, chief clin. resident, rsch. resident dept. urologic surgery, 1979; instr. dept. urologic surgery U. Minn. Hosps., Mpls., 1979-82, asst. prof. dept. urologic surgery, 1982-84; AUA scholar SW Med. Sch., Dallas, 1984; assoc. prof. dept. surgery and radiology Washington U. Sch. Medicine, St. Louis, 1984-90, prof., 1990—2002; chair Dept. Urology U. Calif. Irvine Med. Ctr., 2002—; clin. prof. U. Calif. Irvine Sch. Medicine, 2002—, interim dean, 2009—10, dean, 2010—. Co-investigator USA Siemens Lithotriptor FDA, 1986. Co-editor Jour. Endourology; contbr. numerous articles, chpts. and revs. to profl. jours., books and procs.; also movie and videocassettes. Recipient Ferdinand C. Valentine award Endourology, 1990, Guiteras award, 2010; Am. Cancer Soc. fellow, 1977-81, Nat. Kidney Found. fellow, 1978-80; Merit Rev. grantee VA, 1980-84; grantee BRSG, 1985. Fellow Royal Coll. Surgeons Edinburgh (hon.); mem. ACS, Am. Urol. Assn. (scholar 1982-84, Disting. Contbns. award 1992, various coms. 1987—), Endourology Soc. (sec. 1985-2009), Endosurg. Soc., Nat. Kidney Found. (rsch. bd. 1988), Am. Assn. Genitourologic Surgeons, Am. Surg. Assn., Clin. Soc., Soc. Internat. d'Urologie, Soc. Minimally Invasive Therapy, Coc. Univ. Urologists, Phi Beta Kappa. Achievements include patent for person and blood identification wrist band, Lapsac, cutting balloon, ureteroscope. Office: U Calif Irvine City Tower, Suite 2100 Irvine CA 92697 Office Phone: 714-456-3329. Office Fax: 714-456-5062. E-mail: rclayman@uci.edu. *

CLAYPOOL, HENRY, federal agency administrator; b. Ft. Collins, Colo. BA, U. Colo., Boulder, 1989. Former staff Ctr. Ind. Living; dir. disability svcs. U. Colo., Boulder, 1993—98; sr. advisor for disability policy Centers Medicare & Medicaid Services, US Dept. Health & Human Services, Washington, 1998—2002, dir. Office Disability, 2009—; sr. advisor Office Disability & Income Support Programs, Social Security Adminstrn., 2005—06; dir. policy Independence Care Sys., NYC, 2007—09. Chair Gov.'s Devel. Disabilities Coun., Colo.,

1993—95. Named Person of Yr., New Mobility, 2004. Office: HHS Office Disability Rm 637D 200 Independence Ave SW Washington DC 20201 Office Phone: 202-205-1016. E-mail: henry.claypool@hhs.gov. *

CLAYTON, DAVID A., lab administrator; b. Joliet, Ill., Feb. 5, 1944; m. Lauretta Swanson, 1965; children: Lindsay, Ryan, Megan. BS, Northern Ill. U., DeKalb, 1965; PhD, Calif. Inst. Tech., Pasadena, 1970. Prof. Stanford U., Calif., 1970—96, program dir., med. scientist tng. program, 1978—96; sr. sci. officer Howard Hughes Med. Inst., Chevy Chase, Md., 1996—99, v.p. sci. devel., 2000—01, v.p., chief sci. officer, 2001—07, v.p. rsch. ops., 2007—08, lab. head Ashburn, Va., 2008—. Mem. adv. com. nucleic acids and protein synthesis, Am. Cancer Soc., 1976-80; mem. molecular biology study sect., NIH, 1982-86, chmn., 1984-86; mem. sci. rev. bd. Howard Hughes Med. Inst., 1993-96; mem. nat. adv. bd. Gen. Med. Sci. Coun., 1996-99; Fisher lectr. So. Ill. U., 1989. Contbr. scientific papers to profl. publs. Active Howard Hughes Med. Inst. Sci. Rev. Bd., Chevy Chase, Md., 1993—96, Nat. Adv. Gen. Med. Scis. Coun., Bethesda, Md., 1996—99; active and chair, adv. bd. academic coun. Stanford U., 1989—92; active U. Md., College Park, 2003—06. Recipient Warner-Lambert/Parke Davis award, 1982. Mem. Inst. Medicine Nat. Acad. Sci., Am. Soc. Biochemistry and Molecular Biology. Episcopalian. Office: Howard Hughes Med Inst 19700 Helix Dr Ashburn VA 20147-2408

CLEARFIELD, HARRIS REYNOLD, physician; b. Phila., Aug. 8, 1933; s. Samuel and Rae (Lewis) C.; m. Louise Libby, June 30, 1957; children: Andrea, Jonathan. BS, Franklin and Marshall Coll., 1955; MD, Jefferson Med. Coll., 1959. Intern Grad. Hosp. U. Pa., Phila., 1959-60, resident in internal medicine, 1960-62, resident in gastroenterology, 1962-63, mem. staff, 1963-72, Episcopalian Hosp., Phila., 1967-72, head sect. gastroenterology, until 1972; sr. attending physician Phila. Gen Hosp., 1972-77; mem. faculty U. Pa. Med. Sch., Phila., 1963-72; clin. asst. prof. medicine Temple U. Med. Sch., Phila., 1967-72; dir. div. gastroenterology Hahnemann Hosp., Phila., 1972—, prof. medicine, 1972—. Lectr., cons. Naval Regional Med. Ctr., Phila., 1976-78; sr. cons. Phila. Gen. Hosp., 1972-74; mem. gov.'s adv. com. of ACP, 1980-88; dir. Krancer Ctr. for Inflamatory Bowel Disease Rsch., 1985—. Author: (with Dinoso) Gastrointestinal Emergencies, 1979, (with Borowsky) Case Studies in Gastroenterology, 1989; editorial cons. Am. Jour. Proctology, 1976-86; contbr. articles to profl. jours. Chmn. sci. adv. bd. Nat. Found. Ileitis and Colitis, 1976-80, trustee, 1990—. Recipient Lindback award Phila. chpt. Nat. Found. Ileitis and Colitis, 1979, named Physician of Yr., 1980, Janssen award, 1998. Fellow ACP (mem. bd. regents 1999-2003, chmn. coun. subspecialty socs. 1999-2003, master, 2008), Phila. Coll. Physicians; mem. Am. Gastroenterologic Assn., Bockus Internat. Soc. Gastroenterology (trustee, v.p., pres. 1993-95), Phila. Gastroenterology Group (pres. 1974-75), Am. Coll. Gastroenterology (Master; gov. Ea. Pa. 1990-92, trustee 1992-96), Pa. Soc. Gastroenterology (pres. 1993-95), Delaware Valley Soc. Gastrointestinal Rsch. Forum, Pa. Med. Soc. (commn. on accreditation 1986-92), Phila. Med. Soc. (bd. dirs. 1996—, sec. 1998—, v.p. 1999-, pres. 2001-02), Musical Fund Soc, Phila. (physician, 2003—). Home: 720 Oxford Rd Bala Cynwyd PA 19004-2112 Office: 219 N Broad St Philadelphia PA 19102-1121 Office Phone: 215-762-6070. Personal E-mail: harris.clearfield@drexelmed.edu.

CLEGG, JAMES STANDISH, physiologist, biochemist, educator; b. Aspinwall, Pa., July 27, 1933; divorced, 3 children; m. Eileen Clegg; 1 stepchild. AA in Biology, Coffeyville Coll., 1953; BS in Zoology, Pa. State U., 1958, PhD in Biology, Johns Hopkins U., 1961. Rsch. assoc. biologist Johns Hopkins U., 1961-62, asst. prof. zoology U. Miami, 1962-64, from assoc. prof. biology to prof., 1964-70; prof. sect. molecular and cellular biology U. Calif., Davis, 1986—, dir. Bodega Marine Lab., 1986-98. With CNRS Thias France, 1983; pres. Nat. Assn. Marine Labs., 1992-94. With US Army, 1953—55. Recipient Fulbright Sr. Rsch. award U. London, 1978, U. Ghent, 1999; Wilson fellow, 1958-59. Fellow AAAS; mem. Soc. Integrative & Comparative Biology, Am. Soc. Cell Biology, Biophys. Soc., Soc. Cryobiology, Cell Stress Soc. Internat., Sigma Xi. Independent. Achievements include research in comparative biochemistry and biophysics; mechanisms of cryptobiosis; properties and role of water in cellular metabolism; cytoplasmic organization. Office: U Calif Bodega Marine Lab PO Box 247 Bodega Bay CA 94923-0247 Home Phone: 707-875-2215; Office Phone: 707-875-2010. Business E-Mail: jsclegg@ucdavis.edu.

CLEGG, MICHAEL TRAN, genetics educator, researcher; b. Pasadena, Calif., Aug. 1, 1941; AA, Sacramento City Coll., 1967; BS, U. Calif., Davis, 1969, PhD, 1972. Asst. prof. Brown U., Providence, 1972—76; assoc. prof. botany and genetics U. Ga., Athens, 1976—82, prof., 1982—84; prof. genetics U. Calif., Riverside, 1984—90, disting. prof. genetics, 1990—2004, dean Coll. Natural & Agrl. Scis., 1994—2000, Presdl. chair, 2000—02; Donald Bren prof. biol. scis. U. Calif., Irvine, 2004—. Mem. Bd. Biology, NRC, 1993—2001, chmn. Bd. Biology, 1993—98, chair Commn. Life Scis., 1998—2000. Assoc. editor Am. Naturalist, 1980—84, Genetics, 1982—88, Theoretical Population Biology, 1984—87, Molecular Phylogenetics & Evolution, 1992—2000, mem. editl. bd. Proceedings NAS, 1995—97, Molecular Ecology, 1993—2000; contbr. articles to profl. jours. Sgt. US Army, 1960—63. Recipient Darwin Prize, Edinburgh U., 1995; fellow John Simon Guggenheim Meml. Found., 1981—82. Fellow: Am. Acad. Arts & Scis., Third World Acad. Scis. (assoc.); mem.: NAS (fgn. sec. 2002—), Genetics Soc. America, Am. Soc. Naturalists, Nat. Acad. Exact Phys. & Natural Scis. Argentina (corr.), Am. Genetic Assn. (coun. mem. 1982—85, 1999—2002, exec. v.p. 1988-1992), Soc. Molecular Biology & Evolution (past pres.). Avocations: skiing, flying. Office: U Calif Sch Biological Sciences Mail Code 2525 Irvine CA 92697-2525 Office Phone: 949-824-4490. Office Fax: 949-824-2181. E-mail: mclegg@uci.edu.

CLEMENDOR, ANTHONY ARNOLD, obstetrician, educator, gynecologist, educator; b. Port-of-Spain, Trinidad, Nov. 8, 1933; came to US, 1954, naturalized, 1959; s. Anthony Arnold and Beatrice Helen (Stewart) C.; m. Elaine Browne, May 31, 1958 (dec. May, 1991); children: Anthony Arnold, David Alan; m. Janat Jenkins, Sept. 23, 1993. AB, NYU, 1959; MD, Howard U., 1963. Diplomate Am. Bd. Ob-Gyn. Intern USPHS, SI, NY, 1963-64; resident Met. Hosp. Ctr., NYC, 1964-68, chief outpatient dept. ob-gyn, 1969-73; med. dir. family planning Human Resources Adminstrn., NYC, 1973-74; assoc. dean student affairs, dir. office minority affairs NY Med. Coll., Valhalla, 1974-97, assoc. clin. prof. dept. ob-gyn., 1978-90, prof. clin. ob-gyn., 1990-98, clin. prof. ob-gyn., 1998—. Bd. dirs. Elmcore, Caribbean-Am. Ctr. N.Y.C., Nat. Assn. Minority Med. Educators, Inc., 1978-88, Empire State Med. Sci. and Ednl. Found., Inc., Caribbean Am. Ctr. N.Y., 1988-91; mem. Nat. Urban League, N.Y. Urban League; life mem. NAACP. Fellow ACOG, APHA; mem. AMA (survey team liaison com. on med. edn. 1989—97, treas. PAC, 1997-2009, liaison com. on med. edn. 1989-97, del. N.Y. State 1998-2005, mem. com. to end ethnic and racial healthcare disparities, 2005—2011), Am. Fertility Soc., Nat. Med. Assn., Med. Soc. State of N.Y. (treas. PAC 1997, councilor 1999-2002, asst. sec. 2002, treas. 2004-05), N.Y. County Med. Soc. (sec. 1989, v.p. 1990, pres. elect 1991, pres. 1992-93, bd. trustees, chmn. bd. trustees 1997-98), N.Y. Acad. Medicine, N.Y. Gynecol. Soc. (v.p. 1986, pres. 1988) Personal E-mail: aclemendor@aol.com.

CLEMENS, ANDREAS, endocrinologist, medical director; b. Hildesheim, Germany, May 6, 1966; s. Herbert and Dorothea Clemens; m. Ulrike Von Reyher, Apr. 14, 1969; children: Oscar K.C. Von Reyher children: Carlo H. H. Von Reyher. MD, U. of Göttingen, Germany, 1993; D in Internal Medicine, U. of Heidelberg, Germany, 2001. Resident in diabetologist Hosp. Ludwigshafen, 2001—02; resident in endocrinology U. Heidelberg, 2000—02; physician, dept. gastroenterology U. of Kiel, Kiel, Germany, 1994—95, pathologist, 1995—97; physician, dept. endocrinology U. of Heidelberg, 1997—2000; physician, team leader dept. of metabolism Klinikum Ludwigshafen, Ludwigshafen, Germany, 2000—01; med. advisor Pfizer GmbH, Karlsruhe, Germany, 2001—05; global med. advisor cardiovascular metabolic hdqrs. Boehringer Ingelheim GmbH, 2005—10; global sr. dir., clin. devel. & med. affairs cardiovasc. metabolic hdqrs. Boehringer Ingelheim Pharma GmbH & Co. KG, 2010—. Contbr. articles to profl. jours. Office: Boehringer Ingelheim Pharma GmbH & Co KG CD Clinical Development and Med Affairs Ingelheim am Rhein 55216 Germany Office Phone: +49 6132 77 90606. E-mail: andreas.clemens@boehringer-ingelheim.com.

CLEMENS, ROSEMARY A., health facility administrator; m. Mitchel Greenfield Garren, Aug. 30, 1985 (dec. Dec. 2006). BA, St. John's U., 1966; MA, NYU, 1968, PhD, 1973. Assoc. prof. Fordham U. Sch. Social Work and Edn., NYC, 1973—83; dir. strategic planning and mktg. NY Hosp., NYC, 1983—88; clin. instr. Cornell Med. Coll., Dept. Pub. Health, NYC, 1983—88; dir. AIDS and adolscent awareness project Women's City Club, NYC, 1988—92; dep. dir. NY State Inst. Basic Rsch. Devel. Disabilities, 1992—96; devel. and program dir. Skin Cancer Found., NYC, 1996—98; pres., CEO N.Y. divsn. Prevent Blindness Am., NYC, 1998—2001; CEO N.Y.Children's Vision Coalition, NYC, 2001—08; mem. curriculum com. Sch. Bus. & Mgmt., Thomas Edison State Coll., Trenton, NJ, 2006—. Author: (book) Lessons to be Learned - Adolescents and AIDS (Cmty. Achievement Award - NYS Optometric Assn, 2004). Bd. mem. Cmty. Bd. #1, Women's City Club, UN Assn., NYC, 1975—2010; rsch. assoc. Gov. Nelson A. Rockefeller Presdl. Campaign, 1968—69, Mayor John Lindsay's Adminstrn., NYC, 1973—75; dir. decentralization studies State Sen. Roy M. Goodman Commn. on N.Y.C. Governance, 1975—77; rsch. asst. Ford Found., 1968. Mem.: Worldview Inst. (UNA-NY) (founder), NY Rotary Found. (trustee), Yale Club of NYC. Avocations: travel, reading, theater. Home: 26 Spring St Sag Harbor NY 11963 also: 138 E 36 St New York NY 10016 Personal E-mail: rosemaryclemens@aol.com.

CLEMENS, THOMAS L., medical educator; b. Sellersville, Pa., July 27, 1951; BS, Goshen Coll., 1973, PhD, U. London, 1980. Prof. Johns Hopkins Sch. Medicine, 2009—. Office: 601 Caroline St Baltimore MD 21287 Business E-Mail: tclemen5@jhmi.edu.

CLEMENT, MONICA LOUISE, neuropsychologist; b. Augusta, Ga., Oct. 27, 1977; d. Jasper and Annie J. Jefferson. BS, SUNY, Stony Brook, 1999; PhD, Ohio State U., Columbus, 2005. Psychology intern Northport VA Med. Ctr., NY, 2004—05; postdoc. fellow clin. neuropsychology Maplewood, NJ, 2005—07; asst. dir. clin. svcs. War Related Illness Injury Study Ctr., 2009—. Contbr. chapters to books. Fellow, NIH, 1997—99, Ohio State U., 1999; scholar, NSF, 1995—99. Mem.: APA (MFP fellow 1999—2002), Internat. Neuropsychological Soc., Nat. Assn. Black Psychologists (chmn. student cir. rsch. com. 2003—05), Psi Chi (dir. undergrad. rsch. conf. 1998—99), Golden Key, Phi Beta Kappa, Phi Kappa Phi. Personal E-mail: scorpiamlj@hotmail.com.

CLEMENTE, CARMINE DOMENIC, anatomist, educator; b. Penns Grove, NJ, Apr. 29, 1928; s. Ermanno and Caroline (Friozzi) Clemente; m. Juliette Vance, Sept. 19, 1968. AB, U. Pa., 1948, MS, 1950, PhD, 1952; postdoctoral fellow, U. London, 1953—54. Asst. instr. anatomy U. Pa., 1950—52; mem. faculty UCLA, 1952—, prof., 1963—95, chmn. dept. anatomy, 1963—73, dir. brain rsch. inst., 1976—87, prof. pathology, neurobiology and anatomy, 1995—, Disting. prof. neurobiology and anatomy, 2004—; prof. surg. anatomy Charles R. Drew U. Medicine and Sci., LA, 1974—. Hon. rsch. assoc. Univ. Coll., U. London, 1953—54; vis. scientist Nat. Inst. Med. Rsch., Mill Hill, London, 1988—89, London, 1991; cons. VA Hosp., Sepulveda, Calif., 1956—96, NIH; mem. med. adv. panel Bank Am.-Giannini Found., 1963—98; chmn. sci. adv. com., bd. dirs. Nat. Paraplegia Found.; bd. dirs. Charles R. Drew U., 1985—94. Author: Aggression and Defense: Neurol Mechanisms and Social Patterns, 1967, Physiological Correlates of Dreaming, 1967, Sleep and the Maturing Nervous System, 1972, Anatomy: An Atlas of the Human Body, 1975, 5th edit., 2006, Clemente's Anatomy Dissector, 2001, 2d edit., 2006; editor: Gray's Anatomy, 1973, 30th Am. edit., 1985; editor-in-chief: Exptl. Neurology, 1973—86, assoc. editor: Neurol. Rsch., Jour. Clin. Anatomy; contbr. articles to sci. jours. Recipient award for merit in sci., Nat. Paraplegia Found., 1973, 23rd Ann. Rehfuss Lectr. and medal, Jefferson Coll., 1986, award for excellence in med. edn., UCLA, 1996, Award of Extraordinary merit, UCLA Med. Alumni Assn., 1997, Significant Early Contributor award, Sleep rsch. Soc., 2003, Disting. Tchr. award, Alpha Omega Alpha, 2006; fellow John Simon Guggenheim Meml. Found., 1988—89. Fellow: Am. Assn. Anatomists (v.p. 1972, pres. 1976—77, Henry Gray award 1993, Disting. Educator award 2009); mem.: NAS (mem. com. on neuropathology, mem. BEAR coms.), Soc. for Neurosci., Japan Soc. Promotion of Sci. (Rsch. award 1978), NY Acad. Scis., Med. Rsch. Assn. Calif. (bd. dirs. 1976—87), AMA-Assn. Am. Med. Colls. (mem. liason com. on med. edn. 1981—87, AOA Robert Glaser Tchg. award 2006), Internat. Brain Rsch. Orgn., Biol. Stain Commn., Assn. Anatomy Chairmen (pres. 1972), Nat. Bd. Med. Examiners (bd. dirs. 1978—84, mem. anatomy test com. 1980—84), Coun. Acad. Socs. (mem. adminstrv. bd. 1973—81, chmn. 1979—80), Assn. Am. Med. Colls. (mem. exec. com. 1978—81, disting. svc. mem. 1982), Am. Neurol. Assn., Am. Assn. Clin. Anatomists (Honored Mem. of Yr. 1993), Am. Acad. Neurology, Am. Physiol. Soc., Brain Rsch. Inst. (dir. 1976—87), Pavlovian Soc. N.Am. (pres. 1972, Ann. award 1968), Am. Acad. Cerebral Palsy (hon.), Inst. Medicine of NAS (mem. sci. adv. bd.), Alpha Omega Alpha, Sigma Xi. Democrat. Home: 11737 Bellagio Rd Los Angeles CA 90049-2158 Office: UCLA Sch Medicine Dept Neurobiology Los Angeles CA 90095-0001 Office Phone: 310-825-9566. Business E-Mail: cdclem@ucla.edu.

CLEMENTE, CELESTINO, physician, surgeon; b. Penns Grove, NJ, June 11, 1922; s. Ermanno and Caroline (Friozzi) C.; m. Marie Ann Strangio, Nov. 16, 1946; children: Jeffrey, Roderick, Mark, Laurie Ann, Jonathan. BS, Rutgers U., New Brunswick, NJ, 1942; MD, U. Pa., Phila., 1945. Diplomate Am. Bd. Surgery. Intern Jersey City Med. Ctr., 1945-46; resident in gen. surgery Martland Med. Ctr., 1950-53; practice medicine specializing in gen. surgery Newark, 1953—; dir. surgery Children's Hosp., Newark, 1962-70, St. Vincent's Hosp., Montclair, N.J., 1972-83; trustee United Hosps. Med. Ctr., Newark, 1972-88, v.p. med. affairs, 1975-88. Assoc. clinic prof. surgery N.J. Med. Sch., Newark, 1975—; dir. surgery Roseland (N.J) Surg. Ctr., 1983—, also chmn. bd. Rep. candidate for U.S. Ho. of Reps, N.J., 1968; active Nat. Ad Council/HEW, 1970-74. Served to lt. USNR, 1946-48. Fellow ACS, Internat. Coll. Surgeons; mem. AMA, AAAS, Essex Club (Newark). Home and Office: 364 Ridgewood Ave Glen Ridge NJ 07028-1513 Office: 556 Eagle Rock Ave Roseland NJ 07068-1500 Office Phone: 973-743-5188. E-mail: ccmdnj@aol.com.

CLEMENTI, FRANCESCO, pharmacologist, educator; b. Verona, Italy, Apr. 22, 1936; s. Clementi Aurelio and Maria (Trabucchi) C.; m. Tullia Scamazzo, May 22, 1963; children: Emilio, Maria, Francesca, Chiara. MD, U. Milan, 1960. Asst. prof. U. Milan, 1962-72, prof., 1978—, U. Sassari, Italy, 1972-73, U. Modena, Italy, 1973-78. Dir. CNR Ctr. Cellular and Molecular Pharm.; mem. high health coun. Min. Health, Italy. Editor several books on cellular pharmacology; contbr. articles to profl. jours. Mem.: Acaddemia Europaea, Acad. Dei Lincei, Com. Biology Nat. Rsch. Coun. Italy, European Cell Biology Orgn. (sec. gen. 1989—95), Internat. Fedn. Cell Biology (pres. 1988—92). Roman Catholic. Office: U Milan Dept Pharmacology Via Vanvitelli 32 20129 Milan Italy E-mail: francesco.clementi@unimi.it.

CLEMENTS, DAVID HARRISON, III, orthopaedic surgeon, educator; MD, Temple U., Phila., Pa., 1982. Lic. Pa., 1983, NJ, 1989, diplomate Am. Bd. Orthopaedic Surgery. Intern gen. surgery Temple Univ. Hosp., 1983, resident orthop. surgery, 1988; fellow Hosp. for Spl. Surgery, 1989; assoc. prof. orthop. surgery Cooper Univ. Hosp., dir. scoliosis program, dir. orthop. spine surgery. Named one of the Top Doctors, Phila. Mag., 2011. Office: Cooper University Hospital Three Cooper Plz Ste 104 Camden NJ 08103 Office Phone: 856-968-7965. Office Fax: 856-968-8697.

CLEMENTS, JOHN ALLEN, physiologist; b. Auburn, NY, Mar. 16, 1923; s. Harry Vernon and May (Porter) C.; m. Margot Sloan Power, Nov. 19, 1949; children: Christine, Carolyn. MD, Cornell U., 1947; MD (honoris causa), U. Berne, Switzerland, 1990, Philipps U., Marburg, Germany, 1992; ScD (honoris causa), U. Manitoba, 1993. Rsch. asst. dept. physiology Med. Coll. N.Y., Cornell U., Ithaca, 1947-49, commd. 1st lt. U.S. Army, 1949, advanced through grades to capt., 1951; asst. chief clin. investigation br. Army Chem. Ctr., 1951-61; assoc. rsch. physiologist U. Calif., San Francisco, 1961-64, prof. pediat., 1964—2004, Julius H. Comroe Jr. prof. pulmonary biology, 1987—2004, mem. staff Cardiovascular Research Inst. Cardiovasc. Rsch. Inst., San Francisco, 1961—2004, mem. grad. group in biophysics, 1987—2004. Career investigator Am. Heart Assn., 1964-93; mem. group in biophysics and med. physics U. Calif., Berkeley, 1969-87; cons. Surgeon Gen. USPHS, 1964-68, Surgeon Gen. U.S. Army, 1972-79; sci. counselor Nat. Heart and Lung Inst., 1972-75; Bowditch lectr. Am. Physiol. Soc., 1961; 2d ann. lectr. Neonatal Soc., London, 1965; Distinguished lectr. Can. Soc. Clin. Investigation, 1973; mem. Nat. Heart Lung and Blood Adv. Coun., 1990-93; Ulf von Euler Meml. lectr. Karolinska Inst., 1996. Mem. editorial bd.: Jour. Applied Physiology, 1961-65, Am. Jour. Physiology, 1965-72, Physiol. Reviews, 1965-72, Jour. Developmental Physiology, 1979-85; assoc. editor: Am. Rev. Respiratory Diseases, 1973-79; chmn. publs. policy com.: Am. Thoracic Soc., 1982-86; assoc. editor: Ann. Rev. Physiology, 1988-93, Am. Jour. Physiology: Lung Cellular and Molecular Physiology, 1988-94. Recipient Dept. Army R & D Achievement award, 1961, Modern Medicine Disting. Achievement award, 1973, Howard Taylor Ricketts medal and award U. Chgo., 1975, Mellon award U. Pitts., 1976, Calif. medal Am. Lung Assn. Calif., 1981, Trudeau medal Am. Lung Assn., 1982, Internat. award Gairdner Found., 1983, J. Burns Amberson lecture award Am. Thoracic Soc. and Am. Lung Assn., 1991, Christopher Columbus Discovery award NIH, 1992, Lasker-DeBakey Clin. Med. Rsch. award, Lasker Found., 1994, Virginia Apgar award Am. Acad. Pediat., 1994, Warren Alpert Found. award, 1995, Discover award Pharm. Rsch. and Mfrs. of Am.; named Mayo Clinic Disting. Lectr. in Med. Sci., 1993, Am. Physiol. Soc. Julius H. Conroe Disting. Lectr., 2000. Fellow AAAS, Am. Acad. Arts and Scis., Am. Coll. Chest Physicians (hon.), Royal Coll. Physicians (London); mem. NAS, Western Assn. Physicians, Western Soc. Clin. Rsch.(Polln prize, 2008), Perinatal Rsch. Soc. (councillor 1973-75), Am. Lung Assn. (hon., life), Nat. Acad. Sci. (elect mem. 1974). Office: U Calif Sch Medicine Cardiovascular Rsch Inst 3333 California St Ste 150 San Francisco CA 94118-1944 Business E-Mail: john.clements@ucsf.edu.

CLEMENTS, LYNNE FLEMING, marriage and family therapist, application developer; b. Bklyn., Aug. 8, 1945; d. Daniel Gillies and Dorothy Frances (Zitzmann) Fleming; m. Louis Myrick Clements, Feb. 19, 1972; children: Ryan Louis, Glenn Fleming. BA in Sociology, Bradley Univ., 1967; MSW, Fordham Univ., 1973; post grad. studies, Columbia Univ., 1970-71; cert. in family therapy, Inst. for Mental Health Edn., 1990. LCSW NJ, cert. social work mgr. Computer programmer Employer's Comml. Union Group Ins. Co., Boston, 1967-69, Harvard Bus. Sch., Cambridge, Mass., 1969-70, Volkswagon of Am., Englewood Cliffs, NJ, 1971; psychiat. social worker Associated Cath. Charities Family and Children's Svc., Paramus, NJ, 1973-74, Christian Health Ctr., Wyckoff, NJ, 1976; owner, mgr. Wicker Wagon, Bergenfield, NJ, 1977-85; psychotherapist The Psychotherapy Counseling Ctr., Bergenfield, NJ, 1982-89; programmer analyst Atlas Computing Svc., Secaucus, NJ, 1984-86; program coord., family therapist Divsn. Family Guidance, Hackensack, NJ, 1986-91; pres. Corp. Family Resources, Ridgewood, NJ, 1989—; family therapist cons. Family Recovery of Valley View, White Plains,

NY, 1992-94, Furman Clinic, Fair Lawn, NJ, 1995-96, Van Ost Inst. for Family Living, Englewood, NJ, 1996; cert. social work mgr., 1997—. Part time family therapist NJ Ctr. Psychotherapy Inc., Ridgefield Pk., NJ, 1990; mem. Ridgewood Guild, 2010; founder, chmn. Ridgewood Guild Film Festival, 2011. Chmn. curriculum enhancement com. Bergen County Acad. Advancement Sci. and Tech., NJ, 1992—96; chmn. entertainment Bergen County Children's Festival, 1993; founder, chmn. Bergenfield Coun. of the Arts, 1993; chmn., designer Bergenfield Coun. Arts, 1993—99, chmn. author and poet program, 1996—2007, Bergenfield Coun. of the Arts, 1996—; mem. fundraising com., arts programming chmn. Bergenfield Cmty. Ctr., 2000—; co-chmn. Bergenfield Film Festival, 2004—; co-chmn., designer Bergenfield A Taste of the Arts Festival, 2003—10; sec. Mayor's Beautify Bergenfield Com., NJ, 1991—95; chmn. bd. cmty. play ctr. All Saints Ch., 1977—78, Sunday sch. tchr., 1982—89; mem. Twin Boro Youth Ministry Coun., 1989—. Recipient First and Second Pl. awards, Bergenfield Art Contest, 1980, Best Practice Award for Author/Poet Program, N.J. Dept. Edn., 2003; grantee NIMH, 1973. Mem.: NASW, AAUW, N.J. Coalition Mental Health Profl., N.J. Soc. Clin. Social Workers (bd. dir., chmn. mktg. and vendor 1999—2003, membership chmn. 2003—), N.J. Commerce and Indsl. Assn. (child care com. 1990—, human resources com. 1990—), Fordham U. Alumni Assn., Am. Orthopsychiatric Assn., Acad. Cert. Social Workers, Gifted Child Soc. (parent workshop coord. 1989—, bd dir.), Women of Accomplishments (founder, pres. 1990—95, chmn. women's coalition conf. 1993), Zonta (Amelia Earhart chmn. 1987—88, chmn. status women com. 1993—94, lit. com. 1995—2011, Ridgewood Guild 2010—, chmn. Ridgewood Guild Film Festival 2011). Episcopalian. Avocations: walking, art, music, crafts, boating, acting. Home: 148 Harcourt Ave Bergenfield NJ 07621-1917 Office: Corp Family Resources 15 Godwin Ave Ste 1 Ridgewood NJ 07450-3739 Office Phone: 201-670-0269. Personal E-mail: lynne.clements@att.net.

CLEMENTS, MICHAEL CRAIG, health services consulting executive, retired renal dialysis technician; b. Cin., Sept. 17, 1945; s. Marvin Hubert and Mildred Helen (Rabe) C.; m. Minnie Faye Pospisil, Dec. 1, 1972; children: Melissa Ayn, Michael Aaron. Student, U. Cin., 1968-70; EMT/paramedic, Good Samaritan Health Ctr., 1980. Cert. renal dialysis technician. Hemodialysis technician Christ Hosp., Cin., 1968-79; tech. svcs. dir. Dialysis Clinic, Inc., Cin., 1980-91; pres. Critical Care Svcs., Inc., Mason, Ohio, 1987—. Firefighter/paramedic Mason Vol. Fire Co., 1978-85, EMS tng. officer, 1984, EMS capt., 1985; coop employers environ. and sci. lab. tech. programs Cin. State Coll. Contbr. articles to profl. jours. Mem. Mason Environ. Adv. Commn., 1990—, vice chmn., 1992-93, bus. and parent curriculum review com. Mason City Schs., 1992; employer advisor coop. program Cin. Tech. Coll. Biomed. Engring. Tech., 1986-91; with U.S. Naval Sea Cadet Corps, 2002—, comdg. officer Cin. divsn., 2006—09, house staff 2009-. With USN, 1964-70. Mem.: Nat. Assn. Nephrol. Tech., Ohio Acad. Sci., Assn. Advancement of Med. Instrumentation. Mem. Ch. of Christ. Office: Critical Care Svcs Inc 7562 Central Parke Blvd Mason OH 45040-6816 Office Phone: 513-573-9901. Business E-Mail: michael.clements@criticalcareservicesinc.com.

CLEVELAND, WILLIAM LOUIS, biologist; s. Alfred Eugene Cleveland and Marjorie Jeter Pipkin; m. Fay Ray Hallen, Mar. 2, 1973; 1 child, Jonathan Hallegua. BS in Physics, Columbia U., NYC, 1967; PhD in Chemistry, Rutgers U., NB, NJ, 1974. Instrument maker, physics dept. Columbia U., 1965—68, sr. staff assoc. microbiology, 1980—81, asst. prof. microbiology, 1982—90, rsch. scientist microbiology, 1990—2000, rsch. scientist medicine, 2000—08; dir. rsch. lab. St. Luke's-Roosevelt Hosp. Ctr., NYC, 1985—2009; pres. Behaviorome Scis., Inc., NYC, 2009—. Mem.: Harvey Soc. NY. Achievements include first to use high-dose glycine treatment for refractory obsessive-compulsive disorder and body dysmorphic disorder, object recognition algorithms to replace human observer in biological microscopy; idiotypic network theory for immune system, multistate allosteric model for t-cell antigen receptor, protein-free culture medium for hybridoma and other types of cells. Office: Behaviorome Scis Inc PO Box 250495 New York NY 10025-1525 Business E-Mail: wlcleveland@behavioromesciences.com.

CLEVER, LINDA HAWES, physician; b. Seattle; d. Nathan Harrison and Evelyn Lorraine (Johnson) Hawes; m. James Alexander Clever, Aug. 20, 1960; 1 child, Sarah Lou. AB with distinction, Stanford U., 1962, MD, 1965. Diplomate Am. Bd. Internal Medicine, Am. Bd. Preventive Medicine in Occupl. Medicine. Intern Stanford U. Hosp., Palo Alto, Calif., 1965—66, resident, 1966—67, fellow in infectious disease, 1967—68; fellow in cmty. medicine U. Calif., San Francisco, 1968—69, resident, 1969—70; med. dir. Sister Mary Philippa Diagonostic and Treatment Ctr. St. Mary's Hosp., San Francisco, 1970—77; chmn. dept. occupl. health Calif. Pacific Med. Ctr., San Francisco, 1977—99. Clin. prof. medicine U. Calif. Med. Sch., San Francisco; founder pres. RENEW, 1999—; NIIH rsch. fellow Sch. Medicine, Stanford U., 1967—68; mem. nat. adv. panel Inst. Rsch. on Women and Gender, 1990—, chair panel, 1998—2000; mem. San Francisco Comprehensive Health Planning Coun., 1971—76; bd. dirs., mem. Calif.-OSHA Adv. Com. on Hazard Evaluation Sys. and Info. Svc., 1979—85, Calif. Statewide Profl. Stds. Rev. Coun., 1977—81, San Francisco Regional Commn. on White House Fellows, 1979—81, 1983—89, 1992, 95, chmn., 1977—81, 2001—02; bd. sci. counselors Nat. Inst. Occupl. Safety and Health, 1995—2001. Editor We. Jour. Medicine, 1990—98; contbr. articles to profl. jours. Trustee Stanford U., 1972—76, 1981—91, v.p., 1985—91; pres. RENEW, 2000—; bd. dirs. Sta. KQED, 1976—83, chmn., 1979—81; bd. dirs. Ind. Sector, 1980—86, vice chmn., 1985—86; bd. dirs. San Francisco U. H.S., 1983—90, chmn., 1987—88; active Womens Forum West, 1980—, bd. dirs., 1992—93; mem. Lucile Packard Children's Hosp. Bd., 1993—97, Lucile Packard Found. Children, 1997—99; mem. policy adv. com. U. Calif. Berkeley Sch. Pub. Health, 1995—, chair, 1995—2000; bd. dirs. The Redwoods Retirement Cmty., 1996—2001, Buck Inst. for Rsch. in Aging, 2000—; bd. govs. Stanford Med. Alumni Assn., 1997—2002, 2003—, pres., 2003—05; bd. dirs. No. Calif. Presbyn. Homes and Svcs., 2000—, No. Calif. Presbyn. Homes and Svcs. Found., 2004—, chair, 2008—. Master: ACP (gov. No. Calif. region 1984—89, chmn. bd. govs. 1989—90, regent 1990—96, vice chair bd. regents 1994—95); fellow: Am. Coll. Occupl. and Environ. Medicine; mem.: APHA, We. Assn. Physicians (pres. 2003), We. Occupl. Medicine Assn., Calif. Acad. Medicine, Calif. Med. Assn., Inst. Medicine NAS, Stanford U. Women's Club (bd. dirs. 1971—80), Chi Omega. Office: 2300 California St Ste 202 San Francisco CA 94115 1931 Office Phone: 415-600-3321. Business E-Mail: linda.clever@ucsf.edu.

CLICQUÉ, GUY MARCEL, minister; b. Berlin, Sept. 11, 1959; s. Manfred Wilhelm and Rosemarie (Steinecke) Clicqué; m. Regina Kerstin Korn, July 31, 1998. Diploma in chemistry, Friedrich-Alexander U., Erlangen, Germany, 1985, D in Theology, 2000; diploma in theology, Georg-August U., Göttingen, Germany, 1996. Ordained Evang.-Reformed Ch., Germany, 1993. Asst. min. Evang.-Reformed Ch., Erlangen, 1993—96; sci. asst. U. Bayreuth, Germany, 1996—2002; min. Evang. Ref. Ch., Leipzig, Germany, 2002—03; part-time lectr. Luth. U. Applied Scis., Nuremburg, 1999—2008, U. Bayreuth, 2002—, U. Erlangen, 2009—. Cons. Dept. Environment, City of Erlangen, 1989—92; student tutor Inst. Social Ethics, U. Erlangen, 1990—93; part-time secondary sch. tchr. religious pedagogy, 2003—. Author: (book) difference and Parallelism on the Understanding of the Connection Between Theology and Science Using Günther Howe's Reflections, 2000 (Karl-Heim award, 2000); rev. editor, mem. editl. bd.: Evangelium und Wissenschaft, 2000—, mem. editl. adv. bd.: European Jour. Sci. and Theology, 2005—. Recipient Sci. & Religion Course award, Ctr. Theology and Nat. Scis., 2001; scholar Bursary, Ch. Scotland, 1988—89. Mem.: Sci. and Religion Forum, Inst. Religion Age of Sci., European Soc. Study Sci. and Theology, Inst. Ecol. Chemistry (mem. mng. com., sec. 1983—88). Avocations: reading, music, walking, voluntary work. Home: Rathenaustrasse 11 Erlangen 91052 Germany

CLIFTON, JAMES ALBERT, physician, educator; b. Fayetteville, NC, Sept. 18, 1923; s. James Albert Jr. and Flora M. (McNair) Clifton; m. Katherine Rathe, June 25, 1949; children: Susan M.(dec.), Katherine Y., Caroline M. BA, Vanderbilt U., 1944, MD, 1947. Diplomate Am. Bd. Internal Medicine (mem. 1972-81, mem. subsplty. bd. gastroenterology 1968-75, chmn. 1972-75, mem. exec. com. 1978-81, chmn. 1980-81). Intern U. Hosps., Iowa City, 1947—48, resident dept. medicine, 1948—51; staff dept. medicine Thayer VA Hosp., Nashville, 1952—53; asst. clin. medicine Vanderbilt Hosp., Nashville, 1952—53; cons. physician VA Hosp., Iowa City, 1965—93; assoc. medicine dept. internal medicine Coll. Medicine, U. Iowa, 1953—54, chief divsn. gastroenterology, 1953—71, asst. prof. medicine, 1954-58, assoc. prof., 1958—63, prof., 1963—91, prof. emeritus, 1991—, traveling fellow, 1964, vis. prof. dept. physiology, 1964, vice chmn. dept. medicine, 1967—70, chmn. dept. medicine Coll. Medicine, 1970—76, Roy J. Carver prof. medicine, 1974—91, Roy J. Carver prof. emeritus, 1991—, dir. James A. Clifton Ctr. Digestive Diseases, 1985—90, interim dean, 1991—93. Investigator Mt. Desert Isle Biol. Lab., Salisbury Cove, Maine, 1964; vis. faculty mem. Mayo Found. and Mayo Clinic, 1966; vis. prof. dept. medicine U. N.C. Chapel Hill, 1970; cons. gastroenterology and nutrition tng. grants com. Nat. Inst. Arthritis and Metabolic Diseases, NIH, 1964—68, chmn., 1965—68; mem. Nat. Adv. Arthritis and Metabolic Diseases Coun., 1970—73; mem. gastroenterology tng. com. VA, Washington, 1967—71, chmn. tng. grants com., 1971—73; mem. med. adv. bd. Digestive Disease Found., 1969—73; vis. prof. gastroenterology U. London (St. Marks Hosp.), 1984—85; mem. sci. adv. com. Ludwig Inst. Cancer Rsch., Zurich, 1984—95. Internat. editl. bd. Italian Jour. Gastroenterology, 1970—90, Gastroenterology, 1964—68. Recipient Disting. Alumnus of Yr. award, Vanderbilt U. Sch. Medicine, 1984, Disting. Alumnus of Yr. Achievement award, U. Iowa Coll. Medicine, 2000, Disting. Mentoring award, 2002, Disting. Alumni award, U. Iowa Alumni Assn., 2004; fellow, NIH, USPHS, 1955—56, Evans Meml. Hosp., Mass. Meml. Hosps., also Boston U. Sch. Medicine, 1955—56; Phi Connell scholar, Vanderbilt U., 1943—44. Fellow: ACP (bd. regents 1972—79, pres. 1977—78, Alfred Stengel award 1984, Laureate award 1989); mem.: AAUP, AAAS, AMA (liaison com. grad. med. edn. 1976—77), Internat. Soc. Internal Medicine (exec. com. 1978—80), Assn. Profs. Medicine (councillor 1972—73, sec.-treas. 1973—75), Assn. Am. Med. Colls., Am. Physiol. Soc., Soc. Exptl. Biology and Medicine, Assn. Am. Physicians, Am. Clin. and Climatol. Assn. (v.p. 1984), Am. Fedn. Clin. Rsch., Am. Soc. Internal Medicine (Internist of Yr. award Iowa chpt. 1986), Am. Assn. Study Liver Disease, Am. Heart Assn., Am. Gastroent. Assn. (pres. 1970—71), Inst. Medicine NAS, U. Iowa Assn. Emeritus Faculty (pres. 1999—2000), U. Iowa Retirees Assn. (pres. 1999—2000). Home: 39 Audubon Pl Iowa City IA 52245-3437 Office: U Iowa Hosp and Clinics 4 JCP Hawkins Dr Iowa City IA 52242 Home Phone: 319-351-1561; Office Phone: 319-356-1771. Personal E-mail: zybumjim@mchsi.com. Business E-Mail: james-clifton@uiowa.edu.

CLIFTON, NELIDA, retired social worker; b. Buenos Aires, Aug. 16, 1944; arrived in U.S., 1968; d. Juan Antonio and Zaira Elizabeth (Vera) Tovar; m. Mark Earl Jolls, Nov. 8, 1968 (div. July 1984); children: Patricia Elizabeth, Michael Thomas, Diana Marie Kathleen; m. Anthony Gene Clifton, June 19, 1993. BA in Bus. Adminstrn., Nat. Sch. Commerce, Tucuman, Argentina; BA in Psychology magna cum laude, Fairleigh Dickinson U., 1986; postgrad., William Paterson Coll., 1988—89. Cert. diplomate Am. Psychotherapy Assn.; lic. cert. social worker Bd. Social Work Examiners, N.J.; cert. bilingual. Social worker Bergen County Bd. Social Svcs., Rochelle Pk., NJ, 1987—2009. Crisis intervention counselor; phone counselor; cmty. resources referral profl. Mem. APA, NASW, Am. Assn. Christian Counselors, Phi Zeta Kappa, Phi Omega Epsilon, Psi Chi Nat. Honor Socs. Republican. Avocations: reading, chess, tennis, gardening.

CLIFTON, SHAW, retired relief organization administrator; b. Belfast, Northern Ireland, Sept. 21, 1945; m. Helen Ashman, July 5, 1973; 3 children. LLB, U. London, BD with first class honours; PhD in Hist. of Religion, King's Coll., U. London. Commd. officer Salvation Army, 1973, apptd. Burnt Oak corps London, 1973, staff Lit. Dept., Internat. Hdqs., then corps mem. Zimbabwe (then Rhodesia), 1975, vice-prin. Mazowe Secondary Sch., corps officer Bulawayo Citadel Zimbabwe, then corps officer Enfield, North London, 1979, Internat. Hdqs. legal/parliamentary sec., 1982—89, corps officer Bromley Temple, South London, 1989—92, divisional comdr. Durham & Tees divsn., UK Ter., 1992—95, apptd. lt. col., divisional comdr. Mass. divsn., USA Eastern Ter., 1995—97, apptd. col., 1997, territorial comdr. Islamic Republic of Pakistan, 1997—2002, apptd. commr., 2000, territorial comdr. New Zealand, Fiji & Tonga Ter., 2002—04, territorial comdr. UK Ter. with Republic of Ireland, 2004—06, gen. elect, 2006, internat. gen., 2006—11. Author: What Does the Salvationist Say?, 1977, Growing Together, 1984, Strong Doctrine, Strong Mercy, 1985, Never the same again: Encouragement for new and not-so-new Christians, 1997, Who Are These Salvationists?: An Analysis for the 21st Century, 2004, New Love Thinking Aloud About Practical Holiness, 2004. *

CLINE, CAROLYN JOAN, plastic and reconstructive surgeon; b. Boston, May 15, 1941; d. Paul S. and Elizabeth (Flom) Cline. BA, Wellesley Coll., 1962; MA, U. Cin., 1966; PhD, Washington U., 1970; diploma, Washington Sch. Psychiatry, 1972; MD, U. Miami, 1975. Diplomate Am. Bd. Plastic and Reconstructive Surgery. Rsch. asst. Harvard U. Dental Sch., Boston, 1962-64; rsch. asst. physiology Laser Lab., Children's Hosp. Rsch. Found., Cin., 1964, psychology dept. U. Cin., 1964-65; intern in clin. psychology St. Elizabeth's Hosp., Washington, 1966-67; psychologist Alexandria (Va.) Cmty. Mental Health Ctr., 1967-68; rsch. fellow NIH, Washington, 1968-69; chief psychologist Kingsbury Ctr. for Children, Washington, 1969-73; sole practice clin. psychology Washington, 1970-73; intern internal medicine U. Wis. Hosp. Ctr. for Health Sci., Madison, 1975-76; resident in surgery Stanford U. Med. Ctr., 1976-78; fellow microvasc. surgery dept. surgery U. Calif., San Francisco, 1978-79; resident in plastic surgery St. Francis Hosp., San Francisco, 1979-82; practice medicine specializing in plastic and reconstructive surgery, San Francisco, 1982-95; free-lance writer profl. and popular publs., 1995—. Contbr. chpts. to plastic surgery textbooks, articles to profl. jours. Mem. Am. Soc. Plastic and Reconstructive Surgeons, Royal Soc. Medicine, Calif. Medicine Assn., Calif. Soc. Plastic and Reconstructive Surgeons, San Francisco Med. Soc.

CLINE, JOHN CARROLL, psychologist; b. Staunton, Va., Sept. 6, 1955; s. Carroll Hubert and Naomi Edith (Hevener) C.; m. Diane Jeannette Goudreau, May 21, 1983; 1 child, Virginia Goudreau Cline. BA, U. Va., 1977; PhD, U. Toledo, 1984. Lic. psychologist, Conn.; cert. biofeedback; clin. assoc. Am. Bd. Med. Psychotherapists; diplomate Am. Acad. Pain Mgmt., diplomate Am. Acad. Sleep Medicine. Psychology intern U. Toledo, 1980-81; predoctoral intern VA Med. Ctr., West Haven, Conn., 1981-82, attending psychologist, 1984-85; clinician Alcohol Svcs. Orgn., New Haven, 1982-85; team leader, staff psychologist Elmcrest Hosp., Portland, Conn., 1985-86, asst. unit chief, 1986, dir. behavioral medicine svc., 1986-90; pvt. practice psychologist Hamden, Conn., 1986-94; dir. adult outpatient svcs. Inst. of Living, Hartford, Conn., 1990-93; psychol. svcs. cons. Hamden, Conn., 1994—; clin. dir. dept. counseling and psychiat. svcs. Grove Hill Med. Ctr., New Britain, Conn., 1994-2000, chair quality assurance & outcomes mgmt. dept. psychiat. svcs., 1995-2000; psychologist Gaylord Hosp., Wallingford, Conn., 2000—06, sleep psychologist, 2006—08; cons. Conn. Edn. Svcs., Middletown, 2000—; pvt. practice Affiliated Clin. Therapists, Middletown, 1999—2002; sleep psychologist Gaylord Sleep Medicine, North Haven, 2006—08, Alliance Med. Group, Waterbury Sleep Lab., Middlebury, Conn., Hamden Sleep Disorders Ctr., Conn., 2008—, psychologist, behavioral health cons., 2009—. Clin. affiliate Yale Psychol. Svcs. Clinic, Yale U., New Haven, 1985—; cons. psychologist VA Med. Ctr., West Haven, 1985—91; asst. prof. clin. psychiatry U. Conn. Med. Sch., Farmington, Conn., 1991—94; adj. asst. prof. phys. therapy, orthop. phys. therapy program Sch. Grad. and Continuing Edn. Quinnipiac U., Hamden, Conn., 1992—2006; sr. cons. network devel. Inst. of Living, Hartford, 1993—94; affiliate clin. faculty, Grad. Inst. Profl. Psychology U. Hartford, Conn., 1997—99, 2001—06; asst. prof. clin. psychiatry, dept. psychiatry Yale U. Sch. Medicine, New Haven, 2002—. Mem. mission study com. 1st Presbyn. Ch., New Haven, 1990-91; mem. Conn. Coun. Mental Health Providers, 1993-96, chair, 1993-94. Recipient Karl F. Heiser Pres. award, 1996. Fellow Conn. Psychol. Assn. (chair hosp. practice com. 1990-92, practice directorate coord. 1993, pres.-elect 1994, pres. 1995-96, past pres. 1997); mem. AAAS, APA (coun. rep. 1997-99, Karl F. Heiser Presdl. award, 1996), N.Y. Acad. Scis., Assn. Psychiat. Clinics of Conn. (mem. polit. com. 1993-94, mem. edn. com. 1993-94), Fellow Am. Acad. Sleep Medicine, Sr. Fellow Bioreed Back Cert., Inst. Am. Home: 4 Lamkin St Hamden CT 06517-3309 Office: Hamden Sleep Disorders Ctr 2573 Dixwell Ave Hamden CT 06514 Office Phone: 203-668-2813. Personal E-mail: jcclineusa@netscape.net.

CLINE, TERRY LEE, state agency administrator, public health service officer; b. Ardmore, Okla., July 31, 1958; BS in Psychology, U. Okla., 1980; MS in Clin. Psychology, Okla. State U., PhD. Clin. instr. dept. psychiatry Harvard Med. Sch., Boston; staff psychologist McLean Hosp., Belmont, Maine; clin. dir. cmty. health ctr. Cambridge, Mass.; commr. Okla. Dept. Mental Health & Substance Abuse Services, Oklahoma City, 2001—04; sec. health State of Okla., Oklahoma City, 2004—06; adminstr. Substance Abuse and Mental Health Services Adminstrn. (SAMSHA), US Dept. Health & Human Services, Rockville, Md., 2006—08, health attache, US Embassy Baghdad, Iraq, 2008—09; commr. health State of Okla., Oklahoma City, 2009—. Office: Okla Dept Health 1000 NE 10th Oklahoma City OK 73117 Office Phone: 405-271-5600.

CLINTON, LAWRENCE PAUL, psychiatrist; b. Lubbock, Tex., Apr. 27, 1945; s. Lewis Paul Clinton and Dorothy E. (Higgins) Clinton-Billingslea; m. Bonnie Gail Orenstein, June 22, 1969; children: Kerry Elizabeth, Andrew James, Alexander Geoffrey, Kaylin Lee. BA with honors, So. Conn. State Coll., 1966; postgrad., Ohio State U., 1966-68; MD, Hahnemann U., 1972. Diplomate Am. Bd. Psychiatry and Neurology, Am. Bd. Forensic Examiners, Am. Acad. Experts in Traumatic Stress, Am. Bd. Psychotherapy, 2000, Am. Psychiat. Assn. Teaching asst. Ohio State U., Columbus, 1966-68, research fellow, 1966-68; clin. instr. psychiatry Hahnemann U., Phila., 1975-82, asst. clin. prof., 1982—. Chief exec. officer Bldg. Mgmt. Group, Vineland, NJ, 1986—; psychiat. dir. James Guiffre Med. Ctr., Phila., 1976-79; med. dir. PSI Group, 1990-2003; cons. Superior Ct. NJ, 1975—, Ranch Hope, Alloway, NJ, 1989-92, founder Am. Air Mus. Duxford, Pacific Aviation Pearl Harbour, 2008, Elizabeth the Queen Mother M'Nidou-M'Nissing Provincial Pk., 2005, Nat. World War II Mus., 2009, numerous pres. advisor. Contbr. articles to profl. jours. Mem. Am. Security Coun., 1975—, Rep. Senatorial Com., 1978—, Rep. Nat. Com., 1978, The Pres. Club, 1990—. Recipient awards Am. Security Coun., 1982, Buena Regional Sch. Dist., NJ, 1983, Vineland Parent Support and Adv. Group, 1990, Rep. Presdl. Legion of Merit medal, 1992; decorated Chevalier Comdr. Ordre Souverain et Militaire de la Milice du Saint Sepulcre, 1990—, The DaVinci Diamond award, Cambridge Eng., 2004, Named Americas Top Psychriat, 2008; Disting. fellow, 2009. Fellow Am. Bd. Forensic Examiners, Phila. Coll. Physicians and Surgeons, Am. Psychiat. Assn. (disting.); mem. AMA, Internat. Assn. Group Psychotherapy, NJ Psychiat. Soc., Med. Club Phila., World Fedn. Mental Health, InterAm. Coll. Physicians and Surgeons, Hahnemann Undergrad. Rsch. Soc. (treas. 1971-72), Confedn. of Chivalry, Am. Chem. Soc., Soc. d'Chemie (pres. 1965-66), South Jersey Psychiat. Soc. (sec.-treas. 1994-2001, pres. 2001-03, exec. program chmn. 2003—, Disting. Svc. award 2006), Internat. Churchill Soc., The Heritage Found., SPQR Club (pres. 1961-62) (Milford, Conn.), Union League Phila., Union League Phila. Yacht Club, Phi Lambda Kappa (v.p. 1972). Avocations: gardening, art collecting, book collecting, historical biography, golf, sailing. Office: 1138 E Chestnut Ave Bldg 6 Ste A Vineland NJ 08360-5053 Office Phone: 856-696-2660. Personal E-mail: lpclinton@mindspring.com.

CLODIUS, LEO, retired plastic reconstructive surgeon; b. Osnabruck, Germany, Apr. 29, 1930; MD, U. Zurich, Switzerland, 1955. Dipolomate Am. Bd. Plastic Reconstructive Surgery; Swiss Bd. Plastic Reconstructive Surgery. Resident Boston City Hosp., Mass. Meml. Hosp., 1957-60; plastic reconstructive surgeon St. Barnabas Med. Ctr., 1960-63, Roswell Pk. Meml. Inst., 1963; mil. Swiss Army Med. Corps; head plastic surgery U. Zurich, Switzerland, 1964-87. Docent Plastic Surgery Univ., 1983; Swiss Nat. Rsch. grantee, 1973-82; recipient Asellius ring, Tucson, 1973, Scudo D'oro award, 1979, Purkinje medal, 1982, Dieffenbach medal, 1990, Golden Question Mark, Am. Ignorance Soc., 2006. Mem. Swiss Med. Assn. (hon.), Swiss Soc. Plastic Reconstructive Surgery (hon.), Swiss Soc. Aesthetic Surgery, Internat. Soc. Lymphology, Swiss Soc. Lymphology (hon.), Brit. Assn. Plastic Surgeons (hon.), German Assn. Plastic Surgeons (hon., citation 1992), Univ. Catolica Argentina (hon. fgn. mem.). Home: Weid 17 8126 Zumikon Switzerland Home Phone: 0041 44 91821 13.

CLONINGER, CLAUDE ROBERT, psychiatrist, epidemiologist, educator, researcher; b. Beaumont, Tex., Apr. 4, 1944; s. Morris Sheppard and Marie Concetta (Mazzagatti) Cloninger; m. Sharon Lee Rogan, July 11, 1969; children: Bryan Joseph, Kevin Michael. BA, U. Tex., 1966; MD, Washington U., St. Louis, 1970; MD, PhD (hon.), U. Umea, Sweeden, 1983. Diplomate Am. Bd. Psychology and Neurology. Instr. psychiatry Washington U., St. Louis, 1973—74, asst. prof., 1974—78, assoc. prof., 1978—81, prof., 1981—, prof. genetics, 1978—, prof. psychology, 1989—, Wallace Renard prof. psychiatry, 1991—, head dept. psychiatry, 1989—94, dir. ctr. psychobiology personality, 1994—, dir. Ctr. Well-Being, 2002 . Psychiatrist in chief Barnes and Renard Hosps., St. Louis, 1989—94; vis. prof. U. Hawaii, Honolulu, 1978—79, U. Umea, Sweden, 1980; chmn. NIMH Psychopathology Rev. Com., Washington, 1980—84; cons. WHO, Geneva, 1981—, Am. Psychiat. Assn., Washington, 1978—, Nat. Inst. on Alcohol Abuse and Alcoholism, 1984—99, Inst. Medicine, 1986; chmn. genetics initiative schizophrenia NIMH, 1989—97; mental health commr. State of Mo., 1990—95; taskforce mem. psychiatry for person World Psychiatric Assn., 2006—; dir. Anthropedia Inst., 2008—. Author: Feeling Good: The Science of Well-Being, 2004, Know Yourself DVD series of Anthropedia Inst.; editor: Jour. Behavior Genetics, 1980—86, Am. Jour. Human Genetics, 1980—83; assoc. editor Genetic Epidemiology, 1983—92, Jour. Clinical Genetics, 1981—87, Human Heredity, 1989—2000, mem. editl. bd. Arch. Gen. Psychiatry, Comprehensive Psychiatry, Neuropsychopharmacology, Jour. Comprehensive Psychiatry, Jour. Psychiat. Rsch., Jour. Med. Genetics; contbr. articles to profl. jours. Recipient Rsch. Scientist award, NIMH, 1975, 1980, 1985, Strecker award, Inst. Pa. Hosp., 1988, James B. Isaacson award, ISBRA, 1992, Lifetime Achievement award, Am. Soc. Addiction Medicine, 2000, Finnish Psychiatry Assn. Annual medal, Lifetime Achievement award, Internat. Soc. Psychiat. Genetics, 2003. Fellow: AAAS, Am. Psychopathol. Assn. (treas. 1984—89, v.p. 1990, pres. 1991—93, sec. 1994 96, Samuel Hamilton award 1993), Am. Psychiat. Assn. (Adolf Meyer award 1993, Judd Marmor award 2009); mem.: Rsch. Soc. Alcoholism (bd. dirs. 1987—90), Inst. Medicine of NAS, Behavior Genetics Assn. (editl. bd. 1980—), Am. Soc. Human Genetics (editl. bd. 1980—83). Avocations: gardening, reading, travel. Home: 12950 Huntbridge Forest Dr Saint Louis MO 63131 Office: Wash Univ Dept Psychiatry Campus Box 8134 660 S Euclid Saint Louis MO 63110-1002 Home Phone: 314-863-1338; Office Phone: 314-362-7005. Business E-Mail: clon@tci.wustl.edu.

CLOSE, LANNY GARTH, otolaryngologist, educator; b. San Antonio, Aug. 13, 1946; s. James Garth and Nona Lee (Galbraith) C.; m. Sharron Maredith Smith, Nov. 22, 1980; children: Hunter, Maredith. BA summa cum laude, Tex. Tech. U., 1968; MD cum laude, Baylor Coll. Medicine, 1972. Diplomate Am. Bd. Otolaryngology. Resident in surgery Johns Hopkins Hosp., Balt., 1972-74; resident in otolaryngology Baylor Affiliated Hosps., Houston, 1974-77; asst/assoc. prof. otolaryngology U. Tex., Houston, 1977-82; asst. surgeon dept. head & neck surgery M.D. Anderson Hosp., Houston, 1978-79; from assoc. prof. to prof. otolaryngology U. Tex. Southwestern Med. Sch., Dallas, 1982-94; prof., chmn. dept. otolaryngology/head and neck surgery Columbia U., NYC, 1994—. Guest examiner Am. Bd. Otolaryngology, 1993, 94, 96, 97; pres. Columbia-Presbyn. Med. Bd. Contbr. numerous articles to profl. jours. Fellow ACS, Am. Laryngological Assn., The Triological Soc., Am. Rhinological Assn., Am. Broncho Esophageal Assn., Am. Soc. for Head and Neck Surgery, Soc. of Head and Neck Surgery; mem. Royal Soc. Medicine, Johns Hopkins Soc. Scholars, Alpha Omega Alpha. Office: Coll Physicians & Surgeons Columbia U 630 W 168th St New York NY 10032-3702 Business E-Mail: lgc6@columbia.edu.

CLOUGH, DOUGLAS F., internist, educator; MD, Ohio State U. Diplomate Am. Bd. Internal; Medicine-geriatric medicine. Intern Mercy Hosp. of Pitts., resident; fellow in medicine Drexel Univ., clin. asst.prof. medicine; physician Allegheny Gen. Hosp. Named one of Top Doctors, Pitts. mag., 2011. Office: Allegheny General Hospital 320 E N Ave Pittsburgh PA 15212 Office Phone: 412-359-3131. Office Fax: 412-359-4108.

CLOVER, RICHARD D., dean; MD, U. Okla. Assoc. v.p. health affairs/health infomatics U. Louisville, Ky., dean, Sch. Pub. Health and Info. Sciences Ky. Mem. Nat. Bd. Pub. Health Examiners, Nat. Vaccine Adv. Com., 2007—, Am. Bd. Family Medicine. Fellow: Am. Acad. Family Physicians; mem.: Inst. Medicine, Alpha Omega Alpha. Mailing: 485 E Gray St Louisville KY 40202 Office Phone: 502-852-3297. Office Fax: 502-852-3291. E-mail: rclover@louisville.edu.

CLOWES, ALEXANDER WHITEHILL, surgeon, educator; b. Boston, Oct. 9, 1946; s. George H.A. Jr. and Margaret Gracey (Jackson) Clowes; m. Monika Meyer (dec.); m. Susan E. Detweiler. AB, Harvard U., 1968, MD, 1972. Resident in surgery Case Western Reserve, Cleve., 1972-74, 76-79; rsch. fellow in pathology Harvard Med. Sch., Boston, 1974-76; fellow in vascular surgery Brigham and Womens Hosp. Harvard Med. Sch., 1979-80; asst. prof. surgery U. Wash., Seattle, 1980-85, assoc. prof., 1985-90, prof., 1990—, assoc. chmn. dept., 1989-91, acting chmn. dept., 1992-93, adj. prof. pathology, 1992, chief divsn. vascular surgery, 1995—2007, dept. vice chmn., 1995—, V. Paul Gavora and Helen S. and John A. Schilling prof. surgery, 2005—. Contbr.;, author (numerous sci. papers). Trustee Marine Biol. Labs, Woods Hole, Mass., 1989—2000, Seattle Symphony, 1994—2006, v.p., 1998—2006, 2008—; bd. dirs. Seattle Chamber Music Festival, 1990. Recipient Rsch. Career Devel. award, NIH, 1982—87; Tng. fellow, 1974—77, Loyal Davis Traveling Surg. scholar, ACS, 1987. Mem.: N.Am. Vascular Biology Orgn. (pres. 2001-02), Soc. Vascular Surgery, Seattle Surg. Soc., Internat. Soc. Applied Cardiovasc. Biology, Am. Soc. Cell Biology, Am. Heart Assn. (coun. on arteriosclerosis), Am. Assn. Pathologists, Am. Surg. Assn., Quisset Yacht Club, Cruising Club Am., Sigma Xi. Episcopalian. Home: 3425 Perkins Ln W Seattle WA 98199-1858 Office: U Wash Dept Surgery PO Box 356410 Seattle WA 98195-6410 Office Phone: 206-598-9760.

CLUNIE, GORDON JAMES AITKEN, surgeon, researcher; b. Suva, Fiji, Mar. 29, 1932; s. Thomas Anderson Clunie and Agnes Smith Aitken; m. Jess Anne Crozier, Dec. 29, 1957; children: David Alexander, Christine Louise, Pamela Elizabeth. MB ChB, U. Edinburgh, Scotland, 1956, ChM, 1968, DSc, 1993. Fellow Royal Coll. Surgeons, Edinburgh, 1961, Eng., 1962, Royal Australian Coll. Surgeons, Melbourne, 1969. Lectr. surg. sci. U. Edinburgh, 1964-67; reader in surgery U. Queensland, Brisbane, Australia, 1968-73, prof. surgery, 1973-78, U. Melbourne, 1978-95; deputy dean Faculty of Medicine, U. Melbourne, 1986-95; dean Faculty of Medicine, Dentistry & Health Scis. U. Melbourne, 1995-97; sr. med. cons. Anti-Cancer Coun. Victoria, Carlton, Australia, 1998—2003. Sr. examiner gen. surgery Royal Australian Coll. Surgeons, Melbourne, 1988-92, chmn. bd. basic surg. tng., 1995-99, chmn. ct. of examiners, 1999-2000; chmn. med. and sci. com. Anti-Cancer Coun. Victoria, Australia, 1984-88. Editor-in-chief Australian & New Zealand Jour. of Surgery, 1990-95; editor Integrated Therapy of Cancer, 1984, Textbook of Surgery, 1997. Capt. Royal Army Med. Corps, 1957-59. Mem. Surg. Rsch. Soc. Australia and New Zealand (pres. 1975-77), Clin. Oncological Soc. Australia (pres. 1983-85), Internat. Surg. Soc., Transplantation Soc., Australian Soc. Immunology, Internat. Assn. Endocrine Surgeons, Transplantation Soc. Australia and New Zealand. Avocations: reading, music, swimming. E-mail: gclunie@bigpond.com.

CLUSIN, WILLIAM T., physician, neuroscientist, cardiologist, educator; b. Chgo., Mar. 31, 1949; s. Edward M. and Lorena M. Clusin; children: Jonathan A., Daniel P, Joshua D, Audrey A. BS, MIT, Cambridge, MA, 1970; MD, Albert Einstein Coll. Medicine, Bronx, NY, PhD, 1976. Diplomate Nat. Bd. Med. Examiners, 1977, Am. Bd. Internal Medicine, 1981, cardiovascular disease Am. Bd. of Internal Medicine, 1993. Resident medicine Stanford Med. Sch., Calif., 1976—81, fellow cardiology; attending physician Stanford Hosp.; asst. prof. medicine Stanford U., assoc. prof. medicine with tenure, 1989—. Contbr. book, articles to profl. jours. Fellow: ACP, Royal Soc. Medicine; mem.: Nat. Insts. Health Study Sect., Biophysical Soc., Soc. Gen. Physiologists, Am. Heart Assn. (Established Investigatorship 1984—89), Alpha Omega Alpha. Achievements include discovery of calcium activated potassium channels in the nervous system; calcium transients in intact hearts; over 2000 citations to published work. Home: 946 Valdez Pl Stanford CA 94305 Office: Stanford Univ Med Ctr 300 Pasteur Dr Stanford CA 94305 Office Phone: 650-723-7395. Home Fax: 650-725-7568.

CLUTTER, WILLIAM EDWARD, endocrinologist, educator; BS, Ohio State U., 1972, MD, 1975. Diplomate Am. Bd. Internal Medicine, 1978, Am. Bd. Internal Medicine-endocrinology, diabetes and metabolism, 1981. Fellow metabolism and endocrinology Barnes Hosp. at Wash. Univ. Sch.l of Medicine, St. Louis, 1980; resident internal medicine Barnes Hosp., St. Louis, 1981; hosp. affiliation includes Barnes-Jewish Hosp.; assoc. prof. medicine Wash. Univ., St Louis. Recipient Maurice B. Rusoff award, Disting. Svc. Tchg. award, Wash. Univ. Sch. of Medicine, 1993, 1994, 1996, 1997, John P. Atkinson Outstanding Tchr. award, 1997, Sr. Class Tchr. of the Year award, 1998, Clin.Tchr. of the Year award, 1999; named one of Best Doctors in America, Best Doctors, Inc., 2003—10, America's Top Doctors, Castle Connolly Med. Ltd., 2005—10. Office: Wahington University School of Medicine Campus Box 8121 660 S Euclid Ave Saint Louis MO 63110 Office Phone: 314-362-8064. Office Fax: 314-747-1080. E-mail: wclutter@wustl.edu.

COAN, RICHARD WELTON, psychologist, educator; b. Martinez, Calif., Jan. 24, 1928; s. Otis Welton and Esta Dorothy (Wilson) C.; m. Edith Margaret Vedova, Oct 17, 2003; children: Lisa Anderson, Cynthia, Angela Lambert, Abbie. BA in Psychology, U. Calif., Berkeley, 1948, MA in Psychology, 1950; PhD in Psychology, U. So. Calif., 1955. Psychology instr. L.A. City Coll., 1950-55; rsch. assoc. psychology U. Ill., Urbana, 1955-57; from asst. prof. to prof. psychology U. Ariz., Tucson, 1957-89, prof. emeritus, 1989—. Author: (books) The Optimal Personality, 1974, Hero, Artist, Sage, or Saint?, 1977, Psychologists: Personal and Theoretical Pathways, 1979, Psychology of Adjustment, 1983, Human Consciousness and Its Evolution, 1987, A Princess for Larkin, 2001, Shaul of Tarsos, 2004, Horatio, 2006, Masculine, Feminine and Fully Human, 2008. Democrat. Avocations: musical composition, writing novels and poetry. Home: 2992 W Royal Copeland Dr Tucson AZ 85745 E-mail: rwcoan@cox.net.

COATES, THOMAS DUANE, pediatrician, hematologist, educator; b. Bay City, Mich., 1945; MD, U. Mich., 1975. Cert. Pediat., 1980, Pediatric Hematology-Oncology, 1982. Intern pediat. Riley Children's Hosp., Ind., 1975—76, resident pediat. hematology Ind., 1976—78, fellowship Ind., 1978—81; assoc. prof. pediat. and pathology Keck Sch. Medicine, U. So. Calif.; head hematology Children's Ctr. for Cancer and Blood Diseases Children's Hosp. LA. Contbr. articles to med. jours. Office: Childrens Hosp LA 4650 Sunset Blvd, MS #54 Los Angeles CA 90027 Office Phone: 323-361-2352. Office Fax: 323-660-9321. E-mail: tcoates@usc.edu.

COBABE, ALVIN FRED, retired surgeon, small business owner; b. Slatterville, Utah, Nov. 7, 1917; s. Fredrick James and Hazel (Hudman) Cobabe; m. June Heslop, Nov. 10, 1937; children: Carolyn, Gayla, Shawna, Aleta. AS, Weber State Coll., Ogden, 1957; BS, U. Utah, Salt Lake City, 1960, MD, 1963. Cert. Am. Soc. Clin. Hypnosis, 1966, lic. Calif., 1968; private pilot 1942, cert. basic sci. law State of Utah, 1963, physicians and surgeons State of Calif., 1968, in airplane instrument rating, single engine land 1980. Elec. engr. KLO Radio Sta., Ogden, 1936—37; owner, operater, ranching and equipment co. Weber and Cache County, Utah, 1937—; owner, operater, earth moving constrn. co. Utah, 1950—, Ariz., 1950—, Nev., 1950—, Calif., 1950—; owner, operater Powder Mountain Ski Resort, Weber and Cache County, 1957—2007; pvt. practice Weber County, 1963—; intern Thomas D. Dee Meml. Hosp., 1963—64; pvt. practice Ogden, Utah, 1963—88. Recipient Honored History Maker, U. Utah, Utah Ski Archives Sect., J. Willard Marriott Libr., 2007; named to Intermountain Ski Hall of Fame, Alf Engen Ski Mus. Found., 2008. Mem.: Inter Mountain Ski Area Assn. (founding mem. 1965—2007), Am. Soc. of Clinical Hypnoses, Presidents Club Weber State U., Ogden Exec. Assn. (pres.), Utah Ski Assn. (bd. mem. 1971—79, exec. com. mem. 1974—78), Weber County Med. And Surg. Soc. Achievements include first person to ever have angioplastic surgery performed on July 6, 1967 at Cleveland Clinic as experimental surgery. Avocation: flying. Personal E-mail: acobabe@relia.net.

COBB, JOHN CANDLER (JACK COBB), medical educator; b. Boston, July 8, 1919; s. Stanley and Elizabeth Mason (Almy) C.; m. Helen Imlay-Franchot, July 27, 1946; children: Loren, Nathaniel, Bethany, Julianne. BS in Astronomy cum laude, Harvard U., 1941, MD, 1948; MPH, Johns Hopkins U., 1954. Diplomate Nat. Bd. Med. Examiners, Am. Bd. Preventive Medicine and Pub. Health; lic. physician, Conn., Md., N.Mex. Intern Yale New Haven Hosp., 1948-49, fellow in pediatrics, 1949-50; jr. asst. resident Yale Psychiatric Clinic, 1950-51; instr. pediatrics and psychiatry Johns Hopkins U., 1951-56, asst. prof. maternal & child health, 1954—56, cons. Indian Health divsn. USPHS, Albuquerque, 1956-60; prof. preventive medicine U. Colo., Denver, 1965-85, emeritus prof., 1985—, chmn. dept., 1966-73. Dir. med. social rsch. project on population Govt. of Pakistan, 1960-64; cons. Am. Friends Svc. Com., Algeria, 1964; short term cons. WHO, Indonesia and Western Pacific Region, 1969, 70-73, USAID, Togo and Niger, 1979; exch. prof. Guangxi Med. Coll., Nanning, China, 1985-86; coord. ethics seminars U. Health Scis. Ctr., 1980-85; pres. World Hand Assocs., 1985--; cons. in field. Contbr. numerous articles to profl. jours. Bd. dirs., pres. Am. Assn. Planned Parenthood Physicians, 1966-67; bd. dirs., Planned Parenthood Fedn. Am., 1972-73, chmn. Task Force for Preparing 314(b) Agy. Grant Application, 1969; mem., chmn. health com. of Gov. Lamm and U.S. Congressman Wirth's Task Force on Rocky Flats Nuc. Weapons Plant, Denver, 1974-75; mem. Gov.'s Task Force on Health Effects of Air Pollution, 1978-79; commr. Air Pollution Control Commn. of Colo., 1976-79; mem. air quality policy com. Denver Regional Coun. of Govts., 1978-80, environ. council, U. Colo., 1970-75, Gov.'s Sci. adv. Counc., Colo., 1973-80, Gov.'s Blue Ribbon Task Force on Transp., Colo., 1977; bd. dirs. ROMCOE Ctr. for Environ. Problem Solving, 1978-81, Colo. Coalition for Full Employment, 1978-80; mem. Am. Friends Svc. Com. Adv. Group on Rocky Flats/Nuclear Weapons Project, 1979-86; mem. sci. adv. bd., Three Mile Island Pub. Health Fund, 1982-86, owning mem. Chaordic Commons., vol. Internat. Red Cross, 1942-44 Recipient Florence Sabin award Colo. Pub. Health Assn., 1979, Jack Gore Meml. Peace award Am. Friends Svc. Com., 1980; U.S. EPA grantee, 1975-82. Mem. AAAS, WHO, Internat. Solar Energy Soc., Am. Solar Energy Soc., bd. dir., N.Mex Solar Energy Assn., 1990-96, Internat. Physicians for Prevention of Nuclear War (del. to Congresses in Moscow and Montreal), Appropriate Rural Tech. Assn. (bd. dirs. 1987-2002, v.p. 1991-92), Nat. Resources Def. Coun. (bd. advisors 1991-92), N.Mex. Solar Energy Assn. (bd. dirs. 1995-98), Physicians for Human Rights, Physicians for Social Reponsibility.

COBBS, PRICE MASHAW, social psychiatrist; b. LA, Nov. 2, 1928; s. Peter Price and Rosa (Mashaw) C.; m. Evadne Priester, May 30, 1957 (dec. Oct. 1973); children: Price Priester, Marion Renata; m. Frederica Maxwell, May 26, 1985 AB, U. Calif. Berkeley, 1953; MD, Meharry Med. Coll., 1958. Intern San Francisco Gen. Hosp., 1958-59; psychiat. resident Mendocino State Hosp., Talmage, Calif., 1959-61, Langley Porter Neuro-Psychiat. Inst., San Francisco, 1961-62; pres., CEO Pacific Mgmt. Systems, San Francisco, 1967—; CEO Cobbs, Inc. Mgmt. cons. in workforce diversity numerous cos., govt. agys. and community projects; conducted seminars UN, Dept. State; guest lectr. leading colls. and univs.; chair 1st Ann. Nat. Diversity Conf., San Francisco, 1991; speaker 1st Internat. Diversity Conf., Johannesburg, South Africa, 1991; vis. cons., lectr. workforce diversity, South Africa, 1993; co-founder, pres. Renaissance Books, Inc.; adv. bd. Black Scholar. Author: My American Life: From Rage to Entitlement, 2005, (with William H. Grier) Black Rage, 1968, The Jesus Bag, 1971, (with Judith L. Turnock) Cracking the Corporate Code: From Survival to Mastery, 2000; contbr. State of Black America 1988, 89. Bd. dirs. Shared Interest; founding mem. Diversity Collegium. Served to cpl. U.S. Army, 1951-53 Recipient Pathfinder award Assn. Humanistic Psychology, 1993, Al Martins Heritage award, The Exec. Leadership Coun., Harvey Russell award, PepsiCo, 2003. Fellow Am. Psychiat. Assn.; mem. Nat. Med. Assn., NAACP (life), Nat. Acad. Scis.; charter mem. Nat. Urban League. Achievements include pioneering in discipline of ethnotherapy to understand differences in race, culture and ethnicity. Office: Pacific Mgmt System 3528 Sacramento St San Francisco CA 94118-1850 Personal E-mail: cozycobbs@aol.com.

COBELLI, NEIL J., orthopedist, surgeon, educator; MD, Dartmouth Med. Sch., 1976. Diplomate Am. Bd. of Orthopaedic Surgery. Intern Geisinger Med. Ctr.; resident orthopaedic surgery Montefiore Med. Ctr., 1979—83; fellow Univ. of Wash.; Mary and David Hoar rsch. fellow NY Acad. of Medicine; tng. orthopaedic trauma Harborview Med. Ctr.; tng. orthopaedic surgery Albert Einstein Coll. of Medicine, 1983, assoc. prof. orthpaedic surgery; chair orthopedics dept. Montefiore Med. Ctr. Co-author: (publs.) Immunogenecity of modified alkane polymers is mediated through TLR1/2 activation, 2008, Endosomal damage and TLR2 mediated inflammasome activation by alkane particles in the generation of aseptic osteolysis, 2009, Dendritic cell-mediated in vivo bone resorption, 2010. Office: Montefiore Medical Center Department of Orthopaedics 2nd Fl 1695 Eastchester Rd Bronx NY 10461 Office Phone: 718-920-2060. Office Fax: 718-653-1587. E-mail: NCOBELLI@montefiore.org.

COBURN, MARJORIE FOSTER, psychologist, educator; b. Salt Lake City, Feb. 28, 1939; d. Harlan A. and Alma (Ballinger) Polk; m. Robert Byron Coburn, July 2, 1977; children: Robert Scott, Kelly Anne; children: Polly Klea Foster, Matthew Ryan Foster. BA in

Sociology, UCLA, 1960; Montessori Internat. Diploma with honors, Washington Montessori Inst., 1968; MA in Psychology, U. No. Colo., 1979; PhD in Counseling Psychology, U. Denver, 1983. Lic. clin. psychologist. Probation officer Alameda County, Oakland, Calif., 1960—62; dir. Friendship Club, Orlando, Fla., 1963—65; probation officer Contra Costa County, El Cerrito, Calif., 1966, Fairfax County, Va., 1967; tchr. Va. Montessori Sch., Fairfax, 1968—70; spl. edn. tchr. Leary Sch., Falls Church, Va., 1970—72, sch. administr., 1973—76; tchr. Aseltine Sch., San Diego, 1976—77, Coburn Montessori Sch., Colorado Springs, 1977—79; pvt. practice psychotherapy Colorado Springs, 1979—82, San Diego, 1982—. Cons. in field. Author (with R.C. Orem): Montessori: Prescription for Children with Learning Disabilities, 1977; contbr. articles to profl. jours. Mem.: APA, Mensa, The Charter 100, San Diego Psychol. Assn., Calif. Psychol. Assn., Coun. Exceptional Children, Phobia Soc., Am. Orthopsychiat. Assn., Rotary. Episcopalian. Office: 836 Prospect St Ste 101 La Jolla CA 92037-4206 Home Phone: 858-454-0817; Office Phone: 858-456-5065.

COBURN, RONALD MURRAY, ophthalmologist, surgeon; b. Detroit, Aug. 25, 1943; s. Sidney and Jean (Goldberg) C.; m. Barbara Joan Levy, Feb. 21, 1969; children: Nicholas Scott, Lauren Joy. BS, Wayne State U., 1965, MD, 1969; postgrad., Kresge Eye Inst., 1971—74. Diplomate Am. Bd. Ophthalmology, Am. Bd. Eye Surgery (surg. examiner). Dir. The Coburn Clinic, Dearborn, Mich., 1976—; chief ophthalmology Straith Hosp. for Spl. Surgery, Southfield, Mich., 1985—2000; dir. Cataract Specialty Surgery Ctr., Berkley, Mich., 2003—. Cons. CooperVision, Inc., Bellevue, Wash., 1985-88, Alcon Surg., Inc., Ft. Worth, 1988—. Co-author: Lens-Stat Intraocular Lens Modeling System; editorial advisor Phaco and Foldables, 1990. Trustee Straith Hosp. for Spl. Surgery, 1986—. Capt. Mich. N.G., 1969-76. Fellow: Rsch. Prevent Blindness, Soc. Excellence Eyecare, Soc. Eye Surgeons, Royal Soc. Medicine (London), Internat. Coll. Surgeons, Am. Coll. Surgeons; mem.: Leadership Soc., Internat. Glaucoma Congress, Soc. Geriatric Ophthalmology, Internat. Eye Found., Internat. Assn. Ocular Sci., NY Acad. Sci., Wayne County Medical Soc., Michigan Ophthalmological Soc., Am. Diabetes Assn., Am. Soc. Cataract and Refractive Surgery, Am. Assn. Advancement Scis., Phi Beta Kappa. Achievements include design of Am. Med. Optics PC19LB intraocular lens, CILCO CPLU CP20 intraocular lenses, CooperVision CP10BG posterior chamber intraocular lens, Alcon CZ20BD intraocular lens. Home: 1490 W Long Lake Rd Bloomfield Hills MI 48302-1340 Personal E-mail: ronaldcoburn@mac.com.

COCCHIARO, ANTONIO, physician; b. Torrecuso, Italy, Oct. 19, 1947; s. Luigi and Rosaria Cocchiaro; m. Antonietta Orlanda Macri, June 16, 1974; children: Rosalie Maria Josephine, Luigino Anthony, Vanessa Marie. MBBS, U. Adelaide, 1973. Intern Royal Adelaide Hosp., 1974; sr. ptnr. Midwest Health, Beverley, South Australia, Australia, 1975—. Elected del. Constn. Conv., Australia, 1998; convenor Australian Rep. Mvmt., South Australia, 1999; mem. Profl. Svcs. Rev. Panel, Adelaide, South Australia, 2000—; sr. dep. chair Fedn. Ethnic Cmtys. Couns. Australia, 1999—2001; pres. Multicultural Cmtys. Coun. Southern Australia, 2005—09, Coordinating Italian Com., South Australia, 1989—97; chairperson Tertiary Multicultural Edn. Com., South Australia, 1993—99; v.p. Multicultural Cmtys. Coun., South Australia, 1995—2001; chairperson South Australian Multicultural and Ethnic Affairs Commn., South Australia, 2001—02; dir. Nat. Australia Day Coun., Canberra, Australian Capital Territory, Australia, 2002—07; chair Australia Day Coun., 2007—; chairperson Strata Corp. Hindmarsh Sq. Car Pk., Adelaide, South Australia, 1995—. Recipient Citizen of Yr., City of Charles Sturt, 1999, Cavaliere of Italian Republic, 2007, Officer Order of St. Lazarus of Jerusalem, 2008—; named Mem. Order of Australia Honors, 2004. Mem.: Australian Med. Assn., Royal Australian Coll. Gen. Practitioners. Office: Midwest Health 678 Port Rd 5009 Beverley SA Australia Office Phone: 610883480000.

COCEANI, FLAVIO, medical scientist; b. Trieste, Italy, Jan. 3, 1937; s. Marino Coceani and Tosca Priora; m. Maria Antonietta Romanelli, May 24, 1969; children: Lorenzo, Michele. MD, U. Bologna, 1961, docent in Human Physiology, 1968. Asst. prof. physiology U. Bologna, 1965-66; scientist Rsch. Inst. Hosp. for Sick Children, Toronto, Can., 1968-78; sr. scientist Ibidem, 1978-99; prof. physiology U. Toronto, 1983-99; prof. pediat. Ibidem, 1983-99; prof. physiology Scuola Sup. S.Anna Pisa, 1999—. Dir. div. neurosci. Hosp. Sick Children, 1977-97, head integrative biology programme, 1998-99. Recipient Chevalier of Order to Merit, Republic of Italy, 1993, Annual Govs. award Leonardo Da Vinci Acad. Toronto, 1995.

COCHRAN, JOHN HOWARD, plastic and reconstructive surgeon; b. Muncie, Ind., Sept. 6, 1946; s. John H. and Lois M. (Woolridge) C.; 1 child, Ryan K. BS cum laude, Colo. State U., 1968; MD, U. Colo. Sch. Medicine, 1973. Intern surgery U. Calif., San Diego, 1973-74; resident head and neck surgery Stanford U., Palo Alto, Calif., 1974-77; resident plastic surgery U. Wis., Madison, 1979-81; pvt. practice plastic surgery Denver, 1981-90; chief plastic surgery St. Joseph Hosp., Denver, 1987-93, Colo. Med. Group, Denver, 1990-95; chmn. dept. surgery St. Joseph Hosp., 1993-99; exec. med. dir. Med. Group, Denver, 1999—2007; exec. dir. The Paramounte Fedn., 2007—10. Pres. bd. trustees Kilimanjaro Children's Hosp. Tanzania, E. Africa, 1989—. Fellow Am. Soc. Plastic and Reconstructive Surgery, Am. Coll. SUrgeons, Acad. Otolaryngology, Head and Neck Surgery; mem. Am. Assn. Plastic Surgeons. Avocations: fly fishing, skiing. Office: 1 Kaiser Plaza 27th Fl Oakland CA 94612

COCHRAN, KENNETH WILLIAM, toxicologist; b. Chgo., Nov. 2, 1923; m. Martha Louise Wells, May 10, 1945; children: Kenneth W. III, Kimberley W. Cochran Nelson (dec.). SB, U. Chgo., 1947, PhD, 1950. Rsch. asst. to instr., toxicity lab. and dept. pharmacology U. Chgo., 1946-52; from rsch. assoc., instr. to prof. emeritus U. Mich., Ann Arbor, 1952—. Contbr. articles to profl. jours. Pvt. 1st lt. US Army, 1943—46. Fellow AAAS; mem. Am. Soc. for Microbiology, Am. Soc. for Pharmacology and Exptl. Therapeutics, Mycol. Soc. of Am., N.Am. Mycol. Assn. (exec. sec. 1988-97, award for contributions to amateur mycology, 2004). Home: 3556 Oakwood St Ann Arbor MI 48104-5213 Office Phone: 734-971-2552. Personal E-mail: kwcee@umich.edu.

COCHRAN, LYNN S., medical association administrator; b. Bryson City, NC, Mar. 7, 1955; Degree in HIT & Med. Coding, Southwestern CC, 2007. Dir. practice ops. WNC Internal Medicine, PLLC, 2006—. Recipient Outstanding Academic Achievement award, Southwestern CC. Mem.: AAPC. Office: 63 Healthcare Dr Sylva NC 28779 Office Fax: 828-586-7902. Business E-Mail: lynn_cochran@westcare.org.

COCHRAN, ROBERT CARTER, surgical educator; b. Newton, Mass., Oct. 9, 1932; s. Williams and Mary Faith (Williams) C.; m. Norma Rae Creighton, Aug. 27, 1958 (div. Aug. 1986); children: Barbara, Gwen, Williams; m. Rebecca Anne Fain, Feb. 3, 1990. BA, Princeton U., NJ, 1955; MD, Boston U., 1960. Diplomate Am. Bd. Surgery. Intern Mass. Meml. Hosp., Boston, 1960-61; resident Bethesda (Md.) Naval Hosp., 1963-67; commd. ensign USN, 1956, advanced through grades to capt.; intern Mass. Gen. Hosp.; resident in surgery N.H. Bethesda Hosp.; mem. surg. staff USN, Bethesda, Md., 1961-80; chief of surgery USN Hosp., Bethesda, 1980-83; pvt. practice Hygeia Med. Specialist Group, Charleston, W.Va., 1983-86; prof. Med. Sch. W.Va. U., Charleston, 1986. Asst. prof. surgery Uniformed Svcs. Univ. of Health Scis. Decorated Cross of Gallantry (Vietnam), Meritorious Svc. medal USN. Episcopalian. Avocations: fishing, skiing. E-mail: drbobinwv@frontier.org.

COCHRANE, PAUL HOLLIS, general practice physician; b. Boston, Oct. 23, 1953; s. Joseph Xavier and Bernadette Anne (Abbott) C.; children: Gregory, Jennifer, Amanda, Casey; m. Dorian Cochrane, Oct. 22, 1999; 1 child, Katie. BA, U. Mass., 1974; OD, N.Eng. Coll. Optometry, 1979; D Naturopathy, Clayton Sch. Natural Healing, Birmingham, Ala., 1986; D Chiropractic, Palmer Coll. Chiropractic, 1988; A in Paralegal Sci., Southland U., 1983; DO, New England Coll. Osteopathic Medicine, 1992; JD, Monticello U., 1997. Cert. 8th black belt. Resident in osteopathy Community Hosp. R.I., Cranston, 1992-93; med. examiner Nicholas County, W.Va., 1995-96; physician pvt. practice, 1997—; rschr. Pastoral Ministry, Newsburgh. Real estate developer, Mass., 1981—; instr. diagnosis Palmer Coll. Chiropractic, Davenport, Iowa, 1986-88; instr. U. N.Eng. Coll. Osteopathic Medicine, Biddeford, Maine, 1990—. Coord. glaucoma, pediatric eye screenings, Lions Club, Arlington, 1980— (disting. svc. award 1984); player, coach pro baseball Bangor Blue Ox Northeast League, 1996. Fellow Internat. Acad. Clin. Acupuncture; mem. Am. Osteopathic Assn., Am. Acad. Osteopathy, Am. Coll. Osteopathic Family Physicians, Mass. Osteopathic Soc. (v.p.), N.Eng. Coll. Osteopathic Medicine, Hyannis Med. Ctr. (dir. 2007-), Hyannis Mets Cape Cod League (team physician 2008). Democrat. Roman Catholic. Achievements include 1st, 2nd and 3rd degree in black belt karate. Avocations: sports, reading. Home: 34 Snow Creek Dr Hyannis MA 02601 Office Phone: 508-771-4413.

COCHRANE, ROBERT LOWE, biologist; b. Morgantown, W.Va., Feb. 10, 1931; s. Thomas Joseph and Isabelle Durston (Lowe) C. BA, W.Va. U., 1953; MS, U. Wis., 1954, PhD, 1961. Rsch. asst. genetics U. Wis., Madison, 1953—55, rsch. asst. zoology, 1957—60; with Fur Animal Exptl. Sta., Petersburg, Alaska, 1955; agt. in animal husbandry USDA, Madison, Wis., 1955—61; biologist FDA, Washington, 1961—62; sr. research fellow dept. anatomy U. Birmingham (Eng.), 1962—65; project assoc. dept. physiology U. Pitts., 1965—66; sr. endocrinologist Eli Lilly & Co., Indpls., 1966—80; rsch. assoc. G.D. Searle & Co., Skokie, Ill., 1980—81; with Short's Fur Farm, Granton, Wis., 1981—83; rsch. assoc. Marshfield (Wis.) Med. Found., 1983—84; biologist Northwood Fur Farms, Inc., Cary, Ill., 1984. Participant Internat. Mink Show, Wis., 1976—2006, W.Va. Fox Show, Morgantown, 1989; FAO cons. Wildlife Inst. India, Dehra Dun, 1985; adj prof. divsn. animal and vet. sci. W.Va. U., Morgantown, 1987—; ad hoc reviewer competitive rsch. grants U.S. Dept. Agr. Ad hoc reviewer (various sci. jours.). Recipient Knight of Golden Horse Shoe award W.Va. Pub. Sch. System, 1945, W.Va. Boy's State, 1948; U. Birmingham (Eng.) sr. rsch. fellow, 1962-65. Mem. AAAS, Am. Inst. Biol. Scis., Soc. Exptl. Biology and Medicine, Soc. Reprodn. and Fertility, Soc. Study Reprodn., Am. Soc. Animal Sci., Endocrine Soc., N.Y. Acad. Sci., Soc. Endocrinology, Coun. Agrl. Sci. and Tech., Internat. Platform Assn., NRA (life), Sigma Xi, Pi Kappa Alpha, Gamma Sigma Delta. Presbyterian. Achievements include discovery of the ovarian hormonal requirements for ova-implantation and embryonic diapause in the rat, the elucidation of the role played by prostaglandins in corpus luteum function, parturition and ductus arteriosus closure in the rat; discovery of timing, duration and pattern of reproductive cycles in martens; development of steroid synthesis inhibitors for controlling reproduction in mammals; rsch. in the successful raising of ruffed grouse in captivity, dissemination of scientific information on fur farming and raising ruffed grouse to the commercial trade and public. Home: 404 Junior Ave Morgantown WV 26505-2208 Office Phone: 304-293-1966. Business E-Mail: rcochra2@wvu.edu.

COCKBURN, MYLES, epidemiologist, educator; BA in Geography/Math, Otago U., Dunedin, New Zealand, 1991, PGDip in Geography, 1992, PhD in Epidemiology, 1999. Health Rsch. Coun. of New Zealand Overseas fellow/post-doctoral fellow, dept. preventative medicine U. Southern Calif. Sch. Medicine, U. Southern Calif./Norris Cancer Ctr., 1996—99, rsch. assoc., dept. preventative medicine, 1999—2001, vis. asst. prof. rsch., 2001, asst. prof. rsch., 2003—, assoc. prof. rsch., dept. preventative medicine, 2008—; post-doctoral rsch. in epidemiology U. Southern Calif., Keck Sch. Medicine, 1999—2000; assoc. prof. rsch., dept. geography, Coll. Letters, Arts and Sciences U. Southern Calif., 2008—. Mem. Nat. Inst. Environ. Health Sciences Southern Calif. Environ. Health Sciences Ctr., 2003, Norris Comprehensive Cancer Ctr., 2004—; chair Human Genome Rsch. Inst. Demographics Working Group (PhenX), 2008—. Contbr. several articles to peer-reviewed journals; chair editl. bd. N.Am. Assn. Cancer Registries, 2006—. Recipient John Young award for Excellence in Cancer Rsch., 2002. Office: Univ Southern Calif Dept Preventive Medicine 1441 Eastlake Ave MC 9175 Los Angeles CA 90089-9175 Office Phone: 323-865-0322. Office Fax: 323-865-0141. Business E-Mail: mylesc@usc.edu.

COCKE, WILLIAM MARVIN, JR., plastic surgeon, educator; b. Balt., Aug. 2, 1934; s. William M. and Clara E. (Bosley) C.; m. Sue Ann Harris, Apr. 25, 1981; children: Gregory William, Laura Marie, Julie Ann; children by previous marriage: William Marvin III, Catherine Lynn, Deborah Kay, Brian Thomas. BS with honors in Biology, Tex. A&M U., 1956; MD, Baylor U., 1960. Diplomate: Am. Bd. Plastic Surgery (guest examiner 1978). Intern surgery Vanderbilt U. Hosp., Nashville, 1960-61; fellow gen. surgery Ochsner Clinic and Found. Hosp., New Orleans, 1961-64; chief resident surgery Monroe (La.) Charity Hosp., 1963-64; resident reconstructive surgery Roswell Park Meml. Inst., Buffalo, 1965-66; chief resident plastic surgery VA Hosp., Bronx, NY, 1966; practice medicine specializing in plastic surgery Nashville, 1968-75, Sacramento, 1976-79; pvt. practice medicine specializing in plastic surgery Bryan, Tex., 1980-92; prof. surgery, head div. plastic/reconstructive surgery Marshall U. Sch. of Medicine, Huntington, W.Va., 1992—. Mem. staff Cabell-Huntington Hosp., Huntington Vets. Med. Ctr.; asst. prof. plastic surgery Vanderbilt U. Sch. Medicine, Nashville, 1968-69, asst. clin. prof. plastic surgery, 1969-75; assoc. prof. plastic surgery Ind. U. Sch. Medicine, Indpls., 1975-76; chief plastic surgery service Wishard Meml. Hosp., Ind. U., 1975-76; assoc. prof. surgery U. Calif. Sch. Medicine, Davis, 1976-79, chmn. dept. plastic surgery, 1976-79; prof. surgery, chief div. plastic surgery Tex. Tech. U. Sch. Medicine, Lubbock, 1979-80, dir. Microsurg. Research Lab., 1979-80; clin. prof. surgery Tex. A&M U. Sch. Medicine, 1983-92; prof. plastic surgery, 1986-89; chief plastic surgery svc., dept. surgery, Olin Teague VA Med. Ctr., Temple, Tex., 1986-92; prof. Marshall U. Sch. Medicine, 1992—. Author textbooks on plastic surgery; contbr. articles to profl. jours. Served with M.C. USAF, 1966-68. Recipient Dean Echols award Ochsner Hosp. Found., 1963 Mem. ACS, Am. Assn. Plastic Surgeons, Soc. Head and Neck Surgeons, Assn. Acad. Surgery, Alton Ochsner Surg. Soc., Alpha Omega Alpha. Episcopalian. Home: 45 Olde Farm Rd Ona WV 25545-9747 Office: VA Med Ctr 1540 Spriing Valley Road Huntington WV 25704

COCKERHAM, LORRIS G., radiation toxicologist; b. Denham Springs, La., Sept. 27, 1935; s. Warren Conrad and Leda Frances (Scivicque) C.; m. Patricia Ann Stagg, Aug. 16, 1957; children: Michael B., Richard L., Ann E., Joseph D. BA, La. Coll., 1957; MS, Colo. State U., 1973, PhD, 1979. Diplomate Am. Bd. Forensic Examiners, cert. instr. basic disaster life support AMA, instr. advanced disaster life support AMA. Commd. 2d lt. USAF, 1961, advanced through grades to lt. col., 1977, instr. James Connelly AFB, Tex., 1963-66, squadron electronic warfare officer Fairchild AFB, Wash., 1966-71, asst. prof. dept. chemistry and biology USAF Acad. Colo., 1973-77, wing electronic warfare officer Griffiss AFB, N.Y., 1977-78, comdr. 416 Munitions Maintenance Squadron, 1978-80; Armed Forces Radiobiology Rsch. Inst., Def. Nuc. Agy., Bethesda, Md., 1980-86; Air Force Office of Sci. Rsch., Bolling AFB, D.C., 1986-87; ret., 1987; exec. dir. NCTR-Associated Univs., Little Rock, 1988-89; pres. The Delta Agy., Little Rock, 1989-93, Phenix Cons. and Svcs. Ltd., Little Rock, 1993—. Dir. Product Safety Labs., East Brunswick, N.J., 1994-95; dir. Toxicol. SITEK Rsch. Labs., Rockville, Md., 1997-99; asst. prof. physiology Sch. Medicine, Uniformed Svcs. U. Health Scis., 1981-87; assoc. prof. U. Ark. for Med. Scis., 1988-89, bd. dirs., Shepherd Ministres Internat., 2009-. Troop com. chmn. Iroquois coun. Boy Scouts Am., 1978-80. Decorated D.F.C. (2), Airman's medal, Air medal (12), Air Force Commendation medal, Joint Svc. Achievement medal; Air Force Logistics Command Dioxin Rsch. grantee, 1974-79; recipient Order of Arrow, Boy Scouts Am.; named Disting. Alumnus La. Coll., 1989. Mem. Soc. Neurosci., Internat. Brain Rsch. Orgn., World Fedn. Neuroscientists, Am. Coll. Toxicology, Disting. Flying Cross Soc., Sigma Xi, Phi Kappa Phi, Internat. Soc. Genetic. Genealogy, Sons Am. Revolution. Republican. Baptist. Personal E-mail: phenixltd@aol.com.

COCULESCU, MIHAIL, JR., clinical endocrinologist, educator; b. Bucharest, Romania, Sept. 5, 1943; s. Grigore Gr. Coculescu and Elena Gh. Aposteanu; m. Lucia Silvia C.; children: Ilinca Lucia, Ana Mihaela. Med. diploma, Univ. Med. Pharm. "C.Davila", Bucharest, 1966; DSc, Romanian Acad. Med. Scis., Bucharest, 1976. Intern, resident in internal medicine, endocrinologist Romanian Ministry Health, Bucharest, 1965-72; univ. asst. dept. endocrinology U. Med. Pharm., Bucharest, 1973-81, lectr., 1981-90, reader, 1991-93, prof., 1994—; cons. endocrinology, diabetes, metabolic diseases Nat. Inst. Endocrinology, Bucharest, 1979—; dep. dir. Inst. Endocrinology, Bucharest, 1997—2004. Pro-rector U. Medicine and Pharmacy C. Davila, Bucharest, 2000-08; gen. dir. Nat. Ctr. Postgrad. Tng. in Healthcare, 2005-06; head, dept. endocrinology Davila U. Medicine Nat. Inst. Endocrinology, 2002-; editor-in-chief Acta Endocrinologica, Bucharest, 2005-. Author: Clinical Neuroendocrinology, 1986; contbr. articles to profl. jours. including Cell Tissue Rsch., Jour. Clin. Endocrinology Metabolism, others. Lt. Romanian Army, 1967. Recipient GH Marinescu prize Romanian Acad., 1990, Nat. Order, Sanitary Merit, 2004. Fellow: Romanian Acad. Med. Scis. (pres. sect. basic med. sci.), Am. Coll. Endocrinology (internat. com. mem. 2003—10, Internat. Clinician award 2002), Royal Coll. Physicians (London); mem.: Internat. Soc. Psychoneuroendocrinology, Internat. Neuroendocrine Fedn. (com. bd. mem. 2006—), Romanian Soc. Endorcinology (pres. 2004—07), European Pineal Soc. (founder), Brit. Soc. Endocrinology, Romanian Soc. Psychoneuroendocrinology (founding mem. 1990, hon. pres. 1998—). Achievements include first identification of angiotensin I in pineal gland, arginine vasotocin effects on human REM sleep, blood-cerebrospinal fluid barrier for pituitary hormones. Home: 10 Maria Rosetti Str 020485 Bucharest Romania Office Phone: 4021-3198718, 40722244220. Business E-Mail: m.coculescu@uni-davila.ro.

CODEN, DANIEL JAY, ophthalmologist; b. Detroit, Feb. 20, 1958; s. Theodore Paul and Barbara Joan Coden; m. Elizabeth Ann Nederlander-Coden, June 1, 1984; children: Lauren, Jacqueline, Benjamin. BS, U. Mich., Ann Arbor, 1980; MD, Wayne State U., Detroit, 1984. Diplomate Am. Acad. Ophthalmology. Resident ophthalmology U. Calif., San Diego, 1988; fellow oculoplastic surgery Manhattan Eye, Ear and Throat Hosp., NYC, 1989; sr. staff surgeon Henry Ford Hosp., Detroit, 1989—90; med. dir. La Jolla Laser Vision, Calif., 1990—. Named Young Leader in Ophthalmology, Ophthalmology Mgmt., 1989. Fellow: ACS; mem.: Am. Soc. Cataract and Refractive Surgery, Am. Acad. Ophthalmology (Honor award 2002), Am. Soc. Ophthalmic Plastic and Reconstructive Surgery, Alpha Omega Alpha (pres. 1983). Office: LaJolla Laser Vision 9850 Genesee Ste 310 La Jolla CA 92037 Office Phone: 858-457-3010.

CODISPOTI, ANDRE JOHN, allergist, immunologist; b. Bklyn., Apr. 27, 1938; s. Bruno Mario and Antoinette (Savarese) C.; m. Miranda Babini, June 14, 1967; children: Rita, Elisa, Andrew. BA, Coll. of Holy Cross, 1959; MD, U. Bologna, Italy, 1965. Diplomate Am. Bd. Pediatrics, Am. Bd. Allergy and Immunology. Rotating intern Long Island Coll. Hosp., Bklyn., 1966, resident in pediatrics, 1967-69, fellow in allergy and immunology, 1971-73; pvt. practice Suffern, NY, 1972—. Maj. M.C., U.S. Army, 1969-71. Fellow Am. Coll. Allergy, Asthma and Immunology, Am. Acad. Allergy, Asthma and Immunology. Republican. Roman Catholic. Avocations: reading, music, travel, tennis, skiing. Office: 7 Hemion Rd Suffern NY 10901-4903 also: 70 Gilbert St Monroe NY 10950-1538 Personal E-mail: ascmn@verizon.net. Business E-Mail: ajcmd@frontiernet.net.

CODISPOTI, MAURIZIO, psychology professor; b. July 31, 1965; Laurea, U. Padova, Italy, 1991; PhD, U. Bologna, Italy, 1997. Assoc. prof. U. Bologna, 2002—. Mem.: SPR. Office: Viale Berti Pichat Bologna 40127 Italy Business E-Mail: maurizio.codispoti@unibo.it.

CODNER, MARK ALLEN, plastic surgeon; b. Atlanta, Oct. 9, 1961; BA summa cum laude, Emory U., 1982; MD, Emory Sch. Medicine, 1987. Cert. Am. Bd. Surgery, 1993, Am. Bd. Plastic Surgery, 1997. Resident in gen. surgery NY Hosp.-Cornell Med. Ctr. and Meml. Sloan-Kettering Cancer Ctr., 1987—92; resident in plastic surgery Emory U., 1992—94; fellow in oculoplastic surgery Southeastern Oculoplastic Ctr., Atlanta, 1994—95; fellow in aesthetic surgery Baker, Gordon & Stuzin Plastic Surgers Assocs., Miami, 1995; pvt. practice Paces Plastic Surgery, Atlanta, fellowship dir., 1994—; asst. clin. prof. plastic surgery Emory U. Co-chmn. Atlanta Breast Surgery Symposium, 1998—2004, chmn., 2005; assoc. editor Plastic and Reconstructive Surgery, 2001—08; chmn. Atlanta Oculoplastic Surgery Symposium, 2008. Recipient Best Presentation award, Royal Can. Soc. Plastic Surgery, 2003, Pathways to Leadership award, 2006. Fellow: Am. Coll. Surgeons; mem.: AMA, Am. Fedn. Clin. Rsch., Ga. Med. Assn., Southeastern Soc. Plastic and Reconstructive Surgeons (Best Paper 1995, 1996), Am. Soc. Aesthetic Plastic Surgery (Best Journal article 1997, Sherrel Aston award 2001, 2006), Am. Soc. Plastic and Reconstructive Surgeons, Am. Assn. Plastic Surgeons, John Gordon Stipe Soc. Scholars, Sigma Xi, Phi Beta Kappa, Alpha Omega Alpha. Office: Paces Plastic Surgery Ste 640 3200 Downwood Cir Atlanta GA 30327 Office Phone: 404-351-0051. Office Fax: 404-351-0632.

COE, FREDRIC L., internist, educator, researcher; b. Chgo, Dec. 25, 1936; s. Lester J. and Lillian (Chaitlen) C.; m. Eleanor Joyce Brodny, May 5, 1965; children: Brian, Laura. AB, U. Chgo., 1955, MS, 1957, MD, 1961. Diplomate Am. Bd. Internal Medicine. Intern Michael Reese Hosp., Chgo., 1961-62, resident, 1962-65, U. Tex. S.W. Med. Sch., 1967-69; chmn. nephrology Michael Reese Hosp., 1972-82; prof. medicine U. Chgo., 1977—, prof. physiology, 1979—; chmn. nephrology A.M. Billings Hosp., Chgo., 1982—; founder, pres. Litholink Corp., 1995—. Author: Nephrolithiasis, 1978, 2d edit. (with J. Parks), 1987, (with B. Brenner and F.C. Rector) Renal Physiology, 1986, Clinical Nephrology; editor: Renal Therapeutics, 1978, Nephrolithiasis, 1980, Hypercalciuric States, 1983, (with M. Favus) Disorders of Bone and Mineral Metabolism, 1993, 2d edit., 2001; editor-in-chief Yearbook of Nephrology, 1991-96; editor: (with others) Kidney Stones: Medical and Surgical Management, 1996. Served to capt. USAF, 1961-67. Recipient Belding Scribner medal for lifetime achievement in clin. rsch. Am. Soc. Nephrology, 2000; Univ. of Chgo. Distingguished Svc. Award, 2001; grantee NIH, 1977-. Fellow ACP; mem. Am. Soc. Clin. Investigation, Am. Physiol. Soc., Assn. Am. Physicians Jewish. Achievements include first evidence for hyperuricosuria as cause of calcium renal stones; discovery of nephro calcin a protein inhibitor of crystal growth; first demonstration that human idiopathic hypercalciuria is hereditary. First evidence that apatile plaque begins inthe basement membranes of the renal thin limbs of Henle's loop. Home: 5490 S Shore Dr Chicago IL 60615-5984 Office: U Chgo Med Ctr 5841 S Maryland Ave Chicago IL 60637-1463 Office Phone: 773-702-1475. Business E-Mail: f-coe@uchicago.edu. *

COENEGRACHTS, KENNETH LOUIS, radiologist, researcher; b. Tongeren, Limburg, Belgium, Sept. 28, 1974; s. Jan Coenegrachts and Anne Vanherle; m. Ilse Christine Vincent, Aug. 8, 1972. MD, Cath. U. Leuven, 2004; PhD in Med. Scis., U. Amsterdam. Resident Cath. U. Leuven, Brabant, Belgium, 1999—2004; staff mem. dept. radiology AZ St.-Jan AV, Bruges, West-Flandres, 2004—. Mgmt. tng. Vlerick Sch. Mgmt., Ghent, East-Flandres, Belgium, 2005—05. Mem.: Internat. Soc. Magnetic Resonance Medicine, Société Française de Radiologie, Am. Roentgen Ray Soc., European Soc. Gastrointestinal and Abdominal Radiologists, European Congress Radiology, Royal Belgian Soc. Radiology. Office: AZ St-Jan Brugge-Oostende AV Ruddershove 10 West Flandres Bruges 8000 Belgium Office Fax: 0032 50/45 21 46; Home Fax: 0032 50/34 02 57. Personal E-mail: kenneth.coenegrachts@gmail.com. E-mail: kenneth.coenegrachts@azbrugge.be.

COESTER, ARIANE, emergency physician, educator; b. Porto Alegre, Brazil, Feb. 14, 1977; Degree in Medicine, U. Fed. Rio Grande do Sul, 2003. Cert. emergency phycisian Hosp. Pronto Socorro Porto Alegre. Emergency physician Hosp. Pronto Socorro Porto Alegre, 2006, prof., 2007. Home: David Francisco Maurício 85 Porto Algre Rio Grande do Sul 92760-220 Brazil Personal E-mail: arianecoester@yahoo.com.br.

COFFEY, BARBARA JANE, psychiatrist; b. Schnectady, NY, Jan. 24, 1949; AB, U. Rochester, 1971; MD, Tufts U., 1975; MS, Harvard U., 2000. Diplomate Am. Bd. Psychiatry and Neurology, Child Psychiatry. Dir. Child Psychiatry Clin. Tufts - New Eng. Med. Ctr., Boston, 1980-87, dir. tng. for child psychiatry, 1987-92; dir. pediatric psychopharmacology McLean Hosp., Belmont, Mass., 1992—. Fellow Am. Acad. Child and Adolescent Psychiatry; mem. Am. Psychiat. Assn. Office: NYU Child Study Ctr 577 First Ave New York NY 10016 Office Fax: 212-263-8662. Business E-Mail: barbara.coffey@nyumc.org.

COFFEY, PETE, optometrist researcher, professor of visual sciences; BSc, PhD. Prof. U. of Sheffield; prof. Cellular Therapy and Visual Sciences Inst. of Ophthalmology, U. Coll. London. Founder, dir. London Project to Cure Blindness. Contbr. Office: Divsn Cellular Therapy Inst of Ophthalmology 11-43 Bath St London EC1V9EL England Office Phone: 020 7608 4039. E-mail: p.coffrey@ucl.ac.uk.

COFFIN, JOHN MILLER, medical researcher, biology professor; b. Boston, Apr. 20, 1944; s. Louis Fussell and Mary Elizabeth (McCarthy) C.; m. Marion Clair Szurek, June 22, 1968; children: Erica Mary, Heather Rachel. BA, Wesleyan U., 1967; PhD, U. Wis., 1972. Fellow U. Zurich, Switzerland, 1972—75; asst. prof. molecular biology to assoc. prof. Tufts U. Sch. Medicine, Boston, 1975—82, prof., 1982—, Am. Cancer Soc. Rsch. Prof. Molecular Biology and Microbiol., 1994—; dir. HIV Drug Resistance Program Ctr. Cancer Rsch., Nat. Cancer Inst., NIH, Bethesda, Md., 1997—2006, spl. advisor to dir. HIV Drug Resistance Program, 2006—. Mem. virology study sect. NIH, Bethesda, Md., 1980-84; mem. sci. adv. bd. Viagene, Inc., San Diego, 1988. Editor: RNA Tumor Viruses, 2 vols., 1985, Retroviruses, 1997; mem. editl. bd. Jour. Virol, Virology, Oncogene, Oncogene Res., Leukemia; editor Jour. Virol, 1991-97; contbr. articles to profl. jours. Trustee Leukemia Soc. Am., NY, 1987. Recipient Outstanding Investigator award Nat. Cancer Inst., 1987, Method to Extend Rsch. in Time (MERIT) award NIH, 2006. Mem. AAAS, NAS, Am. Soc. Microbiol. Office: Tufts U Sch Medicine Dept Molecular Biology and Microbiol 136 Harrison Ave Boston MA 02111 also: HIV Drug Resistance Prog Nat Cancer Inst Bldg 535 Rm 109 PO Box B Frederick MD 21702-1201 Office Phone: 617-636-6526, 301-846-5943. Office Fax: 617-636-4086, 301-846-6013. E-mail: jcoffin@ncifcrf.gov, john.coffin@tufts.edu. *

COFFMAN, ROBERT LEE, pharmaceutical executive; AB, Ind. U.; PhD, U. Calif., San Diego. Postdoctoral fellow Stanford U. Med. Sch., Calif.; various positions through disting. rsch. fellow DNAX Rsch. Inst., Palo Alto, Calif., 1981—2000; v.p., chief sci. officer Dynavax Technologies Corp., Berkeley, Calif., 2000—. Contbr. articles to sci. jours.; adv. editor: Jour. Exptl. Medicine. Co-recipient William S. Coley award for rsch. in basic and clin. immunology, Cancer Rsch. Inst., NYC, 1997. Mem.: NAS. Achievements include fundamental discoveries about regulation of immune responses in allergic and infectious diseases. Office: Dynavax Technologies Corp 2929 Seventh St Ste 100 Berkeley CA 94710 Office Fax: 510-848-1327. Business E-Mail: rcoffman@dynavax.com.

COFIELD, ROBERT HAHN, orthopedic surgeon, educator; b. Cin., Oct. 24, 1943; s. Robert Hedrick and Virginia (Hahn) C.; m. Pamela Joyce Haarbauer, Aug. 12, 1967; children: Robert, Stacey, Virginia. BA, Washington and Lee U., 1965; MD, U. Ky., 1969; MS, Mayo Grad. Sch. Medicine, 1976. Diplomate Am. Bd. Orthopedic Surgery. Intern Charity Hosp./Tulane U., New Orleans, 1970; cons. Mayo Clinic, Rochester, Minn., 1975—; from instr. to assoc. prof. Mayo Med. Sch., Rochester, 1975-88, prof., 1988—; vice chmn. dept. orthopedics Mayo Clinic, Rochester, 1992-97, Frank R. and Shari Caywood prof. orthopedic surgery, 1993, chmn. dept. orthopedics, 1997—2005; assoc. dean Mayo Grad. Sch., Rochester, 1992-94, dean 1994-98; pres. Am. Bd. Orthopaedic Surgery, Chapel Hill, 1999-2000. Editor-in-chief Jour. Shoulder and Elbow Surgery, 1990-96; contbr. chpts. to books, more than 200 articles to profl. jours.; co-inventor humeral resect. guide; co-designer Cofield total shoulder sys. Lt. comdr. USNR. Mem. AMA, Am. Acad. Orthopedic Surgery, Am. Bd. Orthopedic Surgery (dir. 114—), Am. Orthopedic Assn., Am. Shoulder and Elbow Surgeons (founding sec.-treas. 1982-87, pres. 1988-89). Republican. Presbyterian. Office: Mayo Clinic 200 1st Ave NW Rochester MN 55901-3004 Office Phone: 507-284-2995.

COGGIN, CHARLOTTE JOAN, cardiologist, educator; b. Takoma Park, Md., Aug. 6, 1928; d. Benjamin and Nanette (McDonald) C. BA, Columbia Union Coll., 1948; MD, Loma Linda U., 1952, MPH, 1987; DSc (hon.), Andrews U., 1994. Diplomate Am. Bd. Pediatrics. Intern L.A. County Gen. Hosp., 1952-53, resident in medicine, 1953-55; fellow in cardiology Children's Hosp., LA, 1955-56, White Meml. Hosp., LA, 1955-56; rsch. assoc. in cardiology, house physician Hammersmith Hosp., London, 1956-57; resident in pediatrics and pediatric cardiology Hosp. for Sick Children, Toronto, Ont., Canada, 1963-64; cardiologist, asst. prof. medicine, co-dir. heart surgery team Loma Linda (Calif.) U., 1961-73, assoc. prof., 1973-91, prof. medicine, 1991—. Asst. dean. Sch. Medicine Internat. Program, 1973—75; v.p. for global outreach Loma Linda U. Health Scis. Ctr., 1998—; assoc.dean. Sch. Medicine Internat. Program, 1975—, spl. asst. to univ. pres. for interat. affairs, 1991; co-dir., cardiologist heart surgery team missions to, Pakistan and Asia, 63, Greece, 67, Greece, 69, Saigon, Vietnam, 1974—75, Saudi Arabia, 1976—87, China, 1984, China, 1989—91, Hong Kong, 1985, Zimbabwe, 88, Zimbabwe, 93, Kenya, 88, Nepal, 92, China, 92, Myanmar, 95, North Korea, 96. Author: Atrial Septal Defects, motion picture (Golden Eagle Cine award and 1st prize Venice Film Festival 1964); contbr. articles to med. jours. Recipient award for service to people of Pakistan City of Karachi, 1963, Medallion award Evangelismos Hosp., Athens, Greece, 1967, Gold medal of health South Vietnam Ministry of Health, 1974, Charles Elliott Weinger award for excellence, 1976, Wall Street Jour. Achievement award, 1987, Disting. Univ. Svc. award Loma Linda U., 1990; named Honored Alumnus Loma Linda U. Sch. Medicine, 1973, Outstanding Women in Gen. Conf. Seventh-day Adventists, 1975, Alumnus of Yr., Columbia Union Coll., 1984, Outstanding Achievement in Edn., Adventist Alumni Achievement award, 1999. Mem. AAUP, AAUW, Am. Coll. Cardiology, AMA (physicians adv. com. 1969—), Calif. Med. Assn. (com. on med. schs., com. on member svcs.), San Bernardino County Med. Soc. (chmn. comm. com. 1975-77, mem. comm. com, 1987-88, editor bull., 1975-76, William L. Cover, M.D. Outstanding Contbn. to Medicine award 1995), Am. Heart Assn., Med. Rsch. Assn. Calif., Calif. Heart Assn., Am. Acad. Pediatrics, World Affairs Coun., Internat. Platform Assn., Calif. Museum Sci. and Industry MUSES (Outstanding Woman of Yr. in Sci. 1969), Am. Med. Women's Assn., Loma Linda Sch. Medicine Alumni Assn. (pres. 1978), Alpha Omega Alpha, Delta Omega. Democrat. Home: 25052 Crestview Dr Loma Linda CA 92354-3415 Personal E-mail: jcoggin@verizon.net.

COHEN, ADIR, oral surgeon; b. Israel, Jan. 29, 1975; DMD, Hebrew U.; MSc, Hadassah-Ein Kerem, 2003, degree in Maxillofacial Surgery, 2009. Maxillofacial surgeon Hadassah-Ein Kerem, 2009, Tel Aviv Sourasky Med. Ctr., Ichilov. Home: Pri megadim 17 Mevasseret Zion Jerusalem 90805 Israel Personal E-mail: dr.adir.cohen@gmail.com.

COHEN, ALAN BARRY, researcher, educator; b. Bklyn., Nov. 3, 1952; s. Max B. and Blanche (Katz) C.; m. Helaine Francine Hartman, Dec. 22, 1973; children: Jeremy Todd, Bradley Daniel, Melanie Ann, Brandon Adam. BA, U. Rochester, 1973; MS, Harvard U., 1975, ScD, 1983. Rsch. asst. Beth Israel Hosp. and Harvard Med. Sch., Boston, 1974-75; sr. analyst Urban Systems Rsch. & Engring. Inc., Cambridge, Mass., 1975-79; rsch. assoc. Harvard Sch. Pub. Health, Boston, 1979-81, Johns Hopkins Sch. Hygiene and Pub. Health, Balt., 1981-82, asst. prof., 1982-84; assoc. dir. John Hopkins Ctr. for Hosp. Fin. and Mgmt., Balt., 1983-84; program officer Robert Wood Johnson Found., Princeton, NJ, 1984-87, sr. program officer, 1987-88, v.p., 1988-92; rsch. prof. Heller Grad. Sch. Brandeis U., 1992-94; prof. health policy and mgmt. Boston U. Sch. Mgmt., 1994—, dir. health care mgmt. program, 1994—2003; exec. dir. Health Policy Inst. Boston U., 2003—. Nat. program dir. Robert Wood Johnson Found. Scholars in Health Policy Rsch. Program, 1992—; investigator Ctr. Org. Leadership Mgmt. Res., Va. Boston Healthcare Sys.; William Evans vis. fellow, U. Otago, New Zealand, 2010, mem. nat. adv. com. Robert Wood Johnson Found. Info. for State Health Policy Program, 1994-98; cons. NJ Dept. Health, 1993; chmn. commr.'s cardiac svc. com. State of NJ, Trenton, 1990-92; mem. Inst. Medicine, Tech. Monitoring Panel on Access to Care, 1989-91; cons. DC State Health Planning and Devel. Agy., 1984, Nat. Ctr. Health Svc. Rsch., 1984. Mem. editl. bd. Inquiry; contbr. articles to profl. jours. Recipient Charles F. Wilinsky award Harvard Sch. Pub. Health, 1979; Kaiser fellow in health policy and mgmt., 1973-74; Dissertation grantee Nat. Ctr. Health Svc. Rsch., 1979-80. Fellow Acad. Health; mem. APHA, Am. Soc. Health Economists, Assoc. Pub. Policy Analysis & Mgt., Am. Econ. Assn., Am. Polit. Sci. Assn., Nat. Acad. Social Ins., Health Tech. Assessment Internat., Zeta Beta Tau (pres. Gamma Pi chpt. 1972-73, treas. 1970-72), Beta Gamma Sigma. Jewish. Avocations: reading, travel, cinema, basketball, gardening. Office: Boston U Health Policy Inst 53 Bay State Rd Boston MA 02215

COHEN, ALAN SEYMOUR, internist; b. Boston, Apr. 9, 1926; s. George I. and Jennie (Laskin) C.; m. Joan Elizabeth Prince, Sept. 12, 1954; children: Evan Bruce, Andrew Hollis, Robert Adam AB magna cum laude, Harvard Coll., Cambridge, Mass., 1947; MD magna cum laude, Boston U., 1952. Intern Harvard Med. Svc., Boston City Hosp., 1952-53, resident, 1953-55; exch. registrar in medicine Dundee Royal Infirmary and U. St. Andrews, Scotland, 1955-56. Rsch. and clin. fellow in rheumatology Mass. Gen. Hosp., Boston, 1956-58; instr. Med. Sch. Harvard Coll. and Mass. Gen. Hosp., 1958-60; head arthritis and connective tissue disease sect. Evans dept. clin. rsch. Mass. U. Hosp., Boston, 1960-72; Conrad Wesselhoeft prof. medicine Sch. Medicine Boston U., 1972-93, prof. pharmacology, 1974-92, disting. prof. medicine in rheumatology, 1993—; dir. Arthritis Ctr., 1977-94; dir. divsn. medicine Boston City Hosp., 1973-93; dir. Thorndike Meml. lab., 1973-93; bd. dirs. Hemagen Diagnostics Inc.; scientific bd. Neurochem. Inc., Can., 1997-2001. Editor: Laboratory Diagnostic Procedures in the Rheumatic Diseases, 1967, rev. edit., 1975, 3d edit., 1985, (with others) Symposium on Amyloidosis, 1968, (With R. Friedin and M. Samuels) Medical Emergencies: Diagnostic and Management Procedures from Boston City Hospital, 1977, (with J. Combes and H. Koh) 2d edit., 1983, Rheumatology and Immunology, 1979, (with J.C. Bennett) 2d edit., 1986, Progress in Clinical Rheumatology, 1984, (with D. Goldenberg) Drugs in the Rheumatic Diseases, 1986, Amyloidosis, 1986, Clinical Problems in Acute Care Medicine (J.J. Heffernan, R.A. Witzburg, A.S. Cohen), 1989; founder, editor-in-chief Amyloid Jour. Protein Folding Disorders, 1994—; contbr. more than 700 articles to profl. jours. Trustee Arthritis Found., Atlanta, 1976-82, trustee Mass. chpt., 1966-85, vice chmn., 1971-84, pres., 1981-94; vice sec. for N.Am., mem. exec. com. Pan Am. League Against Rheumatism, 1982-85; chmn. Boston City Hosp. Physician Alumni Reunion Com., 1992; pres. Boston City Hosp. Fund for Excellence, 1992. Served to surg. USPHS, 1953-55. Recipient Outstanding Alumnus award Boston U. Sch. Medicine, 1975, Purdue Frederic Arthritis award, 1979, James H. Fairclough Jr. award for disting. svc. to Mass. chpt. Arthritis Found., 1981, Alumni award for spl. distinction Boston U., 1981, Jan Van Bremeen Gold medal Dutch Rheumatism Soc., 1990, Commrs. Disting. Physician award Boston City Hosp., 1991, Gold medal Am. Coll. Rheumatology, 1994, Dr. Marian Ropes award Arthritis Found., 1995, Socius Honoris Causa, Hungarian Amyloid Soc., 2001, Hero award Arthritis Found., 2001, Millenium Medal of Hungarian Rsch. Group Amuloidosun, HSFR, 2001, Outstanding Achievement award Internat. Soc. Amyloidosis 2006. Master Am. Coll. Rheumatology (pres. 1978-79); fellow ACP; mem. Internat. Soc. Amyloidosis (bd. dirs. 2004—), Am. Soc. Clin. Investigation, Assn. Am. Physicians, Am. Fedn. Clin. Rsch., Am. Soc. Exptl. Pathology, Soc. Exptl. Biology and Medicine, Electron Microscopy Soc. Am., New Eng. Soc. for Electron Microscopy, Am. Soc. Cell Biology, N.Y. Acad. Sci., AMA, Mass. Med. Soc., New Eng. Rheumatism Assn. (past pres.), Italian Rheumatism Soc. (hon.), Spanish Rheumatism Soc. (hon.), Finnish Rheumatism Soc. (hon.), Brazilian Rheumatism Soc. (hon.), Irish Soc. Rheumatism and Rehab. (hon.), Italian Soc. Amyloidosis (hon.), Boston U. Sch. Medicine Alumni Assn. (past pres.), Harvard Club (Boston), Wightman Tennis Ctr. (Weston, Mass.), Interurban Clin. Club, Boulders Club (Carefree, Ariz.), Phi Beta Kappa, Alpha Omega Alpha. Jewish. Home Phone: 617 527 1121; Office Phone: 617 638 8900. Personal E mail: aljo2@mac.com. Business E-Mail: jlienert@bu.edu. *

COHEN, ARNOLD NORMAN, gastroenterologist; b. NYC, Nov. 5, 1949; s. Norman and Edna C.; m. Colleen Ruth Carey; children: Eric Arnold, Leslie Carey. BA summa cum laude, Hobart Coll., 1971; MD, Harvard U., 1975. Diplomate Am. Bd. Internal Medicine, Am. Bd. Gastroenterology. Resident internal medicine U. Pa., Phila., 1975-78, asst. instr. medicine, 1977-78; fellow gastroenterology, instr. medicine Northwestern U., Chgo., 1978-80; assoc. clin. prof. medicine U. Wash. Med. Sch., Seattle, 1980—2007; mem. faculty Spokane (Wash.) Family Medicine Residency, 1980—; pvt. practice gastroenterology Spokane, 1980—. Mem. various coms. St. Lukes-Deaconess Hosp., Spokane, 1980—; pres. med. staff St. Lukes Hosp., 1985-86; clin. assoc. prof., medicine U. Washington Sch. Medicine, 2007-. Contbr. articles to profl. jours. and textbooks. Fellow ACP, Am. Coll. Gastroenterology; mem. Am. Soc. Gastrointestinal Endoscopy, Am. Gastroent. Soc., Wash. Med. Soc., Spokane Internal Med. Soc., Phi Beta Kappa, Alpha Omega Alpha. Avocations: shooting sports, martial arts, swimming. Home: 3514 S Jefferson St Spokane WA 99203-1441 Office: Spokane Digestive Disease Ctr 801 W 5th Ave Spokane WA 99204-2823 Office Phone: 509-747-5145. *

COHEN, ARNOLD W., gynecologist, obstetrician; MD, Cornell U., Ithaca. Intern Hosp. Of the Univ. Pa., resident, fellow; dir. women's health Aetna, US Healthcare; dir. obstetrics maternal- fetal medicine Hosp. Of the Univ. Pa.; chmn. divsn. maternal-fetal medicine Albert Einstein Med. Ctr. Prof. ob-gyn. Thomas Jefferson Univ. Hosp.; chmn. com. on course coordination ACOG; bd. mem. Soc. for Maternal Fetal Medicine; chmn. Med. Liability Com.; chmn. nat. adv. com. Victor Centers for Jewish Genetic Diseases; clin. adv. bd. Sequenom. Mem.: Coding and Govt. Rels. com. Office: Albert Einstein Medical Center Klein Bldg Ste 410 5501 Old York Rd Philadelphia PA 19141 Office Phone: 215-456-6991. Office Fax: 215-456-2386.

COHEN, BERNARD A., pediatric dermatologist; b. Balt., Apr. 2, 1951; BA, U. Pa., 1973; MD, Johns Hopkins U., 1977. Cert. Am. Bd. Pediat., 1981, Am. Bd. Dermatology, 1984. Residency in pediat. Johns Hopkins U. Sch. Medicine, Balt., fellowship in dermatology, dir. pediatric dermatology Johns Hopkins Children's Ctr., 1991—, assoc. prof. pediat. and dermatology Johns Hopkins Hosp.; dir. pediatric dermatology Children's Hosp., Pitts., 1984-91. Contbr. articles to profl. jours. Fellow Am. Bd. Pediat., Am. Bd. Dermatology; mem. Soc. Pediatric Dermatology, Md. Dermotology Soc., Am. Acad. Dermatology, Am. Acad. Pediatric Dermatology Found. Office: John Hopkins Hosp 601 N Wolfe St Rm 208 Baltimore MD 21287-0004

COHEN, BERNARD H., dermatologist, educator; MD, Columbia U., 1967. Diplomate Am. Bd. Dermatology, 1972, cert. hair restoration surgery. Resident dermatology NYU Med. Ctr., NYC, 1968—71; clin. prof. dermatology and cutaneous surgery dept. Univ. of Miami Sch. Med., dir. surg. tng. dermatology and cutaneous surgery dept., voluntary prof.; hosp. affiliation include Univ. of Miami Jackson Meml. Hosp. Office: Cole Instruments Ste 230 4425 Ponce De Leon Blvd Miami FL 33146 Office Phone: 305-476-9544.

COHEN, BRUCE ARNOLD, nuerologist; b. Chgo., Nov. 6, 1949; s. Norman and Frances (Fisher) C.; m. Susan Sackheim, Aug. 18, 1974; children: Danielle, Michael, Benjamin. BA in psychology, Univ. Ill., 1971, MD, 1978. Diplomate Am. Bd. Psychiatry & Neurology, Am. Bd. Internal Medicine. Resident in internal medicine Luth. Gen. Hosp., Park Ridge, Ill., 1978-81; resident in neurology Northwestern U. Med. Ctr., Chgo., 1981-84; instr. neurology Northwestern U. Med. Sch., 1984-88, asst. prof. neurology, 1988-92, assoc. prof. neurology, 1992—99, prof. neurology, 1999—; attending neurologist Northwestern Meml. Hosp., Chgo., 1984—; cons. neurologist Rehab. Inst. Chgo., 1987—; dir., co-founder Northwestern Comprehensive Multiple Sclerosis Program. Cons. neurology AMA, 1991—; neurology bd. examiner Am. Bd. Psychology and Neurology; ad hoc reviewer Neurology Jours.; clin. practice, dir. dept. neurology Northwestern Med. Faculty Found., 1990-95. Contbr. articles to profl. jours. Spl. review com. AIDS grant NIMH, Washington, 1987-89; profl. adv. com. Chgo-Ill. MS Soc., 1991—; chair Clin. Care Com., Nat. Multiple Sclerosis Soc., 2006-, Multiple Sclerosis Sect., Am. Acad. Neurology, 2008-10. Recipient Edmund James scholar Univ. Ill., 1967-71. Fellow ACP, Am. Acad. Neurology; mem. Am. Neurologic Assn., Phi Beta Kappa. Office: # 1121 710 N Lake Shore Dr Chicago IL 60611-4542

COHEN, BRUCE HOWARD, neurologist; b. St. Louis, Apr. 9, 1956; m. Sheryl Markowitz, Nov. 11, 1989; children: Jordan Benjamin, Arielle Gaila. AB summa cum laude in chemistry, Washington U., St. Louis, 1978; MD, Albert Einstein Coll. Medicine, 1982. Intern, pediatrics Children's Hosp. Phila., 1982—83, resident, neurological pediatrics and neurology, 1983—84, pediatric neuro-oncology fellowship, 1987-89, cons. in neurology to Neuro-Oncology Clinic, 1987-89; pediatric neurology onclogy fellowship Neurol. Inst. and Babies Hosp., Columbia-Presbyn. Med. Ctr., NYC, 1984-87; asst. attending physician Harlem Hosp. Med. Ctr., NYC, 1985-87; instr. in pediatrics Children's Hosp. of Phila., U. Pa., 1988-89; clin. assoc. dept. neurology Cleve. Clinic Found., 1989, asst. staff dept. neurology, 1989-91, staff dept. neurology, 1991—; assoc. prof. divsn. neurology, dept. pediatrics Ohio State U. Coll. Medicine, 1992—. Chmn. infant brain tumor study, Childrens Cancer Group; trustee United Mitochondrial Disease Found. Contbr. articles to profl. jours. Recipient Am. Cancer Soc. Clin. Oncology Fellow grant, 1988-89, Peter Preuss Found. grant, 1987-88, John C. Sowden Meml. award (chemistry dept. Washington U.), 1978. Fellow Nat. Bd. Med. Examiners, Am. Bd. Pediatrics, Am. Bd. Psychiatry and Neurology; mem. AMA, Child Neurology Soc. (vice chmn. practice com. 1996—), Am. Acad. Neurology, Alpha Omega Alpha, Sigma Xi. Office: Cleve Clinic Found S80 9500 Euclid Ave Cleveland OH 44195 Office Phone: 216-444-9182.

COHEN, BRUCE MICHAEL, psychiatrist, educator, scientist, health facility administrator; b. Univ. Heights, Ohio, Sept. 1, 1947; s. Herschel and Natalie (Marshall) C.; m. Marian A. Oliner, July 11, 1970; children: Matthew, Laura. BS, MIT, Cambridge, Mass., 1969; MD, Case Western Res. U., Cleveland, Ohio, 1975; PhD, Case Western Res. U., Dept. Biology, Cleveland, Ohio, 1975. Diplomate Am. Bd. Psychiatry and Neurology, 1979, Nat. Bd. Med. Examiners, 1976, Mass. Lic., 1976. Clin. fellow in psychiatry Harvard Med. Sch., Boston, 1975—78, instr. in psychiatry, 1978-81, asst. prof. psychiatry, 1981-85, assoc. prof. psychiatry, 1985-95, prof. psychiatry, 1995—, Robertson-Steele chair, prof. psychiats., 2007—; resident in psychiatry McLean Hosp., Belmont, Mass., 1975-78, chief resident in psychiatry, 1977-78, asst. psychiatrist, 1978—83, assoc. psychiatrist, 1984—88, spec. asst. to the gen. dir./psychiatrist-in-chief, 1987—88, assoc. gen. dir., 1988-94, psychiatrist, 1988—, sr. v.p. rsch. & tng., 1994-97, pres., psychiatrist in chief, 1997—2005, head dept. psychiatry Med. Sch. Harvard U., 1997—2005, dir. Shervert Frazier Rsch. Inst., 2006—; dir. adult psychiatry residency tng. program combined Mass. Gen. Hosp./McLean Hosp., Belmont, Mass., 1995—97. Vis. physician MIT Clin. Rsch. Ctr., Cambridge, Mass., 1979—85, vis. sci., 1993—; asst. chief clin. rsch. sect. Mailman Rsch. Ctr., Belmont, 1979—81, assoc. chief clin. rsch. sect., 1981—85, chief clin. rsch. sect. Clin. Biochemistry Lab., 1981—85, dir. Molecular Pharmacology Lab., 1985—; cons. psychiatrist Westwood Lodge, Westwood, Mass., 1986—88; assoc. dir. Mental Health Clin. Rsch. Ctr. McLean Hosp., Belmont, 1981—88, program dir. Biomedial Rsch. Support Grant, 1988—92, dir. residency training program, 1993—97, dir. brain imaging program, 1993—97; pres. McLean Health Svcs., Belmont, 1998—99, dir. & CEO, 1999—2006. Contbr. numerous sci. articles and abstracts to peer-reviewed jours.; author 20 book chpts.; adv. editor, Psychopharmacology, 1980-2002; assoc. editor Am. Jour. of Psychiatry, 2000- Laureate investigator Nat. Alliance for Rsch. on Schizophrenia and Depression, 1989. Predoctoral fellow NSF, Case Western Res. U., 1971-73, Ethel duPont Warren fellow in psychiatry Harvard Med. Sch., McLean Hosp. 1977-78, fellowship, Scottish Rite Schizophrenia Rsch. Program, NMJ, USA, 1978-80, recipient 11 grants NIMH, 3 grants, 1 grant NSF, NCRR, Ctr. grant SMRI, Scottish Rite Schizophrenia Program, 11 projects program grants NIMH, Named Psychiatrist of Yr., Nat. Alliance Mentally Ill, Mass., 2005, Jullius Axefrod Mentorship award, Am. Coll. Neuropsychopharmacology, 2008 Fellow Mass. Psychiatric Soc., Soc. Magnetic Resonance, Am. Psychiat. Assn., Am. Coll. Neuropsychpharmacology; mem. AAAS, AMA, Soc. Biological Psychiatry Office: McLean Hosp Mailman Rsch Ctr 115 Mill St Belmont MA 02478-1048 Office Phone: 617-855-3227. Office Fax: 617-855-3670. Business E-Mail: cohenb@mclean.harvard.edu.

COHEN, BURTON JACK, otolaryngologist, educator; b. Louisville, 1936; MD, U. Louisville, 1962. Diplomate Am. Bd. Otolaryngology. Intern Detroit Receiving Hosp., 1962-63; resident in ear nose and throat U. Louisville Hosp., 1965-69; staff Jewish Hosp., Louisville, 1969—. Clin. prof. U. Louisville. Fellow: ACS, Am. Neurotologic Soc., Am. Acad. Otolaryngology-Head and Neck Surgery, Assn. Acad. Physicians, Am. Acad. Pediat. Home Phone: 502-426-2371; Office Phone: 502-583-9425, 502-894-8441, 502-583-7722. Personal E-mail: burton.cohen@insightbb.com.

COHEN, DAVID HARRIS, neuroscientist, educator, academic administrator; b. Springfield, Mass., Aug. 26, 1938; s. Nathan Edward and Sylvia (Golden) C.; m. Arline Wyler, June 17, 1960 (div. Aug. 1980); children: Bonnie, Daniel, Ian; m. Anne Helena Remmes, Jan. 17, 1981; 1 child, Kaitlin. BA, Harvard U., 1960; PhD, U. Calif., Berkeley, 1963. Postdoctoral fellow UCLA, 1963—64; asst. prof. physiology Western Res. U., Cleve., 1964—68; assoc. prof. to prof. physiology U. Va. Med. Sch., Charlottesville, 1968—79; prof., chmn. neurobiology SUNY, Stony Brook, 1979—86; v.p. rsch., dean grad. sch. Northwestern U., Evanston, Ill., 1986—91, provost, 1992—95, prof. neurobiology and physiology, 1986—95; v.p. arts and scis., dean of faculty Columbia U., NYC, 1995—2003, prof. biol. scis. and psychiatry, 1995—2008, v.p. arts and scis., dean faculty emeritus, 2003—, Alan H. Kempner prof. emeritus biol. scis. and prof. emeritus neurosci. psychiatry, 2008—; provost U. People, 2009—. Mem. adv. com. directorate biol., behavioral and social scis. NSF, 1982-89; mem. life scis. rsch. adv. bd. Air Force Office Sci. Rsch., 1985-91; mem. bd. govs. Argonne Nat. Lab., 1986-92; bd. dirs. Zenith Electronics, Inc., 1990-95, Rsch. Librs. Group, 1993-97, 2001—06, Columbia U. Press, 1996-2005, Thuris Corp., 2000—, Trevor Day Sch., 2000-08, Socratic Arts, 2003—, KLi, 2004-06, The Grass Found., 2006—09, Eduventures, 2006—, Schiller Internat. U., 2007-08; ptnr. Knowledge Investment Ptnrs., 2003—09, Identity Theft 911, 2004—; bd. dirs. Oak Tree Ednl. Ptnrs., Inc., 2010-. Mem. various editl. bds. profl. jours.; contbr. articles to profl. jours. Bd. overseers Fermi Nat. Accelerator Lab., Batavia, Ill., 1987-94; exec. com. Ill. Gov.'s Sci. Adv. Com., 1989-95; mem. Liaison Com. Med. Edn., 1987-89; bd. dirs. N.Y. Structural Biology Ctr., 1999-2003. Fellow AAAS; mem. Soc. Neurosci. (pres. 1981-82), Pavlovian Soc. (pres. 1978-79), Assn. Neurosci. Depts. and Programs (pres. 1981-82), Nat. Soc. Med. Rsch. (v.p. 1984-85), Nat. Assn. Biomed. Rsch. (bd. dirs. 1985-87), Coun. Acad. Socs. (adminstrv. bd. 1982-87, chmn. 1985-86), Assn. Am. Med. Colls. (exec. coun. 1984-91, chmn. 1989-90), Internat. Brain Rsch. Orgn. (ctrl. coun. 1978-82), Inst. Medicine Forum on Neurosci. Nervous Sys. Disorders. Jewish. Home: 445 Riverside Dr Apt 72 New York NY 10027-6801 Home Phone: 212-316-6242. Business E-Mail: dhc14@columbia.edu.

COHEN, DAVID JOEL, medical educator; b. New Haven, Nov. 2, 1960; AB summa cum laude, Harvard U., 1982, MD, 1986, MSc, 1994. Diplomate Am. Bd. Internal Medicine; lic. physician, Mass. Intern then resident Brigham and Women's Hosp., Boston, 1986-89; clin. rsch. fellow Beth Israel Hosp., Boston, 1989-94, now asst. dir. interventional cardiology; fellow Harvard Sch. Pub. Health, Boston, 1992-94, instr. health policy and mgmt., 1995—; instr. medicine Harvard Med. Sch., Boston, 1993-96, asst. prof., 1996—. Asst. dir. invasive cardiology sect. Beth Israel Hosp., 1994—. Contbr. chpts. to books and numerous articles to profl. jours. Grantee Johnson and Johnson, 1993-94, Am. Heart Assn., 1995—. Mem. Phi Beta Kappa. Home: 824 W 56th St Kansas City MO 64113-1111 *

COHEN, DAVID JOHN, cardiothoracic surgeon; b. San Antonio, Jan. 13, 1947; s. Melvin David and Betty (Brown) C.; m. Deborah Milton, May 29, 1976; children: John, Christopher, Scott, Joshua, Benjamin. BA in Biochemistry, Rice U., Houston, 1968; MD, Washington U., 1972; BS in Mech. Engring. summa cum laude, U. Tex., San Antonio, 1999; grad., US Army Command and Gen. Staff Coll., 2001; MPA, Harvard U., Cambridge, Mass., 2003. Intern Johns Hopkins Hosp., Balt., 1972-73, resident in gen. surgery, 1973-74, U. Wash. Affiliated Hosps., Seattle, 1976-79; resident in cardiothoracic surgery Hosp. of U. Pa., Phila., 1979-81; chief dept. cardiovasc. physiology Walter Reed Army Inst. of Rsch., Washington, 1981-83; staff Brooke Army Med. Ctr., Ft. Sam Houston, Tex., 1983-84, asst. chief cardiothoracic surgery San Antonio, 1992-93, dir. heart transplant program, 1994—2001, chief cardiothroacic surgery, 1993—2002, cardiothoracic surgeon, 2005—06, ret., 2006; staff U. Wis. Hosp., Madison, 1984-87, William S. Middleton VA Hosp., Madison, 1984-87, chief thoracic surgery svc., 1986-87; staff Med. Ctr. Hosp., San Antonio, 1987-92, Audie L. Murphy VA Hosp., San Antonio, 1987-92, chief cardiothoracic surgery, 1991-92, dir. surg. ICU, 1988-92; sr. clin. cons. for combat doctrine and devel. US Army Med. Ctr. and Sch., Ft. Sam Houston, 2003—05; dep. comdr. for clin. svcs. 86th Combat Support Hosp., Iraq, 2004—05; pvt. practice cardiothoracic surgery San Antonio, 2006—. Bd. dirs. Tex. Organ Sharing Alliance, San Antonio, 1994—2002; cardiac transplant fellow Tex. Heart Inst., Houston, 1993; cons. thoracic and cardiovasc. surgery US Army Surgeon Gen., 1999—2002; pres. Alamo Cardiothoracic Surg. Assocs., P.A., San Antonio, 2006—. Mem. nat. health and safety com. Boy Scouts Am., 2006—, asst. scoutmaster San Antonio, 1990—2002; dep. chief med. officer External Interface, Boy Scout Nat. Jamboree, 2010, Boy Scouts America Southern Region Bd., 2010—, Rotary Club San Antonio, 2005—. Col. Tex. State Guard US Army, 2009—. Decorated Legion of Merit, Bronze Star, Meritorious Svc. medal (4), Army Commendation medal (6), Order of Mil. Med. Merit; recipient Nat. Collegiate Engring. award, US Achievement Acad., 1998. Fellow ACS, Am. Coll. Cardiology, Am. Coll. Chest Physicians; mem. Am. Assn. Thoracic Surgeons, Soc. Thoracic Surgeons, San Antonio Cardiology Soc. (sec.-treas. 1997-98, pres. 1998-99), Golden Key, Rotary Internat., Tau Beta Pi. Jewish. Avocations: horseback riding, camping, skiing. Office: Alamo Cardiothoracic Surgery Assocs PA 525 Oak Ctr Ste 270 San Antonio TX 78258-3917 Office Phone: 210-495-4200. Personal E-mail: david_j_cohen@hotmail.com.

COHEN, DAVID LEON, physician; b. St. Louis, Feb. 2, 1947; s. Benjamin David and Hannah (Finfer) C.; m. Sheila Zeisel, July 2, 1974; children: Robin, Lori, Jonathan, Jennifer. BS, Roosevelt U., 1967; MS, Chgo. Med. Sch., 1972; MD, Mt. Sinai Sch. Medicine, 1976. Diplomate Am. Bd. Dermatology. Intern in internal medicine Michael Reese Hosp., Chgo., 1976—77; resident Mt. Sinai Hosp., NYC, 1977—80; pvt. practice Hewlett and Jamaica, NY, 1980—. Clin. pfof. dept. dermatology Mount Sinai Sch. Medicine, NYC, 1980—. Office: 1800 Rockaway Ave Ste 208 Hewlett NY 11557-1645: 175-61 HIllslide Ave Ste 404 Jamaica NY 11432 Office Phone: 516-887-4343. Business E-Mail: david.l.cohen@mssm.edu.

COHEN, DAVID WALTER, academic administrator, educator, periodontist; b. Phila., Dec. 15, 1926; s. Abram and Goldie (Schlein) C.; m. Betty Axelrod, Dec. 19, 1948 (dec. Mar. 1992); children: Jane Ellen, Amy Sue, Joanne Louise. DDS, U. Pa., 1950; DSc (hon.), Boston U., 1975; PhD (hon.), Hebrew U., Jerusalem, 1977, U. Athens, 1979; Dr Honoris Causa, U. Louis Pasteur, Strasbourg, France, 1986; DHL (hon.), U. Detroit, 1989; DSci with honoris causa, Carol Davilla Med. Sch., Bucharest, Romania, 2008; DSc (hon.), Drexel U., Coll. Medicine, 2009; DHEB (hon.), Grat2 Coll., 2009. Diplomate: Am. Bd. Periodontology (chmn. 1972). Research fellow pathology and periodontia Beth Israel Hosp., Boston, 1950-51; mem. faculty U. Pa. Sch. Dentistry, Phila., 1951—, prof. periodontics, 1962-86, chmn. dept., 1962-73; dean Sch. Dental Medicine U. Pa., Phila., 1972-83; dean emeritus U. Pa. Sch. Dentistry, Phila., 1983—; pres. Med. Coll. Pa., 1986-93; chancellor Allegheny U. of Health Scis., 1993-98; chancellor emeritus Coll. Medicine Drexel U., 1998—, trustee, 2009; mem. staff Albert Einstein Med. Center, Phila., Children's Hosp., Phila.; pres. Jewish Publ. Soc., 1993-96. Vis. prof. Boston U. Sch. Grad Dentistry, 1972—; nat. cons. periodontics USAF, 1965-70; bd. govs. Hebrew U., Jerusalem, Betty and Walter Cohen chair in periodontal rsch., 1986; D. Walter Cohen endowed chair in periodontics U. Pa., 1995. Author: (with H.M. Goldman) Periodontia, 1957, (with others) An Introduction to Periodontia, 1959, Periodontal Therapy, 1960, (with R. Genco and Goldman) Contemporary Periodontics, 1990, (with Genco, L. Rose and B. Mealey) Periodental Medicine, 1999, Periodontics, Medicine Surgery and Implants, 2001; also numerous articles and chpts. V.p. Jewish Publ. Soc., 1985-89, pres., 1993-96; pres. Nat. Mus. Am. Jewish History, Phila., 1996—2006. Served with USN, 1944-45, NMASH chmn. emritus, 2008. Named to Ctrl. H.S. Hall of Fame, 1976; 1st Presdl. scholar U. Calif., San Francisco, 1985-86; named for him Hebrew U. Betty and D. Walter Cohen Chair in Periodontal Rsch., 1986, U. Pa. D. Walter Cohen Endowed Chair in Periodontics, 1995; D. Walter Cohen Mid. East Ctr. for Dental Edn. dedicated by Hebrew U. of Jerusalem, 1997. Fellow AAAS, Am. Acad. Oral Pathology, Am. Acad. Periodontology, Inst. of Medicine of Nat. Acad. Scis.; mem. Am. Soc. Periodontists (pres. 1967), Friends of Nat. Inst. Dental Rsch. (pres. 1998—2000). Office: Drexel Univ Coll Medicine 1601 Cheery St Ste1050 Philadelphia PA 19102

COHEN, ELAINE HELENA, pediatrician, cardiologist, educator; b. Boston, Oct. 14, 1941; d. Samuel Clive and Lillian (Stocklan) C.; m. Marvin Leon Gale, May 7, 1972; 1 child, Pamela Beth Gale. AB, Conn. Coll., 1963; postgrad., Tufts U., 1963—64; MD, Woman's Med. Coll. Pa., 1969. Diplomate Am. Bd. Pediat. Pediat. intern Children's Hosp. of L.A., 1969-70, resident in pediat., 1970-71; fellow in pediat. cardiology UCLA Ctr. Health Scis., 1971-72, L.A. County/U. So. Calif. Med. Ctr., LA, 1972-74; pediatrician Children's Med. Group of South Bay, Chula Vista, Calif., 1974—. Clin. instr. dept. pediat. UCLA Sch. Medicine, 1971-72, U. So. Calif., L.A., 1972-74; asst. clin. prof. dept. pediat. U. Calif., San Diego Sch. Medicine, San Diego, 1974-98, preceptor dept. pediat., 1992—, assoc. clin. prof. dept. pediat., 1998—. Fellow Am. Acad. Pediat.; mem. Calif. Med. Assn., San Diego County Med. Soc. Office: Children's Med Group South Bay 280 E St Chula Vista CA 91910-2945 Office Phone: 619-425-3951.

COHEN, FRED EHRENKRANZ, biophysics professor; b. Miami Beach, Fla., Sept. 10, 1956; s. James Cohen and Ruth Belle (Ehrenkranz) Levkoff; m. Carolyn Beth Klebanoff, July 19, 1981; 1 child, Alison. BS, Yale U., 1978; MD, Stanford U., 1984; PhD, Oxford U., Eng., 1980. Asst. prof. U. Calif., San Francisco, 1985-91, assoc. prof., 1991—94, prof. Medicine, Cellular & Molecular Pharmacology, Pharm. Chemistry, and Biochemistry & Biophysics, 1994—, chief, Div. of Endocrinology and Metabolism, 1995—96. Mem. sci. and med. adv. bd. Chrion Corp., Emeryville, Calif., 1988—, sci. adv. bd. Procept, Inc., Cambridge, Mass., 1988—. Assoc. editor Jour. Molecular Biology, London, 1990—; mem. editorial bd. Protein Engring., 1992—, Perspectives in Drug Discovery & Design, 1993—. Recipient Silver Knight in Math. award The Miami Herald, 1974, Robert C. Bates fellowship Yale U., 1977, Merriman prize Yale U., 1978; Rhodes scholar, 1978, Searle scholar, 1988. Fellow ACP, Am. Acad. Arts and Sciences; mem. Am. Soc. Clin. Investigation, Endocrine Soc. (Weitzman Young Investigator award 1992), Western Assn. of Physicians, Biophys. Soc., Inst. Medicine (2004). Office: U Calif San Francisco 600 16th St N472J Box 2240 San Francisco CA 94143-2240 E-mail: cohen@cmpharm.ucsf.edu.

COHEN, GORDON S., health products executive; b. NYC, May 18, 1937; s. Leon Lewis and Irene (Lipton) C.; m. Marjorie Rennick, June 12, 1960; children: Terri Susan, Lisa Michelle, Bonnie Lynne. AB, Brown U., 1959; MD, Yale U., 1963. Diplomate Am. Bd. Pathology, Anatomic Pathology and Clin. Pathology. Instr. dept. pathology Yale U., New Haven, 1967-70, asst. prof. pathology, 1970-71, asst. clin. prof. pathology, 1971-76; pres. Jeneric Industries, Wallingford, Conn., 1975-86; chmn. Pentron Corp., Wallingford, 1977—2008; pres. Jeneric Pentron Inc., Wallingford, 1987—2008. Attending pathologist Yale-New Haven Hosp., 1970-71, Hosp. St. Raphael, New Haven, 1971-76; pathologist The Charlotte Hungerford Hosp., Torrington, Conn., 1967-70, mem. adv. coun. biology and medicine, Brown U., 2007-, libr. adv. coun. mem., 2009-; mng. dir. Tartan Ltd, LLC, 2008-. Author numerous articles in field. Sr. edn. officer Milford (Conn.) U.S. Power Squadron, 1987; mem. Congressman DeNardis's Small Bus. Adv. Com., 1982; bd. dirs. Mary Wade Home, 2002—. Capt. (M.C.) USAR, 1964-70. Mem. Internat. Acad. Pathology, NY Acad. Scis., Phi Beta Kappa, Sigma Xi, Alpha Omega Alpha. Avocations: sailing, shooting, book collecting. Office Phone: 203-245-5120. Business E-Mail: gordon@tartanltd.com.

COHEN, HARRIS L., diagnostic radiologist, consultant; b. Bklyn., Sept. 18, 1951; s. Samuel G. and Lola Estera (Altman) C.; m. Sandra Wilensky, Oct. 18, 1979; children: David Matthew, Lauren Elizabeth, Benjamin Adam. BA cum laude in Chemistry, CUNY, Bklyn., 1969—73; MD in Medicine, SUNY, Bklyn., 1972—76. Diplomate Am. Bd. Radiology, Nat. Bd. Med. Examiners; cert. added qualifications in pediatric radiology Am. Bd. Radiology. Asst. prof. radiology SUNY Health Sci. Ctr., Bklyn., 1981-88; asst. chief of imaging Brookdale Hosp. Med. Ctr., Bklyn., 1983-85; med. dir. diagnostic med. imaging program Coll. Health Related Professions, SUNY Health Sci. Ctr., Bklyn., 1985—88, 1994—; assoc. prof. radiology Cornell U. Med. Coll., NYC, 1988-93; chief pediatric CT and ultrasound North Shore U. Hosp.-Cornell, Manhasset, NY, 1988-93, assoc. dir. divsn. CT/ultrasound/magnetic resonance imaging, 1988-93; assoc. dir. radiology Kings County Hosp., Bklyn., 1993-2000; prof. radiology SUNY Health Sci. Ctr., Bklyn., 1993-2000, assoc. chmn. acad. affair and clin. rsch., 1998-2000; vis. prof. radiology, dir. divsn. pediat. imaging Johns Hopkins U., Balt., 2000—02; prof. radiology, vice chmn. dept. radiology, dir. divsn., body imaging, chief pediatric body imaging SUNY, Stony Brook, 2002—08, dir. abdominal imaging fellow program, 2003—08; med. dir. radiology LeBonheur Children's Hosp., Memphis, 2008—; exec. vice chmn. radiology, prof. radiology, ob-gyn. and pediat. U. Tenn. Sch. Medicine,

2008—09; chmn., dept. radiology U. Tenn. Health Sci. Ctr., 2009. Dir. divsn. ultrasound U. and Kings County Hosps., Bklyn., 1985-88, 93-2000, dir. divsn. pediat. radiology, 1999-2000; cons. ultrasound and pediatric imaging Brookdale Hosp. Med. Ctr., Bklyn., 1988-2009; RSNA internat. vis. prof., India, 2005; RSNA Eyler editl. fellow, 2004-05; editor-in-chief, continuous profl. improvement program Am. Coll. Radiology, editor-in-chief ACR PSE Series Author, editor, co-editor: Ultrasonography of the Prenatal and Neonatal Brain, 1996, 2d edit., 2002, Spanish transl., 2002, Obstetrics & Gynecology (Ultrasound), 1997, Fetal and Pediatric Ultrasound, 2001, Chinese Transl., 2003, Spanish Transl., Ecografia Fetal y Pediatrica, 2004, Gastrointestinal Disease VI, 2004, Ultrasound III, 2005, Neuroradiology III, 2006, Chest Disease VI, 2007; author, editor, co-editor Bone Disease, 2010; mem. editl. bd.: Jour. Diagnostic Med. Sonography, 1985—2000, Jour. Ultrasound in Medicine, 2002—, Ultrasound Quarterly, 2002—, reviewer: Radiographics, 1991— (Editors cert. recognition, 1990-2003); contbr. chapters to books, articles to profl. jours., ednl. CDs and videos. Recipient Master Tchr. award in radiology, SUNY Health Sci. Ctr. at Bklyn. Alumni Assn., 1996, Tchr. of Yr. award, SUNY Stony Brook Radiology, 2006; named one of Best Drs. in NY, Castle Connoly, 2003—, Radiology Editors Forum, 2006—, NY Mag., 2003—08, Best Drs. in Am., Castle County, 2007—, America's Top Radiologist, Consumer's Rsch. Coun. America, 2007. Fellow: Am. Inst. Ultrasound in Medicine (chmn. pediat. sect. 1994—95, chmn. ctrl. program com. 1995—97, bd. dirs. 1999—2002, bd. govs. 1999—2002, co-chair emergency ultrasound 2001—04), Am. Acad. Pediat. (chmn. radiology sect. 1992—94, exec. coun. sect. radiology 2008—, grand round contbg. editor radiology), Am. Coll. Radiology (stds. and accreditation com. 1992—98, commn. ultrasound edn. com. 1998—, task force on disaster planning 2001—05, assoc. editor, ACR Case in Point 2010, disting. com. svc. award 1998, 2004), Soc. Radiologists in Ultrasound (chmn. constn. com. 1996—98, program com. 2004—07); mem.: Radiologic Soc. N.Am. (audiovisual com. 1992—96, exhibits com. 2002—04, coord. ultrasound cases of day 2004—06, exhibits com. 2007—, Eyler editl. fellow 2004—05, internat. vis. prof., India 2006), Soc. Pediat. Radiology (liaison to Am. Acad. Pediat. 1993—94, liaison to Am. Inst. Ultrasound in Medicine 1995, program com. 2004—08, nom. com. 2007—, chmn., SRU futures ultrasound com. 2008—09, bd. dirs. 2009—, bd. dir. 2009—), SUNY-Downstate Alumni Assn. (councillor, bd. mgrs. 1998—2001), Alpha Omega Alpha. Avocations: basketball, baseball. Home: 5639 Ashley Sq S Memphis TN 38120-2470 Personal E-mail: hcohenmb@optonline.net.

COHEN, HARVEY JAY, geriatrician, hematologist, oncologist, educator; b. Bklyn., Oct. 21, 1940; s. Joseph and Anne (Margolin) C.; m. Sandra Helen Levine, June 1964; children: Ian Mitchell, Pamela Robin. BS, Bklyn. Coll., 1961; MD, Downstate Med. Coll., Bklyn., 1965. Diplomate Am. Bd. Internal Medicine, Am. Bd. Hematology. Intern, then resident internal medicine Duke U. Med. Ctr., Durham, NC, 1965-67, fellow hematology and oncology, 1969-71; chief hematology-oncology VA Med. Ctr., Durham, NC, 1975-76, chief med. svc., 1976-82, assoc. chief staff-edn., 1982—2007, geriatric rsch., edn. and clin. ctr.; assoc. prof. medicine Duke U. Med. Ctr., Durham, 1976-80, Walter Kempner prof. medicine, 2007—, also dir. Ctr. for Study of Aging, 1982—, chair dept. medicine, 2006—10, prof. med., 1980—2007. Chair bd. sci. counselors Nat. Inst. Aging, 1999—2003; chair Women's Health Initiative, Observational Study Monitoring Bd., 2005—. Author: Medical Immunology, 1977, co-author: (with H.G. Koenig) The Link Between Religion and Health: Psychoneuroimmunology and the Faith Factor, 2002, Taking Care After 50, 2000, Practical Geratric Oncology, 2010; editor: Cancer I and II, 1987, Jour. Gerontology: Med. Scis., 1988-92, Geriatric Medicine, 1997; contbr. 300 articles to profl. jours. Served as surgeon USPHS, 1967-69. Fellow ACP, Am. Geriat. Soc. (bd. dirs. 1987-96, chair bd. dirs. 1995-96, sec. 1991-93, ethics com. 1992-96, pres. 1994-95, Dennis W. Jahnigen Meml. award 2005), Gerontology Soc. Am. (clin. sec., rsch. com. 1987-92, chair publs. com. 1996-98, program chair 1994, pres. 2000, Joseph Freeman award, 1998, Donald P. Kent award, 2005); mem. Am. Soc. Clin. Oncology, BJ Kennedy award, 2010, Am. Soc. Hematology, Am. Assn. Cancer Rsch., Cancer and Acute Leukemia Group B (chair, Cancer in Elderly Com.), Assn. Am. Physicians, Internat. Soc. Geriat. Oncology (bd. dirs. 2000-06, pres. 2004-06, Paul Calabresi award, 2009). Home: 2811 Friendship Cir Durham NC 27705-5521 Office: Duke U Med Ctr for Study Aging & Human Devel Box 3003 Durham NC 27710-0001 Business E-Mail: cohen015@mc.duke.edu.

COHEN, HARVEY JOEL, pediatric hematology and oncology educator; b. NYC, July 4, 1943; s. Phillip and Ida (Teitel) C.; m. Ilene Verne Boskeger, Aug. 15, 1965; children: Philip Jason, Jonathan Todd. BS, Bklyn. Coll., 1964; MD, PhD, Duke U., 1970. Intern Children's Hosp., Boston, 1970-71, resident, 1973-74; instr. pediatrics Harvard U. Med. Sch., Boston, 1974-76, asst. prof., 1976-79, assoc. prof., 1979-81; assoc. prof. pediatrics U. Rochester (N.Y.) Med. Ctr., 1981-84, prof., 1984-93, assoc. chmn. dept., 1987-93, chief pediatric hematology and oncology, 1981-93; chmn. dept. pediatrics Stanford (Calif.) U. Sch. Medicine, 1993—2006, prof., 1993—2006; chief staff Lucile Salter Packard Children's Hosp. at Stanford, 1993—2006. Med. advisor Montgomery Med. Ventures, San Francisco, 1984—97; sci. advisor St. Jude Children's Rsch. Hosp., Memphis, 1985—90, 2001—; chmn. hematology study sect. NIH, Washington, 1986—88. Editor: Hematology: Basic Principles and Practice, 1991, 94, 99, 2005. Med. dir. Camp Good Days and Spl. Times, Rochester, 1981—93, Monroe County chpt. Am.Cancer Soc., Rochester, 1983—93; med. dir. Rochester br. Cooley's Anemia Found., 1984—93; bd. dirs. Lucile Pakcard Children's Hosp., 1993—97, Lucile Packard Found. for Children's Health, 1997—2000, Lucile Pakcard Children's Hosp., 2000—06, Ronald McDonald House of Palo Alto, Calif., 1995—2005, Children's Health Coun., 1996—2005. Tng. grantee Nat. Inst. Gen. Med. Scis., 1983-90, Nat. Inst. Child Health and Human Devel., 1990-94. Mem. Soc. for Pediatric Rsch. (pres. 1988-89), Am. Soc. for Clin. Investigation, Am. Pediatric Soc. Democrat. Jewish. Achievements include research in on continuous assay for superoxide production, effect of selenium on synthesis of glutatnione peroxidase; relationship of in vitro and in vivo killing of leukemic cells by asparaganse clinical trials in childhood leukemia; comparative proteomics in pediatric diseases. Office: Stanford U Sch Medicine Dept Pediatrics Rm H-310 Stanford CA 94305 Office Phone: 650-723-5104 can't process batch details. Business E-Mail: punko@stanford.edu.

COHEN, HERBERT JESSE, pediatrician, educator; b. NYC, Apr. 27, 1935; s. Barnet and Edith (Lepolstat) C.; m. Marion E. Finger, Aug. 29, 1960; children— Linda Elizabeth, Gerald Daniel, Seth Michael. BA (Ford Found. scholar), Columbia, 1955; MD, State U. N.Y., 1959. Intern Bellevue Hosp., NYC, 1959-60; resident NY Hosp., 1960-62; asst. instr. Cornell Med. Sch., 1961-62; instr. Tulane Med. Sch., 1962-64; NIH fellow Albert Einstein Coll. Medicine, 1964-66, asst. prof. pediatrics and rehab. medicine, 1966-71, assoc. prof., 1971-76, prof., 1976—; dir. Children's Evaluation and Rehab. Ctr., Rose F. Kennedy Center for Mental Retardation and Human Devel., Bronx, NY, 1968, 1978—2006, emeritus dir., 2006—; dir. Bronx Developmental Services, N.Y. State Dept. Mental Hygiene, 1971-80, Rose F. Kennedy U. Ctr. for Excellence in Devel. Disabilities Tng. Svcs. and Rsch., 1974—2006, dir. div. child devel. and devel. disabilities dept. pediatrics, 1981—2006. Vice chmn. Pres.'s Com. on Mental Retardation, 1978-81; mem. study sect. human devel. NIH, 1978-82; bd.mem. sci. advisor Coord. Ctr. Health Promotion US Ctr. Disease Control & prevention, 2008-; mem. profl. adv. bd. various founds. and profl. orgns., mem. bd. sci. counselors Coordinating Ctr. Health Promotion, Ctr. Disease Control & Prevention, 2008-11. Author 4 books; contbr. over 87 articles to profl. pubs. With USPHS, 1962—64. Recipient Disting. Humanitarian R&D awards Mental Retardation Svc. Orgns., Disting. Svc. award Assn. of Univ. Ctrs. on Disability, 2005; United Cerebral Palsy Rsch. and Edn. Found. fellow, 1966-68 Fellow Am. Acad. Pediatrics (chmn. child devel. sect., chmn. com. on children with disabilities, Arnold J. Capute award sect. on children with disabilities 2004) Assn. U. Ctrs. Disabilities (Disting. Svc. award); mem. AAAS, Am. Acad. Cerebral Palsy, Am. Assn. Univ. Affiliated Facilities (pres. 1980-81, dir. 1977-84), Am. Assn. Mental Retardation (Leadership award 1996), Am. Assn. Ctrs. on Disability (Disting. Leadership award). Office: R F Kennedy Ctr 1410 Pelham Pky S Bronx NY 10461-1101 Office Phone: 718-430-8522.

COHEN, HOWARD A., cardiologist; B cum laude, Yale U.; MD, NYU, 1970. Intern internal medicine Bellevue Hosp., resident internal medicine, chief resident; fellow cardiology Johns Hopkins Hosp.; cardiologist Nat. Naval Med. Ctr., Bethesda, Md.; dir. interventional cardiology St. John's Hosp., Calif., dir. Cardiac Catheterization Lab. Calif., chief of staff Calif.; prof. medicine U. Pitts., dir. clin. cardiology, dir. The Cardiac Catheterization Lab., assoc. dir. Cardiovascular Inst.; dir. cardiac catheterization lab. Lenox Hill Hosp., NYC, dir. divsn. cardiovascular intervention. Med. adv. bd. Biopure Corp.; lectr. area percentaneony left venticular assist, radial artery access; prin. investigator Nat. Heart, Lung and Blood Inst. Dynamic Registry. Named Best Doctor, NY Mag., 2003—06. Fellow: Soc. Cardiac Angiography and Interventions, Am. Coll. Cardiology; mem.: So. Calif. Soc. Interventional Cardiology (founder and pres.). Office: Lenox Hill Hosp 100 East 77th St New York NY 10021 Office Phone: 212-434-2400.

COHEN, JEFFREY K., urologist, educator; MD, SUNY. Diplomate Am. Bd. Urology. Intern Univ. Hosps. of Cleve., resident, San Bernadio County Med. Ctr.; fellow Grace Hosp., Univ. Tex. Hosp.; practice Triangle Urological Group; assoc. prof. surgery Drexel Univ.; co dir. prostate ctr. Allegheny Gen. Hosp., dir. divsn. urology. Named one of Top Doctors, Pitts. mag., 2011. Office: Allegheny General Hospital 320 E N Ave Pittsburgh PA 15212 Office Phone: 412-359-3131. Office Fax: 412-359-4108.

COHEN, JERRY A., anesthesiologist, educator; MD, U. Miami Sch. Medicine, Fla., 1973. Rotating internship anesthesiology continuum Emory U. Affiliated Hospitals, Atlanta, residency in anesthesiology; NIH fellowship divsn. anesthesiology rsch. Emory U. Dept. Anesthesiology; assoc. prof. anesthesiology U. Fla. Sch. Medicine, Gainesville. Vice chmn. hosp. accreditation program profl. tech. adv. com. Joint Commn., 1990, mem. stds. and survey procedures com.; mem. adv. panel Anesthesia Quality Inst., 2009—. Mem.: American Soc. Anesthesiologists (chmn. sect. on profl. stds. 1990, pres. 2011—, mem. bd. dirs.), Fla. Soc. Anesthesiologists (pres. 1990). Office: University Fla Dept Anesthesia Coll Medicine Health Sci Ctr PO Box 100254 Gainesville FL 32610-0254 Business E-Mail: jcohen@anest.ufl.edu. *

COHEN, JOEL EPHRAIM, biologist, educator, demographer; b. Washington, Feb. 10, 1944; s. Hymen Ezra and Alice. C.; children: Zoe, Adam. BA, Harvard U., 1965, MA, 1967, MPH, PhD, Harvard U., 1970, DrPH, 1973; MA (hon.), Cambridge U., 1974. Jr. fellow in math. biology and sociology Soc. of Fellows Harvard U., 1967-71, asst. prof. biology, 1971-72, assoc. prof., 1972-75; prof. populations Rockefeller U., NYC, 1975—, Abby Rockefeller Mauzé prof., 1996—; prof. populations Columbia U., NYC, 1995—; dir.'s visitor Inst. for Advanced Study, Princeton, 1989-90. Chmn. bd. Societal Inst. Math. Scis., 1973—88; mem. ednl. adv. bd. John Simon Guggenheim Meml. Found., 1985—2001, mem. com. selection of fellows, 1990—99; mem. Mayor's Commn. for Sci. and Tech. City of N.Y., 1984—90; mem. sci. adv. bd. Inst. Sci. Interchange, Torino, Italy, 1991—2007; mem. bd. math. scis. NRC, 1991—92, mem. exec. com, panel on sci., tech. and law, 2000—09, mem. governing bd., 2001—05; mem. bd. dir. The Nature Conservancy, Arlington, Va., 2000—09; trustee NY Nature Conservancy, 2001—10; mem. exec. com. Tyler Prize for Environ. Achievement, 2001—04, 2005—06; mem. adv. bd. Sci. for Judges Project Bklyn. Law Sch., 2002—07, Internat. Perspectives Goals Universal Basic & Secondary Edn., 2010. Author: A Model of Simple Competition, 1967, Casual Groups of Monkeys and Men, 1971, Food Webs and Niche Space, 1978, Community Food Webs, 1990, Absolute Zero Gravity, 1992, How Many People Can the Earth Support?, 1995, Comparisons of Stochastic Matrices, 1998, Plants and Population: Is There Time?, 1999, Forecasting Product Liability Claims in the Manville Asbestos Case, 2004, Educating All Children: A Global Agenda, 2007; mem. editl. bd.: Am. Scholar, 1994—99; author: International Perspectives on the Goals of Universal Basic and Secondary Education, 2009. Trustee Russell Sage Found., 1989-99, vice chmn. bd., 1996-99; trustee Black Rock Forest Preserve, 1989—, Population Reference Bur., Washington, 2004-10. Recipient Mercer award Ecol. Soc. Am., 1972, disting. statis. ecologist award 6th Internat. Congress of Ecology, 1994, Olivia Nordberg award for excellence in writing on population scis. Population Coun., N.Y.C., 1997, Fred L. Soper award Pan Am. Health & Edn. Found., Washington, 1998, Tyler prize Environ. Achievement, 1999, N.Y.C. Mayor's award for excellence in sci. and tech., 2002; fellow Ctr. for Advanced Study in Behavioral Scis., Stanford, 1981-82, John Simon Guggenheim Meml. fellow, 1981-82, MacArthur Found. fellow, 1981-86. Fellow AAAS, Am. Acad. Arts and Scis. (mem. coun. 2000—04), Am. Statis. Assn.; mem. Population Assn. Am. (Mindel Sheps award 1992), Cambridge Philos. Soc., Am. Philos. Soc. (mem. coun. 2008-), U.S. Nat. Acad. Scis. (mem. coun. 2001—04). Office: Rockefeller U 1230 York Ave Ste 20 New York NY 10065-6399

COHEN, KAREN R., medical association administrator; PhD in Clin. Psychology. Post-doctoral tng. in rehab. and neuropsychology; various clin. and adminstrv. positions at a rehab. ctr.; assoc. exec. dir., registrar Can. Psychol. Assn., exec. dir. Office: Can Psychol Assn 141 Laurier Ave W Ste 702 Ottawa ON K1P 5J3 Canada Office Phone: 613-237-2144 ext. 331. *

COHEN, LAUREN ANN, psychologist; b. Albany, NY, Mar. 23, 1949; d. David and Sylvia (Bernstein) Cohen; m. Irving A. Cohen, May 29, 1983; children: David, Benjamin. BA, U. Rochester, 1971; MA, U. Md., 1975, PhD, 1977. Lic. psychologist, Md., NY, Kans. Psychologist Kennedy Inst., Balt., 1978-85, Children's Hosp. of Buffalo, N.Y., 1985-89; chief psychologist Children's Hosp. Rehab. Ctr., Buffalo, 1989—; psychologist Sunrise Mental Health Assn., West Seneca, N.Y., 1987—. Cons. Parents Anonymous, Buffalo, 1989-, Disability Determination Svcs., Topeka, 2003-. Mem. Am. Psychol. Assn., Am. Orthopsychiatric Assn. Avocations: travel, reading. Office: 2820 Sw Fairlawn Topeka KS 66614

COHEN, LAWRENCE ALAN, health facility administrator; b. NYC, Nov. 29, 1953; s. Irwin Wolf Cohen and Ernestine Jacqueline (Rosenbloom) Chaut; m. Ilene Beth Rosen, May 27, 1979; children: Bari, Kerri, Andrew. BBA in Acctg., George Washington U., 1975; JD, St. Johns U., 1979; LLM in Taxation, NYU, 1982. Bar: N.Y.; CPA. Assoc. Rogers & Wells, NYC, 1979-82, Battle Fowler, NYC, 1982-84; 1st v.p. VMS Realty Ptnrs., NYC, 1984-88, exec. v.p. PaineWebber Properties Inc., NYC, 1989-90, pres., CEO, 1991-96; vice chmn., CFO Capital Senior Living Corp., NYC, 1996-98, CEO, 1999—. Mem. Nat. Realty Com. (exec. com. 1990—), Nat. Multi Housing Coun. (exec. com. 1992—), Am. Srs. Housing Assn. (exec. bd. dirs. 1992—). Jewish. Home: 1365 Harbor Rd Hewlett NY 11557-2640 Home Phone: 516-374-1549; Office Phone: 212-551-1770. E-mail: lcohen@capitalsenior.com.

COHEN, LAWRENCE B., gastroenterologist, educator; MD, Drexel U., 1978. Diplomate Am. Bd. Internal Medicine, 1981, Am. Bd. Internal Medicine-gastroenterology, 1983. Intern Mt. Sinai Hosp., 1979, resident internal medicine, 1981, fellow gastroenterology, 1983; assoc. clin. prof. Mt. Sinai Sch. of Medicine. Author: (articles) Non-anesthesiologist administration of propofol for gastrointestinal endoscopy, 2009, NSAID-induced antral ulcers are associated with distinct changes in mucosal gene expression, 2009, A randomized, placebo-controlled study of the effect of naproxen, aspirin, celecoxib, or clopidogrel on gastroduodenal healing, 2009, Endoscopist-directed administration of propofol: a world-wide safety experience, 2009, Prospective Randomized Controlled Trial of an Injectable Esophageal Prosthesis versus Sham Procedure for Endoscopic Treatment of GERD, 2009. Named one of Best Doctors in NY, NY Mag., 2010. Fellow: ACP, Am. Soc. for Gastrointestinal Endoscopy, Am. Gastroent. Assn., Am. Coll. of Gastroenterology. Office: Mount Sinai Medical Center 311 E 79th St Ste 2A New York NY 10021-0903 Office Phone: 212-996-6633.

COHEN, LAWRENCE SOREL, internist, educator; b. NYC, Mar. 27, 1933; s. Max and Fannie (Cooper) C.; m. Jane Abramson, Aug. 5, 1961; children: Melanie, Wendy. AB, Harvard U., 1954; MD, N.Y. U., 1958; MA (hon.), Yale U., 1970. Diplomate: Am. Bd. Internal Medicine, Sub Bd. Cardiovascular Diseases. Intern, then resident in medicine Yale-New Haven Hosp., 1958-60, 64-65; asst. in medicine Harvard U. Med. Sch., 1962-64; sr. investigator Nat. Heart, Lung and Blood Inst., 1965-68, mem. task force on arteriosclerosis, 1978-80, chmn. clin. trials rev. com., 1984-85, 87-89; assoc. prof. medicine U. Tex. Med. Sch., Dallas, 1968-70; prof. medicine Yale U. Med. Sch., 1970-81, Ebenezer K. Hunt prof. medicine, 1981—2007, Ebenezer K. Hunt emeritus prof. medicine, 2007—, dep. dean, 1991-95, spl. advisor to dean, 1995—2006. Mem. editorial bd. Circulation, Am. Jour. Cardiology, Am. Heart Jour.; contbr. over 160 articles to med. jours. Active Am. Heart Assn., chpt. pres., 1980-81, affiliate pres. Conn. chpt., 1984-86. With USPHS, 1960-62. Recipient Francis Gilman Blake award for Teaching of Med. Scis., 1973 Fellow ACP, Am. Coll. Cardiology (trustee 1978-83, mem. editorial bd. jour.); mem. Assn. Univ. Cardiologists (pres.-elect 1990, pres. 1991), Brit. Cardiac Soc., Ombudsman Assn., Interurban Clin. Club (pres. 1988), Alpha Omega Alpha. Home: 633 Whitney Ave New Haven CT 06511-2218 Office: Yale U Sch Medicine 333 Cedar St I-207 New Haven CT 06510-3289 Office Phone: 203-785-4128, 203-785-4683. Business E-Mail: lawrence.s.cohen@yale.edu.

COHEN, LEE STUART, psychiatrist, educator; BS, U. Mich.; MD, Albany Medical Coll. Intern St. Elizabeth's Hosp., Brighton, Mass.; resident psychiatry Mass. Gen. Hosp., dir. perinatal and reproductive psychiatry clinical rsch. program; assoc. prof. psychiatry Harvard Medical Sch. Recipient NIH Mental Health Faculty Scholar award, Young Investigator award, Nat. Assn. Rsch. Schizophrenia Depression, Independent Investigator award, Outstanding Psychiatrist award for Rsch., Mass. Psychiatric Soc. Office: Mass Gen Hosp WAC 812 15 Parkman St Boston MA 02114 Office Phone: 617-726-3488. Office Fax: 617-726-7541. Business E-Mail: lcohen2@partners.org.

COHEN, LOIS RUTH KUSHNER, health research consultant; b. Phila., May 31, 1938; d. Joseph George and Doris (Bronstein) Kushner. Tchr.'s diploma, Gratz Coll., Phila., 1957; BA, U. Pa., 1960; MS, Purdue U., 1961, PhD, 1963, LittD (hon.), 1989. Rsch. coord. dept. sociology Purdue U., 1963-64; social sci. analyst div. dental health USPHS, Washington, 1964-70; chief applied behavioral studies div. dental health USPHS, NIH, Bethesda, Md., 1970-71; chief Office Social and Behavioral Analysis, 1971-74; spl. asst. to dir. Div. Dentistry, 1974-76, Nat. Inst. Dental Rsch., 1976-83, chief Office Planning, Evaluation and Comms., 1983-89, dir. div. extramural rsch., 1989-98; assoc. dir. internat. health Nat. Inst. Dental and Craniofacial Rsch., 1998—2006; Paul G. Rogers ambassador Global Health Rsch., 2006—. Vis. lectr. Howard U., spring 1964, health policy and social medicine Harvard U., 1981-88; Percy T. Phillips vis. prof. Columbia U. Sch. Dental and Oral Surgery, N.Y.C., 1988; cons. WHO, 1970, 74, 75, dental health unit WHO, 1970—, Inst. Medicine Nat. Acad. Sci., 1977-80; co-dir. Internat. Collaborative Study Dental Manpower Systems in Relation to Oral Health Status, 1970-84; sr. exec. Svc. Performance Award, 1992, 98, Fed. Dental Internat. Merit Award, 1995. Co-editor: Toward a Sociology of Dentistry, 1971, Social

Sciences and Dentistry, Vol. I, 1971, Vol. II, 1984, Disease Prevention and Oral Health Promotion, 1995; editorial reviewer Social Sci. and Medicine, 1975—, Jour. Preventive Dentistry, 1973—, Scandinavian Jour. Dental Rsch., 1973—, Com. Dental Oral Epidemiology, 1999—; mem. editl. bd. Oral Diseases, 2000—05, Jour. Am. Dental Assn., 2005-, African Jour. Oral Health, 2005—; contbr. numerous articles to profl. jours., books. Recipient Phila. High Sch. for Girls Rowen stipend, 1956, Superior Svc. awards Pub. Health Svc., 1988, 93; Senatorial scholar U. Pa., 1960; David Ross Fellow NSF, 1963. Fellow AAAS (gov. coun. 1971), Am. Coll. Dentists (hon.), Internat. Coll. Dentists (hon.); mem. APHA, ADA (hon.), Am. Sociol. Assn., Behavioral Scientists in Dental Rsch. (founder, pres. 1971-72), Federation Dentaire Internationale (cons.), Internat. Assn. Dental Rsch. (dir. 1976-77, chmn. internat. rels. com. 1979-83, disting. sr. scientist award 1987, 96), Am. Assn. Dental Rsch. (dir. 1980-81), Alpha Omega. Address: NIDCR NIH Room 4B62 Bldg 31 Center Dr Bethesda MD 20892-2290 Office Phone: 301-594-2613. Personal E-mail: lkcohenl@verizon.net. Business E-Mail: lois.cohen@nih.gov.

COHEN, MALCOLM MARTIN, psychologist, researcher; s. Nathan and Esther Cohen; m. Marilyn Jerrow, Jan. 2, 1959 (dec. 1967); m. Eleanor Johnson, June 30, 1969 (div. 1988); m. Suzana Gal, Feb. 14, 1988. BA, Brandeis U., Waltham, Mass., 1959; MA, U. Pa., Phila., 1961, PhD, 1965; ScD (hon.), SUNY, Oneonta, 2011. Lic. psychologist, Pa. Asst. instr. U. Pa., Phila., 1961-63; rsch. psychologist Naval Air Engring. Ctr., Phila., 1963-67; supervisory rsch. psychologist Naval Air Devel. Ctr., Warminster, Pa., 1967-82; asst. chief biomed. rsch. divsn. NASA-Ames Rsch Ctr., Moffett Field, Calif., 1982-85, chief neuroscis. br., 1985-88, rsch. scientist, 1988—2005, chief human info. processing rsch., 2000—05, Ames assoc., 2005—07; pvt. practice, 2006—. Lectr. dept. aeros. and astronautics Stanford U., 1983—92, lectr., cons. prof. human biology program, 1994—2005; cons. in field. Assoc. editor Habitation Jour., 2004-2007; contbr. articles to profl. jours. Founding mem. Common Cause of Phila., 1973. Recipient Exceptional Sci. Achievement medal NASA 1994. Fellow AIAA (assoc., Jeffries Aerospace Medicine & Life Scis. Rsch. award, 2008), Aerospace Med. Assn. (editl. bd. Aviation Space and Environ. Medicine 1985-93, 2010-, assoc. editor 2001-03, Environ. Sci. award 1985, William F. Longacre award, 1989, Kent K. Gillingham award, 2011), Aerospace Human Factors Assn. (pres. 1992, Henry L. Taylor Founder award 2009); mem. AAAS, Nat. Space Biomed. Rsch. Inst. (external adv. coun. 2009-), NASA Sensorimotor Risk Standing Review Panel, Sigma Xi. Jewish. Achievements include patents for light bar to monitor human acceleration tolerance. Avocations: scuba diving, photography, chess. Personal E-mail: malcohen@aol.com.

COHEN, MARC, cardiologist, educator; MD, NYU Sch. Med. Lic. NJ, diplomate Am. Bd. Internal Med., Bd. Cardiovascular Diseases, Bd. Interventional Cardiology. Intern, resident & fellow Mount Sinai Med. Ctr.; former dir. clinical rsch. Hahnemann U. Hosp., former dir. Cardiac Cath Lab; chief div. cardiology Newark Beth Israel Med. Ctr., dir. cardiology fellowship; prof. med. Mount Sinai Sch. Med. Cons. Nat. Heart, Lung & Blood Inst. Clinical Trial Rev. Com.; lead investigator ESSENCE Trial, ACUTE I & II, TETAMI Trial; co-lead investigator PRISM Trial. Contbr. chapters to books;, co-author various scientific articles. Fellow: Soc. for Cardiac Angiography & Interventions, Am. Coll. Physicians, Am. Coll. Cardiology); mem.: Am. Heart Assn. (coun. clinical cardiology). Office: Thrombosis Clinic 685 Rte 202/206 Bridgewater NJ 08807 Office Phone: 888-338-3673. Office Fax: 888-583-3828.

COHEN, MARK S., orthopedist, medical educator; BS in Bio. Sci., Stanford U., 1982; MD, Harvard Med. Sch., 1986. Lic. Calif., 1987, Ill., 1993. Clin. instr., dept. orthopaedics U. Calif., San Diego, 1991—92; clin. instr., dept. orthopaedic surgery Ind. U. Med. Ctr., 1992—93; asst. prof., dir. orthopaedic edn., dir. hand and elbow section, dept. orthopaedic surgery Rush U. Med. Ctr., 1993—98, assoc. prof., 1998—2004, prof., 2004—. Surg. internship Univ. Calif., San Diego, 1986—87, orthopaedic surgery residency, 1987—92, spine rsch., clin. fell., 1988—89; hand and microvascular fell. Ind. Hand Ctr. Contbr. articles to numerous profl. jours. Recipient Russell S. Hibbs award Best Clin. Paper, Scoliosis Rsch. Soc., 1986, Alfred V. Bateman award, Univ. Calif. San Diego, 1988, 1992, Acromed award Best Rsch. Paper, No. Am. Spine Soc., 1989, Henry W. Meyerding Meml. Essay Contest award, Am. Fracture Assn., 1990, Excellence award, New Orleans Orthopaedic Clinic, 1992, Chmn. Prize for Outstanding Achievement as a Resident, UCSD Dept. Surgery, 1992, Cum Laude Ribbon Best Tech. Exhibit, Radiological Soc. No. Am., 1997, Excellence in Tchg. award, Rush, 2001, 2003, Emmanuel Kaplan award Anatomical Excellence in Surgery, Am. Soc. Surgery of the Hand, 2002; named Best Sci. Poster, Am. Assn. Hand Surgery, 1999. Office: Midwest Orthopaedics at Rush Ste 1063 1725 W Harrison St Chicago IL 60612 Home Phone: 312-280-0886; Office Phone: 312-243-4244.

COHEN, MARK STEVEN, dentist; b. NYC, Dec. 10, 1948; s. Lawrence and Yetta (Grossman) C.; m. Arlene Debbie Deutsch, Aug. 23, 1970 (div. May 1984); 1 child, Aaron Philip; m. Donna Lynn Poissonnier, Nov. 27, 1985. BS, CCNY, 1971; DDS, Columbia U., 1975, cert. in Pedodontics, 1976. Practice dentistry, Yonkers, NY, 1975-76, Bristol, Conn., 1976-79, Brookfield, Conn., 1977—. Dir. dental service N.Y. Inst. for the Edn. Blind, Bronx, 1976-78; assoc. attending dentist Danbury (Conn.) Hosp., 1976-82, Blythdale Children's Hosp., Valhalla, N.Y., 1986-87; assoc. clin. prof. dentistry Columbia U., N.Y.C., 1976—, mem. quality assurance com., 1982-85. Patentee in field. Active Dental Guidance Council for Cerebral Palsy, N.Y.C., 1976-81. Chemistry fellow NSF, Washington, 1969-71, research fellow NIH, 1971, United Cerebral Palsy, 1975-76; named one of Am. Top Dentist, Consumers Rsch. Coun., 2007. Mem. ADA, Conn. State Dental Assn., Greater Danbury Dental Soc., Am. Dental Vols. for Israel, OKU Dental Honor Soc. Democrat. Jewish. Avocations: travel, photography, biking, collecting antiques. Office: Mark S Cohen 940 Federal Rd Brookfield CT 06804-1144 Office Phone: 203-775-5533. Personal E-mail: mscddspc@aol.com, mscddspc@mindspring.com.

COHEN, MARLENE LOIS, pharmacologist; b. New Haven, May 5, 1945; d. Abraham David and Jeanette (Bader) C.; m. Jerome H. Fleisch, Aug. 8, 1976; children: Abby F. Fleisch, Sheryl B. Fleisch. BS, U. Conn., 1968; PhD, U. Calif., San Francisco, 1973. Registered pharmacist, Calif., Conn. Postdoctoral fellow Roche Inst. of Molecular Biology, Nutley, NJ, 1973-75; sr. pharmacologist Eli Lilly & Co., Indpls., 1975-80, rsch. scientist, 1980-85, sr. rsch. scientist, 1985-89, rsch. advisor, 1989-94, disting. rsch. fellow, 1994—2002; co-founder Creative Pharmacol. Solutions LLC, Carmel, Ind., 2002—. Adj. asst. prof. dept. pharmacology and toxicology Ind. U. Sch. Medicine, Indpls., 1976-82, adj. assoc. prof., 1982-86, adj. prof., 1987—; rsch. asst. Pfizer Labs., Groton, Conn., 1967; cons. Drug Dependence Inst., Yale U., New Haven, 1974. Mem. editl. bd. Jour. Clin. and Exptl. Hypertension, 1978—99, Procs. of the Soc. for Exptl. Biology and Medicine, 1979-84, Life Sci., 1984—, Jour. Pharmacology and Exptl. Therapeutics, 1987-2006, Current Drugs: Serotonin 1992-2000, Current Topics in Pharmacology, 1994-2000; mem. Molecular Interventions Adv. Bd., 1999-2005; ad hoc reviewer for profl. jours.; author: (with others) Principles of Medicinal Chemistry, 1974, 3d edit., 1989, New Antihypertensive Drugs, 1976, The Serotonin Receptors, 1988, The Peripheral Actions of 5-Hydroxytryptamine, 1989, Central and Peripheral 5-HT3 Receptors, 1992; contbr. articles to profl. jours. Recipient Disting. Alumni award, U. Conn. Sch. Pharmacy, 2002. Mem. Soc. for Exptl. Biology and Medicine, Am. Soc. for Pharmacology and Exptl. Therapeutics (chair subcom. on women in pharmacology 1984-89, chairperson nominating com. 1984, com. on profl. affairs 1984-89, membership com. 1989-92, bd. publs. trustees 1989—95, pres. 2001), Serotonin Club (councilor 1987-90, nomenclature com. 1988—2000), Alpha Lambda Delta, Phi Kappa Phi, Rho Chi. Office: Creative Pharmacol Solutions LLC 10532 Coppergate Ste 101 Carmel IN 46032 Office Phone: 317-571-9878. Personal E-mail: marlenelcohen@aol.com.

COHEN, MARTIN B., cardiac electrophysiologist; Grad., SUNY Downstate Med. Ctr. Diplomate Am. Bd. Internal Medicine, Am. Bd. of Internal Medicine-cardiovasc. disease, Am. Bd. of Internal Medicine-clin. cardiac electrophysiology, Am. Bd. of Internal Medicine-interventional cardiology. Fellow SUNY Downstate Med. Ctr.; assoc. prof. NY Med. Coll. Mailing: Westchester Medical Center Cardiology 19 Bradhurst Ave Suites 3850 Hawthorne NY 10532 Office Phone: 866-962-4327.

COHEN, MITCHELL B., pediatric gastroenterologist; MD, Mt. Sinai Sch. of Medicine, 1977. Diplomate Am. Bd. Pediatrics, 1981, Am. Bd. Pediatrics-pediatric gastroenterology, 2005. Resident pediatrics Johns Hopkins Hosp., 1978—80; fellow pediatric gastroenterology Children's Hosp. Med. Ctr., 1983—86; vice chair pediatrics Cin. Children's Hosp. Med. Ctr., dir. gastroenterology divsn. Prof. Univ. of Cin. Office: Cincinnati Childrens Hospital Medical Center 3333 Burnet Ave MLC 2010 Cincinnati OH 45229 Office Phone: 513-636-4415.

COHEN, MITCHELL J.M., psychiatrist, educator; MD, The Med. Coll. of Pa., Phila., 1984. Diplomate Am. Bd. Psychiatry and Neurology, Am. Bd. Psychiatry and Neurology-pain medicine, Am. Bd. Pain Medicine. Resident John Hopkins Univ., 1988; vice chair edn. dept. of psychiatry and human behavior Thomas Jefferson Univ., assoc. prof. psychiatry and human behavior, dir. Pain Medicine Program. Author: (publs.) Identity transformation in medical students, Cortical activation during executed, imagined, and observed foot movements, Effects of motor imagery training after chronic, complete spinal cord injury, Calming the plaque to delay intervention for 24 hours in acute coronary syndromes., numerous publs. Office: 833 Chestnut St Suite 210 Philadelphia PA 19107 Office Phone: 215-955-6592. Office Fax: 215-503-2853.

COHEN, MURRAY J., surgeon, educator; BA in Biology, U. Pa.; MD, Temple U., 1981. Diplomate Am. Bd. Surgery, Am. Bd. Surgery-surg. critical care. Intern Albert Einstein Med. Ctr., resident; fellow in trauma critical care Hartford Hosp.; fellow Am. Coll. of Surgeons; clin. assoc. prof. surgery Jefferson Med. Coll.; dir. trauma and surg. critical divsn. Thomas Jefferson Univ. Hosp. Mem.: Soc. of Critical Care Medicine, Ea. Assn. for the Surgery of Trauma. Office: Thomas Jefferson University Hospital - Center City Campus 111 S. 11th St Philadelphia PA 19107 Office Phone: 215-955-6000.

COHEN, NEIL D., endocrinologist; MD, Med. Coll. Pa. Hosp. Diplomate Am. Bd. of Internal Medicine, endocrinology. Resident North Shore Univ. Hosp., fellow, Albert Einstein Coll. of Medicine. Office: Staten Island University Hospital 475 Seaview Ave Staten Island NY 10305 Office Phone: 718-226-8851.

COHEN, NICHOLAS, immunologist, educator; b. NYC, Nov. 20, 1938; s. Saris and Frances (Pakett) C.; m. Jayne Sevin Rogal, July 1, 1962 (div. 1972); children: Jaime Anne, Jessica Sevin; m. Catharina Johanna van der Harst, Oct. 23, 1974; children: Misha Thomas, Mark Sebastian. AB, Princeton U., 1959; PhD, U. Rochester, 1965. Asst. prof. microbiology and immunology Sch. Medicine and Dentistry U. Rochester, NY, 1967-73, assoc. prof. NY, 1973-80, prof. microbiology, immunology and psychiatry NY, 1980—2004, dir. divsn. immunology, microbiology & vaccine biology cluster NY, 1998—2004, prof. oncology NY, 1997—2004, prof. emeritus NY, 2004—; assoc. dir. Ctr. for Psychoneuroimmunology Rsch., Rochester. Vis. prof. Agrl. U., Wageningen, The Netherlands, 1982-83; mem. Basel Inst. for Immunology, Switzerland, 1975-76; mem. peer rev. bds. NIH, 1976-80; cons. NIH study sects., NIMH study sects., NSF. Assoc. editor Brain, Behavior and Immunity Jour., Devel. Comparative Immunology; editor 5 books; contbr. articles to profl. jours. Postdoctoral scholar in immunology UCLA, 1965-67, Fulbright scholar, 1982-83; grantee NIH, NIMH, NSF, 1967—2006; recipient Rsch. Career Devel. award NIH, 1974-78, NIH Merit award, 1987-97. Mem. Am. Soc. Zoologists (chmn. divsn. comparative immunology 1977-79), Transplantation Soc., Am. Soc. Immunologists, Brit. Soc. Immunology, Internat. Soc. Devel. and Comparative Immunology (v.p. the Americas 1994-2000), Psychoneuroimmunology Rsch. Soc. (councilor 1993-97). Democrat. Avocations: music, travel. Home: 211 Highland Pkwy Rochester NY 14620-2544 Business E-Mail: n.cohen@rochester.edu.

COHEN, NOEL LEE, otolaryngologist, educator; b. NYC, Sept. 20, 1930; s. Victor Max and Esther Lily (Schonfeld) C.; m. Baukje Philippina Boersma, June 1, 1957; 1 child, Mark Bennett. AB, NYU, 1951; MD, U. Utrecht, The Netherlands, 1957; MD (hon.), U. Freiburg, Germany, 2002. Cert. Am. Bd. Otolaryngology, 1963. Intern Stads-en Academi Ziekenhuis, Utrecht, 1955-57; resident in otolaryngology Bellevue Med. Ctr. NYU, NYC, 1959-62, instr. Sch. Medicine, 1962-64, asst. prof., 1964-69, assoc. prof., 1969-73, clin. prof., 1973-80, prof. otolargyngology, 1980—, chmn. dept. otolaryngology, 1981—2003, interim dean, provost Sch. Medicine, 1997-98, vice dean for clin. affairs, 1998-99, Mendik Found. prof., 1999—2003, sr. advisor to dean, 2000—07, prof. otolaryngology, 2003—; pres. NYU Hosp. Ctr., 1998. Bd. dir. Ctr. for Hearing & Communication023; mem. adv. bd. Self Help for Hard of Hearing People, 1995; sci. adv. bd. Sci. Deafness Rsch. Found., 2000-11; mem. med. adv. bd. Cochlear Corp., 1986-2007; bd. trustees NY Sch.for Deaf, 2010-; lectr. in field, spkr. at profl. confs. Mem. editl. bd. Jour. of Otology & Neurotology, 1986-2004, Otolaryngology-Head and Neck Surgery, Internat. Cochlear Implant Jour., 1999—; reviewer articles and books for profl. jours.; contr. chpts. to books, articles to profl. jours. Lt. USNR, 1957—59. Fellow: ACS; mem.: N.Y. Acad. Scis., N.Y. Otol. Soc. (pres. 1998—99), Soc. Acad. Depts. Otolaryngology, Soc. Univ. Otolaryngologists, Am. Neuro-Otol. Soc., N.Am. Skull Base Soc., N.Y. Head and Neck Soc. (charter mem., pres. 1984), N.Y. State Soc. Otolaryngology-Head and Neck Surgery (pres. 1988—89), N.Y. Acad. Medicine, Am. Otol. Soc., Am. Bronchoesophagol. Assn., Am. Soc. Head and Neck Surgery, Rhinol. and Otol. Soc., Am. Laryngol., Am. Acad. Otolaryngology-Head-Neck Surgery (Honor award 1985, Disting. Svc. award 2001). Democrat. Jewish. Avocations: tennis, skiing, gardening, carpentry. Office: NYU Langone Med Ctr Dept Otolaryngology 560 1st Ave New York NY 10016 Office Phone: 212-263-3301. Business E-Mail: noel.cohen@nyumc.org.

COHEN, RAPHAEL M., nephrologist, educator; AB, Harvard Coll., 1973; MD, Harvard Med. Sch., 1977. Diplomate Am. Bd. of Internal Medicine, 1980, Am. Bd. of Internal Medicine-renal/nephrology, 1984. Intern Tufts New Eng. Med. Ctr., resident in internal medicine, 1977—80; fellow in nephrology Hosp. of the Univ. of Pa., 1981—84, clin. assoc. prof. medicine. Office: Penn Presbyterian Medical Center 240 Medical Office Bldg Philadelphia PA 19104 Office Phone: 215-662-8730. Office Fax: 215-243-4686. E-mail: cohenr@uphs.upenn.edu.

COHEN, ROBERT, medical device, biotechnology manufacturing and marketing executive; b. Glen Cove, NY, Sept. 23, 1957; s. Alan and Selma (Grossman) C.; m. Nancy A. Arey, Jan. 17, 1981. BA, Bates Coll., 1979; JD, U. Maine, 1982. Bar: NY 1983, US Dist. Ct. (so. and ea.) NY 1983. Atty. Pfizer Inc., NYC, 1982-86; asst. corp. counsel, asst. sec. Pfizer Hosp. Products Group, Inc., NYC, 1986-88; v.p. bus. devel., dir. for med. device mfr. and marketer Deknatel Inc., Fall River, Mass., 1988-92; pres., CEO GCI Med., Braintree, Mass., 1992-93; v.p. bus. devel. Sulzermedica USA, Inc., Angleton, Tex., 1993-94, group v.p., 1994-98; v.p. bus. & tech. devel. St. Jude Med., Inc., St. Paul, 1998—2002; CEO, dir. Advanced Circulatory Sys., Inc., Eden Prairie, Minn., 2003—04; dir. Horizon Med. Products, Inc., Atlanta, 1998-2001, CardioFocus, Inc., Boston, 1999-2000; pres., CEO, bd. dirs. Travanti Pharma Inc., Mendota Heights, 2004—09, Miromatrix Med. Inc., Mpls., 2009—. Author: 19th Century Maine Authors, 1978. Mixed Emotions, 2009 Mem.: ABA. Republican. Home: 18683 Bearpath Trl Eden Prairie MN 55347-3476 Office: Miromatrix Med Inc 18683 Bearpath Trail Eden Prairie MN 55347 Personal E-mail: robert.cohen1328@gmail.com.

COHEN, ROBERT M., endocrinologist, educator; MD, U. Rochester, 1978. Diplomate Am. Bd. Internal Medicine, 1981, Am. Bd. Internal Medicine-endocrinology, diabetes and metabolism, 1983, lic. Pa. Intern Rush Presbyn. St. Lukes Hosp., Chgo., 1979, resident internal medicine, 1979—81; fellow endocrinology Univ. of Chgo., 1981—84; hosp. affiliation includes Univ. Hosp., Cin.; assoc. prof. medicine Univ. of Cin., Ohio. Office: University of Cincinnati Physicians Ste 6300 222 Piedmont Ave Cincinnati OH 45219 Office Phone: 513-475-7400. Office Fax: 513-475-7414.

COHEN, ROGER B., oncologist, educator; AB in Biochemical Sciences (magna cum laude), Harvard Coll., 1976, MD, 1980. Diplomate Am. Bd. Internal Medicine, 1984, Am. Bd. Internal Medicine-hematology, 1986, Am. Bd. Internal Medicine-med. oncology, 1993, Am. Bd. Internal Medicine-med. oncology, 2005. Intern medicine Mt. Sinai Hosp., NYC, 1980—81, resident medicine, 1981—82, clin. fellow hematology, 1985—86; rsch. fellow, gene structure and expression Sloan-Kettering Cancer Rsch. Inst., NYC, 1982—85; fellow, lab. molecular hematology Nat. Heart, Lung, and Blood Inst. (NHLBI), Bethseda, Md., 1986—89; clin. fellow, med. oncology Nat. Cancer Inst., Bethseda, Md., 1991—93; prof. medicine Univ. Pa.; hosp. affiliation includes Hosp. of Univ. Pa. Co-author: (publs.) Analysis of ERCC1 (excision repair cross complementing group 1) in squamous cell carcinoma of the head and neck (SCCHN) by quantitative immunohistochemistry (IHC) using FL297, 2010, Phase I study of the investigational drug MLN8237, an Aurora A kinase (AAK) inhibitor, in patients (pts) with solid tumors, 2010, Long-term results in a cohort of medullary thyroid cancer (MTC) patients (pts) in a phase I study of XL184 (BMS 907351), an oral inhibitor of MET, VEGFR2, and RET, 2010, Phase I Assessment of New Mechanism-Based Pharmacodynamic Biomarkers for MLN8054, a Small-Molecule Inhibitor of Aurora A Kinase, 2011, Activity of XL184 (Cabozantinib), an Oral Tyrosine Kinase Inhibitor, in Patients With Medullary Thyroid Cancer, 2011, and numerous other publs. Office: University of Pennsylvania School of Medicine Ste 240 3600 Market St Philadelphia PA 19104 Office Phone: 215-662-4469.

COHEN, SAMUEL MONROE, physician, pathologist, researcher; b. Milw., Sept. 24, 1946; s. David A. and Harriett (Goldman) C.; m. Janet L. Olson, Jan. 27, 1968; children: Sheri Lyn, Benjamin A., Daniel E., Erica A. BS, U. Wis., 1967, MD, PhD, U. Wis., 1972. Diplomate Am. Bd. Anatomic and Clin. Pathology, Acad. Toxicological Scis., Internat. Acad. Toxicologic Pathology. Staff pathologist St. Vincent Hosp., Worcester, Mass., 1975-76, 77-81; assoc. prof. pathology U. Mass. Med. Sch., Worcester, 1977-81; vice chmn. dept. pathology U. Nebr. Med. Ctr., Omaha, 1981-92, chmn. dept. pathology and microbiology, 1992—2007, prof. dept. pathology & microbiology, 2007—. Vis. prof. 1st dept. pathology Nagoya (Japan) City U. Med. Sch.; mem. study sect. NIH, Bethesda, Md., 1982-86, 88, 89-91, chmn., 1991-93; mem. expert panel Flavor and Extracts Mfg. Assn., 2002—; mem. bd. sci. counselors Nat. Toxicology Program, 2002-04; bd. mem. Nat. Inst. Environ. Health Sci., 2008-; panel mem., reviewer, bd. trustees Internat. Life Scis. Inst./Health and Environ. Scis. Inst., 2002-, chmn. 2006-08; bd. trustees Internat. Life Scis. Inst., 2008-, vice chmn., 2010-; expert cons. to several cos. Assoc. editor & editor, several sci. jours. bd.; editor: Pathology of Bladder Cancer, 1983; contbr. articles to profl. jours. Recipient Outstanding Rsch. and Creativity award U. Nebr., 1990; named a disting. scientist in cancer rsch., Japanese Found. for Cancer Rsch., 2004. Fellow Acad. Toxicological Sci., Internat. Acad. Toxicologic Pathology; mem. Am. Assn. Cancer Rsch., Soc. Toxicology (Arnold J. Lehman award 2001), Soc. Toxicologic Pathologists, Am. Soc. Clin. Pathologists, Coll. Am. Pathologists, Am. Soc. Investigative Pathologists (panel mem. rev. for

Environ. Protection Agy.), Food Drug Adminstrn., Internat. Agy Rsch. Cancer, Internat Program Chem. Safety. Avocations: reading, travel. Home: 2721 S 101st St Omaha NE 68124-2618 Office: 983135 Nebr Med Ctr Omaha NE 68198-3135 Office Phone: 402-559-6388.

COHEN, SANFORD IRWIN, physician, educator; b. NYC, Sept. 5, 1928; s. George A. and Gertrude (Slater) C.; m. Jean Steinbruecker, Nov. 30, 1952; children— Jeffrey, Debra, John, Robert. AB magna cum laude, N.Y. U., 1948; M.B., MD, Chgo. Med. Sch., 1952. Intern Jackson Meml. Hosp., Miami, Fla., 1952-53; resident psychiatry U. Colo. Med. Center, 1953-54; resident Duke Med. Center, 1954-55, 57-58, mem. faculty, 1956-68, prof. psychiatry, 1964-68, head div. psychosomatic medicine and psychophysiol. research, 1964-68, lectr. psychology, 1960-68; instr. Washington Psychoanalytic Inst., 1964-68; cons. VA Hosp., Durham, NC, 1957-65, NIMH, 1963-66; prof. psychiatry Boston U. Med. Sch., 1970-86, chmn. dept., 1970-86; vis. research scientist health and behavior br., div. basic scis. NIMH, 1986-88; prof. psychiatry U. Miami (Fla.) Sch. Medicine, 1988-2000, vice chmn. dept., 1990-2000, prof. emeritus, 2000—. Markle scholar med. sci., 1957-62; Commonwealth fellow, Czech Republic and USSR, 1966. Contbr. articles to profl. jours., chpts. to books. Recipient Robert Morse award excellence in sci. writing, 1965 Fellow Am. Psychiat. Assn. (disting. life), Am. Coll. Clin. Pharmacology (life); mem. AAAS, Am. Psychosomatic Soc., Acad. Behavioral Medicine Rsch. Home: 15 Laurel Lake Dr Hudson OH 44236-2140 Home Phone: 330-528-6161. Business E-Mail: scohen@med.miami.edu.

COHEN, SEYMOUR MARTIN, oncologist, hematologist, educator; b. NYC, Dec. 19, 1936; s. Harry and Rose (Ehrlich) C.; m. Carole J. Pomerantz, Aug. 16, 1976; children: Roger, Michael. BA, Bklyn. Coll., 1957; MD, U. Pitts., 1962. Diplomate Am. Bd. Internal Medicine and Subspecialty in Med. Oncology. Intern Montefiore Hosp., NYC, 1962-63, asst. resident in medicine, 1963-64; resident in medicine Mt. Sinai Hosp., NYC, 1964-65, Am. Cancer Soc. fellow in hematology, 1965-66, mem. staff, 1969—. Fellow in hematology L.I. Jewish Hosp., 1968-69; pvt. practice medicine specializing in med. oncology and hematology, N.Y.C., 1969—; clin. assoc. in medicine Mt. Sinai Med. Sch., 1969-73, sr. clin. asst. physician in medicine, 1969-73, asst. clin. prof. medicine, 1973-78, assoc. clin. prof. medicine, 1979—; bd. dirs. Cmty. Oncology Alliance, 2004-08, Lung Cancer Alliance, 2001-04. Assoc. editor Cancer Investigation, 1993-2002; contbr. articles to profl. publs., research on malignant melanoma. Mem. exec. com. Jewish Am. Polit. Action Com., 1975-79, v.p., 1979-81, pres., 1981-83; bd. govs. State of Israel Bonds, 1979-92. Capt. M.C., USAF, 1966-68. Fellow A.C.P.; mem. AMA, Am. Soc. Clin. Oncology, Internat., Am. Socs., Hematology, NY Cancer Soc. (sec. 1983-86, v.p. 1987, pres. 1989), NY State Soc. Med. Oncologists and Hematologists (pres. 1989-92, bd. dirs. 1992—), NY Alliance of Physicians and Surgeons (bd. dirs. 1988-89, co-chmn. 1990-2008), NY County Med. Soc. Office: 1150 5th Ave New York NY 10128 Office Phone: 212-249-9141. Business E-Mail: smonc@aol.com.

COHEN, SEYMOUR STANLEY, biochemist, educator; b. NYC, Apr. 30, 1917; s. Herman and Lena (Tanz) Cohen; m. Elaine Pear, July 12, 1940; children: Michael, Sara. BS, CCNY, 1936; PhD in Biol. Chemistry, Columbia U., 1941; Dr.h.c., U. Louvain, 1972, U. Kuopio, 1982. NRC fellow Rockefeller Inst., 1941—42; mem. faculty U. Pa., 1943—71, prof. biochemistry in pediat., 1954—71, Charles Hayden-Am. Cancer Soc. prof. biochemistry, 1957—71, Hartzell prof., chmn. dept. therapeutic research Sch. Medicine, 1963—71; Am. Cancer Soc. prof. microbiology U. Colo. Sch. Medicine, Denver, 1971—76, disting. prof., Am. Cancer Soc., prof. pharm. scis. SUNY, Stony Brook, 1976—85, prof. emeritus, 1985—. Chmn. coun. analysis and projection Am. Cancer Soc., 1972—74, adviser rsch., 1974—76; Guggenheim fellow Pasteur Inst., Paris, 1947—48; Jesup lectr. Columbia U., 1967; guest investigator Institut du Radium, Paris, 1967—68; vis. prof. Collège de France, Paris, 1970; vis. fellow Smithsonian Instn., 1973—74, 1986; vis. prof. U. Tokyo, 1974, Hadassah Med. Sch., 1974, Zuckerman lectr. tropical disease, 79; Guggenheim and Lady Davis fellow Faculty Agr., Israel, 1983; fellow Nat. Humanities Ctr., NC, 1982—83, NC, 1985; rsch. assoc. history of sci. Smithsonian Instn., 1986; presdl. scholar U. Calif., San Francisco, 1988; lectr. Academia Sinica, Taiwan, 1989; trustee Marine Biol. Lab., Woods Hole, Mass.; bd. sci. cons. Sloan-Kettering Inst. Author: Virus-Induced Enzymes, 1968, Introduction to the Polyamines, 1971, Guide to the Polyamines, 1998, Biography of Thomas Cooper, 1999; editl. bd.: Virology, 1954—59, Jour. Biol. Chemistry, 1959—65, Jour. Cell Physiology, 1966—71, Bacteriol. Revs, 1969—73, Hist., Philos. Life Scis., 1985. Recipient cert. for war research, OSRD, 1945, War Manpower Commn., 1945, War Research medal, Columbia U., 1943, Eli Lilly award and medal, Am. Soc. Bacteriology, Immunology and Pathology, 1951, 1st Mead Johnson award, Am. Acad. Pediatrics, 1952, medal, Soc. de Chimie Biologique France, 1964, Borden award, Am. Assn. Med. Colls., 1967, Passano award, 1974, Townsend Harris medal, CCNY Alumni Assn., 1978, Forster award, German Acad. Sci. and Letters, Mainz, 1978; named Fogarty scholar, NIH, 1973—74. Master: Am. Acad. Arts and Scis.; fellow: AAAS (Newcomb Cleveland award 1955), Am. Acad. of Microbiology; mem.: NAS, Am. Assn. Cancer Rsch. (bd. dirs. 1974—77), French Soc. Microbiology (hon.), Inst. Medicine, Soc. Gen. Physiologists (councilor, pres. 1967—88), Phi Beta Kappa. Home: 10 Carrot Hill Rd Woods Hole MA 02543-1206

COHEN, SHELDON, psychologist, psychology professor; b. Detroit, Oct. 11, 1947; PhB, Monteith Coll., Wayne State U., 1969; PhD, NYU, 1973. Asst. to assoc. prof., dept. psychology U. Oreg., 1973—82; prof., dept. psychology Carnegie Mellon U., Pitts., 1982—, Robert E. Doherty prof. psychology, 2003—; co-dir. U. Pitts.-Carnegie Mellon U. Brain, Behavior & Immunity Ctr., 1989—; adj. prof. pathology & psychiatry U. Pitts. Sch. Medicine, 1990, mem. Pitts. Cancer Inst., 1992—; interim dir. behavioral medicine program Pitts. (Pa.) Cancer Inst., 1992—93. Contbr. articles, chapters to books, scientific papers; mem. editorial bd. scientific journals. Recipient Patricia R. Barchas award, Am. Psychosomatic Soc., 2006, Sr. Scientist award, NIMH, 1997—2002, Rsch. Scientist Devel. awards, 1987—97; named one of 20 psychologists with greatest impact on field, Inst. Scientific Info., 1996, world's most cited authors, 2003. Fellow: Soc. Behavioral Medicine, Acad. Behavioral Medicine Rsch. (exec. com. 1989—2002), Am. Psychological Soc. (James McKeen Cattell fellow award 2002—03), APA (Disting. Scientist Lectr. 1997, Disting. Scientific Contbn. award 2004); mem.: Soc. Exptl. Social Psychology, Inst. Medicine. Office: Dept Psychology Carnegie Mellon U 5000 Forbes Ave Baker Hall Rm 335-D Pittsburgh PA 15213 Office Phone: 412-268-2336, 412-268-2781. E-mail: scohen@cmu.edu.

COHEN, SHELDON GILBERT, physician, historian, immunologist; b. Pittston, Pa., Sept. 21, 1918; s. Samuel H. and Dorthy (Goldberg) C. Grad., Wyo. Sem., 1936; student, Syracuse U., 1936-37; BA, Ohio State U., 1940; MD, NYU, 1943; DSc (hon.), Wilkes U., 1976. Diplomate Am. Bd. Allergy and Immunology. Intern Bellevue Hosp., NYC, 1944; resident internal medicine Ft. Howard VA Hosp., Balt., 1947-48; resident in allergy VA Hosp., Aspinwall, Pa., 1948-49, U. Pitts. Med. Ctr., 1948-49; rsch. fellow U. Pitts. Sch. Medicine, 1949-50; rsch. assoc. U. Pitts., 1950-51; attending physician Allergy Clinic, Falk Clinics, 1950-51; chief of allergy Mercy Hosp., Wilkes-Barre, 1951-72; attending physician in allergy VA Hosp., Wilkes-Barre, 1951-60, cons. in internal medicine and rsch., 1960-72; assoc. prof. biol. rsch. Wilkes U., Wilkes-Barre, 1952-62, prof. biol. rsch., 1962-68, prof. exptl. biology, 1968-72, adj. prof. immunology, 1991—; cons. extramural programs Nat. Inst. Allergy and Infectious Diseases, 1972-73, chief allergy and immunology br., 1973-76, dir. immunology, allergic and immunologic diseases program, 1977-88, sci. advisor div. of intramural rsch. office of dir., 1988—; bd. sci. advisors Allergy and Immunology Inst. of Internat. Life Scis. Inst., 1989-97; sr. staff physician NIAID-NIH Clin. Ctr., 1974—; 21. Adj. prof. medicine Northwestern U., 1988-98; scholar Nat. Libr. Medicine, 1988-99, vis. scholar history of medicine, 1999--; regional med. cons. Children's Asthma Research Inst. and Hosp., Denver, 1969-72; mem. medico adv. bd. CARE, 1977-89; cons. to Ministry Public Health, State of Kuwait, 1981-83; mem. expert adv. panel on immunology WHO, Geneva, Switzerland, 1979-2004, dir. WHO Collaborating Ctr. for Allergy, 1985-89; bd. dirs. Asthma and Allergy Found. Am., 1969-81, mem. com. public edn., 1976-81; bd. dirs. Lupus Found. Am., 1978-85, exec. v.p., 1981-85, mem. med. council, 1978-93; mem. aeroallergens com. NRC, 1976-80. Author: Excerpts from Classics in Allergy, 2d edit., 1992, 3rd edit., 2011, Asthma Among the Famous, 1995—2002; mem. editl. bd. Jour. Devel. and Comparative Immunology, 1976—81, Allergy Proc., 1983—93; editor: Hist. Notes, Allergy and Asthma Proc., 1988—93, Allergy Archives, Jour. Allergy and Clin. Immunology, 2001—; cons. editor Am. Jour. Rhinology, 1986—93; contbr. articles to profl. jours., chapters to books. Trustee Marywood Coll., Scranton, Pa., 1983-89; bd. govs. adv. coun. Wilkes U., Wilkes-Barre, 1991-92. Capt. M.C., USAF, 1944-46. Recipient Disting. Svc. award Wyo. Sem., 1978, Asthma and Allergy Found. Am., 1981, Clemens von Pirquet award Georgetown U., 1981, NIH Centennial award, Terri Gottheif Lupus Rsch. Inst., 1987, NYU Med. Alumni Achievement award in health sci., 1988, Achievement award Internat. Assn. Allergology and Clin. Immunology, 1988, Spl. Recognition award Am. Acad Allergy and Immunology, 1989, 2002, recognition citation ILSI Allergy and Immunology Inst., 1992. Fellow: Am. Acad. Allergy (chmn. rsch. coun. 1963—66, historian 1963—69, v.p. 1979—80, Disting. Svc. award 1971), ACP, Coll. Physicians Phila., Am. Coll. Allergists (hon.), mem.. Washington Soc. History of Medicine (v.p. 1993—94, pres. 1994—96), Am. Assn. History of Medicine, Am. Fedn. Clin. Rsch., Collegium Internat. Allergologicum, Soc. Exptl. Biology and Medicine, Am. Coll. Rheumatology, Clin. Immunology Soc., Assn. Am. Physicians, Am. Assn. Immunologists, Cosmos Club, Alpha Omega Alpha (NYU alumni), Sigma Xi. Home: 5500 Friendship Blvd Apt 1927N Chevy Chase MD 20815-7272 Office: Nat Libr Medicine Bldg 38 HMD Room 1 E21 Bethesda MD 20892 Office Phone: 301-402-0269. Business E-Mail: scohen@niaid.nih.gov.

COHEN, STANLEY, pathologist, educator; b. NYC, June 4, 1937; s. Herman Joseph and Eva (Lapidus) C.; m. Marion Doris Cantor, Aug. 30, 1959; children: Laurie Ellen, Ronald Nelson, Kenneth Stuart. AB, Columbia U., 1957, MD, 1961. Diplomate Am. Bd. Pathology (mem. immunopathology com.). Intern Albert Einstein Med. Ctr., Bronx, NY, 1961-62, resident Mass. Gen. Hosp., 1962-64, fellow NYU Med. Ctr., 1964-66; prof. pathology SUNY, Buffalo, 1968-74; acting dir. Ctr. for Immunology, Buffalo, 1973-74; prof. pathology U. Conn. Health Ctr., Farmington, 1974-87, assoc. chmn., 1976-80; prof., chmn. bd. Hahnemann U., Phila., 1987-94; prof., chmn. U. Medicine Dentistry-N.J. Med. Ctr., 1994—. Mem. study sect. allergy and immunology, 1981-85; chair study sect. tumor immunology ahd therapy TRDRP, 1992-94; co-chmn. 3d, 4th and 5th Internat. Lymphokine Workshops, 1982, 84, Congress on Cytokines, 1987, UCLA colloquium: molecular pathways of cytokines, 1990—, Keystone Symposium, 1992. Author: Mechanisms of Cell-Mediated Immunity, 1974, Mechanisms of Tumor Immunity, 1976, Mechanisms of Immunopathology, 1978, Biology of the Lymphokines, 1979, Interleukins, Lymphokines and Cytokines, 1983, Molecular Basis of Lymphokine Action, 1987, Role of Lymphokines in the Immune Response, 1989; assoc. editor-in-chief Clin. Immunology and Immunopathology; mem. editorial bds. 8 profl. jours.; contbr. more than 195 articles to profl. jours. Served to capt. U.S. Army, 1966-68. Recipient Kinne award, 1954, Borden award, 1961, Parke-Davis award in Exptl. Pathology, 1977, Outstanding Investigator award Nat. Cancer, Inst., 1986; Witobsky Meml. lectr., 1995. Mem.: Assoc. Maleo Pathologist (sec. treas. 2011—), Am. Soc. Investigative Pathology, Fedn. Am. Socs. Exptl. Biology (treas. 2008—), Pluto Soc., Am. Soc. Exptl. Biology (fin. com. 2001—), Am. Soc. Investigative Pathology (sec.-treas. 2001—07, v.p. 2007—, pres. 2009—10), Clin. Immunol. Soc. (councilor), Am. Assn. Immunologists, Am. Assn. Pathologists. Home: 79 Ettl Cir Princeton NJ 08540-2334 Office: UMDNJ Med Sch Newark NJ 07103 Personal E-mail: cohenstan@comcast.net. Business E-Mail: cohenst@umdmj.edu, cohenstan@verizon.net.

COHEN, STANLEY, retired biochemistry educator; b. Bklyn., Nov. 17, 1922; s. Louis and Fannie (Feitel) Cohen; m. Olivia Larson, 1951 (div.); children: Burt, Kenneth, Cary; m. Jan Elizabeth Jordan, 1981. BA in Chemistry and Zoology, Bklyn. Coll., 1943; MA in Zoology, Oberlin Coll., 1945; PhD in Biochemistry, U. Mich., 1948; PhD (hon.), U. Chgo., 1985, Oberlin Coll., 1989, Washington U., 1993. Instr. dept. biochemistry and pediat. U. Colo., Denver, 1948-52; Am. Cancer Soc. fellow in radiology Washington U., St. Louis, 1952-53, assoc. prof. dept. zoology, 1953-59; asst. prof. biochemistry Vanderbilt U. Sch. Medicine, Nashville, 1959-62, assoc. prof., 1962-67, prof. biochemistry, 1967-86, disting. prof., 1986-2000, disting. prof. emeritus biochemistry, 2000—. Charles B. Smith vis. rsch. prof. Meml. Sloan-Kettering Cancer Ctr., 1984; Feodor Lynen lectr. U. Miami, Fla., 1986; Steenbock lectr. U. Wis., 1986. Contbr. articles to profl. jours. Recipient William Thomson Wakeman award, Nat. Paraplegia Found., 1974, Earl Sutherland rsch. prize for achievement in rsch., Vanderbilt U., 1977, Albion O. Bernstein, MD award, NY State Med. Soc., 1978, Lewis S. Rosenstiel award, Brandeis U., 1982, Alfred P. Sloan award, GM Cancer Rsch. Found., 1982, Louisa Gross Horwitz prize, Columbia U., 1983, Disting. Achievement award, Lab. Biomed. & Environ. Scis., UCLA, 1983, Lila Gruber Meml. Cancer Rsch. award, Am. Acad. Dermatology, 1983, Bertner award, M.D. Anderson Hosp./U.Tex., 1983, Gairdner Found. Internat. award, 1985, Nat. Med. Sci., 1986, Fred Conrad Koch award, Endocrine Soc., 1986, Nobel prize in physiology/medicine, 1986, Albert Lasker award for basic med. rsch., 1986; named to Hall of Honor, Nat. Inst. Child Health & Human Devel., NIH, 2007. Fellow: Jewish Acad. Arts & Scis.; mem.: NAS (H.P. Robertson Meml. award 1981), Internat. Inst. Embryology, Am. Chem. Soc., Internat. Acad. Sci. (hon.), Am. Acad. Arts & Scis., Am. Soc. Biol. Chemists. *

COHEN, STANLEY ALLEN, pediatric gastroenterologist; b. Columbus, Ohio, June 3, 1947; s. Norman Saul and Esther (Schlansky) C.; m. Judith Dee Adler, Mar. 22, 1970 (div. 1997). m. Jamie Ann Golsen, Nov. 10, 2002; children: David, Adam, Lauren BS, Case Western Res., 1969; MD, Ohio State U., 1972. Diplomate Am. Bd. Pediat. and Pediatric GI/Nutrition. Intern Johns Hopkins Hosp., Balt., 1972-73, resident, 1973-75; pediatrician USAF, Langley AFB, Va., 1975-77; fellow Mass Gen. Hosp., Boston, 1977-80; pediatrician Roswell Pediat., Ga., 1980-87; physician, dir. Ctr. Pediatric Gastroenterology/Nutrition, Atlanta, 1987-99; physician Children's Ctr. Digestive Healthcare, 1999—; adj. clin. prof. pediatrics Emory U., Atlanta, 2001—. Med. dir. Healthfield/Hug Ctr., Altanta, 1989-2005; dir. Combined Ctr. for Inflammatory Bowel Disease, Children's Healthcare Atlanta, 2006-09. Author: Healthy Babies, Happy Kids, 1985, poem Two, 1990, Seeping Into/Out of the Well, 1991, Beyond Hell, 1992, Re-Re-, 1995, In Celebration, 2002, Measured Words, 2007; editor: Pediatric Emergency Mgmt., 1983. Chmn. 20th Century Art Acquisition Fund High Mus., Atlanta, 1985-86; pres. Scottish Rite Childrens Med. Ctr., Atlanta, 1986. Maj. USAF, 1975-79 Recipient Premiere Physicians award Crohn's and Colitis Found. Ga. chpt., 1995, Atlanta Alliance Devel. Disabilities award, 1999 Fellow Am. Acad. Pediatrics (chmn. com. on nutrition Ga. chpt., lay edn. award 1997, chmn. sect. subspecialists); mem. Greater Atlanta Pediatric Soc., N.Am. Soc. Pediatric Gastroenterology and Nutrition Achievements include patents in field. Office: Children's Ctr Digestive Healthcare Ste 440 993-D Johnson Ferry Rd Atlanta GA 30342-4722 Office Phone: 404-257-0799.

COHEN, STANLEY NORMAN, geneticist, educator; b. Perth Amboy, NJ, Feb. 17, 1935; s. Bernard and Ida (Stolz) Cohen; m. Joanna Lucy Wolter, June 27, 1961; children: Anne, Geoffrey. BA, Rutgers U., NJ, 1956, ScD (hon.), 1994; MD, U. Pa., 1960, ScD (hon.), 1995. Intern Mt. Sinai Hosp., NYC, 1960-61; resident Univ. Hosp., Ann Arbor, Mich., 1961-62; clin. assoc. arthritis & rheumatism br. Nat. Inst. Arthritis & Metabolic Diseases, NIH, Bethesda, Md., 1962-64; sr. resident medicine Duke U. Hosp., Durham, NC, 1964-65; Am. Cancer Soc. postdoc. rsch. fellow Albert Einstein Coll. Medicine, Bronx, NY, 1965-67, asst. prof. devel. biology & cancer, 1967-68, faculty Stanford U., Calif., 1968—, prof. medicine, 1975—, prof. genetics, 1977—, chmn. dept. genetics, 1978-86, K.-T Li Prof., 1993—. Mem. com. recombinant DNA molecules NAS-NRC, 1974; mem. com. genetic experimentation Internat. Coun. Sci. Unions, 1977—96. Mem. editl. bd. Jour. Bacteriology, 1973—79, Molecular Microbiology, 1986—2005, Procs. Nat. Acad. Sci., 1996—, Current Opinion in Microbiology, 1997—. Trustee U. Pa., 1997—2002. With USPHS, 1962—64. Recipient Burroughs Wellcome Scholar award, 1970, Mattia award, Roche Inst. Molecular Biology, 1977, Albert Lasker award for basic med. rsch., 1980, Wolf Found. prize in medicine, Israel, 1981, Marvin J. Johnson award, 1981, Disting. Grad. award, U. Pa. Sch. Medicine, 1986, Disting. Svc. award, Miami Winter Symposium, 1986, Nat. Biotech award, 1989, de la Vie prize, LVMH Inst., 1988, Nat. Medal of Sci., 1988, City of Medicine award, 1988, Nat. Medal of Tech., 1989, Spl. award, Am. Chem. Soc., 1999, Lemelson MIT Prize, 1996, Albany Med. Ctr. prize in medicine & biomed. rsch., 2004, Shaw prize in life sci. & medicine, 2004, Innovation Biosci. award, The Economist, 2005, Cold Spring Harbor Lab. Double Helix medal, 2009, John Stearns Medicine Lifetime Achievement award, NY Acad. Medicine, 2007; named Einstein Prof., Chinese Acad. Scis., 2006; named to Nat. Inventors Hall of Fame, 2001; Guggenheim fellow, 1973, Josiah Macy, Jr. faculty scholar, 1975—76. Fellow: AAAS, Am. Acad. Microbiology; mem.: NAS (chmn. genetics sect. 1988—91), Am. Philos. Soc., Inst. Medicine, Assn. Am. Physicians, Am. Soc. Clin. Investigation, Am. Soc. Pharmacology & Exptl. Therapeutics, Am. Soc. Microbiology (Cetus award 1988), Genetics Soc. America, Am. Soc. Biol. Chemists, Am. Philos. Soc., Alpha Omega Alpha, Phi Beta Kappa, Sigma Xi. Achievements include obtaining, with Herbert Boyer, first patent in the field of recombinant deoxyribonucleic acid (DNA), 1980. Office: Stanford U Sch Med Dept Genetics Rm M-322 Stanford CA 94305

COHEN, STEVEN, plastic surgeon, director; b. Washington, Apr. 9, 1954; m. Sheri Cohen; children: Joshua William, Hannah Rose, Kyoko. BA in English Summa Cum Laude, Emory U., Atlanta, Ga., 1976; MD, George Washington U. Sch. Medicine, Washington, 1980. General surgery internship Columbia-Presbyn. Med. Ctr., NY, 1980—81, general surgery residency, fellowship, 1981—82; clin. assoc. cardiac surgery Cardiac Surgery Branch, Nat. Heart, Lung and Blood Inst., Nat. Inst. Health, 1982—84; general surgery residency Dartmouth-Hitchcock Med. Ctr. Hanover, 1984—87; plastic and reconstructive surgery residency hosp. U. Pa., Phila., 1987—89; craniomaxillofacial and facial plastic surgery fellow. UCLA, Med. Ctr., 1989—90; plastic surgeon and medical dir. FACES plus Aesthetic Facility and The La Jolla Plastic Surgery, Skin and Laser Ctr.; chief Craniofacial Surgical Svcs. Ctr. Craniofacial Disorders Children's Hosp. and Health. Office: 4510 Exec Dr Ste 200 San Diego CA 92121 Business E-Mail: scohen@facesiows.com.

COHEN, STEVEN C., oncologist, educator; MD, Johns Hopkins U., 1980. Diplomate Am. Bd. Internal Medicine, 1983, Am. Bd. Internal Medicine-hematology, 1985, Am. Bd. Internal Medicine-oncology, 1985. Intern Univ. Hosps., Cleve., resident; fellow Hosp. of Univ. Pa.; clin. asst. prof. medicine Thomas Jefferson Univ.; hosp. affiliation include Bryn Mawr Hosp., 1986—, Lankenau Med. Ctr., 1994—, Paoli Hosp., 2001—. Contbg. (publs.) Internal Medicine Bulletin, W.B. Saunders Co., 1994—96; co-author: (publs.) Peripheral Stem Cell Transplantation in Lymphoma, Semin, 1995. Mem. adv. The Wellness Cmty. Mem.: Am. Soc. of Hematology, Am. Soc. of Clin. Oncology. Office: Bryn Mawr Hospital 933 Haverford Rd Bryn Mawr PA 19010 Office Phone: 610-525-4511. Office Fax: 610-525-8561.

COHEN, STEVEN ROBERT, dermatologist, educator; b. Phila., Pa., Apr. 28, 1946; MD, U. Pa., 1971; MPH, Yale U., 1978. Asst. prof. Yale Med. Sch., 1977; assoc. prof. Cornell Univ. Sch. of Medicine, 1984; chair dermatology dept. Israel Med. Ctr., 1988; prof. dermatology Mount Sinai Sch. of Medicine, 1988, prof. and dep. chair dermatology dept., 2001, resident program dir. and co-chief dermatopharmacology sect., 2001; prof. dermatology Albert Einstein Coll. of Medicine, 1994, prof. and chief dermatology dept., 2006—. Vis. physician Rockefeller Univ., 1984. Co-author: (publs.) Genetic association of cutaneous neonatal lupus with HLA class II and tumor necrosis factor alpha: implications for pathogenesis, 2004, A retrospective analysis of 103 patients with emphasis on practical aspects for the clinician, 2005, Etanercept monotherapy for a pateint with psoriasis, psoriatic arthritis, and concomitant hepatitis C infection, 2006. Recipient Outstanding Sci. Alumni award, Pa. State Univ., 1997, Parker J. Palmer Courage to Teach award, 2006. Mem.: Am. Dermatol. Assn., Am. Coll. of Occupl. and Environ. Medicine, NY Acad. of Medicine, Am. Acad. of Dermatology, NY Dermatol. Soc., Soc. for Investigative Dermatology. Office: Montefiore Medical Center 111 East 210th St Bronx NY 10467 Office Phone: 718-920-2680. E-mail: steven.cohen@einstein.yu.edu.

COHEN, TAMMY SUSAN, pharmacist, educator; b. Orange, Calif., Sept. 8, 1972; d. Thomas Joseph and Catherine Doris Shallow; m. Brian Adam Cohen, Oct. 8, 1974; 1 child, Allyson Nicole. BS in Biology, Ill. State U., 1994; MS in Pharmacy Adminstrn., U. Kans., 1999; PharmD, U. Ill., Chgo., 2001. Registered pharmacist Kans. State Bd. Pharmacy, 1999, Tex. State Bd. Pharmacy, 2003. Pharmacy clin. practice mgr. U. Kans. Hosp., Kansas City, 2001—03; pharmacy asst. dir. Tex. Children's Hosp., Houston, 2003—. Peer reviewer Am. Jour. Health-System Pharmacists, Bethesda, Md., 1999—; adj. clin. prof. U. Kans., Lawrence, 2001—, pharmacy practice mgmt. residency preceptor, Kansas City, 2002—03; liason U. Health-System Consortium, Chgo., 2002—02. Recipient Cmty. Pharmacy award, Ill. Assn. Cmty. Pharmacy, 1998, Innovative Clin. Practice award, Bd. Kans. Soc. Health-System Pharmacist, 2001, Bd. Kans. Soc. Health Sys. Pharmacists, 2001; named Outstanding Leader, Pfizer Pharmaceuticals, 1999; ACCP Meeting scholar, Aventis Pharmaceuticals, 2000. Mem.: Gulf Coast Soc. Health Sys. Pharmacists (assoc.; com. mem. 2003—03), Tex. Soc. Health Sys. Pharmacists (assoc.; com. mem. 2003—03), Ill. Coun. Health Sys. Pharmacists (assoc.; student pres., v.p., coms. 1995—98), Kans. Soc. Health-System Pharmacists (assoc.), Inst. for Healtcare Improvement (assoc.), U. Health-System Consortium (assoc.), Am. Soc. Health Sys. Pharmacists (assoc.; coun. mem. 1997—98, Outstanding Student Leadership award 1998, 1999), Phi Lambda Sigma. Office: Texas Children's Hosp 6621 Fannin Houston TX 77030 Personal E-mail: drsbtcohen@earthlink.net. E-mail: tscohen@texaschildrenshospital.org.

COHEN, WILLIAM, cosmetic dentist; Grad., U. Ill.; DDS. Taught Univ. Ill. Dental Sch.; cosmetic dentist Glen Dental Ctr., Chgo. Featured in New Beauty Mag., 2005, 2006. Served US Army. Fellow: Acad. GEn. Dentistry; mem.: Pierre Fauchard Acad., Odontographic Soc. Chgo., Am. Equilibration Soc., Crown Coun., Chgo. Dental Soc., Ill. State Dental Soc., ADA, Am. Acad. Cosmetic Dentistry (pres. Chgo. chapter 1995—, Outstanding Contribution to Cosmetic Dentistry award 2002). Office: Glen Dental Center 2222 Chestnut Ave Ste 220 Glenview IL 60026 Office Phone: 888-781-9069.

COHEN, WILLIAM NATHAN, radiologist; b. Balt., Dec. 10, 1935; s. Herbert and Lillian (Goldberg) C.; m. Sylvia Weinstein, Feb. 9, 1964; children: Elaine, Shirah, Jonathan. Student, Johns Hopkins U., 1952—55; MD, U. Md., 1959. Intern U. Mich. Hosp., Ann Arbor, 1959-60; resident in radiology Mallinckrodt Inst., Washington U., St. Louis, 1960-63; chief radiology sect. Gallup Indian Hosp., USPHS, 1963-65; asst. prof. radiology U. Iowa, Iowa City, 1965-69, asso. prof., 1969-73, prof., 1973-76; prof. radiology SUNY Upstate Med. U., Syracuse, 1976-83, clin. prof. radiology, 1983—. Attending radiologist Crouse Hosp., Syracuse; vis. prof. radiology Hebrew U., Jerusalem, 1971-72; examiner Am. Bd. Radiology, 1981-87. Contbr. articles in field to med. jours. Fellow Am. Coll. Radiology; mem. Radiol. Soc. N. Am., Am. Roentgen Ray Soc., Am. Inst. Ultrasound in Medicine (sr.), Alpha Omega Alpha. Business E-Mail: wcohen1@twcny.rr.com.

COHEN-MAITRE, STACEY ANN, psychologist; b. NYC, June 25, 1963; MA, Loma Linda U., 1998, PhD, 2002. Postdoc. fellow Children's Hosp. LA, 2001—04; vendored psychologist Harbor Regional Ctr. and Tri-Counties Regional Ctr., 2002—, lic. psychologist, 2002—; cons. United Cerebral Palsy, 2004. Profl. advisor Shane's Inspiration, 2003. Contbr. articles to sci. profl. jours. Recipient award, Pepperdine U.; Rsch. grant, Loma Linda U. Mem.: APA, Psi Chi. Avocations: dance, exercise, reading. Office: 5530 Corbin Ave Ste 315 Tarzana CA 91356 E-mail: msmaitre@aol.com.

COHN, AARON I., anesthesiologist, educator; b. LA, Sept. 8, 1959; s. Alan Franklin and Louise Christine (Huff) C.; m. Nicola Ann Bernau, July 1984 (div. Aug. 1986). BS, U. Calif. Riverside, 1980; MA, Rice U., 1984; MD, U. Tex. Galveston, 1987. Diplomate Am. Bd. Anesthesiology. Med. intern Montefiore/Univ. Hosp., Pitts., 1987-88; postdoctoral fellow Ctr. for Med. Informatics, Yale U. Med. Sch., New Haven, 1988-90; resident in anesthesiology Yale-New Haven Hosp., New Haven, 1990-91, St. Elizabeth's Med. Ctr., Boston, 1991-93; asst. prof. dept. anesthesiology U. Tex. Med. Br., Galveston, 1993-96; anesthesiologist North Tex. Anesthesia, Dallas, 1996-97; asst. prof. dept. anesthesiology U. Okla., Oklahoma City, 1997-99, U. Colo., Denver, 1999—2006; anesthesiologist Harlingen Anesthesia Assocs., 2006—07, ptnr., 2007—. Member biomed. computing and health informatics study section (formerly SSS-9), NIH, Bethesda, Md., 1993-2004; reviewer Jour. Clin. Anesthesia, 1998-99. Contbr. articles to profl. jours. Mem. Internat. Anesthesia Rsch. Soc., Am. Soc. Anesthesiologists. Republican. Jewish. Avocations: bicycling, pistol shooting, computers, scuba diving, underwater photography. Home: 2929 Cypress Dr Harlingen TX 78550 Office: Harlingen Anesthesia Assocs 1702 Ed Carey Harlingen TX 78550 Personal E-mail: aaron_cohn@cyberdude.com. Business E-Mail: aaron.cohn@alumni.rice.edu.

COHN, ISIDORE, JR., surgeon, educator; b. New Orleans, Sept. 25, 1921; s. Isidore and Elsie (Waldhorn) C.; m. Jacqueline Heymann, July 4, 1944 (div. Aug. 1971); children: Ian Jeffrey, Lauren Kerry; m. Marianne Winter Miller, Jan. 3, 1976. BS in Chemistry with honors, Tulane U., New Orleans, 1942; MD, U. Pa., Phila., 1945; M.Med. Sci. in Surgery, U. Pa., 1952, DMS in Surgery, 1955; LHD (hon.), U. SC, 1995. Diplomate Am. Bd. Surgery (bd. dirs. 1969-75). Intern Grad. Hosp. U. Pa., 1945-46, resident in surgery, 1949-52; fellow dept. surg. rsch. U. Pa., 1947-48; vis. surgeon Charity Hosp., New Orleans, 1952-62, sr. vis. surgeon, 1962-2000, hon. sr. vis. surgeon, 2000—; surgeon in chief La. State U. Svc., Charity Hosp., New Orleans, 1962-89; prof. surgery La. State U. Sch. Medicine, New Orleans, 1959-2000, emeritus chmn., emeritus prof. surgery, 2000—. Cons. surgeon VA Hosp., New Orleans, Touro Infirmary, New Orleans; instr. surgery La. State U. Sch. Medicine, New Orleans, 1952-53, asst. prof., 1953-56, assoc. prof., 1956-59, prof., 1959-2000, chmn. dept. surgery, 1962-89; mem. surg. rsch. rev. com. VA, Washington, 1967-68; dir. Nat. Pancreatic Cancer Project, 1975-84; mem. Soc. Surg. Chairmen, 1962-89. Mem. editl. bd. Am. Surgeon, 1963-87, Current Surgery, 1964-90, Am. Jour. Surgery, 1968-96, emeritus, 1997—, Digestive Diseases and Scis., 1978-82, Surg. Gastroenterology, 1982—, Cancer, 1992—2002, Digestive Surgery, 1995—. Bd. dirs. New Orleans Met. Conv. and Visitors Bur., 1998-2000, New Orleans Mus. Art, 2004—09, hon. life mem., 2010-, Jewish Endowment Found., 2006—. Served to capt. M.C., AUS, 1946-47. Isidore Cohn, Jr. Professorship named in his honor at La. State U., 1987, Isidore Cohn, Jr., M.D. Student Learning Ctr. at La. State U. Health Sci. Ctr. Sch. Medicine dedicated in his honor, 2002, Spirit of Charity award Med. Ctr. La., 2003; named Outstanding Alumnus, Isidore Newman Sch., New Orleans, La., 2003, Role Model, Young Leadership Coun. New Orleans, 2006, Tzedakah award, Jewish Endowment Found, 2009. Fellow ACS (exec. com., bd. govs. 1987-91, vice-chmn. 1989-90, chmn. 1990-91, 1st v.p. 1993-94), Southern Surg. Assn. (hon; 1st v.p. 1979-80, treas.-recorder 1981-82, pres. 1982-83, hon. mem. 2009-); mem. AMA, Am. Surg. Assn., La. Surg. Assn. (pres. 1968), So. Med. Assn., La., Orleans Parish med. socs., Soc. Univ. Surgeons, Southeastern Surg. Congress (chmn. forum on progress in surgery 1967-69, councillor for La. 1967-73, pres. 1972), Surg. Biology Club II, Assn. Acad. Surgery, Isidore Cohn, Jr.-James D. Rives Surg. Soc., Internat. Surg. Soc., Am. Gastroenterol. Assn., Bockus Soc. Gastroenterology, Soc. Surgery Alimentary Tract (trustee 1969-80, recorder 1973-76, pres. 1976-77, chmn. bd. 1977-78, Founders medal 2004), Am. Soc. Microbiologists, Soc. Surg. Oncology, NY Acad. Scis., Am. Assn. Cancer Research, Southeastern Cancer Research Assn. (pres. 1975), Collegium Internationale Chirurgiae Digestivae, Am. Cancer Soc. (vice chmn. clin. investigation adv. com. 1969, chmn. clin. investigation adv. com. 1969-73), Tex. Surg. Soc. (hon.), Sigma Xi, Phi Beta Kappa, Alpha Omega Alpha, Omicron Delta Kappa, Home: 510 Iona St Metairie LA 70005-4430 Office: La State U Med Sch New Orleans LA 70112 Home Phone: 504-835-6135. Personal E-mail: drdrdrjr@aol.com.

COHN, JOHN R., allergist, immunologist; MD, Thomas Jefferson U., 1976. Diplomate Am. Bd. Allergy and Immunology, Am. Bd. Internal Medicine, Am. Bd. Internal Medicine-pulmonary medicine. Intern Thomas Jefferson Univ. Hosp., resident; fellow allergy and immunology and pulmonary medicine Duke Univ. Med. Ctr.; prof. medicine Jefferson Med. Coll., asst. prof. pediat.; hosp. affiliation includes Thomas Jefferson Univ. Hosp. Named one of Top Docs, Phila. Mag, 2010. Mem.: Am. Acad. of Asthma, Allergy and Immunology (chair practice, diagnostics and therapeutics com.). Office: Thomas Jefferson University Hospital Ste 1300 1015 Chestnut St, Philadelphia PA 19107 Office Phone: 215-955-7410. Office Fax: 215-923-8230.

COHN, JOSEPH DAVID, surgeon; b. NYC, Jan. 26, 1937; s. Samuel Theodor and Gertrude (Emsheimer) C.; m. Barbara Ester Forst, July 27, 1966; children: Michael, Russell. SB, MIT, 1957; MD, NYU, 1961; MBA, Rutgers U., 1993. Diplomate Am. Bd. Surgery, Am. Bd. Thoracic Surgery, Am. Bd. Critical Care Surgery. Intern Duke Hosp., Durham, NC, 1961-62; surg. resident Bronx Mcpl. Hosp. Ctr., NY, 1962-67; thoracic surgery resident U. Calif., San Diego, 1969-71; from asst. dir. surgery to dir. St. Barnabas Med. Ctr., Livingston, NJ, 1971-83; thoracic surgeon Northfield Surg. Assn., Livingston, 1978-99; mem. staff Santa Rosa Meml. Hosp. Sutter Med. Ctr., Santa Rosa, Calif., 2001—. Clin. asst. prof. surgery UMDNJ, Newark, 1972—79, assoc. prof., 1979—90, prof., 1990—99. Editor sci. jours.; author software programs, 1988; contbr. articles to profl. jours. Capt. USAF, 1967-69. Fellow Am. Heart Assn. 1966-67, NIH 1964-66. Fellow ACS, Am. Coll. Critical Care Medicine; mem. Sigma Xi, Phi Lambda Upsilon, Alpha Omega Alpha. Avocations: skiing, scuba, flying. Office: 5773 Shiloh Ridge Road Santa Rosa CA 95403-7802 Office Phone: 707-578-6714. Business E-Mail: jcohn@alum.mit.edu. *

COHN, LAWRENCE H., cardiothoracic surgeon; b. San Francisco, Mar. 11, 1937; s. Harold Edward and Dorothy Harriet Cohn; m. Roberta Lee Cohn, June 26, 1960; children: Leslie Anne, Jennifer Lynne. BA, U. Calif., Berkeley, 1958; MD, Stanford U. Sch. Medicine, 1962; MA (hon.), Harvard U. Sch. Medicine, 1989. Diplomate Am. Bd. Surgery, Am. Bd. Thoracic Surgery. Intern surgery, jr. resident Boston City Hosp., 1962—64; surgeon, surgical assoc. US Pub. Health Svc. Nat. Humanities Inst., 1964—66; fellowship Nat. Heart Inst., 1966; resident thoracic surgery U. Calif., San Francisco Sch. Medicine, 1966—69; resident cardiothoracic surgery Stanford U. Sch. Medicine, 1969—71; cardiothoracic surgeon Brigham & Woman's Hosp., Boston, 1980-87, chief div. cardiac surgery, 1987—2005. Bd. trustees Brigham & Women's Hosp.; prof. cardiac surgery Harvard Med. Sch.; internat. adv. bd. World-Heart Found.; past pres. Thoracic Surgery Found. Rsch. Edn. Contbr. articles to profl. jours. Fellow: Am. Surg. Soc., Soc. Thoracic Surgeons, Am. Coll. Chest Physicians (pres. 1987), Am. Coll. Cardiologists; mem.: Western Thoracic Surgical Assn., French Soc. Thoracic Cardiovascular Surgery, European Assn. Cardiothoracic Surgery, Cardiothoracic Surgery Network (editorial bd.), Am. Assn. Thoracic Surgery (pres. 1998—99). Office: Brigham Womens Hosp Div Cardiac Surgery 75 Francis St Boston MA 02115-6106 Office Phone: 617-732-6569. Office Fax: 617-264-6369. Business E-Mail: lcohn@partners.com.

COHN, RICHARD ALLAN, pediatrician, educator; b. Bronx, NY, May 30, 1946; BA, U. Chgo., 1968; MD, Albert Einstein Coll. Medicine, 1972. Prof. pediat Northwestern U. Feinberg Sch. Medicine, 1980—. Med. dir., kidney transplantation Children's Meml. Hosp., 1995. Named Tchr. of the Yr., Dept. Pediat. Mem.: Am. Soc. Transplantation. Avocations: racquetball, reading. Office: Children's Memorial Hosp 2300 Childrens Plz Mail Code 37 Chicago IL 60614 Office Fax: 773-327-3937. Business E-Mail: r-cohn@northwestern.edu.

COHN, STANLEY ALAN, cell biology educator; b. Denver, Nov. 12, 1957; s. Louie and Evelyn (Shames) C.; m. Sara Hurwitz Cohn, Aug. 11, 1985; children: Rachel Beth, Jacob Samuel. BS in Chemisty with honors, Calif. Inst. of Tech., 1979; PhD in Biology, U. Colo., 1986. Postdoctoral rschr. Nat. Jewish Ctr. for Immunology and Respiratory Medicine, Denver, 1986-89; asst. prof. DePaul U., Chgo., 1989-96, assoc. prof., 1996—2005, chair, dept. biol. scis., 2001—10, prof., 2005—. Bd. dirs. Niles Twp. Jewish Congregation, Skokie, Ill., 1992-99, Jewish Reconstructionist Congregation, Evanston, Ill., 2005-. Postdoctoral fellowship Am. Cancer Soc., 1987-89; rsch. grant NSF, 1994-97, 2000—04. Fellow Royal Soc. of Arts (Silver medal 1979); mem. AAAS, Am. Soc. for Cell Biology, Internat Soc. for Diatom Rsch., Coun. for Undergrad. Rsch., Phycol. Soc. Am. Democrat. Home: 8033 Tripp Ave Skokie IL 60076-3247 Office: DePaul Univ Dept of Biol Scis 2325 N Clifton Ave Chicago IL 60614-3207 Office Phone: 773-325-7595. Business E-Mail: scohn@depaul.edu.

COHN, STEVEN MARK, medical educator; b. Chgo., Nov. 26, 1954; BS, Duke U., 1976; MD, Wash. U. Sch. Medicine, PhD, 1985. Asst. prof. medicine Wash. U., 1992—98; prof. medicine U. Va., 1998—. Fellow: Am. Gastroenterology Assn. Office: Digestive Health Ctr Excellence Charlottesville VA 22908 Office Fax: 434-924-0841. Business E-Mail: sc6w@virginia.edu.

COHN, WILLIAM ETTLINGER, cardiologist, thoracic surgeon, product designer; b. New York, Ny, Sept. 2, 1960; s. Hugh Karl and Judith Ettlinger Cohn; m. Mishaun Victoria Drever, May 30, 1961; children: Benjamen Mycroft, Elizabeth Emily, William Ettlinger, Robert Huntington, Christopher Michael. Grad., Oberlin Coll.; MD, Baylor Coll. of Medicine, Houston, Tex., 1982—86. Diplomate Board of Thoracic Suregry Soc. of Thoracic Surgery, 1994. Assoc. prof. Harvard Med. Sch., Boston, 1991—2002; chief of minimally invasive cardiac surgery Beth Israel Deaconess Med. Ctr., Boston, 2001—04; dir. Minimally Invasive Surgical Tech.; co-dir. Cullen Cardiovascular Rsch. Lab, Tex. Heart Inst., St. Luke's Episcopal Hosp., Houston, 2004—. Author (investigator): (scientific publications) 1)use of ultrasonic welding in cardiac surgery, 2) myocardial revascularization with a pedicaled gastric submucosal flap 3)The Hgraft as a varient of minimally invasive coronary artery bypass; mem. med. team Miracle Workers (ABC), 2006, guest appearance The View, 2006. Achievements include invention of Coronary artery stabilizer to allow bypass surgery without stopping the heart; Nextstitch suture chain for cardiac valve implantation; Catheters For Percutaniously Attaching One Blood Vessel To Another Without Requiring An Operation; Distinguished Inventor of the year, 2000, Intellectual Property Owner's Association; Multiple Patents For Cardiac Valve Procedures Without Stopping The Heart. Office: St Luke's Episcopal Health Sys 6770 Bertner Ave Houston TX 77030 Office Fax: 832-355-9004. Business E-Mail: wcohn@heart.thi.tmc.edu. E-mail: wcohn@caregroup.harvard.edu.

COHNERT, TINA U., surgeon; b. Braunschweig, Germany, Jan. 16, 1963; d. Albrecht and Renate Cohnert. MD, Ludwig-Maximilians U., Munich, 1986. Resident Grosshadern U. Hosp., Munich, 1986—96; vascular fellow Hannover (Germany) Med. Sch. U. Hosp., 1997—99; cons. U. Hosp. Fr.-Schiller U., Jena, Germany, 2000—. Mem.: German Surg. Soc., German Soc. Vascular Surgeons, Internat. Soc. Endo-Vascular Specialists. Office: Cardiothoracic and Vascular Surgery Bachstr 18 D07743 Jena Germany

COIRO, VITTORIO, physician, educator; b. Salerno, Italy, Feb. 11, 1950; Diploma in Classical Lycee, Torquato Tasso Lyceum, Salerno, 1968; D in Medicine and Surgery, U. Parma, Italy, 1974. Rsch. assoc., postdoc. fellow, lectr. U. Mass., Med. Sch., Worcester, 1976—83; postdoc. scholar U. Parma, Med. Sch., 1976—80, rschr., 1980—2006, adj. prof., 1980—, aggregate prof., 2006—. Avocations: tennis, mountain climbing. Office: A Gramsci 14 Parma 43100 Italy Office Fax: 0039-0521033296. Business E-Mail: vittorio.coiro@unipr.it.

COIT, DANIEL G., surgeon, educator; MD, U. Cin., 1976. Diplomate Am. Bd. Surgery. Resident in internal medicine New Eng. Deaconess Hosp., Boston, 1977—78; resident in surgery Meml. Sloan- Kettering Cancer Ctr., NYC, 1978—83, fellow in surgical oncology, 1983—85; prof. surgery Cornell Univ.; surgeon Meml. Sloan- Kettering Cancer Ctr. Office: Memorial Sloan- Kettering Cancer Center 1275 York Ave New York NY 10065 Office Phone: 212-639-2000. Office Fax: 212-639-3576.

COKER, DONALD WILLIAM, banking, management and economic consultant, expert witness; b. Mobile, Ala., Nov. 26, 1945; s. William Mack and Gloria Antoinette (Croker) C.; m. Linda Carol Sandlin, July 12, 1969; children: Caroline Tiffany, Brittany Blaire. BA, postgrad., U. Ala., 1968, U. Houston, 1973, Spring Hill Coll., 1995—96, Harvard Bus. Sch., 2005. Trust mortgage officer Regions Fin. (formerly AmSouth Bank), Mobile, 1968—72; sr. loan officer Bank of America (formerly Gibraltar Savs.), Houston, 1972—73; mortgage officer, asst. treas. Citicorp Real Estate, Houston, 1973-74; comml. loan officer JPMorgan Chase Bank (formerly SW Bancshares and M Bank-Houston and Bank of SW), 1974—77; regional mgr. Citigroup (formerly Comml. Credit Co.), Houston, 1977—83, Ford Motor Credit, Houston, 1983-84; sr. v.p., mgr. lending and mortgage banking BBVA (formerly First Fed. Savs.), San Antonio, 1984—85; exec. v.p., bd. dirs. Home Savs. (now Citigroup), Houston, 1985-86; Don Coker Consulting Woodstock, 1986—. Cons. Prentice-Hall Pub., IRS, FDIC, USAID, Internat. Acctg. Stds. Bd., Resolution Trust Corp., World Bank; cons. to fin. instns., attys., corps. and govt. agys.; nat. healthcare and profl. practice valuation cons.; expert witness on bus. and intangible asset valuation, econ., fin., real estate and banking. Author: Complete Guide to Income Property Financing & Loan Packaging, 1984; tech. editor: Complete Real Estate Computer Workbook, 1986; contbr. over 70 articles to profl. jours. Trustee Katy Sch. Dist., Houston, 1987; treas. Nottingham Country Civic Club, Houston; precinct leader, del. and dep. voters registrar Rep. party. With USAR, 1966—68. Named Expert Cons., DRI & AAJ. Mem. Nat. Hosp. Assn., Am. Bankruptcy Inst., Nat. Assn. State Savs. and Loan Suprs., Am. Mortgage Bankers Assn., Tex. Mortgage Bankers' Assn., Am. Bankers Assn., Greater Grady Meml. Hosp. Task Force, U.S. Savs. and Loan League, Houston C. of C. (bus. devel. com.), Fulton Dekalb Hosp. Authority, Sweetwater Country Club. Republican. Episcopalian. Achievements include development of a patented check fraud prevention system. Office Phone: 770-852-2286. Personal E-mail: bankexpert@cs.com.

COKINOS, STEPHAN GEORGE, cardiologist; b. Bklyn., Aug. 28, 1949; s. George Stephan and Katina Olga (Papanastasopoulos) C.; m. Paula Panagopoulos, Jan. 10, 1982; children: George, Katina, James. BA, Adelphi U., 1971; MD, SUNY, Stony Brook, 1974. Diplomate Am. Bd. Internal Medicine. Intern in internal medicine Nassau County Med. Ctr., East Meadow, N.Y., 1974, resident in internal medicine, 1975-77, cardiology fellow, 1977-79, dir. cardiac catherization lab., 1979-81, dir. coronary care unit, 1981-85, attending cardiologist, 1979-85; cardiologist in group practice Ea. Cardiac Group, PC, West Islip, N.Y., 1985—; attending cardiologist Good Samaritan Hosp., Southside Hosp.; West Islip, N.Y., 1985—; cardiologist Southbay Cardiovascular Assocs., West Islip, N.Y., 1994—; asst. prof. SUNY Sch. Med.; attending cardiologist St. Francis Heart Ctr., NY. Apptd. clin. asst. prof. NY Coll. Osteopathic Medicine; asst. prof. SUNY Sch. Medicine, Stony Brook. Fellow Am. Coll. Cardiology, Am. Coll. Angiology, N.Y. Cardiologic Soc.; mem. AMA, Am. Soc. Internal Medicine, Am. Heart Assn., Am. Soc. Nuclear Cardiology., Medical Soc. NY., Hellenic Med. Soc., Soc. Cardivasc. Computed Tomography. Greek Orthodox. Avocations: swimming, skiing. Office: Southbay Cardiovascular Heart Ctr St Francis Hosp 540 Union Blvd West Islip NY 11795 Business E-Mail: scokinos@aol.com.

COKUSLU, LYNDA ELIZABETH MCCORD, medical assistant; b. Atlanta, June 11, 1956; d. Joseph Adair and Yvonne (Champagne) McCord; m. Fethi Cokuslu, Aug. 24, 1985; children: Sasha, Sedef, Samantha. MS in Mental Health, Capella U.; cert. med. asst., Bryman Sch., 1975; MBA/MHA, U. Phoenix. Lic. GAINS for Health and Life Ins. 2007; cert. med. asst. 2004, AAS, 2006, BAS, 2007. Casuality/liability claims processor Continental Ins./UAC, Atlanta, 1978—82; nutrition asst. Fayette County Edn., Peachtree City, Ga., 2001—03; med. asst. GAINS for Health and Life Ins. Segate Travel, Turkey, 2007—09. Mem. adv. bd. Clayton State U. Host benefit Hapeville Hist. Soc., Ga., 1988; officer PTA, Hapeville, 1997; catechist Youth/Adult Sch. Religion, Hapeville, 1996—2002, Fayetteville, 2003—04. Mem.: Am. Health Info. Mgmt. Assn., Am. Med. Asst. Assn., Travelers Protective Assn., Midtown Bus. Assn., Internat. Poet Soc. Roman Catholic. Home: 105 Buckeye Ln Fayetteville GA 30214 Office: Audvi Electronics 720 Glynn St N Ste D Fayetteville GA 30214-6706 Personal E-mail: lcokuslu@bellsouth.net.

COLAIZZI, JOHN LOUIS, medical educator; b. Pitts., May 10, 1938; s. Peter Richard and Lena M. (Sebastian) C.; m. Maria Rose Santoro, Aug. 12, 1967; children: James J., Patricia R., John Louis. BS, U. Pitts., 1960; MS, Purdue U., 1962, PhD, 1965. Asst. prof. Sch. Pharmacy, W.Va. U., Morgantown, 1964—65; asst. prof., assoc. prof. Sch. Pharmacy, U. Pitts., 1965—76, prof., chmn., assoc. dean, 1976—78; prof., dean Sch. Pharmacy Rutgers U., Piscataway, NJ, 1978—2007, acting v.p. acad. affairs, 2003, prof., 2007—. Bd. dirs. Rahway Hosp., N.J., 2003—; bd. dirs. Robert Wood Johnson Univ. Hosp., New Brunswick, N.J., 1984—, chmn., 1997-2000; mem. Medicaid Drug Utilization Rev. Bd. N.J., 1996-97; bioavailability cons. Drug Utilization Rev. Coun. N.J., 1997 2000. Mem. Am. Pharm. Assn., Am. Assn. Pharm. Scis., Am. Soc. Health-Sys. Pharmacists, Am. Assn. Coll. Pharmacy, Pharm. Care Mgmt. Assn. (dean's adv. coun. 1998-2003), Somerset County Tech. Inst. (pharm. techn. adv. bd. 2007—), Am. Inst. History of Pharmacy, Rho Chi, Alpha Zeta Omega, Sigma Xi. Democrat. Roman Catholic. Home: 21 Jason Dr East Brunswick NJ 08816-3342 Office: Rutgers U Sch Pharmacy 160 Frelinghuysen Rd Piscataway NJ 08854-8020 Office Phone: 732-445-5215. Personal E-mail: j.colaizzi@comcast.net. Business E-Mail: john.colaizzi@pharmacy.rutgers.edu.

COLAK, ALKIN, anesthesiologist, educator; b. Bulgaria, Nov. 11, 1975; D, Trakya U., 1998. Asst. prof., anesthesiology dept. Trakya U., 2007—. Office: Trakya University Edirne 22030 Turkey Personal E-mail: alkincol@yahoo.com.

COLASURDO, GIUSEPPE N., dean, pulmonologist, educator; b. Morrone Del Sannio, Italy; arrived in USA, 1988, naturalized; B, Liceo Scientifico Galileo Galilei, Pescara, Italy; MD summa cum laude, G. D'Annunzio Sch. Medicine, Chieti, Italy. Cert. in pediatric pulmonology, lic. Italy, Tex., Colo. Residency U. Tex. Med. Br., Galveston; fellowship U. Colo. Health Sci. Ctr., Nat. Jewish Med. and Rsch. Ctr., Denver; lab. asst. to Dr. Gary L. Larson Denver; clin. pulmonologist; joined as asst. prof. pediat. in the divsn. pulmonary medicine U. Tex. Med. Sch. at Houston, 1995, head divsn. pulmonary medicine, 1997—2001, dir. fellowship tng. program in pediatric pulmonary medicine, 2001—05, chmn. dept. pediat., 2005—07, dean, H. Wayne Hightower disting. prof. in the med. sciences, 2007—; interim pres. U. Tex. Health Sci Ctr. at Houston, 2011—; CEO UT Physicians; physician-in-chief Children's Meml. Hermann Hosp., Houston. Editl. reviewer: American Jour. Physiology, American Jour. Respiratory and Critical Care Medicine, Pediatric Pulmonology; contbr. articles to profl. jours., chapters to books. Decorated Knight of Order of Merit of Italian Republic Consul Gen. Italy; recipient David W. Smith Trainee award, We. Soc. Pediatric Rsch., Basic Scientist Devel. award, NIH, Facolta di Medicinee Chirurgia award, G. D'Annunzio Sch. Medicine, Exec. communicator of Yr. award, Houston, Internat. Assn. Bus. Communicators, 2008; grantee, NIH, Children's Miracle Network, Cystic Fibrosis Found. Mem.: American Thoracic Soc., Soc. Pediatric Rsch., Alpha Omega Alpha, Houston Delta Chpt. Office: University Tex Med Sch Houston Office of Dean 6431 Fannin MSB G150 Houston TX 77030 Office Phone: 713-500-5010. Office Fax: 713-500-0602. Business E-Mail: med.dean@uth.tmc.edu. *

COLBERG, JOHN W., urologist, educator; BS in Microbiology, ND State U., Fargo, 1981; MD, Wash. U. Sch. of Medicine, St. Louis, Mo., 1985. Lic. no. 03667 Conn., diplomate Am. Bd. of Urology, 1992, Am. Bd. of Urology-recertified, 2001. Intern dept. of surgery Yale-New Haven Hosp., 1985—86, resident dept. of surgery, 1986—87, resident divsn. of urology dept. of surgery, 1987—90, with sect. of urology dept. of surgery, 1998—, with credentials com., 1998—2000; IPA bd. mem. Yale-New Haven Med. Staff, 1999—2000; hosp. appointments include divsn. of urology dept. of surgery Barnes West County Hosp., St. Louis, 1990—98, John Cochran Veterans Adminstrn. Hosp., 1990—98, St. Louis Children's Hosp., 1990—98, Barnes-Jewish Hosp., 1990—98, Wash. Univ. Sch. of Medicine, 1990—98, West Haven Veterans Affairs Hosp., Conn., 1998—. Instr. divsn. of urology dept. of surgery Wash. Univ. Sch. of Medicine, St. Louis, 1990—98; chief divsn. of urology dept. of surgery John Cochran Veterans Adminstrn. Hosp., St. Louis, 1995—98; asst. prof. surgery, dir. urologic oncology sect. of urology Yale Univ. Sch. of Medicine, New Haven, 1998—2000, assoc. prof. surgery, dir. urologic oncology sect. of urology, 2000—; mem. south ctrl. sect. Am. Urological Assn., 1992—98. Co-author: (publs.) Iodine-125 versus palladium-103 implants for prostate cancer: clinical outcomes and complications, 2004, The effect of age on prostate implantation results, 2006, Surgery versus implant for early prostate cancer: results from a single institution 1992-2005, 2007, Whole pelvic radiation therapy versus prostate only radiation therapy of locally advanced or aggressive prostate adencarcinoma, 2009, and numerous others. Fellow: ACS; mem.: Am. Soc. of Clin. Oncologist, The Soc. of Urologic Oncology, The Soc. of Univ. Urologists, Am. Assn. of Clin. Urologists, Am. Urological Assn. Office: Yale Urology Group 800 Howard Ave YPB-3 New Haven CT 06519 Office Phone: 203-785-2815. Office Fax: 203-785-4043.

COLBERT, MARVIN JAY, retired internist, educator; b. Spokane, Wash., Nov. 6, 1923; s. John B. and Elizabeth (Peters) C.; m. Eleanor Ruth Rott, June 2, 1951 (dec. July 2000); children: Janet Lynn, James Lee, Lawrence Jay. Student, U. Utah, 1940-43; BS, Yale U., 1946; MD, Boston U., 1949. Diplomate: Am. Bd. Internal Medicine. Intern, resident in internal medicine Presbyn. Hosp., Chgo., 1949-50, VA Hosp., Boston, 1953-54, U. Ill. Rsch. and Ednl. Hosp., 1954-55; pvt. practice internal medicine Belmond, Iowa, 1955-56; mem. faculty U. Ill., Chgo., 1956-58; dir. health svc. Med. Ctr., 1959-78, prof. medicine, 1969-78; dir. employee health svcs. Evang. Hosp. Assn., Oak Brook, Ill., 1978-86. Cons. internal medicine radiol. and environ. rsch. div. Argonne (Ill.) Nat. Lab., 1978-79. Pres. Hillcrest PTA, Downers Grove, Ill., 1960-62; Parent-Tchrs. Group Chiengmai Co-Ednl. Ctr., Thailand, 1965-66. Capt. M.C. AUS, 1943-46, 50-52. Fellow ACP; mem. Assn. for Advancement of Automotive Medicine (dir. 1969-76). Home: 3195 Rio Dosa Dr # 2102 Lexington KY 40509-1736 Home Phone: 859-335-6807. Personal E-mail: ercolbert@aol.com.

COLBERT, STEPHEN, surgeon, educator; b. Sikeston, Mo., Oct. 22, 1970; BS, Stanford U., 1994; MD, U. Mo., 1999. Fellow, hand & microsurgery Wash. U., St. Louis, 2005—06; resident physician, integrated plastic surgery U. Mo. Sch. Medicine, 1999—2005, chair, faculty affairs com., 2007—09, asst. prof., hand & microsurgery head, 2006—. Chief, plastic surgery Harry S. Truman Meml. Veterans Hosp., 2006—11; chair, fin. & contracting com. U. Physicians, Mo., 2010—11; assoc. editor Jour. Hand Surgery Am., 2011. Recipient 2nd prize, Mo. chpt., ACS. Fellow: ACS; mem.: Am. Soc. Reconstructive Microsurgery, Am. Assn. Hand Surgeons, Am. Soc. Surgery Hand, Am. Soc. Plastic Surgeons. Avocations: baseball, winemaking. Office: 1 Hospital Dr M349 Columbia MO 65212

COLBORN, GENE LOUIS, anatomy educator, researcher; b. Springfield, Ill., Nov. 23, 1935; s. Adin Levi and Grace Downey (Tucker) C.; divorced; children: Robert Mark, Adrian Thomas, Lara Lee Colborn Russell; m. Sarah Ellen Crockett, Aug. 14, 1976; children: Jason Matthew, Nathan Tucker. BA with honors, Ky. Christian Coll., Grayson, 1957; BS with honors, Milligan Coll., Tenn., 1962; MS in Anatomy, Wake Forest U., Winston-Salem, NC, 1964, PhD in Anatomy, 1967. Postdoctoral fellow U. N.Mex. Sch. Medicine, Albuquerque, 1967 68; asst. prof. U. Tex. Health Sci. Ctr., San Antonio, 1968—72, assoc. prof., 1972—75; assoc. prof. anatomy Med. Coll. Ga., Augusta, 1975—88, prof. anatomy, 1988—2000, prof. surgery, 1993 2000, emeritus prof. anatomy and surgery, 2000—, dir. Ctr. for Clin. Anatomy, 1987—2000, dir. med. gross anatomy, 1975—2000, cons. dept. surgery, 1977—2000; clin. prof. surgery Emory U. Sch. Medicine, Atlanta, 1996—; chmn. divsn. anat. scis. Ross U. Sch. Medicine, Dominica, 2000—01; prof. Am. U. Caribbean Sch. Medicine, St. Maarten, Netherlands Antilles, 2002—04, chmn. anatomy, 2002—04. Pres. Ga. State Anat. Bd., 1983-93; cons. Eisenhower Army Med. Ctr., 1990-96; founder, pres. Gelco Med. Pub. Co., 2004-. Author: Practical Gross Anatomy, 1982, Surgical Anatomy, 1987, Hernias, 1988, Musculoskeletal Anatomy, 1989, Workbook of Surgical Anatomy, 1990, Clinical Gross Anatomy, 1993, Modern Hernia Repair, 1996, The Embryological and Anatomical Basis of Surgery, 2002, Benchmark Questions in Clinical Anatomy, 2008, Gray's Anatomy for Students- A Study Guide, 2008; mem. editl. bd.: Clin. Anatomy Jour.; contbr. numerous articles on cardiac conduction, nervous sys., primate anatomy, cell culture and clin. and surg. anatomy to profl. jours. Active San Antonio Symphony Mastersingers, 1970-75, Augusta Opera, 1975—2011, Augusta Choral Soc., 1975-95, Augusta Opera Guild, 2009-; judge Regional Sci. Fairs, Augusta, 1978-90, elder, Presbyn. Ch., 2008-. Recipient Golden Apple award, U. Tex. Health Sci. Ctr., 1975, Outstanding Med. Educator award, Med. Coll. Ga., 1976, 1977, 1978, 1982, 1987, 1988, 1990, 1991, 1997, Disting. Faculty award, 1978, 2000, Excellence in Tchg. award, 1997, 1999, Regents' award in tchg., 1998, others. Mem. AAUP, Am. Assn. Clin. Anatomists (membership chmn. 1982-86, mem. editl. bd. Jour. Clin. Anatomy 1994—), Am. Assn. Anatomists, Columbia County Choral Soc. (founding mem.), KC (4th degree). Republican. Avocations: opera, chess, tennis, camping. Address: Med Coll Ga 178 Creekview Ct Martinez GA 30907 Office Phone: 706-868-9290. Personal E-mail: glcolb@yahoo.com.

COLBURN, HAROLD LEWIS, dermatologist, state legislator, state legislator; m. Jane Harrison, 1949; children: Robert, Suzanne. AB, Princeton U., 1947; MD, Albany Med. Coll., 1949. Diplomate Am. Bd. Dermatology. Intern Hosp. Ctr., Orange, N.J., 1949-50; resident in dermatology U. Pa., 1952-55; dermatologist Moorestown and Mt. Holly, N.J., 1955-95; sec. chief emeritus of dermatology Meml. Hosp. Burlington County, Mt. Holly, 1955-92; sect. chief dermatology Zurbrugg Meml. Hosp., Riverside, N.J., 1955-92; asst. clin. prof. dermatology Thomas Jefferson U., 1971; rep. N.J. Assembly, 1984-95, chmn. health and human svcs. com., 1986-89, 91-95, fin. instns. com., 1993-95, drug and alcohol abuse com., 1987-89; ret., 1997. Med. dir. N.J. State Bd. Med. Examiners, 1995-97, ret., 1997. Freeholder Burlington County, 1971-84, freeholder dir., 1976, 80, 84. Mem. Burlington County Med. Soc. (past pres.), Med. Soc. N.J. (past trustee), Nat. Assn. Counties (chmn. subcom. for health resources 1977-80). *

COLBURN, NANCY DOUGLAS, social worker, educator; d. Cleaveland Fisher Colburn and Virginia Bahrs. BA, Rutgers U., 1963; MSW, U. Ill., Chgo., 1971; MDiv, McCormick Theol. Sem., 1971; MPA, San Diego State U., 1997. LCSW Calif.; Ordained to ministry Vineyard Christian Fellowship 1990, cert. tchr./adminstr. child devel. programs Calif. Social worker Dept. Social Svcs. County of San Diego, 1979—92; social worker Family Advocacy, DOD, USN, San Diego, 1992—97; spl. edn. technician San Diego Unified Sch Dist, 2007—09, in home caregiver, 2009—.

COLBURN, NANCY HALL, medical researcher; b. Wilmington, Del., May 15, 1941; d. Robert Turner and Alice (Edwards) Hall; m. Willis S. Colburn, Aug. 29, 1964 (div. 1976); children: Carolyn Churchill, Christine Hall; m. Thomas D. Gindhart, May 30, 1981 (dec. 1985); m. John P. Farrell, Nov. 14, 1999. BA in Chemistry, Swathmore Coll., Pa., 1963; PhD in Biochemistry, McArdle Lab., U. Wis., 1967. Asst. prof. dept. biol. sci. U. Del., Newark, 1968-72; NIH spl. rsch. fellow dept. dermatology U. Mich., Ann Arbor, 1972-74, asst. prof. depts. dermatology and biol. chemistry, 1974-75; expert lab. exptl. pathology DCCP, Nat. Cancer Inst., Bethesda, Md., 1976-79; chief cell biology sect. Lab. Viral Carcinogenesis, BCP, DCE, Nat. Cancer Inst., NIH, Frederick, Md., 1979-84; chief gene regulation sect. of Lab. Biochemical Physiology Nat. Cancer Inst., NIH, Frederick, Md., 1996—, joined Basic Rsch. Lab, 1999, chief Lab. Cancer Prevention, Ctr. Cancer Rsch., 2003—; chair NCI Cancer Prevention Faculty, 2001—. Vis. scientist and cons. dept. environ. and indsl. health U. Mich., 1975-76; cons., chair Site Visit Teams for NIH Grants, Bethesda, 1985—; cons. Am. Cancer Soc. Study Sect., Atlanta, 1990-93, coun., 1996—; cons., sci. adv. bd. Eppley Inst. for Cancer Rsch., Omaha, 1991—, Mich. State U. Cancer Ctr. 1991—, Genetics Inst. Yonsei U. Medical Sch., Seoul, Koea; adj. prof. genetics George Washington U., pathology U. Md; chair Internat. Union Against Cancer Fellowships Commn., 1990-99. Editor, author: Growth Factors, Tumor Promoters and Cancer Genes, 1988, Genes and Signal Transduction Multistage Carcinogenesis, 1989; mem. editorial bd. Teratogenesis, Carcinogenesis and Mutagenesis, 1980-89, Internat. Jour. Cancer, 1984—, Molecular Carcinogenesis, 1986—, Oncology Rsch., 1988—, Cancer Rch., 1989—, Jour. Cancer Rsch. and Clin. Oncology, 1990, Biochem. Biophys. acta, 1998—, Cancer Prevention Rsch., 2008-; organizer, Keystone Conf. AACR, FASEB, Symposia on Oncogenes, Tumor Suppressors & Molecular Targets Cancer Prevention, 1986-; contbr. articles to profl. jours. Mem. vestry Episcopal Ch., Braddock Hts., Md., 1986-88. NIH grantee, 1972, 76, 79; Conte Inst. for Environ. Studies fellow. Mem AAAS, NOW, N.Y. Acad. Sci., Am. Assn. Cancer Rsch. (bd. dirs. 1990-93), Am. Soc. Biochem. and Molecular Biology, Common Cause, Sierra Club, Sigma Xi. Democrat. Avocations: hiking, backpacking, running, skiing, singing, piano. Office: Nat Cancer Inst Bldg 576 Rm 101 Frederick MD 21702-1201 Office Phone: 301-846-1342. Office Fax: 301-846-6907. Business E-Mail: colburna@mail.nih.gov. *

COLBY, KAREN LYNN See WEINER, KAREN

COLDITZ, PAUL BERNARD, perinatal medicine educator, medical researcher; b. Australia, Dec. 30, 1951; s. Bernard Trevor and Doris (Wright) C.; m. Rhonda Kathleen Jarrett, Dec. 30, 1972; children: Stephen, Michael, Jennifer. MB BS, U. NSW, 1977, M in Biomed. Engring., 1985; PhD, Oxford U., Eng., 1988. Registrar The Children's Hosp., Sydney, 1980-83, neonatal fellow, 1984; rsch. scholar Oxford U., 1985-88; dir. Neonatal Care Unit King George V Hosp./, Sydney, 1989-91; prof. perinatal medicine U. Queensland, Brisbane, 1992—. Mem ANZ Trustees Med. Rsch. com., 2005—, chair, 2007—. Author: Obstetrics and the Newborn, 1997, (interactive CD ROM) Clinical Examination of the Newborn, 1998; contbr. articles to profl. jours. Bd. dirs. SIDS and Kids Australia, Queensland, 1994—, dep. chair 2005-; mem. sci. com. Bonnie Babes Found., 2000-; mem. Royal Brisbane and Women's Hosp. Found., 2002-. Fellow Royal Coll. Physicians (chair sci. program com., pediats. and child health divsn., dep. chair rsch. working party 2005-10, jour. rsch. com. 2011-, mem. policy advocacy com., 2010-, coun. mem., 2011-); mem. Internat. Soc. Perinatal Medicine, Paediatric Rsch. Soc. Australia and New Zealand (pres. 1994-97), Perinatal Soc. Australia and New Zealand (Queensland state chmn. 2000—06), Neonatal Soc. (Eng.), Australian Soc. Med. Rsch., NHMRC (chair 2006, mem. healthy start to life review panel 2006, Australia fellowship review panel 2007, NZ HRC project and program review panel 2000, 02, 05, NHMRC Practioner fellow 2008-), UQCCR Royal Brisbane Womens Hosp. Avocation: running. Office: Royal Brisbane and Womens Hosp Perinatal Rsch Ctr 4029 Brisbane QLD Australia Business E-Mail: p.colditz@uq.edu.au.

COLE, ANN HARRIET, psychologist, consultant; b. Phila., Feb. 27, 1949; d. Albert and Deborah (Mann) Brawerman; m. Stephen Cole, June 4, 1969 (div. June 18, 1987); children: Richard David, Robert Walter; m. Allan J. Besbris, Aug. 4, 1998. BA, SUNY, Stony Brook, 1971, MA, 1975. Dir. field rsch. Opinion Rsch. Assocs., 1974-76; v.p. Social Data Analysts, Inc., 1976-86; rsch. assoc. Jay Schulman, Inc., NYC, 1986-87; cons. Litigation Scis., Inc., NYC, 1988-90, Stanley S. Arkin, P.C., NYC, 1990, Chadbourne & Parke, NYC, 1990-91; pres. Ann Cole Opinion Rsch. and Analysis, 1991—. CBS news cons., 1994-95. Mem. Am. Soc. Trial Cons. (bd. dirs. 1994-99, v.p. 1996-97, pres. 1997-99), Qualitative Rsch. Cons. Am. Office: Ann Cole Opinion Rsch and Analysis 860 Crow Hill Rd Arlington VT 05250-9043 Office Phone: 802-375-6314. Business E-Mail: ahcole@acoraweb.com.

COLE, BRIAN JARED, orthopedist, educator; b. Chgo., Ill., Dec. 7, 1962; m. Emily Cole; children: Ethan, Adam. BS in Bio., Psychol., U. Ill., 1985; MBA in Health Admin., U. Chgo., 1989; MD, U. Chgo. Pritzker Sch. Medicine, 1990. Cert. Advanced Cardiac Life Support, 1992, Am. Bd. Orthop. Surgery, 1999, National Bds. Parts 1-3, 1991, lic. Ill., 1990, NY, 1992, Penn., 1996, Ind., 2000. Intern orthop. Loyola U. Med. Ctr, Maywood, Ill., 1990—91; resident sports medicine Hosp. Spl. Surgery, Cornell U., NYC, 1992—96; sports med. fellow U. Pitts., 1996—97; staff mem. Rush U. Med. Ctr, Chgo., 1997—, asst. prof. Dept. Orthopedic Surgery, 1997—2004, assoc. prof. Dept. Anatomy and Cell Biology, prof. Dept. Anatomy and Cell Biology, assoc. prof. Dept. Orthopedic Surgery, 2002, prof. Dept. Orthop.; dir. sports med. divsn. Cartilage Restoration Ctr., Rush U. Med. Ctr., Chgo., 1997—2004, sect. head cartilage rsch. program, 2004—. Com. mem., cost containment Hosp. Spl. Surg., 1991—96, med. records, 1993—96; med. care evaluation Rush Presbyterian-St. Luke's Med. Ctr., 1997; dir., exec. com. Midwest Orthopaedics, Rush U. Med. Ctr., 1998—2000, dir., coding practices com., 1997, dir. mktg. com., 98; subcommittee sports evaluation AAOS, 2000, com. elec. media, 00; exec. mem. Univ. Chgo. Grad. Program Health Admin., 1997; consul. The Pitts. Ballet Co., 1997—98, Elmhurst Coll., 2001; team doctor Univ. Pitts. Football, 1997—98, NE Ill. Univ. Basketball, 1997—98; team orthopedic surgeon Chgo. Rush Profl. Arena Football, 2001—; team physician Chgo. Bulls, 2004—; co-team physician Chgo. White Sox, 2001—. Contbr. articles to numerous profl. jours.; editor: (profl. jours.) Sports Med. Reports, 2001, Atlas Surg. Techniques in Sports Med., 2001, Sports Med., Arthroscopy, 2001, Orthopedic Quarterly; reviewer: profl. jours. Am. Jour. Sports Med., 2002, Jour. Knee Surgery, 2003. Recipient Golden Key,

Univ. Ill., 1985, Lewis Clark Wagner award, 1996, Best Rsch. Project award, Rush Univ., 2001, 2003, 2004, 2005, OREF Career Devel. award, 2001, Clin. Rsch. Poster award, AMSA, 2002; named Chicago's Top Doctor (placed on cover), Chgo. Mag., 2006; named one of Best Doctors in Am., 2004, 2005, Top Doctor in the Chgo, Metro Area, 2003, 2004, 2005. Mem.: Mid Am. Orthop. Assn., Chgo. Sports Med. Soc., Ill. Orthop. Soc., NY State Orthop. Soc., Chgo. Med. Soc., Ill. State Med. Soc., NBA Team Physicians Society, Am. Orthop. Soc. Sports Med., Internat. Soc. Arthroscopy, Knee Surgery and Orthop. Sports Med., Am. Shoulder and Elbow Soc., Orthop. Rsch. Soc., Am. Orthop. Soc. Sports Med., Arthroscopy Assn. No. Am., Internat. Cartilage Repair Soc., Am. Acad. Orthop. Rsch., Am. Soc. Bone Mineral Rsch., AMA. Office: Rush Univ Hosp Ste 1063 1725 W Harrison Chicago IL 60612 Office Fax: 312-432-2381, 312-942-1517.

COLE, DAVID A., psychology professor, department chairman; BA in Psychology, St. Olaf Coll., Northfield, Minn., 1976; MA in Clin. Psychology, U. Houston, 1980, PhD in Clin. Psychology, 1983. APA clin. intern U. Minn., Mpls., 1983, adj. faculty mem., dept. ednl. psychology, 1983—85, assoc. dir. rsch., Minn. Consortium Inst. the Edn. Severely Handicapped Learners, 1983—85; asst. prof. psychology U. Notre Dame, Ind., 1985—91, program dir. grad. program in counseling and devel. psychology, 1991—95, assoc. prof. psychology, 1991—96, faculty fellow, Urban Inst., 1994—96, dir. lab. social rsch., 1995—2000, prof. psychology, 1996—2001, faculty fellow, Inst. Ednl. Initiatives, 1997—2001; prof. psychology and human devel. Vanderbilt U., Nashville, 2001—, sr. fellow, Kennedy Ctr., 2002—, dir. quantitative methods program, 2002—03, dir. grad. studies, psychology and human devel., 2003—07, chmn. psychology and human devel., 2008—. Mem. bd. editors, cons. editor: Jour. the Assn. Persons with Severe Handicaps, 1985—89, Jour. Cons. and Clin. Psychology, 1988—89, 2003—, Psychol. Assessment, 1989—94, Jour. Child Clin. Psychology, 1993—97, Jour. Abnormal Psychology, 1993—, Applied & Preventive Psychology, 2002—, assoc. editor: Jour. Abnormal Psychology, 1997—2002; contbr. articles to profl. jours. Office: Dept Psychology and Human Devel Peabody Coll Box 512 Vanderbilt Univ Nashville TN 37250 Office Phone: 615-343-8712. Office Fax: 615-343-9494. Business E-Mail: david.cole@vanderbilt.edu.

COLE, JAMES S., dean, dental educator; b. Mpls. m. Barbara Cole. BS, Stephen F. Austin State U., 1967; DDS, Baylor Coll. Dentistry, 1975. Instr., restorative sciences Baylor Coll. Dentistry, Texas A&M U., Dallas, 1977—81, v.p., dir. computer services, 1981—92, prof., restorative sciences, 1992—, interim pres. and dean, 1990, exec. v.p., assoc. dean, CFO, COO, vice dean, interim dean, 1999—2000, dean, 2000—; pres., treas. Baylor Oral Health Found., 1997—99; interim pres. Tex. A&M U. Sys. Health Sci. Ctr., 2000—01. Bd. mem. Friends of the Nat. Inst. of Dental and Craniofacial Rsch., 2005—. Lt. USN, 1967—71. Recipient Dentist of Yr., Dallas County Dental Soc., 2000. Fellow: Internat. Coll. Dentists, Am. Coll. Dentists. Office: 3302 Gaston Ave Dallas TX 75246 Office Phone: 214-828-8300. Office Fax: 214-828-8496. Business E-Mail: JCole@bcd.tamhsc.edu.

COLE, JAMES W., retired dean; BS, Northeast Mo. State U., Kirksville, 1963; DO, Kans. City Coll. Osteo. Medicine, Mo., 1967. Intern Tucson Gen. Hosp., 1967—68; resident in pathology and lab. medicine Cherry Hill Med. Ctr., NJ, 1976—79; fellow in fed. health care policy Ohio U. Coll. Osteo. Medicine, Athens, 1994—95; dean Midwestern U. Ariz. Coll. Osteo. Medicine, Glendale, 1996—2007.

COLE, JEFFREY L., physiatrist; MD, Autonomous U. Guadalajara, Mexico, 1977. Diplomate Am. Bd. Physical Medicine and Rehab., 1983, cert. pain mgmt. Resident internal medicine NY Hosp. Queens, Flushing, NY, 1977—79; resident physical medicine & rehab. Montefiore Med. Ctr., Bronx, NY, 1979—82; fellow electrodiagnosis Booth Meml. Med. Ctr., Flushing, NY, 1982—83; clin. assoc. prof. Coll. of Ostheopathic Medicine NY Inst. of Tech., lectr. electrodiagnostic medicine and pain mgmt. Coll. of Ostheopathic Medicine, tchr. pharmacology Coll. of Ostheopathic Medicine; clin. assoc. prof. physical medicine & rehab. Univ. of Medicine and Dentistry of NJ; dir. electrodiagnostic medicine and musculoskeletal rehab. Kessler Inst. for Rehab., West Orange, NJ. Sys. engr. Apollo Lunar Project NASA. Author numerous articles in prestigious med. jours., various chpts. on the field of electrodiagnostics for physical medicine and rehab., gastrointestinal med. textbooks. Recipient Declaration of Honor, fomer pres. of Queen Borough (NY), 1994; named a Best Doctor, NY Mag.; named one of Top Doctors: NY Metro Area, Castle Connoly. Mem.: Am. Med. Assn., Inst. of Elec. and Electronics Engrs., Am. Acad. of Physical Medicine and Rehab. Office: Kessler Institute for Rehabilitation 1199 Pleasant Valley Way West Orange NJ 07052 Office Phone: 973-243-6343.

COLE, JESSIE MAE, nursing assistant, freelance/self-employed writer; b. McGehee, Ark., Nov. 19, 1925; d. Alonso Smith and Estelle Hursey; m. Amos Burns, May 15, 1942; children: Bobbie D., Joyce R.; m. Mose Eddie Cole (div. Nov. 1972). AA, Fresno City Coll, 1985; BA, Charter Oak State Coll., 1999. Cert. tchr. Calif., 1979. Beautician Beauty Culture, Chgo., 1956—76; nursing asst. Hope Manor Facility, Fresno, Calif., 1983—. Pvt. piano tchr., Fresno, 1981—. Author: (website) How to Read Sheet Music, 1997, Happy-CNA-Appreciation Day FReSND, 1987; contbr. articles; author: They Longed For Home-And Opened A Small Health County Clinic- They Longed For Home-And Opened A Small Health Country Clinic-For Women Men And ChildrenFreelance. Mem. Wall of Tolerance Nat. Campaign for Tolerance, 2002—03; bible study instr. Coll. Ch. of Christ, Fresno, 1975—. Recipient Employee of Year, Calif. Assn. Health Facilities. Mem.: Nat. Assn. Black Journalists. Home: 284 N Logsdon Pky Radcliff KY 40160 Home Phone: 270-272-1244.

COLEMAN, ALBERT MARK ESSAW, medical educator, consultant; b. Sekondi, Western Region, Ghana, July 1, 1953; s. Joseph Simon and Araba Baako Coleman; 1 child, Andrew. MPH, Sch. Pub. Health, U. Tex. Health Scis. Ctr., Houston, 1988. Diploma in medicine Inst. Medicine and Pharmacy, Carol Davilla, Bucharest, Romania, 1980. Med. intern Bucharest Mcpl. Tchg. Hosp., 1981—82; med. officer 37 Mil. Hosp., Accra, Greater Accra, Ghana, 1982—84; typhoid prevention program, med. coord., UNDP Ministry of Health, Savana-la-mar, Westmorland, Jamaica, 1991—92, specialist psychiatrist Mandeville, Manchester, Jamaica, 1998—99, med. officer Accra, 1984—86, Port Antonio, Ochio Rios, Portland, St. Ann, Jamaica, 1989—91, Ringway Clinic, Accra, 1988—89; resident, Kings County Hosp. Psychiatry Residency Program SUNY, Downstate Med. Sch. Ctr., NYC, 1993—94; resident, chief resident., sch. medicine. psychiatry residency program Yale U., New Haven, 1993—97; fellow, child and adolescent psychiatry St. Lukes-Roosevelt Hosp., NYC, 1997—98; sr. house officer, psychiatry Worthing Priority NHS Trust, West Sussex, England, 2000—01, staff grade psychiatrist, 2001—02; locum assoc. specialist psychiatrist Worthing Priority Care NHS Trust, 2002—03; locum staff grade psychiatrist Avon and Wiltshire NHS Trust, Salisbury, England, 2002; assoc. specialist Sussex Partnership NHS Trust, Worthing, 2003—07; locum cons. Hampshire Partnership NHS Trust, Eastleigh, Southampton, England, 2007—08; locum cons., old age psychiatey TEWV NHS Found. Trust. Bowes Lyon Unit, Durham, County Durham, England, 2008—; sr. lectr., psychiatry & med. ethics U. Cape Coast, Sch. Med. Scis., Central Region, Ghana, 2007—. Contbr. scientific papers to conf. presentation, articles to numerous profl. jours. (Mead Johnson fellowship, Am. Psychiatric Assn., 1996). Recipient Svc. Health award, Lions Club, Port Antonio, Jamaica, 1989, Rotary Club, Ochio Rios, Jamaica, 1990, Med. Officer of Dental Health Yearly award, Ministry of Health, 1990, Paul Kaunitz Liaison Psychiatry award, Yale U. Psychiatry Residency Program, 1997. Mem.: Brit. Med. Assn. Avocations: flying, skydiving, Tae Kwon Do, travel. Home and Office: Univ Cape Coast Med Sch Medicine Pvt Mail Bag Cape Coast Ghana Personal E-mail: albert.coleman@gmail.com.

COLEMAN, ANDREA, health care transportation executive; m. Barry Coleman. Former profl. motorcycle rider; dir. Team Castrol-Herron; pub. rels. mgr. to Randy Mamola (motorcycle racing champion); cofounder (with Barry Coleman) Riders for Health, 1989, CEO. Recipient Sage bus. award, leader of yr., 2005. Office: Riders for Health 3 New St Daventry Northamptonshire NN11 4BT England Business E-Mail: rfh@riders.org.

COLEMAN, ARLENE FLORENCE, pediatrics nurse practitioner; b. Braham, Minn., Apr. 8, 1926; d. William and Christine (Judin) C.; m. John Dunkerken, May 30, 1987. Diploma in nursing, U. Minn., 1947; student, Moody Bible Inst., Chgo, 1951; BS, U. Minn., 1953; MPH, Loma Linda U., 1974. RN, Calif., PNP, Loma Linda U., 1972. Operating room scrub nurse Calif. Luth. Hosp., LA, 1947-48; indsl. staff nurse Good Samaritan Hosp., LA, 1948-49; staff nurse Passavant Hosp., Chgo., 1950-51; student health nurse Moody Bible Inst., Chgo., 1950-51; staff nurse St. Andrews Hosp., Mpls., 1951-53; pub. health nurse Bapt. Gen. Conf. Bd. of World Missions, Ethiopia, Africa, 1954-66; staff pub. health nurse County of San Bernadino, Calif., 1966-68, sr. pub. health nurse Calif., 1968-73, pediatric nurse practitioner Calif., 1973—. Contbr. articles to profl. jours. Mem. bd. dist. missions Bapt. Gen. Conf., Calif., 1978-84; mem. adv. coun. Kaiser Hosp., Fontana, Calif., 1969-85, Bethel Sem. West, San Diego, 1987—; bd. dirs. Casa Verdugo Retirement Home, Hemet, Calif., 1985—; active christ Cmty. Ch., Redlands, Calif., 1974—; mem. S.W. Bapt. Conf. Social Ministries, 1993—. With Cadet Nurse Corps USPHS, 1944-47. Calif. State Dept. Health grantee, 1973. Fellow Nat. Assn. Pediatric Nurse Assocs. and Practitioners; mem. Calif. Nurses Assn. (state nursing coun. 1974-76). Democrat. Avocations: gardening, travel, reading. Home: 622 Esther Way Redlands CA 92373-5822

COLEMAN, BARRY, health care transportation executive; m. Andrea Coleman. BA in Philosophy, Manchester U. Feature writer and motorcycling corr. Guardian newspaper, England; journalist BBC, Forbes mag.; cofounder (with Andrea Coleman) Riders for Health, 1989, exe. dir. Office: Riders for Health 3 New Street Daventry Northamptonshire NN11 4BT England Business E-Mail: rfh@riders.org.

COLEMAN, BERNELL, physiologist, educator; b. Jefferson County, Miss., Apr. 26, 1929; s. Percy and Julia (Nailor) C.; m. Annie C. Richardson, Jan. 30, 1962; children— Rochelle, Ronald. BS, Alcorn A&M Coll., 1952; PhD, Loyola U., 1964. Rsch. asst. in biochemistry U. Chgo., 1956-57; rsch. in cancer Hines (Ill.) VA Hosp., 1957-59; instr. St. Louis U. Sch. Medicine, 1963-65, asst. prof. physiology, 1965-67; asst. prof. Chgo. Med. Sch., 1967-69, assoc. prof., 1969-76, prof., 1976, Howard U. Coll. Medicine, Washington, 1976—, chmn. dept. physiology and biophysics, 1979—. Lectr. Cook County Grad. Sch. Medicine, U. Ill. Med. Sch.; vis. prof. Rush Med. Coll.; external examiner Godfrey Huggins Sch. Medicine, U. Zimbabwe, Salisbury, 1981; mem. cardiovasc. and pulmonary study sect. Nat. Heart, Lung and Blood Inst./NIH, 1982-83, rsch. tng. rev. com., 1990-94. Peer rev. com. Am. Heart Assn., 1988-93, 95—, rsch. com., 1993—. With U.S. Army, 1953-56, Korea. Recipient rsch. award Chgo. Med. Sch. Bd. Trustees, 1975; NIH rsch. fellow, 1960-61; NIH grantee, 1966-68, 69-74, 74-76, 79—; USPHS fellow, 1961-63; Univ. fellow Loyola U., 1964; Dept. Def. grantee, 1965-67 Mem.: AAAS, AAUP, Heart Failure Soc. Am., Am. Soc. Hypertension (charter), N.Y. Acad. Scis., Internat. Soc. of Hypertension in Blacks, Assn. Black Cardiologists, Fedn. Am. Socs. Exptl. Biology (vis. scientist for minority instns. programs 1982—83, 1989—90), Am. Heart Assn. (basic sci. coun.), Am. Physiol. Soc. (cardiovascular fellow 1985), Phi Rho Sigma, Sigma Xi. Democrat. Achievements include research numerous publs. in cardiovascular physiology. Home: 14200 Myer Ter Rockville MD 20853-2350 Office: 520 W St NW Washington DC 20001-2337 Office Phone: 202-806-6330. Business E-Mail: bcoleman@howard.edu.

COLEMAN, BEVERLY G., diagnostic radiologist; MD, Harvard U., 1974. Diplomate Am. Bd. of Radiology-diagnostic radiology, 1978. Intern internal medicine Mich. Hosp., 1974—75; resident radiology Univ. of Pa., 1975—77, fellow, 1977—78; assoc. radiologist Hosp. Univ. of Pa. Sch. of Medicine; dir. ultrasound imaging dept. of radiology Univ. of Pa. Med. Ctr., assoc. chmn. abdominal imaging divsn. dept. of radiology. Prof. radiology Hosp. of the Univ. of Pa. Author: (articles) Congenital high airway obstruction syndrome: MR/US findings, effect on management, and outcome. Office: HUP 1 Silverstein 3400 Spruce St 4283 Philadelphia PA 19104 Office Phone: 215-662-3046.

COLEMAN, DONALD JACKSON, ophthalmologist, educator; b. Waverly, NY, Dec. 1, 1934; s. Max Elliot and Frances Agnes (Henton) C.; m. Jane Marie Holmes, July 6, 1963; children: Jeffrey, Jonathan, Jeremy. BS, Union Coll., 1956; MD, U. Buffalo, 1960. Bd. cert. opthalmology. Intern Columbia Med. Div., Bellevue Hosp., NYC, 1960-61; lt. comdr. USPHS Bur. State Services Heart Disease Control Program, Washington, 1961-64; resident in ophthalmology Edward S. Harkness Eye Inst., Columbia Presbyn. Med. Center, NYC, 1964-67, mem. faculty, staff, 1967-79; John Milton McLean prof. Cornell U. Med. Coll., NYC, 1979—; chmn. dept. ophthalmology N.Y. Hosp.-Cornell Med. Ctr., 1979—2006, ophthalmologist-in-chief, 1979—2006; chmn. emeritus, 2006—. Sr. author: Ultrasonography of Eye and Orbit, 1977, 2d edit., 2006; contbr. articles to med. jours. Recipient Wacker award of Club Jules Gonin Internat. Retina Soc., 1976, Lucien Howe medal, 1988, Weisenfeld award, Assn. Vision and Rsch. in Opthalmology; named hon. doctor of med. sci., U. Ferrara; NIH grantee. Fellow ACS, Am. Acad. Ophthalmology; mem. Am. Inst. Ultrasound Medicine (bd. govs. 1970-73), Am. Ophthamolgy Soc., Am. Retina Soc. (v.p. 1989-91, pres. 1991-93), Assn. Rsch. Ophthamology (Weisenfeld award 1996), Societas Interationalis de Diagnostic Ultrasonica in Ophthalmology (exec. bd. 1971-81), World Fedn. Ultrasound Medicine and Biology (exec. bd. 1973-82, sec.treas. 1973-77, treas. 1977-82), Am. Intraocular Lens Soc. (sci. advisor 1976-79), Am. Soc. Ophthalmic Ultrasound (bd. govs. 1976—), AMA, N.Y. County Med. Soc., Am. Eye Study Club, Jules Gonin Club (exec. com. 1992—, v.p. 1993-98, pres. 1998-2004). Republican. Methodist. Office: NY-Presbyterian Hosp-Weill-Cornell Med Ctr 1305 York Ave New York NY 10021-4870 Office Phone: 646-962-5588, 646-962-2020. Business E-Mail: djceye@aol.com.

COLEMAN, DOROTHY CHARMAYNE, nurse; b. July 13, 1958; BS in Nursing, Mich. State U., 1981; MS in Nursing, Wayne State U., Detroit, 1988. RN. Obstet. high risk staff nurse Hutzel Hosp., Detroit, 1983—; ob-gyn. nurse practitioner The Wellness Plan, Detroit, 1991-98; clin. nursing instr. Wayne State U., Detroit, 1994, 95, 99. Named Nurse of Yr., Hutzel Hosp., 2001. Home: 20801 Kipling St Oak Park MI 48237-2747

COLEMAN, DOUGLAS L., research scientist; b. Stratford, Ont., Can., 1931; BS, McMaster U., Hamilton, Ont., 1954; PhD in Biochemistry, U. Wis., 1958. Staff Jackson Labs., Bar Harbor, Maine, 1958—97, sr. staff scientist emeritus, 1997—. Recipient Claude Bernard Medal, Royal Soc., 1977, Gairdner Found. Internat. award, 2005, Albert Lasker Basic Med. Rsch. award, Lasker Found., 2010; co-recipient Shaw prize in life scis. & medicine, Hong Kong, 2009. Mem.: NAS. Achievements include research in the existence of a hormone system that contributed to controlling fat cell homeostasis. Office: c/o Jackson Lab 600 Main St Bar Harbor ME 04609-1500 Office Phone: 207-288-6000. *

COLEMAN, ERIC NORMAN, pediatrician, cardiologist; b. Ayr, Scotland, June 22, 1925; s. Philip Norman and Marion (Nisbet) C. MBChB, U. Glasgow, Scotland, 1948, MD, 1961. Ho. physician Royal Hosp. for Sick Children, Glasgow, 1948-49, registrar, 1954-58, sr. registrar, 1958-59, head cardiology svc., 1961-90; ho. surgeon Hairmyres (Scotland) Hosp., 1949; sr. ho. officer City Hosp., Nottingham, Eng., 1951-52, So. Gen. Hosp., Glasgow, 1952-54; lectr. in child health U. Glasgow, 1959-61; sr. physician Royal Hosp. for Sick Children, Glasgow, 1988-90. Regional postgrad. advisor Com. on Medicine and Pediatrics, Glasgow, 1975-90; Leonard Gow lectr. in child health U. Glasgow, 1988-90. Contbr. articles to profl. publs., chpt. to book. Capt. RAMC, 1949—51. Fellow Royal Coll. Physicians, Royal Coll. Paediats. and Child Health ()hon.; founder, Soc. Cardiol. Sci. and Tech.; mem. Brit. Pediatric Assn. (hon.), Brit. Cardiac Soc., Scottish Pediatric Soc., New Club. Roman Catholic. Avocations: music, art, theology. E-mail: dr.ericcoleman@btinternet.com.

COLEMAN, JACQUELYN T., medical association administrator; B, Middlebury Coll., Vt.; M in Pub. Policy, Trinity Coll., Hartford, Conn. Broadcast journalist; grant adminstr. U. Hartford; sr. v.p. S&S Mgmt. Services, Inc.; exec. dir. Am. Clin. Neurophysiology Soc., Am. Assn. Emergency Psychiatry, Am. Acad. Psychiatry and the Law, Am. Acad. Psychoanalysis and Dynamic Psychiatry. Mem.: Conn. Soc. Assn. Execs. (past. pres., Assn. Exec. of Yr. award). Office: S&S Mgmt Services Inc 1 Regency Dr Bloomfield CT 06002 Office Phone: 860-243-3977. Office Fax: 860-286-0787. Business E-Mail: jcoleman@ssmgt.com. *

COLEMAN, JEAN BLACK, nurse, physician assistant; b. Sharon, Pa., Jan. 11, 1925; d. Charles B. and Sue E. (Dougherty) Black; m. Donald A. Coleman, July 3, 1946; children: Sue Ann Lopez, Donald Ashley. Grad., Spencer Hosp. Sch. Nursing, Meadville, Pa., 1945; student, Vanderbilt U., 1952-54. RN, Ga. Nurse, dir. nursing Bulloch Meml. Hosp., Statesboro, Ga, 1948-51, nurse supr. surgery, 1954-67, dir. nursing, 1967-71; physician's asst., nurse anesthetist Office Dr. Robert H. Swint, Statesboro, 1971-96; physician asst. Office Dr. Earl L. Alderman, Statesboro, 1996-98, Dr. Swaroop Reddy, Statesboro, 1998—. Mem. physician's asst. adv. com. Ga. Med. Bd., 1989-97; mem. physician assts. adv. com. Ga. Bd. Med. Examiners, 1987-97, ex-officio mem., 1994-95. Recipient Dean Day Smith Svc. to Mankind award, 1995; named Woman of Yr. in med. field Bus. and Profl. Women, 1980; Paul Harris fellow Rotary Club. Mem. ANA, Am. Acad. Physician Assts., Ga. Nurses Assn., Ga. Assn. Physician Assts. (bd. dirs. 1975-79, v.p. 1979-80, pres. 1980-81). Republican. Roman Catholic. *

COLEMAN, JOHN JOSEPH, III, plastic surgeon, educator; b. Boston, Nov. 15, 1947; Grad., Harvard U., 1969, MD, 1973. Intern Emory U. Affiliated Hosp., Atlanta, 1973-74, resident in gen. surgery, 1974-78, resident in plastic surgery, 1978-80; fellow in surg. oncology U. Md., Balt., 1980; prof. surgery Ind. U., Indpls.; chief plastic surgery Ind. U. Med. Ctr., Indpls., James E. Bennett prof. of plastic surgery, 1995—, prof. of surgery & chmn. plastic surgery, 1991—; Wadley R. Glenn chair surgery Energy U., 1986—91. Mem.: Am. Head and Neck Soc. (pres. 2006), Am. Bd. of Plastic Surgery (chmn. 2002—03). Office: Ind U Sch Medicine EH 252 545 Barnhill Dr Indianapolis IN 46202 Office Phone: 317-274-8106. Office Fax: 317-274-7612. E-mail: jjcolema@iupui.edu.

COLEMAN, LAURA A., nutritionist, researcher; b. June 13, 1960; PhD, Tufts U., 1995. Rsch. specialist Marshfield Clinic Rsch. Found., 2004—07, project scientist, 2007—10, assoc. rsch. scientist, 2010—. Mem.: Am. Soc. Nutrition. Office: 1000 N Oak Ave ML-2 Marshfield WI 54449 Business E-Mail: coleman.laura@mcrf.mfldclin.edu.

COLEMAN, LAUREL, geriatrician, internist; MD, U. Calif. Sch. Med. Lic. Calif., Maine. Resident U. Calif., San Francisco; fellow UNC Sch. Med.; attending physician Maine Med. Ctr. Office: Central Maine Medical Center 300 Main St Lewiston ME 04240 Office Phone: 207-724-2688.

COLEMAN, MARY SUE, academic administrator; b. Richmond, Ky, Oct. 2, 1943; m. Kenneth Coleman; 1 child, Jonathan. BA, Grinnell Coll., 1965; PhD, U. N.C., 1969; DSc (hon.), Dartmouth Coll., 2005, U. Notre Dame, 2007. NIH postdoctoral fellow University of North Carolina, Chapel Hill, 1969—70, U. Ky., 1971—72, instr., rsch. assoc. depts. biochemistry and medicine, 1972—75, asst. prof. dept. biochemistry, 1975—80, assoc. prof. dept. biochemistry, 1980—85, prof. dept. biochemistry, 1985—90; prof. dept. biochemistry and biophysics University of North Carolina, Chapel Hill, 1990—93; provost, v.p. for academic affairs, prof. biochemistry U. N.Mex., 1993—95; pres., prof. biochemistry, prof. biol. scis. U. Iowa, Iowa City, 1995—2002; pres. University of Michigan, Ann Arbor, 2002—. NSF summer trainee Grinnell Coll., 1962; acting dir. basir rsch. U. Ky. Cancer Ctr., 1980—83; scientific cons. Abbott Labs., 1981—85, Collaborative Rsch., 1983—88; assoc. dir. rsch. L.P. Markey Cancer Ctr. U. Ky., 1983—90, dir. grad. studies biochem., 1984—87, trustee, 1987—90; assoc. provost, dean rsch. U. N.C., 1990—92; scientific cons. Life Techs., Inc., 1992; vice chancellor grad students and rsch. U. N.C., 1992—93; pres. Iowa Health Sys., 1995—2002; mem. Big Ten Coun. Pres.'s, 1995—2002; chair undergrad. edn. com. Am. Assn. Univs., 1997—; bd. trustees Univs. Rsch. Assn., 1998—; mem. task force on tchrs. edn. Am. Coun. Edn., 1998—; mem. Gov.'s Strategic Planning Coun., 1998—2000, Imagining Am. Pres.'s Coun., 1999—, Bus.-Higher Edn. Froum, 1999—; mem. rsch. accountability task force Am. Assn. Univs., 2000—; mem. stds. success adv. bd. Am. Assn. Univs. and he Pew Charitable Trusts, 2000—; co-chair Inst. Medicine Com. on Consequences of Uninsurance, 2000—; mem. Knight Commn., 2000—01; mem. exec. com. Am. Assn. Univs., 2001—; bd. dirs. Meredith Corp., 1997—, Johnson & Johnson, 2003—, Am. Coun. Edn.; presenter in field. Mem. editl. bd.: Jour. Biol. Chemistry, 1989—93; contbr. articles to profl. jours. Trustee Crinnell Coll., 1996—; mem. bd. govs. Warren G. Magnuson Clin. Ctr., NIH, 1996—2000, State of Iowa Gov.'s ACCESS Edn. Commn., 1997; bd. dirs. United Way, Albuquerque, 1995; trustee John S. and James L. Knight Found., 2005—. Named one of The 10 Best Coll. Presidents, TIME mag., 2009; fellow postdoctiral fellow, Clayton Found. Biochem. Inst., U. Tex., 1970—71. Fellow: AAAS, Am. Acad. Arts and Scis.; mem.: Nat. Coll. Athletic Assn. (bd. dirs. 2002—), Nat. Assn. State Univs. ans Land Grant Colls. Coun. Cchief Acad. Officers (exec. com. 1993—95), Am. Soc. Biochem. and Molecular Biology, Am. Assn. Cancer Rsch. Office: University of Michigan Office of President 503 Thompson St 2074 Fleming Administration Building Ann Arbor MI 48109-1340 Office Phone: 734-764-6270. Office Fax: 734-936-3529. E-mail: presoff@umich.edu. *

COLEMAN, MARY THOESEN, physician, educator; b. Valparaiso, Ind., Dec. 21, 1949; PhD, Ohio State U., 1976, MD, 1981. Sr. vice chair clin. affairs family medicine U. Louisville, 2003—06; dean, sch. medicine Ross U., 2006—11, prof. family medicine, 2006—; dir. cmty. clinics La. State U., 2011—. Recipient Kathryn T Schoen award, Ohio State U. Fellow: Exec. Leadership Academic Medicine Women. Avocations: reading, hiking. Home: 6231 Marquette Pl New Orleans LA 70118 Office Phone: 504-568-6248. Personal E-mail: coleman.mary@gmail.com, mcolem@isuhsc.edu.

COLEMAN, MORTON, oncologist, educator; b. Norfolk, Va., Sept. 15, 1939; s. Isadore and Bessie (Levin) C.; m. Joyce Goodman, May 26, 1968; children: Ingrid Alexandra, Benjamin Lee, Abigail Rachael. AA, Coll. William and Mary, 1958; BA, Johns Hopkins U., 1959; MD, Med. Coll. Va., 1963. Diplomate Nat. Bd. Med. Examiners, Am. Bd. Internal Medicine, Am. Bd. Hematology, Am. Bd. Clin. Oncology. Intern Grady Meml. Hosp.-Emory U. Med. Ctr., Atlanta, 1963-64, resident, 1964-65, N.Y. Hosp.-Cornell U. Med. Ctr., NYC, 1967-68; NIH fellow in hematology Cornell U. Med. Coll., 1968-70, asst. prof. medicine, 1970-74, assoc. prof., 1974-86, clin. prof., 1986—; asst. attending N.Y. Hosp., NYC, 1970-74, assoc. attending, 1974-86, attending, 1986—97, assoc. dir. oncology svc., 1974-86; assoc. program dir. Nat. Cancer Inst. Clin. Chemotherapy Program Cancer Control, 1974-80; attending, dir. Ctr. for Lymphoma and Myeloma divsn. hematology-oncology N.Y. Presbyterian Hosp., 1997— Attending staff Manhattan Eye and Ear Hosp., 1972—82, Doctors Hosp., 1973—90, Beth Israel NorthMed. Ctr., 1990—94; cons. Genzyme Genetics, Inc., 2006—10, Metronics, Inc., 2006—09; assoc. editor Clin. Hymphoma Nyelma Leukewa, 2009—. Assoc. editor: Cancer Investigation, 1987—2006; mem. editl. adv. bd., sec. editor (hematologi maligrancies) Hem/Onc Today, 1999—, internat. adv. bd. Indian Jour. Med. and Pediatric Oncology, 1994—, mem. editl. bd. Acta Haematologica, 2005—; contbr. articles to rsch. publications on blood and cancer. Chmn. new agts. com. Cancer and Leukemia Group B, 1975—82; chmn. bd. dir. Fund for Blood and Cancer Rsch., 1975—; sci. advisor United Leukemia Fund, 1976—82; co-chmn. clin. rsch. rev. com. Israel Cancer Rsch. Fund, 1988—93; mem. exec. com. NY State Soc. Med. Oncology and Hematology, 1991—99; program chmn. NY Cancer Soc., 1993—94, sec., 1994—95, treas., 1995—96, v.p., 1996—97, pres.-elect, 1997—98, pres., 1998—99, coun. of advisors, 2002—; chmn. Lymphoma/Hodgkins' Diseases symposium com. Internat. Union Against Cancer Congress, 1993—94; internat. adv. bd. Cancer Care Trust and Rsch. Found., India, 1995—; chmn. bd. dir. Affiliated Physicians Network, 1996—2001; mem. clin. practice com. Am. Soc. Clin. Oncology, 1997—2001, mem. pub. com., 2001—04, mem. program com., 2001—03, chmn. policy and procedures subcom., 2002—04, chmn. hematol. malignancy subcom., 2002—03; bd. dir., chmn. med. affiliates bd. Cure for Lymphoma Found., 1997—2001; mem. sci. adv. com. Lymphoma Rsch. Found., 1998—, exec. com. bd. dirs., chmn. med. affiliates bd., 2001—; bd. dirs. Immunomedics Inc., 2000—, BML Pharmaceuticals Inc., 2003—05; mem. adv. bd. The Lymphoma Found., 2006—; med. adv. coun. Israeli Children's Cancer Found., 2004—; med. bd. advisors SASS Found. Med. Rsch., 2007—; sci. advisor Internat. Waldenstrom's Macroglobulinemia Found., 2003—. Lt. comdr. USN, 1965—67. Recipient Disting. Alumni award, Old Dominion U., 1994, Together award, Cure for Lymphoma Found., 2000, 2001, Rosetta Cir. award, Lymphoma Rsch. Found., 2002, Leadership award, 2010. Fellow: ACP; mem.: AMA, AAAS, NY County Med. Soc., NY State Med. Soc., Soc. Study of Blood, NY Acad. Sci., Internat. Soc. Hematology, Harvey Soc., NY Hosp. Cornell Med. Ctr. Alumni Assn., (v.p., 1992-1994, pres., 1994-1996), Am. Soc. Hematology(mem. devel.), Am. Radium Soc., Am. Fedn. Clin. Rsch., Am. Assn. Cancer Rsch., Am. Soc. Clin. Oncology, Am. Soc. Hematology, Explorers Club, Sigma Zeta, Alpha Omega Alpha. Office: 407 E 70th St 3rd fl New York NY 10021-5302 also: NY Presbyn Hosp-Weill Cornell Univ Med Ctr Div Hematology-Oncology 525 E 68th St New York NY 10021-4870 Office Phone: 212-517-5900, 212-746-6822, 212-746-6889. Personal E-mail: mortoncolemanmd@aol.com.

COLEMAN, PAULA LYNNE, ophthalmologist; b. Peoria, Ill., Sept. 3, 1946; d. Paul Luther and Dorothy June Coleman; m. Dennis Anthony Pastena, Oct. 26, 1974; children: Lauren Pastena, Ryan Pastena. BS in Biology, Loyola U., Chgo., 1969, MD, 1974. Cert. Am. Bd. Ophthalmology. Intern St. Vincents Hosp. and Med. Ctr., NY, 1975, resident, 1975—78; pvt. practice N.E. Eye Care, Carmel, 1978—89, Mahopac Ophthalmology, 1989—. Fellow: Am. Acad. Ophthalmology; mem.: NY State Ophthalmology Soc., Am. Soc. Cataract and Refractive Surgery. Avocations: antiques, skiing. Office: Mahopac Ophthalmology 410 Rte 6 Delamere Blvd Mahopac NY 10541 Office Phone: 845-628-8788. E-mail: plceyemd@aol.com.

COLEMAN, ROBERT L., obstetrician, gynecologic oncologist; b. San Diego, Nov. 3, 1961; s. Gary A. and Marlene Beatty; m. Fay K. Leiting, July 23, 1982; children: Kay, Joe, Mary, Theresa children: Jay, Christina. BS in Math., Creighton U., Omaha, 1983; MD, Creighton U. Sch. Medicine, 1987. Diplomate Am. Bd. Med. Examiners, Am. Bd. Ob-Gyn., cert. in gynecologic oncology; ob-gyn. gyn. oncologist. Ob-gyn. residency Northwestern U. Med. Ctr., Chgo., 1987—91; gynecologic oncology fellowship U. Tex. MD Anderson Cancer Ctr., Houston, 1991—93, assoc. prof. dept. gynecologic oncology, 2004—06, prof., dir. clin. rsch., dept. gynecologic oncology, 2006—; asst. prof., dir. dept. ob-gyn. Creighton U. Sch. Medicine, 1993—96; asst. prof. ob-gyn. U. Tex. Southwestern Med. Ctr., Dallas, 1996—2000, assoc. prof. dept. ob-gyn., 2000—04, Patricia Duniven Fletcher prof. gynecologic oncology & ob.-gyn., vice chmn. gynecologic svcs. Dallas, 2001—04. Examiner Am. Bd. Ob-Gyn., 2001—, examiner divsn. gynecologic oncology, 2006—; bd. dirs. Gynecologic Cancer Found., Chgo., 2006—, Ann Rife Cox chair gynecology, 2010—. Author: Handbook of Gynecologic Oncology, 2001; contbr. articles to profl. jours., chapters to books. Fellow: ACS, Am. Gynecol. & Obstetrical Soc., Am. Coll. Obstetricians & Gynecologists; mem.: Western Assn. Gynecologic Oncologists, Soc. Gynecologic Oncologists, Internat. Gynecologic Cancer Soc., Assn. Professors Gynecology & Obstetrics, Am. Soc. Clin. Oncology (mem. grants selection com. 2006—), Am. Assn. Cancer Researchers, Am. Assn. Cancer Rsch., Felix Rutledge Soc. (program chmn. 2003). Office: U Tex MD Anderson Cancer Ctr 1155 Herman Pressler Dr Unit # 1362 Rm CPB6 3244 Houston TX 77030 Office Phone: 713-792-6810. Office Fax: 713-792-7586. Business E-Mail: rcoleman@mdanderson.org.

COLEMAN, SYDNEY REESE, plastic surgeon, educator; b. Nov. 10, 1954; Grad., U. Tex., Austin, 1974; MD, U. Tex. Med. Br., Galveston, 1978. Cert.: Am. Bd. Plastic Surgery. Resident gen. surgery Ochsner Found. Hosp., New Orleans, 1978—81; resident plastic surgery St. Francis Meml. Hosp., San Francisco, 1982—85; fellow microsurgery R.K. Davies Hosp., San Francisco; fellow aesthetic surgery Manhattan Eye, Ear, & Throat Hosp., NYU Med. Ctr., 1985; pvt. practice Tribeca Plastic Surgery, 1985—. Staff Manhattan Eye, Ear, & Throat Hosp., 1997—, NY Eye & Ear Infirmary, NY Downtown Hosp.; clin. asst. prof. surgery NYU Med. Ctr., 2005—. Contbr. articles to profl. jours. Mem.: Harry Buncke Microsurgical Soc. (founding mem.), NY State Med. Soc., NY County Med. Soc., Internat. Soc. Aesthetic Plastic Surgery, Northeastern Soc. Plastic Surgeons, Plastic Surgeons Assn. Las Americas, Internat. Consortium Aesthetic Plastic Surgeons (founding mem.), Am. Soc. Plastic & Reconstructive Surgery, Am. Soc. Aesthetic Plastic Surgery. Achievements include invention of Lipostructure and designer of the patent-pending instruments necessary to perform this technique; LipoStructure receives ongoing national and local media coverage by CBS, NBC, ABC, Elle, Allure, Esquire, Details, Self, W, NY Times and others. Office: Tribeca Plastic Surgery 44 Hudson St New York NY 10013 Office Phone: 212-571-5200. Office Fax: 212-571-5255. *

COLEN, HELEN SASS, plastic surgeon; b. Bytom, Poland, Jan. 9, 1947; came to the U.S., 1963; m. Stephen Robert Colen, Mar. 25, 1972; children: Kari, Michael. BA, NYU, 1968, MD, 1972. Diplomate Am. Bd. Plastic Surgery. Intern Jefferson U. Hosp., 1972-74; gen. surgeon U. Colo., Denver, 1974-79; plastic surgeon U. Columbia-St. Lukes, NYC, 1979-81; microsurgeon Bellevue Hosp., NYC, 1981-82; practice medicine specializing in plastic surgery NYC, 1982—. Fellow ACS; mem. Am. Soc. Plastic Surgeons, Am. Soc. Aesthetic Plastic Surgery, Phi Beta Kappa. Office: Plastic Surgury Ste 742 Park Ave New York NY 10021-3553 Office Phone: 212-772-1300.

COLEN, STEPHEN R., plastic and reconstructive surgeon; b. NYC, Feb. 11, 1947; s. Leslie Colen and Ruth Mintz; m. Helen Sass, Mar. 25, 1972; children: Kari, Michael. Bachelor's degree, St. Lawrence U., 1967; DDS, NYU, 1971; MD, Hahnemann U., 1974. Cert. Am. Bd. Surgery, Am. Bd. Dental Surgery, Am. Bd. Plastic Surgery. Surgeon NYU Hosp., NYC, 1982—; clin. asst. plastic surgery Bellvue Hosp., NYC, 1982—; attending physician plastic surgery NY Vets. Hosp., NYC, 1993—; attending surgeon Manhattan Eye, Ear & Throat, NYC, 1983—, Beth Israel North Hosp., NYC, 1994—; assoc. prof. plastic surgery NYU Med. Ctr., 2003—; chief dept. plastic surgery Hackensack U. Hosp., 2003—; prof. plastic surgery Med. Coll. Touro. Attending NY Eye and Ear Infirmary, NYC, 1983—; mem. surg. case rev. com. NYU Med. Ctr., NYC, 1987—, mem. ednl. com., 1988—; mem. utilization rev. com. Bellvue Hosp., NYC, 1984—. Mem. Am. Assn. Plastic Surgeons, Am. Soc. Plastic Surgeons, NY Regional Med. Soc., Westchester Country Club, Olde Fla. Golf Club, Univ. Club. Office: 742 Park Ave New York NY 10021 Home Phone: 212-249-8376; Office Phone: 212-988-8900. E-mail: scolen47@aol.com.

COLENDA, CHRISTOPHER COLUMBUS, III, academic administrator, psychiatrist; b. Baltimore, Md., Feb. 14, 1952; s. Christopher Columbus Colenda, Jr. and Janet A. Colenda; m. Kathyryn Winckl-hofer Colenda, July 24, 1976; children: Meredith Lee, Stephanie Adair. BA, Wittenberg U., 1970—73; MD, Med. Coll. of Va., 1973—77; MPH, Johns Hopkins U., 1981—82. Geriatric Psychiatry Am. Bd. of Psychiatry and Neurology, 1991, Psychiatry Am. Bd. of Psychiatry and Neurology, 1986. Dir. of geriatric psychiatry Med. Coll. of Va., Commonwealth U., Richmond, Va., 1985—90; vice chmn. and sect. head, geriatric psychiatry Wake Forest U. Sch. of Medicine, 1990—96; chmn., dept. of psychiatry Mich. State U., 1997—2002; acting dean Mich. State U., Coll. of Human Medicine, 2000—01; Jean and Thomas McMullin dean medicine Tex. A&M U. Health Sci. Ctr. Coll. Medicine, 2003—09; chancellor health sciences W.Va. U. Robert C. Byrd Health Sciences Ctr., 2009—. Vice-chairman, geriatric psychiatry test writing com. Am. Bd. of Psychiatry and Neurology, Deerfield, Ill., 2000—; faculty fellow Liason Com. for Med. Edn., Washington, 2001—02. Author: (health services and policy research) American Journal of Geriatric Psychiatry. Mem.: AMA, Am. Assn. for Geriatric Psychiatry (treas. elect and treas. 2002—, bd. dirs. 2000—01), Am. Psychiat. Assn. (chair, coun. of aging 1997—2000). Office: W Va U Robert C Byrd Health Sciences Ctr G-106 Health Sciences N PO Box 9008 Morgantown WV 26506 *

COLENDA, MARYANN, pediatrician, allergist, immunologist, educator; Attended, NY Med. Coll., 1971. Resident pediat. Columbia Presbyn. Med. Ctr., 1972—74, fellow allergy & immunology, 1976—78; assoc. clin. prof. pediat. Columbia Univ.; with Englewood Hosp. & Med. Ctr., Meadowlands Hosp. Med. Ctr. Office: Englewood Hospital & Medical Center 811 Abbott Blvd Fort Lee NJ 07024-4116 Office Phone: 201-224-2256.

COLES, ANNA LOUISE BAILEY, retired dean, nurse; b. Kansas City, Kans., Jan. 16, 1925; d. Gordon Alonzo and Lillie Mai (Buchanan) Bailey; children: Margot, Michelle, Gina. Diploma, Freedmen's Hosp. Sch. Nursing, 1948; BSN, Avila Coll., Kansas City, Mo., 1958; MSN, Cath. U. Am., 1960, PhD in Higher Edn., 1967. Instr. VA Hosp., Topeka, 1950—52, supr. Kansas City, Mo., 1952—58; asst. dir. in-service edn. Freedmen's Hosp., Washington, 1960—61, adminstrv. asst. to DON, 1961—66, assoc. dir. nursing services, 1966—67, DON, 1967—69; dean Howard U. Coll. Nursing, Washington, 1968—86, dean emeritus, 1986—; pvt. practice Kansas City, Kans.; dir. minority devel. U. Kans., 1991—95. Pres. Nurses Examining Bd., 1967—68; cons. Gen. Rsch. Support Program, NIH, 1972—76; mem. Inst. Medicine, NAS, 1974—; cons. VA Ctrl. Office continuing edn. com., 1976—; mem. D.C. Health Planning Adv. Com., 1967—68, Tri-State Regional Planning Com. for Nursing Edn., 1969, Health Adv. Coun., Nat. Urban Coalition, 1971—73; bd. dirs. Hilton Grand Vacation CLub Seaworkd Internat. Ctr. Contbr. articles to profl. jours. Trustee Cmty. Group Health Found., 1976—77, cons., 1977—; bd. regents State Univ. Sys. Fla., 1977; adv. bd. Am. Assn. Med. Vols., 1970—72; bd. dirs. Iona Whipper Home for Unwed Mothers, 1970—72, Nursing Edn. Opportunities, 1970—72. Recipient Sustained Superior Performance award, HEW, 1962, Meritorious Pub. Svc. award, Govt. of D.C., 1968, medal of honor, Avila Coll., 1969, Disting. Alumni award, Howard U. Nat. Assn. for Equal Opportunity in Higher Edn., 1990, Cmty. Svc. award, Black Profl. Nurses Kansas City, 1991, Lifetime Achievement award, Assn. Black Nursing Faculty in Higher Edn., 1993, Svc. award, Midwest Regional Conf. on Black Families and Children, 1994, Alumni award in Nursing, Avila U., 2006. Mem.: ANA, Avila U. (bd. trustees 2008), Am. Assn. Colls. Nursing (sec. 1975—76), Am. Congress Rehab. Medicine, Nat. League Nursing, Societas Docta (pres. 1996—99, charter), Freedmen's Hosp. Nursing Alumni Assn., Alpha Kappa Alpha, Sigma Theta Tau. Home: 15107 Interlachen Dr Apt 315 Silver Spring MD 20906-5627

COLES, ROBERT, child psychiatrist, educator, writer; b. Boston, Oct. 12, 1929; s. Philip and Sandra (Young) C.; m. Jane Hallowell; children— Robert, Daniel, Michael. AB, Harvard U., 1950; MD, Columbia U., 1954; MD (hon.), Temple U., 1972, Bates Coll., Notre Dame U., Holy Cross Coll.; MD, Wayne State U., 1973, Western Mich. U., 1974, Hofstra U., 1975, Coll. William and Mary, 1976, Rutgers U., 1977, Knox Coll., 1978, Colby Coll., 1981, Sienna Heights Coll., 1983, Beloit Coll., 1984, Emory U., 1986, Dartmouth Coll., 1987. Intern U. Chgo. Clinics, 1954-55; resident in psychiatry Mass. Gen. Hosp., Boston, 1955-56, McLean Hosp., Belmont, Mass., 1956-57, Judge Baker Guidance Center-Children's Hosp., 1957-58; mem. staff children's Unit Met. State Hosp., Waltham, Mass., 1957-58; mem. staff alcoholic clinic Mass. Gen. Hosp.; teaching fellow in psychiatry, mem. psychiat. staff and clin. asst. in psychiatry Harvard Med. Sch., 1955-58; research psychiatrist Harvard U. Health Services, 1963—; lectr. gen. edn. Harvard U., 1966—, prof. psychiatry and med. humanities, 1977—; founder and editor DoubleTake Magazine, 1995—. Child psychiat. fellow Judge Baker Guidance Center, Children's Hosp., Boston, 1960-61; mem. Nat. Adv. Com. on Farm Labor, 1965—; cons. Appalachian Vols., 1965—, Rockefeller Found., 1969—, Ford Found., 1969—; mem. Inst. of Medicine, Nat. Acad. Scis., 1973-78; vis. prof. public policy Duke U., 1973—; cons. supr. dept. psychiatry Cambridge (Mass.) Hosp., 1976—; cons. Center for Study of So. Culture, U. Miss., 1979—; bd. dirs. Ctr. for Documentary Studies, Duke U.; vis. prof. psychiatry, Dartmouth Coll., 1989. Author: Children of Crisis: A Study of Courage and Fear, 1967, Dead End School, 1968, Still Hungry in America, 1969, The Grass Pipe, 1969, The Image is Yours, 1969; Wages of Neglect, 1969, Uprooted Children: The Early Lives of Migrant Farmers, 1970, Teachers and the Children of Poverty, 1970, Erik H. Erikson: The Growth of His Work, 1970, The Middle Americans, 1970, Migrants, Sharecroppers and Mountaineers, 1972, The South Goes North, 1972, Saving Face, 1972, Farewell to the South, 1972, A Spectacle Unto the World, 1973, Riding Free, 1973, The Darkness and the Light, 1974, The Buses Roll, 1974, Irony in the Mind's Life: Essays on Novels by James Agee, Elizabeth Bowen and George Eliot, 1974, Headsparks, 1975, The Mind's Fate, 1975, Eskimos, Chicanos and Indians, 1978, Privileged Ones, Vol. V of Children in Crisis book series, 1978, (with Jane Hallowell Coles) Women of Crisis Lives of Struggle and Hope, 1978, Walker Percy: An American Search, 1978, Flannery O'Connor's South, 1980, Women of Crisis; Lives of Work and Dreams, 1980, Dorothea Lange: Photographs of a Lifetime, 1982, (with Ross Spears) Agee, 1985, The Political Life of Children, 1986, Dorothy Day: A Radical Devotion, 1987, Simone Weil: A Modern Pilgrimage, 1987, Times of Surrender: Selected Essays, 1988, Harvard Diary, 1988, That Red Wheelbarrow, 1988, The Call of Stories: Teaching and the Moral Imagination, 1989, Rumors of Separate Worlds, 1989, The Spiritual Life of Children, 1990; contbg. editor: The New Republic, 1966—, Am. Poetry Rev, 1972—, Aperture, 1974—, Lit. and Medicine, 1981—, New Oxford Rev, 1981—; mem. editorial bd.: Integrated Edn., 1967—, Child Psychiatry and Human Devel., 1969—, Rev. of Books and Religion, 1976—, Internat. Jour. Family Therapy, 1977—, Grants mag., 1977—, Learning mag., 1978—, Jour. Am. Culture, 1977—, Jour. Edn., 1979—; bd. editors: Parents' Choice, 1978—; editor: Children and Youth Services Rev., 1978—. Bd. dirs. Field Found., 1968—; trustee Robert F. Kennedy Meml., 1968—, Robert F. Kennedy Action Corps, State of Mass., 1968—, Miss. Inst. Early Childhood Edn., 1968—, Twentieth Century Fund, 1971—; bd. dirs. Reading is Fundamental, Smithsonian Inst., 1968—, Am. Freedom from Hunger Found., 1968—, Am. Parents Com., 1971—; mem. corp. Boston Children's Service, 1970; mem. adv. council Inst. for Non-violent Social Change of Martin Luther King, Jr. Meml. Center, 1971—, Ams. for Children's Relief, 1972—; mem. nat. com. for Edn. of Young Children, 1972—; mem. nat. adv. council Rural Am.,

1976—; trustee Austen Riggs Found., Stockbridge, Mass., 1976—; mem. nat. adv. com. Ala. Citizens for Responsive Public Television, 1976—; mem. adv. com. Nat. Indian Edn. Assn., 1976—; visitor's com. mem. Boston Mus. Fine Arts, 1977; bd. dirs. Boys Club Boston, 1977; vis. com. Boston Coll. Law Sch., 1977; adv. Center for So. Folklore, 1978—; mem. children's com. Edna McConnell Clark Found., 1978—; bd. dirs. Lyndhurst Found., 1978—; mem. nat. adv. bd. Foxfire Fund, Inc., 1979—. Recipient Ralph Waldo Emerson prize Phi Beta Kappa, 1967; Anisfield-Wolf award in race relations Saturday Rev., 1968; Hofheimer award Am. Psychiat. Assn., 1968; Sidney Hillman prize, 1971; Weatherford prize Berea Coll. and Council So. Mountains, 1973; Lilliam Smith Award So. Regional Council, 1973; McAlpin medal Nat. Assn. Mental Health, 1972; Pulitzer prize, 1973 (all received for Children of Crisis, Vols. II, III); disting. scholar medal Hofstra U., 1974; William A. Shonfeld award Am. Soc. Adolescent Psychiatry, 1977; MacArthur Found. award, 1981; Josepha Hale award, 1986; fellow Davenport Coll., Yale U., 1976— Fellow Am. Acad. Arts and Scis., Inst. Soc., Ethics and the Life Scis.; mem. Am. Psychiat. Assn., Am. Orthopsychiat. Assn. (past dir.), Acad. Psychoanalysis, Nat. Orgn. Migrant Children. Home: PO Box 674 Concord MA 01742-0674

COLE-SCHIRALDI, MARILYN BUSH, medical educator; b. NYC, Jan. 29, 1945; d. George Lyman and Theis (Maurer) Bush; m. Carl E. Cole, Aug. 31, 1968 (div. June 1981); children: Charlot E. Sleeper, Bradley Eric Cole; m. Martin M. Schiraldi Sr., July 3, 1982. BA, U. Conn., 1966; grad. cert., U. Pa., 1969; MS, U. Bridgeport, 1982. Registered occupl. therapist, Conn. Staff occupational therapy Ea. Pa. Psychiat. Inst., Phila., 1968-69; dir. occupational therapy Middlesex Meml. Hosp., Middletown, Conn., 1973-76; supervising occupational therapist Lawrence & Meml. Hosps. Day Treatment Ctr., New London, Conn., 1976-79; staff occupational therapist Newington Children's Hosp., Newington, Conn., 1980-82; asst. prof. occupational therapy Quinnipiac Coll., Hamden, Conn., 1982-95, assoc. prof., tenured, 1995—2007, prof. emeritus occupl. therapy, 2007—. Vis. faculty fellow Yale U., 1999-2001; cons. psychiat. svcs. VA Med. Ctr., West Haven, Conn., 1983-91; cons. Fairfield Hills Hosp., Newtown, Conn., 1989-91. Author: (textbook) Group Dynamics in Occupational Therapy, 1993, 3d edit., 2005, 4th edit., 2011; co-author: Structured Group Experiences, 1982, Applied Theories in Occupational Therapy, 2008, Social Participation in Occupational Contests, 2010, guest editor, Ot Internat. Jour., 2011, contbr. chpts. to books, articles to profl. jours. Grantee Quinnipiac Coll, 1986, 2004, 2005; recipient Best Seller award Slack, Inc., 1999, 2005. Fellow: Am. Occupl. Therapy Assn. (Comms. award 1976, Svc. awards 1998, cert.); mem.: AAUW (cultural chair 1972, publicity chair 1973—76, edn. chair 1989—91, nominations 1993—96, membership treas. 1998—2001, fin. com. 2004—), Stratford Lifelong Learners (bd. mem. 2008—), Ctr. Study Sensory Integrative Dysfunction (cert. 1979), World Fedn. Occupl. Therapists (ednl. program reviewer 2010—), Conn. Occupl. Therapy Assn. (sec. 1978, nominations chair 1982—89, state mental health chair spl. interest sect. 1999—2005), Nat. League Am. Pen Women, U.S. Sailing Assn. Republican. Episcopalian.

COLETTI, DOMENICK, oral surgeon; b. NYC, Aug. 12, 1968; MD, Med. Coll. Va., DDS, 1997; degree in Med., U. Md., 2000. Assoc. prof., divsn. chief dept. oral & maxillofacial surgery U. Md., 2003—09; oral and maxillofacial surgeon, ptnr. Ctrl. Md. Oral and Maxillofacial Surgery PA, 2009—. Fellow: ACS, Am. Bd. Oral and Maxillofacial Surgeon, Am. Assn. Oral and Maxillofacial Surgery (Faculty Educator Devel. award). Office: 10710 Charter Dr Ste 330 Columbia MD 21044 Office Fax: 410-997-0807. Business E-Mail: dcoletti@comcast.net.

COLGAN, JOHN D., medical educator, researcher; b. Trenton, NJ, Sept. 14, 1964; BS, Rutgers U., 1987; PhD, Columbia U., 1994. Asst. prof. internal medicine, rschr. U. Iowa, 2005—. Mem.: AAAS, FASEB, ASBMB, AAI. Office: 375 Newton Rd CBRB 3270 Iowa City IA 52242 Office Fax: 319 353-4728. Business E-Mail: john-colgan@uiowa.edu.

COLIZZA, WAYNE ANTHONY, orthopaedic surgeon; b. Hamilton, Ont., Can., Sept. 12, 1958; came to the U.S., 1992; s. Vincent Patrick and Velma Louise C.; m. Marlene Catherine Morin, Aug. 13, 1983; children: Wayne Jr., Christina, Michael. BSc in Biochemistry with honors, McGill U., Montreal, 1982, MD, 1987. Diplomate Am. Bd. Orthopaedic Surgery, cert. additional qualified sports medicine. Fellow Insall Scott Kelly Inst. for Orthopedics and Sports Medicine, NYC, 1992-93; attending surgeon St. Clares Med. Ctr., Denville, NJ, 1993—2006, Beth Israel Med. Ctr., NYC, 1995-99, Morristown (N.J.) Meml. Hosp., 1996—; pvt. practice Sparta, Morristown, NJ, 1996—. Contbr. articles to profl. jours. Pres. Canadian Orthopaedic Residents Assn., 1992. Recipient Zimmer Travelling Fellows award Am. Orthopaedic Assn., 1994. Fellow ACS, Internat. Coll. Surgeons, Royal Coll. Surgeons Can. (cert.), Am. Acad. Orthopaedic Surgeons, Am. Orthop Assn. Sports Medicine; mem. Can. Orthopaedic Assn., Can. Med. Assn., N.J. Med. Soc., N.J. Orthopedic Soc. (bd. pres.). Office: Tri-County Orthopaedics and Sports Medicine 160 Hanover Ave PO Box 1446 Morristown NJ 07962 Address: 540 Lafayette Ave Sparta NJ 07871

COLLEN, MORRIS FRANK, retired medical administrator, physician, consultant, researcher; b. St. Paul, Nov. 12, 1913; s. Frank Morris and Rose Collen; m. Frances B. Diner, Sept. 24, 1937; children: Arnold Roy, Barry Joel, Roberta Joy, Randal Harry. BEE, U. Minn., 1934, MB with distinction, 1938, MD, 1939; DSc (hon.), U. Victoria, BC, Can., 2004. Diplomate Am. Bd. Internal Medicine. Intern Michael Reese Hosp., Chgo., 1939—40; resident LA County Hosp., 1940—42; chief med. service Kaiser Found. Hosp., Oakland, Calif., 1942—52, chief of staff, 1952—53; physician in chief San Francisco Med. Ctr.; med. dir. West Bay divsn. Permanente Med. Group, 1953—62, dir. med. methods rsch., 1962—79, dir. tech. assessment, 1979—83, cons. divsn. rsch., 1983—. Chmn. exec. com. Permanente Med. Group, Oakland, 1953—73; dir. Permanente Svcs., Inc., Oakland, 1958—73; adj. asst. prof. biomed. informatics Uniformed Svcs. U. Health Scis., 2000—05; chmn. health care sys. study sect. USPHS, 1968—72, mem. adv. com. demonstration grants, 1967, advisor VA, 68; mem. adv. com. Automated Multiphasic Health Testing, 1971; discussant Nat. Conf. Preventive Medicine, Bethesda, Md., 1975; mem. com. on tech. in health care NAS, 1976; mem. adv. group Nat. Commn. on Digestive Diseases, U.S. Congress, 1978; mem. adv. panel to U.S. Congress Office of Tech. Assessment, 1980—85; mem. peer rev. adv. group TRIMIS program Dept. Def., 1978—90; program chmn. 3rd Internat. Conf. Med. Informatics, Tokyo, 1980; chmn. bd. sci. counselors Nat. Libr. Medicine, 1985—87, mem. lit. selection tech. rev. com., 1997—2002, chmn., 2000—02; chmn. tech. evaluation group Application of Advanced Network Infrastructure in Health and Disaster Mgmt., 2002, chmn. tech. group, 02; program chmn. Internat. Conf. Health Promotion, Atlanta, 2003. Author: Treatment of Pneumococcic Pneumonia, 1948, Hospital Computer Systems, 1974, Multiphasic Health Testing Services, 1978, History of Medical Informatics, 1995; editor: Permanente Med. Bull., 1943—53; mem. editl. bd.: Preventive Medicine, 1970—80, Jour. Med. Sys., Methods Info. Medicine, 1980—97, Diagnostic Medicine, 1980—84, Computers in Biomed. Rsch., 1987—94; contbr. more than 200 articles to profl. jours., chpts. to books. Fellow Ctr. Advanced Studies in Behavioral Scis., Stanford U., 1985—86; scholar Johns Hopkins Centennial scholar, 1976, scholar-in-residence, Nat. Libr. Medicine, 1987—2002. Fellow: ACP, Am. Coll. Med. Informatics (pres. 1987—88, Morris F. Collen medal named in his honor 1993), Am. Inst. Med. and Biol. Engring., Am. Coll. Chest Physicians, Am. Coll. Cardiology; mem.: NAS, AMA, Salutis Unitas (v.p. 1972), Internat. Health Evaluation Assn. (pres. 1995—96, Lifetime Achievement award 1992, Computers in Health Care Pioneer award 1992, David E. Morgan award for achievement in health care info. 1998, Japan Shigeaki Hinohara award for preventive medicine 2001, Cummings Psyche award for behavioral medical rsch. 2001, Morris F. Collen Permanente Rsch. award named in his honor 2003, 2009), Am. Med. Informatics Assn. (bd. dirs. 1985—96), Nat. Acad. Practice in Medicine (chmn. 1982—88, co-chmn. 1989—91), Soc. Adv. Med. Sys. (pres. 1973), Am. Fedn. Clin. Rsch., Inst. Medicine (chmn. tech. subcom. for improving patient records 1990, chmn. workshop on informatics in clin. preventive medicine 1991), Internat. Med. Informatics Assn. Sr. Officers Club, Tau Beta Pi, Alpha Omega Alpha. Achievements include named a library after his name at Kaiser Permanente, Oakland, California. Office: 2175 Ygnacio Valley Rd #228 Walnut Creek CA 94598 also: 2000 Broadway Oakland CA 94612

COLLER, BARRY SPENCER, internist, pathologist, hematologist, educator, department chairman; b. NYC, Nov. 21, 1945; s. Arthur L. and Ruth Coller; m. Barbara Nan Gelfand; children: Hilary Ann, Alyssa Brook. BA magna cum laude, Columbia U., 1966; MD, NYU, 1970; DSc (hon.), Mount Sanai Sch. Medicine, 2002, SUNY Stony Brook, 2003. Diplomate in internal medicine and hematology Am. Bd. Internal Medicine, 1973, in hematology Am. Bd. Pathology, 1974, Am. Bd. Pathology, 1975. Intern, resident Bellevue Hosp., NYC, 1970—71, resident in medicine, 1971—72; clin. assoc., hematology svc., clin. pathology dept. NIH, Bethesda, Md., 1972—74, staff physician, hematology svc., clin. pathology dept., 1974—76; asst. prof. medicine SUNY Health Scis. Ctr., Stony Brook, 1976-78, clin. chief hematology lab., 1976-93, assoc. prof., 1978-82, clin. dir. hematology div. dept. medicine, 1978-83, prof. medicine and pathology, 1982-93, head hematology div., 1984-93, Disting. Svc. prof., 1993, adj. prof.; assoc. dir. biomed. rsch. Advanced Ctr. Biotech. SUNY, 1992-93; Murray M. Rosenberg prof. medicine Mt. Sinai Sch. Medicine, NYC, 1993—2001, chmn. dept. medicine, 1993—2001, clin. prof. medicine, 2001—; dir., chief medicine Mt. Sinai Hosp., NYC, 1993—2001; David Rockefeller prof. medicine, head lab. blood and vascular biology, v.p. med. affairs Rockefeller U., NYC, 2001—; physician-in-chief Rockefeller U. Hosp., NYC, 2001—. Surgeon USPHS, NIH, Bethesda, Md., 1972—76; clin. instr. Georgetown U. Sch. Medicine, Washington, 1972—76; Anna and Leo Roon lectr. Scripps Clinic and Rsch. Found., La Jolla, Calif., 1986; Martin Rosenthal lectr. Mt. Sinai Hosp., NYC, 1991; vis. prof. Cornell U., Ithaca, NY, 1992, Ithaca, 96, U. Nebr., Omaha, 1994, SUNY, Bklyn., 1994, U. Wash., 1999, U. Utah, 2002, U. Calif., San Francisco, 2002; Hymie Nossel Meml. lectr. Columbia U., NYC, 1994; Herion-Walker lectr. U. N.C., Chapel Hill, 1997; Oscar D. Ratnoff lectr. Case Western Reserve U., 1997; vis. lectr. U. Okla., 1997; Teichman lectr. Tel Aviv U., 2002; dir. Stony Brook Found., 1991—93, 2001—, L.I. High Tech. Incubator Facility, Stony Brook, 1991—93; sci. advisor Ariad Pharm., Cambridge, Mass., 1991—2000; cons. Centocor Inc., Malvern, Pa., 1986—95, Northport VA Med. Ctr., NY, 1986—94, Genentech, South San Francisco, 1994—95; scientific adv. bd. mem. Otsuka Pharm. Co., Rockville, Md., 1985—93, N.Y. Blood Ctr., NYC, 1994—, N.Y. Biotech. Assn,, 1995—99, Oxford Found., 1996—98, Accumetrics, San Diego, 1996—2001, 2002—; bd. extamural express Nat. Heart, Lung and Blood Inst., 2000—06, bd. external advisors, 2007—; bd. govs. Clin. Ctr. NIH, 2002—05, mem. adv. bd. clin. rsch., 2005—; Lilly lectr. Royal Coll. Physicians, 2009. Editor: Progress in Hemostatis and Thrombosis, Vol. 8, 1986, Vol. 9, 1988, Vol. 10, 1990, Williams' Hematology, 5th edit., 1995, 6th edit., 2000; mem. editorial bd. Blood, 1981-85, Current Opinion in Hematology, 1991-2005, Blood Cells, Molecules & Diseases, 1999-, Circulation, 1993-2004, Mt. Sinai Jour. Medicine, 1994-2001, Haemostasis, 1996-2002, Thrombosis and Haemostasis, 1999-2003; reviewing editor Jour. Lab. and Clin. Medicine, 1991-; cons. editor Jour. Clin. Investigation, 1992-97; contbr. over 100 articles, revs. and abstracts to sci. jours., chpts. to books. Councilor east sect. Am. Fedn. Clin. Rsch., 1981—86; adv. in field. Recipient citation Fight for Sight, 1977, Jane Nugent Cochems prize, 1977, Internat. Investigator recognition award, 1987, Solomon A. Berson Med. Alumni Achievement award NYU Med. Ctr., 1991, Inventor of Yr., N.Y. Intellectual Property Law Assn., 1997, Jacobi medallion Mt. Sinai Sch. Medicine, 1997, Disting. Career award Internat. Soc. on Thrombosis and Haemostasis, Nat. Rsch. Achievement award Am. Heart Assn., 1998, Therapeutic Frontiers award, Am. Coll. Clin. Pharmacy, Alexander Richman award Humanism, Mount Sanai Sch. Medicine, Spl. Achievement award, 2001, Warren Alpert Found. award, 2001, Cotlove award, Acad. Clin. Lab, Physicians and Scientists, Gold Humanism Hon. Soc., Arnold P. Gold Found., medal Royal Coll. Physicians, 2009, named Man of Year Village Times Pub., 1998; grantee NIH, 1976—, Am. Heart Assn., 1983-86, SUNY, 1987-89; Guggenheim fellow Weizmann Inst. Sci., Rehovot, Israel, 1982. Master: Am. Coll. Physicians; fellow: AAAS, Coll. Am. Pathologists, NY Acad. Medicine; mem.: NAS, Am. Heart Assn., Soc. Clin. Translational Sci. (founding pres. 2009—), Am. Acad. Arts & Scis., NY Acad. Sci., Inst. Medicine, Assn. Profs. Medicine (bd. dirs. 2000—01), Internat. Soc. on Thrombosis and Haemostasis (councilor 1986—92, publs. com. 1986—92, chmn., fin. com. 1990—92), Harvey Soc., Am. Soc. Hematology (treas. 1983—87, fin. com. 1983—90, exec. com. 1984—87, corp. adv. com. 1986—87, adv. com. 1987—92, com. on pub. info. and govtl. affairs 1988—98, chmn., com. on pub. info. and govtl. affairs 1992—94, fin. and investment audit com. 1993—2007, v.p. 1995—96, pres.-elect 1996—97, exec. com. 1996—98, edn. com. 1996—98, com. on practice 1996—98, pres. 1997—98, adv. com. 1998, chair, adv. com. 1999—2000, Stratton medal 2005), Am. Fedn. Med. Rsch. (councilor, ea. sect. 1981—86), Assn. Am. Physicians, Am. Soc. Clin. Investigation, Alpha Omega Alpha (sec.-treas., MU chpt. 1985—86, councilor, MU chpt. 1985—90), Phi Beta Kappa (v.p., Alpha Beta N.Y. 1990—91, pres., Alpha Beta N.Y. 1991—92). Achievements include discovery of a monoclonal antibody that was modified to produce the drug abciximab which was approved by the FDA in 1994 and the verify now rapid platelet function assays approved by the FDA in 1999-2005; patents in field. Office: Rockefeller U Lab Blood/Vasc Bio 1230 York Ave New York NY 10021

COLLEY, ANN M., medical association administrator, psychology professor; Prof. psychology U. Leicester, UK, emeritus prof.; CEO Brit. Psychol. Soc., Leicester, 2008—. Mem.: Brit. Psychol. Soc. (former pres., hon. gen. sec.). Office: Sch Psychology Univ Leicester Lancaster Rd Leicester LE1 9HN England also: Brit Psychol Soc St Andrews House 48 Princess Road East LE1 7DR Leicester England Business E-Mail: aoc@le.ac.uk. *

COLLIER, ALBERT M., pediatrician, educator, director; b. Elba, Ala., May 3, 1937; s. Milford William and Ida Ruth C.; m. Mary Gaynell Wehler, July 17, 1960; children: Albert Mark, Dennis Murray, Jonathan Lee. BS, U. Miami, 1959, MD, 1963. Pediatric resident U. Miami, Coral Gables, Fla., 1963-66; fellow infectious diseases U. NC, Chapel Hill, 1968-70, from asst. prof. to assoc. prof., 1971-80, prof., 1980—, chief divsn. infectious disease, 1980—2004, assoc. dir. Ctr. Environ. Med. Lung Bio, 1980—2004, acting dir. Frank Porter Graham Child Devel. Ctr., 1990-92, assoc. chmn. pediat. rsch., 1997—2003, med. sch. res. integrity officer, 2000—. Contbr. over 100 articles to profl. jours. Recipient Louis Dienes award Internat. Orgn. Mycoplasmology, Vienna, Austria, 1988. Mem. Gideons (zone leader 1990-93). Baptist. Office: U NC Chapel Hill Dept Pediatrics Sch Medicine 413 Mac Nider Blvd CB 7231 Chapel Hill NC 27599 E-mail: uncacl@med.unc.edu.

COLLIER, ANN, epidemiologist, researcher; b. Nov. 27, 1953; 3 children. MD, Dartmouth Med. Sch., 1978. Cert. Am. Bd. Internal Medicine, Am. Bd. Internal Medicine with subspecialty Pediatric Infectious Disease. Intern, internal medicine NC Meml. Hosp., Chapel Hill; resident, infectious disease U. Wash., fellow, prof. medicine, dir. AIDS Clinical Trials Unit, 1985—; attending physician Harborview Med. Ctr., 1985; dir. Harborview Med. Ctr. AIDS Clinic, 1987—90. Office: Harborview Medical Center W Clinic Wing 2nd Fl 325 9th Ave Box 359929 Seattle WA 98104

COLLIER, EARL MILLER, JR., former biotechnology company executive; b. Richmond, Va., Aug. 31, 1947; s. Earl Miller and Emily Wallace (Webb) Collier; m. Frances C. Utterback, June 11, 1978 (div. Apr. 1991); children: Emily F., Braxton L.; m. Maren D. Anderson, Aug. 23, 1992; children: Maxwell A. Brooks, William E. BA, Yale U., 1969; JD, U. Va., 1973. Law clerk US Ct Appeals (DC cir.); assoc. Covington & Burlington LLP, 1974—77; dep. adminstr. Health Care Financing Adminstrn. US Dept. Health Edn. & Welfare (HEW), Washington, 1977—79; ptnr. Hogan & Hartson LLP, Washington, 1981-91; pres. Vitas Healthcare, Miami, Fla., 1991-95, Clark Point Co., Washington, 1995-97; exec. v.p. Genzyme Corp., Cambridge, Mass., 1997—2010; sr. advisor life sciences group Polaris Venture Partners, Boston, 2010—. Bd. dirs. deCode Genetics, Pervasis, Inc., Newton Wellesley Hosp., Arsenal Medical, Inc., TransMedics, Beacon Hospice, Boston Athenaeum. Mem. Yale Club NY, Causeway Club, DC Bar Assn. Office: Polaris Venture Partners 1000 Winter St Ste 3350 Waltham MA 02451 Office Phone: 781-290-0770. Office Fax: 781-290-0880. *

COLLIER, HELEN VANDIVORT, psychologist; b. Nagpur, India; d. William Boardley and Stephena Ruth (Hecker) C.; children: Keith Vandivort (dec.), Daniel Vandivort, Heidi Vandivort Zalobowski. BA, Ohio Wesleyan U., 1950; MEd, U. Toledo, 1968, EdD, 1974; postgrad., San Diego Gestalt Tng. Ctr., 1980—90. Lic. psychologist, Ohio, marriage and family therapist, Nev. Tchr. elem. schs., Itasca, Ill.; ednl. cons. Toledo Bd. Edn., 1960-67; elem. counselor Toledo Pub. Schs., 1968; counseling psychologist, asst. prof. U. Toledo, 1968-74; pvt. practice psychotherapy and counseling cons. Bloomington, Ind., 1974—83. Asst. dir. adult counseling project Sch. Continuing Studies Ind. U., Bloomington, 1975-76; rsch. assoc. Ctr. for Human of Human Mobility, Ind. U., 1974-75, cons., adj. faculty, 1976-80; ptnr. Nat. Ct. Svcs., Inc., Reno; adj. faculty Nat. Jud. Coll., Reno, 1984-97; dir. HVC Assocs. Psychotherapy and Orgnl. Cons., 1983-. Author: Freeing Ourselves: Removing Internal Barriers to Equality, 1979, Counseling Women: A Guide for Therapists, 1982; co-editor: Meeting the Educational and Occupational Planning Needs of Adults, 1975; contbr. articles to jours. Women's Ednl. Equity Act Office of Edn. grantee, 1977—. Mem. Am. Psychol. Assn., Am. Assn. Marriage and Family Therapists. Address: 370 Wheeler Ave Reno NV 89502-1614 Office Phone: 775-786-3097. Office Fax: 775-786-1442. Personal E-mail: hvcollier@charter.net.

COLLIER, WILLIAM GAYLE, psychology professor, researcher; b. Albuquerque, July 31, 1970; s. William Robert and Judith Church Collier. BS in Psychology, Okla. Christian U., 1992; MA in Exptl. Psychology, U. Ctrl. Okla., 1994; MS in Exptl. Psychology, Tex. Christian U., 1997, PhD in Gen. Exptl. Psychology, 1998. Grad. asst. Multimedia Ctr., Coll. Edn., U. Ctrl. Okla., Edmond, 1994; dep. asst. dept. psychology Tex. Christian U., Ft. Worth, 1995-96, acad. tutor athletic dept., 1997-98, dep. asst. dept. psychology, 1998; lectr. psychology U. Tex., Tyler, 1998-99, vis. asst. prof., 1999—2002; asst. prof. cognitive psychology U. NC, Pembroke, 2002—08, assoc. prof. cognitive psychology, 2008—, undergrad. student advisor dept. psychology, 2003—. Undergrad. student advisor dept. psychology U. Tex., Tyler, 1999-2002. Author poetry; contbr. articles to profl. jours. Mem.: Soc. Edn., Music and Psychology Rsch., Southwestern Psychol. Assn., Assn. Psychol. Sci., European Soc. Cognitive Scis. Music (assoc.; affiliate mem.), Psi Chi, Alpha Chi. Avocations: science fiction, history, poetry, music, theater. Office Phone: 910-521-6458. Business E-Mail: william.collier@uncp.edu.

COLLIGNON, FREDERIC PIERRE, neurosurgeon; b. Liège, Belgium, July 27, 1969; s. Pierre Jean Collignon and Jacqueline Brach; m. Caroline Françoise Geuzaine, June 11, 1999; children: Raphael Charles, Anais Claire. MD, Liege State U., Belgium, 1994, speciality in neurosurgery, 2000. Fellow in vascular and skull base surgery Mayo Clinic, Rochester, Minn., 2000—02; fellow in neurooncological surgery Meml. Sloan Kettering Cancer Ctr., NYC, 2002—03; cons. Brussels Neurosurg. Ctr., Clinique du Parc Léopold,

2003—. Asst. prof. in neurosurgery Liege State U., Liège, Belgium, 2004—. Contbr. articles to profl. jours. Grantee, Mayo Clinic and Leon Fredericq Found., Belgium, 2002. Mem.: Belgian Soc. Neurosurgery, European Assn. Neurosurgery, Congress Neurol. Surgeons, Am. Assn. Neurol. Surgeons, European Assn. Neurooncology. Achievements include research in gap junctions in epilepsy. Home: Rue Du Laveu 215 Liège 4000 Belgium Office: Clinique du Parc Léopold Rue Froissart 38 Brussels 1040 Belgium Office Fax: 02 287 56 54; Home Fax: 043490949. Business E-Mail: f.collignon@neurobrussels.be.

COLLIN, HERMANN BARRY, retired optometrist, retired medical educator; b. Melbourne, Victoria, Australia, Jan. 21, 1933; s. Herman Emil Collin and Kathleen Langsford Collins; m. Berverley Ann Wilkinson, Dec. 28, 1957; children: Shaun Patrick, Luke Anthony, Marice Kathleen, Thea Majella Loiterton. BSc in Pathology, U Melbourne, Australia, 1956; M of Applied Sci., U. Melbourne, Australia, 1966, PhD in Physiology, 1970; DSc in Optometry, U. NSW, Australia, 1995; DUniv (hon.), Queensland U. Tech., 2003. Lic. optometric science Australian Coll. Optometry, 1954, registered Optometrists Registration Bd., Victoria, 1955, Optometrists Registration Bd., NSW, 1982. Optometric practice H Collin & Co., Melbourne, 1955—61; asst. lectr. Victorian Coll. Optometry, Melbourne, 1962—64, lectr., 1964—66, sr. lectr., 1966—72; rsch. fellow physiology lab., Sir William Dunn Sch. Pathology U. Oxford, England, 1967—68; reader, dept. optometry U. Melbourne, 1973—81; corneal fellow, dept. ophthalmology Harvard Med. Sch. Eye Rsch. Inst. Retina Found., Boston, 1975; sr. rsch. assoc. Eye Rsch. Inst. Retina Found., Boston, 1986; head, sch. optometry U. NSW, Sydney, 1982—92, prof. optometry, 1982—94, emeritus prof., 1994—; Hon. Prof. Hong Kong Polytechnic U., Hong Kong, 2000—. Vis. scientist, dept. neurosci. Scripps Instn. Oceanography, San Diego, 1986; hon. vis. prof. U. NSW, 1994—95; hon. prof. U. Melbourne, 1995—99; vis. prof. U. Auckland, New Zealand, 1997—99, Hong Kong Poly. U., 1999—, hon. prof., 2000—. Editor: Clin. and Exptl. Optometry Jour., 1993—; contbr. numerous articles to profl. jours. Bd. mem. Nat. Vision Rsch. Inst. Australia, Melbourne, 1975—96, Pank Ophthalmic Trust, Australia, 1982—90; commr. declarations and affadavits State Govt., Victoria, 1956—81, justice of peace NSW, 1982—95; bd. mem. Optometrists Registration Bd. NSW, 1982—94, Optometric Vision Rsch. Found., NSW, 1982—92, Australasian Coun. on Chiropractic Edn., Australia, 1977—2005, pres., 1995—2001, 2004—05. Decorated Nat. Svc. medal Australian Govt.; recipient medal, Internat. Optical League, 1969, Shorney prize Ophthalmology award, U. Adelaide, Australia, 1971, Tchg. Excellence award, U. NSW, 1992, Mem. Order of Australia award, Australian Govt., 1997, HB Collin Rsch. medal, Optometrists Assn. Australia, 1977; grantee, Royal Soc., Nufflield Found., 1968, Rsch. grants, Nat. Health and Med. Rsch. Coun. Australia, 1968—88; vis. scholar, Sharp Cabrillo Hosp., San Diego, 1990; Travel grant, Brit. Coun., 1967, Sr. fellow, Fulbright Orgn., 1986, Rsch. grants, Australian Rsch. Coun., 1991—94. Fellow: Royal Coll. Pathologists, Am. Acad. Optometry, New Zealand Coll. Optometrists (hon.), mem.: Victorial Coll. Optometry (councillor 1963—81, hon. life 1981—), Hong Kong Soc. Profl. Optometrists (hon.; life), Optometrists Assn. Australia (hon.; life). Roman Catholic. Achievements include first to establish that lymphatic vessels can grow into the cornea following corneal injury. Also established many aspects of the structure and mode of growth of lymphatic vessels into the cornea; established that preservatives in eye drops can damage the corneal endothelium and retard epithelial healing. Avocations: golf, travel, stamp collecting/philately. Home and Office: 11 Bella Vista Rd North Caulfield Victoria 3161 Australia Business E-Mail: hbcollin@unsw.edu.au.

COLLINE, MARGUERITE RICHNAVSKY, maternal, women's health and pediatrics nurse; b. Bayonne, NJ, Nov. 30, 1953; d. John P. and Margaret M. (Conaghan) Richnavsky; m. Richard L. Colline, Oct. 8, 1977; children: Jennifer, Nicole, Danielle, James Michael. Diploma in practical nurse, Union County Tech. Inst., Scotch Plains, NJ, 1973; BSN, Seton Hall U., 1978. RN NJ, Md. Practical nurse oncology unit John E. Runnell's Hosp., Berkley Heights, N.J.; staff nurse infant unit Johns Hopkins Hosp., Balt.; staff nurse neonatal unit Overlook Hosp., Summit, N.J.; parish nurse Somerville, NJ. Mem. Sigma Theta Tau. Personal E-mail: magee1130@aol.com, mickic1@verizon.net.

COLLINS, ALLAN MEAKIN, education educator; b. Orange, NJ, Aug. 7, 1937; s. Clinton and Sarah Amy (Meakin) C.; m. Anne Marjorie Linstead, Aug. 24, 1963; children: Antony, Elizabeth. MA in Comm. Scis., U. Mich., Ann Arbor, 1962, PhD in Psychology, 1970. Sr. scientist Bolt, Beranek & Newman Inc., Cambridge, 1967-82, prin. scientist, 1982-2000; prof edn. and social policy Northwestern U., Evanston, Ill., 1989—2005, emeritus, 2005—. Co-dir. Ctr. for Tech. in Edn., Bank St. Coll. Edn., NYC, 1991—94; rsch. prof. edn. Boston Coll., 1998—2002; vis. sr. lectr. Harvard Grad. Sch. Edn., 2005—06; lectr. various colls. and univs. Editor: Representation and Understanding, 1975, Cognitive Science, 1976-80, Readings in Cognitive Science, 1988; author: The Cognitive Structure of Emotions, 1988; Rethinking Education in the Age of Technology, 2009. Guggenheim fellow, 1974, Sloan fellow, 1980. Fellow AAAS; mem. Nat. Acad. Edn., Cognitive Sci. Soc. (chmn. 1979-80, goving. bd. 1979-87, fellow 2007), Am. Assn. for Artificial Intelligence (fellow 1990), Am. Ednl. Rsch. Assn. (fellow 2008) Achievements include launched research on human semantic memory (with R. Quillian); development of first intelligent tutoring system (with J.R. Carbonell); development of cognitive apprenticeship (with J.S. Brown). Home: 135 Cedar St Lexington MA 02421-6516 Business E-Mail: collins@bbn.com.

COLLINS, ALLEN HOWARD, psychiatrist; b. Washington, Sept. 6, 1942; s. Murray and Bertha (Baccalman) C.; m. Stephanie Evelyn Awn, May 22, 1976; children: Sasha Marie, Matthew Allen, Alyssa Beth. AB, Columbia Coll., 1964; MD, Tufts U., 1968; MPH, Columbia U., 1974. Diplomate Am. Bd. Psychiatry and Neurology, Nat. Bd. Med. Examiners; cert. in psychoanalysis. Mental health career develop. fellow NIMH, Rockville, Md., 1968—74, staff psychiatrist Region II NYC, 1972—74, psychiat. cons., 1974—90; chief psychiat. consultation liaison svcs. Lenox Hill Hosp., NYC, 1974—76, chief psychiat. inpatient svc., 1976—78, chief psychiatry svc., 1978—86, chmn. dept. psychiatry, 1986—2005, pres. med. bd., 1994—96, 2000—02. Examiner in psychiatry Am. Bd. Psychiatry and Neurology, Evanston, Ill., 1979-2005, chief proctor, 1991-2005; clin. prof. psychiatry N.Y. Med. Coll., Valhalla, 1988-90; tng. and supervisory psychoanalyst divsn. psychoanalytic tng., 1986-90; assoc. clin. prof. psychiatry Cornell U. Med. Coll., 1990-93; clin. prof. psychiatry NYU Med. Ctr., 1993—; vis. prof. psychiatry SUNY/Downstate Health Sci. Ctr., 1998—. Author: (with others) Provider's Guide To Hospital-Based Services, 1986; contbr. articles to profl. jours. Trustee Lenox Hill Hosp., 1994-2004. With USPHS, 1968-74. Fellow Am. Psychiatr. Assn., Am. Acad. of Psychoanalysis, N.Y. Acad. Medicine. Avocations: golf, reading non-fiction biographies, history. Office Phone: 212-588-1205. Personal E-mail: ahcolmd@aol.com.

COLLINS, BOBBY MCMANUS, II, dental educator; s. Bobby McManus Collins, Sr. and Gail Patrick Collins; m. Lisa Joye Dixon, Oct. 14, 1978. BA in Chemistry, Biology, U. NC, Chapel Hill, 1978, DDS in Dental Surgery, 1983; MS in Clinical Med. Edn., U. Pitts. Sch. Medicine, 2004. Diplomate Am. Bd. of Oral and Maxillofacial Pathology, 1998, cert. Oral and Maxillofacial Pathology U. Fla. Coll. Dentistry, 1995. With US Army Dental Corps, 1984, advanced through grades to maj., 1989, dental officer, 1984—92; resident in oral pathology U. Fla., Gainesville, 1992—95; fellow in head and neck pathology U. Pitts. Med. Ctr., 1995—96; asst. prof. U. Pitts. Sch. Dental Medicine, 1996—2005, assoc. prof., 2005—11, East Carolina U. Sch. Dental Medicine, 2011—, assoc. prof. section chief oral & maxillofacial pathology. Guest lectr. US.-Saudi Aramco, Dhahran, Saudi Arabia, 1997, Pa. Dental Assn., 2004—; cons. US Army Dental Corps, 1999—, USN Dental Corps, Bethesda, Md., 2000—; oral pathology cons. VA Med. Ctr., 2005—11, Allegheny Gen. Hosp., 2007—11; keynote spkr. Light Force Am., The Big Show, 2008, 09, 3 Rivers Dental Conf., 2008. Contbr. articles to profl. jours., chapters to books. With dental corps USAR, 1984—92. Decorated 2 Army Commendation medals, Expert Field Med. badge US Army 18th Airborne Corps, 5 Army Achievement medals, Nat. Def. Svc. medal, Meritorious Svc. medal; recipient Faculty Award of Excellence/Appreciation, U. Pitts. Sch. Dental Medicine, 2000, 2001, 2003, 2004, 2005, Graduation Grand Marshal, 2006, 2009, Grad. Hooder, 2000, 2002, 2005, 2008, 2010; named to Best Dentists in Am., Woodward/White, 2004—05, Best of US Dentists/Oral and Maxillofacial Pathology, Pittsburgh's Best Dentists, 2007, 2008, 2009. Fellow: Acad. of Gen. Dentistry (Master 2004); mem.: Student Clinicians of the ADA, Am. Acad. of Oral and Maxillofacial Pathology (chmn., profl. and pub. rels. 2004—05), Omicron Kappa Upsilon (chmn. membership com. 2004—09). Avocations: guitar, travel, volksmarching. Office: East Carolina University Sch Dental Medicine 8 Lake Side Annex Greenville NC 27834-4354 Business E-Mail: bcollins@pitt.edu.

COLLINS, FRANCIS SELLERS, federal agency administrator, geneticist; b. Staunton, Va., Apr. 14, 1950; m. Diane Lynn Baker; children: Margaret, Elizabeth. BS in Chemistry, U. Va., Charlottesville, 1970; PhD in Physical Chemistry, Yale U., New Haven, 1974; MD with honors, U. NC Sch. Medicine, Chapel Hill, 1977; DSc (hon.), Baylor Coll. Medicine, 2004, U. Miami Sch. Medicine, 2007. Diplomate American Bd. Internal Medicine, American Bd. Med. Genetics, lic. NC, Conn., Mich. Inter, resident, chief resident internal medicine NC Meml. Hosp., Chapel Hill, 1977—81; fellow human genetics Yale U., 1981—84; asst. prof. internal medicine/human genetics U. Mich. Med. Sch., Ann Arbor, 1984—88, assoc. prof., 1988—91, prof., 1991—93, chief divsn. med. genetics, Dept. Internal Medicine, 1987—91; dir. Nat. Human Genome Rsch. Inst., Bethesda, Md., 1993—2008, founder divsn. Intramural Rsch.; dir. NIH, 2009—. Asst. investigator Howard Hughes Med. Inst., 1987—88, assoc. investigator, 1988—91, investigator, 1991—93; founder, pres. BioLogos Found., 2007—09. Author: The Language of God: A Scientist Presents Evidence for Belief, 2006, The Language of Life: DNA and the Revolution in Personalized Medicine, 2010; contbr. articles to profl. jours., chapters to books. Recipient Guthrie Family Humanitarian award, Huntington's Disease Soc. of America, 2001, Disting. Achievement & Leadership award, Am. Skin Assn., 2001, Lifetime Achievement award, Va. Biotech. Assn., 2002, Internat. award of merit, Gairdner Found., 2002, Col. Sanders Lifetime Achievement award, March of Dimes, 2004, Antonie Marfan award, 2006, Presdl. Medal of Freedom, 2007, Nat. Medal Sci., NSF, 2009, Philip Hauge Abelson prize, AAAS, 2009; co-recipient Albany Med. Ctr. prize, 2010; named Va.'s Outstanding Scientist, 2001; named one of America's Best Leaders, US News & World Report/Harvard Ctr. Pub. Leadership, 2005. Mem.: NAS, AMA (Scientific Achievement award 2001). Office: NIH 9000 Rockville Pike Bethesda MD 20892 Office Phone: 301-496-2433. Office Fax: 301-402-2700. Business E-Mail: francisc@mail.nih.gov. E-mail: execsec1@od.nih.gov. *

COLLINS, FRANK, JR., dentist, educator; b. Jackson, Miss., Mar. 1, 1965; s. Frank Collins, Sr. and Emma H. Collins. BS in Biology, U. So. Miss., 1988; DDS, Howard U., 1996; cert. in gen. dentistry, Luth. Med. Ctr., Bklyn., 2002. Instr. Hinds C.C., Raymond, Miss., 1997—2000; gen. practice resident St. Mary's Hosp., Waterbury, Conn., 2001. Mem.: ADA (Am. Dental Assn.), Acad. Gen. Dentistry. Avocations: music, jogging.

COLLINS, JAIME A., physician; b. Lima, Peru, Oct. 4, 1971; MS in Epidemiology, San Marcos Nat. U., 2007, MS in Health Policies and Planning, 2010. Attending physician dept. internal medicine Guillermo Almenara Gen. Hosp., 2002—. Med. dir. San Camilo Found., 2004—07. Recipient The Humanitarian award, Ancient Mystical Order Rosae Crucis, 2006. Mem.: Internat. Retrovirology Assn. Avocations: music, movies, football. Office: Av Grau Lima Peru E-mail: jcollinslp@hotmail.com.

COLLINS, JAMES WILLIAM, health science association administrator, epidemiologist, mechanical engineer; b. Atlanta, Oct. 19, 1962; s. Thomas Allen and Mary Frank Collins; m. Maria Joao Ponte, Oct. 25, 1992; children: Karina Maria, James Seth. B of Mech. Engring., Ga. Inst. Tech., 1984; MSME, W.Va. U., 1989; PhD in Health Policy and Mgmt., Johns Hopkins U., 1998. Rsch. mech. engr. Ctrs. Disease Control and Prevention, Nat. Inst. Occupl. Safety and Health, Morgantown, W.Va., 1984—90, rsch. epidemiologist, 1992—2004; assoc. dir. sci. Ctrs. Disease Control and Prevention, Nat. Inst. Occupl. Safety and Health, Divsn. Safety Rsch., 2004—. Bd. editors Jour. Injury Control and Safety Promotion, Amsterdam, 2004—; guest lectr. occupational epidemiology Johns Hopkins U; guest lectr. occupational safety and health W.Va. U. Pres. Exch. Club, Fairchance, Pa., 2000—06; fin. com. Mt. Moriah Bapt. Ch., Smithfield, 2004—06. Capt. USPHS, 1984—2005. Recipient Spl. Assignment award, USPHS, 1991, Surgeon Gen Exemplary Svc. medal, 1992, Achievement medal, 1996, Pub. Health Svc. citation, 1996, Crisis Response Ribbon, 2002, Outstanding Unit citation, 2002, U. S. Pub. Health Svc. Engring. Lit. award, Chief Engr. USPHS, 2000, Partnering award Worker Safety and Health, Nat. Inst. Occupl. Safety and Health, 2003, 2006, Alice Hamilton Excellence in Occupl. Safety and Health Human Studies Rsch. award, 2005. Mem.: Commd. Officers Assn. USPHS (pres., v.p., treas. 1984—2005, Mem. of Yr. 1988). Conservative. Baptist. Achievements include research in intervention trials demonstrating highly effective programs to prevent back and other musculoskeletal injuries among health care workers due to patient lifting and slips and falls. Avocations: travel, hunting, fishing, softball, coaching. Office: Ctrs Disease Control & Prevention 1095 Willowdale Rd Mail stop 1900 Morgantown WV 26505 Home: 3415 Halleck Rd Morgantown WV 26508-3643 Business E-Mail: jcollins1@cdc.gov.

COLLINS, JANET L., psychiatrist; B in Clin. Psychology, San Diego State U., 1975, M in Clin. Psychology, 1977; PhD in Ednl. Psychology, Stanford U. Recruited Centers for Disease Control and Prevention, 1990, acting dir. Nat. Ctr. for HIV, Sexually Transmitted Diseases and Tuberculosis Prevention, acting dir. Adolescent and Sch. Health Divsn., dep. dir. Nat. Ctr. Chronic Disease Prevention and Health Promotion, dir. Nat. Ctr. Chronic Disease Prevention and Health Promotion, 2005—09, assoc. dir. for program, 2009—. Named a Disting. Alumnus (Monty award), San Diego State U., 2009. Office: Centers for Disease Control & Prevention Office of Assoc Dir for Program 1600 Clifton Rd Mail Stop D14 Atlanta GA 30333 *

COLLINS, JOHN ALFRED, retired obstetrician, gynecologist, educator; s. John Bandel and Vera Collins; m. Carole Joanne Sedwick West; children: John, Blayne, Anne. MD, U. West Ont., 1960. Resident ob-gyn. U. West Ont., 1961—65; McLaughlin Found. fellow U. Coll. Hosp., London, U. Edinburgh, Scotland, Middlesex Hosp., London, 1965—67; clin. rsch. fellow Ont. Cancer Found. London Clinic, 1967—76; with dept. ob-gyn. U. West Ont., 1967—77, asst. dean undergrad. edn. faculty medicine, 1975—77; prof., head dept. ob-gyn. Dalhousie U., 1977—83; prof., chmn. dept. ob-gyn. McMaster U., Hamilton, Ont., 1983—93; vis. chair internat. Francqui Found. Brussels Free U., 2000—01. Mem. editl. bd. New Eng. Jour. Medicine, 1991-96, Fertility and Sterility, 1991-96, Obstetrics and Gynecology, 2004—07; editor-in-chief Human Reproduction Update, 2007—; contbr. articles to profl. jours. Mem. Royal Coll. Physicians and Surgeons Can., Royal Belgium Acad. Medicine, Royal Coll. Ob-Gyn. U.K., Am. Coll. Ob-Gyn., Am. Soc. Reproductive Medicine, Can. Fertility and Andrology Soc., Soc. Ob-Gyn. Can. Home: 400 Maders Cove Rd RR 1 Mahone Bay NS Canada B0J 2E0 *

COLLINS, JOHN F., hospital administrator; B in Acctg., Queens Coll., Charlotte, NC, 1976. CPA 1982. V.p. Winthrop-Univ. Hosp., Mineola, NY, 1997, CFO, 2007—08, COO, 2007—08, exec. v.p., 2008, Pres., 2009—, CEO, 2009—. Past pres. met. NY chpt. Healthcare Fin. Mgmt. Assn.; past chmn. Nassau-Suffolk Hosp. Coun. Com. on Fin. Mem.: Greater NY Hosp. Assn. (mem. fin. com.), Healthcare Assn. of NY State (mem. fin. com.), AICPA, NY State Soc. of CPAs, Am. Coll. of Healthcare Professionals. Office: Winthrop-University Hospital 259 First St Mineola NY 11501 Office Phone: 516-663-0333. Office Fax: 516-663-2946.

COLLINS, JOHN VINCENT, physician; b. London, Eng., July 16, 1938; s. Thomas Ernest Vincent and Zillah Phoebe Collins; m. Helen Eluned Cash, Oct. 5, 1963; children: Jonathan James, Philippa Helen. MD, Guy's U., 1966. Sr. lectr., cons. physician St. Bartholomews Hosp. & Med. Sch., London, 1973—76; cons. physician Royal Promotion Hosp., 1976—, St. Stephen's Hosp., 1979—88, Westminster Hosp., 1988—94, Chelsea & Westminster Hosp., 1993—. Med. dir. Chelsea & Westminster Hosp., 1994—; med. advisor Benenden Healthcare Soc., York, 1979—, group med. advisor Smith & Nephew plc, London, 1987—. Contbr. articles to profl. jours., chpts. to books. Fellow: Brit. Thoracic Soc. (asst. treas. 1989). Avocations: guitar, painting, tennis. Home Phone: 01580 76 4304; Office Phone: 0207 351 8030, 020 8746 8000. Office Fax: 0207 351 8030. Business E-Mail: john.collins@chelwest.nhs.uk.

COLLINS, MICHAEL F., academic administrator, medical educator; m. Maryellen Collins; children: Michael Jr., Elizabeth. BS cum laude, Coll. of Holy Cross, 1977; MD, Tufts U., 1981. Asst. prof. internal medicine, asst. dean patient care resources Tex. Tech U. Health Scis. Ctr.; clin. prof. internal medicine, assoc. dean govt. and med. affairs Tufts U. Sch. Medicine; sr. fellow U. Coll. Citizenship and Pub. Svc.; pres. St. Elizabeth's Med. Ctr., Brighton, Mass., 1994—2001; pres., CEO Caritas Christi Health Care Sys., 1994—2004; chancellor U. Mass., Boston, 2005—07, sr. v.p. health scis., 2007—; interim chancellor U. Mass. Med. Sch., 2007—08, chancellor, 2008—. Fellow: Am. Coll. Physicians. Office: Office of Chancellor U Mass Med Sch 55 Lake Ave N Worcester MA 01655 Office Phone: 508-856-8100. Office Fax: 508-856-8181. E-mail: michael.collins@umassmed.edu.

COLLINS, MICHAEL J., orthopedist; MD, Loyola Univ. Stritch Sch. Med., Maywood, Ill. Cert. Am. Bd. Orthopaedic Surgery Examiners. Staff physician Hinsdale Hosp., Good Samaritan Hosp., Salt Creek Surgery Ctr., Hinsdale Surg. Ctr.; ptnr. Hinsdale Orthopaedic Assoc., 1983—. Intern, resident Mayo Clinic, St. Paul. Mem.: Internat. Arthroscopy Assn., Ill. State Med. Soc., Arthroscopic Assn. No. Am., Am. Orthopaedic Soc. Sports Medicine, Am. Coll. Sports Med., Am. Acad. Orthopaedic Surgeons. Office: Hinsdale Orthopaedic Assoc 550 W Ogden Ave Hinsdale IL 60521

COLLINS, RICHARD FRANCIS, microbiologist, educator; b. St. Paul, Minn., Jan. 22, 1938; s. Francis Bernard and Maude Roegene (Night) C.; m. Deanne Margaret Scafati, Dec. 28, 1960 (div. 1970); children: Lisa, Mark, Michael; m. Judy A. Wright, Feb. 15, 1978; children: Kristyn, Todd. AB, Shepherd Coll., 1962; MA, Wake Forest U., 1968; PhD, U. Okla., 1973. Tchr. Alexandria (Va.) Schs., 1962-66; instr. U. Okla., Oklahoma City, 1972-73; lab. dir. Infectious Disease Svc. U. Ill./Rockford Sch. of Medicine, 1974-80; asst. prof. U. Ill., Rockford, 1973-80; assoc. prof. U. Osteo. Medicine and Health Scis., Des Moines, 1980-85, faculty pres., 1990-91, pres.-elect, 1997-98, prof., dept. head, 1985-95; prof. Midwestern U., Glendale, 1997—; divsn. head, 1997—2005. Cons. U.S. EPA, Washington, 1975-81; mem. Nat. Bd. Podiatry Examiners, Princeton, N.J., 1983-96, Nat. Bd. Osteo. Med. Examiners, Des Plaines, Ill., 1994-97; participant mission project Christian Med. Soc., Dominican Republic, 1977. Mem. editorial bd. African Jour. Clin. Exptl. Immunology, 1979-83; contbr. articles to profl. jours. Vol. Blank Guild, Iowa Meth. Hosp., Des Moines, 1988-91. Recipient awards NSF, 1962-67, fellowship NIH, 1969-70, Gov.'s Vol. awards State of Iowa, 1988, 89. Mem. Am. Soc. for Microbiology, Am. Soc. Tropical Medicine and Hygiene, Sigma Xi (pres. 1987-90, 96-97, treas. 1990-91). Avocations: photography, auto restoration. Home: 4131 W Tierra Buena Ln Phoenix AZ 85053-3717 Office: Midwestern U Ariz Coll Osteo Medicine 19555 N 59th Ave Glendale AZ 85308-6813 Office Phone: 623-572-3258. Business E-Mail: rcolli@midwestern.edu.

COLLINS, ROBERT ELLWOOD, surgeon; b. Cottage City, Md., Aug. 4, 1932; s. Edward Clarence and Edith (Blough) C.; m. Barbara Kauffmann Murray, June 28, 1964; children: Garret, Randy, Robin, Bill, Bruce, Brad, Beth. BS, Ea. Mennonite Coll., 1954; MD, Med. Coll. Va., 1958. Diplomate Am. Bd. Orthop. Surgeons. Intern Washington Hosp. Ctr., 1958-59, orthopaedic resident, 1961-64; pvt. practice medicine Broadway, Va., 1959-60; resident in gen. surgery Med. Coll. Va., Richmond, 1960-61; pvt. practice medicine specializing in orthop. surgery Washington, 1964—. Acting orthopaedic chief Children's Hosp., 1970—72; chief orthopaedics Washington Hosp. Ctr., 1973—75, vice-chmn. dept. orthopaedics, 1975—80, bd. dirs., pres. med. and dental staff, 1981, 1983—85; assoc. prof. Georgetown U. Hosp., 1975—; courtesy staff Sibley Meml. Hosp.; pres. med. staff Nat. Rehab. Hosp., Washington, 1988—2001; bd. dirs. Medlantic Health Corp., Washington. Bd. dirs. Easter Seal Soc. of Washington and Md., 1986—, chmn. bd. dirs., 1990—92; bd. dirs. Nat. Orthopedic Hosp., Washington, 1990, Nat. Easter Seals Soc., 1995—2001. Recipient Tchg. award Georgetown U., Washington, 1985; Children's Orthop.'s fellow Children's Hosp., 1963, Cerebral Palsy fellow Children's Rehab. Inst. Johns Hopkins U., 1965. Fellow ACS (chmn. DC trauma com.), Am. Acad. Cerebral Palsy, Am. Acad. Orthop. Surgeons, Am. Acad. Orthop. Foot Surgeons; mem. Med. Soc. DC (pres. 1985-86), Washington Clin. Club (past pres.), Georgetown Club, Congl. Country Club (Bethesda, Md.). Presbyterian. Office: Nat Orthopaedics Inc Drs Collins Johnson & Tozzi PC 106 Irving St NW Ste 215 Washington DC 20010-2993 Home Phone: 703-237-5329. E-mail: granbobc@aol.com.

COLLINS, RONALD LESLIE LEOPOLD, neurosurgeon; b. Nov. 19, 1944; Came to U.S., 1979; MB BS, U. W.I., Kingston, Jamaica, 1968. Diplomate Am. Bd. Neurological Surgery, Am. Bd. Minimally Invasive Spinal Surgery. Intern Harlem Hosp. Ctr., 1979-80, resident, 1980-81, King/Drew Med. Ctr., 1985-88; fellow Cook County Hosp., 1984-85, Robert Wood Johnson U. Hosp., 1988-89; neurosurgeon NYC, 1989—. Contbr. articles to profl. jours.; inventor in field. Fellow Royal Coll. Surgery (Edinburgh), Internat. Coll Surgeons, Oxford Med. Alumni, Masons.

COLLINS, STEPHEN BARKSDALE, retired healthcare executive; b. Houston, Mar. 14, 1932; s. Ray George and Ruth Ella (Davis) C.; m. Katherine Jane Justice, June 6, 1955; children: Nancy Catherine, Rebecca Jane, Ruth Anne, Stephen Barksdale, Cynthia Marye. BA, Baylor U., 1954; M.H.A., Washington U., 1956. Asst. adminstr., adminstr. Good Samaritan Hosp., Vincennes, Ind., 1959-65; adminstr. Rosewood Gen. Hosp., Houston, 1965-72; chief exec. officer Lake Charles Meml. Hosp., La., 1972-85; v.p. shareholder rels. and membership VHA, Inc., Irving, Tex., 1985-97; ret., 1997. Bd. dirs. Better Bus. Bur. Served with USAF, 1956-59. Decorated Meritorious Service medal, Commendation medal. Fellow Am. Coll. Hosp. Adminstrs.; mem. C. of C. (dir.), Southeastern Hosp. Conf. (bd. dirs. 1981-82, exec. com. 1983, chmn.-elect 1984), La. Hosp. Assn. (chmn.-elect 1981, chmn. 1982), Am. Hosp. Assn. Clubs: Rotary. Baptist. Home: 1009 Inwood Ln Colleyville TX 76034-3848 Home Phone: 817-281-4150. Personal E-mail: scollins7@sbcglobal.net.

COLLINS, TERRY, health educator; b. Ventura, Calif., Sept. 10, 1950; s. C.E. and Frances Collins; m. Deborah Louise Stonesifer, Dec. 3, 1983; children: Christi, Jeff, Erin. BA in Phys. Edn., Calif. State U. Stanislaus, Turlock, 1972; MEd in Phys. Edn., Azusa Pacific U., Calif., 1990, MA in Sch. Adminstrn., 1992; EdD in Ednl. Leadership, Calif. Coast U., Santa Ana, 2004. Profl. adminstrv. svcs. credential Azusa Pacific U., cert. health specialist Calif., std. secondary edn. Calif. State U.-Stanislaus, pub. safety, accident prevention Calif. Luth. U. Tchr. coach Ventura Unified Sch. Dist., Ventura, Calif., 1973—74; tchr., coach Modesto City Schs., Calif., 1974—85, Oxnard HS, 1985—2010; dir. spl. projects Oxnard Union HS, Oxnard, Calif., 1996—97, summer sch. prin., 1993—96; adminstr. Azusa Pacific U., 1991—2009, assoc. prof., 1991—2009. Editor: (textbook) Health - Making Life Choices, 1999; contbr. articles to health publs. Mem.: CAHPERD, AAHPERD, Am. Fedn. Tchrs.

COLLINS, WILLIAM EDWARD, JR., aeromedical administrator, psychologist, researcher; b. Bklyn., May 16, 1932; s. William Edward and Loretta Agnes (Brasier) C.; m. Corliss Jean Barnes, June 20, 1970; 1 child, Corliss Adora. BS, St. Peter's Coll., Jersey City, 1954; MA, Fordham U., Bronx, NY, 1956, PhD, 1959. Lic. psychologist, Okla. Psychol. rsch. asst. Fordham U., 1954-56, tchg. fellow, 1958, grad. instr., 1958-59, rsch. asst., 1958-59; rsch. psychologist US Army Med. Rsch. Lab., Ft. Knox, Ky., 1959-61; rsch. psychologist Aviation Psychology Lab. FAA Civil Aeromed. Inst., Oklahoma City, 1961-63, chief sensory integration sect., 1963-65, lab. supr., 1965-86, human resources rsch. br. mgr., 1986-88, inst. dep. dir., 1988—89, dir., 1989-2001; tech. profl. Chickasaw Nation Industries-Aviation, 2002—; with FAA Rsch., Engrng. & Devel. Adv. Com.'s, Subcom. Aircraft Safety, 2008—; adj. assoc. prof. psychology U. Okla., Norman, 1963-70, adj. prof., 1970-89; adj. assoc. prof. rsch. psychology dept. psychiatry and behavioral scis. U. Okla. Health Scis. Ctr., Oklahoma City, 1965-71, adj. prof., 1971—; tech. profl. Chicksae Nation Industries, 2002—. Mem. Nat. Acad. Sci.-NRC Com. on Vision, 1963-82, mem. exec. coun., 1973-81; mem. Nat. Acad. Sci.-NRC Com. on Hearing, Bioacoustics and Biomechanics, 1963-87; appearances before House Sub-Com. on Pub. Health and Environ., 1971, House Sub-Com. on Investigations and Oversight, 1983, House Sub-Com. on Transp., Aviation and Materials, 1987, 88; judge Okla. State Sci. and Engrng. Fair, Ada, 1980, 81, 82; mem. Okla. Bd. Examiners Psychologists, 1981-84, chmn., 1982-84; evaluator proposals NSF, 1968-82, HEW, 1971-80; presenter, lectr. in field. Contbr. articles to profl. jours., chapters to books. Served to res. capt. Med. Services Corps, US Army, 1959-61. Recipient Outstanding Achievement award Okla. City Federally Employed Women, 1986, Dept. Transportation Sec. award, 1986, citation for svc. to aviation medicine Okla. State Legislature, 1999, Disting. Career Svc. award FAA, 2001; named to Okla. Aviation and Space Hall of Fame, 2004; named Fed. Employee of Yr. Okla. City Fed. Exec. Coun., 1985, in his honor Ann. award Most Outstanding Scientific, Tech. FAA Pub. Aerospace Medicine, 2003. Fellow AAAS, APA (abstractor Psychol. Abstracts 1962-2002, citation 1973), NY Acad. Scis., Aerospace Med. Assn. (Raymond F. Longacre award 1971, presdl. exec. com. 1982-84, exec. coun. 1982-85, editl. bd. Aviation, Space and Environ. Medicine 1974-2000, assoc. editor 1980-2000, Pres.'s Citation 1993, Harry G. Moseley award 1998, Life Scis. and Biomed. Engrng. Profl. Excellence award 1989, Pres.'s award 1999, Louis H. Bauer Founders award 2007), Am. Psychol. Soc. (charter), Aerospace Human Factors Assn. (charter, Paul T. Hansen award 1998, William E. Collins award publ. excellence in human factors named in his honor 2002); mem. Assn. Aviation Psychologists (pres. 1974-75), Okla. Psychol. Assn. (Disting. Psychologist award 1984), South African Soc. Aerospace and Environ. Medicine (Silver Medal award 1998), Nat. Mus. Am. Indian (charter, cert. of appreciation 1995), US Holocaust Meml. Mus. (charter mem.), Nat. Mus. African Am. History & Culture (charter mem.). Home: 8900 Sheringham Dr Oklahoma City OK 73132-4764 Office: Dept Psychiat Behavior Sci Okla U Health Sci Ctr Williams Pavillion Oklahoma City OK 73190-3048

COLLIS, STEVEN H., pharmaceutical executive; b. South Africa; B in Commerce with honors, U. the Witwatersrand, Johannesburg. Lic. in charter accountancy, 1986. Mem. Johannesburg Stock Exch.; prin. and gen. mgr. Sterling Med., Irvine, Calif.; gen. mgr. ASD Specialty Healthcare, Inc., 1994—96, exec. v.p., 1996—2000, sr. exec. v.p., pres., 2000—01; pres. AmerisourceBergen Specialty Group, Dallas, 2001—09, AmerisourceBergen Drug Corp., 2009—10; exec. v.p. AmerisourceBergen Corp., Valley Forge, Pa., 2007—10, pres., COO, 2010—11, pres., CEO, 2011—. Bd. dirs. Thoratec Corp., 2008—. Active Am. Cancer Soc. Office: AmerisourceBergen Corp 1300 Morris Dr Chesterbrook PA 19087-5594 Office Phone: 610-727-7000. Office Fax: 610-647-0141. *

COLMAN, JENNY MEYER, psychiatrist; b. Livingston, NJ, Apr. 23, 1968; d. Robert Osborne and Margaret Saur Meyer; m. William Woodruff Colman, June 20, 1998; children: Thomas Emory, Sean Robert, Jackson Schuyler, Anna Rose. BA, Harvard Coll., Cambridge, 1990; MD, Columbia Coll., NYC, 1997. Diplomate Am. Bd. Psychiatry and Neurology. Resident in psychiatry Columbia Presbyn./NY Hosp., NYC, 1997—2000, U. Calif., San Francisco, 2000—01; attending psychiatrist St. Mary's Med. Ctr., San Francisco, 2001—03, med. dir. adolescent inpatient unit, 2002—03; pvt. practice San Francisco, 2001—03, Poughkeepsie, NY, 2003—04, Fishkill, NY, 2004—09, Marist Coll., 2007—. Mem.: Am. Acad. Child and Adolescent Psychiatry, Am. Psychiatric Assn. Avocations: hiking, skiing, running, tennis, yoga.

COLMAN, JON, medical association administrator; Joined Nat. Down Syndrome Soc., NYC, 2001, sr. v.p. programs and ops., acting dir., 2006, COO, 2006—07, pres., 2007—. Office: Nat Down Syndrome Soc 666 Broadway 8th Fl New York NY 10012 *

COLMAN, ROBERT WOLF, hematologist, educator; b. NYC, June 7, 1935; s. Jack K. and Miriam (Greenblatt) C.; m. Roberta Fishman, June 16, 1957; children: Sharon, David. AB summa cum laude, Harvard U., Cambridge, Mass., 1956; MD cum laude, Harvard U., 1960. Cert. Internal Medicine, Hematology. Intern Boston City Hosp., 1960-61; resident Beth Israel, Brookline, Mass., 1961-62; clin. assoc. USPHS, NIH, 1962-64; resident Barnes Hosp., St. Louis, 1964-65, fellow in hematology, 1965-67; assoc. in medicine Harvard Med. Sch., Cambridge, Mass., 1967-69, asst. prof., 1969-73, assoc. prof., 1973, U. Pa., Phila., 1973-77, prof. medicine, 1977-78, Temple U. Sch. Medicine, Phila., 1978—, dir. Sol Sherry Thrombosis Rsch. Ctr., 1979—2005, prof. thrombosis rsch., 1981—, Sol Sherry prof. of medicine, 1989—, prof. physiology, 1992—. Hematology study sect. NIH, Bethesda, Md., 1977-81; parent com. to review SCORs in Ischemic Heart Disease; chemistry spl. emphasis panel to review SBIR, STTR grants, NIH, study sect. rev. therapeutic modulation angiogeneic disease, study sect. to rev. tng. grants and careeer devel. awards; invited lectr. Gordon confs., Internat. Congress Hemostasis and Thrombosis, Fedn. Am. Socs. Exptl. Biology; plenary lectr. and chair Gordon Conf. Internat. Soc. Kallikreins and Kinins, others. Editor: Hemostasis and Thrombosis, 5th edit., 2005; editor Platelet Jour.; mem. editorial bd. Jour. Clin. Investigation, Blood, Procs. Soc. Exptl. Biology, Thrombosis Rsch. Platelets, Thrombosis Hemostasis; contbr. numerous articles to profl. jours. Surgeon USPHS, 1962—64. Recipient Leon Resnick prize Harvard U., Career Devel. award NIH, Sr. Investigator award S.E. Pa. chpt. Am. Heart Assn., Disting. Career award Internat. Soc. Thrombosis and Hemostasis. Fellow ACP; mem. Assn. Am. Physicians. Am. Soc. Clin. Investigation, Am. Soc. Biochemistry and Molecular Biology, Internat. Soc. Hemostasis and Thrombosis (councillor 1989-95), Peripatetic Club, Interurban Clin. Club, Phi Beta Kappa, Sigma Xi, Alpha Omega Alpha. Achievements include 8 patents in field. Avocation: travel. Office: Temple U Sch Medicine Sol Sherry Thrombosis Rsch Ctr 3400 N Broad St Philadelphia PA 19140-5104 Office Phone: 215-707-2779. Business E-Mail: colmanr@temple.edu.

COLMAN, WENDY See ERSKINE, KALI

COLMERS, JOHN MICHAEL, health facility administrator, former public health service officer; b. 1953; BA, Johns Hopkins U.; MPH, U. NC, Chapel Hill. Various positions including exec. dir. Md. Health Care Commn. and the Health Services Cost Rev. Commn. State of Md., 1981—2000; sr. program officer Millbank Meml. Fund, NY, 2000—07; sec. Md. Dept. Health & Mental Hygiene, Baltimore, 2007—11; v.p. health care transformation & strategic planning Johns Hopkins Medicine, Baltimore, 2011. Bd. dirs. CareFirst Blue Cross Blue Shield, Inc., 2004—07; chmn. Md. Health Services Cost Review Commn. (HSCRC), 2011—. Contbg. editor: Am. Jour. Pub. Health. Past chmn. steering com. Reforming States Group. Mem.: Bd. Acad. Health (treas.). Office: Johns Hopkins Medicine Baltimore MD 21205 Office Phone: 410-767-6500. *

COLOMBO-BENKMANN, MARIO, surgeon, educator, health economist; b. Falkirk, Eng., Sept. 23, 1963; MD, Heidelberg, Germany, 1988; M in Health Bus. Adminstrn., Nürnberg, Germany, 2009. Cert. in surgery Med. Bd., Münster, Germany, 2002, in proctology Med. Bd., Münster, 2006, in visceral surgery Med. Bd., 2006, in medical quality mgmt. Med. Bd., Münster, 2008. Asst. prof. U. Münster, 2004—. Mem.: ACS, Soc. Surgery Alimentary Tract, Endocrine Soc. Achievements include development of new method for resection of skin tumors; score for dysphagia and regurgitation. Office: Univ Münster Dept Surgery Waldeyerst 1 Münster 48149 Germany Home: Warendorfer Str. 100 48145 Münster Germany Business E-Mail: m.colombo.benkmann@uni-muenster.de.

COLON, ENNIO M., pediatrician; b. Mar. 16, 1962; BS in Biology, U. PR Ctrl., 1983; MD, Universidad Central del Caribe Med. Sch., Bayamon, PR, 1987. Cert. Am. Bd. Pediat. Resident, pediat. Miami Children's Hosp.; fellow, pediat. infectious diseases Tulane Med. Sch., New Orleans, 1990—92; staff mem. South Fla. Pediat. Partners, Miami, Fla. Contbr. several articles to profl. jours.; TV appearance focusing on Autism Awardness. Fellow: Am. Acad. Pediat.; mem.: Nat. Alliance for Autism Rsch., AMA, Medico Americano Acad. Inter-American Doctors. Avocations: soccer, bicycling, swimming. Office: South Fla Pediat Partners 7800 SW 87th Ave #C-350 Miami FL 33173 Office Phone: 305-271-4711. Office Fax: 305-271-8732.

COLON, GUSTAVO ALBERTO, plastic surgeon; b. Ponce, PR, June 14, 1938; s. Gustavo Enrique and Araceli (de Ramery) Colon; m. Nairda Muniz, June 23, 1962 (dec. June 16, 1997); children: Gene, Albert, Lisa, Nairda; m. Carvea Colon, Dec. 31, 2005. BA, Johns Hopkins U., 1960; MD, U. Md., 1964. Diplomate Am. Bd. Plastic Surgery. Intern USPHS Hosp., Balt., 1964—65, resident in surgery New Orleans, 1965—69, chief plastic surgery, 1971—72; resident in surgery Tulane U., New Orleans, 1969—71, clin. prof. plastic surgery, 1972—. Mem. staff East Jefferson Gen. Hosp., Touro Infirmary, Lakeside Hosp., Drs. Hosp. Jefferson, chmn. bd., 1982—85. Served with USPHS, 1964—71. Decorated USCG commendation ribbon. Fellow: ACS; mem.: ACS, AMA, New Orleans Surg. Soc., Am. Cleft Palate Assn., Am. Soc. Aesthetic Surgery, Am. Burn Assn., Am. Soc. Plastic & Reconstructive Surgery. Roman Catholic. Home: 321 Rue Saint Peter Metairie LA 70005-3473 Office: 4224 Houma Blvd Ste 120 Metairie LA 70006 Office Phone: 504-888-4297. E-mail: gacolon@bellsouth.net.

COLONE, MARISA, research scientist; b. Sora, Italy, June 23, 1975; Degree in Med. Biotech., Tor Vergata U., Rome, 2006; PhD student in Microbiology, U. Cattolica del Sacro Cuore. Rsch. scientist Inst. Superiore di Sanità, 1999—. Recipient award, Assn. Italiana Colture Cellulari, Soc. Italiana di Sci. Microscopiche. Avocation: scuba diving. Office: Viale Regina Elena 299 Rome 00161 Italy Office Fax: 00390649902137.

COLONIAS, ATHANASIOS, radiation oncologist; MD, Northeastern Ohio U. Diplomate Am. Bd. Radiology-radiation oncology. Practice West Pa. Allegheny Health System Radiation Oncology Network; intern Mercy Hosp. of Pitts.; asst. prof. radiation oncology Drexel Univ.; resident Allegheny Gen. Hosp., physician. Named one of Top Doctors, Pitts. mag., 2011. Office: Allegheny General Hospital 320 E N Ave Pittsburgh PA 15212 Office Phone: 412-359-3131. Office Fax: 412-359-4108.

COLONNA, VITO DE GENNARO, pharmacologist, medical educator, physician; b. Milano, Lombardia, Italy, Sept. 16, 1954; s. Chiara Colonna and Gaetano De Gennaro; m. Franca Morelli, Mar. 9, 1991; 1 child, Federico. MD, Sch. Medicine, U. Milano, 1980. Cert. specialist in pathology 1983, specialist in clin. pharmacology 2001. Asst. prof. pharmacology U. Milano, 1991—2002, assoc. prof. pharmacology, 2002—. Cons. clin. pharmacology Galeazzi Hosp., Milano, 2008—. Fellow: Italian Soc. Dietetics and Clin. Nutrition, Italian Soc. Clin. Pathology, Italian Soc. Pharmacology, Italian Soc. Cardiology. Avocation: painting. Office: Univ Milano Dept Pharmacology Via Luigi Vanvitelli 32 20129 Milan MI Italy Office Phone: 39 02 50317017. Office Fax: 39 02 50316956. Business E-Mail: vito.colonna@unimi.it.

COLONNIER, MARC LEOPOLD, retired anatomist; b. Quebec, Can., May 12, 1930; m. Lise De Gagne, Oct. 24, 1959; 1 son, Jean. BA, B.Ph., U. Ottawa, 1951, MD, 1959, MS, 1960; PhD, U. Coll. London, 1963. Asst. prof. anatomy U. Ottawa, 1963-65; asst. prof. dept. physiology U. Montreal, Que., Canada, 1965-67; assoc. prof., assoc. fellow neurol. scis. group Med. Research Council Can., 1967-69; prof., head dept. anatomy U. Ottawa, 1969-76; prof. dept. anatomy Laval U., Quebec City, Que., 1976-91; ret., 1991. Recipient Lederle Med. Faculty award, 1966, Charles Judson Herrick award Am. Assn. Anatomists, 1967 Fellow Royal Soc. Can.; mem. Am. Assn. Anatomists; Mem. Soc. Neurosci.; mem. Can. Assn. Anatomists (pres. 1973-75) Clubs: Cajal.

COLONY, PAMELA CAMERON, medical researcher, educator; b. Boston, Apr. 18, 1947; d. Donald Gifford Colony and Priscilla (Adams) Pratley; m. E. Paul Cokely Jr., Apr. 26, 1986 (div. 2000); children: Daniel Patrick Cokely, John Travis Cokely; m. Richard M. Sparling, June 1, 2003. BA, Wellesley Coll., Mass., 1969; PhD, Boston U., Mass., 1976. Rsch. asst. sch. medicine Boston U., 1969-71, U. Hosp., 1971-73, Peter Bent Brigham Hosp., Boston, 1973-75; instr. dept. anatomy Harvard Med. Sch., 1975-77; assoc. staff in medicine Peter Bent Brigham Hosp., Boston, 1976-79; sr. fellow, instr. Harvard Med. Sch., Boston, 1979-81; asst. prof. anatomy and medicine Pa. State Coll. Medicine, Hershey, Pa., 1981-88; assoc. prof. rsch., pre-health advisor Franklin and Marshall Coll., Lancaster, 1988-91; adj. assoc. prof. of surgery Pa. State Coll. Medicine, Hershey, 1988-91, sr. rsch. assoc. dept. surgery, 1991-95; asst. prof. SUNY, Cobleskill, 1995-97, assoc. prof., 1997-99, program dir. histotech., 1995—, prof. biology, 1999—, co-dir. Women in Sci., 1996—. Bd. dirs. N.Y. State Histotechnol. Soc.; ind. assessor Nat. Health and Med. Rsch. Coun., Australia, 1985—98; ad-hoc reviewer NIH and Nat. Cancer Inst., Bethesda, Md., 1986; lectr. and adj. instr. Harrisburg Area Cmty. Coll., 1991—95. Contbr. articles to profl. jours. Fellow Nat. Found. Ileitis and Colitis, 1979-81; grantee Fed. Republic Germany, 1978, Cancer Rsch. Ctr., 1982-83, NIH, 1982-91; Chancellor's Excellence Tchg. award, NY, 2010. Mem.: Nat. Soc. for Histotech., NY Histotechnol. Soc. (bd. dirs. 2001—05), Am. Soc. Clin. Pathology. Avocation: horseback riding. Office: SUNY Cobleskill Dept Natural Scis 111 Schenecta 04 Ave Cobleskill NY 12043

COLPI, GIOVANNI M., urologist; b. Milan, Aug. 10, 1945; Degree in Medicine and Surgery, U. Milano, 1970. Specialization in urology U. Milano, 1975. Asst. urology dept. Magenta Hosp., Milan, 1972—79, sr. registrar, urology dept., 1979—88; head, uroandological surgery dept. Valduce Hosp., Como, 1988—2004; head, andrology unit San Paolo Hosp. U. Milano, 1994—2005, vis. prof. in nephrourology, andrology, 3rd specialization sch. in pediats., 2003, head, andrological urology and IVF unit, 2006—. Cons. Inst. per la Sterilità e la Sessualità, Milan, 1980; vis. prof. in andrology, specialization sch. in ob-gyn. U. Milan, 1989—92, U. Pavia, 1994—2009; vis. prof. in andrology, specialization sch. endocrinology U. L'Aquila, 2002—07; sci. dir. Lodovica Med. Ctr.; cons. andrologist Ct. Law Milano, Futura Diagnostica Medica, Florence, Futura PMA, Florence, Procrea, Lugano. Mem.: European Soc. Human Reprodn. and Embryology, European Assn. Urology, European Acad. Andrology, Rotary Club Internat. Office: Via Vincenzo Monti 52 Milan I-20123 Italy Office Fax: 39.02.48017785. Personal E-mail: gmcolpi@yahoo.com.

COLUCCI, WILSON S., cardiologist; b. Elmira, NY, Sept. 4, 1949; MD, Boston U. Sch. Medicine, 1975. Cardiologist Brigham and Women's Hosp., 1981—96; chief, cardiovasc. medicine Boston U. Med. Ctr., 1997—. Fellow: Am. Coll. Cardiology, Am. Heart Assn.; mem.: Heart Failure Soc. America, Am. Soc. Clin. Investigation, Assn. U. Cardiologists. Office: Boston University Med Ctr Boston MA 02118 Office Fax: 617-638-8712. Business E-Mail: wilson.colucci@bmc.org.

COLWELL, JOHN AMORY, physician; b. Boston, Nov. 4, 1928; s. Arthur Ralph and Jeane (Haskins) C.; m. Jane Kuebler, June 19, 1954(deceased); children: John Clayton, Ann Kimbell, Karen Elizabeth, James Lewis; m.Georgia Van Cleve February 14,2010. AB, Princeton U., 1950; MD, Northwestern U., 1954, MS in Medicine, 1957, PhD in Physiology, 1968. Intern Univ. Hosps., Cleve., 1954-55; resident in internal medicine Passavant Meml. Hosp., Chgo., 1955-57, VA Research Hosp., Chgo., 1959-60; from instr. to assoc. prof. medicine Northwestern U. Med. Sch., 1960-71; fellow in endocrinology and diabetes Northwestern U. Med. Ctr., Chgo., 1960-63; clin. investigator, then chief metabolic sect. VA Research Hosp., 1961-71; prof. medicine Med. U. S.C., Charleston, 1971—2008, emeritus prof. medicine, 2009, dir. endocrinology-metabolism-diabetes div., dept. medicine, 1972-94, dir. diabetes ctr. Charleston, 1994—, rsch. coord., 1973-79; assoc. chief staff rsch. and devel. VA Med. Center, Charleston, 1971-93. Bd. dirs. Am. Diabetes Assn., 1982-88, v.p. 1985, pres. elect 1986, pres., 1987; bd. dirs. S.C. Dabetes Assn., 1971-80/ Author: Clinical Recognition and Treatment of Diabetic Vascular Disease, 1975; co-author: Diabetes and Metabolic Disorders, 1975, 82, Diabetes, Endocrinology and Metabolic Disorders, 1981, Diabetes, 2003; contbr. articles med. jours. Served to capt. M.C. USAF, 1957-59. Grantee: NiH, VA, 1962-94. Master ACP; mem. AAAS, Am. Diabetes Assn., Am. Fedn. Clin. Rsch., Am. Physiol. Soc., Ctrl. Soc. Clin. Rsch., Endocrine Soc., So. Soc. Clin. Investigation. Clubs: Skokie Country (Glencoe, Ill.), Carolina Yacht (Charleston), Yeamans Hall (Charleston), Cloister Inn (Princeton U.). Republican. Episcopalian. Home: 182 Broad St Charleston SC 29401-2429 Business E-Mail: colwelja@musc.edu. *

COLWILL, JACK MARSHALL, physician, educator; b. Cleve., June 15, 1932; s. Clifford V. and Olive A. (Marshall) Colwill; m. Winifred Stedman, 1954; children: James F., Elizabeth Ann, Carolyn. BA, Oberlin Coll., 1953; MD (George Whipple scholar), U. Rochester, 1957. Diplomate Am. Bd. Med. Examiners, Am. Bd. Internal Medicine, Am. Bd. Family Practice. Intern Barnes Hosp., Washington U. Sch. Medicine, St. Louis, 1957—58; resident in medicine U. Washington Affiliated Hosps., Seattle, 1958—60; chief resident U. Hosp., 1960—61; instr. medicine, dir. med. outpatient dept. U. Rochester Sch. Medicine and Dentistry, 1961—62, sr. instr. medicine, dir. med. outpatient dept., 1962—64; asst. dean, asst. prof. medicine, asst. prof. cmty. health and med. practice U. Mo. Sch. Medicine, Columbia, 1964—67, assoc. dean, asst. prof., 1967—69, assoc. dean for acad. affairs, asst. prof., 1969—70, assoc. dean, assoc. prof., 1970—76, interim chmn. dept. family and cmty. medicine, 1976—77, prof., 1976—97, prof. emeritus, 1999—, chmn. dept., 1977—97, interim dean, 2000. Cons. Bur. Health Manpower, NIH, 1969—75, Office Divsn. Dir. USPHS, 1977—; mem. Coun. on Grad. Med. Edn. Health Resources and Svcs. Adminstrn., 1990—96. Contbr. articles to profl. jours. Chair commn. on Gulf War and Health Inst. of Medicine, NAS, 1999—2003; dir. Robert Wood Johnson Found. Generalist Physician Initiative, 1991—2000; bd. dirs. Am. Bd. Family Medicine, 1998—2003. Mem.: AMA, Inst. Medicine NAS, Am. Acad. Family Physicians (commn. on govtl. legis. affairs 1984—87), Soc. Tchrs. Family Medicine (bd. dirs. 1978—82, 1983—87, pres.-elect 1987—88, pres. 1988—89), Assn. Med. Am. Colls. (chmn. Midwest-Gt. Plains Group on Student Affairs 1971—73, nat. vice chmn. group 1973—74, chmn. working group on non-cognitive assessment 1974—77, adv. to com. on admissions assessment 1974—77), Alpha Omega Alpha. Office: U Mo-Columbia Sch Medicine Dept Family And Medicine Columbia MO 65212-0001 Office Phone: 573-882-2165. Business E-Mail: colwillj@health.missouri.edu.

COMBS, STEPHEN PAUL, pediatrician, health facility administrator; b. Bristol, Tenn., Feb. 11, 1966; s. Paul Willis and Janis Rose C. BS, East Tenn. State U., 1988, MD, 1992; M in Fin., U. NC, 2008. Cert. physician exec. Am. Coll. Physician Execs.; diplomate Nat. Bd. Med. Examiners. Resident pediat. Duke U., Durham, NC, 1992—95, chief pediat. residents Duke Children's Hosp., 1994—95; ptnr. Mountain Region Pediats., Kingsport, Tenn., 1995—98, sec., 1998—; pediatrician Gray Sta. Pediat., Tenn., 1999—; v.p. med. affairs Holston Valley Med. Ctr., 2006—09. Dir. pediat. intensive care Wellmont Health Sys., 1998—2006, chmn. pediat. critical care, 1996—2006, chief med. office, 2008—10; chmn. dept. pediat. Indian Path Med. Ctr., 1999—2003; mem. med. adv. bd. Am. Homepatient, Nashville, 1995—98; mem. child fatality rev. bd. jud. Dist. II State of Tenn., 1995—; bd. dirs. Wellmont Holston Valley Med. Ctr., chief staff, 2006; med. dir. clin. trials program Highlands Physicans Inc., 2001—04, bd. dirs., mem. various coms.; assoc. clin. prof. pediat. East Tenn. State U., 2002—05, clin. prof. pediat., 2005—; bd. dirs. Highlands Wellmont Health Network, vice chmn., 2008—; vice-chair, physicians exec. com. Wellmont Physician Svcs., 2005—, pres., CEO, 2007—, sys. sr. v.p. for med. affairs, 2007—, chief med. officer, chief acad. officer, 2009—. Contbr. articles to profl. jours. Recipient Forty Under 40 award, Bus. Jour., Health Care Hero award, 2003, 2007. Fellow Am. Acad. Pediat. (resident rep. 1993-95, program chmn. Tenn. chpt. 2000, nominating chair Tenn. chpt. 2001, fellow at large 2005—), Am. Soc. Clin. Pediat., Am. Bd. Pediat., Am. Bd. Forensic Examiners, Am. Soc. Clin. Pediat.; mem. AMA, Tenn. Med. Assn., N.C. Med. Assn., Duke Med. Alumni Assn., East Tenn. State U. Med. Alumni Assn. (rep. 1992—), Alpha Omega Alpha. Republican. Baptist. Avocations: revolutionary war, skiing, golf. Home: 405 Westfield Pl Kingsport TN 37664-6410 Office: Gray Sta Pediat 2103 Forest Dr Ste 5 Gray TN 37615-8423 Business E-Mail: stephen_p_combs@wellmont.org.

COMBS, THOMAS J., retired insurance company executive, museum director; BA, Union Coll., Schenectady, NY, BSEE, 1970—74; MBA, U. Pa., Phila., 1975—77. Trainee Gen. Elec. Co., 1974—75; mgr. bus. planning PEPSICO Inc., 1977—84; regional controller Ecolab Inc., 1985—87; dir. fin. Ecolab Canada Ltd., 1987—90; gen. mgr. G.H.Wood & Co. - div Ecolab Inc., 1990—91; sr. v.p., CFO MVP Health Care (merged with Preferred Care), Rochester, NY, 1994—2005, exec. v.p., CFO, 2006—10; dir. ops. and fin. George Eastman House, 2011—. Office: Preferred Care 259 Monroe Ave Rochester NY 14607 also: George Eastman House 900 E Ave Rochester NY 14607 Office Phone: 585-271-3361. *

COMEROTA, ANTHONY JAMES, vascular surgeon, biomedical researcher; b. Newark, Aug. 4, 1948; s. Louis Anthony and Eleanor Dorothy (Dombroski) C.; m. Elsa Benavides, Aug. 18, 1973; children: Anthony James, Maya Christine, Mark Anthony. BA, Millikin U., 1970; MD, Temple U., 1974. Diplomate Am. Bd. Surgery. Surg. resident Temple U. Hosp., Phila., 1974-78; vascular surgery fellow Good Samaritan Hosp., Cin., 1979-81; from asst. prof. to prof. surgery Temple U. Hosp, Temple U. Sch. Medicine, Phila., 1981-88, prof. surgery, chief vascular surgery, 1988—2002; dir. Ctr. for Vascular Diseases Temple U. Hosp., Temple U. Sch. Medicine, Phila., 1995—2002; dir., chief vascular surgery Jobst Vascular Ctr., Toledo; clin. prof. U. Mich., Ann Arbor, 2002—. Editor: Thrombolytic Therapy for Peripheral Vascular Disease, 1995; co-editor: Prevention of Venous Thromboembolism, 1994. Named America's Top Drs., Castle Connolly; named one of Top 25 Most Influential Drs., Vein Mag., 2009. Fellow ACS, Royal Australian Coll. Surgeons; mem. Am. Surg. Assn., Soc. Vascular Surgery, Peripheral Vascular Soc. (pres. 1988-89), Am. Venous Forum (pres. 2000-01), Phila. Acad. Surgery (pres. 1996-97), Temple U. Sch. Medicine Alumni Assn. (pres. 1993-95), Alpha Omega Alpha. Office: Jobst Vascular Ctr 2109 Hughes Dr # 400 Toledo OH 43606 Office Phone: 419-291-2088. Business E-Mail: anthony.comerotamd@promedia.org.

COMI, RICHARD J., endocrinologist; MD, Harvard Coll., 1980. Diplomate Am. Bd. Internal Medicine, 1983, Am. Bd. Internal Medicine-endocrinology, diabetes and metabolism, 1987, lic. NH. Resident internal medicine Mass. Gen. Hosp., 1981—83; fellow endocrinology and metabolism NIH, Bethseda, Md., 1983—86; sect. chief, endocrinology, diabetes and metabolism Dartmouth-Hitchcock Med. Ctr., 1988—. Office: Dartmouth-Hitchcock Medical Center Endocrinology One Medical Center Dr Lebanon NH 03756 Office Phone: 603-650-8630. Office Fax: 603-650-2240.

COMINS, JONATHAN DAVID, physical therapist; b. Watertown, Mass., June 30, 1960; BSc in Phys. Therapy, U. Copenhagen, 1993, PhD student. Staff phys. therapist Copenhagen U. Hosp., Bispebjerg, 1992—2005; rsch. coord. Sahva Inc., 2005—. Avocations: skiing, soccer, basketball. Office: Borgervaenget 5 Copenhagen 2100 Denmark Business E-Mail: jonathan.comins@sahva.dk.

COMITER, CRAIG, medical educator; b. NYC, Sept. 6, 1966; MD, Harvard Med. Sch., 1992. Assoc. prof., urology Stanford U. Sch. Medicine, 2008—. Mem.: Internat. Continence Soc., Soc. Female Urology and Urodynamics, Am. Urol. Assn. Office: 300 Pasteur Dr Rm S-287 Stanford CA 94305-5118 Business E-Mail: ccomiter@stanford.edu.

COMLEY, ANITA LOUISE, oncological nurse; b. Allentown, Pa., July 17, 1956; d. Daniel Stanley and Marion Louise (Schrope) Graver; m. John Alec Comley, Jr., July 12, 1980; children: Eric John, Scott Daniel. BSN, Ind. U., Pa., 1978; MSN, Gwynedd-Mercy Coll., 1988; postgrad., Tex. Women's U., 1992—. RN, Tex., cert. oncology nurse. Supr., staff devel. critical care Suburban Gen. Hosp., Norristown, Pa., 1978-87; critical care nurse Skilled Nursing, Inc., Flourtown, Pa., 1987-89, oncology nurse HCA Med. Ctr. of Plano, Tex., 1990-94; prof. nursing Collin County C.C., McKinney, Tex., 1989-94; grad. teaching asst. Tex. Women's U., Dallas, 1994-95; oncology nurse Baylor U. Med. Ctr., Dallas, 1993—. Lectr. Baylor U. Sch. Nursing, Dallas, 1995—. Authur: (with others) Theory Construction and Testing, 1995, contbr. articles to profl. jours. Chair adminstrv. coun. 1st United Meth. Ch., Lucas, Tex. 1993—, mem. archtl. control bd. Seis Lagos Homeowner's Assn., Lucas, 1993-94. Recipient Outstanding Faculty Sci. and Health award Nat. Inst. for Staff Devel., 1991, Amgen Rsch. grant Oncology Nursing Found., 1995, Profl. Nurse Traineeship grant, 1994-95. Mem. ANA, Tex. State Nurses Assn., Oncology Nursing Soc., Sigma Theta Tau (Beta Beta chpt.). Republican. Avocation: aerobic dance. Home: 202 Carriage Trl Wylie TX 75098-8248 Office: Baylor Sch Nursing 3700 Gaston Ave Dallas TX 75246-1505 *

COMMONER, BARRY, biologist, educator; b. Bklyn., May 28, 1917; s. Isidore and Goldie (Yarmolinsky) C.; m. Lisa Feiner, 1980; children by previous marriage: Lucy Alison, Frederic Gordon. AB with honors, Columbia U., 1937; MA, Harvard U., 1938, PhD, 1941; DSc (hon.), Hahnemann Med. Coll., 1963, Clark U., 1967, Grinnell Coll., 1968, Lehigh U., 1969, Williams Coll., 1970, Ripon Coll., 1971, Colgate U., 1972, Cleve. State U., 1980; LLD (hon.), U. Calif., 1974, Grinnell Coll., 1981; DSc (hon.), St. Lawrence U., 1988; DHL (hon.), Lowell U., 1990; DSc (hon.), Conn. Coll., 1992, Queens Coll., 2001. Asst. biology Harvard, 1938-40; instr. biology Queens Coll., 1940-42; asso. editor Sci. Illus., 1946-47; asso. prof. plant physiology Washington U., St. Louis, 1947-53, prof., 1953-76, chmn. dept. botany, 1965-69; dir. Washington U. (Center for the Biology of Natural Systems), 1965-81, Univ. prof. environ. sci., 1976-81; prof. dept. geology Queens Coll., Flushing, NY, 1981-87, prof. emeritus, 1987—, dir. Center for the Biology of Natural Systems, 1981-2000, sr. scientist, 2000—. Vis. prof. cmty. health Albert Einstein Coll. of Medicine, N.Y.C., 1981-87; disting. univ. prof. indsl. policy U. Mass., Lowell, 1992-95; pres. St. Louis Com. for Nuclear Info., 1965-66, bd. dirs., 1966; mem. Nat. Tb Commn. on Air Conservation, 1966-68; bd. dirs. Scientists Inst. Pub. Info., 1963—, co-chmn., 1967-69, chmn., 1969-78, chmn. exec. com., 1978—; chmn. spl. cons. group sonic boom Dept. Interior, 1967-68; mem. adv. coun. on environ. edn. Office Edn., HEW, 1971; mem. internat. sponsoring com. Chaim Weizmann Centenary Celebration, 1974-75; mem. adv. com. Coalition Health Communities, 1975; mem. sec.'s adv. coun. Dept. Commerce, 1976; mem. sci. adv. coun. on dioxin Vietnam Vets. Am. Found., 1985—; mem. sci. adv. bd. N.Y. State Com. on Sci. and Tech., 1981—; mem. adv. bd. Com. for Responsible Genetics, 1983—. Author: Science and Survival, 1966, The Closing Circle, 1971 (Phi Beta Kappa award), (Internat. prize City of Cervia, Italy), La Technologia del Profitto, 1973, The Poverty of Power, 1976 (Premio Iglesias award, Sardinia, Italy 1978), Ecologia e Lotte Sociali, 1976, l'energia alternativa, 1978, The Politics of Energy, 1979 (Premio Iglesias award 1982), Se Scoppia La Bomba, 1984, Il Cerchio Da Chiudere, 1986, Making Peace With the Planet, 1990; editorial bd. World Book Ency., 1968-73, Environment mag., 1977; mem. adv. bd. Science Year, 1967-72; editorial adv. bd. Hon. Chemosphere, from 1972; bd. sponsors In These Times, 1976—. Bd. cons. experts Rachel Carson Trust for Living Environment, 1967—; adv. com. Center for Devel. Policy, 1978; mem. bd. Univs. Nat. Anti-War Fund; adv. bd. Fund for Peace, 1978, Citizens Party candidate for pres. of U.S., 1980. Served to lt. USNR, 1942-46. Recipient Newcomb Cleveland prize AAAS, 1953; 1st Humanist award Internat. Humanist and Ethical Union, 1970; medal AIA, 1979; decorated comdr. Order of Merit Italy, 1977 Fellow AAAS (chmn. com. sci. in promotion of human welfare 1958-65, dir. 1967-74, chmn. com. on environ. alterations 1969-72), Am. Sch. Health Assn. (hon.); mem. Soc. Biol. Chemists, Soc. Gen. Physiologists, Am. Soc. Plant Physiologists, Sierra Club, Nat. Parks Assn. (trustee 1968-70), Soil Assn. Eng. (hon. life v.p.), Am. Chem. Soc., Am. Soc. Biol. Chemists, Fedn. Am. Scientists, Ecol. Soc. Am., Inst. Environmental Edn. (trustee), Phi Beta Kappa, Sigma Xi. Office: Queens Coll Ctr for Biol Natural Systems Flushing NY 11367 E-mail: commoner@qc.cuny.edu.

COMMONS, GEORGE W., plastic surgeon; b. Johnstown, Pa., 1942; BS, Allegheny Coll., Meadville, Pa.; MD, U. Pa. Sch. Medicine, 1968. Cert. Am. Bd. Plastic Surgery. Intern, plastic surgery Stanford U. Med. Ctr., Calif., 1968—69, fellow plastic surgery, rehabilitation, resident gen., plastic surgery, 1969—74, chief resident plastic, reconstructive surgery; med. dir. Plastic Surgery Ctr., Calif., 1990—2008, Palo Alto Ctr. for Plastic Surgery, Calif., 2008—; staff appointments Menlo Park Surgical Hosp., 1994—2008, Sequoia Hosp., 1976—2008, El Camino Hosp., 1976—2008. Adjunct clinical asst. prof. plastic surgery dept. Stanford U. Hosp.; cons. in field; cons., plastic and reconstructive surgery US Army, USAF, and USN in the Far East, Ctrl. Luzon Gen. Hosp., San Fernando, Republic Philippines, Philippine Air Force; cons., lectr. U. Far East, Manila, Republic Philippines; surgeon-in-charge, plastic and reconstructive Surgery, rehabilitation program for underprivileged children USAF, Philippine Air Force. Contbr. articles to profl. jours. Maj. USAF, chief, plastic and reconstructive surgery USAF Hosp., Clark AFB, Republic Philippines, med. civic action program dir., Clark AFB. Decorated USAF Accommodation medal. Fellow: ACS; mem.: Internat. Soc. Plastic Surgery, AMA, Calif. Soc. Plastic Surgeons, Calif. Med. Assn., Am. Soc. Aesthetic Plastic Surgery, Am. Soc. Plastic Surgery, Military Plastic Surgical Assn., Santa Clara County Med. Soc. Assn., Philippines Plastic Surgical Assn. (hon.), Alpha Omega Alpha. Office: Palo Alto Ctr Plastic Surgery 1515 El Camino Real Ste C Palo Alto CA 94306 Office Phone: 650-328-4570. Office Fax: 650-322-8481. Business E-Mail: gcommons@pacfps.com.

COMO, JOHN J., surgeon; b. NYC, Sept. 18, 1965; MD, U. Medicine and Dentistry, Robert Wood Johnson Med. Sch., NJ, 1995; MPH, Case Western Res. U., 2011. Assoc. dir., trauma surgeon MetroHealth Med. Ctr., 2003—. Assoc. prof. Case Western Res. U., 2003—11. Fellow: ACS. Office: 2500 MetroHealth Dr #H-945 Cleveland OH 44113 Office Fax: 216-778-1351. Personal E-mail: jjc0965@aol.com.

COMP, PHILIP CINNAMON, medical researcher; b. Kewanee, Ill., Feb. 28, 1945; s. Franklin Howard and Alberta (Cinnamon) C.; m. Carol Lee Winter, May 11, 1974; children: Vanessa Cinnamon, Justin Philip, Aubrie Elizabeth. BA, Reed Coll., 1967; MD, U. Wash., 1971; PhD, U. Okla., 1978. Intern, then resident U. Pa. Hosp., Phila., 1971-74; fellow allergy sect. U. Okla. Health Sci. Ctr., Oklahoma City, 1974-76, asst. prof. medicine, 1976-82, assoc. prof. medicine, 1982-88, prof. medicine, 1988—, dir. thrombosis/coagulant lab., 1979—99, dir. gen. clin. rsch. ctr., 2000—04; attending physician med. svc. VA Med. Ctr., Oklahoma City, 1976—, assoc. chief of staff rsch., 1992—; dir. adult sect. Okla. Comprehensive Hemophilia Treatment Ctr., Oklahoma City, 1980—. Affiliated mem. cardiovasc. biology rsch. program Okla. Med. Resident Found., Oklahoma City, 1988—; program dir. Gen. Clin. Rsch. Ctr., 2000—04. Avocation: compost making. Office: VA Med Ctr 921 NE 13th St (151) Oklahoma City OK 73104 Home Phone: 405-720-9326; Office Phone: 405-271-6466.

COMPAGNONE, GAETANO, medical physicist; b. Telese, Italy, Apr. 4, 1963; s. Alfonso Compagnone and Maria D'Andrea; m. Alessandra Morgagni, July 30, 1994. BSc in Physics, U. Bologna, 1988, PhD in Med. Physics, 1991. Qualified expert in radiation protection Italy, 1989. Med. physicist S. Maria Nuova Hosp., Reggio Emilia, Italy, 1988—93, S. Orsola-Malpighi U. Hosp., Bologna, Italy, 1993—. Lectr. U. Bologna, 1996—. Contbr. articles to profl. jours. Mem.: Italian Phys. Soc., Italian Assn. Med. Physics (regional coord. 2002—05), Italian Touring Club. Roman Catholic. Avocations: chess, guitar, sports, travel, movies. Office: UO Fisica Sanitaria Policlinico S Orsola Via Massarenti 9 Bologna 40138 Italy Office Fax: 390516363571. Personal E-mail: gcompa@libero.it. Business E-Mail: gaetano.compagnone@aosp.bo.it.

COMPTE, MARIA EMILIA, physician, educator, administrator; b. Buenos Aires, Jan. 17, 1958; arrived in U.S., 1989, naturalized, 2002; d. Alberto J. Compte and Hilda M. Hostansky. MD, U. Buenos Aires, 1984; MPH, TM, Tulane U., 1992. Cert. Ednl. Commn. for Fgn. Med. Grads., 1995, in tropical medicine and travel health Am. Soc. Tropical Medicine and Hygiene, 2000, lic. Ministry of Health, Argentina, 1984, physician U.S. Med. Licensing Exam. Bd., 1997. Pvt. med. practice, Buenos Aires, 1985—87; med. dir. & program adminstr. Dooley Found. -Intermed, Departamento de Gracias a Dios, Honduras, 1988—91; dep. med. dir. Item Home-Hosp. Corp., Buenos Aires, 1993—94; vol. program dir. Dooley Found.-Intermed Internat., NYC, 1994—2003, v.p. for programs, 2004—; dir. cmty. medicine Mercy Coll., Dobbs Ferry, NY, 1998—2004, asst. prof., 1998—2004; v.p. programs Intermed Internat., 2004—. Bd. dirs. Intermed Internat., NYC; adj. assoc. prof. St. John's U., NYC, 1998—2000, CUNY, NYC, 1998—2001, Adelphi U., Garden City, NY, 1999; asst. prof. LI U., 2007—. Recipient Excellence in Vol. Med. Work award, Friends of the Americas, 1991; fellow, NY Acad. Medicine, 2002. Fellow: Royal Acad. Medicine (UK); mem.: AAUP, APHA, Royal Soc. Tropical Medicine, Argentine-Am. Med. Soc., The Global Health Coun., Infectious Disease Soc. Am. (assoc.), Soc. Tchrs. of Family Medicine (assoc.), Am. Com. on Clin. Tropical Medicine & Traveler's Health, Am. Soc. Tropical Medicine & Hygiene, Tulane Med. Alumni Assn., The Cornell Club, Tulane Club NY. Independent. Roman Catholic. Achievements include design, development, implementation, and evaluation of comprehensive rural health and emergency programs for refugees in Central America. Avocations: anthropology, tennis, trekking. Office: Dooley Found Intermed Internat 420 Lexington Ave Rm 2331 New York NY 10170

COMPTON, PEGGY, dean, educator; b. Inglewood, Calif., July 6, 1959; PhD, NYU, 1993. Prof. & assoc. dean UCLA Sch. Nursing, 1997—. Office: UCLA Sch Nursing 700 Tiverton Ave Los Angeles CA 90266 Business E-Mail: pcompton@sonnet.ucla.edu.

CONACCI-SORRELL, MARALICE, medical researcher; b. Sao Paulo, Brazil, Nov. 15, 1972; PhD, Weizmann Inst. Israel, 2004. Postdoc. rschr. Fred Hutchinson Cancer Rsch. Ctr., 2005—10, staff scientist, 2010—. Office: 1100 Fairview Ave N Seattle WA 98109 Business E-Mail: mconacci@fhcrc.org.

CONAWAY, CARSON CLIFFORD, biochemical toxicologist; b. Alva, Okla., Feb. 19, 1939; s. Carson Henry and Eula Vivian (Sears) C.; m. Donna Rae Bell, May 27, 1968 (dec. Nov. 28, 1990); children: Christin A., Jessica C.; m. Yang-Ming Yang, June 18, 1994. AB in Chemistry, Southwestern Coll., 1960; postgrad., Yale U., 1960-62; MS in Entomology, U. Mo., 1969; PhD, U. Wis., 1974. Diplomate Am. Bd. Toxicology. Toxicologist Texaco, Inc., Beacon, N.Y., 1977-80, project toxicologist, 1980-84; sr. toxicologist Clement Assocs., Arlington, Va., 1984-85; rsch. assoc. Am. Health Found., Valhalla, N.Y., 1986-88, assoc. rsch. scientist, 1988-90, rsch. scientist, 1990—2004. Vis. lectr. N.Y. Med. Coll. Sch. Health Scis. & Practice, Valhalla, 1994—2009, sr. lectr., 2010-, adj. assoc. prof. dept. pharmacology, 1985—, adj. prof. dept. biol. health scis. Pace U., NYC, 2005-; cons. in field; cons. toxicology Conaway Consulting Svcs., 2004-; reviewer ATSDR Toxicol. Profiles, EPA IRIS and PTV risk assessment Documents. Contbr. articles to profl. jours, chpts. to books. Mem. Drew U. Meth. Ch., Carmel, N.Y., 1982-, pres., Drew U. Meth. Mens Group, 1990-96, chmn. staff, Parish Rels. Com., 1999-2001, chmn., Fin. Com., 2001—04, lay leader, 2006-10; co-chmn., Stewardship Com., 2011-. Mem. Am. Chem. Soc., Soc. Toxicology. Avocations: jogging, gardening, cello, church choir. Home and Office: 80 Watermelon Hill Rd Mahopac NY 10541-3918 Home Phone: 845-628-0669. Business E-Mail: ccconaway@verizon.net.

CONCEIÇÃO, ANDRÉ LUIZ COELHO, research scientist; b. Santa Rosa de Viterbo, Brazil, Feb. 14, 1984; PhD, U. Sao Paulo, 2006. Postdoc. rschr. U. Sao Paulo, 2011—. Home: Rua José Chieramonte 21 Santa Rosa de Viterbo SP 14270-000 Brazil Personal E-mail: andre_conceicao@yahoo.com.br.

CONDÉ GREEN, ALEXANDRA, plastic surgeon, researcher; b. Montreal, Que., Can., June 29, 1974; BS, Nat. Bd. Edn., Haiti; MD, Faculte Medecine et de Pharmacie d'Etat d'Haiti, 1998; degree in Plastic and Reconstructive Surgery, Ivo Pitanguy Inst., 2009. Resident in gen. surgery Dept. Digestive Surgery-Laparoscopy, Ctr. Hosp. U. Pointe-a-Pitre, 2005, Hosp. l'Universite d'Etat d'Haiti, 2001—05, chief resident in gen. surgery, 2004—05, plastic surgery cons., 2010; emergency physician, gen. surgeon Drs. without Borders, Medecins sans Frontieres, France, 2005—06; resident in plastic and reconstructive surgery Ivo Pitanguy Inst., 2006—09, chief resident in plastic and reconstructive surgery, 2008—09, fellow in rsch.-prin. investigator, 2009—10; fellow in cranio-maxillofacial surgery Mass. Gen. Hosp. & Boston Ctr., 2010. Prof. surg. anatomy Faculte Medecine et Pharmacie d'Etat d'Haiti, 2003—05; plastic surgery rsch. investigator ADIPOSE stem cells U. Md., Balt. Contbr. articles to profl. jours., chapters to books. Fellow: Internat. Coll. Surgeons; mem.: AMA, Ex-Alumni Assn. Prof. Illouz, Haitian Med. Assn., Ex-Alumni Assn. Prof. Pitanguy. Avocations: writing, dance, travel, languages. Home: 1875 Leclair Cres Ottawa ON Canada K1E 3S2 Personal E-mail: acondegreen@yahoo.com.

CONDON, ROBERT EDWARD, surgeon, educator, consultant; b. Albany, NY, Aug. 13, 1929; s. Edward A. and Catherine (Kilmartin) C.; m. Marcia Jane Pagano, June 16, 1951; children: Sean Edward, Brian Robert. AB, U. Rochester, 1951, MD, 1957; MS, U. Wash., 1965. Diplomate Am. Bd. Surgery, Nat. Bd. Med. Examiners. N.Y. Bd. Regents scholar U. Rochester, 1957; intern King County Hosp., Seattle, 1957-58; resident dept. surgery U. Wash. Sch. Medicine (and affiliated hosps.), 1958-65; postdoctoral rsch. fellow Nat. Heart Inst., 1961-63; asst. prof. surgery Baylor Coll. Medicine, Houston, 1965-67; assoc. prof. surgery U. Ill. Coll. Medicine, Chgo., 1967-69, prof., 1969-70; prof., head dept. surgery U. Iowa Coll. Medicine, Iowa City, 1971-72; prof. surgery Med. Coll. Wis., Milw., 1972—98, prof. emeritus, 1998, chmn. dept. surgery, 1979-95; chief surg. svcs. Wood VA Hosp., Milw., 1972-81. Attending surgeon Froedtert Meml. Luth. Hosp., 1982-98; cons. Columbia Hosp., Milw., St. Joseph Hosp., Milw.; clin. prof. surgery U. Wash., 2000-08, clin. prof. emeritus, 2008-. Author: (with others) Abdominal Pain: A Guide to Rapid Diagnosis, 2d edit., 1995, Manual of Surgical Therapeutics, 9th edit., 1996, Hernia, 4th edit., 1995, Surgical Care, 1980. Recipient sr. class award as Outstanding Faculty Mem. Baylor U. Coll. Medicine, 1966, Excellence in Tchg. award Phi Chi, 1967, Cert. Appreciation U. Iowa Coll. Medicine, 1971, Tchr. of Yr. award U. Iowa Coll. Medicine, 1972, Tchr. of Yr. award Med. Coll. Wis., 1983, 95, Disting. Svc. award Med. Coll. Wis., 1993, Disting. Alumnus award U. Wash., 1998; rsch. fellow Guggenheim Found., 1963-64. Mem. ACS (bd. govs.), Am. Surg. Assn. (v.p.), Surg. Infection Soc. (pres.), Am. Assn. Surgery of Trauma, Internat. Soc. Surgery, Collegium Internationale Chirurgiae Digestivae (pres.), Assn. for Acad. Surgery, Ctrl. Surg. Assn. (pres.), So. Surg. Assn., We. Surg. Assn., Wis. Surg. Soc. (pres.), Milw. Surg. Soc. (pres.), Chgo. Surg. Soc., Soc. Univ. Surgeons, Soc. Clin. Surgery, Milw. Acad. Medicine, Soc. Surgery Alimentary Tract (v.p.), Milw. Acad. Surgery (pres.). Mailing: 725 9th Ave Apt 605 Seattle WA 98104 Personal E-mail: recrecmd@comcast.net.

CONDON, STANLEY CHARLES, retired gastroenterologist; b. Glendale, Calif., Feb. 1, 1931; s. Charles Max and Alma Mae (Chinn) C.; m. Vaneta Marilyn Mabley, May 19, 1963; children: Lori, Brian, David. BA, La Sierra Coll., 1952; MD, Loma Linda U., Calif., 1956. Diplomate Nat. Bd. Med. Examiners, Am. Bd. Internal Medicine, Am. Bd. Gastroenterology; recertified Nutritional Support Physician 2008. Intern LA County Gen. Hosp., 1956-57, resident gen. pathology, 1959-61, active jr. attending staff, 1964-65; resident in internal medicine White Meml. Med. Ctr., LA, 1961-63, attending staff out-patient clinic, 1963-64; dir. intern-resident tng. program Manila Sanitarium and Hosp., 1966-71, med. dir., 1971-72; chief resident internal medicine out-patient clinic Loma Linda U. Med. Ctr., 1972-74, attending staff, asst. prof. medicine, 1976-91, med. dir. nutritional support team, 1984—2007, assoc. prof. medicine, 1991—2010; fellow in gastroenterology Barnes Hosp./Wash. U., 1974-76. Contbr. articles to profl. jours. Capt. U.S. Army, 1957-59. Fellow: ACP; mem.: AMA, San Bernardino County Med. Soc., So. Calif. Soc. Gastroenterology, Calif. Med. Assn., Am. Gastroent. Assn., Am. Soc. for Parenteral and Enteral Nutrition. Republican. Seventh-day Adventist. Avocations: trombone, choral singing, camping, hiking, gardening. Home: 11524 Ray Ct Loma Linda CA 92354-3630 Office: Loma Linda U Med Ctr 11370 Anderson St Loma Linda CA 92354-3450 Office Phone: 909-558-4000 ext. 4905. Business E-Mail: vcondon@llu.edu.

CONDRY, ROBERT STEWART, retired hospital administrator; b. Charleston, W.Va., Aug. 16, 1941; s. John Charles and Mary Louise (Jester) C.; m. Mary Purcell Heinzer, May 21, 1966; children: Mary-Lynch, John Stewart. BA, U. Charleston, 1963; MBA, George Washington U., 1970. Asst. hosp. dir. Med. Coll. of Va., Richmond, 1970-73, assoc. adminstr., 1973-75; assoc. hosp. dir. McGaw Hosp., Loyola U., Maywood, Ill., 1975-84, hosp. dir., 1984-93, ret., 1993. Pres. Inter-Hosp. Planning Assn. of Western Suburbs, Maywood, 1983-93; bd. dirs. PentaMed, Inc., San Antonio. Bd. dirs. Met. Chgo. Healthcare Coun., 1985-93, mem. exec. com., 1989-93; bd. dirs. Cath. Hosp. Alliance, 1992, chmn. bd. dirs., 1992, mem. exec. com. 1988-94; mem. Ill. Gov.'s Adv. Bd. on Infant Mortality Reduction, 1988-93, Rev. Bd. on Emergency Medicine Svcs., 1989-93. With U.S. Army, 1964-66. Recipient preceptorship George Washington U., 1985, U. Chgo., 1984, St. Louis U., 1984, Tulane U., 1984, Yale U., 1991. Fellow Am. Coll. Healthcare Execs., Am. Acad. Med. Adminstrs.; mem. Am. Hosp. Assn., Cath. Hosp. Assn., Am. Mgmt. Assn. Republican. Roman Catholic. Avocations: golf, tennis, camping, travel. E-mail: carmelcondry@comcast.net.

CONEY, PONJOLA, dean, medical educator; MD, U. Miss. Med. Ctr.; resident, U. N.C. Prof., chmn. dept. obstet. and gynecology So. Ill. U. Sch. Medicine, 1995; dean medicine, sr. v.p. health affairs, prof. ob-gyn. Meharry Med. Coll. Sch. Medicine, 2002—07; sr. assoc. dean faculty affairs, prof. ob-gyn., dir. Ctr. on Health Disparities Va. Commonwealth U. Sch. Medicine, 2007—. Rschr. in field. Contbr. over 40 pubs. in med. lit. Mem.: Hedwig van Amerigen Exec. Leadership Acad. Medicine Program, Soc. Exec. Leadership in Acad. Medicine (founding dir.). Achievements include first to do an invitro-fertilization procedure in the state of Nebraska. Office: Va Commonwealth University Deans Office PO Box 980565 Richmond VA 23298-0501 Office Phone: 804-628-1701. Business E-Mail: pconey@vcu.edu. *

CONG, FU, international organization administrator; b. China; married; 1 child. Grad., Fgn. Affairs Coll., Beijing; student, Polytechnic Ctrl. London. Joined Chinese Fgn. Ministry, 1987, served in posts based in Beijing, Geneva and Vienna, dep. dir. gen., arms control dept., 2003—04, dep. dir. gen., fgn. affairs dept. Xinjiang Autonomous Region, 2004—05, min. counsellor, Chinese Permanent Mission to the UN and Internat. Orgns. Geneva, 2005—07; advisor to the dir. gen. WHO, Geneva, 2007—. Office: WHO avenue Appia 20 1211 Geneva Switzerland *

CONG, HONGLIANG, physician; b. Dalian, June 18, 1962; MD, Tianjin Med. U., 1995. Dr. in chief, head Inst. Cardiology Tianjin City Tianjin Chest Hosp., 2006—. Office: Heping Dist Xi'an Rd 93# Tianjin 300051 China Business E-Mail: hongliangcong@126.com.

CONGDON, CHARLES C., pathologist, researcher; b. Dunkirk, NY, Dec. 13, 1920; s. Charles C. and Jessie Goldie Congdon; m. Margaret Louise Ribble, Apr. 12, 1947 (div. Aug. 1967); children: Dune, Mary Dawn, Claudia, Kyle E., Lara Paige; m. Marjorie Ann Davis, Nov. 18, 1967. BA, U. Mich., 1942, MD, 1944, MS, 1950. Diplomate Am. Bd. Pathology. Intern Bellevue Hosp., NYC, 1944—45; med. officer U.S. Army, 1944—47; instr. pathology U. Mich., Ann Arbor, 1948—51; vis. scientist, med. officer Nat. Cancer Inst., Bethesda, Md., 1951—55; group leader Oak Ridge (Tenn.) Nat. Lab., 1955—73; prof. med. biology U. Tenn., Knoxville, 1966—83, prof. emeritus, 1983—. Contbr. articles and reports to profl. jours. Mem. Inst. Study of Human Knowledge, Los Altos, Calif.; bd. dirs. emeritus Gene Rsch. Access Corp., Oak Ridge; bd. dirs. Ea. Tenn. Alzheimer's Assn., 2000—01. Capt. US Army, 1944—47, U.S. and Europe. Mem.: FASEB (emeritus), AMA (emeritus), Am. Assn. Cancer Rsch., Transplantation Soc., Internat. Soc. Hematology (emeritus), Internat. Soc. Exptl. Hematology (editor Exptl. Hematology 1st series 1957—70, emeritus), Soc. Exptl. Biology and Medicine (emeritus), Am. Soc. Investigative Pathology (emeritus), Am. Soc. Clin. Investigation (emeritus), Knoxville Acad. Medicine (emeritus), Tenn. Med. Assn. (emeritus), Sigma Xi.

CONKLIN, DONALD RANSFORD, retired pharmaceutical executive; b. Bound Brook, NJ, Sept. 10, 1936; s. Walter Ransford and Dorothy Ann (Haase) C.; m. Louise Sealey, July 13, 1960; children: Elizabeth, Edward. BA, Williams Coll., 1958; MBA, Rutgers U., 1961; grad. program for mgmt. devel., Harvard U., 1970. Dir. mktg. Schering Corp. U.S.A. (name changed to Schering-Plough 1971), Kenilworth, NJ, 1970-74; dir. mktg. Europe div. Schering-Plough, Lucerne, Switzerland, 1975-76, v.p. internat. mktg. Kenilworth, 1977-79, regional dir., sr. v.p. Latin Am. div. Miami, Fla., 1980-83, sr. v.p. internat. hdqrs. Kenilworth, 1984—, pres., 1985, group v.p. pharm. ops., 1983, exec. v.p. pharm. ops., 1984—85, pres. pharm. ops., 1985—94, pres. healthcare products, 1994-96; ret., 1996. Home: 66 Youngs Rd Basking Ridge NJ 07920

CONKLIN, SUSAN JOAN, education specialist, psychotherapist, educator, reading specialist, television personality, realtor; b. Bklyn., Feb. 7, 1950; d. Joseph Thomas Hallek and Stella Joan Kuceluk; m. John Lariviere Conklin, July 25, 1961; children: Genevieve Therese, Michelle Therese. BA, CCNY, 1972; MSW, Hunter Coll., NYC, 1975; EdS, Simmons Coll., 2008. Master clin. social worker; lic. NJ Real Estate 2003, cert. high, mid. sch. educator. Shop counselor Assn. for Help of Retarded Citizens, NYC, 1971-75; dir. social svcs., acting exec. dir. North Berkshire Assn. for Retarded Citizens, North Adams, Mass., 1975-77; project dir. Title XX tng. grant State of Mass., North Adams, 1978-79; pvt. practice Williamstown, Mass., 1979—; jr. realtor assoc. Century 21 Alliance. Adj. asst. prof. Mass. Coll. Liberal Art, 1977—2000, Berkshire CC, Pittsfield, Mass., 1985—86, Pittsfield, 1995—; docent Clark Art Inst., 1995—; Therapeutic Touch practitioner, 1978—; talk show host Pub. Access TV, 1998—2003; bd. dirs. Willinet TV Channel 17, 1999—2003; vol. Salvation Army. WTC Disaster Relief Family Assistance Ctr., 2001, 9/11 United Svcs. Group, 2002; adj. faculty Springfield Coll. Sch. Social Work, 2002, Pittsfield, Mass., 2007—09, Baypath Coll., 2009—10, Darrow Sch., 2009—10, Molly Stak Elem., 2010—. Pres. Williamstown PTO, 1989—91; bd. dirs., edn. com., spl. events coord. Hospice No. Berkshire, Inc., 1989—94; fundraising coord. Mainland Regional Edn. Found., Linwood, NJ, 2004—06; sec. bd. trustees Pumpkin Hollow Farm. Recipient Cmty. Svc. award, Salvation Army, North Berkshire, Mass., 2004; named Berkshire County Social Worker of Yr., 1999, Mass. Social Worker of Yr., 2002. Mem.: LWV, NASW (bd. dirs. 1981—83, regional coun. mem. 1980—83, 1993—2003), Nurse Healers-Profl. Assn. (trustee 1981—83, rec. sec., editor-in-chief Coop. Connection newsletter 1983—88). Democrat. Episcopalian. Office: Susan Conklin LICSW BCD 85 Hawthorne Rd Williamstown MA 01267-2700 Office Phone: 413-458-9181. E-mail: conklin.susan@gmail.com.

CONN, HAROLD O., hepatologist, nphologist, educator; b. Newark, Nov. 16, 1925; s. Joseph H. and Dora (Kobrin) C.; m. Marilyn Barr, May 2, 1951; children: Chrysanne, Steven A., Dorianne. BS, U. Mich., 1946, MD, 1950; MS, Yale U., 1972. Diplomate: Am. Bd. Internal Medicine. Intern Johns Hopkins Hosp., 1950-51; asst. resident Grace New Haven Community Hosp., 1951-52, chief resident, 1955-56; James Hudson Browne research fellow, 1952-53; dir. med. edn. Middlesex Meml. Hosp., 1956-57; clin. investigator VA, 1957-61; chief med. svc. VA Hosp., West Haven, Conn., 1959-60, chief hepatic rsch. lab., 1961-89; instr. Yale Sch. Medicine, 1955-58, asst. prof., 1958-66, assoc. prof., 1966-71, prof., 1971-91, prof. emeritus, 1991—, dir. continuing med. edn. program, 1988-91; clin. prof. surgery divsn. liver/intestinal transplantation U. Miami, 1996—99, vol., prof. nephrology, 2009, vol., prof. neurosurgery, 2007—. Vis. assoc. prof. Washington U. Sch. Medicine, 1982-83; CEO, Med., Med.-Legal and Consultations; dir. Continuing Med. Edn. dept. medicine Yale U. Sch. Medicine, 1990-92. Author: (with M.M. Lieberthal) The Hepatic Coma Syndromes and Lactulose, 1979, (with J. Rodes M. Nevasa) Spontaneous Bacterial Peritonitis, The Disease, Pathogenesis and Treatment, 2000; co-author: (with G. Klatskin) Histopathology of the Liver, 1990; editor: Cyanidanol in Diseases of the Liver, 1981; (with J. Palmaz, J. Rösch, and M. Rössle) Transjugular Intrahepatic Partal-Systemic Stent-shunts: TIPS, 1995; mem. editl. bd. Gastroenterology, 1970-80, Italian Jour. Gastroenterology, 1977-90, Jour. Internal Medicine, 1988—; assoc. editor Hepatology, 1980-90; book editor: Hepatology, 1985-91; editor: (with J. Bircher) Hepatic Encephalopathy: Management with Lactulose and Related Carbohydrates, 1988, (with J. Bircher) Hepatic Encephalopathy: Syndromes and Therapies, 1994. Bd. dirs. Am. Liver Found., 1977-80. Ensign USNR, 1943-44; 1st lt. USAR, 1953-54, USAFR, 1954-55. Recipient Rorer award, 1973, William Beaumont award clin. rsch., 1974. Fellow ACP, Royal Coll. Physicians; mem. Assn. Am. Physicians, Am. Soc. Clin. Investigation, Internat. Assn. Study Liver, Sydenham Soc. (sec. 1968-88, mem. med. adv. bd. Seminars and Symposia 1974-80), Am. Assn. Study Liver Disease (v.p. 1971, pres. 1972), Am. Fedn. Clin. Rsch., Am. Gastroenterol. Assn. (councillor 1974-77, Hugh Butt-Myles and Shirley Fiterman award for clinical rsch. in hepatology 1990), Nat. Assn. Va. Physicians (bd. dirs. 1986-88, chmn. continuing med. edn. com. 1987-89); hon. mem. Australian Soc. Gastroenterology, Brazilian Assn. for Study of Liver, China Med. Assn. (Shanghai br.; Taiwan), Hungarian Gastroent. Soc. (hon., trustee, bd. dirs. med. libr.), Hampton Beach Club (bd. dirs. 2002—). Home: 1800 S Ocean Blvd Apt 1109 Pompano Beach FL 33062-7919 E-mail: halcon@aol.com.

CONNELL, ALASTAIR MCCRAE, physician; b. Glasgow, Scotland, Dec. 21, 1929; came to U.S., 1970; s. Alex McCrae and Maud (Crawford) C.; m. Joyce Dethlefs, 1983; children: Stewart, Fiona, Alison, Iain, Andrew. BS, U. Glasgow, 1951, MB, ChB, 1954, MD, 1969. Intern Western Infirmary, Glasgow, 1954-55; resident in gastroenterology Cen. Middlesex and St. Mark's Hosp., London, 1957-60; practice medicine specializing in gastroenterology, 1960—91; mem. med. staff Med. Rsch. Coun., 1960-64; sr. lectr. clin. sci. Queen's U., Belfast, No. Ireland, 1964-70; Mark Brown prof. medicine Med. Ctr., U. Cin., 1970-79, dir. digestive diseases, 1970-79, prof. physiology, 1972-79, assoc. dean, 1975-77; dir. Office Clin. Affairs, 1975-77; dean Coll. Medicine, U. Nebr. Med. Ctr., 1979-84, prof. internal medicine, 1979-84; v.p. health scis. Va. Commonwealth U., Richmond, 1984-88; scholar-in-residence Inst. Medicine, 1988-89; vice chancellor health scis. Ea. Carolina U., 1990—91; dir. Office Healthcare Inspections, Dept. Vets. Affairs, Washington, 1991-96; adj. prof. med. George Washington U., 1992-97; prof. kinesiology and health scis. Coll. William and Mary, 2005—. Vis. prof. dept. moral philosophy U. St. Andrews, Scotland, 1984-86; mem. sci. adv. bd. Nat. Found. for Ileitis and Colitis, 1974-80, chmn. rsch. devel. com., 1974-78; mem. Personal Health Com. Ohio, 1974-76; trustee Medco Peer Rev., 1974-79; adj. prof. health adminstrn. Va. Commonwealth U., 1996-2000; med. dir. Williamsburg Landing, 1999-02; chair Sr. Svcs. Coalition, Williamsburg, Va., 2005-06. Author: Clinical Tests of Gastric Function, 1973; author: (with T. Wan) Monitoring the Quality of Health Care, 2002; author: How The Scots Created America, 2008, Dust in the Veterans Eyes, 2009; assoc. editor Am. Jour. Digestive Diseases; contbr. articles to profl. jours. Served with M.C. Royal Army, 1955-57. Fellow Royal Coll. Physicians (Edinburgh), ACP; mem. Brit. Soc. Gastroenterology, Internat. Group for Study Intestinal Motility (past pres.). Avocations: stamp collecting/philately, painting, piano. Address: 6728 Tarpleys Tavern Rd Williamsburg VA 23188 Business E-Mail: amconn@wm.edu.

CONNELL, BRUCE F., plastic surgeon; b. Gordo, Ala. s. Vester Sloan and Lottie Fowler Connell. MD, SUNY at Buffalo Sch. Medicine & Biomed. Sci. Intern LA County Gen. Hosp., USC Med. Ctr.; resident gen. surgery Erie Co. Med. Ctr., Buffalo; resident plastic surgery Mayo Clinic, Rochester, Minn.; pvt. practice cosmetic surgery Santa Ana, Calif. Clinical prof. surgery U. Calif., Irvine. Contbr. articles to profl. jours. Combat infantryman pvt. first class, Europe US Army, WWII. Mem.: Am. Soc. Plastic Surgeons, Am. Soc. Aesthetic Plastic Surgery. Avocations: gardening, languages. Office: 915 Gaviota Dr Laguna Beach CA 92651-2745 Office Phone: 714-972-0666. Office Fax: 714-569-0081. Personal E-mail: drbconnell@aol.com.

CONNELL, JOHN MUIR COCHRANE, endocrinologist, researcher; b. Irvine, Scotland, Oct. 10, 1954; s. William Muir and Betty Nicol Connell; m. Lesley Elizabeth Armstrong, Apr. 14, 1978; children: David, Andrew, Rachel, Alistair. MBChB, U. Glasgow, 1977. Prof. endocrinology U. Glasgow, 1985—2007, Scotland; dean medicine U. Dundee, 2009—. Contbr. scientific papers to profl. rsch. jours. Fellow: RCP, Glasgow, Am. Heart Assn., UK Acad. Med. Scis., Royal Soc. Edinburgh; mem.: RCP. Office: Ninewells Hosp & Med Sch Dundee DD195Y Scotland

CONNELLY, DEIRDRE P., pharmaceutical executive; b. San Juan, 1961; BA in Economics and Mktg., Lycoming Coll., Williamsport, Pa., 1983; grad. advanced mgmt. program, Harvard U., 2000. Sales rep. Eli Lilly & Co., San Juan, 1983—84, mktg. assoc., 1984—89, sales supr. Phila., 1989—90, product mgr. diabetes San Juan, 1990—91, nat. sales mgr., 1991—92, mktg. & sales dir., 1992—93, mktg. & sales dir. Caribbean region, 1993—95, gen mgr. Eli Lilly PR SA, 1995—97, regional sales dir., exec. dir. global mktg. Evista (osteoporosis drug) Indpls., 1997—2001, leader US women's health bus., 2001—03, exec. dir. human resources, 2003, sr. v.p. human resources, 2004—05, pres. US ops., 2005—09; pres. N.Am. pharmaceuticals GlaxoSmithKline plc, 2009—. Bd. dirs. Macy's, Inc., 2008—. Named Woman of Yr., Healthcare Businesswomen's Assn., 2010; named one of The 50 Most Powerful Women in Bus., Fortune mag., 2006—10, The World's 100 Most Powerful Women, Forbes mag., 2009. Office: GlaxoSmithKline 5 Moore Dr PO Box 13398 Research Triangle Park NC 27709 Office Phone: 317-276-2000, 919-483-2100. Office Fax: 919-549-7459. *

CONNEY, ALLAN HOWARD, pharmacologist, researcher; b. Chgo., Mar. 23, 1930; s. Leo Younkers and Celia (Gasway) Conney; m. Diana Conney, Sept. 5, 1954; children: Michael Raymond, Steven Herbert. BS, U. Wis., 1952, MS, 1954, PhD, 1956. Research asst. McArdle Lab., Madison, Wis., 1952—56; guest investigator Nat. Heart Inst., Bethesda, Md., 1957—58, pharmacologist, 1958—60; head dept. biochem. pharmacology Burroughs Wellcome & Co., Tuckahoe, NY, 1960—70; dir. dept. biochemistry Hoffmann-La Roche Inc., Nutley, NJ, 1970—71, dir. dept. biochemistry and drug metabolism, 1971—83, assoc. dir. exptl. therapeutics, 1979—83, dir. lab. exptl. carcinogenesis and metabolism, 1983—85; head Lab. of Exptl. Carcinogenesis and Metabolism Roche Inst. Molecular Biology, Nutley, NJ, 1985—87; chmn. dept. chem. biology Rutgers U. Coll. Pharmacy, Piscataway, NJ, 1987—2002; NJ Prof. Chem. Biology and Garbe Prof. of Leukemia and Cancer Rsch., Dept. Chem. Biology, Ernest Mario Sch. Pharmacy Rutgers U., The State U. NJ, dir., Susan Lehman Cullman Lab. for Cancer Rsch. Claude Bernard Medal and Claude Bernard Vis. Professorship U. Montreal, 1970. Assoc. editor Cancer Rsch.; contbr. articles to profl. publications. Recipient Achievement award in Pharmacodynamics, Acad. of Pharmaceutical Scis., 1968, Outstanding Investigator award, NCI, 1990, Thomas Alva Edison Sci. award, NJ Acad. Sci. and Gov. NJ, 1992, Ernest H. Volwiler award, Am. Assn. Colleges Pharmacy, 1993. Mem.: AAAS, NAS, Internat. Soc. for the Study of Xenobiotics, Soc. Toxicology, Inc. (Rsch. Achievement award 1968, Arnold J. Lehman award 1980), Am. Assn. Cancer Rsch. (G.H.A. Clowes award 1981, DeWitt S. Goodman Lectr. award 2002), Am. Soc. Pharmacology and Exptl. Therapeutics (award for Rsch. in Exptl. Therapeutics 1977), Am. Soc. Biol. Chemists. Office: Rutgers U Coll Pharmacy/Lab Cancer Rsch 170 Frelinghuysen Rd Rm 129 Piscataway NJ 08854-8020 Office Phone: 908-445-4940. Office Fax: 732-445-0687. Business E-Mail: aconney@rci.rutgers.edu.

CONNEY, NANCE, health facility administrator; b. Utica, NY, Mar. 7, 1966; d. John Conney, BeEtta Conney. AAS Med. Lab. Tech., SUNY; BS in Orgnl. Mgmt., Roberts Weselyan U., 2001. Forensic investigator Onondaga County Med. Examiner, Syracuse, NY, 1989—94; tech. dir. Ctrl. N.Y. Eye Bank, Syracuse, 1994—95; dir. recovery svc. Finger Lakes Donor Recovery Network, Rochester, 1995—2001; transplant coord. Organ Donor Ctr. of Hawaii, Honolulu, 2001—03; ops. mgr. Thomos E. Starzl Transplant Inst. U. Pitts. Med. Ctr., 2003—. Instr. Simmons Sch. Mortuary Sci., Syracuse, 1995—2000, Hawaii Bus. Coll., 2002. Vol. emergency med. tech. Onodaga County EMS, Syracuse, 1995—2000, mem. rope rescue team County Rope Rescue, Syracuse, 1996—2001; vol. firefighter NY, 1995—99. Mem.: Internat. Soc. Heart Lung Transplantation, Transplant Recipients Internat. Orgn. (assoc.; bd. dirs. 1997). Avocations: rappeling, skydiving, scuba diving, woodworking, natural habitat rehabilitation. Home: 3607 E 3rd St Tucson AZ 85716-4609 Office Phone: 412-647-6977.

CONNOLLY, JOHN EARLE, surgeon, educator; b. Omaha, May 21, 1923; s. Earl A. and Gertrude (Eckerman) C.; m. Virginia Hartman, Aug. 12, 1967; children: Peter Hart. John Earle, Sarah. AB, Harvard U., 1945, MD, 1948. Diplomate: Am. Bd. Surgery, 1955, Am. Bd. Thoracic and Cardiovascular Surgery, 1957, Am. Bd. Vascular Surgery, 1982. Intern. in surgery Stanford U. Hosps., San Francisco, 1948-49, surg. research fellow, 1949-50, asst. resident surgeon, 1950-52, chief resident surgeon, 1953-54, surg. pathology fellow, 1954-55, 1957-60, John and Mary Markle Scholar in med. scis., 1957-62; surg. registrar professional unit St. Bartholomew's Hosp., London, 1952-53; resident in thoracic surgery Bellevue Hosp., NYC, 1955; resident in thoracic and cardiovascular surgery Columbia-Presbyn. Med. Ctr., NYC, 1956; from instr. to assoc. prof. surgery Stanford U., 1957-65; prof. U. Calif., Irvine, 1965—, chmn. dept. surgery, 1965-78; attending surgeon Stanford Med. Ctr., Palo Alto, Calif., 1959-65; chmn. cardiovascular and thoracic surgery Irvine Med. Ctr. U. Calif., 1968—; attending surgeon Children's Hosp., Orange, Calif., 1968—, Anaheim (Calif.) Meml. Hosp., 1970—. Vis. prof. Beijing Heart, Lung, Blood Vessel Inst., 1990, A.H. Duncan vis. prof. U. Edinburgh, 1984; Hunterian prof. Royal Coll. Surgeons Eng., 1985-86, Kinmonth lectr., 1987, Hume Lectr. Soc. for Clin. Vascular Surgery, 1998; King James IV lectr. Royal Coll. Surgeons Edinburgh, 2003; Dist. Prof. Lectr. Uniformed Svcs. U. Health Scis., Bethesda, 1998; adv. coun. Nat. Heart, Lung, and Blood Inst.-NIH, 1981-85; Emile F. Holman lectr. Stanford U. Sch. Medicine, 2005; cons. Long Beach VA Hosp., Calif., 1965—. Contbr. articles to profl. jours.; mem. editl. bd.: Jour. Cardiovascular Surgery, 1974-03, chief editor, 1985-96; mem. editl. bd. Western Jour. Medicine, 1975—, Jour. Stroke, 1979—, Jour. Vascular Surgery, 1983-95. Bd. dirs. Audio-Digest Found., 1974—, Franklin Martin Found., 1975-80, regent Uniformed Svcs. U. Health Scis., Bethesda, 1992-2003, bd. regentss, Uniformal Svcs. U. Health Scis, Bethesda, Md., 1995-2003. Served with AUS, 1943-44. Recipient Cert. of Merit, Japanese Surg. Soc., 1979, 90. Fellow ACS (gov. 1964-70, regent 1973-82, vice chmn. bd. regents 1980-82, v.p. 1984-85), Royal Coll. Surgeons Eng., 1982 (hon.), Royal Coll. Surgeons Ireland, 1988 (hon.), Royal Coll. Surgeons Edinburgh, (hon.); mem. Japanese Surg. Soc. (hon.), Vascular Soc. of Great Britian & Ireland (hon.), Bd. of Regents, Nat. Library Medicine NIH, Bethesda, Md., Am. Surg. Assn., Soc. U. Surgeons, Am. Assn. Thoracic Surgery (coun. 1974-78), Pacific Coast Surg. Assn. (pres. 1985-86), San Francisco Surg. Soc., L.A. Surg. Soc., Soc. Vascular Surgery, Western Surg. Assn., Internat. Cardiovascular Soc. (pres. 1977), Soc. Internat. Chirurgie, Soc. Thoracic Surgeons, Western Thoracic Surg. Soc. (pres. 1978), Orange County Surg. Soc. (pres. 1984-85), James IV Assn. Surgeons (councillor 1983—), Am. Bd. Surgery (bd. dirs. 1976-82), San Francisco Golf Club, Pacific Union Club (San Francisco), Bohemian Club (San Francisco), Harvard Club (NYC), Big Canyon County Club (Newport Beach, Calif.), Cypress Point Club (Pebble Beach). Home: 7 Deerwood Ln Newport Beach CA 92660-5108 Office Phone: 714-456-5756. E-mail: jeconnol@uci.edu.

CONNOLLY, JOHN JOSEPH, publishing executive; b. Worcester, Mass., Feb. 4, 1940; s. Nicholas John and Margaret Anne (Flynn) Connolly; m. Ingrid Schlemminger, Apr. 11, 1964; children: Sean Timothy, Cheryl Lea. BS, Worcester State Coll., 1962; MA, U. Conn., 1963; EdD in Coll. and Univ. Adminstrn., Teacher's Coll., Columbia U., 1972; LLD, Mercy Coll., 1980; LHD, Worcester State U., 2011. Pres. Dutchess CC, Poughkeepsie, NY, 1972—81; pres., CEO NY Med. Coll., Valhalla, 1981—92, Castle Connolly Med. Ltd., NYC, 1992—. Bd. dirs. Morton Restaurant Group, Inc., Basent Taylor Inc. Guest appearances on or interviewed by (TV and radio stations nationwide) including Good Morning America, The Today Show, 20/20, Fox Cable News, Morning News (CNN) and Weekend Today in New York., author and/or editor of seven books. Chmn. Dutchess County Indsl. Devel. Agy., 1978—81; hon. chmn. Dutchess/Columbia br. Am. Lung Assn., 1993—; pres. Westchester Hist. Soc., 1985—88; pres.'s adv. coun. United Hosp. Fund; bd. advisors Whitehead Inst. for Biomed. Rsch.; adv. com. Funding First, Inc.; bd. dirs., chmn. Profl. Exam. Svc., 1998—2009; bd. dirs. United Way of Dutchess County, pres., 1978; chmn. bd. trustees St. Francis Hosp., Poughkeepsie, 1976—80; trustee Culinary Inst. Am., 1976—2002, chair, 1996—98, chair-emertius, 1998—; trustee Poughkeepsie Area Fund, 1973—78, St. Agnes Hosp, White Plains, 1988—99; bd. dirs., chmn. Econ. Devel. Corp. Dutchess County; bd. dirs. Westchester County Mental Health Assn., Lupus Found., NY Bus. Group on Health, Am. Lyme Disease Found., 1993—2001, founder, chair, 1994—99. Recipient Disting. Svc. award, Poughkeepsie Jaycees, 1974, Marie Y. Martin award, Assn. CC Trustees, 1978; named Man of the Yr., Dutchess County Legislature, 1980; named one of 100 Outstanding Young Leaders in Higher Edn., Change Mag., 1979. Fellow: NY Acad. Sci., NY Acad. Medicine, Friends Hudson Valley (chmn. 1990), Friends Nat. Libr. Medicine (dir. 1994—96); mem.: Westchester County Assn. (dir.), Assn. Colls. Mid-Hudson Area (pres. 1976—79), Phi Delta Kappa. Roman Catholic. Office: Castle Connolly Med Ltd 42 W 24th 2nd Floor New York NY 10010 Office Phone: 212-367-8400.

CONNOLLY, MARK W., thoracic surgeon; b. Alameda, Calif., Jan. 25, 1955; BS in psychology, U. Calif., Davis, 1977; MD, Northwestern U., 1982. Cert. Am. Bd. Thoracic Surgery, 1993. Intern surgery NYU-Bellevue Med. Ctr., NYC, 1982—83, resident, 1983—88; resident cardiothoracic surgery Emory U. Med. Ctr., Atlanta, 1988—91; chief divsn. cardiothoracic surgery Maimonides Med. Ctr., Bklyn., 1996—98; chief sect. cardiovascular and thoracic surgery Lenox Hill Hosp., NYC, 1999—; chief Dept. Cardiovascular and Thoracic Surgery St. Michael's Med. Ctr., Newark, 2002—, dir. Cathedral Heart and Vascular Inst., 2002—. Spkr. in field. Recipient Physician Yr. honors, Am. Heart Assn., 2006. Mem.: Alpha Omega Alpha Soc. Office: Heart and Vascular Inst St Michael's Med Ctr 111 Central Ave Newark NJ 07102 also: 268 Dr Martin Luther King Jr Blvd Newark NJ 07102 Office Phone: 973-877-5300. Office Fax: 973-877-2621.

CONNOLLY, STUART J., cardiologist; MS, Fordham U.; MD, McGill U. Trained U. Toronto, Stanford U.; prof. cardiology McMaster U., Hamilton, ON, 1994—, dir. arrhythmia svc., cardiology divsn., dir. cardiology divsn., 2005—, Salim Yusuf chair cardiology, 2005—; cardiac electrophysiologist Hamilton Health Sciences. Office: HHSC Gen Divsn McMaster Clniic Rm 501 237 Barton St E Hamilton ON L8L 2X2 Canada Office Phone: 905-521-2100 ext. 44507/44750. Office Fax: 905-521-8820. E-mail: connostu@hhsc.ca.

CONNOR, CHARLES DEAN, medical association administrator, retired military officer; BA in Polit. Sci., U. Ill.; grad. student in mktg. and comm., Portland State U., Oreg.; JD, Loyola U. Law Sch., Chgo., 1983. Bar: Ill., DC. Pub. affairs officer US Navy, dir. nat. advt., head Midwest media rels. program, comm. advisor to the comdr. of the US Third Fleet, comm. mgr. US Space Command/NORAD, sr. pub. rels. officer London, COO global comm program, personal comm. advisor to the sec. of Navy, ret. capt.; first dir. pub. affairs Fed. Judiciary, Washington; prin. client strategy The Dilenschneider Group, Chgo.; sr. v.p. comm. & mktg. American Red Cross, 2002—07; exec. v.p., COO American Lung Assn., Washington, 2007—08, pres., CEO, 2008—. Bd. dirs. American Mktg. Assn. Found. Named PR Profl. of Yr., Pub. Rels. Soc. America, 2005. Office: American Lung Assn 1301 Pennsylvania Ave NW Ste 800 Washington DC 20004 Office Phone: 202-785-3355. Office Fax: 202-452-1805. *

CONNOR, SUSAN BLAKE, perinatal nurse, military officer; b. Colo. Springs, June 5, 1952; d. Clyde Dale and Barbara Lavinia (Jayne) Blake; m. Kevin A. Connor, Aug. 15, 1987. BSN, U. Colo., Denver, 1976; MSN, U. Calif., San Francisco, 1982. Cert. high risk perinatal nurse, ANCC. Commd. 2d lt. USAF, 1983, advanced through grades to major; staff nurse pediat. med. surg. Meml. Hosp., Sarasota, Fla., 1977-78; clin. nurse neonatal ICU Children's Hosp. and Health Care Ctr., San Diego, Calif., 1978-80, U. Calif., San Francisco, 1980-82; staff nurse labor and delivery Meml. Hosp., Colo. Springs, 1982-83; clin. spec. neonatal ICU David Grant Med. Ctr., Fairfield, Calif., 1983-85; staff nurse perinatal unit USAF Hosp., Lajes Field, Azores, 1985-87; staff nurse educator MCH Wilford Hall Med. Ctr., San Antonio, 1987-91; flight nurse, coord. clin. 86th Aeromed Evac Squadron, Ramstein, Germany, 1992—. Contbr. articles to profl. jours. Recipient Jr. Nurse Corps. Officer Assoc. of Women Health, Obstet, Neonatal Nurses, 1990, Clin. Nursing Excellence award Assoc. Mil. Surg. of US, 1994. Mem. ANA, Assn. Mil. Surgeons US (Clin. Nursing Excellence award 1994), Assoc. of Women's Health, Obstetric Neonatal Nurses (named Jr. Nurse Corps. Officer 1990). Avocations: winter sports, volksmarching. *

CONNORS, ALFRED FRANCIS, internist, researcher; b. Bklyn., May 14, 1950; s. Alfred Francis and Mary Elizabeth Connors; m. Mimi Lam, June 10, 1978; children: Lisa Marie, Christopher Hin-Laam. BA, St. Louis U., 1971; MD, Med. Coll. of Ohio, 1974. Diplomate Am. Bd. Internal Medicine, Am. Bd. Pulmonary Diseases. Prof. health evaluation scis. and internal medicine U. Va. Sch. Medicine, Charlottesville, 1996—2002; Charles H. Rammelkamp Jr. prof. medicine Case Western Res. U., Cleve., 2002—09, chmn. dept. medicine Metrohealth campus, 2002—09, chief med. officer, sr. v.p., Med. Affairs Metrohealth Sys., 2009—, sr. assoc. dean, Med. Affairs Metrohealth Sys., 2009—. Contbr. articles to profl. jours. Office: MetroHealth Med Ctr / CWRU 2500 MetroHealth Dr Cleveland OH 44109 *

CONNORS, JACK (JOHN M. CONNORS, JR.), retired advertising executive, board member; m. Eileen M. Ahearn; 4 children. Grad., Boston Coll., 1963, D (hon.) in Bus. Adminstrn., 2007. Founding ptnr. Hill Holliday (formerly Hill, Holliday, Connors, Cosmopulos, Inc.), Boston, 1968, pres., CEO, 1995—2003, chmn., 1995—2006, chmn. emeritus, 2006—. Bd. dirs. Hasbro Inc., 2004—, Covidien plc, 2007—; chmn. bd. dirs. Partners HealthCare Sys., Boston, Dana-Farber/Partners CancerCare, Dana-Farber/Harvard CancerCare. Chmn. bd. trustees Brigham & Women's Hosp., Boston, 1992—97; bd. trustees, past chmn. Boston Coll., Wang Ctr. Performing Arts. Recipient Heritage Soc. award, Brigham & Women's Hosp., 2003, John Joseph Moakley Pub. Svc. award, 2004, Centennial award, Greater Boston C. of C., 2009; named one of The Most Powerful People in Boston, Boston Mag.; named to Advt. Hall of Fame, American Advt. Fedn., 2011. Fellow: Am. Acad. Arts & Sciences. Office: Hill Holliday Connors Cosmopulos Inc 53 State St Boston MA 02109 Office Phone: 617-366-4000. Business E-Mail: jconnors@hhcc.com. *

CONNORS, JOHN (BUDDY) J., neurologist, educator; b. Memphis, Apr. 21, 1949; BE, Vanderbilt U., 1971; MD, U. Miss. Med. Sch., 1975. Asst. prof. U. Miss. Med. Ctr., 1983—93; assoc. prof. La. State U. Med. Ctr., 1994—2000; med. dir. NeuroVascular Rsch. Found., 2001—11; dir. interventional neuroradiology Bapt. Vascular Inst., Miami, Fla., 2003—08; prof. radiology, neurology, neurosurgery Vanderbilt U. Med. Ctr., 2009—. Pres. Soc. NeuroInterventional Surgery, 2003—04; founder, first co-chair NeuroVascular Coalition, 2004—06; bd. dirs. Neurocritical Care Soc., 2004—06; mem. stroke coun. sci. statement oversight com. Am. Stroke Assn., 2005—09; chair Tenn. Stroke Sys. Care, 2009—11. Fellow: Soc. Interventional Radiology; mem.: Am. Acad. Neurology, Am. Soc. Neuroradiology (Michael Bros. award), World Fedn. Interventional and Therapeutic Neuroradiology, Am. Assn. Neurol. Surgery. Office: 1161 21st Ave S Nashville TN 37232 Office Fax: 615-322-6889. E-mail: budmancon@gmail.com.

CONNORS, KENNETH ANTONIO, retired pharmacy educator; b. Torrington, Conn., Feb. 19, 1932; s. Peter Francis and Adeline (Gioia) C.; m. Patricia R. Smart, Dec. 30, 1972. BS, U. Conn., 1954; MS, U. Wis., 1957, PhD, 1959. Rsch. assoc. dept. chemistry Ill. Inst. Tech., Chgo., 1959-60, Northwestern U., Evanston, Ill., 1960-61; asst. prof. U. Wis. Sch. Pharmacy, Madison, 1962-65, assoc. prof., 1965-72, prof., 1972-97, prof. emeritus, 1997—, acting dean, 1991-93. Author: A Textbook of Pharmaceutical Analysis, 3d edit., 1982, Reaction Mechanisms in Organic Analytical Chemistry, 1973, Chemical Stability of Pharmaceuticals, 2d edit., 1986, Binding Constants, 1987, Chemical Kinetics, 1990, Thermodynamics of Pharmaceutical Systems, 2d edit., 2010. Served with U.S. Army, 1961. Fellow AAAS, Acad. Pharm. Scis., Am. Assn. Pharm. Scis.; mem. Am. Chem. Soc. Office: U Wis Sch Pharmacy 777 Highland Ave Madison WI 53705-2222

CONOMY, JOHN PAUL, neurologist, educator, lawyer; b. Cleve., July 31, 1938; s. John and Marie Conomy; m. Sharon Sopata; children: John, Lisa, Christopher, Francesca Maria. BS cum laude, John Carroll U., 1960; MD, St. Louis U., 1964; JD, Case Western Res. U., 1992. Diplomate Am. Bd. Psychiatry and Neurology (examiner 1975—). Student rsch. fellow in neurology St. Louis U., 1963-64; intern in straight medicine St. Louis U. Hosps., 1964; resident in neurology U. Hosps. of Cleve., 1965-68; fellow in neuropathology Cleve. Met. Gen. Hosp. and Case Western Res. U., Cleve., 1968; career teaching fellow U. Pa., 1970; asst. prof. neurology Case Western Res. U. Med. Sch., Cleve., 1972-77, assoc. clin. prof., 1979, prof. clin. neurology, 1992—; chmn. dept. neurology Cleve. Clinic Found., 1975-92, chmn. clin. rsch. projects and instl. rev. com., 1978-82, founder, dir. Mellen Ctr. Multiple Sclerosis Treatment and Research, 1984-92, exec. dir., 1987—, also exec. dir. consortium of multiple sclerosis ctrs.; assoc. prof. neurology Pa. State U., 1989—; prof. clin. neurology, adj. prof. law Case Western Res. U., 1992—; dir. clin. neuroscis., dir. Office of Profl. Affairs Innova Med. Svcs., Cleve., 1994—. Attending physician Highland View Hosp., Cleve., 1968, U. Hosps. Cleve., 1968, attending neurologist, 1972-78, bd. govs. dept. medicine, 1974-75; assoc. neurologist Hosp. U. Pa., 1970; sr. staff neurologist Scott and White Clinic and Hosp., Temple, Tex., 1971; cons. in neurology VA Ctr., Temple, 1971; clins. attending neurologist Parkland Hosp., Dallas, 1971-72; clin. instr. neurology U. Tex. Southwestern Med. Sch., Dallas, 1971-72; vis. lectr. neuroscis. U. Tex. Med. Sch., San Antonio, 1971-72; cons. physician evaluation bd. Whittaker Internat. Services for Saudi Arabia and United Arab Emirates, 1980; physician evaluation bd. Whittaker Corp., 1980-85, sci. adv. bd. Communicative Disorders Found., 1980—; med. advisor Huntington's Disease Found., Cleve., 1984-87; biotech. adv. bd. State of Ohio, 1983-85; cons. HHS, SSA, 1990—; participant Manpower in Neurology Conf., San Diego, 1985; vis. prof. London Hosp. Med. Sch., 1982-83, U. Louvain, Belgium, 1983, Oxford (Eng.) U., 1983, Nat. Ctr. Nervous, Mental and Muscular Disorders, Tokyo, 1984, Kyoto (Japan) U., 1984, Kyushu U., Fukuoka, Japan, 1984, U. Bursa, Turkey, 1985, U. Istanbul, 1985, 86, 88, vis. neurologist Christian Med. Coll., Vellore, India, 1986, vis. export Ministry of Health, Singapore, 1988; hon. cons. London Hosp. and Tower Hamlets Health Dist., 1982-83; co-investigator neurogenic factors in the pathogenesis of arterial hypertension NIH, 1978; sr. investigator Quantitation of Cutaneous Sensation VA Hosp., Cleve., 1974, neuroscis. rsch. program Cleve. Clinic Found., 1975—; adj. prof. law Case Western Res. U., 1992—; pres Health Systems Design Inc., 1992—, CompEval Corp., True North Med. Svcs.; cons. Atty. Gen. State of Ohio, 1992—, FTC, 1994—, U.S. Dept. Justice, U.S. Dept. Social Security. Contbr. articles to profl. jours.; mem. editorial bd. Postgrad. Medicine, 1985—, Jour. Neurologic Rehab., 1987—, Surg. Neurology, 1986—, Health Matrix, 1990; reviewer Neurology, 1977—, Cleve. Clin. Quar., 1977—, Neurosurgery, 1979—Am. Jour. Physiology, 1980-81, Archives of Neurology, 1982—, Residency Rev. Com. in Psychiatry and Neurology, 1983—. Served as capt. USAF, 1968-70. Recipient Francis M. Grogan prize St. Louis U. Med. Sch., 1964, Clin. Tchr. of Yr. award U. Hosps. Cleve., 1973; grantee Mary B. Lee Fund, 1973, Reinberger Found., 1976-82, Mellen Fund, 1976, 84, Hostetler Found., 1989, NIH, 1978—. Fellow ACP (invited speaker 1979, 85, reviewer health care delivery programs 1984), Royal Soc. Medicine (London), Am. Acad. Neurology, Am. Heart Assn. (stroke coun.);

mem. AAAS, AMA (sect. coun. on neurology 1977-81, vice chmn.-sec. 1979-81; del. Health Policy agenda for the Am. People, 1983), Soc. Neurosci. (pres. Cleve. chpt. 1975-79), ABA, Am. Assn. History Medicine, Ohio State Med. Assn., Cleve. Acad. Medicine, No. Ohio Neurologic Soc., Assn. Rsch. in Nervous and Mental Disease, Internat. Soc. Tech. Assessment in Health Care, Am. Neurol. Assn. (chmn. pub. rels. com. 1981-85), Soc. Clin. Neurologists (councillor 1976-79, program chmn. 1982), Assn. U. Profs. Neurology, Am. Electroencephalographic Soc., Internat. Assn. Study Pain, Am. Acad. Neurology, Cleve. Med. Libr. Assn. (trustee 1980—, chmn. pubs. com. 1984), Clin. Neurosci. Soc. (pres. elect 1992), Cleve. Health Scis. Libr. (exec. com. 1984-86), Behavioral Neurology Soc., Nat. Multiple Sclerosis Soc., Worshipful Soc. Apothecaries London, Coun. Med. Specialty Socs., 1985—), Nat. Multiple Sclerosis Soc. (med. adv. bd. 1987-92), Internat. Fedn. Multiple Sclerosis Socs. (med. adv. bd. 1989—), Health Svcs. Rsch. Com. (chmn. 1986), Am. Assn. Neurol. Surgeons (assoc. membership bd. 1982—), Inst. Clin. Neuroscis. London, Internat. Med. Scholar's Program, European Neurol. Soc. (pres. 1991), Can. Neurol. Assn. (hon.), Am. Soc. Law and Medicine, Am. Coll. Legal Medicine, ABA, Ohio State Bar Assn., World Assn. for Med. Law (co-chair sect. history health law), Alpha Omega Alpha. Avocations: travel, bicycling, racquetball, photography, music. Office Phone: 216-765-8393, 216-292-1875. Personal E-mail: 2br02b@msn.com.

CONOVER, LLOYD HILLYARD, retired research scientist; b. Orange, NJ, June 13, 1923; s. John Howard and Marguerite Anna (Cameron) C.; m. Virginia Rogers Kirk, Aug. 24, 1944 (dec. Dec. 1988); children: Kirk Howard, Roger Lloyd, Heather Cameron, Craig Scott; m. Marie Strauss Solomons, Oct. 18, 1990 (dec. May 2003); m. Katharine Miller Meacham, Dec. 29, 2005. BA, Amherst Coll., 1947; PhD, U. Rochester, 1950. Rsch. chemist, mgr. Chas. Pfizer & Co., Bklyn. and Groton, Conn., 1950—68; dir. chem. rsch. chemotherapy Pfizer Cen. Rsch., Groton, 1968-71, rsch. dir. Europe, Sandwich, Eng., 1971-74, v.p. agrl. R & D Groton and Sandwich, 1975-84. Contbr. articles on antibiotics, anthelminics and animal health drugs to sci. jours.; patentee tetracycline and pyrantel. Chmn. Waterford Planning, 1961-63. Lt. (j.g.) USNR, 1943-46, PTO. Recipient Eli Whitney award Conn. Patent Law Assn., 1983, Third Century award Found. Creative Am., 1990; inductee Nat. Inventors Hall of Fame, 1992. Fellow Royal Soc. Chemistry, Royal Soc. Arts; mem. Am. Chem. Soc., Phi Beta Kappa, Sigma Xi. Democrat. Achievements include directing research resulting in new drugs for infectious diseases in people and animals.

CONRAD, HAROLD THEODORE, psychiatrist; b. Milw., Jan. 25, 1934; s. Theodore Herman and Alyce Barbara Conrad; m. Elaine Marie Blaine, Sept. 1, 1962 (dec.); children: Blaine, Carl, David, Erich, Rachel. AB, U. Chgo., 1954, BS, 1955, MD, 1958. Diplomate Am. Bd. Psychiatry. Intern USPHS Hosp., San Francisco, 1958-59, commd. sr. asst. surgeon, 1958, advanced through grades to med. dir., 1967, resident psychiatry Lexington, Ky., 1959-61, Charity Hosp., New Orleans, 1961-62; chief of psychiatry USPHS Hosp., New Orleans, 1962-67, clin. dir., 1967; dep. dir. divsn. field investigation NIMH, Chevy Chase, Md., 1968; chief NIMH Clin. Rsch. Ctr., Lexington, 1969-73; cons. psychiatry region IX USPHS, HEW, San Francisco, 1973-79; dir. adolescent unit Alaska Psychiat. Inst., Anchorage, 1979-81, supt., 1981-85; clin. assoc. prof. psychiatry U. Wash. Med. Sch., 1981-85; psychiatrist pvt. practice, Houma, La., 1985—2004; ret., 2005. Contbr. articles to profl. jours. Recipient cmty. awards for contbns. in field of drug abuse and equal employment opportunity for minorities. Fellow: Am. Psychiat. Assn. (Disting. life), Royal Soc. Medicine; mem.: AMA, Alpha Delta Phi, Alpha Omega Alpha.

CONRAD, JO ANN BROOKS, physician assistant; b. Baton Rouge, Dec. 22, 1954; Cert. radiographer, med. asst. Spencor Coll., 1983. Office mgr., med asst., radiographer Family Clinic, 1983—. Avocations: gardening, fishing. Home: 505 Staring Ln Baton Rouge LA 70810-2602 Personal E-mail: jabcon@cox.net.

CONRAD, JOSEPH HENRY, animal nutrition educator; b. Cass County, Ind., Dec. 7, 1926; s. Ferdinand M. and Marie E. (Hubenthal) C.; m. Frances Ash, June 18, 1950; children: Kenneth A., Leonard J., Carol Ann, Joseph C. BS, Purdue U., 1950, MS, 1954, PhD, 1958; prof. (hon.), Fed. U. Viçosa, Brazil, 1965. Asst. prof. Purdue U., West Lafayette, Ind., 1958-63, assoc. prof., 1963-68, prof., 1968-71; animal scientist Fed. U. Viçosa, 1961-65; prof., coord. tropical animal sci. programs U. Fla., Gainesville, 1971-95. Co-author: Swine Production, 1982; contbr. monographs and numerous articles on animal nutrition and tropical animal prodn. to profl. jours. Served with USN, 1944-46. Recipient Disting. Nutritional award Distillers Feed Rsch. Coun., 1964; Moorman fellow, 1989. Fellow Am. Soc. Animal Sci. (Internat. Animal Agrl. award 1985, Bohstedt award 1987, Internat. Mktg. award 1989); mem. World Assn. Animal Prodn. (v.p.), Latin Am. Soc. Animal Prodn., Sociedade Brasileira de Zootecnia, Purdue U. Alumni Assn. (life, pres.'s coun.), Sigma Xi, Gamma Sigma Delta. Republican. Lutheran. Home: 1824 NW 10th Ave Gainesville FL 32605-5312 Office: PO Box 110910 Gainesville FL 32611-0910 Home Phone: 352-727-8317; Office Phone: 352-727-8317. Personal E-mail: joegogator@hotmail.com.

CONRAD, MARCEL EDWARD, hematologist, oncologist, educator; b. NYC, Aug. 15, 1928; s. Marcel Edward and Lulu Marie (Geraghty) C.; m. Marcia Louise Grove; children: Marcel Edward, III, Mark E., Carol J., Erin E., Julia P. BS, Georgetown U., 1949, MD cum laude, 1953. Diplomate Am. Bd. Internal Medicine, Am. Bd. Hematology. Commd. 1st lt. M.C. U.S. Army, 1953, advanced through grades to col., 1968; intern Walter Reed Gen. Hosp., Washington, 1953-54, resident, then chief resident in internal medicine, 1955-60; commdg. officer Mobile Army Surg. Hosp., Republic of Korea, 1960—61; mem. staff Walter Reed Army Inst. Rsch., 1961-74, chief dept. hematology, 1965-74; chief clin. investigation svc. Walter Reed Army Med. Ctr., 1971-74; clin. asst. prof., then clin. assoc. prof. medicine Georgetown U. Med. Sch., 1964-74; prof. medicine U. Ala. Med. Sch., Birmingham, 1974-83, also dir. div. hematology and oncology, 1974-83; prof. medicine, pathology, dir. divsn. hematology, oncology U. South Ala., Mobile, 1983-2001, dir. USA Cancer Ctr., 1985-2001, disting. prof. medicine, 2001; cons. Mobile, 2001—. Prin. investigator Minority Based Cmty. Cancer Oncology Program, 1990—2004. Contbr. numerous articles to med. publs. Advanced from 1st lt. to col. US Army, 1953—74. Decorated Legion of Merit with oak leaf cluster; recipient Skinner medal U.S. Army, 1955, Hoff medal, 1962, John Shaw Billings award, 1967, William Beaumont award, 1972, Walter Reed award, 1974, Harry Hines award Nat. Cancer Inst., 2003, Eagle Scout; named Best Dr. in America, 1981-. Fellow Internat. Soc. Hematology, ACP (Laureate award 1989, named Disting. Prof. Medicine, 2001); mem. AAAS, Assn. Am. Physicians, Internat. Soc. Hematology, Am. Soc. Clin. Investigation, Am. Physiol. Soc., Internat. Soc. Blood Transfusion, Am. Soc. Hematology, Am. Soc. Clin. Oncology, Am. Chem. Soc., Soc. Exptl. Biology and Medicine, So. Soc. Clin. Investigation, Am. Fedn. Clin. Rsch., Alpha Omega Alpha. Roman Catholic. Achievements include basic and clinical contributions in hematology, hepatology and oncology. Avocation: sailing. Home and Office: 3110 Brick Ln Decatur GA 30033 Personal E-mail: mconrad2@comcast.net.

CONRAD, MICHAEL, nephrologist; MD, U. Mass. Diplomate Am. Bd. of Internal Medicine-nephrology. Intern Univ. Mass. Meml. Med. Ctr., resident; fellow Hosp. of the Univ. of Pa.; chief sect. of nephrology Virtua. Office: Virtua Ste 401 401 Route 73 N Lake Center Bldg Marlton NJ 08053 Office Phone: 856-355-6000.

CONRAD, STEVEN ALLEN, critical care and emergency physician, biomedical engineer, educator; b. St. Martinville, La., Aug. 23, 1953; s. Karl Donovan and Dolores Beatrice (Bienvenu) C.; m. Mona Theresa Hollier, Aug. 9, 1974; children: David, Lesley, Taylor. BS, U. S.W. La., 1974; MD, La. State U., Shreveport, 1978; MS, Case Western Reserve U., Cleve., 1980, PhD, 1985; MS in Engring., La. Tech. U., 1981; MBA, La. State U., 2001, MS in Info. Sys. Tech., 2003; MSc in Bioinformatics, U. Manchester, 2006. Diplomate Am. Bd. Internal Medicine, Critical Care Medicine, Am. Bd. Emergency Medicine; cert. nutritional support physician; cert. clin. rsch. investigator Assn. Clin. Rsch. Investigators, 2004. Postdoctoral trainee in biomed. computing Case Western Res. U., 1979—80; resident internal medicine La. State U., Shreveport, 1981-84; fellow in critical care medicine Mayo Grad. Sch. Medicine, Rochester, Minn., 1984-86; from asst. prof. medicine to prof. bioinformatics and computational biology La. State U. Med. Ctr., Shreveport, La., 1986—2003, prof. medicine, emergency medicine, pediatrics, anesthesiology, bioinformatics and computational biology, 2003—, dir. critical care medicine tng. program, 1987—2007; instr. computer sci. Winona State U., 1985—86, prof. neurosurgery, 2009—. Cons. physician critical care VA Med. Ctr., 1986—2003, dir. extracorporeal life support program, 1993—, co-dir. nutritional support svc., 1994—2007, transplant intensivist Willis Knighton Regional Heart Transplant Program, 1994—2004, attending physician in pediat. ICU, 1994—; mem. emergency med. svcs. task force Shreveport Fire Dept., 1992—; prin. investigator in multiple device and drug trials. Editor: Pulmonary Function Testing: Principles and Practice, 1984; mem. editl. bd. Internat. Jour. Electronic Healthcare, 2003—, ASAIO Jour., 2004—; manuscript reviewer ASAIO Jour., 2004-, Artificial Organs, Intensive Care Medicine, Critical Care Chest Medicine, Chest; abstract reviewer Critical Care Medicine; contbr. chpts. to books and articles to profl. jours. Grantee, Am. Heart Assn., NHLBI. Fellow ACP, Am. Coll. Critical Care Med., Am. Coll. Chest Physicians, Am. Coll. Emergency Physicians, Am. Acad. Emergency Physicians; mem. IEEE (sr.), Biomed. Engring. Soc., Shock Soc., Am. Soc. Artificial Internal Organs, Internat. Soc. for Artificial Organs, Soc. for Acad. Emergency Medicine, Am. Soc. for Parenteral and Enteral Nutrition, Internat. Soc. for Computational Biology, Alpha Omega Alpha, Sigma Xi, Phi Kappa Phi, Beta Gamma Sigma, Sigma Iota Epsilon. Office: La State U Health Scis Ctr 1501 Kings Hwy Shreveport LA 71103-4228 Office Phone: 318-675-6885. Business E-Mail: sconrad@lsuhsc.edu. *

CONRAD-ENGLAND, ROBERTA LEE, pathologist; b. Meriden, Conn., Aug. 25, 1950; d. Hans and Emma Ann (Bort) Conrad; m. Gary Thomas England, June 6, 1976; children: Eric Bryan, Christopher Ryan. BS in Microbiology, U. Ky., 1972, MD, 1976. Diplomate Nat. Bd. Med. Examiners, Bd. Am. Pathologists. Resident anatomic and clin. pathology Emory U. Affiliated Hosps., Atlanta, 1976-80; pathologist Western Bapt. Hosp., Paducah, Ky., 1980—2005. Cons. Marshall County Hosp., Benton, Ky., 1985-2005, chair infection control com., 1985-2005 Mem., com. chairperson PTA, Poducah, Ky., 1993-94; mother's asst. Boy Scouts Am., Poducah, 1991-94. Fellow Coll. Am. Pathologists, Am. Soc. Clin. Pathologists; mem. Ky. Med. Assn., Ky. Soc. Pathologists, Ky. Women Mentors in Sci., Alpha Omega Alpha, Phi Beta Kappa. Avocations: swimming, snorkeling, interior decorating.

CONROY, JOANNE M., dean, medical educator; B in Chemistry cum laude, Dartmouth Coll.; MD, Med. U. SC, 1983. Resident in anesthesiology Med. Univ. SC, Charleston, asst. prof. to assoc. prof. dept. anesthesiology, prof. dept. anesthesiology, 1995, interim chair dept. anesthesia and perioperative medicine, 1996—97, vice chair to chair dept. anesthesia and perioperative medicine, 1997, assoc. v.p. for medical affairs, 1998, sr. assoc. dean Coll. Medicine, 2000—, endowed chair for edn. and leadership devel.; chief med. officer Atlantic Health System, exec. v.p., 2001—08; COO Morristown Meml., 2001—08, pres., 2008; chief health officer Assn. of American Med. Colleges, 2008—. Chair coll. admissions com. Med. Univ. SC, 1992; assisted launch of nat. diversity project Women in Medicine and Sci.; lectr. in field. Contbr. articles, chpts. to profl. pubs. Named one of Top 25 Women in Healthcare, Modern Healthcare mag., 2011. Office: Assn of American Medical Colleges 2450 N St NW Washington DC 20037 *

CONROY, ROBERT JOHN, lawyer; b. Newark, Feb. 17, 1953; s. Michael John and Frances (Goncalves) C.; m. Mary Catherine McGuire, June 7, 1975; children: Caitlin Michaela, Michael Colin. BS, St. Peter's Coll., 1977; MPA, CUNY, 1981; JD, N.Y. Law Sch., 1981; MPH, Harvard U., 1985. Bar: NY 1981, NJ 1981, US Dist. Ct. NJ 1981, Calif. 1982, US Dist. Ct. (so. and ea. dists.) NY 1982, US Dist. Ct. (we. dist.) Calif. 1990, US Ct. Appeals (2d, ed and 11th cirs.) 1982, Fla. 1984, DC, US Supreme Ct 1984, Pa. 2000, US Dist. Ct. (ea. dist.) Pa. 2001, US Dist. Ct. (no. dist.) NY 2005, US Dist Ct (we. dist.) NY 2006. Asst. corp. counsel City of N.Y., 1981-83, dep. chief med. malpractice unit, 1983, chief med. malpractice unit, 1984; assoc. Jones, Hirsch, Connors & Bull, NYC, 1985-88; counsel Kern & Augustine, P.A., Morristown, NJ, 1988-90; prin. Kern Augustine Conroy & Schoppmann, P.C., Bridgewater, NJ, 1990—. Spl. counsel pro bono med. malpractice rsch. project, N.Y.C., 1985-88; gen. counsel Med. Soc. N.J., 2002-06. Decorated knight of merit Sacred Mil. Constantinian Order St. George, 2002; Solomon scholar, NY Law Sch., 1979; recipient Bronze Pelican award Roman Cath. Archdiocese, Newark, 2000, Disting. Svc. award N.J. Podiatric Med. Soc. Fellow: Coll. Law Practice Mgmt.; mem.: ABA (chmn. govt. mgmt. com. 1984—86, chmn. document retrieval com. 1985—86, mgr. products media bd. 1985—92, vice-chmn. ins. and malpractice com. 1986—88, coun. mem. 1989—95, co-chmn. glass ceiling task force 1992—95, vice-chmn. law practice mgmt. phb. bd. 1992—95, co-chmn. law practice mgmt. pub. bd. 1995—98, co-chair litig. sect., health litig. program subcom. 2009—, vice chair health law sects. publs. com., Foonberg award 1998), Am. Healthcare Lawyers Assn., N.Y. Bar Assn. (mem. health law sect. 1996—), Assn. of Bar of City of N.Y., Cmty. Health Law Project N.J., Inc. (trustee 1988—91), Westfield Sr. Citizens Housing Corp., Inc. (trustee 1994—, v.p. 1996—98, pres. 1998—), Soc. Health Care Risk Mgmt. N.J. (chmn. legis. com. 1987—96), N.J. Bar Assn. (dir., chmn. health hosp. sect. 1993—95, del. gen. coun. adminstrn. sect. 1995—97, mem. com. health law litigation, mem. subcom. profl. licensing 1995—), Mensa, Harvard Club. Office: Kern Augustine Conroy & Schoppmann PC 1120 Rt 22 E Bridgewater NJ 08807 Home Phone: 908-654-1965; Office Phone: 908-704-8585. Business E-Mail: conroy@drmail.com. E-mail: conroy@drlaw.com.

CONSERVA, ENRICO, dentist, educator; b. Albenga, Jan. 7, 1964; D, Sch. Dentistry, 1987; MS in Implantology, Genoa U., 2000. Assoc. prof. Genoa U., Sch. Dentistry, 2001—. Fellow: Internat. Coll. Prosthodontists; mem.: European Acad. Osseointegration, Am. Acad. Osseointegration. Avocations: sports, art. Office: Via G Mazzini 45/4 Albenga Savona 17031 Italy Business E-Mail: studioconserva@libero.it.

CONSTANTIAN, MARK BARBOUR, plastic surgeon, educator; b. Worcester, Mass., Dec. 19, 1946; s. Harold Martin and Anahid Berberian Constantian; m. Charlotte Ann Dow, Aug. 28, 1993; children: Christopher James, John Andrew, Ronald Brian Clardy, Brett Andrew Clardy. AB in French, Columbia Coll., NYC, 1968; BA in med. Scis., Dartmouth Med. Sch., Hanover, NH, 1970; MD, U. Va. Sch. Medicine, Charlottesville, 1972. Diplomate Am. Bd. of Plastic Surgery, 1979, lic. NH, Mass. Rsch. fellow, dept. physiology Dartmouth Med. Sch., 1969; Am. Soc. Anesthesiology preceptorship Baptist Med. Ctr., Birmingham, Ala., 1970; intern, surgical U. Va. Hosp., 1971—72; resident, gen. surgery Boston U. Med. Ctr., 1972—75, 1975—76, NIGMS fellow, academic surgery, 1975—76; instr., fellow, divsn. plastic and reconstructive surgery Med. Coll. Va., 1976—78; active staff dept. surgery So. NH Med. Ctr. and St. Joseph Hosp., Nashua, 1978—; clin. instr., surgery Harvard Med. Sch., 1984—91. Adj. asst. prof. surgery (plastic and reconstructive) Dartmouth Med. Sch., 1992—; del. NH Med. Soc., 1981—82; chmn., credentials com. Nashua Meml. Hosp., 1981, chmn., dept. surgery, 82, 83, sec. med. staff, 84, v.p. med. staff, 85; guest examiner Am. Bd. Plastic Surgery, 1996, 97, 99. Contbr. chapters to books, several articles to profl. jours.; assoc. editor Annals of Plastic Surgery, 1992—94, Plastic and Reconstructive Surgery, 1997—2003. Trustee St. Peter's Episcopal Ch., Cape Neddick, Maine, 1995—2003. Recipient 1st prize, James R. McClelland Meml. Essay, No. Va. Acad. Surgery, 1978, 1st prize, Bigger-Lehman award, Va. Surgical Soc., 1978, Carl Moyer award, Am. Burn Assn., 1978; named America's Top Dr.-Plastic Surgery-The Best in Am. Medicine, 2001—05; Surgeons Ednl. Found. Scholarship, 1977, So. Med. Assn. Rsch. Project Grant, 1977, A.D. Williams Rsch. Project Grant, Med. Coll. Va., 1977. Fellow: Am. Coll. Surgeons; mem.: Northeastern Soc. Plastic Surgeons (program chmn. 1990, parliamentarian 1991—92, program chmn., one-day aesthetic symposium 1991—93, sec. 1992—95, v.p. 1995—96, pres. 1996—97, founding mem.), Am. Assn. Hand Surgery, New Eng. Soc. Plastic and Reconstructive Surgeons (mem. exec. coun. 1982—85, membership chmn. 1985, sec./treas. 1986—88, pres. 1990—91, nominating com. chmn. 1991—92, Founder's award 2000, 2001, 2003, 2004), Am. Assn. Plastic Surgeons (v.p. 1989), Rhinoplasty Soc. (parliamentarian 1996—97, treas. 1997—98, sec. 1998—99, pres. 2001—02, v.p. 1999—2000), Am. Soc. for Aesthetic Plastic Surgery (northeast rep., membership com. 1997—2000, mem., chair scientific exhibits com. 1998, chair, time and place com. 1999—2001, Tiffany award 1998, 2003), Am. Soc. Plastic Surgeons (ednl. found. in-svc. examination 1981—83, mem.-at-large, bd. dirs. 1993—96, developer, chair, life members program 1996—98, com. mem., life mem. program 1999—, mem., hand and lower extremity com.). Episcopalian. Avocations: musician, songwriter. Office: Memorial Medical Bldg 19 Tyler St Ste 302 Nashua NH 03060 Office Fax: 603-880-6660.

CONSTANTINESCU, ALEX R., pediatrician, nephrologist; MD, Med. Inst. Timisoara, Romania, 1985. Diplomate Am. Bd. Pediat. Intern Flushing (N.Y.) Hosp., 1989—90; resident in pediat. Westchester County Med. Ctr., Valhalla, NY, 1990—92; fellow in pediat. nephrology Montefiore Med. Ctr., Bronx, NY, 1992—95; physician Robert Wood Johnson U. Med. Group, New Brunswick, NJ, 1995—2002; dir. pediat. nephrology Joe DiMaggio Children's Hosp., Hollywood, Fla., 2003—. Office: PMB 308 3389 Sheridan St Hollywood FL 33021-3606 Home Phone: 954-370-6019; Office Phone: 954-894-9344. Business E-Mail: docs4kidneys@yahoo.com.

CONSTANTINIDES, MINAS SPIROS, otolaryngologist, plastic surgeon, educator; b. Thessaloniki, Greece, Jan. 17, 1961; BA in biochemistry magna cum laude, Brown U.; MD, Coll. Physicians and Surgeongs, Columbia U., 1987. Bd. cert. facial plastic surgery and otolaryngology. Intern and resident in gen. surgery Harvard U. Surgical Svc., New England Deaconess Hosp., Boston, 1987—89; resident in otolaryngology- head and neck surgery NYU Sch. Medicine, 1989—93; fellow U. Toronto, 1993—94; dir. facial plastic and reconstructive surgery Dept. Otolaryngology NYU Med. Ctr., 1994—; asst. prof. otolaryngology NYU Sch. Medicine, 1994—. Named one of Top Cosmetic Surgeons in US, Town and Country Mag., 1999, Top Drs. NY, Converse and Connolly, 2000, NY Mag., 2001, 2004, Best Beauty Drs., 2003. Fellow: ACS, Am. Acad. Otolaryngology - Head and Neck Surgery, Am. Acad. Facial Plastic and Reconstructive Surgery (mem. nat. task force domestic violence 1999); mem.: AMA, Hellenic Med. Soc. NY, Facial Plastic Surgery Soc. NY. Office: NYU Med Ctr 530 First Ave Ste 7U New York NY 10016 Office Phone: 212-263-5882, 212-263-8490. E-mail: minas.constantinides@med.nyu.edu.

CONSTANTINO, PETER, otolaryngologist, educator; MD, Northwestern U., 1984. Diplomate Am. Bd. Otolaryngology, 1991, Am. Bd. Surgery-facial plastic and reconstructive surgery, 2000. Intern Northwestern Meml. Hosp., Chgo., 1985, resident in surgery, 1985—86, resident in otolaryngology, 1986—89, fellow head and neck surgery, 1989—90; fellow skull base surgery Pitts. Univ., 1990—91; sr. v.p. Noth Shore Long Island Jewish Hosp.; dir. ctr. for cranial base surgery

NY Head and and Neck Inst. Lenox Hill Hosp., exec. dir. NY Head and and Neck Inst. Office: Lenox Hill Hospital 110 E 59th St Ste 10A New York NY 10022 Office Phone: 212-787-4379. Office Fax: 212-434-4580.

CONSTANTINO-BANA, ROSE EVA, nursing educator, researcher, lawyer; b. Labangan Zamboanga delSur, Philippines, Dec. 25, 1940; arrived in U.S., 1964, naturalized, 1982; d. Norberto C. and Rosalia (Torres) Bana; m. Abraham Antonio Constantino, Jr., Dec. 13, 1964; children: Charles Edward, Kenneth Richard, Abraham Anthony III. BS in Nursing, Philippine Union Coll., Manila, 1962; M of Nursing, U. Pitts., 1971, PhD, 1979; JD, Duquesne U., Pitts., 1984. Lic. clin. specialist in psychiatric-mental health nursing, RN. Instr. Philippine Union Co., 1963-65, Spring Grove State Hosp., Balt., 1965-67, Montefiore Sch. Nursing, Pitts., 1967-70, U. Pitts., 1971-74, asst. prof., 1974-83, assoc. prof., 1983—, chmn. Senate Athletic Com., 1985-86, 89-90, sec. univ. senate, 1991-92, v.p., 1993-95. Project dir. grant divsn. nursing HHS, Washington, 1983-85; bd. dir. Am. Jour. Nursing; prin. investigator NIH NINR, 1991-94; bd. dir. Internat. Coun. Women's Health Issues, 1986—; CEO PALAW, 1997. Author (with others): Principles and Practice of Psychiatric Nursing, 1982; contbr. chapters to books, articles to profl. jours.;, editor forensic nursing textbook. Fellow: Am. Coll. Forensic Examiners, Am. Acad. Nursing; mem.: ANA, IAFN (chair ethics com.), NG Knowledge Internat. (chair bd. dirs. 2010—), Nursing Found. Pa. (bd. pres. 2007—09), Am. Nurses Found. (v.p. 2004—07), Sexual Assault Nurse Examiners, Am. Assn. Legal Nurse Cons., Allegheny County Bar Assn., Pa. State Nurses Assn. (sec. 1994—98, chairperson area 6), Women in the Profession, Pa. Bar Assn., Allegheny County Bar Assn. (bd. cert. forensic examiner), Pitts. Action Against Rape (BOD pres. 2006—07), U. Pitts. Sch. Nursing Alumni Assn., U. Duquesne Law Alumni Assn., Nat. Coun. Jewish Women (Pitts. sect.), Nursing Knowledge Inst. STTI (bd. chmn. 2010—), Phi Alpha Delta, Sigma Theta Tau. Mem. Seventh Day Adventist Ch. Avocations: cooking, piano. Home: 6 Carmel Ct Pittsburgh PA 15221-3618 Office: U Pitts Sch Nursing 4500 Victoria St Rm 415 Pittsburgh PA 15261-0001 Office Phone: 412-624-2063. Business E-Mail: rco100@pitt.edu, rc@roseconstantino.com.

CONTE, JOHN V., surgeon, educator; b. New Haven, Dec. 1, 1958; BS, Providence, 1981; MD, Georgetown, 1986. Prof. surgery Johns Hopkins U., 1997—. Rsch. grants, NIH. Fellow: STSA, AHA (Rsch. grants), STS, AATS. Avocations: sports, fishing, hiking. Office: Divsn Cardiac Surgery Blalock 618 Ellicott City MD 21042 Office Fax: 410-955-3809. Business E Mail: jconte@jhmi.edu.

CONTRACTOR, SOHAIL, radiologist, educator; b. Mumbai, Apr. 29, 1967; MD, Grant Med. Coll., Mumbai, 1990. Assoc. prof., vice chair, radiology U. Medicine and Dentistry, NJ, 2006—. Named Faculty of Yr., U. Medicine and Dentistry, Dept. Radiology; named one of Americas Top Drs., Consumer Rsch. Coun. Mem.: Soc. Interventional Radiology. Office: University Hosp H 108 150 Bergen St Newark NJ 07101 Business E-Mail: contrasg@umdnj.edu.

CONVERY, FREDRICK RICHARD, retired surgeon, orthopedist; b. Olympia, Wash., June 12, 1932; m. Martha Ann Minteer; children: Kristine Helen, Linda Lea, Mark Richard. BA, U. Wash., 1954, MD, 1958. Diplomate Am. Bd. Orthopaedic Surgery (examiner 1980-91). Intern Mpls. Gen. Hosp., 1958-59; resident U. Wash., Seattle, 1961-66; fellow in arthritis Rancho Las Amigos, Downey, Calif., 1966-67; instr. orthopedics U. Wash., Seattle, 1967-68, asst. prof., 1968-71, assoc. prof., 1971-72, U. Calif., San Diego, 1972-77, surgeon in residence, prof. surgery, 1977-97. Inventor prosthetic fixation technique. Mem. med. and sci. com. Western Wash. chpt. The Arthritis Found., 1968-72, San Diego chpt., 1973, chmn., 1977-78; mem. Calif. State Arthritis Coun., 1974-76. With USNR. Grantee Johnson & Johnson, 1994. Fellow Am. Acad. Orthopaedic Surgeons (exam. and evaluation com. 1974-82, Kappa Delta award 1972); mem. Am. Rheumatism Assn. (sect. arthritis, program com. 1973-75), Western Orthopaedic Assn. (Vernon P. Thompson award for Resident Rsch. 1964), Acad. Orthopaedic Soc., Am. Orthopaedic Assn. (resident guest 1966), Orthopaedic Rsch. Soc., Internat. Soc. of the Knee, Assn. for Arthritic Hip and Knee Soc., Wilson-Bost Interurban Club. E-mail: rcon725286@aol.com. *

CONWAY, JAMES HYDE, pediatrician, educator; s. James A. and Linda Hyde Conway; m. Katherine Elizabeth Trace, June 2, 1990. BS in Biol. Scis., Cornell U., Ithaca, NY, 1986, MD, 1990. Diplomate Am. Bd. Pediat., Am. Bd. Pediat. Infectious Disease 1997. Resident pediat. Northwestern U., Chgo., 1990—93; fellow pediat. infectious disease U. Colo. Health Scis. Ctr., Denver, 1994—97; assoc. prof. clin. pediat. Ind. U. Sch. Medicine-Riley Hosp., Indpls., 1997—2005; assoc. prof. pediat. U. Wis., Madison, 2005—. Fellow: Am. Acad. Pediat. Office: 600 Highland Ave H4/450 CSC Madison WI 53792-4108 Office Phone: 608-265-6488.

CONWAY, JASON, gastroenterologist, educator; b. St. Louis, Dec. 31, 1971; MD, UNC Sch. Medicine, 1999; MPH, UNC Sch. Pub. Health, 2005. Asst. prof. Wake Forest Bapt. Med. Ctr., 2006—. Mem.: NC Soc. Gastroenterology, Am. Coll. Gastroenterology, Am. Soc. Gastrointestinal Endoscopy. Office: Wake Forest Baptist Med Ctr Medical Winston Salem NC 27157 Office Phone: 336-713-7777. Office Fax: 336-713-7322. Business E-Mail: jconway@wfubmc.edu.

CONWAY, PAUL GARY, neuropharmacologist; b. Monson, Mass., July 31, 1952; s. Andrew Paul and Joan Sarah (Haley) C.; m. Malana Frances Seniuk, Aug. 21, 1976. BS in Pharmacy, Ohio No. U., 1975; MS in Pharmacology, U. Toledo, 1978; PhD in Pharmacology, Ohio State U., 1982. Postdoctoral fellow U. Pa., Phila., 1982-84; sr. rsch. pharmacologist Hoechst Roussel Pharm. Inc., Somerville, N.J., 1984-86, rsch. assoc., 1986-88, group leader, 1988-92, project mgr., 1992-95, sr. project mgr., 1995-96; dir. project planning Janssen Rsch. Found., Titusville, N.J., 1996-98; dir. project planning & contract adminstrn. Clin. Studies Ltd., Providence, R.I., 1998—. Adj. asst. prof. Fairleigh-Dickinson U., Madison, N.J., 1986; pharmacology instr. Ohio No. U., Ada, 1975-76. Editor Clin. Neuropharmacology, 1991; contbr. more than 40 articles to profl. jours.; patentee in field. Mem. Am. Soc. Pharmacology and Exptl. Therapeutics, Soc. for Neurosci., Internat. Brain Rsch. Orgn., Drug Info. Assn., Sigma Xi. Avocations: sailing, golf. Office: Clinical Studies Ltd 3 Regency Plz Ste 12 Providence RI 02903-3114 *

CONWAY DE MACARIO, EVERLY, molecular biologist; d. Delfin E. and Maria Gloria (Benatuil) Conway; m. Alberto J. L. Macario, Mar. 16, 1963; children: Alex, Everly. PhD in Pharmacy, Nat. U. Buenos Aires, 1960, PhD in Biochemistry, 1962. Rsch. fellow Nat. Acad. Medicine Argentina, Buenos Aires, 1962-63; head lab. oncology and immunology Argentinian Assn. against Cancer, Buenos Aires, 1966-67; chief of immunology Sch. Medicine, Buenos Aires, 1967-68; rsch. fellow dept. tumor-biology Karolinska Inst., Stockholm, 1969-71; sr. rsch. scientist Lab. Cell Biology, NRC Italy, Rome, 1971-73; vis. scientist Internat. Agy. Rsch. on Cancer, WHO, Lyon, France, 1973-74, Brown U., Providence, 1974-76; rsch. scientist Wadsworth Ctr. NY State Dept. Health, Albany, 1976—2006; prof. dept. biomed. scis. Sch. Pub. Health, Albany, 1986—2002, mem. admission com., 1986-89; scientist U. Maryland Biotechnology Inst., 2004—10; adj. prof. Dept. Microbiol. and Immunology, Sch. Medicine, U. Maryland, Balt., 2010—. Grant referee in field. Editor: Monoclonal Antibodies against Bacteria, 1985-86, vols. I-III, Gene Probes for Bacteria, 1990; assoc. editor profl. jour. 1986—; mng. editor Frontiers on Biosci.; contbr. articles to profl. jours.; contbr. chpts. to books and encyclopedias. Past mem. Scandinavian Soc. Immunology, Italian Assn. Immunologists, French Soc. Immunology. Recipient Prof. J.M. Mezzadra award Nat. U. Buenos Aires, 1969, Travel award 2nd Internat. Immunology Congress, French Soc. Immunology, 1974. Gold medal Argentinian Soc. Biochemistry, 1980, Hans Osterman Found. grantee, Sweden, 1969, Sir Samuel Scott of Yews Trust grantee, Sweden, 1970, Winifred Cullis grantee Internat. Fedn. Univ. Women, 1972, NATO rsch. grantee, 1975, 81, U.S. Dept. Energy grantee, 1981, 84; Travel award to China, 1985, Spain, 1993, South Africa, 1994; Italy, 2008; elected fellow mem. Am. Acad. Microbiology, 1997. Mem. Am. Assn. Immunologists (chmn. com. on status of women 1980-86, edn. com. 1982-87, awards com. 1991-92, travel award to Australia 1977), Am. Soc. Microbiology (sr. editor Manual Clin. Lab. Immunology 4th-5th edits.), Internat. Soc. Microbial Ecology, Cell Stress Soc. Internat., Nat. Acad. Microbiology (chmn. Morrison Rogosa awards com. 2002-06, chmn. internat. subcom. on taxonomy of methanogens). Achievements include patents for micro circle system, micro sample holder and carrier; invention of ultra sensitive micro-immunoenzyamtic assay and multipurpose modular system; discovery of oscillations of antibody affinity during maturation of the immune response, diversity of methanogens in natural and manufactured ecosystems; development of antibodies and immunochemical methods for dissecting the antigenic mosaic of archaeal organisms and determination of the identity of methanogens as a distinct and antigenically coherent group of prokaryotes different from bacteria; first to identification of the predominant archaeal organism in the human colon, periodontal space, and vagina, and ascertainment that it is Methanobrevibacter smithii; elucidation of population dynamics of defined methanogenic species in microbial consortia; discovery of the structural topography of methanogens in microbial consortia; isolation for the first time of the ABC-transporter genes and the genes in the hsp70/dnaK locus from an archaebacterim (archaeon); determination that the archaeal hsp70 genes belong to various evolutionary lineages; a unicelled organism with the main four chaperoning system in the cytoplasm; identification of two new chaperonins in archaea; development of first integration vector for genetically engineering a methanogen useful for waste bioconversion; creation of the concept of sick chaperone or chaperonopathy as a factor contributing to the ageing process and disease; elucidation of the entire set of hsp70 genes in the human genome; characterization of the whole complement of cct Hsp60 genes in the human genome. Home: 9 Travilah Terrace Potomac MD 20854 Office: Sch Medicine University Maryland Balt IMET Columbus Ctr 701 E Pratt St Baltimore MD 21202 Office Phone: 410-234-8886. Business E-Mail: everlyc@gmail.com.

CONWELL, HALFORD ROGER, physician; b. Cin., Jan. 28, 1924; s. Halford Fredrick and Erma Pearl (Cornelius) C.; m. Margaret Ann King, Dec. 15, 1965; children: Mark A., Sherri L., John H. BA, U. Wooster, 1948; MA, U. Louisville, 1950; MD, U. Cin., 1955. ATP; diplomate crew coordination tng. Continental Airlines. Lt. USNR, 1943—54; practice in aviation medicine Huntsville, Tex., 1959—; mem. staff Huntsville Meml. Hosp., chief of staff, 1974-75, chief medicine, 1976-80, bd. trustees, 1991—2005. Locomotive fireman, Pa. RR, 1940-41, sr. U.S. med. officer Brit. Caledonian Airways, 1977-89; cons. Aeromexico; chief flight surgeon Continental Airlines, 1996—; mem. Walker County Hosp. Dist., 1975-79, chmn., 1976-79; asst. dean of men, instr. psychology Heidelberg U., Tiffin, Ohio, 1950-51; instr. psychology Cin. Coll.; sr. med. examiner FAA; sr. examiner C.A.A. (U.K.), C.A.A. (Australia); newspaper columnist, 1992—. Trustee Biol. Analysis and Rsch. Found.; capt. (hon.) Tex. Internat. Airline, Continental Airlines Golden Eagles, 2007; founder Bomber Command Mus. (R.A.F.). Recipient safe pilot award Nat. Pilots Assn., Pilot Proficiency award FAA, Profl. Svc. Citation. Fellow Aerospace Med. Assn., Civil Aviation Assn. (John A. Tamisiea award 2000, Bernice Audie Davis award 2005), Civil Aviation Med. Assn. (v.p. 1968-80, dir. 1968—, pres. 1980-81, award of merit 1994, 97), Airline Pilos Assn.(Lifetime Achievement award 2008); mem. Brit. Assn. Aerospace Medicine, Latin Am. Aviation Med. Assn., Scottish Assn. Aviation Med. Examiners, Airline Med. Dirs. Assn., Mitchell Pediatric Soc., Academie Internationale de Medicine Aeronatque et Spatiale, Aircraft Owners and Pilots Assn. (med. adv. panel), Confederate Air Force (founding mem.), Air Transp. Assn. (med. com.), Order Ky. Cols., Quiet Birdmen, Masons, Psi Chi, Alpha Psi Omega. Office: 2800 Lake Rd Huntsville TX 77340-5632 Office Phone: 936-295-5222.

COOK, COLIN BURFORD, psychiatrist; b. London, Jan. 20, 1927; arrived in U.S., 1952, naturalized, 1975; s. Bertram William and Anna Marie (Forster-Jones) C. MD, London U., 1951. Diplomate Am. Bd. Psychiat. & Neurology, 1979. Rotating intern Bridgeport Hosp., Conn., 1952-53; resident Goodmayes Hosp., Warlingham Park Hosp., London, 1955-57; gen. med. practitioner London, 1960-66; resident in psychiatry Marquette Sch. Medicine, Wis., 1968-69, Cornell U., White Plains, NY, 1969-71; fellow Nat. Hosp. Neurol. Disease, U. London, 1973; practice medicine specializing in psychiatry, Stamford, Conn., 1975—; cons. physician Cologne Life Reinsurance Co., 1976—84. Prof. psychiatry Columbia U., NYC, 1992-95. Author: (as Alan Phillips) Jazz Improvisation and Harmony, 1965, 4th edit., 1998. Served with Brit. Navy, 1953-55. Fellow: Am. Soc. Psychoanalytic Physicians; mem.: AMA, Authors League, Masons (32d degree). Address: 373 Strawberry Hill Ave Stamford CT 06902-2512 Office Phone: 203-348-9091. Personal E-mail: ccookie3210@aol.com.

COOK, DAVID A., state official, public health service officer; Grad., Ga. So. U., 1976, U. Ga., 1982. Clin. prof. sch. law U. Ga., 1982—83; tchr. constl. law Ga. So. U.; mng. ptnr. McGuire, Cook, & Martin, P.C., 1983—92; gen. counsel Med. Assn. Ga., dir. advocacy, exec. dir., 2001—10, CEO, 2001—10; commr. Ga. Dept. Cmty. Health, 2011—. Bd. dirs. Physician's Inst. for Excellence Medicine, Physician Advocacy Inst., Ga. Med. Polit. Action Com.; bd. dirs. advocacy resource ctr. AMA; pres. Am. Soc. Med. Assn. Counsel. Recipient Meritorious Achievement award, AMA, 2009. Office: Georgia Department of Community Health 2 Peachtree St NW Atlanta GA 30303 Office Phone: 404-656-4507.

COOK, DEVON RYAN, orthodontist; b. Flint, Mich., Dec. 1, 1973; DDS, Ind. U. Sch. Dentistry, 2000; MDS, U. Tenn., 2003. Diplomate Am. Bd. Orthodontics. Owner, pres. Cook Orthodontics, P.C., 2003—. Mem.: Ind. Assn. Orthodontists, World Fedn. Orthodontists, Am. Assn. Orthodontists. Avocations: travel, golf. Office: 300 Eagle Crest Dr Evansville IN 47715 Office Fax: 812-402-3482. E-mail: drcook@cook-ortho.com.

COOK, DONALD EVAN, pediatrician, educator; b. Pitts., Mar. 24, 1928; s. Merriam E. and Bertha (Gwin) C.; m. Elsie Walden, Sept. 2, 1951; children: Catherine, Christopher, Brian, Jeffrey. BS, Colo. Coll., 1952; MD, U. Colo., 1955. Diplomate Am. Bd. Pediat., 1961. Intern Fresno County Gen. Hosp., Calif., 1955-56; resident in gen. practice Tulare (Calif.) County Gen. Hosp., 1956-57; resident in pediatrics U. Colo., 1957-59; practice medicine specializing in pediatrics Aurora, Colo., 1959—64, Greeley (Colo). Med. Clinic, 1964—86, Greeley Sports Medicine Clinic, 1988—93; med. adv. Centennial Develop. Svcs., Inc., 1993-95; clin. faculty U. Colo., clin. prof., 1977—; pres. Am. Acad. Pediatrics, Elk Grove Village, Ill., 1999-2000; ret. from practice, 2004. Organizer, dir. Sports Medicine Px Exam. Clinic for Indigent Weld Co. athletes, 1990—96; mem. adv. bd. Nat. Ctr. Health Edn., San Francisco, 1978—80; mem. adv. com. inmaternal and child health programs Colo. State Health Dept., 1981—84, chmn., 1981—84; preceptor Sch. Nurse Practitioner program U. Colo., 1978—88; affiliate prof. nursing U. No. Colo., 1996; vol. physician Monfort Children's Clinic, 2002—05. Mem. Weld County Dist. 6 Sch. Bd., 1973—83, pres., 1973—74, 1976—77, chmn. dist. 6 accountability com., 1972—73, mem. adv. com. dist. 6 teen pregnancy program, 1983—85; mem. Weld County Task Force on Teen-aged Pregnancy, 1986—89, Dream Team Weld County Task Force on Sch. Dropouts, 1986—92; mem.Weld County Interagy. Screening Bd., Weld County Cmty. Ctr. Found., 1984—89; mem. Weld County Task Force Spkrs. Bur. on AIDS, 1987—94, Weld County Task Force Adolescent Health Clinic, Task Force Child Abuse, C. of C.; bd. dirs. No. Colo. Med. Ctr., 1993—98, No. Colo. Med. Ctr. Found., 1994—; med. advisor Weld County Sch. Dist. VI-Nurses, 1987—2004; mem. Sch. Dist. 6 Health Coalition, Task Force on Access to Health Care; group leader neonatal group Colo. Action for Healthy People Colo. Dept. Pub. Health, 1985—86; co-founder Colorodians for Seatbelts on Sch. Buses, 1985—90; co-founder, v.p. Coalition of Primary Care Physicians Colo., 1986; mem. adv. com. Greeley Ctrl. Drug and Alcohol Abuse, 1984—86; bd. dirs. Rocky Mtn. Ctr. for Health Promotion and Edn., 1984—2006, v.p., 1992—93, pres., 1994—95; med. cons. Sch. Dist. 6, 1989—2004; mem. bd. dirs. United Way Weld County, 1993—98; founder, med. dir. Monfort Children's Clinic, 1994—98, vol. physician, 1998—2004. With USN, 1946—48. Recipient Disting. Svc. award, Jr. C. of C., 1962, Svc. to Mankind award, Sertoma Club, 1972, Disting. Citizenship award, Elks, 1975—76, 2000—01, Spark Plug award, U. No. Colo., 1981, Mildred Doster award, Colo. Sch. Health Coun. for Sch. Health Contbns., 1992, Svc. award, Eta Sigma Gamma, 1996, Citizen of Yr. award, No. Colo. Med. Ctr. Found., 1996, Humanitarian of Yr. award, Weld County United Way, 1996, Alfred Winchester Humanitarian award, Greeley/Weld Sr. Found., Inc., 1996, Silver and Gold award, U. Colo. Med. Alumni Assn., 1997, Franklin Geggenbach award, 1997, Denver Children's Hosp. Pediatric Alumni award, 1997, Benezet award, Colo. Coll., 2000, Edn. Ptnr. of the Yr. award, Greeler-Weld C. of C., 2004, 2006, Leeann Anderson Cmty. Care award, Greeley C. of C., 2006. Mem.: AMA (chmn. sch. and coll. health com. 1980—82, James E. Strain Cmty. Svc. award 1987, 1994), Greeley C. of C. (mem. local bus. govt. affairs com., local bus. affairs com.), Centennial Pediatric Soc. (pres. 1982—86), Colo. Med. Soc. (com. in sports medicine 1980—90, com. chmn. 1986—90, chmn. com. sch. health 1988—91, A.H. Robbins Cmty. Svc. award 1974), Weld County Med. Soc. (pres. 1968—69), Adams Aurora Med. Soc. (pres. 1964—65), Am. Acad. Pediat. (chmn. sch. health com. 1975—80, mem. task force on new age of pediatrics 1982—85, chmn. Colo. chpt. 1982—87, media spokesperson Speak Up for Children 1983—, Ross edn. and award com. 1985—86, alt. dist. VIII chmn. 1987—93, mem. coun. sects. mgmt. 1991—92, chmn. alt. dist. chmn. com. 1991—93, dist. chmn. dist. VIII 1993—98, mem. search com., exec. dir. candidate for pres. 1998, pres. elect 1998—99, v.p. AAP 1998—99, pres. 1999—2000, 1999—2000, immediate past pres. 2000—01, dist. VIII catch facilitator 2000—06, tomorrows children's task force 2001—04, reimbursement task force 2002—04), Colo. Med. Soc. Sch. Health Com. (chmn. 1967—78), Colo. Coll. Alumni Assn. (bd. dirs. 2003—, co-chmn. class 52 50th reunion com.), Rotary (bd. dirs. Greely chpt. 1988—91, chmn. immunization campaign Weld County 1994, mem. immunization com. 1994—, mem. adv. bd. Greeley Promises for Children 2001—, bd. dirs. Greely chpt. 2003—05, mem. task force on indigent care 2004—, mem. sch. readiness task force 2004—, William D. Farr award 2007, Cmty. Svc. award 2007). Republican. Methodist. Office: Monfort Children's Clinic 100 N 11th Ave Greeley CO 80631 Office Phone: 970-352-0072. Personal E-mail: ecook4130@msn.com. Business E-Mail: dcook@aap.org.

COOK, EDWIN H., JR., psychiatrist, educator; Dir. Lab. Devel. Neuroscience, autism researcher; prof. psychiatry U. Ill., Chgo. Office: Institute for Juvenile Research UIC Department of Psychiatry 1747 W Roosevelt Rd Rm 155 Chicago IL 60612 Office Phone: 312-413-4537. E-mail: ecook@psych.uic.edu.

COOK, IAN AINSWORTH, psychiatrist, researcher, educator; b. NYC, May 1, 1960; s. Charles David and Bobette Cook; m. Hallie Houck; children: Natalie, Abigail. BS in Engring. magna cum laude, Princeton U., 1982; MD, Yale U., 1987. Diplomate Nat. Bd. Med. Examiners, Am. Bd. Psychiatry and Neurology. Resident in surgery U. Colo., Denver, 1987-88; resident in psychiatry Neuropsychiat. Inst. UCLA, 1991-94, chief resident in liaison psychiatry, 1993-94, instr. dept. psychiatry, 1995-96, assoc. dir. residency edn. dept. psychiatry, 1995-96, asst. prof psychiatry, 1996—2003, assoc. prof. psychiatry, 2003—; registrar Neuropsychiat. Inst., 1999—2001; dir. NPI Acad. Info. Tech. Core, 1999—; assoc. dir. Office of Profl. and Cmty. Edn., 1998—. Examiner Am. Bd. Psychiatry and Neurology, 1998—; chmn. departmental Curriculum Com., 2005-07; assoc. dir. Lab. of Brain, Behavior, and Pharmacology, 2006—; dir. UCLA Depression

Rsch. Program, 2007—; mem. task force on professionalism David Geffen Sch. Medicine, UCLA, 2007—; Joanne and George Miller and Family Endowed chair in depression rsch, UCLA Brain Rsch. Inst., 2008-; dir., UCLA Transcranial Magnetic Stimulation Svc. 2009-. Mem. editl. bd. Jefferson Jour. Psychiatry, 1992-94; editor: Mood Disorders, Cogent Medicine, 2005-; contbr. articles to profl. jours. Rsch. fellow Nat. Inst. Mental Health, 1993-96; recipient Young Investigator award Nat. Alliance Rsch. Schizophrenia and Depression, 1995, 97. Fellow: West Coast Coll. Biol. Psychiatry (mem. exec. bd 2005-, pres. 2007—, Jr. Faculty Rsch. award 2003); mem.: Am. Psychiat. Assn. (Burroughs-Wellcome fellow 1992, mem. com. of resident and fellows 1992-94, mem. steering com./practice guidelines 1994-2008, mem. exec. com. 2002-08, disting. fellow 2009), So. Calif. Psychiat. Soc. (councilor 2004—), Nat. Eagle Scout Assn., Sigma Xi, Tau Beta Pi. Achievements include four patents in biomed. devices and methods. Office: UCLA Neuropsychiat Inst & Hosp 760 Westwood Plz Los Angeles CA 90095-8353

COOK, JAMES, veterinarian; m. Marian Spragens, 1968; children: James O., Amanda Cook Reed. B, M, U. Ky., Lexington; DVM, Auburn U., Ala., 1976. Sci., biology tchr. Jessamine and Marion County Sch. Systems, Ky.; veterinarian Cook Animal Hosp., Lebanon, Ky., 1976—. Mem., elder United Presbyn Ch., Lebanon; mem. Marion County Bd. Health, 1983—, chmn., 1997—2002; past mem. Marion County Shelter Bd.; past mem. Ag adv. com. Marion County HS; mem. Lincoln. Trail Regional Bd. Health, Ky., 1994—2002. Fellow: U. Ky.; mem.: Ky. Vet. Med. Assn. (past pres., Disting. Svc. award 2002, Ky. Veterinarian of Yr. 1988), Am. Vet. Med. Assn. (Ky. rep. 1996—2001, exec. bd. vice chmn. 2005—06, pres. 2008—09), Am. Assn. Equine Practitioners, Am. Assn. Bovine Practitioners, Am. Animal Hosp. Assn., Auburn U. Sch. Vet. Medicine Centennial Club, U. Ky. Agr. Alumni (life). Office: Cook Animal Hosp 1955 Springfield Hwy Lebanon KY 40033-8107 Office Phone: 270-692-6787. Office Fax: 270-692-1721. Business E-Mail: cookanhosp@alltel.net. *

COOK, JOHN Q., plastic surgeon; BA cum laude, Yale U.; MD, Northwestern U. Med. Sch.; M in Surgical Rsch., U. Ill., Chicago. Cert. Am. Bd. of Plastic Surgery. Chief surgical resident Rush Presbyn./St. Luke's Med. Ctr.; plastic surgery resident Northwestern Meml. Hosp.; plastic surgeon Whole Beauty Inst. (formerly Cook Ctr. for Med. Skin Enhancement), Chgo., 1988—. Asst. prof., faculty mem. Dept. Plastic and Reconstructive Surgery Rush U. Med. Ctr. Named Top Doctor, Castle Connelly Guide, Top Surgeon, Consumers' Rsch. Council of Am. Mem.: Chicago Soc. of Plastic Surgery, Am. Soc. of Plastic Surgeons, Am. Soc. for Aesthetic Plastic Surgery. Office: Whole Beauty Inst 737 N Michigan Ave Ste 760 Chicago IL 60611-6662 Office Phone: 312-751-2112.

COOK, JONATHAN L., dermatologist, educator; MD, U. SC, 1999. Diplomate Am. Bd. Dermatology, 2005. Resident internal medicine Harvard Sch. of Medicine, Mass., 1992—93; resident dermatology Emory Univ. Hosp., Ga., 1993—96; fellow mohs and dermatologic surgery Univ. of Pa., 1996—97; prof. dermatology dept. Duke Univ.; hosp. affiliation include Duke Univ. Med. Ctr. Office: Duke Medicine Ste 400 5324 McFarland Drive Durham NC 27707 Office Phone: 919-419-4945. Office Fax: 919-419-4930.

COOK, MARK JAMES, neurologist, educator; b. Salford, Eng., Jan. 18; MBBS, U. Melbourne, Victoria, Australia, 1983, MD, 1999. Prof. neurology St. Vincent's Hosp., Melbourne, 2002—10; prof., chair medicine U. Melbourne, 2010—. Bd. chmn. Epilepsy Found. Victoria, 1998. Grants, NHMRC, ARC, STI grant, DIIRD. Fellow: Royal Australian Coll. Physicians; mem.: Australian and New Zealand Assn. Neurologists. Office: University Melbourne Grattan St Parkville Melbourne Victoria 3052 Australia Office Fax: 61392883350. Business E-Mail: markcook@unimelb.edu.au.

COOK, PHILIP JACKSON, economist, educator; b. Buffalo, Oct. 15, 1946; s. Gerhard Albert and Lura (Lincoln) C.; m. Judith Walmsley, June 27, 1966; children; Elizabeth Camden, Brian Lincoln. BA, U. Mich., 1968; PhD, U. Calif., Berkeley, 1973. Prof. Duke U., Durham, NC, 1973—, dir. Inst. Policy Scis., 1985—89, dir. Sanford Inst. Pub. Policy, 1997—99. Vis. scholar Inst. Rsch. in Social Sci. U. NC, Chapel Hill, 1980, mem. adv. bd. Injury Prevention Rsch. Ctr., 1990—; expert Office Poly. and Mgmt. Analysis, criminal divsn. U.S. Dept. Justice, 1982; mem. rsch. adv. com. U.S. Sentencing Commn., 1986—91, chair rsch. adv. com., 1986; mem. adv. bd. H. John Heinz III Sch. Pub. Policy and Mgmt. Carnegie Mellon U., 1992—; mem. Ctr. Gun Policy Rsch. Johns Hopkins U., 1995—2003; cons. enforcement divsn. U.S. Dept. Treasury, 1999—2000; rsch. assoc. Nat. Bur. Econ. Rsch., 1996—; mem. adv. com. Harvard Injury Control Ctr. Author: Selling Hope, 1989, The Winner-Take All Society, 1995, Gun Violence, 2000, Evaluating Gun Policy, 2003, Paying the Tab: The Economics of Alcohol Policy, 2007. Recipient Sims Award, Economics Dept., U. Mich., 1967, Kenneth J. Arrow award for best paper published in health econ., 1994, Vernon Meml. prize, Jour. Policy Analysis & Mgmt., 1997, 2008, Nat. Sci. Found. fellowship, 1968—70, Richard A. Stubbing Tchr. Mentor Award, Duke U., 2008. Fellow: Am. Soc. Criminology; mem.: Inst. Medicine of NAS, Nat. Rsch. Coun. Com. on Law and Justice (vice chair 2008—), Am. Econ. Assn., Assn. Pub. Policy and Mgmt. (treas. 1985—93, v.p. 2007—09), Phi Beta Kappa. Office: Duke University Sch Pub Policy PO Box 90245 Durham NC 27708-0245 Business E-Mail: pcook@duke.edu.

COOK, STUART DONALD, neurologist, educator; b. Boston, Oct. 23, 1936; s. Martius and Nina (Schwartzman) C.; m. Josepha Emdin, June 26, 1960; children— Andrew, Peter, Jonathan. AB, Brandeis U., 1957; MS, U. Vt., 1959, MD, 1962. Diplomate: Am. Bd. Psychiatry and Neurology. Intern Upstate Med. Center, Syracuse, NY, 1962-63; resident in neurology Albert Einstein Coll. Medicine, Bronx, NY, 1965-67, chief resident, 1967-68, instr. dept. neurology, 1968-69; asst. prof. neurology Coll. Physician and Surgeons, Columbia U., NYC, 1969-71; prof. medicine NJ Med. Sch., Newark, 1971, chmn. dept. neuroscis., 1972-98, prof. neurology, neurosciences, 1972—; chief neurology svc. VA Med. Ctr., East Orange, NJ, 1971-86; acting dean NJ Med. Sch., 1987-89; pres. U. Medicine and Dentistry N.J., 1998—2004. Vis. scientist div. virology Nat. Inst. Med. Research, London, 1977-78; vis. scientist Swiss Inst. for Cancer Research, 1985. Contbr. articles to profl. jours. Served with USN, 1963-65. Mem. Am. Acad. Neurology (S. Weir Mitchell award 1968), AAUP, Harvey Soc., Am. Neurol. Assn., Sigma Xi, Alpha Omega Alpha. Home: 26 Dogwood Dr Morristown NJ 07960-3310 Office: U Medicine and Dentistry Rm 1435 65 Bergen St Newark NJ 07101-1709 Business E-Mail: cooksd@umdnj.edu.

COOK-DEEGAN, ROBERT MULLAN, physician, educator; s. William Raymond Cook and Merry (Mullan) Low. BA in Chemistry, Harvard Coll., 1975; MD, U. Colo., 1979. Intern U. Colo., Denver, 1979-80, postdoctoral fellow, rsch. pathologist, 1980-82; sr. assoc. Office Tech. Assessment, U.S. Congress, Washington, 1982-88; acting exec. dir. biomed. ethics adv. com. U.S. Congress, Washington, 1988-89; expert Nat. Ctr. Human Genome Rsch., Bethesda, Md., 1989-90; dir. div. bio-behavioral scis. and mental disorders Inst. Medicine, NAS, Washington, 1991-94; sr. program officer NAS, 1994-96; Cecil and Ida Green fellow U. Tex., Dallas, 1996; dir. Nat. Cancer Policy Bd., 1996-2000, Robert Wood Johnson Health Policy Fellowship Program, 2001—02, Ctr. Genome Ethics Law and Policy, Duke U., 2002—. Author: The Gene Wars: Science, Politics, and the Human Genome, 1994; contbr. articles and chpts. in field. Bd. dirs. Physicians for Human Rights, Boston, 1987-96; dir. ctr. excellence Ethical, Legal & Social Implications Rsch., NIH, 2004—. Recipient Robert Johnson Health Policy Rsch. Investigator award, 1999—2002; grantee Alfred P. Sloan Found., Georgetown U., 1988—91, NSF, 1990—91, Nat. Cancer Inst. and Robert Wood Johnson, 1992—2000, Burroughs Wellcome Fund, 2000—01. Fellow AAAS. Achievements include research in history of human genome project, public policy in cancer, health policy, tobacco control, neurology, psychiatry, behavioral medicine, neuroscience and addiction; U.S. federal policy on Alzheimer's disease and other dementing disorders, public policy on human gene therapy and bioethics. Office: Duke Univ Box 90141 Durham NC 27708-0141 Office Phone: 919-668-0793.

COOKE, BENSON GEORGE, counseling psychologist, psychology professor, consultant; b. Toledo, June 5, 1953; s. Benjamin George Cooke and Elfreda June (Hocker) Foster; m. Alpha L. Bailey, Jan. 26, 1976 (div. Jan. 1990); children: Dawn M. Cunningham, Daá iyah Suad, Siddeeq Seifuddin. BA in Psychology, Morehouse Coll., 1975; MS in Clin. Psychology, U. Mass., 1978, EdD in Counseling Psychology, 1981. Clin. therapist Hope Haven-Madonna Manor, Marerro, La., 1983; asst. prof., chmn. dept. psychology Xavier U., New Orleans, 1982-85; program psychologist PSI Assocs., Inc., Washington, 1985-86, dir. dually diagnosed programs, 1986-89, program psychologist, program psychol. assoc., 1989-92, devel. trainer Md. Foster Parent Tng. Program, 1992—; counseling psychologist, asst. prof., coord. peer empowerment program, asst. dir. multicultural services George Mason U., Fairfax, Va., 1992—2005; assoc. prof. psychology and counseling, coord. grad. counseling program U. DC, Washington, 2006—. Cons. Benson G. Cooke Cons. Svcs., Washington, 1989—, Washington and Washington, Inc., Washington, 1993—, Cmty. Links, Inc., Washington, 1994-95, Spectrum Care, Inc., Washington, 1994—. Author: Person Growth for People of Color: Keys to Success in Higher Education, 2001; contbr. articles to profl. jours., chapters to books. Program coord./curriculum coord. Manhood Tng./Rites of Passage, Union Temple Bapt. Ch., Washington, 1995—, co-facilitator youth discussion group, 1996—; vol., mentor, program coord. J.O. Wilson Elem. Sch. and Payne Elem. Sch., Washington, 1989—. Mem. ACA, Am. Assn. Mental Retardation, Am. Mgmt. Assn., Assn. Black Psychologists (DC chpt. pres. 1995-96, bd. dirs. 2000-02, 03, 04-06, 06-08, treas., 2003, 04-06, nat. pres. 2009-11; Bobby E. Wright award 2006), Psi Chi, Golden Key Nat. Honor Soc. Office: Dept Psychology & Counseling Bldg 44 Rm 200-32 Univ of the DC Washington DC 20008 Office Phone: 202-274-6439. Business E-Mail: bcooke@udc.edu. *

COOKSEY, JOHN CHARLES, ophthalmologist, former congressman; b. Aug. 20, 1941; s. Henry Oscar and Ruth (Lee) C.; m. Dorothy Ann Grabill, Dec. 30, 1969; children: Karen, Carol Ann, Catherine. MD, La. State U., New Orleans, 1966; MBA, U. Tex., Austin, 1994. Mem. Congress from 5th La. Dist., 1996—2002, mem. agr. and internat. rels. coms.; practice medicine specializing in ophthalmology Monroe, La., 1972—; assoc. clin. prof. La. State U. Sch. Medicine, New Orleans, 1982—90, clin. prof., 1990—. Mem. teaching staff E.A. Conway Hosp., Monroe, 1972—; vis. lectr. Alton Ochsner Med. Found., New Orleans, 1978—; asst. clin. prof. La. State U. Med. Sch., New Orleans, 1979-82. Republican. Address: 1310 N 19th St Monroe LA 71201 Business E-Mail: jcooksey@cookseymd.com.

COOLEY, DENTON ARTHUR, surgeon, educator; b. Houston, Aug. 22, 1920; s. Ralph C. and Mary (Fraley) C.; m. Louise Goldsborough Thomas, Jan. 15, 1949; children: Mary, Susan, Louise, Florence, Helen. BA, U. Tex., 1941; MD, Johns Hopkins U., 1944; Doctorem Medicinae (hon.), U. Turin, Italy, 1969; HHD (hon.), Hellenic Coll., 1984, Holy Cross Greek Orthodox Sch. of Theology, 1984; DSc honoris causa, Coll. of William and Mary, 1987. Diplomate: Am. Bd. Surgery, Am. Bd. Thoracic Surgery. Intern Johns Hopkins Sch. Medicine, Balt., 1944-45, resident surgery, 1945-50; sr. surg. registrar thoracic surgery Brompton Hosp. for Chest Diseases, London, 1950-51; assoc. prof. surgery Baylor U. Coll. Medicine, Houston, 1951—62, prof. surgery, 1962-69; clin. prof. surgery U. Tex. Med. Sch., Houston, 1975—; founder, pres. Tex. Heart Inst., 1962—2004, pres. emeritus, 2004—, surgeon-in-chief, 1962—. Chief cardiovascular surgery St. Luke's Episcopal Hosp.; cons., cardiovascular surgery Tex. Children's Hosp. Contbr. articles to profl. jours. Served as capt., M.C., 1946-48. Named one of ten Outstanding Young Men in U.S., U.S. C. of C., 1955, Man of the Yr. award Kappa Sigma, 1964; named Disting. Alumnus U. Tex, John Hopkins U.; recipient Rene Leriche prize Internat. Surg. Soc., 1967, Billings Gold medal Am. Surg. Soc., 1967, Vishnevsky medal Vishnevsky Inst., USSR, 1971, Theodore Roosevelt Award, 1980, Presdl. Medal of Freedom, presented by Pres. Reagan, 1984, Gifted Tchr. award Am. Coll. Cardiology, 1987, Disting. Svc. award AMA, 1997, Nat. Medal of Tech., U.S. Dept Commerce, 1998 Hon. fellow Royal Coll. Physicians and Surgeons of Glasgow, Royal Coll. Surgeons of Ireland, Royal Australasian Coll. Surgeons, Royal Coll. Surgeons of Eng.; mem. ACS, Am. Surg. Assn., Internat. Cardiovascular Soc., Am. Assn. Thoracic Surgery, Soc. Thoracic Surgery, Soc. Univ. Surgeons, Am. Coll. Cardiology, Am. Coll. Chest Physicians, Soc. Clin. Surgery, Soc. Vascular Surgery, Western Surg. Assn., Tex. Surg. Soc., Halsted Soc. Achievements include performance of numerous heart transplants; implanted 1st artificial heart, 1969; first surgeon to successfully remove pulmonary embolisms, squeezing the lungs flat to remove the inaccessible blood clots. Office Phone: 832-355-4932. Business E-Mail: dcooley@heart.thi.tmc.edu.

COOLEY, JACK CRAIN, cardiovascular surgeon; b. Redfield, SD, Sept. 4, 1924; s. Frank Henry and Crystal Cooley; m. Gloria Gamage Cooley, Dec. 23, 1947; children: Crystal, Carolyn Stamm, Craig. BA, Northwestern U., 1942, MD, 1947; BS, U. Minn., 1954. Diplomate Am. Bd. Surgery, 1954, 1955. Surgery fellow Mayo Clinic, Rochester, Minn., 1949—57; staff surgeon Carle Clinic, Urbana, Ill., 1957—90; assoc. prof. surgery U. Ill., 1965—80. Adv. bd. Mayo Clinic Alumni Bd., Rochester, Minn. Contbr. articles to profl. jours. Bd. governors YMCA, Urbana. Capt. USAF, 1951—53. Mem.: ACS, Ill. Coll. Surgeons, Ill. Surg. Soc., Soc. Thoracic Surgeons, Ctrl. Surg. Assn., Western Surg. Assn. Republican. Presbyterian. Avocations: golf, tennis. Home: 7501 E Thompson Peak Pk Pky Unit 71 Scottsdale AZ 85255 Business E-Mail: jackfrommesa1@cox.net.

COOLEY, VERNON JACKMAN, orthopedic surgeon; b. Salt Lake City, Mar. 28, 1963; B, U. Utah, 1986; MD, Harvard Med. Sch., 1991. Cert. Nat. Bd. Med. Examiners, 1991, in sports medicine Accreditation Coun. for Grad. Med. Edn., 1997, Am. Bd. Orthopaedic Surgery, 1999. Orthopedic surgery internship U. Wash., Seattle, 1991—92, orthopedic surgery residency, 1992—96; sports medicine/arthroscopy fellowship Orthopedic Specialty Hosp., Salt Lake City, 1996—99, chief surgery, 1997—2007; knee specialist Rosenberg Cooley Metcalf Clinic, Park City, Utah. Team physician Olympus HS, 2000—; physician Park City Olympic Venue, 2000—02, US Ski Team, US Snowboard Team, US Speedskating Team. Mem. sports medicine adv. com. Utah HS Activities Assn., 1997—. Mem.: Western Orthopaedic Assn., Utah State Orthopaedic Soc. (pres. 2005—07), Utah Med. Assn., Salt Lake County Med. Soc., Nat. Orthopedic Edn. Soc., Am. Orthopaedic Soc. Sports Medicine, Am. Acad. Orthopaedic Surgeons. Office: Rosenberg Cooley Metcalf Clinic 1820 Sidewinder Dr Park City UT 84060 Office Phone: 435-655-6600. Office Fax: 435-655-2388.

COOLEY, WILLIAM EDWARD, research scientist, consultant; b. St. Louis, Mar. 7, 1930; s. Charles Frederic and Lillian Marie (Williams) C.; m. Marion Grace Sherman, June 5, 1952; children: Charles, Marilyn, Harold, Noele. AB, Cen. Coll., 1951; PhD, U. Ill., 1954. Rsch. chemist Procter & Gamble Co., Cin., 1954-61, product devel. chemist, 1961-65, product devel. group leader, 1965-75, product devel. regulatory sect. mgr., 1975-90, regulatory affairs sect. mgr., 1990-91; worldwide regulatory coordination sect. mgr., 1991-94; pres. Cooley Cons., Inc., 1994—. Contbr. articles to profl. jours. Mem. Am. Assn. Dental Rsch., Internat. Assn. Dental Rsch., Drug Info. Assn., Assn. Food Drug Ofcls., Regulatory Affairs Profl. Soc. (bd. editors 1990), Consumer Healthcare Products Assn. (bd. dirs. 1987-91), Food and Drug Law Inst, Personal Care Products Coun. Independent. Achievements include patents in field. Avocations: music, motorcycling, railroading, flying, astronomy. Home and Office: Cooley Cons Inc 531 Chisholm Trail Wyoming OH 45215-2517 Home Phone: 513-522-2491; Office Phone: 513-522-3797.

COOLEY-PARKER, SHEILA LEANNE, psychologist, consultant, educator; b. Oakland, Calif., July 25, 1956; d. Philips Theadore and Helen Ellene (Newbill) Cooley; m. Kenneth Louis Parker. BA, St. Leo Coll., 1979; MS, U. So. Miss., 1986; PhD, Miss. State U., 1990. Lic. psychologist Ky. Counselor Charter Counseling Ctr., Jackson, Miss., 1988—89; staff psychologist Rivendell Psychiat. Ctr., Bowling Green, Ky., 1989—90; program dir. MidSouth Hosp., Memphis, 1990—91; resource ctr. dir. MidSouth Resource Ctr., Ridgeland, Miss., 1991—92; partial hosp. dir. Pathways Partial Hospitalization, Ridgeland, 1991—92; edn. specialist, sr. position Miss. Dept. of Edn., Bur. Spl. Svcs., Jackson, Miss., 1993—94; psychologist Western State Hosp., Hopkinsville, Ky., 1994—99, Caring Connections, Hopkinsville, 1995; pvt. practice Hopkinsville, 1996—2005; chief psychology Ky. State Penitentiary, Eddyville, Ky., 1999—2005, Behavior Assocs., Owensboro, Ky., 2004—. Adj. prof. Hopkinsville C.C., 2001—05, Murray State U., 2003—07. Campaign organizer Dem. Mayor, Jackson, Miss., 1992. Mem.: APA, Ky. Psychol. Assn., Theta Pi Sigma, Psi Chi, Phi Delta Kappa. Baptist. Home: 310 Juliet Dr Hopkinsville KY 42240

COONEY, GAIL AUSTIN, medical association administrator; b. Cedar Rapids, Iowa, June 20, 1952; m. John Cooney; children: Jack, Ted. BA in biology, Wesleyan U.; MD, Mayo Clinic Med. Sch., 1978. Cert. Neurology, 1985, Pain Medicine, 2002. Intern in internal medicine Emory U., Atlanta, 1978—79, resident in neurology, 1979—80, resident in neurological oncology, 1980—83; fellow Sloan-Kettering Cancer Ctr., NYC, 1983—84; mem. staff Hospice of Palm Beach County, West Palm Beach, 1994—97, med. dir., 1997—2008, med. dir. emeritus; dir., med. dir. Sari Asher Ctr. Integrative Cancer Care Palm Beach Cancer Inst. Found., West Palm Beach, Fla., 2008—. Fellow: Am. Acad. Hospice and Palliative Medicine (bd. dirs., pres. 2009—10). Office: PBCI Found and Sari Ctr Ste 8900B 1411 N Flagler Dr West Palm Beach FL 33401 also: Am Acad Hospice and Palliative Medicine 4700 W Lake Ave Glenview IL 60025 E-mail: gcooney@hpbc.com. *

COONEY, KATHLEEN ANN, oncologist; b. San Jose, Calif., Apr. 15, 1958; AB, Dartmouth Coll., 1980; MD, U. Pa., 2008. Prof., chief, divsn. hematology, oncology U. Mich. Med. Sch., 2009—. Office: 7216 Cancer Ctr 1500 East Med Ctr Dr Ann Arbor MI 48105 Business E-Mail: kcooney@umich.edu.

COONEY, MARY ANN, state agency administrator, public health service officer, community health nurse; B nursing, Saint Anselm Coll.; MS, Univ. N.H. Supr. sch. health Manchester Public Health Dept., NH; adminstr. chronic disease prevention N.H. Dept. Health & Human Svc., Concord, dir. div. public health svc., 2003—08, dep. commr., 2008—. Mem.: Am. Nurses Assn., N.H. Nurses Assn. (Nurse of the Yr. 1995), N.H. Public Health Assn. (past pres.). Office: NH Dept Health & Human Svc 29 Hazen Dr # C Concord NH 03301-6503

COONEY, WILLIAM PATRICK, surgeon; b. Detroit, Apr. 27, 1943; MD, St. Louis U., 1969; MS, U. Minn., 1975. Chair, divsn. hand surgery Mayo Clinic, 1980—95; bd. chmn. Orthop. Rsch. and Edn. Soc., 2007—09. Fellow: Am. Soc. Surgery Hand; mem.: Am. Acad. Orthop. Surgery. Avocations: golf, fishing, skiing. Office: 1355 37th St Ste 301 Vero Beach FL 32960 Business E-Mail: cooney.william@mayo.edu.

COOPER, ALAN MICHAEL, psychiatrist; b. Balt., Mar. 14, 1950; s. William I. and Barbara (Stein) C.; m. Elizabeth Ann Mumper, May 31, 1980; children: William, Leigh. SB, MIT, 1972; MD, Med. Coll. Va., 1976. Diplomate Am. Bd. Psychiatry and Neurology. Intern Med. Coll. Va., 1976—77, resident psychiatry, 1977—78, U. Va. Hosps., 1978—79, fellow pain clinic, 1979—80, fellow child and adolescent psychiatry, 1981; instr. psychiatry Harvard Med. Sch., Boston, 1980—81; assoc. anesthesia (psychiatry) Brigham & Women's Hosp., Boston, 1980—81; dir. diagnostic and evaluation unit David C. Wilson Hosp., Charlottesville, Va., 1982—84; clin. adminstr. psychiatry Va. Bapt. Hosp., Lynchburg, 1984—85; chief psychiatrist Ctrl. Va. Cmty. Svcs., Lynchburg, 1985—92; cons. psychiatrist Ctrl. VA Tng. Ctr., Lynchburg, 1992—2009. Asst. prof. clin. family medicine U. Va. Sch. Medicine, Charlottesville, Va., 1997—2000; faculty Lynchburg Family Practice Residency Program, 1997—2000. Past pres. First Unitarian Universalist Ch. of Lynchburg. MIT Nat. scholar, 1968. Mem. Am. Psychiat. Assn., Psychiat. Soc. Va., Va. Assn. Cmty. Psychiatrists (pres.) Office: Southside Cmty Svcs 424 Hamilton Blvd South Boston VA 24592 Office Phone: 434-572-6916.

COOPER, BARRY ROBERT, physician, geriatrician; MD, U. Pa., 1973; attended, Penn State U. Diplomate Am. Bd. Family Medicine. Tng. family medicine Abington Meml. Hosp., physician; tng. internal medicine Pa. Hosp. Univ. of Pa. Health Sys.; geriatrician Abington, Pa. Office: Abington Memorial Hospital 1200 Old York Rd Abington PA 19001 Office Phone: 215-481-2000.

COOPER, BYRON STANLEY, internist, educator; b. Washington, May 21, 1947; s. Joseph David and Ruth (Zeidner) C.; m. Jane Ann Kanter, Feb. 5, 1978; children: Joseph, Allison. BA, Johns Hopkins U., 1969; MD, Washington U., St. Louis, 1973. Diplomate in internal medicine and pulmonary medicine Am. Bd. Internal Medicine. Clin. prof. George Washington U., Washington, 1981—. Fellow Am. Coll. Chest Physicians; mem. AMA (alt. del. 2000--), ACP, D.C. Thoracic Soc. (pres. 1994), Med. Soc. D.C. (pres. 1998-99). Avocations: photography, running, computers. Office: Capital Pumonary Internists 2440 M St NW Washington DC 20037-1404

COOPER, DAVID NEIL, human molecular genetics researcher and educator; b. Dundee, Scotland, Oct. 31, 1957; s. Neil Louis and Beryl Barwell (Turner) C.; m. Margaret McLaughlin, Sept. 4, 1982; children: Paul, Catrin, Duncan. BSc, Edinburgh U., 1979, PhD in Molecular Biology, 1983. Postdoctoral rsch. worker U. Göttingen, 1983-84, U. Lausanne, Switzerland, 1984, U. London, 1985-87, lectr. in haematology, 1987-89, sr. lectr. in molecular genetics, 1989-95; prof. in human molecular genetics Cardiff U., Wales, 1995—. Curator Human Gene Mutation Database; guest prof. U. Göttingen, 1992. Co-author: Human Gene Mutation, 1993, The Molecular Genetics of Haemostasis and its Inherited Disorders, 1994, Venous Thrombosis: From Genes to Clinical Medicine, 1997; co-editor Functional Analysis of the Human Genome, 1995, Gene Therapy, 1996; mem. editl. bd. Genomics, 1987-97, Annales de Génètique, 1994—2005, Human Mutation, 2000-, Jour. Med. Genetics, 2010-; mem. editl. bd., European editor Human Genetics, 1994—; editor-in-chief Nature Ency. of the Human Genome, 2003; co-editor: Fascioscapulohumeral Muscular Dystrophy: Clinical Medicine and Molecular Cell Biology, 2004, Neurofibromatosis Type 1: From Genes to Clinical Medicine, 1998, Handbook of Human Molecular Evolution, 2008, Copy Number Variation and Disease, 2009; author: Human Gene Evolution, 1999, The Molecular Genetics of Lung Cancer, 2005. Avocations: natural history, classical music, travel, world history. Office: Cardiff Univ Inst Med Genetics Heath Pk Cardiff CF14 4XN Wales Business E-Mail: cooperdn@cardiff.ac.uk.

COOPER, DAVID R., neurosurgeon; b. Boston, Oct. 27, 1931; s. Herbert and Rose R. (Furman) Cooper; m. Sandra S. Rosenberg, Dec. 18, 1954 (dec. Jan. 2007); children: Ron H., Jane R. MD cum laude, Tufts U., Boston, 1956, BS in Med. Sci. magna cum laude, Boston U., 1975. Adj. prof. Fla. Gulf Coast U., Fort Myers, Fla., 2008—. Cons. Niagara Falls Meml. Hosp., NY, 1980—89, Mt. St. Mary's Hosp., Lewiston, NY, 1985—89. Contbr. articles to profl. jours. Mem. Environ. Mgmt. Coun., Niagara County, NY, 1986—, Environ. Commn., Lewiston, NY, 1999—; bd. dirs. Niagara Ednl. Found., Niagara Falls, 1980—2005. Lt. comdr. USNR, 1962—64. Mem.: Niagara Frontier Entomol. Soc. (founder, pres. 1993—). Home: 28621 San Lucas Ln #101 Bonita Springs FL 34135 Office Phone: 239-949-0091.

COOPER, DONALD LEE, physician; b. Columbus, Kans., Aug. 11, 1928; s. Calvin M. and J. Pearl (Mullen) C.; m. Dona Faye Maddux, June 4, 1950; children: Donald Lee, Catherine Susan, Cheryl Lyn, Tad Houston. AB, Pittsburg State U., 1949; MD, U. Kans., 1953. Intern St. Mary's and Childrens Mercy hosps., Kansas City, Mo., 1953-54; pvt. practice medicine Manhattan, Kans., 1956-57; team physician, asst. dir. Health Center Kans. State U., 1957-60; dir. health service, team physician Okla. State U. Hosp. and Clinic, Stillwater, 1960-90, dir. athletic medicine, 1990-98, emeritus dir., 1998—. Vis. lectr. divsn. sportsmedicine, dept. orthopedic surgery Coll. Medicine U. Okla. Health Scis. Ctr., 1974—; liaison officer Am. Coll. Health Assn. to Nat. Athletic Trainers Assn., 1963—; Am. chmn. 1st Am.-Soviet Conf. on Student Health, Moscow, Russia, 1967; team physician U.S. Olympic Team, 1967-68; mem. Pres.'s Coun. Phys. Fitness and Sports, 1981-92, del. to Moscow to rev. phys. culture and olympic tng. sites in Russia, 1989; team physician U.S. Deaf Olympic Team, LA, 1985; elected chmn. Joint Commn. on Competitive Safegaurds and Med. Aspects of Sports, 1986. Author: (with others) Standard Nomenclature of Athletic Injuries, 1966; Contbr. (with others) articles med. jours. Served to capt. USAF, 1954-56. Recipient Pres.'s Challenge Sportsmedicine award Nat. Athletic Trainers Assn., 1974, Bill Coltrin Meml. award Western Athletic Conf. Sports Writers Assn., 1974, Edward Hitchcock award Am. Coll. Health Assn., 1975; named among 10 healthy American fitness leaders Nat. Jaycees, Pres.'s Coun. on Physical Fitness and Sports, Allstate Ins. Co., 1995; inductee Okla. Hall of Fame, 1998. Mem. AMA (chmn. com. med. aspects sports 1971-76, chmn. 1976-77, mem. coun. sci. affairs 1976-79), Nat. Collegiate Athletic Assn. (med. cons. to football rules com. 1969-75), Am. Coll. Health Assn. (past pres., exec. com.), Southwestern Coll. Health Assn. (past pres.), Nat. Athletic Trainers Assn., Alpha Omega Alpha, Nu Sigma Nu. Presbyterian (elder 1971—). Club: Lion. Home: 1001 W Liberty Ln Stillwater OK 74075-2113 Office: Okla State U Hosp & Clinic 1202 Farm Rd Stillwater OK 74078-0001 Office Phone: 405-744-7031. Office Fax: 405-744-6556.

COOPER, EDWARD SAWYER, retired cardiologist, internist, educator; b. Columbia, SC, Dec. 11, 1926; s. Henry Howard and Ada Crosland (Sawyer) Cooper; m. Jean Marie Wilder, Dec. 2, 1951 (dec. May 2006); children: Lisa Marie Cooper Hudgins, Edward Sawyer Jr.(dec.), Jan Ada, Charles Wilder. AB, Lincoln U., Pa., 1946; MD, Meharry Med. Coll., Nashville, 1949; MS (hon.), U. Pa., 1972. Diplomate Nat. Bd. Med. Examiners, Am. Bd. Internal Medicine. Intern Phila. Gen. Hosp., 1949—51, resident in medicine, 1951—54, NIH fellow in cardiology, 1956—57, pres. med. staff, 1969—71, co-dir. Stroke Rsch. Ctr., 1968—74, chief med. svc., 1973—76; prof. Sch. Medicine U. Pa., 1976—96, prof. emeritus medicine Phila., 1996—. Bd. dirs. Independence Blue Cross. Bd. trustees Am. Heart Assn., pres.-elect, pres., chmn. Stroke Coun.; adv. com. NIH; trustee Rockefeller U., 1992—, Hosp. of the U. of Pa., 2002—. Served to capt. USAF, 1954—56. Master: ACP; fellow: Phila. Coll. Physicians (coun.); mem.: Am. Heart Assn. (chmn., bd. dirs., past nat. pres.), Alpha Omega Alpha. Democrat. Methodist. Achievements include research in stroke and hypertension. Home: 6710 Lincoln Dr Philadelphia PA 19119-3155 Personal E-mail: ecoopmdphila@aol.com.

COOPER, EUGENE BRUCE, speech pathology/audiology services professional, educator; b. Utica, NY, Dec. 20, 1933; s. Clements Everett and Beulah (Wetzel) C.; m. Crystal Silverman, Sept. 12, 1965; children: Philip Adam, Ivan Bruce. BS, SUNY, Geneseo, 1955; MEd, Pa. State U., 1957, DEd, 1962. Pathologist speech and lang. Franklin County Schs., Chambersburg, Pa., 1957-59; asst. prof. Ohio U., 1962-64, Pa. State U., 1964-66; program specialist U.S. Office Edn., 1966; exec. sec. sensory study sect., rsch. and demonstrations Rehab. Services Adminstrn., HEW, Washington, 1966-67; faculty U. Ala., Tuscaloosa, 1967-96, prof. speech-lang. pathology, 1969-96, chmn. dept. communicative disorders, dir. Speech and Hearing Ctr., 1967-96, prof., chair emeritus, 1996—; Disting. prof. comm. scis. and disorders Nova Southeastern U., 1997—2009. Chmn. Ala. Bd. Examiners Speech Pathology and Audiology, 1979; cons.-at-large Nat. Student Speech-Lang.-Hearing Assn., 1983-88. Author: Personalized Fluency Control Therapy, 1976, Understanding Stuttering: Information for Parents, 1979, revised edit., 1990; (with Crystal Cooper) The Cooper Personalized Fluency Control Therapy Program, 1985, 2d edit., 2003, Cooper Assessment for Stuttering Syndromes, 1995; contbr. articles to profl. jours. Fellow Am. Speech, Lang. and Hearing Assn. (legis. coun. 1971-72, 85-97), Divsn. Fluency and Fluency Disorders (steering com. 1993-99, divsn. coord. 1994-99), Am. Speech, Lang. and Hearing Found. (chmn. adv. and devel. bd. 1988-89, trustee 1989-94); mem. Coun. Exceptional Children (pres. divsn. children comm. disorders 1975-76), Nat. Coun. Grad. Programs in Speech, Lang. Pathology and Audiology (pres. 1978-80), Nat. Coun. State Bds. Examiners Speech-Lang. Pathology and Audiology (pres. 1980, 91, mem. exec. bd. 1988-91), Nat. Coun. Comm. Disorders (chmn. 1982), Nat. Alliance Prevention and Treatment on Stuttering (pres. 1985-86), Internat. Fluency Assn. (bd. dirs. 1991-96, pres. 2d world congress on fluency disorders 1997, chmn. specialty commn. on fluency disorders 1997-99). Office Phone: 954-385-1422. E-mail: ebcooper@msn.com.

COOPER, GREGORY SCOTT, epidemiologist, gastroenterologist, educator; b. Newark, July 14, 1960; s. Murray and Frances Cooper; m. Cathy Lynne Cooper, Feb. 3, 1991; children: Marissa, Ryan, Nicole. BA, MA, U. Pa., 1982, MD, 1986. Diplomate Am. Bd. Internal Medicine. Intern, resident in internal medicine Univ. Hosps., Cleve., 1986-89, chief resident, 1991-92, fellow in gastroenterology, 1989-91, 92-93; instr. medicine Case Western Res. U., Cleve., 1991-93, asst. prof. medicine, 1993-96, asst. prof. medicine and epidemiology, 1996-98, dir. cancer epidemiology-health rsch., 2000—, assoc. prof. medicine and epidemiology, 1998—2005, prof. medicine and epidemiology, 2005—, staff investigator, 2000—05, leader prevention and control, 2005—. Tng. program dir. Case Western Res. U., 1997—; dir. disease mgmt. U. Hosps. Cleve., 1997-99. Contbr. chpts. to books, more than 100 articles to profl. jours. Grantee Nat. Cancer Inst., 1996—. Fellow ACP (med. sch. rep.), Am. Coll. Gastroenterology; mem. Am. Cancer Soc. (rsch. project grants 1997—), Am. Gastroenterology Assn. Avocation: long distance running. Office: Univ Hosps Cleveland 11100 Euclid Ave Cleveland OH 44106-5066 Home Phone: 216-591-1167, Office Phone: 216-844-5386. Business E-Mail: greg.cooper@case.edu.

COOPER, JACK ROSS, pharmacology educator, researcher; b. Ottawa, Ont., Can., July 26, 1924; came to U.S., 1948; s. Harry and Jean (Levine) C.; m. Helen Achbar, Aug. 14, 1951; children: Marilyn, Sheila, Nancy. BA, Queen's U. Kingston, Ont., 1948; MA, George Washington U., 1952, PhD, 1954; MA (hon.), Yale U., 1971. Instr. Yale U., New Haven, 1956—58, asst. prof. pharmacology, 1958—63, assoc. prof., 1963-71, emeritus prof., 1971—. Author: The Biochemical Basis of Neuropharmacology, 8th edit., 2003. Served with RCAF, 1944. Smith, Kline and French rsch. fellow, 1950-52; USPHS predoctoral fellow, 1952-54; postdoctoral fellow USPHS, 1954-56; spl. fellow USPHS, London, 1965-66. Mem. Am. Soc. Neurochemistry, Internat. Soc. Neurochemistry, Am. Soc. Pharmacology and Exptl. Therapeutics, Soc. Neurosci. Democrat. Jewish. Home: 11 Jenick Ln Woodbridge CT 06525-1935 Office: Yale U Sch Medicine Dept Pharmacology 333 Cedar St New Haven CT 06510-3289

COOPER, JANELLE LUNETTE, neurologist, educator; b. Ann Arbor, Mich., Dec. 11, 1955; d. Robert Marion and Madelyn (Leonard) C.; children: Lena Christine, Nicholas Dominic. BA in Chemistry, Reed Coll., 1978; MD, Vanderbilt U., 1986. Diplomate Nat. Bd. Med. Examiners; diplomate in neurology Am. Bd. Psychiatry and Neurology; registered med. technologist Am. Soc. Clin. Pathologists. Med. technologist Swedish Hosp. Med. Ctr., Seattle, 1978-80, U. Wash. Clin. Chemistry, Seattle, 1980-82, Vanderbilt U. Hosp., Nashville, 1983-84; intern medicine Vanderbilt U. Med. Ctr., Nashville, 1986-87, resident neurology, 1987-90; instr. neurology Med. Coll. Pa., Phila., 1990-91, asst. prof., clerkship dir., 1991—, mem. curriculum com., 1990-91, vis. asst. prof., 1991-95; neurologist Greater Ann Arbor Neurology Assocs., 1991-93; dir. neurol. svcs., med. dir. Indsl. Rehab. Program St. Francis Hosp., Escanaba, Mich., 1993-98; founder, dir. No. Neuroscis., Escanaba, 1993-98; pres. HolderLady, Ltd., 1996—2005; chmn. dept. medicine St. Francis Hosp., Escanaba, Mich., 1998-99; dir. The Memory Ctr., Affinity Health Sys., Oshkosh, Wis., 1998—2008; med. dir. Memory Clinic of the Upper Peninsula, Escanaba, Mich., 1998—2000; chmn. dept. medicine Mercy Med. Ctr., 2002—04. ER physician Tenn. Christian Med. Ctr., 1989—90; physician MCP Neurology Assocs., Phila., 1990—91; neurologist Affinity Med. Group, Oshkosh, Wis., 1998—2008, Gundersen Luth. Health Sys., 2008—; dir. The Memory Ctr., Gundersen Luth. Neuroscis., 2008—; presenter in field. Contbr. articles to profl. jours. Vol. Rape and Sexual Abuse Ctr., Nashville, 1988—90; mem. editl. bd. Nashville Women's Alliance, 1989—90; mem. adv. bd. Perspective Adult Daycare Ctr., 1996—99; founding dir. Memory Clinic of Upper Peninsula, 1998—2000; airport support network vol. Aircraft Owners and Pilots Assn.; mem. adminstrv. bd. Edgehill United Methodist Ch., Nashville; bd. dir. Upper Peninsula Physicians Network, 1995—98; mem. profl. adv. com. NE Wis. Alzheimer's Assn., 1999—2008. Recipient Svc. award for outstanding contbns. Rape and Sexual Abuse Ctr., 1990, Pres. award for Creativity Affinity Health Sys. 2006; named Outstanding Physician Wis. Alzheimer's Assn., 2010; epilepsy minifellow Bowman Gray U., 1995. Mem. AMA (physician's Recognition award 1989—), Am. Acad. Neurology (elected fellow 2006), Wis. State Med. Soc., Upper Peninsula Neuro Assn. (v.p. 1998-99, trustee 1998-99), Aircraft Owners and Pilots Assn., Women in Aviation Internat. (charter), National Association of Rocketry, Air Force Assn. (life patron), Assn. of US Army (life mem.). Methodist. Achievements include first synthesis of Difluoromethanedisulfonic Acid; research on neurobehavioral disorders; on effects of dietary lipids on the etiology of Alzheimer's disease; on the role of pantothenic acid in neurodegeneration; on virtual reality computer simulation for assessment of senior drivers clinical investigation trials for new medications for dementias. Home: 2510 Chicken Ridge Rd La Crescent MN 55947-8708 Office: Gundersen Luth Neuroscis Mail Stop EB3-002 1900 South Ave La Crosse WI 54601 Business E-Mail: jlcooper@gundluth.org.

COOPER, JOEL DAVID, physician, medical educator; b. Jan. 2, 1939; AB, Harvard Coll., 1960, MD, 1964. Diplomate Am. Bd. Surgery, Am. Bd. Thoracic Surgery. Intern Mass. Gen. Hosp., Boston, 1964—65, resident, 1965—68, chief resident; chief divsn. cardiothoracic surg. Sch. Medicine Wash. U., St. Louis, 1997—2005; prof. surgery, chief thoracic surgery divsn. U. Pa., Phila., 2005—. Contbr. more than 325 articles to profl. jours. Mem.: Inst. Medicine, Transplantation Soc., Soc. U. Surgeons, Soc. Thoracic Surgeons, Royal Coll. Surgeons of England, Internat. Soc. for Diseases of the Esophagus, European Soc. Thoracic Surgeons, Am. Soc. Transplant Surgeons, Am. Coll. Chest Physicians, Am. Coll. Surgeons, Am. Assn. Thoracic Surgery, Soc. Cardiothoracic Surgeons, Internat. Soc. Heart Transplantation. Office: Hosp U Pa 6 White 3400 Spruce St Philadelphia PA 19104 Office Phone: 215-615-1793. Office Fax: 215-614-1861. E-mail: joel.cooper@uphs.upenn.edu.

COOPER, JOSHUA M., cardiac electrophysiologist, educator; Grad., Wash. U. Diplomate Am. Bd. Internal Medicine., 1999, Am. Bd. Cardiovasc. Medicine, 2002, Am. Bd. Internal Medicine-clin. cardiac electrophysiology, 2003. Intern Brigham & Women's Hosp., resident, fellow; asst. prof. medicine Hosp. of the Univ. of Pa. Named one of Top Docs, Phila. Mag., 2011. Mem.: Alpha Omega Alpha, Am. Coll. of Cardiology, Am. Heart Assn., Mass. Med. Soc., Heart Rhythm Soc. Office: Penn Heart and Vascular Center Perelman Center for Advanced Medicine E Pavilion 2nd Fl 3400 Civic Center Blvd Philadelphia PA 19104 Office Phone: 800-799-7366.

COOPER, KAREN RENÉ, health facility and nursing administrator; b. Pleasanton, Calif., Oct. 15, 1957; d. Homer L. and Rosa B. (Upton) C.; m. Tommy Joe McCarty, Nov. 1, 1981. BSN, U. Ala., Birmingham, 1980. Cert. in profl. healthcare quality; healthcare cert. Bd. Nat. Commn. Certifying Agencies; cert. in profl. utilization rev.; cert. Interqual Nat. Registry; cert. chemotherapy, rehab. nurse, tissue therapy. Internship in SICU/MICU Cedars of Lebanon Hosp., Miami, Fla., 1980; mem. head injury/CVA and chronic pain team Spain Rehab. Ctr. U. Ala. Hosps., Birmingham, 1980-82, rheumatology charge nurse Spain Rehab. Ctr., 1982-88, staff nurse, 1988 90, coord. utilization rev./quality assurance med. care rev., 1990-91, coord. quality improvement med. care rev., 1991-93, sr. nurse coord. med. care rev., 1993, interim dir. med. care rev., 1993-94, sr. coord. dept. quality resources, 1994-2000; quality improvement coord. Dept. Joint Commn./ Regulatory Affairs, 2000—04, Dept. of Quality Resources, 2004—05; quality improvement coord. dept. quality U. Health Sys., Dept. Quality, Birmingham, 2005—06; dir. quality/risk mgmt. Physicians Carraway Med. Ctr., Birmingham, 2006—; CEO Sowhats Nu LLC. Mem. Com. for Quality Improvement U. Ala. Birmingham Hosps., mem. Discharge Planning Com., Emergency Svcs. Quality Improvement, 1991 93, Key 100 Com., Med./Dental Staff Task Force, Mobile Med. ICU Quality Com. APACHE Study, 1990-92, Neurology Quality Com., 1990-92, Nursing Stds. Com., 1982-85, Nursing Task Force Com., 1984-88, Resuscitation Com., 1990-94, 98--, Skin Care/Tissue Therapy Com., 1986-89, Surg. Quality Improvement Com., 1991-93, mem. Arthritis Newsletter Com. U. Ala. Birmingham Multi-Purpose Arthritis Ctr., 1983-89, Quality Resource specialist, Ala. Quality Assurance Found., 2009; active Value Improvement Project of Birmingham Hosp. Network; participant, presenter numerous confs. and workshops in field. Contbr. articles to Arthritis Today and Arthritis Newsletter of U. Ala. Birmingham Multi-Purpose Arthritis Ctr., 1983-90. Pres. Coalnugget Ala. Mining Mus., 1987-89, chair literacy daycamp, 1990-92; participant Ala. State Fair Family Craft Divsn., 1975-94; co-chair AHPA Nat. Nursing Coun., 1986-88; vol. Children's Hosp., Dixie Wheelchair Assn. Regional Wheelchair Games, Goodwill Industries Doll Sale, Caring and Sharing Drive; troop leader Cahaba Coun. Girl Scouts Am., 1982—, POGO advisor, 1985-93, advisor outdoor interest group, 1995-98, mem. program operating unit, 1984-93, coun. trainer, 1984—, cons. svc. area events/programs, 1984-92, bd. dir., 1992-94, svc. area mgr. Upper 78 West, 1995-98, assn. chair, 1991-92, 2002-04, camp nurse, 1992—, mem. nominating com., 1993-95, facilities com., 1992-94, chair long-range property planning com., 1993, del. to nat. coun., 1993-99, life mem., 1993, mem. World of People Interest Group, 1997-98; mem. Ala. Assn. Healthcare Quality, Am. Juvenile Arthritis Orgn., 1982-88, Arthritis Found., 1982-90, liaison ACT Club support group, 1984-86; mem. UHC: Quality and Risk Mgmt. Com., 1993-2001, United Way/Benevolent Fund com. U. Ala. Birmingham Hosps., 1990, 2000-01; chair Honor the Children NA Festival, 2001—, Williamsburg Farm Fall NA Festival, 2003—, Blackwater Creek AI Fest., 2003—; coord. Hawks in Wind Family Clothing and Food Pantry, 1998—; bd. dirs. Am. Indian Scouting Assn., 2005—; bd. dirs. Walk of Faith Ministry, bd. sec., 2003—. Recipient Thanks award Girl Scouts Am. Cahaba Coun., 1989, Thanks II badge, 2005, Grey Wolf award Am. Indian Scouting Assn., 2004; fellow Girl Scouts U.S.A., 1976. Mem. NAFE, Nat. Assn. Healthcare Quality, U. Ala. Birmingham Alumni Assn. Avocations: painting, poetry, crafts. Office: Carraway Internal Medicine Ste 305 1201 11Th Ave S Birmingham AL 35205-3422

COOPER, LISA ANGELINE, internist, medical educator; b. Monrovia, Liberia, Apr. 12, 1963; BA, Emory U., 1984; MD, U. NC Sch. Medicine, 1988; MPH, John Hopkins U. Bloomberg Sch. Pub. Health, 1993. Cert. Internal Medicine. Intern, internal medicine U. Md. Sch. Medicine Affiliated Hosps., 1988—89, resident, internal medicine, 1989—91; fellow, internal medicine John Hopkins Hosp., Balt., 1991, John Hopkins U., Balt., 1991—94; instr. John Hopkins Sch. Medicine, Balt., 1994—95, assoc. prof., 2002, asst. prof., 1996—2002; prof., divsn. gen. internal medicine, core faculty, Welch Ctr. for Prevention, Epidemiology, and Clin. Rsch. John Hopkins U., Sch. Medicine and Bloomberg Sch. Pub. Health, Balt., prof., dept. epidemiology and health behavior and soc. Contbr. scientific papers articles to profl. jours. Recipient Herbert W. Nickens award for Exceptional Commitment to Cultural Diversity in Medicine and Improving Minority Health, Soc. Gen. Internal Medicine, 2006, George Engel Rsch. award, Am. Acad. Communication in Healthcare, 2008; fellow John D. and Catherine T. MacArthur Found., 2007; Picker/Commonwealth Scholar in Patient-Centered Care Rsch., Commonwealth Fund, 1995—97, Harold Amos Soc., Robert Wood Johnson Found., 1996—2000. Mem.: Inst. Medicine, Am. Soc. for Clin. Investigation, Delta Omega Hon. Soc. Pub. Health. Achievements include identifying the crucial role race, ethnicity and gender play in the physician-patient relationship. Office: John Hopkins U Sch Medicine & Bloomberg Sch Pub Health 2024 E Monument St Ste 2-500 Baltimore MD 21205 Office Phone: 410-614-3659. Office Fax: 410-614-0588. Business E-Mail: lisa.cooper@jhmi.edu.

COOPER, MATTHEW, surgeon, educator; MD, Georgetown U. Sch. Med. Gen. surgery resident Med. Coll. Wis.; multi-organ transplant fellow Johns Hopkins Hosp., surgical dir. Kidney Transplantation & Clinical Rsch.; assoc. prof. surgery U. Md. Med. Ctr.; dir. Kidney Transplantation & Clinical Rsch. U. Md. Transplantation Div. Office: Univ Md Med Ctr 29 S Greene St Ste 200 Baltimore MD 21201-1595 Office Phone: 410-328-5408.

COOPER, REGINALD RUDYARD, orthopedic surgeon, educator; b. Elkins, W.Va., Jan. 6, 1932; s. Eston H. and Kathryn (Wyatt) C.; m. Jacqueline Smith, Aug. 22, 1954; children: Pamela Ann, Douglas Mark, Christopher Scott, Jeffrey Michael. BA with honors, W.Va. U., 1952, BS, 1953; MD, Med. Coll. Va., 1955; MS, U. Iowa, 1960. Diplomate Am. Bd. Orthopedic Surgeons (examiner 1968-70). Orthopedic surgeon U.S. Naval Hosp., Pensacola, Fla., 1960-62; assoc. in orthopedics U. Iowa Coll. Medicine, Iowa City, 1962-65, asst. prof. orthopedics, 1965-68, assoc. prof. orthopedics, 1968-71, prof. orthopedics, 1971—, chmn. orthopedics, 1973-99, prof. emeritus orthopaedics, 2003—. Rsch. fellow orthopedic surgery Johns Hopkins Hosp., Balt., 1964-65; exch. fellow to Britain for Am. Orthopedic Assn., 1969. Trustee Jour. Bone and Joint Surgeons, 1989-94, chmn. 1993-94. Trustee Nat. Easter Seals Rsch. Found., 1977-81, chmn., 1979-81. Served to lt. comdr. USN, 1960—62. Mem. Iowa, Johnson County Med. Socs., Orthopedic Rsch. Soc. (sec.-treas. 1970-73, pres. 1974-75), Am. Acad. Orthopedic Surgeons (Kappa Delta award for outstanding rsch. in orthopedics 1971), Can. Orthopedic Assn., Am. Orthopedic Assn., N.Y. Acad. Sci., Assn. Bone and Joint Surgeons, AMA, Am. Rheumatism Assn., Am. Acad. Cerebral Palsy, Am. Acad. Orthopedic Surgeons (chmn. exams. com. 1978-82, sec. 1982, 2d v.p. 1985-86, 1st v.p. 1986-87, pres. 1987-88, ortho residency rev. com. 1989-95, chmn. 1993-95). Avocations: travel, photography, anthropology, history. Home: 201 Ridgeview Ave Iowa City IA 52246-1625 Office: U Iowa Hosps & Clinics 450 Newton Rd Iowa City IA 52242

COOPER, ROSS GORDON, science educator, researcher, physiologist; b. Harare, Mashonaland, Zimbabwe, Sept. 23, 1970; arrived in Great Britain, 2003, naturalized, 2003; s. Richard Cooper and Doreen Dorothy Louise Tennett. BSc in Biol. Scis. with honors, U. Zimbabwe, Harare, 1994, DPhil in Med. Physiology, 2000, post-grad. cert. diploma in tertiary edn., 2001; diploma in mgmt., Cambridge U., 1997; MBA, Nottingham-Trent U., 1999; post-grad. cert. in tertiary edn., Birmingham City U., 2005, diploma in tertiary edn., 2006; M.Inst. PM, Inst. Profl. Mgrs. and Adminstrs., UK, 1996; MA in Edn., Birmingham City U., England, 2009; diploma in Higher Mgmt., Cambridge Tutorial Coll., England, 1997; diploma in Practice Mgmt., Assn. British Dispensing Opticians, England, 1996; diploma in Marketing Mgmt., London Chamber of Commerce & Industry, England, 1995. Lic. industry diploma London C. of C., 1995; cert. Mgmt. Consult. Cert. Price Waterhouse, Zimbabwe, 1996, Gen. Cert. in Educ. Advanced Level U. Cambridge Local Exam. Syndicate, Zimbabwe, 1989, Gen. Cer. Secondary Educ., Ordinary Level U. Cambridge Local Exam. Syndicate, Zimbabwe, 1986, in mgmt. health and safety events Birmingham City U., 2011, in substance awareness, treatment & referral tng. Birmingham Drug & Alcohol Action, 2010, CoSHH Risk Assessment Tng. Birmingham City U., 2010, Immediate Life Support Course Resuscitation Coun. UCE Birmingham, 2006, manual handling Birmingham City U., 2005, Birmingham City U., 2005, Occpl. Health & Safety Course, Harare, Zimbabwe, 1990. Rsch. assoc. U. Zimbabwe, 1995—98, lectr. in physiology, 1999—2001, mem. Zimbabwe Physiology Soc., 1995—2001; rsch. assoc. St. Thomas Hosp., London, 2001—02; demonstrator, rsch. assoc. U. Bristol, England, 2003—04; sr. lectr. in physiology Birmingham City U., 2004—, curriculum devel., 2004—05; tchr. Human Biology & Sci., 1994—95. Sub-editor Sub-Saharan Jor. Health & Womans Health Mag., Zimbabwe, 2011; reviewer numerous jour. Jour. Pre-Clinical & Clinical Rsch., 2009. Contbr. 65 papers, in renowned jours, 45 papers in review article. Mem. London C. of C. and Industry, 1997—; volunteer Toc-H, Harare, Zimbabwe, 1994—95; colunteer World Trust Internat., 2010; Restoration of Peace & Democracy in Zimbabwe; campaigner Birmingham Residents Assn., 2005, Conservation of Nature, 2005—. Recipient Allied Arts Literary award Grade B, Zimbabwe, Licentiate award, London C. of C. and Industry. Mem.: Inst. Prof. Mgrs. & Admins., Zimbabwean Physiological Soc., U. & Coll. Lectrs' Union, World's Poultry Sci. Assn., London C. of C. (licentiate), Inst. Profl. Mgmt. (life). Reform. Baptist. Achievements include math. Olympiad internat. grade C, Zimbabwe; research in systemic physiology and care of African giant rat Cricetomys gambianus; renal physiology and toxicology, pathological investigations of disease transmission from ostriches to man, especially Avian Influenza; physiological and nutritional importance of ostrich meat for man. Avocations: reading, writing, painting, cycling, fishing, squash, cricket, hiking, theater, poetry. Office: Birmingham City University 030 Bevan House Sch Health Dept Health Scis Westbourne Rd Birmingham West Midlands B15 3TN England Office Phone: 44 121 202 4553. Office Fax: 44 121 331 7073. Personal E-mail: rgcooperuk@yahoo.com.

COOPER, RUBIN SEYMOUR, pediatric cardiologist; b. Bklyn., Mar. 22, 1946; s. Isaac Samuel Cooper and Frances Lillian Podzieba; m. Toby Ann Kaufman, Dec. 28, 1969; children: Shulie, Keli, Daniel, Michael. BA, NY Med. Coll., 1967; MD, NYU, 1971. Diplomate in pediatric cardiology Am. Bd. Pediat. Instr. SUNY Health Sci. Ctr., Bklyn., 1977-78, asst. prof. pediat., 1978-86, assoc. prof. pediat., 1996—, co-dir. divsn. pediatric cardiology; chief divsn. pediatric cardiology Brookdale Hosp. Med. Ctr., Bklyn., 1985-99; chief pediatric cardiology North Shore U. Hosp., Manhasset, N.Y., 1991-99; prof. clin. pediat. Cornell Med. Coll., NYU Sch. Medicine; dir. pediat. cardiology NY Presbyn. Hosp./Weill Cornell Med. Ctr., 1999—; assoc. dir. Pediat. Cardiovasc. Ctr. NY Presbyn. Hosp., 1999—, attending pediatrician; prof. clin. pediat. Cornell U. Joan and Sanford Weill Med. Coll., David Wallace-Starr Found. prof. clin. pediatric cardiology. Adj. prof. clin. pediats. Columbia U. Coll. Physicians and Surgeons; cons. pediatric cardiology Meth. Hosp., Bklyn., 1981-96, Coney Island Hosp., Maimonides Hops., Bklyn., 1985—, Luth. Hosp., Bklyn., 1988—, Hungtington, Glen Cove, South Nassau Cmty. Southside, Jamaica, Good Samaritan Southside Hosp., 1994—. Pres. Holliswood Jewish Ctr., NY, 1988-91. Named Lieberman Meml. Fellow, Yeshiava U., 1967, Samuel Claussen Meml. Fellow, U. Rochester, NY, 1973-75. Fellow Am. Acad. Pediat., Am. Coll. Cardiology, NY Acad. Sci., NY Cardiology Soc.; mem. Pediatric Cardiology Soc. NY (pres. 1989-90). Office: NY Presbyn Hosp Ste F-695 525 E 68th St New York NY 10021-4870 E-mail: rsc2002@med.cornel.edu.

COOPER, SATHS, psychologist, consultant; b. Durban, South Africa, June 11, 1950; children: Divian Jongilizwe, Athisten Kwezi, Oneida. BA, U. South Africa, Pretoria, 1982; BA with honors, U. Witwatersrand, Johannesburg, 1983; MA, Boston U., 1987, PhD, 1989, diploma in Gerontology, 1989. Cert. clin. psychologist Health Professions Coun. South Africa, 1989, advanced hypnotherapist Nat. Guild of Hypnotists, 1989. Lectr. U. Witwatersrand, Johannesburg, 1986, Boston U., 1987—89; asst. dir. Roxbury Comprehensive Cmty. Health Ctr., Boston, 1988—89; sr. lectr. U. Western Cape, Cape Town, South Africa, 1990—94; CEO Inst. Multi-Party Democracy, Johannesburg, 1990, Family Inst., Johannesburg, 1991—95; chairperson Kenako Consulting, Johannesburg, 1999—; vice chancellor & prin. U. Durban-Westville, South Africa, 2003. Dir. Inst. Black Rsch., Durban, 1983—2000, Ctr. Health & Devel., Boston, 1988—2001, Uni-Africa Investment Holdings, Johannesburg, 1998—; chairperson Rd. Accident Fund, Pretoria, South Africa, 2004—05. Prodr.: (various drama) (Best Actor, 1967); contbr. articles to profl. publs. Chairperson Conquest for Life Youth Programs, Johannesburg, 1995—, Medicover Med. Fund, Johannesburg, 2005—09. Recipient Achiever award, Indian Acad. South Africa, 2003, Internat. Humanitarian award, Internat. Festival Com., 2005; fellow, Nat. Acad. Psychology, India, 2008; Paul Harris fellow, Rotary Internat., 2003, Presdl. U. fellowship, Boston U., 1986—89, Fullbright fellow, US Info. Svcs., 1986—89. Fellow: Psychol Soc. South Africa; mem.: Internat. Coun. Sci. (chair SA bd.), Profl. Bd. Psychology (chairperson 1999—2004), Internat. Assn. Applied Psychology (dir. 2006—), Health Professions Coun. (v.p. 2001—04), Internat. Union of Psychol. Sci. (v.p. 2004—08), Psychol. Soc. South Africa (pres. 1986—99). Office: PsySSA PO Box 989 Houghton 2041 South Africa Office Fax: 27114863266.

COOPER, SIGNE SKOTT, retired nursing educator; b. Clinton County, Iowa, Jan. 29, 1921; d. Hans Edward and Clara Belle (Steen) Skott. BS, U. Wis., 1948; MEd, U. Minn., 1955. Head nurse U. Wis. Hosp., Madison, 1946—48; instr. U. Wis. Sch. Nursing, Madison, 1948—51, asst. prof., 1952—57, assoc. prof., 1957—62, prof., assoc. dean, 1962—83, prof. emeritus, 1983. Prof. U. Wis. Extension, 1955-83. Contbg. author: American Nursing: A Biographical Dictionary, Vol. 1, 1988, Vol. 2, 1992, Vol. 3, 2000; contbr. articles to profl. jours. 1st Lt. U.S. Army Nurse Corps, 1943-46. Recipient NLN Linda Richards award, ANA Honorary Recognition award, Adult Edn. Assn. Pioneer award; named to Nursing Hall of Fame, 2000. Fellow Am. Acad. Nursing (named Living Legend 2003); mem. Am. Assn. for History Nursing (Pres.'s award 2003), Wis. Nurses Assn. (pres.).

COOPER, SUSAN R., state agency administrator; b. Tenn. 3 children. B in Nursing, MS in Nursing, Vanderbilt U. Sch. Nursing, Nashville. RN. Emergency and intensive care nurse; faculty Vanderbilt U. Sch. Nursing, co-dir., health systems mgmt. program, asst. dean practice; commr. Tenn. Dept. Health, Nashville, 2007—. Co-creator, Ctr. Advanced Practice Nursing and Allied Health Vanderbilt U. Med. Ctr.; health advisor Tenn Dept. Health, 2005. Office: Tenn Dept Health 425 5th Ave N Cordell Hull Bldg 3rd Fl Nashville TN 37243 Office Phone: 615-741-3111.

COOPERMAN, ALAN S., obstetrician, gynecologist; Attended, U. Bologna, Italy, 1968. Diplomate Am. Bd. Ob-Gyn. Intern Newark Beth Israel Med. Ctr., 1970, resident, 1973; with St. Barnabas Med. Ctr., Overlook Med. Ctr. Office: Overlook Medical Center 99 Beauvoir Ave Summit NJ 07901 Office Phone: 908-522-2000.

COOPERMAN, LEON G., hedge fund executive; b. NYC, Apr. 25, 1943; s. Harry and Martha (Rothenstein) C.; m. Toby F.; children: Wayne M., Michael S. BA, CUNY-Hunter Coll., 1964; MBA, Columbia U., 1967. Cert. fin. analyst. Quality control engr. Xerox Corp., Webster, NY, 1965-67; ptnr. Goldman Sachs & Co., NYC, 1967-90, counsel, 1990—; ptnr. Goldman Sachs Group, LP, 1992—; chmn., CEO Goldman, Sachs Asset Management, NYC, 1989-90, cons., chmn., profit-sharing and pension coms., 1992—; founder, chmn., CEO Omega Advisors, Inc., NYC, 1992—. Bd. dirs. Automatic Data Processing, Inc., 1991—. Trustee United Jewish Appeal, N.J., 1980, St. Barnabas Hosp., Livingston, N.J.; bd. overseers Grad. Sch. Bus. Columbia U., bd. dirs., vice-chmn. finance and treasurer, Damon Runyon Cancer Rsch. Found.; global leadership coun. Building With Books. Named one of Forbes 400: Richest Americans, 2009. Mem. Fin. Analyst Fedn. (dir. 1980-), N.Y. Soc. Security Analysts (pres. 1980) Clubs: Atlantis Yacht (Monmouth Beach, N.J.). Office: Omega Advisors Inc 88 Pine St 3100 New York NY 10005-1805 Office Phone: 212-495-5200. Office Fax: 212-495-5236. Business E-Mail: leon_cooperman@adp.com. *

COOPER-RUSPOLI, ANNIE NATAF, psychiatrist, director; d. Victor and Arlette Nataf; m. Stephane Frank Ruspoli, June 9, 1997; 1 child, Jonathan Cooper. MD, U. Paris, 1975. Resident psychiatry Emory U. Sch. Medicine, Atlanta, 1975—78, fellow child psychiatry, 1978—79; med. dir. child and adolescent unit Ga. Regional Hosp. Atlanta, 1980—91; psychiatrist Piedmont Psychiat. Clinic, Atlanta, 1996—. Mem. Counseil Nat. de l'Ordre des Medecins, Paris, 1991—; sci. adv. bd. mem. Skyland Trails Ctr., Atlanta, 2007—11. Trustee Atlanta Internat. Sch., 1985—97, bd. dirs., 1997—2005; trustee Alliance Francaise d'Atlanta, 1992—95, Ga Casa, Atlanta, 1992—2001. Mem.: AMA, Atlanta Med. Assn., Ga. Med. Assn., Ga. Psychiat. Assn., Am. Psychiat. Assn. Independent. Office: Piedmont Psychiatric Clinic 1938 Peachtree Rd Ste 505 Atlanta GA 30309 Office Fax: 404-355-2917. Personal E-mail: acooperrus@aol.com.

COOTE, JOHN HAVEN, medical scientist, educator; b. London, Jan. 5, 1937; s. Albert Ernest and Elizabeth Mary (Noble) C.; m. Susan Mary Hylton, Dec. 28, 1974; children: Edward John, Rachel Elizabeth, Naomi Caroline.0 BSc, Royal Free Hosp. Sch. Medicine, London, 1961, PhD, 1964; DSc, U. Birmingham, Eng., 1980; Med. Diploma, Jagiellonian U., Krakow, Poland, 1995; CBiol, FSB, 1988. Lectr. U. Birmingham, 1967-70, sr. lectr., 1970-77, reader, 1977-84, prof., head dept., 1984—, emeritus prof., 2003, Bowman prof. physiology, 1985—, head Sch. Basic Med. Scis., 1988-91; vis. prof. cardiology Glenfield Hosp., Leicester, 2003—. Vis. scientist Inst. Exptl. Medicine, Caracas, 1971-72; vis. prof. Inst. Gerontology, Tokyo, 1974-75, Inst. Physiology, Warsaw, Poland, 1976; vis. prof. pharmacology U. Loyola, Chgo., 1988, Shanghai, China, 1984, Nankai, China, 2005; prof. dept. physiology U. Heidelberg, Germany, 1992., cons. scientist, Neurosolutions, Uni-Warwick, 2003—; chair editl. bd., Exp. Physiol., 2001-2006, Coun. British Heart Found. and Rsch. Coms., 1999-2003, Ethics Com. Qinetiq Ltd., 1998-2008; civil cons. applied physiology, Inst. Aviation Medicine; hon. mem. Physiol. Soc., 2004; mem. NY Acad. Sci., 1991-; chair grants com. Coun. Brit. Heart Found; chair ethics com. QinetiQ Ltd., 1998-2008; civil cons. RAF Ctr. Aviation Medicine, 2003-. Editor: Serotonin, CNS Receptors and Brain Function, 1993. Fellow: RCS, Inst. Biology of Britain. Avocation: mountain climbing. Office: Sch Clin experimental Medicine Coll Med and Dental Sci Edgbaston B15 2TT Birmingham England Business E-Mail: j.h.coote@bham.ac.uk.

COPE, DORIS K., anesthesiologist, educator; M in Clin. Psychology, Augusta Coll.; MD, Med. Coll. of Ga. Diplomate Am. Bd Anesthesiology. Resident Univ. South Ala.; pres. Anesthesia History Assn.; prof. anesthesiology dept. Univ. of Pitts. Med. Ctr. Vis. prof. Univ. of Ala., Birmingham, Baylor Coll. of Medicine, Houston, La. State Univ., Shreveport, La., SUNY, Buffalo, Southwest Med. Ctr., Dallas, Med. Coll. of Ga., Augusta, Ga., Univ. of Conn., Bridgeport, Conn., Tianjin, China, Chengdu, China, Shanghai, China. Editor-in-chief (publs.) Am. Soc. of Critical Care Anesthesiologists, 1993—95; editor: (publs.) Bull. of Anesthesia History, 1994—, author publs. 76 sci. papers and abstracts. Bd. trustees The Anesthesia Found.; bd. trustees Wood Libr.-Mus. Am. Soc. of Anesthesiologists. Named one of Best Doctors in America, 1998. Mem.: Acad. of Anesthesiology, C.F. Reynolds Med. History Soc. (former pres.). Office: University of Pittsburgh Medical Center St Margaret 815 Freeport Rd Pittsburgh PA 15215-3399 Office Phone: 412-784-4000.

COPE, RHIAN BRIANNA, toxicologist, educator; b. Brisbane, Australia, Oct. 1, 1965; B in Vet. Sci., U. Queensland, 1989; BSc with 1st class honors, Murdoch U., 1991; PhD, U. Sydney, 1996. Clinician dept. companion animal medicine and surgery U. Queensland, 1990; rsch. asst. Sch. Vet. Sci. Murdoch U., 1991—92; lectr. lab. animal medicine and animal genetics TAFE, Perth, Australia, 1991—92; clinician emergency medicine Ku-Ring-Gai Vet. Hosp., Sydney, 1997—98; postdoctoral rsch. asst. Australian Photobiology Testing Facility, 1997; hon. postdoctoral rsch. fellow dept. animal sci. U. Sydney, 1997; postdoctoral rsch. fellow Commonwealth Sci. and Indsl. Rsch. Orgn., 1998; postdoctoral rsch. assoc. dept. vet. bioscis. U. Ill., Urbana, 1999, asst. prof. morphology dept. vet. bioscis., 1999—2002; asst. prof. toxicology dept. biomed. scis. Oreg. State U., Corvallis, 2002—. Contbr. articles to profl. jours., chpt. to book. Del. People to People Amb. Program, Internat. Union Toxicology, China, 2003. Recipient award for outstanding presentation, Am. Coll. Vet. Microbiologists, 2002; grantee, U. Ill., 2000—01, USDA, 2000—01, Ill. Dept. Agr., 2001, Am. Cancer Soc., 2001—02, Oreg. State U., 2003. Fellow: Am. Acad. Toxicology, Am. Acad. Vet. and Comparitive Toxicology; mem.: Am. Soc. Photobiology, Soc. Toxicology. Office Phone: 541-737-6946. Business E-Mail: rhian.cope@oregonstate.edu.

COPEL, JOSHUA, obstetrician-gynecologist, educator; BA in Psychology, Brandeis U., Waltam, Mass., 1971—75; MD, Tufts U. Sch. of Medicine, Boston Mass., 1975—79. Diplomate Am. Bd. Ob-Gyn, cert. maternal and fetal medicine. Resident obstetrics and gynecology Pennsylvania Hosp., Phila., 1980—83; fellow maternal and fetal medicine Yale-New Haven Hosp., 1983—85, dir. resident edn. dept. of obstetrics and gynecology, 1988—92, dir. obstetrics, 1992—. Instr. dept. of obstetrics and gynecology Univ. of Pennsylvania, Phila., 1982—83, Yale Univ. Sch. of Medicine, New Haven, 1983—85, asst. prof. dept. of obstetrics and gynecology, 1985—89, assoc. prof. dept. of obstetrics and gynecology, 1989—93, section head maternal-fetal medicine dept. of obstetrics and gynecology, 1992—, prof. dept. of obstetrics and gynecology, 1993—, co-dir. high risk pregnancy tng. program in perinatal epidemiology, 1994—99. Co-author: (peer-reviewed articles) Carbon monoxide intoxication in pregnancy: Report of a case, 1982; author: The value of culdocentesis in the diagnosis of ectopic pregnancy, 1985, Delivery of a patient with a single ventricle using intrathecal morphine anesthesia, 1986, Combined echocardiographic and Doppler assessment of fetal congenital atrioventricular block, 1987, and numerous others; co-author: (reviews) Intrauterine fetal demise and hemostatic failure: The fetal death syndrome, 1985; author: The application of fetal echocardiography to prenatal care, 1987, Prevention of Rh isoimmunization and treatment of the compromised fetus, 1988, Fetal heart defect detected, 1989, and numerous others. Fellow: Am. Inst. of Ultrasound in Medicine, Am. Coll. of Obstetrics and Gynecology; mem.: Connecticut State Medical Soc., New Haven County Medical Assn., Soc. of Obstetric Medicine, Internat. Soc. of Ultrasound in Obstetrics and Gynecolgy, New England Perinatal Soc., New Haven Obstetric Soc., Soc. of Gynecologic Investigation, Soc. of Perinatal Obstetricians. Office: Yale University School of Medicine Department of Obstetrics and Gycenology 333 Cedar St Box 208063 New Haven CT 06520-3206 Office Phone: 203-785-5682.

COPELAND, EDWARD MEADORS, III, surgeon, educator; b. Augusta, Ga., Oct. 6, 1937; s. Edward Meadors Jr. and Louise (Leggitt) C.; m. Martha Patterson, Ar. 24, 1964; children: Edward Meadors IV, Catherine Leggitt. BA, Duke U., 1959; MD, Cornell U., 1963. Diplomate Am. Bd. Surgery (bd. dir. 1983-91, chmn. 1990-91). Intern in surgery U. Pa. Hosp., Phila., 1963-64, resident in gen. surgery, 1964-69; resident surg. oncology Anderson Hosp., Houston, 1971-72; asst. prof. to prof. U. Tex. Med. Sch., Houston, 1972-82, U. Tex. M.D. Anderson Hosp. and Tumor Inst., Houston, 1972-82; prof. U. Fla. Coll. Medicine, Gainesville, 1982—, chmn. dept., 1982—2003, disting. prof., 2004—08; disting. prof. emeritus, 2008—. Project dir. Nat. Large Bowel Cancer Project, Nat. Cancer Inst., Houston, 1981-82; bd. dirs. Sun Bank North Ctrl. Fla. Maj. US Army, 1969-71, Vietnam. Decorated Bronze Star Rep. Vietnam; recipient Seale Harris award So. Med. Assn., 1984, Disting. Alumnus award M.D. Anderson Hosp. and Tumor Inst., 1987, Lifetime Achievement award, 2008. Fellow Am. Surg. Assn., So. Surg. Assn. (pres. 1998-99), Texas Surg. Soc., Soc. of Black Academic Surgeons, Royal Acad. of Surgeons, Ireland; mem. ACS (chmn. bd. govs. 1995-96, bd. regents 1997-2007, vice chmn. 2002-03, chmn. 2004-05, pres.-elect 2005-06, pres. 2006-07), Assn. Acad. Surgery (pres. 1978-79), Soc. Surg. Oncology (pres. 1998-99), Soc. Surg. Chmn. (pres. 1996-98), Halsted Soc. (pres. 1993), Southeastern Surg. Congress (pres. 2000-01), Soc. Univ. Surgeons, Gainesville Country Club. Avocations: fishing, golf, tennis. Home: 2605 NW 7th Rd Gainesville FL 32607-2600 Office: Univ Fla Coll Medicine Dept Surgery PO Box 100286 Gainesville FL 32610-0286 Office Phone: 352-265-0169. Business E-Mail: copelem@surgery.ufl.edu.

COPELAND, LOIS JACQUELINE, physician; b. Malden, Mass., Sept. 16, 1943; d. Arnold Alan and Ann Copeland; m. Richard A. Sperling, June 7, 1970; children: Mark Edward, Larissa Lynn, Lauren Anne, Lorraine Elizabeth. BA magna cum laude, Cornell U., 1964, MD, 1968. Intern N.Y. Hosp., NYC, 1968-69, resident, 1969-70, Bellevue Hosp., NYU Med. Ctr., 1970-72; tchg. asst. internal medicine NYU Med. Ctr., 1971—; attending physician Pascack Valley Hosp., Westwood, NJ, 1974—2007. Mem. med. staff Valley Hosp., Ridgewood, N.J., 1980—; med. staff Holy Name Hosp., Teaneck, NJ, 2002-, Hackensack U., Hackensack Med. Ctr., NJ, 2009-. Mem. secondary schs. com. Cornell U., 1978—; bd. dirs. Found. for Free Enterprise, 1994—; steering com. physicians coun. Heritage Found., 1993—; pres. Coun. Cornell Women, 1993-95 Mem. Assn. Am. Physicians and Surgeons (bd. dirs. 1991-99, pres. 1994), Assn. Liberty Choice and Self-Autonomy (pres. 1998—), Phi Beta Kappa, Phi Kappa Phi, Alpha Lambda Delta. Achievements include being originator and physician-plaintiff of landmark constitutional lawsuit Stewart v. Sullivan, which reaffirmed the right of senior citizens to contract privately with physicians, and Amicus in United Seniors v. Shalala for the right to pay privately for medical services. Home: 25 Sparrowbush Rd Upper Saddle River NJ 07458-1400 Office: 47 Central Ave Hillsdale NJ 07642-2118 Office Phone: 201-664-1212. Personal E-mail: loisjcope@gmail.com.

COPELAND, NEAL G., medical researcher; B in Biology, U. Utah, PhD in Biochemistry. Postdoctoral fellow Dana-Farber Cancer Ctr., Harvard Med. Sch.; assoc. staff scientist The Jackson Lab.; assoc. prof. microbiology and molecular genetics U. Cin. Coll. Medicine, Cin.; dir. Mammalian Genetics Lab. (as of 1999 renamed Mouse Cancer Genetics Program) ABL-Basic Rsch. Program (now Ctr. Cancer Rsch.), Nat. Cancer Inst., NIH, 1985—2006, also head Molecular Genetics of Oncogenesis Sect., 1985—2006; exec. dir. Inst. of Molecular Cell Biology, Singapore, 2006—. Office: Inst Molecular Cell Biology 61 Biopolis Drive Proteos 138673 Proteos Singapore 138673 Office Phone: 6586 9789. E-mail: ncopeland@imcb.a-star.edu.sg.

COPELAND, ROBERT BODINE, internist, cardiologist; b. Arab, Ala., Jan. 24, 1938; s. Haden Paul and Jimmie Alice (Bodine) Copeland; m. Virginia (Jenny) Ruth Trammell, June 26, 1960; children: Robert Theodore, Haden McTieyre. BS, Auburn U., 1960; MD, U. Ala., Birmingham, 1963. Diplomate Am. Bd. Internal Medicine, cert. internal medicine, cardiovasc. diseases and geriatrics. Intern then resident, clin. rsch. fellow in cardiology Mass. Gen. Hosp., Harvard Med. Sch., Boston, 1963-67; physician Clark Holder Clinic, LaGrange, Ga., 1967-77; founder, dir. Ga. Heart Clinic, LaGrange, 1972—2006; founder, pres. So. Cardiopulmonary Assocs., LaGrange, 1977—2003, clin. prof. med. U. Ala., Birmingham, 1980—2005, Emory U., Atlanta, 1980—. Bd. govs. Joint Commn. on Accreditation of Healthcare Orgns., Chgo., 1991—97, Am. Bd. Internal Medicine, Phila., 1980—86; trustee West Ga. Med. Sys., LaGrange; co-founder Troup Care Free Med. Clin., LaGrange, 2008. Contbr. Trustee LaGrange Coll.; chmn. bd. trustees ACP-ASIM Found., 1999—2002. Recipient Disting. Alumni award, U. Ala., Birmingham, 1985. Fellow: ACP (gov. Ga. chpt. 1987—91, Master 1993, regent 1993—99, chair bd. regents 1998—99), NAS Inst. Medicine, Am. Coll. Cardiology, Royal Coll. Physicians; mem.: Am. Clin. and Climatological Assn., Am. Heart Assn. (pres. Ga. affiliate 1985—86). Office: 1551 Doctors Dr Lagrange GA 30240-4139 Personal E-mail: rbcopeland1101@gmail.com.

COPELAND, STEPHEN ANDREW, orthopaedic surgeon, consultant; b. Muchwenlock, Shropshire, Eng., May 7, 1946; s. Derek Graham and Peggie (Strangward) C.; m. Jennifer Ryan Almeyda, Apr. 3, 1972; children: Sara, Matthew. MB BS, St. Bartholomew's Hosp., London, 1970. Lectr. Royal Nat. Orthopaedic Hosp., London, 1977-78; sr. registrar St. Bartholomew's Hosp., London, 1975-79; surgeon Royal Berkshire Hosp., Reading, Eng., 1979—. Pres. Brit. Shoulder and Elbow Surgery, 1993-95. Author: Surgical Repair and Reconstruction, 1993, Operative Shoulder Surgery, 1996, Shoulder Surgery, 1997, Joint Stiffness in the Upper Limbs, 1997; contbr. chpts. to books on shoulder surgery; mem. editl. bd. Jour. Bone and Joint Surgery, London, 1990-94. ABC travelling fellow Brit. Orthopaedic Assn., 1982; Johnson & Johnson fellow, 1984. Fellow Royal Coll. Surgeons, Royal Soc. Medicine (coun. orthopaedic sect. 1992-95), Brit. Orthopaedic Assn.; mem. European Shoulder Soc. (edn. com. 1992, exec. bd. 1996, pres. 1998—), Brit. Elbow and Shoulder Surgeons Soc. (past pres.), Internat. Soc. Surgery of Shoulder (chmn. 2004—), European Shoulder and Elbow Surgery Soc. (pres. 1998-2002). Avocation: boating. Office Phone: 0118902 8063. Personal E-mail: Stephen.Copeland@btinternet.com.

COPEMAN, MICHAEL CHARLES, oncologist; b. Broken Hill, NSW, Australia, Apr. 27, 1961; MBBS with honors, U. Sydney, 1984; PhD, U. Oxford, 1990. Oncologist Northern Beaches Cancer Svc., Sydney, 2004—. Senate fellow U. Sydney, 1996. Fellow: Royal Australasian Coll. Physicians; mem.: Royal Coll. Physicians London, Am. Assn. Cancer Rsch., Am. Soc. Hematology, Am. Soc. Clin. Oncology. Avocations: travel, surfing, languages. Home: 45 Baringa Rd Northbridge Sydney NSW 2063 Australia Business E-Mail: mcopeman@bigpond.net.au.

COPIT, DEBRA SOMERS, diagnostic radiologist; MD, Jefferson Med. Coll. of Thomas Jefferson U., 1989. Diplomate Am. Bd. of Radiology-diagnostic radiology. Resident diagnostic radiology Albert Einstein Med. Ctr., Phila., 1993, Univ. of Tex. SW Med. Ctr., 1994; fellow diagnostic radiology Baylor Koman Breast Ctr., 1995; sect. chief of mammography Gershon-Cohen Breast Clinic, dir. Named top dr., Phila. Mag., 2007, 2010. Office: Albert Einstein Medical Center 5501 Old York Rd Philadelphia PA 19141 Office Phone: 215-456-6250. Office Fax: 215-456-7578.

COPIT, STEVEN E., plastic surgeon; Grad., Jefferson Med. Coll., 1988. Diplomate Am. Bd. Surgery, Am. Bd. of Facial Plastic and Reconstructive Surgery. Intern Thomas Jefferson Univ. Hosp., resident; fellow Univ. of Tex. SW Med. Sch. Office: Jefferson University Hospitals 840 Walnut St 15th Fl Philadelphia PA 19107 Office Phone: 215-625-6630. Office Fax: 215-625-6640.

COPLAN, NEIL LAWRENCE, cardiologist; b. Wilkes-Barre, Pa., Aug. 13, 1954; s. Joseph Norman and Surita (Greenberg) C.; m. Carolyn Ellen Levine, June 13, 1976; children: Stephanie Beth, Alison Hayley. BA, Cornell U., 1975; MD, U. Pa., 1980. Bd. cert. in internal medicine and cardiovascular disease; diplomate Nat. Bd. Med. Examiners. Resident in internal medicine Hosp. U. Pa., Phila., 1980-83; fellow cardiology Mt. Sinai Med. Ctr., NYC, 1983-85; rsch. fellow cardiology/sports medicine Lenox Hill Hosp., NYC, 1985-86, pvt. practice cardiology/internal medicine, 1986—, chief cardiology consultation svc., 1986—, assoc. chief cardiology, 1989—; rsch. assoc. Nicholas Inst. of Sports Medicine, NYC, 1986—. Named Allen Tanney Cardiologist for Nicholas Inst. Sports Medicine and Cardiovascular Rsch., 1988. Fellow ACP, Am. Coll. Cardiology, N.Y. Cardiological Soc., Coun. Clin. Cardiology. Jewish. Office: Lenox Hill Hosp 100 E 77th St New York NY 10021 Office Phone: 212-434-2172. Office Fax: 212-434-2111.

COPMAN, LOUIS, radiologist; b. Phila., Jan. 17, 1934; s. Jacob and Eve (Snyder) C.; m. Avera Schuster, June 8, 1958; children: Mark, Linda. BA, U. Pa., 1955, MD, 1959. Diplomate Am. Bd. Radiology; Nat. Bd. Med. Examiners. Commd. ensign Med. Corps USN, 1958; advanced through grades to capt. M.C. USN, 1975; ret., 1975; asst. chief radiology dept. Naval Hosp., Pensacola, Fla., 1966—69; chief radiology dept. Doctors Hosp., Phila., 1969—73; radiologist Mercer Hosp. Ctr., Trenton, NJ, 1973—75; chmn. radiology dept. Naval Hosp., Phila., 1975—84; chief. radiology dept. Naval Med. Clinic, Pearl Harbor, Hawaii, 1984—89; pvt. practice radiologist Honolulu, 1989—92. Cons. Radiology Svcs., Wilmington, Del., 1978-84, Yardley (Pa.) Radiology, 1979-84. Author: The Cuckold, 1974. Capt. med corps USN, 1958—89, ret., 1989. Recipient Albert Einstein award in Medicine, U. Pa., 1959. Mem. AMA, Assn. Mil. Surgeons U.S., Royal Soc. Medicine, Radiol. Soc. N.Am., Am. Coll. Radiology, Photographic Soc. Am., Sherlock Holmes Soc., Phi Beta Kappa, Alpha Omega Alpha. Avocations: photography, hang-gliding, scuba diving. Home: PO Box 384767 Waikoloa HI 96738-4767 Office: 68-1771 Makanahele Pl Waikoloa HI 96738-5128 Office Phone: 808-883-0059. Personal E-mail: louiscopman@earthlink.net.

COPPERMAN, STUART MORTON, pediatrician, educator; b. Bklyn., June 5, 1935; s. Irving and Anne (Reisfield) C.; m. Renee Stein, Aug. 17, 1958; children: Beth, Alan, Cara. BA cum laude, Bklyn. Coll., 1956; MD, SUNY-Bklyn., 1960. Diplomate Am. Bd. Pediatrics. Rotating intern. L.I. Jewish Hosp., New Hyde Park, NY, 1960-61, resident in pediat., 1961-63; practice medicine specializing in pediat. Merrick, NY, 1965-2000; sr. med. cons. Med. Advisers, P.C., 2001—02; mem. staff L.I. Jewish Hillside Med. Ctr., Schneider Children's Hosp., New Hyde Park, Nassau County Med. Ctr., East Meadow, Winthrop U. Hosp., Mineola, North Shore Univ. Hosp., Manhasset; clin. assoc. prof. pediat. SUNY Med. Sch., Stony Brook, 1972-2000; asst. prof. clin. health studies SUNY Sch. Allied Health, Stony Brook, 1977-2000; clin. instr. physicians asst. program Stony Brook Med. Ctr., 1972-2000; prof. pediat. St. George's Med. Coll., St. Vincent, W.I., acting chmn. pediat., 1979-80; healthcare security analyst, healthcare cons., 2000—02; medico-legal expert, 2000—04; physician exec. Health and Info. Svcs., 2001—02; pres. SMCMD, Ltd., 2003—; CEO Profl. Practice Brokers, 2002—; cons. Learning Dynamics, Inc., 2006—. Med. advisor Assn. Children with Downs Syndrome, 1971-98; mem. com. for handicapped Bellmore Sch. Dist., 1976-86; mem. ad hoc com. on cmty. as sch. Merrick-Bellmore Schs., 1976-90; bd. dirs. North Shore-L.I. Jewish I.P.O., L.I. Sch. Health Edn. Coalition, North Shore Physicians Orgn., North Shore - L.I. Jewish PHO; mem. Nassau County Sch. Health Edn. Commn., 1990-93; mem. ad hoc com. on prevention of birth defects March of Dimes; preceptor in pediat. Physicians Asst. Program, Cath. Med. Ctr.; mem. doctor's adv. com. Shaare Zedek Hosp., Jerusalem, 1974-98; med. cons. Matchbox Toys, 1985-88, Proctor & Gamble, 1988, Carnation Co., 1989-90, Disney Ednl. Svcs., 1990-95, vaccine divsn. Merck Corp., 1997—, Sepracor, 1999—; cons., mem. spkrs. bur. N.Y. State Med. Soc., N.Y. State Senate Com. Mental Hygiene, 1988—, Lederle Labs., 1989-95, Merck Labs., 1996—, Wallace Labs., 1996—, ucb Pharma, 1999—, Connaught, 1999—, Abbott Labs., 1996—, Pfizer, 1998—, Sepracor, 1999—; author, co-founder, pres., bd. dirs. Child Health Imagery Prodns., 1997-2000; founder, dir. brokerage website, 2002—, edtl. adv. bd. mem. Am. Express Publ. Physicians Golf and Travel, 1995-98. Author: Buying and Selling a Medical or Dental Practice, 2007, Professional Practice Brokers, Exit Strategy, 2009; co-chair, Am. Cancer Soc. Bate Zaliarius Charity Event, Eastern Divsn., The Greens, 2007-, "Ask a Pedatrician" blog for www.parentsave people.com, 2009-; appearance TV shows on Downs Syndrome, learning disabilities, CPR, first aid, infant exercise programs, TV's effects on children, infectious disease, parent-infant bonding, immunizations, enuresis, toilet training, prevention of cigarette smoking among children, 1972—, also on HealthLinks (Life Time TV), 1990-93; mem. editl. adv. bd. Jour. Assn. for Physician Assts., 1987—; editl. cons. Jour. Pediat. Mgmt., 1991—; contbr. chpt. to Textbook Pediat. Sports Medicine; developer Babycise (infant parent interactive program in video tape and book form), 1985; rschr. on hetacillin, 1966, pyridoxine effect on serotonin level and performance in children with Down's Syndrome, 1970-75, Alice in Wonderland syndrome as presenting sympton of infectious mononucleosis, 1966-77, on transmission of group A Beta hemolytic strep infection from pet reservoirs to children, 1963-81; med. editor Air Fair Mag., 1991-93, L.I. Parent Mag., 1985-93, L.I. Family Mag., 1994-95; editl. bd. mem. Physicians Golf and Thurl, 1995-98; contbr. articles to profl. jours. Mem. sch. bd. Temple Beth Am., Merrick, 1972-78, mem. exec. com., 1973-74, chmn. com. Israel and World Affairs, 1976-78, mem. sch. com., 1976-78, mem. ritual com., 1976-93; mem. N.Y. State Senate com. on mental hygiene, 1990—; mem. profl. adv. bd. So. Shore divsn. YM-YWHA; benefactor Merrick Libr., 1992—. With U.S. Army, 1963-65. Recipient Physician Recognition award AMA, 1966—2000, testimonial dinner and plaque Assn. Children with Down Syndrome, 1972, Best Clin. Tchrs. of Pediat. award Nassau County Med. Ctr., 1981-82; named Merrick Profl. of Yr., 1994. Fellow Am. Acad. Pediat. (chmn. com. TV effects on children 1976—, mem. nat. com. comm. and pub. info. 1984-85, mem. nat. com. on substance abuse 1998-2001, media spokesperson 1988—, tobacco, alcohol and drug-free generation coord. 1988-98, chmn. substance abuse com. 1992—, N.Y. state chmn. substance abuse com. 1992-94, managed care com. chpt. 2 1993-95), Internat. Coll. Pediat.; mem. AMA, N.Y. State Med. Soc. (com. on alcohol 1997—), Nassau County Med. Soc. (com. on mental health 1980—, project assist 1992—, Nassau Acad. Medicine Pub. Health com. 1991—, libr. com. 1993—, chmn. pediat. sect. 1995—), Nassau Pediat. Soc. (mem. exec. bd. 1972—, chmn. com. on mental health 1972-88, v.p. 1994-95, pres. 1996-97). A Non-Smoking Generation Internat. (organizer, med. dir. Am. divsn.), Am. Lung Assn., Nassau-Suffolk Lung Assn. (life mem., dir. 1982-84), Am. Physicians Fellowship for Israel Med. Assn., Assn. Children with Learning Disabilities (mem. profl. adv. bd.), La Leche League, Latin Am. Parents Assn., L.I. Sch. Health Edn. Coun. (bd. dirs. 1989-92), Alpha Epsilon Pi (chancellor Phi Theta chpt. 1955-56), Phi Delta Epsilon (consul Zeta chpt. 1960), B'nai Brith. Office: 676 Balfour Pl Melville NY 11747 Personal E-mail: smcmd@aol.com.

COPPOCK, DONALD, biomedical researcher; PhD in Cell Biology, U. Calif. Postdoctoral fellow Dana-Farber Cancer Inst. and Harvard Med. Sch., Brandeis U., Waltham, Mass.; dir. Oncology Rsch. Lab. Winthrop U. Hosp., Mineola, NY; asst. prof. SUNY, Stony Brook; assoc. prof. Coriell Inst. Med. Rsch., NJ, asst. dir. Coriell Cell Repositories NJ. Office: Coriell Inst Med Rsch 403 Haddon Ave Camden NJ 08103 Office Phone: 856-757-9717. Office Fax: 856-757-9737. E-mail: dcoppock@coriell.org.

COPPOCK, JANET ELAINE, retired mental health nurse; b. Tipton, Ind., June 2, 1954; d. Jack Donavon and Bonnie Ruth (Luse) Weismiller; divorced; children: Jonathan Andrew, Daniel Jason. Student, Ball State U., 1972—73; ASN, Ind. U. Kokomo, 1977. RN, Ind., Mich.; cert. psychiat./mental health nurse ANCC. RN charge staff and med.-surg. Tipton County Meml. Hosp., Ind., 1977—79; RN psychiat. staff Howard Cmty. Hosp., Kokomo, 1987—89; pvt. nurse Kokomo, 1989—95; RN psychiat. and addiction treatment, instr. Koala Hosp. & Counseling Ctr. Behavioral Healthcare Corp., Kokomo, 1995—98; RN psychiat. and addiction treatment Lafayette Behavioral Health System, Ind., 1998—99; RN psychiat. staff, patient care coord. Home Hosp. of Greater Lafayette Health Svcs., Inc., Lafayette, 1999—2007; ret., 2007. Instr. parenting edn. Kinsey Youth Ctr., Kokomo, 1995-96; co-developer Koala Halfway House, Behavioral Healthcare Corp., Kokomo, 1996, house mgr., 1996-98. Author: Poetic Reflections, Expressions and Inspirations, 1986, Faithful Resolutions, 1993, Coming to Terms, 1998. Recipient Golden Poet award World Poetry Orgn., 1987, 88. Mem.: Nurses Svc. Orgn., Internat. Platform Assn, Ind. U. Alumni Assn. (life). Avocations: music, art, movies, basketball. Home: 2711 President Ln Kokomo IN 46902-3066

COPPOLA, JOHN T., cardiologist, educator; Attended, NY Med. Coll. Sch. Medicine, 1974—78. Diplomate Am. Bd. Cardiology-cardiovascular disease, 1983, Am. Bd. Cardiology-intervention cardiology, 1999, Am. Bd. Internal Medicine. Intern in internal medicine St. Vincent Hosp., NYC, 1978—81, resident in internal medicine, 1978—81, clin. fellow in cardiology St. Vincent Hosp. Med. Ctr., 1981—83; with Bellevue Hosp. Ctr., clin. asst. prof. NYU Langone Med. Ctr., cardiologist. Contbr. numerous jour. article including "Triple valve repair for rheumatic heart disease, 2005", "Nitroglycerin, nitroprusside, or both, in preventing radial artery spasm during transradial artery catheterization, 2006" and "Noninvasive Assessment of HIV-related Coronary Artery Disease, 2011". Office. New York University Langone Medical Center New York Cardiovascular Associates PLLC 275 7th Ave New York NY 10001 Office Phone: 646-660-9999.

COPPRIDGE, ALTON JAMES, urological surgeon; b. Roanoke, Va., Dec. 8, 1926; s. William Maurice Coppridge and Ferrie (Patterson) Choate; m. Helen Allen Burnett, June 24, 1950; children: William Allen, Virginia Choate BA, U. N.C., 1949; MD, U. Va., 1953. Diplomate Am. Bd. Urology. Intern N.C. Meml. Hosp., Chapel Hill, 1953—54; surg. resident State U. Iowa, Iowa City, 1954—56; urology resident U. Mich., Ann Arbor, 1956—59; mem. Coppridge Urol. Group, P.A., Durham, NC, 1959—89; ret., 1989. Chmn. dept. Durham County Gen. Hosp., 1978—84; asst. clin. prof. Duke Med. Ctr., Durham, 1970—89; clin. instr. U. N.C. Med. Sch., Chapel Hill, 1960—75. Contbr. articles to urologic lit Served with U.S. Army, 1944-46, Japan Mem.: ACS, NRA, Carolina Urol. Soc. (pres. 1985), N.C. Med. Soc. (pres. sect. urology 1978), Am. Urol. Assn. (exec. com. S.E. sect. 1983—86), Safari Internat. Club (Tucson) (pres. N.C. chpt. 1979—80), Durham Pistol and Rifle Club. Democrat. Presbyterian. Avocation: hunting. Home: A213 - 2600 Croasdaile Farm Pky Durham NC 27705 Office Phone: 919-384-2783. *

COQ, JACQUES-OLIVIER FRANÇOIS, neuroscientist; b. Montmorillon, France, July 19, 1969; PhD, U. Aix-Marseille 1, 1998. Prin. investigator CNRS-Inserm-Aix-Marseille U., France, 2002—. Grant, Internat. Cerebral Palsy Found. Avocation: scuba diving. Office: InsermU641 Neurobiologie Canaux Ioniques Marseille Paca 13344 France Business E-Mail: jacques-olivier.coq@univ-provence.fr.

CORAN, ARNOLD GERALD, pediatrician, surgeon; b. Boston, Apr. 16, 1938; s. Charles and Ann (Cohen) C.; m. Susan Myra Williams, Nov. 17, 1960; children: Michael, David, Randi Beth. AB, Harvard U., 1959, MD, 1963. Diplomate Am. Bd. Surgery, Am. Bd. Thoracic Surgery, Am. Bd. Pediat. Surgery. Intern in surgery Peter Bent Brigham Hosp., Boston, 1963-64, resident in general and thoracic surgery, 1964-69; resident in pediatric surgery Children's Hosp., Boston, 1966-68; chief pediat. surgery, assoc. prof. surgery U. So. Calif. Med. Sch., LA, 1972-74; chief pediat. surgery, prof. surgery U. Mich., Ann Arbor, 1974—2007; surgeon in chief C.S. Mott Childrens Hosp., Ann Arbor, 1981—2005. Contbr. articles to profl. jours. Lt. comdr. USN, 1970-72. Mem.: World Fedn. Pediat. Surgery (pres. 2005—07), Am. Pediat. Surg. Assn. (pres. 2001—02). Avocations: skiing, travel. Home: 505 E Huron St Apt 802 Ann Arbor MI 48104-1553 Office: CS Mott Childrens Hosp Rm F3970 Ann Arbor MI 48109-0245 Office Phone: 734-764-6482. Business E-Mail: acoran@umich.edu.

CORBIER, PHILIPPE, physiologist educator; b. Amiens, France, Mar. 2, 1947; m. Colette Fuzillier, Feb. 28, 1976; children: Christophe, Benoit. DSc, U. Paris XI, 1971. Rsch. scientist in devel.

endocrinology and lab endocrinology Ctr. Nat. Recherche Scientifique, Orsay, France, 1972-94; instr. physiology U. Paris XI. Rsch. scientist lab. neuroendocrinology UCLA, 1983. Contbr. articles to sci. jours. Mem. N.Y. Acad. Scis. Home: 18 rue Charles de Gaulle 91400 Orsay France Office: U Paris XI Fac Pharmacy rue Jean Baptiste Clement 92290 Chatenay-Malabry France

CORDANI, DAVID M., insurance company executive; BS, Tex. A&M U., College Station, 1988; MBA in Mktg., U. Hartford, Conn., 1994. Chartered fin. cons., CPA. With Coopers & Lybrand; contr. CIGNA Corp., v.p. corp. acctg. and planning, 2000—02; pres. SE Region CIGNA HealthCare, CFO field ops., sr. v.p. transformation and prog. mgmt., 2002, sr. v.p., CFO, 2002—04, pres. Health Segments, 2004—05, pres., 2005—08; pres., COO CIGNA Corp., 2008—09, pres., CEO, 2010—. Bd. dirs. NAM. Office: CIGNA HealthCare 900 Cottage Grove Rd Bloomfield CT 06002 Office Phone: 860-726-6000. *

CORDANI, STEFANO ERMENEGILDO, medical researcher; b. Parma, Italy, Jan. 31, 1959; s. Paolo Cordani and Anna Vicini; m. Simonetta La Fagola, Aug. 28, 1992; children: Paolo, Luca. MD, U. Parma, 1984. Pheumonology asst. S. Andrea Hosp., La Spezia, Italy, 1990—94; med. pneumology ofcl. S. Bartolomeo Hosp., Sarzana, 1994—. Cons. in field. Mem.: Italian Jour. Club Infectious Lung Diseases, European Soc. Clin. Microbiology & Infectious Diseases. Avocations: fishing, scuba diving, water-skiing, squash. Office: S Bartolomeo Hosp Via Cisa Vecchia 19038 Sarzana SP Italy Office Phone: 0039 0187604755.

CORDEIRO, PETER GABRIEL, plastic surgeon, medical educator; b. Bombay, Feb. 10, 1958; MD, Harvard Med. Sch., 1983. Cert. Am. Bd. Plastic Surgery, Am. Bd. Surgery. Intern gen. surgery New England Deacones, 1983—84, resident plastic surgery, 1984—89; resident micro surgery NYU Med. Ctr., 1989—91; fellow Meml. Sloan-Kettering Cancer Ctr., NYC, 1991, hosp. appt. plastic reconstructive surgery, 1992—, acting chief plastic & reconstructive, 2001, chief plastic & reconstructive svc. Dept. Surgery, 2001—; prof. surgery Cornell U., NYC. Assoc. prof. surgery Weill Med. Coll. Cornell U. Mem. editl. bd. Annals Surgical Oncology; contbr. articles to profl. jours., chapters to books. Mem.: ACS, Am. Assn. Plastic Surgeons, Soc. Surgical Oncology, Am. Soc. Breast Surgeons, Internat. Acad. Oral Oncology. Achievements include being a leader in the area of oncologic reconstructive surgery at a national and international level. Office: Meml Sloan-Kettering Cancer Ctr 1275 York Ave New York NY 10021 Office Phone: 212-639-2521, 800-525-2225. Office Fax: 212-717-3677.

CORDERO, JOSE FERNANDO, pediatrician, dean; b. Camuy, PR, July 25, 1948; s. Fernando and Ana T. Cordero; m. Milagros J. Garcia, June 18, 1970; children: Jose F., Ana M., Joann M., Maria M. BS in Biology, U. P.R., Rio Piedras, 1969; MD, U. P.R., San Juan, 1973; MPH, Harvard U., 1979. Diplomate Nat. Bd. Med. Examiners, Am. Bd. Med. Genetics, Am. Bd. Pediatrics; lic. physician, Ga. Intern Boston City Hosp., 1973-74, jr. asst. resident dept. pediatrics, 1974-75; clin. and rsch. fellow pediatrics Mass. Gen. Hosp., 1975-77; pediatrician South End Cmty. Health Ctr., Boston, 1977-79; epidemiology intelligence svc. officer Bur. Epidemiology Ctrs. for Disease Control & Prevention, Atlanta, 1979-81, dep. chief birth defects and genetic diseases br., 1985-88, acting chief birth defects and genetic diseases bd., 1988-89, asst. dir. sci. divsn. birth defects and devel. disabilities, 1989-94, dep. dir. nat. immunization program, 1994—2001, dir. Nat. Ctr. on Birth Defects and Devel. Disabilities, 2001—06; asst. surgeon gen. USPHS, 1998—2006; dean U. P.R. Grad. Sch. Pub. Health, San Juan, 2006—. Clin. instr. pediatrics Children's Hosp., Boston, 1978-79; clin. asst. prof. pediatrics Emory U., 1982—. Co-editor jour. Teratology, 1983-86; mem. editl. bd. Birth Defects Ency., 1988; reviewer jours.; contbr. numerous articles and abstracts to publs. Mem. working group cancer chemotherapy Internat. Agy. Cancer Rsch., 1980; mem. task force on child health and related issues FDA, 1980-83; mem. rev. coms. NIH; coord. U.S. Govt. Task Force Premature Thelarche in P.R., 1982-85; trustee Calif. Birth Defects Monitoring Program, 1983-89; mem. adv. bd. TERIS, Seattle, 1986—, Fla. Teratogen Info. System, 1986-90; cons. WHO, Guatemala, 1990, 91, 92, Copenhagen, 1991; founding mem. Emmaus Community, 1992—; mem. troop 547 com. Boy Scouts Am., 1983-94. Recipient Arthur S. Flemming award, 1988, Physician's Recognition award AMA, 1980, 84, 88. Mem. APHA, Am. Soc. Human Genetics, Am. Bd. Med. Genetics, Am. Acad. Pediatrics (nutrition com. 1980, com. on drugs 1988-93, genetic com. 1985), Am. Epidemiology Soc., Mass. Med. Soc., Genetics Soc. Ga., Coalition of Spanish Speaking Mental Health and Human Svcs. Orgn., Teratology Soc., Soc. Pediatric Rsch. Roman Catholic. Avocations: bird watching, flying, painting, travel. Office: U PR Grad Sch Pub Health PO Box 365067 San Juan PR 00936-5067 Business E-Mail: jcordero@rcm.upr.edu.

CORDES, ECKHARD, health products and retail executive; b. Neumünster, Germany, Nov. 25, 1950; Grad., Hamburg U., 1974. Mgmt. trainee Daimler-Benz, 1975, asst. plant mgr. Sindelfingen plant, 1977—81, sr. mgr. investment planning Sindelfingen plant, 1981—83, head product controlling new comml. vehicle projects, 1983—86; dir. acctg. and controlling Mercedes-Benz, Sao Paulo, 1986—89; dir. controlling AEG, Frankfurt, Germany, 1989—91, sr. v.p. controlling, corp. planning and M&A, 1991—94; sr. v.p. corp. planning and controlling Daimler-Benz AG, 1994—95, sr. v.p. corp. devel. (corp. strategy and M&A), 1995—96, mem. bd. mgmt., corp. devel. and directly managed businesses, 1997; mem. bd. mgmt. corp. devel. & IT mgmt. and MTU/Diesel Engines and TEMIC Daimler-Chrysler AG (Daimler-Benz merged with Chrysler in 1998), 1998—2000; mem. bd. mgmt. corp. devel. & IT mgmt. Daimler-Chrysler AG, 2000—04, mem. bd. mgmt. comml. vehicles div., 2000—05, head, Mercedes car group, 2004—05; chmn. bd. mgmt. Franz Haniel & Cie. GmbH, 2006—; CEO, chmn. bd. mgmt. Metro AG, Düsseldorf, Germany, 2007—. Office: Franz Haniel & Cie Franz Haniel Platz 1 Duisburg 47119 Germany

CORDES, EUGENE HAROLD, retired pharmacy and chemistry educator; b. York, Nebr., Apr. 7, 1936; s. Elmer Henry and Ruby Mae (Hofeldt) C.; m. Shirley Ann Morton, Nov. 9, 1957; children: Jennifer Eve, Matthew Henry James. BS, Calif. Inst. Tech., 1958; PhD, Brandeis U., 1962, DSc (hon.), 2009. Instr. chemistry Ind. U., Bloomington, 1962-64, asst. prof., 1964-66, assoc. prof., 1966-68, prof., 1968-79, chmn., 1972-78; exec. dir. biochemistry Merck, Sharp and Dohme Research Labs., Rahway, NJ, 1979-84, v.p. biochemistry, 1984-87; v.p. R & D Eastman Pharms., Malvern, Pa., 1987-88; pres. Sterling Winthrop Pharms. Rsch. divsn. Sterling Winthrop Inc., Collegeville, Pa., 1988-94; prof. U. Mich., Ann Arbor, 1995—2002; chmn. bd. dirs. Vitae Pharma (formerly Concurrent Pharms.), 2002—06. Author: (with Henry Mahler) Biological Chemistry, 1966, 2d. edit., 1971, Basic Biological Chemistry, 1969, (with Riley Schaeffer) Chemistry, 1973, The Tao of Chemistry & Life, 2009; also articles. Recipient NIH Career Devel. award, 1966; Alfred P. Sloan Found. fellow, 1968. Mem.: AAAS, Am. Soc. Biol. Chemists. Home: 3603 Saint Davids Rd Newtown Square PA 19073-1410 Personal E-mail: cordeseh@aol.com.

CORDOBA, OCTAVI, gynecologist, breast surgeon; b. Barcelona, May 15, 1972; MD, U. de Barcelona, 1998. Breast surgery specialist Hosp. Vall d'Hebron, 1994—. Assoc. prof. U. Rovira i Virgili, 2004—08; clin. prof. U. Autónoma de Barcelona, 2009. Master: Centre de càncer de mama Vall d'Hebron. Office: Avda Vall d'hebron 119-129 Barcelona 08035 Spain also: Clínica EUGIN C/ Entenza 293-295 Barcelona 08029 Spain Business E-Mail: ocordoba@vhebron.net.

CORDOVA, MARIA ASUNCION, dentist; b. Punta Arenas, Magallanes, Chile, May 14, 1941; came to U.S., 1972; d. Miguel Cordova and Maria Asuncion Requena; m. Carlos F. Salinas, July 27, 1963; children: Carlos M., Claudio A., Lola. DDS, U. Chile, Santiago, 1965; DMD, Med. U. S.C., 1986. From instr. to assoc. prof. physiology U. Chile, Valparaiso, 1965—72; postdoctoral fellow Johns Hopkins U., Balt., 1972-75; from instr. to asst. prof. dept. physiology Med. U. S.C., Charleston, 1975—86; pvt. practice Charleston, 1986—. Vis. scientist N.Y. Med. Coll., 1975. Contbr. articles to profl. jours. Pres. Circulo Hispanic Charleston; country specialist Amnesty Internat. U.S.A., Spoleto, Charleston, mem. outreach com.; past mem. Charleston C. of C. Hispanic Coun.; past bd. dir. Trident Urban League; bd. dir. YWCA, Robert Ivey Ballet, S.C. Humanities Coun., 1996—2002. Mem. Acad. Gen. Dentists, Governance Credentials & Elections Coun., Am. Dental Assn., Charleston Dental Assn., SC Dental Assn. (alt. del.), Charleston Women's Network (pres. 1989-90), Circulo Hispano americano de Charleston (pres.), YWCA Charleston (pres., bd. dirs. 2010-). Roman Catholic.

CORDOVA, RICHARD D., hospital administrator; b. Montebello, Calif. married; 3 children. BBA, Calif. State U., LA, 1972; MBA, Pepperdine U., 1984. With Dept. Health Svcs., County of LA, 1973—91, assoc. hosp. adminstr. of ops. Olive View Med. Ctr., 1978—86, adminstr. Gen. Hosp. LA County (LAC/USC Med. Ctr.), 1986—91; with Dept. of Pub. Health, City and County of San Francisco, 1991—98, CEO San Francisco Gen. Hosp., 1991—97, exec. adminstr. Cmty. Health Network, 1997—98; chief ops. officer Kaiser Permanente Health Plan, So. Calif., 1999—2002, pres. So. Calif. Region, 2002—04; pres., COO Childrens Hosp. LA, 2005—. Founding mem. San Francisco Pub. Health Authority, 1996—98; mem. Coun. on Grad. Med. Edn., 1996—98; bd. dirs. Inst. Diversity in Health Mgmt. Recipient Top 10 Latinos in Healthcare, LatinoLeaders mag., 2004; named one of Top 100 Hispanic Leaders, Hispanic Bus. Mag., 2003. Mem.: Am. Coll. of Health Care Execs. (diplomat 1980—). Office: Childrens Hosp LA 4650 Sunset Blvd Los Angeles CA 90027

COREY, ELIAS JAMES, chemistry professor; b. Methuen, Mass., July 12, 1928; s. Elias and Tina (Hashem) Corey; m. Claire Higham, Sept. 14, 1961; children: David, John, Susan. BS, MIT, 1948, PhD, 1951; AM (hon.), Harvard U., 1959; DSc (hon.), U. Chgo., 1968, Hofstra U., 1974, Colby Coll., 1976, Oxford U., 1982, U. Liege, 1985, U. Ill., 1985, Kenyon Coll., 1989, Helsinki Coll., 1990, Ariz. U., 1990, Merrimac Coll., 1990, Hokkaido U., 1991, Rennselaer Polytechnic Inst., 1991, Boston Coll., 1992, Tex. A&M U., 1997, Nat. Chung Cheng U., 1999, U. Alicante, 1999, Cambridge U., 2000. Asst. prof. U. Ill., Champaign-Urbana, 1951—55, prof., 1955—59; prof. chemistry Harvard U., Cambridge, Mass., 1959—68, Sheldon Emory prof. chemistry, 1968—, now emeritus prof. organic chemistry. Co-author: The Logic of Chemical Synthesis, 1995, Molecules and Medicine, 2008; edtl. bd. mem. Jour. Organic Chemistry, 1962—65; contbr. articles to profl. jours. Recipient Intrasci. Found. award, 1968, Ernest Guenther award in chemistry, 1968, Centenary Medal, Chem. Soc. London, 1971, Ciba Found. medal, 1972, Evans award, Ohio State U., 1972, Linus Pauling award, 1973, Dickson prize in sci., Carnegie Mellon U., 1973, George Ledlie prize in sci., Harvard U., 1973, Nichols medal, 1977, Buchman award, Calif. Inst. Tech., 1978, Franklin medal in sci., Franklin Inst., 1978, Sci. Achievement award, CCNY, 1979, J.G. Kirkwood award, Yale U., 1980, C.S. Hamilton award, U. Nebr., 1980, Chem. Pioneer award, Am. Inst. Chemists, 1981, Lewis S. Rosenstiel Award, Brandeis U., 1981, Medal of Excellence, U. Helsinki, 1982, Paul Karrer award, U. Zurich, 1982, Tetrahedron prize, 1983, Paracelsus award, Swiss Chem. Soc., 1984, V.D. Mattia award, Roche Inst. Molecular Biology, 1985, Wolf prize in chemistry, Wolf Found., 1986, Silliman award, 1986, Japan prize, 1989, Nat. Med. Sci., 1988, Nobel prize in chemistry, 1990, Janot Medal, U. Paris, 1990, Messel Medallist, Soc. for Chem. Industry, 1994, Gold medal, AIC, 2003; fellow, Swiss-Am. Exch., 1957, Guggenheim Found., 1957—58, 1968—69, Alfred P. Sloan Found., 1956—59. Fellow: AAAS; mem.: NAS (Award in chem. scis. 2002), Royal Soc. London (fgn.), Inst. Medicine, Robert A. Welch Found., Franklin Inst., Am. Acad. Arts & Scis., Soc. Synthetic Organic Chemistry (hon.), Pharm. Soc. Japan (hon.), Chem. Soc. Finland (hon.), Royal Soc. Chemistry (hon. Robert Robinson Medal 1988), Chem. Soc. Japan (hon.), Am. Chem. Soc. (hon. Pure Chemistry award 1960, Fritzche award 1968, Synthetic Chemistry award 1971, Harrison Howe award 1971, Remsen award 1974, Arthur C. Cope award 1976, Willard Gibbs award 1984, Madison Marshall award 1985, Roger Adams award 1993, Priestly medal 2004), Sigma Xi. Office: Harvard U Dept Chemistry 12 Oxford St Cambridge MA 02138-2902

COREY, LAWRENCE, medical educator; b. Detroit, Feb. 14, 1947; s. Aaron Corey; m. Amy Helaine Glasser, June 22, 1969; children: Leslie, Jordon, Daniel. AB with high distinction, U. Mich., 1967, MD, 1971. Diplomate Am. Bd. Internal Medicine. Intern U. Mich. Med. Ctr. Hosps., Ann Arbor, 1971-72, jr. asst. resident, 1972-73; epidemic intelligence svc. officer Ctr. for Disease Control, Atlanta, 1973-75; sr. fellow in medicine dept. internal medicine U. Wash., Seattle, 1975-77; attending physician internal medicine U. Washington Children's Hosp. and Med. Ctr., Seattle, 1977—; asst. prof. depts. lab. medicine, microbiology, immunology U. Wash., Seattle, 1977-81, head diagnostic virology divsn., dept. lab. medicine, 1978—, assoc. prof. depts. lab. medicine and microbiology, 1981-84, prof. depts. lab. medicine and microbiology, 1984—; mem. clin. rsch. divsn. Fred Hutchinson Cancer Rsch. Ctr., Seattle, 1996—, mem. pub. health sciences divsn., 2008—, head program in infectious diseases, 1996—2011, sr. v.p., 2007, co-dir. vaccine and infectious disease inst., 2007—11, pres., dir., 2011—. Co-dir. Vaccine and Infection Disease Inst., sr. v.p. Fred Hutchinson Rsch. Ctr., chair in med. virology, dept. laboratory med. U. Wash., prin. investigator HIV Vacccine Trials Network; cons. physician infectious diseases U. Wash. afiliated hosps., 1977—; chmn., co-chmn. course com. U. Wash., Seattle, 1986—; trustee-at-large U. Physicians, U. Wash., Seattle, 1992; acting dir. U. Wash. Ctr. for AIDS Rsch., 1989-90, head retrovirology core, 1989—; chmn. exec. com. clin. trials group NIAID AIDS, 1988-92; mem. program com. for 29th and 30th ICAAC, 1990-91; mem. subcom. IDSA/FDA guidlines for new anti-infective drugs, 1988-92; moderator panel on devel. of AIDS vaccines Inst. Medicine NAS, 1990, surrogate markers for licensing HIV compounds, 1989; mem. infectious diseases subspecialty com. Am. Coll. Physicians, 1988; mem. exec. com. Am. Venereal Disease Assn., 1988—; chmn. sci. adv. bd. Herpes Resource Ctr. Am. Social Health Assn., 1985—; mem. internat. bd. dirs. Internat. Soc. for Sexually Transmitted Disease Rsch., 1986-91; mem. bd. dirs. Am. Social Health Assn., 1986-90; cons. WHO, 1982. Author: (with others) Medical Microbiology: An Introduction to Infectious Diseases, 1984, Second Edition, 1990; editor: (with others) Medicine in a Changing Soc., Vol. I, 1972, Vol. II, 1977, Antiviral Chemotherapy: New Directions for Clinical Applications and Research, 1986, Second Edition, 1989, Third Edition, 1993, AIDS Dx/Rx, 1990; assoc. editor: Jour. Infectious Diseases, 1989—; editorial bd. numerous jours.; contbr. chpts. to books and articles to profl. jours. Recipient Spl. Svc. award Nat. Reyes Syndrome Found., 1983, Spl. Svc. award Nat. Insts. Allergy and Infectious Diseases, 1992, Pan Am. Soc. Clin. Virology award, Parran award, Am. Soc. for STD Rsch., U. Mich. Med. Sch. Disting. Alumnus award. Fellow Infectious Disease Soc. Am., Am. Coll. Physicians; mem. Inst. Medicine, Internat. Immunocompromised Host Soc., Assn. Am. Physicians, Am. Soc. Clin. Investigation, Western Assn. Physicians, Western Soc. Clin. Investigation, Am. Fedn. Clin. Rsch. (councilor Western sect. 1978-81, nat. councilor 1982-83, nat. sec.-treas. 1983-86), Am. Venereal Diseases Assn. (exec. com. 1989—, Achievement award 1984), Acad. Clin. Lab. Physicians and Scientists, Am. Epidemiological Soc., Washington State Pediatric Soc. Office: Fred Hutchinson Cancer Rsch Ctr 1100 Fairview Ave N Campus Box 358080 PO Box 19024 Seattle WA 98109 Office Phone: 206-667-6770. Office Fax: 206-667-4411. Business E-Mail: lcorey@u.washington.edu. *

CORICA, FRANCESCO, clinician, medical educator; b. Polistena, Jan. 19, 1953; Degree in Medicina e Chirurgia, U. Messina, 1978, degree in Endocrinology, 1985. Assoc. prof. U. Messina, 1994—, adj. prof., faculty medicine, 1994—, prof. geriatrics. Avocation: music. Home: Salita Villa Contino Compl Messina 2/8 Messina 98124 Italy Home Fax: 0390902212395. Personal E-mail: coricaf@unime.it.

CORKIN, SUZANNE HAMMOND, behavioral neuroscientist, educator; b. Hartford, Conn., May 18, 1937; d. Lester Hartz and Mabelle (Dowling) Hammond; m. Charles Corkin II, Sept. 8, 1962 (div. 1986); children: J. Zachary II, Jocelyn H., Damon L. BA, Smith Coll., 1959; MS, McGill U., 1961, PhD, 1964. Lic. psychologist, Mass. Rsch. assoc. dept. psychology MIT, Cambridge, 1964-77, rsch. assoc. Clin. Rsch. Ctr., 1964-79, lectr. dept. psychology, 1977-79, prin. rsch. scientist dept. psychology, 1979-81, sr. investigator Clin. Rsch. Ctr., 1979—, assoc. prof. dept. brain and cognitive scis., 1981-87, prof. behavioral neurosci., dept. brain and cognitive scis., 1987—. Cons. in Psychology (Neurosurgery) Mass. Gen. Hosp., Boston, 1975-82, clin. assoc., 1983—; Nat. Inst. Neurol. and Communicative Disorders and Stroke, spl. rev. com. 1978, spl. study rev. com., 1979; NIMH Psychopharmacological, Biological and Phys. Treatments Panel, 1981; Nat. Inst. Aging, contract rev. com., 1981, evaluation study of Alzheimer's Disease rsch. program, 1985-86, bd. scientific counselors, 1988—; U. Pitts. Alzheimer Rsch. project, 1983-88; Rochester Alzheimer's Disease Project, 1986—. Contbr. chpts. to numerous books; editor: (with others) Alzheimer's Disease: A Report of Progress in Research, 1982, Memory Dysfunctions: An Integration of Animal and Human Research From Preclinical and Clinical Perspectives, 1985, Topics in the Basic and Clinical Science of Dementia, 1987, Handbook of Neuropsychology, 1989; contbr. numerous articles to profl. jours.; editorial bd.: The Clinical Journal of Pain, Developmental Neuropsychology, Neurobiology Aging, and Neuropsycholigia. Recipient merit award NIH, 1986, 92. Fellow APA (div. physiol. and comparative psychology); mem. AAAS, Internat. Neuropsychol. Symposium (N.Am. rep.), Internat. Study Group on Pharmacology of Memory Disorders Associated with Aging, Am. Acad. Neurology, Am. Aging Assn., Gerontological Soc. Am., Soc. for Neuroscience, Eastern Psychol. Assn., Boston Soc. Psychiatry and Neurology, Sigma Xi. Office: MIT Dept Brain & Cognitive Scis Building 46-5121 77 Massachusetts Avenue Cambridge MA 02139-4307 Business E-Mail: corkin@mit.edu.

CORLESS, DOROTHY ALICE, nursing educator; b. Reno, Nev., May 28, 1943; d. John Ludwig and Vera Leach (Wilson) Adams; children: James Lawrence Jr., Dorothy Adele Carroll. RN, St. Luke's Sch. Nursing, 1964. Clinician, cons., educator, grant author, adminstr. Fresno County Mental Health Dept., 1970—94; instr. police sci. State Ctr. Tng. Facility, 1970—94; pvt. practice, mental health cons., educator, 1970—; sr. assoc. guidance distbn. disaster svcs. ARC, 2003—04; mental health nurse, sr. supr. Calif. Dept. Corrections and Rehabilitation, 2006—11. Presenter Internat. Congress of Pain, Glassgow, Scotland, 2008, World Inst. Pain, NYC, 2009. Rcs. officer ARC, Disaster Mental Health Svcs., 1993-2003. Maj. USAFR, 1972-94. Mem. USAF Acad. Assn. Grads. (assoc. life), Forensic Mental Health Assn. Calif., Calif. Peace Officers Assn., Critical Incident Stress Found. Home: 1580 Kallakalla Ct Florence OR 97439 Office Phone: 541-991-7584. E-mail: dorothydmh@aol.com.

CORLEY, DONNA JEAN, nursing administrator; b. Berwyn, Ill., June 7, 1957; Diploma in Nursing, Beth-el Sch. Nursing, 1978; M in Nursing, U. N.Mex, 2009. Staff nurse Routt Meml. Hosp., 1978—88; staff rn Rehoboth Mckinley Christian Healthcare Svcs., 1989—91, dir. emergency svcs., icu, 1991—2004, dir., emergency dept., 1991—. Adj. faculty U. N.Mex. Gallup Nursing Program, 2008—. Mem.: Emergency Nurses Assn. Avocation: gardening. Office: 603 Nizhoni Blvd Gallup NM 87301 Office Fax: 505-863-8920. Business E-Mail: dcorley@rmchcs.org.

CORMACK, RONALD S., retired anesthesiologist; b. Rangoon, Burma, Nov. 11, 1930; s. Harry Slater and Dorothy McRae Cormack; m. April Horton Fox, Jan. 31, 1959; children: Nicholas Bruce, Simon Harry. BA, Oxford U., Eng., BSc, 1953; BM BCh, Oxford U. Med. Sch., 1961. Demonstrator, physiology Oxford U., 1952—53; house surgeon Radcliffe Infirmary, Oxford, 1961—62; lectr., anaesthetics Bristol Royal Infirmary, England, 1968—71; cons. anaesthetist Northwick Pk. Hosp. & Clin. Rsch. Ctr., London, 1972—90, head, obstetric anaesthesia, 1974—84, head, anaesthesia, 1984—88. Contbr. scientific papers. Fellow: Royal Coll. Anaesthetists; mem.: Royal Soc. Medicine. Mem. Ch. Eng. Achievements include work on probability theory; formulating the Cormack/Lehane laryngoscopy grades.

CORMAN, MARVIN LEONARD, surgeon, educator; b. Phila., Dec. 17, 1939; s. Joseph Mayer and Dorothy Frances (Stern) C.; children: John Mayer, Alexander Stern. BA, U. Pa., 1961, MD, 1965. Diplomate Nat. Bd. Med. Examiners, Am. Bd. Surgery, Am. Bd. Colon and Rectal Surgery; lic. surgeon, Calif., N.Y. Sr. registrar, vis. lectr. gen. infirmary, profl. surg. unit U. Leeds, Eng., 1968-69; surg. intern Boston City Hosp.-Fifth (Harvard) Surg. Svc., 1965, surg. resident, 1966-68, surg. resident, chief surg. resident, 1969-71; staff surgeon divsn. colon and rectal surgery, dept. surgery Lahey Clinic Med. Ctr., Boston, 1971-81, Sansum Med. Clinic, Santa Barbara, Calif., 1981-95; surgeon divsn. colon and rectal surgery UCLA, 1996-98; prof. surgery U. So. Calif. Sch. Medicine, 1998—2001; vice chmn. dept. surgery, assoc. surgeon-in-chief L.I. Jewish Med. Ctr., New Hyde Park, NY, 2001—04; prof. surgery Albert Einstein Coll. Medicine, 2001—05, SUNY, Stony Brook, 2004—. Instr. surgery Sch. Medicine Harvard U., Boston, 1972-77, clin. asst. prof. surgery, 1977-82, prof. surgery UCLA, 1996-98; co-dir. tng. program colon and rectal surgery Sansum Med. clinic, 1981-95, chmn. divsn. edn., 1983-90; credentials com. Santa Barbara Cottage Hosp., 1984-95, mem. libr. com., 1985-95, mem. com. on grad. med. edn., 1989-94, vice-chmn. dept. surgery, 1994-95; pres. alumni assn. Harvard Surg. Svc., Boston City Hosp., 1983-84; vis. prof. U. Tex. Health Sci. Ctr., San Antonio, 1982, Throckmorton Surg. Soc., Des Moines, 1985, Ogden (Utah) Surg. Soc., 1985, 20th ann. Surg. Congress Orange County Surg. Soc., Newport Beach, Calif., 1988, Royal Australasian Coll. Surgeons, Adelaide, Australia, 1989, Northwest Permanente Dept. Surgery, Portland, Oreg., 1990, Hahnemann U., Phila., 1991, El Colegio de Cirujanos Generales de Mexicali, Mexico, 1991, Cleve. Clinic Fla., Ft. Lauderdale, Fla., 1992, Univ. Hosp. de Clinicas do Parana, Curitiba, Brazil, 1993; Ralph Coffey vis. prof. Sch. Medicine, U. Mo., Kansas City, 1988; Ralph B. Samson Meml. lectr. Grant Med. Ctr., Columbus, Ohio, 1991; Louis A. Buie vis. lectr. Mayo Med. Sch., Rochester, Minn., 1992; ann. vis. surgeon Queen Elizabeth Hosp. Ctr. of Montreal, Que., 1993; vis. prof. U. So. Calif. Sch. Medicine, L.A., 1995, U. Zurich., 2004, others; Neil Swinton vis. prof. Lahey Clinic, Burlington, Mass., 1997; del. leader Citizen Amb. Program Colon and Rectal Surgery Del. to Russia, Hungary and Czechoslovakia, 1992. Author: (textbook) Colon and Rectal Surgery, 1984, 89, 93, 99, 2005; assoc. editor: Diseases of the Colon and Rectum, 1977-92, Lahey Clinic Bull., 1972-81; contbr. numerous articles to profl. jours. Recipient Hoffman-LaRoche award, 1965, Piedmont Proctologic Soc. award, 1973, 1st prize of Med. Book award, 1985, John C. Goligher Meml. medal Assn. Coloproctology of Gt. Britain and Ireland, 1999, 25th Ann. award Crohn's and Colitis Found. Am., 2000. Fellow ACP, mem. ACS (So. Calif. chpt.), AMA (chmn. residency rev. com. for colon and rectal surgery 1985-86), Internat. Soc. Univ. Colon and Rectal Surgeons, Am. Soc. Colon and Rectal Surgeons (v.p. 1995 96), Am. Surg. Assn., Am. Med. Writers Assn. (hon.), Am. Coll. Gastroenterology, Assn. for Program Dirs. in Colon and Rectal Surgery, We. Surg. Assn., Pan Am. Med. Assn. (coun. sect. on colon and rectal surgery 1989—), Royal Australasian Coll. Surgeons (hon., sect. colon and rectal surgery 1989), New Eng. Surg. Soc., New Eng. Soc. Colon and Rectal Surgeons (sec.-treas. 1977-81), Boston Surg. Soc., Northeastern Soc. Colon and Rectal Surgeons, Soc. Surgery Alimentary Tract, N.Y. Surg. Soc., N.Y. Soc. Colon and Rectal Surgeons,Piedmont Proctologic Soc. (hon.), Argentine Soc. Coloproctology (hon.). Office: Dept Surgery SUNY Stony Brook HSC T 18-060 Stony Brook NY 11794-8191 Office Phone: 631-444-3431. Business E-Mail: marvin.corman@stonybrook.edu.

CORN, MORTON, environmental engineer, educator; b. NYC, Oct. 18, 1933; s. Julius and Sophie (Haber) C.; m. Jacqueline Karnell, Aug. 21, 1955; children: Matthew Irwin, Frederick Eliot. BS in Chem. Engring., Cooper Union, 1955; MS, Harvard U., 1956, PhD, 1961. Asst. san. engr. USPHS, Cin., 1956-58; rsch. assoc. Harvard, 1960-61; asst. prof. U. Pitts., 1962-65, assoc. prof., 1965-66, prof. Grad. Sch. Pub. Health and Sch. Engring., 1967-79; prof. and divsn. head environ. health engring. Sch. Hygiene and Public Health, Johns Hopkins U., Balt., 1980-97; prof. emeritus Johns Hopkins U., Balt., 1997—; pres. Morton Corn; Assocs., Cons. Engrs., 1977—. Cons. divsn. biology and medicine AEC, 1965—74; chmn. air pollution rsch. grants com. EPA, 1968—71, mem. sci. adv. bd., 1978—84; mem. com. no biol. effects air pollution NAS, 1971, mem. com. risk assessment, 1982—83; mem. expert panel occupl. health WHO, 1973—98; asst. sec. labor for occupl. safety and health U.S. Dept. Labor, 1975—77; mem. Allegheny County Air Pollution Adv. Com., 1967—72; mem. nat. adv. com. health vital stats. Dept. HHS, 1979—81; mine health rsch. adv. com. Nat. Inst. Occupl. Safety and Health, 1986—89, GM/UAW joint health and safety adv. com., 1988—92; chmn. OTA Commn. Preventing Injury and Illness in the Workplace, 1982—84; chmn. tech. adv. bd. Clean Sites, Inc., Alexandria, Va., 1984—87; trustee Assoc. Univ., Inc., 1991—93; mem. Hanford tank adv. panel DOE, 1993—99; cons. Health, Safety and Environment, 1993. Chmn. Gov. of Md.'s Toxic Coun., 1986-89. NSF postdoctoral fellow U. London, 1961-62; WHO fellow, 1970; Guggenheim fellow, 1972 Fellow APHA, Argentine Acad. Engring.; mem. Argentine Acad. Scis., Am. Soc. Safety Engrs., Am. Indsl. Hygiene Assn. (bd. dirs. 2000-03), Am. Conf. Govt. Indsl. Hygienists (chmn. 1983-84). Home and Office: 1300 L'Ambiance Cir #202 Naples FL 34108 Office Phone: 410-827-3205. Personal E-mail: mjcorn.com@gmail.com.

CORNBLATH, WAYNE TODD, medical educator; b. Mo., Apr. 21, 1959; BA, UMKC, 1981, MD, 1983. Prof. ophthalmology & visual scis. and neurology U. Mich., 1989. Fellow: N.Am. Neuroophthalmolgy Soc., Am. Acad. Neurology; mem.: Am. Neurologic Assn. Office: 1000 Wall St Ann Arbor MI 48105 Office Fax: 734-936-2340. Business E-Mail: wtc@med.umich.edu.

CORNEHL, JARROD, dentist; DDS, U. Tex. Dental Health Ctr., 2002. Pvt. practice dentist, Austin, Tex., San Francisco. Part-time faculty instr. dental anatomy and local anesthesia U. Pacific Sch. Dentistry. Mem.: Am. Acad. Cosmetic Dentistry, San Francisco Dental Soc., Acad. Gen. Dentistry, Calif. Dental Assn., Am. Dental Assn. Office: 260 Stockton St, Second Fl San Francisco CA 94108 Office Phone: 415-397-1030. Office Fax: 415-397-1032.

CORNEJO, RODRIGO, medical educator; b. Santiago, Chile, Mar. 25, 1973; MD in Internal Medicine, U. Chile, 1998; degree in Intensive Care Medicine, U. Catolica, 2005. Chief Intensive Care Unit Hosp. Clinico U. Chile, 1997—2010, assoc. prof., med. dir., 2010—. Mem.: Soc. Chilena de Medicina Intensiva. Avocation: tennis. Office: Santos Dumont 999 Independencia Santiago CD6531063 Chile Business E-Mail: rcornejo@redclinicauchile.cl.

CORNELIUS, JAMES MILTON, pharmaceutical company executive; b. Kalamazoo, Oct. 28, 1943; s. Charles D. and Eleanor F. (Short) Cornelius; m. Kathleen McGovern; children: Andrew, Lindsay. BA magna cum laude in Acctg., Mich. State U., 1965, MBA in Fin., 1967; D (hon.), Marian Coll., 1996, U. Indpls., 1998, Mich. State U., 2001. Assoc. acct. Eli Lilly & Co., Indpls., 1967, fin. planning analyst, 1969—73, adminstr. corp. fin., 1973—75, mgr. econ. studies, 1975—78, initial dir. acquisitions, med. device and diagnostics divsn., 1978, dir. health care bus. planning, 1978—80, pres. IVAC Corp. subs. San Diego, 1980—82, corp. treas., 1982—83, v.p. fin., CFO, 1983—95; chmn. Guidant, 1994—2000, sr. exec., 1995—2000, non-exec. chmn., 2000—06, interim CEO, 2005—06, chmn. emeritus, 2006—; interim CEO Bristol-Myers Squibb Co., 2006—07, CEO, 2007—08, chmn., CEO, 2008—10, chmn., 2010—, mem. exec. com., 2009—. Ind. dir. Given Imaging Ltd.; bd. dirs., chair bd. audit com. DirectTV Group, Inc.; bd. dirs. Chubb Corp., 1998—2006, Bristol-Myers Squibb Co., 2005—, Hughes Electronic Corp., Am. United Mut. Ins. Holding Co., DowElanco, Ind. Nat. Bank, Ind. Bell Tel. Co., Compuserve, Nat. Bank Indpls. Corp., Leerink Swann & Co.; founder, mng. ptnr. Twilight Venture Ptnrs. Contbg. author: The CFO's Handbook, 1986. Treas. Noyes Found., Indpls., 1983; mem. adv. bd. bus. corp. Mich. State U., 1983; treas. bd. govs. Indpls. Mus. Art; trustee U. Indpls. Zool. Soc.; pres. Cornelius Family Charitable Found.; bd. dirs. Mcpl. Recreation, Inc., 1982, Cmty. Hosp. Found., 1991, Walker Rsch., 1991, United Way Ctrl. Ind. Served to 1st lt. Fin. Corps US Army, 1967—69. Recipient Man of Achievement award, Anti-Defamation League, 2003, Hoosier Heritage Lifetime Achievement award, 2005. Mem.: Pharm. Mfg. Assn. (past chmn. fin. sect.), Fin. Execs. Inst. Republican. Roman Catholic. Avocations: tennis, reading, jogging. Office: Bristol-Myers Squibb Co 345 Park Ave New York NY 10154 *

CORNELIUS, LYNN A., dermatologist, educator; BS, U. Del., Newark, 1977; MD, U. Mo., 1984. Diplomate Am. Bd. Dermatology, 1989. Resident dermatology Barnes-Jewish hosp. Washington Univ. Sch. of Medicine, St. Louis, 1989, asst. prof. dermatology, 1993, assoc. dean faculty affairs, 1998, chief dermatology divsn., 2000—, assoc. prof., 2001, bd. dir. faculty plans, 2002; fellow immunological dermatology Emory Univ. Med. Ctr., Atlanta, 1992; hosp. affiliation include Barnes-Jewish Hosp. Reviewer (jour.) American Academy of Dermatology, Investigative Dermatology, American Journal of Pathology, Microvascular Research, Journal of Orthopedic Research; co author: (books) Melanoma and non-melanoma skin cancer, Cancer of the Skin and Melanoma, In: Immune Mechanisms in Cutaneous Disease, 2000, and numerous others. Recipient Dermatology Found. Career Devel. award, 1994—95, K-08 NIAMS Clin. Investigator award, 1995—2000, Dermatology Found. Rsch. Grant, 1995—96, Barnes-Jewish Hosp. Found. Rsch. Grant, 1996, Monsanto-Searle/Washington Univ. Biomedical Grant, 1998—2001, Barnes-Jewish Hosp. Found. Rsch. Grant, 1998—99; named one of Woodward-White Best Doctors in America, 1996—99, Best Doctors in America, Best Doctors, Inc, 2002—10, America's Top Doctors, Castle Connolly Medical Ltd, 2002—10. Office: General Dermatology Ste 220 969 Mason Rd Saint Louis MO 63141 Mailing: Center for Advanced Medicine Multispecialty Center Melanoma Center 4921 Parkview Place B 5 Saint Louis MO 63110 Office Phone: 314-996-8010, 314-362-2643. Office Fax: 914-275-8892, 314-454-5626.

CORNELL, LOIS DEHLS, insurance company executive; BA, Macalester Coll.; JD, Northeastern U.; completed the Advanced Mgmt. Program, Harvard Bus. Sch. Assoc. Goodwin Procter, Boston; joined Tufts Health Plan, 1991, various positions including asst. v.p., dep. gen. counsel, corp. compliance officer and asst. gen. counsel, sr. v.p. human resources, gen. counsel. Frequent spkr. in field. Author on nonprofit governance and compliance issues. Chairs governance com. U. Mass. Meml. Med. Ctr.; mem. Mass. Taxpayers Found. Mem.: ABA, Mass. Assn. of Health Plans (bd. dirs.), American Health Lawyers Assn., Boston Bar Assn. (mem. law sect. steering com., co-chair health law sect. legis. com.), America's Health Ins. Plans. Office: Tufts Health Plan 705 Mt Auburn St Watertown MA 02472

CORNELL, TIMO, pediatrician, educator; b. Effingham, Ill., Dec. 21, 1966; MD, Southern Ill. U., 1995. Asst. prof. U. Mich., 2007—. Dir., translational rsch. Divsn. Pediatric Critical Care Medicine, 2011. Recipient Med. Humanities award, Southern Ill. U., Immunology Specialty award, Soc. Critical Care Medicine, Career Devel. award, NIH. Mem.: Soc. Critical Care Medicine, Am. Acad. Pediat. Avocation: cooking. Office: Mott Hosp 1500 East Med Ctr Dr F68 Ann Arbor MI 48109 Business E-Mail: ttcornel@med.umich.edu.

CORNWELL, GIBBONS GRAY, III, retired internist, educator; b. West Chester, Pa., Jan. 17, 1933; s. Gibbons Gray and Eva Chambers (Parke) C.; m. Mary Helen Fortmiller, Sept. 13, 1958; children: Gibbons Gray IV, Heidi Cornwell Trout, Holly Fortmiller. BS, Yale U., 1954; MD, U. Pa., 1963; MA (hon.), Dartmouth Coll., 1993. Diplomate Am. Bd. Internal Medicine, Am. Bd. Hematology. Resident in medicine Hosp. U. Pa., Phila., 1963-64, 65-66; research fellow Cambridge U., England, 1964-65; hematology fellow Hosp. U. Pa., Phila., 1966-68; biochemistry fellow Dartmouth Med. Sch., Hanover, NH, 1968-70, asst. prof. medicine, 1971-74, assoc. prof., 1974-80, prof., 1980-95, prof. pathology, 1990-95, prof. emeritus medicine and pathology, 1995—, assoc. dean student and acad. affairs, 1973-76, chmn. sect. hematology-oncology, 1977-84. Vis. prof. Inst. Immunology, Oslo, 1976-77; dir. clin. rsch. Norris Cotton Cancer Ctr., Hanover, 1978-91; bd. dirs. Cancer and Leukemia Group B, Boston, 1978-91; trustee, chmn. Hitchcock Found., Hanover, 1978-90; staff bd. govs. Mary Hitchcock Meml. Hosp., Hanover, 1981-88; vis. scientist Inst. Pathology/Swedish Med. Rsch. Coun., Uppsala, Sweden, 1987. Contbr. articles to profl. jours. Bd. dirs. Upper Valley Hospice, Lebanon, NH, 1980; mem. sch. bd. Town of Lyme, NH, 1973-76, health officer, 1970-74, mem. conservation com., 1970-74, budget com., 1996-2008, rep. com., 2000-, chmn., 2002-; trustee Lyme Found., 1998-2009, chmn., 2000-09. Lt., jet fighter pilot USAF, 1955-59. Clin. rsch. grantee NIH, 1978-91. Fellow ACP; mem. Am. Fedn. Clin. Rsch. (emeritus), Am. Soc. Hematology, N.H. Med. Soc. Republican. Episcopalian. Avocations: bicycling, stamp collecting/philately, scuba diving. Home: 1 Orfordville Rd Lyme NH 03768-3305

COROMILAS, JAMES, cardiologist; b. Bklyn., May 5, 1948; MD, McGill U., 1975. Cert. Internal Medicine, 1979, Cardiovascular Disease, 1981, in clin. cardiac electrophysiology 1992, 2002. Intern North Shore U. Hosp., Manhasset, NY, 1975—76, resident in internal medicine, 1976—78, chief resident, 1978—79, fellow in cardiology, 1979—80; fellow Columbia-Presbyn. Med. Ctr., NYC, 1980—82; asst. attending physician Presbyn. Hosp., NYC, 1983—90, assoc. attending physician, 1990; dir. cardiology fellow training prog. Columbia Presbyn. Med. Ctr., NYC, 1991—2008, dir. clin. electrophysiology lab., 1994—98; asst. prof. Columbia U. Coll. Physicians and Surgeons, NYC, 1983—90, assoc. prof. clin. medicine, 1990—2008; prof. med. chief Divsn. Cardiovascular Diseasea & Hypertension Robert Wood Johnson Med. Sch.; chief Cardiology Robert Wood Johnson U. Hosp., 2009—. Office: UMDNJ-RWJ Med Sch MEB 582B One Robert Wood Johnson Pl New Brunswick NJ 08901 Office Phone: 732-235-7856. Office Fax: 732-235-8722.

CORR, WILLIAM V. (BILL CORR), federal agency administrator, lobbyist; b. 1948; BA in Economics, U. Va., 1970; JD, Vanderbilt U. Law Sch., Nashville, 1973. Dir. non-profit health centers, Tenn., Ky., 1974—77; counsel subcom. health & environment US House Com. Energy & Commerce, Washington, 1977—89; chief counsel, staff dir. subcom. antitrust, monopolies & bus. rights US Senate Judiciary Com., 1989—93; dep. asst. sec. for health US Dept. Health & Human Services, 1993—96, chief of staff to sec., 1996—98, dep. sec. HHS, 2009—; chief counsel, policy dir. to Senator Tom Daschle US Senate, 1998—2000; exec. v.p, then exec. dir. Campaign for Tobacco-Free Kids, 2000—09. Bd. dirs. Ctr. Sci. in Pub. Interest, Washington; mem. Obama-Biden Transition Team, 2008. Office: US Dept Health & Human Services 200 Independence Ave SW Rm 614-G Washington DC 20201 Office Phone: 202-690-6133. *

CORREA, ADOLFO, epidemiologist, educator; s. Adolfo Correa and Estela Villaseñor; m. Ana I. Alfaro-Correa, June 2, 1978. BS, San Diego State U., 1969; MS, U. Calif., La Jolla, 1970, MD, 1974; MPH, Johns Hopkins U., Balt., 1981, PhD, 1987; MBA, U. Ga., Atlanta, 2010. Diplomate Am. Bd. Pediat., 1981, Am. Bd. Preventive Medicine, 1983. Assoc. prof. Johns Hopkins U., Balt., 1987—98; med. epidemiologist CDC, Atlanta, 1998—. Adj. assoc. prof. Johns Hopkins U., Balt., 1998—2008; adj. prof. Emory U., Atlanta, 2004—. Recipient Sec.'s award for Disting. Svc., Dept. HHS, 2000, 2004. Mem.: Am. Heart Assn., Am. Diabetes Assn., Teratology Soc., Soc. Epidemiologic Rsch., Soc. Pediatric and Epidemiologic Rsch., Delta Omega. Achievements include research in Reye's syndrome and medication use; on risk factors of major cardiovascular malformations; diabetes and birth defects. Avocations: philosophy, classical guitar. Office: CDC 1600 Clifton Rd MS E-86 Atlanta GA 30329 Office Fax: 404-498-3040. Personal E-mail: acorrea8404@gmail.com. Business E-Mail: acorrea@cdc.gov.

CORREA, AMPARO MARIA, dermatologist; b. Panaba, Yucatan, Mexico, Oct. 18, 1954; d. Enrique Correa and Ernestina Aranda; m. Raul Capiz, Apr. 6, 1977; children: Benjamin Capiz, Daniel Raul Capiz. Med. Dermatologist, U. Nacional Autonoma Mexico, Mexico City, 1979; Internal Medicine, Hosp. Especialidades Centro Medico La Raza, Mexico City, 1980—82; Dermatologist, Centro Dermatologico Dr. Ladislao de la Pascua, Mexico City, 1982—84. Diplomate Consejo Mexicano de Dermatologia, 1998. Tchr. pharmacology Escuela de Enfermeria, Parral, Chihuahua, Mexico, 1978—79. Fellow: Sociedad Mexicana Dermatologia (corr.), Am. Acad. Dermatology (assoc.); mem.: Sociedad Mexicana de Cirugia Dermatologica y Oncologica (corr.). Roman Catholic. Office: Centro de especialidades medicas Av Kino 12 y 13 83400 San Luis Rio Colorado Mexico Home: Av Juarez # 2771 83400 San Luis Rio Colorado SON Mexico Home Fax: 6535340466. Personal E-mail: corrderm18_@hotmail.com.

CORREA-DE-ARAUJO, ROSALY LIA, medical researcher, educator; arrived in U.S., 1990; d. Creighton Correa-de-Araujo and Maria Rosa Lia de Araujo. MD, Fed. U. Bahia, Salvador, Bahia, Brazil, 1980; MS in Human Pathology, U. São Paulo, Ribeirão Preto, São Paulo, Brazil, 1986, PhD in Morphology & Cell Biology, 1988. Assoc. prof. and chmn. dept. anatomic pathology and forensic medicine, chief univ. hosp. autopsy sect. Sch. Medicine Triangulo Mineiro, Uberaba, Minas Gerais, Brazil, 1986—93; vis. assoc. Nat. Heart, Blood and Lung Inst., Bethesda, Md., 1990—92; fellow cardiovasc. pathology Armed Forces Inst. Pathology, Washington, 1992—94; program dir. for geriat. and med. info. specialist US Pharmacopeia, Rockville, Md., 1994—2000; program dir. geriat. and internat. health Am. Soc. Cons. Pharmacists, Alexandria, Va., 2000—02; dir. women's health and gender-based rsch. Agy. Healthcare Rsch. and Quality, U.S. Dept. HHS, Rockville, 2002—06; dir., Office of The Americas Region, Global Health Office of Sec., US Dept. Health and Human Svcs., Washington, 2006—08; sec. to del. US-Mex. Border Health Comm., 2007—09; dep. dir., office disability Office of Sec., US Dept. Health and Human Svcs., 2009—. Mem. and chair bd. pharm. sciences' pub. policy com. Internat. Pharm. Fedn., Hague, Netherlands, 2000—04; adj. assoc. prof. anatomy Sch. Medicine, George Washington U., Washington, 1993—; clin. asst. prof. experiential learning program Sch. Pharmacy, U. Md., Balt., 2002—07. Contbr. chapters to books, articles to profl. jours.; mem. editl. bd.: Jour. Women's Health, 2005—. Recipient Carlos Chagas award, Nat. Acad. Medicine, Brazil, 1986, Bd. Trustees Performance award, US Pharmacopeia, 1995—2000, Dirs. Citation for Outstanding Performance, Agy. for Healthcare Rsch. and Quality, 2003, 2004, 2005, Commissioner's Spl. Citation, FDA, 2004, Dirs. Merit award, Agy. for Healthcare Rsch. and Quality, 2004, Dir.'s award for excellence, Agy. Healthcare Rsch. and Quality, 2006, Letter of Recognition, USN, 2007, Cert. Spl. Appreciation, Ministry of Health Panama, 2009. Mem.: Acad. Health (mem. and chair gender health interest group 2002—), Am. Med. Dirs. Assn. (mem. and chair medication mgmt. in long-term care com. 2000—), Am. Geriatrics Soc. Democrat-Npl.

Roman Catholic. Achievements include expanding the Women's Health Program at the Agy. for Healthcare Rsch. and Quality to encompass gender-based rsch. and analysis; research in gender differences in drug use and expenditures in a privately insured population of order adults; gender differences across racial and ethnic groups in the quality of care for acute myocardial infarction and heart failure associated with comorbidities; gender differences across racial and ethnic groups in the quality of care for diabetes. Avocations: reading, jewelry making, travel, classical music, jogging, art. Office Fax: 301-260-3053. Business E-Mail: rosaly.correa@hhs.gov.

CORREALE, ERNESTO, cardiologist, consultant; b. NYC, Sept. 7, 1926; arrived in Italy, 1937; s. Antonio and Teresa (Rossano) C.; m. Srinart Suriya, Nov. 11, 1967 Medicine, U. Naples, 1953, Specialist Cardiology, 1960, Professorship in Semeiology, 1968. Rotating intern N.Y. Polyclinic Med. Sch. and Hosp., NYC, 1954—55; asst. resident, resident medicine Goldwater Meml. Hosp. NYU, 1955—57; asst. internal medicine U. Naples, 1957—69; chief cardiology dept. internal medicine Hosp. Caserta, Italy, 1969—93, primario emeritus cardiology dept. internal medicine, 1993—. Mem. monitoring com. Gissi-Prevention Trial, 1993—; lectr. phys. and instrument semeiology Sch. Cardiology U. Naples, 1968-86; chair safety and monitoring bd. European Collaboration on Low Dose Aspirin in Polycytemia Vera; mem. DSM Bd. GISSI-AF Trial, 2005. Contbr. numerous articles to profl. jours. Mem. monitoring and ethical bd. Hosp. Caserta. Decorated commendatore al Merito della Republica Italy, grande ufficiale al Merito della Republica; recipient Castello d'Argento Apudmontem, 1999, Nat. Targa D'Oro award, 2002, Regional Targa award, Found. of Dept. of Cardiology, Hosp. of Caserta, 2003; fellow Paul Harris, Rotary. Fellow Am. Coll. Cardiology; mem. Assn. Nat. Medici Cardiologi Ospedalieri Cardiologist (investigator Mario Negri rsch. group 1984—, regional del. 1983-84, nat. directory 1984-86, sec. gen. 1986-88, elected bd. mem. honest man, 2006-). Roman Catholic. Avocations: reading, gardening. Office: Palazzo Anto Via G M Bosco 81100 Caserta Italy Home: Via Giotto 13 81100 Caserta CE Italy Office Phone: 0823-329684.

CORREIA, LUÍS GARDETE, endocrinologist; b. Lisbon, Aug. 12, 1944; Degree, U. Lisbon, 1969. Cert. specialist in endocrinology Curry Cabral Hosp., 1983. Endocrinology cons. Portuguese Diabetes Assn., 1979—, clin. dir., 1996—2002, pres., 2008—; dir. endocrinology dept. Curry Cabral Hosp., 2003—07. Endocrinology cons. Madeira's Regional Health Svcs., 1988—2000. Mem.: Diabetes Education Study Group, Am. Diabetes Assn., European Assn. Study Diabetes (coun. bd. mem. 2006—09), Portugese Soc. Diabetology, Portuguese Soc. Endocrinology, Diabetes and Metabolism (v.p. bd. 2000—03), Ernesto Roma Found. Avocations: sailing, bicycling. Home: Campo Pequeno 37-3° Dt Lisbon 1000-080 Portugal Office: Portuguese Diabetes Assn R Sali Lisbon 1250-203 Portugal Home Phone: 966025921. Office Fax: 351 213 859 371. Personal E-mail: gardete@apdp.pt. Business E-Mail: diabetes@easd2011-lisbon.org.

CORRIERE, JOSEPH N., JR., urologist, educator; b. Apr. 3, 1937; m. Evelyn Pavia Mossey, June 25, 1960 (div. July 1984); children: Joseph N., Christopher John, Gregory James, Evelyn Anne; m. Eileen Doyle Brewer, Oct. 17, 1987. BA, U. Pa., 1959; MD, Seton Hall Coll. Medicine, 1963. Diplomate Am. Bd. Urology (trustee). Intern Pa. Hosp., Phila., 1963—64; asst. instr. surgery, fellow Harrison Dept. Surgery Rsch. Hosp. U. Pa., Phila., 1964—65, asst. instr. urology, 1965—68, USPHS urol. rsch. trainee, 1967—68, instr. urology, 1968—69, assoc. in urology, 1969—71, asst. prof. urology, 1971—74; veneral disease trainee Phila. Dept. Pub. Health, 1965; radioisotope trainee William H. Donner Ctr. for Radiology, Phila., 1965—66; prof., dir. divsn. urology, dept. surgery U. Tex. Med. Sch., Houston, 0974—1993, interim chmn. dept. surgery, 1980—82, assoc. chmn. dept. surgery, 1984—86; chief urology svc. Hermann Hosp., 1974—93, Tex. Med. Ctr., Houston. Cons. residency rev. com. in urology Lyndon Baines Johnson Hosp., 1993—99, M.D. Anderson Cancer Ctr.; cons. NASA. Contbr. numerous articles to profl. jours. Maj. USAF, 1969—71. Mem.: ACS, Am. Assn. for Surgery of Trauma, Am. Assn. Genitourol. Surgery, Soc. Univ. Urologists, Soc. Univ. Surgeons (sec.-treas. 1984—86, pres. 1987—88, 1987—88), Am. Urol. Assn. (dir. edn. 1993—2002). Roman Catholic. Home: 7511 Morningside Dr Houston TX 77030-3619 Office: MD Anderson Cancer Ctr Unit 1274 1220 Holcombe Blvd Houston TX 77030-4004

CORRIGAN, JAMES JOHN, JR., pediatrician, dean, educator; b. Pitts., Aug. 28, 1935; BS, Juniata Coll., Huntingdon, Pa., 1957; MD, U. Pitts., 1961. Diplomate Am. Bd. Pediats. (hematology-oncology). Intern, then resident in pediat. U. Colo. Med. Ctr., 1961-64; trainee in pediat. hematology-oncology U. Ill. Med. Center, 1964-66; assoc. in pediat. Emory U. Med. Sch., 1966-67, asst. prof. Atlanta, 1967-71; mem. faculty U. Ariz. Coll. Medicine, Tucson, 1971-90, prof. pediat., 1974-90; chief sect. pediat. hematology-ongology, also dir. Mountain States Regional Hemophilia Ctr., U. Ariz., Tucson, 1978-90; chief of staff U. Med. Ctr. U. Ariz., Tucson, 1984-86; prof. pediat., vice dean for acad. affairs Tulane U. Sch. Medicine, New Orleans, 1990-93, interim dean, 1993-94, dean, 1994-2000, v.p., 2000—02, prof. emeritus pediat., 2002—; clin. prof. pediat. U. Ariz. Coll. Medicine, Ariz., 2003—. Assoc. editor Am. Jour. Diseases of Children, 1981-89, 90-93, interim editor, 1993; contbr. numerous papers to med. jours. Grantee NIH, Mountain States Regional Hemophilia Ctr., Ga. Heart Assn., GE, Am. Cancer Soc. Mem. Am. Acad. Pediatrics, Am. Soc. Hematology, Soc. Pediatric Rsch., Western Soc. Pediatric Rsch., Am. Heart Assn. (coun. thrombosis), Internat. Soc. Thrombosis and Haemostasis, Am. Pediatric Soc., World Fedn. Hemophilia, Pima County Med. Soc. (v.p., 1986—, pres. 1988—), Alpha Omega Alpha. Republican. Roman Catholic. Office: Univ Ariz Health Scis Ctr Dept Pediatrics 1501 N Campbell Ave Tucson AZ 85724 Business E-Mail: jcorrig@tulane.edu.

CORRIGAN, JANET M., health science association administrator; MBA, U. Rochester, M in Cmty. Health; M in Indsl. Engring., U. Mich., PhD in Health Svcs. Orgn. and Policy. V.p. planning and devel. Nat. Com. for Quality Assurance, 1991-95; prin. rschr. Ctr. for Studying Health Sys. Change Robert Wood Johnson Found., 1995—98; exec. dir. consumer protection and quality in health care industry Pres.'s Advisory Commn. on Consumer Protection and Quality in the Health Care Industry, 1998; dir. Health Care Svcs. Bd. Inst. Medicine of Nat. Academies, 1998—2005; pres., CEO Nat. Quality Forum, Washington, 2006—. Mem. Nat. Ctr. for Healthcare Leadership, 2003—, Coun. for Accountable Physicians Practices Adv. Coun., 2004—, Kaiser Permanente Inst. for Health Policy Adv. Bd., 2004—, Robert Wood Johnson Found. Regional Market Project Adv. Coun., 2005—, Quality Alliance Steering Com., 2006—, Hosp. Quality Alliance, 2006—, Robert Wood Johnson Found. Aligning Forces for Healthcare Quality Nat. Adv. Coun., 2007—, eHealth Initiative Leadership Coun., 2008—; bd. dirs. Am. Health Info. Cmty. Successor, Inc., 2008—. Recipient Inst. Medicine Cecil award for Disting. Svc., 2002, Am. Coll. Med. Quality Founders' award, 2007, Health Rsch. and Ednl. TRUST award, 2007, Am. Soc. Health System Pharmacists' award of Honor, 2008; Am. Coll. Med. Informatics Fellow, 2006. Office: National Quality Forum 601 13th St NW Ste 500 North Washington DC 20005 Office Phone: 202-783-1300. Office Fax: 202-783-3434.

CORRIGAN, JOHN DUDLEY, physiatrist; Helped establish the brain injury unit Ohio State U., 1983, prof. phys. medicine and rehab., prof. psychology, dir. division of rehab. psychology; founder, dir. Ohio Valley Ctr. Brain Injury Prevention and Rehab. Recipient William Fields Caveness award, Brain Injury Assn. America, 2001, Leonard Diller award, American Psychological Assn., 2007, Robert L Moody prize, U. Tex. Galveston, 2007. Fellow: American Psychological Assn. Office: OSU 2145 Dodd Hall 480 Medical Ctr Dr Columbus OH 43210

CORRY, DALILA BOUDJELLAL, internist, educator; b. El-Arrouch, Algeria, July 7, 1943; came to U.S., 1981; MD, U. Algiers, 1974. Diplomate in internal medicine and nephrology Am. Bd. Internal Medicine. Intern Hosp. Mustapha Algiers, 1972-73; resident Hosp. Tenon, Paris, 1975-79; fellow in nephrology UCLA, 1981-83; chief renal divsn. Olive View-UCLA Med. Ctr., Sylmar, Calif., 1983—; from asst. prof. to prof. clin. medicine UCLA, 1993, prof. clin. medicine, 2001—. Fellow Am. Heart Assn. Office: Olive View-UCLA Med Ctr Dept Medicine 2B182 14445 Olive View Dr Sylmar CA 91342-1437 Business E-Mail: dbcorry@ucla.edu.

CORSER, WILLIAM DAVID, nursing researcher; b. Mpls., June 24, 1956; PhD in Nursing, U. Wis., Madison, 2000; MSN in Nursing Adminstrn., Winona State U., Rochester, 1994. Rsch. specialist Mich. State U. Inst. Health Care Studies, 2011—. Bd. dirs. Midwest Nursing Rsch. Soc., 2009—. Mem.: ANA, Acad. Health, Sigma Theta Tau Internat. (Alpha Psi chpt.) (grant 2009). Avocation: banjo. Office: A134 East Fee Hall East Lansing MI 48824 Office Fax: 517-432-9977. Business E-Mail: corser@msu.edu.

CORTES, ARTHUR RODRIGUEZ GONZALEZ, oral surgeon, researcher; b. Sao Paulo, Brazil, July 11, 1983; DDS, U. Sao Paulo, 2006, MS, 2009, PhD student, 2011—. Oral implantologist CETAO, 2009—11; pvt. practice, 2010—11; rschr., oral radiology dept. Sch. Dentistry U. Sao Paulo, 2011—. Mem.: Acad. Osseointegration. Avocations: music, piano. Office: Rua Teixeira da Silva 34 Conj 84 Sao Paulo 04002-030 Brazil Office Fax: 551132662049. Business E-Mail: arthuro@usp.br.

CORTES, ENGRACIO PADILLA, oncologist; b. Iloilo, Philippines, Jan. 9, 1938; came to U.S., 1965; s. Felix Francisco and Ofelia (Ledesma) Padilla; m. Lilia Serrano Gonzales June 7, 1969; children Carl, Marissa, Alfonso. BA, U. San Agustin, Iloilo City, 1958; MD, Far Eastern U., Manila, 1964. Diplomate Am. Bd. Internal Medicine, Am. Bd. Med. Oncology. Internship Cambridge (Mass.) City Hosp., 1965-66; residency in internal medicine Lemuel Shattuck Hosp., Boston, 1966-68; fellowship in medical oncology Roswell Park Meml. Inst., Buffalo, N.Y., 1969-71; physician-in-charge med. oncology Queens (N.Y.) Med. Ctr., 1972-81; clin. coord. cancer program L.I. Jewish Med. Ctr., New Hyde Park, N.Y., 1975-81; chmn. edn. com. Am. Cancer Soc., Queens, 1985-92; dir. oncology rsch. N.Y. Hosp. Queens, 1998—; clin. assoc. prof. medicine Weil Med. Coll. Cornell U., 2001—. Assoc. clin. prof. medicine SUNY, Stonybrook, 1977—80, Albert Einstein Coll. Medicine, NYC, 1983—2002. Contbr. articles to profl. jours., chpts. to books. Pres. N.Y. Cancer Soc. Fellow ACP; mem. Assn. Am. Cancer Rsch., Am. Soc. Clin. Oncology, N.Y. State Hematology-Oncology Soc., N.Y. State Med. Soc., Philippine Med. Assn. Am. (Best Philipine Physician 1975), Assn. Philippine Physicians N.Y. (pres. 1995-97). Avocations: playing tennis, classical guitar, ballroom dancing. Office: 200-20 44th Ave Bayside NY 11361 Office Phone: 718-279-9101.

CORTESE, DENIS A., healthcare executive, medical educator; b. Phila., Feb. 27, 1944; MD, Temple U., 1970. Cert. Nat. Bd. Med. Examiners, diplomate Am. Bd. Internal Medicine, in pulmonary disease Am. Bd. Internal Medicine, cert. Am. Bd. Laser Surgery. Prof. medicine Mayo Med. Sch.; intern Mayo Clinic, Rochester, Minn., 1970—71; resident, internal medicine Mayo Grad. Sch. Medicine, Mayo Clinic, Rochester, 1970—72, resident, thoracic medicine, 1972—74; fellow, thoracic diseases and bronchoscopy Mayo Clinic, 1976, pulmonary medicine specialist, 1976, pres., CEO, 2003—09. Mem. Ctr. Corp. Innovation; bd. dirs. Pinnacle West Capital Corp., 2010—. Bd. trustees Healthcare Leadership Coun.; mem. Harvard/Kennedy Sch. Healthcare Policy Group; bd. govs. Mayo Clinic, Rochester, 1987—92, trustee, 1990—94, 1997—, chair bd. govs. Jacksonville, 1999—2002; bd. dirs. St. Luke's Hosp., Jacksonville, 1999—2002, chair exec. com., 2002; dir., health care delivery and policy program Ariz. State U. Fellow: Royal Coll. Physicians London; mem.: Inst. Medicine. Office: Mayo Clinic 200 1st St SW Rochester MN 55905 also: Pinnacle West Capital Corp Bd Directors 400 N 5th St Phoenix AZ 85004 Office Phone: 602-250-1000. Office Fax: 602-250-2430. Business E-Mail: denis.cortese@pinnaclewest.com. *

CORTESI, LAURA, oncologist; b. Bologna, Italy, Sept. 5, 1967; d. Alberto Cortesi and Comuni Clementina; m. Andrea Pancotti, July 26; 1 child, Stefano. PhD in Oncology, U. Modena and Reggio Emilia, 1996. Intern in oncology F. Addarii Inst., Bologna, 1989—92; oncologist Poly. Modena, 2002—. Author: Clinical Use of Aromatase Inhibitor, 1994, Hereditary Cancers, 2003. Grantee Oncology fellow, U. Rodeue, 1993—96; Biomed. Sci. fellow, 1997—2001. Mem.: Am. Soc. Clin. Oncology, Assn. Italian Med. Oncologists. Office: Dept Oncology Hematology Via del Pozzo 71 41124 Modena MO Italy

CORTI, LUIGI, medical technician; b. Venice, Italy, Nov. 8, 1953; Specialist in radiotherapy Padova, Italy, 1984. Med. mgr. Radiotherapy Iov Irccs, Padova, 1982—96, dir. sect., 1996—. Contract prof. radiation oncology Sch. Specialization Geriatrics and Gerontology, Sch. Specialty Radiology and Radiotherapy, Sch. Specialization Ob-Gyn. Mem.: IPA. Office: Raditherapy Iov Irccs Via Nicolo Giustiniani 2 35128 Padova PD Italy Office Fax: 390498212958. Business E-Mail: luigi.corti@unid.it.

CORWIN, BERT CLARK, optometrist; b. Rapid City, SD, Oct. 4, 1930; s. Meade and Adeline (Clark) C.; m. Lydia M. Forehand; children: B. Clark II, Kelley Linette Fromm. AS, S.D. State U., 1952; BS, Ill. Coll. Optometry, Chgo., 1956, OD, 1957. Pvt. practice, Rapid City, 1957—. Projects chmn. S.D. Lions Sight and Svc. Found., 1964; chmn. med. adv. com. to S.D. Dept. Pub. Welfare, 1968-76; mem. S.D. Adv. Coun. for Regional Med. and Health Planning, 1971; cons. S.D. Dept. Human Svcs., 1989—; adv. bd. S.D. Dept. of Svc. to Visual Impaired; bd. dirs. Super 8 Motel Developers, Rapid City Regional Airport, v.p., 1999-2000, pres., 2000—; chmn. bd. dirs. Transaction Network, Inc., 1997—; mng. ptnr. Tight Line Lake, 1999-2002. Contbr. articles to profl. jours. Pres. Cleghorn PTA, Rapid City, 1968-70; bd. dirs. Am. Optometric Found., 1989-90, v.p., 1990-94, pres., 1994-96; chmn. bd. dirs. Terry Peak Condominiums, 2001—. Recipient Presdl. medal of honor Pres. of Ill. Coll. of Optometry, 1999, 2002, Spl. honor Am. Optometric Found. Fellow Am. Acad. Optometry (diplomate contact lens sect., sec.-treas. 1985-86, pres.-elect 1987-88, pres. 1988-90, chmn. 1st internat. meeting 1992, nom. com. 2000-02); mem. Am. Optometric Assn. (exec. com. 1974-76, Am. Optometrist of the Yr. 1993), S.D. Optometric Soc. (pres. 1970-71), North Ctrl. State Optometric Conf. (bd. dirs. 1970-71), Black Hills Optometric Soc. (sec.-treas. 1958-69), S.D. State Bd. Examiners (pres. 1982-85), Nat. Acad. Practice Optometry (sec.-treas. 1990-94, Disting. Practitioners award, co-chmn. 1994-96). Clubs: Black Hills Water Ski (pres. 1963). Lodges: Masons, Elks, Lions (pres. Rushmore chpt. 1961-62, Robert Tyler award 1998), Rapid City Regional Airport (pres. 2010), Internat. Soc. Contact Lens Specialists. Republican. Methodist. Avocations: skiing, water-skiing, hunting, piloting, public speaking. Home: 5048 Carriage Hills Dr Rapid City SD 57702 Personal E-mail: bc.corwin@juno.com.

CORWIN, STEVEN JONATHAN, hospital administrator; b. White Plains, NY, Jan. 8, 1956; BS, Northwestern U., 1977; MD summa cum laude, Northwestern U. Sch. Medicine, 1979. Bd. cert. in internal medicine and cardiology. Intern and resident Columbia-Presbyn. Med. Ctr., NYC, 1979—82, chief med. resident, dept. medicine, 1982—83; asst. prof. clin. medicine Coll. Physicians & Surgeons, Columbia U., NYC, 1986—98, assoc. prof. clin. medicine, 1998—; med. dir. Milstein Hosp. Columbia-Presbyn. Med. Ctr., NYC, 1997—98, dir. critical care svcs., 1991—97, dir. cardiac intensive care unit, 1986—91; chief med. officer NY Presbyn. Hosp., NYC, 1998—2005, sr. v.p., 1999—2005, exec. v.p., COO, 2005—11, CEO, 2011—. Office: NY Presbyterian Hospital 161 Fort Washington Ave New York NY 10032 Office Phone: 212-305-6902. *

COSCRATO, VIRGINIA ELIAS, research scientist; b. Guaira, Sao Paulo, Brazil, July 30, 1974; BS, UNESP, Botucatu, Sao Paulo, 1997, PhD, 2006. Rsch. scientist dept. genetica UNESP, 2000—. Avocation: singing. Office: Distrito de Rubiao Junior Botucatu Sao Paulo 18610000 Brazil Business E-Mail: coscrato@ibb.unesp.br.

COSEN-BINKER, LAURA IRIS, biomedical researcher, educator; b. Argentina; m. Marcelo Gustavo Binker; children: Andy, Maky. BD in Lab. Medicine & Clin. Chemistry, 1994; PhD, U. Buenos Aires, 2002, Magister in Med. Molecular Biology, Leloir Inst., Consejo Nat. de Investigaciones Cientificas y Tech, 2005. Lic. in lab. medicine Nat. Ministry of Pub. Health. Clin. intern, dept. lab. medicine Hosp. Zubizarreta, 1993—94; trainer, dept. lab. medicine Hosp. de Clinicas "Jose de San Martin", U. Buenos Aires, 1995—96; dir. & ceo RHC-LICB Biomed. Rsch. Inst., 1997—2003, cons., 2003—; lab. prof. gastroenterology & clin. entomology U. Buenos Aires, 1999—2003, prof. gastroenterology & clin. enzymology, dept. clin. biochemistry & lab. medicine, 1999—2003, prof., 1998—99, lectr., 1995—97, 1993—95, asst. tchr., dept. biol. scis., 1989—90, 1988—91; postdoc. rsch. fellow Toronto Gen. Hosp. and SN Hosp. Ont., Canada, 2003—; sr. postdoc. rsch. fellow, dept. medicine U. Toronto, Ont., Canada, 2005—; sr. scientist CBRCH, 2007—. Reviewer Acta Pharmacologica Sinica, Cellular & Molecular Life Scis., CIHR, Exptl. Lung Rsch., Mediators Inflammation, Pancreatology, Regulatory Peptides, Anti-Cancer Drugs; mng. editor Jour. Pancreas; mem. editl. bd. Open Critical Care Medicine Jour. Contbr. chapters to books, articles to profl. jours. Recipient Postdoc. Rsch. award, KB & Assocs., 2003, Travel award, Am. Pancreatology Assn., 2006—07. Mem.: Am. Pancreatic Assn., Am. Soc. Cell Biology. Avocations: tennis, hockey, jogging, swimming, reading, guitar. Business E-Mail: licb@cbrhc.org.

COSER, PAOLO, physician, consultant, educator; b. Bolzano, Alto Adige, Italy, Sept. 14, 1938; s. Livio And Erina (Corazzola) C.; m. Giuliana Ventrella, May 31, 1965; children: Stefano, Alessandro. MD, U. Padova, Italy, 1963. Asst. physician Regional Hosp., Bolzano, Italy, 1964—71, head physician hematology dept. and blood bank, 1971—95, head physician hematology dept. and bone marrow transplantation, 1995—2005, sci. dir. dept. hematology and bone marrow transplantation, 2006—07; prof. U. Parma, 1989—. Contbr. articles to profl. jours. Mem.: Italian Soc. Hematology. Avocations: skiing, diving, tennis. Office: Regional Hosp 5 L Bohler St 39100 Bolzano Italy Fax: 39-0471-908703.

COSGROVE, DELOS M. (TOBY COSGROVE), hospital executive, surgeon; b. Watertown, NY, July 28, 1940; s. Delos M. and Margaret C.; m. Anita Desiderio, May 8, 1976; children: Nicole Ashley, Britt Lindsey. BA, Williams Coll., Williamstown, Mass., 1962; MD, U. Va., 1966. Diplomate Am. Bd. Surgery, Am. Bd. Thoracic Surgery. Intern Strong Meml. Hosp., Rochester, NY, 1966-67, resident in surgery, 1967-68, Mass. Gen. Hosp., Boston, 1970-72, sr. resident in cardiac surgery, 1973-74; registrar in cardiac surgery Brook Gen. Hosp., London, 1972-73; chief resident Boston Children's Hosp., 1974; assoc. staff dept. thoracic and cardiovascular surgery The Cleve. Clinic, 1975-76, profl. staff, 1976—, chmn. dept. thoracic and cardiovascular surgery, 1990—, CEO, 2004—, chmn., bd. governors, 2004—. Bd. trustees Healthcare Leadership Coun. Contbr. articles to profl. jours. Mem. Am. Assn. Thoracic Surgery (pres. 2000), Internat. Soc. Cardiovascular Surgery, Am. Coll. Cardiology, Am. Coll. Chest Physicians, ACS, Am. Heart Assn., AMA, Am. Surg. Assn., Cleve. Surg. Soc., Ohio State Med. Assn., Ohio Thoracic Soc., Cleve. Acad. Medicine, Soc. Thoracic Surgeons, Soc. for Thoracic Surg. Edn. (chmn. membership com. 1985-87), Peruvian Coll. Angiology (hon.), Chilean Soc. Cardiology (hon.), Dominican Republic Soc. Cardiology (hon.), Argentine Coll. Cardiology (hon., mem. editorial bd. The Annals of Thoracic Surgery). Avocation: sailing. Office: Cleve Clinic Surgery 9500 Euclid Ave Cleveland OH 44195-0001 *

COSIMELLI, MAURIZIO, physician; b. Rome, June 27, 1954; MD, U. Rome, 1978, degree in Gen. Surgery, 1983, degree in Surg. Oncology, 1987. Jr. asst. Regina Elena Nat. Cancer Inst., Rome, 1983—89, sr. asst., 1990—. Prof., surgery La Sapienza U. Rome, 1999—2011, Campus Bio Medico U., Rome, 2003—11. Contbr. 300 articles to profl. publs. Rsch. Project grant, Assn. Italiana Ricerche sul Cancro, Consiglio Nat. delle Ricerche, Ministero della Sanità. Fellow: Soc. Surg. Oncology; mem.: Italian Soc. Locoregional Therapy in Oncology, Italian Soc. Surgery. Avocation: acting. Home: Via Cassia 831 Rome 00189 Italy Home Fax: 390652665378. Personal E-mail: mcosimelli@libero.it.

COSMA, DAN IONUT, surgeon, educator; b. Cluj-Napoca, Cluj, Romania, Jan. 7, 1977; s. Stefan and Maria Cosma; m. Smaranda Adina Moldovan, May 14, 2000; 1 child, Ana Iarina. PhD, U. Medicine and Pharmacy, Cluj-Napoca, 2001. Cert. in pediat. orthop. Cluj, 2007. Asst. prof. U. Medicine and Pharmacy, Cluj-Napoca, 2003—; cons., pediat. orthop. Rehab. Clin. Hosp., Cluj-Napoca, 2008—. Vol. Rehab. Clin. Hosp., Cluj-Napoca, 2007—08. Marie Curie Instrnl. Courses scholar, EPOS, 2007—09. Mem.: ISPO. Achievements include research in conservative treatment of clubfoot. Home: St Observatorului nr 9 Apt 3 Cluj-Napoca Cluj 400500 Romania Office: Rehab Clin Hosp St Viilor nr 46-50 Cluj-Napoca Cluj 400347 Romania Home Fax: 40364814344. Business E-Mail: dcosma@umfcluj.ro.

COSMI, ERICH, obstetrician, educator, gynecologist; b. Rome, Dec. 1, 1973; s. Ermelando Vinicio Cosmi and Vittoria Bastianon. MD, U. Rome Sch. Medicine, 1999. Fellow, Sch. Medicine OB/GYN Maternal Fetal Medicine Yale U., New Haven, 1993, rsch. fellow, Sch. Medicine OB/GYN Maternal Fetal Medicine, 1994—94, 1996, 1998, vis. prof. ob-gyn., Sch. Medicine, 2005; asst. prof., Health Sys., Sch. Medicine OB/GYN Maternal Fetal Medicine Va. U., Charlottesville, Va., 2000—03; asst. prof., Sch. Medicine Pharm. OB/GYN Maternal Fetal Medicine U. Sassari, Italy, 2001—04; asst. prof. ob-gyn., Sch. Medicine U. Padua, Italy, 2004—; dir. prenatal diagnosis and fetal therapy unit U. Padua Sch. Medicine; dir. maternal fetal mgmt. U. Padua, 2010; bd. physician UN Women Health, 2010; dir. Maternal and Fetal Medicine Unit, 2010; physician UN Womens Heart, 2010. Chief fetal therapy and maternal fetal medicine and rsch. U. Padua Sch. Medicine, 2004—; cons. fetal ecocardiography Padua Sch. Medicine, 2004—; dir. rsch. project Yale U. Sch. of Medicine, New Haven, 2003—; mem. Physician's Bd UN Women's Health, 2010. Contbr. articles to profl. jours.; author: 4 books. Dir. rsch. project NIH, 1996 . Recipient Ugo Tropea prize, Soc. Prenatal Medicine, 2000; grantee, U. Rome la Sapienza, 2002, Nat. Coun. Rsch., 2001—02; scholar, Yale U., 1993—98. Mem.: Italian Soc. Perinatal Medicine (nat. sec.), Am. Inst. Ultrasound in Medicine, Internat. Soc. Ultrasound in Ob-Gyn, Soc. Perinatal Medicine (gen. sec.), Counselor Soc. Maternal and Fetal Medicine, Soc. Maternal Fetal Medicine. Home: via porta Tiburtina n 36 00185 Rome Italy Office: U Padua Sch Medicine Via Nicolo Giustiniani 3 35128 Padua PD Italy Office Phone: 0039-338146745. Business E-Mail: ecosmi@hotmail.com.

COST, FRANCIS HOWARD, JR., physician; b. Hagerstown, Md., Sept. 24, 1938; s. Francis Howard and Mary Elizabeth C. AB, Gettysburg Coll., 1962; MD, U. Md., 1966. Diplomate Am. Bd. Internal Medicine, Am. Bd. Cardiovascular Disease, Am. Bd. Pulmonary Disease. Resident in internal medicine USPHS, SI, 1967-68, U. Hosp., Balt., 1969-70, fellow in cardiology, 1970-72; fellow in pulmonary disease Temple U. Hosp., Phila., 1972-73; fellow in nuclear medicine/nuclear cardiology Johns Hopkins Hosp., Balt., 1984-85, fellow in med. ICU, 1986-88. Lt. comdr. USPHS, 1967-69. Fellow Am. Coll. Chest Physicians; mem. Am. Coll. Cardiology, Am. Coll. Physicians, Laennec Soc. Phila. Avocations: sailing, music. Home: 1101 North Potomac Ave Hagerstown MD 21742-3439 Office Phone: 301-739-4727.

COSTA, CARLA, biology professor; b. Lisbon, Portugal, June 12, 1975; BSc in Genetics and Microbiology, U. Lisbon, 1998; grad student, Weill Cornell Med. Coll., NY, 2000—03, Inst. Pathology and Molecular Immunology U. Porto, 2004—05; PhD in Human Biology, U. Porto, Portugal, 2005. Postdoc. fellow Faculty Medicine U. Porto, 2005—07, invited prof. cell and molecular biology, 2005—, prin. investigator, 2008, adv. responsibilities-grad. students supr., 2010. Sci. article reviewer European Urology, 2010, Jour. Sexual Medicine, 2010, Internat. Jour. Andrology, 2010, Urology, 2010; abstract reviewer European Assn. Urology, 2010. Grants, Portuguese Assn. Urology, 2008, 2010, Portuguese Found. Sci. and Tech. Mem.: Order of Portuguese Biologists, Portuguese Soc. Andrology (Prof. Alexandre Moreira award 2005), Assn. Advanced Study Human Sexuality (founding mem. iSEX), European Soc. Sexual Medicine (mem. grant com. adv. bd. 2010, mem. exec. com., Rsch. grant 2007). Avocations: sports, travel, movies. Office: Faculty Medicine University Porto Dept Experimental Biology Al Hernani Monteiro Porto 4200-319 Portugal

COSTA, CRISTINA, medical educator; b. Turin, Italy, July 13, 1969; MD, U. Turin, 1993, degree in Microbiology and Virology, 2007. Cert. Italian med. register Ordine dei Medici, 1994. Contract prof., clin. microbiology and gen. virology U. Turin, 2007—. Translator numerous books and jours.; author: (book) Immunofluorescenza per Immagini - Epatogastroenterologia, Malattie Autoimmuni in Epatologia e Gastroenterologia, Dispense di Gastroenterologia ed Epatologia per il corso di Laurea in Scienza Infermieristiche; contbr. scientific papers to profl. jours. Minsiterial fellowship, U. Turin, 2003—07, Rsch. grant, Compagnia di San Pao, 2008. Mem.: Italian Soc. Med. Virology, Italian Soc. Virology, Società Italiana Microbiologia, Assn. Italiana Microbiologi Clin. Achievements include development of LUX real time PCR for the detection of human herpesvirus; RT-PCR for thedetection of human cytomegaloirus lytic gene expression, research in seroprevalence of human herpesvirus-8; occurrence non-organ specific autoantibodies and anti-endothelial antibodies; BK virus replication and relation to lupus nephritis; monitoring human cytomegalovirus infection and polyomavirus BK and JC replication; human cytomegalovirus infection; EBV and relation to lung diseases in transplant recipients; role of human herpesvirus-7, EBV and parvovirus in primary cutaneous lymphomas; pulmonary complication in primary biliary cirrhosis.

COSTA, LUIS ALBERTO, oncologist, researcher; b. Buenos Aires, Mar. 11, 1949; s. Luis Manuel Costa and Concepción Nélida Deleonibus de Costa; m. Beatriz Celia Fuentes, Dec. 23, 1975; children: Luis Atilio, Juan Ignacio, María Eugenia. MD in Medicine, Nat. U. La Plata, La Plata City, Buenos Aires, 1975; MD in Gen. Surgery, Hosp. Marie Curie, Min. Pub. Health, Buenos Aires, Argentina, 1981, MD in Oncology, 1982. Lic. Nat. U. La Plata, 1975, pub. health sec. Min. Social Welfare, 1975, physician Buenos Aires, Argentina, gen. surgery Min. Pub. Health and Environment, 1981, oncologist Min. Pub. Health and Environment, 1982. Gen. surgeon, ho. surgeon Hosp. Marie Curie, Buenos Aires, 1976—86, surgeon emergency unit, gen. surgery area, 1981—86; rschr. Ventech Rsch., Inc., Boston, 1989—96, Onco Venom Rsch., SA, Buenos Aires, 1996—; head oncology Galician Ctr. Buenos Aires, 2007—. Sec. tumor bd. Galician Ctr. Buenos Aires, 2001—; mem. rsch. and tchg. dept. Centro Gallego de Buenos Aires, 2004—; mem. sci. com. Nat. Acad. Medicine, Buenos Aires, 2007—; mem. Assn. Medica Argentina, 1997, Bioabcda Esoana SA, 2000, Assn. Argentina Canarologia, 2010. Achievements include research and development of new drugs; patents in field. Office: Galician Ctr Buenos Aires Avenida Belgrano 2199 Buenos Aires C1094AAD Argentina Office Fax: 5411 4127 1042. Personal E-mail: lcosta@ciudad.com.ar, lacosta@gmail.com. Business E-Mail: l.costa@centrogallegoba.com.ar.

COSTA, MARCIA HELENA SOARES, endocrinologist; b. Sao Luis, Maranhão, Mar. 13, 1974; MD, Fed. U. Maranhao, 1998; PhD in Endocrinology, U. Sao Paulo, 2007. Endocrinologist Fleury, 2007—. Rsch. scientist Fed. U. Rio De Janeiro, 2007. Mem.: Endocrine Soc. Avocations: movies, music, travel. Home: Visconde de silva n33 apt-404 Botafogo Rio de Janeiro 22271091 Brazil Personal E-mail: mhsc@usp.br.

COSTA, PAUL JOSEPH, psychologist; b. Allison Pk., Pa., Mar. 9, 1968; s. Ralph Felix and Therese Marie Costa; m. Rashida Stacy-Ann Campbell, Apr. 16, 2004; 1 child, Antares Dimetrodon Costa. BS in Biology cum laude, Wofford Coll., 1990; MS in Gen. Psychology summa cum laude, Carlos Albizu U., 1996, PsyD in Clin. Psychology summa cum laude, 2001. Lic. psychologist Fla. Dept. Health, 2002. Staff psychologist Ctr. Clin. and Forensic Psychology, Inc., Plantation, Fla., 2002—; designated mental health authority Eckerd Youth Devel. Ctr., Okeechobee, Fla., 2004—06; sr. residential counselor Comprehensive Alcoholism Rehab. Programs Inc., West Palm Beach, Fla., 2006—08; forensic psychologist Treasure Coast Forensic Treatment Ctr., Indiantown, Fla., 2008—10, United States Naval Hosp., Gulfport, Miss., 2010—; staff psychologist Behavioral Health Palm Beaches, West Palm Beach, Fla.; clin. psychologist dept. def. US Naval Branch Health Clinic, Gulfport, Miss., 2010—. Lab. and tchg. asst. Wofford Coll., Spartanburg, SC, 1987—90; psychotherapist Goodman Psychol. Svcs. Ctr., Miami, Fla., 1996—97; psychol. evaluator PsychSolutions, Coral Gables, Fla., 1998; clin. psychology intern Atlantic Shores Hosp., Fort Lauderdale, Fla., 1999—2000; neuropsychol. resident Cognitive Rehabilitative Assoc. South Fla., Inc., Miami, 2001 02; clin. neuropsychologist Ctrs. Psychol. Growth, Inc., Miami, 2002—03; spkr. in field. Musician: The Invertebrates; author: (short stories) Waiting for the Furnace to Kick On (Nat. Honors, Scholastic Writing Awards, 1986), Visions of Terror (Nat. Honors, Scholastic Writing Awards, 1986); composer (musician): (film soundtrack) Frustration; musician: (musical) Grease: The Musical. Benjamin Wofford scholar, Wofford Coll., 1986—90. Roman Catholic. Avocations: singing, music, writing. Office: Ctr Clin and Forensic Psychology Inc 6830 SW 16th St Plantation FL 33325 Home: 1289 Century Oaks Dr # A Gulfport MS 39507-1514 Office Phone: 954-584-6155. Personal E-mail: zepplication@yahoo.com.

COSTA, ROBERTO FERNANDES, medical researcher; b. Santos, Brazil, Nov. 15, 1964; D in Pediat., U. Fed. de São Paulo, 2006. PE tchr. Faculdade de Educação Física da ACM Sorocaba, 1990; prof. U. Santa Cecilia, 2002—10; rschr. U. Fed. do Rio Grande do Sul, 2011—. Master: Ctr. de Estudos e Pesquisas Sanny. Avocation: running. Home: Roque Calage 240/213 D Porto Alegre Rio Grande do Sul 91350090 Brazil Personal E-mail: roberto@robertocosta.com.br.

COSTA, VINICIUS SILVA, medical researcher; b. Mossoró, Apr. 2, 1978; Grad., Fed. U. Rio Grande Do Norte, 2003; PhD, Sao Paulo U. Postdoc. rschr. Sao Paulo U., 2008—. Avocations: soccer, running. Home: Rua Sergio Severo 1327 Natal Rio Grande Do Norte 59063380 Brazil Personal E-mail: vinicius.scosta@usp.br.

COSTA-FELIX, RODRIGO P.B., biomedical engineer; b. São Paulo, Brazil, May 21, 1970; ME, Fed. U. Rio de Janeiro, 2005, DSc in Biomed. Engring., 2005. Head lab. Brazilian Nat. Metrology Inst., Inmetro, 2005—. Assoc. prof. Fed. U. Rio de Janeiro, 2011. Master: Brazilian Soc. Biomed. Engring.; mem.: Brazilian Assn. Non Destructive Testing and Essay. Avocations: sailing, mountain climbing, diving. Office: Ave Nossa Sra das Graças 50 Predio 1 Duque de Caxias Rio de Janeiro 25.250-020 Brazil Office Fax: 55-21-2145 3245. Business E-Mail: rpfelix@inmetro.gov.br.

COSTANZA, MICHAEL C., retired statistics professor; b. NYC, May 3, 1947; m. Judith Ann Chapman. PhD, UCLA Sch. Pub. Health, 1977. Stats. prof. U. Vt., Burlington, 1977—99; editor, stats., Preventive Medicine Elsevier, NYC, 2005—; sr. biostatistician Geneva U. Hosp., 1999—2008; emeritus prof. stats. U. Vt., 2000. Mem. Pl. Biostatistics Core Resources Vt. Cancer Ctr., U. Vt. Pulmonary Sci. Ctr. Rsch., Breast Screening Program Projects; co pl. Swiss Nat. Sci. Found., NIH Cmty. Prevention & Control Study Sect., 1985—89. Contbr. 150 articles to profl. jours. on medical, pub. health, epidemiology, and stat. Grants, NIH, 1997—99. Personal E-mail: michael.c.costanza@uvm.edu.

COSTEA, DANIELA ELENA, dentist, researcher; b. Onesti, Romania, Apr. 4, 1973; d. Costache and Fevronia Radu; life ptnr. Helge Opegal. D in Medicine, Stomatology with honors, Carol Davilla U., Bucharest, Romania, 1997; D in Odontology, U. Bergen, Norway, 2005. Lic. Scandinavian Bd. Oral Pathology and Oral Medicine, 2006. Tchg. asst. Carol Davilla, Bucharest, 1998—2002; rsch. fellow U. Bergen, 2000—05; rschr. King's coll. U. London, 2005; postdoctoral rsch. fellow U. Bergen, 2005—; rsch. fellow Queen Mary U., London, 2007—. Contbr. articles to profl. jours. Dep. female student rep. Ctr. Internat. Health, Bergen; vol. Haydom Hosp., Haydom, Tanzania, 2003. Recipient Young Investigator award, Australia and New Zeeland Assn., 2003, Spanish Soc. Oral Medicine, 2004, Hatton award, Scandinavian Assn. Dental Rsch., 2004, Best Sci. Poster award, Internat. Congress Oral Cancer, 2005, Tchg. and Rsch. in Odontology prize, Norwegian Assn. Dentists, 2005, Meltzer Young Rschrs. prize, U. Bergen, 2006. Fellow: Bergen Oral Cancer Group, Scandinavian Fellowship Oral Pathology and Oral Medicine; mem.: Internat. Assn. Oral Pathologists (Young Investigator award 2006), Internat. Assn. Dental Rsch. Home: Fantoftasen 30A Bergen 5072 Norway Office: Univ Bergen Haukeland Univ Hosp Pathology 5021 Bergen Norway Office Fax: 004755973158. Business E-Mail: daniela.costea@odfa.uib.no.

COSTELLO, JACLYN, pharmacist; b. Brisbane, Queensland, Australia, June 13, 1980; PharmB, U. Queensland, 2006, BS, 2003. Intern pharmacist Clin. Pharmacist, 2007—08; clin. pharmacist Queensland Health, 2008—. Recipient Eleanor Chalmers prize, U. Queensland; grant, Merck Sharp & Dohme. Mem.: Australian Assn. Cons. Pharmacy, Soc. Hosp. Pharmacists Australia. Home: 7/20 Dethridge St Northgate Brisbane Queensland 4109 Australia Personal E-mail: jackie.costello@gmail.com.

COTE, RICHARD JAMES, pathologist, researcher; b. LA, May 10, 1954; s. Richard Patrick and Katherine C.; m. Anne L. Foxen, Feb. 8, 1992; children: Nicholas Foxen, Juliet Anne, Grace Elizabeth. BS in Biology, U. Calif., Irvine, 1976, BA in Chemistry, 1976; MD, U. Chgo., 1980. Diplomate Am. Bd. Pathology. Intern in surgery U. Mich. Hosp., Ann Arbor, 1980-81; rsch. fellow, immunology Meml. Sloan-Kettering Cancer Ctr., NYC, 1981-83; rsch. assoc., immunology Meml. Sloan-Kettering Hosp., NYC, 1983-85, fellow, pathology, 1987-88, chief fellow, pathology, 1988-90; resident, pathology Cornell U. Med. Ctr., NYC, 1985-87; asst. prof., pathology Keck Sch. Medicine, U. So. Calif., LA, 1990-95, assoc. prof., 1995-99, prof., 1999—2009; dir. genitourinary program Keck Sch. Medicine, U. So. Calif./Norris Cancer Ctr., 1997—2009; chair biomed. nanosci. initiative U. So. Calif., 2005—09; attending pathologist Kenneth Norris Cancer Ctr., 1990—2005, dir. lab. immuno and molecular pathology, 1991—2005; prof., chmn., Miller Sch. Medicine U. Miami, 2009—, dir., Biomed. Nanosci. Inst., 2009—, dir., Genitourinary Cancer Program, Sylvester Comprehensive Cancer Ctr., 2009—. Founder, dir. IMPATH, Inc., NYC, 1988—2003; chief med. officer Chromavision Med. Sys. (now Clarient Inc.), 2004—05; mem. numerous nat. and internat. adv. bds.; sci. cons. Roche Molecular Sys., 2000—, MD Anderson Cancer Ctr., Houston, 2002—; founder Filtini Inc., 2008. Author: Immunomicroscopy, 1994, 2006; editor Modern Surg. Pathology; assoc. editor Applied Immunohistochemistry; mem. editl. bd. Jour. Clin. Oncology, 2007—; contbr. articles to profl. jours., book chpts. Patentee in field. Am. Cancer Soc. fellow, 1988; named one of Best Doctor's in Am., 2005 , Am's. Top Doctor's, 2001 ; recipient rsch. grants, awards NIH, ACS, others, 1981—. Mem.: Am. Assn. Cancer Rsch., Alpha Omega Alpha Med. Honor Soc., Phi Beta Kappa. Home: 4050 Battersea Rd Miami FL 33133 Office: University Miami Miller Sch Medicine Dept Patholgy R-5 1120 NW 14th St Ste 1416 Miami FL 33136 Office Phone: 305-243-2683. Business E-Mail: rcote@med.miami.edu.

COTOGNI, PAOLO, anesthesiologist; b. Rome, July 21, 1961; children: Giulio, Lavinia. Degree in Medicine, Cath. U., Rome, 1986. Cons. surgeon Trauma Ctr., Turin, Piedmont, Italy, 1996—99; head dept. surgery Unit Acute Pancreatitis U. Hosp. Turin, 1999—2001, coord. dept. surgery Surg. ICU, 2000—01, coord. ICU dept. anesthesiology & critical care medicine, 2001—08, head dept. medicine Unit Parenteral Nutrition Oncology, 2009; resident anesthesiology & intensive care State U. Turin, 2004. Course dir., instr. ATLS, ALS, BLSD, 1996—2011; mem. Advanced Trauma Life Support State Faculty Italy Am. Coll. Surgeons Com. Trauma, 1999 2011; adj. prof. anesthesiology & intensive care U. Turin, 2002—11, nat. coord. Italy project genetics sepsis & septic shock Europe - genosept European Soc. Intensive Care Medicine, 2005—08. Fellowship, Italian Group of Surg. Intensive Care, Pub. Health State Office, grant, 2003 04, 2007. Mem.: Italian Resuscitation Coun., Italian Soc. Intensive Care, European Soc. Artificial Nutrition and Metabolism, Italian Soc. Artificial Nutrition and Metabolism (mem. bd. dirs. 2009—11). Avocations: history, movies, football. Home: Via G Giolitti 9 Turin Piedmont 10123 Italy Personal E-mail: paolo.cotogni@unito.it.

COTRONE, JANICE LYNNE, nursing consultant; b. Arlington, Va., Sept. 11, 1956; d. James Franklin and Ferne Smith Cooper; m. Mitchell John Cotrone, July 6, 1996; children: Philip Joseph, Joshua John, Francia Marie. BSN, Ind. Wesleyan U., 1978, MS in Cmty. Health Nursing, 1995. RN Va. Charge nurse Shenandoah County Meml. Hosp., Woodstock, Va., 1978—79; asst. head nurse Arlington Hosp., 1979—81; staff nurse, cardiac ICU Fairfax (Va.) Hosp., 1981—84; dir. mission clinic Petit Goave, Haiti Wesleyan World Missions, Indpls., 1981, missionary nurse to Haiti, 1984—94, 1997—2001; nurse case mgr. Samaritan Bethany Home Health Agy., Rochester, Minn., 1995—96; RN cons. Hope Wesleyan Ch., Naples, Fla., 2002—. Dir. mission clinic in Haiti Wesleyan World Missions, Indpls., 1981, adminstr. La Gonave (Haiti) Wesleyan Hosp., 1984—94, prof. nursing La Gonave (Haiti) Wesleyan Hosp., 1985—88, med. dir. Wesleyan Ch. Haiti, 1986—88, DON Wesleyan Hosp. La Gonave, 1984—94, dir. surgery Wesleyan Hosp. La Gonave, 1984—94, mission sta. mgr. Wesleyan Mission Haiti, 1991—94, mission/hosp. bookkeeper and acct. Wesleyan Mission Haiti, 1985—2001; spkr. seminars, confs., retreats, and convs. Author: (book) Nutritional Assessment of American School-Age Children; contbr. articles to mags.; featured on radio and TV interviews regarding work in Haiti. Transl., cons. local health dept., physician's and dentist's offices, local nursing homes, Naples, 2002—05; vol. liaison Am. and Haitian comty., 2002—05; poll worker, poll inspector, Creole transl. for 2004 presdl. election, 2004; English tchr. to Haitian nurses Wesleyan Mission to Haiti, Petit Goave, La Gonave, 1981—2001, vol. meal server to 9 Haitian sch. children, 1984—94, funded sch. for 15 Haitian children, 1984—2004; field dir. child-sponsorship program World Hope Internat., Haiti, 1997—2001. Recipient Continuing Edn. scholarship, Ind. Wesleyan U., 1994. Mem.: Wesleyan Women (work dir. 2004 05), Wesleyan Med. Fellowship (Continuing Edn. scholarship 1994), Sigma Theta Tau. Republican. Avocations: knitting, travel, composing music and writing lyrics, piano. Home: RR 2 Box 2468 Mansfield MO 65704

COTRUVO, JOSEPH ALFRED, water, environmental and public health consultant; b. Toledo, Aug. 3, 1942; s. Nicholas and Angela (Campanale) C.; m. Karen Shrum, June 18, 1983; 1 child, Joseph Alfred Jr. BS in Chemistry, U. Toledo, 1963; PhD, Ohio State U., 1968; postgrad., U. Bologna, Italy, 1969. Mgr. R & D ChemSampCo, Columbus, Ohio, 1970-72; programs analyst EPA, Washington, 1973-76, dir. drinking water criteria and stds. divsn., 1976-90, dir. health and environ. rev. divsn., 1990-92; dir. risk assessment divsn., 1992-96; sr. regulatory exec. NSF Internat., Washington, 1996-98. V.p. environ. health scis. NSF Internat., 1998—2000; coun. pub. health cons. Nat.

Sanitation Found., Ann Arbor, Mich., 1980—96; dir. NSF Internat./WHO Collaborating Ctr. Water Safety & Tech., 1996—2010; adj. prof. environ. scis. Am. U., 1997; mem. sci. adv. bd. Santa Ana River Water Quality and Health; mem. rsch. adv. bd. Nat. Water Rsch. Inst., Orange, Calif., Ground Water Replenishment Study; ind. adv. bd. Tampa Water Resource Reuse Panel, 1997—98; pres. Joseph Cotruvo & Assocs. LLC; mem. sci. adv. bd. Cal-Fed Delta Water Quality Project; rsch. adv. bd. Water Reuse Found.; sci. panel on water sys. security rsch. NAS, 2003, Heterotrophic Plate Counts, 2003, Emerging Pathogen, 2004; mem. San Diego Water Reuse Adv. Com., 2004—; vis. prof. environ. sci. Tech. U. Bari, 2005. Co-editor: Ozone/Chlorine Dioxide, 1978, Water Chlorination, 1983, Procs. Safe Drinking Water in Small Sys.: Tech., Ops. and Econs., 1999; chmn., editor: NATO/CCMS Drinking Water Pilot, 1980; co-editor: Emerging Pathogens in Drinking Water, Bromate Health Rsch. Strategy, Toxicology and AWWARF, 2005; editor: Desalination Technology: Health and Environmental Impacts, 2010; mem. editl. bd. Am. Water Works Assn. Jour., 1987-90; contbr. articles to jours. in field. Bd. dirs. D.C. Water and Sewer Authority, 2006—. Recipient Environ. Leadership award Nat. Sanitation Found., Ann Arbor, 1988, Donald R. Boyd award Assn. Met. Water Agys., 1990; named Meritorious Exec., Pres. US, 1983, Outstanding Alumnus U. Toledo, 2009, Nat. Environment Agy. Singapore, 2007-. Mem. Internat. Desalination Assn., Am. Chem Soc., Am. Water Works Assn. (hon. life), InterAm. Assn. Sanitary and Environ. Engrng. (dir. at large 2000-02, v.p. 2003, pres. 2007-08). Roman Catholic. Avocations: woodworking, light construction. Office Phone: 202-362-3076. Personal E-mail: joseph.cotruvo@verizon.net.

COTTAM, HOWARD B., chemist; b. Kanab, Utah, July 13, 1952; BS, Ariz. State U., 1977; PhD, Brigham Young U., 1983. Head, immunochemistry ICN Nucleic Acid Inst., 1985—90; project medicinal chemist U. Calif., San Diego, 1990—. Bd. dirs. Immune Modulation Inc., 1995—2011. Mem.: Am. Chem. Soc. Avocations: trombone, golf. Office: Moores UCSD Cancer Ctr 3855 Health Scis Dr 901 La Jolla CA 92093-0820 Office Fax: 858-534-5399. Business E-Mail: hcottam@ucsd.edu.

COTTEN, ANNIE LAURA, psychologist, educator; b. Oxford, NC, Nov. 18, 1923; d. Leonard F. and Laura Estelle (Spencer) Cotten; children: Hollis W., Rebecca Ann, Laura Cotten. Diploma, Hardbarger Bus. Coll., 1944; AB, Duke U., 1945; MEd, U. Hartford, Conn., 1965; PhD, The Union Inst., 1979. Diplomate Am. Bd. Sexology, lic. Am. Assn. Marriage & Family Therapists, 1987. Asst. to pres. So. Meth. U., 1953; rsch. asst. Duke U., 1947-49; exec. sec. Ohio Wesleyan U., 1955-56, Conn. Coun. Chs., 1958-60; adj. prof. U. Hartford, 1976-78, 1976-78; clin. pastoral counselor Hartford Hosp., 1962-65; asst., then assoc. dir. social svcs. Hartford Conf. Chs., 1965-67; tchg. fellow U. NC, 1970-71; assoc. prof. Ctrl. Conn. State U., New Britain, 1967-93, adj. prof., 1994—2002. Adj. prof. St. Joseph Coll., 1986-96; clin. intern Montefiore Med. Ctr., 1995; dir. elderhostel programs Ctrl. Conn. State U., 1989-93, organizer ctr. adult learners, 1991-93; cons. Somers Correctional Ctr., Conn., 1980-81, instr./rschr., 1980-81; cons. Conn. Life Ins. Mktg. Rsch., 1981-1982; amb. to China, spring, 1986; presenter 3d Internat. Interdisciplinary Cong. on Women, 1987; vis. prof., scholar Duke U., 1989; adj. prof. health and human svcs. Ctrl. Ch. St. U., 1995-2002; vis. prof. Conn. Coll., New London, 1990; mem. clin. faculty, Am. Bd. Sexology, 1994; land developer NC Triangle, 1995—, presenter World Assn. Svc. Health SWeden, 2009, dept. com. AASECT, 2009-; presenter WHS, Sweden, 2009. Author: Comparisons of Gender Differences in Sexuality 1970s/1990s; cons. editor: Jour. Feminist Family Therapy, 2000—, reviewer: Contemporary Sexuality, 2003, Sexual and Relationship Jour., 2005. Fellow: Am. Acad. Clin. Sexologists (clin. faculty 1994—, founder), Nat. Coun. Family Rels.; mem.: APA (chair divsn. 1987—91), AASECT, Devel. Com., HASECT (devel. com. 2008—), Soc. Sci. Study of Sexuality (presenter ann. meeting 2003), Conn. Assn. Marital and Family Therapists (clin.) (bd. dirs. 2000—02, 2007), Sex Info. and Edn. Coun. of Conn. (bd. dirs. 1994—2002, Human Sexuality Leader of Yr. 1997), Conn. Psychol. Assn., Am. Assn. Sex Educators Counselors and Therapists (sex therapy cert. com. 2005, supr. sex therapy 2005—, Disting. Svc. award 1998), Hartford Women's Network. Personal E-mail: anniecotten@nc.rr.com.

COTTER, JOHN BURLEY, ophthalmologist; b. Zanesville, Ohio, Sept. 14, 1946; s. John Burley and Evelyn Virginia (Ross) C.; m. Perrine Abauzit, Aug. 17, 1977; children: Neils John, Jeremy Pierre. BA, U. Kans., 1968; med. degree, U. Kans., Kansas City, 1968-72. Ophthalmology resident U. Mo., Kansas City, 1976-79; family practice Ashland Hosp., Kans., 1973-74; emergency room physician Providence-St. Margaret Hosp., Kansas City, Kans., 1974-75; family orthopedic practice Mountain Med. Assocs., Vail, Colo., 1975-76; ophthalmologist, pvt. practice Duluth, Minn., 1979-82; surgeon-chief out-patient clinic King Khaled Eye Specialist Hosp., Riyadh, Saudi Arabia, 1983-90, mem. exec. com., 1985-90; asst. clin. prof. King Saud U., Riyadh, Saudi Arabia, 1985-90; corneal splst., refractive surgeon in assn. Greensboro, NC, 1990—2006; corneal sugeon San Luis Obispo, Calif., 2006—. Seminar chmn. Status of Refractive Surgery, Riyadh, 1986; active Nat. Survey Eye Disease and Ea. Province Survey Coun., Saudi Arabia, 1984, 90; assoc. med. dir. NC Eye Bank, 2004—, adj. asst. prof. Dept. Family Med. U. NC Sch. Med., 2005—. Author: (booklet) Radial Keratotomy, 1986; contbr. articles to profl. jours. Rsch. grantee Contact Lens Assn. of Ophthalmology, 1981, Lasers Steering Com. King Khalid Eye Hosp. at Hosp. Hotel Dieu, Paris, 1988; ORBIS fellow Baylor U., Houston, 1982. Fellow Am. Acad. Ophthalmology; mem. AMA, Internat. Assn. Ocular Surgeons, Internat. Soc. Refractive Keratoplasty, Societe Francaise D'Ophthalmologie, Saudi Ophthalmologist Soc., Am. Soc. Cataract and Refractive Surgery. Avocations: wind surfing, scuba diving, hiking, math games. Office: 1270 Peach St San Luis Obispo CA 93401 Office Phone: 805-541-1342. Personal E-mail: cotterjbc@yahoo.com.

COTTON, ROBIN T., pediatric otolaryngologist, surgeon; b. Manchester, Eng., May 13, 1941; arrived in USA, 1972; m. Cindi Fitton; 1 child, Colin; children from previous marriage: Sian, Sally, Stephanie, Stephen. Student, U. Cambridge, Eng., 1959-62; MB, BChir, U. Cambridge, 1965, MA, 1966; student, U. Birmingham, Eng., 1962-65. Diplomate Am. Bd. Otolaryngology, 1972. Intern United Birmingham Hosps., England, 1965-66, gen. surgery resident, 1966-68; otolaryngology resident U. Toronto, Canada, 1968-71, otolaryngology fellow, 1971-72; head and neck fellow U. Cin., 1972-73; prof., dir. pediat. otolaryngology head and neck surgery Children's Hosp. Med. Ctr., Cin., 1973—, dir., aerodigestive and sleep ctr. Lectr. in field. Contbr. articles to profl. jours., chapters to books; mem. editl. bd.: Archives of Otolaryngology, mem. internat. adv. bd.: Saudi Jour. Otolaryngology and Head and Neck Surgery, editl. advisor: Internat. Jour. Pediatric Otolaryngology, The Laryngoscope, Jour. Respiratory Diseases, Otolaryngology-Head and Neck Surgery, Jour. Otolaryngology, Am. Jour. Otolaryngology, Annals Otology, Rhinology and Laryngology, Head and Neck Surgery, Cleft Palate Jour., examiner: Am. Bd. Otolaryngology, 1979, 1998—99. Program chair Cin. Soc. Otolaryngology and Maxillofacial Plastic Surgery, 1979—; US del. European Working Group in Pediatric Otolaryngology, 1981—; adv. bd. Ronald McDonald House, 2001—. Recipient Harris P. Mosher award, 1991, Friend of Children PTA award, 2002, deRoaldes award, 2003, Karl Storz award, 2004, Chevalier Jackson award, 2004, Ronald McDonald Lifetime Achievement award, 2004, Robert Ruben award, SENTAC, 2005, Presdl. award, 2006, Health-care Care Hero Innovator Winner award, Cin. Bus. Courier, 2005, Bruce Benjamin award, 2005, James Yearsley medal, 2005; named to Best Doctors in America, 2002—08, Cin. Top Doctors, 2002—07. Fellow: ACS, Royal Coll. Surgeons, Can., Am. Acad. Pediat., Pediatric Otolaryngology and Bronchoesophagology Sect. (assoc.); mem.: AMA, ACS, Ohio Chpt., Am. Acad. Facial Plastic and Reconstructive Surgery (mem. cleft lip and palate com. 1988—), Am. Acad. Otolaryngology, Head and Neck Surgery, Am. Broncho-Esophagol. Assn. (bd. govs. 1988—), Am. Cleft Palate Assn., Am. Head & Neck Soc., Assn. Rsch. in Otolaryngology, Brit. Med. Assn., Butler County Med. Soc., Can. Otolaryngol. Assn., Cin. Acad. Medicine, Cin. Soc. Otolaryngology and Head and Neck Surgery, Internat. Assn. Dento-Facial Abnormalities, Ohio State Med. Assn., Pan Am. Otolaryngology Assn., Royal Coll. Physicians and Surgeons, Can., Royal Soc. Medicine, Soc. Ear, Nose and Throat Advances in Children, Southwestern Ohio Speech and Hearing Assn. (hon.), Soc. Univ. Otolaryngologists, Am. Soc. Laser Medicine and Surgery, Am. Auditory Soc., Am. Soc. Pediatric Otolaryngology (chair nominating com. 1989—), Am. Laryngol. Rhinol. and Otol. Soc., Inc., Am. Laryngol. Assn., Brit. Assn. Paediatric Otolaryngology, European Soc. Pediatric Otorhinolaryngology. Office: Cin Childrens Hosp Med Ctr 3333 Burnet Ave Cincinnati OH 45229-3026 E-mail: robin.cotton@cchmc.org.

COTTON, SUE MAREE, psychologist, researcher; b. Preston, Australia, Feb. 20, 1971; MS in Applied Sci., Swinburne U. Tech., 2002; PhD, La Trobe U., 2007. Prin. rsch. fellow, Ronald Phillip Griffith fellow Orygen Youth Health Rsch. Ctr., U. Melbourne, 2002—. Recipient Dean's TNT Internat. Mail award, La Trobe U., Westpac Banking award. Mem.: Australasian Soc. Psychiat. Rsch., Internat. Early Psychosis Assn., Schizophrenia Internat. Rsch. Soc., Australian Psychol. Soc. (Early Career Rsch. award). Office: Locked Bag 10 35 Poplar Rd Parkville Victoria 3052 Australia Office Fax: 6193422941. Business E-Mail: smcotton@unimelb.edu.au.

COTTON, WILLIAM ROBERT, retired dentist; b. Miami, Fla., Nov. 29, 1931; s. Robert Lee and Mamie Bell (Daniel) Cotton; m. Marye Ruth Hartz; children: Caroline Ruth Vance, William Robert Jr., David Michael, Lynn Cathryn Tavel. DDS, U. Md., 1955; MS, Northwestern U., Chgo., 1963; MA, Roosevelt U., 1973; EdS, George Washington U., 1980. With USN, 1955-81, commd. capt., 1973, ret., 1981; asst. dental officer Marine Corps Schs. and USS F.D. Roosevelt CVA 42, Quantico, Va. and Mayport, Fla., 1957-61; head exptl. pathology div. Naval Med. Rsch. Inst., Bethesda, Md., 1963-67; dental officer USS Fulton AS-11, New London, Conn., 1967-69; chief histopathology div. Naval Dental Rsch. Inst., Great Lakes, Ill., 1969-72, exec. officer, 1972-73, dep. comdg. officer, 1973-76; chmn. dental scis. dept. Naval Med. Rsch. Inst., Bethesda, Md., 1976-79; dir. Casualty Care Rsch. Program Ctr., Naval Med. Rsch. Inst., Bethesda, Md., 1979-81; assoc. prof. dept. operative dentistry Temple U., Phila., 1981-83; prof., chmn. dept. operative dentistry Georgetown U., Washington, 1983-90; pvt. practice Rockville, Md.; ret., 1999; dentist Mission of Mercy, Frederick, Md., 2001—. Adv. com. dental tech. program So. Ill. U., Carbondale, 1976—85; cons. Naval Dental Rsch. Inst., Great Lakes, 1981—85, Dentsply Internat., York, Pa., 1984—88; mem. spl. study sect. NIH, Washington, 1984, Washington, 87; clin. dentist Mission of Mercy, Brunswick, Md., 2001—; adj. clin. prof. dept. restorative dentistry U. Md. Dental Sch., Balt., 2004—. Contbg. author: book Biology Dental Caires, 1968, Dental Clinics of North America, 1986, editl. bd.: Jour. Dental Rsch., 1976—86, 1988, Jour. Operative Dentistry, 1986—92. Elder Presbyn. Ch. Fellow: Internat. Coll. Dentists (life), Am. Coll. Dentists (life); mem.: ADA (life), D.C. Dental Soc. (life; bd. dirs. 1986—89). Democrat. Home: 11816 Winterset Ter Potomac MD 20854-2846 Personal E-mail: wmrc@comcast.net.

COUCH, DANIEL MICHAEL, healthcare executive; b. Chgo., July 1, 1937; s. Arthur Daniel and Helen Margret (Kreamer) C.; m. Marilee Hermon, Sept. 12, 1958; children: Laura Ann, Mark Allen, Kristina Lynn, Michelle Louise, Daniel Michael Jr. BS in Bus., Ind. U., 1958; MBA, Butler U., 1977. Field examiner Ind. State Bd. Accounts, Indpls., 1959-61; controller Community Hosp., Anderson, Ind., 1961-67; field rep. Am. Hosp. Assn., Chgo., 1967-68; treas./controller Health & Hosp. Corp. of Marion County, Indpls., 1968-71; assoc. adminstr. Winona Meml. Hosp., Indpls., 1971-78; pres. Huntington (Ind.) Meml. Hosp., 1978-80; dep. exec. dir. Truman Med. Ctr., Kansas City, Mo., 1980-99; CFO Health Care Found. Greater Kansas City, 2005—07. Bd. dirs. Nat. Pub. Health and Hosp. Inst., Washington, 1987-90, chmn., 1989. Bd. dirs, mem. exec. com. Labor-Mgmt. Coun., Kansas City, Mo., 1982—2006, co-chmn, 1991—97; bd. dirs. Greater Kansas City Mental Health Found., 1984—93, pres., 1992—93; bd. dirs. Kansas City Care Ctr., 1990—, treas., 1999—2008; bd. dirs. Resource Devel. Inst., Kansas City, 1998—2005, pres., 2002—04; bd. dirs. Vis. Nurse Home Care Svcs., Kansas City, 1991—98, chmn., 1993—98; bd. dirs. The Greater Kansas City Healthcare Found., 2003—05, 2009—, Support KC, 2008—09; treas. Six-State Rally Assn., 2010—11. 1st lt. USAR, 1958—67. Fellow Am. Coll. Healthcare Execs. (life fellow, nominating com. 1995-99); mem. Am. Hosp. Assn. (ho. of dels. and Regional Policy Bd. 7 1989-92, governing coun. sect. met. hosps. 1990-93, chmn. 1993), Nat. Assn. Pub. Hosps. (bd. dirs. 1981-99, chmn. 1989), Kansas City Area Hosp. Assn. (bd. dirs. 1990-96), Greater Kansas City C. of C. (various coms. 1985-99), Healthcare Fin. Mgmt. Assn. (advanced), Kansas City Care Network (bd. dirs. 1995-99, pres. 1995-99), Family Health Ptnrs. (bd. dirs. 1995-99), Masons, Rotary. Episcopalian. Avocations: golf, bowling, reading. Personal E-mail: danmcouch@gmail.com.

COUCH, DEBORAH LYNN, psychiatrist, educator; MD, U. Wis., Madison, 1980. Lic. Ill., 1983, diplomate Am. Bd. Psychiatry and Neurology-psychiatry, 2005. Resident psychiatry Loyola Univ. Med. Ctr., Maywood, Ill., 1981—85, hospital affiliations includes; asst. clin. prof. psychiatry Strict Sch. Medicine Loyola Univ. Chgo. Office: Loyola University Chicago Strict School of Medicine 2160 S First Ave Bldg 54 Maywood IL 60153 Office Phone: 708-216-3750.

COUCH, ROBERT BARNARD, physician, scientist, microbiologist, educator; b. Guntersville, Ala., Sept. 25, 1930; s. Ezekiel Harvey and Frances Jane (Barnard) C.; m. Katherine Frances Klein, Apr. 23, 1955; children: Robert Steven, Leslie Ann, Colleen Frances, Elizabeth Lee. BA, Vanderbilt U., 1952, MD, 1956. Diplomate Am. Bd. Internal Medicine. Intern Vanderbilt U. Hosp., Nashville, 1956—57, resident in medicine, 1959—60, chief resident in medicine, 1960—61; clin. assoc. NIH, Washington, 1957—59, sr. investigator, 1961—65, head clin. virology sect., 1965—66; assoc. prof. Baylor Coll. Medicine, Houston, 1966—71, prof. microbiology, immunology and medicine, 1971—2000, Disting. prof., 1995—, head infectious diseases sect. medicine, 1987—92, chmn. dept. microbiology and immunology, 1989—2000, dir. influenza rsch. ctr., 1974—91, dir. acute viral respiratory diseases unit, 1991—96, dir. respiratory pathogens rsch. unit, 1996—, dir. Ctr. for Infection and Immunity Rsch., 1999—, prof. molecular virology, microbiology and medicine, 2000—. Mem. rsch. rev. panels infectious diseases; cons. NIH, Dept. Def., FDA, various others. Contbr. articles to profl. jours. Served to sr. surgeon USPHS, 1957-66. Mem. ACP, AAAS, Soc. Exptl. Biology and Medicine, Am. Soc. Microbiology, Infectious Diseases Soc. Am., Am. Assn. Immunologists, Am. Fedn. Clin. Rsch., Am. Soc. Clin. Investigation, So. Soc. Clin. Investigation, Am. Assn. Physicians, Am. Soc. Epidemiology, Am. Soc. Virology. Office: Baylor Coll Medicine MS 280 One Baylor Plaza Houston TX 77030 Office Phone: 713-798-4474. Business E-Mail: rcouch@bcm.edu.

COUCH, SANDRA LUAN, medical/surgical nurse, nursing administrator; b. Burlington, Iowa, Apr. 27, 1956; d. Virgil David and Arlene Lois Couch. BS in Edn., Ill. State U., 1978; BSN, St. Francis Med. Ctr. Coll. Nursing, Peoria, Ill., 1989; completed tng. as legal nurse cons., Joliet Jr. Coll., 2004. RN Ill., cert. CPR instr., EMT, CPDN, PICC, PALS, ACLS, BTLS. Tchr., coach Pekin and Morton Sch. Dists., Ill., 1977—91; RN St. Francis Med. Ctr., Peoria, Ill., 1989—91, Loyola U. Med. Ctr., Maywood, Ill., 1991—92, Sherman Hosp., Elgin, Ill., 1993—97; RN, supr. Stateville Penitentiary Ill. Dept. Corrections, Joliet, Ill., 1997—2001, RN DuPage County Jail, 2001, RN Ill. Youth Ctr.-Warrenville, 2002—04; risk mgmt. nurse RSA Med., Naperville, Ill., 2004; nursing supr. Will County Adult Detention Facility, Joliet, 2005—; nurse Cmty. Nursing and Rahab., Napervilie, 2007. Swim instr., lifeguard YMCA/YWCA, Peoria, 1982—91; instr. ARC, Peoria, Pekin, 1973—93; substitute tchr. Naperville Sch. Dist., 1992—; vol. EMT Tremont Rescue 702, Ill., 1982—91, Peoria County Fair, 1983—93; nurse Maxim Staffing Solutions, Oak Pk., 2007—, Temps Inc., 2007—, Brightstar Health Care, Naperville, 2008—, Nurse Staffing, Oak Pk., 2008—. Supr., leader Pioneer Girls, Naperville, 1993, 1994; tchr. Peoria South Side Mission, 1988—91; vol. Naperville Police Dept. Cmty. Radio Watch, 2005—. Mem.: Windridge Naperville Condominium Assn (bd. dirs., sec. 2006—08, bd. dirs., treas. 2011—). Democrat. Avocations: canoeing, swimming, Norman Rockwell collectibles & art, outdoor activities, football. Home: 2903 Bartlett Ct # 201 Naperville IL 60564 Personal E-mail: sndrcch@yahoo.com.

COUDERT, JEAN, physiologist, researcher; b. Saint Alyre d'Arlanc, France, Nov. 16, 1934; s. Paul Coudert and Marie Louise Cartier; m. Jean Coudert, Sept. 18, 1959; children: Yves, Laurent. Asst. physiology Med. Faculty, Paris, 1958—62, co-dir. high altitude biology inst. La Paz, Bolivia, 1968—75. Prof. physiology and dir. lab. Med. Faculty, St. Etienne and Clermont-Ferrand, France, 1975—2002. Pres. of comité contre les maladies respiratoires Comité, Clermont-Ferrand, 2002—07. Recipient Bronz medal, Ministére Jeunesse Et Sport. Fellow: European Coll. Sport Scis. (pres. 2002—). Roman Catholic. Avocations: tennis, literature. Home: 15 Chemin de Mosset Manson Auvergne Saint Genes Champanelle 63122 France Office: Faculté de Médecine 28 Place Henri Dunant Clermont-Ferrand 63001 France Home Phone: 33473358618; Office Phone: 33473178221. Office Fax: 33473448319; Home Fax: 33473448319. Personal E-mail: coudertjean@wanadoo.fr. Business E-Mail: physio.sport@u-clermont1.fr.

COUGHLAN, GARY PATRICK, pharmaceutical executive; b. Fresno, Calif., Feb. 14, 1944; s. Edward Patrick and Elizabeth Claire (Ryan) C.; m. Mary Cary Kelley, Dec. 21, 1967; children: Christopher, Sarah, Laura, Claire, Moira. BA, St. Mary's Coll., 1966; MA in Econs., UCLA, 1967; MBA, Wayne State U., 1971. Sr. fin. analyst Burroughs Corp., Detroit, 1969-72; with Dart Industries, LA, 1972-81, group v.p. field services, 1978-81, v.p. ops. services, 1981, Dart & Kraft Inc., Northbrook, Ill., 1981-82, v.p. fin., contr., 1984-85, sr. v.p. fin. affairs, 1985-86, sr. v.p., CFO, 1986; v.p. fin. retail food group Kraft Inc., Glenview, Ill., 1982-84, sr. v.p., CFO, 1986-88; sr. v.p. fin. Kraft Gen. Foods, Glenview, 1989-90; sr. v.p. fin., CFO Abbott Labs., Abbott Park, Ill., 1990-2001, ret., 2001. Instr. prof. fin. ext. program UCLA, 1974—80; bd. dirs. VISA Inc., San Francisco, Chgo. Hort. Soc., Glencoe, Ill.; mem. adv. coun. Coun. Fgn. Rels., Chgo. Com. Mem. Fin. Execs. Inst. Republican. Roman Catholic. Home: 1135 Central Rd Glenview IL 60025-4432 Office: Ste 306 1200 Central Ave Wilmette IL 60091 Office Phone: 847-920-1677. Personal E-mail: gcoughlan@earthlink.com.

COUGHLIN, FRANCIS RAYMOND, JR., surgeon, educator, lawyer; b. NYC, Feb. 22, 1927; s. Francis Raymond and Isabel (Archibald) C.; m. Barbara Ann Blunt, June 9, 1951; children: Hilary, Mary, Patricia, Christopher Francis, Geoffrey Blunt, Daniel Taylor, Isabel, David Carleton. BS, Fordham U., Bronx, NY, 1948; MD, Yale U., New Haven, Conn., 1952; MS, McGill U., Montreal, Que., Can., 1955, diploma in surgery, 1959; JD, Quinnipiac U., Conn., 1988. Bar: N.Y., Conn., D.C., U.S. Supreme Ct.; diplomate Am. Bd. Surgery, Am. Bd. Thoracic Surgery; pharmacist-purser, US Merchant Marines 1945-46; Cold War. Intern N.Y. Hosp., NYC, 1952-53; resident McGill U. Teaching Hosp., Montreal, 1953-57, Overholt Thoracic Clin., Boston, 1958-60; mem. staff Stamford (Conn.) Hosp., 1960—; practice medicine specializing in thoracic surgery Stamford, 1960—88; medico-legal cons., 1988—. Dir. thoracic and vascular surgery St. Josephs Hosp., Stamford, 1970-73, 80-85, assoc. chief surgery, 1971-73, chief surgery, 1973-77; assoc. prof. clin. surgery N.Y. Med. Coll., 1981-; mem. staff Norwalk Hosp., 1965-89; vice chair Conn. State Commn. Medicolegal Investigations, 1990-2002. With U.S. Maritime Svc., 1945-46. Recipient Encaenia award Fordham U., NYC, 1958, Cold War Commendation Cert., US Dept. Def.; Teaching fellow Harvard U., 1958. Fellow ACS (sec.-treas. Conn. chpt. 1966-70), Royal Coll. Surgeons (Can.), Am. Coll. Cardiology, Am. Coll. Chest Physicians, Royal Soc. Medicine; mem. Soc. Thoracic Surgeons (founding mem.), NY Acad. Medicine, Conn. Heart Assn. (dir. 1961-64), Conn. Lung Assn. (dir. and exec. com. 1963-69, v.p. 1967-69), Lung Assn. So. Fairfield County (pres. 1963-68, dir. 1960-70), Soc. Med. Jurisprudence (v.p. 1992-93, pres. 1995-97), English-Speaking Union, Scottish-Am. Found., Can. Soc. NY, Yale Club NY, Army Navy Club (Washington), Defense Orientation Conf. Assoc., Washington, Yale Med. Sch. Alumni Assn. (v.p. 1999-01, pres. 2001-03, Disting. Alumni Svc. award 2006, trustee Yale Med. Sch. Whitney Cushing Libr. 2004-08), AMA, Mass. Med. Soc., Ct. Med. Assn. Republican. Office: 20 Mead St New Canaan CT 06840-5701

COUGHLIN, SHAUN R., research scientist, medical professor; BS, MS, MIT, 1976, PhD, 1981; MD, Harvard Med. Sch., 1982. Intern, resident Mass. Gen. Hosp., 1982—84; postdoc. asst. rsch. cardiologist, clin. fellow Cardiovasc. Rsch. Inst., U. Calif., San Francisco, 1984—86; dir. Cardiovascular Rsch. Inst., U. Calif., 1997—; asst. prof. U. Calif., San Francisco, 1986—91, assoc. prof., 1991—96, prof. medicine, 1996—, prof. cellular & molecular pharmacology, 1997—. Recipient Jeffrey M. Hoeg award, Am. Heart Assn., 2000, Bristol-Myers Squibb award for disting. achievement in cardiovasc. rsch., 2004. Mem.: NAS, Inst. Medicine. Office: UCSF Dept Biopharm Scis Box 2240 Genentech Hall Rm S 472D San Francisco CA 94143 Office Phone: 415-476-6174. Office Fax: 415-476-8173. Business E-Mail: coughlin@cvrimail.ucsf.edu. *

COUKOS, GEORGE, gynecologic oncologist, educator; MD cum laude, U. Modena Sch. of Medicine, Modena, Italy, 1987; PhD in Reproductive Biology, U. Patras Sch. of Medicine, 1990. Diplomate Am. Bd. Ob-Gyn, 2002, Am. Bd. Ob-Gyn-gynecologic oncology, 2004. Intern Hosp. of the Univ, of Pa., resident ob-gyn, fellow gynecology oncology; rsch. fellow Mellon Found., 1991—93; prof. reproductive biology dept. of ob-gyn Univ. Pa. Sch. of Medicine; dir. gynecologic cancer rsch. Abramson Cancer Ctr. of the Univ. of Pa., Celso Ramon Garcia assoc. prof. divsn. of gynecologic oncology. Contbr. (publs.) Rapid isolation of high-affinity human antibodies against the tumor vascular marker Endosialin/TEM1, using a paired yeast-display/secretory scFv library platform., Jour. of Immunological Methods, Clinical predictors of bevacizumab-associated gastrointestinal perforation., Identification of MicroRNAs Regulating Reprogramming Factor LIN28 in Embryonic Stem Cells and Cancer Cells., The Jour. of Biol. Chemistry, Double-negative feedback loop between reprogramming factor LIN28 and microRNA let-7 regulates aldehyde dehydrogenase 1-positive cancer stem cells., Angiogenesis and the Tumor Vasculature as Antitumor Immune Modulators: The Role of Vascular Endothelial Growth Factor and Endothelin., and numerous others. Recipient 1st Rsch. prize, Phila. Area Reproductive Endocrinology Soc., 1997, Phillip F. Williams prize, Dist. III Am. Coll. of Ob-Gyn, 1997, Glaxo-Wellcome Oncology Clin. Rsch. Scholar award, Am. Assn. for Cancer Rsch., 1998, 1st prize "Virus Vectors and Gene Therapy" Sect., 23rd Internat. Herpes Virus Workshop, 1998, Basic Sci. award, Berlex Found., 2000, Bristol Meyers Immunology Oncology award, Gynecologic Cancer Found., 2001, Greenfield award for "Excellence in Ovarian Cancer Rsch., 2005, Sydney-Kimmel Scholar award, Ovarian Cancer Rsch. Fund, 2002, Liz Tiberis award, 2003, Judah Folkman award, Alliance for Cancer Gene Therapy, 2006, Sir William Osler award for Excellence in Patient Oriented Rsch., Univ. Pa., 2006, Crystal Ball Phila. award for Rsch. Achievement in Ovarian Cancer, 2007; scholar, Am. Assoc. of Ob-Gyn Founds., 2000; Mellon Found Rsch. Fellow, 1991—93, American Assoc. of Ob-gyn. Found. Scholar, 2000. Office: Hospital of the University of Pennsylvania 3400 Spruce St Philadelphia PA 19104 Office Phone: 215-662-4000. E-mail: gcks@mail.med.upenn.edu.

COUNILLON, LAURENT, science educator; b. Neuilly sur Seine, July 1, 1966; PhD, U. Nice-Sophia Antipolis, 1993, HDR, 1997. Prof. U. Nice-Sophia Antipolis, 2003—. Office: Parc Valrose Nice 06108 France Business E-Mail: laurent.counillon@unice.fr.

COUPEY, SUSAN MCGUIRE, pediatrician, educator; b. Montreal, Que., Can., June 29, 1942; came to U.S., 1978; d. Clarence Herbert and Paulette (Lefevre) McGuire; m. Pierre M.L. Coupey, July 1964 (div. 1981); children: Marc M.R., Ariane S.; m. James R. English III, Nov. 23, 1988. BA, Queen's U., Kingston, Ont., Can., 1962; postgrad., McGill U., Montreal, 1962-63; MD, U. B.C., Vancouver, Can., 1975. Diplomate Am. Bd. Pediatrics, subboard in adolescent medicine. Devel. chemist Merck, Sharp & Dohme, Ltd., Montreal, 1963-64; rotating intern Montreal Gen. Hosp., 1975-76; resident in pediatrics Montreal Children's Hosp., 1976-78; fellow in adolescent medicine Montefiore Med. Ctr., Bronx, NY, 1978-79, attending pediatrician, 1980—; rsch. asst. Cancer Rsch. Ctr., U. B.C., 1967-72; instr., asst. prof. pediatrics Albert Einstein Coll. Medicine, Bronx, 1979-85, assoc. prof., 1985-93, prof., 1993—, assoc. dir. div. adolescent medicine, 1984—2001, course dir. introduction to clin. medicine, 1989—2007, mem. faculty senate, 1983-84, 88-90, co-chair divsn. edn., 2000—07, chief adolescent medicine, 2002—. Attending pediatrician North Ctrl. Bronx Hosp., 1979-97; cons. in adolescent medicine Flushing (N.Y.) Hosp. and Med. Ctr., 1982-96; Maricopa-Pima vis. prof. U. Ariz., 1989; vis. prof. Children's Hosp. Ea. Ont., U. Ottawa and Ea. Can. chpt. Soc. for Adolescent Medicine, 1990; vis. prof. Philippine Children's Med. Ctr., U. Philippines Coll. of Medicine, 1997; chmn. health svcs. adv. com. Children's Aid Soc., 1985—, bd. trustees, 1993—; mem. adv. bd. Office Substance Abuse Ministry, Archdiocese of N.Y., 1983-85; spkr. Hosp. Italiano, Buenos Aires, Argentina, 1999, Israeli Soc. Adolescent Medicine, Jeruseleum, Israel, 2000, Greek Soc. Adolescent Med., Athens, Greece, 2000. Editor: Primary Care of Adolescent Girls, 2000; assoc. editor Adolescent Medicine Clinics, 1990—2008; assoc. editor Jour. Devel. & Behavioral Pediatrics, 1992-96, editl. bd., 1996-00; assoc. editor Jour. Pediat. & Adolescent Gynecology, 1992-98, editl. bd. 1998—; editl. bd. Jour. of Youth and Adolescence, 1998-04; contbr. articles to med. jours., also chpts. to books and monographs. Fellow Am. Acad. Pediatrics (exec. com. sect. on adolescent health 1993-96, Adele Dellenbaugh Hofman award for excellence in adolescent health, 2005); mem. Soc. for Adolescent Medicine (nominations com. 1984-85, chmn. jour. adv. com. 1987-97, program com. 1991-93, awards com. 1992-95, bd. dirs. 1997-2000), Am. Pediat. Soc. (abstract review com. 1999—2001), Soc. for Behavioral Pediatrics, N.Am. Soc. Pediat. and Adolescent Gynecology (bd. dirs. 1993-96, sec. 1996-2001, chair publs. com. 1996-2001, pres.-elect 2001-02, pres. 2002-03), Sex Info. and Edn. Coun. U.S., Am. Acad. on Comm. in Healthcare, Albert Einstein Coll. Medicine Alumni Assn. (v.p. pediatrics 1983-84, pres. 1984-85), Alpha Omega Alpha (Kappa chpt. councilor, Harry F. Gordon award for outstanding clin. tchg. at Albert Einstein Coll. Medicine, 2002). Office: Albert Einstein Coll Medicine Montefiore Med Ctr 111 E 210th St Bronx NY 10467-2401 Office Phone: 718-920-6781. Business E-Mail: scoupey@montefiore.org.

COURCOULAS, ANITA PAULINE, surgeon; b. Buffalo, Aug. 10, 1961; d. John H. and Tena (Leonidas) C. BS, Brown U., 1983; MD, Boston U., 1988; MPH, U. Pitts., 1993. Lic. physician, Pa. Resident in surgery U. Pitts., 1988-95, fellow in pediat. surgery, 1995-96, rschr. in epidemiology and outcomes, 1992—. Contbr. articles to profl. jours., chpts. to books. Home: 5222 Wilkins Heights Rd Pittsburgh PA 15217 Office: 3380 Blvd Allies Ste 390 Pittsburgh PA 15213 Home Phone: 412-362-1002.

COUREY, MARK S., otolaryngologist, educator; BA magna cum laude, Boston U., Mass., 1983; MD, Sch. of Medicine and Biomedical Sciences SUNY, Buffalo, 1987. Diplomate Am. Bd. Otolaryngology, 1993. Resident gen. surgery Beth Israel Hosp., Boston, 1987—89; resident otolaryngology - head and neck surgery SUNY, Buffalo, 1989—92; fellow dept. of laryngology Vanderbilt Univ. Med. Ctr., Nashville, 1992—93; dir. Vanderbilt Voice Ctr.; dir. laryngology, med. dir. Univ. of Calif. San Francisco Voice and Swallowing Ctr.; prof. clin. otolaryngology Univ. of Calif. San Francisco Med. Ctr., 2004. Office: University of California San Francisco Voice and Swallowing Center 2330 Post St Fifth Fl San Francisco CA 94115 Office Phone: 415-885-7700. Office Fax: 415-885-7800.

COURTNAY, WILIAM GERARD, osteopathic physician; b. Guthrie, Okla., Aug. 22, 1962; s. Clarence Clive and Patricia Ann (Pike) C.; m. Sandra Louise Ferrell, June 4, 1994. BS, U. Ctrl. Okla., Edmond, 1986; DO, Okla. State U., Tulsa, 1994. Emergency dept. technician Midwest City (Okla.) Meml. Hosp., 1979-88; med. examiner investigator Office of Chief Med. Examiner, Oklahome City, 1988-90; intern Hillcrest Health Ctr., Oklahome City, 1994-95; physician in pvt. practice Moore, Okla., 1995—. Vol. med. examiner Office of Chief Med. Examiner, Oklahoma City, 1995; dir. Mercy Health Network. Mem. AMA, Am. Osteo. Assn., Grady County Med. Soc. Republican. Roman Catholic. Avocations: percussion/music, woodworking, forensic sciences.

COURY, ROBERT J., pharmaceutical executive; BS in Indsl. Engrng., U. Pitts., 1984. Founder, CEO, prin. owner Coury Cons., L.P., Pitts., 1989—2002; dir., vice-chmn. of bd., CEO Mylan Labs Inc., Canonsburg, Pa., 2002—09; chmn., CEO Mylan Laboratories, Canonsburg, Pa., 2009—. Mem. Allegheny Conference on Community Develop. Office: Mylan Labs Inc 1500 Corp Dr Ste 400 Canonsburg PA 15317 Office Phone: 724-514-1800. *

COUSER, WILLIAM GRIFFITH, nephrologist, academic administrator, educator; b. Lebanon, NH, July 11, 1939; s. Thomas Clifford and Winifred Priscilla (Ham) C. BA, Harvard U., 1961, MD, 1965; BMS, Dartmouth Med. Sch., 1963. Diplomate Am. Bd. Internal Medicine. Intern Moffitt Hosp./U. Calif. Med. Ctr., San Francisco, 1965-66, 66-67; resident Boston City Hosp., 1969-70; asst. prof. medicine U. Chgo., 1972-73; asst. prof. Boston U., 1972-77, assoc. prof., 1977-82; prof., head divsn. nephrology U. Wash., Seattle, 1982—2002, Belding Scribner prof. medicine, 1995—2004, affiliate prof. medicine, 2004—. Mem. sci. adv. bd. Kidney Found. Mass., Boston, 1974—82, mem. rsch. grant com. Nat. Kidney Found., NYC, 1981—86; mem. rev. bd. for nephrology VA, Washington, 1981—84; mem. exec. com. Coun. on Kidney in Cardiovasc. Disease, Am. Heart Assn., Dallas, 1982—85; mem. pathology A study sect. NIH, chmn., 1988—89; subsplty. bd. in nephrology Am. Bd. Internal Medicine, 1988—92; dir. George M. O'Brien Kidney Rsch. Ctr. U. Wash., 1993—2003. Co-editor: Immunologic Renal Diseases, 1997, 2d edit. 2001; contbr. numerous articles, chpts., abstracts to profl. publs.; mem. editl. bd. Kidney Internat., 1982-96, Am. Jour. Kidney Diseases, Am. Jour. Nephrology, Jour. Am. Soc. Nephrology, editor-in-chief, 2001-07. Served to capt. U.S. Army, 1967-69, Vietnam. Recipient Purple Heart, Bronze Star awards, Rsch. Career Devel. award NIH, 1975-80, Method to Extend Rsch. in Time award, 1991-97; fellow Nat. Kidney Found., 1971, David Hume award, 2007, NIH, 1973; grantee, 1974-2004. Fellow: ACP, AAAS, Am. Heart Assn., Royal Coll. Physicians, Western Assn. Physicians (cons.), Internat. Soc. Nephrology (coun. 1999, v.p. 2001—03, exec. com. mem. 2001—, pres.-elect 2003—05, pres. 2005—07, chmn. global outreach programs 2007—), Am. Soc. Nephrology (coun. 1991—98, pres. 1996), Am. Assn. Physicians, Am. Soc. Clin. Investigation (v.p. 1983—84). Mailing: 16050 169th Ave NE Woodinville WA 98072 Business E-Mail: wgc@u.washington.edu.

COUSINS, SCOTT WILLIAM, ophthalmologist, educator; b. Ohio, Feb. 27, 1955; AB, Dartmouth U., 1977; MD, Case Western Res. U., 1982. Prof. Bascom Palmer Eye Inst., 1988—2005; prof., vice chair rsch. Duke Eye Ctr., 2005—. Recipient Dolly Green Scholar award, Rsch. Prevent Blindness, 1994, Lew R. Wasserman Merit award, 2003, Clinician Scientist award, Alcon Rsch. Inst., 2006; Heed Ophthalmic Found. fellowship, 1986. Fellow: Assn. Rsch. Vision and Ophthalmology; mem.: Retina Soc., Am. Soc. Retina Specialists, Am. Assn. Immunologists, Am. Acad. Ophthalmology, Phi Beta Kappa. Office: Duke Eye Ctr 2351 Erwin Rd DUMC 3802 Durham NC 27705 Office Fax: 919-684-9016. Business E-Mail: scott.cousins@duke.edu.

COUTINHO, ERIDAN MEDEIROS, retired medical educator, medical researcher; b. Recife, Brazil, Aug. 7, 1931; d. Heli Cavalcanti Gomes and Maria Do Carmo De Medeiros Coutinho; children: Frederico Guilherme, Carlos Gustavo, Ronaldo Cesar. MD, Fed. U., Recife, 1954, M, 1974, PhD, 1997; splty. degree in pathology, Harvard U., Boston, 1958. Instr. pathology Fed. U., Recife, 1955—60, asst. prof., 1965—67, assoc. prof., 1970—76; asst. prof. State U., Recife, 1966—72; prof. Inst. Biol. Scis., Recife, 1976—82, Sch. Med. Scis., Recife, 1982—92. Dir. Aggeu Magalhaes Rsch. Ctr., Recife, 1993—97, sci. cons., 2002; sr. rschr. Oswaldo Cruz Found., Rio de Janeiro, 1987—2006, emeritus rschr., 2004; vis. prof. Fed. U. Bahia, 1978—90. Author: Bogliolo's Pathology, 1987; contbr. articles to profl. jours. Recipient Raul Leite award, Fed. U. Pernambuco, Recife, 1954, Carlos Chagas award, 1962, Maciel Monteiro medal, Med. Soc. Pernambuco, Recife, 1994. Mem.: Brazilian Soc. Tropical Medicine, Brazilian Soc. Pathology (emeritus), Internat. Acad. Pathology. Roman Catholic. Avocations: reading, photography. Office: Ctr Pesguisas Aggeu Magalhaes Campus da UFPE Recife Brazil Home: Rua Laurindo Coelho 52060-340 Recife PE Brazil

COVEN, ROGER A., obstetrician, gynecologist; Attended, U. Medicine and Dentistry Of NJ. Diplomate Am. Bd. Ob-Gyn. Resident Thomas Jefferson Univ. Hosp.; with Valley Hosp., Hackensack Univ. Med. Ctr. Office: Valley Hospital 223 N Van Dien Ave Ridgewood NJ 07450-2736 also: Hackensack University Medical Center 30 Prospect Ave Hackensack NJ 07601 Office Phone: 201-447-8000.

COVERT, DEREK F., insurance company executive; BA in Acctg., U. Akron, 1976, JD, 1981. CPA Calif. With tax division dept. Arthur Anderson and Co., San Francisco and Oakland; sr. v.p., gen. counsel Catholic Healthcare West, 1987—. Mem.: Calif. Soc. for Healthcare Attorneys (former bd. dir.), American Health Lawyers, Healthcare Financial Mgmt. Assn. (past bd. mem. Northern Calif. Chpt., founded and served as the first chairperson of the tax com.). Office: Catholic Healthcare West 185 Berry St Ste 300 San Francisco CA 94107 *

COVIN, THERON MICHAEL, psychotherapist; b. Repton, Ala., Feb. 27, 1947; s. Fisher Burt Covin and Doris (Salter) Knight; m. Charlotte R. Covin, June 13, 1981; children: Caroline, Michelle. MS, Troy State U., 1971; specialist in Edn., U. Ala., Tuscaloosa, 1973; EdD, U. Sarasota, Fla., 1975. Diplomate Am. Bd. Med. Psychotherapists. Instr. psychology Troy (Ala.) State U., 1971-75, Lomax Hannon Jr. Coll., Greeville, Ala., 1975-78; asst. prof. Auburn U., Montgomery, Ala., 1978-80; staff psychologist S.E. Ala. Youth Svcs., Dothan, Ala., 1978-81; with Ctr. for Counseling and Human Devel., Ozark, Ala., 1981—. Contbr. articles to profl. jours. Mem. Am. Counseling Assn., Am. Assn. Family and Marriage Therapy, Rotary (Paul Harris fellow 1987). Office: 191 Katherine Ave Ozark AL 36360-1976

COWAN, DALE HARVEY, internist, lawyer; b. Cleve., Jan. 25, 1938; s. Milton Jerome and Clara (Umans) C.; m. Deborah Wolowitz, Jan. 28, 1967 (div. Aug. 1, 2008); children: Rachel, Morris Benjamin, William Ezra; m. Susan Henderson, June 20, 2009. AB, Harvard U., Cambridge, Mass., 1959, MD, 1963; JD, Case Western Res. U., Cleve., 1981. Diplomate Am. Bd. Internal Medicine with subspecialty cert. in hematology and med. oncology. Bar: Ohio 1981. Intern Cleve. Met. Gen. Hosp., 1963-64, resident, 1964-65, 67-70; practice medicine specializing in internal medicine, hematology and oncology; dir. hematology and oncology Marymount Hosp., Cleve., 1982-2001; asst. prof. medicine Case Western Res. U., Cleve., 1970-75, assoc. prof., 1975-84, clin. prof. environ. health scis., 1985—; assoc. Health Sys. Mgmt. Ctr., 1982-90; of counsel Burke, Haber & Berick, 1984-86; pres. med. staff Parma Cmty. Gen. Hosp., Ohio, 1997-98; med. dir. Cmty. Oncology Group Cleve. Clinic Found., Cleve., 1999—2006; dir. dept. regional oncology Cleve. Clinic Cancer Ctr., 2006—07; 2010sr. med. dir. Oncol Aleve Med., 2009—10. Spl. cons. President's Commn. on Bioethics, Washington, 1981-82; nat. adv. coun. Nat. Heart Lung and Blood Inst., Bethesda, Md., 1982-85. Author: Preferred Provider Organizations, 1984; co-editor: Human Organ Transplantation, 1987; contbr. articles to profl. jours. Bd. dirs. Bur. Jewish Edn., 1977-87, Northeast Ohio affiliate Am. Heart Assn., 1982-86; pres Ohio/W.Va. Oncology Soc., 1990-94; trustee No. Ohio Cancer Resource Ctr., 1998-2001, chmn. 1999-2001. Lt. comdr. USPHS, 1965-67. Recipient David J. Greenburg Service Award, Am. Health Lawyers Assn., 1995, Spl. Honors award, Acad. Med. Cleveland Northeast Ohio, 2008, Clin. Yr. award, Acad. Med. Cleve. Northeast Ohio, 2010. Fellow ACP, Am. Health Lawyers Assn., Am. Coll. Legal Medicine (bd. govs. 2001-07, sec. 2007, mem. exec. com., 2007—, treas. 2008, pres. elect 2009, pres. 2010), Am. Health Lawyers Assn. (bd. dirs. 1988-94); mem. Am. Soc. Hematology, Am. Soc. Clin. Oncology, Am. Assn. Cancer Rsch., Am. Soc. Law and Medicine, Acad. Medicine Cleve. (pres. 1997-98), Cleve. Med. Libr. Assn. (pres. 2004-05), Greater Cleve. Bar Assn. Office: 6525 Powers Blvd Ste 30 Parma OH 44129 Office Phone: 440-842-6011. Personal E-mail: cowand@hotmail.com, dhcmdjd@yahoo.com.

COWAN, MORTON J., medical educator; b. Cleve., Jan. 5, 1945; BSEE, Mass. Inst. Tech., 1966; MD, U. Pa., 1970. Prof. U. Calif. San Francisco Med. Ctr., 1979—. Chief, blood and marrow transplant divsn. UCSF Benioff Children's Hosp., 1982. Primary Immune Deficiency Treatment Consortium grant, NIH, Office Rare Diseases Rsch., Nat. Inst. Allergy & Infectious Diseases. Mem.: Am. Soc. Blood & Marrow Transplantation. Office: 505 Parnassus Ave San Francisco CA 94143-1278 Business E-Mail: mcowan@peds.ucsf.edu.

COWEN, BARRETT STICKNEY, microbiology educator, researcher; b. Lebanon, NH, May 23, 1939; s. Frank Young and Elsie (Stickney) C.; m. Ruth Maria Consuegra, Sept. 3, 1966; children: Marcella Lucia, Matthew Alfredo. BS, U. Vt., 1963; MS, U. N.H., 1968; PhD, Cornell U., 1973. Lic. CIA vaccines USDA, 2001. Lab. asst. Hubbard Farms, Inc., Walpole, NH, 1963-65; grad. asst. U. N.H., Durham, 1965-67; rsch. specialist Cornell U., Ithaca, NY, 1967-73, rsch. assoc., 1973-78; lab. dir. Cobb, Inc., Concord, Mass., 1978-82; assoc. prof. vet. sci. Pa. State U., University Park, 1982-97; dir. rsch. Biomune Co., Lenexa, Kans., 1997—2001. Cons. microbiology dept., 1983, Cobb, Inc., 1983, Pilch, Inc., Troutmen, NC, 1984, Croton Egg Farms, Ohio, 1985, Laverlaim S.A., Calif., Columbia, 2002—05; tech. advisor Pa. Egg Producers, Lancaster, 1984, Biomune, Inc., Lenexa, Kans., 1989-96, Super Pollo, Rancaqua, Chile, 1993—2002, Incubator Anhalzer, Quito, Ecuador, 1994, Grandparents Poultry (PVT) Ltd., Lahore, Pakistan, 1995, edtl. bd. mem. Avian Diseases, 1994-2003, Jour. Applied Poultry Rsch., 1992-2001, mem. emeritus award Northeastern Conf. Avian Disease, 2004 Contbr. articles to profl. jour. With US Army, 1960. Pa. Dept. Agr. grantee, 1984-97; J. William Fulbright Fgn. scholar, 1994. Mem.: World Vet. Poultry Assn., Am. Assn. Bct. Lab. Diagnosticians, Conf. Rsch. Workers in Animal Diseases, Am. Soc. Microbiology, Am. Assn. Avian Pathologists, St. John's Lodge, Masons, Phi Kappa Phi, Sigma Xi. Republican. Methodist. Avocations: hunting and fishing, tennis, skiing, stamp collecting/philately. Home: 621 Benjamin Ct State College PA 16803-2666 Office Phone: 814-238-8651. Personal E-mail: bcowen@msn.com.

COWGILL, URSULA MOSER, biologist, educator, environmental consultant; b. Bern, Switzerland, Nov. 9, 1927; came to U.S., 1943, naturalized, 1945; d. John W. and Mara (Siegrist) Moser. AB, Hunter Coll., 1948; MS, Kans. State U., 1952; PhD, Iowa State U., 1956. Staff MIT, Lincoln Lab., Lexington, Mass., 1957-58; field work Doherty Found., Guatemala, 1958-60; research assoc. dept. biology Yale U., New Haven, 1960-68; prof. biology and anthropology U.

Pitts., 1968-81; environ. scientist Dow Chem. Co., Midland, Mich., 1981-84, assoc. environ. cons., 1984-91; environ. cons., 1991—. Environ. measurements adv. com. Sci. Adv. Bd. EPA, 1976-80; Internat. Joint Commn., 1984-89. Contbr. articles to profl. jours. Trustee Carnegie Mus., Pitts., 1971-75. Grantee NSF 1960-78, Wenner Gren Found., 1965-66, Penrose fund Am. Philos. Soc., 1978; Sigma Xi grant-in-aid, 1965-66 Mem. AAAS, Am. Soc. Limnology and Oceanography, Internat. Soc. Theoretical and Applied Limnology. Achievements include research in ecology, biology and minerology. Home and Office: PO Box 1329 Carbondale CO 81623-1329 Office Phone: 970-963-2488. Personal E-mail: ucowgill@hughes.net. Business E-Mail: ucowgill@direcway.com.

COWIN, STEPHEN CORTEEN, biomedical engineering educator, consultant; b. Elmira, NY, Oct. 26, 1934; s. William Corteen and Bernice (Reidy) C.; m. Martha Agnes Eisel, Aug. 10, 1956; children: Jennifer Marie, Thomas Burrows. BCE, Johns Hopkins U., 1956, MCE, 1958; PhD in Engring. Mechanics, Pa. State U., 1962. Registered profl. engr., La. Prof. mech. engring. Tulane U., 1969-77, prof. mechanics dept. biomed. engring., 1977-85, adj. prof. orthopedics, 1978-88, prof.-in-charge Tulane-Newcomb Jr. Yr. Abroad program, 1974-75, chmn. applied math. program, 1975-79, prof. applied stats., 1979-88, Alden J. Laborde prof. engring., 1985-88; disting. prof. CUNY, 1988—, chmn. dept. biomed. engring., 2002—03; dir. NY Ctr. for Biomed. Engring., 2000—. Sci. Rsch. Coun. Gt. Brit. sr. vis. fellow U. Strathclyde, 1974, 80; vis. research prof. Instituto de Matematica, Estatistica e Ciencia de Computanao, Universidade Estadual de Campinas, Brazil, 1978; adj. prof. orthopaedics, Mt. Siani Sch. Medicine, NY, 1989; participant U.S. Nat. Acad. Scis. interacad. exch. program with Bulgaria, 1983; fellow Japan Soc. for the Promotion Sci., 1987; sr. internat. Fogarty fellowship, Nederlandse Organisatie voor Wetenschappelijk Onderzoek fellowship, Vrije U., Amsterdam, 1996-97; mem. bd. advisors in biomedical engring., Tulane U., 2001-; editl. bd. mem. Mechanics of Multi-Canparent Materials, 2008-, Computers in Biology and Medicine, 2010-. Editor: (with M. Satake) Continuum Mechanical and Statistical Approaches in the Mechanics of Granular Materials, 1978, Mechanics Applied to the Transport of Granular Materials, 1979, (with M.M. Carroll) The Effects of Voids on Material Deformation, 1976, Bone Mechanics, 1988, Bone Mechanics Handbook, 2001, (with J. Humphrey) Cardiovascular Soft Tissue Mechanics, 2001, (with J. Huyghe and P. Raats) IUTAM-Proceedings on Physicochemical and Electromechanical Interaction in Porous Media, 2005, (with S. Doty) Tissue Mechanics, 2007, (with Gailanu G. and Cardoso L.) Russian Poll Poroclastiily Lacombert, 2009; assoc. editor: Jour. Applied Mechanics, 1974-82, Jour. Biomech. Engring., 1982-88; editl. adv. bd. Handbook of Materials, Structures and Mechanics, 1981—, Handbook of Bioengineering, 1981, Acta Biomechanica, 1986—; editl. bd. Annals Biomed. Engring., 1985—, Mechanics Rsch. Comm., 2005—; editl. cons. Jour. Biomechanics, 1988— Served to capt. U.S. Army, 1957-64 Recipient Maurice A. Biot medal ASCE, 2004; grantee NSF, NIH, NASA, U.S. Army Rsch. Office, Edward G. Schlieder Found.; fellow Fogarty Internat. Ctr., Amsterdam, 1996-97, Johns Hopkins U., 1958; Md. state scholar, Ambrose Howard Carner scholar. Fellow AAAS, ASME (Melville medal 1993, H.R. Lissner medal 1999), Am. Inst. Med. and Biol. Engring., European Soc. Biomechanics (Rsch. award 1994), Am. Acad. Mechanics; mem. Nat. Acad. Engring., Orthopedic Rsch. Soc., Soc. Rheology, Soc. Natural Philosophy (treas. 1977-79), Soc. Engring. Sci., Math. Assn. Am., NY Acad. Scis., Sigma Xi. Home: 2166 Broadway Apt 12D New York NY 10024 Office Phone: 212-650-5208. Personal E-mail: scowin@earthlink.net. Business E-Mail: cowin@ccny.cuny.edu.

COWLEY, BENJAMIN DOLLAR, JR., nephrologist, educator; b. Louisville, Ky., Oct. 18, 1956; MD, Baylor Coll. Medicine, 1981. Guest scientist Nat. Heart, Lung & Blood Inst., 1987—89; asst. to assoc. prof. U. Kans. Med. Ctr., 1989—2002; prof., nephrology sect. chief U. Okla. Health Scis. Ctr., 2002—. Pres. & mem., bd. dir. Okla. Found. Kidney Disease, 2006; UNOS designated kidney transplant physician OU Med. Ctr., 2006, pancreas transplant physician, 07; chair, sci. adv. cmty. & mem., bd. trustees Polycystic Kidney Disease Found., 2010; mem., bd. dirs. LifeShare, Transplant Donor Svcs. Okla., 2010. Recipient John Gammill Prof. award, U. Okla. Health Scis. Ctr. Mem.: Sigma Xi Sci. Rsch. Soc., Am. Soc. Transplantation, Internat. Soc. Nephrology, Am. Soc. Nephrology, Am. Soc. Advancement Sci. Avocations: scuba diving, travel, skiing. Office: Nephrology WP2250 OUHSC 920 S L Young Blvd Oklahoma City OK 73104 Office Fax: 405-271-6496. Business E-Mail: ben-cowley@ouhsc.edu.

COWLING, TERIANNE, medical researcher; d. Delta Ray and Madge Faye Cowling. BA, U. Tex., 1988; student, U. NC, 2007. Cert. core pub. health concepts U. NC, Chapel Hill, 2007. Rsch. analyst health care rsch. improvement Baylor Health Care Sys. Inst., Dallas, 2006—08; rsch. analyst Baylor U. Med. Ctr., Dallas, 1994—96, rsch. assoc., 1996—2006; rschr. Health Svcs., 2008—. Contbr. articles to profl. jours., chapters to books. Office: Inst for Health Care Rsch and Improvement Ste 500 LB81 8080 N Central Expressway Dallas TX 75206 Home: 4309 LaGuardia Ln # 1309 Fort Worth TX 76155 Personal E-mail: tericowling@yahoo.com. Business E-Mail: teric@baylorhealth.edu.

COWSER, DANNY LEE, lawyer, mental health specialist; b. Peoria, Ill., July 7, 1948; s. Albert Paul Cowser and Shirley Mae (Donaldson) Chatten; m. Nancy Lynn Hatch, Nov. 11, 1976; children: Kimberly Catherine Hatch Cowser, Dustin Paul Hatch Cowser. BA, No. Ill. U., 1972, MS, 1975; JD, DePaul U., 1980; AA in Nursing, Pima CC, 2009. Bar: Ill. 1980, Wis. 1981, U.S. Dist. Ct. (no. dist.) Ill. 1981, U.S. Ct. Appeals (7th cir.) 1983, U.S. Dist. Ct. (ea. and we. dists.) Wis. 1984, U.S. Supreme Ct. 1984, Ariz. 1985, U.S. Ct. Appeals (9th cir.) 1987, U.S. Dist. Ct. Ariz. 1989, U.S. Tax Ct. 1990, U.S. Ct. Claims 1990, Colo. 2000; RN 2009. Adminstr. Ill. Dept. Mental Health, Elgin, 1972-76, psychotherapist, 1976-79; assoc. Slaby, Deda & Henderson, Phillips, Wis., 1982-83; ptnr. Slaby, Deda & Cowser, Phillips, 1983-86; asst. atty. City of Flagstaff, Ariz., 1986-88; pub. defender Coconino County, Flagstaff, 1988-89; pvt. practice Flagstaff, 1989-97. Atty. City Park Falls, Wis., 1982-86; spl. dep. Mohave County capital def., 1989-90; instr. speech comms. No. Ariz. U., 1992-93; adminstrv. law judge Ariz. Dept. Econ. Security, 1997—. Bd. dirs. DeKalb County (Ill.) Drug Coun., 1973-75, Counseling and Personal Devel., Phillips, 1985-86. Reginald Heber Smith fellow, 1980-81; C.J.S. legal scholar, 1979. Mem. Ariz. Bar Assn., State Bar Ariz. (cert. specialist in criminal law 1993-98), State Bar Wis. Democrat. Avocations: skiing, photography, bicycling.

COX, CARRIE S., pharmaceutical executive; b. 1957; m. Ken Cox; 2 children. BS, Mass. Coll. Pharmacy & Health Sci., 1981. With Sandoz Pharm. (now Novartis), 1982—92; v.p. women's healthcare Wyeth-Ayerst, 1990—97; sr. v.p. & head global bus. mgmt. Pharmacia & Upjohn, 1997—99, exec. v.p., 1999—2002; exec. v.p., pres. global prescription bus. Pharmacia Corp., 2002—03; exec. v.p., pres. global pharm. Schering-Plough Corp., 2003—09; CEO Humacyte, Inc., 2010—. Bd. dirs. Texas Instruments Inc., 2004—, Cardinal Health, Inc., 2009—, Celgene Corp., 2009—. Mem. health coun. & mgmt. exec. coun. Harvard Sch. Pub. Health. Named Healthcare Businesswoman of Yr., Healthcare Businesswomen's Assn., 2001; named one of The 50 Most Powerful Women in Bus., Fortune mag., 2005—09, The 10 Most Powerful Women in NJ Bus., Star-Ledger, 2006. Office: Humacyte Inc 7020 Kit Creek Rd Morrisville NC 27560 *

COX, CLAIR EDWARD, II, urologist, medical educator; b. Lawrenceville, Ill., Sept. 2, 1933; s. Clair Edward and May E. (Judy) C.; m. Clarice Wicks, Aug. 23, 1958; children— Clair Edward III, Daniel Paul, Kevin Christopher, Kenneth Harold. Student, U. Mich., 1951-54, MD, 1958. Diplomate Am. Bd. Urology. Intern U. Colo. Med. Center, Denver, 1958-59, surg. resident, 1959-60; resident urology U. Cal. Med. Center at San Francisco, 1960-63; mem. faculty Bowman Gray Sch. Medicine, Wake Forest U., Winston Salem, NC, 1963-72, assoc. prof., 1967-70, prof. urology, 1970-72; prof., chmn. dept. urology U. Tenn. Med. Sch., Memphis, 1972—99, prof., 1999—2009, prof. emeritus, 2009—. Contbr. profl. jours. Fellow ACS; mem. AMA, Am. Assn. Genito-Urinary Surgeons, Am. Urol. Assn., Internat. Soc. Urology, N.Y. Acad. Scis., Infectious Disease Soc. Am., Soc. Univ. Urologists, Am. Assn. Med. Colls., Am. Soc. Microbiology. Achievements include research in urinary tract infectious disease. Home: 6011 Sweetbriar Cv Memphis TN 38120-2514 Office Phone: 901-490-1690. E-mail: icox@uthsc.edu.

COX, SIR DAVID, statistician, educator; b. Birmingham, Eng., July 15, 1924; s. Sam and Lilian Esther (Braines) C.; m. Joyce Drummond, Aug. 22, 1948; children: Joan, Malcolm, Andrew, Steven. MA, St. John's Coll., Cambridge, England, 1950; PhD, U. Leeds, Eng., 1949; DSc (hon.), U. Reading, Eng., 1982, U. Bradford, 1982, U. Helsinki, 1986, Heriot-Watt U., 1987, Limburgs U., 1988, Queen's U., Kingston, Ontario, 1990, U. Neuchatel, 1992, U. Minn., 1993, U. Dundee Abertay, 1994, U. Toronto, 1994, Tech. U. Crete, 1995, U. Bordeaux 2, 1998, U. Elche, 1999, Harvard U., 1999, Fed. U. Rio de Janiero, 2000, U. Leeds, 2004; degree in Maths (hon.), Waterloo U., Ontario, 1991; hon. Doctorate in Statistics and Demography, U. Padua, 1993; doctorate (hon.), U. Athens Econs. Bus., 1998; doctorate, U. Southampton, 2007; doctorate (hon.), U. Gothenburg, 2008, U. Glasgow, 2011. Jr. sci. officer Royal Aircraft Establishment, Farnborough, England, 1944-46; jr. sci. officer, prin. sci. officer Wool Industries Rsch. Assn., Leeds, 1946-50; asst. lectr. U. Cambridge, 1950-5; vis. prof. dept. biostats. U. NC, Chapel Hill, 1955-56; reader in statistics Birkbeck Coll., London, 1956—60, prof. in statistics, 1966—88; mem. tech. staff Bell Labs., NJ, 1965; prof. in statistics Imperial Coll. of Sci. and Tech., London, 1966-88, dept. head, math., 1970—74; warden Nuffield Coll., Oxford, England, 1988-94. Editor Biometrika, 1966-91, chmn. of trustees, 1994-2005; contbr. articles to profl. jours.; author books on theoretical and applied stats. and applied probability. Pres. Royal Statis. Soc., 1980-82, Bernoulli Soc., 1979-81 Recipient Weldon prize Oxford U., 1984, Guy Medal in Silver, Royal Statis. Soc., 1961, Gold, 1973, Charles F. Kettering prize GM Cancer Rsch. Found., 1990, Gold Medel for Cancer Rsch.,1990, Max Planck Forschungspreise, 1992; fellow Imperial Coll., 1994. Sr. Rsch. Fellow, SERC, 1983-88; Fellow Royal Soc. London, 1973, Inst. of Actuaries (hon.), 1990, St. John's Coll. (hon.), 1990, Nuffield Coll. (hon.), 1994, British Acad. (hon.), 1997, Birkbeck Coll., 2001; knighted, 1985; mem. Internat. Statis. Inst. (pres.-elect 1993-1995), Companion of Operational Rsch. Soc., Royal Danish Acad. Scis. and Letters (hon. fgn.), Am. Philos. Soc. (hon. fgn.), US NAS (hon. fgn.), Finnish Statis. Soc. (hon. fgn.), Am. Acad. of Arts and Sciences(hon. fgn.), Internat. Biometric Soc. (hon. life), I.S.I. (pres. 1995-1997); mem. of coun. Royal Soc. (Copley medal, 2010); for. assoc., Indian Nat. Acad. of Sci. Office Phone: 44 1865 278690. Office Fax: 44 1865 278621. Business E-Mail: david.cox@nuffield.ox.ac.uk. *

COX, ELAINE, epidemiologist, educator; b. Indpls., Apr. 11, 1964; BS in Biochemistry, Ind. U., 1986, MD, 1990. Assoc. prof. pediat. Ind. U. Sch. Medicine, 1995—. Chairwoman One Test Two Lives: Prevent HIV Ind., 2009. Recipient Spirit Svc. award, Ind. Perinatal Network; Emergency Services grant, Elizabeth Glaser Pediatric AIDS Found. Fellow: Am. Acad. HIV Medicine, Am. Acad. Pediat.; mem.: Infectious Disease Soc. Am. Avocations: reading, travel. Office: ROC 4380 705 Riley Dr Indianapolis IN 46202 Office Fax: 317-948-0860. Business E-Mail: elmcox@iupui.edu.

COX, GEOFFREY F., pharmaceutical executive; Gen. mgr. U.K. ops. Gist Brocades; joined Genzyme Corp. (UK), 1984; sr. v.p., ops. to exec. v.p., ops. and pharm., diagnostic and genetics bus. Genzyme Corp. (US), 1988—97; chmn. bd. dirs., CEO Aronex Pharm., Inc., Spring, Tex., 1997—2001; chmn., pres., CEO GTC Biotherapeutics, Framingham, Mass., 2001—. Bd. dirs. BIO, mem. emerging companies sect. and healthcare sect. governing body com.; non-exec. chmn. Nabi Biopharmaceuticals.

COX, JAMES SIDNEY, physician; b. Homer, La., Nov. 17, 1950; s. Sidney and Rita (Haynes) C.; m. Judy Katherine Vickers, Oct. 21, 1984; children: Shannon Ruth, Sarah Anne, Megan Elizabeth. Student, La. State U., 1968-71; MD, Tulane U., 1971-75. Diplomate Am. Bd. Family Practice, Am. Bd. of Emergency Medicine. Intern, resident in family practice John Peter Smith Hosp., Ft. Worth, 1975-78; city health officer family practice City of Athens, Tex., 1978-84; pvt. practice Athens, 1978-84, Ft. Worth, 1984—; mem. staff Henderson County Meml. Hosp., Athens, vice chief med. staff, 1981-82; mem. staff Lakeland Med. Ctr., Athens, chief med. staff, dir., 1983-84; vice chief emergency medicine dept. Harris Meth. Hosp., Ft. Worth, 1988-91, dir. occupational medicine, 1989—2008, chief emergency dept. Ft. Worth, 1992-93, 98-2000, sec. med. staff, 1994-95, sec. emergency medicine divsn., 1996-97. Pres., chmn. bd. dirs. Occuhealth Physicians Group, P.A., 1989-2009, Ft. Worth; mem. faculty U. Tex. Health Sci. Ctr.-Dallas Cmty. Medicine Dept., John Peter Smith Hosp., Ft. Worth, 1978-96, course dir. ACLS, 1989-1998, mem. affiliate faculty ACLS, 1991-95, med. rev. officer for urine drug testing, 1992-2009; med. bd. Harris Meth. Hosp., 1992-95, 98-2000; team chmn. emergency dept. redesign Rochester Inst. Tech. Coll. Bus., 1996; v.p. for physician affairs Emergency Medicine Cons., 1998-2005, exec. dir., 2005-06, cief adminstrv. officer, 2006—; assoc. med. dir. Harris Meth., Ft. Worth, 2000-2007; med. dir. ACLS, Campbell Health Sys., 1997-98. Author: Intestinal Obstruction: A Programmed Text, 1975. Recipient Quality Cup award of Excellence, USA Today, 1996. Fellow Am. Acad. Family Physicians, Am. Coll. Emergency Physicians; mem. AMA (Physician's Recognition award), Tex. Med. Assn. (alt. del. 1994-96, 2003-05, del. 2005-), Tarrant County Med. Soc. (bd. dirs. 1994-96, 2003—, sec. treas. 2008-, v.p. 2008-09, pres. elect 2009-10, pres., 2010-11), Rotary (bd. dirs. Athens chpt. 1983-84), Alpha Epilson Delta., Tex. Med. Assn.(vice-chair., Physicians Health and Rehab. Comm., 2008-, com. emergency med. svc. & truma, 2010-, pres., med. dir. project access Tarrant County, 2011-), Tarrant County Med. Soc.(bd. trustee, 2011-) Presbyterian. Avocations: reading, skiing, bonsai, horticulture, astronomy. Home: 3458 Lantern Holw Fort Worth TX 76109-2411 Office: Emergency Medicine Cons 6451 Brentwood Stair Rd Ste 200 Fort Worth TX 76112-3200 Office Phone: 817-496-9700. Business E-Mail: jcox@emdocs.com.

COX, JIM, retired physician; s. Michael Ievers and Betty Cox; m. Fiona Rolland, Feb. 1, 1975; children: Tamsin, Charlie. MBBS, U. Newcastle Upon Tyne, 1972, MD, 1993. Asst. prof. SIU Sch. Medicine, Springfield, Ill., 1976—78; assoc. advisor gen. practice U. Newcastle Upon Tyne, 1988—97; gen. practitioner Caldbeck, Cumbria, England, 1980—2002; assoc. dir. Nat. Clin. Assessment Authority, England, 2002—05; med. dir. Cumbria Ambulance Svc., England, 2005—07. Bd. mem. Countryside Agy., England, 2005—07; commr. Commn. Rural Cmtys., England, 2007—, OBE, 2003; Deputy Lieutenant Cumbria, 2004; bd. mem. Cumbria Partnership NHS Found. Trust, 2011—. Author: (book) Rural Healthcare, Understanding Doctors' Performance. Fellow: RCP, Royal Coll. Gen. Practitioners. Home: The Barn Caldbeck Wigton Cumbria CA7 8DP England

COX, JOHN SAMUEL TWEEDALE, retired surgeon; b. Jamestown, Australia, Aug. 8, 1931; s. Robert Malcolm Tweedale and Irene Anne (Poling) C.; m. Carola Ray McAuley, Sept. 24, 1963; children: Henry, Simon, Henrietta, Julius, Naomi. MB BChir, Adealaide U., Australia, 1955, M of Surgery, 1964. Cert. specialist surgeon. Vascular fellow Harvard U., Boston, 1960-61; sr. surg. registrar Queen Elizabeth Hosp., Adelaide, 1963-66; clin. asst. Royal Adelaide Hosp., 1966-72; sr. vis. surgeon Modbury Hosp., Adelaide, 1972-98. Chmn. staff soc. Modbury Hosp., Adelaide; clin. tutor Adelaide U., 1980-98; vis. surgeon Samrong Hosp., Cambodia,, 2001, 2002. Contbr. articles to profl. jours. Fellow Royal Coll. Surgeons (London), Royal Australian Coll. Surgeons; mem. Royal Adelaide Golf Club. Roman Catholic.

COX, KAY LORRAINE, physiologist, researcher; b. Perth, Western Australia, Jan. 10, 1949; d. Francis Henry and Frances Elizabeth Grimshaw; m. Walter Jacob Cox, Oct. 6, 1973; children: Grant Justin, Natalie Jayne, Dean Anthony. Diploma, Secondary Tchr. Coll., Nedlands Western Australia, 1969; BEd in Human Movement Studies, U. Western Australia, Perth, 1971, MPE in Human Movement Studies, 1977, PhD, 1993. Phys. edn. tchr. Dept. Edn., Perth, 1970—73; lectr. Churchlands Coll. Advanced Edn., 1974—79; rsch. fellow U. Western Australia, 1994—. Author: (text book) Teaching Adults to Swim; contbr. articles to profl. sci. jours., chapters to books (Eunice Gill Merit award, Svc. Australian Coaching Coun., 1993). Chairperson Kununurra Swimming Pool Com., Western Australia, 1982—84; v.p., pres. Sorrento Kindergarten, 1985—87; com. mem. Sports Fedn. WA Mature-Age Adv. Com., Perth, 1998—2008; co founder, bd. mem., v.p. Masters Swimming Australia, Perth, 1977—99, coaching dir. Victoria, Australia, 1993—2004. Recipient Australian Sports medal, Commonwealth Govt. of Australia., 2000, Eunice Gill award, Confederation of Australian Sport, 2003, Wendy Ey Women Sport award, Sports Medicine Australia, 2005, Young Australian of Yr. award, Jaycees WA Br., 1986, Rsch. Project gGrant, Healthway, 2007—, AUSSI Masters Swimming Coach of Yr., Masters Swimming Australia, 1990, Young Sci. Investigators award, Royal Perth Hosp. Med. Rsch. Found., 1991, Eunice Gill Merit award, Australian Coaching Coun., 1993, Young Sci. Investigators award, Med. Rsch. Found. Royal Perth Hosp., 1994; named Ofcl. of Yr., AUSSI Masters Swimming WA, 2003; Rsch. grant, Healthway, 1993—95, 1999—2001, 2003—05, Rsch. Project grant, Nat. Health Med. Rsch. Found. Australia, 2004—06. Fellow: Females Austswim; mem.: Australian Coun. Health Phys. Edn. and Recreation, Sports Medicine Australia, Australian Assn. Exercise and Sports Sci., Masters Swimming Australia. Mem. Church Of England. Achievements include research in to the role of physical activity on blood pressure and cardiovascular health and cognitive decline. Interventions and strategies to increase physical activity levels in older adults; development of fitness and education programs for adult swimmers. Avocations: swimming, recreation, research, reading. Office: Univ Western Australia Rear 50 Murray St Perth Western Australia 6000 Australia Office Fax: 61 8 92240243. Business E-Mail: kay.cox@uwa.edu.au.

COX, NANCY JANE, microbiologist; b. Emmetsburg, Iowa, July 21, 1948; d. Emmett Stanley and Verna Lucille (Olson) Cox; m. Evan Lindsay Cox, Apr. 11, 1981; 1 child, Julia Claire Lindsay. BS with honors, Iowa State U., 1970; PhD, Cambridge U., Eng., 1975. Postdoctoral fellow Muscular Dystrophy Assn., Balt., 1975—77; staff fellow Ctrs. for Disease Control, Atlanta, 1978—80, rsch. chemist, 1980—, now dir. influenza divsn. Contbr. articles to profl. jours. and books. Named one of 100 Most Influential People, Time mag., 2006; Marshall scholarship, 1970. Mem.: AAAS, Am. Soc. microbiology, Am. Soc. Virology, Sigma Xi. Methodist. Office: Div Viral Diseases 7-111 Centers for Disease Control 1 600 Clifton Rd Atlanta GA 30316-2228

COX, PAUL ALAN, ethnobotanist, educator; b. Salt Lake City, Oct. 10, 1953; s. Leo A. and Rae (Gabbitas) C.; m. Barbara Ann Wilson, May 21, 1975; children: Emily Ann, Paul Matthew, Mary Elisabeth, Hillary Christine, Jane Margaret. BS, Brigham Young U., 1976; MSc, U. Wales, 1978; AM, Harvard U., 1978, PhD, 1981; DSc (hon.), U. Guelph, Can., 2000. Teaching fellow Harvard U., Cambridge, Mass., 1977-81; Miller research fellow Miller Inst. Basic Research in Sci., Berkeley, Calif., 1981-83; asst. prof. Brigham Young U., Provo, Utah, 1983-86, assoc. prof., 1986-91, prof., 1991—98, dean gen. edn. and honors, 1993-97; King Gustav XVI prof. environ. sci. Swedish Biodiversity Ctr., 1997—98; dir. Nat. Tropical Botanical Garden, Kalaheo, Hawaii, 1998—2004, Inst. for Ethnomedicine, Provo, 2004—. Disting. prof. Brigham Young U., Hawaii, 2000—; ecologist Utah Environ. Coun., Salt Lake City, 1976; project ecologist Utah MX Coordination Office, Salt Lake City, 1981. Mem. editl. bd. Pacific Studies. Recipient Bowdoin prize, The Goldman Environ. prize, 1997;

Danforth Found. fellow, 1976-81, Fulbright fellow, 1976-77, NSF fellow, 1977-81, Linnean Soc. fellow, named NSF Presdl. Young Investigator, 1985-90, Hero of Medicine, Time Mag., 1997, Rachel Carson award, 1999. Mem. AAAS, Brit. Ecol. Soc., Internat. Soc. Ethnopharmacology (former pres.), Am. Soc. Naturalists, Assn. Tropical Biology, Soc. Econ. Botany (former pres.), Seacology Found. (founder and chmn.), AIDS Rsch. Alliance (bd.), Ctr. for Plant Conservation (bd.). Mem. Lds Ch. Office: Inst for Ethnomedicine PO Box 3464 Jackson WY 83001 Office Phone: 801-375-6214.

COX, ROBERT ASHLEY, medical researcher, consultant; b. Rhymney, UK, Aug. 25, 1928; s. Herbert Ashley and Mary Jane (Henry) Cox; m. Isobel Terry Pepper, Mar. 30, 1957; children: Simon Ashley, Isobel Jane, Robert Ian Ashley, Timothy John Ashley. BSc, U. Birmingham, 1952, PhD, 1955, DSc, 1971. Cert. chartered chemist Royal Soc. Chemistry. Rsch. scientist Tube Investments, Cambridge, England, 1955—58, Weizmann Inst., Rehovoth, Israel, 1958—59; rsch. fellow Harvard U., Cambridge, Mass., 1959—60; rsch. scientist Nat. Inst. Med. Rsch., London, 1960—. Editor Biochemical Jour., London, 1967—74, Nucleic Acids Rsch., Birmingham, 1974—77. Co-author: Protein Biosynthesis: In Focus, 1992; contbr. chapters to books, scientific papers to prof. jours. Chmn. of govs. Local Schs., Hertfordshire, England, 1971—94. Fellow: Royal Soc. Chemistry, Harvard Assn. Chemists. Avocations: chess, tennis, history. Home: Netherstone 8 Gills Hill Ln Radlett WD7 8DF England Office: Nat Inst Med Rsh The Ridgeway NW7 1AA London England Office Phone: 44 2089593666. E-mail: rcox@nimr.mrc.ac.uk.

COX, RODY POWELL, internist, educator; b. New Brighton, Pa., June 24, 1926; s. Raymond James and Hazel (Powell) C.; m. Jane Beverly Birks, Sept. 5, 1953 (dec. Apr. 1995); children: Shelley Lea, Rody Powell, Sue Ellen; m. LaVaun Jeanne Sears, Mar. 1, 1997. Student, Franklin and Marshall Coll., 1946-48; MD, U. Pa., 1952. Diplomate Am. Bd. Internal Medicine. Intern U. Mich., 1952-53, resident in medicine, 1953-54, U. Pa., Phila., 1953-57, asst. prof. medicine, 1957-60; rsch. assoc. U. Glasgow, Scotland, 1960-61; prof. medicine NYU, NYC, 1961-79, prof. pharmacology, 1972-79, chief div. human genetics, 1972-79; prof., vice chmn. dept. medicine Case-Western Res. U., Cleve., 1979-88; chief med. svc. VA Med. Ctr., Cleve., 1979-88; dean Med. Sch. U. Tex. Southwestern Med. Ctr., Dallas, 1988-89, prof. internal medicine, 1988—. Mem. metabolism study sect. NIH, 1970-74, chmn. genetics study sect., 1978-79, chmn. mammalian genetics study sect., 1979-81; mem. panel on clin. scis. NRC, 1976-86. Editor: Cell Communication, 1974; co-editor: Epithelial Cell Culture, 1981; contbr. articles to profl. publs. Sgt. U.S. Army, 1944-46, NATOUSA. Fellow Royal Soc. Medicine (Eng.); Master ACP; mem. Am. Soc. Clin. Investigation (emeritus), Assn. Am. Physicians, Ctrl. Soc. Clin. Rsch., John Morgan Soc. U. Pa., Harvey Soc., Am. Clin. Climatol. Assn., Am. Soc. Human Genetics, Interurban Clin. Club, Alpha Omega Alpha (councillor NYU chpt. 1970-76). Home: 5 Connaught Ct Dallas TX 75225-2459 Office: U Tex Southwestern Med Ctr 5323 Harry Hines Blvd Dallas TX 75390 8880 Home Phone: 214-363-4329; Office Phone: 214-648-7805. Business E-Mail: rcox@mednet.swmed.edu, rody.cox@utsouthwestern.edu.

COX, THOMAS, principal; b. DC, Apr. 16, 1946; BA, Hofstra U., 1969; PhD, Va. Commonwealth U., 2004. Prin. GTC, 1969—. Office: 1711 NW 55 Ter Gainesville FL 32605 E-mail: nurse.statistician@yahoo.com.

COXON, ANN YVONNE, physician, consultant; b. Saigon, Indochina, Oct. 11, 1940, arrived in Eng., 1947. d. James Stanley and Elizabeth Ann (Traute) C. MB, BS, London U., 1963, DCH, 1965, MRCS, 1961. MRCP. Gen. med. tng. Guy's Hosp., Hammersmith Hosp., Great Ormond St. Childrens, 1963-70; specialist tng. Hammersmith Hosp., Nat. Hosp. Queen Square, 1971-83; cons. physician Portman Clinic, London, 1983—; ind. physician London, 1983—. Dir. medicine and rsch. Howard Found. Rsch., 1983—; founder Brit. Islamic Ctr. Contbr. articles to profl. jours. Mem. Harveian Soc., Med. Soc. of London. Muslim. Avocation: comparative religion. Office: 101 Harley St London W1G 6AH England Office Phone: +44 207 486 2534. Personal E-mail: coxon@easynet.co.uk.

COYLE, JOSEPH THOMAS, psychiatrist; b. Chgo., Oct. 9, 1943; s. Joseph Thomas and Mercedes (Sartor) Coyle; m. Genevieve Sansoucy, Aug. 19, 1968; children: Andrew, Peter, David. AB, Coll. of the Holy Cross, Worcester, Mass., 1965; MD, Johns Hopkins U., Balt., 1969; MA (hon.), Harvard U., Cambridge, Mass., 1991. Diplomate Am. Bd. Psychiatry and Neurology. Asst. prof. pharmacology Johns Hopkins Sch. of Medicine, Balt., 1974—76, asst. prof pharmacology and psychiatry, 1976—78, assoc. prof pharmacology and psychiatry, 1978—80, prof of neurosci., psychiatry and pharmacology, 1980—91, dir. divsn. child psychiatry, 1982—91, Disting. Svc. prof. of child psychiatry, 1985—91; Eben S. Draper prof. of psychiatry and neurosci. Harvard U., Boston, 1991—; chair consol. dept. psychiatry Harvard Med. Sch., Boston, 1991—2001. Co-dir. outpatient pharmacotherapy clinic Johns Hopkins Hosp., Balt., 1977—82; mem. sci. adv. bd. Pfizer Scholars Program, NYC, 1989—94, John F. Merck Found., Boston, 1990—2000, Abbott Pharms., North Chicago, Ill., 1990—, Guilford Pharms., Balt., 1992—98. Contbr. articles to profl. jours.; editor: Archives of General Psychiatry, 2002—. Mem. adv. bd. NIMH, Washington, 1990—94. Recipient AE Bennett award, 1978, Gold Medal award, 1991, EA Strecker award, Inst. Pa. Hosp., 1993, Thomas Salmon lecture, NY Acad. Medicine, 1993, Passarow Found. award, 1997, Lieber award, Nat. Alliance Rsch. Schizophrenia and Depression, 2004, Sanctae Crucis award, Coll. Holy Cross, 2006. Fellow: Am. Acad. of Arts and Scis., Am. Psychiat. Assn. (Found. Fund prize 1985, Adolph Meyer award 1994, Kemp Fund award 1996); mem.: Inst. of Medicine of the Nat. Acad. Sci., Am. Soc. Pharmacology and Exptl. Therapeutics (John Jacob Abel award 1979), Am. Acad. Child and Adolescent Psychiatry, Am. Coll. Neuropsychopharmacology (pres. 2001, Effron award 1982), Soc. Neurosci. (pres. 1991—92, Spl. Achievement award 2001). Avocations: reading, fishing. Office: Harvard Med Sch Dept Psychiatry 115 Mill St Belmont MA 02478-1041 Business E-Mail: joseph_coyle@hms.harvard.edu.

COYLE, MARIE BRIDGET, retired microbiologist, lab administrator; b. Chgo., May 13, 1935; d. John and Bridget Veronica (Fitzpatrick) Coyle; m. Zheng Chen, Oct. 30, 1995 (div. Aug. 2000). BA, Mundelein Coll. (now part of Loyola U.), Chgo., 1957; MS, St. Louis U., 1963; PhD, Kans. State U., Manhattan, 1965. Diplomate Am. Bd. Med. Microbiology. Sci. instr. Sch. Nursing Columbus Hosp., Chgo., 1957-59; research assoc. U. Chgo., 1967-70; instr. U. Ill., Chgo., 1970-71; asst. prof. microbiology U. Wash., Seattle, 1973-80, assoc. prof., 1980-94, prof., 1994-2000; ret., 2000. Assoc. dir. Univ. Hosp., Seattle, 1973—76; dir. microbiology labs Harborview Med. Ctr. U. Wash., Seattle, 1976—, co-dir. postdoctoral tng. clinic microbiology, 1978—96, dir. postdoctoral tng. clinic microbiology, 1996—2000. Contbr. articles to profl. jours. Recipient Pasteur award, Ill. Soc. Microbiology, 1997, Profl. Recognition awards, Am. Bd. Med. Microbiology, Am. Bd. Med. Lab. Immunology, 2000. Fellow: Am. Acad. Microbiology; mem.: Am. Soc. Microbiology (chmn. clin. microbiology divsn. 1984—85, mem. coun. policy com. 1996—99, bd. govs. 2000—, bioMerieux Vitek Sonnenwirth Meml. award 1994), Acad. Clin. Lab. Physicians and Scientists (sec.-treas. 1980—83, mem. exec. com. 1985—90), Kappa Gamma Pi. Avocation: hiking.

COYNE, BRIAN J(OSEPH), pharmaceutical researcher; b. Belfast, No. Ireland, Dec. 5, 1961; s. Edward Anthony and Mary H. Coyne; m. Katharine Brunner, Apr. 11, 1992; children: Patrick Michael, Caroline Genevieve. BA, Ctrl. Conn. State U., New Britain, 1987; MA, Montclair State U., Upper Montclair, NJ, 1995; MPA, Seton Hall U., South Orange, NJ, 2002. Cert. med. rep. Cert. Med. Rep. Inst., 1992, Coun. Accreditation Pharm. Mfrs. Reps. Can. Coun. Continuing Pharm. Edn. Can., 1997, mem. Med. Rep. Inst. of Ireland, 2000, clin. rsch. assoc. Assn. Clin. Rsch. Profls., 2005, med. investigator Am. Coll. Forensic Investigators, 2003. Country study mgr. The Clin. Resource Network, NYC, 2003—04; sr. clin. rsch. scientist Novartis Pharmaceuticals Corp., East Hanover, NJ, 2004—05, Forest Labs. Inc., Jersey City, 2005—; clin. rsch. assoc. Kendle Internat., 2008—. Mgr. clin. rsch. Knoll Pharm. Co., Mount Olive, NJ, 1988—2000, Cordis Corp., Warren, 2001—02; study mgr. North Am. ops. Aventis Pharmaceuticals Inc., Bridgewater, 2000—01; mgr. clin. ops. U.S. clin. rsch. assoc. Hemosol Inc., Parsippany, 2002—03; clin. rsch. assoc. Kendle Internat. With USN, 1981—85. Decorated Battle E Ribbon U.S. Navy, Expeditionary medal, Rifle and Pistol Marksmanship medals, others; Fellowship, Royal Acad. Medicine, Ireland, 2002. Mem.: AMVETS, VFW, Am. Cold War Veterans, Am. Coll. Forensic Examiners, Assn. Mil. Surgeons US, Royal Soc. Medicine, UK, Am. Coll. Clin. Pharmacology, Mil. History Soc. Ireland, Soc. Mil. History, US Naval Inst., Am. Legion, Friendly Sons St. Patrick, Naval Order US. Avocations: running, weightlifting, history, scuba diving, reading.

COZZANI, EMANUELE, medical researcher; b. Lyon, July 19, 1961; MD, U. Genoa, 1989; PhD, U. Lyon, 1995. Rschr. U. Genoa, 1993—. Home: via Montallegro 23 Genoa 16132 Italy Personal E mail: emanuele.cozzani@unige.it.

CRABTREE, BEN C., neuromuscular therapy clinic director; b. Las Vegas, Sept. 11, 1964; s. Ben C. and Jaynelle (Felix) C.; m. Virginia Kathryn Vance, Feb. 7, 1988 (div. Nov. 1989); m. Tania Oylan Tason, May 5, 1992; children: Greta, Bryan. AS, Panama Canal Coll., La Boca, Rep. of Panama, 1993, Austin Peay State U., 1995; BBA, Our Lady of the Lake U., 1995. Cert. concealed firearms permit instr., firearms instr.; lic. massage therapist; cert. neuromuscular therapist; lic. massage therapy instr.; cert. neuromuscular therapy instr., advanced myoskeletal alignment therapist. Software tech., adminstr. asst. Ace Personal Health Care, Inc., San Antonio, 1994-95; dir. info. systems River City Fin. Health Group/Home Health Care Solutions, San Antonio, 1995; chief fin. officer, alt. adminstr. A&E Quality Home Health Care, San Antonio, 1996-99; pres. Oylan, Inc., San Antonio, 1997-99; pres., owner Antonian Bodyworks, 1999-2001; instr. neuromuscular therapy Neuromuscular Therapy Ctr. N.Mex., 2000—07, chief instr. massage therapy Austin Sch. Massage, San Antonio, 2001—03. Profl. adv. com. Silver Days Home Health Care, San Antonio, 1996-97, Responsive Health Svcs., 1997-99. Mem. Dist. 128 State Budget Adv. Com., San Antonio, 1995. Ssgt. U.S. Army, 1984-92. Mem.: Internat. Defensive Pistol Assn., Nat. Rifle Assn., Soc. Ortho-Bionomy Internat., U.S. Practical Shooting Assn. Avocations: practical shooting, web page design. Home: 12221 Blanco Rd Apt 4003 San Antonio TX 78216 Office: San Antonio Neuromuscular Therapy Ctr 900 NE Loop 410 Ste E115 San Antonio TX 78209 E-mail: massagebyben@yahoo.com.

CRACCO, ROGER QUINLAN, neurologist, educator; b. June 1, 1934; s. Frederick A. and Ruby Ann (Quinlan) C.; m. Joan Marie Bender, June 9, 1962. AB, Cornell U., 1956; MD, N.J. Med. Sch., 1960. Diplomate Am. Bd. Psychiatry and Neurology, Am. Bd. Electrodiagnostic Medicine, Am. Bd. Clin. Neurophysiology (bd. dirs. 1984-88). Intern Phila. Gen. Hosp., 1960-61; resident in neurology Jersey City Med. Ctr., 1961-64; fellow in neurophysiology Mayo Grad. Sch., Mayo Clinic, 1964-66; asst. prof. neurology Jefferson Med. Coll., Phila., 1968-71, assoc. prof., 1971-73; prof. neurology SUNY Health Sci. Ctr. at Bklyn., 1973-80, prof., chmn. neurology, 1980—2006, Disting. Svc. prof. neurology, physiology and pharmacology, 2005—. Head neurology service State U. Hosp.-Kings County Hosp. Ctr., Bklyn., 1980—2006; vice dean Coll. Medicine SUNY Health Sci. Ctr., Bklyn., 1997—, dir. Robert F. Furchgott Ctr. for Neural and Behavioral Sci., 2007—; mem. program project rev. com. Nat. Inst. Neurology, Communicative Disease and Stroke, NIH, USPHS, 1984-88, chmn. 1987-88. Editor: (with I. Bodis-Wollner) Evoked Potentials, 1986; mem. editl. bd. Ann. Neurology, Electroencephalography Clinical Neurophysiology, Muscle and Nerve jour., others; contbr. articles to profl. jours. Capt. M.C., U.S. Army, 1966-68. NIH grantee, 1970-86. Fellow Am. Acad. Neurology; mem. Am. Neurol. Assn., Am. Clin. Neurophysiol. Soc. (pres. 1981-82), Ea. Assn. Electroencephalography (pres. 1979-80), Am. Assn. Electromyography and Electrodiagnosis, Am. Epilepsy Soc., Soc. for Neurosci., Assn. U. Profs. of Neurology, Am. Clin. Neurophysiologic Soc. (Herbert A. Jasper award for lifetime achievement 2002), Am. Acad. Clin. Neurophysiology (pres. 1987-89), Alpha Omega Alpha. Office: SUNY Health Sci Ctr Bklyn Dept Neurology 450 Clarkson Ave Dept Brooklyn NY 11203-2056 Office Phone: 718-270-1355.

CRAFT, CHERYL MAE, neurobiologist, anatomist, researcher; b. Lynch, Ky., Apr. 15, 1947; d. Cecil Berton and Lillian Lovelle C.; m. Laney K. Cormney, Oct. 14, 1967 (div. Sept. 1980); children: Tyler Craft Cormney, Ryan Berton Cormney (dec.); m. Richard N. Lolley (dec.). BS in Biology, Chemistry and Math., Valdosta State Coll., 1969; cert. in Tchg. Biology and Math., Ea. Ky. U., 1971; PhD in Human Anatomy and Neurosci., U. Tex., San Antonio, 1984. Undergrad. rsch. asst. Ea. Ky. U., Richmond, 1965-67; tchg. asst. dept. cell-structural biology U. Tex. Health Sci. Ctr., San Antonio, 1979-84; postdoctoral fellowship lab. devel. neurobiology NICHD and LMDB/NEI, Bethesda, Md., 1984-86; instr. dept. psychiatry U. Tex. Southwestern Med. Ctr., Dallas, 1986-87, asst. prof., 1987-91; dir. lab. Molecular Neurogenetics Schizophrenia Rsch. Ctr., VA Med. Ctr., Dallas, 1988-94; dir. Lab. Molecular Neurogenetics Mental Health Clinic Rsch. Ctr., U. Tex. Southwestern Med. Ctr., 1990-94; assoc. prof. U. Tex. Southwestern Med. Ctr., 1991-94; Mary D. Allen chair Doheny Eye Inst. U. So. Calif. Keck Sch. Medicine, LA, Calif., 1994—, founding chmn. dept. cell and neurobiology, 1994—2004. Ad hoc reviewer NEI/NIH, Bethesda, 1993—; reviewer Molecular Biology, NSPB Fight for Sight Grants, 1991-94; STAR-sci. adv. bd. U. So. Calif./Bravo Magnet H.S., L.A., 1995—. Contbr. author: Melatonin: Biosynthesis, Physiological Effects, 1993; exec. editor Exptl. Eye Rsch. jour., 1993—; editor Molecular Vision. Recipient Merit award for rsch. VA Med. Ctr., 1992, 93, 94, nomination for Women in Sci. and Engring. award Dallas VA, 1992, 93; NEI fellow, 1986, NICHD/NIH fellow, 1986. Mem. AAAS, AAUW, Assn. for Rsch. in Vision and Ophthalmology (chair program planning com. 1991-94), Am. Soc. for Neurochemistry (Jordi Folch Pi Outstanding Young Investigator 1992), Sigma Xi (sec./treas. 1986-93, pres. 1993-94), MUSES Calif. Sci. Mus. (Woman of Yr. 2009), John Douglas French Assoc.; fellow. ARVO Found. (Silver award 2009, Gold award 2010). Avocations: reading, travel. Office: U So Calif Keck Sch Medicine 1355 San Pablo St Rm 405 DVRC Los Angeles CA 90033 Personal E-mail: eyesightresearch@hotmail.com. Business E-Mail: ccraft@usc.edu.

CRAFT, PHILLIP R., plastic surgeon; BS, U. Ala., 1985—89; post-grad., U. Ala., 1989—90; MD, U. Tenn., 1990—94. Lic. Fla. Resident gen. surgery U. Tenn., 1994—97, burn fellow, 1997—98, resident in plastic surgery, 1998—2000; hyperbaryc oxygen tng. cours Columbia, SC, 1997; microsurgery tng. course, 1999; plastic surgeon. Author: (publs.) Traumatic and Pseudocyst of the Spleen, 1996, Steriotactic and Ultrasound Core Needle Breast Biopsy Performed by Surgeons, 1997. Mem.: Fla. Med. Assn., Am. Soc. of Plastic Surgeons. Office: 1441 Brickell Ave 3rd Fl Sky Lobby Miami FL 33131 Office Phone: 305-624-0009. Office Fax: 305-373-1175.

CRAFT, SUZANNE, neuroscientist, educator; b. Cin., June 10; d. Charles and Anne Fallon Craft. BA, U. Va., Charlottesville, 1976; PhD, U. Tex. Austin, 1984. Cert. Wash. Bd. Psychology, 2001. Clin. intern Boston VA Med. Ctr., 1984—85; fellow in neuropsychology and behavioral neuroscience Boston U. Sch. Medicine, 1985—86, Mailman Rsch. Ctr., Harvard Med. Sch., 1986—87, asst. prof. psychology, dir. grad. clin. neuropsychology Washington U., St. Louis, 1987—94, assoc. prof. psychology, 1994; adj. rsch. assoc. prof. psychology U. Wash., Seattle, 1994—, rsch. assoc. prof. psychiatry and behavioral sciences, 1994—98, assoc. prof. psychiatry and behavioral sciences, 1998—2002, prof. psychiatry and behavioral sciences, 2002—; rsch. clin. neuropsychologist and dir. memory disorders clinic/memory wellness prog. VA Puget Sound Health Care System, Seattle, 1994—, acting dir. geriatric rsch. edn. and clin. ctr., 1999—2002, assoc. dir. geriatric rsch. edn. and clin. ctr., 2002—. Contbr. scientific papers. Grantee, NIH, 1992—. Mem.: Cognitive Neuroscience Soc., Internat. Neuropsychological Soc., Soc. Neuroscience. Office Phone: 206-277-1156.

CRAIG, EDWARD VINCENT, orthopedic surgeon, educator; b. Bklyn., May 5, 1947; s. Edward Vincent and Lorraine (Youngkin) C.; m. Kathryn Ann Davis, July 4, 1982. BA, Princeton U., 1969; MD, Columbia U., 1973; MPH, Columbia U., NY, 2008. Diplomate Am. Bd. Orthopaedic Surgery. Intern Columbia-Presbyn. Med. Ctr., NYC, 1973-74, resident in internal medicine, 1975-76, resident in orthopaedic surgery, 1977-80, fellow in shoulder surgery, 1980-81, fellow in hand surgery, 1981-82; attending surgeon U. Minn. Hosp., Mpls., 1982-94, Hosp. Spl. Surgery, NYC, 1994—, New York Hosp., NYC, 1994—; prof. clin. surgery Cornell Med. Coll., NYC, 1994—. Cons., designer Biomet Atlas Total Shoulder Replacement Sys., Warsaw, Ind., 1985—, Comprehensed Primary and Comprehensive Reverse Total Shoulder Replacement; cons. Minn. Twins Baseball Club, 1993-94. Author: The Shoulder, 1995, Clinical Orthopaedics, 1999, The Unstable Shoulder, 1999, An Atlas of Replacement Surgery, 2006, Shoulder, Replacement Surgery, 2007, TOtal Shoulder Replacement, 2008, Designer Comprehensive Total Shoulder System Designer; contbr. articles to profl. jours. Bd. dirs. Waveny Day Care Ctr., New Canaan, Conn., 1996, New Canaan Country Sch., 2002, Juvenile Diabetes Found. Fairfield County, New Canaan Basketball Assn., AmeriCares. Fellow Am. Acad. Orthopaedic Surgeons; mem. AMA, Am. Shoulder and Elbow Surgeons (pres. 1985—), Am. Orthopaedic Soc. for Sports Medicine (rsch. grantee 1995), Am. Soc. Surgery of the Hand, Am. Orthopaedic Assn. (ABC Traveling fellow 1980). Republican. Roman Catholic. Achievements include design of comprehensive fracture prosthesis. Avocations: piano, skiing, golf, tennis, running. Office: Hosp Spl Surgery 535 E 70th St New York NY 10021-4872 also: Hosp Spl Surgery Affiliate Office 143 Sound Beach Ave Old Greenwich CT 06870 Home Phone: 203-966-0045; Office Phone: 212-606-1966. Business E-Mail: craige@hss.edu.

CRAIG, JAMES LYNN, physician, health services administrator; b. Columbia, Tenn., Aug. 7, 1933; s. Clifford Paul and Maple (Harris) Craig; m. Suzanne Anderson, July 20, 1957; children: James Lynn, Margaret; m. Roberta Annette Craig, May 17, 1980. Student, Mid. Tenn. State U., 1953; MD, U. Tenn., 1956; MPH, U. Pitts., 1963. Diplomate Am. Bd. Preventive Medicine. Intern U. Tenn. Meml. Hosp., Knoxville, 1957; resident in occupl. medicine U. Pitts., 1962-64, TVA, Chattanooga, 1964-65, physician, 1966-69, chief med. officer, 1969-74; corp. med. dir. Gen. Mills Corp., Mpls., 1974-76, v.p. corp. med. dir., 1976-80, v.p., dir. health and human svcs., 1980-98; adj. clin. prof. U. Minn., Mpls., 1979—, chmn. cmty. adv. com. Ctr. for Environ. and Health Policy, 1994-97, mem. adv. coun. health in scis., 1992-95, chmn. adv. bd. Ctr. for Environ. and Health Policy, 1994-97; pres. Family and Preventive Health Svcs., Inc., Mpls., 1998—. Clin. instr. U. Tenn., Memphis, 1970—74, Meharry Med. Sch., Nashville, 1972—74; mem. adv. bd. to dir. Ctr. Disease Control and Prevention, 1996—99; nat. adv. bd. Internat. Health and Media Awards, 1996—2006. Contbr. articles to profl. jours. Bd. dirs. Mpls. Blood Bank, 1976—88, Minn. Safety Coun., 1981—90, Minn. Heart Assn., Mpls., 1976—87, Children's Heart Fund, 1976—88, Meth. Hosp. Found., 1979—87, Park Nicollet Med. Found., 1987—93, Altcare, 1983—95, Meth. Hosp. Health Assn., 1987—93, Minn. Wellness Coun., 1986—91, Health Sys. Minn. Assocs., 1993—94, Health Sys. Minn. Inst. Rsch. and Edn., 1996—2000, chmn., 1997—2000, Park Nicollet Inst., 2000—01; trustee Minn. Med. Found., 2001—09; trustee bd. dirs. Crossroads Coll., Rochester, 2007—; trustee Crossroads Found., 2009—, bd. dirs., 2009—; exec. com. Crossroads Coll., 2010—; bd. dirs. Minn. Bible Coll., Rochester, 1978—83. Recipient Cmty. Svc. award, Park Nicollet Med. Ctr.,

1995, Knudsen award in occupl. medicine, Am. Coll. Occupl. and Environ. Medicine, 2000; named Legacy Laureate, U. Pitts., 2000. Fellow: Am. Acad. Family Practice, Am. Acad. Occupl. Medicine (treas. 1982—83, sec. 1983—84, v.p. 1984—85, pres. 1986—87), Am. Occupl. Medicine Assn. (bd. dirs. 1974—78); mem.: AMA (alt. del. Ho. Dels. 1990—92, del. 1992—96, Recognition award 1975, 1978, 1981, 1985, 1989, 1993, 1996, 1999, 2002, 2005, 2011), Minn. Med. Found. (bd. dirs. 2001—), Emergency Physicians Assn. (bd. dirs. 1984—92), Mpls. Acad. Medicine (sec. 1983—85, pres. 1985—86), Minn. Acad. Medicine, North Ctrl. Occupl. Medicine Assn. (pres. 1977), Occupl. Health Inst. (chmn. 1983—84), Mpls. Kiwanis Club (trustee 2004—09). Home: 10008 S Shore Dr Minneapolis MN 55441-5011 Office: PO Box 270330 Minneapolis MN 55427-6330 Personal E-mail: jimlcraig@aol.com.

CRAIG, ROBERT MONTGOMERY, medical educator; b. Pitts., Dec. 3, 1941; BA, Colgate U., 1963; MD, Northwestern U., 1967. Prof. Northwestern, 1974—. Recipient AGA Disting. Clinician award, Am. Gastroent. Assn., 2009, Disting. Physician award, Northwestern Feinberg Sch. Medicine. Fellow: Am. Gastroent. Assn. Avocation: tennis. Office: 233 E Erie Ste 206 Chicago IL 60611 Office Fax: 312-503-1881.

CRAIGEN, WILLIAM JAMES, clinical geneticist, educator; BS, BA, U. Tex., 1981; PhD, Baylor Coll., 1987, MD, 1988. Lic. Tex., 1991, cert. Am. Bd. Clin. Genetics-Med. Genetics, 2010, Am. Bd. Clin. Biochemical Genetics-Med. Genetics, 2010. Resident pediat. Baylor Coll. Medicine, 1988—92, fellow clin. genetics, 1988—90, assoc. prof. clin. genetics, asst. prof. molecular and human genetics and pediat. depts.; hosp. affiliation includes St. Luke's Hosp., Woman's Hosp., Tex., Harris Couonty Hosp. Dist.; staff physician genetics ctr. Tex. Children's Hosp. Office: Texas Children's Hospital Clinical Care Center 6701 Fannin St 16th Fl Houston TX 77030 Office Phone: 832-822-4280. Office Fax: 832-825-4294.

CRAIGHEAD, EDWARD, psychology professor; AA in Liberal Arts and Sciences, Freed-Hardeman Coll., Tenn., 1962; BA in Religion, minor in Psychology, Abilene Christian Coll., Tex., 1965; MA in Psychology, U. Ill., Urbana-Champaign, 1967, PhD in Psychology, 1970. Asst. prof. Dept. Psychology Pa. State U., University Park, 1970—74, assoc. prof., 1974—79, prof., 1979—86; vis. prof. Dept. Psychiatry Divsn. Med. Psychology Duke U. Med. Ctr., Durham, NC, 1985—86, prof. Dept. Psychiatry, 1986—95; prof. Dept. Psychology: Health and Social Sciences Duke U., Durham, NC, 1990—95; prof. Dept. Psychology U. Colo., Boulder, 1995—2006, chmn. Dept. Psychology, 2003—06; prof. psychology, prof. psychiatry and behavioral sciences Emory U., Atlanta, 2006—, J. Rex Fuqua chair, dir. child and adolescent mood program. Office: Emory Univ Dept Psychology 468 Psychology Bldg 36 Eagle Row Atlanta GA 30322 Office Phone: 404-712-8383. Office Fax: 404-727-3233. Business E-Mail: ecraigh@emory.edu.

CRAM, L. SCOTT, research scientist; b. Emporia, Kansas, Oct. 21, 1942; BS, Emporia State U., 1964; PhD, Pa. State U., 1969. Dep. divsn. dir. Los Alamos Nat. Lab., 1995—2000, office sci. program dir., 2000—04; rsch. scientist Bio-5 Inst., U. Ariz., 2005—11. Rsch. grant, NIH, Disting. Rsch. Assoc. fellowship, Max-Planck Gesellschaft. Mem.: Internat. Soc. Advancement Cytometry. Avocations: skiing, canoeing, mountain climbing. Office: 14029 N Running Brook Ln Marana AZ 85658 Personal E-mail: scottcram42@gmail.com.

CRAMARIUC, DANA, cardiologist; b. Suceava, Romania, Jan. 4, 1980; MD, U. Medicine Cluj, Romania, 2004; PhD, U. Bergen, Norway, 2009. Fellow cardiology and postdoc. fellow Haukeland U. Hosp., Bergen, Norway, 2010—. Recipient C. Walton Lillehei Young Investigator award, Scandinavian Assn. Thoracic Surgery. Office: Jonas Liesvei 65 Bergen Hordaland 5021 Norway Business E-Mail: dana.cramariuc@helse-bergen.no.

CRAMER, PHEBE, psychologist; b. San Francisco, Dec. 30, 1935; children: Mara, Julia. BA, U. Calif., Berkeley, 1957; PhD, NYU, 1962. Clin. psychologist Malmonides Hosp., Bklyn., 1962-63; asst. prof. Psychology Barnard Coll., NYC, 1963-65; vis. asst. prof. Psychology U. Calif., Berkeley, 1965-70; assoc. prof. Psychology Williams Coll., Williamstown, Mass., 1970-73, prof. Psychology, 1973—. Pvt. practice in clin. psychology, Williamstown, 1970—; chief psychologist Berkshire Mental Health Ctr., Pittsfield, Mass., 1978-86. Author: Word Association, 1968, Understanding Intellectual Development, 1972, The Development of Defense Mechanisms, 1991, Story-telling, Narrative, and the Thematic Apperception Test, 1996, Protecting the Self, 2006; mem. editl. bd. Jour. of Personality, 1987-96, assoc. editor, 1991-96; mem. editl. bd. Jour. of Personality Assessment, 1989—, European Jour. Personality, 2000—, Jour. Rsch. Personality, 2003—2009, assoc. editor 2009-. Judge U.S. Figure Skating Assn., 1989—. Mem.: APA, Assn. Rsch. Personality, Soc. for Personality Assessment. Office: Williams Coll Dept Psychology Bronfman Sci Ctr Williamstown MA 01267 Home: 20 Forest Rd Williamstown MA 01267-2029 Office Phone: 413-597-2463. Business E-Mail: phebe.cramer@williams.edu.

CRANDALL, BLANE MITCHELL, obstetrician, gynecologist; b. Atlanta, Ga., Dec. 4, 1970; s. Blane Milton and Doshie Ruth Crandall; m. Montese Marie Miller, June 12, 1993; children: Greyson Marie, Scarlett Cay. MD, U. Of South Fla., 1993—98. Diplomate Am. Bd. Ob-Gyn. Ob-gyn. resident U. Chgo., 1998—2000, Northshore U., 2000—02; pvt. practice Blane M. Crandall, MD, Clinton, Okla., 2002—06, Naples, Fla., 2006—. Featured spkr. Symposium On Metal Ions In Biology And Medicine, Barcelona, 1996; vis. rschr. Royal Free Hosp., London, 1996; adj. prof. Southwestern Okla. State U., 2003—. Contbr. articles to profl. jours. Active mem. Noon Lions Club, Clinton, Okla., 2002—06; vol. dr. Clinton Free Clinic, Okla., 2002—06; bd. mem. Sunnyside Therapeutic Riding Ctr., Clinton, Okla., 2002—06. Recipient Most Humanistic Resident, U. Of Chgo. Hospitals, 1999, Outstanding Tchg. award, 2000, Humanism And Excellence In Tchg. award, Arnold P. Gold Found., 2000, Physician's Recognition award, AMA, 2001, 2002, 2003. Fellow: Am. Coll. Of Obstetricians And Gynecologists; mem.: AMA, Fla. State Med. Assn. Collier County Med. Soc., Soc. Of Med. Educators, Am. Assn. Of Gynecologic Laparoscopists, Nat. Assn. Of Doctors. Avocations: travel, golf, boating. Office: 1660 Med Blvd St 101 Naples FL 34110-1415 Address: 206 Flamingo Ave Naples FL 34108-2106

CRANE, DANIEL BEVER, dentist, former United States Representative from Illinois; b. Chgo., Jan. 10, 1936; s. George Washington III and Cora Ellen (Miller) C.; m. Judy Ann Van Brunt, June 13, 1970; children: Bo, Joshua, Kimberly, Beth, Emily, Heidi. AB, Hillsdale Coll., 1958; DDS, Ind. U., Indpls., 1963; grad. work, U. Mich., 1964—65; DSc (hon.), Georgetown U., 1982. Pres. Dental Staff St. Elizabeth Hosp.; dir. Crane Clinic, Hillsboro, Ind., 1963-67; mem. US Congress from 22nd Ill. Dist., 1979—83, US Congress from 19th Ill. Dist., 1983—85; dentistry practice Danville, Ill., 1984—. Cons. research Ind. U., Indpls., 1961-67, in dentistry Ind. State Bd. Health, Indpl., 1963-67. Co-Author: Psychology Applied, 1974, Liberal Cliches, 1984; contbr. articles to profl. mags., jours. Chmn. 22d dist. for Reagan, Ill., 1976. Served to capt. US Army, 1967—70. Named one of The Outstanding Young Men of America, 1970. Mem. Assn. American Dentist (pres. 1976, dir. humanitarian studies 1978), American Legion (life). Republican. Methodist. *

CRANE, DAVID L., hospital administrator; Grad., Union Coll.; MBA, Rollins Coll. With Centura Health, Denver, Mercy Health Ptnrs.Toled, Toledo; pres. and CEO Littleton Adventist Hosp., Colo., Adventist Midwest Health, 2006—. Office: Adventist Hinsdale Hospital 120 N Oak St Hinsdale IL 60521 Office Phone: 630-856-9000.

CRANE, STEPHEN CHARLES, medical association executive; b. Waterbury, Conn., Oct. 4, 1946; s. Homer and Edna Crane; children: Russell, Elizabeth. BA, Princeton U., NJ, 1969; MPH in Health Planning, U. Mich., 1973, PhD in Pub. Health Adminstrn., 1981. Legis. analyst, mgmt. intern Dir.'s office NIH, Bethesda, Md., 1969; project dir. Columbia Rsch. Assocs., Inc., Cambridge, Mass., 1970; prog. analyst HEW, 1972; sr. rsch. assoc., rsch. assoc. then grad. rsch. fellow U. Mich. Sch. Pub. Health, 1973-79, lectr. program and bur. hosp. adminstrn., 1979-80, asst. prof., lectr. dept. med. care orgn., 1980-83; dir. Pew Health Policy doctoral prog. Boston U., 1983-90, asst. prof. Sch. Pub. Health, 1984-93, asst. academic v.p. health affairs, 1986-88; v.p. Assn. Health Svcs. Rsch. & Found. Health Svcs. Rsch., Washington, 1990-93; exec. v.p. Am. Acad. Physician Asst., Alexandria, Va., 1993—2007; exec. dir. Am. Thoracic Soc., NYC, 2007—. Staff Mich. Pub. Health Statue Revision Project, 1975—78; mem. adv. com. Mercy Coll. Physician Asst. Prog., Detroit, 1979—83, Western Mich. Physician Asst. Prog., Kalamazoo, 1981—85; mem. Mayor's Com. Access Health Care, Boston, 1984—86; nat. dir. prog. investigator grants in health policy rsch. Robert Wood Johnson Found., 1992—93; former mem. Mass. Com. Medically Uninsured. Contbr. articles to profl. jours. Recipient John H. Romani Disting. Alumni award, U. Mich. Sch. Pub. Health, 1996; grantee U. Mich. Ctr. Rsch. Learning & Tchg., 1982; fellow USPHS, 1972—73. Fellow: Mich. Acad. Physician Assts. (hon.). Office: Am Thoracic Soc 61 Broadway New York NY 10006-2755 Office Phone: 212-315-8600. Office Fax: 212-315-6498. *

CRANNY, THERESA M., veterinarian; b. Ames, Iowa, Dec. 10, 1965; d. Charles Joseph and Beverly Jean Cranny. BS in Biology, Bowling Green State U., 1987; DVM, Ohio State U., 1991. Veterinarian Animal Clinic of Butler, Renfrew, Pa., 1991—93, Woodmar Animal Clinic, Hammond, Ind., 1993—2000, Lincolnway Animal Hosp., Matteson, Ill., 2000—05, South Suburban Animal Hosp., 2005—. Panelist Vet. Medicine Roundtable Discussion, 2002. Office: South Suburban Animal Hosp 5100 Brockway Perrysburg OH 43551 Office Phone: 419-872-0920. Personal E-mail: tmcdvm@msn.com.

CRATER, TIMOTHY ANDREWS, internist; b. Winston-Salem, NC, Aug. 27, 1966; s. John Lee Crater and Nancy Denton Crater; m. Debra Marie Schuh, Feb. 14, 1992; children: Reed Brooks, Zoe Emerson, Grace Warren, Isabelle Holton. BA in History magna cum laude, Wake Forest U., 1989; student field arty. officers basic course, Ft. Sill Arty. Sch., Okla., 1990; officer's tng., U.S. Army Airborne Sch., Ft. Benning, Ga., 1990, 1st Infanty Divsn., 1991; MD, U. Kans., 1998. Commd. 2d lt. US Army, 1989, advanced through grades to 1st lt., 1992, fire support officer hdqs. battery 1/5 field arty. Ft. Riley, 1990-91, fire direction officer bravo battery 1/5 field arty., 1991-92, targeting officer hdqs. battery 1/5 field arty., 1992-93; resigned, 1993; resident in internal medicine U. Ala. Birmingham Hosp., 1998-2001; staff physician internal medicine Hutchinson Clinic, Kans., 2001—, bd. dirs., 2004—10, pres., 2008; clin. asst. prof. internal medicine U. Kans. Sch. Medicine, Wichita, 2002—; vice chief of staff Hutchinson Hosp., 2005—09, chmn. utilization rev., 2005—07, chief of staff, 2008. Bd. dirs., trustees Hutchinson Hosp., 2005—09; med. coord. Reno County Health Dept. Bd. dirs. New Beginnings Homeless Shelter, 2005—07. Decorated Bronze Star medal for valor, Army Commendation medal, Army Achievement medal with oak leaf cluster; fellow, Am. Coll. Physicians; History of Medicine grantee, U. Kans., 1995. Fellow ACP; mem. AMA, VFW (life), Kans. Soc. SAR, Am. Legion (life), Officers of the 1st Divsn., U. Kans. Med. Hon. Soc. (Paul Harris fellow Rotary Internat.), Promise Regional Med. Ctr. (chief med. staff 2011), Phi Beta Kappa, Phi Alpha Theta, Alpha Omega Alpha. Republican. Avocations: reading, running. Home: 3504 Thunderbird Dr Hutchinson KS 67502 Office: Hutchinson Clinic PA 2101 N Waldron Hutchinson KS 67502 Office Phone: 620-694-4225. Personal E-mail: cratermd@aol.com. Business E-Mail: craterta@hutchclinic.com.

CRAVEN, E. RANDY, ophthalmologist, educator; b. Denver, Sept. 14, 1956; BS, Regis U., 1979; MD, U. Colo., 1983. Pres. Splty. Eye Care, 1996—; assoc. clin. prof. U. Colo., 2000—10, Rocky Vista U., 2009. Mem. bd. dirs. Ophthalmic Mut. Ins. Co., 1991—2000; editl. bd. mem. Ophthalmology Mgmt. Mag., 1997; assoc. examiner Am. Bd. Ophthalmology, 2005. Recipient Lewis Rudin prize, NY Acad. Medicine, James Doyle award, James Doyle Soc.; named Best Doctors in Am.; grant, Shell Found. Fellow: Am. Soc. Cataract and Refractive Surgery, Am. Acad. Ophthalmology (Sr. Achievement award); mem.: Assn. Rsch. in Vision, Am. Glaucoma Soc. Avocations: bicycling, fly fishing, winemaking. Office: 11960 Lioness Way 190 Parker CO 80138 Office Fax: 303-347-1341. Personal E-mail: ercraven@yahoo.com.

CRAWFORD, E. DAVID, urologist, surgeon, researcher; b. Cin., June 6, 1947; s. Elward G. and Gertrude E. (Wagner) C.; m. Barbara Schoborg, June 28, 1969; children: Michael, Marc, Ryan. BS, U. Cin., 1969, MD, 1973. Intern Good Samaritan Hosp., Cin., 1973-74, resident, 1974-77; asst. and assoc. prof. urology U. N.Mex. Sch. Medicine, Albuquerque, 1978-83; assoc. prof. to prof. surgery/urology U. Miss. Med. Ctr., Jackson, 1983-86; prof., chmn. div. urology U. Colo. Denver, Sch. Medicine, Denver, 1986—. Chmn. genitourinary com. S.W. Oncology Group, 1979—. Editor: (textbook) Genitourinary Cancer Surgery; contbr. numerous articles to profl. publs. Chmn. Prostate Cancer Edn. Coun., N.Y.C., 1989. Fellow ACS; mem. Am. Soc. Clin. Oncology. Office: U Colo Denver Mail Stop F710 PO Box 6510 Aurora CO 80045 Office Phone: 720-848-0195. Business E-Mail: david.crawford@ucdener.edu.

CRAWFORD, FRED ALLEN, JR., cardiothoracic surgeon, educator; b. Columbia, SC, Oct. 17, 1942; s. Fred Allen and Susan Valery Floyd C.; m. Mary Jane Dantzler, June 11, 1966; children: Fred Allen III, Mary Elizabeth. MD, Duke U., 1967. Diplomate Am. Bd. Surgery, Am. Bd. Thoracic Surgery. Intern Duke U. Med. Ctr., Durham, NC, 1967-68, resident in surgery, 1971-76, instr. surgery, 1975-76; asst. prof. surgery, chief divsn. cardiac surgery U. Miss., Med. Ctr., Jackson, 1976-79; prof. surgery pediat., chief divsn. cardiothoracic surgery Med. U. of S.C., Charleston, 1979—, chmn. dept. surgery, 1988—. Contbr. numerous articles to profl. jours. Maj. U.S. Army, 1969-71. Decorated Bronze Star. Mem. ACS, Am. Surg. Assn., Charleston County Med. Soc., S.C. State Med. Assn., Soc. Thoracic Surgeons, So. Surg. Assn., So. Thoracic Surg. Assn., Am. Heart Assn., Am. Assn. Thoracic Surgery (pres. 2003), Am. Bd. Thoracic Surgery (bd. dirs. 1991-2002, chmn., 2001), Am. Coll. Cardiology, Phi Beta Kappa, Alpha Omega Alpha. Presbyterian. Office: 25 Courtney Dr Ste 7018 MSC 295 Charleston SC 29425-2950 Home Phone: 843-884-0361; Office Phone: 843-876-4840. Business E-Mail: crawfrdf@musc.edu.

CRAWFORD, GLEN H., dermatologist, educator; BA, Wesleyan U., 1992; MD, NYU, 1996. Diplomate Am. Bd. Dermatology. Intern Wilford Hall USAF Med. Ctr.; resident tng. Pa. Hosp., chief dermatology, founder Pa. Centre for Dermatology; dir. resident surgery clinic Hosp.of the Univ. of Pa.; clin. assoc. prof. Univ. of Pa. Co-author: (publs.) Brod BA, Szapary PO. Characterization of adverse dermatologic reactions to a commonly used complementary and alternative medicine: results from a randomized, placebo controlled trial of Guggulipid, Disorganization syndrome, Use of aromatherapy products is associated with increased risk of hand dermatitis in massage therapists, Erythematous facial plaques in a patient with leukemia, and numerous others. Capt. USAF. Named one of Top Doctors, Phila. Mag., 2009—11. Office: Perelman Center for Advanced Medicine S Pavilion 1st Fl 3400 Civic Center Blvd Philadelphia PA 19104 Mailing: PA Hospital PA Centre for Dermatology 822 Pine St Ste 2A Philadelphia PA 19107 Office Phone: 800-789-7366.

CRAWFORD, J. BROOKS, ophthalmologist, educator; b. San Francisco, Aug. 2, 1933; s. Joseph William Crawford and Ora Amanda Brooks; m. Christine Mayne, Sept. 12, 1964; children: Catherine Helene Crawford Bradford, Peter Brooks. B Engring, Yale U., New Haven, 1955; MD, U. Calif. San Francisco, 1960. Diplomate Am. Bd. Ophthalmology. Intern Columbia Presbyn. Med. Ctr., NYC, 1960—61; resident ophthalmology U. Calif. Med. Ctr., San Francisco, 1961—64; clin. assoc. NIH, Bethesda, Md., 1964—66; NIH Spl. fellow eye pathology Armed Forces Inst. Pathology, Washington, 1966—67; chief ophthalmology Children's Hosp., San Francisco, 1978—92; clin. prof., dir. eye pathology U. Calif., San Francisco, 1992—; pvt. practice ophthalmology San Francisco, 1967—. Asbury lectr. U. Cin., 2004; guest lectr. Japanese Ophthalmic Pathology Soc., Osaka, 1998, European Ophthalmic Pathology Soc., Stockholm, 2003; bd. dirs. That Man May See, San Francisco; dir. Eye Pathology Lab. Dept. Ophthalmology U. Calif. Sch. Medicine, San Francisco, 1972—. Contbr. articles to profl. jours. Bd. trustees Town Sch. Boys, San Francisco, 1976—85; bd. dirs. Am. Bd. Ophthalmology, 1976—93, chmn., 1993; bd. dirs. No. Calif. Soc. Prevention Blindness, pres., 1992—93. Lt. cmdr. USPHS, 1960—66. Recipient Charlotte Baer Meml. award, U. Calif. San Francisco, 1995, Crowell Beard award Dept. Ophthalmology, 1995, 2010. Fellow: ACS; mem.: Beard-Quickert Soc., Cordes Eye Soc. (pres. 1981—82, Hogan lectr. 1992), Verhoeff Soc. (pres. 1988), Am. Assn. Ophthalmic Pathologists, Am. Ophthalmol. Soc. (editor Trans. 1997, pres.-elect 2003—04, pres. 2004—05), Am. Acad. Ophthalmology (assoc. sec. 1993—97, Zimmerman lectr. 2000), Armed Forces Inst. Pathology Alumni Assn., Pacific Union Club, Bohemian Club, Gold Headed Cane Soc., Tau Beta Pi, Alpha Omega Alpha, Sigma Xi. Office: 3838 California St San Francisco CA 94118 Office Phone: 415-387-8808.

CRAWFORD, LESTER MILLS, JR., scientific consultant, former federal agency administrator; b. Demopolis, Ala., Mar. 13, 1938; s. Lester Mills and Susan Doris (Mitchell) C.; m. Catherine Walker, July 27, 1963; children: Catherine Leigh, Mary Stuart. DVM, Auburn U., Ala., 1963; PhD in Pharmacology, U. Ga., Athens, 1969; MDV (hon.), Budapest U., Hungary, 1987. Pvt. practice vet. medicine, Meridian, Miss. and Birmingham, Ala., 1963-64; R & D staff agrl. divsn. Am. Cyanamid Co., Princeton, NJ, 1964-66, cons.; assoc. dean Coll. Vet. Medicine, U. Ga., 1970-75, head dept. physiology-pharmacology, 1980-82; dir. Ctr. Vet. Medicine, FDA, Dept. Health and Human Svcs., Rockville, Md., 1978—80, 1982—85; assoc. adminstr. food safety & inspection svc. USDA, Washington, 1986-87, adminstr., food safety & inspection svc., 1987-91; exec. v.p. sci. affairs Nat. Food Processors Assn., Washington, 1991-93; exec. dir. Assn. Am. Vet. Med. Colls., Washington, 1993—97, 2001—02; dir. Ctr. Food and Nutrition Policy, Georgetown U., Washington, 1997-2001; dir. Ctr. Food and Nutrition Policy Va. Tech., 2001—02; dep. commr. FDA, US Dept. Health & Human Services, Rockville, Md., 2002—04, acting commr., 2004—05, commr., 2005; sr. counsel Policy Directions, Inc., Washington, 2006—. Cons. pharm. industry, agribus. FDA, 1992-2002, WHO, 1985-86, 1998-2007; mem. Health Professions Commn., Pew Meml. Trust, 1990-93; bd. dir. BT safety Cary Pharm. and Immunobiosciences; mem. sci. adv. bd. Inst. Food Tech., 1999-2002; chmn. dept. physiology-pharmacology, U. Ga. Contbr. sci. articles to profl. jours. Vice chmn. Codex Alimentarius Commn., 1991-93; bd. dir. Food and Drug Law Inst., 1988-2002; expert advisor food safety WHO 1999-2007. Recipient A.M. Mills award, 1979, K.F. Meyer award, 1980, U.S. Presdl. Rank award of Meritorious Exec., 1988, Disting. Alumnus award, Auburn U., 1989, Wooldridge Meml. medal, Brit. Vet. Assn., 1991, Commrs. Spl. citation FDA, award of merit, 1983. Fellow: Internat. Acad. Food Sci. and Tech., Royal Soc. Medicine (U.K.); mem.: WHO (mem. expert adv. panel food safety), AVMA, AAAS, NAS Inst. Medicine, Fedn. Am. Sch. Health Professions (pres. 1997), French Acad. Vet. (hon.), Nat. Acad. Practice, Cosmos Club (Washington), Phi Kappa Phi, Phi Zeta, Sigma Xi. Republican. Office: Policy Directions Inc 818 Connecticut Ave NW Ste 950 Washington DC 20006 Office Phone: 202-776-0071.

CRAWFORD, MARIA LUISA BUSE, geology educator; b. Beverly, Mass., July 18, 1939; d. William Theodore Buse and Barbara (Kidder) Aldana; m. William A. Crawford, Aug. 29, 1963. BA, Bryn Mawr Coll., 1960; postgrad., U. Oslo, 1960-61; PhD, U. Calif., 1965.

Asst. prof. Bryn Mawr (Pa.) Coll., 1965-73, assoc. prof., 1973-79, prof., 1979-92, prof. environ. studies and sci., 1992—2006, William R. Kenan Jr. prof., 1985-92, chmn. dept. geology, 1976—88, 1998—2005, rsch. prof., 2006—10, prof. emerita, 2006—; ret., 2006. Curator mineral collection Bryn Mawr Coll.; chmn. women geoscientists com. Am. Geol. Inst., 1976-77; mem. U.S. Nat. Com. Geochemistry, 1980-82, U.S. Nat. Com. Geology, 1994-97; organizing com. 28th Internat. Geol. Cong., 1987-89. MacArthur fellow, 1993-98; grantee NASA, 1973-76, NSF, 1967-2007. Fellow Geol. Soc. Am. (councillor 1982-85), Mineral Soc. Am. (councillor 1989-92);mem. Mineral Assn. Can. (councilor 1985-87), Am. Geophys. Union, Norwegian Geol. Soc., Phila. Geol. Soc. Office: Bryn Mawr Coll Dept Geology Bryn Mawr PA 19010 Office Phone: 610-526-5111. Business E-Mail: mcrawfor@brynmawr.edu.

CRAWFORD, MARK E., psychologist; b. Nashville, Feb. 21, 1962; s. W. Edward and Joan (English) C.; m. Dana Elaine Frizzell, May 23, 1992; children: Caleb, Benjamin. BA, U. Tenn., 1984; MS, St. Louis U., 1987, PhD, 1989. Lic. psychologist, Ga. Clin. dir. Rapha USA, Atlanta, 1989-91; psychologist Atlanta Counseling Ctr., 1990-97; pres. Lyles and Crawford Clin. Consulting, P.C., 1997—. Mem. Am. Psychol. Assn., (Divsn. 12, 29), Ga. Psychol. Assn., Am. Assn. Christian Counselors, Soc. for Personality Assessment. Avocations: tennis, swimming. Office: Lyles & Crawford Clin Consulting PC Ste 320 11111 Houze Rd Roswell GA 30076 Office Phone: 770-993-0051. Office Fax: 770-993-0052. E-mail: drcrawford@lylesandcrawford.com.

CRAWFORD, MICHAEL HOWARD, cardiologist, educator, researcher; b. Madison, Wis., July 10, 1943; s. William Henry and A. Kay (Keller) C.; m. Janis Raye Kirschner, June 23, 1968; children: Chelsea Susan, Dinah Jaye, Stuart Michael. AB, U. Calif., Berkeley, 1965; MD, U. Calif., San Francisco, 1969. Diplomate in internal medicine and cardiovasc. disease Am. Bd. Internal Medicine. Med. resident, internal medicine U. Calif. Hosps., San Francisco, 1969-71; sr. med. resident, internal medicine Beth Israel Deaconess Med. Ctr., Boston, 1971-72; tchg. fellow Harvard Med. Sch., Boston, 1971-72; cardiology fellow U. Calif. Hosps., San Diego, 1972-74; asst. prof. medicine U. Calif. Sch. Medicine, San Diego, 1974-76, U. Tex. Health Sci. Ctr., San Antonio, 1976-78, assoc. prof. medicine, 1978-82, prof. medicine, 1982-89; Robert S. Flinn prof. cardiology U. N.Mex. Sch. Medicine, Albuquerque, 1989—2001; prof. medicine Mayo Med. Sch., Minn., 2001—03, U. Calif., San Francisco, 2003—, Lucie Stern chair cardiology, 2005—. Asst. dir. Ischemic Heart Disease Specialized Ctr. Rsch., San Diego, 1975—76; adj. scientist S.W. Found. Biomedical Rsch., San Antonio, 1980—89; co-dir. div. cardiology U. Tex. Health Sci. Ctr., San Antonio, 1983—89; chief div. cardiology U. N.Mex. Sch. Medicine, Albuquerque, 1989—2001; cons. cardiovasc. diseases Mayo Clinic, Scottsdale, Ariz., 2001—03; chief clin. cardiology U. Calif. San Francisco Med. Ctr., 2003—07; chief divsn. cardiology U. Calif., San Francisco, 2007—. Editor: Current Diagnosis and Treatment in Cardiology, 1995, 3d edit., 2009, Cardiology, 2001, 3d edit., 2009, 3rd edit., 2009; editor Clin. Cardiology Alert newsletter, 1990—; cons. editor (periodical) Cardiology Clinics, 1989-; mem. editl. bd. Circulation Jour., 1990-99, Jour. Am. Coll. Cardiology, 1992-95, 2003-; contbr. several articles to profl. jours. Pres. Am. Heart Assn., San Antonio, 1981, Austin, Tex., 1987, chmn. coun. clin. cardiology, Dallas, 1989, pres., Albuquerque, 1995-96. Recipient Paul Dudley White award, Assn. Mil. Surgeons of U.S., 1981; Merit Review grantee, Dept. VA, 1983—91, Rsch. Tng. grantee, Nat. Heart Lung Blood Inst., 1993—2001. Fellow: ACP, Am. Heart Assn. (chmn., coun. on clin. cardiology), Am. Coll. Cardiology (bd. trustees 1998—2003); mem.: Western Assn. Physicians (pres. 2008—09), Assn. Univ. Cardiologists (pres. 2005—06), So. Soc. Clin. Investigation, Am. Soc. Echocardiography (bd. dirs. 1980—83). Avocation: skiing. Office: U Calif Divsn Cardiology 505 Parnassus Ave Box 0124 San Francisco CA 94143-0124 Home: 5 Cecilia Ct Belvedere Tiburon CA 94920-2190 Office Phone: 415-502-8584. Business E-Mail: crawfordm@medicine.ucsf.edu.

CRAWFORD, RICHARD BRADWAY, biologist, biochemist, educator; b. Kalamazoo, Feb. 16, 1933; s. Kenneth and Alma (Smith) C.; m. Betty J. Jacobs, Jan. 30, 1954; children: Kathleen, Christine, Kevin, Nancy. AB, Kalamazoo Coll., 1954; PhD in Biochemistry, U. Rochester, 1959. Postdoctoral fellow U. Rochester, NY, 1959; instr. to assoc. prof. U. Pa., 1959-67; assoc. prof. to prof. biology Trinity Coll., Hartford, Conn., 1967-98, prof. emeritus, 1998—, chmn. dept., 1978-87, resuming chmn., 1996-97. Asst. dir., trustee Mt. Desert Island Biol. Lab., Salsbury Cove, Maine, 1966-82; vis. scientist Jackson Lab., Bar Harbor, Maine, 1988; vis. prof. biology U. Warwick, Eng., 1988; vis. prof. marine biology U. Calif. San Diego, 1974; vis. prof. U. Edinburgh, 1996; mem. faculty and curriculum com. Acadia Sr. Coll., 2000—, v.p. bd. dirs. Contbr. articles to profl. jours. Mem. Inlands, Wetlands and Water Courses Commn., Wethersfield, Conn., 1976-81, Wethersfield Conservation Commn., 1995-98; bd. dirs. Mt. Desert Island Hist. Soc., sec., 2001—; v.p. bd. dirs. Acadia Sr. Coll., 2003-08. Mem. Beatrix Farrand Soc. (bd. dirs. 2006—, V.p. 2007-), Rotary Club Hartford (pres. 1994-95), Mount Desert Island Rotary. Democrat. Congregationalist. Home: PO Box 826 Mount Desert ME 04660-0826

CRAWFORD, SUSAN, library director, educator, editor, writer; d. James Y. and S. Young; m. James Weldon Crawford, July 5, 1955; 1 son, Robert James. BA, U. B.C., 1948; MA, U. Toronto, 1950, U. Chgo., 1954, PhD, 1970. With bur. libr. and indexing svc. ADA, 1954-56; with office exec. v.p. AMA, Chgo., 1956-60, dir. divsn. libr. and archival svcs., 1960-81; assoc. prof. Sch. Libr. Sci., Columbia U., NYC, 1972-75; prof., dir. Sch. Medicine Libr. and Biomed. Comm. Ctr. Washington U., 1981-92; adj. prof. dept. psychiatry U. Ill., Chgo., 1994—; rsch. asst. Northwestern U. Kellogg Sch. Mgmt., 2005—06. Internat. steering com. Royal Coll. Physicians and Surgeons. Mem. internat. steering com. Universal Guide Sci. Publs.; mem. editl. bd. Med. Socioecon. Rsch. Sources, Index to Sci. Revs., Jour. Am. Soc. Info. Sci., Med. Libr. Assn. News, Health and Info. Librs., Budapest, Health Librs. Rev., London, Health Info. and Librs. Jour., Oxford, Eng., 2003—; assoc. editor Jour. Am. Soc. Info Sci. Tech., 1979-82; editor Med. Info. Sys., 1988-90; editor-in-chief Jour. Med. Libr. Assn., 1982-88, 91-92; author of books; contbr. more than 140 articles to profl. jours.; mem. editl. bd. of 10 scientific jours. Bd. regents US Nat. Libr. Medicine, NIH, 1971-75; mem. bd. overseers Tufts U., 1988-89; cons. for grants rev., Nat. Sci. Found., Nat. Libr. Medicine Recipient Eliot award for scientific pubs., Disting. Alumni award U. Toronto, 1987, Grad. medal U. Toronto, 1989, McGovern award, Med. Libr. Assn., 1986, Pres.'s award Med. Libr. Assn., Noyes award, Speciality Group award Am. Soc. for Info. Sci.; named Janet Doe hon. lectr., 1983; grantee NIH, Inst. for Scientific Info., Majors Scientific Publications, St. Louis Metro. Med. Soc., St. Louis Sch. Dental Medicine. Fellow AAAS (chmn. coms.), Med. Libr. Assn. (life, Eliot award 1976, chmn. com. on surveys and stats. 1966-75, publs. panel 1977-80, chmn. consulting editors panel 1981-88, 91-92, spl. award to editor of bull. 1988, Noyes award 1992, Pres.'s award 1992, Centennial award), Med. Libr. Assn. (100 Most Notable 1998); mem. ALA, Soc. Social Studies Sci., Am. Soc. Info. Sci. and Tech. (chmn. med. info. sys. 1987-88, outstanding splty. group award 1988, 89, edn. com., publications com., bd. and program chair Chgo. chpt. 1993-95), Am. Med. Informatics Assn., Acad. Health Info. Profls. (disting. mem.), European Assn. Health and Info. Librs. (U.S. rep. 1989-94), Sigma Xi (chmn. coms.). Achievements include research in scientific and biomedical communication, statistical surveys, information networks, group practice in psychiatry and co-citation analysis. Home: 2418 Lincoln St Evanston IL 60201-2151 Office Phone: 847-869-3108. Personal E-mail: sjcrawf@aol.com.

CRAWFORD, VICKY CHARLENE, perinatal clinical nurse specialist, nursing administrator; b. Waynesville, NC, Aug. 20, 1959; d. Jerry Harrell and Geneva Pauline (Parker) C. BSN, Med. U. of S.C., 1981; MS in Maternal/Infant Nursing, Clemson U., 1991. Cert. in inpatient obstet. nursing. Staff nurse II ob Greenville (S.C.) Gen. Hosp., 1981-83; staff nurse labor and delivery Lexington County Hosp., West Columbia, S.C., 1983-84; staff RN III high risk ob-gyn Greenville Meml. Hosp., 1984-85, ob-gyn. clinician, 1985-91, ob-gyn. clin. nurse specialist, 1991-94; perinatal clin. nurse specialist Ctr. for Women's Medicine-Maternal Fetal Medicine Divsn., Greenville, 1994-2000; clin. nurse specialist, clin. mgr. high risk pregnancy unit Gwinnett Women's Pavilion, Lawrenceville, Ga., 2000—. Counselor, program coord. Resolve Through Sharing Bereavement Svcs.; developer Mother-Baby Care Cross-Tng. Program, 1989. Contbr. articles to profl. jours. Mem. Assn. Women's Health, Obstetrics and Neonatal Nursing (conv. speaker), Sigma Theta Tau. Office Phone: 678-442-3075. E-mail: vcrawford@ghsnet.org.

CREANGA, ANDREEA A., epidemiologist; b. Calarasi, Romania, Mar. 21, 1978; MD, Carol Davila Sch. Medicine, 2002; PhD, Johns Hopkins Bloomberg Sch. Pub. Health, 2009. Rsch. asst. Johns Hopkins U., 2005—09, sr. rsch. scientist, 2009; epidemic intelligence svc. officer Ctrs. Disease Control and Prevention, 2009—11, med. epidemiologist, 2011—. Cons. UNFPA, 2007; adj. prof. Emory U., 2010; tech. cons. Bill and Melinda Gates Inst. Population and Reproductive Health, 2009. Recipient Effective Pub. Health Practice award, Coalition Excellence in Maternal and Child Health Epidemiology, 2009, Excellence award, Ctrs. Disease Control and Prevention, 2009, Paul A. and Esther C. Harper award, Johns Hopkins Bloomberg Sch. Pub. Health, Edward J. Dehne award. Mem.: AAAS, Population Assn. America, Internat. Obstetric Fistula Working Group. Home: 3974 Kendall Cove Atlanta GA 30340 Business E-Mail: acreanga@cdc.gov.

CRÉANGE, ALAIN, neurologist, researcher; b. Neuilly-sur-Seine, France, Oct. 2, 1964; m. Françoise Slotto, Sept. 7, 1996. Med. studies, Paris VII U., 1987; MD in Neurobiologist, Nat. Diploma, France, 1993; PhD in Neuroimmunol. Specialty (hon.), Paris XII U., 2000, ability to conduct rsch. (hon.), 2001. Prof. neurology Paris XII U., 2002—; sr. resident Hopital Henri Mondor, Creteil, France, 1993—. Mem.: French Neurol. Soc. Achievements include research in peripheral neuropathies; neuroimmunology; neurophysiology; neurofibromatoses. Avocations: violin, cycling, photography. Office: Hopital Henri Mondor 51 av du maréchal de Lattre de Tassigny 94000 Creteil France

CREASIA, DONALD ANTHONY, toxicologist, researcher; b. Milford, Mass., Mar. 28, 1937; s. Dominic and Minnie (Bufalo) C.; m. Joan La Belle, June 29, 1963; children: Karen Joan, Tracey Dawn. BS in Biology, U. Vt., 1961; MS, Harvard U., 1967; PhD, U. Tenn., 1981. Rsch. assoc. Sch. Pub. Health, Harvard U., Cambridge, Mass., 1963-69; toxicologist Oak Ridge (Tenn.) Nat. Lab., 1970-77; program dir. Frederick (Md.) Cancer Rsch. Ctr., 1977-83; rsch. chemist U.S. Army R&D, Frederick, 1983-98; cons. Knoxville, Tenn., 1998—. Cons. toxicology. Author: (chpts. in books with others) Internat. Symposium on the Biological Effects of Ozone and Related Photochemical Oxidents, 1983, Trycothecine Mycotoxicosis: Pathophysiological Efffects, 1989; contbr. over 120 articles to profl. jours. NSF scholar, 1965-67; NRC fellow, 1981-83. Mem. AAAS, Soc. Toxicology, Am. Coll. Toxicology, Soc. Govt. Toxicologists, Internat. Soc. Toxicology, Sigma Xi. Achievements include patents for use of castor bean protein as an immunological adjuvant; patents pending for nose-only and body plethismograph animal holder used in inhalation toxicology studies; discovery that insulin is equally effective in lowering blood glucose when inhaled into deep lung as when it is administered intramuscularly. Home: 605 Scotswood Cir Knoxville TN 37919-7457 Personal E-mail: dcreasia@comcast.net.

CREASIA, JOAN CATHERINE, dean, nursing educator; b. Burlington, Vt., Aug. 14, 1941; d. Ramon J. and Marjorie E. (Rising) LaBelle; m. Donald A. Creasia, June 29, 1963; children: Karen, Tracey. BSN, U. Vt., Burlington, 1964; MSN, U. Tenn., 1978; PhD, U. Md., 1987. Staff nurse psychiat. unit Mass. Mental Health Ctr., Boston, 1964-65; instr. D'Youville Sch. Nursing, Cambridge, Mass., 1965-66; staff nurse Boston Lying-In Hosp., 1966-67; staff nurse med. surg. units Norwood Hosp., Mass., 1967-70; staff nurse, nursing supr. Oak Ridge Hosp., Tenn., 1971-74; staff nurse, supr. Frederick Meml. Hosp., Md., 1977-78, 86-92; instr. in nursing U. Tenn., Knoxville, 1974-77; rsch. asst. U. Md., Balt., 1980-83; instr., coord., asst. prof. med. surg. nursing Frederick (Md.) C.C., 1978-80, 81-83; asst. prof., coord. RN BSN program U. Md. Sch. Nursing, Balt., 1983-90, assoc. prof., chair RN-BSN/MS programs, 1990-94, dir. statewide programs, 1991-94; assoc. dean for acad. programs and interim dean Med. U. SC Coll. Nursing, Charleston, 1994-95; dean, Coll. Nursing, U. Tenn., Knoxville, 1995—. Cons. in field. Author: Conceptual Foundations of Professional Nursing Practice, 1991, 96 (Book of Yr. award Am. Jour. Nursing 1992), Conceptual Foundations: The Bridge to Professional Nursing Practice, 2001, 4th edit., 2006, 5th edit., 2010; contbr. articles to profl. jours. and books. Bd. dirs. Tenn. Ctr. for Nursing. Recipient Outstanding Achievement in Indirect Nursing Rsch. award, 1987, Nat. Rsch. Svc. award, 1982, 83, Profl. Nurse Traineeship award, 1981, Outstanding Leadership award Md. Nurses Assn., 1990, Excellence in Nursing Leadership award Tenn. Orgn. Nurse Execs., Knoxville Coun., 2006, Excellence in Edn. award Sigma Theta Tau, Gamma Chi chpt., 2010. Mem.: ANA, Am. Assn. Colls. Nursing, Nat. League Nursing, Phi Kappa Phi, Sigma Theta Tau (award 2010). Home: 605 Scotswood Cir Knoxville TN 37919-7457 Office Phone: 865-974-7583. Personal E-mail: joan.creasia@comcast.net. Business E-Mail: jcreasia@utk.edu.

CREASMAN, WILLIAM THOMAS, obstetrician-gynecologist, educator; b. Miami, Ariz., Sept. 3, 1934; s. George Dewey and Pauline (Cate) C.; m. Erble Jeannie Garrett, Aug. 29, 1958; children: Valrie Kay, William Scott. BA, Baylor U., 1956, MD, 1960. Intern Jefferson Davis Hosp., Houston, 1960-61; resident U. Rochester, N.Y., 1963-67; asst. prof. M.D. Anderson Hosp., Houston, 1969-70; asst. prof. dept. ob-gyn Duke Med. Ctr., Durham, N.C., 1970-74, assoc. prof., 1974-78, prof., 1978—, James Ingram prof., 1982—; Sims-Hester prof., chmn. dept. ob-gyn Med. U. S.C., Charleston, 1986. Key investigator Duke Comprehensive Cancer Ctr., 1971-86; trustee N.C. Cancer Inst., 1976-86. Author: Gynecologic Oncology, 1981; contbr. articles to profl. jours. Recipient Pres's award Am. Coll. Obstetricians and Gynecologists, 1973; recipient First Prize paper Am. Coll. Obstetricians and Gynecologists, 1980; Robertson Meml. lectr. Dundee, Scotland, 1976 Fellow Am. Coll. Obstetricians and Gynecologists, Am. Gynecol. and Obstetrical Soc.; mem. Soc. Gynecologic Oncologists (sec-treas. 1975-78, pres. 1988), Am. Radium Soc., Soc. Pelvic Surgeons Republican. Baptist. Home: 906 Red Coat Run Mount Pleasant SC 29464-9220 Office: OBGYN Dept Med Univ SC Charleston SC 29425 *

CREATH, CURTIS JANSSEN, pediatric dentist; b. Lynwood, Calif., Mar. 10, 1958; s. Ronald J. and Madelyn W. (Chryst) C.; m. Deborah Ann Lipari, June 23, 1990; 1 child, Andrew. Student, UCLA, 1976-81; DMD, Oral Roberts U., 1985; MS, U. Ala., 1988. Asst. prof. Sch. Dental Medicine SUNY, Stony Brook, 1988-91, Sch. Dentistry U. Ala., Birmingham, 1991-94; staff pediat. dentist Family Dental Care Assocs., Cin., 1994-95; pvt. practice Milford, Ohio, 1995—. Team leader dental mission trips to Mex., Jamaica, Peru, 1982-84. Contbr. chpt. to: Special and Medically Compromised Patients in Dentistry, 1989, Clark's Clinical Dentistry, Vol. 2, 1994; contbr. articles, revs. on tobacco control, pediat. dentistry, and preventive medicine to profl. jours. Mem. ADA, Am. Acad. Pediat. Dentistry (mem. edn. com.), Am. Assn. Dental Schs. (v.p. 1986-88), Ala. Soc. Pediat. Dentistry (sec.-treas. 1992-94), Christian Med. and Dental Soc., Omicron Kappa Upsilon. Republican. Presbyterian. Avocations: vocal music, preaching, missionary work, woodworking, gardening. Home: 6514 Tulip Ct Liberty Township OH 45044-9726 Office: 1106-C Main St PO Box 267 Milford OH 45150-0267 Personal E-mail: curtjcre@aol.com.

CREAVEN, PATRICK JOSEPH, pharmacologist; b. London, Jan. 31, 1933; MBBS, St. Mary's Hosp. Med. Sch., U. London, 1956, PhD in Biochemistry, 1964. House surgeon Bedford Gen. Hosp.; also house physician Barnet Gen. Hosp., Eng., 1956-57; asst. lectr. biochemistry U. London, St. Mary's Hosp. Med. Sch., 1963-64, lectr., 1964-66; chief biochemistry Tex. Rsch. Inst. Mental Sci., 1966-69; head, pharmacology lab. Nat. Cancer Inst., VA Med. Oncology Br., 1969-75; assoc. chief, cancer rsch. clinician Roswell Park Meml. Inst. (now Roswell Park Cancer Inst.), Buffalo, 1975-79, chief cancer rsch. clinician, 1979—, chmn. dept. clin. pharmacology and therapeutics, 1979-89, chief div. clin. pharmacology and therapeutics, Dept. Medicine, 1989—91, sr. investigator dept. investigational therapeutics, 1991—97; dir. Phase I Program Roswell Park Cancer Inst., 2001—; rsch. prof. medicine dept. medicine SUNY Med. Sch., Buffalo, 1994—, prof. oncology Roswell Pk. Cancer Inst., 2006—. Contbr. articles to profl. jours. 1st. lt. Royal Army Med. Corps, 1957—58, capt. Royal Army Med. Corps, 1958—60. Fellow Am. Coll. Clin. Pharmacology, Royal Soc. Health; mem. Am. Assn. Cancer Rsch., Am. Soc. Clin. Oncology, Am. Soc. Pharmacology and Exptl. Therapeutics, Am. Soc. Clin. Pharmacology and Therapeutics.

CREE, MICHELE L., pharmacist; b. Lismore, NSW, Australia, Oct. 3, 1965; BSc, U. Queensland, B in Pharmacy, 1989, diploma in Clin Pharmacy, 1999. Clin. team leader Queensland Health Royal Children's Hosp., 2008—10; mem. bus. reference group ICU CIS Project, Queensland Health, Spring Hill, 2008—, clin. pharmacist, 2010—. Mem.: Australian Pain Soc., Soc. Hosp. Pharmacists. Avocations: skiing, running, swimming. Office: Queensland Health Gloucester St Spring Hill Queensland 4000 Australia Office Fax: 07 31460576.

CREECH, CLARENCE BUDDY, pediatric epidemiologist, educator; b. July 16, 1973; Grad. cum laude, MPH, Vanderbilt U.; MD, U. Tenn. Coll. Medicine, 1999. Cert. Pediatrics. Pediatric staff mem. Vanderbilt Children's Hosp., 1999, chief resident, pediatrics, 2002, pediatric infectious disease fellow, asst. prof., pediatric infectious diseases, 2006—. Contbr. articles to profl. jours. Office: Monroe Carell Jr Childrens Hosp at Vanderbilt 2200 Childrens Way Nashville TN 37232 Office Phone: 615-936-6772. Business E-Mail: buddy.creech@vanderbilt.edu.

CREEL, PATRICIA ANN, nursing researcher; b. Springfield, Vt., June 5, 1963; ADN, U. Vt., 1983; BSN, NC Ctrl. U., 2000. Nurse mgr., oncology Duke U. Med. Ctr., 2001—03, sr. lead clin. rsch. coord., 2004—. Nurse, adv. bd. Kidney Cancer Assn., 2004—11. Mem.: Sigma Theta Tau. Home: 180 Denada Path Roxboro NC 27574 Business E-Mail: creel003@mc.duke.edu.

CREER, THOMAS LASELLE, psychologist, educator, writer; b. Lund, Idaho, Nov. 2, 1934; s. Laselle Lewis Creer and Naomi Johanna Jones; m. Patricia J. Plummer, July 7, 1961; children: Jennifer, Matthew. BS, Brigham Young U., 1956; Master's, Utah State U., 1961; PhD in Psychology, Fla. State U., 1967. Lic. psychologist Colo. Prof. psychology Ohio U., Athens, 1980—96; pres. Creer Sys., Inc., Provo, Utah, 1995—2002. Co-exec. dir. Nat. Asthma Ctr., Denver, 1977—80. Author: Chronically Ill and Handicapped Children, 1976, Asthma Therapy: A Behavioral Health Care System for Respiratory Disorders, 1979, Self-Management of Chronic Disease, 1986, Psychology of Adjustment, 1997, Respiratory Disorders and Behavioral Medicine, 2002, others; contbr. 200 articles, revs., writings and chpts. 12 books in field. Bd. dirs. Am. Lung Assn. Ohio, Columbus, 1983—93, Am. Lung Assn. Utah, 2002—; pres. Am. Lung Assn., Utah, 2004—05. With US Army, 1956—58. Recipient Pre-doctoral Internship award, VA, 1966—67; fellow Pre-doctoral fellow, U.S. Pub. Health Svc., 1963—66. Liberal. Avocation: reading. Home: 144 E 4620 N Provo UT 84604 Personal E-mail: tcreer@comcast.net.

CRESSWELL, PETER, immunobiologist, educator; BS, U. Newcastle upon Tyne, 1966, MS, 1967; PhD, U. London, 1971. Postdoc. fellow Harvard U., Cambridge, Mass., 1971—73; faculty, chief divsn.

immunology Duke U. Med. Ctr., Durham, NC, 1973—91; prof. immunobiology Yale U. Sch. Medicine, New Haven, 1991—, Eugene Higgins prof. immunobiology, 2009—. Mem. NRC Com. on Recommendations for US Army Basic Sci. Rsch., 1987—90; mem. allergy and immunology study sect. NIH, 1987—91; investigator Howard Hughes Med. Inst., 1991—; fellow Silliman Coll., Yale U., 1999, Lincoln Coll., U. Oxford, England, 2007; mem. sci. adv. bd. Jane Coffin Childs Meml. Fund, 2002—10, Ctr. HIV/AIDS Vaccine Immunology (CHAVI), U. NC, 2005—; Newton-Abraham vis. prof. U. Oxford, 2007. Assoc. editor Immunity, 1994—, mem. editl. bd. Human Immunology, 1983—97, Ann. Rev. Immunology, 1998—2002, Traffic, 1999—, Immunological Reviews, 2002—08, Tissue Antigens, 2002—, Ann. Rev. Cell & Devel. Biology, 2003—, Immunology, 2004—07; contbr. articles to profl. jours. Fellow: Royal Soc.; mem.: NAS, Am. Acad. Arts & Scis., NY Acad. Scis., Inst. Medicine, European Molecular Biology Orgn. (assoc.), American Soc. Cell Biology, American Soc. Histocompatibility & Immunogenetics (Rose Payne Disting. Scientist award 1995), American Assn. Immunologists. Office: Yale Univ Sch Medicine PO Box 208084 New Haven CT 06520 *

CRETAN, DONNA, neonatal nurse, consultant; b. Mpls., May 18, 1939; d. Howard Robert and Frances E. (Warner) Bjerke; m. Nestor Nicholas Cretan, Jan. 24, 1959; children: Colette, John, Christopher, Bernadette. ADN, Contra Costa Coll., 1973; BSN, Sacred Heart U., Fairfield, Conn., 1986. RN Conn. Nurse mgr., cons. St. Joseph Med. Ctr., Stamford, Conn., 1974-89; staff nurse Cmty. Hosp., Santa Rosa, Calif., 1989-93, Greenwich (Conn.) Hosp., 1993—2002, Mark Twin St. Joseph Hosp., San Andreas, Calif., 2002—. ESL tutor LVA, 1997—. Host parent A Better Chance, New Canaan, Conn., 1982-84, Am. Field Svc., 1983-84, Calif., 1991-93, Cultural Homestay, Cohasset, Mass., 1991-95, People Link, Petaluma, Calif.; sec. Hist. Soc., Sebastopol, Calif., 1989-92; vol. nurse Americares Free Clinic Norwalk, 1994—; literacy vol. ESL Inst., 1997-98. Mem.: ANA, Internat. Lactation Cons. Assn. (cert.), Neonatal Network, Obstetrics and Neonatal Nurses, Assn. Women's Health. Avocations: lactation promotion, photography. Office: Mark Twain St Joseph Hosp San Andreas CA Home: 22865 Northrup Ct Columbia CA 95310-9419

CRIDER, RUDYARD LEE, psychotherapist; b. Abilene, Kans., Oct. 16, 1942; s. Clarence A. and Myrtle (Cox) C.; m. Doris Elaine Heisey, Aug. 3, 1962; 1 child, Michele Renee. BA, Messiah Coll., 1971; MS, Shippensburg U., 1978. Cert. clin. mental health counselor; nat. cert. counselor; cert. diplomate in psychotherapy; lic. profl. counselor; approved clin. supervisor. Mental health worker King's View Hosp., Reedley, Calif., 1966-68; crisis intervention counselor Holy Spirit Hosp. Mental Health, Camp Hill, Pa., 1974-78, sr. psychotherapist, 1978—, asst. coord. outpatient svcs., 1989—2001, program supr. behavioral health svcs., 2001—06, clin. supr. behavioral health svcs., 2006—; pvt. practice psychotherapy, 1992—. Sr. peer reviewer Holy Spirit Hosp. Mental Health, Camp Hill, 1990-96, quality assurance com., 1990—, clin. site supr., 1983—, mem. extended mgmt. team, 1994—. Recipient Recognition for Outstanding Svc. award Cumberland Perry County Mental Health-Mental Retardation Program, 1993. Mem. Acad. Clin. Mental Health Counselors, Am. Counseling Assn., Am. Mental Health Counselors Assn., Am. Psychotherapy Assn., Pa. Counselors Assn., Pa. Psychol. Assn. Lutheran. Avocations: photography, bicycling, hiking, drawing, backpacking. Home: 438 Parkside Rd Camp Hill PA 17011-2127 Office: Holy Spirit Hosp 21st St Camp Hill PA 17011

CRINO, MARJANNE HELEN, anesthesiologist; b. Rochester, NY, Aug. 18, 1933; d. Michael Jay and Helen Barbara (Kennedy) C.; m. Michael Anthony La Iuppa, Nov. 12, 1960 (dec. Feb. 1996); children: James Michael, Barbara Helen, John Christopher. BS, Coll. St. Teresa, 1955; MD, Marquette U. Sch. Medicine, 1959; MA in Theology, St. Bernard's Inst., 1991. Diplomate Nat. Bd. Med. Examiners. House staff Genesee Hosp., Rochester, 1959—61; perinatal mortality rsch., resident in anesthesiology Jackson Meml Hosp.-U. Miami, 1962—65; attending staff in anesthesiology Genesee Hosp., Rochester, 1969—2000, mem. exec. com., med. staff sec., 1980, Rochester, 1982, acting chmn. dept. anesthesiology, 1989, 1991, chmn. pain control com., 1989—95; clin. instr. anesthesiology U. Rochester Sch. Medicine, 1983—99; ret., 1999. Cons. anesthesiology Rochester Psychiat. Ctr., 1975-85; instr. anesthesiology U. Miami Sch. medicine, 1966, 67; attending staff anesthesiology Jackson Meml. Hosp., Miami, 1966, 67. Mem. adv. bd. Isaiah House Hospice, 1994-2000, com. Pittsford Rep. Party, NY, 1970's-80's; vol. chaplain Genesee Hosp. Mem. NY State Soc. Anesthesiologists (bd. dirs., vice spkr. 1983-86, del. 1971-82, 87-2002), Am. Soc. Anesthesiologists (del. 1979-86, 97), AMA, NY State Med. Soc., Med. Soc. County of Monroe, Rochester Acad. Medicine, Cath. Physicians Guild Rochester (bd.dirs., pres. 1988-89), Margaret Roper Guild (pres. 1975-76), Cath. Women's Club (Diocese of Rochester). Roman Catholic. Avocations: reading, gardening, music. Home Phone: 585-381-9663.

CRIPE, MARK, surgeon; b. Ind., Mar. 8, 1973; DO, Midwestern U., 2000. Dir. Breast Health Drs. Hosp., 2006—; breast surgeon Ohio Health, 2011—. Dir., Breast Sugery Fellowship Grant Med. Ctr., 2011—. Office: 285 East State St Ste 300 Columbus OH 43215 Office Phone: 614-566-0774. Office Fax: 614-566-0762. Business E-Mail: mcripester@pol.net.

CRIPPA, STEFANO, surgeon; b. Monza, Milano, Italy, July 11, 1978; s. Guglielmo Crippa and Franca Redaelli; life ptnr. Claudia Bonardi. Diploma in classical studies, Liceo Classico Zocchi Monza, 1997; MD, U. Milan-Bicocca Med. Sch., Italy, 2003. Intership genral surgery San Raffaele Hosp., Milano, Italy, 2003—04; resident surgery U. Verona, Italy, 2004—06; rsch. fellow Mass. Gen. Hosp., Boston, 2006—. Contbr. articles various medical papers. Mem.: Italian Assn. for the Study of the Pancreas (assoc.). Office: U Verona Piazzale LA Scuro 10 Verona 30700 Italy Home: Via Achille Grandi 8 20871 Vimercate MB Italy Personal E-mail: ste.crippa@libero.it.

CRISI, LOUISE-MARIE, oral and maxillofacial surgeon; b. London, Apr. 22, 1959; arrived in Netherlands, 1977; d. John Oreste Edgar Crisi and Louise-Marie Reintjens; 1 child, Sara Giovanna Raphaela. MD, Rijksuniversiteit Limburg, Maastricht, Netherlands, 1988; DMD, Katholieke U., Nymegen, Netherlands, 1995. Speciality in maxillofacial surgery U. Med. Ctr., Utrecht, Netherlands, 1999, mem. staff pediat. maxillo-facial surgery, 1999—2001; pvt. practice pediat. maxillo-facial surgery, surgeon various hosps., Utrecht, 2001—. Mem. Bd. Dentists, Utrecht, 2000—. Mem.: Dutch Assn. Oral and Maxillofacial Surgeons, Dutch Soc. Oral Implantology, EAO, Dutch Soc. Cleft and Craniofacial Anomalies (bd. mem. post-acad. edn. for maxillofacial surgeons). Home: Zevenwouden 22 3524CT Utrecht Netherlands Office: Med Ctr Bilstraat Biltstraat 397 3572AV Utrecht Netherlands Office Phone: 00-31-302333542. Business E-Mail: kaakchicurgie@medischcentrumbiltstreat.nl. E-mail: louisecrisi@hotmail.com.

CRISMON, MILES LYNN, clinical psychopharmacologist, dean, educator; b. Tulsa, Feb. 13, 1951; s. Isaac Edward and Geneva Angeline (Pate) Crismon; children: Teresa Lynne, Anthony Edward, Olya Grace, Sensey Alexander. BS in Pharmacy, U. Okla., 1974; PharmD, U. Tex. Health Sci. Ctr., San Antonio, 1979. Diplomate Am. Bd. Clin. Pharmacology, lic. pharmacist Tex., N.Mex. Resident hosp. pharmacy USPHS Gallup Indian Med. Ctr., 1974-75; resident psychopharmacology U. Tex. Health Sci. Ctr., 1979; asst. prof. U. Tex. Coll. Pharmacy, Austin, 1979-85, assoc. prof., 1985—91, prof., 1991—, asst. dean, 1984-85, head clin. divsn., 1985-96, assoc. dean. clin. programs, 2004—07, dean Coll. Pharmacy, 2007—. Clin. pharmacologist Austin State Hosp., 1979—2004, Healthcare Rehab. Ctr., Austin, 1985—98; cons. Tex. Dept. Mental Health, 1983—91, 1996—2006, Healthcare Financing Adminstrn., Balt., 1986—98, Okla. Dept. Mental Health, 1988; vis. prof. Coll. Arts Sci. & Tech., Kingston, Jamaica, 1989, 91, Nat. Mental Health Inst., Singapore, 2007; co-dir. Tex. Medication Algorithm Project, 1996—2006; dir. Children's Medication Algorithm Project, 1998—2006. Contbr. articles to profl. jours., chapters to books. Lt. sgt. USPHS, 1974—76. Recipient Janssen Pharmaceutica Partnering Rsch. award for mental health, 1998; named Tchr. of Yr., Child Psychiatry Presidency Program, UTSCUMC, Austin, 2010; grantee NEH, 1981, Robert Wood Johnson Found., 1997, Meadows Found., 1997, 1999, Hogg Found., 1999, Houston Endowment, 1999. Fellow: Am. Coll. Clin. Pharmacy Rsch. Inst. (bd. regents 2002—05, bd. trustee 2010—, CNS Rsch. award 1989); mem.: Acad. Pharm. Rsch. & Sci., Tex. Soc. Health-Sys. Pharmacists (bd. dirs. 1981—84, 1986—89, treas. 1987—89, bd. dirs. 1992—95, pres. 1993—94), Coll. Psychiat. & Neurologic Pharmacists (founding mem.), Am. Soc. Health-System Pharmacists (chmn. psychopharmacy splty. practice group 1991). Democrat. Roman Catholic. Avocations: hiking, camping, scuba. Office: U Tex Coll Pharmacy 1 University Sta MC A 1900 Austin TX 78712 Office Phone: 512-471-3718.

CRIST, WILLIAM MILES, academic administrator, pediatrician, educator; b. Florence, SC, July 21, 1943; s. Harry Brogan and Rosemary (Reid) C.; m. Helen Lucille Valle, June 5, 1971; 1 child, Brian. BA cum laude, Cen. Meth. Coll., 1965; MD, U. Mo., 1969. Intern in pediatrics Mott Children's Hosp., Ann Arbor, Mich., 1969-70; resident fellow in pediatrics and pediatric hematology St. Louis Children's Hosp., 1971-72; trainee Nat. Cancer Inst. Wash. U. Sch. Medicine, St. Louis, 1974-75; asst. prof. pediatrics U. Ala., Birmingham, 1975-78; assoc. scientist Comprehensive Cancer Ctr. U. Ala., Birmingham, 1975-78; acting dir., then dir. hematology/oncology Children's Hosp. U. Ala., Birmingham, 1976-85; prof. pediatrics, dir. pediatrics, hematology/oncology U. Tenn., Memphis, 1985—2000; chmn. dept. hematology/oncology St. Jude Children's Rsch. Hosp., Memphis, 1985—94, dep. dir., 1994—97; chair dept. pediats. and adolescent medicine Mayo Clinic, Rochester, 1997—2000; dean U. of Missouri-Columbia Sch. of Med., 2000—08, Hugh E. & Sarah D. Stephenson dean, 2004—08; v.p. health affairs Ariz. Health Scis. Ctr., U. Ariz., 2008—. Mem. Children's Oncology Group, 1976—. Maj. USAF, 1972-74. Mem. Am. Soc. Hematology, Sigma Epsilon Pi, Omicron Delta Kappa. Office: Ariz Health Scis Ctr Drachman Hall, Rm B-207 1295 N Martin Ave / PO Box 210202 Tucson AZ 85721-0202 Office Phone: 250-626-1197. Office Fax: 250-626-1460. E-mail: wcrist@email.arizona.edu. *

CRISTEA, AURELIA NICOLETA, pharmacologist, educator, researcher; b. Turnu Severin, Romania, Nov. 18, 1941; d. Gheorghe Ion and Alexandra Aida (Buica) C.; m. Adrian Gratian Restian, Mar. 10, 1989. Student, U. Romania, 1964, DSc, 1974. Chemist diplomat. Chemist Chemist's Shop, Fetesti, Romania, 1964-67, Ampula Factory, Bucharest, Romania, 1967-68; chemist rschr. Faculty Pharmacy, Bucharest, 1968-73, asst. prof., 1973-93, prof., 1994—, head dept. pharmacology and clin. pharmacy, 1997—2011. Pres.-elect Romanian Clin. Pharmacy sect. Romanian Soc. Pharm. Scis., 1998—2004; sci. chancellorship Faculty of Pharmacy, 2000. Contbr. Elabor (the first applied book of clin. pharmacy in Romania), vol. 1, 2006, vol. 2, 2009; contbr. articles to profl. jours. Recipient Romanian Acd. prize for informational concept in pharmacology, 1994. Mem.: Internat. Assn. Cybernetics, European Soc. Clin. Pharmacy, Internat. Rsch. Group on Very Low Dose Effects, European Coll. Neuropsychopharmacology, Nat. Acad. Pharmacy France, Romanian Med. Sci. Acad. Avocations: meditation, reading philosophy, admiration of nature, pictures and music. Office: U Medicine & Pharmacy Carol Davila/Traian Vuia 6 Bucharest Romania Home: Str Horia Macelariu 23-25 11/5 a 13933 Bucharest Romania Home Phone: 4021-2327256; Office Phone: 4021-3180738. Personal E-mail: anicoletacristea@yahoo.com. Business E-Mail: farmacol_farmbuc@yahoo.com.

CRISWELL, ELEANOR CAMP, psychologist; b. Norfolk, Va., May 12, 1938; d. Norman Harold Camp and Eleanor (Talman) David; m. Thomas L. Hanna (dec. 1990), P.E. Roberts, 2000 BA, U. Ky., 1961, MA, 1962; EdD, U. Fla., 1969. Asst. prof. edn. Calif. State Coll., Hayward, 1969; prof. psychology, former chair Calif. State U., Sonoma, 1969—2008; emeritus prof. Sonoma State U., 2008. Faculty adviser Humanistic Psychology Inst., San Francisco, 1970-77; dir. Novato Inst. Somatic Rsch. and Tng.; editor Somatics jour.; cons. Venturi, Inc., Autogenic Sys., Inc.; clin. dir. Biotherapeutics, Kentfield Med. Hosp., 1985-90; founder Humanistic Psychology Inst. (now Saybrook U.), 1970. Author: How Yoga Works, 1987, Biofeedback and Somatics, 1995; editor: Cram's Introduction to Surface Electromyography, 2010; co-editor: Biofeedback and Family Practice Medicine, 1983; patentee optokinetic perceptual learning device. Mem. APA (past pres. divsn. 32), Biofeedback Soc. Calif. (past pres.), Assn. for Humanistic Psychology (past pres.), Somatic Soc. (pres.), Equine Hanna Somatics (founder), Internat. Assn. Yoga Therapists (pres.). Office: Novato Inst 1516 Grant Ave #212 Novato CA 94945 Home Phone: 415-897-6044; Office Phone: 415-897-0336. Business E-Mail: ecriswel@ix.netcom.com.

CRNIC, KEITH A., psychology professor, department chairman; Attended, Menlo Coll., Atherton, Calif., 1968—70; BA in Psychology, cum laude, U. So. Calif., LA, 1972; PhD in Clin. Psychology, U. Wash., Seattle, 1976. Intern San Fernando Valley Child Guidance Ctr., Northridge, Calif., 1975—76; instr. in psychiatry and behavioral sciences U. Wash., 1976—79, asst. prof. psychiatry and behavioral sciences, 1979—84, affiliate faculty, child devel. and mental retardation ctr., 1979—87, assoc. prof. psychiatry and behavioral sciences, 1984—87, adj. assoc. prof. psychology, 1986—87; assoc. prof., dept. psychology Pa. State U., 1987—91, prof., dept. psychology, 1991—2004, head, dept. psychology, 1998—2003, prof. & dir., dept. psychology child study ctr., 2003—04; prof. psychology Ariz. State U., Tempe, 2004—, chmn., dept. psychology, exec. co-dir., family and human dynamics rsch. inst. Contbr. articles to profl. jours. Recipient Dir. award, US Pub. Health Svc. Maternal and Child Health Bur. Mem.: Soc. Rsch. in Child Devel. Office: Ariz State Univ Psychology Dept 950 S McAllister PO Box 871104 Tempe AZ 85287-1104 Office Phone: 480-965-3061. Business E-Mail: keith.crnic@asu.edu.

CROCK, HENRY VERNON, surgeon, writer; b. Perth, Australia, Sept. 14, 1929; arrived in Eng. 1986; s. Vernon John and Annie (Doyle) C.; m. Mary Carmel Shorten, Mar. 15, 1958; children: Catherine, Elizabeth, Carmel, Vernon, Damian. Student in Dental Sci., U. Western Australia, 1947—48; MB, BS in Anatomy, Physiology, Bacteriology, Medicine and Surgery with honors, U. Melbourne, Victoria, Australia, 1953, MD, 1967, MS, 1977; DSc (hon.), Melbourne U., 2008. Jr. resident med. officer with med. and surg. rotations St. Vincent's Hosp., U. Melbourne, 1954, sr. resident med. officer gen. urol. and orthop. surgery, 1955; sr. demonstrator anatomy dept. U. Melbourne, 1956; resident tutor in anatomy Newman Coll, U. Melbourne, 1956; sr. surg. registrar St. Vincent's Hosp., U. Melbourne, 1957, sr. hon. orthopaedic surgeon, 1961-86; Nuffield Dominions clin. asst. orthop. surgery Nuffield Orthop. Ctr., U. Oxford, 1957-60; lectr. in orthop. surgery Oxford U., 1959-60; assoc. prof. dept. surgery U. Melbourne, 1978-85; hon. cons., hon. sr. lectr. orthop. surgery Royal postgrad. Med. Sch., Hammersmith, 1986-96; hon. rsch. fellow anatomy dept. Royal Coll. Surgeons, England, 1986—88. Spl. lectr. orthop. surgery U. Melbourne, 1961-86, Naughton Dunn lectr. Birmingham Royal Infirmary, 1988; guest lectr. U. Dusseldorf, Japanese Orthop. Assn., U. Nottingham, Norfolk and Norwich Hosps., U. Oporto, U. Bologna, U. Manchester, Internat. Soc. Study of Lumbar Spine, Japan, Switzerland, Saudi Arabia. Author: The Blood Supply of the Lower Limb Bones in Man, 1967, Practice of Spinal Surgery, 1984, A Short Practice of Spinal Surgery, 1992; co-author: (with Yoshizawa) The Blood Supply of the Vertebral Column and Spinal Cord in Man, 1977, (with Yamagishi and M C Crock) The Conus Medullaris and Cauda Equina in Man, 1986, An Atlas of the Vascular Anatomy of the Skeleton and Spinal Cord, 1996; contbr. numerous chpts. in books (with others) including Spinal Stenosis, 1991, The Lumbar Spine and Back Pain, 1991, The Adult Spine: Principles and Practice, 1991; contbr. articles to numerous profl. jours. Pres. DISCS Charitable Trust, London, 2009. Decorated officer Order of Australia; recipient Prosector and Gold medal (with G. W. Crock) U. Melbourne, 1949, Gold medals in Medicine and Surgery St. Vincent's Hosp. Clin. Sch., 1953, L. O. Betts Meml. Gold medal Australian Orthop. Assn., 1976; Michael and Margaret Ryan scholar. Fellow Royal Coll. Surgeons Edinburgh (hon.), Royal Coll. Surgeons (Wood Jones medal 1981, Arnott Demonstrator, 1988), Royal Australasian Coll. Surgeons (Sir Allan Newton prize 1977), Brit. Orthop. Assn., Internat. Soc. Study of Lumbar Spine (pres. 1985). Achievements include research in Anatomical Studies on the Blood Supply of the Human Skeleton and Spinal Cord. Developed new equipment for the internal fixation of bones with special application to the correction of spinal deformities. (With Dr. R. V. Dickens) described the Anatomy of Venous Subchondral Circulation in the human femoral head. Personal E-mail: hvcrock@bigpond.net.au.

CROCKETT, DENNIS M., pediatrician, otolaryngologist, educator; MD, Univ. of Southern Calif. Keck Sch. of Medicine. Resident, intern Univ. of Southern Calif. Keck Sch. of Medicine; fellow pediatric otolaryngology Boston Children's Hosp., Harvard Med. Sch.; assoc. prof. Univ. of Southern Calif. Keck Sch. of Medicine, LA; med. staff Children's Hosp. of Orange County Children's at Mission; joined Head and Neck Assocs., Mission Viejo. Named one of the America's Top Doctors, Castle-Connolly, the America's Top Doctors for Cancer. Fellow: ACS, Am. Acad. of Otolaryngology-Head and Neck Surgery, Am. Acad. of Pediats. Office: Childrens Hospital of Orange County Childrens at Mission Hospital 27700 Medical Center Rd Mission Viejo CA 92691 Office Phone: 949-364-1400.

CROFT, HARRY ALLEN, psychiatrist; b. Houston, July 2, 1943; s. Louis and Ida (Kaplan) C.; m. Benay Bleacher, Dec. 27, 1964; children: Jamie Sue, Bradley Lane, Chasen Ashley. BS, So. Meth. U., 1964; MD, U. Tex. at Galveston, 1968. Intern Brackenridge Hosp., Austin, 1968-69; resident in obstetrics and gynecology U. Tex. Med. Br., 1969-70, resident in psychiatry, 1970-73; dir. methadone program Galveston County, Tex.; dir. sex therapy program U. Tex., Galveston, 1972-73; commd. capt. U.S. Army, 1973, advanced through grades to maj., 1975; chief (Mental Hygiene Service, Brooke Army Med. Center), Houston, 1973-76; pvt. practice, 1976—; med. dir. San Antonio Psychiat. Rsch. Ctr., 1988—. Clin. asst. prof. psychiatry and ob-gyn. Med. Sch. San Antonio, 1973-75; columnist San Antonio Express-News, 1975-76; weekly contbr. Sta. KMOL-TV (NBC) newscast, also KENS TV, 1988-90, KMOL TV, 1990-92; dir. rsch. and edn. Covenant Behavioral Health; med. dir. Healthy Pl.; host Healthy Pl. TV Show 2007-. Contbr. articles to profl. jours. Recipient physician's recognition award AMA, 1974, awards for med. TV work Nat. Healthcare Assn., 1988, Women in Comm., 1988; Meritorious Svc. medal U.S. Army, 1976, Ware 1st place audio-visual award Dept. Army, 1976, Gov.'s award State of Tex., 1991, award City of San Antonio, award Acad. Radio and TV Health Comm., Jules Bergman award-Broadcaster of Yr. award, 1995, Best Radio Show In U.S., Nat. Mental Health Assn., 1996; named Honoree, Am. Heart Assn., 2003. Mem. Am. Psychiat. Assn. (award 1991), Tex. Med. Assn. (award 1988), Am. Soc. Sex Educators, Counselors and Therapists, Am. Soc. Addiction Medince (cert. addictionist). Home: 12738 Hunters Chase St San Antonio TX 78230-1930 Office: 8038 Wurzbach Rd Ste 570 San Antonio TX 78229-3815 Home Phone: 210-602-9418; Office Phone: 210-692-1222. Personal E-mail: hacmd@aol.com.

CROITORU, MIRCEA DUMITRU, pharmacist, educator; b. Baia Mare, Apr. 20, 1977; PhD, UMF Tirgu Mures, 2010. Lectr. UMF Tirgu Mures, 2008—. Avocation: movies. Home: B-dul 1 Dec 1918 187/30 Targu Mures 540000 Romania Personal E-mail: croitorumircea@yahoo.com.

CROMBLEHOLME, TIMOTHY MATTHEUS, pediatric and fetal surgeon; b. New Bedford, Mass., Jan. 6, 1958; s. William J. and Therese L. (Gosselin) C.; m. Peggy Anne Orlando, June 10, 1989; children: Caitlin, Hayley, McCoy. BA, U. Pa., 1980; MD, Tufts U., 1984. Resident U. Calif., San Francisco, 1984-91; asst. prof. surgery Tufts U. Sch. Medicine, Boston, 1993-96; dir. New England Med. Ctr., Boston, 1995-96; asst. prof. surgery U. Pa. Sch. Medicine, Phila., 1996—, assoc. prof., 2000—; investigator strokes inst. Children's Hosp. Phila., 1996—2000. Adj. asst. prof. Wistor Inst., Phila., 1997—. Contbr. articles to profl. jours. Fellow U. Calif., 1987-89, Tufts U., 1991-93. Fellow Am. Coll. Surgeons, Assn. Pediatric Oncology; mem. AM. Soc. Gene Therapy. Office: Childrens Hosp Phila 34th St & Civic Ctr Blvd Philadelphia PA 19104 Home: 8680 Indian Hill Rd Cincinnati OH 45243-3708

CROMWELL, FLORENCE STEVENS, occupational therapist; b. Lewistown, Pa., May 14, 1922; d. William Andrew and Florence (Stevens) Cromwell. BS in Edn., Miami U., Oxford, Ohio, 1943; BS in Occupl. Therapy, Washington U., St. Louis, 1949; MA, U. So. Calif., 1952; cert. in health facility adminstrn., UCLA, 1978. Mem. staff, then supervising therapist Los Angeles County Gen. Hosp., 1949—53; occupl. therapist Goodwill Industries, LA, 1954—55; staff therapist Vis. Nurse Assn., Phila., 1955—56; rsch. therapist United Cerebral Palsy Assn., LA, 1956—60; dir. occupl. therapy Orthopaedic Hosp., LA, 1961—67; coord. occupl. therapy Rsch. and Tng. Ctr. U. So. Calif. Med. Sch., LA, 1967—70; assoc. prof. U. So. Calif., LA, 1970—76, acting chmn. dept. occupl. therapy, 1973—76, mem. adv. bd. project SEARCH, Sch. Medicine, 1969—72; founding editor Occupl. Therapy in Health Care jour., 1984—88, editor emerita, 1988—. Assoc. dir. L.A. Job Corps Ctr., 1977—78; cons. in edn. and program devel., 1976—95; freelance editor, 1986—. Author: Manual for Basic Skills Assessment, 1960; contbr. articles to profl. jours. Mem. scholarship com. L.A. March of Dimes, 1963—70; mentor U. Tex.-Galveston Class 1990 Occupl. Therapy; bd. dirs. Am. Occupl. Therapy Found., 1965—69, v.p., 1966—69; bd. dirs. Nat. Health Coun., 1975—78. Served to lt. (j.g.) WAVES USNR, 1943—46. Recipient Disting. Alumni award, Washington U., 1978, Disting. Lectr., Calif. Occupl. Therapy Found., 1986. Fellow: Am. Occupl. Therapy Assn. (pres. 1967—73, Pres.'s WLWest commendation AOTA-AOTF 1999); mem.: Assn. Schs. Allied Health Professions (dir. 1973—74), Coalition Ind. Health Professions (chmn. 1973—74), So. Calif. Occupl. Therapy Assn. (pres. 1950—51, 1975—76), Inst. Medicine NAS (emerita 2002), Cwen, Kappa Kappa Gamma, Kappa Delta Pi, Mortar Bd. Personal E-mail: fscromwell@aol.com.

CROMWELL, RONITA L., technologist; b. Elmhurst, Ill., Nov. 26, 1958; PhD, U. Ill. at Urbana Champaign, 1996. Rsch. technologist Northwestern U., 1991—93; asst. prof. Temple U., 1993—2000; assoc. prof. U. Tex. Med. Br., 2000—08, adj. assoc. prof., 2008; sr. scientist III U. Space Rsch. Assn., 2008—. Recipient Outstanding Rschr., Tex. Phys. Therapy Assn., UTMB Sch. Allied Health Professions. Fellow: Gerontol. Soc. America. Home: 207 Sleepy Hollow Ct Seabrook TX 77586 Business E-Mail: ronita.l.cromwell@nasa.gov.

CRONAN, JOHN J., radiologist, educator; b. Providence, Sept. 2, 1950; BA, Providence Coll., 1972; MD, Albany Med. Coll., 1976. Prof., chmn. Brown U., 1982—. Named Alumnus Of Yr., Albany Med. Coll. Fellow: Am. Coll. Radiology, Soc. Radiologist Ultrasound, Soc. Uroradiology. Home: 6 Atlantic Crossing Barrington RI 02806 Business E-Mail: jcronan@lifespan.org.

CRONAN, KERRY RICHARD, psychologist; b. Melbourne, Australia, Aug. 14, 1938; s. Alphonsus Richard and Catherine Dorothy (nee Egan) Cronan. BA in Psychology and Sociology, Swinburne Coll Advanced Edn., Victoria, 1975; BEd. in Counselling, La Trobe U., Victoria, 1977, M in Psychology, 1982. Ordained Cath. priest. Asst. priest South Yarra Parish, Victoria, 1965—66, Sunshine Parish, Melbourne, 1967—70, Wattle Park, Melbourne, 1971; Cath. chaplain Collingwood Tech. Sch., Victoria, 1972—75; asst. priest Collingwood Parish, Melbourne, 1972—75, Footscray Parish, Victoria, 1975, adminstr., 1976; asst. priest Doncaster, Victoria, 1977; lectr. Royal Melbourne Inst. Tech., Victoria, 1977; asst. priest Preston, Victoria, 1978, Moreland, Victoria, 1979; clin. dir. pyschiat. unit Mackay Base Hosp., Queensland, 1980—83; clin. psychologist Calvary Hosp., Canberra, 1983—84; area mental health coord. Clarence Valley Area Health Com., NSW, 1984—85; temp. specialist tutor U. Queensland Psychology Clin., 1985; lectr., tutor Queensland Inst. Tech., Coll. Advanced Edn., Kedron, 1986—87; cons. psychology Self Agys., 1987—96; clin. cons. psychologist Pvt. Practice, Brisbane, 1986—. Presenter in field. Resident psychologist: In Queensland Tonight ABC 4QR, 1993—95. Recipient Exemplary Impact Commendation award, Soc. Consulting Psychology, APA, 2007; HOM grant, Australian Embassy, 1994. Fellow: Australian Coll. Clin. Psychologists (chair 1987, found. chair 1987—89); mem.: External Comm. Coll. Orgnl. Psychologists (nat. coord. 2009—10), Acad. Mgmt., Bd. Clin. Psychologists (nat. chair 1992—93), Internat. Coun. Psychologists, Coll. Org. Psychologists, Assn. Pvt. Practicing Psychologists Inc., U. Queensland Alumni Assn., Australian Psychol. Soc. (regional sec. 1987—89, chair 1990, rep. 1991—93, com. mem. 1991—93, chair 1992, found. chair. 1994—97). Catholic. Avocations: walking, exercise. Business E-Mail: kerrycronan@hotmail.com.

CRONCE, PAUL CALVIN, retired dermatologist; b. Trenton, NJ, Dec. 25, 1931; s. Paul I. and Rachie Cathryn (Allen) C.; m. Nancy Elizabeth Dorrien, Aug. 27, 1960 (div. Aug. 1979); children: Paul Allen, Charles Scott, Thomas Taylor. BA summa cum laude, Duke U., Durham, NC, 1954; postgrad., Duke U. Grad. Sch. Arts & Scis., Durham, NC, 1954—55; MD, Duke U. Sch. Medicine, Durham, NC, 1960. Diplomate Am. Bd. Dermatology, 1965. Rotating med. intern USPHS Hosp., Boston, 1960-61; acting dermatology resident USPHS Hosp., Staten Island, 1961—62, dermatology resident, 1962—65, asst. chief dermatology, 1965—66; vis. fellow in dermatology Columbia-Presbyn. Med. Ctr., NYC, 1964-65; ptnr. Alden & Cronce Dermatology, Atlanta, 1966-73; pres. and treas. Alden Dermatology Assocs., P.A., Atlanta, 1973-99; ret., 1999. Instr. medicine, dermatology Emory U. Sch. Medicine, 1967-71, asst. clin. prof. dermatology, 1971-78, assoc. clin. prof. dermatology, 1978-89, clin. prof. dermatology, 1989-2001, prof. emeritus dermatology, 2001-. Contbr. articles to profl. jours. Fellow Am. Acad. Dermatology; mem. Southeastern Dermatological Assn., Ga. Soc. Dermatologists (vice chmn. 1971), Med. Assn. Ga., Internat. Soc. Dermatologic Surgery, Atlanta Dermatological Assn. (sec.-treas. 1967, pres. 1968), Med. Assn. Atlanta, Phi Beta Kappa, Alpha Omega Alpha. Republican. Presbyterian. Avocations: travel, gardening.

CRONE, EUGENE N., addictions specialist, retired educator; b. Newton Falls, Ohio, Apr. 17, 1929; s. Clarence Bennet and Violet Richards Crone. BM, Youngstown U., 1954; MA, Columbia U., 1958; PhD, Nat. U. Grad. Studies, Dallas, 1974. Cert. addiction profl., MAC-master addiction counselor, nat. cert. addiction counselor II, internat. cert. alcohol and drug counselor. Tchr., prof. various pub. schs. and colls., 1952—78; dir. addictions Horizon Psychiatric Hosp., Clearwater, Fla., 1978—95, Nat. Deaf Acad., Mt. Dora, Fla., 1995—, La Amistad Health Svcs., Maitland, Fla., 1999—2003; with Nat. Deaf Acad., Mt. Dora, Fla., 2003—; substance abuse intensive outpatient therapist Life Stream Behavioral Ctr., Leesburg, Fla., 2007. Presenter in field. Author: They Hear Through Their Eyes, 2003, To Russia With Hope, 2006; contbr. articles to profl. jours. PFC US Army, 1950—52. Recipient Profl. of Yr. Nat. award, NAADAC Nat. Conv., 1997, Profl. of Yr. award, Fla. NAADAC, 1996; named one of 10 addiction profls. to tour Russian Addiction Treatment Centers in Moscow and St. Petersburg, 2005. Mem.: NAADAC, Addiction Profls. of Fla., Internat. Cert. Alcohol & Drug Counselors (presenter). Methodist. Home: 1001 Bristol Lake Rd #212 Mount Dora FL 32757 Office: Nat Deaf Acad 19650 US Hwy 441 Mount Dora FL 32757 Office Phone: 352-360-6680. Personal E-mail: ecrone17@msn.com.

CRONENWETT, JACK LEMOYNE, vascular surgeon educator; b. Ludington, Mich., Dec. 13, 1946; s. Jack L. and K. Marie (Grundmark) C.; m. Linda R. Houk, 1969 (div. 1980); children: Sara, Molly; m. Debra A. Cote, Sept. 26, 1981. BS, U. Mich., 1969; MD, Stanford U., 1973. Diplomate in gen. surgery and vascular surgery Am. Bd. Surgery. Resident in gen. surgery U. Mich., Ann Arbor, 1973-79; resident in vacsular surgery U. Tenn., Memphis, 1979-80; asst. prof. surgery U. Mich., Ann Arbor, 1980-84; assoc. prof. surgery Dartmouth Coll., Hanover, NH, 1984-89, prof. surgery, 1989—. Editor Jour. Vascular Surgery, 2003—08. Mem. Am. Surg. Assn., New Eng. Soc. Vascular Surgery (sec. 1991-96, pres. 1997-98), Soc. Vascular Surgery (recorder 1996-2001, pres. 2002-03), Soc. Univ. Surgeons, Ea. Vascular Soc., Midwestern Vascular Soc., Assn. Program Dirs. in Vascular Surgery (sec.-treas. 1993-97, pres. 2000-02). Office: Dartmouth-Hitchcock Med Ctr 1 Medical Center Dr Lebanon NH 03756-0002 Home Phone: 603-448-1886; Office Phone: 603-650-8670. Business E-Mail: j.cronewett@hitchcock.org.

CRONENWETT, LINDA R., dean, educator, hospital administrator; BSN, U. Mich., 1966, PhD in Nursing, 1983; MSN in Maternal-Child Nursing, U. Washington, 1970. Dir. profl. nursing, dir. nursing rsch. and edn. Mary Hitchcock Meml. Hosp., Lebanon, NH, Dartmouth-Hitchcock Med. Ctr., Lebanon; mem. faculty U. Mich., U. NH, Dartmouth U.; Sarah Frances Russell disting. prof. nursing systems U. NC Sch. Nursing, 1998—99, prof., dean, 1999—; chief nursing officer academic affairs U. NC Chapel Hill Hospitals, 2003—. Bd. dirs. Inst. Healthcare Improvement, NC Inst. Medicine; nat. adv. com., Transforming Care at the Bedside Project Robert Wood Johnson-IHI; pres. NC Deans and Dirs. Baccalaureate and Higher Degree Nursing Programs, NH Nurses Assn., mem. NIH Nat. Adv. Coun. Nursing Rsch.; chair ANA Congress Nursing Practice. Mem. editl. bd. Jour. Nursing Measurement; contbr. articles to profl. hours. Served with USN Nurse Corps. Recipient Disting. Profl. Svc. award Assn. Women's Health, Obstetric and Neonatal Nurses, 1993, Disting. Scholar Nursing award NYU, 1997, NH Nursing Leadership award, Disting. Contbn. to Nursing Rsch. award Eastern Nursing Rsch. Soc., Dissemination award Sigma Theta Tau. Fellow Am. Acad. Nursing (sec.), Nat. Academies of Practice. Office: Univ NC Sch Nursing Carrington Hall CB 7460 Chapel Hill NC 27599-7460 Office Phone: 919-966-3731. Business E-Mail: lincron@email.unc.edu.

CROOKE, ROSANNE M., pharmacologist; b. Pittsfield, Mass., Oct. 30, 1955; d. Myron Michael and Marian Geneva (Russell) Muzyka; m. Stanley T. Crooke, Sept. 5, 1986. BA, Williams Coll., 1978; PhD, U. Pa., 1986. Rsch. asst. endocrine sec. dept. medicine U. Pa., Phila., 1978-81; fellow Wistar Inst. Anatomy and Biology, Phila., 1986-89; dir. antisense drug discovery ISIS Pharms., Carlsbad, Calif., 1989—, v.p. cardiovasc. rsch., 1989—. Contbr. articles to profl. jours. Mem.: AAAS, Am. Heart Assn. Avocations: hiking, gourmet cooking, bicycling. Home: 3211 Piragua St Carlsbad CA 92009-7840 Office: ISIS Pharms 2855 Gazelle Ct C217 Carlsbad CA 92008 Business E-Mail: rcrooke@isisph.com.

CROOKE, STANLEY THOMAS, pharmaceutical executive; b. Indpls., Mar. 28, 1945; m. Nancy Alder (dec.); 1 child, Evan; m. Rosanne M. Snyder. BS in Pharmacy, Butler U., 1966; PhD, Baylor Coll., 1971, MD, 1974. Asst. dir. med. rsch. Bristol Labs., NYC, 1975-76, assoc. dir. med. rsch., 1976-77, assoc. dir. R&D, 1977-79, v.p. R&D, 1979-80, Smith Kline & French Labs., Phila., 1980-82; pres. R&D Smith Kline French, Phila., 1982-88; chmn. bd., CEO ISIS Pharms., Inc., Carlsbad, Calif., 1989. Chmn. bd. dirs. GES Pharms., Inc., Houston, 1989-91; adj. prof. Baylor Coll. Medicine, Houston, 1982, U. Pa., Phila., 1982-98; chmn. bd. dirs. GeneMedicine, Houston, 1996-98; bd. dirs. Calif. Healthcare Inst., 1993-2003, Indsl. Biotech. Assn., Washington, Idun Pharms., San Diego 1997-2002, Epix Med., Cambridge, Mass., 1996-2005, BIO, Washington, 1993-94; mem. sci. adv. bd. SIBIA, La Jolla, Calif. 1992-99; adj. prof. pharmacology UCLA, 1991, U. Calif. San Diego, 1994; bd. dirs. Synsorb Biotech Inc., Calgary, Can., 1999-2002; bd. dirs. Axon Instruments, Inc., Foster City, Calif. 1999-2004, Valentis, Inc., Burlingame, Calif., 1999-2002, Antisense Therapeutics Ltd., Toorak, Victoria, Australia, 2002-06, Applied Molecular Evolutions, Inc., San Diego, Calif., 2001-02, Biocom/San Diego, Calif., 2003—; mem. arts and scis. adv. coun. No. Ariz. U., 2002- Mem. editl. adv. bd. Molecular Pharmacology, 1986-91, Jour. Drug Targeting, 1992; editl. bd. Antisense Rsch. and Devel., 1994; sect. editl. bd. for biologicals and immunologicals Expert Opinion on Investigational Drugs, 1995. Trustee Franklin Inst., Phila., 1987-89; bd. dirs. Mann Music Ctr., Phila., 1987-89; children's com. Children's Svcs., Inc., Phila., 1983-84; adv. com. World Affairs Coun., Phila. Recipient Julius Stermer award, Phila. Coll. Pharmacy and Sci., 1981, Outstanding Lectr. award, Baylor Coll. Medicine, 1984, Disting. Prof. award, U. Ky., 1986. Mem. AAAS, Am. Assn. for Cancer Rsch. (state legis. com.), Am. Soc. for Microbiology, Am. Soc. Pharmacology and Exptl. Therapeutics, Am. Soc. Clin. Pharmacology and Therapeutics, Am. Soc. Clin. Oncology, Indsl. Biotech. Assn. (bd. dirs. 1992-93). Achievements include numerous patents in field. Office: ISIS Pharms Inc 1896 Rutherford Rd Carlsbad CA 92008-7208 E-mail: scrooke@isisph.com.

CROOKS, C. THOMAS, III, optometrist, educator; BS, Univ. Ala., 1975, BS in Optometry, 1977, OD, 1979. Ptnr. Drs. Renaud & Crooks, PA, Bessemer, Ala., 1979—89, Hueytown Eye Clinic, PC, 1989—95; pres., CEO EyeCare Assocs., Inc., Birmingham, Ala., 1996—. Clin. asst. prof. Univ. Ala., Birmingham, 1990—. With US Air N.G., 1972—79. Named Ala. Optometrist of Yr., 1985, Univ. Ala. Birmingham Alumnus of Yr., 1990. Mem.: Birmingham Area Optometric Soc. (sec-treas. 1982—83, bd. dir. 1984—86), So. Coun. Optometrists (bd. trustees 1991, pres. 1997—98), Am. Optometric Assn. (bd. trustees 1999—, pres.-elect 2005—06, pres. 2006), Ala. Optometric Assn. (bd. dir. 1984—86, sec.-treas. 1986—87, 2nd v.p. 1987—88, 1st v.p. 1988—89, pres.-elect 1989—90, pres. 1990—91, past. chmn.). Office: EyeCare Assoc Inc Ste 155 One Perimeter Pk Birmingham AL 35243 Office Phone: 205-968-9196.

CROOP, JAMES MERRILL, pediatrician, educator; b. Jan. 25, 1953; BA, U. Pa., 1974, MD, PhD, 1980. Diplomate Am. Bd. Pediatrics. Asst. prof. Med. Sch. Harvard U., Boston, 1988-97; assoc. prof. Ind. U., Inpls., 1997—2003, prof., 2003—. Contbr. articles to profl. jours. Mem. Am. Soc. Pediatric Hematology/Oncology. Achievements include patents (with other) DNA Sequence that Encodes the Multidrug Resistance Gene, Antibodies for P-glycoprotein Encoded by the MDR1 Gene and Uses Thereof. Office: Ind U Riley Hosp Children 702 Barnhill Dr Rm 4340 Indianapolis IN 46202-5128

CROPP, MICHAEL W., physician, insurance company executive; BA, Brown U., 1976, MD, 1979; MBA, State U. of NY Buffalo, 2003. Cert. American Bd. of Family Medicine. Resident family practice Meml. Hosp.; assoc. med. dir., family physician Harvard Cmty. Health Plan, Health Care Plan, Buffalo; assoc. med dir. Health Partners, Minneapolis, 1993—95; med. dir., COO Millard Fillmore Health Sys.; chmn. HEALTHeLINK; exec. v.p., chief med. officer Ind. Health Assn. Inc., Buffalo, 1996—2004, pres., CEO, 2004—. With variety of nat. bds. including Alliance of Cmty. Health Plans, America's Health Insurance Plans; bd. Olmsted Ctr. for Sight Impaired, bd. chmn. Bd. mem., founding chmn. P2 Collaborative of Western NY. Recipient Finger Lakes & WNY's Svc. to Mankind award, Leukemia & Lymphoma Soc. Mem.: American Coll. Physician Exec., American Acad. Family Physicians. Office: Independent Health Association Inc 511 Farber Lakes Dr Buffalo NY 14221 Office Phone: 716-631-3001. *

CROSBY, JAMES, physician; b. Pa., Dec. 12, 1946; MD, Upstate Med. U. Syracuse, 1972. Faculty physician United Health Svcs., 1977—, med. dir. sr. living at ideal, 2000—11. Mem.: Am. Geriat. Soc., Am. Bd. Family Medicine. Avocation: music. Office: 40 Arch St Johnson City NY 13790 Business E-Mail: james_crosby@uhs.org.

CROSBY, JOHN BARTLETT, lawyer, health science association administrator; b. South Bend, Ind., Mar. 25, 1947; s. John Strong and Dorothy (Bartlett) C.; m. Mary Jo Knaup, Dec. 27, 1969; children: Lara, Patrick, Anne. BA in History, Washington U., St. Louis, 1969; JDS cum laude, Ohio State U., 1972. Assoc. Thompson & Mitchell, St. Louis, 1972-77; adminstrv. asst. Congressman Richard A. Gephardt, Washington, 1977-81; dir. Project Hope Ctr. for Health Info., Millwood, Va., 1982-83; sr. v.p. and gen. counsel Nat. Assn. of Ind. Insurers, Des Plaines, Ill., 1983-89; sr. v.p. health policy AMA, Chgo., 1989-97; exec. dir. Am. Osteo. Assn., Chgo., 1997—. Bd. dirs. Chgo. Health Policy Rsch. Coun., 1993-2000, Health Care Quality Alliance, 1993-99, Nat. Health Coun., 2004-06. Mem. ABA, Mo. State Bar Assn. Office: Am Osteopathic Assn 142 E Ontario St Chicago IL 60611 Office Phone: 312-202-8001. E-mail: jcrosby@osteopathic.org. *

CROSS, JENNIFER, pediatrician, educator; Attended, U. Bristol Med. Sch., UK, 1983. Diplomate Am. Bd. Pediatrics, Am. Bd. Pediatrics-devel.-behavioral pediat. Resident in pediat. Lenox Hill Hosp., NY, 1986—88; fellow neonatal-perinatal medicine NY Hosp., 1990—91; fellow devel. pediat. Westchester Co. Med. Ctr., Valhalla, NY, 1992—94; asst. prof. pediat. Cornell Univ. Weill Med. Coll.; pediatrician NY Presbyn. Hosp./Weill Cornell. Office: NewYork-Presbyterian Helmsley Medical Tower 3rd Fl 505 E 70th St New York NY 10021 Office Phone: 646-962-4303. Office Fax: 646-962-0259.

CROSSER, CARMEN LYNN, marriage and family therapist, social worker, consultant; b. Iowa Falls, Iowa, Jan. 17, 1970; d. Gary Laverne Sr. and Karen Dorothy (Ulrich) C. AA, Ellsworth C.C., 1990; BS, Iowa State U., 1993; MSW, U. Iowa, 1995. Lic. clin. social worker, marriage and family thrapist, Ill.; ACSW; diplomate Am. Family Therapy Acad. Grad. teaching asst. U. Iowa, Iowa City, 1994-95; mental health therapy intern Mid-Eastern Cmty. Mental Health Ctr., Iowa City, 1994-95; clin. social worker Sinnissippi Ctrs., Inc., Dixon, Ill., 1995-97; family therapist Ctr. for Counseling, DeKalb, Ill., 1997—2005; pvt. practice DeKalb, 2005—, St. Charles, Ill., 2005—. Cons. sexual abuse svcs. Sinnissippi Ctrs. Inc., 1997—98; rsch. asst. U. Chgo., 1998—2000, tchg. asst., 1999—2001; revs. asst. Jour. of Marital and Family Therapy, 1999—2000; adj. prof. Dominican U., River Forest, Ill., 2002—04, Am. Family Therapy Acad., 2003—. Mem. instnl. rev. bd. No. Ill. U., DeKalb, 1997—2000. All-Am. scholar, 1995. Mem. ACA, NASW, NOW, Am. Assn. Marriage and Family Therapy (clin. mem.), Am. Coll. Counselors, Internat. Assn. Marriage and Family Counselors, Ill. Soc. Clin. Social Work, Nat. Fedn. Socs. for Clin. Social Work, Golden Key, Phi Kappa Phi, Phi Alpha. Office: 400 E Hillcrest Dr Ste 100A Dekalb IL 60115 Office Phone: 630-845-1529. Business E-Mail: c-crosser@uchicago.edu. *

CROSSETT, LAWRENCE S., orthopaedic surgeon; Attended, Temple U., Phila. Cert. orthopaedic surgery. Resident Temple Univ. Sch. of Medicine, Phila.; with orthopaedic surgery dept. Univ. of Pitts. Med. Ctr. Office: University of Pittsburgh Physicians Joint Reconstruction Center 5200 Centre Ave Ste 415 Pittsburgh PA 15232 Office Phone: 412-802-4100.

CROSSLEY, GEORGE HINTON, III, physician, medical association administrator; b. Johnson City, Tenn., Dec. 14, 1954; s. George Hinton and Anne McLellan Crossley; m. Elizabeth Schubring Crossley, June 28, 1984; children: Benjamin Atkinson, Robert Hardeman. BS, U. Ga., Athens, 1974—77, MS, 1980; MD, Med. Coll. Ga., Augusta, 1984. Diplomate in cardiac electrophysiology Am. Bd. Internal Medicine, 1994, in cardiology Am. Bd. Internal Medicine, 1991, Am. Bd. Internal Medicine, 1985. Pres. Mid-State Cardiology, Nashville, 2004—07, St. Thomas Heart, Nashville, 2007—. Contbr. more than 100 articles to profl. jours. Bd. gov. Am. Coll. Cardiology,

Washington, 2009—; chair, perioperative mgmt. writing group Heart Rhythm Soc., Washington, 2009—, Govt. Affairs Com. Heart Rhythm Soc. Fellow: Am. Heart Assn., Am. Coll. Cardiology (pres. tenn. capter 2009—), Heart Rhythm Soc. Conservative. Methodist. Achievements include research in cardiac electrophysiology. Avocations: woodworking, wine collecting, writing. Office: St Thomas Heart 276 Stratton Ct Brentwood TN 37027 Office Fax: 615-327-0216; Home Fax: 615-370-3049. Personal E-mail: ghcmd@comcast.net.

CROSSNO, RONALD J., health services company executive, physician; BS in Zoology, Tex. A&M U., 1977; MD, U. Tex. Med. Sch., San Antonio, 1981. Part-time med. dir. cmty-based hospice, Tex.; regional med. dir. VistaCare, 2002—08; nat. med. dir. Odyssey Healthcare, 2008—11; sr. nat. med. dir. hospice divsn. Gentiva Health Services, Austin, 2011—. Mem. speaker's bur. American Med. Dir. Assn. Inst. Long-Term Care; mem. ethics com., bd. mem. Tex. Pain and Advocacy Info. Network. Fellow: American Acad. Hospice and Palliative Medicine (mem. edn. com. 2004—06, mem. hospice med. dir. course planning com. 2005, co-chmn. rural spl. interest group steering com. 2005—, mem. hospice-based physician edn. task force 2006, chmn. pub. policy com. 2006—07, co-chmn. long-term care spl. interest group steering com. 2006—07, dir.-at-large 2006—08, alt. del. to the AMA 2006—10, mem. pub. policy com. 2006—, treas. bd. dirs. 2008—09, pres. 2011—), American Acad. Physicians; mem.: Nat. Hospice and Palliative Care Orgn. (bd. dirs.), Tex. Med. Dir. Assn. (mem. pub. policy com.), American Med. Dir. Assn. (mem. pub. policy com.), Tex. Acad. Palliative Medicine (bd. dirs., chmn. edn. com.). Office: Gentiva Health Services Hospice Divsn 4201 W Parmer Ln Bldg C Ste 100 Austin TX 78727-4161 Office Phone: 512-310-0214. Office Fax: 512-310-9328. *

CROSWELL, THOMAS A., insurance company executive; Completed the Wharton Advanced Mgmt. Program, U. Pa.; BA, Syracuse U. Chartered life underwriter. Sr. leadership roles Prudential Ins. Com.; sr. v.p. med. mgmt. and specialty businesses CIGNA Healthcare; COO Tufts Health Plan, 2007—. Bd. dirs. Nat. Com. on Quality Assurance. Mem.: Alzheimer Assn. of Mass. and NH (bd. dirs.). Office: Tufts Health Plan 705 Mt. Auburn St Watertown MA 02472 *

CROTTY, JOHN T., investment advisor; BA in Econs., Grinnell Coll.; MBA, U. Chgo. V.p. planning and bus. devel. Am. Hosp. Supply Corp.; co-founder CroBern, Inc., 1986, former pres., CEO; mng. ptnr. CroBern Management Partnership LLP, 1986—. Bd. dirs. Owens & Minor, Inc., 1999—, Omnicare Inc., 2004—, non-exec. chmn., 2008—10. Office: CroBern Mgmt Partnership LLP PO Box 577 Lake Bluff IL 60044 also: Omnicare Inc 100 E Rivercenter Blvd Covington KY 41011 *

CROUSE, BYRON J., physician, academic administrator; b. May 23, 1951; BA, St. Olaf Coll., 1973; MD, Mayo Med. Sch., 1977. Pvt. practice N.E. Med. Ctr., Spooner, Wis., 1980-87; asst. program dir. Duluth (Minn.) Family Practice Residency, 1987-93; dept. head, asst. dean U. Minn. Sch. Medicine, Duluth, 1993-2001; pvt. practice Moose Lake, Minn., 1994-2001, Belleville, Wis., 2001—; asst. dean rural and cmty. health U. Wis. Med. Sch., Madison, 2001—. Co-chmn. rural med. educators group Nat. Rural Health Assn.; chmn. nat. adv. com. Nat. Health Svc. Corps. Mem. Minn. Acad. Family Physician Found. (pres. 1996-2000), Minn. Acad. Family Physician (pres. 1992). Office: University Wis Sch Medicine & Pub Health 4117 Health Sciences Learning Ctr 750 Highland Ave Madison WI 53705-2221 Office Phone: 608-265-6727. E-mail: bjcrouse@wisc.edu. *

CROUT, J. RICHARD, pharmacologist, researcher; b. Portland, Oreg., Dec. 30, 1929; s. John and Georgia Crout; m. Carol Keith, June 19, 1954; children: Linda, Keith, Andrew. AB, Oberlin Coll., 1951; MD, Northwestern U., 1955, MS, 1956; DMed (hon.), U. Uppsala, Sweden, 1977. Intern Passavant Meml. Hosp., Chgo., 1955-56; asst. resident in internal medicine VA Rsch. Hosp., Chgo., 1956-57; clin. assoc. Nat. Heart Inst., Bethesda, Md., 1957-60; asst. resident in Medicine NYU-Bellevue Med. Ctr., NYC, 1960-61; USPHS fellow, instr. pharmacology Harvard U., 1961-63; asst. prof. pharmacology and internal medicine U. Tex. Southwestern Med. Sch., Dallas, 1963-65, assoc. prof., 1965-70; prof. pharmacology and medicine Mich. State U., 1970-71; dep. dir. Bur. Drugs FDA, Rockville, Md., 1971-72, dir. office sci. evaluation Bur. Drugs, 1972-73, dir. Bur. Drugs, 1973-82; dir. Office of Med. Applications of Rsch. NIH, 1982-84; v.p. med. and sci. affairs Boehringer Mannheim Pharms., 1984-94; scholar in residence Inst. Medicine, 1994-95; pres. Crout Cons., Bethesda, 1994—. Mem. drug resch. bd. NAS-NRC; cons. WHO, 1974—84; trustee U.S. Pharmacopeia, 1985—95; mem. coms. Inst. Medicine, 1990, 1992—93, 1998, 2000. Contbr. articles to profl jours. Served to sr asst surgeon USPHS, 1957—60, asst surgeon gen USPHS, 1976—84. Recipient Dist Svc. award, USPHS, 1977, Spec Citation, Comnr FDA, 1981, 1982, Distinguished Career award, Drug Info. Assn., 1994, Oscar B Hunter Therapeutics award, Am Soc. Clin. Pharm. and Therapeutics, 1997; scholar Burroughs Wellcome, 1965—70. Fellow: ACP, Soc. Clin. Trials; mem.: Am. Soc. Clin. Pharmacology and Therapeutics, Am. Soc. Clin. Investigation, Am. Soc. Pharmacology and Exptl.Therapeutics, Alpha Omega Alpha, Phi Beta Kappa. Home and Office: 701 King Farm Blvd Apt 202 Rockville MD 20850 Home Phone: 301-330-3650. Personal E-mail: jrcrout@gmail.com.

CROUZET, SEBASTIEN, surgeon; b. Lyon, France, Jan. 19, 1977; MD, U. Lille, 2003. Surgeon Hospices Civiles Lyon, U. Lyon, 2009—. Office: 5 pl d'Arsonval Lyon Rhone 69003 France Business E-Mail: sebastien.crouzet@chu-lyon.fr.

CROVETTO, MIGUEL ANGEL DE LA TORRE, otolaryngologist; b. Bilbao, Vizcaya, Spain, Nov. 6, 1951; Degree, U. Basque Country, 1977; D, U. Zaragoza., Spain, 1985. Clin. chief ENT Basurto Hosp., 1993—. Prof., physician U. Basque Country, 1985—2011. Recipient award, Soc. Española Otorrinolaringolgía. Mem.: Real Academia Medicina del País Vasco. Office: Reina Maria Cristina 10 Las Arenas Getxo Vizcaya 48930 Spain Business E-Mail: macdlt@telefonica.net.

CROW, HAROLD EUGENE, physician, educator; b. Farber, Mo., Jan. 17, 1933; s. Leslie J. and Laura L. (Sparks) C.; m. Mary Kay Krenke, July 5, 1974; children: Janet L., Jason P. MD, U. Mo., 1963. Diplomate Am. Bd. Family Practice, Am. Bd. Med. Examiners. Intern E.W. Sparrow Hosp., Lansing, Mich., 1963-64; pvt. practice medicine specializing in family practice Lansing, 1964-70; dir. family practice residency E.W. Sparrow Hosp., Lansing, Mich., 1970-82; chmn. dept. family and community medicine Sch. Medicine, U. Nev., Reno, 1982-87, dir. office Rural Health Sch. Medicine, 1984-87; med. dir. S.W. Med. Assocs., Reno, 1987-88; dir. Lynchburg (Va.) Family Practice Resident Program, 1988-96; patient advocate Cons. for Caring, Sun City Center, Fla., 1996—98; dir. Outer Banks Edn. and Program Devel. Project, East Carolina U. Sch. Medicine, Nags Head, NC, 1999—. Dir. Outer Banks Edn. and Program Devel. Project. Developer non-rotational residency model for family practice tng., tng. model for rural med. practice; innovator computerized health info. systems for family physicians. Numerous civic activities. With U.S. Army, 1955-57. Mem.: Am. Coll. Physician Exec. Presbyterian. Home: 408 Stoneham Dr Sun City Center FL 33573-5841 E-mail: hecrow@pol.net.

CROW, MARY KUNTZ, rheumatologist; b. Aug. 22, 1947; BA, Manhattanville Coll., 1972; MD, Cornell U. Med. Coll., 1978. Diplomate Am. Bd. Internal Medicine, cert. in rheumatology. Intern internal medicine NY Hosp., 1978—79, resident, 1979—81; fellow in immunology rsch. Rockefeller U., 1981—84; fellow in rheumatology Hosp. Spl. Surgery, NYC, 1981—84, co-dir. Mary Kirkland Ctr. Lupus Rsch., dir. Autoimmunity & Inflammation Rsch. Program, assoc. chief divsn. rheumatology, dir. rheumatology rsch., 2001—10, Benjamin M. Rosen chair in autoimmunity & inflammation rsch., 2002, physician-in-chief, chair divsn. rheumatology, 2010—. Prof. medicine Weill Cornell Med. Coll.; attending physician NY Presbyn. Hosp.; mem. scientific adv. bd. Alliance Lupus Rsch., Arthritis Nat. Rsch. Found. Mem. editl. bd. Arthritis & Rheumatism, Annals of Rheumatic Diseases & Autoimmunity; contbr. articles to profl. jours. Named an Arthritis Hero, Arthritis Found., 2001. Mem.: Am. Coll. Rheumatology (pres. 2005—06), Henry Kunkel Soc. (pres.). Office: Hosp Spl Surgery 535 E 70th St New York NY 10021

CROWELL, DAVID HARRISON, clinical professor pediatrics, retired biomedical researcher; b. Trenton, NJ, July 19; m. Doris Collins; children: Michael David, Sandra Crowell Lupton, Shannon Kathleen Atkinson, Megan Crowell Sheridan. Ph. D., State U. of Iowa, Iowa City, Iowa, 1946—50. Internship-fellowship U. Iowa 49;Yale 66, Scientist Commd. Corps,USPHS, 1954. Rsch. cons. Straub Clinic and Hosp., Honolulu, Hawaii, 1983—; prin. investigator Kapiolani Med. Crnter, Honolulu, 1991—2002; rsch. cons. Nat'l Inst. Health, Washington, DC, 1973—89; prof. emeritus U. of Hawaii, Honolulu. Author: (scientific articles) Psychophysiology; dir.(researcher): (experimental studies) Scientific Articles (Continuing Grants, 1963). Grantee Clin Home Infant, Clin. Study, Nichd, Nih, 1999-2000. Fellow: Amer Psychol. Assn., Amer Assn Adv Sci. (life); mem.: Population Assoc Am. (assoc.), Hawn Acad Sci. (assoc.; pres. 1953—54), Soc Rsch Child Devel (assoc.), Amer Acad Sleep Med (assoc.), Amer Clin Neurophysiology Soc (assoc.), Sigma Xi (assoc.). Business E-Mail: crowell@hawaii.edu.

CROWLEY, JEFFREY S., federal official; b. 1965; BA in Chemistry, Kalamazoo Coll., Mich., 1988; MPH, Johns Hopkins U. Sch. Hygiene & Pub. Health, Balt., 1994. Chemist sect. analytical biochemistry, Lab. Clin. Sci. NIMH, Washington, 1991—93; pub. policy intern, spl. asst. to exec. dir. Nat. Assn. People with AIDS (NAPWA), 1994, asst. exec. dir., sr. policy assoc., 1994—95, assoc. exec. dir., 1995—97, dep. exec. dir. programs, 1997—2000; project dir., sr. rschr. Inst. Health Care Rsch. & Policy, Georgetown U., 2000—09; dir. Office Nat. AIDS Policy, sr. advisor on disability policy Exec. Office of the Pres., Washington, 2009—. Mem. Families USA Medicaid Coalition, 1995—; mem. steering com. Patient's Bill of Rights Coalition, Nat. Partnership Women & Families, 1998—, Consumer Coalition Health Privacy, 1999—; bd. dirs. Consortium Citizens with Disabilities, 1999—. Vol. sci. tchr. Nsongweni HS, Swaziland, South Africa, 1988—91. Office: The White House Office Nat AIDS Policy 1600 Pennsylvania Ave NW Washington DC 20500 *

CROWLEY, RICHARD WEBSTER, neurosurgeon, researcher; b. Washington, May 11, 1976; MD, George Wash. U. Sch. Medicine, 2005. Resident U. Va. Dept. Neurosurgery, 2005—11; fellow Barrow Neurol. Inst., 2011—. Mem.: Am. Heart Assn., Congress Neurol. Surgeons, Am. Assn. Neurol. Surgeons. Avocations: sports, travel. Office: Barrow Neurosurgical Assoc 2910 No Phoenix AZ 85018 Business E-Mail: webster.crowley@bnaneuro.net.

CROWTHER, BRUCE K., hospital administrator; MBA, Va. Commonwealth U. Dir. Barrington Bank; exec. v.p. and COO Northwest Cmty. Hosp., 1989—91, pres. and CEO, 1992—; dir. Wintrust Fin. Corp., 1998—. Bd. mem. Max McGraw Wildlife Found. Fellow: Am. Coll. of Healthcare Execs.; mem.: Ill. Hosp. Assn. (past chmn.). Office: Northwest Community Hospital 800 W Central Rd Arlington Heights IL 60005 Office Phone: 847-618-1000.

CROYLE, BARBARA ANN, health facility administrative executive; b. Knoxville, Tenn., Oct. 22, 1949; d. Charles Evans and Myrtle Elizabeth (Kellam) C. BA cum laude in Sociology, Coll. William and Mary, 1971; cert. corp. tax and securities law, Inst. Paralegal Tng., 1971; JD, U. Colo., 1975; cert. program mgmt. devel., Colo. Women's Coll., 1980; MBA, U. Denver, 1983. Cert. nursing home adminstr., lectr. Bar: Colo. 1976, Pa. 1990. Paralegal Holland & Hart, Denver, 1972-73; law clk. Colo. Ct. Appeals, Denver, summer 1976; assoc. firm Shaw Spangler & Roth, Denver, 1976-77; mgr. acquisitions/lands Petro-Lewis Corp., Denver, 1977-85; mgr. strategic planning Westinghouse, Transp. Divsn., Denver, 1985-87; mng. dir. Benefit Resource Mgmt. Group subs. Blue Cross We. Pa., 1987-92; COO, v.p. D.T. Watson Rehab. Hosp., 1992-93; v.p. ambulatory care svcs., compliance officer Franciscan Med. Ctr., Dayton campus, Ohio, 1994-2000; exec. dir. Swedish Am. Ctr. for Complementary Medicine, Rockford, Ill., 2000—02; exec. v.p. Peninsula United Meth. Homes, Inc., Hockessin, Del., 2003—10; exec. dir. Lutheran Sr. Svcs. Southern Chester Co., 2010—. Tchr. oil and gas law Colo. Paralegal Inst., 1978, 79; arbitrator Am. Arbitration Assn.; mediator Dayton Mediation Ctr. Mem. ABA, Del. Bar Assn., Inst. Noetic Scis., Del. Forum for Exec. Women, PA. Bar Assn.(bd. mem. DE Forum exec. women) Home: 150 Mercer Mill Rd Landenberg PA 19350 Office: 122 Jenners Pond Rd West Grove PA 19390 Home Phone: 610-274-8439. Personal E-mail: bcroyle@earthlink.net.

CROYLE, ROBERT T., federal agency administrator, psychologist, educator; b. Seattle, Jan. 19, 1956; s. William R. and Elcena (Torrance) C.; m. Carol Jackson, Aug. 8, 1981; children: Kaitlin, Thomas. BA in psychology, U. Wash., 1978; MA in psychology, Princeton U., 1981, PhD in social psychology, 1985. Asst. prof. psychology Williams Coll., Williamstown, Mass., 1983-86; vis. investigator Cancer Prevention Rsch. Program Fred Hutchinson Cancer Rsch. Ctr., Seattle, 1987—89; asst. prof. psychology U. Utah, Salt Lake City, 1989—91, assoc. prof., 1991—98, prof., 1998—99, mem. Huntsman Cancer Inst., 1994—98, head social psychology program, 1992—95, acting chair dept. psychology, 1994; assoc. dir. behavioral rsch. program Nat. Cancer Inst., 1998—2002; acting dir. Divsn. Cancer Control & Population Sciences, Nat. Cancer Inst., 2002—03, dir., 2003—. Co-editor: (books) Mental Representation in Health and Illness, 1991; editor: Psychosocial effects of screening for disease prevention and detection, 1995. Recipient NIH Merit Award, 1999, 2002, NIH Dir.'s Award, 2000. Fellow: Soc. Behavioral Medicine; mem.: APHA, Soc. Pub. Health Edn., NY Acad. Sciences, Soc. Exptl. Social Psychology, Am. Psychol. Assn., Am. Soc. Preventive Oncology, Acad. Behavioral Medicine Rsch. Office: Nat Cancer Inst Divsn Cancer Control and Popluation Sci 6130 Executive Blvd EPN Rm 6138 Rockville MD 20852 Office Phone: 301-594-6776. Office Fax: 301-594-6787. E-mail: croyler@mail.nih.gov. *

CROZIER, WALTER RAYMOND, psychology professor; b. Belfast, Northern Ireland, July 27, 1945; s. Walter Thomas and Elizabeth Jane Lavinia (McClintock) C.; m. Sandra Ann Hamilton, Aug. 19, 1972; children: John, Beth. BA with honors, Queens U., Belfast, 1968; MSc, Stirling U., Scotland, 1969; PhD, Keele U., Eng., 1974. Chartered psychologist. Sr. lectr. South Glamorgan Inst., Cardiff, Wales, 1972-83, Lancashire Poly., Preston, 1983-90, U. Wales, Cardiff, 1990-98, reader, 1998—2003, prof., 2003—06, U. East. Anglia, Norwich, England, 2006—09, vis. fellow, 2009—; hon. prof. Cardiff U., 2010—. Editor: Shyness and Embarrassment, 1990, Shyness: Development, Consolidation and Change, 2000; author: Manufactured Pleasures, 1994, Individual Learners, 1997, Understanding Shyness, 2001, Blushing and the Social Emotions, 2006; co-author (with L. E. Alden): Coping with Shyness and Social Phobia, 2009; co-editor: (with R. Ranyard & O. Svenson) Decision Making, 1997, (with L.E. Alden) International Handbook of Social Anxiety, 2000, The Essential Handbook of Social Anxiety for Clinicians, 2005; mem. editl. bd. Empirical Studies of Arts, 1995—. Fellow Brit. Psychol. Soc. (com. mem. Welsh br. 1994—2003); mem. Internat. Assn. Empirical Aesthetics (v.p. 1983-96). Church Of Wales. Avocations: rambling, reading, sports. Business E-Mail: crozierr@cardiff.ac.uk.

CRUCIANI, RICARDO ALBERTO, physician; arrived in US, 1983; MD, PhD, Buenos Aires U., 1979. Lic. dr. Buenos Aires, 1980, philosophy dr. Buenos Aires, 1996. Dir. rsch. divsn. dept. pain medicine & palliative care Beth Israel Med. Ctr., NYC, 2001—, vice-chairman dept. pain medicine & palliative care, 2005—. Assoc. prof. Albert Einstein Coll. Medicine, Yashiva U., Bronx, NY, 2003—. Contbr. articles to profl. jours. Grantee R21, NIH, 2003, 2004, Grant, Beth Israel Med. Ctr., 2003. Mem.: Am. Pain Soc. Business E-Mail: rcrucian@bethisraelny.org. E-mail: rcrucian@chpnet.org.

CRUESS, RICHARD LEIGH, orthopedic surgeon, dean; b. London, Ont., Can., Dec. 17, 1929; s. Leigh S. and Martha A. (Peever) C.; m. Sylvia Crane Robinson, May 30, 1953; children: Leigh S., Andrew C. BA, Princeton U., 1951; MD, Columbia U., 1955; DSc (hon.), U. Laval, 2004. Diplomate Am. Bd. Orthopedic Surgery. Intern Royal Victoria Hosp., Montreal, Que., 1955-56, resident surgery, 1956-57, N.Y. Orthopedic Hosp., 1959-60, asst. resident orthopedic surgery, 1960-61, resident orthopedic surgery, 1961-62, Annie C. Kane fellow orthopedic surgery, 1961-62; research asso. depts. orthopedic surgery and biochemistry Columbia U., NYC, 1962-63; John Armour Travelling fellow, 1962-63; Am.-Brit.-Can. Travelling fellow, 1967; practice medicine specializing in orthopedic surgery Montreal, 1963-95; orthopedic surgeon Royal Victoria Hosp., orthopedic surgeon-in-charge, 1968-81, asst. surgeon-in-chief, 1970-81; chief surgeon Shriner's Hosp. for Crippled Children, Montreal, 1970-82; prof. surgery McGill U., Montreal, 1970—, chmn. div. orthopedic surgery, 1976-81, dean faculty medicine, 1981-95, prof. Ctr. for Med. Edn., 1995—. Hon. cons. orthopedic surgery Queen Elizabeth Hosp., 1972-95; mem. clin. grants com. Med. Rsch. Coun., 1972-75, mem. coun., 1980-86, mem. exec., 1983-86. Contbr. articles on surgery to profl. jours.; mem. editl. bd. Jour. Internat. Orthopedics, 1976-85, Jour. Bone and Joint Surgery, 1977-83, Current Problems in Orthopedics, 1977-83, Jour. Orthopaedic Rsch., 1986-88. Served to lt. M.C., USN, 1957-59. Decorated mem. and officer Order of Can., officer Order of Que. Fellow Royal Coll. Physicians and Surgeons Can. (chief examiner orthopedic surgery 1970-72), ACS, Am. Acad. Orthopedic Surgeons, Royal Soc. Can.; mem. Can. Orthopedic Assn. (sec. 1971-76, pres. 1977-78), Can. Orthopedic Rsch. Soc. (pres. 1971-72), Am. Orthopedic Rsch. Soc. (pres. 1975-76), Am. Orthopedic Assn., Am. Orthopedic Surgeons Province Que. (treas. 1971-72), Société Française de Chirurgie Orthopedique (hon.), McGill Osler Reporting Soc., Assn. can. Med. colls. (pres. 1987-89). Home: Apt 903 2333 Sherbrooke St W Montreal PQ Canada H3H 2T6 Office: McGill U 1110 Pine Ave W Montreal PQ Canada H3A 1A3 Home Phone: 514-732-0670; Office Phone: 514-398-7331. E-mail: richard.cruess@mcgill.ca.

CRUM, ALBERT B., psychiatrist, consultant; b. Omaha, Nov. 17, 1931; s. J. Rufus and Alberta (McCreary) C.; m. Rosa Maria Hennessy y Sinclair; children: Rosa Maria Crum O'Brien, Elsie Crum McCabe, Alberta Crum Fousek. BS, U. Redlands, Calif., 1953, DSc (hon.), 1974; MD, Harvard U., 1957; MS, NYU, 1987. Diplomate Am. Bd. Forensic Medicine, in Psychotherapy Am. Psychotherapy Assn., Am. Bd. Forensic Examiners. Med. intern Columbia U. divsn. Bellevue Med. Ctr., NYC, 1957—58; rsch. fellow, psychiat. resident Creedmoor Inst. for Psychobiol. Studies, Queens Village, NY, 1958—59; chief, neuropsychiatric svcs. Continental Air Command Hdqs. 2500 USAF Hosp., 1959-61; psychiat. resident Columbia U. Psychiat. Inst. of Columbia-Presbyn. Hosp., NYC, 1961—63; pvt. practice Brooklyn Heights, NY, 1963—. Co-chmn. US Coordinating Commn. for Nomination of His Holiness the Dalai Lama of Tibet for the Nobel Peace Prize, Brooklyn Heights, 1986; chmn. Human Behavior Found., Bklyn. Heights, 1968—; chmn. selection com. Human Behavior Found.'s Albert Schweitzer Humanitarian Award, Bklyn. Heights, 1986—; expert Nat. Forensic Ctr.; pres. Stress Watchers, Inc., The ProImmune Co., LLC., Y.F. One/NY, Ltd., 1991—; advisor Office of Tibet, NYC, 1984—; clin. prof. mgmt. sci., adj. prof. anatomy and neuroanatomy NYU, 1987-2002. Author: The 10-Step Method of Stress Relief: Decoding the Meaning and Significance of Stress, CRC Press, 2000; contbr. articles and abstracts to profl. jours. Bd. dirs. Albert Schweitzer Fellowship, NYC, 1982—2002, Burdick Internat. Ancestry Library, Sarasota, Fla., 1985—; mem., chmn., adv. bd. NYU's Coll. of Dentistry, 1988-96; mem. Bklyn. Heights Assn.,

1970-96; class agent Harvard Med. Sch. Class of 1957; pres. Stress Watchers, Inc. Capt. USAF, 1959-61. Recipient Disting. Svc. award Bklyn. Jr. C. of C., 1966, Bicentennial award Nat. Jogging Assn., 1976; Citizen of Yr. award, Achievements in Medicine and Human Understanding, Bklyn. Philharm., 1986; named Disting. Lectr., NYU Coll. Dentistry, Omicron Kappa Upsilon lect., 1986. Fellow Royal Coll. Physicians and Surgeons in Psychiatry; mem. Sci. Rsch. Soc. (life), Am. Acad. of Forensic Scis. (assoc.), Nat. Bd. Med. Examiners, Med. Coun. of Can., Am. Physicians Art Assn., Harvard Med. Soc., Harvard Club of N.Y., MENSA (life, nat. coord. 1980-84), Phi Beta Kappa (councillor 1981-84), Sigma Xi (life). Achievements include patents for nutritional or therapeutic composition; nutritional or therapeutic supplement and method. Avocations: jogging, studying world religions, history. Home and Office: 64 E Market St Rhinebeck NY 12572 Office Phone: 845-876-3222. Personal E-mail: albertbcrum@aol.com.

CRUM, JOHN EVAN, physician, executive; b. Mpls., Dec. 5, 1953; s. Gerald Pollert and Vivian Dorothy (Wonning) Crum; m. Kimberly Anne Garts, Sep. 10, 1983; children: Susanna, Elizabeth. BS in Biol. Scis., Ind. U., 1973; MD, Ind. U., Indpls., 1978. Diplomate Am. Bds. Family Practice, Med. Mgmt.; lic., Ky.; cert. physician exec. Family practice resident U. Iowa, Iowa City, 1978—81; pvt. practice family medicine Williamsburg, Iowa, 1981—86; med. dir. Maxicare Ky. HMO, Louisville, 1987—88, Humana Health Plan HMO, Louisville, 1988; physician dir. Humana Inc., Louisville, 1988—95; chief med. officer Humana Mil. Healthcare Svcs., Inc., Louisville, 1995—99, 2005—, Emphesys Inc., 1999—2001; pres. John Crum MD, PLC healthcare cons., 2001—05. Bd. mem. Chance Sch., Louisville, 1989-90, Bingham Child Guidance Ctr., 1997-99. Fellow Am. Acad. Family Physicians; mem. Am. Coll. Physician Execs. Presbyterian. Avocation: auto restoration. Office: 500 W Main St Louisville KY 40202 Home: 1448 St James Ct Louisville KY 40208 Office Phone: 502-580-4005. Business E-Mail: jcrummd@humana.com.

CRUMLEY, ROGER LEE, surgeon, educator, otolaryngologist; b. Perry, Iowa, Oct. 8, 1941; s. Dwight Moody and Helen Ethelwyn (Anderson) C.; m. Janet Lynn Conant, Nov. 13, 1987; children: Erin Kelly Helen, Danielle Nicole. BA, Simpson Coll., 1964; MS, U. Iowa, 1975, MD, 1967; MBA, U. Phoenix, 1999. Diplomate Am. Bd. Otolaryngology (dir. 1992—2004). Intern LA County Gen. Hosp., 1967-68; resident in surgery Highland-Alameda Hosp., Oakland, Calif., 1968-69; bn. surgeon 1st Marine Div., Vietnam, 1968-69; resident in otolaryngology U. Iowa, Iowa City, 1971-75; chief otolaryngology San Francisco Gen. Hosp., 1975-81; assoc. prof., then prof. U. Calif., San Francisco, 1981-87, prof., chief otolaryngology-head and neck surgery Irvine, 1987—2007. Guest prof. Humboldt U., East Berlin, 1982, M.S. McLeod vis. prof. S. Australian Postgrad. Edn. Ctr., Adelaide, 1988; treas., pres. Am. Acad. Facial Plastic Surgeons, 1994-95, Triological Soc., 2002-03; McBride lectr. U. Edinburgh, 1998. Contbr. articles and book chpts. to profl. pubs. With UGN, 1969-71, Vietnam. Recipient Alumni Achievement award Simpson Coll., 1984. Fellow ACS, Am. Acad. Otolaryngology (bd. dirs. 1988—, award 1989); mem. Soc. Univ. Otolaryngologists, Triological Soc. (pres. 2002-), Am Laryngol. Assn. (pres. 2009), Bohemian Club (San Francisco), Center Club (Costa Mesa, Calif.). Republican. Methodist. Avocations: music, piano, jazz flügelhorn, running, skiing. Office: U Calif-Irvine Med Ctr Dept Otolaryngology Head & Neck 101 The City Dr S Orange CA 92868-3201 Home Phone: 714-289-0253, Office Phone: 714-456-7017.

CRUSE, JULIUS MAJOR, JR., pathologist, educator; b. New Albany, Miss., Feb. 15, 1937; s. Julius Major and Effie (Davis) C. BA, BS with honors, U. Miss., 1958; DMS with honors, U. Graz, Austria, 1960; MD, U. Tenn., 1964, PhD in Pathology (USPHS fellow), 1966, USPHS postdoctoral fellow, 1964-67; DD (hon.), Gen. Theol. Sem., NYC, 1999. Prof. immunology and biology Grad. Sch. U. Miss., 1967—74, prof. pathology, 1974—, assoc. prof. microbiology, 1974—, dir. grad. studies program in pathology, 1974—, dir. clin. immunopathology, 1978—, dir. immunopathology sect., 1978—, dir. tissue typing lab., 1980—, assoc. prof. medicine, 1989—, prof. medicine, disting. prof. history medicine Med. Sch., 2003—, Guyton disting prof., 2004—09, 2010—, prof. microbiology, 2010, vice chair pathology, dir. anatomic pathology. Lectr. pathology U. Tenn. Coll. Medicine, 1964-74; adj. prof. immunology Miss. Coll., 1977-92; mem. NIH study section on transplantation immunology, 1992; mem. sci. adv. bd. Immuno Tech. Corp., LA; active FDA Expert Panel on Alternatives to Silicone Breast Implants, 1994—. Author: Immunology Examination Review Book, 1971, rev. edit., 1975, Introduction to Immunology, 1977, Principles of Immuno-pathology, 1979; editor-in-chief Immunologic Rsch., 1981—, Pathology and Immunopathology Rsch., 1982-90, Concepts in Immunopathology, 1985—, The Year in Immunology, 1984—, Pathobiology: Jour. Immunopathology, Molecular and Cellular Biology, 1990-98, Exptl. & Molecular Pathology, 1999—, Transgenics: Biological Analysis Through DNA Transfer, 1992-; immunology cons.: Dorland's Illustrated Medical Dictionary, 1967-1994; contbns. to Microbiology and Immunology; editor Immunomodulation of Neoplasia, Antigenic Variation: Molecular and Genetic Mechanisms of Relapsing Disease, 1987, Autoimmunoregulation and Autoimmunity 1987; The Year in Immunology, vol. 1, 1984-85, vol. 2, 1985-86, The Year in Immunology, vol. 3, 1987, The Year in Immunology, vols. 4, 5, 1988, vol. 6, 1989-90, Genetic Basis of Autoimmune Disease, 1988, Cellular Aspects of Autoimmunity, 1988, Therapy of Autoimmune Diseases, 1989, B Lymphocytes: Function and Regulation, Conjugate Vaccines, 1989, Molecules and Cells of Immunity, 1990, Immunoregulation and Autoimmunity, 1986, Organ-Based Autoimmune Diseases, 1985, Autoimmunity: Basic Concepts, Systemic and Selected Organ-Specific Diseases, 1985, Clinical and Molecular Aspects of Autoimmune Diseases, 1990, Immunoregulatory Cytokines and Cell Growth, 1989, Complement Profiles, 1992; co-editor: Self-Nonself Discrimination in the Immune System, 1992, Complement Profiles, vol. 1, 1992, Illustrated Dictionary of Immunology, 1995, 2d edit., 2003, 3d edit., 2009, 10, Atlas of Immunology, 1998, 2d edit., 2003, 3rd edit., 2010, Immunology Guidebook, 2004, Historical Atlas of Immunology, 2005, T.S. Eliot Bibliography, 2003, Historical Atlas of Immunology, 2005; editor-in-chief: Experimental and Molecular Pathology, 1999—; mem. editl. bd. Human Immunology, 2007-; contbr. chpts. to books and articles to profl. jours. Recipient Pathologists award in continuing edn. Coll. Am. Pathologists-Am. Soc. Clin. Pathologists, 1976; Julius M. Cruse collection in immunology established in his honor Middleton Med. Libr., U. Wis., Madison, 1979, Julius M. Cruse collection of T.S. Eliot's works, St. Mark's Libr., Gen. Theol. Sem. (Episcopal), NYC, Julius M. Cruse collection in history of immunology Rowland Med.

Libr., U. Miss. Med. Ctr., 2004, Julius M Cruse Collection of T.S. Eliot, Emory U. Woodruff Libr., Atlanta, 2008; Wilson Found. grantee, 1990-95, 93-94, 95-98, 99-2003; B.S. Guyton lectr. on history of medicine, 1998; Fulbright scholar U. Graz, Austria, 1958-60. Fellow AAAS, Royal Soc. Medicine, Royal Soc. Promotion Health, Am. Acad. Microbiology, Am. Soc. for Histocompatibility and Immunogenetics (chmn. publs. com. 1987-95, councillor 1997-99, historian 2000—), Intercontinental Biog. Assn.; mem. AMA (Physicians Recognition award 196-75), Clin. Immunology Soc., Am. Inst. Biol. Scis., Am. Soc. Clin. Pathologists, Can. Soc. Microbiologists, NY Acad. Scis. Exptl. Biology and Medicine, Am. Diabetes Assn., Soc. Francaise d'Immunologie, Reticuloendothelial Soc., Transplantation Soc., Electron Microscopy Soc. Am., Am. Assn. History Medicine, The Paul Ehrlich Soc., Am. Soc. Investigative Pathology, Am. Assn. Pathologists, Am. Chem. Soc., Brit. Soc. Immunology, Can. Soc. Immunology, Am. Soc. Microbiology, Internat. Acad. Pathology, Am. Assn. Immunologists (historian 1990—), T.S. Eliot Soc., Soc. of Mary, Mariological Soc. Am., Sigma Xi, Phi Kappa Phi, Phi Eta Sigma, Alpha Epsilon Delta, Gamma Sigma Epsilon, Phi Chi. Anglican Catholic. Office: U Miss Med Ctr Dept Pathology 2500 N State St Jackson MS 39216-4500 Office Phone: 601-984-1565. Business E-Mail: jcruse@umc.edu.

CRUSIO, WIM E., biomedical researcher; b. Bergen op Zoom, Netherlands, Dec. 20, 1954; s. Kees Crusio and Annie Crusio-Jordans. PhD, U. of Nijmegen, The Netherlands, 1984. Sr. rsch. scientist U. of Heidelberg, Germany, 1987—90, Centre National de la Recherche Scientifique, Paris, 1991—94; rsch. dir. Centre Nat. de la Recherche Scientifique, Orleans, France, 1994—2000; prof. psychiatry Brudnick Neuropsychiatric Rsch. Inst., U. of Mass., Worcester, 2000—04; rsch. dir. Ctr. Nat. Rsch. Sci., Talence, France, 2005—. Editor-in-chief Genes, Brain and Behavior, Oxford, 2001—; organiser Ann. Internat. Summer Sch. on Behavioral Neurogenetics, 1995—2002; assoc. editor neurobehavioral genetics Behavioral and Brain Sci., 1991—2008. Editor: (book) Handbook of Molecular Genetic Techniques for Brain and Behavior Research, 1999; assoc. editor Genetics and Neurosci. ScientificWorld Jour., 2002—, mem. editl. bd. Behavior Genetics, 1991—95, Psycology, 1991—, Behavioural Brain Rsch., 1997—2007, Physiology and Behavior, 1997—, Neurogenetics, 1998—2006, BMC Neuroscience, 2002—, Behavioral Brain Functions, 2004—, Frontiers Behavior Neurosci., 2007—, Open Behavior Sci. Jour., 2006—, Jour. Visual Exp., 2006—, Behavioural Brain Science, 2009—; academic editor: PLoS ONE; contbr. over 100 articles to profl. jours. Fellow, Alexander von Humboldt Found., 1984—87. Mem.: Inst. Neuroscis. Cognitives Integratives of Aquiframe (adj. dir. 2011—), Behavior Genetics Assn. (mem. at large 1993—96), Dutch Behavior Genetics Contact Group (pres. 1987—97, 2007), Internat. Soc. for Psychiatric Genetics (mem. program com. 2000, 2002), Fedn. of European Neurosci. Socs. (coun. mem. 1998—2000), European Brain and Behaviour Soc. (mem. at large 1996—99), Internat. Behavioural and Neural Genetics Soc. (pres., treas., mem. at large 1996—2001), Internat. Behavioral Neurosci. Soc. (coun. mem. 1999—2002, mem. program com. 2008—, chair program com. 2010—11). Office: Inst Neuroscis Cognitives Integratives d'Aquitaine CNRS UMR 5287 Bat B2-Avenue des Facultes 33405 Talence France Office Phone: 33 5 4000 8900. Personal E-mail: wim_crusio@yahoo.com.

CRUTCHFIELD, CHARLES E., III, dermatologist, educator; b. Mpls. m. Laurie Crutchfield; children: Olivia, Charles IV. BA, Carleton Coll.; M in Molecular Biology, Mayo Clinic, 1993, MD, 1994. Diplomate Am. Bd. Dermatology, Nat. Bd. of Med. Examiners. Intern Gundersen Clinic, 1993; resident in dermatology Univ. Minn., 1998; founding bd. mem. FindaBlackDoctor.com; distinguished Benedict prof. biology Carleton Coll.; clin. assoc. prof. dermatology med. sch. Univ. Minn.; owner Crutchfield Dermatology Clinic, Eagan, med. dir. Co-author (with Bernie Ackerman): (dermatology textbook) A Clin. Atlas of 101 Common Skin Diseases; co-author: various others. Recipient Karis, Mayo Clinic, Distinguished Tchg. award, Minn. Med. Found., Gold Triangle award, Am. Acad. of Dermatology, Clin. Faculty Tchr. of the Yr., AOA; named 1st Expert njector in Minn.; named one of Top Doctors, Mpls.-St Paul Mag., 5 Best Dermatologists for Women, Minn. Monthly Mag., Best Doctors in America, Best Dermatologist, Castle Connolly, 2011. Mem.: Minn. Assn. of Black Physicians (v.p.), Doctors Mayo Soc., Mayo Alumni Assn., Ramsey County Med. Soc. (treas.), Minn. Med. Assn., Minn. Dermatol. Soc., Nat. Med. Assn., O'Leary Dermatol. Soc., Am. Soc. of Dermatologic Surgery, Am. Acad. of Cosmetic Surgery, Am. Soc. of Cosmetic and Aesthetic Surgery, Am. Acad. of Dermatology, Ramsey Med. Assn., Nat. Med. Assn., AMA. Avocations: painting, photography, baseball. Office: Crutchfield Dermatology Clinic 1185 Town Centre Dr Ste 101 Saint Paul MN 55123 Office Phone: 651-209-3600. Office Fax: 651-209-3601.

CRUTCHFIELD, SUSAN RAMSEY, neurophysiologist; b. Pasadena, Calif., Oct. 7, 1941; d. Henry Colwell Ramsey and Rowena Ruth (Lockett) Banning; m. Ralph L. Crutchfield, Sept. 26, 1964 (div. Sept. 1973); children: Pamela Montague, Ashley Noland. AA, Pine Manor Coll., 1961; student, Sorbonne U., Paris, 1961-62; BA, George Washington U., 1964; MA, U. Calif., San Diego, 1978; PhD, Aston U., Birmingham, Eng., 1986. Rsch. assoc. U. Calif. Med. Ctr., San Diego, 1978-80, rschr., 1986-89, clin. instr. dept. pediats. divsn. neonatology, 1989-94, asst. clin. prof. depts. ophthalmology and pediat., 1994-98, clin. prof. dept. pediat., 1998—2004; rschr. Birmingham U., England, 1980-86. Mem. AAAS, NY Acad. Scis., European Neurosci. Soc., Internat. Soc. Clin. Electrophysiology Vision, Assn. Rsch. Vision and Ophthalmology, Brit. Soc. Neurophysiology, U. Club San Diego, U. Calif. San Diego Emeriti Assn., U. Calif. Berkeley Emeriti Assn., Jr. League San Francisco. Avocations: hiking, photography, gardening, reading, painting. Home Phone: 415-383-1133. Personal E-mail: srcridgewood@gmail.com.

CRUZ, ANTONIO MIGUEL, biomedical engineer, educator; b. Ciudad Habana, Cuba, July 2, 1971; s. Delgado Enma Cruz and Miguel Fleitas Antonio. PhD in Bioengring., ISPJAE U., Habana, Cuba, 2001. Cert. in nuc. engring., ISCTN, Havana, 1995. Prof. ISPJAE U., Habana City, 1995—2006, Rosario U., Bogota D.C, Colombia, biomed. eng. program designer team leader, 2006—. Prof. cons. Unexpo U., Venezuela, 1997—2001, CUAO, Cali, Colombia, 2001, Proinsal Gtz-Chile, 2001, DOSIMET, Santiago de los Caballeros, Dominican Republic, 2004—05; rschr. Hosp. Sick Children, Toronto, Canada, 2005—. Author: Instrumentacion, biomed. eng. Soc., 1995, 2006. Mem.: IEEE-EMBS, Advance Assn Medical Instrumentation. Achievements include research in technology management

and computer sciences. Home: CRA15 # 142-45 Apt 603 Cedritos Bogota DC Colombia Office: Univ Rosario Calle 63d 24-31 Quinta de Mutis Bogota Colombia Personal E-mail: fleitas10@yahoo.com. Business E-Mail: antonio.cruz43@urosario.edu.co.

CRUZ, DAVID, biologist; b. Mex. City, Jan. 1, 1967; PhD, Met. Autonomous U., 2008. Biologist Nat. Autonomous U. Mex., 1985—88. Contbr. chapters to books, articles to profl. jours. Mem.: Mexican Assn. Human Genetics. Office: Juan Badiano 1 Mexico 14080 Mexico E-mail: crumis1@yahoo.com.mx.

CRUZ, MAURO, dentist, oral surgeon, orthodontist, implantologist; b. Santo Antonio, Minas Gerais, Brazil, Aug. 3, 1954; s. Clóvis Cruz Reis and Maria José Cruz; married; children: Silvia, Gustavo, Victoria. DDS, Juiz de Fora Fed. U., Brazil, 1976; splty. degree in Oral Surgery, Rio de Janeiro State U., 1978; splty. degree in Orthodontics, Pontifical Cath. U., Rio de Janeiro, 1979; MDSci, Camilo Castelo Branco U., 2001. Dir. Clin. Ctr. Rsch. in Stomatology, Juiz de Fora, 1990—. Sci. cons. Bioform Implant and Allumina Membrane, Rio de Janeiro, 1990—; asst. prof. dept. orthodontics Pontifical Cath. U., Rio de Janeiro, 1979—83; dir. 2d Internat. Orthodontic Congress, Juiz de Fora, 1999; lectr. in field. Author: The Little Creek, 2001; contbr. articles to profl. jours., mags. Permanent mem. City Civic Coun. 1st lt. Brazilian Army, 1977—78. Recipient award, Italian Implant Study Group, 1984, Hypnosis Brazilian Assn., 1985, Developing Inst. of Personality, 1985, Internat. Order Journalists, 1990, Dental Syndicate of Juiz de Fora, 1992, Tiradents Acad., 1999, Mcpl. Chamber of Juiz de Fora, 1999, Tribuna de Minas Jour., 2001. Fellow: Fedn. Dental Internat., Brazilian Acad. Dentistry, Internat. Coll. Dentists, Brazilian Oral Surgery Assn., Brazilian Dental Assn. (pres. Juiz de Fora chpt. 1997—2000), Pierre Fauchard Acad. Office: Clinest Av Rio Branco 2288/1203 - Centro 36016-310 Juiz de Fora Brazil Office Phone: 55 32 3215-3957. Office Fax: 55 32 3215-3957. Business E-Mail: clinest@terra.com.br.

CRUZ, NELSON XAVIER, healthcare executive; b. NYC, June 30, 1950; s. Jaime and Angela (Diaz) C.; m. Asuncion Rosado, July 10, 1971 (div. 1976); children: Celena, Jasmin; m. Lydia Cordero, 1987; 1 child, Lauren A. BA, Hunter Coll., 1974; MS, Herbert H. Lehman Coll., 1978; MBA, Manhattan Coll., 1985; JD, Rutgers U., 1998. CLU, ChFC. Recreation therapist Bronx (N.Y.) Children's Psychiat. Hosp., 1974-78; dir. rehab. svc. Rockland Children's Psychiat. Hosp., Orangeburg, NY, 1978-79; dir. mkgt. Fordham-Tremont Community Mental Health Ctr., Bronx, 1979-83; administr. dept. emergency Woodhull Hosp., Bklyn., 1983-85, assoc. dir. quality assurance, 1985-86; dir., fin. CFO Promesa, Inc., Bronx, 1986-87; administr. ambulatory care network Bronx-Lebanon Hosp. Ctr., 1987-92; exec. dir. United Cmty. Health Plan/United Hosps. Med. Ctr., Newark, 1992-95; dir. network devel. PruCare HMO, Prudential Life Ins. Co. of Am., Iselin, NJ, 1995-97; v.p., COO Universal Inst., Inc., Livingston, NJ, 1997-98; mgr. St. Mary's Hosp. Family Health Ctr., 1998-2000; pres., CFO Henry I Austin Health Ctr. Inc. Trenton, NJ, 2001—04; dir. Hurtado Health Ctr., Rutgers U. Health Svcs., New Brunswick, NJ, 2000-01; CEO Jewish Renaissance Med. Ctr., 2004—07; dir. Englewood Health Dept., 2007—, dir. and health officer. Project coord., cons. Inst. Puerto Rican Hispanic Elderly, N.Y.C., 1983; account exec. Medi-Span, Inc., Worcester, Mass., 1983; healthcare mktg. cons. BSquared Comm., Inc., 1999-2000. Adv. bd. Bronx Legal Aid Soc.; bd. dirs. Community Planning Bd. 6, 1981-82; mem. Bronx-Boro Wide Mental Health Svcs. Com., 1979-81. Leadership Mgmt. Urban Execs. Inst. fellow, Rutgers U., 1996; Leadership N.J. fellow, 1994—; Hispanic Leadership Opportunity Program fellow, 1993-94. Fellow Am. Managed Care and Rev. Assn. (cert.); mem. Am Coll. Healthcare Execs. (diplomate, cert. health care exec.), Assn. Healthcare Execs. of N.J., Med. Group Mgmt. Assn., Am. Coll. Med. Practice Execs., Group Health Assn. Am., Am. Coll. CLUs and ChFCs, N.J. Med. Group Mgmt. Assn., Am. Coll. Healthcare Mktg., Hispanic Assn. Health Svcs. Execs. (mktg. cons. 1986-87), N.Y. Assn. Ambulatory Care, Health Adminstrs. Assn. N.Y., Acad. Health Svcs. Mktg., Nat. Assn. Health Svcs. Execs. Democrat. Roman Catholic. Avocations: running, squash, swimming, music. Office: Englewood Health Dept 73 S van Brunt St Englewood NJ 07631 Office Phone: 732-293-0135. Personal E-mail: nelxav@aol.com. Business E-Mail: ncruz@cityofenglewood.org.

CRUZ, RICARDO M., orthodontist, educator; b. Brasília, Fed. Dist., Brazil, Mar. 30, 1966; DDS, U. Brasília, Brasília, 1987; MS in Orthodontics, Fed. U. Rio de Janeiro, 1995; PhD in Genetics, U. Brasília, 2005. Cert. in dental surgery U. Brasília, 1987. Ceo Machado Cruz Odontologia Especializada, Brasília, 1987—; prof. orthodontics U. Brasília, 1995—2000, CESUBRA, Brasília, 2000—04; coord. orthodontic program Dentistry Sector Fed. Dist. Justice Dept., Brasília, 2001—; chmn. dept. orthodontics Paulista U., Brasília, 2003—. Mem. editl. bd. revisors Dental Press, Curitiba, Brazil. Sec. Coll. Diplomates Brazilian Bd. Orthodontics, Rio de Janeiro, 2008—. Fellow: World Fedn. Orthodontists; mem.: Fed. Dist. Orthodontic Soc. (pres. 1999—2001), Alumni Assn. Orthodontics, Brazilian Assn. Orthodontics and Dentofacial Orthoped. (pres. 2010—). Roman Catholic. Avocations: travel, windsurfing, tennis, saxophone, photography. Office: Machado Cruz Odontologia Especializada SHIS QI9/11 Bloco L sala 101 Lago Sul Fed Dist Brasília 71-625-125 Brazil Office Fax: 55-61-3248-6500. Business E-Mail: ricardomcruz@uol.com.br.

CRUZ, RUY JORGE, JR., surgeon, researcher; b. Santo Andre, Sao Paulo, Brazil, Nov. 14, 1970; s. Ruy Jorge and Cleonice Beccheri Cruz. MD, Faculdade de Medicina de Santo Amaro, Sao Paulo, 1994; PhD, U. Sao Paulo, 2002. Diplomate Brazilian Coll. of Digestive Tract Surgeons, in gen. surgery Sao Paulo Med. State Coun., 2002. Resident in gen. surgery Faculdade de Ciências Médicas da Santa Casa de Sao Paulo, Sao Paulo, Sao Paulo, Brazil, 1995—97, resident in digestive tract surgery, 1997—99; fellowship in pancreas transplantation Beneficiência Portuguesa Hosp., Sao Paulo, 2000—01; rschr. U. of Sao Paulo Med. Sch. / Heart Inst., 1999—; attending surgeon U. of Santo Amaro Med. Sch., Sao Paulo, 1999—; assoc. U. Pitts., 2003—05. Mem. editl. bd. (jour.) Acta Cirurgica Brasileira; mem. editl. bd.: Brazilian Med. Assn. Jour.; contbr. articles to profl. jours. Recipient Young Investigator award, Brazilian and Internat. Shock Soc., 1994, Rubens Monteiro de Arrudap prize, U. of Santo Amaro Med. Sch., 1993, 1994, Golden-Cross prize, Golden-Cross Health Care Sys., 1993, award, Brazilian Coll. Surgeons, 2000, 2002, 2003, Am. Soc. Critical Care Medicine, 2004, 2005. Mem.: Brazilian Soc. for Devel. of Rsch. in Surgery (bd. dirs., nat. sec. 2000—), Brazilian Shock Soc. (bd. dirs., coun. mem. 2001—03), Soc. Complexxity Acute Illness, Soc. Surgery Alimentary Tract, Soc. Critical Care

Medicine, Interantional Shock Soc. (assoc.), Brazilian Soc. Integrated Mgmt. for Trauma Patients (assoc.), Internat. Hepato-Pancreato-Biliary Assn. (assoc.), Brazilian Coll. Digestive Tract Surgery (assoc.). Roman Catholic. Avocations: volleyball, tennis, squash, swimming. Office: Heart Inst Univ São Paulo Av Dr Eneas de Carvalho Aguiar 44 São Paulo 05403-000 Brazil Home: Rua Marivaldo Fernandes 140 04792-060 São Paulo SP Brazil Office Fax: 55-11-30857887. E-mail: ruycruzjunior@yahoo.com.br, expcruzjr@incor.usp.br.

CRUZ, THERESA LAVAINA, mental health services professional, educator; d. Roy Lee Campbell and Bloneva W. Montgomery; 1 child, Micheal Jarodd Campbell. MA in Counseling, Liberty U., Lynchburg, Va., 2004; MSc in Criminal Justice, Capella U., 2006. Cert. forensic cons. 1999, conflict resolution specialist, anger mgmt. facilitator. Forensic specialist Mental Health Ctr., Jacksonville, Fla., 1996—; prof. Fla. Met. U., Orange Park, 2005—, U. Phoenix, Columbia Coll., U. Phoenix, Baker Coll., U. Ashtoo. Forensic evaluator, 2005; counselor Fla. Met. U., 2005. Recipient Prof. of Month, Fla. Met. U., 2005. Mem.: Nat. Assn. Against Sexual Violence, Am. Assn. Sch. Counselors, AAUP, Fla. Comm. Assn., Soc. for the Advancement of Behavioral Econs., Am. Sociol. Assn., Nat. Assn. Cognitive Behavioral Specialists, Anger Mgmt. Assn., Nat. Assn. Against Domestic Violence (corr.). Democrat. Achievements include development of college counseling program and Community Competency Restoration program. Avocations: sewing, reading, cooking. Office Fax: 904-695-2465; Home Fax: 904-743-6706. Personal E-mail: theresacruz@bellsouth.net.

CRUZ, WILHELMINA MANGAHAS, critical care physician; b. Bulacan, Philippines, July 20, 1942; d. Rectorino Bernardo and Mercedes Correa (Mangahas) C.; m. Antonio I. Lee, May 28, 1977; children: Richard Anthony, Alexander Victor. AA, U. Santo Tomas, The Philippines, 1960, MD, 1965. Diplomate in internal medicine and critical care medicine Am. Bd. Internal Medicine; diplomate Am. Bd. Nephrology. Intern Meml. Hosp., Albany, NY, 1967-68; resident in internal medicine Coney Island Hosp., Bklyn., 1968-71; fellow in nephrology VA Hosp., Bronx, 1971-72, SUNY Downstate Med. Ctr., Bklyn., 1972-73; attending physician King's County Hosp. Ctr., Bklyn., 1973-76; coord. in medicine Kingsbrook Jewish Med. Ctr., Bklyn., 1976—. Assoc. med. dir. ICU Drs. Cmty. Hosp., Lanham, Md., 1977-; clin. asst. prof. SUNY Downstate Med. Ctr., 1977—; med. dir. Critical Care Svcs., 1999-. Mem. ACP, Med. and Chirurg. Soc. Md., Prince George's Med. Soc., Soc. Critical Care Medicine, Philippine Med. Assn. Washington. Roman Catholic. Office: PO Box 34534 Bethesda MD 20827 Office Phone: 301-552-5693. *

CRUZ CRUZ, LUIS R., physicist, researcher; s. Luis O. Cruz Soto and Julie E. Cruz Perez; m. Brigita Urbanc, Apr. 17, 1999; children: Marguerita Malina Cruz-Urbanc, Francisco Julian Cruz-Urbanc. BS, U. P.R., Rio Piedras, 1985, MS, 1989; BM, Conservatory of Music of P.R., 1989; PhD, MIT, 1994. Lab. tech. physics dept. U. PR, Rio Piedras, 1985—86, rsch., tchg. asst. physics dept., 1986—89; rsch. asst. MIT, Cambridge, Mass., 1991—94; rsch. assoc. physics dept. Boston U., 1994—2005, sr. rsch. assoc. physics dept., 2005—08; assoc. prof. physics dept Drexel U., 2008—. Systems adminstrn. Ctr. Polymer Studies, Boston U., 1994—2005. Contbr. scientific papers. Recipient Highest Acad. Achievement, U. PR, Rio Piedras, 1985, Coll. Natural Scis. medal Acad. Excellence, 1985, Facundo Bueso Physics medal, 1985, Jose E. Pedreira Piano medal, Conservatory Music, PR, 1989. Achievements include research in possible mechanism of formation of senile plaques in the Alzheimer Brain using an aggregation-disaggregation dynamics model; discovery of relationship between loss of neuronal coherence in a microcolumn and behavioral decay with age; research using computer molecular dynamics, the initial folding behavior of a protein segment that may be key in the formation of the toxic forms of Abeta in the Alzheimer Brain. Office: Drexel Univ Physics Dept 3141 Chestnut St Philadelphia PA 19104 Office Phone: 215-895-2739. Office Fax: 215-895-5934. Business E-Mail: ccruz@drexel.edu.

CRUZEIRO, CELSO, plastic surgeon; b. Cajadaes, Portugal; s. Celso Augusto Cruzeiro and Orsina Rocha; m. Clarinda Silva, Sept. 20, 1975; children: Maria João, Afonso Daniel. MD, U. Coimbra; degree in Plastic Surgery, Coimbra U. Hosp. Resident Plastic Surgery Svc., Coimbra, 1981—85, asst. plastic surgeon, 1981—95, grad. asst. surgeon, 1995—; burns unit dir. Coimbra Burns Unit, 2004—. Plastic surgery Plorfis, Coimbra, 1990—; v.p. Portuguese Burns Soc., Coimbra, 1995—, Plastic Surgery Soc., Coimbra, 2004—. V.p. Coimbra Tennis Club. Mem.: Plastic Surgery Br. of Portuguese Med. Assn., Portuguese Burns Soc. (v.p. 1995), Portuguese Plastic Surgery Soc. (v.p. 2004). Avocations: soccer, reading, tennis. Home: R Daniel Rodrigues 83 13 DTO A 3020 Coimbra Portugal Office: Unidade de Queimados Av Bissaya Barreto 3000-075 Coimbra Portugal Office Phone: 351-239-834615. Personal E-mail: cruzeiroc@hotmail.com.

CRYER, PHILIP EUGENE, endocrinologist; b. El Paso, Ill., Jan. 5, 1940; s. Clifford Eugene and Carol Ruth (Cherry) C.; m. Susan Odette Shipman, Dec. 23, 1963 (div. May 1990); children: Philip Clifford, Justine Laurel; m. Carolyn Elizabeth Havlin, Sept. 16, 1994. BA, Northwestern U., 1962, MD, 1965; MD (hon.), U. Copenhagen, 2000. Diplomate Am. Bd. Internal Medicine, diplomate Am. Bd. Endocrinology and Metabolism. Intern, resident Barnes Hosp., St. Louis, 1965-67; fellow in endocrinology Barnes Hosp./Washington U., 1967-68, resident in medicine, 1968-69, 71-72; investigator Naval Med. Rsch. Inst., Bethesda, Md., 1969-71; from instr. to assoc. prof. Washington U. Sch. Medicine, St. Louis, 1971-80, prof., 1981—, Irene E. and Michael M. Karl prof. endocrinology/metabolism, 1995—, dir. gen. clin. rsch. ctr., 1978—2006, dir. divsn. endocrinology, diabetes and metabolism, 1985—2002. Connaught-Novo lectr. Can. Diabetes Assn., 1987; Pimstone lectr. Soc. Endocrinology, Metabolism and Diabetes, South Africa, 1989; Kellion lectr. Australian Diabetes Soc., 1992; Plenary lectr. Japan Diabetes Soc., 1994, plenary lectr. Argentine Diabetes Assn., 1998, plenary lectr. Asean Fed. Endocrine Socs., 1999. Author: Diagnostic Endocrinology, 1976, Diagnostic Endocrinology, 2d edit., 1979, Hypoglycemia, 1997; editor: Diabetes; author: Hypoglycemia in Diabetes, 2009; mem. editl. bd.: Jour. Clin. Investigation, Am. Jour. Physiology; contbr. 85 chapt. to books, over 350 articles to profl. jours. Lt. comdr. M.C. USNR, 1969—71. Recipient Rorer Clin. Investigator award Endocrine Soc., 1988, Rumbaugh Sci. award Juvenile Diabetes Found., 1989, Banting medal Am. Diabetes Assn., 1994, Excellence in Clin. Rsch. award NIH, 1994, Claude Bernard medal European Assn. Study Diabetes, 2001, Merit award NIH, 2001., Novartis prize, 2008; grantee Am. Diabetes Clin., 1988-, NIH, 1980—; named Disting. Alumnus, Northwestern U. Med. Sch., 2006. Fellow ACP; mem. Am. Fedn. Clin. Rsch. (councilor 1979-80), Am. Soc. Clin. Investigation (v.p. 1985-86), Assn. Am. Physicians, Am. Diabetes Assn. (pres. 1996-97, Albert Renold award 2010), Phi Beta Kappa, Alpha Omega Alpha. Office: Washington U Sch Medicine 660 South Euclid Ave Box 8127 Saint Louis MO 63110 Office Phone: 314-362-7635. Business E-Mail: pcryer@wustl.edu.

CRYER, THEODORE HUDSON, retired ophthalmologist, educator; b. Chgo., May 8, 1946; s. Arthur William and Maxine (Ritter) Cryer; children: Timothy Hudson, Jordan Tinley, Megan Elizabeth, Rebecca Jeanne. AB in Chemistry, Taylor U., 1968; MD, U. Md., 1972. Diplomate Am. Bd. Ophthalmology. Straight med. intern South Balt. Gen. Hosp., 1972-73, jr. asst. resident, 1973-74; asst. resident U. Md. Hosp., Balt., 1974-76, resident, 1976-77; pvt. practice Waynesboro, Pa., 1977—2009, Westminster, Md., 1977-85. Instr. U. Md. Sch. Medicine, 1979—91, clin. asst. prof. ophthalmology, 1991—; chmn. com. ethics Waynesboro Hosp., 1984, trustee, 1991—97, chmn. com. quality assurance, 1996—97, v.p. med. staff, 1988—89, 1999, pres., 1990—91, 2000—01, treas. med. staff, 2001—03, chmn. com. credentialing, chmn. bylaws com., 2003—09, chief of surgery, 1992—96, 2004—07. Clk. session Westminster Reformed Presbyn. Ch., 1980—83; trustee Christ United Meth. Ch., 1997—2000. Fellow: ACS, Am. Acad. Ophthalmology; mem.: AAAS, AMA, Opthal. Assn. Rsch. to Prevent Blindness, Nat. Soc. to Prevent Blindness (charter mem.), Pa. Acad. Otolaryngology and Ophthalmology, Md. Eye Physicians and Surgeons, Franklin County Med. Soc., Pa. Med. Soc. Republican. Methodist. Home Phone: 717-765-9271. Personal E-mail: cryergroup@embarqmail.com.

CRYSTAL, RONALD G., medical geneticist, educator; MS, U. Pa., 1963; MD, U. Pa. Sch. Med., 1968; MD (hon.), Johann Wolfgang Goethe U., Frankfurt, Germany, 1992. Intern & resident Mass. Gen. Hosp.; fellow Harvard U.; rsch. assoc. on molecular hematology Nat. Heart & Lung Inst., head. pulmonary biochemistry; clinical fellow in chest med. U. Calif., San Francisco; chief pulmonary branch Nat. Heart, Lung & Blood Inst., spl. vol. pulmonary branch; prof. genetic & internal med. Weill Cornell Med. Coll. Former surgeon to sr. surgeon USPHS Commissioned Corps, ret. med. dir. Fellow: Royal Coll. Physicians of Ireland (hon.); mem.: Assn. Am. Physicians, Am. Soc. Clinical Investigation, Alpha Omega Alpha. Office: 520 E 70th St Starr Pavilion 505 New York NY 10021 Office Phone: 646-962-4363. Office Fax: 646-962-0220.

CSABA, GYORGY, biologist, educator; b. Torokszentmiklos, Hungary, May 31, 1929; s. Jozsef and Rozalia (Pollak) C.; m. Klara Hegyi, Dec. 5, 1954 (sep. 1969); children: Aniko, Klara; m. Katalin Kallay, Aug. 5, 1970; children: Gyorgy, Tamas. MD, Budapest Med. U., 1953; PhD, Hungary Acad. Sci., Budapest, 1957, DS, 1969. Asst. to prof. Semmelweis U. of Medicine, Budapest, 1953-59, first asst., 1959-63, assoc. prof., 1963-70, prof., 1970-99, dir. dept. biology, 1971-94, prof. emeritus, 2000—. Author: Regulation of Mast Cell Formation, 1972, Ontogeny and Phylogeny of Hormone Receptors, 1981, and other books; editor: Development of Hormone Receptors, 1982, Singaling Mechanisms in Protozoa and Invertebrates, 1996, and other books; contbr. 850 articles to profl. jours. Chmn. book com. of Scientific Rsch. Coun., Budapest, 1980-88; chmn. editl. com. of Semmelweis Pub., Budapest, 1989-2001. Recipient Huzella prize Hungarian Biol. Soc., 1983, Pal Bugat award Sci. Ednl. Soc., Budapest, 1989, Hungarian Higher Edn. medal Min. of Edn., Budapest, 1994, Khwarizmi Internat. award, 2000. Avocation: writing books and papers on the biol. problems of modern men. Home: 1124 Budapest, Vas Gereben U-36 Budapest Hungary Office: Semmelweis U Cell & Immunobiology/Dept Genetics Po Box 370 1445 Budapest Hungary Home Phone: (36-1) 319-6757; Office Phone: (36-1) 210-2950. Business E-Mail: csagyor@dgci.sote.hu.

CSÁNGÓ, PÉTER ANDRÁS, microbiologist; b. Budapest, Hungary, May 14, 1942; s. Ferenc and Magda (Herczeg) C.; m. Gerda Patricia Dub, Oct. 25, 1969; children: Monica, Miriam, Michelle. MD, U. Medicine, Pécs, Hungary, 1967; postgrad., U. Birmingham, Eng., 1972-73. Registrar County Lung Hosp., Szombathely, Hungary, 1967-68, Semmelweis Hosp., Budapest, 1968-69, State Lung Hosp., Tromsø, Norway, 1969-70, Nat. Inst. Pub. Health, Oslo, 1970-73, sr. registrar, 1973-78, virologist, 1978; dir. dept. clin. microbiology Ctr. Hosp., Kristiansand, 1978—2004; cons. dept. clin. microbiology Univ. Hosp., Tromsø, 1996—2003, Sörlandet Hosp., Kristiansand, 2005—06; cons. dept. microbiology divsn. lab. sci. Sykehuset Innlandet Trust, Lillehammer, 2006—08; cons. dept. microbiology Aalesund Hosp.; med. dir. Unilabs Telelab, Skien, Norway, 2008—. Cons. microbiologist Nordland Ctr. Hosp., Bodø, Norway, 1975—78, U. Northern Norway, Tromsø, 1996—2004. Contbr. articles to profl. jours. Lt. Border Guard Hungarian Army, 1967—68. Grantee Royal Ministry Social Affairs, Norway, 1972, Royal Ministry Fgn. Affairs, Norway, 1986, Mid. East Eye Rsch. Inst., Israel, 1987. Mem. Norwegian Med. Assn., Norwegian Soc. Infectious Diseases, Norwegian Soc. Med. Microbiology (chmn. 1989-91), Swedish Soc. Med. Microbiology, Scandinavian Soc. of Bacterial Vaginosis, N.Y. Acad. Scis., Scandinavian Soc. Genitourinary Medicine (bd. dirs. 1986-92), European Soc. Chlamydia Rsch. (bd. dirs. 1987-96), Am. Soc. Microbiology, Internat. AIDS Soc. Avocations: reading, travel, languages, genealogy, sports. Office: Helse Sunnmøre Trust Dept Lab Aalesund Hosp No 6026 Aalesund Norway also: Unilabs Telelab Skien Norway Office Phone: 4735505703. Personal E-mail: csango@gmail.com.

CSERHÁTI, ENDRE FRIGYES, pediatrician; b. Budapest, Apr. 20, 1932; s. Endre and Karolina Ruperta (Tonkres) C.; m. Zsuzsanna Katalin Berzsenyi, June 21, 1968; 1 child, Nóra. MD, Semmelweis U., Budapest, 1956; ScD, Hungarian Acad. Sci., Budapest, 1989. Jr. rsch. fellow Inst. Physiology, Budapest, 1952-56; clin. physician dept. pediats. Semmelweis U., Budapest, 1956-60, asst. prof., 1960-74, sr. lectr., 1974-82, assoc. prof., 1982-90, univ. prof. dept. pediats., 1990—, dep. dir. dept. pediats., 1982—2002. Editor/co-author: Diseases of the Airways in Childhood, 2002; co-author: History of Hungarian Paediatric Society, 1924-1999, 1999, The Heritage of the Past: HIstory of the Hospital for Poor Children 1839-2006, 2007, Practical of Airway's Disease; contbr. articles to profl. jours. Dep. officer Hungarian Army, 1951-52, 53-56. Recipient Purkynye award Czechoslovakian Med. Assn., 1989; Markusovszky award, Görgényi-Göttche award, Comdr. Ordre de la Couronne Royaume Belgique, 2002, Flesch Armin award, 2004. Mem. Hungarian Acad. Scis. (corp. mem.), Hungarian Pediat. Soc. (sec.-gen. 1981-91, Schoepf-Merei Meml. medal 1991), Austrian Pediat. Assn. (hon.), Hungarian Assn. Allergology and Clin. Immunology (mem.-at-large 1983—), European Respiratory Soc., Hungarian Soc. Med. History Achievements include research in late prognoses of bronchial asthma in childhood; cytokines in allergic inflammation; consensus statement in the treatment of allergic diseases, quality of life in bronchial asthma. Office: 1st Dept Pediat Semmelweis Med U Bókay János u 53 H-1083 Budapest Hungary also: Oroszveg U4 H-1112 Budapest Hungary Office Phone: 003613138212, 0036 30 2419906. Personal E-mail: cser@gyer1.sote.hu.

CSERR, ROBERT, psychiatrist, physician, hospital administrator; b. Perth Amboy, NJ, May 29, 1936; s. Frank Joseph and Helen (Bodzany) C.; m. Helen Fitzgerald, May 28, 1962; 1 dau., Ruth. AB magna cum laude, Harvard U., 1958, MD, 1962. Med. intern U. Va. Hosp., 1962-63; resident, fellow in psychiatry Mass. Gen. Hosp., Harvard Med. Sch., 1963-66; alcohol coordinator Mass. Gen. Hosp., 1967-68, clin. assoc. psychiatry, 1968—; asst. supt. Medfield State Hosp., Harding, Mass., 1968-70, supt., 1970-74, area program dir., 1970-74; dir. Outlook Psychiat. Facility, Hampstead, NH, 1974-76; med. dir. Charles River Hosp., Wellesley, Mass., 1976-80, psychiatrist-in-chief, 1980-87, Hahnemann Hosp., Boston, 1982—; med. dir. Taunton Hosp. and Regional Svc. Ctr., 1990-92; assoc. med. dir. psychiatry PHCS, Lexington, Mass., 1991-93, v.p., med. dir. mental health svcs. Waltham, Mass., 1993-96. V.p. clin. affairs Cmty. Care Systems Inc., 1979-86, sr. cons., 1986—; asst. clin. prof. psychiatry Boston U. Sch. Medicine, 1968-74, assoc. clin. prof., 1979—; asst. psychiatrist Beth Israel Hosp., 1970—; lectr. in psychiatry Harvard Med. Sch., 1972-89; cons. Med. Mgmt., Managed Care Programs, 1986—. Pres. Medfield Found.; bd. overseers Mt. Desert Island Biol. Lab. Served with AUS, 1966-68. Mem. Am. Coll. Mental Health Adminstrn., Mass. Med. Soc., BCN Med. Soc. Office: 707 Green Acres North Dighton MA 02764 Business E-Mail: bob@cesrr.com.

CSIKSZENTMIHALYI, MIHALY, psychology professor; b. Fiume, Italy, Sept. 29, 1934; came to U.S., 1956; s. Alfred and Edith (Jankovich) C.; m. Isabella Selega, Dec. 30, 1961; children: Mark, Christopher. BA, U. Chgo., 1960, PhD, 1965. Reporter European News Service, Rome, 1952-56; free-lance artist Rome, 1954-56; translator U.S.A. Pubs., Chgo., 1958-64; prof. sociology Lake Forest (Ill.) Coll., 1965-70; prof. psychology human devel., edn. U. Chgo., 1971—90; prof. psychology Claremont Grad. U., 1990—. Adv. bd. Ency. Britannica, Chgo., 1985—, J.P. Getty Mus., Malibu, Calif., 1985—. Author: Beyond Boredom and Anxiety, 1975, Flow: The Psychology of Optimal Experience, 1990, The Evolving Self, 1993, Creativity, 1996, Finding Flow in Everyday Life, 1997, Good Business, 2003; (with others) The Creative Vision, 1976, The Meaning of Things, 1981, Being Adolescent, 1984, Optimal Experience, 1988, Television and the Quality of Life, 1990, The Art of Seeing, 1990, Talented Teenagers, 1993, Creating Worlds, 1994, Becoming Adult, 2000, Good Work, 2001, A Life Worth Living, 2006, Experience Sampling, 2006. Fulbright Sr. scholar, 1984, 1990, Fellow Ctr. for Advanced Studies in the Behavioral Sci., 1994-95. Fellow Am. Acad. Arts and Scis., Am. Acad. Edn., Am. Acad. Leisure Scis., Am. Acad. Polit. and Social Scis.; mem. Quadrangle Club. Avocations: mountain climbing, reading, art, chess. Home: 700 Alamosa Dr Claremont CA 91711 Office: 1021 N Dartmouth Ave Claremont CA 91711 Home Phone: 909-621-7345. Business E-Mail: miska@cgu.edu.

CSILLIK, BERTALAN BERTRAM, anatomist; b. Szeged, Hungary, Nov. 10, 1927; s. Bertalan sen. and Alice (Csiky) C.; m. Elizabeth Knyihár, Apr. 30, 1972; children: Eva, Peter, Anita, Andrea. MD, U. Med. Sch., 1954; PhD, Hungarian Acad. of Scis., 1962, ScD, 1968. Demonstrator of anatomy U. Med. Sch., Szeged, Hungary, 1950-54, asst. prof. anatomy, 1954-62, assoc. prof. anatomy, 1964-68, prof. anatomy & chmn., 1962—63; asst. prof. pharmacology U. Pa., Phila., 1962-63; project dir. Bay Zoltán Inst. Biotechnology, Szeged, 1993-2001; prof. emeritus anatomy, project dir. U. Szeged, 2001—. Vis. prof. Harvard Med. Sch., Boston, 1974-74, 77-78, 93-94; vis. prof. neuroanatomy Yale Med. Sch., New Haven, Conn., 1982, 92-95; chmn. dept. anatomy Univ. Med. Sch., Szeged, 1968-93; Fogarty sr. rsch. fellow Yale Med. Sch., 1992-94; bd. dirs. of the presidium of the PhD com. Albert Szent-Györgyi Med. U. Author: The Post-Synaptic Membrane, 1965, 2d edit. 1967; co-author: The Protean Gate, 1986 (Pub. Niveau award 1988), Topographical Anatomy, 1988, 2d edit. 1992 (Pub. Niveau award 1991); patentee in field. Recipient Silver Order of Labour Hungarian Govt., 1986, Grand Cross of Merit, Hungarian Republic, 2002. Mem. Hungarian Acad. Sci. (bd. dirs. doctoral com. 1985—93, Laureate 1993), European Fedn. for Exptl. Morphology (bd. dirs. of the presidium 1991—2008), Internat. Brain Rsch. Orgn., Hungarian Anat. Soc. (past pres.), Szeged Acad. Com. (pres. 1983-93, hon. pres.), Soc. Friends of the Albert Szent Gyorgyi Med. U. (chmn. 1997—2011, hon. pres. 2011-), Dugonics Soc. Arts and Letters (chmn. 1994-), Acad. Royale de Medicine de Belgique (hon.), German Acad. Scis. Leopoldina. Avocation: violin. Home: Pillich Kalman u 24 H-6726 Szeged Hungary Office: Dept Anatomy Kossuth L sgt 40 Szeged Hungary Office Phone: 36-62-544-918. Office Fax: 36-62-545-707. Business E-Mail: csillik@anatomy.szote.u-szeged.hu.

CSOKA, ANTONEI BENJAMIN, medical researcher; b. Aug. 25, 1969; BS, Newcastle U., 1991; MS, U. Leicester, 1993; PhD, U. Debrecen, 1998. Postdoc. rsch. assoc. Roswell Pk. Cancer Inst., 2009—. Home: 285 Babcock St Buffalo NY 14210 Personal E-mail: antonei@csoka.us.

CSUTAK, ADRIENNE, ophthalmologist; b. Debrecen, Mar. 29, 1971; MD, U. Debrecen, 1996; MS, Semmelweis U. Health Svcs. Mgmt. Tng. Ctr., 2008. Instr. ophthalmology dept. U. Debrecen Med. and Health Sci. Ctr., 2003—. Fellow Wilmer Eye Inst. Johns Hopkins U., Balt., 1998, fellow APL, 2004; fellow U. Degli Studi Genova, Italy, 2002; mgr. dir. InnoTears-LLC, 2006—08; fellow Moorfields Eye Hosp., London, 2009. Recipient Millennium award, András Berta, József Tozsér, Innovational award, U. Debrecen, Young Investigator award, First Singapore Eye Rsch. Inst.; named Invention of Yr., Johns Hopkins U. Applied Physics Lab. Mem.: European Soc. Ophthalmology, Hungarian Assn. Rsch. in Vision and Ophthalmology, Assn. Rsch. in Vision and Ophthalmology. Avocations: skiing, roller-skating. Office: Nagyerdei krt 98 Debrecen Hajdú Bihar megye 4032 Hungary Office Fax: 36 52 320-852. Business E-Mail: acsutak@dote.hu.

CUALING, HERNANI DEL MUNDO, physician, researcher; s. Pablo Mateong and Flor Del Mundo Cualing; m. Rawia Salem Yassin, Dec. 20, 1989; children: Kareem Yassin Khozaim, Phillip, Andrew. BS, U. Philippines, 1974, MD, 1978. Diplomate Am. Bd. of Pathology, 1991, Am. Bd. of Hematology, 1992. Chief resident Nassau County U. Med. Ctr., East Meadow, NY, 1990—91; fellow dept. pathology Ind. U. Med. Ctr., Indpls., 1991—92; asst. prof. U. Cin. Med. Ctr., 1992—2002; assoc. prof. dept. pathology U. Cin., 2002—02; assoc. prof. U. South Fla./Moffitt Cancer Ctr., Tampa, 2002—. Consulting hematopathology staff VA Med. Ctr., Cin., 1993—2002; med. dir. U. Cin. Med. Ctr., 1993—96, Diagnostic Immunology and Flow Cytometry Interpretation of Leukemias and Lymphomas, Diagnostic Flow Cytometry by Health Alliance, 2000—02; med. dir. immunohistochemistry/histology Moffitt Cancer Ctr. and Rsch. Inst., Tampa, Fla., 2002—. Period furniture, Queen Anne Desk; contbr. articles to profl. jours. Mem. Clin. Cytometry Soc., 2002—03; pres. Med. Student Soc., 1977. Recipient First prize Paper, Fla. Soc. Pathologists, 2004, Tchr. of Yr., U. South Fla. Pathology Residents, 2004, Internat. Rschr. award, U.P. Med. Alumni, 2003; grantee Biomedical Engrng. of Leukemia/Lymphoma, Whitaker Found., 1997-2000; Pioneering grant, U. Cin. Biomed. Engrng., 1994. Fellow: Internat. Acad. Pathologists/Coll. Am. Pathologists (assoc.); mem.: Coun. Health Care Advisors (assoc.), Am. Soc. Hematologists (assoc.). R-Liberal. Catholic. Achievements include invention of computerized virtual flow cytometry of immunostained cells. Avocations: woodworking, sailing, fishing, history. Home: 18804 Chaville Rd Lutz FL 33558 Business E-Mail: cualinhd@moffitt.usf.edu.

CUATRECASAS, PEDRO MARTIN, research biochemist, educator; b. Madrid, Sept. 27, 1936; arrived in US, 1947, naturalized, 1954; s. Jose and Martha Cuatrecasas; m. Carol Zies, Aug. 15, 1959; children: Paul, Lisa, Diane, Julia. AB, Washington U., St. Louis, 1958, MD, 1962; DSc (hon.), U. Barcelona, 1984, Mt. Sinai Sch. Medicine, 1985, U. Buenos Aires, 1990, U. Naples, Italy, 1990. Intern/resident internal medicine Johns Hopkins U. Hosp., Balt., 1962-64, asst. physician, 1972-75; clin. assoc. endocrinology br. Nat. Inst. Arthritis & Metabolic Diseases (NIAMS), NIH, Bethesda, Md., 1964-66, USPHS postdoc. fellow, NIAMS Lab. Chem. Biology, 1966-67, med. officer, Lab. Chem. Biology, 1967-70; assoc. prof. pharmacology, exptl. therapeutics & medicine, Burroughs Wellcome prof. clin. pharmacology, dir. divsn. clin. pharmacology Johns Hopkins U. Sch. Medicine, 1970-72, prof. pharmacology/exptl. therapeutics, assoc. prof. medicine, 1972-75; adj. prof. dept. medicine, dept. pharmacology/physiology Duke U., Durham, NC, 1975—89; adj. prof. U. NC, Chapel Hill, 1975—92, U. Mich. Med. Sch., Ann Arbor, 1990—97; adj. prof. dept. pharmacology, dept. internal medicine U. Calif., San Diego, 1997—. Profl. lectr. biochemistry George Washington U. Sch. Medicine, 1967—70; v.p. rsch. & devel. dept. molecular biology Wellcome Rsch. Labs., Rsch. Triangle Pk., NC, 1975—86; dir. Burroughs Wellcome Co., Rsch. Triangle Pk., 1975—85; sr. v.p. rsch. & devel. dir. Glaxo Inc., Rsch. Triangle Pk., 1986—89; dir. Glaxo Internat. Rsch., Ltd., London, 1988—89; pres. pharm. rsch. divsn. Parke-Davis, Ann Arbor, Mich., 1989—97; v.p. Warner-Lambert Co., Morris Plains, NJ, 1989—97. Editor: Internat. Jour. Biochemistry, 1973, Molecular & Cellular Endocrinology, 1973—77, Biochimica Biophysica Acta, 1973—79, Jour. Solid-Phase Biochemistry, 1975—80, Life Scis., 1978—88, Jour. Applied Biochemistry, 1978—91, Neuropeptides, 1979—99, Cancer Rsch., 1980—81, Jour. Applied Biochemistry & Biotech., 1980—98; contbr. articles to profl. jours. Recipient John Jacob Abel prize in pharmacology, 1972, Beerman award, Soc. Investigative Dermatology, 1981, ISCO award, U. Nebr., 1985, Dupont Splty. Diagnostics award, Clin. Ligand Assay Soc., 1986, Alumni Achievement award, Washington U. Sch. Medicine, 1987, Gov.'s award in sci., State of NC, 1988; co-recipient Wolf Found. prize in medicine, Israel, 1987; named to Soc. of Scholars, Johns Hopkins U., 1990. Fellow: Royal Soc. Medicine, Am. Acad. Arts & Scis.; mem.: Am. Diabetes Assn. (Eli Lilly award 1975), Am. Chem. Soc., Endocrine Soc., Am. Cancer Soc., Md. Acad. Scis. (Outstanding Young Scientist of Yr. 1970), Spanish Biochem. Soc., Am. Soc. Clin. Rsch., Am. Soc. Clin. Investigation, Am. Soc. Pharmacology & Exptl. Therapeutics (Goodman & Gilman award for receptor rsch. 1982), Inst. Medicine, Nat. Acad. Scis., Am. Soc. Biol. Chemists, Sigma Xi. Office: U Calif Sch Medicine 6039 Lago Lindo PO Box 2249 Rancho Santa Fe CA 92067 Personal E-mail: pedrocuatrecasas@znet.com. *

CUCCO, ULISSE P., retired obstetrician, gynecologist; b. Bklyn., Aug. 19, 1929; s. Charles and Elvira (Garafalo) C.; children: Carl, Richard, Antoinette Marie, Michael, Frank, James; m. Bobby Gene Frazier, 2002. BS cum laude, L.I. U., 1950; MD, Loyola U., Chgo., 1954. Diplomate Am. Bd. Ob-Gyn. Intern Nassau County Hosp., Hempstead, NY, 1954-55; resident in ob-gyn Lewis Meml. Mercy Hosp., Chgo., 1955-58; practice medicine specializing in ob-gyn Des Plaines, Ill., 1960—2001. Past pres. med. staff, chmn. dept. ob-gyn. Holy Family Hosp., Des Plaines, Ill.; clin. asst. prof. Stritch Sch. Medicine, Loyola U. Contbr. articles to med. jours. Chief ob-gyn USAF, 1958—60, Ellsworth AFB, Rapid City, SD. Recipient Mother Francis award, Holy Family Med. Ctr. Mem. ACS, Am. Fertility Soc., Ctrl. Assn. Ob-Gyn., Ill. Med. Soc., Chgo. Med. Soc., Chgo. Gynecol. Soc. (past pres.), Chgo. Inst. Medicine, Sunset Ridge Country Club. Roman Catholic. Home: 665 Midfield Ln Northbrook IL 60062-5507

CUCIN, ROBERT LOUIS, plastic surgeon, lawyer; b. NYC, Apr. 17, 1946; s. Robert and Julia C. BA magna cum laude, Cornell U., 1967, MD, 1971; JD, Fordham U., 1985; MBA, Columbia U., 2003. Bar: N.Y. 1983, N.J. State Sureme Ct., Washington Ct. of Appeals; bd. cert. legal medicine, diplomate Am. Bd. Surgery, Am. Bd. Plastic Surgery, lic. physician NJ, N.Y. State, Calif., Va., gen. socs. prin.; securities license series 4, 7, 24, 27, 63, 79, 86 and 87. Intern Cornell-N.Y. Hosp., NYC, 1971-72, resident in gen. surgery, 1972-76, resident in plastic surgery, 1977-79; fellow in surgery Meml.-Sloan Kettering Found., 1972-76, 77-79; practice medicine specializing in plastic surgery Columbia MBA, NYC, 1979—; instr. surgery Cornell U. Med. Coll., 1980—; asst. attending plastic surgeon Beth Israel North, N.Y. Downtown Hosp., 1979—, N.Y. Hosp., 1980—, Drs. Hosp., 1987—. Pres. Esquire Cadillac Limousine Svc. Inc., 1977—93, Beaux Arts Holdings, 1979—, Rocin Labs., Inc., 1981—; pres., CEO Biosculpture Tech., Inc., 2001—. Author: The Kindest Cut, Keeping Face, Medical Malpractice: Handling Plastic Surgical Cases; contbr. articles to profl, jours. Mem. N.Y. County Health Svc. Rev. Orgn., 1976—; founder, dir Rocin Found. for Plastic Surg. Rsch., 1979—; Maj. M.C., USAF, 1976-77; Japan. Fellow: ACS, Am. Coll. Legal Medicine, Internat. Coll. Surgeons; mem.: ABA, ATLA, AMA (Physicians Recognition award 1978, 1981), N.Y. Acad. Scis., N.Y. County Med. Soc. (health systems, pub. rels., peer rev. coms.), N.Y. State Med. Soc., Royal Soc. Medicine, Am. Soc. Plastic and Reconstructive Surgery, Am. Mensa, Cornell Club, N.Y. Athletic Club, Phi Beta Kappa. Republican. Home: 1701 S Flagler Dr Apt 607 West Palm Beach FL 33401-7341 Office Phone: 212-586-9500.

CUETTER, ALBERT CAYETANO, neurologist; b. Cartagena, Colombia, Aug. 7, 1938; MD, Med. U. Cartagena, Colombia, 1963. Diplomate Am. Bd. Neurology, Bd. of Electrodiagnostic Medicine. Intern Hosp. Santa Clara, Cartagena, Colombia, 1963-64; resident in neurology Northwestern U., 1965-68, fellowship in electromyography, 1968-69; prof. neurology Tex. Tech U. Health Scis. Ctr., El Paso, 1990—. Office Phone: 915-545-6703. Business E-Mail: albert.cuetter@ttuhsc.edu.

CUEVA, ROBERTO ALEJANDRO, otolaryngologist; b. Boston, June 29, 1957; BSc in Biology, U. Calif., Irvine, 1979; MD, U. Calif., San Francisco, 1983. Regional neurotologist, skull base surgeon Southern Calif. Permanente Med. Group, 1992—. Voluntary clin. prof. U. Calif., San Diego, 1988—2011. Recipient Golden Scapel Tchg. award, Neurosurg. Residents U. Calif., San Diego, Otolaryngology Resident Tchg. award, U. Calif., San Diego. Fellow: ACS, Am. Laryngol., Rhinol. and Otol. Soc., Am. Neurotology Soc., Am. Acad. Otolaryngology-Head and Neck Surgery; mem.: Am. Otol. Soc. Avocations: opera, theater, winemaking. Office: Dept Head and Neck Surgery 589 San Diego CA 92111 Office Fax: 858-616-5140. Business E-Mail: roberto.a.cueva@kp.org.

CUEVAS, EDUARDO SAMANIEGO, internist; b. Manila, Oct. 7, 1958; came to U.S., 1985; s. Porfirio Carmona and Erlinda Samaniego Cuevas; m. Gigi Mariette Delos Reyes, Aug. 19, 1985; children: Elizabeth Grace, Edilene Gayle, Edward Gabriel, Emmanuel Gregory. BS in Psychology, U. of the Philippines, Quezon City, 1979; MD, Feu Inst. of Medicine, Manila, 1983. Diplomate Am. Bd. Internal Medicine. Intern San Juan de Dios Hosp., Pasay City, The Philippines, 1983-84, surg. resident, 1985; internal medicine resident Bklyn. Hosp. Ctr., 1989-92; pvt. practice Tacoma, 1992—; med. dir. & prin. investigator Mylar Rsch., 2011—. Dir., chair membership com. Southcare HMO, Tacoma, 1995—98; mem. policy bd. Doctors Health Plan, Auburn, Wash., 1996—98, mem. exec. com., chair pharmacy and therapeutics com. Puget Sound Hosp., Tacoma, 1996—97; mem. oper. bd., bd. mem. Physicians Health Network, Tacoma, 2001—03; adj. faculty sch. medicine U. Fla., 2007—; prin. investigator Radiant Rsch. Phase 2-4 Clin.; int. med. cons. Pierce County Human Svc.; with Spkrs. Bur. - Forrest, Pfizer, Ortho-McNeil; cons. Boehringer Ingelheim. Reviewer, contbr. Am. Bd. Internal Medicine, 1997—. With U.S. Army, 1986-88. Recipient Army Achievement award, 1988. Fellow: ACP; mem.: ACP-ASIM, AMA (Physicians Recognition award 1999—), Catholic Physicians Guild of Washington, Filipino Am. Physicians of Wash., Tacoma Acad. Internal Medicine, Tacoma Jour. Club, Beta Sigma (grand princep 2001—07). Avocations: piano, travel. Home: 6306 89th Ave W University Place WA 98467-1044 Office: Allenmore Med Ctr 1901 South Union St Ste A-114 Tacoma WA 98405 Office Phone: 253-472-8389.

CUI, FUQIANG, medical association administrator; b. Gansu, Sept. 15, 1971; M, Hebrew U., 2003. Dir. hepatitis divsn., nat. immunization programme Chinese Ctr. Disease Control & Prevention, 2005—. Office: 27 Nanwei Rd Xicheng Dist Beijing 100050 China E-mail: cuifuq@126.com.

CUI, QUANJUN, orthopedist, educator; b. Henan, China, Feb. 7, 1963; MD, Henan Med. U., 1984, MSc, 1989. Cert. orthop. surgeon, in adult reconstrn. Assoc. prof. U. Va. Sch. Medicine, 2006. Med. dir. U. Va. Med. Ctr., 2006. Recipient Dean's award, U. Va. Sch. Medicine, Patients' Choice award, Am. Registry, OREF/Zachary B. Friedenberg, MD Clinician Scientist award, Orthop. Rsch. and Edn. Found., Career Devel. award, Musculoskeletal Transplant Found.; named one of Top Orthopaedist, Consumers Rsch. Coun. America. Fellow: Am. Assn. Hip and Knee Surgeons, Am. Acad. Orthop. Surgeons; mem.: AO N.Am., Orthop. Trauma Assn., Orthop. Rsch. Soc. Avocations: golf, ping pong/table tennis, reading. Office: University Va Sch Medicine PO Box 800159 Charlottesville VA 22908 Office Fax: 434-243-0242. Business E-Mail: qc4q@hscmail.mcc.virginia.edu.

CUI, RONGJUN, medical association administrator; b. Wudalianchi, Heilongjiang, China, May 23, 1974; B, Mudanjiang Med. Coll., China, 1998; M, Jiamusi U., China, 2004. Sec., dept. biochemistry and molecular biology Mudanjiang Med. Coll., China, 2002—11, dep. dir., dept. biochemistry and molecular biology, 2011—. Recipient Tchg. Achievement 2nd prize, Heilongjiang Provincial Dept. Edn., China, 2007, Multiple Media Tchg. 2nd prize, 2007, 2nd prize, 2009, 3rd prize, 2010, China Reflexology Assn., 2008. Mem.: Chinese Soc. Biochemistry and Molecular Biology. Avocations: movies, computers, sports. Office: 3 Tongxiang Rd Mudanjiang Heilongjiang 157011 China Personal E-mail: jkl305@163.com.

CUKROWSKI, IGNACY, chemistry professor, researcher; b. Szczecin, Poland, Mar. 24, 1951; s. Karol Cukrowski and Maria Cukrowska; m. Ilse Keuler, Oct. 20, 2007; children: Olga Maria Cukrowska, Adam Andrzej. MSc in Chemistry, Maria Curie-Sklodowska U., Lublin, Poland, 1974, PhD in Chemistry, 1982; DSc in Electrochemistry, Nicholas Copernicus U., Torun, Poland. Lectr. Maria Curie-Sklodowska U., 1981—82, sr. lectr., 1983—88; lectr. U. Transkei, Umtata, South Africa, 1989—91; sr. lectr. U. Witwatersrand, Johannesburg, 1992—97, assoc. prof., prof., mgr. electrochemistry rsch. labs., 2002—05; head chemistry dept. U. Pretoria, South Africa, 2005—08, prof., 2008—. Supr. PhD and MSc students, South Africa, 1989—; project leader numerous rsch. projects, South Africa, 1989—; reviewer rsch. project applications, South Africa; evaluator peer rev. rschrs., South Africa; cons. chem. industry, South Africa. Contbr. numerous rsch. articles to internat. jour. (Paul Ehrilch Magic-Bullet award, 2008). Recipient Rector award, Maria Curie-Sklodowska U., 1970—74, 1977—80, 1983, 1987, Student Rsch. Coun. award, 1974, Postgrad. Mentoring Programme award, Mellon Found., 2001—04, award, Thuthuka Mentoring Programme, 2004—08, Exceptional Academic Achiever, U. Pretoria, 2008, Exceptioanl Achiever award, Dept. Chemistry, U. Pretoria, 2006—07, award, Claude Leon Found., 2006—07; Rsch. grants, Nat. Rsch. Found. South Africa, 1992—2008, Postdoc. fellowship, Kosciuszko Found., NY, U. Witwatersrand, 1995, Contracted Rsch. grant, Sasol, South Africa, 2002—07, Chrome Internat. South Africa, 2005—07, Vice Chancellor Rsch. grant, U. Pretoria, 2005, 2008, U. Witwatersrand, Contracted Rsch. grant, PBMR South Africa, 2006—08. Mem.: Internat. Union Pure and Applied Chemistry, South African Chem. Inst. (Merck Gold medal for Best Publs., South African Journ. Chemistry), Electrochem. Soc. South Africa (pres. 1997—2007). Achievements include patents for field of voltammetric measurements, new kinds of electrodes, sensors and microprocessor controlled voltammetric analyser; deriving the most general equation and developed most powerful procedures to study metal complexes by voltammetry; discovering and defining a concept of virtual potential - applicable in the study of metal complexes by voltammetry; re-defining Nernstian slope - applicable in studying metal complexes by voltammetry; first applications of artificial neural networks in prediciton of stability constants and crystalographic structures. Office: Univ Pretoria Dept Chemistry Lynnwood Rd 2 Pretoria South Africa Office Fax: 27 12 420 4687. Business E-Mail: ignacy.cukrowski@up.ac.za.

CULBERTSON, RICHARD ALLEN, healthcare educator, health facility administrator; b. Fremont, Ohio, Aug. 13, 1946; s. Raymond Clark and Ruth Elizabeth Culbertson; m. Linnea VanDyne, July 11, 1970 (div. Dec. 1981); m. Susan Mary Leary, May 3, 1986. BA, Lawrence U., 1967; MDiv, Harvard U., 1970; M in Health Adminstrn., U. Minn., 1973; PhD, U. Calif., San Francisco, 1993. Cert. healthcare exec. Am. Coll. Health Execs. Asst. prof. U. Minn., Mpls., 1976—78; dep. dir. and COO St. Paul-Ramsey Med. Ctr., 1978—84; hosp. dir. and CEO Kaiser Found. Hosp., LA, 1984—87; dir. adminstrn. U. Calif. San Francisco Med. Group, 1987—92; assoc. dean and vice chancellor U. Wis., Madison, 1992—95; assoc. prof. and dir. Ind. U., Indpls., 1995—97; assoc. prof. Tulane U., New Orleans, 1997—2009, prof., 2009—. Chmn. bd. dirs. Aurora Health-Care Inc., Milw., 1994—2007; spl. asst. to pres. for NCAA cert. Tulane U., New Orleans, 1999—2008, 2008—, chair senate com. on intercollegiate athletics, 2002—05; cvc cvc, 2010—; chair sch. pub. health and tropical medicine faculty Tulane U., 2005—07; cert. site reviewer NCAA, Indpls., 2001—; mem. governing bd. Touro Infirmary, New Orleans, 2004—07. Contbg. author The Nation's Health, 6th edit., 2001; contbr. articles to profl. jours. Mem. Mardi Gras Krewe of Mid-City; pres. Humane Soc. Ramsey County, St. Paul, 1981—84; bd. dirs. Touro Found., New Orleans, 2004—07, Wis. Profl. Rev., Madison, 1994—95, Eldercare Dane County, Madison, 1994—95. Recipient Spurgeon award for cmty. svc., Explorer Scouts, St. Paul, 1983; named Emerging Leader in Healthcare, Healthcare Forum, San Francisco, 1986; Nat. Leader fellow, W.K. Kellogg Found., 1985—88. Mem.: Am. Hosp. Assn. Chgo. (regional policy bd. 2006—09, governance com. 2006—09, leadership devel. coun. 2009—), U. Minn. Pres. Club, Harvard Club (La.), Delta Omega Soc. (Eta chpt.), Phi Beta Kappa (La. Alpha chpt.), Beta Theta Pi. Avocations: swimming, Tae Kwon Do, sports. Office: Tulane Univ Sch Pub Health 1430 Tulane Ave SL-29 New Orleans LA 70112 Office Phone: 504-988-6247. Business E-Mail: rculber@tulane.edu.

CULKIN, DANIEL JOSEPH, urologist, educator, department chairman; s. Lawrence Francis and Madeline Culkin; m. Jane Marie Graham, July 10, 1981; children: Matthew Lawrence, Daniel James. BS, Creighton U., Omaha, Nebr., 1968—72, MD, 1975—79; MS, Loyola U., Chgo., 1972—75; MBA/HCM, U. Phoenix, 2003—05. Lic. dr. Okla. State Bd. Med. Licensure, 2009, La. State Med. Licensure Bd., 2009, Ill. State Med. Bd., 2009. Fellow endourology and neurourology Loyola U. Med. Ctr., Maywood, Ill., 1982—85, urology instr., 1985—87; asst. prof. urology La. State U. Med. Ctr., Shreveport, La., 1987—88, assoc. prof. urology, 1988—91, prof. urology, 1991—94; chief urology Shreveport Va. Med. Ctr., 1987—88; prof., chair dept. urology Okla. U. Health Sci Ctr., Okla. City, 1994—. Pres.'s Assoc. Presdl. prof., 2006. Mem. SW Oncology Group, San Antonio, 1991—. Mem.: AMA (assoc.), Soc. U. Urology (pres. 2003—04), Am. Paraplegic Soc. (dir. 1988—91). Catholic. Avocations: water sports, golf, fishing. Home: 6104 LaQuinta Dr Edmond OK 73025 Office: Univ Okla Health Sci Ctr PO Box 26901 Oklahoma City OK 73190 Office Fax: 405 271 3118. Business E-Mail: daniel-culkin@ouhsc.edu.

CULL-CANDY, STUART G., neuroscientist, educator; MSc in Physiology, Univ. Coll. London, 1971; PhD in Synaptic Physiology, U. Glasgow, Scotland, 1974; FRS, 2002, FMedSci, 2003. From Beit Meml. fellow dept. biophysics to prof. Univ. Coll. London, 1975—80, Gaddum prof. pharmacology, prof. neurosci., 2006—; post doctoral Royal Soc. Exch. fellow, Pharmacology Inst. U. Lund, Sweden, 1975. Mem. grants com. Wellcome Trust Internat. Group, Royal Soc. Univ. Rsch. Fellows; mem. sr. rsch. fellowship com. Leverhulme Trust. Editor: Neuron, Jour. Physiology; contbr. articles to profl. jours. Named Howard Hughes Internat. Rsch. scholar. Fellow: Brit. Pharmacol. Soc., Acad. Med. Sci., Royal Soc. Achievements include research in glutamate receptor channels and fast synaptic transmission in the brain. Office: Univ Coll London Dept Pharmacology Gower Street WC1E 6BT London England Office Phone: 44 20 7679 3766. Office Fax: 44 20 7639 7298. Business E-Mail: s.cull-candy@ucl.ac.uk.

CULLEN, KEVIN JOSEPH, oncologist, educator; b. Glen Rock, NJ, 1957; m. Lisa Brown, Jan. 3, 1998. MD, Harvard Med. Sch., 1983. Diplomate Am. Bd. Internal Medicine. Intern Beth Israel Hosp., Boston, 1983-84, resident, 1984-86, Hammersmith Hosp., London, 1985; fellow in oncology Nat. Cancer Inst., Bethesda, Md., 1986; staff Georgetown U. Hosp., Washington; prof. medicine, oncology and otolaryngology Georgetown U. Sch. Medicine, interim dir. Lombardi Cancer Ctr., 2000—02; dir. Greenebaum Cancer Ctr., prof. medicine, head oncology program U. Maryland Sch. Medicine, Balt., 2004—. Office: U Md Greenebaum Cancer Ctr 22 S Green St Baltimore MD 21201

CULLETON, JAMES FREDERICK, neurologist; b. Sewickley, Pa., Apr. 6, 1918; s. James and Jessie (Scragg) C.; m. Flora McDonald Stuart Brown, Mar. 22, 1943; four children. BS, U. Pitts., 1940, MD, 1943. Diplomate Am. Bd. Psychiatry and Neurology. Intern, resident in pathology U. Pitts. Med. Ctr., 1943-44; fellow in neuropsychiatry Inst. Living, Hartford, Conn., 1947-49; resident in neurology Neurol. Inst. N.Y.C., 1949-51, attending neurologist, 1951-84; assoc. in neurology Columbia-Presbyn. Med. Ctr., NYC, 1951-84; dir. EEG and Neurology, New Rochelle Hosp. Med. Ctr., 1954-82; cons. in neurology Miami VA, 1984-95. Maj. M.C. US Army, 1944—47. Mem. AMA, Am. Acad. Neurology, N.Y. State Med. Soc., Westchester County Med. Soc., Westchester Acad. Medicine, Scottish Rite, Masons. Home: 87 Chase Point Rd Mirror Lake NH 03853-6152 Office Phone: 603-569-2472. E-mail: jimflo1@adelphia.net.

CULP, RANDALL, orthopaedic surgeon; Attended, Hershey Sch. Medicine, Pa., 1982. Diplomate Am. Bd. Orthopaedic Surgery-hand surgery, Am. Bd. Orthopaedic Surgery. Intern Univ. Pa. Hosp., resident, fellow; hosp. affiliations include Methodist Hosp., Jefferson Univ. Hosp. Named one of the Top Doctors, Phila. Mag., 2010—11. Office: Jefferson University Hospital Ben Franklin House Ste G114 Chestnut St Philadelphia PA 19107 Office Phone: 800-971-4263.

CULPEPPER, GUY LEE, physician; b. Dallas, June 14, 1957; s. Pat McPherson; m. Deborah Mills, Oct. 4, 1986; children: Dillon, Justin, Logan. BS in Biology, SMU, 1980, BA in Psychology, 1980; MD, U. Tex., Houston, 1984. Lic. dr. Am. Bd. Family Medicine, 1984. Pres. Bent Tree Family Physicians, Dallas, 1987—; CEO Jefferson Physician Grp., Dallas, 1995—. Found. bd. Dallas County Cmty. Coll., 2003—07. Fellow: AAFP. Home: 5353 Spanish Oaks Dr Frisco TX 75034 Office: Bent Tree Family Physicians 3550 Parkwood Blvd #600 Frisco TX 75034 Office Fax: 972-377-8808. Personal E-mail: glcdlc@aol.com. *

CULTON, PAUL MELVIN, retired counselor, educational administrator, professor, interpreter; b. Council Bluffs, Iowa, Feb. 12, 1932; s. Paul Roland and Hallie Ethel Emma (Paschal) C. AB, Crossroads Coll., 1955; BS, U. Nebr., Omaha, 1965; MA, Calif. State U., Northridge, 1970; EdD, Brigham Young U., 1981. Cert. tchr., Iowa. Tchr. Iowa Sch. for Deaf, Council Bluffs, 1956-70; ednl. specialist Golden West Coll., Huntington Beach, Calif., 1970-71, dir. disabled students, 1971-82, instr., 1982-88; counselor El Camino Coll., Via Torrance, Calif., 1990-93, acting assoc. dean, 1993-94, counselor, 1994-97, lectr., 1997—2009; prof. First Global C.C., Nong Khai, Thailand, 2006. Interpreter various state and fed. cts., Iowa, Calif., 1960-90; asst. prof. Calif. State U., Northridge, Fresno, Dominguez Hills, 1973, 76, 80, 87-91, L.A., 1999—; vis. prof. U. Guam, Agana, 1977; prof. First Global C.C., NongKhai, Thailand, 2006; mem. allocations task force, task force on deafness, trainer handicapped students Calif. C.C.s, 1971-81 Editor: Region IX Conf. for Coordinating Rehab. and Edn. Svcs. for Deaf proceedings, 1970, Toward Rehab. Involvement by Parents of Deaf conf. proceedings, 1971; composer Carry the Light, 1986. Bd. dirs. Gay and Lesbian Cmty. Svcs. Ctr., Orange County, Calif., 1975-77; founding sec. Dayle McIntosh Ctr. for Disabled, Anaheim and Garden Grove, Calif., 1974-80; active Dem. Cent. Com. Pottawattamie County, Council Bluffs, 1960-70; del. People to People N.Am. Educators Deaf Vis. Russian Schs. & Programs for Deaf, 1993. League for Innovation in Community Coll. fellow, 1974. Mem. Calif. Assn. Postsecondary Edn. and Disability (founding v.p.), Registry of Interpreters for Deaf, Am. Sign Lang. Tchrs. Assn., Nat. Assn. Deaf. Mem. Am. Humanist Assn. Avocations: vocal music, languages, community activism, travel, politics. Personal E-mail: pmculton@socal.rr.com.

CUMMINGS, CHARLES WILLIAM, otolaryngologist, educator; b. Boston, Nov. 16, 1935; s. Harry Blanchard and Madge (Frey) C.; m. Jane Drake Cummings, July 1, 1983; children: Charles William, Lee Blanchard, Evelyn Howard. AB, Dartmouth Coll., 1957; MD, U. Va., 1961. Intern Mary Hitchcock Meml. Hosp., Hanover, NH, 1961-62; resident otolaryngology Harvard U. Med. Sch., 1965-68; assoc. prof. otolaryngology Upstate Med. Sch., SUNY, Syracuse, 1976-78; prof., chmn. dept. otolaryngology-head and neck surgery U. Wash. Med. Sch., Seattle, 1978-91, Johns Hopkins Hosp. and Med. Ctr., Balt., 1991—93; disting. svcs. prof., med. dir. Johns Hopkins Internat., Balt., 2003—08. Chief staff Johns Hopkins Hosp., 1996-98; bd. dirs. Am. Bd. Otolaryngology Author: Atlas of Laryngeal Surgery; co-author: Comprehensive Text of Otolaryngology-Head and Neck Surgery; contbr. sci. articles to profl. jours. Served to capt., M.C. USAF, 1963-65. Mem. ACS (chmn. adv. coun.), Soc. Head and Neck Surgeons, Am. Soc. for Head and Neck Surgery (sec., pres.), Soc. Univ. Otolaryngologists, Assn. Acad. Depts., Otolaryngology (past pres.), Triological Soc., Laryngological Soc., Bronchoesophagological Soc. (past pres.), Am. Acad. Otolaryngology-Head and Neck Surgery (bd. dirs., past pres.). Episcopalian. Office: Johns Hopkins U Dept Otolaryngology/Head/Neck/Surgery 601 N Caroline St Baltimore MD 21287-0006 Home Phone: 410-833-4458; Office Phone: 410-955-7400. Business E-Mail: ccumming@jhmc.edu.

CUMMINGS, JEFFREY L., neurologist, educator; B with high honors, U. Wyo., Laramie; MD, U. Wash. Sch. Medicine, Seattle, 1974. Cert. Am. Bd. Psychiatry and Neurology, 1974. Intern Hartford Hosp., Conn., 1974—75; residency in neurology Boston Med. Ctr., 1975—78; residency in neurology & behavioral neurology Dept. Vet. Affairs Med. Ctr., Boston, 1978—79; fellow in neuropathology Nat. Hosp. Neurol. Diseases, London, 1980; asst. prof. neurology UCLA David Geffen Sch. Medicine, 1980—96, prof. psychiatry and biobehavioral sciences, 1992—, Augustus S. Rose prof. neurology, 1996—, exec. chmn., dept. neurology, 2002—; dir. Deane F. Johnson Ctr. Neurotherapeutics, 2003—, Mary S. Easton Ctr. Alzheimer's Disease Rsch. at UCLA; physician Ronald Reagan UCLA Med. Ctr., Stewart and Lynda Resnick Neuropsychiatric Hosp. at UCLA. Mem. R&D adv. bd. Prana Biotechnology, Ltd.; mem. clin. and devel. adv. bd. EnVivo Pharm., Inc. Author and editor: 20 books; contbr. articles to profl. jours. Mem.: Am. Neurolpsychiatric Assn. (past pres.), Behavioral Neurology Soc. (past pres.). Office: UCLA Dept Neurology 710 Westwood Plz Ste 2-238 Los Angeles CA 90095-1769 Office Phone: 310-794-3665.

CUMMINGS, JOAN E., health facility administrator, educator; BA, Trinity Coll., 1964; MD, Loyola U., 1968. Diplomate Am. Bd. Internal Medicine, Geriatric Medicine. Med. intern St. Vincent Hosp., Worcester, Mass., 1968-69; med. resident Hines VA Hosp., Hines, Ill., 1969-71, sr. resident in nephrology, 1971-72, ambulatory care svc. chief gen. med. sect., 1971-84, med. dir., hosp. based home care, 1972-87, chief, intermediate care svc., 1984-87, assoc. chief of staff, extended care and geriatrics, 1987-90, med. dir., extended care center, 1987-90, dir., 1990—; asst. prof. clin. medicine U. Ill., 1976-82, Loyola U., 1983-91, assoc. prof. clin. medicine, 1991—; network dir. Dept. Vet. Affairs, Hines, Ill., 1995—2005. Ad hoc com. on primary care U. Ill., 1980-82, coll. edn. policy com. U. Ill., 1980-82, State Ill. Emergency Med. Svc. Coun., 1981-83, Comprehensive Health Ins. Plan Bd. State Ill., 1990—, Med. Licensing Bd. State Ill., 1992—, exec. com. Chgo. Fed. Exec. Bd. State Ill., 1992—; program dir. Loyola/Hines Geriatric Fellowship Program, 1987-90; bd. trustees Rosalind Franklin U. Medicine and Sci., 2005-; bd. dirs. Ismie Mutual Ins. Co., 2003-. Contbr. to profl. mags. and jour. Recipient Disting. Svc. award Abraham Lincoln Sch. Med. Univ. Ill., 1979, 81, Leadership award VA, 1980, Certificate of Appreciation award VA, 1980, Laureate award Am. Coll. Physicians, 1990. Fellow ACP; mem. AMA (Ill. delegation 1985—, vice speaker ho. of dels. 1987-89), Chgo. Med. Soc. (pres. Hines-Loyola br. 1982-83), Ill. State Med. Soc. (trustee 1984—, chmn. com. on Ill. med., 1988—, spkr. ho. of dels. 1989-91, exec. com., 1989-91, policy com., 1989—), Chgo. Geriatric Soc., Am. Geriatric Soc. Office: 772 St Charles Rd Glen Ellyn IL 60137 Office Phone: 630-858-7716. Personal E-mail: joanecum@msn.com.

CUMMINGS, MARTIN MARC, physician, educator, academic administrator; b. Camden, NJ, Sept. 7, 1920; s. Samuel and Cecelia (Silverman) Cummings; m. Arlene Sally Avrutine, Sept. 27, 1942; children: Marc Steven, Lee Bernard, Stuart Lewis. BS, Bucknell U., 1941, DSc, 1969; MD, Duke U., 1944, DSc (hon.), 1985; DHL (hon.), Georgetown U., 1976; DSc (hon.), U. Nebr., Emory U.; MD (hon.), Karolinska Inst., 1972, U. Lvov, 1975. Diplomate Am. Bd. Microbiology. Intern, resident Boston Marine Hosp., 1944—46; resident Tb Grasslands Hosp., Valhalla, NY, 1946—47; dir. Tb evaluation lab. Communicable Disease Ctr., USPHS, Atlanta, 1947—49; instr. medicine Emory U. Sch. Medicine, 1948—50, assoc. medicine, 1950—52, asst. prof., 1953; chief Tb sect., also dir. Tb rsch. lab. VA Hosp., Atlanta, 1949—53; dir. rsch. svcs. VA Ctrl. Office, Washington, 1953—59; prof. microbiology, chmn. dept. Okla. U. Sch. Medicine, 1959—61; chief Office Internat. Rsch., NIH, USPHS, 1961—63; dir. Nat. Libr. Medicine, 1964—84, dir. emeritus, 1984—; cons. Coun. on Libr. Resources, 1984—, chmn., bd. dirs., 1994—96. Assoc. dir. rsch. grants NIH, 1963—64; chmn. com. med. rsch. Nat. Tb Assn., 1958—59; chmn. panel Sarcoidosis NRC-NAS, 1958—60; dist. prof. cmty. medicine Georgetown U. Sch. Medicine, 1986—90. Author (with Dr. H.S. Willis): Diagnostic and Experimental Methods in Tuberculosis, 1952, The Economics of Research Libraries, 1986; editor: Influencing Change in Research Libraries, 1989; contbr. chpt. on Tubercle Bacilli Diagnostic Procedures and Reagents, 1950. With AUS, 1943—44. Recipient Exceptional Svc. award, VA, 1959, Disting. Svc. award, HEW, 1968, Rockefeller Pub. Svc. award, 1973, Disting. Achievement award, Modern Medicine, 1976, Disting. Svc. award, Am. Coll. Cardiology, 1978, John C. Leonard award, Assn. Hosp. Med. Edn., 1979. Fellow: AAAS, Phila. Coll. Physicians, Med. Libr. Assn., Royal Soc. Medicine, N.Y. Acad. Medicine (hon.); mem.: NAS, Inst. Medicine, Am. Fedn. Clin. Rsch., Am. Soc. Clin. Investigation (sr.). Home: 700 John Ringling Blvd Apt 1407 Sarasota FL 34236-1555 Personal E-mail: martincummings@comcast.net.

CUMMINGS, NICHOLAS ANDREW, psychologist; b. Salinas, Calif., July 25, 1924; s. Andrew and Urania (Sims) C.; m. Dorothy Mills, Feb. 5, 1948; children: Janet Lynn, Andrew Mark. AB, U. Calif., Berkeley, 1948; MA, Claremont Grad. Sch., 1954; PhD, Adelphi U., 1958. Chief psychologist Kaiser Permanente No. Calif., San Francisco, 1959-76; pres. Found Behavioral Health, San Francisco, 1976—; chmn., CEO Am. Biodyne, Inc., San Francisco, 1985-93, Kendron Internat., Ltd., Reno, 1992-95; chmn. Nicholas & Dorothy Cummings Found., Reno, 1994—; chmn., pres. UK Behavioural Health, Ltd., London, 1996-98; Disting. prof. U. Nev., 1997—; chmn., CEO DynaMed Integrated Care, Inc., 1998—; clin. prof. Ariz. State U., 2009—. Co-dir. South San Francisco Health Ctr., 1959-75; pres. Calif. Sch. Profl. Psychology, LA, San Francisco, San Diego, Fresno campuses, 1969-76; chmn. bd. Calif. Cmty. Mental Health Ctrs., Inc., LA, San Diego, San Francisco, 1975-77; pres. Blue Psi, Inc., San Francisco, 1972-80, Inst. for Psychosocial Interaction, 1980-84; mem. mental health adv. bd. City and County San Francisco, 1968-75; bd. dirs. San Francisco Assn. Mental Health, 1965-75; pres., chmn. bd. Psycho-Social Inst., 1972-80; dir. Mental Rsch. Inst., Palo Alto, Calif., 1979-80; pres. Nat. Acads. of Practice, 1981-93. Served with U.S. Army, 1944-46. Fellow APA (dir. 1975-81, pres. 1979); mem. Calif. Psychol. Assn. (pres. 1968). Office: Nicholas & Dorothy Cummings Found 4781 Caughlin Pkwy Reno NV 89509 Office Phone: 775-826-3311. Personal E-mail: cummfound@aol.com.

CUMMINGS ROCKWELL, PATRICIA GUILBAULT, psychiatric nurse; b. Ludlow, Mass., June 22, 1939; d. Lee Allen and Mavis Isabella (White) Guilbault; m. Philip W. Cummings, Oct. 23, 1960 (dec. Jan. 1978); children: Sharon Ellen Timmons, Geoffrey Scott Cummings, Susan Mavis Lornitzo, Lee Millett Cummings, Mary Rockwell Thon; m. William Leonard Rockwell Jr., Aug. 18, 1990. ADN, Vt. Coll., 1982; BSN, Norwich U., 1987. RN, Vt. Staff nurse Ctrl. Vt. Hosp. Nursing Home, Berlin, 1982-84, 87—; staff psychiat. nurse Va. Hosp. Ground East, White River Junction, Vt., 1987-94; owner Globe Travel, Bradford, Vt., 1988-94; rschr. Norwich U., Northfield, Vt., 1988—. Nurse-entrepeneur Globe Travel, 1988—. Tchr. adult edn. ARC, Bradford, Vt., 1988, 89; bd. dirs. Fedn. of Vt. Lakes and Ponds, Inc.; v.p. Vale Hospice Internat.; dir. Fedn. Vt. Lakes and Ponds Inc. Mem. ANA (nat. and Vt. chpts.), AAUW, New Eng. Hist. Geneal. Soc. Avocations: writing, travel, medical genealogy, genetics and geneology. Home: 307 Godfrey Rd East Thetford VT 05043-9517 Office Phone: 802-785-4812. Personal E-mail: patsy@together.net.

CUMMINS, FERGAL HENRY, emergency physician, consultant; b. Devon, Eng., Nov. 2, 1968; s. Henry and Mary Cummins; m. Rossann McEnerney, May 19, 2000; children: Saidhbh, Luí, Siún. MB BCh BAO, U. Coll. Cork, Ireland. Cert. European master in disaster medicine U. Eastern Piedemont, Free U. Brussels, 2007, DMMD IPA, Ireland, 2005. Retrieval physician Careflight, Sydney, 2008—09; staff specialist emergency medicine Royal North Shore Hosp., Sydney, 2009—10; clin. sr. lectr. Sydney Med. Sch., U. Sydney, 2010. Recipient Gold medal, South Infirmary Victoria Hosps.; named Intern of Yr., 1995. Fellow: RCS (Ediburgh), Australian Coll. Emergency Medicine; mem.: Coll. Emergency Medicine. Office: Royal North Shore Hosp Emergency Dept St Leonards 2065 Sydney NSW Australia Office Phone: 0061299267922. Personal E-mail: cumminsfergal@hotmail.com.

CUMMINS, THOMAS KENNETH, psychiatrist; MD, U. Wis. Med. Sch., 1990. Cert. Psychiatry, 1996, Child & Adolescent Psychiatry, 1997. Resident, psychiatry Emory U. Affiliated Hospitals, 1990—94; fellow, child and adolescent psychiatry UCLA Neuropsychiatric Inst., 1994—96; med. dir., impatient psychiatry Children's Meml. Hosp., Chgo.; asst. prof., psychiatry and behaviorial scis. Northwestern U. Feinberg Sch. Medicine. Mem.: Am. Acad. Child and Adolescent Psychiatry. Office: Childrens Meml Hosp 2300 Childrens Plz Chicago IL 60614-3363

CUNDRLE, IVAN, anesthesiologist; b. Brno, S. Moravia, Czech Republic, Jan. 9, 1947; s. Ivan and Vera C.; m. Jitka Kubinova, July 2, 1971; 1 child, Ivan. MD, Masaryk U., Brno, 1971, PhD, 1992, asst. prof., 1995. Med. doctor City Hosp., Ostrava, Czech Republic, 1971-73, U. Hosp. Brno, 1973-88, head ICU, 1988—2004; cons. Hosp. Boskovice, Czech Republic, 2006—11; assoc. prof. Masaryk U., Brno, 2006—11. Contbr. articles to profl. jours. Recipient Czech Soc. Anesthesia, Resuscitation and Intensive Medicine prize, 1993, 95. Mem. European Soc. Regional Anesthesia, European Soc. Anesthesia, Network Advancement Transfusion Alternatives, European Soc. Computing Tech. Anesthesia and Intensive Care (rep. Czech Republic), European Soc. Jet Ventilation, Czech Bloodless Medicine Soc. (head). Achievements include research in intraaortal baloon contrapulsation in sepsis bloodless medicine, peroperative autotransfusion and anesthesia in orthopaedic surgery and orthopedic anesthesia, influence of IABP in sepsis. Home: Ukrajinská 9 625 00 Brno South Moravia Czech Republic Office: Univ Hosp Jihlavská 20 639 00 Brno South Moravia Czech Republic Office Phone: 516491442, 420532233850. Office Fax: 516491606. Personal E-mail: doc.cundrle@seznam.cz. Business E-Mail: icundrle@fnbrno.cz.

CUNHA, FERNANDO JOSÉ MELO DA, ophthalmologist, director; b. Recife, Nov. 15, 1983; MS, Fed. U. Pernambuco, 2004. Physician Fed. U. Pernamuco, 1988, Brazilian Coll. Ophthalmology. Ophthalmologist Altino Ventura Found., 1997—2007; dir., cornea transplantation and intraocular rings implant Real Hosp. Portuguese Beneficence, 2007—10; dir. Vision Hosp. Pernambuco HVisão, 2010—. Recipient Merit Honor award, XXX Brazilian Congress Ophthalmology, Directory Assessor award, Brazilian Coll. Ophthalmology. Mem.: Brazilian Soc. Cataract and Intraocular Implants, Brazilian Soc. Refractive Surgery, European Soc. Cataract and Refractive Surgery, Brazilian Soc. Organ Transplantation, Ferrara's Ring Friends Club. Home: Rua Zeferino Galvão 68/701 Boa Viagem Recife Pernambuco 51111110 Brazil Home Fax: 55 (81) 32681796. Personal E-mail: fernandojmcunha@uol.com.br.

CUNHA, PAULO FERRARA, ophthalmologist; b. Belo Horizonte, Mar. 8, 1950; MD, UFMG, 1973, PhD, 1981. Bd. dirs. Ferrara Ophthalmics Ltda, 1999, pres., 1999—. Recipient Outstanding Innovator, wipo. Avocations: motorcycling, tennis, music. Office: Av Contorno 4747 sl 615 Belo Horizonte Mg 30110100 Brazil E-mail: pferrara@ferraraing.com.br.

CUNNINGHAM, ALEC R., health products executive; B, Okla. St. Univ.; MBA, Univ. So. Calif. Mgmt. positions Okla. Health Care Authority, 1994—96; mgmt. positions through v.p. bus. develop. & compliance WellPoint Health Networks, 1996—2004; v.p. bus. develop., sr. v.p. govt. rels., divsn. pres. Fla. & Hawaii WellCare Health Plans, Tampa, Fla., 2005—09; CEO WellCare Health Plans, Inc., Tampa, Fla., 2009—. Office: WellCare Health Plans 8725 Henderson Rd Tampa FL 33634 Mailing: WellCare Health Plans PO Box 31372 Tampa FL 33631-3372 *

CUNNINGHAM, CALHOUN D., III, otolaryngologist, educator; b. Columbia, SC, Sept. 13, 1969; BA in Chemistry, Citadel U., 1991; MD, Med. U. SC, 1996. Assoc. physician Carolina Ear & Hearing Clinic, P.C., 2004—. Cons. asst. prof. otolaryngology Duke U. Med. Ctr., 2004—. Fellow: Am. Neurotology Assn., Am. Acad. Otolaryngology; mem.: NC Soc. Otolaryngology. Office: Carolina Ear & Hearing Clinic 3100 Dura Raleigh NC 27612 Office Fax: 919-876-4327. E-mail: cunningham@carolinaear.us.

CUNNINGHAM, JACQUELINE LEMMÉ, psychologist, educator, researcher; b. Biddeford, Maine, Apr. 22, 1941; d. S. James and Alice (Fréchette) Lemmé; m. Seymour Cunningham II, Dec. 16, 1960 (dec. 1987); children: Macklin Todd, Danielle, Alyssa. BA in Psychology cum laude, U. Maine, Orono, 1963; MS in Psychology, U. South Ala., Mobile, 1983; PhD in Ednl. Psychology, U. Tex., 1994. Tchr. Mobile Pub. Schs., Ala., 1976—81; psychology intern Devereux Found., Devon, Pa., 1988-89; fellow in developmental disabilities Children's Hosp. Harvard Med. Sch., Boston, 1990; prof. U. SD, Vermillion, 1994-95; fellow in pediat. neuropsychology Children's Nat. Med. Ctr., George Washington U. Med. Ctr., Washington, 1995—97; psychologist pvt. practice, Wilmington, Del., 1997—2000, Children's Hosp. of Phila., Phila., 2000—. Cons. in field. Contbr. articles to profl. jours., chapters to books. Mem. Am. Psychol. Assn. (outstanding dissertation of yr. award 1994), Internat. Neuropsychol. Soc., Nat. Acad. Neuropsychology, Soc. History Behavioral Scis., Phila. Neuropsychology Soc. (bd. dirs. 1998-2002), Phi Kappa Phi. Avocations: travel, writing. Office: Children's Hosp of Phila 34th St & Civic Ctr Blvd Philadelphia PA 19104

CUNNINGHAM, JASON, dentist; m. Angela R. Cameron; children: Andrew, Alexis. Dentist, Erwin, Tenn.; part time assoc. dentist Sophisticated Smiles, Johnson City, Tenn., 2004—. Mem.: Am. Acad. of Dental Sleep Medicine, Acad. of Gen. Dentistry, Am. Acad. of Cosmetic Dentistry, Tenn. Dental Assn., ADA. Office: Sophisticated Smiles 189 Corporate Dr Ste 20 Johnson City TN 37601 Office Phone: 423-928-8359. Office Fax: 423-282-6018.

CUNNINGHAM, JOHN, nephrologist, educator; b. Oxford, June 27, 1949; s. Daniel John C. and Judith Cunningham; m. Deborah A. Cunningham (div.); children: Alastair, Oliver, Andrew; m. Caroline A.H. Hewitt; 1 child, Lucy. BA, Cambridge U., 1970; BM, Oxford U., 1973, MD, 1986. Prof. Univ. Coll. London; physician to Her Majesty the Queen; head of the med. household. Address: The Centre for Nephrology Royal Free and Univ Coll Med Sch Rowland Hill St London NW3 2PF England Personal E-mail: arjohncunningham@gmail.com.

CUNNINGHAM, KAREN LYNN, social worker; b. Chapel Hill, NC, Dec. 12, 1975; d. Timothy Clontz and Wendelin Jones McBride; m. John David Cunningham, Oct. 8, 2005. BA in Internat. Studies, U. N.C., Chapel Hill, 1998; MSW, U. Md., Balt., 2001. Lic. ind. clin. social worker. Case worker Bread for the City/Zacchaeus Free Clinic, Washington, 1998—99; social worker intern Yorkwood Health Ctr., Balt., 1999—2000; rsch. asst. Family Connections U Md., Balt., 2000—01; social work intern Adoptions Together, Silver Spring, Md., 2000—01, contract social worker, 2001—02; clin. case mgr. PSI Family Svcs., Lanham, Md., 2001—02; social worker Child and Family Svcs. Agy., Washington, 2002—07. Author: Stay-at-home Mom, 2007—. Recipient Ruth H. Young Endowment award for excellence in child welfare, U. Md., Balt., 2001. Mem.: Nat. Assn. Social Workers. Democrat. Mem. United Ch. Of Christ. Avocations: reading, singing, crafts.

CUNNINGHAM, MARY ELIZABETH (MARY CUNNINGHAM-LUSBY), physician; b. Newark, Apr. 21, 1931; d.

William Rutherford and Mary Agnes Veronica (Harvey) C.; m. Perry Minor Lusby, Nov. 30, 1996. AB, Mount Holyoke Coll., 1953; MS, U. Ill., 1957; PhD, U. Oregon, 1964; MD, U. Conn., 1982. Sr. physicist Lawrence Livermore Nat. Lab., Livermore, Calif., 1964-78; residency in emergency medicine Mich. State U. Affiliated Hosp., 1982—85, chief resident, 1984—85; sr. physician The Permanente Med. Group, Sacramento, 1985—96, ret., 1996, vol. physician, 1996—. Cons. emergency medicine King Faisal Specialist Hosp. and Rsch. Ctr., Jeddah, 2000-01. Contbr. articles to profl. jours. Physician Flying Samaritans-Mother Lode chpt., Sonoma, Calif., 1991—. Fellow Am. Coll. Emergency Physicians (life); mem. AMA, Am. Phys. Soc., Calif. Chpt. Am. Coll. Emergency Physicians, Calif. Med. Assn., NY Acad. Scis., Phi Beta Kappa, Sigma Xi (grant-in-aid-of-rsch. award 1963-64). Roman Cath. Office: Kaiser Permanente Med Ctr 6600 Bruceville Rd Sacramento CA 95823-4671

CUNNINGHAM, MICHAEL, medical association administrator, educator; b. Washington, Mar. 31, 1966; BA, Morehouse Coll., 1989; PhD, Emory U., 1994. Exec. dir., assoc. prof. Tulane U., 1996—. Recipient Suzanne and Stephen Weiss Presidential fellowship, Tulane U. Mem.: Soc. Rsch. Child Devel. Avocations: reading, writing. Office: Center Engaged Learning & Tchg New Orleans LA 70118 Office Fax: 507-862-8744. Business E-Mail: mcunnin1@tulane.edu.

CUNNINGHAM, MICHAEL J., pediatric otolaryngologist, educator; Attended, Princeton U.; MD, U. of Rochester Med. Sch. Diplomate Am. Bd. Otolaryngology, 1988. Hosp. affiliation includes Mass. Gen. Hosp., resident pediats. Boston, 1981—83; resident otolaryngology Univ. of Pitts., 1984—88; pediatric otolaryngologist, mem. full time faculty, mem. bd. surgeons, chief divsn. of pediatric otolaryngology Mass. Eye and Ear Infirmary; assoc. prof. otology and laryngology Harvard Med. Sch.; dir. otolaryngology Harvard Residency Program; otolaryngologist-in-chief Children's Hosp. Boston. Pres. Am. Soc. of Pediatric Otolaryngology; chair Am. Acad. of Pediats. Surgery Adv. Panel. Co-editor: (books) Otolaryngology Prep and Practice. Office: Childrens Hospital Boston 300 Longwood Ave Boston MA 02115 Office Phone: 617-355-6000.

CUNNINGHAM, MILAMARI ANTOINELLA, retired anesthesiologist; b. Cody, Wyo., Oct. 4, 1949; d. Milo Leo and Mary Madeline (Haley) Olds; m. Michael Otis Webb, June 4, 1970 (div. Feb. 1971); m. James Kenneth Cunningham, June 14, 1975. BA with honors, U. Mo., 1971, MD, 1975. Diplomate Am. Bd. Anesthesiologists. Intern and resident U. Mo., Columbia, 1975—78; jr. ptnr. Anesthesiologist, Inc., 1979—82, ptnr., 1982—86; owner Cunningham Anesthesia, 1986—2003; dir. anesthesia dept. Ellis Fischel Cancer Ctr., 1991—92; acting chief anesthesia Harry S. Truman Meml. Vets. Hosp., 1994—95; instr. U. Mo. Columbia Anesthesia Dept. Mem. med. staff U. Mo. Hosp. and Clinics, Columbia; vice chair Mo. Health Facilities Rev. Com., 2001—05. Mem. editl. bd.: Mo. Medicine Jour., 2001—06; contbg. editor, 2007—. Active Mo. Med. Polit. Action Com., 1991-2000, Friends of Music, Friends of Libr.; Mo. bd. dirs. A Call to Serve, 1996-2007, program mgr., 2004-07. Recipient Disting. Svc. award, U. Mo. Med. Alumni Assn., 2007; named Lifetime Senator, World Nations Congress, 2003; fellowship, Am. Coll. Anesthesiologists, 1977. Mem.: AMA (life Physicians Recognition award 1978, 1985, 1987, 1991, 1995), Vis. Nurses Assn. (bd. dirs. 1982—89, adv. bd. 1989—93), Am. Soc. Anesthesiologists (alt. dir. dist. 17 2003, Mo. dist. dir. 2003—05), Mo. State Med. Assn. (commn. econs. 3d party payors 1986—89, del. 1996—2004), Boone County Med. Soc. (sec. treas. 1996, bd. dirs. 1996—99, pres. 1998), Mo. Soc. Anesthesiologists (membership chair 1982—94, v.p. 1986—87, pres. 1988—89, spkr. ho. dels. 1992—2002, bd. dirs. 1996—99), Phi Beta Kappa. Home and Office: 8202 S Bennett Dr Columbia MO 65201-9178 Business E-Mail: milamari@centurytel.net.

CUNNINGHAM, PAUL RAYMOND GOLDWYN, dean, medical educator; b. Jamaica, July 28, 1949; came to U.S., 1974; s. Winston Pommells and Sylvia Fenella (Marsh) C.; m. Bridget Ann Mulvany, 1974 (div. 1985); children: Rachel Louise, Lucinda Jane; m. Sydney Louise Keniston, Feb. 14, 1987; Shawn Alan, Tifanie Dawn. MB, BS, U. of West Indies, Jamaica, 1972. Diplomate Am. Bd. Surgery. Commd. maj. US Army Res. Med. Corp., 1990-98; resident surgeon Mt. Sinai Hosp., NYC, 1974-78, chief resident surgery, 1978-79, clin. instr., 1978-81; asst. dir. surgery and joint diseases North Gen. Hosp., NYC, 1979-81, instr., 1981-84; attending surgeon Bertie County Meml. Hosp., Windsor, NC, 1981-84, vice chief of staff, 1981-84; clin. instr. surgery Brody Sch. Medicine, East Carolina U., Greenville, NC, 1981-84, asst. prof. surgery Dept. Surgery, 1984-89, med. dir. trauma svc., 1986-90, assoc. prof. and tenure, 1989-93, prof., 1993—, chief divsn. gen. surgery, 2000—02, dean, sr. assoc. vice chancellor med. affairs, 2008—; prof., chair Dept. Surgery SUNY Upstate Med. U., Syracuse, 2002—08. Med. dir. Pitt County Meml. Hosp. Trauma Svc., Greenville, 1986-99, chief of staff, 1991, various coms.; mem. N.C. Com. on Trauma, 1985—; cons., mem. Bertie County Dept. Health, Windsor, 1982-84. Contbr. articles to profl. jours. Mem. AMA, Am. Coun. on Transplantation, N.C. Med. Soc., Pitt County Med. Soc. A. Trauma Soc. (pres. N.C. chpt. 1989-91), Ea. Assn. for Surgery of Trauma (pres. 2000), So. Surg. Assn. Avocations: nature appreciation, reading, music, painting, photography. Office: Brody Sch Medicine, East Carolina U Brody AD-52 East Fifth St Greenville NC 27858-4353 Office Phone: 252-744-2201. E-mail: CUNNINGHAMP@ecu.edu.

CUNNINGHAM, TERENCE THOMAS, III, hospital administrator; b. Bell, Calif. BS in Microbiology, Calif. State U., Long Beach; MA in Hosp. Adminstrn., George Washington U., Washington, 1974. Commd. 2d lt. USAF, advanced through grades to col., 1989; adminstrv. resident MacDill Hosp., Tampa, Fla., 1973-74; adminstr. Rhein-Main Clinic, Frankfurt, Germany, 1974-79; hosp. cons. Air Force Med. Inspection Ctr., San Bernardino, Calif., 1979-81; CFO, David Grant Med. Ctr., Fairfield, Calif., 1981-82; CEO, Torrejon Hosp., Madrid, 1982-85; COO, CFO, materials officer Office Command Surgeon, Hdqrs. Mil. Airlift Command, Bellville, Ill., 1985-87; CEO, Wright Patterson Med. Ctr., Dayton, Ohio, 1987-92; adminstr. Wilford Hall Med. Ctr., San Antonio, 1992-94; v.p. adminstrn. Johns Hopkins Hosp., Balt., 1994-2000; CEO Ben Taub Gen. Hosp., Houston, 2000—06, Shriners Hosps. Children, LA, 2006—. Instr. grad. program health care adminstrn. Chapman Coll., Calif., 1981—82; preceptor grad. students in hosp. and health care adminstrn. Xavier U., Cin., 1987—, Baylor U., San Antonio, 1988—, George Washington U., Washington, 1995—, Johns Hopkins U., Balt., 1995—, assoc. prof. dept. health policy and mgmt. Sch. Pub. Health and Hygiene; asst. clin. prof. Wright State U. Sch. Medicine, Dayton, Ohio, 1990—; clin. instr. Baylor Coll. Medicine, 2001; adj. prof. Grad. Sch. Mgmt. Rice U., Houston, 2003—06; cons. to Surgeon Gen. USAF, 1986—. Book reviewer: Hosps. and Health Svcs. Adminstrn., Jour. Quality Assurance, Mil. Medicine; mem. editl. bd. Frontiers Health Svcs. Mgmt., Health Adminstrn. Press. Bd. dirs. Am. Red Cross, Houston. Fellow: Am. Coll. Healthcare Execs. (mem. various coms., regent to USAF); mem.: Assn. Mil. Surgeons US (Young Fed. Healthcare Adminstr. of the Yr. 1983, Fed. Healthcare Adminstr. of the Yr. 1989, Sr. Fed. Healthcare Adminstr. of the Yr. 1992), Tex. Hosp. Assn. (mem. edn. com., mem. disaster readiness task force), Greater Dayton Area Hosp. Assn. (bd. dirs.), Hosp. Assn. So. Calif., Ohio Hosp. Assn. (chmn. accreditation com.), Interagy. Inst. Fed. Health Care Alumni Assn. Avocations: bicycling, photography, sailing, reading.

CUNNINGHAM-RUNDLES, CHARLOTTE, physician, educator; b. Ann Arbor, Mich., July 12, 1943; d. R. Wayne Rundles and Mary Alice (Cunningham) Cunningham-Rundles; m. James B. Bussel, Nov. 13, 1982; 1 child, A. Christine. BS, Duke U., 1965; MD, Columbia U., 1969; PhD, NYU, 1974. Diplomate Am. Bd. Internal Medicine. Intern Bellevue Hosp., NYU, NYC, 1969-70, resident, 1970-72; with dept. immunology NYU Med. Ctr., 1972-74; assoc. Sloan Kettering Inst., NYC, 1974-86, dir. biochem. immunology, 1982-86; assoc. attending physician Meml. Hosp., NYC, 1978-86, adj. assoc., 1986—; prof. biochemistry, medicine and pediatrics Mt. Sinai Med. Ctr., NYC, 1986—, assoc. prof. Immunobiology Inst., 1986—; prof. Immunology Inst., 1994—. Bd. dirs. Immunodeficiency clinic; speaker various nat. and internat. mtgs. on immunology, program dir., Allergy Immunology Fellowship, 2001-, mem. blood safety adv. com. FDA, 2002-04; bd. med. advisors Primary Immunodeficiency Found., 1988—, Modell Found., 1989—; adv. NASA Contbr. numerous articles to sci. and med. jours., chpts. to books. Recipient Best Drs., 2001-08, Lifetime Achievement award Modell Found.; grantee NIH, Nat. Cancer Inst., Am. Cancer Soc., Nat. Found. March of Dimes, Multiple Sclerosis Soc. Fellow ACP; mem. Am. Fedn. Clin. Rsch., Am. Assn. Immunologist, Mucosal Immune Soc., Clin. Immunology Soc. (pres. 2003-04), The Harvey Soc. Episcopalian. Avocations: painting, drawing, computer graphics. Office: Mt Sinai Med Ctr 1 Gustave L Levy Pl New York NY 10029-6500

CUNNINGHAM-WILLIAMS, RENEE MICHELLE, social worker, educator; b. St. Louis, June 26, 1966; BSW, Howard U., 1988; PhD, Wash. U., 1994. Faculty, Sch. Medicine Wash. U., 1996—2005, assoc. prof., George Warren Brown Sch. Social Work, 2005—. Cons. NIH, 1996—. Recipient Young Investigator award, Am. Soc. Addiction Medicine, Nat. Ctr. Responsible Gaming, Inst. Rsch. Gambling and Related Disorders, Eli Robins and Samauel Guze award, Am. Psychopath. Assn. Mem.: Soc. Social Work and Rsch., Coll. Porblems Drug Dependence (Young Investigator award), Gamma Omega chpt., Alpha Kappa Alpha Sorority, Inc. Avocations: history, scrapbooks, crafts. Office: One Brookings Dr CB 1196 Washington Saint Louis MO 63130 Office Fax: 314-935-8511. Business E-Mail: williamsr@wustl.edu.

CUPARENCU, BARBU MILTIADE, pharmacologist; b. Cluj-Napoca, Cluj, Romania, Nov. 2, 1928; s. Miltiade Ioan and Livia Andrei (Bugnariu) C.; m. Maria Ferenc Szöcs, Sept. 16, 1952. Medical diplomate. Instr. U. Med. Pharmacology, Cluj, 1949-52, asst. prof., 1952-55, lectr., 1955-61, assoc. prof., 1961-68, prof., head of dept., 1968-94, U. Oradea, Romania, 1994—. Dir. Ctr. of Exptl. Medicine, Oradea, 1995. Author scientific papers in field. Roman Catholic. Avocations: literature, art, trips. Office: Univ Oradea Faculty Medicine Pharmacy Piata 1 Decembrie 1918 Oradea Romania Home Phone: 40264530074.

CURATI-ALASONATTI, WALTER, radiologist, educator, writer; b. Geneva, Nov. 8, 1943; arrived in U.K., 1984; s. Mario A. and Clotilde N. (Alasonatti) C.-A. MD, U. Geneva, 1970. Cert. foedoeratio medicorum helveticorum in radiology and nuc. medicine, European C.C.S.T. Clin. fellow dept. radiology McGill U., Montreal, Que., Can., 1974-76; resident dept. radiology Univ. Hosp., Geneva, 1971-73, resident dept. medicine, 1973-74, chief resident dept. radiology, 1977, cons. dept. radiology, 1978-83; jr. rsch. fellow Hammersmith Hosp., London, 1976, sr. rsch. fellow, 1984-86; mem. faculty of medicine Imperial Coll. Coll. Medicine, Sci. and Tech., 1990—2003. Prof. Z. Zeit U. Mainz (Germany), 1987-89, Swiss Paraplegic Ctr., Nottwil, Switzerland, 1989-90, The Robert Steiner MRI Unit Project Coord., London, 1990-2003; pub. med. and philosophy books Les Editions du Triangle d'Or, Geneva. Editor: The Imaging of Cancer, 1998, Imaging of the Elderly, 2002; pub., editor Les Editions du Triangle d'Or, 1999—; contbr. more than 200 med. articles to profl. jours. Fellow Royal Coll. Radiologists, Swiss Soc. Radiology, Royal Soc. Medicine; mem. Radiol. Soc. N.Am. Home and Office: Place Camoletti 4 CH 1207 Geneva Switzerland Personal E-mail: waltercurati@aol.com.

CURB, JESS DAVID, medical educator, researcher; b. Raton, N.Mex., Dec. 29, 1945; s. Leslie Calvin and Evelyn Lula (Lindley) C.; m. Beatriz Lorenza Rodriquez; children: Jess Calvin, William Noa, Maria Lorenza, Isabel Alani. BA, U. Colo., 1967; MD, U. N.Mex., Albuquerque, 1971; MPH, U. Tex., Houston, 1974. Diplomate, cert. geriatric medicine Am. Bd. Internal Medicine. Intern Harlem Hosp., Columbia U., NYC, 1971-72; rsch. assoc. U. Tex. Sch. Pub. Health and Medicine, Houston, 1973-76, asst. prof., 1978-80; resident internal medicine Northwestern U. Sch. Medicine, Chgo., 1976-78; asst. prof. Baylor Coll. Medicine, Houston, 1980-83; assoc. prof. U. Hawaii, Honolulu, 1983-85, prof., 1985-87; assoc. dir. Nat. Inst. on Aging, Bethesda, Md., 1986-89; prof. geriatric medicine, chief divsn. clin. epidemiology U. Hawaii, Sch. Medicine, Honolulu, 1989—2007, dir. transitional rsch., 2007—; CEO, med. dir. Pacific Health Rsch. Inst., 1995—2003, pres., 2003—07. Mem. bd. dirs. Kuakini Health Sys., 2004—; chair, bd. dirs. Geriatric Care Sys. Inc., 2007—; mem. bd. dirs. Hawaii Life Sci. & Tech. Coun., Honolulu, 2007. Contbr. articles to profl. jours. Grantee Honolulu Heart Program, Nat. Heart, Lung and Blood Inst., Honolulu, 1989-2003, Hawaii Asia Aging Study, Nat. Inst. on Aging, Honolulu, 1994-2002, Women's Health Initiative, NIH, Honolulu, 1994—, Family Blood Pressure Program, 1995—. Fellow ACP, Am. Heart Assn. (coun. on epidemiology), Gerontol. Soc. America; mem. Am. Geriatric Soc. Office: U Hawaii 651 Ilalo St MEB 223 Honolulu HI 98613 Business E-Mail: curb@hawaii.edu.

CURCILLO, PAUL G., surgeon; MD, U. Pa., 1989. Diplomate Am. Bd. Surgery, 2008, recertified, Am. Coll. of Surgeons, Am. Cadiac Life Support, 1991, cert. Advanced Trauma Life Support, 1994. Fellow Hosp. of the Univ. of Pa., 1989—91; resident in surgery Thomas Jefferson Univ. Hosp., Phila., 1992—96. Bd. dirs. Breast Health Inst., 2004—; bd. visitors Temple Univ., 2006—; pres. Temple Univ. Coll. of Arts and Sciences Alumni Assn., 2007—. Bd. dirs. Breast and Prostrate Health Found., 2005—. Recipient Gallery of Success, Temple Univ., 2009, Paul G Curcillo II Biology Award, 2007; named Top Docs, Castle Conelly, 2008; named one of Best Doctors, 2007—10, Top Surgeons, Consumer Rsch. Coun. for America, 2007, 2008, Top Doctors in Phila., Phila. Mag., 2009, America's Best Surgeons; fellow, Assn. of Minimal Access Surgeons of India, 2009. Mem.: Am. Coll. of Surgeons (chmn. young surgeons com. 1996—, councilor at large 1998, com. on applicants Pa. dist. 5 2000—, treas. 2002, sec. 2003, v.p. 2004, pres. elect 2005—06, pres. 2006—07, past pres. 2007—08), Phila. Acad. of Surgery, Soc. of the Gastroenterologic and Endoscopic Surgeons (SAGES), Soc. for Surgery of the Alimentary Tract. Office: Fox Chase Cancer Center 333 Cottman Ave Philadelphia PA 19111-2497 Office Phone: 215-728-6900.

CURD, JOHN GARY, physician, scientist; b. Grand Junction, Colo., July 2, 1945; s. H. Ronald and Edna (Hegsted) C.; m. Karen Wendel, June 12, 1971; children: Alison, Jonathan, Edward, Bethany. BA, Princeton U., 1967; MD, Harvard U., 1971. Diplomate Am. Bd. Internal Medicine, Am. Bd. Rheumatology, Am. Bd. Allergy and Immunology. Rsch. assoc. NIH, Bethesda, Md., 1973-75; fellow in rheumatology U. Calif., San Diego, 1975-77; fellow in allergy-immunology Scripps Clinic, La Jolla, Calif., 1977-78, fellow in allergy-immunology Stanford Exec. Program, 2000, asst. mem. rsch. inst., 1978-81, mem. div. rheumatology, 1981-91, head div. rheumatology, vice chmn. dept. medicine, 1989-91; pres. med. staff Green Hosp., La Jolla, 1988-90; clin. dir. Genentech Inc., South San Francisco, Calif., 1991-96, sr. dir., head clin. sci., 1996-97, v.p. clin. devel., 1997—99; sr. v.p. pres. Vaxgen, 1999—2001; pres. chief med. officer Novacea, 2001—. Author numerous. sci. papers in field. Med. dir. San Diego Scleroderma Found., 1983-91; sec. San Diego Arthritis Found., 1986-87. Lt. comdr. USPHS, 1973-75. Mem. Princeton Club No. Calif. Republican. Home: 128 Reservoir Rd Hillsborough CA 94010-6957 Office Phone: 650-228-1810. Business E-Mail: curd@novacea.com.

CUREOGLU, SEBAHATTIN, otolaryngologist, educator, researcher; b. Malatya, Turkey, July 1, 1963; s. Kemal Cureoglu, Muazzez Cureoglu; m. Hatice Zehra Akyol; children: Suanur, Abdullah, Mehmet Turhan. MD, Hacettepe U., Turkey, 1989. Diplomate otolaryngology specialization. Med. doctor Hacettepe U., Ankara, Turkey, 1982—89; otolaryngology specialist Erciyes U., Kayseri, Turkey, 1990—94; assoc. prof. Dicle U., Diyarbakir, Turkey, 1997—; rsch. fellow U. Minn., Mpls., 2000—02, instr., 2002—. Med. doctor Turkish Navy, 1993—94, Istanbul. Mem.: Turkish Med. Doctor's Assn., Assn. Rsch. in Otolaryngology, Minn. Electron Microscopy Soc., Otolaryngic Allergy Found. Office Phone: 612-626-9883. Business E-Mail: scureoglu@hotmail.com.

CURETON, CLAUDETTE HAZEL CHAPMAN, retired biology professor; b. Greenville, SC, May 3, 1932; d. John H. and Beatrice (Washington) Chapman; m. Stewart Cleveland Cureton, Dec. 27, 1954; children: Ruthye, Stewart II, S. Charles, Samuel. AB, Spelman Coll., Atlanta, 1951; MA, Fisk U., Nashville, Tenn., 1966; DHum (hon.), Morris Coll., Sumter, SC, 1996. Tchr. North Warren H.S., Wise, NC, 1952-60, tchr. Sterling H.S., Greenville, 1960-66, Wade Hampton H.S., Greenville, 1967-73; instr. Greenville Tech. Coll., 1973-95, ret., 1995. Bd. dirs. State Heritage Trust, 1978-91; commr. Basic Skills Adv. Program, Columbia, 1990—; mem. adv. bd. Am. Fed. Bank, NCNB Bank, Greenville, 1991—; mem. Higher Edn. S.C. Com. for Selection Prof. of Yr., 1995 Mem. Greenville Urban League, NAACP, SC Curriculum Congress; pres. Woman's Bapt. E.& M. Conv. SC, 2008; mem. SC Commn. on Higher Edn. Com. for Selection of Gov.'s Prof. of Yr., 2005, Gov.'s Task Force on Juvenile Crime, SC, Best Chance Network Task Force of Am. Cancer Soc., 1995-, Gov.'s Juvenile Justice Youth Coun., SC, 1996—, Gov.'s Juvenile Justice Task Force, 1997, SC, Piedmont Mental Health Bd., Simpsonville, SC, 2006; bd. dirs. Sisters Saving Sisters, Roper Mountain Sci. Ctr., 2003-. Recipient Presdl. award Morris Coll., 1987, 91, Svc. award SC Wildlife and Marine Dept., 1986, Outstanding Jack and Jill of Am. citation, 1986, Excellence in Tchg. award Nat. Inst. for Staff and Orgnl. Devel., U. Tex., Austin, 1992-93, Educator of Yr. award Greenville chpt. Am. Cancer Soc., 1994, Outstanding Svc. award Best Chance Network/Am. Cancer Soc., 1994, Citation SC Ho. of Reps., 1995, Outstanding Svc. award Reedy River Bapt. Assn., 2001; named Unsung Hero of the Cmty. for Outstanding Svc. to Humankind Greenville Tech. Coll., 1999. Mem. AAAS, AAUW, Nat. Assn. Biology Tchrs., SC Curriculum Congress, Nat. Coun. Negro Women, Inc., Delta Sigma Theta (past v.p. Greenville chpt. alumnae), Benedict Coll. (Columbia, SC) (mem. bd. trustees, Outstanding Support award, 2009-11), Morris Coll. (Sumter, SC) (mem. bd. trustees). Home: 501 Mary Knob Ct Greenville SC 29607-5242

CURIE, CHARLES G., former federal agency administrator; b. Ind., July 22, 1955; m. Candace Curie. Grad., Huntington Coll., 1977; MA, U. Chgo., 1979. Cert. Acad. Cert. Social Workers. Exec. dir., CEO Sandusky Valley Ctr., Tiffin, Ohio; pres., CEO Helen H. Stevens Cmty. Mental Health Ctr., Carlisle, Pa., 1988—90; dir. risk mgmt. services Henry S. Lehr Inc., Bethlehem, Pa., 1990—95; dep. sec. for mental health and substance abuse services Dept. Pub. Welfare, State of Pa., 1995—2001; adminstr. Substance Abuse and Mental Health Services Adminstrn. US Dept. Health & Human Services, Rockville, Md., 2001—06. Recipient McGovern Award for Leadership in Drug Abuse Prevention, Inst. for Behavior and Health, 2005; named Alumnus of Yr., Huntington Coll., 1996. Mem.: Rotary Internat.

CURRE, CORA LEE, medical laboratory manager; b. Baltimore, Md., Mar. 29, 1956; d. Edward William and Polly Pintler Digges; m. Joe Scott Curre, Mar. 1, 1980; children: Erik Alan, Kyle Adam. AA and Sci. in Med. Tech., Shoreline CC, Seattle, Washington, 1975—77. Health Care Assistant-Category A State of Wash. Health Professions Quality Assurance Divsn., 2009, X-Ray Technician-Registered State of Wash. Health Professions Quality Assurance Divsn., 2009; cert. in maintenance program MLT (ASCP) Am. Soc. Clin. Pathology, 2004. Lab. asst., phlebotomist Anne Arundel Gen. Hosp., Annapolis, Md., 1972—74; lab asst., phlebotomist, admitting clk. Valley Gen. Hosp., Renton, Wash., 1975—77; med. lab. technician (ASCP) Eastside Med.

Lab., Inc., Redmond, Wash., 1977—81; med. lab. technician (ASCP), registered x-ray technician Des Moines Way Clinic, Des Moines, Wash., 1981—82; med. lab. technician (ASCP), med. asst. Pediatric Associates, Inc., Bellevue, Wash., 1982—87; med. lab. technician (ASCP), med. asst., registered x-ray technician Family Medicine of Redmond, Redmond, Wash., 1987—89; med. lab. technician (ASCP), lab lead Group Health Coop., Bellevue, Wash., 1989—97; med. lab. technician (ASCP), chief tech, lab. supr., registered x-ray technician UW Medicine Issaquah Clinic, Issaquah, Wash., 1997—. Safety coord. UW Medicine Issaquah Clinic, Issaquah, Wash., 1998—2002, clin. staff trainer, 2001—03; lab. mgr. UW Medicine Neighborhood Clinics, 2008—. Archtl. control com. mem. Klahanie Assn., Issaquah, Wash., 1993—96. Recipient UW AMC Svc. Excellence, Go The Extra Mile (GEM) Award, UW Medicine Neighborhood Clinics, 2002, ASCP Thirty Yr. Mem. Recognition, Am. Soc. for Clin. Pathology, 2007, Ten Yr. Svc. Recognition, UW Medicine Neighborhood Clinics-Issaquah Clinic, 2007, Five Yr. Svc. Recognition, Group Health Coop. Factoria Med. Ctr., 1994. Mem.: Am. Soc. for Clin. Pathology (assoc. Thirty Yr. Mem. Recognition 2007). Achievements include development of UW Medicine Neighborhood Clinics Laboratory Training Program; Group Health Cooperative Factoria Medical Center Laboratory Orientation Program; UW Medicine Neighborhood Clinics Laboratory Procedures and Quality Assurance Program; Family Medicine of Redmond Laboratory Training Program for Nurses. Avocations: skiing, camping, reading, travel, biking. Office: UW Medicine Issaquah Clinic 1455 11th Ave NW Issaquah WA 98027-5319 Personal E-mail: currec@comcast.net. Business E-Mail: currec@uwpn.org.

CURRERI, PETER WILLIAM, health facility administrator, consultant; b. Milw., Sept. 2, 1936; s. Anthony Rudolph and Dorothea Christiana (Heubsch) C.; m. Patricia Ann Egry, Aug. 14, 1958 (div. 1975); children: Charles Anthony, James Bradley, Regina Dawn. BA, Swarthmore Coll., 1958; MD, U. Pa., 1962. Intern Hosp. of U. Pa., 1962-63, resident in surgery, 1963-68; asst. prof. surgery U. Tex., Southwestern Med. Ctr., Dallas, 1971-74; assoc. prof. surgery U. Wash. Med. Sch., Seattle, 1974-77; prof. surgery Cornell U. Med. Ctr., NYC, 1977-81; prof., chmn. surgery U. South Ala. Med. Sch., Mobile, Ala., 1981—88; chmn. Strategem of Ala., Inc., Daphne, 1988—. Mem. surgery anesthesiology and trauma study sect. NIH, Washington, 1980-84, chmn., 1986-88; commr. Physician Payment Rev. Commn., Washington, 1988-97; mem. Medicare Payment Adv. Com., 1997-99. Contbr. articles to profl. jours. Lt. col. U.S. Army, 1968-71. Decorated Meritorious Svc. medal; recipient Rsch. Career Devel. award NIH, 1972, Curtis P. Artz award Am. Trauma Soc., 1989. Mem. Am. Assn. for Surgery of Trauma (pres. 1989-90), Am. Burn Assn. (pres. 1983-84), Am. Coll. Surgeons (sec. bd. govs. 1987-89), Halstead Surg. Soc. (pres. 1988-89), Soc. Univ. Surgeons (pres. 1980-81), Assn. Acad. Surgery (recorder 1972-74). Avocations: golf, walking. Office: Strategem Inc 26064 Capital Dr Ste A Daphne AL 36526-6166 Office Phone: 251-625-2205. *

CURREY, THOMAS ARTHUR, ophthalmologist; b. Itawamba County, Miss., July 9, 1933; s. Charles Edward Currey and Anna L. (Williams) C; m. Carol Ann Clabough, Nov. 7, 1959; children: Thomas A. Jr., C. Russell. Degree, U. Miss., 1955; MD, U. Tenn., 1958. Diplomate Am. Bd. Ophthalmology. Intern City of Memphis Hosps., 1958-59; resident in ophthalmology U. Tenn., Memphis, 1962-65; pvt. practice Memphis, 1965—; mem. staff St. Francis Hosp., 1965—, pres. med. staff, 1985. Assoc. instr. ophthalmology dept. family practice, 1990—, asst. clin. instr. ophthalmology U. Tenn., 1965—. Fellow ACS; mem. Tenn. Med. Assn. (v.p. 1987), Tenn. Acad. Ophthalmology (pres. 1975), Memphis & Shelby County Med. Soc. (treas. 1983-86). Office: Eye Specialists Assoc PC 1900 Kirby Pky Memphis TN 38138-3690 Office Phone: 901-754-0930. Personal E-mail: tcurrey901@aol.com.

CURRIE, JOHN L., gynecologic oncologist; MD, U. NC, 1967. Diplomate Am. Bd. Ob-Gyn-gynecologic oncology, 1982, Am. Bd. Ob-Gyn, 1991, lic. Conn. Resident gynecologic oncology Hosp. Univ. Pa., Phila., 1968—72; fellow gynecologic oncology Duke Univ. Med. Ctr., Durham, 1978—80; hosp. affiliations include Mary Hitchcock Meml. Hosp., Med. Ctr.; dir. women's health and gynecologic oncology dept. John B. Amos Cancer Ctr.; gynecologic oncologist. Office: c/o John B Amos Cancer Center 1831 5th Ave Columbus GA 31904 Office Phone: 860-545-4341.

CURRIER, BRADFORD LEONARD, spine and orthopedic surgeon; s. Malcolm and Evelyn Currier; m. Nancy Romness Currier; children: Sarah, Michael, Thomas. BS in Biology, Emory U., 1977; MD, Georgetown U., 1981. Diplomate Am. Acad. Orthop. Surgeons, lic. Fla., Minn. Intern in gen. surgery Mayo Grad. Sch. Medicine, Rochester, Minn., 1981—82, resident in orthop. surgery, 1984—88; fellowship in spine surgery U. Miami, Fla., 1988—89; spine/orthop. surgeon Mayo Clinic, Rochester, Minn., 1989—, prof. orthop., 2006—, vice chmn. practice dept. orthop., 2003. Dir. spine fellowship Mayo Clinic, 1993—. Contbr. numerous articles to profl. jours. Mem.: AMA, Soc. Minimally Invasive Spine Surgery, Lumbar Spine Rsch. Soc. (treas. 2008—11, pres. 2011—), Am. Orthop. Assn., Zumbro Valley Med. Soc., N.Am. Spine Soc., Minn. Orthop. Soc., Minn. Med. Soc., Mid-Am. Orthop. Assn., Cervical Spine Rsch. Soc. (pres. 2004—05), Am. Acad. Orthop. Surgeons, Sigma Xi. Office: Mayo Clinic 200 First St SW Rochester MN 55905 Office Phone: 507-284-0412. Office Fax: 507-284-5539. *

CURRIER, MARY MARGARET, public health service officer; b. Ann Arbor, Mich., 1956; Attended, Trinity Coll., 1977—78; BA, Rice U., 1978; MD, U. Miss. Sch. Medicine, 1983; MPH, Johns Hopkins Sch. Hygeine & Pub. Health, 1987. Cert. gen. preventive medicine and pub. health. Resident pub. health Johns Hopkins U.; served various capacities Miss. Dept. Health, Jackson, 1984—, staff physician prenatal care, family planning, sexually transmitted disease and pediat. program, state epidemiologist, 1993—2003, 2007—09, state health officer, 2010—. Mem.: APHA, AMA, Miss. Ctrl. Med. Soc. Office: Mississippi Department of Health 570 East Woodrow Wilson Dr Jackson MS 39216 Office Phone: 601-576-7634. Office Fax: 601-576-7931. *

CURRY, KELLY EDWIN, hospital administrator; b. Owensboro, Ky., Jan. 19, 1955; s. Martha (Fogle) C.; m. Susan Marie Miller, July 23, 1977; children: Natalie Marie, Leah Sloane. BS in Acctg., U. Ky., 1977. CPA, Ky. Sr. auditor Touche Ross & Co. CPA's, 1977-79, Humana, Inc., 1979-82; chmn., pres., founder Found. in Christ Ministries Ltd., Ireland, 1995—2007; dir., internal audit Health Management Associates, Inc., Naples, Fla., 1982, dir., reimbursement, 1983-84, hosp. ops. cons., 1985-87, v.p., fin. ops., 1987-92, CFO, 1987—94, sr. v.p., fin., CFO Naples, 1992—94, COO, 2007—08, chief adminstrv. officer, 2008—10, exec. v.p., CFO, 2010—. Mem. AICPA, Ky. Soc. CPAs, Fla. Soc. CPAs. Republican. Baptist. Avocations: golf, fishing, running. Office: Health Management Associates Inc 5811 Pelican Bay Blvd Naples FL 34108-2710 Office Phone: 239-598-3131. Office Fax: 239-598-2705. Business E-Mail: kelly.curry@hma.com. *

CURRY, NANCY ELLEN, psychologist, psychoanalyst, educator; b. Brockway, Pa., Jan. 26, 1931; d. George R. and Mary F. (Covert) C. BA, Grove City Coll., 1952; MEd, U. Pitts., 1956, PhD, 1972; grad., Pitts. Psychoanalytic Inst., 1988, grad. child analytic program, 1992. Lic. psychologist, Pa. Tchr. public schs., East Brady and Oakmont, Pa., 1952-55; presch. demonstration tchr. Arsenal Family and Children's Center, U. Pitts., 1955-79, assoc. dir., 1971-79; from instr. in psychiatry to prof. child devel. Sch. Social Work, U. Pitts, 1957-93; prof. emeritus Sch. Social Work, U. Pitts.; mem. faculty U. Pitts Sch. Medicine, Sch. Edn., Sch. Health Related Professions., Pitts. Psychoanalytic Soc.; pvt. practice in psychanalysis and psychotherapy; ret., 2000. Supr., cons.; Fulbright exchange tchr. North Oxford Nursery Sch., Oxford, Eng., 1957-58; vis. prof. Oreg. State U., summer, 1964, Ariz. State U., summer, 1969; assoc. dir. early childhood project Edn. Professions Devel. Act, U.S. Office of Edn., 1970-74; cons. in field. Co-producer 12 films on children's play; co-author Beyond Self-esteem, 1990; editor The Feeling Child; author numerous articles on child devel. Adv. bd. Fred Rogers Ctr.; bd. mem. Fred Rogers Co. Mem. APA, Assn. Child Psychoanalysis Home: 149 Shadow Ridge Dr Pittsburgh PA 15238-2133 Personal E-mail: NCU149@comcast.net.

CURRY, NANCY S., radiologist, educator; b. Rochester, NY, Jan. 11, 1947; d. Melvin Stuart and Alvina Christine (Scherer) S.; m. Robert Wilker Curry, Aug. 16, 1969; children: Scott, Ryan, Laurel. BA, U. Rochester, 1968; MD, Med. Coll. Pa. (Drexler), 1972. Diplomate Am. Bd. Radiology. Residency internal medicine Med. Coll. Pa. (Drexler), Phila., 1972—74; residency radiology U. Rochester, Rochester, NY, 1975—79; fellowship uroradiology UCLA, Los Angeles, Calif., 1979—80; prof. radiology and urology Med. U. SC, Charleston, SC, 1980—. Contbr. chapters to books, over 60 articles to profl. jours. Fellow Am. Coll. Radiology; mem. S.C. Radiol. Soc. Achievements include 1st female chief resident in radiology program U. Rochester; 2nd female president of the Soc. Uroradiology 2007-08; 1st female president of the South Carolina Radiologic Society. Avocation: competitive running. Office Fax: 843-792-5067.

CURRY, RAYMOND HOWARD, physician; b. Lexington, Ky., June 5, 1956; s. Howard Jr. and Venita (Dawson) C. AB, U. Ky., 1977; MD, Washington U., St. Louis, 1982. Diplomate Am. Bd. Internal Medicine. Resident in internal medicine McGaw Med. Ctr. Northwestern U., Chgo., 1982-85; internist Northwestern Med. Faculty Found., Chgo., 1985—; instr. Northwestern U. Med. Sch., Chgo., 1985-89, asst. prof., 1989-96, assoc. prof., 1996—2002, prof., 2002—, dir. undergrad. edn. dept. medicine, 1992—98, vice dean for edn., 1998—; mem. staff Northwestern Meml. Hosp., Chgo., 1985—; pres. McGaw Med. Ctr. NW U., 2004—. Mem. ACP, Soc. Gen. Internal Medicine, Am. Acad. Physician and Patient, Phi Beta Kappa. Office: Northwestern U Feinberg Sch of Medicine 420 E Superior St Chicago IL 60611

CURRY, SUSAN J., health psychologist, health policy researcher; b. Springfield, Mass., Jan. 8, 1954; m. Clifford R. Curry, Nov. 21, 1984; children: Sarah Elizabeth, Paul Michael. BA in Psychology, magna cum laude, U. Mass., 1976; MA in Psychology, U. NH, 1979, PhD in Psychology, 1981. Postdoc. rsch. assoc. U. Wash., 1981-84; staff scientist Fred Hutchinson Cancer Rsch. Ctr., Seattle, 1984-86; asst. prof. dept. health svcs. U. Wash., Seattle, 1987—91, assoc. prof., 1991—95, prof., 1995—2001; prof. health policy and adminstrn., dir. Inst. Health Rsch. & Policy U. Ill., Chgo., 2001—08; disting. prof. health mgmt. & policy, dean. Coll. Pub. Health U. Iowa, 2008—. Asst. sci. investigator Ctr. Health Studies Group Health Coop., 1986—91, assoc. sci. investigator, 1991—94, sr. investigator, 1994—2001, dir., 1998—2000; mem. external adv. bd. MD Anderson Cancer Ctr., U. Tex., 2002—, U. Wis. Comprehensive Cancer Ctr., 2004—; mem. sci. adv. bd. Nat. Cancer Inst., 2005—. Editor: Psychology Addictive Behaviors, 1994—99; assoc. editor Health Psychology, 1995—98, American Jour. Preventive Medicine, 2005—; contbr. articles to profl. jours. Fellow: Inst. Medicine Chgo., American Psychol. Assn., Soc. Behavioral Medicine (Disting. Scientist award 2001); mem.: APHA, Assn. Health Svcs. Rsch., Assn. Advancement Behavior Therapy, Inst. Medicine (mem. Nat. Cancer Policy Bd. 1999—2002), Soc. Rsch. Nicotine & Tobacco, American Soc. Preventive Oncology (Joseph R. Cullen Meml award 2000). Avocations: swimming, weaving, reading. Office: U Iowa Coll Pub Health E220 H1 GH 200 Hawkins Dr Iowa City IA 52242 Office Phone: 319-384-5452. E-mail: sue-curry@uiowa.edu. *

CURT, GREGORY A., clinical researcher; b. Mass., July 26, 1952; m. Suzanne Grealy, Aug. 18, 1979. BS summa cum laude, Providence Coll., 1973; MD with distinction, U. Rochester Sch. Medicine, NY, 1977. Diplomate Am. Bd. Internal Medicine, Am. Bd. Clin. Oncology. Gordan & Viola Leak rsch. fellow Childrens Cancer Rsch. Found., Boston, 1974, Charing Cross Hosp., London, 1975—76; intern, resident internal medicine New Eng. Deaconess Hosp./Harvard Med. Sch., Boston, 1977—80; rsch. fellow Peter Bent Brigham Hosp., Boston, 1979—80; fellow in med. oncology Nat. Cancer Inst. (NCI), Bethesda, Md., 1980—83, spl. asst. clin. affairs, divsn. cancer treatment, 1983—84, asst. dir. divsn. cancer treatment, 1984—85, dep. dir. divsn. cancer treatment, 1985—88, clin. dir. NCI, 1989—2002, assoc. dir. clin. oncology program, 1989—95, dep. dir. clin. affairs, divsn. clin. scis., 1995—2002; sr. dir., alliance mgr. for NIH AstraZeneca Pharm., 2002—, US med. sci. lead for emerging products, 2007—. Dir. med. edn., chief clin. pharmacology Roger Williams Hosp.-Brown U., Providence, 1988—89; chmn. Life Scis. Consortium Task Force CEO Roundtable. Mem. editl. bd. Cancer Treatment Reports, 1985—88, founding editor The Oncologist, 1995—; contbr. articles to profl. jour., chapters to books. Capt. USPHS. Recipient Outstanding Svc. medal, USPHS, 1992. Roman Catholic. *

CURTIN, BRIAN JOSEPH, retired ophthalmologist; b. NYC, July 25, 1921; s. James Joseph and Julia Margaret (Smith) C.; m. Claire Margaret Flood, June 18, 1955; children: Edward Brian, James Martin, Thomas Hayes, Deirdre Claire. BS, Fordham U., NYC, 1942; MD, NYU, 1945. Intern St. Vincent's Hosp., NYC, 1945-46; resident surgeon Manhattan Eye, Ear and Throat Hosp., 1950-53, asst. attending surgeon, asso. attending surgeon, 1953-74, surgeon dir., 1974-89, surgeon dir. emeritus, 1990—, pres. med. bd., 1977-79, vice chmn. dept. ophthalmology, 1983-89, med. dir., 1989-91; attending ophthalmologist, chief svc. Misericordia-Lincoln Affiliated Hosps., 1958-79; attending ophthalmologist N.Y. Hosp., 1969-84; assoc. attending ophthalmologist Columbia Presbyn. Med. Ctr., 1985-92; asst. prof. clin. ophthalmology NYU, 1954-70; assoc. prof. clin. ophthalmology Cornell Med. Coll., 1970-84, Columbia U. Coll. Physicians and Surgeons, 1985-98; pvt. practice NYC. Med. adv. bd. Eye Bank for Sight Restoration, N.Y.C., 1978-90, chmn., 1988-90; attending ophthalmologist, chmn. dept. St. Clare's Hosp. and Health Ctr., 1978-81. Author: The Myopias: Basic Science and Clinical Management, 1985; mem. editorial bd. Cornea, 1981-85; contbr. chpts. to textbooks, articles to med. jours. With U.S. Navy, 1946-48. Recipient Achievement award Fordham U., 1976. Mem. ACS, AMA, AAAS, Am. Ophthalmol. Soc., N.Y. State Med. Soc., N.Y. County Med. Soc., N.Y. Acad. Medicine, N.Y. Acad. Scis., Am. Acad. Ophthalmology, N.Y. Ophthal. Soc. (v.p. 1981-82, pres. 1982-83), Am. Eye Study Club. Home: 4402 Theall Rd Rye NY 10580-1480 Personal E-mail: bcurti85@hotmail.com.

CURTIN, LEAH LOUISE, publisher, nurse, educator; b. Chgo., Mar. 8, 1942; d. Jean Wilson and Veronica Eloise (Dunst) Sutter; m. Peter Joseph Curtin, Apr. 15, 1966 (div. May 1990); children: Peter James, Rose Mary, Christopher Charles, Joseph Wilson. Diploma in nursing, Good Samaritan Hosp. Sch. Nursing, Cin., 1965; BS in Community Health Planning, U. Cin., 1976, MS in Health Planning and Adminstrn., 1977; MA in Philosophy, Athenaeum of Ohio, 1977; Doctorate (hon.), Med. Coll. Ohio, 1986, SUNY, Buffalo, 1990; DS (hon.), SUNY, Utica, 1990, Med. Coll. Ohio, 2002. RN, Ohio. Staff nurse Vets. Hosp., Cin., 1965-66, Vis. Nurses' Assn., Cin., 1966-67; instr. No. Ky. U., Highland Heights, 1974-76; asst. prof. Coll. Mt. St. Joseph-On-The-Ohio, Cin., 1976—98; editor Nursing Mgmt. Springhouse Corp., Phila., 1979-98; ptnr. Metier Cons., Cin., 1988—; clin. prof. nursing Coll. Nursing and Health, U. Cin. Orgnl. cons. Franciscan Sisters of Poor Health System, N.Y.C., 1987-96; cons. on nursing ethics Nurse Corps, USAF, Washington, 1991—, exec. editor Am. Nurses Today, 2009-. Author: Nursing Ethics: Theories and Pragmatics, 1982 (Am. Jour. Nursing Book of Yr. award 1982), DRGS: The Reorganization of Health, 1984, Curtin Calls, 1986, Cornerstones of Healthcare in the '90s, 1991, Sunflowers in the Sand: Children's Stories of War, 2000; contbr. articles to profl. jours, 1998-2004; editor, pub. Jour. Clin. Systems Mgmt. Recipient Disting. Nurse award Virginia Mason Med. Ctr., 2007, Mary Hammer Greenwood award Ohio Nurses Assn., 1990, Outstanding Svc. award Franciscan Sisters of Poor Health System, 1991; Am. Acad. Nursing fellow, 1983. Mem. ANA, Internat. Acad. Nursing Editors, Nat. League for Nursing, N.Y. Acad. Polit. and Social Scis., Sigma Theta Tau. Home: 5932 Rapid Run Rd Cincinnati OH 45233-4852 Office: Metier Pub PO Box 11054 Cincinnati OH 45211-0054 Office Phone: 513-941-2888. E-mail: curtncal@one.net.

CURTIN, THOMAS LEE, ophthalmologist; b. Columbus, Ohio, Sept. 9, 1932; s. Leo Anthony and Mary Elizabeth (Burns) C.; m. Constance L. Sallman; children: Michael, Gregory, Thomas, Christopher, Kenton. BS, Loyola U., LA, 1954; MD, U. So. Calif., 1957; cert. navy flight surgeon, US Naval Sch. Aerospace Med., 1959. Diplomate Am. Bd. Ophthalmology. Intern Ohio State U. Hosp., 1957-58; resident in ophthalmology U.S. Naval Hosp, San Diego, 1961-64; pvt. practice medicine specializing in ophthalmology Oceanside, Calif., 1967—. Mem. staff Tri City, hosps.; sci. adv. bd. So. Calif. Soc. Prevention Blindness, 1973-76; bd. dirs. North Coast Surgery Ctr., Oceanside, 1987-96; cons. in field. Trustee Carlsbad Unified Sch. Dist., 1975—83, pres., 1979, 1982, 1983; trustee Carlsbad Libr., 1990—99, pres., 1993, 1998; bd. dirs. Mission San Luis Rey, Oceanside, Calif., 2006—08. Officer MC USN, 1958—67. Mem. AMA, Calif. Med. Assn., San Diego County Med. Soc., Am. Acad. Ophthalmology, Aerospace Med. Assn., San Diego Acad. Ophthalmology (pres. 1979), Carlsbad Rotary, El Camino Country Club. Repubican. Roman Catholic. Personal E-mail: curtintc@gmail.com.

CURTIS, CHRIS, state agency administrator; BS, W.Va. U.; MPH in Health Policy and Adminstrn., U. NC, Chapel Hill. Asst. commr. W.Va. Bur. Pub. Health, dep. commr., acting commr.; dir. health resources devel. W.Va. Dept. Health & Human Resources, 2011—. Office: West Virginia Dept Health & Human Resources Staate Capitol Complex Bldg 3 Rm 206 Charleston WV 25305 *

CURTIS, DEBBIE, legislative staff member; b. Arlington, Va. BA, Boston U., 1988. Staff asst. to Representative Ed Markey US House of Reps., Washington, 1987—88, legis. aide to Representative Ron Wyden, 1988—91; legis. affairs dir. Citizen Action, Washington, 1993—95; legis. asst. to Representative Jim Moody US House of Reps., Washington, 1991—93, legis. asst. to Representative Ben Cardin, 1995—98, chief of staff to Representative Pete Stark, 1998—. Office: Office of Representative Pete Stark 239 Cannon House Office Bldg Washington DC 20515-0513 Office Phone: 202-225-5065. E-mail: debra.curtis@mail.house.gov.

CURTIS, JAMES L., psychiatrist; b. Jeffersonville, Ga., Apr. 27, 1922; s. Will and Francis (Hall) C.; m. Vivian Alzine Rawls, Dec. 11, 1948; children: Lawrence, Paul. BA, Albion Coll., 1943; MD, U. Mich., 1946; cert. psychoanalysis, Columbia U., 1954. Diplomate Am. Bd. Psychiatry and Neurology, Am. Bd. Addiction Psychiatry. Intern Wayne County Gen. Hosp., Eloise, Mich., 1947, resident in psychiatry, 1948, SUNY, Bklyn., 1949-50, from instr. to clin. asst. prof. SUNY Dowstate Med. Ctr., Bklyn., 1954-68; assoc. dean, assoc. prof. psychiatry. Cornell U. Med. Ctr., NYC, 1968-80; clin. prof. psychiatry NY Med. Coll., NYC, 1980-82, Columbia U. Coll. Physicians & Surgeons, NYC, 1982—2000, clin. prof. emeritus, 2000—; dir. dept. psychiatry Harlem Hosp. Ctr., NYC, 1982-2000. Author: Blacks, Medical Schools and Society, 1971, Affirmative Action in Medicine, 2003; contbr. articles to profl. jours. Capt. USAF, 1952-54. Fellow Am. Psychiat. Assn., Am. Orthopsychiat. Assn., Am. Psychoanalytic Assn., Am. Acad. Psychoanalysts. Democrat. Congregationalist. Home Phone: 517-629-8117. Personal E-mail: jcurtismd@hotmail.com.

CURTIS, JEPTHA P., cardiologist, educator; BA, Yale U., 1993; MD, Columbia Coll. Physicians and Surgeons, 1997. Intern and resident in internal medicine Duke U. Med. Ctr., 2000; fellow in cardiovascular disease Yale U., 2004; asst. prof. medicine Yale Sch. Medicine. Office: Yale U Sch Medicine Box 207017 New Haven CT 06520-8017 Office Phone: 203-785-4114. E-mail: jeptha.curtis@yale.edu.

CURTIS, LYNDA D., hospital administrator; Sr. v.p. South Manhattan health network NYC Health and Hosps. Corp.; exec. dir. Bellevue Hosp. Ctr., NYC. Office: Bellevue Hospital Center 462 First Ave New York NY 10016 Office Phone: 212-562-1000.

CURTISS, ROY, III, life sciences professor; b. May 27, 1934; m. Josephine Clark, Dec. 28, 1976; children: Brian, Wayne, Roy IV, Lynn, Gregory Clark, Eric Garth, Megan Kimberly. BS in Agr., Cornell U., 1956; PhD in Microbiology, U. Chgo., 1962; DSc (hon.), So. Ill. U., Edwardsville, 2003. Diplomate Am. Coll. Vet. Microbiologists, 2010. Instr., rsch. asst. Cornell U., 1955-56; jr. tech. specialist Brookhaven Nat. Lab., 1956-58; fellow microbiology U. Chgo., 1958-60, USPHS fellow, 1960-62; biologist Oak Ridge Nat. Lab., 1963-72; lectr. microbiology U. Tenn., Knoxville, 1965-72, lectr. Grad. Sch. Biomed. Scis. Oak Ridge, 1967-69, prof., 1969-72, assoc. dir., 1970-71, interim dir., 1971-72; Charles H. McCauley prof. microbiology U. Ala., Birmingham, 1972-83; sr. scientist Inst. Dental Rsch., 1972-83, Comprehensive Cancer Ctr., 1972-83, dir. molecular cell biology grad. program, 1973-82; dir., sr. scientist Cystic Fibrosis Rsch. Ctr., 1981-83; prof. cellular and molecular biology Sch. Dental Medicine Washington U., St. Louis, 1983-91, George William and Irene Koechig Freiberg prof. biology, 1984—2005, chmn. dept. biology, 1983-93, dir. Ctr. Plant Sci. and Biotech., 1991-94, George William and Irene Koechig Freiberg prof. emeritus, 2005—; prof. life scis. Ariz. State U., Tempe, 2004—, co-dir. Ctr. Infectious Diseases and Vaccinology, Biodesign Inst., 2004—06, dir. Ctr. Infectious Diseases and Vaccinology, Biodesign Inst., 2007—, directorate mem. Biodesign Inst., 2007—09; hon. prof. East China U. Sci. & Tech., Shanghai, 2010—; dir. Ctr. Microbial Genetic Engring., 2011—. Mem. Ctr. Infectious Disease, Washington U., St. Louis; vis. prof. Inst. Venezolana de Investigaciones Científicas, 1969, U. P.R., 1972, U. Católica de Chile, 1973, U. Okla., 1982; recombinant DNA molecule program adv. com. NIH, 1974-77, genetic basis disease rev. com., 1979-83, chmn., 1981-83, vaccine study panel, 2001-04, chmn. bacterial biodefence rev. com., 2003-2004, Immune Def. Mechanisms, Mucosa Rev. Com., 2009-; genetic biology com. NSF, 1975-78; mem. diseases rsch. adv. bd. Midwest Regional Ctr. Excellence in Biodefense and Emerging Infections, 2003-05; mem. exec. com. Sch. Life Sci. Ariz. State U., 2005-07. Editor: Jour. Bacteriology, 1970-76, Infection and Immunity, 1985-92, Escherichia coli and Salmonella: Cellular and Molecular Biology, 1993-96, 2006-, exec. editor-in-chief, 2000-05, exec. editor, 2006—. Active Oak Ridge City Coun., 1969-72, Cystic Fibrosis Found., rsch. devel. program rev. com. 1981-89, Conf. Rsch. Workers on Animal Diseases, Heiser Found. Sci. Adv. Bd., 1996-2004; bd. dirs. Am. Type Culture Collection, 1989-99, presdl. adv., 2003—; bd. dirs. Whitfield Sch., 1997-2005, exec. com., 2002-2005; founder, dir. and sci. adv. MEGAN Health, Inc., 1992-2000, v.p. rsch., 1998-99, bd. govs. Ariz. Arts Sci. Tech. Acad., 2006-09; mem. Mo. Seed Capital Investment Bd., 2000-03. Recipient Sardinia Sci. award, 2003, Outstanding Alumni award Cornell U., 2009; named Mo. Inventor of Yr., 1997, Ariz. Biosci. Rschr. of Yr., 2007; Global Health grant, Bill & Melinda Gates Found., 2005-11. Fellow: AAAS, Acad. Sci. St. Louis, Am. Acad. Microbiology; mem.: NAS, Ariz. Arts, Sci. and Tech. Acad., Internat. Soc. Vaccines, World Health Orgn. (steering com. immunology of TB 1982—85), Coun. Advancement Sci. Writing (dir. 1976—82, v.p. 1978—82), N.Y. Acad. Scis., Am. Soc. Microbiology (parliamentarian 1970—75, dir. 1977—80, editl. bd. ASM News 1987—99, dir. 1989—94, 1999—2004), Soc. Gen. Microbiology, Internat. Soc. Mucosal Immunology, Am. Assn. Avian Pathologists, Genetics Soc. Am. (chmn. genetics stock ctrs. com. 1987—89), Gateway Strikers Soccer Club (pres. 1995—2001, chmn. bd. dirs. 2001—05, founder), Sigma Xi. Home: 6732 N Joshua Tree Ln Paradise Valley AZ 85253-3243 Office: CIDV The Biodesign Inst Ariz State U Tempe AZ 85287-5401

CURY, MARCELO S., physician; b. Brazil, Sept. 10, 1972; MD, U. Católica Pelotas, 1996; PhD, U. Fed. São Paulo, 2001. Endoscopist SCOPE, 2004. Mem.: SOBED, ESGE, ASGE. Office: Maracaju 1148 Campo Grande 79002212 Brazil Business E-Mail: mscury@uol.com.br.

CURZI-DASCALOVA, LILIA, neurophysiologist, researcher, consultant; b. Pavlikeni, Bulgaria, Oct. 3, 1935; arrived in France, 1967; m. Lucien Curzi, May 23, 1963; children: Catherine, Muriel. MD, Med. Sch. Sofia, Bulgaria, 1961, splty. neurology, 1967; PhD of Neurophysiology, U. Paris 6, 1971; DSc, U. Paris 12, 1976; Habilitation Rsch. Direction, U. Paris 5, 1987. Med. dr. State Ry. Soc., Bulgaria, 1961-64; resident Inst. Postgrad. Med. Tng., Sofia, 1961-67; med. dr. U. Hosp. Cochin, Paris, 1967-70; rsch. fellow Inst. Nat. Santé et de la Recherche Med., Paris, 1971-76; sr. rschr. INSERM, Paris, 1976—. Cons. Paris U. Hosp., 1980—; head rsch. staff U. Paris-INSERM, 1980—; bd. dirs. European club Sleep Rsch. in Infants and Children. Author: Manual of Methods for Recording and Analyzing Sleep-Wakefulness States in Preterm and Full-term Infants, 1996; co-editor: Sleep and Cardiorespiratory Control, 1991; contbr. critical revs. to Pediat. Rsch., Jour. EEG Clin. Neurophysiol., Sleep; contbr. sci. articles to profl. jours. Sci. grantee INSERM and corr. state rsch. direction, Belgium, Italy, Chile, The Netherlands, Brazil, Austria, Bulgaria, 1983—. Mem. European Neuroscis. Assn., European Sleep Rsch. Soc., Am. Sleep Rsch. Soc., Neonatal Soc. London. Avocations: fine arts, music, reading, mountains, bridge. Office: Hosp R Debré INSERM U676 48 bd Sérurier 75019 Paris France E-mail: lilia.curzi@wanadoo.fr.

CUSHING, GARY W., endocrinologist, educator; MD, U. Mass., 1980. Diplomate Am. Bd. Internal Medicine, 1983, Am. Bd. Internal Medicine-endocrinology, diabetes and metabolism, 1985, lic. Mass. Resident internal medicine St. Vincent Hosp., Worcester, Mass., 1981—83; fellow endocrinology Beth Israel Hosp., Boston, 1983—85, Harvard Med. Sch., 1985—86, clin. instr.; clin. assoc. prof. medicine Tufts Univ., Medford, Mass.; hosp. affiliation includes Lahey Clinic, 1988—. Office: Lahey Clinic Medical Center 41 Mall Rd Burlington MA 01805 Office Phone: 781-744-2088. Office Fax: 781-744-5348.

CUTLER, DAVID M., economics professor; b. 1965; BA in Economics, summa cum laude, Harvard U., 1987; PhD in Economics, MIT, 1991. Asst. prof. economics Harvard U., Cambridge, Mass., 1991—95, John L. Loeb assoc. prof. social sciences, 1995—97, prof. economics, 1997—2005, assoc. dean, faculty of arts & sciences, 2003—08, Otto Eckstein prof. applied economics, 2005—; sr. staff economist Coun. Econ. Advisers, Exec. Office of the Pres., 1993; dir. Nat. Econ. Coun., 1993; rsch. assoc. Nat. Bur. Econ. Rsch. Mem. govt. adv. panel NIH, Social Security Adminstrn., Health Care Fin. Adminstrn.; sci. adv. bd. Alliance for Aging Rsch.; bd. dirs. Nat. Acad. Social Ins. Editor: (jour.) Jour. Health Econ.; author: Your Money or Your Life: Strong Medicine for America's Health Care System, 2004. Recipient Outstanding Mentor award, Harvard U. Grad. Sch. Arts & Sciences, 1999, Griliches prize for best paper, Quarterly Jour. Economics, 1999, Kenneth Arrow award, 2000, Eugene Garfield award, Research!Am., 2003, John Eisenberg Mentoring award, Agy. Health Care Quality & Rsch., 2004, David Kershaw prize, Assn. Pub. Policy & Mgmt., 2004, Biennial award for Disting. Contribution to the Literature in Population, Am. Sociological Assn., 2006; named one of The "30 For The Future", Modern Healthcare mag., 2006, The 50 Most Influential Men Under Age 45, Details mag., 2007; fellow Ctr. Advanced Study in Behavioral Sciences, 2000—01. Fellow: Am. Acad. Arts & Scis., Employee Benefit Rsch. Inst.; mem.: NAS, Inst. Rsch. Poverty, Inst. Medicine, Phi Beta Kappa. Avocations: history, running, ultimate Frisbee, walking along the Charles River. Office: Harvard U Dept Economics Littauer Ctr 1875 Cambridge St Cambridge MA 02138 Office Phone: 617-496-5216. Office Fax: 617-495-7730. Business E-Mail: dcutler@fas.harvard.edu.

CUTLER, JONATHAN M., podiatrist; m. Hope Cutler; children: Jacob, Samuel. BA, Washington U., St. Louis, Mo.; MD, Dr. William M. Scholl coll. Podiatric Medicine, Chgo. Cert. Am. Bd. Podiatric Surgery, Foot Surgery. Surgical resident John Hopkins U., Liberty Med., Baltimore, Md.; podiatrist South Fla. Foot & Ankle Ctrs. Featured on Miracle Workers (ABC), 2006. Mem. exec. bd. Jewish Cmty. Ctr. West Palm Beach. Fellow: Am. Coll. Foot and Ankle Surgeons; mem.: Fla. Podiatric Med. Assn., Am. Podiatric Med. Assn. Avocations: golf, baseball. Office: South Fla Foot & Ankle Ctr 11412 Okeechobee Blvd Royal Palm Beach FL 33411 Office Phone: 561-793-6170.

CUTLER, KENNETH B., JR., dermatologist, educator; b. Sept. 12, 1968; m. Emmy L. Cotler, MD. BA in Econ., Amherst Coll., Mass., 1990; MD cum laude, SUNY, Bklyn., 1994. Intern Columbia Presbyn. Med. Ctr., NYC, 1994—97; resident in dermatology NY Med. Coll., Valhalla, NY, 1997—2000; pvt. practice Stamford, Conn., 2000—01; pres., owner Stamford Dermatology Cons. PC, 2001—08. Prof. dermatology NY Med. Coll., Valhalla, 2000—. Commr. pub. health City of Stamford, 2006—; active Nat. Rep. Congrl. Com., 2004—. Recipient Congl. Merit award, Nat. Rep. Congl. Com., 2006, Congl. medal Distinction, 2008; named Physician of Yr., Nat. Rep. Congl. Com., 2005; named one of America's Top Physicians, Nat. Consumer Rsch. Assn., 2004, 2007, 2008. Fellow: Am. Acad. Dermatology; mem.: AMA, Fairfield County Med. Assn., Conn. State Dermatology and Dermatologic Surgery Soc., Conn. State Med. Assn., Stamford C. of C., Nat. Eagle Scout Assn., Met. Club (NY), Alpha Omega Alpha. Home: 295 Rocky Rapids Rd Stamford CT 06903 Office Phone: 203-254-2292. Personal E-mail: cutlerk@aol.com.

CUTROPIA, JUAN CARLOS, surgeon, department chairman; b. Mendoza, Argentina, Feb. 25, 1940; s. Juan and Elsa (Zambrano) Cutropia. MD Nat. U. Cuyo, Mendoza, Argentina, 1966. Surgeon Hosp. Ctrl., Mendoza, Argentina, 1968—92, coord. residencies, 1993—96; surgeon Hosp. Espanol, Mendoza, 1968—, chief exptl. surgery, 1968—, head physician, 1984—92, chmn. dept. surgery, 1994—. Tng. asst. Sch. Medicine U. NC, Mendoza, Argentina, 1968—92, asst. prof., 1992—; vis. prof. Transplant Divsn. Carnegie Mellon U. Hosp., Pitts., 1987, rsch. fellow, 90. Author: (book) Liver Transplantation, 1991, Laproscopic Biliary Surgery, 1994. Named Leone D'Oro Medicine, Fonditalia, 2003, Gen. Jose San Martin, Mendoza Legislature, 2004. Mem.: Argentina Assn. Surgeons (Special Distinction 1970, Gold medal 1971), Am. Soc. Transplantation, Internat. Hapato Pancreatic Biliary Assn., Am. Soc. Transplant Surgeons (corr.). Office: Hosp Espanol de Mendoza Ave San Martin 965 5501 Mendoza Argentina Home: Calle Tiburcio Benegas 1494 M5502AHT Mendoza Argentina Office Fax: 54-261-4490382.

CUTTNER, JANET, hematologist, educator; b. NYC; d. William Robert and Ida Edith C. BA, NYU, 1953; MD, Med. Coll. of Pa., 1957. Diplomate Am. Bd. Internal Medicine, Am. Bd. Hematology. Intern, resident King's County Hosp., Bklyn., 1957-61; hematology fellow Mt. Sinai Med. Ctr., NYC, 1961-63, rsch. assoc. hematology, 1963-65, asst. prof. medicine, 1965-72, assoc. prof. medicine, 1972-86, prof. medicine, 1986—. Recipient Jacobi Medallion, Alumni Mt. Sinai Med. Ctr., 1999, Catherine Margaret Pasmantier award, NY Cancer Soc., 2007. Fellow N.Y. Acad. Scis.; mem. Am. Soc. Hematology, Am. Soc. Clin. Oncology, Am. Assn. for Cancer Rsch. Office: 1735 York Ave Ste P2 New York NY 10128 Office Phone: 212-860-9055.

CVJETKO, IVAN, vascular surgeon; b. Frankfur, Germany, Mar. 18, 1975; MD, Med. Sch., U. Zagreb, 1999. Gen. surgeon U. Hosp. Traumatology, 2001—07; vascular surgeon U. Hosp. Merkur, 2007. Recipient Outstanding Achievement award, Ann Arbor Bd. Edn., Dean's award, U. Zagreb, Med. Sch.; named Best Young Author, Croatian Soc. Atherosclerosis; AGA fellowship, Deutschsprachige Arbeitsgemeinschaft für Arthroskopie. Mem.: Croatian Soc. Vascular Surgery, Internat. Union Angiology, European Soc. Vascular Surgery. Office: Zajceva 19 Zagreb 10 000 Croatia Office Phone: 585/99/9888-525. Personal E-mail: ivancvjetko@yahoo.com.

CYNADER, MAX SIGMUND, neuroscience professor, researcher; b. Berlin, Feb. 24, 1947; arrived in Can., 1951; s. Samuel and Maria (Kraushar) C.; m. Ann Lynn Langford, Sept. 26, 2004; children: Madeleine Maria, Rebecca Kay, Alexandra Josephine. BSc, Mc Gill U., Montreal, Que., Can., 1967; PhD, MIT, 1972. Fellow neuroanatomy Max-Planck Inst. Psychiatry, Munich, 1972-73; asst. prof. psychology Dalhousie U., 1973-77, assoc. prof., 1977-81, assoc. prof. physiology, 1979-84, prof. psychology, 1981-84, Killam rsch. prof., 1984-88, prof. physiology, 1984-88; prof. psychology U. B.C., 1988—, prof. physiology, 1988—, prof. dept. ophthalmology, 1988—, dir., 1997—; dir. Brain Rsch. Ctr., U. B.C. and Vancouver Coastal Health, 1997; dir. Ctr. Brain Health, 2009. Mem. pres.'s workshop on five yr. plan strengthening sci. support in Can. Natural Scis. and Engring. Rsch. Coun. Can., 1984, workshop for Steacie fellows, 1988; mem. task force on curriculum devel. in Can. neurosci., 1984; mem. spl. adv. panel on rsch. preparedness USAF, 1985; rep. Internat. Human Frontiers Sci. program Med. Rsch. Coun. Can., 1988; mem. grants com. behavioural scis. Med. Rsch. Coun. Can., program grants com. 1989—; referee senate rev. grad. program in neurosci. U. Western Ont., 1989; mem. math., computational and theoretical spl. rev. com. NIMH, 1989—; external reviewer Med. Rsch. Coun. Can., Alta. Heritage Fund Med. Rsch., NIH, NSF, USAF Office Sci. Rsch., Multiple Sclerosis Soc. Can., Vancouver Found., March of Dimes, Fight for Sight; CRC chair in brain devel., 2001-08. Mem. editorial bd. jours. Behavioral Brain Rsch., Clin. Vision Scis., Concepts in Neurosci., Devel. Brain Rsch., Exptl. Brain Rsch., Neural Networks, Visual Neurosci.; mem. adv. bd. series Rsch. Notes in Neural Computing; contbr. articles to profl. jours. Recipient Killam Rsch. prize U. B.C., 1989—; E.W.R. Steacie fellow Natural Sci. and Engring. Rsch. Coun. Can., 1979, Can. Inst. Advanced Rsch. fellow, 1986—, Bank of Montreal fellow Can. Inst. for Advanced Rsch., 1998, BC Biotech award, 2007; grantee Med. Rsch. Coun. Can., 1973—, Natural Sci. and Engring. Rsch. Coun. Can., 1975—, NIH, 1978-81, Killam Rsch. Prof., 1984, B.C. Sci. & Tech. Champion, 2004; Order Brit. Columbia, 2008; Order of Can., 2009. Fellow Can. Inst. Advanced Rsch., Royal Soc. Can.; mem. Soc. Neurosci. (Halifax chpt., pres. 1985, edn. com. 1986-89), Can. Assn. Neurosci. (pres. 1986), Assn. Rsch. Otolaryngology, Assn. Rsch. in Vision and Opthalmology, Can. Physiol. Soc., Internat. Brain Rsch. Orgn., Internat. Soc. Devel. Neurosci., Internat. Strabismol. Assn., World Fedn. Neuroscientists, Can. Acad. health Svc.(elect-mem., 2006, Order of BC, 2007, inducted Order of Can., 2008) Achievements include being named semifinalist Can. Astronaut program, 1983. Office: U BC Vancouver Hosp Brain Rsch Ctr 2211 Wesbrook Mall Vancouver BC Canada V6T 2B5 Home Phone: 604-921-2418; Office Phone: 604-822-1388. Business E-Mail: cynader@brain.ubc.ca.

CYNTHIA, AYRES GUERRERO, medical educator; b. NJ, June 16, 1971; PhD, State U. NJ, Rutgers, 2002. Senate mem. State U. NJ, project dir., 2000, asst. prof., 2005—; rsch. scientist NJ Dept. Health and Sr. Svcs., 2002; cons. NJ. Assn. Health Plans, 2003; state dir., health sys. and collaborations Am. Cancer Soc., Eastern Divsn., 2003. Recipient Faculty Rsch. award, State U., Coll. Nursing, Hurdis M. Griffith Rsch. award, Faculty award, Kirby Found., award, Nat. Coalition of Ethnic and Minority Nurses. Mem.: Nat. Acads. Practice (nursing acad. mem.), NJ Commn. Cancer Joint Psychosocial and Nursing Adv. Group, NJ Commn. Cancer Breast Cancer Rsch. Adv. Group, NJ Comprehensive Cancer Control Evaluation Com. (Disting. Practitioner award). Office: 180 University Ave Ackerson Hall 228 Newark NJ 07102-1803 E-mail: cynthia.ayres@comcast.net.

CYPESS, AARON M., endocrinologist; m. Leah Suslovich, Sept. 18, 2005. AB, Princeton U.; PhD, Rockefeller U.; MD, Cornell U., 2000. Resident in internal medicine Beth Israel Deaconess Med. Ctr., Boston, fellow in endocrinology, diabetes and metabolism Beth Israel Deaconess Med. Ctr./Joslin Diabetes Ctr., Boston; rsch. assoc. Joslin Diabetes Ctr., Boston. Office: Joslin Diabetes Ctr 1 Joslin Pl Boston MA 02215 Office Phone: 617-732-2400.

CYPHER, RONALD L., obstetrician, gynecologist; m. Debbie Cypher; children: Heather, Kristin. Premedical tng., Westminster Coll.; completed gynecologic cancer studies, MD Anderson Hosp. and Tumor Inst.; MD, MCP Hahnemann U., Phila. Diplomate Am. Bd. Ob-Gyn. High risk obstetrics tng. Pa. Hosp., Phila.; resident ob-gyn. Western Pa. Hosp., Pitts., staff, Butler Meml. Hosp., Magee Women's Hosp. Bd. trustee Butler Meml. Hosp. Named one of Top Doc, Pitts. Mag. Fellow: Am. Coll. Obstetrics and Gynecologists; mem.: The Christian Med. and Dental Soc., Am. Fertility Soc. Avocations: tennis, photography. Office: Advanced OB/GYN Associates 901 E Brady St Butler PA 16001 Office Phone: 724-285-9200. Office Fax: 724-285-9288.

CYRIAC, SANJU, oncologist; b. Kottayam, Feb. 28, 1980; MD, Kasturba Med. Coll., 2007; DM, Cancer Inst., 2011. Resident Cancer Inst., 2007—11. Home: Pandarakalam Ettumanoor Kottayam Kerala 68631 India Personal E-mail: drsanpan80@yahoo.com.

CZACHOR, JOHN S., physician, educator; b. Port Chester, NY, Aug. 3, 1957; MD, Wright State U. Sch. Medicine, 1983. Prof. medicine, exec. vice chair clin. affairs, divsn. chief infectious diseases Wright State U. Boonschoft Sch. Medicine, 1989—. Recipient A. Robert Davies award, 1992, 1993, Outstanding Alumni award, Wright State U. Boonschoft Sch. Medicine Com., 2006. Fellow: ACP (Ohio Master Tchr. award 2003), Soc. Healthcare Epidemiology Am., Infectious Diseases Soc. Am.; mem.: Alpha Omega Alpha Med. Honor Soc., Phi Beta Delta Honor Soc. Avocations: golf, reading. Office: 128 East Apple St 2nd Fl Weber Bldg Dayton OH 45409 Office Fax: 937-208-2621. Business E-Mail: john.czachor@wright.edu.

CZECZUGA, BAZYLI, biologist, educator; b. Plutycze, Bialystok, Poland, Oct. 30, 1930; s. Jerzy and Anna (Popławska) C.; m. Ada Matusewicz, July 15, 1956. MSc, U. Minsk, Belarus, 1956. Asst. Med. Acad., Białystok, 1956-61, asst. prof., head biology dept., 1962-71, prof., head gen. biology dept., 1972—2001; prof. Białystok Sch. Econs., Białystok, 2002—06, Higher Sch. of Menegers, Białystok, 2005—. Expert Fed. Univ., Parana, Brazil, 1995. Contbr. numerous articles to profl. jours. Adviser U. Wales Icelandic Expedition, 1970; expert U. La Laguna, Canary Islands, 1983; chmn. Białystok Com. of Defenders of Peace; corres. Ctr. for Short Lived Phenomena, Smithsonian Inst., Washington, 1970-73. Recipient Gold Order of Merit, Order Polonia Restituta, 1988, Order of Merit Tchr., 1978; prize Polish Acad. Sci., 1975, 17 prizes Health Ministry. Mem. AAAS, Nat. Geographic Soc., Polish Bot. Soc., Polish Hydrobiol. Soc., Polish Parasitological Soc., Polish Natural Soc., Soc. Scientarum Bialostaocensis, Am. Soc. Photobiology, Belarus Acad. Scis., N.Y. Acad. Scis., Internat. Assn. Limnology, Internat. Assn. Ecology, Slavobaltiska Sallskapet Vid Lunds U. (hon., Sweden), Paleolimnological Working Group (Japan). Avocation: nature. Office: Med Acad Dept Gen Biology Kilinskiego 1 15-089 Białystok Poland Home: Ul. Szpitalna m 50 15-295 Białystok Poland Home Phone: 0-85-742-79-83; Office Phone: 0-85-748-54-83. Personal E-mail: bazzylio@poczta.onet.pl. Business E-Mail: czecz@umwb.edu.pl.

CZECZUGA-SEMENIUK, EWA, physician, researcher; b. Mińsk, Belarus, Apr. 13, 1957; d. Bazyli Czeczuga and Ada Matusewicz; m. Janusz Włodzimierz Semeniuk, Sept. 11, 1982; 1 child, Adrianna. Med. degree, Med. U., Białystok, Poland, 1982, PhD in Medicine, 1986. Jr. rschr., microbiology Med. U., Białystok, Poland, 1982—83, lectr., microbiology, 1983—85, lectr., gyn. dept., 1985—2003, sr. lectr., gyn. dept., 2003—05, sr. lectr. reproduction and gyn. endocrinology dept., 2005—. Contbr. articles to profl. jours. Recipient award

I, Med. U. Bialystok, 2000, 2006, Award II, 2005, 2010, Award III, 2008. Mem.: Polish Soc. Endocrinology, Polish Soc. Gynecology. Avocations: reading, gardening, classical music, cooking, nature. Office: Dept Reprodn and Gyn Endocrinology Skłodowska-Curie 24 A 15-276 Bialystok Poland Home: Ul. Legionowa 9/54 15-281 Bialystok Poland Personal E-mail: czeczuga@wp.pl.

CZEISLER, CHARLES ANDREW, neuroscientist, educator; b. Chgo., Nov. 7, 1952; s. Tibor and Victoria Wanda (Murzyn) Czeisler. AB in Biochemistry and Molecular Biology, magna cum laude, Harvard Coll., 1974; PhD in Neuro- and Bio-behavioral Scis., Stanford U., Calif., 1978, MD, 1981. Cert. Am. Bd. Sleep Medicine. Rsch. fellow Stanford U., 1974-75; rsch. assoc. in neurology Montefiore Hosp., Bronx, NY, 1976-78; rsch. assoc. in physiology Harvard Med. Sch., Boston, 1979-80, sr. rsch. fellow, Ctr. Health Policy & Mgmt., 1981-83, rsch. assoc. in medicine, 1982-83, asst. prof. medicine, 1983-87, assoc. prof., then prof., 1987—, dir. divsn. sleep medicine, 1997—, Frank Baldino, Jr., prof. sleep medicine, 2004—. Physician Brigham and Women's Hosp., Boston, 1982—, chief divsn. sleep medicine; Elliot David Weitzman lectr. Cornell Med. Coll., NYC, 1988; keynote spkr. Japanese Soc. Sleep Rsch., 1996, Assn. Profl. Sleep Societies, 1997, Patient Safety Rsch. Conf., Agy. Healthcare Rsch. & Quality, 2003, Com. Interns & Residents, 2005, X Internat. Congress, Brazilian Sleep Rsch. Soc., 2005, New Zealand Resident Doctors Assn. Profl. Conf. Safer Working Hours in Medicine, 2005; lectr. World Congress Chronobiology, Sapporo, Japan, 2003, Sanofi Aventis Internat. Forum Sleep Disorders, Paris, 2004, World Fedn. Sleep Rsch. & Sleep Medicine Societies, Australia, 2007. Co-author: REM Sleep: Its Temporal Distribution, 1980, Mathematical Models of the Circadian Sleep-Wake Cycle, 1994; contbr. articles to profl. jours. Recipient Robert R.J. Hilker award, Ctrl. States Occupl. Medicine Assn., 1991, E.H. Ahrens, Jr. Lecture award, Assn. Patient Oriented Rsch., 2002, Director's award, Nat. Inst. Occupl. Safety & Health, 2005, Healthy Sleep Cmty. award, Nat. Sleep Found., 2006, Lifetime Achievement award, 2008, J. Gerald Reves Duke Heart Ctr. Lecture award, Duke Med. Ctr., Durham, NC, 2007, Dorcas Cummings Meml. Lecture award, Cold Spring Harbor Lab., NY, 2007. Fellow: Royal Coll. Physicians, Assn. American Physicians, Acad. Behavioral Medicine Rsch., American Sleep Disorders Assn., American Soc. Clin. Investigation; mem.: AAAS, American Clin. & Climatological Assn., Inst. Medicine, Sleep Rsch. Soc. (Disting. Scientist award 2008), American Acad. Sleep Medicine (William C. Dement Academic Achievement award 2002), Soc. Rsch. Biological Rhythms (Aschoff's Rule 2001), American Physiol. Soc., Soc. Neuroscience, Internat. Soc. Chronobiology. Achievements include research focused on understanding the neurobiology of the human circadian pacemaker, located in the suprachiasmatic nucleus (SCN) of the hypothalamus, and its interaction with the sleep homeostat, and on applying that knowledge to clinical medicine and occupational health. Office: Brigham & Womans Hosp Divsn Sleep Medicine Rm 438A 221 Longwood Ave Boston MA 02115 E-mail: caczeisler@hms.harvard.edu. *

CZEKAJ, HANNA, medical educator; b. Lublin, Poland, July 9, 1955; DVM, U. Life Scis., 1979; PhD, Nat. Vet. Rsch. Inst., 1997. Asst. prof. Nat. Vet. Rsch. Inst., 1997—. Recipient award, Ministry Agrl. Mem.: Polish Soc. Vet. Scis., World Poultry Vet. Assn. Avocation: sailing. Office: Partyzantow 57 Pulawy Lublin 24-100 Poland Business E-Mail: h.czekaj@piwet.pulawy.pl.

CZERKINSKY, CECIL, immunologist, researcher; b. Algiers, France, Sept. 15, 1953; s. Gregori and Jacqueline (Millot) C.; m. Kari Elizabeth Jantzen (div. Oct. 1990); 1 child, Sofia Stefania; m. Anna-Lena Cyrene Karlsson (div. 1999); children: Karolina, Stefan; m. Julie Anne Weindling. DMD, Med. and Dental Sch., Lyon, France, 1980; MBH, Med. Sch., Lyon, France, 1980; PhD, DMS, Med. Sch., Göteborg, Sweden, 1987. Rsch. fellow Guy's Hosp., London, 1980-82, Inst. Med. Microbiology, Göteborg, 1982-84, assoc. prof., 1991—98; asst. prof. U. Ala., Birmingham, 1984-85; sr. investigator Swedish Med. Rsch. Coun., Sweden, 1986-90; rsch. dir. Nat. Inst. Med. Rsch., Lyon, France, 1992—98, dir. Nice, France, 2002—; dep. dir. gen. Internat. Vaccine Inst., Seoul, 2005—; prof., dept. biol. scis. Seoul Nat. U., 2006—. Affiliate prof. Coll. Veterinary Medicine, Seoul Nat. U., 2007—. Contbr. articles to profl. jours. Inventor of the Elispot, a method to measure immune responses. Office: Internat Vaccine Inst Kwanak-gu SNU Research Park 151-818 Seoul Republic of Korea Business E-Mail: cczerkinsky@ivi.int. E-mail: czerk@wanadoo.fr.

CZERNIAWSKI, AMANDA M., sociologist; BA, Princeton U., 2003; PhD, Columbia U., 2009. Asst. prof. Temple U., 2009—. Office: 738 Gladfelter Hall 1115 W Polett Walk Philadelphia PA 19122 Business E-Mail: aczernia@temple.edu.

CZERNICKI, JACEK, orthopedist, sports medicine physician; b. Piekary, Poland, July 25, 1957; s. Jan and Henryka Czernicki; m. Barbara Alexandra Skrzypek, June 12, 1981; 1 child, Michael. Grad., Silesian Med. U., Poland, 1982. Asst. Clinic Traumatology and Orthop., Poland, 1982—85, Clinic Dr. Muschinsky, Bad Lauterberg, Germany, 1986—87, Alpha Clinic, Munich, 1988—89, U. Munster, Brakel, Germany, 1989—90; pvt. practice Munich, 1991—. Co-founder German-Polish Orthopaedics Orgn., Germany, 1993—. Vol. J. Czernicki Found., Munich; disting. adv. Polish politics in Germany Polish Consulate, Munich. Mem.: Orthop. Union Germany. Roman Catholic. Achievements include invention of device for joint diagnosis, acoustic signals of moved joint analyzed and transformed in 3D animation of joint. Avocations: Karate (black belt), skiing, cross country skiing, squash. Office: Praxis J Czernicki Lindwurmstr 75 80337 Munich 80337 Germany Office Phone: 0049/89-532-523. E-mail: czernicki@t-online.de.

CZERNILOFSKY, ARMIN PETER, biochemist; b. Puchberg, Noe, Austria, Mar. 28, 1945; came to US, 1976; s. Josef and Paula (Gut) C.; m. Barbara Baker, 1982 (div. 1989); children: Daniel Josef, Felix David; m. U. Weyer, 1994. Univ. Dozent, PhD, U. Vienna, 1974-91. Biochemist U. Vienna, Austria, 1972-77; postdoctoral fellow, adj. asst. prof. U. Calif., San Francisco, 1976-77, 78-81; postdoctoral fellow U. Vienna, 1977-78; staff scientist Acad. Sci., Salzburg, Austria, 1981-82, Max Planck Soc., Köln, Federal Republic of Germany, 1982-87; cons. Cal-Bio and AGS, Calif., 1987-88; head external rsch. office Boehringer Ingelheim/Austria, Vienna, 1989—2004; founder PCz Consulting, Baden, Austria, 2004—. Prof. biochemistry Rheinisch-Westf. Tech. U., Aachen, Fed. Republic of Germany, 1986-87, pvt. dozent molecular biology, 1987—, dozent biochemistry, U. Vienna, 1991. Contbr. articles to profl. jours. on biochemistry and molecular biology. Rsch. grantee Am. Rsch. Fund, 1977, 81, Austrian Sci. Fund, 1981, European Community, 1986; fellow European Molecular Biology Orgn., 1973, 74-75, 81; recipient Honor award for Sci. and Arts The Körner Stiftung, 1974; grantee EU-Consortium. Mem. AAAS, NY Acad. Scis., Soc. Neurosci., Am. Microbiology Soc., Austrian Biochemistry Soc., German Cancer Soc. Office: PCz Consulting Klesheimstr 28 A 2500 Baden Austria Home Phone: 43225246717; Office Phone: 43664 4108498. Business E-Mail: armin.czernilofsky@aon.at.

CZERWINSKI, HENRYK MATEUSZ, internist; b. Krukienice, Poland, June 16, 1931; s. Kazimierz Casimir and Janina (Balkowska) C.; m. Jadwiga Piatek, Jan. 22, 1955; children: Marek, Ireneusz. MD, PhD, Med. Acad., Krakow, Poland, 1975. Cert. specialist I and II grade of internal medicine and lab. diagnostic, Silesian Acad. Medicine, 1954. Head Lab. Diagnostic Dept., Sanok, Poland, 1967-71; head internal medicine dept. Lesko Hosp., Poland, 1971-75, Sanok Hosp., Poland, 1975-97, emeritus, 1997—. Vice-dir. Hosp. and Internal Medicine Dept., Sanok, 1976-78. Author: Doctor's Epidemiologic, 1975; contbr. articles to profl. jours. Mem. bd. Polish League Environment Conservancy, Krosno, Polish Red Cross, vice chmn.; mem. Polish Lab. Diagnostic Assn., Sanok. Capt. Med. Res. Officer. Recipient Gold Cross of Merit, Knight of Order Poland, Gold Cross of Merit, Polish Red Cross, Gold Medal of Merit, Polish Environment Conservancy. Mem. Polish Acad. Scis. (bd. 1993—96), Commn. Pub. Health, Polish Med. Assn. (hon., mem. ctrl. presidim bd., 1999—, chmn. Carpathian region, Gloria Medicinae medal 1995, Bene Meritus badge 1999), NY Acad. Scis. Roman Catholic. Avocations: spending time in a lakeside cottage, listening to opera and symphonic music, reading books, swimming. Home: Ul. Mickiewicza 5 38-500 Sanok Krosno Poland E-mail: jzagaska@op.pl.

DAAR, ERIC STEVEN, medical educator; b. LA, Oct. 21, 1959; s. David and Thelma Daar; m. Judith Freedel Daar, Dec. 25, 1983; children: Evan, Jared, Adam, Ryan. BA, UCLA, 1981; MD, Georgetown U., Washington, 1985. Intern and resident Cedars-Sinai Med. Ctr., LA, 1985—88, fellow infectious diseases, 1988—91, dir. AIDS program, 1991—2001, chief infectious diseases, 1994—2000; prof. medicine David Geffen Sch. Medicine, UCLA, 2000—; chief divsn. HIV medicine Harbor-UCLA Med. Ctr., Torrance, Calif., 2001—. Contbr. numerous articles to profl. jours. Bd. dirs. LA Biomed. Rsch. Inst., 2001—. Grantee, NIH, State of Calif. Office: Harbor-UCLA Med Ctr 1124 W Carson St N24 Torrance CA 90502 Office Phone: 310-222-2467. Fax: 310-533-0447.

DABROW, SHARON, medical educator; b. Phila., Apr. 30, 1960; BA, U. Pa., 1981; MD, Boston U., 1985. With U. Fla, 1990—95; pediat. prof. U. South Fla, 1995—. Exec. bd. Fla. AAP, 2001, Cont. Clinic Rsch. Network APA, 2011; mentor APA Faculty Scholars Program, 2010. Fellow: AAP; mem.: AAPD, Acad. Pediatric Assn. Avocations: bicycling, reading, travel. Office: 2 Tampa General Cir 5th Fl Tampa FL 33606 Business E-Mail: sdabrow@health.usf.edu.

DABROWSKA-KUGACKA, ALICJA, medical educator; b. Gdynia, Poland, Oct. 24, 1966; MD, Med. U. Gdansk, 1991, PhD, 1998. Assoc. prof. Med. U. Gdansk, 2003—. Mem.: Polish Soc. Cardiology. Avocation: sailing. Office: Debinki 7 Gdansk 80-210 Poland Office Fax: 48586224910. Business E-Mail: alidab@gumed.edu.pl.

DACBERT-FRIESE, SHARYN VARHELY, social worker, evangelist; b. Utica, NY, Dec. 10, 1947; d. Henry Alexander Varhely and Elouise Fulmore; m. Thomas Jewett Mitchell III, Oct. 20, 1968 (div. Dec. 1982); children: Sharyn Mitchell, James Bailey Mitchell, Jaclyn Ashley Mitchell; m. Guenther Roland Friese, Dec. 16, 1998. BA, U. Ala., 1968; MSW, Our Lady of the Lake U., San Antonio, Tex., 1991. Lic. master social worker Advanced Clin. Practitioner, 1991, cert. clin. supr. 1998, LCSW 2003. Entrepreneur, Laredo, Tex., 1972—85; founder, owner Jacob's Well, Laredo, 1980—87; corp. v.p. Dacbert Music Co., San Antonio, 1992—94; psychotherapist individual and family Fuller & Assocs., San Antonio, 1991—94; pvt. practice San Antonio, 1994—; sr. pastor, founder, pres., chmn. Sheepgate Fellowship, San Antonio, 1997—; dir., founder, pres., chmn. Christian Family Counseling Ctr., San Antonio, 1997—. Radio personality, counselor Sta. KSLR-AM, San Antonio, 1997—2001; individual and family psychotherapist Adult Parent Child, San Antonio, 1991—92. Contbr. articles to profl. jours. Mem.: NASW, Nat. Assn. Bus. and Profl. Women, Am. Assn. Christian Counselors, Play Therapy Assn., Tuesday Musical Club. Avocations: painting, camping, drawing, cooking, quilting. Office: Christian Family Counseling Ctr 233 Carolina St San Antonio TX 78210 Office Phone: 210-426-2772.

DACEY, RALPH GERARD, JR., neurosurgeon, educator; b. Boston, Aug. 7, 1948; BA, Harvard U., 1970; MD, U. Va., Charlottesville, 1974. Diplomate Am. Bd. Internal Medicine, Am. Bd. Neurol. Surgery. Intern Strong Meml. Hosp., Rochester, NY, 1974—75, resident internal medicine, 1975—77; resident neurosurgery U. Va., Charlottesville, 1977—83; asst. prof. neurol. surgery U. Wash., Seattle; prof., chief divsn. neurosurgery U. NC, Chapel Hill; prof., chmn. dept. neurol. surgery Washington U. Sch. Medicine, St. Louis, 1989—, Henry G. & Edith R. Schwartz prof. Mem. adv. coun. Nat. Inst. Neurol. Disorders & Stroke, NIH, 2006—; neurosurgeon-in-chief Barnes-Jewish Hosp., St. Louis; neurosurgery cons. NFL St. Louis Rams, NHL St. Louis Blues, MLB St. Louis Cardinals. Mem. editl. bd. Contemporary Neurosurgery, Jour. Neurosurgery, Neurobiology of Disease, Neurosurgery, Perspectives in Neurol. Surgery; contbr. articles to profl. jours. Named one of America's Top Doctors, Castle Connolly Med. Ltd., 2002—08; named to Best Doctors in America, Best Doctors, Inc., 2002—10. Mem.: ACS, AMA, Inst. Medicine, Southern Neurosurgical Soc., Am. Bd. Neurol. Surgery (bd. dirs. 1999—, chmn. 2004—05), Neurosurgical Soc. America, Congress Neurol. Surgeons (pres. 1995), American Heart Assn., American Surg. Assn., American Assn. Neurol. Surgeons (dir.-at-large 2002—), Soc. Univ. Surgeons, Soc. Neurol. Surgeons (Grass award 2003), Rsch. Soc. Neurol. Surgeons, American Acad. Neurol. Surgery. Achievements include development of a device that uses magnets to guide surgical instruments through the brain, performing the first human magnetic surgery in 1998; a patent for methods of and materials for treating vascular defects with magnetically controllable hydrogels. Office: Washington U Sch Medicine Dept Neurol Surgery 660 S Euclid Ave Campus Box 8057 Saint Louis MO 63110 E-mail: dacey@wustl.edu. *

DACORONIAS, DIMITRI, physician, researcher; b. Rome, May 26, 1956; s. Antonio Dimitri and Adele (Guerrini) D. MBChB, State Med. Sch., Rome, 1982, diploma in vascular surgery, 1987. Asst. biomed. rschr. Coun. Nat. Rsch., Rome, 1978-79; intern State Med. Sch., Rome, 1979-82; house surgeon Addolorata Hosp., Rome, 1982-87; physician Italian NHS, Rome, 1986-87, asst. pub. medicine, 1988; clin. monitor, proj. team leader, clin. supr. Bracco Spa, Milan, 1988-2000; med. affairs mgr. CVS Drugs Chiesi Group, Parma, 2000—; head clin. rsch. cardiovasc. and metabolism drugs, project coord. Chiesi Spa, Parma, 2000—. Vis. tchr. G.P. Assn., Rome, 1986-87; vis. prof. Med. Sch., Rome, 1996; prof. faculty pharmacy U. Parma. With Italian Mil., 1982—83. Fellow Internat. Coll. Angiology, Royal Coll. Physicians (faculty pharm. medicine); mem. Ordine Dei Medici, Am. Heart Assn. Avocations: golf, sailing, bridge. Office: Chiesi Group R&D Divsn Palermo 26/A 43100 Parma Italy Home: Piazza Bainsizza 10 195 Rome RM Italy Home Phone: 39-3471441648. Personal E-mail: dimitri.dacoronias@virgilio.it. Business E-Mail: d.dacoronias@chiesigroup.com.

DA CUNHA, ELAINE FONTES FERREIRA, chemist, researcher; d. Izaias Ferreira and Sebastiana Fontes Ferreira da Cunha; m. Teodorico de Castro Ramalho, Oct. 13, 2000; 1 child, Ana Sophia da Cunha Ramalho. BSc, U. Brasília, 1999; MSc, U. Fed. Rio de janeiro, 2002; DSc with honors, U. Fed. Rio de Janeiro, 2005. Vis. rschr. German Acad. Exch., 2004. Singer Bapt. Ch., Rio de Janeiro, 1992—2005. Scholar, Ministery Sci. and Tech., 1996. Mem.: Brazilian Chem. Soc. (assoc.). Achievements include patents for Serine Protease Inhibitor (treatment of flavirisose): design, synthesis and biological application; design of new and more selective drugs against Mycobacterium tuberculosis; development of structure-reactivity, structure-property relationships and theoretical studies; a new molecular descriptor denominated LIV. Avocations: music, swimming, art. Home: Sqs Quadra 407 Bloco M 70256-130 Brasilia DF Brazil E-mail: effcid@dacafe.com.

DADA, RIMA, medical educator, researcher; b. New Delhi, July 8, 1968; d. Vijay Kumar and Kamlesh Dada; m. S. Vijay Rao. MBBS, MAMC, New Delhi, 1992; MD, UCMS, New Delhi, 1996; PhD, AIIMS, New Delhi, 2003; MAMS, DNB, New Delhi, 2007. Task Force mem. ICMR, New Delhi, 2001—, bd. mem., 2001—; sr. resident AIIMS, 1996—98, rsch. assoc., 1998—2001, asst. prof., 2001—05, assoc. prof., 2005—. Contbr. scientific papers to profl. jours. (Young Scientist award, 2003). Recipient G. P. Talwar Gold Medal, Indian Soc. Rsch. Reproduction, New Delhi, 2007. Mem.: Asian Soc. Andrology, Indian Soc. Human Genetics. Avocations: tennis, music, meditation, reading, gardening. Office: All India Inst Med Sci Ansari Nagar New Delhi 110029 India

D'ADAMO, DAVID RALEIGH, physician; b. NYC, June 2, 1966; BS, Yale U., New Haven, 1988; MD, NYU, PhD, 1997. Attending physician Meml. Sloan Kettering Cancer Ctr., 2003—. Med. Scientist Tng. Program fellow, NIH. Mem.: AMA, Connective Tissue Oncology Soc., Am. Soc. Clin. Oncology. Avocation: running. Office: 1275 York Ave New York NY 10021 Office Fax: 212-639-4802. Business E-Mail: dadamod@mskcc.org.

DADMARZ, KEWMARS EBRAHIM, physician, educator; b. Tehran, Iran, Mar. 13, 1928; s. Ebrahim and Nosrat (Hooshyar) D.; m. Lili Azmoudeh; children: Mitra, Ali. MD, U. Tehran, 1955. Diplomate Am. Bd. Surgery, Am. Bd. Disability Analysts. Intern Nashville Gen. Hosp., 1955—56, resident in surgery, 1956—57; resident in gen. surgery Meharry Med. Coll., Nashville, 1957—62; resident in cancer surgery Meml. Ctr. Cancer and Allied Diseases, NYC, 1960-61; resident in thoracic and cardiovascular surgery U. Alta., Edmonton, Canada, 1962-64, fellow in surg. pathology, 1964-65; staff surgeon Wilmington (Del.) VA Med. Ctr.; ret.; assoc. prof. surgery, former chief dept. thoracic surgery U. Tehran; instr. surgery Thomas Jefferson U. Fellow ACS; mem. Assn. Iranian Surgeons, Matthew Walker Surg. Soc. Home and Office: 7 Stabler Cir Wilmington DE 19807 Office Phone: 302-691-5179. Personal E-mail: kewmars@comcast.net.

DADYAN, TAHEREH MITRA, pharmacist; b. Iran, Sept. 14, 1966; PharmD, USP, 1999. Clin. pharmacist Baylor U. Med. Ctr., 2000—10, clin. coord. cardiology, critical care, 2010—. Mem.: ACCP. Home: 2628 Timber Hill Dr Flower Mound TX 75028 Business E-Mail: mitrad@baylorhealth.edu.

DAE, MICHAEL W., cardiologist, medical educator, researcher; BS, NC State U., 1972; MD, Duke U., 1976; MBA, U. San Francisco, 1998. Assoc. prof. U. Calif., prof. radiology medicine, sr. mem. cardiovasc. rsch. inst., 1995—. Cons. chief med. officer Radiant Med., Redwood City, Calif., 1998—. Fellow: Am. Coll. Cardiology. Office: Univ Calif San Francisco 185 Berry St Ste 350 San Francisco CA 94107

DAEGU, SON, plastic surgeon, educator; b. Gyeongju, Aug. 14, 1963; MD, Keimyung U., 1988; PhD, Kyungpook Nat. U., 2002. Rsch. fellowship U. Tex. MD Anderson Cancer Ctr., 2002—03; dir., dept. plastic surgery, Dongsan Med. Ctr. Keimyung U., 2004, assoc. prof., dept. plastic surgery, Sch. Medicine, 2004—09, prof., dept. plastic surgery, 2010—. Mem.: Korean Soc. Hand Surgery (Academic award 2009), Korean Microsurg. Soc., Plastic Surgery Rsch. Coun., Am. Soc. Plastic Surgeon, Korean Soc. Plastic and Reconstructive Surgeons (Academic award 2009). Avocation: music. Office: 194 Dongsan-Dong Daegu 700-712 Republic of Korea Office Fax: 82-53-255-0632. Business E-Mail: handson@dsmc.or.kr.

DAE KEUN, KIM, pharmacist, educator, researcher, dean; b. Jeonju, Republic of Korea, Feb. 10, 1962; s. Kim Hyeong Bong and Kim Ye Sik; m. Hwang Eun Sook, Feb. 23, 1992; children: Kim Geun Ho, Kim Jeong Won. PhD in Pharmacy, SungKyunKwan U., Suwon, Gyeonggi, Republic of Korea, 1997. Lic. pharmacist Ministry Health & Welfare, Seoul, 1987. Chief Coll. Pharmacy, Woosuk U., Wanju, Jeonbuk, Republic of Korea, 1997—99, dean, 2002—, assoc. prof., 2003—. Com. Ctrl. Pharm. Affairs Coun., Eunpyung Gu, Seoul, Republic of Korea, 2003—; with Korea Food and Drug Adminstrn., Eunpyung Gu, Seoul, Republic of Korea. Avocations: mountain climbing, fishing. Office: Coll Pharmacy Woosuk Univ 490 Samrye 565-701 Republic of Korea E-mail: dkkim@woosuk.ac.kr.

DAGENHART, BETTY JANE MAHAFFEY, nursing educator, administrator; b. Welch, W.Va. d. Charley F. and Edith L. (Lucas) Mahaffey; divorced; 1 child, Cynthia Leigh. BA in Health Care Adminstrn., Mary Baldwin, Staunton, Va., 1991; postgrad., St. Joseph's Coll. Cert. nursing adminstr., ANA, nurse examiner Va., elder care coord., U. Fla., 2010. Nurse mgr. ortho. and emergency svcs. Cmty. Hosp. of Roanoke (Va.) Valley, Va., 1967-77; asst. dir. nursing svc. Cmty. Hosp. of Roanoke Valley, Va., 1977-83, coord. quality mgmt., dir. occupl. health svcs., dir. emergency svc. Va., 1983-92, dir. med./surg. nursing Va., 1992-94; dir. nursing edn. City of Salem Sch. Sys., Va., 1994—; dir. med. office asst. program Dominion Coll., Roanoke, 1997; dir. Nurses Dean Allied Health ECPI Med. Cariers Coll., Roanoke, 2003—07; dir. med. program Miller-Molle Tech. Coll., Roanoke, 2007—. Mem. disaster planning coun. City of Roanoke, 1980-90, pre-hosp. care providers, 1982-88, chmn. pers. com.; organized free standing clinic Cmty. Hosp. Roanoke, 1986; dir. med. program Miller Motte Tech. Coll., Roanoke, Va. Bd. dirs. Emergency Med. Svcs. Western Va., 1979-92, Citizens Coalition Responsible Healthcare Inc.; mem. pers. com. Cave Spring Bapt. Ch., Roanoke, 1991-92, fin. com.; pres. Homeplace Homeowners Assn., Salem, Va., com. mem. Tabernacle Bapt. Ch., bd. dir. Citizens Coalition Responsible Healthcare, nurse examiner Naces Plus Found. Svc., elder care coord. King Law Group Mem. ANA, Va. Orgn. Nurse Execs., Exec. Females, Health Occupation Educators, Accrediting Coun. Ind. Colls. and Univs. (accreditation team). Avocations: golf, walking, cooking, dance. Home: 139 Ferrum Drive Salem VA 24153 Office: Miller-Motte Technical Coll 4444 Electric Rd Roanoke VA 24018

DAGGETT, WILLARD M., medical educator, cardiac surgeon, consultant; b. LaCrosse, Wis., June 13, 1933; s. Willard M. and Vida Sherman Daggett; m. Rosemary H. Howard, Sept. 9, 1989; children: Susan E., Emily E., Willard M. Daggett III, Mary P. Brown; m. Margaret Taylor, Aug. 25, 1956 (div.). AB, U. Calif., Berkeley, 1954; MD, 1958; MA (hon.), Harvard U., Cambridge, Mass., 1991. Cert. Am. Bd. Surgery, 1968, Am. Bd. Thoracic Surgery, 1969. Prof. surgery Harvard Med. Sch., Boston, 1978—2000, prof. surgery emeritus, 2000—; vis. surgeon Mass. Gen. Hosp., Boston, 1980—2000, sr. surgeon, 2000—. Cons. Guidant Cardiac Surgery, Santa Clara, Calif., 2000—03. Contbr. scientific papers to profl. jours. including cardiac surgery. Surgeon US Pub. Health Svc., 1963—64, NIH. Recipient Young Investigator award, Am. Coll. Cardiology, 1965; named Established Investigator, Am. Heart Assoc., 1970; Fellow, Am. Surg. Assn., 1970. Fellow: Am. Assn. Thoracic Surgery (com. on ethics 1990—91). Avocations: fly fishing, hunting, swimming, skiing. Office: Massachusetts General Hosp 55 Fruit St Cox Bldg 656 Boston MA 02114 Office Phone: 617-726-8840. Office Fax: 617-726-5804; Home Fax: 508-785-9049. Personal E-mail: wmdcardsurg@aol.com. Business E-Mail: wdaggett@partners.org.

DAGHIO, MARIA MONICA, communications expert, methodologist, medical educator, consultant; b. Mirandola, Italy, Nov. 14, 1960; d. Bruno Daghio and Vittoria Chiozzini. B in social work, Cath. U., 1984, degree in religious Scis., 1990; degree in Philosophy, Federico II State U., 2000; M in Edn. Mgmt., State U. and C. of C., 2002; degree in Comm. sci. and Pub. Health, 2004. Tchr. Pub. H.S., Meta di Sorrento, Italy, 1984—99; educator and methodologist Local Health Unit, Azienda USL, Modena, Italy, 1999—. Cons. health edn. Ministry of Edn., Meta di Sorrento, Italy, 1991—99; directorship Ednl. Lab. for Citizen Empowerment, Local Health Unit, Modena, Italy, 1999—; adv. bd. of the local health plan Local Health Unit, Modena, Italy; adv. bd. of the alliance between patients associations and sci. societies program Outcome Rsch. Unit, Mario Negri Inst., Milan, 2003—; cons. Continuing Med. Edn. at the Local Health Unit, Modena, 2000—. Contbr. articles to profl. jours., chapters to books. Directorship Ednl. sch. for exec. cadres voluntary orgns., Vico Equense, Naples, Italy, 1990—93; adv. bd. and coord. Internat. Volunteers Edn. Non Govt. Org., Naples, Italy, 1987—94. Mem.: Italian Educator Assn. (assoc.). Achievements include development of health literacy promotion; public health services improvement through citizens involvement. Avocations: painting, reading, music, theater. Office: Local Health Unit Azienda USL Viale Muratori 201 Modena 41100 Italy E-mail: m.daghio@ausl.mo.it.

DAGILAS, AGGELOS, physician, consultant; b. Thessaloniki, Greece, Nov. 22, 1952; s. Dimitrios and Eleni Dagilas; m. Eleni Markovitis, July 30, 1977; 1 child, Antonia. Med. degree, Aristotelian U., Greece, 1977. Specialist registrar Papanikolau Hosp., Thessaloniki, Greece, 1986—89, sr. specialist registrar, 1989—98, cons. in neurotology, 1998—, mem. sci. coun., 2002—. Sec. ENT Assn. No. Greece, Thessaloniki, 1991—99; v.p. Greek ENT Assn., Athens, 1997—99. Author: (book) Acoustic Evoked Potential, Clinical Audiology, (booklet) Diagnosis of Auditory Problems in Paediatric Patients. Mem. coun. responsible for human activities of people with spl. needs Ministry of Health, Athens, 1996—99; rschr. program protection against noise European Commn., Thessaloniki, Greece; tchr. program social rehab. of people with needs Sch. Philosophy, Aristotelian U. Thessaloniki, 1997—98. Squadron leader, med. doctor Airforce, 1978—80, Greece. Office: Papanikolau Hosp Exohi Thessaloniki 570 10 Greece Home: Selefkou Pylea 6 555 35 Thessaloniki Greece Office Fax: 0030 2310 350310; Home Fax: 0030 2310 203538. Personal E-mail: adagilas@hol.gr.

DAGLAS, MARIA, academic midwife; b. Athens, Greece, Aug. 19, 1976; Degree in Midwifery, Technol. Ednl. Inst. Athens, 2002; MSc in Bioethics, U. Crete, 2007; MSc in Pub. Health, Nat. Sch. Pub. Health, 2009. Clin. lectr., midwifery Dept. Midwifery Technol. Ednl. Inst. Athens, 2003—10, lectr., midwifery, 2010—; midwife Mitera Midwifery and Surg. Ctr., 2004; pvt. practice, 2006—10; dir., clin. svcs. Day Ctr. Womens Mental Health Care Postnatal Disorder, 2008. Founding mem., pres. NGO Fainareti, 2006. Mem.: NGO Friends Breastfeeding, Greek Assn. Midwives. Home: Paradeisou 38 Athens Nea Smyrni 17123 Greece Home Fax: 0030-2109319056. Personal E-mail: daglam@fks.uoc.gr.

DAGOGO-JACK, SAMUEL E., physician, educator, endocrinologist; b. Nigeria, 1954; came to U.S., 1990; s. Karibi Jim and Titt. D.-J.; m. Agbani D.-J.; children: Karibi, Ibi, Alali, Tari. MBBS, Ibadan U., Nigeria, 1978, MD, 1994; MSc, Newcastle U., Eng., 1988. Diplomate Am. Bd. Internal Medicine, Am. Bd. Endocrinology, Am. Bd. Diabetes and Metabolism. Rsch. assoc. U. Newcastle Upon Tyne (U.K.), 1983—85; cons. physician U. Port Harcourt (Nigeria), 1985—89; chief resident endocrinologist King Faisal Specialist Hosp., Riyadh, Saudi Arabia, 1989—90; from rsch. fellow to assoc. prof. medicine Washington U. Sch. Medicine, St. Louis, 1990—2000; assoc. chief internal medicine svc. Barnes-Jewish Hosp., St. Louis, 1996—2000; prof. medicine, endocrinology, diabetes and metabolism, prof. physiology and biophysics, dir. diabetes programs U. Miss. Med. Ctr., Jackson, 2000—01; dir. minority health rsch. Montgomery VAMC, Jackson, 2000—01; prof. medicine, endocrinology, diabetes and metabolism U. Tenn. Coll. Medicine, Memphis, 2001—, dir. endocrinology fellowship tng. program, dir. divsn. endocrinology, diabetes & metabolism, 2009—; assoc. dir. Gen. Clin. Rsch. Ctr., 2001—, A.C. Mulling Endowed chair transational rsch., 2009—; prin. investigator DCCT/EDIC NIH Diabetes Rsch. Study, 2001—. Endocrinology and diabetes grant rev. study sect. NIH, 2000-04, chair NIH spl. emphasis panel grants rev. study sect., 2004—; Todd Brown Disting. Heritage lectr. Meharry Med. Sch., Nashville, Tenn., 2003, 07; Beverly Towery vis. prof. U. Louisville, 2004; Charles Drew vis. prof. Charles Drew U. Sci. and Medicine, 2000; extra-mural rschr. diabetes drugs devel. programs for pharm. cos.; chair Excellence Diabetes Mgmt. Symposium, 1998-99, 2002; dir. sophomore endocrine pathophysiology course U. Tenn., 2002—; Kroc vis. prof. Ohio State U., 2011; ad-hoc reviewer of grants and manuscripts in field; lectr. in field. Author: The Diabetes Guide, 1992; (with others) The Washington Manual, 2002, The Uncomplicated Guide to Diabetes Complications, 1999, Multicultural Medicine and Health Disparities, 2005, Diabetes and Nutrition, 2005, Clinical Diabetes, 2006, Medications and Diabetes Risk, 2010-; assoc. editor: Diabetes Care Jour., 2006—; mem. editl. bd. Kuwait Med. Jour., 1995-98, Current Drug Targets, 2000—, Cardiology Spl. Edit., 2001—06, Jour. of Clin. Endocrinology and Metabolism, 2004—, Medicinal Chemistry, 2004—, Cardiology Quarterly, 2006—; contbr. articles to profl. jours. Diabetes Rsch. and Tng. Ctr. grantee, 1999—; recipient Young Investigator Travel award Internat. Soc. Endocrinology, 1987, Outstanding Tchr. of Yr. award U. Tenn., 2004. Fellow ACP (co-dir. workshop urban health 1998), Royal Coll. Physicians London, Am. Coll. Endocrinology (Distinction in Clin. Endocrinology award 2008); mem. Nat. Med. Assn. (Meritorious Achievement award 2009), Am. Diabetes Assn. (sec. St. Louis chpt. 1997-98, pres. 1998-00, sci. and med. adv. grp., rsch. fellow 1990-91, Clin. Rsch. award 1997-2000), Endocrine Soc., Am. Fedn. for Med. Rsch., Southern Soc. Clin. Investigation, Am. Assn. Clin. Endocrinologists, Alpha Omega Alpha. Office: U Tenn Coll Medicine Dept Med Endocrinology 920 Madison Ave Memphis TN 38163 Business E-Mail: sdagogojack@utmem.edu.

D'AGOSTINO, RALPH BENEDICT, mathematician, statistician, educator, consultant; b. Somerville, Mass., Aug. 16, 1940; s. Bennedetto and Carmela (Piemonte) D'A.; m. Lei Lanie Carta, Aug. 28, 1965; children: Ralph Benedict, Lei Lanie Maria. AB, Boston U., 1962, MA, 1964; PhD, Harvard U., 1968. Lectr. math. Boston U., 1964-68, asst. prof., 1968-71, assoc. prof., 1971-76, lectr. law, 1975-91, assoc. dean Grad. Sch., 1976-78, prof. math. and stats., 1976—, prof. pub. health, 1982—, dir. data analysis and stats. Framingham Heart Study, 1985—, chmn. dept. math., 1986-91, 2006—11, dir. stats. cons. unit, 1986—, dir. Biostats MA/PhD Program, 1988—, prof. law, 1991—; adj. prof. Tufts U., 2004—; sr. rschr. scientist Forsyth Inst., 1992—. Mem. clin. care rsch. Tufts U., 1990—; exec. dir. data mgmt. and biostats. Harvard Clin. Rsch. Inst., 2002—; vis. lectr. Am. Statis. Assn., 1975-86, 88-92; vis. prof. biostats. clin. epidiology unit Univ. Hosp., Geneva, 1993; Rankin vis. prof. U. Wis., 1995; spl. lectr. clin. trials symposium U. Fla., 1995; spl. lectr. U. Mo., 2000, Johnson & Johnson, 2007; vis. scientist NHLBI, 1993; Lowell Reed lectr. APHA, 1996; Remington lectr. AHA CV-EPI, 2006; spl. scientist Boston City Hosp., 1981-95, Boston Med. Ctr., 1996—, New Eng. Med. Ctr., Tufts Med. Sch., 1990—; mem. Health Inst. New Eng. Med. Ctr., 1990—; cons. stats. United Brands, 1968-76, Diabetes and Arthritis Control Unit, Boston, 1971-75, City of Somerville, Mass., 1972, ednl. Harvard U. Dental Sch., 1969, Lahey Clinic Found., 1973-85, Walden Rsch., 1974-79, FDA Biometrics Divsn. and Over-the-Counter Divsn., 1975—, FBI cons. social sci. unit 1982, Cardio and Renal Divsn. FDA, 1987—, Gastrointestinal Drug Divsn., FDA, 1994-96, Medical Devise Divsn. 1999—, Oncology Drugs Divsn., 2002—, Arnold & Porter, 1980, Bedford Rsch. Assn., 1976-81, Corneal Scis., 1976, Biotek, 1979-88, GCA, 1979-87, Lever Bros., 1982-87, Conrail, 1981, FBI, 1984, Ctr. Psychiat. Rehab., Boston U., 1985-2001, 2006-, NIMH, 1985, Dade Clin. Assays, 1986-90, Millipore, 1983-92, VLI Corp., 1985-90, New Eng. Coll. Optometry, 1985-93, Dupont Corp., 1985, Bristol Myers, 1986, 93, Cheeseborough Ponds, 1987-96, med. decision making divsn. and health svcs. rsch. unit Tufts New Eng. Med. Ctr., 1986—, Am. Inst. Rsch. in Social Scis., 1983-88, New Eng. Rsch. Insts., 1987-92, Thompson Med., 1987-96, Merck, Sharpe and Dohme, 1988-94, Carter Ctr., Emory U., 1969-75, Unilever, 1991-96, 99-, Miles, 1991-95, Ultra Fem., 1991-93, Health Effects Inst., 1992-2001, Forsyth Dental Clinic, 1992-93, 95-2007, Bard Vascular, 1990-95, Ultra Slim Fast, 1990-95, Block Med., 1993-95, Bayer Pharm., 1993-98, 2004-, Astra Pharm., 1993-97, Cytyc, 1993-97, Regua, 1994-96, SmithKline Beechman, 1994-95, Proctor and Gamble, 1994-96, 2000—09, Sandoz, 1994-96, R W Johnson Pharms., 1997, Mass. Med. Assistance, 1995-97, Cambridge Heart, 1996—2000, Merck/ Johnson & Johnson, 1999—2007, Aventis, 2000—, Ajinomoto, 2000, Discovery Lab, 2000—, Genzyme, 2000-, Pfizer, 2000-06, Vertex, 2005-, Gentium, 2005-, Sanofi, 2004-; mem. various FDA coms. including fertility and maternal health drugs adv. com, 1978-81, life support subcom., 1979-81, drug abuse adv. com., 1987-90, gastrointestinal drugs adv. com., 1990-94, nonprescriptive drug adv. com., 1995-99, 2007-08, chair, 1996-98, with dental plague & oral health com, 1997-2000; cons. various FDA coms., Cardio-Renal com., 1995-, arthritis com., 1997-, ob-gyn. devices, 2002-, oncological drugs com., 2004-, anti-infective drugs com., 2008-, OB/GYN Device Com., 2000-, Respiratory Devices Com., 2009-, anesthetas & respiratory drugs, 2009, Genetic Devices, 2011-, Cell Biologies, 2011-; mem. task force on design and analysis of dental and oral rsch., 1979-2003, Harvard U. health tech. com., 1986-90; mem. Honolulu Heart Study Adv. Com., NIH, 1989-96, Balt. Longitudinal Study of Aging Adv. Com., 1990, NIH Consensus Panel on Liver Transplantation, 1983, Consensus Panel on Fresh Frozen Plasma, 1984, Consensus Panel on Geriatric Assessment Methods for Clin. Decision Making, 1987; mem. task force Office Tech. Assessment, 1980; mem. consensus panel on intraoral techniques ADA, 1990; mem. study sect. Agy. for Health Care Policy and Rsch., 1990-94; mem. Bethesda Conf. on Matching Intensity of Risk Factor Mgmt. With the Hazard for Coronary Disease Events, 1996, chair data safety monitoring com., Bayer Arrive Study, 2005-, mem. NIH, CVD Risk Assesment Work Group and Integrative, CVD Risk Panel, 2007-, Inst. Medicine Missing Data In Clinical Trial Panel, 2009; prin., co-prin. investigator or sr. statistician on grants Nat. Ctr. Health Svcs. Rsch., 1976-82, NHLBI, 1982—, USAF, 1980-85, Nat. Cancer Inst., 1985—, Nat. Inst. Criminal Justice, 1982-85, Nat. Ctr. Child Abuse and Neglect, 1982-85, Robert Wood Johnson Found., 1981-85, Social Security Adminstrn., 1982-86, 90-93, Motor Vehicles Mem. Assn., 1987, NIOSH, 1985, Nat. Insts. Aging, 1986—, Agency for Health Care Policy and Rsch., 1989-2000; grant and contract reviewer NAS, 1979—, Nat.Ctr. Health Svcs.Rsch.,1976, 89, NIH, 1983—, NSF, 1987-95, AHCPR, 1990; co-prin. investigator Framingham Heart Study, 1993-; chair spl. emphasis panel reviewing small bus. grant proposal Nat. Inst. Dental Rsch., 1996. Author: (with E.E. Cureton) Factor Analysis, An Applied Approach, Erlbaum Pub., 1983, (with Shuman and Wolf) Mathematical Modeling, Applications in Emergency Health Services, Hawthorne Pub., 1984, (with Stephens) Goodness of Fit Techniques, C. M. Dekker Pub., 1986, (with D. Schiff) Practical Engineering Statistics, Wiley Pub., 1996, (with Sullivan and Beiser) Introductory Applied Biostatistics, Thompson Pub., 2004, Tutorials in Biostatistics, Wiley Pub., 2005, Pharmaceutial Statistics using SAS, 2008, (with I. Graham) Therapeutic Strategies in Cardiovascular Risk, 2008; assoc. editor Am. Statistician, 1972-76, Jour. Am. Statis. Assn., 1993-96; editor Emergency Health Svc. Rev., 1981-88, Stats. in Medicine (biostat. tutorials), 1993—, Stats. in Medicine, 1997—; mem. editl. bd. Biostatistica, 1990-99, Jour. Hypertension, 2004—09; cons. Jour. New Eng. Medicine, 2007-; editor (with L. Sullivan and J. M. Massaro) Encyclopedia of CLinical Trials, 2007; book reviewer Houghton-Mifflin, Holden, Day, Duxbury Press, Prentice Hall, 1969; contbr. over 600 articles to profl. jours. Recipient Spl. citation FDA Commr., 1981, 95, Metcalf awrd for excellence in teaching Boston U., 1985; Am. Heart Assn. fellow, 1991; pre-doctoral fellow NIH, 1962-68. Fellow Am. Statis. Assn. (pres. Boston chpt. 1972, v.p. 1971, mem. nat. coun. 1973-75, vis. lectr. 1976-78, 80—, Statistician of Yr. Boston chpt. 1993, chmn. sect. Health Policy Stats. 1996, chmn. sect. Epidemiology 2003); mem. APHA (Lowell Reed lectr. 1996, chmn. sect. emergency health svcs. 1982-83, governing coun. 1983-85), Am. Heart Assn. (Remington lectr., mem. cardiovasc. epidemiology coun. 2006), Inst. Math. Stats., Am. Soc. Quality Control, Biometrics Soc. (mem. regional adv. com. 1989-94), Phi Beta Kappa, Sigma Xi. Roman Catholic. Achievements include development of instrument for predicting acute ischemic health disease; stroke health risk appraisal function and coronary heart disease risk assessment function; global cardiovacular disease risk function. Home: 5 Everett Ave Winchester MA 01890-3523 Office: Boston U Statistics & Cons Unit 111 Cummington St Boston MA 02215-2411 Office Phone: 617-353-2767. Business E-Mail: ralph@bu.edu.

D'AGOSTINO, RHONDA LYNN, nursing administrator; b. Middletown, NY, Oct. 30, 1980; MSN, NYU, 2006. ICU nurse practitioner coord. Meml. Sloan Kettering Hosp., 2007—. Adj. prof. NYU, 2009. Mem.: Soc. Critical Care. Office: 1275 York Ave New York NY 10065 Business E-Mail: rlb273@nyu.edu.

DAGUM, ALEXANDER B., plastic surgeon; BSc, Queen's U., Kingston, 1982; MD, U. Ottawa, 1987. Diplomate in plastic surgery and surgery of the hand Am. Bd. Plastic Surgery. Surg. intern Ottawa Civic Hosp., 1987—88; resident in plastic surgery U. Toronto, 1988—93, fellow in microsurgery, hand and microsurgery, 1993—94; fellow hand and microsurgery SUNY, Stony Brook, 1994—95, assoc. prof., 2000—09, prof., 2009—. Lectr. U. Toronto, 1995—2000; pres. Ont. Soc. Plastic Surgeons, 1999—2000; sect. chair plastic surgery Ont. Med. Assn., 1999—2000. Vol. surgeon E.M.A.S., Kunming, China, 2005—10; co-dir. Stony Brook U. Craniofacial-Cleft Palate Multidisciplinary Team; vol. surgeon Smile Train Med. Exchange Nairobi, Kenya, 2010. Recipient Leonard Tow Humanism Medicine award, 2009, Surgery award, Stony Brook, 2010; named one of Medical Marvels, NY Mag., 2006, America's Top Plastic Surgeons, 2006—10, Castle Connolly's Top Doctors NY Metro, 2006—10, Best Drs., NY Mag., 2007—10. Fellow: ACS, Royal Coll. Physicians and Surgeons (Can.) (cert. in plastic surgery); mem.: Northeastern Soc. Plastic Surgeon, Groupe pour l'Avancement de la MicroChirugie Can., Am. Cleft Palate-Craniofacial Assn., Can. Soc. Plastic Surgeons, Am. Soc. for Surgery of the Hand, Am. Soc. Plastic Surgeons, Gold Humanism, Alpha Omega Alpha (elected faculty mem. 2003). Office: Stony Brook Univ T-19 Rm 60 Health Sciences Ctr Stony Brook NY 11794-8191 also: 24 Research Way East Setauket NY 11733-3465 Office Phone: 631-444-4666. Office Fax: 631-444-8894. Business E-Mail: alexander.dagum@stonybrook.edu.

DAHER, EDOUARD, cardiologist; b. Kobayat, Akkar, Lebanon, Sept. 11, 1965; arrived in US, 1990; s. Raymond and Marie Daher. BS, Am. U., Beirut, 1986; MD, St. Joseph U., Beirut, 1990. Cert. Am. Bd. Internal Medicine, 1994, in Cardiovasc. Medicine Am. Bd. Cardiovasc. Disease, 1998, Am. Soc. Nuc. Cardiology, 1997, in Endovascular Medicine Am. Bd. Vascular Medicine, 2005. Resident Yale U. Sch. Medicine, New Haven, 1991—94, cardiovasc. fellow, 1994—98; asst. prof. medicine Wayne State U., Detroit, 1999—2004; attending cardiologist John D. Dingell VA Med. Ctr., 1999—2005; interventional peripheral fellow St. Elizabeth Med. Ctr., Boston, 2005; interventional cardiology fellow New Eng. Med. Ctr., 2005—. Dir. nuc. cardiology John D. Dingell VA Med. Ctr., Detroit, 1999—2004, chief sect. cardiology, 2001—04, dir. clin. rsch. ctr., 2002—04; staff physician Children's Hosp. Mich. PET Ctr., Detroit, 2001—04; dir. nuc. cardiology Harper U. Hosp., 2002—03. Contbr. chapters to books, scientific papers, articles to profl. jours. Recipient Process Improvement award, Vets. Integrated Svc. Network II, 2003, Rsch. Protected Time award, Wayne State U. Dept. Internal Medicine, 2000; Seed Money grant, 2000. Fellow: Am. Coll. Cardiology; mem.: Am. Heart Assn., Am. Soc. Nuc. Cardiology (dir. Mich. working group 2001—04, Young Investigator award 1997).

DAHL, GERALD LUVERN, psychotherapist, educator; b. Nov. 10, 1938; s. Lloyd F. and Leola J. (Painter) Dahl; m. Judith Lee Brown, June 24, 1960; children: Peter, Stephen, Leah. BA, Wheaton Coll., 1960; MSW, U. Nebr., 1962; PhD Psychotherapy (hon.), Internat. U. Found., 1987. Diplomate Am. Psychotherapy Assn. Officer juvenile probation Hennepin County Ct. Svcs., 1962—65; cons. Citizens Coun. on Delinquency and Crime, Mpls., 1965—67; dir. patient svcs. Mt. Sinai Hosp., Mpls., 1967—69; clin. social worker Mpls. Clinic Psychiatry, 1969—82, G.L. Dahl & Assocs., Inc., Mpls., 1983—; founder, pres. Strategic Team-Makers, Inc., 1985—. Assoc. prof. social work Bethel Coll., St. Paul, 1964—83; spl. instr. sociology Golden Valley Luth. Coll., Minn., 1974—83; pres. Strategic Team-Makers, Inc., 1985—; adj. prof. U. Wis., River Falls, 1988—90. Author: Why Christian Marriages Are Breaking Up, 1979, Everybody Needs Somebody Sometime, 1980, How Can We Keep Christian Marriages from Falling Apart, 1988, The Sandwich Generation, 1995; contbr. articles to profl. jours. Founder, bd. stewards Family Counseling Svc., Minn. Bapt. Conf., 1994—; dir., spkr. Profl. Referral Orgn., 2001; bd. dirs. Edgewater Bapt. Ch., 1972—75, chmn., 1974—75; vice chmn. bd. stewards Minnetonka Bapt. Ch., 1995; bd. mem.

Stewards Ridgewood Ch. Mem.: AAUP, Am. Assn. Behavioral Therapists, Pi Gamma Mu. Achievements include design of portrait predictor - personality assessment instrument. Office: 7575 Golden Valley Rd Ste 130 Golden Valley MN 55427 Office Phone: 763-542-1199. Personal E-mail: jerryd@stmi.biz.

DAHL, MARILYN GAIL, psychotherapist; b. Louisville, Dec. 6, 1946; d. James Blair and Dorothy Emma (McDermott) Swartzwelder; m. Charles Dalton Weaver, Dec. 30, 1967 (div. Apr. 1969); m. Donald Allan Dahl, Sept. 18, 1985 (div. Oct. 2005). BSN, U. Ky., 1968; MEd in Clin. Counseling, The Citadel, 1987. Lic. profl. counselor, Ill. Instr. med.-surg. nursing Sch. Nursing Ky. Bapt. Hosp., Louisville, 1973-79; child psychiat. nurse Norton's Children's Hosp., Louisville, 1980-81; asst. prof., psychiat. nurse Sch. Nursing, U. Louisville, 1981-82; primary therapist/child psychiat. nurse Children's Treatment Svc., Louisville, 1982-83; instr. psychiat. nursing Sch. Nursing Bellarmine Coll., Louisville, 1983-84; adult and geriat. therapist Seven Counties Svcs., Louisville, 1984; psychiat. nurse So. Pines Hosp., Charleston, SC, 1985-86; rev. specialist S.C. Peer Rev. Orgn., Charleston, 1986-87; psychotherapist Ctr. for Change, Charleston, 1987-88; pvt. practice North Charleston, 1988-94; hospice nurse Condell Home Health Agy., Libertyville, Ill., 1994-95; home health nurse Manpower Temporary Agy., Waukegan, Ill., 1996-97; staff nurse Hospice of Highland Park (Ill.) Hosp., 1996-99; pvt. practice psychotherapy Goshen, Ky., 1999—; home health nurse Manpower Temp. Agy., Waukegan, 1996-97. Hospice nurse Hospice of Charleston, Inc., 1991-92; pub. health nurse Trident Home Halth Svcs., 1992; mental health profl. Charleston/Dorchester Mental Health Ctr., 1993. Vol. Hospice of Louisville, Inc., 1978-85, ARC State and Nat. Response Team, 1996—, Hospice and Palliative Care Louisville, Inc., 1999—; mem. steering com. Highlands Adult Day Ctr., Louisville, 1984-85; bd. dirs. Ashley River Fire Dept., Charleston, 1986-90, chair, 1989-90, mem. ladies aux., 1985-94; mem. test rose panel Jackson & Perkins, 1989-91. Named to Honorable Order Ky. Cols., Commonwealth of Ky., 1977. Mem. ACA, Am. Assn. for Mental Health Counselors. Avocations: cross stitching, raising roses, wildflower gardening, singing, making stained glass projects. Home and Office: 3525 Ephraim McDowell Dr #114 Louisville KY 40205 Personal E-mail: marilyndahl@insightbb.com.

DAHL, MARK VICTOR, dermatologist, educator; b. Mpls., Aug. 24, 1942; s. Victor E. and Edith M. D.; m. Arlene C., July 1, 1966; children: Kristian Mark, Jonathan Mark. BA, Wesleyan U., 1964; MD, U. Minn., 1968. Diplomate in dermatology, immunodermatology and dermatopathology Am. Bd. Dermatology. Intern U. Ore. Med. Sci. Ctr., Portland, 1968-69; fellow in dermatology U. Copenhagen, 1969-70; rsch. assoc. Walter Reed Army Med. Ctr., Washington, 1970-72; resident dermatology U. Calif., San Francisco, 1972—74; from asst. prof. to prof. dermatology U. Minn. Med. Sch., Mpls., 1974—2000, chmn. dept. dermatology, 1995—2000, prof. emeritus, 2000—; prof. dermatology Mayo Clinic Ariz., Scottsdale, 2000—10, chmn. dept. dermatology, 2000—07, prof. emeritus, 2011—. Pres. Mark Dahl & Assocs., Inc., 1994-2002, Mark V. Dahl LLC, 2011-. Author: Clinical Immunodermatology, 1981, 3d edit., 1996, Common Office Dermatology, 1983, Clinical Dermatology, 1990, 4th edit., 2008, Dermatology, 1991; mem. editl. bd. jours. in field; contbr. articles to profl. jours. Founder Camp Discovery for children with severe skin diseases. Maj. M.C., U.S. Army, 1970-72. Mem. Am. Soc. Allergy and Immunology (pres. 1981-82), Am. Acad. Dermatology (hon., pres. 1993-94, Henry Stelwagen award 1972, Gold Triangle award 1998, Gold medal 2002, Master Dermatologist 2006), Am. Dermatol. Assn., Internat. Soc. Dermatology, Soc. Investigative Dermatology (v.p. 1994-95), Br. Dermatol. Assn. (hon.), Mex. Acad. Dermatology (hon.), Can. Dermatol. Assn. (hon.), Minn. Dermatol. Soc., Phoenix Dermatol. Soc., South Africa Dermatology Soc. (hon.), Pacific Dermatology Assn. (hon.), Chilian Dermatol. Soc. (hon.). *

DAHL, OLE-PETTER, physician; b. Namsos, Norway, Jan. 30, 1952; MD, Münster U., Germany, 1980; degree in Neurology, St. Olavs Hosp., 1994. Chief physician Hosp. Namsos, 1993—. Mem.: Norwegian Med. Assn. Avocations: exercise, diving. Home: Nordahl Griegs veg 36 Namsos 7800 Norway Home Fax: 4774215949. Personal E-mail: olepetter.dahl@hnt.no.

DAHLBEN, SALIN ABRAHAM, neuropsychiatrist; b. Rio de Janeiro, Nov. 2, 1945; came to U.S., 1973; s. Abraham and Emilia D.; m. Sonia Sapolnik, July 8, 1971 (div. 1975); m. Jean Annette Leupold, Nov. 7, 1982 (div. 1996); children: Deborah, Rachael Emily, Lindsay Johanna, Joshua Robert, Brian Andre. BS, Hebrew Coll., Rio de Janeiro, 1963; MD, Fed. U., Rio de Janeiro, 1969. Cert. Bd. Med. Quality Assurance, Calif.; diplomate Am. Bd. Psychiatry and Neurology in gen. psychiatry and with added re-cert. in geriatric psychiatry. Mem. med. staff Naval Hosp., Rio de Janeiro, 1970-71; surgery intern Mt. Sinai Hosp. Svcs., NYC, 1973—74; neurosurgery resident Boston City Hosp., 1974—75; fellow in neurosurgery Lahey Clinic, Boston, 1975-76; resident in neurosurgery U. Iowa Hosps., Iowa City, 1976-78, VA Hosp., Iowa City, 1978; resident in psychiatry Mt. Sinai Hosp. Med. Ctr., Chgo., 1979-80, chief resident, 1981; med. unit dir. Bridgewater State Hosp., 1983-85; med. dir. Dorchester Mental Health Ctr., Mass., 1985-87; asst. psychiatrist McLean Hosp., Belmont, Mass., 1983—; asst. clin. prof. Tufts U. Sch. Medicine, Boston, 2005—. Clin. instr. psychiatry Harvard Med. Sch., Boston, 1983—; clin. assoc. Mass. Gen. Hosp., 1988—98, Mass. Mental Health Ctr., 1999—; assoc. Cambridge Hosp., 1990—; unit med. dir. psychiatry Metro Boston Lemuel Shattuck Hosp., Boston, 2001—; asst. clin. prof. Tufts U. Sch. of Medicine, 2005—; course dir. Harvard Med. Lang. Initiative. 1st lt. M.D. Brazilian Navy, 1970-71. Recipient prize Assn. Med. Students, Rio de Janeiro, 1968, 69, Abbey Norman Prince award Mt. Sinai Hosp. Med. Ctr., Chgo., 1981; named one of Am.'s Top Psychiatrists in Neuropsychiatry, Consumers Rsch. Coun. Am., 2003, 2009-2010; scholar Nat. Coun. for Rsch., 1969-70. Mem. NY Acad. Scis. (emeritus mem.), Am. Mensa, Harvard Faculty Club, Harvard Club NY, Sigma Xi (M.I.T. chpt.) (emeritus mem.). Office: 25 Mount Alvernia Rd Chestnut Hill MA 02467-1057 Business E-Mail: sdahlben@hms.harvard.edu.

DAHLE, JOSTEIN, hospital administrator, researcher; b. Haugesund, Norway, Oct. 10, 1972; MSc, Norwegian U. Sci. and Tech., 1995; PhD, U. Oslo, 2000. Postdoc. rschr. Norwegian Radium Hosp., 2000—04, scientist, group leader, 2004—10; chief sci. officer Nordic Nanovector AS, 2011—, CEO, 2011—. Rsch. grant, Health Enterprise South Eastern Norway, Postdoc. fellowship, Norwegian Cancer Soc., OFU Contract grant, Innovation Norway. Home: Vallerveien 106 A Haslum Akershus 1344 Norway Personal E-mail: jd@nordicnanovector.no.

DAHLSTROM, JANE ESTHER, pathologist; b. Parramatta, N.S.W., Australia, Apr. 12, 1961; d. Peter Jon and Gyllian Summerfield (Cowell) Yeend; m. Stephen William Dahlstrom, Dec. 18, 1982 (div. 1991); children: Clare, Nicholas; m. Mark Llewellyn Bassett, Apr. 29, 1992; children: Hamish, Camilla, Katharine, Peter. MBBS with honors, U. Sydney, Australia, 1985, Grad. Cert. Higher Edn., 2002; PhD, Australian Nat. U., Canberra, 1992. Cert. in family planning. Resident Woden Valley Hosp., Canberra, 1986-87; anatomical pathology registrar ACT Health, Canberra, 1992-99, coord. pathology breast cancer screening program, 1993-96. Clin. tchr. U. Sydney, 1995-96; vis. fellow JCSMR, Australian Nat. U., 1992—; acad. pathologist, conjoint appt. Canberra Clin. Sch., U. Sydney, The Canberra Hosp., Woden, ACT, Australia, 2000-2003; sr. lectr. U. Sydney, 2000-03; assoc. prof. Australian Nat. U., 2003-06, prof. anatomical pathology, 2006—; assoc. prof. U. Sydney, 2003-06. Contbr. articles to profl. jours. Chair bd. edn. RCPA, 2006—08, chair, cancer svcs. adv. com., 2011—. Australian Nat. U. scholar, 1988-91; recipient Vice Chancellor's award for excellence in tchg. Australian Nat. U., 2005, Carrick award for excellence, Australian U. Tchg., 2007. Fellow: Royal Coll. Pathologists Australasia (fellow faculty oral pathology 2007, Faculty Sci., Found. fellowship 2011, David Nelson Meml. Trainee award 1985, 1998); mem.: ANZ Pediat. Pathology Group (chairperson 2011—), Canberra Medico-Legal Soc. (pres. 1999), ACT Women's Med. Soc. (pres. 2002—03), Australian Soc. Cytology (state councillor 1999). Avocations: music, sewing. Home: 14 Melbourne Ave Deakin ACT 2600 Australia Office: ACT Pathology Anatomical Pathology PO Box 11 Woden ACT Australia

DAHUT, WILLIAM L., oncologist, researcher; MD, Georgetown U., Washington. Clin. med. tng. in internal medicine Nat. Naval Med. Ctr., Bethesda, Md.; tng. in hematology and med. oncology Bethesda Naval Hosp. and the Nat. Cancer Inst. Medicine Br.; attending physician Nat. Cancer Inst.-Navy Med. Oncology Br.; faculty mem. Georgetown U. Lombardi Cancer Ctr., Washington; head prostate clinic Nat. Cancer Inst. Medicine Br., Bethesda, 1998—2002; chief GU/GYN clin. rsch. sect. in the med. oncology clin. rsch. unit Nat. Cancer Inst., NIH, Bethesda, 2002—, clin. dir. Ctr. Cancer Rsch., sr. investigator Med. Oncology Br. and Affiliates. Achievements include development of novel therapeutic strategies for the treatment of adenocarcinoma of the prostate. Office: Nat Cancer Inst Cancer Rsch Ctr Bldg 10 Rm 12N226 10 Center Dr Bethesda MD 20892 Office Phone: 301-435-8183. Office Fax: 301-435-3854. Business E-Mail: dahutw@mail.nih.gov. *

DAI, WANGDE, vascular surgeon; b. Hubei, China, May 25, 1967; MD, Shanghai Med. U., 1999. Rsch. scientist Heart Inst., Good Samaritan Hosp., 2006—. Office: Heart Inst Good Samaritan Hosp 1225 Wilshire Blvd Los Angeles CA 90017 E-mail: wangdedai@yahoo.com.

DAI, YUCHENG, hematologist; b. Tianshui City, Ganshu Province, Nov. 28, 1936; MD, Jiangxi Med. Sch., 1963. Dir. hematology dept. Med. Sch. Nanchang U., 2002—11. Office: 1 Minde Rd Nanchang Jiangxi 330006 China Office Fax: 086-0791-6252326. Business E-Mail: daiyucheng136@163.com.

DAI, YUN, physician, educator; b. Fujian, China, July 27, 1962; MD, Southern Med. U., 1983, PhD, 1994. Postdoc rsch. fellow U. Pa., 1999—2000; postdoc rsch. assoc. Med. Coll. Va. Va. Commonwealth U., 2000—02, instr. Med. Coll. Va., 2002—03, asst. prof. Massey Cancer Ctr., 2003—10, assoc. prof. Massey Cancer Ctr., 2010—. Recipient award, Leukemia and Lymphoma Soc. America; grant, NIH. Mem.: Am. Soc. Hematology, Am. Assn. Cancer Rsch. Avocations: soccer, tennis. Office: 234 Goodwin 401 College St Richmond VA 23298 Office Fax: 804-827-3781. Business E-Mail: ydai@vcu.edu.

DAIF, EMAD TAWFIK, medical educator; b. Cairo, Oct. 11, 1963; BDS, Cairo U., MSc, 1986; PhD, Bucharest U., 1995. Prof. Cairo U., 2006—. Office: 2 Street No 100 Maadi Cairo 202 Egypt Personal E-mail: daif_emad@yahoo.com.

DAIGER, STEPHEN P., ophthalmologist, educator; AB in Experimental Psychology, Johns Hopkins U., 1965; PhD in Human Population Genetics, Stanford U., 1975. Fellow U. Wash., Seattle, 1976—78; dir. Lab. Molecular Diagnosis of Inherited Eye Diseases; prof. human genetics ctr. U. Tex. Sch. Pub. Health, prof. dept. ophthalmology & visual sci.; adj. prof. dept. pediatrics Baylor Coll. Med.; vice chmn. & scientific adv. bd. Found. Fighting Blindness. Office: 1200 Herman Pressler St Houston TX 77030 Office Phone: 713-500-9829. Office Fax: 713-500-0900. E-mail: Stephen.P.Daiger@uth.tmc.edu.

DAILEY, DAWN ELAINE, public health service official; b. Berkeley, Calif., Feb. 2, 1965; d. Stanley Wilfred Anderson Sr. and Mercedes Anderson; m. Kenneth Lamar Dailey, Apr. 19, 1986; 1 child, Mariana. BSN, U. San Francisco, 1988; MSN, Samuel Merritt Coll., 1997; PhD, U. Calif., San Francisco, 2006. RN Calif., cert. clin. nurse specialist, advanced practice nurse in cmty. health nursing. Nurse Alta Bates Hosp., Berkeley, 1988-91; home health nurse Kaiser Permanent, Martinez, Calif., 1992-94; mgr. Contra Costa SIDS Program, Martinez, 1995—; coord. Fetal Infant Mortality Review Program, Martinez, 1998—2007, Medically Vulnerable Infant Program, Martinez, 2006—. Pub. health nurse Contra Costa County, Martinez, 1989—2002; mgr. Pub. Health Nurse Program, Martinez, 2002—; asst. adj. prof. U. Calif. San Francisco, 2009—; instr. univ. ext. U. Calif. Davis; 2mem. SIDS/OID adv. com. Nat. Ctr. on Cultural Competence Georgetown U., 1999—2005; cons. Calif. SIDS Program, Fair Oaks, 1994—98; mem. Calif. SIDS Adv. Coun., Sacramento, 1996—; pres. No. Calif. Regional SIDS Adv. Coun., Berkeley, 1993—98; mem. Contra Costa Immunization Coalition, Martinez, 1996—97, Childhood Injury Prevention Coalition, Contra Costa County, 1993—97; bd. mem. No. Calid. SIDS Alliance, Berkeley, 1997—2001; v.p. Assn. SIDS and Infant Mortality Program, 1998—2002. Bd. dirs. Child Abuse Prevention Coun., Contra Costa County, 1994—2000; mem. profl. edn. com. Bay Area chpt. March of Dimes, 1999—. Recipient Outstanding Grad. award, Samuel Merritt Coll., 1997, Excellence award, Contra Costa County, 1998, Senator Daniel E. Boatwright award, 2001, Svc. Excellence award, Contra Costa Health Svcs., 2001, 2007, 2009—10, Nat. Rsch. Svc. award, NIH, 2002, Mable Keaton Staupers scholarship award, 2002, Vol. award, Welcome Home Baby Program, 2002; Shirley C. Titus scholar, Calif. Nurses Assn., 1995, Nursing Edn. scholar, 1996, Eugene Cota-Robles fellow, U. Calif. San Francisco, 2001, Pre-doctoral fellow Nat. Inst. Nursing Rsch., NIH, 2002, Grad. nursing scholar, March of Dimes, 2003, M. Elizabeth Carnegie scholar, Nurses' Ednl. Funds, Inc., 2004. Mem.: APHA, ANA, Assn. SIDS and Infant Mortality Programs (v.p. 2000—02), Chi Eta Phi (Basileus 1997, Omicron Phi chpt., Mable Keaton Staupers scholarship 2002, Basileus 1997), Sigma Theta Tau. Avocations: boating, quilting. Home: 980 Cashel Cir Vacaville CA 95688-8572

DAILIANA, ZOE H., orthopedist, surgeon, educator; d. Harilaos A. Ntailianas and Anastasia Ntailiana. MD, U. Ioannina, Greece, 1990, PhD, 1996, postgrad., 1997—98. Fellow Inst. de la Main, Paris, 1997—98, Duke U. Med. Ctr., Durham, NC, 1998—2001; lectr. dept. orthop. surgery U. Thessaly, Larissa, Greece, 2001—05, asst. prof. dept. orthop. surgery, 2006—. Recipient Raoul Tubiana award, GEM, 2001. Mem.: Am. Acad. Orthop. Surgeons (corr.). Office: Dept of Orthop Surgery 22 Papakyriazi St Larissa 41222 Greece Office Fax: 30-2410-670107. Business E-Mail: dailiana@med.uth.gr.

DAILY, DEIRDRE LYNN, systems analyst; b. Santa Monica, Calif., Sept. 28, 1976; d. Karen Lynn Daily. AA, Moorpark Coll., 1997; BS, Calif. State U., Northridge, 1999, postgrad., 2006—. Intern managed care West Hills Hosp., Calif.; provider rels. rep. Family Healthcare Med. Group, Simi Valley, Seaview IPA, Oxnard, 2002; regional sales rep. CIMS- a Wellpoint subsidiary; lead user applications analyst Wellpoint, Inc., Newbury Park, 2005—06; contract compliance advisor Compliance WellPoint, Inc., 2006. Vol. ONE Adult Day Care, Northridge. Personal E-mail: deirddaily@aol.com.

DAISUKE, TACHIKAWA, oncologist, surgeon, consultant; b. Miyazaki, Japan, Oct. 18, 1967; s. Tachikawa Toshio and Tachikawa Chizuko. MD, PhD, Fukuoka U., Japan, 2000. Lic. physician. Intern Dept. of Surgery Chikushi Hosp. Fukuoka (Japan) U., 1983—85; sr. dir. Matsuzaki Meml. Hosp., Ogoori, Japan, 2000—. Consulting Ventuno, Fukuoka, 2001—; sr. gen. mgr. Fucoidan Lab., Fukuoka, 2002—. Author: (book) Miracle marine power of Fucoidan; editor: Amazing Sea Power of Fucoidan, Marverous Marine Power of Fucoidan. Recipient Silver award, Fukuoka (Japan) U. Medicine, 2000. Avocations: racing, body board. Office: Fucoidan Laboratory 1-6-14 Shirogane Chuo-Ku Fukuoka 810-0012 Japan Office Fax: +81 92-523-5500.

DAJANI, ESAM ZAPHER, pharmacologist; b. Jaffa, Palestine, May 30, 1940; arrived in U.S., 1958, naturalized; s. Zapher Rageb and Mamdouha Dajani; m. Najwa Said Beidas, July 16, 1964; children: Mona, Zapher, Noura. BS in Pharmacy, U. Mo., 1963; MS in Pharmacology and Med. Chemistry, Auburn U., 1966; PhD in Pharmacology and Toxicology, Purdue U., 1969. Sr. pharmacologist Rohm and Hass Co., Spring House, Pa., 1968-72; sr. rsch. investigator G.D. Searle and Co., Chgo., 1972-74, group leader, 1974-80, chmn. G.I. diseases, 1974-80, sect. head, 1980, asst. dir., 1980-82, assoc. dir., 1982-85, dir. Cytotec sci. and med. affairs, 1985-87, dir. clin. rsch., 1987-93; founder, pres. Internat. Drug Devel. Cons. Corp.-IDDC, Long Grove, Ill., 1993—. Editl. adv. bd. Drug Devel. Rsch., Dallas, 1983—93, Jour. Assn. Acad. Minority Physicians, Bklyn., 1992—, Jour. Physiology and Pharmacology, Krakow, Poland, 1993—; adj. prof. medicine UCLA, 1984—95, Loyola U., Chgo., 1995—; adj. prof. pharmacology Chgo. Med. Sch., 1983—90; sci. adv. bd. Atlantic Pharm., Inc., C. V. Therapeutics, Inc.; presenter in field. Author (with others): Prostaglandins and GI Mucosa, 1987, Pharmacology of Misoprostol, 1989, Prostaglandins and Esophagus, 1991, Pharmaceutical Industry Perspective, 1991, Prevention and Treatment of Ulcers induced by NSAIDS, 1995, EGF Prevents Esophogeal Ulcers Induced by Sclerotherapy, 1995, Drug Induced Ulcers, 1998, Gastrointestinal Toxicity of Over the Counter Analgesics, 1998, Idiopathic Esophageal Ulceration in HIV Patients, 1998, Gastroesophageal Reflux Disease: Pathophysiology and Pharmacology, 2000; editor: Gastrointestinal Cytoprotection, 1987, Over-the Counter Drugs, 2004, Cardiovascular and Gastrointestine Toxicity of selective Cyclo-Oxygenase Inhibitors in Man, 2008; assoc. editor: Med. Sci. Monitor, Warsaw, Poland, 2003—, Progress in Med. Rsch., 2004—, Spl. Govt. Employee, 2006—; contbr. articles to prof. jours. Mem. Arab-Am. Anti-Discrimination Com., Washington, 1972. Recipient Edward M. Queeny award, Monsanto Corp., 1991; named Disting. Alumnus, Purdue U., 1991. Fellow: Am. Coll. Gastroenterology; mem.: Chgo. Biotech Network (founder, bd. dirs.), N.Y. Acad. Scis., Assn. Acad. Minority Physicians (councillor), European Soc. Gastroenterology and Endoscopy, Am. Pharm. Assn., Drug Info. Assn., Soc. Exptl. Biology and Medicine, Gastroenterology Rsch. Group, Am. Gastroent. Assn., Am. Soc. Pharmacology and Exptl. Therapeutics, Arab-Am. Univ. Grads., Phi Kappa Phi, Rho Chi. Achievements include patents in field; co-discovery and development of Cytotec, the first commercial prostaglandin anti-ulcer drug; directed pre-clinical and clinical research at multinational pharmaceutical companies; considerable expertise in worldwide drug development and pharmacological consulting services. Office: IDDC Corp 1549 RFD Long Grove IL 60047-9532 E-mail: EsamD@comcast.net.

DAKE, MARCIA ALLENE, retired nursing educator, dean; b. Bemus Point, NY, May 22, 1923; d. Earl B. and Bernice DeLeo (Haskin) D. Diploma, Crouse Irving Hosp., 1944; BS, Syracuse U., 1951; MA, Columbia U., 1955, EdD, 1958. RN. Tchr., sch. nurse various locations, 1946—48; chmn. health dept. SUNY, Oneonta, 1952—56; dean coll. nursing U. Ky., Lexington, 1958—72; dir. dept. nursing edn. ANA, Kansas City, 1972—74; project dir. program devel. nursing ARC, Washington, 1975—79; dir. nursing edn. James Madison U. Coll. Nursing, 1979—81; prof. dean Coll. Nursing, 1981—88; ret., 1988. Editor, resident photographer: Greenspring Village Photo Directories, 2000—; programmer, host Closed Circuit TV Studio, 2000. Mem. Ky. Bd. Nursing Edn. Nurse Registration, 1969-72, pres., 1970-72; pres. Va. Coun. Deans of Baccalaureate Nursing Programs, 1981-84; nurse officer Civil Def. Otsego County, N.Y., 1953-56; mem. Def. Adv. Com. on Women in Svcs., 1963-65; mem. Ky. Comprehensive Health Planning Coun., 1968-71; pres. Ky. League for Nursing, 1961-65; bd. dir. Cmty. Ch. Coll., Sun City Ctr., Fla., 1989-92, Sun City Ctr. Guardianship Found., 1990-98; trustee United Cmty. Ch., Sun City Ctr., 1993-96, chmn. pers. com., 1994-96, fin. com., 1994-95, vice chmn. bd. trustees, 1995-96, stewardship com., 1996-98, mem. pastoral rels. com., 1996-98, mem. long range planning com., 1996-97, chmn. pastoral rels. com., 1998—; sec. Caloosa Women's Golf Assn., Sun City Ctr., 1991-92; treas. Greater Sun City Ctr. Disaster Coun., 1992-94; mem., vice chmn. resident adv. com.

Greenspring Village, Springfield, Va., 1999-2000, corr. sec. resident adv. com., 2001; prodr., host Channel 6 T.V Greenspring Village, 2001; prodr., pub. resident/staff photo directories, 2000-. 1st lt. U.S. Army Nurse Corps., 1945—46. Recipient 4th Gold award, Pres.'s Coun. Svc. and Civic Participation, 2008, Lifetime award, 2009, 5th Gold award, Pres. Coun. Civic Participation, 2011. Fellow Nat. League Nursing; mem. ANA, Va. Nurses Assn. (pres. dist. 9 1983-85), Va. Soc. Profl. Nurses (treas. 1983-88), Va. Assn. Colls. Nursing (sec. 1980-82, pres. 1982-85), Alliance Nursing Orgns. (chmn. Va. 1985-88), LWV, Delta Kappa Gamma, Kappa Delta Pi, Pu Lambda Theta. Address: 222 7442 Spring Village Dr Springfield VA 22150-4444

DALAL, HASNAIN, physician; s. Mohamed Suleman and Leila Dalal; m. Naznin Dalal; 2 children. MB ChB, Sheffield U. Med. Sch., Eng., 1981; MD, Penisula Med. Sch., Exeter, Eng., 2007. Ho. officer Royal Hallamshire Hosp., Sheffield, England, 1981—82; sr. ho. officer: gp vocat. tng. scheme Royal Cornwall Hosp., 1983—86; prin. gen. practice Dr. Vowles and Ptnrs., Truro, England, 1986—. Lead investigator, REACH Heart Failure Study Nat. Inst. Health Rsch., 2010—11. Contbr. innovative health care delivery (NHS Beacon Award, 1999). Grantee, NHS R&D South West Directorate, 2000—04. Fellow: Royal Coll. Gen. Practitioners. Achievements include research in randomised trial with patient preference comparing home based versus hospital based cardiac rehabilitation. Office: Three Spires Med Practice Truro Health Pk Truro TRI 2JA England Personal E-mail: hmdalal@doctors.net.uk.

DALAL, PRAFULCHANDRA M., neurologist, researcher; MB BS, U. Bombay, 1955, MD, 1958. Registrar in gen. medicine T.N. Med. Coll. and Nair Hosp., Bombay, 1956-58, tutor in medicine, 1958-62, asst. prof. medicine, 1962-65, prof. head of medicine, neurologist, 1965-69, prof. head of neurology/neurosci., 1963-90. Mem. expert panel neuroscis. WHO Internat., 1980-86; dir. rsch. Sir H.N. Med. Rsch. Centre, Bombay, 1983-87; vis. neurologist Sir N.H. Hosp. Rsch. Ctr., Bombay, 1983—, Li lavati Hosp. Rsch. Centre, Bombay, 1995—; vis. scientist NIH, Bethesda, Md., 1983; guest prof. Wayne State U., Detroit, 1968-69, Wake Forest U., 1978. Author: (with others) Handbook of Clinical Neurology, 1989, Infections and Subcortical Infarctions, 1995; editor: Medicine Update, Current Concepts in Medicine, 1991; contbr. articles to profl. jours. including Nature, Year Book of Neurology and Psychiatry, Lancet, Am. Heart Jour., JAMA, among others. Fellow Rockefeller Found., 1960-62, Wellcome Found., 1968-69; recipient Manorama Vijay Hazrat scholar Bombay U., 1955; Sr. commonwealth fellow Oxford (Eng.) U., 1967-68. Fellow Royal Soc. Medicine (London), Nat. Acad. Med. Scis. (India), Am. Heart Assn. (hon. stroke coun.); mem. Indian Acad. Med. Scis., Am. Coll. Chest Physicians, Internat. Coll. Angiology, Assn. of Physicians of India (pres. 1993), Indian Coll. Physicians (pres. 1993), Acad. Med. Specialists (chmn. 1996), Internat. Stroke Soc. (bd. dirs. 1995, Dr. B.C. Roy Nat. award in neuroscis. 1995). Avocations: chess, watching cricket, tennis, and football games, theater. Home and Office: Clerk Rd Off Colony Ln Mcpl Bldg No 3 Flat 18 2dFl Bombay 400034 India Office Phone: 91-22-23530934.

DALAMAGA, MARIA ANNA, clinical biochemistry professor; b. Athens, Greece, May 8, 1971; d. Antonios Dalamagas and Vassiliki Kostoula-Dalamaga; m. Charry Chavelas (div. 2003); m. Mark Nikolopoulos, Oct. 21, 2005. MD, Ioannina U., Greece, 1995; MPH, Nat. Sch. Pub. Health, Athens, 1997; MSc, Harvard U., 2000; PhD, Athens U., 2002. Resident clin. pathology NIMTS-Evangelismos Hosps., Athens, 1997—2002, fellow clin. chemistry, 2008, cons. physician Iaso Gen. Hosp., Athens, 2002—03, Attikon U. Gen. Hosp., Athens, 2003—05, lectr., 2005—09. Tchr., cons. Attikon U. Gen. Hosp.-Athens U. Med. Sch., 2003—, asst. prof. clin. biochemistry, 2009—. Author: HIV and AIDS, 1995. Active civic, polit. and social work Health Ctr. Metsova, Greece, 1995—96. Recipient Empirikion award, Empirikion Found., Athens, 1999, Choremio award, Pediat. Soc. Greece, 2000, award in sci., Acad. Athens, 2001. Fellow: Coll. Am. Pathologists, Am. Soc. Clin. Pathology, Onassis Found., Virology Soc. Greece, Immunology Soc. Greece, mem.: European Bd. Med. Biopathology. Avocations: tennis, badminton, literature. Office: Attikon Univ Gen Hosp Rimini 1 Chaidari 12462 Athens Greece Home: Thessalias 47 153 54 Athens Greece

DALE, LOWELL C., geriatrician, educator; AA, Bethany Lutheran Coll.; BA in Chemistry and Biology, Augsburg Coll.; MD, U. Minn. Diplomate Am. bd. Internal Medicine, 1984. Resident internal medicine Mayo Clinic, Rochester, Minn., 1982—84, fellow internal medicine, 1984—85; asst. prof. Mayo Med. Sch. Office: Mayo Clinic 13400 E Shea Blvd Scottsdale AZ 85259 Office Phone: 480-301-8000.

DALEN, JAMES EUGENE, cardiologist, educator; b. Seattle, Apr. 1, 1932; s. Charles A. and Muriel E. (Joanise) Robinson. BS, Wash. State U., 1955; MA, U. Mich., 1956; MD, U. Wash., 1961; MPH, Harvard U., 1972. Intern and asst. med. resident Boston City Hosp., 1961—63; sr. resident New Eng. Med. Ctr., Boston, 1963—64; rsch. fellow in cardiology Harvard Med. Sch., Peter Bent Brigham Hosp., Boston, 1964—67, assoc. dir. cardiovasc. lab., 1967—75; instr., asst. prof., assoc. prof. medicine Harvard Med. Sch., 1967—75; chmn. dept. cardiovasc. medicine U. Mass. Med. Sch., 1975—77, prof., chmn. dept. medicine, 1977—88; physician-in-chief U. Mass. Hosp., 1977—88; acting chancellor U. Mass., Worcester, 1986—87; editor Archives Internal Medicine, 1987—2004; dean, vice provost med. affairs U. Ariz. Coll. Medicine, Tucson, 1988—95, dean, v.p. health scis., 1995—2001. Mem. editl. bd. Jour. AMA, 1987—2004, exec. dir. The Weil Found., 2009—; contbr. articles to profl. jours. With USN, 1951—53. Mem.: ACP, Am. Coll. Chest Physicians (pres. 1985—86), Am. Coll. Cardiology, Assn. Univ. Cardiologists. Home: 5305 N Via Velazquez Tucson AZ 85750-5989 Office: 1840 E River Rd Ste 120 Tucson AZ 85718 Office Phone: 520-577-8180. Personal E-mail: jamesdalen@yahoo.com.

DALEN, KNUT, psychologist; b. Hol, Dec. 3, 1954; PhD in Psychology, 1992. Assoc. prof. U. Bergen, 1988—2009, prof., 2009—. Rschr. U. Oslo, 2010. Mem.: Internat. Neuropsychol. Soc. Avocations: cross country skiing, photography, hiking. Home: Haakonsetgutu 8 Hovet Buskerud N-3577 Norway Personal E-mail: knut.dalen@psych.uib.no.

DALES, SAMUEL, microbiologist, virologist, educator; b. Warsaw, Aug. 31, 1927; emigrated to Can., 1948, naturalized, 1953; s. James and Helen (Ochs) D.; m. Laura L.R.J. Fischer, Dec. 28, 1952 (dec.); children: Adam Charles, Pamela Ann. BA with honors, U. B.C., 1951, MA, 1953; PhD, U. Toronto, 1956. Postdoctoral fellow Nat. Cancer Inst. Can., 1957-60; rsch. assoc., asst. prof. Rockefeller U., NYC, 1960-66; assoc. mem., mem., chief cytobiology Pub. Health Rsch. Inst. City of N.Y., Inc., 1966-76; prof. U. Western Ont., Can., London, Can., 1975-93, prof. emeritus, 1993—, chmn. microbiology and immunology, 1975-80. Research prof. NYU Med. Sch., 1969-75; mem. adv. bd. spl. virus cancer program Nat. Cancer Inst., NIH, 1969-73; mem. virology study sect. NIH, 1971-75, ad hoc, 1977, 79; mem. sci. adv. bd. Banting Rsch. Found., 1978-80; mem. rev. panels virology and cancer USPHS, Med. Rsch. Coun. Can.; adj. prof. Rockefeller U., 1996—. Author: Biology of Poxviruses, 1981; mem. editl. bd. Virology, 1963—, Jour. Cell Biology, 1973-76, Intervirology, 1973-91, Virus Rsch., 1983-92, Microbial Pathogenesis, 1985—, Jour. Virology, 1989-97, Ency. Virology, 1990-95; contbr. sci. articles and revs. to profl. publs. Fellow Royal Soc. Can.; Macy Found. scholar, 1981-82; rsch. grantee USPHS; rsch. grantee Med. Rsch. Coun. Can.; rsch. grantee Multiple Sclerosis Soc. Fellow AAAS; mem. Fedn. Am. Socs. for Exptl. Biology, Harvey Soc., Am. Soc. Cell Biology, N.Y. Soc. Electron Microscopy (coun. 1968-70), Amyotrophic Lateral Sclerosis Soc. An. (sci. adv. bd.) Home: 262 Central Park W Apt 4C New York NY 10024-3512 Office Phone: 212-321-8101. Business E-Mail: daless@mail.rockefeller.edu.

D'ALESANDRO, PHILIP ANTHONY, parasitologist, immunologist, retired medical educator; b. Bound Brook, NJ, Apr. 2, 1927; s. Philip and Antoinette Ann (Vaccaro) D'A.; m. Rosemary Natale Falzarine, Nov. 25, 1961. BSc, Rutgers U., 1952, MSc, 1954; PhD, U. Chgo., 1958. Rsch. assoc. U. Chgo., 1958-59; assoc. prof. Rockefeller U., NYC, 1959-75; assoc. prof., acting head divsn. tropical medicine Columbia U., NYC, 1975-92, emeritus prof., 1992—. Chmn. tropical medicine and parasitology study sect. NIH, Bethesda, Md., 1976-80. Author: (with others) Immunity to Parasitic Animals, 1970, Pathogenicity of Trypanosomes, 1979, Parasitic Protoza, Vol. 1, 1991; editor Jour. Protozoology, 1980-88; contbr. articles to profl. jours. Sgt. U.S. Army Air Corps, 1945-46. Grantee NIH, 1972-90, 79-82. Fellow AAAS; mem. Phi Beta Kappa. Avocations: photography, antiques, railroading, model building. E-mail: pdalesand@aol.com.

DALESSANDRI, KATHIE MARIE, breast cancer researcher, surgeon, educator; b. Stambaugh, Mich., May 4, 1947; m. Gordon William Frost, 1986 (dec. 2005). BS, Mich. Technol. U., 1969; MS, Purdue U., 1971; MD, U. Mich., 1976. diplomate, Am. Bd. Surgery. Intern. Martinez VA Hosp., Calif., 1976-77; gen. surgeon Martinez VA Hosp., Calif., 1982—92; resident U. Calif., Davis, Calif., 1977-81, asst. prof. surgery, 1983—89, assoc. clin. prof. surgery, 1989—93, assoc. rsch. sci. Berkeley, Calif., 2001—04; staff surgeon Palo Alto VA Hosp., Palo Alto, Calif., 1992—98; assoc. clin. prof. Stanford U., Calif., 1993—2005; with Calif. Breast Cancer Rsch., 2001—; breast cancer rschr. U. Calif. Berkeley, U. Calif. San Francisco, Buck Inst. for Aging Rsch. Gen. surgeon Project Hope, Grenada, 1984, 89; vol. surgeon Hosp. Albert Sweitzer, Haiti, 1986. Contbr. articles to profl. jours. Vol. Calif. Breast Cancer Rsch., 2007—. Grantee VA, 1983, Calif. Breast Cancer Rsch., 2001-03, Zero Breast Cancer award, 2009, Komen Translational Rsch. award, 2008, Innovative Rsch. award, Calif. Breast Cancer Rsch. Program, 2010. Fellow: ACS; mem.: Assn. Academic Surgeons, S.W. Surg. Soc., Assn. Women Surgeons. Avocations: hiking, art, walking.

D'ALESSIO, DAVID A., endocrinologist, educator; Grad., Carleton Coll.; MD, U. Wis., 1983. Diplomate Am. Bd. Internal Medicine, 1986, Am. Bd. Internal Medicine endocrinology, diabetes and metabolism, 1989. Resident internal medicine Temple Univ. Med. Ctr., Phila., 1983—86; fellow endocrinology Univ. Wash., Seattle, 1987—90, staff physician Cin. Univ. Hosp.; assoc. prof. medicine Univ. of Cin., Albert Vontz chair in diabetes rsch., faculty mem. pathobiology and neuroscience programs. Co-author: (publs.) Benefits of high-protein weight loss diets: enoughevidence for practice?, 2008, Central control of body weight and appetite, 2009;: One-year comparison of a high-monounsaturated fat diet with ahigh-carbohydrate diet in type 2 diabetes, 2009, Treatment with the dipeptidylpeptidase-4 inhibitor vildagliptin improves fasting islet cell function insubjects with type 2 diabetes, 2009. Mem.: Am. Fedn. for Med. Rsch., Am. Diabetes Assn., Endocrine Soc. Office: University of Cincinnati Medical Center Rm 6065 231 Albert B Sabin Way PO Box 670557 Cincinnati OH 45267 Office Phone: 513-558-6689. E-mail: david.d'alessio@uc.edu.

DALESSIO, DONALD JOHN, internist, neurologist, educator; b. Jersey City, Mar. 2, 1931; s. John Andrea and Susan Dorothy (Minotta) Dalessio; m. Jane Catherine Schneider, Sept. 4, 1954 (dec. Mar. 1998); children: Catherine Leah, James John, Susan Jane. BA, Wesleyan U., 1952; MD, Yale U., 1956. Diplomate Am. Bd. Internal Medicine. Intern N.Y.C. Hosp., 1956—57, asst. resident in medicine and neurology, 1959—61; resident in medicine Yale Med. Ctr., 1961—62; pres. med. staff Scripps Clinic, La Jolla, Calif., 1974—78; chmn. dept. medicine Scripps Clin., La Jolla, 1974—89, chmn. emeritus, 1989—, cons., 1982—, pres. med. group, 1980—81; clin. prof. neurology U. Calif., San Diego, 1973—. Physician in chief Green Hosp., La Jolla, 1974—89; pres. Am. Assn. Study Headache, Chgo., 1974—76; chmn. Fedn. We. Soc. Neurology, Santa Barbara, Calif., 1976—77; Musser-Burch lectr. Tulane U., 1979; Kash lectr. U. Ky., 1979. Author: (book) Wolff's Headache, 7th edit., 2001, Approach to Headache, 1973, Approach to Headache, 6th edit., 1999; editor: Headache jour., 1965—75, 1979—84, Scripps Clinic Personal Health Letter; mem. editl. bd. Jour. AMA, 1977—87; columnist: San Diego Tribune. Pres. Nat. Migraine Found., Chgo., 1977—79. Capt. US Army, 1957—59. Recipient Disting. Alumnus award, Wesleyan U., 1982. Fellow: ACP; mem.: World Fedn. Neurology (Am. sec. 1980—90, rsch. group migraine), Am. Acad. Neurology (assoc.), La Jolla Beach/Tennis Club, La Jolla Country Club. Avocations: tennis, squash, piano. Home: 8891 Nottingham Pl La Jolla CA 92037-2131 Office: Scripps Clinic & Rsch Found 10666 N Torrey Pines Rd La Jolla CA 92037-1092 *

DALEY, GEORGE QUENTIN, hematologist, biomedical research scientist; b. Catskill, NY, Nov. 13, 1960; s. Frank Leonard and Natalie Alcine (Evans) Daley; m. Amy Claire Edmondson, 1995. AB, Harvard U., 1982; PhD in Biology, MIT, 1989; MD summa cum laude, Harvard U., 1991. Diplomate Am. Bd. Internal Medicine. Chief resident in internal medicine Mass. Gen. Hosp., Boston, 1994-95; fellow Whitehead Inst. for Biomedical Rsch., MIT, Cambridge, Mass., 1995; clin. rsch. fellow hematology/oncology Children's, Brigham, Women's and Dana Farber Cancer Ctr. Inst.; assoc. prof., biol. chemistry and molecular pharmacology Harvard Med. Sch., 2002—; with divsn. hematology/oncology Children's Hosp., Boston, 2003—, assoc. dir. stem cell/devel. biology rsch., assoc. prof., pediatrics. Chmn. pre-med. adv. com. Quincy House, Harvard U., Cambridge, 1987-95. Contbr. articles to sci. jours. Recipient rsch. award for Clin. Trainees NIH, 1992, Burroughs-Wellcome Fund Career award, Scholar award, Leukemia and Lymphoma Soc. Am., Pioneer award, NIH, 2004; nat. scholar Harvard U., 1978-91. Mem. AAAS, Am. Soc. Clin. Investigation. Achievements include creation of mouse model for chronic myelogenous leukemia; research in stem cells of the blood to define the molecular basis for human leukemia; self-renewal and differentiation of human ES cells, target directed chemotherapy for chronic myelogenous leukemia (CML); first creation of functional sperm cells from embryonic stem cells (cited a "Top Ten" breakthrough for 2003 by Science magazine). Office: Childrens Hosp Boston 300 Longwood Ave Karp-7 Boston MA 02115 also: HHMI/Childrens Hosp Boston Karp Bldg 7th Fl One Blackfan Cir Boston MA 02115 Office Phone: 617-919-2013, 617-919-2015. Office Fax: 617-730-0222. E-mail: daley.lab@childrens.harvard.edu, george.daley@childrens.harvard.edu.

DALEY, JENNIFER, internist, educator; b. Springfield, Mass., Sept. 10, 1949; d. Edward Murray and Elizabeth (Bloom) D.; children: John, Benjamin, Sarah, Beth, Liane. BA magna cum laude, Brown U., 1972; MD, Tufts U., 1976. Diplomate Am. Bd. Internal Medicine. Resident in internal medicine New Eng. Med. Ctr., Boston, 1976-79; fellow in gen. medicine Harvard Med. Sch., Boston, 1985-87; asst. prof. Tufts U. Sch. Medicine, Boston, 1979-87; staff physician Beth Israel Hosp., Boston, 1987-99; asst. prof. medicine Harvard Med. Sch., Boston, 1991-98, assoc. prof., 1998—2002; dir. Ctr. for Health Sys. Design, Mass. Gen. Hosp., Boston, 1999—2002; chief medical officer Tenet Healthcare Corp., Dallas, 2002—07, Partners Cmty. Healthcare, Boston, 2007—; exec. v.p. & COO U. Mass Meml. Med. Ctr., 2010—. Health svcs. rschr. VA, West Roxbury, Mass., 1990; v.p. health care quality Beth Israel Deaconess Med. Ctr., Boston, 1996-99; health care cons. Author: Using Hospital Mortality Data, 1991; editor: Through the Patient's Eyes, 1994; contbr. over 140 articles to med. jours. Grantee VA, 1990. Fellow ACP, Am. Assn. Health Svcs. Rsch.; mem. AMA, Soc. Gen. Internal Medicine. Office: UMass Memorial Med Ctr Memorial Campus 119 Belmont St Worcester MA 01605

DALEY, KAREN, nursing association administrator, nurse, researcher; Diploma in nursing, Catherine Laboure Sch. Nursing; BS in Nursing, Curry Coll., Milton, Mass.; MPH, Boston U.; MS in Nursing, PhD in Nursing, Boston Coll. RN. Staff nurse Brigham and Women's Hosp., Boston, 1973—99. Bd. dirs. American Nurses Credentialing Ctr., ANA-Polit. Action Com.; past pres. Mass. Ctr. Nursing. Staff writer: Bay State Nurse News, reviewer: Jour. Emergency Nursing, American Jour. Nursing, American Jour. Infection Control; contbr. articles to profl. jours. Project prin. Mass. Dept. Pub. Health Nurses Edn. Hepatitis C Project; project coord. trauma rsch. study Harvard Injury Control Ctr. at the Harvard U. Sch. Pub. Health. Fellow: American Acad. Nursing; mem.: ANA (pres. 2010—), Mass. Nurses Assn. (past pres.), Mass. Assn. Registered Nurses (past pres.). Office: American Nurses Assn 8515 Georgia Ave Ste 400 Silver Spring MD 20910 Office Phone: 301-628-5000. Office Fax: 301-628-5001. *

DALEY, ROBERT, orthopedist; MD, Loyola Univ. Stritch Sch. Medicine. Cert. Am. Bd. Orthopaedic Surgery Examiners. Former team physician Chgo. White Sox; team physician United States Soccer Team; staff physician Provena St. Joseph Med. Ctr., Silver Cross Hosp., Hinsdale Hosp., Hinsdale Surg. Center, Salt Creek Surgery Ctr.; ptnr. Hinsdale Orthopaedic Assoc. Intern Loyola Univ. Med. Ctr.; fellow in reconstructive surgery Brigham and Women's Hosp., Boston. Office: Hinsdale Orthopaedic Assoc 550 W Ogden Ave Hinsdale IL 60521 Office Phone: 630-323-6116. Office Fax: 630-323-6169.

DALING, JANET R., epidemiologist, researcher; BS in Math., Wash. State U., 1957; MS in Biostatistics, U. Wash., 1973, PhD in Epidemiology, 1977. Rsch. analyst divsn. health Wash. State Dept. Social Health Svcs., 1967—76, chronic disease epidemiologist, 1977—78; asst. prof. dept. epidemiology U. Wash. Sch. Pub. & Cmty. Medicine, 1978—81, assoc. prof., 1981—83, prof., 1986—. Assoc. in epidemiology Fred Hutchinson Cancer Rsch. Ctr., Seattle, 1978—81, asst. mem. pub. health scis. divsn., 1981—83, assoc. mem. pub. health scis. divsn., 1983—86, mem. pub. health scis. divsn., 1986—. Contbr. articles to profl. jours. Mem.: Soc. Epidemiologic Rsch., Pub. Health Assn., Am. Epidemiological Soc. Achievements include research in breast cancer and assessing risk factors for the disease, the relationship of risk factors to tumor markers and prognosis, and the role of genetics and gene-environment interactions. Office: Fred Hutchinson Cancer Rsch Ctr 1100 Fairview Ave N PO Box 19024 Seattle WA 98109 Office Phone: 206-667-4630. Office Fax: 206-667-5948. E-mail: jdaling@fhcrc.org. *

DALKIN, ALAN C., endocrinologist, educator; MD, U. Mich., 1984. Diplomate Am. Bd. Internal Medicine, 1987, Am. Bd. Internal Medicine-endocrinology, diabetes and metabolism, 1990, lic. Va. Intern internal medicine Univ. of Chgo. Hosps., 1984—85, resident internal medicine, 1985—87; fellow endocrinology and metabolism Univ. of Mich. Med. Ctr., Ann Arbor, 1987—90, asst. prof. internal medicine, 1990—91, Univ. of Va. Health Sciences Ctr., Charlottesville, 1991—97, assoc. prof. internal medicine, 1997—2007, interim chief, divsn. clin. rheumatology, 1991—, prof. internal medicine, 2007—. Co-author: (publs.) Pituitary follistatin gene expression in female rats: Evidence that inhibin regulates transcription, 2004, Testosterone stimulates FSH beta transcription via activation of extracellular signal-regulated kinase (ERK) in rat pituitary cells, 2005, The sensitivity of Fibroblast Growth Factor 23 measurements in tumor induced osteomalacia, 2006, Hypercalcemia: A practical approach to a surprising condition, 2007, Combination therapy for treatment of osteoporosis: A review, 2007. Mem.: ACP, Soc. for the Study of Reproduction, The Pituitary Soc., Endocrine Soc. Office: University of Virginia Fontaine Research Pk 450 Ray C Hunt Dr PO Box 801412 Charlottesville VA 22908 Office Phone: 434-243-2603. Office Fax: 434-243-9143. E-mail: acd6v@virginia.edu.

DALLA-FAVERA, RICCARDO, pathologist, educator; MD, U. Milan, 1976. Hematology/oncology residency U. Milan; vis. fellow Nat. Cancer Inst., Bethesda, Md.; asst. prof. NYU Sch. Medicine, 1983—91; prof. Columbia U. Coll. Physicians & Surgeons, NYC, 1991—, co-founder, dir. Inst. Cancer Genetics, 1999—, Percy & Joanne Uris prof. pathology and genetics & devel. Dep. dir. Columbia-Presbyn. Cancer Ctr., 1992—98; dir. Herbert Irving Comprehensive Cancer Ctr. (HICCC) Columbia U. Med. Ctr. & NY-Presbyn./Columbia, 2005—; bd. dirs. Callisto Pharmaceuticals, Inc., 2005—; co-founder, bd. dirs. Therasis, Inc., 2007—; mem. sci. adv. bd. TrovaGene, Inc., 2010—. Assoc. editor Jour. Clin. Investigation; contbr. articles to profl. jours. Recipient MERIT Award, NIH, 1987, 2002. Fellow: American Assn. Physicians; mem.: Leukemia Soc. America (Stohlman award 1987), Inst. Medicine. Achievements include recognition as a leader in molecular pathology of lymphoid malignancies; first investigator to identify and clone several human protooncogenes and to demonstrate their involvement in cancer-associated chromosomal amplifications and translocations. Office: Inst Cancer Genetics Irving Comprehensive Rsch Ctr Rm 508 A 1130 St Nicholas Ave New York NY 10032 Office Phone: 212-851-5273. Office Fax: 212-851-5256. E-mail: rd10@columbia.edu. *

DALLA VECCHIA, MARCELO, medical educator; b. Pato Branco, Paraná, Brazil, Sept. 15, 1977; D, U. Estadual Paulista, Botucatu, 2011. Prof. U. Fed. Sao Joao del-Rei, 2009—. Office: Rua Sebastiao Goncalves Coelho 400 Chanadour Dist Divinopolis Minas Gerais 35501-296 Brazil Business E-Mail: mdvecchia@yahoo.com.br.

D'ALLEST, ANNE-MARIE, physician; b. Aups, France, Nov. 3, 1934; d. Raymond and Joséphine Morel; m. Frédéric JP d'ALLEST, Mar. 8, 1963; children: Pierre, Vincent, Christophe. MD in Pediatrics & Neurophysiology, Faculté de Médecine, Marseille, 1964; grad in Pediatrics, Faculté de médecine de Marseille, 1963. Cert. neurology, neurophysiology hosps. practician Assistance Publique-Hôpitaux de Paris, 1986; applied statistics to medicine & biology ISUP, 1966. With Inst. Nat. de la Santé et Recherche Médicale, 1965—70, Trousseau Hosp., Hôpitaux de Paris, 1972—84; pratician physiology lab. & neonatal intensive care unit Antoine Béclère Hosp., 1978—2000; physiology asst. U. Paris XI, 1979—81; neurophysiology Béclère Hosp., 1981—86, neurophysiology médecin des hôpitaux, 1986—2000, epileptic deseases children & youngsters clin. follow up & treatment, 1984—2000; hon. medicine physician Assistance Publique- Hôpitaux de Paris, 2000—. Clin. neurophysiology prof. Pierre et Marie Curie in Paris VI, 1985—92. Contbr. articles to profl. publs. Sec. Groupe Tiers Monde Meudon. Mem.: Ligue française contre l'épilepsie, Epilepsies- France Assn. (cons.). Achievements include advances in EEG of the very premature newborn; advances in electroencephalography in premature and full-term infants. Avocations: skiing, mountain climbing, sailing, music, theater. Home: 6 Rue Marcel Allegot 92190 Meudon France Home Phone: 33685077644. Personal E-mail: annemariedallest@orange.fr.

DALLI, MEHMET, dental educator; b. Diyarbakir, Turkey, Jan. 16, 1976; PhD, Inst. Health Scis., 2009. Asst. prof., faculty dentistry University Dicle, 2005—. Co-dir. Inst. Health Scis., 2010. Avocations: travel, reading. Home: University Dicle Faculty Dentistry Diyarbakir 21280 Turkey Home Fax: 904122488100. Business E-Mail: mdalli@dicle.edu.tr.

DALLOS, PETER JOHN, neurobiologist, educator; b. Budapest, Hungary, Nov. 26, 1934; arrived in US, 1956, naturalized, 1962; s. Ernest and Maria Dallos; m. Joan Usis, Aug. 18, 1977; 1 child by previous marriage, Christopher. Student, Tech. U. Budapest, 1953-56; BS, Ill. Inst. Tech., 1958; MS, Northwestern U., 1959, PhD, 1962. Rsch. engr. Am. Machine and Foundry Co., 1959; cons. engr., 1959-60; mem. faculty Northwestern U., 1962—, prof. audiology and elec. engring., 1969—, prof. neurobiology and physiology, 1981—, chmn., 1981-84, 86-87, assoc. dean Coll. Arts and Scis., 1984-85, John Evans prof. neurosci., 1986—, Hugh Knowles prof. audiology, 1994—2003, acting v.p. for rsch., 2003—. Vis. scientist Karolinska Inst., Stockholm, 1977-78; chmn. behavioral and neuroscis. rev. panel No. 5 Nat. Inst. Neurol., Communicative Disorders and Stroke, NIH, 1982-85, mem. nat. adv. council, 1984-87 Author: The Auditory Periphery: Biophysics and Physiology, 1973; editor: The Cochlea, 1996, Audition, The Senses, 2008; contbr. articles to profl. jours. Recipient 12th ann. award Beltone Inst. Hearing Rsch., 1977, Internat. prize Amplifon Rsch. and Study Ctr., 1984, Senator Jacob Javits Neurosci. Investigator award, 1984, Honors of Assn. award Am. Speech-Lang.-Hearing Assn., 1994, Bekesy medal of Acoustical Soc. Am., 1995, Sigma Xi Disting. Nat. lectr., 1997-98, Acta Otolaryngologica Internat. prize, 1997, Kresge-Mirmelstein prize La. State U., 2000; Guggenheim fellow, 1977-78; McKnight sr. fellow, 1997-2000, Guyot prize, 2004, Hugh Knowles prize, 2005, Lifetime Achievement award, Am. Auditory Soc., 2008. Fellow IEEE (life), AAAS, Acoustical Soc. Am., Am. Acad. Arts and Scis.; mem. Soc. for Neurosci., Assn. for Rsch. in Otolaryngology (pres. 1992-93, award of merit 1994), Am. Physiological Soc., Collegium Otolaryngologicum Amicitae Sacrum, Hungarian Acad. Scis., Sigma Xi, Tau Beta Pi, Eta Kappa Nu. Office: Northwestern U 2240 Campus Dr Evanston IL 60208-0837 Business E-Mail: p-dallos@northwestern.edu.

DALLURA, SAL ANTHONY, physician; b. Flushing, NY, Nov. 7, 1960; s. Russ and Mayann (Taranto) D.; m. Donna Ann Baldassare, Aug. 6, 1983 (div. Mar. 1993); children: Christopher Anthony, Corinne Elizabeth; m. Stacy Elizabeth Carberry, July 1, 1995 (div. Jan. 1999); 1 child, Matthew Anthony; m. Tammy L. Chance, Dec. 27, 1999. BS in Pre-Profl. Studies cum laude, U. Notre Dame, South Bend, Ind., 1982; DO with honors, NY Coll. Osteo. Medicine, Old Westbury, 1986. Diplomate Am. Acad. Family Physicians, 1990, 1996, 2002, 09, Am. Acad. Urgent Care Medicine, 2009. Mng. ptnr. Flashner Med. Ptnrship., Babylon, NY, 1989-91; assoc. physician Moriches Med. Care, Center Moriches, NY, 1989-91, Digiovanna, Massepequa Park, NY, 1991-92, Tippecanoe Family Physicians, Tipp City, Ohio, 1992-98, Milton Union Med. Ctr., West Milton, Ohio, 1998-2000; physician mng. ptnr. After Hours Family Care, Tipp City, 1994-98; physician Upper Valley Profl. Corp., 1994-2000, Kenbrook Med. Ctr., 2000—02, St. Marys Family Practice, Ohio, 2002—05, Holzer Clinic, Jackson, Ohio, 2005—08, Premier Health Care Svcs., Inc., 2007—09, Emcare, Inc., 2009—10, Cape Fear Valley Med. Ctr., 2010—; urgent care physician Mercer County Cmty. Hosp., Midwest Emergency Physician Svcs., 2002—06; urgent, emergency care physician Miami Valley Hosp., 2002—06. Expert witness malpractice def., case revs., depositions, testimony for family practice. Recipient Excellence in Gastroenterology award, 1986. Fellow Am. Acad. Family Practice; mem. Am. Osteo. Assn., Am. Acad. Urgent Care Medicine, NC Osteo. Med. Assn., Ohio Osteo. Assn., Alpha Epsilon Delta. Republican. Roman Catholic. Avocations: model railroading, reading, audio and video entertainment, computer research, med. drama writing. Office: Cape Fear Valley Med Ctr 1638 Owen Dr Fayetteville NC 28304 Office Phone: 910-615-4374. Personal E-mail: doclovesthefightingirish@gmail.com. Business E-Mail: sdallura@nc.rr.com.

DALRYMPLE, CHRISTOPHER GUY, chiropractor; b. Beaumont, Tex., Sept. 2, 1958; s. Guy H. and Betty Jane (Williams) D.; m. Angela Hackley, Dec. 15, 1979; children: Sarah E., William C., Clayton G. Student, Baylor U., 1976-78; D in Chiropractic Medicine, Tex. Chiropractic Coll., 1982. Diplomate Nat. Bd. Chiropractic Examiners, Tex. Bd. Chiropractic Examiners; ordained Baptist Deacon, 1988. Chiropractor Brassard Chiropractic Clinic, Beaumont, 1982-85; chiropractic physician, adminstr. Brenham (Tex.) Chiropractic Clinic, 1985—. Host Back Talk, 1987-88; chair Tex. Chiropractic PAC; cons., lectr. in field. Author: Brenham & Masonry...150 Years Together, 1995, San Felipe Secrets Unveiled, 2008; editor Mind and Thought Series; contbr. articles to profl. jours. Team chiropractor track team Blinn Coll., Brenham, 1987-94, Tex. track and field participants Olympics, 1992; Sunday sch. dir. First Bapt., 1986-87, 90-93, Sunday sch. tchr., 1987-89, bd. trustees Calvary Bapt. Ch., Brenham, 1992-94, Sunday sch. tchr. youth, 1993-94, actor, playwright ch. pageants, 1993-94, 96, 98, 99, 03, deacon, chmn., 1994-98, chmn. pers. com., 1995-98, chmn. long range planning com., 1995-98, adult Sunday sch. tchr., 1995-99; treas. Brenham Ind. Sch. Devel.-PAC, 1994; participant Health Occupation Students of Am. Program, Brenham H.S. Recipient State Sweepstakes Winner "Jake", Tex. Jaycees, 1984, Outstanding Officer, 1984. Fellow: Internat. Coll. Chiropractors; mem.: Grand Priory N.Am. (Templar Order), Tex. Chiropractic Assn. (labor rels. 1983, dist. 9 sec. 1983—84, chmn. publ. com. 1987—99, editor-in-chief 1987—99, membership com. 1994—95, dist. 8 state dir. 1996—99, state sec. 1999, pres.-elect 2000, pres. 2001, internal affairs coord. 2002—11, comm. dir. 2009—11, Young Chiropractor award 1997, Pres.'s award 1999, 2004, 2006, 2010), Am. Chiropractic Assn., Masons (Knight Comdr., Knight Templar), K.T., Baylor Alumni Assn. (life), Tex. Chiropractic Coll. Alumni Assn., Gideons Internat. (Bible chmn. 1994—2005), Masons, Graham Masonic Lodge (various offices), Delta Sigma Chi (sec. 1981, bd. dirs. 1982). Republican. Baptist. Avocations: kendo, Aikido. Office: Brenham Chiropractic Clinic PO Box 2350 Brenham TX 77834-2350 Office Phone: 979-836-4610. Business E-Mail: cdal@fixback.com.

DALSING, MICHAEL CLETUS, surgeon, educator; s. Vincent John and Nellie Mary Dalsing; m. Rosa Marie Olejniczak, May 20, 1978; children: Jessica Rose, Rachael Augusta, Heather Matilda. BA in Biology, St. Mary's Coll., Winona, Minn., 1974; MD, The Med. Coll. Wis., Milw., 1978. Cert. in vascular surgery Am. Bd. Surgery, 1986, in gen. surgery Am. Bd. Surgery, 1984, in surg. critical care Am. Bd. Surgery, 1992. Internship in surg. Sch. Medicine, Indiana U., Indpls., 1978—79, residency in surg., 1979—82, chief residency in surg., 1982—83; fellowship in vascular surgery Northwestern U., Chgo., 1983—84; from asst. prof. to prof. surgery Sch. Medicine Ind. U., Indpls., 1984—2004, E. Dale and Susan E. Habegger prof. surgery Sch. Medicine, 2004—, dir. vascular surg. residency program Sch. Medicine, 2001—. Contbr. chapters to books, over 100 articles to profl. jours. Named alumnus mem., Alpha Omega Alpha, 1988; Conrad Jobst fellow, Northwestern U., 1983. Fellow: ACS (gov. from ind. 2004—); mem.: Am. Bd. Surgery (Vascular Surgery Bd.), Assn. Prof. Vascular Surgery (pres. elect), Assn. Program Dirs. Vascular Surg. (pres.), Midwestern Vascular Surg. Soc. (pres. 2005—06), Am. Venous Forum (pres. 2006—07), Ctrl. Surg. Assn., Soc. Clin. Vascular Surg., Soc. Vascular Surg., Am. Surg. Soc. Roman Cath. Achievements include research in vascular surgery esp regarding venous valves, carotid artery surgery, collateral blood vessel development and other unusual vascular disorders. Avocations: travel, tennis, football. Office: Indiana University School of Medicine 1801 North Senate Blvd MPC-2 S-3500 Indianapolis IN 46202 Office Fax: 317-962-0289. Business E-Mail: mdalsing@iupui.edu.

DALTON, CLAUDETTE ELLIS HARLOE, anesthesiologist, educator, dean; b. Roanoke, Va., Jan. 18, 1947; d. John Pinckney and Dorothy Anne (Ellis) Harloe; m. Henry Tucker Dalton, May 17, 1973 (div. 1979); 1 child, Gordon Tucker; m. H. Christopher Alexander, III, Apr. 29, 2000 (div. 2010). BA, Sweet Briar Coll., Va., 1969; MD, U. Va., Charlottesville, 1974. Resident anesthesiology U. N.C., Chapel Hill, 1974—77; med. edn. Lenoir County Meml Hosp./East Carolina U., Kinston, 1978—80; med. edn. intensive care Presbyn Hosp., Charlotte, NC, 1981—82; practice anesthesiology Charlotte Eye, Ear, Nose and Throat Hosp., 1982—85, Medivision Charlotte and Orthop. Hosp. Charlotte, 1985—89; asst. prof. U. Va. Health Scis. Ctr., Charlottesville, Va., 1992—2006; dir. Office Cmty. Based Med. Edn., Charlottesville, 1994—2006; asst. dean cmty. based med. edn. U. Va., Charlottesville, 1996—2006, med. dir. Pre-Anesthesia Clinic, 1996—2006, asst. prof. anesthesiology and med. edn., 1996—2006; med. dir. perioperative svcs. Rockingham Meml. Hosp., 2006—10, cons. in surg. efficiency, 2010—11; founder med. team for the remote area med. clinic in Wise Cmty. Svc./Outreach, 1999—; cons. Intermittent Domestic Joint Commn. Resources, 2011—. Adv. bd. Nat. Bd. Med. Examiners, 2004—10; exec. com. Accreditation Coun. Continuing Med. Edn., 2004—09; mem. Va. Bd. Medicine, 2005—, chair credentials com., 2008—10, chair competency com., 2008—, v.p., 2010—, pres., 2011—, chair, legis. com., 2010; spkr. in field; elected AMA Coun. Med. Edn., 2004—11, chair, 2008—09, past chair, 2009—10, chair nominating com., 2006; chair Subcom. on Continuing Med. Edn., 2005—07, Task Force on Rules & Regulations, 2006, Reentry Task Force, 2007—08, MOC/MOL Task Force, 2008—11, cons., surg. efficiency & productivity, 2010—. Author: emergency med. svc. tng. program, 1981, patient edn. materials for illiterate patients, 1979—. Bd. dirs. Charlottesville Family Svcs., Family Svcs. Albemarle County, 1992—93, Coun. Aging, Am. Cancer Soc.; exec. dir. Cmty. Involvement Coun. Lenoir County, Kinston, 1979; county coord. Internat. Yr. of Child, Kinston, 1979; bd. dirs. U. Va. Women's Ctr., Lenoir County CC; mem. sch. medicine com. women U. Va. Med. Sch. Recipient Gov.'s award, State of NC, 1980, Outstanding Tchg. award, U. Va. Sch. Medicine, 1993, Sharon L. Hostler U. Va. Outstanding Woman in Medicine award, 2002, Svc. to Disadvantaged Populations award, AMA-Hosp. Rsch. and Edn. Trust, 2005, Pres.'s award, Va. Acad. Family Physicians, 2006. Mem.: AMA (Coun. on Med. Edn.), Rockingham Med. Soc., Va. Soc. Anesthesiology, Albemarle County Med. Soc., Med. Soc. Va. (bd. dirs. Va. Health Quality Coun. 1995—97, chair ad hoc com. on telemedicine 1996—99, 2d v.p. 1998—99, chair scope of practice com. 1999—2002, dist. dir. 1999—2005, editor med. news Va. Med. Quar., legis. com., health access com., strategic planning and implementation com., women's com., med. affairs com., bd. medicine adv. com., Cmty. Svc award 2003), Alpha Omega Alpha, U. Va. Med. Alumni Assn. (assoc. bd. dirs. 1989—92, chair women in medicine leadership conf. 1998—99). Avocations: dance, writing, gardening, history.

DALTON, JACK F., oncologist, educator; MD, U. Pitts. Intern Geo Wash. Univ. Hosp., 1972; radiation oncologist Lenox Hill Hosp.; asst. clin prof. Mt. Sinai Sch. of Medicine; resident in hematology Mt. Sinai Hosp., 1972—75, radiation oncologist, resident in diagnostic radialogy, 1979—81. Recipient Castle Connolly Top Doctors award, NY Metro Area, 1998—2010, 2011. Mem.: Am. Soc. for Therapeutic Radiology and Oncology, Am. Soc. of Clin. Oncology. Office: Mount Sinai Medical Center One Gustave L. Levy Pl New York NY 10029

DALTON, JAMES EDGAR, JR., health facility administrator; b. Gretna, Va., Sept. 17, 1942; married. Bachelors degree, Randolph-Macon Coll., 1964; Masters degree, Va. Commonwealth U., 1966. Adminstrv. resident Lynchburg (Va.) Gen. Hosp., 1965-66, adminstrv. asst., 1966-69, asst. adminstr., 1969-70; adminstr. Princeton (W.Va.) Cmty. Hosp., 1970-72; regional adminstr. Humana, Inc., Dallas, 1972-73, regional v.p. Tampa, Fla., 1973-76; dir. hosp. svcs. Am. Medicorp Inc., Atlanta, 1976-77, Dallas, 1977-78; v.p. Hosp. Corp. Am., Nashville, 1978-79, Arlington, Tex., 1979-87, HealthTrust, Inc., Arlington, 1987-89, Nashville, 1989-90; pres., CEO Quorum Health Group, Inc., Brentwood, Tenn., 1990-2001; pres. Edinburgh Assocs., Inc., 2001—07. Chmn. Signature Hosp. Corp., 2006—. Home and Office: 6505 Edinburgh Dr Nashville TN 37221-3707 Home Phone: 615-661-9790. Personal E-mail: jdalton561@aol.com.

DALTON, MARTIN L., retired dean, thoracic surgeon; b. Columbus, Ga. B, Auburn U., 1953; MD, U. Ala., Birmingham, 1957. Rotating intern Carraway Meth. Med. Ctr., Birmingham, Ala.; surgical resident U. Miss. Med. Ctr., resident in thoracic and cardiovascular surgery; chief thoracic sect. Dept. Surgery Walter Reed Army Inst. Rsch., Washington; asst. prof. divsn. thoracic and cardiovascular surgery U. Tex. Southwestern Med. Sch., Dallas; pvt. practice in thoracic and cardiovascular surgery Lubbock, Tex., 1966; clin. prof. Tex. Tech U. Sch. Med., 1973—83, chief divsn. thoracic surgery, 1973—83; prof. surgery U. Miss., 1983—90, Mercer U. Sch. Med., 1990—2008, chmn. Dept. Surgery, 1991—2008, dean, 2005—08, dean & prof. emeritus, 2008—; chief surgery and program dir. surgery residency Med. Ctr. Ctrl. Ga., Macon, 1991—2008. Mem.: Will C. Sealy Surg. Soc., James D. Hardy Surg. Soc., Atlanta Vascular Soc. (former pres.), Am. Coll. Surgeons (former pres. Ga. Chpt.), Ga. Surg. Soc. (former pres.), Southeastern Surg. Congress, Am. Assn. for Vascular Surgery, Internat. Surg. Soc., Soc. Thoracic Surgeons, Am. Assn. for Thoracic Surgery, So. Surg. Assn., Am. Surg. Assn. Achievements include being a member of team that performed first successful human lung transplant, June 11, 1963. Office: Mercer Univ Med Sch 1550 College St Macon GA 31207-0001 *

D'ALTON, MARY, obstetrician-gynecologist, educator; MD, Ireland, 1976. Cert. maternal and fetal medicine, diplomate Am. Bd. Ob-Gyn. Resident obstetrics and gynecology Ottawa Gen. Hosp., Ont., Canada, 1977—82; fellow Tufts-New Eng. Med. Ctr., Boston, 1982—84; chair dept. of obstetrics and gynecology Columbia Univ. Med. Ctr., 1993; prin. investigator first and 2nd trimester evaluation of risk Nat. Inst. of Child Health and Human Devel. (NICHD), mem. coun.; staff ob-gyn. NY Presbyn. Hosp., NY. Clin. prof. obstetrics and gynecology Columbia Univ. Coll. of Physicians and Surgeons. Office: NewYork-Presbyterian Hospital 622 W 168th St New York NY 10032 Office Phone: 212-305-2500.

DALTON, WILLIAM STEVEN, hospital administrator, oncologist, educator; b. Ft. Worth, 1949; BA in Chemistry/Philosophy, U. N.Mex., 1971; MD, Ind. U., 1980, PhD in Toxicology/Med. Life Scis., 1976. Diplomate Am. Bd. Internal Medicine, Am. Bd. Oncology. Intern Ind. U., Indpls., 1980-81; resident in internal medicine U. Ariz., Tucson, 1981-83, fellow in oncology, 1983—; assoc. dir. clin. investigations H. Lee Moffitt Cancer Ctr., Tampa, Fla., 1997—99, dep. dir., 1999—2001, pres., CEO, dir., 2002—. Faculty medicine, pharmacology U. Ariz. Coll. Medicine, 1985—96, prof., 1993—96, dean, 2001—02; prof. oncology, medicine, and biochemistry U. South Fla., 1997—99, prof., chmn. Dept. Interdisciplinary Oncology, 1999—2001. Mem. ACP, Am. Osteo. Assn., Sigma Xi. Office: H Lee Moffitt Cancer Ctr 12902 Magnolia Dr Tampa FL 33612-9416 E-mail: dalton@moffitt.usf.edu. *

DALY, BENEDICT DUDLEY THOMAS, JR., cardiothoracic surgeon, educator; b. Boston, Nov. 28, 1939; s. Benedict Dudley Thomas and Alice Margaret (Groden) Daly; m. Joan Marie Behenna, Sept. 25, 1971; children: Jennifer, Benedict, Matthew. AB, Georgetown U., 1961; MD, Boston U., 1965. Intern, Boston City Hosp., 1965—66, resident, 1966—72; assoc. surgeon Tex. Heart Inst., Houston, 1972—75; dir. cardiothoracic surgery St. Elizabeth Hosp., Brighton, Mass., 1976—78; surgeon New Eng. Med. Ctr., Boston, 1978—87, sr. surgeon, 1987—; chief cardiothoracic surgery VA Med. Ctr., Boston, 1987—2002, Newton Wellesley Hosp., 1986—93; clin. dir. gen. thoracic surgery Boston Med. Ctr., 2002—; dir. Ctr. Thoracic Oncology, 2003—; assoc. prof. Tufts U., Boston, 1976—84, prof. cardiothoracic surgery, 1984—2002, Boston U. Sch. Medicine, 2003—; chief cardiothoracic surgery Boston Med. Ctr., 2008—; chmn. dept. cardiothoracic surgery Boston U. Sch. Medicine, 2008—. Contbr. articles to profl. jours. Grantee, NIH-NHLBI, 1978—84, Am. Heart Assn., 1973—74. Fellow: ACS, Am. Coll. Cardiology, Coll. Chest Physicians; mem.: Am. Assn. Thoracic Surgery, Soc. Thoracic Surgeons. Home: 12 Wildwood Cir Wellesley MA 02482-6465 Office: Boston Med Ctr Ctr Thoracic Oncology Robinson B405 88 E Newton St Boston MA 02118 Office Phone: 617-638-5600. Business E-Mail: benedict.daly@bmc.org.

DALY, JOHN M., surgeon, educator; b. Phila., Dec. 10, 1947; m. Mary F. Bonner, Aug. 1971; children: John M. Jr., William L., Brian P., Timothy J., Patrick T., Maureen P. BA cum laude, LaSalle Coll., 1969; MD, Temple U., 1973. Diplomate Am. Bd. Surgery. Intern Hermann Hosp. U. Tex. Med. Sch., Houston, 1973-74; resident in gen. surgery U. Tex. Med. Sch., Houston, 1974-78, chief resident in gen. surgery, 1977-78, instr. surgery, 1978; faculty assoc. in surgery M.D. Anderson Hosp., Houston, 1978-79; asst. prof. surgery U. Tex. Med. Sch., Houston, 1978-80, M.D. Anderson Hosp. and Tumor Inst., Houston, 1979-80; assoc. attending surgeon Meml. Sloan-Kettering Cancer Ctr., NYC, 1980-85; prof. surgery, chief div. surgical oncology U. Pa., Phila., 1986—93; asst. prof. surgery Weill Med. Coll. of Cornell U., NYC, 1980-81, Lewis Atterbury Stimson prof., 1993—2002, prog. dir., gen. surgery residency prog., 1993—2002, chair, surgery dept., 1993—2002; surgeon-in-chief NY Presbyterian Hosp., 1993—2002; dean Temple U. Med. Sch., Phila., 2002—11, Harry C. Donahoo prof. surgery, dean emeritus, 2011—, surg. dir. William Maul Measey Inst. Clin. Simulation and Patient Safety, 2011—. Asst. mem. Sloan-Kettering Inst., 1981-84, assoc. mem., 1984-85; assoc. attending physician N.Y. Hosp., 1983; Jonathan E. Rhoads prof. surgery U. Pa. Sch. Medicine, Phila., 1986; cons. in surgery Meml. Sloan-Kettering Cancer Ctr., N.Y.C., 1986. Contbr. numerous articles in sci. and profl. jours. Rsch. grantee Smith Kline and French, 1967; named one of Outstanding Young Men of Am., 1972; recipient Rsch. award So. Med. Soc., 1974, Resident Rsch. award, 1977-78, George Waldren award for Outstanding Chief Resident in Surgery, U. Tex. Med. Sch., 1978, Sam E. Roberts Nutrition Found. medal U. Kans. Sch. Medicine, 1981. Mem. AMA (Joseph B. Goldberger Rsch. award 1970-72), Am. Cancer Soc. (bd. dirs. Phila. divsn., nominating com., profl. edn. com., pub. edn. com., Clin. Rsch. award 1977-78, jr. faculty clin. fellowship 1979-82), ACS (Schering Rsch. award 1977-78), AAAS, Am. Assn. Cancer Rsch., Am. Gastroent. Soc., Am. Soc. for Parenteral and Enteral Nutrition (program chmn. 4th clin. congress, chmn. edn. com. 1980-81, treas. and exec. com. 1981-83, pres. 1985-86), Am. Soc. Clin. Oncology, Am. Soc. Clin. Nutrition, Am. Surg. Assn., Assn. Acad. Surgery (program com. 1979-80, 80-81, com. on issues 1980-82, nominating com. 1983-84, councilman 1984-86), Collegium Internationale Chirurgiae Digestivae, Fedn. Am. Socs. Exptl. Biology and Medicine, Am. Inst. Nutrition, Internat. Soc. Surgery, Internat. Soc. Parenteral Nutrition, N.Y. Cancer Soc., N.Y. Surg. Soc., Phila. Acad. Surgery, Phila. Coll. Physicians, Soc. Surgery of Alimentary Tract, Soc. Clin. Surgery, Soc. Surg. Oncology (pres. 2002-03), Soc. Univ. Surgeons. Clubs: Surg. Biology III. Office: Temple U Sch Medicine 3400 N Broad St Philadelphia PA 19140 Office Phone: 215-707-8773. Business E-Mail: johndaly@temple.edu. *

DALY, MARK J., medical educator; BS in Physics, MIT; PhD in Genetics, Leiden U. Dir., human genetics informatics group Whitehead Inst. Ctr. for Genome Rsch., 1996; Pfizer fellow in computational biology Whitehead Inst. Ctr. for Biomedical Rsch., 2001—04; asst. prof. medicine Harvard Med. Sch./Mass. Gen. Hosp.; assoc. mem. Broad Inst. of Harvard and MIT. Contbr. several articles to profl. jours. Office: Ctr for Human Genetic Rsch Mass Gen Hosp Richard B Simches Rsch Ctr 185 Cambridge St CPZN-6818 Boston MA 02114 Office Phone: 617-643-3290. E-mail: mjdaly@chgr.mgh.harvard.edu.

DALY, MIRIAM SHAMER, retired family physician; b. Balt., Jan. 26, 1925; d. Maurice Emory and Bertha (Tapman) Shamer; m. Harold L. Daly, Jr., June 28, 1948 (dec. July 2, 1989); children: John, Martha, Thomas, David. AB, Goucher Coll., 1946; MD, U. Md., 1950. Diplomate Am. Bd. Family Practice. Intern Luth. Hosp. of Md., Balt., 1950-51, resident, 1951-52; clinic physician Balt. City Health Dept., Md. State Health Dept., 1952-55; practicing physician Balt., 1952-55; physician pvt. practice Albion, Mich., 1955-93; ret., 1993. Leader, camp counsellor Girl Scouts, South Ctrl. Mich., 1955—, pres. Irish Hills Coun., 1993-97, coord. Albion ARC blood drives, 1994—; mem. Sweet Adelines, 2003-05; bd. dir., 1990-97, Albion Ambulance Svc., 1989-95, ARC Calhoun County chpt., 1993—, Great Lakes Region Blood Svcs., ARC, 1994-95; bd. dirs. Albion Homer United Way, 1999-2005, pres., 2001, 02; mem. adv. com. Calhoun County Sr. Millage, 2000-07. Recipient Girl Scouts Thanks Badge, Irish Hills Girls Scouts Coun., 1977, 1993, Cmty. Recognition award, Albion Coll., 1996, Athena award, Greater Albion C. of C., 2000. Mem. AMA, AAUW (albion br., pres. 2006-08), NAACP (exec. bd. 2005—, bd. dirs. Albion br.), AALL (curriculum com., 2002-, coun., 2004-2011), Mich. State Med. Soc. (Frederick and Besse Moulton Plessner Meml. award 1996), Calhoun County Med. Soc., Am. Acad. Family Practice, Mich. Acad. Family Practice, Rotary, SIS(mentor to teenage girls, 2010-) Avocations: piano, photography, gardening. Personal E-mail: msdaly@hotmail.com.

DALY, WALTER JOSEPH, medical educator; b. Michigan City, Ind., Jan. 12, 1930; m. Joan Brown, June 12, 1953; children: Lois Kay, Alice Louise. AB, Ind. U., 1951, MD, 1955, ScD, 1998. Diplomate Am. Bd. Internal Medicine. Intern Ind. U., 1955-56, resident, 1956-57, 59-62, instr. medicine, 1962-63, asst. prof., 1963-65, assoc. prof., 1965-68, prof., 1968-77, John B. Hickam prof., 1977-80, J.O. Ritchey prof., 1980-95, J.O. Ritchey prof. emeritus, 1995—; chmn. dept. medicine, 1970-83; dean Sch. Medicine, 1983-95; dean emeritus Ind. U., 1995—. Dir. Regenstrief Inst. Health Rsch., 1976-83. Capt. M.C., U.S. Army, 1957-59. Master ACP (gov. 1980-84), Am. Physiol. Soc., Ctr. Soc. Clin. Rsch. (pres. 1980-81), Am. Soc. Clin. Investigation, Am. Clin. and Climatol. Assn. (v.p. 2004-05), Assn. Am. Physicians. Office: Ind U Sch Medicine 1120 South Dr Indianapolis IN 46202-5135 Office Phone: 317-274-5261.

DAMADE, RICHARD, physician; b. Paris, Aug. 16, 1960; MD, U. Paris VII, 1990. Svc. de médecine interne rhumatologie, Praticien hospitalier Hôpiltal louis Pasteur, Chartres, France, 1993—. Mem.: Soc. Nat. Française Médecine Interne. Office: Bp 30407 Chartres F-28018 France Business E-Mail: rdamade@ch-chartres.fr.

DAMADIAN, RAYMOND VAHAN, biophysicist; b. Forest Hills, NY, Mar. 16, 1936; s. Vahan and Odette (Yazedjian) Damadian; m. Elizabeth Donna Terry, June 4, 1960; children: Timothy, Jevan, Kiera. Attended studied violin, Juilliard Sch. Music, 1944—52; BS in Math., U. Wis., 1956; MD, Albert Einstein Coll. Medicine, 1960. Univ. rsch. fellow in biophysics Harvard U., Cambridge, Mass., 1963—65; sr. investigator Sch. Aerospace Medicine, USAF, 1965—67; asst. prof. SUNY, Bklyn., 1967—71, assoc. prof., 1971—80; founder, pres., chmn. Fonar Corp., Melville, NY, 1978—. Career investigator Health Rsch. Coun., NYC, 1967—72, Capt. USAF, 1963—65. Recipient Lawrence Sperry award, 1984, Nat. medal of Tech., 1988, Lemelson-MIT Lifetime Achievement award, 2001, Benjamin Franklin medal and Bower award for Bus. Leadership, Franklin Inst., 2004, Nat. Inventor of Yr. award, Intellectual Property Owners Edn. Found., 2007; named to National Inventors Hall of Fame, 1989; Ford Found. Scholar, U. Wis., 1944—52. Mem.: AAAS, Soc. for Med. Innovation and Tech., Internat. Soc. for Magnetic Resonance in Medicine, Biophys. Soc., Am. Chem. Soc., Sigma Xi. Achievements include development of MRI (detecting cancer in tissue) in 1980; Upright Multi-Position (tradmarked) Magnetic Resonance Imaging (MRI) technology; holds over 45 patents for improvements to MRI scanner. Office: Fonar Corp 110 Marcus Dr Melville NY 11747-4292

DAMASIO, ANTONIO R., psychology and neurology professor, researcher; b. Lisbon, Portugal, Feb. 25, 1944; arrived in US, 1975, naturalized; m. Hanna Damasio. MD, U. Lisbon, 1969, DMS, 1974. Intern U. Hosp., Lisbon, 1969-72; chief Language Rsch. Lab., Ctr. de Estudos Egas Moniz, 1971—75; prof. auxiliar in neurology U. Lisbon Med. Sch., 1974—75; vis. asst. prof. U. Iowa, Iowa City, 1975—76, assoc. prof. dept. neurology, 1976-80, chief Divsn. of Behavioral Neurology & Cognitive Neuroscience, 1977—2005, prof. neurology, 1980—2005, dir. Alzheimer's Disease Rsch. Ctr., 1985—2005, head Dept. Neurology, 1986—2005, M.W. Van Allen Disting. prof., 1989—2005, dist. adj. prof. neurology, 2005—; prof. psychology, neuroscience and neurology U. So. Calif., LA, 2005—, dir. Brain and Creativity Inst., 2005—, David Dornsife prof. neuroscience Coll. of Letters, Arts and Scis., 2006—. Adj. prof. Salk Inst., San Diego, 1989—; mem. planning subcom. Nat. Adv. Neurol. Disorders Stroke Coun. Author: Lesion Analysis in Neuropsychgology, 1989 (award Assn. Am. Pubs. 1990); mem. editorial bd. Trends in Neuroscis., 1986-91, Behavioral Brain Rsch., 1988—, Cerebral Cortex, 1990—, Jour. Neurosci., 1990, Cognitive Brain Rsch., Learning and Memory, spl. brain issue Sci. Am, 1992, Descartes' Error: Emotion, Reason, and the Human Brain, 1994, The Feeling of What Happens: Body and Emotion in the Making of Consciousness, 1999. Recipient Disting. prof. award U. So. Calif., Prix Plasticite' Neuronale, Ispen Found., 1997, Golden Brain award, 1995, The Reenpää prize, Finland, 2000, Arnold Pfeffer Prize, 2002, Dr. William Beaumont award AMA, 1990, Pessoa prize Portuguese govt., 1992, Prince of Asturias Award for Sci. and Tech. Rsch., 2005, Presdl. Medal of the Am. Psychoanalytic Assn., 2006. Fellow Am. Acad. Neurology, Am. Neurol. Asns.; mem. NAS Inst. Medicine, Soc. for Neurosci., Acad. Aphasia (pres. 1983), Behavioral Neurology Soc., (pres. 1985), Royal Soc. Medicine Belgium (elected), European Acad. Arts and Scis. (elected), Am. Acad. Arts and Scis, Acad. Scis., Lisbon. Office: Brain and Creativity Inst U So Calif 3641 Watt Way Ste 126 Los Angeles CA 90089-2520 Office Phone: 213-821-2377. Office Fax: 213-821-3099. E-mail: damasio@usc.edu.

DAME, CATHERINE ELAINE, acupuncturist; b. Holyoke, Mass., Oct. 1, 1951; d. Josaphat Charles and Lillian Geneva (Archer) Boulanger; m. William Henry Dame, Jan. 9, 1970 (div. May 1999), Jayden D. Charbonneau, 2007; 1 child, Cristinna Lian. Acupuncture Diplomate, N.E. Sch. Acupuncture, Watertown, Mass., 1992; student, Ind. U., 1988-93; MEd, Cambridge Coll., 1994. Lic. acupuncturist, Mass.; nat. bd. diploma in acupuncture, Nat. Cert. Commn. Acupuncture & Oriental Medicine. Dept. mgr. Zayre Dept. Store, Chicopee, Mass., 1969; retail sales clk. Woodward & Lothrop Store, Alexandria, Va., 1971-72; dept. mgr. Steiger Dept. Store, Enfield, Conn., 1972-73; retail sales clk. Point Dept. Store, Ft. Walton Beach, Fla., 1973-74; assembly, repair mfg. Texas Instruments, Ft. Walton Beach, 1974-75; tller Third Nat. Bank, Springfield, Mass., 1975-81, customer svc. rep., 1981-82; teller Bank of N.E./Fleet Bank, Springfield, 1990-93; owner, mgr. Acupuncture Svcs., Chicopee, 1994—. Cons. Cambridge Coll., Springfield, Mass., 1994-95; bus. office liaison Cambridge Coll., 1995-98, Acupuncture Cancer Patient, Meml. Sloan Kettering Cancer Ctr., Integrative Med. Svc., 2011; Traditional Chinese Med. tour, China, 2001. Mem. People to People Internat. Mem.: Acupuncture Soc. Mass., Nat. Commn. Cert. of Acupuncturists Directory, Am. Assn. Oriental Medicine, Assn. Profl. Genealogists, New Eng. Hist. Geneal. Soc., Chicopee C. of C., Kings Bridge Equine Rescue, Inc., Granby Regional Horse Coun. Office: Acupuncture Svcs Chicopee 665 Prospect St Chicopee MA 01020-3064 Office Phone: 413-536-4534.

DAMESHEK, H(AROLD) LEE, retired physician; b. Balt., Mar. 16, 1937; s. Samuel and Rose (Rudick) D.; m. Michelle Zubasic, Sept. 12, 1965; children: Lynne R. Shine, Amy D. Brumbaugh, David, Deborah. BS in Chemistry, Franklin and Marshall Coll., 1959; MD, Tufts U., 1963. Diplomate Am. Bd. Internal Medicine. Intern Presbyn.-Univ. Hosp., Pitts., 1963-64, resident in internal medicine, 1966-68; hematology fellow Ohio State U. Hosp., Columbus, 1968-69; practice medicine specializing in hematology and oncology Pitts., 1969—. Clin. instr. medicine U. Pitts., 1969-74, clin. asst. prof., 1974-81, clin. assoc. prof., 1981—; instr. West Penn Hosp., Pitts., 1969-77; chmn. cancer com. Presbyn.-Univ. Hsop., 1980—; cons. various hosps.; bd. dirs. Physicians' Health Plan Pa., 1986—. Contbr. articles to med. jours. Bd. dirs. Leukemia Soc. West Pa., 1971—, v.p., 1977-79, Am. Cancer Soc.; treas. Presbyn.-Univ. Hosp., 1984-86, v.p., 1986-88, pres. med. staff, 1988-90, mem. med. quality improvement com., 1991—; mem. med. adv. com. Cancer Support Ctr., 1987—; vol. faculty promotions com. U. Pitts. Med. Ctr., 1994—. Capt. U.S. Army, 1964-66. Fellow ACP; mem. AMA, Am. Soc. Hematology, Allegheny County Med. Soc. (treas. 1980-81, v.p 1982, pres. 1984, bd. dirs., 1996-99, peer rev. bd. 1991-94, Frederick Jacob award 1988), Pa. Med. Soc., Pitts. Acad. Medicine (treas. 1981—), Westmoreland Country Club (sec., bd. dirs.), Univ. Club Pitts. Home: 1630 Vineseian Pl Turtle Creek PA 15145 Personal E-mail: michellelee35@msn.com.

D'AMICO, GIUSEPPE, nephrologist; b. Messina, Italy, Sept. 6, 1929; s. Gaetano D'Amico and Gaetana Trifiletti; m. Anna Maria Allegri, July 11, 1957; 1 child, Stefano. MD, U. Milan, 1952. Diplomate Italian Bd. Internal Medicine. Trainee NIH, Chgo., 1957-58; tng. in internal medicine U. Milan, 1957, tng. in clin.pathology, 1962, prof. medicine, 1962; head divsn. nephrology San Carlo Hosp., Milan, 1967-95, dir. dept. nephrology and urology, 1995—2000, emeritus head nephrology, 2001—. Pres. Fondozione Damico Ricerca Sulle Malattie Renali, 2004—. Author 35 books on nephrology; contbr. over 400 articles to profl. jours., chpts. to books. Recipient Internat. Ganassini award, Milan, 1961, Ambrogino d'Oro Mayor of City of Milan, 1974, Disting. Internat. medal Nat. Kidney Found., 1997. Fellow Royal Coll. Physicians (London), Royal Coll. Physicians (Edinburg); mem. Internat. Soc. Nephrology (coun. 1984-93), European Soc. Nephrology (exec. coun. 1981-84), Italian Soc. Nephrology (pres. 1981-83). Business E-Mail: giuseppe.damico@fondazionedamico.org.

D'AMICO, RICHARD, plastic surgeon; b. NYC, May 2, 1951; MD, NYU Sch. Med., 1976. Cert. Am. Bd. Plastic Surgery, Advanced Edn. Cosmetic Surgery. Intern, surgery Georgetown U. Med. Ctr., Washington, 1976—77; resident, surgery U. Okla.-Tulsa Med. Ctr., 1978—79; resident, plastic and reconstructive surgery U. Rochester, NY, 1979—81; fellow plastic surgery Columbia Presbyn. Med. Ctr., NYC, 1981—83; plastic & reconstructive surgeon, dir. pvt. practice Plastic Surgery Skin Care Ctr., Englewood, NJ. Asst. clinical prof., dept. plastic surgery Mt. Sinai Med. Ctr., NYC; chief plastic surgery Englewood Hosp. Med. Ctr.; lectr. in field. Contbr. articles to profl. jours.; provides expert commentary media including Today Show, FOX News Channel, BBC as well as French TV. Surgical dir., vol. Healing The Children, Midlantic Chpt. Named one of Best Doctors in New York, New York Mag., Best Doctors in New Jersey, New Jersey Monthly. Mem.: NJ Soc. Plastic Surgeons (past pres.), Am. Soc. Aesthetic Plastic Surgery (innovative tech. com.), Soc. Plastic Surgery Skin Care Specialists (bd. dirs.), Am. Soc. Plastic Surgeons (bd. dirs., pres.). Achievements include traveling to developing countries in Central America, Asia & Africa to perform surgery on children who suffer with deformities as a result of birth defects, accidents or disease. Office: 180 N Dean St Ste 3N Englewood NJ 07631 Office Phone: 201-567-9595.

DAMJANOV, IVAN, pathologist, educator; b. Subotica, Yugoslavia, Mar. 31, 1941; came to U.S., 1967; s. Milenko and Ana (Pavkovic) D.; m. Andrea Zivanovic, Jan. 18, 1964; children: Nevena, Ivana, Milena. MD, Zagreb U., Croatia, 1964, PhD, 1971; PhD (hon.), Novi Sad U., Serbia, 2008. Lic. physician, Croatia, Pa., Kans.; diplomate Am. Bd. Pathology, 1975. Intern Gen. Hosp., Zagreb, 1964-65; resident in pathology U. Zagreb, 1966-67; intern in pathology Cleve. Met. Gen. Hosp., 1967-68; resident in pathology Mt. Sinai Hosp., NYC, 1968-69; asst. in pathology U. Zagreb, 1969-71; postdoctoral fellow Fels Rsch. Inst., Temple U., Phila., 1971-72; asst. prof. pathology U. Zagreb, 1972-73; from asst. prof. to assoc. prof. U. Conn., Farmington, 1973-77; from assoc. prof. to prof. Hahnemann Med. Coll. and Hosp., Phila., 1977-86; prof. pathology Jefferson Med. Coll. of Thomas Jefferson U., Phila., 1986-94; prof. pathology, chmn. U. Kans. Sch. Med., Kansas City, 1994-98, prof. pathology, 1998—. Cons. pathologist VA Hosp., Newington, Conn., 1975-77, Cancer Info. Dissemination and Analysis Ctr. for Virology, Immunology and Cancer-Related Biology, Franklin Inst., Phila., 1977-82, VAMC, Kansas City, Mo., 1995—, Pathology Stedman's Med. Dictionary, Phila., Pa., 2001-06; group for rsch. in pathology edn. U. Iowa, 1977-82; ad hoc reviewer, site vis. teams and study sects. NIH, Bethesda, Md., 1978—94; basic sci. merit award bd. VA, 1989-92; corr. mem. Croatian Acad. Arts and Scis., 1992; mem. coun. U.S.-Can. Acad. Pathology, 1996-99; vis. prof. U. Novi Sad, Serbia, 2007—, physician 2008, fgn. mem. Voivodina Acad. Arts & Scis., 2010. Mem. editl. bd. Ultrastructural Pathology, 1985-96, Virchows Archiv, 1986-2003, In Vivo, 1988—2009, Modern Pathology, 1989—, Hosp. Physician, 1990-96, Human Pathology, 1991—2008, Croatian Med. Jour., 1992-2006, Lab. Investigation, 1994—2008, Pathology Rsch. Practice, 1998-2002, Jour. Urologic Pathology, 1991-2000, editor-in-chief, 2000-02, Internat. Jour. Devel. Biology, 2005-, Ann. Clin. Lab. Sci., 2005-2009; mem. editl. bd. Am. Registry of Pathology, Washington, 2000—; assoc. editor Lab. Investigation, 1982-94; regional editor N.Am. Differentiation, 1985-96; co-editor Anderson's Pathology, 10th edit., 1996; mem. editl. rev. group chair for pathology/surg. pathology Doody's Health Sciences Book Rev. Jour., 1998—. Recipient Christian R. and Mary F. Lindback award Jefferson Med. Coll., Phila., 1988, Tom Kent award Group for Rsch. in Pathology Edn., 2007, Student Voice Tchg. award U. Kans. Sch. Medicine, 2008-09, Chancellor award U. Kans., 2010. Mem. Am. Soc. Investigative Pathology, Internat. Acad. Pathology, European Soc. Pathology. Office: U Kansas Sch Med Dept Pathol & Lab Med 3901 Rainbow Blvd Kansas City KS 66160-0001 Personal E-mail: idamjanov@kc.rr.com. Business E-Mail: idamjano@kumc.edu.

DAMON, CHRISTOPHER ANDREW, health association executive, lawyer; b. Milw., Nov. 9, 1951; s. Andrew Christ and Katherine John (Vangalis) D., m. Connie Henderson, July 23, 1983; 1 child, Laura Katherine. BA, Beloit Coll., 1973; MA, U. Wis., 1974, JD, 1977. Bar: Wis. 1977. Assoc. dir. for legal affairs Wis. Bankers Assn., Madison, 1977-80; legis. atty. AMA, Chgo., 1980-86, dir. dept. health care rev., 1986-90; exec. dir. Accreditation Assn. for Ambulatory Health Care, Skokie, Ill., 1990, Am. Med. Technologiests, Park Ridge, Ill., 2000—. Trustee Oak Park (Ill.) Pub. Libr., 1993—. Mem. Chgo. Assn. Healthcare Execs. (pres.-elect 1995-96, pres. 1996—). Office: Am Med Technologists 710 Higgins Rd Park Ridge IL 60068 Office Phone: 847-823-5169. *

DAMORE, DOROTHY, emergency physician; b. Kingston, NY, Dec. 1, 1966; BS, Union Coll., 1988; MD, Upstate Med. U., 1992. Attending physician in emergency medicine and pediat. Albany Med. Ctr., 2009—, assoc. prof. in clin. emergency medicine, 2009—11. Fellow: Am. Acad. Pediat.; mem.: Soc. Academic Emergency Medicine, Am. Coll. Emergency Physicians, Academic Pediat. Assn. Avocations: skiing, reading, running. Office: 43 New Scotland Ave MC 139 Albany NY 12208-3479 Office Fax: 518-262-3236. Business E-Mail: damored@mail.amc.edu.

DAMROSE, EDWARD JOSEPH, otolaryngologist, educator; b. NJ, Oct. 21, 1969; MD, UCLA Sch. Medicine, 1995. Asst. prof. Stanford U. Med. Ctr., 2003—. Chief, divsn. laryngeal surgery Stanford U. Med. Ctr., 2003. Fellow: ACS, Am. Acad. Otolaryngology-Head & Neck Surgery; mem.: Am. Laryngol. Assn., Am. Bronchoesophagological Assn., Triological Soc. Office: Stanford University Dept Otolaryngology 801 Welch Rd Stanford CA 94305 Office Fax: 650-725-8502. Business E-Mail: edamrose@stanford.edu.

DAMSBO, ANN MARIE, psychologist; b. Cortland, NY, July 7, 1931; d. Jorgen Einer and Agatha Irene (Schenck) D. BS, San Diego State Coll., 1952; MA, U.S. Internat. U., 1974, PhD, 1975. Diplomate Am. Acad. Pain Mgmt., Am. Coll. Forensic Examiners, Am. Bd. Psychol. Spltys. Commd. 2d lt. U.S. Army, 1952, advanced through grades to capt., 1957; staff therapist Letterman Army Hosp., San Francisco, 1953—54, 1956—58, 1961—62, Ft. Devers, Mass., 1955—56, Walter Reed Army Hosp., Washington, 1958—59, Tripler Army Hosp., Hawaii, 1959—61, Ft. Benning, Ga., 1962—64; chief therapist U.S. Army Hosp., Ft. McPherson, Ga., 1964—67; ret. U.S. Army, 1967; med. missionary So. Presbyn. Ch., Taiwan, 1968—70; psychology intern So. Naval Hosp., San Diego, 1975; pre-doctoral intern Naval Regional Med. Ctr., San Diego, 1975—76, postdoctoral intern, 1975—76, chief, founder pain clinic, 1977—86. Adj. tchr. U. Calif. Med. Sch., San Diego; lectr., U.S., Can., Eng., France, Australia; cons. forensic hypnosis to law enforcement agys.; approved cons. in hypnosis. Contbr. articles to profl. jours., chapters to books. Tchr. Sunday Sch. United Meth. Ch., 1945—; Rep. Nat. Candidate Trust Presdl. adv. com., platform planning commn. at-large-del.; ARC psychology vol. Naval Hosp., San Diego; vol. VA Hosp., La Jolla, Calif. Fellow Am. Soc. Clin. Hypnosis (psychology mem.-at-large, exec. bd. 1989-90), San Diego Soc. Clin. Hypnosis (pres. 1980); mem. AAUW, Am. Phys. Therapy Assn., Calif. Soc. Clin. Hypnosis (bd. govs.), Am. Soc. Clin. Hypnosis Edn. Rsch. Found. (trustee 1992-94),

Internat. Platform Assn., Mil. Officers Am. (past pres. local chpt.), Ret. Officers Assn. (bd. dirs. Hidden Valley chpt., rep. presdl. task force, pres. adv. com.), Toastmasters (local pres.), Job's Daus. Republican. Home and Office: 1062 W Fifth Ave Escondido CA 92025-3802 Office Phone: 760-745-6640.

DAN, LUO, physician; b. Liaoning, China, Oct. 16, 1958; PhD, MD, Pekin Union Med. Coll., 1997. Dir. Jiangsu Province Hosp., 1997—. Recipient Nat. Med. Sci. and Tech. Advancement award, Chinese Med. Assn., Sci. and Tech. Advancement award, Jiangsu Med. Assn., 2009, Nanjing Med. Assn., 2009, Wuzhou Female Tech. Advancement award, Chinese Female Med. Assn., 2010. Home: Guangzhou Rd 300# Nanjing Jiangsu 210029 China Personal E-mail: bingrong.2002@163.com, daniluo2005@yahoo.com.cn.

D'ANCA, JOHN ARTHUR, psychotherapist, educator; b. Chgo., Apr. 19, 1950; s. John Joseph and Josephine Rose (Bartolotta) D.; m. Carol Amendola; 1 son, Matthew John; stepdaughters, Ingrid, Heidi. BA, DePaul U., 1972; MA, Governors State U., 1975; CAS, No. Ill. U., 1978, EdD, 1982; PsyD, Chgo. Sch. Profl. Psychology, 1996; studied, Harvard U., 1994-95. Cert. eye movement desensitization and reprocessing; lic. clinician, Ill. Mem. counseling faculty Fenwick H.S., Oak Park, Ill., 1973-75; instr. psychology, counselor Triton Coll., River Grove, Ill., 1975-78; assoc. dir. Ball Found., Glen Ellyn, Ill., 1978-79; prof. student devel. Oakton Coll., Des Plaines, Ill., 1979—; pvt. practice psychology Park Ridge, Ill., 1975—. Extern John J. Madden Mental Health Ctr., Dept. of Psychiatry Chgo. Osteo. Hosp.; intern in psychology svc. Edward Hines Jr. VA Hosp., Hines, Ill., 1990—; mem. staff Bayside Clinic, Kenosha, Wis., 1993-97, mem. staff, psychiat. svcs., 1998—; cons. Molex Internat., 1986; lectr. in field; cons. Ill. Dept. Edn., Am. Med. Technologists, Goodwill Industries Internat.; cons., expert witness Ill. Dept. Profl. Regulation; mem. bd. Healthy Cmtys. Program Mental Health; mem. crisis response team psychol. trauma and mental health Des Plaines, Park Ridge, Ill. Contbr. articles to profl. jours. Bd. dirs. Chgo. Bd. of Mental Health, Northwest, 1974-75; mem. Oakton Coll. Crusade of Mercy Appeal, 1982; mem. Regional Med. Reserve Corps, 2006; eucharistic min. Roman Cath. Ch.; lector Roman Cath. Ch. Sears grantee, 1986—; recipient NISOD award for Coll. Tchg. Excellence, U. Tex., Austin, 2003, Silent Benefactor award Shrine of Our Lady of Pompeii, Chgo., 2006. Mem. NEA, APA, Internat. Soc. Traumatic Stress Studies (presenter 1996), Ill. Edn. Assn., Ill. Counseling Assn. (gov. coun. mem.), Ill. Mental Health Counselors Assn. (exec. bd. mem.), Am. Soc. Clin. Hypnosis, Soc. Clin. and Exptl. Hypnosis, Joint Civic Commn. Italian Americans, Midwest Psychol. Assn., N.Am. Assn. Adlerian Psychology, Ill. Guidance and Pers. Assn., Ill. Coll. Pers. Assn., Ther Pompeii Soc., Phi Delta Kappa. Home: 935 Evergreen Way Highland Park IL 60035-3739 Office: 1600 E Golf Rd Des Plaines IL 60016-1234 Office Phone: 847-635-1966. E-mail: johnd@oakton.edu.

DANDAMUDI, GOPI, cardiologist; b. San Diego, Oct. 30, 1974; MD, Ross U. Sch. Medicine, 2001. Assoc., cardiac electrophysiology Geisinger Heart Inst., 2008—. Dir., med. student cardiology clerkship program Geisinger, 2009; asst. clin. prof. Temple U. Sch. Medicine, 2009; dir., telemetry medicine Geisinger, 2010. Fellow: Heart Rhyhtm Soc.; mem.: Golden Key Nat. Honors Soc. Avocations: sports, travel. Home: 709 ICe House Dr Mountain Top PA 18707 Office Phone: 570-808-6020. Business E-Mail: gdandamudi1@geisinger.edu.

DANDY, ROSCOE GREER, author, psychotherapist, educator, retired public health service analyst; b. LA, Dec. 20, 1946; s. Roscoe Conkling and Doris L. (Edwards) D.; m. Lesley A. Dandy, Oct.,2007. BA, Calif. State U., 1970; MSW, U. So. Calif., 1973; MPH, U. Pitts., 1974, MPA, 1975, DPH, 1981; cert., Harvard U., 1981. Lic. clin. social worker. Youth counselor Calif. State Youth Authority, Ontario, Calif., 1971; pub. health intern Colo. State Dept. Health, Denver, 1974; health planning intern Green Engring Corp., Pitts., 1975; adminstrv. health intern Kane Hosp., Pitts., 1979; assoc. dir. U.S. Pub. Health Clinic, Washington, 1980-81; asst. chief trainee VA Hosp., Washington, 1981-83, asst. chief med. adminstrn. svc. Ft. Howard, Md., 1983-85, clinical social worker, 1985-93; psychotherapist Columbia Inst. of Psychotherapy, Inc., 1989-91, D.A. Wynne & Assocs. Inc., 1991-94; pub. health analyst USPHS, 1993—2007; asst. prof., health care mgmt. Indian River State Coll., Ft. Pierce, Fla., 2011—. Instr. U. Pitts., 1977-80, Grad. Sch. Washington ext. campus Cen. Mich. U., 1980—, Columbia Pacific U., San Rafael, Calif., 1990—, Nova U., Ft. Lauderdale, Fla., 1991—; vis. instr. Andrews AFB, Washington, Walter Reed Army Med. Ctr. Hosp., Washington, Aberdeen Proving Ground, Md., Ft. Meade, Md., Ft. Hamilton, N.Y.; mem. Nat. Review Panel for Substance Abuse Contracts, 1991-93; adj. prof., pub. health Nova Southeastern U., 2010-. Author: (book) Board and Care Homes in Los Angeles County, 1976. Police cmty. liaison Howard County Police Dept., 1989-93; vol. deployment, Emergency Response Team, Hurricane Katrina, Gulfport, Miss., 2005. Recipient cash award, Dept. Health and Human Svc., 2005, Outstanding Performance evaluation, USPHS, 2005, 2006, Spl. Adminstr. award, 2007, Special Citation award, Sec. award, HHS, 2006; named Project Officer of Yr., Inst. Coll. Rsch. Devel. and Support, 1999; nominee Expert Peer Review panelist, Dept. Health and Human Svc., 2009—11. Mem. APHA, NASW. Avocations: reading, poetry, music, track. Home: 23 Reybury Ln Palm Coast FL 32164

DANERMARK, BERTH DAVID, sociology educator, audiology researcher; b. Älvsbyn, Sweden, July 15, 1951; s. Eskil Nils and Britt Gunborg Danermark; m. Monica Anna Eckestam, Dec. 17, 1972 (div.); children: Stefan, Fredrik; m. Gunilla Britta Ohlson, Mar. 21. BA in Social Scis., Örebro U., Sweden, 1979, PhD in Sociology, 1986. Rsch. asst. Örebro U., 1978—83, lectr., 1983—92, assoc. prof., 1992—97, prof., 1997—. Chmn. Swedish Sociol. Assn., Stockholm, 1988—90; bd. dirs. Faculty Bd., Uppsala, 1990—96; pro-vice chancellor Örebro U., 1990—96. Author: Explaining Society, 2002; contbr. articles to profl. jours. Mem.: Swedish Inst. Spl. Edn. (bd. dirs. 2001—), Swedish Inst. Disability Rsch. (vice chmn. 2000—), Internat. Assn. Critical Realism (chmn. 2000—). Office: Urebro U Dept Health Scis 701 82 Örebro Sweden E-mail: berth.danermark@hi.oru.se.

DANFORTH, JEFFREY SCOTT, psychologist, educator; b. Providence, July 10, 1957; s. Guy Sage and Helen Mott Danforth; m. Julie Ann Polaski, Aug. 21, 1982; children: Nathaniel, Christopher, Nicholas. BA in English and Psychology, Marietta Coll., 1979; MA in Clin. Psychology, We. Mich. U., 1982; PhD in Clin. Psychology, W.Va. U., 1987. Lic. child psychologist 1989. Psychology intern U. Miss. Med. Sch., Jackson, 1986—87; assoc. dir. child inpatient mental health unit U. Mass. Med. Sch., Worcester, 1987—89; clin. dir. The Learning Clinic, Brooklyn, Conn., 1989—92; prof. dept. psychology Ea. Conn. State U., Willimantic, 1992—. Cons. in field. Co-author: The Treatment of Severe Behavior Disorders: Behavior Analysis Approaches, 1989, Handbook of Behavior Modification with the Mentally Retarded, 1990, Dialogues on Verbal Behavior, 1991, Handbook of Child and Adolescent Outpatient, Day Treatment and Community Psychiatry, 1998, Handbook of Parent Training: Helping Parents Prevent and Solve Problem Behaviors; mem. editl. bd.: The Analysis of Verbal Behavior, 2001—10, Clin. Psychology Rev., 2002—, Behavior Analysis in Offender Treatment and Prevention, 2006—; contbr. articles to profl. jours., chapters to books. Soccer coach Neconn Soccer Club, Woodstock, Conn., 1991—2004, Woodstock Mid. Sch., 2002—06, Woodstock Acad., 2006—11. Grantee, U. Mass., 1989, Conn. State U., 1993, 1998. Mem.: Assn. Behavior Analysis. Office: Ea Conn State U Dept Psych 83 Windham St Willimantic CT 06226 Home Phone: 860-974-3432; Office Phone: 860-465-4553. Business E-Mail: danforthj@easternct.edu.

DANFORTH, WILLIAM HENRY, retired academic administrator, physician; b. St. Louis, Apr. 10, 1926; s. Donald and Dorothy (Claggett) D.; m. Elizabeth Anne Gray, Sept. 1, 1950; children: Cynthia Danforth Prather, David Gray, Maebelle Reed, Elizabeth D. Sankey. AB, Princeton U., 1947; MD, Harvard U., 1951. Intern Barnes Hosp., St. Louis, 1951—52, resident, 1954—57; now mem. staff; asst. prof. medicine Washington U., St. Louis, 1960—65, assoc. prof., 1965—67, prof., 1967—, vice chancellor for med. affairs, 1965—71, chancellor, 1971—95, chmn., bd. trustees St. Louis, 1995—99, vice-chmn. bd. trustees, chancellor emeritus, 1999—. Pres. Washington U. Med. Sch. and Assoc. Hosps., 1965-71; program coord. Bi-State Regional Med. Program, 1967-68. Trustee Danforth Found., Am. Youth Found., 1963—, Princeton U., 1970-74, St. Louis Christmas Carols Assn., 1958-74, chmn., 1975—; co-chmn. Barnes/Jewish Hosp., 1996-2002; chmn. bd. trustees Donald Danforth Plant Sci. Ctr. Named Man of Yr., St. Louis Gloe-Democrat, 1978. Fellow: AAAS, Am. Acad. Arts and Scis.; mem.: Inst. Medicine. Home: 10 Glenview Rd Saint Louis MO 63124-1308 Office: Washington U West Campus Campus Box 1044 7425 Forsyth Blvd Ste 262 Saint Louis MO 63105-2161

DANG, LEI, orthopedist, consultant; b. Beijing, Aug. 15, 1972; MD, Peking U., 1996; PhD, U. Birmingham, 2007. Cons. Peking U. Third Hosp., 2011—. Office: Peking University Third Hosp 49 N Garden Rd Haidian Dist Beijing 100191 China E-mail: danglei_2000@yahoo.com.

DANG, TUAN DUC, optometrist; b. Saigon, Vietnam, Jan. 30, 1969; arrived in U.S., 1975; s. Trinh Duc Dang and Nhu Lan (Thi) Nguyen; m. Bich Ha Thi Nguyen, Dec. 31, 1999. BS, U. Houston, 1991, MBA, 1994, OD, 2001. Cert. therapeutic optometrist, optometric glaucoma specialist Tex., Calif. Vietnamese med. interpreter M.D. Anderson Cancer Ctr., Houston, 1992—94; project dir. Asian Am. Health Coalition, Houston, 1996—97; program coord. R&D Inst., Houston, 1995—96; divsn. officer, staff optometrist Naval Med. Ctr., San Diego, 2001—05. Adj. clin. asst. prof. U. Houston, Coll. Optometry, 2003—; adj. clin. instr. So. Calif. Coll. Optometry, Fullerton, 2002—, Pa. Coll. Optometry, Elkins Park, 2001—05. Contbr. articles to profl. jours. Vision coord. Health Edn. for Asian League, Houston, 1998—2001; pub. health coord. Vietnamese Am. Cmty. Health Network, Houston, 1995—98. Lt. USN, 2001—05. Fellow: Am. Contacat Lens Soc., Am. Acad. Optometry; mem.: Mil. Officers Assn. Am., Am. Optometric Assn., Golden Key. Avocations: camping, fishing, basketball.

D'ANGELO, PAOLO, physician; b. Palermo, Italy, July 30, 1959; grad., postgrad., MD, 1985. Cert. pediat. and pediatric hematology oncology specialist. Physician ARNAS Ospedali Civico Di Cristina e Benfratelli, 1991—, staff head, 1998. Avocations: fishing, tennis, football. Office: Piazza Nicola Leotta 4 Palermo Sicilia 90127 Italy Office Fax: 0039-91-6664127. Personal E-mail: papagisa@libero.it.

D'ANGIO, CARL T., pediatrician, educator; b. Boston, Mar. 27, 1957; s. Giulio John and Jean Terhune D'Angio; m. Donna D. D'Angio, Aug. 22, 1981; children: Sara Jean, Rachel Anne. AB, Princeton U., NJ, 1979; MD, Johns Hopkins U., Balt., 1983. Diplomate Am. Bd. Pediat., 1989, Am. Bd. Pediat. (Neonatology), 1995. Chief pediat. Ft. Defiance Indian Hosp., Ariz., 1989—91, staff pediatrician, 1998—99; asst. prof. pediat. U. Rochester, NY, 1995—2001, assoc. prof. pediat., 2001—. Contbr. chapters to books. Lt. comdr. USPHS, 1988—91. Recipient Nat. Rsch. Svc. award, Nat. Heart, Lung and Blood Inst., 1995; grantee Mentored Clin. Scientist Devel. award, 1997—2002, Indian Health Svc., 1989—90, Am. Heart Assn., 1997—99, Nat. Inst. Allergy and Infectious Diseases, 1998—2007, Nat. Inst. Child Health and Human Devel., 2001—06, Thrasher Rsch. Fund, 2007—09. Fellow: Am. Acad. Pediat.; mem.: Perinatal Rsch. Soc., Soc. Pediatric Rsch. Office: Golisano Children's Hospital at Strong 601 Elmwood Avenue Box 651 Rochester NY 14534

D'ANGIO, GIULIO JOHN, radiation oncologist; b. NYC, May 2, 1922; s. Carlo and Rosa (Calderazzo) D'A.; m. Jean Chittenden Terhune, Aug. 27, 1955 (dec. Nov. 2004); children: Carl, Peter; m. Audrey E. Evans, Feb. 1, 2005. AB, Columbia U., 1943; MD, Harvard U., 1945; D. Medicine and Surgery (hon.), U. Bologna, 1983. Diplomate: Am. Bd. Radiology, Am. Bd. Therapeutic Radiology. Surg. intern Children's Hosp., Boston, 1945-46, tng. in pathology, 1948-49; resident in radiology Boston City Hosp., 1949-53; also mem. staff; radiation therapist Children's Hosp., Boston, 1956-62; researcher Donner Lab., also Lawrence Radiation Lab., U. Calif., Berkeley, 1962-63; dir. divsn. radiation therapy U. Minn. Med. Sch., 1964-68; chmn. dept. radiation therapy Meml. Hosp., NYC, 1968-76; dir. children's cancer rsch. ctr. Children's Hosp., Phila., 1976-89; prof. radiation oncology Hosp. of U. Pa., Phila., 1976-92, vice chmn., clin. dir. dept. radiation oncology, 1989-92, prof. emeritus, 1992—; prof. pediatric oncology U. Pa. Med. Sch., Phila., 1976-92. Chmn. Nat. Wilms Tumor Study Com., 1968-91; past chmn. cancer clin. investigation rev. com. Nat. Cancer Inst. Editor-in-chief Med. and Pediat. Oncology, 1996-2003; contbr. numerous articles to med. jours. Capt. M.C. AUS, 1946-48. Decorated Commendation medal; recipient ann. award Am. Cancer Soc., 1978, Heath Meml. award M.D. Anderson Tumor and Cancer Inst., 1979, Am. Soc. Therapeutic Radiation Oncologists Gold medal, 1999, U., Prague Gold medal, 2003, cert. merit Pres. Italian Republic, 2003. Fellow Royal Coll. Radiology, Am. Acad. Pediatrics; mem. Am. Acad. Pediat. (past chmn. sect. oncology-hematology), AAAS, Am. Coll. Radiology, Am. Soc. Therapeutic Radiologists, Mass. Med. Soc., Pa. Med. Soc., Royal Soc. Medicine, Internat. Soc. Pediat. Oncology (pres. 1987), Radiol. Soc. N.Am., Soc. Pediat. Radiology (Gold medal, 2000), Phi Beta Kappa. Episcopalian. Home: 201 S 18th St # 1818 Philadelphia PA 19103 Office: Perelman Ctr for Advanced Medicine Dept Radiation Oncology Civic Center Blvd Philadelphia PA 19104-4206

DANI, CHRISTIAN, medical researcher; b. St. Raphael, France, May 23, 1956; PhD, U. Montpellier, 1985. Rsch. dir. Nat. Inst. Health and Med. Rsch., 1986—. Office: 28 Ave Vallombrose Alpes-Maritimes Nice 06107 France Business E-Mail: dani@unice.fr.

DANIEL, J. CHRISTOPHER, health facility executive, family medicine physician, military officer; b. Phila., Apr. 15, 1958; s. Frank V. and Regina Luff Daniel; m. Lorraine Yetsuko Higa, June 19, 1993; children: Penelope Nicole Michiko, Nicholas Wayne. AB cum laude, Princeton U., 1980; MD, Jefferson Med. Coll., Phila., 1984; MBA, Yale U., 2007. Diplomate Am. Bd. Family Medicine (added qualification in adolescent medicine). Spl. asst. for health care matters Office of Sec. of Navy, Washington, 1981—82; basic surgery intern Naval Hosp., San Diego, 1984—85; flight surgeon U.S Naval Hosp., Subic Bay, Zambales, Philippines, 1986—89, Fleet Composite Squadron FIVE, Naval Air Station Cubi Point, Zambales, 1989—90; family practice resident Naval Hosp., Camp Pendleton, Calif., 1991—93; family physician U.S. Naval Hosp., Naval Air Station Sigonella, Catania, Italy, 1993—96; adolescent medicine fellow Naval Med. Ctr., San Diego, 1996—98; chief med. staff, family and adolescent medicine physician Naval Med. Clinic, Annapolis, Md., 1998—2002; exec. officer U.S. Naval Med. Rsch. Unit Two, Jakarta, Indonesia, 2002—04; commdg. officer Naval Submarine Med. Rsch. Lab., Groton, Conn., 2004—06, Naval Med. Rsch. Ctr., Silver Spring, Md., 2006—09; dep. comdr. US Army Med. Rsch. & Material Command, 2009—. Sr. med. officer, dir. Br. Med. Clinic, NAS Cubi Point, 1987—90; AHA ACLS affiliate faculty, program dir. U.S. Naval Hosp., Naval Air Station Sigonella, 1994—96; founder, dir. Travel Medicine Clinic, U.S. Naval Hosp., Naval Air Station Sigonella, 1994—96; co-founder, dir. San Diego H.S. Football Head Injury Project, 1997—98; clin. instr., dept. family and preventive medicine U. Calif., San Diego, 1997—98; assoc. prof. dept. family medicine Uniformed Svcs. U. Health Scis., Bethesda, Md., 1997—2002; mem. editl. adv. bd. Am. Family Physician, Leawood, Kans., 2002—07. Capt. USN, 1980—. Recipient Outstanding Scholar Athlete award, Phila. Evening and Sunday Bull., 1976, 1st prize staff rsch. project, Naval Med. Ctr., San Diego, 1999; named one of America's Top Family Drs., Consumer's Rsch. Coun. Am., 2002—. Fellow: Am. Acad. Family Physicians; mem.: Naval Submarine League, Uniformed Svcs. Acad. Family Physicians, Aerospace Med. Assn. (life), Am. Coll. Physician Execs. (life), Soc. for Adolescent Medicine (chair internat. adolescent health profls. in tng. 1996—98). Roman Catholic. Avocations: sports, travel. Office: USAMRMC 504 Scott St Frederick MD 21702

DANIEL, LAUREN C, psychologist; b. Richmond, Va., Jan. 30, 1981; BS, Davidson Coll., 2003; PhD, Drexel U., 2011. Postdoc. rsch. fellow Children's Hosp. Phila., 2011—. Home: 304 S 10th St Unit C Philadelphia PA 19107 Personal E-mail: lauren1daniel@gmail.com.

DANIEL, MARANHO AUGUSTO CARVALHO, orthopedist; b. Duartina, Brazil, Apr. 7, 1979; MD, Ribeirao Preto Med. Sch., 2003, PhD, 2011. Orthop. surgeon Hosp. Das Clínicas Ribeirao Preto Med. Sch. U. de Sao Paulo, 2008—. Mem.: Brazilian Soc. Orthops. and Traumatology. Office: Ave Bandeirantes 3900 11st Fl Campus Ribeirao Preto Sao Paulo 14048-900 Brazil Office Fax: 16-36330336. Personal E-mail: danielmaranho@hotmail.com.

DANIEL, REGINALD, retired ophthalmologist; b. London, Dec. 7, 1939; s. Reginald and Alice (Youell) D.;m. Carol Ann Bjorck, July 10, 1943; children: Lorne Piers, Claire Suzanne. MB BS, Westminster Med. Sch., London, 1964; DO, U. London, 1968. Sr. registrar Moorfields Hosp., London, 1966—70; lectr. U. London, 1981—96; cons. ophthalmic surgeon Guys and St. Thomas' Hosp., London, 1970—2010. Tchr. U. London. Contbr. chpts. to books; contbr. articles to profl. jours. Freeman, City of London, 1981. Fellow Royal Coll. Surgeons, Royal Coll. Ophthalmologists; mem. Am. Acad. Ophthalmologists, Moorfields Surgeon's Assn., Worshipful Co. Spectacle Makers (liveryman), City Livery Club. Avocations: tennis, skiing, golf. Home Phone: 020 8508 2042.

DANIEL, ROLLIN KIMBALL, plastic surgeon; b. Montgomery, Ala., Aug. 14, 1943; BA cum laude, Vanderbilt U., Nashville, 1965; MD, Columbia U. Coll. Physicians & Surgeons, NYC, 1969; MSc in Experimental Surgery, McGill U., Montreal, Quebec, Canada, 1974. Cert. Am. Bd. Plastic Surgery. Intern, gen. surgery Barnes Hosp., St. Louis, 1969—70; resident, plastic surgery McGill U., Montreal, Canada, 1971—73, resident, hand surgery, 1973—75; resident, craniofacial surgery U. Louisville, Ky., 1975—76; fellow U. Toronto, Canada, 1984; pvt. practice rhinoplasty Newport Beach, Calif. Chief plastic surgery Hoag Meml. Hosp. Presbyterian, Newport Beach, 1998—2000, Royal Victoria Hosp.; prof. surgery McGill U.; clinical prof. plastic surgery U. Calif, Irvine. Contbr. articles to profl. jours., chapters to books;, author med. textbooks. Fellow: ACS, Quebec Coll. Physicians & Surgeons, Royal Coll. Surgeons Canada; mem.: Am. Soc. Aesthetic Plastic Surgery, Am. Soc. Plastic Surgeons, Am. Bd. Plastic Surgery. Office: 1441 Avocado Ste 308 Newport Beach CA 92660 Office Phone: 949-721-0494. Office Fax: 949-721-4138.

DANIEL, SAMUEL J., hospital administrator, medical educator; b. Leeward Islands, Sept. 13, 1950; BA in Chemistry, CUNY, 1974; MD, Columbia U., 1978. Diplomate Am. Bd. Internal Medicine, Am. Bd. Gastroenterology. Intern Roosevelt Hosp., NYC, 1978—79, resident in internal medicine, 1979—80, St. Lukes-Roosevelt Hosp., NYC, 1980—81, resident in gastroenterology, 1981—83; dir. medicine N. Gen. Hosp., NYC, 1995—2001, CEO, 2001—. Asst. clin. prof. Columbia U.; assoc. clin. prof. Mt. Sinai Sch. Medicine, 2001—; assoc. dean North Gen. Hosp., Mt. Sinai, 2008. Office: 1789 Madison Ave New York NY 10035 Address: 1879 Madison Ave New York NY 10035-3832 Business E-Mail: samuel.daniel@ngsc.org.

DANIEL, VOLKER RUEDIGER MARIA, immunologist, researcher; b. Hadamar, Hessen, Germany, Feb. 24, 1955; s. Oskar and Gertrud (Tkotz) D.; m. Dinara Kaioumova, Aug. 2001; children: Alice Vanessa Friederike, Annika Grace Fabienne. MD, U. Giessen, Germany, 1981; doctorate (hon.), U. Pleven, Bulgaria, 2003. Sci. asst.

dept. internal medicine U. Giessen, 1980-81; sci. asst. dept. transplantation immunology Inst. Immunology, U. Heidelberg, Germany, 1982-94, lectr. dept. transplantation immunology, 1994-2000, prof. immunology, 2000—; hon. dr. Univ. Sch. Medicine, Pleven, Bulgaria, 2003—. Contbr. articles to profl. jours. Deutsche Forschungsgemein Schaft rsch. fellow, 1982-84. Mem. Transplantation Soc., Internat. AIDS Soc. (advisor), German Assn. for Immunology, NY Acad. Scis. Roman Catholic. Avocations: science, sports, history, music. Office: Inst immunology Im Neuenheimer Feld 305 69120 Heidelberg Germany Personal E-mail: volker.daniel@t-online.de. Business E-Mail: volker.daniel@med.uni-heidelberg.de.

DANIELL, HERMAN BURCH, pharmacologist; b. Cadwell, Ga., May 25, 1929; s. Walter and Ruby Florence (Burch) Daniell; m. Mickey Marucheau, May 24, 1952 (dec.); m. Lorraine Smith, June 30, 1957 (dec.); children: Kimberley Ann, Anthony Burch, Walter Herman. BS in Pharmacy, U. Ga., 1951, MS in Pharmacology, 1964; PhD in Pharmacology, Med. U. S.C., 1966. Owner-operator retail pharmacies, Savannah, Ga., 1953-62; instr. U. Ga., 1962-64; USPHS trainee Med. Coll. S.C., Charleston, 1964—66; mem. faculty Med. U. S.C., 1966-92, prof. pharmacology, 1978-92, prof. emeritus, 1992—. Contbr. articles to profl. jours. Served to capt. M.S.C. US Army, 1951—53. Grantee, USPHS, 1966—85, S.C. Heart Assn., 1966—73. Mem.: Am. Soc. Pharmacology and Exptl. Therapeutics, Sigma Xi, Kappa Sigma, Rho Chi. Episcopalian. Home: 1549 Burningtree Rd Charleston SC 29412-2630

DANIELS, CHERYL LYNN, pediatrics nurse; b. Paterson, NJ, June 15, 1951; d. Nathan and Frances Avonna (Bradshaw) D. RN, Martland Hosp. Sch. Nursing, Newark, 1971; AAS in Health and Community Svc., NYU, 1984, BA in Journalism, 1987. Cert. in pediat. nursing. Evening charge nurse Martland Hosp. Unit, Newark, 1971-73; staff nurse Heal Econs. Advancement League, Paterson, NJ, 1972-74; neonatal intensive care nurse St. Joseph's Hosp. & Med. Ctr., Paterson, NJ, 1973-77, charge nurse neonatal intensive care, 1977—79, pediat. neonatal ICU, 1979-89, intensive care nurse, pediatric HIV outpatient nurse, 1989-90; rsch. outpatient HIV/SJH case mgmt. nurse Aids Clin. Trial Group, 1990-2001; case mgr. outpatient pediat. HIV Clinic, 1989—; pediat. sedation nurse for CT scan procedures, 2001—02. Mentor Career Beginning Program, Paterson, 1988-90. Recipient Gobetz award, NYU, 1984. Mem. ARC, Alpha Sigma Lambda. Baptist. Avocations: clarinet, swimming, reading, writing, painting. Office: Saint Joseph Hosp 703 Main St Paterson NJ 07503-2691 Office Phone: 973-754-4703. Personal E-mail: danielscheryl@msn.com, dcheryl@hotmail.com. Business E-Mail: danielsc@sjhmc.org.

DANIELS, JOSEPH, neuropsychiatrist; b. Linden, NJ, Mar. 18, 1931; s. Bennie and Dora (Chese) D.; m. Shirley Perkins, July 20, 1996; children: Joan Marie, Jean Dorene. BA cum laude, Lincoln U., 1953; MD, Howard U., 1957. Rotating intern Med. Ctr. Jersey City, 1957—58; resident internal medicine Worcester City Hosp., Worcester, Mass., 1958—59; resident psychiatry Ancora Hosp., NJ, 1962—65; dir. outpatient clinic Christian Health Care Ctr., Wyckoff, NJ, 1966—70; dir. outpatient dept. Cmty. Mental Health Ctr., N.J. Coll. Medicine, Newark, 1970—79; med. dir., pres. Ctr. for Growth and Reconciliation, East Orange, NJ, 1979—87; sr. staff psychiatrist Pine Rest Christian Hosp., Grand Rapids, Mich., 1987—96; cons. Kent County Cmty. Mental Health Ctr., Grand Rapids, 1996—. Mem. Healthy Kent 2000 Health Com., 1993-94; cons. psychiatrist Newark Bd. Edn., 1976-84, East Orange Bd. Edn., Victory House, Newark, 1976-82, Project Rehab, Grand Rapids, 1990-91. Author: The Urban Mission, 1974. Founder, pres., chmn. bd. Ministry Reconciliation Fellowship, 1980-87; bd. dirs. Grand Rapids Reach Inc., pres., 1991-93; selected mem. Leadership Grand Rapids, 1993-94. Capt. M.C., U.S. Army, 1959-62. Fulbright Sr. scholar U. Zimbabwe Sch. Medicine, 1998-99; decorated Am. Medal of Honor, 2001 Mem.: Beta Kappa Chi. Baptist. Avocations: sports, writing, reading. Office: 901 Eastern Ave NE Grand Rapids MI 49503-1201 Personal E-mail: drsdsapd@juno.com, jdaniels1054@sbcglobal.net.

DANIELS, KURT R., retired speech and language pathologist, consultant; b. Chgo., Oct. 22, 1954; s. Donald R. and Phyllis D. (Lenz) D.; m. Renee Perry, July 5, 1980. BS, Ea. Ill. U., 1976, MS, 1977. Cert. clin. competence speech/lang. pathology; lic. speech/lang. pathologist, nursing home adminstr; tchr's. cert. spl. K-12th grades. Hearing and speech specialist Shapiro Devel. Ctr., Kankakee, Ill., 1977-80; dysphagia specialist lead profl. W.A. Howe Ctr., Tinley Pk., Ill., 1980—2008. Adv. bd. program in comm. disorders Govs. State U., clin. adj. prof.; cons., presenter in field. Recipient Editor's Choice award Nat. Libr. Poetry, 1994, 95. Mem. Am. Speech, Lang. and Hearing Assn., Ill. Speech, Lang. and Hearing Assn., Internat. Soc. Poets. Achievements include research in dysphagia and developmental disabilities. Home Phone: 815-469-7091.

DANIELS, MADELINE MARIE, clinical & forensic psychologist, educator, author, intelligence analyst; b. Newark, Oct. 14, 1948; d. William and Dorothy Barlow; m. Peter W. Daniels, Oct. 18, 1976 (div. July 27, 1988); children: Jonathan, Jedediah, Jeremiah. BA cum laude, CCNY, 1971; PhD, Union Grad. Sch., Yellow Springs, Ohio, 1975, Union Inst., Cin., 1988. Diplomate Am. Bd. Forensic Examiners; cert. med. investigator; diplomate in forensic psychology Am. Bd. Psycol. Spltys; lic. psychologist, Calif. Mem. adj. faculty SUNY, Purchase, 1974-76; data processing coord. GTE Internat., 1976-78; lectr. U. N.H., 1979-87; exec. dir. Crossroads Ctr. Human Integration, East Kingston, N.H., 1979-88; adminstr. Spectrum Cross-Cultural Inst. Youth Inc., East Kingston, 1988-93; rsch./comm. cons. Metis Assocs., No. Calif., 1994-96; staff psychologist region III Parole Outpatient Clinic, Calif. Dept. Corrections, Eureka Station, 1998—99; registered psychol. asst. Eureka, Calif., 1996-2000; lectr. Humboldt State U., 1998—2001; pvt. forensic practice Visala, Calif., 2000—04; clin. practise Paradise, Calif., 2005—09; clin.-forensic practise San Jose, Calif., 2009—10; founder CEO Spectrum Cultural Inst., Inc., 2010—. Lectr., author, spkr., cons. in field., intelligence analyst. Author: Realistic Leadership, 1983, Living Your Religion in the Real World, 1985, A Culturally Different Perspective on Psychology, 1989, (video) The Rainbow Classroom, 1991, Surviving Human Venom, 2008. Fellow Am. Coll. Forensic Examiners(life), Am. Bd. Forensic Examiners(life); mem. APA, Phi Beta Kappa, Am. Bd. Intelligence Analysts (bd. mem.). Mailing: 1608 West Campbell Ave # 313 Campbell CA 95008 Office Phone: 530-873-4543. Office Fax: 408-247-1697.

DANIELS, NORMAN, philosopher, educator; b. NYC, June 30, 1942; s. Manus and Evelyn (Auerbach) D.; m. Anne L. Hooker; 1 child, Noah. AB summa cum laude, Wesleyan U., 1964; BA, MA, Balliol Coll., Oxford, Eng., 1966; PhD, Harvard U., 1970. Asst. prof. philosophy Tufts U., Medford, Mass., 1970-76, assoc. prof. philosophy, 1976-81, prof. philosophy, 1981—2002, chmn. philosophy dept., 1983—92; Mary B. Saltonstall prof., sch. pub. health Harvard U., Boston, 2002—. Spl. investigator RWJ, 1998—2000; ethics adv. bd. PAHQ, CDC; editl. bd. of numerous jours. Author: (book) Thomas Reid's Inquiry: The Geometry of Visibles and the Case for Realism, 1974, Reading Rawls: Critical Studies of John Rawls' A Theory of Justice, 1975, Just Health Care, 1985, Am I My Parent's Keeper? An Essay on Justice Between the Young and the Old, 1988, Seeking Fair Treatment: From The AIDS Epidemic to National Health Reform, 1995, Just Health: Meeting Health Needs Fairly & numerous others, 2008. Fellowship NEH, NSF, Harvard Ethics & Professions, grants NIH, NSF, Ret. Rsch. Found., Harvard Pilgrim Found., ELSI, Rockfeller Found., Greewall Found., RWJ Found. Fellow: Hastings Ctr.; mem.: Internat. Soc. Equity Health & Nat. Acad. Social Insurance (founding mem.), IOM. Office: Harvard Sch Pub Health Dept Global Health & Population 665 Huntington Ave Bldg 1 Rm 1210D Boston MA 02115

DANIELS, W. PETER, hospital administrator; With Meridian Health, 2002, Meml. Sloan Kettering Cancer Ctr., NYC; pres. Southampton Hosp., CEO, Winthrop Univ. Hosp., Mineola; sr. v.p. for ops. Our Lady of Mercy Med. Ctr., Bronx; pres. Ocean Med. Ctr., NJ, Elmhurst Meml. Hosp., 2010—, Elmhurst Meml. Healthcare, 2010—, CEO. Mem.: Am. Coll. of Healthcare Execs. Office: Elmhurst Memorial Healthcare 155 E Brush Hill Rd Elmhurst IL 60126 Office Phone: 311-221-1000.

DANIELSON, GORDON KENNETH, JR., cardiovascular surgeon, educator; b. Burlington, Iowa, Dec. 5, 1931; s. Gordon Kenneth and Helen H. (Hill) Danielson; m. Sondra Jean Bolich, Jan. 21, 1961; children: Gordon Kenneth III, Laura, Karen, Keith, Bruce, Susan, Jennifer. BA in Chemistry, U. Pa., Phila., 1953, MD summa cum laude, 1956, postgrad., 1960. Diplomate Am. Bd. Surgery, Am. Bd. Thoracic Surgery. Intern U. Mich. Hosp., Ann Arbor, 1956-57; asst. resident in surgery Hosp. of U. Pa., 1957-61, chief resident in surgery, 1961-62, gen. and thoracic surgeon, 1962-65, asst. chief surg. div. I, 1962-65; vis. fellow in thoracic surgery Thorax Kliniken, Stockholm, 1963-64; practice medicine specializing in thoracic and cardiovascular surgery Phila., 1963-65, Lexington, Ky., 1965-67, Rochester, Minn., 1967—2003. Assoc. prof. surgery U. Ky. Med. Sch.; chief cardiac surgery Univ. Hosp., 1965-67; faculty Mayo Grad. Sch. Medicine, Rochester, Minn., 1967-2003, prof. surgery, 1975—2003, Joe M. and Ruth Roberts prof. surgery, 1987-2004; past chmn. divsn. thoracic and cardiovascular surgery, cons. cardiovascular and thoracic surgery Mayo Clinic/Mayo Found., 1967-2003, St. Mary's Hosp., Meth. Hosp., Rochester, 1967-2003; Am. Heart Assn. vis. tchr., Singapore, 1975, Amman, Jordan, 1981, W.W.L. Glenn lectr., 1999. Editor: Cardiovascular Surgery, 1972—78; contbr. numerous articles to profl. jours. Recipient Albert Einstein award, 1956, Roche award, 1956, Spencer Morris prize, 1956; Markle Acad. Medicine scholar, 1962—67, Congenital Heart Disease Fellow, US USSR Health Exch. Program, 1973. Fellow ACS, Am. Coll. Cardiology; mem. Am. Assn. Thoracic Surgery, Am. Surg. Assn., Am. Heart Assn. (fellow coun. cardiovascular surgery), Soc. Thoracic Surgeons (a founder), Soc. Univ. Surgeons, Soc. Vascular Surgery, Mexican Soc. Cardiology (hon.), Assn. Thoracic and Cardiovascular Surgeons of Asia (hon.), India (hon.), Chile Soc. Cardiology and Cardiovascular Surgery (hon.), Colombian Soc. of Cardiology (hon.), Congenital Heart Surgeons Soc., Peruvian Soc. of Cardiology (hon.), World Soc. Pediat. & Congenital Heart Surgery (hon. founding mem.), Phi Beta Kappa, Alpha Omega Alpha. Home: 6000 16th Ave NW Rochester MN 55901-2107 Office: Mayo Med Ctr Plummer N-10 Rochester MN 55905-0001 Business E-Mail: danielson.gordon@mayo.edu.

DANIELSON, JAMES WALTER, retired research microbiologist; b. Miller, SD, June 6, 1940; s. Walter Henry and Florence Marie (Manning) Danielson. BS, S.D. State U., 1968. Microbiologist FDA, Mpls., 1969—80, rsch. microbiologist, 1980—2000; ret., 2000. Germicide testing project officer FDA, 1990—92; study dir. Sporicidal Testing Disinfectants and Sterilants Under AOAC Method Com., 1993—2000. Contbr. articles to profl. jour. Recipient Pub. Health Svc. Spl. Recognition award, Washington, 1988. Mem.: Am. Soc. for Microbiology, Assn. Ofcl. Analytical Chemists. Democrat. Roman Catholic. Achievements include development of methods for detecting ethylene oxide residuals in plastics and other materials; determination of effects of disinfectants on dialyzer membranes; determining leached compounds from rubber and plastic in parenteral solutions; sporicidal testing of germicides and determination of glutaraldehyde and phenol in germicides. Avocations: dance, tennis, volleyball. Home: 5925 Halifax Ave N Minneapolis MN 55429-2424 Personal E-mail: jwdan2@netzero.net.

DANILENKO, GEORGY IVANOVICH, pharmaceutical chemist, researcher; b. Kyiv, Ukraine, Oct. 9, 1934; s. Ivan and Valentina Danilenko; m. Valentina Pylypivna Dranyk, Sept. 22, 1957; children: Valentina, Anna Pukish. D in pharm. scis., Med. Inst., Lviv, 1960. Pharm. chemist Med. Inst., Lviv, 1960. Jr. rschr., sr. rschr., leading rsch. asst. Inst. of Organic Chemistry NAS, Kyiv, Ukraine, 1962—; dr. pharm. sci Pharm. Inst., Charkiv, Ukraine, 1980—82. Achievements include invention of anti-HIV isoniazid and antirabies immunoglob; anti-inflammatory drug; anti-influenza drug; research in predicting antiviral activity. Home: Zhukova 51 flat 53 Kyiv 02166 Ukraine Office: Inst Organic Chemistry NAS Murmanska 5 Kyiv 02094 Ukraine Business E-Mail: rostov@bpci.kiev.ua.

DANISMEND, NUR, pediatric surgeon, consultant; b. Istanbul, Turkey, May 18, 1943; s. Ali Bulent Danismend and Hayriye Sara Atak; m. Ayse Hale Agalday, Apr. 18, 1968; children: Emin Emre, Emin Serdar, Halenur Ayse. Cert. in pediat. surgery U. Istanbul, 1988. Prof. pediatric surgery Cerrahpasa Med. Faculty, Istanbul, 1969—2007, head dept. pediatric urology, 1999—2007; pvt. practice Istanbul, 2007—. Mem.: Galatasaray Sports Club, Galatasaraylilar Dernegi. Home: Emin Onat sokak ModaIstanbul Istanbul 34710 Turkey Home Fax: 90 212 2488830. Personal E-mail: danismend@turk.net.

DANJO, YUKITAKA, ophthalmologist; b. Fukuyama, Japan, Dec. 6, 1962; s. Takanobu and Yoshiko (Ando) D.; m. Yukiko Ishida, Sept. 8, 1991; children: Momoko, Rika Marie. BS, Osaka U., 1983, MD, 1987, postgrad., 2005—. Resident Osaka U. Med. Sch., Japan, 1987-89; asst. surgeon Osaka Seamen's Ins. Hosp., 1989-91; instr. Osaka Nat. Hosp., 1991-96; asst. prof. Osaka U. Med. Sch., 1996-2000; rsch. assoc. Schepens Eye Rsch. Inst. and Harvard Med. Sch., 1996-99; dir. Osaka Seamen's Ins. Hosp., 2000—. Fellow Schepens Eye Research Inst., 1996-99. Mem. Assn. for Rsch. in Vision and Ophthalmology, N.Y. Acad. Sci. Avocation: fishing. Home and Office: 3-2-20 Mino-o Mino 562-0001 Japan E-mail: danjo@papa.email.ne.jp.

DANN, FRANCIS JOSEPH, dermatologist, educator; b. NYC, Aug. 26, 1946; s. Richard William and Helen (Brennan) D. BA, Columbia U., 1968, MD, 1972. Bd. cert. dermatologist Am. Bd. Dermatology. Pvt. practice specializing in dermatology, 1976—2005; prof., vice chmn., dermatology UCI; prof. dermatology UCLA, Irvine, 2009—. Recognized expert med. reviewer State of Calif., 1995; specialized tng. in leprosy USPHS Hosp., Carville, La., 1972, 95. Contbr. articles to profl. and med. jours. Recipient Cert. of Appreciation for charitable med. missions to The Philippines, 1986, 88, 92. Mem. AMA, Am. Acad. Dermatology, Philippine Med. Assn. Hawaii, L.A.-Metro Dermatology Soc., Pacific Dermatology Soc., L.A. Acad. Medicine (bd. dirs. 1995-99), Aloha Med. Mission. Roman Catholic. Avocations: sports, photography, swimming, travel. *

DANNENBERG, ARTHUR MILTON, JR., experimental pathologist, immunologist, educator; b. Phila., Oct. 17, 1923; s. Arthur Mansbach and Marion (Loeb) D.; m. Aileen Rose Hart, Mar. 30, 1948; children: Arlene Dannenberg Bowes, Andrew Loeb, Audrey Ann. AB, Swarthmore Coll., 1944; MD, Harvard U., 1947; MA, U. Pa., 1951, PhD, 1952. Diplomate: Nat. Bd. Med. Examiners. Intern Albert Einstein Med. Ctr., Phila., 1947-48; rsch. resident Children's Hosp., Phila., 1948-49; fellow Henry Phipps Inst. U. Pa., Phila., 1950-52, asst. prof., 1956-64; fellow U. Utah, 1952-54; assoc. prof. environ. health scis. Johns Hopkins U. Bloomberg Sch. Pub. Health, Balt., 1964-73, prof., 1973—, prof. joint faculty sch. medicine dept. pathology, 1976—. Mem. editl. bd. Am. Rev. Respiratory Diseases, 1973-75, 79-84, Infection and Immunity jour., 1976-78; contbr. articles to profl. jours. and chpts. to books. Lt. comdr. Med. Rsch. Unit 1, USN, 1954-56. Mem. Am. Soc. Investigative Pathology, Histochem. Soc., Am. Soc. Microbiology, Soc. for Leukocyte Biology (sec. 1975-76), Am. Assn. Immunologists, Am. Thoracic Soc., Soc. Investigative Dermatology. Home: 12 Lake Manor Ct Baltimore MD 21210-1017 Office Fax: 410-955-0105. Business E-Mail: artdann@jhsph.edu.

DANNON, PINHAS N., psychiatrist, researcher; b. Istanbul, Turkey, Mar. 26, 1968; MD, Istanbul U., 1990. Cert. assoc. prof. Tel Aviv U., 2007. Head, rsch. dept., brain stimulation unit Beer Yaakov MHC, 2007—. Mem.: APA, Am. Acad. Clin. Psychiatrists. Office: Tel Aviv University Beer Yaakov 1 Mental Health Ctr Beer Yaakov 70350 Israel Office Fax: 97289212570. Business E-Mail: pinhasd@post.tau.ac.il.

DANNULL, JENS O., medical educator; b. Duisburg, Germany, Aug. 31, 1963; MSc, U. Tuebingen, 1989; PhD, Free U. Berlin, 1993. Asst. prof. surgery DUKE U. Med. Ctr., 2001—. Avocation: piano. Home: 24 Barnsdale Ct Durham NC 27713 Business E-Mail: dannu001@mc.duke.edu.

DANS, PETER EMANUEL, medical educator; b. NYC, June 17, 1937; s. Emanuel and Filomena (Lisanti) Dans; m. Colette Lumina Lizotte, May 28, 1966 (dec. 2004); children: Maria Cristina, Paul Edouard, Thomas Emanuel, Suzanne Elise. BS in Chemistry, Manhattan Coll., 1957; MD, Columbia U., 1961; DSc (hon.), Manhattan Coll., 2003. Intern, resident medicine Johns Hopkins Hosp., Balt., 1961-63; resident medicine Presbyn. Hosp., NYC, 1963-64; fellow rsch. NIH, Bethesda, Md., 1964-67; infectious diseases fellow Harvard U., Boston, 1967-69; asst. prof. medicine U. Colo., Denver, 1969-74, assoc. prof., 1974-78; Robert Wood Johnson health policy fellow Inst. Medicine, Washington, 1976-77, sr. prof. assoc., 1977-78; assoc. prof. medicine Johns Hopkins U. Sch. Medicine and Health Policy and Mgmt., Balt., 1978—, Johns Hopkins U. Sch. Hygiene and Pub. Health, Balt., 1978—; clin. prof. Marshall U. Sch. Medicine, 1995—. Mem. Md. Physician Bd. Quality Assurance, sec., 1988—92; ind. cons. disease mgmt., outcomes, ethics, 1996—; med. cons. CUS/Caremark, 1996—. Author: Doctors in the Movies: Boil the Water & Just Say Aah!, 2000, Perry's Baltimore Adventure: A Bird's Eye View of Charm City, 2003, Christians In The Movies, 2009, Colette's Story, 2011; co-author: New Medical Market Place: A Physician's Guide to the Health Care Revolution, 1988, Life on the Lower East Side: Photographs By Rebecca Lepkoff 1937-1950, 2006; dep. editor: Annals of Internal Medicine, 1991—94, assoc. med. dir.: GMIS, Inc., 1994—95, mem. editl. bd.: Pharos, 1988—; film reviewer Physician at the Movies, Pharos, 1990—; contbr. articles to profl. jours., chpts. to books. Pres. Falls Rd. Cmty. Assn., 1980—84, 1987—90; mem. adv. com. on gifted talented program Baltimore County, 1981—90, mem. zoning adv. com., 1985—86, mem. commn. on aging, 1996—98; pres. parish coun. Shrine of Sacred Heart, Balt., 1981—83; lector St. Francis Xavier, Balt., 1997—, Cath. Com. Hunt Valley, Md.; bd. dirs. Ctr. Profl. Ethics U. Balt., 1999—2001. Fellow: ACP; mem.: Alpha Omega Alpha, Epsilon Sigma Pi. Roman Catholic. Avocations: films, birdwatching. Home and Office: 11 Hickory Hill Rd Cockeysville Hunt Valley MD 21030-1624 Home Phone: 410-667-9049; Office Phone: 410-560-3618. Personal E-mail: pdans@comcast.net.

DANSE, ILENE HOMNICK RAISFELD, physician, educator, toxicologist, designer, sculptor; b. NYC; d. Jack and Henrietta Homnick; m. James Atherton Danse, Aug. 10, 1982; children: Arthur Raisfeld, Robin Raisfeld. BS, CUNY, 1960; MD, NYU, 1964; student, Pratt Inst., Art Students League, Bklyn. Mus. Art Sch. Diplomate Nat. Bd. Med. Examiners, Am. Bd. Internal Medicine, Am. Bd. Toxicology. Assoc. prof. internal medicine SUNY, Stony Brook, 1975-83, assoc. prof. pharmacology, 1977-83, dir. clin. pharmacology and toxicology Sch. Medicine, 1978-83; acting chairperson clin. pharmacology Northport VA Hosp., LI, N.Y., 1978-83; sr. advisor Chevron Environ. Health Ctr., San Pablo, Calif., 1982-84; prin. ENVIROMED Health Svcs., Inc., Novato, Calif., 1984-99; ind. med. examiner toxicology and internal medicine Dept. Indsl. Rels., State of Calif., 1985—; assoc. clin. prof. dept. medicine div. occupl. and environ. medicine U. Calif., San Francisco, 1986—2006, assoc. clin. prof. dept. epidemiol. and preventive medicine Davis, 1991—. Cons. in fields of toxicology, pharmacology, environ., occupl. and internal medicine, 1984-2000; mem. bd. sci. advisors Am. Coun. Sci. and

Health; mem. sci. rev. panel Hazardous Substances Data Base, Nat. Libr. Medicine. Author: Common Sense Toxics in the Workplace, 1991; contbr. articles to sci. publs.; exhibitions include Sonoma Mus. Visual Art, Santa Rosa, Calif., Bolinas Mus., Calif., Ohr-O'Keefe Mus. Art, Biloxi, Miss., Kellogg Gallery, Pomona, Calif., John Toki Gallery, Richmond, Calif., Calif. Clay Competition, Davis, Feats of Clay, Lincoln, Calif. Recipient various art awards. Fellow ACP, Am. Coll. Clin. Pharmacology; mem. AAAS, Am. Acad. Clin. Toxicology, Am. Chem. Soc. (environ. health and safety sect.), Am. Coll. Occupl. Medicine, Am. Indsl. Hygiene Assn. (occupational medicine sect.), Am. Coll. Toxicology, Am. Soc. Pharmacology and Therapeutics, Soc. Toxicology, Western Occupational Med. Assn. Achievements include patent for epithelial cell growth-regulating composition containing polyamines, and method of its use. Office Phone: 415-868-1043.

DANZER, HAL C., reproductive endocrinologist; BS in Biology, U. San Francisco, 1967; MD, St. Louis U. Sch. Medicine, 1971. Diplomate American Bd. Ob-Gyn. Intern U. So. Calif. Med. Ctr., LA; resident ob-gyn. Cedars-Sinai Med. Ctr., LA, reproductive endocrinology fellowship, 1976—78, attending physician, reproductive endocrinologist, 1978—88; co-founder, ptnr. Southern Calif. Reproductive Ctr., Beverly Hills, 1983—. Asst. clin. prof. dept. ob-gyn. David Geffen Sch. Medicine, UCLA, faculty Reproductive Endocrinology & Infertility Fellowship program. Co-author: The Complete Guide to the Treatment of Premenstrual Problems, 1984, The Fertility Awareness Workbook, 1990, Fertility Awareness Handbook: The Natural Guide to Avoiding or Achieving Pregnancy, 1992, Getting Pregnant & Staying Pregnant: Overcoming Infertility and Managing Your High-Risk Pregnancy, 1999, Natural Birth Control Made Simple, 2003, others; contbr. articles to profl. jours., chapters to books. Named one of Top 10 Fertility Specialists in the Country, Parent Mag. Achievements include research in strategies that enhance a patient's chances of having a successful pregnancy, reduce the potential for miscarriages, lower the risk of genetic disorders and avoid the complications associated with multiple births. Office: Southern California Reproductive Center 450 N Roxbury Dr Ste 500 Beverly Hills CA 90210 *

DANZIG, VILÉM, cardiologist; s. Vilém Danzig and Marie Danzigová; m. Zdenka Nováková, Sept. 4, 1990; children: Vilém, Jan, Jakub. MD, Charles U., Praha, 1988, PhD, 2004. ICU cardiologist VFN, Praha, Czech Republic, 1994—2003, sr. cardiologist, head outpatients dept., 2003—. Fellow: ESC. Office: VFN Fakultní Poliklinika Karlovo námestí 32 12000 Prague 2 Czech Republic E-mail: danzig@centrum.cz.

DANZL, DANIEL FRANK, emergency physician; b. Cin., Apr. 2, 1950; s. Frank Bernard and Mary Ellen (Doerger) D.; m. Joanna Colosimo Danzl, Nov. 25, 1978; children: Maggie, Julia. BS magna cum laude, U. Cin., 1972; MD, Ohio State U., 1976. Diplomate Am. Bd. Emergency Medicine. Intern St. Francis Med. Ctr., Peoria, Ill., 1976-77; resident in emergency medicine U. Louisville, 1977-79, asst. prof. emergency medicine, 1979-83, assoc. prof. emergency medicine, 1983-89, prof. emergency medicine, 1989-91, prof., chair, 1991—. Bd. dirs., councilman-at-large Univ. Assn. for Emergency Medicine, 1988-89, indsl./govtl. rels. com., 1984-85, nominating com., 1987-88; bd. dirs. Soc. for Acad. Emergency Medicine, 1989, mem. annals of emergency meidcine task force, 1989; bd. dirs. Am. Bd. Emergency Medicine, sec.-treas., 1995-96, pres.-elect, 1996-97, pres. 1997—, mem. ad hoc com., oral examiner, 1982—; mem. Com. to Advise the Nat. ARC, 1984-87; reviewer for various med. jours. Author book chpts., monographs and textbooks including Airway Management in the Trauma Patient in the Clinical Practice of Emergency Medicine, 1991; editl. bd. Jour. Emergency Medicine, 1983—, Poisindex-Emergindex, 1982—, Jour. Wilderness Medicine, 1991—; contbr. more than 70 articles to Jour. Wilderness Medicine, Jpur. Emergency Medicine, Annals of Emergency Medicine, Am. Jour. Emergency Medicine, others. Mem. Water Safety Com. Nat. Safety Coun.-Pub. Safety Div., 1981-84; alternate med. dir. Jefferson Vocat. Edn.-Louisville EMS Paramedic Tng. Program, 1989-90, 90-91. Recipient Silver Tongue Orator award Soc. Tchrs. of Emergency Medicine, 1986, 88; grantee Office of Naval Resources, 1983-85, Key Pharmaceuticals, 1985, Hoffman-LaRoche, Inc., 1988, 89. Fellow Am. Coll. Emergency Physicians (nat. coun. mem. 1981-93, reference com. mem. 1981, 85, 89, rsch. com. mem. 1982-83, 83-84); mem. AMA (Physician's Recognition awards), NAS, Am. Soc. Circumpolar Health, Soc. for Acad. Emergency Medicine (bd. dirs. 1989, task force 1989), Nat. Rsch. Coun., Undersea and Hyperbaric Oxygen Med. Soc., Ky. Chpt. Am. Coll. Emergency Physicians (councillor 1981-93, sec.-treas. 1983-84, pres.-elect 1984-85, pres. 1985-86), Wilderness Med. Soc., Phi Beta Kappa, Beta Theta Pi, Alpha Omega Alpha, Phi Eta Sigma. Roman Catholic. Achievements include research on hypothermia. Home: 4804 Smith Rd Floyds Knobs IN 47119-9238 Office: U Louisville Dept Emergency Med 530 S Jackson St Louisville KY 40202-1675

DAO, HANH HUNG, physician; b. Hung Yen, Vietnam, Mar. 16, 1966; MD, Hanoi Med. Sch., 1991; PhD, U. Paris 6, 2003. Physician rheumatology dept. Bach Mai U. Hosp., 1995—2006, dep. chief outpatient dept., 2006—. Mem.: Vietnam Rheumatology Assn. Office: 78 Giai Phong Ave Hanoi 04 Vietnam Office Fax: 0438689713. E-mail: hunghanhdao@yahoo.com.

DAO, TAM KHOA, medical educator; b. Vietnam, Apr. 5, 1975; PhD, Fla. State U., 2007. Prof. U. Houston, 2009—. Adj. asst. prof. Baylor Coll. Medicine, 2007. Recipient Faculty Excellence award, U. Houston, Walter Klopfer award, Soc. Personality Assessment. Mem.: APA, Asian APA. Office: 4800 Calhoun Rd Houston TX 77004 Business E-Mail: tkdao@uh.edu.

DAOCHENG, WU, dean; b. Zhenjiang, June 22, 1962; PhD, Xi'an Jiaotong U., 2000. Vice dean Sch. Life Sci. and Tech., 2006—. Recipient award, Chinese Acad. Scis. Mem.: Biomed. Assn. China. Avocation: Go. Office: 28 West Xianing Rd Xi'an Shanxi 710049 China Office Fax: 86-29-82663941. Business E-Mail: wudaocheng@mail.xjtu.edu.cn.

DAOUST, DONALD ROGER, pharmaceutical executive, microbiologist, cosmetics executive; b. Worcester, Mass., Aug. 13, 1935; s. G. Arthur and Alice Anne (Lavalee) D.; m. Johanna K. Kalinoski, May 30, 1959 (div. 2003); children: Donna Jean, Stephen Michael, Sandra Marie; m. Barbara Neubert, 2005. BA, U. Conn., 1957; MS, U. Mass., 1959, PhD, 1962. Sr. rsch. microbiologist Merck Sharp & Dohme, Rahway, NJ, 1962-70, rsch. fellow, 1970-72, mgr. biol. quality control West Point, Pa., 1972-75; dir. quality control Armour Pharm. Co., Kankakee, Ill., 1975-76, v.p. quality assurance and regulatory compliance Phoenix, 1976-78; v.p., quality control Carter-Wallace, Inc., Cranbury, NJ, 1978—2001. Contbr. articles o profl. jours., chapters to books. Mem. Borough Coun., South Plainfield, N.J., 1970-72; treas. George Washington coun. Boy Scouts Am., 1981-84, pres., 1984-87, area v.p., bd.dirs. NE region U.S., 1987—2004. Recipient Disting. Svc. award South Plainfield Jaycees, 1969, silver Beaver award Boy Scouts Am., 1988, Silver Antelope award N.E. region, 1992; named Outstanding Young Man, N.J. Jaycees, 1970. Mem.: AAAS, Pharm. Mfrs. Assn. (quality control adminstrn. 1979—82, adv. bd. 1982—94, vice chmn 1988—90, chmn. 1990—92), Am. Soc. for Quality Control, Am. Soc. Microbiology, Laurel Oak Country Club (Sarasota, Fla.) (bd. govs. 2009—, pres. 2010—). Achievements include patents in field. Avocations: golf, jogging, reading, gardening. Home: 3254 Chas MacDonald Dr Sarasota FL 34240 Personal E-mail: dondaoust@comcast.net.

DA PAZ, REGINA CELIA RODRIGUES, veterinarian, researcher; Degree, U. Estadual de Londrina, 1995; M, U. São Paulo, 2000, PhD, 2004. Lic. vet. Conselho Regional de Medicina Veterinária, São Paulo, 1996. Vet. Clinvet, Sorocaba, Brazil, 1996—98; prof. U. Fed. de Mato Grosso, Cuiabá, Brazil, 2005—. Cons. Assn. Mata Ciliar, Jundiaí, Brazil, 1999—2004. Recipient Best Student Report award, 5th Internat. Symposium Canine and Feline Reproduction, 2004; grantee, Fundação de Amparo a Pesquisa do Estado de São Paulo, 1998—2004; fellow, Fossil Rim Wildlife Ctr., 1995. Mem.: Brazilian Vet. Wildlife Animals Assn. (assoc.). Achievements include research in in vitro fertilization, embryo cryopreservation and embryo transfer for the conservation of the ocelot (Leopardus pardalis); clinical and reproductive evaluation in wild cats at São Paulo Zoo; Rhea Americana semen cryopreservation, Brazilian Pantaneiro horse semen cryopreservation; artificial insemination in jaguars (Panthera onca) in captivity; reproductive biotechnology for the conservation of the ocelots (Leopardus pardalis) and tigrinas (Leopardus tigrinus) in Brazil; Nutritional influence on quality of semen of jaguars (Panthera onca)and coatis(Nasua nasua) in captivity; penetration assay of frozen jaguar (Panthera onca) sperm in heterologous oocytes; seminal analyses in captive capuchin monkey (Cebus apella), ocelot (Leopardus pardalis) and crab-eating poa (Cerdocyun thous) and tayra (Eira barbara); vasectomy evaluation on fertility control in captivity jaguars (Panthera onca) and capuchin monkey (Cebus apella). Office: Universidade Federal de Mato Grosso Avenida Fernando Correia da Costa Mato Grosso Cuiabá 78060-600 Brazil Office Fax: 55 21 65 36158614.

DAPENG, SHI, hospital administrator; b. Weihui, China, Dec. 15, 1956; D, Huazhong U. Tech. and Sci., 2009. Dir. Henan Provincial People's Hosp., 1993—. Master: Henan Provincial Radiol. Physician Assn.; mem.: Chinese Med. Assn. Office: Henan Provincial People's Hosp 7# Weiwu Rd Zhengzhou Henan 450003 China Business E-Mail: cjr.shidapeng@vip.163.com.

DARCY, MICHAEL, radiologist; b. Cleve., Aug. 31, 1954; MD, Ohio State U., 1979. Prof., chief interventional radiology Wash. U. in St Louis, 1989—. Fellow: ACR, SIR. Avocation: model building. Office: Dept Radiology 510 S Kingshighway Blvd Saint Louis MO 63110 Business E-Mail: darcym@mir.wustl.edu.

DARDIK, HERBERT, general and vascular surgeon; b. Long Branch, NJ, May 17, 1935; s. Morris and Sarah D.; m. Janet E. Goldstein, June 23, 1958; children: Alan, Michael, Sharon. BA magna cum laude, NYU, 1956, MD, 1960. Diplomate Am. Bd. Med. Examiners, Am. Bd. Surgery, cert. spl. competency in vascular surgery; lic. physician NJ, NY. Intern Montefiore Hosp. and Med. Ctr., NYC, 1960-61, asst. surg. resident to chief surg. resident, 1961-65; instr. surgery Albert Einstein Coll. Medicine, NYC, 1964-65, asst. prof. surgery, 1967-77; clin. assoc. prof. surgery N.J. Coll. Medicine, Newark, 1981-91; clin. prof. in surgery Sch. Medicine U. Pa., Phila., 1991—2002, clin. prof. surgery Sch. Medicine, 2003—; clin. prof. surgery Mt. Sinai Sch. Medicine, NYC, 1991—2008, prof. surgery, 2008—; staff surgeon USAF Hosp. Andrews AFB, Washington, 1965-67; assoc. dir. surgery to dir. surgery Montefiore-Morrisania Affiliate, NYC, 1967-71, cons. in surgery, 1971-76; assoc. attending surgeon Montefiore Hosp. and Med. Ctr., NYC, 1970-77; cons. surgery North Ctrl. Bronx Hosp., NY, 1976; assoc. attending surgeon Englewood (NJ) Hosp., 1973-79, active attending surgeon and chief vascular surg. svc., 1979—, chief dept. surgery, 1984, 1995, 2000—. Sr. rsch. scientist Lab. for Exptl. Medicine and Surgery in Primates, NYU Med. Ctr., 1973-78; numerous visiting professorships, 1976-95, at Good Samaritan Hosp., Cin., U. Munich, U. Laval, Que., Can., Rigshospitalet, Copenhagen, Karolinska Inst., Stockholm, Semmelweis Med. U., Budapest, First Internat. Course on Vascular Traumatology, Mexico City, Inst. of Vascular Surgery of U. Milan, Groote Schuur Hosp., Cape Town, South Africa, U. Orange Free State, Bloemfontein, South Africa, Johannesburg Hosp. of U. of Witwatersrand, South Africa, Allegheny Gen. Hosp., Pitts., Wilmington (Del.) Med. Ctr., Mercy Hosp., Pitts., U. Cologne, Germany, Jewish Gen. Hosp., Montreal (Harry C. Vallon Vis. Prof.), U. Md., Balt., Maritime Vascular Soc., North Sydney Hosp., N.S., Can., Pa. Hosp., Phila., U. Colo. Health Sci. Ctr. and Affiliated Hosps., Denver, Mary Imogene Basset Hosp., Cooperstown, N.Y., Cooper Hosp./Univ. Med. Ctr., Camden, N.J., Gulf Coast Vascular Soc., Tulane U., La. State U. Ochsner Med. Clinic, New Orleans, St. Vincent's Med. Ctr., N.Y.C., U. Trondheim, Norway, Broadgreen Hosp., Liverpool, Eng., U. Colo. Rose Med. Ctr. (guest lectr.), Queen Elizabeth Hosp., Montreal, Wright State U., Dayton, Ohio, Cleve. Vascular Soc., N.Y. Meth. Hosp., Bklyn.; surgeon by invitation Mass. Gen. Hosp., Bosotn, 1979, Milan, 1981, Sydney, N.S., 1985, Colo. Health Sci. Ctr., 1985, U. Trondheim, 1992, Paul Brousse Hosp., Paris, 1995, Utrecht, The Netherlands, 1997; internat. adv. com. Internat. Vascular Symposium, London, 1981, Internat. Coll. Angiology, Athens, 1985, 14th World Congress Internat. Union Angiology, Munich, 1986. Contbr. over 300 articles and abstracts to profl. jours., chpts. to books; presenter in field; creator exhibits in field; dir. numerous symposia in field; patentee in field; editor SCVS Newsletter, 1987—; editl. bd. Jour. Englewood Hosp., 1989—, Fitness Swimmer, 1992-95, Vascular Forum, 1993-95, guest editor 1994, Vascular Surgery, 1995—; Creativity editor Jour. Am. Coll. Physician Inventors, 1992-95; invited reviewer Jour. Vascular Surgery, European Jour. Vascular Surgery, Am. Jour. Surgery. Capt. USAF Med. Corps, 1965-67. Recipient George Schwartz prize in biology, 1954, Wortis Biol. prize, 1956, Herbert Dardik awards, Ann. Vascular Fellows Abstract Presentation, Humanitarian award, Retired Sr. Vol. Program, 2001. Mem. ACS (bd. govs. 1991-94, adv. coun. vascular surg. 1995—), ACP, AMA (Hektoen Gold medal 1976), Assn. Acad. Surgery, Soc. Vascular Surgery, Internat. Soc. Cardiovasc. Surgery, Soc. Internat. de Chirurgia, Soc. Clin. Vascular Surgery (hon., various offices and coms., pres. 1984-85, exec. com. 1982—, Lifetime Achievement award 2001), Soc. Surgery of the Alimentary Tract, Am. Coll. Gastroenterology, Collegium Internat. Chirurgia Digestive, Am. Coll. Physician Inventors (founding mem., sec. 1992—), Eastern Vascular Soc. (adv. coun. 1991—, exec. com. 1996-95, pres. 1990-91), NJ Vascular Soc. (pres.-elect 1983-84, pres. 1984-85, dir. exec. com. 1982-83, postgrad. surg. edn. award 1983), NY Soc. Cardiovasc. Surgery, NY Surg. Soc., Bergen County Med. Soc., Maine Vascular Soc. (hon.), Mex. Soc. Angiology (hon.), Israel Soc. Vascular Surgery (hon.), Rocky Mountain Vascular Soc. (hon.), Cleve. Vascular Soc. (hon.), Phi Beta Kappa. Office: Englewood Hosp & Med Ctr Dept Surgery 350 Engle St Englewood NJ 07631-1823 E-mail: hdardik@ehmc.com.

DARKOVICH, SHARON MARIE, nursing administrator; b. Ft. Wayne, Ind., Dec. 10, 1949; d. Gerald Antone LaCanne and Ida Eileen (Bowman) LaCanne Cutler; m. Robert Eliot Ness, July 17, 1971 (dec. Aug. 1976); m. Paul Darkovich, Jan. 23, 1981 (div. May 1994); 1 child, Amy Elizabeth. BSN, Case Western Res. U., 1973, BA in Psychology, 1978; cert. in advanced bioethics, Cleve. State U., 1990, MA in Philosophy and Bioethics, 1994. RN, Ohio, cert. profl. in health care quality. Staff nurse Univ. Hosps., Cleve., 1973, asst. head nurse, 1973-76; quality improvement coord. St. Luke's Med. Ctr., Cleve., 1976-83, 84-97, dir. nursing, 1983-84, quality improvement dir., 1997-98; dir. quality svcs. Lake Hosp. Sys., Inc., Painesville, Ohio, 1998-2000, corp. quality and compliance officer, 2000—07; dir. quality improvement UH Bedford Med. Ctr., 2008—. Cons. to long-term care facilities, 1986-92, pressure ulcer dressing devel. B.F. Goodrich Co., 1988-92; cons. to ambulatory facility for Joint Commn. for Accreditation of Health Care Orgns., Oakbrook, Ill., 1994, cons. to cmty. hosp. med. staff, bylaws, 1996; lectr. U. Akron, 1992-93, Northeast Ohio U. Coll. Medicine, 1993-95; bd.dir. Bioethics Network Ohio. Mem. ANA, Am. Soc. for Bioethics and Humanities, Greater Cleve. Nurses Assn. (mem. dist. coun. on practice, 1982-84), Sigma Theta Tau. Avocations: reading, needlecrafts, sewing, camping, jewelry making. Office Phone: 440-735-3578. Business E-Mail: sharon.darkovich@uhhospitals.org.

DARLAMETSOS, IOANNES, biomedical researcher, educator; b. Messolonghi, Etoloakarnania, Greece, June 3, 1958; s. Evangellos Darlametsos and Maria Makri-Darlametsou. B in Physics, Aristotle U., 1981; M in Biomed. Engring., U. Paris VII, 1983; D, Athens U. Med. Sch., 1997. Co-op. rschr. U. Nati. Inst. of Health and Med. Rsch., Paris, Ile de France, 1982—85; adj. prof. Technol. Ednl. Instn., Messolonghi, Etoloakarnania, Greece, 1985—; prin. H.S., Etoliko, Greece, 2002—. Rschr. French-Hellenic Biomed. Rsch. Inst., Agrinion, Etoloakarnania, Greece, 1989—. Contbr. chpts. in books, articles to profl. jours. Mem.: Soc. Exptl. Biology and Medicine (New Jersey, USA 2001—02), Greek Soc. Biomed. Tech. (Athens, Greece 1994—2002), Union Greek Med. Physicists (Athens, Greece 1990—2002). Orthodox Christian. Avocations: swimming, fishing, travel. Office: French-Hellenic Biomedical Research Inst 6 Lorentzou Mavili Etoloakarnania Agrinion 301 00 Greece Home: Elefteron Poliorkmenon 12 302 00 Messolonghi 302 00 Greece Home Phone: (011) 302 6310 22385; Office Phone: (011) 2631022385. Home Fax: (011) 30 6310 55157. Business E-Mail: idarlame@otenet.gr.

DARLING, HELEN, health services consultant; b. Fla., Mar. 1, 1942; d. Henry B. and Ann B. D.; m. John M. Nail Jr., Aug. 31, 1961 (div. Aug. 1970); children: John M. III, Ann Darling Nail Turner; m. Bradford H. Gray, Jan. 15, 1983. BA, Memphis State U., 1965, MA, 1970. Rsch. assoc. R.I. Health Svcs. Rsch., Providence, 1970-75; spl. asst. Dept. health, Edn. & Welfare, Washington, 1975-78; study dir. Inst. Medicine, Nat. Acad. Scis., Washington, 1979-82; v.p. Govt. Rsch. Corp., Washington, 1982-86; sr. policy advisor U.S. Senate, Washington, 1986-88; sr. cons. William M. Mercer, Stanford, Conn., 1988-92; mgr. health care benefits Xerox Corp., Stanford, Conn., 1992-98; sr. cons. Watson Wyatt Worldwide, Stanford, Conn., 1998—2002; pres. Nat. Bus. Group on Health, Washington, 2002—. Bd. trustees Gaylord Rehab. Hosp., Conn., 1993-97, 99—; pres. citizenz bd. Providence Hosp., Washington, 1985-88; pres ARPHA Ctr., Washington, 1980-95. Episcopalian. Office: National Bus Group in Health 20 F St NW Ste 200 Washington DC 20001-6700 *

DARLINGTON, RICHARD BENJAMIN, retired psychologist, neuroscientist, educator, researcher; b. Woodbury, NJ, Nov. 16, 1937; s. Charles Joseph and Eleanor (Collins) D.; m. Elizabeth Day, June 13, 1959; children: Jean Susan, Lois Heather. BA, Swarthmore Coll., 1959; PhD, U. Minn., 1963. Asst. prof. psychology Cornell U., Ithaca, NY, 1963—68, assoc. prof., 1968—80, prof., 1980—2005, rschr. neurosci., prof. emeritus, 2005—. Author: Radicals and Squares, 1975, (with others) Lasting Effects of Early Education, 1982, (with Patricia M. Carlson) Behavioral Statistics: Logic and Methods, 1987, Regression and Linear Models, 1990; contbr. articles to profl. jours.; contbr. chpts. to books. Project dir. Am. Friends Svc. Com., 1960, 61. Fellow NSF, 1959-60, Woodrow Wilson Found., 1959-60; grantee HEW, 1977-81, Office of Edn., 1966-67, 70-71, Dept. of Labor, 1980-81 Fellow AAAS; mem. Phi Beta Kappa Mem. Soc. Of Friends. Avocation: folk dancing. Home: 204 Fairmount Ave Ithaca NY 14850-4804 Business E-Mail: rbd1@cornell.edu.

DARNELL, JAMES EDWIN, JR., molecular biologist, educator; b. Columbus, Miss., Sept. 9, 1930; s. James Edwin and Helen (Hopkins) D.; m. Jane Roller, 1957; children: Christopher, Robert, Jonathan; m. Kristin Holby, 2002. BS, U. Miss., 1951; MD, Washington U., 1955, DSc, 1996. Intern Barnes Hosp., 1955-56; asst. to sr. surgeon USPHS, Bethesda, Md., 1957-60; asst. and assoc. prof. MIT, Cambridge, 1961-64; prof. Albert Einstein Coll. Medicine, NYC, 1967, Columbia U., 1968-74, chmn. dept. biol. scis., 1971-74; Vincent Astor prof. Rockefeller U., NYC, 1974—, v.p. acad. affairs, 1990-91. Co-author: (textbooks) General Virology, 1967, 77, Molecular Cell Biology, 1986, rev. edits., 1990, 1995, 2000, 03. Recipient H.T. Rickets award U. Chgo., 1979, Internat. award Gairdner Found., Toronto, Ont., Can., 1986, Paul Janssen prize in Advanced Biotech. and Medicine, 1994, Bertner award in cancer rsch., 1996, Passano award, 1997, Milstein award, 1997, City of Medicine, 1998, E.B. Wilson award, 1998, Lynen medal, 1999, Dickson Prize in Medicine, 1999, William B. Coley award, 1999, Gerald D. Aurbach lecture award The Endocrine Soc., 1999, Novartis/Drew award in biomed. rsch., 2000, N.Y. Acad. Medicine medal for disting. contbns. in biomed. sci., 2002, Lasker-Koshland award for Spl. Achievement in Med. Sci., Lasker Found., 2002, Nat. Medal of Science award, 2002. Mem. NAS, Am. Acad.

Arts and Scis. (award 1973), Royal Soc. (fgn.), Japanese Biochem. Soc. (hon.), Royal Swedish Acad. Aci. (fgn.), European Acad. Scis. Office: Rockefeller U Molecular Cell Biology 1230 York Ave New York NY 10021-6399 *

DARNELL, ROBERT BERNARD, neurologist, researcher, medical educator; b. Washington, Oct. 29, 1957; s. James Edwin Jr. and Jane (Roller) Darnell; m. Jennifer Cordes, Sept. 26, 1987; children: Alicia Marie Cordes, Andrew James Eugene, Paul Matthew Alexander, Peter Michael Robert. BA in Biology and Chemistry, Columbia U., NYC, 1979; MD, PhD in Molecular Biology, Washington U. Sch. Medicine, St. Louis, 1985. Diplomate Nat. Bd. Med. Examiners, Am. Bd. Psychiatry & Neurology. Intern, resident internal medicine Mt. Sinai Hosp., NYC, 1985-87; resident neurology Weill Cornell Med. Coll., NYC, 1987-89, chief resident neurology, 1989-90, assoc. faculty neurology and neuroscience, 1990—; clin. asst. neurologist Meml. Sloan-Kettering Cancer Ctr., NYC, 1990-92, affiliate clin. asst. neurologist, 1992—; asst. prof. Rockefeller U., NYC, 1992-96, assc. prof., 1997—2000, prof., 2000—, Robert & Harriet Heilbrunn prof. cancer biology, 2002—. Assoc. physician Rockefeller U. Hosp., 1992—2000, sr. physician, 2000—; investigator Howard Hughes Med. Inst., 2002—. Contbr. articles to profl. jours., chapters to books. Recipient Career Scientist award, Irma T. Hirschl Trust, 1996, Clin. Scientist award in translational rsch., Burroughs Wellcome Fund, 2000. Fellow: AAAS; mem.: American Neurol. Assn. (Derek Denny-Brown Neurol. Scholar award 1998), Assn. American Physicians, Inst. Medicine, Harvey Soc., Henry G. Kunkel Soc., Phi Lambda Upsilon. Democrat. Achievements include research in paraneoplastic neurologic disorders (PNDs), a group of diseases thought to arise when tumors—typically breast, ovarian or lung cancers—start making proteins that are normally only made by the brain. Office: Rockefeller Univ Box 226 1230 York Ave New York NY 10021-6399 E-mail: Robert.Darnell@rockefeller.edu. *

DARNERUD, PER OLA, toxicologist; b. Falun, Sweden, Jan. 11, 1953; s. Sune and Anna-Lisa Darnerud; m. Ebba Stålhandske, Oct. 25, 1986; children: Anna Stålhandske, Thomas Stålhandske, Peter Stålhandske. B in Natural Scis., Uppsala U., Sweden, 1977, assoc. prof., 1991; PhD, Swedish U. Agrl. Scis., 1985. Asst. prof. Swedish U. Agrl. Scis., Uppsala, Sweden, 1979—86; sr. rsch. fellow Uppsala (Sweden) U., 1986—92; sr. toxicologist Swedish Nat. Food Adminstrn., Uppsala, 1992—. Office: Swedish National Food Administration Box 622 751 26 Uppsala Sweden Business E-Mail: poda@slv.se.

DARNEY, PHILIP DEMPSEY, gynecologist, educator; b. Granite, Okla., Feb. 27, 1943; s. Walter Preston and Corene (Barton) D.; m. Virginia Grant (div. 1981); children: Blair, Barton; m. Uta Landy, Oct. 13, 1984; 1 child, Undine. AB, U. Calif., Berkeley, 1964; MD, U. Calif., San Francisco, 1968; MSc, London Sch. Hygiene, 1972. Diplomate Am. Bd. Preventive Medicine, Am. Bd. Ob-Gyn. Intern USPHS Hosp., San Francisco, 1968-69; resident in ob-gyn Brigham and Women's Hosp., Boston, 1973-76; dep. dir. div. reproductive health Ctrs. Disease Control, Atlanta, 1971-73; asst. prof. ob-gyn Harvard Med. Sch., Boston, 1976-78; assoc. prof. ob-gyn Oreg. Health Scis. U., Portland, 1978-80, prof. ob-gyn U. Calif. Sch. Medicine, San Francisco, 1981—. Cons. AID, Washington, 1971-74, Pathfinder Internat., Boston, 1973-83, The Population Coun., Family Health Internat., Internat. Projects Assistance Svc., Family Planning Internat. Assistance, Johns Hopkins U., 30 countries;lectr., writer in field. Author: Protocols for Office Gynecologic Surgery, 1996, Clinical Guide for Contraception, 1992, 4th edit., 2005; contbr. chpts. to books, reviewer 20 med. jours.; contbr. over 200 articles to profl. jours Bd. dirs. Engender Health, Planned Parenthood Fedn. Am., Alan Guttmacher Inst. Named Outstanding Young Profl. Am. Pub. Health Assn., 1984, recipeint Schultz award 2004. Fellow Am. Coll. Obstetricians and Gynecologists, Am. Coll. Preventive Medicine, Am. Gyn. and Obstetric Soc., Inst. Medicine. Democrat. Avocations: surfing, sailing, sculling. Office: San Francisco Gen Hosp Dept Ob-Gyn San Francisco CA 94110 Business E-Mail: darneyp@obgyn.ucsf.edu.

DAROFF, ROBERT BARRY, neurologist, educator; b. NYC, Aug. 3, 1936; s. Charles and May (Wolin) D.; m. Jane L. Abrahams, Dec. 4, 1959; children: Charles II, Robert Barry, Jr., William Clayton BA, U. Pa., 1957, MD, 1961. Cert. in Neurology Am. Bd. Psychiatry and Neurology, 1969. Intern Phila. Gen. Hosp., 1961-62; resident in neurology Yale-New Haven Med. Ctr., 1962-65; fellow in neuro-ophthalmology U. Calif. Med. Ctr., San Francisco, 1967-68; prof. neurology, assoc. prof. ophthalmology U. Miami Med. Sch.; dir. ocular motor neurophysiology lab. Miami Va. Med. Ctr., 1968-80; Gilbert W. Humphrey prof., chmn. dept. neurology Case Western Res. U. Med. Sch.; dir. dept. neurology Univ. Hosps., Cleve., 1980-93; prof. neurology Case Western U., 1980—, assoc. dean, 1994—2003, interim vice dean edn. and acad. affairs, 2004—06, interim chair, 2006—07; assoc. dean Devel. and Alumni Affairs; staff neurologist Cleve. Va. Med. Ctr., 1980-93; chief of staff, sr. v.p. acad. affairs U. Hosp., Cleve., 1994—2003; chief med. officer St. Vincents Charity, St. Johns West Shore Hosps., 2004—05; ptnr. Sci. Ptnrs., LLC, 2004—. Med. sci. adv. bd., chmn. sci. program com. Myasthenia Gravis Found., 1984—87, exec. com., 1992—2003, sec., 1995—96, vice chair, 1997—99, chair, 1999—2001, chair nominating com., 2002—03; adv. bd. Nat. Multiple Sclerosis Found., 1988—90, Soc. Progressive Supranuclear Palsy, 1991—94; nat. adv. eye coun. sensory and motor disorders vision panel NIH, 1980—83; steering com. neurological disorders in comml. drivers US Dept. Transp., chmn. task force, 1987; lectr. T.S. Srinivasan Endowment, Madras, India, 1994; Cumings lectr. Migraine Trust, London, 1994; lectr. Am. Coun. Headache Edn., 1996, vice chair, 2000—02; Soriano lectr., 2001; prof. (hon.) Astana-State Med. Acad., Kazakhstan, 1999; bd. advisors Capnia, Inc., 2000—07; lectr. 7th Ann. Vijjajiva, Mahidol U., Bangkok, 2006; Daniel M. Jacobson meml. lectr. N.Am. Neuro-Ophthalmology Soc., 2009—. Book rev. editor: Neuro-ophthalmology, 1981-86, mem. editl. bd., 1987-2003; assoc. editor Jour. Biomed. Sys., 1970-72; editor Neurol. Progress, Anns. Neurology, 1981-84; editor-in-chief Neurology, 1987-96, sci. integrity adv., 2004-; co-editor World Neurology, 1991-98, editl. adv. bd. 1998—2003; mem. editl. bd. Archives of Neurology, 1976, Annals of Neurology, 1977-86, Neurology and Neurosurgery Update Series, 1978-93, Headache, 1980-86, sr. edit. advisor, 2004-; Contemporary Neurology Series, 1989-93, Neurosci., Saudi Arabia, 2003-06, consulting sr. editor, 2007—, Practical Neurology, 2003—; mem. editl. adv. bd. Jour. Neuro-ophthalmology, 2001—09; mem. editl. coun. Neurologia Croatica, 1991-2004; mem. editl. commn. Valeology, Kazakhstan, 2002-05, The Scientific World Neurology Jour., 2006-11; pub. & sci. integrity advisor Cephalalgia, 2009-; assoc. editor Frontiers in Neurotology, 2010-; contbr. articles to profl. jours. Chmn. Young Tae Kwon Do Acad., North Miami, 1977-80; bd. dirs. Benign Essential Blepharospasm Rsch. Found., 1983-, sr. cons., med. adv. bd., 2007-; trustee Fairhill Ptnrs., 1988—, The Learning Corp., 1992-00, Edison Bio Tech. Ctr., 1994-01, Great Lakes Sci. Ctr., 1994-01, Myasthenia Gravis Found. Am., 1999-01; mem. tech. adv. coun. BIOMEC, Inc., 1999-2007; bd. trustees Greater Cleve. chpt. ARC, 1999-05, mem. exec. com., 2000-03; mem. cmty. bd. St. Vincent Charity Hosp., 2003-05, St. John West Shore Hosp., 2003-05; emeritus mem., Soc. Med. Cons. to Armed Forces, Assn. Mil. Surgeons US, Nat. Assn. Uniformed Svcs., Am. Med. Found. Peer Review & Edn., adv. com. neurology. Recipient Ernst Jung-Medaille Für Medizin in Gold, 1993, Silver Jubilee Oration award Med. Coll. Trivandrum, India, 1994, John H. Budd Disting. Mem. award Cleve. Acad. Med., 2002, Disting. Grad. award U. Pa., 2003, Lifetime Achievement award, Neurosciences India Group, 2005, A.B. Baker award for lifetime achievement in Neurol. Edn., Am. Acad. Neurol., 2006, U. Pa. Sch. Medicine Parade Grand Marshall, Med. Alumni Weekend, 2011; named hon. dir. life Fairhill Ctr., 2006. Fellow: Am. Headache Soc. (pres. 2002—04, bd. dirs., sec., John R. Graham Svc. Clin. Forum award 2005); mem.: AMA, Saudi Alzheimer Assn. (chair, sci. adv. coun. 2010—), Hadassah Med. Ctr. (rsch. com. 2008), World Neurology Found. (bd. dirs. 2006—08), Internat. Neurology Forum (chair internat. organizing com. 2004—07), World Assn. Med. Editors, Internat. Headache Soc., Neuromuscular Disease Assn. Romania (internat. sci. com. 1991—93), Acad. Med. Scis. Kazakhstan, Alliance Brain Initiatives (founding mem.), Dana Found., Coun. Sci. Editors (com. publ. ethics), World Fedn. Neurology (fin. com. 1985—, exec. com. Rsch. group on Neuro-Ophthalmology 1987—95, publs. com. 1987—, chmn. 1990—2001), Clin. Eye Movement Soc. (founder), Barany Soc., Internat. Neuro-Ophthalmology Soc. (organizing com. 1986), N.Am. Neuro-Ophthalmology Soc. (bd. dirs. 1986—94, chair cert. and accreditation com. 1997—98, publs. com. 1999—2001), Rocky Mountain Neuro-Ophthalmology Soc. (bd. dirs. 1980—86), Assn. Colombiana Neurologia (hon.), Am. Acad. Neurology (hon.; chmn. sci. program com. 1973—75, exec. bd. 1987—96, Netter lectr. 1989, pub. com. 1993—2001), Am. Neurol. Assn. (hon.; program adv. com. 1977—78, chmn. 1978, councillor 1980—82, membership adv. com. 1980—83, chmn. 1981—83, nominating com. 1984, chmn. Annals of Neurology oversight com. 1984—86, sec. 1985—89, pres. elect 1989—90, pres. 1990—91, past pres. 1991—92, history com. 2004—06), Vietnam Vets. Inst. (hon.; bd. scholars 1998—, united coun. of neurolgic subspecialists, alternate dir. 2005—08, Ea. Med. Assn. Med. Editors, ethics and sci. misconduct com. 2005—10, mem., publ. ethics sub-com. 2011—), Alpha Omega Alpha. Office: Univ Hosp CASE Med Ctr 11100 Euclid Ave Cleveland OH 44106 Office Phone: 216-368-2500. Business E-Mail: robert.daroff@case.edu, rbd2@case.edu.

DA ROS, CARLOS TEODOSIO, medical association administrator; b. Santo Angelo, RS, Brazil, Nov. 12, 1963; Degree in Medicine, UFSM, 1988; PhD, UFCSPA, 1999. Dir. Ctr. Andrology & Urology, 2000—. Pres. Brazilian Soc. Urology, RS Sect., 2004—05, Associação Brasileira para Estudo das Inadequações Sexuais, 2006—07; coord. andrology dept. Brazilian Soc. Urology, 2008—09. Named Young Urologist, 1995. Mem.: Internat. Soc. Sexual Medicine, Am. Urol. Assn., Brazilian Soc. Urology. Avocation: tennis. Office: Soledade 569 Rm 907B Porto Alegre RS 90470340 Brazil Office Fax: 555133789996. Business E-Mail: carlos.da.ros@terra.com.br.

DARRAH, THOMAS, research scientist, educator; b. Centralia, Pa., Oct. 11, 1981; BS, U. Rochester, 2004, PhD, 2009. Rsch. asst. prof. U. Mass., Boston, 2009—. Chief rsch. officer GeoMed Analytical, LLC, 2009. Grant, NCS-NIH. Mem.: Internat. Med. Geology Assn. Office: Earth Environ and Ocean Scis Boston MA 02125 Business E-Mail: thomas.darrah@umb.edu.

DARROW, DAVID H., pediatric otolaryngologist, educator; MD, Duke U. Diplomate Am. Bd. Otolaryngology, 1994. Resident otolaryngology Univ. of Calif. San Diego Med. Ctr.; fellow pediatric otolaryngology Children's Meml. Ctr., Chgo.; hosp. affiliations include Children's Hosp. of The King's Daughter, Sentara Leigh Hosp., Sentara Norfolk Gen. Hosp.; assoc. prof. otolaryngology Eastern Va Med. Sch. Office: Childrens Hospital of The Kings Daughters 601 Childrens Ln Norfolk VA 23507 Office Phone: 757-668-7000.

DARWISH, ATEF MOHAMMAD, physician, educator; b. Assiut, Egypt, July 7, 1961; s. Mohammad Mostafa Darwish and Atyaat Bayomi Mohammad; m. Wafa Ali Gadallah, Aug. 20, 1990; children: Dina Atef, Atef Zolfa, Ahmad Atef. PhD, Assiut U., 1995. Resident Assiut U. Hosp., Assiut, Egypt, 1986—89, asst. lectr., 1989—94. Cons. Police Hosp., Assiut, Egypt, 1997. Mem.: Assiut Univ. Club. Achievements include patents for Creation of a novel drug used for treating hyperprolactinemia. Home: ElHelaly St Assiut 71111 Egypt Office: Assiut University Hospital Assiut Assiut 71112 Egypt Office Fax: 020882333327. Personal E-mail: a_darwish@mailcity.com.

DARZI, ARA, surgeon; b. May 7, 1960; MD, Trinity Coll., Dublin, Ireland. Fellowship Am. Coll. of Surgeons, Royal Coll. of Surgeons and Physicians, Glasgow, England, Royal Coll. of Surgeons, England, Edinburgh, England; with Ctrl. Middlesex Hosp., England; head surgery, oncology, reproductive biology and anaesthetic divsn. Imperial Coll. London; hon. cons. surgeon Royal Marsden NHS Found., England. Mem.: The Inst. of Cancer Rsch. (trust and chm. surgery sec.). Achievements include Pioneered innovative work in the devel. of minimally invasive surgery. Mailing: c/o The Institute of Cancer Research 123 Old Brompton Rd London England Office Phone: 4402073528133. Office Fax: 4402073705261. *

DAS, ASHOKE KUMAR, internist, consultant; b. Calcutta, W. Bengal, India, Nov. 1, 1934; came to U.S., 1974; s. Srikrishna and Durgeshnandini (Bose) D.; m. Geeta Mukhopadhyay, Aug. 15, 1961 (dec. 1993); 1 child, Arnab. MBBS, Calcutta U., 1957, MD, 1962, PhD, 1971. Diplomate Royal Coll. Physicians London, Am. Bd. Internal Medicine. Rotating intern NRS Med. Coll. Hosp., Calcutta, 1956, resident, 1957-58; chief resident Stafford Gen. Infirmary UK, 1970; chief resident internal medicine and cardiology Rush Green Hosp. UK, 1971-74; attending physician Our Lady Mercy Med. Ctr., Bronx, 1976—; chief sect. internal medicine Morrisania Clin., Bronx, 1980-83; pvt. practice Bronx, 1983—; attending physician St. Barnabas Hosp., Bronx, 1983—, Bronx Lebanon Hosp. Ctr., 1983—. Clin. asst. prof. medicine NY Med. Coll.; cons. in field. Indian Coun. Med. Rsch. grantee, 1958-59. Fellow ACP, Royal Coll. Physicians. (Eng.), Royal Soc. London; mem. AMA, NY State Med. Soc., Bronx Med. Soc., U. Calcutta Med. Assn. Am., Assn. Physicians India (US), Lions Club (mem. fundraising campaign 1995—, v.p. 1999, pres. 2001, dir. 2005-). Avocations: walking, travel. Office: 2940 Grand Course Apt SA Bronx NY 10458 Office Phone: 718-933-6655.

DAS, GOKUL M., research scientist, educator; arrived in U.S., 1983; s. Sivarama Menon; m. Lekha G. Nair, Apr. 25, 1965; children: Anagha M., Ananth M. BSc, U. Calicut, Kerala, India, 1975, EdB, 1977; MSc, Jawaharlal Nehru U., New Delhi, India, 1979, MPhil, 1982; PhD, Baylor U., 1988. Head Gene Regulation Lab. Cancer Therapy & Rsch. Ctr., San Antonio, 1994—2000; mem. San Antonio Cancer Inst., 1995—2002; asst. mem. Roswell Pk. Cancer Inst., Buffalo, 2002—; sr. mem. SUNY, Buffalo, 2002—. Adj. asst. prof. U. Tex. Health Sci. Ctr., San Antonio, 1995—2000, asst. prof., 2000—02; cons. InCell, San Antonio, 1998—2002. Recipient Rsch. Excellence award, Mead Johnson, 1988; grantee, San Antonio Area Found., 1995, San Antonio Cancer Inst., 1995, Am. Cancer Soc., 1996, Cancer Ctr. Coun., 1998, Charlotte Geyer Found., 1999, Nat. Cancer Inst., NIH, 1999, Wendy Will Case Cancer Fund, 1999, U.S. Army Breast Cancer Rsch. Program, 2001; fellow, Leukemia Soc. Am., 1988; Jr. Rsch. fellow, U. Grants Commn., India, 1979—82, Sr. Rsch. fellow, 1982—83, Rsch. fellow, L.I. Biol. Assn., Merit scholar, Jawaharlal Nehru U., 1977—79. Mem.: AAAS, Am. Assn. for Cancer Rsch. Achievements include discovery of transcription of U6 gene by RNA ploymease III; U6 gene in fruit fly (drosophila); tRNA gene upstream of U6 gene cluster in fruit fly genome; alternatively spliced vaiant of human homeo domain protein Oct-1; p53 tumor suppressor protein induced in response to genomic damage is active for gene transcription; elucidated the mechanism underlying activation of a gene by an oncoprotein and a tumorsuppressor protein. Office: Roswell Pk Cancer Inst Elm & Carlton Sts Buffalo NY 14263 E-mail: gokul.das@roswellpark.org.

DAS, MALAY KUMAR, pharmacist, educator; b. West Bengal, India, July 2, 1970; PhD, Jadavpur U., 1996. Asst. prof., dept. pharm. scis. Dibrugarh U., 1999—. Mem.: Dibrugarh U. Tchrs. Assn., Indian Pharm. Assn. Avocations: reading, music, gardening, travel, dance. Office: Rajabeheta Dibrugarh University Dibrugarh Assam 786004 India Home Phone: 0373 2371145; Office Phone: 0373-2370254. Office Fax: 0373-2370323. Personal E-mail: malaydas2002@yahoo.com. Business E-Mail: du_mkd@yahoo.co.in.

DAS, SANJITA, pharmacologist, educator; b. Baripada, Orissa, India, May 16, 1975; PharmM, Birla Inst. Tech., 2002, PhD, 2008. HOD, pharmacology Noida Inst. Engring. and Tech., 2006—. Guiding phd students Bit, Utu, Soa U., India, 2010—11. Mem.: ICS, APTI, IGPA, IPS, IPA. Office: Plot 19 Knowlwdgw Park-II Noida Uttar Pradesh 201306 India Office Fax: 01202320062. Personal E-mail: sanjita8@yahoo.co.in.

DAS, SUBINOY, surgeon; b. Atlanta, May 1, 1975; MD, U. Va., 1997. Dir. sinus and allergy, dept. otolaryngology-head and neck surgery Ohio State U., 2008—. Prin. investigator NIH, 2008—. Named one of America's Top Drs., Best Drs., Inc. Fellow: ACS; mem.: Am. Acad. Otolaryngology-Head and Neck Surgery. Office: 915 Olentangy River Rd 4th Fl Dublin OH 43016 Office Fax: 614-293-9698. Business E-Mail: subinoy.das@osumc.edu.

DAS, SUBIR KUMAR, medical educator; b. Kolkata, Oct. 1, 1968; MSc, U. Coll. Sci., 1991; PhD, North Bengal U., 1997. Asst. prof. Sikkim Manipal Inst. Med. Scis., 2000—03; assoc. prof. Amrita Inst. Med. Scis., 2004—08, Agartala Govt. Med. Coll., 2008—10, ESI-PGIMSR, 2010—, Coll. Medicine, JNM Hosp., WBUHS, 2011—. Recipient AACC VSF POCT Rsch. award. Avocation: stamp collecting/philately. Home: 2/120 Paschim Putiary Kolkata West Bengal 700041 India Personal E-mail: drsubirkdas@yahoo.co.in.

DAS, SUMAN KUMAR, plastic surgeon, researcher; b. Calcutta, India, came to U.S., 1980; s. Bisweswar and Devi Rani (Ghosh) D.; m. Carole Ellen Simmons, July 10, 1976 (div. Apr. 1984); children: Louise Angelique, Natalie Krishna; m. Rosyln Tanner, Mar. 22, 1991. B of Medicine and Surgery, Calcutta U., India, 1967; MD, Ednl. Commn. Fgn. Med. Grad., 1981. Diplomate Am. Bd. Plastic Surgery. Intern R.G. Kar Med. Coll. and Hosp., Calcatta, 1966-67, resident in gen. surgery, house officer, 1967-68; sr. house officer in accident and emergency, orthopaedics Royal Infirmary, Bolton, Lancs, Eng., 1968-69, house surgeon in gen. surgery, 1969-70; sr. house officer in gen. surgery Royal United Hosp., St. Martins's Hosp., Bath, Eng., 1970-72; house officer in medicine Whiston Hosp., Prescot, Liverpool, Eng., 1970; registrar in gen. surgery Frenchay Hosp., Bristol, Eng., 1972-73, sr. house officer in plastic surgery, 1973-74; registrar in plastic surgery Frenchay Hosp., Bristol, Eng., 1974, Royal Victoria Infirmary, Fleming Meml. Children's Hosp., Newcastle-Upon-Tyne, Eng., 1974-77; fellow in plastic and reconstructive surgery Hosp. for Sick Children, Toronto, Ont., Can., 1978; fellow in micro and hand surgery St. Vincent's Hosp., Melbourne, Australia, 1979-80, asst. plastic surgeon, 1979-80; rsch. assoc. in plastic surgery UCLA Med. Ctr., 1980-82; co-dir. microsurgery tng. program Harbor/UCLA Med. Ctr., 1980-82; dir. plastic surgery rsch. VA Wadsworth Med. Ctr., LA, 1980-82; resident in plastic surgery U. Miss. Med. Ctr., Jackson, 1982-83, sr. and chief resident in plastic surgery, 1983-84; pvt. practice Jackson, 1984-86; chief and asst. prof. div. plastic surgery U. Miss. Med. Ctr., Jackson, 1986-87, chief and assoc. prof. div. plastic surgery, 1987-90, prof. plastic surgery, chief div. plastic surgery, chief, 1990-95, clin. prof. plastic surgery, 1995—. Cons. plastic surgery Miss. Bapt. Med. Ctr., River Oaks Hosp.; attending Meth. Rehab. Ctr., U. Miss. Med. Ctr., River Oaks East Hosp., St. Dominiso Hosp.; vis. prof. dept. surgery divsn. plastic surgery U. Calif., San Francisco, 1981, U. Ala., 1992; mem. patient care com. U. Miss., Jackson, 1990—92; pres. internet co. Nxmed.com. Inc., 1999—2003; dir. St. Dominic Ambulatory Surgery Ctr., 1999—2004; med. dir. St. Dominic's Ambulatory Surgery Ctr., 1999—2004, pres., 2003—04; dir. outreach program St. Dominic Hosp.; presenter and exhibitor in field at numerous profl. meetings. Author: (with others) Manual of Operative Plastic and Reconstructive Surgery, 1980, Textbook of Surgery, 2nd edit., 1988, Ency. of Flaps, 1990; mem. editorial bd. So. Med. Jour., 1993-1999; contbr. articles to Brit. Jour. Surgery, Brit. Jour. Plastic Surgery, Indian Jour. Dermatology, Hand, Plastic Surgery Forum, Jour. Singapore Acad. Sci., Jour. Oral Surgery, Plastic Reconstrn. Surgery, Acta Anatomica, Jour. Clin. Pathology, others; inventor turmeric on wound healing. Pres. NxMed.com Internet Distant Edn., 2000—. Recipient prize North Eng. Surg. Soc., 1977, Plastic Surgery Ednl. Found. Rsch. grant 1983-84, other grants Eli Lilly 1989, Tyra, 1989, Collagen Corp. 1989, 90-91, NIH, 1989, Am. Soc. Aesthetic

Plastic Surgery, 1990, 91. Fellow ACS, Royal Coll. Surgeons London, Royal Coll. Surgeons Edinburgh (traveling scholarship 1976); mem. AMA, AAAS, Am. Fedn. for Clin. Rsch., Am. Assn. Hand Surgery (rsch. grant com. 1990-91, chmn. rsch. grant com. 1992), Am. Assn. Acad. Plastic Surgeons (fellowship com. 1990), Am. Soc. Plastic and Reconstructive Surgeons, Am. Assn. Plastic Surgeons, Internat. Soc. Burn Injuries, Internat. Soc. Reconstructive Microsurgery, Internat. Soc. Surgery, Internat. Soc. Emergency Medicine and Critical Care (charter), Brit. Assn. Plastic Surgeons (best prize and cert. 1967), Brit. Soc. Surgery of Hands (European traveling scholarship 1977), Soc. N.Am. Skull Base Surgery (founding), Miss. State Med. Assn., Plastic Surgery Rsch. Coun., N.Y. Acad. Sci., S.E. Soc. Plastic and Reconstructive Surgeons (program com. 1990—, trustee 1997-2000, historian 2000-01, chmn. CME com. 1999—, asst. sec. 2001—, v.p. 2005-06, pres. elect 2006-07, pres. 2007—), Miss. Acad. Scis. (chmn. 1992), Acad. Surg. Rsch., Assn. for Acad. Surgery, Southeastern Surg. Congress, Internat. Fedn. Surg. Colls., So. Med. Assn. (chmn. 1992), Cmty. Outreach Prof. St. Dosh Hosp.(bd. mem. 2003-), Miss. Children's Mus. (ptnrs. adivsory bd. mem.) 2007, Cmty. Found. of Greater Jackson (trustee 2007-, Smile Train ptnr. 2008-), Miss. Symphony (bd. mem. 09-), Lions Club (Flora), Sigma Xi. Achievements include discovery that silicone does not elicit any change in T cell population; that capsular contracture with silicone implant is not an immunological effect; rsch. on best treatment for finger tip amputation in children, size and lengthening of human omentum, muscle transplantation by microvascular technique fatigue like normal muscle. Home: 242 Highland Hills Ln Flora MS 39071-9613 Office: 2629 Ct House Cir Flowood MS 39232 Office Phone: 601-362-0611. Office Fax: 601-362-0192. Personal E-mail: Sushrata@aol.com.

DASARI, BOBBY V. M., physician; s. Rao P. and Lakshmi R. Dasari. MBBS, Manipal Acad. Higher Edn., India, 2001, MS, 2004. Splty. registrar gen. surgery Northern Ireland Med. and Dental Tng. Agy., Belfast, Northern Ireland. Contbr. articles to profl. jour., chapters to books. Fellow, Acad. Gen. Edn., 2001. Fellow: Acad. Gen. Edn.; mem.: RCS (Edinburgh). Achievements include surgclinics-a 68 min video CD demonstrating the methods of examination of surgical patients aimed at teaching undergraduate and post graduate medical students. Personal E-mail: bobby.dasari@yahoo.com.

DASCHLE, TOM (THOMAS ANDREW DASCHLE), former United States Senator from South Dakota; b. Aberdeen, SC, Dec. 9, 1947; m. Linda Hall Daschle; children: Kelly, Nathan, Lindsay. BA, S.D. State U., 1969. Fin. investment rep.; chief legis. aide, field coord. to Senator James Abourzek US Senate, 1973-77; mem. US Congress from 1st S.D. Dist., 1979—83, US Congress from S.D. at-large Dist., 1983-87; US Senator from S.D., 1987—2005; minority leader US Senate, 1996—2001, 2003—04, majority leader, 2001—03; spl. policy adv. Alston & Bird LLP, Washington, 2005—09; sr. policy adv. DLA Piper, Washington, 2009—. Disting. sr. fellow, Ctr. for American Progress, 2005-, co-founder, Bi-Partisan Policy Ctr., 2007-, vis. prof., Georgetown U. Pub. Policy Inst., 2008-, Richard von Weizsäcker Disting. Visitor, American Acad., Berlin, 2008-; bd. dirs. CB Richard Ellis Group, Inc., 2005-, Prime BioSolutions, Mascoma Corp., 2007-. Co-author (with Michael D'Orso): Like No Other Time: The Two Years That Changed America, 2004; co-author: (with Scott S. Greenberger & Jeanne M. Lawbrew) Critical: What We Can Do About the Health-Care Crisis, 2008. Founder Am. Grown Found., 1987. Served to 1st lt. USAF, 1969-72. Recipient Nat. Commdr.'s award Disabled Am. Vets., 1980, Disting. Alumni award S.D. State U., 1997, VFW Congl. award VFW, 1997, Legislator of Yr. award Vietnam Vets. Am., 1997, Cert. Appreciation, Nat. Assn. Federally Impacted Sch., 1997, Congl. Leadership award Cmty. Anti-Drug Coalitions Am., 1997, Golden Triangle award Nat. Farmer's Union, 1997-98, Outstanding Vets. Adv. of Yr. award Disabled Am. Vets. Dept. S.D., 1998, Pres. Recognition award Nat. Indian Impacted Schs. Assn., 1998, Cert. Appreciation, Nat. Assn. Alcoholism and Drug Abuse Counselors, 1998, Diplomat award Rapid City C. of C., 1998, Disting. Svc. award Nat. Rural Electric Coop. Assn., 2000; named Outstanding Young Man of Yr., U.S. Jaycees, 1981, Friend of Edn., S.D. Edn. Assn., 1997, Person of the Yr., Nat. Assn. Concerned Vets., 1997, Legislator of Yr., Renewable Fuels Assn., 1998, Maj. Gen. Williamson's S.D. Nat. Guard Militia Man of 1998, S.D. Nat. Guard. Mem.: Coun. Fgn. Rels. Democrat. Roman Catholic. Office: DLA Piper 500 8th St NW Washington DC 20004 Office Phone: 202-799-4370. Office Fax: 202-799-5370. E-mail: tom.daschle@dlapiper.com.

DAS GUPTA, AMAR, hematologist, consultant; s. Kshitindra Nath and Chinmayee Das Gupta; m. Nandita Sarkar, June 14, 1956; children: Anirban Amar Dasgupta, Antara Amar Dasgupta. MB BS, Prince Wales Med. Coll., 1972; MD, Postgrad. Inst. Med. Edn. & Rsch., 1977; PhD, U. Mumbai, 1987. Resident tchg. fellow Post grad. Inst. Med. Edn. & Rsch., Chandigarh, India, 1976—77; rsch. officer Inst. Immunohematology, Mumbai, Maharashtra, India, 1978—81; asst. hematopathologist Tata Meml. Hosp., Mumbai, 1981—87; cons. hematologist P.D. Hinduja Nat. Hosp. & MRC, Mumbai, 1987—. Dir. dept. of lab. medicine P. D. Hinduja Nat. Hosp. & MRC, Mumbai, 1989—99; cons. WHO, Govt. of Myanmar, Yangon, 1991—92; rsch. guide P.D. Hinduja Nat. Hosp. and MRC U. Mumbai, 1985—; =. Contbr. numerous articles to profl. jours. Recipient Blood Group Reference Centre Oration, Bombay Hematology Group, 1993; Talent Search Scheme Fellowship, Indian Coun. Med. Rsch., 1976—77, John Fogarty Internat. Fellowship, NIH, 1982—84, Yamagiwa-Yoshida Fellowship, Internat. Union Against Cancer, 1988—89, Reach-The- World Grant, Internat. Soc. Thrombosis and Hemostasis, 2003. Fellow: Indian Soc. Hematology and Transfusion Medicine (hon.); mem.: South Asian Soc. for Atherosclerosis and Thrombosis (life). Achievements include research in Acquired Abnormalities of Hemoglobin and Red Cell Enzymes; Production and Characterization of Hemopoietic Lineage-associated Monoclonal Antibodies; Flow Cytometric Immunophenotyping of Normal Leucocytes and Leukemic Cells; Prognostication of Hematologic Malignancies on the Basis of Transferrin Receptor Expression; Pathogenesis of Inherited and Acquired Thrombophilic & Bleeding Disorders. Office: PD Hinduja Nat Hosp & MRC Veer Savarkar Marg Mahim Mumbai 400 016 Maharashta India Office Fax: 091-022-24442318. Business E-Mail: dr_adasgupta@hindujahospital.com.

DASGUPTA, INDRANIL, physician, educator; b. Barielly, India, May 24, 1960; arrived in US, 1961; s. Sunil Pryia and Krishna Dasgupta. BA in Philosophy, Duke U., 1982; MPH in Internat. Health, Loma Linda U., 1987; cert. epidemiology, Johns Hopkins U., 1987; MBA in Fin., George Washington U., 1989; MD, St. George U., Grenada, 1994. Diplomate Am. Bd. Internal Medicine, 1999, Am. Bd. Cardiovasc. Disease, 2005, ACP. Congl. intern US Ho. of Reps., Washington, 1983; rsch. asst. Harvard Med. Sch., Boston, 1983-84, Dartmouth U. Med. Sch., Hanover, NH, 1985-86; rsch. assoc. Loma Linda Sch. Pub. Health, Calif., 1986-87; congl. intern US Senator Ed Kennedy, Washington, 1988-89; med. resident Med. Coll. Pa.-Hahnemann U. Hosps., Phila., 1995-98, rsch. assoc., 1998-99, geriatric fellow Phila., 1998-99; cardiology fellow Robert Wood Johnson Med. Sch. U. Medicine and Dentistry NJ, Camden, 1999—2002, rsch. assoc., 1999—2002; clin. asst. prof. divsn. cardiology Jefferson Med. Coll., Phila., 2002—; attending cardiologist Thomas Jefferson U. Hosp., Phila., 2002—. Contbr. articles to profl. jours. Vol. Muscular Dystrophy Assn., Winston-Salem, NC, 1981, US Spl. Olympics, Wilmington, Del., 1985, Dem. Fund Raising, Washington, 1988; rsch. intern Select Com. Aging US House of Reps., 1983. Fellow: Royal Soc. Medicine, Am. Coll. Physicians, Soc. Geriatric Cardiology, Am. Coll. Cardiology, Am. Heart Assn.; mem.: ACP, AHA, Am. Soc. Nuclear Cardiology, Internat. Soc. Heart and Lung Transplantation, NY Acad. Scis., NJ Acad. Sci., Nat. Assn. Advancement Sci., Delta Omega, Sigma Alpha Epsilon. Republican. Avocations: travel, sailing, snorkling, soccer. Office: Thomas Jefferson U Hosp Jefferson Heart Inst 925 Chestnut St Mezzanine Level Philadelphia PA 19107 Home: 941 Lombard St Philadelphia PA 19147 Personal E-mail: indranildasgupta@aol.com.

DASH, ALEKHA K., pharmaceutical scientist, educator; b. Gobindapur, Orissa, India, Aug. 1, 1954; came to the U.S., 1984; s. Jagannath Dash and Flurence Panda; m. Kanchanbala Mohapatra, May 9, 1984; children: Debleena, Rohan Dipak. B in Pharmacy, Jadavpur U., Calcutta, 1981, M in Pharmacy, 1983; PhD, U. Minn., 1990. Registered pharmacist Nebr. Registered pharmacist, Orissa, India, 1975-77; pharmacy technician U. Minn. Med. Ctr., Mpls., 1984-90; tchg. and rsch. asst. U. Minn., Mpls., 1984-90; asst. prof. Creighton U., Omaha, 1990-95, assoc. prof., 1995—2003, prof., 2003—, chair dept. pharmacy, 2003—; adj. asst. prof. U. Nebr., Omaha, 1994—. Gilbert F. Taffe chair pharmacy. Editor-in-chief Orissa Soc. of Ams., 1993-95; contbr. chpts. to books. Recipient John C. Kenific awards Health Future Found., Omaha, 1991, 93, Pharmaceutics award Pharm. Mfrs. Assn., Washington, 1993. Mem. AAAS, Am. Assn. Pharm. Scientists (award and publ. com. 1994—), Am. Assn. Colls. Pharmacy. Achievements include development of implantable delivery system for bone infections; use of microdialysis in implantable dosage form design; solid state characterization of tobramycin. Home: 13518 Sahler St Omaha NE 68164-6025 Office: Creighton Univ 2500 California Plz Omaha NE 68178-0001 Business E-Mail: adash@creighton.edu.

DASH, ASHUTOSH, research scientist; b. Sambalpur, May 18, 1960; PhD, 1979. Sci. officer Bhabha Atomic Rsch. Ctr., 1982—. Adj. prof. HBNI, 2010. Office: Radiopharmaceuticals Divsn Radiology Mumbai Maharastra 400085 India Business E-Mail: adash@barc.gov.in.

DASHASH, NOHA AHMAD, physician, educator; b. Riyadh, Central, Saudi Arabia, Oct. 6, 1966; d. Ahmed Ayesh Dashash and Nour Hamza Khomais; m. Jamal Jumaan Hejres, Aug. 20, 1992; children: Jehad Jamal Hejres, Ahmad Jamal Hejres, Yousuf Jamal Hejres. MBChB, King Saud U., 1992, diploma in Primary Health Care, 1997. Arab Bd. Family Medicine, 1999, Saudi Bd. Family Medicine, 1999. Intern King Fahad Hosp. and Maternity and Children's Hosp., Jeddah, 1993—94; resident King Khalid U. Hosp., Riyadh, Saudi Arabia, 1995—99; family physician Primary Health Care Directorate, Ministry of Health, Jeddah, 1999—; postgrad. trainer Joint Program Family Cmty. Medicine, Jeddah, Western, Saudi Arabia, 2001—; dep. dir. primary health care Jeddah Governorate, Saudi Arabia, 2004. Organizer courses Joint Program Family Cmty. Medicine, Jeddah, 2001—. Author: Notes For Postgraduate Exams in Family Medicine. Master: Jeddah Evidence Based Medicine Working Group (mgr. 2002—03); mem.: Am. Acad. Family Physicians, Saudi Soc. Family Cmty. Medicine (head health edn. com. 2002—03), Gulf Countries Coun. (assoc.; rep. 2003), Nat. Com. Family Cmty. Medicine (assoc.; mem. com. 2003, organizer courses 2002). Achievements include research in Quality of Health Care of Astmatic Patients; Quality of Life with Asthma; Breast Feeding; Burnout in Physicians; Menoupause; first to Evidence Based Healthcare Working Group. Avocations: swimming, reading. Office: Joint Program Family Cmty Medicine PO Box 15814 Palastine St Western Jeddah 21454 Saudi Arabia Office Fax: +966 2 672-5232. Personal E-mail: drnohadashash@yahoo.com.

DA SILVA, ELOÍSIO ALEXSANDRO, urologist; b. Governador Valadares, MG, Brazil, Feb. 12, 1971; MD, U. Fed. Espírito Santo, 1995; PhD, U. Fed. São Paulo, 2001. Asst. prof. U. Estado do Rio de Janeiro, 2006—. Mem. reviewer bd. Jour. Urology, 2008, Yonsei Med. Jour., 2008, Indian Jour. Urology, 2008, Urology Annals, 2010; bd. dirs. Urologia Essential, 2011. Mem.: Soc. Brasileira Urologia (Young Talent 2005), Soc. L.Am. Medicina Sexual (Rsch. grant 2009), World PA Transgender Health, Am. Urol. Assn. Avocations: history, aquariums. Office: Blvd 28 de setembro 77 5th fl Rio de Janeiro 20551-030 Brazil Office Fax: 55 21 35182642. Business E-Mail: alex@uerj.br.

DA SILVA, ERCIO MARIO, physician; b. Catajuczes, Minas, Brazil; s. Mario and Rosa (Pinto) da S.; m. Doris Hale da Silva, Aug. 22, 1953; children: Robert, Suzanne. MD, U. Mines, Brazil, 1949. Diplomate Am. Bd. Colon Rectal Surgery. Physician U.S. Mil. Base, Columbia, SC, 1988—. Mem. Am. Soc. Colon Rectal Surgery, Columbia Med. Soc. Home: 413 Brookshire Dr Columbia SC 29210-4203

DA SILVA VAZ, ITABAJARA, JR., veterinarian, educator; b. Brazil, June 26, 1967; DVM, U. Fed. Pelotas, 1988; PhD, U. Fed. Rio Grande do Sul, 1997. Prof. U. Fed. Rio Grande do Sul, 1995—. Fellow: Conselho Nat. Desenvolvimento Sci. e Tech. Office: Av Bengo Goncalves 9500 CP 15005 Porto Alegre Rio Grande do Sul 91501970 Brazil Office Fax: 55-51-33087309. Business E-Mail: ita@cbiot.ufrgs.br.

DASKALAKI, IRINI, medical educator; MD, U. Athens Med. Sch., Greece, 1994. Cert. Ednl. Comm. Fgn. Med. Grads., 1998, in gen. pediat. Am. Bd. Pediat., 2006, in pediatric infectious diseases 2007, lic. Med. Bd. State Pa., 2008. Pub. svc. med. officer Nat. Health Sys., Zoniana, Crete, Greece, 1995—96; rsch. fellow Sch. Medicine, Nat. U. Athens, Greece, 1996—98; resident, pediat. Agia Sophia Children's Hosp., Athens, Greece, 1998—2001, Monmouth Med. Ctr., Long Branch, NJ, 2001—03; fellow, pediatric infectious diseases St Christopher's Hosp. Children, Phila., 2003—06, rsch. fellow, pediatric infectious diseases, 2006—07; asst. prof. Drexel U. Coll. Medicine, Phila., 2008—; attending physician St Christopher's Hosp. Children, Phila., 2008—; med. epidemiologist Phila. Dept. Pub. Health, 2008—. Contbr. chapters to books, articles to profl. jours. Sunday sch. tchr. Holy Trinity Greek Orthodox Ch., Wilmington, Del., 2006. Recipient Outstanding Fellow's abstract award, Pediatric Infectious Diseases Soc., 2006, Outstanding Abstract award, Coll. Physicians Phila., 2007. Fellow: Am. Acad. Pediat.; mem.: Infectious Diseases Soc. America, Pediatric Infectious Diseases Soc. Achievements include research in vaccine preventable diseases. Office: St Christopher's Hosp Children Erie Ave Front St Philadelphia PA 19134

DASMAHAPATRA, ASOK KUMAR, biomedical researcher; b. Panchrol, India, Feb. 1, 1949; PhD, U. Calcutta, 1981. Sr. rsch. scientist U. Miss., 2011—. Mem.: Rsch. Inst. Alcoholism, Am. Assn. Coll Pharmacy, Soc. Toxicology. Avocation: sports. Office: 313 Faser Hall University MS 38677 Office Fax: 662-915-5148. Business E-Mail: asok@olemiss.edu.

DASSOPOULOS, THEMISTOCLES, gastroenterologist, educator; b. Athens, Greece, 1965; BS, Brown U., 1988, MD, 1991. Assoc. prof. medicine, dir. inflammatory bowel diseases Wash. U. Sch. Medicine, 2008—. Mem.: Am. Soc. Gastrointestinal Endoscopy, Am. Coll. Gastroenterology, Am. Gastroent. Assn. Office: 660 S Euclid Ave Box 8214 Saint Louis MO 63110 Office Fax: 314-454-8289. Business E-Mail: themos@dom.wustl.edu.

DATE, ELAINE SATOMI, physiatrist, educator; b. San Jose, Calif., Feb. 19, 1957; BS, Stanford U., 1978; MD, Med. Coll. Pa., 1982. Diplomate of Nat. Bd. Med. Examiners. Diplomate Am. Bd. Phys. Medicine and Rehab. Dir. phys. medicine and rehab. Stanford U. Sch. Medicine, Calif., 1985—, rehab. medicine sect. chief, 1988-90, head phys. medicine and rehab. div., 1990—, assoc. prof. dept. functional rehab., 1995—; rehab. medicine chief Palo Alto VA Med. Ctr., Calif., 1988—. Fellow Am. Acad. Phys. Medicine and Rehab., Am. Assn. Electromyography and Electrodiagnosis. Avocations: reading, jogging.

DATILES, MANUEL BERNALDES, III, ophthalmologist, researcher; b. Manila, Feb. 26, 1951; arrived in U.S., 1979; s. Roberto Aguiling and Loretta (Bernaldes) Datiles; m. Jacqueline Romero, Mar. 13, 1976; children: Michelle, Joyce, Margaret, Jennifer, Manuel IV, Michael. BS cum laude, U. Santo Tomas, 1970, MD cum laude, 1974. Intern Jose Reyes Meml. Hosp. (North Gen. Hosp.); rsch. fellow Philippine Eye Rsch. Inst. U. Philippines, Manila, 1975—76; resident in ophthalmology U. Philippines-Philippine Gen. Hosp., Manila, 1976—79; rsch. scholar, vis. scientist Lab. Vision Rsch. Nat. Eye Inst.-NIH, Bethesda, Md., 1979—82; clin. fellow corneal and cataract surgery Wilmer Eye Inst.-Johns Hopkins U. Hosp., Balt., 1982—83; sr. staff ophthalmologist Nat. Eye Inst.-NIH, Bethesda, 1983—88, acting chief cornea and cataract sect., clin. svc. br., 1989—92, chief cornea and cataract sect., clin. svcs. br., 1992—2006; chmn. surg. adminstrv. com. NIH Clin. Ctr. Hosp., 1994—95; clin. staff & lectr. Wilmer Eye Inst., Johns Hopkins U., Balt., 2007—; med. officer, sr. clin. investigator Nat. Eye Inst., NIH, 2007—. Vis. lectr. Wilmer Eye Inst.-Johns Hopkins U., Balt., 1984, Osaka U., Japan, 1986, U. Munich, 1988, Harkness Eye Inst., Columbia U., NYC, 1994—97, Washington Hosp. Ctr., 2006, Wilmer Eye Inst., Johns Hopkins U., Balt., 2007—; cons. on eye/cataract rsch. NASA, VA, pharm. cos.; presenter in field; cons. Radiation Injury Rsch. Consotium, 2011—. Editor: cataract sect. Duane's Clinical Ophthalmology Textbook series, 1989—; guest editor: Jour. Investigative Ophthalmology and Visual Sci., 1999, 2000; contbr. chapters to books, articles to profl. jours.; reviewer jours. in field:. Recipient Most Outstanding Silver Jubiliarian in Med. Rsch. award, U. Santo Tomas Alumni Assn. Am., 1999, Cert. Appreciation For Work With Indigents, James Cardinal Hickey and Archdiocese of Washington, Ophthalmology Rsch. award, Assn. Philippine Ophthalmologists in Am., 2001, US Dept. Health & Human Svcs. Innovator award, Sec. Kathleen Sebellius, 2011. Mem.: Philippine Am. Acad. Sci. and Engring., Contact Lens Assn. Ophthalmologists, Wilmer Eye Inst. Residents' Assn., Md. Soc. Eye Physicians and Surgeons, Washington Acad. Ophthalmology, Internat. Assn. Ocular Surgeons, Johns Hopkins Med. Surg. Assn., Castroviego Soc. Corneal Surgeons, Am. Acad. Ophthalmology, Assn. Rsch. in Vision and Ophthalmology, Johns Hopkins Alumni Assn. Roman Catholic. Achievements include research in medical nonsurgical treatment cataracts and early detection and documentation of cataracts; causes of cataracts; development of NASA-NEI dynamic light scattering device for early cataract detection. Avocations: sketching, soap carving, target shooting, guitar, chess. Office: NIH Nat Eye Inst Rm 10n226 Bethesda MD 20892-1860 Office Phone: 301-594-7052, 301-496-3577. Business E-Mail: datilesm@nei.nih.gov, mbdatiles3@jhmi.edu.

DATTA, SOUMITRA SHANKAR, psychiatrist, researcher; b. Calcutta, India, June 6, 1973; s. Pankaj Kumar and Madhabika Datta; m. Debjani Das, May 1, 2000. MBBS, R.G. Kar Med. Coll., 1998; diploma in Psychol. Medicine, Christian Med. Coll., 2001, MD in Psychiatry), 2003. Diplomate in psychiatry Nat. Bd. Examinations, 2003. Intern R.G. Kar Med. Coll., Calcutta, India, 1997—98; lectr. Christian Med. Coll., Vellore, India, 2003—04; specialist registrar Carol Kendrick Unit, Wythenshawe Hosp., Manchester, England, 2007—. V.p. Trineer, Calcutta, India, 1995—98. Recipient Kalyani Nandi Gold medal, R.G.Kar Med. Coll., 1999, Florence Nichole prize, Christian Med. Coll., Vellore, India, 2001, Rose Chacko prize, 2003; fellow, Jawaharlal Nehru Ctr. Advanced Sci. Rsch., 1994; bursary fellow, Royal Coll. Psychiatrists, 2003, Donald Cohen fellow, Internat. Assn. Child & Adolescent Psychiatrists & Allied Profls., 2008. Mem.: Royal Coll. Psychiatrists UK, Brit. Med. Assn., Internat. Headache Soc. (assoc.), Indian Psychiatry Soc. (life). Achievements include research in neuropsychiatry related to epilepsy. Office: Carol Kendrick Unit Dept Child & Adolescent Psychiarty Wythenshaw Hosp Manchester M23 9LT England Personal E-mail: ssdatta2000@yahoo.com.

DATTA, SUBHAS CHANDRA, research scientist, educator; b. Burdwan Dist., West Bengal, India, Dec. 3, 1967; BSc in Zoology with honors, U. Burdwan, 1988, MSc in Zoology, Entomology, 1990, EdB in Sci., 1992; PhD in Zoology, Visva Bharati U., Santiniketan, Birbhum, India, 2001. Jr. rsch. fellow Visva Bharati U., 1993—96; rschr., asst. tchr. Life Sci. Unit, Ajodhya HS, Burdwan Dist., 1996—2007; headmaster, rschr. Eco-Club Rsch. Unit, Kanchannagar D. N. Das HS, Burdwan Dist., 2007—. With Birbhum Janaseva Pratisthan, 1980—; with, lit. programme West Bengal State,

1988—91. Grant, U. Grant Commn. India, Ctrl. Silk Bd. India. Master: West Bengal Bd. Secondary Edn. (cons., rschr., resource person, policy 1996—, Life Style Edn. award, Cpl. Punishment and Disaster Mgmt. award); fellow: Rsch. Coop. Assn., Social And Environ. Biol. Assn.; mem.: Soc. Biol. Chemist, Calcutta U. (life), Zool. Soc. (life), Paschim Banga Vigyan Mancha, Nat. Green Crop., Indian Sci. Congress Assn. Avocation: gardening. Home: Katwa Rd Bajeprotappur Nr Hanuman Mandir Burdwan West Bengal 713101 India

DATTATREYUDU, NORI, radiation oncologist, educator; B, Andhra U., 1965; MB, BChir, Kurnool Med. Coll., 1971; MD, Osmania U., 1976. Diplomate Am. Bd. Radiology, 1979, lic. NY, 1979. Intern Gandhi Hosp., 1973; resident in radiation oncology Meml. Sloan-Kettering Cancer Ctr., 1973—75, clinical asst. radiation therapist, 1978—79, asst. attending radiation therapist, 1980—85; assoc. mem. Meml. Sloan-Kettering Cancer Rsch. Inst., 1985—89; assoc. attending radiation oncologist Meml. Sloan-Kettering Cancer Ctr., 1985—89, dir. of brachytheraphy dept. of radiation oncology, 1988, chief brachytheraphy svc. dept. of radiation oncology, 1988—89; prof. radiation oncology Cornell Univ-Weill Med. Coll.; asst. prof. of radiology Cornell U. Med. Coll., 1980—85; assoc. prof. dept. of medicine Cornell Univ. Med. Coll., 1985—89, assoc. prof. of radiation oncology, 1985—90, prof. of radiology, 1996—, NJ Univ. of Medicine and Dentistry, 1987—90; prof. of clin. radiology NYU Med. Ctr., 1990—96; assoc. attending dept. of medicine The NY Hosp., 1985—89; chmn. dept. of radiation oncology The NY Hosp. Med. Center of Queens, 1989—, dir. of oncology, 1991—; chmn. dept. of radiation oncology The NY Hosp. Med. Ctr., 1996; radiation oncologist NY- Presbyn. Hosp. Fellow: Am. Soc. of Therapeutic and Oncology, Am. Coll. of Radiology Oncology, Am. Coll. of Radiology; mem.: Connective Tissue Oncology Soc., NY Cancer Soc., Soc. of Surgical Oncology, NY Roentgen Soc., NY County Med. Soc., Am. Soc. of Therapeutic Radiology and Oncology, Am. Med. Assn., Am. Cancer Soc., Am. Brachytheraphy Soc., Am. Soc. of Clin. Oncology, Indian Soc. of Clin. Oncology, NY Radiological Soc., Radiology Soc. of North America, Am. Radium Soc. Office: New York- Presbyterian Hospital 525 E. 68th St New York NY 10021

DAULAIRE, NILS MAARTEN PARIN, federal agency administrator; b. 1948; BA summa cum laude, Harvard Coll., 1970; MD, Harvard Med. Sch., 1976; MPH, Johns Hopkins U., Balt., 1978. Bd. cert. gen. preventive medicine & pub. health. Health care advisor People's Health Ctr., Bangladesh, 1976; dir. Bur. Handicapped Children, NH Dept. Health & Human Services, 1978—79; pub. health advisor Ministry Health, Mali, 1979—80; dir. internat. divsn. John Snow Pub. Health Group Inc., Boston, 1983—84; sr. health adminstrn. advisor Nepal Ministry Health & Population, Kathmandu, 1984—89; dir. Internat. Ctr. Prevention & Treatment Major Childhood Diseases (INTERCEPT), Hanover, NH, 1989—93; dep. asst. adminstr. policy, sr. internat. health advisor US Agy. for Internat. Devel. (USAID), Washington, 1993—98; pres., CEO Global Health Coun., 1998—2011; dir. Office Global Health Affairs US Dept. Health & Human Services, Washington, 2011—; mem. exec. bd. WHO US Dept. State, Geneva, 2011—. Lead US negotiator Cairo Internat. Conf. Population & Devel., 1994, Beijing World Conf. Women, 1995, Rome World Food Summit, 1996; mem. bd. overseers Dartmouth Med. Sch. Mem.: Inst. Medicine, Coun. Fgn. Rels. (life). Office: US Dept Health & Human Services Office Global Health Affairs 200 Independence Ave SW Rm 639H Washington DC 20201 Office Phone: 202 690 6174. Office Fax: 202-690-7127. E-mail: ogha.os@hhs.gov. *

DAUNCEY, MARGARET JOY, biomedical scientist, nutritionist, science educator; BSc in Nutrition, with hon., U. London, 1970; PhD, U. Cambridge, 1974, ScD, 1996. Rsch. scientist Med. Rsch. Coun., Dunn Nutrition Unit & U. Cambridge, 1973—79, Biotech. & Biological Scis Rsch. Coun., Babraham Inst., Cambridge, Dept. Applied Biology, Cell Biology, Molecular & Cellular Physiology, Neurobiology, Develop. Genetics, Molecular Immunology, 1979—2005; scientific advisor, internat. visiting prof. in nutritional, med. & veterinary scis. Wolfson Coll, U. Cambridge, 2005—. Fel. Wolfson Coll, U. Cambridge, 2002—; mem. Regent House U. Cambridge; mem. Gov. body Wolfson Coll, U. Cambridge; European Sci. Adviser Núcleo-Nutrição em Pauta, Sao Paulo, Brazil; supervisor in physiology Gonville & Caius Coll, U. Cambridge, 1983—2001; vis. prof. U. London, Guelph, Milan, UNESP Jaboticabal; invited lectr. Australia, Brazil, Canada, Denmark, Egypt, France, Germany, Holland, Italy, Japan, USA. Contbr. chapters to books. Recipient Internat. Peter Debye Prize for outstanding contribution & significant advance in the biomed. scis., 1989. Fellow: Royal Soc. Med., Soc. Biology; mem.: Nutrition Soc. Achievements include breakthroughs in the impact of nutrition, cell, gene interactions on development, health & disease. Office: Wolfson College Cambridge CB3 9BB England Business E-Mail: mjd4@cam.ac.uk.

DAUS, ARTHUR STEVEN, neurological surgeon; b. Louisville, Feb. 6, 1957; s. Arthur Theodore Daus Jr. and Marilyn Ann (McCord) Hanish; m. Victoria Lynn Schilla, July 10, 1982; children: Arthur S. Jr., Haley N. BS in Physics magna cum laude, Vanderbilt U., 1977; MD, St. Louis U., 1981. Diplomate Nat. Bd. Med. Examiners, Am. Bd. Neurol. Surgery, Fedn. State Licensing Examiners; lic. physician, Ky., N.Mex., Ariz., Mo., Calif. Rotating intern in surgery U. Ky. Med. Ctr., Lexington, 1981-82, resident neurosurgeon, 1982-88; pvt. practice Midwest Neurosurgery Ctr., Joplin, Mo., 1988—. Instr. cervical spine instrumentation A.M.E. Med. Co., Kansas City, Mo., 1992. Mem. Nat. Coalition of Physicians Against Family Violence, Chgo., 1994—. Recipient Ky. State Residents award ACS com. on trauma, 1985; named Ky. Col. State of Ky., 1985—. Mem. AMA (Physician's Recognition award 1990-94, 2003-05, 06-08, 09, Physician's Recognition award with spl. commendation 1993-2003), So. Med. Assn., Jasper-Newton County Med. Soc., So. Neurosurg. Soc., Congress Neurol. Surgeons, Am. Assn. Neurol. Surgeons (Continuing Edn. award 1990-2010), Nat. Audubon Soc., Phi Beta Kappa, Phi Eta Sigma. Republican. Roman Catholic. Avocations: chess, swimming, archery, riflery, horseback riding. Home: 5 Teal Dr Joplin MO 64804-5816 Office: Midwest Neurosurgery Ctr 1111 McIntosh Cir Ste 305 Joplin MO 64804-3693 Office Phone: 417-624-7700.

DAUTRY-VARSAT, ALICE, cell biologist, medical association administrator; b. 1950; MS in Molecular Biology, SUNY, Stony Brook; PhD in Solid-State Physics, U. Paris. Prof. cell biology Institut Pasteur, Paris, 1977—, head Biology of Cell Interactions Lab., 1992, dir. gen., 2005—. Mem. Lab Molecular Biology, Cambridge, England, 1980—81; bd. dirs. Institut Curie; vis. sci. MIT; bd. trustees École Polytechnique, France, Inst. Sci. & Tech., Austria, Drugs for Neglected Diseases Initiative; mem. external rsch. group for health rsch. strategy WHO. Decorated Chevalier de la Legion d'honneur France, Chevalier de l'Ordre National du Mérite. Office: Institut Pasteur 25, 28 rue du Docteur Roux 75724 Paris France Business E-Mail: adautry@pasteur.fr. *

DAVE, KARTIK JANAK, lab administrator; b. Rajkot, India, Mar. 19, 1967; MBBS, B. J. Med. Coll., 1990; MD, Sheth K. M. Sch. Med. Rsch. V. S. Hosp., 1993. Asst. prof. Gujarat Cancer and Rsch. Inst., 1993—97, cons. pathologist, hematology, 2006—07; chief pathologist Annab Labs., 1997—2000; med. dir. Sci. Diagnostic Ctr., 2000—06; assoc. dir. Quintiles Transnational Pvt. Ltd., 2008—09; lab. dir. Lambda Therapeutic Rsch. Ltd., 2006—. Cons. pathologist Hematology & Oncology Assocs., 2007—08. Mem.: IAPM, AACC. Avocations: reading, art, classical music. Office: Plot 38 Lambda Therapeutic Rsch Lab Ahmedabad Gujarat 380061 India Office Fax: 91-79-40202023. Personal E-mail: kartikdeval@gmail.com. Business E-Mail: kartikdave@lambda-cro.com.

DAVENPORT, ANN ADELE MAYFIELD, retired home care agency administrator; b. New Orleans, Nov. 12, 1941; d. Henry Louis and Myrtie Iola (Cason) Mayfield; m. John Wayne Davenport, June 18, 1966; children: Steven Lyle, Daniel Ryan, Elaine Adele. BA, Southeasten La. Coll., 1963; MA in Edn., George Peabody Coll., 1965; MA in Sociology, Tex. Tech. U., 1971. Tchr. various schs., 1963—70; instr. of sociology Tex. Tech. U., Lubbock, 1970—74, James Madison U., Harrisonburg, Va., 1981—82, Ga. So. Coll., Statesboro, 1982—84; 5th grade tchr. Bulloch County Schs., Statesboro, Ga., 1985—87; gerontology project coord. Dept. of Nursing Ga. So. Coll., 1987—89; project dir. Sr. Companion Program Ctr. for Rural Health and Rsch., Ga. So. U., Statesboro, 1988—93; instr. dept. health sci. edn. Ga. Southern U., Statesboro, 1993—95; exec. dir. Ogeechee Home Health Agy., Statesboro, 1995—96, Homebound Svcs., Statesboro, 1996—2002; ret., 2002. Editor various newsletters, 1987-2002. Bd. dirs. Citizens Against Violence, Statesboro, 1987-88, Habitat for Humanity, 1990-2002; pres. Coun. on Children and Parents, Statesboro, 1988-89, 93-94; mem. steering com. Bulloch County Commn. on Human Svcs., 1989-2002; adminstrv. bd. dirs., coun. on ministries, nominating com. Pittman Park United Meth. Ch.; pres. Ogeechee Wellness Coun., 1992-2002; bd. dirs. Ogeechee Home Health Agy., 1989-93. Mem. Ga. Rural Health Assn. (sec. 1988-89, editor state newsletter 1989-96), So. Sociol. Soc., Ga. Gerontol. Assn., Ga. Sociol. Assn., AAUW (newsletter editor Statesboro 1987-89), Am. Soc. on Aging, Nat. Coun. on the Aging, Am. Rural Health Assn. Avocations: tennis, reading.

DAVENPORT, ANTHONY PETER, pharmacologist, educator; b. Edinburgh, Nov. 27, 1955; s. Peter Thomas and Kathleen Cynthia (Buckley) D.; m. Ann Judith Payne, July 17, 1982; children: Emma Elisabeth, Rebecca Ann, James Anthony. BS, Nottingham U., Eng., 1978; PhD, London U., 1983; MA, Cambridge U., 1995. Postdoctoral fellow U. Cambridge, England, 1981—86, rsch. assoc. Parke-Davis Rsch. Unit, 1988, lectr., 1988—2004, reader in cardiovascular pharmacology, 2004—. Ofcl. fellow St. Catherine's Coll., Cambridge, 1995—, dir. studies in pharmacology and preclinical medicine. Contbr. chapters to books, articles to profl. jours. Bd. dirs. human cardiovascular rsch. group British Heart Found., 1994—. Rsch. grantee Brit. Med. Rsch. Coun. Heart Found., Sci. and Engring. Rsch. Coun., 1992; Rsch. fellow Hughes Hall, Cambridge, 1992-95. Fellow: Brit. Pharmacological Soc. (trustee, coun. and exec. mem. 2004), Cambridge Philos. Soc.; mem.: Internat. Union Pharmacology (com. receptor nomenclature and drug classification 2003—, co-vice chair 2006—), Pharmacology Soc. Mem. Ch. of England. Avocation: skiing. Office: U Cambridge Level 6 Ctr Clin Invest Box 110 Addenbrooke's Hosp Cambridge CB2 2QQ England Business E-Mail: apd10@medschl.cam.ac.uk.

DAVERAT, JEAN VINCENT, surgeon, educator; b. Orthez, France, Feb. 2, 1927; s. Andre and Madeleine (Aran) Daverat; m. Nicole Bebear, Sept. 23, 1956; children: Pierre, Bernard, Vincent. MD, U. Bordeaux. Resident med. surgeon U. Faculty Medicine, Bordeaux, 1950—54, anatomic asst., 1955, house surgeon, 1956—57; head surgical dept. Hosp. Dax, France, 1958—; chmn. med. cons. com., 1979—; mem. Council Tchg. Faculty Bordeaux, 1979—. Mem. Town Coun., Dax, 1965—, dep. mayor, 1971—77. Lt. Med. Svc., 1951—52. Recipient Silver medal, French Sport & Cultural Fedn., 1974, Medal, Youth & Sport, 1978, French Bridge Fedn., 1985. Mem.: Local Sport Soc. (Dax) (pres. 1978), French Surgery Assn., Surgery Soc. Bordeaux, Bridge Club (pres. 1963), Rotary (pres. 1973—74). Avocations: bridge, tennis. Office: Hosp Dax Ave Yves du Manoir 40100 Landes France Home: Dax 36 Rue de la Republique 17380 Landes France Home Phone: 0558741180.

DAVEY, KENNETH GEORGE, biologist, educator, academic administrator; b. Chatham, Ont., Can., Apr. 20, 1932; s. William and Marguerite (Clark) D.; m. Jeannette Isabel Evans, Nov. 28, 1959 (separated); children: Christopher Graham, Megan Jeannette, Katherine Alison. BSc, U. We. Ont., 1954, MSc, 1955, DSc (hon.), 2002; PhD, Cambridge U., 1958. NRC Can. fellow U. Toronto, Ont., 1958—59; Drosier fellow Gonville and Caius Coll., Cambridge U., 1959—63; assoc. prof. parasitology McGill U., Montreal, Que., Canada, 1963—67, prof. parasitology and biology, 1967—74, dir. Inst. Parasitology, 1964—74; prof., chmn. dept. biology York U., Downsview, Ont., 1974—81, dean of sci., 1982—85, disting. rsch. prof., 1984—2000, disting. rsch. prof. emeritus, 2001—, v.p. acad. affairs, 1986—91; bd. dirs. Canadian Sci. Pub., 2010—, vice-chair, 2011—. Past pres. Huntsman Marine Lab.; pres. Biol. Coun. Can., 1979-81; mem. animal biology grant selection com. Natural Scis. and Engring. Rsch. Coun. Can., 1980-83, group chmn. life scis., 1983-86, mem. com. grants and scholarships, 1983-86; mem. panel on tropical health NIH, 1978-82; pres. World Exec. Coun., Inst. de la Vie, 1987-2003; coun. Royal Can. Inst., 1996—, v.p., 1998-2000, pres. 2000-02; mem. Nat. Coun. on Ethics in Human Rsch., 1998—2005, pres., 2002—04. Author: Reproduction in the Insects, 1965; editor Internat. Jour. Invertebrate Reprodn., 1978-86; mem. editl. bd. Internat. Jour. Parasitology, 1973-80, Exptl. Parasitology, 1970-76, Can. Jour. Zoology, 1966-76, editor, 1994—2004; assoc. editor Ency. Reprodn., Co-Author: Biology: Exploring the Diversity of Life, 2009; contbr. articles to profl. jours. Decorated officer Order of Can., 1997; recipient Queen's Jubilee medal Govt. Can., 1977, 2002, Hitschfeld award Can. Assn. Rsch. Adminstrs., 1997, Wigglesworth medal Royal Entomol. Soc. London. Fellow Royal Soc. Can. (sec. Acad. Sci. 1979-85), Entomol. Soc. Can. (Gold medal 1985), Royal Entomol. Soc. (hon. fellow); mem. Soc. Exptl. Biology, Internat. Union Biol. Scis. (Can. nat. com. 1977-82), Can. Soc. Zoologists (pres. 1981-82, Fry medal 1987), Can. Com. Univ. Biology Chmn. (chmn. 1975-77, Disting. Biologist medal 1992), Biol. Coun. Can. (Gold medal 1987). Office: York Univ Dept Biology North York ON Canada M3J 1P3 Office Phone: 416-736-2100 33804. Personal E-mail: davey@yorku.ca.

DAVEY SMITH, GEORGE, epidemiologist, educator; b. Warrington, Cheshire, Eng., May 9, 1959; s. George and Irmgaard Davey Smith; life ptnr. Helen Lambert; children: Jacob Davey Lambert, Zachary Davey Lambert. BA (hon.), Oxford University, 1981; MB, BChir with distinction, Cambridge U., 1983; MA, Oxford U., 1984; MSc in Epidemiology with distinction, London Sch. Hygiene, 1988; MD in Epidemiology, Cambridge U., 1991; DSc, Oxford U., Uk, 2000. Clin. rsch. fellow Welsh Heart Programme, 1985—86; wellcome rsch. fellow in clin. epidemiology dept. cmty. medicine U. Coll. and Middlesex Sch. Medicine, Middlesex, 1986—89; lectr. epidemiology London Sch. Hygiene and Tropical Medicine, 1989—92; sr. lectr. in pub. health and epidemiology, hon. sr. registrar, cons. pub. health medicine dept. pub. health U. Glasgow, Scotland, 1992—94; prof. clin. epidemiology U. Bristol, England, 1994—. Hon. prof. dept. pub. health U. Glasgow, Scotland; vis. prof. dept. epidemiology and population health London Sch. Hygiene & Tropical Medicine; hon. rsch. fellow dept. epidemiology and pub. health U. Coll., London. Contbr. articles to profl. jours. Fellow: Royal Coll. Physicians; mem.: Inst. Medicine (fgn. asswoc.), Acad. Med. Scis. Office: Univ Bristol Canynge Hall Whiteladies Rd BS8 2PR Bristol England Office Fax: +44 (0)117 927325.

DAVID, DAVID JOHN AC, craniomaxillofacial surgeon, educator; b. Adelaide, South Australia, Dec. 21, 1940; MBBS, Adelaide U., 1966, MD, 1998. Sr. vis. craniomaxillofacial surgeon Meml. Hosp., North Adelaide; sr. vis. plastic surgeon Royal Adelaide Hosp., 1974—, Women's & Children's Hosp., North Adelaide, 1974—, head Australian craniofacial unit, 1975—; clin. prof. craniomaxillofacial surgery Adelaide U., 1998—. Founder Internat. Soc. Craniofacil Surgeons, past pres., councillor; pres. Australian Craniomaxillofacial Found., North Adelaide, 1984—, Inst. Craniofacial Studies, North Adelaide, 1990—2007; councillor Asia Pacific Craniofacial Assn., 1994—, past pres., 1994—, Australian & New Zealand Soc. Craniomaxillofacial Surgeons, 2000—, councillor, 2000—; rsch. fellow U. Adelaide Alumni Assn., 2006—. Fellow: RCS (England), RCS (Edinburgh), RACS, RCS (Thailand) (hon.). Office: Craniofacial Australia 226 Melbourne St North Adelaide South Australia 5006 Australia Office Fax: 61882673403. Business E-Mail: ddavidpa@ddms.com.au.

DAVID, L. RODGERS, medical educator; b. Huntingdon, Pa., July 8, 1959; EdD, Marshall U., 2007. Assoc. dir. edn. Charleston Area Med. Ctr., 1986—2007; cons., owner Healthcare Simulation Strategies, 2007—11; clin. educator Children's Hosp. Pa., 2009—. Adj. prof. Marshall U. Grad. Sch. Edn. and Profl. Devel., 2005—11. Recipient William H. Montgomery Excellence Edn. award, Citizen CPR Found., 2008. Mem.: Am. Mensa, Soc. Simulation Healthcare, Am. Heart Assn. Home: PO Box 288 Ardmore PA 19003 Business E-Mail: rodgers1@marshall.edu.

DAVID, ODILE, pathologist, educator; b. Montreal, Can., Jan. 3, 1969; BA, Northwestern U., 1990; MD, U. Ill., Chgo., 1994. Assoc. prof. pathology, dir. cytopathology U. Ill., 2005—. Fellow: Coll. Am. Pathologists; mem.: Am. Assn. Cancer Rsch. Office: 840 S Wood St Rm 130 CSN Chicago IL 60612 Business E-Mail: odavid@uic.edu.

DAVID, ONORATA, retired pathologist; b. Gassino, Torino, Italy, July 25, 1944; d. Giuseppe David and Maria Stella Muzio. D in Biol. Scis., U.Turin, Italy, 1968. Biol. asst. pediat. lab. U. Turin, Regina Margherita Hosp., Italy, 1970—89; head hemathological lab., dept. clin. pathology Regina Margherita S.Anna Hosp., Turin, 1990—2003; ret. Tchr. integrative didactics, clin. biochemistry specialty U. Turin, 1994—99, tchr. integrative didactics, hematology speciality, 1995—97, clin. (hemathology) pediat. specialist, 1988—2003; tchr. hemathology CEFAR, Turin, 2001—04. Contbr. numerous sci. papers and articles to profl. jours. Home: Via Beaulard 53 10139 Turin TO Italy Personal E-mail: onorata1@virgilio.it.

DAVID, PENNEY P., retired pathologist; b. Waltham, Mass., Dec. 11, 1933; AB, Eastern Nazarene Coll., 1956; MS, Boston U., 1957, PhD, 1962. Prof. emeritus pathology U. Rochester Med. Ctr., 1964—66. Mem.: Microscodical Soc. America, Biol. Stain Commn. (treas. 1988—), Am. Assn. Anatomists. Avocations: golf, reading, sports. Office: Dept Pathology & Lab Medicine Box 626 Rochester NY 14642-0001 Office Fax: 585-442-8993. Business E-Mail: david_penney@urmc.rochester.edu.

DAVID, RICHARD JOSEPH, pediatrician; b. Jacksonville, Fla., Jan. 29, 1949; AB, Dartmouth Coll., 1970; MD, Duke U., 1974. Attending neonatologist Children's Meml. Hosp., 1979—87; co-dir., neonatal ICU Stroger Hosp. Cook County, 1987—. Assoc. prof. pediat. Northwestern U., 1979—87; prof. pediat. U. Ill., Chgo., 1987. Fellow: Am. Acad. Pediat.; mem.: APHA, Soc. Pediatric Rsch., Soc. Epidemiologic Rsch. Achievements include research in social epidemiologic studies birth outcomes; impact of race and racism on infant mortality in the United States. Avocation: sports. Office: Stroger Hosp Cook County Dept Pediat 1 Divsn Neonatology Chicago IL 60612 Office Fax: 312-864-9943. Business E-Mail: rdavid@uic.edu.

DAVID, RIESE J., dean; b. Sheboygan, Wis., Apr. 11, 1965; AB, Wabash Coll., 1987; PhD, Yale U., 1993. Assoc. prof. Purdue U. Coll. Pharmacy, 1997—2010; assoc. dean, rsch. & grad. programs Auburn U. Harrison Sch. Pharmacy, 2010—. Recipient Career Devel. award, Dept. Def. Breast Cancer Rsch. Program, Tchg. award, Purdue U. Coll. Pharmacy, Cancer Rsch. award, Purdue U. Ctr. Cancer Rsch. Mem.: Am. Assn. Colls. Pharmacy, Am. Chem. Soc., Biochem. Soc., Am. Soc. Microbiology, Am. Assn. Cancer Rsch. Avocation: golf. Office: 2316 Walker Bldg Auburn University Auburn AL 36849-5501 Office Fax: 334-844-8353. Business E-Mail: driese@purdue.edu.

DAVID, TAYLOE T., JR., pediatrician; MD, U. NC. Resident St. Christopher's Hosp. for Children, NC Meml. Hosp.; pres. Am. Acad. Pediat., 2008—09. Fellow: AAP NC chpt. (pres. 1993—95). Office: Goldsboro Pediats PA 2706 Medical Office Pl Goldsboro NC 27534

DAVIDSON, BRUCE ALAN, biomedical researcher, educator; b. Lakewood, Ohio, Aug. 11, 1953; BS, U. Mich., 1977; PhD, SUNY, Buffalo, 2010. Rsch. asst. to assoc. U. Mich., 1979—87, rsch. assoc. ii, 1987—92, sr. rsch. assoc., 1992; rsch. instr. SUNY, Buffalo, 1992—2001, rsch. asst. prof., 2001—. Mem.: Am. Thoracic Soc. Avocations: golf, rock climbing, kayaking. Office: University Buffalo 247 BRB 3435 Main St Buffalo NY 14214 Office Fax: 716-829-3889. Business E-Mail: bdavidso@buffalo.edu.

DAVIDSON, BRUCE J., otolaryngologist, educator; MD, W.Va. U. Sch. of Medicine, 1987. Diplomate head and neck surgery Am. Bd. Otolaryngology, 1993. Intern NYU Med. Ctr., 1988; resident otolaryngology Georgetown Univ. Med. Ctr., 1992; fellow head and neck surgery Meml. Sloan-Kettering Cancer Ctr., 1994; chmn. dept. of otolaryngology - head and nech surgery Georgetown Univ. Hosp.; asst. prof. otolaryngology Georgetown Univ. Fellow: ACS. Office: Georgetown University Hospital 3800 Reservoir Rd Washington DC 20007 Office Phone: 202-444-2000.

DAVIDSON, EUGENE ABRAHAM, biochemist, educator, academic administrator; b. NYC, May 27, 1930; s. Jack and Sophie Miriam (Deutsch) D. BS, UCLA, 1950; PhD, Columbia U., 1955. Postdoctoral fellow, instr. U. Mich., 1955-58; asst. prof. biochemistry Duke U., 1958-62, assoc. prof., 1962-65, prof., 1965-67; prof., chmn. dept. biol. chemistry M.S. Hershey Med. Center, Pa. State U., 1967-87, assoc. dean for edn., 1975-87; chmn. dept. biochemistry and molecular biology Georgetown U., Washington, 1988—2002, prof., 2003—, prof. emeritus, 2008—. Mem. Nat. Bd. Med. Examiners, Part I; cons. in field. Author: Carbohydrate Chemistry, 1967; contbr. numerous articles to profl. publs.; Editorial reviewer for numerous jours. Guggenheim fellow, 1965-66; NIH grantee, 1958— Mem. AAAS, Am. Soc. Biol. Chemists, Assn. Med. Sch. Depts. Biochemistry, Biochem. Soc., Glycoconjugate Soc. (pres. 1985-87). Office: Georgetown U Dept Biochem/Molecular Biology Washington DC 20057 Office Phone: 202-687-1100. Business E-Mail: davidson@georgetown.edu.

DAVIDSON, EZRA C., JR., obstetrician, gynecologist, academic administrator, educator; b. Water Valley, Miss., Oct. 21, 1933; s. Ezra Cap and Theresa Hattie (Woods) Davidson; children: Pamela, Gwendolyn, Marc, Ezra K. BS cum laude, Morehouse Coll., 1954; MD, Meharry Med. Coll., 1958. Diplomate Am. Bd. Ob-Gyn. (examiner 1973-). Intern San Diego County Gen. Hosp., 1958—59; resident in ob-gyn. Harlem Hosp., NYC, 1963—66, asst. attending ob-gyn, obstet. coordinator maternal and infant care clinics, 1967—68; dir. departmental research, assoc. attending, acting chmn. ob-gyn, co-dir. coagulation research lab. Roosevelt Hosp., NYC, 1968—70; fellow blood coagulation, asst. ob-gyn Columbia U. Coll. Physicians and Surgeons, NYC, 1966—67, instr. dept. ob-gyn, 1967—69, asst. clin. prof., 1970; cons. ob-gyn Office Health Affairs, OEO, Washington, 1970—72; prof. Charles R. Drew U. of Medicine and Sci., LA, 1971—, acad. v.p., 1982—87, chmn. dept. ob.-gyn., 1971—96, assoc. dean primary care, 1997—; prof. U. So. Calif., Los Angeles, 1971—80, UCLA, 1980—. Chief svc. dept. ob-gyn. King/Drew Med. Ctr., LA, 1971—96; attending physician dept. ob-gyn. L.A. County-U. So. Calif. Med. Ctr., 1971—80; mem. nat. med. adv. com. nat. found. March of Dimes, 1972—76; bd. cons. Internat. Childbirth Edn. Assn., 1973—81; mem. sec.'s adv. com. population affairs HEW, 1974—77, chmn. svcs. task force, 1975—77; chmn. bd. dirs. L.A. Regional Family Planning Coun., 1975—77; bd. dirs. Nat. Alliance Sch. Age Parents, 1975—79; mem. corp. bd. Blue Shield, Calif., 1989—; chair DHHS Sec.'s Adv. Com. on Infant Mortality, 1990—93; active FDA, 1990—96, chmn. fertility and maternal health drugs adv. com., 1992—96; mem. adv. com. to the dir. NIH, 1995—98, mem. dirs. adv. panel on clin. rsch., 1995—98; mem. roundtable on health care quality Inst. on Medicine, 1995—98; mem. coun. grad. med. edn. HHS, 1997—2000; bd. dirs., chair med. policy com. Blue Shield of Calif., 1998—2002. Bd. dirs. The Calif. Wellness Found., 1995—, chmn., 1996—98; bd. dirs. Children's Bur. So. Calif., 1999—, v.p., 1995—99, pres., 1999—2002; bd. dirs. Jacobs Inst. of Womens Health, 1999—; chmn. bd. trustees Blue Shield Calif. Found., 2004—. With USAF, 1959—63. Fellow Johnson Found. Health Policy, Inst. Medicine, NAS, 1979—80. Fellow: ACS, L.A. Ob-Gyn. Soc. (pres. 1982—83), Royal Coll. Ob-Gyn., Am. Coll. Ob-Gyn. (nat. sec. 1983—89, pres.-elect 1989—90, pres. 1990—91); mem.: Calif. Tech. Assessment Forum (chair 2002—), Assn. of Acad. Minority Physicians (pres. 2002—03), Golden State Med. Assn. (pres. 1989—90), Assn. Profs. Ob-Gyn. (pres. 1989—90), Nat. Med. Assn. (chmn. nat. sect. ob-gyn. 1975—77, mem. sci. coun. 1979—88, bd, trustee 1989—95, chmn. bd. trustees 1992—95), Ob-Gyn. Assembly So. Calif. (chmn. 1989—90), Pacific Coast Ob-Gyn. Soc., N.Am. Soc. Pediatric and Adolescent Gynecology (pres.-elect 1993—94, pres. 1994—95), Am. Ob-Gyn. Soc. Office: 12021 Wilmington Ave Los Angeles CA 90059-3019

DAVIDSON, JEFFREY M., medical educator; b. Providence, Jan. 14, 1946; BS, Tufts U., 1967; PhD, Stanford U., 1975. Sr. staff fellow NIH, 1978—81; assoc. prof. pathology U. Utah, 1981—85; sr. rsch. career scientist Dept. Vets. Affairs, 1981; prof. pathology Vanderbilt U. Sch. Medicine, 1986—. Mem. editl. bd. Internat. Wound Jour., 2006; assoc. editor Jour. Investigative Dermatology, 2006, Wound Repair and Regeneration, 2007; pres.-elect Am. Soc. Matrix Biology, 2011—. Recipient Founders award, Symposium on Advanced Wound Care; Sr. Rsch. grant, Dept. Vets. Affairs. Mem.: AAAS, Soc. Investigative Dermatology, Wound Healing Soc. (past pres. 2005—06). Avocations: skiing, bicycling. Office: Dept Pathology 3321a MCN Vand Nashville TN 37232-2561 Business E-Mail: jeff.davidson@vanderbilt.edu.

DAVIDSON, MAYER B., endocrinologist, educator, researcher; b. Balt., Apr. 11, 1935; s. David and Esther (Crockin) D.; m. Naomi Berger, Nov. 25, 1961 (div. 1977); children: Elke W., Seth J.; m. Roseann Herman, Aug. 31, 1980. AB, Swarthmore Coll., 1957; MD, Harvard U., 1961. Diplomate Am. Bd. Internal Medicine, Am. Bd. Endocrinology and Metabolism. Intern Bellevue Hosp., NYC, 1961-62, jr. asst. resident, 1962-63; sr. asst. resident U. Wash. Affiliated Hosps., Seattle, 1963-64; rsch. fellow dept. endocrinology and metabolism King County Hosp., U. Wash., Seattle, 1964-66; asst. prof. medicine UCLA Sch. Medicine, 1969-74, acting chief div. endocrinology and metabolism, 1973-74, from assoc. prof. to prof., 1974—78, clin. prof., 1996—2006; with Drew U., 1998—. Dir. diabetes program Cedars-Sinai Med. Ctr., L.A., 1979-95; assoc. dir. clin. diabetes City of Hope Nat. Med. Ctr., 1995-98; dir. clin. trials unit Charles R. Drew U.; nat. advisor Diabetes Ctr. Humana Hosp., Phoenix, 1985-91; attending physician diabetic clinic Boston City Hosp., 1966-68; clin. asst. Harvard Med. Sch., 1968-69; cons. AMA Dept. Drugs. Author: Diabetus Mellitus: Diagnosis and Treatment, 4th edit., 1998, The Complete Idiot's Guide to Type 2 Diabetes, 2nd edit., 2009, Meeting the American Diabetes Association Standards of Care: an Algorithmic Approach to Clinical Care of the Diabetes Patient, 2010; founding editor: Current Diabetes Reports, 2000—02, editor-in-chief: Diabetes Care, 2002—06; contbr. chapters to books. Co-founder, bd. dirs. free med. facility Venice (Calif.) Family Clinic, 1970. Maj. Med. Svc. Corps U.S. Army, 1966-69. USPHS rsch. fellow Nat. Inst. Arthritis and Metabolic Diseases, 1965-66; recipient Upjohn award for Outstanding Diabetes Educator, 1990, Robert H. Williams/Rachmiel Levine award for sci. contbns. and humanism in tng. young rschrs., 1995, Banting medal for Disting. Svc., 1998, Arabella Carter award, 2007, Local Hero award Bank of America, 2007, Jefferson award, 2010; named to Best Doctors in Am., 1992-93, 95-96, 96-97. Fellow ACP; mem. AAAS, Am. Diabetes Assn. (rsch. prizes 1965, 66, R&D award 1974-75, rsch. 1978-81, bd. dirs. 1986-89, 93-99, v.p. 1995-96, pres.-elect 1996-97, pres. 1997-98), Am. Fedn. Clin. Rsch., Western Soc. Clin. Rsch., Endocrine Soc., Am. Soc. Clin. Investigation, Western Assn. Physicians, Am. Assn. Diabetes Educators (editl. bd. jour. 1980-83), Boylston Med. Soc., Am. Diabetes Assn. (pres. 1997-98), Sigma Xi. Democrat. Jewish. Office Phone: 323-357-3439.

DAVIDSON, NANCY ELLEN, oncologist; b. Denver, 1954; BA in Molecular Biology, Wellesley Coll., Mass., 1975; MD, Harvard U., 1979. Diplomate Am. Bd. Internal Medicine, Am. Bd. Med. Oncology. Internal medicine intern U. Pa., Phila., 1979-80; internal medicine resident Johns Hopkins Hosp., Balt., 1980-82; med. staff fellow Nat. Cancer Inst., Bethesda, Md., 1982—85; rsch. asst. prof. dept. pharmacology Uniformed Svcs. U. Health Scis., Bethesda, 1985—86; asst. prof. to assoc. prof. oncology Johns Hopkins U., 1986—99, Breast Cancer Rsch. chair in oncology, 1995—, dir. Breast Cancer Rsch. Program, 1994—, prof. oncology, 1999—. Mem. exec. bd. sci. advisors Breast Cancer Rsch. Found. Mem. editl. bd.: Jour. Clin. Oncology, 1993—95, Cancer Rsch., 1995—, The Breast Jour., 1995—, The Breast, 1996—, Am. Jour. Medicine, 1997—, Clin. Cancer Rsch., 1999—; contbr. articles to profl. publs. Recipient Merck Clinician Scientist award, 1989—90, Susan G. Komen Found. award, 1987, Rsch. award, Am. Cancer Soc., 1998, Brinker Internat. award for breast cancer rsch., 1999, Wellesley Coll. Alumnae award, 2000; named William L. McGuire Meml. lecture, 2001. Mem. Am. Assn. Cancer Rsch. (bd. dirs. 2002-), Am. Soc. Clin. Oncology (pres. 2007-08, Young Investigator award 1986-87, Career Devel. award 1988-91), Phi Beta Kappa, Sigma Xi. Achievements include research in the biochemical pathways by which breast cancer cells die. Office: Johns Hopkins Oncology Ctr 1650 Orleans St Baltimore MD 21231-1000 Office Phone: 410-955-8489. Office Fax: 410-614-4073. Business E-Mail: davidna@jhmi.edu.

DAVIDSON, RICHARD J., retired medical association administrator; b. Phila., 1936; m. Janet Davidson. BA in Secondary Edn., West Chester U., Pa.; EdM, Temple U., Phila.; PhD in Edn., George Washington U. Former tchr., prin., Del.; dir. edn. Md.-DC-Del. Hosp. Assn.; pres. Md. Hosp. Assn., 1969—91, Am. Hosp. Assn., Chgo. & Washington, 1991—2007, ret., 2007. Bd. dirs. Health Rsch. & Ednl. Trust, Internat. Hosp. Fedn. Founding. dir. Inst. Diversity. Recipient Bd. Dirs. award, Healthcare Fin. Mgmt. Assoc., 2000; co-recipient Nat. Healthcare Leadership award, Nat. Ctr. for Healthcare Leadership, 2006.

DAVIDSON, RICHARD S., orthopaedic surgeon, educator; MD, NYU, 1976. Lic. NJ, 1982, Pa., 1982, diplomate Am. Bd. Orthopaedic Surgery. Intern gen. surgery Bellevue Hosp. Ctr., 1976, resident, NYU, Cornell Univ.; resident orthop. surgery Hosp. for Spl. Surgery, 1981; fellow pediatric orthopaedics Hosp. for Sick Children, 1982; assoc. prof. orthop. surgery Univ. Pa.; hosp. affiliation include Pa. Hosp.; attending surgeon Children's Hosp., Phila., 1982. Co-author: (papers) Fibrous lesion of the distal femur associated with angular deformity, 1999, Diagnosing anerurysmal and unicameral bone cysts with magnetic resonance imaging, 1999, Growth disturbances after distal tibial physeal fractures, 2000, When does the flat-top talus lesion occur in idiopathic clubfoot: evaluation with magnetic resonance imaging at three months of age, 2001, Angular deformity in pediatric transtibial amputation stumps, 2009, and numerous others. Named one of the Top Doctors, Phila. Mag., 2007, 2010—11. Office: Children's Hospital of Philadelphia 210 Mall Blvd King Of Prussia PA 19406 Office Phone: 610-337-3232.

DAVIDSON, STEVEN J., physician; b. Phila, Pa, Mar. 9, 1950; s. Jay Howard and Claire Beverly (Silverman) D.; m. Simone F. Mogul, June 21, 1987; children: Zoey Samuel, Masha Kalinkina. BA in Chemistry, Temple U., Phila., 1971; MD, Temple U., 1975; MBA, U. Pa., 1989. Diplomate Am. Bd. Emergency Medicine. Intern in acute care Med. Coll. Pa., 1975-76, resident in emergency medicine, 1976-78, instr., asst. prof., assoc. prof. surgery Phila., 1978-84, assoc. prof. emergency medicine, 1984-89, prof. emergency medicine, 1989-97, vis. prof., 1997—, head divsn. emergency med. svc., 1988-96; chmn. emergency medicine Maimonides Med. Ctr., Bklyn., 1995—2010, chief med. informatics officer. Med. dir. Phila. Emergency Med. Svc., 1983-94; oral examiner Am. Bd. Emergency Medicine, 1980—, bd. dirs., 1986-95. Assoc. editor Yearbook of Emergency Medicine, 1981-99; guest reviewer Annals of Emergency Medicine, 1983-99, Prehosp. and Disaster Medicine, 1992-97, Acad. Emergency Medicine, 1993-99; mem. editl. bd. Preshosp. Emergency Care, 1997-99. Recipient ACEP EMS award, 1992, Modern Physician 2001, Phys. Exec. award of Excellence, 2001. Fellow Am. Coll. Emergency Physicians (bd. dirs. Pa. chpt. 1979-85, Emergency Svc. award 1992), Soc. Acad. Emergency Medicine (pres. 1985-86), Nat. Assn. Emergency Med. Svc. Physicians. Office: Maimonides Med Ctr 4802 10th Ave Brooklyn NY 11219-2844 *

DAVIDSON, TERRY LEE, experimental psychology educator; b. Vassar, Mich., June 1, 1951; s. George Louis and Helen Marsha (Laskey) D.; m. Cheryl Joan Gohm, June 23, 1973; children: Tyler Louis, Dena Lynn. BA, Mich. State U., East Lansing, 1973; MA, Cal State U., Fullerton., 1977; PhD, Purdue U., West Lafayette, Ind., 1981. Asst. prof. St. Olaf Coll., Northfield, Minn., 1981-83; rsch. scientist Inst. Neurol. Sci., Phila., 1983-86; lectr. U. Pa., Phila., 1984-86; asst. prof. Va. Mil. Inst., Lexington, 1986-90; editor Va. Mil. Inst. Undergrad. Rsch. Rev., Lexington, 1987—90; assoc. prof. exptl. psychology Purdue U., West Lafayette, 1990—, prof. psychology, grad. neurosci., 1995; convener Grad Neurosci. Prog., 2001—03; dir. Ingestive Behavior Rsch. Ctr., 2003—08; fellow Ctr. Behavioral and Social Sci., 2004, 2010. Cons. Cancer Rsch. Ctr., Children's Hosp., Phila., 1984-87 Recipient Acad. Rsch. Enhancement award, 1987, Nat. Rsch. Svc. award NIH, 1984, grant, 1991-. Mem. AAAS, Soc. for Study Ingestive Behavior, Am. Psychol. Soc., Va. Acad. Scis. (vice chmn./sec. 1988-90), NSF (affiliate mem. Neurobiology and Learning and Memory, Sigma Xi. Achievements include development of research paradigm to study associative and biological controls of feeding; provided evidence, that obesity can occur as a consequence of memory deficits produced by hipoocampal dvsfunction, discovery of link between intake of noncaloric sweeteners and overeating. Office: Purdue University 703 Third St West Lafayette IN 47907

DAVIES, HERBERT OLADELE, medical educator, department chairman; b. Nigeria, Aug. 13, 1961; MD, U. Toronto, 1985, MS, 1993. Prof., chair MSU Dept. Pediat. and Human Devel., 2003—. Office: MSU Dept Pediatrics and Human Devel East Lansing MI 48824 Business E-Mail: daviesde@msu.edu.

DAVIS, BARRY, critical care specialist; MD, Tufts U., 1974. Diplomate Am. Bd. Internal Medicine, 1977, Am. Bd. Internal Medicne- pulmonary disease, 1980, Am. Bd. Internal Medicne-critical care medicine, 2009. Intern Jackson Meml. Hosp., Miami, Fla., 1975, resident in internal medicine, 1975—77; fellow in pulmonary disease Mass. Gen. Hosp., Boston, 1977—79; critical care specialist Bora Raton Cmmty. Hosp. Office: Bora Raton Community Hospital 951 NW 13th St Ste 2A Boca Raton FL 33486 Office Phone: 561-391-1666.

DAVIS, BRANTLEY PIERCE, retired physician; b. June 29, 1925; s. Frank Pierce Cleveland and Mary Hamilton Keen Davis; m. Frances Marie Stirrett, June 26, 1954; children: Paula Leigh Misner, Loren Brantley, Natalie Ann Jones. AA, Lower Columbia Coll., Longview, Wash., 1947; BS, U. Wash., Seattle, 1949, MD, 1953. Pvt. practice, Bellingham, Wash., 1955—77; plant physician Arco Refinery, Ferndale, Wash., 1976—82. County jail physician Whatcom County, Bellingham, 1957—67; plant physician Intalco Aluminum Co., Ferndale, 1967—86; staff physician We. Wash. U., Bellingham, 1968—69; v.p., med. dir. Whatcom Med. Bureau, Bellingham, 1971—93; chief of staff St. Luke's Hosp., Bellingham, 1966; pres. Whatcom County Med. Soc., 1969—. Sgt. US Army, 1943—46, ETO. Mem.: AMA, Am. Coll. Occup. and Environ. Medicine, Am. Acad. Family Physicians, Wash. State Med. Assn., Whatcom County Med. Soc. (pres. 1969), Phi Theta Kappa, Phi Chi, Pi Kappa Alpha (v.p. 1949). Protestant. Home: 501 Park Ridge Rd Bellingham WA 98225-7914

DAVIS, BRIAN, medical association administrator; b. South Africa, June 9, 1960; PhD, Pa. State, 1991. V.p. med. device devel. ctr. Austen BioInnovation Inst. Akron, 2010. Office: Austen BioInnovation Inst Akron 1 S Main St Ste 601 Akron OH 44308 Business E-Mail: bdavis@abiakron.org.

DAVIS, DANIEL G., surgeon; BS, SUNY, Stony Brook, 1990; DO, NY Coll. Osteopathic Medicine, Old Westbury, 1994. Diplomate Am. Bd. Surgery, cert. Nat. Bd. Osteopathic Med. Examiners, Advanced Trauma Life Support, Advanced Cardiac Life Support. Rotating internship Maimonides Med. Ctr., NY, 1995; resident, gen. surgery Stamford Hosp./Columbia U. Coll. Physicians & Surgeons, Conn., 1995—2001; fellow, advanced laparoscopic surgery Legacy/Oregon Health Sciences U., Portland, Oreg., 2001—03; surgical dir., Ctr. for Obesity Surgery Lawrence Hosp., Bronxville, NY, 2002—; asst. prof. surgery Weill Med. Coll., Cornell U., NY, 2002—; asst. clin. prof. surgery NY-Presbyn. Hosp./Columbia U. Med. Ctr., NY, 2002—; surgical dir., Ctr. Obesity Surgery Valley Hosp., Ridgewood, NJ, 2002—; attendant surgeon Hackensack Med. Ctr./Advanced Laparoscopic Associates, NJ, 2002—03. Presenter in field. Contbr. several articles to profl. jours. Fellow: ACS; mem.: Am. Osteopathic Assn., AMA, Soc. for Surgery of the Alimentary Tract, Am. Soc. for Bariatric Surgery, Soc. Am. Gastrointestinal Endoscopic Surgeons, Am. Soc. for Bariatric Surgeons, Soc. Am. Gastrointestinal Endoscopic Surgeons. Office: NY-Presbyterian Hosp/Columbia Irving Pavilion Room 620 161 Fort Washington Ave New York NY 10032 Office Phone: 212-305-9506, 201-251-3480. Office Fax: 212-342-1996.

DAVIS, DAWN BELT, medical educator; b. Berwyn, Ill., May 21, 1973; MD, U. Chgo., PhD, 2003. Asst. prof. U. Wis., 2009—. Recipient Clin. Scientist Career Devel. award, NIH - NIDDK, Early Career Devel. award, Ctrl. Soc. Clin. Rsch. Mem.: Am. Diabetes Assn., Endocrine Soc. Office: H4/526 CSC MC5148 600 Highland Ave Madison WI 53792 Personal E-mail: dawnbeltdavis@yahoo.com.

DAVIS, DORINNE SUE, audiologist; b. East Orange, NJ, Mar. 29, 1949; d. William Henry and Evelyn Doris (Thorp) Taylor; children: Larissa Louise, Peter Alexander. BA, Montclair State Coll., 1971, MA, 1973. Cert. tchr. of hearing impaired, speech correctionist, tchr. speech and drama, supr. nursery sch. endorsement, N.J. Ednl. audiologist Kinnelon (N.J.) Bd. Edn., 1972-94, kindergarten tchr., 1994-97; ednl. audiologist Inst. for Career Advancement, Inc., 1980-82, Dover Gen. Hosp., 1984-86; pres. Hear You Are, Inc., 1987-98, Davis Ctr. Hearing Speech and Learning, Inc., Budd Lake, NJ, 1998—2002; with Davis Ctrs., Inc., 2002—05, The Davis Ctr., 2005—. Adj. prof. Kean Coll., Union, NJ, 1993—95, Ctr. Mich. U., 2005—07, Davis Sound Rsch. Assocs. LLC, 2006—09. Mem. NEA, Am. Speech and Hearing Assn. (cert. clin. competence in audiology), Am. Acad. Audiology, N.J. Speech and Hearing Assn., N.J. Edn. Assn., Ednl. Audiology Assn. (past pres.), Internat. Soc. Study Subtle Energy and Energy Medicine. Methodist. Home: 15 Ridgeview Ln Mount Arlington NJ 07856 Office: The Davis Ctr 19 State Rt 10E Ste 25 Succasunna NJ 07876 Home Phone: 973-277-4663; Office Phone: 862-251-4637. Business E-Mail: ddavis@thedaviscenter.com.

DAVIS, DWIGHT, cardiologist, educator; b. Winston-Salem, NC, Apr. 11, 1948; s. James C. Davis; m. Lorna Jean Enck, July 30, 1988; 1 child, Nathan James. BS, N.C. A&T State U., 1970; MD, U. Rochester, 1975. Rsch. asst. U. Rochester, NY, 1970-71; intern in medicine Boston U. Hosp., 1975-76, resident in medicine, 1976-78; cardiology fellow Duke U. Med. Ctr., Durham, NC, 1978-81; asst. prof. medicine, cardiology divsn. Pa. State U., Hershey, 1981-87, assoc. prof., 1987-92, disting. lectr., 1986, prof. medicine, 1992—, cardiology dir. heart transplantation, artificial organs and preclinical tchg. program, dir. cardiology preclinical tng. program, 1984—, dir., cardiology fellow tng. program, 1984-87, dir. cardiac catheterization lab., 1987—, med. dir. cardiac rehab. program, 1988—, dir. clin. cardiology program, 1991—, asst. dean for admissions, 1994-99, assoc. dean admissions and student affairs, 1999—. Vice chmn. faculty affairs faculty senate Pa. State U., University Park, 1988—; mem. med. alumni coun. U. Rochester Sch. Medicine and Dentistry, 1992—; various disting. lectureships. Contbr. numerous articles to profl. jours.; editorial reviewer Annals Internal Medicine, 1983—; editorial adv. bd. Primary Cardiology, 1985—. Mem. Pa. Coun. on Aging, Harrisburg, 1989—. Recipient Outstanding Physician award Pa. State U. Sch. Medicine, 1984, Disting. Tchg. awards, 1988-89, Tchr. of Yr. award, 1991, Disting. Prof. award for tchg., 1991, Outstanding Tchr. of Yr. award med. sch. class of 1995, 93, Outstanding Tchr. of Yr. award med. sch. class of 1997, 1995, Alumni Excellence award N.C. A&T State U., 1986, Disting. Alumni award Nat. Assn. Equal Opportunity in Higher Edn., 1987, Disting. Educator award Penn State Coll. Medicine; Joy McCann scholar, 2005. Fellow Am. Coll. Cardiology, Am. Coll. Angiology; mem. AAAS, Am. Heart Assn. (fellow coun. on clin. cardiology, rsch. com. Pa. affiliate 1992—, pres. elect Pa. affiliate 1997, pres. elect Pa./Del affiliate 1998, Disting. Svc. award Pa. Del. affiliate 2000), Am. Fedn. Clin. Rsch., Am. Assn. Med. Colls. (pres. elect North East group on student affairs 1998, GSA Exemplary Svc. award 2009), Am. Assn. Cardiovasc. and Pulmonary Rehab. (expert panel cardiac rehab. guidelines project 1992—, chair cardiac rehab. criteria devel. panel 1995—), N.Y. Acad. Scis., Alpha Omega Alpha. Mem. United Ch. of Christ. Achievements include discovery that abnormalities of the sympathetic nervous system in patients with heart failure is due to an increase in norepinephrine spillover and a decrease in norepinephrine clearance from the circulation. Office: Pa State U Coll Medicine Divsn Cardiology PO Box 850 Hershey PA 17033-0850 Office Phone: 717-531-1790.

DAVIS, EDGAR GLENN, healthcare executive, educator; b. Indpls., May 12, 1931; s. Thomas Carroll and Florence Isabelle (Watson) Davis; m. Margaret Louise Alandt, June 20, 1953 (dec. Sept. 2008); children: Anne-Elizabeth, Amy Alandt, Edgar Glenn Davis Jr.; m. Joanne Warvel Davis, Apr. 4, 2009. AB, Kenyon Coll., 1953; MBA, Harvard U., 1955. With Eli Lilly & Co., Indpls., 1958—63, mgr. budgeting and profit planning, 1963—66, mgr. econ. studies, 1966—67, mgr. Atlanta sales dist., 1967—68, dir. market rsch. and sales manpower planning, 1968—69, dir. mktg. plans, 1969—74, exec. dir. pharm. mktg. planning, 1974—75, exec. dir. corp. affairs, 1975—76, v.p. corp. affairs, 1976—90, v.p. health care policy, 1990; pres., chmn. bd. dirs. Centre for Health Sci. Info., Boston, 1990—; fellow Ctr. for Bus. and Govt. Kennedy Sch. of Govt. Harvard U., 1991—95; adj. prof. Butler U., Indpls., 1995—. Exec. in residence Butler U. Coll. Bus., 1995—2009; mem. Inst. Ednl. Mgmt., Harvard U. Grad. Sch. Edn., 1987; chmn. staff Bus. Roundtable Task Force on Health, 1981—85; U.S. rep. UN Indsl. Devel. Orgn. Conf., Lisbon, 1980, Casablanca, 81, Budapest, 83, Madrid, 87; participant meeting of experts on pharms UNIDO, 1981; rep. to UN Commn. on Narcotic Drugs, Vienna, 1981, UN Econ. and Social Coun., NYC, 1981, UN Indsl. Devel. Orgn. Conf.; Ctr. for Bus. and Govt. fellow Kennedy Sch. Govt., Harvard U.; co chmn. Harvard Conf. on Govt. Role in Civilian Tech., 1992, Harvard Conf. Pharmaceutical Rsch., Innovation and Pub. Policy, 1993, Harvard Biotech. Roundtable, 1991—96; vis. scholar, advisor Health and Welfare Unit, Inst. for Econ. Affairs, London; vis. scholar Green Coll. Oxford (Eng.) U., 1994—; chmn. Nat. Fund for Med. Edn., 1994—; dir. English Speaking Union, Indpls.; gov. Soc. Indiana Pioneers; lectr. in field. Contbr. articles to profl. jours. Pres. Eli Lilly and Co. Found., 1976—88; trustee Indpls. Symphony Orch., 2010—, life trustee; pres., chmn. bd. Indpls. Health Inst., 1988—91; trustee Kenyon Coll., Gambier, Ohio, Ind. Hist. Soc., 2000—10, pres. bd. trustees Boston Biomed. Rsch. Inst., 1991—95, trustee emeritus; chmn. Nat. Fund for Med. Edn., 1996—; bd. dirs. Carnegie Coun. on Ethics and Internat. Affairs, 1985—92; accredited nongovtl. observer rep. to UN Goodwill Found. Ind. Inc., 1987—95; bd. dirs. Sta. WFYI Pub. TV, Indpls., 1983—91, Am. Symphony Orch. League, 1987—92, mem. dirs. coun., 1987—; bd. dirs. Nat. Health Coun., 1984—91, Pub. Affairs Coun., Washington, 1984—92, Nat. Fund for Med. Edn.; bd. advisors Christian Theol. Sem., Bishops Sch., LaJolla, Calif.; chmn. bd. dirs. Ind. Repertory Theatre, 1979—85; vice chmn., exec. com., bd. dirs. Indpls. Symphony Orch. and Ind. State Symphony Soc., 1977—91; chmn. task force on fine arts Commn. for Future of Butler U.; chmn. exec. com. Pan Am. Econ. Leadership Conf. 10th Pan Am. Games, Indpls.; bd. govs. Soc. Ind. Pioneers. Mem.: NAM (vice-chmn. health policy com. 1987—91, bd. dirs.), Am. Symphony Orch. League N.Y. (mem. dir. coun.), Inst. Medicine NAS, Ind. Soc. Pioneers (bd. govs.), Indian Lake Yacht Club (Mich.), Svc. Club Indpls., Dramatic Club of Indpls., Univ. Club (Indpls.) (bd. dirs.), Literary Club Indpls., Reform Club London, Edgartown Golf Club, Contemporary Club, Woodstock Club, Naples Yacht Club, Edgartown Yacht Club (Martha's Vineyard), Met. Club (Washington). Office: 7941 Clearwater Pky Indianapolis IN 46240

DAVIS, FAITH G., epidemiologist; b. Alberta, Can., Sept. 20, 1949; PhD, Yale U., 1984. Assoc. dean, rsch. U. Ill., Chgo., 2009—. Fellow: Am. Coll. Epidemiology (pres. 2010—). Office: 1603 West Taylor St Chicago IL 60612 Business E-Mail: fayed@uic.edu.

DAVIS, GLEN ANTHONY, pediatrician; b. Kalamazoo, Mar. 18, 1972; s. Charles Alexander and Clementine Johnson Davis; m. Tamera Raeann Davis, Aug. 19, 2005. BS in Biomedical Scis., U. Mich., Ann Arbor, 1998, MD, 1998. Resident Children's Hosp. Mich., Detroit, 1998—2001; pediatrician Elkhart Gen. Hosp., Ind., 2001—04, South Bend Clinic, 2005—. Mag. columnist Ask the Pediatrician Gt. Lakes Family Mag., 2004—05; TV host Ask Dr. D, WSBT-TV, 2005—. Recipient Charles Gibson award, U. Mich. Med. Sch., 1998. Fellow: Am. Acad. Pediat.; mem.: AMA. Avocations: running, reading. Office: South Bend Clinic 211 N Eddy St South Bend IN 46617 Office Phone: 574-233-7337. Personal E-mail: gdavismd98@msn.com.

DAVIS, GLENN CRAIG, psychiatrist; b. Columbia, Mo., Apr. 26, 1946; s. Morris S. and Dorothy (Hall) Davis; children: Jason Michael, Galen Brent. BA, Reed Coll., 1968; MD, Duke U., 1972. Diplomate Am. Bd. Psychiatry and Neurology. Intern, then resident Duke U. Med. Ctr., Durham, NC, 1972-75; clin. assoc. NIMH, Bethesda, Md., 1975-77, chief of drug abuse unit, biological psychiatry br., 1977-79; assoc. prof. U. Tenn. Ctr. Health Scis., Memphis, 1979-81; assoc. prof. then prof. Sch. of Medicine Case Western Reserve U., Cleve., 1981-87; dir. psychiat. rsch. to chief of staff Cleve. VA Med. Ctr., 1981-87; chair psychiatry Henry Ford Med. Ctr., Detroit, 1987-92; v.p. behavioral svcs. Henry Ford Health System, Detroit, 1991-94, v.p. acad. affairs, 1992—2001, chief med. officer suburban regions, 1996-98, assoc. dean Case Western Reserve U., 1993—2001; prof. psychiatry Case Western Reserve U., Cleve., 1994—2001; pres. Am. Bd. Psychiatry & Neurology, Deerfield, Ill.; dean coll. of human medicine Mich. State U., East Lansing, Mich., 2001—05; sr. client ptnr. Korn Ferry Internat., Phila., 2005—. Clin. prof. U. Mich. Sch. Medicine, Ann Arbor, 1988—2001. Author numerous sci. rsch. papers and book chpts.; contbr. articles to profl. jours. Lt. comdr. USPHS, 1975—79. Fellow: Am. Psychopathological Assn., Am. Psychiat. Assn.; mem.: AMA, AAAS, Am. Bd. Med. Specialties, Am. Bd. Psychiatry and Neurology (dir. 1996—2003, pres. 2000), Alpha Omega Alpha, Sigma Xi. Office: Korn Ferry Internat 1835 Market St Philadelphia PA 19103 Office Phone: 215-656-5356. Business E-Mail: gdavis@kornferry.com.

DAVIS, IRENE S., rehabilitation executive; BS in Exercise Sci., U. Massachusetts, 1977; BS in Phys. Therapy, U. Fla., 1978; MEd in Biomechanics, U. Virginia, 1984; PhD in Biomechanics, Pennsylvania State U., 1990. Phys. therapist Woodrow Wilson Rehab. Ctr., Fishersville, Va., 1979—82, Blue Ridge Rehab. Assocs., Charlottesville, 1983—85; rsch & tchg. asst. rehab. engrng. ctr. U. Virginia, 1982—85; rsch. asst. ctr. for locomotion studies Pennsylvania State Univ., 1985—89; asst. prof. Univ. of Delaware, 1989—97; dir. rsch. Joyner Sportymedicine Inst., 2004—; dir. Spaulding Nat. Running Ctr., 2011—. Office: Spaulding Rehabilitation Center 125 Nashua St Boston MA 02114 Office Phone: 617-573-7000.

DAVIS, JACK, biotechnology company executive; Various exec. positions including v.p. and gen. mgr. worldwide diagnostics products Abbott Laboratories; CEO, dir. Infant Advantage, Inc., Genica Pharmaceuticals, Calpyte Biomed. Corp.; co-founder, CEO, chmn., dir. Dianon Systems; chmn. Asterand, Inc., 2008—, interim CEO, 2011—. Bd. dirs. Claros, Inc., Collages.net, Inc., Laboratory Partners, Inc., RedPath Integrated Pathology, Inc., HistoRx, Inc. Office: Asterand Inc TechOne Ste 440 Burroughs Detroit MI 48202-3420 Office Phone: 313-263-0960. *

DAVIS, JAMES, physician, educator; Grad., Lafayette Coll.; MD, George Washington U. Sch. Medicine. Fellow U. Wis., chief resident, founding dir. dept. family medicine rsch. divsn., clinical ops. dir., prof. & acting chmn. dept. family medicine; physician & dir. Wingra Family Med. Ctr., Madison; prof. & chmn. dept. family medicine U. Wash., Seattle. Office: University of Washington Dept Family Medicine Box 356390 Seattle WA 98195-3101

DAVIS, JESSICA G., geneticist; b. Bklyn., Apr. 3, 1934; d. Nathan S. and Sylvia (Teplitz) Grosof; m. Andrew P. Davis, June 17, 1956; children: Jennifer Davis Hall, David. BA, Wellesley Coll., 1955; MD, Columbia U., 1959. Diplomate Am. Bd. Med. Genetics. Intern pediatrics St. Luke's Hosp.-Columbia U.; fellow Albert Einstein Coll. Medicine Yeshiva U., NYC, 1961-68, instr. Albert Einstein Coll. Medicine, 1962, asst. prof. Albert Einstein Coll. Medicine, 1968-74; assoc. prof. clin. pediatric Weill Coll. Medicine Cornell U., NYC, 1974—. Cons. March of Dimes, N.Y.C., 1974—, Hastings Inst., Garrison, N.Y., 1979—; mem. sickle cell adv. com. NIH, co dir. Ctr. skeletal dysplasias, Hosp. Spl. Surgery, 2001—. Contbr. articles to profl. jours. Recipient Antoine Marfan award Nat. Marfan Found., 2005, numerous grants. Fellow: Am. Coll. Med. Genetics (founding fellow, CME officer); mem.: N.Y. Acad. Medicine, Coun. Regional Genetics Network (pres. 1991—94), Am. Soc. Human Genetics. Office: Weill Med Coll Cornell U NY-Presbyn Hosp 525 E 68th St Rm Box 128 New York NY 10021-4870 Office Phone: 646-962-2205. Business E-Mail: jgdavis@med.cornell.edu.

DAVIS, JO, naturopathic physician; b. Pecos, Tex., Jan. 6, 1937; d. Johnnie Rex and Laura (Swann) D.; children: Cassandra Ann, Charles Rex. AA in Nursing, N.Mex. State U., 1992; BS in Nutrition, Clayton Coll. Naturahealth, 1995, MS in Nutrition, 1996, DD, Am. Inst. Theology, 1996; PhD in Nutrition, Clayton Coll. Naturahealth, 1997; PhD in Hypnotherapy, Am. Pacific U.; D Naturopathy, Clayton Coll. Natural Health, 1995. Diplomate Am. Psychotherapy Assn., cert. hypnotherapist, advanced therapy Emotional Freedom Technique, 2004, LNHA; RN Kans., Mo., Tex., N.Mex., cert. resdl. assessment coord., Am. Assn. Nurse Assessment Coords., lic. nursing home adminstr., cert. nurse exec., lic. nursing home adminstr. Asst. coord. Carlsbad Hospice, Inc., N.Mex., 1992—98; prin., owner Natural Health Tng. and Resource Ctr., Carlsbad, 1994—98; dir. New Directions, Inc., Oak Grove, Mo., 1999—. Cons. Westbrooke Chiropractic, Lee's Summit, Mo., 1999—, Chiropractic Physicians, Independence, Mo., 1999—; instr. Continuing Edn. RN, Tex.; cert. trainer Neuro-Linguistic Programming, Inst. for Time Line Therapy Tng. Contbr. articles to newspapers; newsletter editor, 1994-96. Mem. Internat. Good Neighbor Coun., Mex., U.S.A., 1994-96; pres. Wildlife Rescue, Inc., Carlsbad, 1992-96; ordained min. Reverend Universal Life Ch. Named N.Mex. Woman of Yr. State of N.Mex., 1992. Mem. AAUW, Am. Assn. Nurse Assessment Coords. (cert.), Internat. Guild Hypnotists, Am. Bd. Hypnotherapy, Am. Holistic Health Assn., Nat. Audubon Soc., The Nature Conservancy, Order Ea. Star. Avocations: raising horses, shaman studies, native american culture. Home and Office: 8311 S Hillside School Rd Oak Grove MO 64075-8245 Personal E-mail: doctordavis@gmail.com.

DAVIS, KAREN, foundation administrator, educator, economist; b. Blackwell, Okla., Nov. 14, 1942; d. Walter Dwight and Thelma Louise (Kohler) Padgett; 1 child, Kelly Denise Collins. BA, Rice U., 1965, PhD, 1969; LHD (hon.), Johns Hopkins U., 2001; PhD (hon.), U. Md., 2009; PhD of Civil Law (hon.), Newcastle U., UK, 2009. Asst. prof. economics Rice U., 1968—70; econ. policy fellow Social Security Adminstrn. Brookings Instn., Washington, 1970—71, rsch. assoc., 1970—74, sr. fellow, 1974—77; dep. asst. sec. for planning and evaluation, health US Dept. Health and Human Services, Washington, 1977—80; adminstr. health resources adminstrn. USPHS, US Dept. Health and Human Services, Washington, 1980—81; prof. economics Johns Hopkins U., Balt., 1981—92, chmn. dept. health policy and mgmt., Sch. of Hygiene and Pub. Health, 1983—92; exec. v.p. Commonwealth Fund, NYC, 1992—94, pres., 1995—. Vis. lectr. Harvard U., 1974—75; dir. Commonwealth Fund Commn. on Elderly People Living Alone, 1985—91; mem. Physician Payment Rev. Commn., 1986—94, Kaiser Commission on Medicaid and the Uninsured, 1991—, President's Coun., Health Policy Forum, United Hosp. Fund, 1992—, Health Care Exec. Forum, 1993—; bd. dirs. Geisinger Health Sys., 2004—; disting. fellow AcademyHealth, past pres.; former mem. Nat. Adv. Com. Agy. for Healthcare Quality and Rsch.; mem. Panel of Health Advisors Congressional Budget Office, 2007—. Author: Net Income of Hospitals, 1961-1969, 1970, Community Hospitals: Inflation in the Pre-Medicare Period, 1972, National Health Insurance: Benefits, Costs and Consequences, 1975, Health and the War on: A Ten Year Appraisal, 1978, Medicare Policy: New Directions for Health and Long-Term Care, 1986, Health Care Cost Containment, 1990; contbr. articles pub. in sci. journals. Bd. visitor Columbia U. Sch. of Nursing, 2001—09; mem. NYC Commission on Women's Issues, 2002—06; bd. dirs. Employee Benefit Rsch. Inst., 2003—05. Recipient Disting. Investigator award, AcademyHealth, 2006, Disting. Alumna award, 1991, Baxter-Allegiance Found. prize for Health Services Rsch., 2000, AcademyHealth Disting. Investigator award, 2006, Picker Inst. Ann. award for Excellence in the Advancement of Patient Centered Care, 2006, BioMed San Antonio Inaugural Julio Palmaz award for Innovation in Healthcare and the Biosciences, 2007, Healthcare Fin. Mgmt. Assn. Bd. of Directors award, 2009; named one of The 100 Most Influential Bus. Women, Crain's NY Bus., 2005—07, Top 100 Most Influential People in Health Care, Modern Healthcare mag., 2008, 2009, 2011, Top 25 Women in Healthcare, 2008, 2009, 2011. Fellow: Royal Soc. for the Encouragement of Arts, Manufactures & Commerce, NY Acad. of Medicine, Royal Coll. of Physicians (hon.), American Acad. of Arts and Sciences; mem.: Inst. of Medicine (mem. governing coun. 1986—90, 1997—2000, Adam Yarmolinsky medal 2007), Nat. Acad. of Social Ins. (founding mem. 1991—), American Pub. Health Assn., Assn. of Health Svcs. Rsch. (pres. 1995—96, pres.-elect 1994—95), Delta Omega, Delta Phi Alpha, Alpha Omega Alpha (hon.), Phi Beta Kappa. Democrat. Meth. Office: The Commonwealth Fund 1 E 75th St New York NY 10021 Home: 1365 York Ave Apt 23f New York NY 10021-4036 Office Phone: 212-606-3825. Business E-Mail: kd@cmwf.org. *

DAVIS, KAREN SUE, hospital nursing supervisor; b. Owensboro, Ky., June 5, 1950; d. Robert J. and Mona F. (Urlaub) D. Diploma, Deaconess Sch. Nursing, 1971. RN, Ky.; cert. in pediatric nursing; cert. PALS. Supr. pediatrics Daviess County Hosp., 1971-89; clin. supr. pediat, 11-7 shift Owensboro Med. Health Sys., 1989—2005, charge nurse pediat., 2005—09, pediat. family care unit, 2009—. Named Nurse's Of Yr., State of Ky., 2006. Republican. Lutheran. Avocations: needlecrafts, reading, travel, cooking. Home: 686 N Fairview Ct Rockport IN 47635 Office Phone: 270-688-6100.

DAVIS, KENNETH L., hospital administrator, educator; MD, Mt. Sinai Sch. Medicine. Diplomate Am. Bd. Psychiatry and Neurology. Resident psychiatry Stanford Univ., fellow clin. pharmocology; resident rotating Stanford Univ. Hosp.; chief psychiatry dept. Bronx Veterans Adminstrn. (VA) Med. Ctr.; prof. psychiatry dept. Mt. Sinai Sch. of Medicine, prof. pharmacology and sys. therapeutics dept., chmn. psychiatry dept., dean, 2003—07; pres. Mt. Sinai Med. Ctr., CEO, 2003—. Pres. Am. Coll. of Neuropsychopharmacology, 2006. Recipient Career Development award, Veterans Adminstrn., Joel Elkes Research award, Daniel H. Efron Research award, Paul Hoch Distinguished Service award, George H. W. Bush '48 Lifetime of Leadership award, Yale Univ., 2009, A. E. Bennett award. Office: Mount Sinai Medical Center 1425 Madison Ave New York NY 10029 Office Phone: 212-659-8888. Office Fax: 212-659-9800. E-mail: kenneth.davis@mssm.edu.

DAVIS, KENNETH LEON, hospital administrator, psychiatrist, medical educator; b. NYC, Sept. 10, 1947, married, 1972, 2 children. BA, Yale U., 1969; MD, Mt. Sinai Med. Sch., 1973. Diplomate Am. Bd. Psychiatry and Neurology. Intern Stanford U., 1973-74, resident, 1973-76, life sci. rsch. assoc., 1975-76; rsch. assoc. Stanford Psych. Clin., 1974-79; asst. dir. Stanford Psych. Clin. Rsch. Ctr., VA Med. Ctr., 1975-79; clin. psychiat. cons. Santa Clara Valley Med. Ctr., 1976-79; chief dept. psychiat. VA Med. Ctr., 1979-87; assoc. prof. psychiatry and pharmacology Mt. Sinai Sch. Medicine, 1979-84, dir. schizophrenia biol. rsch. ctr., 1981-91, prof., 1984—, chair dept. psychiatry, 1987—, Esther and Joseph Klingenstein prof., 1994—2003, dean, 2003—06, Gustave L. Levy disting. prof.; pres., CEO Mt. Sinai Med. Ctr., 2003—. Editor Alzheimer's Disease and Associated Disorders, Biol. Psychiatry, Clin. Neuropharmacology, Harvard Review of Psychiatry, Internat. Jour. Geriatric Psychiatry, Internat. Jour. Geriatric Psychopharmacology, Jour. Geriatric Psychiatry & Neurology, Jour. Psychiatric Rsch., Jour. Am. Geriatrics Soc., Schizophrenia Rsch., Neuropsychopharmacology, Jour. Exptl. Cognitive and Behavioral Neurosci., Molecular Psychiatry, Sociedade de Psiquiatria Do Rio Grande Do Sul; author, co-author over 500 sci. articles. Recipient A. E. Bennett Clin. Sci. Rsch. award, 1977, Saul Horowitz Jr. Meml. award, 1977-78, Solomon Silver award, 1981, Joel Elkes Internat. award ACNP, 1986, Daniel H. Efron Excellence in Rsch. award, 1990, Rita Hayworth award Alzheimer's Assn., 1991, Lifetime Sci. award Inst. Advanced Sci. in Immunology and Aging, 1992. Mem. NAS, Am. Coll. Neuropsychopharmacology (pres.-elect 2004-05, pres. 05-06), Am. Psychiat. Assn. (APA/KEMPF award 1999), Soc. Biol. Psychiatry (Gold medal award 1999, APA award Rsch. in Psychiatry 2001), Inst. Medicine of NAS. Achievements include research in the biological basis of senile dementia of the Alzheimers' type, and schizophrenia. Office: Mount Sinai Med Ctr - Mount Sinai Sch Medicine Presidents Office One Gustave L Levy Pl Box 1220 New York NY 10029-6574 Business E-Mail: kenneth.davis@mssm.edu. *

DAVIS, LAWRENCE WILLIAM, radiation oncologist; b. North Braddock, Pa., Sept. 5, 1935; s. William Paul Davis and Julia Helen Zukas; children: James G., Karen E. BS, Juniata Coll., Huntington, Pa., 1957; MA, U. Pa., 1969; MBA, Temple U., 1984; MD, Georgetown U., 1961. Diplomate Am. Bd. Radiology (trustee 1981-95, asst. exec. dir. radiation oncology 1994-04, assoc. exec. dir. 2004—), lic. physician Pa., Md., I, NY, Ga. Asst. instr. radiology U. Pa., Phila., 1962-66, instr. radiology, 1966, 68-69, asst. prof. radiology, 1969-72, assoc. prof. radiology, 1972-75; prof. radiation therapy Thomas Jefferson Sch. Medicine, 1975-84; prof. and chmn. radiation oncology Albert Einstein Coll. Medicine, Bronx, 1984-91, Emory U., Atlanta, 1991—2009. Cons. Armed Forces Radiobiology Rsch. Inst., Bethesda, 1968-70; exec. com. of med. staff Montefiore Med. Ctr., 1984-87, 1990-91, div. coun., 1988-89; prof. svc. com. Phila. div. Am. Cancer Soc., 1970-75; trustee 1981-95, asst. exec. dir. radiation oncology 1994-09, assoc. exec. dir. radiation oncology, Am. Bd. Radiology, 2003-. Assoc. editor Internat. Jour. Radiation Oncology, 1986—, mem. editl. bd. Neuro Oncology, 1989—99, assoc. editor, 1991—2003, mem. editl. bd. Am. Jour. Clin. Oncology, 1991—2003; contbr. numerous articles to profl. jours. Capt. USAF, 1966—68. Recipient Gold medal Am. Coll. Radiology, 2008; fellow Am. Cancer Soc., Phila., 1963-64, NIH, 1964-66, Am. Cancer Soc. traineeship, 1968-71. Fellow Am. Coll. Radiology; mem. AAAS, Am. Assn. Cancer Rsch., Am. Coll. Radiology (commn. on radiation oncology 1981-90, bd. chancellors 1993-99), Am. Soc. Therapeutic Radiology and Oncology (chmn. bd. 1988-89, pres. 1987-88), Am. Radium Soc.

(pres. 1992-93), Radiol. Soc. N.Am., Alpha Omega Alpha. Office: Emory Clinic 1365 Clifton Rd NE Atlanta GA 30322-1013 Office Phone: 404-778-3463. Personal E-mail: larry@lwdavis.com. Business E-Mail: lawrence.davis@emory.edu.

DAVIS, LINDA LENNON MCCONNELL, critical care nurse; b. Kingstree, SC, Mar. 1, 1943; d. Murdoch and Vandetta (Vandergrift) Lennon; m. Robert John McConnell, Apr. 20, 1963 (div. 1971); children: Susan McConnell Kennedy, Amber Virginia Smith; m. S.E. Felkel, 1974 (div. 1984); m. Hal Davis, 1998. Grad. with honors, Mercy Sch. Nursing, 1968; student, U. NC, 1972; BS in History with honors, Charleston So. U., 1990. Cert. BLS; RN SC, NC, Fla. Head nurse neurosurgery intensive care Med. U. Hosp., Charleston, SC, 1968—70; head nurse respiratory intensive care Duke U. Med. Ctr., 1971—73. Author: Charleston's Historical Churches and Chapels of Ease, 1998; co-author: Angel Oak Story, 1981. Hist. guide City of Charleston, 1983; active Gibbes Mus. Art Women's Coun., 1978—; vol. Hospice, Jacksonville, Fla., 2001; women's council Gibbes Mus. Art; women's coun. membership chair Unitarian Ch., Charleston, SC, 1979, religious edn. tchr., 1980. Recipient Svc. award, Gibbes Mus. Art Women's Coun., 1997. Mem.: AAUW.

DAVIS, MARY HELEN, psychiatrist, educator; b. Kingsville, Tex., Dec. 2, 1949; d. Garnett Stant and Emogene (Campbell) D. BA, U. Tex., 1970; MD, U. Tex., Galveston, 1975; grad. in adult and child psychoanalysis, Inst. for Psychoanalysis, Chgo., 1982-92. Cert. Nat. Bd. Med. Examiners, Am. Bd. Psychiatry and Neurology, Child and Adolescent Psychiatry. Intern, then resident in psychiatry SUNY, Buffalo, 1975-78; fellow in child psychiatry U. Cin., 1978-80; asst. prof. Med. Coll. Wis., Milw., 1980-89, clin. assoc. prof., 1989-93; med. dir. adolescent treatment unit Milw. Psychiat. Hosp., 1981-86, Schroeder Child Ctr., 1986-89; pvt. practice, 1989-93; med. dir. Devereux-Victoria (Tex.) Psych. Residential Treatment Ctr., 1993-94; pvt. practice Lancaster, Pa., 1995—. Cons. Milw. Mental Health Cons., 1980-93, Children's Svc. Soc., Milw., 1982-93, Cath. charities, Harrisburg, Pa., 1996—, Sch. Dist. Lancaster, 1998—. Bd. dirs. Next Generation Theatre, Milw., 1988-90, Next Act Theatre, Milw., 1990-92, Lancaster Guidance Ctr., 2002-06. Mem. Am. Med. Women's Assn., Assn. for Child Psychoanalysis, Am. Psychoanalytic Assn., Am. Acad. Child and Adolescent Psychiatry. Baptist. Avocations: science fiction, music, computers, crochet. Office Phone: 717-392-7062.

DAVIS, MELLAR PILGRIM, oncologist; b. Columbus, Ohio, Dec. 22, 1951; s. Mellar and Lola (Zimmerman) D.; m. Deborah Doan, Aug. 21, 1976; children: Luke, Amanda, Meghan, Jessamyn. BA, Otterbein Coll., 1974; MD, Ohio State U., 1977. Diplomate Am. Bd. Internal Medicine. Intern, then resident Riverside Meth. Hosp., Columbus, 1977-80; fellow in oncology/hematology Mayo Clinic, Rochester, Minn., 1980-83; pvt. practice Toledo Clinic, 1983-84, Millhon Clinic, Columbus, 1984-87, Columbus Oncology Assocs., 1987—2006; dir. rsch. Harry R. Horvitz Ctr. for Palliative Medicine, Cleve. Clinic Found., 2006—. Instr. medicine Mayo Med. Sch., 1982; mem. community adv. bd. James Comprehensive Cancer Ctr., Ohio State U., Columbus; mem. rsch. com. Riverside Regional Cancer Inst., Columbus; mem. residence evaluation com. Riverside Meth. Hosp.; mem. Taussig Cancer Ctr., Cleve. Clinic.; mem. dept. bioethics Cleve. Clinic. Contbr. articles to profl. jours. Fellow Am. Coll. Chest Physicians; mem. Am. Soc. Hematology, Am. Soc. Clin. Oncology Business E-Mail: davismb@ccf.org.

DAVIS, OWEN KIDDER, physician, reproductive endocrinologist; b. NYC, Aug. 16, 1956; s. Stephen Edward and Joyce Baldwin (Kidder) D.; m. Marianne Alida Gawain, Nov. 19, 1983; children: Zoe Catherine, Alida Ashby. BA, Swarthmore Coll., 1978; MD, Bowman Gray Sch. Medicine, 1982. Diplomate Am. Bd. Ob-gyn., Am. Bd. Reproductive Endocrinology. Intern, resident N.Y. Hosp., Cornell Med. Ctr.; fellow Brigham and Women's Hosp., Boston; instr. Harvard U., Boston, 1986-88; assoc. prof. Cornell U. Med. Coll., NYC, 1988—2009, prof., 2009—; assoc. ob-gyn. Brigham & Women's Hosp., Boston, 1986-88; assoc. attending ob-gyn. N.Y. Presbyn. Hosp., 1988—; prof. ob-gyn & reproductive medicine Weith Med. Coll., Cornell U., 2009—; attending ob-gyn. NY Presby. Hosp., 2009—. Acting chief gynecology Cornell Med. Ctr., assoc. dir. In Vitro Fertilization; assoc. editor Fertitily & Sterility. Contbr. articles to profl. jours. Med. dir. Am. Fertility Assn.; chair instl. rev. bd. N.Y. Presbyn. Hosp.; chief of gynecology Cornell Med. Ctr. John Lockwood Meml. fellow Swarthmore Coll., 1978, Family Building award Am. Fertility Assn., 2000. Fellow: NY Acad. Medicine (sec. sect. ob-gyn. 1991—92), Am. Coll. Ob-Gyn.; mem.: AMA, NY Obstetrical Soc. (mem. editl. bd. of fertility and sterility), Soc. for Reproductive Endocrinologists, Soc. Assisted Reproductive Tech. (pres., exec. coun., past chair membership and practice com.), Am. Soc. for Reproductive Medicine (legis. monitor, practice com., govt. rels. com. 1987—, bd. dirs., assoc. editor fertility and sterility), Alpha Omega Alpha. Avocations: music, travel, tennis. Home: 165 E 72d St Apt 16A New York NY 10021 Office: Weill Med Coll of Cornell U 1305 York Ave New York NY 10021 Office Phone: 646-962-3765. E-mail: okdavis@med.cornell.edu.

DAVIS, PAMELA BOWES, pediatric pulmonologist, dean; b. Jamaica, NY, July 20, 1949; d. Elmer George and Florence (Welsch) Bowes; m. Glenn C. Davis, June 28, 1970 (div. Mar. 1987); children: Jason, Galen. AB, Smith Coll., 1968; PhD, Duke U., 1973, MD, 1974. Cert. Am. Bd. Internal Medicine, 1977, in Pulmonary Diseases 1980, Am. Bd. Pediat., 1996, in Pediatric Pulmonology 2000. Internal medicine intern Duke Hosp., 1973-74, resident in internal medicine, 1974-75; sr. investigator NIAMD/NIH, Bethesda, Md., 1977-79; asst. prof. U. Tenn. Coll. Medicine, Memphis, 1979-81, Case Western Res. U. Sch. Medicine, Cleve., 1981-85, assoc. prof., 1985-89, vice chmn. rsch. dept., 1994—96, prof., 2002—, Arline H. and Curtis F. Garvin Rsch. prof., 2005—, vice dean rsch., 2005—, interim dean, v.p. med. affairs, 2006—07, dean, v.p. med. affairs, 2007—; chief pediatric pulmonary divsn. Rainbow Babies and Children's Hosp., 1985—2007. Pres. Am. Fedn. for Clin. Rsch., Thorofare, NJ, 1989—90; trustee Rsch. Am, Arlington, Va., 1989—90; mem. adv. coun. Nat. Inst. Diabetes, Digestive and Kidney Diseases, 1992—96; mem. bd. sci. counselors NHLBI, 2001—06, chmn., 2004—06; founding scientist Copernicus Therapeutics, Inc., Cleve. Contbr. articles to profl. jours. Chmn. med. adv. coun. Cystic Fibrosis Found., Bethesda, 1988-90. With USPHS, 1975—79. Recipient Samuel Rosenthal award in acad. pediat., 1996, Maurice Saltzman award, Mt. Sinai Health Care Found., 1998, Smith Coll. medal, 2001, Paul di Sant'Agnese award, Cystic Fibrosis Found., 2006, Doris Tulcin award, 2008, AMSA Raising Our Voices award, 2008; named Rainmaker of Yr., Edn. Rsch. Northeast Ohio Live Mag., 2002; named to, Clevel. Med. Hall of Fame, 2001, Ohio Womens Hall of Fame, 2009. Fellow ACP; mem. Am. Pediatric Soc., Am. Acad. Pediatrics, Am. Physiol. Soc., Am. Thoracic Soc., Am. Soc. Gene Therapy, Biophys. Soc., Soc. for Pediatric Rsch., Assn. Am. Physicians, Phi Beta Kappa, Sigma Xi, Alpha Omega Alpha. Achievements include 7 patents in field. Office: Case Western Res University School Medicine 10900 Euclid Ave Cleveland OH 44106 Office Phone: 216-368-4370. Business E-Mail: pamela.davis@case.edu. *

DAVIS, PAMELA MEYER, hospital administrator; BA in Economics and Social Studies, U. Iowa, MA in Hosp. and Health Svcs. Adminstrn. Asst. adminstr. Lutheran Gen. Hosp., Park Ridge; COO and sr. adminstrv. positions Christ Hosp. and Med. Ctr., Oak Lawn; bd. mem. Haris Bank; pres. and CEO Edward Health Svcs. Corp., 1988—. Editl. bd. Frontiers of Health Svc. Mgmt. Chairperson Gift of Hope Organ and Tissue Donor Network. Recipient Bus. Ledger's award, Anti-Defamation League, 2003, Maimonides Health Care Leadership award, 2003; named Person of the Year, Daily Herald, 2005. Fellow: Am. Coll. of Healthcare Execs. Office: Edward Hospital & Health Services 801 S Washington Naperville IL 60540 Office Phone: 630-527-3000.

DAVIS, PAUL JOSEPH, endocrinologist; b. Chgo., Oct. 28, 1937; s. Paul Albert and Maxine Lydia (Mason) D.; m. Faith Ainsworth Baker, Dec. 8, 1962; children: Matthew, John, Sarah. BA magna cum laude, Westminster Coll., 1959; MD cum laude, Harvard U., 1963. Intern Bronx Mcpl. Hosp. Ctr., 1963-64, resident in medicine, 1964-67; clin. assoc. NIH, Bethesda, Md., 1967-69, sr. staff assoc., 1969-70; head endocrinology div. Balt. City Hosps., 1970-75; prof. medicine, head endocrinology div. SUNY, Buffalo Med. Sch., 1975-90, also vice chmn. dept. medicine; prof., chmn. dept. medicine Albany Med. Coll., Albany Med. Ctr., NY, 1990-99, sr. assoc. dean for clin. rsch., 1998—; chief med. svc. VA Med. Ctr., Buffalo, 1980-90. Mem. merit rev. bd. endocrinology, oncology VA; bd. dirs. Am. Bd. Internal Medicine; mem. nat. adv. coun. W.Va. U. Health Sci. Ctr.; dir. Ordway Rsch. Inst., Albany, N.Y., 1999—; bd. dirs. Hauptman Woodward Med. Rsch. Inst., Buffalo. Editor-in-chief Immunology, Endocrine and Metabolic Agents in Medicinal Chemistry, 2007—. Trustee Westminster Coll., Fulton, Mo., 2000—; sci. dir. Charitable Leadership Found. Master ACP (gov. Upstate N.Y. region, pres. N.Y. chpt.), Gerontol. Soc.; mem. Am. Fedn. Med. Rsch., Am. Soc. Biochemistry and Molecular Biology, Am. Thyroid Assn. (bd. dirs., pres. 1997-98, Disting. Svc. award 2003), Endocrine Soc., Bd. Sci. Counselors, Nat. Inst. Aging. Achievements include research and publs. on mechanisms of action of thyroid hormone, effects of aging on endocrine function. Home: 35 Old South Rd West Sand Lake NY 12196-2104 Office: Ordway Research Inst Inc 150 New Scotland Ave Albany NY 12208 Home Phone: 518-674-3383; Office Phone: 518-641-6410. Business E-Mail: pdavis@ordwayresearch.org.

DAVIS, RAPHAEL, neurosurgeon; Studied, Mt. Sinai Sch. of Medicine, 1981. Diplomate Am. Bd. Neurol. Surgery. Resident Mt. Sinai Sch. of Medicine, 1982—87; with St. Charles Hosp.; chmn. dept. of neurol. surgery Stony Brook Univ. Med. Ctr. Office: Stony Brook University Medical Center Ste 200 24 Research Way East Setauket NY 11733-3453 Office Phone: 631-444-1213. Office Fax: 631-444-9310.

DAVIS, RICHARD M., medical educator, researcher, physician; b. Chgo., July 13, 1956; MD, Northwestern U., 1982. Assoc. prof. Wake Forest U. Eye Ctr., 1993—96; founder Carolina Eye Consultants, 1996—99; asst. prof. U. SC, 1988—93, prof., chair, 1999—2009; prof. U. NC, 2009—. Founder Advanced TeleCare, LLC, 2009. Recipient Herschel medal, Internat. Soc. Contact Lens Specialists. Mem.: Am. Acad. Ophthalmology, Am. Diabetes Assn., Am. Telemedicine Assn. Office: 5151 Bioinformatics Bldg CB #7040 Chapel Hill NC 27599-7040 Business E-Mail: richard_davis@med.unc.edu.

DAVIS, RUSSELL HADEN, school administrator, consultant; b. Washington, Nov. 26, 1940; s. Walter Haden Davis and Virginia (Russell) Edge; m. Iva Lee Crocker, 1964; children: Brandon Denise, Haden Arnold. BA, U. Va., 1962; MDiv, Union Theol. Sem., NYC, 1965, STM, 1978, PhD, 1986; ThM, So. Bapt. Theol. Sem., Louisville, 1966. Ordained to ministry So. Bapt. Ch., 1961, endorsed to chaplaincy Alliance of Baptists in the USA, 2000. Clin. chaplain Ky. State Reformatory, LaGrange, 1966-71, Ctrl. State Hosp., Milledgeville, Ga., 1971-77; assoc. min. The Riverside Ch., NYC, 1977-86; pvt. practice pastoral psychotherapy, 1974-98; asst. prof. psychiatry and religion Union Theol. Sem., NYC, 1986-91; mem. faculty Blanton-Peale Grad. Inst. Pastoral Psychotherapy, NYC, 1989-91; dir. Psy-Law, NYC, 1989-91; asst. prof. U. Va., 1994, assoc. prof., 1994-95; exec. dir. Assn. for Clin. Pastoral Edn., Inc., Decatur, Ga., 1995-98; pres. Legacy Group Internat., 1998—; founder sch. clin. pastoral edn. Sentara Norfolk (Va.) Gen. Hosp., 2001—. Adj. prof. Va. Commonwealth U., 2001—06, John Leland Ctr. Theol. Studies, 2004—06. Author: Freud's Concept of Passivity, 1993; also articles. Exec. sec. CCAPS, Comn. Accreditation Pastoral Svc., 2009; founder Sch. of Clin. Pastoral Edn., Sentara Hosps., Norfolk, 2001; bd. dirs. Tidewater Pastoral Counseling Svcs., Norfolk, 2001—09, Inst. for Relationship Therapy, NY, 1981—88, Counseling Ctr., Riverside Ch., NY, 1978—82. Named Ky. Col., State of Ky., 1970; fellow Union Theol. Sem., 1979-81, rsch. grantee, 1987-90; fellow Oaklawn Found., 1980. Mem.: Commn.'s Network (mem.-at-large 2010—11), Assn. Profl. Chaplains (bd. cert. chaplain 1974—99), Assn. for Clin. Pastoral Edn. (v.p. racial, ethnic, multicultural network 2006—07). Office: Sch Clin Pastoral Edn Sentara Norfolk Gen Hosp 600 Gresham Dr Norfolk VA 23507 Office Phone: 757-388-2850. Business E-Mail: rhd.uts.psr@gmail.com.

DAVIS, RUTH CAROL, pharmacist, educator; b. Wilkes-Barre, Pa., Oct. 27, 1943; d. Morris David Davis and Helen Jane Gillis. BS, Phila. Coll. Pharmacy and Sci., 1967; PharmD, Ohio State U., 1970; AA in Elec. Engring., ITT Tech. Inst., 1999. Cert. pharmacist, Pa., Md. Mgr. pharmacist Fairview Pharmacy, Etters, Pa.; mgr., pharmacist Neighborcare Pharmacy, Balt.; dir. ambulatory svcs. Rombro Health Svcs., Balt.; tchr., pharmacist Boothwyn Pharmacy, Phila.; pharm. cons. Nat. Rx Svcs. of Pa.; Eagle Managed Care, 1996; pharmacist Pharmastat Inc., 1996—; pharmacy supr. Johns Hopkins Hospice Pharmacy, 2000—; asst. prof. pharmacy Anne Arundel C.C., 2001—; pharmacy instr. Johns Hopkins Hosp., 2000—, Sojourner-Douglass Coll., Balt., 2008—; prof. pharmacy tech. tng. program Sqourner-Douglas Coll.; MD for pharm. tech. Carroll Comm. Coll. Westminster, 1995—. Adj. prof. Essex C.C., 1999, Balt. City C.C., 2000; pharmacy instr. Sch. Sisters of Notre Dame, 2003. Republican. Baptist. Avocations: music, reading. Home and Office: 75 Lion Dr Hanover PA 17331-3849 E-mail: ladypharm@hotmail.com.

DAVIS, SAMUEL, hospital administrator, educator, consultant; b. NYC, Sept. 30, 1931; s. Morris and Ethel (Levowitz) D.; m. Ellen Darce Kalker, June 16, 1957; children: Joseph Evan, Thomas Adam, Jonathan Edward, Jessica Ann. BA, CCNY, 1952; MS, Columbia U., 1957. Acct. Roosevelt Hosp., NYC, 1954-55; relief adminstr. Meml. Center Cancer and Allied Diseases, NYC, 1955-56; adminstrv. resident, then adminstrv. asst. to dir. and dir. ambulatory care services Roosevelt Hosp., 1956-59; mem. adminstrv. staff Hillside Hosp., Glen Oaks, NY, 1959-72, exec. v.p., 1970-72; exec. cons. L.I. Jewish-Hillside Med. Center, New Hyde Park, NY, 1972; exec. pres. Mt. Sinai Hosp., Mpls., 1972-75, dir. NYC, 1975-81, pres., 1981-85; sr. v.p. Mt. Sinai Med. Center, NYC, 1975-77, exec. v.p., 1978-84; pres. EcuMed, NYC, 1984-85; prin. Sam Davis & Assocs., Rye, NY, 1986—; sr. dir. Delta Cons. Group, NYC, 1990-98; assoc. prof. adminstrv. medicine Mt. Sinai Med. Sch., 1975-79, acting chmn., 1977-79, Edmond A. Guggenheim prof. health care mgmt., chmn. health care mgmt., 1979-84, disting. service prof. health care mgmt., 1984—; adj. prof. health care adminstrn. Baruch Coll., CUNY, 1978-87; prof. mgmt., clin. prof. Sch. Pub. Health Columbia U., 1988—; cons. health care strategy and orgnl. change, 1976—; pres. Sam Davis & Assoc., 1999—. Dir. health care research, The Ctr. for Mgmt., CUNY; vice chmn. bd. dirs. Hennepin County (Minn.) Health Coalition, 1973-75; mem. health adv. com. Minn. Met. Health Bd., 1974-75; mem. Hennepin County Health and Social Services Adv. Bd., 1974-75. Author: Decision Analysis in Hospital Administration, 1974; contbr. articles to profl. jours. Trustee Mpls. Fedn. Jewish Service, 1973-75; chmn. health and welfare div. N.Y.C. Fedn. Jewish Philanthropies, 1975-76; trustee, mem. exec. com. Montefiore Med. Ctr., Bronx, N.Y., 1985—. Served with AUS, 1952-54. Recipient Humanitarian award NCCJ, 1984; fellow social studies and humanities CCNY, 1952; WHO fellow, 1970; sr. fellow Wharton Sch. U. Pa., 1986—. Fellow Am. Coll. Hosp. Adminstrs., Am. Pub. Health Assn.; mem. Am. Assn. Hosp. Planning, Am., Am. Acad. Dramatic Arts (bd. dirs., exec. com., chmn.), N.Y. State hosp. assns., Am. Mgmt. Assn., Herman Biggs Soc.

DAVIS, STEPHEN N., endocrinologist; m. Frances Louise Hunt, Sept. 17, 1982; children: Ian, Stuart, Hugh. MBBS, London U., 1979; MD, Vanderbilt U., Nashville, 1993. Cert. endocrinology, diabetes and metabolism Royal Coll. Physicians and Surgeons Eng., 1982. Qualified Royal Free Hosp., Sch. Medicine, London, 1979; ho. physician acad. depts. diabetes and nephrology Royal Free Hosp., London, 1979—80; ho. surgeon acad. depts. surgery and gynecology Royal Free Hosp., London U., 1980, sr. ho. officer accident, emergency and ICU, 1980—81, sr. ho. officer acad. depts. diabetes, medicine, rheumatology and respiratory medicine, 1981—83; med. registrar acad. depts. gen. medicine, diabetes, endocrinology, geriatric medicine and cardiology Newcastle Gen. and Freeman Hosps., U. Newcastle upon Tyne, England, 1983—84; Eli Lilly rsch. fellow dept. medicine Royal Victoria Infirmary, U. Newcastle upon Tyne, 1984—85, med. rsch. coun. dept. medicine, 1985—87, hon. sr. registrar dept. medicine, 1985—87; sr. registrar infirmary Freeman Hosps., U. Newcastle upon Tyne, 1987—88; Med. Rsch. Coun. traveling fellow dept. molecular physiology and biophysics Vanderbilt U. Sch. Medicine, Nashville, 1988—89, Juvenile Diabetes Found. fellow depts. molecular physiology, biophysics and medicine, 1989—91, asst. prof. dept. medicine Diabetes Rsch. and Tng. Ctr., 1991—94, assoc. prof. dept. medicine Diabetes Rsch. and Tng. Ctr., 1994—99, assoc. prof. dept. molecular physiology and biophysics, 1994—99, chief divsn. diabetes, endocrinology and metabolism, 2000—, prof. dept. molecular physiology and biophysics, 2000—, Rudolph Kampmeier prof. dept. medicine, 2000—06, Mark Collie prof. dept. medicine, 2006—; assoc. dir. Diabetes Rsch. and Tng. Ctr. Vanderbilt U., Nashville, 1999—, assoc. dir. Gen. Clin. Rsch. Ctr., 1999—; dir. Nashville VA/Juvenile Diabetes Found. Internat. Diabetes Rsch. Ctr., Nashville, 1997—2002. Mem. med. bd. Vanderbilt U., Nashville, mem. dept. medicine awards com., mem. physicians scientist awards com., mem. masters clin. investigation entry and rev. com., mem. clin. rsch. scientist entrance and rev. com.; mem. exec. com. Vanderbilt U. Sch. Medicine, Nashville; mem. nat. organizing com. Veterans Affairs Coop. Study #565; chair hypoglycemia and clin. complications Annual Am. Diabetes Assn. Meeting, 2005. Contbr. articles to profl. jours. Recipient Peel Med. Rsch. award, 1986, award, Mason Med. Rsch. Found., 1987, Newcastle Rsch. and Sci. Com. Rsch. award, 1988, So. Sect. AFCR Young Faculty award, 1993, Novartis award for Diabetes Rsch., Am. Soc. Clin. Investigation, 2000, Mary Jane Kugel award, Juvenile Diabetes Rsch. Found. Internat., 2002, Grant W. Liddle award for clin. rsch., Vanderbilt U., 2005; grantee, NIH/Nat. Inst. Diabetes and Digestive and Kidney Diseases, 1997—, 2004—, 2004—, Dept. Veterans Affairs, 2000—, NIH/Nat. Heart, Lung and Blood Inst., 2002—, NIH/ Nat. Heart, Lung and Blood Inst., 2005—, 2006—, NIH/Nat. Ctr. for Rsch. Resources, 2002—, NIH, 2005—. Fellow: Am. Coll. Endocrinologists, Am. Assn. Clin. Endocrinologists, Royal Coll. Physicians; mem.: ACP, Am. Physiology Soc., Endocrine Soc., Am. Soc. Clin. Investigation, So. Soc. Clin. Investigation, Juvenile Diabetes Found. Internat., Brit. Med. Assn., Am. Fedn. Clin. Rsch., Brit. Diabetes Assn., Am. Diabetes Assn. (chair hypoglycemia and clin. complications annual meeting 2005, chair hypoglycemia and complications annual meeting 1997). Office Fax: 615-936-1250. Business E-Mail: steve.davis@vanderbilt.edu.

DAVIS, STEVEN EUGENE, radiographer, consultant; b. Dillon, SC, June 8, 1968; s. Willie and Dianne Davis; m. Dian Graham, Dec. 4, 1992; children: Courtney Gibbs, Jenny Gibbs. AS Radiology, Florence Darlington Tech. Coll., 1992. Registered ARRT Am. Registry of Radilogic Tech. Diagnostic and oper. rm. tech. McLeod Regional Med. Ctr., Florence, SC, 1991—96; chief CT and oper. tech. Carolinas Hosp. Sys., Lake City, SC, 1996—99; dir. imaging Clarendon Meml. Hosp., Manning, SC, 1999—. Cons. in field. Contbr. articles pub. to profl. jour. Team mem. Relay for Life, 2002; polit. action com. S.C. Hosp. Assn., 2000—. Sgt. E-5 US Army, 1987—93. Decorated Army Achievement award. Mem.: Soc. for Computer Applications in Radiology, Am. Soc. of Radiology Tech., Am. Health Care Radiology Adminstr., S.C. Soc. Radiologic Tech. Bapt. Achievements include instituted radiology information system and picture architecture and communications system; development of customer service initiative for hospitals. Avocations: hunting, fishing, finance, computing. Office: Claredon Meml Hosp 10 Hosp St Manning SC 29102 Office Phone: 803-435-3121.

DAVIS, W. JACKSON, environmental services administrator; b. Portsmoutn, Va., Feb. 7, 1942; PhD, U. Oreg., 1967. Prof. U. Calif., 1969—2004; founder, pres. Environ. Studies Inst., 1981—; Gordon Paul Smith prof., founding dir. internat. environ. policy program Monterey Inst. Internat. Studies, 1995—2002. Contbr. scientific papers, articles to profl. sci. jours. Recipient Humboldt prize, Germany. Avocations: movies, art, exercise. Office: 7298 Siena Way Boulder CO 80301 Office Fax: 303-530-3135. E-mail: jacksondavis@earthlink.net.

DAVIS-LEWIS, BETTYE, nursing educator; b. Egypt, Tex., Sept. 19, 1939; d. Henry Sr. and Eliza (Baylock) Davis; divorced; children: Kim Michelle, Roderick Trevor. BS, Prarie View A&M U., 1959; BA in Psychology, U. Houston, 1972; MEd, Tex. Southern U., 1974, EdD, 1982. Dir. edn. Houston Internat. Hosp., 1987—; dir. nurses Mental Health & Mental Retardation Auth. Harris County, Houston, 1982-87, Riverside Gen. Hosp., Houston; CEO, owner Diversified Health Care Systems, Inc., Houston, 1985—; asst. clin. prof. psychiat. nursing U. Tex., 1987-88; asst. prof. allied health sci. Tex. So. U., Houton, 1989—. Adj. prof. Coll. Nursing, Prairie View A&M U., 1986—; lectr. in field; leadership extern. Mem. Harris County Coun. Orgns., 1987—; mem. polit. action com. Coalition 100 Black Women, 1988—; founder, mem. Hattie White Aux. br. NAACP, 1988; mem. grievance com. State Bar Tex., 1988—; chmn. S.W. Regional Nat. Black Leadership Initiative on Cancer, 1988—; grad. Leadership Tex.; bd. dirs. Theatre Under the Stars. Recipient Disting. Rsch. award Internat. Soc. Hypertension, Disting. Crystal award, Impact award Wheeler Ave. Bapt. Ch.; fellow Internat. Leadership Forum, Am. Leadership Forum; named one of Most Influential Black Americans, Ebony mag., 2005, 06. Fellow Internat. Soc. Hypertension in Blacks; mem. ANA, Nat. Black Nurses Assn. (past mem. bd. dirs., past pres.), Sigma Theta Tau, Chi Eta Phi. Office: Diversified Health Care Sys Inc #2 4811 Jackson Houston TX 77004 also: Nat Black Nurses Assn 8630 Fenton St, Ste 330 Silver Spring MD 20910-3803

DAVISON, GERALD C, dean, psychology professor; BA magna cum laude, Harvard U., 1961; PhD, Stanford U., 1965. Mem. psychology faculty SUNY, Stony Brook, 1966—79; vis. assoc. prof. Stanford U., 1969—70; Nat. Inst. Mental Health spl. fellow Harvard U., 1975—76; dir. clin. tng. U. So. Calif., 1979—84, chmn. dept. psychology, 1984—90, 2001—06, interim dean, Anneberg Sch. Comm., 1994—96, interim dean, Sch. Architecture, 2005—06, prof. gerontology and psychology, dean, Leonard Davis Sch. Gerontology, 2007—, exec. dir., Ethel Percy Andrus Gerontology Ctr., 2007—, William and Sylvia Kugel dean's chair. Co-author (with Marvin Goldfried): Clinical Behavior Therapy, 1976 (named a Citation Classic by Social Sciences Citation Index); co-author: (with Ann Kring, John Neale and Sheri Johnson) (textbook) Abnormal Psychology; editl. bd. Behavior Therapy, Cognitive Therapy and Rsch., Jour. Cognitive Psychotherapy, Journal Psychotherapy Integration, Jour. Clinical Psychology, In Session: Psychotherapy in Practice, Clinical Psychology: Science and Practice. Recipient Disting. Psychologist award, LA County Psychol. Assn., 1995. Fellow: Acad. Cognitive Therapy, Am. Psychol. Soc., APA (exec. com. divsn. clin. psychology, bd. sci. affairs, com. sci. awards, coun. representatives, Outstanding Achievement award, Bd. Social and Ethical Responsibility 1988); mem.. Assn. Advancement Behavior Therapy (past pres., publications coord., Outstanding Educator award 1997, Lifetime Achievement award 2003), Soc. Exploration Psychotherapy Integration (adv. bd.). Office: Univ So Calif Davis Sch Gerontology 3715 McClintock Ave Los Angeles CA 90089-0191 Office Phone: 213-740-1354. Business E-Mail: gdaviso@usc.edu.

DAVTYAN, TIGRAN KAMO, immunologist, researcher; b. Yerevan, Armenia, Dec. 1, 1966; s. Kamo Hovak Davtyan and Svetlana Aram Zalibekyan; m. Hasmik Aram Arakelyan, Aug. 20, 1988; children: Araks Tigran, Arusyak Tigran. Degree in pharmacology, Yerevan State Med. U., 1988; PhD in Genetics and Immunology, Yerevan State U., 1993; D in Biol. Scis. Molecular Biology, Buniatian Inst. Biochemistry, Nat. Acad. Scis., Armenia, 2003. Bd. cert. immunopathologist Armenia, state cert. neuroimmunopathologist World Congress of Immunology, Moscow, cert. Nat. Viral Infectious Disease Ctr., Armenia. Sr. technician lab. molecular and cellular immunology Inst. Molecular Biology, NAS, Yerevan, 1988—89; rsch. scientist lab. genetic mechanisms of cell malignization and differentiation Inst. Cytology, St. Petersburg, Russia, 1989—92; rsch. scientist lab. immunology Hosp. of Yerevan State Med. U., 1998—; sr. rsch. scientist lab. neurohormones biochemistry Buniatian Inst. Biochemistry, NAS of Armenia, 1998—; head HIV-clical trial lab. Armenicum Rsch. Ctr., Yerevan, 1999—; sr. rschr., lab. immunology Inst. Epidemiology Ministry of Health, Yerevan, 2002—04. Lab specialist clin. immunology and allergology Sochi Dept. of Health, Russia, 2001; lectr. in field. Lt. med. duty US Army, 1985—87, Yerevan. Recipient Workshop award, Inst. Physics Academia Sinica, 2003. Achievements include research in molecular and cellular immunology and HIV/AIDS. Office: Dept Neurohormone Biochem 5/1 Sevag St Yerevan 375014 Armenia Office Fax: 374-548013. Business E-Mail: tigdav@excite.com.

DAVYDOV, DMITRY M., psychiatrist, researcher; b. Nakhabino, Moscow Province, Russia, Mar. 20, 1963; m. Tatiana I. Luchkina, June 9, 1966; 1 child, Aksinia D. Davydova. MD, Sechenov Moscow Med. Acad., 1986, PhD in Physiology and Medicine, 1986—89. Diplomate in psychiatry Sechenov Moscow Med. Acad., 1998, psychiatry and narcology Russian Med. Acad. Posdoctoral Edn., 2006. Sr. scientist Serbsky Nat. Rsch. Centre for Social & Forensic Psychiatry, Moscow, 1990—2001; rsch. fellow U. Southampton, England, 2001—02; leading scientist Moscow Rsch. Centre of Narcology, 2003—. Vis. scholar psychophysiology UCLA, 1997, 2000, 04, UCL Belgium, 2006—07; head, rsch. projects in human well-being and human factors Nonprofit Org. for Info. and Expertise, Moscow, 2004—. Contbr. papers to profl. jours. and pubs. Home: 12-5-84 Planernaya ulitsa Moscow 125481 Russia Personal E-mail: dadimati@mail.ru, d.m.davydov@gmail.com.

DAWE, GAVIN STEWART, pharmacology educator, researcher; b. Mwanza, Tanzania, June 30, 1969; arrived in Singapore, 2001; s. Michael Charles Stewart and Jennifer Anne (Beveridge) Dawe; m. Siew Noi Choo, July 10, 1999; children: Hamish Stewart, Iain Stewart, Megan Kirsty. BSc in Neurosci. with honors, U. Edinburgh, Scotland, 1990; PhD in Pharmacology, London U., 1995. Sr. scientist, investigator ReNeuron Ltd., London, 1998—2000; cons. Eli Lilly and Co., Erl Wood, England, 2000—01; asst. prof. Dept. Pharmacology Yong Loo Lin Sch. Medicine Nat. U. Singapore, 2001—09, assoc. prof. Dept. Pharmacology, 2009—. Recipient Young Investigator award, Nat. U. Singapore, 2002—05, GSK Rsch. award, Glaxosmithkline, 2010. Achievements include research in neural stem cells and the neuropsychopharmacology of antidepressant and antipsychotic drugs. Avocations: scuba diving, wildlife observation, painting. Business E-Mail: gavindawe@nus.edu.sg.

DAWES, CAROL J., retired psychologist; b. Villa Park, Ill., June 15, 1931; d. John I. and Anna J. (Eggum) Postula; children: Jennifer H., Molly M. BA, Kalamazoo Coll., 1954; PhD, U. Mich., 1965. Psychology intern U. Mich. Psychology Clinic, 1959—65; staff psychologist U. Mich. Children's Psychiat. Hosp., 1965—67; pvt. practice psychology Eugene, Oreg., 1969—95, Corvallis, Oreg., 1979—93; ret., 1995. Specialist in psychology Oreg. State Sys. Higher Edn., 1968-94. Democrat. *

DAWES, CHRISTOPHER, hospital administrator; Unit mgr., asst. dir. nursing Stanford U. Med. Ctr., dir. Hosp. Modernization Project; exec. v.p., COO Lucile Packard Children's Hosp., 1997, sr. v.p., COO, pres., CEO, 2000—. Office: Lucile Packard Children's Hosp 725 Welch Rd Palo Alto CA 94304

DAWSON, GERALDINE, psychologist, educator; b. Cobleskill, NY, Mar. 29, 1951; d. Frank Gates Dawson Jr. and Beta (Holmes) Dale; m. Charles Joseph Coates, July 21, 1985; children: Christopher Staats, Margaret Coates. BS in Psychology, U. Wash., 1974, PhD in Psychology, 1979. Lic. Psychologist, NC, Develop. Disabilities, Clin. Psychologist, Wash. State. Postdoctoral fellow, Neuropsychiaitric Inst. U. Calif., LA, 1979—80; rsch. assoc., divsn. TEACCH, dept. psychiatry U. NC, Chapel Hill, 1980, asst. prof. psychology, 1980-85, rsch. prof., dept. psychiatry, 2008—; dir., child clin. psychology program U. Wash., Seattle, 1985—91, dir., UAP Autism Clin. Program, Ctr. on Human Develop. and Disability, 1997—99, dir., autism clin. program, Ctr. on Human Develop. and Disability, 1997—2000, dir., child clin. psychology grad. program, 1999—2004, co-dir., Integrated Brain Imaging Ctr., 2003—05, assoc. prof. psychology, 1985—90, prof. psychology, 1990—2007, dir. child clin. psychology program, 1985-91, prof. emeritus psychology, 2008—; chief sci. officer Autism Speaks, NYC, 2008—. Dir. NICHDC/NIDCD Ctr. on the Neurobiology and Genetics Autism, 1996—2006, U. Wash. Ctr. Excellence in Autsim Rsch., part of NIMH STAART, 2003—08, U. Wash. Autism Ctr. Excellence, Part of NIH ACE program, 2007—08; founding dir. U. Wash. Autism Ctr., 2000—07; adj. prof. psychiatry and behavioral scis. U. Wash., 2003—07; consensus panelist NIH Consensus Conf. on PKU, 1999—2000; mem. strategic planning com. Autism Treatment Network, 2007—; mem. NIH Baby Siblings Rsch. Consortium, 2005—07; mem. Ctr. on Disease Control workgroup on early child develop., 2005—08; advisor/cons. John D. and Catherine T. MacArthur Found., 1996—2000, Ctr. for Disease Control in Atlanta, 2002, Ctr. for Children's Environ. Health and Disease Prevention, U. Calif. Davis M.I.N.D. Inst., 2002—06, Inst. Medicine, 2003, Nastech, Inc., 2007—08, Integragen, Inc., 2006—, mem. profl. adv. bd., 2008—, State of the Art, Inc., Project on Early Detection of Autism, 2003—06, First Signs: Early Signs of Autism, 2004—, Austism Spectrum Quarterly, 2004—, Guildford Press, Inc., NYC, 2005—, TeachTown, Inc., 2004—, Autism Speaks 100 Day Kit for Families, 2007, Northwest Acad. for Exceptional Children, 2007; mem. sci. adv. bd. Vanderbilt U. Kennedy Ctr., 2002—07, M.I.N.D. Inst., U. Calif., Sacremento, 2002—07, Cure Autism Now Found., 1998—2007, bd. dirs. U. Wash. Found., 2003—06; mem. Wash. State Task Force on Autism, 1997—99, 2005—07, Wash. State Task Force on Edn. for Children with Autism, 1990—93. Editor: Autism: Nature, Diagnosis and Treatment, 1989; co-editor Human Behavior and the Developing Brain, 1994, A Parent's Guide to Asperger Syndrome and High-Functioning Autism: How to Meet the Challenges and Help Your Child Thrive, 2002, Human Behavior and the Developing Brain, 2nd edit.:Atypical Development, 2007, Human Behavior and the Developing Brain, 2nd edit.: Typical Development, 2007, assoc. editor Journal of Autism and Developmental Disorders, 1996-2000; mem. editl. bd. Autism Rsch. 2007-; ad hoc reviewer for several profl. jours.; contbr. articles to profl. jours. Mem. profl. adv. bd. Autism Soc. Wash., 1990—2007, Autism Soc. Am., 2004—. Grantee NIH; Child Develop. and Mental Retardation Fellowship award, U. Wash., 1976-77, Gatzert Child Welfare award, 1977-78, Wash. Autism Soc. Achievement award for Outstanding Svc., 1996, NICHD and NIDCD award for U. Wash. Collaborative Program of Excellence in Autism, 1996, Autism Soc. Am. Honoree Rsch. Contbns. to Autism Cmty., 2004, Autism Soc. Wash. Med. Profl. of Yr., 2004, Autism Hero award Cure Autism Now Found., 2006. Fellow APA, Am. Psychol. Soc.; mem. Soc. Rsch. in Child Devel., Internat. Soc. for Autism Rsch. (mem. exec. com. 2002-2003), Internat. Soc. on Early Intervention, Soc. for Rsch. in Child Develop., Soc. for Rsch. Child Psychopathology, Soc. for Rsch. in Child and Adolescent Psychiatry, Soc. for Rsch. in Psychopathology. Achievements include research in areas of autism and childhood depression. Office: U Wash Dept Psychology Office CHDD-CD386 Box 351525 Seattle WA 98195-1525 also: Autism Speaks 2 Park Ave 11th Fl New York NY 10010 Office Phone: 206-543-1051, 212-252-8584. Office Fax: 206-685-3157, 212-252-8676. Business E-Mail: dawson@u.washington.edu.

DAWSON, GERALDINE, medical educator, social worker; b. Huntington, Pa., Oct. 2, 1945; d. Donn and Evelyn Koontz; m. Nathan Maniam. BA, Pa. State U., 1967; MSW, Smith Coll., 1969; MD, Albert Einstein Coll. Medicine, 1988. Fellow Harvard Med. Sch.-Mass. Gen. Hosp., Boston, 1980—82, All India Inst. Med. Sci., New Delhi, 1987—88; med. resident Lenox Hill Hosp., NYC, 1988—89; cons. Dept. of Def., Washington, 1990—92; assoc. prof. Marywood U., Scranton, Pa., 1993—. Contbr. articles to profl. jours. Mem. adv. coun. Regional Health Edn. Ctr. N.E. Pa., Scranton, 2001—; mem. Pa. Health Edn. Interdisciplinary Task Force, Hershey, 2002—. Named N.E. Woman, Scranton Times, 2000, Excellence in Their Field, Johnstown Tribune Democrat, 2000. Mem.: Pa. Nat. Alliance Mentally Ill, Pa. Nat. Assn. Social Workers (chairperson profl. stds. com. 1997—2003), Am. Psychotherapy Assn. (diplomate). Office Phone: 570-348-6282 ext 2390. Business E-Mail: dawson@marywood.edu.

DAWSON, PATRICIA LUCILLE, surgeon; b. Kingston, Jamaica, W.I., Sept. 30, 1949; arrived in U.S., 1950; d. Percival Gordon and Edna Claire (Overton) D.; children: Alexandria Z. Rooney, Wesley Gordon Hiserman BA in Sociology, Allegheny Coll., 1971; MD, N.J. Med. Sch., Newark, 1977; MA in Human and Orgn. Devel., The Fielding Inst., 1996, PhD in Human and Orgnl. Sys., 1998. Membership dir. N.J. ACLU, Newark, 1972; resident in surgery U. Medicine and Dentistry N.J. Med Sch., 1977-79; resident in surgery Virginia Mason Med. Ctr., Seattle, 1979-82; pvt. practice specializing in surgery Arlington, Wash., 1982-83; dir. med. staff diversity Group Health Coop., Seattle, 1993-98, staff surgeon, 1983-98; pvt. practice Seattle, 1998—2003; breast surgeon Swedish Cancer Inst., 2004—. Author: Forged by the Knife—The Experience of Surgical Residency from the Perspective of a Woman of Color, 1999 Fellow ACS, Seattle Surg. Soc.; mem. Physicians for Social Responsibility, Assn. Women Surgeons, Wash. Black Profls. in Health Care, NOW. Avocations: walking, cooking. Office: Cherry Hill Campus Comp Breast Ctr Jefferson Twr 1600 E Jefferson St Ste 300 Seattle WA 98122-5645 Home Phone: 206-725-1223; Office Phone: 206-320-4880.

DAWSON, STEVEN LEE, radiologist, researcher; b. Corning, NY, Feb. 26, 1952; s. Douglas and Lena Dawson; m. Debra Rowen, May 28, 1978; 1 child, David Douglas. BA in Biology, SUNY, 1974; MD, Tufts U., Boston, 1978. Intern Newton-Wellesley Hosp., Newton, Mass., 1978—79; resident in radiology Mass. Gen. Hosp., 1979—82, fellow, interventional radiology, 1982—84, interventional radiologist Boston, 1984—; rsch. lead, med. simulation MGH - Cimit, Cambridge, Mass., 1994—; assoc. prof. Harvard Med. Sch. Founder, chair Advanced Initiatives in Med. Simulation, DC, 2004—07. Recipient Edward M. Kennedy award, Cmit, 2003, Satava award, Medicine Meets Virtual Reality, 2004, Army's Top Ten Greatest Inventions award, US Dept. Def., 2004. Fellow: Soc. Interventional Radiology, Cardiovasc. and Interventional Radiology Soc. Europe (corr.). Achievements include first computer-based training system for high-risk cardiac interventions; invention of simulation system for training high-risk interventional procedures in the brain; simulation system for training in treatment of chest trauma; simulation system for training in minimally invasive surgery; first commercialized simulation system for trauma drawing. Office: SimGroup MGH - CIMIT 65 Landsdowne St Cambridge MA 02139

DAY, CAROL R.T., nursing educator, director; d. Paul Robert and Ray Rita Tyler; m. Robert Dwain Day, Sept. 8, 1973; children: Leslie Carroll, Ryan Tyler. BSN, Radford Coll., Va., 1973; MS in Nursing, U. SC, Columbia, 1977. Cert. Bd. Nutrition Specialists, 1995. Adj. asst. prof., sch. nursing and health studies Georgetown U., Washington, 1980—, dir. health edn. svcs., 1989—, prin. investigator rsch. emotional intelligence and coll. health, 2006—; faculty advisor Georgetown Emergency Response Med. Svc., 2000—, hon. mem., 2011. Recipient Student Affairs award, Georgetown U., 1995, 1998, Outstanding Contbn. award, 2001, Vicennial medal, 2010, Elizabeth Cady Stanton award, Feminists Life, 2005, Outstanding Cmty. Based Learning award, Georgetown U. Ctr. Social Justice Rsch., Tchg. & Svc., 2011; Harm Reduction grant, Ctr. Social Norms, U. Va., 2001—, Innovative Practices grant, ACHA, Koster Ins., 2004—05, grant, Dept. Justice, 2003—04, Engelhard Found., 2007—08, Curriculum Infusion grant, 2006—. Mem.: NASPA, Am. Assn. U. Women, Am. Coll. Nutrition, Am. Coll. Health Assn., Sigma Theta Tau. Office: Georgetown Univ Village C W 207 Washington DC 20057 Office Phone: 202-687-8942. Office Fax: 202-687-8948. Business E-Mail: daycr@georgetown.edu.

DAY, MARY ANN, medical/surgical nurse; b. Covington, Tenn., Apr. 9, 1944; m. George Day, Jan. 17, 1980; children: Maurice, Michele, Shawn, Corey. AAS, Joliet Jr. Coll., Ill., 1989; BSN, Lewis U., 1995; student, U. St. Francis, 1998—; BSN, CRNI. RN, Ill.; cert. emergency nurse pediat. course. Staff nurse Michael Reese Hosp., Chgo., 1989-91, MacNeal Hosp., Berwyn, Ill., 1991-99, Westlake Hosp., Melrose Park, Ill., 1999—; adj. faculty/LPN program Triton Coll., River Grove, Ill., 1996—, instr. RN continuing edn. course, 1998—; asst. patient care mgr. St. Joseph Hosp., Joliet, Ill., 1999—; IV therapist Ctrl. Dupage Hosp., Winfield, Ill., 1999—, nursing supr. St. Anthony's Hosp., Chgo., 2001—. Mem. diversity task force com., Westlake Hosp., 1999; instr. in nursing assistance Waubonsee Coll., 2002; weekend supr. VNA Home Health; adj. faculty nurse asst. program, Moraine Valley CC, 2005. Nominee Black Profl. Female scholarship, Minority Student of Yr., 1989. Mem.: CRNI-INS, Ill. Chpt. Avocations: classical music, classical pianist. Home: 6 Puffin Cir Bolingbrook IL 60440-1236

DAY, PETER RODNEY, geneticist, educator; b. Chingford, Essex, Eng., Dec. 27, 1928; came to U.S., 1963; m. Lois Elizabeth Rhodes, May 26, 1951; children: Susan Catherine, Rupert Peter, William Rodney. BS in Botany, Birkbeck Coll., Eng., 1950; PhD, U. London, 1954. Sr. scientific officer John Innes Inst., Hertford, Eng., 1957-63; assoc. prof. Ohio State U., Columbus, 1963-64; chief, genetics dept. Conn. Agrl. Expt. Sta., New Haven, 1964-79; dir. Plant Breeding Inst., Cambridge, Eng., 1979-87; prof. genetics, dir. Rutgers U., New Brunswick, NJ, 1987—2002, prof. emeritus, 2002—. Sec. Internat. Genetics Fedn., 1984-93; trustee Internat. Ctr. for Maize and Wheat Improvement, Mexico City, 1986-92; chmn. Mng. Global Genetic Resources Bd. on Agrl., NAS, Washington, 1986-93. Author: Genetics of Host-Parasite Interaction, 1974; co-author: (with J.R.S. Fincham) Fungal Genetics, 1963, (with H.H. Prell) Plant-Fungal Pathogen Interaction, 2001. Commonwealth Fund fellow U. Wis., 1954-56; Guggenheim Meml. fellow U. Queensland, 1972. Home: 8200 Tarsier Ave New Port Richey FL 34653 E-mail: p1rd@verizon.net.

DAY, STACEY BISWAS, physician, educator; b. London, Dec. 31, 1927; came to U.S. 1955, naturalized 1977. s. Satis B. and Emma L. (Camp) D.; m. Ivana Podvalova, Oct. 18, 1973; children Kahil Amyn, Selim. MD, Royal Coll. Surgeons, Dublin, Ireland, 1955; PhD, McGill U., 1964; DSc, Cin. U., 1971. Intern King's County Hosp., SUNY Downstate Ctr., 1955-56; resident fellow in surgery U. Minn. Hosp., 1956-60; hon. registrar St. George's Hosp., London, 1960-61; lectr. exptl. surgery McGill U., Montreal, Que., Canada, 1964; asst. prof. exptl. surgery U. Cin. Med. Sch., 1968-70; assoc. dir. basic med. rsch. Shriner's Burn Inst., Cin., 1969-71; from asst. to assoc. prof. pathology, head Bell Mus. Pathobiology U. Minn., Mpls., 1970-74; dir. biomed. comm. and med. edn. Sloan-Kettering Inst., NYC, 1974-80; mem. Sloan-Kettering Inst. for Cancer Rsch., 1974-80; mem. adminstrv. coun., field coordinator, 1974-75; prof. biology Sloan Kettering divsn. Grad. Sch. Med. Sci. Cornell U., 1974-80; clin. prof. medicine divsn. behavioral medicine NY Med. Coll., 1980-92; prof. biopsychosocial medicine, chmn. dept. cmty. health U. Calabar Sch. Medicine, Nigeria, 1982-85; prof. internat. health, dir. Internat. Ctr. for Health Scis. Meharry Med. Coll., Nashville, 1985-89, dir. WHO Collaborating Ctr. ICHS, 1987-89; founding dir. WHO Collaborating Ctr., Nashville, 1987-89, emeritus dir., 1989; adj. prof. family and cmty. medicine U. Ariz. Coll. Med. Scis., Tucson, 1985-89; univ. prof. internat. health U. Calabar, Nigeria, 1989—; permanent vis. prof. med. edn. Oita Med. U., Japan, 1992-99. Arris and Gale lectr. Royal Coll. Surgeons, England, 1972; vis. lectr., Ireland, 72; vis. prof. U. Bologna, 1977, Kyushu, Japan, 90, U. Mauritius, 1991, Bratislava U., 1991, U. Tokyo, Japan, 1992—93, U. Nagasaki, Japan, 1992—93, Beijing, 1993; vis. prof. health comm. U. Santiago, Chile, 1979—80, Colombo, Sri Lanka, 1996; vis. prof. Oncologic Rsch. Inst., Tallinn, Estonia, 1976, All India Insts. Health, 1976, U. Maidugari, 1982, Vellore U., India, 1996, De Quito, Ecuador, 1996; vis. acad. Oxford (Eng.) U., 1993—95; moderator med. cartography and computer health Harvard U., 1978, Acad. Scis., Czech Republic, 1987, Australia, 88; Fulbright prof. Charles U., Czech Republic, 1989; prof. (hon.) Coll. Health Scis. U. San Francisco de Quito (Ecuador), 1996; cons. Pan Am. Health Assn., 1974—90, US-USSR Agreement for Health Cooperation, 1976, WHO Collaborating Ctr. Meharry Med. Coll., Nashville, 1985, NAFEO/USAID, 1986—89; mem. expert com. for health, manpower devel. WHO, 1986—90, cons. divsn. strengthening health care resources, 1987—90, UN-FSSTD, 1987, AID/Joint Memorandum of Understanding Africa, Kenya, 1987—89, West Africa, 1987—89, Sudan, 1985—89; cons. to dean med. coll. faculty med. and health scis. ABHA, Asir, Saudi Arabia, 1981; cons. to dir. High Tatras symposia Post Grad. Med. Inst., Bratislava, 1990—; cons. to rector U. Autónoma Agraria Antonio Narro, Saltillo, Mexico, 1987—89; pres., chmn. Pub. Cultural and Ednl. Prodns., Montreal, Canada, 1966—85; bd. dirs., v.p. Am. Sci. Activities Mario Negri Found., 1975—80; bd. dirs. Internat. Health, African Health Consultancy Svc., Nigeria, Ekologia & Zivot, Slovakia; founding chmn. (hon.), bd. dirs. Lambo Found. U.S.; v.p., trustee Cancer Relief Found., Calabar; pres., exec. dir. Internat. Found. Biosocial Devel. and Human Health, 1978—86, chmn., 1986—; mem. Medzinárodny Poradny Vybor Nadácie Ekológia Zivot, Slovakia, 1995—; cons. Inst. Health, Lyfford Cay, Bahamas, 1981, Govt. Cross River State, Nigeria, Itreto State and H.H. Obong of Calabar, Nat. Bd. Advisors, Am. Biog. Inst., 1982—; cons. cmty. health and health comms. Navaho Nation, Sage Meml. Hosp., Ganado, Ariz., 1984; founder, cons. Primary Self-Health Clinics, Oban, Ikot Oku Okono and Ikot Imo, Nigeria, 1982—84; cons. High Tatras Internat. Health Symposia, Slovakia, 1990—; apptd. ab. Gov. State of Tenn., 1986—; adj. clin. prof. medicine NY Med. Coll.; prof. (hon.) Colegio Ciencias Salud U. San Francisco, Quito, 1965—. Author: (verse) Collected Lines, 1966, (plays) By the Waters of Babylon, 1966, (verse) American Lines, 1967, (plays) The Music Box, 1967, Three Folk Songs Set to Music, 1967, Poems and Etudes, 1968, (novels) Rosalita, 1968, The Idle Thoughts of a Surgical Fellow, 1968, Edward Stevens-Gastric Physiologist, Physician and American Statesman, 1969, Letters to Ivana from Calabar, 2001, (novella) Bellechasse, 1970, A Leaf of the Chaatim, 1970, Ten Poems and a Letter from America for Mr. Sinha, 1971, Curling's Ulcer: An Experiment of Nature, 1972, Tuluak and Amaulik: Dialogues on Death and Mourning with the Innuit Eskimo of Point Barrow and Wainwright, Alaska, 1974, East of the Navel and Afterbirth: Reflections from Rapa Nui, 1976, Health Communications, 1979, The Biopsychosocial Imperative, 1981, What Is Survival: The Physician's Way and the Biologos, 1981, Developing Health in the West African Bush, 2 parts, 1995; author: (in Czech) Moudrost Samuraju, 1998; author: Selected Poems and Embers of a Medical Life, 1999, In the Shadow of the Bush - Letters from Calabar, 2000, Vitaesophia of Integral Humanism, 2001, The Klacelka in a Slavic Woodland, 2003, The Wisdom of Hagakure, 1996, Nensokan: Moon in a Dewdrop, 2007; editor: Death and Attitudes Toward Death, 1972, Membranes, Viruses and Immune Mechanisms in Experimental and Clinical Disease, 1972, Ethics in Medicine in a Changing Society, 1973, Communication of Scientific Information, 1975, Trauma: Clinical and Biological Aspects, 1975, Molecular Pathology, 1975; editor: (with Robert A. Good) (series) Comprehensive Immunology, 9 vols., 1976—80; editor: Cancer Invasion and Metastasis-Biologic Mechanisms and Therapy, 1977, Some Systems of Biological Communication, 1977, Image of Science and Society, 1977, What Is A Scientist?, 1978, Sloan Kettering Inst. Cancer Series, 1974—80; editor: (with K. Inokouchi) Selections from the Chronicle of the Hagakure as Wisdom Literature: The Way of The Samurai of Saga Domain, 1993; editor-in-chief, mem. editl. bd. Health Communications and Informatics, 1974—80, editor in chief The American Biomedical Network: Health Care System in America Present and Past, 1978, A Companion to the Life Sciences, Vol. 1, 1979, A Companion to the Life Sciences, Vol. 2, Integrated Medicine, 1980, A Companion to the Life Sciences, Vol. 3, Life Stress, 1981, Advance to Biopsychosocial Health, 1984, editor in chief, mem. editorial bd. Health Communications and Biopsychosocial Health; editor (with others): Cancer, Stress and Death, 1979, 2nd edit., 1986; editor: Computers for Medical Office and Patient Management, 1981, Readings in Oncology, 1980, Biopsychosocial Health, 1981, Primary Health Care Guidelines: A Training Manual for Community Health, 2nd edit., 1986; editor: (with T.A. Lambo) Contemporary Issues in International Health, 1989; sr. editor, with Salat and others Health and Quality of Life in Changing Europe in the Year 2000, 1992, sr. editor, with H. Koga Hagakure-Spirit of Bushido, 1993, sr. editor, with K. Inokuchi Selections from the Chronicles of the Hagakure as Wisdom Literature: The Way of the Samurai of Saga Domain, 1993, sr. editor, with Salát Health Management, Organization, and Planning in Changing Eastern Europe, 1993, sr. editor, with M. Kobayashi and K. Inokuchi, in Japanese The Medical Student and the Mission of Medicine in the Twenty First Century, 1995, sr. editor Letters of Owen Wagensteen to a Surgical Fellow: with a memoir, 1996, Man and Mu: The Cradle of Becoming and Unbecoming, 1997, Czech Caesura: Golden Prague and the Black Years (Notes from Diaries 1970-1990), 1998, Moudrost Samuraju Trigon (in Czech), 1998, Poems and Embers of a Medical Life, 1998, The Surgical Treatment of Ischaemic Heart Disease with An Account of the Coronary and Intercoronary Circulation in Man and Animals, 1999, Introduction-Comprehensive Medicine (Oriental-Occidental Overview), 2000, Letters to Ivana from Calabar, 2001, Purkynje Address and Other Health Care Lectures Czechoslovakia 1989-1999, 2002, Pliskova's Butterflies-When God Says Enough, 2003, mem. editl. bd. Annual Reviews on Stress, Jour. Stress, cons. editl. bd. Comprehensive Medicine (Japan), Wilhelm Von Humboldt Über Die Unter Dem Namen Bhagavad Gita with commentary, 2001, Purkyne Address and Other Healthcare Lectures, 1989-1999; co-editor: various publs.; contbr. articles; prodr.: TV and health edn. programs, 1982—85, (TV film) Onchocerciasis-River Blindness in Africa, 1988; co-author: A Season of Flowers in Death Valley and the California Deserts, 2005; co-author: (with Ivana P. Day) In Search of the Desert Five Spot, 2006; translator: Problem of a Small Nation, 2010. Served with Brit. Army, 1946-49. Recipient Moynihan medal Assn. Surgeons Gt. Britain and Ireland, 1960, Reuben Harvey triennial prize Royal Coll. Physicians, Ireland, 1957, Arris and Gale award Royal Coll. Surgeons, Eng., 1972, disting. scholar award Internat. Communication Assn., 1980, Sama Found. medal, 1982, disting. citation Hagakure Soc., 1992, Nat. Svc. medal Royal Brit. Legion, 1993; named to Hon. Order Ky. Cols., 1968; named Chieftan Ntufam Ajan of Oban Ejagham People, Cross River State, Nigeria, 1983; hon. prof. Del Colegio De Ciencas De La Salud De La Universidad San Francisco De Quito, 1996; recipient Chieftan Obong Nsong Idem Ibibio Nigeria, 1983, Mgbe (Ekpe) honor Nigeria, commendation WHO address Fed. Govt. Nigeria, Calabar, 1983, Leadership in Internat. Med. Health citation Pres. US, 1987, WHO medal, 1987, Agromedicine citation Commr. of Agr., State of Tenn., 1987, Assembly citation State of N.Y., 1987, Citation Congl. Record., 1987; Maestro Honorifo, U. Autonoma Agraria, Coahuila, Mex., 1987; presented Key to the City of Nashville, 1987; recipient Vice-Chancellor's Citation and Presentation for Primary Health Care Teaching in Nigeria, U. Calabar, 1988; Pamétni medal Postgrad. Med. Coll., Prague, 1991, Gold medal U. of Bratislava, 1991, Disting. Citation Hagakure Rsch. Soc., Japan, 1992, Nat. Svc. medal Royal Brit. Legion, 1993, Citation Commendation from Pres. Kyoto Prefectural U. Medicine, Japan, 1993, Citation Commendation on Contbn. to Med. Edn. from Pres. Oita Med. U., Japan, 1997; addresses presented by people of Ikot Imo, Nsit Anyang, Oban, 1982-84, Commendation from King of Calabar, 1984; Ciba fellow Can., 1965; Stacey Day Ward named in his honor by Fed. Min. and Gov. of Cross River State, Calabar Med. Ctr., Nigeria, 1986; charter mem. U.S. Normandy Com., 1988; 1st fgn. hon. mem. Hagakure Res. Soc. (Samurai), Kyushu, Japan, 1991. Fellow: African Acad. Med. Scis. (founder), African Acad. Sci., World Acad. Arts and Scis., Japanese Found. for Biopsychosocial Health (internat. hon. fellow and most disting. mem.), Zool. Soc. London Royal Micros. Soc., Royal Soc. Health; mem.: APHA, AMA, AAS, Adelaide Hosp. Soc. (Ireland), Soc. Med. Geographers USSR, Am. Rural Health Assn. (v.p. internat. sci. affairs, bd. dirs.), Am. Anthrop. Assn., Am. Inst. Stress (bd. dirs.), Am. Assn. History Medicine, NY Acad. Scis., Can. Authors Assn., Internat. Burn Assn., Am. Burn Assn. Home: 6 Lomond Ave Chestnut Ridge NY 10977 Home (Summer): Ruzinovska 1228 14200 Prague Czech Republic E-mail: camp27day@yahoo.com.

DAY, TERRENCE A., otolaryngologist, educator; MD, U. of Okla., Okla. City, 1989. Resident otolaryngology La. State Univ. Med. Ctr., Shreveport, 1990—95; fellow craniomaxillofacial surgery Univ. Hosp., Bern, Switzerland, 1994; fellow head and neck oncologic surgery Univ. of Calif. Davis Med. Ctr., Davis, Calif., 1995—96; prof. otolaryngology - head and neck surgery College of Medicine Med. Univ. of SC, vice chair for clin. affairs dept. of otolaryngology - head and neck surgery. Co-author: (publs.) Head and neck cancer disparities in South Carolina: descriptive epidemiology, early detection, and special programs, 2006, Driving performance in patients with cancer in the head and neck region: a pilot study, 2007, Effect of body mass index on chemoradiation outcomes in head and neck cancer, 2008, Effectiveness of calcium hydroxylapatite paste in vocal rehabilitation, 2009, Use of alpha,25-dihydroxyvitamin D3 treatment to stimulate immune infiltration into head and neck squamous cell carcinoma, 2010, and numerous others. Office: Medical University of South Carolina Hollings Cancer Center 86 Jonathan Lucas St Charleston SC 29425 Office Phone: 843-792-0700.

DAYA, SHERAZ MANSOOR, ophthalmic surgeon, health facility administrator; b. Nairobi, Kenya, Feb. 1, 1960; arrived in U.K., 1973; s. Mansoor Mohemadali and Sakerkhanoo (Tejani) D.; m. Marcela Milagros Espinosa-Lagana, Sept. 25, 1998; children: Olivia Sheherezadh, Fernando Sheraz. MB, BChir, BAO with honors, Royal Coll. Surgeons, 1984. Diplomate Am. Bd. Internal Medicine, Am. Bd. Ophthalmology. Resident in internal medicine N.Y. Infirmary-Beekman, 1988-91; fellow in cornea U. Minn., Mpls., 1991-92; resident in ophthalmology Cath. Med. Ctr., NY, 1991-98, dir. corneal svcs. NY, 1992-94; dir., cons. Corneoplastic Unit Eye Bank, Queen Victoria Hosp., 1994—; dir. Ctr. for Sight, East Orinstead, England, 1997—. Ocular tissue adv. group U.K. Transplant Spl. Svcs., Bristol, Eng., 1994—; vis. prof. Mil. Hosp., Alexandria, Egypt, 1997, U. Pitts., 2003; Tom Casey lectr. Contbr.: The Eye and Skin, 1995; chief med. editor Cataract and Rep. Surgery (Europe); contbr. articles to profl. jours. Recipient Sr. Achievement award Am. Acad. Ophthalmology, 1999, 2009, Silver award Dept. of Health, South East Winner Leadership impovement award, 2008. Fellow Royal Coll. Surgeons, ACS, ACP, Internat. Coll. Surgeons, Royal Coll. Ophthalmologists; mem. Internat. Soc. Refractive Surgery (internat. coun. 1997—), European Soc. Cataracts/Refractive Surgery (refractive com. 1997—), U.K. Soc. Cataract and Refractive Surgery (coun. 1995—, mem. cornea com.), Ganea Soc. (bd. dirs.). Avocations: squash, art, travel. Office: 38 Queen Anne Street W1G 8HZ London England Business E-Mail: sdaya@centreforsight.com.

DAYANANDA, GIRIYAPPA, physiologist, physician, diabetologist, researcher; s. Giriyappa and Lakshmamma; m. Suma Dayananda, Oct. 17, 2004; 1 child, Mohith. MBBS, Sree Siddhartha Med. Coll. & Rsch. Hosp., Tumkur, Karnataka, India, 2001; MD in Human Physiology, M. S. Ramaiah Med. Coll., Bangalore, Karnataka, 2006; postgrad. diploma in Diabetes Mellitus, Vinayaka Missions U., Salem, Tamilnadu, India, 2007—08; postgrad. diploma in Med. Law and Ethics, Nat. Law Sch. India U., Bangalore, 2009—. Cert. in clin. electro-physiology Nat. Inst. Mental Health and Neuro Scis., Bangalore, 2005, in nat. sleep medicine Indian Soc. Sleep Rsch., Nat. Inst. Mental Health and Neuro Scis., Bangalore, 2007, in basic trauma and life support M. S. Ramaiah Med. Coll. & Hosp., 2008, in diabetology Cleve. Clinic, 2010, registered Med. Coun., Bangalore, 2003, Med. Coun., Bangalore, 2006. Tutor M. S. Ramaiah Med. Coll. and Hosp., Dept. Physiology, 2003—06, sr. resident, 2006, asst. prof., coord., 2008—, mem. grad. day com., 2009—; asst. prof. Sree Siddhartha Med. Coll. & Rsch. Hosp., Tumkur, 2006—08, mem., med. edn. com., 2006—08; mem. bd. studies Sri Siddhartha Acad. Higher Edn., 2006—08. Recipient Letter of appreciation for the attempts at rsch. publ., M S Ramaiah Med. Coll., Bangalore, India. Master: Indian Soc. Pain Rsch. & Therapy (life); fellow: Acad. Gen. Edn. (Manipal, Karnataka); mem.: Indian Assn. Biomed. Scientists (life), Zydus Pharma (life; CND academic mem.), Rsch. Soc. Study Diabetes India (life), Indian Med. Assn. (life), Assn. Physiologists and Pharmacologists India (life). Hindu. Avocations: drawing, painting, mountain climbing. Home: 624 8th B Main 3rd Stage 2nd Block West of Chord Rd Basaveshwarnagar Bangalore Karnataka 560079 India Office: M S Ramaiah Med Coll and Hosp MSRIT Post Mathikere Bangalore Karnataka 560054 India Personal E-mail: dr.daya@rediffmail.com. Business E-Mail: g.dayananda@gmail.com.

DAYANGAC, MURAT, transplant surgeon; b. Kayseri, Turkey, Jan. 1, 1972; MD, Ege U. Sch. Medicine, 1995. Surgery resident Ege U. Sch. Medicine, 1996—2002, cons., dept. gen. surgery, 2002—04; fellow Florence Nightingale Hosp., Ctr. Organ Transplantation, 2005—07, surgeon, 2007—. Mem.: European Asian Liver Transplantation Soc., Liver Transplantation Soc., Internat. Assn. Surgeons, Gastroenterologists and Oncologists, European Soc. Transplantation. Avocation: baroque music. Office: Abide-I Hurriyet Cad 290 Sisli Istanbul 34381 Turkey

DAYEM, MOHAMED KHAIRY ABDEL, cardiologist, educator; b. Cairo, Feb. 5, 1937; s. Mahmoud Helmy Abdel Dayem and Hanem Mohamed Rizk; m. Kouka Saad El Din Abdel Wahab, Apr. 16, 1964; children: Hoda Mohamed Khairy children: Tarek Mohamed Khairy, Hesham Mohamed Khairy. MB BCh, U. Cairo, 1959; PhD, U. London, 1966. Lic. physician Min. Public Health, Egypt, 1960. Intern Kasr El Aini Hosp., 1960; resident Kasrel Aini Hosp., 1961—63; rsch. fellow postgrad med. sch. U. London, 1964—66; lectr. U. Ain Shams, Cairo, 1966—72, asst. prof. cardiology, 1972—78, prof. cardiology, 1978—86; chmn. Dept. Cardiology U. Of Ain Shams, Cairo, 1986—92; vice dean Faculty Of Medicine U. Ain Shams, Cairo, 1995—97, prof. cardiology, 1997—. Chief Dept. Cardiology Misr Internat. Hosp., Cairo, 1983—. Author: Understanding Cardiology, 1977 (Ideal Dr. award, 1995), 7th edit., 2004; contbr. over 100 articles to profl. jours. Fellow, Royal Coll. Physicians Edinburgh, 1978, Royal Coll. Physicians London, 1985. Fellow: Am. Coll. Cardiology; mem.: Panarab Soc. Cardiology (past pres., chmn. Egyptian working group electrophysiology and pacing), Egyptian Soc. Cardiology (vice chmn.), European Soc. Cardiology. Home: 32 Babel St Dokki Cairo 12311 Egypt Office: Misr Internat Hosp Saraya St Dokki Cairo Egypt Home Fax: (202)3373547. Personal E-mail: mkhairy@idsc.net.eg.

DAYNARD, RICHARD ALAN, law educator; b. NYC, July 19, 1943; s. David M. and Sarah (Weidenbaum) D.; m. Carol S. Iskols, Aug. 9, 1975; children: David J., Gabriela C. BA, Columbia U., 1964, MA in Sociology, 1970; JD, Harvard U., 1967; PhD in Urban Studies and Planning, MIT, 1980. Bar: N.Y. 1967, U.S. Ct. Appeals (6th cir.) 1986, U.S. Supreme Ct. 1986, U.S. Ct. Appeals (11th cir.) 1987, U.S. Ct. Appeals (5th cir.) 1996. Law clk. 2d cir. US Ct. Appeals, NYC, 1967-68; tchg. fellow Columbia U., NYC, 1968-69; asst. prof. law Northeastern U., Boston, 1969-71, assoc. prof. law, 1971-73, prof. law, 1973—, assoc. dean acad. affairs, 2004—06; William Cahan disting. prof. Flight Attendants Med. Rsch. Inst., Miami, Fla., 2005—. Chmn. law and obesity project Pub. Health Advocacy Inst., 2002—; lectr., cons. in field. Editor-in-chief Tobacco Products Litigation Reporter, 1985-2006; assoc. editor: Tobacco Control: An Internat. Jour., 1998—; contbr. articles to profl. jours. Chmn. Tobacco Products Liability Project, Boston, 1984—; pres. Group Against Smoking Pollution of Mass., Boston, 1983-, Clean Indoor Air Ednl. Found., Boston, 1983-92, Tobacco Control Resource Ctr., Inc., Boston, 1993-2006, Pub. Health Advocacy Inst., 2006—; pres. Stop Teenage Addiction to Tobacco, 1996-98; chair lay adv. bd. Flight Attendants Med. Rsch. Inst., 2003-05; bd. mem. Framework Conv. Alliance, 2006—, exec. com., 2007-, vice chair, 2009-11. Mem. ABA, Am. Pub. Health Assn., Law and Soc. Assn., Phi Beta Kappa. Home: 90 Commonwealth Ave Boston MA 02116-3040 Office: Northeastern U Sch Law 400 Huntington Ave Boston MA 02115-5005 Office Phone: 617-373-2026. E-mail: r.daynard@neu.edu.

DAY-SALVATORE, DEBRA LYNN, medical geneticist; b. Hoboken, NJ, Oct. 23, 1953; m. Francis P. Salvatore, Sr., Dec. 24, 1988. BA in Biology, Harvard U., 1975; MS in Pharmacology, NYU, 1979, PhD in Pharmacology, 1982; MD, Case Western Res. U., 1986. Diplomate Am. Bd. Med. Genetics, Am. Bd. Pediats. Grad. fellow dept. pharmacology NYU Med. Ctr., 1978-79; sr. rsch. asst. dept. medicine Case Western Res. U., Cleve., 1979-82, rsch. assoc. dept. molecular biology and microbiology, 1982-84; pediatric and adolescent medicine resident Cleve. Clinic Found., 1986-89; med. genetics fellow Robert Wood Johnson Med. Sch., New Brunswick, NJ, 1990-91, asst. prof. pediatrics, 1990—, coord. perinatal genetics dept. ob-gyn., 1991-92, dir. divsn. reproductive and perinatal genetics dept. ob-gyn., 1992—, asst. prof. ob-gyn. and reproductive scis. and pediatrics, 1992—, acting chief divsn. clin. genetics, dept. ob-gyn. and reproductive scis., 1993—; physician Robert Wood Johnson Univ. Hosp., New Brunswick, 1990—, St. Peter's Med. Ctr., 1992—, chief divsn. clin. genetics, 1996—. Mem. genetic adv. bd. N.J. State Dept. Health's Parental and Child Adv. Com.; mem. med. adv. bd. Cryo-Cell Internat. Genetics editor Jour. of Perinatology, 1993—; contbr. articles, abstracts to profl. jours. Cons. N.J. Interagency Adoption Coun. Mem. AAAS, AMA, Am. Acad. Pediatrics (mem. N.J. chpt.), Am. Soc. Cell Biology, Am. Soc. Human Genetics, Human Genetics Assn. N.J. (mem. legis. com.), N.Y. Acad. Sci. Office: Saint Peter's Univ Hosp 254 Easton Ave # 4410 New Brunswick NJ 08901-1766 Home Phone: 732-274-1192. E-mail: Day-Salva@comcast.net.

DAZZAN, PAOLA, psychiatrist, educator; Degree in Medicine, U. Cagliari, Italy, 1991; MSc, Inst. Psychiatry King's Coll. London, 2002, PhD, 2006. Cert. CCST London Deanery, 2003. Rsch. fellow, psychiatry U. Cagliari, 1991—95; sr. house officer Maudsley Hosp., London, 1996—98; postgrad. fellow Johns Hopkins U., Balt., 1997—98; clin. lectr. Inst. Psychiatry King's Coll. London, 1998—2007, undergrad. psychiatry tchg. coord., 2005—, clin. sr. lectr., 2007—; cons. psychiatrist South London and Maudsley NHS Trust, 2005—. Recipient Young Scientist award, 11th Biennial Winter Workshop, 2002, Internat. Congress Schizophrenia Rsch., 2003, 13th Biennial Winter Workshop, 2005, Young Investigator award, NARSAD, 2003, 2006, Ind. Investigator award, 2009; Project grant, UK Med. Rsch. Coun., 2006, BIAL Found., 2007, Translational Rsch. grant, King's Coll. London, 2008. Mem.: Schizophrenia Internat. Soc., Am. Psychiat. Assn. (internat. mem. 2006, Young Minds Psychiatry award 2006), Royal Coll. Psychiatrist, European Psychiat. Assn. Avocations: travel, scuba diving. Office: Inst Psychiatry De Crespigny Pk London SE5 8AF England Business E-Mail: paola.dazzan@kcl.ac.uk.

DAZZO, OLGA, public health service officer, state official; b. 1950; BA in Acctg., Mich. State U., MBA in Finance. Pres., CEO Physicians Health Plan (PHP), Health Reform Innovations; founder East Lansing Co.; sr. v.p., exec. dir. Jackson Health Plans, Miami, 2007—10; dir. Mich. Dept. Cmty. Health (MDCH), Lansing, 2011—. Trustee Ferris State U., 1998—2006; bd. dirs. Lansing Capital Area United Way, Lansing Latino Health Alliance, Capital Area Health Alliance Bus. Coalition. Recipient Ellis J. Bonner Outstanding Achievement award, Mich. Assn. Health Plans, 2002; named Career Woman of the Yr.,

Lansing Founding Chpt. of the Nat. Assn. Career Women, 1998. Office: Michigan Department of Community Health Capitol View Bldg 201 Townsend St Lansing MI 48913 Office Phone: 517-373-3740. *

D'COSTA, GRACE, medical educator; b. Apr. 30, 1955; MBBS, Bombay U., 1978, MD in Pathology, 1982; diploma in Pathology & Bacteriology, Coll. Physicians & Surgeons, 1982. Cert. FICP, 2008. Resident pathologist Grant Med. Coll. J. J. Group of Hosps., Mumbai, 1980—81, lectr. pathology, 1981—88, assoc. prof. pathology, 1988—2009; prof. & head pathology Grant Med. Coll. J. J. Group Hosps., 2009—. Contbr. posters and presentations, articles to profl. jours. Fellow: Coll. Pathologists; mem.: Bombay Pediat. Pathologists Group, Assn. Med. Women, India (life), Mumbai Hematology Group (life), Indian Assn. Pathologists & Microbiologists (life), Internat. Acad. Pathologists (life), Indian Assn. Cytologists (life), Bombay Breast Pathologists Group. Achievements include work in neonatal and pediatric pathology; breast pathology. Home Phone: 02222046311; Office Phone: 022 23735555 ext 2345. Business E-Mail: dr_grace@vsnl.com.

DEAL, WILLIAM BROWN, medical school dean, physician, educator; b. Durham, NC, Oct. 4, 1936; s. Harold Albert and Louise (Brown) D.; m. April Autrey, May 2, 1998; children: Kimberly Deal Wolpert, Kathleen Louise. AA, Mars Hill Coll., 1956; AB, U. N.C., 1958, MD, 1963. Intern in medicine U. Fla. Hosp., Gainesville, 1963-64, asst. resident, 1966-68, fellow in infectious diseases, 1968—69, chief resident, instr. dept. medicine, 1969-70; asst. prof. dept. medicine U. Fla., 1970-73, assoc. dean Coll. of Medicine, 1973-77, assoc. prof. dept. cmty. health and family medicine, 1973-75, assoc. prof. dept. medicine, 1973-75, prof., 1975-88, acting dean Coll. of Medicine, 1977-78, dean Coll. of Medicine, v.p. clin. affairs, 1978-88, clin. prof. medicine, 1988—; assoc. dean, prof. medicine U. Ala. Sch. of Medicine, 1991-96, sr. assoc. dean, prof. medicine, 1996-97, dean, 1997—2004, prof. medicine Birmingham; interim CEO UAB Health Sys., 1998-99; v.p. medicine U. Ala., Birmingham, 2000—, sr. v.p., dean emeritus, 2004—. Pres. Maine Med. Ctr. Found., Portland, Maine, 1988—90; asst. to sr. v.p. AMA, 1980; lectr. Northwestern U., 1980; vis. clin. tutor City Hosp. U. Edinburgh, Scotland, 1967; chair nat. adv. com. Summer Med. Dental Edn. Program; bd. dirs. PNP Pharm., Inc., 2004—. Contbr. articles to numerous profl. jours. Fellow: ACP, Royal Soc. Medicine; mem.: AMA (liaison com. on med. edn. 1982—87, chmn. governing coun. sect. on med. schs. 1986—87, exec. com. AAMC 1986—88, disting. svc. mem. AAMC 2005—), Med. Assn. State of Ala., Jefferson County Med. Soc., Zool. Soc. of Ala., Noble Order of the Flea, Alpha Omega Alpha (bd. dirs. 1986—95, pres. 1993—95), Beta Theta Pi, Phi Chi. Office: Sch of Medicine FOT 856 UAB Birmingham AL 35294-0001 Office Phone: 205-934-9401. Business E-Mail: wdeal@uab.edu.

DEAL, WILLIAM THOMAS, retired school psychologist; b. Dec. 18, 1949; s. Richard Lee and Rheta Lucille (Gerber) Deal; m. Paula Nespeca, Aug. 5, 1972. BS, Bowling Green State U., 1972; MA, John Carroll U., 1977; postgrad., Kent State U., 1979—. Sci. tchr. Westlake Schs., 1972-76; intern sch. psychologist Garfield Heights Schs., 1976-77; pvt. practice Parma Heights, Ohio, 1982—84; sch. psychologist, 1977—2007; ret., 2007; pvt. practice PSI Assoc., 2007—. Recipient cert. of Recognition, Garfield Heights Bd. Edn., 1980, Outstanding Achievement award, Cleve. Assn. Children with Learning Disabilities, Inc., 1980; named Psychologist of the Yr., Cleve. Sch., 1990. Mem.: Cleve. Assn. Sch. Psychologists, Ohio Sch. Psychology Assn., Nat. Assn. Sch. Psychologists, Phi Delta Kappa. Independent. Mem. Christian Ch. Home: 3290 Kings Hwy Cleveland OH 44126-3059

DE ALARCON, PEDRO ANTONIO, pediatric oncologist, educator; b. Guatemala, Dec. 13, 1945; BA, Harvard U., Boston, 1968; MD, George Washington U. Sch. Medicine, 1972. Diplomate Am. Bd. Pediat., cert. in pediatric hematology-oncology. Intern/resident internal medicine Washington Hosp. Ctr., 1973—74; fellow pediat. U. Vt. Sch. Medicine, 1975—76, SUNY Upstate Med. U., 1977—79; clin. instr. pediat. Columbia U., NYC, 1980-83; attending pediatrician Mary Imogene Bassett Hosp., Cooperstown, NY, 1980-83; asst. prof. U. Iowa, Iowa City, 1983-88, assoc. prof., 1988-91, SUNY, Buffalo, 1991-92; prof. pediat., divsn. head U. Va. Med. Ctr., Charlottesville; dep. chief med. officer St. Jude's Children's Rsch. Hosp., Memphis; William H. Albers prof. & chair, dept. pediat. U. Ill. Coll. Medicine, Peoria, 2007—. Editor: Neonatal Hematology, 2005; contbr. articles to profl. jours. Mem.: Pediatric Oncology Group. Office: U Ill Coll Medicine Dept Pediat 530 NE Glen Oak Ave Peoria IL 61637 Office Phone: 309-655-4242. Office Fax: 309-655-2565. Business E-Mail: pdealarc@uic.edu.

DEAMER, RICHARD MORRIS, psychiatrist; b. South Bend, Ind., July 1, 1941; s. David Wilson and Zena Morris Deamer; m. Harriet Ann Griffith, July 3, 1965; children: Kelly, Julie. BS, Purdue U., Ind., 1963; MD, Ohio State U., 1967; residency in psychiatry, UCLA, 1971. Med. dir. Vista del Mar Hosp., Ventura, Calif., 1969—98; clin. instr. in medicine Ventura (Calif.) County Med. Ctr., UCLA, 1984—98. Pres., CEO Limbic Sys., Inc., Ventura, Calif., 1994—2003. Pres. Child Abuse & Neglect, Ventura, Calif., 1976—80. Lt. comdr. USN, 1971—73. Grantee Small Bus. Innovative Rsch. Grant, Nat. Inst. Musculoskelatal Diseases, 1993; Fellowship in Child Psychiatry, UCLA, 1974. Fellow: Am. Psychiat. Assn. (Disting. fellow 2003). Democrat. Methodist. Achievements include patents for stoop labor body support; stoop labor assist device. Avocations: classical guitar, scuba diving, private pilot.

DEAN, DOROTHY G., psychologist, social sciences educator, researcher; b. Oyster Bay, NY, Jan. 28, 1919; d. William Miles and Georgiana Goodrich Dean; widowed; children: Ellen, Arthur, Robert. BA, St. Lawrence U., 1940; MA in Religion, Yale U., 1973; EdD, Boston U., 1985. Personnel testing R.H. Macy & Co., NYC, 1940—41; advt. rsch. Newell-Emmett Co., NYC, 1941—44; mem. Robert Shaw Collegiate Chorale, 1942—44; coll. admissions Albertus Magnus Coll., New Haven, 1964—65; ref. asst. Yale U. Libr., New Haven, 1966—70; chaplain trainee Boston City Hosp., 1971—72; clinician trainee Conn. Mental Health Ctr., New Haven, 1972—73; therapist intern Cambridge (Mass.) Family & Children's Svc., 1975—76; pvt. practice Brookline, Mass., 1975—86. Family counselor First and Second Ch., Boston, 1975—85; rsch. fellow, Bainton assoc. Yale Divinity Sch., New Haven, 1984; presenter in field. Contbr. articles to profl. jours. and mags.; author: Transforming Violence: Teaching Democracy and Civility, The Growing Seeds of Hospice; report (global climate change) Residence Green Com., 2008, mem.; contbr. numerous confs. Del. Nat. Impact, Washington; mem. great decisions com. Learning in Ret., 2002—05; mem. Faithful Security, 2008, Conf. Yale Div. Sch., 2008, Are We Safe Yet?, 2008, Nat. Women's Hist. Mus., 2010—11; physicians social responsibility mem. Petition to Senator Scott Brown, 2010—11; with Learning Ret. Seminar on Risk, 2010. Mem.: AAUW (pub. chair 1955—56, pres. 1956—57), LWV (v.p. 1950—52, co-founder Rutland chpt. 1950—52), Rutland Players (v.p. 1950—52), Pi Lambda Theta. Mem. United Church Of Christ. Avocations: singing, acting, music, theater, bridge. Home: 52 Firethorn Ln Northampton MA 01060 Personal E-mail: dorothyd52@comcast.net.

DEAN, LLOYD H., insurance company executive; BS in Comm., Western Mich. U., 1972, MEd, 1978; grad. in Exec. Mgmt. Program, Pa. State U.; LHD (hon.), U. San Francisco, 2009. Exec. and operational mgmt. Health Care Svcs. divsn. Upjohn Co., exec. v.p. mktg., nat. v.p. sales; exec. v.p., COO Advocate Health Care; pres., CEO Cath. Healthcare West, 2000—. Dir., chmn. corp. responsibility Wells Fargo & Co., 2005—, com. mem. audit & exam., 2005—, com. mem. credit com., 2005—, mem. risk com., 2005—; dir. Cytori Therapeutics, Inc., 2010, chmn. bd. dirs., mem. governance nominating com., 2011—. Mem. bd. Cath. Health Assn. USA, Premier, Inc., Coalition Nonprofit Healthcare, Alliance Cath. Healthcare, Consol. Cath. Healthcare, Mercy Housing, Inc., Seton Inst. Adv. Bd., Bay Area Sports Organizing Com., Calif. Commn. Jobs & Econ. Develop., 2004; co-chair San Francisco Universal Healthcare Coun., 2006, Healthy San Francisco Program Adv. Com., 2006. Recipient Cmty. Svc. award, 100 Black Men of the Bay Area, Inc., 2004, 100 Black Men in the Bay Area award, 2005, Mathies award, Partners in Care, 2007, MoAD Corp. Leadership award, 2009; named one of the nation's Top 100 Integrated Networks, Modern Healthcare mag., 100 Most Powerful People in Healthcare, Modern Healthcare Mag., 2005, 2006, 2007, 2008, Top 25 Minority Leaders in Healthcare, 2006, 2007, 2008, 2010. Mem.: Am. Hosp. Assn., Health Rsch. & Develop. Inst., Am. Coll. Healthcare Exec. Office: Catholic Healthcare West 185 Berry St San Francisco CA 94107 Office Fax: 415-438-5724. *

DEAN, RICHARD HENRY, surgeon, educator; b. Radford, Va., June 16, 1942; s. Howard Lee and Minnie Yates (Crowder) D.; children: Richard Lancaster, Harrison Blaylock, Howard Lee Alexander, Williams Cabler. BA, Va. Mil. Inst., 1964; MD, Med. Coll. Va., 1968. Diplomate Am. Bd. Surgery (bd. dirs. 1993—), Am. Bd. Gen. Vascular Surgery, Am. Bd. Plastic Surgery. Surg. intern Vanderbilt U. Hosp., 1968-69, surg. asst. resident, 1969-73, chief. surg. resident, 1973-74, asst. prof. surgery sch. medicine, 1975-77, assoc. prof. surgery, 1977-81, prof. surgery, 1981-86, head divsn. vascular surgery sch. medicine, 1978-86; vascular rsch. fellow, instr. surgery Northwestern U. Hosp, 1974-75; Richard T. Meyers prof. and chmn. surgery Bowman Gray Sch. Medicine Wake Forest U., Winston-Salem, NC, 1987-89, dir. divsn. surg. scis., chmn. dept. gen. surgery Bowman Gray Sch. Medicine, 1989-97, sr. v.p. health affairs, 1997—2001; dir. Wake Forest U. Baptist Med. Ctr., 1997—; pres. Wake Forest U. Health Scis., 2001—. Vis. prof. U. Vienna, Austria, 1980, U. NSW, Sydney, Australia, 1982, U. Queensland, Brisbane, Australia, 1984, U. Rochester (N.Y.) Med. Ctr., 1986, 2nd Internat. Symposium on Ischemia, Madrid, 1986, U. Health Scis., Bethesda, Md., 1987, East Carolina U., Greenville, N.C., 1987, Ga. Bapt. Med. Ctr., Atlanta, 1988, Roanoke (Va.) Meml. Hosp., 1988, Ea. Va. Med. Sch., Norfolk, 1988 (two lectures), Mayo Clinic, Rochester, Minn., 1989, Med. Coll. Va., Richmond, 1990, W.Va. U. Health Sci. Ctr., Charleston, 1990, Va. Vascular Soc., Hot Spring, 1990, First All-Union Congress Cardiovascular Surgery, Moscow, 1990, Carolinas Heart Inst., Charlotte, 1991, U. Miami Sch. Medicine, 1991, Allegheny Gen. Hosp., Pitts., 1992, Northwestern U. Med. Sch., Chgo., 1992, U. Minn., Mpls., 1992, Nat. Naval Med. Ctr., Bethesda, 1992, Emory U. Sch. Medicine/Emory Hosp., Atlanta, 1992, Internat. Symposium Hosp. Universitario, Madrid, 1993, Ruprect-Karls-Universitat Heidelberg, Germany, 1993, La. State U. Med. Ctr., Shreveport, 1993, U. N.C., Chapel Hill, 1993, U. Man., Winnipeg, Can., 1993, U. Cin. Med. Ctr., 1993; Paul Dudley White vis. prof. U. Sao Paulo and Campinas, Brazil, 1982; Deryl Hart lectr. Duke U. Med. Sch., 1991; mem. Coun. on Cardio-Thoracic and Vascular Surgery, 1990-91; dir. Am. Bd. Plastic Surgery, 1995—; guest lectr. in field. Editor: (with J.A. O'Neill Jr.) Vascular Disorders of Childhood, 1983, (with W.P. Ritchie and G. Strele Sr.) General Surgery, 1994, (with J.S.T. Jao and D.C. Brewster) Current Diagnosis and Treatment in Vascular Surgery, 1995; mem. editl. bd. Jour. Vascular Surgery, Annals of Vascular Surgery; contbr. numerous chpts. to books and articles to sci. and profl. jours. Recipient Superior Performance award, 1997. Fellow: ACS (N.C. chpt., cardiovascular com. 1987), Am. Heart Assn. (stroke coun., coun. high blood pressure rsch.); mem.: AMA, Nat. Libr. Medicine (bd. regents 2001—), H. William Scott, Jr. Soc. (sec. 1982—87, pres. 1988—89), S.E. Surg. Congress, So. Surg. Assn. (v.p. 1997—98), So. Med. Assn., Forsyth-Stokes-Davie County Med. Assn., So. Assn. Vascular Surgery (program com. 1982—85, exec. coun. 1985—88, pres.-elect 1988—89, pres. 1990—91), Va. Surg. Assn. (hon.), So. Calif. Vascular Surgery Soc. (hon.), Assn. Acad. Surgery (exec. coun. 1978—80, nominating com. 1980), Soc. Vascular Surgery (publs. com. 1992—, recorder), Soc. Univ. Surgeons, Internat. Soc. Surgery, Internat. Soc. Cardiovascular Surgery (vis. prof. First Sci. Congress 1992), Am. Surg. Assn. (adv. membership com. 1991—), Am. Bd. Surgery (cons. com. on vascular surgery 1986—92, dir. 1993—). Office: Wake Forest Univ Sch Medicine Medical Center Blvd Winston Salem NC 27157-0001 Home: 2551 Warwick Rd Winston Salem NC 27104-1943

DEANE, DEBBE, psychologist, journalist, editor, consultant; b. Coatesville, Pa., July 30, 1950; d. George Edward and Dorothea Alice (Martin) Mays; widowed; children: Theo, Vonisha, Lorise, Voniece. AA in Psychology, Mesa Coll., 1989; BA Psychology, San Diego State U., 1993; MA in Psychology, Nat. U., 1995; D of Psychology, Calif. Sch. Profl. Psychology, 2005. Cert. in geropsychology U. Calif. San Diego, 2009. Announcer Sta. KBPI, Denver, 1969-70, Sta. WKXI, Jackson, Miss., 1970-72; news anchor Sta. WNGE-TV, Nashville, 1973-76; news dir. Sta. KLDR, Denver, 1976-78; host, reporter Sta. KMGH-TV, Denver, 1978-81; news anchor, editor Sta. KHOW, Denver, 1978-79; news & pub. affairs dir. Sta. KLZ, Denver, 1979-80, Sta. KCBQ, San Diego, 1980-82; news anchor Sta. KOGO, San Diego, 1983-84; news anchor, reporter Sta. KCST-TV, San Diego, 1984-87; dir. comm. Omni Corp., San Diego, 1987—; news anchor Sta. KFI, LA, 1990-91; sr. psychiat. therapist Behavioral Health Group, San Diego, 1993—. Media liaison United Negro Coll. Fund, San Diego, 1990-92; dir. comm. United Chs. of Christ, San Diego, 1989-92; cons. San Diego Assn. Black Journalists, 1985-92, San Diego Coalition Black Journalists, 1985-92, Alafia Wellness Ctr., Lemongrove, Calif.; cons. in field. Campaign fin. analyst San Diego County Registrar of Voters, San Diego, 1990; cons. San Diego County Office Disaster Preparedness, 1990-91, Nu Way Youth Ctr. & Neighborhood House, Inc., San Diego, 1991-92; counselor Project STARRT, San Diego, 1991-92; cons. United Way Home Start, Inc. Family Self-Sufficiency Program, 1996—; cons. and program coord. San Diego Healthy Start, Inc., 1997—, Samuel L. Gompers Secondary Inst. Math., Sci. & computer Tech., 1997—; coord. Clin. program rsch. treatment, TeleCare, Inc., 1999-; Heritage Clinic, 2007, ALAFIA Wellness Ctr., 2006-, cons., 2006-, clin. psychologist, 2010, Heritage Clinic, 2011. Recipient San Diego Black Achievement award Urban League, 1989, Best News Show & Spot News award San Diego Press Club, 1985, Golden Mike award So. Calif. Broadcast Assn., L.A., 1986; named one of Top 25 Businesswomen Essence Mag., 1978, Outstanding Humanitarian Worldvision, 1993, Outstanding Humanities Alumna Mesa Coll., 1993, Woman of Yr., ABI, 2010, Outstanding Humanitarian, Habitat for Humanity, Outstanding Humanitarian, Feed-the-Children, Outstanding Humanitarian, Teach Tolerance Project. Mem. AFTRA, APA, AAUW, Am. Women in Radio & TV, Women in Comm., Black Students Sci. Orgn. (sec. 1989-91), Africana Psychol. Soc. (media coord. 1990-92), San Diego Assn. Black Psychologists (media coord. 2007—, media dir. 2010-), Nat. Assn Broadcast Engrs. and Technicians, Psi Chi. Democrat. Achievements: first African-Am. in U.S. lic. to teach radio & TV broadcast prodn. Home: 3545 Valley Rd Bonita CA 91902-4164

DEANE, LELAND MARC, plastic surgeon, director; b. NYC, June 18, 1952; s. Maurice Allen and Barbara Elaine (Ushkow) D.; m. Danielle Anne Sheft, Nov. 21, 1993; children: Ashby Bennett, Galen Ames. BS, Union Coll., 1974; MD, SUNY, Bklyn., 1978; MBA in Finance, NYU, 2010. Diplomate Am. Bd. Surgery, 1984, Am. Bd. Plastic Surgery. Intern, then resident in surgery New Eng. Med. Ctr., 1978-83; resident in plastic surgery Ea. Va. Grad. Sch. Medicine, 1983-85; fellow in hand surgery Jefferson Med. Coll., 1986; pvt. practice LI Plastic Surg. Group P.C., Garden City, NY, 1986—; chief divsn. plastic surgery North Shore/LI Jewish Southside Hosp., Bayshore, NY, 2006—. Instr. surgery Cornell Med. Coll., 1989—. Contbr. articles to profl. jours. Advisor Mothers of Super Twins, LI, 1995—. Grantee So. Med. Assn., 1984. Fellow ACS; mem. Am. Soc. Plastic and Reconstructive Surgeons, Northea. Soc. Plastic Surgeons, NY Regional Soc. Plastic and Reconstructive Surgery, Seawanhaka Corinthian Yacht Club, NY Yacht Club. Office: LI Plastic Surg Group PC 999 Franklin Ave Garden City NY 11530-2913 Office Phone: 516-742-3404.

DEANE, SALLY JAN, health facility administrator, consultant; b. Downey, Calif., Sept. 24, 1948; d. Virgil Eldred and Pearl Jan (Kettell) D. BA, Whittier Coll., 1970; MEd, Boston U., 1971, MPH, 1988. Mgr. community health Peter Bent Brigham Hosp., Boston, 1974-76; coord. WIC program Martha Eliot Health Ctr., 1976-78; dir. S.W. Boston WIC program Shattuck Hosp. Corp., 1978-80; exec. dir. Fenway Community Health Ctr., 1980-84; exec. asst. commr. Boston Dept. Health & Hosps., 1984-86; assoc. dir. spl. projects Health Policy Inst. Boston U., 1986-87; dir. ambulatory reimbursement Mass. Medicaid, 1987-88; assoc. Cambridge (Mass.) Mgmt. Group, 1989; ptnr. Integrated Health Strategies Inc., Cambridge, Mass., 1990-96; adj. asst. clin. prof. Pub. Health Boston U., 1994—; v.p. Chadwick Martin Bailey, Boston, 1996-98; mng. ptnr. Strategic Healthcare Innovations LLC, Boston, 1999—; instr. Boston U., 1999—; chief exec. officer Outer Cape Health Svcs. Cons. Mass. Dept. Pub. Health, Boston, 1978-80, Citicorp Corp. Hdqrs., N.Y.C., 1986; lectr. Grad. Sch. Mgmt., Boston U., 1999—; bd. visitors Boston U. Sch. Pub. Health, 1999-07; innkeeper Charles St. Inn, 1999—. Mem. Mayor's Task Force on AIDS, Boston, 1983—86; v.p. Trustees Charitable Donations, Boston, 1984—88; chair bd. dirs. Boston Women's Health Book Collective, 2000—05; chmn. bd. dirs. N.E. Eye Inst., 2001—08; mem. bd. dirs. Associated Early Care Edn., 2008—10. Presbyterian. Office Phone: 508-240-0208. Personal E-mail: sallydeane@yahoo.com. Business E-Mail: sdeane@outercape.org.

DEAR, RONALD BRUCE, retired social work educator; b. Phila., Sept. 23, 1933; s. John David and Margaret (McDade) D.; 1 child, Bruce. BA, Bucknell U., 1955; honors cert., U. Aberdeen, Scotland, 1955; MSW, U. Pitts., 1957; PhD in Social Work, Columbia U., 1972. Cert. social worker, N.Y., Wash. Chief social worker Mental Hygiene Cons. Svc., Aberdeen Proving Ground, Md., 1958-60; chief Neuropsychiat. Clinic, 7th Inf. Divsn., Korea, 1960-61; residence dir. Horizon House, Inc., Phila., 1961-64; prof. U. Wash., Seattle, 1970—2003, prof. emeritus, 2003—. Vis. prof. U. Bergen, Norway, 1984, U. Trondheim, Norway, 1996; faculty lobbyist U. Wash., 1983-85, 88-91, faculty pres., 1993-95; master tchr. Coun. on Social Work Edn., 1991, 93, 94, 97; mem. adv. bd. Internat. Population and Family Assocs. Author: Social Welfare Policy: Trends and Issues, 6th edit., 2001, Teaching Social Policy in Social Work Education: Model Syllabus, 2003; editor: Poverty in Perspective, 1973; mem. The Social Policy Jour., 2002—; contbr. articles to profl. jours. and encys. Apptd. by gov. to income assistance adv. com., 1987-93, to adv. com. for Dept. Social and Health Svcs., 1980-83, Human Svcs. Policy Ctr., 1996—, adv. com. Wash. State Econ. Svcs., 1996-2004; mem. nat. adv. bd. Influencing State Policy, 1997—; appeared in centennial program of Columbia U. Sch. Social Work, 1998; pres. U. Wash. Ret. Assn., 2007—08. 1st lt. U.S. Army, 1957-61. Mem. NASW (charter mem. 1968-69, staff legis. NYC chpt., Social Worker of Yr. Wash. State 1981), Acad. Cert. Social Workers. Avocations: travel in over 50 countries, photography, hiking. Home: 7328 16th Ave NE Seattle WA 98115-5737 Business E-Mail: rdear@u.washington.edu.

DE ARAUJO, DANIEL BRITO, rheumatologist; b. Brazil, Feb. 15, 1977; MD, U. Fed. de Pelotas, 2001. Rheumatology asst. Hosp. do Servidor Público Estadual de São Paulo, 2009. Mem.: Brazilian Coll. Rheumatology. Office: Rua Pedro de Toledo 1800/9 Central São Paulo 04039-004 Brazil E-mail: araujodb@gmail.com.

DEARBORN, MAUREEN MARKT, speech and language clinician; b. Brockton, Mass., Jan. 19, 1948; d. Francis Joseph and Marjorie Agnes (White) M.; m. James Clement Bovin, Nov. 6, 1970 (div. June 1973); m. David C. Dearborn, Jan. 14, 1989. BA in Speech Pathology and Audiology, U. Mass., 1970; MA in Ednl. Psychology, Am. Internat. Coll., Springfield, Mass. Speech and lang. clinician Holyoke (Mass.) Pub. Schs., 1970—2009; speech and lang. clinician mansfield chpt. DAR, 1984—2007; C.E adminstr. Mass Speech Hearing and

Lang. Assn.; historian Evnice Day DAR, 1984—2009; co-registrar Mansfield Chpt., 2009—; admin. Massspeed Hearing & Lang. Assn., 2009—. Chmn. Holyoke Cancer Crusade, 1985; voter registration chmn. Holyoke Dem. Com., 1987; chmn. deaconesses 2d Congl. Ch. Holyoke. Mem.: DAR (historian Mary Mattson 1984—2008, historian Eunice Day 1984—2009, Mansfield chpt. 2009—), Mass. Tchrs. Assn., Mass. Speech, Hearing and Lang. Assn. (CE adminstr. 2009—), Am. Speech, Hearing and Lang. Assn. (congl. action contact 1988—90, continuing edn. adv. bd. 1988—91), Holyoke Tchrs. Assn., Hampden County Tchrs. Assn. (pres. 1981, sec. 1982, v.p. 1984—86, pres. 1987, treas. 1988—2010), Dorchester Hist. Soc., Wrenthan Hist. Soc., Assn. for Gravestone Studies, Friends of the Libr. Coun. (treas. 1992—2000), Mass. Geneal. Soc., New Eng. Hist. and Geneal. Soc. Avocations: bicycling, antiques, genealogy, aerobics. Home: 257 W Franklin St Holyoke MA 01040-2210 also: 104 Mountain St Sharon MA 02067 E-mail: dearborn@massed.net.

DE ASA, VIRGILIO CORTEZ, physician; b. Manila, Philippines, July 7, 1947; s. Mauro Estrada and Salome (Cortez) De A.; m. Nora Aquino, Dec. 16, 1967; 3 children. BSc, Far Eastern Univ., Manila, 1966; MD, Far Eastern Univ. Nicanor Reyes Med. Found., Manila, 1972. Sr. rschr. United Labs. Inc., Philippines, 1973-75, rsch. project supr., 1975-76; sr. med. officer CWM Hosp., Suva, Fiji, 1981-84; lectr. pharmacology and therapeutics Fiji Sch. of Medicine, 1980-83, 86-88; chief med. officer A&E Dept. Colonial War Meml. Hosp., Suva, Fiji, 1984-88; pvt. practice Suva, 1988—; U.N. examining physician, 1999—; physician to pres. Republic of Fiji Islands, 1996—2001. Gen. sec. Fiji Chess Fedn., 1979-88, pres., 1991-94, 96—. Mem. Filipino Assn. Fiji (pres. 1993-2000), Philippine Soc. Microbiology and Infectious Diseases, Fiji Coll. Gen. Practitioners, NY Acad. Scis., Fiji Med. Assn. Avocations: chess, research. Office: GPO Box 12408 Suva Fiji

DEB, RAJIB, medical researcher; b. Agartala, Tripura, India, Apr. 5, 1981; BVSc, CAU, India, 2005; MVSc, Indian Vet. Rsch. Inst., 2008. Postdoc. scholar Indian Vet. Rsch. Inst., 2009—. Sr. Rsch. fellowship, ICAR. Avocation: travel. Home: C/O Prasanta Kumar Pal Advocate N Agartala West Tripura 799001 India Personal E-mail: drrajibdeb@gmail.com.

DEBAKEY, LOIS, science administrator, educator; b. Lake Charles, La. d. S. M. and Raheeja (Zorba) DeBakey. BA in Math., Tulane U., MA in Lit. and Linguistics, 1959, PhD in Lit. and Linguistics, 1963. Asst. prof. English Tulane U., 1963—64; asst. prof. sci. communication Tulane U. Med. Sch., 1963-65, assoc. prof. sci. communication, 1965-67, prof. sci. comm., 1967-68, lectr., 1968-80, adj. prof., 1981-92; prof. sci. comm. Baylor Coll. Medicine, Houston, 1968—. Mem. biomed. libr. rev. com. Nat. Libr. Medicine, Bethesda, Md., 1973-77, bd. regents, 1981-86, cons., 1986-, co-chmn. permanent paper task force, 1987-, lit. selection tech. rev. com., 1988-93, chmn., 1992-93, outreach planning panel, 1988-89; dir. courses in med. comm. ACS and other orgns.; trustee DeBakey Med. Found., 1995-; mem. exec. coun. Commn. on Colls. So. Assn. Colls. and Schs., 1975-80; mem. nat. adv. coun. U. So. Calif. Ctr. Continuing Med. Edn., 1981; mem. steering com. Plain English Forum, 1984; mem. founding bd. dirs. Friends Nat. Libr. Medicine, 1985-, chmn. med. media award of excellence com., 1992-, bd. dirs., 2009, Friends Tex. med. Ctr. Libr. Adv. Com., 2008-; with cmty. coun. Methodist DeBakey Heart & Vascular Ctr., 2008-; mem. adv. com. Soc. for Preservation English Lang. Lit., 1986; mem. nat. adv. bd. John Muir Med. Film Festival, 1990-92; mem. The Internat. Health and Med. Film Festival, Acad. of Judges, 1992-93; mem. adv. bd. U. Tex. at Austin Sch. Nursing Found., 1993-; cons. legal writing com. ABA, 1983-, Ency. Brit. Biomed. and Health Database, 1999-; former cons. Nat. Assn. Std. Med. Vocabulary; pioneered instrn. in sci. comm. in med. sch.; mem. editl. bd. Meth. DeBaker Cardiovasc. Jour., 2008-. Sr. author: The Scientific Journal: Editorial Policies and Practices, 1976; co-author: Medicine: Preserving the Passion, 1987; Medicine: Preserving the Passion in the 21st Century, 2004; mem editl. bd.: Tulane Studies in English, 1966-68, Cardiovasc. Rsch. Ctr. Bull., 1971-83, Health Comms. and Informatics, 1975-80, Forum on Medicine, 1977-80, Grants Mag., 1978-81, Internat. Jour. Cardiology, 1981-86, Excerpta Medica's Core Jours. in Cardiology, 1981—, Health Comm. and Biopsychosocial Health, 1981-82, Internat. Angiology, 1985—, Jour. AMA, 1988-2002. CV Network, 2003-; editl. bd. mem. Meth. Debakey Cardiovasc. Jour., 2008-; mem. usage panel Am. Heritage Dictionary, 1980—; cons. Webster's Med. Desk Dictionary, 1986; editl. advisor Ency. Brit.; contbr. articles on biomed. comm. and sci. writing, literacy, also other subjects to profl. jours., books, encys., and pub. press. With Found. for Advanced Edn. in Sci., 1977—. Recipient Harold Swanberg Disting. Svc. award, Am. Med. Writers Assn., 1970, Bausch & Lomb Sci. award, 1st John P. McGovern award, Med. Libr. Assn., 1983, 50 Outstanding Women, Houston Ctr. for Humanities, 1990—91, Outstanding Alumna award, Newcomb Coll., 1994, Svc. Recognition award for 40 yrs., Baylor Coll. Medicine, 2008, Proclamation award, Lois & Selma DeBakey Family Day, Houston, 2008, Selma & Lois DeBakey Lectrs. award, Meth. DeBakey Heart & Vascular Ctr., 2009; Endowed Med. Humanities scholarship, Baylor U. Waco, 2009. Fellow Am. Coll. Med. Informatics, Royal Soc. for Encouragement of Arts, Mfrs., and Commerce; mem. Internat. Soc. Gen. Semantics, Med. Libr. Assn. (hon.), Coun. Biology Editors (dir. 1973-77, chmn. com. on editl. policy 1971-75), Coun. Basic Edn. (spl. com. writing 1977-79), Assn. Tchrs. Tech. Writing, Dictionary Soc. N.Am., Nat. Assn. Sci. Writers, Soc. for Health and Human Values, Com. of Thousand for Better Health Regulations, Golden Key, Phi Beta Kappa.

DE BEER, FREDERICK C., dean, internist, educator; arrived in USA, 1989; MD, U. Pretoria, South Africa; attended, Royal Postgraduate Med. Sch., London. Prof. medicine U. Stellenbosch, South Africa; prof. internal medicine U. Ky. Coll. Medicine, Lexington, positions including chief divsn. endocrinology and molecular medicine, vice chmn. dept. internal medicine, dir. grad. ctr. nutritional svcs., 1993—2003, chmn. dept. internal medicine, 2003—, Jack M. Gill prof. medicine, 2003—, v.p. clin. academic affairs, 2011—, dean, 2011—; chief of medicine Vets. Affairs Med. Ctr., Lexington. Contbr. articles to profl. jours., chapters to books. Office: University Ky Coll Medicine Office of Dean 138 Leader Ave Lexington KY 40506-9963 Office Phone: 859-323-6582. Business E-Mail: fcdebe1@uky.edu. *

DEBIEC, JACEK, psychiatrist, research scientist, educator; s. Henryk Debiec and Barbara (Malinowska) Malinowska-Debiec; m. Monika Isabella Tang. MD, Jagiellonian U., Cracow, Poland, 1994, PhD in Med. Sci., 2000; MA, Pontiff Acad. Theology, Cracow, 1997, PhD in Philosophy of Sci., 2000. Cert. psychiatrist Cracow. Attending psychiatrist, academic instr. dept. psychiatry Jagiellonian U. Coll. Medicine, Cracow, 1997—2002; rsch. scientist NYU Ctr. for Neural Sci., NYC, 2003—. Author: Possession: A Psychopathological Approach To The Problem, 2000, Mathematics And The Brain, 2002, The Self: From Soul to Brain, 2003. Recipient Neal E. Miller New Investigator award, Acad. Behavioral Medicine Rsch., 2007; Herder fellow, Alfred Toepfer Stiftung, Hamburg, Germany and Vienna U., Austria, 1998—99, Fulbright fellow, Polish-Am. Fulbright Commn., 2000—03. Mem.: NY Acad. Scis., Neuroethics Soc., Am. Psychiat. Assn., Soc. Neurosci. Achievements include research in neural basis of fear and fear learning, mechanisms of memory consolidation and reconsolidation. Office: Ctr for Neural Sci NYU 4 Washington Pl Rm 809 New York NY 10003 Office Fax: 212-995-4704. Business E-Mail: jacek@cns.nyu.edu.

DE BITTENCOURT, PAULO ROGÉRIO MUDROVITSCH, neurologist, researcher, writer; b. Curitiba, Brazil, Dec. 4, 1953; s. Paulo Orlando (M.) and Udine Vera Meri M. De Bittencourt; m. Lilian Dias Pereira, July 27, 1980 (div. 1984); m. Maristela Catarina Simioni, Mar. 18, 1989 (div. 2002); children: Dante Paolo, Paulo Rogério, Sofia, Mateus. MD, Fed. U. Paraná, 1976; PhD, U. London, 1981. Rsch. asst. Inst. Neurology, London, 1977-81; registrar Chalfont Ctr. for Epilepsy, Chalfont St. Peter, Eng., 1978-80; sr. house officer The Nat. Hosp., London, 1981; head of neurology svc. Hosp. Nossa Senhora das Graças, Curitiba, 1982—2004; exec. dir. Unidade de Neurologia Clinica Ltd., Curitiba, 1986—. Vis. prof. UCLA, 1980, U. London, 1984, U. Wales, 1984, U. Cin., 1987; prof. neurology Fed. U. Parana, Curitiba, 1991; pres. Brazilian League of Epilepsy, Curitiba, 1986-90; 1st v.p. Internat. League against Epilepsy, Washington, 1989-93, chmn. commn., 1989-97; sec. gen. 19th Internat. Epilepsy Congress, Rio de Janeiro, 1991; sec.-gen., founder Inst. Amazon Studies, Curitiba, 1990-93; lectr. in field. Chief editor: Jour. Brazilian League of Epilepsy, 1986—91, mem. editl. bd.: Epilepsia Jour., 1989—93, Acta Neurologica (Bogota), 1985—95, Archivos de Neuroscis. (Mex.), 1993—2001, Neurol. Infections and Epidemiology, 1996—2000; contbr. 150 articles to profl. jours. and books. Recipient Ednl. award Rotary Found., 1976, Amb. award Internat. League and Bur. for Epilepsy, 1991; Rsch. grantee Thorn Epilepsy Rsch. Fund, 1979, Wellcome Found., 1980. Fellow Am. Acad. Neurology; mem. Brazilian Soc. Multiple Sclerosis (coun. mem. 1990—), Brazilian Acad. Neurology, NY Acad. Scis., Cuban Neurosci. Soc. Avocations: travel, reading, music, swimming. Office: Rua Padre Anchieta 155 80410030 Curitiba Parana Brazil Office Phone: 55-41-32228801. Business E-Mail: unineuro@unineuro.com.br.

DE BOLD, ADOLFO J., pathologist, educator, physiologist, researcher; b. Paraná, Argentina, Feb. 14, 1942; arrived in Can., 1968; s. Adolfo E.G. and Ana (Patriarca) deB.; m. Mercedes L. Kuroski; children: Adolfo A., Alejandro J., Cecilia I., Gustavo A., Pablo G. B.Sc. (hon.), Faculty Chem. Sci., Cordoba, Argentina, 1968; M.Sc. in Pathology, Queen's U., Kingston, Ont., 1971, PhD in Pathology, 1973. Cert. clin. chemist. Demonstrator in physics Nat. U. Cordoba, 1961-62, demonstrator normal and path. histology, 1964-67; resident, chief resident Nat. Hosp., Clinicas, Cordoba, 1966-68; asst. prof., lab. scientist Queen's U. and Hotel-Dieu Hosp., Kingston, 1974-82, assoc. prof., 1982-85, prof., 1985-86; prof. pathology and physiology U. Ottawa, Ont., Canada, 1986—. Bd. dirs. research U. Ottawa Heart Inst. at Ottawa Civic Hosp., 1986—. Discovered Atrial Natriuretic Hormone, 1981, patented, 1986; contbr. over 100 sci. articles and chpts. to books in field. Bd. dirs. Heart Inst., Ottawa, 1986-93. Decorated officer Order of Can.; recipient Queen Elizabeth II Golden Jubilee medal, Gairdner Internat. award Gairdner Found., Toronto, 1986, Manning Prin. award Manning Found., Alta., Can., 1986, Sci. Achievement award Am. Soc. Hypertension, 1986, rsch. achievement award Can. Cardiovasc. Soc., 1986, CIBA award Am. Heart Assn., 1994; Disting. Rsch. Prof. award Ont. Heart and Stroke Found. Fellow Royal Soc. Can.(McLaughin medal of excellence in rsch. 1988), Royal Coll. Physicians and Surgeons (Can.), AAAS; mem. Can. Hypertension Soc., Am. Soc. for Hypertension, Internat. Soc. Hypertension (Rsch. Achievement award), Internat. Soc. Heart Rsch., Am. Sect. Can. Fedn. Biol. Socs., Histochem. Soc., U.S. Acad. Pathology, Can. Acad. Pathology, Am. Soc. Cell Biology, Can. Soc. Cell Biology, Internat. Acad. Pathology, Am. Assn. Pathology, Fedn. Am. Soc. Exptl. Biology, Microscopial Soc. Can., Soc. Exptl. Biology and Medicine, Can. Soc. Anatomy, N.Y. Acad. Sci. Roman Catholic. Avocation: classical guitar. Office: U Ottawa Heart Inst 40 Ruskin St Ottawa ON Canada K1Y 4W7 Home Phone: 613-761-4326. E-mail: adebold@ottawaheart.ca.

DEBOLD, JOSEPH FRANCIS, psychologist, educator; b. Boston, Nov. 3, 1947; s. Joseph Francis and Patricia (Miltimore) DeB.; m. Carol Lynn Hook, Dec. 20, 1969. AB, UCLA, 1969; PhD, U. Calif., Irvine, 1976. Trainee U. Calif. NICHD Devel. & Reproductive Biology, Irvine, 1971-75; instr., rsch. assoc. Mich. State U., East Lansing, 1975-77; asst. prof. Carnegie-Mellon U., Pitts., 1977-79, Tufts U., Medford, Mass., 1979-83, assoc. prof., 1983-91, prof., 1991—, chmn. dept. psychology, 1990-93, 2002—05; vis. rsch. assoc. Children's Hosp. Med. Ctr., Boston, 1981-85. Advisor NSF, Washington, 1989-92. Mem. editl. bd. Hormones and Behavior, 1987-92; contbr. articles to profl. jours., chpts. to books. Grantee NSF, 1986-99, Nat. Inst. Alcoholism and Alcohol Abuse, 1980-2002, 03—, Biomed. Rsch. Support Program, 1990-91. Mem. AAAS, Soc. for Neurosci., Nat. Assn. Advisors for Health Professions, NY Acad. Scis., Rsch. Soc. on Alcholism, Sigma Xi, Psi Chi. Avocations: motorcycling, tennis, volleyball. Office: Tufts U Dept Psychology 490 Boston Ave Medford MA 02155 Office Phone: 617-627-5901.

DEBONO, MIGUEL, endocrinologist, researcher; b. St. Julian's, Malta, Mar. 8, 1975; s. Anthony and Maria Concetta Debono. MD, U. Malta, 1999; Postgrad. Diploma, Roehampton U., Eng., 2007. Specialist registrar endocrinology & diabetes U. Malta, 2005—06; specialist registrar endocrinology Luton & Dunstable Hosp., Luton, England, 2006—07; academic clin. fellow endocrinology U. Sheffield, South Yorkshire, England, 2007—. Contbr. articles to profl. med. jours. Mem.: RCP, London, Endocrine Soc., Soc. Endocrinology. Office: Royal Hallamshire Hosp Academic Unit of Diab Endo Etab Royal Hallamshire Hospital Glossop Road S10 2JF Sheffield S10 2JF England Business E-Mail: m.debono@sheffield.ac.uk.

DEBOWSKA, RENATA MONIKA, lab administrator; b. Minsk Mazowiecki, Poland, Feb. 10, 1972; PhD, Warsaw U., 2002. Chief rschr. Dr Irena Eris Cosmetic Lab., 2008—. Primary sch. tchr., 1995—97. Grant, Ministry Edn. Mem.: European Soc. Dermatology Rsch. Avocations: theater, bicycling. Office: Pulawska Armii Krajowej Warsaw Mokotow 02-595 Poland Office Fax: 48228441724. Business E-Mail: renata.debowska@eris.pl.

DEBRINCAT, SUSAN JEANNE, nutritionist; b. Detroit, Oct. 7, 1943; d. Lloyd Brode and Florence Claire Greenleaf; m. Raymond Frank DeBrincat, June 19, 1965; children: David Lloyd, Mark Joseph. BS magna cum laude, Mich. State U., 1965. Cert. med. technologist, Am. Soc. Clin. Pathologists. Med. technologist Harper Hosp., Detroit, 1965-66, South Macomb Hosp., Warren, Mich., 1966; art tchr. YWCA, Berkley, Mich., 1969-80; master coord. Shaklee Corp., 1977—, sr. master coord., facilitator Pacific Inst., 1987—, lifetime master, 1990—, nutritional counselor, fashion, color, image and makeup counselor, mgmt. and leadership trainer, motivational spkr., 1977—2007. Interior designer. Painter oil, acrylic, watercolors. Mem. Rep. Nat. Com. Pres.'s Club, Found. Club, Phi Kappa Phi, Delta Zeta. Avocations: painting, art and antiques, reading, travel, boating. Office Phone: 770-538-9982. Personal E-mail: susan@debrincats.com.

DEBUONO, BARBARA ANN, epidemiologist; b. NYC, Apr. 13, 1955; d. Richard Francis and Catherine (Brutto) DeB.; m. David Lavington Farren, June 1, 1980; children: Adam, Douglas. BS, U. Rochester, 1976, MD, 1980; MPH, Harvard U., 1984. Diplomate American Bd. Internal Medicine, Nat. Bd. Med. Examiners. Intern in internal medicine New Eng. Deaconess Hosp., Boston, 1980-81, jr. med. resident, 1981-82, sr. med. resident, 1982-83; clin. fellow Brown U., Providence, 1984-86, clin. instr. dept. medicine, 1987-90, clin. asst. prof. medicine, 1990; med. epidemiologist R.I. Dept. Health, Providence, 1986, state epidemiologist, med. dir. Office Disease Control, 1986-91, dir., 1991—95; commr. NY State Dept. Health, Albany, 1995—98; CEO NY Presbyn. Healthcare Network, 1998—2000; exec. dir. pub. health & govt. Pfizer Inc., 2001—09; chief medical officer Porter Novelli, 2009—10, chief medical officer, global dir. health & social mktg., 2010—11; pres., CEO ORBIS Internat., 2011—. Lectr. in field; adv. com. to dir. Ctrs. for Disease Control; bd. mem. Ctr. Health Policy Devel.; nat. adv. com. Healthy Steps; sr. cons. WHO and Robert Wood Johnson Found. Contbr. articles to profl. jours. Robert Wood Johnson Found. Ednl. scholar U. Rochester Sch. Med., 1976-80; recipient James L. Tulis Disting. Study Lectureship award New Eng. Deaconess Hosp., 1992; named Women of Yr. by Bus. & Profl. Women's Club Providence, 1989, Person of Yr. by The Women's Youth League R.I., 1990, Woman of Yr. by R.I. Fedn. Bus. and Profl. Women's Clubs, 1991. Fellow American Coll. Internat. Physicians, American Coll. Physicians; mem. AMA, APHA, American Soc. Microbiology, Infectious Disease Soc. America, Providence Med. Assn., R.I. Med. Soc., R.I. Med. Women's Assn. (R.I. Women Physician of Yr. 1988), R.I. Environ. Health Assn., Hosp. Assn. R.I., Women Execs. in Govt. Avocations: swimming, tennis, gardening. Office: ORBIS International 520 8th Ave 11th Fl New York NY 10018 Office Phone: 800-672-4787. *

DEC, G. WILLIAM, cardiologist, educator; b. Washington, Sept. 6, 1952; s. George W. Sr. and Sarah Jane Dec; m. Donna M. Dec; children: Sarah, Jonathan. BSc in Chemistry, Georgetown U., Washington, 1974; MD, Johns Hopkins, Balt., 1978; MA (hon.), Harvard U., Cambridge, Mass., 2005. Diplomate Am. Bd. Internal Medicine. Resident Mass. Gen. Hosp., Boston, 1975—81, fellow, 1981—84, physician, 1984—; asst. prof. medicine Harvard Med. Sch., 1988—96, assoc. prof. medicine, 1996—2004, prof. medicine, 2004; chief cardiology divsn. Mass. Gen. Hosp., 2004—; Roman DeSanctis prof. medicine Harvard Med. Sch. Med. dir. heart transplant program Mass Gen. Hosp., 1984—2004, dir. clin. cardiology, 1998—2004; chief Cardiology Divsn., Mass. Gen. Hosp., 2004—; co-dir. Mass. Gen. Hosp. Heart Ctr., 2007—. Editor: Cardiac Allograft Rejection, 2001, Heart Failure: Diagnosis and Management, 2005. Recipient Nathaniel Bowditch award, Mass. Gen. Hosp., 2006. Fellow: Am. Coll. Cardiology, Am. Heart Assn.; mem.: Assn. Univ. Cardiologists, Alpha Omega Alpha, Phi Beta Kappa. Achievements include development of highly successful heart failure and heart transplant program at Mass. Gen. Hosp; heart center for integrated multidisciplinary cardiac care. Avocation: reading. Office: Mass Gen Hosp Bigelow 800 55 Fruit St Boston MA 02114 Office Phone: 617-726-8237. E-mail: gdec@partners.org.

DECAMPLI, WILLIAM MICHAEL, surgeon, researcher; b. Allentown, Pa., Dec. 7, 1951; s. William John and Bernadine Louise (Diehl) DeCampli; m. Kristi Lynn Peterson, May 29, 1989; children: Elissa Cale, William Grant. BS in Physics, MIT, 1973; MA in Astrophysics, PhD in Astrophysics, Harvard U., 1978; MD, U. Miami, 1982; surg. residency, Stanford U., 1982—92. Diplomate Am. Bd. Thoracic Surgery, 1993, Am. Bd. Surgery, 1989, Am. Bd. Med. Examiners, 1983. Attending surgeon Children's Hosp., Oakland, Calif., 1992—95, The Children's Hosp. of Phila., 1996—2004, The Children's Cardiac Ctr., Newark, N.J., 1996—2004; asst. prof. of surgery U. of Pa. Sch. of Medicine, Phila., 1997—2003; co-dir. Ctr. for Adult Congenital Heart Disease, Newark, 1997—2004; rsch. scientist Stokes Rsch. Inst., The Children's Hosp. of Phila., 1998—; assoc. prof. of surgery U. of Pa., Phila., 2003—; attending surgeon The Congenital Heart Inst., Orlando, Fla., 2004—; prof. surgery Coll. Medicine, U. Ctrl. Fla.; dept. surgery Arnold Palmer Hosp. Children. Mem. strategic planning U.S. space program NASA, Mass., 1982—84, mem. space life sciences strategic planning subcom., 1984—87, mem. radiation biology rev. team, 1987—88; mem. performance subcom. cardiovasc. health adv. panel N.J. Dept. of Health and Sr. Svs., Trenton, 2002—04; guest reviewer Jour. of Thoracic and Cardiovasc. Surgery, Annals of Thoracic Surgery, Circulation, Anesthesia and Analgesia. Author: (peer-reviewed publs.) Journal of Thoracic and Cardiovascular Surgery, Annals of Thoracic Surgery, Circulation, Annals of Surgery, and others, Astrophysical Jour., Icarus, Moon & Planets, and others, (book chpts.) Gardner and Spray's Operative Cardiac Surgery, Current Pediatric Therapy, Pediatric Cardiac Surgery Annual, Yearbook of Medicine 1996, Endovascular Surgery, The Human Quest of Space, and others; contbr. Surgeon internat. vol. med. orgn. Heart to Heart, Inc. Fellow Paul Harris, Rotary Internat., 2000, Carl and Leah McConnell Surg. Rsch. fellow, Stanford U., 1986, Chaim Weismann Rsch. fellow, Calif. Inst. of Tech., 1979-80, ACS, 1996—, Am. Coll. Chest Physicians, 1996—, Am. Coll. Cardiology, 2001—; scholar Lee A. Loomis scholar, Harvard U., 1973. Mem.: Congenital Heart Surgeons Soc., Norman E. Shumway Surg. Soc., Internat. Soc. Adult Congenital Cardiac Disease, Soc. Thoracic Surgeons, Am. Assn. Thoracic Surgery. Achievements include patents for #5571127, scalpel handle having retractable blade support and method of use; #5797879 adjustable vascular shunt for control of pulmonary blood flow and method of use; #6053891 apparatus and methods for providing selectively adjustable blood flow through a vascular graft; participation in the greatest distance land-to-sea rescue mission in the history of the U.S. Air Force, 1987; primary authored the first paper analyzing ten year followup of survivors of heart transplantation, reprinted in the 1996 Year Book of Medicine. Home: 314 Salvadore Square Orlando FL 32789 Office: Congenital Heart Institute 50 Sturtevant St Orlando FL 32806 E-mail: wdecampli@orhs.org.

DE CANDIA, ERICA, medical educator, researcher; b. Italy, May 12, 1961; MD, Cath. U. Sch. Medicine, PhD, 1985. Asst. prof. internal medicine Cath. U. Rome, Sch. Medicine, 1996—2006; vis. asst. prof. U. Calif. San Francisco, Cardiovasc. Rsch. Inst., 2007—10. Contbr. articles to profl. jours. Marie Curie Action, Internat. Outgoing fellowship, European Commn. Mem.: Internat. Soc. Haemostasis and Thrombosis. Avocations: sailing, reading, sports. Home: Via della Mendola 185 Rome 00135 Italy Business E-Mail: edecandia@rm.unicatt.it.

DECARLI, JAMES MAX, neuroepidemiologist; b. Ont., Aug. 23, 1960; s. Condy Max and Anita Marie DeCarli; life ptnr. Ivette Isabel Sandoval; 1 child, Andrea Isabel Zometa. BS, Calif. Poly. U., Pomona, 1986; Diploma, Oxford U., Eng., 1988; MPA, U. Southern Calif., LA, 1989; MPH, George Washington U., Washington, 2000; Attended in Neurosci., U. Southern Calif., LA, 2002—11. Cert. CPS technician Safe Kids Worldwide, Calif., 2001, master health edn. specialist Soc. Pub. Health Edn., 2011, in trauma model therapy 2008. Program grant mgr. State of Calif., San Bernardino, 1989—92; pres., owner Health Svcs. Rsch. Consultants, Loma Linda, Calif., 1992—96; mgmt. cons. JLP Veterans Med. Ctr., Loma Linda, Calif., 1992—93; health educator U. Southern Calif., U. Pk. Student Health Ctr., LA, 1999—2000; evidenced-based cons. APHA, Adherence to Chronic Disease Treatment Task Force, Washington, 1999—99; grad. rsch. asst. George Washington U., Pub. Health & Health Svcs., Prevention & Cmty. Health, Washington, 1998—99, tchg. asst., 1999—2000; rsch. analyst III, behavioral sci. neuroepidemiologist, dept. pub. health Chronic Disease & Injury Prevention, LA, 2000—; intern Intergovt. Affairs, White House, 1998—99. Student intern White House, Office Mgmt. & Budget, Washington, 1988—89; grad. project rev. Nat. SAFE KIDS Campaign, Washington, 1999—2000; sci. evaluator mem., dept. pub. health Rsch. & Evaluation Com., LA, 2001—04; pub. health rep. Child and Adolescent Suicide Rev. Team, LA, 2002—, Prevention & Early Intervention, Mental Health Svcs. Act, LA, 2007—, Assn. Batterers Intervention Programs, LA, 2007—, Inter-Agency Coun. Child Abuse and Neglect, LA, 2004—; grant reviewer Office Adolescent Pregnancy Programs, Washington, 2002—; exec. bd. mem. ABC's of Safe Summer, Burbank, Calif., 2002—; editl. bd. mem. Public's Health Rx for Prevention, Newsletter Med. Profls., LA, 2003—; bd. mem. Safe Kids LA, LA, 2003—; spkr. Am. Youth Leadership Found. Medicine, LA, 2004—06; sci. rsch. assoc. USC Davis Sch. Gerontology - Ethel Percy Andrus Gerontology Ctr., LA, 2006—; co-leader Challenge Area 4 Rsch. Team, Calif. State Hwy. Safety Plan, LA, 2006—; rsch. mem. LA County Elder Abuse Forensic Ctr., 2007—; chmn. Safe Kids Coalition, LA, 2007—09; scientist reviewer Deployment Related Med. Rsch. Program, HDA-Trauma Treatment & Rehab., Washington, 2008; co-leader Injury Prodn. Alliance or LA County Children's Hosp., 2008—; sci. mem. Child Injury Policy Com. State Calif. Dept. Pub. Health, 2010; coord. Safe Kids LA, 2010—; com. mem. Calif. Childhood Injury Policy Com., CDC, Calif. Dept. Pub. Health, 2010. Contbr. scientific papers to profl. jours. Recipient Award, Am. Coll. Physician Exec., 1994; named Outstanding Young Am., Outstanding Young Am., 1996—98. Mem.: Soc. Neuroscience, Am. Profl. Soc. Abuse Children, Internat. Positive Psychology Assn., Am. Pub. Health Assn.-Mental Health Sect., Psychoneuroimmunology Rsch. Soc., Eta Sigma Gamma. Achievements include research in preventing listeriosis among pregnant women; occupational injury prevention among child passenger safety technicians: An ergonomic approac; driver distraction: an evidenced-based review; injury risks and prevention among children Ages 1-15 in LA county; applied neuroscience to public health intervention strategies to modify risky behaviors; adult manifestations of childhood sexual abuse; elder abuse assessment and cognitive interviewing; atrophy of hippocampus due to elevated glucocorticoids: a biomarker for Alzheimer's Disease; elevated glucocorticoids among victims of intimate partner violence as a biomarker for alzheimer's disease; genetic Predisposition of Alzheimer's Disease", Alzheimer's Disease International, Cochin, Indi; trauma and early abuse as a biomarker for the development of anxiety disorders; neuropsychobiological prevention model linking early childhood and lifetime Exposure to abuse and Neglect to elder maltreatment; creation of a neuropsychobiological prevention & assessment model for elder maltreatment; establishment of phases of opportunities for effective interventions to reduce adolescent risky behavior; identification of a model five neurodevelopmental predisposing factors to risky behaviors in adolescence; identification of an adolescent protective neurodevelopmental pathway for primary prevention of risk taking in adolescent. Office: LA County Pub Health IVPP 3530 Wilshire Blvd Ste 800 Los Angeles CA 90010 Office Phone: 213-351-7846. Office Fax: 213-351-2714. Business E-Mail: jdecarli@ph.lacounty.gov.

DE CAROLIS, CATERINA, gynecologist; b. Rome, June 23, 1957; MD, La Sapienza U. Rome, 1981. Specialist in pediat. ob-gyn. 1985. Head operative unit recurrent spontaneous abortion ASL Roma C, 2002—05; head ob-gyn. San Giovanni Hosp., 2005—. Prof. U. Rome Tor Vergata, Cath. U. Rome, 1992. Grant, Cenci Bolognetti, 1981, Minerva, 2006. Avocation: music. Office: Via Amba Aradam 9 Rome 00184 Italy Office Fax: 00390677055861. Business E-Mail: caterina.decarolis@fastwebnet.it.

DE CASTRIES, HENRI, corporate financial executive; b. Bayonne, France, Aug. 15, 1954; married; 3 children. Grad. law degree, ENA; attended, Ecole des Hautes Etudes Commerciales. With French Fin. Ministry Inspection Office, 1980-84, TF1-French Nat. TV Network, 1986; dep. sec. Inter-Ministerial Com. on Indsl. Restructuring; with AXA, 1989—, corp. sec., 1991—93, sr. exec. pres., 1993—2000, chmn. mgmt. bd., 2000—; chmn. AXA Fin., 1997. Chmn. The Equitable Cos., US; treas. AXA Atout Coeur.; city councilor Abitain, Pyrenees, 1983-; mem. bd. Assn. pour l'Aide aux Jeunes Infirmes. Recipient Chevalier de l'Ordre National du Mérite, 1996, Chevalier de la Légion d'Honneur, 2001. Office: AXA Group 25 Avenue Matignon 75008 Paris France

DECASTRO, ALFREDO P., physician, consultant; b. Ibaan, Batangas, Philippines, Apr. 30, 1943; arrived in U.S., 1971; s. Joaquin Guerra and Graciana P. DeCastro; m. Leonora DeCastro, July 21, 1976; 1 child, Elaine. BS, Univ. St. Thomas, Manila, 1964, MD, 1969. Diplomate Am. Bd. Radiology. Cons. Ellenville (NY) Med. Group, 1976—97; med. staff St. Francis Hosp., Port Jervis, NY, 1976—89, Ellenville Cmty. Hosp., 1976—97, chmn. dept. radiology, 1990—97; pvt. practice Port Jervis, NY. Cons. in field. Home: 11 Tommy Ln Port Jervis NY 12771 Office: 6 Skinner St Port Jervis NY 12771 Office Phone: 845-355-1617.

DE CHERNEY, ALAN HERSH, obstetrics and gynecology educator; b. Phila., Feb. 13, 1942; s. William Aaron and Ruth (Hersh) De Cherney; m. Deanna Faith Saver, June 26, 1966; children: Peter, Alexander. BS in Natural Scis., Muhlenberg Coll., 1963; MD, Temple U., 1967; MA (hon.), Yale U., 1985. Diplomate Am. Bd. Ob-Gyn (examiner 1984-, bd. dirs. 1995-), Am. Bd. Reproductive Endocrinology (bd. dirs. 1988-94), Nat. Bd. Med. Examiners (examiner 1987-90). Intern in gen. medicine U. Pitts., 1967-68; resident in ob-gyn. U. Pa., Phila., 1968-72, instr. dept. ob-gyn, 1970-72; asst. prof. ob-gyn. Yale U. Sch. Medicine, New Haven, 1974-78, assoc. prof., 1979-84, prof., 1984-91, John Slade Ely prof. ob-gyn, 1987-92, dir. div. reproductive endocrinology, dept. ob-gyn, 1982-92, lectr. dept. biology, 1985-92; Louis E. Phaneuf prof., chmn. dept. ob-gyn. Tufts U. Sch. Medicine, 1992-96; prof. dept. ob-gyn. UCLA, 1996—2006; chief Reproductive Biology and Medicine Br. NIH, Bethesda, Md., 2006—. Editor-in-chief: Fertility and Sterility, 1996—. Maj. US Army, 1972—74. Recipient Disting. Alumni award, Temple U., 1989, 2002, Muhlenberg Coll., 1994. Fellow: IOM, ACOG, Soc. Gynecologic Investigation (pres. 1994—95), Soc. Study Reproduction, Soc. Gynecologic Surgeons, European Soc. Human Reproductions and Embryology, Endocrine Soc., Soc. Reproductive Surgeons (charter, pres. 1991), Soc. Reproductive Endocrinologists (pres. 1988), Soc. Assisted Reproductive Tech. (pres. 1987—88), Am. Assn. History Medicine, Am. Fertility Soc. (pres. 1994—95). Office: NIH Reproductive Biology and Medicine Br Nat Inst Child Health and Human Devel Bldg 10 CRC 1 E Rm 1-3140 10 Center Dr M Bethesda MD 20892-5800 Office Phone: 301-496-5800. Personal E-mail: decherney@gmail.com. Business E-Mail: decherney@nih.mail.gov, dcherney@mednet.ucla.edu, decherna@mail.nih.gov.

DECHURCH, STEPHANIE J., pediatrician; b. Mt. Clemens, Mich., Mar. 31, 1974; m. James DeChurch. MD, U. Fla. Coll. Medicine, Gainesville, 2000. Resident, pediat. Miami Children's Hosp., Fla.; staff mem. South Fla. Pediat. Partners, 2000—, Baptist Children's Hosp., Miami, 2003—, South Miami Hosp., 2003. Office: South Fla Pediat Partners 7800 SW 87th Ave #C-350 Miami FL 33173 Office Phone: 305-271-4711. Office Fax: 305-271-8732.

DECI, EDWARD LEWIS, psychologist, educator; b. Clifton Springs, NY, Oct. 14, 1942; s. Charles Henry and Janice Margaret (Upchurch) Deci. AB, Hamilton Coll., 1964; postgrad., London Sch. Econs., 1965; MBA, U. Pa., 1967; PhD, Carnegie-Mellon U., 1970. Postdoctoral fellow Stanford U., 1973-74; mem. faculty U. Rochester, NY, 1970—, prof. psychology, 1978—, chair dept. psychology, 1993—94, Helen F. and Fred H. Gowen prof. social scis., 2005—; pvt. practice psychotherapy, 1975—; pres. Inst. for Rsch. and Reform in Edn., 1995-97, chmn., 1997—2008. Hon. pres. Can. Psychol. Assn., 2006—07; lectr. in field; cons. in field. Author: (book) Intrinsic Motovation, 1975, The Psychology of Self-Determination, 1980; co-author: Industrial and Organizational Psychology, 1977, Intrinsic Motivation and Self-Determination in Human Behavior, 1985, Why We Do What We Do, 1995. Pres. Monhegan Mus. Assn., 1984—; trustee Monhegan (Maine) Conservation Assocs., 1982—89, 1992—95, Monhegan Artist Residency Corp., Maine, 1998—, Monhegan Island Sustainable Cmty. Assn., 2001—06. Grantee NIMH, 1977—78, 1989—94, NSF, 1981—83, Nat. Inst. Child Health and Human Devel., 1986—89, 1990—96, US-Israel Bi-Nat. Sci. Found., 2004, Bill and Melinda Gates Found., 2006—08, Inst. Edn. Scis., 2007—. Fellow: APA, Assn. Psychol. Sci. Office: U Rochester Psychology Dept Rochester NY 14627 Business E-Mail: deci@psych.rochester.edu.

DECIUTIIS, ALFRED CHARLES MARIA, oncologist, television producer; b. NYC, Oct. 16, 1945; s. Alfred Ralph and Theresa Elizabeth (Manko) deCiutiis; m. Catherine L. Gohn. BS summa cum laude, Fordham U., 1967; MD, Columbia U., 1971. Diplomate Am. Bd. Internal Medicine, Am. Bd. Med. Oncology. Intern N.Y. Hosp.-Cornell Med. Ctr., NYC, 1971-72, resident, 1972-74; fellow in clin. immunology Meml. Hosp.-Sloan Kettering Cancer Ctr., NYC, 1974-75, fellow in clin. oncology, 1975-76, spl. fellow in immunology, 1974-76; guest investigator, asst. physician exptl. hematology Rockefeller U., NYC, 1975-76; pvt. practice specializing in med. oncology LA, 1977—. Mem. adult bone marrow transplant team Memorial Sloan-Kettering Cancer Ctr., 1974—76; chief oncology svc. Misericordia Hosp. (now Mercy Hosp. Cornell Med. Ctr.), Bronx, NY, 1976; mem. med. adv. com. Olympics, 1984; co-founder Medtrina Med. Ctr., Torrance, Calif., physician asst. supr., 1984; mem. fgn. policy leadership project Ctr. Internat. Affairs, Harvard, Ill. Host cable TV shows, 1981—, med. editor Cable Health Network, 1983—, Lifetime Network, 1984—; syndicated columnist: Coast Media News, 1980; prodr.: numerous med. TV shows; interviewed: numerous stars; author: (Landmark sci. paper) Defects in the Alternate Pathway of Complement Activation post Splenectomy; contbr. articles to profl. jours. Mem. gov. bd. med. coun. Italian-Am. Found.; mem. Italian-Am. Civic Com., LA, 1983, Cath. League Civil and Rel. Liberty, World Affairs Coun., LA, Boston Mus. Fine Arts, Met. Mus.; founder Italian-Am. Med. Assn., 1982; co-founder Italian-Am. Legal Alliance, LA, 1982—; mem. UCLA Chancellor's Assocs. Served to capt. M.C. US Army, 1972—74. Leukemia Soc. Am. fellow, 1974—76. Fellow: ACP, Internat. Coll. Physicians and Surgeons; mem.: AAAS, AMA (Physician's Recognition award 1978—80, 1982—85, 1986—89, 1989—91, 1991—94, 1994—96, 1996—99, 1999—2002, 2002—04), Am. Soc. Hematology (emeritus), Internat. Platform Assn., Drug Info. Assn., Chinese Med. Assn., Am. Geriat. Soc., Am. Pub. Health Assn., N.Y. Acad. Sci. (life), Internat. Health Soc., Am. Union Physicians and Dentists, Los Angeles County Med. Assn., Calif. Med. Assn., Am. Soc. Clin. Oncology, Mensa, Smithsonian Instn., Nat. Geog. Soc. (life), Fondazione Giovanni Agnelli, Nature Conservancy, Nat. Wildlife Fedn., Sigma Xi, Alpha Omega Alpha, Phi Beta Kappa. Achievements include participated on some of the first bone marrow transplants in the USA; 1st comprehensive clinical description of chronic fatigue syndrome as a neuro-immunologic acquired disorder, probably induced by a retrovirus, 1991 Audio Digest. Office: PO Box 384 Agoura Hills CA 91376-0384

DECKER, MARK JONATHAN, radiologist; b. Suffern, NY, Oct. 3, 1966; s. Alan Barry and Shelley Decker; m. Dina Loren, June 12, 1993; children: Jake, Alexandra, Nicholas, Christopher. BS, Union Coll., Schnectady, NY, 1988; postgrad., NYU, NYC, 1988—89; MD, Mt. Sinai Sch. Medicine, NYC, 1993. Diplomate Am. Bd. Radiology. Radiology resident Mt. Sinai Hosp., Miami, Fla., 1993—97; musculoskeletal fellow Hosp. Spl. Surgery, NYC, 1997—98; dir. MRI Radiologic Health Sci., Smithtown, NY, Port Jefferson, NY, 1998—2001; dir. orthop. radiology Zwanger & Peseri, Plainview, NY, Massapequa, NY, 2001—04; dir. MRI & orthop. radiology Met. Diagnostic Imaging P.C., NYC, Forest Hills, Garden City, Bklyn., 2004—. Mem.: Pediatric Soc. N. Am., Radiologic Soc. N.Am., Am. Coll. Radiology, Soc. Skeletal Radiology. Avocations: hockey, soccer, lacrosse, baseball, drums.

DECKER, MICHAEL D., medical epidemiologist; b. Chgo., Sept. 26, 1946; BS, Calif. Inst. Tech., 1969; MD, Rush Med. Coll., 1978; MPH, U. Ill. Sch. Pub. Health, 1982. Prof. preventive medicine and infectious diseases Vanderbilt U. Sch. Medicine, 1984—2000, adj. prof. preventive medicine, 2000; v.p., sci. & med. affairs Sanofi Pasteur, 2000—. Editor-in-chief Infection Control and Hosp. Epidemiology, 1993—2001; mem. Nat. Vaccine Adv. Com., 1996—2000, Vaccines and Related Biol. Products Adv. Com., 2001—04. Recipient Alexander D. Langmuir award, CDC EIS Alumni Assn., Stephen R. Preblud award, Ctrs. Disease Control and Prevention. Fellow: ACP, Am. Coll. Epidemiology, Infectious Diseases Soc. America; mem.: Am. Epidemiol. Soc., Pediat. Infectious Diseases Soc., Delta Omega Pub. Health Honor Soc. Avocation: fencing. Office: 1 Discovery Dr Swiftwater PA 18370

DECKERS, PETER JOHN, surgeon, former dean; b. Boston, Feb. 13, 1941; married, 1964; 7 children. BA cum laude, Coll. of the Holy Cross, 1962; MD cum laude, Boston U., 1966. Diplomate Nat. Bd. Med. Examiners, Am. Bd. Surgery. Med. intern Boston City Hosp., 1966—67; jr. asst. resident gen. surgery Boston U. Med. Ctr., Univ. Hosp., 1967—68; clin. assoc. surgery br. Nat. Cancer Inst., NIH, Bethesda, 1968—70; resident gen. surgery Boston U. Med. Ctr., U. Hosp., 1971, UPSHS trainee in acad. surgyer, 1971—72, resident in gen. surgery, 1972—73, chief resident in gen. surgery, 1973—74; staff surgeon Boston City Hosp., 1974—84; asst. to assoc. prof. surgery Boston U. Sch. Medicine, 1974—78; dean U. Conn. Sch. of Medicine, 1995—2008, exec. v.p. health affairs, 2000—08; staff surgeon U. Conn. Health Ctr. Attending staff gen. surgery John Dempsey Hosp./U. Conn. Health Ctr., 1984—, VA Med. Ctr., 1984-89; sr. staff dept. surgery Hartford Hosp., 1984—; program dir. Hartford Hosp.-U. Conn. Integrated Surg. Residency Program, 1984-94; dir. divsn. of gen. surgery Hartford Hosp., 1984-87; sr. staff dept. surgery New Britain Gen. Hosp., 1989—, Dept. Surgery, Mt. Sinai Hosp., 1989—, St. Francis Hosp. and Med. Ctr., 1988—; chmn. dept. surgery Hartford Hosp., 1987-94, Murray-Heilig prof., chmn. dept. surgery U. Conn. Sch. of Medicine, 1987-95; surgeon-in-chief John Dempsey Hosp., 1990-94; program dir. U. of Conn. Integrated Gen. Surg. Residency Tng. Program, 1990-94; interim dean, 1992-94; exec. v.p. for clin. affairs U. Conn. Health System, 1994-95; exec. v.p. for physician practice orgn. U. Conn. Health System, 1995—. Editl. bd. Breast Surgery: Index and Reviews, 1993, Surg. Oncology, 1991; contbr. numerous articles to profl. jours. Recipient First Prize James Ewing Resident Rsch. award, 1971; recipient numerous grants. Mem. Transplantation Soc., Am. Assn. for Cancer Rsch., Eastern Coop. Oncology Group, Assn. for Acad. Surgery, Am. Assn. for Cancer Edn., Am. Fedn. for Clin. Rsch., Mass. Med. Soc., Am. Radium Soc. (exec. com. 1989-91), Am. Soc. of Clin. Oncology, Soc. of Surg. Oncology (mem. coms.), Soc. of Univ. Surgeons, New England Cancer Soc. (pres. 1993, pres.-elect, 1992, exec. coun. 1991-94), Boston Surg. Soc., Societe Internationale de Chirurgie, Bay State Health Care, Soc. for the Surgery of the Alimentary Tract, New England Surg. Soc. (treas. 1996-98, pres. 1999), Assn. of Program Dirs. in Surgeons (pres.-elect 1990-91, pres. 1991-92), Conn. State Med. Soc. (mem. cancer coordinating com. 1990-91), Am. Cancer Soc. (Hartford chpt.), Connecticare, Hartford County Med. Assn., Soc. of Surg. Chmn. Office: U Conn Health Ctr L1096 / MC3804 263 Farmington Ave Farmington CT 06030-3800 Office Phone: 860-679-3880. E-mail: deckers@nso.uchc.edu.

DECKING, ULRICH KARL MARIA, physiologist, researcher; b. Lippstadt, Germany, Jan. 20, 1963; s. Alexander Decking and Helene Dr. Decking. MD, Rheinisch-Westfaelische Technische Hochschule, Aachen, Germany, 1989. Diplomate Germany, 1989, lic. physician Germany, 1991. Rsch. asst. dept. radiol. scis. Guy's Hosp., London, 1989—90; rsch. asst. dept. physiology Heinrich-Heine-U., Duesseldorf, Germany, 1990—96, asst. prof., 1996—2001, assoc. prof., 2001—, dep. dean edn., 2006—. Cons. NIH, Bethesda, Md., 2001—02; spkr. Pax Christi Cologne, Cologne, Germany, 1998—. Contbr. articles to profl. jours. Recipient Borchers-Plakette award, Rheinisch-Westfaelische Technische Hochschule, Aachen, 1991, Edens prize, U. Dusseldorf, 2001; scholar, Cusanuswerk, 1984—89, German Academic Exch. Svc., 1986. Mem.: German Physiol. Soc., German Cardiac Soc. (chmn. working group 2003—05, Oskar-Lapp prize 1997). Achievements include research in cardiac metabolism and function; discovery of hypoxia-induced inhibition of adenosine kinase; spatial heterogeneity of flow, metabolism and protein expression in the heart. Office: Dept Cardiovasc Physiology Heinrich-Heine-Univ Düsseldorf PO Box 101007 40001 Düsseldorf Germany Office Phone: 49-211-81-12651, 49-211-81-14576. Office Fax: 49-211-81-10562. Personal E-mail: ulrich.decking@t-online.de. Business E-Mail: decking@uni-duesseldorf.de.

DECLEVES, XAVIER, medical educator; b. Paris, July 7, 1970; PhD, Pharmacy Paris Descartes, PharmD, 2000. Assoc. prof., pharmacokinetics U. Paris Descartes, 2004—. Office: Faculty Pharmacy 4 Ave de l'obser Paris 75006 France Business E-Mail: xavier.decleves@parisdescartes.fr.

DE COCK, KEVIN, public health service officer; b. Belgium; B in Surgery, U. Bristol, UK, MD; diploma in tropical medicine and hygiene, Liverpool U., UK. Lic. in medicine UK, Calif., registered specialist in infectious and tropical diseases UK. Svc. in various positions and med. schools in the UK, US and sub-Sahara Africa; dir. divsn. HIV/AIDS prevention surveillance and epidemiology Centers

Disease Control and Prevention, Atlanta, dir. Kenya, 2000—06, 2009—10, dir. Ctr. Global Health Atlanta, 2010—; dir. dept. HIV/AIDS WHO, 2006—09. Vis. prof. medicine and internat. health London Sch. Hygiene and Tropical Medicine; ex-officio mem. adv. bd. NIH Fogarty Internat. Ctr. Co-editor: AIDS in Africa, Second Edit., 1997; mem. editl. bd.: AIDS, The Lancet, The New Eng. Jour. Medicine; contbr. articles to profl. jours., chapters to books. Decorated Comdr. of Order Pub. Health Côte d'Ivoire; recipient Chalmers medal, Royal Soc. Tropical Medicine and Hygiene, Internat. Health Honor award, CDC, ATSDR, Mackel award, CDC, William C. Watson Jr. medal. Fellow: Royal Coll. Physicians, UK. Office: Centers Disease Control and Prevention Ctr Global Health 1600 Clifton Rd Atlanta GA 30333 *

DE CORBIERE, STEPHANE PIERRE, surgeon, editor; b. St. Sever, France, Sept. 13, 1957; s. Pierre Marie and Anne De Corbiere; m. Virginie Marie Lecoquiere, June 28, 1980; children: Cecile Aude, Romaric, Louis, Robin, Faustine. D with honors, Med. Faculty Broussais, Paris, 1987. Diplomate Université René Descartes, Paris, cert. ENT Med. U. Paris, head and neck surgery Med. U. Paris. Asst. dept. ENT surgery Foch Hosp., Suresnes, France, 1989—99; med. practician cancer dept. René Huguenin Hosp., Saint-Cloud, France, 1994—2004; head ENT dept. Am. Hosp. Paris, Neuilly-sur-Seine, France, 1998—, head stomatology dept., 2004—. Editor: French ENT Soc. rev., 1989—2003; contbr. articles to profl. jours. Maj. M.C. French Army, 1984—86. Recipient award, Med. Sch. Paris, 1987. Fellow: ACS (life); mem.: Am. Acad. Otolaryngology Head and Neck Surgery (corr.), Romanian Acad. Sci. (hon.), French Acad. Surgery (assoc.). Roman Catholic. Achievements include development of use of Dye Laser and Phototherapy in Ortorhinolaryngology for the treatment of tumors; phase I multicentre, open labelled, light dose ranging study into the effect of foscan-medicated photodynamic therapy (PDT) on primary laryngeal cancer. Avocations: travel, tennis. Office: Am Hosp Paris 63 Blvd Victor Hugo Neuilly-sur-Seine 92200 France Home: 36 Rue de Lubeck 75116 Paris France Home Fax: 00 33 1 56 28 17 85. Personal E-mail: solecorbiare@gmail.com. Business E-Mail: stephane.decorbiere@online.fr.

DE COURTEN, BARBORA, medical educator; b. Bratislava, Slovakia, Nov. 8, 1973; MD, Comenius U., 1998, PhD, 2002. Resident, dept. internal medicine, diabetes and metabolic sect. Derer Tchg. Hosp. Med. Faculty, Bratislava, 1998—99; US fogarty vis. fellow Nat. Inst. Diabetes, Digestive and Kidney Diseases NIH, Phoenix, 1999—2003; sr. rsch. officer Baker IDI Heart and Diabetes Inst., Melbourne, Australia, 2004—07, head, assoc. prof., clin. endocrinology and metabolic studies, 2008—; advanced trainee Professorial Gen. Med. Unit Alfred Hosp., Melbourne, 2009—10. Hon. vis. physician Gen. Med. Ward Colonial War Meml. Hosp., Suva, Fiji, 2003—04; supr., dept. physiology Monash U., 2005—06; hon. sr. lectr., dept. epidemiology and preventive medicine Faculty Medicine Nursing and Health Sci. Monash U., Melbourne, 2005—10. Recipient Career Devel. award, NHMRC, Millennium award, Diabetes Australia Rsch. Trust, Slovak Diabetes Assn. award; Rsch. Excellence fellowship, NIH. Fellow: Royal Coll. Physicians; mem.: Australian Diabetes Assn., Am. Diabetes Assn. Avocations: skiing, scuba diving, travel. Home: 25/49 Head St Brighton Victoria 3186 Australia Personal E-mail: bdecourten@mac.com.

DE CRÉE, CARL, reproductive endocrinologist; b. Elsene, Brussels, June 19, 1962; s. Isidoor Willem De Crée and Amelia Louisa Huybrechts. MD cum laude, U. Brussels, 1985; M of Phys. Edn. and Sports Medicine cum laude, U. Leuven, Belgium, 1985, MA in Asian Lang. and History, 1986, MSc in Med. Sci. cum laude, 1992. Cert. in ob-gyn., sexology, exercise physiology, electrocardiography, judo and jujutsu coach and referee, cert. FAA comml. pilot, instr. Sci. asst. rsch. unit St. Bartholomew's Hosp., Antwerp, Belgium, 1981-83; med. advisor Takeda Pharms., Osaka, Japan, 1987; rsch. scientist U. Maastricht, 1991-92; mgr. exec. seminars Assn. Ind. Health Ins., Malines, 1992-93; assoc. prof. Inst. Gynecol.-Endocrinol. Rsch., Leuven, 1992-99, rsch. prof., 1999-2000; assoc. prof. De Montfort U., Bedford, U.K., 1995-99; dept. clin. biostats. and rsch. data analysis Merck Inc., 2001—02; ops. mgr. Lang. and Computing, Inc., Ghent, 2002—03, U. Puget Found., Tacoma, 2003—10. Vis. prof. U. Copenhagen, 1986-87, U. Coimbra, Portugal, 1992, U. Kyoto, 1993-94; chmn., founder Med. Commn. of Belgian Jujutsu Fedn., 1989-93, Flemish Martial Arts Assn., 1989-94, Cultural Assn. for Japanese Studies and Martial Arts; mem. med. commn. Flemish Sports Fedn., 1989-93; mem. Flemish Anti-Doping Commn. of Ministry of Nat. Health, 1990-93; prof. judo and jujutsu, ofcl. referee; mem. tchg. staff Belgian Govtl. Inst. for Tng. and Coaching Edn., Brussels; dir. Multicenter Interuniv. Project on Reproductive Endocrinology in Women in Sport and Exercise; adj. chief reproductive endocrinology Inst. for Gynecol.-Endocrinol. Rsch., Leuven. Author: The Mechanisms, Monitoring and Management of Exercise-Related Disorders of Estrogen Metabolism in Women, 1998; contbr. articles to profl. jours. Under-lt. Med. Svc., Belgian Army, 1988-89. Recipient Minority Scientist Devel. award Regional Scientist Support Found., 1988-89; vis. scientist grant Dutch Govt., 1987, 90, Clin. Rsch. fellow CVAM, 1989-91. Mem. ACOG, Am. Coll. Sports Medicine, Am. Reproductive Soc., Brit. Assn. Sports and Exercise Sci., Brit. Assn. Sports and Medicine, Brit. Royal Soc. Medicine, Dutch Soc. for Exercise Physiology, Am. Endocrine Soc., Flemish Assn. for Sports Medicine, Flemish Assn. Sexology, Internat. Soc. Gynecol. Endocrinology, N.Y. Acad. Scis., French Soc. Wilhelm Furtwängler, Friends of the London Philharm., Sports Medicine Australia, Dutch Vereiniging Vrienden van het Concert gebouworkest. Avocations: japanese martial arts and culture, music, literature, wine, calligraphy. Home: Zakstraat 12 B-2800 Mechelem Belgium Office: Postbus 125 2800 Mechezen Belgium E-mail: cdecree@earthlink.net.

DEDDENS, ALAN EUGENE, otolaryngologist, head and neck surgeon; b. Louisville, Aug. 17, 1959; s. Eugene H. and Patricia A. (Silliman) D.; m. Ann Marie Gwynn, May 22, 1987; children: Kelci M., Marissa A. BS in Biomed. Engring., Tulane U., 1981; MD, U. Louisville, 1987. Field design biomed. engr. Med. Sys. divsn. GE Co., 1981-83; intern Barnes-Jewish Hosp., St. Louis, 1987-88; resident in otolaryngology Barnes Hosp.-Wash. U., St. Louis, 1988-93, fellow, 1993-94. Recipient Resident Tchg. award Dept. Otolaryngology, HNS, Continuing Med. Edn. Achievement award AAO-HNS, 1997—; named Ky. Col., 1987. Fellow ACS, Am. Acad. Otolaryngology-Head and Neck Surgery, Am. Acad. Otolaryngologic Allergy (examiner oral bd. 1995-97, 99, 2001, 03, 05-06), Am. Acad. Facial Plastic and Reconstructive Surgery, Tau Beta Pi, Alpha Eta Mu Beta, Alpha Omega Alpha (Outstanding Sr. Student award 1987). Achievements include research in design of implantable stimulator; influence of an environment on the developing vestibular system; implantable middle ear hearing aid project. Office: Piedmont Health Care Oto-Head Neck Surgery 707 Bryant St Statesville NC 28677-4142 Office Phone: 704-873-5224.

DEDIO, ROBERT, otolaryngologist; BA, Colgate U., Hamilton, NY, 1981; MD, NYU, 1985. Intern Hosp. U. Pa., 1985—86, resident, 1986—90; staff otolaryngology divsn. Leigh Valley Hosp., Allentown, Pa., 1991—. Fellow: ACS, Am. Acad. Otolaryngology. Office Phone: 610-366-1366.

DEDIU, MIRCEA, physician, researcher; b. Bucharest, Romania, Aug. 30, 1956; m. Ileana Grigorescu, Apr. 19, 1980; children: Stefan, Mihai, Matei. MD, U. Medicine and Pharmacy Carol Davila, Bucharest, 1981. Intern Inst. Medicine and Pharmacy, Bucharest, 1981-84; gen. practitioner Village Surgery Gostinu (Romania), 1984-89; emergency dr. Ambulance Svc., Bucharest, 1986-90; med. oncology sr. cons. Inst. Oncology Bucharest, 1989—. Author: Guideline for Treatment and Diagnosis of Lung Cancer, 1999, Bronchopulmonary Cancer, 2000; contbr. articles to profl. jours. Mem. European Soc. Med. Oncology, Internat. Assn. Study Lung Cancer, Olimpia Karate Sport Club. Achievements include research in advances for the treatment of lung cancer. Black belt in shodan, karate, shotokan. Home: D-na Ghica Nr 3 BL 2 Ap 34 Sector 2 Bucharest 72404 Romania Office: Inst Oncology Bucharest Sos Fundeni Nr 252 Bucharest 72425 Romania

DEDKOV, EDUARD I., medical educator, researcher; b. Sevastopol, Crimea, Ukraine, July 28, 1969; s. Ivan S. Dedkov and Tamara V. Dedkova; m. Alla Ye Amelina; children: Alexandra E. Dedkova, Vladlena E. Dedkova. MD, Orenburg State Med. Inst., Russia, 1993; PhD, Orenburg State Med. Acad., Russia, 1996. Asst. prof. Orenburg State Med. Acad., 1996—96; postdoc. rsch. fellow U. Mich. Med. Sch., Ann Arbor, 1996—2003; asst. rsch. scientist U. Iowa Carver Coll. Medicine, 2003—06; asst. prof. biomed. scis. NY Coll. Osteo. Medicine NY Inst. Tech., Old Westbury, 2006—. With Armed Forces, 1988—89, USSR. Recipient Award, Am. Assn. Anatomists, 2002; Govt. scholarship, Dept. Higher Edn. Russian Fedn., 1995, Pres. scholarship, Dept. Higher Edn. Russian Fed., 1996. Mem.: North Am. Vascular Biology Orgn., Soc. Exptl. Biology & Medicine, Am. Physiol. Soc., Am. Heart Assn., Am. Assn. Anatomists. Avocations: reading, swimming, travel, camping. Office: NY Coll Osteopathic Medicine Northern Blvd / NYIT Old Westbury NY 11568-8000 Office Fax: 516-686-3832. Business E-Mail: ededkov@nyit.edu.

DE DOMENICO, IVANA, medical educator; b. Italy, June 1, 1978; BS, U. Messina, 2002, PhD, 2005. Asst. prof. U. Utah, 2008—. Mem.: Internat. BioIron Soc. (Hiromi Gunshin award 2009, Young Investigator award 2007—09). Avocations: piano, reading, travel. Office: 30 N 1900 E SOM Rm #5B313 Salt Lake City UT 84106 Business E-Mail: ivana.dedomenico@path.utah.edu.

DEDONATO, DONALD MICHAEL, obstetrician, gynecologist; b. Bridgeport, Conn., Apr. 25, 1952; s. Michael Anthony and Mary Jane (Zawacki) DeDonato; m. Susan Mary Naulty, June 15, 1974; children: Mark Dominic, David Nicholas. BA in Chemistry cum laude, Coll. Holy Cross, 1974; MD, Loyola U., Maywood, Ill., 1977. Intern Loyola Foster McGaw Hosp., Maywood, Ill., 1977-78; resident Ohio State U. Hosp., Columbus, Ohio, 1978-81; ob-gyn. Ob-Gyn. Assocs., Arlington Heights, Ill., 1981-87, DeDonato, Goodnough and Geittmann, Ob-Gyn., Arlington Heights, 1987-92; pres., CEO N.W. Women's Cons., Arlington Heights, 1993—. Clin. instr. Northwestern U. Med. Ctr., Chgo., 1981—; chmn. dept. ob-gyn. N.W. Cmty. Healthcare, 1998—2000. Mem. alumni bd. Loyola Stritch Sch. of Medicine, Maywood, Ill. Recipient CIBA award. Mem. AMA, Am. Assn. Med. Colls. (Loyola rep.), Chgo. Med. Soc., Ill. State Med. Soc., Am. Bd. Ob-Gyn., Am. Assn. Gyn. Laparoscopists, Garden Camera (pres. 1985-86, 92-93), Phi Beta Kappa, Alpha Sigma Nu. Avocation: photography. Office: NW Womens Cons 1630 W Central Rd Arlington Heights IL 60005-2407 Office Phone: 847-394-3553.

DE DUVE, CHRISTIAN RENÉ, chemist, educator; b. Thames-Ditton, Surrey, Eng., Oct. 2, 1917; s. Alphonse and Madeleine (Pungs) de Duve; m. Janine Herman de Duve, Sept. 30, 1943 (dec. 2008); children: Thierry, Anne, Françoise, Alain. MD, U. Louvain, Belgium, 1941, MS in Chemistry, 1946; PhD (hon.), U. Turin, 1969, U. Leiden, 1970, U. Sherbrooke, 1970, U. Lille, 1973, Cath. U. Santiago, Chile, 1974, U. René Descartes, Paris, 1974, State U. Liege, 1975, State U. Ghent, 1975, Gustavus Adolphus Coll., St. Peter, Minn., 1975, U. Rosario, Argentina, 1975, U. Aix-Marseille II, 1979, U. Keele, 1982, Katholieke U. Leuven, 1984, Karolinska Inst., Stockholm, 1986, U. Montreal, 1992, Rockefeller U., 1997. Lectr. physiol. chemistry faculty medicine Cath. U. Louvain, 1947—51, prof., head dept. physiol. chemistry, 1951—85, emeritus prof., 1985—; prof. biochem. cytology Rockefeller U., NYC, 1962—74, Andrew W. Mellon prof., 1974—88, prof. emeritus, 1988—. Vis. prof. Albert Einstein Coll. Medicine, Bronx, NY, 1961—62, Chaire Francqui State U. Ghent, 1962—63, Free U., Brussels, 1963—64, State U., Liège, 1972—73, Facultés U. Notre-Dame de la Paix, Namur, 1990—91; Mayne guest prof. U. Queensland, Brisbane, Australia, 1972; pres. Internat. Inst. Cellular & Molecular Pathology, Brussels, 1974—91. Author: The Lysosome, 1963, Lysosomes in Biology and Pathology, 1975, Cellular and Molecular Biology of the Pathological State, 1979, A Guided Tour of the Living Cell, 1984, Blueprint for a Cell: The Nature and Origin of Life, 1991, Vital Dust: Life As a Cosmic Imperative, 1995, Life Evolving: Molecules, Mind, and Meaning, 2002, Singularities: Landmarks on the Pathways of Life, 2005; mem. editl. bd.: Subcellular Biochemistry, 1971—87, Preparative Biochemistry, 1971—80, Molecular and Cellular Biochemistry, 1973—80. Mem. adv. bd. Ciba Found., 1960—85; mem. adult devel., aging rsch. and tng. rev. com. Nat. Inst. Child Health & Devel., NIH, 1970—73; mem. adv. com. med. rsch. WHO, 1974—79; mem. sci. adv. com. Max Planck-Inst. Immunbiology, Freiburg, Germany, 1975—78, Ludwig Inst. Cancer Rsch., 1985—91, Mary Imogene Bassett Rsch. Inst., Cooperstown, NY, 1986—90, Clin. Rsch. Inst. Montreal; mem. biology adv. com. NY Hall Sci., 1986—; mem. sci. adv. com. Basel Inst. Immunology, 1989—93. Recipient Francqui prize for biol. and med. scis., Belgium, 1960, Merit award, Gairdner Found. Internat., Can., 1967, Dr. H.P. Heineken prize, The Netherlands, 1973, Nobel prize for physiology/medicine, 1974, Theobald Smith award, Albany Med. Coll., 1981, Jimenez Diaz award, Spain, 1985. Fellow: AAAS; mem.: NAS, Soc. Belge Physiology, NY Acad. Scis., Internat. Soc. Cell Biology, European Cell Biology Orgn., European Molecular Biology Orgn., European Assn. Study Diabetes, Soc. Belge Biochim. (pres. 1962—64), Am. Soc. Cell Biology (coun. mem. 1966—69, E.B. Wilson award 1989), Pontifical Acad. Sci., Am. Soc. Biol. Chemists, Am. Philos. Soc., Biochem. Soc. (Harden award 1978), Am. Chem. Soc., Royal Acad. Belgium, Royal Acad. Medicine, German Assn. Cell Biology (assoc.), Acad. Europaea (assoc.), Acad. Scis. d'Athénes (assoc.), Acad. Scis. Paris (assoc.), Royal Soc. Can. (assoc.), Royal Soc. London (assoc.), Am. Acad. Arts and Scis. (assoc.), Sigma Xi. Address: Rockefeller U 1230 York Ave New York NY 10021-6399 Mailing: ICP avenue Hippocrate 75 1200 Brussels Belgium *

DEEB, LARRY CHARLES, pediatric endocrinologist, epidemiologist; b. Tallahassee, Fla., July 2, 1947; s. Charles Hobeica and Carol Anna (Goll) D.; m. Josephine Marie Sutter, Oct. 7, 1978; children: Michael Larry, Laura Elzabeth. BA in History, Emory U., 1969, MD, 1973. Diplomate Am. Bd. Pediatrics. Pediatric resident U. Minn., Mpls., 1973-75, pediatric endocrine fellow, 1975-77; epidemic intelligence svc. officer, diabetes control activity Ctrs. for Disease Control, Atlanta, 1977—79, head, epidemiology and statistics group, diabetes control activity, 1979—80; ckin. asst. prof., dept. pediatrics Coll. Medicine, U. Fla., 1981—88, assoc. clin. prof., dept. pediatrics, 1988—93, clin. prof., dept. pediatrics, 1993—; pediatric endocrinology Childrens Clinic, Tallahassee, 1980—; rsch. assoc. Ctr. for Study of Populations, Fla. State U., 1987—; assoc. in medicine Fla. State U., 1993—. Epidemiologist cons. State of Fla., Tallahassee, 1980-, Internat. Diabetes Fedn.; clin. prof. pediatrics U. Fla., Gainesville, 1980-; med. dir. Diabetes Ctr. at Tallahassee Meml. Hosp.; epidemiologist NIH, Bethesda, Md., 1988-93; bd. dirs. Fla. Camp for Children and Youth with Diabetes; assoc. in medicine Fla. State U. Coll. Medicine, 1993-, courtesy assoc. prof. behavioral and social medicine, 2004-, courtesy asst. prof., pediatrics, 2004-. Mem. editl. bd. practical Diabetes, 1987—, Clin. Diabetes, 1988-92, 96—, Meml. Hosp. 1992-, Diabetes Spectra, 1992; contbr. articles to profl. jours. Lt. comdr. USPHS, 1965-77. Recipient Frederick Clifton Moor award, Tallahassee Rotary Club, 2006. Fellow Am. Acad. Pediatrics, Lawson Wilkins Pediatric Endocrinology Soc., Internat. Soc. Pediatric and Adolescent Diabetes, Am. Assn. Clin. Endocrinologists; mem. Am. Diabetes Assn. (mem. programs com., 1984-85, chair, coun. on health care delivery and pub. health, 1986-87, chair, com. on affiliate edn. and program services, 1986-87, mem task force on epidemiology and statistics, 1988-, mem. publications com., 1989-91, bd. dir., 1990-93, chair, non-periodicals review panel, 1991-93, chair elect coun. on clin. endocrinology, 1992-94, mem. nominating com., 1993-95, chair coun. on clin. endocrinology and metabolism, 1994-96, chair coun. on diabetes in youth, 1996-97, publications policy com., 1996-97, chair publications policy com., 1997-97, mem. diabetes quality improvement com., 1998-2000, provider recognition com., 2000-2001, fin. com., 2002-2004, v.p., 2004-2005, pres.-elect, medicine and sci., 2005-2006, pres. medicine & sci., 2006-07), Safe at Schs. (co-chair 2008-) Internat. Diabetes Fedn. (chair task force insulin & other diabetes supplies, 2006-09), Rotary (Paul Harris fellow). Episcopalian. Home: 2307 Trescott Dr Tallahassee FL 32308-0929 Office: Children's Clinic 2416 E Plaza Dr Tallahassee FL 32308-5384 Address: Diabetes Ctr at Tallahassee Meml Hosp 1221 Hodges Dr Tallahassee FL 32308 Office: 2804 Remination Green Cir Tallahassee FL 32308 Office Phone: 850-878-0184. Office Fax: 850-216-1537. E-mail: lcdeeb@attglobal.net, lcdeeb@deeb.org.

DEES, TOM MOORE, II, retired internist; b. Dallas, Mar. 4, 1931; s. Tom Hawkins and Maida Elizabeth (Board) D.; m. Suzanne Settle, Feb. 20, 1971; children: Tom Moore III, David Walsh. BA, Johns Hopkins U., 1952; MD, Southwestern Med. Sch., 1956. Intern Bellevue Hosp., NYC, 1957, resident, 1958-59; rsch. fellow in cardiology Southwestern Med. Sch., Dallas, 1961; internist, ptnr. pvt. practice medicine MedProvider, Dallas, 1962—2007; ret., 2007. Dir. and mng. ptnr. Swiss Ave. Med. Bldg., Dallas, 1984—2004; clin. asst. prof. medicine Southwestern Med. Sch., Dallas, 1962—; attending physician Baylor Med. Ctr., Dallas, 1962—. Mem. dist. commn. Boy Scouts Am., Dallas, 1963-72; mem. ofcl. bd. Highland Park Meth. Ch., Dallas, 1963-72. Capt. USAF, 1959-61. Mem. ACP (life), AMA, Am. Soc. Internal Medicine, Johns Hopkins U. Alumni Assn. (pres. North Tex. chpt 1964-68), Tex. Club of Internists (pres. 1992-93). Republican. Avocations: hunting, fishing, gardening. Home: 3649 Stratford Ave Dallas TX 75205-2810

DE FALCO, MARIA, research scientist; b. Naples, Italy, Dec. 5, 1972; Degree in Biol. Scis., Liceo Specialing Classical Studies, 1996, 2010, PhD in Molecular Systematics, 2001. Rschr., adj. prof. U. Federico II Naples, 2005—. Recipient Young Histochemist award. Mem.: Histochem. Italian Soc. Office: Via Mezzocannone 8 Naples 80134 Italy Office Fax: 390812535035. Business E-Mail: madefalco@unina.it.

DEFRANCIS, SUZANNE COX, international relief organization executive, former federal agency administrator; b. 1948; m. Phillip J. Wakelyn; children: James, Mark, Will. BA, U. Colo. Speechwriter for Nixon Adminstrn., US Senator Robert P. Griffin, US Sec. Interior Rogers C.B. Morton; dep. dir. comm. and Congl. affairs Rep. Nat. Com.; sr. v.p., dir. pub. affairs Porter Novelli; dep. asst. to Pres. for comm. The White House, Washington, 2002—05; asst. sec. for pub. affairs US Dept. Health & Human Services, Washington, 2005—07; chief pub. affairs officer Am. Red Cross, Washington, 2007—. Office: American Red Cross Nat Hdqs 2025 E St NW Washington DC 20006 Office Phone: 202-690-7850. Office Fax: 202-690-5673.

DEFRANZO, ANTHONY JOHN, surgeon, educator; b. Hartford, Conn., Sept. 24, 1947; BA, Trinity Coll., 1969; MD, George Wash. U, 1973. Prof., surgery Wake Forest U., 1981—. Mem.: ABA, ASRM, AAPS, ASSH, ASPS. Avocation: antiques. Office: Med Ctr Blvd Winston Salem NC 27157 Office Fax: 336-716-8759. Business E-Mail: adefranz@wfubmc.edu.

DEGANN, SONA IRENE, obstetrician, gynecologist, educator; b. Homs, Syria, 1952; d. Papken Stephan and Helen Irene (Wadsworth) Mugrditchian; m. A. David Degann, May 11, 1983; children: Alexander, Seta. BSc, Am. U. Beirut, Lebanon, 1975; MS, U. Mich., 1976; MD, Johns Hopkins U., 1983. Diplomate Am. Bd. Ob-Gyn. Resident in ob-gyn. NY Hosp., NYC, 1983-87, staff. Clin. instr. Cornell U. Sch. Medicine, NYC, attending Ob-Gyn NY Presbyn. Hosp., NYC Fellow Am. Coll. Ob-Gyn.; mem. AMA, Med. Soc. State NY, NY County Med. Soc.

DE GAUDIO, RAFFAELE ANGELO, anesthesiologist, educator; b. Florence, Sept. 26, 1950; MD, U. Florence, 1950. Prof. U. Florence, 2001—. Dir., anesthesia and intensive care unit Azienda Ospedaliero, U. Careggi Florence, 2003—. Home: Viale del Poggio Imperiale 64 Florence 50125 Italy Office Phone: 0039055434807. Personal E-mail: rdegaudio@tin.it.

DE GEEST, KOEN, gynecologic oncologist, educator; BS in Basic Sciences in Medicine, U. Gent, Belgium, 1970—73, MD, 1973—77. Diplomate Belgian Bd. Ob-Gyn, 1982, Am. Bd. Ob-Gyn, 1987, Am. Bd. Ob-Gyn, 1994, Am. Bd. Ob-Gyn-gynecologic oncology, 1997, Am. Bd. Ob-Gyn, 2008, Am. Bd. Ob-Gyn-gynecologic oncology, 2008, lic. physicians and surgeons Belgium, 1977, obstetricians and gynecologists Belgium, 1982, ednl. comm. for fgn. med. graduates 1984, visa qualifying examination 1984, fed. licensuring examination 1985, med. physician and surgeon Pa., 1985, physicians and surgeons Ill., 1990, Iowa bd. of med. examiners 2003. Rsch. asst.pharmacology Heymans Inst. Univ. Gent., Belgium, 1974—76, rsch. asst. biochemistry, 1978—80; lt. Mil. Hosp. of Cologne, Germany, 1982—84, Mil. Hosp., Brussels, 1982—84; rschr. ob-gyn. dept. Hershey Med. Ctr. Pa. State Univ., Hershey, 1984—85, full-time asst. prof. ob-gyn. dept., 1985—87, Rush-Presbyn. St. Luke's Med. Ctr., Chgo., 1990—2003, dir. gynecologic oncology sect., 1995—2003, full-time assoc. prof. ob-gyn. dept., 1999—2003; prin. investigator Gynecologic Oncology Group, Buffalo, 1996—2003; vice-chmn. ob-gyn. dept. Rush, 2000—03; clin. prof. ob-gyn. dept. Univ. Iowa, 2003—, dir. divsn. gynecologic oncology, 2004—; gynecologic oncologist Univ. Iowa Hosps. and Clinics. Office: University of Iowa Hospitals and Clinics 200 Hawkins Dr Iowa City IA 52242-1009 Office Phone: 319-356-1616.

DEGEN, ROLF, child neurologist, researcher; b. Chemnitz, F Sachsen, Germany, July 25, 1926; Paul and Nella (Vogel) D.; m. Hanna-Elisabeth Schulz, June 18, 1955; children: Angela Plöger, Heike Eckard. DrMed, U. Leipzig, 1954. Asst. Univ. Children's Hosp., Leipzig, Germany, 1956—66, head dept. child neurology, 1966—73; head EEG dept. and dept. outpatient epileptic children Epilepsy Ctr. Bethel, Bielefeld, Germany, 1973—91, head practice for epileptic outpatients Halle, Westfalen, Germany, 1991—95. Author: Das Anfallskranke Kind in der Sprechstunde, 1970, Die Kindlichen Anfallsleiden, 1976, Praxis der Epileptologie, 2d edit., 1993; co-editor: (with Niedermeyer) Epilepsy, Sleep and Sleep Deprivation, 1981, rev. 2d edit., 1991, (with Rodin) The Lennox Gastaut Syndrome, 1988, (with Dreifuss) The Benign Localized and Generalized Epilepsies in Early Childhood, 1992, Epilepsien und Epileptische Syndrome im Kindes-und Erwachsenenalter, Klinische und Elektroenzephalographische Differentialdiagnose, 1998, Epilepsien und Epileptische Syndrome im Kindes-und Erwachsenenalter, Elektroenzephalographie, 1999; contbr. over 140 articles to profl. jour., articles to books on epilepsy. Mem. German Neuropediat. Assn., Internat. League Against Epilepsy (hon.; German sect.), German EEG Assn. (dir.). Christian Social Union. Lutheran. Avocations: classical music, psychology. Home: Telgter Str 42, 33619 Bielefeld Germany

DEGENKOLB, JOCHEN, biologist, researcher; b. Oberkotzau, Germany, Oct. 1, 1963; s. Walter and Luise Degenkolb; m. Heike Rückert Degenkolb; children: Irina Rückert, Fabio Rückert. Diploma, U. Entrance, 1982; PhD, Friedrich-Alexander-U., Erlangen, Germany, 1992. Sales rep. Kabi Pharmacia GmbH, Erlangen, 1993; clin. rsch. assoc. Pharmacia GmbH, Erlangen, 1993—95, sr. clin. rsch. assoc., 1995, clin. rsch. mgr., 1995—98; head clin. rsch. Novo Nordisk Pharma GmbH, Mainz, Germany, 1998—. Avocation: travel. Office: Novo Nordisk Pharma GmbH Brucknerstr 1 55127 Mainz Germany Home: Jakob-Degen St 3 D-96317 Kronach Germany

DEGIOVANNI-DONNELLY, ROSALIE FRANCES, biologist, educator; b. Bklyn., Nov. 22, 1926; d. Frank and Rose (Quartuccio) DeGiovanni; m. Edward Francis Donnelly, Sept. 23, 1961; children: Edward F. Jr., Francis M. BA, Bklyn. Coll., 1947, MA, 1953, PhD, Columbia U., 1961. Adj. prof. microbiology, genetics George Washington U., Washington, 1968—; rsch. biologist FDA, Washington, 1968-88. Contbr. articles to profl. jours. Recipient Merit award FDA, 1970. Mem. AAAS, AAUW, Italian Cultural Soc., Environ. Mutagen Soc., NY Acad. Scis., Am. Soc. Microbiology, McLean Indoor Club, Women's Club McLean, Sigma Xi, Sigma Delta Epsilon. Democrat. Roman Catholic. Avocations: theater, swimming, tennis, travel, photography. Home: George Washington University 1712 Strine Dr Mc Lean VA 22101-4744 Personal E-mail: edndol@earthlink.net.

DEGOS, LAURENT, hematology professor, public health administrator; b. Paris, July 9, 1945; s. Robert Degos and Monique Lortat-Jacob; m. Françoise Fouchard, Dec. 22, 1971; children: Juliette, Cécile, Vincent. MD, U. Paris, 1972, PhD, 1973. Intern Hosp. de Paris, 1966; asst. prof. hematology U. Paris VII, 1979—86, prof., 1986—, dir. Inst. Universitaire d'Hematologie, 1993—2003; dir. transplantation immunity unit Nat. Inst. Health and Med. Rsch. (INSERM), Paris, 1985—97; chief svc. Hosp. St. Louis, France, 1990—2004; pres. Supreme Authority Health (HAS), 2005—. Pres. sci. bd. GENSET, France, 1989—2003, Inst. Etudes Politique de la Santé, 1993—2004, Hosp. de Paris, 1995—2000; Eisenberg lectr., 2008. Author: ABCD de HLA, 1988, Le Don Recu (award Acad. des Sci., 1992), Greffes d'organes, 1994, Textbook on Malignant Hematology, 1998—2004, Nouvelles Aventures de Candide, 1999, Promenades dans la cellule, 1999, Cloner est-il immoral?, 2002, Vaincre le Cancer?, 2004; chief editor chief editor The Hematology Jour., 1999—2002. Decorated officier Ordre du Merite, chevalier Legion d' Honneur; recipient Svan Killman award, Leukemia Jour., 1992, Ligue Contre. de Cancer, 1993, Charles F. Kettering award, GM Cancer Rsch. Found., 1994, Inst. Curie Loubaresse award, 1996, Perrine Tennis Cup, 1996, Charles-Rodolphe Brupbacher award, 1997, Gagna and Van Heck award, 2003, Mitjaville award, 2004; named Dr. of Yr., Impact Medicin, 1991. Mem.: Am. Soc. Hematology, Am. Assn. Cancer Rsch., French Acad. Scis. (corr.). Avocations: violin, tennis. E-mail: l.degos@has-sante.fr.

DE GREGORIO, CESARE, medical educator; b. Messina, Italy, Oct. 3, 1961; s. Giovanni de Gregorio and Orsola Cento; m. Donatella De Maria, Oct. 26, 2000; 1 child, Mariagiovanna. Degree, U. Sch. Medicine, Messina, 1986, specialization in cardiology, 1990, specialization in sports medicine, 1994. Med. asst. trainer Cath. U. Sch. Medicine, Rome, 1988—89; tchr. cardiology. U. Med. Sch. Cardiology, Messina, 1999—; prof. sports cardiology and diving medicine U. Sch. Sports Sciences, Messina, 2004—. Emergency med. asst. U. Hosp., Messina, 1990—91, cardiology med. asst., 1995—99; cardiology med. asst. and aggregate prof. U. Hosp. and Sch. Medicine, 1999—; responsible for faculty of medicine and surgery web page U. Messina, 2005—. Contbr. articles to profl. jours. Recipient Best Oral Presentationn award, Internat. Congress on Echocardiography, 1993; grantee, Bonino-Pulejo Found., Messina, 1988. Mem.: Italian Cardiology Assn. (nat. coord. study group echocardiography 2006—), Italian Soc. Cardiology (assoc.; mem. nat. study group echocardiography 2004—, mem. nat. study group cardiomyopathies 2004—), Italian Fedn. Cardiology (assoc.), European Soc. Cardiology (assoc.), Lions (assoc.; coord. organ transplantation policy and rare disease svc. 2003—06). Achievements include research in Carvedilol vs Metoprolol European Trial, IN-CHF database of the ANMCO, the MAVI study of the AMNCO, ACLS provider, hospital disaster manager. Home: Via dei Mille no 230 Messina 98123 Italy Office: Univ Hosp Dept Medicine Via Consolare Valeria Messina 98125 Italy Office Phone: 390902213531. Personal E-mail: cesaredegregorio@tiscali.it.

DE GROAT, WILLIAM CHESNEY, pharmacology educator; b. Trenton, NJ, May 18, 1938; s. William Chesney and Margaret (Welch) de Groat; m. Dorothy Marion Albertson, June 13, 1959; children: Allyson L. DeGroat, Cynthia L. DeGroat, Jennifer L. DeGroat. BSc, Phila. Coll. Pharmacy and Sci., 1960, MSc, 1962; PhD, U. Pa., Phila., 1965, postgrad., 1965-66, Australian Nat. U., Canberra, 1966-67. Vis. research fellow John Curtin Sch. Med. Research, Canberra, 1967-68; asst. prof. U. Pitts. Med. Sch., 1968-72, assoc. prof., 1972-77, prof. pharmacology, 1977; disting. prof., 2009; acting chmn. dept. pharmacology U. Pitts. Med. Sch., 1978-80, adj. prof. pharmacy, 1978-88, prof. psychology, 1982-86, mem. ctr. of neurosci., 1984—, prof. dept. behavioral neurosci., 1986-94, prof. dept. neurosci., 1995-96. Vis. prof. U. Coll., London, 1998; mem. neurobiology study sect. NIH, 1983-88; vis. scientist NIAAA-NIH, 1989-90. Mem. editl. bd. Jour. Pharmacology and Exptl. Therapeutics, 1975—, Jour. Autonomic Nervous Sys., 1979—, assoc. editor, 1985-94, Neurourology and Urodynamics, 1982—2009, Am. Jour. Physiology, 1983-94, Life Scis., 1993—, Urology, 1996-98, Current Opinion in Central and Peripheral Nervous System Investigational Drugs, 1999-2006; editl. cons. profl. jours.; contbr. articles to profl. jours., chpts. in books. NSF fellowship, 1962-63; pharmacology fellowship, Riker Pharm. Co., 1966-67; NSF fellowship, 1966-67; recipient Rsch. Career Devel. award, NIH, 1972-77, NIH Merit award, 2000, Reeve-Irvine Rsch. medal, 2007. Fellow: AAAS; mem.: Dana Alliance for Brain Initiatives, Soc. for Urodynamics and Female Urology, Internat. Continence Soc., Internat. Soc. for Autonomic Neurosci. (exec. v.p.), Am. Autonomic Soc., Am. Motility Soc., Soc. for Basic Urologic Rsch., Internat. Med. Soc. of Paraplegia, Urodynamics Soc. (Lifetime Achievement award 1995), Am. Gastroent. Assn., Internat. Brain Rsch. Orgn., Soc. for Neurosci. (treas. 1994—95), Am. Soc. Pharmacology and Exptl. Therapeutics (award for exptl. therapeutics 2003), NY Acad. Scis., Am. Urol. Assn. (hon.), Japanese Urol. Assn. (hon.), Rho Chi, Sigma Xi. Republican. Methodist. Home: 6357 Burchfield Ave Pittsburgh PA 15217-2732 Office: U Pitts Med Sch W-1352 Biomed Sci Tower Terrace St Pittsburgh PA 15213 Business E-Mail: wcd2@pitt.edu.

DEGROOT, LESLIE JACOB, medical educator; b. Ft. Edward, NY, Sept. 20, 1928; BS, Union Coll., 1948; MD, Columbia U., 1952. Intern, asst. resident in medicine Presbyn. Hosp., NYC, 1952-54; health physician Nat. Cancer Inst., 1954-55; physician U.S. Mission, Afghanistan, 1955-56; clin. and research fellow medicine Mass. Gen. Hosp., Boston, 1956, 58-60, resident, 1957-58, asst., 1960-64, asst. physician, 1964-66; assoc. prof. exptl. medicine MIT, 1966-68, assoc. dir. dept. nutrition and food sci. Clin. Research Ctr., 1966-68; prof. endocrinology Pritzker Sch. Medicine, U. Chgo., 1968—2005, chief thyroid study unit, 1968—2005, chief endocrinology sect., 1980—87; prof. medicine rsch. Brown U., Providence, 2005—08; rsch. prof. U. RI, 2008—. Nat. Cancer Inst. clin. fellow, 1954-55 Mem. Assn. Am. Physicians, Am. Thyroid Assn., Endocrine Soc., Am. Soc. Clin. Investigation, Am. Fedn. Clin. Research Home: PO Box P94 South Dartmouth MA 02748-0301 Office: Univ RI Rm 308 80 Washington St Providence RI 02903 Office Phone: 508-525-2870.

DEGRUY, FRANK VERLOIN, III, physician, educator; m. Geri deGruy; children: Mariah, Frank IV, Kalyn, Kyra. AB, Princeton U., NJ, 1970; MD, U. South Ala. Coll. Medicine, Mobile, 1977. Resident family medicine The Med. Ctr., Columbus, Ga., 1977—80; Robert Wood Johnson fellow family medicine Case Western Reserve U., Cleve., 1980—82; prof. dept. family medicine Duke U., Durham, NC; disting. prof., chair dept. family practice & cmty. medicine U. South Ala. Coll. Medicine, 1996—99; Woodward Chisholm chair & prof. dept. family medicine U. Colo. Sch. Medicine, Denver, 1999—. Mem. editl. bd. Families, Systems & Health, Gen. Hosp. Psychiatry, Annals Family Medicine; contbr. articles to profl. jours., chapters to books. Recipient Outstanding Teacher award, Duke U., Disting. Faculty, U. South Ala., 1990, 1998, 1999. Mem.: Assn. Family Medicine Organizations, Inst. Medicine, Assn. Departments Family Medicine (liaison rep.). Office: U Colo Sch Medicine Dept Family Medicine Mail Stop F 496 12631 E 17th Ave Aurora CO 80045 E-mail: frank.degruy@ucdenver.edu. *

DEGUN-MATHER, MARCIA DIANA, psychologist; b. Hampstead, London, England, Apr. 27, 1935; d. Gilbert Mather and Emmie Berry; m. Gian Singh Degun, Oct. 27, 1982 (div. July 1992). BA in Psychology with honors, U. Reading, Eng., 1956; postgrad., U. Liverpool, Eng., 1960; specialized hypnosis tng., Ctrl. Psychiat. Hosp., Warwick, Eng., 1972. Chartered clin. psychologist. Sr. head clin. psychology dept. Hollymoor and Warley Tchg. Psychiat. Hosps., Birmingham and Brentwood, England, 1964—69; prin. head clin. psychology Warley Tchg. Hosp., Brentwood, 1969—74; prin. head psychol. svcs. Barking, Havering and Brentwood Health Authority, Brentwood, 1974—87, prin. head adult mental health psychology svcs., 1988—97, cons. clin. psychologist, 1991—2004; head eating disorder svc. North East London Mental Health Trust, Romford, England, 1998—2004, pvt. cons., 2004—. Examiner, clin. supr., founding mem. doctorate course in clin. psychology U. East London, Stratford, England, 1975—97, specialist lectr. clin. hypnosis clin. psychology course, 1981—2004; course organizer, specialist lectr., founding mem. diploma in clin. hypnosis U. Coll., London, 1992—; clin. supr. postgrad. counselling psychology course City U., London, 2000—04; cons. clin. psychologist pvt. practice, 1994—. Author: (book) Hypnosis, Dissociation, and Survivors of Child Abuse: Understanding and Treatment, 2006; contbr. chapters to books. Fellow: Royal. Soc. Medicine, Brit. Psychol. Soc. (assoc.); mem.: Internat. Soc. Traumatic Stress Studies, Brit. Soc. Exptl. and Clin. Hypnosis (founding mem., br. sec.). Avocations: theater, music, travel, gardening, comparative religions and philosophies.

DEGUTIS, LINDA CHRISTINE, public health service officer, epidemiologist, researcher; b. Chgo., Dec. 16, 1953; d. William Joseph and Genevieve (Karons) D.; m. Robert F. Miller, Aug. 16, 1975 (div. Mar. 1983); m. Bruce Fenton Carmichael, Mar. 26, 1988. BS, DePaul U., 1975; MSN, Yale Sch. of Nursing, 1982; DrPH, Yale Sch. of Medicine, 1994. Cert. RN Conn., Ill. Staff nurse Rush-Presbyn. St. Luke's Med. Ctr., Chgo., 1975-78, Yale-New Haven Hosp., Conn., 1978-81; trauma program coord. Yale Sch. Medicine, New Haven, 1982-91, 92-95, lectr. in surgery, 1984-95, asst. prof. sect. of emergency medicine, 1995—2003, assoc. prof. emergency medicine, pub. health, 2003—10; trauma coord. Bridgeport Hosp., Conn., 1991-92; Robert Wood Johnson Health Policy fellow Office of Senator Paul Wellstone, Washington, 1996-97; dir. Nat. Ctr. Injury Prevention and Control Centers Disease Control and Prevention, Atlanta, 2010—. Adv. mem. Conn. State com. on trauma; exec. com. mem. Conn. Adv. for Highway Safety, Hartford, Conn., 1995—. Contbr. articles to profl. jours. Founding mem. MADD-New Haven Chpt., 1983; vol. Conn. Spl. Olympic Games, New Haven, 1990-94, Internat. Spl. Olympic Games, New Haven, 1995; pres. Lake Point Condominium Assn. Bd., 1991. Mem. ACS, AAAS, Am. Pub. Health Assn. (exec. bd., chmn. injury control and emergency health svcs. sect.), Am. Trauma Soc., Nat. Assn. for Pub. Health Policy, Soc. Acad. Emergency Medicine. Office: Centers Disease Control and Prevention Nat Ctr Injury Prevention and Control 1600 Clifton Rd Atlanta GA 30333 *

DE HAAN, HENRY JOHN, research psychologist; b. St. Clair County, Ill., Nov. 23, 1920; s. Henry J. and Fanny Haislip de H.; m. Mary J. Farrell, Oct. 22, 1943. AB, Washington U., St. Louis, 1942, AM, 1949; PhD, U. Pitts., 1960. Postdoctoral Coatesville VA Hosp., Pa., 1960—62; rsch. scientist George Washington U., Washington, 1962—64; rsch. psychologist Armed Forces Radiobiol. Rsch. Inst., Bethesda, Md., 1965—69, U.S. Army Rsch. Inst., Alexandria, Va., 1969—86; external rsch. prof. Krasnow Inst. for Advanced Study, George Mason U., Fairfax, Va., 2001—04. Mem. faculty USDA Grad. Sch., Washington, 1967-77. Author 10 U.S. govt. sci. and tech. reports, 1951-82; contbr. articles to Perception and Psychophysics, Jour. Comparative and Physiol. Psychology, Internat. Jour. History of Neurosci. and other jours. With USN, 1944-46, PTO. Mem. AAAS (emeritus), APA (life), Fa. Psychol. Assn. (life), Soc. Neurosci. (emeritus), US Tennis Assn. (life), Internat. Primatol. Soc. (life), Psychonomic Soc. (life), Sigma Xi (emeritus). Achievements include research on perceptual and cognitive capacities of retarded children and adult psychotics, on effects of temperature on food intake and brain self & stimulation (in the rat), on effects of ionizing radiation on primate perceptual and cognitive capacities, and research on speech technology and speech compression, including a speech-rate intelligibility threshold. Home: 5403 Yorkshire St Springfield VA 22151-1203

DE HAAS, DAVID DANA, emergency physician; b. Hollywood, Calif., May 31, 1956; S. Martin and Norma (Deutsch) De H.; m. Mary Danuta Przybylowski, June 27, 1982; children: Lindsay Alexandra, Heather Brittany, Lance Austin. BS in Biochemistry, UCLA, Westwood, Calif., 1979, MD, Chgo. Med. Sch., 1983. Diplomate Am. Bd. Internal Medicine, Am. Bd. Emergency Medicine, Nat. Bd. Med. Examiners; cert. provider advanced trauma life support, ACLS, Pediatric Advanced Life Support, BCLS, Med. Disaster Response, instr. ACLS, Pediatric Advanced Life Support, Med. Disaster Response. Resident emergency medicine/internal medicine Kern Med. Ctr., Bakersfield, Calif., 1983-87; assoc. med. dir. Family Care Med. Assocs., Huntington Beach, Calif., 1987—; asst. clin. prof. medicine dept. internal medicine U. Calif.-Irvine Med. Ctr., Orange, 1989—; emergency physician St. Bernardine Med. Ctr., San Bernardino, Calif., 1991—; ptnr. Calif. Emergency Physicians Med. Group, San Bernardino, 1991—. Expert reviewer Med. Bd. Calif.; affiliate faculty ACLS, Pediatric Advanced Life Support, Am. Heart Assn.; vice chmn. dept. emergency medicine St. Bernardine Med. Ctr., ACLS dir., dir. quality assurance/continuous quality improvement dept. emergency medicine; mem. edn. com. Med. Disaster Response; ptnr.Calif. Emergency Physician Med. Group. Fellow ACP, Am. Coll. Emergency Physicians; mem. AMA, Calif. Med. Assn., Orange County Med. Soc., Soc. Orange County Emergency Physicians (bd. dirs.), Assn. Clin. Faculty U. Calif., Irvine Coll. Medicine. Avocations: gardening, pin collecting, reading. Home: 26882 Via La Mirada San Juan Capistrano CA 92675-4935 Office: St Bernardine Med Ctr 2101 N Waterman Ave San Bernardino CA 92404-4836

DEHECQ, JEAN-FRANÇOIS, pharmaceutical executive; b. Nantes, France, Jan. 1, 1940; Grad., Ecole Nationale des Arts et Métiers. Prof. math., 1962-64; with Soc. Nat. des Petroles d'Aquitaines, Paris, 1965-73, adminstr., 1969-70, ops. engr., 1970-71, dir. devel., 1971-73; CEO Sonofi, Paris, 1973—88, vice chmn., 1982-88; mng. dir. healthcare div. Elf Aquitaine, Paris, 1988—; chmn., CEO Sanofi, 1988—99, Sanofi-Synthélabo, 1999—, Sanofi-Aventis, 1999—2006, chmn., 2006—10. Bd. dirs. Diagnostics Pasteur, Chory S.Am., Sanofi Inc. U.S.A., Air France, Pechiney. Served with French army, 1964-65. Mem. Sovereign Order of Malta (officer of merit), Nat. Order Merit (knight), Chevalier de la Confrérie Internationale. Office: Sanofi-Aventis 174 avenue de France 75013 Paris France

DE HEER, EMILE, medical educator; m. Maria Schoemaker. MS in Med. Biology cum laude, U. Utrecht, 1980; PhD in Medicine cum laude, U. Leiden, 1986. Cert. in immunology SMBWO (Dutch Soc. Biomedical Rsch.), 1986, in exptl. pathobiology 1995. Asst. prof. Leiden U. Med. Ctr., Netherlands, 1997—98, assoc. prof., 1999—. Mem.: Renal Pathology Soc., Am. Soc. Nephrology.

DEHMER, GREGORY JOSEPH, cardiologist; b. Milw., Sept. 26, 1949; s. Joseph Anton and Bernadine Elizabeth (Bloom) D.; m. Sue Jane Vencil, Jan. 21, 1977; children: Jeffrey, Laura. BS, Carroll Coll., 1971; MD, U. Wis., 1975. Diplomate Am. Bd. Internal Medicine; cert in medicine, cardiology, and interventional cardiology. Dir. cardiac catheterization lab., asst. prof. medicine U. Tex. Health Sci. Ctr., Dallas, 1984-88; assoc. prof. medicine U. NC, 1988—2001; dir. cardiac catheterization lab U. NC Hosp., 1988—2001; prof. medicine, dir. cardiology divsn. Scott & White Clinic Tex. A&M U. Coll. Medicine, 2001—. Mem. editl. bd. Am. Jour. Cardiology, 1990—, Jour. Am. Coll. Cardiology, 1999-2003, Circulation, 1993-2004. Maj.

USAF, 1981-83. Fellow ACP, Am. Coll. Cardiology, Am. Heart Assn. (past pres.), Soc. Cardiovascular Angiography and Interventions; mem. Med CAC, Am. Coll. Cardiology(bd. trustees 2009-) Mem. Ch. of Christ. Avocation: skiing. Office: 2401 South 31st St Temple TX 76508 Office Phone: 254-724-6782. Business E-Mail: gdehmer@swmail.sw.org.

DEHN, CATHLEEN PATTERSON, health facility administrator; b. Akron, Feb. 25, 1958; d. James Edward and Doris Elizabeth (Boyd) P.; m. James Keith Dehn, June 27, 1981; children: Benjamin Jameson and Alexander Hudson (twins). BSN, U. Akron, 1980; MSN, Case Western Res. U., 1988; MA Applied Psychology, NYU, 1995; PhD in Applied Psychology, 2010. RN, NY; cert. PNP, ANCC. Nurse technician Children's Med. Ctr. Akron, 1979-80, staff nurse, 1980-81; pediatric and advanced clin. nurse, asst. head nurse, clin. nurse specialist Rainbow Babies and Children's Hosp., Cleve., 1981-91, edn. coord., 1991-93; pediat. nurse practitioner, project coord. divsn. nursing NYU The Child Health Ctr., Bklyn., 1994—96; pediat. nurse practitioner, dept. pediat. Inst. for Neurology and Neurosurgery Beth Israel Med. Ctr., NYC, 1996—2000; case mgr. dept. pediats. St. Vincent Hosp. and Med. Ctr., NYC, 2001—05, nurse mgr. NICU, pediat. divsn., 2005—07; nurse mgr. neonatal CCU and pediat. Lenox Hill Hosp., NYC, 2007—08; dir. NICU, Progressive Care Nursery & Gen. Nursery Henrico Dr.'s Hosp., Richmond, Va., 2008—09; mgr. NCCC, U. NC Healthcare, Chapel Hill, 2009—; mem. Instutional Rsch. Review Bd., U. NC, Chapel Hill, 2011. Lectr., clin. instr. Frances Payne Bolton Sch. Nursing, Case Western Res. U., Cleve., 1990-93; mem. adj. faculty divsn. nursing NYU, 1994-96; project coord. Dance Cleve., 1989; nat. instr. Neonatal Resuscitation Program, 1990-91; regional instr. Neonatal Resuscitation Program, Am. Heart Assn., Am. Acad. Pediatrics, exec. com. mem. family adv. bd. NCCC UNC Health Care Exec. prodr. videos: Getting to Know the Unique Behavioral Capabilities of the Newborn, 1987, One Step at a Time: A Family's Guide to the Neonatal Intensive Care Unit, 1991. Co-founder Sick Kids Need Involved People, Cleve., 1987; team-walk capt. March of Dimes, Cleve., 1989-92 (Edn. grantee 1991); mem. Nat. Mus. Women in Arts. Recipient Samuel E. and Rebecca Elliott award for Cmty. Svc. Case Western Res. U., 1988; named One of Outstanding Young Women of Am., 1988; Fed. Profl. Nurse Trainee scholar, 1986-87. Mem. APA, Am. Ednl. Rsch. Assn., Kappa Delta Pi, Sigma Theta Tau, Pi Lambda Theta. Avocations: health outcomes research, teaching, educational evaluation. Home: 303 Copperline Dr Apt Q Chapel Hill NC 27516-0419 Office Phone: 919-843-0954. Business E-Mail: cep1@nyu.edu.

DEHORATIUS, RAPHAEL JOSEPH, rheumatologist; b. Phila., Sept. 16, 1942; s. Pasquale P. and Edith R. DeH.; children: Nicole, Danielle. BS, St. Joseph's U., Phila., 1964; MD, Jefferson Med. Coll., 1968. Med. intern Jefferson Med. Coll., Phila., 1968-69, asst. prof. medicine, 1976-78, assoc. prof. medicine, 1978-82; med. resident U. N.Mex., Albuquerque, 1969-70, rheumatology fellow, 1972-74, asst. prof. medicine, 1974-76; prof. medicine Hahnemann U., Phila., 1982-92, Jefferson Med. Coll./Thomas Jefferson U., Phila., 1992—2006; assoc. dir. med. group med. affairs Centocor Inc, Johnson & Johnson Pharms. Contbr. articles to profl. jours./publs. Maj. USAF, 1970-72. Recipient Lupus Rsch. grant Commonwealth of Pa., Arthritis Rsch. grant. Fellow: ACP, Am. Coll. Rheumatology (chmn. profl. meetings 1988—91, edn. coun. 1988—91, v.p. 2000—01, pres.-elect 2001—02, pres. 2002—03, chmn. nominations com. 2003—04); mem.: Assn. Am. Immunologists. Office: Centocor Inc Johnson & Johnson Pharms 800 Ridgeview Dr Horsham PA 19044 Home Phone: 215-805-4877; Office Phone: 215-325-4209. E-mail: rdehor@comcast.net.

DEICKEN, RAYMOND FRIEDRICH, neuropsychiatrist, neuroscientist; b. Honolulu, June 28, 1957; (parents Am. citizens); s. Raymond T. and Miriam (Ogata) D. AB, MS, Stanford U., 1980; MD, U. Calif., San Francisco, 1984. Diplomate Nat. Bd. Med. Examiners, Am. Bd. Psychiatry and Neurology; lic. physician Med. Bd. Calif. Resident physician U. Calif., San Francisco, 1984-88, rsch. fellow, 1988-91, asst. prof. psychiatry, 1991-97, assoc. prof., 1997—2003, prof., 2003—; staff physician VA Med. Ctr., San Francisco, 1991—2007, med. dir. Partial Hosp. Program, 2002. Lectr. in field; cons. Exodon Neurosci., 2001, Roche Biosci., 2001, Bristol-Myers Squibb, 2003. Reviewer manuscripts Biol. Psychiatry, 1987—, Psychiatry Rsch., 1992—; contbr. articles to profl. jours; mem. editl. bd. Jour. Integrative Neuroscis. Alumni mentor Stanford U. Student Alumni Mentor Program, 1993—. Recipient Young Investigator award Nat. Alliance for Rsch. on Schizophrenia and Depression, 1992, 94, Ind. Investigator award, 2000, 04, Stanley Found. rsch. award Nat. Alliance for Mentally Ill, 1997, 98, VA Physician Rsch. Assoc. Career Devel. award, 1991-95; Dista fellow Soc. Biol. Psychiatry, 1991. Fellow Collegium Internat. Neuro-psychopharmacologicum, Royal Soc. Medicine (London), Internat. Soc. for Affective Disorders; mem. AMA, Soc. for Neuroscience, Soc. Biol. Psychiatry, Internat. Soc. Magnetic Resonance in Medicine, Am. Psychiat. Assn., Internat. Soc. Neuroimaging in Psychiatry, N.Y. Acad. Scis. Episcopalian. Office: 90 Parkridge Dr #2 San Francisco CA 94131-1424 Office Phone: 415-401-6642. Business E-Mail: rfdeicken@gmail.com.

DEIRO, JUDITH ANNE, chemical dependency educator; d. Guido and Ruby Margaret Deiro. BA, Okla. State U., Stillwater, 1968; MA, U. Fla., 1970; PhD, U. Wash., 1994. Cert. alcohol studies Seattle U., developing capable young people Empowering People Inc., addiction sci. U. of Miami, chem. dependency counselor State of Wash. Vocat. rehab. counselor Dept. of Vocat. Rehab., Gainesville, Fla., 1970—72; rsch. assoc. State of Fla., Office of Drug Abuse, Tallahassee, 1972—73; clin. supr. Whatcom County Alcohol Ctr., Bellingham, Wash., 1974—77; mem. faculty Whatcom C.C., Bellingham, 1977—97; rsch. asst. U. of Wash., Seattle, 1991—94; mem. faculty Western Wash. U., Bellingham, 1997—. Cons. U.S. Office of Edn., Divsn. Addiction Scis., Miami, 1973; cons. to ednl. orgns., Seattle, 1977—; adj. faculty Western Wash. U., Bellingham, 1978—86, Seattle U., 1984—97; advisor Wash. State DSHS Adv. Bd., Olympia, 1980—84. Author: (book) Teachers DO Make a Difference, Teaching with Heart, Handbook for Portfolio Process -ERIC, Handbook for Learning Contracts; contbr. articles to profl. jours., chapters to books. Pres. N.W. Consortium of Chem. Dependency Educators, 1996; mem. Wash. State Adv. Bd. for Dept. Social and Health Svcs., 1980—84, Statewide Steering Com. for Presdl. Candidate, Seattle, 2002—04. Recipient Full-time Faculty Excellence award, Whatcom C.C., 1995, Excellence Among Women in Cmty. Colls. award, Assn. of Women in Cmty. and Jr. Colls., 1984; named Chem. Dependency Educator of Yr., State of Wash., N.W. Consortium of Chem. Dependency Educators, 1996; Rachel Royston scholar for Women Leaders in Edn., Rachel Royston Statewide Scholarship Com., 1992, 1993, 1994, James I. Doi Rsch. scholar, U. Wash., 1994, Fund for the Improvement of Postsecondary Edn. grantee, Post-secondary Consortium for Prevention, Prevention Program in Post-Secondary Sch. Mem.: NW Consortium of Chem. Dependency Educators (pres., (2 times) 1996—97). Democrat. Avocations: exercise, skiing, piano, beading, weightlifting.

DEISSEROTH, KARL A., psychiatrist, neuroscientist, educator; AB in Biochemical Scis., Harvard Coll., 1992; MD, Stanford U., Calif., 2000, PhD in Neuroscience, 2000. Diplomate American Bd. Psychiatry & Neurology. Intern, resident, postdoc. fellow Stanford U., 2000—04, asst. prof. bioengineering and psychiatry, 2005—08, assoc. prof. bioengineering and psychiatry, 2009—. Early career scientist Howard Hughes Med. Inst., 2009—. Contbr. articles to profl. jours. Recipient Resident award, West Coast Coll. Biol. Psychiatry, 2003, Culpepper Scholar award, Rockefeller Brothers Fund, 2004, Early Career Translational Rsch. award, Coulter Found., 2005, NIH Dir.'s Pioneer award, 2005, Klingenstein Fellowship award, 2005, Whitehall Found. award, 2005, Young Faculty award, American Psychiat. Inst. Rsch. & Edn., 2005, Robert H. Ebert Clin. Scholar award, 2006, Presdl. Early Career award, The White House, 2006, Scholar award, McKnight Endowment Fund for Neuroscience, 2007, Top 10 Technologies award, MIT Tech. Rev., 2007, Med. Rsch. award, William M. Keck Found., 2008, Brilliant 10 award, Popular Sci. mag, 2008, Lawrence C. Katz prize in neurobiology, Duke U., 2008, Schuetze prize in neurobiology, Columbia U., 2008, Nakasone award, Internat. Human Frontier Sci. Program Orgn., 2010. Mem.: Soc. Neuroscience (Young Investigator award 2009), American Psychiat. Assn. (Lilly Resident Rsch. award 2004), American Coll. Neuropsychopharmacology, Biomedical Engring. Soc., Inst. Medicine. Achievements include research in developing optical, molecular and cellular tools to observe, perturb, and re-engineer brain circuits; development of optogenetics, a technology that uses light to control millisecond-precision activity patterns in genetically defined cell types within the brains of freely moving mammals. Office: Stanford U Clark Ctr W083 318 Campus Dr W Stanford CA 94305 Office Phone: 650-736-4325. E-mail: deissero@stanford.edu. *

DEITELZWEIG, STEVEN, medical association administrator; b. Dec. 6, 1963; MD, SUNY, Stonybrook, 1989; MMM, Tulane U., New Orleans, 2008. Chmn., hosp. medicine, v.p., med. affairs Ochsner Health Sys., 1993—. Named Physician Leader of Yr., Ochsner. Fellow: Soc. Hosp. Medicine; mem.: Delta Omega. Avocation: sports. Office: 1516 Jefferson Hwy 11th Fl V New Orleans LA 70121 Business E-Mail: sdeitelzweig@ochsner.org.

DEITERS, SISTER JOAN ADELE, psychoanalyst, nun, chemistry professor; b. Cin., Apr. 28, 1934; d. Alfred Harry and Rose Catherine (Rusche) Deiters. BA, Coll. Mt. St. Joseph, Cin., 1963; PhD, U. Cin., 1967; M in Christian spirituality, Creighton U., Omaha, 1985. Joined Sisters of Charity, Roman Cath. Ch., 1952; cert. psychoanalyst, Westchester Inst. for Tng. in Psychoanalysis and Psychotherapy, 2000. Prof. chemistry Coll. Mt. St. Joseph, Cin., 1969-78; Matthew Vassar Jr. chair Vassar Coll., Poughkeepsie, NY, 1978-96. Contbr. articles to profl. jours. Mem. Am. Chem. Soc., Sisters of Charity, Sigma Xi; Nat. Assn. for Advancement of Psychoanalysis. Home: 10 Drouilhet Ln Apt 2 Poughkeepsie NY 12603 Office: 39 Collegeview Ave Poughkeepsie NY 12603-2415 Office Phone: 845-489-2401.

DEITRICK, GEORGE ALBERT, III, physician, surgeon; b. Ashland, Pa., Apr. 17, 1946; s. George Albert and Sabina Mary (Cortellini) Deitrick; m. Tara Lynne Gleason, Nov. 28, 1981; 1 child, Taryn Christine. BA, Gettysburg Coll., Pa., 1970; MD, Temple U., Phila., 1976. Cert. Nat. Bd. Med. Examiners, 1981, Am. Bd. Surgery, 1983, 1993, 2003, in spinal cord injury medicine Am. Bd. Phys. Medicine and Rehab., 2003. Intern and resident surgery Pa. Hosp., U. Pa., Phila., 1976—81, attending surgeon, asst. prof. surgery Sch. Medicine, 1981—91; v.p. med. affairs Curative Health Svcs., Curative Techs., East Setauket, NY, 1991—97; prin. InterLink Healthcare Consulting, Garden City, 1997—2000; attending surgeon, spinal cord injury physician James J. Peters Veterans Affairs Med. Ctr., Bronx, NY, 2000—. Cons. Integrated Med. Svcs., Highwood, Ill., 2000—, Gerson Lehrman Group, NYC, 2002—; assoc. prof. surgery Mt. Sinai Sch. Medicine, NY, 2000—; mem. editl. bd. European Jour. Wound Mgmt., 2009; editor European Jours. Wound & Burn Mgmt. Contbg. editor: (med. jour.) Advances in Wound Care, 2001—; contbr. articles to profl. jours. Fellow: ACS; mem.: Alpha Kappa Kappa (life), Sigma Alpha Epsilon (life). Achievements include research in blood flow to the lower extremities and the skin in spinal cord injured patients; role of anabolic steroids in the healing of pelvic pressure ulcers in spinal cord injured patients; patents pending for a hands on clinical measuring device for immediate prescription for patients with chronic non healing wounds of the feet. Home: 17 Kenwood Rd Garden City NY 11530 Office: James J Peters VA Med Ctr 130 W Kingsbridge Rd Bronx NY 10468 Office Phone: 718-584-9000 ext. 5410. Personal E-mail: gad3rd@aol.com, gadeitrick@gmail.com. Business E-Mail: george.deitrick@va.gov.

DEJONCKERE, PHILIPPE HENRI, otolaryngologist; b. Ronse, Belgium, July 11, 1949; s. Edouard Dejonckere and Marthe Van Nerum; m. Suzanne Thiry, Sept. 2, 1978; children: Laurence, Aurélie. Grad., Conservatory of Music, Louvain, Belgium, 1971; degree in sexology, U. Louvain, 1971, MD, 1973, MSc in Occupl. Medicine, 1975, PhD in Medicine, 1981; MSc in Forensic Medicine, U. Liège, Belgium, 1986; degree in stats., U. Paris VI, 1978. Resident U. Hosp. St. Luc., Brussels, 1976-81, sr. resident, 1981-83; lectr. U. Louvain, 1983-86, assoc. clin. prof., 1986-89; assoc. prof. U. Utrecht, The Netherlands, 1989-91, prof., chmn. dept. phoniatrics, 1991—, full prof., 2002—. Med. expert Fund Occupl. Diseases, Brussels, 1987—; gen. coord. sci. coun., Fed. Inst. Occupl. Diseases, 2007-, invited prof. U. Lille, France, 1984—; vis. prof. U. Kurume, Japan, 1996; guest prof. U. Leuven, Belgium, 2001—. Author 7 books; contbr. articles to profl. jours., editor numerous jours. Past pres. Collegium Medicorum Theatri, 1999. Hon. lt. col. Belgian Army Res. Decorated officer Crown Order, officer Order of King Leopold, Comdr. Order of King Leopold II, Belgium. Mem. European Laryngol. Rsch. Group (past pres.), Dutch Soc. Logopedics and Phoniatrics (disting.), Austrian Voice Inst. (disting.), Dutch Soc. Voice, Speech and Lang. Pathology (pres. 2005, Van Lawrence prize 1997, Marie Curie award 2006, chmn. COST action 2006-11, mem. COST 2011-). Office: Inst Phoniatrics Utrecht U PO Box 85500 3508 GA Utrecht Netherlands also: Fed Inst Occupl Diseases Ave de l'Astronomie B 1210 Brussels Belgium Office Phone: 31887557729. Business E-Mail: ph.deJonckere@umcutrecht.nl.

DEJUD, CARLOS, psychologist; b. David, Panama, June 26, 1964; s. Luis Dejud and Abelina Dejud-Valenzuela; 1 child, Brian. BA, U. Ariz., Tucson, 1991, MA, 2000; EdS, U. Ariz, Tucson, 2004, PhD, 2007—. Cert. sch. psychologist Ariz. Dept. Edn., spl. edn. tchr. k-12 Ariz. Dept. Edn. Counselor II La Frontera Ctr., Tucson, 1991—94, child family specialist, 1994—96, clinician III, 1996—98; grad. tchg. asst. U. Ariz., Tucson, 2000—04, rsch. asst., 2004—06; project coord U. Ariz, 2007—; asst. prof. U. Wis., Stout, 2007—. Cons. Tucson Urban League, 2006—; lectr., spkr. U. Med. Ctr., Tucson, 2003—. Contbr. articles to profl. jours. Bd. mem. Tucson Internat. Mariachi Conf., 1999—. Recipient Centennial Achievement award, U. Ariz., 1991, Advisor of Yr., Order of Omega, 2004. Mem.: APA, NASP, Omega Delta Phi (regional dir. 2007—), Omega Delta Phi Alumi Assn. (chmn. 2004—).

DEKKERS, MARIJN E., chief executive officer; b. Tilburg, The Netherlands, Sept. 22, 1957; married; 3 children. B in Chemistry and Chem. Engring., U. Nijmegen, The Netherlands; MS in Chem. Engring., PhD in Chem. Engring., U. Eindhoven. Scientist at the corp. rsch. ctr. Gen. Electric Co., Schenectady, NY, 1985—87, plastics rschr. Bergen op Zoom, Netherlands, 1987—88, head polymer materials rsch. and further mgmt. positions in various polymers rsch. units Schenectady, 1988—95; head specialty films & fluorine chemicals bus. groups and electronic materials divsn. Honeywell Internat., Inc. (formerly Allied Signal), 1995—2000; COO Thermo Fisher Sci. Inc. (merger between Thermo Electron Corp. and Fisher Sci. Inc.), Mass., 2000—02, pres., CEO, 2002—10; mem. & chmn. bd. of mgmt. CEO Bayer AG, 2010—, interim CEO Bayer HealthCare AG, mem. bd. mgmt., 2010, CEO, 2010—; rsch. scientist R & D Ctr. Gen. Electric Co., Schenectady, NY, various rsch. & mgmt. positions, 1985—95. Bd. dirs. Spectra-Physics, Inc., 2000, Thermo Fisher Sci. Inc., 2000—09, Biogen Idec Inc., 2007—09, Fisher Sci. Internat. Inc. Contbr. articles to profl. jours. Achievements include patents in field. Office: Bayer AG Bayerwerk Gebäude W11 Kaiser-Wilhelm-Al 51368 Leverkusen Germany Office Phone: 01149214301. Office Fax: 011492143066328.

DEKOSKY, STEVEN TRENT, dean, neurologist; b. Camden, NJ, Mar. 23, 1947; s. Aaron and Evelyn (Gorlen) DeK.; m. Beverly Nelson; children: Allison. Lauren. AB in Psychology, Bucknell U., 1968; MD, U. Fla. Coll. Medicine, 1974. Diplomate in neurology Am. Bd. Psychiatry and Neurology. Resident in internal medicine John Hopkins Hosp., 1974—75; resident, neurology U. Fla., 1975—78; postdoctoral fellow, instr. neurology, neurochemistry U. Va. Sch. Medicine, Charlottesville, 1978-79; asst. prof. neurology, anatomy U. Ky. Coll. Medicine, Lexington, 1979-85, assoc. prof. anatomy and neurology, 1985-90, interim chmn. dept. neurology, 1985-87; grad. faculty U. Ky. Grad. Sch., Lexington, 1981-90; prof. psychiatry U. Pitts. Sch. Medicine, 1990—2008, prof. neurology, neurobiology, 1990—2008, grad. faculty, 1991—2008, interim chair dept. neurology, 2000—01, chair dept. neurology, 2002—08; v.p., dean U. Va. Sch. Medicine, 2008—. Vis. prof. psychology U. Calif., Irvine, 1983; co-dir. Alzheimer's Disease Rsch. Ctr. U. Pitts. Med. Ctr., 1990-94, dir., 1994-2008, U. Ky. Med. Ctr., 1985-90; task force on Alzheimer's disease State of Ohio, Columbus, 1986-92; head, divsn. geriatrics and neuropsychiatry, dept. psychiatry, U. Pitts and Western Psychiatric Inst. and Clinc and Inst.: chair med. sci. adv. bd. Alzheimer's Assn., 1997-2002, nat. bd. dirs., vice-chair bd. dirs.; dir. behavioral neurology of aging tng. program U. Pitts., 1990-2008; bd. dirs. Alzheimer's Disease Internat., chair med. sci. adv. panel, 2002-; chair profl. adv. bd., Greater Pitts. Chpt. Alzheimer's Assn.; founding mem. Lexington-Blue Grass Chpt. Alzheimer's Assn. Mem. editl. bd. of several leading neurology and Alzheimer's clin. publications, Ad Hoc reviewer for several clin. jours.; contbr. chapters to books, several articles to profl. jours. Named Best Doctors in America. Mem. Am. Neurol. Assn. (Presd. award 1988), Am. Acad. Neurology (chair, sect. on geriatrics, chair practice parameters com. for early detection, diagnosis and mgmt. of dementia), Am. Soc. Neurochemistry, Am. Heart Assn. (stroke coun.), N.Y. Acad. Scis., Soc. Neurosci., Soc. Exptl. Neuropathology (councillor 1990-92), Behavioral Neurology Soc., Am. Bd. of Psychiatry and Neurology (chair strategic planning com., examiner in neurology, mem. Part I (written) Examination Com, mem. neurology coun. 2002), Am. Coll. Neuropsychopharmacology, Am. Neurological Assn., Am. Soc. Neurological Investigation, Behavioral Neurology Soc., Internat. Soc. Neurochemistry, Internat. Soc. Neuropathology, Nat. Neurotrama Soc. Office: U Va Sch Medicine PO Box 800793 Charlottesville VA 22908 Office Phone: 434-924-5118. Business E-Mail: dekosky@virginia.edu.

DE LA CUEVA, MARIO A., ophthalmologist; b. Xalapa, Mexico, Apr. 21, 1954; s. Victor De La Cueva and Dionisia Hernandez. MD, Veracruz U. Med. Sch., Xalapa, Mexico, 1976; FACS, U. Mexico, 1983. Cert. Ophthalmology Mexican Ophthalmology Med. Coun., 1986. Ophthalmologist IMSS, Cardel, Mexico, 1987—88, Xalapa, 1989—93; pvt. practice Xalapa, 1994—; ophthalmologist Medica Millennium, Xalapa, 2002—. Cons. Laser Excimer del Golfo, Veracruz, 2002—. Mem.: Am. Soc. Cataract and Refractive Surgery, PanAm. Assn. Ophthalmology, Am. Acad. Ophthalmology. Avocation: gardening, swimming, reading, classical music. Office: Medica Millennium Maestros Veracruzanos 104 Fracc Pomona 91040 Xalapa Mexico

DE LA FUENTE RAMIREZ, JUAN RAMON, psychiatrist, former academic administrator; b. Mexico City, Sept. 5, 1951; married; 3 children. MB, MD, Nat. Autonomous Univ. Mex., 1976. Postgrad. psychiatry Mayo Clinic, Rochester, Minn.; founding head Clin. Rsch. Unit, Mex. Inst. Psychiatry; lectr. Med. Sch., dir. health rsch. prog. Nat. Autonomous Univ. Mex., vice-chancellor sci., 1989, dean Med. Sch., 1991—94, rector, 1999—2007; Min. of Health Govt. of Mex., 1994—99; coun. mem. UN Univ., 2008—. V.p. Internat. Assn. Universities, 2004—08, pres., 2008—; bd. dirs. Cervantes Inst., El Universal (daily newspaper); investigator Nat. Inst. Nutrition. Contbr. articles to profl. jours., chapters to books. Recipient Eduardo Liceaga prize, Nat. Acad. Medicine, Disting. Alumnus award, Mayo Clinic. Office: UN Univ Shibuya-ku Jingumae 5-53-70 Tokyo 150-8925 Japan also: Internat Assn Universities UNESCO House 1 rue Miollis 75732 Paris France

DELAHAY, JOHN N., orthopedist, surgeon; b. 1943; MD, Georgetown U., 1969. Cert. Orthopaedic Surgery, 1975. Intern Georgetown U. Med. Ctr., 1970, resident, 1974, prof., vice-chair edn. Dept. Orthopaedic Surgery; prof., orthop. surgery Peter Rizzo, 1996. Named one of Top Doctors, Washingtonian.com. Mem.: Pediatric Orthopaedic Soc. N.Am. Office: Pasquerilla Healthcare Ctr Ground Fl Georgetown U Med Ctr Washington DC 20007 Business E-Mail: delahayj@georgetown.edu.

DELAND, JONATHAN T., orthopedist, surgeon, educator; MD, Columbia U., 1980. Diplomate Am. Bd. of Orthopaedic Surgery. Resident Mass. Gen. Hosp., 1982—87, Children's Hosp. Med. Ctr., Harvard Orthopedic Program, Beth Israel Hosp., Brigham and Women's Hosp.; fellow with William Hamilton MD and Francesca Thompson MD St. Luke's-Roosevelt Hosp. Ctr.; fellow with Arthur Boland MD Mass. Gen. Hosp.; assoc. prof. orthopaedics surgery Weill Cornell Med. Coll.; assoc. attending orthopaedic surgeon Hosp. for Spl. Surgery, chief foot and ankle svc. Author: (publs.) Cosmetic Foot Surgery, 2004, Posterior Tibial Tendon Insufficiency (Adult Acquired Flatfoot): An Overview, 2008, 2010, and numerous other publications. Recipient Dow Corning award, Research, Foot and Ankle Soc., 1990, Excellence award, Healthnetwork Found., 2009; named one of Best Doctors in NY, NY Mag., 2009—11, Best Doctors in America; grantee Orthopedic Rsch. and Edn. Found. Rsch. Grant, 1992, Winner Nat. Inst. of Health Grant, 1997. Achievements include research in Early Mobilization following Adult Acquired Flatfoot Deformity Reconstruction; In Vivo Radiographic Validation of Novel EMED Plantar Pressure Masking Algorithm; Development of a Geometric Foot Model: A Tool for Clinical Decision Making. Office: Hospital for Special Surgery East River Professional Bldg 523 E 72nd St New York NY 10021 Office Phone: 212-606-1665. Office Fax: 212-794-4291.

DE LANDTSHEER, JEAN-PIERRRE, health services administrator, educator; b. Bruxelles, Brabant, Belgium, July 21, 1946; s. Pierre and Léonie De Landtsheer; m. Asima Burzic, Sept. 1, 1973; children: Pascal, Vincent. MD, Free U. Brussels, 1973, Occupl. Health Specialist, 1984; MPH, Johns Hopkins U., 1986. Médecin associé Pub. Health Dept. Canton de Vaud- Switzerland, 1999. Med. asst. Hôpital pub. d'Etterbeek, Brussels, 1975—77; med. officer SYBETRA, Alkaïm, Iraq, 1977—78; med. mgr. Qatar Petrochemical Co., Umm Saïd, 1979—85; med. officer Pub. Health Dept., Lausanne, Switzerland, 1987—92; med. dir. Fondation pour le dépistage du cancer du sein, Lausanne, 1993—. Accredited physician French Embassy, Doha, Qatar, 1980—85; tchg. asst. Sch. Pub. Health, Brussels, 1987—87; expert UN Fund for Developing Population, Alger, Algeria, 1987—87. Contbr. articles to profl. jours. Recipient Pink award, Swiss League Against Cancer, 2001. Mem.: European Breast Cancer Screening Network, Internat. Breast Cancer Screening Network. Achievements include development of Integrated Software For Management And Evaluation (Database) Of An Organised Breast Cancer Screening Programme. Office: Fondation pour le dépistage du cancer du Rue César Roux 19 1005 Canton de Vaud Lausanne Switzerland Office Fax: +/41/21/3160851. Personal E-mail: j-pdelandtsheer@bluewin.ch. E-mail: jean-pierre.de-landtsheer@inst.hospvd.ch.

DELANEY, BRIAN, physician, educator; Studied, Yeshiva U., 1983. Diplomate Am. Bd. Family Practice, cert. geriatric medicine. Resident family medicine Montefiore Univ. Hosp.; physician Montefiore Med. Ctr., St. Barnabas Medical Ctr., St. Barnabas Hosp., Met. Podiatry Assocs.; asst. prof. family medicine Albert Einstein Coll. Med. Office: Montefiore Medical Center Henry and Lucy Moses Division 111 E 210 St Bronx NY 10467 Office Phone: 718-364-6199. Office Fax: 718-364-6502.

DELANEY, WAYNE EDWARD, retired surgeon; b. Sherman, Tex., Sept. 5, 1933; s. Milton Loyd and Laura Alice Delaney; m. Mary Maxine Leslie Delaney, Aug. 15, 1953. BA, Tex. U., Austin, 1955; MD, U. Tex., 1959. Diplomate Am. Bd. Surgery, 1965. Intern Parkland Hosp., Dallas, 1959—60, gen. surgery resident, 1960—64. Bd. dirs. Smith Found., Denison, 1985—. Mem.: Chirugio Soc., Denison Country Club. Republican. Baptist. Avocations: tennis, golf. Home: 1201 South Lang Ave Denison TX 75020

DE LANGE, TITIA, cell biologist, research scientist, educator; b. The Netherlands, 1955; BA, U. Amsterdam, 1977, MS, 1981, Nat. Inst. Med. Rsch., London, 1981; PhD in Biochemistry, U. Amsterdam, Netherlands Cancer Inst., 1985; D (hon.), U. Utrecht, The Netherlands. Grad. tchg. asst., dept. biochemistry, U. Amsterdam, 1081—1985; postdoc. fellow U. Calif., San Francisco, 1985—90; asst. prof. Rockefeller U., NYC, 1990—94, assoc. prof., 1994—97, prof., 1997—, Leon Hess prof., 1999—, asst. dir. Anderson Cancer Ctr., 2006—. Mem. bd. sci. consultants Meml. Sloan-Kettering Cancer Ctr., NYC, 2001—; mem. sci. adv. bd. Inst. Molecular Pathology, Vienna, 2003—08, MIT Cancer Ctr., 2003—, Netherlands Cancer Inst., 2005—. Mem. editl. bd. Molecular & Cellular Biology, 1997—, Trends in Biol. Sci., 2000—, Genes & Devel., 2008—; contbr. articles to profl. jours. Mem. bd. trustees Cold Spring Harbor Lab., Nassau County, NY, 2003—. Recipient Scholar award, Lucille P. Markey Charitable Trust, 1987—95, Irma T. Hirschl & Monique Weill-Caulier Charitable Trust award, 1993—98, Rita Allen award, 1995—2000, Cancer Rsch. award, NY Cmty. Trust, 1997—99, Toxicology Scholar award, Burroughs Wellcome Fund, 1997—2002, Sr. Scholar award, Ellison Med. Found., 2000—04, Paul Marks prize for cancer rsch., Meml. Sloan Kettering Cancer Ctr., 2001, Charlotte Friend Meml. award, American Assn. Cancer Rsch., 2004, Clowes Meml. award, 2010, Dir.'s Pioneer award, NIH, 2005, Mass. Gen. Hosp. Cancer Ctr. prize, 2008. Fellow: AAAS, American Soc. Microbiology, NY Acad. Scis., Am. Acad. Arts & Scis.; mem.: NAS (fgn. assoc.), Inst. Medicine, European Molecular Biology Orgn. (fgn.), Royal Dutch Acad. Scis. (corr.). Office: Rockefeller Univ Lab Cell Biology & Genetics 1230 York Ave New York NY 10021 Office Phone: 212-327-8146. Office Fax: 212-327-7147. Business E-Mail: delange@mail.rockefeller.edu. E-mail: Titia.de.Lange@rockefeller.edu. *

DELANIAN, SYLVIE, physician, consultant; b. Marseille, France, Oct. 20, 1960; d. Louis-Noel Delanian and Suzanne Shahpazian. MD, U. Aix-Marseille II, 1984; MS in Radiobiology-Radiopathology, U. Paris XII, Creteil, 1991; PhD, U. Paris V, 1994. Lic. biol. scis. U. Paris XI, 1988, oncology-radiotherapy U. Paris XII, 1988, cert. in med. oncology 1990. Resident APHP Hosps., Curie Inst., Gustave Roussy Inst., Paris, 1984—88; fellowship Hôpital Necker, APHP, 1988—90, sr. physician, 1991—94, St. Louis Hosp., Paris, 1994—. Expert cons. radiopathology, Paris. Fellow: ESTRO (Brussels). Office: Hôpital St Louis 1 Ave Claude vellefaux Paris 75010 France Business E-Mail: sylvie.delanian@sls.aphp.fr.

DELAPP, TINA DAVIS, retired nursing educator; b. LA, Dec. 18, 1946; d. John George and Margaret Mary (Clark) Davis; m. John Robert DeLapp, May 31, 1969; children: Julia Ann, Scott Michael. Diploma, Good Samaritan Hosp., Phoenix, 1967; BSN, Ariz. State U., 1969; MS in Nursing, U. Colo., Denver, 1972; EdD in Post Secondary Edn., U. So. Calif., 1986. Health aide instr. Yukon-Kuskokwim Health Corp., Bethel, Alaska, 1970-71; asst. prof. nursing Bacone Coll., Muskogee, Okla., 1972-74; instr. nursing Alaska Meth. U., Anchorage, 1975-76; prof. nursing U. Alaska, Anchorage, 1976—2004, assoc. dean nursing, 1986—96, dir. Sch. Nursing, 1996—2004, emeritus prof., 2004—. Mem. Alaska Bd. Nursing, 1989-92; cons. in field. Mem. editl. adv. bd. Jour. Nursing Edn., 2004-2010, adv. bd. mem. Alaska Nurse Editl., 2011-; contbr. articles to profl. jours. Recipient Chancellor's Tchg. award, 1994; named Legend of Nursing, Alaska March of Dimes, 2004. Fellow: We. Acad. Nursing; mem.: Alaska Nurses Found. (treas. 2004—), Am. Assn. Colls. Nursing (mem. nominating com. 2003, task force 2003—04, emeritus 2005), Nat. League for Nursing Accreditation Comn. (program evaluator 1986—2010, evaluation rev. panel mem. 2000—05, evaluation rev. panel alt. mem. 2008—10), We. Inst. Nursing (chair program com. 1994—95, sec.-treas. 1995—2005, gov.-at-large 2005—07, chair membership com 2006—, Jo Elinor Elliot Leadership award 2002, Anna Shannon Mentorship award 2006, Emeritus award 2007), Sigma Theta Tau (pres. chpt. 1986—88, v.p. 1988—93, counselor 1995—2000). Avocations: knitting, reading, politics. Personal E-mail: tdelapp@ak.net.

DE LA PUENTE LEON, GUILLERMO, plastic surgeon; b. Lima, Peru, May 1, 1928; s. Alejandro De La Puente Ganoza; m. Bebe Louise De La Borda, Jan. 21, 1956; children: Maria Luisa De La Puente, Guillermo De La Puente, Miguel De La Puente, Julio De La Puente, Manuel De La Puente. BS, San Marcos U., Lima, 1946, B in Medicine, 1955, cert. in plastic surgery, 1980; Medico Cirujano, U. San Marcos, Lima, 1954; PhD, Cayetano Heredia U., Lima, 1976. Plastic Surgery San Marcos U. / Peru, 1980. Surg. resident Clinica Anglo Americana, Miraflores, Lima, 1954—57; chief surg. resident Clinica Internacional, Lima, 1958—62, chief plastic surgery, 1965—97, Clinica Benavides, Surco, Lima, 1996—2001, Peruvian Air Force Hosp., Miraflores, 1971—97; assoc. plastic surgeon Clinica Javier Prado, San Isidro, Lima, 1999—. CEO Clinica Benavides, Surco, Lima, 1992—95; v.p. Academia Peruana De Cirugia, Miraflores, 1999—2000. Author: (med. book) Plastic Surgery In Hand Labor Casualties (nat. 1st prize in surgery, 1976); co-author: Cirugia Plastica Latinoamericana. Master: Peruvian Acad. Surgery; fellow: ACS, Federacion Iberoamericana de Cirugia Plastica, Internat. Soc. for Burns and Injuries (assoc.); mem.: Soc. for Hand Surgery (hon.; Lima), Sociedad De Quemados Lima (hon.), Soc. Plastic Surgery Lima (hon.), Internat. Coll. Surgeons (assoc.; pres. plastic surgery chpt. XIX World Congress 1964), Club De Regatas Lima (hon.; v.p. 1979—82, pres. 1986—90). Achievements include research in silicone in hand surgery; liophylisete porcine skin in burns. Office: Av Benavides 264 - 703 Lima Miraflores 18 Peru Office Fax: 511-446-4940. E-mail: gpuentemd@hotmail.com.

DE LA ROCHA, CARLOS A., retired physician; b. Santo Domingo, Dominican Republic, Aug. 12, 1934; s. Carlos A. and Germania (Contin) de la R.; m. Penelope Lynn Lansing, May 20, 1961; children: C. Andrew, Maria L., Michael J., David L., Alicia M., Juan A. MD, Univ. de Santo Domingo, 1958. Diplomate Am. Bd. Surgery. Rotating intern City Hosp. at Elmhurst, Queens, NY, 1958-59; asst. resident surgery Albert Einstein Med. Ctr., Phila., 1959-60, Ellis Hosp., Schenectady, NY, 1960-62, chief resident surgery, 1962-63; tchg. fellow surgery St. Clares Hosp., Schenectady, 1963-65; asst. attending surgeon St. Clares and Ellis Hosp., 1965-69, attending surgeon, 1969-98; ret., 1998. Chmn. tissue unit Ellis Hosp., 1985-90; mem. Ellis Hosp. Found. Bd., 1988-94. Fellow Am. Coll. Surgeons; mem. AMA, Am. Soc. Gen. Surgeons, N.Y. State Soc. Surgeons, N.Y. State and County Med. Soc. Republican. Roman Catholic. Avocations: travel, classical music. Home: 44 Van Voast Ln Scotia NY 12302-9621

DELATEUR, BARBARA JANE, medical educator; b. Hoquiam, Wash., Nov. 17, 1936; Student, Marylhurst Coll., Oreg., 1954-56; BS in Philosophy, St. Louis U., 1959; MD, U. Wash., 1963, MSc, 1968. Diplomate Am. Bd. Phys. Medicine and Rehab.; lic. physiatrist, Wash., Md. Rotating intern U. Hosp., U. Wash., 1963-64, resident dept. phys. medicine and rehab., 1964-67; instr. dept. phys. medicine and rehab. U. Wash. Sch. Medicine, 1967-68, asst. prof., 1968-71, assoc. prof., 1971-76, prof. dept. rehab. medicine, 1976-93; prof., dir. dept. phys. medicine and rehab. Johns Hopkins U. Sch. Medicine, Balt., 1993—2003, Lawrence Cardinal Shehan chair phys. medicine and rehab., 1993—2003, joint prof. health policy & mgmt. Sch. Hygiene & Pub. Health, 1994—; acting physiatrist-in-chief Rehab. Medicine Svc. Harborview Med. Ctr., Seattle, 1970-72, physiatrist-in-chief, 1972-93; dir. Muscular Dystrophy Clinic Meml. Hosp., Yakima, Wash., 1979-88; dir. dept. phys. medicine and rehab. Johns Hopkins Hosp., Balt., 1993—2003; med. dir. dept. rehab. medicine Good Samaritan Hosp., Balt., 1993—2003, disting. svc. prof. phys. medicine & rehab., 2006—, Lawrence Cardinal Shehan prof. emeritus phys. medicine & rehab., 2006—. Vis. prof. dept. rehab. medicine and dept. internal medicine SUNY, Syracuse, 1988; cons. physiatrist Johns Hopkins Geriatrics Ctr., Johns Hopkins Bayview Med. Ctr., Balt., 1994—; vis. lectr. dept. phys. medicine Coll. Medicine, Ohio State U., 1985; Arthur Grant lectr. U. Tex., San Antonio, 1992; Marquette lectr. Jefferson Med. Coll., Phila., 1993; spkr. various univs. and orgns.; pres. Phys.Medicine and Rehab./Edn. and Rsch. Found., 1990-94; mem. governing coun. sect. rehab. hosps. and programs Am. Hosp. Assn., 1993—; mem. adv. bd. Wash. State Divsn. Vocat. Rehab., 1979-84; vis. prof. U. Wash., 2005, Rehab. Inst. Chgo., 2005; spkr. in field. Contbr. articles to profl. jours.; mem. editl. bd. Archives Phys. Medicine and Rehab., 1978-84, Health After 50, Johns Hopkins Hosp., 1994—; reviewer Jour. Am. Geriatrics Soc., 1994—. Recipient Elizabeth and Sidney Licht award for sci. writing, 1990, Excellence in Tchg. award N.J. Med. Sch., 1992, Excellence in Rsch. Writing award Assn. Acad. Physiatrists and Am. Jour. Phys. Medicine and Rehab., 1992, Golden Goniometer award Phys. Medicine and Rehab. Residents, 1995, 2002, 04, 05, Labe Scheinberg award, Meeting of Consortium of MS Ctrs., Portland, Oreg., 1995. Fellow Am. Acad. Phys. Medicine; mem. AMA, Am. Acad. Phys. Medicine and Rehab. (bd. govs. 1983-90, v.p. 1986-887, pres-elect 1987-88, pres. 1988-89, Disting. Clinician award 1998, Frank M. Krusen award 2004), NAS, Am. Burn Assn., Am. Congress Rehab. Medicine (Gold Key award 2003-04), Assn. Acad. Physiatrists (Disting. Academician award 1998), Internnt. Assn. for Study of Pain, King County Med. Assn., Am. Geriatric Soc., Wash. State Med. Assn. Office: Johns Hopkins Bayview Med Ctr PM&R AA Bldg Rm 1654 4940 Eastern Ave Baltimore MD 21224

DE LA TORRE, JACK CARLOS, clinical neuroscientist; b. Paris, Dec. 2, 1942; s. Rafael de la Torre, Maria de la Torre; m. Helene de Socarraz; 1 child, Lauren Nicole. BS in Biology, Am. U., 1961; MD, U. Madrid, 1979; PhD, U. Geneva, Switzerland, 1969. Asst. prof. neurosurgery and psychiatry U. Chgo., 1969—75, assoc. prof. neurosurgery and psychiatry, 1975—77; assoc. prof neurosurgery U. Miami, Fla., 1979—82; prof. neurosurgery, anatomy and pharmacology U. Ottawa, Ont., Canada, 1983—94; prof. neurosurgery and neurosci. U. N.Mex., Albuquerque, 1994—99; vis. prof. pathology U. Calif., San Diego, 1999—2001; adj. prof. pathology Case Western Res. U., Cleve., 2001—06; sr. scientist Sun Health Rsch. Inst., Sun City, 2007—10; adj. prof. psychology U. Tex., Austin, 2010—. Author: Dynamics of Brain Monoamines, 1972; translator: The Neuron and the Glial Cell, 1984; editor: Biological Actions and Medical Applications of Dimethyl Sulfoxide, 1983, Cerebrovascular Pathology in Alzheimer's Disease, 1997, Vascular Pathophysiology in Alzheimer's Disease, 2000, Pathology of the Aging Human Nervous System, 2001, Alzheimer's Disease: Vascular Etiology and Pathology, 2002, Vascular Dynamics in Alzheimer and Vascular Dementia, 2004, Impact of Heart Disease and Stroke on Alzheimer's Disease, 2006, Basics of Alzheimer's Disease Prevention, 2010; contbr. articles to profl. jours. Grantee Head Injury Ctr., NIH, 1970—80, Can. Heart Assn., 1983—88, Heart & Stroke Found. Ont., 1986—91, Internat. Spinal Rsch. Trust, 1989—94, Alzheimer's Assn., 2000—. Fellow: Am. Heart Assn. (stroke coun.); mem.: Interam. Coll. Physicians and Surgeons, Coll. Physicians and Surgeons Ont., N.Y. Acad. Sci., Soc. Neurosci. Avocations: photography, chess, tennis. Office Phone: 760-703-0585. Personal E-mail: jcdelatorre@comcast.net.

DELATTRE, EDSON, physiologist, educator; b. Imbituva, Paraná, Brazil, May 4, 1953; s. Aquiles Desidério and Zilda Alves Delattre; 1 child, Isis Ceribelli. B in Biomedical Scis., State U. Londrina, Brazil, 1975; MS in Biology, Physiology and Biophysics, State U. Campinas, Brazil, 1981, PhD in Physiology, 1998. Aux. tchr. State U. Londrina, 1976—85, asst. prof., 1985—86, State U. Campinas, Campinas, 1986—98, prof. physiology and chronobiology, 1998—. Contbr. articles various profl. jours. Founder queimadasurbanas.bmd.br, Campinas and Londrina, São Paulo(SP) and Paraná(PR), Brazil, 1997—. Recipient Incentive to Rsch. prize, Unicamp's Sr. Rsch. Com., 1983. Mem.: Fedn. Soc. Exptl. Biology (assoc.). Achievements include development of multiple-choice, objective question, by using the addition of the numerical values, in a geometrical progression, which precedes each alternative. Avocations: music, photography. Office: State U Campinas 255 Monteiro Lobato St São Paulo Campinas 13083-970 Brazil Home Phone: 55-19-33862382; Office Phone: 55-19-35216191. Office Fax: (19) 37 88 61 85. Personal E-mail: delattre@queimadasurbanas.bmd.br.

DELAUNEY, SOPHIE, medical relief organization executive; M in Internat. Bus., U. Le Havre, France; M in Polit. Sci., Yonsei U., Seoul, Republic of Korea. Head program dept. ESTHER, France; adminstrv. & fin. dir., Epicentre Medecins Sans Frontieres/Doctors Without Borders, 1995—98, country adminstr. Thailand, Rwanda, head of mission China, Democratic Peoples Republic of Korea, sr. program officer NYC, 2008—09, exec. dir., US sect., 2009—. Bd. mem. Medecins Sans Frontieres/Doctors Without Borders Epicentre, Medecins Sans Frontieres/Doctors Without Borders, France. Office: Doctors Without Borders Medecins Sans Frontieres 333 7th Ave 2d Fl New York NY 10001-5004 Office Phone: 212-679-6800. Office Fax: 212-679-7016. *

DEL CAÑIZO-GÓMEZ, FRANCISCO JAVIER, endocrinologist; b. Avila, Spain, Feb. 9, 1954; s. Manuel del Cañizo-Suarez and Francisca Gómez-Martín; m. Maria Natividad Moreira-Andrés, Dec. 31, 1980; children: Maria Del Cañizo-Moreira, Francisco Javier Del Cañizo-Moreira, Jorge Del Cañizo-Moreira. Degree (hon.), Complutense U., Madrid, 1977, PhD in endocrinology and nutrition, 1980, MD (hon.), 1999; M in Clin. Investigation (hon.), Autonoma U., Madrid, 1998. Cert. endocrinology, diabetes and nutrition European Bd. Endocrinology, 2001. Rsch. fellow exptl. endocrinology Complutense U., 1980—86; endocrinologist 12 de Octubre U. Hosp., Madrid, 1987—95; head endocrinology Virgen de la Torre Hosp., Madrid, 1995—2001, med. sub-dir., 1999—2001; head med. formation Hosp. Virgen de la Torre, Madrid, 1996—99, endocrinologist, 2001—, head endocrinology, 2005—. Editor: (book) Diabetes para Educadores, 1990; author: Lecciones Sobre Hipertensión, 1985—88; editor: Diabetes Mellitus: Teoría y Práctica, 1996; author: Guía Práctica para el Tratamiento de la Hipertensión Arterial, 1986—88, Curso Teórico-Práctico sobre Evaluación de la Talla baja, 1994; editor: Diabetes mellitus tipo 2 y Factores de Riesgo Cardiovascular, 2003; contbr. articles to profl. jours, chapters to books. Fellow Fondo de Investigaciones Sanitarias de la Seguridad Social, 1981—84. Mem.: Sociedad Castellano-Leonesa de Endocrinología, Diabetes y Nutrición, Sociedad Madrileña de Endocrinología, Diabetes y Nutrición, Sociedad Española de Endocrinología y Nutrición. Avocations: football, basketball, hiking, travel, bicycling. Office: Hospital Virgen de la Torre Puerto Lumbreras 5 Madrid 28031 Spain Personal E-mail: fjdelcanizogomez@hotmail.com. E-mail: fjcanizo@arrakis.es.

DEL CURA, JOSE LUIS, radiologist; b. Barakaldo, Spain, July 24, 1960; s. Jorge del Cura and Basilisa González; m. Amelia Allende, May 1, 1986; 1 child, Gorka. Certificado Estudios Superiores, La Salle Sch., Bilbao, 1977; MD, Basque Country U., 1983, PhD, 2000. Registered Radiologist Ministerio de Educación Spain, 1989. Resident radiology Hosp. de Cruces, Barakaldo, 1985—89, radiologist, 1989—90, AEGON, Bilbao, Spain, 1989—96; chief radiology Clinica Guimon, Bilbao, 1992—, Clínica Indautxu, Bilbao, 2001—; assoc. prof. Basque Country U., Bilbao, 2001—; radiologist Hosp. de Basurto, Bilbao, 1990—2007, chief radiology, 2007—; dir. Postgrad. Med. Edn. Basurto Hosp., 2010. Master: SERAM, FORA, Assn. Radiólogos Euskadi, SEUS; mem.: SEDIA, SERVEI, European Assn. Radiology. Avocations: sports, reading, mountain climbing. Personal E-mail: jlcura@euskalnet.net. Business E-Mail: joseluis.delcurarodriguez@osakidetza.net.

DE LEO, ROBERTO V., neurosurgeon; b. Mexico City, Aug. 12, 1952; s. Ruben V. De Leo and Margarita G. Vargas; m. Ana Maria S. Spindla De Leo, May 24, 1977; children: Roberto, Juan Pablo, Fernando. MD summa cum laude, LaSalle U., Mexico City, 1976; postgrad., U. Rochester, 1977—78, U. Alta., Edmonton, Can., 1978—82. Cons. Nat. Med. Ctr., Mexico City, 1982—84; prof. LaSalle U., Mexico City, 1982—87; cons. ABC Hosp., Mexico City, 1982—, chief neurosurgery, 2003—. Chmn. Think First Found., 2003—; founder Mexican Inst. Neurosci., 2003. Author: The Greatest Neurosurgeon in Earth, 1998. Dir. Mexican Assn. Against Trauma, 1986—. Named Leader in Worldwide Injury Prevention, Nat. Injury Prevention Found., 2005. Fellow: ACS; mem.: Am. Assn. Neurol. Surgeons, Congress Neurol. Surgeons. Roman Catholic. Avocations: Tae Kwon Do, sports. Home: Bosque de Robles 138 11700 Mexico City Mexico Office: ABC Hosp and Med Ctr Sur 136 Observatorio 203 1120 Mexico City Mexico Office Phone: 5255 52723811.

DELEO, VINCENT A., dermatologist, educator; Attended, La. State U. Med. Ctr., 1969. Diplomate Am. Bd. Dermatology, 1977. Resident Columbia Presbyn. Med. Ctr., NYC, 1972—76, fellow dermatology; fellow NY photobiology Columbia Univ., NY, 1975, fellow dermatology rsch. NY, 1982—84, clin. prof. coll. of physicians and surgeons; chmn. dermatology dept. founding dir. skin of color ctr. St. Luke's-Roosevelt Hosp. Ctr., Beth Israel Med. Ctr. Named one of Best Doctors, NY Mag., 2008, Top Doctors-New York Metro Area, Castle Connolly's, 2009. Office: Continuum Health Partners 10 Union Sq East 3C New York NY 10003 Office Phone: 212-844-8800. Office Fax: 212-844-8801. E-mail: vdeleo@slrhc.org.

DELEON, PATRICK HENRY, legislative staff member, lawyer; b. Waterbury, Conn., Jan. 6, 1943; s. Patrick and Catherine (Dzubay) D.; m. Jean Louise Murphy; children: Patrick Daniel Nainoa, Katherine Malia Malie. BA, Amherst Coll., 1964; MS, Purdue U., 1966, PhD in Clin. Psychology, 1969; MPH, U. Hawaii, 1973; JD, Catholic U., 1980. Bar: Hawaii 1981, U.S. Dist. Ct. Hawaii 1983, U.S. Ct. Appeals (9th cir.) 1983; diplomate Am. Bd. Profl. Psychology, Am. Bd. Forensic Psychology. Tng. psychologist Peace Corps Tng. Ctr., Hilo, Hawaii, 1969-70; staff psychologist Diamond Head Mental Health Ctr., Hawaii State Hosp., Honolulu and Kaneohe, Hawaii, 1970-73; chief of staff to Senator Daniel K. Inouye US Senate, Washington, 1973—. Fellow APA (pres. 2000, assoc. editor American Psychologist Jour. 1981—, editor Profl. Psychology Rsch. and Practice 1995-2000), Hawaii Psychol. Assn. (Disting. Svc. award 1981), Hawaii Bar Assn.; mem. Inst. Medicine. Democrat. Office: US House of Representatives 722 SHOB Washington DC 20510-1102 Office Phone: 202-224-3934. Business E-Mail: patrick_deleon@inouye.senate.gov. *

DELGADO, ELIANA, orthopedic surgeon; BA in Philosophy and Religion, San Francisco State U., 1972, BS in Med. Sci., 1977; AA in Nursing, Coll. San Mateo, Calif., 1974; MPH, U. Calif., Berkeley, 1982; MD, U. Calif. Sch. Medicine, San Francisco, 1989. Cert. in orthopaedic surgery 2002. Internship in gen. surgery Highland Gen. Hosp. Dept. Gen. Surgery, Oakland, Calif., 1982—85; residency in orthopaedic surgery U. Calif., San Francisco, 1985—89, clin. instr., 1989—2000, prof. orthopaedic surgery, 2000—, assoc. clin. prof. pediatrics, orthopedic surgeon; orthopaedic trauma fellowship San Francisco Gen. Hosp., 1989—90; pediatric orthopaedic fellowship St. Louis Shriners Hosp., St. Louis, 1992—93. Contbr. articles to profl. jours. Office: Univ Calif San Francisco Box 0728 MU 320 500 Parnassus Ave San Francisco CA 94143-0296 Office Phone: 415-353-9372. Office Fax: 415-476-1304. Business E-Mail: delgadoe@orthosurg.ucsf.edu.

DELGADO-MARTINEZ, ALBERTO D., orthopedic surgeon, educator; b. Jaen, Spain, Oct. 2, 1966; life ptnr. MD, U. Granada, Spain, 1990; PhD, U. Autonoma de Madrid, Spain, 1995. Cons. dept. orthop. Hosp. Universitario Neurotraumatologico, Jaen, 1996—; prof. U. Jaen, 1999—. Contbr. articles to profl. jours. Grantee, Fondo de Investigación sanitaria, 1993, 2000. Fellow: European Bd. Orthop. and Traumatology; mem.: SECOT, AOFAS, AAOS. Office: Hosp Universitario Neurotraumatologico Carretera de Madrid S/N E-23009 Jaen Spain Office Phone: +34953008100. Business E-Mail: adelgado@ujaen.es.

DEL GAUDIO, MASSIMO, surgeon, researcher; b. Bologna, Italy, Aug. 25, 1974; s. Mariano Del Gaudio and Raffaela Morra; m. Federica Ugolini, Aug. 30, 2003; children: Benedetta, Alessandra. Lic. E. Fermi Sci. Liceum, Bologna, 1992, diplomate Bd. U. Bologna, 1999. Resident gen. surgery U. Bologna, 1999—2005, physician, 2005—; gen. and transplant surgeon S. Orsola Malpighi Hosp., Bologna, 2005—. Office: S Orsola Malpighi Hosp Via Massarenti 9 Bologna 40138 Italy Home: Via Bellaria 35 40139 Bologna BO Italy Office Fax: 0039 51 304902. Business E-Mail: m_delgaudio@hotmail.com.

DEL GIGLIO, AURO, oncologist, hematologist; b. São Paulo, Brazil, Oct. 17, 1962; s. Alfredo Fiederer and Norma del Giglio; m. Sandra Braz, Oct. 6, 1987; children: Adriana, Eduardo, Adriana, Eduardo, David, Denise. MD, São Paulo U., 1985. Diplomate Am. Bd. Internal Medicine, 1989, cert. clin. oncology Am. Bd. Internal Medicine, 1991, hematology Am. Bd. Internal Medicine, 1996, Sociedade Brasileira de Cancerologia, 1998. Chmn. hematology and oncology Faculdade de Medicina da Fundação ABC, Santo André, São Paulo, 1996—. Recipient Outstanding Achievement in Cancer Rsch., MD Anderson Cancer Ctr., 1992. Fellow: ACP. Jewish. Avocation: classical music. Office: Clioh Avenida Rebouças 3387 São Paulo 05410-040 Brazil Office Fax: 55-11-38195007. E-mail: sandrabr@netpoint.com.br.

DEL GIUDICE, STEPHEN M., dermatologist; MD, Tufts Univ. Sch. of Medicine, Boston, 1981. Diplomate Am. Bd. Dermatology, 1987. Intern internal medicine Yale-New Haven Hosp., Boston, 1981—82, resident dermatology, 1984—87; with Dartmouth-Hitchcock Concord, 1987—; hosp. affiliation include Concord Hosp. Office: Dartmouth Hitchcock Concord Dermatology 253 Pleasant St Concord NH 03301 Office Phone: 603-226-6119. Office Fax: 603-229-5119.

DEL GUERCIO, LOUIS RICHARD MAURICE, surgeon, educator; b. NYC, Jan. 15, 1929; s. Louis and Hortense (Ardengo) Del G.; m. Paula Marie Helene de Vautibault, May 18, 1957; children: Louis, Francsca, Paul, Catherine, Maria, Michelle, Christopher, Anthony. BS cum laude, Fordham U., 1949; MD, Yale U., 1953. Diplomate Am. Bd. Surgery, Am. Bd. Thoracic Surgery. Intern Columbia-Presbyn. Med. Ctr., NYC, 1953—54; resident St Vincent's Hosp., NYC, 1954—58, Cleve. City Hosp., 1958—60; practice medicine specializing in thoracic surgery, 1960—; assoc. prof. Albert Einstein Coll. Medicine, NYC, 1966—70, prof. surgery, 1970—71, dir. Clin. Rsch. Ctr.-Acute, 1967—71; clin. prof. surgery NJ Coll. Medicine, Newark, 1971—76; prof. surgery NY Med. Coll., NYC, 1976—, chmn. dept., 1976—2001, emeritus prof. surgery, 2001—; chief surgery Westchester County Med. Ctr., 1976—2001; instr. Yale Sch. Nursing, 1953. Mem. surg. study sect. NIH, 1970-74; mem. com. on shock NRC-NAS, 1969-71; merit rev. bd. VA, 1971-74; mem. health care tech. study sect. Dept. HHS, 1980-84; cons. Nat. Ctr. Health Svcs. Rsch., 1980-84, NY State Office Profl. Med. Conduct, 2004—; chmn. bd. dirs. Daltex Med. Scis., Inc.; cons. in field. Author: (with B.G. Clarke) Urology, 1956, The Multilingual Manual for Medical History Taking, 1972, (with S.G. Hershey, R. McConn) Septic Shock in Man, 1971; editor-in-chief Critical Care Monitor, 1980-85, Complications in Surgery, 1990—; contbr. articles to med. jours.; patentee in field. Bd. trustees Maria Fareri Children's Hosp., Westchester Med. Ctr., 2006—. With Mcht. Marine, 1946-47; with AUS, 1949-51; col. med. dept. USAR, 1990—. Recipient award in medicine Fordham U. Alumni Assn., 1974, Gold award Am. Acad. Pediat., 1973, Humanitarian award Boys' Towns of Italy, 1994; grantee Health Rsch. Coun. NY, 1965-71, NIH, 1962-71. Fellow ACS, Coll. of Critical Care Medicine, Am. Thoracic Soc.; mem. Am. Trauma Soc. (founder), Soc. Critical Care Medicine (founder, pres. 1976), Am. Surg. Assn., Am. Physiol. Soc., Soc. Univ. Surgeons, French Nat. Acad. Surgery, Equestrian Order of Holy Sepulchre Jerusalem, Yale U. Sch. Medicine Alumni Assn. (exec. com. 2001—); hon. police surgeon City of N.Y. Home and Office: 14 Pryer Ln Larchmont NY 10538-4021 Office Phone: 914-834-8265. Business E-Mail: lou@delguercio.com.

DELHAYE-BOUCHAUD, NICOLE PAULE, neurobiologist; b. Malakoff, France, Oct. 29, 1936; d. Georges Louis Delhaye, Jeanne Juliette Lefèvre; m. Claude Jean-Louis Bouchaud; children: Valérie Bouchaud, Agnès Bouchaud, Cécile Bouchaud, Nicolas Bouchaud. DSc, U. Pierre et Marie Curie, Paris, 1963. Asst. Faculty of Scis., Paris, 1961—70; maitre-asst. U. Pierre et Marie Curie, Paris, 1970—85, prof., 1985—99, hon. prof. Dir. Developmental Neurobiology Lab., U. Paris, 1988—99. Contbr. Book Dictionnaire Le Cerveau, 1998. Home: 5 bis rue Bronzac 94240 L'Hay-les-Roses France Office: U Pierre et Marie Curie 4 Place Jussieu 75252 Paris Cedex 05 France Home Phone: 33 1 46634737. Home Fax: 33 1 46634737. Personal E-mail: nicolebouchaud@club-internet.fr.

DE LIMA, MAURÍCIO SILVA, medical director, researcher, psychiatry professor; b. Pelotas, Rio Grande do Sul, Brazil; MD, Universidade Fed. Pelotas, 1983, degree in psychiatry, 1987, M in Epidemiology, 1995; PhD in Psychiatry, Fed. U. São Paulo, Brazil, 1996; postgrad., U. London, 1996—97. Cert. psychiatrist Ministry Edn., Brazil, 1998. Assoc. prof. psychiatry Universidade Fed. Pelotas, 1993—, dir. Ctr. Evidence Based Medicine, 1997—2003; med. dir. Ely Lilly Brazil, São Paulo, 2005—. Hon. sr. lectr. Inst. Psychiatry, London, 1999—; clin. rsch. physician Eli Lilly Brazil, 2003—05; rschr. in field. Recipient Best Poster Presentation award, Internat. Fed. Epidemiol. Psychiatry, 1999, 2001, Kenneth Warren award systematic revs. developing world, 2000, 2003; PhD fellow, CAPES, Ministry Edn., 1995—96, Postdoctoral fellow, 1996—97, Rsch. fellow, Brazilian Nat. Coun. Rsch. Ministry Edn., 2000—. Home: Rua Gaivota 1359 ap 31 São Paulo Brazil Office: Eli Lilly Brazil Avenida Morumbi 8264 04703-002 São Paulo SP Brazil Office Fax: +55 1155326966. Personal E-mail: msilvadelima@yahoo.com.br. Business E-Mail: limama@lilly.com.

DELIS, KONSTANTINOS TRIANTAFYLLOS, vascular surgeon, consultant; s. Triantafyllos John Delis. MB BS, U. Athens, 1985, MD with distinction, 1993; MSc in Vascular Tech. and Medicine with distinction, Imperial Coll. U. London, 1994, PhD in Vascular Surgery, 1999, M of Surgery, 2004. Cert. European Bd. Vascular Surgery Qualification, 2002. Gen. surgery registrar Evangelismos Gen. Hosp. Athens, 1988—93; rsch. registrar St. Mary's Hosp., Imperial Coll. Sch. Medicine, London, 1993—96, vascular/surg. registrar, 1996—97, sr. clin. vascular fellow, 1998—2003; vascular registrar Ealing (Eng.) Gen. Hosp., 1997—98; Marco Polo fellow Vascular surgery Mayo Clinic, Rochester, Minn., 2004—05, academic collaborator divsn. vascular surgery, 2005—; vascular surgeon cons. Athens Med. Ctr. Marousi, Greece, 2005—. Contbr. articles to profl. jours. Lt., med. officer Greek Army, 1986—88. Recipient Lars-Eric award original study, European Soc. Microcirculation, 2000, Marco Polo Scholarship award, European Soc. Vascular Surgery, 2003. Fellow: Royal Coll. Surgeons (Dublin); mem.: European Venous Forum, Internat. Union Angiology. Achievements include research in intermittent pneumattic compression in the treatment of arterial claudication, chronic venous disease and microcirculation; middle aortic syndrome, carotid body tumors, endovascular therapy in aortic, carotid and peripheral aortic disease and ilio femoral venous stenting. Avocations: photography, basketball, jazz. Office: Imperial Coll Saint Marys Hosp Regional Vascular Surgery London W2 1NY England Home: Agias Varvaras 56 152 31 Athens Greece Home Phone: 001144 20 8998 8685, 30210 6717 488; Office Phone: 30 69722222 18. Business E-Mail: k.delis@ic.ac.uk. E-mail: delis.kostas@mayo.edu.

DE LISA, JOEL ALAN, rehabilitation physician, research executive; b. Seattle, Mar. 18, 1942; s. Joseph Phillip and Alice Georgia (Jensen) DeL.; m. Janet Hopper, July 25, 1971. BS in Zoology, Wash. State U., 1964; MD, U. Wash., 1968, MS, 1976. Diplomate Am. Bd. Phys. Medicine and Rehab. (chmn. 1993-98); diplomate spinal cord injury medicine. Intern St. Josephs Hosp., Phoenix, 1968-69; resident in phys. medicine and rehab. U. Wash., Seattle, 1972-75; med. dir., chief med. officer Kessler Inst. Rehab., West Orange, NJ, 1987-93; sr. v.p., chief med. officer Kessler Rehab. Corp., West Orange, 1994-2000; pres., CEO Kessler Med. Rehab. Rsch. and Edn. Corp., West Orange, 1998—2008; founding dir. Kessler Found. Rsch. Ctr., 2009—. Prof., chmn. dept. phys. medicine and rehab. U. Medicine and Dentistry NJ, Newark, 1987—, interim dean, 2000; chmn. dept. phys. medicine and rehab. St. Barnabas Med. Ctr., Livingston, NJ, 1990-98, chair. ednl. commn. fgn. med. grad., 2005-06; chmn. Am. Bd. Med. Specialties, 2008-; chair coun. academic socs. Assn. Am. Med. Colls., 2008. Author: Principles and Practice of Physical Medicine and Rehabilitation, 2004, Manual of Nerve Conduction Study and Surface Anatomy and Needle Electromyography, 2004. Mem. AMA, Assn. Acad. Physiatrists, Am. Acad. Phys. Medicine and Rehab., Am. Congress Rehab. Medicine, Am. Paraplegic Soc. (hon., pres. Jackson Heights chpt. 1989-91, Excellence award 1995). Office: Kessler Med Rehab Rsch and Edn Corp 1199 Pleasant Valley Way West Orange NJ 07052-1424 Home Phone: 973-635-6200; Office Phone: 973-243-6806. Business E-Mail: delisaja@umdnj.edu.

DELISI, KRISTIN, adult nurse practitioner; b. Lebanon, Pa., Mar. 10, 1973; BSN, Pa. State U., 1995; MSN, U. Pitts., 1999. RN. Nurse practitioner Adagio Health, 1999—2004, Children's Hosp. Pitts., UPMC, 2004—08, rsch. interventionist, 2006—08, U. Pitts. Med. Ctr., 2009—, nurse practitioner, 2008—. Adj. clin. faculty Duquesne U., 2003—04. Mem.: Sigma Theta Tau. Office: 3601 5th Ave Ste 562 Pittsburgh PA 15213 Business E-Mail: kristin.delisi@chp.edu.

DELIVORIA-PAPADOPOULOS, MARIA, pediatrician; b. Athens, Greece, Feb. 23, 1931; MD, Nat. U. Sch. Medicine, 1957. Chief, neonatal perinatal medicine St. Christopher's Hosp. Children, 1996—. Prof. pediat. & physiology Drexel U. Coll. Medicine, 1996. Recipient Roosevelt award, Mar. of Dimes, Dr. Honoris Causa, U. Athens Med. Sch., Lifetime Achievement award, Castle Connolly Med. Ltd., President's Disting. Scientist award, Soc. Gynecologic Investigation. Mem.: Am. Acad. Pediat., Soc. Gynecologic Investigation, Am. Physiol. Soc., Soc. Pediatric Rsch., Am. Pediatric Soc. Avocations: history, literature. Home: St Christopher's Hosp Children Philadelphia PA 19134 Home Fax: 215-427-8192. Business E-Mail: delivoria@drexelmed.edu.

DELL, MICHAEL S., pediatrician; b. Mpls., Sept. 30, 1965; MD, Harvard Med. Sch., 1992. Cert. Am. Bd. Pediat. Resident Children's Hosp. Phila., 1992—96; staff mem. U. Hospitals-Rainbow Babies & Children's Hosp., Cleve., 1998—; asst. to prof., pediat. Case Western Reserve U. Sch. Medicine, Cleve., 1998—. Office: Rainbow Babies & Childrens Hosp 11100 Euclid Ave Cleveland OH 44106 Office Phone: 216-844-8260.

DELL, RALPH BISHOP, retired pediatrician, researcher; b. Mt. Village, Alaska, July 31, 1935; s. Elwin B. and Elizabeth B. (Bishop) D.; m. Kathryn M. Bownass, June 17, 1957 (div. Dec. 1982); children: Laura, Kenneth; m. Karen K. Hein, Aug. 28, 1983; stepchildren: Ethan Hein, Molly Hein. BA, Pomona Coll., Claremont, Calif., 1957; MD, U. Pa., Phila., 1961. Diplomate Am. Bd. Pediat. Intern and resident Children's Hosp. Med. Ctr., Boston, 1961-63; NIH postdoctoral fellow Coll. Physicians and Surgeons, Columbia U., NYC, 1963-66, assoc., 1966-67, asst. prof. pediat., 1967-72, assoc. prof., 1972-78, prof., 1978-97; dir. Inst. for Lab. Animal Rsch. NRC, Washington, 1997-2000, ret., 2000. Author: 3 books, 100 rsch. papers; co-inventor amino acid solution. Program chair Windham World Affairs Coun., 2006—; trustee Whitingham Hist. Soc. Recipient Rsch. Career Devel. award NIH, 1966-71, Career Scientist award Health Rsch. Coun. N.Y., 1972-75; Fogarty Sr. Internat. fellow NIH, 1975-76. Mem. Am. Pediat. Soc., Am. Physiologic Soc., Am. Soc. Clin. Investigation, Soc. for Pediat. Rsch., Assn. for Computing Machinery, Am. Coll. Lab. Medicine (hon.), Am. Assn. Accreditation Lab. Animal Care (emeritus mem., coun. on accreditation), Lions Club. Democrat. Avocation: woodworking. Home: PO Box 607 Jacksonville VT 05342 Personal E-mail: rbdell@hughes.net.

DELL, THOMAS CHARLES, nurse anesthetist; b. Port Huron, Mich., May 28, 1959; s. John W. and Lois M. (Bell) D.; children: Adam, Aubree, Andrea. AS, St. Clair County Community Coll., Port Huron, Mich., 1979; BSN, No. Mich. U., 1981; BS, Mercy Coll. Detroit, 1985; MS, Gooding Inst. Nurse Anethesia, Panama City, Fla., 1998. RN, Mich.; cert. nurse anesthetist. Nurse Marquette (Mich.) Gen., 1981-83, Mercy Hosp., Port Huron, 1983-85, nurse anesthetist, insvc. coord., 1985-88; nurse anesthetist Saber Salisbury and Assoc., Southfield, Mich., 1988—; chief nurse anesthetist McKenzie Meml. Hosp., Sandusky, Mich., 1989-98; clin. and didactic instr. U. Mich./Hurley Med. Ctr. Sch. Nurse Anesthesia, Flint, 1998—2001; staff nurse anesthetist Marlette (Mich.) Cmty. Hosp., 2001—04; staff anesthetist Port Huron (Mich.) Hosp., 2004—09, St. John River Dist. Hosp., 2004—. Mem. Am. Assn. Nurse Anesthetists, Mich. Assn. Nurse Anesthetists. Avocations: ping pong/table tennis, bicycling, trumpet playing. Personal E-mail: tdell1@comcast.net.

DELL'ACQUA, RENE, cosmetic dentist; m. Joe Dell'Acqua; children: Courtland, Aubrey, Joey. Grad., U. Pacific Sch. of Dentistry. Cosmetic dentist Dell'Acqua Dental Studio. Mem.: ADA, Calif. Dental Assn., Am. Acad. Cosmetic Dentistry. Office: Dell'Acqua Dental Studio 74133 El Paseo Suite D Palm Desert CA 92260 Office Phone: 760-346-8056.

DELL'ANTONE, PAOLO, physics educator; b. Padua, Italy, Apr. 6, 1941; s. Guido Dell'Antone and Jolanda Turolla. Grad. in physics, U. Padua, 1966. Assoc. prof. U. Padua, 1983—. Mem.: AAAS. Home: Via Valeggio 3 Padua Italy Office: Dept Sci and Biomedicine Sperimentali Via Colombo 3 35171 Padua Italy Office Fax: 049 8276049. E-mail: paolo.dellantone@unipd.it.

DELLAVECCHIA, MICHAEL ANTHONY, ophthalmologist, pathologist educator, scientist; BA in Physics and Math., LaSalle Coll., Phila., 1970; MS in Biomed. Sci. and Engring., Drexel U., 1972, PhD in Biomed. Sci. and Engring., 1984; MD, Temple U., 1976. Diplomate Am. Bd. Med. Examiners, Am. Bd. Ophthalmology, lic. physician Pa., NJ. Resident in anatomical and clin. pathology Temple U. Hosp., Phila., 1977-80, chief resident, 1979-80, fellow in surg. pathology, 1980-81, resident in ophthalmology, 1981-84; fellow in ophthalmology Project Orbis, Inc., NYC, 1985; v.p., med. dir., co-founder Mega Med. Electronics, Hatfield, Pa., 1984—95; assoc. John Reichel MD, Ltd., Bryn Mawr, Pa., 1984-95; assoc. staff, clin. instr. Temple U. Hosp., Phila., 1986—; instr. Wills Eye Hosp., Phila., 1986—, Scheie Eye Inst., Phila., 1986-96; prof. dept. biomed. engring. Drexel U., Phila., 1991—, disting. rsch. prof. dept. biomed. engring., 2006—; attending staff ophthalmology Grad. Health Sys. Phila. Coll. Osteo. Medicine, 1995—2002; assoc. surgeon Wills Eye Hosp., 2001—07, attending surgeon, emergency rm., 2002—, dir. emergency dept., 2004—, full attending surgeon, 2007—; clin. asst. prof. Thomas Jefferson U., 2007; resident mem. edn. com., 2005—. Med. dir. Interstate Blood Bank, Inc., 1977—80; dir. med. info. Info. Mgmt. Corp., 1984—87; dir. med. rsch. Sonic Techs., Inc., 1984—86; med. dir., med. adv. bd. Lehigh Ultrasonics Group, 1985—87; pres., founder Dell Med. Inc., 1985—; pres., treas., co-founder Med. Design Assocs., 1985—86; co-founder, med. dir. Omega Nutrients, Inc., 1987—89; tech. advisor Project Orbis, Inc., 1986—; clin. instr. ophthalmology svc. Willis Eye Hosp., 1986—97, asst. prof., 1997—2000, assoc. prof., 2000—07, prof., 2007—, dir. emergency dept., 2003—, mem. resident edn. and sup. com., mem. edn. com., 2006—; clin. instr. ophthalmology svc. U. Pa., 1986—95, Temple U.,

1984—; dir. labs. Am. Clin. Labs., 1985—94, Phila. Union Health Ctr., 1988—96; radiol. officer Emergency Mgmt. Assn., State of Pa., 1993—; co-founder Med. Surveillance Group, 1993—95; cons. Keystone Clin. Labs., 1994—95, NASA, 1992—; adj. prof. surgery dept. ophthalmology Phila. Coll. Osteo. Medicine, 1995—99; mem. editl. bd. laser medicine divsn. Emergency Care Rsch. Inst., 1995—2002; cons. Sensar divsn. Sarnoff Labs., 1993—2000, chmn. med. adv. bd., 1996—2000; mem. emergency mgmt. com. Thomas Jefferson Hosp., 2005—, clin. asst. prof., 2007—, mem. physician computerization com., 2006—; mem. emergency response Del. Valley Hosp. Coun., 2005—. Contbr. articles to profl. jours.; reviewer Physician's Info. and Ednl. Resources, 2005—, peer reviewer Jour. Biomed. Optics, 2006—; editor: Physicians Info. & Ednl. Resources ACP. Vol. counselor Boy Scouts Am.; chmn. instl. rev. bd. Phila. Retinal Endowment Fund, 2002—. Recipient numerous certs., Fed. Emergency Mgmt. Assn., Graduating Resident Tchg. Appreciation award, Wills Eye Inst., 2009; named America's Top Drs., Castle Connolly, 2009; named one of Best Dr.'s in Am., 2003—; Presdl. Acad. scholar, LaSalle Coll., 1966—70, Pa. State Senatorial scholar, Temple U. Sch. Medicine, Rsch. fellow, Drexel U., 1976—77, Surg. Pathology fellow, Temple U. Hosp., 1980—81, numerous rsch. grantees. Fellow: ACS (bd. dirs. Phila. met. chpt. 2004—, treas. 2006—07, editl. cons. physicians info. and edn. resource 2006—, sec 2007—08, v.p. 2008—09, 2008—09, 2008—09, pres. elect 2009—10, bd. regents 2010—), Coll. Physicians Phila. (mem. centenial and sesquisentenial com. 2007—, bd. trustees 2009—, devel. com. mem. 2009—, libr. restoration com. F.C. wood com. 2009—), Phila. Metro Div. Am. Coll. Surgeons (bd. dirs. 2002—04, treas. 2005—06, sec. 2006—07, v.p. 2007—08, pres. elect 2010—11, pres. 2011—), Internat. Coll. Surgeons (mcpl. bd. regents 2009—, bd. regents 2010—), Am. Acad. Ophthalmology (laser & light safety working group 2010—, Lifetime Edn. in Ophthalmology award 1996—99); mem.: AMA (Physician Recognition award 1990—), IEEE, Soc. Photoinstrumentation Engrs. (sr. exec. 2011—), Greater Phila. Ophthalmic Soc., Lifelong Edn. Ophthalmology (with distinction 1999—), Chymian Soc., Newtonian Soc., Montgomery County Med. Soc., Pa. Med. Soc., Phila. County Med. Soc., Intercounty Opthal. Soc., Del. Vally Opthal. Soc., NY Acad. Scis., Am. Soc. Clin. Pathology, Engring. Medicine and Biology, Lase and Electro-Optics Soc., Internat. Biomedical Optics Soc. (inaugural), Internat. Soc. Photoinstrumentation Engrs. (elected sr. mem. 2011), Internat. Bioelectrochem. Soc., Am. Soc. Laser Medicine and Surgery (mem. com. laser safety 2005—06, mem. com. constn. and by-laws 2006—07, mem. budget and fin. com. 2006—, bd. mem. iomed. engring. 2010—, bd. dirs. biomed. engring. 2011—), Phila. Med. Club (bd. dirs. 2003—, chmn. membership com. 2004—, v.p. 2008—, mem. devel. com. 2009, pres. 2009—11), Brit. Officers Club (hon.), Lions, Sigma Xi, Alpha Epsilon Delta, Kappa Mu Epsilon. Achievements include patents for in engineering and medical devices; ophthalmic shield with removable compression device; medicament delivery systems and adaptive optics, and biometric identification and photonics. Office Phone: 215-503-8081. Business E-Mail: mdellavecchia@willseye.org.

DELL'EDERA, DOMENICO, biologist; b. Matera, Italy, Nov. 27, 1968; Laurea, Scienze Biologiche, 1992; genetica, Genetica Medica, 1996. Responsabile Laboratorio Di Genetica Medica, 2001—11. Bd. dirs. Genetica Medica, 2007—11. Home: via Taranto 15/I Matera 75100 Italy Home Fax: 0835253863. Personal E-mail: ducati98@libero.it.

DELL'OSSO, LOUIS FRANK, neuroscience educator; b. Bklyn., Mar. 16, 1941; s. Frank and Rose (Perrone) Dell'O.; m. Aquilina Marie Ferlo, May 22, 1965 (div. 1976); single ptnr. Charlene Hale Morse, Sept. 30, 1977. BEE, Bklyn. Poly. Inst., 1961, postgrad., 1961-63; PhD, U. Wyo., 1968. Co-dir. Ocular Motor Neurophysiology Lab. VA. Med. Ctr., Miami, Fla., 1972-80; asst. prof. biomed. engring. and surgery U. Miami, 1970-72, asst. prof. neurology, 1972-75, assoc. prof. neurology, 1975-79, prof. neurology, 1979-80; dir. Ocular Motor Neurophysiology Lab. VA Med. Ctr., Cleve., 1980—2004; prof. neurology and biomed. engring. Case Western Res. U., Cleve., 1980—2010, prof. emeritus neurology, 2010—, dir. Daroff-Dell'Osso Ocular Motility Lab., 2004—10, dir. emeritus, 2010—. Cons. Westinghouse Research Lab, Pitts, 1966-67, 70-71, Mt. Sinai Hosp., Miami, Fla., 1972-75. Bd. dirs. Vineland Galloway Civic Assn., Miami, 1973-76. Grantee NIH, 1971-77, VA Med. Ctr., 1972—, NSF, 1970. Fellow N.Am. NeuroOphthalmology Soc., Assn. Rsch. Vision and Ophthalmology; mem. IEEE, Engring. in Medicine and Biology Soc. (sr., chpt. chmn. 1977-78), Soc. Neurosci., NY Acad. Scis., Train Collectors Assn., CCCC Rod & Gun Club. Democrat. Home: 2356 Tudor Dr Cleveland OH 44106-3212 Office Phone: 216-421-3224. Business E-Mail: lfd@case.edu.

DELLUC, GILLES, physician, researcher; b. Périgueux, Dordogne, France, Aug. 22, 1934; s. Paul and Geneviève D.; m. Brigitte Antoine, Sept. 15, 1962; 1 child, Sophie. MD, Sch. of Medicine, Paris, 1967; D in Quaternary Geology, Anthropology, Prehistory, Paris VI Univ., 1985. Intern, asst. dr. various hosps., Paris, 1958—70; clinic chief Medical Sch., Paris, 1968—70; chief dept. of medicine Périgueux Hosp., France, 1970—99; rschr. lab. prehistory Nat. Mus. Natural History, Paris, 1985—. Dir. of clinic teaching Sch. of Medicine of Bordeaux, 1980-99; v.p. Hist. Fedn. of the S.W. of France, 1988—, European Ctr. Prehistoric Researches, Vezere Valley. Author: (with wife) Lascaux inconnu, 1979, Lascaux un nouveau regard, 1986, Les Chasseurs de la Préhistoire, 1979, Connaitre Lascaux, 1990, 2d edit., 2006, L'Art Pariétal archaique en Aquitaine, 1991, Connaitre la Préhistoire en Périgord, 1993, 2nd edit., 2011, La Nutrition Préhistorique, 1995, Préhistoire de l'Art Occidental, 1995, Léo Drouyn en Dordogne 1845-1851, 2001, Louis Delluc 1890-1924: l'Eveilleur du Cinema Francais au Temps des Annees Folles, 2002, La vie des hommes de la Prehistoire, 2003, Lascaux retrouvé, 2003, Jean Filliol du Périgord a la Cagoule, de la Milice a Oradour, 2005, Le Sexe au Temps des Cro-Magnons, 2006, Les Recherches d'André Glory à Lascaux (1952-1963), 2008, Dictionnaire de Lascaux, 2008, Petites Enigmes et grands mysteres, 2008-10. Named officer Palmes Académiques, 1997, Chevalier Arts and Letters, 2001. Mem.: Historic and Archeologic Soc. of Perigord, Soc. Prehistorique Francaise, Groupe de Recherche Pedagogique en Diabetologie, Speleoclub de Perigueux. Avocations: speleology, research of caves with prehistoric paintings or engravings, photography. Office: Musée de l' Abri Pataud 24620 Les Eyzies France Home: Lieu Dit le Bourg 24380 Saint Michel France

DELMAR, CHARLOTTE, nursing administrator, researcher; b. Aalborg, Denmark, May 13, 1959; d. Tonni Kähler and Erik Jensen; m. Mads Villi Delmar, July 13, 1985; children: Anna Christine Penthien, Christoffer Penthien. B in Nursing, Sch. Nursing, Aalborg, 1982; diploma in nursing edn., Aarhus U., Denmark, 1987, diploma in nursing, 1992, MSN, 1994; PhD, Aalborg U., Denmark, 1999. Theatre nurse Aalborg Hosp., 1982—83, Old Addenbrookes Hosp., Cambridge, England, 1984; nurse specialist Rogaland Hosp., Stavanger, Norway, 1984—86; dist. nurse Municipality of Aalborg, 1987; tchr. Sch. of Nursing, Hjørring, Denmark, 1987—94; v.p. Aalborg Hosp., 1994—99; rsch. dir. Aalborg U. Hosp., 2000—. Adv. bd. Novo Nordisk Found., Bagsværd/Copenhagen, Denmark, 2005—; judgement for rsch. dir. applicants Bispebjerg Hosp., Copenhagen, 2004; judgement for post docs applicants State Hosp. in Denmark, Copenhagen, 2006; adv. bd. new edn. master in clin. nursing Aarhus U., Århus, Denmark, 2003—; collaborator prof. Kari Martinsen, U. of Bergen, Bergen, Norway, 1992—; adv. bd. Danish Coun. Nurses, Copenhagen, 2003—; collaborator Prof. Jean Watson, Caritas Consortium, Denver, 2003—, prof. Chris Johns. Luton U., Luton, United Kingdom, 2005—, ass. prof. Kerstin Sivonen, Helsinki, Finland, 2005—, ass.professor Ewa Rundqvist,, Inst. for Caring sci., Stockholm, 2005; adv. bd. Århus U. Hosp., Denmark, 2005—, U. Coll., North Jutland, Aalborg, Denmark, 2003—, Sch. of Nursing, Hjørring, Denmark, 2003—04; adv. bd. establishment of local clin. ethical com. Danish Ministry Health, Denmark, 2005—; judgement for ass. prof. applicants Sch. Nursing in Viborg & Deakin U., Australia, Denmark, 2004; presenter, cons., reviewer in field. Contbr. articles to profl. jours. Amb. Municipality of Aalborg, 1996; bd. govs. Klostermarken, Aalborg, 1996—99. Master: Danish Soc. Nursing Rsch. (licentiate); mem.: Internat. Assn. for Human Caring (assoc.), Nordic Coll. Caring Sci. (assoc.), Danish Soc. Nursing Rsch. (assoc.). Home: Højdevej 1 Aalborg 9000 Denmark Office: Aalborg Univ Hosp Sdr Skovvej 15 Aalborg 9000 Denmark Office Fax: 4599326801. Business E-Mail: c.delmar@rn.dk.

DEL MORAL, TERESA, physician; MD, U. Granada, MPH, 1980, PhD, 1988. Physician U. Miami, 2000—. Fellow: AAP. Avocation: skiing. Office: University Miami PO Box 016960 Miami FL 33129 Business E-Mail: tdelmoral@miami.edu.

DELOACHE, JUDY SPRAGUE, psychology professor; BA, Ga. State U., Atlanta, 1967, MA, 1969; PhD, U. Ill., 1973. Asst. prof., psychology dept. Fla. Atlantic U., Boca Raton, Fla., 1973—74; rsch assoc., psychology dept. U. Ill., 1974—76, vis. rsch. asst. prof., Ctr. the Study of Reading, 1977—79, asst. prof. to prof., Human Devel. and Family Studies, 1979—91, chair, Human Devel. and Family Studies, 1988—91, prof., Beckman Inst. Advanced Science & Tech., 1989—, prof., psychology dept., 1991—, alumni prof. psychology, 1999—2000; rsch fellow, psychology dept. Ill. State Pediat. Inst., 1974—76; vis. asst. prof., psychology dept. Ill. State U., Normal; William R. Kenan, Jr. prof. psychology U. Va., Charlottesville, 2000—. Mem. editl bd.: Child Devel., 1984—87, Cognitive Devel., 1986—98, Brit. Jour. Devel. Psychology, 1988—94, Devel. Psychology, 1993—95, Jour. Applied Devel. Psychology, 1995—, Jour. Cognition and Devel., 1999—2002, Monographs the Soc. Rsch. in Child Devel., 1999, Jour. Exptl. Psychology: Gen., 2002—05, Science, 2004—07; editor: Current Readings in Child Development, 1992, 2d edit., 1994; co-editor (with E. Pomerantz). Current Readings in Child Development, 1998; co-editor: (with A. Gottlieb) A World of Babies. Imagined Child Care Manuals from Other Cultures, 2000, co-author (with R.S. Siegler, N. Eisenberg): How Children Develop, 2003, 2d edit., 2006; contbr. articles to profl. jours., chapters to books. Vis. scholar, Stanford U., 1980, Oxford U., 1986—87, Harvard U., 2003. Fellow: AAAS, APA, Am. Psychol. Soc.; mem.: Am. Acad. Arts & Sciences, Jean Piaget Soc., Internat. Soc. Infant Study, Soc. Rsch. in Child Devel., Zero to Three. Office: Dept Psychology Univ Va PO Box 400400 Charlottesville VA 22904 4400 Office Phone: 434-243-3577. Business E-Mail: jdeloache@virginia.edu.

DELONG, MAHLON R., neurologist, educator; b. Des Moines, Iowa, Mar. 17, 1938; MD cum laude, Harvard U., 1966. Lic. Am. Bd. Psychiatry and Neurology, Nat. Bd. Med. Examiners. Asst. resident, intern Harvard Svc./Boston City Hosp., 1966—68; rsch. assoc. NIMH/Clin. Sci. Lab., Bethesda, Md., 1968—70, sr. staff fellow, 1970—71, NIMH/Neurophysiology Lab., Bethesda, Md., 1971—73; resident neurology Johns Hopkins U., Balt., 1973—76, asst. prof. neurology and physiology, 1975—80; chief neurology svc. Columbia (Md.) Med. Plan, 1976—80; dir. phys. diagnosis course Johns Hopkins Hosp., Balt., 1977—80; chief dept. neurology Baltimore City Hosps., 1980—85; assoc. prof. neurology and neurosci. Johns Hopkins Sch. Medicine, 1980—85, prof. neurology and neurosci., 1986—90; chmn. dept. neurology Emory U. Sch. Medicine, Atlanta, 2001—, prof. dept. neurology, 2001—, William Timmie Professor, dept. neurology; sect. chief dept. neurology Emory Clinic, Atlanta, 2001—. Mem. editl. bd.: Critical Revs. in Neurobiology, 1997—, Archives of Neurology, 1996—, mem. manuscript rev. com.: Sci., Jour. Neurophysiology, Annals of Neurology, others. Recipient Tchr.-Investigator award, Nat. Inst. Neurol. and Communicative Disorders and Stroke, 1974—79, Javitz Neuroscis. Investigator award, 1986, Fred Springer award, Am. Parkinson Disease Found., 1997, Disting. Leadership award, Huntington's Disease Soc. Am., 1998; named William Patterson Timmie chair neurology, 1993—, Ga. Biomed. Rsch. scientist, 1995; named to Soc. Scholars, Johns Hopkins U., 1998. Mem.: AAAS, Am. Acad. Arts & Sciences, Inst. Medicine, Assn. Univ. Profs. Neurology, Soc. for Neurosci., Am. Parkinson's Disease Assn. (sci. adv. bd. 1990—), Nat. Inst. Neurol. Disorders and Stroke (counselor 1993—99), Dystonia Med. Rsch. Found. (mem. grant rev. 1990—), Am. Neurol. Assn. (chmn. fin. com. 1995—96, 1994—96, councilor 1994—95, mem. fin. com. 1993—), Internat. Basal Ganglia Soc. (sec. 1995—98), Movement Disorder Soc. (mem. internat. exec. com. 1997—). Achievements include research in structure and focus of basal ganglia, motor functions of the basal ganglia; motor system physiology, movement disorders in man, pathophysiology of movement disorders, basal forebrain cholinergic system, and Alzheimer's Disease and related dementia. Office: Emory U Dept Neurology Ste 6000 1639 Pierce Dr Atlanta GA 30322

DEL PORTILLO, PATRICIA, medical researcher; b. Bogotá, DC, Colombia, Aug. 12, 1953; Degree in Microbiology, U. de los Andes, Bogotá, 1976. Asst. rschr. U. de los Andes, 1976—78; assoc. rschr. Inst. de Inmunología, Hosp. San Juan de Dios, Bogotá, 1979—95; sci. dir. Corp. CorpoGen., Bogotá, 1995—2004, exec. dir., 2004—. Fellow Harvard U., Boston, 1985; invited scientist Chiron Corp. Emeryville, Calif., 1993—93, Inst. de Parasitología y Biomedicina López-Neyra, Ecuador, 1994—95, U. Fed. de Sao Paulo, Brasil Disciplina de Microbiologia & Escuela Paulista de Medicina, 2000—00; bd. dirs. Nat. Programme Biotech., Colciencias, 2001—05. Recipient Dermatology Internat. award, Mayo Clinic, Jacksonville, Fla., Premio Nat. award, Fundación Alejando Angel Escobar, Colombia, Premio Internat. L.Am. Fernando D Gómez award, Union L.Am. de Lucha Contra la Tb, Uruguay, award, Fundación Mujeres de Exito en Colombia, 2010. Mem.: WHO (com. resistant strain mycobacterium tuberculosis), European Soc. Mycobacteriology, L.Am. and Caribbean Network Tb RELAC TB, Am. Soc. Microbiology. Avocations: reading, travel. Office: Carrera 5 # 66A-34 Bogotá DC 110231 Colombia Office Fax: 571 3484607. Business E-Mail: pdelportillo@corpogen.org.

DEL RIO, MARCELA, medical educator; b. Buenos Aires, Apr. 12, 1960; MPharm, 1985; PhD in Pharmacy, Medicine. U. Complutense de Madrid, 1993. Head regenerative medicine unit CIEMAT, 1997—; prof., dept. bioengring. U. Carlos III de Madrid, 2011—. Recipient award, DEBRA bd. Patient Assn. Epydermolysis Bullosa; Rsch. grant, Ministery of Sci. & Innovation, Spain, European Commn. ERA-Net Scheme. Mem.: European Soc. Dermatol. Rsch. Office: Avda Universidad 30 Rm 21A08 Leganés Madrid 28911 Spain

DEL SER, TEODORO, neurologist; b. Leon, Spain, Apr. 12, 1950; s. Teodoro Del Ser and Asunción Quijano; m. Maria Pilar Bartolome, Feb. 27, 1974; children: David, Pablo, Jaime Marcos. Licenciatura en psicologia, U. Complutense, Madrid, 1973, licenciatura en medicina, 1976, MD, 1987; grad. en sociologia politica, Escuela Estudios Politicas, Madrid, 1975. Resident Hosp. Iz de Octubre, Madrid, 1977-81; stagier Unité Izi INSERM, Paris, 1981-82; assoc. prof. psychology U. Complutense, Madrid, 1984-87; chief sect. Hosp. Severo Ochoa, Leganes, Spain, 1987—. Editor: Demencias Conceptos Actuales, 1992, Evaluacion Neuropsicologica y Funcionsl de la Demencia, 1994. Mem. Soc. Española Neurologia, European Neurol. Soc. Office: Hosp Severo Ochoa Avda Orellana S/N 28911 Leganès Madrid Spain

DEL SORBO, ANTONIO, dermatologist; b. Italy, Feb. 28, 1974; PhD in Dermatology, 1998. Physician specialist Dermatology and Venereology, 2002—. Home: Via Del Monte 21 Angri Salerno 84012 Italy Office Phone: 00393386422985. Office Fax: 0039898422310. Business E-Mail: info@ildermatologorisponde.it.

DE LUCA, ANTONIO, anatomist, educator; b. Naples, Italy, July 23, 1966; s. Bruno De Luca and Silvia Messuri. MD, U. Naples, 1991; PhD of Morphology, U. Bari, 1995. Post-doctoral fellow Fels Inst. Molecular Biology Temple U., Phila., 1992—94; post-doctoral fellow Jefferson Cancer Inst. Thomas Jefferson U., Phila., 1994—96, post-doctoral fellow Pathology, Anatomy and Cell Biology dept., 1996—97, instr., asst. prof., assoc. prof. Pathology, Anatomy and Cell Biology dept., 1997—2003; rschr. Medicine and Pub. Health dept. 2d U. Naples, 1998—. Cons. Regina Elena Cancer Inst., Rome, 1998—. Author: (book) The retinoblastoma gene and its role in cancer, Expression pattern of the retinoblastoma-related genes, Expression of tumor suppressor genes in malignant, Simian Virus 40-like DNA sequences and large T antigen, mem. editl. bd. Jour. Digestive Protection, 1998—. Recipient Mario Malzoni Award, 1993, Young Histochemist award, Intern. Fedn. Histochemistry and Cytochemistry, 1996, Rodolfo Cheli Award, 1999, Young Histochemist award, Internat. Fedn. Histochemistry and Cytochemistry, 2000, Carlo Chianiello award, 2001. Mem.: Italian Soc. Neuromorphology, Italian Soc. Histochemistry, Italian Soc. Anatomy. Office: Second Univ Naples Via Luciano Armanni 5 80138 Naples Italy Office Fax: +39 081 458225. E-mail: antonio.deluca@unina2.it.

DE LUCA, CARLO JOHN, biomedical engineer, educator; b. Bagnoli del Trigno, Italy, Oct. 12, 1943; came to the U.S., 1973; s. John and Josephine (De Blasio) De Luca. B in Applied Sci., U. B.C., Can., 1966; MS, U. N.B., Can., 1968; PhD, Queen's U., 1972. Dir. Neuromusclar Rsch. Lab., 1980-84; adj. assoc. prof. biomed. engring. Boston U., 1977-84, prof. biomed. engring., 1984—, rsch. prof. neurology, 1985—, prof. elec. and chem. engring., 2007-, dir. NeuroMuscular Rsch. Ctr., 1984—, chmn. dept. biomed. engring., 1986; dean Coll. Engring., Boston U., 1986-89; founder, pres. DelSys, Inc., 1993-, Altec Inc., 1997-; cons. Liberty Mut. Rsch. Ctr., Hopkinton, Mass., 1973-94; rsch. mem. Harvard-MIT divsn. health sci. and tech., 1978-84; affiliated scientist New Eng. Regional Primate Ctr., 1977-87; mem. nat. and internat. coms.; apptd. dir. Inst. Disability Prevention and Wellness, U. Medicine and Dentistry of N.J., 1999; mem. nat. adv. coun. Nat. Inst. Biomed. Imaging and Engring., NIH, 2002. Founding editor-in-chief Jour. Electromyography and Kinesiology, 1990; mem. editl. bds. sci. jours.; co-author: Muscles Alive; contbr. articles on biomed. engring. and neurophysiology to sci. publs. Founder, pres. Neuromuscular Rsch. Found., 1985—. Recipient Volvo award Internat. Soc. for Study of Lumbar Spine, 1989, Wartenweiler Lecture award Internat. Soc. Biomechanics, 1993, Stuart Reiner Meml. Lectr. award Am. Assn. Electrodiagnostic Medicine, 1994, United Cerebral Palsy Found. Tech. award, 1999, Delsys Prize for Innovation in Electromyography, 2003, Emerging Scientist award, Internat. Soc. Biomechanics, Tibbets award, Small Bus. Tech. Coun., 2006; named to Italian Cultural Ctr. Hall of Fame, Vancouver, Can., 1991; grantee RSA, VA, NIH, NASA, US Army, USAF. Fellow IEEE, Am. Inst. Med. and Biol. Engring. (founding fellow 1993, Basmajian Lectr. award 1998), Biomed. Engring. Soc. (founding fellow 2005); mem. AAAS, Internat. Soc. Electrophysiol. Kinesiology (sec. gen. 1976-80, sec. 1980-84, v.p. 1985-88, pres. 1988-92), Soc. Neuro-Sci., Dante Alighieri Soc. (bd. govs. 1986-88), Mass. Tech. Park Corp. (bd. govs. 1987-90), Harvard Club Boston. Achievements include established Delsys prize for innovation in electromyography and emerging scientist award at the International Society of Biomechanics. Home: 107 Livingston Rd Wellesley MA 02482-7308 Office: Boston U NeuroMuscular Rsch Ctr 19 Deerfield St Boston MA 02215-1904 Business E-Mail: cjd@bu.edu.

DE LUCA, ITALO, cardiologist; b. Maddaloni, Italy, Mar. 18, 1942; s. Leonardo De Luca and Ilda Luciano; m. Giuseppina D'Ardes, Aug. 26, 1972; children: Ylenia, Leonardo. MD, U. Naples, 1966; degree in Internal Medicine, U. Torino, 1971; degree in Cardiology, U. Bologna, 1974. Lic. physician Med. Assn. Bari, Italy, 1967. Asst. Divsn. Cardiology Azienda Policlinico Hosp., Bari, Italy, 1972—87, chief Divsn. Cardiology, 1988—97, dir. Dept. Cardiology, 1998—2009, prof. Sch. Cardiology, 1999—; dir. Clinica L. De Luca, Foggia, Italy, 2009—. Co-author: Trattato di Ecocardiografia, 1984, Cardiopatie Congenite in Utero, 1996, Trattato di Ecocardiografia Clinica, 1999; editor: Ecocardiografia, 1988, Giorn Ital Cardiologia, 2004, Supplement American Jour. Cardiology, 2003. Paul Harris fellow, Rotary Internat., 2003. Mem.: Italian Soc. Echocardiography (pres.

1988—89), Italian Fedn. Cardiology (assoc.). Roman Catholic. Achievements include research in POSTEC trial, Echocardiography, atrial fibrillation. Avocations: sailing, skiing, chess. Office: Clinica L De Luca Foggia Italy Home: Via Delle Murge 59A 70124 Bari BA Italy Office Fax: 00390881559053. Personal E-mail: i_deluca@tin.it. Business E-Mail: clinicaseluca@libero.it.

DE LUCA, LEONARDO, cardiologist; b. Bari, Italy, Dec. 7, 1976; s. Italo De Luca and Giuseppina D'Ardes; m. Rachele Adorisio. MD, U. Bari, 2001. Lic. cardiologist Rome, 2005. Intern Policlinico Hosp., Bari, resident; attending physician La Sapienza U., Rome, 2001—05, interventional cardiologist, 2002—. Fellow, Italian Soc. Hosp. Cardiology, 2005. Mem.: European Soc. Cardiology. Roman Catholic. Achievements include research in functional assessment of coronary artery anomalies; glycoprotein IIb/IIIa inhibitors; acute myocardial infarction; acute heart failure. Avocation: travel. Office: La Sapienza U Vle del Policlinico 155 Rome 00100 Italy Home: Via Alessandro Cialdi 34 154 Rome RM Italy Office Fax: 0039-06-65975724. Personal E-mail: leo.deluca@libero.it. Business E-Mail: leodeluca@virgilio.it.

DELUCA, PATRICK PHILLIP, pharmacist, pharmaceutical educator; b. Scranton, Pa., Sept. 7, 1935; m. Judy Beitzel, June 16, 1956; children: Paul, Thomas, Patrick, Donald, Michelle, Michael. BS in Pharmacy, Temple U., 1957, MS in Pharmacy, 1960, PhD in Pharmacy (SKF W.G. Karr fellow), 1963; Doctorate (hon.), U. Perugia, Italy, 2006. Analytical chemist SKF Co., 1957-59; sr. rsch. pharmacist CIBA Co., Summit, NJ, 1963-66, plant mgr., 1966-69, dir., 1969-70, Cormedics Corp., Somerville, NJ; faculty U. Ky. Coll. Pharmacy, 1970—, prof., assoc. dean, 1972-87, dir. ctr. for pharmaceutical sci. and tech., 1987-88, chmn. faculty pharm. scis., 1998-2000, emeritus prof., 2010—. Pharm. sci. adv. com. FDA, 2003-06; cons. to pharm. industry and FDA., editor-in-chief AAPS Pharm Sci. Tech., 1999-2007 Editor-in-chief: Jour. Pharm. Devel. and Tech., 1995—99; contbr. more than 230 articles to sci. and profl. jours. Recipient Leo G. Penn award Temple U., 1957, Lunsford-Richardson Pharmacy Rsch. award Richardson Merrell Co., 1960, 62, Best Paper Toward Advancement Indsl. Pharmacy award N.J. Pharmacy Discussion Group, 1965, Outstanding Educator award in U.S., 1974, Disting. Alumni award Temple U., 1989, Sturgill Rsch. award U. Ky., 1995, Advisory Com. Svc. award FDA, 2005; also numerous grants. Fellow: Am. Assn. Indian Pharm. Scientists, Acad. Pharm. Sci. (pres. 1979—80), Inst. for Advanced Biotech. (sr.), Am. Assn. Pharm. Scientists (bd. dirs. 1986—88, 2005—10, pres. 2008—09, Rsch. Achievement award 1988, Outstanding Manuscript award in pharm. devel. and technology 1998, Outstanding Educator award 2000, Sullivan medallist at UK 2001, Ky Pharmacist of Yr. 2002, Outstanding Manuscript award in pharm. devel. and technology 2002, Swintosky Disting. lectr. 2003, Outstanding Manuscript award in pharm. devel. and technology 2006, Dale Wurster Rsch. Achievement award 2006); mem.: N.Y. Acad. Sci., Am. Soc. Hosp. Pharmacists (Rsch. award 1975), Parenteral Drug Assn. (Rsch. Achievement award 1975), Am. Pharm. Assn., Rho Chi, Sigma Chi. Achievements include research in pharmaceutical technology and novel drug delivery; co-founder Faith Pharmacy. Home: 3292 Nantucket Dr Lexington KY 40502-3269 Office: U Ky Coll Pharmacy Rose St Lexington KY 40536-0001 Business E-Mail: ppdelu1@email.uky.edu, ppdelu1@uky.edu.

DELUKE, DEAN M., oral surgeon; b. Schenectady, NY, Jan. 16, 1952; s. Dominick J. and Virginia D. (Anderson) DeLuke; m. Theresa S. Slowey, Oct. 6, 1984; 1 child, Deanna Marie. BA, St. Michaels Coll., Burlington, Vt., 1974; DDS, Columbia U., 1978; MBA, Union Coll, 2008. Diplomate Am. Bd. Oral and Maxillofacial Surgery. Pvt. practice oral and maxillofacial surgery, Schenectady, 1982—; chief dept. dentistry St. Clare's Hosp., 1989—93. Cons. Sunnyview Hosp., Schenectady, 1982—2000, VA Med. Ctr., Albany, NY, 1988—2001; pres. N.Y. State Soc. Oral and Maxillofacial Surgeons, 1994; mem. nat. adv. bd. OMS Nat. Ins. Co., 1994—. Contbr. articles to profl. jours. Trustee Albany (N.Y.) Acad. for Girls, 1996—; bd. dirs. St. Clares Hosp. Found., Schenectady, NY, 1987—93, Oral and Maxillofacial Surgery Polit. Action Com., 1996—98. Fellow: Internat. Assn. Oral and Maxillofacial Surgeons, Am. Assn. Oral and Maxillofacial Surgeons (del. 1992—96), Am. Coll. Dentists; mem.: Am. Assn. Dental Cons., Am. Med. Writers Assn., Am. Cleft Palate-Craniofacial Assn. Avocations: skiing, boating, thoroughbred horse racing. Home: 25 Robinwood Dr Clifton Park NY 12065 Office: 1070 Nott St Schenectady NY 12308

DELURGIO, DAVID, cardiac electrophysiologist, educator; MD, U. Calif., 1990. Diplomate AM. Bd. Internal Medicine-cardiovasc. disease, 2007, AM. Bd. Internal Medicine-clin. cardiac electrophysiology. Intern UCLA Med. Ctr., 1991, fellow cardiovasc. disease Calif., 1993—95; resident internal medicine Emory Univ. Med. Ctr., Ga., 1991—93; joined Emory Univ., 1996, assoc. prof. medicine; hosp. affiliations include Emory Univ. Hosp., Emory Univ. Hosp Midtown. Mem.: ACP, Heart Rhythm Soc., Heart Failure Soc., Am. Coll. of Cardiology. Office: Emory University Hospital Midtown 550 Peachtree St NE Fl 6 Atlanta GA 30308 Office Phone: 404-686-2504.

DEL VECCHIO, LUCIA, nephrologist; b. Milan, Mar. 15, 1966; Degree in Medicine, Milan, 1991, degree in Nephrology, 1996. Rschr. Manzoni Hosp., 1997—. Contbr. to profl. publs. Recipient Young Investigators award, Akzo, ERA-EDTA. Mem.: Italian Soc. Nephrology. Avocations: tennis, sailing, mountain climbing, flying. Office: Via Dell'Eremo Lecco 23900 Italy Office Fax: 390341489860. E-mail: luciadelvecchio@yahoo.com.

DELWEL, ERNST JAN, neurosurgeon, consultant; b. Rotterdam, Netherlands, Jan. 1, 1959; s. Johannes Wilhelmus Delwel and Ernestine Beverloo; m. Elizabeth Josina den Uil; children: Ruben Jakob, Valerie Esther, Casper Reinier. MD, Erasmus U., Rotterdam, 1978—85. Resident, gen. surgery Havenziekenhuis, Rotterdam, Netherlands, 1988—89, resident neurosurgery, 1989—93; cons. neurosurgeon Erasmus U., Rotterdam, Netherlands, 1993—, Albert Schweitzer Hosp., Dordrecht, 1993—. Contbr. articles to profl. jours. Mem.: Dutch Soc. Endoscopic Surgery, European Assn. for Rsch. and Treatment of Cancer (assoc.), Dutch Soc. Neurosurgeons (assoc.). Achievements include invention of the iIntervertebral disk chisel; development of the in vitro model mimicking shunt function in hydrocephalus; research in the shunt-valve for normal pressure hydrocephalus; the prospective multi-center study on programmable shunt-valve for normal pressure hydrocephalus. Home: Rivierdijk 656 Hardinxveld-Giessendam 3371 EG Netherlands Office: Erasmus Med Ctr Dr Molewaterplein 40 Rotterdam 3315 MR Netherlands Office Fax: (31)10 4633735. Personal E-mail: delwel@xs4all.nl. E-mail: e.j.delwel@erasmusmc.nl.

DELYE, HANS, neurosurgeon, researcher; b. Leuven, Belgium, Sept. 29, 1978; s. Roger and Marie-Anne (Van Rafelghem) Delye; m. Lien Van den Putte, Oct. 20, 2007; 1 child, Daan. MD, Cath. U., Leuven, Belgium, 2003, postgrad., 2004—, PhD, 2010. Bd. certified neurosurgeon Cath. U., 2010. Neurology trainee U. Hosp. Gasthuisberg, Leuven, 2003—04, neurosurgical trainee, 2005—; gen. surgery trainee Dodoenshosp., Mechelen, Belgium, 2004—05; pediatic neurosurgeon UMC St Radboud, Nijmegen, 2010—. Neuroanatomy lab tchr. Cath. U., Leuven, 2003—04. Contbr. chapters to books. Rsch. grant, Rsch. Found. Flanders, 2004—08, fellowship, CHRU Lille, 2010. Mem.: European Assn. Neurosurgical Soc., Belgian Soc. Neurosurgery (assoc.). Achievements include patents for helmet liner to decrease rotational acceleration of the head after impact; research in role of skull bone vibration in pathogenesis of brain contusions; role of superior sagittal sinus-bridging vein complex in pathogenesis of ASDH. Avocations: soccer, snowboarding, windsurfing, travel. Office: UMC St Radboud Dept Neurosugery Reinier Postlaan 4 Nijmegen Netherlands Personal E-mail: tmdcyberdocem@yahoo.com, hans.delye@gmail.com.

DEMAIN, ARNOLD LESTER, microbiologist, educator; b. NYC, Apr. 26, 1927; s. Henry and Gussie (Katz) D.; m. Joanna Kaye, Aug. 2, 1952; children: Pamela Robin Demain McCloskey, Jeffrey Brian. BS, Mich. State U., East Lansing, 1949, MS, 1950; PhD, U. Calif., Berkeley, 1954; Doctorate (hon.), U. Leon, Spain, 1997, Ghent U., Belgium, 1999, Technion-Israeli Inst. Tech., 2000, Mich. State U., 2000, U. Muenster, Germany, 2003; PhD, Drew U., 2009. Rsch. asst. U. Calif., Davis, 1952-54; rsch. microbiologist Merck & Co., Inc., Danville, Pa., 1954-56, Rahway, NJ, 1956-65, founder, head of dept. ferm. microbiology, 1965-69; prof. of ind. microbiology MIT, Cambridge, 1969—2001; fellow Charles A. Dana Rsch. Inst., Drew U., Madison, NJ, 2001—. Author or editor 14 books; contbr. more than 500 articles to profl. jours. With USN, 1945—47. Recipient Hotpack award Can. Soc. Microbiology, 1978, Rubro award Australian Soc. Microbiology, 1978, Indsl. Microbiology award Italian Pharm. Assn., 1989, Hans Knoll meml. award, Germany, 1990, G. Mendel award Czech Acad. Sci., 1998, Andrew Jackson Moyer award USDA, 1998, Internat. Achievement award Shanghai Inst. Pharm. Industry, 2005, Arima award in Applied Microbiology, IUMS, 2005 Mem.: NAS, Am. Chem. Soc. (Marvin Johnson biotech. award), Am. Soc. Microbiology (Waksman award N.J. br. 1975, Biotech. award 1990, Disting. Svc. award 1994, Alice C. Evans award 1998, hon. mem. N.E. br. 1999, Charles Porta award 2006), Soc. Indsl. Microbiology (pres. 1990, Charles Thom award 1978, Waksman Tchg. award 1995, Porter award 2006), Hungarian Acad. Sci., Mex. Acad. Sci., Croatian Soc. Biotech. (hon.), Czech Soc. Microbiology (hon. Patocka medal 2006), Soc. Actinomycetes Japan (hon.), French Soc. Microbiology (hon.). Achievements include 21 patents; elucidation of biosynthetic pathway to penicillins and cephalosporins; recognition of phenomenon of biochemical regulation of secondary metabolism; discovery of role of lysine and amino adipic acid in penicillin biosynthesis. Office: Drew Univ RISE HS-330 Madison NJ 07940 Office Phone: 973-408-3937. Business E-Mail: ademain@drew.edu.

DEMAIO, MARLENE, orthopedist, surgeon; b. Phila., Dec. 18, 1958; d. Frank Joseph and Grace Marlene (Landrum) DeM. BS in Biology with honors, Brown U., 1981; MD, Hahnemann Med. Sch., 1985. Diplomate Nat. Bd. Med. Examiners, Am. Bd. Orthop. Surgeons. Resident in orthop. Yale U., New Haven, 1985-90, clin. asst., 1990; fellow in sports medicine Cin. Sports Medicine and Orthop. Ctr., 1991-92; staff dept. orthop. Naval Hosp., Oakland, Calif., 1992-95, Bethesda, Md., 1995—, asst. dept. head, 1995—. Asst. prof. dept. surgery Uniformed Svcs. U. Health Scis., Bethesda, Md., 1995—; thesis reader dept. mech. engring. Naval Postgrad. Sch., Monterey, Calif., 1994—2001; vice chmn. inst. rev. bd. Nat. Naval Med. Ctr., 1995—98; libr. com., mgr. equipment and materials dept. orthop. surgery Naval Hosp., Oakland, Calif., 1992—95, dir. resident rsch. and pub. dept. orthop. surgery, 1993—98, mem. intern edn. com., Calif., 1993—95, coord. ninth annual rsch. symposium, 1995, dir. rsch. and pub. dept. orthop. surgery, 1995—98; mem. Multidisciplinary Complex Pain Mgmt. Program, 1993—95; dept. head USNS Mercy, Oakland, 1992—95; reviewer Extramural Women's Health Def. Fund, Dept. Def. Rsch. Grants, 1996; head tissue com. for implants Nat. Naval Med. Ctr., 1995—98; dept. head USNS Comfort, Bethesda, 1995—98; bd. dirs. Am. Jour. Sports Medicine; cons. orthopedics Office of Attending Physician, U.S. Congress, 1999—2004, U.S. Pentagon, 1996—2004; dir. ballistics and biomechanics Inst. Pathology Lab. Armed Forces, 1998—2004; advisor enhanced human performance USMC, 1999—; head football team physician, dept. head orthop., sports medicine, podiatry US Naval Acad., 2002—04; dir. surg. svcs. Expeditionary Med. Facility, Kuwait, 2005—06; oral examiner Am. Bd. Orthop. Surgery, 2005—06. Reviewer: Am. Jour. Sports Medicine, 1996—, editl. bd.:, 2001, mng. editor:, 2000—02. Coord. Celebration of Women in Medicine, Am. Med. Women's Assn., Hahnemann U., Phila., 1984. Capt. USN, 1992—. Decorated Navy Achievement medal, 1992, Navy Commendation medal, 1995, 98, 2004, 06, Meritorious Svc. medal, 1998, Joint Commendation, 2004, Def. Meritorious medal, 2004; recipient Bronze award Nat. Soc. SAR, 1977, Excellence in Rsch. award Am. Orthopaedic Soc. Sports Medicine, 1997, Frank Berry award Delta Dental (Calif.) & U.S. Medicine, 2004; grantee Oakland Naval Hosp., 1993, Nat. Naval Med. Ctr., 1995-98, USMC, 1998, US Army, 1998-2003, Naval Med. Ctr. Portsmouth, 2005-06. Mem.: Am. Orthopaedic Soc. for Sports Medicine (chair edn. subcom. 2006, mem. exec. com. 2005—06, coun. of dels. 2000—06), Orthopaedic Rsch. Soc., Assn. Bone and Joint Surgeons, Am. Orthopedic Foot and Ankle Soc., Am. Coll. Sports Medicine, Soc. Mil. Orthop. Surgeons, Am. Acad. Orthop. Surgeons, Alpha Omega Alpha. Avocations: tennis, piano, cooking, swimming. Office: Naval Med Ctr Dept Orthop Surgery 620 John Paul Jones Cir Portsmouth VA 23708 Business E-Mail: mdemaio@mar.med.navy.mil.

DEMANGE, MARCO KAWAMURA, surgeon; b. Sao Paulo, Brazil, Jan. 14, 1978; Degree in Medicine, State U. Campinas, 2000; MSc, U. São Paulo, PhD, 2011. Attending orthop. surgeon HCor, 2004; sr. surgeon Hosp. Das Clinicas U. São Paulo, 2008—. Mem.: AAOS, Soc. Brasileira de Artroscopia e Trauma Ortopedico, ISAKOS, Soc. Brasileira de Cirurgia do Joelho, Soc. Brasileira de Ortopedia e Traumatologia. Avocations: running, movies. Home: Rua Mateus Grou 57 Apt 183 Sao Paulo 05415050 Brazil Personal E-mail: demange@me.com.

DEMARCO, VOLEEN, medical researcher; b. Aug. 8, 1968; adopted d. John and Susanne Berrytin; m. Shawn DeMarco; children: Eva, Mark, Richard. BS in Biology, U. N.C., 1990, MS in Biology, 1992. Biol. lab rschr. asst. Med. Biological Lab, U. N.C., 1993—95, jr. biol. lab rschr., 1996—99; adj. prof. U. N.C., 1998—2001, full prof., 2010—; sr. rschr. Meriks and Melina Lab, Ronda, NC, 2002—. Rsch. lab asst. U. N.C., 1989—92. Contbr. articles to profl. med. jours.; dir.: (films) Researching Inside You, 2005; co-editor: (textbook) Your Body: Life versus Death, 2006, Your Body: Life versus Death, Updated Ed., 2010. Avocations: album collecting, bonsai, gin rummy. Office: Meriks and Melina Lab 185 Hill Top Cir Ronda NC 28670-8950

DEMARIA, ANTHONY NICHOLAS, cardiologist, educator; b. Elizabeth, NJ, Jan. 12, 1943; s. Anthony and Charlotte DeMaria; m. Delores Horn; children: Christine, Anthony, Jonathon. BA, Coll. Holy Cross, 1964; MD, N.J. Coll. Medicine, 1968; degree (hon.), Kagawa Med. U., Japan, U. Bordeaux, France. Diplomate Am. Bd. Internal Medicine, Am. Bd. Cardiovascular Disease, Am. Bd. Cardiovascular Medicine. Intern St. Vincent Hosp., Worcester, Mass., 1968-69; resident USPHS Hosp., Staten Island, NY, 1969-71; fellow cardiology U. Calif., Davis, 1969-73, asst. prof. medicine, 1972-77, assoc. prof. medicine, 1977-81, prof. medicine, 1977-81; prof. medicine, chief cardiology div. U. Ky., Lexington, 1981-92; dir. Ky. Heart Inst., Lexington, 1989—; prof. medicine, chief cardiology U. Calif. Sch. Medicine, San Diego, 1992—2004, vice chmn. internal medicine, 1998—2001, dir., Sulpizio Family Cardiovasc. Ctr., 2004—, Judith and Jack White chair cardiovasc. medicine. Mem. rev. bds. Vets. Adminstrn. Med. Research Merit in Cardiovascular Studies, Nat. Inst. Health, NSF, NIH, NHLBI, U. Calif., U.S. FDA; chmn. Diagnostic Radiology Study Sect. NIH; vice-chmn. dept. medicine U. Calif., San Diego, 1998-2001. Mem. editl. bd. Am. Heart Jour., Am. Jour. Cardiac Imaging, Circulation, Am. Jour. Cardiology, Jour. Am. Coll. Cardiology, Health News from New Eng. Jour. Medicine; assoc. editor, Jour. Am. Coll. Cardiology, editor-in-chief 2001—; editl. cons. Am. Jour. Physiology, Annals Internal Medicine, Archives Phys. Medicine and Rehab., Catheterization and Cardiovascular Diagnosis, Jour. Clin. Investigation, New Eng. Jour. Medicine; contbr. numerous articles to profl. jours.; host Cardiology Update, Lifetime Med. TV. Recipient Humanitarian award Theodore and Susan Cummings, 1978, Disting. Alumnus award Coll. Medicine and Dentistry of N.J., 1988, Echocardiography award Tufts U., 1988, award of excellence Am. Acad. Med. Adminstrs., 1994, William Harvey award Am. Med. Writers Assn., 1996; named one of Best Doctors in Am., Best Heart Doctors in Am., Good Housekeeping mag., 1996; Golden Empire Heart Assn. grantee, Am. Heart Assn. grantee, Ky. Heart Assn. grantee, Vet. Adminstrn. grantee, Nat. Heart, Lung and Blood Inst. grantee; teaching scholar Am. Heart Assn. Fellow ACP, Am. Coll. Cardiology (chmn. 27th ann. scientific session 1978, cardiovascular procedures com., govt. rels. com., v.p. elect 1986, pres. elect 1987-88, pres. 1988-89, active various coms., Young Investigator award 1976), Am. Coll. Chest Physicians; mem. Am. Heart Assn. (bd. dirs. work evaluation unit Yolo Sierra chpt., Ky. chapter, active various coms., Teaching scholar 1979-82), Am. Fedn. Clin. Rsch., Yolo County Med. Socs., Am. Inst. Ultrasound in Medicine (bd. dirs.), Am. Soc. Echocardiography (bd. dirs. 1975-87, v.p. 1983-85, pres. 1985-87, assoc. editor), N.Am. Soc. for Cardiac Radiology, Assn. U. Cardiologists. Roman Catholic. Office: U Calif San Diego Med Ctr Divsn Cardiology 200 W Arbor Dr #8411 San Diego CA 92103-8411 Office Phone: 619-543-6031, 619-543-6163. Business E-Mail: ademaria@ucsd.edu.

DE MARNEFFE, FRANCIS, psychiatrist, hospital administrator; b. Brussels, May 7, 1924; arrived in Eng., 1940; came to US, 1950; s. Armand Gustave and Esther Magdalen (Loveday) de M.; m. Nancy Marie Edmonds, Aug. 5, 1955 (div. Sept. 1967); children: Peter Loveday, Daphne Elizabeth, Colette; m. Barbara Rowe Hopkins, Dec. 5, 1969. MB, BS, U. London, 1950. Diplomate Am. Bd. Psychiatry Neurology. Intern Muhlenberg Hosp., Plainfield, NJ, 1950-51; asst. resident psychiatry Mass. Gen. Hosp., Boston, 1952; tchg. fellow psychiatry Med. Sch. Harvard U., Boston, 1955-56, rsch. fellow, 1955-56; resident psychiatry McLean Hosp., Belmont, Mass., 1953-54, staff psychiatrist, 1955-90, cons. psychiatrist, 1990—, gen. dir., 1962-87, gen. dir. emeritus, 1987—, pres., CEO McLean Health Svcs., Inc., 1986-89; med. dir. Holly Hill Mental Health Svcs., Raleigh, NC, 1990-93; pvt. practice, 1993—. Instr. psychiatry Med. Sch. Harvard U., 1961-66, lectr. 1966—; mem. accreditation coun. psychiat. facilities Joint Commn. Accreditation Hosps., Chgo., 1979-84, mem. tech. adv. com., 1979-84, chmn. accreditation, 1970-72, mem. coun., 1970-79; adminstr. McLean divsn. Hall-Mercer Hosp., Phila., 1969-87; v.p. Hall-Mercer Hosp., 1980-87; exec. v.p. Belmont programs Mass. Gen. Hosp., Boston, 1986-87; clin. prof. psychiatry U. NC, Chapel Hill, 1991-93; assoc. cons. prof. psychiatry Duke U. Med. Sch., 1991-93, v.p. Wake County Mental Health Assn., 1992-93, med. staff Rex Hosp., Raleigh, NC, 1993; mem. Corp. Ptnrs. Health Care Inc., Boston, 1994—; trustee working group McLean Hosp., 1996, co-chair com. expanding svcs. revs.; cons. Exec. Svcs. Corps., Boston, 1996-2000; cons. Mass. Soc. Prevention of Cruelty to Children, 2004-06. Author: (non-fiction) Introduction to Adolescent Patients in Transition, 1974; author: (contbg.) The Changing Mental Health Scene, 1976; author: Last Boat From Bordeaux, 2001; mem. editl. bd. (jour.) McLean (Hosp.) Jour., 1976—90. Trustee Guidance Camps, Inc., Boston, 1968-90, Preschool, Inc., Cambridge, Mass., 1961-62, Concord Acad. Mass., 1975-78, Nat. Assn. Pvt. Psychiat. Hosps., Washington, 1982-85, 93-94, McLean Hosp. Corp., Belmont, 1985-87; mem. Corp. Family Svc. Assn. Greater Boston, 1978-81; hon. trustee Concord Acad., 1978—; bd. dirs. Mass. chpt. Nat. Com. Prevention Child Abuse, Boston, 1979-81, Health Planning Coun. Greater Boston, 1972-76; chmn. med. divsn. United Way, 1986; mem. Mass. Gen. Hosp. Corp., 1988-94, coll. Des Conseillers French Libr. & Cultural Ctr., Boston, 1995-99; bd. dirs. Friends McLean, 1995-2005, 1st v.p., 1997-99, pres., 1999-2005, co-chmn. 2005-09; co-chmn. Boston chpt. French Heritage Soc. (formerly Friends of Vieilles Maisons Françaises), 2000—; cons. Mass. Soc. Prevention of Cruelty to Children, 2004-05. Served as flying officer RAF, 1943-46. Recipient Presdl. award Nat. Assn. Pvt. Psychiat. Hosps., 1991, Chevalier, l'Ordre Nat. Mérite, France, 2009. Fellow: Am. Coll. Mental Health Adminstrn., Mass. Med. Soc., Royal Coll. Psychiatrists, Am. Coll. Psychiatrists, Am. Psychiat. Assn. (life), Royal Coll. Physicians (licentiate); mem.: Ctrl. Neuropsychiat. Hosp. Assn. (pres. 1986—87),

Royal Coll. Surgeons, The Royal Air Force Club (London), Lake (Dublin, N.H.) Club, Thames Rowing Club (London), Leander (Henley-on-Thames, Eng.) Club, The Country Club (Brookline). Office: McLean Hosp 115 Mill St Belmont MA 02478-9106 Home: 10 Longwood Dr Apt 437 Westwood MA 02090-1145 Office Phone: 617-855-3802.

DEMATTIA, AMY, pediatrician; b. Sept. 15, 1967; MD, Cornell U., 1999; MPH, Mt. Sinai, 2005. Pediatrician Westside Pediats., 2005—. Office: Westside Pediats 620 Columbus Ave New York NY 10024 Business E-Mail: demattia@wppc.pcc.com.

DEMAUSE, LLOYD, psychologist; b. Detroit, Sept. 19, 1931; s. Leon and Martha (Koren) DeM.; m. Susan Hein; children: Neil, Jennifer, Jonathan. Student, GM Inst., 1948-52; AB, Columbia U., 1957, postgrad., 1957-61, Nat. Psychol. Assn. for Psychoanalysis, 1959-60. Founder Atcom Inc. (pub.), 1959; chmn. bd., dir. Inst. for Psychohistory; pub. Psychohistory Press; mem. faculty N.Y. Center for Psychoanalytic Tng. Editor, author: Jimmy Carter and American Fantasy, The History of Childhood, The New Psychohistory, A Bibliography of Psychohistory, Foundations of Psychohistory, Reagan's America: The Emotional Life of Nations, The Origin of war on Child Abuse; editor: Jour. Psychohistory. With AUS, 1952-54. Mem. Internat. Psychohist. Assn. (pres.). Home and Office: Inst for Psychohistory 140 Riverside Dr New York NY 10024-2605 Office Phone: 212-799-2294. E-mail: psychhst@tiac.net.

DEMAY, RICHARD MAC, pathologist; b. Omaha, Sept. 15, 1951; s. Richard F. and Gloria L. DeMay; m. Valerie DeMay; children: Alexander Mac, David Portis, Jacqueline Gail. BA, Hastings Coll., Nebr., 1973; MD, Northwestern U. Med. Sch., Chgo., 1976. Cert. in anatomic & clin. pathology 1981, in cytopathology 1989. Prof. U. Chgo., 1994—, dir., 1994—. Author: (textbook) Art & Sci. Cytopathology, Practical Principles Cytopathology, The Pap Test; contbr. 33 sci. articles in peer-reviewed med. jours., chapters to books. Decorated Commd. Ky. Col.; recipient Excellence in Edn., Am. Soc. Cytopathology, 2006; named one of America's Top Physicians, Consumers' Rsch. Coun. America, 2007. Fellow: Coll. Am. Pathologists, Am. Soc. Clin. Pathology (mem., various coms.); mem.: Internat. Acad. Cytology, Papanicolaou Soc. Cytopathology (bd. mem. 2001—04), Am. Soc. Cytopathology. Avocations: reading, drawing, painting. Office: Univ Chicago MARP212 MC2050 5841 S Maryland Ave Chicago IL 60637 Home: 340 E Randolph St Chicago IL 60601 Office Fax: 773-702-6570. Business E-Mail: rdemay@uchicago.edu.

DEMEO, PATRICK J., orthopaedic surgeon, educator; MD, Wayne State U.; Cert. orthopaedic surgery; Intern SUNY, resident, Ohio State Univ. Med. Ctr.; fellow Cleve. Clinic; practice Allegheny Orthopaedic Surgery; asst. prof. orthopaedic surgery Drexel Univ.; med. dir. Pitts. Pirates; chmn. dept. orthopaedic surgery Allegheny Gen. Hosp., dir. divsn. sports medicine. Named one of Top Doctors, Pitts. mag., 2011. Office: Allegheny General Hospital 320 E N Ave Pittsburgh PA 15212 Office Phone: 412-359-3131. Office Fax: 412-359-4108.

DEMERS, LAURENCE MAURICE, medical educator, biomedical researcher, editor, biochemist, endocrinologist, editor, biochemist; s. Laurence Onezime and Doris Corrine (Goulet) D.; m. Susan Ruth Bernard, Sept. 29, 1962; children: Laurence H., Michele L., Marc B., Christpher J., Andrew J. AB, Merrimack Coll., 1960, ScD (hon.), 2011; PhD, SUNY Upstate Med. Ctr., Syracuse, 1970; DSc (hon.), Merrimack Coll., 2011. Postdoctoral fellow Med. Sch. Harvard U., Boston, 1970-72, instr., 1972-73; asst. prof. M.S. Hershey Med. Ctr. Pa. State U., Hershey, 1973-76, assoc. prof., 1976-80, prof., 1980—, disting. prof., 1997—. Cons. Robert Wood Johnson Pharm Rsch. Inst., Raritan, N.J., 1978-2005; bd. dirs. dBi Labs. Inc., Harrisburg, Pa.; vis. prof. U. Oxford, Eng., 1981-82; bd. dirs. Autogenomics, Inc., 2000-. Editor: Liver Function Testing, 1978, Premenstrual Syndrome, 1985, Premenstrual Syndrome and Menopausal Mood Disorders, 1989, Biomarkers of Disease, 2002; editl. editor Clin. Chemistry Jour., 1990-2000. Eucharistic min. St. Joan of Arc Cath. Ch., Hershey, 1981—, mem. Knights of Malta, 1990—; trustee Merrimack Coll., 2000; chair, bd. trustees, Merrimack Coll., 2007-10. Capt. Med. Svc. Corps US Army, 1961—65. Recipient Lalor award Lalor Found., 1973, Fogarty Internat. award Fogarty Ctr., NIH, 1981, Pharm. Mfrs. Assn. award, 1974, Siemens award, 1986 AACC, Morton Schwartz Cancer Diagnostics award, 2010, Dubin award, 1991 NACB. Fellow Nat. Acad. Clin. Biochemistry (pres. 1984-85, Dubin award 1991); mem. Endocrine Soc., Am. Assn. Clin. Chemistry (pres. 1997, Ames award 1986), Am. Soc. Clin. Pathology, N.Y. Acad. Scis., Assn. Clin. Scientists, Acad. Clin. Lab. Physicians and Scientists, Knights of Malta, Country Club of Hershey (bd. govs. 2000—). Republican. Roman Catholic. Avocations: golf, tennis. Home: 1175 Stonegate Rd Hummelstown PA 17036-9776 Office: Pa State University MS Hershey Med Ctr University Dr Hershey PA 17033 Office Phone: 717-531-8316. Business E-Mail: lmd4@psu.edu.

DEMERS, NANCY KAE, nursing educator; b. Manchester, NH, Oct. 18, 1938; d. Paul E. and Nellie (Matijas) Watts; m. Raymond Joseph Demers, Feb. 13, 1960; children: Paula, John, Diane. RN, Elliot Hosp. Sch. Nursing, Manchester, NH, 1959; BSN, St. Anselm Coll., 1969; MSN, Boston U., 1978; postgrad., Nova U., 1994—. Social and health edn. tchr. NH Youth Devel. Ctr., Manchester, 1969—74; dir. nursing svcs. Hanover Hill Nursing Home, Manchester, 1974—75; asst. prof. St. Anselm Coll., Manchester, 1974-82; maternal and child health coord. Concord (N.H.) Hosp., 1982-83; assoc. prof. NH Tech. Coll., Manchester, 1983—88; prof. nursing NH Cmty. Tech. Coll., Manchester, 1988—2000; adminstr. Regency Nursing Care, LLC, Bedford, NH, 2000—. Panel item writer Nat. Coun. Licensure Exam, 1993; developer evaluation component for an ongoing AIDS edn./prevention program for youths between the ages of 14 and 19, Claremont Coll. and Fed. U. Ceara, Brazil. Recipient Ptnrs. of the Ams. award W.K. Kellogg Found., 1996. Mem. N.H. Am. Diabetes Assn. (bd. mem. 1988-93, Disting. Svc. award 1993), N.H. Nurse Educators, N.H. Ptnrs. of Americas (corr. sec. 1992-2005, travel awards 1991, 93, 95, Internat. award 1996), Transcultural Nursing, Sigma Theta Tau. Home and Office: 501 Route 101 Bedford NH 03110-4710 Personal E-mail: ndemers501@aol.com. *

DEMETIS, SPIRO, pulmonologist, educator; Attended, U. Monterey, Mexico, 1983. Diplomate Am. Bd. Internal Medicine, Am. Bd. Internal Medicine-pulmonary disease, Am. Bd. Internal Medicine-critical care medicine. With Lutheran Med. Ctr., Bklyn.; assoc. prof. medicine SUNY Health Sci. Ctr.; intern SUNY Downstate Med. Ctr., resident in internal medicine, 1984—88, fellow in pulmonary disease, 1988—90, fellow in critical care medicine, 1990—91, pulmonologist. Office: SUNY Downstate Medical Center University Hospital Bklyn 445 Lenoc Rd Brooklyn NY 11203 Office Phone: 718-270-1821. Office Fax: 718-270-1733.

DEMETRI, GEORGE DANIEL, oncologist, medical researcher, educator; b. Poughkeepsie, NY, Sept. 28, 1956; MD, Stanford U. Sch. Med., 1983. Cert. in Internal Medicine 1986, in Med. Oncology 1989. Intern in internal medicine U. Washington, Seattle, 1983—84, resident in med. oncology, 1984—86; fellow Dana-Farber Cancer Ctr., Boston, 1986—89, dir. Ctr. Sarcoma and Bone Oncology, sr. v.p. experimental therapeutics; asst. prof. medicine Harvard Med. Sch., Boston, assoc. prof.; exec. dir. clin. and translational rsch. Ludwig Inst. Cancer Rsch., 2006—. Office: Dana-Farber Cancer Ctr Shields-Warren 530 44 Binney St Boston MA 02115 Office Phone: 617-632-3985. Office Fax: 617-632-3408. E-mail: gdemetri@partners.org.

DE MEYTS, PIERRE MARCEL JOSEPH, biochemist, endocrinologist; b. Verviers, Belgium, Nov. 17, 1944; s. Antoine and Marie-José (Zangerlé) De M.; m. Madeleine Graitson, Mar. 15, 1972 (div. 1981); 1 child, Daniel; m. Ewa Rajpert, Sept. 6, 1986. MD, U. Liege, Belgium, 1969; PhD, Cath. U. of Louvain, Brussels, 1995. Resident in internal medicine Hosp.of Baviere, U. of Liege, Belgium, 1969-72; postdoctoral fellow NIH, Clin. Endocrinology Br., Bethesda, Md., 1973-75; Solomon A. Berson rschr. NIH, Bethesda, Md., 1975-76; rsch. assoc. of Belgian Nat. Fund for Sci. Rsch. Internat. Inst. of Cellular and Molecular Pathology, Brussels, 1977-86; dir. Dept. Diabetes, Endocrinology and Metabolism City of Hope Nat. Med. Ctr., Duarte, Calif., 1986-90; dir. Hagedorn Rsch. Inst., Gentofte, Denmark, 1990-2000, sci. dir. Receptor Sys. Biology Lab., 2000—10; prof. dept. chemistry Cath. U. of Louvain, Louvain-la-Neuve, Belgium, 1984—2010; mng. dirs. De Meyts R & D Cons. SPRLU, Kzaeinem, Belgium. Adj. prof. exptl. endocrinology Copenhagen U., 2000-05. Contbr. 190 articles to profl. jours. Comdr. (res.) Health, Belgian Army, 1976-77, Brussels. Recipient Alumni prize, Fondation Universitaire, 1978, Diaz Cristobal prize, Spanish Diabetes Assn., 1979, Oskar Minkowski prize, EASD, 1981, Assubel prize, 1983, prize, Joseph Maisin FNRS, 1995, Christoffel Plantin, 2002, gold medal, Liege U. Alumni Assoc., 2004, Frontiers in science award, Am. Assn. Clin. Endocrinologists, 2005. Fellow: Am. Coll. Endocrinology; mem.: Scanbalt Acad., Am. Soc. Biochemistry and Molecular Biology, Am. Assn. Clin. Endocrinologists, European Assn. Study Diabetes, U.S. Endocrine Soc., Am. Diabetes Assn. Achievements include research on structure-function relationships of insulin and related molecules; introduction of concept of negative cooperativity in insulin receptors. Office: Hagedorn Rsch Inst Niels Steensens Vej 1 2820 Gentofte Denmark Home: Ave Reine Astrid 10 1950 Kraainem Belgium Home Phone: +45 43693912; Office Phone: +45 44439167. E-mail: pdm@novonordisk.com.

DEMICHELE, DOMENIC JOHN, neurologist, neuroradiologist; b. Utica, NY, Apr. 2, 1951; s. Joseph John DeMichele and Mary JoAnn Urgo; children: Carrie, Kristan. BS in Biology cum laude, Syracuse U., 1974; PhD, Georgetown U., 1981, MD, 1984. Cert. in nuc. medicine, positron emission, tomography imaging, magnetic resonance imaging NIH, Bethesda, Md, lic. physician Md., NY, SC. Instr. human anatomy Syracuse U., 1972—75, instr. comparative anatomy, 1974; instr. human histology Georgetown U., Washington, 1977—78, instr. human neurobiology, 1977—80; dir. neurology critical care nursing Georgetown U. Med. Ctr., Washington, 1979—81; asst. prof. biology Cath. U., Washington, 1980—82; intern St. Joseph's Hosp., Syracuse, 1984—85; resident dept. neurology Georgetown U. Med. Ctr., Washington, 1987—90; med. staff fellow Nat. Inst. Neurol. and Communicative Disorders and Stroke, NIH neuroimaging sect., Bethesda, 1986—87; pvt. practice neurologist Florence, SC, 1990—94; founder, dir. Carolinas Hosp. Systems Sleep Disorders Ctr., Florence, 1990—; chief resident dept. neurol. Geotown U., 1983—89. Med. dir. Open MRI of Florence; med. dir., dir. nuc. medicine In-Med; presenter in field; active guest staff, neuro-imaging sec. NIH, Bethesda, Md., 1990—96. Author (with F. Suarez, H.K. Huang, J. Mazziotta): Cross Sectional Anatomy, 1978; editor (with Ampara Escarilla): General Chemistry: A Laboratory Experience, 1973; contbr. articles to profl. jours., chapters to books; author 9 novels, photographer; program of health care issues & diseases, Local & Regional TV Channels, 1990—. Mem. Senate subcom. Senate Majority Trust, 2004—, Senate subcom. Medicare/Medicaid Reform, 2004—; elected state chmn. Nat. Rep. Com. to Pres. for Medicare/Medicaid Reform, 2003—04; state cons. SC, 1996—; with Pres. Bush Sr.; inaugural balls gov. David Blasky SC instr., critical care for nurses Pres. Bush Jr., 1991—97. Recipient Tchr. Recognition award, McLeod Regional Med. Ctr., 1990—93; named Hometown Hero, 1990, Physician of Yr., Pres. George Bush Jr., Washington, 2004. Mem.: ACP (exec. com. mem. 2008), Am. Acad. Neurology, Soc. Neuroimaging, Florence County Med. Assn., SC Med. Assn., Psi Chi. Avocations: coin collecting/numismatics, stamp collecting/philately, guitar, keyboard playing, flying. Home: 2416 Windsor Forest Dr Florence SC 29501-2093 Office: Domenic Demichele 125 S Cashua Dr Florence SC 29501-4001 Office Phone: 843-669-1615. Personal E-mail: domenicddmmdphd@aol.com.

DEMIDOV, VADIM V., biotechnologist, inventor, writer; MS in Phys.-Chem. Engring., Moscow Phys-Tech. Inst., 1977; PhD in Biophysics, Inst. Molecular Genetics, Moscow, 1980. Named to rank of sr. scientific worker USSR Superior Certifying Comm., 1990. Jr. rschr. Rsch. Inst. for Biol. Testing of Chem. Compounds, Moscow, 1980—85; rschr. Moscow Inst. Biotech., 1985—87; sr. rschr. Inst. Mineralogy, Geochemistry and Crystallochemistry of Rare Elements, 1987—90, Inst. Molecular Genetics, Moscow, 1990—93; vis. asst. rsch. prof. dept. biology George Mason U., Fairfax, Va., 1993; vis. rsch. prof. Panum Inst. Copenhagen U., 1993—94; sr. rsch. assoc., group leader, prin. investigator, cons. biotechnologist Ctr. Advanced Biotech. Dept. Biomedical Engring. Boston U., 1994—2007; sr. biotechnology analyst Global Prior Art Inc., Boston, 2008—. Participant 3 sci. ecol. expeditions on peninsulas Kamchatka and Taimyr and Russian Far East, 1990—92; mem. internat. working group experts on planetary protection, 1991—92; mem. sci. bd. on problem of gene targeted drugs Russian Acad. Sci., 1992—93. Co-editor: DNA Amplification: Current Technologies & Applications, 2004; contbg. editor: Drug Discover & Development, 2004; mem. editl. bd.: Trends in Biotechnology, 2003—09, Expert Rev. Molecular Diagnostics, 2003—09, Current Medicinal Chemistry, 2006—09, Open Medicinal Chemistry, 2007—09, Expert Opinion on Medical Diagnostics, 2007—08, reviewer: jours. in field; contbr. chapters to books, articles to profl. jours. Recipient Silver medal, All-Union Nat. Exhbn. Econ. Achievements, Moscow, 1988, Medal of Hon., Internat. Biographical Ctr., Cambridge, Eng., 2007; grantee, Russian State Com. Natural Resources and Environment, 1991—93, St. Jude Children's Rsch. Hosp., Memphis, 2006—07. Mem.: Soc. Chem. Industry, Planetary Soc., Amnesty Internat. Achievements include US and international patents on nucleic acids biotechnology and environmental monitoring. Avocations: travel, pets. Office: Global Prior Art Inc 21 Milk St 6th Fl Boston MA 02109 Business E-Mail: vdemidov@globalpriorart.com.

DEMIR, HAKAN, medical educator; b. Antalya, Turkey, Sept. 5, 1971; MD, Akdeniz U. Sch. Medicine, 1995. Assoc. prof. Kocaeli U. Sch. Medicine, 2008—. Office: Kocaeli University Sch Medicine Kocaeli TR-41380 Turkey Office Fax: 90-2623038003. Personal E-mail: hakandemir99@yahoo.com.

DEMIRALP, BURAK, dentist; b. Istanbul, June 8, 1972; DDS, Hacettepe U., 1996, PhD, 2000. Rschr., lectr., clin. asst. prof. U. Mich. Sch. Dentistry, 1999—2001; rsch. asst. Hacettepe U. Faculty Dentistry Dept. Periodontology, 1996—2005, asst. prof., 2005—06, assoc. prof., 2006—09; owner, periodontist Dentina Agiz ve Dissagligi Poliklinigi, 2009—. Dentist Office Pres., Health Care Unit, 2009. Recipient Young Investigator award, Am. Soc. Bone and Mineral Rsch., Hatton award, Am. Acad. Dental Rsch., BANAT Best Presentation award, Turkish Soc. Periodontology. Mem.: Turkish Soc. Periodontology, ICOI, Acad. Osseintegration. Avocation: scuba diving. Office: Mithatpasa Caddesi 62 / 8 Kizi Ankara 06100 Turkey Personal E-mail: burakdemiralp@yahoo.com.

DEMIRCI, SENEM, oncologist; b. Izmir, Turkey, Nov. 10, 1976; MD, Pamukkale U., 2000. Physician, faculty medicine, dept. radiation oncology Ege U., 2005—11. Office: Ege University Faculty Medicine Dept Radiation Oncology Izmir 35100 Turkey Business E-Mail: senem.demirci@ege.edu.tr.

DEMIRCIOGLU, FATIH, medical educator; b. Adana, Apr. 10, 1977; D, Çukurova U., 2000. Asst. pediat. edn. Dokuz Eylul U., 2001—05, pediat. hematology fellow, 2005—08, assoc. prof., 2010. Mem.: Turkish Soc. Hematology. Avocations: fishing, travel. Home: Ihsaniye Mahallesi Emniyet Caddesi Nilüfer Bursa 16110 Turkey Business E-Mail: fatih.demircioglu@deu.edu.tr.

DEMIRHAN, MEHMET S, orthopedist, surgeon; b. Istanbul, Turkey, Apr. 12, 1960; s. Fettah and Gulsum Demirhan; m. Ebru Kiper, Nov. 5, 2001; 1 child, Haluk Cem. MD, Istanbul U., 1984. Assoc. prof. dept orthopaedics and traumatology Istanbul U., Istanbul Med. Faculty, Istanbul, Turkey, 1996—2001, prof. dept orthopaedics and traumatology, 2001—. Exec. com. mem. Turkish Shoulder and Elbow Surgery Soc., Istanbul, 1996—, pres. Turkish Bd. Orthopedic Edn., Ankara, Turkey, 2001—03; exec. com. mem. Turkish Assoc. Orthopaedics and Traumatology, Ankara, Turkey, 2004—; editor Acta Orthop. Traumatologica Turcica, Istanbul, Turkey; delegate EBOT, 2002—. Author (several orthopaedic journal articles) see pubmed list. Mem.: European Soc. Surgery of Shoulder and Elbow (licentiate; france 1998), Am. Acad. of Orthopedic Surgery (assoc.; usa 1995). Achievements include patents for Orthopaedic devices. Avocation: sailing. Office: Istanbul Univ Istanbul Med Faculty Dept Orthopedics Trauma Capa Istanbul 34390 Turkey Business E-Mail: demirhan@istanbul.edu.tr.

DEMLING, JOACHIM HEINRICH, psychiatrist, psychotherapist; b. Fuerth, Bavaria, Germany, June 2, 1947; s. Ludwig and Elisabeth (Renner) D.; m. Antonie Staedele; 7 children. MD, U. Erlangen-Nürnberg, Germany, 1974, Prof., 1996. Intern depts. surgery, internal medicine and psychiatry Univ. Hosp, Wuerzburg, Germany, 1974-75; registrar State Mental Hosp.-U. Ulm, Gunzburg, Germany, 1976-78, 3d Med. Clinic, Augsburg, Germany, 1978-79; registrar dept. neurology U. Saarbrücken, Homburg, Germany, 1979-81; scholar Max-Planck Inst. Biophys. Chemistry, Göttingen, Germany, 1982-83; staff physician dept. psychiatry U. Erlangen, 1983-98, acting dir., 1999-2000. Translator, reviser: Reactions to Psychotropic Medication, 1991; contbr. articles to med. jours., including Neuroendocrinology, Amino Acids, Biol. Psychiatry, Med. Hypotheses, Complementary Therapies in Medicine. Sgt. German Air Force, 1966-68. Lutheran. Avocations: psychotherapy, german and english literature, religion, psychopharmacology, philosophy of science. Office: U Erlangen Dept Psychiatry and Psychothe Schwabachanlage 6 D-91054 Erlangen Germany Business E-Mail: joachim.demling@uk.erlangen.de.

DEMOPOULOS, HARRY BYRON, retired pathologist, pharmaceutical researcher; b. NYC, Feb. 14, 1932; m. Rita Margarite Iovine, July 24, 1956; children: Thomas, Laura, Richard, Byron. Student, NYU, 1949-52; MD, SUNY, NYC, 1956. Diplomate Am. Bd. of Pathology. Intern Kings County Hosp., Bklyn., 1956-57; resident, tng. fellow in rsch. NYU Med. Ctr., NYC, 1957-61; sr. asst. surgeon USPHS NIH, Bethesda, Md., 1961-63; assoc. prof. U. So. Calif., LA, 1963-67; tenured assoc. prof. NYU Med. Ctr., NYC, 1967—2000; chmn., CEO Antioxidant Pharm. Corp., Elmsford, NY, 1982—, ThyoGen Pharm., 1993—. Exec. dir. Internat. Study Ctr. for Environ. Health Scis., Rye, NY, 1980-83; founding trustee Doris Duke Charitable Found., 1996—. Editor: (book) Cancer and the Environment, 1980, Thresholds for Carcinogens, 1983; contbr. 92 sci. publs. to profl. jours. Recipient Rsch. Career Devel. award Nat. Cancer Inst., NIH, 1963-67. Mem. N.Y. Acad. Scis. Achievements include the founding of the sci. of Free Radical Pathology acknowledged by Nobel winner Dr. Gerhard Herzberg; founding of the sci. of antioxidant pharmacology. Office: ThyoGen Pharmaceuticals 7 Westchester Plz Elmsford NY 10523-1603 Office Phone: 914-261-5855. Business E-Mail: hdemopoulos@thyogen.com.

DEMOREST, ALLAN FREDERICK, retired psychologist; b. Omaha, Dec. 20, 1931; 1 child, Steven M. BA, U. Omaha, 1957; MA, U. Mich., 1959, postgrad., 1960. Lic. psychologist, Iowa, Nat. Register Health Svc. Providers. Counselor Mayor's Com. on Skid Row Problems, Detroit, 1959-61; psychologist Macomb County Schs., Mt. Clemens, Mich., 1961-64; chief psychologist Jasper County Mental Health Ctr., Newton, Iowa, 1964-68; exec. dir. North Cen. Iowa Mental Health Ctr., Ft. Dodge, 1968-75; pvt. practice Ft. Dodge, 1968-85; psychologist Iowa Luth. Hosp., Des Moines, 1985-87; clin. dir. United Behavioral Systems, Des Moines, 1987-94, sr. psychologist, 1994-96; cons. pvt. practice, Des Moines, 1996—. Adj. prof. psychology Buena Vista U., Ft. Dodge, 1974-2002; substitute tchr. Des Moines Pub. Schs., 1999-05; chief trainer AARP Iowa Driver Safety Program, 2005—. Contbr. articles on rational therapy to profl. jours. Founding bd. dirs. Rape and Sexual Assault Victim

Program, Ft. Dodge, 1976-85, Family Violence Ctr., Ft. Dodge, 1976-85, Youth Shelter Svcs., Ft. Dodge, 1979. With U.S. Army, 1952-54, Korea. Recipient appreciation award Community Mental Health Ctrs. Assn., 1968, community svc. award Iowa Dept. Human Svcs., 1985. Fellow Albert Ellis Inst.; mem. APA, VFW (quartermaster 2006-08, trustee 2009-10), Iowa Psychol. Assn., Adminstrv. Mgmt. Soc. (pres. Ft. Dodge 1979-80, 84-85), Iowa Assn. for Advancement Psychology (pres. 1984, appreciation award 1988), Elks (exalted ruler 1979, trustee 2002, Elk of Yr. 2004). Home and Office: 2929 Beaver Ave 203 Des Moines IA 50310-4058 Personal E-mail: Ademorest@aol.com.

DE MORICZ, ANDRÉ, surgeon, educator; b. Rio de Janeiro, Apr. 26, 1969; Grad., Faculdade Medicina ABC, 1993; degree in Gen. Surgery, Gastroent. Surgery, Faculty Med. Scis. Santa Casa São Paulo, 1997. Asst. prof. Dept. Surgery, Faculty Med. Scis. Santa Casa São Paulo, 1998—, mem. sci. commn., 2001; pres., dir. dept. surgery Alipio Corrêa Netto Edn. and Rsch. Ctr., 2005. Chief surgeon São Luiz Itaim Hosp., Sao Paulo, 2008. Master: Colégio Brasileiro de Cirurgiões (São Paulo); mem.: Soc. Brasileira para Desenvolvimento Pesquisa em Cirurgia, Internat. Hepato-Pancreato-Biliary Assn. Avocations: windsurfing, drawing, reading. Office: R Cesario Mota Jr112 São Paulo 01221020 Brazil Office Fax: 5511 33378164. Business E-Mail: amoricz@uol.com.br.

DEMORO, ROSE ANN, nursing administrator; Grad., So. Ill. U. Former dir. collective bargaining Calif. Nurses Assn. (CNA), Oakland, Calif., exec. dir., 1993—, Nat. Nurses United (NNU), 2009—; nat. v.p. AFL-CIO. Named one of 100 Most Influential People in Healthcare, Modern Healthcare mag., Top 25 Women in Healthcare, 2005. Office: Calif Nurses Association 2000 Franklin St Oakland CA 94612 also: National Nurses United 8630 Fenton St, Suite 1100 Silver Spring MD 20910 Office Phone: 510-273-2200. Office Fax: 510-663-1625. *

DEMOSS, LISA SEWELL, lawyer, director, educator, former insurance company executive; BA summa cum laude, Mich. State U., East Lansing; JD, Wayne State U., Detroit, Mich., 1977. Assoc. Fitzgerald, Peters, Dakmak and Bruno LLP, 1977—80, ptnr., 1980—84; litigation counsel Blue Cross Blue Shield of Mich., Detroit, 1984—98, v.p., dep. gen. counsel litigation, prin. counsel auto-nat. divsn., 1998—2003, corp. sec., sr. v.p., corp. compliance officer, gen. counsel, 2003—09; vis. prof. Thomas M. Cooley Law Sch., Lansing, 2011—, dir. grad. ins. program, 2011—; health care cons. Strategic adv. bd. mem. Health Data Insights Inc. Fellow: State Bar of Mich.; mem.: Detroit Met. Bar Assn. (past pres. 1998—99), American Corp. Counsel Assn., American Health Lawyers Assn. Office: Health Data Insights Incorporated 7501 Trinity Peak St Ste 210 Las Vegas NV 89128 also: Thomas M Cooley Law School 300 S Capitol Ave PO Box 13038 Lansing MI 48901 Office Phone: 517-371-5140. Office Fax: 702-639-1515. *

DEMOSTHENES, PANAGIOTAKOS, biostatistician, epidemiologist, educator; b. Athens, Greece, July 17, 1967; s. Basilios Panagiotakos and Helen Koliopoulou; m. Christina Chrysohoou, Apr. 20, 1996. MPhil in Applied Stats., Sch. Math., 1991; MS in Biostats., Sch. Medicine, 2001, D Medicine, 2003. Rsch. scientist Sch. Medicine, U. Athens, Greece, 1996—2003; lectr. TEI Piraeus, 1998—2003, Hellanion Coll./U. Portsmouth, Portsmouth/Athens, 1996—98; rsch. scientist A Cardiology Clinic, Sch. Medicine, U. Athens, 2003—. Rsch. cons. U. Athens, Sch. Nursing, 2000—03, 2003—; lectr. Harokopio U. Athens, 2004—. Contbr. articles to profl. jours. Recipient Young Investigator award, European Soc. of Hypertension, Internat. Epidemiological Assn., Hellenic Cardiological Soc. Mem.: Am. Epidemology, European Soc. Atherosclerosis, European Soc. Cardiology, Internat. Epidemiol. Assn. Home: 46 Paleon Polemiston Attica Glyfada 16674 Greece Home Fax: 0302109600719. Personal E-mail: d.b.panagiotakos@usa.net.

DE MOUZON, JACQUES, medical educator; b. Creil, France, Dec. 23, 1948; MD, Toulouse U., France, MPH, 1979. Assoc. prof. INSERM, 1980—. Chmn. European Register ART (formerly ESHRE), 2009—. Home: 15 rue Guilleminot Paris 75014 France Personal E-mail: jacques.demouzon@inserm.fr.

DEMUNBRUN-HARMON, DONNE O'DONNELL, retired family physician; b. St. Paul, Aug. 26, 1926; d. Francis Joseph and Julia (Hoffmann) O'Donnell; m. Truman Weldon DeMunbrun, Mar. 17, 1948 (dec. Aug. 1996); children: Michael J., Steven M., Julie F., Suzanne B.; m. Donald Laurance Harmon, Aug. 26, 1997. BS, U. Ky., 1948, MS, 1949; MD, U. Louisville, 1954. Diplomate Am. Bd. Family Practice. Rotating intern St. Anthony Hosp., Louisville, 1955—56; pvt. practice Louisville, 1956—85; med. dir. St. Mary and Elizabeth Hosp., Louisville, 1971—76, Parkway Med. Ctr., Louisville, 1976—99, Family Health Ctrs., Louisville, 1985—90; ret., 1999. Case reviewer Health Care Rev., Louisville, 1995-96; criteria writer Nat. Health Svc., Louisville, 1995-96; asst. clin. prof. family practice, U. Louisville Med. Sch., 1987-90. Contbg. author: Tales From Kentucky Doctors, 2008. Pres. Jacques Timothe Boucher Sieur de Montbrun Heritage Soc., Nashville, 1996-97. Recipient mayor's citation, City of Louisville, 1990, proclamation of tribute, Jefferson County, Ky., 1990. Mem.: Jefferson County Med. Soc. (life; v.p. 1976—77), Ky. Acad. Family Practice (life), Ky. Med. Assn. (life; del.), Am. Acad. Family Practice (life), Frazier Arms Mus., Filson Club, Execs. Club, Univ. Club, Sigma Pi Sigma, Pi Mu Epsilon, Alpha Lambda Delta. Avocations: gardening, dogs, reading. Home: 3004 Beals Branch Dr Louisville KY 40206-2902 Home Phone: 502-895-5682. Personal E-mail: donneharmon@insight-bb.com.

DEMURA, YOSHIKI, medical association administrator; b. Japan, Mar. 14, 1966; MD, U. Fukui, 1990, PhD, 1998. Chief dir., dept. respiratory medicine Ishikawa Prefectural Ctrl. Hosp., 2009—. Office: Ishikawa Prefectural Ctrl Hosp Kanaawa Ishikawa 920-8530 Japan Personal E-mail: dem2180@aol.com.

DENARDO, JOHN J., hospital administrator, educator; BS in Pharmacy, U. of Ill., Chgo., 1971, MS in Pharmacy, 1974; MPH, U. of Mich., Ann Arbor, 1984. Registered pharmacist NW Hosp., Chgo., 1971—73; pharmacy resident Hines Veterans Adminstrn. Hosp., Ill., 1973—74, staff pharmacist, 1974—75, supr. pharmacist, 1975—77, assoc. dir. (trainee), 1981—82, asst. med. ctr. dir., 1984—86, dir. Ill., 1996—2000; supr. pharmacist Big Spring Veterans Adminstrn. Hosp., Tex., 1977—78; chief, pharmacy svc. Clarksburg Veterans Adminstrn. Med. Ctr., W.Va., 1978—80, Ann Arbor Veterans Adminstrn. Med. Ctr., Mich., 1980—81; med. dist. coord. Med. Dist. 17 Chgo., Hines, Ill., 1982—84; assoc. dir. Lakeside Veterans Adminstrn. Med. Ctr, Chgo., 1986—92; acting dir. West Side Veterans Adminstrn. Med. Ctr., 1992, dir., 1992—96; exec. dir. hosp. and clinics Univ. of Ill. at Chgo., 2000—, assoc. vice chancellor health affairs, 2003—05, CEO health care sys., 2005—. Chair Greater Chgo. Area Combined Fed. Campaign; member adv. coun. Univ. of Ill. Chgo. Coll. of Pharmacy; adj. clin. prof. Govs. State Univ. Recipient Disting. Cmty. Svc. award, DuPage County NAACP. Fellow: Am. Coll. Healthcare Execs. Office: University of Illinois at Chicago Office of Public Affairs MC 288 601 S Morgan St Chicago IL 60607-7113 Office Phone: 312-996-3456.

DENENBERG, STEVEN M., otolaryngologist, educator; MD, U. of Nebr. Med. Ctr., 1980. Diplomate Am. Bd. Otolaryngology, 1984, cert. facial plastic and reconstructive surgery 1992. Resident otolaryngology Stanford Univ. Med. Ctr., Palo Alto, Calif., 1981—84; fellow facial plastic surgery McCollough Ctr., Birmingham, Ala., 1984—85; hosp. affiliations include Meth. Hosp., Alegent Health Bergan Mercy Med. Ctr.; asst. clin. prof. otolaryngology Univ. Nebr. Coll. of Medicine. Office: Methodist Hospital 8303 Dodge St Omaha NE 68114-4108 Office Phone: 402-354-4000.

DENG, DAJUN, oncologist, researcher; b. Ruijin, Jiangxi, China, Jan. 3, 1961; s. Zhenmao Deng and Xiuyin Zhu; m. Yiming Zhu, Jan. 3, 1988; 1 child, Zhiyuan. MD, Jiangxi Med. Coll., Nanchang, China, 1983; MS, Peking Union Med. Coll., Beijing, 1986. Head dept. cancer etiology Peking U. Sch. Oncology, Beijing, 1994—, prof., 1998—. Contbr. articles to profl. jours. Mem. AACR, Internat. Gastric Cancer Assn. (Poster prize 1995), China Anti-Cancer Assn. (vice chmn. com. etiology 1997—). Achievements include research on characterization of N-nitrosamide (N-nitrosomethylurea) in nitrosated foods and human stomach; inventor of setup of method to detect methylation of CpG islands by denaturing high performance chromatography. Office: Peking U Sch Oncology Fu-Chen-Lu St Beijing 100036 China Home Phone: 8610 88125649; Office Phone: 8610 88196752. Office Fax: 8610 88122437. Personal E-mail: dengdajun@hotmail.com. Business E-Mail: dengdajun@bjmu.edu.cn.

DENG, LIANG, biomedical engineer, researcher; b. Nanchang, Jiangxi, China, Jan. 30, 1981; MS in Engring., Northwestern Poly. U., Xi'an, Shaaxi, China. Prodr.: (exhn.) Flow Reposition Bioreactor with Pressure Gradient (Gold medal, 10th Chinese Patents Exhbn., 2002). Recipient Sci. Rsch. award, Nat. Aeronautics and Astronautics Found. China, 2002. Achievements include patents in field. Personal E-mail: denglsilva@hotmail.com.

DENG, LINHONG, biomedical engineer, engineering educator, director; b. Jiajiang, Sichuan, China, July 4, 1960; arrived in Can., 1996, 2005; s. Zhenghe Deng and Zhongrui Fan; m. Xiaoyan Fan, June 10, 1986 (div. Jan. 5, 2000); 1 child, Paul Tiange; m. Youqin Li, Jan. 26, 2006; 1 child, Yanzhi. BS in Engring., Chongqing U., China, 1982; MS in Engring., Chongqing U., 1986; PhD in Bioengring., U. Strathclyde, Glasgow, Scotland, 1998. Gen. mgr., founder Chongqing Vital Biotech., Ltd., 1986—90; lectr. bioengring. coll. Chongqing U., 1988—90, prof., dir. bioengring. coll., 2006—; vis. scholar, bioengring. unit. U. Strathclyde, Glasgow, 1990—92, rsch. asst., bioengring. unit, 1996—98; postdoctoral fellow, sch. biomed. engring. Dalhousie U., Halifax, Canada, 2000—03; rsch. assoc., sch. pub. health Harvard U., Boston, 2003—06. Sci. advisor Halifax Biomed. Inc., Halifax, Nova Scotia, Canada, 2005—; bd. dir. Weiduo Biomed., Ltd., Chongqing, 2006—; vis. scientist, sch. pub. health Harvard U., 2006—. Recipient Travel award, Internat. Soc. Biorheology, 1992, Young Investigator award, Fedn. Am. Socs. Exptl. Biology, 2003, Cheung Kong Professorship award, Ministry Edn., China, 2007, Fast Breaking Paper award, Sci. Watch, 2007; grantee Legacy 2000 award, NS Lung Assn., 2002; vis. scholar, Strathclyde U., 1990—92; scholarship, Sino-British Friendship Scholarship Found., 1990. Mem.: IEEE, Fedn. Am. Socs. Exptl. Biology, Optical Soc. China (councillor biophotonics divsn.), Biophys. Soc. China (exec. mem.), Chinese Soc. Biomaterials, NY Acad. Scis. Achievements include discovery of fast and slow dynamics of the living cytoskeleton; universal physical response to transient stretch in the living cell. Home: Apt 24-1 68 Baishulin Shapingba Chongqing 400044 China also: 68 Bashulin Shapingba Chongqing 400030 China Office: Chongqing Univ Bioengring Coll 174 Shazhengjie St Shapingba Dist 400044 Chongqing Chongqing China Office Phone: 86 23 65112670. Office Fax: 86 23 65102507. Business E-Mail: denglh@cqu.edu.cn.

DENG, WENLI, engineering educator, researcher; b. Chongqing, China, Oct. 1, 1963; PhD, U. Electronic Sci. and Tech. China, 1995. Prof. South China U. Tech., 2004—. Dir. Lab. Nanotechnology and Molecular Sci., 2004—. Recipient Ann. Personality award, Sci. Chinese. Mem.: Chinese Chem. Soc. Avocations: basketball, ping pong/table tennis, badminton. Office: Wushan Rd 381# Tianhe Dist Guangzhou Guangdong 510640 China Business E-Mail: wldeng@scut.edu.cn.

DENG, WEN-TAO, medical researcher; b. Gansu, China, Sept. 14, 1969; BS, Lanzhou U., 1991; PhD, U. Fla., 2000. Rsch. scientist Dept. Ophthalmology, 2002—. Office: Dept Ophthalmology 1600 SW Archer Rd Gainesville FL 32610 Business E-Mail: wdeng@ufl.edu.

DENITTIS, ALBERT STEPHEN, oncologist; b. Phila., Mar. 22, 1965; s. Albert Peter and Theresa DeNittis; m. Lisa Bassano, Oct. 14, 1995; children: Andrew Stephen, Julianna Lisa. MS, Rutgers U., 1990; MD, Robert Wood Johnson Med. Sch., 1995. Diplomate Am. Bd. Radiology, 2000. Med. intern Cooper Hosp., Camden, NJ, 1996; resident U. Pa., Phila., 1998—2000; chief dept. radiation oncology Lankenau Hosp., Wynnewood, Pa., 2001—. Prin. investigator Radiation Therapy Oncology Group, Wynnewood, Pa., 2002—; co-dir. Man to Man, 2003—. Contbr. chapters to books, more than 35 articles to profl. jours. Mem.: AMA, Am. Coll. Radiology, Am. Soc. Clin. Oncology, Am. Soc. Therapeutic Radiation Oncology. Achievements include research in recipiant of Sharp grant for prostate research. Office: Lankenau Hosp 100 Lancaster Ave Wynnewood PA 19106 E-mail: denittisa@mlhs.org.

DENMARK, STANLEY JAY, orthodontist; b. Queens, NY, May 26, 1927; s. Jack and Frieda (Kirschenbaum) D.; m. Florence Levin, June 7, 1953 (div. June 1973); children: Valerie (dec.), Pamela (dec.) and Richard (twins); m. Anita Goodman, Jan. 2, 1983. BS, Queens Coll., 1950; MSc, NYU, 1955; DDS, U. Pa., 1955, orthodontics cert., 1957. Diplomate Am. Bd. Orthodontics. Practice dentistry specializing in orthodontics, Westbury, NY, 1955-91; asst. prof. orthodontics Fairleigh Dickinson U., Hackensack, NJ, 1974-79; clin. assoc. prof. growth and devel. scis. orthodontics Sch. Dentistry NYU, 1991—. With USN, 1945-47. Mem. ADA, Am. Assn. Orthodontists, Northeastern Soc. Orthodontists, Coll. Diplomates of Am. Bd. Orthodontists, Sigma Xi. Jewish. Avocations: painting, woodcuts, tennis, cross country skiing. Home: 228 E 46th St Apt 5C New York NY 10017-2968 Personal E-mail: denmarknewyork@aol.com. *

DENNESS, RICHARD P., foundation administrator; married; 2 children. V.p., gen. mgr. ctrl. nervous divsn. UCB, Inc.; pres., CEO Epilepsy Found. America, Landover, Md., 2011—. Bd. dirs. Epilepsy Found. America, 2007—. Office: Epilepsy Found America 8301 Professional Pl Landover MD 20785 *

DENNISTON, GEORGE CLINTON, medical activist; b. Phila., Apr. 10, 1934; s. George Clinton Denniston and Martha Mosby Averett; m. Martha Cryer Kent, July 5, 1974 (dec.); stepchildren: Peter, Matthew, Thomas, Stephen; m. Tina Palmer, Jan. 30, 2009; stepchildren: Terence, Michael, Jonathan, Adrian. AB, Princeton U., NJ, 1955; MD, U. Pa. Sch. Medicine, Phila., 1959; MPH, Harvard U., Boston, 1961. Diplomate in gen. preventive medicine; cert. flight instr. glider. Ford fellow U. Wash., Seattle, 1965—67; assoc. med. dir. Planned Parenthood Fedn. America, NY, 1968; med. dir. pres. Population Dynamics Non Profit, Seattle, 1970—95; founder & pres. Drs. Opposing Circumcision, Seattle, 1995—. Author: (book) Joy of Ballooning, 1999; editor (anti-circumcision): Flesh & Blood, numerous med. training films; co-prodr.: Birth As We Know It, 2006. Dir., prodr. and editor Documentary Film, Beyond Conception, 1968. Lt. comdr. USPHS, 1961—63, Ctrs. Disease Control, Atlanta. Recipient Patent award, VASSECT, 1978, Humanitarian award, NOCIRC, 1996, Achievement award, Princeton U. Class 55, 2004. Achievements include initiating 7 birth control clinics in Seattle. Avocations: mountain climbing, sailing, ballooning, film producing, flying. Business E-Mail: george_denniston@post.harvard.edu. *

DENNY, DONALD FRANCIS, JR., radiologist; BA, U. Pa., 1973; MD, Hanemann Med. Coll., Phila., 1978. Cert. Diagnostic Radiology, Vascular & Interventional Radiology. Intern, internal medicine Yale-New Haven Hosp., resident, diagnostic radiology, co-chief resident, 1981—82; clin. fellow, cardiovascular radiology Brigham and Women's Hosp. and Harvard U. Sch. Medicine, 1982—83; clin. asst. prof., radiation medicine Brown U., 1983—85; staff mem. RI Hosp., Providence, 1983—85; chief, vascular and interventional radiology Yale U., 1985, clin. dir., dept. diagnostic imaging, assoc. prof., diagnostic radiology, dir., diagnostic radiology rsch. lab.; physician Princeton Radiology Assocs., 1991—. Lectr. in field. Contbr. several articles to profl. jours., chapters to books. Fellow: Soc. Cardiovascular and Interventional Radiology; mem.: Radiol. Soc. NJ (officer 2007—08). Office Phone: 609-497-4310. Office Fax: 609-683-8769. Business E-Mail: ddenny@prada.com.

DENOFRIO, DAVID, cardiologist, educator; MD, Tufts U., 1988. Diplomate Am. Bd. Internal Medicine, 2001, Am. Bd. Internal Medicine-cardiovasc. disease, 2005. Resident internal medicine Barnes Hosp., St. Louis, 1988—91; fellow cardiology Duke Univ. Med. Ctr., Durhan, NC, 1991—94; assoc. prof. Tufts Univ. Sch. of Medicine, Boston; staff cardiologist Tufts Med. Ctr., Boston. Coauthor: (publs.) Left ventricular assist device therapy normalizes inducible nitric oxide synthase expression in failing human hearts, 2005, Cyclosporine monitoring with two-hour post-dose levels in heart transplant recipients, 2005, The economic effect of a tertiary hospital-based heart failure program, 2005, Treatment of hypercholesterolemia with ezetimibe in cardiac transplant recipients, 2007, The effect of ventricular assist devices on post-transplant mortality: Analysis of the UNOS Thoracic Registry, 2009. Named one of the Top Doctors List for Cardiology, Boston Mag., 2006, 2007. Fellow: Am. Coll. of Cardiology; mem.: Mass. Med. Soc., Internat. Soc. of Heart and Lung Transplantation, Am. Soc. of Transplantation, Heart Failure Soc. of America. Office: Tufts Medical Center Number 5931 800 Washington St Boston MA 02111 Office Phone: 617-636-8068. Office Fax: 617-636-6030. Business E-Mail: ddenofrio@tuftsmedicalcenter.org.

DENSEN, PAUL MAXIMILLIAN, retired health facility administrator; b. NYC, Aug. 1, 1913; s. Charles Edwin and Carrie (Weinberg) Densen; m. Elizabeth A. Reed, Dec. 19, 1939; children: Rebecca E., Peter. AB, Bklyn.Coll., 1934; DSc, Johns Hopkins U., 1939; MA (hon.), Harvard U., 1968. From instr. to assoc. prof. preventive medicine Vanderbilt U. Med. Sch., 1939—46; chief div. med. research statistics VA, Washington, 1946—49; assoc. prof., then prof. biometry Grad. Sch. Pub. Health, U. Pitts., 1949—54; dir. div. research and statistics Health Ins. Plan Greater N.Y., 1954—59; dept. commr. N.Y.C. Dept. Health, 1959—66; dept. adminstr. N.Y.C. Health Services Adminstrn., 1966—69; dir. Harvard Center Community Health and Med. Care, 1968—85; prof. community health Harvard Sch. Pub. Health, 1968—85, prof. emeritus, 1985—. Fellow: AAAS, APHA, Am. Statis. Assn.; mem.: Inst. Medicine of NAS, Am. Epidemiol. Soc. Home: Apt 1019 350 Dublin Dr Iowa City IA 52246

DENTON, DEREK ASHWORTH, medical researcher, foundation administrator; b. Launceston, Tasmania, Australia, May 27, 1924; s. Arthur A. and Catherine (Edwards) D.; m. Margaret Catherine Scott, Mar. 13, 1953; children: Matthew, Angus. MBBS, Melbourne U., 1947; LLD (hon.), U. Melbourne, Australia, 2006. Haley Rsch. Fellow Walter and Eliza Hall Inst., Melbourne, 1948; med. rsch. fellow, sr. med. rsch. fellow Nat. Health and Med. Rsch. Coun., Melbourne, 1948—, prin. med. rsch. fellow, 1970; founding dir. Howard Florey Inst. Exptl. Physiology and Medicine, Melbourne, 1971-89, emeritus dir., 1990—; pres. Howard Florey Biomed. Found., Melbourne, 1997—. Bd. dir. David Syme Ltd. Pubs. The Age, 1984-93; invited OECD examiner of sci. and tech. policy Govt. Sweden, 1985-86; 1st v.p. Internat. Union of Physiol. Scis., 1983-89 (chmn. nominating com. and com. on commns. 1986-93), jury Albert and Mary Lasker Found. awards in med. sci., 1979-90; fgn. assoc. NAS of U.S., 1995; adj. scientist Southwest Found. Biomed. Rsch., San Antonio, 1994—; fgn. assoc. Inst. France Acad. Scis., 2000. Author: The Hunger for Salt, 1982, The Pinnacle of Life: Consciousness in Animals and Humans; editor: Olfaction and Taste, 1985, Les Emotions Primordiales et L'Eveil de la Conscience, 2005, The Primordial Emotions: The Dawning of Consciousness, 2006. Decorated Companion Order of Australia. Fellow Royal Soc. London, Royal Coll. Physicians (hon.) London and Australia, Am. Physiol. Soc. (hon.), Am. Acad. Arts and Scis. (fgn.); mem. Royal Swedish Acad. Scis. (fgn. med. mem.). Avocations: wine, tennis, fly fishing. Home: 816 Orrong Rd Toorak

3142 Melbourne Australia Office: Univ Melbourne 4th Fl 766 Elizabeth St 3010 Melbourne Australia Home Phone: 61398272640; Office Phone: 61383445639. Business E-Mail: ddenton@unimelb.edu.au.

DE NUNZIO, ALESSANDRO MARCO, biomedical engineer, researcher; b. Teano, Italy, Sept. 22, 1979; s. Giuliano De Nunzio and Angela Piciocchi. Degree in Biomedical Engring., U. Genoa, Italy, 2002; PhD in Physiology, U. Pavia, Italy, 2005, diploma, 2005. Registered profl. engr., Nat. Coun. Engrs., 2002. Rschr. neurophysiology and biomechanics Salvatore Maugeri Found., Veruno, Italy, 2002—04, Pavia, 2005—; rschr. neurophysiology U. Pavia, 2004—05, asst. prof. faculty motor sci., 2006—. Contbr. articles to profl. jours. Founder mem. Ius Gentium, Soc. for the Protection of the Citizen's Rights, Teano, Italy, 2006. Fellow, Salvatore Maugeri Found., 2002—04; Degree scholar, Italian Govt., 1997—2002, Doctorate scholar, 2002—05, Advanced Sch. scholar, Scuola Avanzata di Formazione Integrata, Pavia, 2002—05, Fondo Investimenti Ricerca di Base grantee, Italian Ministry Edn., 2005—07. Mem.: Am. Physiol. Soc. (assoc.), Engr. Register Pavia (assoc.). Achievements include patents for programmable device for muscular vibratory stimulation; project developer for the use of the human muscular vibratory device to study the importance of proprioceptive input during locomotion; responsible for a programmable mobile platform for the study and rehabilitation of balance disorders; research in normal and pathological human movement with special interest in locomotion and dynamic posture; expert devices used to collect biomechanics and physiological data; development of models for human equilibrium; devices for balance rehabilitation. Avocations: cooking, reading, music. Office: Salvatore Maugeri Foundation Scientific Inst Telese Terme (BN) Via Bagni Vecchi 82037 Telese Italy Office Phone: 0039-0824803507. Home Fax: 00390824909507. Business E-Mail: marco.denunzio@fsm.it.

DE NUNZIO, COSIMO, urologist, consultant; b. Benevento, Italy, May 27, 1973; s. Pasquale De Nunzio and Anna Bologna. MD, U. La Sapienza Med. Sch., Rome, 1997, PhD in advanced surg. techs., 2003. Specialization in urology U. La Sapienza, 2002. Registar in urology policlinico Umberto 1 U. La Sapienza, Rome, 1991—2002, cons. urol. surgeon Ospdale Sant'Andrea, 2001—. Mem.: Italian Soc. of Urology (assoc.), European Soc. of Urology (assoc.). Office: Azienda Ospedaliera sant'Andrea Via Di Grottarossa 1035 Rome 00100 Italy Home: Via Giuseppe Piermarini 32 82100 Benevento BN Italy Personal E-mail: cosimodenunzio@virgilio.it.

DEO, SURYANARAYANA SV, oncologist, consultant; b. Salur, Andhra Pradesh, India, Nov. 13, 1963; s. Deo Vikram and Deo Dhiraj Kumari; m. Prabha Kanta, Jan. 15, 2004; 1 child, Deo Harshita. MB BS, MS, All India Inst. Med. Scis., New Delhi, 1995. Cert. in surg. oncology All India Inst. Med. Scis., 1995. Asst. prof., surg. oncology All India Inst. Med. Scis., New Delhi, 1995—2002, assoc. prof., surg. oncology, 2002—. Full time acad. cons. All India Inst. Med. Scis., New Delhi, 1995—2005. Contbr. over 99 articles to profl. jours. Treas. Surg. Oncology Rsch. Soc., New Delhi, 2001—05. Recipient Young Scientista award, Indian Soc. Oncology, 1999. Fellow: ACS (Internat. guest scholar), Internat. Union Against Cancer - Geneva (life ICRETT fellowships 199, 2003); mem.: Indian Assn. Surg. Oncology (life; exec. mem. 2001—03, Detroit fellowship 2002), Assn. Surgeons India (life). Achievements include research in new surgical techniques for breast cancer surgery; mandibular reconstruction; fertility-preserving surgery in young cancer patients; intra-operative radiotherapy for advanced cancers. Home: E- 14 Ayur Vigyan Nagar Khel Gaon Road Delhi New Delhi 110049 India Office: Surgical Oncology IRCH AIIMS Ansari Nagar 110 029 New Delhi 110029 India Office Fax: 91-11-26588663. Personal E-mail: svsdeo@yahoo.co.in.

DE OLIVEIRA, FERNANDO ROCHA, gynecologist; b. Porto Alegre, Brazil, Oct. 26, 1967; MD, UFRGS, 1992, PhD, 2005. Ob gyn. U. Fed. do Rio Grande do Sul, 1993—. Attendant physician Hosp. de Clinicas de Porto Alegre, 2004—11. Avocation: literature. Home: Gonçalo de Carvalho 471 Porto Alegre RS 90035-170 Brazil Home Fax: 555132229074. Personal E-mail: oliveirafr@terra.com.br.

DE OLIVEIRA FILHO, GETÚLIO RODRIGUES, anesthesiologist, researcher; s. Getúlio Rodrigues and Núbia Rodrigues de Oliveira; m. Maria Katuyo Motooka, July 20, 1984. MD, U. Fed. de Pelotas, 1980; PhD, São Paulo Sch. Medicine, 2006. Cert. Brazilian Bd. Anesthesiology, 1986. Residency Hosp. Governador Celso Ramos, Florianópolis, Brazil, 1981—82; pvt. practice, 1983—85; clin. dir. Sãos Hosp., Ponta Grossa, Brazil, 1983—85; anesthesiologist Hosp. Governador Celso Ramos, 1986—, rschr., 1986—, sr. rschr., 1999—. Chief Dept. Anesthesiology Hosp. Governador Celso Ramos, 1999—, sr. rschr., 1999—. Mem.: Soc. Anesthesiology (sci. dir. Santa Catarina chpt. 2004—05), Brazilian Soc. Anesthesiology (assoc.). Office: Hospital Governador Celso Ramos Rua Irmã Benwarda 297 Florianopolis 88015270 Brazil Office Fax: 554832820376. Business E-Mail: grof@th.com.br.

DEORIO, ANTHONY JOSEPH, surgeon; b. Chgo., June 27, 1945; s. Joseph John and Catherine Marie Deorio; m. Janet Ann Balskus, Jan. 10, 1970; children: Joseph, Catherine. BS, Loyola U., Chgo., 1967; MD, Loyola U., Maywood, Ill., 1971. Diplomate Am. Bd. Surgery. Intern St. Joseph Hosp., Chgo., 1971-72; resident in surgery Loyola Med. Ctr., Maywood, 1972-76, clin. instr. surgery, 1976-77, asst. prof. surgery, 1977—; pvt. practice Resurrection Hosp., Chgo., 1977—, dir. surg. edn., 1977—, chmn. dept. surgery, 1984-88, sec. med. staff, 1986-88. Assoc. examiner Am. Bd. Surgery, 1993, 96. Contbr. articles to profl. jours. Fellow ACS (com. on applicants 1990—); mem. AMA, Ill. Med. Soc., Chgo. Med. Soc., Chgo. Surg. Soc., Ill. Surg. Soc., Alumni Assn. Stritch Sch. Medicine (bd. govs.), Columbian Club, KC, Blue Key, Alpha Omega Alpha. Roman Catholic. Avocations: model railroads, sports, fishing. Office: 7447 W Talcott Ave Chicago IL 60631-3745 Home Phone: 708-435-3039; Office Phone: 773-631-9699. Business E-Mail: TonyD453@Ameritech.net.

DE PÁDUA, FERNANDO, cardiology educator, internist; b. Faro, Algarve, Portugal, May 29, 1927; s. Carlos Paraiso and Irene Archer (Moreira) De P.; m. Maria Mauela Vieira Pinto, June 2, 1952; children: Josè Manuel, Fernando Manuel, João Manuel Pinto. Grad. in Medicine, U. Lisbon, Portugal, 1950; grad. student in Cardiology, Harvard U., Boston, 1952-53; specialist in Cardiology, Med. Assn., Lisbon, 1954; PhD, U. Lisbon, 1959. Intern Univ. Hosps. St. Marta, Lisbon, 1950-53; asst instr. U. Hosp. St. Maria, Lisbon, 1952-59, asst. prof., 1959-63, assoc. prof., 1963-67, dir. dept. medicine, 1964, full prof. internal medicine, 1967, full prof. cardiology, 1988, pres. sci. coun. faculty of medicine, 1989-91, dean faculty of medicine, 1991-97, ret., 1997. Dir. Ctr. Studies of Preventive Cardiology, Lisbon, 1976-88, Nat. Inst. Preventive Cardiology, Lisbon, 1986—; pres. Portugese Heart Found., Lisbon, 1979-87. Editor: Electrocardiology New Frontier, 1980, Update, 1992; author and editor: Cindi-Portugal 2nd Quinquenium, 1994, Cindi Portugal 3rd Quinquenium, 1998; dir. Rev. Portugese Terapeutica Medica, 1967, Rev. Portugese Clin. Terapeutics, 1972. Creator, pres. Prof. Fernando de Pádua Found., 2002. Lt. Portugese Army Med. Forces 1951-52. Named Hon. Pres. Soc. Cardiology, 1983, Hon. Mem. Soc. Rheumatology, 1991, Hon. Pres. Portuguese Heart Found., 1994; recipient Gold medal Min. Health; decorated Star and Grand Collar of Order of St. James adn Sward, Pres. of Portuguese Republic, 2005. Fellow European Heart Assn., Internat. Soc. and Fedn. Cardiology-Epidemiology and Prevention; mem. Cindi-European WHO Program, Acad. Medicine, Portugese Soc. Cardiology (pres. 1977-80), Internat. Coun. Cardiology (bd. dirs., pres. 1992-94), Internat. Soc. Electrocardiology (founder). Achievements include leadership in nat. fight against hypertension and stroke and in countrywide integrated non-communicable diseases intervention program (Cindi-Euro-WHO), founding of World Movement Heart and Health in Portugese in 1995. Office: Ave Fontes Pereira de Melo 35-2C 1050-118 Lisbon Portugal Home: R das Amoreiras 72-E-4 Dto 1250-024 Lisbon Portugal Office Phone: (351) 968096966. Fax: 351.21.3530866. Business E-Mail: fernando.pádua@incp.pt.

DE PAIVA, TEREZINHA MARIA, biomedical researcher, virologist; d. Massilon Dias and Izabel Cecilia R. De Paiva. MS, Sao Paulo U., 1988, PhD, 2001. Biologist Inst. Adolfo Lutz, Sao Paulo, 1982—84, rsch. virologist, 1984—2008, head respiratory virus sec., 2005—08; biomed. scientists Faculty Ciencias Biol. Araras, Sao Paulo, 1984; sci. rschr. IAL Sao Paulo Govt., 1984—2008; trainee influenza Nat. Influenza Ctr., Lyon, France, 1995, Influenza Br. CDC, Atlanta, 2000. NIC dir. WHO, Geneva, 1996—2008, temporary adv., 2006; virologic surveillance coor. Ministry Health, Brazil, 2002—08; cons. PAHO, Wash., 2008. Recipient award, Adolfo Lutz, 2007, Ministry Health Brazil, Dept. Sci. & Tech., 2008. Mem.: Brazilian Soc. Virology, Rio De Janeiro. Avocations: travel, reading, gardening, volleyball. Office: Inst Adolfo Lutz Avenida Doutor Arnaldo 355 01246-902 Sao Paolo SP Brazil

DE PALMA, GIOVANNI DOMENICO, radiologist, educator; b. Napoli, Oct. 9, 1955; MD, U. Naples Federico II, Sch. Medicine, 1981. Chief sect. diagnostic & therapeutic endoscopy U. Naples Federico II, Sch. Medicine, 2002, assoc. prof. surgery, 2011—. Mem.: ASGE. Avocations: antiques, photography. Office: Via Pansini 5 Naples 80131 Italy Office Fax: 39-81-7462752. E-mail: giovanni.depalma@unina.it.

DEPALMA, RALPH GEORGE, surgeon, educator, medical administrator; m. Maleva Tankard, Sept. 17, 1955; children: Ralph L., Edward F., Maleva B., Malinda G. AB, Columbia U, 1953; MD, NYU, 1956. Diplomate Am. Bd. Surgery, Am. Bd. Vascular Surgery. Resident in surgery Univ. Hosps., Cleve., 1962-64; from instr. to prof. surgery Case Western Res. U., Cleve., 1964-80; prof., chmn. surgery U. Nev., Reno, 1980-82, George Washington U. Sch. Medicine, Washington, 1982-92; Lewis B. Saltz prof. of surgery George Washington U. Med. Ctr., Washington, 1992-94; prof. surgery, vice-chmn. dept. surgery, assoc. dean U. Nev., Reno, 1994-2000; nat. dir. surgery US Dept. Vets. Affairs, Washington, 2000—08, Nat. Dir. Transplantation, 2007—10; prof. surgery Uniformed Svcs. U. Health Scis., Bethesda, Md., 2000—; spl. operations officer Va. Office R & D, 2010—. Chair nat. surg. quality program Dept. Vet. Affairs, 2005—08; faculty surg. complications collaborative Inst. for Health Care Improvement, 2007—08. Author: Practicing and Other Stories, 2005, Xlibris: Lives and Loves in Cars, 2006, Xlibris: Saeta for a Son, 2008; editor: (with J.M. Giordano) Reoperative Vascular Surgery, 1987, Chief Complaints Surgery and Dilemmas in Health Care, 2009, Basic Science of Vascular Surgery, 1988; assoc. editor: Haimovici Vascular Surgery: Principles and Techniques, 1989; co-editor: Basic Science in Vascular Disease, 1997, Vascular Surgery, Internat. Jour. Impotence Rsch.; mem. editl. bd. Vascular and Endovascular Surgery, 2003; contbr. 278 chapters to books; articles to profl. jours. Bd. dirs. Reno Opera, 1980-83, Reno Chamber Orch., 1999-00; stroke liaison nat. chpt. Am. Heart Assn., 1992-94; tech adv. group Nat. Quality Found., 2004, steering com. Surg. Complications Improvement Project, 2004-06, tech. adv. group Venous Thromboembolism, DOD Expert Panel Brain Injury, 2010 Capt. aviation med. examiner USAF, 1957—60, with USAFR, 1960—63. Recipient Founder's Honor award Am. Venous Forum, 2008, Alumni award NYU Coll. Medicine; name to Best Doctors in Am., 1994, named lectureship and surg. svc. GWN Hosp.; grantee USPHS, 1974-82, Lifetime Achievement award award, Assn. VA Surgeons, 2010 Fellow ACS (mem. com. trauma 2007-, expert panel DOD brain injury modeling 2009-); mem. Cleve. Vascular Soc. (pres. 1977-78, registry 1978-80), Rocky Mt. Vascular Soc. (pres. 1981-82), Am. Surg. Assn., Soc. Vascular Surgery, Washington Acad. Surgery (sec. 1991-92, v.p. 1992-93, pres. 1993-94), Am. Venous Forum (sec. 1991-94, bd. dirs. found. 1992-95), Am. Coll. Healthcare Execs. (assoc.), 1996, Cosmos Club (admissions com. 1992-94, chair awards com. 1998, awards com. 2001, chair 2003—), Western Vascular Soc., Surgical Soc. Inst. Health Care Improvement(faculty 2006-), Prospectors Club Reno, Phi Beta Kappa, Alpha Omega Alpha. Episcopalian. Achievements include research in atherosclerotic plaque dynamics, observations on regression of atherosclerosis in animal models and in men with PAD; effect of cigarette smoking on patency of vascular grafts; definition of cellular and subcellular changes in shock; altered mitochondrial metabolism; diagnosis and treatment of vasculogenic erectile dysfunction; treatment of limb ulceration due to advanced chronic venous disease; role of iron storage, inflammatory cytokines and survival in atherosclerosis; surgical quality assurance and reduction of surgical complications; injury due to exlosions and blasts. Avocations: sailing, literature, writing. Office Phone: 202-433-5612. Personal E-mail: docdepalma@msn.com. Business E-Mail: ralph.depalma@va.gov.

DE PASCHALE, MASSIMO ENZO ALFREDO, microbiologist; b. Milan, Aug. 17, 1959; s. Pietro De Paschale and Rosalia Alabiso. Grad. in Biology with honors, State U. Milan, 1983, postgrad. in Hygiene with honors, 1990, postgrad. in Microbiology and Virology with honors, 1998; postgrad. in Clin. Pathology with honors, State U. Pavia, Italy, 1994. Cert. biologist Bd. Italian Biologists, 1985, in Chromatography Lombardy Region, 1985, in Clinical Chemistry Lab. 1987; U. d'Enseignement Européen de Transfusion Sanguine, U. Louis Pasteur, Strasbourg, France, 1995. Rschr. Virology Inst., State U. Milan, 1983—86; internat. coop. biologist Blood Transfusion Svc., Mogadishu, Somalia, 1987; biologist Clin. Chemistry and Microbiology Lab., Cassano d'Adda Hosp., Cassano d'Adda, Milan, 1988—89, Blood Transfusion Ctr., Legnano Hosp., Milan, 1989—2004; head Serology Lab. Microbiology Unit, Legnano Hosp., 2004—. Tchr. natural sci., chemistry and geography HS Alfieri, Magenta, Milan, 1986—88; tchr. periodic serological virology Legnano Hosp., 1990—; guest tchr. virology and immunology State U. Milan, 1991—92; tchr. seminars transfusion-related infections Bd. Italian Biologists, Milan, 1993—95. Author la trasfusione del sangue; contbr. articles to profl. jours. Expert biologist Regional Infection Diseases Monitoring A, 1985—86, Rozzano Milan. Lab. grant, Blood Transfusion Ctr. and Transplant Immunology, Policlinic Hosp., Milan, 1987—88. Mem.: Italian Soc. Med. Virology, Italian Assn. Clin. Microbiology (AMCLI), Italian Soc. Immunohematology and Blood Transfusion (SIMTI) (past mem.). Office: Microbiology Unit Legnano Hosp via Papa Giovanni Paolo II Legnano MI 20025 Italy Office Fax: 0039(0)331449578. Business E-Mail: massimo.depaschale@ao-legnano.it.

DE PAULA, AUREO LUDOVICO, surgeon, director; b. Goiania, Goias, Brazil, Mar. 22, 1962; MD, U. Goias, 1986; PhD, U. Sao Paulo, 1997. Dir. surgery Hosp. de Especialidades, 2000—. Office: Ave 136 n°961 14° andar Setor Marista Goiania Goias 74.093-250 Brazil Office Fax: 55.62.3241.7344. Business E-Mail: adepaula@uol.com.br.

DE PETRO, GIUSEPPINA, science educator, researcher; b. Piacenza, Italy, May 13, 1954; d. Giorgio De Petro and Carmela Vigilia; m. Roberto Ing. Volpini, Oct. 6, 1985; 1 child, Arianna Volpini. Degree in Biol. Sciences, U. Pavia, Italy, 1977. Rsch. fellow NRC (CNR), Pavia, 1977—79, U. Helsinki, Finland, 1980—82, U. Brescia, Italy, 1982—86, scientist, 1986—98, assoc. prof., 1998—2004, prof., 2004—. Mem. ctr. study & rsch. hereditary diseases EULO- U. Brescia, Italy, 1995—; mem. sci. & adv. bd. italian found. liver FISF Onlus, Firenze, 1996—; mem. bd. molecular biology tech., hepatic physiopathology Italian Assn. liver studies, AISF, Rome, 1998—2004; mem. integrated academic senatus U. Brescia, 1992—96, mem. rsch. coun., 2000—01, mem. doctorate sch. molecular genetics, med. sciences, 1998—, mem. dept. fund com., 2004—, mem. dept. biomedical sciences & biotechnology, 2004—; lab. incharge, rna interference & microrna, biomedical sciences & biotechnology dept. U. Brescia, Divsn. Biology & Genetics, 2003—. Mem. Nat. Red Cross, Piacenza, Italy, 1973—75. Mem.: European Cell Biology Assn., Italian Assn. Biology & Devel., ECBO, European Assn. Cancer Rsch., Italian Assn. Oncology, EACR, SIC, ABCD, Italian Assn. Biology & Genetics. Roman Cath. Office: Unive Brescia Viale Europa n11 25100 Brescia Brescia Italy Office Phone: 390303717 264 241. Business E-Mail: depetro@med.unibs.it.

DEPINHO, RONALD A., health facility administrator, research scientist, medical educator; s. Alvaro DePinho; m. Lynda Chin. MD, Albert Einstein Med. Coll., 1981. Feinberg scholar Albert Einstein Med. Coll.; prof. medicine (genetics) Harvard Med. Sch., Boston, 1998—2011, American Cancer Soc. rsch. prof.; mem. Dept. Adult Oncology Dana-Farber Cancer Inst., Boston, 1998—2011, dir. Belfer Inst. for Applied Cancer Sci.; pres. U. Tex. MD Anderson Cancer Ctr., 2011—. Co-founder, scientific adv. bd. AVEO Pharm. Inc., Cambridge, Mass.; bd. dirs. Am. Assn. Cancer Rsch. Bd. dirs. Am. Assn. Cancer Rsch., 2001. Recipient American Soc. Clin. Investigation award, 2000, Steven and Michele Kirsch Found. Investigator award, 2000, AACR-GHA Clowes award, 2003, Albert Szent-Gyrgyi Prize for Progress in Cancer Rsch., 2009. Mem.: Inst. Medicine. Office: University of Texas MD Anderson Cancer Center Office of President 1515 Holcombe Blvd Houston TX 77030 Office Phone: 713-792-2121. E-mail: rdepinho@mdanderson.org. *

DE PINIES, FELIX, retired physician; b. Madrid, Feb. 14, 1925; came to U.S., 1950; s. Vicente and Mercedes (Rubio) De P.; m. Carmen De Pinies, Sept. 1, 1955; children: Carmen, Carlos. MD, U. Madrid; postgrad., NYU, 1956. Resident in ear nose and throat N.Y. Eye and Ear Infirmary, NYC, 1951-55, surgeon, dir., 1960—2006, also chmn. med. bd., dir. H.O.L.A. program; clin. asst. attending physician St. Vincent Med. Ctr., NYC; assoc. clin. prof. N.Y. Med. Coll., Valhalla; ret., 2006. Office: 208 Ludlow Ave Spring Lake NJ 07762-1550 Home Phone: 732-449-4705. Business E-Mail: fdpr@optonline.net.

DEPONDT, JOËL PIERRE DENIS, surgeon, educator; b. Paris, May 8, 1956; s. Claude Depondt and Christiane Pieyre; m. Martine Gadet, Sept. 14, 1985; 1 child, Claire. MD, Unité d'Enseignement et de Recherche X Bichat, Paris, 1987; MPhil in Biology, U. Paris VII, 1992, PhD, 2000. Intern Assistance Publique-Hosp., Paris, 1980-87; asst. prof. Bichat Hosp., Paris, 1987-90, assoc. prof., 1990—. Legal expert Expert près la cour d'appel de Paris. Contbr. articles to profl. jours. Mem. French Soc. Head and Neck Plastic Surgery, French Soc. ENT-Head Neck Surgery, French Soc. Head Neck Oncology. Roman Catholic. Avocations: aviation, Judo, scuba diving. Home: 14 Rue de Thann 75017 Paris France Office: Bichat Hosp-Head/Neck Surg 46 Rue H Huchard 75018 Paris France Office Phone: 33-140257751. Personal E-mail: joel.depondt@wanadoo.fr. Business E-Mail: joel.depondt@bch.aphp.fr.

DEPUE, JUDITH DIANE, psychologist, educator; b. NY, Oct. 3, 1946; BA, Syracuse U., 1968; EdD, Boston U., 1977. Rsch. psychologist Meml. Hosp. RI, 1981—86; clin. prof. Miriam Hosp. & Alpert Med. Sch. at Brown U., 1987—. Recipient Tchg. Recognition award, Brown Med. Sch. Mem.: APHA, APA, Assn. Cognitive and Behavioral Therapies, Soc. Behavioral Medicine. Avocation: travel. Office: Miriam Hosp CBPM 1 Hoppin St Coro W Providence RI 02903 Office Fax: 1-401-793-8078. Business E-Mail: jdepue@lifespan.org.

DE QUADROS, CIRO A., epidemiologist, educator; MD, Cath. Sch. Medicine, Brazil; MPH, Nat. Sch. Pub. Health, Rio de Janeiro, 1968. Chief epidemiologist Smallpox Eradication Prog., WHO, Ethiopia, 1970; Expanded Prog. on Immunization Pan Am. Health Orgn., 1991, dir. Div. Vaccines and Immunization Washington; dir. Internat. Progs. Sabin Vaccine Inst. (SVI), Washington, 2003—, interim pres., CEO, 2006. Assoc. adj. prof. Johns Hopkins Sch. Hygiene and Pub. Health; assoc. prof. Sch. Medicine, Case Western Reserve U.; adj. prof. Dept. Tropical Medicine Sch. Medicine, George Washington U. Author:

Vaccines: Preventing Disease Protecting Health; presented papers in over 100 confs. Mem. bd. Internat. AIDS Vaccine Initiative; chmn. ind. rev. com. Global Alliance for Vaccines & Immunization; chmn. tech. adv. group on vaccines & immunizations Pan. Am. Health Orgn. Recipient Order of the Bifurcated Needle, WHO, Internat. Child Survival Award, UNICEF and the Carter Ctr., Prince Mahidol Award, Thailand, 1993, Order of Rio Branco, Govt. Brazil, 1999, Albert B. Sabin Gold Medal, 2000, Order of Pub. Health, Govt. Bolivia, 2003, Internat. Pub. Health Hero award, U. Calif., Berkeley. Mem.: AAAS, Inst. Medicine, NY Acad. Scis., Am. Soc. Tropical Medicine & Hygiene, Nat. Coun. Internat. Health, Am. Pub. Health Assn. Achievements include participating in the organization of the first national epidemiology center in Brazil. Office: Sabin Vaccine Institute STE 7100 2000 Pennsylvania Ave NW Washington DC 20006-1894

DER, DAVID F., family practice physician, retired general surgeon; married. MD, Howard Univ. Sr. ptnr., chief surgeon Bay Valley Med. Group, Hayward, Calif.; ret.; exec. dir. Chinese Am. Physicians' Soc.; currently family physician Alta Bates Summit Med. Ctr., Oakland, Calif. Asian Outreach Adv. Com. Alta Bates Summit Med. Ctr. Founder Asian Health Svcs., Oakland, 1974, Hong Fook Senior Health Care Ctr., Oakland, 1986. Recipient Benjamin Rush award for Citizenship and Comty. Svc., AMA, 2006. Mem.: Calif. Med. Assn. (bd. trustee 2006—08), Fedn. Chinese Am. and Chinese Canadian Med. Societies (sec.). Office: Prime Med Assocs Inc 817 Harrison St Oakland CA 94607 Office Phone: 510-451-8088. E-mail: daveder44@hotmail.com.

DEREKLIS, DIMITRIOS, ophthalmologist, educator; b. Greece, Apr. 11, 1944; Degree in Medicine, Aristotle U. Thessaloniki, Greece, 1974. Prof. ophthalmology, physician Aristotle U. Thessaloniki, 1981—2011. Home: 26 Patriarhou Ioakeim Thessaloniki 54635 Greece Home Fax: 2310207767. Personal E-mail: derec@tellas.gr.

DEREMEE, RICHARD ARTHUR, retired internist, educator, researcher; b. Red Wing, Minn., July 4, 1933; s. Arthur Eugene and Anna Helen (Vinquist) DeR.; m. E. Lucille Fogelstrom, Mar. 17, 1956; children: Lisa C., Brita L., Bo A. BA, Gustavus Adolphus Coll., 1955; BS, MD, U. Minn., 1959. Diplomate Am. Bd. Internal Medicine. Intern William Beaumont Gen. Hosp., El Paso, 1959-60; resident, fellow in internal medicine and pulmonary disease Mayo Clinic, Rochester, Minn., 1962—66, cons. in internal medicine and pulmonary disease, 1966—96; ret., 1996. Assoc. prof. medicine Mayo Med. Sch., Rochester, 1977-83, prof. medicine, 1983-96; Friedrich Wegener Meml. lectr. Lübeck, Germany, 1992. Author: (books) Time and the Mystery of Consciousness, 2003, The Mick-Rick Debates: Controversies in Contemporary Christianity, 2007, Mick-Rick Essays on the Sacred & Profane, 2007, From a Solitary Room, 2008; contbr. articles to profl. jours. Pres. South Woodly Civic Assn., Va., 1960-62. Capt. med. corp. US Army, 1959—62. Recipient cert. of achievement U.S. Army, 1962; Judson Daland travel award Mayo Found., 1966; Alumni citation Gustavus Adolphus Coll., 1982; named to Red Wing H.S. Wall of Honor, 2000. Mem.: Gustavus Adolphus Alumni Assn. (pres. 1979—80), Sigma Xi (pres. Mayo chpt. 1988—89). Republican. Lutheran. discovered the use of trimethoprim/sulfa as a new treatment for Wegener's granulomatosis. Home: 2209 5th Ave NE Rochester MN 55906-4017 Home Phone: 507-288-3745. Personal E-mail: radrst@aol.com.

DERINSU, UFUK EMINE, audiologist, educator; b. Adapazari, Sept. 20, 1958; Degree in Psychology, Hacettepe U., 1983; degree in Audiology, Marmara U., 1995. Asst. prof. Marmara U., 1997—. Home: Itirli sokak 4/13 Acibadem Istanbul Kadiköy 34718 Turkey Personal E-mail: uderinsu@yahoo.com.

DE RIVAS, CARMELA FODERARO, retired psychiatrist, health facility administrator; b. Cortale, Italy, Nov. 25, 1920; arrived in U.S., 1935, naturalized, 1942; d. Salvatore and Mary (Vaiti) Foderaro; m. Aureliano Rivas, Oct. 30, 1948; children: Carmen, Norma, Sandra, David. Student, U. Pa., 1940—42; MD, Women's Med. Coll. Pa., 1946. Diplomate Am. Bd. Psychiatry and Neurology. Intern women's health Med. Coll. Pa. Hosp., 1946—47; resident gen. medicine Chestnut Hill Hosp., Phila., 1947—48; gen. practice Tex., 1948—49; mem. staff Norristown State Hosp., Pa., 1949—63, supt., 1963—70, dir. family planning, 1979—87, clin. dir. spl. assignments, 1979—82. Psychiatrist Penn Found. Mental Health, Sellersville, Pa., 1970—72; dir. intake coping svcs. Ctrl. Montgomery Mental Health/ Mental Retardation Ctr., Norristown, 1972—77, med. dir., 1977—82, psychiatrist, 1980—82; cons. surveyor Health Care Fin. Adminstrn., 1987—2001; dir. program evaluation Norristown State Hosp., 1979—82, med. dir., 1982—87; assoc. psychiatry U. Pa., 1963—75. Named to Hall of Fame S. Phila. H.S., 1968; recipient citation Women's Med. Coll. Pa., 1968, Amita achievement award, 1976, achievement award Grad. Club Phila., 1976; named Woman of Yr. Pa. Fedn. Bus. and Profl. Women, 1979. Disting. life fellow Am. Psychiat. Assn., Pa. Psychiat. Soc. (rep. assembly of dist. brs. 1979-88); mem. AMA, Phila. Psychiat. Soc. (councilor), Montgomery County Med. Soc. (bd. dir., past pres.), Pa. Med. Soc. (chmn. adv. com. to aux. 1981-88, ho. of dels., commn. med. edn. 1991-94, com. continuing med. edn. 1994-98) Home: Dunwoody Village-Woodlea 107 3500 W Chester Pike Newtown Square PA 19073-4101

DER KALOUSTIAN, VAZKEN MOVSES, pediatrics and medical genetics educator; b. Musa Dagh, Turkey, Oct. 27, 1937; arrived in Can., 1986; s. Movses and Anahid (Khatchadourian) Der K.; m. Lena Sethian, June 21, 1970; children: Sarine, Daria. BSc, Am. U. Beirut, Lebanon, 1959, MD, 1963; MSc, Johns Hopkins U., 1968. Diplomate Am. Bd. Pediats., Am. Bd. Med. Genetics, Can. Coll. Med. Geneticists. Asst. prof. pediatrics Am. U. Beirut, 1970-75, assoc. prof. pediatrics, 1975-76, 78-81, prof., 1981-86; prof. pediat. and human genetics McGill U., Montreal, 1988—2009, emeritus prof. pediat. & human genetics, 2009—. Cons. WHO, Geneva, Kuwait, Oman and Alexandria, Egypt. Author: Genetic Diseases of the Skin, 1979, The Kidney in Genetic Disease, 1986, Congenital Anomalies of the Ear, Nose and Throat, 1997; contbr. over 150 artcles to med. jours., contbr. chapters in book. Mem. ctrl. coun. Armenian Catholicosate, Antelias, Lebanon, 1983-86; pres. ctrl. exec. Hamazkayin Armenian Cultural Assn., Beirut, 1986-88. Mem. Am. Coll. Med. Genetics (founding), Can. Coll. Med. Geneticists, Alpha Omega Alpha. Business E-Mail: vazken.derkaloustian@mcgill.ca.

DERMKSIAN, GEORGE, cardiologist; b. NYC, Nov. 10, 1927; s. Yervant Edward and Mariam Dermksian; m. Tamara Manookian Dermksian, June 13, 1954; children: Gregory Edward, Jeffrey Vahe. AB, Columbia Coll., NYC, 1948; MA, Columbia U., 1950; MD, Cornell U., 1954. Diplomate Nat. Bd. Med. Examiners, Am. Bd. Internal Medicine. Intern St. Lukes Hosp. Ctr., NYC, 1954, resident in internal medicine, 1955, 1958—60; pvt. practice, 1960—2000; sr. attending physician and cardiologist emeritus St. Luke's/Roosevelt Hosp. Ctr., NYC, 2000—; clin. prof. medicine Coll. Physicians and Surgeons, Columbia U., NYC, 1994—, emeritus clin. prof. medicine, 2001—. Cons., flight surgeon, lectr. USAF Sch. Aviation Medicine, Randolph AFB, Tex., 1956—58; physician Union Theol. Sem., NYC, 1960—70, Collegiate Sch., NYC, 1962—92; med. staff St. Luke's/Roosevelt Hosp. Ctr., NYC, 1960—; faculty Columbia U. Coll. Physicians & Surgeons, NYC, 1960—. Contbr. articles to profl. jours. Mem. N.Y. State Senate Adv. Com. on Legis. Issues, 1985; vol. physician Airlift Project (Armenian Earthquake), 1988; bd. dirs. Am. Assn. to Aid Armenian Nat. Sanatarium in Lebanon, 1986—90, Armenian Am. Med. Philanthropic Fund, 1990—2005, Armenian Med. Fund, 2005—. Capt. USAF, 1956—58. Recipient Mosby Scholarship Book award for scholastic excellence, Cornell U. Med. Coll., 1954, Cert. of Merit for outstanding clin. and rsch. contbns., USAF Sch. Aviation Medicine; Alumni scholar, Boston U. Med. Sch., 1951—52. Fellow: ACP, Am. Heart Assn., N.Y. Acad. Medicine; mem.: Begg Honor Soc. (hon.), Alpha Omega Alpha (Disting. Alumnus award, St. Luke's Roosevelt Hosp. Ctr. 2009). Armenian Apostolic. Avocations: fishing, stamp collecting/philately, exercise. Home and Office: 1115 5th Ave New York NY 10128-0100 *

DERMODY, WILLIAM CHRISTIAN, biomedical consultant; s. William Frederick and Ann Drusilla Dermody; m. Lynne Heringer, Sept. 19, 1964; 1 child, Christina. BS, Calif. State Polytechnic U., 1964; MS, Utah State U., 1968, PhD, 1970; postdoc, Cornell U., 1970. Postdoctoral fellow Cornell U., Ithaca, NY, 1969-70; sr. rsch. physiologist Parke-Davis & Co., Ann Arbor, Mich., 1970-76; sect. head cancer markers Frederick (Md.) Cancer Rsch. Ctr., 1976-81; dir. biotech. Am. Dade, Miami, Fla., 1981-84; mktg. mgr. ICN Biomed./Miles Sci., Lyle, Ill., 1984-86; mgr. tech. resources Difco Labs., Ann Arbor, 1986-88; assoc. dir. sci. Am. Type Culture Collection, Rockville, Md., 1988-90; pres. Bio World Assoc., Gaithersburg, Md., 1990—. Adj. prof. U.Miami Cancer Ctr., 1982-84, Fla. Internat. U., Miami, 1982-84; proposal reviewer Advanced Tech. Program, NIST, Gaithersburg, 1995-2004, 2007; mem. steering com. Molecular Biology Ctr., Wayne State U., Detroit, 1987-88; pub. spokesperson to civic and sci. orgns. Pres. Homeowners Assn., North Potomac, Md., 1990-92; bd. dirs. Hyde Park Condominium Assn. Grantee NSF, 1967-70. Mem. Alpha Zeta. Avocations: antiques, photography. Home and Office: 405 Christopher Ave Apt 34 Gaithersburg MD 20879-3539 Office Phone: 301-947-6914.

DEROGATIS, LEONARD R., psychologist, educator; b. Wilmington, Del., Sept. 24, 1938; BA, U. Del., 1961; PhD, Cath. U., 1965. Assoc. prof. psychiatry Johns Hopkins U. Sch. Medicine, 1969—; dir. ctr. sexual medicine Sheppard Pratt Health Sys., 2006—. Grant, NIMH, NCI. Office: 6501 N Charles St Rm A302 Baltimore MD 21285 Office Fax: 410-938-4340. Business E-Mail: lderogatis@sheppardpratt.org.

DE ROSA, CHRISTOPHER THOMAS, biomedical researcher; b. Cin., June 18, 1949; s. Frank P. and Mary Lorean De Rosa; m. Yolan Susan De Rosa, Aug. 25, 1979; children: Brian, Erin, Phillip, Joel. BA, Ohio Weslyan U., 1971; MS Ecology, Miami U., Oxford, Ohio, 1974, PhD Biology, 1977. From instr. to asst. prof. biology U. Va., Charlottesville, 1976—80; sr. scientist U.S. EPA, Cin., 1980—82, br. chief, 1984—88, dir. Nat. Ctr. Environ. Assessment, 1988—91; asst. prof. botany and zoology U. Maine, Orono, 1982—84; dep. assoc. adminstr. sci. Ctr. Disease Control, Atlanta, 1991—92, dir. divsn. toxicology, 1991—2005, dir. divsn. toxicology and environ. medicine, 2005—. Tchr. St. Bernard's Parish Sch., Cin., 1986—88; mem. steering com. risk assessment WHO, Geneva, 1992—, cons., State Dept., NASA, Dept. Energy, Dept. Def., NATO, Pan Am. Health Orgn.; reader, contbr. Ednl. Testing Svc., Princeton, NJ, mem. test devel. com.; presenter in field; credentialed mem. Sr. Biomed. Rsch. Svc. Editor: Toxicology Letters, 1995; reviewer: Jour. Ambulatory Pediat., Quar. Rev. Biology, Oxford U. Press.; contbr. articles to profl. jours.; mem. editl. bd. Environ. Rsch., Environ. Health Perspectives, Toxicology and Indsl. Health, Environ. Rsch., Human and Ecological Risk Assessment. Mem. bd. edn. Hampden Sch. Dist., Maine, 1982—84. Recipient Bronze medal, U.S. EPA, 1981, 1986, 1988, 1998, Publ. award, Ctr. Disease Control, 1998, Hammer award, U.S. V.P. Al Gore, 2000; grantee, Am. Philos. Soc., 1977, Exxon Found., 1983, U.S. EPA, 1989, NSF, 1975, 1978; fellow, 1975; Faculty Rsch. grantee, U. Maine, 1982, Faculty Equipment grantee, 1983. Fellow: Collegium Ramazzini; mem.: AAAS, Soc. Occupl. and Environ. Health, N.Y. Acad. Scis., Animal Behavior Soc., Rsch. Soc. N.Am., Soc. Integrative and Comparative Biology, Ecol. Soc. Am., Soc. Risk Analysis, Am. Coll. Toxicology, Sigma Xi (grantee 1975). Avocations: landscape design, fly fishing, natural history. Office: CDC F32 Divsn Toxicology and Environ Medicine 1600 Clifton Rd Atlanta GA 30333 Home: 5305 Burdock Creek Acworth GA 30101

DEROSE, JOSEPH JOHN, thoracic surgeon, educator; BS in Biology summa cum laude, Georgetown U., 1989; MD, Columbia U., 1993. Diplomate Am. Bd. Medical Specialties, Am. Bd. Surgery, 2000, Am. Bd. Thoracic Surgery, 2002, registered NY, 1996. Intern NY Presbyn. Hosp./Columbia Univ. Med. Ctr., 1993—99, resident in gen. surgery, 1993—99, chief resident in gen. surgery, 1998—99, fellow in cardiothoracic surgery, 1999—2001, postgrad. fellow in robotic cardiothoracic surgery, 2001—02; asst. prof. clin. surgery Coll. of Physicians and Surgeons Columbia Univ., 2001—06; attending cardiothoracic surgeon St. Luke's-Roosevelt Hosp. Ctr., NY, 2001—06, robotics dir. cardiothoracic surgery, 2001—06, asst. chief cardiothoracic surgery, 2003—06; assoc. prof. cardiovascular and thoracic surgery Albert Einstein Coll. of Medicine Yeshiva Univ., 2006—; dir. minimally invasive and robotic cardiac surgery Montefiore Med. Ctr., 2006—, chief adult cardiac surgery Weiler divsn., 2008—. Co-author: Lung reduction surgery and resection of pulmonary nodules in patients with severe emphysema, Current perspectives on sudden death in hypertrophic cardiomyopathy. Progress in Cardiovascular Diseases, 1994, Implantable left ventricular assist devices: An evolving long-term cardiac replacement strategy, 1997, Mechanical unloading with a miniature axial flow pump as an alternative to cardiopulmonary bypass, 1997, Retinoic acid suppresses intimal hyperplasia and inhibits vessel remodeling following arterial injury, 1999, various others. Recipient Allen O. Whipple award for Excellence in Surgery, 1993, Blakemore Rsch. award, 1997, Blakemore Rsch. prize, 1999, Sr. Resident Tchr. of the Yr., 1999; named one of Best Doctors in America, 2005—07, Top US Surgeons, 2006—07, numerous others. Fellow: ACS; mem.: Soc. of Thoracic Surgeons. Address: Montefiore Medical Center Weiler Division 1575 Blondell Ave Bronx NY 10461 Office Phone: 718-405-8371. Office Fax: 718-405-8253. Business E-Mail: jderose@montefiore.org.

DEROSE, KATHRYN PITKIN, medical researcher, minister; d. Roy MacBeth and Marcia Jenkins Pitkin; m. Stephen Francis Derose, Apr. 10, 1999; children: Nathanael Pitkin, Leander Pitkin. BA, Duke U., 1985; MPH, UCLA, 1992, PhD, 2003. Program officer MAP Internat., Quito, Ecuador, 1986—90; project coord. Harbor UCLA Rsch. and Edn. Inst., Torrance, Calif., 1992—94; project dir. RAND Corp., Santa Monica, Calif., 1994—99, soc. rsch. analyst, 1999—2003, assoc. social sci., 2003—05, social scientist, 2005—06, health policy rschr., 2006—, sr. policy rschr., 2009—. Cons. UCLA Ctr. Health Policy Rsch., 2001—02. Contbr. articles to profl. jours. Deacon Episc. Diocese of LA, 1998. Recipient PResdl. Early Career award Scientists & Engrs., 2005, Beverlee Myers award, UCLA Sch. Pub. Health, 2000-2001; Celia and Joseph Blann fellow, 2000-2001, Maternal and Child Health Econs. Tng. grantee, UCLA Child and Family Health Program, 1999-2000, Cmty. Health Promotion grantee, UCLA Cmty. Health Promotion Program, 1998-1999, Health Svcs. Rsch. predoc. trainee, Agy. Health Care Rsch. and Policy, 1996-1998, Learning fellow on Social Change, Inter-Am. Found., 1991, Unrestricted Grad. fellow, UCLA Sch. Pub. Health. Mem.: APHA, N.Am. Assn. for Diaconate, Acad. Health. Office: RAND Health 1776 Main St PO Box 2138 Santa Monica CA 90407-2138 Business E-Mail: derose@rand.org.

DE ROSE, SANDRA MICHELE, psychotherapist, supervisor, education administrator, coach; b. Beacon, NY; d. Michael Joseph Borrell and Mabel Adelaide Edic Sloane; m. James Joseph De Rose, June 28, 1964 (div. 1977); children: Stacey Marie, Harrison Marquisa. Diploma in Nursing, St. Luke's Hosp., 1964; BA in Child and Cmty. Psychology, Albertus Magnus Coll., 1983; MS in Counseling Psychology with Honors, Century U., 1986, PhD in Counseling Psychology with Honors, 1987. Cert. Am. Nurses Credentialing Com., 1975. Gen. duty float nurse St. Luke's Hosp., Newburgh, N.Y., 1964-65; supr. nurses Craig House Hosp., Beacon, NY, 1965—70; pvt. practice New Haven, 1975—; psychotherapist, inpatient unit Conn. Mental Health Ctr., Outpatient Unit, 1970—71; psychotherapist, out-patient unit Conn. Mental Health Ctr., Outpatient Treatment Svc., 1971—75, head nurse, outpatient unit, 1975—80, clin. instrn., outpatient divsn., 1980—86, dir. staff devel., team dir. unit, 1986—94; dir. edn. Conn. Mental Health Ctr., Outpatient Unit, 1994—95; clin. instr., sch. nursing Yale U., New Haven, 1979-84, clin. instr., dept. psychiatry, 1989-96. Clin. dir. Comprehensive Psychiat. Care, Norwich, Colchester and Willimantic, Conn., 1994-96; group practice Comprehensive Psychiat. Care, Norwich, Conn., 1995-2003, Alternative Paths, Yalesville, Conn., 1995-97. Mem. AAUW, ANA (cert.), Conn. Nurses Assn., Conn. Nurse Psychotherapists Assn., Western New Eng., Psychoanalytic Psychologists Soc., New Haven C. of C., Yale Sch. Nursing, Sigma Theta Tau, Delta Mu, Alpha Sigma Lambda. Avocations: music, antiques, writing, interior design/architecture, travel, anthropology, movies. Office: 129 Church St Ste 609 New Haven CT 06510 Office Phone: 203-787-5381. Office Fax: 203-624-0862.

DE ROSSI, GIULIO, physician; b. Bellano, Italy, July 7, 1944; Cert. Med. Diplomate 1968. Asst. in hematology U. Rome, 1971—80, prof. hematology, 1980—; chief hematology Bambino Gesu Childrens Hosp., Vatican City, 1994—. Contbr. articles over 250 articles to profl. jours. Mem.: European Hematology Assn., Am. Soc. Hematology, Italian Soc. Hematology. Office: Via Arno 62 198 Rome RM Italy Office Phone: 00393292064084. E-mail: giulio.derossi@alice.it.

DE RUITER, CORINE, clinical and forensic psychologist, researcher; b. Wisch, The Netherlands, Aug. 17, 1960; d. Peter de Ruiter and Betsy Alie Duitshof; m. Joseph Rogers Wiggins, May 27, 1992 (dec. July 2007); 1 child, Julian Alexander Isaäc Wiggins. MSc, Utrecht U., The Netherlands, 1986; PhD, U. Amsterdam, The Netherlands, 1989. Lic. clin. psychologist. Rsch. clin. psychologist Utrecht U., 1986-90; postdoc. fellow Leiden U., Netherlands, 1990-92; sr. rschr. U. Amsterdam, 1992-95; head dept. rsch. Dr. Henri van der Hoeven Clinic, Utrecht, 1995—; prof. forensic psychology U. Amsterdam, 1999—2004, Maastricht U., 2006—. Editl. bd. Dutch Jour. Psychotherapy, 1990—, Dutch Jour. Behavior Therapy, 1992-95; contbr. articles to profl. jours., book chpt. Mem. Soc. Personality Assessment, Am. Psychology and Law Soc., European Assn. for Psychology and Law, Internat. Assn. Forensic Mental Health Svcs. (pres. 2011-)., Internat. Assn. Forensic mental Health Svcs.(pres., 2011-) Avocations: jogging, reading. Office: Maastricht Univ Dept Clin Psychol Sci PO Box 616 6200 MD Maastricht Netherlands Office Phone: 31-43-3881905. Business E-Mail: corine.deruiter@maastrichtuniversity.nl.

DERUSSO, PATRICIA, gastroenterologist; b. Boston, Aug. 26, 1957; MS, Boston U., 1982; MD, George Wash. U., 1990. V.p. Pfizer Pharmaceuticals, 2006. Faculty divsn. pediatric gi & nutrition Johns Hopkins Sch. Medicine, 1996—2006. Mem.: Am. Acad. Pediat. Home: 86 E Princeton Rd Bala Cynwyd PA 19004 Personal E-mail: patricia.derusso@pfizer.com.

DERVAN, PETER BRENDAN, chemistry professor; b. Boston, July 28, 1945; s. Peter Brendan and Ellen (Comer) D.; m. Jackqueline K. Barton; children: Andrew, Elizabeth. BS in Chemistry, Boston Coll., 1967, DSc, 1997; PhD in Chemistry, Yale U., New Haven, Conn., 1972. NIH postdoctoral fellow Stanford University, 1973; asst. prof. chemistry Calif. Inst. Tech., Pasadena, 1973—79, assoc. prof. chemistry, 1979—82, prof. chemistry, 1982—88, Bren prof., chemistry, 1988, chmn. div. chemistry & chem. engring., 1994—99. Bd. trustees Yale U.; bd. dirs. Beckman Coulter Inc., 1997—. Mem. Nat. Acad. of Sciences, Am. Acad. of Arts and Sciences, Am. Philos. Soc., Inst. of Medicine; mem., sci. adv. bd. Robert A. Welch Found. Alfred P. Sloan Rsch. fellow, 1977; Camille and Henry Dreyfus Tchr.-Scholar, 1978; John Simon Guggenheim Meml. Fellow, 1983; Arthur C. Cope Scholar award, 1986; recipient Maison de la Chimie Found. prize, 1996, Max Tishler prize, 1999; named 2006 Nat. Medal Sci. Laureate, NSF, 2007. Office: Beckman Coulter Inc Bd Directors 250 S Kraemer Blvd Brea CA 92822 Office Phone: 714-993-5321, 714-773-8111. Business E-Mail: pdervan@beckmancoulter.com.

DERWINGER, KRISTOFFER JOHAN, surgeon, researcher; b. Stockholm, Mar. 11, 1969; s. Ted Derwinger and Elisabeth Ekman; life ptnr. Sophie Wallman; children: Ludwig, Jonathon. MD, Karolinska Inst., Stockholm, 1996, PhD in Surgery, 2009. Lic. dr. Swedish Nat. Bd. Health, 1998, specialist surgery Swedish Nat. Bd. Health, 2003, cert. European Bd. coloproctology, 2008. Internship Oskarshamns Sjukhus, Sweden, 1996—98; resident surgery Dept. Surgery, Linköping, Sweden, 1998—2003; colorectal surgeon Sahlgrenska U. Hosp., Östra, Gothenburg, Sweden, 2003—. Cons. sports medicine Fighter Ctr., Gothenburg, 2003—. Contbr. articles to profl. publs. 2nd lt. inf., 1989—91. Fellow: Swedish Surg. Soc.

DERYABIN, DMITRII GENNADIEVICH, microbiologist, educator; b. Orenburg, Russia, July 26, 1963; MD, Chelyabinsk Med. Acad., 1997. Sci. sec. Inst. Cellular and Intracellular Symbiosis Russian Acad. Scis., 1991—2000; head, microbiological dept. Orenburg State U., 2001—, prof., 2003—. Office: Prospect Pobedi 13 16209 Orenburg Ural 460018 Russia Office Fax: 7-3532-723701. E-mail: dgderyabin@yandex.ru.

DESAI, VEENA BALVANTRAI, obstetrician, gynecologist, educator; b. Karvan, Gujarat, India, Oct. 5, 1931; arrived in U.S., 1973; d. Balvantrai P. and Maniben (Vashl) Desai; m. Vinay D. Gandevia, Sept. 19, 1964. MBBS, Seth G.S. Med. Coll., Bombay, 1957, MD, 1961. Jr. resident Bombay U., 1957-59; house officer gyn. Chalmer's Hosp., Edinburgh, Scotland, 1962-63; registrar ob-gyn. Neath Gen. Hosp., England, 1963-64, Scunthorpe Gen. Hosp., England, 1964-66; chief resident ob-gyn. St. John Gen. Hosp., Canada, 1973-74; attending ob-gyn. Portsmouth Hosp., NH, 1975-84; assoc. prof. Boston U., 1985-86; sr. staff ob-gyn. Santa Clara Valley Med. Ctr., Calif., 1986-87; mem. staff ob-gyn. West Anaheim Med. Ctr., Calif., 1988-98, chief dept. ob-gyn., 1992-93, vice chief of gen. med. staff, 1994—95; ob/gyn Bay State Med. Ctr., Springfield, Mass., 1998—; chief ob-gyn. Mercy Med. Ctr., Springfield, 2002—03. Pres. Desai Med. Corp., Anaheim, 1989—; assoc. clin. prof. ob-gyn. U. Calif., Irvine, 1990—98. Chmn.'s advisor NSC; charter mem. Presdl. Task Froce; mem. Reps. Inner Cir., 1984—2003; bd. dirs. ARC Pioneer Valley Chpt., Springfield, Mass., 2007. Recipient Presdl. medal of Merit, 1982, award, Spl. Congl. Adv. Bd., 1984, Order of Liberty, US Congress, 1995, medal of Freedom, US Senate, 1994, medal, Ronald Wilson Reagan Eternal Flame of Freedom, 1996, Millennium medal of Freedom, Rep. Senate, 1999, Internat. Peace prize, United Cultural Conv., 2003, Congl. Order of Merit, 2004, Dame, Confedn. Chivalry, Sydney, 1989, Outstanding Achievement in Poetry award, Internat. Soc. Poets, 2005; named Pioneer of Healthcare Reform, Nat. Rep. Congl. Com., 2004, Merit for Life, Confedn. Chivalry, Sydney, 1989; named to Hall of Fame, Am. Biog. Inst., 2006—07; Paul Harris fellow, Buena Pk. Rotary Club, 1993—94. Fellow: ACOG, ACS, Royal Coll. Ob-Gyn. (chmn. Am. rep. com. 1997—2002), Western Mass. Ob-Gyn. Soc. (pres. 2002—), Internat. Coll. Surgeons; mem.: ARC, Clara Barton Soc., Rotary Club West Springfield (bd. dirs. 2008—, Distinguished Svc. Spirit award 2007—08), Rotary Club Springfield (bd. dirs. 2006—), Buena Park Rotary (chair internat. svc. 1992—93, pres., 1994). Avocations: international politics, travel, poetry. Home: 35 Sean Louis Cir West Springfield MA 01089-4347 Personal E-mail: veenadesai@comcast.net.

DE SALVA, SALVATORE JOSEPH, retired pharmacologist, toxicologist; b. NYC, Jan. 14, 1924; s. Nicola Carlo and Frances Agnes (Caldarella) De S.; m. Elaine Mae Radloff, June 14, 1948; children: Salaine Claire De Salva Bonanne, Christopher Joseph, Stephanie De Salva, Steven William, Gregory Vincent, Peter Nicholas, Philip Anthony, Deidre De Salva Berry. BS, Marquette U., 1947, MS, 1949; postgrad., U. Ill., Chgo., 1951-53; PhD, Stritch Sch. Medicine, Loyola U., Chgo., 1958. Research and teaching asst. Marquette U., Milw., 1947-49; research biochemist Milw. County Gen. Hosp., 1954, instr. U. Ill., Chgo., 1951-52; asst. prof. Chgo. Coll. Optometry, 1951-53; pharmacologist Armour Pharm. Lab., Chgo, 1953-59; sect. head Colgate Palmolive Co., Piscataway, NJ, 1959-66, sr. research assoc., 1966-72, mgr., 1972-76, assoc. dir. research for pharmacology and toxicology, 1976-83, dir. research pharmacology and toxicology, 1983-88, worldwide ops. dir., 1988-90, corp. dir. human and environ. safety worldwide, 1990-92; pres. Salva Cons. Svcs., Somerset, NJ, 1992-99; ret., 1999. Lectr. Loyola U., 1957-59; mem. technician tng. N.J. Council for Research and Devel., Rutgers U., 1969-72. Editor: Symposium for Biomedical Electronic Instrumentation, 1965; contbr. articles to profl. jours.; patentee in field; current work in pharmacotoxicology of flourides, sequestering agts. and surfactants, nitrosamine risk assessment, alternative safety testing method devel., safety of triclosan and use in dental therapeutic products. Mem. Park Forest (Ill.) Mosquito Abatement Program, 1952-55, Franklin Twp. (N.J.) Sch. Bd., 1969-70, Somerset (N.J.) Bd. Health, 1965-67, Cath. Youth Orgn., Somerset; v.p. Cedar Hill Swim Club, Somerset; active Boy Scouts Am., Somerset, 1965-67; trustee Franklin Twp. Day Care Ctr., 1969. Served with USN, 1942-46. Mem. AAAS, Soc. Exptl. Biology and Medicine, Am. Soc. Pharmacology and Exptl. Therapeutics, Soc. Toxicology, Internat. Union Pharmacology (toxicology sect.), N.Y. Acad. Scis., Internat. Soc. Regulatory Pharmacology and Toxicology, Internat. Soc. Study of Xenobiotics, Sigma Xi. Roman Catholic. Home: 83 Demott Ln Somerset NJ 08873-1604 Office Phone: 732-545-8785.

DESANCTIS, ROMAN WILLIAM, cardiologist, educator; b. Cambridge Springs, Pa., Oct. 30, 1930; s. Vincent and Margherita (Marini) DeSanctis; m. Ruth Ann Foley, May 7, 1955; children: Ellen Ruth, Lydia Marie, Andrea Jean, Marcia Louise. BS summa cum laude, U. Ariz., 1951, DSc (hon.), 1999; MD magna cum laude, Harvard U., 1955; DSc (hon.), Wilkes Coll., 1984, U. Ariz., 1998. Diplomate Am. Bd. Internal Medicine, Sub Bd. Cardiovasc. Diseases. Intern medicine Mass. Gen. Hosp., Boston, 1955—56, from asst. resident to sr. resident medicine, 1958—60, fellow cardiology, 1960—62; dir. CCU, 1967—80, dir. clin. cardiology, 1980—98, emeritus, 1998—, physician, 1970—. Mem. faculty Harvard U. Med. Sch., 1962—, Evelyn and James Jenks and Paul Dudley White prof. medicine, 1998—. Co-author: Cardiac Clinico-Pathological Conferences of the Massachusetts General Hospital, 1972, The Practice of Cardiology, 1989; contbr. articles to med. jours. Officer M.C. USNR, 1956—58. Decorated Order of Dynasty of Alouite Morocco; recipient Excellence in Clin. Tchg. award, Harvard U. Med. Sch., 1990, Centennial Achievement award, U. Ariz., 1989, Alumni Achievement award, 2001, Letterman's Lifetime Achievement award, 2010, Glorney-Raisbeck award, NY Acad. Medicine, 2003, Trustee's award, Mass. Gen. Physician's Orgn., 2006. Fellow: ACP (master coll. 1994), Am. Coll. Cardiology (Gifted Tchr. award 1991, Disting. Fellow award 1999); mem.: N.Y. Acad. Medicine (Glorney-Raisbeck award 2003), Am. Clin. Climatol. Soc., New Eng. Cardiovasc. Soc. (pres. 1979—80), Inst. Medicine, Assn. Am. Physicians, Am. Heart Assn. (David Littmann award 1996, Paul Dudley White award 1999, Master Clinician award 2003, Trustee's Gold medal 2006), Knights of Malta, Aesculapian Club, Winchester Country Club, Phi Gamma Delta (Disting. Fiji award 2008). Roman Catholic. Home: 5 Thoreau Cir Winchester MA 01890-3340 Office: Mass Gen Hosp Yawkey Bldg 55 Fruit St Ste 5700 Boston MA 02114 Home Phone: 781-729-1453; Office Phone: 617-726-2889.

DE SANTO, NATALE GASPARE, nephrologist, educator; b. Cosenza, Italy, Oct. 23, 1937; s. Salvatore De Santo and Rosina Reda; m. Amalia Virzo, Jan. 3, 1966; children: Rosa Maria, Luca Salvatore. MD, U. Naples, Italy, 1963; specialist in cardiology, U. Turin, Italy, 1966, specialist in internal medicine, 1974; specialist of nephrology, U. Naples, Italy, 1976; prof. in medicine (hon.), U. Slovak Republic, Kosice, 1999; prof. in nephrology (hon.), U. Varna, Bulgaria, 1999. Investigator U. Berlin, 1966—69; asst. prof. U. Naples, 1973—80, prof. pediat. nephrology, 1980—90, prof. nephrology, 1990—. Chief divsn. pediat. nephrology, 1984—90; chief divsn. adult and pediat. nephrology, 1990—; chmn. PhD Program Nephrology, 1990—2005, Postgrad. Sch. Nephrology, 1999—; chief Ctr. Clin. Rsch., 2003—. Co-editor: History of Nephrology (Karger) vols. 1-4, author 30 books; contbr. 500 articles to profl. jours. Recipient Taormina award, U. Messina, 1998, Arethusa medal, 2001, Nat. Kidney Found. award, U.S.A., 1996. Mem.: Slovack Soc. Nephrology, Romanian Soc. Nephrology, German Soc. Nephrology, Italian Soc. Pediat. Nephrology, Internat. Assn. Hist. Nephrology, Internat. Soc. Peritoneal Dialysis, Internat. Soc. Pediat. Nephrology. Home: Salita Scudillo 20 Naples 80131 Italy Office: 2d U Naples Via Sergio Pansini 5 80131 Naples NA Italy Office Fax: +39 081 566 66 55. Business E-Mail: nataleg.desanto@unina2.it.

DESARDA, MOHAN PHULCHAND, surgeon, consultant; b. Changatpuri, Maharashtra, India, Jan. 5, 1946; s. Phulchand Rupchand and Harakubai Phulchand Desarda; m. Mangla Mohan Desarda, Mar. 23, 1951; children: Mrunali, Mahavir. M.B.BS, B.J.Med. Coll., Pune, India., 1970; MS in Gen. Surgery, B.J. Med. Coll. and Sassoon Gen. Hosp., 1972. Lectr. in gen. surgery Bharati Vidyapith Med. Coll., Pune, Maharashtra, India, 1992—97, assoc. prof. surgery, 1997—; prof., head dept. surgery Poona Hosp. and Rsch. Ctr., Pune, 2001—10; prof. emeritus Galaxy Case Group Hosps., Pune, 2010—. Hon. cons. surgeon Kamala Nehru Gen. Hosp., Pune, Maharashtra, India, 1980—; cons. gen. surgeon Poona Hospital and Rsch. Ctr., Pune, 1985—; panel cons. Life Ins. Corp. of India, Pune, 1975—, Tata Engring. and Locomotive Co. Ltd., Pune, 1989—, Film and TV Inst. of India, Pune, 1985—, KSB Pumps Ltd., Pune, 1985—, Ruby Hall Nursing Home, Pune, 1975—84, Jahangir Nursing Home, Pune, 1975—84; cons. vis. surgeon Medinova Diagnostic Svcs. Ltd., Pune; bd. mem. Med. Sci. Monitor, 2001, Sci. Adv. Bd., 2001, SAACOR, 2002; vis. lectr. in hernia repair, Poland, 05; lectr. in field. Contbr. articles to profl. jours. Mng. trustee Dr.M.P.Desarda Charitable Trust and Rsch. Inst., Pune, 2001—; chmn., med. dir. Indian Hernia Inst., Pune, 2001—; chmn. Vasundhara Inst. for Edn. and Social Welfare, Pune, 1995—2000, pres., 2001—, Vasundhara Primary Sch., Pune, 2001—, New Little Angels Pre-Primary Sch., Pune, 2001—, Nalini Bal Sadan (Orphanage), Pune, 2001—. Recipient Spl. Cert. for 1st in university in 1st MBBS, U. of Pune, 1965, Spl. Cert. for 1st in university in Anatomy, 1965, Spl. Cert. for 1st in university in forensic medicine, 1968, The Shri Dutt prize (gold medal), 1965, The Dr.N.W.Joshi prize, 1965, Univ. 1st award, All India Student Fedn., 1966, Gold Medal for Distinction in Forensic Medicine, U. Pune, 1968, Best Student award, Rotary Club of Poona, 1968, 'Gaurav-Patra' for best family planning work, Mcpl. Corp. of Pune, 1973, Spl.l Silver Jubillee award, Silver Jubillee World Congress of Medicina Alternativa Holistic Health Spiritual Scis., 2002; named Dr. of Yr., Medi-Jain, Pune, 2002; scholar Nat. scholar, Govt. of India, 1963—68, The Dr.S.B.Gadgil scholar in anatomy, U. of Pune, 1965—68. Fellow: Internat. Coll. Angiology, Internat. Coll. of Surgeons; mem.: The Royal Soc. of Health, Pune Surg. Soc. (life), Assn. of Sugeons of India (life), Indian Med. Assn. Jain. Achievements include development of Desarda Repair technique of groin hernia operation providing a physiologically dynamic posterior wall for complete hernia cure, this operation now called as br Desasda technique followed in 53 centters all over the world in many countries. Avocation: Yoga (Spiritual Science) and Travel. Office: I Indian Hernia Inst c/o Dr Desarda 1273 Shiwajinagar Opp DG Post Office Maharashtra Pune 411004 India Home: Vishwa Laxmi Housing Society Kothrud Pune 411029 India Office Phone: +91 93 73322178. Personal E-mail: desarda@gmail.com. Business E-Mail: desarda@hotmail.com.

DE SAVORGNANI, ADRIANE ALDRICH, healthcare administrator, nurse; d. Merritt James Aldrich and Edith Carolyn (Borrebach); m. Luciano de Savorgnani, Aug. 1, 1979 (dec. Aug. 2002); children: Andrew, Alexia, Miranda. AB, Radcliffe Coll., 1962; diploma in nursing coord. program, Radcliffe Coll./Mass. Gen Hosp, 1965; MPH, U. Hawaii, 1974; DBA, Nova U., 1992. RN Hawaii, cert. nursing adminstrn. advanced., Am. Nurses Credentialing Ctr., Silver Spring, Md. Clin. nurse Dept. Public Health, Washington, 1966-67; staff nurse pediat., obstetrics, nursery, med.-surg. US Naval Hosp., Naples, Italy, 1967-69; pub. health nurse Dept. Human Resources, Washington, 1969-72; staff nurse, ob-gyn., nursery, recovery rm. Kapiolani Hosp., Honolulu, 1972-75; rsch. nurse U. Hawaii Newborn Psychology Rsch. Lab, Honolulu, 1974-75; staff nurse, med. and gynecol. oncology Naval Regional Med. Ctr., San Diego, 1975-78; staff nurse emergency rm. Naval Aerospace Reg. Med. Ctr., Pensacola, Fla., 1978-79; charge nurse, emergency rm. outpatient-inpatient care coord. US Naval Hosp., Naples, Italy, 1979-83; charge nurse military med. dept., utilization rev., discharge planning Naval Hosp., Newport, RI, 1983-86; head, Reg./Fleet Support, Naval Med. Command N.E. Region, Great Lakes, Ill., 1986-89; head health care plans spl. projects, head preventive med. health promotion br. Bur. Medicine and Surgery, Washington, 1989—92; exec. officer Naval Med. Clinic, Key West, Fla., 1993—. Asst. dir. nursing svcs. Naval Hosp., Jacksonville, Fla., 1992—95; exec. officer Naval Hosp., Lemoore, Calif., 1995—98; comdg. officer US Naval Med. Clinics, UK, 1998—2001; head clin. plans and mgmt., acting asst. dep. chief med. ops. support Bur. Medicine and Surgery, Washington, DC, 2001—03; adminstrv. asst. to Def. Attaché Office Am. Embassy, London, 2003—. Contbr. articles to profl. jours. Lector, lay eucharistic minister, choir accompanist; vol. local sch.; vol. tchr. ESL; vol. women's homeless shelter. Capt., Nurse Corps, US Navy, 1975-2003. Decorated Legion of Merit, Meritorious Svc. medal (5), Navy and Marine Corps Commendation medal (2), Nat. Def. medal one star, Global War on Terrorism Svc. medal, Navy and Marine Corps Overseas Svc. Ribbon (7 stars); recipient Clara Barton award, ARC, Naples, 1983, Cert. of Appreciation award, Operation Desert Storm, Wash., 1991, Jane A. Delano award, ARC London, 2001, Dir.'s award, Human Resources Svc. Ctr., Europe, 2001, Incentive award, 2007, 2009, 2010, Qualitative Step Increase award, 2008, 2010. Fellow Am. Coll. Healthcare Execs.; mem. ANA, APHA, Assn. Mil. Surgeons US (life), Acad. Mgmt., Internat. Tng. in Comm., ARC (instr.), Navy Nurse Corps. Assn., Sigma Theta Tau Internat. Phi Mu Chpt. (v.p. nurses), Coll. Alumnae Assns., Mensa (life), Sigma Theta Tau. Republican. Roman Catholic. Avocations: piano, theater, art, travel, exercise. Home: 14 Bardsley Ln London SE10 9RF England Office: US Defense Attache Am Embassy 24 Grosvenor Sq London W1A IAE England

DESBRÉE, AURÉLIE, research scientist; b. Montargis, France, Sept. 29, 1979; PhD, U. Paris, 2005. Rschr. nuc. medicine Inst. de Radio Protection et de Sûreté Nuclear, 2006—. Office: 31 Ave de la Divsn Leclerc Fontenay-aux-Roses 92260 France Business E-Mail: aurelie.desbree@irsn.fr.

DESCHAMPS-BRALY, JORDAN, plastic surgeon, educator; b. Norman, Okla., Apr. 8, 1979; BS in Biochemistry with Summa Cum Laude, U. Okla., 2001; MD, U. Okla. Coll. Medicine, 2005. Resident-plastic surgery & gen. surgery U. Okla. Dept. Surgery, Divsn. Plastic Surgery, 2005—10, clin. instr. plastic surgery, 2010—; craniofacial surgery fellow Children's Hosp. Wis., Med. Coll. Wis., 2010—. Organic chemistry tchg. asst., lab instr. U. Okla. Coll. Arts and Scis., 1999—2001; course instr. Princeton Rev., 2000—01. Rsch. grant, U. Okla. Honors Coll., Marchac fellowship, Dr. Daniel Marchac. Fellow: Am. Soc. Maxillofacial Surgery (resident mem.), Am. Soc. Craniofacial Surgeons; mem.: AMA, Aircraft Owners and Pilots Assn., Phi Beta Kappa. Avocations: aviation, piano. Office: 5030 N May Ave #321 Oklahoma City OK 73112 Business E-Mail: jdbraly@me.com.

DESCO, CARMEN, ophthalmologist, consultant; b. Valencia, Spain, Oct. 10, 1972; MD, U. Valencia, 1996, PhD, 1998. Cons. Ophthalmological Found. Mediterranean, 2005—. Home: Valle De La Ballestera 13-9 Valencia 46015 Spain Business E-Mail: carmen.desco@uv.es.

DE SERRES, FREDERICK JOSEPH, geneticist, toxicologist; b. Dobbs Ferry, NY, Sept. 24, 1929; s. Frederick J. and Helen Marie (Henshaw) de S.; m. Christine Marie Covone, Sept. 18, 1954; children: Mark, John, Paul, David, Jonathan, Lianne. BS in Biology, Tufts U., Medford, Mass., 1951; MS in Botany, Yale U., 1953, PhD, 1955; Doctorate (honoris causa), Cath. U. of Louvain, 1987. Research assoc. biology div. Oak Ridge Nat. Lab., 1955-57, sr. staff biologist, 1957-72; experimenters rep. NASA biosatellite program, 1964-68; coord. environ. mutagenesis program Oak Ridge Nat. Lab., 1969-72; lectr. U. Tenn., 1971-73; adj. prof. dept. pathology U. N.C., Chapel Hill, 1973-90; chief environ. mutagenesis br. Nat. Inst. Environ. Health Scis., Research Triangle Park, N.C., 1972-76, assoc. dir. genetics, 1976-86, guest rschr., 1994-98, rsch. dir. Ctr. for Life Scis. and Toxicology Rsch. Triangle Inst., Research Triangle Park, N.C., 1986-93, prin. sci., 1993-94; guest rschr. Nat. Toxicology program Nat. Inst. Environ. Health Scis., Research Triangle Park, N.C., 1994—; sr. cons. Tech. Planning & Mgmt. Corp., 1996—97, program mgr., 1998. U.S. coord. biol. and genetic consequences project U.S.-USSR Environ. Protection Agreement, 1972-78; chmn. panel mutagenesis and carcinogenesis U.S.-Japan Coop. Med. Sci. Program, 1972-87; chmn. subcom. environ. mutagenesis, com. to coordinate toxicology and related programs Dept. Health and Human Svcs., 1972-85; mem. com. on assessment nitrate accumulation in environ., divsn. biology and agr. NAS/Nat. Rsch. Coun., 1970-72; mem. com. chem. toxicity and aging, commn. on life scis. Nat. Rsch. Coun., 1986-87; cons. in govt., chmn. workshops on environ. pollutants and mutagenesis, 1961-86; vis. prof. U. Zagazig, Egypt, Ain-Shams U., Cairo, 1982, Case We. Res. U., 1983. Mem. editl. bd. Radiation Botany, 1965-74, Mutation Rsch., 1969-72, Jour. Toxicology and Environ. Health, 1975-78, Carcinogenesis, 1979-85, editor Jour. Environ. and Exptl. Botany, 1975-77, Mutation Rsch., 1973-98; sect. editor: Jour. Environ. Pathology and Toxicology, 1979, Jour. Toxicology and Indsl. Health, 1984-88; co-editor: Chemical Mutagens, Vol. 5, 1978, Vol. 6, 1980, Vol. 7, 1982, editor Vol. 8, 1983, vol. 9, 1985, vol. 10, 1986; cons. editor: Environmental Research, 1981-86; contbg. editor: Environmental Mutagenesis, 1979-81; contbr. over 500 articles to profl. jours. Recipient Dir.'s award NIH, 1976; Univ. Scholar Yale U., 1951-52, Wadsworth fellow, 1954-55; Nat. Cancer Inst. predoctoral fellow, 1952-54. Mem. AAAS, Genetic Soc. Am. (rep. to NRC 1970-73), Internat. Assn. Environ. Mutagen Socs. (v.p. 1985-89), Radiation Rsch. Soc., Am. Soc. Cancer Rsch., Environ. Mutagen Soc. (coun. 1969-72, v.p., 1972-73, pres. 1973-76, editor newsletter 1969-72, ann. award 1979, contbg. editor jour. 1979), Internat. Commn. Protection Against Environ. Mutagens and Carcinogensis (vice-chmn. 1976-84, commn. 1985-89), Environ. Mutagen Soc. (pres. 1991-93), European Environ. Mutagen Soc., Japanese Environ. Mutagen Soc., Alpha-1 Nat. Assn. (bd. dirs. 1998-2000), Alpha One Found. (med. and sci. adv. com. 1999-2002, bd. dirs. 1999-2004). Home: 632 Rock Creek Rd Chapel Hill NC 27514-6716 Office: NIEHS Ctr Evaluation Risks Human Reprodn MSC-K204 Research Triangle Park NC 27709-2233 Office Phone: 919-541-3455. Personal E-mail: deserres@bellsouth.net.

DESFORGES, JANE FAY, retired internist, hematologist, educator; b. Melrose, Mass., Dec. 18, 1921; d. Joseph Henry Desforges and Alice Maher Fay; m. Gerard Desforges, Sept. 11, 1948; children: Gerard Joseph, Jane Alice. BA cum laude (Durant scholar), Wellesley Coll., 1942; MD cum laude, Tufts U., 1945; ScD (hon.), Holy Cross Coll., 1990. Diplomate Am. Bd. Internal Medicine, Am. Bd. Hematology. Intern in pathology Mt. Auburn Hosp., Cambridge, Mass., 1945—46; intern in medicine Boston City Hosp., 1946—47, resident in medicine, then chief resident, 1948—50; USPHS rsch. fellow in hematology Salt Lake Gen. Hosp., Salt Lake City, 1946—47; rsch. fellow in hematology hosp. Thorndike Lab., 1950—52; physician-in-charge RH lab., 1952—53; faculty Tufts U. Med. Sch., 1952—72, prof. medicine, 1972—92, disting. prof., 1992—94, prof. emerita, 1994—; asst. dir. Tufts Med. Svc., Boston City Hosp., 1952—67; assoc. dir. Tufts Med. Svc., 1967—68, acting dir., physician in charge, 1968—73, dir., 1968—69; ret., 1999. Sr. physician in hematology New Eng. Med. Ctr. Hosp., Boston, 1973—, rsch. assoc. blood resch. lab, 1973—92; attending physician VA Hosp., Jamaica Plain; cons. in hematology to various area hosps., 1955—72. Assoc. editor New Eng. Jour. Medicine, 1960—93, mem. editl. bd. Blood, 1976—79; contbr. numerous articles to med. jours. Bd. dirs. Med. Found., Inc., 1976—82; bd. trustees Boston Med. Libr., 1977—81; chmn. automation in med. lab. scis. rev. com. Nat. Inst. Gen. Med. Scis., 1974—76; chmn. consensus com. of infectious disease testing for blood transfusions NIH, 1995—96; mem. subcom. on hematology Am. Bd. Internal Medicine, 1976—82, bd. dirs., 1980—88, exec. com., 1984—88; chmn. blood diseases and resources adv. com. Nat. Heart, Lung and Blood Inst., 1978—81. Recipient Disting. Alumna award, Wellesley Coll., 1981; named to Internat. Women in Medicine Hall of Fame, Am. Med. Women's Assn., 2003; grantee NIH, 1955—88. Fellow: AAAS; mem.: Inst. Medicine, Am. Assn. Physicians, N.Y. Acad. Scis., Mass. Med. Soc. (mem. publs. com. 1995—99, Lifetime Achievement award 2001), Internat. Soc. Hematology, Am. Soc. Hematology (exec. com. 1975—78, adv. bd. 1980—82, v.p. 1982—83, pres. 1984—85), Am. Soc. Clin. Pathology, Am. Fedn. Clin. Rsch., ACP (chmn. med. knowledge self assessment program IX 1989—92, Master 1983, Disting. Tchr. award 1987), Alpha Omega Alpha (Outstanding Tchr. award 1994), Phi Beta Kappa.

DESHAZO, RICHARD DENSON, medical educator, academic administrator; b. Birmingham, Ala., Apr. 4, 1945; s. Hyman Denson and Agnes L. (Carr) de S.; m. Gloria L. Jenkins, June 4, 1967; children: Melanie, Mollie, Matthew. BA in Chemistry, Religion, Birmingham So. Coll., 1967; MD, U. Ala., 1971. Diplomate Am. Bd. Internal Medicine, Am. Bd. Allergy and Immunology, Am. Bd. Rheumatology, Am. Bd. Geriatrics, Nat. Bd. Med. Examiners. Lt. col. U.S. Army Med. Corp., 1972-80; intern in pediat. Children's and Univ. Hosp., Birmingham, 1971-72; resident in internal medicine Walter Reed Army Med. Ctr., Washington, 1972-74, fellow in immunology, microbiology, 1974-75, fellow in clin. immunology, 1975-77; clin. asst. prof. medicine U. Colo. Sch. Med., Denver, 1977-78; asst. prof. medicine and pediatrics Uniformed Svcs. Univ. Health Scis., Bethesda, Md., 1978-80; assoc. prof. medicine and pediat. Tulane U. Sch. Medicine, New Orleans, 1980—89, prof. medicine and pediat., 1985-89, vice chair, clin. ops., 1986—89; prof., chmn. dept. medicine U. South Ala. Coll. Medicine, Mobile, 1989-97; prof. medicine and pediat., chmn. dept. medicine U. Miss. Med. Ctr., Jackson, 1997—2010, Billy Guyton disting. prof. medicine and pediat., 2004—; exec. prodr. health programming Miss. Pub. Broadcasting, 2010—. Clin. immunologist Fitzsimmons Army Med. Ctr., Denver, 1977-78; staff attending internal medicine, asst. chief, clin. immunologist, dir. lab. exptl. immunology, allergy, clin. immunology Svc. Walter Reed Army Med. Ctr., Washington, 1978-80; staff internist S.E. Cmty. Hosp., Washington, 1978-80; chief allergy and rheumatology dept. pediat. Tulane U. Sch. Med., New Orleans, 1980-89, adj. assoc. prof. microbiology, 1983-85, vice chair clin. ops. dept. medicine, 1985-89, dir. immunology program AIDS clin. trials unit, 1987-89; attending physician VA and U. Hosps., New Orleans, 1980-89, St. Jude Hosp., Kenner, La., 1987-89; mem. Nat. Sci. Adv. Com. on AIDS, NIH, 1987-91, study sect. on epidemiology of AIDS, 1987-91, AIDS clin. trials group, 1987-89, reviewers res., 1990-94; chief clin. immunology and allergy VA med. Ctr. New Orleans, 1985-89, assoc. chief staff edn., 1988-89; dir. tng. program internal medicine, v.p. health svcs. found., chief divsn. allergy depts. medicine and pediat., mem. various com. U. South Ala. Hosps. and Clinics, Mobile, 1989-97; chief clin. immunology, allergy and rheumatology dept. medicine VA Med. Ctr., Biloxi, Miss., 1989-97; mem. expert panel allergenic products FDA, 1991-96; asst. clin. coord. Health Care Financing Agy. coop. cardiovasc. project Ala. Quality Assurance Found, Birmingham, 1993-94, bd. dirs., 1994-95, fin. and planning com., 1995-96; pres. UMC Faculty Practice Plan, 2001-; guest prof. Children's Hosp. Kansas City, St. Louis U. Med. Sch., Walter Reed and Brooke Army Med. Ctr., Nat. Jewish Hosp., U. South Fla., U. Tex. Med. Br. at Galveston, Houston, Boston U., others; presenter in field. Assoc. editor, editl. bd. So. Med. Jour., 1995—, Am. J. Med., 2005-; mem. editl. bd. Jour. Allergy and Clin. Immunology, 1986-89, Postgrad. Medicine, 1986-94, Jour. Investigational Allergology and Clin. Immunology, 1987-93, Am. Jour. Med. Scis., 1989—, Annals of Allergy, 1991-96, Clin. Immunotherapeutics, 1993-99; host: (med. lit. project) Miss. Pub. Broadcasting-Weekly Statewide Audio Program, Southern Remedy, 2007-; contbr. 25 chpts. to books, over 175 articles to profl. jours. Elder Cumberland Presbyn. Ch., 1986-89; mem. adminstrv. bd. Christ United Meth. Ch., Mobile, 1990-97, chmn., 1993-96, chmn. coun. on ministries 1993-95; bd. dirs. Leadership Mobile, 1994-97; bd. stewards Galloway United Meth. Ch., 1999-2002, Mission MS, 1999-; bd. adv. Millsaps Coll. Sch. Bus., 1999-. Optimist Club scholar, 1963-67; Caduceus Club Travel fellow St. George Hosp. Med. Sch., London, 1970; grantee NIH, 1981-89, NIAID, 1985-88, Cancer Assn. New Orleans, 1982, 83, La. Lung Trust, 1982, 83, others; recipient Armed Forces Meritorious Svc. medal, 1980, Cert. Merit Cmty. Svc., City New Orleans, 1983. Fellow ACP (program com. 1993-95), Am. Coll. Rheumatology, Am. Coll. Chest Physicians, Am. Acad. Allergy, Asthma and Immunology (program and workshop com. 1985, chmn. 1986, grad. edn. com. 1988-89, allergy and immunology program dirs. assn. 1989-2005, standing com. fellowship programs 1990-97, standing com. immunology in med. schs. 1993, chmn. primer adv. com. 1992-93, co-chair com. on allergy in VA Med. Ctr. 1995-96, chair com. med. sch. 1994, Young Investigators award, 1979, Special Svc. award, 1993, 1996, 2006), Am. Coll. Allergy, Asthma, Immunology (editl. bd. 1995, Bernard Burman Lecturship 2002, Harold Nelson Leadership 2009), Am. Thoracic Soc. (program and workshop com. 1986-87, sec.-treas. 1987, nat. program com. 1988-90, vice-chmn. 1989, chmn. 1989, chair sect. immunology 1992), So. Med. Assn. (Morton Rsch. medal, 2004); mem. AMA (editor Primer on Allergy 1994), Am. Assn. Immunology, Clin. Immunology Soc. So. Med. Assn., Am. Assn. Med. Colls. (coun. acad. socs. 1994—, coun. academic specialists 1997-, adminstrv. specialist 2010-), Am. Fedn. Clin. Rsch. (coun. so. sect. 1984-87, 93), Assn. Profs. Medicine (bd. dirs. 1995—2004, nat. manpower com. 1994-96, pres. 2001, fin. com. 2009, diversity com. 2010), Am. Bd. Med. Specialists (coun. bd. reps. and adminstrn. 1996-99), 2 Carnival Orgns., Am. Bd. Internal Medicine (bd. dirs. 2000-04), So. Soc. Clin. Investigation (coun. 1998—, pres. 2001, adv. council 2001-, Founder's medal 2004), Am. Bd. Allergy-Immunology (bd. dirs. 1995-2004, sec., 2003); Am. Clin. and Climatol. Assn. Avocations: gardening, swimming, youth work, writing. Office: U Miss Med Ctr Dept Internal Medicine 2500 N State St Jackson MS 39216-4105 Office Phone: 601-815-3865. Business E-Mail: rdeshazo@umc.edu.

DESHMUKH, VIVEK R., neurosurgeon, medical educator; MD, U. Fla. Coll. Medicine, Gainesville, 1998. Diplomate Am. Bd. Neurol. Surgery. Intern gen. surgery Barrow Neurol. Inst., Phoenix, resident neurosurgery, 2003—05, fellow cerebrovascular/endovascular neurosurgery, 2005—06; asst. prof. neurosurgery George Washington U.; dir. endovascular/vascular neurosurgery George Washington U. Hosp. Contbr. articles to profl. jours., chapters to books. Mem.: Congress Neurol. Surgeons, Am. Assn. Neurol. Surgeons. Achievements include recognition as one of the few neurosurgeons in the Mid-Atlantic region who offer both direct surgical and minimally invasive endovascular treatment of cerebrovascular disorders. Office: GWU Hosp Dept Neurosurgery 2150 Pennsylvania Ave NW Washington DC 20037 Office Phone: 202-741-2750.

DESHPANDE, BIPIN BHASKAR, dermatologist, researcher, educator; b. Pune, Maharashtra, India, Nov. 4, 1962; s. Bhaskar Shripad and Sushanta Bhaskar Deshpande; m. Anjali Bipin Kirane, Jan. 27, 1993; 1 child, Ruchir Bipin. HSC, St. Vincent's Jr. Coll., Pune Cantonment, 1980; MBBS, Pune U., 1986, DVD in Dermatology and Venereology, 1988. Pvt. practice Chaitanya Clinic, Pune, Maharashtra, 1988—98; dermatology practical rschr. Chaitanya Clinic & DermaClass Clinic, 1996—; dermatologist DermaClass Clinic, Pune, 1998—; dermatologic surgeon, 1999—; hon. prof. dermatology Sancheti Coll. Physiotherapy, Pune, 1999—2001, Maharashtra Inst. Med. Edn. and Rsch., 2002—, med. tchr., rschr., 2002—; cons. cosmetic dermatologist Noble Hosp., 2008—. Dir. Ruby Health Care Pvt. Ltd., Pune, 1997—; spkr. in field. Contbr. articles to profl. jours., newspapers, 50 rsch. paper, 20 tchg. workshops, chapters to books. Active Dahanukar Colony Progress Com., Pune, 1994—95. Recipient Best Paper prize, Ann. Gen. Practitioners' Conf., 1994, 5th Biennial Conf. of Cutaneous Surgeons of India, 2002, Rashtriya Ratna award Outstanding Achievements & Selfless Svcs. to Nation, India Internat. Soc. Unity, 2002. Fellow: Am. Acad. Dermatology; mem.: Indian Assn. Dermatology, Venereology & Leprology (life), Cosmetology Soc. India (life), Indian Med. Assn. (life). Hindu. Achievements include first to introduce and establish Two New Therapies in Indian Dermatology viz. Photobiomodulation with 660nm Red Light & Radiofrequency Surgery; development of new applications of Red Phototherapy & Radiofrequency Surgery; patents for instrument for use in facial scar resurfacing technique with radiosurgery on face. Avocations: music, singing, photography, sports, collecting quotations. Office: Chaitanya Clinic 8th Ln Dahanukar Colony Kothrud Pune 411038 India Home: 474 H 3 Bldg Mhada 411 009 Pune India Office Phone: 0091-20-9823071379. Personal E-mail: rabipin@vsnl.com. E-mail: rabipin@eth.net, rabipin@vsnl.com.

DESILVEY, DENNIS LEE, cardiologist, educator, academic administrator; b. May 17, 1942; m. Kathleen Selkirk, Aug. 28, 1965; children: Ethan Selkirk, Caitlin O'Brian, Sarah Candace Shaw. BA in History and Religion magna cum laude, Yale U., 1964; MD, Columbia U., 1968. Lic. Vt., Va., Maine; cert. Advanced Trauma Life Support instr. Intern medicine Cornell Med. Ctr., NYC, 1968-69, resident medicine, 1969-71, resident medicine, cardiology, 1971; chief med. resident medicine North Shore U. Hosp., Manhasset, NY, 1972-73, instr. medicine, 1972-73; mem. staff Rancocas Valley Hosp., Willingboro, NJ, 1973-75; cardiologist Brachfeld Med. Assocs., Willingboro, NJ, 1974-75, Castleton (Vt.) Med. Assocs., 1975-77; attending physician Rutland Regional Med. Ctr., Rutland, Vt., 1975-92; pvt. practice Rutland, Vt., 1977-92; adj. asst. prof. clin. medicine Dartmouth Hitchcock Med. Ctr., Hanover, NH, 1979-92; asst. prof. medicine U. Vt., Burlington, 1983-92; mem. staff Dwight David Eisenhower Med. Ctr., Ft. Gordon, Ga., 1991; dir. ambulatory cardiology, dir. cardiology consult svc., mem. clin. faculty cardiovascular divsn., dept. medicine Health Scis. Ctr. U. Va., Charlottesville, 1992—2001, assoc. prof. medicine Health Scis. Ctr., 1992—. Cons. Southwestern Vt. Med. Ctr., Bennington, 1986—, Keller U.S. Army Hosp., West Point, NY, 1985—, internal medicine Veteran Affairs Med. Ctr., Salem, Va., 1993—, Consultants in Cardiology, Lexington, Va., 2001-05, Waldo CU Medicine, Belfast, Maine, 2005—; critical care com. Rutland Regional Med. Ctr., pharmacy and therapeutics com., investigational review bd., ethics com.; mem. pharmacy and therapeutics com. Health Scis. Ctr. U. Va., nutrition com., health care evaluation com., ambulatory policy com.; bd. dirs., profl. affairs com., bylaws com. Blue Cross/Blue Shield Vt.; bd. dirs., founding mem. Vt. Cardiac Network; presenter New Eng. regional meeting Am. Coll. Physicians, Hanover, N.H., 1976, Advanced Concepts Shock and Trauma, Woodstock (Vt.) Inn, 1982; dir. ACLS Tng. Ctr.; chmn. Resolution Com. Contbr. articles to profl. jours. Med. advisor skiing svcs. Killington Ski Area, 1975-92, Smokey House Found., 1975-80, Farm and Wilderness Camps, 1975-85; steering com. Vt. Med. Practice Variation Assessment Program, 1988; cardiology study sect. Vt. Program Quality Care, 1988-92, Vt. Gov.'s Coun. Phys. Fitness, 1985-88; vestry Trinity Episcopal Ch., 1986-89; bd. dirs. Vermont Diabetes Assn., 1975-79, Rutland Mental Health Svc., 1975-82, Rutland Area Vis. Nurses Assn., 1975-77, chmn. profl. affairs com., mem. utilization review com.; bd. dirs. Barstow Sch., 1986-90; town health officer Wallingford, Vt., 1975-80. Maj. U.S. Army, 1973-75; col. USAR, 1985—. Decorated Nat. Def. Svc. medal, Reserve Achievement medal, Army Commendation medal; recipient Physician Recognition award Am. Med. Assn., Exceptional Svc. award, Spiritual Aims award Kiwanis Club Am., 1983, U. Va. Pres.'s Report award, 1992. Fellow Am. Coll. Physicians, Am. Coll. Cardiology, N.Am. Soc. Pacing and Electrophysiology; mem. Am. Heart Assn. (ACLS instr., BCLS instr., nat. faculty ACLS Vt., mem. mil. tng. network ACLS, Advanced Trauma Life Support; bd. dirs. 1978-80, bd. dirs., at large appointee 1988-93, agenda planning com. 1986-89, affiliate relations com. 1986-88, sci. pub. com. 1989-93, "heart and stroke" planning com. 1989-90, participant edn. and inf. group heart guide consumer health and info. program, 1989-91, chmn. task force mission to elderly 1989-90; v.p.-elect New Eng. region 1986-87, regional v.p. 1987-88, fellow coun. clin. cardiology, bd. dirs. Charlottesville divsn. 1992—, bd. dirs. Va. affiliate 1992—, bd. dirs. Rutland, Vt. divsn. 1986-92, program coun. 1986-92, bd. dirs. Vt. affiliate 1975-92, exec. com. 1978-92, pres.-elect 1982-83, pres. 1983-85, co-chair capital campaign 1988-90, nominating com. 1984-86, cardiac rehab. com. 1982-85, program coun. 1978-90, ACLS com. 1978-90, cardiac critical care com. 1978-82, hypertension com. 1975-82, chmn. emergency cardiac care com. region V 1976-80, bd. dirs. N.J. affiliate 1973-75, BCLS com. 1973-75, mem. greater N.Y. affiliate 1966-72, BCLS instr. 1968-72, del. N.E. regional heart com. 1985-91, reaffiliation com. 1987-89, nominating com. 1987-88, Pysician of Yr. award 1992), Am. Soc. Echocardiology, N.Y. Acad. Scis., Vt. Cardiac Network (vice chmn. 1982-86), Phi Beta Kappa. Avocations: bicycling, running, cross country skiing, hiking, mountain climbing, theology. Office Phone: 540-982-8204, 207-338-1838. E-mail: ddesilvey@wchi.com.

DESJARDINS, CLAUDE, physiologist, dean; b. Fall River, Mass., June 13, 1938; s. Armand Louis and Marguerite Jean (Mercier) D.; m. Jane Elizabeth Campbell, June 30, 1962; children: Douglas, Mark, Anne. BS, U. R.I., 1960; MS, Mich. State U., 1964, PhD, 1967. Asst. prof. dept. physiology Okla. State U., Stillwater, 1968-69, assoc. prof., 1969-72; assoc. prof. physiology U. Tex., Austin, 1970-75; prof. physiology Inst. Reproductive Biology, Patterson Labs., 1975-86, U. Va. Med. Sch., Charlottesville, 1987-96, dir. Ctr. Rsch. Reprodn., 1990-96; prof. physiology and biophysics, sr. assoc. dean Med. Coll., U. Ill., Chgo., 1996—, dean, dir. program for rsch. in acad. medicine and clin. scholar project, 2005—. Mem. Ctr. for Advanced Studies, 1986; cons. NIH, ASA, VA, FDA. Author: Cell and Molecular Biology of the Testis, 1993, Molecular Physiology of Testicular Cells, 1996; editor-in-chief Am. Jour. physiology: Endocrinology and Metabolism, 1991-95; editor-in-chief Jour. Andrology, 1989-91, Ency. of Reprodn., 1997-98; mem. editl. bd. Biology Reprodn., Endocrinology; contbr. articles to profl. jours.; patentee techs. for male contraception, mechanisms of peptide hormone transport in the microcirculation and ligand-dependent and ligand ind. action of steroid hormones in peripheral vasculature. Fellow The Jackson Lab., Bar Harbor, Maine, 1967, NIH Sr. fellow U. Va. Med. Sch., 1983-84, Danforth Found. fellow, 1960; Cornell U. fellow, 2004-05; C.F. Wilcox Found. scholar, 1958. Mem. Am. Physiol. Soc., Soc. Neurosci., Soc. Study Reprodn. (pres. 1982-83), Endocrine Soc., Am. Soc. Cell Biology, The Microcirculatory Soc. Office: U Ill at Chgo Coll Medicine M/C 955 820 S Wood St Chicago IL 60612-4325 Office Phone: 312-355-0916. Business E-Mail: clauded@uic.edu.

DESJARDINS, RAOUL, medical association administrator, financial consultant; b. Montreal, Quebec, Can., Oct. 8, 1933; came to U.S., 1962; s. Elso and Blanche (Lemieux) D.; m. Regina Turgeon, Oct. 10, 1961; children: Bryan-Claude, John Andrew. BA, U. Montreal, 1953, MD, 1958; MS, Baylor U., 1964, PhD, 1966; MBA, Rutgers U., 1990. Diplomate Am. Bd. Medicine. Chief intern, resident St. Joan of Arc Hosp., Montreal, 1958-59; med. dir. Candiac (Can.) Med. Clinic, 1953-62, Ortho Research Found., Raritan, NJ, 1966-72; pres. Raoul Desjardins Assocs. Inc., Mendham, NJ, 1972-83, Research Cons. Inc., Mendham, 1983—, APG Internat., Inc., 1991—. Med. dirs. Iroquois Class Co., Candiac, 1959-62; asst. prof. Hahnemann Hosp. and U., Phila., 1976-80; bd. govs. Internat. Medicines Exch. and Devel., Georgetown, Ga., 1986—; chmn. bd. advisors Fed. Inst. Health, 1991—; chmn. bd. govs. Grand Masters Found., 1989—. Prodr. video: The Apgram: A New Tool to Measure Cardiovascular Performance, 1995. Recipient physician's recognition award AMA, 1969. Fellow: N.Y. Acad. Medicine, Am. Coll. Clin. Pharmacology, The Royal Soc. Health, Am. Coll. Angiology; mem.: Petroleum Club Houston, Doctors Club, Met. Club (membership com. 1991—), Med. Execs. Club, Beta Gamma Omega, Sigma Xi. Roman Catholic. Avocations: safaris, history. Office: Fed Inst Health 35 Stonecroft Pl The Woodlands TX 77381-5226 Office Phone: 281-298-9205. E-mail: doctord@fih.ky.

DESKIN, WILLIAM C., healthcare educator; b. Des Moines, Sept. 9, 1947; s. Jack L. and Iris E. Deskin; m. Patricia L. Snyder, Feb. 2, 1970; children: William C. Jr., Catherine D. Deskin-Constantine. BS in Health Planning, U. of Minn., 1976; MS in Health Svcs. Adminstrn., U. of St. Francis, Joliet, Ill, 1989; Exec. MBA, U. of Iowa, 1992; PhD, Walden U., Mpls., 2001. Cert. FACHE. V.p. Ottumwa (Iowa) Regional Health Ctr., 1989—96; dir. quality mgmt., utilization and planning Bay Med. Ctr., Bay City, Mich., 1997—2001; educator Cen. Mich. U. Coll. of Extended Learning, Lansing, Mich., 1998—, Delta Coll., University Center, Mich., 1998—, Bay City, 1998—, Spring Arbor U., Flint, Mich., 2001—, Walden U., Kaplan U., Grad. Courses Bus., Healthcare, Mgmt. & Doctoral Studies. Sculptures in stone and hard wood, various. Long range planning YMCA, Bay City, 1998—2002. Sgt. USMC, 1966—70. Fellow: Am. Coll. of Healthcare Execs. (profl. exam. com. 2000—, rep. Health Leadership Alliance 2004—05, product planning com. 2004—); mem.: Nat. Coun. Quality Assurance (cert. profl. healthcare quality, cert. profl. in healthcare). Methodist. Avocations: racquetball, guitar, sculpting. Office: 4724 Tolley Creek Dr Winston Salem NC 27106 Personal E-mail: w_deskin@hotmail.com.

DESLOGE, ROSEMARY BYRNE, otolaryngologist, educator; b. Tallahassee, Fla., Feb. 25, 1962; d. Edward Augustine and Moira Dunne Desloge; m. John M. Wassem, July 8, 2005; 1 child, Moira Wassem. BS in Biology, U. Notre Dame, 1984; MD, U. Miami, 1989. Diplomate Am. Bd. Otolaryngology, Nat. Bd. Med. Examiners. Resident in gen. surgery U. SC, Columbia, 1989—91; resident in internal medicine NYU/Bellevue Hosps., NYC, 1992—93; ENT resident/fellow Manhattan Eye/Ear/Throat Hosp., NYC, 1993—98; laryngology fellow Harvard U., Boston, 1993—99; asst. prof. dept. otorhinolaryngology Weill Med. Coll., Cornell U., NYC, 1999—2005. Contbr. articles to profl. jours. Fellow: ACS; mem.: AMA, Am. Acad. Otolaryngology Head and Neck Surgery. Office: 969 Park Ave Ste 1C New York NY 10028 Office Phone: 212-717-2700. Business E-Mail: rdesloge@desloge.md.

DESMARTEAU, JOHN KENTON, personal care industry executive; b. Montreal, Can., July 18, 1949; MD, Queen's U., Kingston, Ont., Can., 1974. Regional dir., outpatient surgery Mid-Atlantic Permanente Med. Group PC, 2000—03, bd. dirs., 1998—2004, chmn., bus. & investment com., 2000—04; chmn., pres., CEO LAXOR Inc., 2006—10; pres., CEO Life-Prints Solutions LLC, 2010—. Keynote spkr., MDP XI Proton Bus. Sch., Indore, Ahmedabad, India; chmn., anesthesia dept. Loudoun Hosp. Ctr., Leesburg, Va., 1986—89, Kaiser Permanente Mid-Atlantic States, 1997—2003, Jefferson Meml. Hosp., Charles Town, W.Va., 1989—92; regional dir., HIPAA Kaiser Permanente Mid-Atlantic States, 2000—04. Scholarship, Province of Ont. Fellow: Am. Bd. Anesthesiology; mem.: NY Acad. Scis., Am. Soc. Composers Authors and Pubs., Am. Soc. Anesthesiologists, Am. Coll. Physician Execs. Avocations: music, travel, gardening. Home: 4651 Mass Ave NW Washington DC 20016-2361 Home Fax: 202-558-6742. Personal E-mail: john@jdesmarteau.com.

DESMOND-HELLMANN, SUSAN, academic administrator, oncologist; b. 1957; BS in Pre-Medicine, U. Nev., Reno, MD; MPH, U. Calif., Berkeley. Cert. American Bd. Internal Medicine, in med. oncology. Oncology residency U. Calif., San Francisco; assoc. dir. clin. cancer rsch. Bristol-Myers Squibb Pharm. Rsch. Inst., 1993—95; clin. scientist Genentech, Inc., San Francisco, 1995-96, sr. dir. clin. sci., v.p. med. affairs, 1996, chief med. officer, 1996—97, sr. v.p. devel., 1997—99, exec. v.p. devel. and product ops., 1999—2004, pres. product devel., 2004—09; chancellor U. Calif., San Francisco, 2009—, Arthur & Toni Rembe Rock disting. prof. Adj. assoc. prof. epidemiology and biostats U. Calif., San Francisco; vis. faculty Uganda Cancer Inst., 1991—93; bd. dirs. Biotechnology Industry

Orgn., 2001—09, Affymetrix Corp., 2004—09, The Procter & Gamble Co., 2010—, American Assn. Cancer Rsch., 2005—08; bd. trustees Calif. Acad. Scis., 2008—; mem. econ. adv. coun. Fed. Reserve Bank San Francisco, 2009—. Named Woman of Yr., Healthcare Businesswomen's Assn., 2006; named one of The 50 Most Powerful Women in Bus., Fortune mag., 2001, 2003, 2004, 2006, 2007, 2008, The 100 Most Powerful Women in World, Forbes mag., 2005, 2007, 2008, 50 Women to Watch, The Wall St. Jour., 2004, 2005, 2006, 50 Who Matter Now, CNNMoney.com Bus. 2.0, 2006; named to Biotech Hall of Fame, 2007. Mem.: American Acad. Arts & Scis., Inst. Medicine. Office: U Calif San Francisco Office of Chancellor 513 Parnassus Ave S 126 San Francisco CA 94143-0560 Office Phone: 415-476-4285. *

DESNICK, ROBERT JOHN, human geneticist; b. Mpls., July 12, 1943; s. Theodore David and Celia Janice (Marcus) D.; Julie E. Herzig, Oct. 23, 1988; 1 child, Jonathan Phillips. BA, U. Minn., 1965, PhD, 1970, MD, 1971; DSc (hon.), Mt. Sinai Sch. Medicine/NYU, 2004. Diplomate Am. Bd. Med. Examiners, Am. Acad. Pediat., Am. Bd. Med. Genetics (bd. dirs. 1990-93, treas. 1991-93). Rsch. assoc. U. Minn., 1970-72, intern and resident dept. pediat., 1972—73, asst. prof. lab. medicine and pathology, 1973-75; asst. prof. pediat. U. Minn. Dight Inst. Human Genetics, 1973-75, assoc. prof. pediat., 1975—77; assoc. prof. genetics and cell biology U. Minn. Coll. Biological Sci., 1975-77. Arthur J. and Nellie Z. Cohen prof. pediat. and genetics Mt. Sinai Sch. Medicine, NYC, 1977—2000, chief divsn. med. and molecular genetics, 1977—93, chair dept. human genetics (renamed genetics and genomic scis. 2007), 1993—2011, dean, genetics and genomics, 2009—11, dean genetic and genomic medicine, 2011—; med. adv. bd. Nat. Neurofibromatosis Found., 1978—81; dir. Mt. Sinai Ctr. Jewish Genetic Diseases, 1981—; program dir. Mt. Sinai Gen. Clin. Rsch. Ctr., 1990—99; attending physician pediat. Mt. Sinai Hosp., 1977—; physician-in-chief Dept. Med. Genetics and Genomics, Mt. Sinai Hosp., 2007—; cons. physician pediat. Beth Israel Med. Ctr., NYC, City Ctr. Hosp., Elmhurst, NY; med. adv. bd. Nat. Found. Jewish Genetic Diseases, 1981—2002; mem. NY Gov.'s Adv. Com. on Genetics, 1982—92; med. adv. bd. Mucolipidosis IV Found., 1984—2004; sci. adv. bd. Dysautonomia Found., 1990—2005, Nat. Niemann-Pick Found., 1992—2011; med. adv. bd. Internat. Incontinenta Pigmenti Found., 1993—; mem. mental retardation study sect. NIH, 1995—98; sci. adv. bd. Ara Parshegian Med. Rsch. Found., 1995—2002, Bachman-Strauss Dystonia & Parkinson Found., 1997—2005; chmn. organizing com. Internat. Congresses Inherited Metabolic Diseases, 1990—2006; mem. NCRR adv. coun. NIH, 2000—04; med. adv. bd. Am. Porphyria Found., 1984—; adj. prof. Tokyo Jikei U. Sch. Medicine, 2006—. Editor: Enzyme Therapy in Genetic Diseases, 1973, Molecular Genetic Modification of Eucaryotes, 1978, Enzyme Therapy in Genetic Diseases, 1980, Gaucher Disease: A Century of Delineation and Research, 1982, Animal Models of Inherited Metabolic Disorders, 1982, Assays of Heme Biosynthetic Enzymes, 1984, Recent Advances in Inborn Errors of Metabolism, 1987, Treatment of Genetic Diseases, 1991, Tay-Sachs Disease, 2001; mem. editl. bd. Enzyme, 1979—98, Am. Jour. Human Genetics, 1980—84, Pediatrics, 1991—96, Human Mutation, 1991—2007, Biochem. Medicine and Metabolic Biology, 1991—97, Jour. Clin. Investigation, 1992—97, Jour. Inherited Metabolic Disease, 1996—, Jour. Human Genetics, 1998—, Molecular Genetics and Metabolism, 1998—, Molecular Medicine, 2002—, Human Genome, 2003—, Pharmacogenetics, 2008—, Personalized Medicine, 2008—; contbr. articles to profl. jours. Pres. fifth Internat. Congress Inborn Errors Metabolism, 1990. Recipient Ross award Soc. Pediat. Rsch., 1972, C.J. Watson award U. Minn. Med. Sch., 1973, E. Mead Johnson award Am. Acad. Pediat., 1981, Outstanding Faculty award Mt. Sinai Sch. Medicine, 1991, NIH Merit award, 1992, J. Lester Gabrilove award med. rsch., 2003, Jacobi award Mt. Sinai Sch. Medicine Alumni Assn., 2003, E.H. Ahrens Jr. Disting. Rsch. award Assn. Patient-Oriented Rsch., 2004, Disting. Alumni award U. Minn. Med. Sch., 2004, Clin. Rsch. Excellence award Nat. Ctr. Clin. Rsch., NIH, 2005, Albion O. Bernstein award NY State Med. Soc., 2005, Disting. Svc. award, Assn. Am. Med. Colls, 2010; USPHS fellow, 1968-70; grantee NIH, 1975-. Fellow AAAS (sr.); mem. Nat. Acad. Scis. (mem. inst. medicine 2004), Am. Soc. Human Genetics, Genetics Soc. Am., Am. Acad. Pediat., Minn. Human Genetics League (dir. 1970-77), Soc. Complex Carbohydrates, Behavior Genetics Assn., Am. Fedn. Clin. Rsch., Am. Coll. Med. Genetics (founding fellow, chair hon. membership com. 1990-98, chair biochem. and molecular resource com. 1993-2002, chmn. accreditation com. 1998-2000), Am. Coll. Med. Genetics Found. (bd. dirs. 1998-08), Am. Soc. Biochem. and Molecular Biology, Am. Soc. Clin. Pharmacology and Therapeutics, Assn. Profs. Human/Med. Genetics (co-founder 1994, pres. 1996-98), Eastern Soc. Pediatric Rsch., Soc. Pediatric Rsch., Soc. Exptl. Biology and Medicine, Am. Soc. Exptl. Pathology, Ctrl. Soc. Clin. Rsch., Soc. Study Social Biology, Soc. Study Inborn Errors of Metabolism, NY Acad. Sci., European Soc. Human Genetics, Harvey Soc. (sec. 1984-89), Soc. Inherited Metabolic Diseases (bd. dirs. 1983-92, pres. 1989-91), Am. Pediatric Soc., Am. Soc. Microbiology, Assn. Am. Med. Colls. (adminstrv. bd., coun. acad. socs. 2001—05, chmn.-elect, 2004, chmn., 2005, coun. mem.Acad. Soc. AANC, chair ASPC Am. Med. Coll. exec. coun., chair-elect 2007-08, chair 2008-09, bd. dirs. 2008-09), Nat. Tay-Sachs and Allied Diseases Assn. (med. adv. bd. 1975—, chmn. 1990-92), Nat. MPS Soc. (med. adv. bd. 1987—), Am. Assn. Physicians, Am. Soc. Clinical. Investigation, Assn. Patient-Oriented Rsch. (founding mem. 1998—), Am. Soc. Gene Therapy, Japanese Soc. Inherited Diseases (hon.), Societá Italiana di Pediatrica (hon.), Sigma Xi, Inst. Medicine Nat. Acad. Svcs., 2004, Am. Bd. Med. Genetics (bd. dirs. 1990-95, treas. 1990-93), Am. Bd. Med. Specialist (del. 2007-). Office: Mt Sinai Sch Medicine Dept Genetics & Genomic Scis 5th Ave & 100th St New York NY 10029 Office Phone: 212-659-6700.

DE SOUZA, JOAO FABIO RAMOS, medical researcher; b. Rio de Janeiro, June 23, 1983; Degree in Pharmacy, U. Fed. Fluminense, 2006; degree in Toxicology, FIOCRUZ, 2007. Rsch. scientist, 2008—. Avocation: poetry. Home: Rua Gen Andrade Neves 275/1003 Niteroi Rio de Janeiro 24210-001 Brazil Personal E-mail: joaofabiodesouza@hotmail.com.

DE SOUZA, MARK STEPHEN, lab administrator; b. Port of Spain, Trinidad and Tobago, Mar. 20, 1958; BSc, U. Essex, 1980; PhD, Yale U., MPH, 1990. Internat. lab. dir. US Mil. HIV Rsch. Program, 2001—. Mem.: Am. Soc. Virology. Office: 315/6 Rajvithi Rd Bangkok 10400 Thailand Office Fax: 6626444824. Business E-Mail: desouzams@afrims.org.

DESPER, BEATRICE S., obstetrician, gynecologist; b. Mass. 1 adopted child. Student, Brandeis U., Waltham, Mass.; BS in Chemistry, U. Mass., Amherst; MD, Tufts U. Sch. Medicine, Boston, 1979. Diplomate Am. Bd. Obstetrics & Gynecology. Intern, resident obstetrics & gynecology St. Francis Hosp. & Med. Ctr., Hartford, Conn., 1979—83; pvt. practice obstetrician/gynecologist Mandeville, La. Mem.: Am. Med. Women's Assn. (pres. 2009—10). Office: Dr Beatrice S Desper 1120 N Causeway Blvd Ste 1 Mandeville LA 70471 Office Phone: 985-674-4434. Personal E-mail: bsdesper@yahoo.com. *

DESPOMMIER, DICKSON DONALD, microbiology educator, parasitologist; b. New Orleans, June 5, 1940; s. Roland Medd and Beverly (Wood) D.; children— Bruce, Bradley BS, Fairleigh Dickinson U., 1962; MS, Columbia U., 1964; PhD, U. Notre Dame, 1967. Postdoctoral fellow Rockefeller U., 1967-71; Asst. prof. pub. health Columbia U., NYC, 1971-75, assoc. prof., 1975-77, prof. pub. health and microbiology, 1982—. Cons. NIH, 1980-84, Gen. Food Corp., 1976, Cordis Corp., 1973-74, Bionetics Rsch. Inc., 1986-89, Eco-Chem, Inc., 1993; Theobald Smith lectr. 1993; pres. Apple Trees Prodns., LLC, NYC; dir. Vertical Farm Project; pres. Vertical Farm Tech., LLC. Author: Parasitic Diseases, 5th edit., 2005, Parasite Life Cycles, 1988, West Nile Story, 2001, The Vertical Farm: Feeding the World in the 21st Century, 2010. Bd. dirs., chmn. edn. com. Catskill Flyfishing Ctr. and Mus., 1994—, dir., 1994—. Named Tchr. of Yr. Columbia U., 1980, 81, 83, 84; recipient Career Devel. award Nat. Inst. A.I.D., 1971-75, Disting. Tchr. award Med. Coll. Ohio, 1980, Deans' Disting. Tchr. award Columbia U., 1989, Golden Apple Tchr. of Yr. award Am. Med. Students Assn., 2003. Mem. AAAS, Am. Soc. Parasitologists, Brodheads Forest and Stream Assn., Am. Soc. Tropical Medicine and Hygiene, Am. Soc. Microbiology, Am. Chem. Soc., Harvey Soc., N.Y. Soc. Tropical Medicine (pres. 1980), Internat. Commn. on Trichinellosis East Jersey, Trout Unltd. (bd. dirs. 1976-78), Salmagundi Club, Anglers Club NY, Sci Barge (adv. bd.). Business E-Mail: ddd1@columbia.edu.

DESPOSITO, FRANKLIN, clinical geneticist, educator; Grad., Finch U. Health Scis./Chgo. Med. Sch., 1957. Diplomate Am. Bd. Pediatrics, cert. pediatric hematology/oncology, clin. genetics, in Clin. Cytogenetics, in Molecular Genetics. Intership, residency tng. LI Jewish Hosp.; pediatric hematology fellowship Univ. Wis., Madison, Wis., 1963; with pediat. dept. Univ. of Medicine & Dentistry of NJ - NJ Med. Sch., 1971, dir. human genetics divsn., 1981, prof. pediat., 1989, acting chmn. pediat., interim chmn., 1992—2002; dir. Univ. Regional Newborn Screening Network, 2002; chmn. Am. Acad. of Pediatric's Com.; chair NJ Adv. Panel; advisor, com. mem. Health Resources and Svcs.Adminstrn. Region II; with Saint Barnabas Med. Ctr. Office: University of Medicine & Dentistry of NJ - NJ Medical School 185 South Orange Ave Newark NJ 07103 Office Phone: 973 972-3300

DESUTER, GAUTHIER R.R., ear, nose and throat surgeon; b. Brussels, Mar. 12, 1968; s. Roland Maximilien Desuter and Antonia Yvette Van Den Bossche; m. Angelica T. Chiarini, Aug. 12, 2000; children: Maximilien M., Leopold M. MD, U. Louvain, Brussels, 1994; MS, Harvard Sch. Pub. Health, 2007. Resident Cliniques U. Saint-Luc, Brussels, 1994—99, chef de clinique adjoint, 1999—, clin. adminstr., 2004—08. Risk mgmt. cons., Brussels, 2003—. Scholar, Fondation Saint-Luc, 2004—05, Eisenhower fellow, 2003. Home: Chaussée de Boitsfort 154a Brussels 1170 Belgium Office: Clin U Saint-Luc 10 av Hippocrate Brussels 1200 Belgium Office Fax: 322 764 8935; Home Fax: 322 764 8935.

DETELS, ROGER, epidemiologist, retired dean; b. Bklyn., Oct. 14, 1936; s. Martin P. and Mary J. (Crooker) D.; m. Mary M. Doud, Sept. 14, 1963; children: Martin, Edward. BA, Harvard U., 1958; MD, NYU, 1962; MS in Preventive Medicine, U. Wash., 1966. Diplomate Am. Bd. Preventive Medicine. Intern U. Calif. Gen. Hosp., San Francisco, 1962—63; resident U. Wash., Seattle, 1963—66; med. officer, epidemiologist Nat. Inst. Neurol. Diseases, Bethesda, Md., 1969—71; assoc. prof. epidemiology Sch. Pub. Health UCLA, 1971—73, prof. Sch. Pub. Health, 1973—, dean, 1980—85, head divsn. epidemiology Sch. Pub. Health, 1972—80, chair, dept. epidemiology, 2001—05, 2010—; Hsu-Li disting. lectr. epidemiology U. Iowa, 2008. Guest lectr. various univs., profl. confs. and med. orgns., 1969—; sci. adv. com. Am. Found AIDS Rsch.; dir. UCLA/Fogarty AIDS Internat. Tng. and Rsch. Program, 1988—, Tng. Program in Epidemiology of HIV/AIDS, 1995—2000; cons. Ministries of Health, Thailand, Myanmar, Philippines, 1989, Global Program on AIDS, 1995, Singapore, 1996, 2006, China, 2002-, WHO, 1999, U.S. AID, 1998, 99, 2000, 01, Cambodia, 1998, 99, 2000, 02, 03, 04, 05, 06, 07, UN Devel. Program, 2001, St. Thomas Med. Sch., London, 1993-94, Myanmar, 1997, UN Devel. Program, Myanmar, 2001, UNICEF, 2005; mem. Nat. Adv. Environ. Health Scis. Coun., 1990-94; com. to study transmission of HIV through blood products Inst. Medicine, 1994-95; external examiner Nat. U. Singapore, 1994, 2004. Editor: Oxford Textbook of Public Health, 1985, 2d edit. 1991, 3d edit., 1997, 4th edit., 2002, 5th edit., 2009; contbr. articles to profl. jours. Lt. comdr. M.C. USN, 1966-69. Grantee in field; recipient Sahametry award, Gov. Cambodia, 2007, Abraham Lilienfeld award, Am. Coll. Epidemiology, 2008, Disting. Tchg. award, UCLA Academic Senate Common Tchg., 2009 Fellow AAAS, Am. Coll. Preventive Medicine, Am. Coll. Epidemiology (coun. 1987-89), Faculty Pub. Health Medicine Royal Coll. Physicians of U.K. (hon.); mem. Am. Epidemiol. Soc., Soc. Epidemiologic Rsch. (pres. 1977-78), Assn. Tchrs. Preventive Medicine (chmn. essay com. 1969-75), APHA, Am. Assn. Cancer Edn. (membership com. 1978-85), Internat. Epidemiol. Assn. (exec. com. 1984-99, treas. 1984-90, pres. 1990-93), Assn. Schs. Pub. Health (sec.-treas. 1980-85), Sigma Xi, Delta Omega. Office: UCLA Dept Epidemiology Ctr for Health Scis Box 951772 Los Angeles CA 90095-1772 Office Fax: 310-206-6039. Business E-Mail: detels@ucla.edu.

DETER, RUSSELL LEE, II, obstetrical ultrasonographer; b. Dallas, Jan. 14, 1936; s. Russell Lee and Virginia (Peden) D.; m. Susan Tipery, Dec. 14, 1981. BS, Baylor U., Waco, Tex., 1958; MS, MD, Baylor U., Houston, 1963. Postdoctoral fellow Rockefeller U., NYC, 1964-66, U. Louvain, Belgium, 1966-67; asst. prof. anatomy Baylor Coll. Medicine, Houston, 1967-72, asst. prof. cell biology, 1973—, asst. prof. ob-gyn., 1975-80, dir. obstet. ultrasonography, 1977-95, assoc. prof. ob-gyn., 1981-84, prof., 1985—. Med. dir. outpatient ultrasound program Harris County Hosp. Dist., Houston, 1986-2005. Co-author: Quantitative Obstetrical Ultrasonography, 1986; editor-in-chief Jour. Clin. Ultrasound, 1982-96; contbr. articles to profl. jours., chpts. to books. Recipient rsch. grants Frankel Found., 1979-84, March of Dimes, 1979-83, 84-87, Joseph H. Holmes award Jour. Clin. Ultrasound, 1987. Mem. ACOG, Am. Inst. Ultrasound in Medicine (assoc.), Soc. Maternal-Fetal Medicine (assoc.), Internat. Soc. Ultrasound in Ob-Gyn. Home: 1721 Hawthorne St Houston TX 77098-1605 Office: Baylor Coll Medicine Dept Ob Gyn 1 Baylor Plz Houston TX 77030 Office Phone: 713-524-2877. Business E-Mail: russelld@bcm.tmc.edu.

DE-THÉ, GUY BLAUDIN, research scientist, educator; b. Marseille, France, May 5, 1930; s. François De-The and Madeleine (Du Verne) De-T.; children: Hughes, Beatrice, Catherine. MD, U. Marseille, 1954; PhD, U. Paris-Sorbonne, 1966. Rsch. assoc. Duke U., Durham, NC, 1961—63; vis. scientist Nat. Cancer Inst./NIH, Bethesda, Md., 1963—65; unit rsch. dir. Internat. Agency Rsch. on Cance (IARC)r-WHO, Lyon, France, 1967—78; rsch. dir. Nat. Ctr. Scientific Rsch. (CNRS) Univ. A. Carrel, Lyon, 1979—; prof., head epidemiology Inst. Pasteur, Paris, 1990—98, prof. emeritus, 1998—. Co-chair Inter Acad. Med. Panel. Author: Sur la Piste du Cancer, 1984, Modes de Vie et Cancer, 1988, others; contbr. articles to profl. jours.; author: Le Souple et le Dur CNRS Editions, 2009. Decorated comdr. Order of Merite (France); recipient numerous sci. awards. Mem.: Acad. Techs., Chinese Acad. Sci., NAS Inst. Medicine (US), French Acad. Sci., Nat. Acad. Medicine. Roman Catholic. Home: 14 Rue Le Regrattier 75004 Paris France Office: Inst Pasteur 28 Rue Dr Roux 75015 Paris France Home Phone: 33-1-43540122. E-mail: dethe@pasteur.fr.

DE THÉ, HUGUES, medical educator, researcher; b. Marseille, France, Jan. 18, 1959; MD, U. Paris V, 1989; PhD, U. Paris VI, 1990. Staff scientist INSERM, 1991—95; prof. U. Paris VII, 1995—. Pres. sci. coun. ARC-French Cancer Charity, 2003—06. Decorated Legion of Honor French Republic; recipient Griffuel award, ARC, Claude Bernard award, City of Paris, Mergier-Bourdeix award, French Acad. Sci.; Sr. grant, European Rsch. Coun. Mem.: European Molecular Biology Assn., French Acad. Sci. Avocations: gardening, painting. Home: 146 Rue De L'Université Paris 75007 France Business E-Mail: hugues.dethe@inserm.fr.

DETMER, DON EUGENE, health informatics, management and policy researcher; b. Winfield, Kans., Feb. 3, 1939; s. Lawrence Oscar and Esther Beulah (McCormick) Detmer; m. Mary Helen McFerson, Aug. 26, 1961; children: Mary Catherine, Emily Anne. Student, U. Kans., Lawrence, 1957—59, U. Durham, NC, 1959—60; MD, U. Kans., Kansas City, 1965; MA, U. Cambridge, Eng., 2002. Intern, then resident in surgery Johns Hopkins U., Balt., 1965—67; clin. assoc. surg. br. Nat. Heart Inst. NIH, Bethesda, Md., 1967—69; resident in surgery Duke U., Durham, NC, 1969—72; Global Cmty. Health fellow Dept. HEW, Inst. Medicine/NAS, Washington DC, 1972—73; prof. preventive medicine and surgery U. Wis., Madison, 1973—84; v.p. health scis., prof. surgery and med. info. U. Utah, Salt Lake City, 1984—88; univ. prof. health policy, prof. surgery and health evaluation scis. U. Va., Charlottesville, 1988—93, v.p., provost for health scis., 1988—96, sr. v.p., 1996—98, Louise Nurancy prof. health scis. policy, 1996—99, prof. emeritus, prof. med. edn., 1999—; Dennis Gillings prof. health mgmt. Cambridge U., 1999—2003; dir. Cambridge U. Health, 1999—2003; sr. assoc. judge bus. sch. Cambridge U., 2004—07; pres. and CEO Am. Med. Informatics Assn., Bethesda, Md., 2004—09, sr. advisor, 2009—. Mem. commn. on systemic interoperability US Dept. HHS, Washington DC, 2004—05, mem. Am. health info. cmty. workgroup confidentiality, privacy and security, 2006—08; bd. sci. counselors Nat. Ctr. Pub. Health Informatics, 2008—; chmn. bd. dirs. MedBiquitious, 2006—; vice chmn. China Med. Bd. NY, Inc., 2002—04; chmn. bd. healthcare svcs. Inst. Medicine, Washington DC, 1994—2000; chmn. nat. com. vital health stats. HHS, Washington DC, 1996—99; chmn. Blue Ridge Acad. Health Grp., 1997—, co-chmn., 2002—; regent Nat. Libr. Medicine, NIH, Bethesda, Md., 1987—91; trustee Nuffield Trust, 2000—06; bd. dirs., developer adminstrv. medicine U. Wis., Madison; membership com. chmn. sect. 12 Inst. Medicine, Washington DC, 2002—04, 2009—, chair Iom Membership com.; chair Nat. Libr. Medicine NIH, Bethesda, 1989—91; assoc. Nat. Acads., 2002; vis. prof. Chime U. Coll. London, 2005—; health IT steering com. Agy. Healthcare Rsch. and Quality Nat. Resource Ctr., Rockville, Md., 2005—; healthcare IT adv. panel Joint Commn. Accreditation Healthcare Orgns., Oakbrook, Ill., 2005—08; cons. in field; vice chmn. Friends of Nat. Libr. Medicine, Bethesda, Md., 2006—09; dir. Corp. Nat. Rsch. Initiative, 2008, IBM Healthcare & Life Scis. Adv. Coun., 2006—. Contbr. articles on nat. health info. sys., compartment syndromes, health svcs. rsch. and policy to profl. jours. Chmn. pub. svc. com. bd. dir. United Way, Salt Lake City, 1986—88, Charlottesville, 1992—97; active USPHS, 1967—69; pres. Peace Luth. Ch., 1996—99. Recipient Global Cmty. Health fellowship, HEW, 1972—73; fellow, Clare Hall, Cambridge U., 2000—05. Fellow: ACS (vice chmn. com. allied health pers. 1989—90, chmn. 1990—94, internat. health com. 1996—2002, informatics com. 2004—, web portal com. 2004—), AAAS; mem.: HHS (bd. mem. 2008—), NAS Inst. Medicine (chmn. Cecil awards com. 2004—06, Walsh McDermott medal 2009), Sci. Counselors Nat. Ctr. (bd. mem. 2008—), Coun. Med. Splty. Socs., Lake Bluff (treas. 2007—09), Royal Soc. Medicine, Soc. Med. Adminstrs. (treas. 1997—2000), Am. Hosp. Assn. (chmn. coun. hosp. med. staffs 1984—87), Assn. Acad. Health Ctrs. (bd. dir. 1996—98), Am. Med. Informatics Assn. (bd. dir. 1996—98, chair internat. com. 2004), Am. Acad. Physician Assts. (hon.), Clare Hall Cambridge U. (life), Alpha Omega Alpha. Methodist. Avocations: fly fishing, painting, horseback riding, crafts, reading. Home: 5245 Browns Gap Tpke Crozet VA 22932-1613 Office Phone: 434-823-1742. Business E-Mail: detmer@virginia.edu.

DE TOMMASI, ANTONIO ROSSANO, neurosurgeon, educator; b. Bari, Italy, July 6, 1947; s. Domenico De Tommasi and Addolorata Mattiace; m. Vittoria Sportelli, Jan. 9, 1999; children: Claudio, Anthony, Raffaella, Flavia. Degree in Medicine and Surgery, U. Bari, 1972; degree in Neurosurgery, U. Turin, 1977; degree in Oncology, U. Bari, 1986. Lic. neurosurgeon Italy, 1972. U. intern physician U. Bari, Italy, 1972—73, ministry bursar, 1973—81, rschr. neurosurgery, 1981—2001; assoc. prof. neurosurgery U. Foggia, Italy, 2001—. Cons. in field. Mem.: Internat. Biomed. Inst., Regional Paraplegic Assn., Nat. Paraplegic Assn. (pres. 1986—95), Congress Neurol. Surgeons (assoc.), Am. Assn. Neurosurgical Socs. (assoc.), European Assn. Neurosurgical Socs. (assoc.), Internat. Med. Soc. Paraplegia (assoc.), Italian Soc. Neurosurgeons (assoc.), Rotary (assoc.; pres. 2000—01, Recognition award 2001). Roman Catholic. Avocations: opera, music, golf, tennis, skiing. Home: Via Delle Azalee N 16

(Parchitello) Noicattaro Bari 70016 Italy Office: Universita' Degli Studi-Policlinico Piazza Giulio Cesare N 11 Bari 70124 Italy Office Fax: 0039-080-5592001; Home Fax: 0039-080-543-2305. Personal E-mail: detosport@libero.it. Business E-Mail: adetommasi@neurosurgery.uniba.it.

DE TRUCHIS, PIERRE, medical doctor; b. Boulogne, France, May 21, 1958; s. Gérard de Truchis and Marie-Thérèse d'Indy; m. Thuy-Anne Pham, Feb. 3, 1989; children: Tanguy Bret, Camille, Aurélien, Théophile. BSc, St. Croix de Neuilly, Neuilly, France, 1975; MD, U. Paris VII, Bichat, France, 1987. Med. practitioner Hosp. R. Poincaré, Garches, France, 1992—. Cca Hosp. Bichat-Claude Bernard, Paris, 1987—90; med. chief Svc. des Grandes Endémies, Franceville, Haut-Ogooué, Gabon, 1984—85. Mem.: RVH ValdeSeine, EACS, Internat. AIDS Soc., Entraide Santé 92 (v.p.). Home: 8 rue des Erables 78150 Rocquencourt France Office: Hopital R Poincaré 104 bd R Poincaré Ile de france Garches 92380 France Office Fax: 33-1-47107767. Business E-Mail: p.de-truchis@rpc.aphp.fr.

DETTWYLER, WILLIAM KARL, medical technologist; b. Silverton, Oreg., Mar. 24, 1933; s. Karl Henry and Lydia Mae (Stadeli) D.; m. Mary Jane Kaufman, May 7, 1960; children: Nancy, Brian, Kelvin, Judith, Marlin, Arden, Roseann, Mark, Karla, Melissa. AAS, Oreg. Inst. Tech., 1959. Registered med. technologist. Med. technologist Salem Meml. Hosp., Oreg., 1959—65; lab. dir. D.F. Taylor Med. Lab., Salem, 1965—75; sr. technologist Ctrl. Clin. Lab., Salem, 1975—79; lab. cons. Aetna Oreg. Med. Carrier, Portland, Oreg., 1981—83; procedure code analyst Wolfgang Assocs., Portland, 1986—88, Medicode, Salem, 1971—99; lab. and x-ray cons. State of Oreg., Salem, 1971—86; med. technologist West Salem Clinic, 1984—91; sr. coding analyst Health Sys. Concepts, Inc., Longwood, Fla., 1989—; pres. Codus Medicus, Inc., 1999—. Med. asst., instr. Cascade Vocat. Ctr., Salem, 1972-75; bd. dirs. Northwest Human Svcs., Salem, 1994—. Contbr. articles to profl. jours. Mem. adv. com. Sheriff's Adv. Commn., Salem, 1980-84, Marion County Traffic Safety, Salem, 1984-90; With U.S. Army Med., 1956-58. Recipient Disting. Achievement award Am. Med. Technologists, 1961, Charles E. Martin award Oreg. State Soc., 1988. Mem. Am. Med. Technologists, Oreg. State Soc. (pres. 1959-60), Am. Soc. Clin. Lab. Scientists, Am. Assn. Clin. Chemists, Med. Group Mgmt. Assn., Clin. Lab. Mgmt. Assn. Avocations: history, silviculture, genealogy, parasitology. Home and Office: 5555 Sunnyview Rd NE Salem OR 97305-3264 Home Phone: 503-399-9774; Office Phone: 503-399-9656, 503-871-5259. E-mail: wdettwcpt@aol.com.

DETURK, NANETTE, insurance company executive; B in Acctg., Ohio State U.; MBA in Fin., Pa. State U. CPA Pa. Joined Highmark Inc., 1993, mgr. fin. reporting Pa. Blue Shield, exec. v.p., chief adminstrv., treasurer, CFO, 2006—. Bd. dirs. Highmark Vision Companies, KHPWest, Mountain State BCBS, Highmark Sr. Resources, United Concordia Ins. Co. and Subsidiaries, HM Health Ins. Co., Gateway Health Plan. Vol. Highmark Caring Place; dir. Western Pa. chpt. Juvenile Diabetes Rsch. Found., chmn. corp. gala com. Office: Highmark Fifth Ave Place 120 Fifth Ave Pittsburgh PA 15222-3099 Office Phone: 412-544-7000. *

DEURA, SHIGEYUKI, anatomy educator, researcher; b. Yokohama, Japan, May 30, 1926; s. Toshichika and Umeko Deura; m. Nobuko Shimonishi, May 5, 1974; 1 child, Tomoyuki. MD, Keio U., 1949, PhD, 1956. Asst. dept. physiology Keio U. Sch. Medicine, Tokyo, 1950-53, Kobe (Japan) Med. Coll., 1953-55, lectr., 1955-57; asst. dept. anatomy Kyoto (Japan) U., 1957-63, lectr., 1963-64, asst. prof., 1964-71; prof. dept. anatomy Kawasaki Med. Coll., Kurashiki, Okayama, Japan, 1971-74; prof. Gifu (Japan) U. Sch. Medicine, 1974-90; prof. emeritus, 1990; prof. Fujita Health U. Sch. Medicine, Toyoake, Aichi, Japan, 1990-96; head rsch. staff, dir. sanitary inst. aged people Kawamura Hosp., Akutami, Japan, 1996—2007, vice head, 2007—; pres. Favor-Clinic, affiliated Kawamura Med. Soc. Outpatient Divsn., 2010—. Vis. prof. U. Santo Tomas, Manila, 1984—, Perpetual Help Coll. Medicine, Binãn, Laguna, The Philippines, 1994—. Author: Morphol. Biochem. Correlates of Neural Activity, 1964, Note of Anatomy of the Central Nervous System, 2003. Rsch. grantee NIH, 1965, Japanese Med. Assn., 1975, Kato Meml. Rsch. Fund, 1977, Recipient of Third Order of Merit by Japanese Govt., 2006. Mem. Japan Assn. Anatomists, Physiol. Soc. Japan, Japan Assn. Physiol. Scis., Internat. Brain Rsch. Orgn. Avocations: classical music, photography. Home: 15 Higashi Komazume-cho Gifu 500-8168 Japan Office: Kawamura Hosp Neurol Rsch 1-84 Dai-hannya Akutami Gifu 501-3144 Japan Office Phone: 058-241-3311, 058-244-1151.

DEUTSCH, ALEXANDRU, cardiologist, educator; b. Slobozia, Ialomita, Romania, Jan. 24, 1972; s. Tiberiu and Mihaela Deutsch; m. Crinuta Florentina Diaconu, Nov. 25, 1995; 1 child, Ana. Degree, U. Medicine and Pharmacy, Bucharest, Romania, 1996. Cert. cardiologist Ministery Health Romania, 2002, in accreditation cardiac pacing and electrophysiology Ministery Health Romania, 2004. Rezident cardiology Theodor Burghele Hosp., Bucharest, Romania, 1997—2002; asst. prof. U. Medicine and Pharmacy, Bucharest, 1999—; cardiologist Caritas Hosp., Bucharest, 2002. Mem.: Romanian Soc. Cardiology, European Hearth Rhythm Assn. (Electrophysiology fellowship 2007—). Orthodox. Office: Univ klinikum Mannheim Theodor-Kutzer-Ufer 1-3 Mannheim Baden-Wurtemberg 68167 Germany Personal E-mail: alexandru_deutsch@yahoo.com.

DEUTSCH, DANIEL J., dental educator; Grad., SUNY. Diplomate Am. Bd. Anesthesiology. Lectr.; host advanced dental edn.; fellow gen. anesthesia; dentist Washington Ctr. for Dentistry. Named Best Dentist, Washingtonian Mag. Mem.: ADA, DC Dental Soc., Am. Soc. of Dental Anesthesiology, The Acad. of Gen. Dentistry, Am. Acad. of Cosmetic Dentistry, Washington Study Club. Office: Washington Center for Dentistry 8th Fl 1430 K St NW Washington DC 20005 Office Phone: 202-223-6630.

DEUTSCH, MARSHALL E(MANUEL), medical products company executive, inventor; b. NYC, Aug. 17, 1921; s. David and Madeline Lea (Roth) D.; m. Judith Greene, June 27, 1947; children: Pamina Margret, Ethan Amadeus, Freeman Sarastro. BS, CCNY, 1941; PhD, NYU, 1951. Tech. dir. NEN-Picker Radiopharms., Boston, 1966-68, Picker-Hoechst Inc., Bedford, Mass., 1968-70, Mead Diagnostics, Inc., Bedford, 1970-72, CIS Radiopharms., Bedford, 1972-74, Thyroid Diagnostics Inc., Bedford, 1972-85; chmn. Marshall Diagnostics Inc., Bedford, 1985-87; tech. adv. J&S Med. Assocs., Framingham, Mass., 1989—2004, cons., 2004—. Bd. dirs., corp. sec., v.p. Health Svcs. Internat., Washington, 1983-96; contractor Joint Publs. Rsch. Svc., Arlington, Va., 1984-92. Inventor self-contained technetium generator, 1971, various radiopharm. products, 1973, various clin. chem. test kits, devices, 1953-96; contbr. articles to mags. Cons. AID, Zaire, 1979, UN Capital Devel. Fund, Benin, 1977. 1st lt. A.C., U.S. Army, 1942-45, ETO. Fellow AAAS (life); mem. Am. Assn. Clin. Chemistry (emeritus, chmn. pub. rels. com. 1962), Am. Chem. Soc. (sr., emeritus), Am. soc. Nutrition, Sci. Rsch. Soc. Am. Unitarian Universalist. Avocations: folk dancing, growing exotic mushrooms. Home: 41 Concord Rd Sudbury MA 01776-2328 Home Phone: 978-443-5837; Office Phone: 978-443-5837. E-mail: med41@aol.com.

DEUTSCH, MAURICE MAYER, healthcare educator, consultant, medical librarian; s. Armand and Rosalie Deutsch; m. Diane Perkins, June 15, 1971. BSc magna cum laude, Bklyn. Coll., 1966; MLS, Pratt Inst., 1967; MSc in Zoology, U. Toronto, 1970; grad., B.C. Conservation and Outdoor Recreation, 1976. Sr. libr., tchr., cons. Simon Fraser U. Libr., Burnaby, 1971—97, acting dir. distance edn. info. svc., 1990—95; weight-loss cons., lectr. Creative Weight Loss Techniques., Tucson, 2000—. Portrait photographer MD Studios, Burnaby, B.C., Canada, 1978—82; sci. info. resources cons., 1986—93; weight-loss cons., tchr. Oasis Inst., Tucson, 2002—05, Tucson Open U., 2003—05, Pima CC, 2004—05; cons. Take Off Pounds Sensibly, Tuscon, 2004; host TV show Lose Weight Forever Access Tucson, 2004—05; weight-loss cons., workshops U. Ariz. CampusLink Program, 2008—09. Author: Lose Weight Forever-Take It Off & Keep It Off! Success Strategies for Permanent Weight Loss, 2005—. Vol. Carnegie Cmty. Ctr. Kitchen, Vancouver, 1999—2000; weight-loss cons. El Pueblo Clinic Pima County Health Dept., Tucson, 2004—, Beta Sigma Phi, 2006—08; weight-loss cons., tchr. St. Philip's Episcopal Ch., 2003—05. Mem.: Tucson Macintosh Users Group, Beta Phi Mu, Phi Beta Kappa. Avocations: weightlifting, walking, music, gardening. Home and Office: Creative Weight Loss Techniques 2660 W Dante Way Tucson AZ 85741-2516 Business E-Mail: maurice@loseweightforever.us.

DEUTSCH, MELVIN, medical educator; b. Bklyn., Dec. 27, 1938; AB, Columbia Coll., 1960; MD, NYU Sch. Medicine, 1964. Prof. radiation oncology U. Pitts. Med. Ctr., 1971—. Decorated Bronze Star US Army, Medic Badge. Fellow: Am. Coll. Cardiology. Office: 5230 Centre Ave Pittsburgh PA 15232 Business E-Mail: deutschm@upiTic.edu.

DEUTSCH, PAUL M., psychologist; b. Bronx, NY, May 23, 1949; MS, U. Fla., 1972, PhD, 1983. Rehab. counselor, mental health counselor Paul M. Deutsch & Assocs. PA, 1972—, cons., catastrophic disability, 1972—2011. Contbr. articles to profl. jours. Recipient Life Time Achievement award, Internat. Symposium Life Care Planning & Co-Sponsoring U.; named Alumni of Yr., U. Fla. Coll. Pub. Health and Health Related Professions, 1987, 2007. Fellow: Internat. Assn. Life Care Planners; mem.: APA, Am. Mental Health Counselors Assn., Internat. Assn. Rehab. Profls. (Lifetime Achievement award), Am. Congress Rehab. Medicine. Avocations: horseback riding, ballroom dancing. Office: 10 Windsormere Way Ste 400 PO Box 6 Oviedo FL 32765 Office Fax: 407-977-0311. E-mail: pdeutsch@mac.com.

DEUTSCH, THOMAS ALAN, ophthalmologist, educator, dean; b. Nagoya, Japan, Aug. 11, 1954; (parents U.S. citizens); William E. and Natasha S. (Sobotka) D.; m. Judith Silverman, Dec. 6, 1986. AB, Washington U., 1975; MD, Rush Med. Coll., Chgo., 1979. Diplomate Am. Bd. Ophthalmology. Intern Presbyn.-St. Luke's Hosp., Chgo., 1979-80; resident U. Ill. Eye and Ear Infirmary, Chgo., 1980-83; asst. prof. ophthalmology U. Ill., Chgo., 1983-84, Rush Med. Coll., Chgo., 1984-87, assoc. prof., 1987-94, prof., 1994—, chmn. ophthalmology, 1996—2004, assoc. dean grad. med. edn., 2000—03, acting dean, 2002—03, dean, sr. v.p., 2003—, provost, 2004—. Lectr., U. Ill., Chgo., 1984-96; adj. asst. prof. biomed. engri., Northwestern U. Evanston, Ill., 1986-87, adj. assoc. prof., 1987-94, adj. prof., 1994-97. Assoc. editor Key Ophthalmology, 1986-88, Year Book Ophthalmology, 1986-88; author 6 books; contbr. articles to profl. jours. Recipient Chancellor's award Washington U., 1975, Henry Lyman award Rush Med. Coll, 1978, Mark Lepper tchg. award, 1994, Disting. Alumnus award Rush Med. Coll., 1998. Fellow: ACS, Am. Acad. Ophthalmology (sec. for instrn. 2001—02, sec. for new ophthalmic info. 2002—03, Honor award 1990, Sr. Honor award 2003); mem.: Rush Alumni Assn. (pres. 1990—93, James A. Campbell award 1990), Chgo. Ophthalmol. Soc. (chmn. clin. conf. 1986, councillor 1988—89, sec.-treas. 1989—91, pres. 1994—95), Assn. Rsch. Vision Ophthalmology. Office: Rush U Med Ctr 1725 W Harrison St Ste 918 Chicago IL 60612-3835 Office Phone: 312-942-5567. *

DEUTSCHMANN, HANNES ALEXANDER, radiologist; b. Graz, Austria, Nov. 10, 1970; MD, Med. U. Graz, 1997. Head, tchg. unit dept. radiology Med. U. Graz, 2009, vice head, divsn. neuroradiology dept. radiology, 2009, vice head, divsn. vascular and interventional radiology dept. radiology, 2009—. Fellow: Austrian Soc. Neuroradiology; mem.: Austrian Roentgen Soc. (Schering prize 2001), Austrian Soc. Interventional Radiology. Office: Auenbruggerplatz 9 Graz 8036 Austria Office Fax: 4331638513851. Business E-Mail: hannes.deutschmann@medunigraz.at.

DEVARIS, JEANNETTE MARY, psychologist; b. Burbank, Calif., Jan. 7, 1947; d. Nicholas Propper Klein and Elizabeth (Von Lichtenberg) Schaeffer; 1 child: Brendon. BA, Adelphi U., 1968; MA, Fairleigh Dickinson U., 1977; PhD, Seton Hall U., 1987. Lic. psychologist, N.J. Caseworker N.Y.C. Welfare Dept., 1968-72; alcohol and drug rehab. counselor U.S. Army, Ft. Monmouth, NJ, 1972-76; psychol. intern N.J. State Intern Program, Trenton, 1977-78; psychologist Greystone Psychiat. Hosp., Greystone Park, NJ, 1979; sr. psychologist R. Hall Cmty. Mental Health Ctr., Bridgewater, NJ, 1979-90; pvt. practice South Orange, NJ, 1988—2006, Summit, 2006—. Tng. supr. Grad. Sch. Applied and Profl. Psychology; adj. prof. Seton Hall U.; sponsor and participant in Cable TV program; mem. South Orange Critical Support Team Vol. Group of Psychologists; founder One Braine Integration. Contbr. articles to profl. jours. Mem. APA, Nat. Register Health Svc. Providers, N.J. Psychol. Assn. (bd. dirs., interprofl. rels. com.), Soc. Psychologists in Pvt. Practice (bd. dirs., spkrs. bur. com.). Achievements include founding of emotional Integration Psychotherapy Technique. Avocations: travel, reading. Office Phone: 908-522-0800. Personal E-mail: drdevaris@yahoo.com.

DEVARO, JOHN MICHAEL, ophthalmologist; b. Rochester, NY, Feb. 23, 1962; m. Josepha Bueno, Oct. 7, 1990. AB, Dartmouth Coll., 1984; MD, U. Pa., 1988. Diplomate Am. Bd. Ophthalmology, Nat. Bd. Med. Examiners. Intern Pa. Hosp., Phila., 1988-89; resident in ophthalmology U. Pitts., 1989—92, chief resident, 1991; gen. ophthalmologist Danville Eye Ctr., Va., 1992-94; fellow pediat. Ophth. & Strabismus Duke U. Eye Ctr., Durham, NC, 1994-95; assoc. in pediat. and neuro-ophthalmology Nevyas Eye Associates, Bala Cynwyd, Pa., 1995—97; ophthalmologist Meml. U. Med. Ctr. Ga. Eye Inst., Savannah, Ga., 1997—2008; faculty, pediat. Mercer U. Sch. Medicine, Savannah, Children's Eye Inst., 2008—. Instr. Wills Eye Hosp., Phila. Contbr. chpt. to book Ophthalmology: A Comprehensive Text, 1995; contbr. articles to profl. jours. including Archives of Ophthalmology, Jour. of Pediat. Ophthalmology. Rufus Choate scholar Dartmouth Coll., 1984; short-term experimental rsch. fellow NIH, 1987. Fellow Am. Acad. Ophthalmology, Am. Acad. Pediat.; mem. Am. Assn. Pediatric Ophthalmology and Strabismus. Avocations: skiing, ice skating, scuba diving, piano, trumpet. Office: Children's Eye Inst 836 E 65th St Ste 36A Savannah GA 31405 Office Phone: 912-353-1001. Office Fax: 912-353-1026.

DEVEREAUX, ASHA V., medical association administrator; b. Calif., July 11, 1964; BA, UCSD, 1986; MD, Tulane U., 1991, MPH. Past-pres. Calif. Thoracic Soc., 2006—. Bd. mem. Am. Lung Assn., Calif., 2009—. Decorated Navy Commendation medal US Navy. Fellow: Am. Coll. Chest Physicians. Office: 1224 10th St 205 Coronado CA 92118 Business E-Mail: adevereaux@pol.net.

DEVERTS, DENISE JANICKI, health psychology researcher; b. Pitts., Dec. 14, 1973; m. Andrew Joseph Deverts, May 20, 2006. BA, Duquesne U., Pitts., 1995; MA, Bucknell U., Lewisburg, Pa., 1999; PhD, U. Pitts., 2006. Rsch. asst. Carnegie Mellon U., Pitts., 1999—2001, postdoc. fellow, 2006—09, rsch. psychologist, 2009—. Contbr. articles to psychology and med. jours. Cardiovasc. Behavioral Medicine Tng. grant, Pitts. Mind-Body Ctr., 2004—06. Office Phone: 412-268-3295. Personal E-mail: denisedeverts@hotmail.com.

DEVEYDT, WAYNE S., health insurance company executive; b. 1970; m. Judith DeVeydt. Various positions PricewaterhouseCoopers, LLP, 1996—2005; sr. v.p., chief acctg. officer WellPoint, Inc. (formerly Anthem, Inc.), Indpls., 2005—07, chief of staff, 2006—07, exec. v.p., CFO, 2007—. Office: WellPoint Inc 120 Monument Cir Indianapolis IN 46204 E-mail: wayne.deveydt@wellpoint.com. *

DEVI, MULLAPUDI LALITHA, chemist; b. Tanuku-Westgodavari, Andhra Pradesh, India, Nov. 4, 1979; MS in Organic Chemistry, Andhra U., 1999; PhD in Chemistry, JNTUA, 2011. Jr. scientist Dr. Reddy's Labs., 2001—07; sr. scientist US Pharmacopeia-India Pvt. Ltd., 2007—. Home: 304 Ushodaya Residency Hyderabad Andhra Pradesh 500072 India Personal E-mail: mullapudilalitha@yahoo.co.in.

DEVILLE, CURTILAND, oncologist, educator; b. Washington, July 20, 1978; BA, Brown U., 2000; MD, Brown Med. Sch., 2005. Resident physician U. Pa., 2006—10, asst. prof., 2010—. Fellow Doris Duke Clin. Rsch. Fellowship, Doris Duke Found. Mem.: Am. Soc. Radiation Oncology. Home: 3154 W Master St Philadelphia PA 19121 Home Fax: 215-349-8975. Personal E-mail: curtiland@gmail.com.

DE VILLIERS, FRANÇOIS PIERRE ROUSSEAU, pediatrician, educator, researcher; b. Swakopmund, S.W.A., South Africa, May 10, 1950; s. Charl Johannes and Elena Susanna (Gardiner) De Villiers; m. Gai Talbot, Dec. 1, 1979 (dec. Aug. 2001); children: Gillian Katinka, Tertius Gregoire; m. Mariana Viljoen, Sept. 3, 2004. MB, B of Surgery, U. Stellenbosch, South Africa, 1974; BA in Philos. Logic, U. South Africa, 1982; M of Medicine in Pediat., U. Witwatersrand, South Africa, 1987, PhD, 1990, DS, 2005. Cert physician, specialist in paediats. and endocrinology South African Med. and Dental Coun.; lic. tchr. music, U. South Africa, 2001. Intern/med. officer Edendale Hosp., Pietermaritzburg, South Africa, 1974-77; med. officer/sr. med. officer George Stegmann Hosp., Moruleng, South Africa, 1978-82; resident in pediat. Baragwanath Hosp., Johannesburg, South Africa, 1983-87; specialist in pediat. Johannesburg Hosp., 1987-90, sr. cons. in pediat., 1990-94; prof., chair pediat. and child health Med. U. So. Africa, Pretoria, 1995—. Dir. MSc course U. Witwatersrand, 1991—94; med. assessor Regional Ct., Pretoria, 1994—98; examiner South Africa Coll. Medicine, 1994—98, 2000—; ethics com. Med. U. South Africa, 1995—2003; rheumatic fever policy com. Dept. Health, Pretoria, 1995—2002; dep. dean rsch. faculty medicine Med. U. South Africa, 1997—2001; tech. task team Integrated Mgmt. of Childhood Illness, Dept. of Health, Pretoria, 1997—2003; dep. dean acad. affairs, faculty medicine Med. U. South Africa, 2004—06. Editor: Practical Management of Paediatric Emergencies, 1989, 3d edit., 1999, 4th edit., 2004, 5th edit., 2008; contbr. over 70 articles to profl. jours. Recipient Silver medal for family practice rsch. Noristan, Pretoria, 1983, Rsch. Excellence award Med. U. South Africa, 1998, 2001. Fellow: ACP, Coll. Family Practitioners of South Africa, Coll. Pediatricians of South Africa; mem.: Soc. for Endocrinology, Metabolism and Diabetes of South Africa, Internat. Soc. Pediat. and Adolescent Diabetes. Methodist. Office: PO Box 221 204 Medunsa South Africa Office Phone: +27-12-521-4445. E-mail: johnchild@medunsa.ac.za.

DEVINE, DUSTIN VANCE, veterinarian, educator; b. Weatherford, Okla., Aug. 4, 1976; DVM, Okla. State U., 2002, MS, 2006. Cert. in large animal surgery Am. Coll. Vet. Surgeons, 2007. Asst. prof. equine surgery Okla. State U. Ctr. Vet. Health Scis., 2008—. Recipient America's Next Top Surgeon, Ethicon, Excellence award, Am. Coll. Vet. Surgeons. Home: 2608 N Pk Cir Stillwater OK 74075 Business E-Mail: dustin.devine@okstate.edu.

DEVINE, PATRICIA G., psychology professor, department chairman; BA in Psychology summa cum laude, SUNY, Plattsburgh, 1981; MA in Social Psychology, Ohio State U., Columbus, 1983, PhD in Social Psychology, 1986. Rsch. asst. SUNY Plattsburgh, 1979, 1981; summer rsch. asst. SUNY Plattsburgh Rsch. Found., 1980; grad. rsch. assoc. Ohio State U., Columbus, 1982—83, 1984, grad. tchg. assoc., 1983—84; asst. prof. U. Wis., Madison, 1985—91, assoc. prof., 1991—95, prof., 1995—, dir., Ctr. the Study of Prejudice and Intergroup Conflict, 2001—, chair dept. psychology. Vis. fellow Yale U., New Haven, 1994. Assoc. editor: Encyclopedia of Psychology, 1996—2000, Jour. Personality and Social Psychology: Attitudes and Social Cognition, 1996—2000; editor, 2000—05; contbr. articles to profl. jours. Fellow: APA (Soc. the Psychol. Study Social Issues,

Divsn. 9, Soc. Personality and Social Psychology, Divsn. 8), Am. Psychol. Soc. Office: Dept Psychology 1202 W Johnson St Univ Wis Madison WI 53706 Office Phone: 608-262-2815. Office Fax: 608-262-4029. Business E-Mail: pgdevine@wisc.edu.

DEVINSKY, ORRIN, neurologist, medical educator; b. Bklyn., Feb. 12, 1957; BS, Yale U., New Haven; MS, Yale U., 1977; MD, Harvard U., 1982. Diplomate Am. Bd. Neurol Psychiatry, Am. Bd. Clin. Neurophysiology. Internship in medicine Beth Israel Hosp., Boston, 1982—83; residency tng. in neurology NY Hosp. Cornell Med. Ctr., NYC, 1983—86; clin. fellowship in neurology NIH, 1986—88; attending physician U. Medicine and Dentistry NJ, Newark, 1988-89; chief in neurology Hosp. for Joint Diseases, NYC, 1989-98; dir. Comprehensive Epilepsy Ctr., prof. neurology, neurosurgery and psychiatry NYU Med. Ctr., NYC, 1998—; dir. St. Barnabas Med. Ctr. Inst. Neurology, Livingston, NJ. Co-editor: Reviews in Neurological Diseases, Epilepsy and Behavior, Epilepsy.com; reviewer: more than 30 profl. jours.; contbr. articles to numerous profl. jours., chapters to books. Active Epilepsy Found. Mem.: Am. Acad. Neurology, Am. Epilepsy Soc. (former bd. mem., committees chair). Office: NYU Med Ctr Epilepsy Ctr 223 E 34 St New York NY 10016 Office Phone: 646-558-0803. E-mail: od4@is4.nyu.edu.

DE VIRGILIO, CHRISTIAN MIGUEL, surgeon; married. BS, Loyola Marymount U., LA, 1982; MD, UCLA, 1986. Diplomate Am. Bd. Surgery, 1993, cert. in vascular surgery 1994. Co-chair, coll. applied anatomy UCLA Sch. Medicine; vice-chair edn. Harbor-UCLA Med. Ctr., Torrance, dir., gen. surgery residency, 2003—. Contbr. articles to profl. jours. Bd. mem. UCLA Med. Alumni Assn., 2005—08; internat. med. mission HELPS Internat., Guatemala. Recipient Golden Apple Tchg. award, UCLA Sch. Medicine, 1998, 2000—06, 2008, ACGME Courage to Teach award; named Faculty Tchr. of Yr., Harbor-UCLA Med. Ctr., 1995, Nat. Faculty Tchr. of Yr., Am. Med. Sch. Assn., 2007. Fellow: ACS; mem.: Southern Calif. Vascular Surg. Assn., Pacific Coast Surg. Assn., Southwestern Surg. Congress, Assn. Program Dir. Surgery, Alpha Sigma Nu, Alpha Omega Alpha. Office: Harbor-UCLA Med Ctr 1000 W Carson St Torrance CA 90509

DEVITA, VINCENT THEODORE, JR., oncologist; b. Bronx, NY, Mar. 7, 1935; s. Vincent Theodore and Isabel DeVita; m. Mary Kay Bush, Aug. 3, 1957; children: Ted(dec.), Elizabeth. BS, Coll. William and Mary, 1957; MD with distinction, George Washington U., 1961; DSc (hon.), NY Med. Coll., 1987, Georgetown U., 1989. Diplomate Nat. Bd. Med. Examiners, Am. Bd. Internal Medicine (subspecialty hematology, med. oncology). Sr. investigator Solid Tumor Svcs., Medicine Br., Nat. Cancer Inst., 1966—68, head, 1968—71; chief Medicine Br., Nat. Cancer Inst., 1971—74; dir. Divsn. Cancer Treatment, Nat. Cancer Inst., 1974—80, pres., dir. Nat. Cancer Inst., 1980—88; physician-in-chief, 1988—93; physician VA Medical Ctr., New Haven, 1993—; dir. Yale Cancer Ctr., New Haven, 1993—2003, chair, bd. dirs., 2003—. Bd. dir. ImClone Systems Inc., 1992—2006; scientific adv. cons. The Immunotherapy Rsch. and Treatment Inst., St. Luke's Med. Ctr., 2002—09; chmn., scientific adv. bd. Sci. Adv. Bd. Am.-Italian Cancer Found., 2003—09. Co-editor: (textbooks) Cancer: Principles and Practice Oncology, edits. 1-6, Progress in Oncology, edits. 1-4, (jours.) The Cancer Jour., 1995—; editor-in-chief The Cancer Jour., —; co-editor: (jours.) Principles and Practice Oncology updates, 1987—; assoc. editor Online Jour. Current Clin. Trials, 1991—94; assoc. editor: Cancer Investigation, 1983—87, Am. Jour. Medicine, 1983—88, adv. bd.: Am. Health Mag., 1995—99; editor-in-chief Nat. Clinical Practice Oncology, Yale. U. Sch. Medicine, 1997—2000; contbr. articles to profl. med. jours. Mem. Awards Assembly, GM Cancer Rsch. Found., 1981—85; mem. adv. coun., 1984—; chair med. adv. bd. CancerSource.com, 1999—; bd. advisors Breast Cancer Alliance, Inc., 1999—; mem. Armand Hammer Cancer Award Com., 1983—86. With USMC, 1955—61, with USPHS, 1963—88. Decorated Oren del Sol en el Grando de Official Govt. of Peru; recipient Albert and Mary Lasker Med. Rsch. award, 1972, Superior Svc. award, HEW, 1975, Esther Langer Found. award, 1976, Alumni medallion, Coll. William and Mary, 1976, Jeffrey Gottlieb award, 1976, Bronze medal, Am. Soc. Therapeutic Radiology, 1978, Karnofsky prize and lectr., 1979, Griffuel prize, Assn. for Devel. Rsch. on Cancer, 1980, James Ewing award, Soc. Surg. Oncology, 1982, Meml. Sloan-Kettering Cancer Ctr. award, 1972, DSM, USPHS, 1983, Meyer and Anna Prentiss award, 1984, Second Emmanuel Cancer Found. award, 1984, Pierluigi Nervi award, Rome, 1985, Medal of Honor, Am. Cancer Soc., 1985, Barbara Bohen Pfeifer award, Am.-Italian Found. Cancer Rsch., 1985, Tenth Richard and Hilda Rosenthal Found. award, Am. Assn. Cancer Rsch., Inc., 1986, Stanley G. Kay Meml. award, D.C. Am. Cancer Soc., 1986, Sci. award, Brady Cancer Rsch. Inst., 1987, Prix Cino del Duca, Paris, 1988, Pezcoller award, European Soc. Oncology, Trento, Italy, 1988, Surgeon Gen.'s Exemplary Svc. medal, 1988, Armand Hammer Cancer prize, 1990, Outstanding Achievement in Clin. Rsch. award, Assn. Cmty. Cancer Ctrs., 1992, City of Medicine award, 1995, Presdl. award, New Eng. Cancer Soc., 1997, Key to Cure award, Cure for Lymphoma Found., 1997, Mary Waterman award, Breast Cancer Alliance, 1999, 50th Anniversary Leukemia Soc. Am., 1999, Saul Rosenberg Rsch. award, Lymphoma Rsch. Found. Am., 2000; named Stratton lectr., Am. Soc. Hematology, 1985, Leukemia Rsch. Fund lectr., London, 1985; named to, Conn. Acad. Sci. and Engring., 1994, Commendatore of Italian Rep. order of merit, Pres. Italy, 1998, European Acad. Scis. for outstanding and lasting contbn. to cancer rsch. edn., 2002; Tobacco Rsch. Industry fellow, 1959. Fellow: ACP, NY Acad. Medicine; mem.: AMA, Assn. Am. Cancer Insts. (bd. dirs. 1999—, co-chmn., Nat. Cancer Legis. adv.com. 2000—02, policy and planning com. 2000—, mem., award panel for Pollin Prize in Pediatric Rsch. 2000), Internat. Coun. for Coordinating Cancer Rsch. (pres. Am. bd. 1989—92), Smith-Reed-Russel Med. Soc., Soc. Surg. Oncology, Assn. Am. Physicians, Am. Soc. Clin. Investigation, Am. Fedn. Clin. Rsch., Am. Assn. Cancer Rsch. (dir. 1976—79, Gertrude B. Elion cancer rsch. award com. 1999—2000), Am. Soc. Hematology, Am. Cancer Soc., Am. Soc. Clin. Oncology (chmn. program com. 1972, dir. 1973—76, pres. 1977—78), Alpha Omega Alpha. Achievements include development of the first successful combination cancer chemotherapy program, which ultimately led to effective regimens of curative chemotherapy for a variety of cancers; developer of the four combination drug, known as the acronym MOPP, which increased the cure rate of patients with advanced Hodgkin's disease; co-developer of the combination chemotherapy CMF, which still remains useful for theraphy for breast cancer. Business E-Mail: vincent.devita@yale.edu.

DEVORE, KIMBERLY K., healthcare executive; b. Louisville, June 19, 1947; d. Wendell O. and Shirley F. DeVore. Student, Xavier U., 1972-76; AA, Coll. Mt. St. Joseph, 1979; BA, Internat. U. Metaphysics, 1999. Lic. ins. agent. Patient registration supr. St. Francis Hosp., Cin., 1974-76; cons., bus. mgr. Family Health Care Found., Cin., 1976-77; exec. dir. Hospice of Cin., Inc., 1977-80; pres. Micro Med, 1979-86; v.p. Sycamore Profl. Assn., 1979-86; ptnr. Enchanted House, 1979-86, sec., 1979-80, treas., 1980-83; dist. sales rep. Control-O-Fax, 1986; br. sales mgr., 1987; nat. dealer devel. rep., 1987; nat. computer field sales trainer, 1987-90; pres. U.S. Exec. Leasing and U.S. Med. Leasing, Inc., 1991—2001, Accu Svcs., Inc., 1993—2003, US Med. Mgmt., Inc., 1994—98; lic. ins. agt. United Am. Ins. Co., Orlando, Fla., 2005—06; mng. ptnr. DKN Ins. Agy., LLC, 2006—; divsn. mgr. Americas Health Team, 2006—08; pres. DKN Mktg., Inc., 2009. Pres. U.S. Med. Mgmt Ga., Inc., 1996—2006. Pres. Saddle Creek Homeowners Assn., Inc., 1992-95, parliamentarian, 1995-96; chairperson Citizen's Police Adv. Com. City of Roswell, 1997-99; chairperson found. grants Orch. Atlanta, 1998-99, pres., 1999-03, vice-chmn., pres. & CEO, chaplin Unity N. Atlanta, 2000-02, emeritus, 2003; bd. dirs., membership chairperson Smith Plantation City of Roswell, 1996-97; pres. Roswell Citizen's Police Acad., Inc., 1994-95; mem. City of Roswell Med. Devel. Dist. Coun., 1995—2001; mem. North Fulton Civic League, Inc., 1995-96, 2001-; bd. dirs. Nat. Hospice Orgn., 1979-82, chmn. long-term planning com., fin. com., ann. meeting com., 1979-82, sec., 1980-81, treas., 1981-82; bd. dirs. Hospice of Miami Valley, Inc., 1982-86, also chmn. pers. com., by-laws com.; bd. dirs. Orch. Atlanta, 1998—. Mem. Greater Clin. Soc. Fund Raisers, Better Housing League; mem. service and rehab. com. Hamilton County Unit, Am. Cancer Soc., 1977 78; chair road com. Saddle Creek Homeowners Assn., 1991-92. Mem. Ohio Hospice Assn. (co-founder, state chmn., pres., 1978-83), Nat. League for Nursing, Ohio Hosp. Assn., Nat. Fedn. Bus. and Profl. Women's Clubs, Ohio Fedn. Bus. and Profl. Women's Clubs, Cin. Bus. and Profl. Women's Clubs (pres. 1973-75).

DE VROEGE, ROEL, perfusionist; b. Delft, The Netherlands, Nov. 16, 1961; s. Jan de Vroege and Ria van der Meer; m. S. Kaewwan, July 6, 1992; children: Jiraphorn Vroege, Winly Vroege, Johnny Vroege. BSc, Poly. Faculty, Delft, 1985; European clin. perfusionist, Perfusion Sch., Leiden, The Netherlands, 1993; PhD, Free U., Amsterdam, 2001. Lab. tech., haemaphereses asst. Leyenburg Hosp., The Hague, 1986—89; clin. perfusionist Acad. Med. Ctr., Amsterdam, 1989—94, Cardiac Ctr. BDF, Bahrain, 1994—96, Vrije U. Med. Ctr., Amsterdam, 1996—97, chief perfusionist, 1997—. Mem. ednl. bd Netherlands Soc. Extracorporeal Circulation, Utrecht, 1998—2000, mem. exec. com. Editor: Netherlands Soc. Extracorporeal Circulation Jour., 1992—94; contbr. articles to profl. jours. Recipient sci. award, Netherlands Soc. Extracorporeal Circulation, 2001; grantee, Dutch Heart Found., 1997—2001. Mem.: European Soc. Perfusionists, Dutch Soc. Perfusionists. Home: Roland HolstLaan 1067 2624 KL Delft Netherlands Office: Vrije U Medisch Centrum De Boelelaan 1117 1081 HV Amsterdam Netherlands Fax: 020 4444450.

DE WAAL, FRANS B.M., biologist, psychology professor; b. Netherlands, 1948; B in Biology, U. Nijmegen, Netherlands, 1970; D in Biology, U. Groeningen, Netherlands, 1973; PhD in Biology, U. Utrecht, Netherlands, 1977. Rsch. assoc., lab. comparative physiology U. Utrecht, 1973—81; vis. asst. scientist Wis. Nat. Primate Rsch. Ctr., 1981—82, asst. scientist, 1982—85, assoc. scientist, 1985—91, affiliate scientist, 1991—; assoc. prof. psychology Emory U., 1991—93, prof. psychology, 1993—96, dir. grad. studies: Program in Population Biology, Ecology, & Evolution, 1996—2000, Charles Howard Candler prof. primate behavior, dept. psychology, 1996—; affiliate scientist Yerkes Nat. Primate Rsch. Ctr., 1989—91, rsch. prof. psychobiology, 1991—, dir. Living Links Ctr., 1997—. Adj. assoc. prof., biol. sciences U. Wis., Milw., 1988—91; spkr. in field. Author: Chimpanzee Politics: Power and Sex Among Apes, 1982, Peacemaking Among Primates, 1989 (LA Times Book award, 1989), Good Natured: The Origins of Right and Wrong in Humans and Other Animals, 1996, Bonobo: The Forgotten Ape, 1997, The Ape and the Sushi Master: Cultural Reflections by a primologist, 2001, My Family Album: Thirty Years of Photgraphy, 2003, Our Inner Ape: A Leading Primatologist Explains Why We are Who We Are, 2005, Primates and Philosophers: How Morality Evolved, 2006; consulting editor Zoo Biology, 1988—93; consulting editor: Jour. of Comparative Psychology; mem. editl. nd. Jour. of Comparative Psychology, 1993—, assoc. editor Am. Jour. Primatology, 1997—2003, mem. editl. bd. De Levende Natuur (Dutch), 1980—82, Animal Behavior, 1985—88; mem. editl. bd.: Primatologie, 1987; mem. editl. bd. Politics and the Life Sciences, 1991—; mem. editl. bd.: Primates, 1998—, Evolutionary Psychology, 2001—, PloS Biology, 2003—, Internat. Jour. of Primatology, Politics, and the Life Sciences; mem. editl. bd. Internat. Jour. of Primatology, Politics, and the Life Sciences, 1995—; contbr. articles to peer-reviewed jours., chapters to books. Recipient Presdl. Citation, APA, 2001, Arthur W. Staats award, 2005; named Carl Friedrich von Siemens Stiftung fellow, 1995; named one of The World's Most Influential People, TIME mag., 2007. Fellow: Am. Acad. Arts & Scis., Carl Friedrich von Siemens Stiftung (Germany), Japan Soc. for the Promotion of Sci.; mem.: Am. Philos. Soc., NAS (fgn. assoc.), Royal Dutch Acad. Scis. (corr.). Office: Living Links Ctr Yerkes Nat Primate Ctr 954 N Gatewood Rd Atlanta GA 30329 also: Dept Psychology Emory Univ Atlanta GA 30322 Office Phone: 404-727-3695, 404-727-7898. Office Fax: 404-727-3270, 404-727-0372.

DEWALD, PAUL ADOLPH, psychiatrist, educator; b. NYC, Mar. 12, 1920; s. Jacob Frederick and Elsie (Wurzburger) D.; m. Eleanor Whitman, Sept. 1, 1961; children: Jonathan S., Ellen F. BA, Swarthmore Coll., 1942; MD, U. Rochester, 1945; cert. psychoanalysis, SUNY, 1960. Intern, Strong Meml. Hosp., Rochester, NY, 1945-46, resident, 1948-52; instr. U. Rochester, 1952-57, asst. prof. psychiatry, 1957-61; pvt. practice psychoanalysis St. Louis, 1961-99; asst. clin. prof. psychiatry Washington U., St. Louis, 1961-65, 96—; asso. clin. prof. St. Louis U., 1965-69, clin. prof. psychiatry, 1969—. Dir. treatment svc. Psychoanalytic Found. St. Louis, 1961-72, med. dir., 1972-83 St. Louis Psychoanalytic Inst., 1973-83, supervising and tng. analyst, 1973—; mem. faculty Chgo. Inst. Psychoanlysis, 1961-75, supervising and tng. analyst, 1965-73; vis. prof. U. Cin., 1968-80; mem. Mo. State Mental Health Commn., 1978-83, chmn., 1981-83; asst. prof. clin. psychiatry Washington U., 1995—. Author: Psychotherapy: A Dynamic Approach, 1964, 2d edit., 1969, The Psychoanalystic Process, 1972, Learning Process in Psycho-analytic Supervision, 1987; co-editor: Ethics Case Book of the American Psychoanalytic Assn., 2001; contbr. articles to profl. jours. Served to capt. M.C., AUS, 1946-48. Fellow Am. Psychiat. Assn. (life); mem. Mo. Psychiat. Assn. (pres. 1970-71), Eastern Mo. Psychiat. Assn. (pres. 1969-70), Am. Psychoanalytic Assn. (life), St. Louis Psychoanalytic Soc. (pres. 1970-71, 86-88) Home: Apt 3H 8600 Delmar Blvd Saint Louis MO 63124-1961 Office: 8600 Delmar Blvd Saint Louis MO 63124 Office Phone: 314-994-9608. Personal E-mail: padewald@charter.net.

DEWANI, CHANDRAPAL, urologist, surgeon; b. Sukhar, Sindh, Pakistan, Jan. 3, 1942; MBBS, Gandhi Med. Coll. Bhopal, Vikram U., Ujjain, Madhya Pradesh, India, 1967, MS, 1972; postgrad., Allegmien Policlinic Vienna, 1982. Asst. surgeon Dist. Hosp., Chhindwara, Madhya Pradesh, 1973—75, surgeon Nagadeh, West Azarbaizan, Iran, 1975—81; dir. Dewani Hosp. and Rsch. Ctr., Bhopal, 1982; urologist, surgeon Dewani Hosp., Bhopal, 1982—. Intern, Hamidia Hosp. Gandhi Med. Coll., 1968—69, demonstrator in surgery, 1970—72; house surgeon Dept. Surgery, 1969—70; asst. surgeon Primary Health Ctr., Raisen, Madhya Pradesh, 1972—73; hon. prof. surgery Pandit Khushilal Sharma Ayurvedic Med. Coll., Bhopal, 2002—04. Contbr. articles to numerous profl. jours. Organising pres. pulse polio programme Rotary Club, Dist. 3040. Recipient Med. Achievements award, Madhya Pradesh Sindhu Bhawan Trust, Bhopal, Sinddhu Ratna, Akhil Bhartia Sindhi Samaj India; named one of Best Pres., State Br. I.M.A. Madhya Pradesh. Mem.: Assn. Pvt. Practitioners (Bhopal) (past pres., silver jubilee yr.), Pvt. Hosps. and Nursing Home Assn. India (past pres.), Am. Med. Soc. Vienna, Urol. Soc. India, Indian Med. Assn. Avocations: painting, writing, photography. Home: Hig -454 E-7 Arera Colony Bhopal Madhya Pradesh 462016 India Personal E-mail: cpdewani@yahoo.com.

DEWERD, LARRY ALBERT, medical physicist, educator; b. Milw., July 18, 1941; s. Anthony Lawrence and Dorothy M. (Heling) DeW.; m. Vada Mary Anderson, Sept. 14, 1963; children: Scott, Mark, Eric. BS, U. Wis., Milw., 1963; MS, U. Wis., 1965, PhD, 1970. Rsch. assoc. U. Wash., Seattle, 1970-72, rsch. asst. prof., 1973-75; vis. asst. prof. U. Wis., Madison, 1975-76, clin. asst. prof., 1976-79, clin. assoc. prof., 1979-86, prof., 1990—. Mgr. product devel. Radiation Measurements, Middleton, Wis., 1986-90; dir. Radiation Calibration Lab., Madison, 1983-86, 90—; cons. Instrumentarium, Milw., 1990; v.p. Standard Imaging, Madison, 1990—; presenter in field; cons. IAEA. Contbg. author: Brachytherapy, Ionization Chambers and Dosimetry, Thermoluminescence and Mammography; also numerous articles. Science chmn. Am. Cancer Soc. State of Wis., 1986-90. Nat. Cancer Inst. grantee, 1979-86, 94-98, F. Daniels Best Paper award, AAPM, 2008. Fellow Am. Assn. Physicists in Medicine (pres. 1990-92, L. Lanzl hon. award 2005), Health Physics Soc., Am. Phys. Soc., Coun. Ionizing Radiation Measurements and Standards (pres. 1995-98, R. Cashwell hon. award, 2008), Sigma Xi (bd. dirs. 1984-86). Avocations: golf, fishing, backpacking, hunting. Home: 13 Pilgrim Cir Madison WI 53711-4033 Office: U Wis 1530 Med Sci Ctr 1300 University Ave Madison WI 53706-1510 Office Phone: 608-262-6320. Business E-Mail: ladewerd@wisc.edu.

DE WIT, RONALD, oncologist; b. Amsterdam, The Netherlands, Aug. 8, 1955; s. Jaap and Tiny (van Langelaan) de W.; married (widower); two children. MD, U. Amsterdam, 1982, degree in internal medicine, 1987, degree in med. oncology, PhD, 1990. Internist Acad. Med. Ctr., Amsterdam, 1985-90; med. oncologist Erasmus U. Med Ctr Rotterdam (The Netherlands), Rotterdam Cancer Inst., 1990—. Mem. editl. bd. Brit. Jour. Cancer, 2001—, Jour. Clin. Oncology, 2002-2005; author several textbooks, reviewer and au. articles to profl. jours. Mem.: Dutch Cancer Soc. (mem. sci. bd. 1998—2001), European Orgn. Rsch. Treatment Cancer (chmn. and cons. chemotherapy com. genitourinary group 1995—, mem. early clin. study group 1997—2000), European Soc. Med. Oncology (mem. sci. bd. 1999—, reviewer, program chmn. genitourinary cancer 2000—, European cancer conf. 2000—), Am. Assn. Cancer Rsch., Am. Soc. Clin. Oncology (meeting presenter 1996—, faculty mem. 1997—). Office: Erasmas Univ Med Ctr Rotterdam Cancer Inst PO Box 5201 3008 AE Rotterdam Netherlands

DEWITT, THOMAS G., pediatrician; b. Greenfield, Mass., Sept. 2, 1949; m. Florence L. DeWitt. BA, Amherst Coll., Mass., 1971; MD, U. Rochester, NYC, 1976. Diplomate Am. Bd. Pediat. 1982. Resident, pediat. Yale-New Haven Hosp., Conn., 1976—79, chief resident, pediat. Conn., 1979—80; fellow, gen. academic pediat. Robert Wood Johnson Found., Yale U. Sch. Medicine, Conn., 1980—82; prof. and dir., gen. pediat. Univ. Mass. Med. Ctr., Worcester, 1982—95; Carl Weihl prof. pediat. and dir., gen. and cmty. pediat., assoc. chair edn. Cin. Children's Hosp., 1995—. Co-investigator Health Found. Greater Cin., Ctr. for Promotion of Lifelong Health, 1998—2002; co-principle investigator Health Found. Greater Cin., Rockdale Sch.-Based Health Ctr., 1998—2002; cons. Agy. for Healthcare Rsch. and Quality. Primary Care Practice-Based Rsch. Networks, 2000—01; bd. on children, youth, and families Inst. Medicine, Washington, 2001—; prin. investigator NIH, Enhancement of the Technology Interface for Cin. Pediat. Rsch. Group, 2002; med. dir. Every Child Succeeds; invited presenter in field. Editor (author): (manual) Pediatric Education in Community Settings:A Manual, 1996; contbr. articles to profl. jours.; editl. position Clinical Pediatrics, 2001—, Ambulatory Pediatrics, 2003—. Named one of Best Doctors, 2004, 2005, Best Doctors in America, 2008; Pub. Health Svc. Pub. Policy Fellow, 1995, Health Resources and Svcs. Administn. Pediat. Faculty Develop. Scholar, 1999—2000, Pub. Health Svc. Primary Care Policy Fellow. Fellow: Am. Acad. Pediat. (chair com. on pediat. edn. 2001—, Profl. Edn. award 1995, Med. Edn. Profl. award); mem.: Ambulatory Pediat. Assn. (pres. 1992—93, Tchg. award 1993), Am. Pediat. Soc., Primary Care Fellowship Soc. Office: Cincinnati Children's Hosp 3333 Burnet Ave Cincinnati OH 45229 Office Phone: 513-636-5932. Office Fax: 513-636-7247. E-mail: tom.dewitt@chmcc.org

DEWJI, NAZNEEN N., medical educator, small business owner; d. Nurdin and Gulshan Dewji. PhD, U. London, 1982. Asst. prof. U. Calif., La Jolla, 1989—97, assoc. prof., 1998—. Pres., CEO Cenna Bioscis., Inc., San Diego, 2006—. Contbr. articles to profl. jours. Bd. mem. Aga Khan Edn. Bd., 1996—99. Grantee Rsch. grants, NIH, 1989—. Mem.: Soc. Neuroscis. Achievements include patents pending in field. Business E-Mail: ndewji@ucsd.edu.

DEWS, P(ETER) B(OOTH), retired pharmacology educator, physician; b. Ossett, Yorkshire, Eng., Sept. 11, 1922; s. G.A. and E. (Booth) D.; m. Grace Miller, Dec. 1949; children: Pamela, Kenneth, Alan, Michael. MBChB, U. Leeds, Eng., 1944; PhD, U. Minn., 1952; MA, Harvard U., 1959. House physician Grimsby Hosp., England, 1944-

45; lectr. pharmacology U. Leeds, England, 1945-47; rsch. assoc. Wellcome Rsch. Labs., Tuckahoe, NY, 1948-49, Mayo Found., Rochester, Minn., 1950-52; from instr. to prof. Harvard Med. Sch., Boston, 1953-93, prof. emeritus, 1993—. Mem. Nat. Adv. Mental Health Coun., Washington, 1985-88, Nat. Adv. Space Coun., Washington, 1982-86; v.p. Internat. Life Scis. Inst., Washington, 1977-97. Mem.: Inst. of Medicine. Home: 99 Norumbega Rd Apt 231 Weston MA 02493-2485 Home Phone: 617-244-0663. Personal E-mail: peter_dews@hms.harvard.edu.

DEWSBURY, DONALD ALLEN, psychologist; b. Bklyn., Aug. 11, 1939; s. Edwin Leroy and Carol Wieler (Neil) D.; m.; children: Bryan Bradley, Laura Alison. AB, Bucknell U., 1961; PhD, U. Mich., 1965. NSF postdoctoral fellow U. Calif., Berkeley, 1965-66; mem. faculty dept. psychology U. Fla., Gainesville, 1966—, prof., 1973—2007, ret. prof. emeritus, 2007—. Author: Comparative Animal Behavior, 1978, Comparative Psychology in the Twentieth Century, 1984, Monkey Farm: A history of Yerkes Laboratories of Primate Biology, 1930-1965, 2006; editor (with D. Rethlinghshafer): Comparative Psychology: A Modern Survey, 1973; editor: (with T. McGill, B. Sachs) Sex and Behavior: Status and Prospectus, 1978; editor: Mammalian Sexual Behavior, 1981, Foundations of Comparative Psychology, 1984, Leaders in the Study of Animal Behavior, 1985, Studying Animal Behavior, 1989, Contemporary Issues in Comparative Psychology, 1990, Unification Through Division: Histories of the Divisions of the American Psychological Association, vol. 1, 1996, vol. 2, 1997, vol. 3, 1998, vol. 4, 1999, vol. 5, 2000; editor: (with W. Pickren) Evolving Perspectives on the History of Psychology, 2002; editor: (with L.T. Benjamin, Jr. and M. Wertheimer) Portraits of Pioneers in Psychology, vol. 6, 2006; editor: (with L C Drickamer) Leaders in Animal Behavior, The Second Generation, 2010. Recipient Wainwright D. Blake prize in Psychology, Bucknell U., 1961, Phi Sigma award Biological Sci., U. Mich., 1962, Lifetime Achievement award, Soc. History of Psychology, 2008. Fellow APA (pres. divsn. 6 1992-93, pres. divsn. 26 1997-98, 2008-, Clifford T. Morgan Disting. Svc. to divsn. 6 award, 1998, pres. divsn. 1 2008-09), AAAS, Animal Behavior Soc. (pres. 1978-79, Exemplar award, 1998, Exceptional Svc. award, 2003); mem. Assn. Psychological Sci., History of Sci. Soc., Cheiron Soc., Phi Beta Kappa, Psi Chi, Phi Eta Sigma, Sigma Xi (U. Fla. Sr. Rsch. award 1997). Avocations: opera, baseball, photography, jazz. Home: 4004 NW 59th Ave Gainesville FL 32653-8358 Office: Univ Fla Dept Psychology Gainesville FL 32611-2250

DEXTER, DONALD HARVEY, surgeon, educator; b. Maywood, Ill., Apr. 8, 1928; s. Harry Malcolm and Theodora Jane (Trelawny) D.; m. Esther Ruth Reeve, May 16, 1953; children: Donald Harvey, Scott Reeve, Bryce Malcolm, Margaret Helen. BS, Tulane U., 1948; MD, Northwestern U., 1950; LHD (hon.), Western Ill. U., 1993. Diplomate: Am. Bd. Surgery. Intern Cook County Hosp., Chgo., 1950-51; resident in surgery Ill. Central Hosp., Chgo., 1951-52, Cook County Hosp., 1955-58; practice medicine specializing in surgery Macomb, Ill., 1958—89; prof. dept. health scis. Western Ill. U., 1975—89; physician surveyor Joint Commn. on Accreditation Healthcare Orgns., 1989-93; chief of staff Beu Health Ctr., Western Ill. U., 1993-2001, physician, 2001—07. Sr. mem. Macomb Clinic; team physician; coroner McDonough County, Ill., 1964-76; mem. gov. bd., chmn. devel. coun. McDonough Dist. Hosp., 1995—. Mem. Western Ill. U. Found. Served with USNR, 1953-54. Named Outstanding Citizen of Macomb Jaycees, 1972, Outstanding Citizen of Macomb Macomb Area C. of C., 1973; recipient award of recognition Devel. Center of Western Ill. U. and Macomb Area C. of C., 1977, Hon. Alumni award Western Ill. U., 2004; named to Hall of Fame Western Ill. U., 1991. Fellow ACS (pres. Ill. chpt. 1972, gov.-at-large Ill. chpt. 1983-88), state chmn. field liaison program commn. on cancer, 1983-89); mem. AMA, Ill. Med. Soc., (Outstanding Team Physician award 1985), Ill. Surg. Soc., M.W. Surg. Assn., Rotary (Paul Harris fellow 1987), Phi Beta Kappa. Republican. Episcopalian. Home: 1601 Tower Rd RR 1 Macomb IL 61455-9801 Personal E-mail: dondex@macomb.com.

DEY, CHARLOTTE JANE, retired community health nurse; b. Benson, Minn., Dec. 14, 1927; d. Elmer Ellsworth and Charlotte Iona (Eastman) Bowers; m. Thomas A. Dey, June 25, 1948 (dec. Mar. 1973); children: Thomas A. Jr., Scott E. (dec.). Grad., St. Luke's Hosp. Sch. Nursing, 1948; student, Kans. City CC, 1968; BS in Nursing with distinction, U. Kans., 1970; MPA, U. Mo., Kansas City, 1975. RN, Mo.; ordained deacon, Episcopal Ch., 1993. Head nurse communicable disease ward St. Luke's Children's Hosp., Kansas City, Mo., 1948-49; head nurse newborn nursery Providence Hosp., Kansas City, Kans., 1949-51; pub. health nurse Johnson County Health Dept., Olathe, Kans., 1951-52, 66-68, pub. health nurse, supr., 1970-72; evening supr. Olathe Community Hosp., 1953-55; office nurse B. Albert Lieberman, Jr., MD, Kansas City, Mo., 1960-66; coord. clin. confs. ANA, Kansas City, 1973-76; chief Bur. Community Health Nursing Mo. Dept. Health, Jefferson City, 1976-93; ret., 1993. Sem. expert panel to review and update criteria to estimate future requirements for nursing pers. div. nursing Dept. Health and Human Svcs., 1984, mem. nat. adv. coun. nursing edn. and practice div. nursing, 1998-2002; chair Mid-Am. Community Health Nursing Leadership Group. Recipient award of merit Assn. State and Territorial Dirs. Nursing, 1992. Mem. ANA (cert. nursing adminstrn. advanced, chairperson exec. com. coun. community health nursing 1989-92), APHA, Nat. League Nursing, Nat. Perinatal Assn., Am. Acad. Health Adminstrn. (pres. Mo. chpt. 1980-82), Mo. State Nurses Assn. (coun. nursing svc. facilitors exec. com. 1983-92), Mo. Pub. Health Assn., Mo. League Nursing, Mo. Perinatal Assn., Kans. State Nurses' Assn. (vice chairperson community health conf. group), Kans. Pub. Health Assn. (legislative com.), Sigma Theta Tau. Mem. Episcopal Ch. Home: 8090 Granite Falls Ct Redmond OR 97756-7389 Personal E-mail: janedey@bendcable.com.

DEY, RADHESHYAM CHANDRA, supervisory cytologist; b. Calcutta, India, Jan. 30, 1950; arrived in US, 1978; s. Bhairab and Satyabala D.; m. Indrani Roy Chowdhury, July 5, 1981; children: Smita, Anita, Ishan. BSc, Bangabasi Coll., Calcutta, 1970; MSc, U. Calcutta, 1972, cert. in life sci., 1974; CT, Brooke Army Med. Ctr., San Antonio, 1983; cert. leaderhsip mgmt., ednl. devel., quality improvement and equal opportunity, Walter Reed Army Med. Ctr., 1989; postgrad., Laval U., Quebec City, Can., 1995, Albert Einstein Sch. Medicine, NYC, 1997. Cert. in quality assurance, Inspector's Inspection Lab., Coll. Am. Pathologists, 2005, 2008, basic Am. sign lang. course, Gallaudet U., 1989; Registered cytotechnologist, Am. Soc. Clin. Pathologists, Internat. Acad. Cytology, Calif., Md. Rsch. fellow U. Calcutta, 1975-77; with Anthropol. Survey of India Indian Mus. Calcutta, India, 1977—78; biol. sci. asst. Army Inst. Rsch., Washington, 1980—83; cytology specialist U.S. Army Hosp., Ft. Campbell, Ky., 1983-85, SHAPE Med. Ctr., Mons, Belgium, 1985—87; cytotechnologist Nat. Health Lab., Vienna, Va., 1988; supervisory cytologist Walter Reed Army Med. Ctr., Washington, 1988—2007; chief cytotechnologist United Med. Lab., McLean, 2007—08; health sci. specialist, supervisory cytologist Vets. Affairs Med. Ctr., Balt., 2008—. Vis. Indian Statis. Inst., Calcutta, 1999; presenter in field; mem. European Congress Cytology, Athens, Greece, 2004, Lisbon, 09, Edinburgh, 10. Contbr. articles to profl. jours., numerous pathological conf. Decorated U.S. Army Commendation medal, Achievement medal, Good Conduct medals; recipient Decree of Merit for outstanding contbn. to medicine and health care, 1995, Excellence in Tchg. award Nat. Capital Region Consortium Pathology Residency, 1997, Comdr.'s award US Army Walter Reed Med. Ctr., 1997; Anthrop. Survey of India fellow U. Calcutta, 1976, Leadership Symposia award, Balt., 2010. Fellow: Internat. Acad. Cytology; mem.: AAAS, Washington Met. Assn. Cytology, Indian Anthropol. Soc., Ind. Sci. Congress, Belge de Cytologie Clinique, Soc. of Armed Forces Med. Lab. Scientists, N.Y. Acad. Scis., Am. Soc. for Cytotech., Am. Soc. Clin. Pathologists, Am. Soc. Cytopathology, Am. Anthropol. Assn., Am. Legion. Avocations: soccer, swimming, running, travel, theater. Home: 10110 Treble Ct Rockville MD 20850 Office: Cytology & Histology Svcs Dept Pathology & Lab Medicine Vet Adminstrn Med Ctr Baltimore MD 21201 Home Phone: 301-838-0341; Office Phone: 410-605-7000 ext. 5316. Personal E-mail: dey_rad@hotmail.com.

DEZUBE, BRUCE JEFFREY, internist, oncologist, hematologist; b. Bklyn., Nov. 21, 1955; MD, Tufts U., 1983. Diplomate Am. Bd. Internal Medicine, Am. Bd. Oncology, Am. Bd. Hematology. From intern to resident in internal medicine New Eng. Med. Ctr., Boston, 1983-86; fellow Beth Israel Hosp., Boston, 1986-89; med. staff Beth Israel Deaconess Med. Ctr., Boston; assoc. prof. medicine Harvard Med. Sch., 1993—. Mem. ACP, Am. Soc. Clin. Oncology, Am. Soc. Hematology, Mass. Med. Soc. Office Phone: 617-632-9258. *

DHAFAR, KHALID OBAID, surgeon, consultant; s. Obaid Ahmad Dhafar and Amina Ahmad Khayat; m. Olfat Jameel Alfi, Oct. 10, 1996; children: Nadir Khalid, Alaa Khalid, Safaa Khalid, Mohammad Khalid. MBBS, BAO, U. Coll. Galway, Ireland, 1984. Diplomate in healthcare quality Am. U. Cairo, 2007. Programme dir. Al-Noor Spec. Hosp., Makka, Saudi Arabia, 1999—2007; gen. dir. health affairs Ministry of Health, Makka, 2007—. Bariatric surgeon King Abdalla Med. City, Makka, 1996—. Contbr. scientific papers. Mem. Makka Coun., 2007—. Peace Party. Office: Ministry of health Al Hamra Western Makka Saudi Arabia Office Fax: 00966 2 5422696.

DHALL, DHARAM PAL, retired surgeon, consultant; b. Meru, Kenya, Dec. 8, 1937; s. Surjan Dass and Ram Pyari (Puri) D.; m. Tehseen Zehra Muzaffar, Dec. 28, 1973; children: Amar, Shammah. MB, BChir, U. Manchester, Eng., 1961; PhD, U. Aberdeen, Scotland, 1968, MD with honors, 1969. Lectr. surgery U. Aberdeen, 1966-67; clin. tutor in surgery Aberdeen U., 1967-70; sr. registrar Aberdeen Royal Infirmary, 1970-72; prof. surgery U. Nairobi, Kenya, 1972-74; dir. vascular, thrombosis rsch. Canberra, Australia, 1975-98; sr. cons. surgeon Canberra Hosp., 1975-98; ret., 1998. Vis. fellow John Curtin Sch. Med. Rsch., Canberra, 1975-98; adj. prof. bioethics U. Canberra, 2003—06; referee Nat. Heart Found., Australia, 1978-2000, others; bd. dirs. Satpal Holdings Pty. Ltd., Saishah Pty. Ltd., Total Bldgs. Solutions Trust, Palsat Pty. Ltd., Educare Internat. Ltd.; past examiner in surgery Australian Med. Entry Cert. Fgn. Grads.; past acad. advisor U. Ctrl. Queensland, Australia; cons. UN Habitat. Author: Sri Sathya Sai Human Values Programme: Lesson Plans Group 3, 1991, Sai Awareness Programme Vol. I, 1992; author: (with M. Bhuller) Sai Awareness Program Vol. II, 1993; author: Divinity and Love - The Essence of Human Values, 1993, Sai Vision Vol. I, 1994, Sai Vision Vol. II, 1995, Sai Vision Vol. III, 1995, ACT and NSW Teacher's Workshop - Focus on Syllabus and Lesson Plans, 1996, Dynamic Dharma for Integrated Living, 1997, Stepping Stones to Peace, 1998, My Work is My Blessing, 1999; author: (with T.Z. Dhall) Dynamic Parenting, 1999, Workshops on Dynamic Parenting, 1999, Towards Balance in Education, 2007; editor: East African Med. Jour., 1973—74, Fibrinolysis, 1996; contbr. articles to profl. jours. Spiritual coord. Sri Sathya Sai Orgn., 1992—95, edn. coord., 1992—95, edn. coord. in human values, 1994—98; pres. Australian Soc. Advancement of Ea. and We. Music, Canberra, 1996; co-devel. Edn. in Human Values for Parents Program; chmn. internat. zone 3 Sai Sathya Sai Orgn., 2004—; organizer Oriental Rug Soc., Canberra, 1993; co-organizer 1st Sri Sathya Sai Symposium on Values Parenting, Puttaparthi, India, 1999; edn. com. Sathya Sai Found.; mem. edn. com. Sri Sathya Sai World Found., 2006—; organizer Interfaith Forum, Canberra, 1993; dir. Inst. Sathya Sai Edn. Australia, Canberra; co-dir. Educare Internat. Ltd. Recipient Hallett award Royal Coll. Surgeons, London, 1963; grantee Nat. Heart Found., Australia, Nat. Health and Med. Rsch. Coun., Australia, Inst. Rsch. Internat. Servier, France, Pharmacia AB, Uppsala, Sweden. Fellow: Royal Australian Coll. Surgeons (Edinburgh), Royal Coll. Surgeons; mem.: Australian Coll. Edn. Avocations: music, antique textiles, chess. Home: PO Box 697 Queanbeyan NSW 2620 Australia Personal E-mail: paldhall@aol.com.

DHALL, ROHIT, neurologist; b. Jalandhar, Punjab, India, Sept. 4, 1977; arrived in US, 2001, permanent resident, 2008; s. Harish Chander and Usha Rani Dhall; m. Suzanne Jay Roseman; 1 child, Samir Benjamin. MBBS, All India Inst. Med. Scis., New Delhi, 2001; MS in Epidemiology, U. Tex., Houston, 2008. Diplomate Am. Bd. Psychiatry Neurology, 2008. Resident physician dept. psychiatry All India Inst. Med. Scis., Delhi, 2001; grad. rsch. asst. Mickey Leland Nat. Urban Air Toxics Rsch. Ctr., Houston, 2001—03; resident physician PGY1 dept. internal medicine U. Tex., Houston, 2003—04; resident physician dept. neurology U. Birmingham, Ala., 2004—07, instr., fellow dept. neurology, movement disorders divsn., 2007—09; attending physician, dir. DBS Clinics Movement Disorder & Deep Brain Stimulation Mohammed Ali Parkinson Disease Ctr. Barrows Neurol. Inst., Phoenix, 2009—. Recipient Nat. Talent Search scholarship, Nat. Coun. for Edn., Rsch. and Tng., India, 1993—2000; Schumann fellowship Neurology, 2007—09. Mem.: Movement Disorder Soc., Am. Acad. Neurology (mem. 2004), Internat. Restless Leg Study Group. Hindu. Avocation: reading. Home: 5830 N 24th St Phoenix AZ 85016

DHANANJAYAN, VENUGOPAL, medical researcher; b. Panruti, Tamil Nadu, India, May 22, 1978; MSc, State Bd., PhD, 1998, 2009. Rsch. fellow Salim Ali Ctr. Ornithology and Natural History, Anaikatty, Coimbatore, India, 2001—09; rschr. Regional Occupl. Health Ctr. (S), 2009—. Mem.: Regional Occupl. Health Ctr. Avocation: painting. Office: Regional Occupational Health Ctr (S) Bangalore Karnataka 562110 India Office Fax: 91 (080) 28477102. E-mail: dhananjayan_v@yahoo.com.

DHANESHWAR, SUNEELA SUNIL, pharmacist, educator; b. Mumbai, July 21, 1963; PharmM, SGSITS, DAVV, Indore, 1991, PhD, 1996. Lectr. Bharati Vidyapeeth's Inst. Pharmacy, 1994—99; asst. prof. Poona Coll. Pharmacy, Bharati Vidyapeeth Deemed U., Maharashtra, India, 1999—2005, assoc. prof., 2006—. Cons. Lg Life Scis., Republic of Korea, 2008—10; mem., bd. studies Bharati Vidyapeeth Deemed U., U. Pune, 2009—; mem., editl. bd. Indian Jour. Pharm. Scis., 2010; A grade light music artist All India Radio. Recipient Rsch. Project of the Yr. award, 54th Indian Pharm. Congress Trust, Pune, Best Rsch. Project award, Ranbaxy Rsch. Found., India, 2009, Disting. Educator and Rschr. award, Am. Assn. Indian Pharm. Scientists, USA, 2010. Mem.: Indian Soc. Tech. Edn., Assn. Pharmacy Tchrs. India, Am. Assn. Pharm. Scientists, Indian Pharm. Assn. Achievements include research in gastrosparing mutual prodrugs of NSIDS for rheumatoid arthritis, osteoarthritis; colon-specific prodrugs for IBD, highly bioavailable antimicrobial prodrugs, antihypertensive prodrugs. Avocations: singing, painting, calligraphy. Office: Poona College Pharmacy Erandwane Paud Rd Pune Maharashtra 411 038 India Office Phone: 912025437237. Personal E-mail: suneeladhaneshwar@rediffmail.com.

DHARMESH, SHYLAJA MALLAIAH, medical researcher; b. Mysore, Karnataka, India, June 1, 1957; d. Mallaiah Mysore Adappa and Puttavenkatamma Mysore Mallaiah; m. Dharmesh Thirumalanahalli Kullegowda, Nov. 11, 1984; 1 child, Akshatha Mysore. BSc, Sharada vilas coll., Mysore, 1977; MSc, Manasagangotri, Mysore, 1979; PhD, Mysore U., 1986; PDF, MS, Harvard Med. Sch., Boston, 1991, Wash. U. Sch. Medicine, St. Louis, 1993. Temp. lectr. Mysore U., 1979—80, jr. rsch. fellow, 1980—82, sr. rsch. fellow, 1983—86, lectr., Manasagangotri, 1986—87, pool officer, 1993—96, sr. rsch. assoc., 1996—99; scientist CFTRI, Mysore, 1987—89, sr. scientist, 1999—. Contbr. scientific papers. Recipient Best Rschr., 1984, Best Rschr. appreciation letter, 1991, Best Paper award, 1993, Project award, DBT, 2003—05, Porject award, CSIR, 2003—, DST, 2004—, Best Poster award, 2006, Merit award, 2005, Best Scientist award, 2008, Best Paper award, 2008, 2009; Jr. rsch. fellowship, UGC, 1980—82, Sr. Rsch. fellowship, 1983—86, Postdoc. fellowship, Harvard med. Sch., USA, 1989—91, Sr. Postdoc. fellowship, Wash. U. sch. Medicine USA, 1991—93. Mem.: Nat. Acad. Scis. (India), Indian Assn. Cancer Rsch., NMRS, Alll India Assn. Microbiol. Soc. (life), BARC (life), Soc. Biol. Chemists (life). Office: CFTRI Chelumba Mansion Mysore 570020 India Home Phone: 91-821-2418434; Office Phone: 91-821-2514876. Office Fax: 91-821-2517233. Personal E-mail: cancerbiolab@gmail.com, shylaakshu@yahoo.com.

DHIB-JALBUT, SUHAYL S., physician; b. Khiam, Lebanon, Oct. 2, 1954; came to U.S., 1980; s. Samih and Nahia (Gaith) Dhib-J.; m. Mary Maral Mouradian, June 29, 1982; 1 child, Marla. MD, Am. U. Beirut, 1980. Diplomate Am. Bd. Psychiatry and Neurology. Resident in medicine Am. U. Beirut Hosp. and Med. Sch., 1980-81; resident in neurology Am. U. Beirut Hosp. and Med. Sch. & U. Cin. Hosp., 1981-84; fellow neuroimmunology NIH, Bethesda, Md., 1985-90, sr. staff fellow, 1989-90; asst. prof. neurology U. Md., Balt., 1990-94, assoc. prof., 1994-99, prof., 1999—2003; prof., chmn. dept. neurology U. Med. Dentistry N.J., Robert Wood Johnson Med. Sch., New Brunswick, NJ, 2003—. Guest rschr. NIH, Bethesda, 1990—; prin. investigator awards from NIH and Dept. Vets. Affairs, 1991—. Assoc. editor Jour. Neuroimmunology, 2003—; contbr. articles to profl. jours., chpts. to books. Recipient Career Devel. award Dept. Vets. Affairs, Washington, 1992—, Merit Rev. award, 1992—; NIH Ctr. grantee, Bethesda, 1992—; NIH Mid-Career Investigator awardee 1999-2006. Mem. Am. Acad. Neurology, Am. Neurol. Assn., Am. Assn. Immunologists, Internat. Soc. Neuroimmunology. Achievements include research interest in the cause and treatment of Multiple Sclerosis. Office: U Medicine Dentistry NJ-Robert Wood Johnson Med Sch 97 Paterson St Rm 205 New Brunswick NJ 08901 Office Phone: 732-235-7732.

DHUNGANA, GOVINDA PRASAD, science educator; b. Raipur, Oct. 12, 1978; B, Tribhuvan U., 2002, M, 2005. Faculty mem. Tribhuvan U., 2006—. Prof. Tribhuvan U., 2006—. Office: Shree Siddhanath Sci Campus Katan Mahendranagar Kanchanpur 00977 Nepal Office Fax: 97799521304. Business E-Mail: dhunganagovinda7826@yahoo.com.

DIAB, MOHAMMAD, orthopedic surgeon; b. Cairo, May 6, 1964; B in Classics, Stanford U., Calif., B in Biology; MD, Stanford U. Sch. Medicine, Calif., 1990. Cert. in orthopaedic surgery 2000. Internship in orthopedics U. Wash. Sch. Medicine, Seattle, 1990—91, residency in orthopaedic surgery, 1993—97, asst. prof., dept. orthopedics, physician, 1998—2002; fellowship in pediatric orthopaedic surgery Harvard U., Boston, 1997—98; physician Children's Hosp. & Regional Med. Ctr., Seattle, 1998—2002, Overlake Hosp, Bellevue, Wash., 2000—02; assoc. prof. orthopaedic surgery and pediat. U. Calif., San Francisco, 2002—, paediatric orthopaedic surgeon, 2002—, chief, pediatric orthopedics. Mem.: AMA, Scoliosis Rsch. Soc., Pediatric Orthopedic Soc. North America, Am. Acad. Pediatrics, Am. Acad. Orthopedic Surgery. Office: Univ Calif San Francisco Dept Orthopaedic Surgery 400 Parnassus Ave, 2nd Fl San Francisco CA 94143 Office Phone: 415-353-2967. Office Fax: 415-353-2299.

DIAMANTI-KANDARAKIS, EVANTHIA, endocrinologist, educator; b. Amaliada, Elias, Greece, June 18, 1948; d. Dimitrios Diamantis Georgios and Eleni Giannakopoulou Dionysios; m. Artemios Stylianos Kandarakis, Sept. 15, 1979; children: Helen, Stylianos, Anna. MD, U. Athens, Greece, 1972, PhD, 1973. Rsch. fellow U. Milw., 1980—82; clin. fellow Milw. Med. Sch., 1980—82, Oschner Found., New Orleans, 1983—84; sr. endocrinologist Gen. U. Hosp., Athens, 1984—92, First Pathology Clinic, U. Athens, 1992—94; instr. endocrinology pathology unit U. Athens, 1992—, supr. PhD students in medicine, 1994—; assoc. prof. U Athens Med. Sch., 1999—. Instr. medicine La. State U., New Orleans, 1983—84. Author: Cushing Syndrome and Androgen Excess, 1997; mem. editl. bd.: Jour. Endocrinological Investigation, 1999; contbr. chapters to books, articles to profl. jours. Organizer Med. Support, Servia, 1994; dir. Sci. Update, Lesbos, Greece, 1996, Sci. Comm., Elias, Greece, 1997. Recipient 1st award, ACP, 1983, Rsch. award, Internat. Endocrine Soc., 1984, Hellenic Endocrine Soc., 1992, 1998. Mem.: Mediterranean Group Study of Diabetes, N.Y. Acad. Scis., Endocrine Soc. Home: Zefiru 1A 145 78 Ekali Greece

DIAMOND, FRANK B., pediatric endocrinologist, educator; BA, Yale U., 1970; MD, Pa. State U., 1974. Diplomate Am. Bd. Pediatrics, 1979, Am. Bd. Pediatrics-pediatric endocrinolgy, 1980. Resident pediatrics Children's Hosp.-Univ. Ala., Birmingham, 1975—76; fellow pediatric endocrinology Children's Hosp.-Univ. Pa., 1976—78; pvt. practice Diagnostic Clinic, Largo, Fla.; asst. med. dir. Children Med. Svcs., Pasco County, Fla.; prof. pediatric endocrinology Universidad de San Francisco de Quito, Av Pampite, Ecuador; med. dir. All Children's Hosp. Weight Mgmt. and Fitness Program (Kidshapers); prof. pediatrics Univ. South. Fla., 1988—; hosp. affiliations include Tampa Gen. Hosp., All Children's Hosp., St. Petersburg, Fla. Mem.: Fla. Camp for Children and Youth with Diabetes (pres.), Human Growth Found. (pres.), Lawson Wilkins Pediatric Endocrine Soc. (dir.), Genentech Endowment for Growth Disorders (pres.). Office: All Children's Hospital Dept 6900 501 6th Ave S Saint Petersburg FL 33701 Office Phone: 727-767-4233. Office Fax: 727-767-3275.

DIAMOND, JASON BRETT, plastic surgeon; b. NJ, Dec. 21, 1970; MD, U. Rochester Sch. Medicine, 1997. Diplomate Am. Bd. Facial Plastic and Reconstructive Surgery, Am. Bd. Otolaryngology. Fellow Am. Coll. Surgeon; pvt. practice Beverly Hills. Featured facelift, rhinoplasty and eyelid expert on Dr. 90210, 2005—, guest appearances Discovery Health Channel, Entertainment Tonight, NBC, and E! Channel, ABC, CBS, Access Hollywood, others, featured in Harpers Bazaar, Life & Style, People. Office: The Diamond Inst 9400 Brighton Way Penthouse Suite Beverly Hills CA 90210 also: 14th E 96th St, Ste #C1 New York NY 10128 Office Fax: 310-859-9815. Business E-Mail: drdiamond@jasonbdiamond.com.

DIAMOND, SEYMOUR, physician; b. Chgo., Apr. 15, 1925; s. Nathan Avruum and Rose (Roth) D.; m. Elaine June Flamm, June 20, 1948; children: Judi, Merle, Amy Student, Loyola U., 1943-45; MB, Chgo. Med. Sch., 1948, MD, 1949. Intern White Cross Hosp., Columbus, Ohio, 1949-50; gen. practice medicine Chgo., 1950—; founder, dir. emeritus Diamond Headache Clinic, Ltd., Chgo., 1970—; dir. inpatient headache unit St. Joseph Hosp., Chgo., 2001—09; prof. neurology Chgo. Med. Sch. at Rosalind Franklin U. Medicine and Sci., 1970-82, 85—, adj. prof. cellular and molecular pharmacology, 1985—, clin. prof. family medicine, 1999—; clin. prof. dept. family medicine U. Medicine and Dentistry N.J. Sch. Osteo. Medicine, Stratford, NJ, 1994-98; cons. mem. FDA Orphan Products Devel. Initial Rev. Group; lectr., dept. family medicine, neurology Loyola U. Chgo. Stritch Sch. Medicine, 2009—. Lectr. dept. cmty. and family medicine Loyola U. Stritch Sch. Medicine, 1972-78; lectr. Falconbridge lecture series Laurentian U., Sudbury, Ont., Can., 1987; disting. lectr. neurology U. Tenn., 1992; AMA cons. on drug evaluation, 1993; mem. sci. com. neurology Internat. Jour. Pain Therapy, 1993; mem. panel Nat. Ctr. on Addiction and Substance Abuse, Columbia U., N.Y.C., 2003. Author: A Pain Specialist's Approach to the Headache Patient, 1994; (with Bill and Cynthia Still) The Hormone Headache, 1995; Diagnosing and Managing Headaches, (with Merle L. Diamond)7th edit., 2009; (with Donald J. Dalessio) The Practicing Physician's Approach to Headache, 5th edit., 1992, More Than Two Aspirin: Help for Your Headache Problem, 1976, (with Judi Diamond-Falk) Advice from the Diamond Headache Clinic, 1982, (with Mary Franklin Epstein) Coping with Your Headaches, 1982, 2d edit., 1987, (with Arnold P. Friedman MD) Headache in Contemporary Patient Management series, 1983; (with Amy Diamond Vye) Headache and Diet, 1990; (with Michael Maliszewski) Sexual Aspects of Headaches, 1992; (with Mary A. Franklin) Conquering Your Migraine, 2001; (with Amy Diamond) Headache and Your Child, 2001; (with Merle L. Diamond) Contemporary Diagnosis and Management of Headache and Migraine, 2d edit., 2000, (with Mary A. Franklin) Headache Through the Ages, 2005; contbg. author: Wolff's Headache and Other Head Pain, 6th edit., 1993, Handbook of Pain Management, 2d edit., 1994, Nonsteroidal Anti-Inflammatory Drugs, 2d edit., 1994, Current Review of Pain, 1994, New Advances in Headache Research, 1994, Conn's Current Therapy, 1998, Advanced Therapy of Headache, 1999, Diamond and Dalessio's Practicing Physician's Approach to Headache, 6th edit., 1999; editor: Migraine Headache Prevention and Management; editor-in-chief Headache Quar., 1990-02; editor-in-chief Headache and Pain, 2003-08; mem. internat. editl. bd. Pediat. Drugs, 2001-; editl. cons. BIOSIS, 1986-90; contbr. numerous articles on headache and related fields to profl. jours. Bd. govs. Chgo. Med. Sch. at Rosalind Franklin U. Medicine & Sci. Recipient Disting. Alumni award Chgo. Med. Sch., 1977; Nat. Migraine Found. lectureship award, 1982, award Headache Consortium of New Eng., 1997, Cert. Appreciation, Chgo. Med. Soc., 1998, Presdl. award Alumni Assn. Chgo. Med. Sch., 2002; 1st recipient Migraine Trust lectureship, 1988; Brit. Migraine Trust 7th Internat. Migraine Symposium, London; Nat. Headache Found. Seymour Diamond fellow, 1993; Headache fellowship, United Coun. Neurologie Subspacialties Headache Medicine fellowship Loyola U. Chgo. Stritch Sch. Medicine; Disting. lectr. in neurology U. Tenn., 1992. Fellow Royal Soc. Medicine; mem. AMA (Physicians Recognition awards 1970-73, 74, 77, 79, 82, 87, del. sect. clin. pharmacology and therapeutics 1987-89, mem. health policy agenda for Am. people, mem. cost effectiveness conf., del. reference com. "C" on edn., reference com. C, 1988), Am. Coun. on Sci. and Health (bd. sci. and policy advisors), Am. Assn. Study of Headache (exec. dir. 1971-85, pres. 1972-74, #1 regent mem. 1984, svc. award 1971-85, Lifetime Achievement award 1999), Nat. Headache Found. (pres. 1971-77, exec. dir. 1977-95, exec. chmn. 1995—, 1st recipient cert. of added qualification in headache mgmt. Nat. Bd. Cert. in Headache Mgmt. 2001), Assn. Applied Psychophysiology and Biofeedback (Presdl. Recognition award 2005), World Fedn. Neurology (exec. officer 1980-95, rsch. group on migraine and headache), Ill. Acad. Gen. Practice (chmn. mental health com. 1966-70), Ill. Med. Soc., Chgo. Med. Soc., Assn. Applied Psychophisiology and Biofeedback, Internat. Assn. Study Pain, Am. Soc. Clin. Pharmacology and Therapeutics (chmn. headache sect. 1982-89, mem. com. coordination sci. sects. 1983-89), Postgrad. Med. Assn. (pres. 1981). Office: 1460 N Halsted St Ste 501 Chicago IL 60642 Office Phone: 773-388-6390. *

DIANZANI, FERDINANDO M., physician, researcher; b. Grosseto, Italy, Sept. 12, 1932; s. Edgardo Dianzani and Irma Bocelli; m. Giuliana Bini, Dec. 2, 1961; children: Lorenzo, Caterina. MD, U. Siena, Siena, Italy, 1959, PhD in Microbiology, 1964, PhD in Virology, 1968. Profl. Accreditation Italy, 1960. Asst. prof. of microbiology U. Siena, Siena, Italy, 1959—69; prof. microbiology U. Turin, Italy, 1969—76, U. Tex. Med. Br., Galveston, 1976—80, 1981—; prof., chmn. virology U. Rome La sapienza, Rome, 1981—99; prof. virology, emeritus U. Rome La Sapienza, Rome, 2004; prof. virology and dean medicine U. Campus Biomedico, Rome, 1999—2004. Sci. advisor for clin. virology Nat. Inst. for Infectious Diseases, Rome, 2004—; pres., nat. aids com. Italian Ministry of Health, Rome, 2004—06, mem., nat. aids com., 1986—2006; dir. of the aimed rsch. program for infectious diseases NRC, Rome, 1982—87; mem. Higher Health Coun., Rome, 1991—93. Editor: (several books on microbiology) both Italian and English; contbr. scientific papers more than 200 pub. to profl. jour. Vis. scholar Wellcome Vis. Prof. in Microbiology, Americal Acad. of Microbiology, 1990. Mem.: Internat. Soc. for Interferon and Cytokine Rsch. (hon.; pres. 1990—92). Roman Catholic. Avocations: history, antiques, classical music, swimming. Office: Natl Inst for Infectious Diseas 292 via Portuense Rome 00149 Italy Office Fax: 39-06-5594224. Business E-Mail: dianzani@inmi.it.

DIAREME, STAVROULA, clinical psychologist, lecturer, therapist, researcher; b. Athens, Greece, Sept. 12, 1967; d. Panayiotis and Margarita (Vassalou) D. BA, U. Athens, 1989; MS with distinction, U. Warwick, Eng., 1990; MA, Calif. Sch. Profl. Psychology, 1993, PsyD, 1995. Lic. clin. psychologist. Psychologist Greek Ministry of Health-European Econ. Communities, Leros Asylum & Deinstitutionalization Project, Leros Island, Greece, 1991; intern in clin. psychology The Children's Village, Dobbs Ferry, N.Y., 1994-95; clin. psychologist, rschr. The Counseling Ctr., Assn. Psychol. Health of Children and Adolescents, Athens, 1995—99, coord. edn. and rsch. projects, 1996—2001, coord. ednl. & rsch activities BIOMED II, 1998—2001. Lectr. U. Athens, Med. Sch. U. Athens, child psychiat. dept Ag. Sophia Childrens Hosp., 2004-2007, Aristotelian U. Thessaloniki, Greece, 1998, coord. clin. rsch. COSIP project, 5th Framework European Programmes & U. Athens Med. Sch., 2001-2004; cons., supr. Child Guidance Ctr. Municipality of Rhodes, Rhodes Island, Greece, 1997—2007, supr. rsch. activities DAPHNE II Program, Athens, Greece, 06-08, lectr.-staff MA Program Infant Mental Health U. East London Taristock & Portman NHS Found. Trust, Athens, 09-, pvt. practice, Athens, 1996-. Fulbright scholar Internat. Inst. Edn., San Francisco, 1991-95, Grad. scholar Greek State Scholarship Found., 1992-95. Mem. APA, Greek Psychol. Assn. Personal E-mail: sdiareme@gmail.com.

DIAS, CRISTIANE MARIA CARVALHO COSTA, psychotherapist, educator; b. Itabuna, Bahia, Brazil, July 20, 1957; Degree in Physiotherapy, Bahia Sch. Medicine and Pub. Health, 1979, M, 2008. Lead physiotherapist Alliance Hosp., 1991; tchr. Bahia Sch. Medicine and Pub. Health, 2000—. Avocations: reading, travel, dance. Home: da Taquara 550 LT 78 Casa 1 Colina C Salvador Bahia 41680-450 Brazil Home Fax: 71 32404928. Personal E-mail: cristianedias7@yahoo.com.br.

DIAS, FERNANDO SUPARREGUI, critical care physician; b. Itaqui, Brazil, Mar. 27, 1953; s. Sydney Santos and Pastorinha Suparregui Dias, m. Zilda Fontana, June 16, 1955 (div. June 30, 1987), children: Rafael Fontana, Kelli Fontana, Fernando Fontana. MD Universidade Fed. de Santa Maria, 1977, Specialist Associação de Medicina Intensiva Brasileira, 1983. Dir. gen. ICU Hosp. São Lucas da PUCRS, Porto Alegre, Brazil, 1991—, dir. cardiac surg. ICU, 1989—97; critical care physician Instituto de Cardiologia do Rio Grande do Sul, Porto Alegre, Brazil, 1983—89. Prof. Pontifícia Universidade Católica do Rio Grande do Sul, Porto Alegre, Brazil, 1991—; dir. critical care med. residency program Hosp. São Lucas da PUCRS, Porto Alegre, Brazil, 2000—. Author: (book) Shock. Pres. vi brazilian congress of critical care medicine Associação de Medicina Intensiva Brasileira, Porto Alegre, Brazil, 1993—93; pres. Sociedade de Terapia Intensiva do Rio Grande do Sul, Porto Alegre, Brazil, 1996—97, v.p., 1994—95. Mem.: Associação de Medicina Intensiva Brasileira (assoc.), Soc. Critical Care Medicine (assoc.), European Soc. Intensive Care Medicine (assoc.). Avocations: travel, history, movies, soccer, music. Office: Hospital São Lucas da PUCRS Av Ipiranga 6690 Rio Grande do Sul Porto Alegre 90610-000 Brazil Office Fax: 55-51-33360304; Home Fax: 55-51-33360304. Personal E-mail: fersdias@via-rs.net.

DIAS, RICARDO AUGUSTO, medical educator; b. Sao Paulo, Brazil, Mar. 26, 1975; Degree in Vet. Medicine, U. Sao Paulo, 1999, PhD in Vet. Medicine, 2004. Fed. agt. Ministry of Agr., Livestock and Food Supply, 2004—05; prof. Faculty Vet. Medicine, U. Sao Paulo, 2005—. Office: Av Prof Dr Orlando Marques Paiva 87 São Paulo 05508-270 Brazil Office Fax: 55(11)30917928. Business E-Mail: dias@vps.fmvz.usp.br.

DIAS JUNIOR, LEONIDAS BRAGA, pathologist; b. Rio de Janeiro, Nov. 6, 1958; MD, U. Fed. do Pará, 1983; PhD, U. São Paulo, 2006. Adj. prof., anathomic pathology dept. U. Estado Pará, 1988—. Dir. Lab. Patologia Clínica Dr. Paulo C. Azevedo, 1988—2011. Mem.: Soc. Brasileira Patologia Clínica, Soc. Brasileira Citopatologia, Soc. Brasileira Patologia. Avocation: running. Office: Ave Brás de Aguiar 99 Belém Pará 66035-000 Brazil Business E-Mail: leonidas@supridados.com.br.

DIAZ, ANGELA, pediatrician, educator; b. Dominican Republic, Oct. 2, 1954; MD, Columbia Coll. Physicians and Surgeons, 1981; MPH, Harvard U. Diplomate Am. Bd. Pediatrics with subspecialty in adolescent medicine. Intern Mt. Sinai Med. Ctr., NYC, 1981—82, resident in pediats., 1982—84, fellow, 1984—85, prof. dept. pediats., 1985—, Jean C. and James W. Crystal prof. pediatrics, vice-chair pediatrics; dir. Mt. Sinai Adolescent Health Ctr., NYC White House fellow, 1995; bd. trustees Children's Aid Soc., v.p. bd. trustees, 1996—2004, pres. bd. trustees, 2004—; mem. NYC Bd. Health. Recipient Alexander Richman Commemorative award for Ethics and Humanism in Medicine, Mt. Sinai Sch. Medicine, Dr. Sidney Grossman Humanitarian award, Mt. Sinai Sch. Medicine Alumni Assn.; named one of the 100 Most Influential Hispanics in the US, Hispanic Bus. Mag., 2008. Mem.: SAM, Inst. Medicine, Am. Acad. Pediats. (Founders of Adolescent Health award 2001). Office: Mount Sinai Med Ctr 320 E 94th St New York NY 10128-5604 Office Phone: 212-423-2900. Office Fax: 212-423-2920. E-mail: angela.diaz@mountsinai.org.

DIAZ, FERNANDO GUSTAVO, neurosurgeon; s. Fernando Diaz Calderon and Susana (Barriga) D.; children: Fernando Austin, David Frederick, Sean Christopher, Patrick Aaron, Johnathan Paul. BS, Centro Universitario Mex., 1963; MD, Univ. de Mex., 1969; MA, U. Kans., Kansas City, 1973; PhD, U. Minn., 1979; MA in Bus., Cen. Mich. U., Mt. Pleasant, 1987; JD, Wayne State U., 1995. Diplomate Am. Bd. Neurol. Surgery; bar: Mich. 1995. Intern Regina Gen. Hosp., Sask., Can., 1969-70, resident in anethesia Sask., 1971; resident in gen. surgery U. Kans., Kansas City, 1971-73; resident in neurosurgery U. Minn. Hosps., Mpls., 1973-78; staff neurosurgeon Henry Ford Hosp., Detroit, 1978-87; chmn. Neurosci. Inst. Santa Fe, Gainesville, Fla., 1987-90; prof., chmn. dept. neurol. surgery Wayne State U., Detroit, 1990—; chief med. officer Detroit Med. Ctr., 2000—; cert. physician exec. ACPE, 2002. Neurosurg. nat. cons. to U.S. Surgeon Gen., USAF, 1991; coord. neurosurgery resident edn. Henry Ford Hosp., 1979—; clin. assoc. prof. surgery U. Mich., 1986—; mem. working group in neurosurgery WHO. Mem. editl. bd. Neurosurgery Jour.; contbr. articles to profl. jours. Lt. col. USAFR. Recipient awards Lily Pharms., Merck, Sharp & Dome Pharms., Organon Labs. Fellow Am. Chem. Soc., Interam. Coll. Physicians, Internat. Coll. Surgeons (vice regent U.S. sect. 1985); mem. AMA, Neurosurg. Soc. Am., Soc. Neurol. Surgeons, Mich. Med. Soc., Wayne County Med. Soc., Am. Assn. Neurol. Surgeons (cerebrovascular sect.), Congress Neurol. Surgeons, Mich. Assn. Neurol. Surgeons (sec.-treas. 1984-86, v.p. 1986, pres. 1997-98), Detroit Neurosurg. Acad. (v.p. 1986-90), Soc. Critical Care Medicine, Mich. Heart Assn. (chmn. stroke com. 1984-86, cmty. site ad-hoc com. 1984, cmty. programs and edn. com. 1986), Mich. Assn. Neurosurgery (chmn. bd.), L.Am. Fedn. Neurosurgery (sec. gen., 1999-2002), Coun. State Neurol. Soc. (vice chair) U. Minn. Alumni Assn. Roman Catholic.

DIAZ, JOHN, plastic surgeon; MD, Albert Einstein Coll. Medicine, 2000; BS, Cornell U., 1996. Resident, plastic surgery Albert Einstein Coll. Medicine, Montefiore Med. Ctr., NY, 2000—05; fellowship in advanced cosmetic surgery Beverly Hills, Calif., 2005; with Beverly Hills Body; med. staff mem. Cedars Sinai Med. Ctr., LA; pvt. practice Beverly Hills. Presenter in field; dir. Age Defying Inst. Contbr. articles to profl. jours. Recipient NY Regional Soc. of Plastic Surgeons award, Montefiore Med. Ctr. Investigator's Symposium award; Albert Einstein Scholarship, 1996—98, Montefiore Med. Ctr. House Staff and Alumni award, Frank H.T. Rhodes Scholarship, 1999. Mem.: LA Soc. Plastic Surgery (mem. exec. bd.), Alpha Omega Alpha. Office: 436 N Roxbury Ste 205 Beverly Hills CA 90210 Office Phone: 310-770-9949. Office Fax: 800-880-9324.

DIAZ, PAUL J., health products executive; With Arthur Andersen LLC; atty. pvt. practice; CEO Allegis Health Svcs., Inc.; exec. v.p., COO Mariner Health Group, Inc., 1996—98; chmn., CEO Capella Sr. Living, LLC; mng. mem. Falcon Capital Partners, LLC; pres., CEO Kindred Healthcare, Inc., Louisville, 2002—. Mem.: Johns Hopkins Bloomberg Sch. Pub. Health. Office: Kindred Healthcare 680 S Fourth St Louisville KY 40202 *

DIAZ, VICTOR A., physician, educator; MD, Cath. U. Madre y Maestra, Dominican Republic, 1986. Intern Chestnut Hill Hosp., resident family practice; fellow Dept. Family Medicine Thomas Jefferson Univ. Hosp.; physician Thomas Jefferson Univ., asst. prof. Dept. Family Medicine; asst. med. dir. Jefferson Med. Coll., dir. quality improvement, Leadership fellow Nat. Hispanic Med. Assn., Wash., DC, 2010—11. Author: (publs.) Hispanic Male Health Disparities Primary Care: Clinics in Office Practice, 2006; co-author: Oral Health Care Issues in HIV Disease: Developing a Core Curriculum for Primary Care Physicians, 1998, Cultural Factors in Preventive Care. Primary Care: Clinics in Office Practice, 2002, The Red Eye. Family Medicine-Ambulatory Care and Prevention, 2005, HIV-Related Oral Lesions: Clues for Early Diagnosis, 2009, Essential Evidence Plus, 2010, Male Sexual Dysfunction. Primary Care: Clinics in Primary Care Urology, 2010. Mem.: Team Physician, Phila. Phillies, Jefferson Family Medicine Assocs. (assoc.). Office: Thomas Jefferson University Hospital Department of Family and Community Medicine 833 Chestnut St Ste 301 Philadelphia PA 19107 Office Phone: 215-955-7190. Office Fax: 215-955-8600.

DIAZ-ARIAS, ALBERTO A., pathologist, educator; b. Lima, Peru, Jan. 12, 1958; MD, U. Mo., 1985. Assoc. prof., U. Mo. Pathology and Anat. Scis., 1989—. Staff pathologist Harry S. Truman Vets. Hosp., 1989—. Fellow: CAP. Avocations: running, travel. Office: University Mo Pathology and Anatomical Scis One Hosp Dr - M263 Columbia MO 65212 Business E-Mail: diazariasa@health.missouri.edu.

DÍAZ-MUÑOZ, MAURICIO, biomedical sciences professor, researcher; b. Mexico City, Distrito Fed., Mex., Feb. 17, 1959; s. Juan and Ofelia (Muñoz-Aguilar) Díaz-Romero; m. Virginia Echaniz-Hernández, Apr. 4, 1987; 1 child, Dalia Díaz-Echaniz. Degree in biology, U. Nacional Autonoma Mex., Mexico City, 1981, MS, 1984, PhD, 1988. Asst. prof. IFC, U. Nacional Autonoma Mex., Mexico City, 1993; assoc. prof. INB, U. Nacional Autonoma Mex., Querétaro, 2001, prof., 2005. Office: U Nacional Autonoma Mex Querétaro Mexico

DIAZ PEREZ, GILMER ARCENIO, oncologist; b. Peru, Nov. 23, 1973; MD, Nat. U. Trujillo, MBA, 2000. Cert. oncologic surgeon UPCH, 2005. Oncologic urologist Santa Rosa Gen. Hosp., 2008. Recipient 1st Pl., Residence Oncologic Surgery, Residences Med. Rsch. award. Avocations: swimming, literature. Home: Calle Green Mz T Lt 17 Calera Surquillo Lima 34 Peru Personal E-mail: gilmeruro@yahoo.com.

DIB, JUAN CARLOS, physician, director; b. Santa Marta, Magdalena, Colombia, Jan. 5, 1967; MD, CES U., 1991; MPH in Tropical Medicine, Tulane U., PhD, 1997. Dir. Tropical Health Found., 2000—, Ctr. Investigación en Enfermedades Tropicales, 2003. Adj. prof. SUE Caribe U., 2000. Recipient Humanitarian awards, Indigenous Orgn.; grants, Colciencias. Mem.: Am. Tropical Medicine Assn., Lion Club. Avocations: piano, swimming. Home: Calle 17 N° 22-94 Santa Marta Magdalena 1794 Colombia Personal E-mail: juandib@hotmail.com.

DIB, LUCIANO LAURIA, medical educator; b. Sao Jose do Rio Pardo, São Paulo, Brazil, Dec. 1, 1963; Degree in Odontology, U. Sao Paulo, 1984, PhD, 1997. Prof. U. Paulista, 1988—. Cons. Pvt. Clinic, 1985; dir., dept. stomatology Cancer Hosp. Sao Paulo, 1992—2003. Mem.: Assn. Paulista de Cirurgioes Dentistas, Colegio Brasileiro de Cirurgia Bucomaxilofacial, Sociedade Brasileira de Estomatologia e Patologia. Avocations: tennis, Tae Kwon Do, literature. Office: Rua Afonso Bras 525 cj 81 Sao Paulo 04511011 Brazil Office Fax: 55 11 30453846. Business E-Mail: lldib@uol.com.br.

DIB, NABIL, cardiologist, researcher; b. Toumin, Syria, Nov. 24, 1961; U.S. m. Cheryl A. Brandt, Apr. 12, 1996; children: Dib, Lauren. MD, U. Damascus, Syria, 1985; cardiologist, U. Wis., Milw., 1997; MSc, Harvard U., 1999. Lic. Mass., Wis., Ariz., diplomate Am. Bd. Internal Medicine, Am. Bd. Cardiovasc. Disease, Am. Bd. Interventional Cardiology. Dir. cardiovasc. rsch. Ariz. Heart Inst., Phoenix, 1998—; investigational interventional cardiology fellow Harvard Med. Sch., Boston, 1999; also dir., cardiovascular rsch. Mercy Gilbert (Ariz.) Hosp., Phoenix; and assoc. physician diplomate, dir. clin. cardiovascular cell therapy Univ. Calif., San Diego. Spkr. in field; advisor Radi Med., 1995—, Possis Med., Minn., 1998—; cons. in field. Contbr. articles to profl. jours.; editl. cons.: Catheterization and Cardiovasc. Jour., 1996—. Recipient Med. Staff Sci. award, Tufts U., Boston, 1994; Med. scholar, Damascus U., 1985. Fellow: Am. Coll. Cardiology; mem.: ACP, Internat. Soc. Endovascular Interventionists. Avocations: swimming, fishing, travel. Office: Perlman Ambulatory Care Ctr 9350 Campus Point Dr La Jolla CA 92037 Home: 3951 E Paradise View Dr Paradise Valley AZ 85253-3808

DIBAISE, JOHN, gastroenterologist, educator; b. Omaha, Nov. 26, 1965; MD, U. Nebr., 1992. Prof. medicine, divsn. gastroenterology Mayo Clinic, 2005—. Fellow: Am. Coll. Gastroenterology; mem.: Am. Soc. Parenteral and Enteral Nutrition, Am. Gastroent. Assn. Office: 13400 E Shea Blvd Scottsdale AZ 85259 Business E-Mail: dibaise.john@mayo.edu.

DIBERARDINO, MARIE ANTOINETTE, developmental biologist, educator; b. Phila., May 2, 1926; d. Henry and Adelina (Belfi) DiB. BS in Biology, Chestnut Hill Coll., 1948, JD (hon.), 1990; PhD in Zoology, U. Pa., 1962. Rsch. asst. Fox Chase Cancer Ctr., 1948—58, rsch. assoc., 1960—64, asst. mem., 1964—67; assoc. prof. anatomy Drexel U. Coll. Medicine, Phila., 1964—67, prof. anatomy, 1971-81, prof. physiology, 1981-92, prof. biochemistry, 1992-96, prof. emerita, 1996—. Adv. bd. Internat. Rev. of Cytology, 1976-2000, Differentiation, 1981—2008, Series: Developmental Biology, A Comprehensive Synthesis, 1982-94; assoc. editor Jour. Exptl. Zoology, 1984-86; Contbr. articles on devel., genetics and cell biology to sci. jours.; contbr. book revs. in field. Mem. NIH Fogarty Internat. Fellowship Study Group, 1984. NSF grantee, NIH grantee; recipient Jean Brachet Meml. award. Fellow AAAS; mem. Am. Soc. Cell Biology (emerita), Soc. for Devel. Biologists (emerita, treas., trustee 1975-78), Internat. Soc. Devel. Biologists, Internat. Soc. of Differentiation (emerita, exec. com. 1978-85, 87-90, bd. dirs. 1980-94). Home: The Quadrangle 7311 #3300 Darby Rd Haverford PA 19041 E-mail: mdiberar@drexelmed.edu.

DI BIASE, MATTEO, cardiologist, educator; b. Canosa, Feb. 27, 1947; MD, U. Bari, 1971. Assoc. prof. U. Bari, 1988—2002; prof. U. Foggia, 2002—. Office: Viale Pinto 1 Foggia 71100 Italy Office Fax: 390881745424. Business E-Mail: dibiama@tiscali.it.

DI BLASI, ZELDA MARIA, psychologist, researcher; b. Messina, Sicily, Italy, Sept. 29, 1970; d. Ignazio Di Blasi and Musetta Joyce. BA in Applied Psychology with honors, U. Coll. Cork, Ireland, 1992; MPsychSc, U. Coll. Galway, Ireland, 1996; PhD, U. of York, Eng., 2003. Rsch. fellow Dept. of Health Scis., U. of York, Northern Yorkshire, England, 1997—2000; postdoctoral rsch. fellow Osher Ctr. for Integrative Medicine, U. Calif., San Francisco, 2003—. Cons. Harvard Med. Sch., Cambridge, Mass., 2003—; health psychology lectr. Dept. of Health Scis. of York, York, 1998—2000. Mem.: Brit. Psychol. Soc. (mem. 1996—). Achievements include research in Studies on the placebo effect and doctor-patient interactions published in the Lancet and the British Medical Journal.

DI CANDIA, MICHELE, medical researcher; b. Bari, Sept. 23, 1977; Degree in Medicine & Surgery, U. Bari, 2003, specialist in Plastic, Reconstructive & Aesthetic Surgery, 2008. Rschr., plastic surgery dept. U. Bari, 2010—. Fellowship, Plastic Surgery Dept., Addenbrooke's Hosp., Cambridge U., Eng., Plastic Surgery Dept., Broomfield Hosp., Chelmsford, Eng., Canniesburn Hosp., Glasgow, Eng. Mem.: GMC, Eng., Ordine dei medici chirurghi di Bari. Avocations: golf, sailing, soccer. Office: Via Melo da Bari Bari Puglia 70122 Italy Business E-Mail: mdicandia@doctors.net.uk.

DICANDILO, MICHAEL D., pharmaceutical executive, accountant; BSc in Acctg., U. Pa. Wharton Sch. CPA. With Ernst & Young LLP, 1982—90; regional v.p. fin. AmeriSource, Thorofare, NJ, 1990—95, v.p., 1995—2001; v.p., corp. contr. AmerisourceBergen Corp., 2001—02, sr. v.p., CFO, 2002—05, exec. v.p., CFO, 2005—; COO AmerisourceBergen Drug Corp., 2008. Office: AmerisourceBergen Corp 1300 Morris Dr Ste 100 Chesterbrook PA 19087 Office Phone: 610-727-7000, 800-829-3132. Office Fax: 800-829-3132. *

DI CARO, SIMONA, gastroenterologist; b. Agrigento, Italy, Sept. 30, 1975; d. Diego Di Caro and Angela Lombardo; m. Gianluca Bonanomi, Nov. 20, 2004; children: Gabriele Bonanomi, Lorenzo Bonanomi. Degree in Medicine, Cath. U. Sch. Medicine, Rome, 2000; attending in Nutrition, Tor Vergata U., Rome, 2007—. Cert. in medicine Cath. U. Sch. Medicine, 2001; specialist in gastroenterolgy & digestive endoscopy Cath. U., Gemelli Hosp., Rome, 2004. Residency gastroenterology Cath. U., Gemelli Hosp., 2000—04; postdoc. fellow U. Pitts. Med. Ctr., 2002—03; cons. gastroenterology San Raffaele U. Hosp., Cefalù, Italy, 2005—08; locum cons. gastroenterology Royal Berkshire Hosp. Found. Trust, Reading, England, 2008—09; sr. clin. rsch. fellow gastroenterology U. Coll. London Hosp., 2010—. Cons. San Raffaele U. Hosp., Cefalù, Italy, 2005—08; presenter & moderator lab. & clin. rsch. projects Internat. Profl. Meetings. Author: (novels) A Chick in Parliament; dance, Sicilia Antica Folkloristic Group. Mem. Vernice Fresca, Agrigento, Italy, 1993—94, Tamburino Orgn. Devel., Agrigento, 2009. Recipient Best Poster Presentation award, U. Pitts. Med. Ctr., 2003, United European Gastroenterology Week, 2004, Best Poster award, 2003, 2007; Young Investigator grant, Cath. U. Rome, 2002, Rsch. fellowship, Human Frontiere Sci. Programme, U. Pitts. Med. Ctr., 2003, fellowship, Human Forntiere Sci. Programme, 2003, Travel grant, United European Gastroenterology Week, 2003—04, 2007, UCLH Charities Fast Track grant, U. Coll. Hosp., London, 2011. Mem.: Italian Soc. Young Gastroenterologists, Italian Soc. Digestive Endoscopy, Italian Soc. Gastroenterology, Brit. Med. Assn., Gen. Med. Coun. Avocations: writing, reading, travel, painting, bicycling.

DI CEGLIE, DOMENICO, psychiatrist, educator; b. Cassano, Italy, Jan. 17, 1947; s. Angelantonio Di Ceglie and Amalia Lastray; m. Giovanna Rita Di Giacomo, Aug. 19, 1972; children: Angelo Antonio, Margherita. Degree in Medicine with honors, U. Perugia, Italy, 1972, Specialization in Psychiatry, 1976. Asst. dept. neurology and psychiatry U. Perugia, Italy, 1973—76; registrar psychiatry Ctrl. Middlesex Hosp., Northgate Clinic, London, 1976—79; sr. registrar Tavostock Clinic, London, 1979—85; founder Gender Identity Devel. Unit, England, 1989—; cons. child psychiatrist Croydon Child and Family Clinic, London, 1985—94, Tavistock and Portman NHS Trust, London, 1994—. Mem. Patron of Mermaids. Recipient Highly Commended Health and Social Care awards, London Region, 2004. Fellow: Royal Coll. Psychiatrists. Achievements include development of models of care and treatment for children and adolescents with gender dysphoria; in 2008 he led a successful application for national designation and funding of the Gender Identity Development service by the NSCG. Office: Gender Identity Devel Svc Tavistock & Portman NHS Trust The Tavistock Centre 120 Belsize Lane NW3 5BA London England Office Phone: 0044 20 7435 7111. Business E-Mail: gidu@tavi-port.nhs.uk.

DICHEK, DAVID A., cardiologist, educator; AB in Romance Langs. and Literatures magna cum laude, Princeton U., 1976; MD, UCLA, 1984. Diplomate Am. Bd. Internal Medicine, 1999, Am. Bd. Internal Medicine-cardiovasc. disease, 2004. Resident internal medicine Mass. Gen. Hosp., 1984—87; clin. fellow cardiology Johns Hopkins Hosp./Nat. Insts. of Health, 1990—92; assoc. dir. rsch. Univ. of Wash. Sch. of Medicine, Seattle, prof. medicine, adj. prof. pathology, edowed chair cardiovasc. rsch. and treatment John L. Locke, Jr. Family. Editl. bd. Circulation, 1996—2008, Circulation Rsch., 1996—2008, Human Gene Theraphy, 1998—2009, Artherosclerosis, Thrombosis and Vascular Biology, 2001—. Co-author: (publs.) Improved vascular gene transfer with a helper-dependent adenoviral vector, 2004, Macrophage-targeted overexpression of urokinase causes accelerated atherosclerosis, coronary artery occlusions, and premature death, 2004, Overexpression of urokinase by macrophages or deficiency of plasminogen activator inhibitor type 1 causes cardiac fibrosis in mice, 2004, Transforming growth factor ß1 induces neointima formation through plasminogen activator inhibitor-1-dependent pathways, 2006, Mechanisms of cardiac fibrosis induced by urokinase plasminogen activator, 2006, Plasminogen mediates the atherogenic effects of macrophage-expressed urokinase and accelerates atherosclerosis in apoE-knockout mice, 2008, TGF-ß1 limits plaque growth, stabilizes plaque structure, and prevents aortic dilation in Apolipoprotein E-null mice, 2009, Overexpression of urokinase by plaque macrophages causes histological features of plaque rupture and increases vascular matrix metalloproteinase activity in aged Apolipoprotein E-null mice, 2010. Recipient Special Recognition award, ATVB Coun. Am. Heart Assn., 2008. Fellow: Am. Heart Assn. Office: University of Washington Medical Center 1959 NE Pacific St Seattle WA 98195 Office Phone: 206-685-6959. Office Fax: 206-221-6346. Business E-Mail: ddichek@uw.edu.

DI CIANNIK, GRAZIANO, physician, director; b. San Marco Argentano, Italy, Feb. 5, 1958; MD, U. Pisa, 1983, degree in Internal Medicine, 1989. Physician U. Pisa, 1991—2010; dept. dir. Livorno Hosp., 2010—. Bd. dirs. U. Hosp. Pisa, 1999—2010. Master: Italian Diabetes and Pregnancy Study Group; mem.: European Diabetes and Pregnancy Study Group. Avocations: football, reading. Office: Dept Diabetology and Metabolic Livorno 57100 Italy Office Fax: 390586223380. Business E-Mail: dicianni@immr.med.unipi.it.

DICICCO, MICHAEL P., chemist; b. Phila., Sept. 14, 1975; BS, Temple U., 2000, PhD, 2005. Rsch. scientist Orthovita, Inc., 2000—02; scientist Johnson & Johnson, 2004—07, sr. scientist, 2007—. Mem.: AAMI Stds. Working Group 63 on Ethylene Oxide Residuals. Avocation: travel. Home: 146 Kinsman Rd Florence NJ 08518 Personal E-mail: mikedicicco2001@yahoo.com.

DICK, BARRY LEE, surgeon; b. Cin., Feb. 23, 1954; MD, U. Cin., 1987. Diplomate Am. Bd. Surgery with added qualifications in vascular surgery. Intern U. Cin., 1987-88, resident in gen. surgery, 1988-92; fellow in vasc. surgery St. Louis U., 1992-93; attending Good Samaritan Hosp., Cin., 1993—; attending, v.p. med. staff St. Elizabeth Hosps., Edgewood, Ky., 1993-95, bd. trustees, 2000—. Chmn. surgery St. Luke's Hosps., Florence, Ky., 1997-99. Fellow ACS; mem. Ohio Med. Assn., No. Ky. Med. Assn., Ky. Med. Assn., Mid West Vascular Surg. Soc. Office: Cranley Surg Assocs Inc 20 Med Village Dr # 394 Edgewood KY 41017 Office Phone: 859-578-0442. *

DICK, JOHN E., medical geneticist, educator; Prof. U. Toronto Dept. Molecular Genetics; dir. cancer stem cells program Ontario Inst. Cancer Rsch.; sr. scientist Toronto Gen. Rsch. Inst. Div. Cellular & Molecular Biology; affiliate scientist Ontario Cancer Inst. Div. Stem Cell & Devel. Biology. Recipient Michael Smith prize, Canadian Inst. for Health Rsch., 1997, Robert L. Noble prize, Nat. Cancer Inst. Canada, 2000, Herman Boerhaave medal, Leiden U., Netherlands, 2002, William Dameshek prize, Am. Soc. Hematology, 2005, Premier's Summit award, Province of Ontario, 2007. Fellow: Royal Soc. Canada Acad. Sciences. Office: Toronto Medical Discovery Tower 101 College St 8th Fl Rm 8-401 Toronto ON Canada M5G 1L7 Office Phone: 416-581-7466. E-mail: jdick@uhnres.utoronto.ca.

DICK, MACDONALD, II, pediatrician; b. Wilmington, Del., July 24, 1941; s. Alexander Colclough and Dorothy Quarles Dick; m. Carolin Kirkpatrick, Apr. 12, 1975; children: Alexander, Eliza. BA, Williams Coll., Williamstown, Mass., 1963; MD, U. Va., Charlottesville, 1967. Diplomate Am. Bd. Pediat., 1989, Am. Bd. Pediatric Cardiology, 1989. Pediatric intern U. Va. Hosp., Charlottesville, 1967-68, pediatric resident, 1968-70, fellow in pediatric cardiology, 1970-71; fellow in cardiology Children's Hosp. Med. Ctr., Boston, 1971-74; instr. in pediat. Children's Hosp. Med. Ctr., Harvard Med. Sch., 1974-77, asst. prof. pediat., 1977; asst. prof. dept. pediat. and communicable diseases U. Mich. Health Sys., Ann Arbor, 1977-88, assoc. prof. dept. pediat. and communicable diseases, 1988-93, prof., dept. pediat. and communicable diseases, 1994—, Amnon Rosenthal Collegiate prof. pediatric cardiology, 1994—. Dir. pediatric cardiology fellowship program U. Mich. Health Sys., dir. pediatric electrophysiology lab. and svc. Contbr. articles to profl. jours. Mem. Am. Acad. Pediat., Midwest Pediatric Cardiology Soc., N.Am. Soc. Pacing and Electrophysiology, Am. Coll. Cardiology, Internat. Soc. Heart Rsch., Pediatric Electrophysiology Soc. (pres. 1991) Am. Pediatric Soc., Soc. Pediatric Rsch., Soc. Pediatric Cardiology Fellowship Directors (tres. 2003, sec. 2004). Avocations: fly fishing, tennis, hiking, skiing. Office: Univ Mich Health Sys F1310 Box 0204 1500 E Med Ctr Dr Ann Arbor MI 48109-0005 E-mail: mdick@umich.edu.

DICKENS, JOYCE REBECCA, retired addictions therapist, educator; b. Roanoke Rapids, NC; d. Leslie and Lydia Marie Dickens. M in Addiction Psychology with honors, Capella U., 2000, PhD in Psychology with honors, 2003. Cert. addiction profl. Adj. prof. Broward Coll., Ft. Lauderdale, Fla., 1991—; primary therapist addictions Treatment Works, Ft. Lauderdale, 1962—2008. Mem.: AAUW, Phi Theta Kappa, Alpha Chi. Avocations: tennis, travel, public speaking. Office Phone: 954-201-7396. Personal E-mail: joycedickens@bellsouth.net.

DICKERSIN, KAY, researcher, educator; b. Phila., Nov. 10, 1951; d. George Richard and Barbara (Bray) D.; m. Robert Alan Van Wesep, June 30, 1973; children: Isaac, Edward. BA in Zoology, U. Calif., Berkeley, 1974, MA in Zoology, 1975; PhD in Epidemiology, Johns Hopkins U., 1989. Asst. prof. U. Md. Sch. Medicine, Balt., 1989-96, assoc. prof., 1996—98, Brown U. Sch. Medicine, Providence, 1998—2002, prof., 2002—05; dir. Balt. Cochrane Ctr., 1993-98; co-dir. New Eng. Cochrane Ctr., 1998—2002, US Cochrane Ctr., 2002—; prof. Johns Hopkins Bloomberg Sch. Pub. Health, 2005—, dir. Ctr. Clin. Trials. Bd. dir. Nat. Cancer Adv. Bd., 1994-2000. Recipient Ellen Barnett Meml. award Susan B. Komen Found. Race for the Cure, 1995; named to Women's Hall of Fame, Balt. City Commn. for Women, 1996; named one of Md.'s Top 100 Women, Md. Daily, 1998, 2005. Mem. Am. Epidemiol. Soc., Soc. Clin. Trials, Inst. Medicine. Office: Dept Epidemiology Rm 5010 615 N Wolfe St Baltimore MD 21205 Home: 1402 Bolton St Baltimore MD 21217 Office Phone: 410-502-4421. Fax: 410-502-4621. E-mail: kdickers@jhsph.edu.

DICKEY, BURTON F., critical care specialist, educator; MD, U. Conn., 1980. Diplomate Am. Bd. Internal Medicine, 1983, Am. Bd. Internal Medicine- pulmonary disease, 1988, Am. Bd. Internal Medicine- critical care medicine, 1999. Resident in internal medicine Temple Univ. Hosp., Phila.; fellow in pulmonary disease Univ. Conn. Health Ctr., Farmington; prof. in medicine Case West Res. Univ.; hosp. affiliation include Univ. Tex. MD Anderson Cancer Ctr. Office: University of Texas MD Anderson Cancer Center 1515 Holcombe Blvd Houston TX 77030-4000 Office Phone: 713-792-6161.

DICKEY, NANCY WILSON, chancellor, physician; b. Watertown, SD, Sept. 10, 1950; m. Franklin Champ; children: Danielle, Wilson, Elizabeth. BA, Stephen F. Austin State U.; MD, U. Tex., 1976. Diplomate Am. Bd. Family Practice. Resident family medicine Meml. Hosp. System, Houston, 1976-79; pres., vice chancellor health affairs TAMUS Health Sci. Ctr.; prof. family medicine TAMUS Coll. Med., College Station, Tex., 1996—, pres., 2006—. Hon. staff Polly Ryon Meml. Hosp., Richmond; active staff Coll. Sta. (Tex.) Med. Ctr., St. Josephs Hosp., Bryan, Tex. Reviewer Jour. of AMA; editl. adv. bd. Patient Care, Med. World News, Med. Ethics Advisor, Archives of Family Medicine. Coach youth soccer, 1986-88; sponsor United Meth. Youth Fellowship, 1991-95; bd. dirs. Hastings Ctr., Office of Early Childhood Devel., Am. Heart Assn.; mem. Christ United Meth. Ch., College Station. Recipient Disting. Alumni award U. Tex. Med. Sch., Citation of Merit Tex. Soc. of Pathologists, 1995. Mem. AMA (pres. elect 1997, pres. 1998, chair bd. trustees 1995-97, vice chair 1994-95, bd. trustees 1989-97, sec. treas. 1993-94, exec. com. 1991, other coms.), Inst. Medicine, Tex. Acad. of Family Physicians, Tex. Med. Assn., Alpha Omega Alpha. Office: 301 Tarrow St #7th Flr College Station TX 77840-7896

DICKINSON, CHRISTINE Z., nuclear medicine physician, cardiologist; b. American Fork, Utah, Oct. 23, 1952; d. James Hershel and Helen Evatz Zunich; 1 child, William Claiborne. BS, U. Utah, 1974, MD, 1978; cardiology fellow, U. Calif. Davis, 1990. Diplomate Am. Bd. Internal Medicine, Am. Bd. Nuclear Medicine. Resident in internal medicine Vanderbilt U. Sch. Medicine, Nashville, 1981, fellow in nuc. medicine and nuc. cardiology, 1981—85; fellow in cardiology U. Calif., Davis, 1990; asst. prof. radiology, divsn. nuc. medicine U. Calif. Davis Med. Ctr., Sacramento, 1985—87; dir. nuc. medicine San Jose Imaging Ctr., Calif., 1990—92; asst. clin. prof. radiology U. Calif. Davis, Sacramento, 1991; staff physician nuc. medicine Covina Intercmty. Hosp., 1992; dir. nuc. cardiology, dept. nuc. medicine William Beaumont Hosp., Royal Oak, Mich., 1992—. Clin. asst. prof. dept. radiology Mich. State U., Lansing, 2000—; mem. admissions com., cardiology fellowship program William Beaumont Hosp., Royal Oak, Mich., 2000—, lectr. nuc. medicine residency tng. and oncology fellowship tng., 1999—, coord. nuc. cardiology faculty/divsn. cardiology, 1992—; sci. program com. moderator Soc. Nuc. Medicine, 2001. Contbr. articles to profl. jours. Mem. Joint Rev. Com. on Ednl. Programs in Nuc. Medicine Tech., Mont., 2003—; mem. women's legacy luncheon Am. Heart Assn., Detroit, 2002—03, bd. dirs., 2003—. Grantee, Am. Heart Assn., 1989—90; Presdl. scholar, U. Utah, 1974—78. Mem.: Am. Coll. Nuc. Physicians, Am. Soc. Nuc. Cardiology, Soc. Nuc. Medicine, Mortar Board, Phi Kappa Phi. Office: William Beaumont Hosp 3601 West 13 Mile Rd Royal Oak MI 48073 Business E-Mail: cdickinson@beaumont.edu.

DICKSHEET, SHARADKUMAR, plastic surgeon; b. Pandharpur, Mumbai, India, Dec. 13, 1930; s. Sitaram Ganpat and Malathibai Dixit; children: Shari, Sharad, Supriya. BMus, Bhatkhande U., 1943; BS, Osmania U., Hyperabad, India, 1951; MBBS, Naqpur U., India, 1956. Pvt. practice, Fairbanks, Ala., 1969—78; fellow cosmetic surgery Guadalahara Inst. of Plastic Surgery, Mexico, 1979—80, Manhattan EET Hosp., NYC, 1980—81, Trudi Vogt Inst., Zurich, Switzerland, 1981—82; resident plastic surgery Downstate Med. Ctr., Bklyn., 1982—84; pvt. practice Bklyn., 1984—94. Residency tchg. Downstate Med. Ctr., Bklyn., 1984—94; classical music vocalist, India, 1948—58; founder Plasti Surgery India Project, 1968. Contbr. articles to profl. jours. Recipient Internat. award for child advocacy, Hannah Neil Ctr. Found. Bd., 2001, Sheikh Hamdan Bid Rashid Al Maktoum award, 2001—02, Dr. Nathan Davis Internat. Humanitarian award in medicine, AMA Found., 2005, Internat. Humanitarian award, Am. Soc. Plastic Surgeons, 2005, award, Rotary Internat., 2005, Bharat Gaurav award, Friends India Internat. Soc., 2007, citation by, Internat. Soc. Laryngectomees, 2005, MRI of Yr., Dubai, 2002. Mem.: Bhavatiya Jaih Soc., Giants Club, Lions Club, Rotary Club. Hindu. Avocation: music. Office Phone: 718-871-0280. Personal E-mail: murphy.pianoman@att.net.

DICLAUDIO, JANET ALBERTA, health information administrator; b. Monroeville, Pa., June 17, 1940; d. Frank and Pearl Alberta (Wolfgang) DiC. Cert. in Med. Rsch. Libr. Sci., Luth Med. Ctr., 1962; BA, Thiel Coll., 1975; MS, SUNY, Buffalo, 1978. Registered record adminstr. Dir. med. records Bashline Hosp., Grove City, Pa., 1962, St. Clair Meml. Hosp., Pitts., 1963-73; asst. prof. Ill. State U., Normal, 1976-81; corp. dir. med. records Buffalo Gen. Hosp., 1981-85; dir. med. records Candler Hosp., Savannah, Ga., 1985-94, med. records analyst, 1994-98; pres. prn Assocs., Savannah, Ga., 1998—2003. Med. record cons. White Cliff Nursing Home, Greenville, Pa., 1973—75; mgmt. cons. Gifford W. Lorenz MD, Savannah, 1992—94; Medicare compliance officer and coder Health Claims, Inc., Savannah, 1999—2001; mgmt. cons. John D. Northup, Jr., MD, Savannah, 2001—02; auditor, cons. Healthpac Computer Sys., Inc., 2001—. Contbr. articles to periodicals. Bd. dirs. Mid-Ill. Areawide Health Planning Corp., Normal, 1979-81. Mem. Am. Health Info. Mgmt. Assn., Ga. Health Info. Mgmt. Assn., S.E. Ga. Health Info. Mgmt. Assn. Avocations: painting, reading. Personal E-mail: jdcprn@aol.com.

DIECKMANN, KLAUS PETER, urologist, educator; b. Bremen, Germany, June 12, 1950; s. Johann Heinrich and Hermine (Unrecht) D.; m. Monika Nowack, May 21, 1987; children: Thomas, Andreas, Oliver. MD, U. Göttingen, Germany, 1977. Diplomate in urology, Germany. Resident in surgery Krankenhaus Weende, Göttingen, 1977-80; vol. dr. German Vol. Svc., Tunduru, Tanzania, 1981-82; resident in urology Free U., Berlin, 1983-87, staff urologist Klinikum Steglitz, 1987-91, dep. head dept. Klinikum Steglitz, 1992-93; head dept. Albertinen-Krankenhaus, Hamburg, Germany, 1993—. Contbr. over 180 articles to profl. jours. Sgt. German Army, 1970-71. Mem. German Urol. Soc., European Soc. Urology, Assn. Urol. Oncology, European Assn. Urology, Internat. Soc. Urology. Avocations: sports, stamp collecting/philately, collecting old urologic books. Office: Albertinen-Krankenhaus Süntelstr 11 D-22457 Hamburg Germany Office Phone: 40-55882253. Business E-Mail: dieckmannkp@t-online.de.

DIEHL, JAMES T., thoracic surgeon; MD, Yeshiva U., NYC, 1978. Diplomate Am. Bd. Thoracic Surgery, lic. Pa., 1992. Intern gen. surgery Montefiore Med. Ctr., Albert Einstein Coll. Medicine, NYC, 1979; resident gen. surgery Cleve. Clinic, 1984; resident cardiothoracic surgery Univ. Toronto Med. Ctr., 1986; hosp. affiliations includes Thomas Jefferson Univ. Hosp. Named one of Top Doctors, Phila. Mag., 2007, 2010—. Office: Thomas Jefferson University Hospital 5th Fl 1100 Walnut St Philadelphia PA 19107 Office Phone: 215-955-6996. Office Fax: 215 955-6010.

DIEHL, LOUIS F., hematologist; b. Trenton, NJ, Apr. 8, 1948; s. Louis and Anna D.; m. Anna Mae, Dec. 3, 1973, children: Megan, Erin. BS, Georgetown U., 1970, MD, 1975. Oncologist Johns Hopkins Oncology Ctr., Balt., 1999—2004, Duke U. Med. Ctr., 2004—. *

DIELMAN, RAY WALTER, health physics, nuclear medicine and radiologic scientist, natural hygienist; b. Napoleon, Ohio, Dec. 25, 1938; s. Walter Carl and Gail Ann (Fenstermaker) D.; m. Diane Tahy, June 1961 (div. 1968); children: Joseph Scott, David Jon; m. Roberta Schreiber, June 1968 (div. 1980); m. Beverly Beavers Bryan, Oct. 16, 1994. Student, Defiance Coll., 1956-59; radiologic technologist diploma, St. Joseph Hosp. Sch., Ft. Wayne, Ind., 1962; nuclear medicine technologist cert., U. Mich., 1962; OPM, Harvard U., 1975; doctor of Naturopathy, Trinity Coll. Natural Health, 1997. Cert mgmt. cons., radiologic, nuclear medicine technologist, bd. eligible nuclear medicine scientist. Supt. nuclear medicine U. Mich. Hosp., Ann Arbor, 1962-63; dir. nuclear medicine Mercy Hosp & Med. Ctr., Chgo., 1963-64; cons., nuclear medicine Picker Corp., White Plains, N.Y., 1964-67; pres. Dielman Cons., Inc., Chgo., 1967-88; dir. dept. of radiology Loyola U. Med. Ctr., Chgo., 1980-83; co-owner Island Cinema & Theatre, Sanibel Isle, Fla., 1983-87; mgr. Fla. Dept. Health Bur. Radiation Control, Tampa, 1988—2005; health physics and radiation medicine scientist cons., 2005—. Assoc. mem., com. Conf. Radiation Control Program Dirs., Frankfort, Ky., 1989-; vice chmn. Radiation Control Rsch. and Edn. Found.; del. Internat. Com. of Radionuclide Metrology, London, 1976-85; chmn. Manatee County Health Care Adv. Bd., 1995—2005; instnl. biosafety com. U. South Fla., 1999—2005, instnl. rev. bd., 2002-06; chair City of Palmetto Employee Pension Fund, 2002—; chair bd. suprs. Palms of Terra Ceia Bay Cmty. Devel. Dist., 2007—. Co-editor/author: Essentials Nuclear Medicine Technology, 1970; contbr. articles to profl. jours. Am. Cancer Soc. scholar, 1962, Pub. Health Leadership Inst. scholar U. South Fla., 2003-04. Avocations: tennis, golf, sailing, skiing, travel. Home: 2725 Terra Ceia Bay Blvd Unit 208 Palmetto FL 34221-5934 Office: Radiation Safety Advisors LLC PO Box 2082 Palmetto FL 34220-1224 Office Phone: 813-493-5443. Personal E-mail: raydielman@verizon.net.

DIENER, ERWIN, immunologist; b. Lucerne, Switzerland, Jan. 6, 1932; arrived in Can., 1970; m. Eva Schaufelberger, 1957. PhD, U. Zurich, 1963. Rsch. fellow Inst. for Radiobiology, Zurich, 1960-64; Roche fellow Walter and Eliza Hall Inst., Melbourne, Australia, 1964-67, rsch. fellow, 1967-70; prof. U. Alta., Edmonton, Can., 1970-73, prof., head dept. immunology, 1973-88, prof. emeritus, 1989—. Fellow Royal Soc. Can.

DIENSTAG, JULES LEONARD, dean, hepatologist, researcher; b. NYC, Dec. 10, 1946; m. Judy Iris Gordon, Feb. 3, 1974; children: Josh, Jonathan. AB magna cum laude, Columbia Coll., 1968; MD, Columbia U., 1972. Diplomate Am. Bd Internal Medicine. Intern in medicine U. Chgo., 1972-73, resident in medicine, 1973-74; postdoctoral fellow, rsch. assoc. NIH, Bethesda, Md., 1974-76; clin. and rsch. fellow Mass. Gen. Hosp., Boston, 1976-78, clin. asst. medicine, 1978-79, asst. in medicine, 1979-82, asst. physician, 1983-87, assoc. physician, 1988-93, physician, 1993—; asst. prof. of medicine Harvard Med. Sch., Boston, 1978-82, assoc. prof., 1982—2002, faculty assoc. dean for admissions, 1998—2004, prof. medicine, 2002—, assoc. dean Academic and Clin. Programs, 2003—05, dean Med. Edn., 2005—, Carl W. Walter prof. medicine, 2005—. Expert panelist on viral hepatitis Lister Hill Nat. Ctr. Biomed. Comm., Nat. Libr. Medicine, 1980-82, advisor, 1982-86; numerous tchg. appointments; lectr. in field Mem. editl. bd. Jour. Clin. Microbiology, 1977-86, Hepatology, 1980-86, Infectious Disease Series, Marcel Dekker Med. divsn., 1981-85, Gastroenterology, 1981-86, Jour. Viral Hepatitis, 1993—2007; editor: Gastroenterology Series, Marcel Dekker, 1983-86, Mass. Gen. Hosp. Liver-Biliary-Pancreas Ctr. Newsletter, 1990-05; assoc. editor: Gastroenterology, 1986-91, 96-01. Recipient Clin. Investigator award USPHS, 1978-79. Fellow ACP; mem. AAAS, Internat. Assn. Study of the Liver, European Assn. Study of the Liver (corr.), Am. Soc. Microbiology, Am. Fedn. Clin. Rsch. Am. Assn. Immunologists, Am. Assn. Study Liver Diseases, Am. Gastroent. Assn., Mass. Med. Soc., Phi Beta Kappa. Office: Harvard Med Sch Off Dean for Med Edn / Gordon Hall 25 Shattuck St Boston MA 02115 also: Mass Gen Hosp 55 Fruit St Boston MA 02114-2696 Office Fax: 617-432-6253. Personal E-mail: jdienstag@partners.org. Business E-Mail: jdienstag@hms.harvard.edu.

DIESFELD, KATE, lawyer, educator; b. Buffalo, Sept. 20, 1960; arrived in Eng., 1992, arrived in New Zealand, 2000; d. Gerard and Mildred Diesfeld. BA, Colgate U., 1982; JD, U. San Diego, 1988. Bar: Calif. 1989. Atty. Protection Advocacy, Inc., LA, 1989—92; legal supr. Kent Law Clinic, U. Kent, England, 1992—2000, Nat. Ctr. Health, Law and Social Ethics, Auckland (New Zealand) U. Tech., 2001—10, assoc. prof. social justice, assoc. dean, 2011—. Co-editor: Involuntary Detention and Therapeutic Jurisprudence: International Perspectives on Civil Commitment, 2003. Nominee Vice Chancellors Woman in Leadership Program, New Zealand, 2008. Office: Te-Piringa Faculty Law Private Bag 3105 Hamilton 3240 New Zealand Office Phone: 6478562889 ext. 8976. Business E-Mail: kate.diesfeld@aut.ac, kated@waikato.ac.nz.

DIETER, RAYMOND ANDREW, JR., physician, thoracic general and vascular surgeon; b. Chebanse, Ill.; June 19, 1934; s. Raymond Augustus Sr. and Emma Rose Mayme (Witt) D.; m. Bette Renéé Myers, Sept. 29, 1961; children: Raymond III, David, Lisa, Lynn, Deanna, Robert. Student, U. Ill., 1952-56, Olivet Nazarene Coll., 1954; MA in Physiology, U. Ill., Chgo., 1966; BS in Chemistry, U. Ill., Champaign, 1994; MD, Loyola U., 1960. Diplomate Am. Bd. Thoracic Surgery, Am. Bd. Surgery. Intern Cook County Hosp., Chgo., 1960-61; resident in gen. surgery VA Hosp., Hines, Ill., 1963-67, sr. resident in cardiopulmonary surgery, 1967-69; practice specializing in thoracic, cardiovascular surg. DuPage Med. Group, 1999—; practice specializing in thoracic, cardiovas. gen. and oncologic surg. Glen Ellyn Clinic, Ill., 1969—, pres., 1982-85, also bd. dirs.; mem. staff Hines VA Hosp., Ill., 1963-74, Cen. DuPage Hosp., Winfield, Ill., 1969—, pres. staff, 1987-89; mem. staff Loyola U. Med. Ctr., Maywood, Ill., 1969-80, Meml. Hosp. DuPage County, Elmhurst, Ill., 1969—, Delnor Hosp., St. Charles, Ill., 1970—, Community Hosp., Geneva, Ill., 1970—79, Good Samaritan Hosp., Downers Grove, Ill., 1976—, Glendale Heights (Ill.) and Glen Oaks Cmty. Hosp., 1980—, St. Mary's Hosp., Streator, Ill., 1997—, Alexian Bros. Med. Ctr., Elk Grove Village, Ill., 1975—79, 1993—2009, emeritus, 2009—; pres. staff Good Samaritan Hosp., Downers Grove, Ill., 1979. Clin. instr. Stritch Sch. Medicine Loyola U., 1966-71, clin. asst. prof., 1971-80, Edward Hosp., Naperville Ill., 1985-; trustee Ctr. Bank, Glen Ellyn, 1978-90, Lake Shore Bank, Glen Ellyn Found.; internat. lectr. on med. and outdoor topics; chmn. Glen Ellyn Clinic Facilities, 1987-98, Physicians Benefit trust, 1988-92; pres., chmn. bd. No. Ill. Surg. Ctr., 1989—; pres. DuPage Doctors, Inc., Ctr. for Surgery, 1989-; co-founder Cmty. Banks of Wheaton/Glen Ellyn, 1993-, dirs., vice chmn., 2005—; co-founder, pres. Northeast DuPage Surgicenter, 1997—2009; chmn. bd. dirs., CEO, pres. Masterile, Inc., 1997-99; mem., chmn. negotiating com. Glen Ellyn Clinic, 1999; officer Internat. Healthcare Cons., LLC, 2002—. Author: (with B.R. Dieter and A.C. Mickelson) Mickelson and Peterson Family Sketch, 1970, (with M.C. Sorensen and E.R. Dieter) A Sorensen and Jensen Family Tree, 1975, (with B.R. Dieter, C. Myers, U. Myers, and D. Dieter) A Myers and Remley Family Tree, 1978, (with others) A Witt and (von) Ruehle Family Sketch, 1976, A Hofeling, Janssen, Lehnert, and Meier Family Sketch, 1979, A Dieter Family Tree: Sketches of German Families, 1981, Thoracoscopy for Surgeons, 1994; editor: Thoracoscopy for Surgeons-Diagnostic and Therapeutic Text, 1995; co-editor (with Robert and Raymond Dieter III): Peripheral Arterial Diseases Text, 2009, (with Robert & Raymond Dieter III) Vermont and Lymphatic Disease Text, 2011; contbr. numerous articles to profl. jours. and chpts. in med. books, numerous TV and radio interviews. Mgr. Glen Ellyn baseball team, 1970, 71, 78-82; asst. leader 4-H Club, 1975-83; mem. Glenbard South High Sch. Boosters, World Fedn. Drs. Who Respect Human Life, 1980—; pres., bd. dirs. DuPage Med. Found.; mem. Econ. Devel. Coun. Glen Ellyn, sec., 2000, v.p., 2001-02, pres., 2003; bd. dirs. Farm Safety Just 4 Kids, 2004-07. Served with USPHS, 1961-63, with Res., 1982—. Recipient Key to City of Manila, Philippines; named Hon. Citizen, Quito Ecuador, La Paz, Bolivia. Fellow ACS, Internat. Coll. Angiology (editl. bd. 1995—, co-chair membership com. 2007—), Internat. Coll. Surgeons (exec. com. 1991—, treas. 1993-94, pres. elect 1995-96, pres. 1997-98, U.S. sect., corp. sec. 1997-2000, pres.-elect 2001-02, pres. 2003-04, immediate past pres. 2005-06, chmn. internat. surg. teams. program 2005-06, World body ICS to WHO:NGO, del. 2001-06); mem. AMA (Physician's Recognition awards, mem. ho. dels.), Internat. Mus. Surg. Sci. (chmn. bd. dirs. 1991—), Internat. Soc. Circumpolar Health (reviewer), Internat. Soc. Outdoor Health, Global Acad. for Tropical Surgery (co-founder 2004), Am. Coll. Angiology, Am. Coll. Chest Physicians, Assn. Acad. Surgeons, Am. Soc. Circumpolar Health (charter, 1964), Alaska Cmty. Found. (bd. mem. 2008-), Assn. Mil. Surgeons, Assn. Res. Officers, Am. Heart Assn. (coun. 1974—), Soc. Med. Hist. Chgo., Soc. Critical Care Medicine, Soc. Thoracic Surgeons (membership com.), Ill. State Med. Soc. (trustee 1983-92, chmn. Ill. hosp. med. staff sect. 1985-87, pres., med. adminstrs. ctr. for surgery 1994—, award 2011), Ill. Thoracic Surg. Soc. (sec. 1981-83, pres. 1984-85), DuPage County Med. Soc. (pres. 1977, mem. govtl. com., numerous others), Chgo. Med. Soc., Charles B. Puestow Surg. Soc. (sec., treas. 1966-67, v.p. 1968), Good Samaritan Soc., Ala. Geographic Soc., Kankakee Valley Geneal. Soc., Ill. Geneal. Soc., U. Ill. Alumni Assn. (bd. dirs. 2002-09), Am. Rabbit Breeders Assn., Silver Marten Club, Century Club (Elmhurst), Chebanse Lions (charter), Resurrection Bay (Alaska) Lions, Internat. lions Club (50 yr. mem.), Alaska Found. (bd. dir., 2008-). Republican. Roman Catholic. Avocations: exercise, farming, fishing, hunting, writing. Office: Glen Ellyn Clinic DuPage Med Group 430 Pennsylvania Ave Glen Ellyn IL 60137-4496 Office Phone: 653-790-1700. Office Fax: 630-545-7531.

DIETERICH, DOUGLAS THOMAS, gastroenterologist, researcher; b. Queens, NY, Mar. 1, 1951; s. Albert Frederick and Florence Anna (Kilroy) D. BS, Yale U., 1973; M in Health Adminstrn., C.W. Post Coll., 1974; MD, NYU, 1978. Diplomate Am. Bd. Internal Medicine and Gastroenterology. Intern, then resident Bellevue Hosp., NYC, 1978-81, fellow gastroenterology, 1981-83; attending physician NYU Hosp., 1983; clin. instr. medicine NYU, 1983—88, clin. asst. prof., 1988—93, clin. assoc. prof., 1993—2003, adj. prof., 2003—. Teaching asst. NYU, NYC, 1979—83; mem. AIDS Clin. Trials Group NIH, 1986-97, Internat. AIDS Soc. U.S.A.mem., 1986—97; pres. Liberty Med. LLP, NYC, 1996—2002; vice chair medicine Mt. Sinai Sch. Medicine, NYC, 2002—; chmn. HIV Ind. Physicians Assn.; bd. dirs. Cmty. Rsch. Initiative on AIDS. Contbr. articles to profl. jours. Fellow ACP, Am. Coll. Gastroenterology; mem. AMA, Am. Gastroent. Assn., Am. Soc. Gastrointestinal Endoscopy, Am. Soc. Internal Medicine, Internat. AIDS Soc. U.S.A., N.Y. County Med. Soc., N.Y. Liver Found. (bd. dir.), N.Y. State Med. Soc., N.Y. Acad. Gastroenterology, Yale Club, Cherry Valley Club, Grand Harbor Club. Republican. Lutheran. Home: 62 Saint James St S Garden City NY 11530-6344 Office: Mt Sinai Sch Medicine One Gustav Levy Pl New York NY 10128 Office Phone: 212-241-7270. E-mail: douglas.dieterich@mountsinai.org.

DIETERT, RODNEY REYNOLDS, immunology and toxicology educator; b. Ft. Lee, Va., Dec. 6, 1951; s. Ralph O. and Beverly (Reynolds) D.; children: Grant C., Matthew W; m. Janice M. Dietert. BS, Duke U., 1974; PhD, U. Tex., 1977. Asst. prof. immunogenetics Cornell U., Ithaca, NY, 1977-83, assoc. prof., 1983-89, prof., 1989—, prof. immunotoxicology, 1997—; adj. prof. N.C. State U., 1992—2000; head grad. program in immunology Cornell U., Ithaca, NY, 1989-92, dir. Inst. for Comparative and Environ. Toxicology, 1992-97, prof. immunotoxicology, 1997—, dir. program on breast cancer and environ. risk factors, 2000—04; sr. fellow Ctr. for the Environment, 1993-96, Inst. Medicine, Agt. Orange Panel, 2010—; editor Toxicology Book Series, Springer, 2010—; pres. immunotoxicology Speciality Sect. Soc. Toxicology, 2011—. Cons. Burleson Rsch. Techs., 2005-10, World Health Orgn. Immunotoxicity Risk Assessment Panel, 2007-, Nat. Toxicology Program Panel, Immunotoxicology Criteria Document, 2008-09; panelist Nat. Inst. Environ. Health Scis. (AIDS Therapeutics), Research Triangle Park, 1988, mem. oxidative damage panel, 1997; USDA grant panel mgr., Washington, 1993-94; mem. Am. Inst. Biol. Scis.-Gulf War Illnesses panel Dept. Def., 1995, 97; invited testimony U.S. Congress Clean Water Act, 1995; spkr. at profl. confs. Author: Strategies for Protecting Your Child's Immune Systemn 2010; jour. editor CRC Press, Inc., Boca Raton, Fla., 1986-90, editor book series, 1990—; editor jour. Elsevier Sci. Publs., Ltd., Oxford, U.K., 1990-95. Chmn. Minority Edn. Com., Ithaca, 1980; chmn. Environ. Com. on Native Americans, Ithaca, 1994-95. Mem. Assn. Immunologists, Soc. Toxicology. Office: Cornell U Dept Microbiology/Immunol Coll Vet Med C5-135 UMC Ithaca NY 14853-5601 Home Phone: 607-257-1156; Office Phone: 607-253-4015. Business E-Mail: rrd1@cornell.edu.

DIETHELM, ARNOLD GILLESPIE, surgeon; b. Balt., Jan. 13, 1932; s. Oskar Arnold and Grace (Gillespie) D.; m. Nancy Lee Lane, June 21, 1951; children: Nancy Elizabeth, Linda Lane, Eugene Arnold (dec.), Ellen Jeanette, Richard Gillespie. AB, Wash. State U., 1953; MD, Cornell U., 1958; DSc (hon.), U. Ala., 1993. Intern, then resident in surgery NY Hosp., 1958-65; asst. in surgery, research fellow Peter Bent Brigham Hosp., Boston, 1965-66; research fellow surgery Harvard U. Med. Sch., 1966-67; instr. Cornell U. Med. Sch., 1964-65; mem. faculty U. Ala. Med. Center, Birmingham, 1967—, prof. surgery, 1973—, vice chmn. dept., 1973-82, chmn. dept. surgery, 1982-2000; prof. emertius dept. surgery U. Ala. Sch. Medicine. Mem. residency rev. com. for surgery Accreditation Coun. for Grad. Med. Edn., 1994—, chmn., 1997-99. Contbr. articles med. jours. Mem. AAAS, ACS, AMA, Am. Soc. Nephrology, Am. Soc. Transplant Surgeons (pres. 1991-92), Am. Surg. Assn., Am. Bd. Surgery (dir. 1987-93), Assn. Acad. Surgery, Transplantation Soc., So. Surg. Assn. (pres. 1989). Home: 3248 Sterling Rd Birmingham AL 35213-3508 Office: U Ala Hosp Dept Surgery 619 19th St S Birmingham AL 35233-0001 *

DIETRICH, ROBERT ANTHONY, pathologist, consultant, medical association administrator; b. Buffalo, May 24, 1933; s. Charles Thomas and Mary Evelyn (Shoecraft) D.; m. Alison Elinor D'Arcy, June 13, 1959; children— Anne Marie, Alison D'Arcy, Karen Elizabeth, Kathleen Murray, Patricia Evelyn, Ellen Kiley BS, Canisius Coll., Buffalo, 1955; MD, Georgetown U., Washington, 1959; MS in Surg. Pathology, U. Minn., Mpls., 1964; JD, George Washington U., Washington, 1974. Diplomate Am. Bd. Pathology, Am. Bd. Nuclear Medicine. Intern D.C. Gen. Hosp., Washington, 1959-60; resident Mayo Clinic, Rochester, Minn., 1960-64; chief pathology svc. U.S. Army Hosp., Fort Gordon, Augusta, Ga., 1964-66; pathologist O.B. Hunter Meml. Lab., Washington, 1966-78; chmn. dept. pathology, chief div. nuclear medicine Montgomery Gen. Hosp., Olney, Md., 1972-78; vice chmn. dept. pathology, chief divsn. nuclear medicine Sibley Meml. Hosp., Washington, 1978-89; sec. Am. Soc. Clin. Pathologists, Chgo., 1981-88, exec. v.p./chief staff, 1982-92; cons., 1992—. Served to capt. U.S. Army, 1964-66. Noble Found. grantee Mayo Clinic, 1964 Fellow Am. Coll. Legal Medicine, Coll. Am. Path., Am. Soc. Clin. Path.; mem. Med. Soc. D.C. (sec. 1984-86, pres. 1988). Home and Office: 5506 Parkston Rd Bethesda MD 20816-3326

DIETZ, DAIVD W., colon and rectal surgeon; Attended in Biology, Wash. and Lee U., Lexington, 1989; MD, Thomas Jefferson U., Phila., 1993. Diplomate Am. Bd. Surgery, Am. Bd. Colon and Rectal Surgery. Intern in gen. surgery Allegheny Univ. Hosp.-East Falls, Phila., 1994; resident in in gen. surgery Cleve. Clinic, Ohio, 2000, fellow in colon and rectal surgery, 2001, staff surgeon colorectal surgery dept., vice chair. Co-author: Clinical Implictions of Acellular Mucin Pools in Resected Rectal Cancer with Pathologic Complete Response to Neoadjuvant Chemoradiation, 2010, Downstaging after chemoradiotherapy for locally advanced rectal cancer: is there more (tumor) than meets the eye?, 2010, Prone or lithotomy positioning during an abdominoperineal resection for rectal cancer results in comparable oncologic outcomes, 2011, Pathologic complete response after neoadjuvant treatment for rectal cancer decreases distant recurrence and could eradicate local recurrence, 2011, Response to letter to the editor: neoadjuvant therapy for rectal cancer: the impact of longer interval between chemoradiation and surgery, 2011. Fellow: Am. Soc. Colon and Rectal Surgeons, ACS; mem.: Internat. Soc. for Gastrointestinal Hereditary Tumors, Assn. for Acad. Surgery, Am. Gastrointestinal Endoscopic Surgeons, Soc. for Surgery of the Alimentary Tract. Office: Cleveland Clinic 9500 Euclid Ave Cleveland OH 44195 Office Phone: 216-444-5404.

DIETZ, FREDERICK R., orthopaedic surgeon; b. Akron, Ohio; MD, Columbia Coll. Physicians & Surgery, NYC, 1977. Cert. in orthopaedic surgery 2007. Internship in pediatric orthopedic surgery U. Iowa Hosps. and Clinics, Iowa City, 1977—78, residency in pediatric orthopedic surgery, 1978—83, clin. rschr., pediatric orthopaedics, 1981—82, fellowship in pediatric orthopaedics, 1983—84, asst. prof. orthopaedics, divsn. pediatric orthopaedics, 1984—89, assoc. prof. orthopaedics, divsn. pediatric orthopaedics, 1989—93, prof. orthopaedics, divsn. pediatric orthopaedics, 1993—. Guest lectr. Latin Am. Soc. Orthopaedics and Traumatology, Lima, Peru, 1998;

vis. prof. New Zealand Pediatric Orthopaedic Assn., Christchurch, 2001, Children's Hosp. Med. Ctr. Dept. Pediatric Orthopaedics, Cin., 2002, West Penn Hosp. Dept. Foot and Ankle Surgery, Pitts., 2002, Hosp. for Sick Children, Dept. Orthopaedic Surgery, Toronto, Canada, 2003; co-dir. orthopaedic gait lab. U. Iowa Hosps. and Clinics. Contbr. articles to profl. jours., chapters to books. Named to Best Doctors in Am., 2007. Fellow: Am. Acad. Pediat.; mem.: Am. Acad. Cerebral Palsy and Devel. Medicine, Iowa Orthopaedic Soc, Pediatric Orthopaedic Soc. North America, Orthopaedic Rsch. Soc., Am. Acad. Orthopaedic Surgeons, Am. Soc. Human Genetics. Office: Dept Orthopaedics and Rehab Univ Iowa Hosps and Clinics 200 Hawkins Dr 01008 JPP Iowa City IA 52242-1009 Office Phone: 319-356-3523. Office Fax: 319-353-6754. Business E-Mail: frederick-dietz@uiowa.edu.

DIETZ, HARRY C., pediatrician, educator; b. 1958; BS, Duke U., 1980; MD, SUNY: Upstate, 1984. Cert. Pediat., 1989. Resident in pediats. Johns Hopkins Hosp., Balt., 1984—87, fellow in cardiology, 1988; postdoc. Johns Hopkins U., Balt., 1989; Victor A. McKusick prof. genetics and medicine Inst. Genetic Medicine, Johns Hopkins U. Sch. Medicine, Balt.; investigator Howard Hughes Med. Inst., 1997—. Bd. govs. Nat. Human Genome Rsch. Inst. Recipient Richard D. Rowe award for outstanding rsch. in pediatric cardiology, Young Investigator award, Soc. Pediatric Rsch., Antoine Marfan award, Nat. Marfan Found., Curt Stern award, Am. Soc. Human Genetics. Fellow: AAAS; mem.: NAS, Inst. Medicine, Am. Soc. Pediatric Rsch., Am. Soc. Clin. Investigation. Office: Inst Genetic Medicine 539 Broadway Rsch Bldg 733 N Broadway Baltimore MD 21205 also: Med Genetics Clinic Johns Hopkins Outpatient Ctr 601 N Caroline St 8th Fl Baltimore MD 21205 Office Phone: 410-955-3071. Office Fax: 410-614-9246. E-mail: hdietz@jhmi.edu. *

DIETZ, WILLIAM HARRY, pediatrician; b. Phila., Oct. 6, 1944; s. William H. and Margaret (Shoemaker) Dietz; m. Nancy Fenn, May 6, 1966. BA, Wesleyan U., 1966; MD, U. Pa., 1970; PhD, MIT, 1981. Diplomate Am. Bd. Pediatrics. Intern Children's Hosp. Phila., 1970-71; resident Upstate Med. Ctr., Syracuse, NY, 1974-76; rsch. assoc. NIH, 1971-74, MIT, Cambridge, 1976-81; assoc. prof. Tufts U. Sch. Medicine, Boston, 1986-96, prof., 1996-98; dir. clin. nutrition New England Med. Ctr., Boston, 1983-97. Adj. prof. Tufts U. Sch. Medicine, Boston, 1998—. Fellow: Am. Acad. Pediat. (chmn. task force on children and TV, Elk Grove Village, Ill. 1984—87); mem.: Nat. Acad. Scis., Inst. Medicine, Am. Dietetic Assn. (hon.), N.Am. Assn. Study Obesity (pres. 1993—94), Am. Soc. Clin. Nutrition (v.p. 1998—99, pres. 1999—2000, counselor). Office: CDC Divsn Nutrition Phys Act Obesity 4770 Buford Hwy NE # MS-K24 Atlanta GA 30341-3717 Office Phone: 770-488-6042. Business E-Mail: wcd4@cdc.gov.

DIETZEK, ALAN M., surgeon; b. NY, Feb. 15, 1956; MD, Loyola Stritch Sch. Medicine, 1983. With North Shore U. Hosp., Manhasset, NY, 1990—93, Vascular Assocs. LI, Gt. Neck, 1993—97, Integrated Cardiovasc. Therapeutics, Woodbury, 1997—2000; chief DOPS Vascular Surgery, 2000—. Pres. Vascular Surg. Soc. So. Conn., 2004; chair two spl. interest groups so. conn. Ann. Meeting Soc. Clin. Vascular Surgery, 2006; membership com. Soc. Clin. Vascular Surgery, 2007—10; adv. bd. Jour. Ctr. Vascular Awareness, 2010; coun. mem. Ea. Vascular Soc., 2010. Recipient hon., SUNY, Albany, Academic Achievement award, Dept. Surgery, LI Jewish Med. Ctr., Danbury Hosp. Surg. Tchg. Attending of Yr., Sound Shore Med. Ctr., Westchester, NY, Endowed Chair, 'The Linda & Stephen R. Cohen Chair Vascular Surgery'. Mem.: Vascular Surg. Soc. So. Conn. (pres.), New Eng. Soc. Vascular Surgery, Ea. Vascular Soc., Soc. Clin. Vascular Surgery. Office: 111 Osborne St Ste 131 Danbury CT 06810 Business E-Mail: alan.dietzek@danhosp.org.

DIETZEL, LOUISE ALVERTA, psychologist; b. Canton, Ohio, Nov. 18, 1937; d. Daniel Walter and Velma Irene Bender Miller; m. Cleason Samuel Dietzel, June 18, 1960; children: Laurie Christine, Rebecca Doreen, Beth Ann. BS, Goshen Coll., Ind., 1960; MS, St. Michaels Coll., 1976. Lic. psychologist, lic. clin. mental health counselor, Vt. Dir. day care, Mt. Pleasant, Mich., 1965-67, E. Lansing, Mich., 1967-71, Winooski, Vt., 1972-73; sch. cons. Essex Junction (Vt.) Schs., 1976-77; rsch. asst. U. Vt., Burlington, 1976-77; pvt. cons. practice Essex Junction, 1974—. Chair counselor Vt. Clin. Mental Health Counselors, Montpelier, 1989-95, elem. counselor Essex Junction Schs., 1977-94, cons. Head Start, Burlington, Vt., 1992-99; psychology instr. St. Michael's Coll., 1999—. Author: Parenting With Respect and Peacefulness, 1995. Mem. Am. Mental Health Counselors Assoc., Vt. Psychol. Assn., Am. and Vt. Counseling Assn. Avocations: cooking, camping. Home: 37 Prospect St Essex Junction VT 05452-3612 Office: Psychol Svcs 6 Hillcrest Rd Essex Junction VT 05452-3611 Home Phone: 802-878-8439; Office Phone: 802-878-2118. Personal E-mail: ldietzel@comcast.net.

DIFABRIZIO, LARRY, pulmonologist; Grad., Wash. U. Sch. Medicine, 1984. Lic. NY, cert. AMA, diplomate Am. Thoratic Soc., Am. Bd. Internal Medicine-critical care medicine, Am. Bd. Internal Medicine-pulmonary disease, Am. Bd. Internal Medicine-sleep medicine, Am. Bd. Internal Medicine. Resident in internal medicine Brigham & Womens Hosp., Boston, 1985—87, fellow in pulmonary critical care medicine, 1987—88; fellow in rehumatology Columbia-Presbyn. Med. Ctr., NY, 1988—90; pulmonologist Lenox Hill Hosp. Fellow: Am. Coll. Chest Physicians; mem.: Am. Coll. Physicians. Office: Lenox Hill Hospital 111 E 80th St New York NY 10075 Office Phone: 212-517-8488. Office Fax: 212-517-5129.

DIFEDE, JOANN, psychologist; BA, George Washington Univ., 1982; MA, New Sch. for Social Rsch., 1986, PhD, 1992. Assoc. prof. psychology, dept. of psychiatry Weill Cornell Medical Coll., NYC; and assoc. attending psychologist NY Presbyn. Hosp./Weill Cornell Medical Ctr., NYC; also dir., program for anxiety, traumatic stress studies Payne Whitney Clinic, NYC. Cons. NY Presbyn. Hosp. Burn Ctr. Author: (numerous articles, chapters) on assessment, treatment of PTSD. Recipient numerous NIH grants; named one of Best Doctors, NY Mag., 2005; grantee Aaron Diamond Fellowship award, 1992—95. Achievements include publishing first report of successful use of virtual reality tech. for treatment of PTSD following 9/11. Office: Dept Psychiatry & PTSD Program NY Presbyn/Weill Cornell Med Ctr 525 E 68th St New York NY 10021 Office Phone: 212-821-0783. Office Fax: 212-821-0994.

DIGEL, ILYA, biomedical engineer, biophysicist, educator; s. Svetlana and Edgar Digel; m. Marina Dolgova, Nov. 13, 2001. Diploma in Biology and Chemistry with honors, Kazakh Nat. State U., Almaty, 1995; PhD in Microbiology, Inst. Microbiology and Virology, Kazakhstan, 1998. Cert. pre-print specialist, Almaty Digital Printing Assn., 2001, digital print specialist, Almaty Digital Printing Assn., 2001. Rschr. Inst. Microbiology and Virology, Acad. Sci., Almaty, 1993—99; chief cons., deputy dir. Nat. Sci. Agrl. Libr., Almaty, 1999—2001; sr. resercher Aachen U. Applied Scis., Juelich, Germany, 2002—. Editor: Food Industry and Packaging Magazine, 2001—02. Recipient Gold medal, Acad. Sci. Republic of Kazakhstan, 1996, 1st pl., Modern Am. Poetry Translation Competition, 2002, Grand prize, Wipe Out Poverty poster exhbn., 2002; grantee, Ministry Sci. and Edn., Republic of Kazakhstan, 1996; scholar, Pres. Republic of Kazakhstan, 1997; postdctoral rsch. fellow, German Academic Exch. Svc., 2003. Fellow: European Fedn. Biotechnology. Achievements include patents for new method of yeast cells (Torulopsis kefyr) immobilization; new method of ethanol production using immobilized yeast cells; first to find mechanisms of antimicrobial action of clustered air-ions. Avocations: badminton, calligraphy. Office: Aachen University Applied Scis Dept Biomed Engring Heinrich-Mussmann St N1 NRW Jülich 52428 Germany Office Fax: +49 (0)241600953273. Business E-Mail: digel@fh-aachen.de.

DIGGS, WALTER WHITLEY, health science facility administrator; b. Memphis, Tenn., June 8, 1932; s. Lemuel Whitley and Beatrice (Moshier) D.; m. Ann C. Thobae, Nov. 29, 1958; children: Jennie, Thomas, Andrew. BS, Washington and Lee U., 1954; MHA, U. Minn., 1956. Adminstrv. resident Stormont-Vail Hosp., Topeka, 1955-56; asst. dir. The Johns Hopkins Hosp., Balt., 1959-66; adminstr. Med. Coll. Ga. Hosp., Augusta, 1966-70; asst. prof. Med. Coll. Ga., Augusta, 1970-71, U. Tenn. and U. Memphis, 1971-97; field rep. Joint Commn. Hosps., Chgo., 1981—88, 1993—2011; supt. Memphis Mental Health Inst., 1987-93. Cons. Tenn. Dept. Mental Health, 1993-95. Pres. Delta Found., Miss., 1987—, Ballet South, Memphis Ballet, Augusta Civic Ballet. Lt. USNR, 1956-59. Recipient Peter Cooper award, Unitarian Ch., Memphis, 1975, Forrest Fletcher, Washington and Lee, Lexington, Va., 1954. Fellow Am. Coll. Healthcare Execs. (life). Avocation: seniors track and field. Home: 204 Main St Harwich MA 02645 Personal E-mail: cordwawwd@aol.com.

DIGIOIA, JULIA M., surgeon, educator; MD, Universidad Di Roma-La Sapienza, 1979. Diplomate Am. Bd. Surgery. Asst. clin. prof. surgery Univ. of Medicine and Dentistry of NJ; resident in surgery Jersey City Med. Ctr, NJ, 1980—84, surgeon, Overlook Med. Ctr. Office: Overlook Medical Center 33 Overlook Rd Ste 205 Summit NJ 07901 Office Phone: 908-522-3200.

DIGREGORIO, VINCENT R., plastic surgeon; s. Nicholas J. and Anne M. DiGregorio; m. Jennifer E. Ruys, Apr. 26, 2003; 1 child, Nicole C. BA, Hobart Coll., Geneva, NY, 1964; MD, Albany Med. Coll., 1968. Plastic surgeon Long Island Plastic Surgery Group, Garden City, NY, 1978—; chief plastic surgery Winthrop U. Hosp., Mineola, NY, 1978—, pres. med. staff, 1984—88. Pres. Day Op Ctr. of L.I., Mineola, NY, 1988—. Oils and watercolors. Maj. Us Army, 1970—71, m. Home: 110 Sixth St Garden City NY 11530 Office: Long Island Plastic Surgery Group 999 Franklin Ave Garden City NY 11530 Office Phone: 516-742-3404. Personal E-mail: vincentdig@cs.com.

DI GUARDO, GIOVANNI, veterinary pathologist; b. Turin, Piedmont, Italy, July 4, 1958; s. Giuseppe and Giovanna (Marino) Di G.; m. Letizia Curini, July 12, 1987; children: Cecilia, Benedetta. DVM, U. Bologna, Italy, 1982. Diplomate European Coll. Vet. Pathologists, 1995. Tng. pathologist Faculty Vet. Medicine, U. Bologna, 1982-85; state veterinarian Health Ministry, Rome, 1985-87; vis. prof. dept. vet. clin. scis. Iowa State U., Ames, 1987-88; asst. vet. pathologist Istituto Zooprofilattico Sperimentale delle Regioni Lazio e Toscana, Rome, 1987—93, chief vet. pathologist, 1993—; assoc. prof. dept. comparative biomed. sci. Faculty Vet. Medicine, U. Teramo, Italy, 2002—. Contbr. articles to profl. jours. Cpl. Maj. Italian Army, 1983-84. Fulbright scholar, 1987-88, Coun. for Internat. Exch. Scholars. Mem. European Soc. Vet. Pathology, European Coll. Vet. Pathologists, Fulbright Alumni Assn. Avocations: art, music, tennis, skiing, flying, reading. Office: Faculty Vet Medicine Dept Comp Biom Sci U Teramo Piazza Aldo Moro 45 64100 Teramo Italy Home: Via dei Mulini Snc 64100 Teramo Italy Office Phone: 011 39 861 966933. Business E-Mail: gdiguardo@unite.it.

DIKTABAN, THEODORE, plastic surgeon; b. Queens, NY, Mar. 11, 1951; BS in Biology, Colgate U., Hamilton, NY; MD, NY Med. Coll., Valhalla, 1976. Cert. Am. Bd. Plastic Surgery, Am. Bd. Otolaryngology. Resident, gen. surgery Lenox Hill Hosp., NYC, 1976—78, resident, plastic surgery, 1981—83; resident, otolaryngology Mt Sinai Hosp., NYC, 1978—81; fellow, reconstructive microsurgery U. Louisville, 1984; practicing cosmetic surgeon Sadick Dermatology Ctr., NYC. Instr. microsurgery Kings County Hosp., 1987—92. Contbr. articles to profl. jours. Named one of Best Plastic Surgeons in NY, Castle Connolly Med. LTD, 2001—06. Fellow: ACS; mem.: Am. Acad. Otolaryngology, Hellenic Med. Soc., NY State Med. Soc., NY County Med. Soc., NYS Regional Soc. Plastic Surgery, Am. Soc. Plastic & Reconstructive Surgeons, Lipoplasty Soc. N. Am. Office: Sadick Dermatology 911 Park Ave New York NY 10021 Office Phone: 212-772-7242. Business E-Mail: tdiktaban@sadickdermatology.com.

DILCHER, DAVID LEONARD, paleobotany educator, researcher; b. Cedar Falls, Iowa, July 10, 1936; m. Katherine Swanson, 1961; children: Peter, Ann. BS in Natural History, U. Minn., 1958, MS in Botany, Geology and Zoology, 1960; postgrad., U. Ill., 1960-62; PhD in Biology, Geology, Yale U., 1964; participant OTS course field dendrology, Costa Rica, 1968; D honoris causa (hon.), Lyon U. 1, France, 2007. Teaching asst. U. Minn., Mpls., 1958-60, U. Ill., Urbana, 1960-62, Yale U., New Haven, Conn., 1962-63, Cullman-Univ. fellow, 1963-64, instr. biology, 1965-66; NSF postdoctoral fellow Senckenberg Mus., Frankfurt am Main, Fed. Republic of Germany, 1964-65; asst. prof. botany Ind. U., Bloomington, 1966-70, assoc. prof., 1970-76; Guggenheim fellow Imperial Coll., Univ. London, 1972-73; assoc. prof. geology Ind. U., Bloomington, 1975-77, prof. paleobotany, 1977-90, adj. prof. biology, adj. prof. geology, 1990—; grad. rsch. prof. Fla. Mus. Natural History, U. Fla., Gainesville, 1990—. Panel mem. for systematic biology program, NSF, 1977-79, panel mem. for selecting NATO postdoctoral fellow, 1982, mem. adv. com. Earth Sys. History, 1997-2000, bd. mem. on earth scis. and resources NRC, 2001-04; vis. lectr. to People's Republic of China Nat. Acad. Sci. com. on scholarly communications with China, 1986; corr. mem. Senckenberg Mus., Frankfurt, Fed. Republic Germany, 1989; hon. prof. Nanjing Inst. Geology and Paleontology, Acad. Sinica, China, 1998—, Jilin U., Changchau, China, 2001—; adj. prof. biology U. Tenn., Martin, 2000—; hon. prof., vice chmn. sci. com. rsch. ctr. paleontoloty and stratigraphy Jilin U., Changchun, China, 2001—; bd. dirs. Smithsonian Inst., 1998-2006; prof. Rsch. Found. Univ. Fla., 2004—. Author: (with D. Redmon, M. Tansey and D. Whitehead) Plant Biology Laboratory Manual, 1973, 2d edit., 1975; editor: (with Tom Taylor and Theodore Delevoryas) Plant Reproduction in the Fossil Record, symposium vol., 1979; (with T. Taylor) Biostratigraphy of Fossil Plants: Successional and Paleoecological Analysis, 1980; (with William L. Crepet) Origin and Evolution of Flowering Plants, Symposium Volume, 1984; (with Michael S. Zavada) Phylogeny of the Hamamedidae, symposium vol., 1986; (with Patrick S. Herendeen) Advances in Legume Systematics Part 4, The Fossil Record, 1992; mem. edilt. bd. Taxon, 2004—; contbr. over 200 articles to profl. jours. Mem. utilities bd. City of Bloomington, 1974-76; ruling elder First Presbyn. Ch. Bloomington, 1975-77; bd. dirs. United Campus Ministries, 1971-72, Smithsonian Mus. Natural History, 1998—; mem. coun. Monroe County United Ministries, 1975-77. Dist. Vis. Rsch. scholar U. Adelaide, Australia, 1981, 88; Vis. Rsch. scholar Birbal Sahni Palaeonbot. Inst., Lucknow, India, 1992; grantee Sigma Xi, 1961-62, 66, Ind. U., 1967-68, Orgn. Tropical Studies, 1971, Travel grantee Ind. U., 1968, 71, 77, 80, Rsch. grantee NSF, 1966-89, 96—, Amax Coal Found., 1980-81, NATO Coop, 1991-93; Eaton-Hooker fellow, 1963, Cullman-Univ. fellow, 1963-64, Guggenheim fellow, Giessen, Fed. Republic of Germany, 1972-73, Ind. U., 1972-73, Brit. Mus. Natural History, London, 1988-89; recipient Tracey M. Sonneborn award for disting. rsch. and excellenc in tchg. Ind. U., 1978-88, Bot. Soc. Am. Merit award, 1991, Birbal Sahni Found. award, 1998, U. Fla. Rsch. Found. Professorship award, 2004-06, Outstanding Palaeobotanist award Indian Palaeontological Soc., 2005, Mt. Changbai Friendship cup, Jilin Province China, 2006; hon. prof. Honzhou U., China, 2007; Doctorats Hon. Causa 2, U. Claude Bernard Lyon 1, France. Fellow Ind. Acad. Sci.; mem. NAS, AAAS, Bot. Soc. Am. (chmn. paleobot. sect. 1974, sec.-treas. 1975-77, rep. to jour. editl. bd. 1978-79, jour. editl. bd. 1981-82, conservation com. 1978-81, chmn. conservation com. 1981, 82, program dir. 1982-84, exec. bd. 1982-91, sec. 1984-88, pres.-elect 1988-89, pres. 1989-90), Paleontol. Soc., Paleontol. Assn., Internat. Orgn. Paleobotany (N.Am. rep. 1975-81, v.p. 1987-93), Assn. Tropical Biology, Am. Inst. Biol. Scis., Am. Assn. Stratigraphic Palynologists, Internat. Assn. Angiosperm Paleobotany (pres. 1977-80), Geol. Soc. Am. (com. on collection and collecting 1978-85), Ky. Acad. Scis., Senckenberg Natur Mus. und Forschungsgeshellshaft Frankfurt am Main (corr. mem. 1990), Sigma Xi (pres.-elect Ind. chpt. 1985-86, pres. 1986-87). Office: 2260 E. Cape Cod Dr Bloomington IN 47401

DI LEONARDO, ALDO, biology professor; b. Palermo, Dec. 3, 1952; Laurea, U. Palemo, Italy, 1977. Asst. prof. U. Palermo, 1984—2001, assoc. prof., 2002—; asst. prof. Salk Inst., San Diego, 1992—93. Long term fellowship, Fondazione Italiana Ricerca sul Cancro. Avocations: gardening, motorcycling. Office: Viale delle Scienze Palermo 90128 Italy Business E-Mail: adileon@unipa.it.

DILEONE, CARMEL MONTANO, retired dental hygienist; b. New Haven, Aug. 24, 1926; d. Nicholas and Martha (Ercolano) M.; m. Eugene Francis Dileone, Jan. 28, 1948; children: Gina, Richard. Dental Hygienist, Temple U., 1945; AA, Albertus Magnus Coll., 1980; BS, U. Bridgeport, 1983; MS, So. Conn. State U., 1985. Registered dental hygienist. Dental hygiene practitioner George M. Montano, DDS, New Haven, 1946-50, George V. Montano, DDS, Orange, 1959-2000, Francis R. Mullen, DDS, West Haven, 1950-55; dental hygiene practioner Herbert Saunders, DDS, Orange, Conn., 1958-63, Children's Dental Assocs., Hamden, 2000—03, Children's Dental Group, New Haven, 2000—09; ret., 2010. Instr. Huntington Inst., North Haven, Conn., 1983; adj. assoc. prof. U. Bridgeport, Conn., Fones Sch. Dental Hygiene, 1985-96; adj. faculty U. New Haven, 1994—. Dir., treas. Conn. Hygienists' Polit. Action Com., 1996—2002. Recipient Profl. Recognition award U. New Haven, 1999, Hon. award, New Haven Dental Hygienist Established, The Carmel DiLeone RDH, 2010. Mem.: Ct. Pub. Health Assn., New Haven Dental Hygienists Assn. (pres. 1949, 1975), Conn. Dental Hygienists Assn. (treas. 1986—88, v.p. 1988—89, pres.-elect 1989—90, pres. 1991, Mabel C. McCarthy award 1983, Pres. award 1994, Outstanding Svc. Recognition award 2008), Am. Dental Hygienists Assn., Am. Soc. Dentistry for Children, Conn. Pub. Health Assn., Sigma Phi Alpha. Roman Catholic. Achievements include New Heaven dental association established the carmes Dileane RDH, MPH scholarship in honor.

DILER, RASIM SOMER, psychiatrist, researcher; s. Kemal and Leman Cercel Diler; m. Hacer Aytas, Sept. 3, 1995; 1 child, Simge Su. MD, Istanbul U., Turkey, 1993. Cert. specialist in child and adolescent psychiatry Child and Adolescent Psychiatry Bd., 1999, Crisis Mgmt. in Psychiatry U. of Pitts., 2000, eye movement desensitization and reprocessing Internat. Soc. EMDR, 2001, Autism Diagnostic Interview Turkish Soc. of Child and Adolescent Psychiatry, 2003, Treatment of Pervasive Developmental Disorders Turkish Soc. of Child and Adolescent Psychiatry, 2003. Asst. prof. psychiatry Cukurova U. Faculty of Medicine, Child and Adolescent Psychiatry, Adana, Turkey, 1999—2003, assoc. prof. psychiatry, 2003—. Dir. outpatient svcs. Cukurova U. Faculty of Medicine, Child and Adolescent Psychiatry, Adana, Turkey, 1999—, co-dir. and supr. of rsch. studies, 1999—, co-dir. residency tng., 1999, web dir. of ofcl. child psychiatry univ. homepage, 1998—; bd. mem., Ctr. Hearing and Communication Disabilities Cukurova U. Faculty of Medicine, Adana, Turkey, 2003—; site coord. tech. and rsch. cooperation Xi'an U. (China) and Cukurova U., 2003—; bd. mem. and cons. Gov. Oguz Kaan Koksal Residential Treatment Ctr.(the first juvenile residential treatment ctr. of Adana city), Turkey, Adana, Turkey, 2002—; bd. mem. Bridging Ea. and Western Psychiatry Orgn., Pisa, Italy, 2002—. Co-dir. Commn. Planning Core Edn. For Grad. Students, Adana, Turkey, 2002—03; cons., bd. mem., and policy maker State Coun. for Preventing Youth from Harmful Environment and Activities, Adana, Turkey, 2001—03; coord. Commn. Planning Core Edn. For Grad. Students, Adana, Turkey, 2002—03. Recipient Young Minds in CNS (Ctrl. Nervous Sys.) Award in Depressionand Anxiety category, AstraZeneca, 2001; named Hon. Prof. and Prof. Emeritus, Xi'an (China) Jiaoton U., 2003—; fellow XII. World Congress of Psychiatry, World Psychiat. Assn., 2002; Disting. Rsch. grantee, Sci. and Tech. Rsch. Coun. of Turkey (TUBITAK), 2003—. Mem.: AAAS, Pa. Med. Soc. (licentiate), Bridging Ea. and Western Psychiatry (corr.; site coord. 2001), Turkish Psychiatry Soc. (life), Turkish Soc. of Child and Adolescent Psychiatry (life). Achievements include research in Pharmacotherapy and changes in regional cerebral blood flow in children with obsessive compulsive disorder; Emotional and behavioral problems in migrant children; Efficacy of Risperidone in Children with Autism; Efficacy of paroxetine in children with obsessive compulsive disorder; discovery of presence of selective serotonin reuptake inhibitor discontinuation syndrome in children; selective serotonin reuptake inhibitors induced mania in children with obsessive compulsive disorder; an atypical antipsyhotic agent which may be used adjunctively for obsessions, can induce obsessive compulsive symptoms in children; research in efficacy of moclobemide in young adolescents with major depressive disorder. Avocations: music, dance, travel, international cuisine, movies. Office: Cukurova U Faculty Medicine Balcali 01130 Adana Turkey also: 3811 O'Hara St Pittsburgh PA 15213 Personal E-mail: dilerrs@yahoo.com.

DILL, DAVID M., hospital administrator; Exec. v.p., N.Am. Fresenius Med. Care Svcs. (subs. Fresenius Medical Care AG & Co. KGaA.); various fin., acctg. positions Renal Care Group, Inc. (acquired by Fresenius Med. Care Svcs.), 1996—2003, exec. v.p., CFO & treas., 2003—06; CEO, East Divsn. Fresenius Med. Care Svcs. (subs. Fresenius Medical Care AG & Co. KGaA.), 2006—07; CFO LifePoint Hosps., Inc., 2007—09; exec. v.p. LifePoint Hospitals, Inc., 2007—11, COO, 2009—, pres., 2011—. Bd. dirs. Psychiatric Solutions, Inc, 2005. Office: LifePoint Hospitals Inc 103 Powell Ct Ste 200 Brentwood TN 37027 Office Phone: 615-372-8500. Office Fax: 615-372-8575. Business E-Mail: david.dill@lpnt.net. *

DILLARD, JAMES N., physiatrist, educator; MD, Rush U., 1990; DC, Cleve. Chiropractic Coll., Los Angeles; attended, Calif. Acupuncture Coll., Los Angeles. Diplomate Am. Bd. Physical Medicine and Rehab., 2005. Resident physical medicine & rehab. Columbia-Presbyn. Md. Ctr., NYC, 1991—94; asst. clin. prof. physical medicine & rehab. Coll. of Physicians and Surgeons Columbia Univ.; asst. clin. prof. rehab. medicine dept. Neurol. Inst. of NY; med. staff NY-Presbyn. Hosp. Columbia Univ. Med. Ctr.; attending physician pain medicine and palliative care Beth Israel Med. Ctr.; med. dir. Rosenthal Ctr. for Complementary and Alternative Medicine. Author (book): Alternative Medicine for Dummies. Office: Neurological Institute of New York Department of Rehabilitation Medicine 16 E 60th St Ste 440 New York NY 10022 Office Phone: 212-326-8501. Office Fax: 212-326-8580.

DILLE, JOHN ROBERT, retired physician; b. Waynesbur, Pa., Sept. 2, 1931; s. Charles Emanuel and Ruth Emma (South) D.; m. Joan Marie Sirtosky, Dec. 17, 1955 (wid. Mar. 1996); children: Paul Andrew, John Alan. BS, Waynesburg Coll., Pa., 1952; MD, U. Pitts., 1956; M in Indsl. Health, Harvard U., Cambridge, Mass., 1960. Diplomate Am. Bd. Preventive Medicine. Intern Akron City Hosp., 1956-57; resident in aerospace medicine USAF Sch. Aerospace Medicine, San Antonio, 1960-62; program adv. officer FAA Civil Aeromed. Rsch. Inst., Oklahoma City, 1961-64; western region flight surgeon FAA, LA, 1965, chief FAA Civil Aeromed. Inst., US Dept. Transp., Oklahoma City, 1966-87, ret., 1987; med. dir. Okla. Dept. Corrections, Oklahoma City, 1990-93. Assoc. prof. U. Okla., 1961-98, dir. tng. residency in aerospace medicine, 1967-72; state surgeon Okla. Army N.G., 1990-91; surveyor Nat. Commn. on Correctional Health Care, 2000-04. Assoc. editor: Ag Pilot Internat. mag., 1980-98, Conservation Aeronautics mag., 1989-92, Above All mag., 1992; mem. editorial bd. Aviation, Space and Environ. Medicine, 1987-94; contbr. chpts. to textbooks and articles to profl. jours. With USAF, 1957-59; col. M.C., US Army N.G., 1976-91. Recipient Meritorious award William A. Jump Found., 1968; named Army N.G. Flight Surgeon of Yr. 1987, Master Flight Surgeon, 1987. Fellow: Am. Coll. Preventive Medicine (regent 1974—77), Aerospace Med. Assn. (mem. exec. coun. 1978—81, chmn. history and archives com. 1982—90, chmn. sci. program com. 1985, 1st v.p. 1990—91, pres. 1992—93, mem. exec. coun. 1993—98, chmn. nominating com. 1997—98, Theodore C. Lyster award 1978, Harry G. Moseley award 1987, Armstrong lectr. 1997, Marie Marvingt award 2008); mem.: Civil Aviation Med. Assn., Am. Soc. Aerospace Medicine Specialists, Res. Officers Assn. (state surgeon Okla. dept. 2002—07, 2008—10), Am. Air Mail Soc. (bd. dir. 1990—92), Soc. US Army Flight Surgeons (bd. govs. 1990—92, Order Aeromed. Merit), Internat. Acad. Aviation and Space Medicine, Mil. and Hospitaller Order St. Lazarus of Jerusalem commandary of Midwest (knight, hospitaller, commandery Midwest), Sigma Xi, Nu Sigma Nu. Presbyterian. Home: 335 Merkle Dr Norman OK 73069-6429 Personal E-mail: jrobtdille@aol.com.

DILLON, KRISTIN A., research scientist; b. St. Paul, Apr. 1, 1982; PhD, U. Minn., 2010. Rsch. scientist Wilder Rsch., 2008—. Mem.: Minn. Coun. on Family Rels. Office: 451 Lexington Pky N Saint Paul MN 55104 Business E-Mail: kristin.dillon@wilder.org.

DILMEN, UGUR, medical association administrator; b. 1955; married; 2 children. MD, Hacettepe U., 1979, MSc, 1982; PhD, Ataturk U., 1994. Chief resident Hacettepe Childrens Hosp., 1982—83; prof. pediat. Ataurk Univ., 1994—96; dean med. faculty Faith Univ., 1996—, prof. pediat. and neonatology, 1996—. Chief physician Turkish Health and Therapy Found., 1987—94. Recipient Cihad Tahsin Gürson Rsch. award, 1982, TUBITAK (Turkish Scientific and Tech. Rsch. Coun.) award, 1988, Dr. Ibrahim Memorial award, Islamic Academy of Sciences, 1996. Fellow: IAS; mem.: World Med. Assn., Neonatoloji Soc., Perinatology Endockrinolody Soc., Nat. Pediat. Soc., Turkish Med. Soc. Office: c/o World Medical Association 13 ch du Levant CIB Batiment A France Office Phone: 33450407575. Office Fax: 33450405937. *

DILORENZO, CARLO, pediatrician, gastroenterologist, educator; MD, 2nd Univ. Naples, 1984. Cert. Pediat. Gastroenterology. Intern 2nd Univ. Naples, Italy, 1986—88, resident, 1988; fellowship Hosp. Universitaire des Enfants, Brussels, 1986, U. So. Calif. County Hosp., 1998, Harbor UCLA Med. Ctr., 1990; chief, divsn. pediat. gastroenterology Nationwide Children's Hosp., Columbus, Ohio, prin. investigator, ctr. clin. and translational rsch.; prof. clin. pediat. Ohio State U. Coll. Medicine. Mem. functional GI disorders & motility disorders working group Nat. Commn. Digestive Diseases; mem. sci. adv. bd. Children's Digestive Health and Nutrition Found., U. NC Ctr. Functional GI and Motility Disorders; reviewer Internat. Found. Functional Gastrointestinal Disorders Rsch. Awards; chair Adolescent Com., Rome III Criteria; grant reviewer NIH; chair, guidelines com. Am. Acad. Pediat.; coun. mem. Functional Bowel Group. Editl. bd. mem. Jour. Pediatric Gastroenterology, Hepatology and Nutrition, Neurogastroenterology and Motility; contbr. articles to med. jours. Recipient Masters award, Am. Gastroenterol. Assn. Inst., 2008; named to Best Doctors in America, 2008. Mem.: N.Am. Soc. Pediatric Gastroenterology, Hepatology and Nutrition (organizer World Cup Soccer), Am. Bd. Pediat. (mem. pediat. gastroenterology subbd.), Am. Motility Soc. (mem. clin. practice com., mem. testing stds. com.). Office: Nationwide Childrens Hospice 255 E Main St Columbus OH 43215-5222 Office Phone: 614-772-3450. Office Fax: 614-772-3454. E-mail: dilorenzo.8@osu.edu, Carlo.DiLorenzo@nationwidechildrens.org.

DILSIZIAN, VASKEN, cardiologist, nuclear medicine physician; b. Aug. 12, 1956; BSChemE magna cum laude, Tufts U., 1977, MSChemE, 1978, MD, 1982. Diplomate Nat. Bd. Med. Examiners, Am. Bd. Internal Medicine, Am. Bd. Cardiovascular Disease, Am. Bd. Nuclear Medicine; lic. physician Va., Md., Mass. Intern and resident in internal medicine Georgetown U. Hosp., Washington, 1982-85; fellow in cardiology Boston U. Med. Ctr./Boston City Hosp., 1985-87; fellow in cardiovascular and nuclear medicine Mass. Gen. Hosp./Harvard Med. Sch., Boston, 1987-88; sr. staff fellow cardiology br. Nat. Heart, Lung, and Blood Inst., Bethesda, Md., 1988-89, clin. investigator, 1989-92; resident in nuclear medicine NIH, Bethesda, Md., 1991-92, dir. nuclear cardiology, 1992—2001; dir. cardiovasc. nuc. medicine U. Md. Med. Ctr., 2001—, prof. medicine and radiology, chief divsn. nuclear medicine, 2007—. Adj. prof. medicine Sch. Medicine George Washington U., 1994-01; adj. prof. medicine and radiology Georgetown U. Sch. Medicine, 1999-01; spkr., invited lectr. and presenter in field. Editl. cons. Circulation, Am. Jour. Cardiology, Jour. Am. Coll. Cardiology, Annals Internal Medicine, New Eng. Jour. Medicine, Jour. Nuc. Cardiology, assoc. editor Jour. Nuc. Medicine, 1998—99; assoc. editor: Jour. Am. Coll. Cardiology Cardiovasc. Imaging, 2007—; mem. editl. bd. Jour. Nuc. Medicine, 1997—2003, Jour. Nuc. Cardiology, 2004—; mem. editl. bd.: Jour. Thoracic Imaging, 2007—; editor: Myocardial Viability: A Clinical and Scientific Treatise, 2000, Atlas of Nuclear Cardiology, 2003, 2d edit., 2006, 3rd edit., 2009, Cardiac CT, PET and MR, 2006; editor in chief War Cardiovasc. Ing. Rep., 2008—; editor: Noninvasive Imaging of Heart Failure, Heart Failure Clinics, 2006; contbg. editor: Essential Atlas of Heart Diseases, 3d edit., 2005; contbr. over 287 articles and abstracts to profl. jours., 27 chpts. to books. Fellow Am. Coll. Cardiology (editorial cons. jour., abstract reviewer), Am. Heart Assn. (coun. on clin. cardiology, com. on advanced cardiac imaging and tech. 1994-95, abstract reviewer); mem. Am. Soc. Nuclear Cardiology (founding, bd. dirs.), Soc. Nuclear Medicine (bd. dirs cardiovascular coun. 1993—, abstract reviewer). Office: U Md Med Ctr Gudelsky Bldg Rm N2W78 22 S Greene St Baltimore MD 21201-1595

DIMAIO, CHRISTOPHER JOHN, gastroenterologist; b. Huntington, NY, May 26, 1971; BS, Cornell U., 1996; MD, SUNY, Buffalo Sch. Medicine and Biomed. Scis., 2000. Assoc. dir. advanced endoscopy fellowship Meml. Sloan-Kettering Cancer Ctr., 2008—; dir., therapeutic endoscopy Mt. Sinai Med. Ctr., 2011—. Mem.: Am. Coll. Gastroenterology, Am. Gastroent. Assn., Am. Soc. Gastrointestinal Endoscopy. Achievements include research in advanced endoscopic procedures to diagnose and treat benign, pre-cancerous, and cancerous lesions of the pancreas, biliary tree, and gastrointestinal tract. Home: 245 E63rd St Apt 20M New York NY 10065 Personal E-mail: dimaio33@gmail.com.

DIMAIO, MARY F., pediatrician; b. NYC, Oct. 12, 1955; d. Dominick and Violet DiMaio; m. Sahibzada Mustafa Kemal, Dec. 7, 1985 (div.); m. William Michael Ricci, Nov. 18, 1995. AB magna cum laude, Barnard Coll., NYC, 1977; MD cum laude, SUNY Health Sci. Ctr., Bklyn., 1981. Cert. in pediat. 1987, in pediatric allergy & immunology 1999, in pediatric pulmonology 2007. Internship in pediat. NY Presbyn. Hosp./Weill Cornell Med. Ctr., NYC, 1981—82, assoc. attending pediatrician, clin. assoc. prof. pediat.; residency in pediat. Kings County Hosp. Ctr., Bklyn., 1982—83; residency in pediat. pulmonology North Shore U. Hosp., LI, NY, 1983—85; fellowship Mount Sinai Hosp., NYC, 1985; hosp. appointment Mount Sinai Med. Ctr., instr. Contbr. articles to profl. jours. Office: Weill Cornell Med Coll 505 E 70th St New York NY 10021 also: 1440 York Ave New York NY 10021-2577 Office Phone: 212-746-1638.

DIMANCESCU, MIHAI D., neurosurgeon, researcher, educator; b. Maidenhead, Berkshire, Eng., Mar. 27, 1940; arrived in US, 1956, naturalized, 1963; s. Dimitri D. and Alexandra Irina (Radulescu) D.; m. Joan E. Brenner, Mar. 17, 1966; children: Stefan, Marc-Mihai. BA, Yale U., 1962; MD, U. Toulouse, France, 1968. Diplomate Am. Bd. Neurol. Surgery. Rotating intern Purpan Hosp., Toulouse, 1968-69; jr. resident in gen. surgery Hartford Hosp., Conn., 1969-70; jr. resident neurosurgy Albert Einstein-Montefiore Hosp., Bronx, NY, 1970-72; rsch. fellow in spasticity and movement disorders U. Miami VA Hosp., Miami, Fla., 1972-74; sr. resident in neurosurgery U. Miami, 1972-76, asst. instr. in neurol. surgery, 1975-76; pvt. practice Freeport, NY, 1976—2003, Garden City, 1976—2003; v.p. med. affairs Omni-Corder Tech., Inc., Bohemia, NY, 2004—06; pres. Gogosh, Inc., Freeport, 2006—. Dir. Internat. Coma Recovery Inst., Freeport, 1977—2011; faculty, dir. brain studies Internat. Sch. Evan Thomas Inst., Phila., 1980—; staff, dir. dept. neurosurgery Franklin Hosp. Med. Ctr., Valley Stream, NY; staff neurosurgery South Nassau Cmtys. Hosp., Oceanside, NY, Mercy Med. Ctr., Rockville Ctr., NY, St. Francis Hosp., Rockville Ctr., NY, Winthrop U. Hosp., Mineola, NY, North Shore U. Hosp., Manhasset, NY, continuing med. edn. lectr., 1977—2003; cons. neurosurgery Inst. Achievement Human Potential, Phila., 1977—; surg. core faculty Health Sci. Ctr., Sch. Medicine, SUNY Stony Brook, 1980—2003; med. coun. LI Health Network; v.p. med. affairs Advanced BioPhotonics, Inc., Bohemia, NY, 2004—06; bd. dirs. South Nassau Cmty. Hosp.; adj. faculty Molloy Coll., Rockville Ctr., NY, 2007—09; mem. faculty Leeds U. Touro Coll. Campus, Bayshore, NY, 2007—09; sr. neurosurg. cons. Neurol. Surgery PC, 2008—, exec. adminstr. Contbr. articles profl. jours. Bd. dirs. Inst. Achievement Human Potential, 1990—, Princess Margarita Romania Found., chmn., 1998—. Recipient Golden medal, World Orgn. Human Potential, 1978; grantee, VA, 1972—74. Fellow: Royal Soc. Arts, ACS; mem.: Nassau Physicians' Rev. Orgn., Nassau County Med. Soc., World Med. Assn., NY State Head Injury Providers' Council (rotating chmn. 1986—87), Med. Soc. State NY (neurosurg. de. intersplty. com. 1983—88), NY State Neurosurg. Soc. (bd. dirs. 1983—88, pres. elect 1986—87, pres. 1988), Coma Recovery Assn. (chmn. bd. dirs. LI chpt. 1983), Congress Neurol. Surgeons (Sci. Exhibit award 1974), Am. Assn. Neurol. Surgeons, AMA. Office: Neurol Surgery PC 100 Merrick Rd Ste 128W Rockville Centre NY 11570 Personal E-mail: mihaidimancescu@aol.com. Business E-Mail: mihaidimancescu@aya.yale.edu, mdimancescu@nspc.com.

DIMANT, JACOB, internist; b. Rehovot, Israel, Apr. 27, 1947; came to U.S., 1972, naturalized, 1977; s. Simcha and Ita D.; m. Rose Bea Jearolmen, Sept. 11, 1974. MD, Hebrew U., Jerusalem, 1972. Diplomate Am. Bd. Internal Medicine and Rheumatology and Geriatric Medicine, Am. Bd. Quality Assurance and Utilization Rev. Physicians. Intern Maimonides Med. Ctr., Bklyn., 1972-73, resident in medicine, 1973-75, chief resident in medicine Bklyn., 1975-76; fellow in rheumatology SUNY Downstate Med. Ctr., Bklyn., 1976-78; practice medicine specializing in internal medicine and rheumatology Bklyn., 1975—; dir. rheumatology Maimonides Med. Ctr., Bklyn., 1978-89, assoc. dir. med. edn., 1978-80; med. dir. Clove Lakes Nursing Home, SI, N.Y., 1985-97; dir. divsn. of geriatrics Luth. Med. Ctr., Bklyn., 1998—. Med. dir. Prospect Park Nursing Home, Bklyn., 1977—87, Crown Nursing Home, Bklyn., 1983—2001, Hillside Manor Nursing Ctr., Queens, NY, 1993—98, Augustana Luth. Ctr. for Extended Care, Bklyn., 1996—; pres. Crown Nursing Home Assocs., Inc., Bklyn., 1989—; asst. prof. medicine SUNY, Bklyn., 1978—2006, clin. assoc., prof. medicine, 2006—; pres. Crest Hall Care Ctr. and Oak Hollow Nursing Ctr., Middle Island, NY, 1999—. Contbr. articles to profl. jours. Named hon. police surgeon N.Y.C. Police Dept., 1982; fellow Arthritis Found. of N.Y., 1977-78. Fellow: ACP; mem.: N.Y. Med. Dirs. Assn. (bd. dirs. 1990—, pres. 1994—96), Am. Med. Dirs. Assn. (bd. dirs. 1995—97, treas. 1997—99, v.p. 2000—01, pres.-elect 2001—02, pres. 2002—03), Am. Geriatric Soc. Office: Luth Augustana Ctr 5434 2d Ave Brooklyn NY 11220

DIMASI, JOSEPH, economist; b. Boston, Jan. 13, 1954; BA, U. Mass., Boston, 1975; PhD, Boston Coll., 1984. Dir. econ. analysis Tufts Ctr. Study Drug Devel., Tufts U., 1987—. Recipient Donald E. Francke award, Drug Info. Assn. Mem.: Am. Econ. Assn. Office: 75 Kneeland St Ste 1100 Boston MA 02111 Office Fax: 617-636-2425. Business E-Mail: joseph.dimasi@tufts.edu.

DIMBERG, LENNART AXEL, medical researcher, physician; b. Vanersborg, Sweden, Aug. 28, 1947; arrived in U.S., 1998; s. Sven Ingvar and Eva Ingrid Dimberg; m. Kerstin Aline Dimberg, Mar. 31, 1973; children: Asa, Ida, Emelie. DMS in Occpl. Health, Arbet Arskydds Styrelsen, Stockholm, 1973; diploma in Gen. Medicine, Norra Alvsborgs Sjukhus, Trollhattan, Sweden, 1978; PhD in Orthop. Surgery, Goteborg U., Sweden, 1991. Intern then resident Trollhattans Sjukhus, Trollhattan, Sweden, 1975—78; mgr. health promotion Volvo Flygmotor, 1978—98; corp. medical dir. Volvo AB, Goteborg, 1989—94; occpl. health specialist World Bank, Washington, 1998—. Chmn. Assn. Volvo Physicians, Goteborg, Sweden, 1993—98; Swedish coord. Volvo-Renault Heart Study, 1993—2004; assoc. prof. Sahlgrenska Acad., 2004; co-task mgr. first symposium on travel and stress World Bank, Washington, 2004. Contbr. chapters to books, articles to profl. jours. Coord. table tennis team Volvo Aero, Trollhattan, Sweden, 1980—90; vol. instr. Tennis Club, Vanersborg, 1988—89; bd. mem PTA, Vanersborg, 1997—98. Mem.: Swedish Med. Assn. (sec. 1982—85), Am. Coll. Occpl. and Environ. Medicine. Avocations: tennis, ping pong/table tennis, guitar, piano. Office: World Bank Occpl Health Svcs 1818 H St NW Washington DC 20433-0001 Personal E-mail: ldimberg@aol.com. E-mail: ldimberg@worldbank.org.

DIMITRAKAKIS, GEORGIOS, physician, cardiac surgeon; s. Konstantinos Serafim Dimitrakakis and Genny Danelatou. DDS, Aristotelian U., Thessaloniki, Greece, 1988, MD, Democretium U. Thrace, Alexandroupolis, Greece, 1993; diploma in Emergency Medicine, Med. Corp Greek Army, Athens, 1991; diploma in Pre-Hosp. Emergency Medicine, Nat. Ctr. First Aid, Athens, 1997; MSc in Disaster Medicine, U. Eastern Piedmont, Novara, Italy, 2008; MSc in Surg. Sci., U. Coll. London, 2009. Cert. Hellenic Ministry Health Bd. Thoracic Surgery, 2002, registered Gen. Med. Coun., 2004. With Polyklinik Gen. Hosp. Nat. Health Sys., Athens, 1989—90, with Areteion U. Hosp., 1993—94, resident, Sotiria Gen. Hosp. Chest Disease, 1994—97, resident, Onassis Cardiac Ctr., 1998—2000, resident, Evangelismos Gen. Hosp., 2002—02, cons. Onassis Cardiac Ctr. Pvt. Sector, 2003—04, assoc. specialist cardiac surgeon staff U. Hosp. Wales Cardiff, 2005—; cons. cardiac surgeon Met. Hosp. Pvt. Sector, Athens, 2002—04. Contbr. articles to profl. jours. (award, 1996, 1997). Rep. Students Union, Thessaloniki, 1983—88. Capt. Med. Corp Hellenic Ministry Def. Greek Army, 1990—92, Athens. Vis. Postdoc. fellowship, Yale U., New Haven, 2001. Mem.: Soc. Cardiothoracic Surgery (Ireland), Gen. Med. Coun. Avocations: reading, history. Office: Univ Hosp Wales NHS Heath Pk Cardiff CF144XW Wales Home: 506 Heath Park CF14 4XW Cardiff Wales Office Phone: 02920747747, 02420745160. Office Fax: 02920743578; Home Fax: 02920748319. Personal E-mail: gdimitrakakis@yahoo.com.

DIMITRIOU, GABRIEL GABRIEL, pediatrician, neonatologist; b. Athens, Greece, Jan. 17, 1959; s. Gabriel George and Kleopatra Nikitas Dimitriou; m. Vasiliki Nikolaos Kavvadia, Aug. 31, 1996. MD, U. Athens, 1983; PhD, U. London, 2003. Diplomate Greek Bd. Pediat. Resident in pediat. Gen. Hosp., Lesvos, Greece, 1985—86, U. Patras Sch. Medicine, Greece, 1987—90, fellow in neonatology, 1990—93, sr. registrar, 1995—96; clin. rsch. fellow Neonatal ICU, King's Coll. Hosp., London, 1993—95, 1996—2000, mem. staff, 2000—01, spl. registar neonatal ICU, 2001—02; lectr. perinatology, cons. neonatology Guy's King's and St. Thomas Med. Sch., London, 2002—05; assoc. prof. pediat. and neonatology neonatal ICU U. Patras, Greece, 2005—. Grantee, Children's Nationwide Med. Rsch. Fund, U.K., 1996—2000; fellow, Brit. Lung Found., 1995; scholar, U. Athens, 1980—82. Avocations: travel, diving, swimming, music, computers. Office: Neonatal ICU 3rd Fl Univ Gen Hosp Patras RIO 26504 Patras Greece Home: Ammokhostu 30 264 41 Patras Greece Office Phone: 00302610999856. Personal E-mail: gabrieldimitriou@gmail.com. Business E-Mail: gdimitriou@med.upatras.gr.

DIMOND, EDMUNDS GREY, medical educator; b. St. Louis, Dec. 8, 1918; s. Edmunds Grey and Gertrude Ruth (Schmidt) D.; m. Mary Dwight Clark, Nov. 28, 1968 (dec. June 1983); children: Sherri Grey Byrer, Lea Grey Dimond, Lark Grey Dimond-Cates. Student, Purdue U., 1938—39; BS, Ind. U., 1942, MD, 1944. Mem. faculty Med. Ctr., U. Kans., Kansas City, 1950-60, prof., chmn. dept. medicine, 1953-60, dir. cardiovasc. lab., 1950-60; mem., dir. Inst. for Cardiopulmonary

Diseases, Scripps Clinic and Rsch. Found., 1960-67; rsch. assoc. physiology Scripps Inst. Oceanography, La Jolla, Calif., 1960-68; prof. in residence Sch. Medicine, U. Calif., San Diego, 1967-68; scholar in residence Nat. Libr. Medicine, 1967; spl. asst. to asst. sec. HEW, Washington, 1968; Disting. univ. prof. medicine U. Mo., Kansas City, 1968-98, provost for health scis., 1968-79. Fulbright prof., The Netherlands, 1956; vis. prof., Israel, 1978; scholar in residence Rockefeller Found. Study Ctr., Bellagio, Italy, 1978; chmn. overseas edn. team Dept. State, 1962, 64-66, 73; guest lectr. Chinese Med. Assn., 1971-73, 76-80, 82-92; pres. Edgar Snow Fund, Inc., Diastole-Hospital Hill, Inc. Author: Electrocardiography, 1952, rev. edits., 1955, 60, 64, Digitalis, 1957, Exercise Electrocardiograms, 1961, More Than Herbs and Acupuncture, 1975, Inside China Today, 1981, Take Wing, 1991, Dr. Horse of China, 1992, Reverend Whitehead, Mississippi Pioneer, 1987, Letters from Forest Place, 1993, Essays By An Unfinished Physician, 1995, Milepost Eighty, 2000, Milepost Eighty-Five, 2005; editor: Diastole on Hospital Hill Audiotape, 1980-86; editor-in-chief Accel, 1968-77; contbr. articles to profl. jours. Bd. dirs. Truman Med. Ctr., Kansas City, Mo., Eye Found., Kansas City, Sci. Edn. Partnership, Kansas City. With M.C., AUS, 1945-47. Paul Dudley White Traveling scholar, 1956-57. Master Am. Coll. Cardiology (pres. 1962, Disting. Svc. award 1969). Home and Office: 2501 Holmes St Kansas City MO 64108-2742 Office Phone: 816-235-8855. Personal E-mail: gdimond@kc.rr.com.

DIMOPOULOS, PANAGIOTIS G., pharmaceutical product manager, biologist; b. Moschato, Athens, Greece, Mar. 30, 1979; s. George P. and Zoe C. Dimopoulos. Diploma in Biol. Scis., Colchester Study Ctr., Eng., 1997; BSc in Applied Biology, Kingston U., London, 2000; MSc in Biomolecular Archeology and Genetics, UMIST and Sheffield U., 2001. Cert. scuba diver, skipper open sea sailing diploma. Trainee Eyaggelisuos Hosp., Athens, Greece, 1998; biologist asst. Nimits Hosp., 1999; microbiologist asst. Aretaon Hosp, 2000; head biomed. rsch. dept. 251 G.N.A. Military Hosp., 2003; product mgr. Servier Hellas, 2003. Active World Wildlife Fedn., Zakynthos, Greece, 2004, Greenpeace, Athens, 1999—2005. 2d lt. Greek Air Force, 2002—03. Recipient Gold medal under 80 kg., Nat. League Tae Kwon Do, Greece, 1996. Greek Orthodox. Avocations: driving, sailing, scuba diving, martial arts, travel. Office: Servier Hellas Ethn Antrsascos and Agaulunonos 72 Athens Greece Personal E-mail: dimopoulospg@hotmail.com.

DIMOV, GEORGIY P., medical researcher; b. Chelyabinsk, Russia, Jan. 20, 1977; MD in Hematology, Chelyabinsk State Med. Acad., 2000. Rsch. scientist Urals Rsch. Ctr. Radiation Medicine, 2001—. Bd. dirs. Ctr. Innovative Technologies Chelyabinsk State Med. Acad., 2010. Mem.: Chelyabinsk Regional Bd. Experts. Avocations: singing, history. Office: 68 A Vorovsky Str Chelyabinsk 454076 Russia Business E-Mail: dimov@urcrm.ru.

DIMUZIO, PAUL J., vascular surgeon; MD, U. Pa., 1989. Diplomate Am. Bd. Surgery-vascular. Intern Thomas Jefferson Univ. Hosp., resident; fellow Univ, of Calif., San Francisco; physician Thomas Jefferson Univ., William M. Measey prof. surgery, dir. vascular and endovascular surgery divsn., dir. vascular tissue engring. and stem cell rsch. lab. divsn., program dir. vascular surgery fellowship. Named one of the Top Doctor, Phila. Mag., 2011. Office: Thomas Jefferson University Hospital Gibbon Bldg Ste 6270 111 S 11th St Philadelphia PA 19107 Office Phone: 215-955-4912. Office Fax: 215-923-0835.

DINARELLO, CHARLES A., medical educator; b. Boston, 1943; MD, Boston U., 1969; Doctor Honoris Causa, U. Marseille, France, 1997. Clin. tng. Mass. Gen. Hosp.; clin. assoc. NIH, Bethesda, 1971—74, sr. investigator, 1975—77; prof. medicine and pediat. Tufts U. Sch. Medicine; staff physician New England Med. Ctr. Hosp., Boston; prof. medicine U. Colorado Sch. Medicine, Denver, 1996—. Sci. adv, bd. Senesco Technologies, Inc., 2002; mem. bd. scientific advisors Nat. Inst. Allergy and Infections Diseases; dir. Techne Corp. Mem. several editl. bds.; contbr. several articles to profl. jours. Recipient Ernst Jung prize in medicine, 1993, Ludwig Heilmeyer Gold medal, Soc. for Internal Medicine, 1996; co-recipient Crafoord prize in Polyarthritis, Royal Swedish Acad. Sciences, 2009. Mem.: NAS, Internat. Cytokine Soc. (pres. 1995—96), Am. Soc. Clin. Investigations (v.p. 1989—90), European Molecular Biology Organization (EMBO) (assoc.). Achievements include pioneering work with collegues to isolate interleukins, determine their properties and explore their role in the onset of inflammatory diseases. Office: Divsn Infections Diseases 12700 E 19th Ave Box B168 Aurora CO 80045 Office Phone: 303-724-4922. Business E-Mail: charles.dinarello@ucdenver.edu.

DINCECCO, JENNIE ELIZABETH WILLIAMS SWANSON, healthcare administrator, mentor, educator, volunteer; b. Atlanta, Aug. 5, 1932; d. Chester Arthur and Cleo Annie Williams; m. Richard Edward Swanson, Apr. 24, 1954 (dec. 1994); children: Laurel Dee Swanson, Jeffrey Richard Swanson, Scott Edward Swanson; m. Thomas M. Dincecco, Aug. 26, 2000. BS, Northwestern U., 1954; MS, No. Ill. U., 1972, EdD, 1976. Pub. sch. tchr., 1954-69; psychoednl. diagnostician, 1969-72; faculty Loyola U., Chgo., 1976-82, asst. prof. ob-gyn and pediat., 1979-82; dir. pre-start project depts. ob-gyn and pediat. Stritch Sch. Medicine, 1978-82; dir. spl. svcs. Cmty. Unit Sch. Dist. 220, 1982-92. Hospice bereavement vol., 1997—; coun. mem., mentor Cong. Unitarian Ch.; antique dealer; mem. Gov. Ill. Com. Preventive Svcs., 1979-80; chair B-3 subcom. First Chance Consortium, 1978-80; chair INTER-ACT, 1979-80; cons. in field; with prominent alumni Sullivan HS, Chgo., 2009. Author: Dying With Open Eyes: Alzheimer's Disease, 2005, (with others) Wise Words From Women of a Certain Age, 2006; co-author: Partners in Child Development, 1978; columnist: Woodstock Ind. Newspaper, 2006-07. Vol. Latino Coalition, Alzheimer's Assn. Named Sullivan HS Prominent Alumnae, 2008; Grantee HEW, 1973-76, 78-82. Mem.: Ret. Tchrs. McHenry County, Nat. Assn. Edn. Young Child, Nat. Acad. Neuropsychology, Nat. Perinatal Assn., Assn. Maternal and Child Health, Coun. Exceptional Children, Golden Cir., Woodstock Opera House Commn. (chairperson 2001—07), Northwestern U. Alumni Assn , Nu Alumni Club, Delta Kappa Gamma (scholar 1974), Delta Delta Delta (life; golden cir.). Unitarian Universalist.

DINCER, ALP, medical educator; b. Nigde, Turkey, Sept. 4, 1964; MD, Hacettepe U., 1988. Assoc. prof. Acibadem U., 2010—. Office: Okur Sok 1 Acibadem Kozyatgi H Istanbul 34718 Turkey Office Fax: 90-2166589611. Business E-Mail: adincer@asg.com.tr.

DINEEN, JOHN C., health products executive; m. Gina Dineen; 2 children. BS, U. Vt. Mgmt. positions General Electric Co., 1986—2005, telecommunications engr. Rockville, Md., gen. mgr. power equip. Plainville, Conn., gen. mgr. meter bus. Somersworth, NH, gen. mgr. microwave & a.c. Louisville; mgr. of fin. GE Asia, Hong Kong; pres. GE Plastics Pacific; v.p. & gen. mgr. plastics & resins GE Advanced Materials; pres., CEO General Electric Transportation, 2005—08, General Electric Healthcare, 2008—. Office: GE 3135 Easton Tpke Fairfield CT 06431 *

DINES, DAVID MICHAEL, surgeon, educator; b. NYC, Feb. 4, 1948; s. Aaron and Yvette Harriet Dines; m. Judith Lori Dines, Jan. 29, 1973; children: Joshua Scott, Alison Kate. BA in Biology, Lehigh U., Bethlehem, Pa., 1970; MD, NJ Coll. Medicine, 1974. Diplomate Am. Bd. Surgery. Resident in orthop. surgery NY Hosp. Cornell, NYC, 1974—76, Hosp. Spl. Surgery, NYC, 1976—79, fellow, 1980, Am. Acad. Orthop. Surgery, Chgo., 1981; adj. Cornell U. Med. Coll., NYC, 1983—; clin. prof. orthop. surgery Albert Einstein Coll. Medicine, NYC, 1998—2010, chmn. dept. orthop. surgery, 1996—2007; sr. orthop. attending Hosp. for Spl. Surgery, NYC; clin. prof. orthop. surgery Wesll Cornell Med. Coll., NY. Team physician NY Mets, 1991—97, USTA, 1999—; med. advisor Assn. Tennis Profls., Ponte Verde, Fla., 1994—, dir. med. svcs. (Men's Profl. Tennis), 2004—; team physician US Davis Cup Tennis Team, 2000—04; trustee bd. Jour. Shoulder and Elbow Surgery, 2005—; presenter in field. Contbr. more than 100 articles to profl. jours. Fund raiser Hosp. Spl. Surgery, NYC, 1979—. Recipient John Chanley Meml. award, U. Liverpool, Eng., 1996, Lifetime Achievement award, Am. Acad. Orthop., 2010; named one of Best Drs. in NY, NY Mag., 1996—, Best Drs. in Am., 1999—, Best Orthop. Surgeons, 2005—. Fellow: Am. Acad. Orthop. Surgeons (mem. publs. com. 2005—, mem. bd. edn. com. 2005—, Lifetime Achievement award 2010); mem.: Assn. Tennis Profls. (med. dir. 2005—), Assn. Team Profl. Med. Soc. (assoc. dir. 1991), Am. Orthop. Assn. (mem. membership com. 1998—), Acad. Orthop. Soc. Am., Am. Shoulder and Elbow Soc. (mem. exec. com. 1999—, pres. 2005, pres.-elect, Neer award 2004). Avocations: tennis, golf, politics. Office: 935 Northern Blvd Ste 303 Great Neck NY 11021 Office Phone: 516-482-1037.

DINES, JOSHUA S., orthopedist, sports medicine physician; b. NYC, July 29, 1974; BA, Dartmouth Coll., Hanover, NH, 1996; MD, Cornell U. Med. Coll., NYC, 2001. Orthop. surgeon Hosp. Spl. Surgery, NYC, 2002—. Recipient Founders award, Eastern Orthop. Soc., 2006. Office: Hosp Spl Surgery 935 Northern Blvd Great Neck NY 11021 Business E-Mail: dinesj@hss.edu.

DING, ALEXANDER, radiologist; m. Kimberly Ding. BA in Economics, summa cum laude, U. Calif., Berkeley, 2002, MS in Pub. Health, 2005; MD, U. Calif., San Francisco, 2007. Worked in fin. Goldman Sachs; econ. rschr. in the intelligence unit The Economist; med. intern Santa Clara Valley Med. Ctr., San Jose, Calif.; resident physician dept. radiology Mass. Gen. Hosp., Boston, 2008—; clin. fellow Harvard Med. Sch., 2008—. Bd. mem. Physicians Ins. Agy. Mass., Boston Med. Libr.; mem. publications com. The New Eng. Jour., CALPAC. Contbr. articles to profl. jours. Lt. med. corps USNR, 2007—. Mem.: AMA (mem. House Dels. 2004—, bd. trustees 2011—, mem. coun. on legis., mem. PAC bd. dirs., Found. Leadership award 2009), Radiol. Soc. N.Am. (founding mem. resident fellow com.), Mass. Med. Soc. (chmn. resident fellow sect.). Office: Mass Gen Hosp Radiology FND 216 55 Fruit St Boston MA 02114-2622 Office Phone: 617-726-4255. Office Fax: 617-726-3077. Business E-Mail: ading@partners.org. *

DING, DING, medical researcher, educator; b. China, July 15, 1984; MPH, San Diego State U., 2008. Rsch. specialist Rsch. Found. San Diego State U., 2006—, adj. prof. Grad. Sch. Pub. Health, 2008—. Fellowship, Inamori Found. Mem.: Soc. Behavioral Medicine, Delta Omega Hon. Pub. Health Soc., Phi Kappa Phi Honor Soc. Avocations: dance, music, art. Home: 4554 Date Ave La Mesa CA 91941 Business E-Mail: dding@projects.sdsu.edu.

DING, JIANCHI, embryologist, researcher; b. Jiangyin, Jiangsu, Peoples Republic of China, Oct. 24, 1957; came to U.S., 1996; s. Xufu and Xiujin (Gao) D.; m. Mingxian Shen, Nov. 15, 1983; children: Helen Guangning, Jennifer Guangting. BSc, Jiangsu Agrl. Coll., Yangzhou, 1982, MSc, 1985; PhD, U. Alta., Edmonton, Can., 1993. Cert. high complexity lab. dir. Am. Bd. Bioanalysis. Instr. Jiangsu Agrl. Coll., Yangzhou, 1985-87; Natural Sci. and Engring. Rsch. Coun. postdoctoral fellow U. Guelph, Guelph, Ont., Can., 1993-95, rsch. assoc., 1993-96; sr. rschr. Inst. for the Study and Treatment of Endometriosis, Oak Brook, Ill., 1996—; lab. dir. Oak Brook Fertility Ctr., 1996—. Contbr. articles to profl. jours. including Biology of Reprodn., Molecular Reprodn. Devel., and Human Reprodn.; assoc. editor: New Technics to Animal and Poultry Production, 2003. Recipient scholarship Jiangsu Edn. Com., China, 1987-88. Mem. Am. Assn. Bioanalysts, Am. Soc. for Reproductive Medicine, Am. Soc. Andrology, Soc. for Study Reprodn., Coll. Reproductive Biology. Home: 117 Hawkins Cir Wheaton IL 60189 Office: Oak Brook Fertility Ctr 2425 W 22nd St Ste 102 Oak Brook IL 60523-4643 Home Phone: 630-665-8959; Office Phone: 630-954-0054. E-mail: jianchiding@sbcglobal.net.

DING, JINWEN, biomedical researcher; MD, Tongji Med. U., Wuhan, China, 1983; PhD, Lund U., Sweden, 1993. Rsch. scientisit U. of Toronto, Ont., Canada, 1993—99; asst. prof. Loyola U. Med. Ctr., Maywood, Ill., 1999—2004, U. Ill., Chgo., 2004—07, Astellas Pharma, 2007—. Recipient Rsch. award, Am. Cancer Soc., 2004; grantee, Can. Assn. Gastroenterology, 1997, Ill. Transplant Soc., 2002; Sheila Sherlock Basic Rsch. grant, The U. of Toronto, 1997. Mem.: World Assn. of HPB Surgery, Am. Gastroent. Assn. Achievements include research in immunological and molecular mechanisms of liver injury.

DING, LIANSHU, neurosurgeon; b. Shuyang, China, Apr. 25, 1968; MD, Southern Med. U., PhD, 2005. Dir., cons. Huaian No. 1 Hosp., Nanjing Med. U., China, 2005—. Recipient Huaian Sci. Rsch. Excellence award, 2000, 2006. Office: 6 Beijing W Huaian Jiangsu 223300 China Business E-Mail: dlshu@163.com.

DING, SHINN-JYH, materials engineer, educator; b. Yunlin, Taiwan, Oct. 3, 1964; s. Chia-Lin Ding and Zue Ding-Lin; m. Kai-Ling Chen, Oct. 10, 2001; children: Syuan-Chi, Syuan-How. B, Nat. Kaohsiung Normal U., 1988; M, Nat. Cheng-Kung U., Taiwan, 1993, PhD, 1999. Tchr. Sanmin Jr. H.S., Taipei, Taiwan, 1987—92; postdoctoral fellow Nat. Cheng-Kung U., Tainan, Taiwan, 1999—2000; guest rschr. Tissue Engring. Rsch. Ctr., Amagasaki, Japan, 2003; adj. prof. Feng-Chia U., Taichung, Taiwan, 2000—10; prof. Chung-Shan Med. U., 2000—; guest rschr. Biomater Ctr. Tsukuba, Japan, 2008. Sec. gen. Chinese Assn. Chem. Sensors Taiwan, Tainan, 2000—02, dir., 2002—. Author: Surface and Coatings Technology; contbr. articles to profl. jours. Recipient Excellent Rsch., Nat. Sci. Coun. of the Republic of China, 2000. Mem.: Japanese Soc. Dental Materials and Devices, Am. Chemistry Soc., Biomaterials and Drug Delivery Soc. ROC, Chinese Assn. Chem. Sensors in Taiwan, Chinese Soc. Materials Sci., Biomed. Engring. Soc. ROC, Internat. Soc. Electrochemistry, European Soc. Biomaterials, Internat. Assn. Dental Rsch. Achievements include patents for US 6, 344, 276 B1; non-dissolvable amorphous Ti-Ca-P coating for implant application. Avocations: swimming, reading. Office: Chung-Shan Med Univ 110 Section 1 Jianguo North Rd Taichung 402 Taiwan Office Phone: +886-4-24718668 ext. 55529. Office Fax: +886-4-24759065. Business E-Mail: sjding@csmu.edu.tw.

DING, WEI, oncologist; s. Hou Huang Ding and FenLian Hu; m. Ling Li, May 1, 1987; children: YiTong, Jessica. B in Med. Sci., Henan Med. U., Zhengzhou, Henan, China, 1984; M in Applied Physics, RMIT U., Melbourne, Victoria, Australia, 2002. Radiation oncologist Henan Tumor Inst./Hosp., Zhengzhou, Henan, China, 1990—93, jr. radiation oncologist, 1984—90; med. physicist Austin & Repatriation Med. Ctr., Melbourne, Victoria, Australia, 1999—2002, sr. oncologost, 2002—05. Fellow, U. Leuven, Belgium, 1993—94, Geelong Hosp., Victoria, Australia, 1994—96. Mem.: Australasian Brachytherapy Group (assoc.), Australasian Coll. Phys. Scientists and Engs. Medicine (assoc.). Achievements include research in Create in-vivo dosimetry as a quality insurance program in Radiotherapy.

DING, YU, medical researcher; b. JiNan, Shandong, China, Oct. 26, 1972; MS, Peking U., 1999; PhD, Northwestern U., 2006. Rsch. scientist Ohio State U., 2006—. Mem.: Internat. Soc. Magnetic Resonance Medicine. Avocations: history, poetry. Home: 63 McMillen Ave Columbus OH 43201 Personal E-mail: yuding99@yahoo.com.

DINGLEDINE, RAYMOND J., JR., pharmacologist, educator; BS in Biochemistry, Mich. State U., 1971; PhD in Pharmacology, Stanford U., Calif., 1975. Postdoc. fellow U. Cambridge, England, 1975—77, U. Oslo, Norway, 1977—78; rsch. assoc. dept. physiology Duke U., Durham, NC, 1978; asst., assoc., then full prof. dept. pharmacology U. NC, Chapel Hill, 1978—92; prof., chmn. dept. pharmacology Emory U. Sch. Medicine, Atlanta, 1992—, exec. assoc. dean. rsch., 2008—. Vis. scientist Salk Inst. Biol. Studies, La Jolla, Calif., 1990—91; co-founder, mem. sci. adv. bd. NeurOp Inc., Atlanta, 2002—; apptd. sci. coun. Nat. Inst. Neurol. Disorders & Stroke, NIH. Mem. editl. bd. Neuropharmacology, Jour. Molecular Neurosci., Epilepsy Rsch., NeuroMolecular Medicine, former editor Molecular Pharmacology; contbr. articles to profl. jours. Recipient PhRMA Found. Career award in excellence, 1999, John A. Boezi Disting. Alumnus award, Michigan State U., Jacob Javits award in neurosciences, NIH, Bristol-Myers Squibb Neuroscience award; Alfred P. Sloan Fellowship, Klingenstein Fellowship. Fellow: AAAS; mem.: American Soc. Pharmacology & Exptl. Therapeutics, American Epilepsy Soc. (Basic Rsch. award 1995), Soc. Neuroscience, Inst. Medicine. Achievements include research in the pharmacology of neurotransmitter receptors, including glutamate, which are responsible for communication between neurons in the brain; contributions to the current understanding of seizure development in brain cells which has laid the foundation for new approaches to drug therapy for epilepsy. Office: Emory U Sch Medicine Dept Pharmacology 1510 Clifton Rd Atlanta GA 30322 Office Phone: 404-727-5983. Office Fax: 404-727-0365. E-mail: rdingledine@pharm.emory.edu.

DINH, ANTHONY TUNG, internist; b. Jan. 1, 1938; s. Hoan B. and Phieu T. (Nguyen) D.; m. Lisa L. Tran, Jan. 8, 1971; children: Andrew A., Thomas A. BS, U. Saigon, Vietnam, 1959, MD, 1967. Diplomate Am. Bd. Internal Medicine, Am. Bd. Infectious Disease, Am. Bd. Med. Microbiology. Intern in internal medicine Phila. Gen. Hosp., 1976-77; resident in internal medicine Wayne State U., 1977-79; fellow in infectious diseases U. Pa., 1979-81; asst. prof. U. Saigon, 1970-75; chief infectious disease VA Med. Ctr., Beckley, W.Va., 1981-82, chief med. svc., 1982-85, chief staff, 1985—. Adj. clin. prof. medicine W.Va. Sch. Osteopathic Medicine, Lewisburg, 1987—; cons. in infectius disease. Contbr. articles to profl. jours. Mem. ACP, N.Y. Acad. Scis., Am. Soc. Microbiology, Raleigh County Med. Soc. (chmn. continuing med. edn. 1987—), W.Va. State Med. Assn. Office: Beckley Med Arts 2401 S Kanawha St Beckley WV 25801-6905 Home Phone: 304-252-8230; Office Phone: 304-252-5746.

DINH, TRI ANH, oncologist; b. Da Nang, Vietnam, Sept. 6, 1966; MD, Baylor Coll. Medicine, 1992. Chief, divsn. gynecologic oncology Meth. Hosp. Physician Orgn., 2006—. Recipient Golden Apple award, U. Tex. Med. Br., Health Care Hero award, Houston Bus. Jour. Fellow: Tex. Assn. Ob-Gyn.; mem.: Vietnamese Med. Assn., Williard R. Cooke Soc., Am. Coll. Ob-gyn., Tex. Med. Assn. Avocations: tennis, photography. Office: 6550 Fannin Ste 901 Houston TX 77030 Office Phone: 713-441-3095. Office Fax: 713-790-2986. Business E-Mail: tadinh@tmhs.org.

DINI, GAL MOREIRA, plastic surgeon, researcher, university teacher; b. Sorocaba, São Paulo, Brazil, Feb. 24, 1968; s. Gualberto Moreira and Heloisa Santos Dini; m. Erika Neander Trentin, Dec. 22, 2000. MD, São Francisco U., 1992; M in Plastic and Reparative Surgery, Fed. U. São Paulo- Escola Paulista Medicine, 2000, PhD in Plastic and Reparative Surgery, 2004; postgrad. in Psychiatry, 2001, postgrad. in Psychiatry, 2006. Resident in gen. surgery Pontiff Catholic U. São Paulo, Brazil, 1993—95; trained in plastic surgery and other disciplines various med. schs. and hosps., São Paulo, 1995—99; asst. med. dr., founder plastic surgery league Paulista Med. Sch., Fed. U. São Paulo, 1996—97, mem. pub. rels. plastic surgery, 1997—2004, rep. residents' coun., 1998, preceptor plastic surgery, 1998—99, chief officer plastic surgery, 1999—2002. Vol. dr. Insane Hosp. Mental & Teixiera Lima, 1994—98; affiliated prof., orientation tchr. M and PhD programs Fed. U. São Paulo; spkr., presenter in field. Contbr. chapters to books, articles to profl. jours. Vol. Insane Hosp. Mental and Teixeira Lima, 1994—98; mem. Swing Choir, Suring, Wis., Mixed Choir, Suring. Dr. res. lt. Airforce, 1992—97, São Paulo. Recipient 1st prize, 11th Congress Internat. Confederation, Yokohama, Japan, 1995, World Congress Plastic Surgery, 1995, Hon. Mention, Sorocaba City Hall, 2004, prize, Heroes of War Combatants

Assn.; Internat. fellow, Suring Pub. Sch., 1983—84. Fellow: Fed. Ibero-Latino Am. Cirurgia. Plastica, Brazilian Soc. Plastic Surgery, Brazilian Coll. Surgeons; mem.: ISAPS, Future Farmers of Am. Roman Catholic. Achievements include invention of the Rambo technique. Avocations: travel, water-skiing, snowboarding, running. Office: Av Barao de Tatui 1455 Soracaba São Paulo Brazil Office Phone: 55-15-32118840, 55 15 32323311. Personal E-mail: dr.gal@uol.com.br.

DINICHERT, ANTOINE, neurosurgeon; b. Boudevilliers, Switzerland, Aug. 28, 1974; s. Grégoire and Monique Dinichert; m. Constanza Catherine Pournaras, May 27, 2004; children: Paris Adonis, Melia Electra. Dr., Geneva's U., 2001. U. diploma in nervous system radiology Pierre Marie Curie U., Paris, 2003, u. diploma functional and therapeutic stereotaxy Pierre Marie Curie U., Paris, 2004, u. diploma of microsurgical technique René Descartes U., Paris, 2004, u. diploma in spine surgery Paris, 2009. Jr. trainee gen. surgery Moutier Hosp., Switzerland, 2000—01; specialized trainee neurosurgery Lariboisière Hosp., Paris, 2001—04; clin. fellow (specialist registrar) in neurosurgery Charing Cross Hosp., London, 2004—05; specialised trainee neurosurgery Schulthess Clinic, Zürich, Switzerland, 2005—07; neurosurgeon, cons., spine surgery specialist St. Gall Cantonal Hosp., Switzerland, 2007—10; pvt. practice Geneva, 2010—. Home: Florissant 8 Geneva 206 Syria Office: Clinique la Colline Ave de Beau-Sejour 6 Geneva 1206 Switzerland Home Phone: 41794108720. Business E-Mail: antoine@dinichert.com.

DI NICOLA, LUIGI PHILIPPE ROGER, pharmaceutical executive, director; b. St. Germain, France, Sept. 16, 1958; s. Luciano Di Nicola and Genevieve Rouire; m. Caroline Di nicola-Gadet, June 10, 1961; 1 child, Eleonore. MSc in Biochemistry, U. Rome La Sapienza, 1985, PhD in Chemistry, 1985; PhD in Molecular Endocrinology, U. Monpellier, 1997; M in Health Mgmt., U.Paris, 2000; MBA, Paris, 2003. Product mgr. Farmitalia Carlo Erba Onco, Paris, 1987—89, Pharmacia, Paris, 1989—91; bus. unit mgr. Novo Nordisk, Boulogne, France, 1991—98; sci. dir. Sandoz Biopharms Controls SA, Rueil, France, 1998—, gen. mgr., 1998—. Mem.: French Endocrine Soc., Endocrine Soc., Growth Hormone Rsch. Soc. Home: 36 Bis Rue De Dunkerque 75010 Paris France Office: Sandoz Biopharmaceuticals SA 14 Bvd Richelieu F92845 Rueil France

DINIZ, CRISTIANO MENEZES, ophthalmologist; b. Minas Gerais, Brazil, Feb. 28, 1975; Degree in Medicine, Minas Gerais Fed. U., 1999, M, 2009. Ophthalmologist Brazilian Air Force FAB, 2005—07; urgency med. staff ophthalmologist Hosp. João XXIII FHEMIG, 2006—07; oculoplastic surgeon ophthalmologist Hosp. Das Clínicas Minas Gerais Fed. U., 2002—10, Hosp. de Olhos Beira Rio, 2008—. Bd. dirs. Ophthalmology Hosp. Das Clínicas Minas Gerais Fed. U., 2006—08. Mem.: Soc. Brasileira Cirurgia Plástica Ocular, Brazilian Ophthalmology Coun. Conselho Brasileiro Oftalmologia, Brazilian Oculoplastic Soc. Avocation: tennis. Office: Av Mário Padre 185 Góes Calmon Itabuna Bahia 45605415 Brazil Business E-Mail: crismdiniz@yahoo.com.br.

DIOGUARDI, PAUL T., federal agency administrator; m. Kate Schekells; 1 child, Thomas. BA in Polit. Sci., Boston Coll., 1992; MPA, Harvard U., 2002. Chief of staff, spl. asst. Congl. & intergovernmental affairs US Dept. Labor, 1999—2001; field dir. Ohio Dem. Coordinated Campaign, 2002; nat. field dir. Debt, AIDS, Trade, Africa (DATA), 2003—05; acting CEO, exec. v.p. ONE, 2005—07, nat. polit. dir. Dem. Govs. Assn., 2008; indsl. states regional dir. Presdl. campaign Barack Obama, 2008; dir. Office Intergovernmental Affairs, US Dept. Health & Human Services, Washington, 2009—. Office: HHS Intergovernmental Affairs 200 Independence Ave SW Rm 610E Washington DC 20201 Office Phone: 202-690-6060. E-mail: paul.dioguardi@hhs.gov. *

DIORIO, EILEEN PATRICIA, retired medical technologist, philosophy educator; b. Pitts., Mar. 17, 1938; d. Charles Frederick and Elizabeth (Maturkanich) Kozlowski; m. David Robert Kaslewicz, June 21, 1958 (div. May 1965); m. Alfred Frank Diorio, June 11, 1983; children: Suzanne C. Kaslewicz Ickes, Fredric C. Kaslewicz, Warren G. Kaslewicz, Jennifer Kaslewicz Dalessandro. Student, Duquesne U., 1956-58. Reg. Med. Technologist, Pa. Microbiology technician Presbyn. U. Hosp., Pitts., 1967-70; supr. virology/immunology lab. Allegheny Gen. Hosp., Pitts., 1970-90. Co-dir. Himalayan Inst. Yoga Science & Philosophy of Pitts., 1977-96. Vol. med. lab. mgr. Himalayan Inst. Hosp., India, 1992-96. Avocations: violin, cooking, meditation.

DIPALMA, JOSEPH RUPERT, pharmacology educator, dean; b. NYC, Mar. 21, 1916; s. Frank and Anna (Attanasio) DiP.; m. Mary Solowey, June 26, 1948; children: Maria, Dorothea, Joan, Yvonne, Mary-Jo. BS, Columbia U., 1936; MD, SUNY, Bklyn., 1941; DSc (hon.), Hahnemann U., 1980. Intern, resident in internal medicine Kings County Hosp., Bklyn., 1942-44; asst. prof. medicine and pharmacology State U. N.Y. Downstate Med. Sch., 1946; prof. pharmacology, chmn. dept. Hahnemann Med. Coll. and Hosp., Phila., 1951-67, dean, 1967-82, v.p., 1971-82, sr. v.p., 1972-82, prof. pharmacology and medicine, 1982-86, emeritus prof. pharmacology and medicine, 1986—, emeritus dean, 1986—. Bd. dirs. Regional Med. Program Southeastern Pa., 1967-75, Health Sys. Agy., 1977-82, Hahnemann Hosp., 2000-, St. Davids Instnl. Rev., 1975-. Author: Decanus Maximus, The Life and Times of a Medical School Dean, 2004; editor: Pharmacology in Medicine, 1971, Basic Pharmacology in Medicine, 1976, 4th edit., 1994; contbr. articles to med. jours. Bd. dirs. Hahnemann Univ. Hosp., 2003—. Recipient Alumni medallion SUNY, Downstate Med. Sch., 1966, Corp. medal Hahnemann U., 1990 Mem. Coll. Physicians Phila. (council 1969-78), AMA, Pa., Phila. County Med. socs., Am. Physiol. Soc., Am. Soc. Pharmacology and Exptl. Therapeutics, Am. Soc. Clin. Investigation, Am. Soc. Clin. Pharmacology, Alpha Omega Alpha. Home: 100 Pembroke Ave Wayne PA 19087-4819 Office: 235 N 15th St Philadelphia PA 19102-1101 Personal E-mail: josephdipalma@verizon.net, josephdipalma@yahoo.com. *

DI PAOLO, JOSEPH AMEDEO, geneticist; b. Bridgeport, Conn., June 13, 1924; s. John Anthony and Nancy (Montagano) Di P.; m. Arleta Mae Schreib, June 14, 1952; children: Nancy, John. BA, Wesleyan U., 1948; MS, Western Res. U., 1949; PhD, Northwestern U., 1951; MD (hon.), U. Cagliari, Italy, 1991. Instr. genetics bacteriology dept. biology Loyola U., Chgo., 1951-53; instr. clin. and exptl. pathology Northwestern U. Med. Sch., Chgo., 1953-55; sr. cancer research scientist Roswell Park Meml. Inst., Buffalo, 1955-63; research pharmacologist, cell biologist biology br., div. chem. and phys. carcinogenesis program Nat. Cancer Inst., Bethesda, Md., 1963-76, chief lab. biology, divsn. basic scis., 1976—99; emeritus, 1999. Assoc. prof., lectr. anatomy George Washington U., Washington, 1973-96; chmn. U.S.-Germany Cancer Program Area for Environ. Carcinogenesis, 1979-85, U.S.-USSR Mammalian Sometic Cell Genetics Relation to Neoplasia Program, 1973-76; cons. U.S.-Poland Cancer Program, 1979-91; mem. Coun. of the European Rsch. Orgn. on Genital Infection and Neoplasis, 1994; co-chmn. Cervical Cancer Prevention and Therapy Symposium UICC, New Delhi, 1994; co-organizer 16th Internat. Papillomavirus Conf., Siena, Italy, 1997; mem. sci. com. European Environ. Hygiene, 1996, mem. scientific com. 23d Internat. Papilloma Conf., Prague, 2006; sci. advisor divsn. biol. scis. NCI Frontiers in Sci., 1999—. Editor, co-author: Chemical Carcinogenesis, 1974; assoc. editor: Jour. of Nat. Cancer Inst., 1968-71, Cancer Rsch., 1970-78, Teratogenesis, Carcinogenesis, Mutagenesis, 1982-92; editl. acad. Internat. Jour. Oncology, 1992—; guest editor Cancer Investigation, 2000-01; sci. adv. mem. CCR Frontiers in Sci., 2000—. With USN, 1943-46 Fellow N.Y. Acad. Sci., AAAS; mem. Am. Assn. Cancer Rsch. (bd. dirs. 1983-86), Coun. of European Rsch., Orgn. Genital Infection and Neoplasia, Am. Soc. Human Genetics, Am. Soc. for Investigation of Pathology, Genetics Soc. Am., Teratology Soc., Hamster Soc., Tissue Culture Assn., Am. Assn. Pathology, European Assn. for Cancer Rsch., Sigma Xi. Achievements include research on ribozyme and antisense patents for cervical cancer; patent for identification of transforming fragment of HSV-2 and its detection in clinical specimens. Home: 6605 Melody Ln Bethesda MD 20817-3154 Home Phone: 301-469-7003; Office Phone: 301-496-6441. Business E-Mail: jd8la@nih.gov

DIPIETRO, JOSEPH A., academic administrator, medical educator; BS, U. Ill., Urbana, 1974, DVM, 1976, MS, 1980. Assoc. veterinarian Peotone Animal Hosp., Ill., 1976—78; instr. veterinary clin. medicine Coll. Veterinary Medicine, U. Ill., Urbana, 1976—80, asst. prof., 1980—84, assoc. prof., 1984—90, prof. Dept. Veterinary Pathobiology, 1990—97, acting assoc. dean rsch., 1990—91, asst. dean rsch., 1991—92, acting assoc. dean rsch., 1993—94, assoc. dean rsch., 1994—97; acting asst. dir. Agr. Experiment Station Coll. Agr., U. Ill., Urbana, 1993—94, asst. dir., 1994—97; dean Coll. Veterinary Medicine, U. Fla., Gainesville, 1997—2006, prof. Dept. Pathobiology, 1997—2006; prof. Comparative Medicine Dept., Coll. Veterinary Medicine U. Tenn., Knoxville, 2006—, chancellor Inst. Agr., 2006—10, pres., 2011—. Mem. bd. vet. medicine US Pharmacopia; equine adv. com. Fla. Farm Bur.; mem. organizing com. Internat. Cyathostome Workshop; commr. Ill. Racing Bd.; bd. dirs., fin. com. U. Fla. Found.; chmn. coun. on affirmative action U. Fla.; chmn. bd. dir. Vet. Med. Faculty Assn.; mem. Nat. Agrl. Rsch., Edn. and Economics Adv. Bd. Mem.: Tenn. Veterinary Med. Assn., American Veterinary Med. Assn., Assn. American Veterinary Med. Colleges (chmn. rsch. deans and directorss com., sec., bd.dirs., accreditation task force, comparative data com., pres.), Nat. Rsch. Coun. (bd. agr. & natural resources com. future role of pesticides in US agr.), American Assn. Equine Practitioners (biologic and therapeutic com., rsch. com.). Office: University of Tennessee Office of President 831 Andy Holt Tower Knoxville TN 37996-0180 Office Phone: 865-974-2241. Office Fax: 865-974-3753. *

DIPIRO, JOSEPH THOMAS, dean, pharmacy educator; BS in Pharmacy, magna cum laude, U. Conn., 1978; PharmD, U. Ky. Coll. Pharmacy, 1981. Pharmacy resident Albert B. Chandler Med. Ctr., Lexington, Ky., 1981—84; postdoc. rsch. fellow clin. immunology Johns Hopkins U., Balt., 1989—90; clin. prof. surgery Med. Coll. Ga. Sch. Medicine, Augusta; prof. pharmacy, asst. dean, head dept. clin. & adminstrv. pharmacy U. Ga. Coll. Pharmacy, Panoz Prof. pharmacy, 1997—2004; prof., exec. dean SC Coll. Pharmacy, Med. Univ. SC/Univ. SC, 2004—. Editor: Am. Jour. Pharm. Edn., 2002—, Encyclopedia of Clinical Pharmacy; contbr. numerous articles to profl. jours., chapters to books. Recipient Paul Parker award, U. Ky., 2001. Fellow: Am. Coll. Clin. Pharmacy (past pres., Russell R. Miller Lit. award 1998); mem.: Am. Assn. Colleges of Pharmacy (Robert K. Chalmers Disting. Educator award 2002), Am. Soc. Health-Sys. Pharmacists, Surg. Infection Soc. Office: MUSC Campus 171 Ashley Ave Charleston SC 29425 also: USC Campus Columbia SC 29208 Office Phone: 843-792-3740, 803-777-4151. Business E-Mail: jdipiro@sccp.sc.edu.

DIPPENAAR, RICKY, pediatrician; s. Jannie and Denise Dippenaar. MBChB, U. Cape Town, 1998; diploma in Child Health, Coll. Medicine, S. Africa, 2000; Master of Medicine in Pediat., U. Stellenbosch, 2004. Cert. in neonatology Coll. Medicine South Africa. Dir. Neontal Svc., NI City, South Africa, Blaauwberg Neontal Intensive Units, Western Cape, South Africa. Fellow: Fellowship Coll. Pediatricians (assoc.). Achievements include research in use of medicinal leeches, primarily in children.

DIPRIMA, RICHARD JOSEPH, neuropsychologist; s. Michael T. and Kathleen M. DiPrima; m. Erin Kathleen Cashin, Aug. 14, 1999; children: John Patrick, Maria Charlotte, Joseph Michael. BA, Marquette U., 1995; MA, Argosy U., 1999, D Psychology, 2002. Lic. psychologist NY, Minn. Job coach supportive rehab. and tng. Lifetime Asst., Rochester, NY, 1997; psychologist Alexian Bros. No. Mental Health Ctr., Palatine, Ill., 1998—99; psychotherapy/day ctr. practice in neuropsychology Neuropsychol. and Rehab. Cons., Chgo., 1999—2000; cons., diagnostician U.S. Family Counseling Ctr., Chgo., 1999—2001; predoctoral intern U. Rochester Med. Ctr., 2001—02, postdoctoral resident in neuropsychology, 2002—04, faculty mem., sr. instr., 2004—05; neuropsychologist Gillette Childrens, 2005—; with Crestomathy Ctr., Mpls., 1996, counselor Dungarvin, St. Paul, 1996. Program aide in support rehab. and tng. Crestomathy Ctr., Mpls., 1996; program counselor Dungarvin, St. Paul, 1996. Recipient Outstanding Grad. award, Argosy U. Clin. Psychology, 2002; nominee Tzvi Daremblum Excellence Teamwork award, 2010; Acad. scholar, Marquette U., 1991, Deans Acad. scholar, Argosy U., 1999, APA Conf. Student Rep. scholar, 1999, fellow, Psi Chi, Nat. Honor Soc. Psychology, 1997. Mem.: APA (divsn. neuropsychology mem.), AES. Avocations: soccer, tennis, golf, writing, softball, painting. Office: Gillette Childrens Hosp 305 E Nicollet Blvd Burnsville MN 55337 Office Phone: 952-223-3415. Business E-Mail: rdiprima@gillettechildrens.com.

DIRKES, SUSAN, critical care nurse, educator; b. May 16, 1953; BSN, U. Detroit Mercy, 1976; MSA, Madonna U., 1991. Cert. in critical care and dialysis. Clin. educator U. Mich. Health Sys., 1984—. Critical care relationship mgr. NxStage Med. Inc., 2003—09. Mem.: Am. Assn. Critical Care Nurses, Soc. Critical Care Medicine. Avocation: sailing. Home: 6326 Sterling Dr Newport MI 48166 Personal E-mail: susandirkes@gmail.com.

DIRKS, JOHN HERBERT, physician; b. Winnipeg, Man., Can., Aug. 20, 1933; s. Alexander P. and Agnes (Warkentin) D.; m. Fay Ruth Inman, July 3, 1961; children— John Mark, Peter Benjamin, Martha, Carol BSc in Medicine, U. Man., Winnipeg, 1957, MD with honors, 1957. Jr. rotating intern Winnipeg Gen. Hosp., 1957-58, jr. asst. resident, 1958-59; renal fellow Deer Lodge VA Hosp., Winnipeg, 1959-60; med. resident Montreal Gen. Hosp., 1960-62; Med. Research Council fellow McGill U., Montreal, 1960-62, Med. Research Council scholar, 1965-70, dir. nephrology, 1965—76, John Fraser research assoc., 1971-76, prof. medicine, 1971-76, prof. physiology, 1974-76; Med. Research Council fellow, vis. scientist Lab. Kidney and Electrolyte Metabolism/Nat. Heart Inst. Bethesda, Md., 1963-65; Eric W. Hamber prof. medicine, head dept. medicine U. B.C., 1976-87, hon. prof. physiology, 1978-87, head dept. medicine Health Scis. Centre Hosp., 1976—87; physician-in-chief Vancouver Gen. Hosp., 1976-86; mem. staff St. Paul's Hosp., Vancouver, 1976-87; com. mem. Med. Research Coun. Can., 1972-84, mem. council, 1978-87; dean Medicine U. Toronto, 1987—91; sr. fellow Massey Coll.; prof. emeritus medicine U. Toronto. Chmn. sci. adv. com. Kidney Found., 1982—; mem. med. adv. bd. Gairdner Award Found., 1983-; pres., sci. dir. Gairdner Found., 1993—; bd. dirs. B.C. Sci. Council, 1986—; 6th Internat. Urolithiasis Workshop, 1987, program chmn. Am. Soc. of Nephrology, 1987, MRC Peer Rev. Adv. Group, 1986-87; co-chair feasibility study UN Univ., 1992-94, chair on health coun.; dean, rector Aga Khan U., 1994-96. Contbr. numerous articles to profl. jours. Recipient Queen Elizabeth Jubilee award, 1977, Kidney Found. of Can. Med. award, 1985, Nat. Kidney Found. Internat. medal, 2005, Order of Can., 2006. Fellow Royal Soc. Can., Royal Coll. Physicians and Surgeons Can., ACP; mem. Coll. Physicians and Surgeons of Province Que., Fedn. Med. Specialists Que., Can. Soc. Clin. Investigation (sec.-treas. 1972-75, pres. 1976-77), Can. Physiol. Soc., Internat. Soc. Nephrology (coun. mem. 1984-87, co-chair COMGAN 1993, chair 1994-2005, Roscoe Robinson award, 2005), Can. Soc. Nephrology (council), Am. Soc. Nephrology, Am. Heart Assn., Am. Physiol. Soc., Am. Soc. Clin. Investigation, N.Y. Acad. Scis., Internat. Soc. Nephrology (council 1984—), Can. for Health Research, Que. Coll. Physicians (cert. internal medicine and nephrology), Am. Acad. Arts & Scis. (fgn.).

DI ROCCO, VINCENT, psychologist, educator; b. Vincennes, France, June 4, 1957; PhD, U. Lyon 2, 2006. Rsch. prof. U. Lyon 2, 2009. Office: University Lyon 2 5 Av P Mendès Franc Bron Rhône Alpes 69679 France Business E-Mail: vincent.di-rocco@orange.fr.

DIRZO, RODOLFO, biologist, educator, researcher; b. Cuernavaca, Mex., June 26, 1951; s. Felix and Antonia (Minjarez) D.; m. Bertha Guillermina Gomez, Dec. 18, 1986; 1 child, Arturo. BSc in Biology, U. Morelos, Cuernavaca, 1974; MSc in Ecology, U. Wales, Bangor, UK, 1977, PhD in Ecology, 1980. Rsch. asst. Nat. U. Mex., Mexico City, 1974-80, assoc. prof. ecology, 1980-83, prof. ecology, 1983-85; dir. Tropical Rsch. Sta., Veracruz, Mex., 1985-87; dep. chair Inst. Ecology, Nat. U. Mex., 1994-97, full prof. ecology, 1990—, Bing prof. environ. sci., dept. biol. scis. Stanford U., 2004. Prof., instr. Orgn. Tropical Studies, Costa Rica and U.S., 1982-; conservation & environment scholar Pew Charitable Trust, U.S., 1993; nat. rschr. Mex. Coun. Sci., Mexico City, 1990-; cons. Nat. Geographic Soc., Washington, 1995. Author, editor: Perspectives on Plant Population Ecology, 1984, Mexico Faces the Biodiversity Crisis, 1992, Tropical Forests: Biodiversity, 1996; mem. editl. bd. Trends in Ecology and Evolution, 1993—. Mem. Mex. Acad. Sci. (chair biology 1996-97), Ecol. Soc. Am. (mem. pub. affairs com. 1996-98, governing bd. 1999—), Internat. Geosphere-Biosphere Program (mem. scientific com 1997—), Assn. Tropical Biology (pres. 1993-94), NAS (fgn. assoc.), Am. Acad. Arts & Sciences (hon. fgn.). Avocations: children's education, hiking, soccer, music, movies. Office: Stanford U Dept Biol Sciences Gilbert Hall Stanford CA 94305-5020 Business E-Mail: rdirzo@stanford.edu.

DISA, JOSEPH JAMES, plastic surgeon; s. Rose and Ralph Disa; m. Julie Lynn Stebbins, Oct. 2, 1961. MD, U. Mass. Sch. Medicine, Worcester, MA, 1988. Am. Bd. Plastic Surgery, Am. Bd. Surgery. Intern, gen. surgery U. Md. Med. Ctr., Balt., 1988—89, resident, 1989—94, John Hopkins U., Balt., 1994—96; fellow, plastic surgery Meml. Sloan-Kettering Cancer Ctr., 1996, attending surgeon, plastic and reconstructive surgery New York, NY, 1997—; assoc. prof., plastic and reconstructive surgery Cornell Weill Sch. of Medicine, New York, NY, 1997—. Co-author: 100 Questions & Answers About Breast Surgery, 2006; contbr. several articles to profl. jours.; editl. bd. mem. Annals of Plastic Surgery. Fellow: ACS; mem.: Northeastern Soc. Plastic Surgeons (bd. dir. historian 2006—07), Plastic Surgery Edn. Found., Am. Soc. of Reconstructive Microsurgery, Am. Soc. of Plastic Surgeons. Achievements include research in microsurgical reconstruction. Office: Meml Sloan-Kettering Cancer Center 1275 York Ave New York NY 10021 Office Fax: 212-717-3677. Business E-Mail: disaj@mskcc.org.

DISAIA, PHILIP JOHN, obstetrician, gynecologist, radiology educator; b. Providence, Aug. 14, 1937; s. George and Antoinette (Vastano) DiS.; children: John P., Steven D.; m. Patricia June; children: Dominic J., Vincent J. BS cum laude, Brown U., 1959; MD cum laude, Tufts U., 1963; MD (hon.), U. Genoa, Italy, 1999. Diplomate Am. Bd. Ob-Gyn. (examiner 1975—, bd. dirs. 1994, v.p. bd. dirs. 1997—), Am. Bd. Gynecologic Oncology (bd. dirs. 1987—). Intern Yale U. Sch. Medicine, New Haven Hosp., 1963-64, resident in ob-gyn., 1964-67, instr. ob gyn., 1966-67; fellow in gynecologic oncology U. Tex. M.D. Anderson Hosp. and Tumor Inst., Houston, 1969-70, NIH sr. fellow, 1969-70, instr. ob-gyn., 1969-71; asst. prof. ob-gyn. and radiology U. So. Calif. Sch. Medicine, LA, 1971-74, assoc. prof., 1974-77; prof., chmn. dept. ob-gyn. U. Calif. Irvine Med. Ctr., Calif. Coll. Medicine, 1977-88, prof., 1977—, prof. radiology, radiation therapy div., 1978—, assoc. vice chancellor for health scis. Irvine Coll. Medicine, 1987-89, Dorothy Marsh chair of reproductive biology, 1989—; divsn. dir. cancer ctr. U. Calif, Irvine Med. Ctr., Calif. Coll. Medicine, 1989—; pres. med. staff U. Calif. Irvine Med. Ctr., Calif. Coll. Medicine, 1993-97; pres. UCI Clin. Practice Group, 1994—. Dir. div. gynecol. oncology Am. Bd. Obstetrics & Gynecology, 1995—, bd. dirs., 1994—, past chair, current pres.; bd. dirs. U. Calif. Irvine Med. Ctr., 1995, chair health sys. steering com., 1995, chair health sys. capital planning group, 1995, health sys. bd. dirs.,

1995; clin. enterprise adv. coun. to pres. U. Calif., 1995; academic planning task force U. Calif. Irvine, 1994, continuing med. edn. com., 1991-94; cancer liaison commn. on cancer Am. Coll. Surgeons, 1981-94; bd. dirs., dir. at large Am. Cancer Soc., 1985—; clin. prof. dept. ob-gyn. U. Nev. Sch. Medicine, Reno, 1985—; chmn. site visit team for surgery br. Nat. Cancer Inst. NIH, 1983, subcom. surg. oncology rsch. devel., 1982-83, mem. sci. counselors div. cancer treatment, 1979-83; mem. gov.'s adv. coun. on cancer State of Calif., 1980-85; vis. prof., lectr., speaker various sci. meetings, confs., courses. Recipient Disting. Alumnus award M.D. Anderson Hosp. and Tumor Inst. U. Tex., 1980, Silver Apple award U. Calif. Med. Students, 1983, Lauds and Laurels Profl. Achievement award U. Calif. Alumni Assn., 1983, Hubert Haussel's award Long Beach Meml. Hosp., 1983, Dist. Faculty Lectureship award for Teaching, U. Calif. Irvine Acad. Senate, 1993-94, Robert Wood Johnson award, 2003, medal for excellence UIC, 2003, IGS award for excellence in gynecologic oncology Bristol Myers Squibb, 2004, Arise award UCI, 2005, award Women's Cancer Symposium, Amman, Jordan, 2005, Frederick Naptolin award SGI, 2007, also various rsch. awards. Fellow Am. Coll. Obstetricians and Gynecologists (com. on human rsch. for cancer 1979—, chmn. 1984—, chmn. subcom. on gynecologic oncology 1984-85, prolog editorial and adv. com. 1986—, v.p. 1997-99, various others), ACS (bd. govs. 1998—), Commn. on Cancer Liaison, Western Assn. Gynecologic Oncologists (founder 1971, pres. 1978-79), Am. Gynecol. and Obstet. Soc. (exec. coun. 1986—), Am. Gynecologic Soc., Pacific Coast Ob/Gyn Soc., South Atlantic Assn. Obstetricians and Gynecologists (hon.); mem. AMA, Am. Cancer Soc. (bd. dirs. L.A. County unit 1975-77, Orange County 1979, unit pres. 1993—; bd. dirs. Calif. div. 1985—, chmn. med. scientific com. 1993-94), Nat. Am. Cancer Soc. (dir.-at-large, bd. dirs. 1985—, chmn. program com. for nat. conf. 1986, vice-chmn. detection and treatment adv. group gynecol. cancer 1993-94, active in others), Am. Coll. Radiology (commn. on cancer 1984-85), Am. Soc. Clin. Oncologists, Soc. Gynecologic Oncologists (exec. coun. 1975-80, pres. 1982-83), Internat. Gynecologic Oncology Cancer Soc., Italian Soc. Ob-Gyn. (Camillo Golgi prof. U. Brescia 1991), Calif. Med, Assn., NCI, Ctrl. IRB, Academic Senate, (chair 2000-), Gynecologic Oncology Group, (chair 2002-), ABOG, (pres.2002-06, chmn. bd. 2006—), Alpha Omega Alpha. Office: U Calif Irvine Med Ctr 101 The City Dr S Bldg 56 Rm 265 Orange CA 92868-3201 Office Phone: 714-456-5220. E-mail: pjdisaia@uci.edu.

DI SALVO, GIOVANNI, cardiologist, researcher; b. Naples, Italy, Sept. 10, 1971; s. Mario Di Salvo and Naida Corrado. M in Med. Imaging, Cath. U., Leuven, Belgium, 2002; speciality in medicine and surgery, Second U. Naples, 1996, speciality in cardiology, 2000, MD, 2003. Asst. Second U. Naples, 2002—, dir., 2002—. Recipient Young Rschr. award, European Soc. Cardiology, 2002, European Soc. Echocardiography, 2003. Mem.: European Soc. Echocardiography (Young Rschr. award 2003), European Soc. Cardiology (Young Rschr. award 2002), Am. Heart Assn. Office: Second Univ Naples Monaldi Via Pansini 80128 Naples Italy Home: Via Adolfo Omodeo 45 80128 Naples NA Italy Office Fax: 00390815605648. Personal E-mail: giodisal@yahoo.it. Business E-Mail: giovanni.disalvo@unina2.it.

DI SIMONE, ROBERT NICHOLAS, radiologist, educator; b. Canton, Ohio, Nov. 15, 1937; s. Nicholas Joseph and Margaret Elizabeth (Karas) DiS.; m. Patricia Anne Zwigard, June 22, 1963; children: Christopher, Angela, Elizabeth BSc summa cum laude, Ohio State U., 1959, MSc, 1963, MD cum laude, 1963. Diplomate Am. Bd. Radiology, Am. Bd. Nuclear Medicine. Intern, fellow Johns Hopkins U. Hosp., Balt., 1963-64, asst. resident, fellow in internal medicine, 1964-65, asst. resident, fellow in radiology, 1967-70, instr., radiologist, 1970-71; dir. nuclear medicine Aultman Hosp., Canton, 1971-95, pres., med. staff, 1986-87, vice-chmn. dept. radiology, 1988-96, sec.-treas. med. staff, 1977-79; chmn. nuclear medicine sect. Northeastern Ohio Univs. Coll. Medicine, Rootstown, 1979-97; chmn. dept. radiology Northeastern Ohio Univs. Coll. of Medicine (NEOUCOM), Rootstown, 1992-93; diagnostic radiologist Aultman Health Found., Canton, Ohio, 1971-2000; radiology cons. North Canton, Ohio, 2000—. Author: Imaging of the Endocrine System in Organ System Radiology, 1984; contbr. articles to profl. jours Fellow Am. Coll. Radiology; mem. AMA, Soc. Nuc. Medicine (emeritus), Ohio State Med. Soc. (del. 1983-95), Radiol. Soc. N.Am., Stark County Med. Soc. (trustee 1979-95, chmn. bd. censors 1980-82, pres. 1993), Unique Club Stark County, Phi Beta Kappa, Sigma Xi, Alpha Omega Alpha, Phi Lambda Upsilon Avocations: playing bluegrass guitar music, collecting antique toy trains, travel, hiking, gardening. Home and Office: 2465 Oakway St NW North Canton OH 44720-5886

DISPALTRO, FRANKLIN L., plastic surgeon; MD with honors, N.Y. Med. Coll., 1965. Diplomate Am. Bd. Plastic Surgery. Intern New Rochelle Hosp., NY; resident in gen. surgery Met. Hosp. Ctr. N.Y.; resident in plastic surgery St. Barnabas Med. Ctr., Livingston; chief resident plastic surgery Bellevue Hosp. Ctr., NY; fellow in plastic surgery NYU Med. Ctr., 1973; pvt. practice plastic surgery West Orange, NJ. Attending and clin. instr. gen. surgery N.Y. Med. Coll., 1980—90, NYU, 1980—90; cons. in plastic and reconstructive surgery N.J. Rehab. Hosp., East Orange, 1972—2000; full attending St. Barnabas Med. Ctr., Livingston, 1979—, assoc. and clin. chief, chair dept. plastic and reconstructive surgery, 1980—87, chmn. dept. plastic and reconstructive surgery, 1987—93, bd. trustees, 1992—; chmn., founder, CEO Metrowest, 1984—92. Bd. govs. Nat. owment for Plastic Surgery, 1999—; bd. trustees N.Y. Med. Coll., 1982—92. Fellow: ACS; mem.: Internat. Soc. Clin. Plastic Surgery, N.Y. Regional Soc. Plastic and Reconstructive Surgeons (pres. 1983—84), Northeastern Soc. Plastic Surgery, Am. Bd. Plastic Surgery, Internat. Plastic Reconstructive Aesthetic Surgery, Internat. Soc. Aesthetic Plastic Surgery, Aesthetic Surgery Edn. and Rsch. Found. (bd. dirs. 2000—01), Lipoplasty Soc. N.Am., Plastic Surgery Ednl. Found., Am. Soc. Aesthetic Plastic Surgery (pres.-elect 2001—02, v.p. 2000—01, bd. dirs. 1990—, treas. 1999—2000, parliamentarian 1997—98), Am. Soc. Plastic Surgeons. Office: Franklin Dispaltro Mdpa 22 Melrose Ln Green Village NJ 07935-3035

DI SPIGNO, GUY JOSEPH, industrial clinical psychologist, international management consultant; b. Bklyn., Mar. 6, 1948; s. Joseph Vincent and Jeanne Nina (Renna) DiS.; m. Gisela Riba, May 23, 1979; children: Michael Paul, Abie Francis. BS, Carroll U., 1969; MA, No. Ill. U., 1972; MEd, Loyola U., 1974; PhD, Northwestern U., 1977. Instr. No. Ill. U., DeKalb, 1969-70; chmn. humanities dept. Quincy (Ill.) Boys' H.S., 1970-71; dir. religious edn. St. Mary's Ch., DeKalb, 1971-72; dir. edn. Immaculate Conception Parish, Highland Park, Ill., 1972-77; dir. human resources Am. Valuation Cons., Des Plaines, Ill., 1977-79; psychologist Hay Assocs., Chgo., 1979-80; v.p. mktg. Exec. Assets Corp., Chgo., 1980-82; dir. mgmt. devel. and pers. svcs. Borg-Warner Corp., Chgo., 1982-84; ptnr., cons. psychologist Medina & Thompson, Chgo., 1984-91; pres. Exec. Synergies, Inc., Northbrook, Ill., 1991—. Coun. Regents Loyola U., Chgo., 2004—, student affairs com., 2006—; adv. bd. Northwestern U. Sch. Continuing Studies, 2005—07; adv. com. Inst. Pastorial Studies, Loyola U., Chgo., 2007—10; adj. prof. Loyola U., Chicago, Ill., 2008; dir. industrial and orgnl. psychology consulting & clin. prof. psychology Roosevelt U., Chgo., 2008; bd. trustees Carroll U., Waukesha, Wis., 2010—; knight comdr. Equestrian Order of the Holy Sepulchre of Jerusalem, 2008—; knight Knight of Malta, 2008—. Contbr. articles to profl. jours. Mem. Highland Park Human Rels. Commn., 1975-77, Home Owners and Businessmen's Assn., Highland Park, 1976-77; mem. legis. com. Vernon Hills (Ill.) Sch. Bd., alumni coun. Carroll U., 1991-95; benefactor Jesuit Partnership, Chgo. province, 1995—. Clifford B. Scott scholar, 1967; fellow No. Ill. U., 1970-72; named to Order Ky. Cols. Mem. APA, Cmty. Religious Edn. Dirs. (nat. vice chmn. 1971-73), Ill. Psychol. Assn., Nat. Registry Health Svc. Providers in Psychology, Am. Pers. and Guidance Assn., Soc. Indsl. and Orgnl. Psychology, Carroll Coll. Alumni Counsel, Phi Alpha Theta, Sigma Phi Epsilon. Office: 5 Revere Dr Suite 200 Northbrook IL 60062 Office Phone: 847-272-3420. Business E-Mail: guyd@executivesynergies.com.

DITKOFF, EDWARD CHARLES, reproductive endocrinologist; b. NYC, Jan. 12, 1960; s. Jerome Lionel and Adele Helen (Liebermann) D.; m. Patricia Marie Hansen, May 1, 1988; children: Rebecca, Erica. BS in Biology, Emory U., 1981; MD, Chgo. Med. Sch., 1985. Intern. ObGyn. Brookdale Med. Ctr., Bklyn., 1985-86; resident ObGyn. Albany Med. Ctr., NYC, 1986-87; resident Washington Med. Ctr., 1987-90; fellow reproductive endocrinology U. So. Calif., LA, 1990-92; asst. prof., med. dir. divsn. asst. reproduction Columbia U., NYC, 1992-98; physician Advanced Fertility Svcs., NYC, 1998—. Asst. instr. George Washington Med. Sch., 1987-90. Contbr. articles to profl. jours. Fellow Am. Coll. ObGyn.; mem. Am. Soc. Reproductive Medicine, Soc. Laproscopic Surgeons, Endocrine Soc. Office: 1625 Third Ave New York NY 10128 also: 1990 Ctrl Pk Ave Yonkers NY 10710 Personal E-mail: reproed@aol.com.

DITZEL, HERIBERT, sports medicine physician; b. Oberhausen, North-Rhine Wesphalia, Germany, Feb. 24, 1952; s. Anton and Maria Ditzel; m. Renate Johanna Elizabeth Nitsch Ditzel, Sept. 16, 1978; children: Eva-Maria, Roman. MD, U. Aachen Med. Sch., Bochum, Lubeck, Aachen, Germany, 1976. Cert. sports medicine specialty German Fedn. Sports Medicine, 1988. Resident cardiology U. Aachen, Germany, 1978—81; resident radiology U. Hosp., Aachen-Bardenberg, 1981—82, resident gastroenterology Aachen, 1982—84; sr. physician Hosp. Marien Hosp. Recher, Würselen, Germany, 1984—86; pvt. practice internal and sports medicine Mönchengladbach and Rheindahlen, 1986—. Physician internal sports medicine Borussia Mönchengladbach Soccer, 1994—. Mem. directory St. Helens Ch., Mönchengladbach, Germany, 1987—95. Capt. MC German Air Force, 1976—78. Mem.: German Sports Medicine Assn., Borussia Mönchengladbach Sport Club. Roman Catholic. Avocations: running, soccer, golf, tennis. Office: Max Reger Str 37 D41179 Mönchengladbach Germany Office Phone: 0048-2161-580136. Personal E-mail: heribert.ditzel@t-online.de.

DIVERTIE, GAVIN D., critical care specialist; MD, Mayo Med. Sch., 1983. Diplomate Am. Bd. Anesthesiology, 1990, Am. Bd. Internal Medicine, 1987, Am. Bd. Internal Medicine- critical care medicine, 2001. Intern Pacific Med. Ctr., San Francisco; resident in internal medicine Mayo Grad. Sch. Medicine, Jacksonville, Fla., 1986—89, fellow in rsch., 1989—90; hosp. affiliation include Mayo Clinic. Co-author: Lack of effect of hyperglycemia on lipolysis in humans, 1990, Stimulation of lipolysis in humans by physiological hypercortisolemia, 1991, Insulin-like growth factor-binding protein-1 response to insulin during suppression of endogenous insulin secretion, 1993, Cortisol increases plasma insulin-like growth factor binding protein-1 in humans, 1993, Dynamic left ventricular outflow tract obstruction. Diagnosis by transesophageal echocardiography in a critically ill patient, 1993, Lipolytic responsiveness to epinephrine in nondiabetic and diabetic humans, 1997, Clinical relevance of time of onset, duration, and type of pulmonary edema after liver transplantation, 2003, A comparison of intensive care unit physician staffing costs at the 3 Mayo Clinic sites, 2006, Brain injury after cardiopulmonary arrest and its assessment with diffusion-weighted magnetic resonance imaging, 2007, Predictors of poor neurologic outcome after induced mild hypothermia following cardiac arrest, 2009, Safety and efficacy of levetiracetam for critically ill patients with seizures, 2009, Perspectives of Physicians and Nurses Regarding End-of-Life Care in the Intensive Care Unit, 2011. Office: Mayo Clinic 4500 San Pablo Rd S Jacksonville FL 32224-1865 Office Phone: 904-296-5287.

DIX, RICHARD D., medical educator, virologist, researcher; s. Delmas D. and Juanita B. Dix. BS, Youngstown State U., Ohio, 1973; PhD, Baylor Coll. of Medicine, Houston, 1978; post doc., U. Calif., San Francisco, 1978—82, San Francisco Gen. Hosp., 1982—85. Asst. prof. to prof. U. of Miami Sch. of Medicine Bascom Palmer Eye Inst., Miami, Fla., 1985—99; prof. U. of Ark. for Med. Scis. Jones Eye Inst., Little Rock, 1999—2003. Dir., Walker Eye Rsch. Ctr. U. Ark. Med. Scis., Jones Eye Inst., Little Rock, 1999—2003. Grantee Individual Rsch., NIH, 1985—. Office: Jones Eye Inst UAMS 4301 West Markham St #523 Little Rock AR 72205 E-mail: drrichardd@uams.edu.

DIXIT, ALOK, medical educator; b. Uttar Pradesh, India, Oct. 12, 1969; MBBS, Indira Gandhi Med. Coll., Shimla, 2000; MD in Pharmacology, Himalayan Inst. Med. Scis., 2005. Assoc. prof. M. M. Inst. Med. Scis. and Rsch., 2005—. Mem.: Indian Pharmacological Soc. Office: Dept Pharmacology M M Inst Med Scis & Rsch Mullana Ambala Haryana 133203 India Personal E-mail: alkdxt@yahoo.co.in.

DIXON, ANDREW DERART, retired academic administrator; b. Belfast, No. Ireland, Oct. 27, 1925; arrived in came to U.S., 1963, naturalized; s. Andrew and Martha (Stewart) Dixon; m. Mary Elizabeth Hernderson, Oct. 14, 1948; children: Penelope Jane, Melinda Sara, Alison Mary. Licentiate in Dental Surgery, Queens U., Belfast, 1948, B in Dental Surgery, 1949, M.Dental Surgery, 1953, BS (Nuffield Found. dental fellow), 1954, D.Sc., 1965; PhD, U. Manchester, 1958. Asst. lectr. anatomy U. Manchester, 1954—56, lectr., 1956—62, sr. lectr., 1962—63; 1vis. assoc. prof. anatomy U. Iowa, 1959—61; prof. dental sci. U. N.C., Chapel Hill, 1963—65, prof. dental sci., anatomy, 1965—69, prof. oral biology and anatomy, 1969—73, asst. dean, coordinator research Sch. Dentistry, 1966—69, dir. Dental Research Ctr., 1967—73, assoc. dean research, 1969—73; prof., dean UCLA, 1973—80, assoc. dean for faculty affairs, 1985—92, assoc. dean adminstrn., 1989—92; prof. emeritus, 1993—. Chmn. dental tng. com. Nat. Inst. Dental Rsch., 1972—73; mem. No. Ireland Partnership. Author sci. texts; contbr. articles to profl. jours.; Studies on early devel. and growth of the jaws, sex chromatin in oral smears as a diagnostic tool, nerve supply to oral mucous membrane, facial tissues and temporomandibular joint, craniofacial skeletal growth, trigeminal pathway. Grantee Fulbright Sr. Fellow award, 1959—61, Commonwealth Fund Travel fellow, 1961. Fellow: AAAS, Internat. Coll. Dentists, Am. Coll. Dentists; mem.: Pierre Fauchard Acad., Internat. Soc. Craniofacial Biology, N.Y. Acad. Sci., Am. Soc. Cell Biology, AAAS, Internat. Assn. Dental Rsch., Am. Assn. Anatomists, Anat. Soc. Gt. Britain and Ireland (sr.), Western Conf. Dental Examiners and Dental Deans, Pacific Coast Soc. Orthodontists (hon.), Inst. of Medicine, ADA, Psi Omega, Omicron Kappa Upsilon, Sigma Xi. Home: 1200 Mira Mar Ave Apt 1018 Medford OR 97504-8556 Personal E-mail: addixRVM@charter.net.

DIXON, MARTHA LEE, anatomist, physiologist, educator; b. San Diego, Jan. 27, 1944; d. Dick Dixon and Clara Lowe. BA in Physiology, U. Calif., Berkeley, 1966; PhD in Biophysics, U. Calif., 1983; Std. Secondary Tchg. Credential in Biology, San Francisco State U., San Francisco, 1968—70; grad in Physiology & Biophysics, UCB, 1987. Cert. biology tchr. Calif., 1970. Tchr. Lowell HS, San Francisco, 1970—72; postdoctoral fellow, scientist, instr. York U., Toronto, Ontario, Canada, 1983—87; staff scientist Lawrence Berkeley Lab., Berkeley, 1987—89; dir. tissue network Bay Area Tumor Inst., Oakland, Calif., 1989—94; instr. Peralta Cmty. Coll., Oakland, 1989—94; prof. Diablo Valley Coll., Pleasant Hill, Calif., 1994—. Reviewer: Textbook Publishers, 1994—. Fellow Tng. grants, NIH, 1970—80; Individual Postdoctoral fellowship, 1980. Mem.: Am. Assn. Anatomists, Human Anatomy and Physiology Soc. D-Liberal. Avocations: swimming, travel. Home: 4154 Piedmont Ave #2 Oakland CA 94611 Office: Diablo Valley Coll 321 Golf Club Rd Pleasant Hill CA 94523 Office Fax: 925-685-7963. Business E-Mail: mdixon@dvc.edu.

DIXON, MILDRED KELLEY, podiatrist; b. Phila., Sept. 7, 1916; d. Spencer Paul and Annie B. (West) Kelley; widowed; children: James, Denise. DPM, Ohio Coll. Podiatric Med., 1944; MD (hon.), U. St. Kitt. Founder, dir. podiatric residency program VAH, Tuskegee, Ala., 1956—85; pvt. practice Tuskegee Inst., Ala., 1948—. Cons. podiatry VA Montgomery, Montgomery, Ala., 1977—84, VA, Tuscaloosa, 1982—84; presenter in field. Contbr. articles to profl. med. jours. Pres. AARP; vol. RSVP, Tuskegee, Ala.; chaplain Ch. Women United; pres. Missionary Circle. Mem.: AAUW, NAACP, APHA, Nat. Acads. Practice, AWP, Assn. Podiatrists in Fed. Svcs. (past. pres.), Nat. Podiatry Med. Assn. (past pres.). Avocations: travel, reading. Home: 1103 Thompson St PO Box 753 Tuskegee Institute AL 36087

DIXON, ROSINA BERRY, physician, pharmaceutical executive; b. Columbus, Ohio, Dec. 3, 1942; d. Loren C. and Florence H. (Bateson) Berry; m. Richard W. Dixon, July 4, 1970; children: Erica H., Douglas R., Andrew D. BA in Chemistry, Radcliffe Coll., Cambridge, Mass., 1964; MD, Columbia U., NYC, 1968. Diplomate Am. Bd. Internal Medicine. Intern, resident, and chief med. resident Roosevelt Hosp., NYC, 1968-72; from sr. assoc. to exec. dir. Ciba-Geigy, Summit, N.J., 1972-81; med. dir. Schering Labs., Kenilworth, N.J., 1981-84; v.p. Med. Market Spltys., Boonton, N.J., 1985-86; cons. pharm. devel. Bernardsville, NJ, 1986—2006; sr. dir. global pharmacovigilance and epidemiology Sanofi-Aventis, Bridgewater, NJ, 2006—. Bd. dirs. Cambrex Corp., East Rutherford, N.J., Church & Dwight Co., Inc., Princeton, N.J.; instr. medicine Columbia U. Coll. P&S, 1972-99; preceptor in family practice Overlook Hosp., Summit, 1979—; governing bd. Daytop, N.J., 1991—; bd. advisors Fairleigh Dickinson Silberman Coll., 2003— Mem. Am. Coll. Clin. Pharmacology, Am. Soc. Clin. Pharmacology and Therapeutics, Nat. Assn. Corp. Dirs. Home and Office: 43 Old Wood Rd Bernardsville NJ 07924-1416

DJANG, ARTHUR H.K., pathologist, nuclear medicine and preventive medicine physician; b. Beijing, Feb. 12, 1925; arrived in U.S., 1948; s. Wei-Fang DJang and Sujen Liu; m. Mary Helen Winston; divorced; children: Philipp, Douglas, Lincoln, David; m. Tina Marie Barone, 1980-98; 1 child, Anna Claire. MD, Harbin Med. U., China, 1944; MPH, U. Minn., 1951; PhD in Infectious Diseases, UCLA, 1955. Cert. specialist in Clin. Pathology, Anatomic Pathology, Nuclear Medicine Clin. Faculty UCLA Sch. Medicine, 1955. Chief state epidemiologist, dir. chronic & communicable diseases and radiological health State Dept. Pub. Health, Santa Fe, Los Alamos Med. Ctr., 1956—58; pres., dir. Biomedical Sci. Labs., Albuquerque, 1962-74; chmn. dept. pathology & nuclear med. Jamestown Gen. Hosp., NY, 1975-85; clin. prof. of molecular biology SUNY, Fredonia, NY, 1977-86; pres. Internat. Health Inc., Jamestown, 1987—90; pres., CEO Santé Internat. Inc., Jamestown (NY) and Tianjin, China, 1985—; pres. Environ. Scis. Internat., Jamestown and Tianjin, China, 1993—; dir. pub. health, central New Mexico counties including Trinity site and Grants; chief pathologist Dir. Clin. Lab. & Isotope Project, Meml. Gen. Hosp., Univ. Pk.; chief med. examiner and coroner County of Dana Ana, Las Cruces; chief forensic pathologist SW New Mex. Cons. prof. in pathology N. Mex. State U., University Park, 1962-74; cons. physician NASA White Sands Facility, N. Mex., 1966-74; med. dir., cons. physician Medina Meml. Hosp., 1991—93; disting. vis. prof. Grad. Sch. Health Scis. Dalian (China) U., 1988—, bd. dirs.; hon. chmn. Sci. and Tech. Commn., Zhuhai, China, Collaborative Physician, Hosp. Antoine Beclere, U. Hospital, Paris, First Military Med. U., Guangzhou, China, U. of Ioannina Sch. of Medicine, Greece. Author monographs in field; cons. editor Jour. Gerontology, 1988—. Bd. dirs. Am. Heart Assn., Albuquerque, 1965-75, Am. Cancer Soc.,NM, 1965-74, Chautauqua Bd. Health, Mayville, NY, 1976-84; Founding Pres., Chinese Am. Soc. Nuclear Medicine, 1977-78, Founding Bd. Chmn., North Am. Chinese Clinical Chemistry Assn., 1980; coun. mem. SUNY, Fredonia, 1978-86, Honorary Pres. Tianjin First Med. Center, Tianjin, China 1985-92. Named hon. chmn. Scis. Tech. Commn., hon. pres. Yantai Internat. Red Cross Hosp., hon. pres. Dalian Inst. Gerontology, 1988, hon. prof. Harbin Med. U., 1981; recipient First Nation (Can.)Gold Medal award outstanding contbn. health scis., 2004. Fellow Am. Coll. Pathologists, Am. Coll. Nuclear Med. (chmn. Internat. com. 1984-85), Am. Coll. Preventive Med. (mem. by-laws com. 1983-85); mem. AASS, Am. Coll. Physician Execs., NY Acad. Scis., Sigma Xi. Achievements include discovery of main ingredients used in Lysol and Amphyl;

holder of 6 patents related to anti-aging and cancer prevention and treatment; invention of oncolyn, an anti-cancer plant extract; mellinol for blood sugar and weight balance; evergreen green tea for protection of UV damage and antimutation; memory gold+ for prevention and treatment of pre-dementia and Alzheimer; cardio-CP for cardiovascular health; bariatol weight management; rejuvenin and oncolyn creme skin anti-aging and UV damage; viranox HIV and other viral infections; longevity crystal, an anti-radiation and anti-aging properties; nasbesilin, for inhibiting pathogenesis assoc.d with particle-inhalation. Avocations: coins, stamps, paintings. Office: Santé Internat Inc 111 W Second St Jamestown NY 14701 Office Phone: 716-664-7255. Business E-Mail: santedjang@aol.com.

DJANG, DAVID S.W., physician; b. Seattle, Jan. 24, 1970; s. Mary Helen Surovik; m. Eleanor Yu-Chen Lo, Mar. 3, 2001; children: Luke, Michael. BA, U. Tex., 1992; MD, U. Tex. S.W. Med. Sch., 1998. Diplomate Am. Bd. Nuc. Medicine. Intern U. Wash. Med. Ctr., Seattle, 1998—99, resident, 1999—2003; staff physician, nuclear medicine Swedish Hosp., Seattle, 2003—, med. dir. divsn. nuc. medicine, 2004—. Bd. dirs. Brain Imaging Coun. Vol. US Peace Corp., Malawi, Africa, 1992—94. Recipient Rsch. in Tng., RSNA, 2002, WRSNM, 2002, Best Drs. in Seattle, 2006, 2008, 2010. Mem.: Brain Imaging Coun., Soc. Nuc. Medicine, AMA.

DJERASSI, CARL, writer, retired chemistry professor; b. Vienna, Oct. 29, 1923; s. Samuel and Alice (Friedmann) Djerassi; m. Virginia Jeremiah (div. 1950); m. Norma Lundholm (div. 1976); children: Dale, Pamela(dec.); m. Diane W. Middlebrook, 1985 (dec. 2007). AB summa cum laude, Kenyon Coll., 1942, DSc (hon.), 1959; PhD, U. Wis., 1945, DSc (hon.), 1995, Nat. U. Mex., 1953, Fed. U., Rio de Janeiro, 1969, Worcester Poly. Inst., 1972, Wayne State U., 1974, Columbia U., 1975, Uppsala U., 1977, Coe Coll., 1978, U. Geneva, 1978, U. Ghent, 1985, U. Man., 1985, Adelphi U., 1993, U. S.C., 1995, Swiss Fed. Inst. Tech., 1995, U. Md.- Balt. County, 1997, Bulgarian Acad. Scis., 1998, U. Aberdeen, 2000, Polytechnic U., 2001, Cambridge U., 2005, Tech. U. Dortmund, 2009. Rsch. chemist Ciba Pharm. Products, Inc., Summit, NJ, 1942—43, 1945—49; assoc. dir. rsch. Syntex, Mexico City, 1949—52, rsch. v.p., 1957—60; v.p. Syntex Labs., Palo Alto, Calif., 1960—62, Syntex Rsch., 1962—68, pres., 1968—72, Zoecon Corp., 1968—83, chmn. bd. dirs., 1968—86; prof. chemistry Wayne State U., 1952—59, Stanford (Calif.) U., 1959—2002; ret., 2002. Founder Djerassi Resident Artists Program, Woodside, Calif. Author: The Futurist and Other Stories, 1988; author: (novels) Cantor's Dilemma, 1989, The Bourbaki Gambit, 1994, Marx Deceased, 1996, Menachem's Seed, 1997, NO, 1998; author: (poetry) The Clock Runs Backward, 1991; author: (plays) An Immaculate Misconception, 1998, BBC World Svc. Play of Week, 2000, ICSI--a pedagogic wordplay for 2 voices, 2002, Calculus, 2003, (musical version) Music Werner Schulze, 2005, Ego, 2003, Three on a Couch, 2004, Taboos, 2006, Phallacy, 2007, Four Jews on Parnassus, 2000, author: (with Roald Hoffmann) Oxygen, 2001, BBC World Svc.Play of Week, 2001; author: (with Pierre Laszlo) NO--a pedagogic wordplay for 3 voices, 2003; author: (autobiography) The Pill, Pygmy Chimps and Degas' Horse, 1992; author: (memoir) This Man's Pill, 2001; author: (with D. Pinner) Newton's Darkness: Two Dramatic Views, 2004; author: 9 other books; mem. editl. bd. Jour. Organic Chemistry, 1955—59, Tetrahedron, 1958—92, Steroids, 1963—2001, Procs. NAS, 1964—70, Jour. Am. Chem. Soc., 1966—75, Organic Mass Spectrometry, 1968—91, contbr. numerous articles to profl. jours., poems, memoirs and short stories to lit. publs. Decorated Austrian Cross of Honor 1st class, sci. & art, Great Cross of Merit Germany, Silver Cross of Honor Austria; recipient Intrasci. Rsch. Found. award, 1969, Freedman Patent award, Am. Inst. Chemists, 1970, Chem. Pioneer award, 1973, Nat. medal of Sci. for first synthesis of oral contraceptive, 1973, Wolf prize in chemistry, Israel, 1978, John and Samuel Bard award in Sci. and Medicine, 1983, Roussel prize, Paris, 1988, Discovers award, Pharm. Mfg. Assn., 1988, Nat. medal Tech. for new approaches to insect control, 1991, Nev. medal, 1992, Thomson medal, Internat. Soc. Mass Spectroscopy, 1994, Prince Mahidol award, Thailand, 1995, Sovereign Fund award, 1996, Othmer Gold medal, Chem. Heritage Found., 2000, Author's prize, German Chem. Soc., 2001, Erasmus medal, Acad. Europeae, 2003, Gold medal, Am. Inst. Chemists, 2004, Serono prize fiction, Rome, 2005, Lichtenberg medal, Göttingen Acad., 2005; named to Nat. Inventors Hall of Fame. Fellow: Royal Soc. London (fgn. mem.); mem.: NAS (Indsl. Application of Sci. award 1990), Acad. Europeae, Bulgarian Acad. Scis. (fgn. mem.), Mex. Acad. Scis., Brazilian Acad. Scis., Royal Swedish Acad. Engring. (fgn. mem.), Royal Swedish Acad. Scis. (fgn. mem.), Am. Acad. Pharm. Scis. (hon.), German Acad. Leopoldina, Am. Acad. Arts and Scis., Royal Soc. Chemistry (hon. fellow, Centenary lectr. 1964), Am. Chem. Soc. (award pure chemistry 1958, Baekeland medal 1959, Fritzsche award 1960, award for creative invention 1973, award in chemistry of contemporary tech. problems 1983, Esselen award 1989, Priestley medal 1992, Gibbs medal 1997), NAS Inst. Medicine, Sigma Xi (Proctor prize for sci. achievement 1998), Phi Beta Kappa, Phi Lambda Upsilon (hon.). Office: Stanford U Dept Chemistry Stanford CA 94305-5080 Business E-Mail: djerassi@stanford.edu.

DJOHAN, RISAL, plastic surgeon; MD, Chgo. Med. Sch. Finch U. Health Sci. Cert. plastic surgery. Intern & resident Catholic Health Partners Columbus Hosp.; fellow U. Chgo. Hosp.; plastic surgeon Cleveland Clinic, 2003—. Achievements include being on surgical team to perform first facial transplant in U.S. Office: Cleveland Clinic Main Campus 9500 Euclid Ave Mail Code A60 Cleveland OH 44195 Office Phone: 216-445-2433.

DJOKIC, DIVNA, pediatrician; b. Belgrade, Serbia, Mar. 21, 1968; MD, Med. Sch., U. Belgrade, 1992. Pediatrician Primary Care Health Svcs., Inc, 2007—. Mem.: Am. Bd. Pediatric Infectious Diseases, Am. Bd. Pediat. Office: Rankin Health Ctr 300 Rankin Blvd Rankin PA 15104 Home Fax: divnand@yahoo.com.

DJOKIC, MIROSLAV, medical educator; b. Belgrade, Serbia, Jan. 5, 1966; MD, U. Belgrade, 1992; MS, Cornell U., 1996. Asst. prof. U. Pitts. Sch. Medicine, 2006—. Fellow: Am. Soc. Clin. Pathology, Coll. Am. Pathologists (Tng. Tech. award). Avocation: soccer. Office: 200 Lothrop St G316 Pittsburgh PA 15213 Office Fax: 412-647-6332. Business E-Mail: djokicm@upmc.edu.

DJORDJEVIC, DRAGANA, pediatrician, researcher; b. Nis, Serbia, Feb. 15, 1969; d. Radosav and Dusica Djordjevic. MD, U. Nis, 1992, MS in Immunology Studies, 1993; PhD in Psychosomatic, U. Heidelberg, Germany, 2004. Cert. physician Republic Serbia Ministry of Health, Belgrade, 1993, in pediat. U. Nis, 1999, integrative Eltern-Saeuglings-/Kleinkind-Beratung und psychotherapie Deutsche Akademie fuer Entwicklungsfoerderung & Gesundheit des Kindes, 2001, in emotional availability scales Colo. State U., Dept. Human Devel. & Family Studies, 2004. Young investigator & jr. rschr., lab. immunology & genetics Faculty Medicine, U. Nis, 1988—94, tutor, Inst. Histology & Inst. Pathohistology, 1989—92, intern, internal medicine praxis clinic cardiology, 1990; intern dept. surgery San Raffaele Hosp., Milan, 1991; gen. internship U. Clin. Ctr. Nis, 1992—93, clinician & pediatrician, dept. neonatology, clinic ob-gyn., 1994—2000, pediatrician, dept. cardiology, children's clinic, 2000—03, pediatrician, dept. neonatology, children's clinic, 2007—; guest pediatrician Inst. Kooperationsforschung und Familientherapie, Universitaetsklinikum Heidelberg, 2002—03, guest rschr., 2004—06; pediatrician further edn. & tng. for neonatology Universitaetskinderklinik beider Basel, Switzerland, 2003. Contbr. articles to profl. jour. Recipient German Acad. Exchange Svc., DAAD, 2002—03; fellow, Republic Serbia Found. Devel. Young Scientists and Artists, 1988—92, Republic Serbia Ministry of Sci. and Rsch., 1993—94, Hanse Inst. Advanced Study, 2005. Mem.: Internat. Soc. Prenatal & Perinatal Psychology & Medicine, Internat. Union Immunological Socs. and World Allergy Orgn., Serbian Assn. Pediatricians, Serbian Neurocardiol. Soc. & Serbian Autonomic Soc., Serbian Dr.'s Soc., Immunological Soc. Serbia, German-speaking Assn. Infant Mental Health. Avocations: travel, reading, dance, skiing, swimming. Office: Univ Clin Ctr Dr Zorana Djindjica 48 Nis 18000 Serbia and Montenegro Home: Tome Roksandica 3/8 18000 Nis Serbia and Montenegro Office Phone: 381 62 8421 550, 491782086815. Personal E-mail: d_djordjevic@yahoo.com. Business E-Mail: dragana.djordjevic@alumni.uni.heidelberg.de.

DJOUSSE, LUC, epidemiologist, educator, medical researcher; Researcher Harvard U.; prof. preventive med. & epidemiology Boston U.; assoc. epidemiologist Brigham & Women's Hosp.; asst. prof. med. Harvard Medical Sch. Office: Harvard University Office of News and Public Affairs Holyoke Center 1060 Cambridge MA 02138 Office Phone: 617-495-1585, 617-638-8096. E-mail: ldjousse@rics.bwh.harvard.edu.

DLUHY, ROBERT GEORGE, physician; b. Montclair, NJ, Jan. 23, 1937; s. John George and Leona (Fila) D.; m. Deborah Haigh; 1 child, Leonore Alexandra. AB magna cum laude, Princeton U., 1958; MD, Harvard Med. Sch., 1962. Intern/resident Peter Bent Brigham Hosp., Boston, 1962, 65-67, endocrine fellow, 1967-69; instr. med. Harvard Med. Sch., Boston, 1969-74, asst. prof. med., 1974-80, assoc. prof. med., 1980-98, prof. med., 1998—. Assoc. editor New Eng. Jour. Medicine. Capt. med. corp. U.S. Army, 1964-66, Germany. Fellow: Endocrine Soc., Hypertension Coun. AHA; mem.: Phi Beta Kappa. Office: Endocrine Hypertension Divs 221 Longwood Ave # Rfb2 Boston MA 02115-5804 Office Phone: 617-732-5011. E-mail: rdluhy@partners.org.

DMOCHOWSKI, ROGER, urologist, educator; s. Sheila Dmochowski and Leon; m. Suzanne Sykora, Nov. 10, 1986; children: Colin Edward, Nicolas Roman. MD, U. Tex., Galveston, 1983. Diplomate Am. Bd. Urology. Staff urologist Naval hosp. U.S. Navy, Portsmouth, Va., 1989—93; dir. of resident edn. Ea. Va. Med. Sch., Norfolk, 1990—93; clin. instr. in surgery Uniformed Svcs. U. of Health Scis., Bethesda, Md., 1990—91, clin. asst. prof. in surgery, 1991—2006; asst. prof. dept. of urology U. Tenn., Memphis, 1994—95, assoc. prof. depts. of urology/gynecology, dir. divsn. of neurourology, 1996—98; med. dir. North Tex. Ctr. for Urinary Control, 1998—2001; prof. dept. of urology Vanderbilt U. Med. Ctr., Nashville, 2001—. Admissions com. Vanderbilt U. Sch. of Medicine, Nashville, 2004—; vis. prof. Walter Reed Army Med. Ctr., Tulane U. Med. Ctr., Kans. Med. Ctr.; lectr. in field. Contbr. chapters to books, articles to profl. jours. Recipient Zimskind award, Urodynamics Soc., 1999. Fellow: ACS; mem.: Internat. Continence Soc. (sci. com. 2003—06, edn. com. 2003—06), Am. Urogynecologic Soc., Cociete' Internationale d'Urologie, Soc. of Genitourinary Reconstructive Surgeons, Urodynamicc Soc., Soc. of Govt. Svcs. Urologists, Southeastern Sect. Am. Urologic Assn., Soc. of Female Urology and Urodynamics (v.p. 2003—06, pres. 2006—), Am. Urologic Assn. (safety com. 2003—, Blue Ribbon com. 2005—06, chair practice parameters and guidelines com. 2005—06, pub. rels. com. 2005—06). Office: Vanderbilt Univ Med Ctr A-1302 Medical Ctr N Nashville TN 37232-2765

DMOWSKI, W. PAUL, obstetrician, gynecologist, educator, endocrinologist, researcher; b. Lodz, Poland, May 17, 1937; came to U.S., 1964; naturalized 1988; s. Thaddeus and Mirona D.; m. May 20, 1967 (div. 1975); 1 child Andrzej. T. MD, The Warsaw (Poland) Med. Acad., 1962; PhD in Endocrinology, Med. Coll. Ga., 1971. Diplomate in ob-gyn. and reproductive endocrinology/infertility Am. Bd. Ob.-Gyn. Intern Warsaw U. Hosps., 1961-62; resident dept. ob-gyn Ottawa (Can.) Gen. Hosp., 1962-64, Beth Israel Med. Ctr., NYC, 1964-67; Population Coun. rsch. fellow in gynecologic endocrinology Med. Coll. Ga., Augusta, 1967-69; asst. prof. dept. ob-gyn Pritzker Sch. Medicine, U. Chgo., 1971-74, assoc. prof. dept. ob-gyn Pritzker Sch. Medicine, 1974-79; prof. U. Ark. for Med. Scis., Little Rock, 1979-81, Rush Med. Coll., Chgo., 1981—; assoc. attending physician dept. ob-gyn Michael Reese Hosp. and Med. Ctr., Chgo., 1971-76, attending physician, 1976-79, U. Ark. for Med. Scis., 1979-81; sr. attending physician Rush-Presbyn.-St. Lukes Med. Ctr., Chgo., 1981—; attending physician Grant Hosp., Chgo., 1982—. Mem. cons. staff dept. ob-gyn. Christ Hosp., Oak Lawn, Ill., 1982—; mem. courtesy staff MacNeal Hosp., Berwyn, Ill., 1989—; cons. staff dept. ob/gyn Elmhurst (Ill.) Hosp., 1994—; assoc. dept. ob-gyn. Good Samaritan Hosp., Downers Grove, Ill., 1999—; founder, dir. fertility unit Michael Reese Med. Ctr., 1973-79, co-dir. sect. reproductive endocrinology and infertility, 1976-79; dir. div. reproductive endocrinology and infertility U. Ark. for Med. Scis., 1979-81; founder, dir. fellowship tng. program in reproductive endocrinology and infertility Rush Med. Coll., 1982-88, dir. sect. reproductive endocrinology and infertility, 1981-88; founder, dir. in vitro fertilization and embryo transfer program Rush-Presbyn. St. Luke's Med. Ctr., 1983-88; founder, dir. family fertility ctr. Grant Hosp., 1988-95, Inst. for Study and Treatment Endometriosis, 1988—, Oak Brook Fertility Ctr., 1990—; presenter in field. Contbr. over 300 articles to profl. jours., 40 chapts. to books; numerous invited articles, letters to editor in field. Recipient Cert. Appreciation ACS, 1979; grantee, clin. investigator Winthrop Rsch. Inst., 1967—88, Ill. Inst. Tech., 1971-72, Program Applied Rsch. on Fertility Regulation, 1973-75, NICHHD, 1973-75, Carnrick Labs., 1975-79, Organon Internat., 1979-82, Abbott Labs., 1984—, Hoechst-Roussel Pharm., 1985-90, ICI Pharm., 1988-92, Syntex Labs., 1992-94, Ostex Internat., 1993-95, Serono Labs., 1998—2000, Praecis Pharms., 1998—2001, Femme Pharma, 2001—, Immunex Corp., 1999-2001, TAP Pharm., 2002—, Centocor, Inc., 2003—. Fellow Am. Coll. Ob-Gyn. (Prize award 1975, 76, Coll. award 1977); mem. AMA (Cert. Merit 1969, 76, 78), Am. Assn. Gynecologic Laparoscopists, Am. Assn. Tissue Banks, Am. Soc. Reproductive Medicine (Cert. award 1977, Ortho Symposium Award 1980, Poster award 1992), Am. Assn. Reproductive Immunologists, Am. Bd. Specialties, Am. Inst. Ultrasound Medicine, Am. Soc. Reproductive Immunology, Ark. Med. Soc., Assn. Profs. Gynecology and Obstetrics, Chgo. Assn. Reproductive Endocrinologists, Chgo. Gynecol. Soc., Chgo. Med. Soc., Chgo. Assn. Gyn. Endoscopists, Endocrine Soc., Ill. State Med. Soc., Little Rock Gynecol. Soc., N.Y. Acad. Scis., Soc. for Advancement Contraception, Soc. for Gynecologic Investigation, Soc. Reproductive Endocrinologists, Soc. Reproductive Surgeons, Soc. for Study Reprodn., Soc. for Assisted Reproductive Tech., Soc. Laparoendoscopic Surgeons, Polish Am. Med. Soc. Office: Ste 102 2425 W 22nd St Oak Brook IL 60523-4643 Office Phone: 630-954-0054. Business E-Mail: wpdmowski@oakbrookfertility.com.

DN, NANDAKUMAR, medical educator; b. Keragodu, Karnataka, India, June 1, 1975; MBBS, Mysore Med. Coll., 2000; MD in Biochemistry, JIPMER, Pondicherry, 2004. Asst. prof. NIMHANS, Bangalore, India, 2009—. Rsch. assoc. Indian Inst. Sci., Bangalore, 2004—06. Avocations: chess, badminton. Office: NIMHANS Hosur Rd Bangalore Karnataka 560029 India E-mail: drnandn@gmail.com.

DO, DIANA V., ophthalmologist, educator; b. Saigon, Vietnam, Feb. 25, 1973; MD, U. Calif., San Francisco Sch. Medicine, 1999. Asst. prof. ophthalmology Johns Hopkins U. Sch. Medicine, 2005—. Office: Johns Hopkins University 600 N Wolfe St M Baltimore MD 21287 Business E-Mail: ddo@jhmi.edu.

DO, JUN-YOUNG, nephrologist, educator; b. Daegu, Republic of Korea, June 11, 1962; m. Sung Meung-Jin, Jan. 15, 1989; children: Yoon-Sung, Eun-Jung. MD, U. Seoul, 1987; PhD, Kemyung U., 1999. Internal medicine intern and resident Yeungnam U. Hosp., Daegu, Republic of Korea, 1987—91, chief nephrology, 2002—; from instr. to prof. dept. internal medicine Yeungnam U., 1994—. Capt. Korean Army, 1991—94. Recipient Bergstrom award, Internat. Soc. Peritoneal Dialysis, 2004. Mem.: Daegu-Kyungbook Soc. Nephrology (mgr. 2002—05), Am. Soc. Nephrology (assoc.). Office: Yeungnam University Hospital 317-1 Daemyungdong Namgu 705-717 Daegu Daegu Republic of Korea Office Fax: 82-53-654-8386. Business E-Mail: jydo@med.yu.ac.kr.

DO, LAURENT, neurosurgeon; s. Phuoc Hau Do and Thi Mau Phan. MD, Sch. Medicine, Montpellier, France, 1991. Resident Centre Hospitalier Universitaire Marseille Neurosurgery, 1991—97, staff, 1998—2002; head dept. neurosurgery Centre Hospitalier Universitaire Pointe A Pitre, Guadeloupe, 2002—. Contbr. articles. Office: CHU Pointe a Pitre Neurochirurgie Bp 465 Pointe A Pitre 97159 Guadeloupe Office Fax: (590)590891729. E-mail: laurent.do@chu-guadeloupe.fr.

DOBERENZ, ALEXANDER R., retired nutrition educator, chemist; b. Newark, Aug. 17, 1936; s. Alexander J. and Marie (Zink) D.; m. Angela Rajoppi, June 7, 1958; children: Annamarie Wexler, Judith Lynn, Hoke Jr. BS in Chemistry, Tusculum Coll., 1958; MS, U. Ariz., 1960, PhD in Biochemistry and Nutrition, 1963. Rsch. assoc. dept. physics U. Ariz., Tucson, 1963-69, vis. assoc. prof. nutrition U. Hawaii, 1969; assoc. prof. nutritional scis. U. Wis., Green Bay, 1969-71, prof., 1971-76, assoc. dean Coll. and Sch. Profl. Studies, 1969-76, prof. growth and devel., 1975-76; prof. food sci. and human nutrition U. Del., Newark, 1976-97, dean Coll. Human Resources, 1976-93, coord. home econs. rsch., 1978-93, spl. asst. to the pres., 1993, interim v.p. for student life, 1994-95, prof. nutritional scis., Coll. Health Scis., 1997-99, prof. emerita, 1999—. Cons. food industry, 1976-93; nat. steering com. new initiatives for home econs. U.S. Dept. Agr., 1979-81, USDA Planning com. Workshops on Improving Health Maintenance, 1984-87. Contbr. numerous articles on food chemistry and nutrition to profl. publs. Head underwater recovery unit Pima County Sheriff's Dept., 1966-68; warrant officer CAP, 1965-69; mem. Brown County Comprehensive Health Planning Coun., 1973-76; bd. dirs. Pima County Sheriff's Search and Rescue, 1968. Recipient Rsch. Career Devel. award NIH, 1966-69; named Outstanding Educator Am., 1971-72. Fellow Am. Inst. Chemists; mem. Am. Chem. Soc., Am. Home Econs. Soc., Am. Inst. Nutrition (Mead Johnson award nominating com. 1973-76), Nutrition Soc. Today, Soc. for Nutrition Edn., Nutrition Soc. London Soc. Exptl. Biology and Medicine, Am. Soc. Clin. Nutrition, AAAS, Assn. Adminstrs. of Home Econs., Del. Gerontol. Soc. (exec. com. 1978), Nat. Coun. Adminstrs. Home Econs. (exec. bd. 1982-83), APHA, Del.-Panama Ptnrs. of Ams., Assn. for Devel. Computer Based Instruction, Del. Acad. Sci., Univ. and Whist Club, Sigma Xi, Phi Lambda Upsilon., Phi Kappa Phi. Roman Catholic. Business E-Mail: ard@udel.edu.

DOBES, WILLIAM LAMAR, JR., dermatologist, educator; b. Atlanta, Apr. 16, 1943; s. William Lamar and Sara (Wilson) Dobes; m. Martha Husmann, June 16, 1966; children: Margaret Alison Key, William Shane. BA, Emory U., 1965, MD, 1969. Diplomate Am. Bd. Dermatology. Intern Grady Meml. Hosp., Atlanta, 1969-70; fellow in dermatology Mayo Clinic, 1970-71; fellow U. Miami, 1971-73; clin. instr. Emory U. Sch. Medicine, Atlanta, 1973-77, asst. prof. dermatology, 1977-83, assoc. prof., 1983—. Dir. immunofluorescense lab., 1978-85; mem. staff Crawford Long, Grady Meml., Piedmont hosps., Atlanta; dir. Skin Cancer Project, Emory U., 1981-89; chmn. profl. edn. unit Atlanta chpt. Am. Cancer Soc., 1980-86, also bd. dirs., pres., 1986-87, chmn. bd. dirs., 1987-88; pres. Carter's Atlanta, project chmn. Physicians Com., 1992-95. Contbr. articles to profl. jours. and texts. Chmn. Ga. med. bd. Lupus Found., 1988, bd. dirs. Whitney Rsch. Lab., U. Fla., 1998-2002; Emory Yerkes Rsch. Ctr., 2004—, bd. dirs, v.p., 2006-. Dermatology Found. Rsch. award, 1979; named to best Doctors in Am., 2003-08. Fellow Am. Dermatol. Assn.; mem. AMA, ACP, Am. Soc. Cosmetic and Aesthetic Surgery, Soc. Investigative Dermatology, Am. Acad. Dermatology (chmn. com. quality assurance 1982-84, adv. coun. 1985-95, ad coun. exec. com. 1991-95, com. on stds. of care 1987-91, chmn. CLIA task force 1993-97), So. Med. Assn. (vice chmn. 1983), Pan Am. Med. Assn., Am. Soc. Dermatologic Surgery, Ga. Dermatol. Assn. (pres. 1986-87), Atlanta Dermatol. Assn. (pres. 1979), N.Am. Clin. Dermatologic Soc., Soc. Tropical Dermatology, Med. Assn. Atlanta (bd. dirs. 1985-92, chmn.

comm. com. 1985-90, sec. 1988-89, pres.-elect 1989-90, pres. 1990-91), Med. Assn. Ga. (Interspltу. Coun. 1984-97, com. on cancer 1988-93, pub. rels. com. 1988-94, del. to Ga. Med. Assn. 1985—, Outstanding Svc. award 1993), Atlanta Clin. Soc., Atlanta Olympic Med. Com. (chmn. dermatology sect. 1996), Emory U. Med. Alumni Assn. (pres. 1980, 86, exec. com. 1992-97), Phi Delta Theta (past pres.), Phi Chi (past pres.), Cherokee Town & Country Club (Atlanta). Office: 2045 Peachtree St NE Ste 200 Atlanta GA 30309-1414 also: Emory U Sch Medicine Dept Dermatology Atlanta GA 30308 Home Phone: 404-261-1379.

DOBROWOLSKI, JERZY A. (GEORGE), physics researcher; BSc in Physics and Math., U. London, 1953, MSc in Tech. Optics, 1954, PhD in Tech. Optics, 1955. Former rsch. scientist NRC, Ottawa, Ont., Can., former prin. rsch. officer, ret., rschr. emeritus, 1991—. Lectr. and instr. in field. Contbr. articles to profl. jours., chapters to books. Recipient Moet Hennessy-Louis Vuitton Sci. Pour l'Art prize, 1989, Outstanding Achievement medal in Indsl. and Applied Physics Can. Assn. Physicists, 1997. Fellow Optical Soc. Am. (Joseph Fraunhofer award 1987, David Richardson award 1997); mem. Internat. Soc. Optical Engring., Soc. Vacuum Coaters (Nathaniel H. Sugerman award 2005), Order of Can. Achievements include patents in field.

DOBS, ADRIAN SANDRA, endocrinologist, educator; b. June 27, 1952; m. Martin Auster; children: Nina Auster, Becky Auster, Harry Auster, Paul Auster. BS in Nutrition Scis., Cornell U., 1973; MD, Albany Med. Coll., 1978; MHS in Cardiovascular Epidemiology, Johns Hopkins U., 1990. Diplomate Nat. Bd. Med. Examiners, Am. Bd. Internal Medicine, Am. Bd. Endocrinology and Metabolism. Resident in internal medicine Montefiore Hosp. Med. Ctr./Albert Einstein Coll. Medicine, Bronx, NY, 1978-81, chief resident, 1981-82; instr. medicine, physicians asst. program CCNY, NYC, 1981-82; endocrinology fellow Johns Hopkins U., Balt., 1982-84, instr. divsn. endocrinology and metabolism, 1984-87, asst. prof. medicine, 1987-93, assoc. prof. medicine, 1993—2005, prof. medicine, 2006—, vice chair dept. medicine, clin. rsch., 1996—. Mem. study sect., adv. com. Nat. Inst. Aging, 1992, NIH, 1993, 94; lectr. in field. Reviewer Am. Jour. Clin. Nutrition, Am. Jour. Medicine, Diabetes Care, Jour. AMA, Jour. Clin. Endocrinology and Metabolism, New Eng. Jour. Medicine; contbr. articles, abstracts to profl. jours., chpts. to books. Recipient Rsch. award Women Physicians Stetler Found., 1986-87; scholar Leopold Schepp Found., 1975, Vanderbilt U., 1976, Carnegie-Mellon Found., 1984-85, Robert Glassner Found. Diabetes Rsch., 1985-86; grantee Merck, Inc., 1991-93, TheraTech, Inc., 1991-94, NIH, 1992-93, 92—, Diabetes Rsch. and Edn. Found., 1992-93, Johns Hopkins Out-patient Clin. Rsch. Ctr., 1992-93. Mem. ACP, Am. Coll. Nutrition, Am. Diabetes Assn. (award Md. chpt. 1986-87), Am. Fedn. Clin. Rsch. (Johns Hopkins rep. 1990—, sch. coun. 1990—), Am. Heart Assn. (epidemiology coun. 1985, grantee 1990-94), Endocrine Soc. Home: 3510 Anton Farms Rd Baltimore MD 21208-1703 Office: Johns Hopkins Hosp 1830 Monument St Baltimore MD 21287-0005 Office Phone: 410-955-2130. Business E-Mail: adobs@jhu.edu.

DOBSON, RICHARD LAWRENCE, dermatologist, educator; b. Boston, Apr. 12, 1928; s. Joseph William and Celia Beatrice (Siegler) D.; m. Marie C. Mollomo, 1950; children: Richard Lawrence, Pamela Blair, Lisa Marie, Karen Jill, David Scott; m. Rhoda H. Freda, Feb. 14, 2004. MD, U. Chgo., 1953; BS, U. N.H., 1981. Diplomate Am. Bd. Dermatology (v.p. 1987-88, pres. 1988-89). Intern Cin. Gen. Hosp., 1953-54; resident Hitchcock Clinic, Hanover, NH, 1954-57; asst. prof. dermatology U. NC, Chapel Hill, 1957-61; prof. U. Oreg., Portland, 1961-72, SUNY-Buffalo, 1972-79, Med. U. SC, Charleston, 1980-98, acting dean, 1985-86, chmn. dept. anatomy and cell biology, 1991-92; prof. emeritus Med. U. S.C., Charleston, 1998—. Vis. prof. U. Nijmegen, The Netherlands, 1969-70; hon. prof. Shanghai 2d Med. U.; hon. cons. Royal Prince Alfred Hosp., Sydney, Australia. Editor: Year Book of Dermatology, 1979-82, Clinical Dermatology, 1972-82, Contemporary Review, 1973-87; asst. editor: Jour. Am. Acad. Dermatology, 1979-87, editor, 1988-98; mng. editor Arch. Dermatol. Research, 1982-87. Served with USN, 1946-47. Fellow ACP, Am. Acad. Dermatology (pres. 1983-84); mem. Am. Dermatologic Assn. (treas. 1977-82), Soc. Investigative Dermatology (pres. 1975-76), Oreg. Dermatol. Soc. (pres. 1971-72); hon. mem. Brit. Assn. Dermatology, Spanish Assn. Dermatology, French Dermatology Soc., Polish Dermatology Soc., Finnish Dermatology Soc., Dutch Dermatology Soc., German Dermatology Soc., N.Am. Dermatology Soc., Ga. Dermatology Soc., Iowa Dermatology Soc., Snee Farm Club. Republican. Roman Catholic. Home Phone: 843-884-7550. Personal E-mail: rowda@aol.com.

DOCTORS, MARC D., dental educator; Grad. with honors, SUNY, Buffalo. Commd. officer US Pub. Health Svc.; with Nat. Insts. of Health; instr. Clin. Dentistry Georgetown Univ.; dentist Washington Ctr. of Dentistry, DC. Cons. maj. ins. companies. Cons. dental matters US Peace Corps. Mem.: ADA, DC Dental Soc., Am. Acad. of Cosmetic Dentistry. Office: Washington Center for Dentistry 8th Fl 1430 K St NW Washington DC 20005 Office Phone: 202-223-6630.

DODANI, SUNITA, physician, educator; MD, MSc, U. Pitts., PhD, 2006. Diplomate. Asst. prof. Aga Khan U., Karachi, Sindh, Pakistan, 2000—02, U. Pitts., 2003—. Achievements include research in heart diseases in young population. Home: 997 ST Sebastian Way Augusta GA 30912 Home Fax: 412-383-1974. Personal E-mail: sud9@pitt.edu.

DODD, CHRISTOPHER JOHN, motion picture association executive, lobbyist, former United States Senator from Connecticut; b. Willimantic, Conn., May 27, 1944; s. Thomas J. and Grace (Murphy) Dodd; m. Jackie Marie Clegg, 1999; children: Grace, Christina. BA in English Lit., Providence Coll., 1966; JD, U. Louisville, 1972. Bar: Conn. 1973. Vol. Peace Corps, Dominican Republic, 1966-68; atty. Suisman, Shapiro, Wool & Brennan, New London, Conn., 1973-74; mem. US Congress from 2nd Conn. Dist., 1975-80; US Senator from Conn., 1981—2011; chmn. US Senate Rules & Adminstrn. Com., 2001—03, US Senate Banking Housing & Urban Affairs Com., 2007—11; pres., CEO Motion Picture Association America (MPAA), Encino, Calif., 2011—. Gen. chmn. Democratic Nat. Com., 1995—97. Served with USAR, 1969—75. Recipient Excellence in Pub. Svc. award, American Acad. Pediat., 1987, High Tech Legis. of Yr. award, Info. Tech. Industry Coun., 2000, Congl. Recognition award, Internat. Assn. Fire Fighters, 2001, Nat. Family Week award, Alliance Children & Families, 2002, Gerald Solomon Legis. of Yr. award, Independent Ins. Agents & Brokers America, 2002, Pub. Svc. award, U. Minn. Hubert H. Humphrey Inst. Pub. Affairs, Nathan Davis award, AMA. Democrat. Roman Catholic. Office: Motion Picture Association America (MPAA) 15503 Ventura Blvd Encino CA 91436 *

DODD, DARLENE MAE, retired nurse, retired military officer; b. Dowagiac, Mich., Oct. 11, 1935; d. Charles B. and Lila H. Dodd. Diploma in nursing, Borgess Hosp. Sch. Nursing, Kalamazoo, 1957; grad., Air Command and Staff Coll., 1973; BS in Psychology and Gen. Studies, So. Oreg. State Coll., 1987, postgrad., 1987. Commd. 2d lt. USAF, 1959, advanced through grades to lt. col., 1975, staff nurse Randolph AFB, Tex., 1959-60, Ladd AFB, Alaska, 1960-62, Selfridge AFB, Mich., 1962-63, Cam Rahn Bay Air Base, Vietnam, 1966-67, Seymour Johnson AFB, NC, 1967-69, USAF Acad., Colorado Springs, Colo., 1971-72; flight nurse 22d Aeromed. Evacuation, Tenn., 1963-66; chief nure USAF, Danang Air Base, Vietnam, 1968, flight nurse Yokota AFB, Japan, 1969-71, clin. coord. ob-gyn., flight nurse Elmendorf AFB, Alaska, 1973-76; clin. nurse coord. ob-gyn. and pediatric svcs. USAF Med. Ctr., Keesler AFB, Miss., 1976-79; with Bear Creek Corp., Medford, Oreg., 1986—2004. Decorated Bronze Star. Mem. DAV, VFW, Am. Legion (life), Soc. Air Force Nurses, Ret. Officers Assn., Vietnam Vets. Am., Uniformed Svcs. Disabled Retirees, Air Force Assn., Women of Moose, Psi Chi, Phi Kappa Phi. Home: 712 1st St Phoenix OR 97535-9787 *

DODD, GERALD DEWEY, JR., radiologist, educator; b. Oaklyn, NJ, Nov. 18, 1922; s. Gerald Dewey and Anne Aloysius (Keveney) D.; m. Helen Carolyn Glenzing, Apr. 5, 1946; children: Patricia, Michael, Barbara, Gerald Dewey III, Anne, Susan, Thomas. AB, Lafayette Coll., 1945; MD, Jefferson Med. Coll., 1947; DSc (hon.), Lafayette Coll., 1991. Diplomate Am. Bd. Radiology. Intern Fitzgerald Mercy Hosp., Darby, Pa., 1947; resident Jefferson Med. Coll., Phila., 1948—50; asst. radiologist, asst. in radiology Thomas Jefferson Med. Coll. and Hosp., Phila., 1952—54, assoc. in radiology, 1954—55; asst. radiologist, clin. prof. radiology Thomas Jefferson Med. Coll., 1961—66; assoc. radiologist, assoc. prof. radiology U. Tex. M.D. Anderson Cancer Ctr., Houston, 1955—61, prof., 1966—89, chmn. dept. diagnostic radiology, 1966—89, prof., head divsn. diagnostic imaging, 1984—92, Robert D. Moreton Chair Diagnostic Radiology, 1988—93, chair emeritus, 1996—; prof. radiology U. Tex. Med. Sch., Houston, 1971—, chmn. dept. radiology, 1971—74, prof. radiology Sch. Allied Health Scis., 1971—94. Cons. radiologist St. Luke's Hosp., Tex. Children's Hosp., Houston, 1966—, Singleton Prof. Radiology, 1995-99; vis. mem. grad. faculty Tex. A&M U., College Station, 1969-93; adj. prof. radiology Baylor Coll. Medicine, 1983—. Cons. to editor Radiology, 1977—86, cons. editor The Cancer Bull., 1979—89, assoc. editor Cancer, 1991—2000; editor: Breast Diseases, 1993—2004; referee CRC Critical Revs. in Radiol. Scis., 1969—95; contbr. articles to profl. jours. Dir.-at-large Am. Cancer Soc., 1977-90, pres., 1990-91, past officer dir.; mem. coun. Nat. Coun. Radiation Protection and Measurement, 1979-91, bd. dirs., 1981-91. Fellow Am. Coll. Radiology (bd. chancellors, 1971-80, pres. 1984-85, Gold medal 1989); mem. Radiol. Soc. N.Am. (Gold medal 1986), Am. Roentgen Ray Soc. (Gold medal 1992), Soc. Gastrointestinal Radiologists (Cannon medal 1995), Assn. Univ. Radiologists, Tex. Med. Assn., Tex. Radiol. Soc. (Gold medal 1988), Soc. Breast Imaging (Gold medal 1995), Harris County Med. Soc., Houston Radiol. Soc., Phila. Roentgen Ray Soc. (hon.), Gilbert H. Fletcher Soc. (Gold medal 2008), Alpha Omega Alpha, Phi Delta Theta, Phi Chi. Republican. Roman Catholic. Office: M D Anderson Hosp 1515 Holcombe Blvd Houston TX 77030-4009

DODD, JONATHAN DERMOT, cardiac and thoracic radiologist, consultant; b. Dublin, Jan. 1, 1971; s. Christopher and Anne Dodd. MSc in Physiology, Castleknock Coll., Dublin, 1989, MD, 1989; MS in Medicine, U. Coll. Dublin, 2002. Cert. in medicine U. Coll. Dublin, 1995, in internal medicine Royal Coll. Physicians, Ireland, 2000, in radiology Faculty Radiology, Ireland, 2004. Fellow cardiac CT & MRI Harvard Med. Sch.; intern St. Vincent's U. Hosp., Dublin, resident, fellow thoracic radiology, prof., cons. radiologist, 2006—. Author: (med. textbook) Diagnostic Imaging in Cardiovascular Imaging; contbr. scientific papers to profl. publs. Fellow, Radiol. Soc. N.Am., 2004. Office: St Vincent's Univ Hosp Elm Park Dublin D4 Ireland

DODDS, LARRY D., retired insurance company executive; m. Jane Dodds; 2 children. BBA, Union Coll., Lincoln, Nebr.; M, Portland State U. Chair, chmn. Sonora Regional Med. Ctr., Calif.; with health care orgn. Md., 1971; chair, chmn., sr. v.p. Adventist Med. Ctr., Portland, Oreg., pres., CEO, 1983; chair Walla Walla Gen. Hosp., Wash., assoc. adminstr., 1979, pres., CEO, 1983; with Verticare Adventist Health, sr. v.p., 1998—2007, exec. v.p., COO, 2007—11, bd. chmn. facility, dir. Chair Feather River Hosp., Paradise, Calif., Castle Med. Ctr., Kailua, Hawaii, Tillamook County Gen. Hosp., Oreg. Fellow: American Coll. Healthcare Execs. Office: Adventist Health 2100 Douglas Blvd Roseville CA 95661 Office Phone: 916-781-2000. Office Fax: 916-783-9146. *

DODGEN, DANIEL W., health policy advisor, psychologist; s. David W Dodgen and Marye Dodgen Settles. BA in Psychology, U. So. Calif., L.A., 1986, BA in Spanish, 1986; MA in Clin. Psychology, U. Houston, 1990, PhD in Clin. Psychology, 1995. Lic. clin. psychologist D.C., 2000. Clin. psychologist Didi Hirsch CMHC, L.A., 1992—96; congl. fellow U.S. Ho. of Reps., Washington, 1996—97; sr. fed. affairs officer APA, Washington, 1997—2003; emergency mgmt. coord. Office of the Sec., U.S. Dept. HHS, Washington, 2003—. Chair Pentagon Mental Health Response Coalition, Washington, 2001—03, Nat. Child and Adolescent Mental Health Coalition, Washington, 1997—2003; mental health steering com. Met. Wash. Coun. of Govts., Washington, 2003—05. Recipient Early Career Contbn. award, APA, 2005, Scholar in Rehab. Policy, Mary Switzer Found., 2000; fellow Congl. Sci. fellow, APA. Mem.: APA, Smithsonian Instn., US Holocaust Meml. Mus., Phi Beta Kappa.

DODICK, JACK, ophthalmologist; Attended, U. Toronto, 1963. Diplomate Am. Bd. of Ophthalmology. Resident Manhattan Eye, Ear & Throat Hosp., 1964—67; fellow NY Med. Coll., 1967—69; prof. dept. of ophthalmology NYU Langone Med. Ctr., chair dept. of ophthalmology. Office: NYU Langone Medical Center and School of Medicine 550 1st Ave New York NY 10016 Office Phone: 212-263-7300.

DODSON, MICHAEL, pathologist, educator; s. Angelo Debrincat and Diane Dodson; m. Lisa Wang, July 8, 2003. B in Med. Sci., U. Melbourne, Parkville, Victoria, Australia, 1996, MB, BChir, 1999. Registered Med. Bd. Victoria, 2005, NSW Med. Bd., 2004, New Zealand Med. Bd., 2003. Lectr. faculty medicine Otago U., Dunedin, Otago, New Zealand, 2003—04; pathology registrar Dorevitch Pathology, Ballarat, Victoria, Australia, 2004—. Contbr. articles to profl. jours. Named Intern of the Yr., Wangaratta Base Hosp., 2001; scholar, Faculty Medicine, Dentistry & Health Sciences, U. Melbourne, 1994, Faculty Medicine, Dentistry & Health Sciences, U. Melbourne, 1995, Multiple Sclerosis Assn. Australia, 2002. Mem.: Royal Coll. Pathologists Australasia. Achievements include first to identification of vestibular stimulation as a possible treatment for mood disorders. This previously untried technique provided important information regarding neural regulation of mood; research in mechanisms by which we discriminate the shape and orientation of objects using our fingers. Office: Univ Melbourne Grattan St Parkville VIC 3052 Australia Business E-Mail: dodson@ausdoctors.net.

DOERKSEN, ROBERT JOHN, pharmacy educator; s. Daniel William and Nettie Nan Doerksen; m. Yu-Chu Chen, July 3, 1993; children: Rosalie Shinwei, Edmund Siwei. BS, U. NB, Fredericton, NB, Can., 1986; diploma in Christian studies, Regent Coll., Vancouver, 1988; PhD, U. NB, Fredericton, NB, Can., 1998. Postdoctoral fellow U. Calif., Berkeley, 1999—2001, U. Pa., Phila., 2001—04; asst. prof. U. Miss., 2004—10, assoc. prof., 2010—; rsch. asst. prof. Rsch. Inst. Pharm. Sci., 2004—, rsch. assoc. prof., 2010—. Hon. editl. bd. Perspectives in Medicinal Chemistry, North Harbour, Auckland, New Zealand, 2006—. Contbr. articles to profl. jours. Scholar, Natural Scis. Engring. Rsch. Coun., Can., 1995—97. Mem.: Sigma Xi, Am. Assn. Pharm. Sci., ONE, Am. Assn. Colls. Pharmacy, Am. Chem. Soc. (symposium co-chair 2005—). Achievements include patents for methods, systems, and computer program products for computational analysis and design of amphiphilic polymers. Office: Univ Miss Department of Medicinal Chemistry 421 Faser Hall University MS 38677-1848 Office Fax: 662-915-5638. Business E-Mail: rjd@olemiss.edu.

DOERR, HANS WILHELM, virologist; b. Arnstadt, Germany, Jan. 15, 1945; s. Wilhelm and Eva (Neuroth) D.; m. Silvia Middeldorf, June 13, 1975; children: Andrea, Simon. MD, U. Munich, 1971. From asst. to prof. U. Freiburg, U. Heidelberg, U. Frankfurt, Germany, 1972—84; dir. Inst. Med. Virology, Frankfurt, 1985—. Author: Contributions to Epidemiology of Infectious Diseases, 1978; co-author: Virological Safety of Biotechnologic Drugs, 1990, 1997, Clinical Laboratory Diagnostics, 2005, Medical Virology, 2002, 2nd edit., 2010; series editor: Monographs in Virology, 1997-; co-editor: Prions, 2d edit., 2003, Infectiology, 2004. Mem. German Assn. Against Virus Diseases (pres. 1995-2001). Achievements include co-discovery of SARS-Coronavirus, 2003. Avocation: history. Office: U Frankfurt Inst Med Virol Paul-Ehrlich-Str. 40 60596 Frankfurt Germany Office Phone: 49 69 6301 5219. Office Fax: 49 69 6301 6477. Business E-Mail: H.W.Doerr@em.uni-frankfurt.de.

DOERSHUK, CARL FREDERICK, physician, educator; b. Warren, Ohio, Dec. 24, 1930; s. Carl Frederick and Eula Blanche (Mahan) D.; m. Emma Lou Plummer, Aug. 21, 1954 (dec. Feb. 21, 2004); children: Rebecca Lee, John Frederick, David Plummer; m. Marian Marrs, Sept. 22, 2007. BA, Oberlin Coll., 1952; MD, Case Western Res. U., 1956. Intern U.S. Naval Hosp., Camp Pendleton, Calif., 1956—57; resident in pediat. Cleve. Met. Gen. Hosp. and Babies and Children's Hosp., Cleve., 1959-61; postdoctoral pulmonary fellow Babies and Children's Hosp. USPHS, Cleve., 1961-63; sr. instr. to prof. pediatrics specializing in academic pediatric pulmonary medicine Case Western Res. U., Cleve., 1963-98, emeritus prof., 1998—. Co-editor Pediatric Respiratory Therapy, 1974, 3d edit., 1986; editor, contbr.: Cystic Fibrosis in the 20th Century: People, Events and Progress, 2002; contbr. articles to profl. jours. Chmn. med. adv. coun. Cystic Fibrosis Found., Washington, 1966-72, bd. trustees, 1969-81, exec. com., 1969-74, v.p. med. affairs Cleve. chpt., 1965-90. Lt. M.C., USN, 1957-59. Named Young Man Yr. Cystic Fibrosis Found., 1970; recipient Richard C. Talamo Clinician Scientist award Cystic Fibrosis Found., 1997. Mem. Am. Pediatric Soc., Soc. Pediatric Research, Am. Acad. Pediatrics (exec. com. chest sect. Edwin Kendig Pediat. Pulmonology award 2009), Am. Thoracic Soc. (chmn. pediatric pulmonary sect. 1969-70), Acad. Medicine. Avocation: sailing. Office: Rainbow Babies & Childrens Hosp 11100 Euclid Ave Cleveland OH 44106 Office Phone: 216-844-3267. Business E-Mail: carldoershuk@sbcglobal.net.

DOETTL, CHRISTIAN, orthopedic surgeon; b. Steyr, Austria, Oct. 1, 1961; s. Johann and Erika Doettl; m. Sigrid Miesbauer, May 18, 1990; children: Hanna Maria, Sophie Carolin. MD, U. Innsbruck, Austria, 1989. Resident gen. medicine St. Vincent Hosp., Linz, Austria, 1989—93, resident orthop. surgery, 1993—97, specialist orthop. surgery, 1997—. Assoc. lectr. St. Vincent Hosp., 2004—. Contbr. scientific papers. Mem.: Australian Soc. Arthroscopy Europeanship Soc., German Speaking Assn. Arthroscopy, Austrian Soc. Chirotherapie, Austrian Soc. Orthop. Surgery, Am. Assn. Orthop. Surgeons. Office: Krankenhaus Barmherzige Schwestern Seilerstaette 4 Upper Austria Linz 4020 Austria Office Fax: 0043/732/7677/7509; Home Fax: 0043/732/7727284. Personal E-mail: ortho@dr-doettl.at. E-mail: christian.doettl@bhs.at.

DOFT, BERNARD HARVEY, ophthalmologist; b. NYC, Aug. 13, 1946; children: Michelle, Amy, Jennifer. Student, Cornell U., 1964—67; MD, NYU, 1971. Diplomate Am. Bd. Internal Medicine, Am. Bd. Ophthalmology. Intern, asst. resident in internal medicine Barnes Hosp., Washington U. Sch. of Medicine, St. Louis, 1971—73; rsch. assoc. NIH, Nat. Heart & Lung Inst. and Bur. of Biologics, Bethesda, Md., 1973—75; resident in ophthalmology Bascom Palmer Eye Inst., U. Miami Sch. Medicine, 1975—78, fellowship in diseases and surgery of retina and vitreous, 1978—79; asst. prof. ophthalmology U. Pitts. Sch. Medicine, 1979—84, clin. assoc. prof. ophthalmology, 1984—99, clin. assoc. prof. epidemiology, 1989—99, clin. prof. ophthalmology, 1999—; pvt. practice Retina Vitreous Cons, Pitts., 1984—. Cons. vision rsch. rev. com. NIH Nat. Eye Inst., 1985, protocol rev. com, 2003; apptd. ophthalmic steering com., diabetic control and complications trial NIH, 1983; quality assurance com. Bascom Palmer Eye Inst., Ann Bates Leach Eye Hosp., U. Miami Sch. Medicine, 1977—78; co-dir., retina svc. Eye and Ear Hosp., U. Pitts., 1979—84, operating rm. com., 1982—87, chmn. com. on lasers, 1982—85; clinic coord. com. Eye and Ear Hosp., Pitts., 1982—85, ad hoc. com. for adminstrn./staff rels., 1983—85, chmn. oversight com. outpatient testing and laser ctr., 1983—85, med. staff nursing oversight com., 1983—98; study chair the endophthalmitis vitrectomy study Nat. Eye Inst., Bethesda, 1989—99; SurgiCenter task force U.

Pitts. Med. Ctr., 1995, ophthalmology search com. dept. of ophthalmology chmn., 95; network cons. Diabetic Retinopathy Clin. Rsch. Network, 2003; rsch. adv. com. for steroids in ctrl. vein occlusion study NIH, 2003—. Vitreoretinal Surgery and Technology, 1989—99; contbr. articles to profl. jours. Parent coun. Emory U., Atlanta, 1998—2002. With USPHS, 1973—75. Recipient Disting. Tchg. award Dept. Ophthalmology, U. Pitts. Sch. Medicine, 1998, 2000, 2007; named Chief Residents award; named one of Best Drs. in Am., Woodward/White Inc., 1999, 2002, 2003, 2004, 2005, 2006, 2007, 2010; grantee in field. Fellow: ACS, Am. Acad. Ophthalmology; mem.: AMA, Pa. Acad. Ophthalmology (coun. mem. 1990—91), Retina Soc. (chmn. nominating com. 2006—07, exec. com. 2007—, sec. 2011—), Am. Soc. Retinal Specialists, Macula Soc., Allegheny County Med. Soc., Pa. Med. Soc., Pitts. Ophthalmology Soc. (exec. com. 1980—91, program co-chmn. 1982—83, program chmn. 1983—87, v.p., pres.-elect 1987—88, pres. 1989—91, chmn. nominating com. 1991—93), Bascom Palmer Eye Inst. Alumni Assn., Alpha Omega Alpha. Avocation: tennis. Office: Retina-Vitreous Cons Ste 500 3501 Forbes Ave Pittsburgh PA 15213-3317 Office Phone: 412-683-5300. Personal E-mail: bdoft@aol.com.

DOGAN, ALTAN, periodontist, educator; b. Ankara, Turkey, Sept. 28, 1962; s. Kamil and Ayten Dogan; m. Esin Dogan, June 17, 1991; 1 child, Artun. D.D.S., Gazi U., Ankara, 1984, PhD, 1988. Rsch. asst. dept. periodontology Gazi U., Ankara, 1984—94, assoc. prof., dr., dept. periodontology, 1994—2002, prof., 2002—. Contbr. articles to profl. jours. Lt., dentist, 1988—89, Erzurum. Master: Turkish Soc. Periodontology (Ankara sect.). Office: Gazi Univ Faculty Dentistry 84 Ankara 06510 Turkey Office Phone: 0090312 468 94 07. Personal E-mail: doganaltan@gmail.com.

DOGHRAMJI, KARL, psychiatrist, educator; MD, Jefferson Med. Coll., Pa., 1980. Diplomate Am. Bd. Psychiatry and Neurology, Am. Bd. Psychiatry and Neurology-sleep medicine, cert. psychiatry. Intern internal medicine Presbyn.- Univ. of Pa. Med. Ctr., 1981; resident in psychiatry Thomas Jefferson Univ. Hosp., 1984, program dir.; clin. rsch. fellow sleep disorders medicine and polysomnography Montefiore Med. Ctr., Albert Einstein Med. Ctr., 1984; prof. psychiatry and human behavior Jefferson Med. Coll., assoc. prof.; med. dir. Jefferson Sleep Disorders Ctr. Author: (publs.) Assessment of excessive sleepiness and insomnia as they relate to circadian rhythm sleep disorders., The effect of gastro-oesophageal reflux and omeprazole on key sleep parameters, The epidemiology and diagnosis of insomnia, Melatonin and its receptors: A new class of sleep-promoting agents, numerous publs. Office: 211 S Ninth St Suite 500 Philadelphia PA 19107 Office Phone: 215-955-6175. Office Fax: 215-955-9783.

DOGRA, JAIDEEP, physician; b. Jodhpur, Rajasthan, India, Dec. 13, 1958; s. Yogender Pal and Chandan Prabha Dogra; m. Neelam Aneja, Nov. 17, 1987; children: Luvdeep, Pearl. MBBS, S.P. Med. Coll., Rajasthan, 1982, MD, 1986. Med. officer S.P. Med. Coll., Rajasthan, 1986-87, Ctrl. Govt. Health Scheme, Jaipur, 1987-91, sr. med. officer, 1991-96, chief med. officer, 1996—2002, chief med. officer (non functional selection grade), 2002—08, family physician, v.p. India, 2003—07, supertime adminstrv. grade, 2008—, polyclinic in-charge, 2011. Author: Breakthrough in Psoriasis Management, 2005, Breakthrough in Coronary Artery Disease Management By Anti Chlamydia Pneumonia Antibiotic; manuscript reviewer Internat. Journal Dermatology; reviewer DRUGS (Internat.); contbr. articles to profl. journals. Recipient Young Scientist award Indian Coun. Med. Rsch., New Delhi, 1991, Young Investigator award Internat. Soc. Chemotherapy, Sweden, 1993; WHO Tropical Disease Rsch. grantee, 1988; Internat. League Dermatol. Socs. scholar, 1992, Outstanding Young Indian award., Indian Jr. Chamber. Fellow Royal Soc. Tropical Medicine and Hygiene (Pres.'s Fund 1995), Internat. Coll. Nutrition (life); mem. Assn. Physicians of India (life), European Soc. for Dermatol. Rsch.; The Soc. for Investigative Dermatology Inc., Rotary. Achievements include research in 5th Internat Congress on cardiovasc. diseases, Slovakia, highlighting the role of chronic Chlamydia pneumonia infection in causing coronary artery disease and its cure with long term oral azithromycin. Avocations: antique collecting, meditation. Office: Central Government Health Scheme AG Colony Bajaj Nagar Jaipur 302015 India Personal E-mail: jd_4u1958@yahoo.com.

DOHAN EHRENFEST, DAVID MARCEL, dentist, surgeon, researcher; b. Suresnes, France, Dec. 18, 1977; s. Yves André and Simone Régine Dohan. DDS, Paris 5 René Descartes U., 2002, MSc, 2003, PhD, 2005. Asst. prof. Paris 5 René Descartes U., 2003—. Rschr. Sahlgrenska acad. Göteborg U., Sweden, 2007—. Contbr. articles to profl. jours. Achievements include development of platelet rich fibrin, a new generation of platelet concentrates for surgical use. Office: AP-HP Hosp Albert Chenevier 40 rue de Mesly Créteil 94000 France Business E-Mail: radioprotection@mac.com.

DOHERTY, PATRICIA ANNE, psychologist; b. Ottumwa, Iowa, May 25, 1947; d. Russell S. and Dorotha L. (Moehle) Cadwallader; m. Michael Doherty, Sept.6, 1969; 1 child, David M. BA in History, U. Iowa, 1969, MA, 1974, PhD in Counselor Edn., 1979. Lic. profl. counselor Wis., cert. Nat. counselor. Grad. asst. U. Iowa, Iowa City, 1974-78; counseling intern Colo. State U., Ft. Collins, 1978-79; sr. psychologist U. Wis., Stevens Point, 1979—. Co-author: Women, Power and Relationships; contbr. articles to profl. jour. Mem. Wausau (Wis.) Lyric Choir, 1995—, bd. dir., 1999-2003; ofcl. Wis. Spl. Olympics, Stevens Point, 1989-2005. Mem. ACA, Am. Coll. Pers. Assn., Silvan Tomkins Inst., Nature Conservancy, Phi Delta Kappa, Phi Kappa Phi (exec.com. 2001-11), Pi Lambda Theta. Avocations: singing, tennis, swimming, running, skiing. Office: U Wis Stevens Point Counseling Ctr 317 Delzell Hall Stevens Point WI 54481 Home: 9411 Woodland Cir Amherst Junction WI 54407-9169

DOHERTY, PETER CHARLES, immunologist; b. Brisbane, Australia, Oct. 15, 1940; s. Eric C. and Linda Doherty; m. Penelope Stephens, 1965; children: James, Michael. B of Vet. Sci., U. Queensland, Australia, 1963, M of Vet. Sci., 1966; PhD, U. Edinburgh, Scotland, 1970; DSc (hon.), Australian Nat. U., 1996, U. Edinburgh, 1997, Tufts U., 1997, Warsaw Agrl. U., 1998, Latrobe U., 1999, Imperial Coll., U. London, 2000, Autonomous U. Barcelona, 2000, NC State U., 2000, U. Guelph, 2001, U. Pa., 2001, Mich. State U., 2002, U. Ill., 2002. Vet. officer Animal Rsch. Inst., Brisbane, 1963—67; sci. officer, dept. exptl. pathology Moredun Rsch. Inst., Edinburgh, 1967—71; rsch. fellow, dept. microbiology John Curtin Sch. Med. Rsch., Australian Nat. U., Canberra, 1972—75, prof., head dept. exptl. pathology, 1982—88; assoc. prof., prof. Wistar Inst., Phila., 1975—82; chmn. dept. immunology St. Jude Children's Rsch. Hosp., Memphis, 1988—2001, Michael F. Tamer Chair of biomed. rsch., 1988—; laureate prof. dept. microbiology and immunology U. Melbourne, Australia, 2002—. Mem. exptl. virology study sect. NIH, 1982—83, 1990—; bd. dirs. Internat. Lab. Animal Diseases, Nairobi, 1986—92; hon. prof. U. Tenn. Contbr. articles to profl. jours., chapters to books. Recipient Paul Ehrlich prize, Germany, 1983, Gairdner Found. Internat. award, 1986, Albert Lasker award for basic med. rsch., 1995, Nobel prize for medicine/physiology, 1996, Humanitarian award, Memphis City Coun., 1997, Peter Doherty Young Scientist award, Internat. Livestock Rsch. Inst., Kenya, 1998, Gregor Mendel medal, Villanova U., 2000, Vocational Svc. award, Rotary Club Melbourne, 2003, Centenary Medal, 2003, Curtin Medal, 2003; named Australian of Yr., Nat. Australia Day Coun., 1997, Living Nat. Treasure of Australia, 1998. Fellow: AAAS, Am. Soc. Microbiology, Royal Coll. Vet. Surgeons, Australian Soc. Immunology, Am. Coll. Vet. Pathologists, Am. Assn. Vet. Immunologists, Am. Soc. Med. Rsch., Australian Coll. Vet. Sci. (hon.), Scandinavian Soc. Immunology (hon.), Royal Soc. London; mem.: NAS (fgn. assoc.), Neuroimmunology Soc., Am. Assn. Pathologists, Paris Acad. Medicine (assoc.), Inst. Medicine, Internat. Union Immunological Societies (pres. 2008—10), Golden Key Nat. Honor Soc. (hon. life). Avocations: walking, reading. Office: St Jude Childrens Rsch Hosp MS 351 Rm E7062 262 Danny Thomas Pl Memphis TN 38105 also: U Melbourne Dept Microbiology and Immunology 3010 Melbourne VIC Australia Office Phone: 901-495-3470. Business E-Mail: peter.doherty@stjude.org. E-mail: pcd@unimelb.edu.au. *

DOHLSTEN, MIKAEL, pharmaceutical executive, researcher; b. 1959; MD, U. Lund, Sweden; PhD in Tumor Immunology, U. Lund; studied Virology, Cell Biology, Weizmann Inst, Israel. With Pharmacia & Upjohn; v.p., head global discovery AstraZeneca; exec. v.p. pharm. rsch. & devel. Boehringer Ingelheim; pres. Wyeth Rsch., 2008—. Adj. prof. immunology Med. Faculty, Lund; bd. mem. Fenix Ctr. Innovations in Mgmt. Office: Wyeth Worldwide Hdqs 5 Giralda Farms Madison NJ 07940 Office Phone: 973-660-5500. Office Fax: 973-660-7111.

DOHMANN, HANS FERNANDO, cardiologist, director; b. Rio de Janeiro, June 13, 1965; s. Hans Jurgen and Isolda Rocha Dohmann; m. Elizabete Simone Luquetti, Aug. 8, 1998 (dec. Dec. 1, 2005); 1 child, Johann Ferdinand. MBA in Health Mgmt., Fed. U., 1998; MBA in Svc. Mgmt., IBMEC, 2000; PhD, Fed. U., 2005. Dir. New Techs. Devel. Pró-Cardíaco Hosp., Rio de Janeiro, 2004—; CEO Rio de Janeiro (Brazil) Cardiology Inst., 2005—. Contbr. articles to profl. jours. Mem. bd. technol. devel. Rio de Janeiro (Brazil) Industry Fedn., 2004—05. Recipient Hon. Mention award, Ministry Health, 2003. Mem.: Nat. Acad. Medicine (Best Contbn. Improvement Quality Life award 2003), Latin Am. Soc. Interventional Cardiology (Best Poster Comm. award 2003), Brazilian Soc. Cardiology (Best Comm. award 2003, 2004), European Soc. Cardiology (Poster award 2002). Home: Av Nossa Senhora de Copacabana 2 602 Rio de Janeiro 22010 122 Brazil Office: Pró-Cardíaco Hosp Rua General Polidoro 198 Rio de Janeiro 22010 122 Brazil Office Fax: 55 21 2528 1584. Personal E-mail: hans.dohman@globo.com.

DOHN, JULIANNE, child protective services specialist; d. William Henry and Geraldine Mae Dohn. BA, SUNY, Buffalo, 1971. Child protective svcs. supr. Erie County Child Protective Svcs., Buffalo, 1974—2006; coord. Erie County Child Fatality Review Team, Buffalo, 1997—2006. Cons. in field. Recipient Cert. of Hon. Recognition, Erie County, 1999; grantee, N.Y. State Office of Child and Family Svcs., 1997, 1998. Mem.: U.S. Equestrian Fedn. Avocation: riding and showing horses. Office Phone: 716 998-9202. Personal E-mail: jdohn133@hotmail.com.

DOHNER, RUSSELL ROWLAND, physician; b. Astoria, Ill., Feb. 8, 1925; s. David Royer and Ethel Mae Dohner. BA, Northwestern U., Chgo., 1950, MD, 1953, MD (hon.), Western Ill. U., Macomb, Ill., 2006. Med. doctor gen. practice, Rushville, Ill., 1955—. Hosp. staff Culbertson Hosp., Rushville, 1953—. Staff sgt. US Army, 1944—46, Washington. Named Dr. Dohner Day, Gov. Ill., 2005, Rushville, Ill., 2005. Mem.: Masonic Lodge, Am. Legion, Rushville Rotary Club (past. pres., Paul Harris fellow 1960). Avocations: fishing, gardening. Office: Med Office 103 W Wasington Rushville IL 62681

DO HOON, KIM, medical educator; b. Suwon, Kyungki-do, Republic Of Korea, Aug. 24, 1963; s. Kang Suk Ja; m. Moon Yoo Sun, Feb. 23, 1993; children: Kim Min Kyung, Kim Sung Kook. MD, Yonsei U., Seoul, PhD, 1998. Cert. psychiatrist Korean Govt., 1993. Prof. Hallym U., Chuncheon, Kanwon-do, Republic of Korea, 1996—. Dir., med. mission Ch., Chuncheon. Recipient Whanin Neuropsychiatric award, Koran Neuropsychiatric Assn. Office: Sacred Heart Hosp Dept Chuncheon Kyo-Dong 153 200-704 Chuncheon Gangwon-do Republic of Korea Office Fax: 82 33 244 0317.

DOHRMANN, PETER JULIAN, neurosurgeon; b. Melbourne, Victoria, Australia, Nov. 14, 1954; s. John Frederick Dohrmann and Henrietta Deacon; m. Christine Houghton, Apr. 23, 1951; children: Bronwyn, Catherine, Genevieve, Peter William, Jacqueline. Student, Xavier Coll., Australia, 1962—71; MBBS, Monash U., Australia, 1977. Fellow Southwestern Med. Sch., Dallas, 1984; neurosurgery registrar London Hosp., 1985; neurosurgeon Royal Melbourne Hosp., Australia, 1987—93, Alfred Hosp., Prahran, Australia, 1986—87, 1993—96, Epworth Hosp., Richmond, Victoria, Australia, 1986—, chmn. Victorian Neurosci. Ctr., 1996—2002, exec. med. dir., 2002—. Dir. Melbourne Football Club, Victoria, Australia, 2001—08. Recipient prize, Alfred Hosp. Residents and Grads. Assn., 1977; Dilworth S. Hagar fellow, Southwestern Med. Sch., Dallas, 1984. Mem.: Med. Practitioners Bd. Victoria, Kew Golf Club, Melbourne Cricket Club, Melbourne Club. Office: Epworth Centre 32 Erin St Richmond VIC 3121 Australia Business E-Mail: peter.dohrmann@epworth.org.au.

DOI, MASAKO, pharmacologist; PhD, Hokkaido U., Sapporo, Japan, 1990. Rschr. Otsuka Pharm. Factory, Inc., Naruto, Tokushima, Japan, 1990—; sr. mgr. regenerative medicine rsch. Naruto Rsch. Inst., R & D Ctr. Office Fax: 81-88-684-2421. Business E-Mail: doim@otsuka.jp.

DOI, YOSHINORI, gastroenterologist, hepatologist; m. Fumi Doi, Oct. 9, 1993; children: Kazuhiro, Ayaka. MD, Osaka U. Med. Sch., Japan, 1990; PhD, Osaka U. Grad. Sch. Medicine, Japan, 1998. Resident 2nd dept. internal medicine Osaka U., Japan, 1990—91, postdoc. rsch. fellow, 2nd dept. internal medicine, 1998—2001, med. staff dept. gastroenterology and hepatology, 2001—02; med. staff, internal medicine Suita Mcpl. Hosp., Osaka, 1991—93; med. staff internal medicine Itami Mcpl. Hosp., Hyogo, Japan, 2002—05; dir., dept. gastroenterology and hepatology Otemae Hosp., Osaka, 2005—. Lectr. pathology Nursing Sch., Otemae Hosp., Osaka, 2007—. Contbr. scientific papers. Mem.: Japan Soc. Ultrasonic Medicine, Japan Gastroent. and Endoscopy Soc., Japan Soc. Hepatology, Japanese Soc. Gastroenterology, Japanese Soc. Internal Medicine. Avocation: swimming. Office: Otemae Hosp 1-5-34 Otemae Chuo-ku Osaka 540-0008 Japan Office Fax: 81-6-6942-2848. Business E-Mail: ydoi@otemae.gr.jp.

DOKA, KENNETH J., gerontology professor, foundation consultant; b. NYC, Feb. 12, 1948; s. Frank and Josephine (Martin) D.; 1 child, Michael. BA, Concordia Coll., Ft. Wayne, Ind., 1969; MDiv, Concordia Sem., 1973; PhD, St. Louis U., 1978. Assoc. prof. Concordia Coll., Bronxville, N.Y., 1973-81; prof. Coll. of New Rochelle, 1981—. Cons. Thomas M. Quinn and Sons, N.Y.C., 1983—, Nat. Found. of Funeral Svc., Evanston, Ill., 1983—; sr. cons. Hospice Found., Am., 1992—; chair Internat. Work Group on Dying, Death and Bereavement, chmn., 1997-99. Author: Disenfranchised Grief, 1989, Living with Life-Threatening Illness, 1993, Death and Spirituality, 1993, Mourning Children, children Mourning, 1995, Living with Grief After Sudden Loss, 1996, Lifing with Grief When Illness is Prolonged, 1997, AIDS Fear and Society, 1997, Living with Grief: Who We Are, How We Grieve, 1998, Living with Grief: At Work, At School, At Worship, 1999, Living with Grief: Children, Adolescents and Loss, 2000, Aging and Developmental Disabilities, 1999, Men Don't Cry, Women Do: Transcending Gender Stereotypes and Grief, 1999; Caregiving and Loss: Family Needs, Professional Responses, 2001, Disenfranchised Grief: New Directions, Challenges and Strategies for Practice, 2001, Spirituality and End-of Life Care (with Amy Tucci), 2011, Washington, DC: The Hospice Foundation of America. Grieving beyond Gender: Understanding the Ways Men and Woman Mourn (with Terry Martin), 2010, Cancer and End-of Life Care (with Amy Tucci), 2010, Diversity and End-of-Life Care (with Amy Tucci), 2009, Counseling Individuals with Life-Threatening Illness, 2009, Living with Grief: Children and Adolescents. (with Amy Tucci), 2008, Living with Grief: Before and After Death. 2007, Death, Dying and Bereavement: Major Themes in Health and Social Welfare (4 Volumes — edited). 2006. Pain Management at the End-of-Life: Bridging the Gap Between Knowledge and Practice. 2006, Living with Grief: Ethical Dilemmas at the End of Life (with Charles Corr and Bruce Jennings), 2005, Living with Grief: Alzheimer's Disease, 2004, Living with Grief: Coping with Public Tragedy (with M. Lattanzi-Licht). 2003, Living with Grief: Loss in Later Life. Disenfranchised Grief: New Directions, Challenges and Strategies for Practice, 2002 Bd. dirs. Variety Boys and Girls Club of Queens, N.Y., 1975—1990; editl. bd. Nat. Kidney Found., N.Y., 1990-95, bd. dirs. Recipient Program award Boys' Clubs Am., 1981, ADEC award, 1998, Scott and White award for contbns. to thanatology, 2000, Disting. Alumnus award Concordia Coll., 2001. Mem. Gerontol. Soc. Am., Am. Soc. on Aging, Am. Sociol. Assn., Assn. for Death Edn. and Counseling (bd. dirs. 1985-87, v.p. 1991). Republican. Lutheran. Avocations: scuba diving, skiing. Office: Coll of New Rochelle Dept Gerontology New Rochelle NY 10805 E-mail: kndok@aol.com.

DOLAN, PETER ROBERT, former pharmaceutical executive; b. Salem, Mass., Jan. 6, 1956; s. John Ralph and Lois D. (Burkhart); m. Katherine Helen Lange, Sept. 12, 1981; children: Christopher Lange, Timothy Lange. B, Tufts U., 1978; MBA, Amos Tuck Sch. Bus. Dartmouth Coll., 1980. Asst. product mgr. Gen. Foods Corp., White Plains, NY, 1980-81, assoc. product mgr., 1982-83, product mgr., 1983-84, sr. product mgr., 1985, group product mgr., 1986-87, category mgr., 1987-88; v.p. mktg. Bristol-Myers Co., NYC, 1988-90, sr. v.p. mktg. & sales, 1990-91, sr. v.p. mktg., sales & ops., 1991-92, exec. v.p., 1992, pres., 1993-94, Mead Johnson Nutritional Group, Evansville, Ind., 1995-96; group pres. nutritionals and med. devices Bristol-Myers Squibb Co., 1997—98, pres. Europe, Worldwide medicines, 1998, sr. v.p. strategy and orgnl. effectiveness, 1998—2000, pres., 2000—05, chmn., 2001—05, CEO, 2001—06. Bd. dir. Old Nat. Bank, Am. Express Comp., Pharm. Rsch. and Mfrs. of Am., Gemin X Pharmaceuticals; bd. overseers Tufts Medical Sch. Bd.; mem. Bus. Coun., Bus. Roundtable. Co-author: Insider's Guide to the Top Ten Business Schools, 1982. Bd. dirs. NY Botanical Garden, Nat. Center on Addiction and Substance Abuse at Columbia U., C-Change; bd. trustee Tufts U. Mem.: Young Pres. Orgn., Non-Prescription Drug Mfrs. Assn. (bd. dirs. 1993). Avocations: triathlons, tennis, scuba diving.

DOLAN, TERESA A., dean, educator, researcher; MPH, UCLA; BA in Zoology, Rutgers U., 1979; DDS, U. Tex., 1983; cert. gen. practice, L.I. Jewish Med. Ctr., 1985; cert. geriatric dentistry, Vets. Adminstrn., 1989; cert. dental pub. health, U. Fla., 1991; grad., Pub. Health Leadership Inst. Fla., 1998; grad. cert., U. Fla., 2001. Diplomate Am. Bd. Dental Pub. Health, 1994. Resident in gen. dentistry dept. dentistry L.I. Jewish Med. Ctr., 1983—84, chief resident in gen. dentistry dept. dentistry, 1984—85; fellow geriatric dentistry Vets. Adminstrn. Med. Ctr., Sepulveda, Calif., 1987—89; asst. prof. U. Fla. Coll. Dentistry, 1989—93, assoc. prof. with tenure, 1993—98, acting assoc. dean acad. affairs, 1996—97, assoc. dean acad. affairs, 1997—2001, prof. with tenure, 1998—, assoc. dean edn., 2001—03, interim dean, 2002—03, dean, 2003—. Rschr., tchr., spkr. in field, lectr. various seminars; vis. asst. prof. U. Calif., 1985—87, adj. asst. prof., 1987—89; faculty discipline com. Fla. Dept. Edn., Statewide Course Numbering Sys., 1998—; reviewer grants in field; participant NIH Summer Inst. Rsh. on Minority Aging, 1991; pres. Am. Bd. of Dental Pub. Health, 2005—06. Contbr. articles to profl. jours.; exec. prodr.: (ednl. satellite videoconf.) Dental Care for the Developmentally Disabled Patient, 1991, Challenges in Geriatrics: Moving on-Rehabilitation After Stroke, 1991, How Much is Enough? Dental Tretament Decisions for Older Adults, 1992; author (dir.): Five Steps to Improving the Oral Health of Your Older Patients: A Guide for Non-dental Health Professionals, 1994. Adv., treating dentist cmty. nursing homes, 1989—96; dentist to low income elderly participants U. Fla. Geriatric Dental Demonstration Project, Jacksonville, 1990—92; dir. dental svcs. to older and medically compromised patients U. Fla. Geriatric Dental Group, 1990—95. Recipient numerous grants and awards; named honorable mention AARP Healthy Order Adults, 2000 Recognition Programs Exemplary Contbns. to Healthy Aging, 1992; fellow Vets. Adminstrn. Geriatric Dentistry; scholar Rsch., Robert Wood Johnson Found. Dental Health Svcs., 1985—87, L.I. U., 1984—85. Mem.: APHA, Am. Coll. Dentists, Phi Beta Kappa, Am. Soc. Geriatric Dentistry (ad hoc reviewer Spl. Care in Dentistry 1992—93, judge Saul Kamen Sci. Report award competition 1993—, chmn. ann. sci. session 1996), Fla. Coun. Aging, Fla. Pub. Health Assn., Am. Assn. Pub. Health Dentistry (abstract reviewer 1987, co-chmn. local arrangements ann. meeting 1992, ad hoc reviewer Jour. Pub. Health Dentistry 1994, session co-chmn. ann. meeting 1996, judge grad. student merit award projects 1997, mem. at large exec. coun. 1997—2000, mem. awards and nominations com. 2000, Pres.'s award 1999), Am. Dental Assn. (com. G Coun. Dental Edn. and Licensure 1999—, Geriatric Dental Care award 1991), Internat. Assn. Dental Rsch. (v.p. abstract reviewer geriat. oral rsch. sect. 1992—93, dir. behavioral sci. and health svcs. rsch. sect. 1992—95, pres.-elect program chmn. geriat. oral rsch. sect. 1993—94, pres. symposium organizer geriat. oral rsch. sect. 1994—95), Am. Assn. Women Dentists (chmn. com. student and component chpts. 1986—88, trustee dist. XIII Calif. 1986—89, contbg. editor Chronicle 1986—91), Acorn Clinic (v.p., acting pres. 1996—97, pres. 1997—99, past pres. 1999—2000), Fla. Coun. Aging (bd. trustees 1993—95), U. Health Sci. Ctr., Edn. Task Force, U. Curriculum Com., Geriatric Rsch., Edn. and Clin. Ctr., ACORN Clinic, Internat. Assn. Dental Rsch. (session co-chmn., abstract reviewer geriat. oral rsch. sect. 1991—92, immediate past-pres., chmn. nominations com. geriat. oral rsch. sect. 1995—96, mem. awards com. geriat. oral rsch. sect. 1996—97, constn. and bylaws com. 1996—), Am. Bd. Dental Pub. Health (dir.-elect 2000—01, pres. 2005—), Am. Dental Edn. Assn. (chair-elect spl. interest group in geriatric dentistry 1991—92, editl. rev. bd. Jour. Dental Edn. 1991—94, chmn. spl. intertest group in geriatric dentistry 1992—93, immediate past chmn. sect. on gerontology and geriat. edn. 1993—94, abstract reviewer ann. session 1998—2000, ann. session planning com. 2002—), Beta Beta Beta, Omicron Kappa Upsilon (Xi Omicron chpt. 1998), Phi Beta Kappa. Office: U Fla Coll Dentistry 1600 SW Archer Rd D 4-6B Box 100405 JHMH Gainesville FL 32610-0405 Office Phone: 352-392-2911. Office Fax: 352-392-3070. E-mail: tdolan@dental.ufl.edu.

DOLAN, THOMAS CHRISTOPHER, professional society administrator; b. Chgo., Dec. 31, 1947; s. Thomas Christopher and Bernice Mary (Doyle) D.; m. Georgia Ann Siebke, Feb. 14, 1983; children: William, Barbara, Lauren. BBA, Loyola U., Chgo., 1969; PhD, U. Iowa, 1977. Instr. U. Iowa, Iowa City, 1971-72; vis. fellow U. Wash., Seattle, 1973-74; asst. prof. U. Mo., Columbia, 1974-79; assoc. prof., dir. St. Louis U., 1979-86; v.p. Am. Coll. Healthcare Execs., Chgo., 1986-87, exec. v.p., 1987-91, pres., CEO, 1991—. Mem. Accrediting Commn. on Edn. for Health Svcs. Administrn., Washington, 1985-86; chmn. Assn. Univ. Programs in Health Adminstrn., Washington, 1983-84; cons. HEW, Kansas City, Mo., 1974-79, State of Mo., Jefferson City, 1974-79. Author: Systems for Health Care Administration: A Model for the Education of Health Manpower, 1975; contbr. articles to profl. jours. Pres. Mental Health Assn. Boone County, Columbia, Mo., 1977—78, Mental Health Assn. Mo., Jefferson City, 1980—82; chair Inst. Diversity in Health Mgmt., 2002, Assn. Forum, 1999—2000, Am. Soc. Assn. Execs., Washington, 2007—08. Fellow: Am. Soc. Assn. Execs. (pres. designate 2010, chairperson 2010—11), Am. Coll. Healthcare Execs.; mem.: Alexian Bros. Hosp. (St. Louis) (bd. dirs. 1980—86), Internat. Hosp. Fedn. (pres. designate 2010, bd. dirs. 2005—), US Chamber Com. of 100, Baldrige Bd. Overseers (chairperson 2010—11). Roman Catholic. Avocations: golf, motorcycling, photography. Office: Am Coll Healthcare Execs 1 N Franklin St Ste 1700 Chicago IL 60606-4425 Office Fax: 312-424-0023. E-mail: tdolan@ache.org. *

DOLAN, WILLIAM A., orthopedist, medical educator; b. Bklyn., Dec. 29, 1940; m. Brenda Dolan; children: Jeannine, Bill, Carrielyn. MD cum laude, Dalhousie U. Med. Sch., 1967. Intern gen. surgery Victoria Gen. Hosp., 1966—67; resident orthop. surgery U. Rochester Med. Ctr., 1970—72, resident, 1972—74; clin. prof. orthop. U. Rochester; mem. Westfall Orthopaedic & Sports Medicine. Mem. Health Care Reform Act Quality Task Force; founder Med. Quality Assurance Task Force. Lt. comdr. USN. Mem.: AMA (mem. coun. on med. svc., bd. trustees 2007—11). Office: U Rochester Med Ctr Box 665 601 Elmwood Ave Rochester NY 14624 also: Westfall Orthop Ctr Westfall Profl Park 880 Westfall Rd, Ste A Rochester NY 14618 Office Phone: 585-271-4305, 585-271-2022. *

DOLE, ARTHUR ALEXANDER, former psychology professor, department chairman; b. San Francisco, Oct. 25, 1917; s. Arthur Alexander and Ella Elizabeth (Duncan) D.; m. Marjorie Elizabeth Welsh, Mar. 19, 1949; children: Peter, Steven, Barbara. BA, Antioch Coll., 1946; MA, Ohio State U., 1949, PhD, 1951; MA (hon.), U. Pa., 1973. Diplomate Am. Bd. Examiners Profl. Psychology. Asst. psychology, edn. Antioch Coll., 1946-48; counselor Ohio State U., 1948-51; dir. Bur. Testing and Guidance, U. Hawaii, 1951-60, asst. prof., prof. psychology, 1951-67; prof. psychology edn. U. Pa., 1967-88, chmn. divsn., 1967-88, prof. emeritus, 1988—. Mem. internat. adv. bd. Univ MSG, Romero, El Salvador. Author articles in field.; cons. editor profl. jours. Exec. adv. bd., Internat. Cultic Studies Assn. Fellow APA, AAUP, ACA, Am. Ednl. Rsch. Assn., Internat. Coun. Psychologists, Internat. Assn. Applied Psychology, Nat. Rehab. Assn. Home Phone: 207-667-9237. E-mail: aadole@roadrunner.com.

DOLE, WILLIAM PAUL, physician, researcher, biomedical researcher; b. Ellenville, NY, May 31, 1947; BA, Columbia Coll., 1969; MD, NYU, 1973. Head, cardiovasc. devel. Schering AG, 1987—92; v.p., head, cardiovasc. rsch. Berlex Bioscis., 1993—2004; global head, profiling clin. pharmacology, cardiovasc., diabetes & metabolism Novartis Pharms. Corp., 2004—08; exec. dir., translational medicine cardiovasc. Novartis Insts. Biomed. Rsch., 2008—, Novartis disting. investigator. Asst. prof., medicine U. Tex. Health Sci. Ctr. Divsn. Cardiology, 1980—83; assoc. prof., medicine U. Iowa Coll. Medicine Cardiovasc. Divsn., 1983—87. Rsch. Career Devel. grant, NIH, Math. scholarship, NSF. Fellow: Am. Physiol. Soc. Cardiovasc. Sect., Am. Coll. Cardiology, Am. Heart Assn. Avocations: hiking, travel, reading. Office: Novartis Insts Biomed Rsch Cambridge MA 02139 Business E-Mail: bill.dole@novartis.com.

DOLEV, JACQUELINE, physician, researcher; b. Feb. 25, 1975; d. Sharon and Mark Dolev. BA, U. Calif, Berkeley; MD, Yale U. Sch. Medicine. Lic. Calif. Internal medicine resident Stanford U. Hosp., Calif.; dermatology resident and fellow UCSF, San Francisco. Dir., advancement med. edn. dermatology, UCSF, Calif., asst. clin. prof.; healthcare fellow U.S Senate, Washington; co-founder Med. observational skills curriculum, Yale Ctr. for Brit. Art, New Haven; eDerm co-dir. UCSF online curriculum. Contbr. articles various profl. jours. and chpts. to books; author: (resolution) AMA Policy Compendium; author: (illustrator) (children's book) Around the World. Mem.: AMA,

San Francisco Med. Soc. (editor), Am. Acad. Dermatology, Calif. Med. Assn. Office: 2100 Webster St Ste 411 San Francisco CA 94115 Business E-Mail: info@dolevdermatology.com.

DOLGIH, VLADIMIR TERENTIEVICH, physiologist, consultant; b. Vasiss of Omsk, Russia, Jan. 28, 1948; s. Terenty Lukianovich and Marina Semenovna Dolgih; m. Tatiana Ivanovna Dolgih, Aug. 9, 1977; children: Dmitry, Sergey. Diploma with honors, Omsk State Med. Inst., 1972, PhD, 1975, MD, 1988. Cert. prof. Omsk State Med. Inst., 1989. Asst. prof. Omsk State Med. Acad., 1975—79, head main sci. rsch. lab, 1979—85, head pathophysiology dept., 1985—, vice chancellor sci. rsch. work, 1996—2002. Sci. cons. Mcpl. Clin. Hosp. Emergency Medicine, Omsk, 2005—. Author: (book) Molecular Damage of the Heart After Acute Hemorrhage, Different Aspects of Pathophysiology; contbr. articles to profl. jours. Adminstrn. bd. mem. Russian Sci. Soc. Pathophysiology; vice chief External and Terminal Conditions Commn. Russian Acad. Med. Scis. Recipient medal, 1971, award, 1998, Silver medal, European Natural Scis. Acad. Hannover, 2006; Soros Found. grant, 1993. Master: Russian Sci. Soc. Pathophysiology; mem.: Russian Acad. Medico Tech. Scis., Syberian Br. Acad. High Sch. Scis. Office: Omsk State Med Acad Lenina Str 12 Omsk 644043 Russia Home Phone: 7-3812-567919; Office Phone: 7-3812-230378. Office Fax: 7-3812-234632; Home Fax: 7-3812-567919. E-mail: prof_dolgih@mail.ru.

DOLITSKY, JAY NEIL, pediatric otolaryngologist, educator; BA, Yeshiva U., NY, 1980; MD, SUNY, Brooklyn, 1984. Diplomate Am. Bd. Otolaryngology, 1990, cert. NY, 1986, Pa., 1990. Resident gen. surgery NY Univ. Med. Ctr., 1984—86; resident otolaryngology Manhattan Eye, Ear and Throat Hosp., 1987—90, clin. fellow, 1986—87; fellow pediatric otolaryngology Children's Hosp. of Pitts., 1990—92; asst. prof. otolaryngology NY Med. Coll., 1992—2004, dir. med. student edn. otolaryngology, 1992—2004; dir. pediatric otolaryngology NY Eye and ear Infirmary, 1992—2004. Med. record audit com. NY Eye and Ear Infirmary, pediatric task force com. Named one of Best Doctors, NY Mag., 1998—2000, 2003—10, America's Top Doctors, Castle Connolly, 2003—10. Fellow: Am. Acad. of Pediat., Am. Acad. of Otolaryngology-Head and Neck Surgery. Office: New York Eye and Ear Infirmary Department of Otolaryngology 404 Park Ave S 12th Fl New York NY 10016 Office Phone: 212-679-3499. Office Fax: 212-683-4551.

DOLLENS, RONALD W., medical products executive; b. Ind., Dec. 17, 1946; s. William Franklin and Louise Anna (Davis) D.; m. Susan Stanley, Aug. 30, 1969; children: Stephanie, Grant. BS, Purdue U., 1970; MBA, Ind. U., 1972. Sales rep., dir., Bus. Devel. Eli Lilly & Co., Indpls., 1972—85, pres., Med. Devices Divsn., 1991—94; sr. v.p. Advanced Cardiovasc. Sys., Santa Clara, 1985—88, pres., CEO, 1988—94, Guidant Corp., Indpls. 1994—2005; chmn. Kinetic Concepts, Inc. Bd. dirs. Ind. Health Industry Forum, Beckman Coulter Corp. Bd. dirs. Butler U., Indpls., Eiteljorg Mus., Indpls., St. Vincent Hosp. Found.; mem., Adv. Com., Regulatory Health US Dept. Health & Human Svcs., 2002—. Mem.: AdvaMed, Alliance for Aging Rsch., Healthcare Leadership Coun. (chmn. 2003—05, bd. trustees). Office: Kinetic Concepts Inc 8023 Vantage Dr San Antonio TX 78230-4726 Office Phone: 210-255-4726. E-mail: ronald.dollens@kci1.com. *

DOLLIVER, ROBERT HENRY, psychology professor; b. Fort Dodge, Iowa, Oct. 15, 1934; BA, Cornell Coll., 1958; MA, Ohio State U., 1963, PhD, 1966. Social worker Bd. Child Welfare, Elyria, Ohio, 1958-59; social worker Cleve. Boys Sch., 1959-61; asst., then assoc. prof. psychology U. Mo., Columbia, 1966-77, prof., 1977-99, prof. emeritus, 1999—. Office: U Mo Dept Psychology Columbia MO 65211-0001 Personal E-mail: snoopyrhd@aol.com.

DOLUISIO, JAMES THOMAS, dean, pharmacy educator; b. Bethlehem, Pa., Sept. 28, 1935; s. Dominic and Sue (Powell) D.; m. Phyllis M. Sabolski, June 20, 1959; children: Thomas, James, Rebecca. BS in Pharmacy, Temple U., 1957, MS, 1959; PhD, Purdue U., 1962; DSc, Phila. Coll. Pharmacy and Sci., 1983; DSc (hon.), Purdue U., 1995, Wilkes U., 2000. From asst. prof. to assoc. prof. pharmacy Phila. Coll. Pharmacy and Sci., 1961-67, also assoc. dir. dept., 1965-67; prof., chmn. dept. pharmacy U. Ky., Lexington, 1967-73; prof., dean U. Tex., Austin, 1973-98. Bd. dirs. Eckerd Corp., 1986-96, COR Therapeutics, 1994-02; cons. Smith Kline & French Labs., Phila., 1962-67, McNeil Labs., Ft. Washington, Pa., 1967-72, Hoechst Labs., Somerville, N.J., 1973-93, Nat. Inst. Drug Abuse, 1976-78, HEW, U.S. Surgeon Gen., 1975-83; cons. Merck-Medco, Franklin Lakes, N.J., 2000-2001. Contbr. to profl. and sci. jours. Active Pharmacists Against Drug Abuse Found., 1984; chmn. U.S. Pharmacopeial Conv., Inc., 1990-95; v.p. Fedn. Internat. Pharmaceutique, 1994-98. NSF fellow, 1959-61; Am. Found. Pharm. Edn. fellow, 1957-59 Mem. Am. Pharm. Assn. (pres. 1982, Remington Honor medal 1995), Am. Assn. Colls. Pharmacy, Am. Soc. Hosp. Pharmacy, Am. Assn. Pharm. Scientists (pres. 1988), Fed. Internat. Pharmacists (Lifetime Achievement award 2000), Rho Chi. Office: U Texas College of Pharmacy Austin TX 78712 Business E-Mail: doluisio.jt@mail.utexas.edu.

DOMBROWSKI, ANNE WESSELING, microbiologist; b. Cin., Jan. 26, 1948; m. Allan Wayne Dombrowski, Apr. 17, 1982; children: Amy, Alicia. BA summa cum laude, Xavier U., 1970; MS, U. Cin., 1972, PhD, 1974. Fellow Scripps Clinic and Rsch. Found., La Jolla, Calif., 1974-76; sr. rsch. microbiologist Merck & Co., Inc., Rahway, NJ, 1976-87, rsch. fellow, 1987-96, sr. rsch. fellow, 1996—2003, ret., 2003; lab. rschr. Rutgers U., NB, 2008—11, Inst. Hepatitis and Viral Rsch., Doylestown, Pa., 2011—. Contbr. articles to profl. jours. Mem.: Am. Soc. Microbiology, Soc. Indsl. Microbiology (sec. 1982—85, dir. 1998—2001). Achievements include patents in field. Avocations: reading, gardening. Home: 51 Landsdowne Rd East Brunswick NJ 08816-4156 Personal E-mail: annewd@aol.com.

DOMCHEK, SUSAN M., oncologist, educator; Grad., Dartmouth Coll.; MD, Harvard Coll. Diplomate Am. Bd. Internal Medicine, 1998, Am. Bd. Internal Medicine-hematology-oncology, 2001, lic. Pa. Resident internal medicine Mass. Gen. Hosp.; fellow Dana-Farber Cancer Inst.; assoc. prof., medicine Univ. Pa., mem. Abramson cancer ctr.; hosp. affiliation includes Hosp. of Univ. Pa., dir., cancer risk evaluation program. Named Best Doctors in America, 2010; named one of Top Docs, Phila. Mag., 2011. Mem.: Am. Soc. of Clin. Oncology. Office: Abramson Cancer Center 3400 Civic Ctr Blvd Philadelphia PA 19104 Office Phone: 800-789-7366.

DOMENECH, JULIO, orthopedist; b. Guadalajara, Spain, Sept. 18, 1965; Degree in Medicine, U. Navarra, Spain, 1989; PhD, U.

Valencia, 2001. Resident, orthop. surgery Hosp. Ramon Y Cajal, Madrid, 1990—95; cons. orthop. surgeon Hosp. La Fe, Valencia, Spain, 1995—99, Hosp. de la Ribera, Alcira, Spain, 1999—2005, Hosp. Virgen de los Lirios, Alcoy, Spain, 2005—07; cons., orthop. surgery Hosp. Arnau de Vilanova, 2007—. Assoc. prof. U. Cardenal Herrera CEU, Valencia, 2001; prof. Sch. Medicine Cath. U. Valencia, 2008. Mem.: Spanish Spine Soc., Spanish Orthop. Surgery Soc., Spine Soc. Europe, Spanish Soc. Rsch. Orthop. Surgery. Avocations: history, tennis. Office: San Clemente 12 Valencia 46015 Spain Office Fax: 34-963868197.

DOMENICI, ALESSANDRO, medical association administrator, educator; b. Rome, Aug. 7, 1961; Degree in Medicine & Surgery, 'Sapienza' U. Rome, 1988, degree in Nephrology, 1992. Med. dir. Nephrology & Dialysis Unit, Sant'Andrea Hosp., Rome, 1992—. Adj. prof. Sch. Nephrology, 'Sapienza' U. Rome, 2004—. Mem.: Internat. Soc. Peritoneal Dialysis, Italian Soc. Nephrology, European Dialysis & Transplant Assn. - European Renal Assn. Avocations: music, sailing. Office: via di Grottarossa 1035 Rome Lazio 00189 Italy Business E-Mail: alessandro.domenici@ospedalesantandrea.it.

DOMINGO, E. JOSEPH, dental association administrator; b. NYC, Dec. 12, 1969; DDS, NYU, 1996; degree in Oral and Maxillofacial Surgery, Cornell U., 2001. Pres. Oral Surgery Svcs., 2001—. Fellow: Am. Assn. Oral and Maxillofacial Surgeons; mem.: ADA, RI Assn. Oral and Maxillofacial Surgeons, Nat. Dental Bd. Anesthesia, Am. Bd. Oral and Maxillofacial Surgery. Avocations: golf, surfing. Office: 20 Cumberland Hill Rd Ste 101 Woonsocket RI 02895 Personal E-mail: drjdomingo@aol.com.

DOMINGUE, GERALD JAMES, medical researcher, educator, microbiologist, immunologist; b. Lafayette, La., Mar. 2, 1937; s. Edgar Paul and Sarah Ann (Prejean) D.; m. Marie Hazel Dugas, Aug. 30, 1958 (div. 1979); children: Andrea, Yvonne, Michelle, Gerald Jr., Marcel; m. Kathryn H. Colbert, (div. 1985). BS in Bacteriology, U. La., Lafayette, 1959; PhD in Med. Microbiology and Immunology, Tulane U., 1964. Post-doctoral research fellow Children's Hosp., asst. research instr. pediatrics SUNY, Buffalo, 1965-66; dir. microbiol. Snodgras Lab. of Pathology and Bacteriology, St. Louis, 1966-67; instr. microbiology St. Louis U., 1966-67; asst. prof. microbiology, immunology and urology Tulane U., New Orleans, 1967-70, assoc. prof. microbiology, immunology and urology, 1970-74, prof. microbiology, immunology and urology, 1974-97, prof. emeritus, 1997—. Lectr. microbiology sch. dentistry Washington U., St. Louis, 1966-67; vis. prof., lectr. Peruvian Urol. Assn., Lima, 1973, First Internat. Congress Bacteriology, Jerusalem, 1973, Internat. Convocation Immunology, Buffalo, 1974, World Health Orgn. Conf. on Sperm Immunology, Aarhus, Denmark, 1974, European Soc. Exptl. Urol. Research, Wurzburg, Fed. Republic Germany, 1976, Internat. Seminar L-Forms, Montpellier, France, 1976, U. Melbourne, Royal Melbourne Hosp., Australia, 1978, XII Internat. Congress Microbiology, Munich, 1978, Internat. Symposium Vaccines and Vaccinations, Institut Pasteur, Paris, 1985; speaker U. Montpellier Sch. Medicine, 1985, 4th Internat. Congress on Pyelonephritis, Goteborg, Sweden, 1986, Orion Diagnostica, Helsinki, Finland, 1986, Nat. Inst. Hygiene, Warsaw, Poland, 1986, Symposium on Molecular Biology and Infectious Diseases, Institut Pasteur, 1987; com. for infection control So. Bapt. Hosp., 1971-75, Charity Hosp. La., 1977—, Tulane U. Hosp., 1977—; infectious disease com. St. Louis City Hosp., 1966-67; reviewer, visitor project sites NIH Grant Review Study Sects., 1967-97, NSF, Kaiser Rsch. Found., Kidney Found. Can.; cons. bacteriology So. Bapt. Hosp., New Orleans, 1968-84, Tulane U. Hosp., 1978-83, Med. Tech. Corp., Somerset, NJ, 1983—; rsch. cons. VA Hosp., New Orleans, 1970-78; cons., tech. adv. bd. Analytab Products, Inc., NYC, 1972-77; expert witness to subcom. on dept. investigation oversight and rsch. for Animal Cancer Rsch. Act, U.S. Ho. of Reps., 1980; cons. in field Author, editor: Cell Wall-Deficient Bacteria, 1962; (catalogue) Domingue, an abstract expressionist painter, 1997-2000; author: Memories of a Grandson: Echoes and Footprints of Spanish-Isleno French Acadian Families: Domingue-Prejean and Prejean-Castille, Vols. I, II, III, 2006, (poems) Massaging the Intellect, 2007; L'habitation Domingue 1895-1963, 2008; Monotypes, 2009; author numerous poems; contbr. over 160 articles to profl. jours., chpts. to books. Pres. France-Louisiane de la Nouvelle Orleans, 1985—, pres. fondateur, 1988; apptd. mem. Gov.'s Council for Devel. of French Lang. in La., 1985, 88; mem. Met. Area Com., New Orleans, 1987, Bur. Govtl. Research, New Orleans, 1987; mem. Mayor's Com. New Orleans-Paris Cultural Exchange, 1988; chmn. scholar's com. La. Com. on French Revolution, 1988; mem. Alliance for Good Govt., 1980-84; mem. Greater New Orleans French Bd., 1987—; rep. Coun. for Devel. French and France Louisiane for celebration of French Bicentennial, Paris, 1989; pres., bd. govs. Le Petit Theatre du Vieux Carre, New Orleans, 1996-97. Served with La. Nat. Guard 156th Inf. Med. Co. USAR, 1955—63. Guaranty scholar U. Southwestern La., 1958; grantee NIH, 1970-97, Schlieder Found., Armour Pharm. House, VA, Cadwallader Family Found., Med. Tech. Corp., Orion Diagnostica; decorated chevalier Order of Palmes Academiques (France); recipient French Medal, 1996. Fellow Am. Acad. Microbiology, Infectious Disease Soc. Am.; mem. Am. Soc. Microbiology (divisional lectr. 1978, found. lectr. 1979-80, symposium lectr. 1994), Soc. Basic Urologic Rsch. (state of art lectr. 1994), Soc. for Exptl. Biology and Medicine, AAAS, AAUP, Fedn. Am. Scientists, Southwestern Assn. Clin. Microbiology (editor newsletter 1983-85, pres. 1985-86), N.Y. Acad. Scis., Am. Assn. Lab. Animal Sci., Soc. Basic Urological Rsch. (nominating com. 1988), Am. Urol. Assn. (affiliate mem.), French-Am. Bus. Assn., Am. Acad. Poets (assoc.), Sigma Xi, Roman Catholic. Avocations: painting, writing, poetry. Home and Office: Kronleinstrasse 14 8044 Zurich Switzerland

DOMINGUES, MARLOS R., physical education educator; b. Rio Grande, Brazil, Mar. 17, 1974; PhD in Phys. Edn., Fed. U. Pelotas, 2001, degree in Epidemiology, 2007. Tchr. Fed. U. Pelotas, 2009—. Adj. prof. Postgrad. Program Phys. Edn., 2009. Mem.: Brazilian Soc. Phys. Activity and Health. Home: Pedro Armando Gatti 158 Jardim do Sol Rio Grande Rio Grande do Sul 96216-080 Brazil Personal E-Mail: coriolis@vetorial.net.

DOMINGUEZ-BENDALA, JUAN, medical educator; b. Sevilla, Sevilla, Spain, Oct. 12, 1970; s. Juan Dominguez Galiano and Lina Bendala Rodriguez; m. Xiomara Mordcovich, May 1, 2003. BS in Biology, U. Seville, Spain, 1993; MS in Applied Molecular Biology and Biotech., U. Coll. London, 1997; PhD in Cell and Molecular Biology, U. Edinburgh, Scotland, 2000. Postdoctoral assoc. Diabetes Rsch. Inst., U. Miami Leonard M. Miller Sch. Medicine, Fla.,

2001—04, lectr., 2004—06, rsch. asst. prof., 2006—10, rsch assc. prof., 2010—. Dir. stem cell & translational rsch. lab. Diabetes Rsch. Inst., U. Miami Leonard M. Miller Sch. Medicine, 2004—. Contbr. articles to profl. jours. Spokesperson stem cell rsch., therapeutic cloning and diabetes Diabetes Rsch. Inst. Found., Miami, 2000; advisor Genetics Policy Inst., Miami. 2d lt. Spanish Air Force, 1994—95. Grantee, Found. Diabetes Rsch., 2004—07, Juvenile Diabetes Rsch. Found., 2006—07, Peacock Found., 2006—, NIH, 2009; scholar, Biotech. and Biol. Sciences Rsch. Coun., England, 1997—2000. Mem.: Cell Transplantation Soc., Internat. Soc. Stem Cell Rsch., Transplantation Soc. Achievements include research in protein transduction strategies for the differentiation of pancreatic beta cells; strategies for improved gene targeting frequency in mammalian cells; strategies for the efficient differentiation of human embryonic stem cells into insulin-producing cells; patents pending for enhanced oxygenation for the differentiation of pancreatic beta cells. Avocations: music, piano, basketball. Office: Diabetes Research Institute U of Miami 1450 NW 10th Ave Miami FL 33136

DOMINGUEZ ORTEGA, LUIS, medical educator, health facility administrator; b. Barcelona, Oct. 4, 1941; s. Jose Dominguez and Dolores Ortega (Araujo) Dominguez; m. Mercedes Sanchez Tamayo, Jan. 2, 1969; children: Elena, Jose Luis. Cert., Ramiro Maeztu Inst., Madrid, Spain, 1962; MD, Complutense U., Madrid, 1969, diploma in internal medicine, 1975; PhD, Complutense Univ., 1999. Cert. gen. practitioner. Postgrad. Clinico Hosp., Madrid, 1969-73; asst. physician emergency svc. Dept. of Internal Medicine, 12 de Octubre Hosp., Madrid, 1974-77, asst. physician, 1977—, asst. prof., 1977-86, assoc. prof., 1986—98; dir., coord. sleep disorders unit 12 de Octobre Hosp., Madrid, 1990—2001; dir., prof. sleep medicine Complutense U. Madrid, 1996—2004; dir. Ruber Clinic, Madrid, 2001—04, dir. family practice unit, 2002—04; cons. internal medicine Octubre Hosp., 2001—04. Mem. faculty bd. 12 de Octubre Hosp., 1984-88; mem. hosp. bd. Med. Coll., Madrid, 1984-88, candidate to pres. hosp. bd., 1986; organizer, chmn. internat. meeting Advances in Sleep Disorders, Madrid, 1992; mem. project evaluation com. of Nat. Agy. for Evaluation and Prospective in Interministerial Bd. of Sci. and Tech.; dir. univ. course on sleep medicine Complutense U., Madrid, 1996-99; mem. reading com. Vigilia-Sueño Rev.; mem. evaluation-selection com. Anales de Medicina interna Rev. Member Club Liberal, Madrid, 1980-89; founder, v.p. Asociacion Nacional Medicos Empresarios, Spain, 1991—. FISS grantee, 1980-90, 92. Mem. Am. Sleep Disorders Assn., Nat. Assn. Internal Medicine, N.Y. Acad. Scis., Internat. Assn. Internal Medicine, European Sleep Rsch. Soc., European Assn. Internal Medicine, Spanish Assn. of Hypnosis (pres. 2002-2004), Am. Soc. Clin. Hypnosis, Iberian Assn. of Sleep Pathology. Roman Catholic. Avocations: music, literature, tennis, hunting. Office: Clinica Ludor Principe de Vergara 31 28001 Madrid Spain Home Phone: (34) 918593848; Office Phone: (34) 917814280. E-mail: luis.dominguez@clinicaludor.com.

DOMINICI, MASSIMO, oncologist, hematologist; b. Lodi, Italy, Feb. 9, 1972; s. Orlando Dominici and Piera Maria Tacchinardi; m. Elisa Fiumana, May 26, 2001; 1 child, Fransesco. MD (hon.), U. Pavia, Italy, 1996. Resident hematology U. Ferrara, Italy, 1996—2000; post-doctoral assoc. St. Jude Children's Rsch. Hosp., Memphis, 2000—03, U. Modena and Reggio Emilia, Italy, 2003—05, asst. prof., 2005—; founder Soc. Forum Italian Rschr. Stem Cells, 2009; founder v.p. biotech. co. Rigenerand Sr., 2009. Hosp. physician dept. onocology and hematology, divsn. oncology Modena U. Hosp., 2003—; prof. med. oncology, sch. medicine U. Modena and Reggio Emilia, 2005—, prof. cellular and molecular therapies in medicine, faculty biotech., 2005—, prin. investigator, lab. cell biology and advanced cancer therapies, 2005—. Contbr. 45 articles to prof. jours. Recipient Young Investigator award, Italian Assn. Against Leukemia, 2004, 2005; grantee, Ministry Health, 2009—, European Cmty., 2010—; Hematology scholar, Vienna U., 1996, Rsch. grant, Italian Ministry Rsch., 2007—10, Italian Assn. Cancer Rsch., 2007—. Mem.: Italian Assn. Cell Culture (assoc.), Am. Soc. Hematology (assoc.), European Soc. Gene Therapy (assoc.), Internat. Soc. Cellular Therapy (assoc.; treas. 2008—). Achievements include discovery of clonogenic endothelial assay form bone marrow; description of the osteogenic potential of marrow derived cells; research in evaluation of the bone marrow microenvironment in hematological malignancies; biology of adult stem cells; the use of adult stem cells as vehicles for cancer therapeutics; patents in field. Office: Univ Modena and Reggio Emilia Via del Pozzo 71 41124 Modena MO Italy Home Phone: 0039-348-8509755; Office Phone: 05900394222858. Office Fax: 0039-059-4223341; Home Fax: 0039-059-4223341. Business E-Mail: massimo.dominici@unimore.it.

DOMINICZAK, ANNA F., medical educator; b. Gdansk, Poland, Aug. 26, 1954; came to Scotland, 1982; d. Jacob and Joanna (Muszkowska) Penson; m. Marek Henryk Dominiczak, Dec. 26, 1976; 1 child, Peter. MD, Med. Sch. Gdansk, 1978, U. Glasgow, 1989. Registrar MRC Blood Pressure Unit, Glasgow, 1986-89, sr. registrar, 1989-91; from lectr. in medicine to sr. lectr. U. Glasgow, 1991-96, reader in medicine, 1996-97, Brit. Heart Found. prof. cardiovasc. medicine, 1997—2010, Regius chair medicine, vice prin., head, Coll. Medicine, Vet. & Life Scis., 2010—. Chief editor Hypertension Jour., 2011—. Editor: Genetics of Hypertension, 1999; chief editor: (jour.) Clin. Sci., 2004. Officer Order of British Empire, 2005. Project grantee Brit. Heart Found., 1998, The Wellcome Trust, 1999, coop. group grantee Med. Rsch. Coun., 1999. Fellow Acad. Med. Scis., Royal Coll. Physicians, Am. Heart Assn., Royal Soc. Edinburgh; mem. Internat. Soc. Hypertension (sec.) Avocations: reading, modern literature. Office: Wolfson Med Sch Bldg University Glasgow University Ave Glasgow G12 8QQ Scotland Home Phone: 441419423742; Office Phone: 441413305420 or 2738.

DOMINIK, JAN, cardiac surgeon, educator; b. Zlín, Czech Republic, May 15, 1944; s. František D. and Olga (Svobodová) Dominiková; m. Karla Dominiková, Dec. 7, 1968. MD, Masaryk U., Brno, Czech Republic, 1967, PhD, 1988. Registrar, sr. registrar dept. surgery U. Brno, Czech Republic, 1967—77, sr. registrar dept. cardiac surgery, 1978—84; cons. cardiac surgeon, dep. dir. Ctr. Cardiovasc. Transplant Surgery, Brno, Czech Republic, 1985-90; assoc. prof. Masaryks U., Brno, Czech Republic, 1990; assoc. prof. surgery, head, surgeon chief dept. cardiac surgery Charles U. Prague, Hradec Králové, Czech Republic, 1991—2004, vice dean sch. medicine, 1997—2003, prof. surgery, 1998—. Cons. cardiac surgeon Hosp. Sanaà, Yemen Arab Republic, 1987; scientific coun. sch. medicine Charles U., Hradec Králové, Czech Republic, 1994—, scientific coun. ministry health cardiovascular diseases, 1993-03; lectr. in field. Author: Cardiac Surgery, 1998, Interactive Cardiac Surgery, 2005, Heart Valve Surgery, 2008; contbr. articles to profl. jours. Mem.: Am. Heart Assn., European Assn. Cardiothoracic Surgery. Avocations: literature, travel. Home: K Rybníku 180 Hradec Králové 50002 Czech Republic Office Phone: 420 49 5833628. Business E-Mail: dominik@fnhk.cz.

DOMINIQUE, DEVANAND ANTHONY, neurosurgeon; b. Hamilton, Can., Sept. 30, 1967; MBBCh, Med. Sch. U. Coll., Dublin, 1992; Pediatric Neurosurgeon, Harvard Med. Sch., 1998. Asst. prof. surgery U. N.D., Grand Forks, 2001—02; asst. prof. neurosurgery Temple U., Phila., 2002—; dir. spinal neurosurgery Temple U. Hosp., Temple U. Children's Med. Ctr. Fellow: Royal Soc. Medicine; mem.: Am. Assn. Neurol. Surgeons, Congress of Neurol. Surgeons. Office: Temple Hosp Dept Neurosurgery 3401 N Broad St Philadelphia PA 19140 Office Phone: 215-707-2000.

DOMINIS, MARIJA, medical educator, researcher; d. Frano Dominis and Zdenka Marok. Postgrad., Sch. Pub. Health Andrija Stampar, Zagreb, Croatia, 1967; MD, Med. Sch., Zagreb, 1966, MSc, 1973, PhD, 1978. Lic. Ministry Health, Zagreb, 1967, cert. in pathology 1974, in cytology. Resident Gen. Hosp. dr. O. Novosel, later U. Hosp. Merkur, Zagreb, 1968—70, tng. in pathology, 1970—74; asst. prof. Med. Sch., full time prof., vice dean for postgrad. studies, 2000—04; head dept. pathology and cytology U. Hosp. Merkur, Zagreb, 1974—. Contbr. scientific papers. ECFMG fellowship, NIH, 1988—89, fellowship, DCA. Mem.: European Assn. for Haematopathology, European Soc. Pathology, Internat. Acad. Cytology, Croatian Med. Assn. Office: Univ Hosp Merkur Zajceva 19 Zagreb 10 000 Croatia Office Phone: 38512431410. Business E-Mail: mara.dominis@zg.htnet.hr.

DOMINO, EDWARD FELIX, physician, clinical pharmacologist, educator; b. Chgo., Nov. 20, 1924; s. James I. and Mary (Dolerzek) D.; m. Antoinette Frances Kaczorowski, Nov. 20, 1948; children: Karen Barbara, Laurence Edward, Debra Ann, Kenneth Edward, Steven Edward. BS, U. Ill., 1948, U. Ill., Chgo., 1949, MS in Pharmacology, MD with honors, 1951. Diplomate Am. Bd. Med. Examiners, Am. Bd. Clin. Pharmacology. Rotating intern Presbyn. Hosp., Chgo., 1951-52; mem. faculty U. Ill., 1951-53, U. Mich. Med. Sch., 1953—, prof. pharmacology, 1962—; pharmacology cons. Lafayette Clinic, Detroit, 1958-67, dir. pharmacology div., 1967-83; vis. prof. neuropsychopharmacology Wayne State U., 1959-73, clin. prof. psychiatry, 1973-80, clin. prof. pharmacology in psychiatry, 1981-86; vis. prof. pharmacology Dept. Neurosurgery U. Occupational and Environ. Health, Kitakyshu, Japan, 1988-89; vis. scientist Japan Marine Sci. and Tech. Ctr., Yokosuka, 1988; vis. lectr. dept. pharmacology Hiroshima (Japan) U. Med. Sch., 1995-96, Wakayama (Japan) U. Med. Sch., 1996; prof. pharmacology U. Mich. Mem. study sect. pharmacology and chemistry NIMH, 1965-69; vis. pharmacologist U.S.-USSR Cultural Exch. Program, 1971; mem. com. on nicotine and smoking antagonist drugs Nat. Cancer Inst., 1972-76; rep. U.S. Pharmacopeia, 1970-79, 97—2001; spl. fellow Nat. Inst. Gen. Med. Scis., 1972-73; mem. ad hoc com. sci. adv. bd. USAF, 1977-78, mem. med. rsch. and devel. adv. panel to surgeon gen. U.S. Army, 1979-82, nat. sci. adv. bd. Brain Info. Svc., UCLA, 1975-81; mem. ad hoc com. on marijuana and health Nat. Acad. Scis., 1981; cons. Policy Analysis Ctr., The Franklin Inst., Chevy Chase, Md., 1983-87, cons. clin. pharmacology VA Med. Ctr. Dept. Psychiatry, Ann Arbor, Mich., 1980—; cons. clin. pharmacology U. Ill. Inst. Aviation, Savoy, 1981-88; Burroughs Wellcome William N. Creasy vis. prof. clin. pharmacology U. Miss. Med. Ctr., Jackson, 1987; hon. staff Shanghai Clin. Ctr. for Endocrine and Metabolic Diseases, Shanghai No. 2 Med. U., Ruijing Hosp. Group, U. Shanghai, 2004; mem. pharm. del. dept. pharm. People to People Amb.Program, Chongquing and Shanghai, 2005. Author and editor books in field; mem. editl. bd. Jour. Clin. Pharmacology and Therapeutics, 1973-98, Jour. Pharmacology and Exptl. Therapeutics, 1958-65, Drug Metabolism Disposition, 1991-93, Pharmacology, Biochemistry and Behavior, 1973-88, Rsch. Comm. on Drugs and Substance Abuse, 1980-82, Neurobiol. Aging, 1980-82; mem. adv. bd., supporting editor Psychopharmacology, 1966-78, Archives Inter. de Pharmacodynam. et Ther, 1976-90; assoc. editor Exptl. Neurology, 1977-80; contbr. articles to med. jours. With USNR, 1943—46. Recipient Sigma Xi prize medicine, 1951; Research award Mich. Soc. Neurology and Psychiatry, 1955; Sci. Exhibit 1st prize Am. Soc. Anesthesiologists, 1963; Sci. Exhibit cert. of merit AMA, 1964; Kravkov Meml. medal acad. bd. Inst. Pharmacology and Chemotherapy of Acad. Med. Sci., USSR, 1968; Cert. of Merit in Tchg. and Rsch., Mich. Psychiat. Assn., 1981; Alumnus award in rsch. and edn. U. Ill., 1981; Cert. for Service with High Distinction U.S. Med. Rsch. and Svc. Command, 1979-82, Early Contbr. to Dream or REM Sleep award, 2003. Fellow Am. Coll. Neuropsychopharm. (life); mem. Am. Soc. Pharmacology and Exptl. Therapeutics (emeritus), N.Y. Acad. Sci. (emeritus), Internat. Soc. Cerebral Blood Flow and Metabolism (emeritus), Washtenaw County Med. Soc. (emeritus), Soc. Exptl. Biology and Medicine (emeritus), Internat. Soc. Neurochemistry (emeritus), Mich. Psychiat. Assn. (assoc. emeritus), Am. Psychiat. Assn. (emeritus), Soc. Toxicology (emeritus), Sigma Xi (emeritus, councilor 1961-63), Alpha Omega Alpha, Collegium Internat. Neuro-Psychopharmacologicum Home and Office: 3071 Exmoor Rd Ann Arbor MI 48104-4122 Office Phone: 734-764-9115.

DOMITROVIC, ROBERT, medical educator; b. Sisak, Mar. 22, 1968; PhD, Faculty Pharmacy and Biochemistry, 1999. Assoc. prof. Faculty Medicine, 2007—. Office: B Branchetta 20 Rijeka 51000 Croatia Business E-Mail: robertd@medri.hr.

DON, MANUEL, medical researcher; s. Chun and Shee Chin Don; m. Margery Mai Yeung, Aug. 20, 1967; children: Kendra Marie D'Ercole, Erica Lynn Chien, Angela Noelle. BA, U. Calif., Berkeley, 1964; MA, U. Ariz., Tucson, 1966; PhD, Stanford U., Calif., 1971. Asst. rschr. U. Calif., Irvine, 1973—76; dept. head, rschr. House Ear Inst., LA, 1976—. Study sect. mem., chair NIH, Bethesda, Md., 1988—91. Contbr. articles to profl. jours. Ch. officer Cornerstone United Meth. Ch., Placentia, Calif., 1980—2002. Grant, NIH, 1990—94, 2000—04. Mem.: Internat. Evoked Response Audiometry Study Group (treas. 1991—). Achievements include patents for sininger YS, hyde ML: method for detection of auditory evoked potentials using point optimized variance ratio; acoustic tumor detection using stacked derived-band ABR amplitude; method for aligning derived-band responses based on integration of detrended derived-band ABRs; patents pending for diagnosis of the presence of cochlear hydrops using observed auditory brainstem responses. Avocations: crossword puzzles, bowling, tennis, guitar. Office: House Ear Inst 2100 W Third St Los Angeles CA 90057 Office Fax: 213-413-6739. Business E-Mail: mdon@hei.org.

DONAHOE, MICHAEL P., internist; MD, Drexel U., Phila. Diplomate Am. Bd. Internal Medicine, Am. Bd. Internal Medicine-critical care medicine, Am. Bd. Internal Medicine-pulmonary disease. Resident Univ. Pitts., Pa., fellow; hosp. affiliations include Univ. Pitts. Med. Ctr. Magee-Womens Hosp., Univ. Pitts. Med. Ctr. McKeesport, Univ. Pitts. Med. Ctr. Presbyn., Univ. Pitts. Med. Ctr. Shadyside; pulmonary, allergy and critical care medicine divsn. Univ. Pitts. Med. Ctr. Comprehensive Lung Ctr. Office: University of Pittsburgh Medical Center Comprehensive Lung Center 4th Fl 3601 5th Ave Pittsburgh PA 15213 Office Phone: 412-648-6161.

DONAHOO, JAMES SAUNDERS, cardiothoracic surgeon; b. Jackson, Tenn., Sept. 30, 1937; s. Henry Amos and Ruby Burt (Welch) D.; m. Rose Carol Manasco, June 24, 1961; children: Paige, James. AB, Birmingham So. Coll., 1959; MD, Med. Coll. Ala., 1963. Chief resident surgeon Vanderbilt U. Hosp., Nashville, 1969; chief resident cardiac surgery Johns Hopkins U., Balt., 1971; asst. prof. surgery Johns Hopkins U. Sch. of Medicine, Balt., 1971-75; assoc. prof. surgery Johns Hopkins U., Balt., 1975-82, Jefferson Med. Coll., Phila., 1983-89; prof. cardiothoracic surgery Univ. Medicine Dentistry N.J., Newark, 1989—. Chief thoracic surgery East Orange (N.J.) VA Hosp., 1989—; chief divsn. cardiothoracic surgery N.J. Med. Sch., 1999-02. Editor: Practical Reviews in Surgery, 1975-82; contbr. articles to profl. jours. Col. USAR, 1964-92, Op. Desert Storm, 1991. Decorated Army Def. Svc. medal, Army Achievement medal; recipient Gold Medal Paper award S.E. Surg. Conv., 1967, Disting. Alumnus award U. Ala. Sch. Medicine, 2009. Fellow ACS; mem. Am. Assn. Thoracic Surgery, So. Surg. Assn., So. Thoracic Surg. Assn. (coun. mem., Osler Abbott award 1982), N.Y. Soc. Thoracic Surgery, N.J. Soc. Thoracic Surgeons (pres. 1994), Elkridge Harford Hunt Club (exec. com. 1980), Merion Cricket Club, Baltusrol Golf Club, Alpha Omega Alpha. Episcopalian. Avocations: polo, fox-hunting, opera, art. Home: 71 Hillcrest Ave Summit NJ 07901-2012 Office Phone: 973-676-1000 1844. Personal E-mail: jdonahoo37@gmail.com.

DONAHUE, DONALD A., health facility administrator, educator; b. Jersey City, Aug. 11, 1954; MBA, Baruch Coll., 1989; D in Health Edn., A.T. Still U., 2009. Mng. ptnr. Diogenec Group LLP, 2005; sr. fellow and program dir., health policy & preparedness Potomac Inst. Policy Studies, 2006—; asst. prof. U. Md., 2010—. Bd. dir. Melwood, 2008. Dep. surgeon, plans and fiscal adminstrn. USAR, 1997—2004. Decorated Legion of Merit US Army, Meritorious Svc. medal, Joint Svc. Commendation medal, Army Commendation medal, Army Achievement medal; recipient Hammer award, 2000, Excellence award, Dept. Vets. Affairs, 2000. Avocations: painting, travel, sculpting. Home: 911 Massachusetts Ave NE Washington DC 20002 Office Phone: 202-701-6234. Home Fax: 202-543-7113. E-mail: donald.donahue@diogenec.com

DONAHUE, JOHN EDWARD, physician; b. Revere, Mass., Apr. 27, 1966; s. Edward Francis and Camille (Santoro) D BS summa cum laude, Tufts U., Boston, 1988; MD, Tufts U. Sch. Med., Medford, 1992. Diplomate Am. Bd. Psychiatry and Neurology, Am. Bd. Pathology, Nat. Bd. Med. Examiners. Intern St. Elizabeth's Med. Ctr., Boston, 1992—93; resident New Eng. Med. Ctr., Boston, 1993—96; fellow R.I. Hosp., Providence, 1996—99; dir. neuropathology NJ Neurosci. Inst., Edison, 1999—2003, asst program dir. neurology residency program, 2001—03; asst. prof. neuroscience Sch. Grad. Med. Edn. Seton Hall U., South Orange, NJ, 1999—2003; attending neuropathologist RI Hosp., 2003—; assoc. prof. pathology & neurology Warren Alpert Med. Sch. Brown U., 2011—. Asst. prof. pathology & neurology Warren Alpert Med. Sch. Brown U., 2003—11; dir. neuropathology rotation RI Hosp., 2005—; co-dir. brain scis. Alpert Med. Sch., mem. animal welfare com. RI Hosp., 2006—11; mem. awards com. Am. Assn. Nueropathologists, 2010—; mem. AANP, resident In-Svc. Examination Liasion Com., 2011—. Mem. editl. bd. Jour. Neuropathology and Exptl. Neurology, 2007—; contbr. articles to profl. jours.; ad hoc reviewer in field. Recipient David L. Kasdon prize Tufts U. Sch. Medicine, 1992, Second Pl. award Gustaf Retzius Neuroanatomy Competition, 1997, 98, champion 1999, Dean's Tchg. Excellence award Brown Med. Sch., 2004, 05, 06, 07, 08, 10, Alzheimer's Disease Clin. Scientist Devel. award NIH, 2006—10; Recognition Tchg. award, 2009-11. Mem.: AAAS, RI Path. Soc., RI Neurol. Soc., Internat. Soc. Advance Alzheimer Rsch. Treatment, Children's Oncology Group, Brown Inst. Brain Sci., NY Acad. Scis., Neuroplex Inc., Soc. Neurosci., Am. Assn. Neuropathologists, Am. Acad. Neurology, Mass. Med. Soc., Phi Beta Kappa. Roman Catholic. Achievements include breakthroughs in Alzheimer's disease research and neuro-oncology. Avocations: swimming, video games, computers. Office: RI Hosp Dept Pathology 593 Eddy St APC12115 Providence RI 02903 Office Phone: 401-444-7968. Business E-Mail: JDonahue3@Lifespan.org.

DONALD, ALEXANDER GRANT, psychiatrist, educator; b. Darlington, SC, Jan. 24, 1928; s. Raymond George and Chesnut Evans (McIntosh) Donald; m. Emma Louise Coggeshall, Oct. 25, 1958; children: Sandy, Mary Chesnut, Marion Lide. BS, Davidson Coll., 1948; MD, Med. U. S.C., 1952. Diplomate Am. Bd. Psychiatry and Neurology. Intern Jefferson Med. Coll., 1952-53; resident in psychiatry Walter Reed Hosp., 1956-59; dir. Mental Health Clinic, Florence, SC, 1962-66; dept. commr. S.C. Dept. Mental Health, 1966-67; dir. William S Hall Psychiat. Inst., Columbia, 1967-90; prof., chmn. dept. neuropsychiatry and behavioral scis. Sch. Medicine, U. S.C., Columbia, 1975-90, Disting. prof. neuropsychiatry, assoc. dean ednl. planning, 1990-91, Disting. prof. emeritus, 1991—. Bd. dirs. Health Resource Found.; trustee Richland Meml. Hosp., 1993—2002, vice-chmn., 1997, chmn., 1999; bd. dirs. S.C. Inst. Med. Edn. and Rsch., pres., 1992—96; trustee Palmetto Health Alliance, 1999—2004, vice-chmn., 2003; steward United Way of Midlands, 2003—08. Fellow: Am. Psychiat. Assn. (pres. S.C. chpt. 1967), Am. Coll. Psychiatrists; mem.: AMA, So. Psychiat. Assn. (v.p.), Columbia Med. Soc. (v.p. 1981, del. 1981, pres. 1989—90), Evening Music Club, Alpha Omega Alpha. Presbyterian. Office: U SC Sch Medicine 3555 Harden St Ext Ste 104 Columbia SC 29203-6894 Personal E-mail: grantd@bellsouth.net.

DONALDSON, DAVID, pathologist; b. Birmingham, England, Feb. 13, 1936; s. Henry and Esther Donaldson. MB, ChB, U. Birmingham, Eng., 1959. House physician Selly Oak Hosp., Birmingham,

1959—60; house surgeon Children's Hosp., Birmingham, 1960; sr. house officer in clin. pathology Queen Elizabeth Hosp., Birmingham, 1960—61; asst. resident med. officer, registrar in gen. medicine Gen. Infirmary, Leeds, England, 1961-62; registrar in gen. medicine Victoria Hosp., Keighley, England, 1963-64; lectr., hon. sr. registrar in chem. pathology Inst. Neurology, Nat. Hosp Nervous Diseases, London, 1964—70; cons. chem. pathology East Surrey Hosp., Redhill, Surrey, England, 1970—2001, clin. dir. pathology, 1991—94; cons. chem. pathology Crawley Hosp., West Sussex, England, 1970—2001, BUPA Gatwick Park Hosp., Horley, Surrey, England, 1984—2006. Vice chmn. med. sub-com. Marie Curie Meml. Found., London, 1978—83; chmn. South West Thames Chem. Pathology Adv. Group South Thames Regional Health Authority, London, 1995—2000; lectr. clin. biochemistry London South Bank U., 1997—. Author: Psychiatric Disorders with a Biochemical Basis, 1998; co-author: Essential Diagnostic Tests in Biochemistry and Haematology, 1971, Diagnostic Function Tests in Chem. Pathology, 1989; contbr. chapters to books, articles to over 100 profl. jours.; dep. hon. editor, mem. editl. bd. Jour. Royal Soc. for the Promotion of Health, 1997—2004. Fellow: Hunterian Soc., Med. Soc. London, Internat. Coll. Nutrition (life, Mori Felicitation award 2002), Royal Soc. Medicine, Inst. Biology, Royal Soc. for the Promotion of Health, Royal Geog. Soc. (life), Royal Soc. Chemistry, Royal Coll. Pathologists, Royal Coll. Physicians; mem.: AAAS, Brit. Med. Assn. (chmn. East Surrey divsn. 1992—93), N.Y. Acad. Sci., Brit. Assn. Advancement Sci., HEART UK (Hyperlipidaemic Edn. and Rsch. Trust UK), Assn. Clin. Pathologists, Assn. Clin. Biochemists, Harveian Soc. London, Worshipful Soc. of Apothecaries, London (faculty of history and philosophy of medicine and pharmacy). Avocations: piano, music, history of medicine. Home: 5 Woodfield Way Redhill Surrey RH1 2DP England

DONALDSON, JAMES OSWELL, III, neurologist, educator; b. Butler, Pa., July 19, 1942; s. James Oswell Jr. and Estelle Mathilda (Unverzagt) D.; m. Mary Hoopingarner, Aug. 23, 1969 (div. Dec. 1983); 1 child, Andrew Robert; m. Susan McKernin, Nov. 3, 1984; stepchildren: Brendan McDonald, Ian McDonald. BS, Haverford Coll., 1964; MD, U. Pa., 1968. Diplomate Am. Bd. Psychiatry and Neurology, Am. Bd. Internal Medicine. Intern in medicine Hosp. of U. Pa., Phila., 1968-69, resident, 1969-70, resident in neurology, 1974-76; hon. house physician Nat. Hosp. for Nervous Diseases, London, 1973-74, sr. vis. fellow, 1991; asst. prof. neurology U. Conn. Sch. Medicine, Farmington, 1977-82, assoc. prof., 1982-88, prof., 1988—. Author: Neurology of Pregnancy, 1978, 2nd edit., 1989. Maj. M.C., U.S. Army, 1970-73. Fellow ACP, Am. Acad. Neurology; mem. Am. Neurol. Assn. Office: U Conn Health Ctr 263 Farmington Ave Farmington CT 06030-1840 Home Phone: 860-521-8842; Office Phone: 860-679-3186.

DONALDSON, SARAH SUSAN, radiologist; b. Portland, Oreg., Apr. 20, 1939; BS, RN, U. Oreg., 1961; MD, Harvard U., 1968. Intern U. Wash., 1968—69; resident in radiol. therapy Stanford Med. Ctr., Calif., 1969—72; fellow in pediatric oncology Inst. Gustave-Roussy, 1972—73; prof. radiol. oncology Stanford U. Sch. Medicine., 1973—, Catherine and Howard Avery prof., dept. radiation. Recipient Elizabeth Blackwell medal, Am. Med. Women's Assn., 2005. Mem.: NIH. Office: Stanford U Med Ctr Dept Radio/Oncology 875 Blake Wilbur Dr Stanford CA 94305-5847 Business E-Mail: sarah2@stanford.edu.

DONALISIO, MARIA RITA, epidemiologist; b. Cerqueira César, São Paulo, Brazil, Oct. 13, 1957; MD, UNICAMP, PhD, 1995, U. Kans., 2010. Coord., epidemiology Faculty Med. Scientist, 2011—. Avocation: mountain climbing. Office: DMPS FCM UNICAMP Tessalia Vieira Camargo Campinas Sao Paulo 13083887 Brazil Office Fax: 55 19 35218044. Business E-Mail: donalisi@fcm.unicamp.br.

DONELAN, PETER ANDREW, dermatologist; b. Memphis, Nov. 13, 1953; s. Richard T. and Irene M. (Jacobson) D. BA in Chemistry, Wake Forest U., 1975; MD, U. South Fla., 1978. Diplomate, Am. Bd. Dermatology. Intern U. South Fla., Tampa, Fla., 1978-79, resident in internal medicine, 1979-80, resident in dermatology, 1980-83, assoc. clin. prof. medicine, 1984—; instr. dermatologic surgery VA Hosp., 1993—; pvt. practice, Tampa, 1983—. Chief dermatology Tampa Gen. Hosp., 1987-88, U. Conn. Hosp., 1993—. Mem. editorial bd. Bull. Hillsboro County Med. Soc., 1987—. Named to Best Doctors in Am., 1996—. Fellow Am. Acad. Dermatology, Am. Soc. Dermatol. Surgery; mem. Fla. Dermatol. Soc., Leaders Soc. of Dermatology Found., Fla. Med. Soc., Green Jacket Club, Pres.'s Coun. Avocations: golf, skiing. Office: 3000 E Fletcher Ave Ste 200 Tampa FL 33613-4644 Office Phone: 813-972-1229.

DONG, GUO NIAN, cardiologist; b. Ezhou, Hubei, Sept. 3, 1963; BS, Tongji Med. U., 1986; MD, Tongji Med. Coll., 1994. Chief Dept. Cardiovasc. Surgery, Union Hosp., Tongji Med. Coll., Huazhong U. Sci. and Tech., 2008—. Mem., standing com. Chinese Soc. Thoracic and Cardiovasc. Surgery, 2008—, Chinese Assn. Cardiovasc. Surgeons, 2008—; bd. dirs. Jour. Clin. Cardiology, 2008—. Master: Nat. High Tech. R & D Program China. Office: 1277 Jiefang Rd Union Hosp Wuhan Hubei 430022 China Office Fax: 86-027-85351636. E-mail: hh09ronaldo@yahoo.com.cn.

DONG, KYUNG RAE, healthcare educator; b. Seongnam-Si, GyeongGi-Do, Republic of Korea, Mar. 11, 1972; M, Yonsei U., 2002; PhD, Chosun U., 2010. Radiol. technologist Asan Med. Ctr., 1996—2003; asst. prof. Gwangyang Health Coll., 2004—07, Gwangju Health Coll. U., 2008—. Editor Korean Soc. Digital Imaging in Medicine, 2011; editl. staff Korean Assn. Radiation Protection, 2011. Recipient Young Med. Physicist award, Korean Soc. Med. Physics. Mem.: Korean Radiol. Technologists Assn., Korean Soc. Radiol. Sci., Korean Soc. Med. Physics, Korean Assn. Radiation Protection, Korean Soc. Digital Imaging Medicine. Avocation: golf. Office: Dept Radiology 683 Shinchang-Dong Gwangju Gwangsang-Gu 506-701 Republic of Korea Office Fax: 82-62-958-7669.

DONG, ZHENGCHAO, psychology professor, researcher; b. China, Sept. 28, 1955; Dr. rer. nat, U. Bremen, 2002. Asst. prof. Columbia U., 2005. Mem.: Internat. Soc. Magnetic Resonance Medicine. Office: 1051 Riverside Dr Unit 74 New York NY 10032 Personal E-mail: zhengchaodong@gmail.com.

DONG, ZHIHUI, surgeon; b. Jiangsu, China, Nov. 4, 1973; D, Fudan U., 2006. Physician Zhongshan Hosp., Fudan U., 2006—. Recipient 2nd prize, Ministry Edn., China, 3rd prize, Shanghai Mcpl. Sci. and Tech. Commn.; Shanghai Talent Devel. grant, Shanghai Mcpl. Human Resources and Social Security Bur., grant, Nat. Nature Sci. Found. China, Internat. scholar, Soc. Vascular Surgery US. Mem.: Internat. Soc. Endovascular Specialist, Soc. Vascular Surgery. Avocation: ping pong/table tennis. Office: 180 Fenglin Rd Shanghai 200032 China Personal E-mail: dzh926@126.com.

DONG AH, SHIN, neurosurgeon, educator; b. Taegu, Republic of Korea, Dec. 9, 1972; MD, Yonsei U., 1998, PhD, 2009. Asst. prof. CHA U., 2007—. Clin. fellow Yonsei U., 2006—07. Mem.: Korean Spinal Neurosurgery Soc. (Korean Jour. Spine award). Avocation: computers. Office: 351 Yatapdong Bundanggu Seongnam Kyonggido 463-712 Republic of Korea

DONGWU, LIU, engineering educator; b. Heze, Shandong, China, Feb. 16, 1978; MS, Shandong Normal U., 1998. Educator, Analysis and Testing Ctr. Shandong U. Tech., 2006—. Office: 12 Zhangzhou Rd Zibo Shandong 255049 China Office Fax: 86-5332786781. Business E-Mail: liudongwu@sdut.edu.cn.

DONIS, RUBEN, federal agency administrator, researcher, virologist; Molecular genetics team leader Centers for Disease Control & Prevention, Atlanta, mem. influenza branch, swine flu chief, chief molecular virology & vaccines branch. Office: MGS - Influenza Branch MS G/1 1600 Clifton Rd N E Atlanta GA 30333 Office Phone: 404-639-4968. Office Fax: 404-639-2334. E-mail: r.donis@emory.edu.

DONKOV, IVO ILIEV, urologist, researcher; b. Dobrich, Bulgaria, Apr. 14, 1967; s. Iliya Ivanov Donkov and Ganka Todorova Donkova. MD, Med. U. Sofia, Bulgaria, 1994, PhD in Biomaterials Compliance and Use in Urethroplasties, 2006. Cert. Bulgarian Bd. Urology, 1999, Ednl. Commn. Fgn. Med. Grads., 1997, Med. Coun. of Can., 2003, Inst. Clin. Rsch., UK, 2004. Higher urol. trainee Alexander's U. Hosp., Sofia, 1994—2000, cons., attending academic urologist, 2000—04, hon. attending urologist, 2000—01, cons., attending urologist, 2006—; trust urologist U. Coll. London, 2004—05. Attending urologist Lincoln County Hosp., 2007. Contbr. more than 100 articles to profl. jours., chpts. to books. Mem. Internat. Urology Bd., Arthem, Netherlands, 2005—07. Capt. Med. Corps Bulgarian armed forces, 1994—2005. Nominee IBC's Leading Health Profls. of World, 2008; fellow, European Bd. Urology, 2005—06; European scholar, 2002, 2004, 2004, Corp. fellow, 2003, COOK Urol., 2007. Fellow: Inst. Clin. rsch. (hon.). Achievements include invention of implementation of small intestinal submucosa for augmentation urethroplasty for strictures of the bulbar urethra; first to tissue characteristics and complience in endoscopic urethroplasty; development of implementation of S.I.S. in penile thickening. Avocations: travel, wine expert. Home: Kv Hadji Dimitar Block 71 Ent E Sofia 1510 Bulgaria Office: Med U Sofia Dept Urology 1 G Sofiiski Sofia 1431 Bulgaria Personal E-mail: donkow@doctors.org.uk, idonkov@hotmail.com.

DONMA, MUSTAFA METIN, pediatrician, researcher; b. Adana, Turkey, Feb. 26, 1960; s. Mustafa Sadik and Hatice D. Diploma, Faculty of Medicine, Adana, 1982. Physician Min. Health, Trabzon, 1982-85, 86-87; military physician Gendarme Sch. Commandership, Ankara, Turkey, 1985-86; rsch. asst. Faculty of Medicine, Diyarbakir, Turkey, 1987-91; staff pediatrician Min. Health, Bakirkoy State Hosp., Istanbul, 1991—2001; assoc. prof. dr. pediats. Namik Kemel U., Med. Faculty, 2001—11, prof. dr. pediats., 2011—. With Min Health Suleymaniye Ednl. Res. Hosp. Istanbul, 2001- Contbr. articles to prof. jours., including Biol. Trace Element Rsch., Ultrasound Med. Biol., Med. Hypotheses, Brain and Devel., Pediat. Neurology and Pediats. Internat. jours. Lt. Gendarme Sch. Commandership, 1985-86. Recipient Scientific Rsch. award, Ministry Health, awards Turkish Scientific and Tech. Rsch. Fund; grantee Norwegian Ctr. Child Rsch., 1st Grade Sci. Res. Perf., Aknowledgement Cert. Istanbul Govt. Mem. Turkish Med. Assn., Turkish Pediatric Assn. Avocations: composing texts for music, playing guitar, swimming, painting exhibitions, floriculture; achievements include bringing new perspectives to evaluation of pediat. malignancies, first study in clin. use of hair trace element analysis in prognosis of pediat. malignancies, first study on piracetam's mechanisms of action in treatment of breath-holding spells, introduction of values for weight, length and head circumference in Turkish children, head of large scaled study performed on newborns, contributions to trace elements and phyto chemicals fields. Home: Atakoy 11 Kisim-MESA Villa #22 2F6 34158 Istanbul Turkey Office: Namik Kemal University Med Faculty Tekirdag Turkey Business E-Mail: mdonma@nku.edu.tr.

DONNAN, GEOFFREY ALAN, neurology educator, researcher; b. Sydney, Apr. 13, 1948; s. Victor Tennyson and Shirley Isobel (May) Donnan; m. Elizabeth Patricia Ayton, Nov. 6, 1976; children: Clare, Julia. BS in Medicine, Melbourne U., Australia, 1972, MD, 1980. Staff neurologist Austin Hosp., Melbourne, 1983-93; prof. neurology Melbourne U., 1993—; founding dir. Nat. Stroke Rsch. Inst., Melbourne, 1995—2009; dir. dept. neurology Austin Hosp., Melbourne, 1996—; dir. Howard Florey Neurosci. Inst., Melbourne, 2009—. Author: Lacunar and Other Subcortical Infarctions, 1995; co-author: Interventional Therapy in Acute Stroke, 1997. Recipient William M. Feinberg award for excellence in clin. stroke, 2007, Bethlehem Griffiths Rsch. Found. medal, 2008. Fellow: Royal Australian Coll. Physicians; mem.: Australian Assn. Neurologists. Office: Howard Florey Inst Level 2 Alan Gilbert Bldg 161 Barry St Carlton South VIC 3053 Australia *

DONNELLY, BARBARA SCHETTLER, retired medical technologist; b. Sweetwater, Tenn., Dec. 2, 1933; d. Clarence G. and Irene Elizabeth (Brown) Schettler; children: Linda Ann, Richard Michael. AA, Tenn. Wesleyan Coll., 1952; BS, U. Tenn., 1954; cert. med. tech., Erlanger Hosp. Sch. Med. Tech., 1954; postgrad., So. Meth. U., 1980-81. Med. technologist Erlanger Hosp., Chattanooga, 1953-57, St. Luke's Episcopal Hosp., Tex. Med. Ctr., Houston, 1957-58, 62; engrng. R&D SCI Systems, Inc., Huntsville, Ala., 1974-76; cons. hematology systems Abbott Labs., Dallas, 1976-77; hematology specialist Dallas, Irving, Tex., 1977-81; tech. specialist microbiology systems Irving, Tex., 1981-83; coord. tech. svc. clin. chemistry systems, 1983-84; coord. customer tng. clin. chemistry systems, 1984-87; supr. clin. chemistry tech. svcs., 1987-88; supr. clin. chemistry customer support ctr., 1988-93; supr. clin. chemistry and x-systems customer support ctr., 1993-97; ret., 1997. Contbr. articles on cytology to profl. jours. Mem. Am. Soc. Clin. Pathologists (cert. med. technologist), Am. Soc. Microbiology, Nat. Assn. Female Execs., U. Tenn. Alumni Assn., Chi Omega. Republican. Methodist. Home: 204 Greenbriar Ln Colleyville TX 76034-8616

DONNELLY, MARGARET T., state agency administrator, public health service officer, former state legislator; b. Alton, Ill., Jan. 14, 1954; m. David Riedel; children: Julia Riedel, Adam Riedel. B in Social Work, St. Louis U., Mo., 1975, MSW, 1977, JD, 1988. Social worker, Wis., Mo. Dept. Social Services; pvt. practice atty.; mem. Dist. 73 Mo. House of Reps., 2002—08; dir. Mo. Dept. Health & Sr. Services, 2009—. Mem. Ferguson-Florissant Sch. Bd., 1986—92; del. Dem. Nat. Conv., 1996; bd. dirs. Beyond Housing, 1981—84; chair Commn. Abused Women and Children, 1991—92; mem. METRO Bd. Commrs., 1999—2002; bd. dirs. Family Support Network, 2003—. Mem.: Women Lawyers Assn., Mo. Bar (mem., family law sect.), Bar Assn. Met. St. Louis, Richmond Heights Hist. Soc., FOCUS, Family & Domestic Violence Coun. St. Louis County. Democrat. Office: Mo Dept Health & Sr Svcs PO Box 570 Jefferson City MO 65102 Office Phone: 573-751-6400. Office Fax: 573-751-6010.

DONNER, THOMAS W., endocrinologist, educator; MD, U. Va., 1986. Diplomate Am. Bd. Internal Medicine, 1989, Am. Bd. Internal Medicine-endocrinology, diabetes and metabolism, 2007. Tng. Univ. Va., 1986; resident internal medicine Univ. Md., Baltimore, 1986—89, fellow endocrinology, diabetes and metabolism, 1989—91, assoc. prof. medicine; hosp. affiliation includes Johns Hopkins Hosp. Office: Johns Hopkins University Ste 333 1830 E Monument St Baltimore MD 21287 Office Phone: 410-955-7139. Office Fax: 410-614-9586.

DONOFF, R. BRUCE, dean, oral surgeon, dental educator; BSc cum laude, Bklyn. Coll., 1963; DMD, Harvard U., 1967, MD, 1973. Clin. fellow in oral surgery Harvard U. Sch. Dental Medicine, Boston, 1969-71, asst. prof. oral surgery, 1974-78, assoc. prof. oral and maxillofacial surgery, 1978-83, acting chmn. dept. oral and maxillofacial surgery, 1982-83, chmn., 1983-93, prof., 1983—, dean and Walter C. Guralnick disting. prof. oral and maxillofacial surgery, 1991—. Bd. mem. Friends of the Nat. Inst. of Dental and Craniofacial Rsch. Contbr. articles to profl. jours.; editor: MGH Manual of Oral and Maxillofacial Surgery. Mem. of editl. bd. Jour. of Oral and Maxillofacial Surgery, Mass. Dental Soc. Jour. Recipient William J. Gies Found. award, 1993, 2d place award Am. Soc. Oral Surgeons, 1969, Disting. Alumni and Faculty awards from the Harvard Sch. of Dental Medicine. Fellow AAAS; mem. Omicron Kappa Upsilon. Office Phone: 617-432-1401. Office Fax: 617-432-4266. Business E-Mail: bruce_donoff@hsdm.harvard.edu.

DONOGHUE, JOHN PHILLIP, neuroscience educator, neurotechnology company executive; b. Cambridge, Mass., Mar. 22, 1949; s. John P. and Nanette L. (Maxwell) D.; m. Karen L. Kerman, Oct. 9, 1982; children: Jacob, Noah. AB, Boston U., 1971; MS in Anatomy, U. Vt., 1976; PhD in Neurosci., Brown U., 1979. Asst. prof. Brown U. Ctr. Neural Sci., Providence, 1984-88, assoc. prof., 1988-91; chmn., dept. neuroscience Brown U., Providence, 1991—, Henry Merritt Wriston prof., exec. dir., Brain Science Program, 1998—; founder, chief scientific officer, dir. Cyberkinetics Neurotechnology Systems, Inc., Foxborough, Mass., 2001—. Mem. advisory panel NIH Neurology and Mental Health Inst.; mem., space med. panel NASA. Assoc. editor Jour. Neurosci., 1995—, Metabolic Brain Disease, 1989-93; contbr. articles to profl. jours. Basil O'Connor fellow March of Dimes Found., 1985; nominee Rave award in Medicine, WIRED, 2005. Mem. AAAS, Am. Physiological Soc., Soc. Neurosci., Internat. Brain Rsch. Orgn, Fedn. Am. Socs. for Exptl. Biology. Office: Brown U Dept Neurosci PO Box 1953 Providence RI 02912-1953 also: Cyberkinetics STE 101 124 Washington St Foxboro MA 02035-1368 Office Phone: 508-549-9981, 401-863-2701. Office Fax: 508-549-9985. Business E-Mail: John_Donoghue@brown.edu.

DONOGHUE, MICHAEL JOHN, biologist, educator, museum director; b. Chgo., June 14, 1952; BS in Botany and Plant Pathology, Mich. State U., 1976; PhD in Biology, Harvard U., 1982. Asst. prof. biology San Diego State U., 1982—85; asst. prof. Dept. Ecology and Evolutionary Biology U. Ariz., 1985—88, assoc. prof., 1988—90, prof., 1990—92, adj. prof., 1993—99; prof. biology Harvard U., 1993—2000; dir. Harvard U. Herbaria, 1995—99; vis. prof. Stanford U., 1998—99; G. Evelyn Hutchinson prof. Dept. Ecology and Evolutionary Biology Yale U., 2000—, joint faculty, Sch. Forestry and Environment. Studies, 2000—, chmn. Dept. Ecology and Evolutionary Biology, 2001—02; cur. botany Peabody Mus. Natural History, 2000—, dir., 2003—. Fellow: Am. Acad. Arts and Sciences; mem.: NAS. Office: Yale Univ Environ Sci Ctr 21 Sachem St PO Box 208105 New Haven CT 06520-8105 Mailing: Peabody Mus Natural History Yale Univ 170 Whitney Ave PO Box 208118 New Haven CT 06520-8118 Office Phone: 203-432-2074, 203-432-3752. Office Fax: 203-432-3758, 203-432-5176. E-mail: michael.donoghue@yale.edu.

DONOHUE, JOYCE MORRISSEY, biochemist, dietician, educator; b. Holyoke, Mass., Jan. 27, 1940; d. Richard Charles and Anna Elizabeth (Joyce) Morrissey; m. John Thomas Donohue, Jan. 27, 1973; children: Maura Joyce, John Thomas, Sean Richard, Eric Patrick. BS, Framingham State Coll., Mass., 1961; MS, U. Mass., 1964; PhD, U. NH, 1972. Cert. secondary sch. tchr., Mass.; registered dietitian. Tchr. West Springfield (Mass.) H.S., 1962—66; instr. Framingham State Coll., 1966—68, asst. prof. biochemistry and nutrition, 1971—72, assoc. prof., 1972—73; adj. prof. No. Va. C.C., Annandale, 1974—2008, Va. Poly. Inst. and State U., Falls Church, 1979—97; health scientist VJ Cicconi & Assocs., Woodbridge, Va., 1981—89; toxicology svc. mgr. Law Environ. Washington Svc. Ctr., Woodbridge, 1989—90; program mgr., toxicologist ICAIR/Life Sys. Inc., Arlington, Va., 1990—94; mgr. toxicology NSF Internat., Washington, 1994—96; health scientist, Office of Water U.S. EPA, Washington, 1996—. Mem. Prince William County Wetlands Bd., 1989—; mem. dietetics program adv. com. James Madison U., Va., 1997—. Recipient Alumni Achievement award, Framingham State Coll., 1986. Mem. AAAS, Am. Dietetic Assn. (cert.), No. Va. Dietetic Assn., Sigma Xi. Home: 11979 William And Mary Cir Woodbridge VA 22192-1314 Office: USEPA 1200 Pennsylvania Ave NW Mail Code 4304T Washington DC 20460 Business E-Mail: donohue.joyce@epa.gov.

DONOHUGH, DONALD LEE, physician; b. LA, Apr. 12, 1924; s. William Noble and Florence Virginia (Shelton) D.; m. Virginia Eskew McGregor, Sept. 12, 1950; children: Ruth, Laurel, Marilee, Carol, Greg; m. Beatrice Ivany Redick, Dec. 3, 1976 (dec. 2005). BS, U.S. Naval Acad., 1946; MD, U. Calif., San Francisco, 1956; MPH and Tropical Medicine, Tulane U., 1961. Diplomate Am. Bd. Internal Medicine. Intern U. Hosp., San Diego, 1956—57; resident Monterey County Hosp., 1957—58; dir. med. svc. U.S. Dept. Interior, Am.

Samoa, 1958—60; instr. Tulane U. Med. Sch., New Orleans, 1960—63; resident Tulane Svc. VA and Charity Hosp., New Orleans, 1961—63; cons. Internat. Ctr. for Rsch and Tng., Costa Rica, 1961—63; asst. prof. medicine and preventive medicine La. State U. Sch. Medicine, 1962—63, assoc. prof., 1963—65; vis. prof. U. Costa Rica, 1963—65; faculty advisor, head of AID program U. Costa Rica Med. Sch., 1965—67; dir. med. svcs. Med. Ctr. U. Calif. (formerly Orange County Hosp.), Irvine, 1967—69; assoc. clin. prof. U. Calif., Irvine, 1967—79, clin. prof., 1980—85; pvt. practice Tustin, Calif., 1970—80; with Joint Commn. on Accreditation of Hosp., 1981; cons. Kauai, Hawaii, 1981—. Author: The Middle Years, 1981, Practice Management, 1986, Kauai, 1988, 4th edit., 1992, Our Ancestors, 1995, The Story of Koloa, 2001, (second edition, 2002); co-translator; Rashomon (Ryonosuke Akutagawa), 1950; also numerous articles. Lt. USN, 1946-52, capt. USNR, 1966-84. Fellow ACP (life); mem. Delta Omega. Independent. Episcopalian. Personal E-mail: dldondhugh1@gmail.com.

DONOVAN, DONALD T., otolaryngologist, educator; Attended, Harvard U.; MD, Baylor Coll. of Medicine, 1976. Diplomate Am. Bd. Otolaryngology, 1981. Resident surgery Baylor Coll. of Medicine, Houston, 1977—78, resident otolaryngology, 1978—81, prof. Bobby R. Alford Dept. of Otolaryngology - Head and Neck Surgery; fellow head and neck surgery Columbia-Presbyn. Med. Ctr., 1981—82, St. Vincent's Hosp. and Med. Ctr., NY; interim dept. chair, dep. chief otolaryngology svc. Meth. Hosp.; hosp. affiliation includes St. Luke's Episcopal Hosp. Office: The Bobby R. Alford Department of Otolaryngology-Head and Neck Surgery One Baylor Plz Mail Stop NA-102 Houston TX 77030 Office Phone: 713-798-5906. Office Fax: 713-798-3520.

DONOVAN, GAIL F., hospital administrator; married; 2 children. BSBA, Villanova U., Pa.; M in Health Svc. Adminstrn., George Wash. U. Administrative intern St. Vincent's Med. Ctr., NYC, 1983; with Meth. Hosp., Bklyn., 1984—86; assoc. dir. for ops. Beth Israel Med. Ctr., 1986, v.p. for ops. North divsn., 1988—90, sr. v.p. for ops. North divsn., 1988—90, COO, 1994—2003, exec. v.p., 1994—2003, St. Luke's Hosp. Ctr., 2000—01, COO, 2000—01, Continuum Health Ptnrs. Inc., 2001 , exec. v.p., 2001—, interim pres., 2003, CEO, 2003. Named one of Top 25 Women in Healthcare, Modern Healthcare mag., 2011. Mem.: Greater NY Hosp. Assn. (bd. dirs.), Hosp. Assn. NY State (bd. dirs.), American Hosp. Assn. (bd. dirs.), Met. Health Adminstrs. Assn. (past. pres.), Healthcare Exec. Forum. Office: Continuum Health Partners Incorporated 1111 Amsterdam Ave New York NY 10025-1716 Office Phone: 212-523-4000.

DOODY, RACHELLE, neurologist, educator, researcher; b. Pitts., Aug. 12, 1956; d. David and Audrey Margaret (Dixon) Smith; m. Terrence Arthur Doody, Sept. 29, 1979; children: Clare, Robin, Justin, Aleah. BA, Rice U., Houston, 1978, PhD, 1992; MD, Baylor Coll. Medicine, Houston, 1983. Diplomate American Bd. Psychology & Neurology. Intern neurology McGill U., Montreal, Canada, 1983—84; resident neurology Baylor Coll. Medicine, 1984-87, asst. prof. neurology, 1987-96, founding dir. Alzheimer's Disease & Memory Disorders Ctr., 1989—, assoc. prof. neurology, 1996—2003, Effie Marie Cain chair Alzheimer's disease rsch., 2000—, prof. neurology, 2003—. Mem. sci. adv. bd. Anavex Life Scis. Corp., 2011—; med. adv. bd. QR Pharma, Inc., 2011—, Sonexa Therapeutics, Inc.; sic. & clin. adv. bd. Medivation, Inc.; past mem. Texas Coun. Alzheimer's Disease & Related Disorders. Recipient Disting. Alumni award, Assn. Rice Alumni, 2009, Zenith award, Nat. Alzheimer's Assn., Disting. Faculty award, Baylor Coll. Medicine, 2011. Mem.: Alzheimer's Assn. (bd. dirs. Houston/Southwest chpt., Harry E. Walker award). Achievements include research in cognitive aspects of Alzheimer's disease, dementia, and aphasia; development of treatments for memory disorder and Alzheimer's disease. Avocations: fine arts, tennis, literature. Office: Baylor Coll Medicine Dept Neurology 1977 Butler Blvd Suite E5 101 Houston TX 77030-2744 Office Phone: 713-798-7416, 713-798-4734. Office Fax: 713-798-5326. E-mail: rdoody@bcm.edu.

DOOLEY, DIANA S., state official, public health service officer; b. 1951; m. Dan Dooley; 2 children. BA in Social Sci., Calif. State U., Fresno, 1972; LLB, San Joaquin Coll. of Law, 1995. Analyst State Personnel Bd.; legis. dir., spl. asst. to Gov. Jerry Brown State of Calif., Sacramento, 1975—83; v.p., gen. counsel Children's Hosp. Ctrl. Calif., 2000; pres., CEO Calif. Children's Hosp. Assn., 2006—11; sec. Calif. Dept. Health & Human Services, Sacramento, 2011—. Bds. dirs. Maddy Inst.; former pres. Visalia C. of C., Ctrl. Calif. Futures Inst. Bd. dirs. UC Merced Found., Blood Source of Northern Calif. Office: California Dept Health & Human Services Rm 460 1600 Ninth St Sacramento CA 95814 Office Phone: 916-654-3454. *

DOOLITTLE-ROMAS, MONIQUE, health science association administrator; B of Commerce, Laurentian U., Sudbury, Ont., Can.; MPA, Queen's U., Kingston, Ont. Coord. pub. rels. Laurentian Hosp.; dir. orgnl. devel. United Way Can.; regional dir. Can. Hearing Soc., 2000—06; exec. dir, Can. AIDS Soc., 2006—. Office: CAS 190 O'Connor St Suite 800 Ottawa ON K2P 2R3 Canada Office Phone: 613-230-3580. Office Fax: 613-563-4998. *

DOPPALAPUDI, HARISH, medical educator; b. India, Dec. 22, 1972; MBBS, Guntur Med. Coll., 1997. Asst. prof. U. Ala., Birmingham, 2007—. Office: University Ala FOT 930 Birmingham AL 35294 Business E-Mail: harish@uab.edu.

DORAI, THAMBI, oncologist, researcher; b. Tirupattur, India, Feb. 28, 1950; arrived in U.S., 1983, s. Devarajan and Radha; m. Bhuvaneswari Dorai, Sept. 5, 1982; children: Arvind, Vinod. BS, Sacred Heart Coll. (Madras Univ.), 1970; MS, Christian Med. Coll. (Madras Univ.), Vellore, India, 1973; PhD, Madras Univ., 1980. Sr. scientist Indian Inst. Chem. Biology, Calcutta, Ind., 1980—83; rsch. fellow USC, Sch. Medicine, LA, 1980—84; rsch. assoc. Rockefeller Univ., NYC, 1984—88; vis. fellow Mt. Sinai Sch. Medicine, NYC, 1988—91, rsch. asst. prof., 1991—94; sr. rsch. assoc. Columbia Univ. Coll. of Physicians and Surgeons, NYC, 1994—2000; rsch. assoc. prof. N.Y. Med. Coll., NYC, 2000—. Contbr. over 40 articles to profl. jours. Recipient Edwin Beer award, N.Y. Acad. Medicine, 1997; grantee Rsch. in Urology, Elsa U. Pardee Found., 1999; Irwin White Fellowship, Columbia Univ., N.Y., 1995. Mem.: Am. Assn. for Advancement of Sci., Am. Assn. for Cancer Rsch. Achievements include characterization of novel prevention and treatment strategies for bone metastasis in prostate cancer; research in the molecular mechanisms of kidney cancer. Avocation: travel. Home: 92 E Allison Ave Nanuet NY 10954 Office: Comprehensive Cancer Ctr Our Lady of Mercy Med Ctr 600 E 233rd St Bronx NY 10466 Office Phone: 718-920-1137.

DORAISWAMY, VIJAY ARUN, internist; BS in Surgery, Madras Med. Coll., MB, 2003. Diplomate Am. Bd. Internal Medicine. Internal medicine resident Western Pa. Hosp., Pitts., 2005—06, U. Ariz., Tucson, 2008—10; rsch. asst. U. Pa., Phila., 2008; hospitalist Salem Hosp., 2010—11. Elected resident rep. Grad. Med. Edn., Tucson, 2008—09; editor Online Med. Ency., 2008—; bd. dirs. Pima County Med. Soc., Tucson, 2009—10. Contbr. articles to profl. jours. Recipient Arignar Anna award, Tamil Madu Govt., India, 1997, W. Warner Watkins MD award, State Championship Drs. Dilemma Competition, 2009, Norma J. Peal PhD Grad. Med. Edn. Resident award, 2010; Thandai Periyar scholarship, Tamil Nadu Govt., 1997—2002. Mem.: ACP (assoc. coun., Ariz. 2008—10, assoc. coun., Phoenix 2009—10, leadership day capitol, Washington 2010, poster presentation judge 2010, Young Physicians coun., Oreg. 2010—11, Joseph E. Johnson Leadership Day grant 2010), OPUS 12 Found. (pres., Tucson chpt. 2008—10, pres., Oregon chpt. 2010—11, dir., internet publs. 2010—), Am. Heart Assn., Southern Med. Assn. Avocations: painting, driving, sports. Office: Salem Hosp 890 Oak St SE Salem OR 97301

D'ORAZIO, JOHN AUGUST, medical educator; b. NB, NJ, May 7, 1966; PhD, U. Miami, 1994, MD, 1996. Assoc. prof. U. Ky. Coll. Medicine, 2004—. Mem.: Alpha Omega Alpha. Office: Markey Cancer Ctr Combs 204 800 Ros Lexington KY 40536-0096 Office Fax: 859-257-8940. Business E-Mail: jdorazio@uky.edu.

DORFMAN, HOWARD DAVID, pathologist, educator; b. NYC, July 20, 1928; s. Louis and Helen (Weingarten) D.; m. Esther Novick, June 21, 1952; children: Richard H., Peter W., Leslie Jane. BA, NYU, 1947; MD, SUNY, Bklyn., 1951. Cert. in pathologic anatomy Am. Bd. Pathology, 1958. Resident in pathology Mt. Sinai Hosp., NYC, 1952-54, Columbia Presby. Medical Ctr., NYC, 1954-58; dir. pathology Sharon (Conn.) Hosp., 1958-60; assoc. pathologist Sinai Hosp. Balt., Baltimore, Md., 1960-64; dir. pathology Hosp. Joint Diseases, NYC, 1964-74; pathologist-in-chief Sinai Hosp. Balt., 1974-85; prof. orthopedic pathology Johns Hopkins Sch. of Medicine, Balt., 1985; prof. pathology, radiology and orthopaedic surgery Albert Einstein Coll. Medicine, Bronx, NY, 1985—. Walter Putschar lectr. Mass. Gen. Hosp. Harvard Med. Sch., 1983; vis. prof. Wayne State U. Sch. Medicine, 1984, Baylor Coll. Medicine, Houston, 1984, Cleve. Clinic, 1984, SUNY, Stony Brook, 1994, Johns Hopkins U. Sch. Medicine, 1995, U. Mich. Sch. Medicine, 1997, Cornell U. Sch. Medicine, Meml.-Sloan Kettering Cancer Ctr., 1998, U. Pitts. Sch. Medicine, 1998, Brigham and Women's Hosp., Harvard Med. Sch., 1998, Yale U. Sch. Medicine, 2003; Stembridge lectr. Tex. Soc. Pathologists, 2006; 1st P.G. Bullough lectr. Hosp. Spl. Surgery, NYC, 2009; lectr. in field. Author: Bone Tumors, 1998; co-author: Tumors of Bone and Cartilage, 1971. Recipient Henry Jaffe award Hosp. Joint Diseases, 1984, Corinne Farrell award, Internat. Skeletal Soc., 2009, Alan Darby award, 2009, Jean R. Oliver award, SUNY Downstate Med. Sch., 2011. Mem. N.Y. Pathological Soc. (pres. 1989-91), Internat. Skeletal Soc. (pres. 1986-88). Democrat. Home: 201 E 79th St Apt 10G New York NY 10075-0836 Office Phone: 718-920-5622. Business E-Mail: hdorfman@montefiore.org.

DORFMAN, WILLIAM M. (BILL DORFMAN), dentist; b. 1958; children: Anna, Charlotte, Georgia. Grad., UCLA, 1980; DDS, U. Pacific, San Francisco, 1983. Dental resident, Lausanne, Switzerland, 1983—85; pvt. practice aesthetic and gen. dentistry LA, 1985—; founder Discus Dental, Inc., LA, 1989—. Dental cons. ABC's Extreme Makeover, NBC's The Today Show, NBC's Entertainment Tonight, NBC's EXTRA, NBC's The Rosie O'Donnell Show, E! Entertainment TV; founder, program coord. P.A.C.-live, U. Pacific Dental Sch., San Francisco; lectr. in field. Author: The Smile Guide; past editor Jour. Am. Acad. Cosmetic Dentistry; contbr. articles to profl. jours.; guest appearances Channel 4 News, LA, Channel 7 News. Judge Miss S.C. beauty pageant; raised and donated with Crown Coun. of Dentists to St Jude's Children Rsch. Hosp., Children's Dental Ctr., & Garth Brooks' Teammates for Kids Found. Recipient Lifetime Achievement awards (2), Outstanding Sr. award, UCLA, 1980; named Best Aesthetic Dentist in L.A., L.A. Mag. Fellow: Am. Acad. Cosmetic Dentistry; mem.: ADA. Recognized as one of the country's leading dentists and is responsible for creating smiles for famous Hollywood stars; developed products such as: Nite White, Day White, Zoom!, Breath Rx. Office: Discus Dental Inc Century City Aesthetic Dentistry 2080 Century Park E Ste 1601 Los Angeles CA 90067 Office Phone: 310-277-5678. Office Fax: 310-277-3294. Business E-Mail: billd@discusdental.com.

DORIN, MARIAN, surgeon, educator; b. Toplita, Harghita, Romania, Aug. 27, 1958; s. Marian Ioan and Marian Emilia; m. Marian Claudia Boer, Feb. 14, 1994; children: Marian Mihai, Marian Patricia. MD, U. Medicine, Targu Mures, Romania, 1984, PhD, 1997. Prof. Red Cross Soc., San. H.S., Secondary H.S. Group, Targu Mures, 1984—94; sci. rschr. Inst. Pub. Health and Med. Rsch., Targu Mures, 1984—90; asst. prof. of surgery U. Medicine and Pharmacy, Targu Mures, 1991—2001, lectr., physician, 2002—; sr. surgeon U. Hosp. Surg. Clinic, Targu Mures, 1996—. Chief examinator high sch. graduation exam Ministry of Edn., Bucuresti, Romania, 2002—. Author: (monograph) Machanic jaundice: clinical and experimental studies, Surgical Anatomy and Semiology of the Abodmen; co-author (monograph) General pathologic anatomy, Pathology of the striated muscles, Pathology af the digestive system: radiologic, surgical and dermatologic aspects; contbr. articles to profl. publs.; author ednl. materials. Fellow, UNESCO, 2004—. Fellow: Am. Coll. Chest Physicians; mem.: Internat. Assn. Surgeons and Gastroenterologists (corr.), Internat. Assn. Endoscopic Surgery (corr.), Internat Assn. Gastric Cancer Surgery (corr.), Internat. Assn. Colorectal Surgeons (corr.), Am. Coll. Chest Surgeons (corr.), Romanian Soc. Oncologic Surgery (assoc.), Romanian Soc. Gastroenterology (assoc.), Romanian Soc. Liver, Gall, Pancreas Surgery (assoc.), Romanian Med. Assn. (assoc.), Romanian Soc. Surgery (assoc.). Romanian Orthodox. Achievements include experimental surgery in mechanic jaundice, normal and pathologic liver recovery, normal and pathologic pancreas resections and radiofrequency ablation of liver tumors. Avocations: travel, music, movies. Home: Gh Marinescu 49/11 540136 Targu Mures 540136 Romania Personal E-mail: dorinmar@rdslink.ro.

DORLEN, ROSALIND, clinical psychologist, psychoanalyst, medical researcher, educator; MA in Anthropology, Columbia U.; Profl. Diploma in Sch. PSychology, Kean U.; Doctorate in Clin. Psychology, Rutgers U., 1977; post-doctoral cert. in Psychoanalytic Psychotheraphy, Ctr. for Psychoanalytic Tng., NY; post-doctoral cert. in Psychoanalysis, Inst. for Psychoanalysis and Psychotheraphy, NJ. Lic. and bd. cert. Diplomate in Clin. Psychology, cert. school psychologist, psychoanalyst. Pvt. practice, Summit, NJ, 1977—. Pub. edn. chair NJ Working Group on Postpartum Depression, 2005—; bd. dir. Allied Profl. Staff, Overlook Hosp., Summit, NJ, Nat. Register of Health Svc., 1980—; dir. Resilience Project, Overlook Hosp. (sponsored by NJ Psychological Assn.), Summit, NJ; field supervisor Rutgers Grad. Sch. Profl. Psychology; mem. sr. faculty Inst. for Psychoanalysis and Psychotherapy NJ; chairperson adv. bd. for Psychological Well-Being Overlook Hosp., Summit, NJ, mem. adv. bd.; mem. cmty. benefits com. Overlook Adv. Bd., Summit, NJ; psychological health educator and lectr.; spkr. in field; lectured and media appearances about effective parenting, depression, and stress in the workplace. Author: Niche Guide for APA Divsn. 42 (Independent Practice); published and lectured on the subject of strengthening resilience in individuals, children, and communities coping with terrorism, bio-terrorism, and war; contbr. columns in newspapers, articles to profl. jours. Nationally recognized innovator of cmty. initiatives; mem. mcpl. alliance for the Prevention of Drug and Alcohol Abuse; mem. Suburban C. of C., Summit, NJ. Recipient Psychologist Recognition award, NJ Acad. of Psychology, Peterson prize, Rutgers Profl. Sch. Psychology, Disting. Grad. Alumni award, Kean Univ. Dept. of Sch. Psychology, Blousteir award, Rutgers Profl. Sch., 2008. Fellow: APA (mem., Com. for the Advancement of Psychological Practice); mem.: Soc. of Psychologists in Private Practice (past pres.), Am. Bd. Profl. Psychology (fellow in clin. psychology), NJ Psychological Assn. (past pres., mem. ethics com., chairperson, coun. on psychological health, Psychologist of Yr. 2000, Presdl. Citation in Recognition of Outstanding Contribution to Profl. Psychology). Office: 332 Springfield Ave Ste 204 Summit NJ 07901 Office Phone: 908-522-1444. Office Fax: 908-233-9310. Business E-Mail: dorlen@mindspring.com.

DORMAN-RODRIGUEZ, DEBORAH, insurance company executive, lawyer; B in Psychology, Calif. State U.; JD, U. Oreg. Asst. atty. gen. N.Mex. Atty. Gen.'s Office; asst. gen. counsel N.Mex. State Corp. Commn., gen. counsel N.Mex. Supt. Ins.; atty. Simons, Cuddy & Friedman, Santa Fe; v.p., gen. counsel Blue Cross Blue Shield N.Mex., 2000; sr. v.p., chief legal officer Health Care Svc. Corp. Mem.: Assn. Corp. Counsel, Am. Health Lawyers Assn., ABA (health law sect.), Calif. State Bar, N.Mex. State Bar, Ill. State Bar. Office: Health Care Service Corporation 300 E Randolph St Chicago IL 60601 Office Phone: 312-653-6000. Office Fax: 312-938-4209. *

DORMANS, JOHN PAUL, surgeon, educator; b. Ft. Wayne, Ind., Jan. 13, 1957; s. Paul M. and Viginia Ann Dormans; children: Nicholas, Andrea, Laura, Kath. BA magna cum laude, Ind. U., 1979, MD, 1983. Diplomate Am. Bd. Orthop. Surgery, 2002. Resident in orthop. surgery Mich. State U., Grand Rapids, 1988; fellow pediatric orthopedics Hosp. Sick Children, Toronto, Canada, 1988; orthop. surgeon Children's Hosp. Phila., 1989—96, chief orthop. surgery, 1996—, pres. med. staff, 1999—2001, trustee; asst. prof. to assoc. prof. orthop. surgery U. Pa. Sch. Medicine, Phila., 1991—2000, prof. orthop. surgery, 2000—. Pres. Surg. Assoc. Rsch. and Edn. Found., 1997-98; dir. pediatric orthop. fellowship Children's Hosp. Phila. Editor: Caring for the Child with Cerebral Palsy, 1998; sect. editor: The Cervical Spine, 2004; assoc. editor Jour. Bone and Joint Surgery, 2000—; contbr. articles to profl. jours. Fellow ACS, Am. Acad. Orthop. Surgeons (travelling fellow 1996), Scoliosis Rsch. Soc.; mem. Am. Orthop. Assn. (travelling fellow 1996), Pediatric Orthop. Soc. N.Am., Musculoskeletal Tumor Soc., Phi Beta Kappa. Lutheran. Avocations: fly fishing, painting, reading, history of medicine. Office: Childrens Hosp Phila Orthopedics Surgery Wood Bldg Rm 2312 34th and Civic Ctr Blvd Philadelphia PA 19104-4399 Office Phone: 215-590-1534. Business E-Mail: dormans@email.chop.edu.

DORMINEY, HENRY CLAYTON, JR., allergist; b. Tifton, Ga., May 15, 1949; s. Henry Clayton and Virgina (Petty) D. BS, Davidson Coll., 1971; MD, U. Iowa, 1975. Diplomate Am. Bd. Internal Medicine, Am. Bd. Allergy and Immunology; lic. physician, Ga. Med. intern U. Iowa Hosps. and Clinics, Iowa City, 1975-76, med. resident, 1976-78, allergy and immunology fellow, 1978-80; practice medicine specializing allergy and clin. immunology Allergy & Dermatology Assocs. of Tifton, Ga., 1981—99, Allergy, Asthma and Sinus Clinic of Tifton, 1999—. Mem. staff Tift Regional Med. Ctr., 1982-2011; bd. dirs. Brumby's Crossing, Dorminey Enterprises; chmn. and founder Tifton Mus. Arts and Heritage, 1991; mem. Allergy, Asthma & Sinus Clinic of Tifton; pres. ZapAds, Inc., 2006—. Assoc. editor, contbg. author Vital Signs, 1969-71. Bd. dirs. Tift County Found. Ednl. Excellence, 1996—08, chmn. investment com., 1998—, v.p., 2004-05, pres., 2005-06; bd. dirs. Tifton Heritage Found., pres., 1992; bd. dirs. Tifton Mus. Arts and Heritage, 1991—2006, chmn. & pres., 1991-2002. Recipient Physician's Recognition award AMA, 1979, 85, Lee Willingham III trophy Davidson Coll., 1987, Tifton Main Street Program award, 1989, Best Adaptive Re-Use Project, Tifton Historic District, The Coca Cola Bldg., 1993; grantee Am. Coll. Allergy, 1980. Mem. Am. Acad. Allergy (travel grantee 1980), Tift County Med. Soc. (sec., treas. 1983-84, v.p., 1984-85, pres. 1985-86), Med. Assn. Ga., Am. Numismatic Soc., Forward Tifton, Tifton C. of C. Lodges: Rotary (Spl. Merit award, founder Tifton Directory, bd. dirs. 1988-93, 2006-07, pres.-elect 1989-90, pres. 1990-91, Paul Harris fellow 1993). Independent. Home: 21 Duck Dr Tifton GA 31794-3953 Office: 820 Love Ave Tifton GA 31794-4071 Office Phone: 229-382-3720. Personal E-mail: dorminey@friendlycity.net.

DORN, SUE BRICKER, retired hospital administrator; b. Seattle, Apr. 1, 1934; d. Barney and Frances B. (Schnitzer) Bricker; m. Philip Henry Dorn, Dec. 31, 1955 (dec.); children: Charles, Martha Dorn. BA, Stanford U., Palo Alto, 1955; MA, Bank St. Coll., 1973. Cert. tchr., N.Y. Dir. promotion exec. compensation svc. Am. Mgmt. Assn., NYC, 1956-58; tchr. spl. edn. N.Y.C. Bd. of Edn., 1969-77; assoc. dir. Yale U., New Haven, 1977—79; v.p. Bank St. Coll. of Edn., NYC, 1979-81, Aspen Inst. for Humanistic Studies, NYC, 1981-82; assoc. v.p. Yale U., New Haven, 1982-87; dep. dir. devel. and pub. affairs Mus. of Modern Art, NYC, 1987-94; v.p., vice provost for devel. The N.Y. Hosp.-Cornell Med. Ctr., 1994—98. Mem. maj. gifts com. Stanford U.; cons. in field. Pres. LWV, Warren, Mich., 1962-65, Stanford Alumni Club of N.Y., N.J. and Conn., N.Y.C., 1968-70, 25 East 86th St. Corp., N.Y.C., 1989-93, 95—; mem. dirs. adv. bd. Yale Comprehensive Cancer Ctr., Yale U., 1990-94; mem. bd. dirs. Jewish

Women's Archive, 2009-. Named Citizen of the Yr., Warren C. of C., 1962; recipient Citation, City of Warren, 1963, Gold Spike award and Cert. of Outstanding Achievement, Stanford U., 1976. Mem. Stanford Assocs., Univ. Club. Home: 25 E 86th St New York NY 10028-0553 E-mail: sdorn@nyc.rr.com. *

DORNFEST, BURTON SAUL, anatomist, educator; b. NYC, Oct. 31, 1930; s. Irving and Yetta (Rosengarten) D.; m. Eveline Drucker, June 13, 1954; children: Michael Barry. BA, NYU, 1952, MS, 1954, PhD, 1960. Rsch. asst. dept. biostats. Sloan-Kettering Inst. and Meml. Hosp., NYC, 1952-53; rsch. asst. dept. biology NYU, 1953-54, 56-58, instr. gen. sci., 1958-63; instr. anatomy N.Y. Med. Coll., 1963-64, SUNY Health Sci. Ctr., Bklyn., 1964-67, asst. prof., 1967-73, assoc. prof., 1973-91; cons. study sect. Nat. Heart and Lung Inst., 1975; adj. prof. Sophie Davis Sch. Biomed. Edn. CUNY, 1974-97; adj. prof. hematology sch. health scis. Hunter Coll., 1978-82, 90-91; adj. prof. anatomy N.Y. Med. Coll., 1982-85, 91-96, Touro Coll. Ctr. Biomed. Edn., 1983-88, Einstein Coll. Medicine, 1991-99. Contbr. rsch. papers in field of hematology articles to profl. jours. Served with U.S. Army, 1954-56. NIH fellow, 1958-60, 61-63; Leukemia Soc., 1960-61; Nat. Inst. Arthritis and Metabolic Diseases grantee, 1964-71; Nat. Cancer Inst. grantee, 1973-75; Mildred Werner League for Cancer Research grantee, 1976-77; co-prin. investigator NIH Heart, Blood and Lung Inst., 1982-85. Mem. AAAS, Am. Soc. Hematology, Am. Assn. Clin. Anatomists, Sigma Xi. Jewish. Home and Office: 96 Everett Rd Demarest NJ 07627-1225 Personal E-mail: bureve35@aol.com.

DORO, DANIELE, medical educator; b. Verona, Italy, Mar. 3, 1947; s. Fulvia Fraccaroli; m. Pierangela Cimatti, Sept. 26, 1981; children: Filippo, Sara. MD in Ophthalmology, U. Padua, Italy, 1971. Aggregate prof. U. Padua, 1978—. Cons. U. Padua, 1978—2007. Contbr. articles to profl. jours. Home: Via della Pieve 3 Padova 35121 Italy Office: Studio medico Via Barbarigo 41 Padova 35100 Italy Office Phone: 39-049655446. Office Fax: 0039-049655446. Business E-Mail: daniele.doro@unipd.it.

DOROSHOW, JAMES HALPERN, federal agency administrator, oncologist; b. Lynwood, Calif., 1948; MD, Harvard Med. Sch., 1973. Cert. internal medicine, oncology. Intern Mass. Gen. Hosp., Boston, 1973-74, resident, 1974-75; fellow in med. oncology Nat. Cancer Inst., Bethesda, Md., 1975-78; chmn. dept. med. oncology and therapeutics rsch. City of Hope Nat. Med. Ctr., Duarte, Calif.; assoc. dir. clin. rsch. City of Hope Comprehensive Cancer Ctr., Duarte, 1981—2004; dir. divsn. cancer treatment & diagnosis Nat. Cancer Inst., NIH, Bethesda, 2004—, chmn. clin trials working group, dep. dir. clin. and translational rsch. Mem. Am. Assn. for Cancer Rsch., Am. Soc. for Clin. Oncology, Am. Soc. Hematology, Am. Fedn. for Clin. Rsch. Office: Nat Cancer Inst Divsn Cancer Treatment & Diagnosis 31 Center Dr Bldg 31 Rm 3A44 Bethesda MD 20892-2440 Office Phone: 301-496-4291. E-mail: doroshoj@mail.nih.gov. *

DORR, LAWRENCE DOUGLAS, orthopedic surgeon; b. Storm Lake, Iowa, 1941; m. Marilyn Dorr. BA in English, Cornell Coll., 1963; MS, U. Iowa, 1965, MD, 1967. Cert. Orthopaedic Surgery, 1978. Intern, orthopedics LA County, U. So. Calif. Sch. Med., 1967—68, resident, joint replacement surgery, 1974—76; fellow Hosp. Spl. Surgery, NYC, 1976—77; founder (Calif. based inst.), med. dir. Dorr Inst., Centinela Hosp. Med. Ctr., Inglewood, Calif., 2001—; prof. U. So. Calif. Sch. Medicine, LA. Founder, med. staff mem. Operation Walk, 1994—; lectr. in field; researcher in field. Featured on Miracle Workers (ABC), 2006; contbr. articles to profl. jours. Bd. trustee Cornell Coll. Recipient Humanitarian Yr. award, Am. Acad. Orthopedic Surgeons for work with Operation Walk, 2005, Cornell Coll. Disting. Achievement award, 2003, Disting. Alumni award, U. Iowa, 2006. Mem.: Hip Soc. (pres. elect 2006).

DORR, STEPHANIE TILDEN, psychotherapist; b. Orlando, Fla., Sept. 21, 1950; d. Luther Willis Tilden II and Lillian Murfee (Grace) Owen; m. Darwin Dorr, May 21, 1986. AA, El Camino Coll., 1975; BA, U. N.C., 1985; MA, Western Carolina U., 1991. Lic. clin. psychotherapist State Kans. Behavioral Scis. Regulatory Bd., 2000. Cons. psychologist Sylva (N.C.) Psychol. Assocs., 1991-92; staff psychologist Park Ridge Hosp., Naples, N.C., 1992, Blue Ridge Ctr., Asheville, N.C., 1991-93; pvt. practice psychology Asheville, 1991-93; project mgr. Sedgwick County Dept. Mental Health, Wichita, Kans., 1993-95; pvt. practice psychotherapy and psychol. assessment Counseling and Mediation Ctr., Wichita, Kans., 1995-98; therapist United Meth. Youthville Clinic, Wichita, 1998—2001; clin. therapist Wichita (Kans.) Pub. Schs. Greiffenstein Spl. Edn. Ctr., 2001—. Adj. faculty Kans. Newman Coll., Wichita, 1995-2001, Butler County (Kans.) Cmty. Coll., 1996-97; Assertive Cmty. Treatment (ACT) team clinician United Meth. Youthville, Wichita, 1997-98; presenter in field. Contbr. articles to profl. publs. Recipient Excellence in Tchg. award Butler County C.C., 1997, Outstanding Faculty Mem. award Butler County C.C., 1998. Mem. Psychoanalytic Study Group (sec. 1989-93, award 1993), We. N.C. Psychol. Assn. (mem.-at-large 1985-93, pres.-elect 1993), Kans. Assn. Masters Psychologists (bd. mem. 2005, pres. 2006), Psi Chi, Pi Gamma Mu. Democrat. Episcopalian. Avocations: sewing, rock collecting, gardening. Office: Wichita Pub Schs Greiffenstein Alternative Elem 1221 E Galena Wichita KS 67216 Office Phone: 316-973-6400. Personal E-mail: sdorr@usd259.net.

DORSEY, JOHN KEVIN, dean; b. NYC, 1943; B, Fairfield U., Conn., 1964; PhD in physiologic chemistry, U. Wis., Madison, 1968; MD, So. Ill. U. Sch. Medicine, 1978; postgrad., The Johns Hopkins U., 1970—73. Diplomate internal medicine and rheumatology Am. Bd. Internal Medicine. Intern U. Iowa Hosps., Iowa City, 1978—79, resident in internal medicine, 1979—81; fellow in rheumatology U. Iowa, Iowa City, 1981—83; joined faculty as asst. prof. chemistry and biochemistry So. Ill. U., Carbondale, Ill., 1973, rejoined faculty as asst. prof. and coord. clin. affairs, 1983; med. dir. So. Ill. Arthritis Found.; attending rheumatologist Carbondale (Ill.) Clinic; consulting rheumatologist V.A. Hosp., Marion, Ill.; prof. internal medicine So. Ill. U. Sch. Medicine, Carbondale, Ill., assoc. provost so. region, 1998—2001, interim dean and provost Springfield, 2001—02, dean and provost, 2002—. Mem. Nuc. Magnetic Resonance Mgmt. Com. So. Ill. U., mem. Molecular Biology, Microbiology and Biochemistry com.; bd. trustees So. Ill. Healthcare. Co-host (edn. television program) Medically Speaking, reviewer Developmental Biology, Ill. Med. Jour., Tchg. and Learning in Medicine, Academic Medicine; contbr. articles to profl. jours. Recipient John Templeton Spirituality in Medicine Curricular Award, 2000; named a Disting. Alumnus, So. Ill. U. Sch. Medicine, 1993. Fellow: Am. Coll. Rheumatology, Am. Coll. Physicians; mem.: Alpha Omega Alpha, Sigma Xi. Office: So Ill Univ Sch Medicine Office of Dean & Provost PO Box 19620 Springfield IL 62794-9620 Office Phone: 217-545-3625. Business E-Mail: kdorsey@siumed.edu. *

DORTON, TRUDA LOU, medical/surgical and geriatrics nurse; b. Elkhorn Creek, Ky., Aug. 26, 1949; d. Clair Otis Parsons and Joyce Kidd; m. Eugene Anderson, Nov. 26, 1966 (dec. Apr. 1971); children: Gena Lynn, Richard Eugene; m. Leon Dorton, Dec. 15, 1972 (dec. Feb. 2008); children: Leondra Michelle, Jerald Thomas, Jonathan Layne. AS, student, Pikeville Coll., 1993. RN, Ky.; cert. ACLS, PALS. Instr. computer usage Lookout Elem. Sch., Ky., 1983; water/sewage technician McCoy & McCoy Environ. Cons., Pikeville, Ky., 1984; owner Signs of the Times, Elkhorn City, Ky., 1979-89; sec.'s asst. humanities and social scis. divsns. Pikeville Coll., 1989-92; nurse aide Mud Creek Clinic, Grethel, Ky., 1992-93; charge nurse Jenkins Cmty. Hosp., Ky., 1993-94; case mix coord. Parkview Manor Nursing Home, 1994-95, minimum data set and nursing care plan coord., 1995; acute care nurse Harrison Meml. Hosp., Cynthiana, Ky., 1996—2002; dir. nursing Robertson County Health Care Facility, Mt. Olivet, Ky.; long-term care charge nurse Trilogy Health Ctr. at Harrison Meml. Hosp., Cynthiana; med. inpatient svcs. Floyd Meml. Hosp., New Albany, Ind. Vol. nurse aide Mud Creek Clinic, Grethel, 1989-92. Founder free blood pressure clinic H.E.L.P.S. Community Action Program, Hellier, Ky., 1983; co-founder H.E.L.P.S. Community Action Group, Hellier, 1983; mem. Ellis Island Centennial Commn., N.Y., 1986. Appalachian Honors scholar Pikeville Coll., 1989-92. Mem. Nat. Geog. Soc., Ky. Nursing Assn., Order Ky. Cols. (Honorable Ky. Col. 1989), Smithsonian Inst., Nat. Trust Hist. Preservation, World Wildlife Fund, Pikeville Coll. Alumni Assn., Mountain Assembly Ch. God (Living Water fellow). Democrat. Avocations: reading, calligraphy, music. Home: 901 Santa Fe Rd Brooksville KY 41004

DORUK, HASAN ERDAL, medical educator; b. Kayseri, Turkey, Feb. 24, 1966; Degree, 1984, Cukurova U., 1990. Assoc. prof. Mersin U., 1998—. Gen. mgr. Mersin U. Hosp., 2006—10. Mem.: Turkish Urology Assn., European Assn. Urology. Office: Mersin University Medikal Faculty Urology Mersin 33079 Turkey Office Fax: 903243373738. Business E-Mail: edoruk@mersin.edu.tr.

DORWART, BONNIE BRICE, historian, retired rheumatologist; b. Petersburg, Va., Jan. 27, 1942; d. Gratien Bertrand and Myrtle Elizabeth (Houser) Brice; m. William Villee Dorwart, Jr., June 22, 1963; children: William Bertrand, Brice Burdan, Michael Walter. AB, Bryn Mawr Coll., 1964; MD, Temple U., 1968. Diplomate Am. Bd. Med. Examiners, Am. Bd. Internal Medicine, Am. Bd. Rheumatology. Intern then resident in internal medicine Lankenau Hosp., Jefferson Med. Coll., Phila., 1968-72; instr. medicine Hosp. U. Pa., Phila., 1972-74; fellow rheumatology U. Pa. Sch. Medicine, Phila., 1974; instr. medicine Jefferson Med. Coll., Phila., 1974-76, asst. prof., 1976-81, assoc. prof., 1981-95, clin. prof., 1995—2003; assoc. investigator divsn. rsch. Lankenau Hosp., Wynnewood, Pa., 1978—88, chief arthritis clinic, 1982—86, chief connective tissue disorders, 1982—97; Civil War med. historian, writer, 2001—. Assoc. dir. Greater Delaware Valley Arthritis Control Program, 1975; mem. Gov.'s adv. bd. on Systemic Lupus Erythematosus, Phila., 1981-88. Author: Carson's Materia Medica of 1851: An Annotation, 2003, Death is in the Breeze: Disease during the American Civil War, 2009; contbr. articles to med. jours., chpts. to books. Med. career advisor, active cells workshop Merion Elem. Sch., Pa., 1984-90; fund raiser Arthritis Found., Am. Cancer Soc., Phila., 1974-97; mem. resources com. Bryn Mawr Coll., 1985-90; historian Walter and Lenore Annenberg Conf. Ctr. Med. Edn., Lankenau Hosp., 2004—; archivist, Lankenau Hosp., Wynnewood, Pa., 2006— Named to Nat. Med. Honor Soc. Fellow ACP, Coll. Physicians Phila.; mem. AMA, Am. Coll. Rheumatology, Phila. Rheumatism Soc. (pres. 1981-82), Pa. Med. Soc., Philadelphia County Med. Soc. Avocations: cooking, gardening. Home: 124 Maple Ave Bala Cynwyd PA 19004-3031 Office Phone: 610-667-3849. Personal E-mail: dorwart@verizon.net.

DOSS, MOUNIR F., hospital administrator; BS in Acctg., Ein Shams U., Cairo, 1965; MBA, Fordham U., 1974. Cost. acct. pvt. industry; contr. Jamaica Hosp. Nursing Home; joined Jamaica Hosp. Med. Ctr., 1970, rejoined, 1978, exec. v.p. and CFO, Medisys Health Network Inc., Brookdale Univ. Hosp. and Med. Ctr. Active mem. policy devel. Coalition of Financially Distressed Hosps. Office: Jamaica Hospital Medical Center 8900 Van Wyck Expressway Jamaica NY 11418 Office Phone: 718-206-6000. Office Fax: 718-206-8716.

DOSTÁLOVÁ, TATJANA, dentist, researcher, educator; b. Prague, Czech Republic, Oct. 21, 1955; d. Jiri and Tatjana (Trepetova) B.; m. Jan Dostal, July 6, 1974; 1 child, Jana. MD, Charles U., Prague, 1979; degree in Dentistry, 1982, M in Med. Sci., 1989, degree in Prosthetic Dentistry, 1992, DMS, 2001; MBA, Prague Internat. Bus. Sch., 2004. Medical Diplomate Czech Republic, 1979. Rsch. fellow Inst. Dental Rsch., Prague, 1979—93, head clin. ctr., assoc. prof., 1993—2001, assoc. prof., 2000—; head prosthetics dept. stomatology Gen. Faculty Hosp., 1st med. faculty Charles U., 2001—, prof. 1st Med. Faculty, 2004—08, prof. dept. pediatric stomatology 2d Med. Faculty, 2006. Assoc. prof. Postgrad. Med. Sch., Prague, 1992, 1st Med. Clinic, Charles U., 2001—; gen. faculty, head prosthetic dentistry dept. Hosp. Prague. Author (books, articles). Mem. Am. Soc. for Lasers in Medicine and Surgery, European Prosthodontic Assn. Home: Svidnicka 509/8 181 00 Prague Czech Republic Office: Charles Univ 2nd Med Sch Dept Pediat Stomatology V Uvalu 84 150 00 Prague Czech Republic Office Fax: 420224435820. Personal E-mail: tatjana.dostalova@fnmotol.cz.

DOTY, RICHARD L., medical researcher; b. Boulder, Colo., Oct. 14, 1944; s. George David and Frances Amelia (Bradley) D. BS, Colo. State U., 1966; MA, Calif. State U., 1968; PhD, Mich. State U., 1971; postgrad., U. Calif., Berkeley, 1973. Instr. dept. psychology Calif. State U., San Francisco, 1971-72, U. San Francisco, 1971-72; asst. mem. Monell Chem. Senses Ctr., Phila., 1974-76, assoc. mem., head human olfaction sect., 1976-78; dir. smell and taste ctr. Hosp. U. Pa., Phila., 1979—, Sch. Medicine, U. Pa., Phila., 1980—, asst. prof. dept. otorhinolaryngology, human communication, 1983-89, assoc. prof., 1989-93; prof. dept. otorhinolaryngology U. Pa., Phila., 1994—. Cons. in field; lectr. in field; editorial cons. for numerous profl. jours.; external adv. bd. Taste and Smell Ctr. U. Conn./Yale U., 1982-84, Rocky Mountain Taste and Smell Ctr., U. Colo. Sch. Medicine, 1985, Mayo Found. Project, 1989; internat. adv. bd. 1st Internat. Congress on Food and Health, Salsomaggiore Terme, Italy, 1985. Author: The Smell Identification Test (TM) Administration Manual, 1983, 2d edit., 1989, 3d edit., 1995; editor: Mammalian Olfaction, Reproductive Processes and Behavior, 1976; co-editor: (with T.V. Getchell, E.P. Koster) Chemical Senses, spl. edit., 1981, (with D.G. Laing, W. Breopohl) Human Olfaction, 1990, (with L.M. Bartoshuk, T.V. Getchell and J.B. Snow) Smell and Taste in Health Disease, 1991, (with D. Muller-Schwartze) Chemical Signals in Vertebrates VI, 1992, Handbook of Olfaction and Gustation, 1995, 2d edit., 2003. NIH postdoctoral rsch. fellow, 1973-75; grantee Nat. Inst. on Aging, 1989-91, 2000-05, Nat. Inst. Deafness and Other Comm. Disorders, 1980—. Mem. European Chemoreception Rsch. Orgn. (mem. organizational com. 1981), Assn. for Chemoreception Scis. (mem. program com. 1985, 87, mem. elections com. 1987), AAAS, N.Y. Acad. Scis., Assn. for Rsch. in Otolaryngology, Am. Acad. Otolaryngology (head and neck surgery), Am. Psychol. Assn., Internat. Soc. for Chem. Ecology, Phila. Coll. Physicians (mem. adv. com., sect. on geriatrics and gerontology). Home: 125 White Horse Pike Haddon Heights NJ 08035-1909 Office: U Pa Smell & Taste Ctr 5 Ravdin Bldg 3400 Spruce St Philadelphia PA 19104-4206 Office Phone: 215-662-6580. Business E-Mail: doty@mail.med.upenn.edu.

DOUBAL, STANISLAV, gerontologist; b. Cerna za Bory, Czech Republic, Feb. 2, 1946; s. Stanislav and Zdenka Doubal; children: Stanislav, Lucie, Jan, Jana. Ing., Czech Tech. U., 1969; RNDr, Charles U., 1982; PhD, Inst. Biophysics ASCR, 1980. Lectr. Faculty of Pharmacy Charles U., Hradec Kralové, Czech Republic, 1971-90, prof. biophysics, 1990—, head bd. for doctoral study in gerontology, 1991—. Contbr. articles to profl. jours. Mem. Acad. of Scis. Czech Republic (com. for biophysics 1999—), Am. Aging Assn., Czech Gerontol. Soc. Achievements include research on theory of verification in gerontology; biological age determination, biomechanics. Home: Lohenice 43 535 01 Přelouč Czech Republic Office: Charles Univ Fac Pharmacy Heyrovského 1203 50005 Hradec Králové Czech Republic Home Phone: 420 466 955 898; Office Phone: 420 495 067 410. Business E-Mail: doubal@faf.cuni.cz.

DOUBLEDAY, CHARLES WILLIAM, dermatologist, educator; b. Houston, Oct. 1, 1954; s. Leonard Charles and Margaret (Walker) D.; m. Verlinde Van den Berge Hill, June 22, 1985; children: George Marchant, Julia Van den Berge, Walker Hill. BA with honors, U. Tex., Austin, 1976; MD, U. Tex., Houston, 1981. Diplomate Am. Bd. Dermatology, 1987. Rotating intern John Peter Smith Hosp., Ft. Worth, 1981-82; resident in dermatology U. Tex. Med. Sch., 1982-83, 85-87, fellow in dermatology, 1985, clin. asst. prof. dermatology, 1988—; pvt. practice, Houston, 1987—. Bd. dirs. The Park People. Contbr. articles to profl. jours. Recipient high sci. quality award Soc. for Investigative Dermatology, 1986; Rsch. fellow Dermatology Found., 1985. Fellow Am. Acad. Dermatology; mem. Tex. Med. Assn., Harris County Med. Soc., Tex. Dermatol. Soc., Houston Dermatol. Soc. (pres. 2005), U. Tex. Houston Health Sci. Ctr. (devel. coun. 1994-96, devel. bd., 2007-), Houston Country Club. Republican. Episcopalian. Avocations: tennis, golf. Office: 515 Post Oak Blvd Ste 535 Houston TX 77027-9494

DOUGHERTY, CHARLES HAMILTON, pediatrician; b. St. Louis, June 1, 1947; s. Charles Joseph and Suzanne Louise (Hamilton) D.; m. Mary Laverty Peckham, July 7, 1972; children: Bridget, Matthew, Erin, Kelly. BA in Biology, Coll. of the Holy Cross, 1969; MD, U. Rochester Sch. of Medicine, NYC, 1973. Pediatric resident St. Louis Children's Hosp., 1973-76, pres. med. staff, 2005—07; pvt. practice pediatrics Primary Pediatric Care Group, St. Louis, 1976-86, Esse Health, St. Louis, 1986—. Fellow Am. Acad. Pediatrics. Roman Catholic. Avocations: running, travel, water sports. Office: Esse Health 13303 Tesson Ferry Rd Saint Louis MO 63128-4062 Office Phone: 314-842-5239. Personal E-mail: cdoughe103@aol.com. Business E-Mail: cdougher@essehealth.com.

DOUGHERTY, JAMES, cardiologist; b. Washington, Nov. 2, 1948; BS, Villanova U., 1970; MD, Georgetown U., 1974. Pres. Consulting Cardiologists P.C., 1979—. Assoc. clin. prof. medicine U. Conn., 2004. Recipient Top Physician, Hartford Mag. Fellow: ACP, Am. Coll. Cardiology. Avocation: tennis. Office: 85 Seymour St Hartford CT 06106 Office Fax: 860-522-1761. Personal E-mail: jedmd11@gmail.com.

DOUGHERTY, MATTHEW J., vascular surgeon; MD, Harvard Coll. Diplomate Am. Bd. Surgery-gen. surgery, 1991, Am. Bd. Surgery-vascular surgery, 1993. Intern Mass. Gen. Hosp., resident; fellow Mayo Clinic; hosp. affiliation includes Pa. Hosp. Named one of the Top Doctor, Phila. Mag., 2009—11, the Am.'s Top Doctors, 2010. Office: Pennsylvania Vascular Associates PC Ste 101 700 Spruce St Philadelphia PA 19106 Office Phone: 800-789-7366.

DOUGHTY, DOROTHY BECKLEY, nursing administrator; b. Columbia, SC, Aug. 3, 1947; BSN, Med. Coll. Ga., 1969; MN, Emory U., 1972. Dir. Wound, Ostomy, and Continence Nursing Edn. Ctr., Emory U., 1984—. Past pres., mem. various com. WOCN Soc., 1986—2011. Fellow: Am. Acad. Nursing. Office: Emory University WOC Nursing Edn Ctr Atlanta GA 30322 Office Fax: 404-778-4778. Business E-Mail: ddought@emory.edu.

DOUGLAS, BARRY K., plastic surgeon; b. NYC, June 15, 1954; s. Leonard S. and Elaine K. Douglas; m. K. K. Koenigsberg, Mar. 27, 1983; children: Lauren, Robert, Marc. BA, Trinity Coll., Conn., 1976; MD, Wake Forest U., 1980. Diplomate Am. Bd. Plastic Surgery. Residency in gen. surgery and plastic surgery Mt. Sinai Hosp., NYC, 1980—87; fellowship in pediat. plastic surgery Children's Hosp. Akron, 1987; attending physician plastic surgery L.I. Plastic Surg. Group, Garden City, 1991—. Covers for art jours. and programs. Fellow, MEDCOM, 1987. Fellow: Am. Acad. Pediats., Am. Coll. Surgeons; mem.: N.Y. State Med. Soc., Am. Cleft Palate Assn., Am. Soc. Plastic Surgeons, Northeastern Soc. Plastic Surgeons, NY Regional Soc. Plastic Surgeons, Nassau Surg., Nassau County MAD Soc., Phi Beta Kappa. Avocations: painting, piano. Office: LI Plastic Surg Group 999 Franklin Ave Garden City NY 11530 Office Phone: 516-742-3404. E-mail: bdouglas@lipsg.com. *

DOUGLAS, BRUCE LEE, oral and maxillofacial surgeon, occupational and geriatric health educator, consultant; b. NYC, July 14, 1925; s. William and Carrie (Basescu) D.; m. Janet Ramsden; children: Clifford, Steven, Jennifer, Sarah, Sandra. AB, Princeton U., 1947; DDS, NYU, 1948; postgrad. in oral surgery, Columbia U., 1949-51, MA in Edn, 1955, diploma in higher edn, 1957; MPH, U. Calif., Berkeley, 1962. Diplomate Am. Bd. Oral and Maxillofacial Surgery. Prof. oral medicine and community dentistry Coll. Dentistry

U. Ill., 1962-72, prof. preventive medicine Coll. Medicine, 1962-72; prof. health adminstrn. Sch. Pub. Health, 1972-98; prof. dental and oral surgery Rush Med. Coll., 1970-76; clin. prof. environ. and occupl. medicine Sch. Pub. Health, U. Ill. at Chgo., 1998—, health policy rsch., 2001—. Chief dentistry and oral surgery Rush-Presbyn.-St. Luke's Med. Ctr., Chgo., 1968-75; chief divsn. dental health, Ill. Dept. Pub. Health, 1976-78; chief sect. dentistry and oral surgery Lincoln Park Hosp. Chgo. (formerly Grant Hosp.), 1980-90, attending oral and maxillofacial surgeon, 1967-2009; attending oral and maxillofacial surgeon Vista Med. Ctr. Waukegan, Ill., 2005-, vis. prof., U. Haiti Faculty Dentistry, Port Au Prince; Fulbright prof. oral surgery and anesthesiology Okayama U. and Tokyo Med.-Dental U., 1959-61; WHO cons. to U. Antioquia, Colombia, Nat. U. and U. Zulia, Venezuela, 1964-69, Mahidol U., Bangkok, Thailand, 1973, Nat. Health Svc., Gt. Britain, 1977. Mem. Ill. Ho. of Reps., 11th Dist., 1971-72, 12th Dist., 1973-74; chmn. Ill. Coalition Against Tobacco, 1991-93; chief med. advisor, Sedgwick Claims Mgmt. Svcs., 1998-2002; sr. scholar in residence Wash. Bus. Group on Health, 2002-04. With USN, 1951—53, Japan, Korea, with USNR, 1943—53, lt. dental corps. USN, 1951—53. Recipient Hon. award, U. Ctrl. de Venezuela, Ill. Pub. Health Assn., Ill. Gen. Assembly, Lincoln Park (Chgo.) C. of C., William J. Gies Found. Advancement Dentistry, Okayama U. Med. Sch., Japan, Best Legislator award, Ind. Voters Ill., Ill. Vet. Med. Assn., Nat. Hemophilia Found., AFL-CIO Ill., Jewish War Vets. Fellow Chgo. Inst. Medicine (bd. dirs. 1970-80), Am. Dental Soc. Anesthesiology (editor, fellow gen. anesthesia, past pres.), Am. Pub. Health Assn., Internat. Coll. Dentists, Am. Assn. Hosp. Dentists (past pres., editor), Am. Assn. Oral and Maxillofacial Surgeons (assoc. editor Jour. Oral Surgery), Fulbright Assn. (pres. Chgo. chpt. 1990-92), Omicron Kappa Upsilon (hon.), Phi Delta Kappa (hon.), Soc. Sigma X (hon.). Address: 2401 Duffy Ln Riverwoods IL 60015 Personal E-mail: brucedouglas@comcast.net.

DOUGLAS, CAROLYN JORY, psychiatrist; b. NYC, Sept. 27, 1953; BA summa cum laude, Princeton U., 1976; MD, Harvard U., 1980. Diplomate Am. Bd. Psychiatry and Neurology. Resident Payne Whitney Clinic, NYC, 1980-84; assoc. clin. prof. psychiatry Presbyn. Hosp., Columbia U. Coll. Surgeons and Physicians, NYC, 1984—. Dir. Eye-6 inpatient psychiatric unit, Presbyn. Hosp., N.Y.C., 1986—. Contbr. articles to profl. jours. Mem. Am. Psychiatric Assn., Phi Beta Kappa. Office: 122 E 93rd St New York NY 10128-1608

DOUGLAS, JACK FRANK, chemist; b. Richmond, Va., July 2, 1956; s. Frank Henry and Nancy (Miles) D.; m. Kathryn Abernathy, Aug. 16, 1975; 1 child, Gregory Alan. BS in Chemistry, Va. Commonwealth U., 1979, MS in Maths., 1981; PhD in Chemistry, U. Chgo., 1986. Postdoctoral rschr. Cavendish Lab. Cambridge U., England, 1986-87; postdoctoral rschr. NIST, Gaithersburg, Md., 1987-88, rsch. scientist, 1988—. Fellow Am. Phys. Soc. Avocation: fossil and mineral collecting. Office: NIST 100 Bureau Dr Gaithersburg MD 20899-0003

DOUGLAS, JAMES FREDERICK, nephrologist; b. Portadown, Ireland, Sept. 22, 1938; s. James and Annie Hildegarde (Harte) D.; m. Giselle Sook An Lim, Apr. 27, 1973; children: Jeremy, Timothy, Andrew. BA in Jurisprudence, Oxford U., 1959, B in Civl Law, 1960, MA, 1965, BMBCh, 1969, MDBCh, QUB Belfast, UK, 1969. Barrister-at-law Middle Temple, London, 1964; FRCP/U.K., 1986. Lectr. Coll. of Law, London, 1962-64; house officer Royal Victoria Hosp., Belfast, 1969-70, registrar nephrology Belfast City Hosp., 1972-74; No. Ireland Kidney Rsch. Fellow Belfast, 1974-75; cons. nephrologist Belfast City and Royal Victoria Hosps., 1975—2003, dir. nephrology, 1988-96; lectr. clin. pharm. Med. Law & Ethics, Queens U., Belfast, 2003—. Mem. Transplant Regulatory Authority, U.K., 1996-2006, UK Transplant Support Authority, U.K., 1995-2002; vis. physician St. Helena, 2007. Contbr. numerous articles to profl. jours., chpt. to textbook. Fellow Royal Coll. Physicians,; mem. Am. Soc. Nephrology, Renal Assn., European Dialysis and Transplant Soc., Brit. Transplant Soc. (mem. coun. 2002--), Transplantation Soc., Internat. Soc. of Nephrology, British Transplant Games Com. (chmn. Belfast Games 1998). Mem. Ch. of Ireland. Office: Ballyrobert House 5 Coyle's Ln BT19 1UF Ballyrobert Northern Ireland E-mail: jamesfdouglas38@hotmail.com.

DOUGLAS, JOHN SIMONTON, JR., cardiologist, educator; b. Tuscumbia, Ala., Apr. 18, 1941; Grad., U. South; MD, Washington U. Sch. Medicine, St. Louis, 1967. Diplomate Am. Bd. Internal Medicine, Am. Bd. Cardiovascular Diseases, Am. Bd. Interventional Cardiology. Intern, medicine NC Meml. Hosp., Chapel Hill, 1967-68, resident, internal medicine, 1968-69; resident, cardiology Grady Meml. Hosp., Atlanta, 1971-72; fellow, cardiology Emory Affiliated Hosps., Atlanta, 1972-74; mem. staff Emory U. Hosp., Atlanta, 1972—, dir., cardiac catheterization lab., 2001—, dir., interventional cardiology, 2001—; assoc. prof. Emory U. Sch. Medicine, prof., medicine. Dir., Emory Practical Intervention Course Emory U. Contbr. several articles to profl. jours. Lt. comdr. US Navy Med. Corps, Camp Lejeune Marine Corps Base and in An Hoa, S. Vietnam. Named to Castle Connolly Guide to America's Top Doctors, Atlanta's Top Doctors, The Best Doctors in Am. Fellow: Am. Coll. Cardiology (former bd. mem.); mem.: Soc. for Cardiac Angiography and Intervention. Achievements include being the member of the team that performed the first coronary angioplasty at Emory University Hospital and in 1987 the first coronary stent in the US. Office: Emory U Hosp Ste F606 1364 Clifton Rd NE Atlanta GA 30322 Office Phone: 404-727-7040. Business E-Mail: john.douglas@emoryhealthcare.org.

DOUGLAS, PAMELA SUSAN, physician, researcher, educator; b. New Brunswick, NJ, Dec. 2, 1954; d. Jocelyn Fielding and Rose Maria (Terrazzino) D.; m. Geoffrey Steven Ginsburg. AB, Princeton U., NJ, 1974; MD, Med. Coll. Va., 1978. Cert. Nat. Bd. Med. Examiners, Am. Bd. Internal Medicine (subspecialty in cardiovasc. disease), Nat. Bd. Echocardiography. Resident, internal medicine Hosp. U. Pa., Phila., 1978—81, clin. and rsch. fellow, cardiology, 1981—84, physician, 1984—90; asst. instr. medicine U. Pa. Sch. Medicine, Phila., 1979—81, asst. prof. medicine, 1984—90; physician Phila. VA Hosp., 1984—90; assoc. prof. medicine Harvard Med. Sch., Boston, 1990—2000; physician Beth Israel Deaconess Med. Ctr., 1990—2000; Dr. Herman and Ailene Tuchman prof. cardiovasc. medicine, head dept. U. Wis., Madison, 2000—04, assoc. dir. Cardiovasc. Rsch. Ctr., 2000—04; physician U. Wis. Hosp. and Clinics, Madison, 2000—04, William S. Middleton VA Hosp., 2000—; chief, divsn. cardiology Duke U. Med. Ctr., 2004—, Ursula Geller prof. for Rsch. in Cardiovascular Diseases, 2004—, dir., cardiovascular rsch. strategies, 2004—. Adv. bd. Mallinckrodt, 1997—2001, DuPont Pharm., 1998—2001, Premier Innovation Inst., 1999—2001, Nat. Women's Health Report Card, 1998—, Boston Women's Health, 1998—2001, Cardiology Domain, 2000—; mem. sci. adv. coun. Soc. Women's Health Rsch., 2001—. Mem. editl. bd. Am. Jour. Cardiology, 1986—, Jour. Sports Medicine and Physical Fitness, 1991—, Internat. Jour. Sports Cardiology, 1991—, Jour. Women's Health, 1991—, Am. Jour. Geriatric Cardiology, 1992—, Am. Heart Jour., 1996—, Jour. Clin. and Exptl. Cardiology, 1997—, Jour. Clin. and Basic Cardiology, —, Cardiology, 2000—; manuscript reviewer: numerous pubs. in field; contbr. numerous articles to profl. jours., chapters to books; editor: Heart Disease in Women, 1989, Cardiovascular Health and Disease in Women, 1993, 2d edit., 2002. Mem. med. com. USA Triathlon, 1988—, chmn. med. control. com., 1989—; chmn. antidoping control com. Internat. Triathlon Union, 1989—92, mem. med. com., 1989—92; physician, finish line med. team Hawaii Ironman Triathlon, 1984—99; dir. elite med. tent Boston Marathon, 1991—96. Named Best of Boston cardiologist, 1997—2000; nominee IOC Olympic prize for Med. Sci., 2000—; grantee, Commonwealth Pa., 1984—90, A.H. Robins, 1985—87, Echocardiography Rsch. Found., 1986—88, 1990—96, 1993, 1995—97, 1996—98, 1996—, Syntex, 1987—93, SOCAR, 1991—94, Gensia, 1992—93, Merck, 1992—93, 1993—97, St. Jude Med. Ctr., 1993, Women's Aid to Heart Rsch., 1993, 1995, Hewlett-Packard, 1991—96, 1995—98, NIH, 1995—2000, 1999—2000, 2000—, Molecular Biosys. Inc., 1997—99, Nat. Ctr. Excellence in Women's Health, 1998—2000, Nat. Rsch. Consortium Women's Health, 1999—, Agilent Tech., 2000—, Inovise Med., 2000—; fellow, NIH, 1978, Am. Coll. Cardiology/European Soc. Cardiology/Merck, 1992. Fellow: Am. Coll. Sports Medicine, Am. Heart Assn. (session chair and structured sessions spkr. 1988—, bd. dirs. 1991—92, program com. 1993—95, exec. com. 1994—98, nominations com. coun. clin. cardiology 1995—2000, fellowship award 1982—83, 1983—84, grant 1985—86, 1986—87, 1987—88, 1988—89), Am. Coll. Cardiology (com. on women in cardiology 1994—2000, asst. sec. bd. trustees 1995—97, bd. trustees 1995—, audit com. 1996—97, nominating com. 1997—99, chair nominating com. 1998—99, com. expert consensus documents 1998—2001, mem. task force mem. rels. 1999—2000, forum for future writing group 1999—2000, task force for 21st century 1999—2000, chair tax status restructuring task force 2000—01, writing com. to develop clin. competence echocardiography statement 2000—, mem. echocardiography com. 2001—, budget fin. and investment com. 2001—, other coms., mem. editl. bd. 1993—97); mem.: Assn. Profs. Cardiology, Ctrl. Soc. Clin. Rsch., Am. Soc. Echocardiography (bd. dirs. 1993—96, session chair and structured sessions spkr. 1993—, sci. session program com. 1994—, judge young investigator rsch. awards 1995—2000, chair outcomes rsch. awards com. 1996—2001, devel. com. 1996—, sect. editor jour. 1998—, v.p. 1999—2001, strategic planning process co-chair 1999—2001, bd. dirs. 1999—, exec. com. 1999—, pres. 2001—, chair women's health adv. group 2001—, mem. editl. bd. 1993—, rsch. award 1992), Alpha Sigma Chi. Office: Duke U Med Ctr PO Box 17969 7022 N Pavillion DUMC Durham NC 27715 Office Phone: 919-681-2690. Office Fax: 919-668-7059.

DOUGLAS, ROBERT GORDON, JR., physician; b. NYC, Apr. 17, 1934; s. Robert Gordon and Alice (Lewis) D.; m. Sheila Ann Mahoney, Sept. 12, 2007; children: Robert Gordon, 3d, Timothy Stuart, Catherine Lewis. AB, Princeton U., 1955; MD, Cornell U., 1959. Diplomate Am. Bd. Internal Medicine. Successively intern, asst. resident in internal medicine, resident N.Y. Hosp., 1959-61, 62-63; asst. resident Johns Hopkins Hosp., 1961-62; USPHS clin. assoc., clin. investigator Nat. Inst. Allergy and Infectious Disease, 1963-66, asst. prof. microbiology and medicine Baylor Coll. Medicine, Houston, 1966-70; mem. faculty Sch. Medicine and Dentistry U. Rochester, NY, 1970-82, prof. medicine and microbiology Sch. Medicine and Dentistry NY, 1974-82, head infectious disease unit Sch. Medicine and Dentistry NY, 1970-82, sr. assoc. dean cdn. Sch. Medicine and Dentistry NY, 1979-82; prof., chmn. dept. medicine Med. Coll. Cornell U., 1982-90; physician in chief N.Y. Hosp., 1982-90; sr. v.p. medi. and sci. affairs Merck Sharp & Dohme Internat., 1990-91; pres. Merck Vaccines, 1991-99; cons. Vaccine Rsch. Ctr., NIAID, 1999—. Bd. dirs. Elusys Inc., 2000-09, Iomai Inc., 2000-08, VaxInnate Inc., 2005-09; chmn. bd. dirs. Vical Inc., 1999—, Middlebrook Pharm. Corp., 2006—; adj. prof. medicine Cornell U. Med. Coll., 1990—; hon. attending physician N.Y. Hosp., 1990—; chmn. Aeras Global TB Vaccine Found., 2001—; cons. in field. Editor: Principles and Practices of Infectious Diseases, 1979, 2d edit., 1985, 3d edit., 1990; contbr. articles to profl. jours. Recipient Hawkins award Assn. Am. Pubs., 1980. Fellow ACP, Infectious Diseases Soc. Am. (pres. 1991-92, Feldman award); mem. Inst. Medicine, Am. Soc. Clin. Investigation, Assn. Am. Physicians, Am. Clin. Climatol. Assn. (pres. 1999-2000), Nat. Found. for Infectious Disease (Maxwell Finland award 2000). Home and Office: 265 Old Black Point Rd Niantic CT 06357

DOUGLAS, TOBY, public health service officer, state official; BS in Economics, U. Calif., Berkeley, M in Public Health and Public Policy. Rsch. assoc. Urban Inst., Washington; sr. mgr. health access, policy and planning San Mateo County Health Dept., 2001—05; joined Calif. Dept. Health Care Services, 2005, chief dep. dir. health care programs, 2009—11, dir., 2011—. Office: California Department if Health Care Services PO Box 15559 Sacramento CA 95852-0559 Office Phone: 916-445-4171. *

DOUKI DEDIEU, SAIDA, retired medical educator; b. Monastir, Italy, Dec. 27, 1948; PhD in Medicine, 1979. Prof., psychiatry Faculty Medicine, Tunis, 1986—2008, emeritus prof., 2009—; prof., medicine, 1991; assoc. prof. U. Claude Bernard, Lyon, 2006—10. Head, dept. psychiatry Razi Hosp., 1978—2008. Recipient award, Tunisian Govt. Master: Congres De Psychiatrie Et Neurologie De Langue Francaise, Arab Fedn. Psychiatrists, Tunisian Soc. Psychiatry; mem.: Am. Psychiat. Assn. Avocations: writing, music, travel. Home: 15 Rue Gustave Nadaud Lyon Rhone 69007 France Personal E-mail: saida.douki@ch-le-vinatier.fr.

DOUPI, PERSEPHONE, research scientist; b. Athens, Greece, Feb. 15, 1969; d. Vasileios Doupis and Polyxeni Doupi; m. Kristian Lampe, May 27, 2006; children: Aleksi, Vasileios, Peter. MD, Nat. & Kapodistrian U. of Athens, 1996; MS in Med. Informatics, Erasmus U., 1998, DSc in Med. Informatics, 1999, PhD in Med. Informatics, 2005. Cert. physician Ministry of Health, Greece, 1997, lic. Finland, 2008. Sci. rschr. Dutch Burns Found., Beverwijk, 2000—02; rsch. fellow Inst. Med. Informatics Erasmus Med. Ctr., Rotterdam, Netherlands, 2000—02; sr. rschr. Nat. Inst. for Health & Welfare, Helsinki, Finland, 2002—. Mem. support team Tech. Foresight in Greece, Athens, 2002—03; mem. expert team BIOINFOMED, Spain, 2002, Internat. Consensus Workshop on Quality Criteria for Internet Health Info., Heidelberg, Germany, 2000; mem. working group 23 e-business forum, Greece, 04; mem. working group Finnish Nat. Health Portal project, 2006—; mem. Ministerial Group Patient Safety Reporting, 2008—. Co-author (white paper) Synergy between Medical Informatics and Bioinformatics: Facilitating Genomic Medicine for Future Healthcare; mem. editl. bd.: World Hosp. and Health Svcs. Jour., 2004—; contbr. articles to profl. jours.; author: (book) Perspnalised Parent Education & Internat, 2005; co-author: eHealth Policy & Deployment In The European Union, 2008; author: National Repotrting Systems for Patient Safety Incidents, 2009. Grantee, Greek Scholarships Found., 1998—2001, Erasmus U. Inst. for Decision Support and Info. Sys., 1997—98; Gina Bachauer Scholarship, Am. Coll. of Greece, 1980—86. Mem.: IEEE, IEEE Computer Soc., Athens Med. Assn., Soc. Internet in Medicine. Achievements include research in personalized discharge education and support of burn patients; Internet health applications and quality, ehealth strategies monitoring and analysis, information technology and patient safety. Avocations: travel, languages, literature, movies, swimming. Office: Nat Inst Health & Welfare PO Box 30 Linhulahden Kuja 4 Helsinki FL 00271 Finland Office Fax: 358-20-6107443. Business E-Mail: persephone.doupi@stakes.fi.

DOVER, GEORGE JOSEPH, pediatric oncologist; b. Jan. 10, 1947; MD, La. State U. Sch. Medicine, New Orleans, 1972. Cert. in pediat. 1976, in pediatric hematology-oncology 1978. Internship in pediat. Johns Hopkins U. Hosp., Balt., 1972—73, residency in pediat., 1973—74, residency in pediatric hematology, 1974—75, fellowship, 1975—77; prof. pediat., medicine, and oncology The Johns Hopkins Sch. Medicine, dir., divsn. pediatric hematology, 1990—97; dir., pediatrician-in-chief The Johns Hopkins Children's Ctr. Dept. Pediat., 1997—, Given prof. pediat. Bd. mem. Johns Hopkins Children's Ctr., Balt. Contbr. articles to profl. jours., chapters to books. Med. adv. bd. Cooley's Anemia Found. Inc. Recipient George J. Stuart award, Johns Hopkins U., Alexander Schaffer award, Harriet Lane Pediatric Residents, MERIT Rsch. award, Nat. Heart, Lung, and Blood Inst.; grantee, NIH, 1980—. Office: Johns Hopkins Univ Dept Pediat 600 N Wolfe St Baltimore MD 21287 Office Phone: 410-955-5976. Office Fax: 410-614-2079.

DOVEY, MARK EDWARD, pediatric pulmonologist, educator; MD, Duke U., 1989. Diplomate Am. Bd. Pediatrics, Am. Bd. Pediatrics-pediatric pulmonology, lic. Pa., 2007. Resident pediat. Johns Hopkins Hosp., 1992; fellow pediatric pulmonology Children's Hosp.; assoc. prof. pediat. Drexel Univ. Coll. of Medicine; attending pulmonologist St. Christopher's Hospital for Children, acting chief sect. of critical care, chief sect. of pulmonology. Named one of Top Doctors, Phila. Mag., 2010—11. Office: Saint Christopher's Hospital for Children 3601 A St Philadelphia PA 19134 Office Phone: 215-427-5000. Office Fax: 215-427-5555.

DOVEY, SERENA, endocrinologist; b. Auckland, New Zealand, Nov. 2, 1977; BS, Coll. William & Mary, 2000; MD, U. Va. Sch. Medicine, 2004. Endocrinologist U. Pitts. Med. Ctr., 2011—. Office: 300 Halket St Ste 5150 Pittsburgh PA 15213 Business E-Mail: doveysl@upmc.edu.

DOW, DAVID SONTAG, retired ophthalmologist; b. Ann Arbor, Mich., Feb. 15, 1931; s. William Gould and Edna Lois (Sontag) Dow; m. Gail Anita Bade, Feb. 11, 1961 (dec. Feb. 2000); children: Steven Michael, Bonnie Jean, William Herbert, James Patrick; m. Figes Flaherty, Mar. 17, 2001. BS with distinction, U. Mich., 1956, MD, 1958, MS in Ophthalmology, 1964. Diplomate Am. Bd. Ophthalmology. Intern Denver Gen. Comm. Hosp., 1958-59; psychiatrist USAF Med. Svc., Wichita Falls, Tex., 1959-61; resident in ophthalmology U. Mich. Med. Ctr., Ann Arbor, 1961-64; pvt. practice ophthalmology Scruggs, Dow, and Kannwischer ptnr., Waco, Tex., 1964-88, Cen. Tex. Eye Clinic, Waco, 1988-97; pres. Woodway Found., 2006—09. Contbg. editor: Waco Tribune Herald, 1983—2010; author: pamphlets in field. Mem. Waco City Coun., 1977—81; mayor City of Waco, 1980—81; mem. Woodway City Coun., 1997—2001; bd. dir. Waco Symphony Assn., 1970—89, 1994—2001, 2006—09, pres., 1982—83; bd. dir. Tex. Med. Polit. Action Com., Austin, 1973—82; founding bd. dirs., chmn. Greater Waco Arts Coun., 1986—2010, chmn., 1992, 1994—2000, 2007—10. Capt. USAF, 1959—61. Mem.: Tex. Med. Assn., Am. Acad. Ophthalmology, Ridgewood Country Club, Rotary. Presbyterian. Avocations: politics, gardening, singing, musical theater. *

DOW, LOIS WEYMAN, physician; b. Cin., Mar. 1942; d. Albert Dames and Elsie Marion (Krug) Weyman; m. Alan Wayne Dow, 1966 (div. Aug. 1979); children: Elizabeth Suzanne, Alan Wayne; m. William H. Rowe, June 2006. BA summa cum laude, Cornell U., 1964; MD cum laude, Harvard U., 1968. Diplomate Am. Bd. Internal Medicine, Am. Bd. Hematology, Am. Bd. Oncology, Am. Bd. Pathology in Hematopathology. Intern Bronx Mcpl. Hosp. Ctr., NYC, 1968—69; resident internal medicine Presbyn. Hosp., NYC, 1969—70; fellow hematology Columbia U. Coll. Physicians and Surgeons, 1970—72; instr., rsch. assoc. U. Tenn., Memphis, 1972—73, asst. prof., 1973—74; rsch. assoc. hematology and oncology St. Jude Children's Rsch. Hosp., Memphis, 1974—77, asst. mem., 1977—80, assoc. mem., 1980—88; assoc. prof. pediat. U. Tenn., Memphis, 1983—88; mem. staff Bapt. Mem. Hosp., Memphis, 1972—88, St. Jude Children's Rsch. Hosp., 1974—88; pvt. practice Newark, 1988—98; mem. staff Med. Ctr. Del. (now Christian Care Health Ctr.), Wilmington, 1988—98; dir. hematology lab. Med. Ctr. Del. (now Christiana Care Health Ctr.), Newark, Del., 1993—98; mem. staff Alfred I Dupont Inst., 1988—98, St. Francis Hosp., 1996—98. Assoc. prof., Jefferson Med. Coll., Phila., 1988—; cons., Nat. Cancer Inst. Contbr. articles to profl. jours. Fellow ACP; mem. Am. Soc. Clin. Oncology, Am. Fedn. Clin. Rsch., Am. Soc. Hematology, Am. Assn. for Cancer Rsch., Am. Soc. Clin. Pathologists, Cornell Club, Harvard Club.

DOWDELL, MICHAEL FRANCIS, critical care nurse, anesthesia nurse practitioner; b. Cleve., June 5, 1949; s. Harry William and Dorothy May (McGivney) Dowdell; 1 child, Michael Patrick. BSN, Ohio State U., 1975; MA in Counseling, Nat. U., San Diego, 1981; MSN, Calif. State U., Long Beach, 1991; diploma in nursing anesthesia, Kaiser Sch. Anesthesia, LA, 1991; postgrad., Case Western Res. U., Cleve., 1996—. CRNA, ARNP, critical care nurse specialist; cert. c.c. instr. Calif. Enlisted USN, 1968, commd. ensign,

1974, advanced through grades to lt. comdr., 1984, ret., 1988; resident nurse anesthesist Kaiser Sch. Anesthesia for Nurses, 1989-91; staff nurse anesthetist Kaiser Hosp., Panorama City, Calif., 1991-92, HCA Med. Ctr., Largo, Fla., 1992-93, Meml. Mission Hosp., Asheville, N.C., 1993-97; owner Anesthesia Nursing Svcs. P.A., 1998—. Vis. lectr. dept. anesthesia Makerere U., Kampala, Uganda, 1995. Fellow: Am. Acad. Pain Mgmt. (credentialed pain practitioner); mem.: VFW, NRA, AACN, Fleet Res. Assn., Assn. Mil. Surgeons U.S., Am. Assn. Nurse Anesthetists, Single Action Shooting Soc., Ret. Officers Assn., Am. Legion, Sigma Theta Tau. Republican. Avocations: fishing, shooting sports, travel. Office: 10650 Culebra Rd Ste 104 PMB 544 San Antonio TX 78251-4949 Office Phone: 210-845-4480. Personal E-mail: mfdpatexas@yahoo.com.

DOWLING, BRIAN R., medical association administrator; b. Harrisburg, Pa., Jan. 27, 1979; BS, Ind. U., Pa., 2001. Dir. fin. Pa. Psychiat. Inst., 2008—. Mem.: HFMA. Home: 210 N 39th St Harrisburg PA 17109 Business E-Mail: bdowling@papsychinst.org.

DOWLING, MICHAEL J., hospital administrator; Attended, U. Coll. Cork, Ireland; MA, Fordham U.; D (hon.), Hofstra U. State dir. health, edn., and human svcs. NY State Govt., dep. sec. to the gov.; sr. v.p. Empire Blue Cross/Blue Shield; sr. v.p. hosp. svcs. North Shore Long Island Jewish Med. Ctr., 1995, health system exec. v.p., 1997, COO, 1997, pres., 2002—, CEO, 2002—. Prof. social policy Fordham Univ. Grad. Sch. of Social Svcs., asst. dean; dir. Fordham Campus, Westchester County, NY; mem. trust symposium steering com. Harvard Univ.; bd. dirs. Long Island Philharmonic Bd., Biomedical Rsch. Alliance of NY, Academic Medicine Devel. Co., Nat. Ctr. for Healthcare Leadership; mem. N. Am. bd. of the Smurfit sch. of bus. University Coll. Dublin; mem. pres. adv. coun. Adelphi Univ.; chmn. League of Voluntary Hosps. and Homes of NY. Recipient Nat. Human Rels. award, Am. Jewish Com., CEO Info. Tech. award, Modern Healthcare Mag., 2011, Ellis Island Medal of Honor, Distinguished Pub. Svc. award, SUNY Nelson A. Rockefeller Coll. of Pub. Affairs and Policy, Outstanding Pub. Svc. award, Mental Health Assn. of NY State, Mental Health Assn. of Nassau County, Alfred E. Smith award, ASPA, Gold medal, Am. Irish Hist. Soc. Mem.: Econ. Club of NY, Healthcare Rsch. and Devel. Inst., Am. Hosp. Assn. (regional policy bd. mem.), Greater NY Hosp. Assn. (vice chmn.), Healthcare Assn. of NY State (bd. dirs.). Office: North Shore Long Island Jewish Medical Center 270-05 76th Ave New Hyde Park NY 11040 Office Phone: 718-470-7000.

DOWNEY, LAURENCE, retired pharmaceutical executive; b. UK; MD, U. Manchester, UK; diploma, Royal Coll. Physicians; grad. Adv. Mgmt. Program, Harvard Bus. Sch., 1996. Joined Solvay Pharm. Inc., 1981; med. adv. Solvay Healthcare Ltd., Southampton, UK, 1979—86; v.p. med. svcs. to sr. v.p., comml. ops., interim pres., CEO Solvay Pharm. Inc., Marietta, Ga., 1986—2006, pres., CEO, 2006—08; and CEO, chmn. Organics LLC (Solvay subs.), Marietta, Ga., 2006; pres. Berkshire Pharma Consulting, 2008—; CEO Ketal Biomed. Inc. Home: 1124 Berkshire Rd NE Atlanta GA 30306 Home Phone: 404-892-1242.

DOWNEY, ROBERT J., thoracic surgeon; BA, Yale U., 1981; MD, Columbia U. Cert. gen. surgery, diplomate Am. Bd. Surgery, Am. Bd. Surgery-surgical critical care, Am. Bd. Thoracic Surgery. Resident in gen. surgery NY Presbyn. Hosp./Columbia Univ. Med. Ctr., 1991; fellow in cardiothoracic surgery Mayo Clinic, 1992, NY Presbyn. Hosp./Columbia Univ. Med. Ctr., 1994; chest surgeon Meml. Sloan-Kettering Cancer Ctr. Author: (articles) Comparison of patterns of relapse in thymic carcinoma and thymoma, 2009, Video-assisted thoracic surgery (VATS) evaluation of pleural effusions in patients with newly diagnosed advanced ovarian carcinoma can influence the primary management choice for these patients, 2009, Progenitor stem cell marker expression by pulmonary carcinomas, 2010, A differentiation-based phylogeny of cancer subtypes, 2010, A grading system of lung adenocarcinomas based on histologic pattern is predictive of disease recurrence in stage I tumors, 2010. Named one of Best Doctors, NY Mag., 2010. Office: Memorial Sloan-Kettering Cancer Center 1275 York Ave New York NY 10065 Office Phone: 212-639-8124.

DOWNHAM, MAX C., medical association administrator; b. Carroll County, Ind. BSChemE, Purdue U. Coll. Engring., West Lafayette, Ind., 1958; MBA, U. Pa. Wharton Sch. Formerly with Nuc.-Chgo. Corp.; various positions to corp. v.p. NutraSweet Co., ret., 1995; exec. dir. Internat. Coll. Surgeons, 1996—. Lectr. mktg./bus. intelligence Oxford U., Harvard Bus. Sch. Bd. dirs. United Way Met. Chgo.; chair bd. dirs. United Way Ill. Served with USN. Named Disting. Engring. Alumni, Purdue U., 2006. Office: ICS 1516 N Lake Shore Dr Chicago IL 60610 Office Phone: 312-642-3155. Office Fax: 312-787-1624. Business E-Mail: max@icsglobal.org. *

DOWNS, FIONA MARY, physician; b. Campbeltown, Scotland, May 31, 1955; d. Dugald McMillan and Jean Alexander McShannon; m. Alan Stephen Downs, May 4, 1985; children: Thomas Stephen McShannon, Lois Mary. BSc, Glasgow U., 1977, MBChB, 1980. Trainee fellow St. Columba's Hospice, Edinburgh, 1983—87; various gen. practitioner tng. posts Forth Valley and Lanarkshire Heathboards, 1988—90; registrar Med. Rsch. Coun., Edinburgh, 1990—91; cons. palliative medicine Strathcarron Hospice, Denny, 1995—. Home: 28 Griffiths St Falkirk FK1 5AJ Scotland Office: Randolph Hill Denny FK6 5HJ Scotland

DOWNS, KATHLEEN ANNE, retired health facility administrator; b. Toledo, Sept. 20, 1951; d. Keith Landis and Cecelia Josephine Babcock; m. Michael Brian Thomas, July 17, 1971 (dec. Oct. 1973); m. David Michael Downs, Aug. 8, 1981. Student, San Diego Mesa Coll., 1968—70; BS, Union Inst., 1989. Cert. profl. med. staff mgmt., provider credentialing specialist. Sec. Travelodge Internat., Inc., El Cajon, Calif., 1970-73; intermediate stenographer City of El Cajon, 1973-77; adminstrv. asst. MacLellan & Assocs., El Cajon, 1977-78; sr. sec. WESTEC Services, Inc., San Diego, 1978; adminstrv. sec. El Cajon Valley Hosp., 1978-80; asst. med. staff Grossmont Dist. Hosp., La Mesa, Calif., 1980-83, coord. med. staff, 1983-87, mgr., 1987-94; mgr. med. staff Sharp Meml. Hosp., San Diego, 1994; dir. med. staff svcs. Sharp HealthCare, San Diego, 1994-96, sr. specialist med. staff svcs., 1996; dir. med. staff svcs. Alvarado Hosp. Med. Ctr. and San Diego Rehab. Inst., San Diego, 1996-99; mgr. med. staff svcs. Kaiser Permanente Hosp., San Diego, 1999-2001, med. staff svcs. cons., 2001—08; dir. med. staff svcs. Paradise Valley Hosp., National City, Calif., 2001—07; credentialing specialist Scripps Mercy Surgery Pavilion, 2007—; med. staff coord. San Diego Hosp. & Palliative Care, 2007—09. Tchr. The Vogel Inst., San Diego, 1986; mem. med. staff svcs. adv. com. San Diego C.C. Dist.; adj. faculty Union Inst., 1991-96, Chemeketa C.C., 1991-95; credentials verification orgn. surveyor Nat. Com. Quality Assurance, Washington, 1996—2004. Mem. Nat. Assn. Med. Staff Svcs. (edn. coun. 1989-93, faculty 1990—, chmn. 1991-93, bd. dirs. 1991-93, editl. bd. Over View 1993-96), Calif. Assn. Med. Staff Svcs. (treas. San Diego chpt. 1984-86, pres. 1986-87, state sec. 1999-2001, pres.-elect 2001-03, pres. 2003-05, forum com. 2008-11). Avocations: gardening, boating, gourmet cooking, yoga, walking. Personal E-mail: kathydowns51@gmail.com. Business E-Mail: downs.kathy@scrippshealth.org.

DOYLE, CONSTANCE TALCOTT JOHNSTON, physician, medical association administrator, educator; b. Mansfield, Ohio, July 8, 1945; d. Frederick Lyman IV and Nancy Jean Bushnell (Johnston) Talcott; children: Ian Frederick Demsky, Zachary Adam Demsky. BS, Ohio U., 1967; MD, Ohio State U., 1971. Diplomate Am. Bd. Emergency Medicine; bd. cert. in emergency crisis response. Intern Riverside Hosp., Columbus, Ohio, 1971—72; resident in internal medicine Hurley Hosp., U. Mich., Flint, 1972—74; emergency physician Oakwood Hosp., Dearborn, Mich., 1974—76, Jackson County Emergency Svcs., Mich., 1975—95; cons. Region II EMS, 1978—79, disaster cons., 1983—95, St. Joseph Mercy Hosp., Ann Arbor, 1995—, med. flight physician helicopter life support svcs., 1996—; core faculty St. Joseph Mercy Hosp./U. Mich. Emergency Residency, Ann Arbor, 1995—; survival flight physician helicopter rescue svc. U. Mich., 1983—91; course dir. advanced cardiac life support and chmn. advanced life support com. W.A. Foote Meml. Hosp., Jackson, 1979—95; dep. dir. emergency svcs. med. ctrl. bd. Washtenaw Livingston County, 2000—; core faculty St. Joseph Mercy Hosp., Ann Arbor, 1996—. Clin. instr. emergency svcs., dept. emergency med. U. Mich., 1981—; faculty combined emergency medicine residency St. Joseph Mercy Hosp.-U. Mich., Ann Arbor, 1995—; EMS rotation dir., 2002-07, asst. med. dir. Region 2 South Biodef. Network, 2002-03, co-med. dir., 2003-05, dep. med. dir., 2005-06; instr. EMT refresher courses, Jackson County, Jackson C.C.; Med-Flight physician, 1996-99; Washtenaw County Subcom. on Bioterrorism, 2000—; Washtenaw County Local Emergency Planning Com., 1998—; dep. med. dir. Washtenaw/Livingston County Med. Control Authority, 2000—. Contbg. author: Clinical Approach to Poisoning and Toxicology, 1983, 89, 97, May's Textbook of Emergency Medicine, 1991, Schwartz Principles and Practice of Emergency Medicine, 1992, Reisdorff Pediatric Emergency Medicine, 1993; contbr. articles to profl. jours. Mem. Disaster Med. Assistance Team, 2000—; served Ground Zero, 2001, Hurrican Francis, 2004, Hurrican Katrina/Rita, 2005, Hurricane Ernesto. Fellow Am. Coll. Emergency Physicians (life, pres. Mich. disaster com. 1987-88, bd. dirs. Mich. 1979-88, chmn. Mich. disaster com. 1979-85, mem. nat. disaster med. svcs. com. 1983-85, chmn. 1987-88, cons. disaster mgmt. course Fed. Emergency Mgmt. Agy. 1982, treas. 1984-85, emergency med. svcs. com. 1985, pres. 1986-87, councillor 1986-87, chair steering com. policy sect., 1994—, mem. disaster sect., 1995—, exec. com. disaster sect. 1997—2001, chair policy sect. disaster 1995—, vice chair sect. careers in emergency medicine 1997—, chair, 2000-02, past chair 2002-04), Nat. Am. Coll. Emergency Physicians (vice chair sect. of disaster med. svcs. 1990-92, nat. disaster subcom. 1989-90, chair subsect. psychol. rehab. svcs., disaster med. svcs. 1992-94, chair policy and legis. 1994-96, task force on hazardous materials 1993-97, steering com. sect. disaster medicine 1994-2002, exec. com. sect. disaster medicine 1995, disaster com. mem., 2008-, chair task force, 2008-); mem. ACP (disaster com. chair task force pediat spl. needs, 2008-), Am. Med. Women's Assn., Am. Assn. Women Emergency Physicians, Mich. Assn. Emergency Med. Technicians (bd. dirs. 1979-80), Mich. State Med. Soc., Washtenaw County Med. Soc., Sierra Club. Jewish. Office: 1251 King George Blvd Ann Arbor MI 48108 also: St Joseph Mercy Hosp Dept Emergency Medicine Ann Arbor MI 48109 Personal E-mail: cjdoyle@pol.net.

DOYLE, DEREK, physician, consultant; b. Bury, England, July 13, 1931; s. John Patrick and Gladys Doyle; m. Bethia Robb, Sept. 4, 1956; children: Barbara, Elizabeth Brown, Alan, Peter. MB, ChB, Edinburgh U. Med. Sch., Eng., 1955, DSc (hon.), 2001. Missionary surgeon Ch. of Scotland, Sulenkama, South Africa, 1957—66; family physician Edinburgh, 1967—77; assoc. specialist Lothian Health, 1968—77; med. dir. St Columba's Hospice; hon. sr. lectr. U. Edinburgh, 1977—95. Hon v.p. Nat. Coun. Palliative Care, London, 1995—; hon pres. Scottish Partnership Palliative Care, Edinburgh. Editor: Oxford Textbook of Palliative Medicine, 2005 (Lifetime Achievement award, 2005); author, editor: 17 books. Vice chmn. Queen Margaret U., Edinburgh, 1995—2002. Recipient Officer of Noble Order of Brit. Empire, Her Majesty Queen Elizabeth, 1987; named Citizen of Yr., Edinburgh, 1992. Fellow: Soc. Antiquaries Scotland, Royal Colleges Surgeons, Physicians and Gen. Practice (London, Edinburgh) (life). Personal E-mail: derekdoyle@waitrose.com.

DOYLE, EUGENIE FLERI, pediatrician, cardiologist, educator; b. Bklyn., Oct. 19, 1921; d. Paul Charles and Antoinette (Giovannetti) Fleri; m. Joseph Anthony Doyle, Aug. 19, 1944; children: Christopher, Stephen, Eugenie, Jane Marie, Richard. BS, Marymount Coll., Tarrytown, NY, 1943, DSc (hon.), 1993; MD, Johns Hopkins U., 1946; DSc (hon.), Coll. New Rochelle, 1975. Intern in pediatrics Johns Hopkins Hosp., Balt., 1946-47; pediatric resident Bellevue Hosp., NYC, 1947-49; fellow pediatric cardiology NYU Med. Ctr., 1949-53, dir. pediatric cardiology, 1958-93; asst. prof. pediatrics NYU Sch. Medicine, 1953-58, assoc. prof., 1959-70, prof., 1970-92, prof. emerita, 1993—, clin. prof. pediatrics, 1994—, NYU Faculty Senate, 1985—88. Mem. cardiac adv. com. N.Y. State Health Dept., 1983-92; dir. Vis. Nurse Svc., N.Y.C., 1984—. Editor: Pediatric Cardiology, 1985; contbr. articles to profl. jours. Trustee Marymount Coll., 1983-91, vice chair bd., 1988-91. Mem. Am. Acad. Pediatrics, Am. Pediatric Soc., Am. Coll. Cardiology, Am. Heart Assn., N.Y. Heart Assn. (bd. dirs. 1977-84, pres. 1979-81), Cosmopolitan Club. Roman Catholic. Avocations: gardening, travel, ballet. Home: 32 Washington Sq W New York NY 10011-9156 Office: NYU Med Ctr 550 1st Ave New York NY 10016-6402

DOYLE, FRANCES MARY, psychiatric social worker; d. Francis Joseph and Margaret Mary (O'Donnell) Barry; m. Eugene Francis Doyle, Aug. 8, 1997. BS, Adelphi U., 1989, MSW, 1990. LCSW Substance Abuse Svc. NY State Edn. Dept. Alcohol rehab. counselor I Nassau Co. Dept. Drug and Alcohol, Hempstead, NY, 1982—85; alcohol rehab. counselor II Nassau Co. Dept. Drug and Alcohol, Outpatient Unit, 1985—87, alcohol rehab. counselor III, 1987—92; psychiat. social worker I Nassau Co. Dept. Drug and Alcohol, Nassau County Jail, 1992—2001, psychiat. social worker II, 2001—02, dir. Stop DWI program, 2002—05; pvt. practice Uniondale, NY, 2001—. Co-author: (training manual) Treating Mandated Clients, 2003. Vol. Mineola (NY) Mustang Run, Fundraiser, 2000—02; bereavement counselor Sacred Heart Ch., No. Merrick, NY, 1999—. Named Social Worker of Yr., Elizabeth A. Doherty Scholarship Fund, 2002. Mem.: Eye Movement Desensitization and Reprocessing Internat. Assn., NY Fed. of Alcoholism Counselors, Nat. Assn. Social Workers. Avocations: crocheting, dog grooming, running marathon races. Home: 1342 Menard St Uniondale NY 11553 Office: Nassau County Dept Drug and Alcohol Nassau County Jail 100 Carman Ave East Meadow NY 11554 Office Phone: 516-576-7572. Personal E-mail: barrydoyle@msn.com.

DOYLE, MICHAEL PATRICK, microbiologist, educator, director; b. Madison, Wis., Oct. 3, 1949; s. Donald Vincent and Evelyn (Bauer) Doyle; m. Annette Marie Ripple, Dec. 27, 1971; children: Michael Patrick, Patrick Matthew, Kristen Anne. BS in Bacteriology, U. Wis., 1973, MS in Food Microbiology, 1975, PhD in Food Microbiology, 1977. Sr. project leader Ralston Purina Co., St. Louis, 1977-80; asst. prof. U. Wis., Madison, 1980-84, assoc. prof., 1984-88, prof., 1988-91; prof., dir. U. Ga., Griffin, 1991—, dept. head Athens, 1993-99. Mem. sci. bd. U.S. FDA, 2000—03; regents prof. Bd. Regents Ga. U. Sys., 1997—; nat. adv. com. on microbiol. criteria for foods USA, Washington, 1988—90, 1994—2000; trustee Internat. Life Scis. Inst.-N.Am., Washington, 1992—, sci. advisor, 1987—96; mem. Internat. Commn. on Microbiol. Specifications for Foods, 1989—2000; Wis. Disting. prof. bd. regents U. Wis., Madison, 1988—91; James M. Craig Meml. lectr. Oreg. State U., Corvallis, 1990; sci. lectr. Am. Soc. Microbiology Found., 1991—93, 1999—2001; Peter J. Shields lectr. U. Calif., Davis, 1993; G. Malcolm Trout vis. scholar Mich. State U., Lansing, 1994; sci. adv. coun. Refrigeration Rsch. and Edn. Found., 1997—2002; York Disting. lectr. Auburn U., 1999. Editor: Food Microbiology: Fundamentals and Frontiers, 1997, 3rd edit., 2007, Foodborne Bacterial Pathogens, 1989, Emerging Issues in Food Safety, 2004—; contbr. articles to profl. jours. Recipient award for Profl. Excellence, Am. Agrl. Econs. Assn., 1992, Silver Plow Honor award, USDA, 1998, Ptnrs. in Pub. Health award, Ctrs. Disease Control and Prevention, 2001, Commrs. citation, FDA, 2006; named one of Top 100 Most Cited Rschrs. Agrl. Scis., Inst. Sci. Info., 2002. Fellow: AAAS, World Innovation Found., Am. Acad. Microbiology, Inst. of Food Technologists (Fred W. Tanner lectr. 1986, sci. lectr. 1987—90, exec. com. 2000—03, Samuel Cate Prescott award for rsch. 1987, Nicholas Appert award for preeminence in and contbns. to field of food tech. 1996), Internat. Assn. Food Protection (pres. 1992—93, Norbert F. Sherman article excellence award 1993, NFPA food safety award for outstanding contbn. to food safety rsch. and edn. 1999); mem.: NAS (assoc.), Inst. Medicine NAS (food and nutrition bd. 1991—97, com. to ensure safe food from prodn. to consumption 1998, chmn. rev. com. USDA E. coli O157:H7 in ground beef risk assessment 2001—02, chmn. food forum 2003—, com. nat. needs rsch. in vet. scis. 2004—05, vice chmn. food and nutrition bd. 2005—), Am. Soc. for Microbiology (chmn. food microbiology divsn. 1987—89, pub. and sci. affairs bd. 2003—, P.R. Edwards award for outstanding career achievements 1994), Gamma Sigma Delta, Phi Kappa Phi. Roman Catholic. Achievements include patents for for monoclonal antibody to enterohemorrhagic E. coli; competitive exclusion bacteria to reduce carriage of enterohemorrhagic E. coli by cattle and Listeria in floor drains; development of methods to control and detect foodborne pathogens. Office: U Ga Ctr Food Safety 1109 Experiment St Griffin GA 30223-1797 Office Phone: 770-228-7284. Business E-Mail: mdoyle@uga.edu.

DOYLE, PETER M., medical researcher; b. Naperville, Ill., Feb. 20, 1974; BS, U. Ill. Urbana-Champaign, 1997; PhD, Northwestern U., 2009. Postdoc. rsch. fellow U. Chgo., 2009—. Pediatric Rsch. grant, NIH, Ruth L. Kirschstein Nat. Rsch. grant. Mem.: Acad. Eating Disorders. Office: 5841 South Md Ave MC3077 Chicago IL 60637 Business E-Mail: pdoyle@yoda.bsd.uchicago.edu.

DOYLE, ROBERT LLOYD, psychiatrist; b. Baton Rouge, La., May 12, 1956; MD, La. State U. Sch. Medicine, 1993, DDS, 1985. Staff psychiatrist Harvard U. Health Svc., 2008—. Sci. bd. dirs. Mindroom, 2005; editl. bd. mem. Jour. Attention Disorders, 2005, Internat. Jpou. Immunopathology & Pharmacology, 2003, European Jour Inflamation, 2006. Recipient Ptnrs. Excellence award, Mass. Gen. Hosp., McLean Hosp. Achievements include research in Psychopharmacology, ranging from ADHD to Autism, pediatric psychopharmacology unit at MGH. Avocations: guitar, painting, drawing, writing. Office: Harvard University Health Svcs 75 Mt Auburn St 2nd Fl Cambridge MA 02138 Business E-Mail: rdoyle@partners.org, r.doyle@uhs.harvard.edu.

DOZOR, ALLEN J., pediatrician, pulmonologist, educator; Attended, U. Pa., Pa. State U. Diplomate Am. Bd. of Pediatrics-pediatric pulmonology, 1985. Resident St. Vincent's Hosp. & Med. Ctr.; fellow Children's Hosp.; prof. pediat. NY Med. Coll., chief divsn. pulmonology, allergy & sleep medicine Valhalla, NY; dir. Children's Environ. health Ctr., Armond V. Mascia, MD Cystic Fibrosis Ctr.; prin. investigator ALA Asthma Clin. Rsch. Ctr.; assoc. physician in chief maria fareri children's hosp. Westchester Med. Ctr., Valhalla, NY. Office: Children's & Women's Physicians of Westchester LLP Room 123 Munger Pavilion Valhalla NY 10595 Office Phone: 914-594-4280. Office Fax: 914-594-4280.

DRABEK, TOMAS, anesthesiologist, educator; b. Prague, Czech Republic, Nov. 5, 1966; s. Drahomir Drabek and Jarmila Drabkova; m. Tereza Vachova, Oct. 24, 2003; children: Filip C., Lucie Drabkova; m. Katerina Pecenkova, July 22, 1993 (div. Oct. 10, 2000). MD, Charles U., Prague, 1991. Staff anesthesiologist Inst. Clin. & Exptl. Medicine, Prague, 1995—2003; asst. prof. Postgraduate Med. Sch., Prague, 1995—2003, U. Pitts., 2004—; scientist Safar Ctr. Resuscitation Rsch., Pitts., 2008—. Contbr. scientific papers. Fellowship, J.W.Fulbright Commn., 2001, Charles Schertz fellowship, U. Pitts., 2007, Nancy Caroline fellowship, Safar Ctr. Resuscitation Rsch., 2008. Mem.: Am. Heart Assn., Soc. Critical Care Medicine, Shock Soc., Soc. Cardiovasc. Anesthesiologists, Am. Soc. Anesthesiologists. Home: 221 Park Entrance Dr Pittsburgh PA 15228 Office: University Pitts 3434 Fifth Ave Pittsburgh PA 15260 Personal E-mail: tomasdrabek@hotmail.com. Business E-Mail: drabekt@anes.upmc.edu.

DRACEA, LAURA LUANA, gynecologist, educator; b. Iasi, Romania, Oct. 7, 1967; d. Constantin and Emilia Dediu; m. Andrei Mihai Dracea, Sept. 25, 1992; children: Luca Andrei, Anya Carina. MD, U. Medicine and Pharmacy, Iasi Romania, 1992; PhD, Ministry Edn. and Rsch., 2003. Cert. in ob-gyn. Ministry Health, 1996, fertility and IVF specialist Ministry Health & Family, 2002, lectr. Bd. U. Medicine Carol Davila Bucharest, 2004. Resident ob-gyn. U. Hosp., Bucharest, Romania, 1993—98, specialist in ob-gyn., 1998—, head IVF dept., 1998—; asst. prof. U. Medicine Carol Davila, Bucharest, 1998—2004, lectr., 2004—; fertility specialist Gynera Med. Ctr., Bucharest, 2006—. Med. dir. Gynera Med. Ctr., Bucharest, 2006—. Mem.: ESHRE, ASRM, Romanian Gynecology Soc. Office: Gynera Med Ctr Constantin Aricescu 8 Bucharest 011687 Romania Office Phone: 40733682882. Business E-Mail: ldracea@rdslink.ro, office@gynera.ro.

DRACH, JOHN CHARLES, research scientist, educator; b. Sept. 25, 1939; s. Charles Louis and Edrie B. Drach; m. E. Jean Flamm, June 20, 1964; children: Laura J., Diane E. BS in Pharmacy, U. Cin., 1961, MS in Pharm. Chemistry, 1963, PhD in Biochemistry, 1966. From assoc. rsch. scientist to rsch. scientist Parke, Davis and Co., Ann Arbor, Mich., 1966-70; asst. prof. U. Mich. Dental Sch., Ann Arbor, 1970-74; assoc. prof. U. Mich., Ann Arbor, 1974-80; assoc. prof. medicinal chemistry U. Mich. Coll. Pharmacy, Ann Arbor, 1978-80; prof. U. Mich., Ann Arbor, 1980—2008, prof. emeritus, 2008—; chmn. dept. oral biology U. Mich. Dental Sch., Ann Arbor, 1985-87, chmn. dept. biologic and materials scis., 1987-95; vis. prof. divsn. virology Burroughs Wellcome Co., Research Triangle Park, NC, 1994. Cons. Adria Labs., Am. Inst. Chem., Am. Pharm. Assn., AMA, Chartwell, Kimberly-Clark, others, 1976-2008. Author: Clinical Pharmacology, 1986; mem. editorial bd. Elsevier Sci. Pubs., 1984—2007, Antiviral Chemistry & Chemotherapy, 1996—; contbr. articles to profl. jours.; patentee antiviral drugs. NSF summer fellow, 1963; NIH grad. fellow, 1964-66; NIH grantee, 1970—. Fellow: AAAS; mem.: Internat. Soc. Antiviral Rsch. (archivist 1992—, chmn. travel grants com. 1998—2002, pres. 2002—04, chmn. conf. com. 2004—06, chmn. nomination com. 2006—08), Am. Soc. Microbiology (mem. editl. bd. 1982—91), Am. Chem. Soc., Am. Assn. Oral Biology, Dental Edn. Assn. (pres. oral biology sect. 1990—91), Sigma Xi, Omicron Kappa Upsilon, Rho Chi. Home: 1372 Barrister Rd Ann Arbor MI 48105-2875 Office: U Mich 1210 Eisenhower Pl Ann Arbor MI 48108-3218 Office Phone: 734-975-9402. Business E-Mail: jcdrach@umich.edu.

DRACHMAN, DANIEL BRUCE, neurologist, educator; s. Julian Moses and Emily (Deitchman) D.; m. Jephta Piatigorsky, Aug. 28, 1960; children: Jonathan Gregor, Evan Bernard, Eric Edouard. AB summa cum laude (N.Y. State scholar), Columbia Coll., 1952; MD (N.Y. State Med. scholar), NYU, 1956. Cert. Neurology and Psychiatry 1962. Intern in internal medicine Beth Israel Hosp., Boston, 1956 57; asst. resident in neurology Harvard neurol. unit Boston City Hosp., 1957 58, resident in neurology, 1958-59; resident in neuropathology Harvard neurol. unit. and Mallory Inst. Pathology, 1959-60; teaching fellow in neurology Harvard U., 1957-60; clin. assoc. Nat. Inst. Neurol. Diseases and Blindness, NIH, Bethesda, Md., 1960-62, research asso. lab. neuroanat. scis., 1962-63; clin. instr. Georgetown U., 1961-63; asst. prof. neurology Tufts U., 1963-69; assoc. prof. Johns Hopkins U., 1969-73, prof., 1974—, prof. neurosci., 1980—, W.W. Smith Charitable Trust prof. neuroimmunology, 2003—. Attending neurologist Johns Hopkins Hosp.; adv. bd. Multiple Sclerosis Soc., 1981-85; pres. med. adv. bd. Myasthenia Gravis Found.; adv. bd. Familial Dysautonomia Found.; bd. sci. councillors Nat. Inst. Neurol. and Communicative Disorders and Stroke, NIH, 1985-90; med. adv. com. Muscular Dystrophy Assn., 1994-99. Clarinetist; mem. editl. bd. Muscle and Nerve jour., Exptl. Neurology, Autoimmunity; appeared in (film) Two Hands (nominatee Acad. award 2007-, Emmey, 2008); author over 200 publs. on myasthenia gravis, muscular atrophy, muscular dystrophy, clubfoot, devel. disorders, neurology, amyotrophic lateral sclerosis, chamber music. Served with USPHS, 1960-63. Recipient Founders' Day award NYU, 1956, Jacob Javits award, 1986, Berson Disting. Alumnus award NYU Sch. Medicine, 1999, Acad. award 2008; NIH grantee, 1963—, Muscular Dystrophy Assn. grantee, 1969—. Fellow Am. Acad. Neurology, N.Y. Acad. Scis.; mem. AAAS, Internat. Soc. Devel. Biology, Balt. Neurol. Soc., Phi Beta Kappa, Alpha Omega Alpha. Achievements include defining pathogenesis of clubfoot (most common human congenital malformation) and arthrogryposis (rare form of similar disorder); first basic work on the trophic role of nerves in maintaining the integrity of skeletal muscles; first described the only currently useful treatment for Duchenne Muscular Dystrophy; basic work on botulinum toxin demonstrated its use to paralyze individual muscles, and led to the widespread clinical use of Botox; first defined pathogenic abnormalities in myasthenia gravis; development of several immunosuppressive treatments for Myasthenia. Avocations: clarinet, fly fishing, bicycling. Office: Johns Hopkins U Sch Medicine Dept Neurology 600 N Wolfe St Baltimore MD 21287-7519 Office Phone: 410-955-5406. Personal E-mail: dandrac@aol.com.

DRACHTMAN, RICHARD ALLAN, pediatrician, educator; MD, U. Chgo, 1984. Diplomate Am. Bd. Pediat. Intern Northshore U. Hosp., Manhasset, NY, 1984—85, resident in pediat., 1985—88; fellow in pediat. hematology/oncology Mt. Sinai Med. Ctr., NYC, 1988—91; physician divsn. pediat. hematology & oncology Cancer Inst. N.J., New Brunswick, NJ, 1991—. Office: Cancer Inst NJ 195 Little Albany St New Brunswick NJ 08903 Home Phone: 732-613-8795; Office Phone: 732-235-8862. Office Fax: 732-235-8234. *

DRACUP, KATHLEEN ANNE, dean, nursing educator; b. Santa Monica, Calif., Sept. 28, 1942; d. Paul Joseph and Lucy Elizabeth (Milligan) Molloy; children: Jeffrey, Jonathan, Joy, Jan, Brian. BS in Nursing, St. Xavier's Coll., Chgo., 1967; M in Nursing, UCLA, 1974; D in Nursing Sci., U. Calif., San Francisco, 1982. Clin. nurse Little Co. of Mary Hosp., Chgo., 1967-70, UCLA Med. Ctr., 1970-74; asst. clin. prof. UCLA, 1974-78, rsch. fellow, dept. medicine, 1979-81, asst. prof. to prof., 1982-99; clin. nurse, sch. nursing U. Calif. San Francisco Med. Ctr., 1979; dean, sch. nursing U. Calif., San Francisco, 2000—; pvt. practice psychotherapist, 1980—95. Editor Heart and Lung Jour., 1981-91, Am. Jour. Critical Care, 1991—; editor Critical Care Nursing Series; contbr. chpts. to books, articles to profl. jours. Recipient Eugene Brunwald Acad. Mentorship award Am. Heart Assn., 2003; Disting. Practitioner Nat. Acad., Washington, 1987; Fulbright Sr. scholar, 1995. Fellow Coun. Cardiovascular Nursing, Am. Heart Assn., Am. Assn. Cardiopulmonary Rehab.; mem. Inst. of Medicine, Am. Nurses' Assn., Am. Assn. Critical Care Nurses (life), Sigma Theta Tau. Office: U Calif San Francisco Sch Nursing 2 Koret Way Rm N319 San Francisco CA 94143-0604 Office Phone: 415-476-1805. Business E-Mail: kathy.dracup@nursing.ucsf.edu.

DRAEGER, JOERG ALBERT, ophthalmologist educator; b. Germany, Nov. 29, 1929; s. Kurt and Margarete (Arnold) D.; m. Brigitte Altenstein, 1955; children: Annette, Ulrike, Frank. MD, Heidelberg U., Germany, 1955; Univ.-Dozent, Hamburg U., Germany, 1962, Prof. Medizin, 1968. Med. Diplomate. Prof., chmn. Augenklinik Bremen, Germany, 1968-81; prof., chmn. dept. opthalmology Hamburg (Germany) U., 1981—. Author Handapplanat. Tonometer (Martini award 1966), Microsurgical Unit, 1965 (Graefe Doro 1975), Spaceflight Selftonometer, 1992 (Rolex award 1993); author, editor 6 sci. books. Recipient Scientific award Contactlens Soc., 1981. Fellow Royal Coll. Ophthalmology, Royal Soc. Medicine, Aerospace Med. Assn. (v.p. 1999); mem. German Soc. Aviation & Spacemedicine (pres. 1992-95), German Ophthal. Soc. (pres. 1990-91), Swiss, Austrian and Italian Ophthalmol. Socs. (hon.). Achievements include numerous patents in field. Office: Hamburg U Dept Ophthalmology Martinistr 52 D-20246 Hamburg Germany

DRAELOS, ZOE DIANA, dermatologist, consultant; b. Milw., Oct. 13, 1958; d. Dimitri Basil and Lorene June (Legan) Kececioglu; m. Michael Draelos, June 14, 1980; children: Mark, Matthew. BSME, U. Ariz., 1979, MD, 1983. Diplomate Am. Bd. Dermatology. Physician in solo dermatology practice, High Point, NC, 1988—. Cons., owner Dermatology Cons. Svcs., High Point, 1990—. Author: Cosmetics in Dermatology, 1995, Atlas of Cosmetic Dermatology, 2000. Rhodes scholar, Oxford, Eng., 1979. Office: Zoe Diana Draelos MD PA 2444 N Main St High Point NC 27262-7833 Office Phone: 336-841-2040.

DRAGO, CARL JOSEPH, prosthodontist; b. Yonkers, NY, Aug. 14, 1952; s. Rosario Phillip and Elizabeth (Brisgal) D.; m. Kathryn Sue Lammers, Mar. 11, 1978; children: Stephanie Ann, Matthew Brisgal. BA cum laude, Ohio State U., 1974, DDS, 1976; MS, U. Tex., San Antonio, 1981. Diplomate Am. Bd. Prosthodontics. Intern Northwestern U., Evanston, Ill., 1976-77; asst. prof. U. Tex. Dental Sch., San Antonio, 1979-81, resident, 1979-81; staff prosthodontist Gundersen Clinic, Ltd., La Crosse, Wis., 1981—. Cons. St. Paul Dist. Dental Soc., 1982; guest lectr. VA Hosp., Milw., 1986. Author chpt. Advances in Occlusion, 1981, Implant Prosthodontics. Grantee Research and Edn. Found. for Prosthodontics, 1980. Fellow Am. Coll. Prosthodontists. Republican. Roman Catholic. Avocations: photography, racquetball, biking, travel. Office: Gundersen Clinic Ltd 1836 South Ave La Crosse WI 54601 5494 Home: 2727 Bayshore Dr La Crosse WI 54603-1057

DRAGOI, GHEORGHE STEFAN, retired physician; b. Bucharest, June 24, 1938; MD, PhD, U. Medicine and Pharmacy Craiova, 1962. Cert. in pathologist, anatomist, forensic anthropologist Faculty Medicine, 1970. Prof., bd. dirs. U. Medicine and Pharmacy Craiova, 1970—2011. Fellow: Assn. Anatomists; mem.: European Soc. Biomechanics (The Nederland), Internat. Acad. Legal Medicine, European Soc. Pathology (Germany, Kiel), Acad. Med. Scis. Romania (prof. emeritus). Avocations: sculpting, photography, tennis. Home: Maiorescu Ion 7 Bl2 Sc1 Ap3 Craiova Dolj 200760 Romania Personal E-mail: dragoigs@yahoo.com.

DRAKE, AMELIA F., otolaryngologist; b. Nov. 13, 1955; m. Craig Drake; children: Connor, Cliff. B in Biology, Cornell U., Ithaca, NY; MD, U. NC, Chapel Hill, 1981. Cert. in otolaryngology 1987. Residency, dept. surgery U. Mich. Med. Ctr., 1981—83, residency, dept. otolaryngology/head and neck surgery, 1983—87, adj. prof. vocal pedagogy Ann Arbor, 1986—87; fellowship Children's Hosp., Cin., 1987—88; asst. prof. surgery/otolarynogology U. Mich. Sch. Music, Ann Arbor, 1988—94; asst. prof. U. NC Dept. Pediat., 1989—94, assoc. prof., 1994—2001, prof., 2001—; assoc. prof. U. NC Dept. Otolaryngology/Head and Neck Surgery, 1994—2001, Newton D. Fischer disting. prof. surgery, 1999—, prof., 2001—, chief, divsn. pediatric otolaryngology, 2001—; dir. craniofacial ctr. U. NC Sch. Dentistry, 2001—. Dir. residency program, otolaryngology/head and neck surgery U. NC. Contbr. articles to profl. jours. Recipient Gabriel F. Tucker award, Am. Laryngol. Assn., 2006; named to Top Doctors in America, Castle Connolly Med. Ltd., 2002—07, Best Doctors, Bus. NC mag., 2006. Fellow: ACS; mem.: NC Soc. Otolaryngology and Head and Neck Surgery (past pres.), Carolina Masters Crew Club. Avocation: crew. Office: U NC Sch Medicine Dept Otolaryngology 1114 Bioinformatics Bldg CB 7070 Chapel Hill NC 27599-7405 Office Phone: 919-966-8926. Office Fax: 919-966-7656. Business E-Mail: amelia_drake@med.unc.edu.

DRAKE, MICHAEL V., academic administrator, ophthalmologist, educator; b. NYC, 1950; m. Brenda Drake; 2 children. AB in African & African American Studies, Stanford U., 1974; BS in Medical Sciences, U. Calif., San Francisco, MD, 1975. Resident U. Calif., San Francisco, asst. prof. ophthalmology, 1979—87, chief eye clinic, 1979—91, assoc. prof., 1987—93, dir. vision care and rsch. unit, asst. dean student affairs, 1991—93, prof., 1993—98, vice chmn. dept. ophthalmology, assoc. dean admissions and student programs, sr. assoc. dean admissions and extramural academic programs, 1998—2000, Stephen P. Shearing prof., 1998—2005, v.p. health affairs, sys., 2000—05, chancellor, 2005—. Bd. dirs. Bank of the West, 2010—, Commonworth Fund, 2008—. Author: (with D.O. Harrington) The Visual Fields: Text and Atlas of Clinical Perimetry, 1990, (with R. Stamper and M. Lieberman) Becker-shaffer Diagnosis of glaucoma, 1999, 2009. Recipient Herbert W. Nickens award, Assn. Am. Med. Colls., 2004, Burbridge award for Pub. Svc., Michael J. Hogan award, S.J. Kimura Teaching award, U. Calif. San Francisco Sch. of Medicine Alumnus of the Yr. award, Binational Health Pioneer award. Fellow: AAAS; mem.: IOM. Office: University of California The Chancellor's Office Irvine CA 92697-1900 Office Phone: 949-824-5111. Office Fax: 949-824-2087.

DRAKE, STEPHEN DOUGLAS, psychologist, health facility administrator; b. Iola, Kans., Sept. 8, 1947; s. Harry Francis and Emojean (Price) Drake; m. Rebecca Gonzalez, June 1, 1968; 1 child, Michael Paul. BA, U. Tex., 1970; PhD, U. North Tex., 1987. Diplomate Am. Bd. Forensic Examiners, lic. psychologist. Mental health worker Austin (Tex.) State Hosp., 1970-73; claims rep. Social Security Adminstrn., Galveston, Tex., 1974-77, ops. supr. Dallas, 1977-79, staff asst., 1979-80; clin. psychologist Terrell (Tex.) State Hosp., 1987-89, Austin State Hosp., 1989-90, program dir., 1990-92; cons. Tex. Rehab. Commn., 1992-98, chief mental med. cons., 1998—2003, med. adminstr., 2003—. Contbr. articles to profl. jours. Vice-chmn. bd. dirs. Galveston Island Mental Health/Mental Retardation Ctr., 1977. Recipient award, Nat. Assn. Disability Examiners, 2001, Commr.'s citation, Social Security Adminstrn., 2005. Mem.: APA, Tex. Psychol. Assn., Mensa, Phi Kappa Phi. Avocations: Tae Kwon Do, weightlifting, eastern philosophy, languages, travel. Office: Tex Rehab Commn 6102 E Oltorf St Austin TX 78741 Personal E-mail: drakestephen@sbcglobal.net.

DRAKEMAN, DONALD LEE, venture capitalist, educator; b. Camden, NJ, Oct. 21, 1953; s. Fred J. and Jean (Faucett) D.; m. Lisa Natale Drakeman, Aug. 23, 1975; children: Cynthia and Amy. BA magna cum laude, Dartmouth Coll., 1975; JD, Columbia U., 1979; MA, Princeton U., 1984, PhD, 1988. Bar: NJ 1979; US Dist. Ct. NJ 1979, NY 1980; US Supreme Ct. 1984. Assoc. Milbank, Tweed, Hadley and McCloy, NYC, 1979-82; gen. counsel Essex Chem. Corp., Clifton, NJ, 1982-89, v.p., 1987-89; pres. Essex Med. Products, Clifton, NJ, 1988-89; pres., CEO Medarex, Inc., Annandale, NJ, 1987—2006; venture ptnr. Advent Venture Ptnrs., London, 2007—. Adj. prof. polit. sci. Montclair State Coll., NJ, 1984; rsch. cons. Lilly Found., Inc., 1989—90; lectr. politics dept. Princeton U., 1990—93, 1995—2009, co-chair adv. coun. religion dept., 2001—08; chmn. adv. coun. James Madison Program in Am. Ideals and Instn., Princeton Univ., 2000—; mem. adv. coun. Index Ventures, Geneva, 2002—03; chmn. NJ Commn. Sci. and Tech., 2004—06; bd. advs. ETHICA, Asti, Italy, 2008—; fellow Burgon Soc., 2009—; fellow health mgmt. Judge Bus. Sch. U. Cambridge, 2010—. Author: Church-State Constitutional Issues, 1990, Church State & Original Intent, 2009; co-editor Church-State in Am. History, 2d edit., 1986, 3d edit., 2003; contbg. articles to profl. jours. Chmn. Montclair bd. adjustment, 1984; trustee, chair Biotech. Coun. NJ, 1996-98; trustee, U. Charleston, 1999-2003, Drew U., 2002—; adv. coun. Rutgers Bus. Sch., 2002—07; trustee, Woodrow Wilson Nat. Fellowship Found., 2003-06, Am. Coun. Sci. & Health, 2010-. Harlan Fiske Stone Scholar, Columbia Univ., 1976-79; Alumni Svc. award, Princeton U. Alumni Assn., 1999, inducted NJ High Tech. Hall of Fame, 2000. Mem.: John Maclean Soc., Yale Club, Princeton Club, Princeton Alumni Coun. Home Phone: 843-682-3771.

DRAKEMAN, LISA N., biotechnologist; b. Boston, Oct. 30, 1953; d. Paul and Josephine (Covino) Natale; m. Donald L. Drakeman, Aug. 23, 1975. BA, Mt. Holyoke Coll., South Hadley, Mass., 1975, MA, Rutgers U., New Brunswick, NJ, 1983, Princeton U., NJ, 1986, PhD, 1988. Chair, v. chair Monclair Redevelopment Agy., NJ, 1981-84; vis. scholar Dartmouth Coll., 1988-89; lectr. Princeton U., 1989-92; asst. dir. Alumni Coun. of Princeton U., 1991; dir. administrn. Medarex, Inc., Princeton, NJ, 1991-94, v.p. adminstrn., 1994-96, v.p., 1996-98, sr. v.p., head bus. devel., 1998-2000; CEO Genmab A/S, 1999—. Faculty fellow Grad. Coll. Princeton U., 1991-93, mem. adv. coun. dept. religion, 1996-; bd. dir. Medarex Europe, B.V., GenPharm. Internat., Inc., Biotech. Coun. NJ. Mem. biopharm. adv. coun. Tech. Coun. Greater Phila., 1993-96; mem. Gov.'s Biopharm. Task Force NJ Econ. Master Plan Commn., Trenton, 1994-95; mem biotech. adv. com. The Franklin Inst., Phila., 1994-96; commr. Prosperity NJ, 1995-2000; mem. Cancer Inst. NJ Leadership Coun., 2004—06; bd. dirs., mem. exec. com. Biotechnology Coun. NJ, 2005—, sec., 2007—. Garden State grad. fellow State of NJ, 1981-85; named to NJ High Tech. Hall of Fame, 2000. Mem. Soc. Advancement of Women's Health Rsch. (steering com., corp. adv. coun. 1994-97), Biotech. Industry Orgn. (chair nat. capital formation task force 1995-98, Advocate of Yr. award, 1995), Biotech. Coun. NJ (v.p. 1996-2000, sec., 2007-08, vice chair 2009-, Outstanding Industry Woman of Yr 1996, Dr. Sol J. Barer award for Vision, Innovation & Leadership, 2009), European Fedn. Pharm. Industries and Assns. (bd. dir. emerging pharm. enterprises sect. 2004-06, v.p. 2006). Office: 457 N Harrison St Princeton NJ 08540

DRANCE, STEPHEN MICHAEL, ophthalmologist, educator; b. Bielsko, Poland, May 22, 1925; Can. citizen; MB,ChB, U. Edinburgh, Scotland, 1948, MD, 1949; Diploma in Ophthalmology, Royal Coll. Surgeons, London, 1953; LLD (hon.), Dalhousce U., Halifax, 1995; DSc (hon.), U. Oulu, Finland, 1998, U. B.C., Vancouver, 1998. Intern Western Gen. Hosp., Edinburgh, 1948-49; resident County Hosp., York, Eng., 1952-53, Edinburgh Royal Infirmary, 1953-55, Oxford Eye Hosp., Eng., 1955-57, Oxford U., 1955-57; asst. prof. and assoc. prof. medicine U. Sask., Saskatoon, Can., 1957-63; assoc. prof. ophthalmology U. B.C., Vancouver, Can., 1963-66, prof., 1966-90, dir. ophthalmologic research, 1967-73, head dept. ophthalmology, 1973-90. Cons., lectr. medicine; vis. prof., lectr. numerous univs. Author: (with H. Reed) The Essentials of Perimetry, 2d edit., 1971, (with A. Neufeld) Applied Pharmacology of Glaucoma, 1984, (with D.R. Anderson) Automatic Perimetry in Glaucoma, 1985, (with A. Neufeld, M. van Buskirk) Applied Pharmacology of Glaucoma, 1991; assoc. editor Am. Archives Ophthalmology, 1961-74; mem. editorial bd. Can. Jour. Ophthalmology, 1966; mng. editor Albrecht von Graefe's Archive for Clin. and Exptl. Ophthalmology, 1979-90; editl. bd. Am. Jour. Opthalmology, 1994-99; contbr. articles to profl. jours., chpts. to books Pres. Vancouver Summer Festivals Soc., 1997-2002. With RAF, 1949-51. Decorated officer Order of Can., 1987; recipient numerous awards and grants for excellence in medicine. Fellow Royal Australian Coll. Ophthalmologists U.K. (hon.), Coll. Ophthalmology U.K. (hon.), Royal Soc. Medicine, Royal Coll. Physicians and Surgeons Can. (sec. 1976-77), Royal Coll. Surgeons Eng.; mem. Can. Assn. Clin. Rsch., Assn. Ophthalmologic Rsch. (U.K.), Assn. for Rsch. in Vision and Ophthalmology, Can. Ophthalmol. Soc. (pres. 1974-75), B.C. Oto-Ophthalmol. Soc., Ophthal. Soc. U.K., Oxford Ophthalmol. Congress, Am. Acad. Ophthalmology (v.p. 1993), Can. Med. Assn., B.C. Med. Assn., Internat. Perimetric Soc. (pres. 1982-88), Glaucoma Soc. Internat. Congrss (pres. 1983-90), Pan-Am. Ophthalmol. Congress, Pan-Am. Glaucoma Soc., Pan-Am. Assn. Ophthalmology, Assn. N.Am. Glaucomatologists, N.Z. Ophthalmol. Soc. (hon.), Academia Ophthalmol. Internat., Internat. Congress Ophthalmology (pres. 1994), Concillium Ophthalmol. Univaersale (visual function com.) E-mail: smd@interchange.ubc.ca.

DRANITZKE, RICHARD J., surgeon; b. L.I., NY, 1940; MD, Columbia U., 1966. Diplomate Am. Bd. Surgery, Am. Bd. Thoracic Surgery. Intern Columbia-Presbyn. Hosp., NYC, 1966-67; resident in surgery Bellevue Hosp. Ctr., NYC, 1969-73; resident in cardiothoracic surgery Albany (N.Y.) Med. Ctr., 1973—75; chief thoracic and vascular surgery St. Charles Hosp., Port Jefferson, NY, 1991—, St. Charles and J.T. Mather Meml. Hosp., 1985—; clin. instr. dept. surgery Stony Brook U. Hosp., 1994—; chief vascular surgery Mather Hosp., 1991—. Mem. ACP, ACS, AMA, Soc. Thoracic Surgeons,

Eastern Vascular Soc., N.Y. Soc. for Cardiovasc. Surgery. Office: 635 Belle Terre Rd Port Jefferson NY 11777 Home: 635 Belle Terre Rd Ste 102 Port Jefferson NY 11777-1984 Office Phone: 631-473-1602.

DRANNIK, GEORGE NICOLAEVICH, immunologist, researcher; b. Uman, Ukraine, Mar. 16, 1941; s. Nicolai Lukich and Valentina Ivanovna Drannik; m. Ludmila Ivanovna Lazarenko; children: Elena, Anna. Student, Med. Inst., Carckov, Ukraine, 1958—65; Candidate of Sci., Inst. Urology and Nephrology, Acad. Med. Sci., Kiev, Ukraine, 1972, MD, 1980. Jr. sci. rschr. Inst. Urology and Nephrology, Acad. Med. Sci., 1968—72, sr. sci. rschr., 1972—81, chmn. dept. immunology, prof., 1981—; dir. Ukrainian Ctr. for Clin. Immunology, Kiev, 1987—; head chair clin. immunology and allergy, clin. prof. medicine Nat. Med. U., Kiev, 1994—. Mem. spl. sci. coun. for immunology and allergy Nat. Med. U., 1987—, Inst. Urology and Nephrology, Kiev, 1986—; main specialist for clin. and lab. immunology Ministry of Health, Kiev, 1992—2004; mem. Ukrainian Pharmacol. Com. of Ministry of Health, Kiev, 1994—. Author (with E. Baran, A. Rudenko): Immunity and Infection after Kidney Transplantation, 1986; author: Immunonephrology, 1989; author: (with G. Disik) People's Genetic Blood Systems and Diseases, 1990; author: (with Y. Grinevich, G. Disik) Drugs for Immunomodulation, 1994; author: (handbook) Clinical Immunology and Allergology, 1999, 2003, 2006; editor in chief: Jour. Immunology and Alergology, 1998—. Recipient Excellence in Healthcare award, Ministry of Health, Ukraine, 1985. Mem.: Am. Soc. Clin. Immunology, Am. Coll. Allergy, Asthma and Immunology, Russian Assn. Allergology and Clin. Immunology, European Acad. Allergology and Clin. Immunology, Ukrainian Soc. Allergology and Clin. Immunology (pres. 1998). Achievements include patents for diagnostic and treatment of different immunodependent diseases, 14 patents. Avocations: collecting paintings, basketball. Office: Inst Urology and Nephrology Acad Med Sci Yuri Kozubinski 9A 04053 Kiev Ukraine Home: Klovskiy Spusk 4 App 73 1021 Kiev Ukraine Office Phone: (380) 44 486 54 03. Office Fax: (380) 44 486 54 03. Personal E-mail: timgeorge@svitonline.com.

DRAPER, EDGAR, psychiatrist; b. St. Louis, Feb. 5, 1926; s. Neal McLain and Florence Mabel (Meyers) D.; m. Norma Jane Alexander, Mar. 16, 1949; children: Sue Draper, Anne Draper Klevay, Neal Edgar. AB, Washington U., 1946, Duke Div. Sch., 1948; BD, Garrett Biblical Inst., 1949; MD, Washington U. Med. Sch., 1953; grad., Inst. for Psychoanalysis, Chgo., 1966. Diplomate Am. Bd. Psychiatry and Neurology; ordained deacon, elder Meth. Ch., 1946. Asst. pastor Edenton St. Meth. Ch., Raleigh, 1947, Grece Methodist Ch., Rockford, Ill.; pastor Garden Prarie, Ill., 1949; intern Washington U. Svc. City Hosp., St. Louis, 1953-54; resident in psychiatry U. Cin., 1954-55, 57-59; sr. asst. surgeon USPHS, Ft. Worth, 1955-57; from instr. to assoc. prof. U. Chgo., 1959-68; co-dir. psychiat. outpatient dept., prof. psychiatry U. Mich., Ann Arbor, 1968, dir. psychiat. resident edn., 1968-74, prof. postgrad edn., 1970-75; prof., chmn. dept. psychiatry U. Miss. Med. Ctr., Jackson, 1975-93; prof. psychiatry U. Miss., Jackson, 1993-94; prof. emeritus, 1994—. Cons. in field. Contbr. numerous articles to profl. jours. Bd. dirs. Friends Libr. U. Miss. Named Vis. scholar U. Chgo., 1987, Fellow Soc. for Sci. Study of Religion, 1987, Man of Month Pastoral Psychology, 1970; recipient Physicians Recognition award, 1982-85, Cert. Appreciation Mental Health Assn. Hinds County, 1983, Plaque of Commendation Chgo. Acad. Religion and Mental Health, 1966-67. Fellow Am. Psychiat. Assn. (disting. life fellow), Am. Coll. Psychiatry (life), Am. Soc. Psychoanalytic Physicians, Soc. for Sci. Study of Religion (life), Am. Coll. Psychoanalysts (life, program chmn., bd. regents), So. Psychiat. Assn. (parlimentarian 1980—), Soc. for Study of Psychiatry and Culture; mem. Miss. Psychiat. Assn. (past pres., Disting. Svc. award 2001), Miss. State Med. Soc., Mich. Psychiat. Soc., Washtenaw County Med. Soc., Mich. State Med. Soc., So. Psychiat. Assn., Mich. Psychoanalytic Soc., Mental Health Assn. (bd. dirs. Jackson, Spl. Svc. award, 2006, 07). Office Phone: 601-982-2176. Business E-Mail: purpledoced@aol.com.

DRAYER, BURTON PAUL, neuroradiologist; b. NYC, Mar. 19, 1946; s. Alexander and Marion Horowitz; m. Michaele Gerri Cohen, June 13, 1968; children: Aron Stuart, Alex Nathan. AB, U. Pa., 1967; MD, Chgo. Med. Sch., 1971. Diplomate Am. Bd. Psychiatry and Neurology, Am. Bd. Radiology. Intern U. Vat. Med. Ctr., Burlington, 1971—72, resident neurology, 1972—75; fellow, resident radiology Health Ctr. U. Pitts., 1975—78, asst. prof. neurology, 1977—79; dir. neuroradiology Children's Hosp. U. Pitts., 1978—79; assoc prof. radiology and asst. prof. neurology Duke U. Med. Ctr., Durham, NC, 1979, chief sect. neuroradiology, 1981; dir. neuroradiol. rsch. Barrow Neurol. Inst.; Charles M. and Marilyn Newman prof. and chmn. dept. radiology Med. Sch. The Mt. Sinai Med. Ctr., 1995—, exec. v.p. risk; pres. The Mt. Sinai Hosp., 2003—08. Past pres. Neuroradiology Edn. and Rsch. Found. Editor: Neuroimaging Clinics N.Am.; contbr. articles to books and jours. Grantee, Squibb Rsch. Inst., 1982—83, Nat. Heart, Lung, and Blood Inst., 1983. Fellow: Am. Coll. Radiology, Am. Acad. Neurology; mem.: Am. Acad. Neurology, Radiol. Soc. N.Am. (bd. dirs. 2003—, bd. chmn. 2009, pres.-elect. 2010, pres. 2011), Am. Heart Assn. (mem. exec. com. stroke coun.), Am. Roentgen Ray Soc., Soc. for Neuroscis., Am. Soc. Neuroradiology (past pres.), Alpha Omage Alpha, Sigma Xi. Office: Mt Sinai Med Ctr Dept Radiology One Gustave L Levy Pl Box 1234 New York NY 10029 Office Phone: 212-241-6403. Business E-Mail: Burton.Drayer@mountsinai.org. *

DRAZANCIC, ANTE, retired obstetrician, gynecologist, educator; b. Sibenik, Croatia, Nov. 29, 1928; s. Filip and Slavica (Trstenjak) D.; m. Jakica Bilic (div. 1978); children: Filip, Dubravka Drazancic Hrabar; m. Ljiljana Sprihal; 1 child, Marija. MD, U. Med. Sch., 1953, specialist in ob-gyn., 1961; PhD, U. Zagreb, 1965. Resident physician Gen. Hosp., Varazdin, Croatia, 1953-58; asst. physician Univ. Med. Sch., Zagreb, 1958-66, assoc. prof., 1967-76, prof., 1980—94, chmn. ob-gyn, 1991-94. Head divsn. perinatal medicine Clin. Hosp., Zagreb, 1978—94; cons. Clinic for Diabetes, Zagreb, 1965—94. Author: Nutrition in Pregnancy, 1983, Obstetrics, 1994, 2d edit., 1999, Prevention & Diagnostics of Female Genital Tumors, 1998; editor: Gynaecologia & Perinatologia, 1992-2008; contbr. articles to profl. jours. Recipient Golden medal for work, Pres. of Yugoslavia, 1974. Mem. European Assn. Diabetes (mem. diabetic pregnancy study group), European Bd. Ob-gyn., European Coll. Ob-gyn., Croatian Med. Assn. (pres. 1993-96), Croatian Soc. Perinatal Medicine (chmn. 1972-78), N.Y. Acad. Sci. Home: Ulica Jakova Gotovca 7 10-000 Zagreb Croatia Home Phone: 38514664922; Office Phone: 38514604646. Business E-Mail: ante.drazancic@zg.t-com.hr.

DRAZEN, JEFFREY MARK, medical educator; b. St. Louis, May 19, 1946; s. Yale and Sylvia (Wainer) D.; m. Erica Coburn Drazen, July 27, 1969; children: David, Daniel. BS, Tufts U., 1968; MD, Harvard U., 1972. Diplomate Am. Bd. Internal Medicine, Am. Bd. Pulmonary Medicine. Asst. prof. medicine Harvard U., Boston, 1977—81, assoc. prof. medicine, 1981—89, prof. medicine, 1989—90, Parker B. Francs prof. medicine, 1990—2000, prof. medicine, 2000—04, Disting. Parker B. Francis prof. medicine, 2004—; asst. prof. physiology Harvard Sch. Pub. Health, 1980—81, assoc. prof. physiology, 1981—91, prof. physiology, 1991—; chief pulmonary and critical care medicine divsn. Brigham & Women's Hosp., Boston, 1985-2000, sr. physician, 1989—. Mem. respiratory and applied physiology study sect. NIH, 1981-86, pulmonary disease adv. coun., 1988-92, lung bio. & pathology study sec., 1996-2000; Nat. Heart, Lung & Blood Inst. (NHLBI) adv. coun., 2000-2004. Editor-in-chief New England Jour. of Medicine, 2000—. NIH grantee, 1972—. Mem. Am. Soc. Clin. Investigation, Am. Thoracic Soc., Am. Physiology Soc., Am. Fedn. Clin. Rsch., Am. Soc. Clin. Investigation, Am. Soc. Pharmacology and Exptl. Therapeutics, Assn. Am. Physicians, Inst. Medicine., Interurban Clin. Club. Office: Brigham & Women's Hosp 75 Francis St Boston MA 02115-6106 also: New England Journal Medicine 10 Shattuck St Boston MA 02115 Home Phone: 781-721-2333; Office Phone: 781-434-7870. E-mail: jmdrazen@bics.bwh.harvard.edu, jdrazen@nejm.org.

DR. DREW, (DAVID DREW PINSKY), television personality, psychotherapist; b. Pasadena, Calif., Sept. 4, 1958; s. Morton and Helene (Stanton) Pinsky; m. Susan Dr. Drew, July 21, 1991; children: Jordan Davidson, Douglas Drew, Paulina Marie. BS in Biology, Amherst Coll., Mass., 1980; MD, U. So. Calif. Keck Sch. Medicine, 1984. Diplomate American Bd. Internal Medicine, American Bd. Addiction Medicine. Chief resident internal medicine Huntington Meml. Hosp., Pasadena; asst. clin. prof. psychiatry U. So. Calif. Keck Sch. Medicine; co-med. dir. chem. dependency program Aurora Las Encinas Hosp., Pasadena, 1991—2010. Spokesperson Musicians Assistance Program; various vol. activities Advocates for Youth, Ind. Women's Forum, Media Project, Entertainment Industry Coun., Hillside Home for Children. Host (nationally syndicated talk radio show) Loveline, 1984—, Dr. Drew Live, 2007—08, co-host (TV series) Loveline, MTV, 1996—2000, host Strictly Sex with Dr. Drew, Discovery Health Channel, 2005, Strictly Dr. Drew, 2006, Sex...With Mom and Dad, MTV, 2008—, Dr. Drew on HLN, 2011—, exec. prodr., host Celebrity Rehab with Dr. Drew, VH1, 2008—, Sex Rehab with Dr. Drew, 2009, Sober House, 2009—10; author: Cracked: Putting Broken Lives Together Again, 2003, Cracked: Life on the Edge in a Rehab Clinic, 2004, When Painkillers Become Dangerous: What Everyone Needs to Know About OxyContin and Other Prescription Drugs, 2004, The Mirror Effect: How Celebrity Narcissism is Seducing America, 2009; contbr. articles to profl. jours. Recipient Larry Stewart Leadership & Inspiration award, Entertainment Industries Coun. PRISM Awards, 2008, Henry J. Kaiser SHINE (Sexual Health in Entertainment) award. Mem.: AMA, ACP, American Soc. Internal Medicine, Calif. Med. Assn., American Soc. Addiction Medicine. Avocations: opera, running, skiing, surfing. Office: c/o Lapides/Lear Entertainment 14724 Ventura Blvd Penthouse Sherman Oaks CA 91403 *

DREBIN, JEFFREY A., surgeon, educator; MD, Harvard Med. Sch. Diplomate Am. Bd. Surgery-gen. surgery, 1995. Intern Johns Hopkins Hosp., resident, fellow; joined Wash. Univ. Sch. of Medicine; chief divsn. of gastrointestinal surgery Univ. of Pa. Sch. of Medicine, 2004, vice chmn. rsch. dept. of surgery, 2004; chmn. dept. of surgery Hosp. of the Univ. of Pa.; John Rhea Barton prof. of surgery Perelman Sch. of Medicine. Mem.: AMA, St. Louis Surg. Soc., Soc. of Surg. Oncology (councilor at large), Soc. for Surgery of the Alimentary Tract, Am. Surg. Assn., Am. Hepato-Pancreato Biliary Assn. Scientific Program Com., Am. Coll. of Surgeons, Am. Assn. for the Advancement of Sci., Soc. of Clin. Surgery (pres. elect). Office: Hospital of the University of Pennsylvania 3400 Spruce St 4 Silverstein Pavilion Philadelphia PA 19104 Office Phone: 215-662-4000, 215-662-7539. Office Fax: 215-614-0363. E-mail: jeffrey.drebin@uphs.upenn.edu.

DREES, BETTY, medical educator, dean; Interim sect. chair in diabetes, endocrinology, and metabolism Truman Med. Ctr. Hosp. Hill, exec. assoc. dean; assoc. prof., docent U. Mo.-Kansas City Sch. Medicine, 1998, interim dean, 2001—03, dean, prof. medicine, 2003—, interim provost, 2007. Office: U Mo Kansas City Sch Medicine 2411 Holmes Kansas City MO 64108 Office Phone: 816-235-1965. E-mail: DreesB@umkc.edu. *

DREHER, MELANIE CREAGAN, dean, nursing educator; BSN magna cum laude, L.I. U.; D in Anthropology, Columbia U. Mem. faculty Columbia U., NYC; dean Sch. Nursing, William Ryan disting. prof. U. Miami; dean Sch. Nursing, prof. U. Mass., 1988—97; Kelting dean, prof. U. Iowa Coll. Nursing, 1997—2006; John L. and Helen Kellogg dean Rush U. Coll. Nursing, Chgo., 2006—. Mem. NIH Coun. on Pub. Rels., Washington, 1999—2001; adv. bd. mem. Pfizer Fellowship Prog. in Nursing Rsch., 2000—01; dir. Beverly Enterprises, Inc., 2004—. Mem. editl. bds. various profl. jours. Recipient May A. Brunson award, CASE award. Mem. Sigma Theta Tau (pres. Beta Zeta chpt. 1995). Office: Rush Univ Coll Nursing Armour Academic Ctr 600 S Paulina St Ste 1080 Chicago IL 60612 Office Phone: 312-942-7117. Business E-Mail: Melanie_Dreher@rush.edu.

DREICER, ROBERT, oncologist, director, medical educator; b. Brooklyn, NY, May 30, 1955; BS, Colo. State U., Fort Collins; MD, U. Tex., 1983. Intern, internal medicine Ind. U., Indpls., 1983—84, resident, oncology, 1984—86; fellow U. Wis., 1986—89; assoc. prof. medicine U. Iowa, Iowa City, 1989—99; dir. med. oncology Cleve. Clinic Found., 1999—; prof. medicine Cleve. Clinic Lerner Coll. Medicine, 2005, chmn. dept. solid tumor oncology, 2006—. Fellow: Am. Coll. Physicians; mem.: Am. Soc. Clin. Oncology (chair membership com. 1997—2000). Office: Cleve Clinic Found Mail Code R35 9500 Euclid Cleveland OH 44195

DREILING, RICHARD W. (RICK DREILING), retail executive; b. 1953; BA in Industrial Relations, Rockhurst U., Mo. Various mgmt. positions Safeway, Inc., 1969—97; pres. The Vons Companies, Inc. (divsn. Safeway, Inc.), 1998—99; exec. v.p. mfg. & distbn. Safeway, Inc., 2000—03; chief ops. officer, exec. v.p. Longs Drug Stores Corp., 2003—05, COO, 2005; pres., CEO Duane Reade Holdings, Inc., NYC, 2005—07, chmn., pres., CEO, 2007—08; CEO Dollar General Corp., Goodlettsville, Tenn., 2008, chmn., CEO, 2008—. Office: Dollar General 100 Mission Ridge Goodlettsville TN 37072

DRENHAUS, ULRICH KARL GUSTAV, retired anatomist researcher; b. Witten, Germany, June 29, 1946; s. Gustav and Gisela Drenhaus; m. Noboku Omori, Sept. 24, 1976; children: Julia, Mark, Michael, Hanni. D in Natural Scis., Christian-Albrechts U., Kiel, Germany, 1975. Collaborator U. Kiel, 1972-77, U. Bochum, 1977-86; collaborator, lectr. U. Fribourg, Switzerland, 1987-2000, master in tchg. and rsch. (ret.), 2001—08; adv. bd. mem. Optima Living, Berlin, 2004—. Contbr. over 90 publs. related to paleodemography, human biology, anatomy, neuroscience, anthropology and history colonn devel. Recipient 1st prize im microphotography German Assn. Biologists, 1999, 4th prize, 2001, 5th prize, 2003, 2d prize, 2005, spl. prize in microphotography, 1997, 98, 99, 2001. Mem. Am. Assn. Anatomists, NY Acad. Scis. Avocation: genealogy.

DREPAUL, LORIS OMESH, internist, infectious diseases physician; b. Georgetown, Guyana, Feb. 6, 1960; naturalized U.S. citizen; s. Frank Eric and Iris Ismay Etwaria (Masih-Das) D. BA in Philosophy with honors, CUNY, 1985, BS in Biology magna cum laude; MD, NYU, 1989. Lic. NYS, 1994. Intern in internal medicine St. Luke's Hosp.-Columbia U. Coll. Physicians and Surgeons, NYC, 1989-90, jr. resident in internal medicine, 1990—91; sr. resident in internal medicine Booth Meml. Med. Ctr.-NYU Sch. Medicine, Queens, 1991-92; fellow in infectious diseases Bronx VA Med. Ctr.-Mt. Sinai Sch. Medicine, NY, 1992-94, asst. coord. phys. diagnosis course, 1994; attending in infectious diseases Mary Immaculate Hosp, Queens, Cath. Med. Ctr.-Albert Einstein Coll. Medicine, Bronx, 1995-96; faculty, attending in infectious diseases Highland Hosp., Rochester, NY, 1997-98; pvt. practice Rochester, NY, 1997—98, 2007—, Essen Med. Bronx, NYC, 2009—. Founder HIV/AIDS Bilingual Primary Care Outreach Program, Bridge Plaza Rehab. Clinic, Queens, N.Y., 1995-96; med. dir. Cmty. Health Network, Inc., Rochester, 1997-98, adj. attending medicine, Bronx Lebanon Hosp. Ctr., 2009-. Mem. AMA, ACP, Med. Soc. State N.Y., Med. Res. Corps N.Y.C., Phi Beta Kappa, MENSA Avocations: music, bridge, chess, soccer, computers. Home: 952 E 214th St Bronx NY 10469 Business E-Mail: drepaul@pol.net. *

DRESCHER, JOACHIM JOSEPH, virologist; b. Reichenbach, Germany, July 8, 1930; s. Arthur Heinrich and Annelise Drescher; m. Christa Hildegard Haubold, Dec. 23, 1958; 1 child, Bettina. Physician, Freie U. Berlin, 1954, MD, 1955, docent of microbiology, 1962. Rsch. assoc. Robert Koch Inst., Berlin, 1955—59, lab. head, 1959—67; prof. virology, dir. Inst. Virology Hannover (Germany) Med. Sch., 1967—2000, prof. emeritus, 2000—. Contbr. articles to profl. jours. Mem.: AAAS, N.Y. Acad. Scis., Royal Soc. Med. Roman Catholic. Home: 6 Husarenweg D-31303 Burgdorf Germany

DRESKIN, STEPHEN CHARLES, immunologist, allergist; b. Chgo., Aug. 11, 1949; s. E. Arthur and Jeanet (Steckler) D.; m. June Inuzuka, May 8, 1982; children: Andrea T., Samuel M., Lauren F. BA, U. Pa., 1971; PhD, Emory U., 1975, MD, 1977. Diplomate allergy and clin. immunology and diagnostic lab. immunology Am. Bd. Internal Medicine. Intern U. Calif., Davis, 1977-78, resident, 1978-80; med. staff fellow NIH, Bethesda, Md., 1981-85, guest rschr., 1985-87, expert, 1987-88; asst. prof. dept. medicine U. Colo. Health Scis. Ctr., Denver, 1989—96, assoc. prof. dept. medicine, 1996—2004, prof. dept. medicine, 2004—. Contbr. articles to profl. jours. Recipient investigator award Arthritis Found., 1985-88, developing investigator award Bouroughs Wellcome Found., 1990-1994; rsch. grantee NIH, 1991-95, 2003—. Mem. AAAS, Am. Acad. Allergy and Immunology, Am. Fedn. Clin. Investigation, Western Soc. for Clin. Investigation, Clin. Immunology Soc. Avocations: tennis, bridge.

DREW, CLIFFORD JAMES, psychologist, educator; b. Eugene, Oregon, Mar. 9, 1943; s. Albert C. and Violet M. (Caskey) D. BS magna cum laude, Ea. Oreg. Coll., 1965; EdM, U.Ill., 1966; PhD (hon.), U. Oreg., 1968. Asst. prof. edn. Kent State U., Ohio, 1968-69; asst. prof. dir. rsch. and spl. edn. U. Tex., Austin, 1969-71; assoc. prof. spl. edn. U. Utah, Salt Lake City, 1971-76, prof., 1977—, asst. dean Grad. Sch. Edn., 1974-77, assoc. dean, 1977-79, 89-95, prof. spl. edn., ednl. psychology, 1979—, coord. instrnl. tech., acad. v.p. office, 1995-97, assoc. acad. v.p., 1997—2004, assoc. dean Coll. Edn., 2004—09. Cons. HEW, 1969-80. Bd. dir. Far West Lab. Ednl. Rsch. and Devel., San Francisco, 1974-80; mem. exec. bd. Salt Lake County Assn. Retarded Children, 1971-72; mem. adv. com. Mental Retardation Counseling Svc., Tex. Dept. Mental Health Mental Retardation, 1969-70. Author: Intro. to Designing Rsch. and Evaluation, 2d edit., 1976, Designing and Conducting Behavioral Rsch., 1985; co-author (with B. Wampold): Theory and Application of Stats., 1990; co-author: (with M. Hardman and A. Hart) Designing and Conducting Rsch.: Inquiry in Edn. and Social Sci., 1996; co-author: (with D. Gelfand) Understanding Child Behavior Disorders, 2003; co-author: (with M. Hardman) Intellectual Disabilities Across the Lifespan, 2006, 9th edit., 2007; co-author: (with M. Hardman and W. Egan) Human Exceptionality: School, Community, and Family, 2006, Human Exceptionality: School, Community and Family, 2008—; co-author: (with M. Hardman and J. Hosp) Designing and Conducting Research in education, 2008; co-editor (with Robert Zheng & Jason Burrow Sanchez): Adolescent Online Social Communication and Behaviour; contbr. numerous articles to profl. jours. NDEA fellow, 1965-66; U.S. Office Edn. fellow, 1966-68. Fellow Am. Assn. on Intellectual and Devel. Disabilities; mem. Am. Psychol. Assn., Am. Ednl. Rsch. Assn. Office: U Utah Dean's Office 1705 Campus Center Dr Rm 225 Salt Lake City UT 84112-9007 Home Phone: 435-783-2743. *

DREWRY, MARCIA ANN, physician; b. St. Louis, Feb. 15, 1951; d. Owen and Annie Vernell (Smith) Palmer; m. Norman T. Drewry, Sept. 18, 1970 (dec. May 1978); 1 child, Tammy Robbins; m. David W. Worsdell Jr., Dec. 7, 1991. AS with honors, Forest Park Coll., 1989; DO, Kirksville Coll. Osteo. Med., 1993. Diplomate Nat. Bd. Osteo. Med. Examiners; bd. cert. family practice. Intern Riverside Hosp., Wichita, 1993-94; med. transcriptionist Malcolm Bliss Mental Health, St. Louis, 1970-78; asst. adminstr. radiology Incarnate Word Hosp., St. Louis, 1977-79; grant writer molecular virology St. Louis U., St. Louis, 1977-79; med. transcriptionist Neurosurg. Assocs., Inc., St. Louis, 1979-87, Stat Transcription, St. Louis, 1987-88, PRN Transcription, St. Louis, 1988-90; physician Anthony (Kans.) Primary Care Ctr., 1994-96; chief of staff Harper County Hosp. Dist. #6, 1995-96; family practice physician Kiowa (Kans.) Hosp. and Clinic, 1997—2000; staff physician Cen. Fla. Family Health Ctr., Sanford, 2004—; resident Fla. Hosp., East Orlando, 2002—04. Dir. credentials, emergency dept. and med. records Anthony (Kans.) Primary Care Ctr., 1995-96. Capt. Operation Safe St., St. Louis, 1985-89; choir mem.

Dover Place Christian Ch., St. Louis, 1986-93; mem. Careers for Homemakers, St. Louis, 1987-89. Fellow: Fla. Soc. Am. Coll. Family Practice; mem. Am. Coll. Osteo. Family Physicians, Am. Acad. Osteopathy, Am. Osteo. Assn., Fla. Osteopathic Med. Assn. (Sci. Rsch. award 2004), Kans. Assn. Osteo. Medicine, Bus. and Profl. Women, Beta Sigma Phi, Phi Theta Kappa (pres. 1988-89), Alpha Phi Omega (sec. 1990-91), Theta Psi (promotions asst. 1990-91). Avocations: travel, singing. Home: 2664 Shiprock Ct Deltona FL 32738-8803 Office: 2400 SR 415 Sanford FL 32771

DREWS, JÜRGEN, pharmaceutical researcher; b. Berlin, Aug. 16, 1933; came to U.S., 1991; s. Walter and Charlotte (Schneider) D.; m. Helga Eberlein, July 26, 1963; children: Ulrike, Karoline, Bettina. MD, Free U. Berlin, 1959; Professorship, U. Heidelberg, Fed. Republic of Germany, 1973. Head chemotherapy Sandoz Rsch. Inst., Vienna, 1976-79, head of inst., 1979-82; head internat. pharm. rsch. and devel. Sandoz, Ltd., Basel, Switzerland, 1982-85; dir. pharm. rsch. F. Hoffmann-La Roche Ltd., Basel, 1985-86, chmn. rsch. bd., mem. exec. com., 1986-90; pres. internat. rsch. and devel., mem. exec. com. Hoffmann-La Roche Inc., Basel, 1991-97, pres. global rsch., mem. exec. com. Nutley, NJ, 1996-97; chmn. Internat. Biomedicine Mgmt. Ptnrs., Basel, 1998—2000; mng. ptnr. Bear Stearns Health Innoventures, NYC, 2002—. Prof. medicine U. Heidelberg, 1973—; mem. sci. adv. bd. (jour.) Infection, München, Fed. Republic of Germany, 1973-95, Drug News & Perspectives, Barcelona, Spain, 1988—, Klinische Pharmakologie, München, 1989-2000; bd. dirs. Genentech, Inc., South San Francisco, 1990-97, Protein Design Labs., Mountain View, Calif., MorphoSys GmbH, Munich; bd. dirs., internat. bd. advisors Basel Inst. Immunology, 1986-97; mem. dean's coun. Yale U. Sch. Medicine, 1993-96, chmn. sci. panel inter-company collaboration for AIDS drug devel., 1993-96, chmn. bd. participants inter-company collaboration for AIDS drug devel., 1996-97; mem. adv. com. Mass. Gen. Hosp., Boston, 1994-98; chmn. steering com. Sr. Adv. Group Biotech., 1994-96; chmn. bd. mgmt. EuropaBio, 1997-98; bd. dirs. Human Genome Scis., Rockville, Md. Author: Chemotherapie: Grundlagen und Perspektiven, 1979, Immunpharmakologie, Grundlagen und Perspektiven, 1986, Immunopharmacology, Principles and Perspectives, 1990, In Quest of Tomorrow's Medicines, 1999; editor: (with others) Topics in Infectious Diseases, vol. 1, 1975, vol. 2, 1977; also over 250 articles. Home: 6983 Bridgestone Ct Naples FL 34108-6500 Personal E-mail: info@j_drews.de.

DREYER, GRETA, oncologist; b. Boksburg, South Africa, Nov. 24, 1963; d. Gerrit and Laurika Jacoba Grond; m. Jaco Stephanus Dreyer, Apr. 6, 1985; children: Jacob Stephanus, Gerrit Jan. MBChB, U. Pretoria, Gauteng, 1987; MMed, U. Pretoria, South Africa, 1994. Internship 1 Mil. Hosp., Pretoria, South Africa, 1988, med. officer, 1989—90; registrar U. Hosps. Pretoria, 1991—94; specialist, lectr. U. Pretoria, 1995—97, sr. lectr., sr. specialist, 1997—2003; adj. prof., sr. prin. specialist U. Pretoia, Pretoria Academic Hosp., 2004—. Gynaecological oncology fellowship U. Utrecht and Academic Hosp. Utrecht, Netherlands, 1999; mem. nat. coun. Coll. Obstetricians and Gynaecologists, Coll. Medicine South Africa, 2003—; mem. nat. coun. and rsch. com. South Africa Soc. Obstetricians and Gynecologists, 2005—; head gynecologic oncology unit, dept. gynecology, U. Pretoria, 2004—; head familial cancer ctr. U. Pretoria and Netcare Pvt. Hosp. Group, 2004—; founding mem. Pretoria Breast Cancer Forum, Gauteng, South Africa, 2004—06; mem., head rsch. com. South African HPV Adv. Bd., 2005—; founder mem. African HPV Bd., South Africa, 2005—, South African Anaemia Working Group, 2006—; editor Suthern African Jour. Gynecologic Oncology, 2009—; spkr. in field. Author: Guidelines for the Management of the Menopause, 2000, Guidelines for the Use and Management of High Risk HPV Testing and Infection, 2005; contbr. chapters to books, articles to profl. jours. Mem. Nat. Osteoporosis Forum, South Africa, 1999—2006. Travel grant, Flemish-South African Soc., 1996, Gynaecological Oncology fellowship, Netherlands Cancer Soc. and U. Utrecht, 1999, Travel and Rsch. grant, U. Bologne, 2004, 2005, grant, Cancer Assn. South Africa and Med. Rsch. Coun., 1999, 2010—. Mem.: South African Menopause Soc. (Rsch. grant 2005—07), South African Soc. Gynaecologic Oncologists, European Soc. Gynaecologic Oncologists, Internat. Gynaecologic Cancer Soc., Coll. Obstetricians and Gynecologists (hon.; mem. nat. coun. 2003—), South African Med. Assn. Lds Ch. Achievements include development of private public partnership initiated and established between the University of Pretoria and the Netcare hospital group. Avocations: travel, art. Home: 183 Charles St Gauteng Pretoria 0181 South Africa Office: U Pretoria Dr Savage Rd Gauteng Pretoria 0001 South Africa Office Fax: 27 12 329 6258; Home Fax: 27 12 325 0302. Business E-Mail: greta.dreyer@mweb.co.za.

DREYFUS, ANDREW, insurance company executive; B in English, Conn. Coll., New London. Exec. v.p. Mass. Hosp. Assn.; with Commonwealth of Mass. spl. comn. on Health Care Payment System; Mass. undersecretary consumer affairs and bus. regulation, dir. ops., dir. comm. Mass. Exec. Office of Human Services; exec. v.p. health care svcs. Blue Cross Blue Shield of Mass., Inc., pres., CEO, 2010—. Bd. dirs. Kenneth B. Schwartz Ctr.; bd. adv. Brigham and Women's Hosp. Ctr. for Surgery and Pub. Health. Pres. Blue Cross Blue Shield of Mass. Found.; Harvard Risk Mgmt. Found.; United Way of Mass. Bay; Merrimack Valley. Office: Blue Cross and Blue Shield of Massachusetts Inc Landmark Center 401 Pk Dr Boston MA 02215-3326 Office Phone: 800-262-2583.

DREYFUSS, ERIC MARTIN, allergist; b. Bad Homburg, Germany, July 11, 1930; came to U.S., 1934; s. Walter and Hedwig (Herz) D.; m. Sandra Dale Gasul, June 16, 1957; children: Peter, Lisa. AB, Cornell U., 1953; MD, Chgo. Med. Sch., 1957. Diplomat Am. Bd. Allergy and Immunology. Intern Beth Israel Hosp., NYC, 1957-58; resident in pediats. SUNY, Syracuse, 1958-60; fellow in allergy Rochester, NY, 1962-64; allergist Allergy Assocs. Rochester, 1964—. Asst. clin. prof. U. Rochester Sch. Medicine and Dentistry, 1970—. Capt. U.S. Army, 1960-62. Fellow Am. Acad. Allergy and Immunology, Am. Coll. Allergists, Am. Acad. Pediatrics. Office: Allergy Assocs Rochester 300 Goodman St S Rochester NY 14607-3105

DREYLING, MARTIN H., medical educator; b. Wuppertal, Germany, Sept. 9, 1961; married; children: Anna Dominika, Cornelius Carl. Cert. human medicine State Bavaria, 1987. Residency Dept. Internal Medicine, U. Hosp., Bonn, Germany, 1988—90; fellow Dept. Internal Medicine, Clemens Hosp., Münster, 1990—91, Dept. Hematology, Oncology, U. Hosp., Münster, 1991—92; vis. scientist Dept. Hematology, Oncology, U. Chgo., 1992—95; fellow Dept. Medicine, U. Hosp., Göttingen, 1995—98; prof. medicine Dept. Medicine III, U. Hosp. Grosshadern LMU, Munich, 1998—, attending physician, 2002—, prof. medicine, 2007—. Coord. European Mantle Cell Lymphoma Network, 2000; asst. coord. German Low Grade Lymphoma Study Group, 2002—; bd. mem. German Soc. Hematology, Oncology. Recipient Ellen Glesby Cohen Leadership award, Lymphoma Rsch. Found., 2007. Office: Univ Hosp Grosshadern LMU Marchioninistrasse 15 Munich D-81377 Germany Office Fax: 49 89 7095 2201. Business E-Mail: martin.dreyling@med.uni-muenchen.de.

DREZ, DAVID JACOB, JR., orthopedic surgeon, educator; b. Lake Charles, La., Aug. 21, 1938; s. David Jacob and Hester Adele (Bingham) D.; m. Judith Diane Wolfe, June 5, 1963; children: Susan, Catherine Ann Self, David Jacob III. BS, Tulane U., 1959, MD, 1963. Diplomate Am. Bd. Surgery, Am. Bd. Orthopaedic Surgery. Intern Charity Hosp., New Orleans, 1963-64, resident in gen. surgery, 1964-68, resident in orthopaedic surgery, 1968-71; resident Scottish Rite Hosp., Atlanta, 1969, USPHS Hosp., New Orleans, 1970; pvt. practice Orthopaedic Assocs., Lake Charles, 1971-82; pvt. practice Orthopaedic and Sports Injury Clinic Knee and Sports Medicine Ctr., Lake Charles, 1982-94; pvt. practice Ctr. Orthopaedics, Lake Charles, 1994—2006; pvt. practice, orthop. specialists, 2007—. Staff Lake Charles Meml. Hosp., 1973—, bd. trustees, 1973, 80-82, sec.-treas., 1977, pres., 1981, chief surgery, 1984, 85; med. staff dept. orthopaedics Children's Hosp., New Orleans, 1988; La. state chmn. Orthopaedic Rsch. and Edn. Found., 1987, 90-92; network of orthopedic surgeons U.S. Gymnastics Fedn., 1988—; physician U.S. Soccer Assn., 1988—; examiner Am. Bd. Orthopaedic Surgery, 1989, 91, 92, bd. dirs.; vis. prof. numerous hosps. and univs.; speaker in field. Author: (with R. D'Ambrosia) Prevention and Treatment of Running Injuries, 1982, Prevention and Treatment of Running Injuries, 2d edit., 1989, (with D.W. Jackson) The Anterior Cruciate Deficient Knee-New Concepts in Ligament Repair, 1986, Orthopaedic Sports Medicine: Principles and Practice, 1994 (with Jesse DeLee); author 8 chpts. in books; editor Am. Jour. Sports Medicine, 1988—, Jour. Orthopaedic Techniques, 1993—; co-editor Operative Techniques in Sports Medicine jour., 1993—; mem. editl. bd. Orthopaedics, 1983—, Arthroscopy, 1984-89, Sports Medicine News, 1989—; author 5 video tapes, audio tape; adv. bd. Clin. Update, Sports Medicine, 1983—, Clin. Orthopaedics and Related Rsch., 1987-93; con. rev. bd. Jour. Bone and Joint Surgeons, 1989—; contbr. articles to profl. jours. Team orthopaedist athletic dept. McNeese State U., Lake Charles, 1974—, pres. 100 Club, 1979; co-dir. Runner's Clinic, La. State U. Sch. Medicine, New Orleans, 1978-81; chief physician NAAU Boxing Championship, Lake Charles, 1979; mem. Gov.'s Coun. on Phys. Fitness and Sports, 1981; bd. dirs. Lake Area Runners, 1989-92. Maj. La. N.G., 1963-71. Named to La. Athletic Trainers Assn. Hall of Fame, 1989, McNeese State U. Hall of Honors, 1990. Mem. Acad. Orthopaedic Soc., Am. Acad. Orthopaedic Surgeons, Am. Acad. Sports Physicians, Am. Coll. Sports Medicine, Am. Coll. Surgeons, Am. Orthopaedic Assn., Am. Orthopaedic Foot Soc., Am. Orthopaedic Foot and Ankle Soc., Am. Orthopaedic Soc. Sports Medicine, Arthroscopy Assn. N.Am., Assn. Bone and Joint Surgeons, Assn. Sports Medicine Fellowship Dirs., Mid. Am. Orthopaedic Assn., Assn. Arthritic Hip and Knee Surgery, Australian-Am. Orthopaedic Soc., Calcasieu Parish Med. Soc., Clin. Orthopaedic Soc., European Soc. Knee Surgery and Arthroscopy, Herodicus Sports Medicine Soc. (past sec., v.p., pres.), Internat. Arthroscopy Assn., Internat. Soc. Knee, La. Orthopaedic Assn. (pres. 1992), La. State Med. Assn., Oscar Creech Surg. Soc., Orthopaedic Rsch. Soc., Soc. Internat. Chirurgie Orthopedique Traumatologie, Soc. Internat. Recherche Orthopedique Tramatologie. Avocations: reading, jogging, travel. Office: 1717 Oak Pk Blvd FL 3 Lake Charles LA 70601-8990 also: Ctr Orthop 1747 Imperial Blvd Lake Charles LA 70607 Office Phone: 337-494-4900, 337-721-7236. Business E-Mail: drezmd@pol.net.

DRIÁK, DANIEL, surgeon, educator; b. Apr. 29, 1965; MD, Charles U., Prague, 1989; PhD, U. Def., Hradec Kralové, Czech Republic, 2006. Surgeon regional hosps., Melník, Czech Republic, 1989—2002; surgeon ob-gyn. clinic Univ. Hosp. Bulovka, Prague, Czech Republic, 2002—06, head ob-gyn. clinic, 2006—10. Faculty medicine Charles U. Author: Charming Even in Pregnancy, 2004; co-author: Urogynecology, 2004. Mem.: European Soc. Gynecol. Cancer, Czech Ob-gyn. Soc. (bd. dirs. sect. infectious diseases), European Soc. Contraception. Office: Charles Univ Tchg Hosp NA B Dept Ob-gyn/1st Medical Faculty Budinova 2 180 81 Prague 180 81 Czech Republic Office Phone: 420 2 66083229. Office Fax: 420 283840507. Business E-Mail: driak@seznam.cz.

DRIESSEN, BERND, veterinarian, educator; b. Wuppertal, Germany, Sept. 12, 1961; DVM, Free U. Berlin, 1988, Dr. med. vet., 1991. Resident, anesthesia and critical patient care U. Calif., Davis, 1995—98, fellow, vet. anesthesia, 1998—99, adj. prof., anesthesiology, David-Geffen Sch. Medicine LA, 2003—; asst. prof., vet. anesthesiology, chief, svc. large animal anesthesia U. Pa., 1999—2003, assoc. prof., 2003—10, prof., vet. anesthesiology, chief, sect. large animal emergency and critical care medicine, anesthesia, 2010—. Recipient 3rd Pain award, German Soc. Study Pain, Barbaro Meml. Health Study award, Morris Animal Found. Mem.: European Coll. Vet. Pharmacology & Toxicology, Assn. Vet. Anaesthetists, Internat. Vet. Acad. Pain Mgmt., Am. Coll. Vet. Anesthesiologists (ANESCO award). Avocations: music, opera, theater, mountain climbing, skiing. Office: 382 W St Rd Kennett Square PA 19348 Office Fax: 610-925-6820. Business E-Mail: driessen@vet.upenn.edu.

DRINKOVIC, NIKSA, cardiologist, educator; b. Zagreb, Croatia, Oct. 26, 1947; s. Tadija and Marija Drinkovic; m. Violeta Dunkovic, Apr. 18, 1950; children: Nivia, Niksa. MD, U. Zagreb, 1972, cert. specialist in medicine, 1978, cert. cardiology specialist, 1997. Staff specialist dept. cardiology Univ. Hosp. Centre, Zagreb, 1978—94, chief ward, 1994—. Asst. prof. U. Zagreb, 1987—93, prof., 1993—, mem. sci. bd., 1996—98; mem. biomedical coun. Ministry Scis., Zagreb, 1996—98. Author: (book) Advances in Doppler Echocardiography, 1990. John E. Fogarty grantee, U. Ky., 1984—86, A. von Humboldt grantee, 1989. Fellow: Am. Coll. Angiology, Am. Coll. Cardiology; mem.: Croatian Acad. Scis. (mem. cardiovasc. bd. 1998—), N.Y. Acad. Scis. Avocations: skiing, bicycling, fishing. Office: Univ Hosp Centre Dept Cardiology Kispticeva 12 10000 Zagreb Croatia Home: Klanjcic 29 10-000 Zagreb Croatia Office Fax: (+385 1) 487 35 35. Business E-Mail: niksa.drinkovic@zg.tel.hr.

DRISCOLL, COLIN L. W., otolaryngologist, educator; MD, U. of N.Mex., Albuquerque; BA in Geology, Pomona Coll. Diplomate Am. Bd. Otolaryngology, 1998. Hosp. affiliation includes Mayo Clinic, Rochester, Minn., intern gen. surgery Mayo Grad. Sch. of Medicine, resident otorhinolaryngology, 1993—97; fellow neurotology Univ. of Calif. San Francisco Med. Ctr., 1997—98, fellow skull base surgery, 1998—99; assoc. prof. otolaryngology Mayo Med. Sch.; v.p. Minn. Acad. of Otolaryngology, 2005—06, pres., 2006—07. Co-author: (publs.) Long-term clinical course and temporal bone histology after cochlear implantation, 2005, Retrospective analysis of outcomes after stapedotomy with implantation of a self-crimping Nitinol stapes prosthesis, 2007, Surgical approaches to vestibular schwannomas: what the radiologist needs to know, 2009, The use of micro-CT to evaluate cochlear implant electrode position and intracochlear damage, 2010, Implications of minimizing trauma during conventional cochlear implantation, 2011, and numerous others. Office: Mayo Clinic 200 S W First St Rochester MN 55905-0002 Office Phone: 507-284-2511.

DRISCOLL, DANIEL J., medical geneticist, educator; MD, Albany Med. Coll., 1983; PhD, Indiana U., 1983. Lic. Fla., 1989, diplomate Am. Bd. Pediatrics, 1987, cert. Am. Bd. Clin. Genetics-Med. Genetics, 1990, Am. Bd. Clin. Cytogenetics-Med. Genetics, 1990. Intern Johns Hopkins Hosp., 1984, resident pediat., 1984—86, fellow clin. genetics, 1986—89; prof. pediat. Univ. Fla.; hosp. affiliation include Shands Health Care. Office: University of Florida Shands 1600 SW Archer Rd Gainesville FL 32608 Office Phone: 352-265-0111.

DRISCOLL, DAVID JOHN, pediatric cardiologist; b. Milw., June 25, 1945; MD, Marquette U. Sch. Medicine, Milw., 1970. Cert. in pediat., in pediatric cardiology. Internship in pediat. Johns Hopkins U. Hosp., Balt., 1970—71; residency in pediat. Milw. Children's Hosp. Med. Coll. Wis., 1971—72, residency in pediatric cardiology, 1974—75; fellowship in pediatric cardiology Tex. Children's Hosp. Baylor Coll. Medicine, Houston, 1975—78; prof. pediat. Mayo Clinic, Rochester, Minn. Author: Fundamentals of Pediatric Cardiology, 2006; contbr. articles to profl. jours. Office: Mayo Clinic Dept Pediatric Cardiology 200 1st St SW Rochester MN 55905 Office Phone: 507-284-2511.

DRISCOLL, DEBORAH ANNE, gynecologist, obstetrician; b. NYC, Apr. 9, 1955; AB in Biology, Smith Coll., Northampton, Mass., 1977; MD, NYU Sch. Medicine, 1983. Diplomate American Bd. Ob-gyn., cert. in clin. and molecular genetics. Intern ob-gyn. U. Pa. Hosp., 1983—84, resident genetics, 1984—87, fellow ob-gyn., 1987—89, attending physician ob-gyn., 1989—; asst. prof. ob-gyn. U. Pa. Sch. Medicine, 1989—98, assoc. prof., 1998—2005, prof., 2005—08, Luigi Mastroianni, Jr. prof. ob-gyn., 2008—, chair dept. ob-gyn., asst. prof. pediat., 1993—98, assoc. prof., 1998—2007, asst. prof. genetics, 1997—98, prof., 2007—, assoc. prof. ob-gyn. in genetics, 1998—. Contbr. articles to profl. jours. Named a Top Doc, Phila. Mag., 2006—10; named one of America's Top Doctors, Castle Connolly Medical Ltd., 2007, 2008, 2010. Mem.: Inst. Medicine, Assn. Professors Gynecology & Obstetrics, N.Am. Soc. Pediatric & Adolescent Gynecology, American Coll. Ob-gyn., American Soc. Human Genetics, American Coll. Med. Genetics. Office: Univ Pa Hosp Dept Obstetrics & Gynecology 3400 Spruce St Philadelphia PA 19104 Office Phone: 215-662-2459. Office Fax: 215-349-5893. E-mail: driscold@mail.med.upenn.edu. *

DRITSCHILO, ANATOLY, radiologist, educator; b. Reigersfeld, Germany, Oct. 10, 1944; arrived in USA, 1949, naturalized; s. Peter Prokofovich and Maria (Ivanovna) Dritschilo; m. Joy Ann Dritschilo, Apr. 6, 1968; children: Peter Dale, Andrea Beth, Lisa Ann. BS in Engring., U. Pa., 1967; MS in Engring., Newark Coll. Engring., 1969; MD, Coll. Medicine NJ, 1973. Diplomate Am. Bd. Radiology; lic. Mass., DC, Md., Va. Clin. fellow Harvard Med. Sch., Boston, 1974-77; resident, radiation therapy Joint Ctr. Radiol. Therapy, Boston, 1974—77; asst. prof. radiation oncology Tufts U. Sch. Medicine, Boston, 1977-79; assoc. prof. radiation medicine Georgetown U. Sch. Medicine, Washington, 1980—87, chmn. dept. radiation medicine, 1980—2005, prof. radiation medicine, 1987—2005, dean grad. med. edn., 1994-97; med. dir. Georgetown U. Hosp., Washington, 1994-97; dir., radiation oncology, Lombardi Comprehensive Cancer Ctr. Georgetown U., Washington, 1979—2005, acting co-dir., Lombardi Comprehensive Cancer Ctr., 1987—88, clin. dir., Lombardi Comprehensive Cancer Ctr., 1988—94, interim dir., Lombardi Sector and Lombardi Comprehensive Cancer Ctr., 2005—07; interim assoc. v.p. Georgetown U. Med. Ctr., Washington, 2005—, interim chair, dept. oncology, 2005—08, prof. radiation medicine, 2008—10; chairman dept. radiation medicine, 2010—. Chief co-protor, Am. Bd. Radiology, 1986-88; mem. ext. adv. com. U. Wis. Cancer Ctr., Madison, 1992-97; mem. sci. coun. Radiation Rsch., Reston, Va., 2000-; bd. dirs. Neopharm Inc., Bannockburn, Ill, 1990-, Nat. Coalition for Cancer Rsch.; advisor on rsch. funding matters, NIH, Am. Cancer Soc.; mem. NIH (grantee 1987-, mem. radiation study sect. 1990-94, sci. rev. group 1997-); mem. scientific bd., Oxigene Inc., 1992-96; mem. scientific adv. com., U. Wis. Comprehensive Cancer Ctr., 1992-96; reviewer/cons. dept. radiation oncology, U. Mass., 1990, divsn. radiation oncology, Case Western Reserve U., 1997; expert cons. Am. Medico-Legal Found., Phila., PA, 1996-; cons. in rsch., dept. physics, George Washington U., 1996-; spkr. in field. Assoc. editor Radiation Oncology Investigations jour., 1995, assoc. editor, Computerized Tomography, 1980-88; mem. editl. bd. Radiation Oncology Investigations 1992-95, assoc. editor 1995-; manuscript reviewer, Cancer Rsch., Radiation Rsch., Internat. Jour. Radiation Oncology, Biology and Physics, Cancer Comm., The Cancer Jour. for Scientific Am., Oncogene and Gene Therapy, 1987-; reviewer, dept. radiation therapy, U. Tex. Med. Br., Galveston, 1993; contbr. several articles to profl. jours. Bd. dirs. Nat. Coalition for Cancer Rsch., Washington, 2000—. Fellow Am. Coll. Radiology; mem. Am. Soc. Clin. Oncologists, Am. Assn. Cancer Rsch., Am. Radium Soc., Radiation Rsch. Soc.(mem. awards monitoring com., 1989, program com., 1989, rsch. award selection com., 1989, chair nominating com., 1992, chair, fund raising com., 1995-96, mem. rsch. support com., 1997, radiation com. 1997), Am. Soc. Therapeutic Radiation Oncologists, Radiological Soc. N.Am. (dist. sci. advisor), DC Med. Soc., Soc. Chmn. Academic Radiation Oncology Programs, Am. Coll. Radiation Oncology, Am. Cancer Soc. (mem. prevention, diagnosis, and treatment grant review com., 1989-90, com. on clin. investigators II, prevention, diagnosis and therapy, 1990-92, ad hoc reviewer, cancer control and epidemiology com., 1996, ad hoc mem., clin. rsch. cancer control and epidemiology com., 1997), Am. Radiation Soc. (mem. radiation therapy and biology NIH/NCI study sect). Russian Orthodox. Achievements include patents for radiosurgery and sterotactic methods. Avocations: golf, painting. Office: Georgetown University Hosp Dept Radiation Med Ctr 3800 Reservoir Rd NW Washington

DC 20007 also: Georgetown U Med Ctr Lower Level, Bles Building CB-18 Washington DC 20007 Office Phone: 202-444-3320. Fax: 202-687-6402. Business E-Mail: dritscha@georgetown.edu.

DROCIUK, DANIEL, epidemiologist, director; b. Newark, June 1, 1964; MT, Med. U. SC, 1987. Chief med. technologist, spl. chemistry & chemistry Bapt. Med. Ctr., 1987—96; med. technologist Lexington Med. Ctr., 1996—98; rsch. asst. Ctrs. Disease Control and Prevention, Nat. Immunization Program, 1998—99, state rep., 2009—; dir. bioterrorism surveillance and response program SC Dept. Health and Environ. Control, 2000—04, dir. epidemiologic response & enhanced surveillance, 2004—. Recipient Monthly award, SC Dept. Health and Environ. Control, 2005, Outstanding Customer Svc. award, 2005, Michael D. Jarrett Outstanding Customer Svc. award, 2010, Joint Terrorism Task Force Outstanding Svc. award, FBI, 2008. Mem.: SC Pub. Health Assn., Coun. State and Territorial Epidemiologists. Avocation: stamp collecting/philately. Home: 120 Melville Rd Columbia SC 29212 Home Fax: 803-898-0897. Business E-Mail: drociukd@dhec.sc.gov.

DRONAMRAJU, KRISHNA RAO, geneticist; b. Pithapuram, India, Jan. 14, 1937; came to U.S., 1963; s. Bapiraju and Rajeswaramma (Vankayalapati) D.; m. Sheila Marion McHarg, Mar. 31, 1962 (div. 1978); 1 child, Raj Gopal. MSc, Agra U., India, 1957; PhD, Indian Statis. Inst., Calcutta, 1966. Cert. cancer cytogenetics Fox Chase Cancer Ctr., Phila. Rsch. fellow U. Alta., Edmonton, Canada, 1966-68; asst. prof. U. Sask., Saskatoon, Canada, 1968-69; chief geneticist Lancaster (Pa.) Cleft Palate Clinic, 1969-73; writer, lectr. Balt., 1973-77; pers. cons. City of Balt., 1978-79, job devel. advisor, 1979-81; sr. fellow U. Tex., Houston, 1982-85; pres., dir. Found. for Genetic Rsch., Houston, 1985—. Vis. prof. Hershey Med. Ctr., Pa. 1969-73, Osmania U., India, 1995, U. Turin, Italy, 2004, 2005-06, U. Hong kong Med. Ctr., 2005; mem. recombinant DNA adv. com. NIH, Bethesda, Md., 1992—; hon. rsch. fellow U. London, 1994; vis. prof. U. Paris, 1994, Jawaharlal Nehru U., New Delhi, 1994; hon. prof. Albert Schweitzer Internat. U., Geneva, 1996; advisor Tex. State Coun. on Biotech., 2000-; hon. prof. Andhra U., 2003; mem. adv. bd. to U.S. Sec. Agr., 2002-; chmn. internat. adv. bd. Chemtech Found., 2002-; del. 23rd Internat. Congress Sci. and Tech., Beijing, China, 2005; del. Indian Sci. Congress, 2006, chmn. Frontier Techs., 2006, Biotech. Plenary Symposium, 2008; disting. centennial lecturer Tamil Nadu Agrl. U., 2006. Author: Cleft Lip and Palate: Aspects of Reproductive Biology, 1986, The Foundations of Human Genetics, 1989, If I am To Be Remembered, The Life and Work of Julian Huxley with Selected Correspondence, 1993; editor: Haldane and Modern Biology, 1968, Haldane, The Life and Work of J.B.S. Haldane with special reference to India, 1985, Foundations of Human Genetics, 1989, Selected Genetic Papers of JBS Haldane, 1990, The History and Development of Human Genetics: Progress in Different Countries, 1992, Haldane's Daedalus Revisited, 1995, Haldane in India, 1997, Science and Society, 1998, Biological and Social Issues in Biotechnology, 1998, Biological Wealth and Other Essays, 2002, Infectious Disease: Host-Pathogen Evolution, 2004, Malaria: Genetic and Evolutionary Aspects, 2006, Emerging Consequences of Biotechnology, 2008, What I Require from Life: Writing on Science And Life JBS Haldane, 2009, Haldane, Mayr, and Beanbag Genetics, 2011; contbr. articles to profl. jours. Bd. dirs. Sickle Cell Assn., Houston, 1992—; mem. US Pres. del. India, 2000. Recipient Sr. Scientist award NIH, 1982-85, merit award History of Sci. Soc., 1989, Yellapragada Subbarow award for med. rsch., 1997, Y. Nayudamma award for sci. and tech., India, 1997, Welcome Trust Travel awards, 1995-11, Indian Sci. Congress award, 2006; Rockefeller U. Archives grantee, 2002, Chem. Heritage Found. grantee, 2003, 06, 07, 11, Biodiversity Appreciation award, A.P. Govt., India, 2009. Fellow N.Am. Acad. Arts and Scis.; mem. AAAS, Am. Soc. Human Genetics, Asia. Avocations: travel, walking. Office: Found for Genetic Rsch PO Box 27701 Houston TX 77227-7701 Personal E-mail: kdronamraj@aol.com.

DRONCA, MARIA, biochemist, educator; b. Sibiu, Aug. 26, 1949; BS, Babes-Bolyai U., Cluj-Napoca, 1972, PhD in Chemistry, 2000. Rschr. dept. analytical chemistry Chem. and Pharm. Rsch. Inst., 1973—76; jr. asst. I. Hatieganu U. Medicine and Pharmacy, Med. Biochemistry Dept., 1976—80, asst. prof., 1980—90, lectr. med., 1990—2002, assoc. prof., 2002—. Avocations: classical music, travel. Office: 6 Pasteur Cluj_Napoca 400349 Romania Office Fax: 40264597257. Business E-Mail: m_dronca@yahoo.com.

DROSSMAN, DOUGLAS ARNOLD, medical investigator, gastroenterologist, educator; b. Bklyn., Mar. 20, 1946; s. Murray and Ruth (Cohen) D.; m. Deborah Risa Ducoff, June 3, 1970; children: David, Daniel. BA cum laude, Hofstra U., 1966; MD, Albert Einstein Coll., 1970. Diplomate Am. Bd. Internal Medicine, Gastroenterology. Resident N.Y.U.-Bellevue Med. Ctr., NYC, 1972-73; fellow in psychosomatic medicine U. Rochester, N.Y., 1975-76; intern, resident U. NC, Chapel Hill, 1970—72, fellow in gastroenterology, 1976—78, instr. in medicine, 1977—78, asst. prof. medicine & psychiatry, 1978—83, assoc. prof. medicine & psychiatry, 1983—90, prof. medicine & psychiatry, 1990—. Internship selection com. U. NC, 1977-84, housestaff-faculty com., 1980-84,; health promotion/disease prevention steering com., 1983, co-dir. med.-psychiat. liaison program faculty-resident study group in behavioral medicine, 1977-91; vis. prof. med. ctrs. and univs.; chair Functional Brain-Gut Rsch. Group, 1989-1993, Inst. Medicine Com. on Stress and Gulf War 2005-07, 08-09; co-dir. Ctr. Functional GI and Motility Disorders, 1993—; pres., Rome Found., 2003-. Editor: The Functional Gastrointestinal Disorders, 1994, 3d edit., 2006, Functional Brain Gut Rsch. Group Newsletter, 1989—, Participate, 1997—, Handbook of Gastroenterologic Procedures, 2005, The Merck Manual, 15-17th edit., 2006; assoc. editor: Gastroenterology, 2001-06; mem. editl. bd.: Behavioral Medicine Abstracts, 1985-91, Stress Medicine, 1985-92, Current Concepts Gastroenterology, 1986-90, Jour. Clin. Gastroenterology, 1986—, Psychosomatic Medicine, 1998—; ad hoc reviewer over 30 profl. jours.; contbr. over 450 articles to profl. jours., chpts. to textbooks; prodr. 10 edil. videotapes. Maj. Med. Corps USAF, 1973—75. Grantee S.S. Zlinkoff Found., 1979, Smith, Kline, Beckman, 1982, NIH, 1983-86, 91-96, 2003—06, Core Ctr. Diarrheal Diseases, U. NC, 1986, Nat. Found. Ileitis and Colitis, 1987-88; named to Best Doctors in Am., 1992—, Top Gastroenterologist Men's Health, 2007, Women's Health, 2008, Gastroenterology Best Practices Aspatore Press, 2007. Fellow Am. Coll. Gastroenterology (master, Clin. Scholar award, 2004), Am. Gastroenterol. Assn. (program selection com. 1985-86, program selection chmn., coun. co-chair 2001-03, chair nerve-gut 2003-06, Janssen award 1999, Dist. Educator award 2004, Educator award in clin. rsch. 2005, Rsch. Mentor award 2007),; mem. Am. Psychosomatic Soc. (councillor 1985-88, 90-92, 1986 program com. 1985-86, chmn. membership com. 1988-92, sec.-treas. 1992-96, pres. 1997-98, President's award, 2003), Am. Acad. on Phys. and Patient (charter fellow), Am. Fedn. for Clin. Rsch., Am. Soc. for Gastrointestinal Endoscopy, So. Soc. for Clin. Investigation. Avocations: tennis, magic, travel. Office: U NC Div Digestive Diseases # 7080 4150 Bioinformatics Bldg Chapel Hill NC 27599-7080 Office Phone: 919-966-0142. Business E-Mail: drossman@med.unc.edu.

DROUGHT, JAMES HENRY, healthcare business owner, exercise physiologist, writer; b. Aurora, Ill., Mar. 29, 1957; s. James William and Lorna Beryl (Carlson) D.; m. Sarah Jacqueline Drought; children: John Carlson, Daisy Stratton. Student, U.S. Mil. Acad., 1975-77; BS in Phys. Edn., Rutgers U., 1980; MS in Clin. Exercise Physiology, Northeastern U., 1995. Comm. coord. Lake Placid Olympic Organizing Com., NY, 1980-81; dir. Rainmaker Prodns., Boston, 1982-85; health promotion mgr. City of Boston, 1986-87; owner Personal Trainers Strength & Conditioning Consulting, Boston, 1987—2005, Personal Trainers.com, 1995—. Cons. City of Boston, 1988-89, State of Mass., Boston, 1988-89, Lotus Devel. Corp., Cambridge, Mass., 1990-91, Madison Conn. Town Employee Wellness Program, Conn., 2006—; mem. (C.O.R.P.S.) nat. bd. Reebok Internat., Ltd., Stoughton, Mass., 1992-96; articles cons. SHAPE mag., 1995—, Men's Health mag., 1998—. Author: (screenplays) So Long Chgo., 1983, Memories, 1989, Up At The Villa, 1992, Writer in Exile, 1999, (short stories) Walking Manzanillo, 1989, On Meeting John Huston: A Personal Reminiscence, 1998, Bukowski Writing, 1999, Bukowski's Visit, 2000, Changing Time, 2005, Baby Talk, 2008, Jack's Protectors, 2009, Rotten Beer, 2010, (plays) Traveling with Hemingway and Fitzgerald, 1991, (novels) The Picadors, 1996, (poems and quotes to Anthologies) Breaking Chains, 2002, Breaking Chains II, 2008, Breaking Chains III, 2011, Ask the Experts Column, Boston Globe, 1990-92; prodr. (dir., actor): (audio plays) The Wedding, 1982, Sonny Davis Televised, 1982; chpt. author: Essentials of Personal Training; exec. editor Conditioning Instr., 1991-93, (non-fiction) Hank Drought's Football Quarterback Drills, 2011, Hank Drought's Snow Shoveling Tips, 2011; contbr. chpt. to book, articles to profl. jours. Exec. com. Boston vs. Montreal Fitness Challenge, City of Boston, 1989; James Henry Drought collection donated to Howard Gotlieb Archival Rsch. Ctr., Mugar Meml. Libr., Boston U. Named Personal Trainer of Yr., Nat. Strength & Conditioning Assn., 2000; named one of 100 Best Trainers in America, Men's Jour. mag., 2004, New Haven Adv. Reader's Poll Best Personal Trainer, 2010. Mem. Am. Coll. Sports Medicine, Nat. Strength and Conditioning Assn. (Mass. state dir. 1992-98, nat. bd. dirs. 1998-2001, task analysis com. 1992—, nat. conf. com. 1993-95, chmn. personal trainer com. 1991, exam devel. com., 1994-98, exec. coun., state dirs. com. 1997-98, job analysis com., 2007, Challenge Scholarship 1993, State Dir.'s award 1995, Personal Trainer of Yr. award 2000, Cert. Commn. award 1993). Avocations: screenwriting, writing, weightlifting, running, tai chi, golf, swimming. Home and Office: PO Box 1058 Madison CT 06443 Office Phone: 203-245-1199. E-mail: drought@personaltrainers.com.

DROUILLON, VINCENT, clinical biologist; b. Neuilly Sur Seine, France, Oct. 15, 1977; s. Guy Beaubillard and Sylviane Drouillon. D in Pharmacy, René Descartes U., Paris, 2005. Cert. clin. biologist Paris, 2005. Clin. biology resident Paris Hosps., 2001—05; attached practitioner St Louis Hosp., Paris, 2005—06; dir. asst. LABM, Pont Sainte Maxence, France, 2005—06; lab. dir., sci. advisor MDS Pharma Services Ctrl. Lab, Baillet en France, France, 2006—09; global dir. hematology Covance CLS, Geneva, 2009—. Achievements include development of Biological tools to improve diagnosis of Tuberculosis in Human. Office: Covance CLS rue Moise Marcinhes 7 Meyrin 1217 Switzerland Business E-Mail: vincent@drouillon.fr.

DR. PHIL, (PHILLIP CALVIN MCGRAW), television personality, psychologist; b. Vinita, Okla., Sept. 1, 1950; s. Joseph and Jerri (Stevens) McGraw; m. Debbie Higgins, 1970 (div. 1973); m. Robin Jo Jameson, 1976; children: Jay, Jordan. Attended, U. Tulsa, Okla.; BA in Psychology, Midwestern State U, Wichita Falls, Tex., 1975; MA in Clin. Psychology, North Tex. State U., Denton, 1976, PhD in Clin. Psychology, 1979. Pvt. practice psychology, Wichita Falls, 1979—89; co-founder, lectr. Pathways Seminars, 1983—91; co-founder, pres. litig. consulting firm Courtroom Scis., Inc. (CSI), Irving, Tex.; relationship & life strategy expert, regular commentator The Oprah Winfrey Show, 1998—2002; host syndicated daily TV show Dr. Phil, 2002—. Cons., MindFindBind with Dr. Phil match.com, 2006—. Author: Life Strategies: Doing What Works, Doing What Matters, 1999, Relationship Rescue: A Seven-Step Strategy for Reconnecting with Your Partner, 2000, Self Matters: Creating Your Life from the Inside Out, 2001, The Life Strategies Self-Discovery Journal: Finding What Matters Most for You, 2001, Getting Real: Lessons in Life, Marriage, and Family, 2002, The Ultimate Weight Solution: The Seven Keys to Weight Loss Freedom, 2003, The Ultimate Weight Solution Food Guide, 2003, The Ultimate Weight Solution Cookbook: Recipes for Weight Loss Freedom, 2004, Family First: Your Step-by-Step Plan for Creating a Phenomenal Family, 2005 (Publishers Weekly Bestseller list, 2004), Love Smart: Find the One You Want--Fix the One You Got, 2006, Real Life: Preparing for the 7 Most Challenging Days of Your Life, 2008; introduced themes to Dr. Phil Show such as: The Ultimate Weight Loss Challenge, Relationship Rescue Retreat Series, monthly columnist O, the Oprah Mag.; contbr. articles to profl. jours. Founder, chmn. bd. dirs. Dr. Phil Found., 2003—. Named one of Most Intriguing People of 2002, People mag., Ten Most Fascinating People, Barbara Walters TV special, 2002, The 100 Most Powerful Celebrities, Forbes.com, 2007, 2008, 2009. Avocations: golf, tennis, scuba diving, coaching Little League baseball. Office: The Dr Phil Show 5482 Wilshire Blvd 1902 Los Angeles CA 90036 *

DRUGOVA, BELA, radiologist, educator; b. Ohrudum, Czech Republic, Jan. 25, 1941; d. Antonin Radej and Bela Radejova; m. Bela Radejova-Drugova, Nov. 6, 1964; 1 child, Klara. DS, Charles U., 1985. Neurologist Gen. Hosp., Mlada Boleslav, Czech Republic, 1965—67; sr. lectr. Radiologic Clinic Faculty Hosp., Prague, 1967—87; head physician radiology dept. Hosp. Homolce, 1987—90, radiologist, 1990—. Co-author: Radio-Duagnostic, 1967; contbr. articles to profl. jours. Mem.: Radiol. Soc. Prague. Avocations: tennis, skiing, swimming, music. Home: IRbankova 65 14300 Prague 4 Czech Republic Office: Hosp Homolce Dept Radiology Roentgenova Str 2 15030 Prague 5 Czech Republic

DRUKER, BRIAN JAY, medical educator, researcher; b. St. Paul, Apr. 30, 1955; s. Jean S. Druker. BA in Chemistry, U. Calif., San Diego, MD, 1981. Internship and residency in internal medicine Barnes Hosp., Washington Sch. of Medicine, St. Louis; trained in oncology Harvard's Dana-Farber Cancer Inst.; prof. medicine Oreg. Health & Sci. U. Cancer Inst., Portland, 1993—, JELD-WEN chair, dir. leukemia ctr., dir. Knight Cancer Inst. Investigator Howard Hughes Med. Inst., 2002—. Recipient medal of honor, Am. Cancer Soc., 2001, Richard and Hinda Rosenthal award, Am. Assn. Cancer Rsch., 2001, Dameshak prize, Am. Soc. Hematology, 2001, Warren Alpert Found. award, Harvard Med. Sch., 2001, John J. Kenney award, Leukemia and Lymphoma Soc., 2000, Brupbacher Found. Cancer Rsch. award, 2001, Emil J. Freireich award for clin. rsch., MD Anderson Cancer Ctr., 2001, Charles F. Kettering prize, GM Cancer Rsch. Found., 2002, Pioneer Survivorship award, Lance Armstrong Found., 2002, Karnofsky award, Am. Soc. Clin. Oncology; co-recipient Lasker-DeBakey Clin. Med. Rsch. award, Lasker Found., 2009. Mem.: NAS, Inst. Medicine. Avocations: running, bicycling. Office: Oreg Health and Sci U 3181 SW Sam Jackson Park Rd Portland OR 97239-3098 Business E-Mail: drukerb@ohsu.edu. *

DRUMMOND, WILLA HENDRICKS, neonatologist, educator, information technology developer and executive; b. Harrisburg, Pa., Dec. 5, 1945; d. George Edson and Leah Clementine (Connelly) Hendricks; m. Thomas Weston Drummond, June 1966 (div. 1978). BA cum laude, Brown U., 1966; MD, U. Pa., 1970; MS in Med. Informatics, U. Utah, 1999. Resident in pediat. Children's Hosp. Phila., 1970-72, cardiology fellow, 1972-74; instr. pediat. U. Pa., Phila., 1973-74; rsch. fellow perinatology U. Oreg., Portland, 1974-75; staff pediatrician Kaiser-Permanente Clinics, Portland, 1975-76; instr. neonatology, fellow Cardiovasc. Rsch. Inst.-U. Calif., San Francisco, 1976-78; asst. prof. pediat. U. Fla., Gainesville, 1978-82, asst. prof. pediat. and physiology, 1981-82, assoc. prof. pediat. physiology and vet. med. scis., 1982-88, prof., 1988—, Somanetics Inc., Troy, Mich., 2009—10. Cons. Baxter-Travenol Labs., Deerfield, Ill., 1986-88, co-chair Equine Neonatology Study Group, Gainesville, 1981-91; dir. Neonatology Fellowship Program U. Fla., Gainesville, 1981-85; cons., CIO, chief med. info. officer, ICU Data Sys., Inc., Gainesville, 2001-05, interim CEO, exec. v.p. med. affairs, 2004-06, founder, chief med. info. exec., 2006—08; Cert. Commn. Health Info. Tech. CCHIT Inpatient Experts Panel, 2007-10, patent holder Vital Sync, 2005-, Covidien, Inc. Cons., 2010-. Contbr. numerous rsch. papers and abstracts to profl. jours.; poet: Carousel of Progress, 1979. Emily's List, Named Best Dr. in USA, Best Doctors, Inc., 2005-; named one of America's Top Pediatricians, 2007, 08-10; rsch. grantee Am. Heart Assn., NIH, Dept. of Def., others, 1976—2006; sr. fellow Med. Informatics, 1997-99, U. Utah. Mem. Am. Physiologic Soc., Soc. Pediat. Rsch., Am. Pediat. Soc., Am. Acad. Pediat.(exec. steering com. Coun. Clin. Info. Tech. 2005-11), Am. Med. Informatics Assn., Sigma Xi, So. Soc. Pediat. Rsch., Internat. Soc. Vet. Perinatology (bd. dirs., pres. 1995-97), Internat. Physicians Prevention of Nuc. War (collective Nobel Peace prize 1985), Union of Concerned Scientists, Nat. Orgn. Women, Nat. Resources Def. Com., Sierra Club, Greenpeace, Friends Earth, Alaska Wilderness League. Democrat. Office: U Fla Coll Medicine PO Box 100296 Gainesville FL 32610-0296 Office Phone: 352-273-8985. Business E-Mail: drwilla@peds.ufl.edu.

DRUMMOND BORG, LESLEY MARGARET, geneticist; b. Wellington, New Zealand, Oct. 26, 1948; arrived in U.S., 1986; d. Grant Allen and Yolanda Drummond; m. Kenneth Irvin Borg; children: Marc Borg, Kyle Borg. MBChB, Otago Med. Sch., New Zealand, 1971; MD, Otago Med. Sch., 1983; BSc, Auckland U., New Zealand, 1976. Diplomate Am. Bd. Pediat., Am. Bd. Med. Genetics, cert. clin. geneticist. Fellow clin. genetics U. Auckland Med. Sch., 1974—77, med. geneticist, 1977—79; resident pediat. Hosp. Sick Children, Toronto, Ont., Canada, 1980—82; gen. practitioner ARAMCO, Saudi Arabia, 1983—86; sr. fellow med. genetics U. Wash., Seattle, 1986—88; clin. geneticist Genetic Screening and Counseling Svc., Denton, Tex., 1988—95; dir. genetics divsn. Tex. Dept. Health, Austin, 1995—2004; mgr. health screening br. Tex. Dept. State Health Svcs., Austin, 2004—05, physician cons. health screening and case mgmt. unit, 2005—. Clin. asst. prof. Tex. A&M U., College Station, 1991—98; cons. staff Odessa Women's Children's Hosp., Tex., 1991—96, Cook/Ft. Worth Children's Med. Ctr., 1991—98. Contbr. articles to profl. jours. Fellow: Am. Coll. Med. Genetics (founder), Am. Acad. Pediat.; mem.: AMA, Am. Soc. Human Genetics. Avocations: jogging, swimming, hiking.

DRUTZ, JAN EDWIN, pediatrics educator; b. Louisville, Jan. 8, 1942; s. Abe Morris and Lillian (Billig) D.; m. Anne Edwina Sussman, June 7, 1965; children: Jeffrey Benjamin, Lisa Michele, Dana Nicole. BA, U. Louisville, 1964, MD, 1968. Pvt. practice, Houston, 1973-87; intern, then resident Baylor Coll. Medicine, Houston, 1968-71, from clin. asst. prof. to assoc. prof. pediat., 1973—2002, dir. pediat. continuity clinic, 1987—, prof. pediat., 2002—; pres. med. staff Tex. Children's Hosp., 1995, prof. pediats., 2002—. Maj. U.S. Army, 1971-73. Mem. AMA, Harris County Med. Soc., Tex. Pediat. Soc. (adv. com., mem. student preceptorship program 1995-96), Houston Pediat. Soc. (sec. 1984-85, pres. 1988-89), Ambulatory Pediat. Assn. (chmn. continuity clinic spl. interest group 1990-95, edn. com. 1993—). Office: Tex Children Hosp Clin Care Ctr Ste 1540-00 6701 Fannin St Houston TX 77030 Business E-Mail: jdrutz@bcm.edu.

DRUZ, REGINA SHMUKLER, cardiologist, researcher; b. Lvov, Ukraine, Aug. 3, 1968; m. Ari A. Druz, Apr. 8, 1995. BA in Biol. Scis., CUNY, 1987—91; MD, Cornell U. Med. Coll., NYC, 1991—95. Lic. Cornell U., 1995, diplomate Am. Bd. Internal Medicine, 2008, Am. Bd. Med. Subspecialties, Cardiovasc. Disease, 2001, Cert. Bd. Nuc. Cardiology, 2001, cert. bd. cardiac computed Tomography 2008. Asst. physician NY-Presbyterian Hosp., NYC, 1995—2001; assoc. dir. nuc. cardiology St. Francis Hosp., Roslyn, NY, 2001—06; dir. nuc. cardiology North Shore U. Hosp., Manhasset, NY, 2006—. Scholar New Immigrants award, HIAS, 1987—88. Fellow: Am. Soc. Nuc. Cardiology (life; leadership com. 2006, Young Investigator award 2001, Rsch. grant 2004), Am. Coll. Cardiology (life). Jewish. Achievements include research in cardiovascular imaging. Business E-Mail: rdruz@nshs.edu. *

DRYMAN, AMY, epidemiologist; d. Sylvia and Irving Armin Dryman. BA, Yale U., New Haven, Conn., 1977—81; postgrad., Columbia U., NYC, 1981—82; DSc, Johns Hopkins U., Sch. of Hygiene and Pub. Health, Balt., 1982—87. Rsch. scientist, rsch. assoc. Johns

Hopkins U. Sch. Hygiene and Pub. Health, Balt., 1987—88; cons. Pfizer, Inc., NYC, 1993, project leader, 1993—99, asst. dir., 1999—2001, mgr., 2001—04. Contbr. articles to profl. jours. Personal E-mail: amydryscd@aol.com.

DSOUZA, HERMAN, medical educator; b. Udupi, India, Mar. 12, 1971; MSc, Kasturba Med. Coll., 1995; PhD, St. John's Med. Coll., 2005. Assoc. prof. Manipal U., 2011—. Lectr., asst. prof. St. John's Med. Coll., 1996—2005; asst. prof. Manipal Life Scis. Ctr. Manipal U., 2005—11. Project grant, Dept. Biotech. Mem.: Assn. Clin. Biochemists India. Office: Dept Biotech Manipal Life Scis Ctr Manipal Karnataka 576104 India Personal E-mail: hsdsouza@rediffmail.com.

DU, BIN, critical care physician; b. Beijing, Jan. 28, 1968; s. Shiqiang Du and Xiuqing Li; m. Hong Ji; 1 child, Yifan. MD, Peking Union Med. Coll., Beijing, 1994. Resident, fellow dept. critical care medicine Peking Union Med. Coll. Hosp., attending physician, 1997, now dir. Med. ICU. Recipient Nat. Advances Sci. & Tech. award, Ministry Sci. & Tech., 2002. Mem.: Asia Pacific Assn. Critical Care Medicine, Beijing Med. Assn., Beijing Soc. Critical Care Medicine, Chinese Soc. Critical Care Medicine. Office: Peking Union Med College Hosp 1 Shuaifuyuan Wangfujing Beijing 100730 China E-mail: dubin98@yahoo.com. *

DU, WEI, medical researcher; b. China, July 5, 1978; MD, Tohoku U., PhD, 2007. Rsch. assoc. Cin. Children's Hosp. Med. Ctr., 2007—. Recipient Fujino Incentive award, Tohoku U.; FARF fellow. Mem.: ISEH, ASH. Office: 3333 Burnet Ave Cincinnati OH 45229 Business E-Mail: wei.du@cchmc.org.

DU, YONG, medical researcher; b. Public of China, July 17, 1971; MD, PhD, Sun Yat-sen U., 2004. Resident First Hosp. LuZhou Med. Coll., China, 1995—98; fellow 2nd Affiliated Hosp. Zhejiang U., China, 2004—07; postdoc. UT Southwestern Med. Ctr., Dallas, 2007—. Postdoc. fellowship, Nat. Arthritis Found. Mem.: Am. Soc. Nephrology. Avocations: reading, fishing. Office: 5323 Harry Hines Blvd Dallas TX 75390 E-mail: duyong717@hotmail.com.

DUA, PRERNA, engineering educator; b. India, Jan. 28, 1978; PhD, La. Tech. U., 2006. Asst. prof. La. tech U., 2006—11. Mem.: AHIMA. Office: La Tech University 1122 Wyly Tower Ruston LA 71270 Personal E-mail: prerna.dua@gmail.com.

DUANGNET, CHATREE, hospital administrator; MD, Chulalongkorn U. Group chief med. officer Bumrungrad Hosp.; dir. Bumrungrad Hosp. Pub. Co. Ltd., Global Med. Network Co. Ltd., Royal Bangkok Healthcare Co. Ltd., Greenline Synergy Co. Ltd., Phnom Penh Med. Svcs. Co. Ltd., Asia Internat. Healthcare Co. Ltd., Bangkok Helicopter Svcs. Co. Ltd., Bangkok Health Ins. Co. Ltd., Bio Molecular Lab. Co. Ltd., Thailand, Nat. Healthcare Sys. Co. Ltd., Rattanak Med. Svcs. Co. Ltd., Angkor Pisith Co. Ltd., Bangkok Ratchasima Hosp. Co. Ltd.; chief exec. officer Bangkok Hosp., Thailand. Chief exec. adminstr. coll. of medicine Pa. State Univ.; physician exec. Jameson Health System, New Castle, Pa.; faculty of medicine Chulalongkorn Univ. Fellow: Am. Acad. of Pediatrics, Am. Coll. of Med. Quality; mem.: Jameson Physician Hosp. Orgn. (chmn.), Lawrence Ind. Physician Assn. (pres.). Office: Bangkok Hospital 2 Soi Soonvijai 7 New Petchburi Rd 10310 Bangkok Thailand E-mail: info@bangkokhospital.com. *

DUARTE, ANA FILIPA, dermatologist; b. Viana do Castelo, Portugal, Apr. 21, 1978; MD, Coimbra Faculty Medicine, 2002. Physician, dermatology dept. Hosp. de São João & Epidermis ICUF, 2005. Adj. prof. Oporto Faculty Medicine, 2007. Mem.: EADV. Avocation: reading. Office: Rua Fonte das Sete Bicas Sra da Hora - Matosinhos Porto 4460-188 Portugal Office Fax: 00351220033720. E-mail: duarte.af.t30@gmail.com.

DUARTE, JOÃO BOSCO VIEIRA, surgeon; b. Belo Horizonte, Minas Gerais, Brazil, Apr. 9, 1962; s. Hugo Duarte Braga and Olga Vieira Brandão Duarte; m. Denise França Magalhães, July 27, 1986; children: João Victor Magalhães, Gabriel Magalhães, Arthur Magalhães. Degree, Med. Sch. Fed. U. Minas Gerais, Belo Horizonte, 1980. Cert. bd. diplomate Regional Med. Bd. State Minas Gerais, 1985. Staff mem. Belvedere Clinic, Belo Horizonte, Minas Gerais, Brazil, 1997—; mem. icu team Mater Dei Hosp., Belo Horizonte, 1987—96, gen. surgeon, 1987—, staff mem., 1987—, surg. ptnr., 1997—2008; staff mem. Vera Cruz Hosp., Minas Gerais, 2002—, Life Ctr. Hosp., Belo Horizonte, 2002—. Surg. cons. Pvt. Clinic Dr. Múcio Magalhães, Belo Horizonte, 1987—; founder and ceo Clinic Treatment Excessive Sweating, Belo Horizonte, 1991—. Recipient FUPEC award, Surg. Conf. Com., 1998, Best poster award, Brazilian Coll. Surgeons, 1998; Study Myocardial Distbn. Cardioplegic Solution scholership, Fed. U. Minas Gerais Rsch. Ctr., 1984. Mem.: Brazilian Soc. Diabetes, Minas Gerais Soc. Video Laparoscopic Surgery, Brazilian Soc. Clin. Medicine, Brazilian Soc. Video Laparoscopic Surgery. Roman Catholic. Achievements include discovery of surgical treatment for specific forms of hyperhidrosis, compensatory sweating, noninfectitious rhinitis and chronic regional pain syndrome. Avocation: traveling. Office: Clinica Especializada Em Hiperhidrose Avenida Barbacena 906 30190-131 Belo Horizonte MG Brazil Office Phone: 55-31-3292-4613. Office Fax: 55-31-3292-4613. Business E-Mail: duartejb@globo.com.

DUATTI, ADRIANO, chemist, radiochemist; b. Ostellato, Ferrara, Italy, May 17, 1952; s. Alvaro and Liliana (Ricci) D.; m. Maria Grazia Ghisini, Oct. 30, 1976; children: Francesca, Federica. PhD, U. Ferrara, 1976. Rsch. asst. U. Ferrara, 1978-81, sr. rsch. fellow, 1981-86, invited prof., 1990; assoc. prof. U. Bologna, Italy, 1986-98; prof. U. Ferrara, Italy, 1998—. Cons. Internat. Atomic Energy Agy., NIH; head nuc. medicine lab. dept. radiol. scis. U. Ferrara. Mem. editl. bd. Quar. Jour. Nuc. Medicine and Molecular Imaging; contbr. articles to profl. jours.; patentee in field. Sgt. Italian Mil., 1976-77. Nat. Rsch. Coun. rsch. grantee, 1984. Mem. Soc. Nuclear Medicine, Italian Assn. Nuclear Medicine, European Assn. Nuclear Medicine. Avocations: painting, running, tennis. Office: Univ Ferrara Lab Nuc Medicine Dept Radiol Scis Via Luigi Borsari 46 44121 Ferrara FE Italy Office Phone: (39)-0532-455354. Business E-Mail: dta@unife.it.

DUAX, WILLIAM LEO, biologist, researcher; b. Chgo., Apr. 18, 1939; s. William Joseph and Alice B. (Joyce) Duax; m. Caroline Townsend Dowell, May 6, 1966; children: Julia, Sarah, William, Stephen. BA, St. Ambrose Coll., Davenport, Iowa, 1961; PhD, U. Iowa, Iowa City, 1967; DSc (hon.), U. Lodz, Poland, 1999. Postdoctoral research fellow Ohio U., Athens, 1967-68; rsch. assoc. Hauptman-Woodward Med. Rsch. Inst. (formerly Med. Found.), Buffalo, 1968-69; head crystallography dept. Med. Found. Buffalo, 1969-70, head molecular biophysics dept., 1970-88, assoc. dir. research, 1983-88, research dir., 1988-93, exec v.p. rsch., 1993-99, v.p., 1998-99, H.A. Hauptman Disting. Scientist, 2000—. Adj. assoc. prof. dept. medicinal chemistry SUNY, Buffalo, 1973—, assoc. rsch. prof. dept. biochemistry, 1981—, prof. dept. structural biology, 2001-; dir. distbn. Cambridge Database in US, Buffalo, 1983-99; lectr. various internat. confs. Editor: Atlas of Steroid Structure Vol. I, 1975, Vol. II, 1984, Molecular Structure and Biological Activity, 1982, Molecular Structure and Biological Activity of Steriods, 1992, Internat. Union of Crystallography Newsletter, 1993—. Mem. Am. Field Svc., Amherst, NY. Served with USAR, 1961-67. Fulbright scholar Coun. for Internat. Exchange, 1987; grantee NIH, 1971—2003; recipient Spl. Merit award Inst. Arthritis and Metabolic Diseases NIH, 1987—03, Disting. Alumni award, St. Ambrose Coll., 1983, Clin. Ligand Assay Soc. Disting. Scientist award, 1994. Mem. AAAS(fellow, 2007), Am. Crystallographic Assn. (v.p. 1985, pres. 1986, exec. officer 1988—, Am. Chem. Soc., Am. Cancer Soc., Biophys. Soc., Endocrine Soc., Peptide Soc., Protein Soc., Internat. Union Crystallography (charter mem., sec. com. on small molecules 1984-90, exec. com. 1999—2008, pres. 2002-05), Am. Inst. Physics (bd. govs. 1987-94, exec. com. 1992), Coun. Sci. Soc. Pres. (govt. and pub. affairs com. 1987), Saturn Club (Buffalo). Democrat. Office: Hauptman Woodward Med Rsch Inst Inc 700 Ellicott St Buffalo NY 14203-1102 Office Phone: 716-898-8600, 716-898-8616. Business E-Mail: duax@hwi.buffalo.edu.

DUBE, AMOL HARIDAS, physician, educator; b. Bhadrawati, Chandrapur, Jan. 10, 1978; MBBS, VNGMC, Yavatmal, 2001; MD in Medicine, IGGMC, Nagpur, 2006. Jr. resident Indira Gandhi Govt. Med. Coll., Nagpur, 2003—06, asst. prof., 2006—; sr. resident Nkp Salve Inst., Lata Mangeshkar Hosp., Nagpur, Hingana, 2006. Cons. physician Keshav Hosp.-A Group Laxmikeshav Inst. And Rsch., Pvt Ltd, 2009—. Recipient Gold medal, Amaravati U., Maharashtra, 2001. Mem.: Cardiology Soc. India (Nagpur chpt.), Acad. Med. Scis. (Nagpur), Assn. Physician India (Vidarbha chpt.). Avocation: music. Home: Plot 380 Kukade Layout Nagpur Maharashtra 440027 India Personal E-mail: amol_00dube@rediffmail.com.

DUBE, SAMUKELISO, physician; b. Zimbabwe, July 6, 1976; MBChB, U. Zimbabwe, 2000; MPH, U. Limpopo; MBa, Wits Bus. Sch., U. Witwatersrand, 2006. Med. officer Mpilo Hosp., United Bulawayo Hosp., 2001—04; regional HIV coord. Action Aid, 2005—06; project mgr., rschr. SAVIC, 2006—08, africa program leader PATH, 2008—. Mem. bd. dirs. South African Women Migration Affairs, 2006—11, South African Sexual and Reproductive Health Group, 2011; cons. Eastern Cape Provincial Govt., 2010. Mem.: Health Professions Coun. South Africa. Avocation: reading. Office: 47 Bath Ave Rosebank Johannesburg Gauteng 2121 South Africa Office Fax: 114471353. Personal E-mail: samudan2001@yahoo.com.

DUBERNARD, JEAN-MICHEL, surgeon, educator; b. Lyon, Rhone, France, May 17, 1941; s. Maurice and Marie-Louise (Boissel) D.; children: Carole, Gil, Estelle. Student, Lyon Med. Sch., 1959-65, Harvard Med. Sch., Boston, 1965-67; MD, U. Lyon J., 1967, PhD, 1971. Prof. urol. surgery U. Lyon, 1977—; chief dept. urology and transplant surgery Edouard Herriot Hosp., Lyon, 1979—2007; chmn. Medium Devices Assesment Com., 2008. Contbr. numerous articles and books in the field of transplantation and urology; author med. books. Dep. du Rhone, French Nat. Assembly, 1986—, pres. social affairs com., 2002-07; dep. mayor of Lyon in charge of finances and programming, 1983-2001. Decorated chevalier Ordre National du Merite, Ordre des Palmes Academiques. Mem. Gaullist Party. Achievements include France's first pancreas transplant in 1976; being leaderof the team that performed the world's first hand transplant in 1998 and first double hand transplant in 2000; co-leader of world's first face transplant in 2005. Home: 12 Bd des Belges 69006 Lyon France Office: Edouard Herriot Hosp Dept Urology Transplantation 5 Place d'Arsonval 69437 Lyon France Office Phone: 33472110589. Business E-Mail: Jean-Michel.Dubernard@chu-lyon1.fr.

DUBERSTEIN, JOEL LAWRENCE, internist, pulmonologist, educator; b. Bklyn., Jan. 8, 1937; m. Judith Schwartz; children: Laura, Amy. AB, Princeton U., 1957; MD, Columbia U., 1961. Diplomate Am. Bd. Internal Medicine, Am. Bd. Pulmonary Diseases. Intern Mt. Sinai Hosp., NYC, 1961-62, rsch. fellow in medicine, 1962, 65, asst. med. resident, 1963, chief med. resident, 1964, clin. asst., rsch. fellow, 1965-67; asst. chief medicine, chief pulmonary diseases Morrisania Hosp., Montefiore-Morrisania Affiliation, Bronx, N.Y., 1969-71; attending physician dept. medicine Overlook Hosp., Summit, N.J., 1971—, chmn. pulmonary sect., ICU com., med. dir. ICU, 1985-97, divsn. chief pulmonary disease dept. internal medicine; assoc. clin. prof. medicine Columbia U., 1998—2007, Mt. Sinai Sch. Medicine, 2007—. Assoc. vis. physician Morrisania City Hosp., Bronx, 1969-71; mem. staff Morristown Meml. Hosp., 1972—, med. co-dir. respiratory svcs., 1977-82; attending phsician dept. medicine St. Barnabas Med. Ctr., Livingston, N.J., 1971-89, past chmn. pulmonary sect.; mem. staff Newark Beth Israel Med. Ctr., 1971-82; spkr. in field; mem. Essex County Med. Soc. TB Control. Contbr. articles to profl. jours. Maj. U.S. Army, 1967-69. Recipient Recognition award Soc. N.J.'s Physicians. Fellow ACP, Am. Coll. Chest Physicians; mem. AMA (Physician's Recognition award), N.J. Med. Soc., Essex Thoracic Soc., N.J. Acad. Medicine. Address: 1 Springfield Ave 3rd Fl Summit NJ 07901 Office Phone: 908-934-0555.

DUBERT, THIERRY, hand surgeon; b. Paris, Aug. 23, 1957; s. Jean-Marie and Andrée Dubert; m. Véronique Mirlesse, July 1, 1989; children: Léo, Lucie, Gaspard, Marie. MD, U. Paris V, 1986. Fellow Bichat Claude Bernard Hosp., Paris, 1989—91; gen. sec. Fedn. European Depts. for Trauma Hand Surgery, France, 2001—, chmn. hand trauma com. Europe, 2004—. Contbr. articles to profl. jours. Grantee, French Soc. for Orthop. and Trauma Surgery, 1991. Mem.: Am. Soc. for Surgery of Hand, Brit. Soc. for Surgery of Hand, European Rheumatoid Arthritis Surg. Soc., French Coll. Orthop. Surgery, French Soc. for Surgery of Hand (grantee 1992). Achievements include patents pending for wedding ring with breaking device. Office: Clinique La Francilienne 16 Av de l'Hôtel de Ville Pontault-Combault 77340 France Home: 98 Rue de Rennes Paris 75006 France Personal E-mail: thierrydubert@gmail.com, sosmain@club-internet.fr.

DUBEY, MAYA, medical researcher, educator; b. Eng. BS in Biol. Scis., U. Mass., Lowell, 2004, PhD in Biomed. Engring. and Biotech., 2007. Lab. instr. U. Mass., 2004—07, adj. prof., 2008—; rsch. scientist Excelimmune Inc., Woburn, Mass., 2007—. Contbr. articles to publs. Mem.: Neurosci. Soc. Achievements include research in methods for understanding tau-mediated neurodegeneration; Working on recombinant polycolnal antibody expression. Office: Excelimmune Inc 12 B Cabot Rd Woburn MA 01801 Business E-Mail: md@excelimmune.com.

DUBICK, MICHAEL A., scientist; b. Balt., Apr. 8, 1950; BA, UCLA, 1972; PhD, U. Southern Calif., 1978. Chief damage control resuscitation unit US Army Inst. Surg. Rsch., 1988—. Recipient Order of Mil. Med. Merit, US Army Med. Dept, Achievement award, Office of Sec. Army, Commanders award, US Army. Mem.: Western Trauma Assn., NY Acad. Scis., Am. Soc. Nutrition, Soc. Critical Care Medicine, Shock Soc. Office: 3698 Chambers Pass San Antonio TX 78234 Business E-Mail: michael.dubick@us.arm.mil.

DUBIKOV, ALEXANDR IVANOVICH, rheumatologist, researcher; b. Vladivostok, Russia, Sept. 28, 1960; MD, Vladivostok State Med. Inst., 1983, PhD, 1986; MD, Inst. Rheumatology, Moscow, 2005. Asst. prof. Vladivostok State Med. Inst., 1986—97; head Rheumatological City Ctr., Vladivostok, 1991—. Head of rheumatologists Mcpl. Dept. of Healthcare, Vladivostok, 1996—. Cons. Patient Assn., Vladivostok, 1996—. Recipient City prize, 1996. Mem.: Russian Rheumatologists Assn. (presidium 2005—, Best Rsch. of Yr. 2003). Achievements include research in role of apoptosis and nitric oxide in patogenesis of rheumatoid arthritis. Avocations: music, travel, philology, literature, art. Office: Rheumatological City Ctr Russkaya St 57 690105 Vladivostok Russia E-mail: aihavlad@online.vladivostok.ru.

DUBIN, ANNE, medical educator; b. NY; MD, U. Rochester, 1988. Assoc prof. pediat. Stanford U., Palo Alto, Calif., 1995—. Office: Packard Children's Hospital 750 Welch Rd Ste 305 Palo Alto CA 94304 Office Fax: 650-725-8343.

DUBIN, BRUCE, medical educator, dean; Grad., Kirksville Coll. Osteo. Medicine, 1973; JD cum laude, U. Detroit Coll. Law. Bar: Mich. Resident internal medicine Martin Place Hosp., Madison Heights, Mich.; fellow allergy and clin. immunology Nat. Jewish Hosp. / U. Colo. Med. Ctr., 1978; dir. Ctr. for Asthma, Emphysema and Allergic Disorders, Southfield, Mich.; dir. med. edn. Oakland General Hosp., 1989—95; health policy fellow Mich. State U. and Ohio U.; v.p. med. edn. Grandview Hosp. and Med. Ctr., Dayton, Ohio, 1995—98, med. dir. DOPMI; assoc. dean Ohio U. Coll. Osteo. Medicine, 1998—2002; assoc. prof. health policy and med. jurisprudence Dept. Social Medicine Ohio U., 1998—2002; assoc. dean, prof. internal medicine Edward Via Coll. Osteo. Medicine, 2002—03; assoc. dean academic affairs, assoc. prof. internal medicine Tex. Coll. of Osteo. Medicine U. North Tex. Health Sci. Ctr., 2003—, interim dean, 2009—. Mem.: Am. Lung Assn. of Southeast Mich. (former exec. com. mem.).

DUBLIN, SASCHA, epidemiologist, researcher; b. NYC, Aug. 10, 1970; AB in Renaissance Studies, magna cum laude, Brown U., Providence, 1992; PhD in Epidemiology, U. Wash., Seattle, 1999, MD, 2001. Diplomate Am. Bd. Internal Medicine. Intern, residnt internal medicine Oreg. Health & Sci. U., Portland, 2001—04; sr. fellow VA Puget Sound Health Sys., Seattle, 2004—07; asst. investigator Group Health Ctr. for Health Studies, Seattle, 2007—; affiliate asst. prof., dept. epidemiology U. Wash., Seattle, 2008—. Contbr. articles to profl. jours. Recipient Paul Beeson Career Devel. award, Nat. Inst. Aging, 2007. Mem.: ACP, Am. Geriatrics Soc., Am. Heart Assn., Soc. Gen. Internal Medicine, Internat. Soc. Pharmacoepidemiology, Alpha Omega Alpha, Phi Beta Kappa. Office: Group Health Ctr for Health Studies 1730 Minor Ave Ste 1600 Seattle WA 98101 Office Phone: 206-287-2870. Office Fax: 206-287-2871. E-mail: dublin.s@ghc.org. *

DUBNER, PAUL FLOYD, pediatrician; MD, U. Pitts., 1981. Diplomate Am. Bd. Pediatrics, lic. Pa., 1982. Resident Children's Hosp. Pitts., 1984; hosp. affiliations include Western Pa. Hosp., Heritage Valley Beaver, Heritage Valley Sewickley. Office: Heritage Valley Sewickley 720 Blackburn Rd Sewickley PA 15143 Office Phone: 724-774-4070.

DUBOIS, ARTHUR BROOKS, physiologist, educator; b. NYC, Nov. 21, 1923; s. Eugene Floyd and Rebeckah (Rutter) DuB.; m. Roberdeau Callery, June 21, 1950; children: Anne R., Brooks, James E.F. Student, Harvard U., 1941-43; MD, Cornell U., 1946. Intern in medicine NY Hosp., 1946-47; med. research fellow U. Rochester, 1949-51; asst. resident Peter Bent Brigham Hosp., Boston, 1951-52; asst. prof. to prof. physiology and medicine U. Pa., 1952-74; prof. epidemiology and physiology Yale U., 1974—2005, emeritus prof. epidemiology, 2006—. Fellow John B. Pierce Found. Lab., 1974-2005, dir., 1974-88, emeritus fellow, 2006. Author: The Lung, 3d ed. 1986, Body Plethysmography, 1969; contbr. articles to profl. jours. With USNR, 1947—49. Recipient Rsch. Career award NIH, 1963-74; Edward Livingston Trudeau medal Am. Lung Assn., 1989. Mem. Am. Physiol. Soc., Am. Soc. Clin. Investigation, Assn. Am. Physicians, Undersea Med. Soc. Clubs: Harvard, Cosmos. Democrat. Home: 370 Livingston St New Haven CT 06511-1336 Office: 290 Congress Ave New Haven CT 06519-1403 Home Phone: 203-777-8135; Office Phone: 203-562-9901. Business E-Mail: adubois@jbpierce.org.

DUBOIS, MICHEL, anesthesiologist; arrived in U.S., 1978; s. Yvon and Renee Dubois; m. Judith Ray Jamison-Dubois, June 25, 1976; children: Marie-Laure, Matthieu. MD, Paris Sch. Medicine, 1968. Diplomate Am. Bd. Anesthesiology, Am. Bd. Pain Medicine, French Nat. Bd. Anesthesiology, lic. practitioner Gen. Med. Coun., London. Staff anesthesiologist Hopital Henri Mondor, Creteil, France, 1972—74; lectr. in anaesthesia The London Hosp. Med. Sch., 1974—76, sr. lectr. in anaesthesia, 1976—78; instr. anesthesiology Georgetown U. Sch. Medicine, Washington, 1978—80, asst. prof. anesthesiology, 1980—85, assoc. prof. anesthesiology, 1985—92, prof. anesthesiology, 1992—94, NYU Sch. Medicine, 1996—; dir. NYU Pain Program, 1996—. Staff attending NYU Med. Ctr., 1996—; chmn. instl. rev. bd. Georgetown U. Sch. Medicine, 1990—94; dir. clin. investigation unit, dir. pain mgmt. svcs. dept. anesthesia Georgetown U. Hosp., 1988—93; hon. cons. The London Hosp., 1976—77. Editor: Ethics Forum. Mem.: Am. Bd. Pain Medicine (pres. 2010—), Am. Bd. Pain Mgmt. (pres.-elect 2007), Ea. Pain Assn. (pres. 2001—02, chmn. nomination com. 2002—), France-USA Pain Assn.

(pres., founder 1993—95), Am. Acad. Pain Medicine (chmn. ethics com. 1998—2003, chmn. by-laws com.), Am. Soc. Anesthesiolologists (pain therapy com. 1993—94). Avocations: reading, petanque. Office: NYU Pain Mgmt Ctr 317 E 34th St Ste 902 New York NY 10016 Personal E-mail: michel.dubois@med.nyu.edu.

DUBOIS, RAYMOND N., medical educator, researcher; BS in Biochemistry, Tex. A&M U.; PhD in Biochemistry, Tex. Southwestern Med. Sch.; MD, U. Tex. Health Sci. Ctr., San Antonio. Osler medicine intern, resident John Hopkins Hosp., Balt.; with Vanderbilt U. Med. Ctr., 1991—, head divsn. gastroenterology, hepatology, and nutrition Nashville, 1998—2003, Mina. C. Wallace prof. medicine and cell biology, 1998—2003, prof. medicine, cancer biology, cell and devel. biology, 2003—; dir. Vanderbilt Digestive Disease Rsch. Ctr., 1999—; Hortnse B. Ingram prof. molecular oncology Vanderbilt-Ingram Cancer Ctr., Vanderbilt U. Med. Ctr., 2004, dir. cancer prevention program, 2005—07; provost, exec. v.p. academic affairs M.D. Anderson Cancer Ctr., Houston, 2007—. Scientific adv. bd. Nat. Colorectal Cancer Rsch. Alliance Found.; bd. scientific advisors Nat. Cancer Inst.; adv. bd. Nat. Inst. Diabetes and Digestive and Kidney Diseases, NIH; chmn. bd. dirs. Keystone Symposia on Molecular and Cellular Biology. Assoc. editor Gasteroenterology and Cancer Rsch.; contbr. articles to profl. jour. Recipient Outstanding Investigator award, AFMR, 2000, Disting. Achievement award, Am. Gastroenterological Assn., 2004. Fellow: AAAS; mem.: Am. Assn. Cancer Rsch. (pres.-elect 2007—, Dorothy P. Landon prize translational cancer rsch. 2004, Richard and Hinda Rosenthal award 2002), Am. Soc. Clin. Investigation, Am. Assn. Physicians, Royal Coll. Physicians. Achievements include first to report the link between cyclooxygenase-2 (COX-2) enzyme and colon cancer. Office: MD Anderson Cancer Ctr 1515 Holcombe Blvd Unit 118 Houston TX 77030 Office Phone: 615-343-0527. Business E-Mail: raymond.dubois@vanderbilt.edu.

DUBOURG, OLIVIER JEAN, cardiology educator, researcher; b. Orleans, Loiret, France, Mar. 26, 1952; s. Jean Fortune and Arlette (Masson) D.; m. Sylvie Rolet, Sept. 21, 1979; 1 child, Benjamin. MD, Laureat, U. Paris, 1981. Cert. French Bd. Cardiology. Intern Salpetriere Hosp., Paris, 1973—76; resident Assistance Publique Hosp. de Paris, 1977-81; fellow Ambroise Paré Hosp., Boulogne, France, 1981-89, prof. cardiology, chief dept. cardiology, 1989—; vice dean UVSQ, 2010, chief dept. cardiology neurology vascular surgery obesity, 2011. Last pres. med. com., mem. steering com., tech. com., pres. human rels. Ambroise Paré Hosp.; mem. med. com. Assistance Publique Hosp. of Paris; mem. bd. French Soc. Cardiology 2004—; chmn. guideline com. French Soc. Cardiology, 2007-; mem. C.N. U., mem. steering com. U. UVSQ Contbr. articles to med. jours. Decorated chevalier Nat. Order Legion of Honor. Fellow European Soc. Cardiology, Am. Coll. Cardiology, Am. Coll. Chest Physicians, French Soc. Cardiology, Am. Heart Assn. Avocation: golf. Home: 8 rue Barye 75017 Paris France Office: Ambroise Paré Hosp 9 ave Charles de Gaulle 92100 Boulogne 1 France Office Phone: 33149095620. Business E-Mail: olivier.dubourg@apr.aphp.fr.

DUBOUSSET, JEAN, pediatric orthopedic surgeon; b. Montferrand, France, Nov. 16, 1936; s. Marcel Dubousset and Jeanne blanche Thomazet. m. Anne Marie Chognon, Mar. 31, 1959; children: Valerie, François, Pierre. MD, Clermont Ferrand U., Paris, 1953. External resident Assistance Publique, Paris, 1956-70, hosp. physician, 1979—; prof. U. Rene Descartes, Paris, 1991—. Cons. in field. Mem. Adapt, paris, 1985. Recipient Chevalier de la Legion d'Honneur, 2000. Fellow SRS, SICOT, MSTHS. Achievements include research in spinal pathology in children and surgical treatment. Office: Hopital St Vincent dePaul 82 Ave Denfert Rochereau 75014 Paris France Home: 26 Rue des Cordelieres 75013 Paris France Home Phone: 33607635275. Personal E-mail: jean.dubousset@wanadoo.fr.

DUBOWSKI, KURT MAX, toxicologist, educator, consultant; b. Berlin, Nov. 21, 1921; came to U.S., 1935; s. Jacques Dubowski and Gertrud (Baron) Steinberg. AB, NYU, 1946; MSc, Ohio State U., 1947, PhD, 1949; LLD (hon.), Capital U., 1984. Diplomate Am. Bd. Clin. Chemistry (pres. emeritus, sec.-treas. emeritus), Am. Bd. of Forensic Toxicology (founding pres., past pres.). Biochemist, asst. dir. labs. Norwalk (Conn.) Hosp., 1950-53; dir. chemistry Iowa Meth. Hosp., Des Moines, 1953-58; state criminalist State of Iowa Divsn. of Criminal Investigation, Des Moines, 1954-58; assoc. prof. clin. chemistry and toxicology U. Fla., Gainesville, 1958-61; George Lynn Cross disting. prof. medicine U. Okla., Oklahoma City, 1961-98, prof. surgery, prof. pathology, dir. toxicology labs., dir. forensic sci. labs. health scis. ctr., mem. clin. staff Univ. Hosps., 1961-2001, emeritus prof., 1998—; prin. rsch. scientist Civil Aerospace Med. Inst. FAA U.S. Dept. Trans., Oklahoma City, 2001—. Cons. clin. chemistry and toxicology Dept. Vets. Affairs Med. Ctr., Oklahoma City, 1962-2001; cons. lab. medicine Okla. Med. Rsch. Found., Oklahoma City, 1967-2001; state dir. tests for alcohol and drug influence, State of Okla., 1967-97, state dir. emeritus, 1997—; chmn. emeritus Bd. Tests for Alcohol and Drug Influence, State of Okla., 2000—; ret. sci. dir. Okla. Dept. Pub. Safety; ret. criminalist Okla. Dept. Pub. Safety/Okla. Hwy. Patrol, Okla. State Bur. Investigation, Oklahoma City Police Dept.; mem. sci. adv. bd. Armed Forces Inst. Pathology, U.S. Dept. Def., 1991-97; mem. Internat. Coun. Alcohol, Drugs and Traffic Safety; mem. exec. bd., co-chair subcom. alcohol pharmacology, toxicology and tech. com. on alcohol and other drugs Nat. Safety Coun.; past advisor subcom. urine drug testing NCCLS; toxicologist advisor DEC program Nat. Hwy. Traffic Safety Adminstrn., U.S. Dept. Transp.; cons. in field; mem. various fed. adv. groups; vis. lectr. and prof. various colls. and univs.; expert witness in forensic sci. matters. Author numerous books; contbr. chpts. to books and articles to profl. jours.; mem. editl. bd. Jour. Forensic Scis., Therapeutic Drug Monitoring, Forensic Sci. Rev.; past mem. editl. bd. Am. Jour. Forensic Medicine and Pathology, Clin. Chemistry, Internat. Microform Jour. Legal Medicine, Jour. Analytical Toxicology. 1st lt. U.S. Army, 1942-55. Recipient Widmark award Internat. Coun. Alcohol, Drugs and Traffic Safety, 1980, CIIT award Chem. Industry Inst. Toxicology, 1983, Cert. of Merit Forensic Scis. Found., 1984, Robert F. Borkenstein award Nat. Safety Coun., 1992, Disting. Svc. to Safety award NSC, 1995, Outstanding Contbn. to Clin. Chemistry award Am. Assn. for Clin. Chemistry, 1996; Kurt M. Dubowski Award established by Internat. Assn. Chem. Testing, 2002; numerous others; named Disting. Alumnus Ohio State U., 1994, hon. Tex. Ranger, 2007; Nat. Rsch. Coun. fellow in phys. scis. Ohio State U., 1948-49. Fellow Am. Acad. Forensic Scis. (founding fellow, disting. fellow, past pres., editor procs., Award of Merit 1980, Rolla N. Harger award 1983), Am. Inst. Chemists (life), Assn. Clin. Scientists (emeritus), Am. Coll. Forensic Examiners (life, Golden Eagle award 1996); mem. AMA, Am. Chem. Soc. (sr., emeritus mem. com. clin. chemistry), Am. Assn. Clin. Chemistry (emeritus, past pres., chmn. com. constn. & bylaws, assn. parliamentarian, Outstanding Clin. Chemist award Tex. sect. 1981, Past Pres.'s award 1986, Presdl. citation 1992, award for outstanding contbn. to clin. chemistry 1996), Indian Acad. Forensic Scis. (hon. life), Southwestern Assn. Forensic Scientists (charter, emeritus), Internat. Assn. Forensic Toxicologists (founding mem.), Internat. Assn. of Chiefs of Police (life), Internat. Assn. Forensic Scis. (charter), Internat. Soc. Clin. Forensic Medicine (founding mem.), Acad. Clin. Lab. Physicians and Scientists (emeritus), Biomed. Engring. Soc. (founding mem./emeritus), Rsch. Soc. Alcoholism (emeritus), Soc. Forensic Toxicologists (charter, emeritus), Soc. Toxicology (emeritus), U. Okla. Univ. Club, Ind. Univ. Club, Phi Lambda Upsilon, Sigma Xi. Avocations: horology, photography, music, travel. Office: PO Box 7245 Oklahoma City OK 73153-1245 Business E-Mail: kurt-dubowski@ouhsc.edu.

DUBRIN, ANDREW JOHN, management and behavioral sciences educator, writer; b. NYC, Mar. 3, 1935; s. Albert Edward and Louise Theresa (Walsh) D.; m. Drew, Douglas, Melanie. AB, Hunter Coll., 1956; MS, Purdue U., 1957; PhD, Mich. State U., 1960. Diplomate: Am. Bd. Profl. Psychology; cert. psychologist N.Y. state. Psychologist Data Systems div. IBM, Kingston, NY, 1962-63; teaching asst., part-time instr. Purdue U., West Lafayette, Ind., 1956-57; psychol. cons. Clark, Cooper, Field & Wohl, NYC, 1963-64, Rohrer, Hibler & Replogle, NYC, 1964-70, ptnr., 1964-70; assoc. prof. Rochester (N.Y.) Inst. Tech., 1970-72, prof. behavioral sci., 1972—, dept. head mgmt., 1982-84, prof. mgmt., 1984—. Mem. N.Y. State Bd. Psychology, 1979-94; cons. lectr. in field Author: The Practice of Managerial Psychology, 1972, Women in Transition, 1972, The Singles Game, 1973, Fundamentals of Organization Behavior: An Applied Perspective, 1974, Survival in the Sexist Jungle, 1974, The New Husbands and How to Become One, 1976, Casebook of Organizational Behavior, 1979, Human Relations: A Job Oriented Approach, 1978, 8th edit., 2004, 9th edit., 2006, Fundamentals of Organizational Behavior: An Applied Perspective, 2d edit., 1978, Winning at Office Politics, 1979, Contemporary Applied Management, 1982, 4th edit., 1994, Essentials of Management, 1986, 8th edit., 2008, 9th edit., 2011, The Last Straw, 1987, Human Relations for Career and Personal Success, 3d edit., 1992, 8th edit., 2007, 9th edit., 2010, Management and Organization, 1989, 2d edit., 1992, Effective Business Psychology, 1980, 6th edit., 2004, Winning Office Politics: DuBrin's Guide for the '90s, 1990, Bouncing Back: How to Overcome Adversity in the Workplace, 1992, Your Own Worst Enemy: How to Prevent Career Self-Sabotage, 1992, Stand Out! 330 Ways to Gain the Edge with Superiors, Subordinates, Co-workers, and Customers, 1993, Getting It Done: The Transforming Power of Self-Discipline, 1995, The Reengineering Survival Guide, 1995, The Breakthrough Team Player, 1995, Leadership: Research Findings, Practice and Skill, 1995, 6th edit., 2009, Human Relations: Job-Oriented Interpersonal Skills, 2000, 4th edit. 2009, 6th edit., 2011, Fundamentals of Organizational Behavior, 1998, 4th edit., 2007, The 10-Min. Guide to Effective Leadership, Personal Magnetism, 1997, Complete Idiot's Guide to Leadership, 1998, 2000, Looking Around Corners, 1999, The Active Manager, 2000, Political Behavior in Organization, 2008, Impression Management in the Workplace, 2010. Capt. U.S. Army, 1960-62. Mem. Am. Psychol. Assn., Am. Mgmt. Assn., Acad. of Mgmt. Office: 192 Barclay Square Dr Rochester NY 14618 Office Phone: 585-442-0484. Personal E-mail: ajdubrin@frontiernet.net.

DUBUQUE, THEODORE JULIEN, JR., retired surgeon; b. St. Louis, 1927; MD, St. Louis U., 1952. Diplomate Am. Bd. Surgery. Intern, resident St. Louis U. Hosps., 1952-58; prof. surgery St. Louis U., 1958-96, emeritus prof. surgery, 1996—. Fellow ACS; mem. Western Surg. Assn., Alpha Omega Alpha. *

DUBUSKE, LAWRENCE MICHAEL, immunologist, rheumatologist; b. Jersey City, Oct. 16, 1954; BS, Northwestern U., 1976, MD, 1978; diploma (hon.), Polish Allergy Soc., 2001; diploma in medicine (hon.), Crimean Med. U., 2001; diploma (hon.), Belarussian Inst. Epidemiology and Microbiology, Minsk, Belarus, 2001, Ukrainian Med. U., Ukraine, 2001, Russian Fed. Inst. Immunology, Moscow, 2002. Diplomate Am. Bd. Allergy and Immunology, Am. Bd. Internal Medicine, Am. Bd. Rheumatology. Dir. Allergy and Arthritis Family Treatment Ctr., Gardner, Mass., 1984—, Immunology Rsch. Inst. New England, Gardner, 1990—; dir. immunology Ednl. Inst. New Eng., 1999—2003; clin. prof. medicine George Washington U., Washington, 2010—. Clin. instr. Harvard Med. Sch., Boston, 1984—2010; co-dir. allergy fellow tng. program Brigham and Women's Hosp., Boston, 1994—98; adv. bd. Hycor Biomedical, Garden Grove, Calif., 1995—97; hon. prof. Crimean Med. U., 2001, Inst. Immunology, Ministry of Health of Russia, Russia, 2002; cons. Schering Plough, Kenilworth, NJ, 1994—2009, Hoechst Marion Roussel Pharms., Kansas City, Kans., 1995—97, Hycor Biomedical, Garden Grove, 1995—97, Upjohn Pharms., Mich., 1997, Novartis Pharm., East Hanover, NJ, 2002, Sanofi-Aventis Pasteur Inc., Swiftwater, Pa., 2002—03, Genentech, San Francisco, 2002—08, Allergy Theraputics, 2004—. Contbg. editor: Asthma and Allergy Procs., 1994—, Jour. Allergy and Clin. Immunology Supplement, 1996—97, Internat. Allergology Rev., 1997—, Internat. Jour. Immune Rehab., 1998—, Am. Jour. Respiratory Medicine, 2001—; mem. editl. bd. Balkan Allergy Jour., 2002—, Allergy, Hypersensitivity, Asthma; contbr. chapters to books, articles Exercise Induced Allergy Syndromes. Fellow: ACCP, ACAAI (bd. regents 2007—10), ACP, ACR, Am. Acad. Asthma, Allergy and Immunology (chmn. practice and therapeutics com. 1996—2000, chmn. practice stds. coun. 1999—2000); mem.: Interasma (bd. dirs. 2004—, sec. gen. 2006—, v.p. 2011—), Am. Assn. Cert. Allergists (pres. 2004—06, treas. 2007—), Alpha Omega Alipha (pres. northwestern chptr. 1977—78). Office: Immunology Rsch Inst New Eng 358 Elm St Gardner MA 01440-3926 E-mail: ldubuske@aol.com.

DUCHARME, FRANCINE CAROLE, nursing educator, researcher; PhD; BSc in Nursing, U. Montréal, 1977, MSc in Nursing, 1982; PhD in Nursing, McGill U., 1990. RN. Full prof. faculty of nursing U. Montréal; sr. rschr. Inst. U. de gériatrie de Montréal. Postdoc psychosocial rsch. unit Douglas Hosp.; chair Rsch. in Nursing Care of Elderly & Their Families; sr. rschr. Ctr. Excellence for Women's Health. Grantee, MRC-NHRDP, 1995—2000, FRSQ, 2000—06. Office: Faculty Nursing U Montreal PO 6128 Sta Centre-ville Montreal PQ H3C 3J7 Canada *

DUCHARME, JAMES W., health insurance company executive; MBA, U. Pitts., 1981—83; B in Economics, Dickinson Coll. Cert. mgmt. acct. CFO Blue Cross and Blue Shield, Vt., 1989—2004, dir. budgets and acctg. Mass.; CFO Capital Dist. Physicians Health Plan Inc., Albany, NY, 2005—08, sr. v.p. fin., 2005—; CFO Harvard Pilgrim Health Care, 2008—. Mem.: AICPA. Office: Harvard Pilgrim Health Care 93 Worcester St Wellesley Hills MA 02481 Office Phone: 617-509-1000.

DUCKETT, STEPHEN JOHN, health service manager; b. Sydney, Feb. 18, 1950; s. Alan Edward and Ruth Eason (Wilson); m. Terri Jurgens Jackson. B in Econs., Australian Nat. U., 1971; M in Health Adminstrn., U. NSW, Australia, 1973; PhD, UNSW, Australia, 1981, DSc, 2006; DBA, U. Bath, Eng., 2006. Lectr. U. NSW, Australia, 1974-80, sr. lectr., 1980-83; dep. dir. rsch. Health Dept. Victoria, Australia, 1983-85, dep. regional dir., 1985-88, regional dir., 1988-91, dir. policy, 1991-92; dir. acute health Health & Community Svcs., Victoria, 1992-93; dean health scis. La Trobe U., Victoria, 1996—2005; sec. (head) Commonwealth Dept. Human Svcs. and Health, Canberra, Australia, 1994-96; chief exec. Ctr. Healthcare Improved, Queensland Health, 2006—09; pres. & CEO Alberta Health Svc., 2009—10; prof. Sch. Pub. Health, U. Alberta, 2010—. Chmn. bd. dirs. Bayside Health., 2000-06 Bd. dirs. Brotherhood St. Laurence, Melbourne., 2000-05 Fellow Australian Coll. Health Svc. Execs. Anglican. Home: Ste 700 Manuife Pl 10180-101 St NW Edmonton T5I354 Canada

DUCOTE, CHARLOTTE ANNE, allied health services administrator; b. Baton Rouge, Oct. 21, 1951; d. Gaston Camille and Edna Lora (Bossier) D. BA in Speech and Hearing Therapy, La. State U., 1972, PhD in Speech-Lang. Pathology, 1983; MA in Speech and Hearing Scis., Vanderbilt U., 1973. Cert. clin. competence in speech-lang. pathology; lic. speech-lang. pathology, La. Speech-lang. clinician Met. Schs. of Nashville and Davidson County, 1973-74; speech and hearing cons., acad. instr. dept. spl. edn. U. New Orleans, 1974-78; speech-lang. pathologist, coord. speech and hearing svc. dept. pediatrics and adult units Earl K. Long Meml. Hosp., Baton Rouge, 1978-81; head sect. speech-lang. pathology La. Rehab. Inst. of Charity Hosp., New Orleans, 1982-87; asst. prof. medicine rehab. medicine sect./dept. medicine La. State U. Sch. Medicine, 1986-87; assoc. program dir. New Medico Rehab. Ctr. La., Folsom, 1987, program dir., 1987-88; program dir. post-acute brain injury program Touro Rehab. Ctr., New Orleans, 1989-94; dir. divsn. communicative disorders Ochsner Clinic Found., New Orleans, 1994—. Speech-lang. pathology cons. dept. pediat. Ochsner Med. Ctr., 1978; instr. speech dept. La. State U., Baton Rouge, 1979, clin. supr. articulation disorders and cleft palate clinics, 1979, 81-82; speech-lang. pathologist Upjohn Home Health Care Svc. and Americare Home Health Svc., Baton Rouge, 1981-82; speech-lang. pathology cons. Greenwell Springs Hosp., Baton Rouge, 1981-82; mem. utilization review com. St. Tammany Parish Home Health Svcs., Covington, La., 1980, Am. Healthcare Svc., Baton Rouge, 1981-82; clin. supr. off-site clin. tng. program La. State U. Med. Ctr., 1983-86; program com. chair Gov.'s task force La. Conf. for Disabled Persons, 1986; mem. Hosp./Sch. Linkage Com., 1991-95; mem. program com. Internat. Brain Injury Symposium, 1991; adj. instr. comm. disorders La. State U. Med. Ctr., 1992-95. Contbr. articles and revs. to profl. publs. Mem. Coalition for Citizens with Disabilities, 1983-95; vol. speech pathologist Op. Smile, 1996—; chair Op. Smile Speech Pathology Coun., 1998—2006; mem. Ops. Smile's Speech Pathology Coun., 1998-; co-founder & Coord. Op. Smile Speech Therapy, Vietnam, 1998—. Phi Mu-Mary King Shepardson fellow, 1978; recipient Disting. Alumnus award, Vanderbilt U. Med. Ctr., Divsn. Hearing and Speech Scis., 2002. Mem. Am. Speech-Lang.-Hearing Assn. (clin. reviewer 1977-85, assoc. editor 1986-90, spl. interest groups speech scis. and orofacial disorders, neurol. scis. and disorders, swallowing and swallowing disorders, lang. and multicultural populations), Am. Speech and Hearing Found. (Louis DiCarlo award for recent clin. achievement 2001, State award for recent clin. achievement 2001), Brain Injury Assn., La. Speech and Hearing Assn. (rehab. and med. agys. com. 1984-2000, chair 1996-98, Spl. Recognition award 2000, La. DiCarlo Clin. Achievement award 2001), La. Head Injury Found. (co-founder 1983, coord., pres. 1983-86, bd. dirs. 1986-95, sec., bd. dirs. 1987-90, program co-chair ann. conf. 1990, 91, 92, pres. 1993-94, Profl. of Yr. 1991), New Orleans Neuropathology Interest Group. Avocations: travel, reading, music. Office: Ochsner Clinic Found 6-South 1514 Jefferson Hwy New Orleans LA 70121-2483 Office Phone: 504-842-4618, 504-842-4022. Personal E-mail: caducote@yahoo.com. Business E-Mail: cducote@ochsner.org.

DUDAS, MAREK, embryologist, educator; s. Jan Dudas and Lydia Dudasova. MD, Safarik U., Kosice, 1998, PhD, 2001. Cert. Rhodon Inst., Boiron, France, 1997, Women's Health Alliance Nashville, 2007, Healthcare Surveillance Authority Slovak Republic, 1998; State Vet. and Food Agy. Bratislava, 2008. Clin. embryologist L. Pasteur U. Hosp., Kosice, 1998—2001; rsch. scholar U. Southern Calif., Dept. Pathology, LA, 2002—04, Childrens Hosp., LA, 2005—06, rsch. assoc., 2007—08; asst. prof. Safarik U., Inst. Biology and Ecology, Kosice, 2006—08, assoc. prof., 2008—; adj. assoc. prof. Safarik U., Sch. Medicine, Kosice, 2008—. Exec. dir. Persica, Ltd., Presov, 2000—02; exec. dir., projects adminstrn. Safarik U., Rectorate, Kosice, 2007—10; cons., non-agt. ind. contractor Thomson Reuters, Reuters Insight Cmty. Experts, NYC, 2008—; chief embryologist Sanatorium SPLN Ltd., Kosice, 2010—. Contbr. articles to profl. jours. Head Homeowner Cmty. Bd., Kosice, 2009—; vol. physician Various Orgs, Kosice, 1997—2008; mem., regional commn. Slovak Nat. Biology Olympiad, Kosice, 2009—. Recipient Pathway to Independence award, NIH, USA, 2007, award, InnoCentive Inc. Worldwide Challenges, 2010, 2011; fellow Rsch. Career Devel. fellowship, Childrens Hosp. LA, 2003—05; Postdoc. fellowship, U. So. Calif., Keck Sch. Medicine, 2002—04. Mem.: ESHRE, Internat. Com. Red Cross, Soc. Devel. Biology, Slovak Med. Assn., Am. Cleft Palate - Craniofacial Assn., Slovak Histochem. Soc. (pres. 2009—), The Smithsonian Inst. Achievements include development of novel method for human embryo blastomere biopsy and diagnosis; discovery of novel promoter to drive gene manipulations in bone marrow, with implications to hematology; genetic manipulation in bone marrow resulting in depletion of B lymphocytes, with implication to leukemia treatment. Avocations: gardening, reading, travel, hiking. Office: Safarik University UBEV Moyzesova 11 Kosice SK-04001 Slovakia Office Phone: 421-905-513-578. Personal E-mail: marek.dudas.sk@gmail.com. Business E-Mail: marek.dudas@upjs.sk.

DUDDA, MARCEL, trauma surgeon, orthopedist; b. Essen, NRW, Germany, Nov. 22, 1973; s. Klaus Juergen and Monika Dudda; life ptnr. Sophia Luise Goericke. MD, Essen Med. Sch., Germany, 2002. Diplomate Govt. NRW, 2002. Resident, rschr. U. Hosp. Bergmannsheil, Ruhr-U. Bochum, NRW, 2002—, Inselspital, U. Berne, Switzerland, 2007—08; clin. rsch. fellow Childrens Hosp. Boston, Harvard Med. Sch., 2006—07, rschr., 2006—. Rschr. Rsch. Ctr. Orthop. Surgery, Inst. Evaluative Rsch. Orthop. Surgery, U. Berne, 2007—. Mem.: German Soc. Sports Medicine, German Soc. Surgery, German Soc. Trauma and Orthop. Surgery. Office: Univ Hosp Bergmannsheil Buerkle-de-la-Camp Platz 1 Bochum NRW 44789 Germany Business E-Mail: marcel.dudda@rub.de.

DUDGEON, WES, healthcare educator; b. Ind., Oct. 29, 1978; PhD, U. SC, 2006. Asst. prof. The Citadel, 2008—. Office: 171 Moultrie St Deas Hall-Rm 11 Charleston SC 29409 Office Fax: 843-953-6798. Business E-Mail: wes.dudgeon@citadel.edu.

DUDLEY, GARY EDWARD, psychologist; b. Columbus, Ohio, July 19, 1947; s. Ray Leonard and Mary Virginia (Russi) D.; children: Michelle Denise, Karen Elizabeth. BS, Ohio State U., 1969; MS, U. Miami, 1972, PhD, 1975. Lic. psychologist, Ga., Fla. Tchr. Columbus Pub. Schs., 1969—70; intern in clin. psychology Mt. Zion Hosp. and Med. Ctr., San Francisco, 1972—73; clin. psychologist Met. Dade County Jail, Miami, Fla., 1974—76, Southeast Inst. Criminal Justice, Miami, 1974—76, Ga. So. U., Statesboro, 1976—80; pvt. practice Marietta, Ga., 1980—. Cons. Child Devel. Ctr., Ga. Psycho-Ednl. Network, Atlanta; bd. dirs. svcs. Atlanta Area Psychol. Assocs., PC; pres. Accurate Assessment Svcs. Atlanta. Contbr. articles to profl. jours. NIMH fellow, 1971, 73, VA fellow, 1971. Mem. APA, Nat. Acad. Neuropsychologists, Am. Bd. Med. Psychotherapists, Southeastern Psychol. Assn., Ga. Psychol. Assn., Nat. Honor Soc. Psychology, Sigma Xi. Office: Doctors Bldg/Windy Hill 2520 Windy Hill Rd Ste 203 Marietta GA 30067-8650 Home Phone: 404-358-1571; Office Phone: 770-953-6401. Personal E-mail: ged69@hotmail.com.

DUDLEY-GRANT, G. RITA, psychologist; b. St. Thomas, Virgin Islanda, Nov. 2, 1951; d. George H. T. Dudley and Gertude Alethea (Lockhart) Melchior; m. Richard Ernest Wilson, Mar. 26, 1988; children: Stacey, Damien, Jeremy, Megan. BA, Simmons Coll., 1973; MPH, Harvard Sch. Pub. Health, 1984; PhD, Adelphi U., 1980. Diplomate Nat. Register of Health Svc. Providers in Psychology, lic. psychologist Mass., V.I. Infant specialist Solomon Carter Fuller Mental Ctr., Boston, 1977—78; clin. dir. Diagnostic Clinic, Boston City Hosp., 1979—82, dir. tng. Mass., 1982—87; asst. prof. Boston U. Sch. Medicine, 1983—88; chief psychology Boston City Hosp., 1982—87; asst. commr. health V.I. Dept. Health, St. Thomas, 1987—95; clin. dir. V.I. Behavioral Svc., St. Croix, 1995—. Dir. V.I. Coun. Alcoholism, St. Thomas, 1988—90. Co-editor: Psychology & Buddhism, 2003; contbr. chapters to books, articles pub. to profl. jour. Bd. dirs. Mental Health Planning Coun., St. Thomas, 1988—97; chairperson V.I. Victory Partnership Against Drugs, St. Croix, 1991—96; trustee, bd. dirs. St. Croix County Day Sch., 2000—. Recipient Outstanding Women of Am., APA, 1982, Jack Krasner award for outstanding young psychologist, 1984, Outstanding Svc. award, Ptnrs. in Recovery, 1992. Fellow: APA (coun. reps. 2003—, Heiser award 1999), Soc. Psychol. Study of Ethnic Minorities; mem.: Assn. V.I. Psychologists (founding mem.). Democrat. Buddhist. Avocations: walking, theater, swimming, singing. Home: PO Box 24241 Christiansted VI 00824 Office: Virgin Islands Behavioral Svcs 183 Anna's Hope Christiansted VI 00820 Office Phone: 340-773-6445.

DUDRICK, STANLEY JOHN, surgeon, research scientist, educator; b. Nanticoke, Pa., Apr. 9, 1935; s. Stanley Francis and Stephania Mary (Jachimczak) Dudrick; m. Theresa M. Keen, June 14, 1958; children: Susan Marie, Paul Stanley, Carolyn Mary, Stanley Jonathan, Holly Anne, Anne Theresa. BS cum laude, Franklin and Marshall Coll., 1957; MD, U. Pa., 1961; MA (hon.), Yale U., 1999. Diplomate Am. Bd. Surgery. Intern Hosp. U. Pa., Phila., 1961—62, resident gen. surgery, 1962—67; acad. practice specializing in surgery Phila., 1967—72; prof. surgery U. Tex. Med. Sch., Houston, 1972—90, clin. prof. surgery, 1990—95; dir. Med. Edn. St. Mary's Hosp., Waterbury, 1995—2000, 2002—08, chmn. surgery, 2002—04; chmn. surgery dept., dir. surg. edn. Bridgeport Hosp.-Yale U. New Haven Health Sys., 2000—02. Acad. practice specializing in surgery, Houston, 1972—88, Houston, 1990—94, Phila., 1988—90, New Haven, 1994—, Waterbury, 1994—, Bridgeport, 2002—; cons. in surgery M. D. Anderson Hosp. and Tumor Inst., 1973—88, clin. prof. surgery, cons. to pres., 1982—88; chief. surg. svcs. Hermann Hosp., Houston, 1972—80; surgeon-in-chief, dir. Ctr. Cardiovasc. Disease, dir. nutritional support svcs. Nutritional Sci. Ctr., 1990—94; chmn. dept. surgery U. Tex. Med. Sch., Houston, 1972—80; sr. cons. surgery and medicine Tex. Inst. Rehab. and Rsch., 1974—88; mem. anat. bd. State of Tex., 1973—78; examiner Am. Bd. Surgery, 1974—78, bd. dirs., 1978—84, sr. mem., 1984—2002, mem. and chmn. various. com.s; chmn. sci. adv. com. Tex. Med. Ctr. Libr., 1974; mem. food and nutrition bd. NRC-Nat. Acad. Scis., 1973—75; mem. sci. adv. com. Nat. Found. Ileitis and Colitis; mem. surgery, anesthesia and trauma study sect. NIH, 1982—86; chmn. dept. surgery Pa. Hosp., Phila., 1988—90, surgeon-in-chief, 1988—91, hon. surgery staff, 1991—; clin. prof. surgery U. Pa., 1988—93, assoc. chmn. dept. surgery, 1994—2000, 2002—04, chmn. dept. surgery, 2004—08, dir. surgery program, 1994—2000, 2002—08, St. Mary's Hosp., Waterbury; clin. prof. Yale U., New Haven, 1995—99, prof., 1999—; adj. prof. Quinippiac U., 1996—. Editor: Manual of Surgical Nutrition, 1975, Manual of Preoperative and Postoperative Care, 1983, Current Strategies in Surgical Nutrition, 1991, Practical Handbook of Nutrition in Clinical Practice, 1994, Surgical Nutrition: Strategies in Critically Ill Patients, 1995; assoc. editor: Nutrition in Medicine, 1975—; mem. editl. bd. Annals of Surgery, 1975—, Infusion, 1978—, Nutrition and Cancer, 1980—2002, Nutrition Support Services, 1980—86, Jour. Clin. Surgery, 1980—83, Nutrition Rsch., 1981—, Intermed. Comm. Nursing Svcs., 1981—, Postgrad. Gen. Surgery, 1992—, others; contbr. chapters to books, articles to profl. jours. Bd. dirs. Found. Children, Houston, Harris County unit Am. Cancer Soc., Phila., 1988—90; founder Benjamin Rush Soc., 1987, hon. chmn., 1999—; trustee Franklin and Marshall Coll., 1985—, mem. student life, art collection and trusteeship coms., mem. exec. com., mem. overseers bd., 1986—2002, mem. alumni programs and devel. com., 1991—2002, pres. regional adv. coun., 1992—94, vice chmn., 1994—2002, John Marshall Soc., 1993—, campaign nat. chmn., 1995—2002, mem. bldgs. and grounds com., 2002—, acad. investments com., 2002—. Decorated knight Order St. John of Jerusalem Knights Hopitalier; recipient VA citation for Significant Contbn. to Med. Care, 1970, Mead Johnson award for Rsch. in Hosp. Pharmacy, 1972, Seale Harris medal, So. Med. Assn., 1973, AMA-Brookdale award in Medicine, 1975, Great Texan award, Nat. Found. Ileitis and Colitis, 1975, Modern Medicine award, 1977, Disting. Alumnus citation, Franklin and Marshall Coll., 1980, Alumni medal, 2002, Presdl. medal, 2007, WHO, Houston, 1980, Stinchfield award, Am. Acad. Orthopedic Surgery, 1981, Bernstein award, Med. Soc. State of NY, 1986, Alumni Svc. award, U. Pa. Med. Sch., 1996, Excellence in Surgery Tchg. award, St. Mary's Hosp., 1999, 2003, 2008, Roswell Park award, Buffalo Surgery Soc., 2000, Nos Magni Nominis Umbra Tchg. and Rsch. award, Yale Gen. Surgery Residents, 2000, Alumni medal, Franklin and Marshall Coll., 2002, Jacobson Innovation award, ACS, 2005, others, Pres. Medal, 2007; named Stanley J. Dudrick MD Surg. Edn. and Rsch. Fund in his honor, St. Mary's Hosp., 2003, Disting. Alumnus, U. Pa. Med. Sch., 2007. Fellow ACS (vice chmn. pre and post operative com. 1975, gov. 1979-85, com. med. motion pictures 1981-90, SESAP com. 1990-94, co-chmn. multiple choice com. 1993-94), Fellows Leadership Soc. (life, mem. Conn. chpt.), Philippine Coll. Surgeons (hon.), Coll. Medicine and Surgery Costa Rica (hon.), Am. Coll. Nutrition (Grace A. Goldsmith award 1982), Leadership Soc. (life), Phi Beta Kappa; mem. AMA (coun. food and nutrition 1971-76, exec. com. 1975-76, coun. sci. affairs 1976-81, Goldberger award clin. nutrition 1970), AAAS, AAUP, Am. Surg. Assn. (Flance-Karl award 1997), Am. Acad. Pediat. (hon., Ladd medal 1988), Am. Pediat. Surg. Assn. (hon.), Am. Soc. Nutritional Support Svcs. (bd. dirs. 1982-87, pres. 1984, Outstanding Humanitarian award 1984) Soc. Univ. Surgeons (exec. coun. 1974-78), Assn. for Acad. Surgery (founders group), Assn. Polish Surgeons (hon.), Internat. Soc. Surgeons, Internat. Fedn. Surg. Colls., Internat. Soc. Parenteral Nutrition (exec. coun 1975-81, pres. 1978-81), Internat. Fedn. Surgery Soc., So. Med. Assn. (chmn. surgery sect. 1984-85), Houston Gastroent. Soc., Houston Surg. Soc., Tex. Surg. Soc., Tex. Med. Assn. (com. nutrition and food resources), Tex. Med. Found., Harris County Med. Soc., New Haven County Med. Soc., Conn. Soc. Am. Bd. Surgeons, New Eng. Surg. Soc., L.A. Surg. Soc. (hon.), Am. Radium Soc., Am. Soc. Clin. Oncology, Am. Soc. Parenteral and Enteral Nutrition (pres. 1977, bd. advs. 1978—, chmn. bd. advisers 1978, Vars award 1982, Rhoads lectr. 1985, 2005, Dudrick Rsch. Scholar award named in his honor), Pa. Nutritionists Soc. (pres. 1985), Am. Gastroent. Assn., Soc. Surg. Oncology, James Ewing Soc., Ravdin-Rhoads Surg. Assn., Excelsior Surg. Soc. (Edward D. Churchill lectr 1981), Soc. Laparoendoscopic Surgery, Soc. Surg. Chairmen, So. Surg. Assn., Southwe. Surg. Congress, Southea. Surg. Congress, Surg. Biology Club II, Surg. Infection Soc. (chmn. membership com. 1987-90), We. Surg. Soc., Halsted Soc., Allen O. Whipple Surg. Soc., Am. Inst. Nutrition, Soc. Clin. Surgery, Am. Soc. Clin. Investigation, Soc. Surgery Alimentary Tract, Am. Trauma Soc. (founders group), Am. Assn. Surgery Trauma, Soc. Clin. Surgery, Am. Soc. Clin. Nutrition, Fedn. Am. Soc. Exptl. Biology, Am. Burn Assn., Assn. Program Dirs. Surgery (bd. dirs.), John Marshall Soc., Coll. Physicians Phila., Phila. Acad. Surgeons, George Hermann Soc., Polish Soc. Parenteral and Enteral Nutrition (hon.), Polish Soc. Surgery (hon.), Columbian Assn. Surgery (hon.), Columbian Acad. Medicine (hon.), Mexican Acad. Surgery (hon.), Bohemian Soc. Nutrition and Metabolism (hon.), Mexican Assn. Gen. Surgery (hon.), Union League Phila., Med. Club Phila., Franklin Club Phila., Houston Doctors Club (gov. 1973-76), Nat. Alumni Coun. U. Pa. Med. Sch. (chmn. 1994-2001), Conn. United for Rsch. Excellence (bd. dirs. 1995-2001), Waterbury Symphony Orch. (bd. dirs. 1999-, chmn. endowment com. 2002-05), Cosmos Club, Athenaeum, The Penn Club (charter), Phi Beta Kappa Assocs., Sigma Xi, Alpha Omega Alpha. (sec.-treas. Houston chpt. 1982-83) Achievements include invention of new technique of intravenous feeding and anti-cholesterol therapy. Home: 40 Beecher St Naugatuck CT 06770-2721 Office: St Mary's Hosp 56 Franklin St Waterbury CT 06706 Business E-Mail: sdudrick@stmh.org.

DUEL, BARRY P., urologist, pediatrician; MD, Harvard Med. Sch., 1990. Cert. Urology, 2000. Resident in urologic surgery Harvard Med. Sch., Boston Children's Hosp.; fellow in pediatric urology Children's Hosp. Mich., Detroit; assoc. prof. urology and pediat. U. Calif., Irvine; pvt. practice Children's Hosp. Orange County, Calif.; assoc. dir. pediatric urology, mem. surgery dept. Cedars-Sinai Med. Ctr., LA, 2008—. Fellow: ACS, Am. Acad. Pediat.; mem.: Soc. Pediatric Urology, Soc. Fetal Urology. Office: Minimally Invasive Urology Inst Ste 1070 8635 W 3rd St Los Angeles CA 90048 Office Phone: 310-423-4700. Office Fax: 310-423-4711.

DUENAS, OMAR FELIPE, gynecologist, researcher; b. Mexico City, Distrito Federa, June 6, 1979; s. Mike and Lupe Duenas; m. Maricela Same. MD summa cum laude, Benemerita U. Autonoma Pueba, Puebla, Mexico, 2004; MPh, Benemerita U. Autonoma Pueba. Cert. Comego Mex., 2008. Rschr. St. Lukes Hosp., Houston, 2007—08; resident Bronx Lebanon Hosp., NYC, 2008—. Chmn. jr fellows sect. mex. Am. Coll. Ob-Gyn., Mexico, 2007—. Editor (writer): (book) Crossing Borders, Operative Obstetrics For Dummies (Novelist of Yr. BUAP, 2007). Organizer Am. Coll. of Obstetricians and Gynecologysts, Mexico - Washington, DC, 2008—. Recipient Best Med. Essay award, CONACYT, 2005, Donald R. award, Am. Coll. Ob-Gyn., 2006, Chief Residents award, INPer, 2008. Fellow: Internat. Federation Ob-Gyn. (reviewer 2006—07, Jr. Fellow of Yr. 2007). Avocations: hiking, mechanics, travel, photography, painting. Office: Bronx Lebanon Hosp Grand Concourse 1650 Bronx NY 10457 Personal E-mail: dugof1@hotmail.com. Business E-Mail: dugof1@yahoo.com.mx.

DUENSING, LENORE, medical association administrator; MEd. Dir. outreach WNET / Thirteen, NYC; dir. comm. and outreach, interim dir. Am. Pain Found., Balt.; exec. dir. Am. Acad. Pain Mgmt., Sonora, Calif., 2007—. Editor-in-chief: The Pain Practitioner. Office: Am Acad Pain Mgmt 13947 Mono Way #A Sonora CA 95370 Office Phone: 209-533-9744. Office Fax: 209-533-9750. E-mail: lduensing@yahoo.com. *

DUERDEN, BRIAN ION, medical microbiology educator; b. Nelson, Eng., June 21, 1948; s. Cyril and Mildred (Ion) D.; m. Marjorie Hudson, Aug. 5, 1972. BSc in Med. Sci. with honors, Edinburgh U., Scotland, 1970, MB, ChB., 1972, MD, 1979; CBE, 2008. House officer thoracic surgery City Hosp., Edinburgh, 1972-73, house officer infectious diseases, 1973; lectr. bacteriology Edinburgh U. Med. Sch., 1973-76; lectr. med. microbiology Sheffield (Eng.) U. Med. Sch., 1976-79, sr. lectr. med. microbiology, 1979-83, prof. med. microbiology, 1983-90; cons. med. microbiologist Sheffield Children's Hosp., 1979-90; prof. med. microbiology U. Wales Coll. Medicine, Cardiff, 1991—2008; emritus prof. med. microbiology Cardiff U., 2008—; vis. prof. Imperial Coll., London, 2011—. Dir. Pub. Health Lab. Svc., Cardiff, 1991—95, Anaerobe Reference Unit, 1992—2004; dep. dir. and med. dir. Pub. Health Lab. Svc. Bd., Eng. and Wales, 1995—2002, dir. svc., 2002—03; mgr. South Glamorgan Microbiology Svc., Cardiff, 1991—95; mem. adv. com. on dangerous pathogens U.K. Dept. Health, 1989—94, 2003—10, chmn. joint working party on infection in renal units, 1995—2010, mem. prescribing and rsch. sub-groups on antimicrobial resistance, 1999—2002, inspector microbiology and infection control, 2004—10; mem. microbiology adv. com. Govt. of U.K., 1988—95, surveillance group on diseases and infections in animals, 1999—2010, mem. U.K. zoonoses group, 1999—2010, mem. joint com. on vaccines and immunization, 2002—04, mem. specialist adv. com. on antimicrobial resistance, 2002—07; mem. adv. com. Antimicrobial Resistance and Healthcare Associated Infection, 2007—10; dir. clin. governance and quality Health Protection Agy., 2003—04. Editor-in-chief Jour. Med. Microbiology, U.K., 1988-2002, mem. editl. bd., 1977—2006; author: Textbook of Microbial and Parasitic Infection, 1987, 93; author, editor: Topley & Wilson's Principles of Bacteriology, Virology and Immunity, 9th edit., 1997, Anaerobes in Human Disease, 1991; contbr. articles to profl. jours. Fellow Royal Coll. Pathologists (mem. coun. 1986-89, 90-93, mem. exec. com. 1990-93, chmn. exam. panel med. microbiology 1994-99, exam. panel publs. works 1999-2004, mem. specialist adv. com. 1981-89, 90-99, 2004-10), Royal Coll. Physicians Edinburgh, Infectious Disease Soc. Am.; mem. Path. Soc. Gt. Britain and Ireland (editor, com. mem. 1981-2002), Soc. for Anaerobic Microbiology (chmn. 1989-93), Assn. Med. Microbiologists (mem. exec. com. 1984-94), Nat. External Quality Assurance Panel, Anaerobe Soc. Ams., Soc. for Gen. Microbiology. Home Phone: 01291 623310. Personal E-mail: bduerden@doctors.org.uk.

DUERK, HEINZ ALBERT, hematologist, consultant; b. Karlsruhe, Germany, June 30, 1953; s. Isidor and Maria (Goetz) Duerk; 1 child, Maike. Biochemist, Eberhard Karls U., 1980, physician, 1986; PhD, U. Tuebingen, 1988, MD, 1990. Diplomate Bd. Internal Medicine, Hematology and Med. Oncology, Rheumatology. Resident U. Tuebingen, Germany, 1987-93, cons., 1993-95; assoc. chief St. Franziskus Hosp., Flensburg, Germany, 1995-98; head dept. hematology, oncology, immunology St. Marien Hosp., Hamm, Germany, 1998—. Senator U. Tuebingen, 1988—92. Author, editor Manual Rheumatologie, 1997. Sec. Cmty. Cancer Ctr., Flensburg, 1996—98. Mem.: Am. Soc. Clin. Oncology, Bone Marrow and Stem Cell Transplantation Group, German Soc. Rheumatology, Assn. Internal Oncologists, European Soc. Med. Oncology, German Soc. Hematology and Oncology, German Cancer Soc. Avocation: jogging. Home: Weidenhecke 29 D-59069 Hamm Germany Office: St Marien Hosp Knappenstr 19 59071 Hamm Germany Fax: 49-2381-18-2252. Business E-Mail: heinz.duerk@marienhospibe-hamm.de.

DUERKSEN, GEORGE LOUIS, music therapist, educator; b. St. Joseph, Mo., Oct. 29, 1934; s. George Herbert and Louise May (Dalke) D.; m. Patricia Gay Beers, June 3, 1961; children— Mark Jeffrey, Joseph Scott, Cynthia Elizabeth Student, Tabor Coll., 1951-52; BMusEdn, U. Kans., 1955, MMusEdn, 1956, PhD in Music Edn., 1967. Cert. music educator Kans., Mo., registered music therapist Nat. Assn. Music Therapy, 1975, bd. cert. music therapist Cert. Bd. Music Therapists, 1987. Tchr. music Tonganoxie HS, Kans., 1955-56, Stafford Jr. and Sr. HS, Kans., 1959-60, Labette County HS, Altamont, Kans., 1960-62, Shawnee Mission North HS, Kans., 1962-63, asst. prof., dir. psychology of music lab. Mich. State U., East Lansing, 1965-69; prof., chmn. dept. art and music edn. and music therapy U. Kans., Lawrence, 1969-93, dir. Singing Jayhawks, 1979-83, prof., dir. music edn. and music therapy divsn., 1993—2004, prof., interim chair dept. music and dance, 2000-01, prof., dir. grad. studies, music edn. and music therapy, dir. Ctr. for Rsch. on Music Behavior, 2001—; assoc. dir. Kans. North Ctrl. Assn. Colls. and Schs., 1992-2000. Cons., vis. prof. U. Hawaii, Honolulu, summer 1978; cons., vis. prof. U. Melbourne, Australia, summer 1981; cons., lectr. N.Z. Soc. for Music Therapy, Wellington, 1983, Ctr. for Contemporary Music Rsch., Athens, 1991, U. Thessaloniki, Greece, 1993, Korean Assn. for Music Therapy, 1994, 97, Sook Myung U., Seoul, 1997; cons. functional music applications, 1967—, Deakin U., Geelong, Victoria, Australia, 1990. Author: (monograph) Teaching Instrumental Music, 1973; Music for Exceptional Children, 1981; contbr. articles to profl. jours., chpts. to books. Fulbright scholar Inst. for Internat. Edn., Australia, 1956-57; U.Kans. fellow, Lawrence, 1963-64; U.S. Office Edn. grantee, 1966-67, 73-75, 78-81. Mem. AAAS, Music Educators Nat. Conf., Am. Music Therapy Assn.(award of merit, 2000), Music Edn. Rsch. Coun. (chmn. 1980-82), Brit. Soc. for Music Therapy, Coun. for Rsch. in Music Edn., Pi Kappa Lambda, Phi Mu Alpha, Phi Delta Kappa. Avocations: photography, boating, travel. Home Phone: 785-843-0418; Office Phone: 785-864-9632. E-mail: gduerksen@ku.edu.

DUERR, DIANNE MARIE, sports medicine consultant, educator; b. Buffalo, July 14, 1945; d. Robert John and Aileen Louise D. BS in Health and Phys. Edn., SUNY, Brockport, 1967; cert., SUNY, Oswego, 1982; postgrad., Canisius Coll., 1970-71. Cert. tchr. NY. Tchr. North Syracuse (NY) Sch. Dist., 1967—2004; project dir. dept. orthop. surgery SUNY Upstate Med. U., Syracuse, 1982—2003; creator Inst. for Human Performance SUNY Health Sci. Ctr., Syracuse, 1988. Coord. scholastic sports injury reporting system project SUNY, 1985-98; mem. com. on scholastic sports-related injuries NIH Inst. Arthritis, Musculoskeletal and Skin Diseases, 1993-96; project dir. dept. orthop. surgery North Syracuse Ctrl. Sch. Dist., 1967-2004. Author: SSIRS Pilot Study Report, 1987, SSIRS Fall Study Report, 1988, SHASIRS Report, 1991; creator Scholastic Sports Injury Reporting System, 1985, Scholastic Head and Spine Injury Reporting System, 1989. Co-chmn. sports medicine USA Amateur Athletic Union, Nat. Jr. Olympic Games, Syracuse, NY, 1987; vol. sports medicine NY State Sr. Games, 1990—95, sports medicine coord., 1990—95, US Roller Skating Nat. Championships, 1995, NY State Womens Lacrosse Championships, 1995, US Nat. Precision Ice Skating Championships, 1997, Youth Basketball of Am., Northeast Regional Tournament, 1999; co-chmn. healthcare, security Empire State Games, Syracuse, 2002; mem. com. sports injury surveillance Ctrs. for Disease Control, 1995; cons. NY Sci., Tech. and Soc. Edn. Project, 1995. Mem. NY State AAHPERD (pres. exercise sci. and sports medicine sect., 1994-98), Am. Coll. Sports Medicine, United Univ. Profs., Am. Fedn. Tchrs., NY United Tchrs., North Syracuse Tchrs. Assn., Phi Kappa Phi, Sierra Club, Audubon Soc., Nat. Wildlife Found. Avocations: swimming, bicycling, ice skating, reading, photography. Office: 418 Buffington Rd Syracuse NY 13224-2208 Personal E-mail: dmduerr@twcny.rr.com.

DUFAY-DUPAR, BAPTISTE, ophthalmologist; b. Marseille, France, Aug. 11, 1977; Baccalaureat, Lacordaire, 1995; MD, Parish U., 2007. Practitioner Beziers Hosp., 2009—. Mem.: Soc. Francaise D'ophtalmologie. Office: 2 rue Valentin Hauy Beziers 34500 France Business E-Mail: avicenne5@voila.fr.

DUFFNER, LEE R., ophthalmologist; b. June 3, 1936; m. Alvina Bross, Aug. 31, 1957; children: Fay, Rachel, Tamar. BS Engring., Purdue U., 1957; MS Physiology, Marquette U., Milw., 1961; MD, Med. Coll. Wis., 1962. Diplomate Am. Bd. Ophthalmology. Intern Stanford U., 1962—63; resident U. Miami, Fla., 1966—69; practice medicine specializing in ophthalmology Hollywood, Fla., 1969—; clin. prof. ophthalmology U. Miami Sch. Medicine, 1969—; dir. Am. Bd. Ophthalmology, 1995—2002, chmn., 2002. Pres. town coun. Town of Golden Beach, Fla., 1983—95. Capt. USAF, 1963—66. Fellow: ACS, Am. Acad. Ophthalmology; mem.: Miami Ophthal. Soc. (pres. 1983—84). Avocation: racewalking. Home: 185 Ocean Blvd Golden Beach FL 33160-2208 Office: 2740 Hollywood Blvd Hollywood FL 33020-4826 Office Phone: 954-925-2740.

DUFFY, JOHN ALASTAIR, retired chemistry professor, researcher; b. Birmingham, Eng., Sept. 24, 1932; s. John and Edna Frances (Walker) D.; m. Muriel Florence Lyon Ramsay, Dec. 19, 1959; children: Alastair, Penelope. BSc in Chemistry, Sheffield U., Eng., 1955, PhD, 1958; DSc, Aberdeen U., Scotland, 1979. Rsch. chemist Albright & Wilson, Oldbury, Eng., 1958-59; lectr. Wolverhampton Poly., Eng., 1959-61; sr. lectr. N.E. Wales Inst., 1961-65; from lectr. to reader chemistry dept. U. Aberdeen, 1966-96, prof., 1996—2001, emeritus prof., 2001—. Cons. Schott Glaswerke, Germany, 1984-86. Author: General Inorganic Chemistry, 1966, Bonding Energy Levels and Bands in Inorganic Solids, 1990; contbr. articles to profl. jours. Fellow Royal Soc. Chemistry, Soc. Glass Tech. Achievements include discovery of special glasses for drug delivery systems; discovery and development of optical basicity method for technological assessment of molten glass and of slags in the iron and steel industry. Home: 35 Beechgrove Ter Aberdeen AB15 5DR Scotland Office: U Aberdeen Dept Chemistry Meston Bldg Meston Walk Old Aberdeen AB24 3UE Scotland Office Phone: 01224 272914.

DUFFY, JOHN CHARLES, psychiatrist, educator, consultant; b. Cleve., June 19, 1934; s. John Joseph and Hannah (McIllwee) D.; m. Francoise C. Antonini; children: Charles, Robert, John. Grad., Boston Coll., 1956; MD, N.Y. Med. Coll., 1960. Intern Henry Ford Hosp., Detroit, 1960-61; resident Mayo Clinic, Rochester, Minn., 1963-67; exec. dir. Tucson Child Guidance Ctr., 1971-74; commd. med. officer USPHS, 1974; prof., assoc. chmn. Uniformed Svcs. U. Sch. Medicine, Bethesda, Md., 1974-81; assoc. commr. health affairs FDA, cons. Surgeon Gen., Rockville, Md., 1981-88; asst. surgeon gen. USPHS, 1983-92, chief physician officer, 1983-88; dir. C. Everett Koop Inst. Dartmouth Coll., Hanover, NH, 1992-94; prof. psychiatry Uniformed Svcs. U. Sch. Medicine, Bethesda, 1981-94, clin. prof., 1994—. Nat. and internat. surveyor Joint Commn. on Accreditation of Healthcare Orgns., 1998—; founder Integrative Healthcare Solutions; med. cons. Joint Comm. Internat.;internat. cons. Joint Comm. Internat. Author: Psychiatric Morbidity of Physicians, 1964, Psychiatric Issues in the Lives of Physicians, 1966, Child Psychiatry, 1972, 86, Psychiatric Reviews, 1976; founding editor-in-chief Child Psychiatry and Human Devel., 1970-83; editor: Ship's Medical Chest, 1984; mem. editl. bd. MD mag., 1976—. Recipient OutstandingSvc. medal Bd. Regents Uniformed Svcs. U., 1981, Surgeon Gen.'s medallion. Fellow Am. Psychiat. Assn. (life), Aerospace Med. Assn. (assoc.; Longacre medal), mem. Assn. Mil. Surgeons U.S., Sigma Xi. Catholic. Home: 2402 Golf Vista Blvd Viera FL 32955 Home Phone: 321-747-9210; Office Phone: 638-268-2900. Personal E-mail: jcduffy34@hotmail.com. Business E-Mail: jduffy@jcrinc.com.

DUFRESNE, CRAIG ROGER, plastic surgeon, educator; b. Newport, RI, Sept. 20, 1951; s. Roger Joseph and Molly T. Dufresne; m. Katherine Ann Scrive, Aug. 11, 1978; children: Jacqueline Melissa, Elizabeth Ashley, Christopher Scrive. BA in Zoology summa cum laude, U. Vt., 1973; MD, Columbia U., 1977. Diplomate Am. Bd. Plastic Surgery. Intern Johns Hopkins Hosp., Balt., 1977-78, jr., then sr. resident in surgery, 1978-82; registrar in thoracic surgery Frenchay Hosp., Bristol, Eng., 1980-81; jr. res., then sr. resident in plastic surgery NYU Med. Ctr., NYC, 1982-84, fellow in microvascular surgery, 1984, fellow in craniofacial surgery, 1985; asst. prof., dir. Ctr. for Reconstructive Surgery, Johns Hopkins U., 1985-89, dir. Cleft Lip and Palate Clinic, 1985-89, clin. asst. prof. to clin. assoc. prof. Balt., 1989—; pvt. practice, Fairfax and Annandale, Va., 1989—, Chevy Chase, Md., 1989—; dir. craniofacial program Inova Fairfax Hosp. for Children. Clin. instr. George Washington U., Washington, 1990-93; clin. assoc. prof. Georgetown U., Washington, 1994—; numerous presentations in field; chief plastic surgery svc. Loch Raven VA Med. Ctr., 1985-89; clin. assoc. in plastic surgery U. Md. Hosps., 1985-89; attending physician Md. Inst. for Emergency Med. Svcs. Ctr., 1985-89; mem. exec. com., and med. adv. bd. Internat. Craniofacial Found., 1990-92; co-dir. Ctr. for Facial Rehab., Fairfax Hosp., 1989—; vis. prof. U. Rochester, N.Y., 1992, Ea. Va. Med. Coll., Norfolk, 1993; cons. plastic surgery svc. Bethesda Naval Hosp. Co-editor: Complex Craniofacial Problems: Guide to Analysis and Treatment, 1992; contbr. numerous articles to med. jours., chpts. to books. Asst. scoutmaster troop 1449 Boy Scouts Am., Washington, 1994-95. Named One of Best 150 Drs. in Balt., Balt. Mag., 1986; One of Best Regional Breast Surgeons, The Washingtonian, 1986, One Best Plastic Surgeons in Washington Area, 1993, 95, One of Best Doctors in DC Region, Washington Family mag., 2007, also others; grantee AO/ASIF, Howmedica, Inc., Nat. Inst. Dental Rsch., Bowles Fund, Children's Hosp., Storz, Inc. Fellow ACS; mem. AMA, Am. Soc. Aesthetic Plastic Surgery, Am. Soc. Plastic Surgeons, Am. Cleft Lip and Palate Assn., Am. Soc. Plastic and Reconstructive Surgeons (govt. rels. com. 1989—), Internat. Soc. Craniomaxillofacial Surgery, Am. Soc. Maxillofacial Surgeons (govt. rels. com. 1990—, best paper award com. 1993—), Plastic Surgery Rsch. Coun., John Staige David Soc., John M. Converse Soc., Northeastern Plastic Surgery Soc. (sci. program com. 1992-93), Southeastern Med. Soc., Pan-Pacific Plastic Surgery Assn., Fairfax Med. Soc., Nat. Capital Med. Soc., Montgomery Med. Soc., Johns Hopkins Med. and Surg. Assn. Avocations: tennis, golf, art and sculpture. Office: 5530 Wisconsin Ave #1235 Chevy Chase MD 20815 Address: 8501 Arlington Blvd #420 Fairfax VA 22031 Home: 12217 Scarlet Tanager Dr Potomac MD 20854-8306

DUGAN, PATRICK RAYMOND, microbiologist, educator, dean; b. Syracuse, NY, Dec. 14, 1931; s. Francis Patrick and Joan Irma (Clause) D.; m. Patricia Ann Murray, Sept. 22, 1956; children: Susan Eileen, Craig Patrick, Wendy Shawn, Carolyn Paige. BS, Syracuse U., 1956, MS, 1959, PhD, 1964. Assoc. rsch. scientist Syracuse U. Rsch. Corp., 1956-63; mem. faculty Ohio State U., Columbus, 1964—, asso. prof., 1968-70, prof., chmn. dept. microbiology, 1970-73; acting dean Ohio State U. (Coll. Biol. Scis.), 1978-79, dean, 1979-85; prin. scientist EG&G Idaho Nat. Lab., Idaho Falls, 1987-91, sci. and engring. fellow, 1991-94, dir. Ctr. for Bioprocessing Tech., 1987-94; ret., 1994—. Cons., 1994—. Author: Biochemical Ecology of Water Pollution, 1972, Global Warming, a Layman's Guide to Issues, 2008. Trustee Columbus Zool. Assn. and Zoo, 1982—87. Fellow Am. Acad. Microbiology; mem. AAAS, Am. Soc. Microbiology (Ohio pres. 1968-70), Soc. Indsl. Microbiology, Am. Chem. Soc.

DUGAROV, ZHARGAL NIMAEVICH, biologist; b. Ulan-Ude, Nov. 13, 1959; DSc, Irkutsk State U., 1996. Biologist Tomsk State U., 1982. Sr. scientist Inst. Gen. and Exptl. Biology Siberian Br. Russian Acad. Scis., 1983—. Grant, Russian Found. Basic Rschrs. Mem.: Parasitologicheskoe Obzhestvo Russian Acad. Scis. Avocation: reading. Office: Sahjanovoi Ulan-Ude Respublica Buriatia 670047 Russia Business E-Mail: zhar-dug@biol.bscnet.ru.

DUGONI, ARTHUR A., dean emeritus, orthodontics educator; b. San Francisco, June 29, 1925; s. Arthur B. and Lina Maria (Bianco) D.; m. Katherine Agnes Groo, Feb. 5, 1949; children: Steven, Michael, Russell, Mary, Diane, Arthur, James. DDS, Coll. Physicians and Surgeons, San Francisco, 1948; MSD, U. Wash., 1963; BS, Gonzaga U., 1986; DHL honoris causa, U. Detroit, 1997. Diplomate Am. Bd. Orthodontics (bd. dirs., pres. 1979-86). Clin. instr. operative dentistry Coll. Physicians and Surgeons, San Francisco, 1951-55, asst. clin. prof. operative dentistry, 1955-60, asst. clin. prof. orthodontics, 1963-64, chair dept. orthodontics, 1963-67; assoc. prof. orthodontics U. Pacific, San Francisco, 1966-77, prof., 1977—, dean Sch. Dentistry, 1978—2006, dean emeritus, 2006. Chair coun. deans Am. Assn. Dental Schs., 1985; active Pew Commn. for the Health Professions, 1993-96. Recipient Disting. Svc. award San Mateo County Dental Soc., 1971, 1990, Disting. Svc. award Pacific Coast Soc. Orthodontists, 1976, Merit award, 1976, 2001, Disting. Practitioner award Nat. Acads. Practice Press Club, 1987, Hinman medallion, 1989, medallion of distinction U. Pacific, 1989, Orthodontic Edn. and Rsch. Found. disting. merit award, 1993, Albert H. Ketcham award Am. Bd. Orthodontics, 1994, Chmn.'s award Am. Dental Trade Assn., 1994, Dr. Irving E. Gruber award, 1997, List of Honor of FDI World Dental Fedn., 1998; named Person of Yr., South San Francisco, 1960, Alumnus of Yr., U. Pacific Sch. Dentistry, 1983, U. Wash., 1984, U. San Francisco, 1988, Gonzaga U., 1992, Gold medal Pierre Fauchard Acad., 1996, Callahan Internat. award Ohio Dental Assn., 1999, William J. Gies award Am. Coll. Dentists, 2001, Excellence in Dentistry award 13th Dist.'s Internat. Coll. Dentists, 2002, Willard C. Fleming Meritorious Svc. award No. Calif. sect. Am. Coll. Dentists, 2003, Arthur A. Dugoni Lifetime Achievement award Alumni Assn. U. Pacific, Arthur A. Dugoni Sch. Dentistry, 2006; named Arthur A. Dugoni Sch. Dentistry in his honor U. Pacific, 2004. Fellow Pierre Fauchard Acad., Acad. Dentistry Internat. (Internat. Dentist of Yr. 2005), Acad. Gen. Dentistry (hon.); mem. ADA (trustee 1984-87, treas. 1987-88, pres. 1988-89, Found. pres., Pres.'s citation 1994, 99, Disting. Svc. award 1995), Fedn. Dentaire Internat. (councilor 1989-98, treas. 1992-98, List of Honour 1999), Am. Assn. Dental Schs. (pres. 1995, Disting. Svc. award 2000), Calif. Dental Assn. (pres. 1982-83, Dist. Svc. award, 1978, Dale F. Redig Dist. Svc. award, 2003), Am. Dental Assn. (found. pres. 2003-), Peninsula Golf and Country Club, Phi Kappa Phi, Omicron Kappa Upsilon, Tau Kappa Omega, Xi Psi Phi. Republican. Roman Catholic. Avocation: golf. Office: U Pacific Arthur A Dugoni Sch Dentistry 2155 Webster St San Francisco CA 94115-2333 Business E-Mail: adugoni@pacific.edu.

DUGOSH, JEREMY W., medical editor, writer; b. Jourdanton, Tex., Aug. 15, 1972; s. Alfred A. and Deborah L. Dugosh; m. Karen Leggett, Apr. 4, 1998; 1 child, Ezra W. BA summa cum laude, Tex. A&M U., 1995; MS, U. Tex. Arlington, 1998, PhD, 2001. Rsch. asst. U. Tex., Arlington, 1995—98, rsch. assoc., 1998—2001; editor Am. Bd. Internal Medicine, Phila., 2001—05, sr. editor, 2005—10, sr. mng. editor, 2010—. Contbr. articles to profl. jours. Mem.: Coun. Sci. Editors, Am. Ednl. Rsch. Assn., Nat. Coun. Measurement Edn., Am. Med. Writers Assn. Avocations: rock climbing, hiking, art, mountain biking. Home: 413 S Iseminger St Philadelphia PA 19147 Office: Am Bd Internal Medicine 510 Walnut St Ste 1700 Philadelphia PA 19016

DUKE, EDWARD MARION, III, (MICKEY), health facility administrator, consultant; s. Edward M. Duke, Jr. and Margueritte M. (Young) Duke; m. Sharon Diane Page, June 21, 1968; 5 children. AB in Social Sci., San Diego State U., 1970; M in Urban Planning, U. Oreg., 1974. Exec. dir. Oreg. Dist. 4 Health Planning Coun., Corvallis, Oreg., 1972—76, Lane County Med. Soc., Eugene, Oreg., 1976—82; dep. dir., pub. affairs Oreg. Med. Assn., Portland, 1983; dir. med. delivery sys. Health Plan of Am., Emeryville, Calif., 1983—85; exec. dir. med. affairs Sierra Health Svcs., Las Vegas, 1985—94; sr. dir. managed care, we. region Universal Health Svcs., Las Vegas, 1994—2002; CEO Oasis Health System, LLC, Las Vegas, 2002—. Pres. E.M. Duke & Assocs., LLC, Henderson, Nev., 2002—; adj. faculty, guest lectr., healthcare adminstrn. program U. Nev., Las Vegas; guest spkr., workshop presenter various symposia. Contbr. articles to profl. newsletters, jours. Dist. com. commr. Boy Scouts of Am., Boulder Dam Coun., Las Vegas, 2002—05. Mem.: Healthcare Fin. Mgmt. Assn. (pres. Nev. chpt. 2005—06, lead author HFMA Nat. Managed Care Cert. Exam Study Guide 2007—08, region II, regional exec. 2009—10, Follmer Bronze award 2001, Reeves Silver award 2003, Muncie Gold award 2005, Honor medal 2008). Avocations: bicycling, woodworking. Office: Oasis Health System 8801 W Sahara Ave Las Vegas NV 89117-5865 Office Phone: 702-493-0606, 702-894-5549. Personal E-mail: edwardmduke@aol.com.

DUKE, SCOTT A., public health service officer; b. Bethesda, Md., Nov. 13, 1962; BBA, Minot State U., 1987, MS in Mgmt., 2000. Diplomate Am. Coll. Healthcare Execs., 2002. Regional mgr. Team Care, Inc. Med. Arts Clinic, PC, 1993—96, asst. adminstr., 1996—98; dir. physician svcs. Mercy Med. Ctr., 1998—2000, v.p. clinic and ancillary svcs., 2000—02; CEO Glendive Med. Ctr., 2002—. Chair Mont. Health Network, 2002, Dawson County Econ. Devel. Coun., 2004; bd. mem. Mont. Hosp. Assn., 2003; bd. dirs. Am. Hosp. Assn. Bd., 2011. Recipient Regent's award, Am. Coll. Healthcare Execs. Mem.: Dawson County Bd. Health, Glendive Noon Lions Club. Avocations: hunting, fishing. Office: 202 Prospect Dr Glendive MT 59330 Office Fax: 406-345-3378. Business E-Mail: jwoods@gmc.org.

DUKE, STEPHEN OSCAR, physiologist, research scientist, educator; b. Battle Creek, Mich., Oct. 9, 1944; s. Oscar and Azalee Rosa (Tallant) D.; m. Barbara Alice Rowe, June 2, 1967 (div. Dec. 1993); children: Gregory Ivan, Robin Anne; m. Mary Virginia Duke, Jan. 18, 2009. BS, Henderson State U., 1966; MS, U. Ark., 1969; PhD, Duke U., 1975; PhD (hon.), U. Basque Countray Bilbao, 2008. Plant physiologist So. Weed Sci. Lab., USDA, Stoneville, Miss., 1975-84, rsch. leader, 1984-87, lab. dir., 1987-96, rsch. leader Oxford, Miss., 1996—. Adj. prof. U. Miss., Oxford, 1996—. Co-author: Physiology of Herbicide Action, 1993; editor: Weed Physiology, 2 vols., 1985, Pest Control with Enhanced Environmental Safety, 1993, Porphyric Pesticides, 1994, Herbicide Resistant Crops, 1995, Natural Products for Pest Management, 2006; contbr. articles to profl. jours. Lt. US Army, 1968—70, Vietnam. Decorated Bronze Star; recipient Edminster award USDA, 1986, Disting. Alumnus award Henderson State U., 1989, CIBA-GEIGY/Weed Sci. Soc. Am. award CIBA-GEIGY Corp., 1990, Outstanding Sr. Scientist award USDA, Agr. Rsch. Svc., 2001, Extraordinary Prof. award U. Pretoria RSA, 2002-, Molisch award Internat. Allelopathy Soc.; elected Henderson State U. Acad., 2001. Fellow AAAS, Weed Sci. Soc. Am. (assoc. editor 1978-83, pres. 1996, Outstanding Young Scientist award 1984, Outstanding Article award 1984, Rsch. award 1990); mem. Am. Soc. Plant Physiology (chmn. so. sect. 1985-86), Coun. for Agrl. Sci. and Tech. (bd. dirs. 1993-94), Am. Chem. Soc.(Internat. Rsch. award agrochem. divsn. 2004), So. Weed Soc. (pres. 1995, disting. svc. award 1998), Internat. Weed Sci. Soc. (pres. 2000-04), Internat. Allelopathy Soc. (pres. 2008—). Avocations: gardening, writing. Home: 9 Private Rd 3078 Oxford MS 38655 Mailing: PO Box 3964 University MS 38677 Business E-Mail: sduke@olemiss.edu.

DUKES, DEBORAH FEAGANS, counseling administrator; b. Ashland, Ky., June 13, 1952; d. Robert Geary and Anna Louise (McCalvin) Feagans; m. J.W. Buckner, May 22, 1982 (div. Dec. 1989); 1 child, Zachary Robert; m. Jeffery Miram Dukes, May 24, 1996. AA in English, U. S.C., 1972, BA in Psychology, 1974; MA in Profl. Counseling, Liberty U., 1995. Lic. profl. counselor, nat. cert. counselor, S.C. cert. addictions counselor II, nat. cert. addictions counselor II. Clin. counselor State of S.C. Dept. Mental Health, Columbia, 1976-84; alcohol and drug safety action program coord. Rubicon Counseling Ctr., Hartsville, S.C., 1984-87, adolescent counselor, 1986-87; clin. counselor Aiken (S.C.) Ctr. for Alcohol and Drug Abuse, 1987-95; clin. coord. Mentor Inc., Aiken, 1995-96; dir. Shiflet Ctr. John de la Howe Sch., McCormick, S.C., 1996-2000; counselor, dir. child, adolescent, family divsn. Aiken-Barnwell Mental Health Ctr., 2000—09; mgr. inpatient clin. svcs. Ga. Health Scis. U., Med. Coll., 2009—. Mem. adv. bd. Darlington County Youth Home, 1984-87; mem. Darlington County Treatment Adv. Team, 1986-87; mem. dist. core team Aiken County Student Assistance Program, 1990-96; mem. McCormick Cmty. Coordinating Coun., 1996-2000; chair parent adv. coun. John de la Howe Sch., 1996-2000. Mem. child task force Aiken County, 2001—04, mem child advocacy com., 2005—09, mem truancy task force, 2006—08. Mem.: Nat. Assn. Alcohol and Drug Abuse Counselors, SC Assn. Alcohol and Drug Abuse Counselors (Counselor of Yr. 2002). Avocations: reading, swimming, refinishing furniture, quilting. Personal E-mail: jaddukes@gforcecable.com.

DULA, KARL, surgeon, researcher, radiologist, educator; b. Marburg, Hessen, Germany, Mar. 6, 1955; s. Hans Friedrich and Alwine Dula; m. Marianne Ulrike Koch, Apr. 15, 1977; children: Niklas Michael, Jannik Oliver. BS, 1974, DMD, 1982. Asst. prof. sect. oral radiology U. Berne, Switzerland, 1996—99, acting head dept., 1999—2000, assoc. prof., 2001—, head dept., 2001—. Mem. internat. team oral implantology, 1992—; rschr. Fed. Bur. Health (BAG), Berne, 1994—; vis. rsch. prof. dept. oral and maxillofacial radiology U. Amsterdam, 1995—96. Author: (Journal title) Der Ein-fluss verschiedener Zahnbürsten und Zahnreinigungstechniken auf die interdentale Belagsentfernung ohne und mit festsitzenden kieferorthopädischen Apparaturen , 1984, Chirurgische und kieferorthopädische Aspekte zur Erhaltung retinierter Zähne bei der Therapie der Odontome. , 1987, Vergleichende klinische und röntgenologische Untersuchungen nach Antrocystektomien von Kiefercysten., 1988, Zur Häufigkeit und histologischen Differenzierung odontogener Tumoren im Wachstumsalter., 1991, Localized Ridge Augmentation using Guided Bone Regeneration. I. Surgical Procedure in the Maxilla., 1993, Localized ridge augmentation using guided bone regeneration. II. Surgical procedure in the mandible., 1995, Lateral Ridge Augmentation using Autografts and e-PTFE Membranes. A Clinical Study with 40 Partially Edentulous Patients., 1996 (Daniel M. Laskin Award 1997 for the most outstanding article published in J Oral Maxillofac Surg JOMS in 1996.), Longterm stability of osseointegrated implants in bone regenerated with a membrane technique. 5-Year results of a prospective study with 12 implants., 1996, Hypothetical mortality risk associated with spiral computed tomography of the maxilla and mandible., 1996, Hypothetical mortality risk associated with spiral tomography of the maxilla and mandible prior to endosseous implant treatment., 1997, Effects of dose reduction on the detectability of standardized radiolucent lesions in digital panoramic radiography., 1998, Clinical experience with one stage, non submerged dental implants., 1999, Comparatative dose measurements by spiral tomography for preimplant diagnosis: The Scanora machine versus the Cranex Tome radiographic unit., 2001, The radiographic assessment of implant patients- decision making criteria., 2001, Longterm Stability of Osseointegrated Implants in Augmented Bone. 5-Year Prospective Study in Partially Edentulous Patients., 2002, (Book chapter) Localized ridge augmentation using guided bone regeneration. In: Buser D, Dahlin C, Schenk RK(eds.): Guided bone regeneration in implant dentistry. Quintessenz Publishing Co., Inc., Chicago (1994) pp. 189-233, 1994, Funktionsweise von zahnärztlichen Röntgengeräten. In: Lambrecht J Th (ed.): Kompendium für den zahnärztlichen Sachverständigen im Strahlenschutz. Publishing house Schweizerische Zahnärzte-Gesellschaft SSO, Bern, Schweiz, 1997., 1997, Einstelltechnik in der zahnärztlichen Radiologie. In: Lambrecht J Th (ed.): Kompendium für den Zahnärztlichen Sachverständigen im Strahlenschutz. Publishing house Swiss Society of Odontology SSO, Bern, Schweiz, 1997., 1997, Bildqualität konventioneller und digitaler Röntgenaufnahmetechniken. In: Lambrecht J Th (ed.): Kompendium für den Zahnärztlichen Sachverständigen im Strahlenschutz. Publishing house Schweizerische Zahnärzte-Gesellschaft SSO, 1997, The loss of image quality in digital panoramic radiography using image compression. In: Farman AG, Ruprecht A, Gibbs SJ, Scarfe WC (eds.): Advances in Maxillofacial Imaging. Elsevier, Amsterdam-Lausanne-New York, 1997, 1997, OralSurgery, Oral Medicine, Oral Implantology. In: Schweizerische Zahnärzte-Gesellschaft SSO (ed.):

Quality standards in dentistry. Stämpfli AG, Berne, 2000, 2000. Mem.: Swiss Soc. Oral Surgery and Stomatology, European Assn. Osseointegration, Internat. Assn. Dentomaxillofacial Radiology, Swiss Soc. Dentomaxillofacial Radiology (treas. 1987—95, v.p. 1996—2000, pres. 2001—02, del. 2000—), German Soc. Odontology, Swiss Soc. Odontology (mem. Commn. Dental Expert in Radiation Protection 1994—97, mem. working groups 1994—, del. 2000). Office: U Berne Dept Oral Surgery Freiburgstrasse 7 3010 Berne Switzerland Office Phone: 031 632 49 30. Business E-Mail: karl.dula@zmk.unibe.ch.

DULBECCO, RENATO, biologist, educator; b. Catanzaro, Italy, Feb. 22, 1914; arrived in U.S., 1947, naturalized, 1953; s. Leonardo and Maria (Virdia) D.; m. Gulseppina Salvo, June 1, 1940 (div. 1963); children: Peter Leonard (dec.), Maria Vittoria; m. Maureen Rutherford Muir; 1 child, Fiona Linsey. BS in Pathology, U. Torino, Italy, 1932, MD, 1936; DSc (hon.), Yale U., 1968, Vrije U., Brussels, 1978, Ind. U., 1984, U. Bologna, 1988; LLD (hon.), U. Glasgow, Scotland, 1970. Tchr. U. Torino, 1940—43, neurology scholar, 1943—47; bacteriology scholar Ind. U., Bloomington, 1947-49; sr. rsch. fellow Calif. Inst. Tech., 1949-52, assoc. prof., then prof. biology, 1952-63; sr. fellow Salk Inst. Biol. Studies, San Diego, 1963-71; asst. dir. rsch. Imperial Cancer Rsch. Fund, London, 1971-74; dep. dir. rsch. Imperial Cancer Research Fund, 1974-77; disting. prof. cancer rsch. Salk Inst. Biol. Studies, La Jolla, Calif., 1977—2006, pres., 1989-92, pres. emeritus, 1993—. Vis. prof. Royal Soc. Great Britain, 1963—64; mem. Calif. Cancer Adv. Coun., 1963—67; mem. adv. bd. Roche Inst., Nutley, NJ, 1968—71, Inst. Immunology, Basel, Switzerland; Dunham lectr. Harvard U., 1972; prof. pathology and medicine U. Calif. San Diego Sch. Medicine, 1977—81; dir. Italian Genome Project, Italian Nat. Rsch. Coun., 1992—95, pres. Biomedical Technologies, 1995—2006; mem. vis. com. Case Western Res. Sch. Medicine, Cleve. Author: Virology, 1980, The Design of Life, 1987; editor: Encyclopedia of Human Biology, 1991; contbr. articles to profl. jours. Trustee La Jolla Country Day Sch., Am.-Italian Fedn. Cancer Rsch.; bd. mem. sci. counselors dept. etiology Nat. Cancer Inst. Recipient John Scott award, City of Phila., 1958, Kimball award, Conf. Pub. Health Lab. Directors, 1959, Albert & Mary Lasker Basic Med. Rsch. award, 1964, Howard Taylor Ricketts award, 1965, Paul Ehrlich-Ludwig Darmstaedter prize, 1967, Louisa Gross Horwitz prize, Columbia U., 1973, Nobel prize in physiology/medicine, 1975, Mandel Gold medal, Czechoslovak Acad. Scis., 1982, Via de Condotti prize, 1990, Natale Di Roma prize, 1993, Columbus prize, 1993, S. Ambrogio medal, City of Milan, 1993, Italian TV Spl. Oscar, 1999; named Man of Yr., London, 1975, Italian Am. of Yr., San Diego County, 1978; named an Hon. Citizen, City of Imperia, Italy, 1983, City of Arezzo, Italy, City of Catanzaro, Italy, City of Torino. Mem.: NAS, Am. Acad. Arts and Scis., Fedn. Am. Scientists, Royal Soc. (fgn.), Academia Nazionale del Lincel (fgn.), Am. Philos. Assn., Internat. Physicians for Prevention Nuclear War, Am. Assn. Cancer Rsch., Comitato di Collaborazione Culturale (hon.), Academia Ligure di Scienze e Lettre (hon.), Alpha Omega Alpha. Office: Salk Inst PO Box 85800 San Diego CA 92186-5800 also: National Research Council Piazzale Aldo Moro 7 00185 Rome Italy Office Phone: 858-453-4690. *

DUMA, RICHARD JOSEPH, epidemiologist, writer, microbiologist, pathologist, physician, researcher, educator; b. Bethlehem, Pa., Apr. 2, 1933; s. Joseph Anthony and Helen Veronica (Bartek) D.; m. Mary Alyce Fridley, Apr. 18, 1957; 1 child, Scott. BA, Va. Poly. Inst., 1955; MD, U. Va., 1959; PhD, Va. Commonwealth U.-Med. Coll. Va., 1978. Diplomate Am. Bd. Internal Medicine, lic. physician, Fla., Va.; lic. pvt. pilot. Intern, then resident in medicine U. Ala. Med. Center, Birmingham, 1959-60, 62-65; research fellow Harvard U. Med. Sch.-Mass. Gen. Hosp., 1965-67; mem. faculty Med. Coll. Va., Richmond, 1967-91, chmn. div. infectious diseases, 1974-92, prof. medicine and pathology, 1975-92, prof. microbiology, 1977-92. Mem. U. S. Pharmacopeia Adv. Panel on Hosp. Practices, 1971-82, chmn. subcom. rsch., 1976-82, clin. prof. medicine and infectious diseases Med. Coll. Richmond, 1992—; exec. dir. Nat. Found. for Infectious Diseases, 1991-94, v.p. bd. dirs., 1973-75, pres., 1975-91, trustee, 1994-2003, bd. dirs., 2004—09; dir. emeritus, 2010-, chmn. Nat. Coalition for Adult Immunization, 1988-94; didr. infectious diseases and infection control Halifax Med. Ctr., Daytona Beach, Fla., 1995—, editl. bd. mem., Infectious Diseases Clin. Practice (editl. bd. mem. 2005-). Mem. bd. visitors Embry-Riddle Aero. U., 1999—. Served with M.C., USNR, 1960-62. Fellow ACP, Infectious Disease Soc. Am., Royal Soc. Tropical Medicine and Hygiene, Am. Soc. Tropical Medicine and Hygiene, Am. Soc. Rickettsiology, Fla. Infectious Disease Soc. (pres. 1997-99, bd. dirs. 1997-), Fla. Dept. Health Hosp. Acquired Infections (adv. bd. mem.); mem. AAAS, Am. Fedn. Clin. Rsch., Am. Soc. Microbiology, Va. Soc. Microbiology, Am. Soc. Internal Medicine, Va. Soc. Internal Medicine, Richmond Soc. Internal Medicine, So. Soc. Clin. Investigation, Am. Thoracic Soc., Royal Soc. Medicine, Med. Soc. Va., Richmond Acad. Medicine, Acad. of Medicine, Washington, Med. Assn. Fla., Volusia Med. Soc., Daytona Beach Rotary Club, Hammock Dunes Golf & Country Club,, Sigma Xi, Tau Beta Pi. Home: 1 Capri Ct Palm Coast FL 32137- Office: Halifax Medical Ctr 303 N Clyde Morris Blvd Daytona Beach FL 32114-2700 Office Phone: 386-258-4871. Business E-Mail: rjduma@att.net, richard.duma@halifax.org.

DUMANIAN, GREGORY A., surgeon; b. Rochester, Minn., Oct. 7, 1961; BA, Harvard Coll., 1983; MD, U. Chgo. Med. Sch., 1987. Cert. Am. Bd. Surgery, 1993, Am. Bd. Plastic Surgery, 1998, Added Qualification Hand Surgery, 1998, lic. Ill. Surgeon Rehab. Inst. Chgo., Children's Meml. Hosp., VAMC Lakeside, Evanston Northwestern Healthcare, Shriner's Hosp. Children, Northwestern Meml. Hosp.; asst. prof. surgery divsn. plastic surgery Northwestern U. Feinberg Sch. Medicine, 1996—2004, assoc. prof. surgery divsn. plastic surgery, 2004—, program dir. divsn. plastic surgery, 2005, assoc. prof. surgery dept. neurosurgery, 2007. Program dir., gen. surgery Mass. Gen. Hosp., 1986—92; rsch. fell., plastic maxillofacial and reconstructive surgery divsn. U. Pitts., 1992—93, resident plastic surgery, 1993—95; fell., hand surgery, divsn. chmn. Union Meml. Hosp., Baltimore, Md., 1995—96. Contbr. articles to numerous profl. jours. Recipient Excellence in Tchg. award, Dept. Surgery, 2002—06; co-recipient DaVinci award, Ford Motor Co., 2005. Fellow: Am. Coll. Surgery; mem.: Plastic Surgery Rsch. Coun., Lymphology Soc., Am. Soc. Plastic Reconstructive Surgery. Office: Divsn Plastic Surgery 675 N St Clair Ste 19-250 Chicago IL 60611 Office Phone: 312-695-6022. Business E-Mail: gdumania@nmh.org.

DUMAS, SANDRA LEE, medical technician, microbiologist; b. Amsterdam, NY, Nov. 15, 1949; d. Richard Carl and Eunice Yetive Teschka; children: Stacey Ann Warner, Joseph William Hodlin; m. C. Clifford Jr. A in Clin. Lab. Sci., Empire State Coll., Saratoga Springs, NY, 1987, BS in Biology, 1991. Cert. clin. lab. scientist Nat. Cert. Agy. for Med. Lab. Pers.; lic. lab. tech., NY. Med. tech. Johnstown (N.Y.) Hosp., 1968-70, Nathan Littauer Hosp., Gloversville, N.Y., 1967-68, med. tech. in microbiology, 1975—. Mem.: ASCP. Avocations: painting, golf, boating, photography.

DUMITRASCU, DAN L., medical educator; b. Cluj, Romania, Feb. 5, 1957; MD, U. Medicine and Pharmacy, Cluj, 1982; PhD, Iuliu Hatieganu U. Medicine and Pharmacy, Cluj, 1995. Prof., medicine Iuliu Hatieganu U. Medicine and Pharmacy, Cluj-Napoca, Romania, 2007—. V.p. European Soc. Clin. Investigation; pres. Romanian Soc. Neurogastroentreology. Recipient Internat. Rsch. award, Internat. Found. Functional Gastrointestinal Disorders, Milw., 2005. Avocations: stamp collecting/philately, art. Office: 2nd Med Dept Clinicilor 2-4 Cluj RO 400 003 Romania Business E-Mail: dumitras@cluj.astral.ro.

DUMITRESCU, CRISTINA M., intensive care nurse; b. Bucharest, Romania, Mar. 5, 1960; d. Mircea and Margareta Ispas; m. Gabriel N None, June 6, 1989. Degree in biochem. rsch. mgmt., C.A. Rosetti, Bucharest, 1980, BSc in Biochemistry, 1981; ADN, Walla Walla CC, 1986; BS, U. Wash., 1988. RN Wash., 1986, lic. advance cardiac life support, Medic 7 Dist. Snohomish County, 1996. Biochem. rschr. Pharm. Co. Bucharest, Romania, 1981—82; registry relief nurse Kimberly Quality Care, Seattle, 1986—92; RN/charge nurse Swedish Med. Ctr., Seattle, 1988—93; home care ventilator nurse Nurse's Ho. Call, Seattle, 1989—94; registry relief nurse Amserv Western Med., Seattle, 1990—95; case mgr./mktg. dir. Vis. Nurse Svcs., Seattle, 1991—96; ICCU/CO RN Stevens Med. Ctr., Edmonds, Wash., 1996—; ICU RN Cascade Valley Hosp., Wash., 2008—. Marketer Vis. Nurse, Seattle, 1991—96; cmty. health care cons. Walla Walla DSHS, 1986; exec. sec./office mgr. Musica Romanica Inc., Seattle, 2000—; property mgmt. Dumitrescu Fourplex, Kent, Wash., 2002—; cmty. svc. dir. Seventh Day Adventist Ch., Seattle, 1992—. Contbr. articles to profl. jours. Dir. allocation of cmty. resources Cmty. Services Ctr., Seattle, 1992; project mgr. Helping Hands of Am., Seattle, 1993—94, Cmty. Services SDA, Snohomish, Wash., 1994—95. Mem.: NAFE (Excellence in Nursing award 2001), Walla Walla Businesswoman's Assn., U. Wash. Alumni Assn., Sigma Theta Tau Internat. Office: Musica Romanica LLC PO Box 1471 Edmonds WA 98020 Office Phone: 206-228-2873. Personal E-mail: montliv@gmail.com.

DUMITRU, DANIEL, physiatrist; b. Massillon, Ohio; MD, U. Cin., 1980. Diplomate Am. Bd. Phys. Medicine and Rehab. Resident phys. medicine and rehab. VA Hosp., San Antonio, 1980—83; prof. U. Tex. Health Sci. Ctr., San Antonio, 1983—. Attending physician Audie Murphy Vets. Hosp., San Antonio. Mem.: Am. Assn. Neuromuscular and Electrodiagnostic Medicine, Am. Acad. Phys. Medicine and Rehab. (pres. 2002—03). Office: U Tex Health Sci Ctr Dept RM/PMR 7703 Floyd Curl Dr San Antonio TX 78229-3900

DUMMETT, CLIFTON ORRIN, dentist, educator; b. Georgetown, British Guiana, May 20, 1919; s. Alexander Adolphus and Eglantine Annabella (Johnson) Dummett; m. Lois Maxine Doyle, Mar. 6, 1943; 1 child, Clifton Orrin Jr. BS in Psychology, Roosevelt U., Chgo., 1941, DDS, Northwestern U., 1941, MScD, 1942, DSc (hon.), 1976; MPH, U. Mich., 1947; ScD (hon.), U. Pa., 1978; DSc (hon.), Meharry Med. Coll., 2004. Diplomate Am. Bd. Periodontology, Am. Bd. Oral Medicine. Dean, prof. periodontology Meharry Med. Coll., Nashville, 1945-49; chief dental service VA Hosp., Tuskegee, Ala., 1949-65, assoc. chief staff for rsch. and edn., 1958-65, chief dental service Chgo., 1965-66; dental dir., dir. ctr. Watts Health Ctr., LA, 1966-69; assoc. dean, chmn. dept. cmty. dentistry U. So. Calif. Sch. Dentistry, LA, 1969-75, prof., 1969-89, prof. emeritus, 1989-96, disting. emeritus prof., 1997—. Adj. prof. Northwestern U. Dental Sch., 1989; vis. prof., cons. Sch. Vet. Medicine Tuskegee Inst., 1962—65; vis. prof. Meharry Med. Coll., 1989—; trustee Am. Fund Dental Health, Chgo., 1968—78; chem. devel. component rev. panel Calif. Regional Med. Programs, LA, 1975—77; mem. Pres.'s Com. Nat. Health Ins., 1977; sr. reviewer US Surgeon Gen. Report Oral Health, 2000. Author: The Growth and Development of the Negro in Dentistry in the United States, 1952, Proceedings of the First Institute of Public Health in the South, 1952, Community Dentistry, 1974, Afro-Americans in Dentistry: Sequence and Consequence of Events, 1977, Charles Edwin Bentley, 1982, Dental Education at Meharry Medical College: Origin and Odyssey, 1992, Culture and Education in Dentistry at Northwestern University, 1993, NDA.II The Story of America's Second National Dental Association, 2000, (editl.) Nor Yet the Last, 1962 (W.J. Gies award, 1963), The Hillenbrand Era, 1986; editor: Nat. Dental Assn., 1953—75; contbr. chapters to books, more than 300 articles to profl. jours. Chmn. adv. bd. Econ. and Youth Opportunity Agy. Project Head Start, Tuskegee, Ala., 1964—65; mem. spl. health adv. com. Calif. Bd. Edn., LA, 1972—74; mem. L.A. regional hearing planning coun. Pres.'s Com. on Health Edn., LA, 1973—74. Lt. col. USAF, 1955—58. Recipient Alumni Merit award, Northwestern U., 1971, Fones Gold medal, Conn. Dental Assn., 1976, Pierre Fauchard Gold medal, Pierre Fauchard Acad., 1980, Lifetime Achievement award, U. Md., 2000, John R. Callahan award, Ohio Dental Assn., 2003, Presdl. award, U. Southern Calif, 2005, Legend award, Nat. Dental Assn., 2008; named to, U. So. Calif. Dental Hall of Fame, 1997. Fellow: AAAS (chmn. dental sect. 1975—76, 1987—88), APHA (v.p. for U.S. 1995—96, John W. Knutson Disting. Svc. award 1992), Am. Acad. History of Dentistry (pres. 1982—83, Hayden and Harris award 1987), Internat. Coll. Dentists; mem.: ADA (hon.), Am. Dental Edn. Assn. (Presdl. citation 2003), Inst. Medicine of NAS (sr. mem.), Nat. Acads. Practice (Disting. Practitioner 1987), Am. Assn. Dental Editors (editor 1963—72, pres. 1974—75, Disting. Svc. medal 1976), Assn. Mil. Surgeons (life), Internat. Assn. Dental Rsch. (pres. 1969—70), Am. Coll. Dentists (Wm. J. Gies award 1992, Salute of Coll. 1988), Sigma Xi, Omicron Kappa Upsilon (pres., founder Nashville chpt. 1947—49), Delta Omega, Alpha Phi Alpha, Sigma Pi Phi. Democrat. Episcopalian. Avocations: music, politics, track. Home: 5344 Highlight Pl Los Angeles CA 90016-5119 Office: U So Calif Sch Dentistry PO Box 77006 Los Angeles CA 90007-0006

DUMONT, ALLAN ELIOT, retired physician, educator; b. NYC, Oct. 8, 1924; m. Joan Auerbach, Oct. 1, 1949; children: Mark E., James A., David H. BA, Hobart Coll., 1945; MD, NYU, 1948. Diplomate Am. Bd. Surgery. Intern Bellevue Hosp., NYC, 1948-49, resident, 1949-51, 53-54, chief resident, 1954-55; instr. surgery NYU, 1955-59, asst. attending surgeon Univ. Hosp., asst. vis. surgeon 3d and 4th surg. divs. Bellevue, 1955-60, asst. prof. surgery, 1959-62, assoc. vis. surgeon 3d and 4th surg. div. Bellvue, 1961-65; attending surgeon Manhattan VA Hosp., NYC, 1958-67, cons. surgeon, 1967-90; assoc. attending surgeon Univ. Hosp. NYU, 1961-68, attending surgeon, 1968-90, assoc. prof. surgery, 1962-68, prof. surgery, 1968-73, Jules Leonard Whitehill prof. surgery, 1973-90, prof. emeritus, 1990—; clin. prof. surgery U. Conn. Sch. Medicine, 1991. Career scientist N.Y.C. Health Research Council, 1959-62; univ. senate NYU, 1966-69; vis. surgeon Bellevue Hosp., 1965-90, assoc. dir. surg. service, 1975-90. Editor: Lymphology. 1974-84. Served to lt (j.g.) USN, 1951-53. Recipient Research Career Devel. award USPHS, 1961-71, Purkinje medal, Czechoslovakia, 1977. Mem. Am. Coll. Surgeons, New Eng. Surg. Soc., Harvey Soc., N.Y. Surg. Soc. (pres. 1987-88), Am. Physiol. Soc., Soc. Univ. Surgeons, Soc. for Surgery Alimentary Tract, Internat. Soc. Lymphology (pres. 1979-83), Am. Surg. Assn.

DU MONT, NICOLAS, psychiatrist, educator; b. San Juan, Dec. 22, 1954; s. Joseph Henri and Isabel (Solano) Du M. Postgrad. adult psychiatry, Columbia U., 1990; MD, U. P.R., 1986; postgrad. child, adolescent psychiatry, Columbia U., 1992, postgrad. pub. cmty. psychiatry, 1993. Assoc. prof. Polytech. U., San Juan, 1984-88, InterAm. U., San Juan, P.R., 1986-87; med. dir. Holistic Med. Ctr., NYC, 1993-94; asst. prof. Albert Einstein Coll. of Medicine, NYC, 1991-96, Mt. Sinai Sch. of Medicine, NYC, 1993-96, Columbia Physicians and Surgeons Coll. Medicine, NYC, 1997—; asst. attending physician Elmhurst Med. Ctr., NYC, 1993-94; asst. physician Mt. Sinai Med. Ctr., NYC, 1993-96; v.p., CEO Engring. Med. Support, Inc., NYC, 1992—; asst. prof. Columbia Physicians and Surgeons Coll. Medicine, NYC, 1997—. Attending physician Westchester Jewish Med. Svcs., Hartsdale, N.Y., 1990-95, Montefiore Med. Ctr., N.Y.C., 1991-96, Albert Einstein Coll. Medicine, 1991-96, Puerto Rican Family Inst., 1994—; asst. attending physician and med. dir. Tavares Hispanic Mental Health Clin. at Columbia Presbyn. Med. Ctr., 1997—. Mem. editl. bd.: Jour. Pagan Studies, NY edit., 1990—. Vis. fellow N.Y. State Psychiat. Inst., 1992-93. Mem. Assn. Hispanic Mental Health Profls. (exec. bd. dirs. 1999-2003, sr. advisor, 2003—, treas.). Office: Engring Med Support Inc 200 W 70th St Ste 8F New York NY 10023-4326 Home Phone: 212-721-5374; Office Phone: 212-787-8168. Business E-Mail: notes@dumont.org, nd5@columbia.edu.

DUNAGIN, WILLIAM G., dermatologist; b. Topeka, Oct. 2, 1950; s. Jack Allison and Muriel Elaine Dunagin. MD, U. Kans., Kansas City, 1975. Diplomate Am. Bd. Dermatology, 1979. From asst. to assoc. prof. medicine U. Mo., Columbia, 1979—85; chief dermatology VA Hosp., Columbia, 1979—85; pvt. practice Franklin, Pa., 1985—. Summerfield scholar, U. Kans., 1968—72. Fellow: Pa. Acad. Dermatology, Am. Acad. Dermatology; mem.: Am. Conifer Soc., Phi Beta Kappa, Alpha Omega Alpha. Achievements include research in DNCB immunotherapy of verruca resistant to common treatment modalities.

DUNAVAN, CLAIRE PANOSIAN See PANOSIAN, CLAIRE

DUNAWAY, FRANK ROSSER, III, emergency physician; b. Albuquerque, Sept. 2, 1953; s. Frank Rosser and Constance (Durham) D.; m. Marcia Lee Moore, May 24, 1975 (dec. 2006); children: Melissa Sommer, Amanda Durham, Vanessa Lee; m. Amy Jane Rutledge, Apr. 7, 1990; children: Kiera Elizabeth Eirwyn, Reagan Kailean Maira. BS, Duke U., 1975; MD, U. Ill., 1988; M in Theol. Studies, Nashotah House Theol. Sem., 2009. Diplomate Nat. Bd. Med. Examiners, Am. Bd. Emergency Medicine, 1993, 2003. Resident inspector nuclear engr. U.S. Nuclear Regulatory Commn., Glen Ellyn, Ill., 1982-84; resident emergency physician St. Francis Med. Ctr., Peoria, Ill., 1988-91; attending emergency physician Qualified Emergency Specialists Inc., Cin., 1991-93; med. dir. emergency svcs., chmn. dept. emergency medicine Proctor Hosp, Peoria, 1993—2007; attending emergency physician Proctor Hosp., Peoria, 1993—2009, assoc. chmn. interventional dept., 1997—99; v.p. Proctor Emergency Physicians, P.C., Peoria, 1995-97, pres., 1997—2007; consulting physician Hyperbaric Medicine, Peoria, 1996—2000; med.-legal cons. in emergency medicine, 1998—; attending emergency physician Methodist Med. Ctr. Ill., Peoria, 2007—. Mem. faculty Ill. Coll. Emergency Physicians Oral Bd. Rev. Course, 1995—, AHA, 1985—; chmn. dept. emergency medicine Proctor Hosp., 1993—2007; assoc. project med. dir. Peoria Area Emergency Med. Svcs., 1994—2007, Canon to Ordinary, Diocese Quincy Anglican Ch. N. Am., 2010—. Contbr. articles to profl. jours. Priest-in-charge St. Andrews Ch., El Paso, Ill., 2009—; standing com. mem. Diocese Quincy Anglican Ch. N.Am., SC, 2009—, standing com. pres., 2010—; bishop's warden St. Paul's Episc. Cathedral, 2006—07; ordained deacon Anglican Ch., 2008, ordained priest, 2009; vicar St. Johns Ch., Henry, Ill., 2009—. Lt. USN, 1975—82, capt. USNR, 1982—2002. Fellow: Am. Coll. Emergency Physicians; mem.: SAR, Shriners, Masons. Republican. Anglican. Avocations: skiing, sailing, scuba, backcountry canoeing. Office Phone: 309-672-5500.

DUNBAR, ROBERT EVERETT, writer, educator; b. Quincy, Mass., Nov. 24, 1926; s. Charles Wheeler Dunbar and Eva Emma Duquette; m. Thelma Rose Arseneault, June 26, 1954 (div. Apr. 1986); children: Jesse Robert, Yvett Maria. BA, Marietta Coll., 1951; MS, Northwestern U., 1954. Asst. editor publs. Continental Assurance Co., Chgo., 1954—57; dir. comm. Jr. Achievement, Chgo., 1957—58; editor Nat. Sporting Goods Assn., Chgo., 1958—67; dir. comm. Am. Soc. Anesthesiologists, Park Ridge, Ill., 1967—70; dir. pub. info. divsn. Am. Fund for Dental Health, Chgo., 1970—74; owner Dunbar Editl., Nobleboro and Gardiner, Maine, 1974—; internet bookseller Christiesplus, Gardiner, Maine, 2004—. Instr. U. Health Sci., Chgo. Med. Sch., 1973—74, adj. asst. prof., 1974—75; judge HS debate tournaments, 1992—2003; judge nat. tournament Cath. Forensic League, 1995. Columnist: Maine Life Mag., 1981—86; author: Learning How to Cope with Arthritis, Rheumatism, and Gout, 1973 (Beth Fonda award for Excellence, Chgo. area chpt., Am. Med. Writers Assn., 1974), How to Debate, 1987, (15 books including) Homosexuality, 1996 (named one of the Notable Books of 1996, Nat. Coun. Social Studies and Children's Books Coun., 1996), (books for musicals) Vaudeville Gold, 1987, Friends and Lovers, 1988, Folk and Fancy, 1991; co-author: (stage adaptation) It's A Wonderful Life, 1986; actor, singer (plays and musicals) various cmty. theatres, 1984—;, singer ann. concerts. A founder, interim pres., first elected pres. Saint Andrew's Soc. Maine, 1980—81; vol. Maine State Music Theater, 1995—2008, Portland Stage Co., 1998—2009; first selectman Nobleboro, Maine, 1977—78. With USN, 1944—45. Fellow:

Am. Med. Writers Assn. (pres. Chgo. area chpt. 1970—71, gen. chmn. ann. meeting 1971, nat. co-chmn. edn. com. 1971—75, founder, chmn. organizing com. New Eng. chpt. 1975—76, treas. New Eng. chpt. 1976—77, Judith Linn mem. award com. 2001—, judge nat. book awards, judge Will Solermine awards New Eng. chpt.); mem.: DAV (life), Thoreau Soc., Authors Guild, New Eng. Sci. Writers, Nobleboro Hist. Soc. (pres. 1978—79, applefest publicity 2006—08, oral history project 2006—07), Gaslight Theater. Republican. Roman Catholic. Achievements include design of two courses in scientific writing, one basic, one advanced, for The School of Related Health Sciences and The University of Health Sciences/Chicago Medical School. Avocations: singing, acting, writing. Home and Office: 552 Water St Gardiner ME 04345 Business E-Mail: reddunbar@gmail.com.

DUNBAR-JACOB, JACQUELINE, dean, nursing educator, researcher; b. Detroit, Jan. 7, 1942; d. Donald and Margaret Jean (Henderson) Brashley; m. Rolf G. Jacob, Jan. 1, 1989. Diploma, Presbyn. U. Hosp. Sch. Nursing, 1962; BS, Fla. State U., 1968; MS, U. Calif., San Francisco, 1969; PhD, Stanford U., 1977. RN; lic. psychologist Calif., Pa., Fla. Asst. prof. U. Iowa, Iowa City; deputy dir. behavioral sci. Stanford U., Calif.; dir. nursing Western Psychiat. Inst. and Clinic, Pitts.; joined as assoc. prof., dir. rsch. U. Pitts. Sch. Nursing, 1984, founding dir. Ctr. Nursing Rsch., 1987—96, prof. nursing, psychology, epidemiology, and occupl. therapy, dir. Ctr. Rsch. in Chronic Disorders, dean, 2001—. Chair adv. bd. Bayer Inst. Health Care Communication; mem. health career futures exec. adv. bd. Jewish Healthcare; past pres. Acad. Behavioral Medicine Rsch.; bd. mem. Assn. Adults and Children with Learning Disabilities, Beckwith Inst. Innovative Patient Care; mem. quality patient care com. U. Pitts. Med. Ctr. Presbyn. Shadyside, univ. mem. on the bd. dirs. Contbr. numerous articles to profl. jours. Healthcare adv. bd., Rep. T. Murphy US House of Reps.; mem. health profls. study group Pa. Dept. Health, edn./student retention task force; mem. leadership coun. Pa. Ctr. Health Careers, Pa. Workforce Investment Bd. Fellow Am. Acad. Nursing, Soc. Behavioral Medicine (mem. com. 1979, 82-85, publ. com. 1989, 90, program com. 1980, 85, 90, bd. mem. at large 1981-84, editor Behavioral Medicine Update 1982-85, chair edn./tng. com. 1984-85, sec./treas. 1985-88, past pres.); mem. ANA (coun. on rsch. 1984—, coun. adminstrn. 1985-87, bd. dirs.), Soc. Epidemiol. Rsch., Am. Heart Assn., APA Health Psychology Divsn. (program com. 1983, abstract rev. com. 1984), Assn. Advancement Behavior Therapy (program com. 1977, 87, 89), Soc. Clin. Trials (bd. dirs. 1990-93), Am. Diabetes Assn. (ad hoc com. 1983-84, abstract rev. com. 1984-85), Sigma Theta Tau, Phi Kappa Phi. Office: U Pitts Sch Nursing 350 Victoria Bldg 3500 Victoria St Pittsburgh PA 15261 Office Phone: 412-624-7838. Office Fax: 412-624-2401. E-mail: dunbar@pitt.edu.

DUNCALF, DERYCK, retired anesthesiologist; b. York, Eng., Nov. 14, 1926; arrived in U.S., 1956; s. Hubert Claude and Anne Elizabeth D.; m. Mira Novakovic, July 23, 1978; children: Richard Michael, Tamara, Sharon. MB, ChB, U. Leeds, 1950. Diplomate Am. Bd. Anesthesiology. Resident in anesthesia St. James Hosp. and Gen. Infirmary, Leeds, 1950-54, Cardiff Royal Infirmary, Wales, 1954-56; fellow faculty anaesthetists Royal Coll. Physicians and Surgeons, 1954; fellow in anesthesiology Mercy Hosp., Pitts., 1956-57, Montreal Children's Hosp., Que., Can., 1958-59; staff anesthesiologist Kings County Hosp., Bklyn., 1959-62, Montefiore Med. Ctr., Bronx, 1962-97, chmn. dept. anesthesiology, 1975-85; prof. anesthesiology Albert Einstein Coll. Medicine, Bronx, 1971-97, vice-chmn. dept. anesthesiology, 1985-94, emeritus prof., 1997—. Cons. Wyckoff Heights Hosp., Bklyn., 1966-85. Author: (with D.H. Rhodes) Anesthesia in Clinical Ophthalmolgy, 1963; contbr. articles to profl.jours. Fellow Am. Coll. Anesthesiologists; mem. Am. Soc. Anesthesiologists, N.Y. State Soc. Anesthesiologists, Pan Am. Med. Assn. (diplomate and hon. life mem. sect. anesthesiology), Assn. Univ. Anesthetists, Ecuatoriano de Anesthesiologia (hon.). Home: 33 Ferncliff Rd Cos Cob CT 06807-1206 Personal E-mail: ulphus@gmail.com.

DUNCAN, NEWTON O., otolaryngologist, educator; MD, Baylor Coll. of Medicine, 1978; B in Biol. Sciences, Stanford U., Palo Alto, Calif.; postgrad., Letterman Army Med. Ctr., San Francisco, Calif. Diplomate Am. Bd. Otolaryngology, 1986. Resident surgery Baylor Coll. of Medicine, Houston, 1982—83, resident otolaryngology, 1983—86, asst. clin. prof. depts. of otorhinolaryngology and pediats., chief resident dept. of otorhinolaryngology and communicative sciences; intern gen. surgery Letterman Army Med. Ctr., San Francisco, Calif.; fellow pediatric otolaryngology Univ. of Wash., Seattle, 1990—91, Royal Alexandra Hosp. for Children, Sydney, 1991—92; hosp. affiliations include Texas Children's Hosp., St. Luke's Episcopal Hosp., The Meth. Hosp., Columbia Women's Hosp., Doctors' Surg. Ctr. Decorated Army Commendation medal US Army, Meritorious Svc. medal; named one of the Best Doctors in America, 1996—, the America's Top Doctors, 2000. Fellow: ACS, Am. Acad. of Pediats., Am. Soc. of Pediatric Otolaryngology, Am. Acad. of Otolaryngology - Head and Neck Surgery; mem.: AMA, Am. Cleft Palate-Craniofacial Assn., Harris County Med. Soc., Soc. for Ear, Nose and Throat Advances in Children. Office: Baylor College of Medicine One Baylor Plz Houston TX 77030 Office Phone: 713-798-4951.

DUNEA, GEORGE, nephrologist, educator; b. Craiova, Rumania, June 1, 1933; came to U.S., 1964; s. Charles L. and Gerda (Low) D.; 1 dau., Melanie. MD, U. Sydney, Australia, 1957. Diplomate Am. Bd. Internal Medicine, Am. Bd. Nephrology. Intern Royal North Shore Hosp., Sydney, 1958—59; resident internal medicine Australia, 1959—63, England, 1959—63; fellow in nephrology Cleve. Clinic, Presbyn.-St. Luke's Hosp., Chgo., 1964—66; practice internal medicine specializing in nephrology Chgo., 1972—; attending physician Cook County Hosp., Chgo., 1966—, dir. dept. nephrology-hypertension, 1969—2009; prof. medicine U. Ill., Chgo., 1986—; pres., CEO Hektoen Inst. of Med. Rsch., Chgo., 1991—; emeritus founding chmn. Stronger Hosp. Cook County. Vis. prof. medicine Rush Med. Sch., Chgo., 1976—. Contbr. chpts. to books, articles to profl. pubs. Fellow A.C.P., Royal Coll. Physicians (London, Edinburgh); mem. AMA, Am. Soc. Nephrology, Brit. Med. Assn., Soc. Med. History. Office: 222 East Chestnut St Chicago IL 60611 Personal E-mail: gdu222@yahoo.com.

DUNGAN, JOHN RUSSELL, JR., (12TH VISCOUNT DUNGAN OF CLANE, HEREDITARY PRINCE OF FERMOY AND ARRA), anesthesiologist, health facility administrator; b. Boston, Dec. 12, 1953; s. John Russell and Nancy Pauline (Beaton) Dungan; m. Nancy Elizabeth Perkins, July 12, 1986 (div. 1997); children: Elizabeth Adelaide, Thayer Warren, Eleanor Grace Appleton. AB magna cum laude, Harvard U., 1977, EdM, 1978; DDS, Baylor U., 1984; MD cum laude, Creighton U., 1989. Diplomate Nat. Bd. Anesthesiology (dir. 1989-92, 97-, v.p. 1997-), Am. Acad. Pain Mgmt. Instr. anesthesiology Boston U. Sch. Medicine, 1987—88; attending staff anesthesiologist, residency instr. Boston City Hosp., 1986-89; anesthesiologist, chief Tobey Hosp., Wareham, Mass., 1990—91; chief anesthesia Mary Lanning Hosp., Hastings, Nebr., 1991—, chief surgery, 1995, 2001; pres. Hastings Anesthesiology Assocs., 1992—; med. dir. Hastings Surg. Ctr., 2006—. Author: The Kings of the Picts and Dál Riads, 1976, The Beatons, 1976, Angus MacDonald, 1977; contbr. articles to profl. jours. Rschr. nat. trust Restoration of Celbridge Chapel and Cemetery, Kildare, Ireland, 1995. Named to, Honorable Order Ky. Cols.; 13th head and comdr., Mil. Order Knights of Leinster (estab. 1645), John Eliot scholar, 1966, Nat. Merit scholar, 1971, Harvard Coll. scholar, 1976, John Harvard scholar, 1975, 1977. Mem.: Soc. Interventional Pain Physicians (pres. 2003—), Adams County Med. Soc. (pres. 2001—), Nebr. Soc. Anesthesiologists, Am. Soc. Anesthesiologists, Cum Laude Soc. (Tabor chpt.), United Empire Loyalists Assn. (Can.), New Eng. Hist. Geneal. Soc., N.Y. Irish History Roundtable, English-Speaking Union U.S. (Internat. fellow 1971—72), N.Y. Biog. and Geneal. Soc., Harvard Club Nebr., Clan Dungan (clan chief, pres. 1998—), Wild Geese, Old Tonbridgian Soc., Hasty Pudding Inst. 1770, Phi Beta Kappa. Republican. Episcopalian. Avocation: history. Home: Heartwell Park 923 N Elm Ave Hastings NE 68901-4021 Office: Hastings Anesthesiology Ste 101 420 W 5th St Hastings NE 68901-7551 Business E-Mail: jdungan@inebraska.com.

DUNKER, STEPHAN WERNER WILHELM, ophthalmologist, researcher; b. Frankfurt am Main, Hessen, Germany, Mar. 4, 1967; m. Ute Reuter, July 21, 1995; children: Konstanze, Marie. MD, Johann Wolfgang Goeteh U., Frankfurt am Main, 1993. Specialized dr. in Ophthalmology 1999. Intern Philipps U. Marburg; resident Marburg, Graz, Bonn; ophthalmologist, rschr. Philipps U., Marburg, Hessen, Germany, 1993—94, Med. U., Graz, Steiermark, Austria, 1994—95, U. So. Calif., LA, 1995—96, Rheinische Friedrich-Wilhelms U., Bonn, Germany, 1997—2000; ophtholmologist pvt. practice, 2000—. Basketball team sponsor Skyliners, Frankfurt, Germany, 2004—08; sci. advisor German Orgn. of Eye Diagnostic Ctrs., Berlin, 2003—07. Grantee Rsch. grant, German Rsch. Soc., 1995, 1996, 1997; Rsch. fellowship, 1995—98. Mem.: Am. Acad. Ophthalmology (assoc.), Assn. Rsch. in Vision and Ophthalmology (assoc.), German Ophthal. Soc. (assoc.), Assn. of Ophthalmologists (assoc.). Achievements include invention of fundus imaging network; subretinal fluid analysis; discovery of structures of the peripheral vitreoretinal interface. Office Fax: 00492241391188. Business E-Mail: dunker@augenarzt-troisdorf.de.

DUNLAP, ROBERT WILLIAM, retired internist, cardiologist, educator; b. Detroit, Oct. 5, 1939; MD, U. Mich., 1964. Diplomate Am. Bd. Internal Medicine, Am. Bd. Cardiovasc. Medicine. Intern U. Calif. Med. Ctr., 1964-65; resident in internal medicine Mayo Grad. Sch. Medicine, Rochester, Minn., 1965-67, fellow in cardiovasc. disease, 1967-69; cons. cardiologist Keesler AFB, Miss., 1969-71; chief cardiologist Harkness Hosp., San Francisco, 1971-72; mem. active staff St. Mary's Med. Ctr., San Francisco, 1973—, chief cardiology, 1974-80, chief medicine, 1981-86; pvt. practice, cardiology, San Francisco, 1998; assoc. clin. prof. U. Calif., San Francisco. Mem. active staff Seton Med. Ctr., Daly City, Calif., chief medicine, 1992-94, pres.-elect med. staff, 1994-96, chief staff, 1996-98; cons. Cath. Healthcare West (CHW) Bay Region, San Francisco, 1998-99, med. dir. care mgmt., 1999-2005, mem. quality com., 2000-2006; mem. courtesy staff St. Francis Hosp. Fellow ACP, Am. Coll. Cardiology; mem. Alpha Omega Alpha. *

DUNN, DAVID W., psychiatrist, educator; b. Oxford, Miss., June 11, 1948; BA, Tulane U., 1969, MD, 1973. Prof., psychiatry, neurology Ind. U., 1984—, arthur b. richter prof. child psychiatry, 1998—. Recipient Tchg. award, Ind. U., Excellence award, Am. Psychiat. Assn. Home: 702 Barnhill Dr ROC 4300 Indianapolis IN 46202 Business E-Mail: ddunn@iupui.edu.

DUNN, LINDA KAY, retired physician; b. Grand Rapids, Mich., Jan. 11, 1947; d. Roger John and Mary Kathryn (Bouwer) Kloote; m. Jeffrey Marc Dunn, June 3, 1972; children: David Alan, Kathryn Ann. AB in Chemistry, Hope Coll., 1968; MD, U. Mich., 1972. Diplomate Am. Bd. Ob-Gyn, Am. Bd. Maternal-Fetal Medicine, Am. Bd. Med. Genetics. Resident in ob-gyn. U. Mich., Ann Arbor, 1972-75, fellow in maternal-fetal medicine, 1975-77; hon. rsch. registrar St. Mary's Hosp., London, 1977-78; dir. of perinatology Temple U. Sch. Medicine, Phila., 1978-79, assoc. prof. ob-gyn, 1991-97; dir. subsect. on genetics Pa. Hosp., Phila., 1980-90; pres Medigen, Inc., Phila., 1987-90; dir. maternal-fetal medicine and genetics Abington Meml. Hosp., Pa., 1991-97; dir. maternal-fetal medicine, chair dept. ob-gyn. Allegheny U., 1997—99; pres., CEO Allegheny U. Hosp. at City Av.; chair dept. ob-gyn. Chestnut Hill Hosp., Phila., 1999—2007; ret., 2007. Med. dir. Comprehensive Maternal and Infant Svcs., Phila., 1987-90; pres. Abington Perinatal Assocs., P.C., 1993-97. Fellow Am. Coll. Ob-Gyn.; mem. Soc. Maternal Fetal Medicine, Am. Coll. Med. Genetics, Phila. Obstet. Soc., U. Mich. Med. Ctr. Alumni Soc. (chair 1996), Norman Miller Gynecologic Soc. (pres. 1996). Mem. Soc. Of Friends. Avocations: travel, piano. Personal E-mail: dunn.lk@gmail.com.

DUNN, MICHAEL J., former dean; m. Patricia O'Reilly; 5 children. MD, Med. Coll. of Wisconsin, 1962. Intern Johns Hopkins Hosp, Baltimore, 1962—63, resident, 1963—65; asst. prof. & co-dir., nephrology unit U. Vermont Coll. Medicine, 1969—77; various pos. Case Western Reserve, 1977—95; dean, prof. of med. and exec v.p. Med. Coll. Wis., Milw., 1995—2008, dean emeritus, disting. prof. medicine & physiology and dir. of translational rsch. resources office, 2008—. Grantee Fogarty Senior International Fellow. Mem.: Am. Soc. Nephrology (pres. 1989—90). Office: Med Coll Wis 8701 W Watertown Plank Rd Milwaukee WI 53226-3548 Office Phone: 414-955-2524. Business E-Mail: mdunn@mcw.edu. *

DUNN, STEPHEN PHILIP, surgeon; b. Bloomington, Ind., June 1, 1952; BA, Wash. U., 1974; MD, Ind. U., 1978. Chief, pediatric surgery & solid organ transplantation Nemours Clinic's, Wilmington, 2000—. Office: 1600 Rockland Rd Wilmington DE 19899 Office Fax: 302-651-5990. Business E-Mail: sdunn@nemours.org.

DUNN, WILLIAM F., medical association administrator; b. Bellefonte, Pa., Jan. 12, 1958; BS, Penn State U., 1980; MD, Jefferson Med. Sch., 1980. Pulmonologist, intensivist Mayo Clinic, 1989—2011, med. dir., 10-3 multidisciplinary ICU, 1991—2003, program dir., multidisciplinary critical care fellowship, 1991—2006, med. dir., Multidisciplinary Simulation Ctr., 2005—. Past pres. Soc. Simulation Healthcare, 2008—09. Recipient Excellence in Teamwork award, Mayo Clinic, Innovations in Edn. award, Karis award. Fellow: Soc. Critical Care Medicine, Am. Coll. Chest Physicians. Avocation: winemaking. Office: 200 1st St SW Rochester MN 55905 Business E-Mail: dunn.william@mayo.edu.

DUNNE, MYRA SCHLEY, nurse, consultant; b. Stamford, Conn., June 10, 1950; d. Charles Henry and Myra Catherine Schley; m. Frank Edward Dunne, May 23, 1981 (div. Sept. 23, 1997); children: Elizabeth Anne, Michael Edward. BSN, Sacred Heart U., 1972, MBA, 1989. Cert. case mgr. Commn. for Case Mgr. Cert., Rolling Meadows, Ill., 1997, legal nurse cons. Am. Legal Nurse Cert. Bd., Chgo., 2001. Nurse case mgr. CNA Ins., Quincy, Mass., 1996—2000; med. cons. Encompass Ins., Quincy, 2000—05; with Blue Cross Blue Shield Mass., Rockland, 2005—. Trainer Encompass Ins., Quincy, 2003—. Vol. Boston Rescue Mission, 2004—. Mem.: Am. Assn. Legal Nurse Cons. (assoc.). Democrat. Roman Catholic. Avocations: walking, yoga, weightlifting, ballroom dancing. Home: 23 Smith Rd Hingham MA 02043 Office: Blue Cross Blue Shield 1030 Hingham St Rockland MA 02370 Business E-Mail: myra.dunne@bcbsma.com.

DUNNER, DAVID LOUIS, medical educator; b. Bklyn., May 27, 1940; s. Edward and Reichel (Connor) D.; m. Peggy Jane Zolbert, Dec. 27, 1964; children: Laura Louise, Jonathan Michael. AA, George Washington U., 1960; MD, Washington U., St. Louis, 1965. Diplomate Am. Bd. Psychiatry and Neurology. Intern Phila. Gen. Hosp., 1965-66; resident in psychiatry Barnes Renard Hosp. of Washington U., St. Louis, 1966-69; rsch. psychiatrist NY State Psychiat. Inst., NYC, 1971—79; from asst. prof. to assoc. prof. clin. psychiatry Columbia U., NYC, 1972-79; chief psychiatry Harborview Med. Ctr., Seattle, 1979-89, dir. outpatient psychiatry, 1989-97; prof. psychiatry and behavioral scis. U. Wash., Seattle, 1979—2006, prof. emeritus, 2006—, vice chmn. clin. svcs., 1989-97; dir. Ctr. for Anxiety & Depression, 1997—; pvt. practice psychiatry, 2006—. Cons. Found. for Depression and Manic Depression, NYC, 1974—. Editor-in-chief Comprehensive Psychiatry, 1997—; contbr. articles to profl. jours. Served to lt. comdr. USPHS, 1969-71. Fellow Am. Psychiat. Assn., Am. Psychopathol. Assn. (pres. 1986), Am. Coll. Neuropsychopharmacology, West Coast Coll. Biol. Psychiatry (charter, pres. 1987); mem. Psychiat. Research Soc. (pres. 1984). Office: Ctr for Anxiety & Depression 7525 SE 24th St Ste 400 Mercer Island WA 98040 Office Phone: 206-230-0330. E-mail: dldunner@comcast.net.

DUNNICK, N. REED, physician, radiologist, educator; b. Waukegan, Ill., Aug. 23, 1943; s. Paul A. and Marceil H. (Reed) D.; children: Cory, Amanda. BS, Purdue U., 1965; MD, Cornell U., 1969. Intern, resident U. Rochester, N.Y., 1969-71; resident Stanford U., Palo Alto, Calif., 1973-76; mem. staff NIH, Bethesda, Md., 1976-80; mem. faculty Duke U., Durham, N.C., 1980-92; chair dept. radiology, prof. U. Mich., Ann Arbor, 1992—. Author: A Practical Approach to Angiography, 1987, Endourology, 1988, Textbook of Uroradiology, 1991. Served to lt. comdr. USPHS, 1971-73. Mem. Soc. Uroradiology (pres. 1990-91), Soc. Computed Body Tomography (pres. 1991-92), Am. Coll. Radiology, Am. Roentgen Ray Soc. (exec. coun. 1989-98), Assn. Univ. Radiologists (exec. com. 1996-), Soc. Chmn. Acad. Radiology Depts. (pres. 1998-99), American Bd. Radiology (pres. 2009-2010). Office: U Mich Dept Radiology 1500 E Medical Center Dr Ann Arbor MI 48109-0005

DUNNING, PATRICIA LYNETTE (TRISHA DUNNING), nurse, researcher; b. Inverell, NSW, Australia, Dec. 19, 1946; d. Walter William and Rene Madge Brown; m. John Hayward Dunning, Aug. 29, 1970; children: Tracey-Leigh, Althea, Justin James Edward. MEd, PhD, Deakin U. RN Australia. Nurse Inverell Dist. Hosp., Sydney, 1968; midwife The Bankstown Hosp., 1969; nurse Royal Alexander Hosp., 1970, St. Vincent's Hosp., Melbourne, 1981—85, nurse cons. diabetes, 1985—2001; prof. endocrinology, rsch. diabetes nursing U. Melbourne, 2001—07; inaugural chair nursing Deakin U. and Barwon Health, 2007—. Mem. Nurses Bd. Victoria, 2002—04. Author: Care of People with Diabetes 3rd edit., 2009, Care of Older People with Diabetes, 2005, Complementary Therapies in the Management of Diabetes and Vascular Disease, 2006, (book) Essential Oils in Therapeutic Care, 2007, Managing Clinical Problems in Diabetes, 2008, short stories. Counselor Youth for Understanding, Melbourne, 1980—84. Decorated Order of Australia. Fellow: Royal Coll. Nursing Australia (life; disting. mem. 2011); mem.: IDF Consultative Sect. on Diabetes Edn. (chair 2009—), Internat. Diabetes Fedn. (v.p. 2009—, past chair edn. sect.), Australian Plant Soc., Australian Diabetes Educators Assn. (sec., pres.), Order Australia Assn. (life), Sigma Theta Tau. Avocations: Australian plants, horseback riding, reading, Asian cooking, writing. Office: Kitchener House The Geelong Hosp Ryrie St 3220 Geelong VIC Australia Home Phone: 61 03 52811974; Office Phone: +61 03 52465113. Business E-Mail: trisha-dunning@barwonhealth.org.au.

DUNPHY, EDWARD JAMES, science educator, crop extension specialist; b. Frederick, Md., Nov. 14, 1940; s. Edward John and Marie W. (Barlow) D.; m. Judith Kay Mitchell, Aug. 18, 1962; children: Kevin James, Brian Patrick, Cory Edward. MS, U. Ill., 1964; PhD, Iowa State U., 1972. Rsch. asst. U. Ill., Urbana, 1962-64; agronomist Dunphy's Feed & Fertilizer, Sullivan, Ill., 1964-66; rsch. asst. Iowa State U., Ames, 1969-72, crop prodn. specialist Des Moines, 1972-75; extension specialist soybeans N.C. State U., Raleigh, 1975—, prof. crop sci., 1986—. Instr. soybean prodn. N.C., 1975—; mem. N.C. Land Use Value Adv. Bd., Raleigh, 1987—. Author 4 computer programs; contbr. numerous articles to profl. jours. Cubmaster Boy Scouts Am., Raleigh, 1976-81, troop com. chair, 1979-98; officer Athens Dr. Band Boosters, Raleigh, 1983-90. Sgt. U.S. Army, 1966-69. Recipient Meritorious Svc. award N.C. Soybean Producers. Fellow Am. Soc. Agronomy (bd. mem., com. chair, Agronomic Extension Edn. award); mem.Crop and Soil Sci. Socs. Am., Am. Soybean Assn. (Ext. Edn. award, mem. S.Am. soybean mission), Coun. Agrl. Sci. and Tech., Internat. Cert. Crop Advisers (bd. mem., com. chair), Alpha Zeta, Epsilon Sigma Phi, Gamma Sigma Delta, Phi Eta Sigma, Phi Kappa Phi, Sigma Xi. Achievements include research on soybean varieties, production, management and econ. Home: 3708 Swift Dr Raleigh NC 27606-2572 Office: NC State U Box 7620 Raleigh NC 27695-7620 Office Phone: 919-515-5813. E-mail: jim_dunphy@ncsu.edu.

DUNSIRE, DEBORAH, pharmaceutical executive; b. 1963; arrived in US, 1994; MD, U. Witwatersrand, South Africa; DSc (hon.), Worcester Polytechnic U. Gen. practitioner, South Africa; clinical rschr. Sandoz (now Novartis), 1988, head mktg. and sales of specialty brands, Basel, Switzerland, 1991; sr. v.p. oncology bus. unit Novartis AG, 1996—2000; head N.Am. oncology ops. Novartis Pharmaceuticals Corp., 2000—05; pres., CEO Millennium Pharmaceuticals, Inc., Cambridge, Mass., 2005—. Bd. dirs. Allergan Inc., 2006—. Recipient Rising Star award, Health Care Business Women's Assn., 2000, Excalibur Award, American Cancer Soc., 2001, Corporate Leadership award, Multiple Myeloma Rsch. Found. (MMRF), 2009, Creative Spirit award, Creative Ctr. for Women; named Woman of the Yr., Healthcare Businesswomen's Assn., 2009. Office: Millennium Pharmaceuticals Inc 40 Landsdowne St Cambridge MA 02139

DUNSKER, STEWART B., neurosurgeon; b. Cin. s. Shiel and Tillie Dunsker; m. Ellen Lothian Treiman, July 2, 1966. BA, Harvard U., 1956; MD, U. Cin., 1960. Diplomate Am. Bd. Neurol. Surgery (pres.). Intern U. Ill., Chgo., 1960-61; resident in internal medicine U. Cin., 1961-62, resident in gen. surgery, 1964-65; resident in neurol. surgery Washington U., St. Louis, 1965-69; prof. clin. neurosurgery U. Cin.; treas. Mayfield Clinic, Cin. Capt. U.S. Army, 1962-64. Fellow: ACS; mem.: Am. Bd. Neurol. Surgeons (vice chair), Am. Acad. Neurol. Surgeons (v.p.), Am. Assn. Neurol. Surgeons (pres., Harvey Cushing medal 2003), Ohio State Neurosurg. Soc. (pres.), Soc. Univ. Neurosurgeons (pres.), Ohio State Med. Assn. (pres., Ohio Neurosurgeon of Yr. 1992, Evans award 1998). Office: Mayfield Clinic 2123 Auburn Ave # 441 Cincinnati OH 45219-2906

DUNSON, WILLIAM ALBERT, biology professor, ecological consultant; b. Cedartown, Ga., Dec. 17, 1941; s. James Blake and Eleanor (Adams) D.; m. Margaret E. Kvashay, Aug. 19, 1963; children: Mary Elizabeth, William Albert, David Brian. BS in Zoology with honors, Yale U., 1962; MS, U. Mich., 1964, PhD, 1965. Teaching fellow U. Mich., Ann Arbor, 1962-63; mem. faculty Pa. State U., University Park, 1965—, prof. biology, 1974 97, prof. emeritus, 1997—; environ. scientist Seminole Tribe Fla., 1997—2002. Adj. prof. biology U. Miami, Old Dominion U., Fla., Atlantic U. (now Atlantic Coll.); chief scientist various internat. oceanographic expdns.; collaborator Everglades Nat. Park. Author: The Biology of Sea Snakes, 1975; contbr. over 140 articles to profl. jours. Queens marine sci. fellow, 1972, hon. Fulbright fellow, 1972; grantee NSF, U.S. Dept. Interior, U.S. Geol. Survey, U.S. EPA. Mem. Soc. for Study Amphibians and Reptiles (jour. edit. bd.). Achievements include study of ecotoxicology, physiological ecology and wetlands ecology. Office: 577 State Shd Ln Galax VA 24333 Business E-Mail: wad4@psu.edu.

DUNST, KARIN MARIA, surgeon; b. Wr. Neustadt, Austria, Jan. 27, 1972; d. Herbert Gottfried and Theresia Dunst; life ptnr. Georg Michael Huemer. MD, Med. U. Vienna, Vienna, 2000. Resident cardiac surgery Med. U. Innsbruck, Austria, 2002—. Contbr. articles various scientific jours. Home: Untere Hauptstrasse 20 Sieggraben 7223 Austria Personal E-mail: karin.dunst@gmx.at.

DUPAGNE, NESTOR L., gynecologist, oncologist, surgeon; b. Tillier, Namur, Belgium, June 29, 1922; s. Jules and Irma (LaFalize) DuP.; m. Lucy Chatelain, Dec. 26, 1948; children: Michel, Alan. MD, U. Liege, 1948, DDS, 1949. Intern St. Barnabas Hosp., Newark, N.J., 1953-54; resident in obstetrics Margaret Hague, Jersey City, 1954-55; resident in surgery Dr.'s Hosp., NYC, 1955; resident in ob-gyn. Woman's Hosp., NYC, 1955-59; gynecologist, oncology surgeon Brussels, Belgium, 1960—. Fellow ACS; mem. N.Y. Acad. Sci. Avocation: bicycling. Home and Office: 15 Rue du Village 1450 Chastre Belgium Home Phone: 010 65 5212.

DUPIN, JOÃO BOSCO, cardiologist, educator; b. São Sebastião do Maranhão, Jan. 10, 1948; Physician Faculty Scis. Médicas Minas Gerais, 1977, surgeon 1979. Prof. Faculdade Medicina Vale do Aço, 1999—. Master: Founda. Cardiovasc. São Francisco Assis. Avocation: music. Office: Caviuna 206 Ipatinga Minas Gerais 35160295 Brazil Office Fax: 55 31 3824 6060. Business E-Mail: dupinjb@terra.com.br.

DUPLESSIS, HERMAN J.C., surgeon; b. Johannesburg, Feb. 3, 1950; s. Nicolaas Jacobus and Anna Maria Elizabeth DuPlessis; m. Hester Lucia Gous DuPlessis, Dec. 8, 1973; children: Anneke, Nicolaas Jacobus. MB, BChir, U. Pretoria, 1975, MMed in Surgery, 1984. Intern Mil. Hosp., Pretoria, South Africa, 1975—76, med. officer, 1976—79; surgery registrar Pretoria Acad. Hosp., 1980—84; surgeon cons. Mil. Hosp., 1985—88; col. South African Mil. Health Svcs., 1988—2010; chief surgery, head dept. Mil. Hosp., 1989—2010, head multi ICU, 1996—2010. ICU cons. Kalafong Hosp., Pretoria, 1996—, Pretoria Acad. Hosp., 1994—, surgery cons., 1994—; bd. dirs. Unitas Hosp., 2000—06. Contbr. articles to jours. Recipient Southern Cross medal, SANDF, 1998, Mil. Merit medal, 1992, SG Commendation cert., SAMHS, 1989, 1995. Fellow: ACS (gov., South Africa 2006—); mem.: SAMA (pres., Gauteng North Br. 2002, pres., Gauteng Notrh Br. 2008), Critical Care Soc. South Africa (pres. 1993—94), Trauma Soc. South Africa (pres. 1996—99). Avocations: running, clay target shooting, photography, birdwatching, travel. Office: Dept Surgery Sch Medicine University Pretoria Po Box 667 Pretoria 001 South Africa Business E-Mail: colon@ananzi.co.za.

DUPONT, ANNABELLE, pharmacist; b. Mamers, Sarthe, Apr. 30, 1973; Med. biologist, pharmacist MCU-PH, EA 2693 Faculté de Médecine, 2005. Office: EA 2693 Faculté de Médecine Pole Recherche Lille Nord Pas De Calais 59045 France Business E-Mail: annabelle.dupont-2@univ-lille2.fr.

DUPONT, HERBERT LANCASHIRE, medical educator, researcher; b. Toledo, Nov. 12, 1938; s. Robert L. and Martha (Lancashire) DuPont; m. Margaret Wright, June 9, 1963; children: Denise Lorraine, Andrew Wright BA, Ohio Wesleyan U., 1961; MD, Emory U., 1965; doctorate (hon.), U. Zurich, 2004. Diplomate Am. Bd. Internal Medicine. Resident U. Minn. Med. Ctr., Mpls., 1965-67; officer epidemic intelligence svc. CDC Atlanta, infectious disease fellow U. Md. Sch. Medicine, Balt., 1967-69; faculty, prof., dir. Infectious Diseases Program & Clin. Microbiology U. Tex., Houston, 1973—88, dir. Ctr. for Infectious Diseases, Sch. Pub. Health, 2000—, prof. epidemiology, Sch. Pub. Health, 1975—, Mary W. Kelsey chair med. sci., 1988—; chief internal medicine svc. St. Luke's Episcopal Hosp., Houston, 1995—; clin. prof. dept. medicine Baylor Coll. Medicine, Houston, 1995—, vice chmn. dept. medicine, H. Irving Schweppe chair, 1995—; prof. grad. sch. biomed. sci. U. Tex., 2002, Baylor Coll. Medicine, 2004—; adj. prof. infectious diseases, infection control and employee health divsn. internal medicine U. Tex. MD Anderson Cancer Ctr., 2008—; adj. prof. dept. clin. svcs. and adminstrns. U. Houston, Coll. Pharmacy, 2008—. Vaccines and related biologic products adv. com. US FDA, 1989—, cons., 1989—; mid.-east regional infectious disease rsch. program Inst. Medicine, NAS, 1989—94; bd. sci. counselors Nat. Ctr. for Infectious Diseases, CDC, 1992—96; bd. Kelsey Rsch. Found., 2001—, interim pres., 2001, pres., 2008—. Author various med. books; assoc. editor: Am. Jour. Epidemiology, 1978—81, Jour. Infectious Diseases, 1983—88; mem. editl. bd. Clin. Infectious Diseases, 1990—95, Infectious Diseases in Clin. Practice, 1992—, Jour. of Infection, 1997—, Jour. Infectious Diseases, 2006—, mem. editl. adv. bd. Gastroenterology & Hepatology, 2007—, dep. editor Jour. of Travel Medicine, 2003—; contbr. articles to profl. jours. Lt. comdr. USN, 1967—69. Recipient John P. McGovern Outstanding Tchr., U. Tex.-Houston Med. Sch., 1991, Bronze medal of honor, government of France, 1993, Benjy Brooks award, U. Tex.-Houston, 1997, Disting. Achievement citation, Ohio Wesleyan U., 2006, Maxwell Finland award for Scientific Achievement, Nat. Found. Infectious Diseases, Washington, 2007; Rsch. grant NIH, 1975-, Laureate award, TAIM, ACP, 2008, Pres.'s Scholar award, U. Tex. Health Sci. Ctr., Houston, 2009; Disting. Med. Achievement award Emory U. Sch. Medicine, 2009, TIAA Disting. Med. Educator award. Master ACP; mem. Am. Soc. Clin. Investigation, Infectious Diseases Soc. Am. (counselor 1978-81, sec. 1982-87, pres. 1989-90), Nat. Found. Infectious Diseases (bd. dirs. 1981-2002, v.p. 1994-97, pres. 1997-99), Am. Clin. and Climatol. Assn. (recorder 2000-05, coun. mem. 2000-, pres.-elect. 2005-06, pres. 2006-07), Am. Epidemiology Soc., Assn. Am. Physicians, U.S. Mex. Found. Sci. and Tech. (com. chair health 1994-99), Tex. Acad. Internal Medicine (bd. dirs. 2003-07), Internat. Soc. Travel Medicine (pres. 1991-93), Am. Coll. Physicians (gov. S. Tex. bd. govs. 2003-07), Alpha Omega Alpha. Republican. Methodist. Office: St Luke's Episcopal Hosp # MC 1-164 6720 Bertner St Houston TX 77030-2697

DUPONT, ROBERT LOUIS, psychiatrist, physician; b. Toledo, Mar. 25, 1936; s. Robert Louis and Martha Ireton (Lancashire) DuP.; m. Helen Gayden Spink, July 14, 1962; children: Elizabeth, Caroline. BA, Emory U., 1958; MD, Harvard U., 1963. Diplomate in psychiatry and addiction psychiatry Am. Bd. Psychiatry and Neurology; cert. med. rev. officer. Intern Western Res. U., 1963-64; resident in psychiatry Harvard Med. Sch., 1964-66; clin. assoc. NIH, 1966-68; rsch. psychiatrist, assoc. dir. for community services D.C. Dept. Corrections, Washington, 1968-70; practice medicine specializing in psychiatry, 1968—. Adminstr. Narcotics Treatment Adminstrn., D.C. Dept. Human Resources, 1970—73; acting adminstr. Alcohol, Drug Abuse and Mental Health Adminstrn., HEW, Rockville, Md., 1974; dir. Nat. Inst. on Drug Abuse, HEW, Rockville, 1973—78, Spl. Action Office for Drug Abuse Prevention, Exec. Office Pres., Washington, 1973—75; pres. Inst. for Behavior and Health Inc., 1978—, Am. Coun. Drug Edn., 1980—85; U.S. del. UN Commn. on Narcotic Drugs, 1973—78; assoc. clin. prof. psychiatry and behavioral scis. George Washington Med. Sch., 1972—80; clin. prof. psychiatry Georgetown U. Med. Sch., 1980—; vis. assoc. clin. prof. psychiatry Harvard U. Med. Sch., 1978—84; chmn. Ctr. Behavioral Medicine, 1978—89; v.p. Bensinger, DuPont Assocs., Inc., 1982—; chair Prescription Drug Rsch. Ctr., 2004—. Author: The Selfish Brain, 2000, The Anxiety Cure, 2003, The Anxiety Cure for Kids, 2003, Drug Testing in Treatment Settings, 2005, Drug Testing in Schools, 2005, Drug Testing in Correctional Settings, 2005; contbr. articles in fields of drug abuse, criminology and mental health to profl. jours.; appeared on Good Morning Am., ABC-TV, 1978—80. Bd. dirs. Washington Soc. for Performing Arts, 1972-76; mem. adv. com. Washington Jr. League, 1972-76. Served to surgeon (maj.) USPHS, 1966-68. Fellow: Am. Soc. Addiction Medicine (life; diplomate), Am. Psychiat. Assn. (life); mem.: Washington Psychiatric Soc., Am. Med. Assn., Anxiety Disorders Assn. Am. (pres. 1982—85). Home: 8708 Susanna Ln Chevy Chase MD 20815-4714 Office: 6191 Executive Blvd Rockville MD 20852-3901 Home Phone: 301-657-8194; Office Phone: 301-231-9010. Personal E-mail: bobdupont@aol.com.

DURACK, DAVID TULLOCH, medical products executive; b. Perth, Australia, Dec. 18, 1944; s. Reginald Wyndham and Grace Enid (Tulloch) D.; m. Carmen Elizabeth Prosser, July 25, 1970; children: Jeremy, Kimberley, Sonya, Justin. BS, U. Western Australia, MB, 1969; DPhil, Oxford U., Eng., 1976. Diplomate Am. Bd. Internal Medicine, Royal Australasian Coll. Physicians, Royal Coll. Physicians U.K. Chief, resident medicine, asst. prof., medicine U. Wash., 1975—77; chief, infectious diseases and internat. health Duke University, Durham, 1977—94, prof., medicine, microbiology & immunology, 1982—94, cons. prof., medicine, 1994; chmn., dept. medicine, chief, divsn. infectious diseases Health Care Internat., Clydebank, Scotland, 1994—95; worldwide med. dir. Becton Dickinson Microbiology Sys., Balt., 1995—99; v.p., corp. med. affairs Becton, Dickinson & Co., 1999, sr. v.p., corp. med. affairs, 2006—. Co-editor: Infections of the Central Nervous System, 1996; contbr. articles to profl. jours. Rhodes scholar, 1969; NIH grantee, 1980, 86-91, grantee R.J. Reynolds Co., 1983-88, Carnegie Corp., 1989-94, grantee Roche Labs., 1991-94. Fellow Royal Coll. Physicians U.K., ACP, Royal Australasian Coll. Physicians, Infectious Diseases Soc. Am., Am. Soc. Clin. Investigation, Am. Fedn. Clin. Research. Presbyterian. Avocation: flying. Office: Becton Dickinson and Co 1 Becton Dr Franklin Lakes NJ 07417-1880 Office Fax: 201-847-6475. Business E-Mail: david_durack@bd.com.

DURAIRAJ, MANUEL, cardiologist, educator; b. Feb. 5, 1940; married; 2 children. Intermediate degree, U. Madras, 1957, MBBS, 1962; MD, U. Poona, 1969; DM in Cardiology, U. Madras, 1975; postgrad., Armed Forces Med. Coll., 1967—69, Christian Med. Coll. and Hosp., 1975. Intern Govt. Erskine Hosp., Madurai, India, 1962—63; registrar in medicine Armed Forces Med. Coll., Pune, India, 1968—70, instr. medicine, 1970—73; sr. registrar cardiology Christian Med. Coll., Vellore, India, 1973—75; specialist in medicine and cardiology Army Hosp. (Delhi Cantt. affiliated with Delhi and Poona U.), India, 1975—76, cardiologist, 1983—84; reader in cardiology Mil. Hosp. (affiliated with Armed Forces Med. Coll.), India, 1977—82, prof. and head dept. cardiology, 1982—83; dir. cardiology Poona Hosp. and Rsch. Ctr., Pune, 1984—99; prof. cardiology Poona Med. Found., Pune, 1991—. Vis. cardiologist Royal Melbourne Hosp., Australia, 1980; dir. bd. mgmt. Hindustan Antibiotics, Pune; expert mem. selection com. PGI, Chandigarh, India; expert mem. com. under Drug Contr. India; hon. physician Pres. of India; post intermediate and postgrad. tchr. medicine U. Poona, India, 1970—79, postgrad. tchr. cardiology, India, 1979—, prof. cardiology, India, 1982—, chmn. bd. examination DM in Cardiology degree, India, 1982—84; examiner in cardiology for DNB Nat. Bd. Exams., Min. Health and Family Welfare Govt. of India, 1999—; spkr. in field. Mem. editl. bd.: jours. Indian Heart Jour., 1979—81, 1983, mem. editl. com.: jours. Jour. Med. Ultrasound, assoc. editor: jours. Jour. Assn. Physicians India, mem. nat. editl. bd.: jours. Jour. Indian Acad. Echocardiography, mem. nat. adv. bd.: mags. Cardiology Today, 1996—; contbr. articles to profl. jours. Mem.: Am. Heart Assn., Am. Soc. Echocardiography, Am. Coll. Chest Physicans, Am. Coll. Cardiology, Indian Acad. Echocardiography (mem. exec. com., chmn. organizing com. and convenor 6th ann. conf.), Indian Coll. Cardiology (mem. exec. com. 1995—97, pres. 1998—99, sec. organizing com. 3rd nat. conf.), Christian Med. Assn. India, Indian Coll. Physicians, Hypertension Soc. India (chmn. organizing com. 8th nat. conf.), Assn. Agrl. Medicine and Rural Health in India, Indian Coll. Chest Physicians, Indian Soc. Med. Ultrasound (mem. governing body 1983, v.p.), India Soc. Electrocardiology (v.p., mem. governing body, mem. exec. com.), Indian Assn. Advancement Med. Edn., Assn. Physicians India (mem. governing body 1981—82, 1991—97, Emerck award 1979, Dr. J.N. Berry Meml. award 1980), Cardiol. Soc. India (mem. pediat. cardiology coun. 1978—81, mem. exec. com. Pune br. 1980, sec. sci. sub-com. joint annual conf. 1980, mem. exec. com. 1981—82, mem. sci. com. 1981—83, sec. Pune br. 1982, hon. joint sec. 1982—83, v.p. Pune br. 1983, v.p. 1985—86, v.p. 1988—89, pres. Pune br., others, Gold medal 1983), Internat. Soc. Heart Rsch., Internat. Coll. Angiology, Internat. Lipid Info. Bur. Office: Marian Cardiac Ctr and Rsch Found A Wing Fl 1, Thacker's House 2418 East St Pune 411 001 India Home Phone: 91 20 26691590; Office Phone: 91 20 26346867. Business E-Mail: drmdurairaj@eth.net.

DURAN, ENVER, thoracic surgeon; b. June 19, 1945; Attended, Bursa Resit Pasha Primary Sch., 1951—56, Bursa Osmangazi Secondary Sch., 1956—60, Bursa High Sch. for Boys, 1960—63; MB, Ankara U., 1969. Intern Gulhane Med. Mil. Acad., 1970; chief Dr. Izmir Mil. Dispensary, 1971—73; asst. gen. surgery dept. Ankara Gulhane Med. Mil. Acad., 1973—77; assoc. prof. Hacettepe Univ., 1985; assoc. prof. thoracic-cadiovascular surgery Gulhane med. Mil. Acad., 1985—90, prof., 1990; clinic dir. cardiovascular surgery Gulhane Mil. Med. Acad., 1990—98; chmn. dept. of cardiovascular surgery Trakya Univ., 1998—2004. Rector trakya Univ., 2004; pres. interuniversity bd. 55th Interuniversity Bd. Meeting, 2006; dep. rector Namik Kemal Univ., 2006, Kirklareli Univ., 2007—08. Mailing: c/o Trakya University 22050 Elm EDRINE Turkey Office Phone: 902842234210. Office Fax: 902842234203. *

DURANDY, YVES, cardiologist; b. Neuilly sur Seine, France, Feb. 20, 1947; s. Yvon Durandy and Yvette Murat; children: François-Xavier, Axel. BS in Sci., 1965; MD, Pierre and Marie Curie U. Paris 6, 1974 Diplomate internal medicine French Med. Assn., 1994. Resident Welfare Svcs. Paris, 1975—79, chief resident, 1979—82, asst. med. faculty Rene Descartes U., Paris, 1980—83; asst. in intensive care and perfusion Medico Surg. Ctr. Porte de Choisy, Paris, 1982—90; asst. rsch. lab. Unit Rsch. Med. Ctr. Porte de Choisy, Paris, 1982—90; cons. dept. intensive care and perfusion Mediterranean Inst. Cardiology, Marseille, France, 1991—94; chief ICU and perfusion pediat. cardiac surgery Inst. Hosp. Jacques Cartier Inst. Cardiology Paris Sud, Massy, France, 1994—. Intensivist Am. Hosp. Paris, Neuilly sur Seine, France, 1980—84. Capt. med. unit Army, 1974—75, Begin Hosp. Paris. Mem.: Mich. U. Extra Corporeal Life Support Orgn., European Work Group on Cardiothoracic Intensive Care. Achievements include research in new treatment for respiratory failure in pediatric patient: Extra corporeal veno venous single canula assistance; new treatment for post operative mediastinitis in cardiac surgery; research in normothermic perfusion and myocardial protection in pediatric cardiac surgery. Home: 13 rue Moutard Martin Marcoussis 91460 France Office: Inst Hosp Jacques Cartier Avenue du Noyer Lambert Massy 91300 France Office Phone: 0033160134656. Office Fax: 0033(0)160136267. Business E-Mail: iciprea@icip.org.

DURANT, GRAHAM JOHN, medicinal chemist, drug researcher; b. Newport, Gwent, U.K., Mar. 14, 1934; s. Edgar Counsell and Florence (Pocock) D.; m. Rosemary Margaret Towle, Apr. 14, 1962; children: Julian Clive, Adrian Charles. BSc in Chemistry with honors, U. Birmingham, UK, 1955, PhD, 1958; postdoctoral study, State U. Iowa, Iowa City, 1958-59. Sr. rsch. officer Smith Kline & French Rsch., Welwyn Garden City, Hertfordshire, U.K., 1960-75, head dept. medicinal chemistry, 1975-85, head rsch. adminstrn., 1985-86; Disting. prof. medicinal chemistry Coll. Pharmacy, U. Toledo, Ohio, 1987-92, dir. Ctr. for Drug Design and Devel. Ohio, 1987-92; sr. dir. chemistry Cambridge (Mass.) Neurosci., Inc., 1992-98; pharm. cons., 1998—. Contbr. articles to profl. jours.; co-holder over 100 patents. Trustee Inventure Place, Akron, Ohio, 1990-98. Inducted into Nat. Inventors Hall of Fame, 1990. Fellow Royal Soc. Chemistry (Medicinal Chemistry award 1983, mem. fine chems. group com. 1985-87). Avocations: genealogy, travel. Home and Office: GJD Consulting 5 Wingfield TQ7 3TE Kingsbridge England E-mail: gradurant@aol.com.

DURDAHL, CAROL LAVAUN, retired psychiatric nurse; b. Crookston, Minn., Jan. 18, 1933; d. Elmer Oliver and Ovidia (Olson) Durdahl; m. Hans A. Dahl, May 22, 1956 (div. 1983); children: Hana Sorensen-O'Neill, Carla Pederson. RN, St. Lukes Hosp., Duluth, Minn., 1953; BA in Human Svcs., Met. State U., St. Paul, 1982. Staff nurse various hosps., Minn., 1953-59; human svcs. tech. Willmar (Minn.) State Hosp., 1970-74, supplemental tchr., 1974-83; staff nurse Rice Meml. Hosp., Willmar, 1983-86; utilization rev. various nursing homes, Willmar, 1985-86; tchr. Willmar Area Vocat. Tech. Inst., 1986; dir. nurses Glenmore Recovery Ctr., Crookston, Minn., 1986-88; shift supr. Golden Valley (Minn.) Health Ctr., 1988-92; with crisis dept. Hennepin County Med. Ctr., 1988—2006; managed care of psychiat. and substance abuse MCC Managed Behavioral Care, Mpls., 1992; ret., 2006. Contbr. articles to profl. jours. Mem.: AAUW, LWV (pres. and state bd.), Bus. and Profl. Women, Federated Women, Does. Democrat. Lutheran. Avocations: reading, walking, crafts. Home: 1509 10th Ave Southern #212 Minneapolis MN 55404

DURELL, JACK, psychiatrist; b. NYC, July 5, 1928; s. Sam and Helen (Schwartzman) D.; m. Viviane M. diGioja, May 19, 1955. BA summa cum laude, Harvard U., 1949; MD cum laude, Yale U., 1953. Rsch. biochemist NIMH, Bethesda, Md., 1954-57, chief, sect. of psychiatry, 1963-67; v.p. med. affairs, clin. dir. The Psychiat. Inst.,

Washington, 1967-72, pres., med. dir., 1972-78; assoc. dir. sci. Nat. Inst. Drug Abuse, Rockville, Md., 1979-86; med. dir. clin. affairs div. Ea. Va. Med. Authority, Norfolk, 1986-87; chmn. dept. psychiatry Mercy Cath. Med. Ctr., Phila., 1987-92; prof. psychiatry U. Pa., Phila., 1987—. Exec. dir. Treatment Rsch. Inst., 1992—; pres. Delta Metrics, 1994—; pres. The Psychiat. Inst. Found., Washington, 1973-78; trustee Phila. Mental Health Care Connection, 1987-89. Editor: The Changing Clinical Picture of Schizophrenia, 1977; asst. editor-in-chief Jour. Psychiat. Rsch., 1966-82, mem. editorial bd., 1982—; contbr. to numerous med. publs. With USPHS, 1953-86. Fellow Am. Psychiat. Assn.; mem. Am. Acad. Psychiatrists in Alcoholism and Addictions (sec.-treas. 1985-93), Am. Psychopathological Assn., Am. Coll. Neuropsychopharmacology. Personal E-mail: jadurell@aol.com, jadurell@gmail.com. Business E-Mail: jdurell@deltametrics.com.

DURELL, VIVIANE G., psychologist, small business owner; b. Paris, Mar. 22, 1926; d. Andre Di Gioja and Francoise Martinez; m. Jack Durell, May 19, 1955. BSFS, Georgetown U., 1955; MA, George Wash. U., 1958. Cert. Bd. Psychologist, Washington, 1976. Statician IBRD, Washington, 1951—55; rsch. psychologist Gesell Inst. Child Devel., New Haven, 1958—59; psychologist Montgomery Count Bd. Edn., Rockville, Md., 1961—77; cons. psychologist Psychiat. Inst., Washington, 1967—77; group therapist Cmty. Psychiat. Clinic, Bethesda, Md., 1968—73; instr. Montgomery Coll., Takoma Park, 1971—73; pres. Vivianna Inc., McLean, Va., 2002—. Co-author: (book) When Schools Care, Family Therapy Techniques for Problem Behavior of Children and Teenagers. Friends of first ladies Smithsonian Mus. Am. History, 1990—92; pres. bd. trustees Samaritans of Washington, 1980—96; bd. assocs. mem. Nat. Rehab. Hosp., 1995—. Recipient Lifetime Dedication award, Samaritans of Washington, 1984, Blanch Keith Samaritan of the Yr. award, 1986. Mem.: APA, The Hist. Georgetown Club, Sulgrave Club, Capital Speakers Club (life), Psi Chi (life). Avocations: public speaking, music, travel, languages, cooking. Personal E-mail: viviannainc@netzero.net.

DURHAM, LYNN ELLEN, school psychologist; b. Urbana, Ill., Aug. 10, 1954; d. Leonard and Olga Durham; m. Greydon Anthony Smith, Oct. 31, 1992. BS in Edn., Ea. Ill. U., Charleston, 1975, MA, 1983. Cert. sch. psychologist K-12 Utah State Office of Edn., spl. edn. K-12+ Utah State Office of Edn., early childhood edn. Pre K-3 Utah State Office of Edn., elem. edn. 1-8 Utah State Office of Edn., Nat. cert. sch. psychologist 1989. Tchr. spl. edn. Streator (Ill.) H.S., 1975—78, Sterling (Ill.) H.S., 1978—81; intern sch. psychologist Peoria (Ill.) Sch. Dist., 1982—83; sch. psychologist Uinta Sch. Dist., Vernal, Utah, 1983—84, Jordan Sch. Dist., Sandy, Utah, 1984—2010; ret., 2010. Mem. Jr. League of Salt Lake City, 1997—2005, dir. adv. and strategic planning, 2003—04, dir. project evaluation, 2004—05, sustaining mem., 2005—; vol. Salt Lake Olympic Organizing Com., 2002. Recipient Dedicated Svc. award, 2009; named Educator of Month, Sandy C. of C., 1987. Mem.: Utah Assn. Sch. Psychologists (treas. 1989—92, pres. 1993—94, membership chair 1996—2008, bd. mem. 2004—08, dist. rep. 2008—09, Disting. Svc. award 1996), Delta Kappa Gamma Soc. Avocations: stitchery, knitting, miniature houses and interiors, cats. Home: 121 4th Ave Salt Lake City UT 84103 Personal E-mail: 1lynndurham@gmail.com.

DURIE, BRIAN GEORGE MARTIN, hematologist, oncologist; b. Gullane, Scotland, 1942; MD, U. Edinburgh Med. Sch., Scotland, 1966. Diplomate Am. Bd. Internal Medicine, Nat. Bd. Med. Examiners, cert. in hematology/oncology, lic. Minn., Ariz., Calif. Medical intern/resident Wayne State U., Detroit, 1967—69; medical resident-,clin. rsch. fellow hematology & hematologic oncology Mayo Clinic, Rochester, Minn., 1969—72; instr. dept. internal medicine U. Ariz. Coll. Medicine, Tucson, 1972—73, asst. prof. medicine, 1973—76, assoc. prof. medicine, 1976—80, dir. clin. hematology, 1979—89, prof. medicine, hematology/oncology, 1981—92; prof. hematology/oncology Cedars Sinai Med. Ctr., LA, 1992—93, atending physician, 1993—; dir. hematologic rsch. & myeloma programs Aptium Oncology, Inc./Cedars Sinai Comprehensive Cancer Ctr., 1993—. Prof. clin. & lab. medicine/hematology Charing Cross & Westminster Med. Sch., U. London. 1989—92; founder, chmn. sci. adv. bd. Internat. Myeloma Found., Norh Hollywood, Calif., 1990—; co-chmn. myeloma com. Southwest Oncology Group, San Antonio, 2002—; mem. Sutter Western divsn. cancer rsch. group Alta Bates Cancer Care Ctr., Berkeley, Calif., 2005—. Mem. editl. adv. bd. Leukemia Reviews Internat., 1984—92, Molecular Biotherapy, 1987—92; contbr. articles to profl. jours., chapters to books. Recipient Robert A. Kyle Lifetime Achievement award, 2006; scholar Leukemia Soc. America, 1976—81. Mem.: AMA, Scholar Leukemia Soc. America, Soc. Interferon Rsch., Internat. Soc. Exptl. Hematology, Cell Kinetic Soc., Am. Fedn. Clin. Rsch., European Oncology Soc., Am. Assn. Cancer Rsch., Am. Soc. Clin. Oncology, Am. Soc. Hematology, Brit. Oncology Soc., Brit. Soc. Haematology, Brit. Med. Assn., Mayo Alumni Assn. Achievements include patents in field. Office: Aptium Oncology Inc 8201 Beverly Blvd Los Angeles CA 90048 also: Cedars Sinai Outpatient Cancer Ctr 8700 Beverly Blvd Los Angeles CA 90048 also: Internat Myeloma Found 12650 Riverside Dr Ste 206 Valley Village CA 91607 Office Phone: 323-966-3572. Office Fax: 323-966-3685. E-mail: bdurie@aptiumoncology.com. *

DURKEE, WILLIAM ROBERT, retired internist; b. Kansas City, Mo., Apr. 12, 1923; s. Dwight and Bessie Deane (Williams) D.; m. Billie Maxine Schreiner, Sept. 19, 1946; m. Jeanne Elizabeth Wells, June 7, 1975; children— Bruce William, Ellen Jeanne AA, Kansas City Jr. Coll., 1941; student, U. Chgo., 1941-42; MD, U. Kans., 1945. Diplomate Am. Bd. Internal Medicine. Intern U. Kans. Med. Ctr., Kansas City, 1945-46, resident, 1948-51; practice medicine specializing in internal medicine Manhattan, Kans., 1951-91; ptnr. Ball Meml. Clinic, 1951-76, Drs. Durkee and Boese, 1976-91; med. dir. Kans. Farm Bur. Life Ins. Co., Manhattan, 1963-91; ret., 1991. Mem. staff Mercy Health Ctr.; trustee Meml. Hosp., Manhattan, Kans., 1994-03, chmn. 2001-03. Bd. dirs. Friends of McCain, 1988-95, Sunset Zoo Wildlife Conservation Trust, Manhattan, 1995-2002, pres., 1998; mem. adv. bd. Friends of Libr., Kans. State U., 1993-2002. Capt. U.S. Army, 1943-48. Fellow ACP, Am. Coll. Cardiology (assoc.); mem. AMA, Riley County Med. Soc., Kans. Med. Soc., Am. Soc. Internal Medicine, Manhattan C. of C., Pres.'s Club Kans. State U., Manhattan Country Club, Rotary. Republican. Methodist. Home: 2121 Meadowlark Rd Apt 238 Manhattan KS 66502

DURKIN, MICHAEL C., orthopedist; MD, Univ. Ill., Chgo. Cert. Am. Bd. Orthopaedic Surgery Examiners. Staff physician Provena St. Joseph Med. Ctr., Silver Cross Hosp., Hinsdale Hosp., Edward Hosp., Hinsdale Surg. Ctr., AmSurg; physician Hinsdale Orthopaedic Assoc., 2002—. Intern, resident Univ. Ill. Hosp., Clinics. Mem.: DuPage Med. Soc., Ill. State Med. Soc., Am. Acad. Orthopaedic Surgeons. Office: Hinsdale Orthopaedic Assoc 550 W Ogden Ave Hinsdale IL 60521

DUROCHER, ALAIN VICTOR, hospital administrator; b. Crespin, July 3, 1949; MD, U. Lille2, 1976, PhD. Chief, intensive care dept. Calmette Hosp, Lille U. Hosp., 2000—; dean, health mgmt., engring. Lille 2 U., 2010—. Counsellor HAS, 1992; pres. APNET, 2011—. Fellow: SRLF. Office: Intensive Care Dept CHU de Lille Lille Nord 59000 France E-mail: alain.durocher@univ-lille2.fr.

DUROVICH, CHRISTOPHER J., hospital administrator; BA, U. Vt.; MA in Healthcare Adminstrn., U. No. Colo.; MA in Bus. Mgmt., Northwestern U. Diplomate Am. Coll. Healthcare Execs. Chief adminstr. Internal Medicine U. Mich. Health Sys., 1993—98; pres., COO Baylor MedCare Baylor Coll. Medicine, 1998—2000; v.p. U. Tex. M.D. Anderson Cancer Ctr., 2000—02; pres., CEO Children's Medical Ctr., Dallas, 2003—. Adj. prof. Jones Grad. Sch. of Mgmt., Rice U. Pres. Houston Food Bank Bd. Dirs. Capt. Army Med. Svc. Corps. Mem.: Healthcare Fin. Mgmt. Assn., Houston Rotary Club. Office: Children's Med Ctr 1935 Motor St Dallas TX 75235

DURRIEU, ALAIN-JACQUES, diabetologist, nutritionist; b. Cazeres, France, July 22, 1943; s. Jean and Hortense (Duclos) D.; m. July 13, 1966; children: Gilles, Marie-Christine. MD, U. Toulouse, 1971. Registered physician, Conseil de l'Ordre des Médecins. Intern, resident Hosp. Hotel Dieu, Toulouse, France, 1966-67; resident Hosp. Gen., Tarbes, France, 1968-73; pvt. practice diabetes/nutrition Biarritz, France, 1973—. Cons. in occupational medicine and hygiene Social Security, Bayonne, France, 1980—, chem. industry, Tarpos, France, 1973—, others; rschr. in multipurpose computer aided problem solving and nimble network. Contbr. articles to profl. jours. Bd. dirs. Group de recherches pedagogiques en diabétologie. Lt. French Air Force, 1970-71. Decorated Vermeil Cross, Paris, 1991, 92, Gold Cross, 1993. Mem. AAAAs, Rsch. Group in Diabetes Edn., French Nutrition Assn., Hygiene and Pub. Health Assn., Nat. Coun. French Engrs. and Scientists, Union des Ingenieurs et Scientifiques dubassin de l'Adour, Am. Diabetes Assn., Assn. de Langue Française pour l'étude du Diabete et des maladies métaboliques, Internat. Diabetes Fedn., Internat. Soc. for Sys. Scis., Human Factors Soc., Am. Soc. for Quality Control, N.Y. Acad. Scis., Am. Telemedicine Assn. Roman Catholic. Avocation: yachting. Home: Rue Madeleine Villa Argia Bidart France 64210 Office: Résidence Tolédo 1 Rue de la Poste Biarritz France 64200

DURUALP, ENDER, medical educator; b. Çankiri, Jan. 1, 1974; PhD, Ankara U., 2009. Asst. prof. Cankiri Karatekin U., 2010. Office: Devlet Hastanesi Yani Çankiri Merkez 18200 Turkey Business E-Mail: edurualp@karatekin.edu.tr.

DUSE, ADRIAN TRAIAN, surgeon; b. Nucet, Bihor, Romania, Feb. 6, 1963; MD, U. Medecine and Farmacy Iuliu Hatieganu, Cluj Napoca, 1988, PhD, 2005. Trainee Ob-Gyn. Hosp. Oradea, 1988—91; resident, gen. surgery II Surgery Clinic U. Medecine and Farmacy Iuliu Hatieganu, Cluj Napoca, 1991—94; gen. surgeon Emergency County Clinic Hosp., Oradea, 1995—2006, dept. chief, gen., oncological and vascular surgeon, II surgery dept., 2006—, bd. dirs., 2010. Del. Nat. Assembly Romanian Med. Coll., 2004—; mem. Bihor County Bd. Med. Coll., 2004—, Gen. Surgery Com. Romanian Ministery of Health, 2010. Mem.: European Assn. Endoscopic Surgery, European Digestive Surgery, Internat. Soc. Diseases of Esophagus, Romanian Soc. Angiology and Vascular Surgery, Romanian Soc. Surgery. Avocations: mountain climbing, snowboarding. Home: Republicii Nr 51 Oradea Bihor 410167 Romania Personal E-mail: adriantraianduse@yahoo.com.

DUSKA, LINDA, physician, educator; b. Bklyn., Aug. 12, 1965; MD, NYU, 1991. Physician, assoc. prof. U. Va., 2008—. Fellow: ACS; mem.: ACOG, ASCO, SGO. Office: PO Box 800712 Charlottesville VA 22908 Office Fax: 434-982-1840. Business E-Mail: lduska@virginia.edu.

DUTCHER, JANICE JEAN PHILLIPS, oncologist; b. Bend, Oreg., Nov. 10, 1950; d. Charles Glen and MayBelle (Fluit) Phillips; m. John Dutcher, Sept. 8, 1971 (div. 1980). BA with honors, U. Utah, 1971; MD, U. Calif., Davis, 1975. Diplomate Am. Bd. Internal Medicine, Am. Bd. Med. Oncology. Intern Rush-Presbyn. St. Luke's Hosp., Chgo., 1975-76, resident, 1976-78; clin. assoc. Balt. Cancer Rsch., Nat. Cancer Inst., 1978-81, sr. investigator, 1981-82; asst. prof. U. Md., Balt., 1982, Albert Einstein Coll. Medicine, NYC, 1983-86, assoc. prof., 1986-92, prof., 1992-98, course co-dir. Advances in Cancer Treatment Rsch. Manhattan, 1984-96; prof. medicine N.Y. Med. Coll., 1998—; assoc. dir. for clin. affairs Comprehensive Cancer Ctr., Our Lady of Mercy Med. Ctr., 1998—2008; site dir. oncology Montefiore North Divsn., 2009—10; dir. immunotherapy, divsn. hematology-oncology St. Luke's Roosevelt Hosp. Ctr., Continuum Cancer Ctr., NY, 2010—. Chmn. biol. response mod. com. Ea. Coop. Oncology Group, Madison, Wis., 1989-95, mem. exec. com., 1995-97, chair renal subcom., 1998—; mem. data safety com. Nat. Heart Lung Blood Inst., Bethesda, Md., 1990-95; mem. biologic response modifier study sect. Nat. Cancer Inst., Bethesda, 1988, 90, 94, 96; mem. NIH Consensus Panel on Early Melanoma, 1992; mem. FDA Oncology Drug Adv. Bd., 1995-99, chair FDA-ODAC, 1996-99, NCI subcom. D for program project rev., 1995-98, mem. subsplty. med. oncology bd. Am. Bd. Internal Medicine, 1997-2003; mem. NCI subcom. A for Cancer Ctrs., 1998-2002; mem. faculty AACR/ASCO Workshop on Clin. Trials Devel., 1996-2002, NIH Progress Rev. Group on Kidney Cancer, 2001, NIH, CBSS-Biomakers Study Sec., adhoc., 2007, mem. 08-, mem. exam writing com. ASCO-SEP, 2008-11; mem. tng. exam oncology ASCO-NBME, 2009-11. Editor: Handbook of Hematology/Oncology Emergencies, 1987, Modern Transfusion Therapy, 1990; sect. editor: Neoplastic Diseases of the Blood, 3d edit., 1996, 4th edit., 2003, 5th edit., 2011; mem. editl. bd. Jour. Immunotherapy, Med. Oncology, Jour. Clin. Oncology, Jour. Clin. Pharm., Ann. Intern. Med.; sect. editor Current Treatment Options in Oncology, 2000-06, Chronic Leukemia, 2000-06, Leukemia, 2010-; contbr. articles to Blood, Leukemia, Jour. Clin. Oncology, Jour. Immunotherapy, Clin. Cancer Rsch., Soc. Am. Cancer Jour. Recipient Beecham award in Hematology So. Blood Club, 1983, Henry C. Moses Clin. Rsch. award Montefiore Med. Ctr., 1989, Outstanding Alumnus award U. Calif., Davis, 1989; named Outstanding Young Investigator Ea. Coop. Oncology Group, 1993; recipient numerous grants. Mem.: European Soc. Med Onc, Am. Assn. of Blood Banks, Am. Radium Soc., Am. Assn. for Cancer Rsch., Am. Soc. Hematology, Am. Soc. Clin. Oncology, Internat. Soc. Biol. Therapy, Alpha Omega Alpha, Phi Kappa Phi, Phi Beta Kappa. Achievements include findings related to management of alloimmunization to platelet transfusions, intensive maintenance of patients with acute leukemia, studies of new biologic response modifiers as antitumor drugs, management of renal cell cancer, melanoma and breast cancer, study and treatment with biologic antitumor agents, study and treatment of targeted therapies in renal cell cancer and melanoma. Address: Divsn Hematology & Oncology St Lukes Roosevelt Hosp Ctr Continuum Cancer Ctrs 1000 10th Ave Ste 11C02 New York NY 10019 Office Phone: 212-636-3334. Office Fax: 212-523-2004. Personal E-mail: jpd4401@aol.com. Business E-Mail: jdutcher@chpnet.org.

DUTKIEWICZ, JACEK, biologist, researcher; b. Łuck, Poland, July 29, 1934; s. Józef Edward and Jadwiga (Łojasiewicz) D.; m. Elżbieta Perkowska, Apr. 9, 1959; 1 child, Dorota. MS, Jagiellonian U., Cracow, Poland, 1956, PhD, 1965; D Habilitation, Univ. Sch. Medicine, Lublin, Poland, 1977. Scientist Inst. for Environ. Protection, Cracow, 1956-58; asst. Univ. Sch. Medicine, 1958-61, sr. asst., 1961-65; sr. scientist Inst. Agrl. Medicine, Lublin, 1966-71, chief lab., 1971-91, lectr., 1978-91, prof. biology, head dept., 1991—. Lectr., head dept. Univ. Sch. Medicine, Katowice, Poland, 1985; sr. rsch. assoc. Nat. Inst. for Occupational Safety and Health, Morgantown, W.Va., 1987-89. Author: (monograph) Occupational Biohazards, 1989; founding editor-in-chief Annals of Agrl. and Environ. Medicine, 1994—; contbr. numerous articles to profl. jours. Decorated Golden Cross of Merit, Coun. of State, 1986; recipient cert. of appreciation Ctrs. for Disease Ctrl., HHS, 1989. Mem. Internat. Assn. for Aerobiology, Polish Allergological Soc. (pres. Lublin sect. 1983-87), Pan-Am. Biodeterioration Soc., Am. Soc. for Microbiology, N.Y. Acad. Scis., Sci. Soc. Lublin, Polish Soc. Indsl. Hygienists (mem. governing body 2001-05). Roman Catholic. Avocations: travel, mountain climbing, photography, bridge, films. Office: Inst Agrl Medicine Jaczewskiego 2 PL20-950 Lublin Poland Home: Ul. Kleniewskich 6/42 20-093 Lublin Poland Home Phone: 4881 7473314; Office Phone: 4881 7184572. Business E-Mail: dutkiewi@galen.imw.lublin.pl.

DU TOIT, NAGIB, ophthalmologist, consultant; b. Cape Town, Western Cape, South Africa, Apr. 2, 1968; s. Sadick and Miriam Du Toit; m. Amina Bagus-Du Toit; children: Muhammad Sadiq, Athira, Zahra, Matin, Jowwad. MBChB, U. Cape Town, 1992, MMed, 2006. Diploma in ophthalmolgy Coll. Medicine South Africa, 1998. Cons. ophthalmic surgeon Groote Schuur Hosp., Cape Town, 2004—, head glaucoma svc., 2004—; lectr. ophthalmology U. Cape Town, 2004—, course coord. undergrad. ophthalmology course, 2004—. Cmty. upliftment Internal Reformation, Cape Town, 1993—2008. Recipient Distinction, Internat. Coun. Ophthalmology, 1999; fellow, Coll. Ophthalmolgy South Africa, 2003. Fellow: Royal Coll. Surgeons Edinburgh; mem.: South African Glaucoma Soc., Ophthal. Soc. South Africa. Achievements include research in sympathetic ophthalmia. Office: Groote Schuur Hosp Anzio Rd Observatory Cape Town Western Cape 7925 South Africa Home: 1 Klein Constantia Rd Constantia 7806 Cape Town South Africa Personal E-mail: ndutoit@mweb.co.za. Business E-Mail: nagib.dutoit@uct.ac.za.

DUTT, KAMLA, medical educator; b. Lahore, Punjab, India; came to U.S., 1969; d. Gulzari Lal and Raj Bansi Dutt. BS with honors, Panjab U., Chandigarh, India, 1961, MS in Zoology with honors, 1962, PhD, 1970. Rsch. assoc. Harvard Med. Sch. Sidney Farber Cancer Ctr., Boston, 1972-76; rsch. assoc. Eye Inst. Retinal Fedn., Boston, 1977-80; sr. rsch. assoc. Yale Med. Ctr., New Haven, 1980-81, Emory U., Atlanta, 1981-82; asst. prof. Morehouse Sch. Medicine, Atlanta, 1983-89, assoc. prof., 1989—2001, prof., 2001—. Sci. adv. bd. Fernbank Sci. Ctr., Atlanta. Contbr. numerous articles to sci. jours.; author short stories (in Hindi); prodr., actor 3 maj. plays, Atlanta; actor 11 maj. plays, India. Bd. dirs. VSEI (vol. fundraising orgn. for edn. in India), 1973-78; v.p. Indian Am. Cultural Assn., 1985; podium spkr., participant King Week, 1990, 91, 93; spkr. Gandhi Day Celebration, 1984, 85; key participant Intercultural Conf., 1990; main participant joint document Women's Perspective; active human rights issues; stake holder Vision 20/20 Collaborative State of Ga., diversity and edn. coms., 1995. Hindu. Achievements include establishment of human ocular cell lines by gene transfection, used as model for study of eye diseases and tissue engineering. Office: Morehouse Sch Medicine 720 Westview Dr Atlanta GA 30310-1458 Business E-Mail: kdutt@msm.edu.

DUTTA, DEEP, endocrinologist; b. India, Apr. 8, 1983; MBBS, JIPMER, Pondicherry, 2006; MD in Medicine, Calcutta Med. Coll., Kolkata, 2009. Resident, dept. endocrinology & metabolism IPGMER & SSKM Hosp., Kolkata, India, physician, 2010—. Office: Rm 9 4th Fl Ronald Ross Bldg 242 AJC Bose Rd Kolkata West Bengal 700020 India Personal E-mail: deepdutta2000@yahoo.com.

DUTTON, RICHARD P., anesthesiologist, educator; MD, Tufts U. Sch. Medicine. Resident Mass. Gen. Hosp.; assoc. prof. anesthesiology U. Md. Med. Ctr., dir. trauma anesthesiology. Office: 22 S Greene St Baltimore MD 21201 Office Phone: 419-328-8919.

DUVALL, CHARLES PATTON, internist, retired oncologist; b. Evanston, Ill., June 16, 1936; s. Charles Fleming and Edith (Osgood) Duvall; m. Nancy Ash, June 21, 1958; children: Lawrence Charles, Stephen Rogers, Douglas Patton, Lauren Duvall Meacham. AB, Cornell U., Ithaca, NY, 1958; MD, U. Rochester, NY, 1962. Diplomate Am. Bd. Internal Medicine, Am. Bd. Med. Oncology. Intern Yale New Haven Med. Ctr., 1962—63; resident internal medicine U. Rochester, 1963—64; lt. comdr. USPHS, 1964—66; clin. assoc. Nat. Cancer Inst., NIH, Bethesda, Md., 1964—66; resident medicine Georgetown U. Hosp., Washington, 1966—67, USPHS spl. fellow hematology, 1967—68; physician Foxhall Internists, Washington, 1968—2000. Clin. prof. medicine Georgetown U. Hosp., Washington, 1968—2000; chmn. dept. medicine Sibley Hosp., Washington, 1989—90; mem. emeritus staff Washington Hosp. Ctr., 1988—. Contbr. articles to profl. jours. Chmn. bd. dirs. Blue Cross Blue Shield Nat. Capital area, Washington, 1986—94, Bradley Hills Presbyn. Ch., Bethesda, Md.; elder First Presbyn Ch, Hilton Head Island; elder, Stephen min., deacon, pres. Men's group, chair Prayer Mission Ministries, 2005; bd. dir. Lowcountry Cmty. Devel. Corp., 2007—08; bd. dir., vice chair Vols. Med. Inst., 2000—03; chair med. exec. com., bd. dir. Vol Med. Clin., Hilton Head Island, 2007—09. Recipient Mayor's Citizenship award, 2003; named Man of Yr., 1st Presbyn. Ch., 2007, Men of Ch. Master: ACP (Outpatient Tchg. award 1998,

Laureate award 2000, Pres. Emeritus award 2005); mem.: AMA (del. 1988—93, coun. legis. 1991—2000, chmn. 1996—97, chmn. splty. and svcs. soc.), Clin. Pathologic Soc. (pres. 1995—96), Osler Soc. DC (pres. 1978—79), Sect. Coun. Internal Medicine AMA (chmn. 1987—88), Spltys. and Svcs. Soc. AMA (pres. 1990—91, sect. coun. IM), Am. Soc. Internal Medicine (pres. DC chpt. 1977, Spl. Recognition award 1979, pres. rsch. found. 1987—88, pres. ASIM 1989—90, chmn. federated coun. internal medicine 1989—90, spkr. ho. of dels. 1991—95, Spl. Recognition award 1979), Bear Creek Club (pres. SC), Congl. Country Club (hon. life), Sigma Chi (Significant Sig award 2010), Alpha Omega Alpha. Republican. Presbyterian. Avocations: golf, skiing, photography, painting. Home: 316 Seabrook Dr Hilton Head Island SC 29926-1979 Personal E-mail: cduvall636@aol.com.

DUYCK, KATHLEEN MARIE, poet, musician, retired social worker; b. Portland, Oreg., July 21, 1933; d. Anthony Joseph Dwyer and Edna Elisabeth Hayes; m. Robert Duyck, Feb. 3, 1962; children: Mary Kay Boeyen, Robert Patrick, Anthony Joseph. BS, Oreg. State U., 1954; MSW, U. Wash., 1956. Cert. NASW, Oreg. Adoption worker Cath. Svcs., Portland, 1956-61, Cath. Welfare, San Antonio, 1962; musician Tucson Symphony, 1963-65; prin. cellist Phoenix (Ariz.) Coll. Orch., 1968-78, Scottsdale (Ariz.) Symphony, 1974-80; poet, 1993—. Author: (poetry cassettes) Visions, 1993 (Contemporary Series Poet 1993), Visions II, 1996 (Contemporary Series Poet 1996); author numerous poems; contbr. CD Rep. worker Maricopa County Reps., Phoenix, 1974; mem. Scottsdale Cultural Coun.; NASW bd. Cath. Charities Rep., Portland, 1959-61; mem. Signal Soc. of Channel 8, Phoenix., v.p. Friends Family Svc., 2011-12 Recipient Golden Poet award, World of Poetry, 1991-92, Sec. gift, Phoenix Exec. Bd., 1976, Recognition award, Archbishop Howard, 1961, Kathleen Duyck award, Cello Congress V, 1996, Excellence in Music award IBC, 2007, named to Inner Cir., 2010, Order of Distinction, 2010, Lifetime award 2009, ABI Lifetime award 2009, World Forum; named Woman of the Yr., ABI, 2009, Mozart award, IBC, 2010-11, Attache medal, ABI, 2011, Academician award, 2011, Cambridge medal, IBC, 2011. Mem. Internat. Poetry Hall Fame, Ariz. Cello Soc., Nat. Libr. Poetry (Editor's Choice awards, 1993-2003), Internat. Soc. Poets (Internat. Poet of Merit award, 2003, Outstanding Achievement award in Poetry, 2005, 06, 08), Phoenix Symphony Guild (exec. bd. 1970-80), Women in Arts, World War II Mus., St. Mary's Alumni Assn., Phoenix Art Mus., Oreg. State U. Alumni Assn., U. Wash. Alumni Assn., Mental Health Guild, Friends Family Svc (v.p. 2008-09), Phoenix Symphony Orchestra, Internat. Biog. Ctr (hon; inner cir. mem.) (Order of Distinction, 2010). Republican. Roman Catholic. Achievements include Ambassador to World Forum of arts, sciences and communications, 2009, 2010 and 2011. Avocations: piano, photography, poetry, music. Home and Office: 4545 E Palomino Rd Phoenix AZ 85018-1719

DVORAK, DAVID C., medical products executive, lawyer; BS in Fin., Miami U., Ohio; JD magna cum laude, Case Western Reserve U., 1991. Sr. v.p., gen. counsel, corp. sec. STERIS Corp., mem. exec. com.; sr. v.p. corp. affairs, gen. counsel Zimmer Holdings, Inc., Warsaw, Ind., 2001—03, exec. v.p. corp. svcs., chief counsel, sec., 2003—05, group pres. global bus., chief legal officer, 2005—07, pres., CEO, 2007—. Office: Zimmer Holdings Inc 345 E Main St Warsaw IN 46580 *

DVORETZKY, ISRAEL, dermatologist; b. Jerusalem, June 4, 1944; came to U.S., 1976; s. Itzak and Zippora (Levit) D.; m. Ayala Chenstochovsky, Oct. 11, 1970; 1 child, Shay. MD, Tel Aviv U., 1971. Intern Meir Kfar-Saba Hosp., Tel-Aviv, Israel, 1971-72; resident in dermatology Chaim Sheba Med. Ctr., Tel-Aviv, 1973-76; 2d resident in dermatology Yale New Haven Hosp., 1976-78; vis. assoc. At. Cancer Inst. NIH, Bethesda, Md., 1978-82; asst. clin. prof. dermatology Yale U. Sch. Medicine, New Haven, 1982-88, assoc. clin. prof., 1988-97, clin. prof. dermatology, 1997—. Pvt. practice Ansonia, Conn., 1982—. Author: Chemistry and Biology of Interferon, 1982; contbr. articles to profl. jours.; patentee in wart therapy. Fellow Am. Acad. Dermatology, Soc. Dermatol. Surgery, Soc. Pediat. Dermatology, Soc. Internat. Dermatology, Soc. Investigative Dermatology; mem. New Eng. Dermatol. Soc., Am. Contact Dermatitis Soc., Dermatology Found. Avocations: classical music, jazz, international music, reading, writing. Office: 22 Westfield Ave Ansonia CT 06401-1158 Office Phone: 203-735-6144.

DWELLE, TERRY, state agency administrator, public health service officer; b. Garrison, ND; MD cum laude, St. Louis U.; MPH in Tropical Medicine, Tulane U., New Orleans. Cert. Am. Bd. Pediat., in pediat. infectious diseases, in tropical and travel medicine Am. Soc. Tropical Medicine and Hygiene. Pediat. infectious disease fellow St. Louis U. Cardinal Glennon Meml. Hosp. Children; preventive medicine residency Tulane U.; clin. dir. Pub. Health Svc., pediat. cons. Ft. Berthold & Turtle Mountain Reservations Indian Health Svc., Ft. Totten, ND, 1977—80, reserve officer, 1980—; asst. prof. pediat. U. ND Sch. Medicine, Bismarck, 1980—93, asst. clin. prof. pediat., 1997—; pediatrician Bismarck, ND; chief med. officer N.D. Dept. Health, state health officer, 2001—. Chmn. infectious control com. Medcenter One, Bismarck, 1987—91; rural health officer Am Acad. Pediat., 1985—; cmty. health cons. to Romania Med. Ambs. internat., 1994—, East Africa field dir., Cmty. Health Evangelism Program, 1997—. Med. missionary appointment, Africa, 1988—94, 1996—. Recipient Benjamin H. Cohen award, St. Louis U., McCormack award, Assn. State and Territorial Health Ofcls., 2008. Mem.: Delta Omega, Alpha Omega Alpha. Office: ND Dept Health 600 E Blvd Ave Bismarck ND 58505-0200

DWORKIN, MARTIN, retired microbiologist; b. NYC, Dec. 3, 1927; s. Hyman Bernard and Pauline (Herstein) D.; m. Nomi Rees Buda, Feb. 2, 1957; children: Jessica Sarah, Hanna Beth. BA, Ind. U., 1951; PhD (NSF predoctoral fellow), U. Tex., Austin, 1955. NIH research fellow U. Calif., Berkeley, 1955-57, vis. prof., summers 1958-60; asst. prof. microbiology Ind. U. Med. Sch., 1957-61, assoc. prof., 1961-62; from assoc. prof. to prof. U. Minn., 1962—2004, prof. emeritus, 2004—. Vis. prof. U. Wash., 1965, Stanford U., 1978-79, co-dir. Microbial Diversity Course Marine Biol. Lab., Woods Hole, 1990-94; vis. scholar Oxford (Eng.) U., 1970-71; Found. for Microbiology lectr., 1973-74, 76-77, 81-82; Sackler scholar Tel Aviv U., 1992. Author: Developmental Biology of the Bacteria, 1985, Microbial Cell-Cell Interactions, 1991; contbr. numerous articles, revs. to profl. pubs.; mem. editorial bd. Jour. Bacteriology, 1967-74, 86-88, Ann. Revs. Microbiology, 1975-79, The Prokaryotes, 2d edit., editor-in-chief 3d edit. Alt. del. Democratic Nat. Conv., 1968; mem. Minn. Dem. Farm Labor Central Com., 1969-70. Served with U.S. Army, 1946-48. Recipient Career Devel. award NIH, 1963-73; John Simon Guggenheim fellow, 1978-79 Fellow Am. Acad. Arts and Scis. (chmn. Midwest ctr., v.p., 2002), Am. Soc. Microbiology (vice chmn. div. gen. microbiology 1977-78, chmn. 1978-79, div. councillor 1980-82, Roger Porter award 2006); mem. Soc. Gen. Microbiology (Eng.). Home: 2123 Hoyt Ave W Saint Paul MN 55108-1314 Office: U Minn Dept Microbiology Minneapolis MN 55455 Office Phone: 612-624-5634. Business E-Mail: dworkin@umn.edu.

DWORKIN, PAUL HOWARD, pediatrician; b. Paterson, NJ, Oct. 22, 1947; s. Bernard and Ruth (Steinhauer) D.; m. Sheila Ann Maher, Oct. 7, 1979; children: Molly Maher, Eamon Timothy. AB, Rutgers U., 1969; MD, Johns Hopkins U., 1973. Diplomate Am. Bd. Pediatrics, 1979, Devel. and Behavioral Pediat., 2003. Pediatric registrar Paddington Green Children's Hosp./St. Mary's Med. Sch., London, 1976; resident in pediatrics Children's Hosp., Boston, 1973-75, fellow in ambulatory pediatrics, 1976-78; asst. prof. pediatrics W.Va. U. Sch. Medicine, Morgantown, 1978-81; prof./asso. chair pediats., head div. gen. peds., asst. dean U. Conn. Sch. Medicine, Farmington, 1981-98, prof./chair pediats., 1998—. Dir., chair pediats. St. Francis Hosp. and Med. Ctr., Hartford, Conn., 1992-03; physician-in-chief Conn. Children's Med. Ctr., Hartford, 1998—, editor AMSPDC Sec., Jour. Pediat., 2009-. Author: Learning and Behavior Problems of Schoolchildren, 1985; editor: Pediatrics: National Medical Series for Independent Study, 1987, 5th edit., 2009, Jour. Devel. & Behavioral Pediats., 1996-2002; co-editor: Developmental-Behavioral Pediatrics: Evidence and Practice, 2007; mem. editl. bd. Pediats., 1991-98, Ambulatory Child Health, Current Pediatrics, 1991—2005, Jour. Pediat., 2009-; contbr. articles to profl. jours. Vol. Salvation Army Shelter Pediat. Clinic, Hartford, 1991—. Fellow: Am. Acad. Pediats. (chair com. on sci. mtgs. 1994—96); mem.: Soc. Devel. and Behavioral Pediats. (pres. 2005—06), Acad. Pediat. Assn. Office: Conn Children's Med Ctr 282 Washington St Hartford CT 06106-3322 Business E-Mail: pdworki@ccmckids.org.

DWORSKY, BRAD, orthopedist; BS, Wash. U., St. Louis; MS, MD, Rush U. Staff physician Provena St. Joseph's Med. Ctr., Silver Cross Hosp., AmSurg; chmn. orthopedic surgery Provena St. Joseph Med. Ctr., Joliet, dir. sports medicine; ptnr. Hinsdale Orthopaedic Assoc. Intern Rush Presbyterian-St. Luke's Med. Ctr., resident; fell. Cin. Sports Medicine Ctr.; team physician Joliet Township High Sch., Coal City High Sch., Wilmington High Sch., Reed-Custer High Sch. Mem.: Will-Grundy Med. Soc., Ill. State Med. Soc., Am. Coll. Surgeons, AMA, Arthroscopy Assn. No. Am., Am. Acad. Orthopaedic Surgeons Office: Hinsdale Orthopaedic 550 W Ogden Hinsdale IL 60521

DWYER, JOHANNA TODD, nutritionist, educator; b. Syracuse, NY, Oct. 20, 1938; d. M. Harold and Frances (Markey) D. BS with distinction, Cornell U., 1960; MSc, U. Wis., 1962; MS, Harvard Sch. Pub. Health, Boston, 1965, DSc, 1969. Asst. prof. Harvard Sch. Pub. Health, 1969-73; home economist Procter & Gamble, Cin., 1960-61; rsch. asst. U. Wis., Madison, 1960-62; assoc. prof. Tufts Med. Sch., 1974, prof. medicine and nutrition, 1984—; sr. scientist human nutrition rsch. USDA, Boston, 1988—, asst. adminstr. for human nutrition Agrl. Rsch. Svc. Washington, 2001—02; sr. nutrition rsch. scientist Office of Dietary Supplements, NIH, 2003—. Dir. Frances Stern Nutrition Ctr., New Eng. Med. Ctr., Boston, 1974—; adj. prof. Harvard Sch. Pub. Health, 1988—. Author 3 books, 1979, 83; editor Nutrition Today, 1995—, contbr. over 450 articles to profl. jours. Mem. Mass. Nutrition Bd., Boston, 1980-2004; cons. Exec. Office of Pres., Washington, 1976; mem. bd. sci. counselors Nat. Cancer Inst., 1985-89; com. mem. and nutrition work study Am. Cancer Soc., 1990-94; sec. ADA Found., 2004 Robert Wood Johnson Health Policy fellow, 1980-81, John Stalker award Am. Sch. Food Svc. Assn., 1990, Alumni Merit award Harvand Sch. Pub. Health, 2004; named Vol. of Yr., 2010. Fellow: Am. Soc. Nutrition Scis. (Conrad Elvejhem award for pub. policy 2005), Am. Inst. Nutrition (pres. 1994—95, bd. dirs.), Soc. for Nutrition Edn. (bd. dirs. 1975—77, pres. 1976, J. Harvey Wiley award 1983), Am. Soc. Clin. Nutrition (sec. 1990—93); mem.: APHA (program devel. bd. 1990—92), Am. Soc. Nutrition (med. nutrition coun. 2007—, strategic oversight com. chair 2008—), Dannon Inst. (sci. adv. bd. 2003—06), Internat. Life Scis. Inst. (bd. dirs. 1999—, exec. com. 2005—), Food and Drug Law Inst. (bd. dirs. 1980—95), Am. Inst. Food and Wine (bd. dirs. 1991—95), Nutrition Screening Initiative (tech. and sci. rev. com. 1990—2004), Inst. Medicine of NAS (food and nutrition bd. 1990—2000, councilor 2001—03, mil. nutrition com. mem. 2004—09, report renew com. 2005—), Am. Dietetic Assn. (legis. and pub. policy com. 1998—2004, sec. found. 2005—09, lectr., bd. mem. ADA Found., Lenna Frances Cooper award 1980, Medallion award 2002), Am. Soc. Parenteral and Enteral Nutrition (adv. bd. 1978—). Office: Tufts Med Ctr 750 Washington St PO Box 783 Boston MA 02102-0783 Office Phone: 617-636-5273. Personal E-mail: toddyd@msn.com, toddyd@me.com. Business E-Mail: jdwyer1@tuftsmedicalcenter.org.

DWYER, JUDITH MARGARET, health service manager and educator, researcher; b. Brisbane, Australia, Mar. 20, 1951; d. Patrick Francis and Joie Elwyn (Malone) D.; m. Charles Irving Meisner, Oct. 31, 1975 (div. 1982); 1 child, Rachel Sarah Meisner. BA, U. Queensland, 1973; diploma, Victoria Coll., 1981; MBA, U. Adelaide, 1989. Dir. Julia Farr Ctr., Adelaide, 1985-87; CEO Family Planning Assn., Adelaide, 1987-89; dir. health programs S.A. Health Commn., Adelaide, 1989-91; dep. CEO Women's Children's Hosp., Adelaide, 1991-95; CEO Flinders Med. Ctr., Adelaide, 1995-99, So. Health Care Network, Melbourne, 1999-2000; assoc. prof. health svcs. mgmt. LaTrobe U., 2000—05, adj. prof., 2006—; prof. health svcs. mgmt. Flinders U., 2006—; dir. Cancer Coun. South Australia, 2010—; rsch. program leader Co-op Rsch. Ctr. Aboriginal & Torres Strait Islander Health, 2010—. Dir. Australian Inst. Health & Welfare, Canberra, 1995-98, Prince Henry's Inst. of Medical Rsch., Melbourne, 1999-2000; pres. Women's Hosp. Australia, 1994-95; assoc. prof. Flinders U., 1997-99, mem. resources com., 1996-99; adj. prof. Inst. Pub. Health, Monash U., 2000—2005; rsch. program; spkr. at numerous confs.; participant in various convs. Contbr. articles to profl. jours. Mem. AHA Nat. Learning Set, 1993—; justice of peace South Australia, 1986-99; dir. Yarra Valley Water, 2000—2006. Recipient Women's Health award Australian Med. Assn., 1998, MBA Soc. prize, 1989; numerous rsch. grants. Fellow Australasian Coll. Health Sci. Mgmt., Australian Inst. Co. Dirs.; mem. Tandanya Nat. Aboriginal Cultural Ctr. (assoc.). Avocation: walking. Office: Health Care Mgmt Finders Univ Po Box 2100 Adelaide SA 5001 Australia Office Phone: 08-82017762.

DY, DAVID YU, surgeon, oncologist; b. Cebu City, Philippines, June 13, 1958; s. Tiao Un and Lourdes Yu Dy; m. Amy Nierva Goleta, Oct. 3, 1956; children: Catherine Lourdes, Christopher Lawrence. BS, U. Philippines, Quezon City, 1978; MD, U. Philippines, Manila, 1982; CM, U. New South Wales, Sydney, 1992; MA in Buss. Econs., U. Asia Pacific, Philippines, 2006. Diplomate Philippine Bd. Surgery. Intern Philippine Gen. Hosp., Manila, 1982—83; human anatomy preceptor U. Philippines, Coll. Medicine, Manila, 1984—84; gen. surgery resident Philippine Gen. Hosp., Manila, 1985—89; hon. surg. registrar U. New South Wales, St. George Hosp., Sydney, 1990—91; rsch. asst. U. Tex., M.D. Anderson Cancer Ctr., Houston, 1992—93; surg. oncologist St. Luke's Med. Ctr., Quezon City, MetroManila, Philippines, 1994—. Chair instl. rev. bd. St. Luke's Med. Ctr., Quezon City, 1995—96; pres. Cancer Treatment and Support Found., Inc., QuezonCity, 2002—. Scholar, Australian Internat. Devel. Assistance Bur., 1990—91. Fellow: ACS, Philippine Coll. Surgeons, Soc. Surg. Oncology; mem.: Clin. Oncological Soc. Australia, Am. Assn. Cancer Rsch. (corr.), Am. Soc. Clin. Oncology. Office: St Luke's Med Ctr Dept Surg 279 Eulogio Rodriguez Sr Ave 1102 Quezon City Metromanila Philippines Office Fax: (632)7231054. Business E-Mail: surg.onc1@gmail.com.

DYAR, KATHRYN WILKIN, pediatrician; b. Colquitt, Ga., Feb. 20, 1945; d. Patrick McWhorter and Virginia (Wilkin) Dyar; m. James Ansley Patten, Jan. 1, 1985. BS in Biology, Emory U., Decatur, Ga., 1966; MD, Med. Coll. Ga., Augusta, 1970. Resident in pediatrics Eugene Talmadge Meml. Hosp., Augusta, Ga., 1970-72, Georgetown U. Hosp., Washington, 1972-73; pediatrician Children's Clinic, Tifton, Ga., 1973-74, Children and Youth Project, Norfolk, Va., 1974-83, 90-95, dir., 1990-94; pediatrician Hampton (Va.) Health Dept., 1983-90.

DYBELL, ELIZABETH ANNE SLEDDEN, psychologist; b. Buffalo, Sept. 25, 1958; d. Richard Edward and Angela Brigid Sledden; m. David Joseph Dybell, Nov. 30, 1985. BA in Psychology summa cum laude, U. St. Thomas, Houston, 1980; PhD in Psychology, Tex. Tech. U., 1986. Lic. clin. psychologist, Tex. Rsch. asst. health sci. ctr. Tex. Tech. U., Lubbock, 1983-84, psychol. cons. health sci. ctr. neurology dept., 1982-84; psychology intern U. N.Mex. Med. Sch., Albuquerque, 1984-85; psychotherapist Katz & Assocs. P.C., Houston, 1985-88, Meyer Ctr. for Devel. Pediatrics Tex. Children's Hosp., Houston, 1988-92; pvt. practice Houston, 1990—. Author: (monograph) When Will Life Be Normal?, 1989, Myths of the Super Parent: Finding the Power of Real Parenting, 2003; contbr. articles to numerous publs. Choir mem. St. Thomas More Ch., Houston, 1974-87. Mem. APA, Soc. Pediatric Psychology, Tex. Psychol. Assn., Internat. Dyslexia Assn., Am. Psychol. Soc. (charter). Roman Catholic. Avocations: gardening, horticulture, nature studies. Home and Office: 1770 St James Pl Ste 405 Houston TX 77056-3471

DYBKAER, RENÉ, health facility administrator; b. Copenhagen, Feb. 7, 1926; s. Ove and Kirsten Johanne (Nielsen) Dybkaer. MD, U. Copenhagen, 1951, DSc in Medicine, 2004. Cert. specialist in clin. chemistry. Intern Sundby Hosp., Copenhagen, 1951-52, resident, 1952-54, 55, De Gamles By, Copenhagen, 1954-55, Frederiksberg Hosp., Copenhagen, 1955; reader Univ. Inst. Med. Microbiology, Copenhagen, 1956-70; head dept. med. microbiology Royal Dental Sch., Copenhagen, 1959-70; head dept. clin. chemistry De Gamles By, Noerre Hosp., Copenhagen, 1970-77, Frederiksberg Hosp., Copenhagen, 1977-96, head dept. standardization lab. medicine, 2000—; head dept. standardization lab medicine Kommunehospitalet, Copenhagen, 1997-2000. Cons. De Gamles By, Noerre Hosp., Copenhagen, 1959—69; mem. expert adv. panel Health Lab. Svc. WHO, 1992—2003. Author: Quantities and Units, 1967, An Ontology on Property for Physical, Chemical and Biological Systems, 2004; editor: Good Practice in Decentralized Analytical Clinical Measurement, 1992, Continuous Quality Improvement in Clinical Laboratory Sciences, 1996; contbr. articles to profl. jours. Recipient award Commemorative Lecture Enrique Concustell Bas, 1988, Prof. James O. Westgard Quality award, Antwerp meetings on med. lab. accreditation, 1998. Mem.: Nordkem (chmn. standardization lab. medicine 1992—94), European Confed. Lab. Med. (pres. 1994—97), European Coun. Clin. Lab. Standardization (chmn. stand. act. com. good pract. decentr. clin. lab 1984—92), European Cmty. Bur. Ref. (chmn. cert. com. 1983—96), Internat. Fedn. Clin. Chemistry (v.p. 1973—78, pres. 1979—84, past pres. 1985—90, Henry Wishinsky Disting. Internat. Svc. award 1993), German Soc. Lab. Medicine (corr.), Italian Soc. Clin. Biochemistry (hon.), Israel Soc. Clin. Biochemistry (hon.), Austrian Soc. Clin. Chemistry (hon.), Mex. Assn. Clin. Biochemistry (hon.), Columbian Fedn. Clin. Lab. Specialists (hon.), Danish Soc. Clin. Chemistry (hon.; chmn. 1991—93). Avocations: classical jazz, stamp collecting/philately. Office: Frederiksberg Hosp Dept Standard Lab Med Region H Frederiksberg Hosp Nordre Fasanvej 57 DK-2000 Frederiksberg Denmark Home Phone: 0045 39 63 42 22; Office Phone: 0045 38 16 38 70. Personal E-mail: rene.dybkaer@frh.regionh.dk.

DYBUL, MARK RICHARD, immunologist, former ambassador; b. Sept. 23, 1963; AB, Georgetown U., 1985, MD, 1992. Resident internal medicine U. Chgo. Hospitals, 1992—95; fellow Nat. Inst. Allergy and Infectious Diseases, 1998; capt. U.S. Pub. Health Svc. Commissioned Corps; staff clinician lab. immunoregulation Nat. Inst. Allergy and Infectious Diseases/NIH; asst. dir. medical affairs Nat. Inst. Allergy and Infectious Diseases NIH; co-exec. sec. HIV therapy guidelines US Dept. Health & Human Services, head internat. prevention mother and child HIV initiative, mem. emergency plan planning task force; dep. global AIDS coord. US Dept. State, 2005—06, acting global AIDS coord., 2006, global AIDS coord., 2006—09.

DYCK, WALTER PETER, gastroenterologist, educator, academic administrator; b. Winkler, Man., Can., 1935; MD, U. Kans., 1961. Diplomate Am. Bd. Internal Medicine, Am. Bd. Gastroenterology. Intern Henry Ford Hosp., Detroit, 1961—62, resident in internal medicine, 1962-63, 65-66; rsch. fellow gastroenterology U. Zurich, Switzerland, 1963—64; fellow enzymology rsch. U. Toronto, Ont., Canada, 1964—65; fellow gastroenterology Mt. Sinai Sch. Medicine, NYC, 1966—68; mem. sr. staff Scott and White Clinic, Temple, Tex., 1968—2006, chmn. dept. rsch., 1969—72, dir. divsn. gastroenterology, 1972—96; prof. medicine, dir. divsn. gastroenterology Tex. A&M Coll. Medicine, 1978—96, sr. assoc. dean, 1996—2003, exec. assoc. dean, 2003—06, prof. emeritus, 2006—; adminstrv. dir. rsch. and edn. divsns., chief acad. officer Scott and White Meml. Hosp., Temple, 1996—2006; sr. advisor Temple Health and Biosci. Econ.

Devel. Corp., 2006—. Mem. gen. medicine study sect. A NIH, 1973-77. Fellow ACP, Am. Coll. Gastroenterology; mem. AMA, Am. Fedn. Clin. Rsch., Am. Gastroenterology Assn., Am. Physiol. Soc., So. Soc. Clin. Investigation, Soc. for Exptl. Biology and Medicine, Am. Pancreatic Assn., N.Y. Acad. Scis. Home: 9424 Hackberry Rd Holland TX 76534 E-mail: wdyck@swmail.sw.org.

DYE, SHARON ELIZABETH HERNDON, speech pathologist; b. Springfield, Mo., June 14, 1952; d. Leonard Leroy and Virginia Louise (Kennard) Herndon; divorced children: Brian Keith Dye, Johnathan Paul Dye, Christopher Shawn Dye. BS, Marquette U., 1973, MS, 1975. Counselor to supr. Career Youth Devel., Milw., 1973—76; speech pathologist Milw. Pub. Schs., 1976-98; head start speech pathologist Peacé Action Milw.-Milw., Inc., 1998—; speech pathologist Phillis Wheatley Elem. Sch., Milw., 1999—, Clara Barton, Spotted Eagle H.S., Willowglen Acad., Willowglen Cornerstone, Peace Action, Wis., 2004, Barton Elem. Sch., 2006—, Bine Elem. Sch., 2006—. Interant. speech pathologist Wis. Speech Lang. Hearing Assn., 1998-99; speech pathologist North Divn. HS PTA, 1998—, mem. spl. edn. com., 2000-02; part-time resident care worker Bell Therapy, Phoenix., Benton Sch. HR Acad., 2005-; resident care worker Bell Therapy-Phonex Care Sys., 2005-. Author: (poetry) Wind Riders, 1996; guest host area cable TV program MATA. Vol. House of Correction, Franklin, Wis., 1993, glaucoma screenings, 1995, 96; mem. Jobs for Peace, 1994, 95; past mem. Progressive Milw., Jamie's Club Theatre, featured poet, 1999, 2001; mem. spl. edn. com. PTA, 2000-2003; commr. neighborhood perspective com. Fondy Neighborhood Bus. Assn., 2002-2003; mem. In Touch Prayer Ptnrs., 2005-; bd. mem. Wis Edn. Assn. Student Support, 2004-06. Mem. NEA (del. rep. assembly 2000-03), Wis. Speech Lang. Hearing Assn., Wis. Edn. Assn. (del., rep. assembly, student support programs conf. com., 2001-06, student support programs bd. dir., 2003-06), Nat. Assn. Black Speech, Lang. and Hearing, Milw. Tchrs. Edn. Assn. (parent tchr. cmty. partnerships com., speech pathologist alt. bldg. rep., 2006-, spl. edn. com., 2004—), Barton Speech Pathologists, Bruce Speech Pathologists, Milw. Met. Assn. Black Sch. Educators, Marquette U. Alumni Assn., Milkw. Assn. Black Sch. Educators, Jamie's Club Theater, Nat. Assoc. Profl. Women, ETA Phi Beta. Baptist. Avocation: writing inspirational songs and poetry. Personal E-mail: ladydye49@yahoo.com. Business E-Mail: dyese@mail.milwaukee.k12.wi.us.

DYER, RAYMOND B., diagnostic radiology physician; MD, U. Va., 1977. Diplomate Diagnostic Radiology Am. Bd. Radiology, Ariz., 1981. Intern, internal medicine WFUBMC, 1977—78; resident, diag radiol. U. Va., 1978—81; prof. radiology and urology Wake Forest U. Sch. Medicine, Winston-Salem, NC, 1991—. Contbr. articles to sci. jours. Fellow: Soc. Uroradiology (pres. 2008—09), Am. Coll. Radiology. Office: Wake Forest U Sch Med Medical Center Blvd Winston Salem NC 27157 Office Phone: 336-716-2471. Office Fax: 336-716-0555, 336-716-0555.

DYER, WAYNE WALTER, psychologist, writer, radio and television personality; b. Detroit, May 10, 1940; s. Melvin Lyle and Hazel Irene (Vollick) Dyer; m. Marcelene Louise Dyer (div.); children: Shane, Stephanie, Skye, Sommer, Serena, Sands, Saje; 1 child from previous marriage, Tracy. BS, Wayne State U., Detroit, 1965, MS in Counseling and Ednl. Psychology, 1966, EdD in Counseling and Psychology, 1970. Tchr., counselor Pershing HS, Detroit, 1965-67; dir. guidance/counseling Mercy HS, Farmington, Mich., 1967-71; instr. counselor edn. Wayne State U., 1970—73; staff cons. Herman Kiefer Hosp., Detroit, 1974-75; staff cons., instr. guidance and sch. psychol. pers. Half Hollow Sch. Dist., Huntington, NY, 1973-75; mem. tchg. faculty North Shore U. Hosp., Cornell U. Med. Coll., Manhasset, NY, 1974-75; asst. prof. counselor edn. St. John's U., Jamaica, NY, 1971-74, assoc. prof., 1974-77. Author: Counseling Techniques That Work, 1975, Your Erroneous Zones, 1976, Pulling Your Own Strings, 1978, Group Counseling for Personal Mastery, 1980, The Sky's the Limit, 1980, Gifts from Eykis: A Story of Self-Discovery, 1983, What Do You Really Want for Your Children, 1985, Happy Holidays!, 1986, Real Magic: Creating Miracles in Everyday Life, 1992, Everyday Wisdom, 1993, How to Be a No-Limit Person, 1994, You'll See It When You Believe It: The Way to Your Personal Transformation, 1995, Your Sacred Self: Making the Decision to Be Free, 1995, A Promise Is a Promise: An Almost Unbelievable Story of a Mother's Unconditional Love and What It Can Teach Us, 1996, Manifest Your Destiny: The Nine Spiritual Principles for Getting Everything You Want, 1997, Wisdom of the Ages, 1998, There's a Spiritual Solution to Every Problem, 2001, 10 Secrets For Success And Inner Peace, 2002, It's Never Crowded Along the Extra Mile, 2002, Getting in the Gap: Making Conscious Contact With God Through Meditation, 2002, The Caroline Myss & Wayne Dyer Seminar, 2003, The Power of Intention: Learning to Co-Create Your World Your Way, 2004, Staying on the Path, 2004, Incredible You!, 2005, Inspiration: Your Ultimate Calling, 2006, Being in Balance: 9 Principles for Creating habits to Match Your Desires, 2006, Everyday Wisdom for Success, 2006, Making Your Thoughts Work for You, 2007, Change Your Thoughts - Change Your Life: Living the Wisdom of the Tao, 2007, Living The Wisdom Of The Tao: The Complete Tao Te Ching and Affirmations, 2008, Excuses Begone!, 2009; over 4000 appearances on TV/radio programs including Phil Donohue Show, Tonight Show, Dinah Shore Show, Merv Griffin Show, Mike Douglas Show, Good Morning America, Canada AM, Oprah Winfrey Show, others; contbr. numerous articles to profl. jours. Served with USN, 1958—62. Recipient Disting. Alumni of Yr., Wayne State U., 1980, Golden Gavel award, Internat. Toastmasters, 1987.

DYER-COLE, PAULINE, school psychologist, educator; b. Methuen, Mass., Aug. 20, 1935; d. E. Dewey and Rose Alma (Des Jardins) Dyer; m. Richard Grey, Aug. 1, 1964 (dec. 1977); children: Douglas Richard, Christopher Lachlan, Heather Judith; m. Malcolm A. Cole, July 23, 1983. BS in Edn. and Music, Lowell State Coll., Mass., 1957; MEd, Boston State Coll., 1961; EdD, Clark U., Mass., 1991. Lic. ednl. psychologist, Mass.; cert. sch. psychologist, Mass.; nat. cert. sch. psychologist. Supr. music and art Merrimac and W. Newbury (Mass.) Pub. Schs., 1957-59; music editor textbooks Allyn & Bacon, Inc., Boston, 1959-64; prof. music West Pines Coll., Chester, NH, 1969-72; sch. psychologist Nashoba Regional H.S., Bolton, Mass., 1979—2001, chair SPED dept., 1995—2001, dir. SPED dept., 1998—2001; child study dept. Worcester (Mass.) Pub. Schs., 2001—10. Vis. lectr., then vis. prof. Framingham (Mass.) State Coll., 1980—89; dir. psychol. testing Nashoba Regional Sch. Dist., Bolton, Mass., 1980—94; dean adv. bd. U. Mass. Lowell, 2007—. Author: The Play Game Songbook, 1964; singer (soprano): The Worcester Chorus, 2003—; singer: Robert Page Festival Chorus, 2008, Blackstone Valley Chorale, 2008—. V.p., bd. dirs. Timberlane Devel. Ctr., Plaistow, N.H., 1970-73; founder Friends of Kimi Nichols Devel. Ctr., Plaistow, N.H., 1973; chmn. human svcs. St. Ann Parish, Southborough, Mass., 1974-77, active, 1973-85; citizen amb. del. People to People, China, 1995; active The Regional Lab., Andover, Mass., 1993-2001. Fellow Frances L. Hyatt fellow, Clark U., 1977—79. Mem. Nat. Assn. Sch. Psychologists (cert.), Mass. Assn. Sch. Psychologists, Mass. Tchrs. Assn., People to People Internat. Roman Catholic. Avocations: music, boating, swimming, reading, creative writing. Home: 43 Crowningshield Dr Paxton MA 01612-1253 Personal E-mail: dyercole@charter.net.

DYESS, BRIAN NELSON, oral and maxillofacial surgeon; b. Columbus, Ga., Aug. 30, 1956; s. Garon Dempsey and Frances Fortenberry D.; m. Jeanne Billon Dyess, Apr. 20, 1997; children: Christian Brian, Jaime Patricia, Daniel Garon. BS in Zoology, La. State U., 1979; DDS, La. State U., New Orleans, 1983. Diplomate Am. Bd. Oral and Maxillofacial Surgery. Pvt. practice, Baton Rouge, 1988—; clin. asst. prof. Sch. Dentistry La. State U., New Orleans, 1988—. Chief dental svc., med. exec. com. Our Lady of the Lake Hosp., Baton Rouge, 1995-96; program chmn. Greater Baton Rouge Dental Assn., 1995-96; lectr. in field. Contbr. articles to profl. jours. Active free med. and dental clinic, Baton Rouge; fund generator Cmty. Fund for Arts, Baton Rouge, 1992-93, United Way, Baton Rouge, 1994-95. Fellow Internat. Assn. Oral and Maxillofacial Surgeons, Am. Assn. Oral and Maxillofacial Surgeons, La. Assn. Oral and Maxillofacial Surgeons (v.p., pres. elect 1997—); mem. ADA, Am. Cleft-Palate-Craniofacial Assn., La. Dental Assn., Greater Baton Rouge Dental Assn. (pres. 1996), C. Edmund Kelly Hon. Soc. (hon. mem.), Omicron Kappa Upsilon (hon. mem.). Democrat. Baptist. Avocations: outdoor sports, fishing, coaching children sports. Home: 19420 S Muirfield Cir Baton Rouge LA 70810-5989 Office: 7777 Hennessy Blvd Ste 610 Baton Rouge LA 70808-4366

DYKEN, MARK LEWIS, JR., neurologist, educator; b. Laramie, Wyo., Aug. 26, 1928; s. Mark L. and Thelma Violet (Achenbach) D.; m. Beverly All, June 8, 1951; children: Betsy Lynn, Mark Eric, Julie Suzanne, Amy Luise, Andrew Christopher, Gregory Allen. BS in Anatomy and Physiology, Ind. U., 1951, MD, 1954. Diplomate Am. Bd. Psychiatry and Neurology. Intern Indpls. Gen. Hosp., 1954-55; resident in neurology Ind. U. Med. Ctr., 1955-58; clin. dir., dir. rsch. New Castle (Ind.) State Hosp., 1958-61; asst. dept. neurology Ind. U., 1958-61, assoc. prof. neurology, 1964-69, prof., 1969—, chmn. dept. neurology, 1971-94, prof. emeritus, 1994—. Chmn. profl. adv. coun. Nat. Easter Seal Soc., 1974-82; cons., chmn. panel on rev. neurol. devices subcom. FDA, 1979-83; bd. dirs. Am. Bd. Psychiatry and Neurology, 1988-96, pres., 1995. Editor-in-chief Stroke, 1992-2000; contbr. numerous articles on topics including cerebral vascular disease, blood flow, epilepsy, electroencephalography, muscle disease, to profl. jours. With U.S. Army, 1946-48. Recipient numerous grants in cerebrovascular disease. Fellow ACP; mem. AMA, Am. Assn. Univ. Profs. Neurology (pres. 1986-88), Epilepsy Found. Am., Am. Heart Assn (chmn. stroke coun. 1984-86, v.p. for sci. couns. 1988-89), Ind. Neurol. Assn. (charter pres. 1966-68), Am. Acad. Neurology, Am. Neurol. Assn., Sigma Xi, Alpha Omega Alpha. Home: 7406 W 92nd St Zionsville IN 46077-9103 Office: Ind U Med Ctr Neurol Dept 545 Barnhill Dr EM124 Indianapolis IN 46202 Home Phone: 317-873-4211; Office Phone: 317-278-2340. E-mail: mdyken@aol.com.

DYKES, VIRGINIA CHANDLER, occupational therapist, educator; b. Evanston, Ill., Jan. 10, 1930; d. Daniel Guy and Helen (Schnedier) Goodman; children: Ron Lee, Chuch Lee Chandler, james R., Jr. BA in Art and Psychology, So. Meth. U., 1951; postgrad. in occupl. therapy, Tex. Women's U., 1953. Dir. occupl. and recreational therapy Baylor U. Med. Ctr., Dallas, 1956-60, 68-89; pvt. practice Dallas, 1989-92; dir. occupl. and recreational therapy Fla. Hosp., Orlando, 1962-65; staff therapist Parkland meml. Hosp., Dallas, 1965-68. Cons. Arthritis Found., 1974-89, benefactor; Fanny B. Vanderkodi lectr. Tex. Women's U., 1993—, lord lady mayor, Dickens Christmas Party, Dallas Theatre Ctr., 2007. Author: (manual) Lightcast II Splints, 1976; Adult Visual Perceptual Evaluation, 1981; contbr. articles to profl. jours. Sponsor Kimball Art Mus.; mem. bd. regents Tex. Woman's U., 2003—10; mem. coord. bd. allied health adv. com. Tex. Coll. and Univ. Sys., 1980—88; bd. dirs. Tex. Arthritis Found., chmn. patient svcs. com., 1985—89, exec. bd. sec.; bd. dirs. Dallas Opera, also women's bd.; bd. dirs. Dallas Arboretum, Theatre III, Fort Worth Opera, Baylor U. Med. Ctr. Found.; chmn. adv. bd. healing environment program Baylor Med. Ctr.; pres. Diana Dean Head Injury Guild, 1992—93. Recipient Disting. Alumni award, Tex. Women's U., 2010; named Tex. Occupl. Therapist of Yr., 1985, Chi Omega of Yr., 2006; Ann. Virginia Chandler Dykes Leadership award named in her honor, Tex. Women's U. Mem. Tex. Occupl. Therapy Assn. (life mem. award), World Fedn. Occupl. Therapists (participant 8th Internat. Congress, Hamburg, Germany, 1982, del. to 10th European Congress on Rheumatology, Moscow 1983), Boomerang Club (dir. 1971-88), Les Femmes du Monde, Pierian Lit. Club. Home: 8523 Thackery St Apt 2203 Dallas TX 75225-3907

DYKEWICZ, MARK STEVEN, physician; b. Flint, Mich., May 21, 1955; s. Richard Alfred and Evelyn Ellen Dykewicz; m. Lenora-Marya Anop. BS, U. Mich., 1977; MD, St. Louis U., 1981. Resident medicine Northwestern U. Med. Sch., Chgo., 1981-84, fellow allergy-immunology, 1984-86, asst. prof. medicine, 1986-90; asst. prof. internal medicine St. Louis U. Med. Sch., 1990—94, assoc. prof., 1994—2002, prof., 2002—09, dir. allergy immunology postgrad. tng. program, 1997—2009, chief section allergy and clin. immunology, divsn. immunobiology, prof. internal medicine, 2007—09; dir. Allergy & Immunology Fellowship Program; chief allergy & immunology, sec. pulmonary critical care, allergy & immunologic diseases Wake Forest U. Sch. Medicine, 2009—. Mem. pulmonary allergy drug adv. com. FDA, 1999—2003, chmn., 2001—03; bd. dirs. Am. Bd. Allergy and Immunology, 2004—09. Chief editor Joint Task Force Practice Parameters on Rhinitis, 1998—2008. Recipient Disting. Svc. award, Am. Coll. Allergy, Asthma and Immunology, 1999. Fellow ACP, Am. Coll. Chest Physicians, Am. Acad. Allergy-Immunology; mem. Am. Thoracic Soc., Am. Acad. Allergy, Asthma and Immunology (chmn. com. on occupl. lung disease 1998-2000, chmn. com. on adverse reactions to drugs and biols. 2001-03, chmn. com. on rhinitis 2004-05, bd. dirs., 2009-, Spl. Recognition award 1999) Office Phone: 336-713-7520. Business E-Mail: dykewicz@wakehealth.edu.

DYKSTRA, DENNIS DALE, physiatrist; b. Lakewood, Ohio, Feb. 21, 1950; s. Gerald and Grace Maire (Thomas) D.; m. Mary Louise Kerker, May 16, 1992; children: Dorothy, Perry, Caitlin, Patrick. AB in Zoology summa cum laude, Ohio U., 1972; MD, U. Cin., 1976; PhD, U. Minn., 1988, M in Health Adminstrn., 1999. Diplomate Am. Bd. Pediatrics, Am. Bd. Phys. Medicine and Rehab. Intern/resident Cin. Children's Hosp., 1976-81; instr. U. Minn., Mpls., 1981-88, asst. prof., 1988-92, assoc. prof. phys. medicine/rehab./pediatrics/urol. surgery, 1992—, head dept. phys. medicine/rehab., 1992—; assoc. chief staff for rehab. VA Med. Ctr., Mpls., 1994-97. Author: Krusen's Handbook of Phys. Medicine and Rehabilitation, 1991; contbr. articles to profl. jours. Med. advisor Minn. Spasmodic Torticolits Soc., Duluth, Minn., 1991—. Recipient Phys. Med. and Rehab. Investigator award Phys. Med. and Rehab. Rsch. Found., 1984, 85; Spinal Cord Soc. grantee, 1990. Fellow Am. Acad. Phys. Med. and Rehab. (chair edn. com. 1996—), Am. Acad. Pediatrics, Am. Assn. Electrodiagnostic Medicine. Achievements include 2 patents on method of apparatus for mechanical stimulation of nerves, method and device for pharmacological control of spasticity. Office: Univ Minn 420 Delaware St SE Box 297 Mayor Bldg Minneapolis MN 55455 Office Phone: 612-626-5399.

DYLAG, HELEN MARIE, health facility administrator; b. Cleve., Oct. 14, 1950; d. Stanley John and Helen Agnes (Jarkiewicz) D. BSN, St. John Coll., Cleve., 1971; MS, Ohio State U., Columbus, 1973. RN, Ohio. Nurse V.A. Adminstrn. Hosp., Brecksville, Ohio, 1971-72; clin. specialist, psychiat.-mental health nursing Marymount Hosp./Mental Health Ctr., Garfield Heights, Ohio, 1973-78, dir. consultation and edn. dept., 1978-84, dir. Ctr. for Health Styles, 1984-88; adminstrv. dir. Women's Healthcare Ctr./St. Luke's Hosp., Cleve., 1988-90; adminstrv. dir. dept. of psychiatry MetroHealth Sys, Cleve., 1990-97; CEO FarWest Ctr., Westlake, Ohio, 1997—. Mem. adv. coun. Joint Commn. Mental Health Ctrs., 2007—; nat. coun. cmty. behavioural healthcare Adv. Coun. Jr. Commn., 2010—. Contbg. author: Nursing of Families in Crisis, 1974, Distributive Nursing Practice: A Systems Approach to Community Health, 1977; producer and host "Health Styles" TV Talk Show, 1987-88; contbr. articles to profl. jours. Trustee The Stroke Assn. of Ohio, Cleve., 1990-91; mem. Women of Achievement com., Women's City Club, Cleve., 1989-91; officer, bd. dirs. The Littlest Heroes, Inc., 2000—. Recipient award Greater Cleve. Hosp. Assn., 1981, Innovator award Am. Hosp. Assn./Ctr. for Health Promotion, 1985, Disting. Women Healthcare award Healthcare Monitor and Vis. Nurse Assn. Cleve., 2000, Woodruff prize Excellence Behavioral Health, 2005, Lifetime Achievement award Nat. Coun. Cmty. Behavioral Healthcare, 2006; named Woman of Note, Crain's Cleve. Bus., 2007. Mem. Assn. Mental Health Adminstrs., Am. Coll. Healthcare Execs., Healthcare Adminstrs. Assn. of Northeast Ohio, Sigma Theta Tau. Avocations: interior decorating, gardening, jazz, travel, exercise. Office: FarWest Ctr 29133 Health Campus Dr Cleveland OH 44145-5256 Business E-Mail: hmdylag@cox.net.

DY-LIACCO, GABRIEL S., psychotherapist, social sciences educator; BA in Psychology, Ateneo de Manila U., Quezon City, Philippines, 1993; MS in Pastoral Counseling, Loyola Coll., 1999, PhD in Pastoral Counseling, 2006. Cert. Nat. Bd. Cert. Counselors Md., lic. clin. profl. counselor 2002, Va. lic. profl. counselor, 2006. Adult and adolescent psychotherapist Key Point Health Svcs., Inc., Catonsville, Md., 1999—2004; doctral rsch. fellow dept. pastoral counseling Loyola Coll., Columbia, Md., 2002—03, tchg. asst. dept. pastoral counseling, 2003—04, rsch. asst. dept. psychology, 2004—05, asst. prof. dept. pastoral counseling, 2007—; asst. prof. Sch. Psychology and Counseling Regent U. Grad. Ctr., Alexandria, Va., 2005—07; therapist Saint Luke Inst. Patient care monitor Key Point Health Svcs., Inc., Catonsville, Md., 2003—04, clin. peer trainer, 2003—04, clin. internship supr., 2002—03; individual clin. supr. Pastoral Counseling Dept., Loyola Coll. in Md., Columbia, Md., 2002—03; assoc. editor Psychology of Religion and Spirituality; mem. editl. adv. bd. Scientific Jours. Internat. Contbr. articles and revs. to profl. jours.; translator: (Tagalog version) Spiritual Transcendence Scale. Vol. Parish Pastoral Coun. for Responsible Voting, Quezon City, Philippines, 1992, SJ Prison Ministry, Muntinlupa, Metro Manila, 1989—90; mem. Arvisu House SJ Prenovitiate, Quezon City, 1989—91. Recipient William James award, Coun. on Spiritual Practices, 2005. Mem.: APA (exec. com. divsn. 36 2006—07), Am. Counseling Assn., Am. Mental Health Counselors Assn. (clin. mem.), Profl. Assn. Diving Instrs. (life; dive master 1989—), Chi Sigma Iota (founding chpt. faculty advisor), Alpha Sigma Nu. Avocations: scuba diving, travel. Business E-Mail: gdyliacco@loyola.edu.

DZAU, VICTOR JOSEPH, healthcare executive, cardiologist, director, researcher; b. Shanghai, Oct. 23, 1946; MD, McGill U., 1972. Cert. in internal medicine, subspecialty in cardiovasc. disease. With Harvard Med. Sch. Stanford & Duke U.; intern N.Y. Hosp., 1972-73; resident in medicine Peter Bent Brigham Hosp., Boston, 1974-76, chief resident, 1976-78; fellow in rsch. Mass. Gen. Hosp., Boston, 1976-78, fellow in cardiology, 1979-80; chief divsn. vascular medicine and atherosclerosis Brigham & Women's Hosp., 1984-90; dir. cardiovasc. rsch. ctr. Stanford U. Sch. Medicine, chief divsn. cardiovasc. medicine, 1990-96, assoc. chmn. dept. medicine, 1993-96, chmn. dept. medicine, 1995-96; dir. Am. Heart Assn.-Bugher Found. Ctr. for Molecular Biology, 1991-96; chmn. dept. med., dir. rsch. Brigham & Women's Hosp., 1996—2004; chancellor for health affairs Duke University, 2004—; pres., CEO Duke University Health Systems, 2004—. Asst. prof. medicine, assoc. prof. medicine Harvard Med. Sch., 1980—90, Hersey prof. theory and practice of medicine, 1996—2004; William G. Irvin prof. medicine Stanford U. Sch. Medicine, 1990—96, Arthur L. Bloomfield prof., medicine, 1995—96; bd. dirs. Genzyme, 2000—11, Medtronic, Inc., 2002—, Duke U. Health System, 2004—; James B. Duke prof. medicine Duke U., 2004—; bd. dirs. PepsiCo, Inc., 2005—, Alnylam Inc., 2007—. Mem.: Inst. Medicine (coun. mem.). Office: Duke U Med Ctr 1 Davison Blvd Box 3701 Durham NC 27710 Office Phone: 919-684-2255. Business E-Mail: victor.dzau@duke.edu.

DZIEWANOWSKA, ZOFIA ELIZABETH, pharmaceutical executive; b. Warsaw, Nov. 17, 1939; came to U.S., 1972; d. Stanislaw Kazimierz Dziewanowski and Zofia Danuta (Mieczkowska) Rudowska; m. Krzysztof A. Kunert, Sept. 1, 1961 (div. 1971); 1 child, Martin. MD, U. Warsaw, 1963; PhD, Polish Acad. Sci., 1970. MD recert. U.K., 1972, U.S., 1973. Asst. prof. psychiatry U. Warsaw Med. Sch., 1969—71; sr. house officer St. George's Hosp., U. London, 1971—72; assoc. dir. Merck Sharp & Dohme, Rahway, NJ, 1972—76; vis. assoc. physician Rockefeller U. Hosp., NYC, 1975—76; adj. asst.

prof. psychiatry Cornell U. Med. Ctr., NYC, 1978—; v.p., global med. dir. Hoffmann-La Roche, Inc., Nutley, NJ, 1976—94; sr. v.p., dir. global med. affairs Genta Inc., San Diego, 1994—97; sr. v.p. drug devel. and regulatory Cypros Pharms. Corp., Carlsbad, Calif., 1997—99; pres., med. dir. New Drug Assocs., La Jolla, Calif., 1999—; sr. v.p. clin. and regulatory Maxia Pharms, San Diego, 2001—02; v.p. clin. rsch. Ligand Pharm, Inc., San Diego, 2002—09. Lectr. in field. Contbr. articles to profl. publs. Bd. dirs Royal Soc. Medicine Found.; mem. alumni coun. Cornell U. Med. Ctr. Recipient TWIN Honoree award for Outstanding Women in Mgmt., Ridgewood (N.J.) YWCA, 1984. Mem. AMA, AAAS, Am. Soc. Pharmacology and Therapeutics, Am. Coll. Neuropsychopharmacology, N.Y. Acad. Scis., PhRMA. (vice chmn. steering com. med. sect., chmn. internat. med. affairs com., head biotech. working group), Royal Soc. Medicine (U.K.), Drug Info. Assn. (Woman of Yr. award 1994), Am. Assn. Pharm. Physicians. Roman Catholic. Achievements include original research on the role of the nervous system in the regulation of respiratory functions, research and development and therapeutic uses of many new drugs, pharmaceutical medicine and biotechnology; molecular biology derived as well as conventional products including antisense, interferon efficacy in cancer, virology and AIDS and drugs useful in cardiovascular, immunological, neuropsychiatric, infectious diseases, and others; impact of different cultures on medical practices and clinical research; drug evaluation and development management strategies of pharmaceutical industries; treatments against cardiac and brain ischemia, cytoprotection.

EADEN, JAYNE ALISON, gastroenterologist, consultant; b. Barnsley, England, Dec. 12, 1968; d. David and Dorothy Winifred Eaden. MB, BChir, U. Leicester, Eng., 1992, MD, 2000. Ho. officer Leicester Gen. Hosp., England, 1992—93; sr. ho. officer Leicester Royal Infirmary, 1993—95; rschr. East of Eng. Rotation, 1995—97; rsch. fellow Leicester Gen. Hosp., 1997—2000; vis. fellow U. Adelaide, Australia, 2000—01; registrar Leicester Royal Infirmary, Leicestershire, England, 2002—; cons. Walsgrave Hosp., Coventry, England, 2002—. Internat. spkr. on cancer, 2000—. Author: British Guidelines for Cancer Surveillance in Inflammatory Bowel Disease Patients, 2001; contbr. chapters to books. Mem.: Am. Cancer Soc., British Soc. Gastroenterologists, Royal Coll. Physicians. Avocations: golf, gardening, good food and wine.

EAGAN, MARIE T. (RIA EAGAN), chiropractor; b. Rockville Ctr., NY, June 17, 1952; d. John F. and Mary (Ebner) E. BA, Goddard Coll., 1975; D in Chiropractic Medicine, N.Y. Chiropractic Coll., 1983. Pvt. practice chiropractic medicine, NYC, 1983—. Chiropractic examiner N.Y. State Bd. Chiropractic, 1995. Mem.: Internat. Chiropractic Assn., Am. Chiropractic Assn. Democrat. Office: 20E Vanderventer Ave Ste 100 Port Washington NY 11050 Office Phone: 516-944-9460.

EAGLE, KIM ALLEN, cardiologist; m. Darlene Eagle; 1 child, Taylor. Grad., Oreg. State U., 1976; MD, Tufts U. Sch. of Medicine, Boston, 1979. Cert. Internal Medicine, Cardiovascular Disease, 1987. Intern, resident Yale New Haven Hosp., 1979—82, chief resident, 1982—83; rsch. and clin. fellow, cardiology and health svcs. rsch. Harvard Med. Sch. and Mass. Gen. Hosp., Boston, 1983—86; instr. Mass. Gen. Hosp., Boston, 1986—88, asst. prof., 1988—94, assoc. prof., 1994, assoc. dir., clin. cardiology; prof., internal medicine U. Mich., Ann Arbor, 1994—, Albion Walter Hewlett Prof., internal medicine, 1994—, dir., Cardiovasc. Ctr., 1994—, chief, clin. cardiovascular medicine, 1994—. Mem. external adv. com. Nat. Heart, Lung and Blood Inst., 2002—06, study chair, Genetic Causes Aortic Disease Initiative, 2006. Editor: (book) Practice of Cardiology, (jours.) 100 Years of Cardiology, Cardiosource Rev. Jour. Fellow: Am. Coll. Cardiology (life; mem. guideline task force, chair, task force develop. performance measures in cardiovascular care, mem. scientific sessions prog. com., bd. trustee 2001—05).

EAGLE, RALPH C., ophthalmologist; Grad., U. Delaware, 1966; MD, U. Pa., 1970. Diplomate Am. Bd. Ophthalmology, 1976. Resident Univ. of Pa., fellow ophthalmic pathology, 1971; resident Scheie Eye Inst., 1975; fellow ophthalmic pathology Armed Forces Inst. of Pathology, 1976; fellow retina rsch. Wills Eye Hosp., 1976; dir. pathology dept. Wills Eye Inst., attending surgeon, Noel T. Sara L. Simmonds prof. ophthalmic pathology; prof. opthalmology Thomas Jefferson Univ., prof. pathology. Pres. Am. Assn. of Ophthalmic Pathologists. Author: (textbook) Eye Pathology, of more than 350 scientific papers. Fellow: Am. Acad. of Ophthalmology; mem.: Am. Registry of Pathology (sec. treas.), Verhoeff-Zimmerman and Eastern Ophthalmic Pathology Socs., Am. Ophthalmological Soc. Office: Wills Eye Institute 9th Fl 840 Walnut St Philadelphia PA 19107 Office Phone: 215-928-3250. Office Fax: 215-928-3276.

EAGLEMAN, DAVID M., neuroscientist, educator; b. Albuquerque, Apr. 1971; BA in English, Rice U., Houston, 1993; PhD in Neuroscience, Baylor Coll. Medicine, Houston, 1998. Postdoc. fellow Salk Inst. Biol. Studies, La Jolla, Calif.; faculty U. Tex. Health Sci. Ctr., Houston; asst. prof. dept. neuroscience, asst. prof. dept. psychiatry & behavioral scis. Baylor Coll. Medicine, dir. Lab. Perception & Action. Fellow Inst. Ethics & Emerging Technologies, 2011—. Author: (fiction) Sum: Forty Tales from the Afterlives, 2009, (nonfiction) Why the Net Matters: How the Internet will save Civilization, 2010, Incognito: The Secret Lives of the Brain, 2011; co-author: Wednesday is Indigo Blue: Discovering the Brain of Synesthesia, 2009; mem. editl. bd. PLoS One, Jour. Vision; contbr. numerous articles to profl. jours. Bd. dirs. Long Now Found., 2010—. Fellow John Simon Guggenheim Meml. Found., 2011. Office: Baylor College Medicine Dept Neuroscience One Baylor Plz Houston TX 77030 Office Fax: 713-798-6699, 713-798-3946. Business E-Mail: eagleman@bcm.tmc.edu. *

EAGLETON, MATTHEW J., surgeon, educator; b. Geneva, NY, Oct. 10, 1968; BS, U. Rochester, 1990, MD, 1994. Assoc. prof. surgery Cleve. Clinic Lerner Coll. Medicine-CWRU, 2005—. Rsch. grant, NIH. Fellow: ACS; mem.: Soc. Clin. Vascular Surgery, Assn. Academic Surgery, Soc. U. Surgeons, Soc. Vascular Surgery. Avocations: Tae Kwon Do, running. Office: 9500 Euclid Ave H32 Dept Vasc Surg Cleveland OH 44195 Office Fax: 216-444-9324. Business E-Mail: eagletm@ccf.org.

EAGLY, ALICE HENDRICKSON, social psychology educator; b. LA, Dec. 25, 1938; d. Harold Martin and Josara Alberta (Whyers) Hendrickson; m. Robert Victor Eagly, Sept. 8, 1962; children: Ingrid Victoria, Ursula Elizabeth. BA, Radcliffe Coll., 1960; MA, U. Mich., 1963, PhD, 1965. Asst. prof. Mich. State U., East Lansing, 1965-67; asst. to assoc. to full prof. U. Mass., Amherst, 1967-80; vis. asst. prof. U. Ill., Champaign, 1970-71; vis. assoc. prof. Harvard U., Cambridge, Mass., 1974-75; prof. social psychology Purdue U., West Lafayette, Ind., 1980-95, Northwestern U., Evanston, Ill., 1995—, James Padilla chair arts and scis., 2006—, dept. chmn. psychology, 2006—09, prof. mgmt. & orgns. Kellogg Sch.; faculty fellow Inst. Policy Rsch.; disting. vis. prof. U. Southern Calif., 2009—10. MacEachern Meml. lectr. U. Alta., 1985; vis. prof. U. Tuebingen (Germany), 1991-92; vis. scholar Murray Rsch. Ctr., 1998-99, vis. rsch. prof. U Amsterdam, 2005-06; faculty fellow Inst. Policy Rsch. Author: Sex Differences in Social Behavior: A Social Role Interpretation, 1987; co-author: (with Shelly Chaiken) The Psychology of Attitudes, 1993, (with Linda L. Carli) Through the Labyrinth: The Truth About How Women Become Leaders, 2007; cons. editor Jour. Personality and Social Psychology: Attitudes and Social Cognition, 1979—, mem. editl. bd., 1983—; cons. editor Psychology of Women Quar., 1978-86, also others; contbr. articles to profl. jours. Recipient Gordon Allport Intergroup Rels. prize, Soc. Psychol. Study Social Issues, 1976, Disting. Pub. award, Assn. Women Psychology, 1978, Cattell Sabbatical award, Soc. Psychology Women, 2000, Carolyn Wood Sherif award 2005; Nat. Merit scholar, 1956-60, Fulbright fellow, 1960-61, Woodrow Wilson fellow, 1961-62, NSF fellow, 1962-65; various rsch. grants. Fellow: APA (citation as disting. leader for women in psychology com. on women in psychology, Life Achievement Sci. Psychology Gold medal 2008, Disting. Sci. award, 2009), Soc. Personality and Social Psychology (pres. 1981, Donald Campbell award for disting. contbn. to social psychology 1994), Soc. for Exptl. Social Psychology (exec. com. 1973-76, 81-83, Disting. Sci. Contbn. award), Midwestern Psychol. Assn. (pres. 1998-99), Am. Psychol. Soc., Phi Beta Kappa, Sigma Xi. Office: Northwestern U Dept Psychology Swift Hall 2029 Sheridan Rd Evanston IL 60208-0828

EARLE, JEAN BUIST, finance executive; b. Newton, NJ, Oct. 5, 1951; d. Richardson and Jean (Mackerly) Buist; m. Terry Dean Earle, Mar. 4, 1989; children: Morgan, Abigail. AB, Cornell U., 1973; MEd, Coll. William and Mary, 1974; MBA, U. Pa., 1987. Mgr. The Korman Corp., Jenkintown, Pa., 1975-77; v.p. ops. Community Assn. Mgmt. Co., Havertown, Pa., 1977-78; adminstrv. asst. Albert Einstein Med. Ctr., Phila., 1978-83; assoc. adminstr. Meml. Hosp. Burlington County, Mt. Holly, NJ, 1983-87; v.p. Overlook Hosp., Summit, NJ, 1987-95; exec. dir. Summit (N.J.) Child Care Ctrs., Inc., 1995-96; owner, ptnr. Elrae, LLP, Chatham, NJ, 1996—; CFO ECLC of N.J., Chatham, 1998—. Past pres. Family Link of Union and Essex Counties, 1994—96, chmn. Kirby Ctr. YMCA Family Coun., 1996—98. Recipient Diana Cuthbertsen award in health, NJ Statewide Parent Advocacy Network, 2003. Fellow Am. Coll. Healthcare Execs; mem. AICPA, Am. Hosp. Assn., U. Pa. Wharton Sch. Alumni Assn., Cornell Club, Ctr. for Enabling Tech. (trustee 1997-2004, treas. 1999-2004), Chatham Assn. for Support in Edn. (founding mem. 2004-), NJ Chpt. Canine Companions for Independence (treas. 2007-09, pres. 2009-). Home: 37 Rose Ter Chatham NJ 07928-1826 Office: ECLC NJ 100 Passaic Ave Ste 1 Chatham NJ 07928 Home Phone: 973-635-4734; Office Phone: 973-635-1705. E-mail: jbearle@hotmail.com.

EARLEY, LAURENCE ELLIOTT, retired medical educator; b. Ahoskie, NC, Jan. 23, 1931; s. Frank Claxton and Eleanor (Dilday) Earley; m. Joanne Frances Sinclair, Sept. 5, 1953; children: Laurence Elliott Earley Jr., Peter Hunter Earley. BS, U. N.C., 1953, MD, 1956; MA (hon.), U. Pa., 1978. Diplomate Am. Bd. Internal Medicine. Asst. prof. Harvard Med. Sch., Boston, 1967—68; assoc. prof. U. Calif. Sch. Medicine, San Francisco, 1968—69, prof., 1969—73, chief of nephrology, 1968—73; prof., chmn. dept. medicine U. Tex. Health Sci. Ctr., San Antonio, 1973—77; chmn. dept. medicine, Frank Wister Thomas Prof. U. Pa., Phila., 1977—90, chmn. dept. phys. medicine & rehab., 1987—90, Francis C. Wood prof., 1983—95, sr. assoc. dean., 1992—95; clin. prof. medicine U. N.C., Chapel Hill, 1995—2000; ret., 2001. Study sect. NIH, Bethesda, Md., 1969—77; chmn. Am. Bd. Internal Medicine, 1987—88. Editor: Diseases of The Kidney; contbr. articles to profl. jours. Chmn. sci. adv. bd. Nat. Kidney Found., NYC, 1973—74. Sr. asst. surgeon USPHS, 1959—61. Recipient Kaiser award, U. Calif., 1972, Disting. Svc. award, U. N.C., 1976. Master: ACP; mem.: Phila. Coll. Physicians, Assn. Am. Physicians (pres. 1988—89), Inst. Medicine, Am. Soc. Nephrology (pres. 1977—78), Am. Soc. for Clin. Investigation (pres. 1975—76), Assn. Profs. Medicine (pres. 1983—84), Alpha Omega Alpha, Phi Beta Kappa. Achievements include research in kidney disease, physiology. Avocations: photography, woodwork. Home: 436 Saunders Dr Wayne PA 19087 Personal E-mail: jselee@verizon.net, jseleech@aol.com.

EARLL, JERRY MILLER, internist, educator, endocrinologist; b. Hawarden, Iowa, Aug. 15, 1928; s. Harry Ezra and Magdalene Anna (Miller) E.; m. Faith Anne Allbaugh, Sept. 14, 1956; children: Leslie Anne, Nikki Lee, Holly Magdalene. BS, U. Nebr., 1950; MD, U. Iowa, 1958; postgrad., U. Calif., 1965-66. Diplomate Am. Bd. Internal Medicine, Am. Bd. Endocrinology, Am. Bd. Nuc. Medicine, Am. Bd. Geriat. Commd. 2d lt. U.S. Army, 1951, advanced through grades to col., 1972; intern Letterman Gen. Hosp., San Francisco, 1958, resident in internal medicine, 1959-62; chief endocrinology and metabolism William Beaumont Gen. Hosp., El Paso, 1963-65, Tripler Gen. Hosp., Honolulu, 1965-69, Walter Reed Army Inst. Rsch. and Walter Reed Army Hosp., Washington, 1969-76; chief dept. medicine Walter Reed Army Hosp., 1976-79; cons. endocrinology Office Surgeon Gen.; assoc. prof. medicine U. Hawaii, 1967—69; clin. prof. medicine Georgetown U., Washington, 1976—79, prof., 1979—, chief divsn. internal medicine, 1979—94, dir. geriatrics svc. dept. medicine, 1993—2000; prof. medicine, vice chmn. dept. medicine Uniformed Svcs. U. Health Scis., Washington, 1977-79; med. dir. to v.p. med. affairs Washington Home, 1996, 97—. Decorated Legion of Merit, Army Commendation medal, Meritorious Service medal. Fellow ACP (regional laureate); mem. Am. Med. Dirs. Assn., Endocrine Soc., Am. Geriatric Soc. (Clinician of Yr. 2002, 03), Assn. Mil. Surgeons, Acad. Medicine of Washington, Physicians for Nat. Health Program (spkr.). Achievements include research and publs. on pituitary and thyroid physiology. Home: 313 6200 Oregon Ave Washington DC 20015 Office: Georgetown U Hosp 3800 Reservoir Rd NW Washington DC 20007-2113 Office Phone: 202-895-0122. Business E-Mail: jearll@thewashingtonhome.org.

EARP, H. SHELTON, III, endocrinologist, educator; AB in Premed., Johns Hopkins U., 1966; MD, U. NC, 1970. Diplomate Am. Bd. Internal Medicine, 1976, Am. Bd. Internal Medicine-endocrinology, diabetes and metabolism, 1977. Resident internal medicine NC Meml. Hosp., Chapel Hill, 1974—75; fellow endocrinology, diabetes and metabolism Univ. NC Hosp., Chapel Hill, 1975—77; asst. prof., medicine; asst. dir. Univ. NC. Lineberger Comprehensive Cancer Ctr., 1977—82, assoc. prof., medicine, assoc. dir., 1982—88, prof., medicine, pharmacology; dep. dir., 1988—97; dir. Univ. NC. Lineberger Comprehensive Cancer Rsch., 1997—; prof. medicine and pharmacology Univ. NC., 1997—. Co-author: (publs.) Angiotensin II Stimulates Protein-Tyrosine Phosphorylation In A Calcium-Dependent Manner, 1990, Signal transduction by integrins: increased protein tyrosine phosphorylation caused by clustering of ß1 integrins, 1991, Cell adhesion or integrin clustering increases phosphorylation of a focal adhesion-associated tyrosine kinase, 1992, The mouse waved-2 phenotype results from a point mutation in the EGF receptor tyrosine kinase, 1994, Cloning and mRNA expression analysis of a novel human protooncogene, c-mer, 1994, and numerous other publs. Rsch. investigator US Army, 1971—74. Mem.: Am. Cancer Soc. (cell and devel. biology study sect. 1989—93, chair 1990—93), Nat. Cancer Inst. (bd. sci. advisors 2002—07), Assn. of Am. Cancer Insts. (bd. dirs. 2001—, pres.-elect 2003—05, pres. 2005—07). Office: University of North Carolina 4009 Genetic Medicine Campus Box 7365 Chapel Hill NC 27599 Office Phone: 919-966-3036. Office Fax: 919-966-3015. E-mail: hse@med.unc.edu.

EARWAKER, JOHN W.S., radiologist; b. Brisbane, Australia, May 7, 1939; MBBS, U. Qld., 1962; degree, RANX & ZCR, 1968. Dir. radiology Royal Brisbane Hosp., 1971—74; sr. ptnr. Queensland Diagnostic Imaging, 1974—2004; cons. radiologist Princess Alexandra Hosp., 1974—, Mater Childrens Hosp. South Brisbane, 2004—. Assoc. prof. radiology U. Queensland, 1987—; pres. Royal Australian & New Zealand Coll. Radiologists, 1998—2001; adj. prof. boimech. engring. Queensland U. Tech., 2004—. Recipient Gold medal, Royal Australian & New Zealand Coll. Radiologists, Centenary medal, Commonwealth Australia. Fellow: Royal Coll. Radiology, Am. Coll. Radiology (hon.); mem.: Pediat. Spinal Rsch. Group, Internat. Skeletal Soc. Home: 302/49 B Newstead Ter Newstead Queensland 4006 Australia Business E-Mail: j.earwaker@uq.edu.au.

EASON, JAMES DAVID, surgeon; b. Memphis, Tenn., Dec. 27, 1960; MD, U. Tenn., 1987. Cert. Am. Bd. Surgery. Resident, surgery Wilford Hall Med. Ctr., Lackland Air Force Base, San Antonio; clin. and rsch. fellow transplant surgery Mass. Gen. Hosp., Boston; clin. fellow surgery Harvard Med. Sch.; prof. transplant surgery U. Tenn. Health Sci. Ctr., Memphis, chief transplantation; program dir. U. Tenn./Meth. U. Hosp. Transplant Inst. Mem. physician adv. com. Patient Access to Transplantation Coalition; mem. Genzyme Liver Transplantation adv. bd. Assoc. editor, editl. bd. American Journal of Transplantation. Maj. USAF. Fellow: Am. Coll. Surgeons; mem.: Transplantation Soc., Internat. Liver Transplantation Soc., Am. Soc. Transplant Surgeons, AMA, Am. Assn. Study of Liver Diseases. Office: Meth U Hospital Transplant Inst 1265 Union Ave S1011 Memphis TN 38104-3499 Office Phone: 901-516-7070. Office Fax: 901-516-9184. *

EASSON, WILLIAM MCALPINE, psychiatrist, educator; b. Evanston, Ill., July 3, 1931; s. Alexander and Anne Meldrum (Watson) E.; m. Gwendolyn Bowen, May 31, 1958; children: Anne, Jane, David, Michael. M.B., Ch.B., U. Aberdeen, Scotland, 1954, MD, 1967. Fellow in medicine and psychiatry Mayo Clinic, Rochester, Minn., 1956-59; resident in psychiatry U. Sask., 1959-60, instr. psychiatry, 1959-61; fellow in child psychiatry Menninger Clinic, Topeka, 1961-63, staff child psychiatrist, 1963-67; prof. psychiatry, chmn. dept. Med. Coll. Ohio, Toledo, 1967-72; prof., dir. div. child and adolescent psychiatry U. Minn. Med. Sch., Mpls., 1972-74; prof. psychiatry La. State U. Med. Ctr., New Orleans, 1974-96, head dept. psychiatry, 1974-82, prof. emeritus, 1996—. Vis. prof. psychiatry U. Garyounis Med. Sch., Benghazi, Libya, 1979; prof. grad. studies U. Riyadh, Saudi Arabia; U.S.-USSR health scientist, Moscow and Leningrad. Author: The Severely Disturbed Adolescent, 1969, The Dying Child, 2d edit., 1981, Psychiatry Exam. Rev., 5th edit., 1994, Psychiatry Patient Mgmt. Rev., 1977, (with N. Rock) Psychiatry Splty. Bd. Rev., 1991, The Management of the Severely Disturbed Adolscent, 1996; editor: Jour. Clin. Psychiatry, 1977-80. Carnegie fellow, 1956-58; Anderson fellow, 1956-58; WHO fellow, 1976 Fellow Am. Psychiat. Assn. (life). Home: 5218 Saint Charles Ave New Orleans LA 70115-4943

EASTHAM, JAMES A., urologist, educator; MD, U. of SC Sch. of Medicine, LA, 1987; B, U. of California, Irvine. Diplomate Am. Bd. Urology. Resident urology Univ. of SC Med. Ctr., LA, 1988—93; fellow urologic oncology Baylor Coll. of Medicine, Houston; chief urology Overton-Brooks Veterans Adminstrn. Med. Ctr., La.; assoc. prof. dept. of urology Meml. Sloan-Kettering Cancer Ctr., NY, La. State Univ., Shreveport. Recipient Am. Cancer Soc.'s Clin. Fellowship award, Lamar Fleming award for Gene Therapy in Prostate Cancer, first pl. in the Montague Boyd Essay contest. Fellow: ASC; mem.: Societé Internationale D'Urologie, Soc. of Urologic Oncology, Am. Urologic Assn. Office: Memorial Sloan-Kettering Cancer Center 1275 York Ave New York NY 10021 Office Phone: 212-639-2000.

EASTHAM, JOHN HOWARD, pharmacist, educator, missionary; b. San Luis Obispo, Calif., Sept. 2, 1969; s. Howard Ambrose and Linda Jane (Croft) E.; m. Lily Cheng, Aug. 7, 1993; children: Joseph David, Benjamin Samuel, Gabriela Grace. Student, Am. River Coll., 1990; D of Pharmacy, U. of the Pacific, 1994. Resident VA Med. Ctr., Long Beach, Calif., 1994-95; postdoctoral rsch. fellow U. Calif., San Diego, 1995-97; clin. pharmacist Naval Med. Ctr., San Diego, 1997—2002; clin. specialist Pomerado Hosp., Poway, Calif., 2002—05; medication safety specialist Palomar Pomerado Health Dist., Escondido, Calif., 2005—11; intern Far Reaching Ministries, Murrieta, Calif., 2011, missionary Kampala, Uganda, 2011—. Mem. dean's adv. com. U. of Pacific, Sch. Pharmacy, Stockton, Calif., 1991-92, pharmacy student mentor, 2005—, residency adv. coun., 2006—; clin. asst. prof. Western U. Health Scis., Pomona, Calif., 1999—2002; clin. instr. Skaggs Sch. Pharmacy and Pharm. Scis. and Medicine, U. Calif., San Diego, 2007-11. Author: (with others) Clinical Geriatric Psychopharmacology, 1998; contbr. articles to profl. jours., chpt. to book. Pharmacy dir. Project Compassion, San Diego, 1995—2003, pharmacist, 1994—. Recipient Cert. of Appreciation, Project Compassion, 1998, 2000, 2003, Cert. Recognition, U.S. Assn. Mil. Surgeons, 1998, Letter of Appreciation, Comdr. Naval Med. Ctr., San Diego, 2001, Svc. and Dedication award, Project Compassion, 2002. Mem. Christian Pharmacists Fellowship Internat., Acad. Students of Pharmacy (rep. to Calif. Pharmacists Assn. 1991-92, Outstanding Svc. 1992), Acad. of Students of Pharmacy (rep., Award 1992), others. Republican. Business E-Mail: john@frmusa.org.

EATON, RICHARD GILLETTE, retired surgeon, educator; b. Forty Ft., Pa., Dec. 3, 1929; s. Walter L. and Ruth (Shaw) Eaton; m. Du Ree Hunter Eaton, June 13, 1954; children: Bradford(dec.), Holly, Hillary. BA, Franklin & Marshall Coll., 1951; MD, U. Pa., 1955. Diplomate Am. Bd. Orthop. Surgeons. Intern U. Pa. Grad. Hosp., 1956; gen. surg. resident Peter Bent Brigham Hosp., Boston, 1957; orthop. resident Children's Hosp. Med. Ctr., Mass. Gen. Hosp. & Peter Bent Brigham Hosp., Boston, 1959—62; hand surgery fellow J.W. Littler, Roosevelt Hosp., NYC, 1962; orthop. surgery & reconstrn., chief hand surgery svc., ret., 2002; prof. emeritus clin. orthop. surgery Columbia Coll. Physicians & Surgeons. Author: Joint Injuries of the Hand, 1971; contbr. articles to profl. jours. NYC ruling elder Huguenot Presbyn. Ch., Pelham, NY. Capt. MC US Army, 1957—59. NIH fellow, 1963—64. Mem.: ACS, NY Soc. Surgery Hand, J.W. Littler Soc., NY Acad. Medicine, Am. Soc. Surgery Hand, Am. Orthop. Assn., Am. Acad. Orthop. Surgery, Interurban Orthop. Club. Home: 6 Greens Way New Rochelle NY 10805 Personal E-mail: rgehand@aol.com.

EAVES, FELMONT FARRELL, III, plastic surgeon; b. June 8, 1962; MD, U. Tenn. Coll. Medicine, Memphis, 1987. Cert. Am. Bd. Plastic Surgery, Am. Bd. Surgery. Intern U. Tex. Southwestern Med. Ctr.; resident gen. surgery Parkland Hosp. U. Texas Southwestern, Dallas; resident plastic surgery Emory U., fellow endoscopic, minimally invasive plastic surgery; practicing minimally invasive, endoscopic surgery, ptnr. Charlotte Plastic Surgery Ctr. Co-author med. textbook; contbr. articles to profl. jours. Mem.: ACS, Southeastern Soc. Plastic & Reconstructive Surgeons, Internat. Soc. Aesthetic Plastic Surgery, Am. Soc. Aesthetic Plastic Surgery (treas., adminstrv. commr., chair patient safety com. 2006—, Sherrill J. Aston award, Lockwood award, Simon Fredricks award), Am. Soc. Plastic Surgeons, Alpha Omega. Office: Charlotte Plastic Surgery Ctr 2215 Randolph Rd Charlotte NC 28207 Office Phone: 704-372-6846, 800-281-2456. Fax: 704-342-0752. Business E-Mail: tvanneste@charlotteplasticsurgery.com.

EAVES, GEORGE NEWTON, health research administrator, educator; b. Athens, Tenn., Mar. 12, 1935; s. Felmont Farrell and Margaret Isobel (Dobson) E. BA, U. Chattanooga, 1957; MS, U. Tenn., 1959; PhD, Wayne State U. Sch. Medicine, 1962. Postdoctoral fellow Bryn Mawr Coll., Pa., 1963-65; postdoctoral fellow, guest investigator The Rockefeller U., NYC, 1970-71; exec. sec. molecular biology study sect. NIH, Bethesda, Md., 1967-73; exec. sect. Nat. Heart and Lung Adv. Coun., NIH, Bethesda, 1973-74; assoc. staff dir. Pres.'s Biomed. Rsch. Panel, Washington, 1974-76; dep. dir. Divsn. Blood Diseases and Resources, NIH, Bethesda, 1976-83, dep. dir. Divsn. of Stroke and Trauma, 1983-94. Lectr. on tech. writing, grant applications and peer rev.; bd. dirs. Cyclotec Med. Industries, Inc.; asst. prof. Washington and Jefferson Coll., 1962-63. Cons. editor Procs. NAS, 1973-76; mem. editl. bd. Grants Mag., 1978-81, Nonprofit Mgmt. and Fin., 1981—; contbr. articles to tech. jours. and chpts. to sci. books. Mem. adv. coun. Park and Tree Commn., City of Savannah, 1994—. Recipient Citation for Profl. Achievement, McDonnell Douglas Corp., 1968, NIH Dir.'s award, 1976, 86, Sustained High Quality Performance award NIH, 1970, 74, 79, Spl. Achievement award HHS, 1989, Spl. Recognition award Pub. Health Svc., 1990. Mem. Sigma Xi. Republican. Anglican. Avocation: church organist. Home: PO Box 10105 Savannah GA 31412-0305 Personal E-mail: georgeeaves@bellsouth.net. *

EBBESEN, LISELOTTE SABROE, plastic and reconstructive surgery specialist; b. Holstebro, Denmark, June 20, 1966; d. Bent Peter and Elinor (Sabroe) Jensen; m. Ebbe Nils Ebbesen, Aug. 25, 1990; children: Henriette Sabroe, Troels Sabroe, Elisabeth Sabroe. MD, U. Odense, Denmark, 1992; PhD, U. Aarhus, Denmark, 2003. Rsch. fellow U. Hosp. Aarhus, Denmark, 1999—2005, med. residency, 2003—05; specialist in coagulation Novo Nordisk A/S, Denmark, 2005—07; sr. registrar dept. plastic and reconstructive surgery U. Hosp. Copenhagen, 2007—. Avocation: swimming. Personal E-mail: lse@dadlnet.dk.

EBENEZER, ESTHER GUNASELI, psychiatrist, educator; b. Ipoh, Perak, Malaysia, Nov. 8, 1962; MBBS, Stanley Med. Coll., Chennai, India, 1990; M in Psychol. Medicine, U. Malaya, 2000. Fellow old age psychiatry U. Western Australia, 2003; assoc. prof., head dept. psychiatry U. Kuala Lumpur Royal Coll. Medicine, Perak, 2007—. Cons. Ministry Health, 2007—11. Recipient Silver medal, U. Putra Malaysia, Bronze medal. Master: Dementia Soc. Perak; mem.: Alzheimer's Disease Found. Malaysia. Avocations: gardening, travel. Office: University Kuala Lumpur Royal Coll Medicine 3 Jalan Greentown Ipoh Perak 30450 Malaysia Office Phone: 605 - 2432635. Office Fax: 605 - 2343636. Personal E-mail: esthergunamy@yahoo.com.

EBER, ROBERT MICHAEL, dental educator, periodontist; b. Detroit, Mich., Dec. 18, 1958; DDS, Ind. U., Indpls., 1984; MS in Periodontology, Ohio State U., Columbus, 1987. Cert. in periodontics Ohio State U., 1987, diplomate Am. Bd. Periodontology, 2006. Clin. asst. prof. Ohio State U., Columbus, 1987—89; pvt. practice in periodontics Indpls., 1989—95; clin. asst. prof. Ind. U., Indpls., 1990—95; clin. asst. prof., sch. dentistry U. Mich., Ann Arbor, 1995—2001, clin. assoc. prof., sch. dentistry, 2001—07, assoc. chair periodontics and oral medicine, 2002—10, clin. prof., dental sch., 2007—; pvt. practice; oral examiner Am. Bd. Periodontology, 2011—; dir. healthcare delivery pathway U. Mich., Sch. Dentistry, 2010—. Ch. worship team guitarist Crossroads Cmty. Bapt. Ch., Ann Arbor, 2003—08. Named Best Clin. Instr., Grad. Periodontics, 2005, Outstanding Faculty Mem., 2007. Mem.: ADA, Midwest Soc. Periodontology (sec. 2007—08, v.p. 2008—09, pres. elect 2009—10, pres. 2010—11), Internat. Assn. Dental Rsch., Am. Assn. Dental Rsch., Am. Dental Educators' Assn. (sec. periodontics sect. 2001—02, chair-elect periodontics sect. 2002—03, chair periodontics sect. 2003—04), Washtenaw Dist. Dental Soc., Mich. Dental Assn., Mich. Periodontists Assn., Russell W. Bunting Periodontal Soc. (sec. 2004—05, v.p. 2005—06, pres. 2006—07), Am. Acad. Periodontology, Phi Eta Sigma, Omicron Kappa Upsilon, Sigma Nu, Delta Sigma Delta. Baptist. Avocation: guitar. Home: 7219 Quackenbush St Dexter MI 48130 Office: Univ Mich Dental Sch 1101 N University St Ann Arbor MI 48109-1078 Business E-Mail: reber@umich.edu.

EBERHART, ROBERT CLYDE, biomedical engineering educator, researcher; b. Oakland, Calif., Apr. 17, 1937; s. George Perrin and Roberta Eberhart; m. Carol Eberhart, Aug. 4, 1960; 3 children. AB in Applied Physics, Harvard U., 1958; MS in Mech. Engring., U. Calif., Berkeley, 1960, PhD, 1965. Staff scientist Inst. Med. Scis., San Francisco, 1964—70, sr. scientist, 1970—75; assoc. prof. mech. engring. U. Tex., Austin, Tex., 1975—76; assoc. prof. surgery U. Tex. So. Med. Ctr., Dallas, 1976—86; chmn. biomed. engring. U. Tex. So. Med. Ctr. and U. Tex.-Arlington, 1983—2001; prof. engring. in surgery U. Tex. So. Med. Ctr. and U. Tex., Arlington, 1984—2005; adj. prof. surgery U. Tex. So. Med. Ctr., Dallas, 2006—09, prof. emeritus, 2010—; prof. bioengring. and mech. engring. U. Tex., Arlington, 2006—. Pres. Tex. Stent Tech., 2005—; bd. sci. advisors Andev, Inc.; cons. in field. Editor: Heat Transfer in Medicine and Biology, 1985; co-editor: Biomaterials-Living Sys. Interactions, 1993—98; mem. editl. bd.: Jour. Applied Biomaterials, Jour. Biomaterials Sci.; contbr. articles to profl. jours., chpts. in books. Recipient C.W. Hall Rsch. award So. Biomed. Engring. Conf., 1987, Career Achievement award Houston Symposium for Biomed. Engring., 1996. Fellow: ASME (Engr. of Yr. 2007, North Tex. divsn. Engr. of Yr. 2007), Biomed. Engring. Soc. (Inaugural fellow 2005), Am. Inst. Med. and Biol. Engring. (founding fellow 1993—); mem.: Biomaterials Soc., Soc. Critical Care Medicine (editl. bd. 1973—75), Am. Soc. Artificial Internal Organs (pres. 1994—95), Harvard Club. Achievements include patentee nonthrombogenic treatment for med. polymers 1985; patents for expandable biodegradable polymeric stents for combined mechanical support and pharmacological or radiation therapy 2005. Office: U Tex So Med Ctr Dept Surgery 5323 Harry Hines Blvd Dallas TX 75390-9130 Business E-Mail: robert.eberhart@utsouthwestern.edu.

EBERHART, STEVEN WESLEY, psychologist; b. St. Louis, Oct. 12, 1952; s. Carl A. and Cora H. (Kruckeberg) E. BA in Psychology, So. Ill. U., 1974; MS in Psychology, Western Ill. U., 1980; EdS in Sch. Psychology, U. Iowa, 1984, PhD in Sch. Psychology, 1986. Lic. cons. psychologist, Minn.; cert. sch. psychologist Minn., Ill., Iowa, nat. cert. sch. psychologist. Mental health technician Anna (Ill.) State Hosp., 1974-78; clin. psychologist Barren River Comprehensive Care, Bowling Green, Ky., 1980-82; sch. psychologist Meeker and Wright Spl. Edn. Co-op, Cokato, Minn., 1985-92; clin. pvt. practice St. Joseph, Minn., 1990-92; with Ministry of Edn. Govt. of Bermuda, 1992-96; psychologist Tri-County Spl. Edn. Coop., Murphysboro, Ill., 1996—. Adj. faculty mem. Southern Ill. U., 1998—. Contbr. article to profl. jours., author (novel) Makanda dreams, 2010. Ill. State scholar. Mem. APA, Nat. Assn. Sch. Psychologists, Ill. Sch. Psychologist Assn. (governing bd. mem). Avocations: race walking, karate (5th degree black belt), travel, scuba diving. Personal E-mail: eberpsy@frontier.com.

EBERLE, ALEX NIKLAUS, pathobiologist, educator; b. St. Gallen, Switzerland, Nov. 9, 1945; s. August Eugen and Martha (Huber) E.; m. Leni Ruth Jacot, May 26, 1976 (div. June 1993); 1 child, David Andreas; m. Anna Hirt, Aug. 21, 1998. MS, Swiss Fed. Inst. Tech., Zurich, 1971, PhD in Sci., 1976; PD (DSc), U. Basel, Switzerland, 1988. Postdoctoral fellow, asst. Swiss Fed. Inst. Tech., 1976-79; fellow in sci. Med. Rsch. Coun., Lab. of Molecular Biology, Cambridge, Eng., 1980-81; head of lab. Univ. Hosp. Basel, 1982-88, dep. chmn. dept. rsch., 1988-92, prof. pathobiology, chmn. dept. rsch., 1992-2000, pres. univ. planning com., 2006—; vice rector U. Basel, 2009—; fellow Collegium Helveticum ETH, Zurich, 2009—. Author: The Melanotropins, 1988; editor: Perspectives in Peptide Chemistry, 1981, Peptides, 1992, The Melanotropic Peptides, 1993; Contbr. Articles to jours. Capt. Swiss Army, 1966—96. Recipient Robert-Wenner award Swiss Cancer League, 1990, Debio Peptides award, 1994. Mem. Swiss Socs. Biology, Swiss Soc. Chemistry, German Soc. Chemistry, Biochem. Soc. Britain, European Peptide Soc. (Leonidas Zervas award 1988), Am. Peptide Soc., NY Acad. Scis. Avocations: mountain climbing, skiing, jogging, swimming, photography. Office: University of Basel Petersgraben 35 4051 Basel Switzerland Home Phone: 41-61-3619841. Business E-Mail: alex-n.eberle@unibas.ch.

EBERSOLE, JEFFREY LEE, dental educator, researcher; b. Harrisburg, Pa., May 20, 1949; PhD, U. Pitts., 1975. Sr. scientist Forsyth Inst., 1975—85; prof. U. Tex. Health Sci. Ctr., San Antonio, 1985—2000; assoc. dean rsch. U. Ky., 2000—. Cons. NIH, 1980—. Recipient Basic Rsch. grant, Internat. Assn. Dental Rsch., 1983. Master: Am. Soc. Microbiology; mem.: AAAS, Internat. Assn. Dental Rsch. (Periodontal Rsch. award 2000), Am. Assn. Dental Rsch. Avocation: golf. Office: Ctr Oral Health Research HSRB422 Lexington KY 40536 Office Fax: 859-257-6566. Business E-Mail: jleber2@uky.edu.

EBLING, ZDRAVKO, medical educator, researcher; b. St. Djurad, Croatia, Aug. 29, 1938; s. Franjo and Petra (Petrovic) Ebling; m. Anica Adric, Sept. 25, 1965; children: Davor, Barbara. MD, U. Zagreb, 1963, MSc in Gastroent. and Hepatology, 1978, PhD, 1987, MSc in Ultrasound Clin. Gastroent. and Nephrology, 1998, MSc in Course for Mentors in Family Practice, 2002. Cert. gen. practice specialist Ministry of Health, Croatia, 1970. Head, dept. gen. practice Health Ctr., Osijek, Croatia, 1974—2005; head Sch. Med. Assts., Osijek, 1982—86; asst. prof. U. Zagreb, 1991, assoc. prof., 2002, prof., 2005; dean asst. Faculty of Medicine, J. J. Strossmayer U., Osijek, 1998—2003; head, dept. family practice and primary health care Faculty of Medicine, Osijek, 1998—; prof. Assoc. Degree Coll., Vukovar, Croatia, 2007—. Regular mem. Acad. Med. Scis., Croatia, 1997—; mem. Nat. Health Com., Croatia, 2002; dep. chmn. Commn. Prevention and Early Detection of Cancer, Croatia, 2002—; chmn. supervisory bd. Croatian Med. Assn., 2005—; edit. bd. mem. Jour. Medicinski Vjesnik, Jour. Medicina Familiaris Croatica. Co-author: (textbook) Making an Appointment in Primary Health Care, Program of Detecting Cancer Early; editor: Cancer Problems in Primary Health Care, Detecting Cancer Early; co-author: (book) From the Time of Turks to Modern Osijek; editor: Proposal of a Program of Prevention and Early Detection of Cancer, How to Prevent and Detect Cancer Early, Deseases Caused by Smoking; co-author: Psychosocial Oncology and Rehabilitation. Mem. Croatian Assn. Family Practice, Osijek; sec. Osijek League Against Cancer, Croatia, 1984. Mem.: Croatian Med. Assn. (hon.). Achievements include research in prevention and early detection of cancer. Avocations: skiing, photography. Home: Jahorinska 7 Osijek 31000 Croatia Office: Health Ctr K P Kresimira IV nr6 Osijek 31000 Croatia Office Fax: 385 31 225 330. Business E-Mail: zdravko.ebling@os.t-com.hr.

EBRAHEIM, NABIL ANWAR, orthopedist, surgeon; MD, Cairo U., 1975. Lic. NY, 1981, Md., 1983, Ind., 1985, Ohio, 1985, Mich., 1998, diplomate Am. Bd. Orthop. Surgery, 1987, re-cert. 1998, 2004. Intern Ministry Pub. Health, Cairo, 1975—76, surg. resident, 1976—77, St. Clare's Hosp., NYC, 1978—80; orthop. resident Kings County Hosp. Ctr., Bklyn., 1980—83; orthop. trauma fellowship U. Md., Balt., 1983—84; pelvic and acetabular trauma fellowship Sunny Brook Hosp., Toronto, Canada, 1984; spine and acetabular trauma fellowship Pitie Salpetriere, Paris, 1984—85; AO fellowship Kantonsspital Chur, Switzerland, 1985, Hanover Trauma Ctr., Germany, 1985, Divisione Orthopadia E. Traumatologia, Lecco, Italy, 1989; vice chmn. dept. orthop. surgery Med. U. Ohio, Toledo, 1985—97, acting chmn., 1997—98, prof., chmn. dept. orthop. surgery, 1998—. Instr. Internat. Fixation Technique, Toronto, Canada, 1986, 88; orthop. residency program dir. Med. U. Ohio, dir. orthop. trauma fellowship program, chief divsn. orthop. trauma, dir. Office Orthop. for Practicing Physicians, 1995; dir., chmn., moderator numerous seminars in field. Contbr. articles to profl. jours. Recipient Foot and Ankle Rsch. award, 1999. Office Phone: 419-383-3761. Business E-Mail: nabil.ebraheim@utoledo.edu. E-mail: nebraheim@meduohio.edu.

EBRÍ, BERNARDO TORNÉ, internist, researcher; b. Zaragoza, Spain, Oct. 26, 1949; s. Bernardo Ebri and Araceli Torne; m. Inmaculada Casas Verde, June 28, 1975; children: Bernardo, Inmaculada, Pablo, Daniel, Sandra. BSc, U. Maristas, 1985; MD, U. Zaragoza, 1972, PhD, 1978; degree in Biol. Medicine, Homeopathy And Homotoxicology. Specialist in internal medicine. Rsch. fellow Edn. and Sci. Ministry, Madrid, 1973—76; asst. prof. U. Zaragoza, 1973—86; med. resident Miguel Servet Hosp., Zaragoza, 1974—77, med. asst., 1977—; prof. J.R. Santamaría Ctr., Zaragoza, 1986—; assoc. prof. Faculty of Medicine, Zaragoza, 1987—; dir. and prof. postgrad. courses biological medicine, 1999; lectr. Conf. Biotech. and Mech. Source, 1980, Nat. Group Rschs. Cardiovascular Risk Spanish Soc. Internal Medicine, 2002. Cons. internal medicine Miguel Servet Hosp., 1974—, dir. thesis and advisor med. residents, 1977—; med. homeopathic-naturist, Zaragoza, 1993—; lectr. in field, mem., Naturist Doctors Sect. Sch. Doctors Zarojoza, Arag. & Spanish Homeopathy Sci. Soc., assoc. mem., Assn. Aragonesa Escritores, Aragon Writers Assn., Spanish Assn. Writers Doctors, Aragon Encyclopaedia, 2007, Aragon Authors Dictionary, 2008, NY Acad. Scientist. Author (editor): (med. books) Maduracion Osea Sobre Tarso y Carpo, 1988, 14 books; author: Medicina Y Musica, 1996, Etiopatogenia y Fisiopatología de la Hipertensión Arterial Esencial, 1997, La Otra Cara de la Medicina: Qué es el hombre?, 1999, La Otra Cara de la Medicina: El Hombre ante el Dolor y la Muerte. Hay algo despues de la Vida?, 2000, La Otra Cara de la Medicina: Hacia dónde vamos?, 2003, Entre dos Vidas, 2004, Que es el Ser humano?, 2005, Mistica del dia a dia, 2008; contbr. more than 200 articles to profl. jours. Pres. Tng. of Christians, Zaragoza, 1986-90; mem. Life Protection Assn., Zaragoza, 1986—. Served in mil. hosp. Spanish Army, 1973-74. Recipient award for Best Acad. Record, Zaragoza City Coun., 1973, Nat. award, 1975, Best Doctoral Thesis award, Govt. Arajon, 1976-1977. Mem. Acad. of Medicine Zaragoza, Spanish Soc. Internal Medicine, NY Acad. Scis., Hypertension Soc. Arajon & Spanish, Arajon Fedn. Homeo. Drs., Ofcl. Coll. Medicine Drs. (1st award, 1988-89), Semergen Congress Gen. Practitioners (Best Comm. Internal Medicine award, 2004) Roman Catholic. Avocations: bicycling, stamp collecting/philately, tennis, walking. Office: Hosp Miguel Servet Isabel La Catolica 1 50009 Zaragoza Spain Home: Vinedo Viejo 2 13-1d 50009 Zaragoza Spain Personal E-mail: b.ebri@yahoo.es.

ECCLES, NYJON KARL, physician, director; s. Ecton George and Barbara Eccles. BSc, Kings Coll., London, 1982; PhD, Charing Cross Hosp. U. London, 1987; MBBS, U. Coll. London, BS in Medicine, 1992. Mem. Royal Coll. Physician, 1997; chief physician Harley St. Stress Clinic, London, 1999—2002; med. advisor Magnopulse Ltd., London, 2001—; med. dir. Chiron Clinic, London, 1998—. Med. dir. HB Health, London, 2007—. Trustee Cancer Health Anti Aging Rsch. Trust, 2004. Achievements include significant contributions in nutritional and magnetic medicine; first to attempt to establish the adjuntive use of infra-red thermal imaging in breast cancer screening and monitoring in UK & Europe; patents for 3 novel Mechanisms of action of magnetic fields on the human body. Office: Chiron Clinic 104 Harley St London W1G7JD England Personal E-mail: drnyjon@chironclinic.com. Business E-Mail: info@chironclinic.com.

ECHEVERRIA MORAN, VALENTINA, biochemist; b. Concepcion, Chile, Sept. 6, 1966; Degree in Biochemistry, U. Concepcion, 1991, PhD, 1999. Rsch. scientist Nat. Ctr. Biotech., Spain, 1999—2001; postdoc. rsch. fellow McGill U., Canada, 2001—03, Johns Hopkins U., 2003—05; rsch. scientist Columbia U., NY, 2005—06; rsch. chemist Bay Pines VA Healthcare Sys., 2007—. Adj. asst. prof. U. South Fla., 2007. Rsch. grant, Byrd Inst. NIA Subaward, 2007—08, James and Esther King Program Dept. Health Fla., 2007—, New Investigator grant, Am. Alzheimers Assn., 2008—10. Mem.: Soc. Neurochemistry, Soc. Neurosci. Avocation: birdwatching. Office: 10000 Bay Pines Blvd Bldg 23 Rm 123 Bay Pines FL 33744 Personal E-mail: echeverria.valentina@gmail.com.

ECHTERNACH, MATTHIAS, otolaryngologist, singer; married. MD, Heidelberg Med. Sch., 2000, Freiburg Med. Sch., Vienna Med. Sch. Residency otolaryngology Saarland U. Med. Ctr., Homburg, Germany, 2000—05; otolaryngologist Inst. Musicians Medicine, Freiburg U. Med. Ctr., Germany, 2006—. Musician: (singer, tenor) Kammerchor Stuttgart, Kammerchor Saarbrücken (numerous awards). Achievements include research in vocal registers; intubation related morbidity. Office: Inst Musicians' Medicine Breisacherstr 60 Freiburg Baden-Würtemberg 79106 Germany Office Fax: 49-761-270-6169. Business E-Mail: matthias.echternach@uniklinik-freiburg.de.

ECKBERG, WILLIAM ROBERT, biologist, educator, researcher; b. Grand Rapids, Mich., Apr. 29, 1947; s. Robert H. and Irene G. (Swart) E.; m. Susan G. West; children: Cynthia Goodhue, Leighsa Perlish, Amy Curran. BS, U. Mich., 1969; PhD, Mich. State U., 1975. Asst. prof. Howard U., Washington, 1975-81, assoc. prof., 1981-88, prof., 1989—, chmn., 2001—06, assoc. dean, 2007—. Summer investigator Marine Biol. Lab., Woods Hole, Mass., 1977—2003; mem. editorial bd. Biol. Bull., 1987—91; vis. scientist Cold Spring Harbor (N.Y.) Lab., 1993—94; site visit and rev. panel NIH, Bethesda, Md., 1990—. Contbr. more than 45 articles to Devel. Biology, Biol. Bull., The Jour. of Biol. Chemistry, Cell Calcium, The Jour. Exptl. Zoology and Exptl. Cell Rsch. Recipient Rsch. grants NIH, 1979—, Coun. for Tobacco Rsch., 1992—, NSF 2001-. Mem. Am. Soc. for

Cell Biology, Soc. for Devel. Biology, Marine Biol. Lab. Achievements include rsch. in the involvement of protein kinase C in control of cell division; involvement of calcium release in protostones egg activation; purification and biochem. properties of a human protein tyrosine phosphatase. Office: Howard U Grad Sch Washington DC 20059-0001 E-mail: weckberg@howard.edu.

ECKEL, ROBERT H., endocrinologist, educator; married; 5 children. BS in Bacteriology, U. Cin., 1969; MD, U. Cin. Coll. Med., 1973. Intern, medicine U. Wis. Hosp., 1973—74, resident, 1974—76; sr. fellow, metabolism and endocrinology U. Wash. Sch. Med., 1976—79; asst. prof. med. div. endocrinology U. Colo. HSC, 1979—85, assoc. prof. med. div. endocrinology, 1985—89, prof. biochemistry, biophysics & genetics, 1989—95, prof. physiology, 1995—; adj. prof. dept. food sci. & human nutrition Colo. State U., 1987—, grad. faculty appointment, dept. food sci. and human nutrition, 1990—, prof. med. div. endocrinology, metabolism & diabetes, 1989—. Assoc. dir. clinical rsch. ctr. U. Colo. HSC, 1981—93, co-dir. Ctr. for Human Nutrition, 1991—, program dir. gen. clinical rsch. ctr., 1993—; editorial bd. mem. Diabetes, Internat. Jour. Obesity & Obesity Rsch., 1990—94. Recipient Moses Barron award, Am. Diabetes Assn., 1990, Excellence award, Colo. Dietetic Assn., 1991. Mem.: Western Assn. Physicians, Am. Soc. Clinical Investigation, Am. Fedn. Clinical Rsch. (counselor 1982—84, sec. & treas. 1985—88), Alpha Omega Alpha. Office: University of Colorado Campus Box B-151 Dept Physiology & Biophysics BRB Rm #611 12800 E 19th Ave PO Box 6511 Aurora CO 80045 Office Phone: 303-315-8443. Office Fax: 303-315-4525. E-mail: Robert.Eckel@uchsc.edu.

ECKENHOFF, EDWARD ALVIN, health facility administrator, educator; b. Durham, NC, Mar. 4, 1943; s. James Edward and Bonnie Lee E.; m. Judi G. Vicich, May 27, 1978 BA, Transylvania U., 1966, PhD (hon.), 2000; MA, U. Ky., 1968; MHA, Washington U., 1974. V.p., adminstr. Rehab. Inst. Chgo., 1976-82; emeritus pres., founder Nat. Rehab. Hosp., Washington, 1982—; asst. prof. dept. community and family practice Med. Sch., Georgetown U., Washington, 1983-94; v.p. Medlantic Healthcare Group, 1987-99. V.p. Medlantic Healthcare Group, 1987-98; pres. Nat. Rehab. Services Corp., 1987-92; chmn. bd. NASCOTT, IBIS; instr. Med. Sch., Northwestern U., preceptor Grad. Sch. Bus.; mem. Ill. Commn. on Health Assistance Programs; mem. Ill. adv. com., chmn. exec. com. Internat. Yr. of Disabled; surveyor Commn. on Accreditation of Rehab. Facilities; com. on accreditation and edn. Am. Phys. Therapy Assn.; mem. Healthcare Rsch. Devel. Inst Contbr. articles to profl. jours. Bd. dirs. Am. Occupl. Therapy Found., Easter Seal Soc., Boy Scouts Am., Chgo. Area coun., Nat. Area, 1987-87, Operation ABLE Chgo., Access Living of Met. Chgo., Am. Chamber Symphony, Chgo., Nat. Assn. Rehab. Facilities, 1982-83, Am. Med. Rehab. Provider Assn., chmn. bd. dirs., 2000-01 Named Washingtonian of the Yr., Washingtonian Mag., 1989; recipient Citation for Disting. Svc., AMA, 1990, Ann. Healthcare Leader award B'nai B'rith, 2005. Fellow Inst. Medicine Chgo., Am. Coll. Hosp. Execs.; mem. Am. Hosp. Assn. (chmn. governing coun. for rehab. hosps. 1985, trustee 1991-93, chmn. policy com. 1993, exec. com. 1993, Honor award 2007), Am. Congress Rehab. Medicine (chmn. policy and devel. com.), Chgo. Hosp. Coun. (chmn. com. rehab. 1978-82, exec. com. 1983), Healthcare Devel. and Rsch. Inst. (bd. dirs. 2005—), Am. Med. Rehab. Providers Assn. (chmn. bd. dirs. 2000-01), Nat. Orgn. on Disability (bd. dirs. 1992-97, medicare coverage adv. commn. 1999-2002, presdl. appointment commr. commn. on care for Ams. wounded warriors, 2007), DC Hosp. Assn. (bd. dirs. 2003—). Episcopalian. Office: Nat Rehab Hosp 102 Irving St NW Washington DC 20010-2949 Office Phone: 202-877-1674.

ECKER, SIDNEY WOLF, urologist, consultant; s. Morris and Rose Ecker; m. Karen Garber, Mar. 1, 1964; children: Felice Ecker-Ramaikas, Erica. BS, U. Scranton, 1962; MD, Albert Einstein Coll. Medicine, Bronx, NY, 1966. Diplomate Am. Bd. Urology, Diplomate Nat. Bd. Med. Examiners. Surg. intern Georgetown U. Med. Sch., Washington, 1966—67, urology resident, 1967—71; pvt. practice Am. Urol. Assn., 1973—96; chmn. surgery sect. Shady Grove Adventist Hosp., Rockville, Md., 1996—97, chmn. surg. rev., 1991—95; mem. regular affiliate staff Walter Reed Army Med. Ctr., Washington, 1998—; chief of urology Wash. VA Med. Ctr., Washington, 2001—03, surg. cons., 2005—; clin. prof. of urology Georgetown U. Med. Sch., Washington, 2004—; symposium chair Am. Psychiatric Assn., San Fransisco, 2009, Internat. Found. Gender Edn., Alexandria, Va., 2010. Guest worker surgery br. NIH, Bethesda, Md., 1968—69; urol. surgeon to Belize Found. for Global Health, Washington, 1975; vis. urologist to China People to People Med. Ambs., Spokane, 2002; spkr. in fields. Contbr. scientific papers to profl. publs. Maj. USAF, 1971—73. Recipient Residents Sci. Presentation 1st prize, Wash. Urol. Soc., 1969. Fellow: ACS (life); mem.: Wash. Urological Soc. (pres. 1991—92), Med-chi Md. (life), Am. Urol. Assn. (life), Cosmos Club Wash. Avocations: Apple and Mac computers, photography, travel and travel lecturing, international cooking. Home: 132 Silvertail Ln New Hope PA 18938 Personal E-mail: swecker@comcast.net.

ECKHARDT, CRAIG JON, chemistry professor; b. Rapid City, SD, June 26, 1940; s. Reuben H and Hilda W. (Craig) E. BA magna cum laude, U. Colo., 1962; MS, Yale U., 1964, PhD, 1967. Asst. prof. chemistry U. Nebr., Lincoln, 1967-72, assoc. prof., 1972-78, prof., 1978—, interim chmn. dept. chemistry, 1986-87, prof. physics, 1988—. Cons., mem. adv. panel, condensed matter scis. div. materials research NSF, 1976-79 NIH predoctoral fellow, 1964-67; Yale predoctoral fellow, 1967; John Simon Guggenheim fellow, 1979-80; German Acad. Exchange fellow; Fulbright Sr. fellow, 2006; grantee NSF, 1974-84, Dept. Energy, 1979-82, Petroleum Rsch. Fund-Am. Chem. Soc., 1968-72, Rsch. Corp., 1971-74, 3M Corp., 1983-89, Army Rsch. Office, 1989-97, Office Naval Rsch., 2000—09. Mem. Am. Phys. Soc., Am. Assn. Physics Tchrs., Optical Soc. Am., Am. Chem. Soc., Royal Chemistry Soc., Phi Beta Kappa, Sigma Xi, Phi Lambda Upsilon. Achievements include patents in field. Office: U Nebr Dept Chemistry Lincoln NE 68588 Office Phone: 402-472-2734. Business E-Mail: eckhardt@undserve.unl.edu.

ECKHARDT, LAUREL ANN, biologist, researcher, educator; b. Palo Alto, Calif., Sept. 4, 1951; d. Joseph Carl Augustus Eckhardt and Ada Jane Williams Smith; m. Michael Warren Young, Dec. 27, 1978; children: Natalie Alice Eckhardt Young, Arissa Caroline Eckhardt Young. BA summa cum laude, U. Tex., 1974; PhD in Genetics, Stanford U., Calif., 1980. Damon Runyon-Walter Winchell postdoctoral fellow Albert Einstein Coll. Medicine, Bronx, 1980-83; asst. prof. Dept. Biol. Sci., Columbia U., NYC, 1984-88, assoc. prof., 1989-92; prof. Dept. Biol. Sci., Hunter Coll. of CUNY, 1992—, Marie Hesselbach prof. biology, 1999—. Reviewer immunobiology study sect. Dept. Rsch. Grants, NIH, Bethesda, Md., 1993-96; reviewer grand rev. com. Am. Heart Assn., N.Y.C., 1990-93, sci. rev. Immunological Sciences peer rev. com., Dept. of Def. Breast Cancer Rsch. Program, 1998, 2000, 03, rev. panelist for rsch. tng. fellowships for med. students, Howard Huges Med. Student, Howard Hughes Med. Inst., 2002-04; exec. officer CUNY, PhD Program Biology, 2008-. Assoc. editor Jour. Immunology, 1997-2001; contbr. articles to profl. jours. Rsch. grantee NIH-Inst. Allergy and Infectious Diseases, 1984-90, 90—, Am. Cancer Soc., 1990-95, NIH-Nat. Cancer Inst., 1994-99. Mem. Am. Assn. Immunologists (program com. mem. 1995-99, edn. com. 2006-09), N.Y. Acad. Scis., Harvey Soc. Democrat. Avocations: gardening, dance. Office: Hunter College of CUNY Dept Biol Sci 695 Park Ave New York NY 10021-5085

ECKHART, WALTER, molecular biologist, educator; b. Yonkers, NY, May 22, 1938; s. Walter and Jean E. BS, Yale U., 1960; postgrad., Cambridge U., Eng., 1960-61; PhD, U. Calif.-Berkeley, 1965. Postdoctoral fellow Salk Inst., San Diego, 1965-69, mem., 1970-73, assoc. prof. molecular biology, 1973-79, prof., 1979—2009, prof. emeritus, 2010—, cancer ctr. dir. San Diego, 1976—2007. Adj. prof. U. Calif.-San Diego, 1973-2003. Contbr. articles on molecular biology and virology to profl. jours. NIH research grantee, 1967-2008. Mem. AAAS, Am. Soc. Microbiology. Home: 951 Skylark Dr La Jolla CA 92037-7731 Office: Salk Inst PO Box 85800 San Diego CA 92186-5800 Home Phone: 858-454-6566; Office Phone: 858-453-4100 1386. Business E-Mail: eckhart@salk.edu.

ECKSTEIN, JULIE, healthcare administrator, former state agency administrator; m. Mark Eckstein; 3 children. BS, Univ. Mo., Columbia; MBA, Washington Univ., St. Louis. Dir. cmty. prog. SSM St. Joseph Health Ctr.; dir. corp. wellness prog. SSM Health Care; exec. dir. Healthy Communities St. Charles County, 2000—05; dir. Mo. Dept. Health & Sr. Svc., Jefferson City, 2005—06; dir. state ops., Mo. Project Ctr. Health Transformation, St. Louis, 2007—. Founder CommunityCalendars.net LLC; dir. bus. recruitment St. Charles County Govt. and Econ. Devel. Ctr.; dir. mktg. Keystone Partnership. Office: Ctr Health Transformation 111 Westport Plz Ste 600 Saint Louis MO 63146 Office Phone: 314-542-3022.

ECKSTEIN, MARLENE R., vascular radiologist; b. Poughkeepsie, NY, Sept. 6, 1948; d. Marc and Lola (Charm) E. AB, Vassar Coll., 1970; MD, Albert Einstein Coll. Medicine, 1973. Diplomate Nat. Bd. Med. Examiners; cert. Am. Bd. Radiology. Intern in medicine Yale-New Haven Med. Ctr., 1973-74, resident in diagnostic radiology, 1974-77; asst. radiologist, chief vascular radiology sect. South Nassau Cmtys. Hosp., Oceanside, N.Y., 1977-78, assoc. radiologist, chief vascular radiology sect., 1978-81, asst. dir. dept. radiology, chief vascular radiology sect., 1981-83; asst. radiologist Mass. Gen. Hosp., 1983-87, assoc. radiologist, 1987—. Asst. prof. clin. radiology SUNY-Stony Brook Med. Sch., 1980-83; instr. radiology, Harvard Med. Sch., 1983-84, asst. prof., 1984—. Mem. exec. com. and hosp. chmn. United Jewish Appeal of Physicians and Dentists of Nassau County, N.Y., 1981-83. Fellow Am. Coll. Angiology, Soc. Cardiovasc. and Interventional Radiology; mem. AMA, Am. Coll. Radiology, Am. Inst. Ultrasound in Medicine, Am. Assn. Women Radiologists, Am. Med. Women's Assn., Mass. Radiol. Soc., Mass. Med. Soc., New Eng. Soc. Cardiovasc. and Interventional Radiology (pres. 1985-86), Radiol. Soc. N.Am. Achievements include design and development of line of vascular catheters. Office: Mass Gen Hosp Vascular Radiology Sect Boston MA 02114 Home: 6 Merlot Dr Apt 640 Highland NY 12528 E-mail: mreckstein@alum.vassar.edu.

ECONOMOPOULOS, KONSTANTINOS P., physician; b. Athens, Greece, Feb. 11, 1984; s. Panayotis Economopoulos and Vivi Economopoulou; m. Souzana Choussein Economopoulos. MD, U. Athens, 2008, PhD student, 2009—. Lic. examinar Athens, 2008; accredited instr. potential 2009. Gen. sec. Soc. Neoplastic Diseases, 2005—06, vp, 2006—08, founding mem., 2005; asst. Vascular Surgery Dept., Athens Med. Ctr., Athens, 2007—08; fellow rschr. U. Athens, 2009; founding mem. Soc. Jr. Doctors, 2009, pres., 2009—, mem. organizing com., 2010—, pres. sci. com., 2010—; fellow rschr. Prolepsis Med. Group, 2010—; spl. sec. Greek Chpt., Am. Coll. Surgeons, 2010—. Reviewer various jours. Contbr. articles to profl. jours. Airman med. dr. Hellenic Airforce, 2008—09. Recipient 1st Accolade, 12th Panhellenic Competition Piano, 1997, Silver medal, 13th Panhellenic Competition Piano, 1998, Gold medal, 14th Panhellenic Competition, 1999, 9th Panhellenic Junior Chorus Competition, 1999, 10th Panhellenic Chorus Competition, 2000, Best paper award, Nat. and Kapodistrian U. Athens Med. Sch., 2006, ESMO Conference Lugano, 2007. Mem.: AAAS, Soc. Jr. Drs., Soc. Neoplastic Diseases: Akeso, European Assn. Cancer Rsch., Hellenic Am. Soc. Medicine, European Soc. Med. Oncology (ESMO assoc. mem.). Greek Orthodox. Avocations: piano, windsurfing, skiing, basketball, movies. Office: Menalou 5 Athens 15123 Greece Office Phone: 306942462812. Personal E-mail: economopoulos@gmail.com.

ECONOMOS, DOROS, neurosurgeon; s. Spyridon and Aida Economos; 1 child, Katerina. MD, U. Paris, 1950. Resident, Paris, 1944—50; head neurol. ctr. Polyclinic of Athens Hosp., 1953—90; emeritus prof. neurosurgery U. Athens. Cons. neurosurgeon N.I.M.T.S. Hosp., Athens, 1960—86. Fellow, Montreal Neurosurg. Inst., Can., 1951—52, Inst. Marey, Coll. of France, Paris, 1952—53. Avocation: sailing. Home: Rigillis 24 106 74 Athens Greece E-mail: dorosa1@ath.forthnet.gr.

ECONOMOU, EMMANUEL VASILIOS, pharmacologist, researcher, biochemist; b. Athens, Greece, Jan. 30, 1962; s. Vasilios Emmanuel and Metaxia Panagiotis Economou. PharmD, Health Sciences, Greece, 1985, PhD, 1993; postgrad Cert., Nuc. Ctr. For Sci. Rsch. Demokritos, Greece, 2000, Inst. For Nuc. Medicine Kern Forschungs Anlage, Germany, 2002. Rsch. fellow Diabetes Ctr., Kyriakou Children's Hosp., Athens, 1993—94, Dept. Neonatology, Alexandra U. And State Hosp., Athens, 1990—94, Rsch. Lab. For Clin. Biochemistry And Immunology, Hippokration U. and State Gen. Hosp., Athens, 1992—2003; supr. Radioimmunoassay Lab., Hygeia Pvt. Gen. Hosp., Athens, 1997—; lectr. in clin. path. biochemistry Med. Sch., U. Athens, Aretaieion U. and State Hosp., Hormone Lab., Athens, 2003—. Contbr. scientific papers. Sailor Greek Navy, 1991—92, Athens - Greece. Recipient scholarship, State Scholarship's Found., 1981, 1982, 1983, 1984; fellow, Inst. For Nuc. Medicine Kern Forschungs Anlage, 1989—91. Fellow: European Soc. Of Cardiology, Am. Assn. For Clin. Chemistry. Avocations: film production, swimming, tennis, travel. Office: Aretaieion Univ And State Hosp 76 Vas Sofias Attiki Athens 115 28 Greece Home: Thrakis 27 152 35 Vrilissia - Athens 152 35 Greece Office Fax: 0030-210-7286229; Home Fax: 0030-210-6084476. Personal E-mail: eveconom@otenet.gr. Business E-Mail: eveconom@aretaieio.upa.gr.

ECONS, MICHAEL J., endocrinologist, educator; Grad., Johns Hopkins U.; MD, U. Calif., 1983. Diplomate Am. Bd. Internal Medicine, 1986, Am. Bd. Internal Medicine-endocrinology, diabetes and metabolism, 1989. Resident internal medicine Univ. of Md. Hosp., Baltimore, 1984—86; fellow endocrinology Duke Univ. Med. Ctr., Durham, NC, 1986—89, assoc. prof. medicine, 1990—97, Ind. Univ. Med. Ctr., 1997—2002, divsn. dir., divsn. endocrinology and metabolism, 2001—, prof. medicine and med. and molecular genetics, 2002—; hosp. affiliation includes Indiana Univ. Health. Co-author: (publs.) Genome-wide association study of bone mineral density in premenopausal European-American women and replication in African-American women, 2010, Replication of previous genome-wide association studies of bone mineral density in premenopausal American women, 2010, Identification of genes influencing skeletal phenotypes in congenic P/NP rats, 2010, Clinical variability of familial tumoral calcinosis caused by novel GALNT3 mutations, 2010, Heterogeneous stock rat: a unique animal model for mapping genes influencing bone fragility, 2011, and numerous other publs. Recipient Young Investigators award, Am. Soc. for Bone and Mineral Rsch. (ASBMR), 1990, Young Investigator award: Advances in Mineral Metabolism, 1991, Boy Frame award, 2000. Mem.: Assn. of Am. Physicians, Am. Soc. for Clin. Investigation. Office: Indiana University Gatch Clinical Bldg Rm 459 541 N Clinical Dr Indianapolis IN 46202 Office Phone: 317-274-1339. E-mail: mecons@iupui.edu.

EDATHODU, JAMEELA, physician; b. Kozhikode, Kerala, India, Dec. 12, 1960; MBBS, Calicut Med. Coll., 1984. Asst. cons. King Faisal Hosp. & Rsch. Ctr., 2000—. Recipient Best Asst. Cons. award, King Faisal Hosp. Riyadh, 2009. Master: Royal Coll. Physician. Home: Thakasussi St Riyadh 11211 Saudi Arabia Personal E-mail: jameelaedathodu@yahoo.com.

EDDEY, GARY ERWIN, physician, administrator, educator; b. Englewood, NJ, Dec. 10, 1951; s. Erwin Carnes and Emma (Bogart) E.; m. Ilene N. Eddey, July 31, 1976 (div.); children: John, An nMichele, Emily. BS, U. Md., 1976; ScM, U. Pitts., 1978; MD, Cornell U., 1983. Diplomate Am. Bd. Pediats. Intern U. NC, Chapel Hill, 1983-84; resident NY Hosp.-Cornell U., NYC, 1984, chief resident in pediats., 1984; asst. prof. pediats. Cornell Med. Coll., 1986-88; clin. asst. prof. pediats. Columbia U., NYC, 1986-88; from clin. assoc. prof. to assoc. prof. pediats. NJ Med. Sch., Newark, 1997—; assoc. med. dir. Matheny Hosp., Peapack, NJ, 1990—, dir. comprehensive continuum of care, 2001, med. dir., 2005—; assoc. med. dir. Matheny Ctr. Medicine and Dentistry, Peapack, 2002—05; med. dir. Matheny Med. and Ednl. Ctr. (formerly Matheny Hosp.), Peapack, 2001—09, chief med. officer, 2009—. Bd. dirs. Lesch-Nyhan Coun., Matheny. Author: (novel) The Weather House, 2011, Contbr. articles to profl. jours. Pres. Eddy Family Assn., Inc., 2008—; bd. trustees Matheny Med. & Ednl. Court; founding mem., trustee Alliance Disabilities Healthcare Edn. Recipient Outstanding Pediatrician award Morris County Office Hispanic Affairs, 1993. Mem. Am. Acad. Pediats., Am. Acad. Devel. Medicine, Internat. Soc. for the Study of Behavioural Phenotypes. Unitarian Universalist. Achievements include research in culture of disability and medical education; clinical excellence in care of patients with Lesch-Nyhan disease. Avocations: genealogy, history, creative writing, jazz, recording arts, writing. Office: Matheny Hosp Box 339 Main St Peapack NJ 07977 Home: 83 Skyline Dr Morristown NJ 07960 Home Phone: 973-993-8774; Office Phone: 908-234-0011. Business E-Mail: GaryEddey@matheny.org. *

EDDINGTON, NATALIE DAWN, science educator, dean; d. Chester Elwood and Florence Hope Eddington. BS in Pharmacy, summa cum laude, Howard U., Washington, 1982; PhD, U. Md. Sch. Pharmacy, Balt., 1989. Asst. clin. dir. new drug. devel. Pfizer Inc., NYC; faculty U. Md. Sch. Pharmacy, 1991—, assoc. prof., 1993—2002, prof., 2002—, dir. Pharmacokinetics/Biopharmaceutics Lab., 1999, chair dept. pharm. scis., 2003—07, dean, 2007—. Contbr. articles to profl. jours. Mem. Nat. Inst. Pharm. Tech., Lafayette, Ind., 2007—08. Recipient Outstanding Svc. aeard, Fla. Agrl. & Mech. U., 2004, All Star award, Nat. Women of Color in Tech. Conference, 2006. Mem.: AAPS, Am. Assn. Pharm. Scis. Achievements include research in factors that influence drug delivery and pharmacokinetics of drugs across biological membranes using in vitro cell culture and animal models so as to elucidate structure-pharmacokinetic and pharmacodynamic relationships; patents for oral and blood brain barrier delivery. Office: U Md Sch Pharmacy Rm 730 20 N Pine St Baltimore MD 21201 Office Phone: 410-706-6710. Office Fax: 410-706-5017. Business E-Mail: neddingt@rx.umaryland.edu.

EDDY, CHARLES ALAN, chiropractor; b. Kansas City, Mo., Feb. 20, 1948; s. Sam Albert and Ella Louise (Gani) E.; m. Donna Darlene Perry, Oct. 23, 1971. Student, U. Mo., Kansas City, 1967; D in Chiropractic, Cleveland Chiropractic, Kansas City, 1970. Diplomate Nat. Bd. Chiropractic Examiners. Pvt. practice, Kansas City, 1970—. Peer rev. bd. Blue Cross and Blue Shield, Kansas City, 1972; pres. hon. bd. govs. Bapt. Hosp., Kansas City, 1993-94; cons. Quality Corp., Overland Park, Kans., 1988. Res. officer Kansas City Police Dept., 1970—77, sgt., 1977—82, capt., 1982—94; vice chmn. Citizens Assn., 1995—98; mem. pub. improvement adv. com. City of Kansas City, 1997—98; city councilperson 6th Dist., 1999—2007; chmn. bd. Mid. Am. Reg. Coun., Kansas City, 2003—05, 1st v.p., 2001—02; bd. dirs. Econ. Devel. Coun., 1999—2007, 1st v.p., 2001—03; chmn. Mo. Total Transp. Com., 2003—07, with City Coun. 6th Dist. at Large, 2011; candidate for City Coun. Kansas City, 1995; candidate for mayor, 2007; chief staff, city mgr. KCMO, 2009; leader, profl. musician Chuck Eddy Band, Kansas City, 1964—. Mem. Am. Chiropractic Assn., Mo. State Chriopractic Assn., Mo. Dist. II Chiropractic Assn. (bd. dirste., v.p. 1998-2003), Cleve. Chiropractic Coll. (trustee 1990, vice chmn. 1992-03, chmn. 2003—), Cleve. Chiropractic Alumni Assn. (v.p. 1995-97, pres. 1997-99, bd. dirs. 1990—, amb.'s soc. 1983—, chmn. 1990-96, 2001-07, bd. dirs. Truman Med. Ctr.), Optimist Club of Landing (pres. 1980, lt. gov. Mo. dist. 1982), South Kansas City C. of C. (Sml. Bus. of Yr. award 1998), Am. Lebanon Syrian Men's Club (pres. 1988-91, chmn. bd. 1992), St. Andrews Soc. (drummer in pipe band), DeMolay Legion Hon. (sec. 1988, treas. 1990, vice-dean 1991, dean 1992), Pipes and Drums of

Ararat (treas. 1977-90, pres. 1985, dir. 1989, 90), Ctrl. States Shrine Assn. (v.p. 2000-07, pres. 2007-), Elks, Shriners (Potentate of Ararat shrine temple 1999, CSSA officer 2001-, pres. 2008-, publicity chmn. 1991-92), Royal Order Jesters, Order Quetzalcoatl, Rotary Club (bd. mem. 2011-, Paul Harris fellow, bd. mem. 2011-), Shepherd Ctr. Ctrl. (bd. mem., Don Bosco 2005-, mayors prayer breakfast 2002-, pres. 2008-09), Native Sons & Daus. of Greater Kans. City (bd. mem. 2004-10, 2nd v.p. 2011), Kingswood Found. (bd. mem. 2003-, vice chair 2009-10, chair 2011-). Episcopalian. Avocations: photography, guns, stereo and video entertainment. Home: 406 W 109th St Kansas City MO 64114-4910 Office: 8301 State Line Rd Ste 108 Kansas City MO 64114-2019 Office Phone: 816-363-5311. Personal E-mail: dr.eddy@juno.com.

EDDY-JOHNSON, DEANNA M., home health care advocate; b. Bklyn., Aug. 26, 1950; d. Gerharctt W. Gaarde and Virginia Fern (Hoelscher); m. Dennis R. Eddy (div.); children: Denny R. Eddy, Ginger Deann Spillers. Degree in computer programming, Parkland Jr. Coll., Champaign, Ill., 1983; degree in real estate, Parkland Jr. Coll., 1985, nursing cert., 1990. CEO Jenn Swing Co., Urbana, Ill., 1993—; ptnr., owner coord. Helping Hands Eldercare. Inventor Jenn Swing, 1st full body accessible swing, 1996, The Cubby, toddler swing, 2004; author: Idea to Financial Success, 2003, Patty Panda Joins the Circus, 2005; lyricist I Want to Rock with you Jesus, 2005. Recipient Sec. award, Ambucs Assn., Urbana, 1996. Republican. Baptist. Avocations: walking, bicycling, concerts, plays. Home: 306 Dodson Dr E Urbana IL 61802 E-mail: deannajohnson33@yahoo.com.

EDELMAN, GERALD MAURICE, biochemist, neuroscientist, educator; b. NYC, July 1, 1929; s. Edward and Anna (Freedman) Edelman; m. Maxine Morrison, June 11, 1950; children: Eric, David, Judith. BS, Ursinus Coll., Collegeville, Pa., 1950, DSc, 1974; MD, U. Pa., 1954, DSc, 1973; PhD, Rockefeller Inst., NYC, 1960; DSc (hon.), Gustavus Adolphus Coll., 1975, Williams Coll., 1976, U. Paris, 1989; LSc (hon.), U. Cagliari, 1989; DSc (hon.), Georgetown U., 1989, U. degli Studi di Napoli, 1990, Tulane U., 1991, U. Miami, 1995, Adelphi U., 1995, U. Bologna, 1998, U. Minn., 2000, Moscow State U., 2008, Rockefeller U., 2008, U. Louvain, 2009; MD (hon.), U. Siena, Italy, 1974, U de A Coruña, Spain, 2000. Med. house officer Mass. Gen. Hosp., Boston, 1954—55; asst. physician Rockefeller Inst. Hosp., 1957—60; asst. prof., asst. dean grad. studies Rockefeller Inst., 1960—63, assoc. prof., assoc. dean, 1963—66; prof. Rockefeller U., 1966—74, Vincent Astor disting. prof., 1974—92; prof., chmn. dept. neurobiology Scripps Rsch. Inst., La Jolla, Calif., 1992—. Mem. biophysics and biophys. chemistry study sect. NIH, 1964—67; mem. adv. bd. Basel Inst. Immunology, Switzerland, 1970—77, chmn., 1975—77; non-resident fellow, trustee Salk Inst. Biol. Studies, La Jolla, 1973—85, bd. trustees, 1975—85; founder, dir. Neurosciences Inst., NYC, 1981—93, La Jolla, 1993—95, San Diego, 1995—. Author: The Mindful Brain, 1978, Neural Darwinism, 1987, Topobiology, 1988, The Remembered Present, 1989, Bright Air, Brilliant Fire, 1992, A Universe of Consciousness: How Matter Becomes Imagination, 2000, Wider than the Sky: The Phenomenal Gift of Consciousness, 2004, Second Nature: Brain Science and Human Knowledge, 2006. Bd. governors Weizmann Inst. Sci., Israel, 1971—87; trustee Rockefeller Bros. Found., 1972—82; bd. trustees Carnegie Instn., Washington, 1980—87. Capt. US Army Med. Corps, 1955—57. Recipient Spencer Morris award, U. Pa., 1954, Ann. Alumni award, Ursinus Coll., 1969, Nobel prize for physiology/medicine, 1972, Albert Einstein Commemorative award, Yeshiva U., 1974, Buchman Meml. award, Calif. Inst. Tech., 1975, Rabbi Shai Shacknai Meml. prize, Hebrew U.-Hadassah Med. Sch., Jerusalem, 1977, Regents medal of excellence, NY State, 1984, Hans Neurath prize, U. Wash., 1986, Sesquicentennial Commemorative award, Nat. Libr. Medicine, 1986, Cécile and Oskar Vogt award, U. Dusseldorf, 1988, Disting. Grad. award, U. Pa., 1990, Warren Triennial Prize award, Mass. Gen. Hosp., 1992, C.V. Ariens-Kappers medal, Netherlands Inst. Brain Rsch., 1999, Jiménez Díaz Meml. prize, Jiménez Díaz Found., Madrid, 1999, Medal of Presidency of Italian Republic, 1999, Medal of City of Paris, 2002, Cátedra Santiago Grisolia prize, Spain, 2003, Caianiello Meml. Internat. award, Italy, 2003. Fellow: AAAS, Jewish Acad. Arts & Scis. (Albert Einstein Commemorative medal 1986), NY Acad. Medicine, NY Acad. Scis.; mem.: NAS, Am. Chem. Soc. (Eli Lilly award 1965), Coun. Fgn. Rels., Soc. Devel. Biology, Acad. Scis. Inst. France (fgn.), Am. Psychoanalytic Assn. (hon.), Japanese Biochem. Soc. (hon.), Pharm. Soc. Japan (hon.), Am. Soc. Cell Biology, Am. Acad. Arts & Scis., Genetics Soc. America, Am. Assn. Immunologists, Am. Soc. Biol. Chemists, Am. Philos. Soc., Century Assn., Harvey Soc. (pres. 1976—77), Cosmos Club, Alpha Omega Alpha, Sigma Xi, Phi Beta Kappa. Office: Scripps Rsch Inst Mail Drop SBR14 10550 N Torrey Pines Rd La Jolla CA 92037-1000 *

EDELMAN, JOEL, health facility administrator; b. Chgo., Mar. 24, 1931; s. Maurice B. and Ethel J. (Newman) E.; m. Beth L. Sommers, July 31, 1955; children: Peter J., Ann Elizabeth, Deborah S. BA in Spl. Edn., U. Mich., 1952; JD, DePaul U., 1960. Bar: Ill. 1961. Program dir. Chgo. Heart Assn., 1955-61; staff atty. Michael Reese Hosp. and Med. Center, Chgo., 1961-70, exec. v.p., 1971-73; dir. Ill. Dept. Pub. Aid, 1973-74; exec. dir. Ill. Legis. Adv. Com. on Pub. Aid, 1974-77; pres. Rose Med. Ctr., Denver, 1979-95; prin., sr. v.p. Frontier Holdings, Inc., Englewood, Colo., 1995—. Asst. prof. dept. preventive medicine U. Colo.; U.; dir. office legal affairs Am. Hosp. Assn., 1970 Contbr. articles to profl. jours. Served with AUS, 1955. Mem. Soc. Hosp. Attys. (charter) Home: 3156 S Hills Ct Denver CO 80210-6830

EDELMAN, MARIAN WRIGHT, not-for-profit developer, lawyer; b. Bennettsville, SC, June 6, 1939; d. Arthur J. and Maggie (Bowen) Wright; m. Peter B. Edelman, July 14, 1968; children: Joshua, Jonah, Ezra. Merrill scholar, Univs. Paris, Geneva, 1958-59; BA, Spelman Coll., 1960; LLB, Yale U., 1963, LLD (hon.), Smith Coll., 1969, Lowell Tech. U., 1975, Williams Coll., 1978, Columbia U., U. Pa., Amherst Coll., St. Joseph's Coll.; DHL (hon.), Lesley Coll., 1975, Trinity Coll., Washington, Russell Sage Coll., 1978, Syracuse U., Coll. New Rochelle, 1979, Swarthmore Coll., 1980, SUNY Old Westbury, Northeastern U., 1981, Bard Coll., 1982, U. Mass., 1983, Hunter Coll., U. So. Maine, SUNY, Albany, 1984, Bates Coll., Maryville Coll., Bank St., 1986, Claremont Grad Sch., Lincoln U., Georgetown U., Chgo. Theol. Coll., 1987, Wheaton Coll., Tulane U., Grinnell Coll. Brandeis U., Wheelock Coll., Dartmouth Coll., U. S.C., U. N.C., Grad. Ctr. CUNY, U. Wis. Milw., 1988, Interdenom. Theol. Ctr., Hofstra U., Tufts U., Borough Manhattan Community Coll., Wesleyan U., Calif. State U. L.A., Dillard U., U. Md., U. Miami, 1989, Howard U., Beloit Coll., Queens Coll., Am. U., New Sch. of Social Rsch., Coll. of Notre Dame, DePaul U., 1990, Beaver Coll., Fordham U., Simmons Coll., Hamline U., Clark U., Harvard U., Union Coll., 1991, Tuskegee U., Washington U. St. Louis, Hood Coll., Duke U., Mercy Coll., 1992, Princeton U., U. Ill., Calif. State U. San Francisco, Wittenberg Coll., Shaw U., So. Meth. U., 1993, Brown U., U. Balt., Ea. Conn. State U., U. Notre Dame, 1994. Bar: DC, Miss., Mass. Staff atty. NAACP Legal Def. and Ednl. Fund, Inc., NYC, 1963-64, dir. Jackson, Miss., 1964-68; Congl. and fed. liaison Poor People's Campaign, summer 1968; partner Washington Rsch. Project of So. Ctr. Pub. Policy, 1968-73; dir. Harvard U. Ctr. Law and Edn., 1971-73; pres., founder Children's Def. Fund, 1973—. Author: Families in Peril, 1987, The Measure of Our Success: A Letter To My Children and Yours, 1992. Mem. exec. com. Student Non-Violent Coordinating Com., 1961-63; mem. adv. coun. Martin Luther King Jr. Meml. Libr.; mem. adv. bd. Hampshire Coll.; mem. Presdl. Commn. on Missing in Action, 1977, Presdl. Commn. on Internat. Yr. of Child, 1979, Presdl. Commn. on Agenda for 80's, 1980; bd. dirs. NAACP Legal Def. and Ednl. Fund; trustee Spelman Coll., Carnegie Coun. on Children, 1972-77, Martin Luther King Jr. Meml. Ctr.; mem. Yale U. Corp., 1971-77, Aetna Found., Nat. Commn. on Children, 1989—; bd. dirs. Aetna Life Casualty Found., Citizens for Constitutional Concerns, US. com. UNICEF, Robin Hood Found., Aaron Diamond Found., Nat. Alliance Business, City Lights, Leadership Conf. Civil Rights, Skadden Fellowship Found., Parents as Tchrs. Nat. Ctr., Inc.; U.S. rep. UNICEF; active U.S. Olympic Com. Recipient Mademoiselle mag. award, 1965, Louise Waterman Wise award, 1970, Whitney M. Young award, 1979, Profl. of Yr. award, 1979, Leadership award, Nat. Women's Polit. Caucus, 1980, Black Womens Forum award, 1980, Columbia Tchrs. Coll. medal, Barnard Coll., 1984, MacArthur prize fellow, 1985, Eliot award, Am. Pub. Health Assn., John W. Gardner Leadership award, Pub. Svc. Achievement award, Compostela award, Cathedral St. James, 1987, Albert Schweitzer Humanitarian prize, Johns Hopkins U., 1987, Philip Hauge Ahelson award, AAAS, 1988, Hubert Humphrey Civil Rights award, AFL-CIO award, 1989, Radcliffe Coll. medal, 1989, Fordham Stein prize, 1989, Gandhi Peace award, 1990, M. Carey Thomas award, Robie award for humanitarianism; named one of Outstanding Young Women of America, 1966, 100 Most Influential Black Americans, Ebony mag., 2006, America's Best Leaders, US News & World Report, 2008; named to Power 150, Ebony mag., 2008. Mem.: Inst. Medicine, Phi Beta Kappa (hon.). Office: Children's Def Fund 25 E St NW Washington DC 20001-1522

EDELMAN, NORMAN HERMAN, dean, medical educator, academic administrator; b. NYC, May 21, 1937; s. Irving H. and Pearl Ruth (Solomon) E.; m. Ida Nadel, June 1959; children: David, Ruth, Deborah. AB, Bklyn. Coll., 1957; MD, NYU, 1961. Diplomate Am. Bd. Internal Medicine, Am. Bd. Pulmonary Diseases. Intern NYU Med. Sch., NYC, 1961-62, resident, 1962-63; rsch. fellow NIH, Balt., 1963-65; vis. fellow Columbia U., Presbyn. Med. Ctr., Balt., 1965-67; rsch. assoc. Michael Reese Med. Ctr., Chgo., 1967-69; asst. prof. medicine U. Pa. Sch. Medicine, Phila., 1969-72; prof. medicine, chief pulmonary medicine Robert Wood Johnson Med. Sch., U. Medicine and Dentistry of NJ, New Brunswick, NJ, 1972-95, dean, 1988-95; prof. preventive medicine and physiology and biophysics SUNY, Stony Brook, 1996—, dean Sch. Medicine, 1996—2005, v.p. Health Sci. Ctr., 1996—2006. Cons. for sci., chief med. officer, Am. Lung Assn., NYC, 1984—; mem. pulmonary disease adv. com. NIH, 1984-88; adj. prof. dept. health policy & mgmt. Mailman Sch. Pub. Health, Columbia U., 2008-. Contbr. articles, abstracts to profl. jours., chpts. to med. textbooks; mem. editorial bd. Jour. Applied Physiol., Am. Rev. Respiratory Diseases. Served as surgeon USPHS, 1963-65. Recipient MERIT award, NIH, Nat. Heart, Lung and Blood Inst., 1990. Fellow AAAS, Am. Coll. Physicians, Am. Coll. Chest Physicians; mem. Assn. Am. Physicians, Am. Soc. Clin. Investigation, Am. Thoracic Soc., Am. Physiol. Soc. Office: Dept Preventive Medicine SUNY Stony Brook L3 RM Health Sciences Ctr Stony Brook NY 11794-8036 Office Phone: 631-444-3484. Personal E-mail: nedelman@live.com. Business E-Mail: norman.edelman@sunysb.edu, norman.edelman@stonybrook.edu.

EDELMAN, STEVEN V., endocrinologist, educator; BS in Biology, UCLA, 1973—77, MS in Biology, 1977—78; MD valedictorian, U. Calif., 1978—82. Diplomate Am. Bd. Internal Medicine, 1986, Am. Bd. Internal Medicine-endocrinology, diabetes and metabolism, 2003, lic. Calif. Intern internal medicine Univ. Calif., LA, resident internal medicine, 1982—85; clin. fellow in endocrinology and metabolism Joslin Clinic, Boston, 1985—86; fellow endocrinology, diabetes and metabolism Lahey Clinic, Burlington, Mass., 1986—87; rsch. fellow Univ. Calif., San Diego; tchg. asst., dept. human physiology Univ. of So. Calif., LA, 1977—78; clin. asst. prof., dept. medicine, divsn. Univ. of Oreg. Ctr. for Health Sciences, Portland, 1989—90; staff physician Portland Diabetes and Endocrinology Ctr., Oreg., 1989—90; asst. prof. medicine, divsn. endocrinology and metabolism Univ. Calif., San Diego, 1991—95, assoc. prof. medicine, divsn. endocrinology and metabolism, 1995—2001, prof. medicine, divsn. endocrinology and metabolism, 2001—; dir. Veterans Affairs Healthcare System, San Diego, 2001—; founder and dir. Taking Control of Your Diabetes; hosp. affiliations include Univ. Calif. San Diego-Thornton Hosp., La Jolla, Univ. Calif. San Diego Med. Ctr., Hillcrest; tchg. asst. Harvard Med. Sch., Boston, 1985—87. Recipient Chief Resident's Tchr. of the Year award, Univ.Calif., San Diego, 1994, 1996, 1999, 2001, 2002, Whittier Insts. Persistence award for Pub Svc., 2001, Healthcare Found. of NJ's Humanism in Medicine award, 2001, House staff Tchg. award, Univ. Calif., San Diego, 2002, Top Doctors in San Diego County award, San Diego Mag., 2003, 2004, Health Hero award, Combined Health Agencies San Diego Chpt., 2006. Mem.: Internat. Diabetes Fedn., Am. Soc. of Clin. Investigation, Assn. of Clin. Endocrinologists, Insulin Pump Support Group, Am. Physicians Fellowship, Am. Assn. of Diabetic Educators, Am. Diabetes Assn., Juvenile Diabetes Found., Assn. of Academic Profs., Endocrine Soc. Office: University of California Health System 9350 Campus Point Dr La Jolla CA 92037 Office Phone: 858-657-8440. Office Fax: 858-552-8585.

EDELSBERG, SALLY COMINS, retired physical therapist, educator; b. Rowno, Poland, Aug. 6, 1939; came to U.S., 1949; d. Joseph Luria and Chana (Bebczuk) Comins; m. Warde C. Pierson, Oct. 8, 1968 (div. 1978); m. Paul Edelsberg, Feb. 2, 1979; 1 child, Tema. BS in Phys. Medicine, U. Wis., Madison, 1963; MS, Northwestern U., Evanston, Ill., 1972. Lic. phys. therapist. Staff and supervisory phys. therapist Hines VA Hosp., Maywood, Ill., 1963-67; program dir. Health Careers Council of Ill., Chgo., 1967-70; instr., clin. edn. coord. Programs in Phys. Therapy, Northwestern U. Med. Sch., Chgo., 1970—72, dir., assoc. prof., 1972—99, dir. devel. and alumni rels., 1999—2003. Pres. Phys. Therapy Ltd., Chgo., 1986-95; v.p. World Confedn. Phys. Therapy, 1995-99, exec. com., 1991-95. Mem.: Am. Phys. Therapy Assn. (bd. dirs. 1975—78, 1979—82, Ill. pres. 1972—76, Catherine Worthingham fellow 1999). Personal E-mail: sce1323@sbcglobal.net. E-mail: s-edelsberg@northwestern.edu.

EDELSTEIN, BARBARA A., radiologist; b. NYC, 1952; MD, NY Med. Coll., 1977. Cert. diagnostic radiology 1983. Intern Lenox Hill Hosp., NYC, 1977—78; resident Montefiore Hosp., NYC, 1979—82; radiologist Women's Radiology, NYC, 1983—. Office: Womens Radiology 1045 Park Ave New York NY 10028-1030 Office Phone: 212-860-7700. Personal E-mail: b99xray@aol.com. Business E-Mail: barbara@women'sradiology.com.

EDEN, ALVIN NOAM, pediatrician, writer; b. Bklyn., Mar. 21, 1926; s. Emanuel M. and Rae (Taran) Edelstein; m. Elaine R. Jaffe, Nov. 20, 1952; children: Robert, Elizabeth. BA, Columbia Coll., 1948; MD, Boston U., 1952. Intern Bellevue Hosp., NYC, 1952-53; resident in pediat. Univ. Hosp., NYC, 1953-55; pvt. practice specializing in pediat. Forest Hills, NY, 1955—. Assoc. clin. prof. pediat. NYU Sch. Medicine, 1960-84; chmn., dir. dept. pediat. Wyckoff Heights Med. Ctr., Bklyn., 1959—2009, chmn. emeritus, 2009-; lectr. SUNY-Downstate Med. Ctr., Bklyn., 1984-86, assoc. clin. prof. pediat., 1986-90; assoc. clin. prof. pediat. Cornell Med. Coll., 1990-99, clin. prof., 1999—. Author: Growing Up Thin, 1975, Handbook for New Parents, 1978, Positive Parenting, 1980, Dr. Eden's Healthy Kids, 1987, Positive Parenting, 2007; contbr. articles to profl. jours.; author text and reference materials. Mem. med. adv. com. YMCA of U.S., 1987—2003. With USMC, 1944-46. Mem. N.Y. Pediatric Soc. (pres. 1980-81), Queens Pediatric Soc. (pres. 1972-73), N.Y. Acad. Medicine (chmn. pediatric sect. 1985-89), Am. Acad. Pediatrics (chmn. nutrition com. chpt. 2 1985-89). Avocation: tennis. Home: 710 Park Ave New York NY 10021-4944 Office: 10721 Queens Blvd Forest Hills NY 11375-4451 Home Phone: 212-628-4475; Office Phone: 718-261-8989. Personal E-mail: babydoceden@gmail.com.

EDEN, GUINEVERE F., neurologist, educator; BSc in Physiology, U. Coll., London, England; PhD in Physiology, Oxford U., England. Dir. Ctr. for the Study of Learning; assoc. prof. dept. pediatrics Georgetown U., assoc. prof. dept. neuroscience. Mem. Ctr. Neural Injury & Recovery, Ctr. Brain Basis of Cognition. Office: Georgetown University Department of Psychology White-Gravenor Hall 306 Box 571001 Washington DC 20057-1001 Office Phone: 202-687-4042, 202-687-6893. Office Fax: 202-687-6050. E-mail: edeng@georgetown.edu.

EDENS, FRANK WESLEY, physiologist; b. Big Stone Gap, Va., Dec. 18, 1946; s. Frank Ervin and Erma Marie (Daughertry) E.; m. Mary Elizabeth Ayers, June 17, 1977; 1 child, Wesley Aaron. BS, Va. Poly. Inst. and State U., 1969, MS, 1971; PhD, U. Ga., 1974. Asst. prof. N.C. State U., Raleigh, 1973-78, assoc. prof., 1978-84, prof., 1984—. Cons. Embrex Inc., Research Triangle Park, N.C., 1984—99; sci. adv. bd. United EGG Producers, Decatur, Ga., 1987—; pres., owner Edenco Cons.-Sales, Raleigh, 1988—. Contbr. over 700 articles to profl. jours. Deacon Trinity Bapt. Ch., Raleigh, 1990—. Grantee Sterling Drug/Eastman Kodak, 1987-89, S.E. Poultry and Egg Assn., 1981, 84, 89, 91, 93, 94, 2000,02, 04, 06, Schering-Plough, 1985-86, Zoecon, 1988, 89, N.C. Biotech. Ctr., 1989, N.C. Poultry Fedn., 1991, 93, Tex. Gulf, 1993, U.S. Agy. Internat. Devel., 1993, Alltech, Inc., 1994-2011, Restoration Systems, 2011, Novamol GmbH, Novus Internat. 2007-10, Probiotics Inc., 2010-11, BioGaia Eli Metchnikov Probiotics award, 1996, Nat. Turkey Fed. award, 2000, All Tech. medal Excellence, 2002. Mem. AAAS, Am. Physiol. Soc., Poultry Sci. Assn., Am. Assn. Avian Pathologists, So. Poultry Sci. Soc. (2d v.p. 1992, 1st v.p. 1993, pres. 1994), World Poultry Sci. Assn. Republican. Achievements include American and European patents on inovo injection of Lactobacillus reuteri into chicken and turkey embryos; 5 European patents on the use of L.reuteri in chickens and tuskeys; the use of LH RH d-tryptophan-6 to induce molt in laying hens. Home: 326 Northclift Dr Raleigh NC 27609-3723 Office: NC State U Dept Poultry Sci Raleigh NC 27695-0001 Home Phone: 919-847-4190; Office Phone: 919-515-2649. Personal E-mail: fwedens@mindspring.com.

EDERY, PATRICK, physician, educator; b. France, Nov. 11, 1962; MD, Paris XI U., 1995; PhD, Paris V U., 2000. Prof. Lyon Hosps., 2003—. Rsch. scientist Lyon 1 U., 2003. Mem.: Am. Soc. Human Genetics. Avocations: tennis, guitar. Office: 59 Blvd Pinel France Bron 69677 France Personal E-mail: patrick.edery@gmail.com.

EDGAR, TERENCE S., pediatric neurologist; m. Angelika S. Lippert. DDS, UW Hosp. Clinics, Madison, WI. Chief child neurology Med. U. SC., Charleston, 2003—; head child neurology Prevea Health, Green Bay, Wis. Named Top Dr., Castle Connnolly's Am., Best Dr. Am. Office: Prevea Health 1821 S Webster Ave Green Bay WI 54307

EDGE, JAMES EDWARD, health care administrator; b. Anacortes, Wash., Apr. 29, 1948; s. Edward and Carol Marie (Lian) E.; m. Nellie Ruth Horton, Mar. 21, 1970; children: Elissa Marie, Gina Dawn. BS in Pharmacy, U. Wash., 1971; MPH, U. Hawaii, 1979. Registered pharmacist. Commd. USPHS, 1969-2000, advanced through grades to capt.; staff pharmacist USPHS Indian Hosp., Albuquerque, 1971-73; chief pharmacy, lab/x-ray S.W. Indian Poly. Inst., Albuquerque, 1972-73, Neah Bay Indian Health Ctr., Wash., 1973-75; svc. unit dir. Neah Bay Svc. Unit, Indian Health Svc., 1975-78, Western Oreg. Service Unit, Indian Health Svc., Salem, 1980-2000; mgr. policy unit Office of Med. Assistance Programs, State of Oreg., Salem, 2000—02; dep. state Medicaid dir. State of Oreg., 2003—07, state medicaid dir., 2008—10, healthcare cons., 2010—. Cons. in field. Active Combined Fed. Campaign, Salem, 1985-2000. John Quick Pharmacy scholar, U. Wash., 1967, Health Professions scholar, 1969. Mem. APHA, Am. Coll. Healthcare Adminstrs., Am. Acad. Med. Adminstrs., Assn. Mil. Surgeons U.S., Mensa, Res. Officers Assn., Commd. Officer USPHS, Wash. Pharm. Assn., nat. Coun. Svc. Unit Dirs. (chmn. 1986-88). Avocations: running, sculling. Personal E-mail: jeedge@aol.com.

EDGERTON, BRADFORD WHEATLY, plastic surgeon; b. Phila., May 8, 1947; s. Milton Thomas and Patricia Jane (Jones) E.; children: Bradford Wheatly Jr., Lauren Harrington; m. Louise Dungan Edgerton; stepchildren: Catherine Kelleher, Robert Kelleher. BA in Chemistry, Vanderbilt U., 1969, MD, 1973. Diplomate Am. Bd. Plastic

Surgery, Am. Bd. Hand Surgery. Intern U. Calif., San Francisco, 1973-74; resident U. Va., Charlottesville, 1974-78; resident in plastic surgery Columbia-Presbyn., NY, 1979-81; fellow in hand surgery NYU, 1981-82, clin. instr. plastic surgery, 1981-89; ptnr. So. Calif. Permanente Med. Group, LA, 1989—; assoc. prof. clin. plastic surgery U. So. Calif., LA, 1989—. Mem. Pacific Coun. Internat. Policy. Trustee Harvard-Westlake Sch., L.A., 2001—; pres. Edgerton Found., Beverly Hills, Calif, 2001-. Mem. Am. Assn. Hand Surgery, Am. Soc. Plastic and Reconstructive Surgery, Am. Soc. Surgery of Hand, L.A. (Calif.) Tennis Club, L.A. (Calif.) Country Club Episcopal. Home: 494 S Spalding Dr Beverly Hills CA 90212-4104 Office: 6041 Cadillac Ave Los Angeles CA 90034-1702

EDINGTON, HOWARD D.J., plastic surgeon, surgical oncologist; MD, Temple U. Sch. of Medicine, 1981. Diplomate Am. Bd. Plastic Surgery, Am. Bd. Surgery, lic. to practice Pa., 1982. Resident Univ. of Pitts. Med. Ctr. (UPMC), Pitts.; fellow Nat. Cancer Inst., Bethesda, Md.; hosp. affiliations include Magee-Womens Hosp. Univ. of UPMC, UPMC Mercy South Side Surgery, UPMC Presbyn. South Surgery, UPMC Mercy, UPMC Presbyn., UPMC Shadyside. Co-author: (publs.) Effects of high-dose IFNalpha2b on regional lymph node metastases of human melanoma: modulation of STAT5, FOXP3, and IL-17, Impact of IFNalpha2b upon pSTAT3 and the MEK/ERK MAPK pathway in melanoma, SAGE and antibody array analysis of melanoma-infiltrated lymph nodes: identification of Ubc9 as an importasnt molecule in advanced-stage melanomas, Expression analysis of genes identified by molecular profiling of VGP melanomas and MGP melanoma-positive lymph nodes, 2004. Named Top Doc, Pitts. Mag., 2009. Office: Magee-Womens Surgical Associates 300 Halket St Ste 2601 Pittsburgh PA 15213 Office Phone: 412-641-4274.

EDIS, GLORIA TOBY, pediatrician; b. NYC, Dec. 6, 1939; d. Murray Alvin and Anna G. (Goldstein) E.; m. Myron Royal Schoenfeld, June 14, 1959; children: Bradley, Glenn, Dawn, Melody. BA, Cornell U., 1960; MD, NYU, 1963. Intern Montefiore Hosp., NYC, 1963-64; pediatric resident Columbia Presbyn. Med. Ctr., NYC, 1966-68; pediatrician Scarsdale (N.Y.) Pediatric Assocs., 1977—; pediatric attending Albert Einstein Med. Coll., Bronx, 1968-70; pediatrician Barsky Med. Group, NYC, 1970-80. Fellow Am. Acad. Pediatrics; mem. Westchester County Med. Soc., Cornell Alumni Assn. Avocations: hiking, bicycling, reading, weight training, theater. Office: Scarsdale Pediatric Assn 7 Popham Rd Scarsdale NY 10583

EDIVALDO, DE OLIVEIRA HERCULANO CORREA, geneticist, educator; b. Santaré, Brazil, Sept. 9, 1969; B in Biomedicine, U. Fed. do Pará, 1991; PhD in Genetics, U. Fed. do Parána, 2001. Assoc. prof. U. Fed. do Parána, 1997—. Mem.: Brazilian Soc. Genetics. Office: Universidade Federal do Parána Rua Augusto Correa s/n Belém PA 66075-990 Brazil Business E-Mail: ehco@ufpa.br.

EDIZER, DENIZ TUNA, physician; b. Turkey, June 14, 1979; Cert. otorhinolaryngologist Cerrahpasa Med. Sch., 1998. Physician otorhinolaryngology dept. Cerrahpasa Med. Faculty, 2003—09, Bayrampasa State Hosp., 2009—11; physician Istanbul Tng. and Rsch. Hosp., 2011—. Avocation: history. Home: Istanbul Egitim ve Arastirma Hastanesi Istanbul 34098 Turkey Personal E-mail: deniztunaedizer@yahoo.com.

EDLICH, RICHARD FRENCH, biomedical engineer, educator; b. NYC, Jan. 19, 1939; MD, NYU, 1962; PhD, U. Minn., 1973. From instr. to assoc. prof. U. Va. Sch. Medicine, Charlottesville, 1971-76, prof. plastic surgery and biomed. engring., dist. prof. emergency medicine, 1976-82, disting. prof. plastic and maxillofacial surgery and biomed. engring., 1983-96, Raymoon F. Morgan prof. plastic surgery and disting. prof. biomed. engring., 1996—2001; dir. Trauma Prevention, Rsch. and Edn. Trauma Specialist LLP of Legacy Emanuel Hosp., Portland, 2004—09. Founder dept. emergency medicine U. Va., 1973, DeCamp Burn and wound Healing Ctr., 1974—85, Pegasus Air Med. Transp. Sys., 1984; physician tech. adviser Bur. Emergency Svc., HEW, 1974—79; cons. Divsn. Health Manpower and Nat. Ctr. Health Svc. Rsch., 1977—79; founder North Fork Rsch. Pk., Charlottesville, Va., 1991; sect. editor Wound Care, 1990—; edtl. cons. Am. Jour. Emergency Medicine, 2007; editl. bd. mem. Jour. Environ. Pathology, Toxicology & Oncology, 2010. Author: Medicines Deadly Dust, 1997, Citizen's Petition to Ban Cornstarch on Medical Gloves to the CDRH of the FDA, 2008; editor-in-chief: Jour. Long-Term Effects Med. Implants, 2000—06; author: itizen's Petition to Require Surgical Glove Manufacturers to Put a Warning to Put Warning Label On Surgical Glove Packages & on The Surgical Gloves Indicating That There is a 1.5% Glove Hole Leakage Rate, To the CDRH of The FDA, 2010. Recipient Disting. Pub. Svc. award for Contbns. to Emergency Medicine, USPHS, 1979, Outstanding Tchg. award, U. Va., 1989, Thomas Jefferson award, 1991, Outstanding Faculty award, Commonwealth of Va. Coun. Higher Edn., 1989, Disting. Alumni award, U. Minn. Med. Alumni Assn., 2005, The Lawn Soc., U. Va., 2006; named 5th Ann. David Boyd Lectr. in Emergency Medicine, U. Va., 2001, Richard Edlich rsch. prof. plastic surgery, U. Va. Health Sys., 1984, Endowed Edlich Henderson Inventor of Yr., U. Va. Patent Found., 2002—. Mem.: ACS, Am. Surg. Assn., Am. Coll. Emergency Physicians (James D. Mills award 2008), Soc. Acad. Emergency Medicine, Am. Soc. Plastic and Reconstructive Surgeons, Univ. Assn. Emergency Medicine, Am. Burn Assn. (Harvey Stuart Allen award 2000), Am. Assn. Surg. Trauma, Soc. Univ. Surgeons, U. Va. Lawn Soc., Alpha Omega Alpha. Achievements include research in biology of wound repair and infection, systems approach to emergency medical and trauma care; development of Edlich gastric lavage; reinforced steri-strip; CSM gram stain procedure; Shur-Clens; stabilized topical pharmaceutical preparations. Home and Office: 22500 NE 128th Cir Brush Prairie WA 98606 Office Phone: 360-944-7641. Office Fax: 360-944-7612. Personal E-mail: richardedlich@gmail.com.

EDMUNDOWICZ, DANIEL, internist, educator, cardiologist; B in Biology, U. Notre Dame; MS in Human Anatomy, MCP Hahnemann U., MD. Diplomate Am. Bd. Internal Medicine, cert. nuclear cardiology. Resident internal medicine Temple Univ. Sch. Medicine, Phila., 1993; fellow cardiovasc. disease Univ. of Pitts. Med. Sch., 1996, assoc. prof. medicine; dir. preventive cardiology Univ. of Pitts. Med. Ctr. Cardiovasc. Inst., 1996—; dir. cardiovasc. medicine UPMC Passavant; hosp. affiliations include Magee-Womens Hospital of UPMC, UPMC Presbyterian, UPMC Shadyside. Named one of Top Docs, Pitts. Mag. Fellow: Am. Coll. of Cardiology; mem.: Soc. of Atherosclerosis Imaging (pres.). Office: University of Pittsburgh Medical Center Passavant Cardiovascular Institute Ste 700 9365 McKnight Rd Pittsburgh PA 15237 Office Phone: 412-367-8202.

EDREES, AMR, rheumatologist, educator; b. Cairo, July 14, 1964; MD, Cairo U., 1987, PhD in Internal Medicine, 1998. Asst. lectr. internal medicine Cairo U., Dept. Internal Medicine, Rheumatology and Immunology, 1993—98, lectr. internal medicine, 1998—2000; internal medicine resident U. Mo., Kans. City, 2000—03, asst. prof. internal medicine, sect. chief, divsn. rheumatology, 2005—; rheumatology fellow U. Iowa Hosps. and Clinics, 2003—05. Recipient Recognition award, Gold Humanism Honor Soc. Fellow: ACP, Am. Coll. Rheumatology. Avocation: photography. Home: 14728 Eby St Overland Park KS 66221 Business E-Mail: edreesa@umkc.edu.

EDWARDS, BRIAN, health service manager, educator; b. Bebington, Eng., Feb. 19, 1942; s. John Albert and Ethel (Davis) E.; m. Jean Cannon, Nov. 7, 1964; children: Penny, Paula, Christopher, Jonathan. Grad., Wirral Grammar Sch., Bebington, Eng. Mgmt. trainee Ctrl. Wirral H.M.C.; various positions in hosp. adminstrn., 1958—69; lectr. U. Leeds, U.K., 1969-71; prof. health svcs. mgmt. U. Keele, 1991—2000; dep. sec. Hull "A" H.M.C., Hull, U.K., 1971-73; dist. adminstr. Leeds (West) Dist., 1973-76; area adminstr. Cheshire A.H.A., Chester, 1976-81; chief exec. Trent Health, Sheffield, U.K., 1981-92, West Midlands Health, 1992-94; regional dir. NHS Exec., Birmingham, 1994-96; prof. health care devel. U. Sheffield, 1996-2001. Cons. WHO, Geneva, 1970—80; pres. Inst. Health Svc. Mgmt., 1982; chmn. Clin. Pathology Accreditation, Sheffield, 1991—2000, Nottingham Health NHS Trust, 2000—06; chair coun. Professions Supplementary Medicine, 1997—2002; chair ATM Consulting, 2005—09, Pain Mgmt. Sys. Ltd., 2009—10. Author: A Managers Tale of the NHS, 1994, The Executive Years of the NHS, 2005, An Independent NHS, 2007, Acad. Health Sci. Ctrs., 2008. Chmn. Patient Empowerment and Patients Charter Groups; pres. European Hosp. Fedn., 2002—08; trustee Cavendish Hip fellowship, 1998—2005; chmn. Nottinghamshire Health Care Inst., 2000—07; patron NHS Retirement Fellowship, 2001—07. Decorated comdr. and companion Order Brit. Empire. Fellow: Inst. Health Svcs. Mgmt., Royal Coll. Pathologists (hon.); mem.: Assn. Health Svc. Suppliers (pres. 2000—04), Assn. Clin. Pathologists (hon.), Brit. Inst. Mgmt. Assn., Arden Cancer Network (chmn. 2002—03). Anglican. Avocation: golf. Home: 3 Royal Croft Drive DE45 1SN Baslow England E-mail: edwardssheffield@msn.com.

EDWARDS, BRIAN DAVID, physician; b. Luton, Eng., May 17, 1956; s. Alan Millington and Joy Enid Edwards; m. Jennifer Glew; children: Harriet, Toby, Rupert, Bridget, Lily. BSc in Pathology, U. London, 1977; MRCS LRCP, Royal Coll. Physicians, London, 1980, MRCP, 1984; MD Medicine, U. Manchester, 1994. House surgeon West Kent Gen. Hosp., Maidstone, 1980—81; house physician Joyce Green Hosp., Dartford, Kent, 1981; sr. house officer pathology Charing Cross Hosp., London, 1982—83, sr. house officer, 1982—83; sr. house officer accident and emergency Westminster Hosp., London, 1983; sr. house officer med. rotation The Royal and New Cross Hosps., Wolverhampton, 1984—85; med. registrar St. George's Hosp., Tooting, London, 1985—88; lectr. medicine U. Manchester, 1988—94; sr. med. assessor Medicines Control Agy., Vauxhall, London, 1996—99; sr. dir. Parexel Internat., Uxbridge, 1999—2005; sr. med. advisor Janssen-Cilag U.K., 2005—07; prin. cons. NBA Regulatory Sci. Bd. Editor; (book) Pharmacovigiliance: Integrating Effective Safety Surveillance, 2002; author: numerous articles in field. Recipient Beaney Prize in Histopathology, 1978, Dermatology Prize, 1978, Draper's award for study abroad, 1979, Charles Oldham prize in Ophthalmology, 1980. Mem.: Royal Coll. Physicians, British Med. Assn., Internat. Soc. Pharmacovigilance (treas. 2003—09), Drug Info. Assn. (co-chair clin. safety pharm.). Home: 105 Overdale Ashtead KT21 1PX England Home Phone: +44 1372-273789; Office Phone: +44 1494-658308. E-mail: brian.edwards@ndareg.com.

EDWARDS, BRUCE GEORGE, retired ophthalmologist, military officer; b. Idaho Springs, Colo., Apr. 6, 1942; s. Bruce Norwood and Evelyn Alice (Kohut) Edwards. BA, U. Colo., 1964; MD, U. Colo., Denver, 1968. Diplomate Am. Acad. Ophthalmology. Commd. ensign USN, 1964; advanced through grades to capt. US Naval Hosp., 1980, intern San Diego, 1968-69; USN med. officer USS Long Beach (CGN-9), 1969-70; gen. med. officer US Naval Hosp., Taipei, Taiwan, 1970-72, US Naval Dispensary Treasure Island, San Francisco, 1972-73; resident in ophthalmology US Naval Hosp., Oakland, Calif., 1973-76, mem. ophthalmology staff Camp Pendleton, Calif., 1976—83, ophthalmologist, chief of med. staff Naples, Italy, 1983—85; resident in ophthalmology U. Calif., San Francisco, 1973-76; ophthalmology head Camp Pendleton Naval Hosp., 1985-97, dir. surg. svcs., 1990-92, physician advisor quality assurance, 1985-86, ret., 1997. Vol. Internat. Eye Found., Harar, Ethiopia, 1975. Fellow Am. Acad. Ophthalmology (diplomate); mem. AMA, Calif. Med. Assn., Calif. Assn. Ophthalmologists, Am. Soc. Contemporary Ophthalmologists, Assn. U.S. Mil. Surgeons, Pan Am. Assn. Ophthalmology, Order of DeMolay (Colo. DeMolay of Yr. 1961, Idaho Springs Chevalier, Colo. State sec. 1961-62). Republican. Methodist. Avocations: piano, camping, hiking, bicycling, travel.

EDWARDS, CHRISTOPHER LEVON, medical association administrator; PhD, U. Ky., 1997. Dir. Duke U. Med. Ctr., Chronic Pain Mgmt. Program, Durham, NC, 2001—03. Dir. Duke U. Med. Ctr., Neurobehavioral Cognitive Assessment Lab., 2001—. Orgnl. devel. Bridges Point Found., Inc., Durham, 2000—03. Grantee Fin., Nat. Alliance for Rsch. on Schizophrenia and Depression, 1. Mem.: APA (assoc.), Soc. of Behavioral Medicine. Achievements include research in race and pain; race and diabetes; prostate cancer and african am. men; Alzheimer's Disease and african ams; genetics and Alzheimer's Disease. Office: Duke U Med Ctr 932 Morreene Rd Rm 170 Durham NC 27705 Business E-Mail: christopher.edwards@duke.edu.

EDWARDS, FRED HAYDEN, cardiologist; b. Madisonville, Ky., Oct. 20, 1947; m. Linda Edwards. MD, U. Ky., Lexington, 1979. Cert. in thoracic surgery ABTS, 2008. Chief, cardiothoracic surgery U. Fla. Shands Jacksonville, 1998—; Col. Walter Reed Army Med. Ctr., 1984—93. Chmn. Soc. Thoracic Surgeons, Chgo., 2004—. Recipient Disting. Svc. award, Soc. Thoracic Surgeons, 2007. Office: Univ Florida 635 W 8th St Jacksonville FL 32210 Office Phone: 904-244-3418. Business E-Mail: fhe@comcast.net.

EDWARDS, F(REDERICK) GARY, architectural firm executive, architect and health facility planner; b. Melbourne, Australia, Aug. 3, 1943; s. Frederic Kingsley and Dorothy Vernon (Harrison) E.; m. Kathryn Margaret Winford, Nov. 3, 1979; children: Simon John Just, Ingrid Emily Just, Phillipa Claire Edwards. Diploma in architectural design, U. Melbourne, 1974; diploma in architecture, Royal Melbourne Inst. Tech., 1975. Registered architect Victoria (Australia), Archts. Accreditation Coun. Australia. Draftsman then architect Stephenson & Turner, Melbourne, 1961-83, assoc. and sr. health facility planner, 1983-91; co-founding prin. Health Facilities Cons. Archs., Melbourne, 1991—; life gov. mem. and past v.p. Child and Family Care Network, Inc. and Bestchance, Melbourne, 1983—; exec. mem. Free Masons' Victoria Task Force, 2009—; mem. Victoria Br. Assn. Counsulting Archs., Australia, 2009—. Co-founding dir. Health Planners Australia Pty Ltd., Melbourne, 1993-98, Newpolis Ply Ltd., Melbourne, 1996-98, ArcHealth Pty Ltd., Melbourne, 2000—; examiner Architect's Registration Bd. Victoria; exec. mem. Freemasons Victoria Task Forces Com.; mem. Victoria Br. Assn. Consulting Archs., Australia; com. mem. Bestchance Child Family Care; chartered architect and health facility planner major health related bldg. devel. including acute hosps. and aged care facilities throughout Australia and internationally. Recipient Pres. award, Royal Australian Inst. Architects, 1995, Cert. Appreciation award, Victorian Premier's, 2001, Liberal Party Australian Svcs. award, 2005, Lifetime Achievement award, World Congress Arts Scis., 2007, IBC's Internat. Health Profl. of Yr. award, 2007, ABI's Am. Order of Merit award, 2009, UCC's Internat. Peace prize, 2009, Gold medal, ABI, 2010. Fellow: Royal Australian Inst. Architects (convenor complaints com. and fees and conditions com., former councilor, awards assessor, practice bd. mem., Inaugural Victorian Chpt. Pres. award 1995); mem.: Australian Inst. Co. Dirs., Inst. Hosp. Engring. Australia, Royal Melbourne Inst. Tech. (assoc.), Royal Inst. Brit. Architects, Assn. Consulting Architects-Australia, Order of Internat. fellowship, Melbourne and Old Scotch Football Clubs, Citroen Car Club of Victoria (past pres.), Royal Automobile Club of Victoria, Old Scotch Collegians (Masonic) Lodge. Achievements include development of health facility models for optimum functionality, quality care and cost effectiveness, including for day surgery/procedures and first super-clinic integrated acute and primary day care center, multi-purpose health services and "under one roof" model providing integrated facility with single point staff management of multi-houses for both high and low level aged care and acute services, allowing reduced operational costs, improved quality of life and care, and "aging in place" support for residents and quality of care for patients; adviser in preparation of generic guidelines for health facilities for governments and of standard building contracts and architectural practise instruction notes. Office: Health Facilities Cons Arch 10 Cochran Ave Camberwell VIC 3124 Australia Fax: 61-3-98821402. E-mail: hfca@bigpond.com.

EDWARDS, HELEN ETHEL, nurse, educator; married. BA with honors, U. Queensland, Australia, 1996, PhD. RN EM, Queensland, 1973; cert. psychologist 1990. Head sch. nursing Queensland U. Tech., Brisbane, 1997—, prof., 2003—. Dir. Queensland Villages, Brisbane, 1993—2008. Office: Queensland Univ Tech Victoria Pk Rd Kelvin Grove 4059 Brisbane QLD Australia Office Fax: 617 3138 5895. Business E-Mail: h.edwards@qut.edu.au.

EDWARDS, KATHRYN MARGARET, physician, researcher, educator; b. Williamsburg, Iowa, Aug. 27, 1948; d. Glen Wesley and Betty Jeanne (Heitman) Cranston; m. William John Edwards, June 3, 1970; children: Emily, Kevin, Megan, Gretchen. Student, Grinnell Coll., Iowa; grad., U. Iowa Coll. Pharmacy, 1969; MD, U. Iowa Coll. Medicine, 1973. Diplomate Am. Bd. Pediat., cert. in Pediatric Infectious Disease, lic. Iowa, Ill., Tenn. Resident pediat. Children's Meml. Hosp./Northwestern U. Sch. Medicine, Chgo., 1973—76, fellow infectious diseases, 1976—78; postdoc. fellow, instr. immunology Presbyn. St. Luke's Hosp./Rush Med. Sch., Chgo., 1978—80; asst. prof. pediat., divsn. infectious diseases Vanderbilt U. Sch. Medicine, Nashville, 1980—86, assoc. prof., 1986—91, prof., 1991—, vice-chair clin. rsch., 2001—. Mem. adv. com. immunization practices Ctrs. Disease Control & Prevention, Atlanta, 1991—93; mem. vaccines and related biol. products adv. com. FDA, Washington, 1996—2000. Mem. editl. bd. Infection & Immunity, 2005—07, Pediat., Jour. Infectious Diseases, Pediat. Infectious Disease Jour., Infectious Diseases in Children; contbr. articles to profl. jours., chapters to books. Recipient Amos Christie award for Outstanding Tchg., Vanderbilt U. Dept. Pediat., 1983, Stephen R. Preblud award, 2004, Alexander Heard Disting. Prof. award, 2005. Fellow: Am. Acad. Pediat. (mem. exec. com. sect. infectious diseases 1999—2002), Infectious Diseases Soc. America (coun. mem. 2002—05, Mentor award 2006); mem.: Inst. Medicine, Am. Pediatric Soc., Pediatric Infectious Disease Soc. (coun. mem. 1995—99), Soc. Pediatric Rsch., Alpha Omega Alpha. Roman Catholic. Avocations: cooking, reading. Office: Vanderbilt U Sch Medicine Pediat Clin Rsch Office 1116 21st Ave S Nashville TN 37232-0001 Office Phone: 615-322-3078. Office Fax: 615-322-2733. Business E-Mail: kathryn.edwards@vanderbilt.edu.

EDWARDS, MICHAEL GERARD, physician; b. Duluth, Minn., Apr. 27, 1956; s. Charles and Cecelia Edwards; m. Patricia Ann Roedl; children: Matthew, Conor, Anne. BA, U. Notre Dame, 1978; MD, Creighton U., 1982. Resident in radiology SUNY, Buffalo, 1983-86; fellow William Beaumont Hosp., Royal Oak, Mich., 1986-87, staff radiologist, 1987-92, Providence Hosp., Southfield, Mich., 1992—, St. John Macomb Hosp., Warren, 2004—. Mailing: 783 Abbey St Birmingham MI 48009 Office Phone: 586-573-5060. Personal E-mail: medwards533@gmail.com. Business E-Mail: michael.edwards@stjohn.org.

EDWARDS, MORVEN SPENCER, pediatrician, educator; b. Glasgow, Scotland, May 8, 1947; BA, Rice U., 1969; MD, Baylor Coll. Medicine, 1973. Prof., pediat. Baylor Coll. Medicine, 1990—. Fellow: Infectious Disease Soc. America; mem.: Pediatric Infectious Disease Soc. Avocations: jogging, reading. Office: 1102 Bates St Ste 1120 Houston TX 77030 Office Fax: 832-825-1048. Business E-Mail: morvene@bcm.edu.

EDWARDS, ROBERT GEOFFREY, physiologist, human reproduction researcher; b. Manchester, England, Sept. 27, 1925; Grad., U. Wales, Bangor; PhD, Edinburgh U., Scotland, 1955. Faculty mem., rschr. Calif. Inst. Tech., 1953—58; rschr. Nat. Inst. Med. Rsch., London, 1958; faculty Cambridge U., 1963—89, reader, 1968—85, prof. human reproduction, 1985—89; co-founder, head rsch. Bourn Hall Clinic, Cambridge, 1980; ret. Editor: Human Reproduction Jour., 1991—2000; editor emeritus RBM Online. Served with Brit. Army. Recipient Berterelli award in reproductive health, Venice, 2000, Albert Lasker Clin. Med. Rsch. award, 2001, Nobel prize in Physiology/Medicine, Nobel Found., 2010, Pride of Britain award for lifetime achievement; named one of 100 Greatest Living Geniuses, The Daily Telegraph, UK, 2007. Achievements include along with surgeon Patrick Steptoe, successfully pioneering conception through in-vitro fertilization (IVF), which led to the birth of the first test-tube baby, Louise Brown, on 25 July 1978; this scientific breakthrough laid the groundwork for further innovations such as intracytoplasmatic sperm injection, embryo biopsy and stem cell research. Office: RBM Online Duck End Farm Park Lane CB23 8DB Cambridge England Business E-Mail: office@rbmonline.com. *

EDWARDS, ROBERT P., gynecologic oncologist, educator, obstetrician; MD, U. of Pittsburgh School of Medicine, 1984; attended, Gettysburg Coll., Pa. Diplomate Am. Bd. Ob-Gyn, cert. gynecologic oncology. Resident Univ. of Pitts. Med. Ctr. (UPMC), 1989; exec. vice chair gynecologic svcs., dir. Ovarian Cancer Ctr. for Excellence Gynecologic Cancer Program Magee-Womens Hosp. of UPMC; hosp. affiliations include UPMC Horizon, UPMC Mercy, UPMC Passavant, UPMC Presbyn., UPMC Shadyside; bd. dirs. Univ. of Pitts. Physicians. Fellow Univ. of Ala. Birmingham Hosp., Birmingham, Ala., 1993; prof. medicine dept. of obstetrics, gynecology, and reproductive sciences UPMC. Fellow: ACS, Am. Congress of Obstetricians and Gynecologists; mem.: AMA, Internat. Gynecologic Cancer Soc., Am. Assn. for the Advancement of Sci., Internat. Soc. for Biol. Therapy of Cancer, Am. Soc. of Colposcopy and Cervical Pathology, Soc. of Gynecologic Oncologists, Am. Soc. of Clin. Oncology, Am. Assn. for Cancer Rsch., Soc. of Gynecologic Oncologists. Office: Magee Gynecologic Cancer Program 300 Halket St Ste 1750 Pittsburgh PA 15213 Office Phone: 412-641-5411.

EDWARDS, SAMUEL ROGER, retired internist; b. Santa Barbara, Calif., Aug. 11, 1937; s. Harold S. and Margaret (Spaulding) E.; m. Marcia Elizabeth Dutton, June 17, 1961; children: Harold S. II, Charles Dutton. BA, Harvard U., 1960; MD, U. So. Calif., 1964. Intern Presbyn. Hosp., Phila., 1964-65; resident in internal medicine U Calif., San Francisco, 1968-70; fellow in cardiology Pacific Presbyn. Med. Ctr., San Francisco, 1970; pvt. practice specializing in internal medicine Santa Paula, Calif., 1971-94; med. dir. Santa Paula Convalescent, Twin Pines Convalescent Hosps., 1974-95; pres. med. staff Ventura (Calif.) County Med. Ctr., 1979-80, med. dir., 1983-95, hosp. adminstr., 1995—2002; ret., 2002. Chief dept. medicine Ventura County Gen. Hosp., 1975; chief med. staff Santa Paula Meml. Hosp., 1977; mem. clin. faculty sch. medicine UCLA, 1980—95; chmn. Citizens State Bank of Santa Paula, 1994—97; bd. dir. Santa Barbara Bank and Trust, 1998—2006; chmn. Limoneira Co., 2003—04, bd. dirs. Lt. comdr. USNR, 1966-68. Recipient Disting. Svc. award Ventura County Heart Assn., 1974. Fellow: ACP; mem.: AMA, Am. Coll. Hosp. Execs. Episcopalian. Home: 19789 E Telegraph Rd Santa Paula CA 93060-9693 *

EDWARDS, SARAH ANNE, licensed clinical social worker, psychologist; b. Tulsa, Jan. 7, 1943; d. Clyde Elton and Virginia Elizabeth Glandon; m. Paul Robert Edwards, Apr. 24, 1965; 1 son, Jon Scott. BA with distinction, U. Mo., Kansas City, 1965; MSW, U. Kans., 1974; PhD in Applied Ecopsychology, Akamai U., Hilo, Hawaii, 2006. LCSW Calif.; cert. ecopsychologist Inst. Global Edn., 2005. Cmty. rep. OEO, Kans. City Regional Office, 1966-68; social svc./parent involvement and resource specialist Office of Child Devel., HEW, Kansas City, Mo., 1968-73; dir. tng. social svcs. dept., children's rehab. unit U. Affiliated Facility, U. Kans. Med. Ctr., Kansas City, 1975-76; co-dir. Cathexis Inst. S., Glendale, Calif., 1976-77; pvt. practice psychotherapy, tng. and cons. personal and interpersonal, orgnl. behavior, Sierra Madre, Calif., 1973-80; sys. operator CompuServe Info. Svc., 1983-98; faculty mem. grad. dept. applied ecopsychology Akami U., 2005—; NGO cons. UNESCO, 2005—. Prodr., co-host radio show Working From Home, on Bus. Talk Radio, 1988-01; co-host radio show Entrepeneur's Home Business Edition, 2003— co-host cable show Working from Home Scripp's Howard Home and Garden Cable TV Network, 1995-97; commentator CNBC, 1996-99, NPR Marketplace, 1996-97; co-host Entrepreneurs Home Bus. Show, WS Radio, 2000—, trainer US Transition Inst., 2008-; bd. dirs. Let's Live Local Non Profit Corp., 2005-, pvt. psychotherapy practice, 2009-. Columnist for Home Office Computing Mag., 1988-97, Your Home Office, L.A. Times Syndicate, 1997-99, Entrepreneur's Home Office, 1998—, CostCo Connection, 1994—, Inc-Com., 2000—; co-author: How to Make Money with Your Personal Computer, 1997, Getting Business to Come to You, 1998, Working From Home, rev. edit., 1999, Secrets of Self-Employment, 1996, Finding Your Perfect Work, 1996, Teaming Up, 1997, Home Businesses You Can Buy, 1997, Cool Careers for Dummies, 1998, Making Money in Cyberspace, 1998, Best Home Business for the 21st Century, 1999, Working From Home, 1999, The Practical Dreamer's Handbook, 2000, Home-Based Business for Dummies, 2010, Changing Directions without Losing Your Way, 2001, Entrepreneurial Parent, 2002, Sitting with the Enemy, A Novel, 2002, Why Aren't You Your Own Boss?, 2003, Best Home Business for People 50+, 2004, Middle Class Lifeboat, 2008; mem. editl. bd. Jour. Applied Ecopsychology Akamai U., 2005—. Dir. nature-guided continuing edn. programs Pine Mtn. Inst., 2001—; dir. Let's Live Local Transition Initiative, 2008—; trainer Pathways Transitions www.pathwaystotransition.com, 2009. Mem.: Red Cross Provider for Family Care Giving Tng., Red Cross Emergency Response Team for Mental Health, Pine Mountain Club. Address: Box 6775 2624 Teakwood Ct Frazier Park CA 93222 Business E-Mail: sedwards@frazmtn.com.

EDWARDS, WILLARDA V., internist; MBA, Loyola Coll., Balt.; MD, Univ. Md. Staff Bethesda Naval Hosp.; chief internal medicine dept. US Navy Hosp., Annapolis; asst. dean student and faculty devel. U. Md. Sch. Medicine; mng. ptnr., internist Edwards & Stephens, Balt. Bd. mem. Med. Mutual Liability Co., Md. Mem. blood products adv. com. FDA; former commr. Health Services Cost Rev. Commn., Md.; mem. High Blood Pressure Commn., Md. Served with USNR. Recipient Zeta Phi Beta Woman of Yr. in Medicine award, 1997, Md.'s Top 100 Women award, 2003, Girl Scouts Ctrl. Md. award, 2004. Mem.: AMA (pres. Md. chpt. 1996), Sickle Cell Assn. Am. (pres., COO 2004—09), Nat. Med. Assn. (pres. Md chpt. 1996, pres.-elect 2008—09, pres. 2009—10, immediate past pres. 2010—11). Avocations: bicycling, golf, scuba diving, skiing. Office: Edwards & Stephens 1005 N Point Blvd Ste 724 Baltimore MD 21224 *

EDYE, MICHAEL B, surgeon, educator; MD, U. Sydney, 1977; postgrad. in surgical training, Sydney, Australia, 1991. Lic. NY. Resident in surgery St. Vincent's Hosp., 1978—80; resident in pediatric surgery Royal North Shore Hosp., 1981—84; fellow in laparoscopic surgery Univ. Bordeaux, 1991—92; assoc. clin. prof. surgery Mt. Sinai Sch. Med. Ctr.; surgeon Mt. Sinai Med. Ctr. Pub. (numerous original manuscripts). Office: Mount Sinai Medical Center 5 E 98th St 14th Fl New York NY 10029-6574 Office Phone: 212-241-0872. Office Fax: 212-824-2336.

EEDY, DAVID JOHN, dermatologist, consultant; b. Belfast, Northern Ireland, Northern Ireland, Jan. 27, 1957; s. Edward and Ruth Eedy; m. Colette Gillan. MBChB, Queen's U., Belfast, 1981. Chief cons. dermatologist Craigavon Area Hosp., Portadown, Northern Ireland, 1991—. Editor-in-chief British Journal of Dermatology, editl. advisory bd., Clin. and Experimental Dermatology, Jour. Dermatological Sci., Ulster Med. Jour. Author: (book) Surgical Dermatology, Rook's Textbook of Dermatology. Fellow: Royal Soc. Medicine, London, Royal Coll. Physicians, London; mem.: Brit. Assn. Dermatology (treas. 2009—), Brit. Assn. Dermatologists (sec. 2006—, treas. 2009—), Brit. Assn. Dermatologists (hon. sec. 2005—10). Achievements include research in neuropeptides in skin, teledermatology. Home: 77 Balmoral Ave Belfast BT9 6NY Northern Ireland Office: Craigavon Area Hosp 68 Lurgan Rd Portadown BT63 5QQ Northern Ireland Personal E-mail: davidjeedy@gmail.com.

EEG-OLOFSSON, ORVAR, pediatric neurologist; b. Borås, Sweden, Sept. 3, 1932; s. Ansgar Olof and Sonja Margareta (Samuelsson) E-O.; m. Anne-Marie Enander, Aug. 31, 1963 (div. 1986); children: Jens, Måns, Mia; m. Karin Eva Edebol, May 19, 1990(div. 2007). MD, U. Lund, Sweden, 1959; PhD, U. Goteborg, Sweden, 1970. Asst. prof. dept. pediatrics U. Goteborg, 1970-71, assoc. prof. dept. pediatrics, 1971-74, U. Linköping, Sweden, 1974-85; prof. pediatrics Kuwait U., 1985-88; prof. Nat. Epilepsy Ctr., Oslo, 1988-90; prof. pediat. neurology U. Uppsala, Sweden, 1990—, head child neurology unit, 1990-97; cons. child neurology, 1998—. Contbr. over 220 articles to profl. jours. Capt. Swedish armed forces, 1987. Mem. Rotary, Save Children Assn. (bd. mem. Uppsala dist.) Avocations: ornithology, bridge, sports, literature. Office: U Children's Hosp Child Neurology Unit S-75185 Uppsala Sweden Home: Norbyvagen 44A Uppsala S-75239 Sweden Office Phone: 46-18-6110000. E-mail: orvar.eeg-olofsson@kbh.uu.se.

EFREMOV, DIMITAR, hematologist, researcher; b. Skopje, Macedonia, Dec. 26, 1960; m. Marija Apostolska, Nov. 6, 1987; 1 child, Kristian. MD, U. St. Cyril & Methodius, Skopje, Macedonia, 1986; PhD, U. Limburg, Maastricht, The Netherlands, 1994. Vis. scientist Med. Coll. Ga., Augusta, 1987, 1993; rsch. assoc. Rsch. Ctr. New Technologies, MASA, Skopje, Macedonia, 1988—89; resident in hematology Faculty of Medicine, Skopje, 1990—92, asst. prof. hematology, 1998—2001, assoc. prof. internal medicine, 2001—; fellow Internat. Centre for Genetic Engring. and Biotechnology, Trieste, 1992, staff scientist, 1994—98; staff scientist and group leader Internat. Centre for Genetic Engring. and Biotechnology-Monterotondo Outstation, Monterotondo Scalo, Rome, 2002—. Head lymphoma/myeloma bone marrow transplantation program Faculty of Medicine, Skopje, 2000—02; head outstation ICGEB Molecular Hematology Group. Monterotondo Outstation, Monterotondo Scalo, 2002—; external lectr. hematology Sch. Specialization in Hematology, Cath. U. Hosp. A. Gemelli, Rome, 2004—. Contbr. articles to numerous profl. jours. Cons. physician of the european commn., Skopje, 1999—2002; mem. Internat. Ctr. for Genetic Engring. and Biotechnology, Trieste, 1998—2002; mem. prep. com. for the strategy for devel. of health sector Skopje, 2000—02; mem. expert com. for sci. cooperation in SE Europe Unesco Roste, Venice, Italy, 2001. Grantee, Internat. Ctr. Genetic Engring. and Biotech., 1998—2001, Soros Open Soc. Inst., Leukemia & Lymphoma Soc., 2005—. Mem.: European Group for Blood and Marrow Transplantation, Am. Soc. Clin. Oncology, Am. Soc. Hematology. Achievements include first to established the first bone marrow transplantation program in Macedonia, 2000; introduced molecular diagnostics of hematological diseases in Macedonia; research in biology, prognosis and treatment of chronic lymphocytic leukemia; of the hepatitis C virus in the development of certain B-cell lymphoproliferative disorders; performed characterization of immunoglobulin E antibodies and their role in allergy; characterized factors that Determine the severity of the disease in patients with beta-yhalassemia. Avocations: travel, skiing, tennis, jogging. Office: ICGEB Monterotondo Outstation CNR Campus Via E Ramarini 32 Rome Monterotondo Scalo 00016 Italy E-mail: efremov@icgeb.org.

EFRON, JONATHAN EDWARD, colon and rectal surgeon, educator; MD, U. Md., 1993. Diplomate Am. Bd. Surgery, 2008, Am. Bd. Colon and Rectal Surgery, 2009. Resident in surgery LI Jewish Med. Ctr., 1994—99; fellow in colon and rectal surgery Cleve. Clinic, Weston, Fla., 1999—2000, rsch. fellow in colon and rectal surgery, 2000—01; assoc. prof. surgery Johns Hopkins Univ.; hosp. affiliations include Johns Hopkins Bayview Med. Ctr., Johns Hopkins Hosp., Md. Office: Johns Hopkins Hospital 600 N Wolfe St Baltimore MD 21287 Office Phone: 410-955-5000.

EFSTATHIOU, ELENI, oncologist, educator; b. Athens, Greece, Sept. 1, 1972; MD, U. Athens, 1995, PhD, 2003. Asst. prof. U. Tex., 2007—, U. Athens Greece Med. Sch., 2009. Recipient Young Investigator award, Prostate Cancer Found. Mem.: ASCO. Office: MD Anderson Cancer Ctr 1155 Pressler St Houston TX 77030 Business E-Mail: eefstathiou@mdanderson.org.

EFTEKHARI, NASSER, physiatrist; b. Aug. 15, 1940; MD, U. Tehran, 1965. Diplomate AM. Bd. Phys. Medicine and Rehab. Intern Greater Balt. Med. Ctr., 1967-68; resident in phys. medicine and rehab. Temple U. Sch. Med., Phila., 1968-70, Hahneman Med. U., Phila., 1970-71; rsch. fellow SUNY, Bklyn., 1971-72; chief dept. phys. medicine and rehab. Shafa Rehab. Hosp., Tehran, Iran, 1973-75; dean Coll. of Rehab. Scis., Tehran, 1973-79; phys. med. and rehab. cons. Golestan Clinic, Mehr Hosp., Tehran, 1980-84; staff physician VA Hosp., Miami, Fla., 1985—2005, Mercy Hosp., 1989—, Cedars Med. Ctr., 1989—, Bapt. Health Sys. Hosp. South Fla., Miami, 1996—; chief phys. med. and rehab. svc. VA Hosp., Miami, 1997—2005. Clin. assoc. prof. rehab. medicine U. Miami Sch. Medicine, 2003—. Fellow: Am. Assn. Electrodiagnostic Medicine; mem.: Am. Acad. Phys. Medicine and Rehab., Fla. Soc. Phys. Medicine and Rehab. Office: 8600 SW 92 St Ste 201 Miami FL 33156 Office Phone: 305-206-4726. Business E-Mail: dreftekhari@yahoo.com.

EGBERT, BARBARA MAYER, dermatopathologist; b. Cumberland, Md., Aug. 30, 1942; MD, Yale U., 1968. Bd. cert. anatomic pathology & dermatopathology. Resident in pathology Yale U., Stanford U.; physician, prof. Vets. Hosp., Stanford U. Affiliated, 1972—. Mem.: Am. Acad. Dermatology, Internat. Soc. Dermatopathology, Southbay Pathology Soc., Am. Soc. Dermatopathology. Avocation: travel. Office: 3801 Miranda Ave Palo Alto CA 94304 E-mail: barbaraegbert@yahoo.com.

EGBERT, PETER ROY, ophthalmologist, educator; b. Indpls., Dec. 6, 1941; BA magna cum laude, DePauw U., Greencastle, Ind., 1963; MD, Yale U., 1967. Diplomate Nat. Bd. Med. Examiners, Am. Bd. Ophthalmology. Intern Cleve. Met. Gen. Hosp., 1967—68; resident in ophthalmology Yale U., New Haven, 1968—69; acting asst. prof. surgery (ophthalmology Stanford (Calif.) U., 1973—74, dir. Ophthalmic Pathology Lab., 1973—, asst. prof. surgery, 1974—81; acting head divsn. ophthalmology Stanford U. Med. Ctr., 1980—82, assoc. prof. surgery, 1981—88, prof. ophthalmology, 1988—, chmn. dept. ophthalmology, 1992—97; resident in ophthalmology Yale U., New Haven, 1971—73. Recipient Bordon prize, DePauw U., 1960. Mem.: Verhoeff Ophthalmic Pathology Soc., Peninsula Eye Soc., Michael Hogan Eye Pathology Soc., Am. Intra-Ocular Implant Soc., Am. Assn. Ophthalmic Pathologists, Am. Acad. Ophthalmology (Outstanding Humanitarian Svc. award 2004), Phi Beta Kappa, Alpha Omega Alpha. Office: Stanford U Sch Medicine 300 Pasteur Dr Stanford CA 94305-5308

EGELUND, NIELS, psychologist; b. Odense, Funen, Denmark, Aug. 26, 1945; s. Niels and Thora Egelund; m. Jette Gaarsvig Nielsen, May 26, 1977 (div. 1997); children: Kasper, Sofie; m. Camilla Dgssegaard, Nov. 19, 2010. Tchg. cert., Odense Seminarium, 1968; MA, U. Copenhagen, 1976; PhD, Royal Danish Sch. Ednl. Studies, 1982, Dr. Paed. Tchr. Ringe Municipality, Denmark, 1970-72; psychologist Albertslund Municipality, Denmark, 1976-79; asst. prof. Danish Sch. of Ednl. Studies, 1979-82, assoc. prof., 1982-87, doctorate, 1987-95; prof. The Danish U. of Edn., 1996—. Dean studies Danish Sch. Ednl. Studies, 1983—88, 1998—2000, dir. inst., 1997—; cons., Danida, Denmark, 1993—. Contbr. articles to profl. jours. Com. mem. Ministry of Edn., Denmark, 1984—87, 1999, adv. bd., 1999—; peer rev. group mem. OECD, Paris, 2000—. Sgt. Royal Danish Air Force, 1968—70. Decorated Knight of Dannebrog; grantee, Ednl. Rsch. Bd., 1977, Ministry of Edn., 1996, Velux Fond, 1999. Mem.: Consortium Instns. Rsch. Edn. Europe (del. 1998—), Danish Aviators, Danish Assn. Psychologists. Achievements include research in inclusive education, behavioral problems and cross curriculum competences. Avocations: flying, gliders, old military jet aircraft. Office: Danish U of Edn Tuborgvej 164 2400 Copenhagen Denmark Office Phone: 45-87161300. Office Fax: 45-8888-9707. Business E-Mail: egelund@dpu.dk.

EGER, THOMAS, periodontist, researcher; b. Speyer, Germany, June 6, 1962; s. Wolfgang Walter and Kaethi (Waldburger) Eger; m. Eva-Marie Erlemeier; children: Anika, Jens. D in Med. Dentistry, Ruprecht-Karls U., 1987; postgrad., Westfaelische-Wilhelms U., 1993. Col. German Armed Forces Ctrl. Hosp., Koblenz, 1981—, chief periodontist dept. periodontology, 1993—; comdr., head Ctr. for Dental Spltys., dir. periodontology German Armed Forces Ctr. Hosp., Koblenz, 1998—. Cons. periodontology to surgeon gen. German Armed Forces, 2002—. Author: Furkationsbehandlung, 1998; editor Neue Arbeitsgruppe Parodontologie-News, 1996—; contbr. articles to profl. jours. Mem. Internat. Assn. for Dental Rsch., Neue Arbeitsgruppe Parodontology (pres. 1996—), Deutsche Gesellschaft für Parodontologie, Am. Acad. Periodontology. Avocations: curling, painting, tennis. Office: German Armed Forces Hosp Ruebenacherstr 170 56072 Koblenz Germany Business E-Mail: thomaseger@bundeswehr.org.

EGEROD, INGRID, critical care nurse, educator; b. Oakland, Calif., Dec. 5, 1954; d. Soren Christian and Lois Eubank Egerod; m. Finn Collin, July 24, 1999. PhD, U. Copenhagen, 2003. RN Hawaii, 1986, lic. critical care nurse, Calif., 1990. Asst. prof. SF Rigshospitalet 7331 U. Copenhagen, 2003—04, assoc. prof., 2004—. Mem.: AACN. Office: UCSF Rigshospitalet 7331 Blegdamsvej 9 Copenhagen DK-2100 Denmark Office Fax: +4535457399. Business E-Mail: ie@ucsf.dk.

EGERTON, CHARLES PICKFORD, anatomy and physiology educator; b. Toronto, Ont., Can., Mar. 17, 1939; (parents Am. citizens); s. Matthew Davis and Margaret Swain (Pickford) E.; m. Carol Anne Carlson, Dec. 16, 1976; children: Matthew, Andrew, Victoria. BA in Zoology, Duke U., 1962; BS in Medicine, U. Okla., Oklahoma City, 1978; MS in Sci. Edn., U. So. Miss., 1981, PhD in Sci. Edn., 1991, MPH in Health Edn., 1994. Cert. physician asst. Nat. Commn. on Cert. Physician Assts. Commd. 2d lt. USAF, 1962, advanced through grades to maj., 1980, ops. officer, 1962-76, primary care med. officer Keesler AFB, Miss., 1978-88; ret., 1988; instr. anatomy and physiology Miss. Gulf Coast C.C., Gautier, 1992—. Mem. Miss. Health Adv. Coun., Jackson, 1990—; guest lectr. dept. physician asst. studies U. South Ala. Author: Student Study Guide for Anatomy and Physiology; editor: Physician Assistant Handbook, 1995, Principles of Anatomy and Physiology, 9th edit., 2000; contbr. articles to profl. jours. Lectr. Miss. Inst. Drug-Free Sch., Hattiesburg, 1992; lectr. single parent-displaced spouse, Guatier, 1994-97; dir. smoking cessation Keesler AFB Med. Ctr., 1986-88; lay reader St. Luke's Anglican Ch., Gulfport, Miss., 1986-94. Mem. Am. Assn. Anatomists, Am. Acad. Physician Assts., Human Anatomy and Physiology Soc., Miss. Acad. Scis., Miss. Sci. Tchrs. Assn., Phi Delta Kappa, Eta Sigma Gamma. Democrat. Avocation: boating. Office: Miss Gulf Coast CC PO Box 100 Gautier MS 39553-0100 Home: 6008 Moreton Pl Ocean Springs MS 39564-2731 Office Phone: 228-497-7783. E-mail: charles.egerton@mgccc.edu, egerton@cableone.net.

EGGAN, KEVIN C., molecular and cellular biology professor, researcher; BS with Distinction in Molecular Biology, U. Ill., Urbana-Champaign, 1996; PhD in Biology, MIT, 2003. Postdoctoral fellow Whitehead Inst. for Biomedical Rsch., 2002—03; pre-doctoral fellow Nat. Inst. Child Health and Human Develop., Bethesda, Md.; junior fellow, dept. molecular and cellular biology Harvard Soc. Fellow, 2003; asst. prof., dept. molecular and cellular biology Harvard U., 2005. Spkr. in field; founding mem., asst. investigator Stowers Med. Inst., 2005—. Contbr. articles to profl. jours. Named one of Brilliant 10, Popular Sci. mag., 2005; Basil O'Connor Scholar, March of Dimes, MacArthur Fellow, John D. and Catherine T. MacArthur

Found., 2006. Avocation: French cooking. Office: Harvard U 437 Fairchild 7 Divinity Ave Cambridge MA 02138 Office Phone: 617-496-5611. Office Fax: 617-496-8116. Business E-Mail: eggan@mcb.harvard.edu.

EGGERS, GEORGE WILLIAM NORDHOLTZ, JR., anesthesiologist, educator; b. Galveston, Tex., Feb. 22, 1929; s. George William Nordholtz and Edith (Sykes) E.; m. Mary Futrell, Dec. 30, 1955; children: Carol Ann, George William. BA, Rice U., Tex., 1949; MD, U. Tex., Galveston, Tex., 1953. Diplomate Am. Bd. Anesthesiology. Instr. dept. anesthesiology, U. Tex., Galveston, Tex., 1956-59; asst. prof. dept. anesthesiology, U. Tex., Galveston, Tex., 1959-61; assoc. prof. dept. anesthesiology, U. Mo., 1961-67; prof. dept anesthesiology U. Mo., 1967—94, acting chmn. dept. anesthesiology, 1969, chmn. dept. anesthesiology, 1970-94, prof. emeritus, 1994—2001. Vis. instr. USAF Hosp., Lackland AFB, San Antonio, 1956-61; vis. rsch. prof. dept. anesthesiology Northwestern U. Med. Sch., Chgo., 1968-69; rsch. assoc. Space Sci. Rsch. Ctr., U. Mo., 1965-66. Contbr. over 50 articles to profl. jours. Recipient Ashbel Smith Disting. Alumnus Award U. Tex., 1993. Mem. Am. Soc. Anesthesiology (bd. dirs. 1979-86, v.p. 1986-89, 1st v.p. 1990, pres. elect 1991, pres. 1992), Am. Coll. Anesthesiology (bd. govs., 1965-74, chmn. bd. govs., 1973), Soc. Acad. Anesthesiology Chmn. (pres. 1971), Assn. Am. Med. Colls. (adminstrv. bd. coun. acad. socs. 1976-79), Mo. Soc. Anesthesiologists (pres. 1970, Disting. Svc. Award 2001), Tex. Gulf Coast Anesthesiology Soc. (v.p. 1960), Boone County Med. Soc. (pres. 1988), Am. Bd. Anesthesiology (assoc. examiner 1968, joint coun. with Am. Soc. Anesthesiology on in-tng. exams.), Acad. Anesthesiology (pres. 1995, Citation of Merit 1997), Accreditation Coun. Grad. Med. Edn. (mem. residency rev. com. for anesthesiology 1989-94), Anesthesia Found. (trustee 1993-2003), Jefferson Club of U. Mo., Alpha Omega Alpha, Mu Delta, Sigma Xi. Republican. Roman Catholic. Avocations: hunting, astronomy, magic, photography, shooting. Home: 1509 Woodrail Ave Columbia MO 65203-0931 Office: U Mo Dept Anesthesiology 1 Hospital Dr Dept Columbia MO 65201-5276 E-mail: nordholtz@aol.com.

EGGLESTON, PEYTON ARCHER, allergist, immunologist; b. Santa Monica, Calif., Aug. 14, 1939; MD, U. Va. Sch. Med., 1965. Diplomate Am. Bd. Allergy and Immunology. Intern Vanderbilt Hosp., Nashville, 1965-66; resident in pediat. U. Wash., Seattle, 1968-70, fellow in allergy/immunology, 1970-72; assoc. prof. pediat., dir. tng. program allergy and immunology U. Va. Sch. Medicine, Charlottesville, 1972—81; allergist, immunologist Johns Hopkins Hosp., Balt., 1981—; assoc. prof. pediat. Johns Hopkins Sch. Medicine, 1981-93, prof. pediat., 1994—, dir., ctr. childhood asthma in the urban environment, 1998—, interim dir. pediatric allergy and immunology divsn.; prof. environ. health sciences Johns Hopkins Bloomberg Sch. Pub. Health. Temporary reviewer Nat. Heart, Lung, and Blood Inst., Nat. Insts. Environ. Health Sciences; investigator, Home-Based Environ. Adherence Trial Nat. Inst. Allergy and Infectious Diseases, Nat. Heart, Lung, and Blood Inst., Investigator Nat. Inst. Nursing Rsch., Nat. Insts. Health Nebulized Intervention in Minority Children with Asthma. Mem.: AAAI, Am. Assn. Pediat., Soc. Pediat. Rsch. Office: Johns Hopkins Hosp Pediatric Allergy and Immunology Divsn 600 N Wolfe St Baltimore MD 21205 Office Phone: 410-955-5883.

EGI, TAKESHI, orthopedist; b. Itami, Hyogo, Japan, Apr. 23, 1968; s. Yasushi and Chieko Egi; m. Mariko Yokoyama, Dec. 13, 1973; 1 child, Risako. MD, PhD, Osaka City U. Med. Sch., Japan, 1993. Cert. orthop. surgeon, hand surgeon, rheumatologist Joa, Issh, Icr. Asst. prof. dept. orthop. surgery Osaka City U. Grad. Sch. Medicine, 2001—04; assoc. dir., dept. orthop. surgery Osaka Rosai Hosp., Sakai, 2007—. Counsilor Japanese Soc. Surgery of Hand, Nagoya, Aichi, 2008—. Contbr. articles to profl. jours. Recipient Sci. Exhibit award, 60th Am. Soc. Surgery of Hand, 2005. Achievements include patents for finger MP joint prosthesis. Business E-Mail: eggy@orh.go.jp.

EGLY, HANS JOACHIM, chemist; b. Feb. 11, 1949; s. Johann Georg Peter and Anna Elise (Hosch) Egly; m. Christa Heidrun Huebler, Apr. 25, 1975; children: Sven, Jennifer, Sarah, David, Tim, Alina, Christopher. Diploma in engring., Tech. U., Darmstadt, Germany, 1975, Dr Ing, 1977. From sales rep. to product mgr. Schering Ag, Berlin, 1977—84; mktg. mgr. Boehringer Ingelheim, 1984—88; mktg. and sales dir. GD Searle, Dreieich, 1988—90, Grunenthal, Aachen, 1990—98; bus. devel. mgr. Schwarz Pharma Deutschland GmbH, Monheim, 1998—; dir. bus. unit UCB-Schwartz Pharma Deutschland GmbH, 2007—. Stake pres. LDS Ch., Duesseldort, 1994—2001. Mem.: Pharma Lizenz Club Germany (pres. 1999—). Mem. Lds Ch. Home: Kantstrasse 44 Stolberg 52224 Germany Office: UCB Pharma GmbH Alfred-Nobel-Strasse 10 Monheim 40789 Germany

EHIGIE, BENJAMIN ODION, radiographer, technologist; b. Benin-City, Edo, Nigeria, June 14, 1959; arrived in US, 1987; s. John E. and Amen E. Egharevba; m. Colett D. Burnett, Mar. 23, 1991; m. Ivie Ehigie, Dec. 29, 1993; m. Benny Ehigie, May 3, 2000. Nat. Edn. Cert., U. Abraka, Nigeria, 1984; AAS, Malcolm X Coll., Chgo., 1996. Radiographer Chgo. Agy., 1997—2000; spl. procedures technologist Provident Hosp. Chgo., 2000—. Mem. Akugbe-Ortin Club, Chgo., 2003—04. Avocations: photography, travel, sports.

EHLERS, KATHRYN HAWES (MRS. JAMES D. GABLER), physician; b. Richmond Hill, NY, Aug. 22, 1931; d. Albert and Edna (Hawes) E.; m. James D. Gabler, Dec. 5, 1959; children— Jennifer K., Emily E. AB, Bryn Mawr Coll., 1953; MD, Cornell U.; MD (Hannah E. Longshore Meml. Med. scholar 1953-57, Elsie Strang L'Esperance scholar 1956-57), 1957. Diplomate: Am. Bd. Pediatrics, Am. Bd. Pediatric Cardiology. Intern N.Y. Hosp., 1957-58, asst. resident pediatrics, 1958-60; fellow in pediatric cardiology Cornell U. Med. Coll., NYC, 1960-64, instr. pediatrics, 1964-66, asst. prof., 1966-70, asso. prof. pediatrics, 1970-75, prof., 1975-96, prof. emeritus, 1996—, vice-chmn. pediat., 1988-96; practice medicine specializing in pediat. cardiology NYC, 1958-96. Contbr. articles to profl. jours. Research trainee N.Y. Heart Assn., 1960-62, Am. Heart Assn., 1962-64. Fellow Am. Coll. Cardiology; mem. N.Y. Heart Assn., Am. Heart Assn., Harvey Soc., Am. Pediatric Soc., Am. Acad. Pediatrics, Alpha Omega Alpha. Personal E-mail: jkgabler@comcast.net.

EHLINGER, EDWARD, public health service officer; b. Green Bay, Wis., June 22, 1946; BA, U. Wis., MD, 1972; MSPH, U. NC. Dir. personal health services Mpls. Health Dept., 1980—85; dir., chief health officer Boynton Health Svc. U. Minn., 1995—2011; commr. Minn. Dept. Health, 2011—. Adj. prof. epidemiology and cmty. health divsn. Sch. of Pub. Health Univ. Of Minn. Recipient Albert Justus Chesely award, Minnesota Pub. Health Assn., 1989, Advancement of Justice award, Hennepin County Bar Assn., 1997, Ed Ehlinger award, CityMatCH (urban maternal and child health directors), 1996, Physician Communicator award, Minnesota Med. Assn., 2003. Office: Minnesota Department Health PO Box 64975 Saint Paul MN 55164-0975 Office Phone: 651-201-5000, 651-201-5797 TTY. *

EHMAN, RICHARD LORNE, diagnostic radiologist; b. Saskatoon, Saskatchewan, Can., July 29, 1952; BS in Physics, U. Saskatchewan, MD, 1979, DSc (hon.), 2000. Diplomate American Bd. Radiology, cert. in diagnostic radiology Can. Royal Coll. Physicians & Surgeons, lic. Med. Coun. Can. Intern radiology Foothills Hosp., Calgary, Alberta, Canada, 1979—80, resident diagnostic radiology, 1980—83; magnetic resonance imaging (MRI) fellowship U. Calif., San Francisco, 1983—84; faculty Mayo Clinic, Rochester, Minn., 1985—, prof. dept. radiology. Chair med. imaging study sect. NIH, 2002—04, mem. nat. adv. coun., Nat. Inst. Biomedical Imaging & Bioengineering. Assoc. editor Magnetic Resonance in Medicine, mem. editl. bd. Jour. Magnetic Resonance Imaging; contbr. articles to profl. jours. Fellow: American Inst. Med. & Biol. Engring., American Coll. Radiology, Soc. Magnetic Resonance Imaging; mem.: Radiol. Soc. North America (bd. dirs. 2010—, Outstanding Rschr. award 2006), Internat. Soc. Magnetic Resonance in Medicine (pres. 2002—03, Gold medal 1995), Inst. Medicine. Achievements include research in developing methods to reduce or eliminate flow and tissue motion artifacts in MRI, approaches for vascular imaging, and development of MRI-based techniques for characterizing the mechanical properties of tissue; development of magnetic resonance elastography or MRE, which allows physicians to determine the stiffness of internal organs without invasive procedures; patents in field. Office: Mayo Clinic 200 First Street SW Rochester MN 55905 E-mail: ehman.richard@mayo.edu. *

EHMER, BERNHARD, pharmaceutical executive; Grad., U. Munich, U. Heidelberg, Germany, 1982. Resident in internal medicine U. Heidelberg, 1983—86; various clin. R&D and mgmt. positions Boehringer Mannheim GmbH, Germany, Italy, head therapeutics regional office Singapore; head clin. R&D ops. Merck KGaA, 1998—2000, v.p. for bus. area oncology, 2000—05, v.p. corp. strategic planning and alliance mgmt., 2005; mng. dir., CEO Biopheresis Technologies, 2006—07; pres., CEO Fresenius Biotech GmbH, 2007—08; sr. v.p., mng. dir. internat. ops. ImClone Systems, pres. Bd. dirs. Hybrigenics SA, Paris, 2006—. Contbr. articles to profl. jours. Office: ImClone Systems 440 Route 22 E Bridgewater NJ 08807 Office Phone: 908-541-8000. *

EHRENFELD, MICHAEL, physician; b. Jerusalem, Jan. 23, 1943; s. Ernest and Gerda Ehrenfeld; m. Mally Braun, Feb. 29, 1968; children: Michal Lifschitz, Ziv. MD, Hebrew U. Med. Sch., Jerusalem, 1969. Resident Hadassah U. Hosp., Jerusalem, 1973—78; internat. fellow, clin. rheumatology U. Toronto, Canada, 1980—81. Asst. dep. dir. gen. Sheba Med. Ctr., Tel-Hashomer, Israel, 1997—. Contbg. editor chpt. to books, med. papers. Mem. Arthritis & Rheumatism Internat., 1995—2005. Lt. col., 1969—74, Israel Med. Forces. 1st Internat. Metro Ogryzlo fellow, Can. Rheumatism Assn., 1982. Office: Sheba Med Ctr Tel-Hashomer Hosp Tel-Hashomer 52621 Israel Home: 11A, Ussishkin St 55554 Kiryat-Ono Israel Personal E-mail: ehrenfel@post.tau.ac.il. Business E-Mail: ehrenfel@sheba.health.gov.il.

EHRENKRANZ, RICHARD ALLAN, pediatrician; b. Newark, July 28, 1946; s. Robert and Miriam (Wiskind) Ehrenkranz; married, 2000. BS in Life Scis., MIT, 1968; MD cum laude, SUNY Downstate Med. Ctr., 1972. Diplomate Nat. Bd. Med. Examiners, Am. Bd. Pediatrics. Intern in pediatrics Yale-New Haven Med. Ctr., 1972-73, resident in pediatrics, 1973-74; rsch. assoc. pregnancy rsch. br. Nat. Inst. Child Health and Human Devel., NIH, Bethesda, Md., 1974-76; fellow in neonatology divsn. perinatal medicine Yale U. Sch. Medicine, New Haven, 1976-78, asst. prof. pediatrics, 1978-82, asst. prof. ob-gyn, 1979-82, assoc. prof. pediatrics and ob-gyn, 1982-88, prof. pediatrics and ob-gyn, 1988—; attending physician pediatrics Yale-New Haven Hosp., 1978—, clin. dir. newborn spl. care unit, 1982—2005, med. dir. newborn spl. care unit, 2005—. Mem. NIH pulmonary SCOR grant site visit, dept. pediatrics Vanderbilt U. Sch. Medicine, Nashville, 1981; mem. adv. com. perinatal medicine seminars Ross Labs., 1985-89; mem. ad hoc study sect. multictr. trial of cryotherapy for retinopathy of prematurity NEI, 1985, mem. ad hoc rev. group planning grants for retinopathy of prematurity trials, 1989; mem. adv. com. perinatal and devel. medicine symposium Mead Johnson, 1995-2000; prin. investigator NICHD Neonatal Rsch. Network, 1991—, mem. initial review group, pediatrics review subcom., 2003-05; mem. NIDDK Childhood Liver Disease Rsch. & Edn. Network, DSMB-A, 2004-, DSMB, Maternal, Infant and Reproductive Health Unit, Women's Coll. Rsch. Inst., U. Toronto, Can., 2007-, NHLBI Therapeutic Hypothermia After Pediat. Cardiac Arrest, DSMB, 2009-; mem. rev. panel RFA-NICHD Maternal Fetal Medicine Units Network, 2005. Author book chpts., articles, abstracts, procs. in field. Lt. comdr. USPHS, 1974-76. Fellow: Am. Coll. Nutrition; mem.: AAAS, New Eng. Perinatal Soc., Am. Acad. Pediat., Am. Soc. Clin. Nutrition, Am. Pediatric Soc., Soc. for Pediatric Rsch., Alpha Omega Alpha, Sigma Xi. Office: Yale U Sch Medicine 333 Cedar St PO Box 208064 New Haven CT 06520-8064 Home: 25 Kildeer Rd Hamden CT 06517 Personal E-mail: richard.ehrenkranz@yale.edu.

EHRET, JOSEPHINE MARY, retired microbiologist researcher; b. Roswell, N.Mex., Feb. 26, 1934; d. Edward and Glenna (Memmer) E. BS, U. N.Mex., 1955. Med. technologist U. Colo. Health Scis. Ctr., Denver, 1956-75, rsch. microbiologist, 1956—, Denver Dept. Health and Hosps., 1980—2004; instr. Sch. Medicine, U. Colo., 1985—2008. Contbr. articles to profl. publs. Mem. Am. Soc. for Microbiology, Am. Soc. Med. Technologists (cert.), Am. Venereal Disease Assn., Calif. Assn. Continuing Med. Lab. Edn. Democrat. Avocations: reading, birding. Home: 1344 S Eudora St Denver CO 80222-3526 Personal E-mail: JsphnEhret@aol.com.

EHRLICH, GARTH DAVID, molecular biologist; b. Plattsburgh, NY, July 9, 1956; s. Robert Elias and Evelyn Gertrude (Talvitie) E.; children: Ian S.G., Nathan E.G. BA, Alfred U., 1977; PhD, Syracuse U., 1987. Rsch. microbiologist Bethesda Rsch. Labs., Md., 1980-81; rsch. specialist Syracuse U., NY, 1981-83; rsch. scientist C indsl. divsn. Bristol Meyers, 1981-83, rsch. scientist B, 1983-84; tech. specialist I SUNY Health Sci. Ctr., Syracuse, NY, 1984-86, rsch. instr., 1988-89, rsch. asst. prof., 1989-90; tech. specialist II SUNY Rsch. Found., Syracuse, NY, 1986-88; asst. to assoc. prof., dir. PCR facility U. Pitts., Pa., 1990-97; chief microbiology, virology and infectious diseases sect. molecular diogostics divsn. U. Pitts. Med. Ctr., Pa., assoc. prof. Pa., 1995-97; vis. prof. Cleve. Clin., 1992; founder, exec. dir. Ctr. Genomic Sci. Allegheny Singer Rsch. Inst., 1997—, governmental and regional affairs liason officer, 2001—; prof. microbiology, immunology Drexel Coll. Medicine, 1997—, prof., vice-chmn, dept human genetics, 1998—, prof., dir. rsch. dept. otolaryngology, 1997—. Cons. Teltech, Inc., 1990—, Kodak, Rochester, NY, 1991-95, Oncogenetics, Phoenix, 1993-95; Visible Genetics, 1997-99, CL Sci., 1997-99, Quest Diagnostics, 1998-99, Isis-Ibis, 2006-; invited participant NCI Symposia, 1989, NMMS Symposia, 1989, NIAID Symposia, 1991, NIDCA Coun., 1995, NILC Symposiun, 2000; adj. mem. Ctrl. Blood Bank Pitts., 1992—; lectr. Heritage Found. Cross Cancer Ctr., Edmonton, Can.; Feinstein lectr. Alfred U., 1995; invited participant Internat. Chromosome 10 Workshop, Crete, Greece; invited guest spkr. Mexican Infection Disease Soc. Ann. Meeting, 1995; exec. dir. Ctr. for Genomic Sci., Allegheny Singer Rsch. Inst., 1997—; prof. microbiology, immunology, otolaryngology and human genetics Drexel Univ. Coll. of Med., vice-chmn. dept. human genetics, 1998—; hon. prof. med. genetics West China U. of Med. Sci., Chengdu, Sichuan, 1999—; over 100 invited speaking engagements including World Congress of Pediat. Infectious Disease, Acapulco, Mex., 1996, Bicor Conf. on Antiinfective Agents, Leipzig, Germany, 1996, Case Western Res. U., 1997, Bacterial Genome Conf., 2005, USC Biofilms Symposia, 2005, Functional Genotics of Infectious Diseases, Giessen, Germany, 2006, Biofilms in Orthopedics, Naples, Italy, 2006; La Spienza, U. Rome, Italy, 2006, Weill Med. Coll., Cornelll U., 2007, others; lectr. Kaiyuon Bioengring., Xian, China, 1997, Chinese U. Hong Kong, 1999; hon. lectr. West China U. Med. Sci., 1999; vis. prof. Shantou U. Med. Coll., China, 2001; guest prof. Shantou U., 2003; mem. adv. com. Med. Biofilms, Tokyo, 2002, Extraordinary Meeting on Otitis Media, Amsterdam, 2005, MaxPlancx Inst. Marine Biology, Bremen, Germany, 2005, Nat. Inst. Microbiology, Chineses Acad. Sci., China, 2005; organizer symposia in field, 1995-1997, 2000, 2003, ASM Divisn. Symposium Conv., 2006; mem. numerous NIH grant rev. coms.; bd. dirs. Pitts. Tissue Engring. Initiative, 2005-; panel mem. Stryker (Infectious Diseases), 2007, Medtronics Biolfim, 2007. Author, editor: PCR-Based Diagnostics in Infectious Disease, 1994; contbr. 200 articles to profl. jours., chpts. to books, editls. to med. jours. Mem. gifted edn. adv. bd. Syracuse City Sch. Dist., 1989-90; lectr. on AIDS to secondary sch. children, sci. to elem. sch. children, 1989—. Recipient Disting. Alumni citation Alfred U., 1995, Feinstein Lectureship Alfred U., 1995, 4 NIH grants, 2000; named hon. prof. in med. genetics, West China U. of Med. Sci., 1999, keynote spkr. Indian Assn. Med. Microbiology, 2001; finalist Healthcare Hero award, Rsch. and Innovation, Pitts. Bus. Times, 2005. Mem. Soc. for Leukocyte Biology, Assn. for Rsch. in Otolaryngology, Assn. Med. Lab. Immunologists, Acad. Clin. Lab. Physicians and Scientists, Am. Soc. for Microbiology, Assn. Molecular Pathology (co-chair infectious disease sect.), Sigma Xi, Phi Kappa Phi. Democrat. Avocations: sports car racing, skiing, scuba diving. Address: Allegheny Singer Rsch Inst Ctr Genomic Sci 320 E North Ave Pittsburgh PA 15212-4756 Office Phone: 412-359-4228. Business E-Mail: gehrlich@wpahs.org.

EHRLICH, GEORGE EDWARD, rheumatologist, consultant; b. Vienna, July 18, 1928; came to US, 1938, naturalized, 1944; s. Edward and Irene (Elling) E.; m. Gail S. Abrams, Mar. 30, 1968; children: Charles Edward, Steven L. Abrams, Rebecca Sayles. AB cum laude, Harvard U., Cambridge, Mass., 1948; MB, MD, Chgo. Med. Sch., 1952. Intern Michael Reese Hosp., Chgo., 1952; resident Francis Delafield Hosp., NYC, 1955, Beth Israel Hosp., Boston, 1956, New Eng. Center Hosp., Boston, 1957; fellow rheumatology NIH, Bethesda, Md., 1958, Hosp. for Spl. Surgery, NYC, 1959-61, asst. attending physician, 1960-64; spl. fellow Sloan Kettering Inst., 1960-61; instr. medicine Cornell U., 1960-64; dir. Arthritis Center, chief rheumatology Albert Einstein Med. Center and Moss Rehab. Hosp., Phila., 1964-80, asst. prof. medicine Temple U., 1964-67, asso. prof. medicine, 1967-72, prof. medicine, 1972-80, asso. prof. rehab. medicine, 1964-74, prof., 1974-80; vis. lectr. U. Pa., 1964-80; prof. medicine, dir. div. rheumatology Hahnemann U., Phila., 1980-83; v.p. Anti-Inflammatory/Endocrine CIBA-Geigy Pharmaceuticals, Summit, NJ, 1983-86; head med. affairs CIBA-Geigy Ltd., Switzerland, 1987-88; pres. George E. Ehrlich Assocs., pharmaceutical cons. Adj. prof. clin. medicine NYU Med. Ctr., 1984—; lectr. medicine U. Pa., 1989-91, adj. prof. medicine, 1992—; expert advisor, cons. Diabetes and Other Noncommunicable Diseases unit WHO, 1990-98, Chronic Disease Mgmt., 1998—; chmn. Internat. Low Back Pain Initiative; rep. of pres. Internat. League Assns. Rheumatology for Soft Tissue Rheumatisms, 1993-97, exec. com.; liaison to WHO, 1997—; mem. arthritis adv. com. FDA, 1993-96, chmn., 1993-96; expert, FDA, 1997-99; mem. coun. Chairs, FDA, 1996—; chmn. sci. adv. bd. Hochrheininstitut (Rheumatic Disease and Rehab. Rsch. Inst. of Upper Rhine in Germany, France and Switzerland for Treatment, Tchg., and Rsch.), 1993—; bd. dirs. Greenwich Inst. Am. Edn.; chmn., U.S. mem. Expert Adv. Panel on Chronic Degenerative Diseases, WHO, 1996—. Author: Differential Diagnosis of Rheumatoid Arthritis, 1972, Oculocutaneous Manifestations of Rheumatic Diseases, 1973; editor: Total Management of the Arthritic Patient, 1973, Rehabilitation Management of Rheumatic Conditions, 1980, 2d edit., 1986; editor: (with J. Fries) Prognosis, 1981; editor: (with H.E. Paulus) Controversies in the Clinical Evaluation of Analgesic-Anti-Inflammatory-Antirheumatic Drugs, 1981; editor: (with P. Utsinger, N. Zvaifler) Rheumatoid Arthritis, 1985; editor: (with W. Simon) Medicolegal Consequences of Trauma, 1992; editor: (with N. Khaltaev) Low Back Pain, 2000; editor: (with W. Simon A. Sadwin) Conquering Chronic Pain After Injury, 2002; editor: Jour. Albert Einstein Med. Ctr., 1966—71, Arthritis and Rheumatic Diseases Abstracts, 1968—71; mem. editl. bd.: Inflammation, 1974—88, Psychosomatics, 1977—83, Sexual Medicine Today, 1977—84, Jour. Rheumatology, 1982—, Internat. Jour. Immunotherapy, 1984—, Immunopharmacology, 1985—, Med. Problems Performing Artists, 1985—92, Brazilian Jour. Rheumatology, 1992, 1996—99, Italian Jour. Rheumatic Diseases, 1999—; contbr. articles to profl. jours. Pres. Ea. Pa. chpt. Arthritis Found., 1970-72; mem. Phila. Mayor's Sci. and Tech. Adv. Coun., 1972-81; chmn. ad hoc adv. com. Bur. Drugs, FDA, 1971; subcom. on redefinition of disability Social Security Adminstrn., 1982-86. Served to comdr. MC USNR, 1953—55, with USNR, 1975, comdg. officer med. co. 4-3 USNR, 1978—81. Decorated Cavaliere Order of Star of Italian Solidarity; recipient citations, City Phila., 1969, 1974, Distinguished Alumnus award, Chgo. Med. Sch., 1969, Dr. Joseph Lee Hollander award, Ea. Pa. chpt., Arthritis Found., 2004. Fellow ACP, Royal Coll. Physicians Edinburgh, Phila. Coll. Physicians, Am. Coll. Rheumatology (elected master, 1994, com. for publ. Arthritis and Rheumatism, 1977-79, mem. editl. bd. 1980-83), Rheumatism Socs. Ecuador, India (hon.); mem. AMA (editl. bd. Jour. 1972-82), Am. Soc. Clin. Pharmacology and Therapeutics, Assn. Mil. Surgeons (Philip Hench award 1971), Brit. Assn. Rheumatology and Rehab. (overseas mem., editl. bd. 1979-82), Internat. Soc. for Behcet's Disease (hon. life pres.), Harvard Club (Boston, NYC), Alpha Omega Alpha. Office: 1 Independence Pl Ste 1506 241 S Sixth St Philadelphia PA 19106-3731 Home Phone: 215-928-9988. Personal E-mail: g2ehrlich@gmail.com.

EHRLICH, GERALDINE ELIZABETH, management consultant; d. Joseph Vincent and Agnes Barbara (Campbell) McKenna; m. S. Paul Ehrlich, Jr.; children: Susan Patricia, Paula Jeanne, Jill Marie. BS, Drexel Inst. Tech. Nutrition cons. hypertension rsch. team U. Calif. Micronesia, 1970; regional sales mgr. Marriott Corp., Bethesda, Md., 1976-78; dir. sales and profl. svcs. Coll. and Health Care divsn. Macke Co., Cheverly, Md., 1978-79, v.p. ops. divsn., 1979-80, pres. Health Care divsn., 1980-81; regional v.p. Custom Mgmt. Corp., Alexandria, Va., 1981-83, v.p. mktg., 1983-87; v.p. mktg. and healthcare sales Morrison's Custom Mgmt., Mobile, Ala., 1987-88; v.p. sales ARA Svcs., Phila., 1988-93; v.p. bus. devel. ARAMARK, Phila., 1993-95; exec. dir. The Resource Group, Phila., 1995—2001; healthcare mktg. cons., 2001—. Cons. mktg. The Green House, Tokyo, 1987-88; chmn. bd. Mktg. Matrix, Falls Church, Va., 1984—. Mem. Health Systems Agy. No. Va., 1976-77; chmn. Health Care Adv. Bd., Fairfax County, Va., 1973-77; vice chmn. Fairfax County Cmty. Action Com., 1973-77; treas. Fairfax County Dem. Com., 1969-73; trustee Fairfax Hosp., 1973-77; bd. dirs. Tennis Patrons, Washington, 1984-88, Phila. Singers, 1993-98, Physicians for Peace, 1993-98; mem. adv. bd. Nat. Mus. Women in the Arts, 2000—, mem. bd. Fla. State Com., 2005—. Mem. NAFE, AAUW, Internat. Women's Assn., Am. Mgmt. Assn., Soc. Mktg. Profls., Gulfstream Club, Rotary Club. Home: 35 S Ocean Blvd Boca Raton FL 33432 Personal E-mail: gehrlich1@gmail.com.

EHRLICH, GERT, science educator, researcher; b. Vienna, June 22, 1926; arrived in US, 1939; s. Leopold and Paula Maria (Kucera) Ehrlich; m. Anne Vogdes Alger, Apr. 27, 1957. AB in Chemistry with honors, Columbia U., NYC, 1948; AM, Harvard U., Cambridge, Mass., 1950, PhD, 1952. NIH postdoctoral fellow Harvard U., Cambridge, Mass., 1951—52; rsch. assoc. dept. physics U. Mich., Ann Arbor, 1952—53; rsch. staff GE Rsch. Lab., Schenectady, NY, 1953—68; prof. materials sci. Coordinated Sci. Lab. U. Ill., Urbana-Champaign, 1968—. Former mem. editl. adv. bd. Chem. Physics Letters, Jour. Chem. Physics, Jour. Vacuum Sci. & Tech., Surface & Colloid Sci., Progress in Surface & Membrance Sci.; contbr. articles to profl. jours. With US Army, 1945—47, ETO. Guggenheim fellow, 1985. Fellow: Am. Vacuum Soc. (Medard W. Welch award 1979), NY Acad. Scis., Am. Phys. Soc.; mem.: Am. Chem. Soc. (Kendall award 1982), Nat. Acad. Scis., Alexander von Humboldt Found. (Humboldt-Preis 1992), Sigma Xi. Office: U Ill Materials Rsch Lab 104 S Goodwin Ave Urbana IL 61801-2985 Office Phone: 217-333-6448. Business E-Mail: ehrlich@mrl.uiuc.edu.

EHRLICH, PAUL M., pediatrician, allergist, immunologist, educator; b. NY, USA, June 8, 1944; AB, Columbia U., 1962—66; MD, Boston U., 1966—68, NYU, 1968—70. Diplomate Nat. Bd. of Med. Examiners, 1971, Am. Bd. of Pediatrics, 1975, Am. Bd. Allergy and Immunology, 1977. Intern pediat. dept. NY Univ. and Bellevue Hosp., 1970—71, resident pediat. dept., 1971—73; clk. The Hosp. for Sick Children, London, 1972; fellow allergy and immunology dept. Walter Reed Army Med. Ctr., Wash., DC, 1975—76, mil. svcs., 1973—77, Portsmouth Regional Med. Ctr., 1973—77, Nat. Naval Med. Ctr., 1973—77; attending pediat. dept. NY Univ. Sch. of Medicine, 1977—79, clin. assoc. prof., 1979—82, clin. asst. prof., 1982—; full attending divsn. of clin. immunology and allergy Beth Israel Med. Ctr., attending pediats. dept., attending medicine dept., mem. com. on cmty. health edn., 1982—94; clin. asst. attending pediats. dept. Bellevue Hosp. Ctr.; asst. attending pediats. dept. St. Vincent's Hosp.; with NYU Langone Med. Ctr.; assoc. adj. surgeon otolaryngology NY Eye & Ear Infirmary, head and neck surgeon, 2009—; practice allergy and immunology, 1977—. Co-author: (publs.) Biofeedback and Asthma, 1986, Asthma in the Inner City, 1992, Asthma Today: Beyond the Guidelines for Better Care, 1994, and numerous other publications. Mem. pub. health edn. Asthma and Allergy Found. of America, 1980—82, mem. bd. dirs., 1982—83, med. advisor NY, 1980—82; founder and med. advisor Parents of Asthmatic and Allergic Children Support Group, 1981—; mem., med. adv. bd. Allergy and Asthma Network/Mothers of Asthmatics, 1992—, med. editor, 1994—. Recipient Dr. Jose Celso Barbosa award for Health, 1998, Muriel Muñoz award, 2002; named one of The Best Doctors in NY, NY Mag., 1998—2008; grantee Cert. of Commendation, Asthma and Allergy Network/Mothers of Asthmatics, 1998—2005. Fellow: Am. Coll. of Allergy, Asthma and Immunology, Am. Acad. of Allergy, Asthma and Immunology, Am. Acad. of Pediat.; mem.: NY Allergy Soc., Med. Soc. of the State of NY, Am. Thoracic Soc. Office: New York Eye & Ear Infirmary Ste 202 35 E 35th St New York NY 10016 Office Phone: 212-685-4225. Office Fax: 212-696-5682.

EHRLICH, PAUL RALPH, biology professor; b. Phila., May 29, 1932; s. William and Ruth (Rosenberg) E.; m. Anne Fitzhugh Howland, Dec. 18, 1954; 1 child, Lisa Marie. AB, U. Pa., 1953; AM, U. Kans., 1955, PhD, 1957. Rsch assoc. U. Kans., Lawrence, 1958—59; asst. prof. biol. scis. Stanford U., 1959—62, assoc. prof., 1962—66, prof., 1966—, Bing prof. population studies, 1976—, dir. grad. study dept. biol. scis., 1966—69, pres. Ctr. for Conservation Biology, 1988—, dir. grad. study dept. biol. scis., 1974—76. Cons. Behavioral Rsch. Labs., 1963—67; corr. NBC News, 1989—92. Author: How to Know the Butterflies, 1961, Process of Evolution, 1963, Principles of Modern Biology, 1968, Population Bomb, 1968, Population Bomb, 2d edit., 1971, Population, Resources, Environment: Issues in Human Ecology, 1970, 2d edit, 1972, How to Be a Survivor, 1971, Global Ecology: Readings Toward a Rational Strategy for Man, 1971, Man and the Ecosphere, 1971, Introductory Biology, 1973, Human Ecology: Problems and Solutions, 1973, Ark II: Social Response to Environmental Imperatives, 1974, The End of Affluence: A Blueprint for the Future, 1974, Biology and Society, 1976, Race Bomb, 1977, Ecoscience: Population, Resources, Environment, 1977, Insect Biology, 1978, The Golden Door: International Migration, Mexico, and the U.S., 1979, Extinction: The Causes and Consequences of the Disappearance of Species, 1981, The Machinery of Nature, 1986, Earth, 1987, The Science of Ecology, 1987, The Birder's Handbook, 1988, New World/New Mind, 1989, The Population Explosion, 1990, Healing the Planet, 1991, Birds in Jeopardy, 1992, The Birdwatchers Handbook, 1994, The Stork & the Plow, 1995, Betrayal of Science and Reason, 1996, World of Wounds, 1997, Human Natures, 2000, Wild Solutions, 2001, Butterflies: Ecology and Evolution Taking Flight, 2003, On the Wings of Checkerspots, 2004, One with Nineveh, 2004, The Dominant Animal: Human Evolution on the Environment, 2008, Humanity on a Tightrope, 2010; contbr. articles to profl. jours. Recipient World Wildlife Fedn. medal, 1987, Volvo Environ. prize, 1993, World Ecology medal, Internat. Ctr. Tropical Ecology, 1993, UN Sasakawa Environ. prize, 1994, Heinz prize for the environment, 1995, Tyler Environ. prize, 1998, Heineken prize for environ. sci., 1998, Blue Plant prize, 1999, Disting. Achievement award, Kansas U. Alumni, 2003; co-recipient Crafoord prize in population biology and conservation biol. diversity, 1990; fellow MacArthur Prize fellow, 1990—95. Fellow: AAAS, Entomology Soc. Am., Am. Philos. Soc., Am. Acad. Arts and Scis., Calif. Acad. Scis. (Fellows medal 2003); mem.: NAS, Lepidopterists Soc., Am. Mus. Natural History (hon.), Am. Mus. Natural History (life), Brit. Ecol. Soc. (hon.), Am. Soc. Naturalists, Soc. Systematic Biology, Soc. for Study of Evolution, Ecol. Soc. Am. (Eminent Ecologist award 2001). Office: Stanford University Dept Biology Stanford CA 94305

EHRMAN, LEE, geneticist, educator; b. NYC, May 25, 1935; m. Richard Ehrman, 1955 (dec. Mar. 2007); children: Esther, Judith. BS, Queens Coll., Flushing, NY, 1956; MS, Columbia U., 1957; PhD in Genetics, Columbia U., NYC, 1959; DSc (hon.), CUNY, 1989. Mem. faculty Barnard Coll., 1956-58; postdoctoral fellow in genetics Columbia U., NYC, 1959-61; mem. faculty SUNY-Purchase, 1970—, prof. div. natural scis., 1972—; Disting. prof. biology SUNY, Purchase, 1995—; mem. spl. study sect. NIH, NIMH, 1979-80. Vis. disting. prof. U. Miami, Coral Gables, Fla., 1981; vis. lectr. U. Puerto Rico, Rio Piedras, 1987; coord., panelist workshops, programs in field; mem. panels NIH, 2003—. Author: Behavior Genetics and Evolution, 2nd edit., 1981; assoc. editor Evolution; assoc. editor for genetics and cytology Am. Midland Naturalist; co-editor: Behavior Genetics; assoc. editor, exec. com. Soc. Am. Naturalists, 1977-, pres.-elect 1990; contbr. more than 700 articles to profl. jours. Recipient Lit. Soc. Found. medal in German, 1956; Shirley Farr postdoctoral fellow, 1961-62; USPHS postdoctoral fellow, 1959-61; faculty exch. scholar, 1974—; NSF grantee, 1979-84; Sr. Scientist awardee Whitehall Found., 1987, 93; NIH gen. med. scis. grantee, 1987—; SUNY travel grantee, 1988, 93, 96, 2010; Merck rsch. support grantee, 2000-. Fellow AAAS (Rsch. Support award Merck/AAAS, 2001), Inst. Soc. Ethics and Life Scis; mem. AAUW (life), Am. Soc. Naturalists (pres. 1990), Behavior Genetics Assn. (pres. 1978, Dobzhansky award for lifetime resch. 1988), Soc. for Study of Evolution (exec. council 1986), Faculty 1000 Libr., Phi Beta Kappa, Sigma Xi. Home: 2 Jennifer Ln Rye Brook NY 10573-1916 Office: SUNY Div Natural Scis Purchase NY 10577 Office Phone: 914-251-6671. Office Fax: 914-251-6635.

EHRMANN, DAVID A., endocrinologist, educator; BS in Anthropology and Zoology, U. Mich., 1977, MD, 1982. Diplomate Am. Bd. Internal Medicine, 1985, Am. Bd. Internal Medicine-endocrinology, diabetes and metabolism, 1987. Resident internal medicine Univ. Mich. Med. Ctr., Ann Arbor, 1983—85; fellow endocrinology, diabetes and metabolism Univ. Chgo., 1985—87, prof. medicine; assoc. dir. Univ. Chgo. Clin. Rsch. Ctr.; dir. Univ. Chgo. Ctr. for Polycystic ovary syndrome (PCOS). Co-author: (publs.) Heritability of Insulin Secretion and Insulin Action in Women with Polycystic Ovary Syndrome and Their First Degree Relatives, 2001, Insulin Resistance Is Attenuated in Women with Polycystic Ovary Syndrome with the Pro12Ala Polymorphism in the PPAR
Gene, 2002, Relationship of Calpain-10 Genotype to Phenotypic Features of Polycystic Ovary Syndrome, 2002, Insulin secretory responses to rising and falling glucose concentrations are delayed in subjects with impaired glucose tolerance, 2002, Relationship of Insulin Receptor Substrate-1 and -2 Genotypes to Phenotypic Features of Polycystic Ovary Syndrome, 2002. Mem.: Endocrine Soc., Androgen Excess Soc., Am. Diabetes Assn. Office: University of Chicago Medical Center MC 1027 5841 S Maryland Ave Chicago IL 60637 Office Phone: 773-702-6138. Office Fax: 773-834-0486. E-mail: dehrmann@medicine.bsd.uchicago.edu.

EHYA, HORMOZ, pathologist; MD, U. Tehran, Iran, 1974. Diplomate Am. Bd. Pathology, Am. Bd. Pathology-anatomic pathology, Am. Bd. Pathology-cytopathology. Resident pathology Univ. of Miss. Med. Ctr.; fellow cytopathology Meml. Sloan-Kettering Cancer Ctr.; joined Fox Chase Cancer Ctr., 1994, chief cytopathology. Recipient Warren Lang Resident Physician award, 1980, President's award, Am. Soc. of Cytopathology, 1998; named one of Top Doctors, Phila. Mag., 2011. Fellow: Coll. of Am. Pathologists; mem.: Papanicolaou Soc. of Cytopathology, US and Canadian Acad. of Pathology, The Internat. Acad. of Cytology, Am. Soc. for Colposcopy and Cervical Pathology, Am. Soc. of Cytopathology (v.p. 2007—08, pres. 2009—10, exec. bd. 2001—07). Office: Fox Chase Cancer Center 333 Cottman Ave Philadelphia PA 19111-2497 Office Phone: 215-728-3675.

EIBEN, ROBERT MICHAEL, pediatric neurologist, educator; b. Cleve., July 12, 1922; s. Michael Albert and Frances Carlysle (Gedeon) E.; m. Anne F. Eiben; children: Daniel F., Christopher J., Thomas M., Mary, Charles G., Elizabeth A. BS, Western Res. U., 1944, MD, 1946. Diplomate Am. Bd. Pediatrics. Intern medicine Univ. Hosp., Cleve., 1946-47; asst. resident pediatrics and contagious diseases City Hosp., Cleve., 1947; asst. resident pediatrics Babies and Children's Hosp., Cleve., 1948, clin. fellow pediatrics, 1948-49; clin. instr. pediatrics Western Res. U., 1949-50; asst. med. dir. div. contagious diseases City Hosp., 1949-50, visitant in pediatrics, 1949-50; practice medicine specializing in pediatrics Cleve., 1949-90; acting dir. dept. pediatrics and contagious diseases City Hosp., 1950-52; asst. dir. dept. pediatrics and contagious diseases Cleve. Met. Gen. Hosp., 1952-60; med. dir. Respiratory Care and Rehab. Center, 1954-60, pres. med. staff, 1958-60; USPHS fellow in neurology U. Wash., 1960-63; pediatric neurologist Cleve. (Ohio) Met. Gen. Hosp., 1963—90, acting med. dir. comprehensive care program, 1966-67, med. dir., 1968-73, mem. med. exec. com., 1974-76; acting chief, sect. on clin. investigations and therapeutics Developmental and Metabolic Neurology br. Nat. Inst. Neurol. and Communicative Disorders and Strokes, NIH, Bethesda, Md., 1976-77; acting dir. dept. pediatrics Metro Health Med. Ctr., 1979-80; from instr. pediatrics to prof. emeritus Western Res. U., 1950—, prof. emeritus pediatric neurology, 1991—; vis. lectr. pediat. neurology Case Western Res. U., 2008. Cons., project site visitor Nat. Found. Birth Defects Center Programs, 1961-66; mem. adv. com. on grants to train dentists to care for handicapped Robert Wood Johnson Found., 1975-80; emeritus faculty marshall Case Western Res. U., 1992-2007, mem. regional leadership coun., 2003-. Mem. coun. Bratenahl Village-County of Cuyahoga, 1982-98. Recipient Presdl. award Internat. Poliomyelitis Congress, Geneva, 1957, Clifford J. Vogt Alumni Svc. award Case Western Res. U., Cleve., 1985, Robert M. Eiben, MD established annual endowed lectureship, 2009; established Annual Robert M. Eiben, MD. vis. professorship in child neurology MetroHealth Med. Ctr. Dept. Pediat., 1991. Mem.: Child Neurology Soc. (chmn. tng. program com. 1976—77, sec.-treas. 1978—81, pres. 1983—85, Lifetime Career Achievement award 2005), Innominatum Soc., No. Ohio Pediat. Soc., Am. Epilepsy Soc., Am. Pediat. Soc., Am. Soc. Human Genetics, Am. Acad. Neurology (chmn. residence exam. com. 1989—93), Am. Acad. Pediat., Case Western Res. U. Med. Alumni Assn. (pres. 1979, bd. of trustees 2002—), Pasteur Club. Office: MetroHealth Med Ctr 2500 Metrohealth Dr Cleveland OH 44109-1900 Home: 1890 E 107th St Apt 308 Cleveland OH 44106-2249

EICHBAUM, MICHAEL HANS ROBERT, gynecologist, researcher; b. Siegen, Germany, Oct. 1, 1972; s. Kurt Walter and Heidi Eichbaum; life ptnr. Alicia Schmidt; 1 child, Katharina Helena. Med. grad., U. Paris VI, René Descartes, 1998; state exam., med. grad., U. Heidelberg, Germany, 1999, MD, 2001. Cert. breast ultrasound German Assn. Panel Drs., 2003, Doppler sonography of fetomaternal sys. German Assn. Panel Drs., 2004, ob-gyn. specialist German Chamber Physicians, 2005, in anti cancer treatment specialist, in minimally invasive techniques in gynecology European Surg. Inst., 2005, bd. cert. specialist in palliative care German Chamber Physicians, 2007. Intern, resident dept. gynecology and obstetrics U. Heidelberg Med. Sch., 1999—2005, specialist in gynecology and obstetrics, 2005, cons. in gynecol. oncology, 2006—. Lectr. U. Heidelberg Nursery Sch., 2003—; vis. fellow McGill Cancer Ctr., Royal Victoria Hosp., Montreal, Canada, 2005; co-investigator German Adjuvant Breast Cancer Group, Frankfurt, 2002—, German Adjuvant Breast Cancer Group, Breast Cancer Internat. Rsch. Group, Edmonton, Canada, 2002—; co-investigator dept. gynecology and obstetrics U. Heidelberg Med. Sch., 2004—; co-investigator NE German Soc. Gynecol. Oncology, Berlin, 2004—. Contbr. articles to profl. jours., short stories to publs. Chmn. Youth Orgn. Christian Dem. Union, Kreuztal, Germany, 1988—92. Sr. airman Air Force, 1992—93, Erndtebrück, Germany. Recipient Energy technologies, Jugend forscht, 1989, Friedrich-Flick-Found., 1992, cert. of excellence, 16th Symposium Neuradiologicum, Phila., 1998, award, German Soc. Prenatal Medicine, 2005; grantee, Deutsche Forschungsgemeinschaft, German Sci. Found., 2003, Mid-Rhine Soc. of Gynecology and Obstetrics, 2004. Mem.: German Soc. Gynecologic Oncology (assoc.), German Soc. for Ultrasound in Medicine (assoc.; cert.), German Soc. Gynecology and Obstetrics (assoc.), German Cancer Soc. (assoc.), Soc. U. Heidelberg (assoc.), Frankonia Heidelberg (assoc.). Conservative. Achievements include research in molecular basics of the hepatic metastasization of breast cancer; prognostic impact of tumor hypoxia/anemia in the treatment of patients with ovarian cancer; value of locoregional therapies for patients with limited hepatic metastases from breast cancer; innovative zytostatic and immunological therapies for patients with primary and recurrent ovarian cancer. Avocations: literature, piano, cooking. Home: Schillerstraße 9 Heidelberg D-69115 Germany Office: Univ Heidelberg Med Sch Voßstraße 9 Heidelberg D-69115 Germany Office Fax: 0049 6221 568599. Personal E-mail: 113006.3152@compuserve.com. Business E-Mail: michael_eichbaum@med.uni-heidelberg.de.

EICHBERG, RODOLFO DAVID, physiatrist, educator; b. Pforzheim, Germany, July 26, 1937; came to the U.S., 1965; s. Julio and Ilse (Schonfarber) E.; m. Yvette Salama, May 21, 1965; children: William Amadeo, Matias David. Baccalaureate, St. Andrews Scots Sch., Argentina, 1955; MD, U. Buenos Aires, 0963. Diplomate Am. Bd. Phys. Medicine and Rehab., cert. Ind. Med. Rehab. examiner, ringside physician Am. Assn. Profl. Ringside Physicians, diplomate Am. Bd. Disability Analysts, 2008. Intern, resident Grace Hosp. Wayne State U., Detroit, 1965-67; orthopedic surgeon Mar Del Plata, Argentina, 1968-73; resident physical medicine NYU, 1973-75; pvt. practice Rehab. and Electro Diagnosis Assocs., P.C., Tampa, 1975-96, 98—; asst. prof. U. So. Fla., Tampa, 1975-93, clin. assoc. prof., 1994—; chief spinal cord injury rehab. Tampa Gen. Hosp., 1984-96; chief phys. medicine & rehab. VA Med. Ctr., New Orleans, 1997-98; med. dir. Meml. Hosp. Ctr. for Comprehensive Rehab., 1998—2004. Mem. state adv. com. Head Spinal Cord Injuries, Tallahassee, 1976-96; clin. assoc. prof. La. State U. Sch. Medicine, 1997-98; physician advisor State of Fla. Athletic Commn., 1998-99; mem. advisor State of Fla. Agy. for Healthcare Adminstrn., 2001—; cons. MetLife Ins. Co., 2003-, Tech Health, 2010-. Contbr. articles to profl. jours. Bd. trustees Congregation Schaaraizedek, Tampa, 1980-82. Recipient Honors award City of La Paz, Bolivia, 1994, Physician of Yr. award Tampa Bay Latin Am. Med. Soc., 1997. Mem. AMA, Am. Acad. Phys. Medicine and Rehab. (health policy legis. com. 1990-95), Am. Spinal Injury Assn. (internat. rels. rep. S.C. 1990-95), Assn. Med. Latino Americana de Rehab., Colombian Phys. Medicine Rehab. Soc. (corr.), Argentine Soc. Rehab. Medicine (corr.), Fla. Med. Assn., Fla. Soc. Phys. Medicine Rehab. (pres. 1994-96), Hillsborough County Med. Assn. (exec. coun. 2001-03, bulletin editl. bd. 2006-), So. Soc. Phys. Medicine and Rehab. (pres. 1999-2000). Jewish. Avocations: boating, travel, aerobics. Office: Rehab and Electro Diag Assocs PA 2914 N Boulevard Tampa FL 33602-1208 Office Phone: 813-228-7696. Personal E-mail: eichberg@tampabay.rr.com.

EICHEL, EDWARD WILLIAM, psychotherapist, painter; b. Bklyn., June 8, 1932; s. Martin and Elizabeth (Shapiro) Eichelbaum. BFA, Sch. Art Inst. Chgo., 1958; MA, NYU, 1984; LHD (hon.), Med. U. of Americas, Nevis, W.I., 2003. Cert. experiential psychotherapist. Psychotherapist in pvt. practice, NYC, 1969—; group therapy leader Aureon Inst., NYC, 1968-70; founder, dir. Creativity Labs., Inc., 1971-84; pres. Marriage Sci. 2000, NYC, 2001—. Instr. art Ea. Mich. U., Ypsilanti, 1965-66, Queens (N.Y.) Coll., 1966, L.I. U., Bklyn., 1967, St. Vincent's Hosp., N.Y.C., 1967-69, Hartford (Conn.) Art Sch., 1981-83; health educator Medgar Evers Coll., Bklyn., 1984, Flushing (N.Y.) Boys Club, 1985-86; counselor AIDS Hotline, N.Y.C. Health Dept., 1990; faculty 1995 Nat. Clin. Conf., Am. Acad. Clin. Sexologists. Artist: The Glass Cage: The Jerusalem Trial (of Adolf Eichmann), 1962 (original drawings on loan to Dallas Meml. Ctr. for Holocaust Studies), Israel Sketchbook, 1962, The Beast Book (by Jan Wahl), 1964; author: Kinsey, Sex and Fraud: The Indoctrination of a People, 1990, The Perfect Fit: How to Achieve Mutual Fulfillment,

1992; prodr. (video) The Coital Alignment Technique, version 1.1, 2002; contbr. articles to profl. jours. With USCG, 1951-54. Recipient award Oskar Kokoschka Acad., Salzburg, Austria, 1959, medal of merit Painters and Sculptors Soc. N.J., 1968; Louis Comfort Tiffany Fond. grantee for painting, 1967; George D. and Isabella A. Brown Fgn. Travel fellow, 1958. Mem. Soc. for Sci. Study of Sex (com. on sci. and profl. affairs 1986-87), Am. Assn. Sex Educators, Counselors and Therapists, Fedn. Modern Painters and Sculptors (v.p.), Nat. Expressive Therapy Assn. (hon. life; bd. dirs. 1979-83). Office Phone: 212-989-1826. Personal E-mail: eichel@marriagescience.com.

EICHENFIELD, ANDREW HOWARD, pediatric rheumatologist; b. 1955; s. Stuart M. and Frances (Fassler) Eichenfield; m. Nancy Eichenfield. Grad., Wesleyan U., Middletown, Conn.; MD, U. Health Sciences, The Chgo. Med. Sch., 1978. Cert. in pediat., in pediatric rheumatology. Residency in pediat. Mt. Sinai Med. Ctr., NYC, 1979—82; fellowship in pediatric rheumatology Children's Hosp., Phila., 1982—84; dir. clin. services, asst. clin. prof. NY Presbyn. Hosp. Columbia U. Med. Ctr., NYC, clin. assoc. prof. pediat. Med. dir. Camp Sunshine, Sebago Lake, Maine; cons. Blythedale Children's Hosp., Valhalla, NY; intern selection com. NY Presbyn Hosp. Columbia Med. Ctr., com. on residency edn. Contbr. chapters to books. Vol. physician Adolescent Health Ctr.; med. and scientific affairs com. Arthritis Found. NY Chpt. Named to Top Doctors: NY Metro Area, Castle Connolly Med. Ltd., 2006. Fellow: NY Acad. Medicine; mem.: NY Pediatric Soc. (mem. program com.). Office: NY Presbyn Hosp Columbia Med Ctr 3959 Broadway BHN 106 New York NY 10032 Office Phone: 212-305-9304. Office Fax: 212-305-4932.

EICHENWALD, HEINZ FELIX, physician; b. Switzerland, Mar. 3, 1926; came to U.S., 1936, naturalized, 1945; s. Ernst M. and Stella E.; m. Linda E. Moragné, July 20, 1995; children: Kathryn S., Eric C., Kurt A., Michael M. BA in Biochem. Scis. magna cum laude, Harvard U., 1946; MD, Cornell U., 1950. Intern, sr. asst. resident, sr. resident pediatrician N.Y. Hosp., 1950-51; asst. in pediat. Cornell U. Med. Sch., 1951-53, instr., then asst. prof., 1955-58, assoc. prof., then prof. pediat., 1958-64; USPHS instr. pediat. Emory U. Med. Sch., 1953-55; also vis. physician Grady and Crawford Long hosps., Atlanta; mem. staff N.Y. Hosp., 1958-65, attending pediatrician, 1963-65; vis. asst. prof. Albert Einstein Med. Sch., 1956-58; cons. Hosp. Spl. Surgery, NYC, 1956-64, Patterson (N.J.) Gen. Hosp., 1958-64; prof. pediat., chmn. dept. U. Tex. Southwestern Med. Sch., Dallas, 1964-83; chief-of-staff Children's Med. Ctr., Dallas, 1964—83; chief pediat. Parkland Meml. Hosp., Dallas, 1964—83, prof. emeritus, 2006. Cons. St. Paul, Irving Cmty., Presbyn. Hosps., Dallas; chief hepatitis investigation unit, epidemiology br. USPHS, 1954-55; Richard Bruce Miller lectr. Harvard U. Med. Sch., 1960; lectr. Columbia U. Tchrs. Coll., 1960-64; chmn. Internat. Rsch. Confs. Mental Retardation, 1965-66; chmn. panel anti-infectives NAS-NRC, 1966-69; vis. prof. U. Saigon Med. Sch., 1968-72, Wakeman lectr. Princeton U., 1970; bd. dirs. Dallas Free Clinic, 1970-74, Children's Devel. Ctr., Dallas, 1974—; mem. bd. maternal and child health NIH, 1974-78; cons. in field, mem. numerous profl. coms. Assoc. editor Pediatric Therapy, 1974; editor Practical Pediatric Therapy, 1985, Current Therapy in Pediatrics, 1989, Pediatric Therapy, 1993; mem. editorial bd. profl. jours.; contbr. numerous articles in profl. publs. Bd. dirs., chmn. exec. com. Lamplighter Sch., Dallas, 1971—1980; bd. dirs. Winston Sch., 1974. Recipient Career Rsch. award NIH, 1963-65, Alexander von Humboldt prize Govt. of Germany (then Fed. Republic Germany), 1979, Weinstein-Goldenson award United Cerebral Palsy Found., 1980; Markle scholar med. sci., 1953. Mem. Harvey Soc., Soc. Pediatric Rsch., Am. Pediatric Soc., Infectious Disease Soc. Am., N.Y. Acad. Scis., Tex. Pediatric Soc., Phi Beta Kappa, Sigma Xi, Alpha Omega Alpha. Personal E-mail: echo18@swbell.net. *

EICHLER, CRAIG J., dermatologist; BA in Chemistry, Emory U., Atlanta, 1985; MD, U. Fla., Gainesville, Fla., 1989. Diplomate Am. Bd. Dermatology, 1993. Intern internal medicine Univ. of Fla., Gainesville, Fla.; resident dermatology Univ. of Tex., Galveston, Tex.; staff dermatology dept. Cleve. Clinic Fla Weston, 1993—98, Cleve. Clinic Fla Naples, 1998—2006; staff dermatology divsn. Physicians Regional Med. Group, 2006—, chief dermatology divsn., 2009—; hosp. affiliation include Physicians Regional Med. Ctr. - Pine Ridge. Named one of America's Top Doctors, Castle Connolly Medical Ltd., 1998, 2000, 2002—. Mem.: Fla. Soc. of Dermatology and Dermatologic Surgery (pres. 2004—05), Fla. Med. Assn., Collier County Med. Soc., Am. Acad. of Dermatology. Office: Physicians Regional-Pine Ridge 6101 Pine Ridge Rd Desk 12 Naples FL 34119 Office Phone: 239-348-4400. Office Fax: 239-348-4059.

EICHLER, MARC, neurosurgeon; b. Kaisershetern, Germany, Feb. 23, 1966; s. Martin and Paula Eichler. BS, U. Mich., 1988; MD, Wash. U., Mo., 1999. Diplomate Am. Bd. Neurological Surgery. Instr. surgery Harvard Med. Sch., Boston, 1999; neurosurgeon Brigham and Women's Hosp., Boston, 1999, Boston's Children's Hosp., Boston, 1999. Contbr. articles various profl. jours., chapters to books. Fellow: ACS; mem.: AMA, Congress Neurological Surgeons, Am. Assn. Neurological Surgeons. Office: 831 Beacon St Ste 239 Newton Center MA 02459 *

EICHMANN, HAROLD D., laboratory administrator; b. Madison, SD, Sept. 11, 1946; s. Gerhardt Henry and Esther Marie (Haak) E.; m. Jolene Elaine Springer, Nov. 29, 1969; children: Michelle Marie, Lori Lynn. BA, U. S.D., 1969. Cert. med. technologist; cert. lab. mgr. Lab. asst. Madison Cmty. Hosp., SD, 1964-66; rsch. asst. dept. biochemistry Med. Sch., U. S.D., Vermillion, 1966-69; corpsman Naval Hosp., Nat. Naval Med. Ctr., Bethesda, Md., 1969—71, Balboa Naval Hosp., San Diego, 1969—; med. technologist, support lab, dept. exptl. surgery Nat. Naval Med. Ctr., Bethesda, Md., 1971-73; med. technologist, lab. dept. Suburban Hosp., Bethesda, Md., 1971-73; safety dir. Sanford Sheldon Med. Ctr., 1973—92, adminstrv. dir. lab., 1973—. Clin. instr. radiologic tech. program Iowa Ctrl. CC, Ft. Dodge, 1990-2002; clin. instr. med. lab. technician program Minn. West Cmty. and Tech. Coll., Worthington, 1996—; adv. bd. mem. med./biosci. technician program N.W. Iowa CC, Sheldon, 2006-. Foster parent Dept. Human Svcs., State of Iowa, 1975—. Served with USN, 1969-74. Mem.: Nat. Assn. Physician Office Labs., Clin. Lab. Mgmt. Assn., Am. Assn. Bioanalysts, Am. Assn. Blood Banks. Lutheran. Avocations: genealogy, reading, history, working with children. Home: 714 6th St Sheldon IA 51201-1623 Office: Sanford Sheldon Med Ctr 118 N 7th Ave Sheldon IA 51201-1235 Office Phone: 712-324-6351. Business E-Mail: eichmanh@hotmail.com, harold.eichmann@sanfordhealth.org. *

EICK, JOHN DAVID, materials engineer, educator; m. Mary Elizabeth Warren, Sept. 10, 1960; children: Elizabeth Marion, Cynthia Marie, Jennifer. BS, U. Mich., 1963; MS, George Washington U., 1966; PhD, SUNY, Buffalo, 1971. Lab. asst. dept. dental materials U. Mich., Ann Arbor, 1960—63; rsch. assoc. ADA, Chgo., 1963—67; instr., assoc. prof. dept. dental materials SUNY, Sch. Dentistry, Buffalo, 1967—77; assoc. prof., prof., dir. dental biomaterials Oral Roberts U., Tulsa, Okla., 1977—86; prof. dept. oral biology U. Mo., Sch. Dentistry, Kansas City, 1986—89, chair dept. oral biology, 1991—, curators' prof. dept. oral biology, 1989—. Chair Pres.'s Award Rsch. and Creativity Com. U. Mo., Kansas City, 2003—05, mem. Resources for Our Vision Com., 2003—, mem. search com. sys. pres., chancellor, provost, dean Sch. Computing & Engring.; vis. prof., vis. lectr. U. Pacific, San Francisco, 1975. Contbr. articles to profl. jours. Episcopal deacon Diocese of Kans. and West Mo., Kansas City, 1988—2005. Recipient Spl. tchg. award, U. Mo., Sch. Dentistry, 1992, Sauder Disting. Scientist award, Internat. Assn. Dental Rsch., 2004; grantee, NIH, 1996—2001, NIH/NIDCR, 1996—, NIH, 2001—, NIH/NIDCR, 2005—; fellow, U. Mo., 1997, 2002. Fellow: Acad. Dental Materials (assoc.), Soc. Biomaterials (assoc.); mem.: ADA (assoc.), Am. Assn. Dental Schs. (assoc.), Internat. Assn. Dental Rsch. (assoc.), Omicron Kappa Upsilon (hon.). Achievements include patents in field. Office: U Mo 650 E 25th St Kansas City MO 64108 E-mail: eickj@umkc.edu.

EICKHOFF, THEODORE CARL, infectious disease physician, epidemiologist; b. Cleve., Sept. 13, 1931; s. Theodore Henry and Clara (Strasen) E.; m. Margaret Heinecke, Aug. 24, 1952; children: Stephen, Mark, Philip. BA, Valparaiso U., 1953; MD, Case Western Res. U., 1957. Diplomate Am. Bd. Internal Medicine. Intern, then resident Harvard Med. Svcs., Boston City Hosp., 1957-59; fellow in infectious disease Harvard Med. Sch.-Boston City Hosp., 1961-64; epidemiologist Ctr. for Disease Control, 1964-67; prof. medicine U. Colo. Med. Ctr., 1975—2003, prof. emeritus, 2003—, head divsn. infectious disease, 1967-80, vice chmn. dept. medicine, 1976-81; dir. medicine Denver Gen. Hosp., 1978-81; dir. internal medicine Presbyn./St. Luke's Med. Ctr., 1981-92. Cons. FDA, CDC, Am. Hosp. Assn.; mem. nat. commn. orphan diseases HHS, 1986-90, mem. vaccines adv. com., 1995-99. Contbr. over 150 articles to med. jours. Served with USPHS, 1959-61. Recipient Commr.'s Spl. Citation, FDA, 1990, Trustee's award Am. Hosp. Assn., 1993, Dr. Charles Merieux award Nat. Found. Infectious Diseases, 2010. Master ACP (Disting. Internist award Colo. chpt. 1995); mem. Am. Fedn. Clin. Rsch., Am. Soc. Clin. Investigation, Assn. Am. Physicians, Infectious Diseases Soc. Am. (sec. 1978-82, pres. 1983-84, Finland Lectureship award 1995, Soc. Citation award 2010), Am. Epidemiol. Soc. (pres. 1985-86). Home: 5114 Long Meadow Cir Greenwood Village CO 80111-3436 Office: Univ Colo Health Sci Ctr 12700 E 19th Ave Aurora CO 80045 Home Phone: 303-789-0194; Office Phone: 303-724-4928. Business E-Mail: theodore.eickhoff@ucdenver.edu.

EIDE, TOR JACOB, pathologist; b. Bergen, Norway, July 11, 1946; MD, U. Gøttingen, Germany, 1971; PhD, U. Tromsø, Norway, 1984. Resident, rsch. fellow pathology U. No. Norway, Tromsø, 1974—80; cons. pathology asst. prof. U. Hosp. No. Norway, Tromsø, 1980—88, prof., head dept. pathology bd. dirs., 1988—94; prof., head dept. pathology Rikshospitalet, Oslo, Norway, 1994—2005; prof., head sect. gastrointestinal pathology Rikshospitalet, Oslo U. Hosp., Norway, 2005—. Pres. Norwegian Soc. Pathology, 2003—05; vis. scientist Auckland U., 1990, AFIP, Wash., DC, 2005. Contbr. scientific papers. Recipient Honoring Pioneers Telemedicine award, Armed Forces Inst. Pathology Am. Registry Pathology, 1995, Telenors Rsch prize, Norwegian Telecom, 1999. Mem.: European Pathology Soc., Norwegian Pathology Soc. Achievements include development of telepathology in the world. Avocations: music, mountain climbing, reading. Office: Sognsvannsveien 20 Oslo 0424 Norway Office Fax: 4723071410. Business E-Mail: tor.eide@rikshospitalet.no.

EIFUKU, SATOSHI, neuroscientist, educator; b. Ishikawa, Jan. 25, 1965; MD, U. Toyama, 1990, PhD, 1994. Assoc. prof. U. Toyama, 2005—. Mem.: Japan Neurosci. Soc., Physiol. Soc. Japan, Soc. Neurosci. Office: University Toyama 2630 Sugitani Toyama 930-0194 Japan Office Fax: 81-76-434-5013. Business E-Mail: se@med.u-toyama.ac.jp.

EIL, LOIS HELEN, retired physician; b. Ashland, Wis., Dec. 25, 1920; d. Abraham Isaac Latts and Claire Ida Frindell; m. Harry Meyer Eil, Mar. 12, 1944 (dec.); children: Charles, Alison, Mitchell. BS, U. Minn., Mpls., 1942, MS, 1943, MD, 1946; MPH, Columbia U., NYC, 1967. Diplomate bd. cert. pub. health 1975. Supervising physician NYC Health Dept., 1960—65; attending physician, pediatrician Lincoln Hosp., Bronx, 1960—65; med. dir. Am. Pub. Health, NYC, 1968—70; med. dir. regional office NY State Health Dept., White Plains, 1970—83; ret., 1983. Home: 25 Rockledge Ave Apt 903W White Plains NY 10601

EIMERS, JERI ANNE, retired counselor; b. Berkeley, Calif., Jan. 20, 1951; d. Alfred D. Wallace and Marjorie E. (Nordheim) Stevens; m. Roy A. Neiman, June 12, 1969 (div. Aug. 1977); children: Lorien, Arwen; m. Richard A. Eimers, Mar. 2, 1996. AA, Palomar Jr. Coll., San Marcos, Calif., 1977; BA in Psychology with distinction, Calif. State U., Long Beach, 1979, MA in Psychology with distinction, 1981; postgrad. Human Sexuality Program, UCLA, 1991-92. Lic. marriage, family, child therapist, Calif.; cert. community coll. instr., counselor; cert. sex therapist. Rsch. asst. Calif. State U., 1978-82; tchr. Artesia (Calif.)-Bellflower-Cerritos Unified Sch. Dist., 1982-83; dir. Am. Learning Corp., Huntington Beach, Calif., 1983-85; social worker Los Angeles County Children's Protective Svcs., Long Beach, 1986-88; sr. social worker Orange County Social Svc. Agy., Orange, Calif., 1988-90; therapist Cypress Mental Health, Cypress, Calif., 1988—, cons., 1990—. Cons., 1990—; group chair, leader Adults Abused as Children, Los Altos Hosp., Long Beach, 1991—, Coll. Hosp., Cerritos, 1993—; speaker, presenter in field. Mem. Child's Sexual Abuse Network, Orange, 1988—; mem. legis. com. Child Abuse Coun. of Orange County, 1988. Women's League scholar, 1980-81. Mem. APA, AAUW, Am. Assn. Marriage, Family Therapists, Calif. Assn. Marriage, Family Therapists, Am. Profl. Soc. for Abused Children, Calif. Profl. Assn. for Abused Children, Phi Kappa Phi, Psi Chi., Am. Psychological Soc., Am. Psychotherapy Assn., Nat. Assn. Profl. Women. Republican. Methodist. Avocations: writing, theater, classical and jazz music, swimming. Personal E-mail: jaeimers@roadrunner.com.

EIN, DANIEL, allergist; b. Liege, Belgium, Nov. 26, 1938; arrived in U.S., 1941; s. Max Motel and Sabine (Toeman) E.; m. Marion Hess, June 25, 1961 (div. 1978); children: Mark David, Jon Spencer; m. Marina Wallach, Apr. 10, 1988; stepchildren: Jacqueline A. Newmyer, Tory Newmyer. AB, Columbia U., 1959; MD, Albert Einstein Coll. Medicine, 1964. Diplomate Am. Bd. Internal Medicine, Am. Bd. Allergy and Immunology. Intern Bronx Mcpl. Hosp., NYC, 1964—65; staff assoc. Nat. Cancer Inst., Washington, 1965—67, clin. assoc., 1967—68; asst. resident Mass. Gen. Hosp., Boston, 1968—69; sr. investigator Nat. Cancer Inst., Washington, 1969—71; pvt. practice Washington, 1971—2005. Clin. prof. medicine George Washington U., Washington, 1984—, dir. divsn. allergy, 2005—; founder, pres. Capital Physicians Network, 1994-99. Contbr. articles to profl. jours. and newspapers. Fellow ACP, Am. Acad. Allergy (AMA del. 1994), Am. Coll. Allergy (bd. dirs. 2000-03, v.p. 2004, pres. 2007); mem. Joint Coun. Allergy (pres. 1998-2000), Med. Soc. D.C. (pres. 1991), Greater Washington Allergy Soc. (pres. 1979), Cosmos Club. Jewish. Achievements include discovery of OZ factors on human immunoglobulin light chains. Home: 4636 Kenmore Dr NW Washington DC 20007-1924 Office Phone: 202-741-2770. Personal E-mail: danein@verizon.net.

EINHORN, LAWRENCE HENRY, oncologist, medical educator; b. Dayton, Ohio, 1942; BS, Ind. U., 1965; MD, U. Iowa Coll. Medicine, Iowa City, 1968. Diplomate Am. Bd. Internal Medicine, cert. in med. oncology. Intern in medicine Ind. U. Med. Ctr., Indpls., 1967—68, resident hematologic oncology, 1968—69, fellow hematology & oncology, 1971—72; fellow oncology M.D. Anderson Hosp. Tumor Inst., Houston, 1972—73; assoc. prof. medicine, clin. oncology & hematology Ind. U. Sch. Medicine, 1973—87, disting. prof. medicine, 1987—, Lance Armstrong Found. prof. & chair oncology, 2006—. Contbr. numerous articles to profl jours. Capt. Med. Corps USAF, 1969—72. Recipient Richard & Hilda Rosenthal Found. award for Cancer Rsch., Am. Assn. Cancer Rsch., 1981, Disting. Clinician award, Milken Found., 1989, Clin. Oncology award, Assn. Cmty. Cancer Centers, 1991, Charles F. Kettering prize, GM Cancer Rsch. Found., 1992, Glenn Irwin Experience Excellence award, 1996, Herman B. Wells Visionary award, 2001. Mem.: NAS, Am. Philos. Soc. Achievements include development of a chemotherapy regimen to treat testicular cancer increasing the survival rate from 10% to 95%, recognition as the leader of the medical team treating champion cyclist and testicular cancer survivor Lance Armstrong. Office: Ind U Simon Cancer Ctr RT 473 535 Barnhill Dr Indianapolis IN 46202-5289 Office Phone: 317-274-0920. Business E-Mail: leinhorn@iupui.edu. *

EINSPRUCH, BURTON CYRIL, psychiatrist; b. NYC, June 27, 1935; s. Adolph and Mala (Goldblatt) E.; m. Barbara Standen Traeger, Oct. 9, 1960; children: Julia E. Lewis, Alexander Louis, Robert Sands. BA, So. Meth. U., 1956, ScB, 1958; MD, Southwestern Med. Sch., Dallas, 1960. Diplomate Am. Bd. Psychiatry and Neurology (examiner 1974—). Intern Montefiore Hosp., NYC, 1960-61; resident Nat. Hosp. Inst. Neurology, London, 1962; resident, fellow U. Tex., Dallas, 1961—64, adv. devel. bd.; chief resident Parkland Meml. Hosp., Dallas, 1964; instr. psychiatry U. Pa., 1964-66; pvt. practice psychiatry Dallas, 1966—; adv. dir. Am. Nat. Bur. Tex., 2010. Staff Presbyn. and Parkland Hosps.; clin. asst. prof. U. Tex., Health Sci. Center, Dallas, 1966-70, dir. Southwestern Adult Psychiat. Clinic, Dallas, 1966-74; dir. psychiat. service Dallas Geriatric Research Inst., 1974-80; adj. prof. sociology U. North Tex., Denton, 1975-82; cons. staff Baylor U. Hosp., Golden Acres Hosp.; clin. assoc. prof. psychiatry U. Tex. Health Scis. Ctr., Dallas, 1971—; prof. psychiatry U. Tex. Southwestern Med. Ctr., Dallas, 1971—; bd. dirs., founder Dallas Nat. Bank; clin. assoc. prof. psychiatry NYU Med. Ctr., N.Y.C., 1990; adj. prof. Dept. Occupl. and Environ. Med. U. Tex. Med. Ctr., Tyler, Tex., cognitive and neuroscience, U. Tex., Dallas; chmn. bd. dirs. Planned Behavioral Health Care, Inc., Dallas; affiliate Tex. Inst. Rsch. and Edn. on Aging, Health Sci. Ctr. Fort Worth; bd. dirs. Am. Svc. Group; adv. bd. Am. Nat. Bank Tex., 2010. Contbr. articles to profl. jours.; mem. editl. bd.: Tex. Medicine Bd., 1991—2002. Trustee Evans Fedn., N.Y.C., 1986-94, U. Tex., Dallas, 1987—, St. Mark's Sch. Tex., 1987-94, chmn. holocaust studies program bd., 1998—; mem. exec. bd. libr. So. Meth. U., 1992-97; adv. dir. Leonhardt Fedn., N.Y.C., 1990, Children of Alcoholics Fedn., 1991, 1995; arbitrator, N.Y. and Am. Exchs., N.Y.C., 1984; bd. dirs. Wyndham Internat., 1997-2000; dir. Dallas Mus. Natural History, Dallas, Tex., bd. trustees adv. devel., U. Tex., Dallas, 2010. Lt. comdr. M.C., USNR, 1964-66. Fellow Am. Psychiat. Assn. (disting. life, Am. Coll. Psychiatrists, Am. Soc. Adolescent Psychiatry, N. Tex. Soc. Adolescent Psychiatry (past pres.); mem. Royal Coll. Psychiatry London, AMA, Tex. Med. Assn. Home: 3505 Lindenwood Ave Dallas TX 75205-3229 Office: 8330 Meadow Rd Ste 117 Dallas TX 75231-3750 Office Phone: 214-369-1636. Personal E-mail: einspruch@charter.net.

EINSTEIN, ANDREW J., cardiologist, educator; AB, Princeton U.; MD, PhD, Mt. Sinai Sch. Med. Cert. cardiovascular diseases Am. Bd. Internal Med., Bd. Nuclear Cardiology. Intern & resident UMDNJ Robert Wood Johnson Med. Sch.; fellow Mt. Sinai Sch. Med.; asst. prof. clinical med. dept. cardiology & radiology Columbia U. Coll. Physicians & Surgeons, 2006—; attending staff NY Presbyterian Hosp. Reviewer JAMA, Circulation, Jour. Am. Coll. Cardiology. Mem.: Internat. Commn. Radiological Protection, Nat. Coun. Radiation Protection & Measurements, Multi-Specialty Occupational Health Group, Am. Soc. Nuclear Cardiology. Office: 622 W 168th St PH 10-408 New York NY 10032 Office Phone: 212-305-6812. Office Fax: 212-305-4648. E-mail: ac2214@columbia.edu.

EIRIK, NESTAAS, pediatrician; b. Trondheim, Norway, Dec. 20, 1969; s. Lars and Astrid Nestaas; children: Fredrik Nestaas, Kristine Nestaas. MD, U. Oslo, 1997, PhD, 2010. Diplomate U. of Oslo, 1997. Resident Dep of Pediat., Hosp. of Vestfold, Tønsberg, Norway, 1999—2001, Dep of Pediat., Ullevål U. Hosp., Oslo, 2002—03, Hosp. of Vestfold, Tønsberg, 2003—; rsch. fellow Ullevål U. Hosp./U. of Oslo, Oslo, 2005—. Achievements include patents pending for noise quantification in tissue doppler ultrasound cardial imaging; research in neonatal sepsis treatment and neonatal ultrasound cardial imaging. Office: Hosp of Vestfold Tønsberg 3103 Norway Home: Haugakerveien 23 3132 Husoysund Norway Personal E-mail: nestaas@hotmail.com.

EISELE, DAVID W., otolaryngologist, department chairman; b. Watertown, Wis., Mar. 7, 1956; AB, Dartmouth Coll., 1978; MD, Cornell U., 1982. Prof., chmn., dept. otolaryngology-head and neck surgery U. Calif., San Francisco, 2001—. Fellow: ACS. Office: 2233 Post St 3rd Fl San Francisco CA 94115 Business E-Mail: deisele@ohns.ucsf.edu.

EISEN, HERMAN NATHANIEL, immunology researcher, medical educator; b. Bklyn., Oct. 15, 1918; m. Natalie Aronson, 1948; 5 children. AB, NYU, 1939, MD, 1943; ScD (hon.), Washington U., St. Louis, 2003. Asst. in pathology Coll. Physicians and Surgeons, Columbia U., NYC, 1944—46; NIH fellow Coll. Medicine, NYU, 1947—48, fellow in chemistry, 1948—49, asst. prof. indsl. medicine, 1949—53, assoc. prof., 1953—55; prof. medicine Sch. Medicine, Washington U., St. Louis, 1955—61; dermatologist-in-chief Barnes Hosp., St. Louis, 1955—61; prof. microbiology, head dept. Sch. Medicine Washington U., St. Louis, 1961—73; prof. MIT, Cambridge, 1973—82, Whitehead Inst. prof. immunology, 1982—89; prof. emeritus, 1989—. Mem. adv. bd. Mass. Gen Hosp., Yale Med. Sch., Harvard Sch. Pub. Health, Children's Hosp., Boston, Merck, Sharpe, Dohme Rsch. Labs., Roche Inst. for Molecular Biology, Howard Hughes Med. Inst.; chmn. Nat. Inst. Health Study, 1962—66; bd. of sci. counselors Nat. Inst. of Arthritis and Metabolic Dis., 1971—75; chmn. World Health Orgn. Sci. Group on Regulation of Immune Responses, 1969; lectr. Harvey Soc., NYC, 1964; Phillips lectr. Haverford Coll., 1971; Burroughs & Wellcome vis. lectr. Med. Coll. So. Carolina, 1979; Culpepper Found. lectr. State Univ. of N.Y., Stonybrook, 1981; Lowry lectr. Washington Univ., St. Louis, 1989. Recipient Med. Sci. Achievement award, NYU, 1978, Outstanding Investigator award, Nat. Cancer Inst., NIH, 1986—93, Dupont award, Clin. Ligand Soc., 1987, Behring-Heidelberger award, 1993. Mem.: Am. Soc. for Clin. Investigation (v.p. 1965), Am. Assn. Immunologists (pres. 1968, Lifetime Svc./Achievement award 1997), Am. Acad. Arts and Scis., Inst. Medicine, Am. Assn. Physicians, Nat. Acad. Sci. (editl. bd. Procs. of the NAS 1994—2004). Office: MIT Koch Inst Integrative Cancer Rsch 76253D 77 Massachusetts Ave Cambridge MA 02139-4307 Business E-Mail: hneisen@mit.edu.

EISEN, HOWARD JOEL, internist, researcher; b. Forest Hills, NY, May 25, 1956; s. Ezra Michael and Gertrude Margaret (Schmidt) Eisen; m. Judith Ellen Wolf, June 26, 1983; children: Jonathan Ezra, Miriam Sarah. BA in Biology, Cornell U., 1977; MD, U. Pa., 1981. Diplomate Am. Bd. Med. Examiners, Am. Bd Internal Medicine, Am. Bd. Cardiovascular Diseases, in advanced heart failure & transplantation Am. Bd Internal Medicine. Med. intern Hosp. U. Pa., Phila., 1981—82, resident in medicine, 1982—84; fellow in cardiology Washington U. Sch. Medicine-Barnes Hosp., St. Louis, 1984—87; asst. prof. medicine U. Pa., Phila., 1990—93; assoc. prof. medicine and physiology Temple U., Phila., 1993—97, prof. medicine and physiology, 1997—2004, dir. heart failure care unit, 1993—99, med. dir. cardiac transplant program, 1999—2004, assoc. dir. Gen. Clin. Rsch. Ctr., 1995—2002, med. dir. Cardiomyopathy and Transplant Ctr., 1999—2002, med. dir. advanced heart failure and transplant program, 1999—2002, dir. Advanced Heart Failure Ctr., 2002—04; Thomas J. Vischer prof. medicine Drexel U. Coll. Medicine, Phila., 2004—, dir., Ctr. Advanced Heart Failure Care at Hahnemann, dir. Ctr. Cardiovasc. Disorders; chief divsn. cardiology Drexel U. Coll. Medicine and Hahnemann U. Hosp. Mem. cryptosporidiosis adv. com. Dept. Pub. Health, Phila., 1995—2000; mem. study section NIH, 2002—; edtl. cons. edtl. bd. Jour. Heart & Lung Transplantation; assoc. editor Am. Jour. Transplantation; editl. bd. mem. Jour. Cardiac Failure. Fellow: Am. Heart Assn. (clin. coun. 1995—, rsch. com. 1995—, established investigatorship award 1996—2001, chmn. peer-review com. 1996—), Am. Coll. Cardiology, ACP; mem.: Am. Soc. Transplantation (chair thoracic com. 2007—08,), Southeastern Pa. Am. Heart Assn. Affiliate (pres. 2003—05), Internat. Soc. Heart and Lung Transplantation (program com. 2004, 2007), Am. Fedn. Clin. Rsch (mem. nat. coun. 1992—95, H. Christian award 1993, Alumni Svc. award 2006, Phila. Mag. Top Dr. 1996—, Castle & Connolly's Top Dr. in America 1996—, Best Dr. in America 1998—), Phi Kappa Phi, Phi Beta Kappa, Alpha Omega Alpha. Avocations: reading, rowing, classical music, running. Home: 507 Shortridge Dr Wynnewood PA 19096-1609 Office: Drexel Univ Coll Medicine Mail Stop 1012 245 N 15th St Philadelphia PA 19102 Office Phone: 215-762-3829. Business E-Mail: heisen@drexelmed.edu.

EISENBERG, CAROLA, psychiatrist, educator; b. Buenos Aires, Sept. 15, 1917; came to U.S., 1945; d. Bernardo and Teodora (Kahan) Blitzman; m. Manfred Guttmacher, Oct. 11, 1946 (dec. 1966); m. Leon Eisenberg, Aug. 31, 1967; children: Laurence, Alan. M of Social Work, Liceo de Senoritas; MD, U. Buenos Aires, 1945. Resident in psychiatry U. Md., 1946-48; fellow in child psychiatry Johns Hopkins Hosp., 1948-50, asst. prof. psychiatry and pediatrics Balt., 1960-67; psychiatrist MIT, Boston, 1967-72, dean of students, 1972-78; dean student affairs Harvard Med. Sch., Boston, 1978-90, dir. internat. programs for students, 1990-92, lectr. psychiatry, 1970-92, lectr. social medicine, 1992—; hon. psychiatrist Mass. Gen. Hosp., Boston, 2005. Co-chmn. women in biomed. careers workshop Office on Women's Health, NIH, 1992, mem. adv. com. on rsch. and women's health, 1995-98; mem. com. on human rights ACP; mem. com. on women in sci. and engring. NAS, 1992-95. V.p. Physicians for Human Rights, Boston, 1987-. Recipient Morani Renaissance Woman award, Found. for History of Women in Medicine, 2003, George Eastman medal, Rochester U., 2009, award, 2010, Physicians for Human Rights award, 2010. Fellow Am. Psychiat. Assn. (Disting. life fellow 2003, mem. Coun. Internat. Affairs, com. on human rights, Human Rights award 2005, Anthem Return Hon. award, 2011), Am. Orthopsychiat. Assn. (life); mem. AAUP. Avocations: travel, music, reading.

EISENBERG, HOWARD EDWARD, physician, psychotherapist, consultant, educator, author; b. Montreal, Aug. 5, 1946; s. Harold and Elsie (Goldbloom) Eisenberg; m. Susan Doelman; children: Taryn Noelle, Jory Michael, Meredith Kate, Tessa Chloe. BS in Psychology, McGill U., 1967, MS in Psychology, 1971, MD, 1972. Rsch. asst. psychology dept. McGill U., 1966-69, rsch. asst. gerontology unit Alan Meml. Inst. Psychiatry, 1968; lectr. York U. Ctr. Continuing Edn., 1973—78; supr. individual directed study Faculty Environ. Studies York U., 1975; pvt. practice Toronto, 1973—91, 1999—, Stowe, Vt., 1991—98; clin. fellow U. Toronto Clarke Inst. Psychiatry, 1973; instr. ind. studies program U. Toronto Innis Coll., 1975—78; lectr. Sch. Continuing Studies U. Toronto, 1977-89; assoc. staff dept. family practice Drs. Hosp., Toronto, 1987—92; clin. assoc. prof. dept. family practice U. Vt. Coll. Medicine, 1993—99. Assoc. dir. edn. and growth opportunities program York U., 1975—76, dir. E.G.O. program, 1976—78; instr. profl. and mgmt. devel. Humber Coll., 1982—85; pres. Synectia Cons., Inc., Toronto, 1980—84, Syntrek, Inc., Stowe, Vt., 1989—2000, Toronto, 1974—; lectr., presenter, cons. in field. Author: Inner Spaces, 1977, The Tranquility Experience, 1987, Stress Mastery for the Real World, 3d edit., 2004, Fundamentals of High Performance Teamwork, 1995, Creative Thinking Tools for Innovation, 2d edit., 1997; contbr. articles to profl. jours. McGill scholar, 1966—67, Que. scholar, 1967—68, Earle C. Anthony fellow, 1967—68, Med. Rsch. Coun. Can. scholar, 1977. Mem.: Ont. Med. Assn. (former chmn. sect. ind. physicians). Achievements include co-founding Health Care Knowledge Mgmt. Consortium, 1998-2000.

EISENBERG, HOWARD MICHAEL, neurosurgeon; b. NYC, May 4, 1939; s. Monroe L. and Regina (Fish) Eisenberg; children: Nancy M. Hoy, John A. BA, Syracuse U., 1960; MD, SUNY, NYC, 1964. Diplomate Am. Bd. Neurol. Surgery. Intern NY Hosp., 1964-65; resident, fellow Cornell U. Med. Sch., 1964-66; resident neurosurgery Peter Bent Brigham Hosp., Boston, 1966-70; surgery instr. Harvard U., 1972-75; assoc. prof. U. Tex. Med. Br., Galveston, 1975-80, prof., chief neurosurgery, 1980-92; head divsn. neurosurgery U. Md., Balt., 1992-96, dir. med. svcs. Shock Trauma Ctr., 1992-96, prof. chair dept. neurosurgery, 1996—, R.K. Thompson prof., 2000—. Chmn. neurology A study sect. NIH, Bethesda, Md., 1980—87; numerous vis. professorships and guest lectureships. Mem. editl. bd. Jour. Neurosurgery, 1989—99, chair, 1997—99; editor: (book) The Cerebral Microvasulature, 1980, Neurobehavioral Recovery from Head Injury, 1987, Mild Head Injury, 1989, Neurosurgery Clinics of North America-Management of Head Injury, 1991, The Frontal Lobes, 1991; contbr. articles to profl. jours. Mem. devel. bd. Houston Grand Opera, 1989—92. Lt. comdr. USN, 1970—72. Recipient William Cavernes award, Nat. Head Injury Found., 1994, Wakeman award, 1990; numerous grants in field. Mem.: ACGME (mem. residency rev. com. neurosurgery 2001—02, v.p.), ACS (chair neurosurgical adv. coun.), Am. Surg. Assn., Acad. Neurol. Surgeons (v.p.), Soc. Neurol. Surgeons (v.p., pres.-elect, pres.), Am. Bd. Neurol. Surgery (bd. dirs., sec.-treas., bd. dirs. 1990—95, chmn. 1995—96), NY Yacht Club (mem. seamanship com.), Cruising Club Am., Annapolis Yacht. Club, Cosmos Club. Office: U Md Med Systems Dept Neurosurgery 22 S Greene St Ste S12D Baltimore MD 21201-1544 Office Phone: 410-328-3514. Business E-Mail: heisenberg@smail.umaryland.edu.

EISENBERG, JOSEPH MARTIN, psychologist, consultant; b. Bklyn., June 19, 1944; s. David and Dora (Levine) Eisenberg; m. Susan Joan Kahn, Aug. 16, 1980; children: Ian, Lara, Jason, Davida. BA in Psychology magna cum laude, C.W. Post Coll., 1966; MA in Psychology, U. Alta, 1969, PhD in Psychology, 1971. Cert., lic. Md., cert. clin. hypnotherapist Negotiation Inst. Psychol. Psychol. diagnostician, counselor dept. psychology U. Alta, Can., 1969-70; field rschr. Dept. Youth Alta, 1969-70; assoc. dir. Toronto (Ont.) YMCA Ctr. for counseling and Human Rels., 1970-71; chief psychologist Salvation Army House of Concord, Toronto, 1971-72; dir. outpatient svc. St. Vincent Hosp. Cmty. Mental Health Ctr., Erie, Pa., 1972-73; dir. Erie County Ctr. for Learning Disabilities, 1973-74; pvt. practice psychology Erie and Balt., 1972—; v.p. in charge personnel and comm. Bridge Energy Corp., Balt., 1981—, Reason House, Balt., 1981-97. Spl. cons. Md. Children and Family Svcs., Inc.; mem. profl. adv. bd. Balt. Assn. Children with Learning Disabilities; cons. Mormac Ltd., 1979—97; forensic cons. Howard County/Baltimore County/Carroll County, Office Pub. Defenders, Balt. City Solicitor's Office, 1977—. Co-author: computer software; contbr. articles to profl. jours. Chmn. Carroll county Child Abuse Consultation Com., 1978—80; mem. profl. adv. bd. Catonsville Group Home, 1980—81; dir. Psychol. Svcs. Metabolic Nutrition Program, 1986—89. Recipient Richard P. Runyon award, 1966. Mem.: APA, Am. Bd. Cert. Managed Care Providers, Am. Bd. Profl. Disability Cons., Md. Psychol. Assn. (sec. 2003—05, rep. at large 2005—07), Phi Theta, Psi Chi. Office: 1402 York Rd Ste 207 Lutherville MD 21093-6031 Office Phone: 410-321-9101. Personal E-mail: jme@attglobal.net, drjme@verizon.net.

EISENBERG, PATRICIA LEE, retired medical/surgical nurse; b. Benton, Ky., Aug. 25, 1952; d. James and Katherine (Bolton) Goodman; m. Paul Eisenberg, Apr. 24, 1982; 1 child, Jamie. BSN, Murray State U., Ky., 1974; MSN, St. Louis U., 1981. RN; cert. med.-surg. clin. specialist. Charge nurse Mayfield (Ky.) Community Hosp., 1974-75; staff nurse surg. step-down unit Med. U. S.C., Charleston, 1975; charge nurse ICU North Trident Hosp., Charleston; staff nurse ICU VA Hosp., Memphis, 1977-79, staff nurse surg. ICU St. Louis, 1979; staff nurse ICU various hosps., St. Louis, 1979-80; clin. nurse specialist surgery Jewish Hosp. at Washington U., St. Louis, 1981-88, nutritional support clin. nurse specialist, 1989-98; clin. nurse specialist Community Hosp., Indpls., 1998—2008. Cons. Resource Applications/Mosby Year Book, Inc., 1991-98; cons. Am. Healthcare Inst., Silver Spring, Md., 1990, Sheryl A. Fuetz, Atty., Kansas City, Mo., 1984-86; cons. enteral products Argyle div. Sherwood Med., St. Louis, 1984-2000; clin. faculty Sch. Nursing U. Mo., 1989-93; adj. clin. instr. Grad. Sch. Nursing, St. Louis U., 1982-88; advisor Ross Labs., 1989; adj. grad. faculty Ind. U. Sch. Nursing; contr. NCLEX-RN Exam. Nat. Coun. State Bds. of Nursing, Inc., 1998; adj. grad. faculty Ind. U. Sch. Nursing; speaker in field. Reviewer Concept Media, Inc., 1989-90; reviewer, editor Clin. Specialist Jour., 1986—, Nutrition, 1988, Intravenous Nurses Soc., 1999-; contbr. articles to profl. jours. Vol. Ladue Jr. High Sch., 1987-89, Coun. Girl Scouts, St. Louis, 1984-86, March of Dimes, 1984-85; active children and youth com. Jewish Community Ctr. Assn., 1983-85, Family Fair West County Shopping Ctr., 1984; coord. St. Louis Model Health Fair ARC, 1984, 83, Emerson Electric Health Fair, 1984. Capt. USAR, 1981-87. Recipient Mo. Tribute to Nursing Rsch. award, 1991, Jewish Hosp. Nursing Rsch. award, 1995, Commitment to Evidence-Based Practice Nursing Excellence award, 2003, Comm. Health Network. Mem. ANA (coun. clin. nurse specialist, program planning com. 3d dist. 1984-85, hostess state bd. nursing test 1984, proctor state bd. nursing 1984), Mo. Nurses Assn. (chmn. awards com. 1986-88, dir.-at-large 1988-90, achievement in clin. practice award 1987), Am. Soc. Parenteral and Enteral Nutrition (nat. nurses com. 1986, 87, nursing rep. pub. policy com. 1987-89, nursing rep. 2005-2006), Am. Heart Assn. Coun. Cardiovascular Nursing, Midwest Nursing Rsch. Soc., St. Louis Nursing Rsch. Consortium, Am. Nurses Credentialing Ctr., Clin. Specialist in Med. Surgical Nursing Content Expert Panel, Commn. on Collegiate Nursing Edn., Bd. of Commr. Practicing Nurses Rep., Am. Soc. of Parenteral and Enteral Nutrition Publication Review Bd. (mem. abstract rev. com. 2005-07). Home Phone: 805-370-1944.

EISENBERG, PAUL RICHARD, cardiologist, consultant, educator; b. Rome, Mar. 9, 1955; came to US, 1956; s. David Marvin and Sonia Maria (Benedetti) Eisenberg; m. Patricia Lynn Goodman, Apr. 25, 1982; 1 child, Jamie. BS, Tulane U., New Orleans, 1975, MPH, 1980; MD, NY Med. Coll., Valhalla, 1980. Diplomate Am. Bd. Internal Medicine, Am. Bd. Cardiology. Intern in internal medicine Barnes Hosp., St. Louis, 1980-83, fellow in cardiology, pulmonary medicine, 1983-85, asst. dir. CCU, 1986-91, dir. CCU, 1991-98; asst. prof. Washington U., St. Louis, 1985-91, assoc. prof., 1991-97, prof., 1997-98; med. dir. cardiovasc. therapeutics Eli Lilly & Co., Indpls., 1998-2000, exec. dir. cardiovasc. discovery, 2000—01, v.p. med., 2001—02, v.p. global drug safety, 2003—05; v.p. Amgen Global Safety, Thousand Oaks, Calif., 2005—06, v.p. Global Regulatory Affairs Safety, 2007—, sr. v.p. Global Regulatory Affairs Safety, 2008. Asst. editor: Medical Management of Heart Disease; contbr. over 100 articles to profl. jours. Fellow Am. Heart Assn. (clin. cardiology), Am. Coll. Chest Physicians, Am. Coll. Cardiology; mem. Am. Fedn. Clin. Rsch., Internat. Soc. Thrombosis and Haemostasis. Office: Amgen 1 Amgen Ctr Dr Thousand Oaks CA 91320 Home Phone: 805-670-1944; Office Phone: 805-447-6453. Personal E-mail: piesenberg@attglobal.net.

EISENBERG, TED STEVEN, plastic and reconstructive surgeon; b. Phila., June 21, 1952; s. Martin John and Mitzi Eisenberg; m. Joyce Janet Kirschner, Sept. 1, 1973; children: Ben, Samantha. BS, Pa. State U., 1972; DO, Phila. Coll. Osteo. Medicine, 1976. Diplomate Nat. Bd. Examiners for Osteo. Physicians and Surgeons; Bd. cert. in Osteo. Plastic Surgery, Laser Surgery, Gen. Surgery; lic. physician, N.Y., Pa. Intern North Miami Beach Osteo. Gen. Hosp., 1976-77; resident in gen. surgery Met. Hosp., Phila., 1977-81; resident in hand surgery Hand Rehab. Ctr./Jefferson U., Phila., 1981; preceptee in plastic surgery Rolling Hill and Albert Einstein Med. Ctrs., Phila., 1983-85; practice plastic and reconstructive surgery Phila. area, 1985—; assoc. prof. Phila. Coll. Osteo. Medicine, 1991—. Attending staff physician Grad. Hosp., John F. Kennedy Hosp., Northeastern Hosp., Suburban Genl. Hosp., others; cons. staff physician Delaware Valley Med. Ctr., Springfield Hosp.; lectr. in field. Contbr. numerous articles to profl. jours. Recipient numerous awards for sci. exhibits and publs. Fellow Am. Coll. Osteo. Surgeons; mem. Am. Acad. Aesthetic and Restorative Surgery (charter), Am. Osteo. Assn., Jefferson Hand Club (charter), Pa. Osteo. Med. Assn., Philadelphia County Osteo. Soc., Phila. Coll. Osteo. Medicine Alumni Assn. (life), Lambda Omicron Gamma (v.p. 1993-94). Office: Ste 102 2375 Woodward St Philadelphia PA 19115 Office Phone: 215-969-2005.

EISENDLE, KLAUS, dermatologist, immunologist; b. Bolzano, Trentino-Alto Adige, Italy, Apr. 4, 1972; s. Karl and Edith Eisendle; 1 child, Emilia Ruetz. BSc in Microbiology, Innsbruck U., Austria, 1993, MSc in Molecular Biology, 1996, PhD in Immunology, 2003; MD, Innsbruck Med. U., 2001; MBA in Healthcare Mgmt., U. Salzburg Bus. Sch., 2011, Rotman Sch. Mgmt. Toronto, Can., 2011. Cert. in advanced life suport provider Tiroler Ärztekammer Austria, 2003, in Clin. Investigator Austria, 2006. Jr. scientist Med. U. Innsbruck, 1998—2001; physician dept. dermatology Innsbruck Med. U., 2001—07, physician dept. psychiatry, 2007, physician dept. internal medicine, 2007—08, physician dept. vascular surgery, 2008—, physician dept. plastic and reconstructive surgery, 2008, sr. cons., physician dept. dermatology & venereology, 2009—11, asst. prof. dermatology, 2009; dept. head dermatology Ctrl. Hosp. Bolzano, 2011—. Recipient Dako Jr. Flow Cytometry Rsch. award, 2000, Isidor von Neumann Poster award, 2008, 2009, Euroderm Excellence, 2008, Steigleder Dermatohistopathology award, 2009; Anna Dengl Stipendium for Palliative Care, 1998. Mem.: Austrian Sci. Assn. Acupunture, Tyrolean Soc. Promoting Cancer Rsch., Austrian Assn. Flow Cytometry, Austrian Assn. Dermatologists, European Acad. Dermatology and Venerology (edtl. adv. bd. Open Dermatology jour.). Office: Dept Dermatology Lorenz Bohlenstr 5 Bolzano 39100 Italy Home Phone: +436508204956. Personal E-mail: klauseisendle@hotmail.com. Business E-Mail: klaus.eisendle@asbz.it.

EISENMAN, DAVID PAUL, physician, educator; b. NYC, May 19, 1962; MD, U. Pa., 1980; MSHS, UCLA, 2002. Assoc. prof. medicine UCLA Sch. Medicine, 2002—. Mem. editl. bd. Human Rights Rev., 1999, Am. Jour. Disaster Medicine, 2007, Jour. Bioterrorism and Biodef., 2010; bd. dirs. Just Detention Internat., 2002—11; assoc. natural scientist RAND, 2002. Fellow, NRC, Ctr. Disease Control & Prevention, grant, Nat. Inst. Nursing Rsch., NIH, USDA Forest Svc. Fellow: Am. Bd. Internal Medicine. Avocations: surfing, reading. Office: 911 Broxton Plz Los Angeles CA 90024 Business E-Mail: deisenman@mednet.ucla.edu.

EISENMANN-KLEIN, MARITA, plastic surgeon; b. Gars/Inn, Bavaria, Germany, Sept. 5, 1947; d. Johann B. and Therese (Thaler) Eisenmann; children: Julian, Silvan, Konstantin. Degree, Ludwig-Maximilians U., Munich, Germany, 1974; diploma in quality mgmt. Bd. cert. gen. surgeon, plastic surgeon, hand surgeon. Resident Maimonides Med. Ctr., NYC, 1975-76; resident in surgery City Hosp., Muenchen-Schwabing, 1976-83, gen. surgeon Munich, 1983-84, fellow in plastic surgery Muenchen-Bogenhausen, 1984-87, plastic surgeon, 1987; dir. surgery and plastic surgery Kreiskrankenhaus, Nittenau, Germany, 1988-93; dir. dept. plastic surgery, aesthetic, hand & reconstructive Caritas Krankenhaus St. Josef, Regensburg, Germany, 1994—, dep. med. dir., 2008—; cons. Hosp. St. Wolfgang, Bad Griesbach, Germany, 2009—. Pres. European Com. on Quality Assurance and Med. Devices, 1992-98, hon. pres. World Congress, IPRAS, New Delhi, 2009, intern, Congress Facial Pl S Greece, 2011, Armenia, 2011, Ctrl. Asian Congres Tashkent Uzbetistan, 2010. Co-editor: (with Prof. Maria Siemionow) Plastic & Reconstructive Surgery, 2010; editor: (with Dr. C. Neuhann-Lorenz) Innovations in Plastic and Aesthetic Surgery, 2007, editor: Plastische Chirurgie, 2003-07, mem. editl. bd.: Aesthetic Plastic Surgery, 2002—. Pres. Red Cross Kreisverband, Regensburg, Germany, 2001—05, dep. chair, 2005—; founder IPRAS Women for Women Humanitarian Force. Recipient Travel award Bavarian Assn. Surgeons, 1983; decorated US Army Freedom Team Salute Commendation, 2009. Mem. German Soc. Plastic, Reconstructive and Aesthetic Surgeons (bd. dirs. 1990-92, 2002-03, 07-09, v.p. 2004-05, pres. 2005-07), Internat. Confedn. Plastic, Reconstructive and Aesthetic Surgery (dep. gen. sec. 2003-06, gen. sec. 2006-11, pres. 2011-), Internat. Soc. Aesthetic Plastic Surgery, European Soc. Mastology, Internat. Assn. Univ. Plastic Surgeons, Am. Soc. Plastic Surgery (Pres. award 2006), Basrah U. Med. Coll. (hon. prof., 2007), Romanian Assn. Plastic Surgeons(hon-)(hon prof., 2008), Carolus Davila U. Bucharest (hon. dr.), R. N.

Sharma Meml. Oration (Lucknow, India), Kenya Soc. Plastic Surgery (patron 2010). Roman Catholic. Avocations: skiing, golf, contemporary art, windsurfing, dance, jazz. Office: Caritas Krankenhaus St Josef Landshuter Str 65 93053 Regensburg Germany Office Phone: 49 941 7823110. Business E-Mail: plastische.chirurgie@caritasstjosef.de.

EISENSTAT, THEODORE ELLIS, colon and rectal surgeon, educator; b. NYC, Sept. 24, 1942; m. Sharon Diane Leonard, July, 1966; children: Maren Elise, Loren Aline. BA, Vanderbilt U., 1964; MD, N.Y. Med. Coll., 1968. Diplomate Am. Bd. Surgery, Am. Bd. Colon and Rectal Surgery, Nat. Bd. Med. Examiners. Rotating intern St. Vincent's Hosp., Worcester, Mass., 1968-69; resident in surgery Thomas Jefferson U. Hosp., Phila., 1969-71; chief resident in surgery Pa. Hosp., Phila., 1971-73; fellow in colon and rectal surgery Muhlenberg Hosp.-Robert Wood Johnson Sch. Medicine, NJ, 1977-78; dir. surg. endoscopy U. Md., 1975-80, dir. colon & rectal svc., 1976-80; asst. prof. surgery U. Md. Sch. Medicine, 1975-80; sr. attending surgeon Muhlenberg Regional Med. Ctr., Plainfield, NJ, 1979—, John F. Kennedy Med. Ctr., Edison, 1979—; clin. assoc. prof. surgery U. Medicine and Dentistry of N.J., Newark, 1981—, clin. prof. surgery Robert Wood Johnson Med. Sch. New Brunswick, 1979-91, clin. prof. surgery, 1991—, dir. colon and rectal residency program, 1993—2005; dir. colon and rectal surgery Robert Wood Johnson U. Hosp. Cons. surgeon Lock Raven VA Hosp., Balt., 1975-80, U.S. Army, Kimbrough Army Hosp., Ft. Meade, Md., 1975-80; bd. dirs., ACS rep. Am. Bd. Colon and Rectal Surgery, 1990-96, pres., 1995-96; attending surgeon Robert Wood Johnson U. Hosp., New Brunswick, N.J., 1984—; exhibitor and presenter in field; vis. prof. U. Md. Sch. Medicine, 1983, Abington (Pa.) Meml. Hosp., 1985, York (Pa.) Hosp., 1990, Pa. Hosp., Phila., 1990, others. Contbr. articles to profl. jours. Maj. U.S. Army, 1973-75. Fellow ACS (adv. coun. colon and rectal surgery), Am. Soc. Colon and Rectal Surgeons (Walter A. Fansler award 1977, Purdue Frederick fellow 1977, 1st prize sci. exhibit 1979); mem. AMA, Soc. for Surgery of Alimentary Tract, Assn. for Acad. Surgery, Soc. Am. Gastrointestinal Endoscopic Surgeons (founder 1981, bd. govs. 1986-89), Am. Soc. Gastrointestinal Endoscopy, N.Y. Soc. Colon and Rectal Surgeons (mem. coun. 1983-85, sec. treas. 1986-87, v.p. 1988-89, pres. 1990-92, 1st prize film 1978), Pa. Soc. Colon. and Rectal Surgeons, N.J. Soc. Colon and Rectal Surgeons (sec.-treas. 1983-85, pres. 1989-90), N.J. Soc. Gastroenterology, N.J. Soc. Gastrointestinal Endoscopy, Assn. Mil. Surgeons U.S., Soc. Surgeons N.J., Crohn's and Colitis Found. Am.

EISENSTEIN, EDWARD MILTON, neuroscientist, radiologist, educator; b. LA, July 29, 1932; s. Phillip and Yetta Eisenstein; m. Doris L. Woolfe, June 21, 1953; 1 child, Jeremy. BA in Psychology, UCLA, 1956, MA in Psychology, 1959, PhD in Psychology and Physiology, 1962; MD, Mich. State U., East Lansing, 1978. Lic. physician Mich., 1982, NY, 1984. Postdoctoral fellow dept. biology Calif. Inst. Tech., 1961—63, U. Oreg., Eugene, 1963—64; lectr. psychology UCLA, 1963; asst. prof psychology SUNY, Stony Brook, 1964—67, assoc. prof. psychology, 1967—68, rsch. asst. prof., dept. radiology, Med. Sch., 1985—97, asst. prof., dept. neurology, Med. Sch., 1985—97, adj. prof., dept. psychology, 1987—97; rsch. assoc. Brookhaven Nat. Labs., Upton, NY, 1966—67, 1994—97; assoc. prof. biophysics Mich. State U., 1968—70, prof. biophysics, 1970—82, prof., mem. grad. faculty interdisciplinary neuroscience program, 1970—02, adj. prof., Coll. Natural Sci., 1982—85, chmn., biophysics dept., 1969—73, program dir., NIH tng. grant, dept. biophysics, 1969—73; intern, family practice Mich. State U., St. Lawrence Hosps., Lansing, 1980; resident in radiology Wayne State U., Harper-Grace Hosps., Detroit, 1982—85, chief resident, radiology, 1984—85; clin. prof. neurology Sch. Medicine, Wayne State U., 1983—85; radiologist, rschr. VA Med. Ctr., Northport, NY, 1985—97, chief, radiology svc., 1996—97, chmn. IRB com., 2003—, mem. R & D com., 2003—; prin. rschr. West LA VA Med. Ctr., 1998—. Mem. neurobiology study panel NSF, 1971—73. Editor: (book) Aneural Organisms in Neurobiology, 1975; assoc. editor: The Physiology Tchr., 1979—82; contbr. articles to profl. jours. and book chpts. in field. Recipient Ann. Pavlovian Investigator award, 1997. Fellow: Internat. Behavioral Neuroscience Soc.; mem.: AMA, AAAS, APA, Am. Physiol. Soc., Internat. Soc. Magnetic Resonance in Medicine, Pavlovian Soc. N.Am., Soc. Neuroscience. Achievements include research in biological basis of learning and memory. Avocations: piano, nature walks, reading. Office: VA Greater LA Healthcare Sys 11301 Wilshire Blvd Los Angeles CA 90073 Home Phone: 310-207-0453; Office Phone: 310-268-3498. Business E-Mail: edward.eisenstein@med.va.gov.

EISENSTEIN, TOBY K., microbiology professor; b. Phila., Sept. 15, 1942; d. Edward and Sylvia (Mandel) Karet; m. Bruce A. Eisenstein, Sept. 8, 1963; children: Eric, Andrew, Ilana. BA, Wellesley Coll., 1964; PhD, Bryn Mawr Coll., 1969. Instr. Med. Sch. Temple U., Phila., 1969-71, asst. prof., 1971-79, assoc. prof. microbiology and immunology Med. Sch., 1979-84, prof., 1984—, acting chair, 1990-92, co-dir. Ctr. Substance Abuse Rsch., 1992—. Mem. bacteriology and mycology study sect. NIH, 1976—80, 1988—92, mem. drugs abuse and AIDS study sect., 1994—2004. Contbr. articles to profl. jours. Recipient Lindback award, Temple U., 1986, Rsch. prize, 2003; NIH fellow, 1965—69, USPHS grantee, 1971—. Fellow: Coll. Physicians Phila., Coll. Problems Drug Dependence (bd. dirs. 2005—08), Am. Acad. Microbiology; mem.: AAAS, Psychoneuroimmunology Rsch. Soc., Soc. Neuroimmune Pharmacology (pres. 2010—, Joseph Wybran award), Internat. Endotoxin and Innate Immunity Soc., Soc. Leukocyte Biology (sec. 1998—2000), Am. Assn. Immunologists, Am. Soc. Microbiology (pres. eastern Pa. br. 1983—86, mem. coun. policy com. 1993—96, chair membership bd. 2003—, mem. coun. policy com. 2003—), Sigma Xi (pres. Temple U. chpt. 1981—83). Office: Temple U Sch Medicine Dept Microbiology and Immunology 3400 N Broad St Philadelphia PA 19140-5104 Office Phone: 215-707-3585. Business E-Mail: tke@temple.edu.

EISENTAT, STEVEN ALLAN, physician, educator; Studied, Ohio U., 1984. Diplomate Am. Bd. Family Practice, cert. geriatric medicine. Resident family medicine Union Hosp.; asst. clin. prof. family medicine NY Coll. Osteo Med.; physician Overlook Medical Ctr. Office: Overlook Medical Center Ste 202 1050 Galloping Hill Rd Union NJ 07083-7980 Office Phone: 908-688-4845. Office Fax: 908-687-2039.

EISER, ARNOLD ROBERT, physician executive, bioethicist, nephrologist, internist, medical educator; b. Newark, NY, Jan. 2, 1949; s. Harold H. and Anne Eiser; m. Barbara Joyce Andrews, June 15, 1975; 1 child, Arielle Veronica. BA magna cum laude, U. Pa., 1970; MD, Northwestern U., 1974. Intern Pa. Hosp., 1974-75; resident Med. Coll. Pa., 1975-77; fellow Hahnemann U., 1977-79; nephrologist Elmhurst (N.Y.) Hosp. Ctr., 1979-95, assoc. chief nephrology, 1993-95, dir. ambulatory care, 1995-97, dir. med. residency program, 1996-97; chief sect. gen. internal medicine U. Ill., Chgo., 1997—2001, prof. medicine, 1997—2003; v.p. Med. Edn. Mercy Health Sys., Darby, Pa., 2003—; sr. fellow Jeffrson Sch. Population Health, 2009—; assoc. fellow Ctr. Bioethics U. Penna, 2009—. Assoc. prof. medicine Mt. Sinai Sch. Medicine, NYC, 1986-97; adj. assoc. Hastings Ctr., Briarcliff Manor, NY, 1994-98; prof., assoc. dean medicine Coll. Medicine, Drexel U., 2003—. Contbg. author: The Kidney in Collagen Vascular Diseases, 1993, Violence Against Women: Philosophical Perspective, 1998; contbr. articles to profl. jours. Recipient Courage to Lead award, ACGME, 2010, Lead award, Accreditation Coun. Grad. Med. Edn., 2010, Castle Connolly Best Drs. award, 2011. Fellow: ACP (chair, Health Policy Com. 2008—, chair health pub. policy com. Pa. chpt. 2010—, Laureate award, Pa. chpt. 2008), Coll. Physicians Phila. (sec. history sect. 2006—), Inst. Medicine Chgo. (pres. Chgo. clin. ethics program 2001—03). Avocations: travel, exercise, music. Office: 1500 Lansdowne Ave Darby PA 19023 Office Phone: 610-237-5620. Business E-Mail: aeiser@mercyhealth.org, arnold.eiser@drexelmed.edu.

EKBOM, KARL EDVARD, neurologist; b. Stockholm, Oct. 28, 1935; s. Karl-Axel and Hedvig Charlotta (Stalhane) E.; m. Christina Ingrid Bergnas, June 18, 1960; children: Karl-Johan, Anders, Tomas, Helena. MD, PhD, Karolinska Inst., Stockholm, 1970, MEd, 1974. Resident in internal medicine Soder Hosp., Stockholm, 1962-65; resident in neurology Karolinska Hosp., Stockholm, 1965-71; asst. cons. neurology Soder Hosp., Stockholm, 1972-78, head dept. neurology, 1978-96; cons. dept. neurology Huddinge (Sweden) U. Hosp., 1997-2000. Editor: Migraine in General Practice, 1993; contbr. articles to profl. jours. Mem. Swedish Med. Soc., Internat. Headache Soc. (hon. life, bd. dirs. 1987-93), World Fedn. Neurology (bd. dirs. rsch. group 1972-2001), Swedish Migraine Soc. (hon., sec. 1968-88, chmn. 1989-95), Swedish Neurol. Soc. (chmn. 1980-82), European Headache Fedn. (v.p. 1992-94). Avocations: music, literature, photography. Office: Karolinska U Hosp Huddinge Dept Neurology S-14186 Stockholm Sweden Fax: 46-8-7744822. Business E-Mail: karl.ekbom@karolinska.se.

EKE, NDUBUISI, medical educator, urologist, consultant; s. Stephen Onuzuruike and Helen Chijiago Eke; m. Felicia Uchezuba Acholonu; children: Ure, Kechy, Ikedi. MB ChB, U. of Edinburgh, 1972—77. Surgical registrar West Cumberland Hosp., Whitehaven, England, 1983—84; sr. surgical registrar UPTH, Port Harcourt, Rivers, Nigeria, 1985—89; prof. surgery U. Port Harcourt; examiner W. African Coll. Surgeons; external examiner several U., Nigeria. Med. dir. Sophia Clinic, Port Harcourt, Rivers, Nigeria, 1987—97. Author: Paediatrics and Child Health, 1999; contbr. articles to profl. med. jours. and publs. Nat. pres. GSS Afikpo Old Boys' Assn., Afikpo, Ebonyi, Nigeria. Scholar Wien Scholarship, Brandeis U., 1971, Pollock Halls Scholarship, U. of Edinburgh, 1973—75, Fed. Scholarship, Nigerian Govt., 1976—77. Fellow: Internat. Coll. Surgeons Nigerian Sect., Royal Coll. Surgeons Eng., Royal Coll. Surgeons Edinburgh, West African Coll. of Surgeons (Nil). Home: PO Box 5575 27 Old Aba Rd Rivers Port Harcourt Nigeria Office: Dept Surgery Univ Port Harcourt Rivers Port Harcourt Nigeria Home Phone: 234 84 611606; Office Phone: 234 84 8037714188. Personal E-mail: ndubuisi_eke@hotmail.com.

EKELE, BISSALLAH AHMED, obstetrician, gynecologist, educator; b. Ofante, Nigeria, Mar. 8, 1962; s. Moses Ahmed and Rebecca Iyojo Ekele; m. Comfort Eleojo Ogala, Dec. 9, 1995; children: Bissallah Jr. Ahmed, Jemima Mama. B in Surgery, U. of Jos, Nigera, 1985; B in Med., U. of Jos, Nigeria, 1985. Fellow, West African Coll. of Surgeons West African Postgraduate Med. Coll., 1994. Intern U. Tchg. Hosp., Maiduguri, Nigeria, 1985—86; med. resident Jos U. Tchg. Hosp., Nigeria, 1987—94. Cons. obsterician Usmanu Danfodiyo Univ., Sokoto, Nigeria, 1994—, sr. lectr., 1997—2000; assoc. prof. Usmanu Danfodyo Univ., Sokoto, Nigeria, 2000—03; prof., head of dept. Usmanu Danfodiyo Univ., Sokoto, Nigeria, 2003—; dir. clin. svcs. and tng. U. Tchg. Hosp., Sokoto, Nigeria, 1998—2001; vis. cons. Fed. Med. Ctr., Birnin Kebbi, Nigeria, 2000—. Author: (30 publs. in sci. jours.) West African Jour. of Medicine, African Jour. of Medicine and Med. Scis., Tropical Doctor, Brit. Jour of Obstetrics and Gynecology, Acta Obstetricia et Gynecol. Scandnavica, Lancet. Chmn. adolescent and reproductive health com. Nigerian Med. Assn., Abuja, 2002. Recipient Ashok's prize in Anatomy, U. of Jos (Nigeria), 1982, Glazo prize in Anaesthesia, 1985, Fredrick Zuspan award, Internat. Soc. for Study of Hypertention in Pregnancy, 2002. Fellow: Internat. Coll. of Surgeons (hon.; sector sec., soc. of obtetrics and gynaecology of Nigeria 2000—02). Achievements include research in treating ectopic pregnancy and eclampsia using modified protocols that are safe, effective, and feasible in low income settings. Avocations: Scrabble, soccer, travel. Office: Usmanu Danfodiyo Univ Tchg Hosp Pmb 2370 Sokoto Sokoto Nigeria

EKIN, ISMAIL H., microbiologist; b. Siirt, May 9, 1970; PhD, YYU Saglik Bil Enstitusu, 2004. Rsch. scientist Microbiology Dept., U. Yuzuncu Yil, Faculty Vet. Medicine, 1996. Office: Yuzuncu Yil Universitesi Veteriner Fak Merkez VAN 65080 Turkey Business E-Mail: ihekin@yyu.edu.tr.

ELAHI, MAQSOOD MANZOOR, medical researcher; b. Pakistan, Dec. 25, 1974; BSc 1st class hons., Punjab U., Lahore, Pakistan, 1994, MBBS, 1997; MS Thesis, U. Glasgow, Scotland, 2001; postgrad studies toward PhD Cadiovascular Scis. MRCS Royal Coll. Physicians & Surgeons Glasgow, 2002, FICS in cardiovascular surgery Internat. Coll. Surgeons, 2004. Postgrad. rsch. fellow Glasgow U., Scotland, 1998—2000; sr. house officer in cardiac surgery Glasgow Royal Infirmary, 2000—01; surgical trainee U. Hosps., Leicester, England, 2001—02; fellow in cardiac surgery Glenfield Hosp., Leicester, 2002—03; clin. rsch. fellow, registrar U. Leicester Glenfield Hosp., 2003—. Presenter seminars and workshops to medical groups, 2001—. Contbr. articles to profl. jours and chpt. to book. Grantee Astra-Zeneca Rsch. and Devel. fund, 2002—03, Take Heart Charity, 2002—03, Heart-Link charity, 2002—03, Proctor & Gamble, 2002—06. Personal E-mail: manzoor_elahi@hotmail.com.

EL-AHL, MOHAMMAD HAMZA, pediatrician, educator; b. Mansoura, Egypt, June 25, 1936; s. Hamza Ibrahim Sayed El Ahl and Sabra Mohammad Amer; m. Sawasn Ahmed Ragha, Sept. 3, 1970; children: Ahmed, Yahya. B Medicine & Surgery, Alexandria U., 1960, diploma in child health, 1962, MD, 1963. Resident Alexandria U. Hosp., Egypt, 1961—70; registrar Great Ormond St. Hosp., London, 1971—72; cons. Maadi Mil. Hosp., Cairo, 1972—80, head dept., 1980—86; prof. Mil. Med. Acad., Cairo, 1980—; chmn. Tabarak Children's Hosp., Cairo, 1987—. Cons. pediat. svcs. Egyptian Army hosps. Author: (in Arabic) Your Baby in His First Year, 1994, How to Care for Your Sick Child, 2000; co-author jour. Biomed. Optoelectronic Instrumentation, 1995. Gen. Egyptian armed forces, 1986-94. Recipient Egyptian Rep. award Ministry of Def., 1994. Fellow Royal Coll. Physicians (Glasgow); mem. Egyptian Pediat. Assn., Egyptian Neonatology Assn., Internat. Soc. Optical Engring., Royal Coll. Physicians (London). Democrat. Muslim. Avocations: music, meditation, swimming. Office: Tabarak Children's Hosp Golf Land 3 Husain Zuhdi St 11361 Cairo Egypt Home Phone: +202 291 1123; Office Phone: +202 418 11841. Business E-Mail: hamza@tabarakhospital.com. E-mail: tabarak_hamza@hotmail.com.

ELANDER LINDBERG, NOOMI CHRISTIN, psychotherapist; b. Alingsås, Sweden, May 16, 1937; d. Viktor Eugen and Elisabet Elin (Jonsson) Elander; m. Erik Lindberg, May 16, 1964. Grad., Nursing Sch., Gothenburg, Sweden, 1960, Midwife Edn. Instn., Stockholm, 1962; BA, U. Stockholm, 1975, grad. in psychology, 1978; MD, PhD in Psychosomatic Medicine, Karolinska Inst., Stockholm, 1997. RN, Sweden; cert. tchr. psychotherapy and supervision, 1999; registered psychologist, psychotherapist, midwife, Sweden. Oper. room nurse Sahlgrenska Hosp., Gothenburg, 1960-61, Södersjukhuset, Stockholm, 1962-64; nurse Strängnäs Rheuma Hosp., Sweden, 1964-67, Sch. Health Svc., Täby and Danderyd, Sweden, 1969; midwife and oper. room nurse Gävle Hosp., Sweden, 1967-68; midwife Maternity Hosp., Stockholm, 1968-69; pvt. practice psychotherapy, Stocksund, Sweden, 1978—. Psychologist Nat. Bd. Occupl. Health and Safety, Stockholm, 1979-81. Contbg. author: Psychosomatic Medicine, 1991; contbr. articles to profl. jours. including Psychotherapy Psychosomatics, Am. Jour. Indsl. Medicine, Acta Odont Scand, Work and Stress, Zeitschrift Rheumatologie; other Swedish jours. include (series) Power of Spirit, Minstry of Health. Mem. Swedish Psychol. Assn., Swedish Nat. Psychotherapy Ctr., Swedish Soc. Medicine, Assn. Psychosomatic Medicine, Assn. Psychosomatic Ob-Gyn. Mem. Swedish Nat. Ch. Avocations: gardening, literature, opera music, antiques. Office: PsykoSoma Ltd Egilsvägen 5 182 78 Stocksund Sweden Personal E-mail: noomi.lindberg@home.se.

ELASHRY, OSAMA M., urologist, educator; b. El Mahalla El Kobra, Feb. 6, 1962; MD, Tanta U., PhD, 1985. Prof. urology Tanta Faculty Medicine, 2010—. Recipient Best Sci. Publ. award, Tanta U. Mem.: Egyptian Urologic Assn., Soc. Internat. d' Urologie, European Urologic Assn., Am. Urologic Assn. Office: 19 Emoderia St Teeba Tower Ste #10 Tanta Gharbia Egypt Office Fax: 020403312645. E-mail: oselashry@yahoo.com.

EL-BEIALY, WALEED RAGAB, dental educator; b. Norway, Jan. 21, 1975; MDS, Cairo U., DDS, 2002; PhD, Hokkaido U., 2008. Assoc. prof. Hokkaido Grad. Sch. Dental Medicine, 2008—10, Faculty Oral & Dental Medicine, Cairo U., 2010—. Grants, Hokkaido U. Avocation: soccer. Home: Kita-ku Kita 24jo Nishi 12 chome 1-3 Sapporo Hokkaido 001 0024 Japan Home Fax: 011 7096006. Personal E-mail: wbeialy@yahoo.com.

ELBOGEN, ERIC B., psychologist, educator; BA, Cornell U.; M.Ed., Harvard U.; PhD, MLS, U. Nebr. Intern Harvard Med. Sch., Mass. Mental Health Ctr.; fellow Duke U. Med. Ctr., forensic psychologist Ctrl. Regional Hosp., Butner; asst. prof. psychiatry UNC Sch. Med. Office: UNC Department of Psychiatry 3rd Fl Medical School Wing D Campus Box 7160 Chapel Hill NC 27599-7160 Office Phone: 919-966-5540. E-mail: eric.elbogen@unc.edu.

ELCANO, MARY S., international non profit organization executive, lawyer; b. Sept. 12, 1949; BA cum laude, Lynchburg Coll., 1971; JD, Cath. U., Washington, 1976. Litigation atty. Balt. Legal Aide Bur., 1976—79; staff atty. Office Solicitor US Dept. Labor, 1979—82; gen. trial and appellate atty. Office Labor Law US Postal Svc., 1982—84, exec. dir. Office EEO, 1984—87, regional dir. human resources N.E. region, 1987—92, sr. v.p., gen. counsel, 1992-99, exec. v.p., gen. counsel, 1999-2000; ptnr. Sidley Austin Brown & Wood LLP, Washington, 2000—03; gen. counsel, corp. sec. Am. Red Cross, Washington, 2003—, interim pres. & CEO, 2007—08. Office: American Red Cross 430 17th St NW Washington DC 20006 Office Phone: 202-303-5422. Business E-Mail: ElcanoM@usa.redcross.org.

EL CHAAR, EDGARD S., periodontist; b. Beirut, Jan. 27, 1970; Degree in Advanced Edn. Program in Periodontics, NYU, 1997, DDS, 1999. Diplomate Am. Bd. Oral Implantology. Periodontist, owner Edgard El Chaar DDS PC, 1999—. Clin. assoc. prof., dept. periodontics and implant dentistry NYU; surg. dir., continuing edn. dental implant program NYU Coll. Dentistry; dir., founder EEC Inst. Inc., AAID NY, 2010. Recipient 10 Yr. Recognition award, NYU Coll. Dentistry, Appreciation award, DENTAC Ft. Irwin, 2003, Dental Program, Ft. Gordon, Ga., 2006, 2007. Fellow: Am. Acad. Periodontology; mem.: Am. Acad. Implant Dentistry, Am. Acad. Osseointegration, Northeastern Caucus of AAID (treas.), ITI Inst. Avocations: flying, skiing, sailing. Office: 67 Park Ave Ste 1A New York NY 10016 Office Fax: 212-685-5134. Business E-Mail: info@edgardelchaar.com.

ELCIN, MELIH, physician; b. Mugla, Turkey, July 30, 1967; s. Ozer and Nuray Elcin; children: Nehir children: Yagmur. MD, Ege U., Izmir, 1991. Lic. family physician Ministry Health, 1999. Physician Ministry Health, Turkey, 1992—2000; faculty mem. Hacettepe U., Ankara, 2000—08. Head dept. med. edn. and informatics Hacettepe U. Faculty Medicine, Ankara, Turkey, 2006—. Author: (book) The Blueness of My Heart; actor: Beyond Me, Till Me. Served with Turkish Army, 2000, Ankara. Grantee, TUBITAK, 2005—. Mem.: ASPE. Achievements include being the first associate professor of medical education in Turkey. Office: Hacettepe U Faculty Medicine Sihhiye Ankara 06100 Turkey Business E-Mail: melcin@hacettepe.edu.tr.

ELDE, ROBERT P., dean, neuroscientist, educator; Grad. with honors, North Park Coll., Chgo., 1969; PhD, U. Minn., 1974; MD (hon.), Karolinska Inst., Stockholm, 1996. Faculty mem. U. Minn., 1977—, prof. cell biology and neuroanatomy, J.B. Johnston Land Grant prof. neuroscience, dean Coll. Biol. Scis., 1995—. Dir. grad. studies Grad. Program in Neuroscience U. Minn., 1987—89; bd. dirs.

Gel-Del Techs. Contbr. articles to sci. jours. Office: U Minn Coll Biol Scis 123 Snyder Hall 1475 Gortner Ave Saint Paul MN 55108 Office Phone: 612-624-2244. E-mail: elde@umn.edu.

ELDER, DEBORAH A., pediatrician, educator; b. Wayne, Mich., June 21, 1969; MD, U. Ky. Sch. Medicine, 1995. Asst. prof. pediat. Cin. Children's Hosp. Med. Ctr., 2001—. Rsch. grant, NIH. Mem.: Pediatric Endocrine Soc., Endocrine Soc., Am. Diabetes Assn. Office: Cin Children's Hosp Med C Cincinnati OH 45229 Office Fax: 513-636-7486. Business E-Mail: deborah.elder@cchmc.org.

ELDER, JACK S., urologist, educator; s. Stanley Gordon and Alma Westfall Elder; m. Judith Rose Lenobel, June 16, 1973; children: Samuel Isaac, Benjamin Daniel, Kathryn Rachel, Allison Miriam, Abigail Paula. MD with Distinction, U. Okla., Oklahoma City, 1976. Diplomate Am. Bd. Urology, 1984. Internship / residency surgery Yala New Haven Hosp., 1976—78; residency urology The Johns Hopkins Hosp., 1978—82; chief pediat. urology Rainbow Babies and Children's Hosp., Cleve., 1986—2007; Carter Kissell prof. urology Case Sch. Medicine, Cleve., 2003—07, vice chmn. dept. urology, 2004—07; chief, dept. urology Henry Ford Hosp. Sys., Detroit, 2007—; assoc. dir. Vattikuti Urology Inst., 2007—. Pediatric urology editor Jour. Urology, Balt., 1998—2007; physician Perlman Music Program China Trip, NYC, 2002; cons. H. H. Sheikh Zayed, Abu Dhabi, United Arab Emirates, 1992. Contbr. articles to profl. jours., chpts. to books;, author 5 books and monographs in field. Named one of Best Drs. Am., Castle Connolly, 1996, 1998, 2000, 2002, 2004, 2006, 2008; fellow Pediat. Urology, Children Hosp. of Phila., 1985—86; fellowship Pediat. Urology, The Johns Hopkins Hosp., 1982. Fellow: ACS, Am. Acad. Pediat.; mem.: Clin. Soc. Genitourinary Surgeons, Am. Urol. Assn. (chmn. panel on reflux guidelines 1990—97, 1st prize lab. rsch. 1981), Soc. Pediat. Urology (pres. 2006—07), Am. Assn. Genitourinary Surgeons, Alpha Omega Alpha (1st v.p. okla. chpt. 1975—76). Achievements include development of sedation protocol for children undergoing urinary bladder diagnostic testing; research in cryptorchidism, androgenic regulation of the gubernaculum testis. Office: Vattikuti Urology Inst 2799 W Grand Blvd K-9 Detroit MI 48202-2689 Office Fax: 313-916-2956. Personal E-mail: jack.s.elder@gmail.com. *

ELDER, JENNIFER, nursing educator, researcher; b. Atlanta, Mar. 18, 1955; BSN, U. Fla., 1976, PhD, 1992. Prof., assoc. dean rsch. U. Fla., 1992—. Recipient Mentoring award, Howard Hughes Inst., Presdl. Recognition, U. Fla.; named one of 100 Gt. Nurses Fla., Fla. Nurses Assn.; grant, Nat. Inst. Nursing Rsch. Fellow: Am. Acad. Nursing; mem.: ANA, Coun. Advancement Nursing Sci., Internat. Soc. Autism Rsch., Sigma Theta Tau Internat. Honor Soc. Avocations: boating, motorcycling, water-skiing. Office: Box 100187 101 S Newell Dr Gainesville FL 32610-0187 Business E-Mail: elderjh@ufl.edu.

ELDER, STEWART TAYLOR, dentist, retired military officer; b. Darlington, Pa., Aug. 6, 1917; s. William Carl and Olive Gertrude (Taylor) E.; m. Loretta Tersa Vitlo, Apr. 23, 1946; children: Donna Lou, Susan Loretta. BS, Mt. Union Coll., 1940; DDS, Ohio State U., 1945; postgrad., Naval Dental Sch., Nat. Naval Med. Center, Bethesda, Md., 1952-53. With Deming Pump Co., Salem, Ohio, 1935-36, prodn. mgr., 1952-53; commd. lt. (j.g.) U.S. Navy, 1945; advanced through grades to capt. Dental Corps, 1960; prosthetics officer 50th Field Hosp., Paris, 1946-47; asst. dental officer Norfolk Naval Shipyard, Portsmouth, Va., 1948-50, U.S.S. Wisconsin, 1950-52; postgrad. resident in prosthodontics Naval Weapons Plant, Washington, 1953-54; prosthetics officer Norfolk Naval Shipyard, Portsmouth, 1954-55, 57-60; dental officer, prosthetics officer U.S.S. Vulcan, 1955-57; prosthetics officer, exec. officer Naval Dental Clinic, Guantanamo Bay, Cuba, 1960-62; prosthetics officer Naval Dental Clinic Marine Corps Base, Camp Pendleton, Calif., 1962-66; comdg. officer 11th Dental Co., Republic of Vietnam, 1966-67; chief dental service Naval Hosp., Camp Pendleton, 1967-71; exec. officer Naval Dental Clinic, Washington, 1971-73, comdg. officer, 1973-75, Naval Regional Dental Center, Washington, 1975-76, Nat. Naval Dental Center, Bethesda, Md., 1976-79; lectr., instr. Navy Dental Corps Continuing Edn. Program, 1963—, Dental Intern and Postdoctoral Fellowship Programs, 1967—. Practice gen. dentistry, Salem, Ohio, 1947-48, lectr. and condr. clinics in field Mem. ADA (life), Am. Prosthodontic Soc. (life), Fedn. Prosthodontic Orgns. (life). Home: 1436 Patriot Dr Melbourne FL 32940-6818 Personal E-mail: selder1430@earthlink.net.

ELDERS, JOYCELYN (MINNIE JOCELYN ELDERS, MINNIE JOYCELYN LEE), public health service officer, endocrinologist, former Surgeon General of the United States; b. Schaal, Ark., Aug. 13, 1933; d. Curtis and Haller Jones; m. Oliver B. Elders, Feb. 14, 1960; children: Eric D., Kevin M. BA in Biol., Philander Smith Coll., 1952; MD, U. Ark. Med. Sch., 1960; MS in Biochemistry, U. Ark., 1967. Pediatric intern U. Minn. Hosp., Mpls., 1960-61; pediatric resident U. Ark. Med. Ctr., Little Rock, 1961-63, chief pediatric resident, 1963-64, pediatric rsch. fellow, 1964-67, asst. prof. of pediatrics, 1967-71, assoc. prof. of pediatrics, 1971-76, prof. of pediatrics, 1976-87; dir. Ark. Dept. of Health, Little Rock, 1987-93; pres. Assn. of State & Territorial Health Officers, 1992; surgeon gen. US Dept. Health & Human Services, 1993-94; prof. pediatrics Univ. Ark. Med. Ctr., Little Rock, 1994—98, prof. emeritus, pediatric endocrinology, 1998—; medical dir. Apothecus Pharmaceutical Corp., 2006—. Bd. dirs. Nat. Bank of Ark., North Little Rock, 1979-89. Editorial bd. Jour. Pediatrics, 1981—; contbr. articles on pediatrics to profl. jours. Bd. dirs. Northside YMCA, Little Rock, 1973—; vol. vols. in pub. schs., Little Rock, 1973—. 1st lt. U.S. Army, 1953-56. Recipient NIH Career Devel. award, Worthen Bank's Ark. Profl. Woman of Distinction award, 1987; named one of 100 Women of Ark., 1980, Ark. Dem. Woman of Yr. statewide newspaper, 1988, Presdl. award, Ark. Sociological and Anthropological Assn., 1993. Mem. So. Soc. Pediatrics (rsch. pres. 1979-80), Lawson Wilkins Endocrine Soc. (com. chair 1976), Ark. Sci. and Tech. Commn. (sec. 1975-89), Little Rock C. of C. (bd. dirs. 1980—), Endocrine Soc., Acad. Pediatrics, Am. Pediatric Soc. First African Am. US Surgeon General. Office: U Ark Med Ctr 4301 W Markham # 820 Little Rock AR 72205 *

EL-DESOUKI, MAHMOUD IBRAHIM, nuclear medicine educator, physician; b. Cairo, Aug. 20, 1951; s. Ibrahim Mohammad and Faiza Ali (Ahmed) El-D.; m. Mayyada H. Alhomsi, Jan. 27, 1977; children: Majed, Munir, Mohannad. MB BS, King Saud U., Saudi Arabia, 1976. Diplomate Am. Bd. Nuclear Medicine. Intern King Saud U. Hosp., Riyadh, Saudi Arabia, 1976-77, resident in internal medicine, 1977-80, U. Toronto, 1981-83, resident in nuclear medicine, 1983-85; asst. prof., cons. in nuclear medicine King Saud U. Hosp., 1988-92; chief dept. nuclear medicine King Khalid Univ. Hosp. King Khalid U. Hosp., King Saud U., 1988; prof., chief dept. nuclear medicine King Saud U. Hosp., 1992—. Cons. Security Force Hosp. and King Fahd Nat. Guard Hosp., Riyadh, Saudi Arabia. Editor-in-chief Nuclear Medicine newsletter. Mem. Nat. Osteoporosis Found. Fellow Royal Coll. Physicians and Surgeons (Can., diplomate), IBA (life); mem. Radiol. Soc. N.Am., N.Y. Acad. Scis., Brit. Nuc. Medicine Soc., Soc. Nuc. Medicine, Am. Soc. Radiol. Tech., Am. Coll. Nuc. Physicians, Am. Coll. Radiology, European Soc. Nuc. Medicine, Saudi Cardiology Soc., Nat. Geog. Soc., Am. Soc. Nuc. Cardiology, Smithsonian Assn., Nat. Osteoporosis Soc., Nat. Osteoporosis Found., Saudi Osteoporosis Club (pres.).

ELDIB, AHMED, biophysicist, educator; b. Egypt, July 27, 1978; BSc in Biophysics, 1999, PhD in Biophysics, 2008. Lectr., edn. and rsch. Alazhar U., 2002—, lectr., 2009—. Recipient Sun Nuc. award. Mem.: Am. Assn. Physicists Medicine. Avocation: swimming. Home: 7 Nawal St Cairo Giza 12311 Egypt Personal E-mail: ahmedeldeeb2003@yahoo.com.

EL-DOMYATI, MOETAZ MOUSTAFA, medical educator, researcher; b. Cairo, Mar. 31, 1957; s. Moustafa Mahmoud El-Domyati and Tahea Taher Abdel-Salam; m. Iman Fawzy Abdelhamid, June 23, 1993; children: Farah Moetaz, Mohamed Moetaz. MB, Ain Shams U., 1980, MSc in Dermatology, 1984, Diploma of Surgery, 1986, MD, 1989. Ho. officer Ain Shams U. Hosp., Cairo, 1981—82, resident, 1982—85; asst. lectr. Al-Minya U., 1985—89, lectr., 1990—94, assoc. prof., 1995—99, prof., 1999—. Cons. dermatologist Judge Clinic, Min. Justice, Cairo, 2001—; adv. bd. Jour. of Egyptian Women's Dermatologic Soc., Cairo, 2004—, Egyptian Dermatology Online Jour., Jour. Egyptian Soc. Dermatology and Andrology; chmn. dermatology & venereology dept. Al-Minya U., 2005—, laser unit dir., 2005—; presenter in field; mem. Egyptian U. Promotion Com., 2008—, Egyptian Fellowship Bd. Dermatology, 2009—. Contbr. articles and reports to profl. jours. Recipient 18th World Congress Dermatology award, NY, 1992, Egyptian Med. Syndicate award, 2007. Fellow: Internat. Soc. Dermatologic Surgery (Perry Robins award 1987); mem.: Dermatologic & Aesthetic Surgery Internat. League (adv. bd. mem. 2011—, organizing com. mem. 2011—), Promotions Profs. Title Dermatology Venerology (sci. com. mem.), European Acad. Dermatology & Venereology, Egyptian Soc. Dermatology & Venereology. Avocations: swimming, jogging. Home: Nasr City 2 Obour blgs Salah Salem St Apt 53 Cairo Egypt 11371 Office: Al-Minya U Dept Dermatology Fac Medicine Al Minya Egypt Office Phone: (20)12-3121132. Personal E-mail: moetazeldomyati@gmail.com.

ELDRED, KENNETH MCKECHNIE, acoustician, consultant; b. Springfield, Mass., Nov. 25, 1929; s. Robert Moseley and Jean McKechnie (Ashton) E.; m. Helene Barbara Koerting Fischer, May 31, 1957; 1 dau., Heidi Jean. BS, MIT, 1950, postgrad., 1951-53, UCLA, 1960-63. Engr. in charge vibration and sound lab. Boston Naval Shipyard, 1951-54; supervisory physicist, chief phys. acoustics sect. U.S. Air Force, Wright Field, Ohio, 1956-57; v.p., cons. acoustics Western Electro-Acoustics Labs., Los Angeles, 1957-63; v.p., tech. dir. sci. services and systems group Wyle Labs., El Segundo, Calif., 1963-73; v.p., dir. div. environ. and noise control tech. Bolt Beranek and Newman Inc., Cambridge, Mass., 1973-77, prin. cons., 1977-81. Dir. Ken Eldred Engring.; mem. exec. stds. coun. Am. Nat. Stds. Inst., 1979-81, vice-chmn., 1981-83, chmn., 1985-87, bd. dirs., 1983-87; bd. dirs., Ince Found.; mem., past chmn. Acoustical Stds. Bd.; mem. com. hearing, bioacoustics and biomechanics NRC, 1963-88; chmn. Internat. Stds. Orgn. Tech. Com. TC108 Mechanical Shock and Vibration, 1994-99; bd. dirs., treas. Earcraft Tech. Inc., 1999-2003. 1st lt. USAF, 1954-56. Fellow Acoustical Soc. Am. (stds. dir. 1987-93, past chmn. coordinating com. environ. acoustics, Silver Medal in Noise 1994); mem. NAE, Inst. Noise Control Engring. (pres. 1976, bd. dirs. 1987-91), Down East Yacht Club. Home: Meadow Cove East Boothbay ME 04544 Office: PO Box 501 East Boothbay ME 04544-0501 Home Phone: 207-633-5991; Office Phone: 207-633-5991. Personal E-mail: keldred@alum.mit.edu.

ELDREDGE, JONATHAN DEFOREST, medical librarian, educator, social informaticist; s. LeRoy Lincoln Jr. and Elizabeth Belding Eldredge; m. Regina Leslie Wolfe, Nov. 19, 1994; children: Nicolas-Etienne, Gabriela Regina. BA cum laude, Beloit Coll., 1976; MLS, U. Mich., 1978; PhD, U. N.Mex., 1993. Cert. Acad. Health Info. Profls. Med. Libr. Assn., 1989. Disting. level libr. dir. Ea. N.Mex U., Clovis, 1981—83; asst. prof., chief Collections and Info. Resources Devel. U. N.Mex, Albuquerque, 1986—2000, assoc. prof., acad. and clin. svcs. coord., 2001—09; interim coord., assoc. prof. Learning Design Ctr., 2009—. Oversight com. Nat. Libr. Medicine, Bethesda, Md., 2001—; assoc. editor Evidence Based Libr. and Info. Practice, 2009—. Assoc. editor: Biomed. Digital Librs., 2003—, jour. rev. editor: Jour. AMA, 1994—2000, mem. adv. bd.: New Eng. Jour. Medicine, 2001—04; contbr. articles to profl. jours. Sec., bd. mem. Friends Librs., N.Mex., Albuquerque, 1995—2003. Recipient Hippo Excellent Tchg. award, U N.Mex. Sch. Medicine, 2007, 2009. Mem.: ALA (life), Med. Libr. Assn. (Rsch. award 2002, 2006, Louise Darling medal for disting. achievement in collection devel. in health scis. 1999). Unitarian Universalist/Buddhist. Achievements include one of the main founders of the international Evidence-Based library and information practice movement. Avocations: skiing, surfing, bicycling, hiking, travel. Office: Univ NMex Health Sci Lib and Informatics Ctr Albuquerque NM 87131-5686 Business E-Mail: jeldredge@salud.unm.edu.

ELDREDGE, LINDA, psychologist; BS, Howard Payne U., 1980; MA, Tex. Woman's U., 1981; EdD, Baylor U., 1989. Lic. psychologist, Tex.; cert. tchr. hearing impaired, sch. counselor, spl. edn. counselor, Tex.; cert. verbal self def. trainer. Tchr. hearing impaired Waco (Tex.) Ind. Sch. Dist., 1982-85, spl. edn. sch. counselor, cons. hearing impaired, 1986-87; doctoral teaching fellow Baylor U., Waco, 1985-87; dir. regional alcohol and drug abuse svcs. Heart of Tex. Coun. Govts., Waco, 1987; psychotherapist Houston, 1989-91; psychologist, 1991—, Tex. Sch. for the Deaf, Austin, Tex., 1993-95. Mem. APA, Am. Deafness and Rehab. Assn., Internat. Soc. Study Subtle Energies and Energy Medicine. Office: Bldg 4 Ste 200 4601 Spicewood Springs Rd Austin TX 78759

ELDRIDGE, EUGENE JOHN, ophthalmologist; b. Sturgis, Mich., Sept. 5, 1956; s. Eugene Edward and Lorene Patricia E.; m. Paula Marie Capelli, June 21, 1980; children: Mary Patricia, Kathleen Anne, Joseph Paul, Eugene Paul. BS, U. Notre Dame, 1979; MD, Northwestern U., Chgo., 1983. Diplomate Am. Bd. Ophthalmology. Resident Med. Coll. Wis., Milw., 1984-87; ophthalmologist Evanston (Ill.) Ophthalmologists, 1987-88, E. John Eldridge, M.D., S.C., Kenosha, Wis., 1988—; chmn., dept. surgery St. Catherine's Hosp., Kenosha, 1993-94. Pres. St. Catherine's Network Physicians IPA, Kenosha, 1991-93. Fellow Am. Acad. Ophthalmology; mem. Milw. Ophthalmol. Soc., Phi Beta Kappa. Conservative. Roman Catholic. Avocations: golf, tennis, gardening, computer sci., classical music. Office: 1400 75th St Kenosha WI 53143-1522

ELDRIDGE, J. CHARLES, endocrinologist, educator, researcher; b. Chgo., June 7, 1942; s. John Godfrey Eldridge, Carol Boedeker Eldridge; m. Pat Hudler. BA in Biology, North Cen. Coll., Naperville, Ill., 1965; MS in Physiology, No. Ill. U., 1967; PhD in Endocrinology, Med. Coll. Ga., 1971. Instr. biology Orange County C.C., Middletown, NY, 1967—68; rsch. assoc. I.N.S.E.R.M., Bordeaux, France, 1971-72, Med. Coll. Ga., Augusta, 1973; asst. prof. lab. medicine Med. U. S.C., Charleston, 1974-79; asst. prof. physiology and pharmacology Wake Forest U. Sch. Medicine, Winston-Salem, NC, 1979—87, assoc. prof. physiology and pharmacology, 1987—99, prof. physiology and pharmacology, 1999—. Grant reviewer Nat. Inst. Aging, NIH, Bethesda, Md., 1990—93; rsch. cons. EPA, Washington, 1999—, mem. endocrine disruptors methods validation com., 2001—04; ad-hoc mem. Sci. Adv. Panel, 2006—; cons. Internat. Life Scis. Inst., Washington, 1992—94; med. edn. cons. various schs., 1988—; adj. faculty Harvard Macy Inst. Med. Educators, 2001—. Mng. editor: Basic Sci. Educator, 1999—2002, mem. editl. bd.: Biology of Reproduction, 2000—05, Jour. Internat. Assn. Med. Sci. Educators, 2002—04; contbr. articles to profl. jours. Coord. United Way, Winston-Salem, 1986—98; elder, deacon, other positions Presby. Ch., 1992—. Recipient Disting. Alumni award, Med. Coll. Ga., 2002, CIBA Toxicology Rsch. award, Novartis Corp., 1995; grantee, NIH, 1976—97, Nat. Inst. Drug Abuse, 1990—98; Macy fellow in edn., Harvard Med. Sch., 2001. Mem.: Soc. for Study of Reproduction, Internat. Assn. for Med. Sci. Educators, Soc. Neurosci., Endocrine Soc., Shriners (bd. dirs. 1988—91). Presbyterian. Avocations: music, travel, cuisine. Office: Wake Forest U Sch Medicine Dept Physiology and Pharmacology Winston Salem NC 27157-1083 Office Phone: 336-716-8570.

ELENBERG, EWA, pediatrician, educator; b. Wroclaw, Poland, Sept. 24, 1957; MD, Med. U., 1983. Assoc. prof. pediat. Baylor Coll. Medicine, Tex. Children's Hosp., 2001—. Mem.: Internat. Assn. Pediat. Nephrology. Avocation: art. Office: 1102 Bates St Ste 260 Houston TX 77030 Office Fax: 832-825-3889. Business E-Mail: elenebrg@bcm.edu.

ELEQUIN, CLETO, JR., retired physician; b. Antique, Philippines, Oct. 18, 1933; s. Cleto and Enriqueta (Tengonciang) E.; m. Nancy Johnson, May 14, 1958; children: Tracy, Thomas Kyle, Stuart Scott MD, Far Eastern U., Philippines, 1957. Rotating intern Good Samaritan Hosp., Lexington, Ky., 1957-58; gen. practice resident Central Bapt. Hosp., Lexington, 1958-59; psychiat. resident State Hosp., Danville, Pa., 1959-60, 61-62, psychiat. resident with child psychiatry New Castle, Del., 1962-63; staff physician Eastern State Hosp., Lexington, 1960-61, dir. Fayette County Project, dir. intensive treatment service, 1964-67, supt., 1969-71; dep. commr. Dept. Mental Health, State Ky., 1967-69; pvt. practice specializing in family practice and psychiatry Pecos, Tex., 1971-72; practice medicine, specializing in family practice Austin, Tex., 1974-89; ret.; with Umbrella Tex. Integrative Medicine; pvt. practice Tex., 2011; with Tex. Integrative Medicine Holistic Medicine & Psychiatry; founding mem. expert Countries Health Med., Stanford Med. Sch. Cons. psychiatrist Texas Youth Commn., Peyote, Tex., Permian Basin Cmty. Mental Health-Mental Retardation, Odessa, Tex., Prude Ranch for Emotionally Disturbed Children and Adolescents, Ft. Davis, Tex., Dept. Mental Health-Mental Retardation State of Tex.; vis. lectr. in medicine and psychiatry Am. U. of the Caribbean, Plymouth, Montserrat; asst. dep. commr. Tex. Dept. Mental Health and Mental Retardation, Austin, 1973-74, dep. commr. mental health, 1974; pvt. practice family medicine and psychiatry, Austin, 1974-85; mem. attending staff Brackenridge Hosp., St. David Med. Ctr., Seton Med. Ctr., Shoal Creek Hosp.; med. dir. Mary Lee Sch. and Found., 1974-80, bd. trustees, 1980-85; attending psychiatrist U. Ky. Med. Ctr., 1964-71, Good Samaritan Hosp., 1969-71, Ctrl. Bapt. Hosp., 1966-71; cons. psychiatrist U. Ky. Student Health Svc., 1965-71, Peace Corps, 1966-68, Bur. Rehab. State Ky., 1965-71, Blue Grass Cmty. Care Ctr., 1967-71, Covington (Ky.) Cmty. Care Ctr., 1969-71, Hazard Cmty. Care Ctr., 1969-71, Danville (Ky.) Cmty. Ctr., 1969-71, Maysville (Ky.) Cmty. Care Ctr., 1969-71; clin. instr., asst. clin. prof. dept. psychiatry U. Ky. Med. Ctr., 1964-69, assoc. clin. prof., 1969-71; cons. psychiatrist Tex. Youth Commn. Tex. Dept. of MH-MR, State of Tex.; pvt. practice in psychiatry, Austin, 1974-85; attending staff Brackenridge Hosp., St. David Med. Ctr., Seton Med. Ctr., Shoal Creek Hosp.; med. dir. Mary Lee Sch. and Found., 1974-80, bd. trustees, 1980-85, psychiatrist Tex. Cmty., Austin. Profl. adv. coun. Cmty. Mental Health-Retardation Ctr., Lexington, 1967-71; active Lexington Hosp. Coun., 1969-71. Mem. AMA, Am. Psychiat. Assn., Am. Acad. Family Physicians (life), Assn. Med. Supts. Mental Hosps., Tex. Med. Assn., Travis County Med. Soc., Austin Psychiat. Soc. Home: 10101 Jupiter Hills Dr Austin TX 78747-1322 also: 9801 S Interstate Hwy 35 Austin TX 78744 Office Phone: 512-280-9508. Personal E-mail: c1yelequin@aol.com.

EL ETRIBI, MOHAMED ANWAR FATHI, neurology professor; b. Cairo, Aug. 13, 1946; MBBCH, Ain Shams U., Cairo, 1969; DPM&N, MD, MSc, PhD, Ain Shams U., Manchester, 1982. Founder, dir. Heliopolis Neuroclinic, 1984—2011; prof. neurology and psychiatry Ain Shams U. Med. Sch., 1990—, chmn. dept. neurology, 1995—2006; chmn. Egyptian Soc. Neurology, Psychiatry and Neurosurgery, 2001—03, Pan Arab Unions Neurosci., 2003—05. Bd. mem. World Stroke Orgn., 2004—08; v.p. World Fedn. Neurorehab., 2006—09; chmn., founder Brain Care Co., 2009—11; past pres. Heliopolis El Shorouk Rotary Club Dist. 2450, 2009—10. Mem.: Rotary Internat., Enos Study-Nottingham U. (Egypt coord. 2009—11). Avocations: painting, sports. Office: 7 Ahram St Heliopolis Cairo 11341 Egypt Office Phone: 20222908432. Office Fax: 2222908432.

ELEUTHERIO, ELIS CRISTINA ARAUJO, biochemist, educator; b. Rio de Janeiro, Oct. 19, 1965; Degree in Chem. Engring., UFRJ, 1988, PhD, 1997. Investigator UFRJ, 1998, prof., 1998—. Mem.: Brazilian Biochemistry & Molecular Biology Soc. Office: Ave Athos Da Silveira Ramos Ct BL A 547 Rio De Janeiro 21941909 Brazil Office Fax: 55-21-25627826. Business E-Mail: eliscael@iq.ufrj.br.

ELFANT, ADAM B., gastroenterologist, educator; MD, U. Medicine and Dentistry of NJ. Diplomate Am. Bd. Internal Medicine-gastroenterology, Am. Bd. Internal Medicine. Intern Cooper Univ. Hosp., resident; fellow The Wellesley Hosp., Canada; assoc. prof. Medicine; hosp. affiliation includes Virtua Voorhees Hosp. Office: Cooper University Hospital One Cooper Plz Camden NJ 08103 Office Phone: 856-342-2000.

EL GAMMAL, STEPHAN, dermatologist, allergologist, phlebologist; b. London, June 28, 1957; s. Joseph El Gammal and Helga Bremme; m. Claudia Popp. Med. state exam, Ruhr U., Bochum, Germany, 1983, MD, 1984, Priv. Doz. Dr. med. habil., 1998. Sr. doctor Dermatological Clinic Ruhr U., Bochum, chief dept. phlebology, angiology and lymphology, 1995-2000; chief doctor dermatol. clinic Hosp. Bethesda, Freudenberg, Germany, 2000—, prof. hon., 2010. Mem. Internat. Soc. Biophys. & Imaging Skin (treas.). Achievements include research in non-invasive skin imaging methods, biomedical engineering, vascular and inflammatory diseases, skin tumors, operative and aesthetic dermatology. Office: Derma Clinic Hosp Bethesda Euelsbruchstr 39 D-57258 Freudenberg Germany

ELGAZZAR, REDA FOUAD, oral surgeon, educator; b. Tanta, Algharbia, Egypt, Nov. 30, 1963; s. Fouad Mohammed Elgazzar and Soad Rezk Elshorbagy; m. Sahar Elsayed Elmahallawy, July 23, 2003; children: Israa Reda, Omar Reda, Mohammed Reda, Salma Reda. B Dental Surgery, Tanta U., Egypt, 1987; MSc in Dentistry, Tanta U., 1993; PhD in Dentistry, Dundee U., Scotland, 2000. Dental ho. officer faculty dentistry Tanta U., 1988—89, demonstrator, oral surgery, 1990—93, asst. lectr. oral and maxillofacial surgery, 1993—2001, asst. prof. oral and maxillofacial surgery, 2001—06; asst. lectr. oral and maxillofacial surgery Dundee Dental Hosp. and Sch., 1997—2000; assoc. prof. oral and maxillofacial surgery, Coll. Dentistry King Faisal U., Dammam, Saudi Arabia, 2006—08; assoc. prof. faculty, dentistry Manitoba U., OMS Dental Diagnostic & Surg. Scis., 2008—. Contbr. rsch. papers to profl. publs. Chmn. Society Devel. Assn., Tanta, 1990—96. Soldier Air Force, 1989—90, Cairo, Egypt. Grantee, King Faisal U., 2006—. Mem.: Brit. Dental Coun. (temp.), European Assn. Cranial Maxillofacial Surgery (assoc.), Internat. Assn. Oral and Maxillofacial Surgery (assoc.), Egyptian Dental Syndicate (assoc.). Islam. Achievements include research in modefied technique for reconstruction of the lower jaw after TMJ ankylosis using intraoral distractor; prediction and early diagnosis of oral cancer; lip and Maxillary alveolar cleft using ultrasonic waves and Platelet Rich Plasma for enhancing bone healing; impacted lower 3rd molar: difficulty evaluation and complications. Avocations: reading, swimming, travel. Office Fax: 00966 3 8572624; Home Fax: 0020403345314. Personal E-mail: reda_elgazzar@yahoo.co.uk. Business E-Mail: elgazzar@cc.umanitoba.ca.

ELGEE, NEIL JOHNSON, retired internist, endocrinologist, educator; b. Oxford, NS, Can., Apr. 3, 1926; arrived in U.S., 1946, naturalized, 1955; s. William Harris and Lucile (Nevers) Elgee, m. Leona Victoria Karlsson, Aug. 18, 1951; children: Joan, Susan, Laurie, Steven, Karen. BSc, U. N.B., Can., 1946; MD, U. Rochester, 1950. Intern Peter Bent Brigham Hosp., Boston, 1950—51; resident Strong Meml. Hosp., Rochester, NY, 1951—52; fellow in endocrinology U. Wash., 1952—54, co-chief resident in medicine Seattle, 1954—55, clin. prof. medicine, 1968—93, emeritus clin. prof. medicine, 1993—; practice medicine specializing in endocrinology Seattle, 1957—93; retired, 1993. Founder, pres. Ernest Becker Found., 1993—. Capt. USAF, 1955—57. Master: ACP (gov. for Wash. and Alaska 1965—71, regent 1974—78); mem.: Inst. Medicine, Endocrine Soc. Home: 3621 72nd Ave SE Mercer Island WA 98040-3330 Office Phone: 206-232-2994. Business E-Mail: nelgee@u.washington.edu.

EL GHARIB, MOHAMED NABIH, gynecologist, educator; b. Egypt, July 28, 1945; married; 3 children. PhD in Ob-Gyn., 1979, diploma in Gen. Surgery, 1974, diploma in Ob-Gyn., 1971, MBBCH, 1969; diploma in Laparoscopic Surgery, Kiehl U., 1992. Lectr. ob-gyn. Tanta U. Projects Mgmt. Unit, 1979—, asst. prof. ob-gyn., 1984, prof. ob-gyn., 1989; ex chmn. ob-gyn. dept., 1999—2005; exec. dir. Tanta U. Projects Mgmt. Unit, 2003—06; emeritus prof. ob-gyn., 2005—. Evalution asst. prof. Sci. Com.; mem. adminstrn. bd. Egyptian Soc. Ob-Gyn., Egyptian Soc. Fertility & Sterility; editor Gynaecology Book, Obstetrics Book. Contbr. articles to profl. jours. Mem.: Am. Soc. Ob-Gyn. Muslim. Office: Dept Obstetrics Gynaecology Tanta Faculty Medicine Tanta University Tanta Egypt

EL-GOWILLY, SAHAR MAHMOUD, medical educator; b. Alexandria, Egypt, Nov. 7, 1972; BSc, Alexandria U., 1995, PhD, 2004. Asst. prof., pharmacology Faculty Pharmacy Alexandria U., 2004—. Recipient ACDIMA award, Co. Drug Industries and Med. Appliances, Amman, Jordon. Office: Sultan Hussain Alexandria 123456 Egypt Personal E-mail: saharelgowelly@yahoo.com.

EL HADJ OTHMANE, TAHA, physician; b. Damascus, Mar. 20, 1970; MD, Semmelweis Med. U., PhD, 2001. Physician Semmelweis U., 2001. Home: Szigligeti U 5 Budapest 1193 Hungary Personal E-mail: tahaothmane@yahoo.com.

EL HAGE, WISSAM, psychiatrist, researcher; m. Celine Descriaud, July 7, 2000; children: Anice, Lisa. MS in Biology, U. François Rabelais, Tours, France, 1999, MD, 2002, PhD, 2003. Cert. Psychiatrist U. François Rabelais, 2002. Resident U. Hosp Tours, 1997—2002, sr. registrar, assistantship Dept. Psychiatry, 2002—04, med. practitioner Dept. Psychiatry, 2004—; rschr. U. François Rabelais, 2003—. Contbr. scientific papers to profl. jours. Mem.: French Assn. for Study of Stress and Trauma. Office: CPU U Hosp CHRU of Tours Cedex 1 Tours 37044 France Office Fax: + 33 2 47 47 80 43. Business E-Mail: el-hage@med.univ-tours.fr.

EL-HANAFY, EHAB ALI, medical educator; b. Domitte, Dec. 7, 1972; MS, Port Said U., 1996. Lectr. gastrointestinal surgery Mansoura U., Dakahlia, Egypt, 1998. Office: Gehan St Mansoura Dakahlia 35516 Egypt Personal E-mail: dr_ehab_elhanafy@yahoo.com.

EL HASSANE, SIDIBÉ, endocrinologist, researcher; b. Thilene Dagana, Saint-Louis Du Senegal, Senegal, May 12, 1951; s. Sidibé Moussa and Kane Aissatou; m. Amsatou Sow; children: Sidibé Bintou Alice, Sidibé Aissatou, Sidibé Caab Ousmane, Sidibé Hussein Moussa. Aggregated, Cames, Ouagadougou Burkina faso, 1998—2007; MSc, Paris 7, 2001. Endocrinology Metabolism Edn. Nationale France Minstre, 2001, Cames, 1998, Medecine Endo-Metabolism Cmhp, 1986, Medecine Dakar université, 1984. Hosp. intern Ministry Health, Dakar, 1977—84; resident CMhP, Paris, 1984—86; endocrinologist Dakar U., Senegal, 1984—2008; intern asst. resident mc Coll. Med. Hosp. Paris, 1984—; prof. endocrinology metabolism Ouagadougou burkina faso, Cames, 2007—08. Is Senghor Found. grant, 1984. Mem.: Soc. Arts Letters, NY Acad. Sci., Acad. European Sci. Art Letter (paris 1998—2003, prof. endocrinology 2007). Office: Univ Paris 7 Fmpos-Ucad 10 Ave Verdun Paris 75010 France Home: Villa 2a Rue 1xc Point E Dakar Senegal Business E-Mail: sidibeeh@refer.sn.

EL-HEFNAWY, AHMED SOBHY, urologist, educator; b. Mansoura, May 15, 1975; MB BChir, Mansoura Faculty Medicine, 2000, MSc, MD, Mansoura Faculty Medicine, 2009. Resident urology Mansoura UNC, Faculty Medicine, Mansoura U., 2001—05, clin. demonstrator, 2005, asst. lectr. urology, 2005—10, rschr., lectr. urology, 2010—. Recipient Gold medal, Mansoura U., 2000. Mem.: Egyptian Med. Syndicate (Ideal Med. Staff Faculty 2010), Egyptian Urology Assn., European Assn. Urology. Office: El Gomhoria St Mansoura Dakahlia 35516 Egypt Office Fax: 0020502263717. Personal E-mail: a_s_elhefnawy@yahoo.com.

EL HELALI, NAJOUA, microbiologist; b. Fes, Morocco; PharmD, U. Paris, Chatenay Malabry; degree in Med. Biology Specialized Studies, U. Paris, degree in Antibiotics and Antibiotherapy, degree in Nosocomial Infections & Hosp. Hygiene. Cert. med. microbiologist Paris. Former clin. biology resident Paris Hosp.; parasitologist Tenon Hôsp., Paris, 1990—91, microbiologist, 1992—98, Bicêtre Hosp., Paris, Paris St. Joseph Hosp., 2010—. Expert Haute Autorité en Santé, Paris, 2001—02. Pres. Assn. Mosaiques Solidarité Maroc, Paris, 1999—2002. Recipient first award, French Soc. Perinatal Medicine, 2009. Mem.: Club XXI eme Siecle Assn. Office: Paris Saint Joseph Hosp 185 rue Raymond Losserand Paris 75674 France Personal E-mail: najele@gmail.com. Business E-Mail: nelhelali@hpsj.fr.

ELIAN, MARTA, neurologist, medical counsellor; b. Oradea, Romania; d. Laszlo Steiner and Magda Laszlo; m. Ezra Eilender Elian, Aug. 23, 1949 (dec. 1982); children: Amnon, Yoram. MD, Hebrew U., 1958; diploma in hypnotherapy/integral therapy, London, 1989; diploma in reality therapy, Dublin, 1993. Staff neurologist Children Med. Ctr., Boston, 1959-62; neurologist, sr. lectr. Tel Aviv Univ. Hosp., 1962-73; neurologist Hosp. for Epilepsy, Zurich, 1974-75; staff psychiatrist Psychiat. Hosp., Zurich, 1975-76; cons. neurophysiologist Nat. Health Svc., London, 1976-93, cons. neurologist, 1988—98; pvt. practice. Contbr. over 100 neurology med. counselling articles to profl. jours.; author: Research: Epidemiology of Multiple Sclerosis Continuing, I Have Less..., The Twins and I, 2011, A Humoristic Accounts on raising Twins. Avocations: travel, theater, music, languages. Home and Office: 32 A Queens Grove London NW8 6HJ England Office Phone: 0044207 7225508.

ELIANA, MARIA, medical educator; b. Desulo, Sardinia, Italy, July 16, 1948; MD, U. Cagliari, Sardinia, Italy, 1973. Cert. specialist in gastroenterology U. Cagliari, 1979, specialist in internal medicine U. Cagliari, 1984. Rsch. fellow, Inst. Infectious Diseases U. Cagliari, 1973—80, asst. prof. internal medicine Italy, 1975—2000, section head, adult thalassemic unit, 1985—, tchr. sch. infectious diseases, 1986—, tchr. sch. medicine, 1992—2003, assoc. prof. internal medicine, 2000—, dir., liver unit, 2006—, tchr. clin. examination, 2006—, dir., post-graduate sch. infectious disease, 2006—; rsch. fellow Lab Medicine, Viral Hepatitis, U. Calif., San Francisco, 1982—83. Mem.: NY Acad. Scis., Italian Soc. Internal Medicine, Italian Soc. Thalassemia. Achievements include research in HBVDNA sequences in the liver in the absence serological markers HBV infection; occult HBV infection in HBsAg negative sardinian blood donors; tracking the first introduction human immunodeficiency virus (HTV) into Sardinia in 1981. The prevalence increased from 0.7% in 1981 to 57% in 1987; HCV infection does not elicit protective immunity in the host in humans, in a prospective study repeatedly transfused thalassemic children; effect iron overload on the response to recombinant interferon-alpha treatment in transfusion-dependent patients with thalassemia major and chronic hepatitis C. Office: Dept Med Scis University Cagliari SS 554 Bivio Sestu 09042 Cagliari Italy Office Phone: 39-070-51096202. Business E-Mail: laie@medicina.unica.it.

ELIAS, JACK ANGEL, pulmonary care physician, medical educator; b. Fayetteville, Ark., Apr. 10, 1951; s. Gabriel and Alma (Kowalsky) Elias; m. Sandra Gross Elias, Jan. 3, 1981; 1 child, Lauren Rachel. BA, U. Pa., 1973, MD, 1976. Diplomate American Bd. Internal Medicine, American Bd. Allergy & Immunology, cert. in pulmonary and critical care medicine. Intern internal medicine Tufts-New Eng. Med. Ctr., Boston, 1976-77, resident internal medicine, 1977-78; sr. resident internal medicine U. Pa. Hosp., Phila., 1978—79, fellow allergy and immunology, pulmonary and critical care medicine, 1979-82, dir. Sarcoidosis & Interstitial Lung Disease Clinic, 1982—90; asst. prof. U. Pa. Sch. Medicine, Phila., 1982—88, assoc. prof., 1988-90; prof. medicine, chief pulmonary and critical care medicine Yale U. Sch. Medicine, New Haven, 1990—2006, Waldemar Von Zedtwitz prof. medicine, 2000—, chair dept. internal medicine, 2006—, prof. immunobiology, 2007—. Dir. Winchester Chest Clinic, New Haven, 1990—2006; chief pulmonary and critical care medicine Yale-New Haven Hosp., 1990—2006, dir. med. intensive care unit, 1991—92, physician-in-chief, 2006—, chief Beeson Med. Svc., 2006—; Pfizer vis. prof. allergic diseases and asthma U. Iowa, 1998; Harold & Marilyn Menkes Meml. lectr. Bloomberg Sch. Pub. Health, Johns Hopkins U. Sch. Medicine, 2005; coun. mem. Nat. Heart, Lung & Blood Inst., NIH, 2009—; Herbert Y. & Anne L. Reynolds grand rounds lectr. Penn State Milton S. Hershey Med. Ctr., 2010. Assoc. editor American Jour. Respiratory Cell & Molecular Biology, mem. editl. bd. Encyclopedia Respiratory Medicine, Jour. Lab. Investigation, Respiratory Rsch., Jour. Lab. & Clin. Medicine, American Jour. Medicine; contbr. articles to profl. jours. Fellow: ACP, American Coll. Chest Physicians; mem.: New Haven County Med. Assn., Pa. Thoracic Soc., Conn. Thoracic Soc., Laennac Soc., American Soc. Clin. Investigation, Assn. American Physicians, American Thoracic Soc. (v.p. 2010), American Lung Assn., Fedn. Societies Expl. Biology, American Assn. Immunologists, Reticuloendothelial Soc., American Fedn. Clin. Rsch., Inst. Medicine, American Acad. Allergy, Interurban Clin. Club, Alpha Omega Alpha, Phi Beta Kappa. Achievements include research in cellular and molecular pathogenesis of asthma and COPD, the cellular and molecular mechanisms of lung injury, repair and remodeling, and transgenic modeling of pulmonary diseases and disorders. Office: Yale U Sch Medicine PO Box 20856 330Cedar St Boardman Bldg Ste 10 New Haven CT 06520-3289 Office Phone: 203-785-4119. Office Fax: 203-785-6954. E-mail: jack.elias@yale.edu. *

ELIAS, MAURICE JESSE, psychology educator; b. Bronx, NY, Dec. 1, 1952; m. Ellen Sue Rosen, Aug. 7, 1976; children: Sara Elizabeth, Samara Alexandra. BA in Psychology summa cum laude, CUNY, 1974; MA in Clin. Psychology, U. Conn., 1977, PhD in Clin. Psychology, 1980. Psychotherapist mental health svc. U. Conn., Storrs, 1977-78; prevention planning cons. Conn. Dept. Children and Youth Svcs., 1978-79; asst. prof. psychology Rutgers U., New Brunswick, NJ, 1979-85, assoc. prof., 1985—94, prof., coord. internship program in applied-cmty. psychology, 1979—, field supr. psychol. clinic grad. sch., 1979—. Mem. co-adj. faculty dept. psychiatry U. Medicine and Dentistry N.J.-Robert Wood Johnson Med. Sch., 1985, Schwartzman family parenting program Am. Jerusalem Acad. for Contemporary Judaic Studies, 1987—; cons. to numerous pub. sch. dists., pvt. schs., community groups, presenter in field. Author: Social Problem Solving Interventions in the Schools, 1996, Promoting Social & Emotional Learnings: Guidelines for Educators, 1997, Emotionally Intelligent Parenting, 1999, Raising Emotionally Intelligent Teenagers, 2002, The Educator's Guide to Emotional Intelligence and Academic Achievement, 2006, Community Psychology: Linking Individuals and Communities, 2007, Urban Dreams: Stories of Hope Resilience, Character,2008; contbr. articles to profl. jours. Treas., trustee Middlesex County Resources for Menatlly Handicapped, Inc., 1981-83; bd. dirs. Nat. Orgns. Adv. Coun. Children, 1981-85, Prevention Coalition NJ, 1990-92; mem. Interagy. Youth Devel. Consortium, 1982-86, Nat. Coalition Against TV Violence, 1979-95; pres. religious sch. bd. edn. Highland Park Conservative Temple and Ctr., 1992-2004, trustee, 1992-2004; trustee Assn. for Children NJ, 1992—; exec. com. Collaborative for Academic of Social and Emotional Learning, 1995-2005. Grantee Rutgers U., 1979-83, 84-85, 85-87, William T. Grant Found., 1982-90, 99-2002, NIMH, 1982-85, 88, 99—, Middlesex County Mental Health Bd. and Bd. Chosen Freeholders, 1984-87, Schumann Found. NJ, 1987-89, 90-93, Fetzer Inst., 1995-99, John Templeton Found., 2002-07, NJ Dept. Edn., 2005-11; Lilly Endowment grantee, 1991-94, Surdna Found., 1999-2000, Novo Found., 2010-. Mem. ASCD, APA (Nat. Psychology award 1986, 88, Nat. Psychol. Cons. to Mgmt. award 1990, Disting. Contbn. to Practice award 1993, Ethnic Minority Mendoring award, 1998), Soc. Cmty. Rsch. & Action (pres., 2009-11), Nat. Assn. Sch. Psychologists, Phi Beta Kappa. Home: 139 N 5th Ave Highland Park NJ 08904-2924 Office: Tillett Hall Livingston Campus Rutgers U Dept Psychol New Brunswick NJ 08903 Office Phone: 848-445-2444. Business E-Mail: rutgersmjc@aol.com.

ELIASHIV, DAWN, neurologist, educator; b. Jerusalem, Apr. 3, 1960, MD, Sackler Sch. Medicine, 1985. Dir. Epilepsy Program and Neurophysiology Cedars Sinai Med. Ctr.; prof. medicine and neurology, UCLA David Geffen Sch. Medicine, Cedars Sinai Med. Ctr., David Geffen Sch. Medicine, 1994—. Fellow: Am. Clin. Neurophysiology Soc., Am. Acad. Neurology; mem.: Western Clin. Neurophysiology Soc., Am. Soc. Neurophysiol. Monitoring, Am. Epilepsy Soc. Office: 8700 Beverly Blvd Los Angeles CA 90048 Business E-Mail: eliashivd@cshs.org.

ELIASOVA, IRENA, geneticist; b. Prague, Czech Republic, May 24, 1982; MS, Charles U., Prague, 2007. Gennet Reproduction Genetic Co., 2008—. Genetic cons. Home: V Podluzi 5 Prague 14000 Czech Republic Personal E-mail: i.eliasova@seznam.cz.

ELIBOL, TARIK, gastroenterologist, educator; b. Sept. 1, 1939; s. Ismail Cemal and Nuriye (Tutkun) E.; m. Eileen Elibol, Aug. 30, 1997; children: Kimberly, Lisa, David, Adam, John. MD, U. Istanbul, 1964. Resident in internal medicine E.J. Meyer Hosp. U. Buffalo, 1964-66; fellow in gastroenterology Cleve. Clinic, 1966-68; clin. asst. prof. medicine U. Buffalo, 1975—; practice medicine specializing in digestive diseases Buffalo, 1969—97; primary care practice in internal medicine, 2004—. Former chief of staff DeGraff Meml. Hosp. Fellow ACP, Am. Coll. Gastroenterology; mem. Am. Soc. Internal Medicine, Am. Soc. Gastrointestinal Endoscopy, NY State Med. Soc., Erie County Med. Soc., Western NY Soc. Gastrointestinal Endoscopy (past pres.), Western NY Gastrointestinal Liver Soc. (pres. 1980—), Western NY Physician Found. (pres. 1980—). Home: 55 Leicester Rd Buffalo NY 14217-2111 Office: 2949 Elmwood Ave Kenmore NY 14217-1356

ELIDAN, JOSEF, otolaryngologist, educator; b. Jerusalem, July 17, 1945; s. Aahron and Bronia Elidan; m. Sara Frish, Apr. 12, 1967; children: Sharon, Gal, Orly. MD, Hebrew U., Jerusalem, 1970. Resident in otolaryngology Hadassah U. Hosp., Jerusalem, 1977-81, sr. physician, 1981-84, 86-90, head dept. otolaryngology, 1991—. Fellow UCLA, 1984-86; lectr. Med. Sch. Hebrew U., Jerusalem, 1981-86, sr. lectr., 1987-90, assoc. prof., 1991-99, full prof., 1999—. Inventor system for induction of vestibular evoked potentials, 1981, 89, balloon catheter for intraesophageal pressure measurements, 1991. Maj. Israeli Med. Corp, 1971-73. Recipient Outstanding Rsch. award Faculty of Medicine, 1982; grantee Ministry of Sci., 1987-89, Israel-U.S. Binat. Fund, 1991-93, 94-95, Ministry of Health, 1992-93. Mem.: Israeli Soc. Lasers in Surgery and Medicine (pres. 2003—), Israeli Soc. Otolaryngology, Head and Neck Surgery (pres. 1997—2003), Collogium Otorhinolaryngologicum, The Barany Soc., Assn. Rsch. in Otolaryngology, Am. Acad. Otolaryngology, Israel Med. Assn. Avocation: playing violin. Home: 30 Hantke St Jerusalem 96629 Israel Office: Hadassah U Hosp Ein Kerem 91120 Jerusalem Israel Office Phone: 972-2-6776469, 972-2-6419864. Business E-Mail: elidan@hadassah.org.il.

ELIN, RONALD JOHN, pathologist, educator; b. Mpls., Apr. 14, 1939; s. John Matthew and Helen Sophia Elin; m. Susan May Krogh, June 14, 1969; children: Derek, Justin. BA, U. Minn., 1960, BS, 1962, MD, 1966, PhD, 1969. Diplomate Am. Bd. Pathology, Am. Bd. Clin. Chemistry. Intern U. Hosp. Calif., San Diego, 1969-70; commd. med. officer USPHS, 1970, advanced through grades to med. dir., 1975; staff assoc. Nat. Inst. Allergy and Infectious Diseases NIH, Bethesda, Md., 1970-73, resident clin. pathology dept., 1973-74, chief clin. pathology dept., 1975-97, chief chemistry svc., 1977-97; vice chmn.

pathology U. Louisville, Ky., 1997—2001, chmn. dept. pathology and lab. medicine, 2002. Clin. prof. Uniformed Svcs. U. of Health Scis., Bethesda, 1978-97; initiator, first chmn. Gordon Rsch. Conf. on Magnesium in Biomed. Processes and Medicine, 1978. Contbr. more than 230 articles to profl. jours. Decorated Commendation medal USPHS, 1980, Meritorious Svc. medal USPHS, 1984. Fellow Am. Coll. Nutrition, Coll. Am. Pathologists, Am. Soc. Clin. Pathologists; mem. Am. Assn. Pathologists, Am. Assn. Clin. Chemistry (Outstanding Contbns. to Clin. Chemistry in a Selected Area of Rsch. award 1994), Acad. Clin. Lab. Physicians and Scientists (sec.-treas. 1985-87, pres. 1990-91, Gerald T. Evans award 1995). Lutheran. Achievements include research on magnesium metabolism, properties of endotoxin. Office: U Louisville Hosp Dept Pathology and Lab Medicine 627 S Preston St Rm 210 Louisville KY 40202-1675 Home Phone: 502-500-0236; Office Phone: 502-852-4464. Business E-Mail: rjelin01@louisville.edu.

ELINSON, JACK, social sciences educator; b. NYC, June 30, 1917; s. Sam and Rebecca (Block) Elinson; m. May Gomberg, July 5, 1941; children: Richard, Elaine, Mitchell, Robert. BS, CCNY, 1937; MA, George Washington U., 1946, PhD, 1954. Social sci. analyst Dept. Def., Washington, 1942-51; sr. study dir. Nat. Opinion Research Center, 1951-56; asst. prof. sociology U. Chgo., 1954-56; assoc. prof. adminstrv. medicine Columbia U., NYC, 1956-64, prof. adminstrv. medicine, 1964-68, prof. sociomed. scis. and sociology, 1968-86, prof. emeritus, 1986—; Service fellow Nat. Center Health Stats., 1977-81; vis. prof. behavioral scis. U. Toronto, 1969-77; Disting. vis. prof. Inst. Health Care Policy, Rutgers U., 1986-89, Disting. sr. scholar, 1990—; vis. prof. Robert Wood Johnson Med. Sch. (formerly Rutgers Med. Sch.), Univ. Medicine and Dentistry of N.J., 1986—; dir. program evaluation dept. patient care Harlem Hosp. Ctr., 1966-71. Bd. dirs. Med. and Health Rsch. Assn., NYC, 1977—89, Bergen County N.J. Tb and Health Assn., 1960—65; mem. adminstrv. bd. Bur. Applied Social Rsch. Columbia U., 1970—75; co-dir. health care orgn. and adminstrn. track Program for Master's in Pub. Health Rutgers U.-U. Medicine and Dentistry of N.J., 1983—92. Co-author (with R.E. Trussell): Chronic Illness in a Rural Area, 1959; co-author: (with J.J. Williams and R.E. Trussell) Family Medical Care Under Three Types of Health Insurance, 1962; co-author: (with E. Padilla and M. Perkins) Public Image of Mental Health Services, 1967; editor (with A.E. Siegmann): Sociomedical Health Indicators, 1979; editor: (with A. Mooney and A. Siegmann) Health Goals and Health Indicators: Policy, Planning and Evaluation, 1977; editor: (with N.K. Wenger, M.E. Mattson and C.D. Furberg) Assessment of Quality of Life in Clinical Trials of Cardiovascular Therapies, 1984. Recipient Nat. Merit award, Delta Omega Soc., 1982, Festschrift, spl. issue of Social Sci. and Medicine, 1989; named Jack Elinson Sociomed. Scis. Libr., Columbia U. Sch. Pub. Health, 1998. Fellow: APHA (1st award Assn. Social Scis. in Health 1984), Am. Assn. Pub. Opinion Rsch. (pres. 1979—80, Exceptionally Disting. Achievement award 1993), Am. Sociol. Assn. (chmn. med. sociology, Leo G. Reeder award 1985), AAAS; mem.: Med. and Health Rsch. Assn. N.U.C. (bd. dirs.), N.J. Pub. Health Assn. (exec. bd., Dennis J. Sullivan award 1990), N.Y.C. Pub. Health Assn. (bd. dirs.), Inst. Medicine NAS. Office: Columbia U Sch Pub Health Dept Sociomed Scis 600 W 168th St New York NY 10032-3722 Personal E-mail: jelinson@juno.com. Business E-Mail: je7@columbia.edu.

ELITO, JULIO, JR., obstetrician; b. São Paulo, Brazil, Aug. 6, 1966; s. Julio and Naciba Anauate Elito. MD, Fed. U. of São Paulo, 1989. Board Certified Diplomate Ministry of Edn., Brazil, 1989. Chief of videolaparoscopy sector Fed. U. of São Paulo, 1995—, prof. of dept. of obstetrics, 1999—. Directorships First Aid of Obstetrician of Fed. U. of São Paulo, 1996—; cons. Bd. of Medicine, São Paulo, 2000—. Contbr. articles to profl. jours. Pacific. Cath. Achievements include research in predictive score for the systemic treatment of unruptured ectopic pregnancy with a single dose of methotrexate. Avocations: travel, squash. Office: Clinica de GO e Laparoscopia Dr Elito Rua Barata Ribeiro 490 - Cj 101 01308-000 São Paulo Brazil Office Fax: 55-11-31235626. Personal E-mail: elitojjr@hotmail.com.

ELJAMEL, MUFTAH SALEM, neurosurgeon, computer programmer; b. Misurata, Libya, Jan. 1, 1957; s. Salem M. and Amna H. Eljamel; m. Adoracion Rodolfo, May 30, 1985; children: Sarah, Sana, Samir. MB, BCh with honors, Alfateh U., Libya, 1982; MD with distinction, Liverpool U., Eng., 1992. Sr. house officer emergency medicine Tripoli (Libya) Ctrl., 1985; neurosurgical sr. house officer Richmond Hosp., Dublin, 1985—86; surg. sr. house officer Dublin, Ireland, Monklands DG Hosp., Airdrie, Scotland, 1987; neurosurgical registrar Walton Hosp., Liverpool, England, 1987—91; sr. neurosurgical registrar Beaumont Hosp., Dublin, 1991—; cons., surgeon, clin. leader, dept. head Ninewells Hosp. and Med. Sch.; trained in neurosurgery Walton Ctr. for Neurology and Neurosurgery, Liverpool, England, 1987—91, Nat. Ctr. for Neurology and Neurosurgery, Dublin, 1991—94; fellow neurosurgery U. Conn. /Hartford Hosp, 1995—. Nat. panelist. Contbr. more than 100 articles to profl. jours. Recipient First Honor award Nat. Ednl. Bd., Misurata, 1976. Fellow: Am. Biog. Inst. (Man of Yr. 1993), Royal Coll. Surgeons (neurosurgery), Royal Coll. Surgeons (Ireland); mem.: Am. Stergotactic and Functional Neurosurgery Assn., N.Am. Skull Base Soc., Internat. Stereotactic Radiosurgery, Internat. Neuro-Modulation Soc., N.Y. Acad. Scis., Brit. Neurosurgical Soc., Royal Acad. Medicine., Internat. Assn. for Study of Pain. Achievements include research in special rsch. Stergotactic and functional neurosurgery for PD, MS, Dystonia, Skull-base surgery including acoustic neuroma & Meningiomas key-hole and image guided Surgery. Avocations: golf, football, swimming, tennis, computer tech. Office: Ninewells Hosp & Med Sch Dept Neurosurgery S Block 6 Lvl DD1 9SY Dundee Scotland E-mail: m.s.eljamel@dundee.ac.uk.

ELKHADEM, AMR HOSNY, dental educator; b. Giza, Egypt, May 4, 1979; B, Cairo U., 2002, M, 2008. Asst. lectr. prosthodontics, faculty oral and dental medicine Cairo U., 2004—. Avocations: reading, soccer. Home: 5 Jasmine Bldg Zahraa Elmaadi Cairo 11435 Egypt Personal E-mail: amrelkhadem@gmail.com.

EL KHADEM, HASSAN SAAD, chemistry professor, researcher; b. Cairo, Mar. 24, 1923; naturalized, 1975; s. Saad S. and Nimet (Zulficar) El K.; m. Nadia M. Said, Sept. 6, 1951 (dec. 2002); children: Samiha, Saad. DSc Tech., ETH Zurich, Switzerland, 1950; PhD, Imperial Coll., London, 1952; DSc, U. London, 1967; BSc with honors, Cairo U., 1946; DSc, U. Alexandria, Egypt, 1963. Lectr. Alexandria U., 1952-58, asst. prof., 1958-64, prof. organic chemistry, 1964-71; prof. chemistry Mich. Tech. U., Houghton, 1971-74, head dept. chemistry and chem. engring., 1974-80, pres. prof. chemistry, 1980-84; Isbell prof. chemistry The Am. U., Washington, 1984-93, Isbell prof. chemistry emeritus, 1993—. Author: Synthetic Methods for Carbohydrates, 1976, Carbohydrate Chemistry: Monosaccharides and their Oligomers, 1988, Anthracycline Antibiotics, 1982, others; mem. editl. bd. Carbohydrate Rsch., 1966-92; contbr. articles and book chpts. on carbohydrates and medicinal chemistry to profl. jours. Fulbright scholar U.S. Dept. State, Ohio State U., Columbus, 1963-64; recipient Phys. Sci. award Washington Acad. Sci., 1992. Mem. AAAS, Am. Chem. Soc. (chmn. carbonhydrate div. 1984-85, Melville L. Wolfrom award 1989), Sigma Xi. Achievements include discovery of a lost Greek manuscript by Zosimos (300 A.D.) translated to Arabic in a twelveth century Alchemy book (donated to the Libr. of Congress); patents in field. Home: 4948 Sentinel Dr Apt 101 Bethesda MD 20816-3586 Office: Am U Dept Chemistry Beeghly Bldg 4400 Massachusetts Ave NW Washington DC 20016-8001

EL-KHAIRY, LINA YASER, nutritionist, educator; b. Jerusalem, Palestine, Jan. 1, 1974; d. Yaser Jalal and Iffat Ibrahim El-Khairy. MPhil, U. of Bergen, Norway, 2003; PhD, U. Bergen, Norway. Rsch. fellow U. of Bergen, Bergen, Norway, 1999—2003; asst. prof. Al-Quds U., East Jerusalem, Palestine, 2004—. Contbr. articles to profl. jours. Office: Al Quds U Abu dees East Jerusalem Palestine

EL-KHALDY, MONTASER FAYEK, health and safety specialist; b. Tripoli, Libya, Apr. 18, 1975; s. Fayek Erabi El-khaldy and Alba Metawa Abdel Hamid. B Medicine B Surgery, U. Mysore, Karnataka State, India, 1998; diploma in Safety Mgmt., Internat. Air Transp. Assn. Tng. and Devel. Inst., Montreal, Can., 2006, diploma in Aviation Studies, 2009. Rotatory housemanship J.S.S. Hosp., Mysore U., India, 1998—99; med. officer dept. ob-gyn. Victoria Hosp., Mahé, Seychelles, 1999, med. officer dept. pediat., 1999—2000, med. office dept. casualty and emergency, 2000, med. officer dept. pediat., 2000—01, sr. med. officer dept. pediat., 2001; sr. med. officer primary health care divsn. Glacis Clinic, Mahé, 2001—02, sr. med. officer dept. pediat., 2002—03. Presenter in field. Mem.: Internat. Assn. Mil. Flight Surgeon Pilots, Flight Safety Found., Aerospace Med. Assn., Seychelles Med. and Dental Assn. Avocations: bodybuilding, exercise, photography, travel, movies. Home: PO Box 21274 Ajman United Arab Emirates Office Phone: 971 50 4288750. Office Fax: 971 6 7490622. Business E-Mail: drmont75@hotmail.com.

EL-KHAZEN, MARWAN, surgeon; MD, Dusseldorf Germany, 1982. With St. Vincez Hosp., Germany, Lennep Hosp., Germany; orthopedic surgeon Emirates Hosp. Recipient Svc. Excellence award, DOMHS, 2005. Mem.: Aerzte Kammer Assn. Germany Switzerland, AO / ASIF Assn. Internat. Fixation Switzerland, Arthrocopy Assn. Office: Emirates Hospital PO Box 73663 Jumeirah Beach Rd Jumeirah 2 Dubai United Arab Emirates Office Phone: 97143496666. Office Fax: 97143983400. *

ELLEDGE, RICHARD M., oncologist; married; 1 child. BA in Zoology with honors, U. Tex., Austin, 1977; MD, U. Tex. Med. Sch., Houston, 1981. Cert. Am. Bd. Internal Medicine, Am. Bd. Internal Medicine-Med. Oncology, Tex. State Bd. Med. Examiners. Med. dir., Breast Cancer Ctr. Baylor Coll. Medicine, assoc. prof. medicine; intern, internal medicine Methodist Hosp., Dallas, 1981—82, resident, 1982—84; fellow, med. oncology U. Tex. Health Sci. Ctr., San Antonio, 1989—92. Mem. editl. bd. Breast Diseases: A Yearbook Quarterly, 2000—. Recipient Career Develop. Specialized Program for Rsch. Excellence, Breast Cancer, 1993; Tex. Divsn., Am. Cancer Soc. Oncology Fellowship award, 1991. Fellow: ACP; mem.: Am. Soc. Clin. Oncology, Am. Assn. for Cancer Rsch., Southwest Oncology Group, Phi Beta Kappa. Avocations: golf, running, classical music.

ELLENBOGEN, LEON, nutritionist, biochemist, retired pharmaceutical executive; b. NYC, May 3, 1927; s. Martin and Bella (Zalesnick) E.; m. Roslyn Barban, June 30, 1951; children: Kenneth Alan, Richard Glen, Cheryl Sue. BS, CCNY, 1949; MS, NYU, 1951; PhD, Ind. U., 1954. Technician and med. corpsman USN, 1945-47; rsch. technician Columbia U., NYC, 1949-51; teaching asst. gen. chemistry and biochemistry Ind. U., Bloomington, 1951-53; rsch. biochemist Lederle Labs., Am. Cyanamid Co., Pearl River, NY, 1953-59, sr. rsch. biochemist, group leader, 1959-77, chief nutritional sci., sr. assoc. dir. med. pharm. devel., 1977-95; asst. v.p. nutritional scis. Lederle Consumer Health divsn. Whitehall Robins Health Care, Am. Home Products, Madison, NJ, 1995-97; ret., 1997. Adj. prof. nutrition in medicine Cornell U. Med. Coll., 1978—2003; adj. prof. nutrition N.Y. Med. Coll., 1981—; adj. prof., adv. com. intrinsic factor Nat. Formulatory Com.; mem. sci. affairs com. Proprietary Assn., 1980-89. Contbr. numerous articles to profl. jours., tech. books; author, presenter abstracts and papers profl. meetings; editor Contemporary Issues in Clin. Nutrition, 1980—, guest editor vols. 2 and 12; editor Drug Nutrient Interactions, 1982-91; cons. editor Biochemistry, Jour. AMA, Am. Jour. Clin. Nutrition, Sci., The Med. Letter, Nutrition Reports Internat., Thrombosis Rsch., Jour. Medicinal Chemistry, Archives Biochem. and Biophys., Annals Internal Medicine, Jour. Biol. Chemistry, Biochem. Pharmacology. Pharmacists mate USN, 1945-47. Recipient Steuben apple for contbns. to sci. rsch. Coun. for Responsible Nutrition. Fellow Am. Soc. Nutritional Scis., N.Y. Acad. Scis. (steering com. biochem. pharmacology discussion group 1973-77); mem. Am. Heart Assn., Am. Soc. Hematology, Am. Inst. Nutrition (nomenclature com.), Am. Soc. Clin. Nutrition, Am. Soc. Biol. Chemists, Am. Soc. Pharmacology and Exptl. Therapeutics, Am. Chem. Soc. (chmn. biochem. discussion group N.Y. sect. 1959, counselor divsn. biol. labs. 1977-79), Soc. Exptl. Biology and Medicine (editor proc. 1961-62), U.S. Pharmacopeia (com. on revision 1990-95, subcom. for nonprescription drugs and nutritional supplements 1995-2000, U.S. Pharmacopia Nutrition and Electrolytes Expert Com., expert com. on bioavailabilty and nutrient absorption of U.S. pharmacopia 2000-05), Sigma Xi, Phi Lambda Upsilon. Avocation: sports. Office: Wyeth Consumer Healthcare Madison NJ 07940-0871 Home Phone: 845-634-5731. Personal E-mail: ellenblr@aol.com.

ELLENBOGEN, PAUL H., radiologist; b. Port Chester, NY, Apr. 8, 1947; s. Andrew A. and Lillian M. Ellenbogen; m. Maxine Platt Ellenbogen, June 24, 1972; children: Jeffrey, Marc. ScB, Brown U., Providence, 1969; MD, SUNY, NYC, 1973. Diplomate Am. Bd. Radiology. Radiologist Radiology Assocs. North Tex., Dallas, 1978—. Pres. Tex. Radiol. Soc., 2001. Fellow: Am. Inst. Ultrasound in Medicine, Am. Coll. Radiology (spkr. ACR Coun. 2002—04, treas. 2006—, vice chmn. bd. chancellors 2010—). Office: Presbyn Hosp Dallas 8200 Walnut Hill Ln Dallas TX 75231 Office Phone: 214-345-7770.

ELLENBOGEN, RICHARD G., neurosurgeon, educator; b. Suffern, NY, Apr. 10, 1958; BS in Biochemistry, Brown U., Providence, 1980; MD, Brown U. Med. Sch., 1983. Neurol. surgery intern Walter Reed Army Med. Ctr., Washington, 1983—84, chief pediatric neurosurgery, dir. surg. epilepsy program, 1990—97; resident dept. neurol. surgery Children's Hosp./Brigham & Women's Hosp., Harvard Med. Sch., Boston, 1984—89; assoc. prof. neurol. surgery U. Wash. Sch. Medicine, Seattle, 1997—2004, acting chmn. dept. neurosurgery, 2002—04, prof., chmn. dept. neurosurgery, 2004—. Chmn. neurosurgical residency programs Bethesda Naval Hosp./Walter Reed Army Med. Ctr., 1996—97; pediatric neurosurgeon Seattle Children's Hosp. & Regional Med. Ctr., 1997—; chief divsn. neurol. surgery Harborview Med. Ctr., Seattle, 1998—, Theodore S. Roberts endowed chair pediatric neurosurgery, 1999—; co-chmn. NFL Head, Neck, & Spine Medical Com., 2010—. Author/editor (textbook) Principles of Neurosurgery, 2004. Comdr. 252nd Med. XVIII Airborne Corp US Army, Operation Desert Shield/Desert Storm, Saudi Arabia. Recipient Sidney Farber award for Most Outstanding Physician, Harvard Med. Sch., 1989; named a Top Doc in Adult & Pediatric Neurosurgery, Seattle Mag., 2006—08. Fellow: ACS; mem.: Soc. Neurol. Surgeons, Congress Neurol. Surgeons (pres. 2005—06). Office: Harborview Med Ctr U Wash Dept Neurosurgery Box 359924 325 Ninth Ave Seattle WA 98104 also: Ninth & Jefferson Bldg 908 Jefferson St Fifth Fl Seattle WA 98104 Office Phone: 206-987-4525. Office Fax: 206-987-3925. E-mail: rge@u.washington.edu. *

ELLENBY, MILES S., pediatrician, educator; b. Chgo., Aug. 24, 1964; MD, U. Chgo., 1991; MSEE, U. Ill., Urbana-Champaign, 1987. Assoc. prof. pediat. critical care medicine Oreg. Health & Sci. U., 2000—, med. dir. telemedicine program, 2006—. Office: Oreg Health and Sci University 707 SW Gaines St Portland OR 97239-2901 Office Fax: 503-494-4951. Business E-Mail: ellenbym@ohsu.edu.

ELLENSON, LORA HEDRICK, medical educator; b. Oreg., Oct. 13, 1958; AB, U. Calif., Berkeley, 1980; MD, Stanford Sch. Medicine, 1986. Assoc. prof. Johns Hopkins Med. Instn., 1986—97; prof. Weill Cornell Med. Coll., 1998—. Rsch. grant, Nat. Cancer Inst. Mem.: Am. Soc. Investigative Pathology. Office: 525 E 68th St New York NY 10065 Office Fax: 212-746-8079. Business E-Mail: lora.ellenson@med.cornell.edu.

ELLIOTT, CHRISTOPHER ROBERT BYRNE, surgeon; b. Brisbane, Australia, Jan. 15, 1985; B in Vet. Sci., U. Queensland, 2007. Vet. surgeon Blackdown Equine Clinic, 2011—. Mem.: Royal Coll. Vet. Surgeons. Avocation: rugby. Office: Blackdown Equine Clinic Midhurst Rd Fernhurst Surrey GU273EX England Personal E-mail: chrisbvsc@gmail.com.

ELLIOTT, DOUG, nursing educator; b. Australia, Apr. 17, 1960; PhD, U. Sydney, 1998. Prof. U. Tech., Sydney, 2006—. Office: Bldg 10 Level 7 Broadway NSW 2007 Australia Office Fax: 61-2-9514-4835. Business E-Mail: doug.elliott@uts.edu.au.

ELLIOTT, JOHN FOSTER, psychotherapist, writer; b. Pitts., Jan. 21, 1952; s. Victor and Ruth Elliott; m. Beth Tamara Kesselman, Dec. 18, 1982. BSc in Cmty. Devel. cum laude, Pa. State U., 1974; MA, Internat. Coll., LA, 1981. Cert. clin. hypnotist Calif. Bd. Behavioral Scis., 1983. Founder, exec. dir. OD Drug Crisis Intervention, State College, Pa., 1972—74; founder, exec. dir., clin. dir. Sunrise Cmty. Counseling, LA, 1976—82; marriage and family therapist John F. Elliott & Assocs., North Hollywood, Calif., 1982—. Cons. Law Enforcement Assistance Adminstrn., State College, Pa., 1971—72, Nat. Free Clinic Coun., Washington, 1974, Project Heavy, LA, 1976—78, Luth. Social Svcs., LA, 1979—82, Impact Ho., Pasadena, Calif., 1982—84, Calif. State Assembly, Sacramento, 1982, Calif. Bd. Behavioral Sci. Examiners Orals Commn., LA, 1983, Pasadena HS Peer Counseling Program, 1983; mem. psychology grad. and undergrad. faculty Internat. Coll., 1983—85. Author: Grassroots Gestalt in Gestalt Therapy and Beyond, 1980, The Rock and Roll BIble of Collaborative Therapy in Heroic Clients, Heroic Agencies, Partners for Change, 2001, Directions In Life for the Occasionally Confused, 2004. Bd. dirs. LA County Drug Abuse Task Force, 1975, Kadima Conservatory of Music Inc., Sherman Oaks, Calif., 2003—. Recipient Eric Walker award for outstanding sr. grad., Pa. Sate U., 1974, Dist. Ten award, LA City Coun., 1979, Dist. Four award, 1982, citation, California State Assembly, 1979, Diogenes Lantern award, Psychjourney, 2004. Mem.: Calif. Assn. Marriage and Family Therapists (assoc.). Office: 6442 Coldwater Canyon Ste 114 North Hollywood CA 91606 Office Fax: 818-509-9536. Business E-Mail: jfelliott@aol.com.

ELLIOTT, LARRY PAUL, radiologist, educator; b. Manhattan, Kans., Oct. 16, 1931; s. Leonard Paul and Mary Elizabeth (Myers) E.; m. Betty Lou Hawkins, June 23, 1956; children: Laurie Lou, Mary Elizabeth, Larry Paul. BS, U. Fla., 1954; MD, U. Tenn., 1957. Intern John Gaston Hosp., Memphis, 1957-58; resident in pediat. and pediat. cardiology U. Fla. Hosp., 1958-61; resident in cardiac pathology and cardiovasc. radiology U. Minn. Hosp., 1961-65; assoc. prof. cardiac radiology Washington U. Med. Sch., St. Louis, 1966-67; prof. cardiac radiology U. Fla. Med. Sch., 1967-76; prof. radiology, dir. divsn. cardiac radiology U. Ala. Med. Sch., Birmingham, 1976-81; prof., chmn. dept. radiology Georgetown U. Sch. Medicine, 1981—97, clin. prof., chmn. emeritus, 1996—; clin. prof. radiology Emory U. Med. Ctr., Atlanta, 1997—, Med. U. S.C., 1999—. Chmn. Fac. Practice Group, 1989—; clin. prof. Med. U. S.C., 1999—. Author: Pekannens, 1959, The X-Ray Diagnosis Heart Disease, 1968, 79; editor: Radiology, 1967—, Cardiovascular and Interventional Radiology, 1979—, The Fundamentals of Cardiac Imaging in Infants, Children and Adults, 1990; assoc. editor cardiovasc. sect. Taveras Radiology, 1986; contbr. over 200 articles to med. jours. Vol. Charleston Area Therapeutic Riding Group; camp counselor North Charleston Recreation Inner City Group; tutor Gethsesman's Cmty. Ctr., North Charleston, SC. Recipient Disting. Alumnus award U. Fla., 1981, Outstanding Alumnus award U. Tenn. Med. Sch., 1993; grantee cardiac radiology Nat. Heart Inst., 1968-76, Allied Health Profl. Act, 1970. Fellow N.Am. Soc. Cardiac Radiology (pres. 1977-78), Am. Coll. Cardiology; mem. Radiol. Soc. N.Am., Soc. Cardiac Angiography, Am. Heart Assn., Soc. Thoracic Radiology (founding mem., pres. faculty practice group 1989-93). Home: 3 Ocean Point Dr Isle Of Palms SC 29451-3852

ELLIOTT, LESTER FRANKLYN, plastic surgeon; b. Macon, Ga., Oct. 18, 1950; s. Sewell and Mary Grace E.; m. Elizabeth Wilkinson, May 30, 1981; children: Mary Grace, Elizabeth Ballard. BA, Princeton U., 1972; MD, Vanderbilt Sch. Med., Nashville, 1976. Cert. Am. Bd. Plastic Surgery, Am. Bd. Surgery, lic. Ga., Tenn., La. Resident gen. surgery Vanderbilt U. Hosp., 1976—78, Tulane U. Hosp., New Orleans, 1978—80, chief resident gen. surgery, 1980—81; resident plastic surgery Emory U. Hosp., Atlanta, 1981—83; instr. surgery La. State U., New Orleans, 1983—85, asst. clin. prof. surgery, 1985—87; clin. asst. prof. surgery Emory U., 1987—; cosmetic surgeon Atlanta Plastic Surgery, 1987—, pres. Ga., 1995—2004. Researcher in field. Contbr. articles to profl. jours. Bd. dirs. Atlanta Ballet, 1996—. Clin. orthopaedic fellow Sahlgranska Hosp., Gothenberg, Sweden, 1975. Fellow Am. Coll. Surgeons; mem. Am. Soc. Aesthetic Plastic Surgery, Am. Cleft Palate Assn., Am. Soc. Plastic and Reconstructive Surgeons, Am. Soc. Maxillo-Facial Surgeons, Southeastern Soc. Plastic and Reconstructive Surgeons, La. State Med. Soc., Surg. Assn. La., Ga. Surg. Soc., Ga. Plastic Surgery Soc., New Orleans Surg. Soc., Orleans Parish Med. Soc., Maurice J. Jurkiewicz Soc., Alton Ochsner Surg. Soc., Southern Surgical Assn., Oneiro Travel Club, Cap and Gown Club, Kappa Alpha. Avocations: travel, golf, bicycling, mountain climbing, reading, marathons, hunting. Office: Atlanta Plastic Surgery PC 975 Johnson Ferry Rd NE STE 100 Atlanta GA 30342-1618 Office Phone: 404-256-1311, 888-298-0835. Office Fax: 404-250-3380. Business E-Mail: felliott@atlplastic.com.

ELLIOTT, RAY (J. RAYMOND ELLIOTT), biomedical device manufacturing company executive; b. 1950; BA, U. Western Ont., London, Ont., 1972. Various positions sales, mktg., ops., bus. devel., gen. mgmt. Am. Hosp. Supply Corp. (now Baxter Internat.), pres. Far East divsns. Tokyo; group pres. John Labatt Ltd.; pres., chmn. various divsns. Southam Inc., Toronto, Ont.; pres., CEO J.R. Elliott & Associates, Cybex International Inc., Medway, Mass., 1995—97; pres. Zimmer Holdings Inc., Warsaw, Ind., 1997—2001, chmn., pres., CEO, 2001—07; pres., CEO Boston Scientific Corp., Natick, Mass., 2009—. Bd. dirs., chair orthops. sector AdvaMed, Washington, 2003—; bd. dirs. Centerpulse, Ltd., 2003—, Boston Scientific Corp., 2007—, Bausch & Lomb Corp., Rochester, NY, 2008—. Bd. dirs. State of Ind. Workplace Devel. Bd.; trustee Orthop. Rsch. & Edn. Found., Rosemount, Ill., 2003—. Named Best CEO in America for Health Care (Medical Supplies and Devices), Instl. Investor mag., 2005. Office: Boston Scientific Corp One Boston Scientific Place Natick MA 01760-1537 *

ELLIOTT, ROBIN ANTHONY LISTER, foundation administrator; b. Newbury, Berkshire, Eng., Feb. 8, 1941; came to U.S., 1962; s. Dougan Arthur Robert Elliott and Ilene Isobel (Noyes) Paddick; m. Sheila Carol Gordon, July 21, 1974; children: Janna, Caroline. BA, Oxford U., 1962; MA, Columbia U., 1965. Dir. info./edn. Planned Parenthood Fedn. Am., NYC, 1971-79, dep. to chancellor CUNY, NYC, 1979-82, v.p. devel. and external affairs Hunter Coll., 1982-88; v.p. devel. and external affairs Tchrs. Coll., Columbia U., NYC, 1988—95; exec. dir. Parkinson's Disease Found., NYC, 1996—. Mem. bd. Ctr. for Population Options, Washington. Mem. Nat. Soc. Fundraising Execs. Episcopalian. Avocations: music, running. Office: Parkinson's Disease Found 710 West 168th St New York NY 10032 *

ELLIOTT-ZAHORIK, BONNIE, nurse, administrator; b. Algona, Iowa; AAS, Coll. Lake County, Grayslake, Ill.; student, U. Iowa, Iowa City; BS, U. St. Francis, Joliet, Ill.; MS, Nat. Louis U., Evanston, Ill.; grad., Kellogg Inst. Mgmt., Skokie, Ill., 2001. Bd. cert. nurse exec. advanced, 2009, critical incident stress debriefing provider, ACLS provider, 2005-07; cert. legal nurse cons. 2005-09. Chair coordinating coun. Vista Health, Waukegan, Ill., chair managerial coun., dir. telemetry/cardiac step-down unit; dir. med./surg. oncology, pediat. and adolescent units across the life span Vista Health/Victory Meml. Hosp., nursing adminstrn. mgr., 2004; legal nurse cons. Elliott Enterprises and Cons. Preceptor/mentor Graceland U., Parkside and St. Xavier U.; fellow doctorate program adminstrn. Walden U., 1995—96. Contbr. articles to profl. jours. Mem. combined appeal com., vol. Am. Heart Assn.; co-chair Victory Healthcare Svcs. Combined Appeal Campaign; mem. Ill. Gov. Workforce Met. Chgo. Health Care Coun., 2004—06, Workforce Coun. Health Care Leadership, Critical Skills Shortage Initiative, 2004—06; mem. healthcare adv. bd. Ill. Inst. Tech., 2004—06. Mem.: AACN, Ill. Centenial Celebration Licensed Nurses (spkr. on info, definition NPA Changes 2007), Ill. Nurse Practice Act, Sunset Com. (co-chair gen. info intro delinitions 2005—07), Gen. Info. Intro. Definitions, Ill. Orgn. Nurse Leaders (bd. dirs. 1991—, pres. 1998, past pres., state chmn. bylaws com. 1998—99, pres. 2000, strategic planning com. 2000—, pres. IONL region 2-B 2001), Ill. Coalition Nursing Resources (exec. bd. dir. 2000—09, legis. funding com. 2001—06, pres. 2004, co-chair ICNR perpetuity comm. 2006—09, exec. bd. dir. 2007—09), Ill. Coun. Nurse Mgrs. (past pres. Region 2B).

ELLIS, DEMETRIUS, pediatrics nephrologist; MD, State U. NY, 1973. Diplomate Am. Bd. Pediatrics, Am. Bd. Pediatrics-pediatric nephrology. Resident Children's Hosp. of Pitts. of UPMC, 1975, Univ. of Pitts.; fellow Children's Hosp. Nat. Med. Ctr., 1977, George Wash. Univ. Recipient Medical Research award, Gift of Life award. Mem.: Internat. Soc. of Pediatric Transplantation, Am. Soc. of Hypertension. Office: Children's Hospital of Pittsburgh of UPMC 1 Childrens Hospital Drive 4401 Penn Ave Pittsburgh PA 15224 Office Phone: 412-692-5182.

ELLIS, EUGENE JOSEPH, retired cardiologist; b. Rochester, NY, Feb. 23, 1919; s. Eugene Joseph and Violet (Anderson) E.; m. Ruth Nugent, July 31, 1943; children: Eugene J., Susan Ellis Renwick, Amy Ellis Miller. AB, U. So. Calif., LA, 1941; MD, U. So. Calif., 1944; MS in medicine, U. Minn., 1950. Diplomate Am. Bd. Internal Medicine and Cardiovascular Diseases. Intern L.A. County Hosp., 1944, resident, 1946; fellowship Mayo Clinic, Rochester, Minn., 1947-51; dir. dept. cardiology St. Vincent's Hosp., LA, 1953-55, Good Samaritan Hosp., LA, 1955-84, ret., 1984; prof. clin. medicine emeritus U. So. Calif., 1984—. Mem. Med. Bd. of Calif., 1984-91; pres., 1988; pres. Div. of Med. Quality, State of Calif., 1985-89; exec. com. trustees U. Redlands, 1976-86. Lt. USN, 1944-46. Contbr. articles to profl. jours. Bd. dirs. Cancer Found. Santa Barbara, Casa Dorinda Retirement Facility, Alcohol Coun. Santa Barbara; trustee Sansum-Santa Barbara Clinic, 2002-, Santa Barbara Mus. Natural History. Lt. USN, 1944-46. Fellow Am. Coll. Cardiology, Am. Heart Assn., Am Coll. Physicians; mem. L.A. Country Club, Birnam Wood Golf Club (bd. dirs. 1994-95), Valley Club of Montecito. Republican. Avocations: golf, fly fishing. Home: 300 Hot Springs Rd 208 Santa Barbara CA 93108

ELLIS, HAROLD, surgeon; b. London, Jan. 13, 1926; s. Samuel and Ada Ellis; m. Wendy Mae Levine; children: Jonathan, Suzanne. MBBCh, Oxford U., Eng., 1948, ChM, 1956, MD, 1962. Various surg. appointments, 1948—62; prof. surgery U. London, 1962—89; clin. anatomist Cambridge (Eng.) U., 1989—93, King's Coll., London, 1993—. Author 27 textbooks on surgery, anatomy and history. Capt. Royal Army Med. Corps, 1950—52. Named a Comdr. of the British Empire, 1987. Fellow: ACS, Royal Coll. Obstetricians and Gynecologists, Royal Coll. Surgeons (U.K.) (coun. 1974—87). Home: 16 Bancroft Ave London N2 0AS England Office: King's Coll London Dept Anatomy Guy's Campus London SE1 1UL England Home Phone: 0208348 2720; Office Phone: 0207188 2028.

ELLIS, HELENE RITA, social worker; b. St. Paul, Sept. 20, 1935; d. Moe and Cele (Sidletsky) Weisman; m. Bernard M. Ellis, Sept. 30, 1956; children: Miriam, Arienne, Elia, Evie. BS, U. Minn., 1956; MSW, Loyola U., 1974; PhD, Inst. Clin. Social Work, Chgo., 1996. Lic. clin. social worker, Ill.; bd. cert. diplomate. Tchr. Roosevelt High Sch., Mpls., 1957-58, Barrington (Ill.) High Sch., 1958-59; social worker Dist. #39 Schs., Wilmette, Ill., 1974—2003; pvt. practice Wilmette, 1996—. Adj. prof. Loyola U. of Chgo., 1996—; chairperson Dist. 39 Health and Safety Curriculum Project, Wilmette, 1987-92. Named Ill. Sch. Social Worker of Yr., Ill. Assn. Sch. Social Workers, 1997-98. Mem. NASW, Sch. Social Work Assn. Am., Am. Group Psychotherapy Assn., Ill. Assn. Sch. Social Workers (Social Worker of Yr. 1997-98), Pi Lambda Theta, Phi Beta Kappa, Alpha Sigma Nu. Office: 3330 Old Glenview Rd Wilmette IL 60091 Office Phone: 847-800-4408. Personal E-mail: helener18@gmail.com.

ELLIS, LESLIE ELAINE, clinical psychologist; d. Ira Milton and Evelyn Fogel Marks; m. Clyde Arthur Ellis, Jr., Feb. 16, 1969; children: David Michael, Eric Arthur. BA in Psychology, U. Fla., 1969, MA in Rehab. Counseling, 1972; PhD in Theatre, Fla. State U., 1982; MA in Psychology, Fielding Grad. Inst., 2002, PhD in Clin. Psychology, 2004. Cert. Rehab. Counselor Commn. Rehab. Counselor Certification, Rolling Meadows, Ill., Clin. Supr. Fla., lic. Mental Health Counselor, qualified rehab. profl. Instr. acting Fla. State U., 1982; instr. speech North Fla. Jr. Coll., Madison, Fla., 1983; dir. academic svcs. Profl. Employment Tng. Inc., Svcs., Clearwater, Fla., 1988—91; intern rehab. counseling Cognitive Rehab. Inst., Tampa, Fla., 1994—95; pvt. practice counselor, 1995—2003; intern clin. counseling Bay Area Psychol. Svcs., St. Petersburg, Fla., 1996—98; with Wein Ctr. Memory Disorders Mt. Sinai Hosp., Miami, Fla., 2001; intern neuropsychology Rehab. Solutions, Tampa, 2002—03; intern clin. psychology Counseling Ctr. U. South Fla., 2002—03; clin. dir. Genesis Behavioral Healthcare, Tampa; pres., clin. dir. Nat. Ednl. Training Sys. Inc., Lutz, Fla. Adj. instr. St. Petersburg (Fla.) Coll., 1991—94; adj. faculty Argosy U., Tampa, 2004—08; mem. com. Nat. Rehab. Counselors Cert. Exam, Princeton, NJ, 2002, Princeton, 04; cons. in field; presenter in field. Author: Lose Weight By Surgery, 1974, Nutrition Guide to Brand Name Baby Foods, 1977, Teacher's Guide to Dramatic Techniques for Use with Handicapped Students, 1982; actor(dancer): (plays) Desire Under the Elms, 1979; author (dir.): (films) Teenaged and Pregnant, 1982, (plays) Merfel's Magic Wand, 1982; dir.: (plays) Ghost of Canterville Hall, 1984; author: (songs) Theme Song Leon County Spl. Olympics, 1983; co-author: (plays) The Trial of Ruby McCollum, 2003 (Honorable Mention award Sundance, 2003); contbr. articles to profl. jours., newspapers, mags. Mem. spl. events com. Fla. State Spl. Olympics, 1980—83; adv. bd. Thomas County Schs., 1985—86; adv. com. Career Devel. Ctr. Thomas Area Tech. Sch., 1985; chmn. pubs. Am. Theatre Assn., 1982—83. Recipient Disting. Performance Design Spl. Needs Program, Nat. Alliance Bus., 1987, Outstanding Performance award, Gov. Ga., 1987, Gov. Fla., 1989. Mem.: APA (student sci. com. 1999—2003), Phi Kappa Phi, Eta Rho Pi. Democrat. Jewish. Achievements include patents for book hanging device. Office: Nat Ednl Training Sys Inc 207 Crystal Grove Blvd Lutz FL 33548 Personal E-mail: lesliee@tampabay.rr.com.

ELLIS, MATTHEW JAMES, oncologist, educator; b. Romsey, Hampshire, Eng., Mar. 5, 1960; came to U.S., 1991; s. John Charles and Jennifer Monkton (Webb) E. BSc first class, U. London, 1981; MB BChir, U. Cambridge, Eng., 1984; PhD, U. London, 1992. Intern Addenbrookes Hosp., Cambridge, 1984; resident Hammersmith Hosp., London, 1985; sr. resident Hammersmith & Ealing Hosps., London, 1986-88; clin. fellow Imperial Cancer Rsch. Fund, London, 1988-91; fellow Lombardi Cancer Ctr., Washington, 1991-94, instr., 1994-96, asst. prof., 1996—2000; assoc. prof. Duke U. Med. Ctr., Durham, NC, 2000—03; assoc. prof., divsn. oncology, dept. medicine Washington U., St. Louis, 2003—, head section medical oncology, divsn. oncology, dept. medicine, 2003—; co-dir., clinical and translational rsch. Siteman Comprehensive Cancer Ctr., St. Louis, 2003—; dir. breast health program Washington U. and Barnes Jewish Hosp., St. Louis, 2003—; Anheuser Busch prof. medical oncology Washington U., St. Louis, 2003—; U. ambassador to Brazil and U. Campinas McDonnell Internat. Scholars Academy, Washington U., 2007—. External reviewer developmental projects MD Anderson SPORE in Breast Cancer, 2007—; scientific advisory bd. AVON found., 2007—. Contbr.: (books) The Treatment of Cancer, 1989, Molecular Biology in Medicine, 1997, The Encyclopedia of Cancer, 1997, Contemporary Cancer Research, 1998, Diseases of the Breast, 1999. Recipient 1st award NIH, 1996. Mem. Royal Coll. Physicians U.K., Am. Assn. Cancer Rsch., Am. Soc. Clin. Oncology, Endocrine Soc., Cancer and Leukemia Group B (chmn. correlative sci. com. 2001—). Office: Washington U Medical Sch Campus Box 8056 660 S Euclid Ave Saint Louis MO 63110 Office Phone: 314-362-8903. Business E-Mail: mellis@wustl.edu.

ELLIS, R. JOHN, biology professor; PhD, King's Coll. With dept. botany and biochemistry U. Aberdeen, 1964—70; with U. Warwick, Coventry, England, 1970—, sr. lectr., head chloroplast rsch. group, 1996, prof. emeritus. Contbr. articles to profl. jours.; author: How Science Works in Evaluation, 2010. Recipient Gairdner Found. Internat. award, 2004, Internat. medal, Cell Stress Soc., 2007. Mem.: Royal Soc. Achievements include formulation of the general concept of the molecular chaperone function. Office Phone: 44-0-24-7652-3509. Office Fax: 44-0-24-7652-3568. *

ELLIS, THOMAS L., neurosurgeon, educator; married; 4 children. MD, U NC Sch. Medicine, 1993. Cert. Am. Bd. Neurological Surgery. Resident U. Fla., 1993—2000; asst. prof., co-dir., Deep Brain Stimulation Program, Residency Program assoc. Dir. Wake Forest U. Sch. Medicine. Mem. Gamma Knife Ctr., 1999—. Contbr. several articles to profl. jours. Office: Wake Forest U Sch Medicine 300 Medical Center Blvd Winston Salem NC 27157 Office Phone: 336-716-6438. Office Fax: 336-716-3065.

ELLISON, EDWIN CHRISTOPHER, surgeon, educator; b. Columbus, Ohio, Jan. 10, 1950; s. Edwin Homer and Molly (Scheeler) E.; m. Mary Pat Borgess, Dec. 23, 1978; children: Jonathan Scott, Eric Christopher. BS, U. Wis., 1972; MD, Med. Coll. Wis., 1976. Diplomate Am. Bd. Surgery. Resident surgery Ohio State U., Columbus, 1976—83, asst. prof. surgery, 1983—93, assoc. prof., 1993—99, prof., 1999—; chief divsn. gen. surgery, bd. dirs. Ohio Digestive Disease Inst., Columbus, 1987—93; chief of staff Ohio State U. Med. Ctr., Columbus, 1999—2000, vice chmn. dept. surgery, 1996—99, 1interim chair surgery, 0999—2000, chmn. surgery, 2000—, assoc. v.p. health sci., 2002—, vice dean clin. affairs, 2002—. Fellow ACS. Office: Rm 692 395 W 12th Ave Columbus OH 43210-1240 Office Phone: 614-293-8701.

ELLISON, LOIS TAYLOR, internist, educator, medical association administrator; b. Ft. Valley, Ga., Oct. 28, 1923; d. Robert James and Annie Maude (Anderson) Taylor; m. Robert Gordon Ellison, Feb. 11, 1945; children: Robert Gordon, Gregory Taylor, Mark Frederick, James Walton, John Charles. BS, U. Ga., 1943; MD, Med. Coll. Ga., 1950. Fellow, Univ. Hosp., Augusta, Ga., 1950-51; mem. faculty Med. Coll. Ga., Augusta, 1951—, prof. medicine and surgery, 1968—2000, assoc. dean, 1974-75, provost, 1975-84, assoc. v.p. planning (hosps. and clins.), 1984—2000, prof. emeritus medicine and surgery, 2000—, med. historian in residence, 2000—, provost emeritus, 2000—. Attending VA Med. Ctr., Augusta; civilian cons. Eisenhower Army Med. Ctr., Fort Gordon, Ga.; mem. coal mine health research adv. council Nat. Inst. Occupational Safety and Health, 1972-75; bd. dirs. East Central Ga. Health Systems Agy., 1976-80, treas., 1978—80; bd. dirs. Oak Ridge Associated Univs., 1979-84; mem. adv. council Univ. Systems Ga., 1975-84; mem. exec. com. Ga. Health Coordinating Council, 1980 Contbr. articles to profl. jours. Bd. dirs. United Way Greater Augusta, 1975-78, chair div. hosp. and health, 1978, chair div. colls. and univs., 1980; mem. adminstrv. bd. Trinity-on-the-Hill United Methodist Ch., Augusta, 1974-77, mem. pastor-parish com., 1978—90, 1998-2001. Recipient: Hall of Fame Alumni award, U. Sys. Ga. Found. Regents, 2009, NIH Rsch. Career award, Lifetime Achievement award Med. Coll. Ga. Sch. Medicine, 1996, Pres. award, Will Ross medal, Am. Lung Assn., 1998, Gov. award Historic Preservation Stewartship, 2004, Sprit of MCG award, 2010, MCG U., 2010, Career award, Lifetime Achievement award, Ga. Health Scis. U., 2011; named Vessel of Life, 2005; included in NIH Nat. Libr. Medicine exhbn., 2003. Fellow Am. Coll. Chest Physicians; mem. Am. Physiol. Soc., Am. Med. Women's Assn., AMA, Assn. Am. Med. Colls., Am. Lung Assn. (bd. dir. 1974—88, sec. 1982-85, pres.-elect 1985-86, pres. 1986-87), Am. Heart Assn. (pres. Ga. affiliate chpt. 1982-83, bd. dir. 1979—87), So. Soc. Clin. Investigation, Am. Lung Assn. of Ga. (pres. 1984-85), Ga. Heart Assn. Home Phone: 706-210-7816; Office Phone: 706-721-4013. Business E-Mail: ellisonl@georgiahealth.edu.

ELLMAN, MARC, ophthalmologist, writer; BS, Ursinus Coll., 1996; MD, Pa. State U., Hershey, 2000; intern, Pa. State U., 2000—01. Chief resident Albert Einstein Coll. Medicine, Bronx, NY, 2001—04; pvt. practice S.W. Eye Inst., El Paso, Tex., 2004—. Profl. magician. Contbr. articles to mags.

ELLMAN, NORMAN KENNETH, psychologist, psychoanalyst; b. Yonkers, NY, June 29, 1932; s. Sidney Lionel and Sadelle (Volan) E.; children: Deborah, Sharon, Douglas; m. Donna E. Ellman, May 20, 1995; stepchildren: Cheryl Graybush, Christina Graybush. BS Edn., SUNY, New Paltz, 1954; MEd, Queens Coll., 1958; M in Psychology, Yeshiva U., 1967; PhD, NYU, 1972. Lic. psychologist, N.J., Fla.; cert. tchr.; cert. in psychoanalysis; diplomate Am. Bd. Psychoanalysis in Psychology. Tchr. 6th grade Malverne Pub. Schs., NY, 1956—57, East Williston Pub. Schs., NY, 1957—59; sch. psychologist Brentwood Pub. Schs., NY, 1959—62, Wantagh Pub. Schs., NY, 1962—67; pvt. practice psychotherapy Oakland, NJ, 1967—; co-dir. North Jersey Mental Health Assocs., 1972—83, Counseling and Psychotherapy Svcs., Oakland, 1983—. Chief psychologist, dir. child study team Glen Rock (N.J.) Pub. Schs., 1967-72, psychol. cons., 1972-82; head counselor and dir. day camp Long Beach, N.Y., 1959-67; tchr. N.J. Inst. Psycholotherapy, Teaneck, N.J., part-time, 1975; adj. faculty psychology Nassau C.C., Hempstead, N.Y., 1966, Paterson (N.J.) State Tchrs. Coll., 1969; staff therapist Lynbrook (N.Y.) Cons. Ctr., Bi-County Cons. Ctr., Amityville, N.Y., 1963-67. With U.S. Army, 1954-56. Mem. APA, N.J. Psychol. Assn., Bergen County Psychol. Assn., Assn. Advancement of Psychology, Nat. Assn. Advancement of Psycholoanalysis, Am. Bd. Psychoanalysis in Psychology, Acad. Psychoanalysis, meberGreat minds of the 21stCentury,Am. Biographical Inst. Avocations: baseball, softball, chess, piano. Home and Office: 60 Tidy Island Blvd Bradenton FL 34210-3302 Office Phone: 941-720-8277, 941-761-7710.

ELLNER, PAUL DANIEL, retired microbiologist; b. NYC, May 2, 1925; s. George and Cele (Weis) Ellner; m. Estelle Ziswasser, 1948 (div. 1960); 1 child, Diane; m. Cornelia Johns, Jan. 15, 1965; children: David, Jonathan. BS, LI U., 1948; MS, U. So. Calif., 1952; PhD, U. Md., 1956. Diplomate Am. Bd. Med. Microbiology, cert. clin. lab. dir. NYC Dept. Health. Clin. bacteriologist LA hosps., 1948-52; rsch. asst. Mt. Sinai Hosp., NYC, 1952-53; instr. microbiology U. Fla. Coll. Medicine, 1956-60; asst. prof. U. Vt. Coll. Medicine, 1960-63, Columbia U. Coll. Physicians and Surgeons, NYC, 1963-66, assoc. prof., 1966-70, prof., 1971-78, prof. microbiology and pathology, 1978—89, prof. emeritus, 1989, dir. clin. microbiology svc., 1971-89; assoc. microbiologist Presbyn. Hosp., NYC, 1966-70, attending staff, 1971-89; ret., 1989. Cons. in field; vis. prof. NY Med. Coll., Valhalla, 1979, ASM Latin Am., Medellin, Colombia, 1982, Am. Bur. Med. Advancement, Taiwan, 1982; regional coord. Nat. Disaster Med. Sys.; v.p. Am. BioSci. Cons. Author: Current Procedures in Clinical Bacteriology, 1978, Understanding Infectious Disease, 1992, The Biomedical Scientist as Expert Witness, 2006; editor: Infectious Diarrheal Diseases: Current Concepts and Laboratory Procedures, 1984; mem. editl. bd. Sexually Transmitted Diseases, 1982—84, European Jour. Clin. Microbiology, 1985—89; contbr. chapters to books, articles to profl. jours. With AC USN, 1943—44, served to capt. USPHS Res., health project officer USCG, 1982—91. Rsch. fellow, USN, 1954—56. Fellow: Infectious Diseases Soc. Am., Assn. Clin. Scientists, NY Acad. Medicine (assoc.), Am. Acad. Microbiology; mem.: AMA (spl. affiliate), Am. Venereal Disease Assn., Acad. Clin. Lab. Physicians and Scientists, Am. Soc. Microbiology (chmn. clin. divsn. 1980—81, Sonnerwirth Meml. award 1992), Sigma Xi. Republican. Jewish. Avocations: fishing, gardening, photography. Home Phone: 860-496-1207. Personal E-mail: pdel@columbia.edu.

ELLWOOD, PAUL MURDOCK, JR., health policy analyst, consultant; b. San Francisco, July 16, 1926; s. Paul and Rebecca May (Logan) Ellwood; m. Barbara Ellwood; children: David, Cynthia, Deborah. BA, Stanford U., 1949, MD, 1953. Dir. Kenny Rehab. Inst., Mpls., 1962—63; exec. dir. Am. Rehab. Found., Mpls., 1963—73; dir. Inst. Interdisciplinary Studies, Mpls., 1970—73; pres. InterStudy, health policy analysis Excelsior, Minn., 1973—85; pres. Paul Ellwood & Assocs., Excelsior, 1985—87; chmn. bd., pres. InterStudy, 1987—92; pres. Jackson Hole Group, Teton Village, Wyo., 1992—; founding dir. Found. for Accountability/Quality Measure for Healthcare, Portland, Oreg., 1997—. Dir., mem. exec. com. Jackson Hole Ski Corp., Wyo., 1972—87; clin. prof. phys. medicine and rehab., neurology and pediat. U. Minn. Med. Sch.; cons. in health and delivery systems. Co-author: Assuring the Quality of Health Care, 1973; co-editor: Handbook of Physical Medicine and Rehabilitation, 1971. With USNR, 1944—46. Recipient award, Ministry Pub. Health, Republic Argentina, 1957, 1st award sci. exhibit, Am. Acad. Neurology, 1958, citation, Pres.'s Com. Employment Handicapped, 1962, Gold Key award, Am. Congress Rehab., 1971; named Disting. fellow, Am. Rehab. Found., 1973. Mem.: Group Health Assn. Am. (dir. 1975—76), Assn. Rehab. Ctrs. (pres. 1960—61, U.S. Healthcare Quality award 1991), Nat. Health Coun. (dir. 1971—76), Inst. Medicine NAS. Home: PO Box 15 Bondurant WY 82922-0015 Office Phone: 307-734-8520. Business E-Mail: pmellwood@earthlink.net.

ELMA, BAYANI BORJA, physician; b. Manila, Philippines, Nov. 3, 1942; s. Medardo Romero Elma and Hiwaga Rada Borja E.; m. Maria Mercado Chavez-Elma, July 4, 1971; children: Michael Anthony, Mary Anne. Degree in preparatory medicine, U. Philippines, 1963; MD, U. of the East, Quezon City, Philippines, 1968. Diplomate Am. Bd. Quality Assurance, Utilization Review Physicians. Vice-chief of staff Md. Gen. Hosp., Balt., 1985-90, dir., trustee, 1988-95, chmn., prof. affairs com., 1992-95. Panel editl. advisers Internal Medicine for the Specialist, Livingston, NJ, 1990-2003. Mem. editl. bd.: Md. Med. Jour., 1993—96. Pres. U. East Med. Alumni Assn., 1992-94, Assn. Philippine Physicians in Md., 1997-99.; dir., trustee U. East Med. Alumni Found, 1994-2006; vice-chmn. Govs. Commn. on Asian-Pacific Am. Affairs, Balt., 1992-2003; alt. del. House Del. Balt. City Med. Soc., 1997-99; vice-chmn. bd. trustees U. East Med. Alumni Found., 1998-2003, chmn. bd. trustees, 2003-06, chmn. emeritus, 2006—; trustee Found. for Aid to Philippines, Inc., 2002-09. Named One of the Twenty Outstanding Filipino Am. US and Can. Filipino Image mag., 1998-99, Outstanding Leadership Medicine award U. East Med. Alumni Assn., 2007, Recognition award U. East RMMMC Coll. Medicine, 2009. Mem.: Am. Coll. Physician Execs., U. East Med. Alumni Found. (chmn. and advisor 2010, Dedicated Svc. Recognition award). Republican. Roman Catholic. Avocations: reading, writing, travel. Home: 10907 Tony Dr Lutherville MD 21093-3618 Office Phone: 410-296-0573. Personal E-mail: bbelmamd@gmail.com.

ELMAN, IGOR N., addiction psychiatrist; b. Leningrad, Russia, June 13, 1962; MD, Ben-Gurion U. Med. Sch., 1990. Diplomate Am. Bd. Psychiatry, cert. in addiction psychiatry. Intern Gapir Med. Ctr., Kfar Saba, Israel, 1990—91; resident Albert Einstein Coll. Medicine, Bronx, NY, 1991—95; fellowship Nat. Inst. Mental Health, Bethesda, Md., 1994—97, Mass. Gen. Hosp./Harvard Med. Sch., 1997—98; asst. to assoc. prof. psychiatry Harvard Med. Sch., 1997—, dir. Clin. Psychopathology Lab. Editor-in-chief Jour. Psychology Rsch. & Behavior Mgmt.; contbr. articles to profl. jours. Office: McLean Hosp Dept Psychiatry 115 Mill St Belmont MA 02478 Office Phone: 617-855-3692. Office Fax: 617-855-3711. E-mail: ielman@partners.org. *

ELMAN, LAUREN B., neurologist, educator; BA in Psychology, Cornell U., Ithaca, NY, 1994, MD, 1998. Diplomate Am. Bd. Psychiatry and Neurology, 2003. Intern medicine Hosp. of the Univ. Pa., 1998—99, resident neurology, 1999—2002, fellow neuromuscular, 2002—04, asst. prof. neurology; assoc. dir. Muscular Dystrophy Assn. Clinic. Univ. Pa. Med. Ctr., assoc. dir. ALS Assn. Ctr. Named one of Top Docs, Phila. Mag., 2011. Mem.: Am. Assn. Electrodiagnostic Medicine, Am. Acad. Neurology. Office: Hospital of the University of Pennsylvania 330 S 9th St Philadelphia PA 19107 Office Phone: 215-829-8407. Office Fax: 215-829-6606. Business E-Mail: elmanl@uphs.upenn.edu.

EL-MAS, MAHMOUD MOHAMED, pharmacologist; b. Suez, Egypt, Jan. 6, 1960; BS in Pharmacy, U. Alexandria, 1982, M in Pharmacy, 1986, PhD, 1990. Instr., grad. student dept. pharmacology Leeds U. Sch. Medicine, England, 1988—90; rsch. assoc. dept. pharmacology East Carolina U. Sch. Medicine, Greenville, NC, 1991—93, 1996—99; instr. dept. pharmacology faculty pharmacy U. Alexandria, Egypt, 1982—88, asst. prof. dept. pharmacology faculty pharmacy, 1990—91, from asst. prof. to assoc. prof. dept. pharmacology faculty pharmacy, 1993—95, assoc. prof. dept. pharmacology faculty pharmacy, 1999—2000, prof. dept. pharmacology faculty pharmacy, 2000—. Cons. PHARCO Pharm. Co., Alexandria, 1994—95; vis. prof. dept. pharmacology East Carolina U. Sch. Medicine, Greenville, NC, 2002—04. Contbr. articles to profl. jours. Recipient Student Union's award, Alexandria U., 1980, Egyptian Pharm. Cos. award, 1982; grantee, Am. Heart Assn., 1992—93, Biomedical Rsch. Support Grant, East Carolina U. Sch. Medicine, 1992—93. Mem.: Egyptian Syndicate Pharmacists (Gold medal 2002), Egyptian Toxicological Soc., Egyptian Soc. Pharmacology and Exptl. Therapeutics. Office: Univ Alexandria Faculty of Pharmacy Champlion St Alexandria Egypt Office Fax: +203-487-3273. Personal E-mail: mahelm@hotmail.com.

ELMER, LAWRENCE WILLIAM, neurologist, researcher; b. Gainesville, Fla., Jan. 31, 1958; s. Joseph William and Jean (Maguire) Elmer; m. LeAnn Wolitarsky, Jan. 17, 1953; children: Stephen William, Caroline Grace. BA, Davidson Coll., NC, 1980; MS, Fla. State U., 1983; MD, U. Fla., 1987, PhD, 1988. Diplomate Am. Bd. Psychiatry and Neurology. Asst. prof. U. Mich., Ann Arbor, 1994—98, Med. Coll. Ohio, Toledo, 1998—2004; assoc. prof. U. Toledo, 2003—09, prof., 2009—. Dir., Parkinson's Disease and Movement Disorders program Med. U. Ohio, Toledo, 1998—, dir. ctr. for neurol. disorders, 2003—, pres.-elect faculty senate, 2004—05. V.p. Washtenaw Christian Acad., Saline, Mich., 2000—02; bd. dirs. ctrl. Ohio chpt. Huntington's Disease Soc., Columbus, 1999—2001, bd. dirs. Mich. chpt. Lansing, 2001—03; med. dir. NW Ohio Parkinson's Found., Toledo, 1998—2005; APMCO credentials com. mem. Med. Coll. Ohio, Toledo, 2000—04, chair, clin. rsch. ctr. subcom., 2004—04. Recipient Nat. Rsch. Svc. award, NIH, Baylor Coll. Medicine, 1987—88, Humanism in Medicine award, Med. Sch. Class of 2003, 2002, Dean's Tchg. award, Dean's Office, Sch. Medicine, 2003, Golden Apple Tchg. award, 2003—07, 2009; named one of Am. Best Drs., 2001—10; fellow, U. Fla. Sch. of Medicine, 1983—87; scholar, Pfizer Pharms., 1995—97. Mem.: Movement Disorder Soc., Soc. for Neuroscience, NY Acad. Sci., Am. Acad. Neurology. Office: U Toledo Health Sci Campus 3000 Arlington Ave Mail Stop 1195 Toledo OH 43614-2598

ELMES, DAVID GORDON, psychologist, educator; b. Newton, Mass., Feb. 15, 1942; s. Leslie and Ruth (Adams) E.; m. Anne Louise Lawrence, June 7, 1963; children: Matthew David, Jennifer Anne. BA, U. Va., Charlottesville, 1964, MA, 1966, PhD, 1967. Mgmt. trainee C & P of Va., 1963; asst. prof. psychology Washington and Lee U., Lexington, Va., 1967-71, assoc. prof., 1971-74, prof., 1975—2007, prof. emeritus, 2007—, head dept. psychology, 1990-2000, co-dir. cognitive sci., 1987-2000. Rsch. assoc. Human Performance Ctr., U. Mich., 1973-74; vis. fellow Univ. Coll., Oxford U., Eng., 1987. Author: Readings in Experimental Psychology, 1978; contbr. articles to profl. jours. Fellow Assn. Psychol. Sci., Va. Acad. Sci.; mem. Psychonomic Soc., Coun. on Undergrad. Rsch. (past pres.), Phi Beta Kappa. Office: Washington and Lee U Dept Psychology Lexington VA 24450-0303 Business E-Mail: elmesd@wlu.edu.

EL-MOWAFI, HANI MOHAMED ZAKI, surgeon, educator; b. Damieta, Egypt, July 1, 1962; s. Mohamed Zaki El-Mowafi and Fatma Mohamad El-Khiat; m. Mona Ali Hegazi, Oct. 22, 1987. M.B.B.CH., Faculty of Medicine, Mansoura U., 1985, MSc, 1989, MD, 1995. Internship rotation Mansoura U. Hosp., Egypt, 1986—87, resident, 1987—90, asst. lectr., clin. demonstrator, 1990—95, lectr., clin. demonstrator, 1995—2001, asst. prof., 2001—. Cons. surgeon Mansoura U. Hosp., 1995—, asst. prof., 2001—. Contbr. articles various profl. jours. Recipient Best Rsch., Egyptian Orthopaedic Assn., 1998, Ideal Resident, Mansoura U. Hosp., 1988, Best Rsch. award, Egyptian Orthopaedic Assn., 1998; scholar Stiftung Riedrichsheim Ortop. U., Egyptian Govt., Klinik, Germany, 1992-1994. Mem.: Egyptian Orthopaedic Assn. (corr.), European Musculoskeletal Tumor Soc. (corr.), Limb Length And Reconstruction Soc. Of N.Am. (corr.), Egyptian Orthopaedic Assn. (corr.), Limb Length And Reconstruction Soc. Of N.am. (corr.), European Musculoskeletal Tumor Soc. (corr.), Am. Acad. Of Orthopaedic Surgeons (corr.). Achievements include research in extracapsular base of neck osteotomy versus southwick osteotomy in treatment of moderate to sever chronic slipped capital femoral epiphysis; functional outcome following treatment of segmental skeletal defects of the forearm bones by Ilizarov application; the effect of low intensity pulsed ultrasound on callus maturation in tibial distraction osteogenesis; assessment of percutaneous V osteotomy of the calcaneus with Ilizarov application for correction of complex foot deformities; percutaneous destruction and alcoholisation for the management of Osteoid Osteoma; bone transport for Segmental skeletal defects of the forearm bones; staged management of comminuted intra-artcular oilon fracture; treatment of nonunion of the humerus using the ilizarov external fixtor. Office: Mansoura U Al-Gomhoria Mansoura 35516 Egypt E-mail: hanielmowafi@yahoo.com.

EL-NAGGAR, ADEL K., medical educator; b. Cairo, June 1, 1946; MD, Ein-Shams Sch. Medicine, Cairo, PhD, 1970. Prof., pathology U. Tex. MD Anderson Cancer Ctr., 1987—. Office: 1515 Holcombe Blvd Houston TX 77082 Office Fax: 713-745-3356. Business E-Mail: anaggar@mdanderson.org.

ELOFF, JACOBUS NICOLAAS, botanist, educator; b. Johannesburg, Aug. 19, 1939; DSc, U. NW, 1969. Prof., leader, Phytomedicine Programme U. Pretoria, 1995—. Exec. dir. Nat. Bot. Gardens South Africa, 1983—90; rsch. dir. Nat. Bot. Inst., 1991. Contbr. articles to profl. jours., scientific papers. Recipient Havenga Outstanding Biol. Rsch. prize, South African Acad. Sci. and Arts, Gold medal, Bronze medal, Internat. Soc. Hort. Sci. Mem.: Internat. Soc. Ethnopharmacology (bd. mem.), Assn. African Medicinal Plant Stds. (past pres.), South African Assn. Botanists (life; hon. mem., past pres., Sr. medal). Avocation: reading. Office: Phytomedicine Programme Pvt Bag X Onderstepoort Pretoria Gauteng 0110 South Africa Office Fax: 27125298525. Business E-Mail: kobus.eloff@up.ac.za.

ELOWITZ, ERIC H., neurosurgeon, educator; MD summa cum laude, SUNY Downstate Med. Ctr., 1986. Lic. NY, 1987, NJ, 2008, diplomate Am. Bd. Neurol. Surgery. Intern SUNY Downstate Med. Ctr., 1987, resident, 1993; joined Beth Israel Med. Ctr., 1993, dir. neurosurgery, 2004; asst. prof. NY Presbyn./Weill Cornell Med. Ctr., 2010, joined neurosurgical surgery dept., 2010; physician St. Luke's Roosevelt Hosp. Recipient Young Investigator award, Am. Assn. Neurol. Surgeons. Mailing: c/o New York Presbyterian Hospital Department of Neurosurgical Surgery 525 E 68th St Starr 651 Box 99 New York NY 10065 Office Phone: 212-746-2870. Office Fax: 212-746-8387.

EL-RAGGAL, TAMER MOHAMED, medical educator; b. Cairo, Oct. 6, 1970; s. Mohamed Hussein El-Raggal and Wafaa S. Noor El-Din; m. Dalia G. Aly; children: Jana Tamer, Nada Tamer. MD, Ain Shams U., Cairo, 1993, MSc, 1997, PhD, 2002. Ophthalmology resident Ain Shams Hosp., 1995—98; asst. lectr. Ain Shams U., 1998—2002, lectr., 2002—07, assoc. prof., 2007—. Cornea and refractive surgery cons. Magrabi Eye Hosp., Cairo, 2001—. Contbr. articles to profl. jours. Fellow: Royal Coll. Surgeons Edinburgh. Conservative. Office: Magrabi Eye Hosp El-Sayyeda Nafisa Sq Cairo 11361 Egypt Home: 2, Nakhla El-Moteae St Heliopolis 11361 Cairo Egypt Office Phone: 20226363028. Office Fax: 202 22623995. Personal E-mail: telragal@hotmail.com.

EL-SAAIEE, LOTFY TAHA, dermatologist, educator; s. Taha Aly Elsaie and Fatma Mostafa El-Fashny; m. Laila Hussein Meky; children: Mohamed Lotfy Elsaie, Ahmed Lotfy Elsaie, Mostafa Lotfy Elsaie. MBBCh, Cairo U., 1965, D in Deratology and Venereology, 1968; DM, Al Azhar U., 1974; MD in Dermatology and Venereology, Al Azhar U., Egypt, 1975. Ho. officer medicine Cairo Univ., 1965—66; resident dermatology and venereology, faculty medicine Cairo U., 1966—68; asst. lectr. dermatology and venereology Al Azhar U., Cairo, 1968—75, lectr. dermatology and venereology, 1975—81, asst. prof., 1981—86, prof. dermatology, venereology & andrology, 1987—. Sr. cons. dermatology and venereology U. Hosps., Medina, Saudi Arabia, 1979—82; vis. prof. U. Komasi, Ghana, 1986—86; sr. cons. dermatolog and venereology Kuwait Hosp., Dubai, United Arab Emirates, 1993—94; sr. cons. dermatolgy and venereology Gahra Hosp., Kuwait City, Kuwait, 1998—99; sr. cons. dermatology Internat. Hosp. Bahrain, Manama, 2002—04. Author: (book) Spot Lights In Dermatology, 1976; contbr. articles to profl. jours. Recipient Med. Scis. State prize, Egyptian Acad. Sci. and Tech., 1986, Nat. Figure Egypt award, Ministry Info., 1986, Ribbon Excellence 1st degree award, Egyptian Pres., 1995, Internat. Health Physician Yr., IBC, Eng., 2006, Medal of Honor, ABI, 2008, Am. medal honor, 2008, Amb. World Forum, 2009. Fellow: Am. Soc. Dermat. Surgery (corr.); mem.: Egyptian Soc. of Pediat. Dermatology (coun. bd. mem. 2007), Am. Coll. Tropical Medicine, Egyptian Soc. Dermatology and Venereology (bd. dirs. 1975—), Kuwaiti Soc. Dermatology (corr.), Egyptian Soc. Andrology (corr.), Emirates Soc. Dermatology (assoc.; bd. mem. 1993—96), Am. Acad. Dermatology (life), Internat. Soc. Dermatol. Surgery (corr.), Internat. Soc. Dermatology (corr.; bd. dirs. 1992—99), European Acad. Dermatology and Venereology (corr.), Bahrain Soc. Dermatology (corr.), Egyptian Med. Assn. (corr.; editor in chief Jour. Egypt Soc. of Pediat. Dermatology 2008). Home Phone: 202-22721825; Office Phone: 202-23951280, +26328955. Home Fax: 202-26328955. Personal E-mail: egydoc77@yahoo.com, loffyelsaaiee@gmail.com.

EL-SADR, WAFAA MAHMOUD, epidemiologist, medical educator; b. Egypt; MD, Cairo U., 1974; MPH, Columbia U., 1991; MPA, Harvard U., 1996. Diplomate Am. Bd. Internal Medicine, cert. in infectious diseases. Chief divsn. infectious diseases Harlem Hosp. Ctr., 1988—2008; prof. clin. epidemiology Columbia U. Mailman Sch. Pub. Health, dir. Internat. Ctr. for AIDS Care & Treatment Programs (ICAP), also dir. Ctr. for Infectious Disease Epidemiologic Rsch. (CIDER). Mem. WHO Technical Adv. Group on Tuberculosis, 2008—; bd. dirs. Am. Found. AIDS Rsch.; mem. antiviral adv. com. FDA; mem. adv. coun. for elimination of tuberculosis Ctrs. Disease Control & Prevention. Named a MacArthur Fellow, The John D. & Catherine T. MacArthur Found., 2008; named one of 50 Visionaries Changing the World, Utne Reader, 2009, The 100 Agents of Change, Rolling Stone mag., 2009. Fellow: Infectious Diseases Soc. America; mem.: HIV Medicine Assn. (bd. dirs.), Inst. Medicine, Internat. AIDS Soc. Office: Mailman Sch Pub Health 722 W 168th St Rm 715 New York NY 10032 Office Phone: 212-342-0532. Office Fax: 212-342-1824. E-mail: wme1@columbia.edu. *

EL SAIE, LOTFY TAHA, dermatologist, educator; b. Benisuef, Egypt, Aug. 18, 1942; s. Taha Ali El Saie and Fatma Mostafa El Fashny; m. Laila Hussein Meky; children: Mohammed, Ahmed, Mostafa. MbChB, Cairo U., 1965; MD, Al Azhar U., 1975. Sr. cons. Kuwaiti Ministry of Health, 1989—90, Emirates Ministry of Health, Dubai, 1990—91, Bahrain Ministry of Health, 2002—03. Editor: Pan African and Pan Arab Jours. Dermatology. Recipient State Prize of Medicine, Acad. Sci. Rsch., Egypt, 1986, 2nd ribbon of excellence, Pres. of Egypt, 1997; named Nat. Figure of Egypt, Egyptian Govt., 1986. Fellow: European Acad. Dermatology, Am. Acad. Dermatology; mem.: Internat. Soc. Dermatology (bd. advisors). Avocations: travel, reading, music. Home: 15 Tarablos St off Abbas Akkad St Nasr City Egypt Office: Al Azhar Univ Nasr City Egypt Address: Heliopolis W 6 El Sheikh Mahmoud Abou El-Oyoun St Cairo 11351 Egypt

EL-SALAMOUNY, TAREK MOHAMED, urologist, educator; b. Cairo, Mar. 18, 1946; s. Mohamed Mahmoud El-Salamouny and Doria Mohamed El-Sheishaie; m. Sahar Mahamed Anwar, July 19; children: Yomna, Maha. BS with honors in Medicine, Ain Shams U., Cairo, 1968; diploma in Gen. Surgery, Al Azhar U., Cairo, 1971, diploma in Urology, 1972, DSc in Urology, 1979. Cert. in treatment of renal failure and renal transplantation Eng., Ireland, Frace. Ho. officer Ain Shams U., Cairo, 1968—69; resident gen. surgery Ahmed Maher Tchg. Hosp., Cairo, 1969—70; resident urology Al Azhar U. Hosps., Cairo, 1970—73; from tutor to prof. urology Al Azhar U., 1973—89, prof. urology, 1989—; with PCNL-ESWL. Mem. various coms. Al Azhar U., 1979—, Al Azhar U. Hosp., 1979—; examiner Egyptian Med. Bd., 2002; cons. in field. Contbr. articles to profl. jours. Recipient Kidney Transplantation medal, Al Azhar U. Faculty Medicine, 1981, plaque, 2006, Kidney Transplantation medal, Egyptian Urol. Assn., 1981. Mem.: Internat. Soc. Urology, African Urol. Assn., Egyptian Med. Syndicate (named Ideal Physician 1980, named Ideal Tchr. 2003), Am. Urol. Assn. (corr.). Avocations: swimming, tennis, crafts, music, reading. Office: 12 Ahmed Fouad Nassim St 2d Zone Madinet Nasr Cairo 11371 Egypt Office Phone: 20122130942. Personal E-mail: tmsalamony@link.net.

EL SAMAN, ALI MAHMOUD, medical educator, researcher; b. El Minya, Egypt, Aug. 14, 1964; MD, Assiut U., 1988. Cons., prof. Assiut U., 1988—2011, prof., rschr., 2010—. Recipient award, Internat. Fedn. Ob-Gyn. FIGO. Mem.: Egyptian Fertility Soc. Avocations: reading, travel. Home: Kaser Elanii Abd Elraman Off Assiut 030 Egypt Home Fax: 002088354488. Personal E-mail: ali_elsaman@yahoo.com.

ELSAS, LOUIS JACOB, II, physician, educator; b. Atlanta, Feb. 10, 1937; s. Herbert R. and Edith (Levy) E.; m. Nancy Terrell, July 15, 1961; children: Nancy Louise, Margaret Edith, Louis Jacob, III. BA, Harvard U., 1958; MD, U. Va., 1962. Diplomate Am. Bd. Internal Medicine, Am. Bd. Med. Genetics in clin. genetics; clin. biochem. genetics and molecular genetics. Intern Yale-New Haven Hosp., 1962-63, resident in internal medicine, 1963-65; NIH postdoctoral fellow in med. genetics Yale U., 1965-68, from instr. to asst. prof. sect. genetics, dept. medicine and pediatrics, 1968-70; faculty Emory U. Med. Sch., Atlanta, 1970—2002, prof. pediatrics and biochemistry, 1977—2002, prof. emeritus, 2002—; dir., prof. Dr. John T. Macdonald Ctr. Med. Genetics, 2002—08; chmn., dept. biochemistry and molecular biology U. Miami, 2008—10. Dir. Ga. Comprehensive Genetic System, 1978; vis. prof. Japan Soc. Promotion Sci., 1976; Professore a contratto, Italy, 1985—; U.S. advisor Congress of Inborn Errors of Metabolism, 1980-2000; bd. dirs. The Howard Sch., 1994-02; founding pres., Soc. Inherited Metabolic Disorders; bd. dirs., Am. Coll. Med. Genetics. Contbr. numerous articles to profl. jours. Mem. alumni coun. Phillips Acad., 2001—. Recipient Rsch. Career Devel. award NIH, 1972-77, John Horsley Meml. prize U. Va. Med. Sch., 1972,

A.E. Levy Faculty Rsch. award Emory U., 1989, Big Heart award Civitans, 1992, Claude Fuess award Phillips Acad., 2000; named hon. citizen Interlaken, Switzerland, 1980. Fellow Am. Acad. Pediat., Am. Coll. Med. Genetics (founder, bd. dirs. 1996—); mem. UNICEF, Soc. Inherited Metabolic Disorders (founding pres.), Am. Soc. Clin. Investigation, Soc. Pediat. Rsch., Am. Soc. Biol. Chemistry, Am. Soc. Human Genetics, Assn. Am. Physicians, Assn. Profs. Human and Med. Genetics (pres. 1998-2001), S.E. Genetics Group (chmn. 1983-94), Coun. Regional Networks (pres. 1994-2001), Emory U. Faculty Club, The Temple, Sigma Xi (past chpt. pres.). Clubs: Emory U. Faculty, Druid Hills Golf, Civitan (Humanitarian award 1979, Big Heart award 1992). Office: Univ Miami R Bunn Gautier Bldg Dept Biochemistry & Moleculer Biology Rm 109 1011 NW 15th St Miami FL 33136

ELSÄSSER, HANS-PETER, cell biologist; b. Solingen, Nordrheinwestfalen, Germany, Sept. 3, 1955; s. Alois and Eva Elsässer; m. Katharina Ritzel; children: Lea, Marlene. Abitur, Konrad Adenauer Gymnasium, Langenfeld (Rhld), 1966—75; BS in Human Biology, Philipps U., Marburg, Germany, 1984, PhD in Human Biology, 1988, Habilitation, 1995. Nurse applicant Landeskrankenhaus, Langenfeld (Rhld), Nordrheinwestfalen, Germany, 1975—77, U. Clinic, Marburg, 1977—78, nurse surgery, 1978—79; rsch. asst. Philipps U., 1988—95, sr. rsch. asst., 1995—2000, assoc. prof., 2000—. Office: Dept of Cytobiology Robert-Koch-Str. 6 35037 Marburg Germany Office Phone: 06421-2864075. Office Fax: 06421-2866414. Business E-Mail: elsaesse@mailer.uni-marburg.de.

EL-SAYED, IVAN HOMER, otolaryngologist, researcher; s. Mostafa Amr and Janice El-Sayed; m. Belinda Hahn; children: Oliver Clark children: Ava Alexandria. MD (hon.), Boston U., 1996. Diplomate Am. Bd. Otolaryngology, 2002. Attending physician U. Calif., San Francisco, 2002—. Mem. Comprehensive Cancer Ctr. U. Calif., 2002—; dir. Otolaryngology Minimally Invasive Skull Base Program. Fellow: ACS; mem.: Am. Head and Neck Cancer Soc., Am. Acad. Nanomedicine, Am. Acad. Otolaryngology, Alpha Omega Alpha. Achievements include patents for Spectroscopic Diagnosis for Bacteria in Biologic Fluid; patents pending for Detection of Cancer with Metallic Nanoparticles, invention of Photothermal Destruction of Cancer with Immunotarged Nanoparticles. Office: U Calif 400 Parnassus Ave San Francisco CA 94143 Office Fax: 415-353-2603.

EL SAYED, NESRINE SALAH EL DINE, pharmacologist, educator; b. Cairo, Mar. 24, 1970; B in Pharm. Scis., Cairo U., 1993, PhD in Pharmacology & Toxicology, 2004. Lectr. German U., Cairo, 2007—. Mem.: Internat. Soc. Study Xenobiotics. Avocation: basketball. Office: El Tagamoa El Khames Maadi Cairo 11235 Egypt Office Fax: 20-2-7582125. Personal E-mail: nesrine_salah2002@yahoo.com.

EL SAYED, RANIA FAROUK, radiologist, educator; b. Egypt, Sept. 1, 1973; MBBCh, Cairo U., 1995, MSc, PhD, 2005. Lectr. dept. radiodiagnosis faculty medicine Cairo U., 2009—. Reviewer Am. Jour. Roentgenology, 2005—. Mem.: European Symposium on Urogenital Radiology (First prize). Avocation: reading. Home: 8 Abu Zer El Ghafari Nasr City dist Cairo 11511 Egypt Home Fax: 002 02 261 42 31. Business E-Mail: rania729@internetegypt.com.

EL SHAFEI, HASSAN ISMAIL, medical educator, director; b. Egypt, Mar. 26, 1970; MBBch, Cairo U., 1993, MD in Neurosurgery, 2001. Prof., dept. neurosurgery Cairo U. Hosp., 2011—. Dir. Cairo Neuro-Spine Ctr., 2003—. Fellow: Ctr. Minimally Invasive Neurosurgery (Sydney); mem.: Egyptian Soc. Skull & Spine Surgery, Egyptian Soc. Neurosurgeons. Avocations: fishing, diving, surfing, squash, golf. Home: 9A Ahmed Hishmat St Cairo Zamalek 11211 Egypt Home Fax: 202-27369203. Personal E-mail: drhelshafei@hotmail.com.

ELSHAHAT, AHMED MOHAMED FATHY, plastic surgeon, educator; b. Kuwait, Sept. 27, 1970; s. Mohamed Fathy Elshahat and Emtithal Ahmed Elsawi; m. Amani Abdelhadi Mohamed, Mar. 21, 1998; children: Habiba Ahmed, Amr Ahmed. MD, Ain Sham U., Cairo, 1993; MSc in Gen. Surgery, Ain Shams U., 1997; D in Plastic Surgery, Ain Shams U., Cairo, 2003. Resident plastic surgery Ain Shams U., Cairo, 1995—98, asst. lectr. plastic surgery, 1998—2003; fellowship plastic surgery Johns Hopkins Med. Inst., Balt., 2000—02; lectr. plastic surgery Ain Shams U., Cairo, 2003—, assoc. prof. plastic surgery, 2008. Dir. burn unit Ain Shams U., Cairo, 2005—06, dir plastic surgery, 2007—08. Contbr. articles to profl. jours. Fellow, Johns Hopkins Med. Inst., 2000—02. Mem.: Egyptian Soc. Plastic Surgery (Best Presented Papers in Ann. Meetings 2003-2004, 2007). Home: 38 Elshaheed Said Afify Ali Ard Elgof Nasr City Cairo 11371 Egypt Office: Ain Shams U Abbasia Sq Cairo Egypt Personal E-mail: elshahat70@hotmail.com.

EL SHAMY, ABDEL SALAM MAHMOUD, pulmonologist, educator; b. Egypt, Sept. 1, 1953; MBBCh, Al Azhar U., Cairo, MSc, 1978, MD in Chest and Respiratory Diseases, 1991. Chest and respiratory diseases cons. Chest Hosp., Ministry Health, Kuwait, 1996—2011; prof., chest diseases Al Azhar U., Cairo, 1979—. Fellow: Am. Coll. Chest Diseases; mem.: Am. Coll. Chest Diseases, Regent Kuwait Chest Physician. Avocations: football, swimming, surfing, reading. Home: Rigae Dorar Complex Block D Flat 44 Farwanyia 13033 Kuwait Personal E-mail: drshamy2000@yahoo.com.

EL-SHARIF, AMANY, physician, educator; b. Cairo, Nov. 5, 1966; MB BCh, Faculty Pharmacy, 1988, PhD, 2002. Dep. dir. quality assurance edn. unit Faculty Pharmacy, Al-Azhar U., 2007—, coord. students activities. Trainer, expert Nat. Authority Quality Assurance Higher Edn., 2007—11. Mem.: World Islamic Assn. Mental Health, Arab Soc. Infectious Diseases and Antimicrobials, Egyptian Soc. Biotech., El Ahly Club (Cairo) (mem. women com.). Home: El-Sefarat area bld 10/blk1 Cairo Nasr City 11614 Egypt Home Fax: 00202-26716092. Personal E-mail: amanyelsharif@yahoo.com.

EL-SHARKAWY, MAGDY M. SAED, nephrologist, educator; married. MD, Ain-Shams U., Cairo, 1998, PhD. Asst. prof. internal medicine & nephrology Ain-Shams U., 1998—2003, assoc. prof. internal medicine & nephrology, 2003—08, prof. internal medicine & nephrology. Dir. Dept. Nephrology. Office: Ain-Shams Univ Abbasia Sq Cairo 11360 Egypt Office Phone: 202-26844319. Personal E-mail: magdi35@hotmail.com.

EL SHAZLY, OSSAMA, surgeon, educator; b. Cairo, Dec. 1, 1974; MBCh, Ain Shams Med. Sch., 1998; MD in Orthopedic, Ain Shams U., 2007. Lectr. orthop. Ain Shams U. Hosp., 2007—. Cons. foot and ankle arthroscopic surgery, 2007—11. Mem.: ISAKOS. Avocation: reading. Office: Ramses Extension Rd Abassia Sq Cairo Abassia 1234 Egypt Personal E-mail: ossama_elshazly@yahoo.com.

EL-SHINAWI, MOHAMED EL-SAYED, surgeon, educator; b. Cairo, July 6, 1973; B, Ain Shams U., 1997, MD, 2005. Ho. officer Faculty Medicine, Ain Shams U., 1998—99, resident gen. surgery, 1999—2003, asst. lectr. od gen. surgery, 2003—05, asst. prof. gen. surgery, 2005—10, assoc. prof. gen. surgery, 2010. Cons. gen. surgery Ain Shams Specialized Hosp., 2005, El-Nozha Internat. Hosp., Cairo, 2006, Palestine Hosp., 2009; head er dept. Ain Shams U. Hosp., 2011. Co-Investigator grant, Avon Found. Mem.: Egyptian Soc. Intensive Care & Trauma., Colo-rectal Soc. Ain Shams U., Egyptian Med. Syndicate, Egyptian Soc. Laparoscopic Surgery, Am. Assn. Cancer Rsch. Avocations: football, swimming, tennis. Home: 16 Omar Ibn Elkhatab st Masken Sheraton Cairo 11371 Egypt Home Fax: 202 26910605. Personal E-mail: mohamedshinawi@hotmail.com.

ELSON, CHARLES O., gastroenterologist, educator; b. Chgo., Aug. 21, 1942; MD, Wash. U., 1968. Prof. medicine and microbiology, Basil I. Hirschowitz chair gastroenterology U. Ala., Birmingham, 1987—. Recipient Outstanding Alumni award, Wash. U., St. Louis; named one of Best Drs. America. Fellow: ACP, Assn. Am. Physicians, Am. Acad. Microbiology; mem.: Am. Assn. Immunologists, Am. Gastroent. Assn. Office: SHEL 607 1825 University Blvd Birmingham AL 35294 Office Fax: 205-996-9113. Business E-Mail: coelson@uab.edu.

ELTAYEB, EMIL, pharmacist, researcher; b. Salzburg, Austria, May 24, 1975; arrived in U.S., 1975; s. Ali and Maia Eltayeb. BS cum laude, St. John's U., 1998, PharmD, 2002. Intern Mary Immaculate Hosp., Jamaica, NY, 1995—97, Rite Aid, Jamaica, NY, 1999—2000. Author: The Mystery of Cancer and Alzheimer's Disease is Revealed, 2005, Albert Einstein and Diseases, 2008. Mem.: Am. Assn. Pharm. Scientists, Am. Chem. Soc., N.Y. Acad. Scis., Rho Chi Honor Soc., Golden Key Nat. Hon. Soc. Achievements include research in application of Einstein's theory of relativity, law of conservation of energy, and quantum mechanics to the understanding of the pathophysiology of various diseases and their treatment. Avocation: reading. Personal E-mail: meltayeb@msn.com.

ELTAYEB, YOUSIF H., surgeon; s. H. Eltayeb and Batoul A. Elgamal; m. N. K. Akasha; children: A. Y., S. H. MB, BChir, U. Cairo, 1980; M in Clin. Surgery, U. Khartoum, Sudan, 1987. Registered specialist Sudan Med. Coun., surg. splty. Irish Med. Coun., ltd. registration Gen. Med. Coun. UK. Surgeon, lectr. U. Juba, Sudan, 1983—89, Univ. Coll. Hosp., Galway, Ireland, 1991—93, DOHMS, United Arab Emirates, 1994—2000; locum cons. United Arab Emirates and Ireland, 2000—, Observer UNESCO bioethics orgn.; presenter confs. in field. Participant campaign against illiteracy, Greef Sharq -Khartoum North, Sudan, 1970—74. Fellow: Royal Coll. Surgeons (Ireland) (life), Internat. Coll. Surgeons (assoc.). Achievements include patents for laparoscopic surgical trainer; development of mini-laparotomy operation for closure of perforated peptic ulcers; assisted laproscopic repair of incisional hernia and abdominoplasty; simple external fixator for fractures. Avocation: horseback riding. Home: 15338 Jordan's Journey Centreville VA 20120 E-mail: abusaree@hotmail.com.

ELTE, JAN WILLEM FREDERIK, retired internist; b. Amsterdam, The Netherlands, July 25, 1946; s. Philip and Johanna Mathilda Louise (Schulein) E.; m. Elisabeth Alice Pool, Mar. 24, 1973; children: Josine, Derk Jan, Maurits. MD, U. Leiden, The Netherlands, 1972, Internal Medicine, 1978, Endocrinology Diploma, 1991. Staff mem. U. Hosp., Leiden, 1978-83; cons. phys. St. Jozef Ziekenhuis Gouda, Netherlands, 1983-86, St. Franciscus Gasthuis, Rotterdam, Netherlands, 1987—2011; hon. staff mem. U. Hosp., Rotterdam, Netherlands, 1987—2011. Mem. European Bd. Endocrinology, 1995-; del. European Fed. Internal Medicine, 1996-2003, treas., EFIM, 2003-06, sec. gen., 2005—. Founding dep. editor: European Jour. of Internal Medicine, 1989-99; editl. bd. Postgrad. Med. Jour., 1987-2006, Clin. Med., 2003-05; co-editor, author: (book) Differentiele diagnostiek in de interne geneeskunde, 1994; author: (book) Diabetes Mellitus, 1992; co-author (book): Diabetes Mellitus in de Huisartsenpraktyk, 2002, author (book): Schildklierafwykingen, 2003 Lt. med. svc., 1972-73, The Netherlands. Fellow ACP, European Fed. Internal Medicine (hon.), Royal Coll. Physicians; mem. European Assn. Study Diabetes, Endocrine Soc, Romanian Soc. Internal Medicine(hon), European Soc. Endocrinology, Nat. Assn. Internal Medicine (Order of Knighthood, 2011) Avocations: international tie collecting, golf, skiing, reading. Home Phone: 31 18 25 1851. E-mail: j.elte@sfg.nl.

ELTOUKHY, HESAHM MOHAMED, ophthalmologist, educator; b. Alexandria, Nov. 21, 1965; BBCh, Tanta U., 1988, MD, 2000. Asst. prof Tanta U., 2006—. Mem.: Egyptian Soc. Ophthalmology. Home: Mansheiat AlBakry Mahalla Alkobra AlGharbeia Egypt Personal E-mail: eltoukhy65@yahoo.com.

ELWAN, NAGWA MOHAMMAD, dermatologist, educator; d. Mohammad I. Elwan and Hanyia A. Soliman; m. El-Sayed A. Gad; children: Rania E. Gad, Omar E. Gad, Samar E. Gad. MD, Tanta Faculty Medicine, 1990. Residency in dermatology Tanta U. Hosp., 1982—85; asst. prof. Tanta Faculty Medicine, 1990—2000, prof. dermatology, 2000—. Pvt. cons. Egyptian Ministry Health, Tanta, 1996—. Mem. Soc. Care Leprosy Patients, Tanta, Egypt, 1985. Fellowship, Tubingen, Germany, 1994, Zurich, Switzerland, 2001. Fellow: Egyptian Women's Soc. Dermatology, Egyptian Soc. Dermatology, Am. Soc. Dermatopathology, Am. Acad. Dermatology; mem.: Internat. Soc. Cutaneous Lymphoma, Internat. Soc. Dermatopathology. Office: Tanta Dept Dermatology/Faculty Medicine 31527 Tanta Egypt Business E-Mail: elwan2egy@yahoo.com.

ELWATIDY, SHERIF MOHAMED FAHMY, neurosurgeon, educator, neurosurgeon, consultant; b. Meet Ghamr, Dakahleia, Egypt, June 18, 1961; s. Mohamed Fahmy Ibrahim Elwatidy and Amina Ahmed Eisa; m. Hanan Abdullatif Mohsen, Sept. 3, 1987; children: Omar Sherif, Mahmoud Sherif, Hana Sherif, Farah Sherif, Nour Sherif. MD in Neurosurgery, Ain Shams U., Cairo, 1987; MS in Surgery, Alexandria U., Egypt, 1990. Sr. registrar neurosurgery Frenchay Hosp., Bristol, England, 1998—2000; assoc. prof., cons. neurosurgeon Coll. Medicine, King Saud U., Riyadh, Saudi Arabia, 2000—. V.p. Riyadh Neurosci. Club, 2001—03. Fellow: Royal Coll. Surgeons Edinburgh. Achievements include development of new surgical techniques for decompression of lumbar and cervical spine; research in prediction of outcome of surgery for Cerebral aneurysms; brain tumors & pregnancy; craniopharyngiomas; decompressive craniotomy. Office: King Saud Univ Coll Medicine PO Box 7805 Riyadh 11472 Saudi Arabia Home: Kkuh Neurosurgery Dept P.O. Box 7805 11472 Riyadh Saudi Arabia Office Fax: +966 14679493; Home Fax: +966 14679493. E-mail: smfwat@yahoo.com.

ELY, PARRY HAINES, dermatologist, educator; b. Washington, Sept. 19, 1945; s. Northcutt and Marica (McCann) E.; m. Elizabeth Magee, June 24, 1969 (div. June 1998); children: Sims, Rebecca, Meredith, Tess; m. Kathleen O'Brien, May 3, 2000 AB, Stanford U., 1967; MD, U. So. Calif., 1971. Diplomate Am. Bd. Dermatology, Am. Bd. Pathology; lic. dermatologist, Calif. Intern medicine U. So. Calif.-L.A. County Med. Ctr., 1971—72, resident dermatology, 1972—75; clin. prof. dermatology U. Calif., Davis, 1975—. Bd. dirs. Nevada City Wineries Mem. editl. bd. Calif. Physician, 1994—; manuscript reviewer Archives Internal Medicine, 1988—, Annals Internal Medicine, 1980—, Archives Dermatology, 1977—; contbr. articles to med. jours Fellow Am. Acad. Dermatology (asst. editor jour. 1988-94, manuscript reviewer 1994—), Am. Soc. Dermatopathology; mem. AMA, Internat. Soc. Tropical Dermatology, Am. Fedn. Clin. Rsch., Am. Soc. Dermatologic Surgery, N.Am. Clin. Dermatologic Soc., Calif. Med. Assn. (alt. del. 1995—, rep. to Calif. Telehealth/Telemedicine coord. project planning com. 1996—), Pacific Dermatologic Soc. (Nelson Paul Anderson Meml. Essay 1st pl. award 1979, Mini Presentation of Yr. award 1984), Noah Worcester Dermatol. Soc., Cutaneous Therapy Soc., Soc. Investigative Dermatology, Sacramento Valley Dermatol. Soc. (pres. 1990-91), Placer Nev. Med. Soc. (bd. dirs. 1978-79, 91-93, v.p. 1994, pres. 1995), Skin Cancer Found. (med. coun. 1987—), Tri-County Am. Cancer Soc. (bd. dirs. 1978-79, 91-92), Royal Soc. Medicine (London), Dermatology Found., Space Dermatology Found. (founding), Shivas Irons Soc. (founding) Office: 565 Brunswick Rd Ste 7 Grass Valley CA 95945-9053 E-mail: haines@netshel.net.

ELZAY, RICHARD PAUL, retired dean, dental educator, department chairman; b. Lima, Ohio, Dec. 6, 1931; s. Paul William and Edna Virginia (Moyer) E.; 1 child, Mark S. BS, Ind. U., Indpls., 1957, DDS with honors, 1960, MS in Dental Surgery, 1962. Diplomate Am. Bd. Oral Maxillofacial Pathology. Gen. practice dentistry, Brownsburg, Ind., 1960-62; instr. dept. oral pathology Med. Coll. Va. Sch. Dentistry, Richmond, 1962-64; asst. prof. Sch. Dentistry Med. Coll. Va., Richmond, 1964 66, assoc. prof., 1966-69, prof., chmn. dept. oral pathology, 1969-86, asst. dean acad. affairs, 1970-74; prof., dep. v.p. for health scis., dean Sch. Dentistry U. Minn., Mpls., 1986-96. Home Phone: 434-645-9254. E-mail: coe_rpe@meekcom.net.

ELZEIN, CHAWKI FAYEZ, pediatrician, surgeon; b. Saida, Lebanon, July 30, 1967; s. Fayez Najib elZein and Nahla Mostafa Darazi; m. Nadine Alayli Alayli, Mar. 6, 2002; children: Lana Chawki, Talia Chawki. BS, Am. U. Beirut, Lebanon, 1988. Asst. prof. surgery U. Ill., Chgo., 2002—; instr. Rush U. Med. Ctr., Chgo., 2004. Instr. Heart Inst. Children, Oak Lawn, Ill., 2003. Fellow: Am. Coll. Surgeons; mem.: Internat. Soc. Thoracic and Cardiovascular Surgery, Soc. Thoracic Surgeons. Achievements include reconstructive heart surgery on children born with congential defects. Avocations: hunting, reading, music. Home: 8605 west 98 Pl Palos Hills IL 60465 Office: Heart Inst Children 4440 W 95th St Oak Lawn IL 60453 Office Fax: 708-684-4068; Home Fax: 708 684-4068 Personal E-mail: celzein444@hotmail.com. Business E-Mail: chawki@thic.com.

EMANS, SARAH JEAN, pediatrician, educator; MD, Harvard U., 1970. Diplomate Am. Bd. Pediatrics, 1993, Am. Bd. Pediatrics-adolescent medicine, 2009. Resident pediat. Children's Hosp. Boston, 1971—73, fellow, 1973—75, chief divsn. adolescent medicine; co-dir. Ctr. for Young Women's Health, prof. pediat. Harvard Med. Sch. Office: Children's Hospital Boston Department Adolescent Medicine 300 Longwood Ave Boston MA 02115-5742 Office Phone: 617-355-7170. Office Fax: 617-730-0185.

EMANUEL, EZEKIEL JONATHAN (ZEKE EMANUEL), oncologist, bioethicist; b. Israel, Sept. 6, 1957; s. Benjamin and Marsha Emanuel. BA, Amherst Coll., 1979; MSc, Oxford U., Exeter Coll., 1981; MD, Harvard U. Med. Sch., 1988; PhD, Harvard U., 1989. Lic. Mass., diplomate med. oncology, internal medicine. Fellow in ethics & the professions John F. Kennedy Sch. Govt., Harvard U., Cambridge, Mass., 1987—88; med. intern Beth Israel Hosp., Boston, 1988—89, med. resident, 1989—90; med. clin. fellow Harvard Med. Sch., Boston, 1990—92; fellow, med. oncology Dana-Farber Cancer Inst., Boston, 1990—92; instructor Harvard Med. Sch., Boston, 1992—94, asst. prof. medicine, clin. medicine, clin. epidemiology, 1994—97, assoc. prof. social medicine, 1997—98; chair dept. clin. bioethics dept., Warren G. Magnuson Clin. Ctr. NIH, 1998—; spl. adv. for health policy to dir. Office Mgmt. & Budget, Exec. Office of the Pres., Washington, 2009—11; Diane & Robert Levy prof., chair Dept. Medical Ethics & Health Policy U. Pa. Perelman Sch. Medicine, Phila., 2011—. Internat. adv. bd. on bioethics Pan. American Health Orgn., 1999—; med. adv. bd. Cancer Care, Inc., 2000—; chair, Com. to Develop Ethical Guidelines Academy/Health, 2002—; adj. lectr. pub. policy John F. Kennedy Sch. Govt., Harvard U., 2002—03; assoc. editor Jour. Clinical Ethics, Jour. Health Comm.; bd. editors Lancet Oncology, Jour. Law, Medicine & Ethics, American Jour Bioethics; editorial adv. bd. BioMed Ctrl., Medicine, Health Care & Philosophy. Author: The Ends of Human Life, 1991, Healthcare Guaranteed: A Simple, Secure Solution for America, 2008; co-author: No Margin, No Mission, 2003; co editor: Clinical & Epidemiol. Aspects of End-of-Life Decision-Making, 2001. Recipient Career Devel. award, American Cancer Soc., 1992, Baruj Benacerraf Clin. Investigator award, 1994, Clin. Ctr. Director's award, 2000, AMA/Burroughs Welcome Leadership award, 1990, Danforth Teaching award, 1984—86. Fellow. Hastings Ctr.; mem.: Am. Soc. Clin. Oncology (mem. task force on oversight of clin. rsch. 2000—, chair task force on quality of cancer care 2000—, chair ethics com. 2003—04), Inst. Medicine, Phi Beta Kappa. Office: NIH Dept Clin Bioethics Bldg 10 Rm 1C118 10 Ctr Dr Bethesda MD 20892 also: Dept Medical Ethics & Health Policy Perelman School Medicine U Penn 3401 Market St Ste 320 Philadelphia PA 19104 Office Phone: 215-898-7136. Office Fax: 215-573-3036. E-mail: emanuel@nih.gov. *

EMANUELE, MARY ANN, endocrinologist, educator; MD, Loyola U., 1975. Diplomate Am. Bd. Internal Medicine, 1978, Am. Bd. Internal Medicine-endocrinology, diabetes and metabolism, 1983. Resident internal medicine Northwestern Univ. Med. Ctr., Univ. Hawaii, Honolulu, 1976—78; fellow endocrinology Loyola Univ. Med. Ctr./Hines VA Med. Ctr., Ill., 1978—80; prof., dept. medicine, divsn. endocrinology Loyola Univ.; hosp. affiliation includes Loyola Univ. Med. Ctr. Co-author: (publs.) Adverse clinical outcomes associated with elevated blood alcohol levels at the time of burn injury, 2008, Vitamin D and diabetes: let the sunshine in, 2008, Interference at work: a case report of a malfunctioning insulin pump, 2009, Ethanol potentiates the acute fatty infiltration of liver caused by burn injury: prevention by insulin treatment, 2009, Reducing hyperglycemia hospitalwide: the basal-bolus concept, 2009, and numerous other publs. Office: Loyola University Bldg 110 Rm 4231 2160 S First Ave Maywood IL 60153 Office Phone: 708-216-6200. E-mail: memanue@lumc.edu.

EMANUELE, NICHOLAS V., endocrinologist, educator; MD, Northwestern U., 1967. Diplomate Am. Bd. Internal Medicine, 1975, Am. Bd. Internal Medicine-endocrinology, diabetes and metabolism, 1979, lic. Ill. Intern medicine Cook County Hosp., Chgo.; resident internal medicine Edward Hines, Jr. VA Hosp., Chgo., 1972—74; fellow endocrinology Northwestern Univ., Chgo., 1974—76, VA Lakeside Hosp., Chgo.; physician Veterans Affairs Edward Hines, Jr. Hosp.; prof., dept. medicine, divsn. endocrinology and metabolism Loyola Univ., Chgo. Office: Edward Hines Jr VA Hospital 5000 S 5th Ave Hines IL 60141 Office Phone: 708-202-8387. Office Fax: 708-202-7998.

EMARA, ASHRAF MAHMOUD, medical educator; b. Cairo, June 18, 1966; PhD in Medicine, 1998. Prof., dir. tanta poison ctr. faculty medicine Tanta U., Egypt, 2009—. Mem.: Egyptian Soc. Anthropology, Egyptian Soc. Pharmacology and Exptl. Therapeutics, Egyptian Soc. Toxicology, Internat. Soc. Study Xenobiotics (Best Rschr. award). Avocations: reading, movies, travel. Office: El Baher St 12 Mawea St Tanta ElGharbia 66666 Egypt Personal E-mail: ashrafemara99@hotmail.com.

EMBY, DONALD JAN, radiologist; b. Durbann, South Africa, Feb. 19, 1949; s. Gordon Noel and Margaretha Catharina (Buys) Emby; m. Gail Yolanda Simmonds, Aug. 24, 1979 (div. Apr. 10, 1990); children: Gordon Michael, Steven Rex; m. Fiona Elizabeth Welch, June 26, 1993; 1 child, Karen. B in Medicine and Surgery, U. Witwatersrand, Gauteng, South Africa, 1973. Fellow in radiology Coll. Medicine South Africa, 1982; sr. radiologist Chamber of Mines of South Africa, Johannesburg, 1983—96, chief radiologist, 1997—98; cons. radiologist Anglogold Health Svcs., Carltonville, South Africa, 1999—. Hon. tutor U. Witwatersrand, Johannesburg, 1985—98; cons. radiologist mining industry, South Africa, 1997—. Methodist. Achievements include pioneered use of direct coronal C.T. scanning to demonstrate site of CSF leakage; pioneered technique of peritoneo-saphenous shunting. Avocations: road running, birdwatching, hiking. Office: Anglogold Health Svc Western Deep Levels Hosp Carletonville Western Levels 2501 South Africa Office Fax: 2718 788-8298. Business E-Mail: demby@aghs.ashanti.com, demby@anglogoldashanti.com.

EME, ROBERT, psychology professor; b. Chgo., June 24, 1943; BA in Philosophy, St Mary Lake Sem., 1965; PhD in Clin. Psychology, Loyola U. Chgo., 1972. Asst. prof. psychology North Ctrl. Coll., 1972—80; clin. psychologist Forest Hosp., 1980—94; prof. clin. psychology Am. Sch. Profl. Psychology, Argosy U., Schaumburg, 1994—. Profl. adv. bd. mem. Adult Attention Deficit Disorder Assn., 2005—11. Mem.: APA. Avocation: basketball. Home: 731 Grey Evanston IL 60202 Business E-Mail: reme@argosy.edu.

EMERICK, THOMAS H., critical care specialist; MD, U. Calif., 1991. Diplomate Am. Bd. Anesthesiology, 1998, Am. Bd. Anesthesiology- critical care medicine, 1999. Resident in anesthesiology Univ. Calif, San Francisco, 1993—96, fellow in critical care medicine, 1997—98; hosp. affiliation includes Calif. Pacific Med. Ctr. Office: California Pacific Medical Center 2333 Buchanan St Fl 3 San Francisco CA 94115 Office Phone: 415-923-3293.

EMERSON, CHARLES H., endocrinologist, educator; b. India, 1941; BS, Randolph-Macon Coll., 1963; MD, U. Va. Prof. emeritus, medicine U. Mass., 1980—. Mem.: European Thyroid Assn., Am. Assn. Clin. Endocrinologists, Endocrine Soc., Am. Thyroid Assn. (bd. mem. 2002—07, treas. 2003—07, exec. com. mem. 2003—07, editor-in-chief 2008, Disting. Svc. award). Avocation: sailing. Office: University Mass Med Ctr Worcester MA 01655 Business E-Mail: charles.emerson@umassmed.edu.

EMERSON, CHARLES P., JR., research scientist; s. Charles and Annette L. (Bryant) Emerson. PhD. Prof., chair dept. cell & devel. biology U. Pa. Sch. Medicine, 1994—2003; dir. Penn Ctr. Devel. Biology, 1999—2003; sr. scientist, dir. Boston Biomed. Rsch. Inst., 2003—. Author: Methods in Muscle Biology, 1997; contbr. articles to profl. jours. Achievements include research in the studies of muscle regulatory genes that control the formation of muscle stem cells and coordinate the expression of muscle proteins during embryonic development. Office: Boston Biomedical Research Institute 64 Grove St Watertown MA 02472 Office Phone: 617-658-7721. Office Fax: 617-972-1759. Business E-Mail: emersonc@bbri.org. *

EMERSON, STEPHEN G., academic administrator, oncologist, hematologist, educator; b. NYC, Oct. 21, 1953; BA summa cum laude, Haverford Coll., 1974; MS in Molecular Biophysics, Yale U., 1976, PhD in Cell Biology and Immunology, 1980, MD, 1980; MA (hon.), U. Pa., 1994. Intern, resident Mass. Gen. Hosp., Boston, 1980—82; fellow Brigham & Women's Hosp., Dana-Farber Cancer Inst., Children's Hosp., Boston, 1982—86; asst. to assoc. prof. medicine U. Mich., Ann Arbor, 1986—94; prof. medicine U. Pa., Phila., 1994—2007, chief Div. Hematology/Oncology, 1994—2007, assoc. dir. clin./tanslational rsch., Francis C. Wood prof. medicine, pathology and pediatrics; pres. Haverford Coll., Pa., 2007—. Founder Astrom Biosci., Inc., Ann Arbor, 1989. Mem. editl. bd. Jour. Experimental Medicine, Stem Cells, Journal of Clin. Investigation; contbr. articles to profl. jours. Recipient Med. Scientist Trainee Prize, Yale U., Career Achievement award, Rolex Corp., 1999, Stohlman Award, Leukemia and Lymphoma Soc., Bai-Yu Lan Prize, City of Shanghai, Wilbur Lucius Cross Medal, Yale U., 2008; named one of Top Docs, Philadelphia Mag., 2002, 2005, 2006; scholar, Leukemia Soc. Am., 1987—92. Fellow: ACP; mem.: Am. Soc. Blood and Marrow Transplantation (mem. leadership coun.), Am. Soc. Hematology (mem. leadership coun.), Internat. Clin. Club, Am. Assn. Physicians. Office: Haverford College Office of President 370 Lancaster Ave Haverford PA 19041 Office Phone: 610-896-1021. E-mail: semerson@haverford.edu. *

EMERY, HELEN MARGARET, pediatric rheumatologist; b. Adelaide, Australia, Dec. 6, 1947; MD, U. Adelaide Med. Sch. Cert. in pediat., in pediatric rheumatology 2007. Internship in pediat. Royal Adelaide Hosp., Australia, 1971—72; residency in pediatric rheumatology U. Wash. Sch. Medicine Children's Hosp., 1973—75, fellowship in rheumatology, 1975—77, chief, rheumatology clinic, program dir. rheumatology edn., 2003—; prof. clin. pediat. U. Calif., San Francisco, head, pediatric rheumatology. Recipient Clinician Educator award, Am. Coll. Rheumatology; named a Best Doctor, Seattle Mag., 2004—06, Top Doctor, Seattle Met. Mag., 2006. Office: Children's Hosp & Regional Med Ctr Univ Wash Sch Med R-5420 Rheumatology 4800 Sand Point Way NE Seattle WA 98105 Office Phone: 206-987-2380.

EMERY, MICHELLE MIZE, dermatologist; m. Todd Allen Emery, 1988; children: Justin Allen, David Alexander, Stephen Anthony. BA, Cornell U., 1981—85; MD, U. Tex. at Houston, 1989. Dermatology U. of Iowa Hospitals and Clinics, 1993. Dermatologist Tulsa Dermatology Clinic, Okla., 1993—95, Dermatology Assoc., Grand Rapids, Mich., 1996—98, V.A. Outpatient Clinic, Grand Rapids, 1999—2005, Dermatology Ctr. of Grand Rapids, 2005—. Clin. faculty Okla. State U. Med. Br., 1993—95; lectr. Mich. State U. Med. Br., 1996—98, clin. faculty, 2002—03. Educator St Robert Ch., Grand Rapids, VI, 1999—2005. Recipient Alpha Omega Alpha Med. Honor Soc., U. Tex. at Houston, 1988, Janet M. Glasgow Meml. Achievemnt Citation, U. Tex. at Houston Med. Sch., 1989, Departmental award for academic excellence in Dermatology, U. Tex.at Houston Med. Sch., 1989. Fellow: Am. Acad. of Dermatology, Am. Bd. of Dermatology; mem.: AMA, Mich. State Med. Soc., Women's Dermatologic Soc., Am. Soc. Dermatologic Surgery, Alpha Omega Alpha Med. Soc. Achievements include research in the relationship between postnatal skin maturation and electrical skin impedance. Avocations: travel, boating, skiing. Office: 426 Michigan St NE Grand Rapids MI 49503

EMERY, PAUL EMILE, psychiatrist; b. Montreal, May 2, 1922; arrived in U.S., 1951; s. Esdras Fernand and Julia (Benoit) E.; m. Virginia Olga B. Kennick, July 27, 1979. BA, U. Montreal, 1942, MD, 1948. Diplomate in gen. psychiatry and forensic psychiatry, Am. Acad. Experts in Traumatic Stress. Staff psychiatrist Austen Riggs Ctr., Stockbridge, Mass., 1958-60; chief mental hygiene VA, Bridgeport, Conn., 1960-62, staff psychiatrist, chief of psychiatry Manchester, NH, 1988-99; pvt. practice Concord, NH, 1962-85, 99—; clin. dir. Ctr. for Stress Recovery, Brecksville, Ohio, 1985-87, dir., 1987-88. Med. dir. forensic unit N.H. Hosp., Concord, 1980-82; cons. VA med. Ctr., Manchester, 1962-64, 82-85, pub. health State of N.H., Concord, 1962-71, St. Paul's Sch., Concord, 1971-78; mem. faculty Dartmouth Coll. Med. Sch., 1971—, Western Res. Sch. Medicine, 1985—. Contbr. articles to profl. jours.; author: Trauma Psychology Model of the Mind, 1993. Sec. adv. commn. health and welfare State of N.H., Concord. Capt. U.S. Army, 1953-55. Recipient Salutation plaque N.H. Program on Alcoholism, 1971, cert. honor for scholarly achievement Internat. Assn. Psychohistory, 1998. Fellow Am. Psychiat. Assn. (life, disting., founder N.H. dist. br. 1972, chair ethics com.), Am. Acad. Experts in Traumatic Stress; mem. N.H. Med. Soc. (hon.)(cert. commendation 1972), Mass. Psychiat. Soc. (pres. 1965), N.H. Psychiat. Soc. (pres. 1980). Office: 15 Buckingham Dr Bow NH 03304-5207

EMERY, VIRGINIA OLGA BEATTIE, psychologist, researcher; b. Cleve., Apr. 9, 1938; d. W. Joseph P. and Antoinette Pauline (Misjak) Kennick; m. Paul Hamilton Beattie Sr., 1960 (div. 1975); children: Tamsan Beattie Tharin, Paul Hamilton Beattie Jr.; m. Paul E. Emery, 1979. BA, U. Chgo., 1962, PhD, 1982; MA, Ind. U., 1973. Diplomate Am. Bd. Disability Analysts, Am. Acad. Traumatic Stress; lic. psychologist, NH, Ohio; cert. brief therapist Nat. Acad. Brief Therapists; cert. cognitive therapist Nat. Bd. Behavioral Therapists, cert. domestic violence counselor endorsement; cert. expert traumatic stress, cognitive therapist. Asst. prof. psychology Case Western Res. U., Cleve., 1986—89, asst. clin. prof. psychiatry, 1986—89; sr. faculty assoc. Ctr. on Aging and Health, Concord and Hanover, NH, 1986—89, dir., 1989—; adj. clin. asst. prof. psychiatry Dartmouth Med. Sch., Lebanon, NH, 1983—85, clin. assoc. prof., 1989—; lectr. 3rd World Congress Controversies Neurology, Prague, Czech Republic, 2009. Mem. com. human devel. NIMH, Adult Devel. and Aging Traineeship, U. Chgo., 1974-76; sub-project dir. Case Western Res. U. Sch. Medicine, 1986-90; sec. women's faculty assn. Case Western Res. U., 1987-89; cons. Vets. Affairs Med. Ctr., Manchester, NH, 1989—; sub-project dir. NIMH Mental Health Clin. Rsch. Ctr. Grant, Case Western Res. U. Sch. Medicine, 1986-90; mem. Dartmouth Coll. and Dartmouth Med. Sch. Neurosci. Group, 1990—; Dunaway-Burnham vis. scientist Dartmouth Med. Sch., 2005; Paul Janssen lectr. U. Goteberg, Sweden, 1997; Dunaway-Burnham vis. scientist Dartmouth Med. Sch., 2005; lectr. 4th Internat. Congress Vascular Dementia, Porto, Portugal, 2005; lectr. 3rd Cell Stress Soc. Internat. Congress Stress Responses in Biology and Medicine; lectr. in field.; lectr. 61st Ann. Sci. Meeting Gerontol. Soc. America, Nat. Harbor, Md., 2008, lectr. 3rd World Congress, CONy, Prague, 2009, invited grand, Case Western Res. U. Sch. Medicine, 2011. Author: Language and Aging, 1985, Pseudodementia: A Theoretical and Empirical Discussion, 1988, Language Impairment in Dementia of the Alzheimer Type: A Hierarchical Decline, 2000, Interface between Vascular Dementia and Alzheimer Syndrome: Nosologic Redefinition, 2000, Retrophylogenesis of Memory in Dementia of the Alzheimer Type: A New Evolutionary Memory Framework, 2003, Noninfarct Vascular Dementia and Alzheimer Syndrome Spectrum, 2005; editor: Dementia: Presentations, Differential Diagnosis, and Nosology, 1994, 2d edit., 2003; contbr. chapters to books, articles to profl. jours. Bd. dirs. Frontiers of Knowledge Civic Trust, Concord, 1990—, pres. 1990-95. Recipient Adult Devel. and Aging grant, traineeship NIH/NIMH, 1974-76, Rsch. prize Am. Aging Assn., 1983, Havighurst prize for aging rsch. U. Chgo., 1984, NH Hosp. award for outstanding rsch. in dementia, 2003; named Frontiers of Knowledge Atlee Zellers lectr., 1994, Paul Janssen Med. Inst. lectr., 1997; rsch. grantee Western Res. Coll., 1986-87, NIMH Mental Health Clin. rsch. grantee, 1986-89. Fellow Gerontol. Soc. Am. (Disting Creative Contbn. award 1989; clin. medicine membership com. state liaison 1998—; lectr. Boston 2002), Am. Psychol. Assn., NH Psychol. Assn. (bd. dirs. 1991-93, chair com. acad. rsch. interests 1992-94, sec. 1994—, Riggs Disting. Contbn. award 1991, chmn. Women and Minorities com. 2001—), APA (student rsch. award 1984), Am. Acad. Experts in Traumatic Stress; mem. AAAS, AAUW, Internat. Psychiat. Rsch. Soc., Internat. Psychogeriatric Assn. (Pfizer lectr. 1997, 2d place award for rsch. paper 1995, 2nd Pl. Rsch. award in psychogeriatrics for paper 1995, IPA/Bayer Rsch. award in psychogeriat. 1995), Boston Soc. Gerontol. Psychiatry, Acad. Psychosomatic Medicine, NY Acad. Scis., Am. Acad. Experts in Traumatic Stress, Assn. Alzheimer's Disease Scientists, Am. Mensa Ltd. Home: 15 Buckingham Dr Bow NH 03304-5207 Office: Dartmouth Med Sch Dept Psychiatry Box HB 7750 Lebanon NH 03756 Business E-Mail: v.olga.emery@dartmouth.edu.

EMGÅRD, MIA GÖRANSSON, research scientist, educator; b. Visby, Gotland, Sweden, Oct. 28, 1972; d. Marcus Nils Mattson and Ingrid Elin Margareta Emgård. MSc, Lund U., Sweden, 1997, PhD, 2001. Scientist/post-doc Karolinska Inst., Stockholm, 2001—02, sr. scientist, 2004—08, assoc. prof. in clin. neuroscience, 2010; Marie Curie fellow Bologna U., Italy, 2003; scientist and business development mgr. Cellartis AB, Göteborg, Sweden, 2008—, project leader, 2008. Fellow Marie Curie Fellowship, European Union. Avocations: adventurous travel, music, squash, pottery. Office: Arvid Wallgrens Backe 20 Västra Götaland Göteborg SE-413 46 Sweden Office Phone: +46 31 758 0900. Office Fax: +46 31 758 0910. Business E-Mail: mia.emgard@cellartis.com.

EMILSSON, KENT, medical researcher; b. Säffle, Sweden, Aug. 8, 1963; m. Maria Emilsson; children: Elin, Oscar, Viktor. MD, Goteborg U., Sweden, 1989; PhD, Linköping (Sweden) U., 2001. Cert. specialist in clin. physiology, cardiology and internal medicine. Chief physician dept. clin. physiology Karlskoga (Sweden) Hosp., 2002—06; head dept. clin. physiology Orebro Univ. Hosp., Sweden, 2006—. Assoc. prof. Orebro U., 2007. Achievements include research in mitral annulus motion and circumflex artery motion in left ventricular pumping; right ventricular systolic and diastolic function; magnetic resonance imaging and mode of left ventricular pumping; Aortic annulus motion Takotsubo Cardiomyopathy. Home: Myggvägen 15 SE-70230 Orebro Sweden

EMILY, PETER P., retired dentist; b. Denver, June 9, 1932; BS in Biology, Regis Coll., 1955; DDS, Creighton U., 1959. Cert. in periodontology U. Pa., 1964, in pediat. dentistry Denver Gen. Hosp., 1967, in endodontics and oral surgery 1968. Pvt. practice, 1959—2011; dir. exotic animal dentistry Denver Zoo, 1979—2011; founder, co-chmn. Peter Emily Internat. Vet. Dental Found., 2005—. Faculty affiliate physician Colo. State U. Sch. Vet. Medicine, 1987—2011, U. Mo., Columbia, 1989—93; faculty Colo. U. Sch. Dentistry, 2008—11. Working group judge Am. Kennel Club. Recipient Merit award, Am. Animal Hosp. Assn., 1992, Western Vet. Conf., 2002. Mem.: ADA, Am. Vet. Dental Soc., Am. Vet. Dental Coll. Office: 1051 Independence St Lakewood CO 80215 Office Fax: 303-237-4122. Business E-Mail: info@peteremilyfoundation.org.

EMMANOUILIDES, GEORGE CHRISTOS, physician, educator; b. Drama, Greece, Dec. 17, 1926; came to U.S., 1955; s. Christos Nicholas and Vassiliki (Jordanopoulos) E.; married; children: Nicholas, Elizabeth, Christopher, Martha, Sophia MD, Aristotelion U., 1951; MS in Physiology, UCLA, 1963. Diplomate in pediatric cardiology and neonatal-perinatal medicine Am. Bd. Pediat. Asst. prof. UCLA, 1963-69, assoc. prof., 1969-73, prof., 1973-95, prof. emeritus, 1995—. Chief divsn. pediat. cardiology Harbor UCLA Med. Ctr., Torrance, Calif., 1963-95 Co-author: Practical Pediatric Electrocardiography, 1973; co-editor: Heart Disease in Infants, Children and Adolescents, 2d edit., 1977, Moss' Heart Disease in Infants, Children and Adolescents, 5th edit., 1995, Neonatal Cardiopulmonary Distress, 1988; contbr. more than 70 articles to profl. jours. and 25 chpts. to books Served as 2d lt. M.C., Greek Army, 1953-55 Recipient Sherman Mellincoff award UCLA Sch. Medicine, 1982, Rsch. award Am. Heart Assn., 1965-83. Fellow Am. Acad. Pediat. (cardiology sect., chmn. 1978-80, Founders award 1996), Am. Coll. Cardiology; mem. Am. Pediatric Soc., Soc. for Pediatric Rsch., Hellenic-Am. Med. Soc. (pres.), Acad. of Athens (corr.), Hellenic Univ. Club (LA, bd. dirs.) Democrat. Greek Orthodox. Avocation: gardening. Home: 4619 Browndeer Ln Rolling Hills Estates CA 90275-3911 Office: Harbor-UCLA Med Ctr 1000 W Carson St Torrance CA 90502-2004

EMMANUELLI, XAVIER FRANCOIS, social services administrator; b. Paris, Aug. 23, 1938; D in Medicine, Faculté de Médecine de Paris, 1967; Anesthésiste Réanimateur, Faculté de Médecine de Créteil, 1976. Pres., founder Médecins Sans Frontières, 1971—95, Samusocial de Paris, 1993—; min. to prime min., humanitarian action emergency Mem. of French Govt., 1995—97; pres. Samusocial Internat., 1998—. Recipient Légion d'honneur Commandeur du mérite, 2005. Mem.: Conseil Nat. de la Légion D'Honneur. Office: 35 Ave Courteline Paris 75012 France Office Fax: 0033141748811. Business E-Mail: x.emmanuelli@samusocial-75.fr.

EMMENS, MATTHEW W., pharmaceutical executive; b. Pasadena, Calif., June 29, 1951; 3 children. BS in Bus. Adminstrn., Fairleigh Dickinson U., East Rutherford, NJ, 1974. Various sales, marketing, and training positions Merck & Co., 1974—92; founder Astra Merck (joint venture with Astra Pharm.), 1992—97; pres., CEO Astra Merck Inc., 1997—99; joined Merck KGaA; pres., CEO EMD Pharm., 1999—2001; pres., global prescription pharm. bus. Merck, Darmstadt, Germany, 2001—03; CEO Shire Pharmaceutical Group plc, 2003—08, non-exec. chmn., 2008—; pres. Vertex Pharmaceuticals Inc., Cambridge, Mass., 2009, chmn., pres., CEO, 2009—. Bd. dirs. Shire Pharmaceuticals Group plc, 2003—, Vertex Pharmaceuticals Inc., 2004—. Avocation: flying. Office: Vertex Pharmaceuticals Inc 130 Waverly St Cambridge MA 02139 also: Shire Pharmaceuticals Group plc Chineham Basingstoke Hampshire England Office Phone: 484-595-8800. Office Fax: 484-595-8900. Business E-Mail: dmilbourne@us.shire.com.

EMMETT, JOHN COLIN, retired inventor, consultant; b. Bradford, Yorkshire, Eng., Apr. 27, 1939; BS, PhD, London U. Former rsch. team leader SmithKline Beecham Corp.; cons. Euromedica Ltd.; freelance cons., 2001—. Co-inventor over 100 patents in field. Named to National Inventors Hall of Fame, 1990. Office: Nat Inventors Hall of Fame 221 S Broadway St Akron OH 44308-1505

EMOND, JEAN C., surgeon, educator; BA, U. Chgo., 1975, MD, 1979. Cert. Nat. Bd. Med. Examiners, 1980, diplomate Am. Bd. Surgery, 1995. Intern in gen. surgery Cook County Hosp., 1979—80, resident in gen. surgery, 1980—84; fellow in hepatobiliary surgery Hosp. Paul Brousse, 1984—85; dir. pediatric liver transplantation

Univ. Calif., 1992—97; transplant surgeon Calif. Pacific Med. Ctr., 1995—97; cons. liver transplantation Northwestern Univ. Med. Ctr., 1997—98; fellow in liver transplantation Univ. Chgo., 1985—87, dir. liver transplantation and hepatobiliary surgery, 1991—92; prof. surgery in pediat. Columbia Univ., 1999—, Thomas S. Zimmer prof. of surgery, 2000—; attending surgeon NY-Presbyn. Hosp./ Columbia Univ. Med. Ctr., 1999—, vice chair transplantation, 2007—, dir. transplantation, 2007—, exec. dir. transplant initiative, 2010—. Author: What's new in transplantation 2002, 2002, Brown R. Mesenteric venous thrombosis, 2002, Split-Liver Transplantation: A Review, 2003, Living donor liver transplantation and hepatitis C, 2004, Living donor liver transplantation in children: what to recommend?, 2004. Named a Doctor of the Year, Latino Orgn. for liver awareness, 2000; named one of Best Doctors in NY, NY mag.; grantee Fulbright Travel; fellow Eleanor B. Pillsbury; scholar Ray and Joan Kroc Travelling, French Govt. Postgrad. Mem.: Warren H. Cole Soc., Soc. of Univ. Surgeons, Soc. for Surgery of the Alimentary Tract, Societé Internat. de Chirurgie, San Francisco Surgical Soc., Pacific Coast Surgical Assn., Internat. Liver Transplantation Soc., Internat. Hepato-Biliary Pancreatic Assn., Howard C. Naffziger Surgical Soc., Compagnons Hepato-Biliaires, Assn. for Academic Surgery, Am. Surgical Assn., Am. Soc. of Transplant Surgeons, Am. Soc. of Hepato-Pancreato-Biliary Surgery, ACS, Am. Assn. for the Study of Liver Diseases. Office: New York Presbyterian Hospital Columbia University Medical Center 622 W 168th St New York NY 10032 Office Phone: 212-305-2500.

EMSHOFF, RUEDIGER, surgeon, educator; b. Muelheim, Germany, Apr. 5, 1960; s. Horst Werner and Gisela Sophie-Luise Emshoff; m. Iris Marina Brandlmaier-Emshoff; 1 child, Sophia. MD, U. Düsseldorf, Germany; DentalMD, Dental Med. Sch., Budapest. Resident dept. Dental and Maxillofacial Surgery U. Innsbruck, Austria, assoc. prof. in surgery; cons. oral and maxillofacial surgery Innsbruck. Mem.: Soc. Clin. Trials, Philosophy Sci. Assn., NY Acad. Sci. Avocations: swimming, philosophic lecture, travel. Home: Hoehenstrasse 24D Innsbruck 6020 Austria Office: Dept Oral and Maxillofacial Surgery Maximilianstr 10 6020 Innsbruck Austria Office Phone: 0043-512-504-24373. Fax: 0043-512-504-24371.

ENARSON, CAM EDWIN, medical educator, dean; b. Edmonton, Alta., Can., Jan. 11, 1958; arrived in US, 1982; m. Carol Ann Spacht, Oct. 1, 1983; children: Edward, David. BA summa cum laude, Concordia Coll., 1978; MD, U. Alta., 1982; MBA, U. Pa., 1990. Diplomate Am. Bd. Anesthesiology. Asst. prof. pub. health scis. and anesthesiology Bowman Gray Sch. Medicine, Winston-Salem, NC, 1990; dean Sch. Med. Creighton U., Nebr., 2003—08, v.p. health scis., 2003—08, prof. anesthesiology and health policy and ethics; interim dean Sch. Medicine Ctrl. Mich. U., 2009—. Mem. at large Nat. Bd. Med. Examiners. Recipient Charles B. Clark Meml. award, 1994. Mem.: Assn. Am. Med. Colleges, AMA. Republican. Lutheran. Avocation: long distance running. Office: Ctrl Mich U Sch Medicine Rowe 207 Mount Pleasant MI 48859

ENATESCU, VIRGIL, physician, psychiatrist, researcher; b. Brasov, Romania, Nov. 11, 1940; s. Virgil and Aurora Enatescu; m. Maria Faur; children: Emilia Panescu, Virgil. Degree in psychiatry, Inst. Medicine and Pharmacy, Cluj, 1973; PhD in Med. Sci., Inst. Medicine and Pharmacy, Timisoara, 1977; PhD in Anthropology, Romanian Acad., Bucharest, 1998. Head Barza Med. Facility, 1964-67; resident in clin. med. lab. Med. Balnear Svcs. Buzias, 1967-70; resident in psychiatry Clinic of Psychiatry, Cluj, 1970—72, Clinic of Psychiatry, Timisoara, 1972—73; coord. Psychiat. Svc. of the Ambulatory of Satu Mare Hosp., 1973-79; chief Lab. Mental Health, Satu Mare, 1979-83; head dept. acute psychiatry Satu Mare County Hosp., Satu Mare, 1983—2010; head psychiatric dept. West Media Soc., 2010—. Dir. Lab. Med. Informatics, Satu Mare, 1991—; head psychiat. dept. West Medica Soc., 2010—. Author: The Dialogue Physician-Patient, 1981, The Nonverbal Communication, 1987, The Medical Informatics, 1988; contbr. articles to profl. jours. Pres. Fundation The Humanisation of the Hosp., Satu Mare, 1994—, Civical Alliance, Satu Mare, 1991-98; counsellor Satu Mare Mcpl. Coun., 1992-96, 2004-08; bd. dirs. Nat. Physicians Coll., Satu Mare, 1997—, v.p. Satu Mare County Orgn. Nat. Liberal Party. Recipient Knight Art & Letters, Sanitary Merit award Ministry of Health, 1981, gold awards Red Cross, 1977, 2d prize Nat. Contest Tech.-Sci. Creation, 1981, 3d prize Internat. Congress Cybernetics, 1976, Gheorghe Marinescu award Romanian Acad., 1989, Cultural award Satu Mare County, 1996, Gold medal U. West, 2007; named hon. citizen Satu Mare city. Fellow: Romanian Fedn. Psychotherapy (elected pres. 2001), Romanian Med. Informatics Soc. (hon. pres.), NY Acad. Scis., Romanian Acad. Med. Scis.; mem.: Writer Physician Soc., World Psychiatrist Assn., Balcanic Med. Union (Meml. award 1996), Internat. Soc. Cybernetics (Belgium), World Soc. Group Psychotherapy, Rotary (founding pres. Satu Mare 2002—04). Achievements include invention of equipment for analysis of nonverbal communications parameters of gait, gesture, voice, writing and drawing. Avocations: travel, literature. Office: West Medica Druhul Rareiu2u NR1 Satu Mare Romania Fax: 0040261769769. E-mail: virgilenatescu@yahoo.com.

ENATSU, SOTARO, clinical research physician; b. Miyakonojo, Miyazaki, Japan, Feb. 26, 1972; s. Yoriyuki and Yuko Enatsu; m. Megumi Komori, July 29, 2000; children: Noriyuki, Naoya. MD, Fukuoka U., 1997, PhD, 2007. Intern Fukuoka U. Sch. Medicine, Japan, 1997—98, Hyogo Med. Ctr. Adults, Akashi, 1998—99; resident Nat. Cancer Ctr. Hosp., East, Kashiwa, Chiba, 1999—2002; staff gen. thoracic surgery St. Mary's Hosp., Kurume, Fukuoka, 2002—03; fellow dept. surgery Fukuoka U. Sch. Medicine, 2003—04; postdoct. Harvard Med. Dana-Farber Cancer Inst., Boston, 2007—. Coord. Japanese Clin. Oncology Group, Chuo-ku, Tokyo, 2003—. Contbr. articles to profl. jours. Mem.: Japanese Soc. Med. Oncology, Japan Soc. Clin. Oncology, Japan Surg. Assn., Japan Soc. Endoscopic Surgery, Japanese Assn. Thoracic Surgery, Japanese Breast Cancer Soc., Japanese Cancer Assn., Japan Soc. Respiratory Endoscopy (licentiate), Japanese Assn. Chest Surgery (licentiate), Japan Surg. Soc. (licentiate), Japan Broncho-Esophagological Soc. (licentiate). Buddhist. Avocations: swimming, travel, triathlon, jazz, tea ceremony. Home: 2-4-13 Katae Jonan-ku Fukuoka 814-0142 Japan Office: Harvard Med Sch Dana-Farber Cancer Inst Med Oncology 44 Binney St Mayer M549 Boston MA 02115 also: Eli Lilly Kk Sannomiya Plaza Bldg N-1-5 Isogaanidor Chuo-Ku Kobe 6510086 Japan Office Phone: 617-632-2559. Office Fax: 81-92-861-8271; Home Fax: 81-92-874-2460. Personal E-mail: someno@my.0038.net. Business E-Mail: enatsu_sotaro@lilly.com, senatsu@mac.com. E-mail: enatsu_dfci@yahoo.co.jp.

ENDE, JACK, internist, educator; MD, Med. Coll. Va., 1973. Diplomate Am. Bd. Internal Medicine, 1976. Intern medicine dept. Univ. of Chgo., 1973—74, resident medicine dept., 1974—76, chief med. resident, 1977—78; Adele and Harold Schaeffer prof. gen. internal medicine divsn. Penn Presbyterian Med. Ctr. Named one of the Top Doctor, Phila Mag., 2011. Office: Penn Presbyterian Medical Center 130 Wright-Saunders 39th & Market St Philadelphia PA 19104 Office Phone: 215-898-8989. Office Fax: 215-243-3208. E-mail: ENDE@MAIL.MED.UPENN.EDU.

ENDERS, ALLEN COFFIN, anatomy educator; b. Wooster, Ohio, Aug. 5, 1928; s. Robert Kendal and Abbie Gertrude (Crandell) E.; m. Alice Hay, June 15, 1950 (div. Dec. 1975); children: Robert H., George C., Richard S., Gregory H.; m. Sandra Jean Schlafke, Aug. 5, 1976. AB, Swarthmore Coll., 1950; AM, Harvard U., 1952, PhD, 1955. From asst. prof. to assoc. prof Rice Inst., Houston, 1954-63; from assoc. prof. to prof. Washington U., St. Louis, 1963-75; prof., chmn. dept. human anatomy U. Calif., Davis, 1976-86, prof. cell biology and human anatomy, 1986—. Cons. NIH, Bethesda, Md., 1964-68, 70-73, 76-80, 83-93. Author: (with others) Bailey's Microscopic Anatomy, 1984; editor: Delayed Implantation, 1964; contbr. numerous articles on anatomy and reproduction to profl. jours. Nat. pres. Perinatal Rsch. Soc., 1981. Grantee NIH, 1959-99. Fellow AAAS; mem. Am. Assn. Anatomists (v.p. 1980-82, pres. 1983-84), Pioneer Reprodn. Res. Home: 39707 Barry Rd Davis CA 95616-9415 Office: U Calif Sch Medicine Cell Biology & Anatomy Davis CA 95616

ENDO, AKIRA, pharmaceutical executive; b. Japan, Nov. 14, 1933; BA, Tohoku U., Sendai, Japan, 1957; PhD in Biochemistry, Tohoku U., 1966. Rsch. fellow Sankyo Co. Ltd., Tokyo, 1957—66, 1968—69, sr. rsch. fellow, 1969—78; rsch. assoc. dept. molecular biology Albert Einstein Coll. Medicine, NYC, 1966—68; assoc. prof. faculty of agr. Tokyo U. Agr. and Tech., 1979—86, prof., 1986—97, prof. emeritus, 1997—; dir. Biopharm Rsch. Laboratories, Inc., Tokyo, 1997—. Contbr. articles to sci. jours. Recipient Young Investigator award in agrl. chemistry, 1966, Heinrich Wieland prize, Germany, 1987, Toray Sci. and Tech. prize, Japan, 1988, Warren Alpert Found. prize, Harvard Med. Sch., 2000, Japan prize (Category: The Develop. of Novel Therapeutic Concepts and Technologics), Sci. and Tech. Found. Japan, 2006, Lasker-DeBakey Clin. Med. Rsch. award, Lasker Found., 2008. Mem.: NAS (fgn. assoc.). Achievements include significant contributions to the discovery and development of statins, cholesterol-lowering drugs. Office: Biopharm Rsch Laboratories Inc 41-3-501 Shimo Renjaku 3-Chome Mitaka Shi Tokyo 181-0013 Japan *

ENDO, FUMIYASU, physician; b. Japan, July 10, 1968; PhD, U. Tsukuba, MD, 1993. Sr. staff St. Luke's Internat. Hosp., 2006—. Office: 9-1 Akashi cho Chuo Tokyo 104-8560 Japan

ENDO, TOSHIYA, dentist, educator; b. Japan, Dec. 16, 1955; DDS, Nippon Dental U. Sch. Life Dentistry, Niigata, PhD, 1982. Prof., chair Nippon Dental U. Niigata Hosp., 2008—. Office: 1-8 Hamaura-cho Chuo-ku Niigata 951-8580 Japan Business E-Mail: endoto@ngt.ndu.ac.jp.

ENDO, YASUYUKI, chemist, educator; b. Kamakura, Japan, Jan. 1, 1954; BA, U. Tokyo, 1976, MS, 1978. Rsch. assoc. Faculty Pharm. Scis., U. Tokyo, 1979—86, asst. prof., 1986—91, assoc. prof., 1991—2002; postdoc dept. chemistry, Ohio State U., 1988—89, prof. faculty pharm. scis. Tohoku Pharm. U., 2002—. Bd. nat. exam. pharmacist Ministry Health, Labor and Welfare, 2003—09. Recipient Sci. Rsch. award, Uehara Meml. Found., award, Sapporo Biosci. Found. Mem.: Internat. Conf. Boron Chemistry (internat. sci. com. mem.), Pharm. Soc. Japan (exec. com. mem., Young Scientists award). Office: 4-4-1 Komatsushima Aoba-ku Sendai Miyagi 981-8558 Japan Office Fax: 81-22-275-2013. Business E-Mail: yendo@tohoku-pharm.ac.jp.

ENDOH, HIDEKI, thoracic surgeon; b. Japan, May 9, 1972; MD, Gunma U., 1997, PhD, 2004. Resident Aichi Cancer Ctr. Hosp., 2001—05; rsch. fellow Dana-Farber Cancer Inst., 2011—; stuff surgeon Gunma U. Sch. Medicine, 2005—07, Saku Gen. Hosp., 2007—10. Office: 450 Brookline Ave M420 Boston MA 02215 Home Phone: 617-963-6651. E-mail: hideki_endoh1@dfci.harvard.edu.

ENERBÄCK, SVEN, medical geneticist; b. Sweden; MD, PhD. Prof. med. genetics Inst., Med. Biochemistry, Göteborg U., Sweden; mem., fin. officer Diabesity project, Göteborg, Sweden. Mem.: Swedish Royal Acad. Scis. (elec. mem.). Office: Inst Med Biochemistry Box 440 401 26 Göteborg Sweden Office Phone: +46 (0)31 786 3334. Office Fax: +46 (0)31 416108. E-mail: sven.enerback@medgen.gu.se.

ENESEL, MIRCEA, anesthesiologist; b. Sibiu, Romania, Feb. 25, 1951; d. Vasile and Maria Enesel; 1 child, Julia. MD, U. Medicine and Pharmacy, Bucharest, Romania, 1976, specialist in anesthesiology and intensive care, 1982, PhD in Med. Scis., 2004. Sr. physician in anesthesiology and intensive care U. Medicine and Pharmacy, Bucharest, 1990; head intensive care unit and anesthesiology dept. U. Emergency Hosp., Turgu Mures, Romania, 1992—. Internat. scholar Cleve. Clinic Found., 1996; vis. asst. prof. U. Tex., Houston, 1998. Contbr. articles to profl. jours. Mem.: European Soc. Anesthesiology. Achievements include research in immunomodulating in cancer patients. Avocations: psychology, writing beleltristics, history. Office: Emergency U Hosp Targu Mures Strada Marinescu Gheorghe 1 540103 Targu Mures Romania Office Phone: +40-265-262076. Fax: +40-265-262076. E-mail: eneshell@rdslink.ro.

ENG, ANA MAR, dermatologist, dermatologist; b. Manila, Nov. 25, 1939; arrived in US, 1965; d. Sai Ying O'Young and Yee Mar; children: Oliver, Tanya Eng Sun. MD, U. Santo Tomas, Manila, 1964. Intern, Burlington, Vt., 1965—66; resident U. Wis., Madison, 1966—67, U. Chgo., 1967—70. Instr. U. Chgo., 1970—75; attending physician dept. pathology, 1973—93; attending physician, 1974—95; asst. prof. dept. dermatology U. Ill., 1975—80; clin. asst. prof. dept pathology Loyola Med. Ctr., 1981—91, clin. prof. dept pathology, 1992—95; treas. Chgo. Dermatological Soc., 1985—86; attendent Cook County, Chgo., 1986—93; pres. Chgo. Deramatological Soc., 1986—89; faculty Osler Inst., 1996—2004. Fellow: Am. Acad. Dermatology, Chgo. Dermatol. Soc. (pres. 1986—87, Founders award 1998); mem.: Am. Soc. Dermatopathology. Avocations: flower arranging, hula dancing. Personal E-mail: anabrightcloud@gmail.com.

ENG, CHARIS EU LI, geneticist, researcher; b. Singapore, Jan. 17, 1962; s. SooPeck and Siok Mui (Lee) Eng. BA, U. Chgo., 1982, PhD, 1986; MD, U. Chgo. Pritzker Sch. Medicine, 1988. Diplomate American Bd. Internal Medicine. Resident internal medicine Beth Israel Deaconess Med. Ctr., Boston, 1988-91; clin. fellow med. oncology Brigham & Women's Hosp., Boston, 1991—92, Dana-Farber Cancer Inst., Boston, 1992—95, staff physician, 1995-98; fellow clin. cancer genetics U. Cambridge/Royal Marsden Hosp., England, 1992-95; instr. Harvard Med. Sch., Boston, 1994-95, asst. prof. medicine, 1995-98; assoc. prof. medicine Ohio State U., Columbus, 1999—2002, dir. clin. cancer genetics program, 1999—2005, prof. medicine, dir. divsn. human genetics, 2002—05, Dorothy E. Klotz chair cancer rsch., 2002—05; prof., vice-chair dept. genetics Case Western Reserve U., Cleve., 2005—; founding dir., chair Genomic Medicine Inst., Cleve. Clinic, 2005—, Sondra J. & Stephen R. Hardis chair cancer genomic medicine, 2008—, American Cancer Soc. clin. rsch. prof., 2009—10. Disting. lectr. Fox Chase Cancer Ctr., Phila., 2007; apptd. mem. sec.'s adv. com. genetics, health & society US Dept. Health & Human Svcs. (HHS), 2009—. North American editor Jour. Med. Genetics, 1998—2005, sr. editor Cancer Rsch., 2004—09, assoc. editor Jour. Clin. Endocrinology & Metabolism, 2005—09, American Jour. Human Genetics, 2007—09; contbr. articles to profl. jours. Recipient Stephanie Spielman Breast Cancer Rsch. award, James Cancer Hosp. & Solove Rsch. Inst., Ohio State U., 2002, Doris Duke Disting. Clin. Scientist award, 2002, Van Meter award, American Thyroid Assn., 2005, Innovator award, Cleve. Clinic, 2006, 2007, John Peter Minton, MD, PhD Hero of Hope Rsch. Medal of Honor, American Cancer Soc., 2006, Maria and Sam Miller Profl. Excellence award for sci. achievement in clin. rsch., 2009; named a Local Legend from Ohio, American Med. Women's Assn., 2006. Fellow: ACP, AAAS; mem.: Endocrine Soc. (Ernst Oppenheimer Meml. award 2006), American Soc. Clin. Oncology, American Assn. Cancer Rsch., American Soc. Human Genetics, Assn. American Physicians, Inst. Medicine, American Soc. Clin. Investigation. Office: Cleve Clinic Main Campus Mail Code NE5 9500 Euclid Ave Cleveland OH 44195 Office Phone: 216-444-3440. Business E-Mail: engc@ccf.org. *

ENG, TONY, medical educator; b. Hong Kong, Jan. 1, 1960; MD, USUSHC, 1986. Prof. U. Tex. Health Sci. Ctr., San Antonio, 1999—. Named Tchr. of Yr., ARRO. Office: 7979 Wurzbach Rd San Antonio TX 78229 E-mail: tyeng@pol.net.

ENGEBERG, ERIK DANIEL, engineering educator; b. Powell, Wyo., Nov. 6, 1980; PhD, U. Utah, 2008. Asst. prof. U. Akron, 2008—. Office: ASEC 113 Akron OH 44325-3903 Business E-Mail: ee9@uakron.edu.

ENGEL, ANDREW GEORGE, neurologist; b. Budapest, Hungary, July 12, 1930; s. Alexander and Alice Julia (Gluck) E.; m. Nancy Jean Brombacher, Aug. 15, 1958; children: Lloyd William, Andrew George. BSc, McGill U., Montreal, 1953, MD, 1955. Diplomate: Am. Bd. Internal Medicine, Am. Bd. Psychiatry and Neurology. Intern Phila. Gen. Hosp., 1955—56; sr. asst. surgeon, clin. asso. USPHS, NIH, Bethesda, Md., 1958-59; fellow in neuropathology Columbia U., NYC, 1962-64; with Mayo Clinic, Rochester, Minn., 1956-57, 60-62; cons. Rochester, Minn., 1965—; prof. neurology Mayo Med. Sch., Rochester, 1973—, William L. McKnight-3M prof. neurosci., 1984—; disting. investigator Mayo Clinic, 1995—, disting. alumnus, 2008. Mem. sci. adv. com. Muscular Dystrophy Assn., 1973-99, mem. rev. com. NIH, 1977-81. Mem. editl. bd. Neurology, 1973-77, Annals Neurology, 1978-84, 90-95, Muscle and Nerve, 1978-97, 00-, Jour. Neuropathology, 1981-83, 96-00, European Neurology, 1989-2005, Jour. Neuroimmunology, 1991-98, Molecular Neurobiology, 1997—, assoc. editor Neuromuscular Disorders, 1998-, Neurology, 2007—; contbr. over 350 articles to med. jours. Served with USPHS, 1957-59. Mem. Am. Acad. Neurology (hon.), Am. Neurol. Assn. (hon.), Soc. Neuroscis., AAAS, Inst. of Medicine of Nat. Acad. Sci., 2004, European, German and Spanish Neurologic Assoc. (hon.), European Neurol. Soc., German Neurol. Soc., Spanish Neurol. Assn., German Soc. Clin. Neurophys., Prin. Assoc. Neuromascular & Electrolignatic Medicine(hon.). Home: 2027 Lenwood Dr SW Rochester MN 55902-1051 Office: Mayo Clinic 200 1st St SW Rochester MN 55905-0002

ENGEL, BERNARD THEODORE, psychologist, educator; b. Chgo., Apr. 18, 1928; s. Marvin I. and Hannah (Hollander) E.; m. Rae Goldberg, Mar. 10, 1951; children: Sandra E., Jeffrey P., Lauren C. BA, UCLA, 1954, PhD, 1956. Jr. rsch. psychologist UCLA, 1956; rsch. psychologist Inst. Psychosomatic and Psychiatric. Research and Tng., Michael Reese Hosp., Chgo., 1957-58; lectr. med. psychology, mem. sr. staff Cardiovasc. rsch. Inst., Sch. Medicine U. Calif., San Francisco, 1959-67; chief behavioral physiology sect., chief Lab. Behavioral Scis. Gerontology Research Center, Nat. Inst. Aging, NIH, Balt., 1967-95; assoc. prof. behavioral biology Johns Hopkins Sch. Medicine, Balt., 1970-82, prof., 1982—. Bd. dirs. Insts. for Behavioral Resources, Inc.; adj. prof. psychiatry and behavioral scis. Duke U. Sch. Medicine, Durham, N.C., 1999—. Contbr. 175 articles to sci. jours.; editorial bds. Applied Psychophysiology and Biofeedback, Jour. of Behavioral Medicine, Psychosmatic Medicine. Served US Army, 1950—52. Recipient award Pavlovian Soc., 1979; cert. of Appreciation, N.C. State Hwy. Patrol, 2003. Fellow AAAS, Gerontol. Sci.; mem. Soc. Psychophysiol. Rsch. (pres. 1970-71), Assn. Applied Psychophysiology and Biofeedback (pres. 1981-82, Disting. Scientist award 2001), Am. Psychosomatic Soc. (sec.-treas. 1981-85, pres. 1985-86, Patricia R. Barchas award in sociophysiology 1999), Gerontol. Soc. Am., Acad. Behavioral Medicine Rsch., Sigma Xi. Personal E-mail: btere@aol.com.

ENGEL, HEINZ-JÜRGEN, retired cardiologist director; b. Marburg, Germany, May 9, 1941; s. Heinrich and Christa (Vietor) E.; m. Hiltrude Vogel, Dec. 16, 1965; children: Christine, Achim, Brenda. MD, U. Munich, 1965. Cert. internist, cardiologist, Germany. Asst. physician U. Göttingen and Northeim, Germany, 1966-72; fellow in cardiology St. Thomas Hosp., Nashville, 1973-74; asst. physician Hannover (Germany) Med. Sch., 1974-77, lectr., sr. registrar, 1977-81, prof., 1982; chief dept. cardiology Bremen (Germany) Heart Ctr., 1981—2006; ret., 2006. Vis. prof. med. schs. in Can., 1980-82, China, 1994, Moscow and St. Petersburg, Russia, 1999, Kiev, Ukraine, 1999; also lectr., instr. angioplasty courses. Editor books on cardiac drugs and coronary angiography; contbr. numerous articles on coronary artery disease, coronary anomalies, coronary heart disease in women, coronary angioplasty, myocardial infarction, and catheter interventions to med. jours. Fellow Am. Coll. Cardiology; mem. German Soc.

Cardiology (various offices), Rotary (various offices Bremen Neuenlande). Avocations: tennis, sailing, piano. Office Phone: 0049-421-8791430. E-mail: engel.bremen@t-online.de.

ENGEL, JEFFREY P., state agency administrator, public health service officer; B, Johns Hopkins U., Balt., 1977, MD, 1981. Residency, chief residency, fellowship tng. U. Minn., Mpls. Veterans Adminstrn. Med. Ctr., 1981—88; prof. medicine & chief, divsn. infectious diseases East Carolina U. Brody Sch. Medicine, Greenville, 1988—2002; med. dir., hosp. infection control Pitt County Meml. Hosp.; state epidemiologist NC Dept. Health and Human Services, 2002—09, chief, divsn. pub. health epidemiology sect., 2006—09, state health dir. & dir., divsn. pub. health, 2009—. Office: NC Divsn Public Health 5605 Six Forks Rd 1st Fl 1931 Mail Svc Ctr Raleigh NC 27699-1931 Office Phone: 919-707-5000. Office Fax: 919-870-4829.

ENGEL, JEROME, JR., neurologist, neuroscientist, psychiatry professor; b. Albany, NY, May 11, 1938; s. Jerome and Pauline (Feder) E.; m. Catherine Margaret Lambourne, Feb. 26, 1967 (dec. Mar. 10, 2009); children: Sean, Jesse, Anasuya. BA, Cornell U., 1960; MD, Stanford U., 1965, PhD in Physiology, 1966. Diplomate Nat. Bd. Med. Examiners, Am. Bd. Qualification in EEG, Nat. Bd. Psychiatry and Neurology. Intern Ind. U., Indpls., 1966-67; resident in neurology Albert Einstein Coll. Medicine, Bronx, N.Y., 1967-68, 70-72; resident in EEG Nat. Hosp. Nervous and Mental Disease Queen Sq., London, 1971, Maudsley Hosp., London, 1972; attending neurologist, dir. electroencephalography labs. Bronx Mcpl. Hosp. Ctr., Hosp. Albert Einstein Coll. Medicine, 1972-76; attending neurologist, chief of epilepsy, clin. neurophysiology UCLA Hosp. and Clinics, 1976—; assoc. investigator lab. nuclear medicine of Lab. Biomed. and Environ. Scis. UCLA Med. Ctr., 1981—; dir. UCLA Seizure Disorder Ctr., 1994—; prof. psychiatry and biobehavioral medicine UCLA Sch. Medicine, 2005—; Jerome Merlis lectr. U. Md., 2008; Jerome Merlin lectr. U. Calgary, 2008. Staff assoc. NINDS NIH Lab. Perinatal Physiology, San Juan, P.R.; vis. asst. prof. dept. physiology and biophysics U. P.R. Sch. Medicine, 1968-69, Lab. Neural Control, Bethesda, Md., 1969-70; asst. prof. neurology Albert Einstein Coll. Medicine, Bronx, 1972-76, asst. prof. neurosci., 1974-76; assoc. prof. neurology UCLA Sch. Medicine, 1976-80, assoc. prof. anatomy, 1977-80, prof. neurology, neurobiology (formerly anatomy and cell biology), 1980—; assoc. investigator Lab. Nuclear Medicine, Lab. Biomed. and Environ. Scis., 1981—; chmn. internat. and coop. projects study sect. NIH, 1989-90, mem. biomed. scis. study sect., 1985-89, chmn., 1988-89; vis. prof. dept. anatomy Sydney U., 1984, Jonathan Sinay prof., 2002—; prof. psychiatry and behavioral scis., 2005—. Author: Epilepsy and Positron CT, Clinical Relevance for Diagnosis of Epilepsy, 1985, Surgical Treatment of the Epilepsies, 1987, Seizures and Epilepsy, 1989, Surgical Treatment of Epilepsies, 1993, (with others) Neurotransmitters, Seizures and Epilepsy II, 1984, Neurotransmitters, Seizures and Epilepsy II, 1984, Neurotransmitters, Seizures and Epilepsy III, 1986, The Epileptic Focus, 1987, Fundamental Mechanisms of Human Brain Function, 1987, Clinical Use of Emission Tomography in Focal Epilepsy, Current Problems in Epilepsy, Vol. 7, 1990, Neurotransmitters in Epilepsy, 1992, Molecular Neurobiology and Epilepsy, 1992, The Progressive Nature of Epilepsy, 1996, Epilepsy: a Comprehensive Textbook, 1998, Parallel Studies of Epileptogenesis in Human Tissue and Animal Models, 1998, Brain Plasticity and Epilepsy, 2000, 01, The Goal of Epilepsy Surgery, No Seizures, No Side Effects, As Soon As Possible, 2004, Atlas of EEG Patterns, 2004, Epilepsy: Global Issues for the Practicing Neurologist, 2005, Generalized Seizures, From Clinical Phenomenology to Underlying Systems and Networks, 2006, Epilepsy: A Comprehensive Textbook 2nd edit., 2008, The Treatment of Epilepsy, 2009; chief editor: Advances in Neurobiology of Epilepsy, 1989-91, World Federation of Neurology, Seminars in Neurology, 2006-; assoc. editor: Jour. Clin. Neurophysiology, 1983—, Epilepsy Rsch., 1985—, Epilepsy Advances, 1985-87, Brain Topography, 1990—, Epilepsia, 1994—; contbr. over 140 chpts. to books including Functional Brain Imaging, 1988, Anatomy of Epileptogenesis, 1989, EEG Handbook, rev. series vol. 4, 1990, Comprehensive Epileptology, 1990, Generalized Epilepsy, 1990, Neurotransmitters in Epilepsy, Epilepsy Research (Supplement), 1992, Molecular Neurobiology and Epilepsy;, Encyclopedia of the Neurological Sciences, 2003, The Goal of Epilepsy Surgery, 2004; contbr. over 240 articles to profl. jours. including New Issues in Neuroscis., Neurology, Jour. Neurosurg., Jour. Epilepsy, Epilepsia, Can. Jour. Neurol. Sci., Radiology, Jour. Cerebral Blood Flow Metabolism, Acta Neurochirugica, Jour. Clin. Psychiatry. Active profl. adv. bd. Epilepsy Found. Internat. League Against Epilepsy, 1988—. N.Y. State Regents scholar, 1956-60, NIH traineeship, summer 1962, predoctoral fellowship, 1964, postdoctoral fellowship, 1965-66, career devel. award 1972-76; recipient Epilepsy Found. Am. award, 1963, Stiftung Michael prize, 1982; Fulbright scholar, 1971-72, fellow in neurology Sch. Medicine Stanford U., 1965-66, Lab. Applied Neuophysiology, C.N.R.S., Marseilles, France, 1966, Dagan Lectr. Winter Conf. on Brain Rsch., 1981, John Guggenheim fellow, 1983-84, Hanna lectr. Case-Western Reserve, 1983, First Aird lectr. U. Calif. San Francisco, 1985, First Cox lectr. Albert Einstein Coll. Medicine, 1985, First Vaajasalo lectr. and award, Kuopio, Finland, 1987, Aring lectr. U. Cin. Med. Ctr., 1987, First Hans Berger lectr. Internat. Congress of EEG and Clin. Neurophysiology, 1990; Covy Williams lectr. Cleve Clinic, 1992; Hans Berger lectr. Med. Coll. Va., 1993, Javits Investigator award, NIH, 2003, Franklin D. Murphy prize, UCLA, 2010 Fellow: Am. Acad. Neurology (self assessment epilepsy task force chair 1990—96, Mythili Oration 2000, Hoyer lectr. 2002, Mary Ann Lee lectr. U. Calgary 2005); mem.: AAAS, World Fed. Neurology (edn. com. mem. 2003—, web editor 2010—), Liga Chilena contra la Epilepsia, Hong Kong Neurol. Soc., Western Electroencephalography Soc. (Wilder Penfield lectr. 2000), Soc. for Neurosci. (neurobiology of disease workshop organizing com. 1989—90), Nat. Assn. Epilepsy Ctrs. (bd. dirs. 1988—, treas. 1990—94), Ea. Assn. Electroencephalographers (Kershman lectr. 1994, first Judith Hoyer lectr. 2002, Dreifuss lectr. 2003), Epilepsy Support Assn. Ethopia (hon.), Am. Neurol. Assn. (hon.; mem. program com. 1987—90), Australian Assn. Neurologists (hon.), Can. Soc. Clin. Neurophysiologists (hon.), Turkish Epilepsy Soc. (hon.), All-Russian Assn. Neurologists (hon.), Yugoslavian League Against Epilepsy (hon.), Internat. Soc. Cerebral Blood Flow and Metabolism, Internat. League Against Epilepsy (program com. 1986—88, commn. on epilepsy surgery 1989—93, chmn. commn. on neurobiology of epilepsy 1989—93, treas. 1994—97, pres. 1997—2001, co-chair global campaign against epilepsy 2001—05, amb. for epilepsy award 1991), Internat. Fedn. EEG and Clin. Neurophysiology Socs. (program com. 1988—90, chmn. com. on guidelines for long-term monitoring for epilepsy 1989—, Lifetime Achievement award 2011), Internat. Brain Rsch. Orgn., Am. Physiol. Soc., Am. Epilepsy Soc. (sec. 1979—82, 2nd v.p. 1982—83, 1st v.p. 1983—84, pres. 1984—85, councillor 1985—86, v.p. to Internat. League Against Epilepsy 1990—93, William G. Lennox lectr. 1990, Clin. Investigator award 1996, William Lennox award 1999), Am. EEG Soc. (councillor 1984—87, chmn. rsch. fellowship com. 1988—91, pres. elect 1991—92, pres. 1992—93, Pierre Gloor award 1999), Russian League Against Epilepsy. Achievements include research on basic mechanisms of epilepsy and epilepsy related behavior, particularly involving surgical treatment of partial seizures and use of new technology such as positron emission tomography and advanced EEG telemetry. Home: 10521 Seabury Ln Los Angeles CA 90077-2441 Office: UCLA Sch Medicine Reed Neurol Rsch Ctr # 1250 710 Westwood Plz Los Angeles CA 90095-8353 Home Phone: 310-441-7783; Office Phone: 310-825-5745. Business E-Mail: engel@ucla.edu.

ENGEL, MICHAEL E., medical educator; b. Franklin, Ind., Sept. 13, 1965; BS, Purdue U., 1989; MD, Vanderbilt U. Sch. Medicine, PhD, 2001. Adj. asst. prof., cancer biology Vanderbilt U. Sch. Medicine, 2006—10; asst. prof. Vanderbilt Children's Hosp., 2006—10; adj. asst. prof., oncological scis. Huntsman Cancer Inst., Ctr. Children's Cancer Rsch., 2010—11; asst. prof. U. Utah Sch. Medicine, 2010—. Recipient Career Devel. award, St. Baldrick's Found., Young Investigator award, ASPHO. Mem.: FASEB, Am. Soc. Pediatric Hematology-Oncology, Am. Assn. Cancer Rsch., Am. Soc. Hematology, Children's Oncology Group. Office: 2000 Circle Hope Dr Salt Lake City UT 84112 Personal E-mail: engelme@comcast.net.

ENGEL, WILLIAM KING, neurologist, educator; b. St. Louis, Nov. 19, 1930; s. William Ernst and Opal (King) E.; m. Valerie Askanas; children: W. Keith, Peter J., Bradford C., Eve M. Kerr. BA, Johns Hopkins U., 1951; MD, C.M., McGill U., 1955; MD (hon.), L'univ. d'Aix Marseille II, 1987. Diplomate: Am. Bd. Neurology and Psychiatry, Pan. Am. Med. Assn. (hon. life mem.). Intern U. Mich. Hosp., 1955-56; clin. assoc. Nat. Inst. Neurol. Diseases and Blindness, 1956-59; clin. clk. Nat. Hosp., London, 1959-60; with Nat. Inst. Neurol. Diseases and Stroke, 1960-81, chief med. neurology, 1963-78, chief neuromuscular diseases, 1978-81; clin. prof. neurology George Washington U., 1969-81; prof. neurology and pathology, chief div. neuromuscular diseases, dept. neurology U. So. Calif. Sch. Medicine, Los Angeles, 1981—; mem. med. bd. NIH, 1968-69; founding dir. U. So. Calif. Neuromuscular Center, Hosp. of Good Samaritan, 1981—. Mem. med. adv. bd. St. Jude's Children's Rsch. Hosp., Memphis, 1970-76, Myasthenia Gravis Found., 1970—, L.A. chpt. Muscular Dystropy Assn., 1981—, Amyotrophic Lateral Sclerosis Nat. Found., 1971-85, Amyotrophic Lateral Sclerosis Soc. Am., 1980-85, mem. sci. adv. bd., 1982-85; vis. prof., invited lectr., advisor internat. congresses in Europe, S.Am., Can., Australia, Far East; cons. Nat. Naval Med. Ctr. Former mem. editl. bd. Archives of Neurology; contbr. over 900 articles to profl. jours., poems to mags. Past pres. Citizens Assn., Bethesda, Md., Longhouse chief YMCA Indian Guides, 1965-66; past chmn. troop com. Boy Scouts Am.; nat. v.p. Muscular Dystrophy Assn., 1985-88, nat. v.p. 1988—, med. adv. bd. Los Angeles chpt., 1981—, chmn., 2001—; mem. med. adv. bd. The Myositis Assn., 1995—. Recipient Meritorious Service medal USPHS, 1971, Gaetano Conte Gold medal for clin. rsch., 1999, Lifetime Achievement award World Fedn. Neurology, 2002, Lifetime Achievement award Neuropathy Assn., 2006, various awards from Italian me. socs. Fellow Am. Acad. Neurology (S. Weir Mitchell award 1962; pres. VI Internat. Congress Neuromuscular Diseases 1986); mem. AMA, Histochem. Soc., Am. Soc. Cell Biology, Soc. Neurosci., Am. Assn. Neuropathologists, World Commn. Neuromuscular Disease (exec. com.), Am. Neurol. Assn., LA County Med. Assn., Socièté Belge d'Electromyographie (assoc.), Asociación de Distrofia Muscular de la Republica Argentina (hon. pres.), Socièté Française de Neurologie (hon.). Office: U So Calif Neuromuscular Ctr Good Samaritan Hosp 637 Lucas Ave Los Angeles CA 90017-1912

ENGEL-ARIELI, SUSAN LEE, physician; b. Chgo., Oct. 7, 1954; d. Thaddeus S. Dziengiel and Marion L. (Carpenter) Kasper; m. Udi Arieli. BA, Northwestern U., 1975; MD, Chgo. Med. Sch., 1982. Diplomate Am. Bd. Gen. Practice, Am. Bd. Ambulatory Medicine. Med. technician G.D. Searle, Skokie, Ill., 1972, 73, assoc. dir., 1983-84, dir. U.S. Regional Clin. Support, 1984-86; rsch. editorial asst. U. Chgo., 1974; rsch. assoc. Loyola U., Maywood, Ill., 1977-78; intern Rush Presbyn. St. Lukes Hosp., Chgo., 1982-83; resident U. Chgo., 1983; mgr. hosp. products div. Abbott Labs., Abbott Park, Ill., 1986-87. Bd. govs., dep. gov. Am. Biog. Inst. Rsch. Assn., 1988; vis. prof. Rush Presbyn.-St. Luke's Hosp., Chgo., 1985, faculty assoc., 1985; assoc. investigator, asst. prof. medicine King Drew Med. Ctr., UCLA, 1985-90; practical cardiology panel experts, 1988; Med. World News Rev. panel, 1988; bd. dirs. Am. Soc. Handicapped Physicians, acting v.p.; bd. dirs. fundraising, chmn. Vestibular Disorders Assn. Author: How Your Body Works, 1994, C-D Rom version, 1995; contbr. articles to profl. and scholarly jours. Bd. govs. Art Inst. Chgo., 1985—, mem. aux. bd., 1988—, mem. multiple benefit coms., 1984—, vice chmn. Capital Campaign, 1984-85; mem. pres. com. Landmark Preservation Coun., Chgo., 1984-90, chmn. multiple coms. polit. candidates, 1986; bd. dirs. Marshall unit Chgo. Boys Clubs, 1984—; mem. benefit com. Hubbard St. Dance Co. 10th Gala, 1988, Victory Garden's Theatre Ann. Benefit, 1988. Recipient Gold award, 1995, Nat. Health Info. award, 1995; Internat. Coll. Surgeons fellow, 1982. Mem. AMA, ACP, Am. Fedn. for Clin. Rsch., Southern Med. Assn., Ill. State Med. Soc., Chgo. Med. Soc., Am. Acad. Med. Dirs., Nat. Acad. Arts and Scis., Am. Soc. Handicapped Physicians (bd. dirs., v.p.), Vestibular Disorders Assn. (bd. dirs., pub. rels. com., co-chmn. fundraising). Avocations: german language, organ playing, composing music, writing.

ENGELHARDT, HUGO TRISTRAM, JR., physician, educator; s. Hugo Tristram and Beulah Engelhardt; m. Susan Gay Malloy, Nov. 25, 1965; children: Elisabeth, Christina, Dorothea. BA, U. Tex. Austin, 1963, PhD, 1969; MD with honors, Tulane U., New Orleans, 1972; Dr (hon.), U. Medicine and Pharmacy Gr. T. Popa, Iasi, Romania, 2005, U. Alba Iulia, Romania, 2011. Asst. prof. U. Tex. Med. Br., 1972-75, assoc. prof., 1975-77; mem. Inst. Med. Humanities, 1973-77; Rosemary Kennedy prof. philosophy of medicine Georgetown U., 1977-82; sr. rsch. scholar Kennedy Inst. Ctr. for Bioethics, Washington, 1977-82; prof. depts. internal medicine, cmty. medicine and ob-gyn. Baylor Coll. Medicine, Houston, 1983-2001, prof. emeritus, 2001—; mem. Ctr. for Med. Ethics and Health Policy, Houston, 1983-2001; prof. dept. philosophy Rice U., Houston, 1983—. Chmn. adv. panel on infertility prevention and treatment for office of tech. assessment of the U.S. Congress, 1986-87; vis. scholar Internat. Akad. für Philosophie, Liechtenstein, 1997, Liberty Fund, spring, 1998. Author: Mind Body: A Categorial Relation, 1973, The Foundations of Bioethics, 1986, rev. edit., 1996, Bioethics and Secular Humanism, 1991, The Foundations of Christian Bioethics, 2000; co-author: Bioethics: Readings and Cases, 1987; assoc. editor: Ency. of Bioethics, 1978—83; assoc. editor Jour. Medicine and Philosophy, 1974—84; mem. editl. bd. Poiesis & Praxis, 2001—, Chinese and Internat. Philosophy Medicine, 1998—, sr. editor Jour. Medicine and Philosophy, 1984—, Christian Bioethics, 1995—, (series) Philos. Studies in Contemporary Culture, 1992, Philosophy and Medicine series, 1974—; editor: Clin. Med. Ethics, 1987—2002, Evaluation and Explanation in the Biomedical Sciences, 1975, Philosophical Medical Ethics, 1977, Mental Health, 1978, Clinical Judgment, 1979, Concepts of Health and Disease, 1981, New Knowledge in the Biomedical Sciences, 1982, Scientific Controversies, 1987, The Use of Human Beings in Research, 1988, Sicherheit und Freiheit, 1990, Hegel Reconsidered, 1994, The Philosophy of Medicine, 2000, Allocating Scarce Medical Resources, 2002, Global Bioethics, 2006, The Philosophy Medicine Reborn, 2008, Innovation and the Pharmaceutical Industry, 2008. Mem. bioethics com. Nat. Found. March of Dimes, 1975—. Recipient McDonald-Merrill-Ketcham Meml. Excellence award in law and medicine, 2003; Fulbright fellow, 1969-70, Woodrow Wilson vis. fellow, 1988; fellow Inst. for Advanced Studies, Berlin, 1988-89. Mem. Am. Philos. Assn., European Acad. Scis. and Arts. Office: Rice U Dept Philosophy PO Box 1892 Houston TX 77251-1892 Office Phone: 713-348-2491. Business E-Mail: htengelh@rice.edu. *

ENGELMAN, KARL, physician; b. NYC, June 23, 1933; s. Samuel and Lillian (Wachs) E.; m. Elaine Kaufman, June 10, 1956; children: Harold Kent, Ross Mitchell, Jeffrey Steven. BS, Rutgers U., 1955; MD, Harvard U., 1959; MA (hon.), U. Pa., 1971. Diplomate Am. Bd. Internal Medicine. Intern, asst. resident, resident in medicine Mass. Gen. Hosp., Boston, 1959-64; clin. asso., sr. investigator, attending physician Nat. Heart Inst., NIH, Bethesda, Md., 1961-70; assoc. prof. medicine and pharmacology Sch. Medicine U. Pa., Phila., 1971-95; chief hypertension sect., dir. clin. research center Sch. Medicine U. Pa. Cons. physician Phila. VA Hosp., 1971-95, Children's Hosp., Phila., 1971-95; clin. prof. medicine Med. U. of S.C., 1996—; cons. Beaufort-Jasper Comprehensive Health Svcs., 1996—, Vols. in Medicine, 2002—. Patentee in field. Med. staff Vols. in Medicine, 2002--. Served with USPHS, 1961-63. Mem. ACP, Am. Coll. Clin. Pharmacology, Internat. Soc. of Hypertension (sci. coun. on hypertension), U.S. Pharmacopeia and Nat. Formullary (adv. coun.), Coun. for High Blood Pressure Rsch. (adv. bd.), Am. Heart Assn., Phila. Doctors Golf Assn., Sea Pines Club. Jewish. Home: 20 Turnberry Ln Hilton Head Island SC 29928-4108

ENGELMAN, MELVIN ALKON, retired dentist, dental products executive; b. Waterbury, Conn., July 27, 1921; s. Herman B. and Marion (Halpern) E.; m. Muriel Phillips, Aug. 27, 1949; children: Curtis Land, Suzanne Ruth. AB, Ohio U., 1942; DDS, Case Western Res. U., 1944. Diplomate: Am. Bd. Oral Electrosurgery. Pvt. practice dentistry, Wappingers Falls, NY, 1949-89; chmn. oral diagnosis and oral pathology sect., dir. oral diagnostic ctr. St. Francis Hosp., Poughkeepsie, NY, 1963-77, attending dentist, 1963-89, dir. dept. dentistry, 1967, 71-74, 78, hon. staff, 1989—; pres. Di-Equi Dental Products Inc., 1980-99, Dentifax Internat. Inc., 1982-99. Dir. 1st regional sci. fair, Dutchess County, NY, 1960-61; observer Meml. Hosp. Cancer and Allied Diseases, NYC, 1962-66; adv. bd. Dutchess CC, 1963-69; project dir. USPHS cmty. cancer demonstration project, St. Francis Hosp., 1963-66; asst. chief med. officer Dutchess County NY CD, 1963-68; cons. Nat. Cancer Inst., clin. cancer tng. com., 1968-71, profl. edn. com. for cancer control, 1972-73; attending dentist Central Dutchess Nursing Home, 1970-85; cons. VA Hosp., Castle Point, NY, 1976-77, Lactona Corp., divsn. Warner Lambert, 1976-80; lectr. in field Co-author: Oral Cancer Examination Procedure, 1967, 16th edit., 83; contbr. articles to profl. jours. Chmn. Wappinger Red Cross Fund Drive, 1956; troop com. mem., Boy Scouts Am., Chelsea, NY, 1963-67; pres. Dutchess County unit Am. Cancer Soc., 1969-71. With USNR, 1942—81, lt. (j.g.) dental corps USNR, 1944, ret. lt. comdr. USNR, 1981. Fellow AAAS (life), Royal Soc. Health (Eng.), Am. Pub. Health Assn., Acad. Gen. Dentistry; mem. ADA (life), Internat. Assn. Dental Rsch., Mil. Officers Assn., Assn. Mil. Surgeons (life), 9th Dist. Dental Soc. (life), Dutchess County Dental Soc. (pres. 1965), Am. Acad. Dental Electrosurgery (pres. 1983), Wappinger Conservation Assn. (v.p. 1970-71), Wappingers Falls C. of C. (pres. 1952-54), Masons (32 degree), Shriners, B'nai B'rith (pres. So. Duchess lodge 1963-64), Am. Legion, Jewish War Vets., Navy Reserve Assn., Marine Corps League, Alpha Omega. Achievements include patents for feeder bar, spruing assembly, sprue pin, and hollow movable reservoir. Home: 5371 Punta Alta Unit 3H Laguna Hills CA 92637-2588

ENGLAND, ROBERT (BOB), city health department administrator, epidemiologist; m. Nancy Hook; 1 child, Dawn. BS, MD, Univ. Ariz.; MPH, UCLA. Residency in pub. health UCLA & LA County Dept. Health Services; dir. disease control Pima County, Ariz.; med. epidemiologist HIV prog. Ariz. Dept. Health, state epidemiologist; med. dir. Maricopa County Dept. Pub. Health, Phoenix, 2006, acting dir. & dir., 2006—. Mem.: Ariz. Pub. Health Assn., Am. Pub. Health Assn., Nat. Assn. County & City Health Officials, Coun. State & Territorial Epidemiologists, Ariz. Local Health Officers Assn., Ariz. Med. Assn., Physicians for a Nat. Health Plan. Office: Maricopa County Pub Health Ste 1400 4041 N Central Ave Phoenix AZ 85012 Office Phone: 602-506-6900.

ENGLE, JANE, research nurse, artist, chaplain; b. LA, June 15, 1942; d. John Dean and Florence (Updike) E. BA with honors, U. N.C., Chapel Hill, 1965; BSN, Cornell U., Ithaca, NY, 1970; MS in Nursing, U. Ill., Chgo., 1974; MDiv magna cum laude, Wesley Theol. Sem., 1988. RN Md. Tchr., vol., trainer Peace Corps, Afghanistan, 1965—68; pub. health nurse Tufts Delta Health Ctr., Mound Bayou, Miss., 1969; coord. pub. health nursing Ill. Cmty. Clinic, Chgo., 1970—72; nursing cons. rsch. edn. Dept. Pub. Health, Chgo., 1974—78; rsch. nurse AIDS, NIH, Bethesda, Md., 1989—97; abstract artist and paper maker, 1997—; chaplain, 2002—. Mem. AIDS task force Interfaith Conf. Met. Washington, 1988-90. Author: Outcome Measures in Home Care, 1987, Immune-Based Therapy for HIV, 1996; contbr. article to profl. jours. Vol. homeless agys.; v.p. women's bd. Episcopal Ch., Washington, 1981—82; mem. bd. deacons Nat. Presbyn. Ch., Washington, 1982—86; mem. Mayor's Task Force on

Standards, Washington, 1985—87, Foundry Gallery, Washington, 2001. Wesley Theol. Sem. Biblical scholar, 1988; named Person of Week Washington Times, 1992; recipient award for excellence in painting, 2000, The Ethel Lorraine Bernstein Meml. award for excellence in painting Corcoran Coll. Art and Design, 2000. Mem. ANA (pres. local chpt. 1976-78), Assn. Nurses in AIDS Care, Phi Beta Kappa, Sigma Theta Tau. Democrat.

ENGLE, JEANNETTE CRANFILL, medical technician; b. Davie County, NC, July 7, 1941; d. Gurney Nathaniel and Versie Emmaline (Reavis) Cranfill; m. William Sherman Engle (div. 1970); children: Phillip William, Lisa Kaye. Diploma, Dell Sch. Med. Tech., 1960; BA, U. N.C., Asheville, 1976; MS in Biomed. Sci.-Genetics, Marshall U., 1999. Instr. Dell Sch. Med. Tech., Asheville, 1960-67; rotating technologist Meml. Mission Hosp., Asheville, 1967-68, asst. supr. hematology, 1968-71; supr. Damon Subs. Pvt. Clinic Lab., Asheville, 1971-73; chemistry technologist VA Med. Ctr., Durham, N.C., 1973-74, 75-76, supr., 1974-75, asst. supr. microbiology Salem, Va., 1976-79; supr. rsch. Med. Svc. Lab., Salem, 1979-90; flow cytometrist VA Med. Ctr., Huntington, W.Va., 1990-92, cons. to clin. lab. flow cytometry dept., 1992—. Reviewer Jour. Club, Roanoke-Salem, Va., 1980-90. Author: (poem) Reflections on a Comet, 1984; contbr. numerous articles and abstracts on med. tech. to profl. jours., 1982—. Mem. The Acting Co. Ensemble. Democrat. Episcopalian. Avocations: reading, flower arranging, interior design, art, music. Home: 4775 Green Valley Rd Huntington WV 25701-9793 Home Phone: 304-522-9277. Personal E-mail: jeannette.engle@yahoo.com, jeannetterengle@gmail.com.

ENGLE, WILLIAM DOUGLAS, medical educator; b. Dayton, Ohio, Apr. 2, 1948; BA, Dartmouth, 1970; MD, Tufts, 1974. Prof. pediat. UTSW, 1980—2011. Mem.: AAP. Office: 5323 Harry Hines Blvd Dallas TX 75390-9063 Office Phone: 214-648-6378. Business E-Mail: william.engle@utsouthwestern.edu.

ENGLEMAN, EPHRAIM PHILIP, rheumatologist; b. San Jose, Calif., Mar. 24, 1911; s. Maurice and Tillie (Rosenberg) E.; m. Jean Sinton, Mar. 2, 1941; children: Ephraim Philip, Edgar George, Jill. BA, Stanford U., 1933; MD, Columbia U., 1937. Intern Mt. Zion Hosp., San Francisco; resident U. Calif., San Francisco, Jos. Pratt Diagnostic Hosp., Boston; rsch. fellow Mass. Gen. Hosp., Boston, 1937-42; practice medicine specializing in rheumatology San Francisco, 1948—; mem. faculty U. Calif. Med. Ctr., San Francisco, 1949—, clin. prof. medicine, 1965—; dir. Rosalind Russell Arthritis Ctr., 1979—. Staff U. Calif. Hosp.; chmn. Nat. Commn. Arthritis and Related Diseases, 1975-76. Author: The Book on Arthritis: A Guide for Patients and Their Families, 1979; also articles, chpts. in books. Served to maj. M.C. USMCR, 1942—47. Recipient medal of Honor, U. Calif., San Francisco, 1999, citation Arthritis Found., 1973, Gold medal for excellence in clin. medicine Columbia U. P&S Alumni, 2007; Ephraim P. Engleman Disting. Professorship in Rheumatology named in his honor U. Calif., San Francisco, 1991; Nat. Inst. Arthritis grantee. Fellow ACP; mem. Internat. League Against Rheumatism (pres. 1981-85), Am. Coll. Rheumatology (founding fellow, master, pres. 1962-63, Presdl. Gold medal 2002), Nat. Soc. Clin. Rheumatologists, AMA, Am. Fedn. Clin. Rsch.; mem. Japanese Rheumatism Soc. (hon.), Spanish Rheumatism Soc., Uruguay Rheumatism Soc., Australian Rheumatism Assn., Chinese Med. Assn., French Soc. Rheumatology, Internat. League against Rheumatism, Gold-Headed Cane Soc. (U. Calif. San Francisco), Family Club (San Francisco). Republican. Jewish. Office: U Calif Rosalind Russell Med Rsch Ctr Arthritis 350 Parnassus Ave Ste 600 San Francisco CA 94117-3608 Office Phone: 415-476-1141.

ENGLENDER, MOSHE, otolaryngologist; b. Omsk, Russia, Jan. 17, 1946; MD, Med. Sch. Bologna, 1973. Head dept. otolaryngology Ministry Health, 2005—. Adj. prof. Negev U., 2006. Home: Revivim 14 Tel Aviv 69354 Israel Home Fax: 972 3 6471327. Business E-Mail: moshee@barzi.health.gov.il.

ENGLISH, SHARON JEANETTE, neonatologist, consultant; b. London, Eng., Mar. 13, 1971; d. Raymond John English and Ann Susan Full; m. Steven Tsu-Wi Ong, Oct. 28, 2005; children: Arjun Dasgupta, Ella Louise Ong, Amelie Constance Ong. BSc in Physiology and Basic Med. Scis., U. London, 1992, MBBS, 1995. Lic. in paediatrics Royal Coll. Paediatrics and Child Health, 1998. Ho. officer medicine Royal Free Hosp., London, 1995; ho. officer in surgery and orthopaedics Lister Hosp., Stevenage, Hertfordshire, England, 1995—96; sr. ho. officer in paediatrics and neonates East Anglian Deanery, Cambridge, East Anglia, England, 1996—98, specialist registrar in paediatrics and neonates, 1998—2000, Yorkshire Deanery, Leeds, England, 2000—04; cons. neonatologist Leeds Gen. Infirmary, 2004—. Contbr. chapters to books, articles to profl. jours. Fellow: Royal Coll. Paediatrics and Child Health (life); mem.: Brit. Assn. Perinatal Medicine (life). Avocations: travel, photography, scuba diving. Office: Leeds General Infirmary Belmont Grove Leeds LS2 9NS England

ENGS, RUTH CLIFFORD, health educator, historian; b. Ridgeway, Pa., Sept. 15, 1939; d. Theodore Alexander and Elinor Kay Clifford; m. William Denis Engs, July 24, 1965 (div. 1973); m. Jeffrey Lee Franz, Oct. 2, 1987. BA, U. Vt., 1961; diploma in nursing, Merritt Coll., 1968; MA, MS, U. Oreg., 1970; EdD, U. Tenn., 1973. RN Ind. Rsch. asst. Harvard Med. Sch., Boston, 1961-63; asst. prof. Dalhousie U., Halifax, N.S., Can., 1970-71, Ind. U., Bloomington, 1973-80, assoc. prof., 1980-90, prof. applied health sci., 1999—2003, prof. emeritus, 2003—. Vis. prof. U. Queensland, Australia, 1980. Author: Responsible Drug and Alcohol Use, 1979, Alcohol and Other Drugs: Self Responsibility, 1987, Teaching Health Education in the Elementary Schools, 1978, Clean Living Movements: American Cycles of Health Reform, 2000, The Progressive Era's Health Reform Movement: A Historical Dictionary, 2003, The Eugenics Movement: An Encyclopedia, 2005, Conversations in the Abbey: Senior Monks of Saint Meinrad Reflect on their Lives, 2008, Unseen Upton Sinclair: Nine Unpublished Stories, Essays and Other Works, 2009; editor: Controversies in the Addiction Field, 1990, Women: Alcohol and Other Drugs, 1992, 2005; contbr. articles to profl. jours. Mem. Am. Sch. Health Assn. Avocation: model A touring. Office: 615 Poplars 400 E 7th St Ind U Bloomington IN 47405 *

ENGSTROM, JOHN W., neurologist, educator; b. Pomona, Calif., Oct. 23, 1954; BS, U. Calif., Davis, 1976; MD, Stanford U., 1981. Neurology residency program dir. dept. neurology U. Calif., San Francicso, 1994, clin. chief of svc., 2005, prof. neurology, 2005—, Betty Anker Fife disting. chair neurology, dept. neurology. Chair neurology rev. com. Accreditation Coun. Grad. Med. Edn., 2004. Recipient Exceptional Physician award, U. Calif. Med. Ctr., 2006, J. Elliott Royer award, San Francisco Neurologic Soc. Fellow: Am. Acad. Neurology (chair consortium neurology residency program dirs., neurology residency program dir. 2010); mem.: Am. Neurologic Assn. (Disting. Neurology Tchr. award 2010). Avocations: hiking, basketball. Office: 505 Parnassus Ave San Francisco CA 94143 Office Fax: 415-476-3428. E-mail: carmel6237@comcast.net.

ENGSTROM, PAUL F., oncologist, medical educator; b. St. Cloud, Minn., May 28, 1936; m. Janet F. Johnson, Oct. 21, 1961; children: Karin Z. Engstrom Davis, Maria P. Engstrom Pharr, David W. BA, St. Olaf Coll., 1958; MD, U. Minn., 1962. Bd. cert. internal medicine, bd. cert. med. oncology. Intern, resident in internal medicine U. Minn. Hosp., Mpls., 1963-67; chief hematology and oncology sect. Tripler Army Hosp., Honolulu, 1967-70; attending physician medicine Am. Oncol. Hosp., Phila., 1970-72; chmn. dept. medicine Foxchase Cancer Ctr., Phila., 1972-84, v.p. population sci., 1984—. Chmn., mem. intervention rev. com. divsn. cancer prevention and control NCI, Bethesda, Md., 1976-80, mem., chmn. bd. sci. comdrs., 1986-89; mem., chmn. sci. bd. Armed Forces Inst. of Pathology, Washington, 1980-84; mem. adv. com. Can. Ctrl. NCI Can., Toronto, 1992—; prof. medicine Temple U. Sch. Medicine, Phila., 1987-95. Editor, author: Advances in Cancer Control, 1983-90; author (editl.) Cancer Epidemiology Biomarkers and Prevention, 1993; contbr. chpts. to books. Chmn. bd. dirs. Paul's Run Retirement Com., Phila., 1988—. Maj. U.S. Army, 1967-70. Recipient Cancer Ctrl. award Am. Cancer Soc., Phila., 1989. Fellow ACP; mem. AMA, Am. Soc. Clin. Oncology, Am. Fedn. for Clin. Rsch., Am. Assn. for Cancer Edn., Am. Soc. Preventive Oncology, Alpha Omega Alpha. Avocations: music, gardening. Office: Fox Chase Cancer Ctr 333 Cottman Ave Philadelphia PA 19111 Business E-Mail: Paul.Engstrom@fccc.edu.

ENHORNING, GORAN, obstetrician, gynecologist; b. Birkdale, Eng., Mar. 18, 1924; came to US 1986; s. Emil Augustin and Maria Rosina (von Haartman) E.; m. Louise Christina Carlberg, Apr. 16, 1955; children: Ulf, Dag and Peder (twins), Marianne. MD, Karolinska Inst., Stockholm, 1952, PhD in Physiology, 1961. Asst. prof. ob-gyn. Karolinska Inst., Stockholm, 1952—61; Fulbright scholar U. Utah, Salt Lake City, 1961—63, UCLA, 1963—64; assoc. prof. ob-gyn. Karolinska Inst., 1964—71, U. Toronto, Ont., Canada, 1971—75, prof. ob-gyn., 1975—86; prof. ob-gyn. and physiology SUNY, Buffalo, 1986—2002. Contbr. articles to profl. jour. initiation of concept that symptoms of asthma and infectious bronchiolitis may be due to a surfactant dysfunction, caused by airway inflammation, an allergic reaction, an inhalation of cold air, or a hydrolysis of surfactant phospholipids, catalyzed by phospholipase A2 (PLA2) and by lysophospholipase (LPLase) from eosinophils. The way the surfactant dysfunction causes airway blockage, and thus breathing difficulties is demonstrated with the Capillary Surfactometer, an instrument developed to simulate surfactant function in terminal airways.

ENLOW, DONALD HUGH, retired anatomist, dean; b. Mosquero, N.Mex., Jan. 22, 1927; s. Donald Carter and Martie Blairene (Albertson) E.; m. Martha Ruth McKnight, Sept. 3, 1945; 1 child, Sharon Lynn. BS, U. Houston, 1949, MS, 1951; PhD, Tex. A&M U., 1955. Instr. biology U. Houston, 1949-51; asst. prof. biology West Tex. State U., 1955-56, instr. anatomy Med. Coll. S.C., 1956-57; asst. prof. U. Mich. Med. Sch., Ann Arbor, 1957-62, assoc. prof., 1962-67, prof. anatomy, 1969-72; dir. phys. growth program Center for Human Growth and Devel., 1966-72; prof., chmn. dept. anatomy W.Va. U. Sch. Medicine, Morgantown, 1972-77; Thomas Hill disting. prof., chmn. dept. orthodontics Case Western Res. Sch. Dentistry, Cleve., 1977-89, prof. emeritus, 1989—, asst. dean for rsch. and grad. studies, 1977-85, acting dean, 1983-86. Adj. prof. U. NC, 1992—; lectr. in field in 32 fgn. countries. Author: Principles of Bone Remodeling, 1963, The Human Face, 1968, Handbook of Facial Growth, 1975, 3d edit., 1990, Essentials of Facial Growth, 2nd edit., 2008; contbr. chpts. to 30 books, numerous articles to profl. jours. Served with reserves USCG, 1945—46. Recipient Outstanding Research award Tex. Acad. Sci., 1952, Dewel award, 2006, Thomas Graber award, 2006. Fellow Royal Soc. Medicine, Am. Assn. Anatomists, Internat. Assn. Dental Research; hon. mem. Am. Assn. Orthodontists (Mershon Meml. lectr. 1968, Spl. Merit award 1969, award for outstanding contbns. to orthodontia, 1984, Thomas Grober award 2003), Gt. Lakes Orthodontic Soc., Cleve. Dental Soc., Cleve. Orthodontic Soc., Omicron Kappa Upsilon. Republican. Methodist. Home: 4940 Monarch Rd Milton WI 53563 Personal E-mail: donnlo@charter.net.

ENNEZAT, PIERRE VLADIMIR, cardiologist; b. Ermont, France, July 14, 1968; MD, Paris Sch. Medicine, 1998. Médecin des hôpitaux Lille U. Med. Ctr., 2001—. Mem.: European Assn. Echocardiography. Office: Bd Pr J Leclercq Lille Nord 59037 France Personal E-mail: ennezat@yahoo.com.

ENOCH, JAY MARTIN, optometrist, research scientist, educator; b. NYC, Apr. 20, 1929; s. Jerome Dee and Stella Sarah (Nathan) E.; m. Rebekah Ann Feiss, June 24, 1951; children: Harold Owen, Barbara Diane, Ann Allison. BS in Optics and Optometry, Columbia U., 1950; post grad., Inst. Optics U. Rochester, 1953; PhD in Physiol. Optics, Ohio State U., 1956; DSc (hon.), SUNY, 1993, U. Politecnica Catalunya, Barcelona, Spain, 2002. Asst. prof. physiol. optics Ohio State U., Columbus, 1956-58; assoc. supr. Ohio State U. (Mapping and Charting Rsch. Lab.), 1957-58; fellow Nat. Phys. Lab., Teddington, England, 1959-60; rsch. instr. dept. ophthalmology Washington U. Sch. Medicine, St. Louis, 1958-59, rsch. asst. prof., 1959-64, rsch. assoc. prof., 1965-70, rsch. prof., 1970-74; fellow Barnes Hosp., St. Louis, 1960-64, cons. ophthalmology, 1964-74; rsch. prof. dept. psychology Washington U., St. Louis, 1970-74; grad. rsch. prof. ophthalmology and psychology Coll. Medicine U. Fla., Gainesville, 1974-80, grad. rsch. prof. physics, 1979-80; dir. Ctr. for Sensory Studies, 1976-80; dean Sch. Optometry, chmn. Grad. Group in Vision Sci. U. Calif., Berkeley, Calif., 1980-92, prof. optometry and vision sci., 1980-94, prof. of Grad. Sch., 1994—; prof. physiol. optics in ophthalmology U. Calif., San Francisco, 1980—. Exec. sec. subcom. on vision and its disorders of nat. adv. Neurol. Diseases and Blindness Coun., NIH, 1963-66; chmn. subcom. contact lens stds. Am. Nat. Std. Inst., 1970-77; nat. adv. eye coun. Nat. Eye Inst., NIH, 1975-77, 80-84; exec. com., com. on vision NAS-NRC, 1973-76; mem. US Nat. Com. Internat. Commn. Optics, 1976-79, health sci. com. Systemwide Adminstrn. U. Calif., 1989-93, co-chmn. subcom. on immigrant health in Calif., 1993-94, sci. adv. bd. Fight-for-Sight, 1988-92, Allergan Corp., 1991-95, mem. Lighthouse Internat., NY, 1991-95, 2001-05, chair, 1995, Pisart award com., bd. dir. 2001-06, com. on Refractive Errors WHO, 2002-; founder Elite Sch. Optometry, Chennai, Tamil Nadu, India, dedication lectr., 1985, plenary spkr. 20th Ann., 2005, 25th Ann., 2010, Pahlkivala Foundation Oration, Chennai, Tamil Nadu, 2008; Enoch Lecture on Vision Sci., Washington U. Med. Sch., St. Louis, 2007-; spkr. in field. Mem. editl. bd.: Investigative Ophthalmology and Vision Sci., 1965—75, 1983—88, Vision Rsch., 1974—80, Sight-Saving Rev., 1974—84, Sensory Processes, 1974—80, Internat. Ophthalmology, 1977—93, mem. editl. bd. optical scis.: Springer-Verlag, 1978—87, mem. editl. bd.: Binocular Vision, 1984—2004, Clin. Vision Sci., 1986—93, Biomed. Optics, 1988—90, mem. editl. bd. biomed. scis.: Springer-Verlag, 1988—95, assoc. editor: Optometry Today, 2010—, mem. editl. bd.: Annals of Ophthalmology, 1997—2006, assoc. editor for vision: Handbook of Optics, Optical Soc. Am., 1997—2010, mem. internat. editl. bd.: Ophthalmic and Physiol. Optics, 2002—; contbr. articles to profl. jours., chapters to books. Nat. sci. adv. bd. Retinitis Pigmentosa Found., 1977-95; US rep. Internat. Perimetric Soc., 1974-90, also exec. com., chmn. Rsch. Group Standards; bd. dirs. Friends of Eye Rsch., 1977-88, Lighting Rsch. Bd., 1988-95; trustee, dir. Illuminating Engring. Rsch. Inst., 1977-81; mem. bd. counselors U. Calif. San Francisco Sch. Dentistry, 1995-2003. 2d lt. US Army, 1951-52. Recipient Career Devel. award, NIH, 1963—73, Everett Kinsey award, Contact Lens Soc. Ophthalmologists, 1991, Berkeley citation, Festschrift U. Calif. Berkeley, 1996, Pisart award, Lighthouse Internat., 2001, Gaspar de Portola award, U. Calif. and Govt. of Catalunya, 2001, 2004, US Congl. Recognition award, 2005, Spl. Recognition award, Friends Indo-Am. Cmty., 2005, Glenn A. Fry medal, Ohio State U., 2007; named one of 250 Alumni Ahead of Their Time, Columbia Univ., 2004; named to Hall of Fame, UC Berkeley Sch. Optometry, 2009. Fellow AAAS, Am. Acad. Optometry (co-founder eye disease sect., Glenn A. Fry award 1972, Charles F. Prentice medal award 1974, 50 Yr. award 2004), Optical Soc. Am. (chmn. vision tech. sect. 1974-76, mem. book pub. com. 1996-2000, assoc. editor, 2001-10, elected sensor mem. 2011), Am. Acad. Ophthalmology (low-vision com., honor award 1985); mem. Assn. for Rsch. in Vision and Ophthalmology (trustee 1967-73, pres. 1972-73, Francis I. Proctor medal 1977, Silver fellow, 2009, Gold fellow, 2010), Concilium Ophthalmologicum Universale (chmn. visual functions com. 1982-86), Am. Optometric Assn. (low vision sect., Vision Care award 1987), Internat. Perimetric Soc. (hon. mem., chair com. stds.), Ocular Heritage Soc. (medal 1997), Cogan Ophthalmic History Soc. (bd. dirs. 2010-), Optometric Hist. Soc. (trustee 2000-02, 2006—, v.p. 2002-04, pres. 2005), Cosmos Club (Washington), Sigma Xi. Achievements include research in visual sci., photoreceptor optics, perimetry, contact lenses, infant and aged vision, myopia, history of earliest lenses and mirrors. Office: 5537 106th Ave NE Kirkland WA 98033-7413 Business E-Mail: jmenoch@berkeley.edu.

ENOKI, YASUNORI, medical educator, researcher; b. Nara, Japan, Mar. 1, 1931; s. Tomoyoshi and Ikue (Kuromatsu) E.; m. Hisako Uesugi; children: Yasuyuki, Yasuhiro. MD, Nara Med. U., 1954, PhD, 1960. Diplomate in medicine, Japan. Instr. Nara Med. U., 1955-60, asst. prof., 1960-66, prof., 1966-96, prof. emeritus, 1996—. Dir. libr. Nara Med. U., 1973-77, dean, 1977-82. Author: (textbook) Current Physiology, 1994, others; contbr. articles to profl. jours. Mem. N.Y. Acad. Scis. Shintoist. Avocations: music, swimming, antiques. Office: Nara Med U 2d Dept Physiol Shijo cho 840 Kashihara 634-8521 Japan Office Phone: 81-0744 22-3051. Personal E-mail: yasuo.n@nifty.com

ENOMOTO, TAKAYUKI, obstetrician, educator; b. Osaka, Japan, Aug. 21, 1956; MD, Osaka U. Sch. Medicine, 1983; PhD, Osaka U. Grad. Sch. Medicine, 1993. Assoc. prof. dept. ob-gyn. Osaka U., 1996. Mem.: Am. Soc. Clin. Oncology. Office: 2-2 Yamadaoka Suita Osaka 565-0871 Japan Office Fax: 816668793359. Business E-Mail: enomoto@gyne.med.osaka-u.ac.jp.

ENQUIST, LYNN WILLIAM, molecular biologist, educator; b. Denver, Oct. 23, 1945; s. Clarence Andrew and Doris Alice (Hajenga) E.; m. Kathleen Marie Siverson, Aug. 10, 1968; 1 child, Brian Joseph. BS, S.D. State U., 1967; PhD, Va. Commonwealth U., 1971. Postdoctoral fellow Roche Inst. of Molecular Biology, Nutley, N.J., 1971-73; staff fellow NIH, Bethesda, Md., 1973-77, staff scientist, 1977-81; rsch. dir. Molecular Genetics Inc., Minnetonka, Minn., 1981-84; rsch. leader DuPont Cen. Rsch., Wilmington, Del., 1984-90; sr. rsch. fellow DuPont Merck Pharm. Co., Wilmington, 1991-93; prof. molecular biology Princeton (N.J.) U., 1993—, assoc. chair dept. molecular biology, 2003—04, chair dept. molecular biology, 2004—. Mem. Nat. Sci. Adv. Bd. for Biosecurity, 2005—. Editor Jour. Virology, 1994-2001, editor in chief, 2002-; mem. editorial bd. Jour. of Virology, 1979-81, 89-91, 91-94, Virology, 1992-94; contbr. numerous articles to profl. jours.; patentee in field; author: Experiments with Gene Fusions, 1984, Principles of Virology: Molecular Biology, Pathogenesis and Control, 3rd edit., 2009. Named Disting. Alumnus, Va. Commonwealth U., 1983, S.D. State U., 1984; recipient Pres.'s award Disting. Tchg. Princeton U., 2001, Disting. Alumni award, SD State U., 2010. Mem. AAAS (bd. dirs. 2005—), Am. Acad. Microbiology, Am. Soc. for Microbiology, Am. Soc. for Virology, Am. Acad. Arts & Scis., Soc. for Neurosci. Avocations: fly fishing, reading, music, gardening. Office: Dept Molecular Biology Princeton U 314 Schultz Lab Princeton NJ 08544-0001 Home Phone: 609-497-4589; Office Phone: 609-258-2415. Business E-Mail: lenquist@princeton.edu.

ENRIGHT, PAUL LEWIS, pulmonologist; b. LA, Apr. 21, 1950; m. Diane Enright. MD, Loma Linda U., 1975. Cert. Internal Medicine, 1986. Resident in internal medicine U. Hawaii, Honolulu, 1975—77; fellow in pulmonary medicine U. Colo., Denver, 1977—79; pulmonologist Mayo Clinic, Rochester, Minn.; investigator NIH Lung Health Study, 1990; prof. medicine U. Ariz., Tucson, 1993—; investigator Nat. Inst. Occupational Safety and Health, 2000—. Contbr. WebMD, 2001—. Office: U Ariz PO Box 245211 1295 N Martin Ave Tucson AZ 85724 Office Phone: 520-577-8254. E-mail: lungguy@aol.com.

ENROTH-CUGELL, CHRISTINA ALMA ELISABETH, neurophysiologist, educator; b. Helsingfors, Finland, Aug. 27, 1919; came to US, 1956, naturalized, 1962; d. Emil and Maja (Syren) Enroth; m. David W. Cugell, Sept. 5, 1955. MD, Karolinska Inst., 1948, PhD, 1952; Hon. Doctors Degree, U. Helsinki, Finland, 1994. Resident in ophthalmology Karolinska Sjukhuset, 1949-52; intern Passavant Meml. Hosp., 1956-57; with Northwestern U., Evanston, Ill., 1959-91, prof. emeritus, 1991—, prof. dept. neurobiology and physiology and dept. biomed. engring., 1974—78; mem. vision rsch. program com. Nat. Eye Inst., 1974-78, mem. nat. adv. eye coun., 1980-84. Contbr. articles to profl. jours. Recipient Ludwig von Sallman award Internat. Assn. Rsch. in Vision and Ophthalmology, 1982. Fellow Am. Inst. Med. and Biol. Engring., Am. Acad. Arts and Sci.; mem. Am. Assn. Rsch. in Vision and Ophthalmology (co-recipient Friedenwald award 1983, recipient W.H. Helmerich III award 1992), Soc. Neurosci., Am. Physiol. Soc., Physiol. Soc. (U.K.) Business E-Mail: enroth@northwestern.edu.

ENSINA, LUIS FELIPE CHIAVERINI, medical researcher; b. Sao Paulo, Brazil, Apr. 15, 1972; MD, Pontificia U. Catolica De Sao Paulo, 1995; MSc, U. Sao Paulo, 2003. Prin. investigator Cp Alpha Clin. Rsch., 2010—. Asst. prof. allergy and immunology U. Santo Amaro, 2003—11. Mem.: Am. Acad. Allergy Asthma And Immunology. Office: Rua Barata Ribeiro 490 - Cj 67 Sao Paulo 01308000 Brazil Personal E-mail: lfensina@yahoo.com.br.

ENSTROM, JAMES EUGENE, epidemiologist, physicist, educator; b. Alhambra, Calif., June 20, 1943; s. Elmer Melvin, Jr. and Klea Elizabeth (Bissell) E.; m. Marta Eugenia Villanea, Sept. 3, 1978. BS, Harvey Mudd Coll., Claremont, Calif., 1965; MS, Stanford U., 1967; PhD in Physics, 1970; M.P.H., UCLA, 1976. Research assoc. Stanford Linear Accelerator Center, 1970-71; research physicist, cons. Lawrence Berkeley Lab. U. Calif., 1971-75; Celeste Durand Rogers cancer research fellow Sch. Pub. Health, UCLA, 1973-75; Nat. Cancer Inst. postdoctoral trainee, 1975-76; cancer epidemiology researcher, 1976-81; assoc. research prof., 1981—2000; rsch. prof., 2001; rsch. epidemiologist, 1978—. Program dir. for cancer control epidemiology Jonsson Comprehensive Cancer Center, 1978-88, research epidemiologist, 1988—, sci. dir. tumor registry, 1984-87, mem. dean's council, 1976—2000; cons. epidemiologist Linus Pauling Inst. Sci. and Medicine, 1976-94; cons. physicist Rand Corp., 1969-73, R&D Assos., 1971-75; mem. sci. bd. Am. Council on Sci. and Health, 1984—, trustee, 2006-, pres. Sci. Integrity Inst., 2005- Author papers in field. NSF predoctoral trainee, 1965-66; grantee Am. Cancer Soc., 1973—92, Nat. Cancer Inst., 1979—93; Preventive Oncology Acad. award, 1981-87. Fellow Am. Coll. Epidemiology; mem. Soc. Epidemiologic Research, Am. Pub. Health Assn., Am. Phys. Soc., AAAS, N.Y. Acad. Scis., Galileo Soc. Office: U Calif Sch Pub Health Los Angeles CA 90024

ENTE, GERALD, retired pediatrician; b. NYC, July 18, 1930; s. Louis M. and Minnie (Lackfish) E.; m. Phyllis Warch, Aug. 27, 1995; children: Peter, William. BS, Union Coll., 1951; MD, NYU, 1955. Diplomate Am. Acad. Pediatrics. Intern Kings County Hosp., Bklyn., 1955-56, resident in pediat., 1958-59, Bronx Mcpl. Hosp., 1959-60; pvt. practice Westbury, NY, 1960—2003, Mineola, NY, 2003—; clin. instr. pediat. Einstein Med. Sch., 1960-64, Meadowbrook, 1960-65, asst. attending pediat., 1965-68, clin. assoc. dir. of newborn svcs., 1968-70; clin. dir neonatology Nassau County Med. Ctr., 1970-88, attending physician pediat., 1974—; assoc. clin. prof. pediat. emeritus SUNY Med. Coll., Stony Brook, N.Y., 1985-99; attending pediatrician Winthrop U. Hosp., 1997—, Schneider Children's Hosp., 1997—. Med. dir. Trya Hostel, 1974-77, Fellowship Med. Labs, 1974-80; pediatric cons. Project Headstart, 1972, Westbury med. dir., 1966-76; cons. staff physician SUNY Coll. at Old Westbury, 1971-82, physician in-charge, 1972-79; cons. Westinghouse Electric Co., 1971-72, Gen-Tel Electric Co., 1972; mem. Westbury Health Coun., 1974-78; dir. neonatology Ctrl. Gen. Hosp., 1980-90, chmn. pediats., 1990-94; profl. adv. bd. L.I. Inst. for Tng. in the Psychotherapies, 1979-81; mem. rsch. panel Med. World News, 1979-81. Author: (with others) Handbook of Neonatology, 1974, Pediatricians Manual Vol. I & II, 1977, Management of Prader Willi Syndrome, 1988; contbr. numerous articles to profl. jours.; editor Nassau U. Med. Ctr. Procs., Nassau County Med. Soc. Bull., Schneider Children's Hosp. Bull. Bd. dirs. Offspring Dance Group, 1976-92; chmn. L.I. physicians United Way, 1983-84; bd. trustees Long Island Patient Info. Exch., 2008-, Com. Autism Nassau County, 2008-. Capt. U.S. Army Res., 1956-58. Recipient Samaritan award N.Y. Assn. Brain Injured Children, 1968, Man of Yr. N.Y. State Fraternal Order of Police, 2003, Legacy of Light award Westbury Friends Sch., 2005, Resident's Tchg. award Nassau County Med. Soc., 1972, NY State Fraternal Order of Police Found. Humanitarian award 2010; Outstanding Attending of the Yr. Winthrop Univ. Hosp., 1998. Fellow Am. Acad. Pediatrics (PREP fellowship award 1979-85, PREP awards 1980-86, 93, 96, 98, 2000, 02, 04, 06, exec. bd. chpt. 2), Royal Soc. of Pediatrics, Royal Soc. of Health, Internat. Coll. Pediatrics, Nassau Acad. of Medicine; mem. AMA (Physicians Recognition award 1980-84, 86, 87, 89, 91, 93, 96, 98, 2000, 02, 04, 06, 08), N.Y. State Med. Soc., Nassau County Med. Soc. (exec. com., pres, 2008-2009), World Med. Assn., Nassau Acad. Medicine (sect. on pediatrics), Pan Am. Med. Assn. (diplomate), World Med. Soc., Assn. Am. Soc. Photobiology, Internat. Transactional Analysis Assn., Am. Holistic Med. Assn., Nassau Acad. Medicine (pres., 2001-02), Nassau County Med. Soc. Pres. (bd. trustees LIPIX 2008-09), NY State Fraternal Order of Police Surgeons' Lodge (pres. 1998—, Assoc. Mem. of Yr. 2003), NY State Fraternal Order of Police (Found. Humanitarian award 2010). Personal E-mail: entedoc@aol.com.

ENTHOVEN, ALAIN CHARLES, economist, educator; b. Seattle, Sept. 10, 1930; s. Richard Frederick and Jacqueline E.; m. Rosemary Fenech, July 28, 1956; children: Eleanor, Richard, Andrew, Martha, Nicholas, Daniel. BA in Econs., Stanford U., 1952; M.Phil. (Rhodes scholar), Oxford U., Eng., 1954; PhD in Econs, MIT, 1956; PhD in Public Pol. (hon.), RAND Graduate Sch., 2008. Instr. econs. MIT, Cambridge, 1955-56; economist The RAND Corp., Santa Monica, Calif., 1956-60; ops. research analyst Office of Dir. Def. Research and Engring., Dept. Def., Washington, 1960; dep. comptroller, dep. asst. sec. U.S. Dept. Def., Washington, 1961-65, asst. sec. for systems analysis, 1965-69; v.p. for econ. planning Litton Industries, Beverly Hills, Calif., 1969-71; pres. Litton Med. Products, Beverly Hills, 1971-73; Marriner S. Eccles prof. pub. and pvt. mgmt. Grad. Sch. Bus. Stanford (Calif.) U., 1973-2000, prof. health care econs. Sch. Medicine, 1973-2000; sr. fellow Ctr. for Health Policy, Stanford U., 2000—. Cons. The Brookings Instn., 1956-60; vis. assoc. prof. econs. U. Wash., 1958; mem. Stanford Computer Sci. Adv. Com., 1968-73; cons. The RAND Corp., 1969—; mem. vis. com. in econs. MIT, 1971-78; mem. vis. com. on environ. quality lab. Calif. Inst. Tech., 1972-77; mem. Inst. Medicine, Nat. Acad. Scis., 1972—; mem. vis. com. Harvard U. Sch. Pub. Health, 1974-80; cons. Kaiser Found. Health Plan, Inc., 1973—; vis. prof. U. Paris, 1985, London Sch. Hygiene and Tropical Medicine, 1998-99; vis. fellow St. Catherine's Coll., Oxford U., Eng., 1985, New Coll., 1998-99; dir. Hotel Investors Trust, 1986-87, PCS Inc., 1987-90, Caresoft, 1996-2002, Rx Intelligence, 2000-03, eBenX Inc, 2001-03. Author: (with K. Wayne Smith) How Much is Enough? Shaping the Defense Program 1961-69, 71, 2d edit., 2005, Health Plan: The Only Practical Solution to the Soaring Cost of Medical Care, 1980; editor: (with A. Myrick Freeman III) Pollution, Resources and the Environment, 1973, Theory and Practice of Managed Competition in Health Care Finance, 1988, In Pursuit of an Improving National Health Service, 1999, (with Laura A. Tollen) Toward a 21st Century Health System: The Contributions and Promise of Prepaid Group Practice, 2004; contbr. articles to profl. jours. Bd. dirs. Georgetown U., Washington, 1968-73, Jackson Hole Group, 1993-96; bd. regents St. John's Hosp., Santa Monica, 1971-73; chmn. Gov's Taskforce Managed Health Care Improvement, 1997-98, vis. com. Harvard U. Kennedy Sch. Govt., 1998-2003. Recipient President's award for disting. fed. civilian svc., 1963, Disting. Pub. Svc. medal Dept. Def., 1968, Baxter prize for health svcs. rsch., 1994, Bd. Dirs.' award Healthcare Fin. Mgmt. Assn., 1995, Ellwood award Found. for Accountability, 1998, Rock Carling fellow, Nuffield Trust, 1999. Mem. Am. Assn. Rhodes Scholars, Am. Acad. Arts and Scis., Integrated Healthcare Assn. (bd. dirs. 1999—), Phi Beta Kappa. Home: 1 McCormick Ln Atherton CA 94027-3033 Office: Stanford University Grad Sch Business Knight Mgmt Ctr 655 Knight Way Stanford CA 94305-7298 Business E-Mail: enthoven@stanford.edu.

ENWO, OTU NNACHI, anesthesiologist; b. Afikpo, Ebonyi State, Nigeria, Mar. 20, 1958; s. Nnachi and Ogeri Enwo; m. Lois Akama Oti, May 7, 1994; children: Oby Otu, Amaa Otu, Nach Otu. MBBS, U. Ibadan, Nigeria, 1985; FCARCSI, Coll. Anaesthetists, Ireland, 2000. Registrar in anaesthetics U. Port Harcourt, Rivers State, Nigeria, 1989—96; specialist registrar Gt. Western Hosp., Swindon, England, 1999; sr. ho. officer Chase Farm Hosp., London, 1996—97, James Paget Hosp., Great Yarmouth, Norfolk, England, 1997—99; specialist registrar in anaesthetics Southampton U. Hosp., England, 1999—2000; anaesthetist, intensivist Prince Philip Hosp., Llanelli, Carmarthenshire, England, 2000—04; neuroanaesthetist Old Church Hosp., Romford, Essex, England, 2004—. Dir. Nachinex First Aid Tng. Consultants, Nigeria, 1994—96. Contbr. articles. Rd. safety instr. Fed. Rd. Safety Corps, Nigeria, 1992—96. Fellow: Royal Coll. Surgeons Ireland, Internat. Coll. Surgeons, Coll. Anaesthetists; mem.: Med. Defence Union, Brit. Med. Assn., Royal Coll. Anaesthetists, Assn. Anaesthetists Gt. Britain and Ireland. Achievements include research in The Oxygen - Air Equation. Avocations: photography, chess, computing. E-mail: otuenwo@hotmail.com.

EN-YUAN, ZHU, medical educator; b. Wuxi, Jiangsu, China, Jan. 18, 1974; PhD, China Pharmaceutical U., 2001. Assoc. prof. Shanghai U. Traditional Chinese Medicine, 2005—. Avocation: music. Office: Cailun Rd 1200 Shanghai 201203 China Business E-Mail: wxzey@163.com.

ENZI, MICHAEL BRADLEY, United States Senator from Wyoming, accountant; b. Bremerton, Wash., Feb. 1, 1944; s. Elmer Jacob and Dorothy (Bradley) Enzi; m. Diana Buckley, June 7, 1969; children: Amy, Bradley, Emily. BBA, George Wash. U., 1966; MBA, Denver U., 1968. Mayor City of Gillette, Wyo., 1975—82; pres. NZ Shoes, Inc., Gillette, Wyo., 1969-95, Sheridan, Wyo., 1983-96; acctg. mgr. Dunbar Well Svc., Inc., Gillette, 1985-97; mem. Wyo. House of Reps., Cheyenne, 1986—91, Wyo. State Senate, Cheyenne, 1991-96, commr. We. Interstate Commn. Higher Edn., 1995—96; US Senator from Wyo., 1997—; chmn. US Senate Health, Edn., Labor & Pensions Com., 2005—07. Mem. Edn. Commn. States, 1989—93. Pres. Wyo. Assn. Mcpls., Cheyenne, 1980—82; chmn. bd. dirs. First Wyo. Bank, Gillette, 1978—88; bd. dirs. Black Hills Corp., 1992—96. Served as Sgt. Wyo. Air NG, 1967—73. Recipient W. Stuart Symington award, Air Force Assn., 2001, Small Investor Empowerment award, Nat. Assn. Real Estate Investment Trusts, 2002, Congl. Leadership award, Food Industry Assn., 2005, Leadership award, Nat. Orgn. Fetal Alcohol Syndrome, 2005, TechNet Founders Cir. award, 2005; named Legis. of Yr., Am. Soc. Consultant Pharmacists, 2004, Biotechnology Industry Orgn., 2005, Policy Maker of Yr., Assn. Career & Tech. Edn., 2005. Mem.: Lions, Wyo. Jaycees (pres. 1973—74), Shriners, Masons, Wyo. Order of DeMolay (state master councilor 1963—64), Scottish Rite, Sigma Chi. Republican. Presbyn. Avocations: fishing, bicycling, soccer, hunting. Office: US Senate 379A Senate Russell Bldg Washington DC 20510-0001 also: District Office Ste 303 400 South Kendrick Ave Gillette WY 82716-3803 Office Phone: 202-224-3424, 307-682-6268. Office Fax: 202-228-0359, 307-682-6501. Business E-Mail: senator@enzi.senate.gov.

EOH, WHAN, neurosurgeon; b. Seoul, Republic of Korea, May 19, 1953; s. Yak-Sun Eoh and Chang-Sung Lee; m. Hyung-Sook Paek, Dec. 19, 1978; 1 child, June-Soo. BS, Seoul Nat. U., 1978, MS, 1982, PhD, 1989. Instr. Hallym U. Sch. Medicine, Seoul, 1986—87, asst. prof., 1987—91, assoc. prof., 1991—94; neurosurgeon Samsung Med. Ctr., Seoul, 1994—97, chmn. dept. neurosurgery, 2003—, dir., 2001—, chmn., 2003—; prof. Sungkyunkwan U. Sch. Medicine, Seoul, 1997—. Rsch. fellow dept. neurosurgery U. Tokyo, 1990; clin. observer Barrow Neurol. Inst., Phoenix, 1997; reviewer Health Ins. Rev. Agy., Seoul, 2002—. Translator: Brain Tumor, 1991, Neurosurgery Manual, 1992. Capt. Korean Mil., 1983—86. Mem.: Korean Neurosurg. Soc., Am. Assn. Neurol. Surgeons. Avocations: golf, mountain climbing, jogging. Office: Samsung Med Ctr Kangnam-ku Ilwon-dong 50 Seoul 135-710 Republic of Korea

EOM, DAE-WOON, pathologist, educator; b. Gyoung-Ju, GyoungSangbook-do, Republic Of Korea, Sept. 22, 1967; BS in Med. Sci., Dongguk U., Gyoungju, Republic of Korea, 1992, MS in Pathology, 2001; PhD in Pathology, Chungbuk Nat. U., Chungju, Republic of Korea, 2008. Diplomate Ministry Health and Social Affairs, 1992, lic. medical specialist Ministry Health and Social Affairs, 2002. Rsch. fellow Seoul Asan Hosp., Republic of Korea, 2002—04; asst. prof. Uni. Ulsan. Coll. Medicine, Ulsan, Goungsangnamdo, Republic of Korea, 2006—. Dir. pathology dept. Gangneung Asan Hosp., 2004—. Contbr. numerous articles to profl. jours. Mem.: Korean Soc. Cytopathology, Korean Soc. Pathologists. Office: Gang-Neung Asan Hosp 415 Bangdong-ri Gangwon-do GangNeung 210-711 Republic of Korea Office Fax: 82 33 610 3430.

EOM, KEESEON STEPHEN, parasitologist, medical educator; b. Chunchon, Kangwon Province, Republic of Korea, Apr. 26, 1955; s. Yoonseop Eom and Kyungae Park; m. Changhye Lucy Choi, Sept. 26, 1982; 1 child, Hyeseok Angela. VMD, Seoul Nat. U., 1978, MSc, 1984, PhD, 1991. Tchg. asst. dept. parasitology Korea U. Coll. Medicine, Seoul, Republic of Korea, 1982—85, rsch. instr. dept. parasitology, 1986—87; from instr. to prof. dept. parasitology Chungbuk Nat. U. Coll. Medicine, Cheongju, Chungbuk Province, Republic of Korea, 1987—99, prof., chmn. dept. parasitology, 1999—. Vis. scientist Biosystematic Parasitology Lab. and Immunology and Disease Resistance Lab, Beltsville, Md., 1995—96; dir. Chungbuk (Republic of Korea) Nat. U. Med. Rsch. Inst., Republic of Korea, 2002—04; curator Med. Libr. of Chungbuk (Republic of Korea) Nat. U., 1997—2000; leading scientist Korea U. Inst. for Tropical Endemic Diseases, Seoul, 1988—92; scientist Chungbuk (Republic of Korea) Nat. Inst. for Genetic Engring. Rsch., 1990—; adv. bd. Korea Assn. of Health Promotion, Cheongju, 1997—; parasitology specialist Internat. Projects Parasite Control Activities, Republic of Korea, 2000—05, Tanzania, 2005—, Cambodia, 2006—; bd. dirs. Korea-China Internat. Project for Control Activities of Parasitic Infections, Seoul, 2001—04; dir. Parasite Resource Bank of Korea, 2005—; dir. Disability Support Ctr., Chungbuk Nat. U. Editor: (online internet contents) Atlas of Medical Parasitology, 2000—; mem. editl. board Korean Jour. of Parasitology, 1991—93, mem. editl. bd., 2000—01, mem. editl. board Korean Jour. of Veterinary Medicine, 1997—99; contbr. articles to profl. jours.; mem. editl. bd.: Korean Jour. Systematic Zoology, 2003—. Recipient sci. award for outstanding paper, Korean Fedn. Sci. and tech., 2003, Nat. Client award, Internat. Assn. Profl. Congress Organizers, 2009; grantee, Ministry of Edn., 1989—90, Korea Sci. and Engring. Found., 1991—92, Ministry of Edn., 1992—93, 1996—98, Ministry Health and Welfare, 1997—2000, 2001—; scholar, Korean Ministry of Edn., 1995—96. Mem.: Korean Soc. Parasitology (coun. mem. 2001—03, chmn. info. com. 2003, pres. 2010—, Acad. award 1994). Achievements include discovery of a new human tapeworm, Taenia asiatica; research in epidemiological problems for better understanding of human tapeworms distributed in Asia; DNA sequences for differential diagnosis between Taenia species; molecular epidemiological surveys of human tapeworms in China and Laos; phylogenetics of Taenia species; analysis of mitochondrial genomes of cestode parasites. Home: Kaeshindong Chungbuk Cheongju 361 763 Republic of Korea Office: Chungbuk Nat U Coll Med Dept Parasit Gaeshindong 12 Heungdokgu Chungbuk Cheongju 361 763 Republic of Korea Office Phone: 82-43-261-2849. Office Fax: 82-43-272-1603. Business E-Mail: kseom@chungbuk.ac.kr.

EPPERLY, TED, physician, medical association administrator; BS magna cum laude, Utah State U.; MD, U. Wash. Sch. Med. Cert. geriatrics Am. Bd. Family Med. Resident Madigan Army Med. Ctr., Fort Lewis; fellow UNC, Chapel Hill; program dir. & CEO Idaho Family Med. Residency; clinical prof. family med. U. Wash. Sch. Med.; former bd. dir. Am. Acad. Family Physicians, pres., 2007—. Commr. Ctrl. Dist. Bd. Health, Boise; editorial bd. Annals of Family Med.; reviewer Jour. Musculoskeletal Med., Am. Family Physician. Ret. col. US Army. Mem.: Internat. Soc. for Men's Health & Gender (editorial adv. bd.). Office: American Academy of Family Physicians 11400 Tomahawk Creek Pkwy Leawood KS 66211-2680 Mailing: PO Box 11210 Shawnee Mission KS 66207-1210 Office Phone: 913-906-6000. Office Fax: 913-906-6075. E-mail: contactcenter@aafp.org.

EPPS, ANNA CHERRIE, immunologist, educator, dean interim president; b. New Orleans, July 8, 1930; d. Ernest and Anna L. (Johnson) Cherrie; m. Joseph M. Epps, Sr., Nov. 23, 1968. BS, Howard U., 1951, PhD, 1966; MS, Loyola U., New Orleans, 1959. Technologist clin. lab. dept. Our Lady of Mercy Hosp., Cin., 1953-54; asst. prof., acting chmn. dept. med. tech. Xavier U., New Orleans, 1954-60; technologist dept. medicine La. State U. Sch. Medicine, New Orleans, 1954-60; asst. prof. microbiology Coll. Medicine Howard U., Washington, 1961-69; fellow dept. medicine Sch. Medicine Johns Hopkins U., Balt., 1969; asst. prof., USPHS faculty fellow dept. medicine Tulane U. Sch. Medicine, New Orleans, 1969-71, assoc. prof., 1971-75, prof., 1975—97, assoc. dean student svcs., 1970—97; dir. med. edn. reinforcement and enrichment program Tulane U. Med. Ctr., New Orleans, 1969—97; acting dean, v.p. acad. affairs Meharry Med. Coll., Nashville, 1994—96, dean sch. med., sr. v.p. acad. affairs, 1997—2002, dean emerita, sr. advisor to pres., 2002—. Co-author: Medrep, Tulane U.; co-editor: Medical Education: Responses to a Challenge; mem. editorial bd. Jour. Med. Edn., 1980—; contbr. articles to med. jours. Trustee Children's Hosp., New Orleans, 1977-79; regent Georgetown U., Washington, 1975—; bd. dirs. Diabetes Assn. Greater New Orleans, 1978; mem. La. Bd. Health and Rehab. Svcs., 1972; adv. mem. Kellogg Nat. Fellowship Program, 1981. Recipient award for meritorious rsch. Interstate Postgrad. Med. Assn. N.Am., 1966, Scroll of Merit, Nat. Med. Assn., 1980, Herbert W. Nickens award, AAMC, 2003, dr. harold delancy award, Am. Assn. Blacks Higher Edn., 2008. Mem. Am. Soc. Clin. Pathologists (cert. in med. tech. and blood banking), Am. Soc. Med. Technologists, Am. Assn. Blood Banks (cert. in blood banking), Am. Soc. Tropical Medicine and Hygiene, AAUP, Musser-Burch Soc., Albertus Magnus Guild, Washington Helminthol. Soc., Am. Soc. Bacteriologists, Sigma Xi. Home: 769 Sinclair Cir Brentwood TN 37027-2921 Office: Meharry Med Coll 1005 D B Todd Blvd Nashville TN 37208 Home Phone: 615-371-2404; Office Phone: 615-327-5935. Business E-Mail: acepps@mmc.edu.

EPPS, CHARLES HARRY, JR., retired orthopaedic surgery educator, dean; b. Balt., July 24, 1930; BS magna cum laude, Howard U., 1951, MD, 1955. Intern Freedmen's Hosp., 1955-56, resident, 1956-57, mem. staff, 1961—2001; resident D.C. Gen. Hosp., Washington, 1958-60, vis. staff, 1961-98, orthopaedic med. officer for handicapped and crippled children's svc., 1961-98; instr. orthopaedic surgery Howard U., Washington, 1961-64, asst. prof., 1964-68, assoc. prof., 1968-73, prof., 1973-96, prof. emeritus, 1996—2001, chief divsn. orthopaedic surgery, 1968-88, dean Coll. Medicine, 1988-94, exec. dean Coll. Medicine, 1994-95; v.p. health affairs, acting exec. dir., CEO Howard U. Hosp., Washington, 1994-96; spl. asst. to pres. for health affairs Howard U., 1996-2001; ret., 2001. Assoc. prof. Johns Hopkins U., 1971; mem. staff VA Hosp., Washington, Cafritz Meml. Hosp., Providence Hosp.; cons. USN Med. Ctr., Bethesda, Md., Walter Reed Army Med. Ctr. Capt. M.C., U.S. Army, 1961-62. Fellow ACS; mem. AMA, Nat. Med. Assn., Ea. Orthop. Assn., Am. Orthop. Assn., Am. Acad. Orthop. Surgery.

EPPS, ROSELYN ELIZABETH PAYNE, pediatrician, educator; b. Little Rock, Dec. 11, 1930; d. William Kenneth and Mattie Elizabeth (Beverly) Payne; m. Charles Harry Epps, Jr., June 25, 1955; children: Charles Harry III (dec.), Kenneth Carter, Roselyn Elizabeth, Howard Robert. BS, Howard U., 1951, MD, 1955; MPH, Johns Hopkins U., 1973; MA, Am. U., 1981. Intern Freedmen's Hosp., Howard U., Washington, 1955-56, pediatric resident, 1956-59, chief resident,

1958-59; practice medicine specializing in pediatrics Washington, 1960; med. officer, pediatrics D.C. Dept. Pub. Health, Washington, 1961-64, dir. Clinic for Retarded Children, 1964-67, chief Infant and Pre-Sch. div., 1967-71, dir. children and youth project, 1970-71, dir. maternal and crippled children services, 1971-75; chief Bur. Clin. Services D.C. Dept. Human Services, Washington, 1975-80, acting commr. pub. health, 1980; instr., asst. research investigator Howard U. Coll. Medicine, Washington, 1960-61, prof. Dept. Pediatrics and Child Health, 1980-98, chief divsn. child devel., dir., 1985-89, dir. Child Devel. Ctr., 1985-89; rsch. assoc., vis. scientist smoking tobacco and cancer program, div. cancer prevention and control Nat. Cancer Inst. NIH, Washington, 1989-91; expert Nat. Cancer Inst. NIH, Pub. Health Applications Br., Bethesda, Md., 1991-97; scientific program adminstr. Nat. Cancer Inst. Pub. Health Applications Branch, Bethesda, Md., 1997-98; med. pub. hlth cons., 1998—; sr. program advisor for women's health programs Women's Health Inst., Howard U., Wash., 1999—. Chmn. task force to prepare comprehensive child care plan for D.C. Dept. Human Services, 1973-74; mem. nat. task force on pediatric hypertension Heart, Lung and Blood Inst., NIH, 1975; chmn. rsch. grants rev. com. maternal and child health and crippled children's svcs. HEW, Rockville, Md., 1978-80; sec. Commn. Licensure to Practice Healing Arts, Washington, 1980; trustee med. svc. D.C. Blue Shield Plan Nat. Capital Area, 1980; chmn. sec.'s adv. com. on rights and responsibilities of women HEW, Washington, 1981; dir. high-risk young people's project Howard U. Hosp., 1981-85; Washington coord. Know Your Body Program Am. Health Found., N.Y.C., 1982-91; mem. bd. advs. Coll. Home Econs. Ohio State U., Columbus, Ohio, 1983-87; adv. com. Nat. Ctr. for Edn. in Maternal and Child Health Georgetown U., Washington, 1983-89; nat. steering com., subcom. chmn. Healthy Mothers, Healthy Babies Coalition, Washington, 1983-90, mem. nominating com., 1991; cons. sickle cell disease NIH, 1984-88, Govt. Liberia and World Bank, 1984, UN Fund for Population Activities, N.Y. and Caribbean, 1984, filmstrip Miriam Berg Varian/Parents Mag. Films, 1978; bd. dirs. Vis. Nurse Assn., Inc., Washington, 1983-89; pres. bd. dirs. Hosp. for Sick Children, Washington, 1986-90, bd. dirs., 1984-94; frequent guest lectr. Weekly columnist Your Child's Health, Afro-Am. Newspaper, Washington, 1960-63; contbr. articles syndicated column Nat. Newspaper Pubs. Assn., 1982, Nat. Newspaper Assn., 1986-87; co-author audiocassettes; exhibitor sci. program, exhibit: Women Chage the Faces of Medicine; contbr. more than 90 articles to profl. jours. US trustee Children's Internat. Summer Villages, Casstown, Ohio, 1969—76, pres., 1974—75; trustee nat. bd. Palmer Meml. Inst., Sedalia, NC, 1969—71, Ford's Theater, Washington, 1973—79; bd. mgrs. YWCA of DC, 1970—83, vice chmn., 1975—76; v.p. Jack and Jill of Am., Inc., Washington, 1970—71; nat. bd. dir. Ctr. Population Options, Washington, 1980—86, Alexander Graham Bell Assn. for Deaf, Washington, 1974—78; bd. dir. Washington Performing Arts Soc., 1971—81, v.p., 1979—81, hon. dir., 1981—. Recipient Leadership and Meritorious Service in Medicine award Palmer Meml. Inst., 1968, 14th Ann. Fed. Women's award CSC, Washington, 1974, Superior Performance award D.C. Govt., 1975, Meritorious Community Service award Howard U. Sch. Social Work Alumni Assns. and vis. com., 1980, Cert. Commendation Mayor of DC, 1981, Roselyn Payne Epps M.D. Recognition Resolution of 1983 Council DC, 1983, Disting. Vol. Leadership award March of Dimes Birth Defects Found., 1984, Community Svc. award DC Hosp. Assn., 1990, Physician of Yr award Women's Med. Assn. N.Y.C., 1990, 91; named Outstanding Vol. in Leadership category YWCA Nat. Capital Area, 1990, inducted into DC Women's Hall of Fame DC Commn. for Women, 1990, Hall of Fame, DC, 2005; grantee Robert Wood Johnson Found., Princeton, N.J., 1982, div. maternal and child health HHS, Rockville, Md., 1986, honored Tribute Resolution of 1981 declaring Feb. 14 Dr. Roselyn Payne Epps Day, Council of D.C., 1981; recipient Ophelia Settle Egypt award Planned Parenthood of Met. Washington, 1991, Advocacy award Soc. Advancement Women's Health, 1996, Horizon award Nat. Assn. Negro Bus. and Profl. Women's Clubs, 1999, Dorothy I Height award, Nat. Coun. of Negro Women, 2001, Lifetime Achievement award, Girls Inc., 2003. Fellow Am. Acad. Pediatrics (alt. state chmn. D.C. 1973-75, exec. com. D.C. chpt. 1983-94, pres. D.C. chpt. 1988-91, sec. cmty. pediatrics sect. 1973-75, cert. appreciation 1979, mem. coun. of child and adolescent health, cmty. and internat. health sect., charter mem., exec. com. 1992-94); mem. Acad. Medicine, AMA (alt. del. Nat. Med. Assn. 1983-85), Am. Med. Women's Assn. (chmn. pub. health com. 1973-75, pres. br. 1 1974-76, sec. 1988, v.p. 1989, pres-elect nat. 1990, pres. 1991, found. founding pres. 1992, bd. dirs. 1992-97, chmn. nominating com. 1993, Physician of Yr. award 1991, Cmty. Svc. award 1990, Elizabeth Blackwell award 1992), Women's Forum Washington, Med. Soc. D.C. (exec. bd. 1990, sec. 1990, pres.-elect 1991, pres. 1992, chair exec. bd. 1993, ann. Cmty. Svc. award 1982), Am. Pediatric Soc., D.C. Hosp. Assn. (Cmty. Svc. award 1990), Am. Pub. Health Assn. (action bd. 1977-79, joint policy com. 1978-79, gov. council 1978-81), Met. Washington Pub. Health Assn. (gov. council 1975-78, 81-83, ann. award 1981), Nat. Med. Assn. (chmn. pediatric sect. 1977-79, Ross Labs. award 1979, Outstanding Svcs. to Children during Internat. Yr. of Child award 1979, Meritorious Service Appreciation award 1979, W.M. Cobb co-lectr. 1985, mem. Coun. on Maternal and Child Health, 1974-92, chmn. 1979-89, ann. Roselyn Payne Epps Symposium 1994—, Grace Marilyn James award for Disting svc. Pediatric sect. 1991, Achievement award 1993, ann. Roselyn Payne Epps symposium 1994—), Am. Hosp. Assn. (maternal and child health sect. governing coun. 1989, 1992-94, maternal and child health nominating com. 1991), Soc. for the Advancement of Women's Health Rsch. (award for advocacy 1996), The Women's Forum of Washington, Alpha Omega Alpha, Delta Omega, Alpha Kappa Alpha. Mem. United Ch. of Christ. Clubs: Pearls (pres. 1984-86), Carrousels (corr. sec. 1978-80), Links (pres. Met. chpt. 1986-89) (Washington), Cosmos. Lodge: Zonta, Internat. Women's Forum. Home and Office: 1775 N Portal Dr NW Washington DC 20012-1014

EPSTEIN, ANDREW ERNEST, cardiologist, educator; b. NYC, Nov. 30, 1950; s. Frederick Hermon Epstein and Ingeborg Luise (Gunther) Davenport; 1 child, Anne Elizabeth. BA in English, Amherst Coll., 1973; MD, U. Rochester, 1977. Diplomate Am. Bd. Internal Medicine, Am. Bd. Cardiology, Nat. Bd. Med. Examiners, Am. Bd. Clin. Electrophysiology. Intern Barnes Hosp., St. Louis, 1977-78, resident, 1978-80; fellow U. Ala. at Birmingham, 1980-82, chief fellow divsn. cardiovasc. diseases, 1982-83, instr., 1982-83, asst. prof. medicine, 1983-87, assoc. prof. medicine, 1988-91, prof. medicine, 1991—2009, U. Pa., 2009—; chief Phila. Vets. Adminstrn. Med. Ctr. Cardiovasc. Sect., 2009—. Advisor to many mfrs. cardiac rhythm mgmt. devices and pharm. cos. Contbr. more than 270 articles, more than 260 abstracts to profl. jours., chpts. to 30 books in field. Vol. Am. Heart Assn., 1983—, mem. Ala. emergency cardiac care com., 1993-2000, Inst. Med. Com. Soc. Security Cardiovascular Disability Determination, 2009-10; expert advisory panel cardiovasc. and renal drugs US Pharmacopoeia, 1995-00; com. mem. Dept. Transp. on Guildlines on Fitness to Drive, 2001, 06. Fellow Am. Coll. Cardiology (chmn. com. on guideline for implantation of cardiac pacemakers and arrhythmia devices, 2004—), Am. Heart Assn. (fellow clin. coun. 1983—, exec. com. 1992-95, 96-97, chmn. com. on sudden death 1992-95, com. on electrocardiography and arrhythmias 1995-02, com. guideline implantation pacemakers and arrhythmia devices 2000—, chmn. 2004—), Heart Rhythm Soc., Assn. U. Cardiologists. Office: University Pa Cardiovasc Sect Electrophysiology Divsn 3400 Spruce St 9 Founders Philadelphia PA 19104 Office Phone: 215-614-1889. Business E-Mail: andrew.epstein@uphs.upenn.edu.

EPSTEIN, CHARLES MARTIN, medical educator; b. Miami, Fla., Feb. 14, 1947; AB, Harvard Coll., 1969, degree in Medicine, 1973. Prof. neurology Emory U. Healthcare, 1978—. Fellow: Am. Epilepsy Soc., Am. Clin. Neurophysiology Soc., Am. Acad. Neurology. Avocations: electronics, orchids. Office: 1365A Clifton Rd NE Atlanta GA 30307 Business E-Mail: charles.epstein@emory.edu.

EPSTEIN, JEFFREY S., hair restoration, facial plastic surgeon, otolaryngologist, educator; BA, Swarthmore Coll.; MD, U. of Vt. Coll. of Medicine, 1988. Diplomate Am. Bd. Otolaryngology, Am. Bd. Facial Plastic and Reconstructive Surgery, Am. Bd. Hair Restoration Surgery, 1998. Resident otolaryngology Jackson Meml. Hosp., Miami, Fla., 1989—93; clin. instr. otolaryngology, divsn. of facial plastic surgery Univ. of Miami Sch. of Medicine; solo pvt. practice Miami, 1994—, NY, 2005—; hosp. affiliation includes South Miami Hosp. Found. for Hair Restoration and Plastic Surgery, 2008; past pres. Fla. Soc. of Facial Plastic and Reconstructive Surgery. Fellow: ACS, Am. Acad. Facial and Reconstructive Plastic Surgery. Office: South Miami Hospital 6200 SW 73rd St Miami FL 33143-9990 Office Phone: 786-662-4000.

EPSTEIN, JOHN HOWARD, dermatologist; b. San Francisco, Dec. 29, 1926; s. Norman Neman and Gertrude (Hirsch) E.; m. Alice Thompson, Nov. 1953; children: Norman H., Janice A., Beverly A. BA, U. Calif., Berkeley, 1949, MD, 1952; MS, U. Minn., 1956. Diplomate Am. Bd. Dermatology (dir. 1974-84, pres. 1981 82). Intern Stanford U. Med. Ctr., 1952-53; resident in dermatology Mayo Clinic, Rochester, Minn., 1953-56; practice medicine specializing in dermatology San Francisco, 1956—; chief dermatology Mt. Zion Hosp., 1970-80. Clin. prof. U. Calif. Med. Sch., San Francisco, 1972—; cons. Letterman Army Med. Center, U.S. Naval Hosp., San Diego. Chief editor Archives of Dermatology, 1973-78; asst. editor Jour. Am. Acad. Dermatology, 1978-88; contbr. over 275 articles to profl. jours. With USNR, 1944-46. Recipient Finsen medal, Internat. Soc. Photobiology, 2004. Fellow ACP; mem. Am. Acad. Dermatology (pres. 1981-82, Silver award for exhibit 1962, Gold award 1969), Soc. Investigative Dermatology (v.p. 1979-80), Am. Dermatol. Assn. (bd. dirs. 1983-88, pres. 1990-91), N.Am. Dermatology Soc., Pacific Dermatol. Assn. (pres. 1985-86), Brit. Dermatol. Soc., Danish Dermatol. Soc., Polish Dermatol. Soc., San Francisco Dermatol. Soc. (pres. 1963-64), Am. Soc. Photobiology (councilor 1983 86), Academia Mexicana and Dermatologia (hon.), European Acad. Dermatology and Venerology (hon.), La Societe Francaise de Dermatologie & de Syphiligraphie, Spanish Dermatol. Soc. Office: 450 Sutter St Rm 1306 San Francisco CA 94108-4002 Office Phone: 415-781-4083.

EPSTEIN, JONATHAN A., medical educator, researcher; b. New Haven, Conn., May 19, 1961; s. Franklin H. and Sherrie S. Epstein; m. Margaret A. Myers; children: Max, James. AB magna cum laude, Harvard U., 1983, MD magna cum laude, 1988. Diplomate Am. Bd. Internal Medicine, Am. Bd. Cardiovascular Medicine. Intern in medicine Brigham and Women's Hosp., Boston, 1988—89, resident in medicine, 1989—91, rsch./clin. fellow in medicine (cardiology), 1991—94; postdoctoral assoc. dept. physiology Tufts U., 1988—90; clin. fellow in medicine Harvard Med. Sch., 1988—91, rsch. fellow in medicine, 1991—94, instr. medicine, 1994—96; chief med. resident Brockton-West Roxbury (Mass.) VA Med. Ctr., 1990; assoc. in rsch. Howard Hughes Med. Inst. Postdoctoral Fellowship for Physicians, 1992—95; asst. prof. medicine U. Pa., Phila., 1996—2001, asst. prof. cell and devel. biology, 1997—2001, assoc. prof. medicine, 2001, assoc. prof. cell and devel. biology, 2001, William Wikoff Smith prof. medicine, 2004—, sci. dir. Penn Cardiovascular Inst., 2005—, chair cell and devel. biology, 2006—. Assoc. physician divsns. cardiology and genetics Brigham and Women's Hosp., 1994—96; mem. med. staff (cardiology) dept. medicine Hosp. of U. Pa., 1996—; mem. med. staff Dept. VA Med. Ctr., Phila., 1996—; assoc. mem. Pa. Muscle Inst., 1997—; mem. Grad. Group in Cell and Molecular Biology, 1997—, U. Pa. Cancer Ctr., 1998—; ad hoc mem. human embryology and devel. 2 study sect. NIH, 1998; ad hoc mem. Cardiovascular A study sect. NIH, 2002, ad hoc mem. maternal and child health rsch. subcom. study sect., 02; mem. exec. com. Ctr. for Devel. Biology, 1999—; mem. Inst. for Medicine and Engring., 1999—; dir. Cardiovascular Histology and Gene Expression Core Facility, 1999—, Cardiovascular Transgenic and Knockout Care Facility, 2000—; adj. asst. prof. The Wistar Inst., 2000—; mem. study sect. Doris Duke Charitable Found., 2000—; mem. Ctr. for Rsch. on Reprodn. and Women's Health, 2001—; dir. Molecular Cardiology Rsch. Ctr., Divsn. Cardiology, 2001—; external advisor Tulane U., 2001; ad hoc reviewer Wellcome Trust, London, The Med. Rsch. Coun., London, The Health Rsch. Bd., Dublin. Contbr. articles to profl. jours. Recipient travel award, Am. Coll. Cardiology/Bristol Labs., 1993, 1st pl. award, Eli Lilly Scholar-Critical Care Cardiology Case Presentation Competition, New Orleans, 1993, Clinician Investigator Devel. award, NIH, 1995, McCabe Fellow award, 1996, Basil O'Connor Starter Scholar Rsch. award, March of Dimes Birth Defects Found., 1997, Sir William Osler Young Investigator award, Interurban Club, 2001; named Penn/Hughes Scientist, U. Pa./Howard Hughes Med. Inst. Program for Devel. Biology, 1996; finalist Raymond Kalil award for cardiology rsch., 1994; nominee Pfizer Postdoctoral Fellowship award, 1991, Med. Found. New Investigator award, 1995, Charles E. Culpeper Found. Scholarship in Med. Sci., 1995; grantee, W.W. Smith Charitable Trust, 1998. Fellow: Am. Heart Assn. (molecular signaling I study sect. 1997—99, basic sci. coun. 1997—, cardiovascular disease in the young coun. 1997—, ann. sci. sessions abstract rev. com. 1998—, devel. study sect. 1999—, study sect. Southea. Pa. affiliate 1996, Young Investigator award 1995, grantee 1995, 1996, finalist Louis N. and Arnold M. Katz Basic Sci. Rsch. prize for young investigators 1998, spl. rev. panel Greater L.A. cardiovascular rsch. devel. award 1998); mem.: AAAS, Inst. Medicine, Am. Soc. Clin. Investigation, Cardiac Muscle Soc., Am. Soc. Cancer Rsch., Nat. Neurofibromatosis Found. (cardiovascular task force 1999, Peter and Margie Feinberg Family Fund award 1997). Home: 821 King of Prussia Rd Radnor PA 19087 Office: U Pa 1154 Biomedical Rsch Bldg 421 Curie Blvd Philadelphia PA 19104-6140 E-mail: epsteinj@mail.med.upenn.edu.

EPSTEIN, LAURA, speech educator; b. Binghamton, NY, Oct. 14, 1960; PhD, U. Calif., Santa Barbara, 1994. Asst. prof., speech-lang. pathologist San Francisco State U., 2006—. Recipient Diversity award, Calif. Speech-Lang.-Hearing Assn. Fellow: Calif. Healthcare Found. Leadership Program; mem.: Am. Speech-Lang.-Hearing Assn., Calif. Speech-Lang.-Hearing Assn. Office: San Francisco State University SPED/CD San Francisco CA 94132 Office Fax: 415-338-0916. Business E-Mail: lepstein@sfsu.edu.

EPSTEIN, MARSHA ANN, public health physician; b. Chgo., Feb. 4, 1945; 1 child, Lee Rashad Mahmood. BA, Reed Coll., 1965; MD, U. Calif., San Francisco, 1969; MPH, U. Calif., Berkeley, 1971. Diplomate Am. Bd. Preventive Medicine. Intern French Hosp., San Francisco, 1969-70; resident in preventive medicine Sch. Pub. Health, U. Calif., Berkeley, 1971-73; fellow in family planning dept. ob-gyn. UCLA, 1973-74; med. dir. Herself Health Clinic, 1974-79; pvt. adult gen. practitioner, 1978-82; dist. health officer LA County Pub. Health, 1982—2001, area med. dir., 2001—07, chief special projects, chronic disease and injury prevention, 2007—10, rschr., med. educator, 2010—. Part-time physician U. Calif. Student Health, Berkeley, 1970—73; co-med. dir. Monsenior Oscar Romero Free Clinic, LA, 1992—93. Mem.: APHA, Calif. Acad. Preventive Medicine, So. Calif. Pub. Health Assn., LA-Am. Med. Women's Assn., Am. Med. Women's Assn., Am. Coll. Physician Execs. Democrat. Jewish. Avocations: dance, native plants, meditation. Office: South Tower 14 Fl 695 S Vermont Ave Los Angeles CA 90005 Business E-Mail: mepstein@ph.lacounty.gov.

EPSTEIN, MICHAEL A., plastic surgeon; BS in Distinction, U. Mich., Ann Arbor, 1977—81; MD, Wayne State U., Detroit, 1981—85. Diplomate Am. Bd. of Plastic Surgery, cert. Advanced Trauma Life Support, Microsurgical Techniques, Louisville, lic. Ill. Resident gen. surgery Michael Reese Hosp., Chgo., 1985—90; resident aesthetic surgery Manhattan Eye, Ear and Throat Hosp, NYC, 1992; resident plastic and reconstructive surgery sch. of medicine Wayne State Univ., Detroit, 1990—92; hosp. affiliation includes Evanston Hosp., Glenbrook Hosp., Highland Park Hosp., St. Alexius Hosp. and Med. Ctr.; pvt. practice plastic and reconstructive surgery Northbrook Plastic Surgery, 1992—. Vol. Pediatric Plastic and Reconstructive Surgery, Guanajuato, Mexico, 1990; bd. mem. Y-Me, 2002, Sue Duncan Children's Found., 2000—; chmn. med. advisory bd. Y-Me, 2002—. Mem.: Chgo. Soc. of Plastic Surgery, Am. Soc. of Aesthetic Plastic Surgeons, ACS, Am. Soc. of Plastic Surgeons. Office: Northbrook Plastic Surgery Ste 211 1535 Lake Cook Rd Northbrook IL 60062 Office Phone: 847-205-1680. Office Fax: 847 205 9822.

EPSTEIN, RANDY J., physician, ophthalmologist; b. Chgo., Jan. 8, 1955; s. Benita M. LoGiudice; m. Kayla G. Schieber, June 17, 1979; children: Rachel H., Sarah A, Joshua N. BS, U Ill., Urbana, 1976; MD, Rush Med. Coll., Chgo., 1980. Diplomate Am. Bd. of Ophthalmology, 1986. CEO Chgo. Cornea Consultants, Ltd., Highland Pk., Ill., 1986—; prof. Dept. of Ophthalmology, Rush Med. Coll., Chgo., 1986—. Mem. Lions Club, Highland Pk., Ill. Recipient One of Chicago's Top Doctors, Chgo. Mag., 2001, Honor award, Am. Acad. Ophthalmology, Sr. Achievement award, 2004. Office: Chicago Cornea Cons 806 Central Highland Park IL 60035 Personal E-mail: corneas@aol.com.

EPSTEIN, ROBERT MARVIN, anesthesiologist, educator; b. NYC, Mar. 10, 1928; s. Nathan B. and Rebecca Epstein; m. Lillian Ray Cohen, Dec. 31, 1950; children: Judith Susan, Neal Myron, Charles Benjamin. BS with distinction, U. Mich., 1947, MD cum laude, 1951. Diplomate Am. Bd. Anesthesiology (dir. 1972-84, pres. 1979-80). Intern U. Mich. Hosp., 1951—52; resident in anesthesiology Presbyn. Hosp., NYC, 1952—53, 1955—56; instr. in anesthesiology and fellow in medicine Columbia U., NYC, 1956—57, assoc., 1957—59, asst. prof., anesthesiology, 1959—65, assoc. prof., 1965—70, prof., 1970—72, U. Va., Charlottesville, 1972—74, Alumni prof., 1974—87, Disting. prof., 1987—92, Harold Carron prof., 1992—2002, dept. chmn., 1972—96, Harold Carron prof. emeritus, 2002—. Mem. anesthesiology tng. com. Nat. Inst. Gen. Med. Scis., NIH, 1966—69; mem. com. on anesthesia NRC, 1970—71; mem. Nat. Bd. Med. Examiners, 1982—90, Am. Bd. Med. Specialities, 1974—95. Editor: Anesthesiology, 1974—79; contbr. numerous articles to profl. jours. Mem. Ednl. Commn. for Fgn. Med. Grads., 1990—95; bd. dirs., sec. U. Va. Health Svcs. Found., 1980—90, pres., 1990—93; trustee Ednl. Commn. for Fgn. Med. Grads., 1991—95, vice chmn., 1994—95; bd. dirs. QualChoice of Va., 1997—2000. With US Army, 1953—55. Fellow Guggenheim fellow, Oxford U., England, 1966—67, NY Heart Assn., 1956—57; scholar in-residence, Inst. Medicine NAS, 1997, sr. scholar, Va. Health Policy Ctr., 1997—2002. Fellow: Royal Coll. Anaesthetists (Eng.); mem.: W.T.G. Morton Soc., Assn. Univ. Anesthesiologists (pres. 1973—74), Anaesthetic Rsch. Soc. (U.K.), Am. Soc. Pharmacology and Exptl. Therapeutics, Soc. Acad. Anesthesia Chmn. (rep. to Coun. Acad. Soc. Assn. Am. Med. Coll. 1984—91, mem. coun.), Am. Soc. Anesthesiologists, Am. Physiol. Soc., Inst. Medicine NAS, AAAS, Alpha Omega Alpha, Sigma Xi, Phi Beta Kappa. Avocations: sailing, photography. Office: Dept Anesthesiology PO Box 800710 Charlottesville VA 22908-0710

EPSTEIN, SETH PAUL, immunologist, infectious disease researcher; b. NYC, Sept. 11, 1958; s. Donald and Eileen (Schulman) Epstein; m. Ivy Chatanow, June 23, 2002; 1 child, Kaylic. BA in Chemistry with high honors, Brandeis U., Waltham, Mass., 1980; MD, Autonomous U. Guadalajara, Mex., 1984. Med. extern Pontiac (Mich.) Gen. Hosp., 1984; postdoctoral rsch. fellow Mich. Cancer Found., Detroit, 1985-86, NYU Med. Ctr., NYC, 1987-91, asst. rsch. scientist, 1991; rsch. asst. Mt. Sinai Med. Ctr., NYC, 1991-96, instr., asst. prof., 1997—. Contbr. articles to profl. jours. Tng. fellow NIH, 1987; grantee Dermatology Found., Inc., 1990. Mem. Assn. Rsch. in Vision and Ophthalmology, Phi Beta Kappa. Achievements include rsch. on cyclosporine A rapamycin transforming growth factor interferon-gamma relating to cytokine-induced upregulation of Langerhans cells, cell chemotaxis into the cornea and skin and treatment of herpetic keratitis; sunscreen prevention of Ultraviolet-activated herpes simplex; novel treatments for herpes simplex and adenovirus ocular infections, toxicity & efficiency of pharmaceuticals. Office: Mount Sinai Med Ctr Dept Ophthalmology 1 Gustave L Levy Pl New York NY 10029-6500 Business E-Mail: seth.epstein@mssm.edu.

ERB, CARL, ophthalmologist; b. Garmisch-Part., Germany, June 3, 1963; s. Horst and Uta Erb; m. Eleonora Lichtenberg, June 26, 1999; children: Karl, Clivia. Student, Ruhr U., Bochum, Germany, 1984—86; MD, Freie U., Berlin, 1994. Med. resident U. Eye Clinic, Tubingen, Germany, 1991—96, asst. med. dir., 1998—99, rsch. fellow Basel, Switzerland, 1996—98; asst. med. dir. dept. ophthalmology Med. HS, Hannover, Germany, 1999—2004; asst. med. dir. U. Eye Clinic, Rostock, 2004—05; med. dir. Schlosspark Clinic, Dept. Opthalmology, Berlin, 2005—. Editor (with Flammer): Risikofaktoren in der Augenheilkunde, 1999; editor: (with Krieglstein) Glaukom-Fragen Zur Praxis, 2000; editor: Search on Glaucoma, 2000—, Progression Fakoren beim Glaukom, 2005; co-editor (with Schlote): Medikamentöse Augentherapie, 2010. Lt., 1982—84, Germany. Mem.: German Opthal. Soc., Assn. for Rsch. in Vision and Ophthalmology, Am. Acad. Ophthalmology. Mailing: Nussbaumallee 17 Berlin 14050 Germany Office: Eye Clinic Wittenburg Platz Uleiststrasse 23-26 Berlin 10787 Germany Office Phone: 4930244862. Business E-Mail: carl.erb12@yahoo.com.

ERBA, HARRY PAUL, oncologist, educator; b. New Haven, Oct. 3, 1957; BS, Yale U., 1979; MD, Stanford U. Sch. Medicine, 1988, PhD. Instr. medicine Harvard Med. Sch., 1993—96; assoc. prof. internal medicine U. Mich. Med. Sch., 1996—. Exec. officer SW Oncology Group, 2005—. Recipient Spl. Recognition award, Nat. Comprehensive Cancer Ctr. Bd. Prodrs., 2007—08; named Best Tchr., Divsn. Hematology, Oncology, Dept. Internal Medicine, U. Mich., 2002—05, Outstanding Clinician, U. Mich., 2004; Fulbright-Hays fellowship, U. Leicester, Eng., 1979—80. Mem.: Am. Soc. Clin. Oncologists, Am. Soc. Hematologists. Avocation: running. Office: 1500 E Med Ctr Dr C348 MIB Ann Arbor MI 48109-5848 Office Fax: 734-647-8792. Business E-Mail: hperba@umich.edu.

ERBAN, JOHN KALIL, III, medicine educator, cancer specialist, researcher; b. Boston, Aug. 26, 1955; s. John Kalil and Najla Teresa (Maloof) E.; m. Lisa Ann Benoit, Sept. 4, 1982; children: Laura Elizabeth, John Kalil IV, Stephen Benoit. AB, Harvard U., 1977; MD, Tufts U., 1981. Diplomate Am. Bd. Internal Medicine. Intern U. Pa., 1981—82, resident, 1982—84, 1986—87; dir. clin. programs Gillette Ctr. Mass. General Hosp., Boston, 2007—; with Pub. Health Svcs., 1984—86. Med. editor Tufts Medicine, 1991—; contbr. articles to sci. and med. jours. Recipient Disting. Alumni award, Tufts Univ. Sch. Medicine, 2006. Mem. Mass. Soc. Clin. Oncology (pres. 2001). Office: Gillette Center Massachusetts General Hosp 55 Fruit St Boston MA 02111 Business E-Mail: jerban@partners.org.

ERBENICH, LOTHAR, internist; b. Wertheim, Mainz, Baden-Württemberg, Germany, Apr. 19, 1956; s. Helmut Werner and Elfriede Erbenich; m. Irmgard Planko, June 17, 1981; children: Vanessa Ines Philine, Vivian Ives Philipp. Diploma, Adventist Theol. Sem., 1980; MD, Johannes Gutenberg U., Mainz, 1989; specialty in emergency, Chamber Med. Drs. NY, Hessen, Germany, 1992; MD in Internal Medicine, Chamber Med. Drs., Berlin, 2000; student in Pub. Health, Loma Linda U., 2007—. Pastor Seventh-Day Adventist Ch., Nürnberg, Bavaria, Germany, 1980—81, Erlangen and Forchheim, Bavaria, Germany, 1981—83; with Hosp. Waldfriede, Berlin, 1989—90, 1994—98, 1999—, Jewish Hosp., Berlin, 1998—99. Lectr. Sch. Nursing Hosp. Waldfriede, Berlin, 1995—98; med. dir. Health Care Ctr., Berlin, 2000—, Optifast Program Health Care Ctr. Waldfriede, Berlin, 2000—; chief svcs. Internat. Med. Svcs. Hosp. Waldfriede, Berlin, 2000—; panel physician for various embassies, Berlin, 2000—; founding mem. Forum-Rauchfrei, 2000—. Editor: (films) The Search, Health Course of Adventist Media; contbr. articles to profl. jours. Mem. Commn. Smoke Free Hosps., 2002—04, Commn. Smoke Free Hosp. Waldfriede, Berlin Steglitz-Zehlendorf, 2005—; project mgr. Smoke Free Hosps., Germany, 2005—06; mem. fed. workshop addiction Adventist Cmty. Svcs., Germany, 2001—06, mem. fed. handicapped workshop, 2001—04. Mem.: German Soc. Obesity, German Internal Med. Drs., German Soc. Health (licentiate; sci. adv. bd.). Home: Carl-Ulrich-Str 51A Hessen Darmstadt D-64297 Germany Office: Hosp Waldfriede Argentinische Allee 40 Berlin D-14163 Germany Office Fax: 493081810308; Home Fax: 493081810308. Personal E-mail: dr.erbenich@adventisten.de. Business E-Mail: l.erbenich@primavita-berlin.de.

ERBER, WILLIAM FRANKLIN, gastroenterologist; b. NYC, June 1, 1941; s. Sigmund and Marcia (Picard) E.; m. Ingrid Amelia Friedler, Dec. 25, 1967; children: Gregory, Karina, Jonathan, Joanna, Jeremy. BS, Muhlenberg Coll., 1963; MD, U. Health Sci., Chgo., 1967. Diplomate Am. Bd. Internal Medicine and Gastroenterology. Intern Maimonides Hosp., 1967-68, resident, 1968-69, 71-72; fellowship in gastroenterology Albert Einstein Coll. of Medicine, 1973-75; rsch. fellow Hadassah Hosp., Jerusalem, 1971-72; clin. asst. prof. Health Sci. Ctr., Bklyn., 1975—. Cons. Crohn's Colitis Found., N.Y.C., 1975—, H.I.P., N.Y.C., 1975—; attending gastroenterologist Maimonides Med. Ctr., Bklyn., 1975—. Author: Internal Medicine Review, 1979; contbr. articles to profl. jours. Maj. USAF, 1969-71. Fellow: ACP, Am. Coll. Gastroenterology; mem.: Am. Soc. Gastroenterol. Endoscopy, Am. Gastroenterol. Assn. Avocations: music, piano, skiing. Office: 591 Ocean Pkwy Brooklyn NY 11218-5913 Home: 159 Beach 147th St Neponsit NY 11694 Office Phone: 718-972-8500. Personal E-mail: ef591@aol.com. *

ERBIL, GUVEN, medical educator, researcher; b. Izmir, Apr. 24, 1965; MD, Dokuz Eylul Med. Faculty, 1988, PhD in Histology and Embryology, 1999. Assoc. prof., rschr. Dokuz Eylul Med. Faculty, 2000—. Office: 2040 Sk Pamukkale 4 G:60 D:2 Mavisehir Izmir Karsiyaka 35340 Turkey Office Fax: 4124555. Business E-Mail: guven.erbil@deu.edu.tr.

ERDEM, ATILLA, neurosurgeon, educator; b. Gaziantep, Anatolia, Turkey, Nov. 7, 1954; s. Mahmut Sevket and Nezihe (Kuyumcu) E.; m. Hatice Rana Erdem, July 15, 1982; 1 child, Mehmet Can. MD, U. Ankara, Turkey, 1977. Med. diplomate. Resident neurosurgery dept. Ankara U., 1977-83, neurosurgeon, cons., 1983-90, assoc. prof. neurosurgery dept., 1990-96, prof. in neurosurgery, 1996—. Bd. dirs. Epilepsy Surgery Program, Ankara. Collaborator: Microneurosurgery IV B, 1996. Mem. Turkish Neurosurg. Soc. Avocations: playing guitar, photography. Office: Ibn-i Sina Hastahanesi Nörosirürji Kl 06100 Samanpazari Ankara Turkey Home: Sokak 83/3 6540 Ankara Ankara Turkey Home Phone: 90-312-441 3566; Office Phone: 90-312-5082304, 903124683745. Office Fax: 903124683742. E-mail: erdem@medicine.ankara.edu.tr.

ERDMANN, JAMES BERNARD, educational psychologist; b. Oct. 27, 1937; s. George C. and Emma (Hiltebrand) E.; m. Rebecca Susan Lindsay; children: Theodore Michael, Carolyn Louise, Christopher Joseph, Timothy James. Grad. cum laude, Pontifical Coll., Josephinum, 1959; MA, Loyola U., Chgo., 1964, PhD, 1966. Rsch. asst. Psychometric Lab. Loyola U., 1960-63, rsch. assoc., project dir., 1963-65, acting dir., 1965-66, assoc. dir., 1967-69, instr. dept. psychology, 1964-66, asst. prof. measurement program, 1967-69; assoc. prof. Sch. Edn. and Sch. Human Medicine, eval. coord. Office Med. Edn., R & D, Mich. State U., 1969-70; dir. divsn. ednl. measurement and rsch. Assn. Am. Med. Colls., Washington, 1970-87; clin. assoc. prof. psychiatry and behavioral scis. George Washington U. Sch. Medicine and Health Scis., 1973-87; assoc. dean adminstrn. and spl. projects Jefferson Med. Coll., Thomas Jefferson U., Phila., 1987-89, assoc. dean adminstrn. and univ. registrar, 1990-2001, prof. medicine (edn.) dept. medicine, 1993—, sr. assoc. dean faculty affairs, 2001; dean Jefferson Coll. Health Professions Thomas Jefferson U., Phila., 2002—09, assoc. sr. v.p. academic affairs, 2009—. Contbr. articles to profl. jours. Mem. Am. Ednl. Rsch. Assn., Assn. Schs. of Allied Health, Assn. Am. Med. Coll. Roman Catholic. Home: 408 Bickmore Dr Media PA 19086-6909 Office: 130 S 9th St Philadelphia PA 19107-5233 Office Phone: 215-955-4481. Business E-Mail: james.erdmann@jefferson.edu.

ERDÖS, ERVIN GEORGE, pharmacology and biochemistry professor; b. Budapest, Hungary; came to U.S., 1954; naturalized, 1959; s. Andor and Aranka (Breuer) E; m. Sara F. Rabito, May 30, 1986; children from previous marriage: Martin, Peter, Philip. Grad., U. Budapest Sch. Medicine, 1950; MD, U. Munich, 1950. With hosp., Munich, 1951; rsch. assoc. in biochem. rsch. lab. U. Munich, 1952-54; rsch. assoc. Mercy Hosp., Pitts., 1955-58; fellow in biochemistry, ind. rsch. Mellon Inst., Pitts., 1958-63; asst. prof. pharmacology U. Pitts., 1958-61, assoc. prof., 1961-63; prof. pharmacology U. Okla. Sch. Medicine, Oklahoma City, 1963-73, George Lynn Cross rsch. prof., 1970-73; prof. pharmacology, internal medicine U. Tex., Southwestern Med. Sch., Dallas, 1973-85; prof. pharmacology and anesthesiology, dir. Peptide Rsch. Lab. U. Ill. Coll. Medicine, Chgo., 1985—; prof. emeritus U. Ill. Coll. Med., 2007—. Vis. prof. Tulane U., 1963; Disting. Fulbright prof., 1975; vis. scientist U.S.-Japan Coop. Sci. Program, NSF, 1966; vis. prof. dept. pharmacology Rush Med. Coll., Chgo., 1993—; cons. in field; mem. coms. Nat. Heart and Lung Inst. Editor books; mem. editorial bd. jours. Recipient gold medal Frey-Werle Found., Munich, 1988, Disting. Faculty award U. Ill. Coll. Medicine, 1992; Deutsche Forschungsgemeinschaft fellow, 1954; Wellcome Rsch. travel grantee, 1964; Univ. scholar U. Ill., 1990. Fellow: Am. Heart Assn. (mem. Coun. for High Blood Pressure Rsch. 1972—, Ciba award for hypertension rsch. 1994, Rsch. Achievement award 1995); mem.: Am. Physiol. Soc., Am. Soc. Biochemistry and Molecular Biology, Hungarian Acad. Sci. (fgn.) (hon.), Am. Soc. Pharmacology and Exptl. Therapeutics. Office: U Ill Coll Medicine Dept Pharmacology MC 868 835 S Wolcott Ave Chicago IL 60612-7340 E-mail: egerdos@uic.edu.

ERDTMANN, FREDERICK J., physician, retired military officer; b. Mineola, NY, July 28, 1944; m. Jean Erdtmann. BS, Bucknell U.; MD, Temple U. Sch. Medicine, 1970; MPH, U. Calif., Berkeley; grad., Armed Forces Staff Coll., Indsl. Coll. Armed Forces. Intern Allentown Gen. Hosp., Pa., 1970—71; advanced through grades to col. U.S. Army; resident, preventive medicine Walter Reed Army Inst. Rsch., 1974—75; chief, preventive medicine svc. Fitzsimmons Army Med. Ctr., Frankfurt Army Med. Ctr., Germany, Madigan Army Med. Ctr.; divsn. surgeon 2d Infantry Divsn., Tongduchon, Republic of Korea; several tours Office of the Surgeon Gen.; hosp. cmdr. Walter Reed Army Med. Ctr., 1998—99; dir., Health Select Population Bd. Inst. Medicine-Nat. Acads., 2003—. Decorated 5 Legions of Merit, Order of Military Med. Merit, George Sternberg Medal for Excellence in Preventive Medicine. Office: Institute of Medicine 500 Fifth St NW Washington DC 20001 Office Phone: 202-334-1925. Business E-Mail: rerdtmann@nas.edu.

ERDURAN, EROL, pediatrician; b. Samsun, Turkey, July 2, 1960; s. Riza and Nazan (Yendi) E.; m. Gülseren Bilge Abanozoglu, July 7, 1990; 1 child, Ece Nazan. MD, Atatürk U. Med. Sch., 1983. Health mgr. Health Ministry, Maras, Turkey, 1984-85; asst. to head dr. Karadeniz Tech. U. Edn. Hosp., Trabzon, Turkey, 1994-96; head, chamber of med. dr. Turkish Med. Dr. Assn., Trabzon, 1996—. Assoc. sec. Nat. Pediatrics Congress, 1994; editl. bd. Karadeniz Med. Bulletin, 1994—. Editor: (bulletin) Bulletin of Chamber of Med. Dr., 1996—. Recipient Encouragement cert. Karadeniz Tech. U., 1994, 95, 96. Mem. Turkish Hematology Soc., Blood Bank and Blood Transfusion Soc., Nat. Pediatrics Assn., Turkish Club, N.Y. Acad. Scis., Nat. Geog. Soc. Avocations: reading, rsch., social activities, travel. Office: Karadeniz Tech U Medicine 61080 Trabzon Turkey

EREL, OZCAN, medical researcher, educator; b. Konya, Turkey, Jan. 15, 1963; PhD, Firat U., 1993. Prof. Harran U. Med. Faculty, 1993—2008; Ataturk Hosp. Yildirim Beyazit U. Med Faculty, 2008—11. Head prof. Med. Biochemistry Dept., 1993—2011. Recipient Xi. John M. Kinney Internat. award, Best Med. Project award, 2007. Mem.: AACC. Office: Yildirim Beyazit University Medical Faculty Biochem Ankara TR06000 Turkey Personal E-mail: erelozcan@gmail.com.

EREN, BULENT, pathologist; b. Bulgaria, Aug. 11, 1974; MD, Istanbul U., 1999. Cert. in pathology Istanbul U., in forensic medicine Uludag U., 2003. Physician, rschr., neurosurgery dept. Istanbul U. Cerrahpasa Med. Faculty, 1999—2000, physician, pathology, rschr., 2000—03; pathologist Bursa Morgue Dept., Coun. Forensic Medicine Turkey, 2006—08, forensic medicine specialist, 2008—, chmn., 2009—. Contbr. articles to profl. jours. Recipient Spl. Publs. award, Uludag U. Mem.: Turkish Med. Soc., Soc. Forensic Medicine Specialists, Soc. Forensic Medicine, Turkish Soc. Pathology. Office: Coun Forensic Medicine Turkey Bursa South Marmara 16010 Turkey E-mail: bulenteren2000@yahoo.com.

EREN, GÜLAY, anesthesiologist; b. Balikesir, Turkey, May 6, 1971; Degree in Medicine, Maramara U., 1995. Anesthesiology and intensive care physician Sisli Etfal Rsch. Hosp., 2000, Bakirkoy Dr Sadi Konuk Tng. and Rsch. Hosp., 2003—. Cons. Istanbul Simulation Ctr., 2007. Mem.: Turkish Intensive Care Soc., Turkish Anesthesiology Soc. Office: Tevfik Saglam Istanbul Bakirkoy 34147 Turkey Business E-Mail: glyeren@mynet.com.

ERENSTEIN, ALAN, emergency nurse, legal nurse consultant; Grad., Aliquippa Hosp Sch. Radiology, Pa., 1974; student, Aliquippa Hosp. Sch. Radiology, New Wilmington, Pa., 1974; AA in Gen. Studies, LPN, Beaver County C.C., Monaca, Pa., 1977, AS in Nursing, RN, 1979. RN, Fla.; registered radiologic technologist, cert. legal nurse cons. LPN Hamot Med. Ctr., Erie, Pa., 1977-78; team leader Trauma-Neuro ICU and Stepdown Unit Allegheny Gen. Hosp., Pitts., 1979-81, staff nurse Emergency Room, 1981; flight nurse LifeWATCH HCA Wesley Med. Ctr., Wichita, Kans., 1981-91, contigency and float pool, 1991-92, hyperbaric nurse, 1991-92; ER nurse, relief charge nurse, clin. coord., team leader JFK Med. Ctr., Atlantis, Fla., 1992-95; aeromed. specialist Bizjet Air Ambulance, West Palm Beach, Fla., 1994-95; med. edn. cons. Med. Edn. Cons. Am., Tampa, 1994-97; with disaster team Cutler Ridge (Fla.) Field Hosp., 1992; response team Kans. Tornado Wesley Med. Ctr., Wichita, 1991; emergency rm./trauma nurse DelRay Med. Ctr., 1996—. Paramedic clin. coord. Hutchinson (Kans.) C.C., 1989; skills lab coord. Advanced Trauma Life Support Course, HCA Wesley Med. Ctr., Wichita, 1989-92; lectr.in field; cons. in field. Author: Trauma in Pregnancy, 1990; co-author: LifeWATCH Transport Manual, 1988; contbr. Society Trauma Nurses: Instructor's Resource Manual for Trauma Nursing, The Pregnant Trauma Patient Module, 1998.

ERGIL, KEVIN VAHIT, acupuncturist, educator; b. San Rafael, Calif., July 16, 1957; s. Tanju Vahit and Helen Martin Ergil; m. Marnae Crystal Pearlman, July 21, 1990; m. Cecelia Jean Packard, Jan. 18, 1984 (div. July 30, 1987); children: Jacob Vahit, Elizabeth Crystal, Katherine Crystal. BA in Anthropology with highest honors, U. of Calif., Santa Cruz, 1983; MA in Anthropology, U. of Wash., 1986, postgrad., 1984—87; MS in Traditional Chinese Medicine, Am. Coll. of Traditional Chinese Medicine, San Francisco, 1989. Lic. acupuncturist Calif., 1990, aupuncturist NY, 1993, diplomate Nat. Commn. for Certification of Acupuncture & Oriental Medicine. Pres. Am. Coll. Traditional Chinese Medicine, San Francisco, 1990—92; dean and dir. Pacific Coll. Oriental Medicine, NYC, 1992—98; rsch. dir. NY Coll. Health Profession, Syosset, 1999—2000; dir. grad. program in Oriental medicine Sch. Health Scis. Touro Coll., NYC, 2000—06; prof. Finger Lakes Sch.; assoc. prof. Sch. Acupuncture & Oriental Medicine NY Chiropractic Coll., Seneca Falls, 2006—. Editor Clin. Acupuncture and Oriental Medicine: An Internat. Jour., NYC, 1998—2000; dir. Soc. for Acupuncture Rsch., Bethesda, Md., 1994—2001; acupuncturist Huntington Herbs & Acupuncture, NY, 2001—06; chair Core Curriculum Com., Coun. of Colleges Acupuncture and Oriental Medicine, Silver Springs, Md., 1991—2000. Editor: (text book) Practical Diagnosis in Traditional Chinese Medicine, Pocket Atlas of Chinese Medicine; contbr. articles to profl. jours. Fellow Nat. Resource fellow, 1984, Career Devel. fellow, NSF, 1985—88, Pres. Undergrad. fellow, Office of the Pres., U. of Calif., 1982. Mem.: Acupuncture Soc. of NY. Avocations: snowboarding, boating, drawing, gardening, photography. Office: NY Chiropractic Coll State Rt 89 Seneca Falls NY 13148-0800 Office Phone: 315-568-3211. Personal E-mail: kve@pobox.com.

ERHARDT, WALTER L., JR., medical association administrator; m. Carolyn Erhardt; children: Trish, Abbie. BS cum laude, Roanoke Coll., Salem, Va., 1969; MD, U. Va. Sch. Medicine, Charlottesville, 1973. Diplomate Am. Bd. Plastic Surgery 1980, lic. Ga., Va. Resident, gen. surgery, plastic and reconstructive surgery Vanderbilt U., Nashville; chief of surgery Phoebe Putney Meml. Hosp., Albany, Ga., chmn., divsn. plastic surgery; solo private practice Albany, Ga., 1979—. Adv. bd. Consumer Guide to Plastic Surgery; examinar Am. Bd. Plastic Surgery, 1996—, dir., chair, written examination com. Editor: Plastic Surgery News, 1995—99; assoc. adv. editor Plastic Surgery News, 1992—95. Mem. med. mission teams to India and El Salvador. Fellow: ACS; mem.: Southeastern Soc. Plastic and Reconstructive Surgeons, Dougherty County Med. Soc., Med. Assn. Ga., Am. Soc. Plastic and Reconstructive Surgeons (bd. dir. 1992—93, mem. publications com. 1992—, mem. fin. com. 1992—, mem. CPT com. 1992—, bd. dir. 1995—, treas. 1996—98, v.p. 1998—99), Am. Soc. Plastic Surgeons (pres. 2000—01, past pres. 2002), Ga. Soc. Plastic Surgeons, Am. Soc. Aesthetic Plastic Surgery, AMA (mem. specialty soc. adv. com., alternate del. 1992—). Office: 506 West 4th Ave Albany GA 31701 Office Phone: 229-432-9325. Office Fax: 229-439-4396.

ERI, SASABE, dentist; b. Ehime, Japan, Feb. 19, 1974; PhD, Hiroshima U., Japan, 2002. Rsch. assoc. Dept. Oral and Maxillofacial Surgery, Kochi Med. Sch., Kochi U., 2003—. Named Eminent Scientist of Yr., IRPC, 2009. Mem.: Japanese Tissue Culture Soc. Dental Rsch., Japanese Soc. Oral & Maxillofacial Surgeons, Japanese Stomatological Soc. Office: Kohasu Oko-cho Nankoku City Kochi 783-8505 Japan Office Phone: 81-88-880-2423. Office Fax: 81-88-880-2424. Business E-Mail: erinko-arinko.0219@docomo.ne.jp, yoshieri@kochi-u.ac.jp.

ERICHSON, ROBERT B., hematologist, oncologist; b. Bklyn., Aug. 23, 1935; s. Harry L. Erichson and Betty Reichlin; m. Elaine Greenberg Erichson, June 15, 1958; children: Laura, Howard. BA, Columbia U., 1956; MD, Cornell U., 1960. Adj. attending physician Montefiore Hosp., Bronx, NY, 1965; instr. medicine Albert Einstein Coll. Med., 1966; cons. US Army Transfusion Svc., Europe, 1966—69; clin. asst. prof. medicine Yale Med. Sch., New Haven, 1974—80; clin. prof. medicine NY Med. Coll., NYC, 1981—, Columbia U., 1998—; dir. hematology Stamford Hosp., Conn., 1973—, physician-in-chief, 1972—73, pres. med. staff, 1979—82, bd. trustees, 1979—83; bd. dirs. Ctr. Continuing Care, 1986—; dir. Bennett Cancer Ctr., 1996—. Author: Hematologic Problems in Surgery, 1970; contbr. articles to profl. jours. Maj. US Army, 1966—69. Fellow: ACP; mem.: Am. Soc. Hematology (publs. com. 1980—), Am. Soc. Clin. Oncology. Democrat. Jewish. Office: Hematology-Oncology PC 34 Shelburne Rd Stamford CT 06902-3658 E-mail: bobbye2@optonline.net.

ERICKSON, EDWARD LEONARD, biotechnologist, consultant; s. Leonard Gerald and Eleanore Antoinette E.; m. Helen Leonora Masten, Dec. 29, 1979. BS in Math., Ill. Inst. Tech., 1968, MS in Math., 1970; MBA in Gen. Mgmt., Harvard U., 1980. Mktg. rep. IBM, Miami, Fla., 1975-76; sr. systems engr. Advanced Tech., Inc., McLean, Va., 1976-78; cons. Bain & Co., Boston, 1979-80; sr. assoc.

Resource Planning Assocs., Washington, 1980-82; dir. RPA Mgmt. Cons., London, 1982-83; dir. corp. devel. Amersham Internat. plc., Little Chalfont, Eng., 1983-86, gen. mgr. internat. ops., 1986-88; v.p. fin. ops. The Ares-Serono Group, Boston, 1988-90; pres. Serono-Baker Diagnostics (The Ares-Serono Group), Allentown, Pa., 1990-91; pres., CEO, dir. Cholestech Corp., Hayward, Calif., 1991-93; CEO, dir. DepoTech Corp., La Jolla, Calif., 1993—98; CEO, chmn. Immunicon Corp., 1998—2007, Cellatope Corp., 2007—09; dir. BioNanomatrix Inc., 2009—11. Venture ptnr. University City Sci. Ctr., 2006—07; bd. mem. Metabolon Inc., MDx Health; CEO Saladax Biomed., 2011—. Lt. USN, 1970—75. Recipient Small Times Mag. Best Small Tech Bus. Leader award; John L. Loeb fellow Harvard U., 1980, George F. Baker scholar, 1980, NASA fellow, 1968-70. Mem. AAAS, ASHG. Republican. Avocations: tennis, skiing. Personal E-mail: elerickson@comcast.net. Business E-Mail: eerickson@saladax.com.

ERICKSON, RAY CHARLES, retired wildlife biologist; b. St. Peter, Minn., Jan. 30, 1918; s. Isaac and Martha Ernestina (Ziebarth) Erickson; m. Patricia Katherine Miles, Jan. 8, 1950 (div. Nov. 8, 1951); 1 child, Susan Eileen; m. Helen Josephine Haworth, Sept. 10, 1953 (dec. Nov. 16, 1996); children: Joanne Louise, David Wayne, Thomas Alan; m. Grace Marjorie Hayes, May 2, 2001. Student, George Washington U., 1939—40; AB, Gustavus Adolphus Coll., St. Peter, Minn., 1941; MS, Iowa State U., Ames, 1942, PhD, 1948. Wildlife biologist U.S. Fish and Wildlife Svc., Burns, Oreg., 1948—55, chief, sect. habitat mgmt. wildlife refuges divsn., 1955—57, rsch. staff specialist wetland ecology divsn. wildlife rsch. Washington, 1957—65; charter mem. Whooping Crane Recovery Team and the Aleutian Can. Goose Recovery Team; supr. endangered wildlife rsch. program U.S. Fish and Wildlife Svc., Laurel, Md., 1965—80; ret., 1980. Mem., scientist Oreg. Natural Heritage Adv. Coun., Salem, 1990—2002. Contbr. articles to profl. publs. Officer landing craft boat divsn. USN, 1943—46, PTO. Recipient Disting. Svc. award, U.S. Dept. of Interior, 1968, Spl. Conservation award, Nat. Wildlife Fedn., 1975, Wildlife Conservation award, Zool. Soc. San Diego, 1979; named Disting. Alumnus, Gustavus Adolphus Coll., 1991. Mem.: Whooping Crane Conservation Assn. (life), Washington Biologists' Field Club (pres. 1967—70). Lutheran. Achievements include federal refuge management studies of the role of grazing and other agricultural practices in wetland wildlife production; conceiving and directing endangered species research program involving coordinated laboratory and ecological investigations; captive propagation to preserve and restore viable wild populations. Avocations: nature watching, fishing, photography, travel. Home: 3010 Twin Oak Pl NW Salem OR 97304

ERICKSON, ROBERT PORTER, genetics researcher, educator, clinician; b. Portland, Oreg., June 27, 1939; s. Harold M. and Marjorie S. (Porter) Erickson; m. Sandra De'Ath, June 20, 1964; children: Andrew Ian, Colin De'Ath, Tanya Nadene, Tracy Lynn, Michelle Lee, Christof Phillipe. BA, Reed Coll., Portland, 1960; MD, Stanford U., Calif., 1965. Diplomate Am. Bd. Pediat., Am. Coll. Med. Genetics. Asst. prof. pediatrics U. Calif.-San Francisco Med. Sch., 1970-75; vis. scientist Institut Pasteur, Paris, 1975-76; assoc. prof. human genetics and pediat. U. Mich., Ann Arbor, 1976-80, prof., 1980-90, dir. divsn. pediat. genetics, 1985-90. Vis. scientist Imperial Cancer Rsch. Fund, London, 1983-84; Holsclaw Family prof. human genetics and inherited diseases dept. pediat. U. Ariz., 1990—; vis fellow Hughes Hall, U. Cambridge, 1996-97; with Ariz. Biomed. Rsch. Commn., 2008-09. Mem. editl. bd. Jour. Reproductive Immunology, 1978-89, Dictionary of Lab. Tech., 1983, Molecular Reprodn. and Devel., 1989-99, Antisense R&D, 1992-2005, Jour. Rare Diseases, 1995-98, Jour. Applied Genetics, 2000—, Reviews in Mutation Rsch., 2001—; contbr. over 350 articles to sci. jours. and books. With USPHS, 1967-69. Guggenheim fellow, Paris, 1975, Eleanor Roosevelt fellow, London, 1983; Fogarty Sr. Internat. fellow, 1996, Burroughs Wellcome travel fellow, 1996; Fulbright grantee, London, 1983, NIH grantee, 1971—. Mem. Am. Soc. Human Genetics, Soc. Pediat. Rsch., Am. Pediat. Soc. Avocations: hiking, enology. Home: 5200 N Camino Real Tucson AZ 85718-5029 Office Phone: 520-626-5483. Business E-Mail: erickson@peds.arizona.edu.

ERICKSON, SUE ALICE, health educator, consultant, nurse; b. Sailor Springs, Ill., Feb. 3, 1938; d. Charles Ashby and Myra Estella (McPherson) Inskeep; m. Dale Gilbert Erickson, Sept. 25, 1959; children: Erin Erickson Fonken, Kelly, Sean B. Diploma in Profl. Nursing, St. Luke's Hosp., 1959; BA, Stephens Coll., 1981; MS in Cmty. Health Edn., U. N.Mex., 1987, PhD in Cmty. Health Edn., 1992; doctoral student, Trinity Seminary, 2010—. RN; cert. health edn. specialist. Nurse, health educator Sandia Nat. Labs., Albuquerque, 1985-88; cons. Cuidandos Los Ninos, Albuquerque, 1988-90; cons., bd. dirs. Pioneer Bible Translators, Dallas, 1983—95, vice chmn. bd. dirs., 1993—94; owner SAE Health Comms., LLC, 1993—. Asst. matron, health educator Chidamoyo Christian Hosp., Karoi, Rhodesia, 1968-70, vol. nurse tchr., Zimbabwe, 1991; instr. Pioneer Missions Inst., 1982-94; vis. lectr. dept. medicine U. Zimbabwe, 1995, 97-2000, 01, 04, 10; adj. health instr. Equip, Inc., 1994-04; adj. prof. health edn. U. N.Mex., 2001; adj. prof. bioethics Lincoln Christian Sem., Ill., 1996, 2001, 03, 07, Hope Internat. U., Fullerton, Calif., 1997; bd. dirs. Best Choice Ednl. Svc., 2001-06; mem. adv. coun. abstinence edn. State N.Mex., 2004—06; adv. coun. Carenet, Inc., Albuquerque, N.Mex., 2003-07, mem. devel. com., 2008-09; pres. TTL Care Assessment and Edn., LLC, 2006—; instr. primary health care Pioneer Bible Translators, Dallas, 2005—09; nurse tng. cons., provider Aegin Place Home Care, Footprints Homecare, Albuquerque 2005—08; workshop leader on missionary health Nat. Missionary Conv., 2010; mem. bd. N.Mex. Family Coun., 2006-07, mem. bd. Family Lifeline Inc., v.p. 2007, 2009; pres. bd. N.Mex. Youth Families Lifeline, 2008-09; adj. prof. Bioethics U. St. Francis, physician assistant program, 2009-; vis. faculty dept. cmty. health, Malawi Sch. Medicine, 2008. Author: (course for HS students/pregnancy crisis ctrs.) After Abstinence, 2005. Vol. nurse educator New Heart, Inc., Albuquerque, 1975-80; mem. bd. dirs. Covenant Christian Fellowship, Albuquerque, 1984-88; dir. Christian Edn., Hts. Christian Ch., 1992-96; adv. Boy Scouts Am., 1978-86; organize dir. Fibromyalgia Support Group Albuquerque, 1989-95. St. Luke's Hosp. Sch. Nursing scholar, 1959; named Disting. Alumnus, Mt. Vernon Township H.S., 2006. Mem. ACA, AAHPERD, Christian Med. and Dental Assn., Ctr. Bioethics and Human Dignity, N.Mex. Abstinence Edn. Coalition, Nat. Abstinence Edn. Assn., Health Vols. Overseas. Republican. Avocations: backpacking, running, biking, skiing, music. Home: 2904 Calle Grande NW Albuquerque NM 87104-3146 Office Phone: 505-344-3570. Personal E-mail: saede2@gmail.com.

ERICSSON, KJERSTIN ELISABETH, retired neuroscience educator; b. Stockholm, Jan. 5, 1938; d. Bertil Eurenius and Anna Maria (Larsson) E. RN/Midwife, St. Eric Nursing Coll., Stockholm, 1962; Cert. Fin D'Etudes de Annee, Ecole Inter Enseign Inf. Sup., Lyon, France, 1978; cert. in social gerontology, U. Lyon, France, 1979, Maitrise Psychology, 1981, Maitrise Sociology and Ethnology, 1988; M in Social Sci., U. Uppsala, Sweden, 1984, PhD, 1985. Lab. asst. Halland County Coun., Sweden, 1957-58; nurse Dalecarlia County Coun., Sweden, 1962-64; dist. nurse Gavle County Coun., Sweden, 1964-72; geriat. nursing chief adminstr. Stockholm County Coun., Sweden, 1976-88; rschr. Huddinge (Sweden) U. Hosp., 1988-92; sr. lectr. Karolinska Inst., Stockholm, 1992—, asst. prof. geriat. nursing rsch., 1997. Advisor to dir. gen. IBC (AdVah). Contbr. articles to profl. jours. Recipient grant Swedish 3M, Stockholm, 1973, grants European Coun., Lyon, France, Basel, Switzerland, 1974, 91. Mem. AAAS, Internat. Psychogeriatric Assn., Internat. Graphonomics Soc., NY Acad. Scis., Internat. Assn. for Sci. Study of Intellectual Disability, ABIRA (life, dep. bd. govs.), London Diplomatic Acad. (founder diplomatic counsellor).

ERIKSEN, CHARLES WALTER, psychologist, educator; b. Omaha, Feb. 4, 1923; s. Charles Hans and Luella (Carlson) E.; m. Garnita Tharp, July 22, 1945 (div. Jan. 1971); children: Michael John, Kathy Ann; m. Barbara Becker, Apr. 1971. BA summa cum laude, U. Omaha, 1943; PhD, Stanford, 1950. Asst. prof. Johns Hopkins U., Balt., 1949-53, research scientist, 1954-55; lectr. Harvard U., Cambridge, Mass., 1953-54; mem. faculty U. Ill., Urbana, 1956—, prof., 1959-93, prof. emeritus, 1993—. Rsch. cons. VA, 1960-80; mem. psycho-biology panel NSF, 1963; mem. exptl. psychology study sect. NIH, 1958-62, 66-70; Pillsbury Meml. lectr. Cornell U., 1966; keynote address 1st Internat. Congress on Visual Search, U. Durham, U.K., 1988, European Congress for Cognitive Psychology, Elsinore, Denmark, 1993; invited lectr. Max Plank Inst., Munich, 1993, Universidad Autonoma de Madrid, 1993, U. of Salamanca, Spain, 1993. Author: Behavior and Awareness, 1962; editor Am. Jour. Psychology, 1968; prin. editor Perception and Psychophysics, 1971-93; cons. editor Jour. Exptl. Psychology, 1965-71, Jour. Gerontology, 1980—; contbr. articles to profl. jours. Recipient Stratton award Am. Psychopath. Assn., 1964, NIMH Research Career award, 1964 Fellow AAAS; mem. Am. Psychol. Soc., Psychonomic Soc., Soc. Exptl. Psychologists, Midwestern Psychol. Assn., Sigma Xi. Home: 22485 State Highway 133 Oakland IL 61943-6822 Personal E-mail: erikbarb@consolidated.net.

ERIKSEN, ERIK FINK, endocrinologist, internist, researcher; b. O. Jerstal, Denmark, Aug. 2, 1953; s. Christian Frede and Signe Fink Eriksen; m. Catherine Barbara Sundt (Andersen), Mar. 12, 2002; 1 child, Barbara S. stepchildren: Celia Sundt, Athena B. Sundt, Sander N. Sundt;children from previous marriage: Morten, Mads. MD, Aarhus U., Denmark, 1980; Dr in Med. Sci., Aarhus U., 1989. Diplomate Endocrinology and Internal Medicine. Cons. Aarhus U. Hosp., Denmark, 1980-82; rsch. fellow Aarhus Amtssygehus, 1982-85; postdoctoral fellow Mayo Clinic, Rochester, Minn., 1985-87; clin. fellow Aarhus U. Hosp., 1987-89, asst. prof. internal medicine, 1989-96, assoc. prof. internal medicine, 1996—2002, cons. endocrinology and internal medicine, 1994—2001, chmn. dept. endocrinology, 1995—2002; med. dir. Eli Lilly & Co., Indpls., 2002—05; global brand med. dir. Novartis Pharma A.G., Basel, Switzerland, 2005—08, prof. endocrinology, internal medicine Oslo U., Aker U. Hosp., Norway, 2008—. Author: Osteoporosis, 1992, 2002, Histomorphometry, 1993; mem. editl. bd. Osteoporosis Int., 1989, Bone, 1988, Bone Mineral Rsch., 1988-98, Scandinavian Jour. Musculoskeletal Rsch., 1992; sci. editor European Jour. Clin. Investigation; contbr. chpts. to books, articles to profl. jours. Recipient GCP award. Mem. European Calcified Soc., Danish Soc. Internat. Medicine, Danish Endocrine Soc. (bd. dirs.), Am. Soc. Bone and Mineral Rsch. (Young Investigator award 1987), Danish Bone and Tooth Soc. (chmn.), Internat. Osteoporosis Found. (mem. sci. adv. com.). Office: Oslo University Hospital Tronohemlsveien 235 NO-514 Olso Norway

ERIKSSON, SVEN-ERIK, neurologist; b. Stockholm, Dec. 22, 1949; s. Arne Erik and Kerstin Linnea (Jönsson) E.; m. Kristina Marianne Zackrisson, June 17, 1972; children: Emma, Jakob, Susanna. MD, Karolinska Inst., Stockholm, 1975; qualification as specialist in neurology, Univ. Hosp., Linköping, Sweden, 1981. House officer Gävle (Sweden) Hosp., 1975-77; sr. house officer Univ. Hosp., Linköping, 1977-78, registrar, 1979-81, asst. physician dept. neurology, 1981-83, ward physician dept. neurology, 1983-84; chief physician divsn. neurology dept. medicine Falu Hosp., Falun, Sweden, 1984-92, 1993—, Mälar-Hosp., Sweden, 1992. Contbr. articles to profl. publs. Mem. Swedish Soc. Medicine, Swedish Neurology Soc. Avocations: skiing, bridge. Office: Falu Hosp 791 82 Falun Sweden E-mail: sven-erik.eriksson@ltdalarna.se.

ERK, FRANK CHRIS, biologist, educator; b. Evansville, Ind., Dec. 17, 1924; s. Carl Benjamin and Matilda (Schumacher) E.; m. Ruth Parker Hobgood, June 12, 1948; children: Susan Patricia Erk Tierney, Elisabeth Carlene Erk Smith, Stephanie Diane Erk Lutostanski. AB magna cum laude, U. Evansville, 1948; PhD in Genetics, Johns Hopkins U., 1952. Jr. instr. Johns Hopkins U., Balt., 1948-51, Adam T. Bruce fellow, 1951-52, Lalor faculty fellow, 1956; assoc. prof. biology, chmn. dept. Washington Coll., Chestertown, Md., 1952-57, dir. coll. choir, 1952-57; prof. biology SUNY, L.I. Ctr., Oyster Bay, 1957-61, chmn. divsn. sci. and math., 1957—60, chmn. dept. biology, 1958-61, dir. univ. choir, 1957-61; prof. biol. scis. SUNY, Stony Brook, 1962-81, prof. biochemistry and cell biology, 1981-90, prof. emeritus, 1990—, chmn. dept. biology, 1962-67, 76-78. Vis. assoc. prof. biology, Carnegie intern in gen. edn. U. Chgo., 1954-55; rsch. collaborator Masonic Med. Rsch. Lab., Utica, N.Y., 1968-71; vis. investigator Poultry Rsch. Ctr., Agrl. Rsch. Coun., U. Edinburgh, Scotland, 1964-65, Genetics Inst., U. Milan, Italy, 1965, U. Sussex, Eng., 1971-72, 85-86, Galton Lab., U. Coll. London, Eng., 1978-79, U. Edinburgh, 1979; vis. prof. U. Essex, Eng., 1978-79; asst. examiner Internat. Baccalaureate Program, Geneva, 1977-82, cons., 1976-84; cons., writer Biol. Scis. Curriculum Study, Boulder, Colo., 1960-70, 85-90; senator statewide SUNY Faculty Senate, 1967-69, pres., 1969-71; chair Emeritus Faculty Assn. SUNY, Stony Brook, 1990-00, acting master honors coll., 1991-92; dir. Madrigal Singers, Stony Brook, 1963-71, Riderwood Balladeers, Silver Spring Md., 2001—; dir. Riderwood Women's Chorus, 2007-; mem. examining com. Advanced Placement Biology Coll. Entrance Exam. Bd., 1967-71, chmn., 1973-77; genealogy chair Three Village Hist. Soc., East Setauket, N.Y., 1996-00. Author: (with others) Biological Science: Molecules to Man, 1963, 68, (with others) Biological Sciences: Interaction of Experiments and Ideas, 1965, 70, Biological Science: An Ecological Approach, 1987, William Sidney Mount: Family, Friends, and Ideas, 1999; editor: (with others) Evolution, Mammals and Southern Continents, 1972; exec. editor Quar. Rev. Biology, 1966-69, editor, 1969-99; mem. editl. bd. Jour. Biol. Edn., London, 1976-90. 1st lt. USAAF, 1943-46, PTO. Mem. AAAS, AAUP, Am. Genetics Assn. (coun. 1978-81), Genetics Soc. Am., Nat. Assn. Biology Tchrs., Soc. for Study Evolution, Human Biology Coun., SUNY Emeritus Faculty Assn. (chmn. 1990-00), Sigma Xi, Phi Beta Chi, Omicron Delta Kappa. Home: 3118 Gracefield Rd Apt 310 Silver Spring MD 20904-7849 E-mail: frankcerk@earthlink.net.

ERKEKOGLU, PINAR, medical educator; b. Ankara, Jan. 9, 1972; PhD, Hacettepe U., 2009. Asst. prof. Hacettepe U., 2009—. Vis. scientist MIT, 2011. Mem.: ISSX. Office: Mass Ave 77 bldg 56 Cambridge MA 02139-4307 Office Fax: 617-258-8676. Business E-Mail: erkekp@mit.edu.

ERKONEN, WILLIAM EDWARD, radiologist, medical educator; BS, U. Iowa, 1955, MD, 1958. Diplomate Am. Bd. Radiology. Intern U. Oreg., Portland, 1959; family practice, 1961—68; pvt. practice, 1971-87; resident in radiology U. Iowa Coll. Medicine, Iowa City, 1968-71, faculty, 1988-94, asst. prof. radiology, 1994-98, assoc. prof., 1995-98, co-dir. Electric Differential Multimedia Lab., 1993—, assoc. prof. emeritus, 1998—. Rschr. in med. informatics and med. student instrn. and edn.; mem. anatomy and interdisciplinary com. Nat. Bd. Med. Licensure Exam., 1999—2001. Editor: (textbook) Radiology 101 1st edit., 1998, 3rd edit., 2009; contbr. articles to profl. jours.; developer electronic med. textbooks. Capt. US Army, 1959—61. Recipient numerous certs. of merit Radiology Soc. N.Am.; named Tchr. of Yr., U. Iowa Coll. Med., 1990, 93, 96; recipient Disting. Tchr. award for jr. faculty in clin. scis. Alpha Omega Alpha. Fellow Am. Coll. Radiology.

ERMIS, SITKI SAMET, ophthalmic surgeon, researcher; b. Istanbul, Turkey, May 6, 1969; s. Ahmet Ermis and Hatice Saadet (Gulum)E; m. Betul Ugur, Aug. 8, 1996; children: Eymen children: Ahmet, Mustafa. MD, U. of Istanbul, Turkey, 1993. Resident ophthalmology U. Istanbul, 1993—97; ophthalmologist Gulhane Haydarpasa Mil. Hosp., Istanbul, Turkey, 1998—2000; assoc. prof. U. Afyon Kocatepe, Faculty Medicine, Afyon, Turkey, 2000—; fellow Kyoto Prefectural U. Medicine, Dept. Ophthalmology, Kyoto, 2003—. Contbr. chapter in book Progress in Glaucoma Research, Nova Publishers, articles to profl. jours. Mem.: Am. Soc. Cataract and Refractuve Surgery, Istanbul Assn. Med. Doctors, The Assn. for Rsch. in Vision and Ophthalmology, European Soc. of Cataract and Refractive Surgeons, Turkish Ophthalmic Soc. Achievements include Ranks Student Selection and Placement Examination for Universities (1987) and Selection Examination for Medical Doctors (1993); research in Japanese Government Scholarship (2002); Mishima Foundation Award (2003). Avocations: reading, walking, travel. Home: Yusuf Ziya Pasa sk 10/3 Istanbul 34240 Turkey Office: Univ Afyon Kocatepe Faculty of Medicine Afyon 03200 Turkey Personal E-mail: sametermis@yahoo.com.

ERMOLENKO, ALEXANDER, radiologist; b. Gorlivka, Ukraine, Mar. 1, 1942; s. Ermolenko and Davidova; m. Nadezhda Lagushkina, Jan. 18, 1975; children: Elena Perepada, Zhanna, Julia. D of Gen. Practice, Med. State Inst., Donetsk, 1967; PhD, A. V. Vishnevsky Inst. Surgery, Moscow, 1978. Physician gen. practice Hosp., Summa, Ukraine, 1967—69; rsch. fellow A. V. Vishnevsky Inst. Surgery, Moscow, 1969—76, sci. employee, 1976—80, Inst. Transplantology, Moscow, 1980—85, chief nuc. medicine dept., 1985—. Contbr. articles to profl. jours. Recipient Medal of Moscow, Pres. of Russia B. Eltsin, 1997, medal, Pub. Awards Coun. Russia, 2008, medal of Outstanding Scientists medal of 21st Century, Cambridge, 2007, Gold-Gilt Commemorative medal, 2008, 2008. Mem.: Moscow Soc. Nuc. Medicine (assoc.). Achievements include patents for the two-plane symmetry in the structure organization of man; biocrystalloid structure of man (the Extracellular Theory); origin of segmentation in the human structure; origin of vertebrates. Office: Inst Transplantology Schukinskaya 1 Moscow 123182 Russia Home: Fl 19 13 B Sukharevskiy Ln Moscow 127051 Russia Office Fax: 74991902104. Business E-Mail: alex-ermol@yandex.ru, yermola@gmail.com.

ERNST, CALVIN BRADLEY, retired vascular surgery educator; b. Detroit, May 12, 1934; s. Edward William and Irene Marie (Doelker) E.; m. Elizabeth Abbott, Dec. 21, 1957; children: Lisa Anne, Matthew Abbott, David William, Susan Elizabeth. MD, U. Mich., 1959. Diplomate Am. Bd. Surgery (bd. dirs. 1991-97). Intern Ohio State U. Med. Ctr., Columbus, 1959-60; resident U. Mich. Med. Ctr., Ann Arbor, 1960-65; instr. surgery U. Mich., 1968-69, asst. prof., 1969-72, assoc. prof., 1972, U. Ky., Lexington, 1972-74, prof., 1974-79; prof. surgery Johns Hopkins U., 1979-85, surgeon hosp., 1979-85; chmn. surg. scis. Balt. City Hosps., 1979-85; clin. prof. surgery U. Mich., Ann Arbor, 1985-97; prof. surgery Case Western Res. U., Cleve., 1994-97; head vascular surgery Henry Ford Hosp., Detroit, 1985-97; prof. surgery, chief vascular surgery Med. Coll. Pa., Hahnemann Univ., Phila., 1997-99. Cons. surgeon Loch Raven VA Hosp., Balt., 1979-85. Assoc. editor Jour. Vascular Surgery, 1986-91, editor, 1991-97, emeritus editor, 1997—; mem. editl. bd. Archives of Surgery, 1983-93, Surgery, 1983-93; editor 7 vascular surgery textbooks; contbr. chpts. to books. Dir. Am. Bd. Surgery, 1991-97. Served to capt. U.S. Army, 1966-68. Fellow ACS; mem. Soc. Vascular Surgery (sec. 1984-88, pres.-elect 1989-90, pres. 1990-91, Am. Surg. Assn., Internat. Cardiovascular Soc. (recorder 1977-82), So. Assn. Vascular Surgery (sec. treas. 1976-81, pres. 1982-83), Alpha Omega Alpha. Home: 3904 N Fairway Dr Jupiter FL 33477 Office Phone: 561-214-3580. E-mail: cbernst@earthlink.net.

ERNST, JOHN ALLAN, clinical neuropsychologist; b. Seattle, June 27, 1955; s. Gene Allan and Maxine Joan (Weedon) Ernst. BA magna cum laude, U. Calif., San Diego, 1977; MS, San Diego State U., 1979; PhD, U. Mont., 1983. Diplomate Am. Bd. Clin. Neuropsychology, Am. Bd. Profl. Psychology, lic. psychologist Wash. Postdoctoral fellow U. Wash., Seattle, 1983-84; psychologist Western State Hosp., Lakewood, Wash., 1984-85; postdoctoral rsch. fellow U. Queensland, Brisbane, Australia, 1985-87; neuropsychologist St. Joseph Med. Ctr., Tacoma, 1987—. Mem. Wash. State Exam. Bd. Psychology,

1995—2000. Mem. editl. bd.: Rehab. Psychology, 1991—98; mem. editl. bd. SCI Psychosocial Process, 1994—98; contbr. articles to profl. jours. Mem.: Pacific N.W. Neuropsychol. Soc. (pres. 2001—02, rehab psychology edn. bd. 1993—98), Am. Neuropsychiat. Assn., Internat. Neuropsychol. Soc., Am. Acad. Clin. Neuropsychology. Avocations: music appreciation, art appreciation. Office: Saint Joseph Med Ctr Dept Psychology PO Box 2197 Tacoma WA 98401-2197 E-mail: johnaernst@fhshealth.org.

ERNST, RICHARD ROBERT, chemist, educator; b. Winterthur, Switzerland, Aug. 14, 1933; s. Robert and Irma (Brunner) Ernst; m. Magdalena Kielholz, Oct. 9, 1963; children: Anna Magdalena, Katharina Elisabeth, Hans-Martin Walter. Diploma in Chemistry, Swiss Fed. Inst. Tech. (ETH), Zurich, 1956, DSc, 1962, PhD (hon.), 1986, Tech. Coll., Munich, 1989, U. Zurich, 1994, U. Antwerp, 1997, U. Cluj-Napoca, 1998, U. Montpellier, 1999, Charles U., Prague, 2002, Babes-Bolyai U. Scientist ETH, 1962-63, lectr., 1968-70, asst. prof., 1970-72, assoc. prof., 1973-76, prof., 1976—2001, dir. Phys. Chemistry Lab., pres. Rsch. Coun.; scientist Varian Assocs., Palo Alto, Calif., 1963-68. A.D. White prof.-at-large Cornell U., NYC, 1996—2002. Mem. editl bd. Molecular Physics, 1983—2003, Chemical Physics Letters, 1985—2005, Magnetic Resonance Imaging, Applied Magnetic Resonance, Jour. Biomolecular NMR, Jour. Magnetic Resonance, Solid State Magnetic Resonance; contbr. articles to profl. jours. Lt. Swiss Mil., 1953—88. Recipient Ruzicka prize, ETH, 1968, Marcel Benoist prize, Switzerland, 1986, John Gamble Kirkwood medal, Am. Chem. Soc., 1989, AMPERE Prize, Atoms & Molecules by Radio-Electric Studies Group, 1990, Louisa Gross Horwitz prize, Columbia U., 1991, Wolf prize in chemistry, Israel, 1991, Nobel prize in chemistry, 1991, H. R. Schinz medal, 1995. Fellow: Bangladesh Acad. Scis. (fgn.); mem.: NAS (fgn. assoc.), Academia Europaea, Am. Acad. Arts & Scis. (fgn.), Am. Phys. Soc. (fgn.), Am. Soc. Neuroradiology (fgn.), German Acad. Scis. Leopoldina (fgn.), Indian Nat. Sci. Acad. (fgn.), Internat. Soc. Magnetic Resonance in Medicine, Islamic Acad. Scis., Korean Acad. Sci. & Tech. (fgn.), Russian Acad. Scis. (fgn.), Swiss Chem. Soc., Swiss Soc. Radiology, Royal Soc. London (fgn.). Achievements include development of the methodology of high-resolution nuclear magnetic resonance (NMR) spectroscopy, in turn leading to the development of magnetic resonance imaging (MRI). Avocations: tibetan art, music. Home Phone: 41 52 242 7807; Office Phone: 41 1 632 4368. E-mail: ernst@nmr.phys.chem.ethz.ch.

ERON, MADELINE MARCUS, psychologist; b. New Brunswick, NJ, Sept. 8, 1919; d. Israel and Rae (Becker) Marcus; m. Leonard David Eron, May 21, 1950; children: Joni Eron Hobson, Don Marcus, Barbara Eron Christensen. Student, U. Mich., 1937-39; BA, NYU, 1941; MA, Columbia U., 1942. Lic. psychologist, Ill., N.Y.; nat. cert. Sch. Psychologist. Intern in psychology Phila. State Hosp., 1942-43; psychology extern Neurol. Inst. Columbia Presbyn. Med. Ctr., NYC, 1943-44; sr. clin. psychologist Inst. Crippled and Disabled, NYC, 1944-51; cons. psychologist New Haven, 1951-55; clin. psychologist Rip Van Winkle Clinic and Found., Hudson, N.Y., 1958-62; chief psychologist Berkshire Farm for Boys, Canaan, N.Y., 1961-62; pvt. practice psychology specializing in retng. the brain injured Iowa City, 1962-63; cons. Cedar Rapids (Iowa) Community Sch. Dist., 1963-67; dir. psychol. svcs. Comprehensive Evaluation-Rehab. Ctr., U. Iowa Med. Sch., Iowa City, 1968-69; sch. psychologist Winnetka, Glencoe and Skokie (Ill.) Elem. Sch. Dists., 1969-72, Evanston (Ill.) Twp. High Sch., 1972-90. Bd. dirs. Lincoln Ctr. Clin. Services, Highland Park, Ill. Mem. APA (divsn. sch. psychology, rehab. psychology, child and youth service), Iowa Psychol. Assn. (sec. 1965-67), Midwestern Psychol. Assn., Nat. Assn. Sch. Psychologists (charter), Ill. Sch. Psychologists Assn. (charter), Assn. Advancement Psychology, N.Y. State Psychol. Assn., Psi Chi. Achievements include pioneer in retraining of brain-injured and attention deficit disorder; first to retrain the brain injured and treating hyperkinetic impulse disorder. Home: 7700 Nemco Way Apt 219 Brighton MI 48116-9444

EROSS, ERIC JASON, osteopathic physician; b. Pitts., Sept. 9, 1968; s. Bela and Linda Lee (Dreher) E. BS in Neurobiology, Allegheny Coll., 1991; DO, Ohio U. Coll. Osteo. Medicine, 1996. Rsch. asst. dept. medicine U. Pitts., 1991-92; intern Western Pa. Hosp., Pitts., 1996-97. Pa. Osteo. Medicine Assn. scholar, 1995, 96. Mem. Am. Osteo. Assn. Avocations: roller hockey, squash, drawing, volleyball, sportswear design and sales. Home: 13616 N Bonita Dr Fountain Hls AZ 85268-8569

EROZAN, YENER SAHIR, pathologist, educator; arrived in U.S., 1959; s. Celal Sahir and Sevim Erozan; m. Brenda Martin, July 7, 1966. MD, Istanbul U., Turkey, 1954. Cert. practice medicine and surgery Bd. Med. Examiners State Md., 1972, anatomic pathology Am. Bd. Pathology, 1974, added qualification in cytopathology Am. Bd. Pathology, 1989. Resident in pathology Haydarpasa Numune Hosp., Istanbul, 1956—59, Suburban Hosp., Bethesda, Md., 1959—62; fellow in pathology Johns Hopkins U., Balt., 1962—64; instr. pathology Johns Hopkins U. Sch. Medicine, Balt., 1964—65, asst. prof. pathology, 1969—75, assoc. prof. pathology, 1975—95, prof. pathology, 1995—; asst. prof. pathology Hacettepe U. Sch. Medicine, Ankara, Turkey, 1965—68. Dir. The John K. Frost cytopathology lab. The Johns Hopkins Hosp., Balt., 1989—95. Editor: (book) Fine Needle Aspiration of Subcutaneous Organs and Masses, 1996. Recipient Disting. Svc. award, Am. Soc. for Clin. Pathology, 2002, L. C. Tao award - Educator of Yr., Papanicolaou Soc. Cytopathology, 2004; named Otago Trust Vis. Prof., Dunedin Sch. Medicine, New Zealand, 1998; Yener S. Erozan, M.D. fellowship established in his name, Johns Hopkins U. Sch. Medicine Dept. Pathology, 2003. Master: Am. Soc. clin. Pathology; fellow: Am. Coll. Chest Physicians, Internat. Acad. Cytology (Maurice Goldblatt award 2007), Coll. Am. Pathologists; mem.: AMA, Md. Soc. Pathologists, The Johns Hopkins Alumni and Faculty Assn., Am. Soc. Cytopathology (pres. 1985—86, Papanicolaou award 1997), Johns Hopkins Club. Avocations: photography, travel, swimming. Office: The Johns Hopkins Hosp 600 North Wolfe St Baltimore MD 21287 Business E-Mail: yerozan@jhmi.edu.

ERSANLI, DILAVER, ophthalmologist, educator; b. Kilis, Turkey, Aug. 1, 1959; s. Selahattin and Zubeyde Ersanli; m. Semra Derikesen, Jan. 6, 1996; children: Arda, Zeynep, Eren. MD, Edirne Medicine Faculty, 1983. Diplomate in ophthalmology GATA Haydarpasa Tng. Hosp., Istanbul, Turkey, 1989. Asst. prof. GATA Haydarpasa Tng. Hosp., 1993—98, assoc. prof., 1998—2008, prof., 2008—. Contbr. articles to profl. jours. Col. Istanbul Armed Forces, 1983—2005. Mem.: Turkish Ophthalmology Soc. Office: Gata Haydarpasa Egitim Hastanesi Tibbiye Cad Uskudar Istanbul 34668 Turkey Office Fax: +90 216 348 7880; Home Fax: +90 216 348 7880. Personal E-mail: dilavererersanli@ttnet.net.tr.

ERSHLER, WILLIAM BALDWIN, biogerontologist, educator; b. Syracuse, NY, Jan. 13, 1949; s. Irving Leonard and Eunice (Baldwin) E.; m. Joan Lipstein, Nov. 6, 1971; children: Rachel Eve, Leah Rose. BA, Case Western Res. U., 1970; MD, SUNY Upstate Ctr., Syracuse, 1974. Diplomate Am. Bd. Internal Medicine, Am. Bd. Med. Oncology, Am. Bd. Hematology. Asst. prof. U. Vt., Burlington, 1980-85; assoc. prof. U. Wis., Madison, 1985-89, prof. medicine, 1989-96, dir. U. Wis. Inst. on Aging, 1989-96, head geriatrics, 1989-96; dir. geriatric rsch. Edn. and Clin. Ctr. William Middleton VA Hosp., Madison, 1991-96; prof. medicine, dir. Glennan Ctr. Geriatrics & gerontolog Eastern Va. Medical Sch., Norfolk, 1996-97; dir. Inst. Advanced Studies in Aging and Geriatric Medicine, Washington, 1998—, Nat. Geriatrics Rsch. Consortium, 1998—; rsch. edn. dir. Extended Care Info. Network, 1999—. Dir. Geriatric Oncology Consortium, 2001—; sr. investigator Nat. Inst. Aging, NIH, dep. clin. dir., 2006—10. Editor Jour. Gerontology, 1996-2000; contbr. articles to profl. jours. Recipient Geriatric Leadership award NIH, 1990-96; NIH grantee, 1989—. Fellow Gerontologic Soc. Am.; mem. Am. Geriatrics Soc., Am. Assn. Cancer Rsch., Am. Soc. Clin. Oncology, Am. Soc. Hematology, Assn. Dirs. Acad. Geriatrics (councilor). Jewish. Avocations: running, photography, travel. Office: 6400 Arlingron Blvd Falls Church VA 22042 Business E-Mail: wershler@iasia.org.

ERSKINE, JOHN MORSE, surgeon; b. San Francisco, Sept. 10, 1920; s. Morse and Dorothy (Ward) E. BS, Harvard U., 1942, MD, 1945. Diplomate Am. Bd. Surgery. Surg. intern U. Calif. Hosp., San Francisco, 1945-46; surg. researcher Mass. Gen. Hosp., Boston, 1948; resident in surgery Peter Bent Brigham Hosp., Boston, 1948-53; George Gorham Peters fellow St. Mary's Hosp., London, 1952; pvt. practice in medicine specializing in surgery San Francisco, 1954-98; asst. clin. prof. Stanford Med. Sch., San Francisco, 1956-59; asst., assoc. clin. prof. U. Calif. Med. Sch., San Francisco, 1959—. Surg. cons. San Francisco Vets. Hosp., 1959-73, Ft. Miley Vets. Hosp.; disiting. prof. emeritus dept. surgery, U. Calif., San Francisco, 2009; mem. Calif. Pacific Hosp. Hon. Med. Staff. Contbr. articles to profl. jours., chpts. to books. Founder No. Calif. Artery Bank, 1954-58, Irwin Meml. Blood Bank, San Francisco, commr., pres., 1969-74; bd. dirs. People for Open Space-Greenbelt Alliance, 1984-98, adv. coun., 1998—, San Francisco Blood Bank; chmn. adv. coun. Dorothy Enskine Open Space Fund. Capt. with U.S. Army, 1946-48. Named Disting. Prof. Emeritus, U. Calif. Med. Sch. Fellow ACS; mem. San Francisco Med. Soc. (bd. dirs. 1968-72), San Francisco Surg. Soc. (v.p. 1984), Pacific Coast Surg. Assn., Am. Cancer Soc. (bd. dirs. San Francisco br. 1965-75), Calif. Med. Assn., Olympic Club, Sierra Club. Democrat. Unitarian Universalist. Avocations: mountains, tree farming, gardening, walking, reading, music. Office: 233 Chestnut St San Francisco CA 94133-2452 Personal E-mail: john.m.erskine@gmail.com.

ERSKINE, KALI (WENDY COLMAN), psychoanalyst; b. Flushing, NY, July 6, 1950; d. Leo M. and Ray (Fine) Colman BS, Tufts U., Medford, Mass., 1972; MA, NYU, 1977, PhD, 1984; postgrad., Phila. Sch. of Psychoanalysis, 1988—92. Lic. psychoanalyst. With Extended Family Ctr., San Francisco, 1973—74, Roosevelt Hosp., NYC, 1975—77; cons. child abuse San Francisco, 1974-75; adj. instr. NYU, NYC, 1977—80; asst. prof. Boston U., 1980—83; dir. grad. edn., assoc. prof. Temple U., Phila., 1984—87; cons. curriculum design Kean Coll. N.J., Union, 1985-88; cons. spl. projects, vice provost for rsch.- grad. studies Temple U., Phila., 1987-88; evaluation rsch. coord. Nat. Inst. Adolescent Pregnancy, Phila., 1986-90; pvt. practice psychotherapy and psychoanalysis, 1987—. Tng. and supervising analyst Phila. Sch. of Psychoanalysis. Contbg editor: AJOT, editor PSP newsletter, 1990-94, VAPS Aviso newsletter, 1998-2000; contbr. articles to profl. jours. and texts in occupl. therapy and psychoanalysis (under names Wendy Colman and Kali Erskine). Fellow Am. Occupl. Therapy Assn.; mem. APA (Divsn. psychoanalysis), Nat. Assn. Advancement Psychoanalysis, Vt. Assn. for Psychoanalytic Studies, Soc. Phila. Sch. Psychoanalysis. Office: 201 Kildrummy Way Montpelier VT 05062 Office Phone: 802-223-6465.

ERSOY, EREN, medical educator; b. Turkey, Oct. 17, 1970; Degree in Surgery, Ankara U. Med. Sch., 1995. Assoc. prof. surgery & medicine, 2001—11. Office: Ataturk Egitim ve Arastirma Hastane Beytepe Caddersi Bilkent 06820 Turkey Personal E-mail: perenersoy@gmail.com.

ERYILMAZ, MÜJDE, medical researcher; b. Agri, Turkey, 1979; PhD, Ankara U., 2001. Rschr. Ankara U., 2001. Mem.: Antibiyotik ve Kemoterapi Dernegi, Türk Mikrobiyoloji Cemiyeti. Office: Ankara University Faculty Pharmacy Ankara Tandogan 06100 Turkey Personal E-mail: mujdeyuce@yahoo.com.

ESCALLIER, LORI A., medical educator; b. Queens, NY, May 2, 1958; PhD, Adelphi U., 1995. Clin. prof. Stony Brook U., 1981—. Assoc. dean Sch. Nursing. Recipient Champion, Diversity Bus. Avocations: skiing, gardening. Office: Stony Brook University Health Scis Ctr Stony Brook NY 11794 Office Fax: 631-444-3136. Business E-Mail: lori.escallier@stonybrook.edu.

ESCANDE, MICHELE, cardiologist, researcher; d. Tony and Marie Claire (Maurice) Orthlieb; m. Jacques Escande, Apr. 22, 1967; 1 child, Nathalie Beillard. B in Math., U. Marseilles, 1963, MD, 1976. Cert. specialist in internal medicine 1980, European specialist in hypertension 2003, specialist in geriat. 2005, cardiologist France, 1975. Lectr. U. Tchg. Hosp., Marseilles, France, 1966—69, intern, 1970—75, 1975—76, asst. prof., chief clinic, 1976—80; cardiologist Allauch, France, 1980—. Lectr. U. Marseilles, France, 1981—85, dir. clin. tchg., 1985—; attending physician Allauch Hosp., France, 1982—84, head geriatrics dept., 1984—. Fellow Ethical Com. of Med. Faculty of Marseilles, 1985—91, Ethical Com. of Med. Faculty of Marseilles II, 1991—. Master: French Soc. Geriatry and Gerontology (mem. adminstrv. com. 2005—); fellow: Ethical Com. Marseilles, French Soc. Internal Medicine, French Soc. Cardiology, French Soc. Pharmacology, French Coll. Vascular Pathology, European Soc. Cardiology (European Heart House, Nice, France 2001—), French Soc. Hypertension, French Ethical Soc.; mem.: European Soc. Hypertension, Med. Soc. Paris's Hosp. (corr. bd. mem. 2002), N.Y. Acad. Scis., European Working Group Echocardiography. Avocations: music, literature, tennis, drawing. Office: Allauch Hosp Chemin Des Mille Écus bp 28 13718 Allauch France Personal E-mail: micheleescande@hotmail.com. E-mail: escandemichele@aol.com.

ESCARCE, JOSÉ J., medical educator; b. Havana, Cuba, Apr. 30, 1953; BA, Princeton U.; MS in physics, Harvard U.; MD, U. Pa., 1981, PhD in health economics. Cert. Internal Medicine, 1984. Prof. medicine UCLA David Geffen Sch. Medicine; sr. natural sci. RAND; intern in internal medicine Stanford U. Hosp., 1981—82, resident, 1982—84. Mem. health adv. panel Congl. Budget Office; methods coun., bd. dirs. AcademyHealth; co-editor-in-chief Health Services Rsch. jour. Mem.: Inst. Medicine. Office: UCLA Med-GIM-HSR Box 951736 911 Broxton Plz Los Angeles CA 90095-1736 Office Phone: 310-794-3842. Office Fax: 310-451-7062. E-mail: escarce@rand.org, jescarce@mednet.ucla.edu.

ESCARCEGA ALARCON, RICARDO ORLANDO, cardiologist; b. Puebla, Mex., May 11, 1980; MD, Benemerita U. Autonoma Puebla, 2005. Physician, divsn. cardiology, dept. medicine Temple U. Hosp., 2007—. Recipient W. I. Ginsberg award, Temple U. Hosp. Mem.: ACP, AMA, Am. Soc. Nuc. Cardiology, Am. Coll. Cardiology. Avocations: literature, exercise. Office: 3401 North Broad St Parkinson 912 Philadelphia PA 19140 Business E-Mail: orlando.escarcega@tuhs.temple.edu.

ESCH, TOBIAS, medical researcher; MD, U. Goettingen Med. Sch., Germany, 1999; D, U. Goettingen Med. Sch., 2000. Cert. in gen. internal & family medicine Physician's Chamber Westfalen-Lippe, Germany, 2004. Postdoc. rsch. fellow Harvard U., Harvard Med. Sch., Boston, 2001—02; rsch. assoc. SUNY, Old Westbury, 2002—; prof. integrative health promotion Coburg U. Applied Scis., Bavaria, Germany, 2006—, head divsn. integrative health promotion, 2007—10; program dir. Health Promoting U., 2010—. Dir. Inst. Integrative Medicine & Health Promotion, Potsdam, Brandenburg, Germany, 2007—; pres. sci. adv. bd. Inst. Mind-Body Medicine, Potsdam, 2008—; vice chair, bd. dir. Internat. Young Scientist Competition, Smithtown, NY; dep. editor-in-chief Med. Sci. Monitor, NY, 2011—. Mem.: LI Conservatory, Mensa Internat., German Assn. Music Physiology & Musicians' Medicine, Postgrad. Assn. Harvard Med. Sch. (life). Office: Coburg Univ Applied Sci Friedrich-Streib-Str 2 Coburg Bayern-Bavaria D-96450 Germany Office Fax: 49 9561 317 326; Home Fax: 49 331 730 67 58.

ESCHENBACH, DAVID ARTHUR, obstetrician and gynecologist, educator; b. Reedsburg, Wis., Aug. 27, 1942; s. Ivan Henry and Florence Mae (Attridge) E.; m. Ann Cross, June 27, 1964; children: Elizabeth, Eric. BA, Lawrence U., 1964; MD, U. Wis., 1968. Intern King County Hosp., Seattle, 1968-69; resident U. Wash., Seattle, 1969-73, fellow in infectious disease, 1972-74, asst. prof., 1976-79, prof., 1979—, acting chair dept Obstetrics and Gynecology, 2001—02, chair dept Obstetrics and Gynecology, 2002—; mem. Northwest Coast Native Am. & Native Am. Art Collection. Asst. editor Maternal-Fetal Medicine of Gynecology and Obstetrics, 1982—; contbr. articles to profl. jours. Maj. U.S. Army, 1974-76. Named one of Best Doctors for Women, Ob/Gyn Infectious Disease Specialists, Good Housekeeping mag., 1997, Best Doctors in America, Infectious Disease, 1998—, Seattle's Top Physicians in Ob/Gyn, Seattle Mag., 1998, 2008, 2010. Fellow Am. Coll. Ob-Gyn.; mem. Am. Ob-Gyn. Assn., Infectious Disease Soc. Am., Ob-Gyn. Infectious Disease Soc. Avocations: hiking, skiing, bicycling, basketball, football. Office: U Wash Hosp Gynecology Dept 1959 NE Pacific St Seattle WA 98195-0001 also: U Wash Dept Ob Gyn Box 356460 Seattle WA 98195-6460

ESCOBEDO, JORGE, physician; b. Mexico City, Dec. 26, 1965; MD, UNAM, 1978; MPH, INSP, MSc, 1986. Head, CRC IMSS, 2003—. Prof., internal medicine UNAM, 2010. Recipient Honorific Mention award, Escuela de Salud Publica de Mex. Fellow: ACP. Avocation: baseball. Office: Apartado Postal 40-028 Cuauhtemoc 06140 Mexico Office Fax: 525552736679. Business E-Mail: jorgeep@unam.mx.

ESERNIO-JENSSEN, DEBRA, pediatrician, director; b. Bklyn., Feb. 28, 1956; BA in Biology, Harpur Coll., 1978; MD, U. Rochester Sch. Medicine, 1982. Med. dir. U. Fla. Child Protection Team, 2010—. Mem.: Fla. Pediatric Soc., APSAC, AAP Sect. Child Abuse and Neglect, Ray Helfer Soc., Am. Acad. Pediat. Avocations: running, motorcycling, swimming. Office: 1701-A SW 16th Ave Gainesville FL 32608 Office Fax: 352-334-1521. Personal E-mail: dejenssen@aol.com.

ESHAGHIAN, SHAHROOZ, physician; b. Tehran, Iran, June 15, 1980; BS, UCLA, 2002; MD, Albert Einstein Coll. Medicine, 2006. Physician internal medicine Cedars Sinai Med. Ctr., 2006—09; physician hematology & oncology UCLA Med. Ctr., 2009—. Office: 11961 Montana Ave #201 Los Angeles CA 90049 Business E-Mail: seshaghian@mednet.ucla.edu.

ESHIETT, MICHAEL UDOH-AKA, neurologist, educator; b. Ikot Ekpene, Akwa Ibom State, Nigeria, Oct. 27, 1954; s. Udoh-aka Eshiett and Grace Adiaha Eshiett; m. Teresa Michaela Enang; children: Otobong, Michael, Eminimo. BM, BCh, U. Nigeria, 1977; MSc, U. Surrey, Guildford, Eng., 1995; diploma in Tropical Medicine and Hygiene, Sch. Tropical Medicine, London, 1988; diploma in Clin. Neurology, Inst. Neurology, London, 1989; diploma, Inst. Mgmt., 1999. Med. registrar Bedford Gen. Hosp., Bedfordshire, England, 1990—92; neurology registrar Guy's Hosp., London, 1992—93; sr. registrar neuro-rehab. Roehampton and St. George's NHS Trust hosps., London, 1993—95. Lead clinician in neuro-rehab., stroke medicine and assistive tech. WWL (NHS) Trust hosps., Wiagn, Greater Manchester, England, 1996—. Editor: (jour.) W. African Edit. Brit. Med. Jour., 1997. Cmty. leader Akwa Ibom Cmty., U.K., London, 1991—95. Fellow: Royal Coll. Physicians, Ireland, Royal Coll. Physicians, London (regional specialty adviser 1997—2002); mem.: Soc. Rsch. Rehab. Medicine, Brit. Soc. Rehab. Medicine (regional chmn./coord. 1997—2001), Assn. Brit. Neurologists, Inst. Mgmt. Lemurian. Avocations: music, philosophy, lawn tennis. Home: #5 Northam Close, Standish Lancs Wigan WN6 0RN England Office: WWL (NHS) Trust - Whelley Hospital Bradshaw St Lancs Wigan WN1 3XD England Home Phone: +44 (0)1257-472400; Office Phone: +44 1942 822610. Office Fax: +44(0)1942-822630; Home Fax: +44(0)1257-472591. E-mail: eshiett@doctors.org.uk.

ESIRI, MARGARET MIRIAM, neuropathology educator; b. Stanmore, Middlesex, Eng., Oct. 5, 1941; d. William Alfred Evans and

Doreen Mary Bates; m. Frederick Esiri; children: Henrietta Margaret, Mark Leslie, Frederick William. BA, U. Oxford, Eng., 1963, MB BChir, 1967, BSc, 1969, DM, 1976. House officer Radcliffe Infirmary, Oxford, 1969, rsch. officer neuropathology, 1970-72, trainee in pathology, 1978-79; sr. clin. fellow Oxford U., 1980-85, reader in neuropathology, 1986-96, prof. neuropathology, 1996—2007, emeritus prof., 2008—. Author: (books) Diagnostic Neuropathology, 2d edit., 1996 (Brit. Med. Assn. prize short list 1996), (with J. Booss) Viral Encephalitis, 1986, (with D.R. Oppenheimer) Diagnostic Neuropathology, 1989 (Best Illustrated Med. Textbook award short list 1989), (with J. Booss) Viral Encephalitis in Humans, 2003, (with V M-Y Lee and JQ Trojanowski) The Neuropathology of Dementia, 2d edit., 2004, (with D. Perl) Oppenheimer's Diagnostic Neuroipathology, 3d edit., 2006; author, editor: The Neuropathology of Dementia, 1997. Recipient Frewin prize Oxford Regional Health Authority, 1975, "A" Distinction award U.K. Dept. Health, 1999. Fellow Royal Coll. Pathologists. Office: John Radcliffe Hosp Wrest Wing Level 1 Neuropathol Dept Headley Way OX3 9DU Oxford England

ESKANDER, JACQUELINE YOUNAN, medical educator; b. Egypt, Sept. 23, 1972; PhD in Pharmacy, 2005. Lectr. pharmacognosy Helwan U., 2005—. Rsch. scientist coop. with France team U. Reims, Champagne Ardenne-CNRS, 2003—11. Avocation: reading. Office: Ain Helwan Cairo 11795 Egypt E-mail: jacqueline.eskander@hotmail.com.

ESKIIZMIRLILER, SELIM, engineering educator; b. Ankara, Jan. 21, 1961; MSc, Mid. East Tech. U., 1993; PhD, Ecole Nat. Supérieure des Télécomm., 2000. Rsch. scientist, asst. prof. Orebro U., Sweden, 2000—03; assoc. prof. U. Paris Diderot, 2003—. Office: 45 rue des Saints Pères CESEM CNRS UMR Paris 75006 France Office Fax: 0033142863399. Business E-Mail: selim.eskiizmirliler@parisdescartes.fr.

ESMAT, MOHAMED EMAD ESMAT, surgeon, educator; b. Cairo, Oct. 25, 1960; s. Nour El Din Ahmed Esmat and Golshan Abdelaziz Osman; m. Ghada Mounir Yousfi, Sept. 29, 2003; children: Akmal Mohamed Emad, Yara Mohamed Emad. MBBCh, Kasr El Aini Sch. medicine, Cairo U., 1984; MSc, Cairo U., 1990, MD, 1994. Higher diploma in hosp. adminstrn. Helwan U., Cairo, 1999; cert. Internat. Register Cert. Auditors, UK, 2003. Resident in gen. surgery dept. Thoedor Bilharz Rsch. Inst., Cairo, Giza, 1986—90, asst. lectr. dept. surgery, tbri, ministry sci. rsch., 1990—96, lectr. in gen. surgery dept., 1996—2001, asst. prof. in gen. surgery, tbri, 2001—06, prof. in gen. surgery, tbri, 2006—, dep. gen. mgr. of tbri hosp., 2000—, project mgr. for implementing the total quality mgmt. (tqm) sys. in tbri, 2007—, supr. for hosp. mgmt. courses for overseas candidates held in tbri, 2007—; surg. fellow Queen Elizabeth Hosp., Birmingham U., UK. & Heartland and Solihull Hosp., West-Midlands, 2004—06. Internat. cert. auditor quality managment sys. IRCA (Internat. Register of Cert. Auditors), London, 2003—; reviewer for the 'world jour. surgery' Ofcl. Jour. Internat. Soc. Surgeons & Internat. Assn. Endocrine Surgeons & Internat. Assn. for Surgery of trauma and Surg. Intensive Care & the IASMEN & the DSI, Portland, Oreg., 2005—. Contbr. scientific papers to numarous profl. publs., chapters to books. Humanitarian; fin. and tech. support for the poor patients with chronic liver disease who suffers repeated bleeding from esophageal varices Hematemesis Patient Saving Soc., Cairo, 2006. Numarous scholarship, Ministry High Edn. and sci. Rsch., 2001—06. Fellow: RCS (Glasgow) (fellow 1995—2007), Internat. Coll. Surgeons (fellow 1997—99); mem.: Pan Arab Liver Transplantation Soc. (mem. 2007), Egyptian Soc. Surgeons (mem. 2000), Egyptian Med. Syndicate, Mediteranean & Mid. Ea. Endoscopic Surgery Assn. (mem. 2007), internat. register cert. auditors, UK, Shooting Social Club (mem. 1973). Moslem. Avocations: swimming, fishing, football, tennis, target shooting. Office: Theodor Bilharz Rsch Inst Kournash El Nile Cairo Giza-Warak El Hadar-Imbaba 12411 Egypt Home: 20, Khan Younis From Shehab St 12411 Cairo Cairo Egypt Office Fax: 20235408125; Home Fax: 20233021414. E-mail: emadesmat2000@yahoo.com.

ESPANDAR, LADAN, ophthalmologist, researcher; d. Ali Espandar and Zarifeh Niroumand; m. Majid Roohafza, Sept. 20, 2005. MD, Tehran U. Med. sci., 2000; attending in Ophthalmology, Tulane U., New Orleans, 2009—; attending in Clin. & Translational Rsch., 2009—. Cert. ECFMG, 2007, in gen. surgery internship Tulane U., 2009; ophthalmologist Iran, 2005. Gen. practitioner, MD, head staff Darreh-shahr Hosp., Iran, 2000—01; ophthalmology resident Farabi Hosp., Tehran, 2001—05, mem. faculty, 2005—06; rsch. fellow MD Anderson Cancer Ctr., Houston, 2006—07; ocular pathology fellow Moran Eye Ctr., Salt Lake City, 2007—08; eye bank technitian Utah Eye bank, Salt Lake City, 2007—08. Contbr. scientific papers to profl. jours. Recipient Resident Excellent award; Translational Rsch. Project grant, Tulane U., 2009, Rsch. Project grant, ASCRS found., 2009, Travel grant, Contact Lens Assn. Mem.: Assn. Rsch. Vision & Ophthalmology, Am. Soc. Cataract & Refractive Surgery, Am. Acad. Ophthalmology. Avocations: mountain climbing, travel, running, camping.

ESPEN, DAVID, hand surgeon; b. Bolzano, Italy, Jan. 22, 1960; s. Dina Antonia Espen; m. Patrizia Scatola, Mar. 13, 1999; 1 child, Caroline. MD, Innsbruck U. Med. Sch., 1988; postgrad. tng. hand courses, Med. U. Innsbruck-Austria, 1993, postgrad. tng. hand courses, 1995, postgrad. tng. hand courses, 1999. Cert. Specialist Orthopaedics and Traumatologic surgery Italy, 1994. Asst. dr. Dept. Orthopaedics and Traumatologic Surgery, Bolzano, Italy, 1990—94, med. leader first level, 1995—, high splty. holder for hand surgery, 2004—; lectr. U. Innsbruck-Austria, Writst Symposium. Lectr. Master for Hand Surgery U. Verona Med. Sch., Italy, 2003—; local coord. of alumni Assn. for Study of Internal Fixation, Davos, Switzerland, 2004—, faculty mem., instr., 2003—; lectr., presenter workshops in field. Prodr.: (scientific videos) Pi-Plate Fixation of Distal Radius Fractures, 2001, Synovial Flap Plasty for Recurrent Carpal Tunnel Syndrome, 2001, Combined Palmar and Dorsal Approach for Distal Radius Fractures, 2002, Arthroplasty of Metacarpo-Phalangeal Joints in Rheumatoid Hand, 2003, Locking Distal Radius Plate Fixation, 2003, Locking Distal Radius Plating for the American Society for Surgery of the Hand, 2004, Dorsal Nail Plating System for Distal Radius Fractures; contbr. chapters to books, scientific papers. Fellow, Hand Dept. Republic San Marino, 1995, Hand Unit Traumatol. Surgery, 1996, Hand Clinic Lanz, Germany, 2000, Hand Surgery Dept. Baden-Baden, Germany, 2004. Mem.: Internat. Wrist Investigators Workshop, Fedn. European Societies for Surgery of Hand (assoc.), Austrian Soc. for Surgery of Hand (assoc.), German Speaking Soc. for Surgery of Hand (assoc. sponsorship 2001), Italian Soc. for Surgery of Hand (assoc. sponsorship 2001). Personal E-mail: d.espen@handteam.eu.

ESPINOSA, PATRICIO SEBASTIAN, neurologist, researcher; s. Espinosa. MD, U. Ctrl. Ecuador, Quito, 2000; MPH, Johns Hopkins U., Balt., 2001; BS, El Sauce Quito, Ecuador, 1993. Cert. neurologist Ky., 2003. Intern, internal medicine U. Ky., Lexington, resident, neurology, 2003—07, MD, 2002—; Epileptologyst Brigham Women's Hosp. Harvard med. Sch., 2007—08; chmn. Internat, Ctr. Neurosci. Fellow Harvard Med. Sch. Epilepsy, 2007—08. Achievements include research in epidemiology of neurological disease and International Health. Office: 15790 Paul Vega MD Dr Hammond LA 70403 Business E-Mail: ps.espinosa@gmail.com.

ESPINOZA, LUIS ALBERTO, medical educator, researcher; arrived in U.S., 1989; m. Lita Rosa Calagua, Mar. 18, 1988; children: Diego, David. MD, Nat. U. Federico Villarreal, Lima, Peru, 1986. Intern internal medicine Hahnemann U., Phila., 1994—95, resident internal medicine, 1995—97; dir. HIV/AIDS Clin. Edn. MCP Hahnemann U., Phila., 1997—; asst. prof. U. Miami Sch. Medicine, Fla., 2001—, dir. HIV/AIDS tng. program, 2005—, assoc. prof. clin. medicine, 2010. Mem. infection surveillance and policy com. Cedars Med. Ctr., Miami, Fla., 2001—02; mem. med. scis. com. A U. Miami Sch. Medicine, 2004. Contr.: 2005 HIV/AIDS Primary Care Guide; contbr. articles to profl. jours. Named Fellow of Yr. in HIV/AIDS, Ortho Biotech, 1993—94. Mem.: Peruvian Am. Med. Soc. (pres. South Fla. chpt. 2004—), Infectious Diseases Soc. Am., Am. Acad. HIV Medicine. Office: U Miami Sch Medicine Ste 858 1400 NW 10th Ave Miami FL 33136 Office Fax: 305-243-4037. Business E-Mail: lespinoza@med.miami.edu.

ESPLIN, ED, medical educator; b. Utah, Jan. 12, 1975; BA in Biology, U. Utah, 1995; MD, UT Southwestern, PhD, 2005. Asst. prof., internal medicine UT Southwestern, 2009—. Med. Scientist Tng. Program fellowship, UT Southwestern Nat. Insts. Health. Fellow: Am. Bd. Internal Medicine. Avocation: exercise. Office: 4500 Lancaster Rd Dallas TX 75216 Personal E-mail: edesplin@hotmail.com.

ESPOSITO, RICK ANTHONY, thoracic surgeon; b. Chgo., Feb. 24, 1954; s. Anthony and Marie Premetta Esposito; m. Margaret Rose Devito, May 12, 1984; children: Matthew James, Daniel Anthony, Katherine Anne. BS summa cum laude, U. Ill., Urbana-Champaign, 1975; MD with honors, U. Chgo., 1979; MD, U. Bronze Tablet. Cert. Am. Bd. Thoracic Surgery, 1996, Am. Bd. Surgery. Resident surgery NYU Med. Ctr., NYC, 1979—84, fellow cardiothoracic surgery, 1984—86, staff surgeon, 1986—2002, assoc. prof. surgery, 1996—2002; staff surgeon Bellevue Hosp. Ctr., NYC, 1986—2002; chief cardiothoracic surgery NY VA Med. Ctr., NYC, 1988—2002; faculty mem. North Shore U. Hosp., Manhasset, NY, 2002—, vice chmn. cardiothoracic surgery, 2005—. Dir. cardiac surgery quality assurance North Shore U. Hosp., Manhasset, 2002—, dir. cardiac surgery Intensive Care Unit, 2004—. Contbr. articles to profl. jours.; mem. editl. bd.: Jour. Cardiac Surgery; mem. editl. bd. Thoracic and Cardiovascular, Surgeon, ad hoc reviewer Annals Thoracic Surgery, Am. Heart Assn., Circulation and Chest. Recipient Bronze Tablet, U. Ill., 1975. Fellow: ACS, Am. Heart Assn., Am. Coll. Chest Physicians (life); mem., AMA, Northeastern Cardiovasc. Surgery Assn., Med. Soc. NY State, NY Soc. Thoracic Surgeons, NY Assn. Thoracic Surgery (life), European Assn. Cardiothoracic Surgery, Soc. Thoracic Surgeons, Assn. and Soc. Alumni Bellevue Hosp., Alpha Omega Alpha. Achievements include research in heparin usage, reversal, myocardial protection, mitral valve surgery, mitral valve repair, minimally invasive surgery, surgery in the elderly. Office: North Shore Univ Hosp 300 Community Dr Manhasset NY 11030 Office Fax: 516-562-3786. E-mail: resposit@nshs.edu.

ESQUEA, JAMES R., federal agency administrator; b. NYC, Mar. 22, 1967; BA, Wesleyan U., Middletown, Conn., 1990; MPA, Columbia U., NYC, 1994. Dept. paralegal supr. NY County (Manhattan) Dist. Attorney's Office, 1990—92; program examiner White House Office Mgmt. & Budget, 1994—99; income security & veterans affairs analyst US Senate Budget Com., 1999—2001, income security & Medicaid analyst, 2001—10; asst. sec. for legislation US Dept. Health & Human Services, Washington, 2010—. Office: US Dept Health & Human Services 200 Independence Ave NW Washington DC 20201 Office Phone: 202-690-7627. E-mail: Jim.Esquea@hhs.gov. *

ESQUENAZI, ALBERTO, physiatrist; MD, UNAM. Dir. Moss Rehab., Phila., dir. rehab. program, chair. Prof. Jefferson U., Phila. Contbr. articles to profl. jours. Mem.: Internat. Soc. Prosthetics Orthotics, Am. Soc. Biomedicine, Am. Acad. Physical Medicine and Rehab. Office: Moss Rehab 60 Townshipline Rd Elkins Park PA 19027 Office Phone: 215-663-6676.

ESQUIBEL, EDWARD V., psychiatrist, health facility administrator; b. Denver, May 28, 1928; s. Delfino C. and Beatrice (Solis) E.; m. Elaine F. Telk (div. 1961); children: Roxanne, Cyndi, Allen, James; m. Lillian D. Robb, 1961; children: Amanda, Ramona. MD in Healthcare, U. Colo., Denver, 1958. Diplomate Am. Bd. Psychiatry and Neurology. Assoc. chief svc. Ill. State Psychiat. Inst., Chgo., 1964-66; dir. undergrad. program psychiatry, asst. prof. psychiatry Chgo Med. Sch., 1966-68; cons. and supr. group therapy Lake County Mental Health Clinic, Gary, Ind., 1968-72; pvt. practice Daytona Beach, Jacksonville, Fla., 1972-82; chief forensic svcs., dir. div. maximum security and inst. rsch. Colo. State Hosp., Pueblo, 1981; assoc. clin. prof. psychiatry Quillen-Dishner Coll. Medicine, Johnson City, Tenn., 1982-84; clin. psychiatrist VA Outpatient Clinic, Riviera Beach, Fla., 1984-86; mental health coord., supr. VA, Pensacola, Fla., 1986-88; assoc. chief staff, ambulatory care VA Med. Ctr., Ft. Lyon, Colo., 1988-90, Carl Vinson VA Med. Ctr., Dublin, Ga., 1990-91; staff physician VA Med. Ctr., Sheridan, Wyo., 1993—, chief psychiat. svcs. Lake City, Fla., 1993-94; contract physician, 1995—2000. Author: Healthcare Faction; Ticket to Nowhere: Toward Wiser Care of Veterans, 2005; contbr. articles to profl. jours. Sgt. 82nd Airborne Divsn. US Army, 1948—52. Recipient Plaque Recognition award Southeastern Psychiat. Inst., 1964, Internat. Pers. Creative award, 1972, Key to City Daytona Beach, 1975, Hosp. Dirs. commendation VA, 1991. Avocations: gardening, arts and crafts, reading. Home and Office: 801 Gospel Island Rd Inverness FL 34450-3592 Office Phone: 352-637-4749. Personal E-mail: dreesquibel@wmconnect.com.

ESSANI, KARIM, biology professor; b. Karachi, Oct. 30, 1946; PhD, U. Western Ont., Can., 1982. Prof. Western Mich. U., 1989—. Oncolytic Virus Rsch. grant, Nat. Cancer Inst., NIH. Mem.: Am. Soc. Virology. Avocation: gardening. Office: Western Mich University Dept Biological Scis Kalamazoo MI 49008-5410 Office Fax: 269-387-5610. Business E-Mail: karim.essani@wmich.edu.

ESSER, ARISTIDE HENRI, psychiatrist; b. Padalarang, Java, Indonesia, May 11, 1930; came to U.S., 1961; s. Samuel Jonathan and Anganita (Tawalujan) E.; m. Ada Reif; children: Jonathan Hendrik, Jessica. MD, U. Amsterdam, The Netherlands, 1955. Diplomate Am. Bd. Psychiatry and Neurology. Med. dir. N.S. Kline Rsch. Inst., Orangeburg, N.Y., 1962-69; dir. rsch. Letchworth Village, Thiells, N.Y., 1969-71; dir. Ctrl. Bergen Cmty. Mental Health Ctr., Paramus, N.J., 1971-77; med. dir. Mission for Immaculate Virgin, SI, N.Y., 1977-80; dir. quality assurance Bronx (N.Y.) Psychiat. Ctr., 1980-85; unit chief for supportive rehab. Rockland Psychiat. Ctr., Orangeburg, 1985-88, chief geriat. divsn., 1988-90; pvt. practice, 1989; cons. psychiatrist St. Dominic's Home, Blauvelt, 1990—2001; attending psychiatrist Good Samaritan Hosp., Suffern, NY, 1990—2002, Rye (N.Y.) Hosp. Ctr., 1990—. Rsch. prof. NYU Med. Ctr., NYC, 1985-94; pres. Psychiatry PC, 1989—. Co-author: Mental Illness: A Homecare Guide, 1989, Chi Gong: The Ancient Chinese Way to Health, 1990; editor: Behavior and Environment, 1971, Design for Community and Privacy, 1978, Jour. Man-Environment Sys., 1969— (Internat. Design award 1973). Travel grant City of Leyden, The Netherlands, 1960; Lederle Labs. fellow Yale U., 1961. Fellow AAAS (life), Am. Psychiat. Assn. (life); mem. Soc. for Biol. Psychiatry, Soc. for Gen. Systems Rsch., Am. Acad. Acupuncture (founding), Assn. for Study Man-Environment Rels. (founding), Internat. Soc. Neurofeedback & Rsch. Home: 435 S Mountain Rd New City NY 10956-5731 Office: 337 N Main St Ste 2 New City NY 10956-4310 Home Phone: 845-634-8221; Office Phone: 845-639-6723. Office Fax: 845-639-3031. Personal E-mail: pbhppmc@att.net.

ESSERMAN, LAURA JEAN, oncologist, educator; b. Harvey, Ill., Mar. 24, 1957; BS, Harvard U.; MD, Stanford U., 1983; MBA, Stanford Grad. Sch. Bus., 1993. Intern gen. surgery Stanford Med. Ctr., 1983—84, resident med. oncology, 1983—85, fellow surgery, 1985—88, resident, 1988—90, resident gen. surgery, 1990—91; staff mem. Mt. Zion Hosp., San Francisco, 1993; prof. surgery & radiology U. Calif., San Francisco; affiliate faculty Inst. for Health Policy Studies & Med. Informatics Program; co-leader U. Calif. Cancer Ctr. Breast Oncology Program, San Francisco; dir. Carol Franc Buck Breast Care Ctr. Office: 1600 Divisadero St San Francisco CA 94115 Office Phone: 415-567-6600.

ESSLEMONT, IAIN, retired physician; b. Aberdeen, Scotland, Sept. 2, 1932; arrived in Australia, 1977; s. John Connon and Grace Muriel (Née Milne) Esslemont; m. Mary Gibb Mars, Sept. 3, 1966; children: Graeme, Seonaid Mairi, Catriona Muireall. MBChB, Aberdeen U., Scotland, 1956. Diplomate in obstetrics Royal Coll. Obstetricians and Gynaecologists, 1960, Australian Coll. Obstetricians and Gynaecologists, 1980. House surgeon Ayr County Hosp., Scotland, 1956—57; house physician, pediatrician Gen. Hosp., Dewsbury, Yorkshire, England, 1957; house surgeon in obstetrics, jr. house med. officer Ayrshire Ctrl. Hosp., Irvine, Ayrshire, Scotland, 1960; physician Cha'ah, Malaya, 1960—62, with Drs. Allan and Gunstensen, Penang, Malaysia, 1962—77, Wickham, Australia, Port Maquarie, NSW, Australia, 1978, Huntingdale Family Med. Practice, Gosnells, Australia, 1979—99, Gosnells Health Care Practice, 1999; med. officer Kununurra, Australia, 1977—78, Southside After-Hours Med. Svc., Perth, Australia, 1979—83; ret., 1999. Author: Life Is What You Make It, 2009; contbr. articles to profl. jours. Pres. The Dalton Soc. Capt. Royal Army Med. Corps, 1957—59. Fellow: Royal Coll. Gen. Practitioners, Acad. Family Physicians Malaysia, Royal Australian Coll. Gen. Practitioners (examiner 1985—2010, supr. registrar 1986—87, 1993—99, external clin. instr. 2001—02); mem.: Malaysian Coll. Gen. Practitioners, Rotary (Paul Harris fellow 1998). Avocations: painting, gardening. Home: 2 Chardonnay Ave 6285 Margaret River WA Australia Business E-Mail: esslemont@wn.com.au.

ESSNER, ROBERT ALAN, retired pharmaceutical executive; b. NYC, Oct. 26, 1947; s. Arthur and Charlotte (Levy) E.; m. Rosalind Esser, July 24, 1969 (div. June 1986); children: Elizabeth, Emily; m. Anne Essner, May 23, 1987; children: Elizabeth, Emily, Benjamin. Grad., Miami U., Oxford, OH; MA, U. Chicago. Various positions Sandoz Pharms. Corp., East Hanover, NJ, 1978-86, v.p., 1986-87, corp. v.p., COO bus. mgmt., 1987; pres. Sandoz Consumer Health-Care Group, Parsippany, NJ, 1987, Wyeth-Ayerst Labs., 1993—97, Wyeth-Ayerst Global Pharm., 1997; exec. v.p. Wyeth, Madison, NJ, 1997-2000, COO, 2000, pres., 2000—06, CEO, 2001—07, chmn., 2003—08. Bd. dirs. Mass. Mutual Life Ins. Comp., Pharm. Rsch. & Mfr. Am.; mem. Bus. Roundtable, Bus. Coun. Chmn. Children's Health Fund Corp. Coun.; trustee Penn Medicine. Recipient Prix Galien Suisse, 2003, Science/Tech. medal, R&D Coun. NJ, 2003. Mem.: Pharm. Mfr. Assn. Avocation: antique photography.

ESTANI, PATRICIA BEATRIZ, psychologist, researcher; b. Cordoba, Cordoba, Argentina, Mar. 8, 1967; d. Jose Antonio Estani and Beatriz Virginia Giuliani De Estani. B in Humanities, Saul Taborda HS, Cordoba, 1984; Licenciate in Psychology., U. Cordoba, 1990, D in Psychology, 1994. Asst. prof., dept. neuroanatomy and psychophysiology Nat. U. Cordoba, 1990—92; fellow rschr. Martin Ferreyra Rsch. Inst., Nat. Coun. Sci. and Tech. Papers, Cordoba, 1990—94; fellow Fleni Argentina Found. for Neurol. Rsch., Buenos Aires, 1996—98; clin. neuropsychology Pvt. Med. Health Care Svcs., Cordoba, 1998—2006; fellow rschr. Leon S. Morra Neuropsychiatric Hosp., Ministry Health, Cordoba, 2006—. Contbr. scientific papers to profl. jours. Grantee, Ministry Health, Argentina, 2006; Sci. Rsch. in Schizophrenia fellowship, 2006. Fellow: Exptl. Psychopharmacology Assn. Argentina (assoc.); mem.: NIH (mem. alzheimer rsch. forum, mem. schizophrenia rsch. forum), APA (mem. neuropsychology sect.), Behavioral Scis. Assn. Argentina (assoc.), Internat. Schizophrenia Rsch. Orgn. in Process (assoc.). Office Phone: 5451-4822191. Personal E-mail: consulneuropsychology@yahoo.com.

ESTAPE, RICARDO E., gynecologist, educator; b. Rio Piedras, PR, July 20, 1964; BSEE, U. Miami, 1987, MD, 1991. Gynecologic oncology site group dir. U. Miami Sylvester Comprehensive Cancer Ctr., 1999—2002; dir., robotics Bapt. Health and South Miami Hosp., 2006—; mng. ptnr. South Miami Gynecologic Oncology Group, 2001—. Asst. prof. U. Miami, 1995—98, assoc. prof., 1998—2002, voluntary assoc. prof., 2009—. Recipient Outstanding Tchr. award, Assn. Profs. Gynecology and Obstetrics; named Person of Yr., South Miami Hosp. Bd. Dirs. Fellow: Am. Coll. Obstetrics and Gynecology; mem.: Am. Soc. Clin. Oncology, Soc. Robotic Surgeons, Soc. Gynecologic Oncology. Avocations: golf, boating. Office: 8585 Sunset Dr Ste 202 Miami FL 33143 Office Fax: 305-666-1801. Business E-Mail: restape@southmiamigog.com.

ESTELLA, ANGEL, emergency physician, internist; b. Algeciras, Aug. 13, 1976; Degree in Medicine & Surgery, U. Sevilla, 2000; MD summa cum laude given, U. Cadiz, 2007. Intensivist. Hosp. SAS Jerez, 2002—11, hospitalary medicine prof. family medicine residents, 2008—11. Master: Ethics Com. Hosp. SAS of Jerez. Office: Carretera Nat IV Jerez de la Frontera Cádiz 11407 Spain Office Fax: 34956032091. Personal E-mail: litoestella@hotmail.com.

ESTERLY, NANCY BURTON, retired physician; b. NYC, Apr. 14, 1935; d. Paul R. and Tanya (Pasahow) Burton; m. John R. Esterly, June 16, 1957(dec.); children: Sarah Burton, Anne Beidler, John Snyder, II, Henry Clark, II. AB, Smith Coll., 1956; MD, Johns Hopkins U., 1960. Intern, then resident in pediatrics Johns Hopkins Hosp., 1960-63, resident in dermatology, 1964-67; instr. pediatrics Johns Hopkins U. Med. Sch., 1967-68; instr., trainee La Rabida U. Chgo. Inst.; also dept. pediatrics U. Chgo. Med. Sch., 1968-69; asst. prof. Pritzker Sch. Medicine, U. Chgo., 1969-70, assoc. prof., 1973-78; asst. prof. dermatology Abraham Lincoln Sch. Medicine, U. Ill., 1970-72, assoc. prof. dermatology and pediatrics, 1972-73; dir. div. dermatology, dept. pediatrics Michael Reese Hosp. and Med. Ctr., Chgo., 1973-78; prof. pediatrics and dermatology Northwestern U. Med. Sch., 1978; head div. dermatology, dept. pediatrics Children's Meml. Hosp., Chgo., 1978-87; prof. pediatrics and dermatology Med. Coll. Wis., Milw., 1987—2004, prof. emeritus dermatology, 2005—; head div. dermatology, dept. pediatrics Children's Hosp. Wis., Milw., 1987—2004; ret., 2004. Editor-in-chief Pediatric Dermatology, 1983—2006; contbr. articles to profl. jours. Recipient David Martin Carter award, Am. Skin Assn., 2002, Lifetime Career Educator award, Dermatology Found., 2002, Disting. Svc. award, Med. Coll. Wis., 2004, Disting. Alumni award, John Hopkins U., 2007. Mem.: Wis. Pediat. Soc., Women's Dermatol. Soc. (Rose Hirschler award), Soc. Pediat. Dermatology (1st Lifetime Achievement award 1998), Soc. Pediat. Rsch., Am. Acad. Pediatrics, Soc. Investigative Dermatology, Wis. Dermatol. Soc., Am. Dermatol. Assn., Am. Acad. Dermatology, Internat. Soc. Pediat. Dermatology, Sigma Xi. Home Phone: 505-792-1427. *

ESTES, CARROLL LYNN, sociologist, educator; b. Ft. Worth, May 30, 1938; d. Joe Ewing and Carroll (Cox) E.; 1 child, Duskie Lynn Gelfand Estes. AB, Stanford U., 1959; MA, So. Meth. U., 1961; PhD, U. Calif., San Diego, 1972; DHL (hon.), Russell Sage Coll., 1986. Rsch. asst., asst. study dir. Brandeis U. Social Welfare Rsch. Ctr., 1962-63, rsch. assoc., 1964-65, project dir., 1965-67; vis. lectr. Florence Heller Grad. Sch., 1964-65; rsch. dir. Simmons Coll., 1963-64; asst. prof. social work San Diego State Coll., 1967-72; asst. prof. in residence dept. psychiatry U. Calif., San Francisco, 1972-75, assoc. prof. dept. social and behavioral scis., 1975-79, prof., 1979-92, chair dept. social and behavioral scis., 1981-93, coord. human devel. tng. program, 1974-75; dir. Aging Health Policy Rsch. Ctr., 1979-85, Inst. for Health and Aging, 1985-99. Faculty rsch. lectr. U. Calif., 1993; LaSor lectr. Oreg. Health Scis. U, 2005; co-founder Concerned Scientists in Aging, 2005, founder Estes scholars program, Inst. Health Aging, U. Calif., San Fransisco, 2008. Author: The Decision-Makers: The Power Structure of Dallas, 1963; co-author: Protective Services for Older People, 1972, U.S. Senate Special Committee on Aging Report, Paperwork and the Older Americans Act, 1978, The Aging Enterprise, 1979 Fiscal Austerity and Aging, 1983, Long Term Care of the Elderly, 1985, Political Economy, Health and Aging, 1984, The Long Term Care Crisis, 1993, The Nation's Health, 2001, 7th edit., 2003, Critical Gerontology, 1999, Social Policy and Aging, 2001, Social Theory, Social Policy and Aging, 2003, Health Policy, 5th edit., 2008, Social Justice and Social Insurance, 2009; contbr. articles to profl. jours. Mem. Calif. Commn. on Aging, 1974-77; cons. U.S. Senate Spl. Com. on Aging from 1976, Notch Commn. U.S. Commn. Social Security, 1993-94; bd. dir. Nat. Com. to Preserve Social Security and Medicare, 2002—, vice chair, 2006-08, chair 2009-, bd. chair, NC Found., 2009-. Recipient Matrix award Theta Sigma Phi, 1964, award for contbns. to lives of older Californians, Calif. Commn. on Aging, 1977, Helen Nahm Rsch. award U. Calif., San Francisco, 1986, Woman Who Would Be Pres. League of Women Voters, 1998, Lifetime Achievement award Nat. Com. to Preserve Social Security and Medicare, 2006, Improvement of Status of Women award, U. Calif. San Francisco, 2007. Fellow Am. Acad. Nursing (hon.); Mem. Inst. Medicine of NAS, Am. Pub. Health Assn.(Weiler award 2008), Am. Sociol. Assn. (Disting. Scholar award Aging and Life Course 2000), Assn. Gerontology in Higher Edn. (pres. 1980-81, recipient Beverly award 1993, Tibbitts award 2000), Am. Soc. on Aging (pres. 1982-84, Leadership award 1986, Hall of Fame award, 2007), Geronotol. Soc. Am. (Kent award 1992, pres. 1995-96), Older Women's League (v.p. 1994-97), Sociologists Women Soc. (Feminist Activist award 2008, Hockaday medal, 2010, Sr. advocacy award, Meals on Wheels 2010, Social Justice award Goray Panthess 2011), Soc. Study Social Problems, Alpha Kappa Delta, Pi Beta Phi. Office: U Calif San Francisco Inst Health & Aging 3333 California St Ste 340 San Francisco CA 94118-1944 Business E-Mail: carroll.estes@ucsf.edu, carrall.estes@gmail.com.

ESTES, DON MARK, immunologist; b. Waco, Tex., Mar. 28, 1959; BS, Tex. Tech U., 1982; PhD, Tex. A&M U., 1988. Fred L. Davison chair biomed. scis. U. Ga., 2011—. Recipient Disting. Vet. Immunologist, Conf. Rsch. Workers Animal Diseases. Mem.: AAAS, Am. Assn. Immunologists. Office: 327 Vet Medicine 501 DW Brooks Athens GA 30602 Business E-Mail: dmestes@utmb.edu.

ESTEVES, SANDRO C., physician, urologist, male infertility specialist, director; b. Tupa, Sao Paulo, July 19, 1967; MD, MSc, U. Campinas Sch. Medicine, Campinas, Brazil, PhD, 1990, Fed. U. Sao Paulo Sch. Medicine, 2001. Dir. ANDROFERT - Andrology & Human Reproduction Clinic, 1997—. Contbr. scientific papers to profl. jours., chapters to books. Recipient Alumni of the Yr., MerckSerono Internat. Adv. Bd., 2008; fellowship, Cleve. Clinic Reproductive Ctr., 1995—96. Office: Ave Dr Heitor Penteado 1464 Campinas SP 13075-460 Brazil Office Phone: 55 19 3295-8877. Office Fax: 55 19 3294-6992. Business E-Mail: s.esteves@androfert.com.br.

ESTEVES, SÉRGIO CARLOS BARROS, oncologist; b. Brazil, Mar. 6, 1964; Degree in Medicine, Cath. U. São Paulo, 1988; postgrad., U. São Paulo, 2000. Physician UNICAMP, 1995—. Dir. Radiation Therapy Dept., 1995—2011. Avocation: basketball. Office: Avenida Brasil 961 Campinas Sao Paulo 13073-000 Brazil Office Fax: 37416540. Business E-Mail: estevesrt@uol.com.br.

ESTEVEZ, ANNE-MARIE, psychologist, lawyer; b. Hiaieah, Fla., Jan. 3, 1968; d. Antonio Jesus and Linda Francis (Murphy) E. BA in Psychology cum laude, U. Miami, 1990; JD, U. Miami Sch. Law, 1993. Bar: Fla., DC. Acct. asst. Project Advisors Corp., Miami, Fla., 1986-87, bookkeeper, 1987-88, asst. to the pres., 1989-90; ptnr. Labor & Employment Morgan Lewis. Author: (ethnographic rsch.) World-War II Vet--Buster Murphy, 1989 (preserved in U. Miami Libr.). Vol. fundraiser and polit. conv. worker for Democrats. Mem. Women in Communications, Inc., Female Execs. of Am., Phi Kappa Phi, Psi Chi, Phi Kappa Alpha. Roman Catholic. Avocations: scuba diving, volunteer work. Office: c/o Morgan Lewis 5300 Wachovia Financial Ctr 200 S Biscayne Blvd Miami FL 33131-2339 Office Phone: 305-415-3330. Office Fax: 305-415-3001. Business E-Mail: aestevez@morganlewis.com. *

ESTOL, CONRADO JOSE, neurologist; b. NYC, May 28, 1959; s. Jose Estol Conrado and Lilina Guevara Arenas; m. Clarisa Diana Lifsic, Nov. 25, 1988; children: Clara, Maximo, Manuel, Conrado Alfonso. MD, U. Buenos Aires, Sch. Medicine, 1982, PhD, 1994. Lic. Ministry of Pub. Health, Buenos Aires, 1983, cert. Ednl. Commn. Fgn. Med. Grads., 1983, lic. State Pa., 1983, Mass., 1988, cert. Am. Bd. Psychiatry and Neurology, 1990. Internal medicine internship Joint Diseases North Gen. Hosp. and Mt. Sinai Hosp., NYC, 1984—85; neurology residency Presbyn. U. Hosp. (Pitts. U.), 1984—88; stroke fellow New Eng. Med. Ctr. Hosps. (Tufts U.), Boston, 1988—91; stroke rehab. fellow Spaulding Rehab. Hosp. (Harvard U.), Boston, 1988—91; dir. neuroscis., chief, divsn. cerebrovascular diseases and headache clinic Cardiovascular Inst. Buenos Aires, 1991—98; founder Neurologic Ctr. Treatment, Rehab. and Rsch., Buenos Aires, 1996—; chief sci. officer STAT Rsch. Inc., Buenos Aires, 2007—. Advisor Pontificial Acad. Scis., Vatican City, 2005—06; spkr. in fields. Contbr. articles more than 150 publs., chapters to books. Recipient 1st prize, Neurosci. Resident's Day Rsch. Pitts., 1987—88. Fellow: Am. Acad. Neurology, Am. Heart Assn.; mem.: Am. Neurol. Assn., Argentine Cerebrovascular Assn. (pres.), Argentine Med. Assn. (neurosci. sect. 1997—, mem. neurosci. sect 1997—), Neurointensive Care Rsch. Group World Fed. Neurology Exec. Com., Internat. Stroke Soc. (assoc. editor 2006—, exec. com. mem.). Office Fax: 54 11 4816 6668. Business E-Mail: conrado.estol@stat-research.com.

ESTORES, IRENE MISON, physical medicine and rehabilitation physician; b. Quezon City, Philippines, Apr. 14, 1962; MD, Coll. Medicine U. Philippines, 1987. Cert. Phys. Medicine and Rehabilitation, Spinal Cord Injury Medicine. Intern, phys. medicine rehabilitation Sinai Hosp. Balt., Md., 1989—90, resident Md., 1990—93; attending physician U. Miami Hosp., Fla., 2002; staff physician, rehabilitation medicine Miami VA Med. Ctr., 2000—02; project dir. So. Fla. Spinal Cord Injury model system; co-medical dir., spinal cord injury unit Jackson Meml. Hosp. Rehabilitation Ctr.; med. student elective coord., dept. rehabilitation medicine Leonard M. Miller Sch. Medicine, U. Miami, asst. prof., clin. rehabilitation medicine Fla. Office: Jackson Meml Hosp Rehabilitation Ctr Basement Fl 1611 NW 12th Ave Miami FL 33136 Office Phone: 305-585-1320. Office Fax: 305-585-1340.

ESUVARANATHAN, KESAVAN, urologist, educator; s. Ponnusamy and Rasaiah; m. Roshni Pillay. MBBS, Nat. U. Singapore, 1983, MD, 2006. Sr. cons. urologist Nat. U. Hosp., 1998—, dir. rsch., dept. surgery, 1997—, prof., 2008—; chmn. chpt. Urology Acad. Medicine, Singapore, 2009—, head sr. cons. dept. urology, 2010—; prof. surgery, dir. rsch. dept. surgery Nat. U. Singapore, 2006—. Pres. Singapore Urol. Assn., 2007—09; chmn. chpt. urology Acad. Med. Singapore, 2009—. Specialist cons. Sri Satya Sai Baba Free Specialist Clinic, Singapore. Recipient Young Surgeon's award, Acad. Medicine, Singapore, 1993, Best Paper prize, Congress U. Surgeons SE Asia, 1994, Asian Congress Urology, 1998, SUA Book prize, Singapore Urol. Assn., 2000. Fellow: Acad. Medicine, Singapore, Royal Coll. Surgeons, Edinburgh; mem.: Urol. Assn. Asia, Singapore Urol. Assn. (life; pres. 2007—). Achievements include patents for European Union, Australia & Japan for our novel liposomal technique for transfection for gene therapy. Home: 6 Binjai Walk Singapore 589739 Singapore Office: Nat University Health Sys Tower Block Level 8 1E Kent Ridge Rd Singapore 119228 Singapore Office Phone: 67795555, 67725642.

ETEFIA, FLORENCE VICTORIA, retired school psychologist; b. Alton, Ill., Feb. 13, 1946; d. Esau and Pearl (Taylor) Anthony. BA, Mich. State U., 1968; MAT, Oakland U., Rochester, Mich., 1972; EdS, Wayne State U., 1977, MA, 1987, postgrad. Cert. tchr. mentally impaired, Mich.; spl. edn. supr., Mich.; cert. tchr. mentally impaired, learning disabled, K-8 gen. edn., psychology, Mich. Spl. edn. tchr. Sch. Dist. of Pontiac, Mich. Mem. NEA, Mich. Edn. Assn., Pontiac Edn. Assn., Delta Sigma Theta. Home: 3035 Debra Ct Auburn Hills MI 48326-2044

ETEVENON, PIERRE, retired medical researcher; b. Courbevoie, Hauts de Seine, France, Dec. 4, 1935; s. Raymond Etevenon and Marcelle Legrain; m. Brigitte Michel; m. Micheline Hayem Etevenon, June 10, 1967 (dec. May 17, 2001). Baccalaureat, Coll. St. Joseph, Asnieres sur Seine, France, 1955; grad. in Organic Chemistry, U. Paris Sorbonne, 6, 1961; PhD, U. Paris Sorbonne, 1962; DSc, U. Pierre Marie Curie, Paris VI, 1977. Lic. in physics U. Paris Sorbonne, 1960. Tchr., physics, chemistry Coll. St. Francois Salles, Evreux, France, 1960, Coll. ND Bury, Margency, France, 1961—63, Coll. Stanislas, Paris, 1964; rschr. engr. Site Kodak Pathe, Vincennes, France, 1964—65; NATO fellow NJ Neuro Psychiatric Inst., Princeton, 1965; rsch. assoc. NJ Neuro Psychiatric Inst., Princeton, 1966; attached rschr. Inst. Nat. Sante et Rsch. Med., Paris, 1967—69, rsch. in charge, 1970—87; rsch dir. Inst. Nat. Sante et Rsch. Med., U. Basse-Normandie, 1988—99. Vis. assoc. prof. Rutgers U., Piscataway, 1975; cons. Soc. ALVAR Electronics, Montreuil, 1984—85. Author: (book) The Blind Seers, Limit States of Consciousness, 1984, From Dreams to the Awakening, Physiological Bases of Sleep, 1987, The Man Enlightend, Paradoxes of Sleep and Dream, 1990, States of Consciousness, Sophrology and Yoga, 2006; contbr. articles. With Ctr. d'Etudes Aeronautic Medicine, 1962—64, Paris. Recipient Prix Courtade Pharmacology award, Soc. Francaise Pharmacology, 1969, award, French Govt. Rsch. Commn. U. Rsch. Agys., Paris, 1968—99; grant, French Govt. Rsch. Grants. U. Rsch. Agys., 1968—99. Mem.: Soc. Francaise Rsch. Medicine Sommeil, Coll. Internat. Neuro Pharmacology (emerritus mem. 2000), French Soc. Perfumers (sec., Soc. Parfums France 2011), Internat. Pharmaco EEG Group, French Pen Club (sec., Soc. Gens Lettres France 2000). Personal E-mail: pierre.etevenon@noos.fr.

ETIENNE, CARISSA F., international organization administrator; b. Dominica; married; 3 children. MBBS, U. West Indies, Jamaica, 1976; MSc in Cmty. Health in Developing Countries, U. London Sch. Hygiene and Tropical Health, 1982. Med. officer, mem. exec. team Princess Margaret Hosp., Dominica, 1977—86, med. dir., 1986—89; dir. primary health care Ministry of Health, Dominica, disaster coord., coord. nat. AIDS program, chief med. officer, nat. epidemiologist; chairwoman Nat. Adv. Coun. AIDS/HIV, Dominica; asst. dir. Pan Am. sanitary bur., WHO Am. regional office Secretariat of the Pan Am. Health Orgn., 2003—08; asst. dir. gen. health systems and services WHO, Geneva, 2008—. Assoc. prof. Ross U. Sch. Medicine, 1996—. Mem.: Dominica Med. Assn., Caribbean Pub. Health Assn. Office: WHO avenue Appia 20 1211 Geneva Switzerland *

ETINGIN, ORLI R., internist, educator; Grad., Johns Hopkins U., 1975; MD, Yeshiva U., NY, 1980. Diplomate Am. Bd. Internal Medicine, Am. Bd. Hematology. Prof. medicine in clin. ob-gyn. Weill Cornell Med. Coll., prof. clin. medicine, prof. Lisa and Stanford B. Ehrenkranz in women's health; founder and med. dir. Iris Cantor Women's Health Ctr., 1994; resident tng. internal medicine NY-Presbyn. Hosp./Weill Cornell Med. Ctr., subspecialty tng. hematology-oncology, chief resident, 1987, vice chmn. dept. medicine, 1997—2009, attending physician; pvt. practice in internal medicine, 1992. Editor: (newsletters) Women's Health Advisor, Food and Fitness Advisor; contbr. Everyday Health; author: Hematologic Conditions in Women, 1996; assoc. editor Textbook of WomenA's Health, 1996; co-author: (Jour. Articles) Nifedipine Alters Cholesterol Metabolism in Lipid-laden Cells: A Possible Mechanism of Its Anti-Atherogenic Effect, 1985, Cholesterol Metabolism is Altered By Hydrolytic Metabolites of Prostacyclin in Arterial Smooth Muscle Cells, 1986, Platelet-Neutrophil - Smooth Muscle Cell Interactions. Lipoxygenase-Derived Mono-and Di-Hydroxy Acids Activate Cholesteryl Ester Hydrolysis By The Cyclic AMP-Dependent Protein Kinase Cascade, 1989, Evidence For Cytokine Regulation of Cholesterol Metabolism in Herpesvirus Infected Arterial Cells, 1990, Enhanced Cholesteryl Ester Hydrolytic Activity In Aortic Tissue of Patients on Calcium Channel Blockers, 1990, various jour. articles in publs. Recipient Edward Weinstein award in Medicine, 1980, Clin. Investigator award, Nat. Insts. of Health, 1987—92. Mem.: AMA, Am. Med. Women's Assn. (award recipient 1980). Office: New York-Presbyterian Hospital/Weill Cornell Medical Center 425 E 61st St New York NY 10065 Office Phone: 212-821-0296. Office Fax: 212-746-8163.

ETTEMA, SANDRA LYNN, medical educator; b. Blue Island, Ill., Jan. 7, 1969; PhD, U. Ill., 1999, MD, 2002. Asst. prof. divsn. otolaryngology SIU HealthCare and SIU Sch. Medicine, 2008—. Vis. prof. U. Ill. Coll. Medicine, 2008. Recipient Horst R. Konrad Excellence Tchg. award, Divsn. Otolaryngology-Head and Neck Surgery, Excellence Tchg. award, SIU Sch. Medicine, 2010. Mem.: AMA, Am. Cleft Palate-Craniofacial Assn., Am. Speech-Language-Hearing Assn., Am. Acad. Otolaryngologic Allergy, Am. Acad. Otolaryngology. Avocations: fishing, travel. Office: 301 N Eighth St 5th Fl Pavilion Springfield IL 62794-9662 Office Fax: 217-545-7512. Business E-Mail: settema@siumed.edu.

ETTENGER, ROBERT BRUCE, physician, pediatric nephrologist; b. Phila., Sept. 17, 1942; s. Ervin Earl and Sylvia (Goodstein) W.; m. Angela Joan Castellano; children: Allison, Jessica. BA, U. Pa., 1964; MD, 1968. Asst. prof. pediat. Children's Hosp. LA, 1976-80, Sch. Medicine UCLA, 1980-84, asst. prof., 1984-89, prof., 1989—, Casey Lee Ball Disting. prof. pediat., 2005—, head divsn. pediat. nephrology dept. pediat., 1990—2004, vice chmn. clin. affairs, 1990—2004; med. dir. pediat. renal transplant program UCLA Med. Ctr., 1983—, dir. historcompatibility lab., 1987—2001, vice chief med. staff, 2002—04, chief med. staff, 2004—06. Mem., chair sub-bd. nephrology Am. Bd. Pediat., Chapel Hill, N.C., 1986-91; cons. Immunosuppressive Adv. Com. Food and Drug Adminstrn., Bethesda, Md., 1994—, Biologics and Immune Response Modifiers, Food and Drug Adminstrn., Bethesda, 1994—; mem. biol. sci. adv. com. U.S. Renal Data Sys., Ann Arbor, Mich., 1993-2000, Data Safety Monitoring Bd., Dept. Transplantation, Nat. Inst. Immunology Transplant Adv. Group, U.S. Sec. Health and Human Svcs., Am. Soc. Nephrology; mem. Adv. Com. Transplantation. Assoc. editor Am. Jour. Transplantation; mem. editl. bd. Transplantation, Pediat. Nephrology, Pediat. Transplantation; contbr. articles to profl. jours. Coach, mem. exec. bd. AYSO Soccer, Santa Monica, Calif., 1994-2001, Bobby Sox Softball, 1995-97, YWCA Basketball, 1995-2000; mem. med. adv. bd. Nat. Kidney Found., LA, 1993—. Maj. US Army, 1971—73. Recipient Ortho Biotech Lectureship Urologic Soc. for Transplantation, 1990, Continuing Svc. award Nat. Kidney Found., L.A., 1991, 92, 94. Fellow Internat. Soc. Nephrology, Internat. Pediat. Nephrology Assn., Am. Acad. Pediat., Am. Soc. Transplant Physicians (pres. 1984-85), Am. Pediat. Soc., Am. Soc. of Nephrology, Am. Soc. Pediat. Nephrology, Soc. Pediat. Rsch., Transplantation Soc. (Best Drs. in Am. 1992-06, Am.'s Top Drs. 1998-06), United Network Organ Sharing (regional councillor at region 5, bd. dirs. 2000-02). Jewish. Avocations: distance running, youth sports. Office: UCLA Med Ctr A2-383 Dept Pediatrics 10833 Le Conte Ave Los Angeles CA 90095-3075

ETTINGER, DAVID SEYMOUR, oncologist; b. Bklyn., Mar. 16, 1942; s. Harry and Frieda (Rose) E.; m. Phyllis Evellen Katz, June 4, 1964; children: Laura, Daniel, Kathryn. BA, Yeshiva Coll., 1963; MD, U. Louisville, 1967. Intern Albany (N.Y.) Med. Coll., 1967-68; fellow in medicine Mayo Clinic, Rochester, NY, 1968-71; fellow in med. oncology Johns Hopkins U. Sch. Medicine, Balt., 1973-75, instr. oncology, 1975-76, instr. medicine, 1975-77, asst. prof. oncology, 1976-81, asst. prof. medicine, 1977-81, assoc. prof. oncology, 1981-82, assoc. prof. medicine, 1981-93, prof. oncology, 1992—, prof. medicine, 1993—, Alex Grass prof. oncology, 2003—; assoc. dir. for clin. rsch. Johns Hopkins Oncology Ctr., Balt., 1992—2006. Mem. editorial bd. Oncology: Internat. Jour. of Cancer Rsch. and Treatment, Jour. Cancer Rsch. and Clin. Oncology, The Oncologist, Expert Rev. of Anticancer Therapy; editor-in-chief: Current Treatment Options in Oncology; contbr. chpts. to books, numerous articles to profl. jours. Pres. Md. divsn. Am. Cancer Soc., 1994-96. Maj. U.S. Army,

1971-73. Recipient Nat. Divisional award, St. George Medal, Am. Cancer Soc. 1997. Fellow ACP, Am. Coll. Chest Physicians; mem. Eastern Coop. Oncology Group, Radiation Therapy Oncology Group, Am. Soc. Clin. Oncology, Am. Assn. for Cancer Rsch., Internat. Assn. for Study of Lung Cancer, Am. Soc. Therapeutic Radiology and Oncology, Connective Tissue Oncology Soc., Phi Delta Epsilon. Office: Bunting Blaustein CRBI Room G88 1650 Orleans St Baltimore MD 21231 Office Phone: 410-955-8847. Business E-Mail: ettinda@jhmi.edu.

ETTINGER, HARRY JOSEPH, retired industrial hygiene engineer, consultant; b. NYC, July 20, 1934; s. Morris and Pauline (Waxman) E.; m. June Kopf, June 14, 1958; children: Linda E., Steven E., Robert A. BCE, CCNY, 1956; MCE, NYU, 1958. Registered profl. engr., N.Mex.; cert. indsl. hygienist. San. engr. USPHS, Bethesda, Md., 1958-61; staff mem. Los Alamos (N.Mex.) Nat. Lab., 1961-71, alt. group leader, 1971-74, group leader, 1974-80, program mgr., 1981-87, tech. rsch. coord., 1989-91, program mgr., 1991-93, chief scientist environ., safety and health divsn., 1993-97, acting dep. divsn. dir., 1995-96, lab. assoc., 1997-99, cons., 1999—2004; project dir. Occupl. Safety and Health Adminstrn., Washington, 1987-89. Cons. divsn. reactor licensing USAEC, 1970-71, cons. EPA, 1972-74, various industries, 1970—; cons. to adv. com. on nuc. facility safety DOE, 1990-91; mem. adj. faculty U. Ark., Little Rock, 1969-90, San Diego State U., 1981-86; vis. faculty Tex. A&M U., College Station, 1981-99; faculty affiliate Colo. State U., Ft. Collins, 1983-2004; mem. exec. com. toxic substances rsch. and tchg. program U. Calif., 1984-90; mem. stds. steering group DOE Lab. Dirs. Environ. and Occupl. Health, 1990-96; mem. liaison com. NIOSH Nat. Occupl. Rsch. Agenda, 2000-03; reviewer Inst. Medicine, 2006. Mem. editl. bd. Jour. Occupl. and Environ. Hygiene, 2004-2010; contbr. jour. articles and tech. reports on indsl. hygiene, aerosol physics, respiratory protection. Active Los Alamos County Utility Bd., 1968-70, 78-82, chmn., 1970; vice chmn. Los Alamos County Planning and Zoning Commn., 1974-76, mem., 1972-76, 97-2001, 2004-2006, Charter Review Com., 2009- Fellow: Am. Indsl. Hygiene Assn. (chmn. aerosol tech. com. 1968—70, mem. aerosol tech. com. 1968—78, editl. rev. bd. 1979—87, aerosol tech. com. 1980—84, bd. dirs. 1987—90, editl. rev. bd. 1990—91, v.p. 1991—92, pres.-elect 1992—93, pres. 1993—94, editl. rev. bd. 1995—2003, respirator com. 1995—, Edward Baier award 1990, Donald Cummings Lectr. and award 2003, Henry Smyth Lectr. and award 2004); mem.: Internat. Occupl. Hygiene Assn. (bd. dirs. 1994—97), Internat. Soc. Respiratory Protection (bd. dirs. 1985—88, 1995—97, mem. editl. bd. NSC Jour. safety rsch. 2001—07), Am. Conf. Govtl. Indsl. Hygiene (Meritorious Achievement award 1985), Am. Bd. Indsl. Hygiene (bd. dirs. 1979—85, chmn. 1983—85), Am. Acad. Indsl. Hygiene (editor newsletter 1997—2001). Democrat. Jewish. Office Phone: 505-662-7132.

ETTL, ARMIN, ophthalmologist, plastic eye and orbital surgeon; b. Strass, Austria, Feb. 13, 1962; s. Siegfried and Herta Ettl; m. Karin Leibetseder, Mar. 27, 1999; children: Alexander, Christina. MD, U. Graz, Austria, 1987; PhD, U. Amsterdam, 2000. Intern Greys Hosp., Pietermaritzburg, South Africa, 1988-89; asst. U. Innsbruck, Austria, 1989-94; cons. ophthalmic surgeon Gen. Hosp., St. Polten, Austria, 1995-96, head dept. Ophthalmology, Orbital Surgery, 1996—. Lectr. ophthalmology U. Innsbruck, 1999—. Author: High Resolution MRI Anatomy of the Orbit, 1999; contbr. articles to profl. jours. Fellow Orbital Ctr., Amsterdam, The Netherlands, 1995, Moorfields Eye Hosp., London, 1995. Mem.: Austrian Soc. Ophthalmology, European Soc. Ophthalmic Plastic and Reconstructive Surgeons, Internat. Soc. Orbital Disorders. Office: Grillparzerstr 2A A-3100 Saint Poelton Austria also: Dept Ophthalmology & Orbital Surgery Landesklinikum 3100 Saint Poelten Austria Office Phone: 0043-2742-300-17101. Business E-Mail: orbitazentrum@stpoelten.lknoe.at.

ETZ, JANE (HELEN JANE ETZ), hospital clinical review analyst; b. Riverside, Calif., Feb. 21, 1938; d. James Wycoff Van Derpool and Mildred Thelma Carr; m. William Arthur Ward, Aug. 9, 1958 (div. 1978); children: Arthur Scott Ward, Wendolyn Zee (Ward) Warwick; m. Charles Frederick Etz, Jan. 26, 1980 (dec. Aug. 2006). BSN, Calif. State U., Dominguez Hills, 1996. RN Calif., cert. pub. health nurse, Calif., case mgr., Ca;of/. Clinic nurse Gridley (Calif.) Farm Labor Camp, 1965—67; staff nurse Chico (Calif.) Cmty. Hosp., 1972—75, patient care coord., 1975—80; head nurse King Abdulaziz Air Base Hosp., Dhahran, Saudi Arabia, 1980—81; utilization mgr. Chico Cmty. Hosp., 1981—91, dir. quality mgmt., 1991—94; dir. utilization mgmt. discharge planning and social svcs. Chico Cmty. Hosp., Inc., 1994—98; utilization mgr. Enloe Med. Ctr., Chico, 1998—2001, clin. regulatory analyst, 2001. V.p., bd. dirs. Peg Taylor Adult Day Health, Chico, 1996—, sec., 1993-96; pres. elect Butte/Glenn/Tehema County (Calif.) chpt. Am. Diabetic Assn., 1996-99, pres. 1999-2000. Mem. North Sierra Quality/Utilization Assn. (pres. 1981-82), Chico Book Club, Caribou Women's Club, Chico Elks R. V. Club. Presbyterian. Avocations: books, investing, bicycling, birdwatching, gardening. Office: Enloe Med Ctr 1351 Esplanade Chico CA 95926-3330 Office Phone: 530-332-7094. Business E-Mail: jane.etz@enloe.org, jane.etz@sbcglobal.net.

ETZEL, RUTH ANN, public health specialist, pediatrician, epidemiologist, educator; Student, St. Olaf Coll., 1972-73; BA in Biology summa cum laude, U. Minn., 1976; MD, U. Wis., 1980; PhD, U. N.C., 1985. Bd. cert. Am. Bd. Pediat., Am. Bd. Preventive Medicine. Resident in pediat. N.C. Meml. Hosp., Chapel Hill, 1980-83; resident preventive medicine, RobertWood Johnson Clin. Sch., U. NC, 1983—85; adj. asst. prof. pediat. Emory U. Sch. Medicine, Atlanta, 1985-87; epidemic intelligence svc. officer Ctr. Environ. Health Ctrs. Disease Control, Atlanta, 1985-87, med. epidemiologist Ctr. Environ. Health and Injury Control, 1987-90, chief air pollution and respiratory health br., 1991-96, asst. dir. preventive medicine residency program, 1992-97; dir. divsn. epidemiology and risk assessment Office Pub. Health and Sci., Food Safety and Inspection Svc., USDA, Washington, 1998—2001; rsch. dir. Southctrl. Found., 2001—08; adj. prof. environ. and occupl. health George Washington U., Washington, 2000—. Mem. preventive medicine and pub. health test com. Nat. Bd. Med. Examiners, 1992—94; mem. US Med. Licensing Exam. Step 2 Preventive Medicine and Pub. Health Test Material Devel. Com., 1992—94; mem., trustee Am. Bd. Preventive Medicine, 1992—2001, vice chair pub. health and preventive medicine, 1997—2001; commissioned officer US Pub. Health Svc, 1985—2005. Editor: Am. Acad. Pediat., Pediat. Environ. Health, 1999—; assoc. editor: Current Problems in Pediatrics and Adolescent Healthcare, 2005—; contbr. articles to profl. publs. Recipient Don C. Mackel Meml. award, Ctrs. Disease Control, 1987, Arthur S. Flemming award, DC Jaycees, 1991, EPA Children's Environ. Health Champion award, 2007, Disting. Svc. medal, US Public Svc., 2008; MacPherson scholar, 1972. Fellow: Am. Coll. Preventive Medicine (vice chmn., environ. health com. 2002—06), Am. Acad. Pediats. (Ctrs. Disease Control and Prevention liaison 1986—94, chmn. sect. epidemiology 1988—92, ex-officio 1993—94, chmn. com. environ. health 1995—99, mem. com. on native Am. child health 2003—09, mem. exec. com. sect. epidemiology 2005—); mem.: Internat. Soc. Environ. Epidemiology (bd. councillors 1995—98), Academic Pediat. Assn. (mem. rsch. com. 1987—, comms. dir. 2002—05), Sigma Xi, Delta Omega, Phi Beta Kappa. Office: N87-W15905 Belleview Menomonee Falls WI 53051

EUN, BAIK-LIN, medical educator; b. Gobu-myeon, Jeol-la-buk-do, Republic Of Korea, Nov. 22, 1959; s. Jong Suk Eun and Sun Jung Song; m. Ho Sun Kim, May 5, 1986; children: Hae Young, Yong. PhD, Korea U., Seoul, 1993. Cert. dr. Ministry for Health, Welfare and Family Affairs, Republic of Korea, 1984. Postdoc. fellow U. Mich., Ann Arbor, Mich., 1995—97; prof. Korea U., 1993—. Recipient award, Ministry for Health, Welfare and Family Affairs, Republic of Korea, 2008. Mem.: Korean Child Neorology Soc., Korean Pediatric Soc. Office: Korea Univ Guro Hosp Dept Pediatri 80 Guro-Gu Guro-Dong Seoul 152-703 Republic of Korea Office Phone: 82-2-2626-1220. Office Fax: 82-2-2626-1249. Personal E-mail: bleun@chollian.net. Business E-Mail: bleun@korea.ac.kr.

EUN, JONGPIL, medical educator, department chairman; b. Jeongeup, Republic of Korea, Jan. 30, 1962; MD, Hanyang U., 1987; PhD, Chonbuk Nat. U., 2003. Chmn., dept. neurosurgery Presbyn. Med. Ctr., 1996—2003; clin. prof. Med. Sch. Hosp. Chonbuk Nat. U., 2003—04, assoc. prof., chmn., dept. neurosurgery, 2004—. Editl. bd. mem. Korean Spinal Neurosurg. Soc., 2004—11, Korean Neurotraumatology Soc., 2004—11, Korean Neurosurg. Soc., 2009—11; peer rev. mem. Health Ins. Rev. and Assessment Svc., 2007—11; reviewer Spine. Recipient award, Ganwoen Province South Korea, 1989, Academic award, Chonbuk Nat. U. Hosp., Korean Neurosurg. Soc., 2007. Mem.: Korean Soc. Critical Care Medicine, Korean Neurotraumatology Soc., Korean IMS Therapy Soc., Korean Spinal Neurosurgery Soc., Korean Neurosurg. Soc. Avocations: golf, hiking, music. Office: Dept Neurosugery Chonbuk Nat University Hosp 634-18 Geumamdong Deokjingu Jeonju Jeollabukdo 561-712 Republic of Korea Office Phone: 82-63-250-1870 (1580). Office Fax: 82-63-277-3273. Business E-mail: spineeun@chonbuk.ac.kr, spineeun@jbnu.ac.kr.

EUN, SANG SOO, surgeon; b. Seoul, Republic of Korea, Feb. 17, 1979; MD, Ajou U., 2003; M, Seoul Nat. U., 2010. Staff Wooridul Spine Hosp., Seoul, 2009—. Cons. Ministry Def., Republic of Korea, 2011. Recipient Best Acad. Achievement award, Korean Soc. Laser Medicine and Surgery, 2010. Mem.: Korean Orthop. Assn. Avocation: tennis. Home: Tap Mael DaeWoo Apt 211-1602 Bun Dang Seong Nam Si Kyeong Gi Do 463 926 Republic of Korea Office Phone: 82-2-513-8375. Home Fax: 82-2-513-8146. E-mail. erupt0123@naver.com.

EVANS, AUDREY ELIZABETH, physician, educator; b. York, Eng., Mar. 6, 1925; came to U.S., 1957, naturalized, 1962; d. Leonard Llewellyn and Phyllis Mary (Miller) E. Licentiate Sch. Medicine, Royal Coll. Surgeons, Edinburgh, 1950. Intern Royal Infirmary, Edinburgh, 1950-52; physician tumor therapy Children's Hosp., Boston, 1957-65; instr. pediatrics Harvard U. Med. Sch., 1961-65; asst. prof. pediatric hematologist U. Chgo., 1965-69; prof. pediatrics U. Pa., 1969—, now emeritus. Dir. oncology Children's Hosp., Phila., 1969-89. Office: Children's Hosp ARB 902 324 S 34th St Philadelphia PA 19104-4399 Home: 201 S 18th St Apt 1818 Philadelphia PA 19103-5936 Home Phone: 215-735-1835. Personal E-mail: aeevans25@yahoo.com.

EVANS, CHRISTOPHER CHARLES, retired physician; b. Widnes, Lancashire, Eng., Oct. 2, 1941; s. Robert Percy and Nora Carson (Crowther) E.; m. Susan Fuld, Feb. 5, 1966; children: Joanne Victoria, Matthew Richard, Sophie Kate. MB ChB, Liverpool U., Eng., 1964, MD, 1973. House officer Clatterbridge Hosp., Liverpool, 1964-65; med. registrar Royal So. Hosp., Liverpool, 1966-69; sr. med. registrar Liverpool region, 1969-72; Wellcome-Swedish travelling fellow Uppsala, 1972-73; sr. lectr. Liverpool U., 1974-78; cons. physician Cardiothoracic Ctr. and Royal Liverpool U. Hosp., 1978—2003; ret. Bd. dirs. Med. Def. Union, U.K., 1992—; cons. med. officer Royal Life, U.K., 1977-2005, POCSSS, U.K., 1985-2005; chief cons. med. officer Swiss Pioneer, U.K., 1990-2005; chmn., pres. & chmn. Med. Def. Union, 2006-. Co-author Symptoms and Signs in Clinical Medicine, 12th edit., 1997; contbr. articles to profl. publs., chpt. to book. Chmn. N.W. Brit. Lung Found., Merseyside, U.K., 1992, 97. Guy Scadding fellow, 1978. Fellow Royal Coll. Physicians (Dublin), Royal Coll. Physicians (London; v.p. 2001-03), Med. Def. Union (coun. 1984—, mem. bd. dirs. 1992—, v.p. 2001-06); mem. Assn. Physicians, Twenty Club (pres. 1994-95), Artists Club (pres. 2011), Reform Club. Avocations: skiing, fell walking, watching liverpool football, theater, tennis. Home: Lagom Glendyke Rd L18 6JR Liverpool England Personal E-mail: christoffe58@hotmail.com.

EVANS, GREGORY RANDOLPH DEAN, plastic surgeon, educator; b. Lynwood, Calif., Sept. 4, 1958; s. Richard Dean and Lavon Ilene Evans; m. Ruth Ellen Anderson, Mar. 15, 1986; children: Brandon, Brogan. BS in Psychobiology, U. So. Calif., LA, 1980; MD, U. So. Calif., 1985. Cert. Am. Bd. Surgery, Am. Bd. Plastic Surgeons. Resident in gen. surgery LA County, U. So. Calif. Med. Ctr., 1985—90; resident in craniofacial microvascular surgery Md. Inst. Emergency Med. Svcs. Sys., 1992-93; resident in plastic and reconstrv. surgery Johns Hopkins Hosp., U. Md., 1993; clin. assoc. prof. divsn. plastic surgery Baylor Coll. Medicine, Houston, 1993-2000; asst. prof. U. Tex. M.D. Anderson Cancer Ctr., Houston, 1993—97, assoc. prof. dept. plastic surgery, 1997—2000; prof. surgery, chief divsn. plastic surgery U. Calif., Irvine, 2000—. Adj. prof. biomed. engring. U. Calif., Irvine; Adj. prof. bioengring. Rice U., Houston, 1993—2000; visiting prof Ky. Soc. Plastic Surgeons, 2006. Contbr. articles to profl. jours.; reviewer (of sci. jour.). Recipient Jr. Clin. Rsch. award, Johns Hopkins Hosp. U. Med. Combined Programs, 1992. Fellow: ACS; mem.: Am. Bd. Plastic Surgery (elected dir. 2005), Plastic Surgery Rsch. Coun., Tissue Engring. Soc., Soc. of Surg. Oncology, Am. Soc. Plastic and Reconstructive Surgeons. Avocations: golf, skiing. Office: UCI Manchester Pavilion 200 S Manchester Ave Ste 650 Orange CA 92868 Office Phone: 714-456-3077. Office Fax: 714-456-2229. Business E-Mail: gevans@uci.edu.

EVANS, HARRY LAUNIUS, pathology educator; b. Mobile, Ala., June 11, 1948; s. Aurelius A. and Anne (Hathaway) E.; m. Cheryl J. Winfrey, June 6, 1970 (div. Dec. 1990); children: Thomas H., Sarah S. BS, Stetson U., 1970; MD, U. Fla., 1974. Diplomate Am. Bd. Pathology. Resident in pathology Vanderbilt U. Med. Ctr., Nashville, 1974-75; fellow in dermatopathology Mayo Clinic, Rochester, Minn., 1977-78; fellow in pathology U.Tex.-M.D. Anderson Cancer Ctr., Houston, 1975-77, asst. prof. pathology, 1978-82, assoc. prof., 1982-90, prof., 1990—. Contbr. articles to med. jours. Mem. U.S.-Can. Acad. Pathology, Arthur Purdy Stout Soc. Surg. Pathologists. Avocations: mountain climbing, music, crossword puzzles. Office: U Tex-MD Anderson Cancer Ctr Dept Pathology 1515 Holcombe Blvd Houston TX 77030-4009 Office Phone: 713-792-3152. E-mail: hevans@mdanderson.org.

EVANS, JOHN N., medical educator, former dean; PhD in Physiology, U. Fla. Postdoctoral trainee in physiology U. Vt. Coll. Medicine, Burlington, 1976, prof. physiology & biology, 1990—, sr. adv. to dean, sr. adv. to pres. strategic initiatives, acting dean, 2003—04, dean, 2004—06. Office: U Vt Coll Medicine E-126 Given Bldg 89 Beaumont Ave Burlington VT 05405-0068 Office Phone: 802-656-3117. E-mail: joh.evans@uvm.edu.

EVANS, KATHLEEN MARY, literature educator; b. Mullumbimby, Australia, Mar. 7, 1950; d. Robert Henry Khan and Ida Mildred Makin; m. Lawrence Evan Jenkin Evans, Nov. 6, 1984; children: Natalie Anna Morgan, Charlotte Roberta. BA, U. Queensland, 1982, MA in Lit. Studies, 1987, PhD in Psychiatry, Classics and Ancient History, 2000. RN NSW, Australia, 1972. Psychiat. nurse Broughton Hall Psychiat. Clinic, Sydney, Austria, 1969—73; rsch. asst. Dept. Psychiatry U. Queensland, Brisbane, Australia, 1976—86; lectr. Queensland U. Tech., Brisbane, 1993—97, Griffith U., Brisbane, 2000—. Editor: Psychiatric and Mental Health Nursing; contbr. chpt. to Historical Precedents for Mental Illness, articles to profl. jours. Scholar, U. Queensland, 1997—99. Fellow: Australian and New Zealand Coll. Mental Health Nurses (fellow 2003). Green Party. Avocations: travel, literature, opera, painting. Office: Griffith University 213 N48 Nathan Campus 4059 Brisbane QLD Australia Office Fax: +61 (0) 7 37355431. Business E-Mail: k.evans@griffith.edu.au.

EVANS, LOUISE, investor, retired psychologist; b. San Antonio; d. Henry Daniel and Adela (Pariser) E.; m. Thomas Ross Gambrell, Feb. 23, 1960. BS, Northwestern U., 1949; MS in Clin. Psychology, Purdue U., 1952, PhD in Clin. Psychology, 1955. Lic. marriage, family and child counselor Calif.; Nat. Register of Health Svc. Providers in Psychology; lic. psychologist, Calif., N.Y. (inactive); diplomate Clin. Psychology, Am. Bd. Profl. Psychology. Intern clin. psychology Menninger Found. Topeka (Kans.) State Hosp., 1952-53; postdoctoral fellow clin. child psychology Menninger Clinic, Topeka, 1955-56; staff psychologist Kankakee (Ill.) State Hosp., 1954-55; head staff psychologist child guidance clinic Kings County Hosp., Bklyn., 1957-58; dir. psychology clinic Barnes-Renard Hosp.; instr. med. psychology Washington U. Sch. Medicine St. Louis, 1959-60, clin. rsch. cons. Episc. City Diocese, St. Louis, 1959-60; pvt. practice Fullerton, Calif., 1960—93; fellow Internat. Coun. Sex Edn. and Parenthood, 1984, Am. U., Washington. Psychol. cons. Fullerton Cmty. Hosp., 1961-81; staff cons. clin. psychology Martin Luther Hosp., Anaheim, Calif., 1963-70; chair, participant psychol. symposiums, 1956—; spkr., lectr. in field. Contbr. articles on clin. psychology to profl. publs. Elected to Hall of Fame Ctrl. H.S., Evansville, Ind., 1966; recipient Svc. award Yuma County (Ariz.) Head Start Program, 1972, Statue of Victory Personality of Yr. award Centro Studi E. Ricerche Delle Nazioni, Italy, 1985, Alumni Merit award Northwestern U. Coll. Arts and Scis., 1997, Corann Okorodudu Internat Womens Advocacy award, APA, Soc. Psychol. Women, 2009, named Miss Heritage, Heritage Publs., 1965. Fellow AAAS (emeritus), APA Internat. (Internat. Psychology Recognition award for lifelong contbns. to advancement of psychology internationally 2002), Soc. Psychology Women (Corann Okorodudu Internat Womens Advocacy award, 2009), Soc. Clin. Psychology, Soc. Cons. Psychology (dir. exec. bd. 1976-79), Psychotherapy Acad. Clin. Psychology, Am. Assn. Applied and Preventive Psychology (charter), Royal Soc. Pub. Health Eng. (emeritus), Internat. Coun. Psychologists (dir. 1977-79, sec. 1962-64, 73-76, 2 awards 2003, recognition for pioneering leadership in internat. psychology, named amb. for life Recognition Outstanding Leadership & Enduring Commitment award 2003), Am. Orthopsychiat. Assn. (life), World Wide Acad. Scholars of N.Z. (life), Assn. Psychol. Sci. (charter), L.A. Soc. Clin. Psychologists (exec. bd. 1966-67), Internat. Coun. Psychologists, Profl. Orgs. and Socs.; mem. AAUP (emeritus), Calif. Psychol. Assn. (life, ins. com. 1961-65), LA County Psychol. Assn. (emeritus), Orange County Psychol. Assn. (charter founder, exec. bd. 1961-62), Am. Pub. Health Assn. (emeritus), Internat. Platform Assn., NY Acad. Scis. (emeritus), Purdue U. Alumni Assn. (life, past pres. coun., mem. dean's club, Citizenship award 1975, Disting. Alumni award 1993, Old Master 1993), Northwestern U. Past 1851 Soc. (Coll. Arts and Scis. Merit award 1997), Ctr. Study Presidency, Soc. Jewelry Historians USA (charter), Alumni Assn. Menninger Sch. Psychiatry, Soc. Psychology Women, Sigma Xi (emeritus). Achievements include development of innovative theories and techniques of clinical practice; acknowledged pioneer in development of psychology as science and profession both nationally and internationally, and in marital and family therapy, and in consulting to hospitals and clinics. Office: PO Box 6067 Beverly Hills CA 90212-1067 Office Phone: 310-474-1361. Office Fax: 310-474-1361.

EVANS, MARK IRA, obstetrician, geneticist; b. Bklyn., May 14, 1952; s. Robert Bernard and Sonia Beatrice Evans. BS in Psychology, Tufts U., 1973; MD, SUNY, Bklyn., 1978. Diplomate Am. Bd. Ob-Gyn, Am. Bd. Med. Genetics. Resident in ob-gyn. U. Chgo., 1979—82; med. genetics fellow NIH, Bethesda, Md., 1982—84; dir. reproductive genetics Hutzel Hosp. Wayne State U., Detroit, 1984—2001, Charlotte B. Failing prof. ob-gyn. and human genetics Ctr. Molecular Med./Path., 1991—2001, disting. prof., 2000, dir. Ctr. for Fetal Diagnosis and Therapy, 1985—2001, dir. human genetics program, 1996—2001, chmn., chief, 1998—2001; pres. Internat. Fetal Medicine and Surgery Soc., 1996—, Fetal Medicine Found. America, 2001—; prof., chmn. ob-gyn, prof. human genetics, dir. fetal therap Hahnemann Hosp., Phila., 2000—02; dir. fetal therapy program MCP Hahnemann U., 2000—02; dir. Inst. Genetics and Fetal Medicine Columbia U. Coll. of Physicians and Surgeons, NYC, 2002—; prof. ob-gyn St. Lukes Roosevelt Hosp. Ctr./Columbia U., 2002—04, Mt. Sinai Sch. Medicine, 2005—. Mem. adv. bd. Ehlrs Danlos Found., L.A., 1986—2004, Corning Metpath, Quest Diagnostics, 1988-2000, Lab. Corp., 2003-05, Nat. Adv. Bd. on Ethics in Reproduction,

Washington; mem. ethics com. Am. Coll. Ob-Gyn., 1987-90, Molecular Medicine and Genetics, Wayne State U.; dir. sci. adv. bd. Manhatton, Profl Labs., 2008-. Author: (textbooks) Pretest: Obsterics and Gynecology, 6th rev. edit., 1991, 9th edit., 2000, (with C.C. Lin) Intrauterine Growth Retardation, 1984, (with others) Fetal Diagnosis Therapy: Science, Ethics and the Law, 1989, Reproductive Risks and Prenatal Diagnosis, 1992, The New Reproductive Genetics, 1993, Maternal Genetic Disease, 1996, Invasive Outpatient Procedures in Reproductive Medicine, 1997, Principles and Practice of Medical Therapy in Pregnancy, 1998, Study Guide, 1998, The Unborn Patient, 2001, Contemporary Therapy for Obstetrics & Gynecology, 2002; (with Evans and Rodeck) Ultrasound and Fetal Therapy, 2000; (with Evans, Platt and De La Cruz) Fetal Therapy, 2000; editor: (with others) The Genetic Revolution and Obstetrics and Gynecology, 2002, New Genetics for the Clinician, 2002, Prenatal Diagnosis, 2006, Chinese edit., 2010, High Risk Obstetrics, 2009; contbr. articles to profl. jours. Fellow Am. Coll. Ob-Gyn. (course coordination com. 1996-99), Am. Coll. Med. Genetics (founder); mem. AMA (nat. ultrasound task force 1990-91), Internat. Fetal Medicine Surgery Soc. (pres. 1986-87, 96-97), Am. Soc. Human Genetics, Soc. Gynecol. Investigation, Ctrl. Assn. Ob-Gyn. (bd. dirs. 1998-2000, pres. 2007), Soc. Perinatal Obstetricians, Am. Gynecol. and Obstetrics Soc., Ctrl. Assn. Obstetrics and Gynecologists (v.p. 2004). Jewish. Office: Comprehensive Genetics 131 E 65th St New York NY 10065 Office Phone: 212-288-1422. Office Fax: 212-879-2606. Business E-Mail: evans@compregen.com.

EVANS, MARSHA JOHNSON, retired military officer, former non profit and sports association executive; b. Springfield, Ill., Aug. 12, 1947; d. Walter Edward Johnson and Alice Anne Field; m. Gerard Riendeau Evans, June 30, 1979. AB, Occidental Coll., 1968; MA, Fletcher Sch., 1977, MA in Law & Diplomacy, 1977; postgrad., Nat. War Coll., 1988-89. Commd. ensign USN, 1968, advanced through grades to rear admiral, 1993, ret., 1998; mideast policy officer Commander-in-Chief, U.S. Naval Forces, Europe, London, 1977-79; spl. asst. to sec. US Dept. Treasury, Washington, 1979-80; staff analyst Office of Chief Naval Ops., Washington, 1980-81; dep. dir. Pres. Commn. on White House Fellowships, Washington, 1981-82; exec. officer Recruit Tng. Command, San Diego, 1982-84; commanding officer Naval Tech. Tng. Ctr., San Francisco, 1984-86; battalion officer, sr. lectr. polit. sci. U.S. Naval Acad., Annapolis, Md., 1986-88; chief of staff San Francisco Naval Base, 1989-91, US Naval Acad., Annapolis, Md., 1991-92; exec. dir. of the standing com. on mil. and civilian women Dept. Navy, US Dept. Def., 1992-93; comdr. Navy Recruiting Command, Washington, 1993-95; supt. Naval Postgrad. Sch., Monterey, Calif., 1995-97; CEO, nat. exec. dir. Girl Scouts U.S.A., NYC, 1998—2002; pres., CEO Am. Red Cross, Washington, 2002—05; acting commr. LPGA, Daytona Beach, Fla., 2009—10. Mem. bd. visitors U.S. Mil. Acad. at West Point, 2002-06; interim dir. George C. Marshall European Ctr. Security Studies, Garmisch Partenkirchen, Germany, 1996-97; bd. dirs. Weight Watchers Internat., Inc., 2002-, Huntsman Corp., 2005-, Office Depot, Inc., 2006-; mem. advisory coun., LPGA, 2007-08, bd. dirs., 2009-10. Advisory bd. Pew Partnership for Civic Change Pew Charitable Trusts; dir. Naval Acad. Found. White House fellow, 1979; Chief Naval Ops. scholar, 1976; named Exec. of the Yr., Not for Profit Times, 2005 Mem. Mortar Bd., Phi Beta Kappa. Office: c/o Office Depot Inc 2200 Old Germantown Rd Delray Beach FL 33445 Home: 169 Linkside Cir Ponte Vedra Beach FL 32082-2032 Personal E-mail: mevansnps@aol.com.

EVANS, SIR MARTIN J., biomedical researcher, educator; b. Gloucestershire, Eng., Jan. 1, 1941; m. Judith Evans; 3 children. BA in Biochemistry, Christ Coll., U. Cambridge, 1963, MA, 1966, DSc, 1996; PhD in Embryology and Anatomy, Univ. Coll., London, 1969. Lectr. anatomy and embryology Univ. Coll., London; rschr. dept. genetics U. Cambridge, 1978—99; prof. mammalian genetics, dir. Sch. Biosciences Cardiff U., Wales, 1999—2007; ret., 2007. Contbr. articles to profl. jours. Recipient William Bate Hardy prize, 1993, Albert Lasker award in basic med. rsch., 2001, Nobel prize in physiology/medicine, 2007; grantee Walter Cottman Fellowship, 1993. Fellow: Royal Soc. (Copley Gold Medal 2009), Acad. Med. Scis. (founding mem.). Achievements include development of the knockout mouse and the related technology of gene targeting, a method of using embryonic stem cells to create specific gene modifications in mice. Office: Cardiff Sch Biosciences Biomedical Bldg 911 Museum Ave Po Box CF10 3US Cardiff Wales Office Phone: +44 (0) 29 20 874122. Office Fax: +44 (0) 29 20 874116. E-mail: EvansMJ@cardiff.ac.uk. *

EVANS, PAUL, osteopathic physician; b. Nutley, NJ, May 23, 1950; m. Roxanne Romack. BS cum laude in Biology, U. Miami, 1972; DO, Phila. Coll. Osteo. Medicine, 1979. Diplomate Am. Bd. Family Medicine, Nat. Bd. Osteo. Examiners; cert. Am. Osteo. Bd. Family Practice. Commd. 2d lt. U.S. Army, 1972, advanced through grades to col., 1995; asst. chief mil. pers. U.S. Army Med. Svc. Corps, Frankfurt, Fed. Republic Germany, 1972-75; intern Letterman Army Med. Ctr., San Francisco, 1979-80; resident in family practice Womack Army Community Hosp., Ft. Bragg, N.C., 1980-82; dir. family practice quality assurance Tripler Army Med. Ctr., Hawaii, 1982-84, dir. residency tng. dept. family practice Hawaii, 1984-86; asst. prof. family practice, physician Uniformed Svcs. U. Health Scis., F. Edward Hebert Sch. Med., Bethesda, Md., 1986-92, clerkship dir., 1986-88, dir. continuing med. edn., 1987-91, asst. prof. mil. and emergency medicine, 1991-92; chief dept. family practice Reynolds Army Community Hosp., Ft. Sill, Okla., 1992-94, chief primary care, 1994-95, chmn. rsch. com., dir. hosp. continuing med. edn., 1992-95, dir. physicians asst. tng. program, dir. quality improvement, 1992-94; tchg. chief dept. family practice Madigan Army Med. Ctr., Tacoma, 1995-97, dir. primary care projects Tricare N.W., 1997-98, dir. primary care, mem. exec. bd. dirs., exec. adv. coun.; clin. assoc. prof. of family medicine U. Wash., 1996-98; ret. U.S. Army, 1998; assoc. dean curricular affairs, dir. ednl. resources/devel. Okla. State U. Ctr. Health Scis., Tulsa, 1998—2003; prof. family med., exec. coun. curriculum com., learning resources com. Okla. State U. Coll. Osteopathic Med., Tulsa, 1998—2003, dir. dept. edn. resources and devel., 1998—2003, prof. family medicine, 2003—04; chief acad. officer, founding dean Ga. campus Phila. Coll. Osteo. Medicine, Suwanee, Ga., 2004—10, founding dean, 2008—10; v.p., founding dean Marian U. Coll. Osteopathic Medicine, 2010—. Presenter, lectr., cons. in field; clin. faculty, family practice residency DeWitt Army Hosp., Ft. Belvoir, Va., 1986-89, 91-92, Malcolm Grow USAF Med. Ctr., Andrews AFB, Md., 1989-91; mem. Nat. Bd. Osteopathic Med. Examiners Competency and Evidence Based Medicine Com., 2005-09, cabinet mem., Mariam U. Administrv. Coun., mem., Ind. State Med. Assn., Am. Assn. Coll. Osteopathic Med. Deans Coun. Reviewer Am. Family Physician, Patient Care, Military Medicine, Family Medicine, Farmily Practice Mgmt.; mem. editl. bd. Jour. Am. Osteo. Assn., 2003—08; contbr. articles to profl. jours. Asst. med. dir. Old Dominion 100 Mile Run, Front Royal, Va., 1990, med. dir., 1991; asst. med. dir. Am. Diabetes Assn. Youth Camp, Honolulu, 1984, med. dir., 1985. USUHS grantee. Fellow Am. Acad. Family Physicians, Am. Osteo. Assn., Am. Coll. Osteo. Family Physicians; mem. AA Commn. Steering Com. (bd. deans retreat seminars 2008-10), Uniformed Svcs. Acad. Family Physicians (chmn. edn. com. 1993-97, sec.-treas. 1997-98), Soc. Tchrs. Family Medicine (genogram rsch. com. 1989-94, managed care com. 1997-2000, faculty devel. com. 1999-2003), Am. Osteo. Assn. (insp., AOA Commn. on Osteopathic Coll. Accreditation 2009-), Ind. Osteopathic Medicine Assn., Ind. Osteopathic Assn. (bd. trustees 2011-), Ind. Area Health Edn. Consortium (academic com. mem. 2011-), Ga. Osteo. Assn., Phila. Coll. Osteo. Medicine Alumni Assn. (life), Nat. Bd. Osteopathic Med. Examiners (blu ribbon panel mem.), Omicron Delta Kappa, Alpha Epsilon Delta. Avocations: nature art collecting, golf, birdwatching.

EVANS, PETER YOSHIO, ophthalmologist, educator; b. Tokyo, Dec. 19, 1925; came to the U.S., 1957; s. Paul Yuzuru Kawai and Vicki Wichgraf Evans; m. Helga Kemp, Sept. 19, 1953; children: Johannes, Marina, Michael, André, Thomas, Ursula, Christiane. MD, Innsbruck U., 1951. Resident Innsbruck (Austria) and Frankfurt (Germany) Univs., 1951-55; intern Sisters Charity Hosp., Buffalo, 1957-58; chief dept. ophthalmology D.C. Gen. Hosp., 1958-63; fellow Georgetown U., Washington, 1958-59, program dir. div. ophthalmology, 1963-69, chmn., 1969-83, prof., 1973-92, prof. emeritus, 1992—. Cons. D.C. Columbia Lighthouse for the Blind, 1959-63; sr. cons. D.C. Child and Maternal Welfare Dept., 1961-74; exec. v.p. Joint Commn. Allied Health Pers. in Ophthalmology, St. Paul, 1981-96; bd. dirs. Internat. Eye Found., 1999-2006. Author, producer scientific films; contbr. articles to profl. jours.; editor numerous jours. Recipient Man of Decade award, Joint Commn. on Allied Health Pers. in Ophthalmology, 1997, Promotion of Peace and Vision award, Internat. Eye Found., 2002. Fellow Am. Acad. Ophthalmology (Disting. Svc. award 1982), Austrian Ophthalm. Soc. (First Fuchs Meml. Lectr. 1975), German Ophthalm. Soc., Am.Austrian Cultural Soc. (pres. 1989-91), Cosmos Club D.C. Lutheran. Avocations: skiing, violin, photography, bridge, philately. Home and Office: 3113 Lewis Pl Falls Church VA 22042-2511 Home Phone: 703-573-6452. Personal E-mail: pye19@verizon.net.

EVANS, R. LEE, dean; b. Ga. BS in Pharmacy, U. Ga., 1971; PharmD, U. Tenn. Coll. Pharmacy, Memphis, 1973. Cert. psychiatric pharmacist. Resident hosp. pharmacy Med. Univ. SC; faculty U. Tenn. Coll. Pharmacy, 1973—75; various positions including project coord. & sect. head ambulatory care instruction U. Mo., Kansas City, 1975—87, prof. pharmacy practice & psychiatry, chmn. divsn. pharmacy practice, 1987—94; dean Auburn U. Harrison Sch. Pharmacy, Ala., 1994—. Contbr. articles to profl. jours., chapters to books. Recipient U. Kans. City Faculty Fellow award, 1986. Mem.: Ala. Higher Edn. Partnership, Am. Assn. Higher Edn., Ala. Pharmacist Assn., Am. Assn. Colleges of Pharmacy, Ala. Soc. Health Sys. Pharmacists, Am. Pharm. Assn., Am. Coll. Clin. Pharmacists, Am. Soc. Health Sys. Pharmacists. Office: Harrison Sch Pharmacy 2316 Walker Bldg Auburn University AL 36849 Office Phone: 334-844-8348. Office Fax: 334-844-8353. Business E-Mail: evansrl@auburn.edu.

EVANS, RICHARD H., hospital administrator; b. Ogden, Utah, June 13, 1944; s. Hubert H. Evans and Bety Jean (McVean) Roberts; m. Carla Elizabeth Blank, Oct. 18, 1968; children: Eric Richard, Jamie Elizabeth. BS in Bus. Adminstrn., U. Denver, 1966. Chmn. Evans Holdings, LLC., 1999; CEO Madison Sq. Garden Corp., Huizenga Sports, Entertainment Group; COO Gaylord Entertainment Co.; COO, corp. dir. Fla. Panther Holdings; chmn. LifePoint Hospitals, Inc.; With Walt Disney Prodns., Los Angeles and Orlando, 1966-73; dir., Ops. Ringling Bros. & Barnum & Bailey's Circus, Orlando, Fla., 1973-74; asst. mgr., dir., Ops. Marriott's Great America, San Francisco, 1974—75; v.p., prin. XCaliber Corp., Atlanta, 1975—77; pres., CEO & owner Leisure Gen. Corp., Atlanta, 1977—80; chmn., pres. & CEO Radio City Music Hall Prodns., Inc., NYC, 1980. Bd. dirs. Radio City Music Hall TV, N.Y.C. Bd. dirs. N.Y. Conv. and Visitors Bur., N.Y.C., 1982—, Boys Choir of Harlem, N.Y.C., 1984—; co-chmn. arts and entertainment adv. bd. N.Y.C. Partnership, Inc., 1983—; mem. bus. adv. bd. N.Y. State Dept. Commerce, 1984— Mem. Young Pres.' Orgn., Inc. (bd. dirs. Metro N.Y. chpt. 1985—), Assn. for a Better N.Y. Clubs: N.Y. Athletic. Avocations: jogging; swimming; weight-lifting; gardening; family. Office: LifePoint Hospitals Inc 103 Powell Ct Ste 200 Brentwood TN 37027 Office Phone: 614-372-8500. E-mail: richard.evans@lpnt.net. *

EVANS, RONALD M., microbiologist, educator; BA in Bacteriology, UCLA, 1970, PhD in Microbiology and Immunology, 1974. Asst. rsch. prof. dept. molecular cell biology Rockefeller U., NYC, 1975—78; from asst. to assoc. prof. tumor virology lab. Salk Inst. Biol. Studies Howard Hughes Med. Inst., La Jolla, Calif., 1978—84, sr. mem. molecular biology and virology lab. Salk Inst. Biol. Studies, 1984—86, prof. gene expression lab Salk Inst. Biol. Studies, 1986—, investigator, 1985—; prof., March of Dimes Chair in Molecular and Developmental Biology Salk Institute for Biol. Studies, San Diego. Adj. prof. dept. biology U. Calif., San Francisco, 1985—, adj. prof. dept. biomedical scis. Sch. Medicine, San Diego, 1989—, adj. prof. dept. neurosciences, 1995—; chmn. faculty Salk Inst. Biol. Studies Howard Hughes Med. Inst., La Jolla, 1993—94, La Jolla, 1997—98; mem. sci. adv. bd. SIBIA, 1983—; mem. external sci. adv. com. City of Hope, 1987; mem. molecular biology study sect. NIH, 1983—86, mem. molecular neurobiology study sect., 1984—85; mem. nat. adv. com. Pew Scholars Program in Biomedical Scis., 1987—2000; founder and chair sci. adv. bd. Ligand Pharm., 1988—; mem. program com. Searle Scholars, 1989—91; mem. Alfred P. Sloan Jr. selection com. GM Cancer Rsch. Found., 1991; organizer numerous confs. in field; mem. external sci. adv. bd. Mass. Gen. Hosp., 1996—; mem. sci. adv. bd. Dana Farber Cancer Inst., 1996—, Osaka Bioscience Inst., 1999—; S. Richard Hill, Jr. vis. prof. U. Ala., 1995; Woodward vis. prof. Meml. Sloan-Kettering, 1996; Burroughs Wellcome vis. prof. U. Mass., 1998; spkr. in field, lectr. Editor: Molecular Endocrinology, 1993—97; editor: (assoc. editor) Molecular Brain Rsch., 1985—93, Jour. Neuroscience, 1985—90, Neuron, 1987—93; mem. editl. bd. Receptors and Channels, 1992—93, Genes and Development, 1992—, Hormones and Signalling, 1996—; co-editor: Current Opinion in Cell Biology, 1993. Mem. fellowship screening com. Am. Cancer Soc., 1987—90. Recipient Gregory Pincus medal, Laurentian Soc., 1988, Louis S. Goodman and Alfred Gilman award, Am. Soc. Pharmacology and Exptl. Therapeutics, 1988, Van Meter/Rorer Pharm. prize, Am. Thyroid Assn., 1989, Gregory Pincus Meml. award, Worcester Found. Exptl. Biology, 1991, Rita Levi Montalcini award, Fidia Rsch. Found. Neuroscience, 1991, Osborne and Mendel award, Am. Inst. Nutrition, 1992, award for cancer rsch., Robert J. and Claire Pasarow Found., 1993, Transatlantic medal, Soc. Endocrinology, 1994, Dickson prize in medicine, U. Pitts., 1994—95, Morton award, U. Liverpool, Biochemical Soc., 1996, Gerald Aurbach Meml. award, Assn. Bone and Mineral Rsch., 1997, Fred Conrad Koch award, Endocrine Soc., 1999, award for disting. achievement in metabolic rsch., Bristol-Myers Squibb, 2000, Alfred P. Sloan Jr. prize, GM Cancer Rsch. Found., 2003, Albert Lasker award for Basic Med. Rsch., Lasker Found., 2004, Gairdner Found. Internat. award, 2006, Grande Médaille d'Or, France, 2005, Glenn T. Seaborg medal, 2005, Harvey prize in Human Health, 2006, Albany Med. Ctr. prize in Medicine and Biomedical Rsch., 2007; named Calif. Scientist of Yr., Calif. Mus. Sci., 1994, most cited researcher, Inst. Scientific Info., 1997; fellow, NIH, 1975—78; Rsch. Assoc. fellow, Cancer Rsch. Com. Calif., 1975. Mem.: NAS, Am. Philosophical Soc., Inst. Medicine, 2004, Am. Assn. Cancer Rsch. (chair cancer rsch. com. 2001, Pezcoller Internat. award 2001, Eleventh C.P. Rhoads Meml. award 1990), Am. Acad. Arts and Scis. (fellow), Harvey Soc., Am. Acad. Microbiology, Am. Soc. Microbiology (fellow), Soc. Neuroscience, Soc. Devel. Biology, Endocrine Soc. (Edwin B. Astwood Lectureship award 1993). Office: Salk Inst Biol Studies Howard Hughes Med Inst 10010 N Torrey Pines Rd La Jolla CA 92037 Office Phone: 858-453-4100 ext. 1302. Office Fax: 858-455-1349. Business E-Mail: evans@salk.edu. *

EVANS, THELMA JEAN MATHIS, retired internist; b. East St. Louis, Ill., Jan. 29, 1944; d. Clemmie and Catherine (Rose) Mathis; m. Timothy Charles Evans, June 29, 1968; children: Cynthia Marie, Catherine Elizabeth (twins). BS in Zoology with honors, U. Ill., 1967; MD, U. Ill., Chgo., 1969. Intern, then resident U. Ill. Hosp., Chgo., 1969-71, fellow in pulmonary medicine, 1971-73; med. dir., acute care unit Presbyn.-St. Luke's Hosp., Chgo., 1973-75, asst. to dir. emergency svcs., 1975-77; staff physician Health Specialists, S.C., Chgo., 1977-80, AT&T (Western Electric), Cicero, Ill., 1980-85, Health First, Inc., Chgo., 1985-89, Michael Reese Health Plan, Chgo., 1989-98; mem. adv. bd. Advocate Profl. Group, Chgo., 1998—2009; bd. dirs. Advocate Health Care Network, Chgo., 2000—. Instr., Rush Med. Coll., Chgo., 1973-84; tuberculosis control officer, infectious disease sect. Chgo. Dept. Health, 1976-77. V.p., Com. to Elect Timothy C. Evans, Chgo., 1989. Grantee, Chgo. Lung Assn., 1972-73. Fellow: ACP; mem.: AMA, AMWA, NAACP. Democrat. African Methodist Episcopal. Avocations: photography, gardening, collecting thimbles, bells and music boxes.

EVANS, TIMOTHY GRANT, dean, former international organization administrator; b. Jan. 10, 1961; BSS, U. Ottawa, Can., 1984; PhD in Agrl. Econ., U. Oxford, Eng., 1989; MD, McMaster U., Can., 1992. Intern Brigham and Women's Hosp., Boston, 1992—93, rsch. resident, 1992—96, jr. asst. resident, internal medicine, 1993—94, sr. asst. resident, internal medicine, 1994—96, attending physician, dept. gen. internal medicine and primary care, 1996—97; MacArthur fellow Harvard Ctr. for Population and Devel. Studies, 1992—94; asst. prof., internat. health econ. Harvard U. Sch. Pub. Health, 1995—97; team dir., health equity program The Rockefeller Found., 1997—2003; asst. dir. gen. evidence and info. for policy WHO, Geneva, 2003—07, asst. dir. gen. info., evidence and rsch., 2007—10; dean James P. Grant Sch. Pub. Health at Bangladesh Rural Advancement Com. U., 2010—. Fellow, Internat. Exchange of Experts in Rehab., 1994; scholar, Can. Internat. Devel. Agy., 1986—87; Rhodes Scholar, U. Oxford, 1984—88. Office: James P Grant Sch Pub Health BRAC University 66 Mohakhali Dhaka 1212 Bangladesh Office Phone: 88 02 8824051 4 ext. 4135. Business E-Mail: evanst@bracu.ac.bd. *

EVANS, WAYNE, obstetrician, perinatologist; b. Cin., Apr. 13, 1954; s. Johnnie Kate and Wilbur Evans; m. Jacqueline Evette Brown, Apr. 1, 2001; children: Karoline Odessa, David Wayne;. BS in Biology, Marietta Coll., 1976; AAS Physician Asst., Cin. Tech. Coll., 1978; MD, Med. Coll. of Ohio, Toledo, 1981. Diplomate Am. Bd. Ob-Gyn., Am. Bd. Maternal-Fetal Medicine. Resident, ob-gyn. Good Samaritan Hosp., Cin., 1981—85; gen. obstetrician-gynecologist Milw. Comprehensive Cmty. Health, Milw., 1985—86, MetroHealth of Ind., Indpls., 1986—89, USPHS, Carl Albert Indian Health Facility, Ada, Okla., 1989—91; fellow, critical care medicine U. of Md./RA Crowley Shock Trauma Ctr., Balt., 1991—92; fellow, maternal fetal medicine U. of Pitts./ Magee Womens Hosp., Pitts., 1992—94; dir. of perinatology/clin. asst. prof. U. of Wis. Med. Sch.- Milw. Clin. Campus, 1994—. Dir. of perinatology Aurora Sinai Med. Ctr., Milw., 1995—. Author: (novel) I Seek You, 2001. 0-6 comdr. USPHS, 1989—91, Ada, Okla. Mem.: AMA, State Med. Soc. of Wis., Nat. Perinatal Assn., Soc. of Obstetric Medicine, Milw. Gynecologic Soc. (assoc.). Home: 18149 Lake Shore Dr Orland Park IL 60467-5220 E-mail: docdub@hotmail.com.

EVANS, WILLIAM EDWARD, hospital administrator, pharmacist, researcher; b. Clarksville, TN, June 27, 1950; s. Buford Joseph and Wanda (Wilson) Evans; m. Diana D. Miller, Sept. 2, 1972; children: Leslie, Kelli McDonald. Pharm.D., U. Tenn., 1974. Asst. prof. Health Sci. Ctr., U. Tenn., Memphis, 1974—75, assoc. prof., 1976—80, prof., 1983—2002; mem., chair St. Jude Children's Rsch. Hosp., Memphis, 1986—2002, dep. dir., exec. v.p., 1999—2002, sci. dir., dep. dir., 2002—04, dir., CEO, 2004—. Editor Pharmacogenetics Journal, London, 2000—00. Editor: (textbook) Applied Pharmacokinetics, 1981 (Volhwiler Award, 1995); author: Pharmacogenomics (Tyler Prize, 2002). Board of Directors Memphis Area Chamber of Commerce, Memphis, 2000—02. Recipient MERIT Award, NIH, 1987, 1995. Fellow: AAAS (Chair, Pharmaceutical Sciences 1998—99), Am. Coll. Clin Pharmacolog (President 1982—83, Therapeutic Frontier Lecture Award 1992); mem.: Am. Soc. Clin. Pharmacology and Therapeutics, Am. Assn. for Cancer Rsch., Am. Soc. Clin. Oncology. Republican. Methodist. Avocation: Golf. Office: St Jude Children's Rsch Hosp 332 N Lauderdale Memphis TN 38105 Home Phone: 901-386-7829; Office Phone: 901-495-3663. Office Fax: 901-525-6869. E-mail: william.evans@stjude.org.

EVANS, WILLIAM LEE, biologist, educator; b. Calvert, Tex., Aug. 28, 1924; s. James Herman and Lilly Australia (O'Neal) E.; m. Lillian Mary Madden, July 30, 1948; children: Kathy A. Timmons, David C. Evans, Susan D. Hinson. BA with honors, U. Tex., Austin, 1949, MA,

1950, PhD, 1955; cert., Electron Microscope Sch., Berkeley, Calif., 1966. Mem. faculty U. Ark., Fayetteville, 1955-89, prof. zoology, 1968-89, prof. emeritus, 1989, chmn. gen. biology, 1967-70. Mem. health professions adv. com. Fulbright Coll. Arts and Scis., 1982-89, chmn. 1987-89, mem. Coll. Cabinet Author articles, lab. manuals. Capt. AUS, 1942-46, USAF, 1947-52. Decorated Air medal with oak leaf cluster; recipient Classrm. Tchg. award, Omicron Delta Kappa, 1959; grantee, NSF, 1959—62, U. Ark. Found., 1979, Fullbright Coll. Arts and Sci., 1982. Mem. Ark. Acad. Sci. (treas. 1972-82, pres. 1984-85), Am. Philatelic Soc., Nat. Wildlife Fed., Am. Legion, The History Channel Club, Phi Beta Kappa, Sigma Xi, Phi Eta Sigma, Phi Sigma.

EVANS BERNSTEIN, LORI, health care executive; BA, Ohio Wesleyan U.; MPH, George Wash. U. Rschr. ctr. for health svcs. rsch.and policy George Wash. Univ.; health policy analyst inst. for health policy studies Univ. of Calif. San Francisco Sch. of Medicine; with Kaiser Permanente Med. Group; CEO ActiveHealth Mgmt.; founding mng. dir. Manatt Health Solutions; dir. care data exch. divsn. CareScience; dep. commr. Dept. of Health, NY; sr. advisor to Dr. David Brailer US Dept. of Health and Human Svcs.; inaugural mem. Office of the Nat. Coord. for Health Info. Tech.; bd. dirs. National eHealth Collaborative (NeHC); bd. trustees Certification Commn. for HealthCare IT (CCHIT); pres. GSI Health. Named 2007 Rising Star, Modern Healthcare; named to 40 under 40 Bus. Leader, Crain's NY Bus. Publ., 2009. Office: GSI Health 8327 Germantown Ave Philadelphia PA 19118 Office Phone: 888-206-4237. Office Fax: 888-423-8759.

EVARTS, C. MCCOLLISTER, orthopedist, health science association administrator; s. Charles Melville and Laura McCOLLISTER Evarts; m. Nancy L. Lyons, July 2, 1955; children: Cynthia Evarts Goldberg, Charles Mark, Robert Alan. BA, Colgate U., Hamilton, NY, 1953; MD, NY, 1958. Diplomate Am. Bd. Orthopaedic Surgery. Chair, dept. orthopaedic surgery Cleve. Clinic, 1964—74; prof. & chair, dept. orthopaedics U. Rochester Sch. Medicine & Dentistry, NY, 1974—86; sr. v.p. health affairs & dean, Coll. Medicine Pa. State U., Hershey, 1987—2000; sr. v.p. & vice provost health affairs, CEO U. Rochester Med. Ctr., 2003—06; disting. prof. & prof. orthopaedics U. Rochester, 2006—. Cons. NYU, NYC, 2006 09. Author: (orthopaedic text book) Surgery Of The Musculoskeletal System; contbr. articles to profl. jours. Lt. comdr. USN, 1959—61, Pensacola, Fla. Recipient Charnley award, Hip Soc., 1996, Alpha David Kaiser medal, Rochester Acad. Medicine, 2005, Disting. Alumnus award, U. Rochester Sch. Medicine & Dentistry, 2007. Mem.: Inst. Medicine, Hip Soc. (pres. 1984—89), Assoc. Orthopedic Chairmen, Am. Bd. Orthopedic Surgery (pres. 1985—86), Am. Acad. Orthopedic Surgeons, Am. Orthopedic Assn. (pres. 1984—85, Aoa-zimmer award 2006), Alpha Omega Alpha. Avocation: woodworking. Office: University Rochester 601 Elmwood Ave Box Son Rochester NY 14642 Office Fax: 585-276-2322. Business E-Mail: mac_evarts@urmc.rochester.edu.

EVENS, RONALD GENE, radiologist, educator, health facility administrator; b. St. Louis, Sept. 24, 1939; s. Robert and Dorothy (Lupkey) E.; m. Hanna Blunk, Sept. 3, 1960; children: Ronald Jr., Christine, Amanda. BA, Washington U., 1960, MD, 1964, postgrad. in bus. and edn., 1970-71. Intern Barnes Hosp., St. Louis, 1964-65; resident Mallinckrodt Inst. Radiology, St. Louis, 1965-66, 68-70; rsch. assoc. Nat. Heart Inst., 1966-68; asst. prof. radiology, v.p. Washington U. Med. Sch., 1970-71, prof., head dept. radiology, dir., 1971-72, Elizabeth Mallinckrodt prof., head radiology dept. St. Louis, 1972-99, prof. med. econs., 1988—; pres., sr. exec. ofcr. Barnes-Jewish Hosp., St. Louis, 1999—2005. Radiologist-in-chief Barnes Hosp., St. Louis, 1971-99; radiologist-in-chief Children's Hosp., 1971-99, pres., chief exec. officer, 1985-88; vice chancellor fin. Washington U., St. Louis, 1988-91; mem. adv. com. on splty. and geog. distbn. of physicians Inst. Medicine, Nat. Acad. Scis., 1974-76, Hickey lectr., 1976, Carmen lectr. Calif. U., 1985, Kiewit lectr. Eisenhower Med. Ctr., 1986; Hornick lectr. U. Pitts., 1986; ann. orator Can. Radiol. Soc., 1984; Hodes lectr. Jefferson U., 1991—; Smith lectr. Royal Coll. Physicians, Edinburgh, 1992; Seaman lectr. Columbia Presbyn., 1992; dir. Boatmens Bank Inc., Mallinckrodt Group Inc., Right Choice Inc., Blue Choice, Inc.; chmn. bd. Med. Care Group St. Louis, 1980-86. Contbr. over 210 articles to profl. jours. Active Boy Scouts Am., 1975—; elder Glendale Presbyn. Ch., 1971-74, Kirkwood Presbyn. Ch., 1983-86. Served with USPHS, 1966-68. Advance Acad. fellow James Picker Found, 1970; recipient Disting. Svc. award. St. Louis C. of C., 1972; named Disting. Eagle Scout Nat. Coun., 1983. Fellow Am. Coll. Radiology (chair elect 1995, chair bd. chancellors 1996—); mem. AMA (editl. bd. JAMA), Mo. Radiol. Soc. (pres. 1977-78), Soc. Nuclear Medicine (trustee 1971-75), St. Louis Med. Soc., Mo. State Med. Assn., Soc. Chmn. Acad. Radiology Depts. (pres. 1979), Radiol. Soc. N.Am., Assn. Univ. Radiologists (pres. 1988), Am. Roentgen Ray Soc. (pres. 1989), Phi Beta Kappa, Alpha Omega Alpha (Sheard-Sanford award). Address: Barnes-Jewish Hosp One Barnes-Jewish Hospital Plz Saint Louis MO 63110 Office: Mallinckrodt Inst Radiology 510 S Kings Hwy Saint Louis MO 63110-1016

EVERETT, ERIC THOMAS, dental educator; b. Orleans, France, Aug. 2, 1959; MS, U. Fla., 1989; PhD, Med. U. SC, 1993. Assoc. prof. Ind. U., 1996—2004, U. NC, Chapel Hill, 2004—10, prof., 2010—. Recipient Trustees Tchg. award, Ind. U. Sch. Dentistry, Alumni Assn. Disting. Faculty award. Mem.: Nat. Dental Honor Soc., ASHG, IBMS, ASBMR, ACPA, IADR, Omicron Kappa Upsilon, Upsilon Upsilon Upsilon chpt. (hon.). Office: University NC Sch Dentistry CB# 7450 228 Brauer Hall Chapel Hill NC 27599 Business E-Mail: eric_everett@dentistry.unc.edu.

EVERITT, ARTHUR VINCENT, medical educator, physiologist; b. Sydney, Sept. 25, 1924; s. Raymond Vincent Everitt and Elaine Bertha Leahy; m. Joyce Nutt, Feb. 1957; children: Suzanne, Michael. AA, Sydney Tech. Coll., 1949; BSc, U. Sydney, 1953, PhD, 1959. Tchg. fellow in physiology U. Sydney, 1953—55, lectr. in physiology, 1956—58, 1960—64, sr. lectr. in physiology, 1965—72, assoc. prof. physiology, 1973—85, hon. assoc., 1987—2003, hon. assoc. prof. physiology, Sch. Med. Scis., Ctr. Edn. and Rsch. on Aging, 2004—; Nuffield travelling fellow Kings Coll., U. London, 1959; fellow Columbia U., NYC, 1960. Mem. editl. bd. Internat. Jour. Gerontology, 1960—2002; presenter in field. Author (editor): Hypothalamus, Pituitary and Aging, 1976, Calorie Restriction, Aging and Longevity, 2010; editor: Regulation of Neuroendocrine Aging, 1988; contbr. articles to profl. jours. Chmn. biol. scis. sect. Asia/Oceania region Internat. Assn. Gerontology, 1979—88. Recipient Disting. Achievement award, Am. Aging Assn., 2008. Fellow: Australian Assn. Gerontology (co-founder 1964), Gerontol. Soc. Am. Achievements include research in role of pituitary hormones and nutrition on aging; studies on healthy lifestyle in humans. Office: University Sydney Concord Hosp Sch Med Scis & Ctr Edn and Rsch on Aging Hospital Rd Sydney 2006 NSW Australia Personal E-mail: arthureveritt42@bigpond.com.

EVERS, KATHRYN ALICE, diagnostic radiologist; MD, NYU Sch. of Medicine, 1975. Diplomate Am. Bd. of Radiology-diagnostic radiology. Intern internal medicine U. of Conn. Health Ctr., 1976; resident diagnostic radiology Pa. Hosp., 1980, fellow diagnostic radiology, 1981; dir. mammography Fox Chase Cancer Center. Named top. dr., Phila. Mag., 2007, 2010. Mem.: Am. Soc. of Therapeutic Radiology and Oncology, Am. Soc. of Radiologic Technologists, Am. Coll. of Radiology. Office: Fox Chase Cancer Center 333 Cottman Ave Philadelphia PA 19111 Office Phone: 215-728-3024.

EVERSON, MARK WHITTY, commissioner; b. NYC, Sept. 10, 1954; s. Leonard Charles and Marjory (Whitty) Everson; m. Nanette Rutka (div. 2008); 2 children. BA, Yale U., 1976; MS in Acctg., NYU, 1977. Staff acct. Arthur Andersen & Co., NYC, 1976—78, sr. acct., 1978—81, mgr., 1981—82; spl. project officer US Info. Agy. (USIA), 1982—83, spl. asst. to the dir., asst. dir., 1983—85; spl. asst. to Atty. Gen. Edwin Meese US Dept. Justice, 1985—86; exec. assoc. commr. Immigration and Naturalization Svc., 1986—87, dep. commr., 1987—88; various fin. & operations positions in the United States, France and Turkey Pechiney Group, 1988—98; group v.p. fin. SC Internat. Svcs., Inc., 1998—2001; contr. fed. fin. mgmt. Office Mgmt. & Budget, Exec. Office of the Pres., Washington, 2001—02, dep. dir. for mgmt., 2002—03; commr. IRS, Washington, 2003—07; pres., CEO Am. Red Cross, Washington, 2007; commr. dept. administrn. Ind., 2008; sr. advisor Dynamics. Home: 350 N Moridian St Apt 702 Indianapolis IN 46204

EVERT, SANDRA FLORENCE (SANDRA WHEELER), medical/surgical nurse, consultant; b. Saginaw, Mich., Sept. 18, 1949; d. Charles William and Florence Arlene (Babcock) Wheeler; m. Raymond Clyde Evert, Jan. 20, 1968; children: Christine Michelle, Raymond Clyde II. AD cum laude, Lansing C.C., 1986. Phlebotomist, med.-surg. E.W. Sparrow Hosp., Lansing, Mich., 1980—86, staff nurse, 1986, geriatric nurse, 1986—. Mem. 1st United Pentecostal Ch., The Liberty Ch. Grand Ledge, Mich., 1988. Mem. Apostolic Ch. Avocations: Bible reading, Christian music, travel, camping. Home: 10 Willard Ct Grand Ledge MI 48837-1356 Office Phone: 517-230-6981, 517-256-9955. Personal E-mail: sandraevert@comcast.net.

EVETT, RUSSELL DOUGHERTY, internist, educator; b. Norfolk, Va., Feb. 1, 1932; s. Edward Hall and Elizabeth (Dougherty) E.; m. Mary Gail Kirby, Aug. 18, 1956; children: Stephen, Anne, Gail, John. BS, Randolph-Macon Coll., 1953; MD, Med. Coll. Va., 1957; MS in Medicine, Mayo Clinic and U. Minn., 1963. Diplomate Am. Bd. Internal Medicine. Intern DePaul Hosp., Norfolk, 1957-58; fellow in internal medicine Mayo Clinic, Rochester, Minn., 1960-63; pvt. practice internal medicine Norfolk, 1964—98. Pres. med. staff Leigh Meml. Hosp., Norfolk, 1970-72; chmn. dept. internal medicine Norfolk Gen. Hosp., 1972-74; assoc. prof. medicine Ea. Va. Med. Sch., 1974-98; mem. staff Med. Ctr. Hosps., DePaul Hosp., to 1998; mem. Va. Health Info. Bd., 1997—; bd. dirs. Med. Coll. Va. Found., 1998—. Served with USNR, 1958-60. Mem. Va. Health Info. Bd., 1997—, Served with USNR, 1958-60. Fellow ACP (Laureate award 1997); mem. Va. Gastroent. Soc. (pres. 1975-77), Norfolk Acad. Medicine (pres. 1976-77), Med. Soc. Va. (pres. 1994-95), AMA (alt. del. 1985-95, del. 1995-99), Norfolk Cmty. Svcs. Bd.,(chmn. 2007-08), So. Med. Assn., Norfolk Yacht and Country Club, Harbor Club, Phi Beta Kappa, Omicron Delta Kappa, Alpha Omega Alpha, Norfolk Hist. Soc. Bd. Methodist. Home: One Colley Ave Apt 816 Norfolk VA 23510

EVIATAR, LYDIA, pediatrician, neurologist; b. Bucharest, Romania, Apr. 7, 1936; came to U.S., 1966; d. Joseph and Ghitea (Scheinberg) Tamir; m. Abraham Eviatar, Oct. 9, 1956; children: Joseph, Daphne. BSc, Faculte des Scis., Strasbourg, 1954; MD, Hadassah Hebrew U., Jerusalem, 1961. Diplomate Am. Bd. Pediatrics, Am. Bd. Neurology with spl. competence in child neurology. Intern and resident Tel Hashoner Hosp., Tel Aviv, 1961-65; U.C.P. fellow UCLA, 1966-67, fellow in pediatric neurology, 1967-69; pediatric neurologist Bronx (N.Y.) Lebanon Hosp., 1970-79; resident in neurology Montefiore Hosp. Med. Ctr., Bronx, 1973-75; pediatric neurologist L.I. Jewish Med. Ctr., 1979-86; chief pediatric neurology Schneider Children's Hosp., New Hyde Park, NY, 1986-99; from assoc. prof. to prof. pediatrics and neurology Albert Einstein Coll. Medicine, Bronx, NY, 1989-99, chief emeritus Pediat. Neurology Sch., 1999—. Co-author: (with others) Pediatric Neurology, 1988, 2004. Grantee Nat. Inst. Neurol. Disease and Blindness, 1970-77, Acad. Cerebral Palsy, 1980-81, Richmond award, 1981; recipient teaching award Am. Acad. Otolaryngology, 1983. Fellow Am. Acad. Pediatrics, Am. Acad. Neurology (cert. neurologist, child neurologist); mem. Epilepsy Soc., Child Neurological Soc. Office Phone: 516-465-5225.

EVRON, WAYNE A., endocrinologist; MD, U. Pa., 1980. Diplomate Am. Bd. Internal Medicine, Am. Bd. Internal Medicine-endocrinology and metabolism, lic. Pa., 1982. Intern Shands Tchg. Hosp., Gainesville, Fla., Univ. Pitts. Med. Ctr.; resident Univ. Pitts. Med. Ctr. - Presbyn. Hosp. Pitts., fellow; assoc. med. dir. Joslin diabetes ctr. affiliate The Western Pa. Hosp., hosp. affiliations include, Alle-Kiski Med. Ctr., Monongahela Valley Hosp., West Penn Hosp. Forbes Campus, The Western Pa. Hosp. - Forbes Regional Camp. Named one of Top Doctors, Pitts. Mag., 2011. Office: The Western Pennsylvania Hospital 4800 Friendship Ave Pittsburgh PA 15224 Office Phone: 412-683-4550. Office Fax: 412-683-3233.

EWARD, WILLIAM, veterinarian, orthopedist; b. Winter Pk., Fla., May 2, 1974; DVM, Auburn U. Coll. Vet. Medicine, 2000; MD, U. Vt. Coll. Medicine, 2006. Intern, small animal surgery and medicine Ont. Vet. Coll., 2000—01; asst. prof. Auburn U. Coll. Vet. Medicine, 2001—02; staff veterinarian Burlington Emergency Vet. Svcs., 2002—06; resident, orthop. surgery Duke U. Med. Ctr., 2006—11; fellow, orthop. oncology U. Toronto, 2011—. Recipient Young Achiever award, Auburn U. Coll. Vet. Medicine, Harrelson Chief Resident Tchg. award, Duke U., Orthop. Trauma Assn. PGY-3 Resident Tchg. award, James E. Demeules Surg. Rsch. prize, U. Vt. Coll. Medicine. Mem.: AMA, AVMA, Alpha Omega Alpha. Avocations: fishing, sports, languages. Home: 101 Wood Valley Ct Durham NC 27713 Business E-Mail: w.eward@alumni.duke.edu.

EWART-SMITH, MIKE, psychiatrist; b. Edinburgh, Oct. 11, 1937; MBChB, Edinburgh, 1962; M in Med. Psychology, U. Witwatersrand, 1982. Prin. psychiatrist U. Witwatersrand, 1986—95, hon. clin. cons., 2000—. Convenor, task team disability South African Soc. Psychiatrists, 2004, convenor, divsn. ethics & peer rev., 2008—10. Avocations: history, music. Office: PO Box 6109 Weltevredenpark Gauteng 1715 South Africa Office Fax: 086-689-1576. E-mail: mesmith@mweb.co.za.

EWIN, DABNEY MINOR, surgeon; b. New Orleans, Dec. 7, 1925; s. James Perkins and Lucille Havard (Scott) E.; m. Ethelyn Alexander Sherrouse, June 6, 1951 (div. 1968); children: Dabney Jr., Constance, Walton, Christopher, Leila; m. Marilyn Allison Abernathy, June 29, 1968. MD, Tulane U., 1951. Intern Jefferson-Hillman Hosp. U. Ala., Birmingham, 1951, resident, 1951-54, Ochsner Found. Hosp., New Orleans, 1954-56; chief resident Huey P. Long Charity Hosp., Pineville, La., 1956-57; pvt. practice, 1957—99; staff physician Concentra Med. Ctrs., 1999—. Cons. staff Touro Infirmary, New Orleans; staff surgeon Charity Hosp. La.; clin. prof. surgery and psychiatry Tulane Med. Sch.; clin. prof. psychiatry La. State U. Contbr. articles to profl. jours. Bd. dirs. Christ Sch., 1979-85; sr. class Sunday sch. tchr. Trinity Episc. Ch., 1960-66. Fellow ACS; mem. AMA (life), Am. Trauma Soc. (dir. 1975-79), Am. Burn Assn., Am. Coll. Occup. and Environ. Medicine (spkr. Ho. of Dels., 1973-75), Am. Bd. Med. Hypnosis (past pres.), Am. Soc. Clin. Hypnosis (past pres.), La. State Med. Soc., Orleans Parish Med. Soc., Surg. Assn. La., New Orleans Surg. Soc., Alton Ochsner Surg. Soc. (past sec.), So. Med. Assn. (chmn. sect. on indsl. medicine and surgery 1966-67), Soc. for Clin. and Exptl. Hypnosis, La. Psychiat. Med. Assn. Republican. Avocations: fishing, tennis. Office: 318 Baronne St New Orleans LA 70112-1606 Home Phone: 504-861-1751; Office Phone: 504-561-1051. Personal E-mail: dabneyewin@aol.com.

EWING, MARY EILEEN, radiologic technologist; b. Morning Sun, Iowa, Aug. 26, 1926; d. Frank Leeman and Myrtle Marguerite (Mehaffy) Steele; m. Dean Willard Ewing, Mar. 29, 1952; children: John, Eileen, Diane, Denise. BS in Radiologic Tech., St. Louis U., 1948. Registered technologist. Staff technologist Mo. Pacific Hosp., St. Louis, 1948-52, Blanchard Valley Hosp., Findlay, Ohio, 1968-69, asst. chief technologist, 1969-80, asst. dir. dept., 1980-90. Clin. instr. Lima (Ohio) Tech. Coll., 1978-90; sec. N.W. Libr. Dist. Exec. Bd., 1988-97. Trustee McComb Pub. Libr., Ohio 1957-2002; pres. Libr. Bd., McComb, 1967-2002; elder ck. of session, 1994—2007. Mem.: Nat. Soc. DAR (Ft. Findlay chpt. sec. 1993—94, regent 1995—2001, Ft. Findlay chpt. sec. 2001—03, state chmn. Am. heritage com. 2007—10, sec. 2008—09, historian 2010—), Findlay China Painters, Internat. Porcelain Artists and Tchrs. (treas. 2002—04), Mansfield World Orgn. China Painters (pres. 2000—01), Philomath Club (pres. 1958, 1995—98). Democrat. Presbyterian. Avocations: porcelain painting, reading, genealogy, bridge. Home Phone: 419-306-3028. E-mail: Mary_Ewing@woh.rr.com.

EWING, SCOTT EDWIN, physician, psychiatrist, educator; b. Seattle, July 2, 1956; s. Edwin Stanley Jr. and Mary Alice (Castleman) E.; m. Eileen Smith, June 9, 1990; 1 child, Edwin Stanley III. BS, U. Mich., 1980; DO, Midwestern U., 1989. Diplomate Am. Osteo. Bd. Neurology and Psychiatry; MD, Mass. Resident in psychiatry Mass. Gen. Hosp., Boston, 1991-94; clin. fellow in psychiatry Harvard Med. Sch., Boston, 1991-94; chief resident in psychiatry Mass. Gen. Hosp., Boston, 1993-94; fellow in psychopharmacology Harvard Med. Sch., Boston, 1994-95; psychiatrist in charge short term unit McLean Hosp., Belmont, Mass., 1995-96; instr. in psychiatry Harvard Med. Sch., Boston, 1995—; dir. depression and anxiety disorders outpatient clinic McLean Hosp., Belmont, 1996—. Cons. Harvard Pilgrim Health Plan, Boston, 1995-2003. Contbg. author: (book) Challenges in Psychiatric Treatment: Pharmacologic and Psychosocial Strategies, 1996; patentee in field. Mem. Nat. Trust for Hist. Preservation, Washington, 1995—. Recipient Outstanding Resident award NIMH, 1992, Laughlin fellowship Am. Coll. Psychiatrists, 1993, Dupont-Warren fellowship Harvard Med. Sch. Dept. of Psychiatry, 1994-95, Livingston award, 1995. Mem. AMA, Am. Psychiat. Assn., Am. Osteo. Assn., N.Y. Acad. Scis., Am. Coll. Neuropsychiatrists, Harvard Club of Boston, Harvard Faculty Club, Sigma Sigma Phi. Avocations: creative writing, photography, athletics. Office Phone: 617-233-0344.

EWING, SIDNEY ALTON, veterinary medical educator, parasitologist; b. Emory Univ., Ga., Dec. 1, 1934; s. Aubrey Coleman and Grace Eliza (Prickett) E.; m. Margaret Jane Steffens, Aug. 16, 1963; children— Holly Annette, Ann Krull, Leah Grace. BSA, DVM, U. Ga., 1958; MS, U. Wis., 1960; PhD, Okla. State U., 1964. Instr. U. Wis., 1960; mem. faculty Okla. State U., Stillwater, 1960—65, 1968—72, prof., head dept. vet. parasitology, microbiology and public health, 1968—72, 1979—84, prof., 1984—91, interim assoc. dean for acad. affairs, 1991—92, 2001—03, Wendell H./Nellie G. Krull endowed prof. vet. parasitology, 1992—2003, Wendell H./Nellie G. Krull prof. emeritus, 2004—; assoc. prof. Kans. State U., 1965—67; prof., head dept. Miss. State U., 1967—68; prof., dean Coll. Vet. Medicine, U. Minn., St. Paul, 1972—78. Adv. bd. Morris Animal Found., Denver, 1967-69, cons., 1969-78; animal health com. NRC, 1971-75; adv. panel U.S. Pharmacopeial Conv., 1980-95 Recipient Outstanding Tchr. of Yr. award Okla. State U. Coll. Vet. Medicine, 1970, SmithKline Beecham award for rsch. excellence Okla. State U., 1991, A.M. Mills award for outstanding contbns. to vet. medicine, 1993, Good Neighbor award Radio Sta. WCCO, Mpls.-St. Paul, 1978; commendation Gov. Minn., 1978; named Veterinarian of Yr., State of Okla., 1997; named to Okla. Higher Edn. Hall of Fame, 2000, Paul Harris fellowship, 2009 Mem. AAUP, AVMA, Am. Assn. Vet. Parasitologists (Disting. Vet. Parasitologist 2002), Am. Soc. Parasitologists, Am. Vet. Med. History Soc., Am. Soc. Rickettsiology, World Assn. Advancement Vet. Parasitology, Conf. Rsch. Workers in Animal Diseases (coun. 1980-85, v.p. 1983-84, pres. 1984-85, dedicatee, 89th Ann. Meeting, 2008), Soc. Vector Ecology, Soc. Tropical Vet. Medicine, Minn. Vet. Med. Assn., Okla. Vet. Med. Assn., NY Acad. Sci., Southwestern Assn. of Parasitologists (program officer, pres. elect 2001-02, pres. 2002-2003), Sigma Xi, Phi Kappa Phi, Phi Zeta, Alpha Zeta, Alpha Psi (past nat. pres.), Gamma Sigma Delta, Aghon, Omicron Delta Kappa Office: Okla State U Dept Vet Pathobiology Stillwater OK 74078-2005 Office Phone: 405-744-8177.

EXBRAYAT, JEAN-MARIE, biologist, researcher, histologist, educator; b. Besseges, Gard, France, Mar. 30, 1952; s. Fernand and Marie-Rose (Vitalis) Exbrayat; m. Pascale Pionchon, Sept. 16, 1978; children: Philippe, Jean-François. Grad., Acad. Montpellier, France, 1970; MS, U. Montpellier, 1974, PhD, 1977; DSc, U. Paris, 1986. Maitre-asst. Cath. U., Lyon, France, 1979-86, lectr., 1986-87, prof., 1987—, dean sci. faculty, 1997—2005, hon. dean, 2005—; dir. Ecole Pratique Hautes Etudes, Lyon, France, 1991—. Author: Cahier de l'Institut Catholique de Lyon, 1993, Ecotoxicity of Chemicals to Amphibians, 1992, Evolution Biologique, 1989, L'origine des espèces aujourd'hui, 1995, L'evolution biologique, science, histoire ou philosophie?, 1997, Les Gymnophiones ces curieux amphibiens, 2000, Methodes classiques de visualisation du genome en microscopie photonique, 2000, Genome Visualization by Classic Methods in Light Microscopy, 2001, L'èvolution Biologique faits Thèories-èpistèmologie Philosophie, 2002, The Mediterranean Man and His Environment (in French), 2004, Reproductive Biology and Phylogeny of Gymnophiona, 2006, Nature and Creation Between Science and Theology (in French), 2006. Decorated knight Merit Nat. Order, Acad. Palms. Mem.: N.Y. Acad. Scis., Societas Europaea Herpetologica, Zool. Soc. France, French Herpetological Soc. Roman Catholic. Office: Cath Univ 25 Rue Du Plat 69288 Lyon France Office Phone: 33 04 72 32 50 36 Fax: 33-04-72-32-50-66. E-mail: jmexbrayat@univ-catholyon.fr.

EYBL, VLADISLAV, pharmacologist; b. Pisek, Czechoslovakia, June 20, 1932; s. Antonin and Marie E.; m. Marie Lucakova, May 7, 1958; 1 child, Vladislava. MD, Charles U., 1957, PhD, 1964; DSc, Czech Acad. Sci., 1985. From asst. prof. to prof. med. faculty Charles U., Pilsen, Czech Republic, 1957—. Avocation: music. Office: Charles Univ Med Faculty in Pilsen 301 66 Plzen Czech Republic Home Phone: 420 377 374 501; Office Phone: 420 377 593 242. Business E-Mail: vladislav.eybl@lfp.cuni.cz.

EYDELMAN, MALVINA BERTHA, ophthalmologist; b. Tbilisi, Georgia, July 20, 1966; BS in Elect. Engring., Cooper Union, 1987; MD, Harvard Med. Sch., 1991. Intern & resident Long Island Jewish Hosp.; sr. med. adv. Divsn. Opthalmic & ENT Devices FDA Ctr. for Devices & Radiological Health; rep. for WG7-Ophthalmic Implants Internat. Standards Org. Achievements include patents for new instrumentation for testing and treatment of visual dysfunctions. Office: FDA Division of Ophthalmic and ENT Devices 10903 New Hampshire Ave Silver Spring MD 20903-0002 Office Phone: 240-276-4200.

EYO, MARY UMOH, radiologist, consultant; b. Enugu, Nigeria, Nov. 11, 1958; d. Paul Louis and Ekanem Louis Eyo. MBBS, U. Lagos, 1981, FWACS, 1993, MSc in Anatomy, 2003. Med. officer Tchg. Hosp. Lagos (Nigeria) U., 1981—82; med. doctor-in-charge Alpha Hosps., Lagos, 1983—88; jr. registrar Tchg. Hosp. Lagos (Nigeria) U., 1988—92, sr. registrar, 1992—93; cons. radiologist Ojuelegba X-Ray and Scan Ctr. Glory-N-Heritage Hosp., Lagos, 1993—2003; cons. radiologist Nat. Orthop. Hosp., Lagos, 1999—. Nat. youth corp. doctor Ikorodu Maternity, Lagos, 1982—83; cons. in field; mem. Nigerian Med. and Dental Coun., 1981—. Mem. editl. bd.: Igbobi Jour., 2003—; contbr. articles to profl. jours. Fellow: West African Coll. Surgeons; mem.: Med. and Dental Cons. Assn. Nigeria. Avocations: singing, sewing, reading, interior decorating, languages. Home: No 1 Mogaji Close Surulere Lagos Nigeria Office: National Orthopaedic Hospital Igbobi Nigeria Office Phone: 01-5820504 ext. 281.

EYSTER, MARY ELAINE, hematologist, educator; m. Robert E. Dye, Jan. 2, 1965; children: Robert E. Dye, Charles Dye. AB, Duke U., 1956, MD, 1960. Intern. N.Y. Hosp.-Cornell Med. Coll., NYC, 1960-61, resident in medicine, 1961-63, fellow in hematology, 1963-66, instr. medicine, 1966-67, asst. prof. medicine, 1967-70; asst. prof. medicine Milton S. Hershey Med. Ctr. Pa. State U., Hershey, 1970-73, assoc. prof. Milton S. Hershey Med. Ctr., 1973-82, prof. Milton S. Hershey Med. Ctr., 1982—, chief hematology divsn., dept. medicine Coll. Medicine, 1973—96; dir. Hemophilia Ctr. Ctrl. Pa., 1973—, Spl. Hematology Lab., Milton S. Hershey Med. Ctr., 1973—96, med. dir., 1997—, Hemostatsis Lab, Milton S. Hershey Med. Ctr., 1997—. Dir. AIDS Clin. Trials Unit Pa. State U., 1987-2000; faculty rsch. assoc. Am. Cancer Soc., 1966-71; mem. State Hemophilia Adv. Com, 1973-90, chmn., 1977-79, 1988-90; mem. policy bd. Coop. F VII inhibitor study Nat. Heart, Lung and Blood Inst., 1975-79; mem. med. and sci. adv. counc. Nat. Hemophilia Found., 1976-77, 83-89, chmn. med. adv. com. Del. Valley chpt., 1979-82; co-investigator, mem. multi-agy. task force on AIDS HHS, 1982-83; mem. blood products adv. com. FDA, 1985-89; mem exec. com. NIH-NIAID Clin. Trials Group, 1987-89; mem. forum on blood safety and availability Inst. of Med., 1993-95; mem. exec. com. second NCI Hemophilia Study Group 2000-2006. USPHS grantee, 1976-95. Fellow ACP; mem. Am. Fedn. Clin. Rsch., World Fedn. Hemophilia, Am. Soc. Hematology, Internat. Soc. Thrombosis and Haemostasis, Insternat. Soc. Hematology, Pa. Soc. Hematology and Oncology (bd. dirs. 1982-85), Am. Assn. for Study Liver Diseases, Hemophilia and Thrombosis Rsch. Soc., Phi Beta Kappa, Alpha Omega Alpha. Office: Milton S Hershey Med Ctr PO Box 850 Hershey PA 17033-0850 Office Phone: 717-531-8399.

EZEAMUZIE, CHARLES I., medical educator, department chairman; b. Uga, Nigeria, Apr. 14, 1955; BSc, U. Ibadan, Nigeria, 1979; PhD, U. London, 1984. Prof., chmn., dept. pharmacology Faculty Medicine Kuwait U., 2003—. Recipient Disting. Rschr. award, Kuwait U., Elliot Blake prize, U. Coll. London; Med. fellowship, Brit. Commonwealth, Internat. fellowship, Glaxo Pharm. Co. Mem.: NY Acad. Scis., European Histamine Rsch. Soc., Internation Soc. Immunopharmacology, Am. Soc. Pharmacology & Exptl. Therapeutics, Brit. Pharmacological Soc. Avocations: hunting, reading. Office: Faculty Medicine Kuwait University PO Box 24923 Safat Kuwait City Jabriya 13110 Kuwait Personal E-mail: ezeamuzie@yahoo.com.

EZENWA, JOSEPHINE NWABUOKU, social worker; b. Oct. 20, 1959; d. H.M. Eze-Igwe Silas O. and H.R.H. Veronica Ezenwa; children: Bryan, Brenda, Sean. BA in Psychology and Human Svc. (hon.), Fontbonne Coll., St. Louis, 1980; MSW, Washington Univ., St. Louis, 1981; postgrad., St. Louis U., 1991—93. Diplomate Am. Coll. Profl. Mental Health Practitioners, 2002. Rsch. dir. Nat. Benevolent Assn., St. Louis, 1981-89; tchr. U. City Sch. Dist., St. Louis, 1989-94; therapist Presbyn. Children's Home, St. Louis, 1994-95; social worker St. Louis Regional Med. Ctr., 1995-97; founder, chair St. Louis Regional Med. Ctr. Dialysis Support Group, 1995-97; social worker St. Louis U. Hosp., 1997; CEO, pres. BBS Care U.S.A., Inc., St. Louis, 1997—; pres. BBS Charities, Inc., St. Louis, 2000—; chair Bus. Adv. Coun. Nat Rep. Congl. Com., St. Louis, 2002—. Founder and chair St. Louis Regional Med. Ctr. Dialysis Support Group, 1995-97; chair long range planning com. Washington U.; co-chair Bus. Adv. Coun., 2002; presenter in field. Chair bus. adv. coun. Nat. Rep. Congl. Com., 2002—. Recipient Nat. Leadership award, St. Louis Regional Med. Ctr. Dialysis Support Group, 2002, Gold Medal award, Nat. Rep. Congl. Com., 2003; named Businesswoman of Yr., 2003. Mem. NASW, NAFE, Coun. Nephrology Social Workers; Nat. Assn. Forensic Counselors; Nat. Assn. Cognitive Behavioral Therapists, Washington U. Sch. Social Work Alumni Assn. (bd. dir.); Creve Coeur-Olive C. of C.; Lions Club. Avocations: choreography, fashion cons., event coord., design, travel. Office: St Louis U Hosp 3536 Vista Grand Saint Louis MO 63110 also: BBS Care USA Inc 7151-7155 Olive Blvd Saint Louis MO 63130 Office Phone: 314-725-7733. Personal E-mail: bbsooool@msn.com.

EZZAT, WALEED FARAG, otolaryngologist, educator; b. Cairo, May 19, 1967; MD, Ain Shams U., 1991, degree in Pediatric Otolaryngology, 1999. Prof. Ain Shams U., 2009—. Founder & treas. Egyptian Soc. Pediatric Otolaryngology & Allied Scis., 2009. Pediatric Otolaryngology Tng. fellowship, TEMPUS. Mem.: Am. Acad. Otolaryngology Head & Neck Surgery, Ain Shams U. Clin. Soc., Egyptian Soc. Rhinoplasty, Egyptian Soc. Otolaryngology & Allied Scis., Egyptian Soc. Otolaryngology. Office: 56 Ahmed ElZomor St 8th Dist Nasr Cairo 11471 Egypt Personal E-mail: wfezzat@yahoo.com.

FABBRI, ALBERTO, hematologist; b. San Giovanni Valdarno, Aug. 6, 1967; MD, U. Florence, 1994, degree in Hematology, 1999. Physician Azienda Ospedaliera U. Senese, 2001—, sr. cons., hematology. Mem.: Italian Lymphoma Found., Italian Hematology Soc. Avocations: music, travel. Office: Viale Bracci 16 Siena 53100 Italy Office Fax: 390577586185. Business E-Mail: fabbri7@unisi.it.

FABER, ANNE, physiologist; b. Århus, Denmark, Nov. 7, 1958; MSc, U. Copenhagen, 1986. Lectr., physiology & phys. activities Met. U. Coll., 1988—96; rschr., work physiologist Nat. Rsch. Ctr. Working Environment, 1997—2011; sr. cons. Guldmann Consulting, 2011—. Mem.: Dansk Biomekanisk Selskab. Office: Parkalle 382 Copenhagen Brøndby 2605 Denmark Business E-Mail: afh@guldmann.com.

FABIJANIC, IRIS, cytologist; d. Hrvoje and Jelena Fabijanic. MD, Med. U., Zagreb, 1996; MS, Faculty of Sci., Zagreb, 2004. Diplomate Bd. Croatia, 1998. Resident, cytopathology U. Hosp. Merkur, Zagreb, 2000—04, cytopathologist, 2004—. Sec. Croatian Soc. Clin. Soc., Zagreb, 2004—. Contbr. articles to profl. jour. Mem.: Croatian Soc. Genetics. Independent. Roman Catholic. Achievements include research in Sjögren's syndrome. Avocations: classical music, reading, swimming, travel, piano. Office: University Hosp Ctr University Zagreb Med Sch Dept Pathology & Cytology Zagreb Croatia Home: Medvedgradska 70 Zagreb 10 000 Croatia Personal E-mail: iris.fabijanic1@zg.t-com.hr.

FABREGAT, JUAN RAMON, cardiologist, university dean; b. Mexico City, Aug. 29, 1958; s. Francisco Jose and Enriqueta (Ramirez) F.; m. Maria Angeles Trueba, Dec. 3, 1983; children: Nieves, Pedro, Santiago, Nicolas. MD, Nat. Autonoma U. Mex., Mexico City, 1983, specialist in cardiology, 1988; subspecialist in electrophysiology, U. Montpellier, France, 1989. Asst. prof. Nat. Autonoma U. Mex., 1978-85, prof., 1985-87; med. dir. Seguros Tepeyac, Mexico City, 1986-94; rsch. asst. U. Montpellier, 1989-98, assoc. attache, 1989—; dean Panam. U., Mexico City, 1995—. Dir. Lab. Cardiac Electophysiology Spanish Hosp., Mexico City, 1989-96; mem. staff Am. Brit. Cowdray Hosp., Mexico City, 1993—, chmn. cardiology svc., 1999—; CEO, Rithmus Inc., Mexico City, 1994-96. Author: Arrithmias Therapy in Emegency Medicine, 1995; also articles. Bd. dirs. Com. Salubridad de Mixcoac, Mexico City, 1998. Fellow Am. Coll. Cardiology (assoc.); mem. Mexican Soc. Cardiology, N.Am. Soc. Pacing and Elctrophysiology. Roman Catholic. Avocations: airplane models and remote control flying, scale ships and boats construction, golf. Office: Panam U, Col Insurgentes Mixcoac, Donatello 59 03920 Mexico City Mexico Business E-Mail: jfabregat@drfabregar.net.

FABUNAN, RUBEN G., physician, research scientist, inventor; b. San Marcelino, Zambales, Philippines, Mar. 15, 1945; arrived in U.S., 1979; s. Roman Battad Fabunan, Sr. and Feliza Pescador Garcia; m. Annie Pilapil Fabunan, Dec. 1973; children: Maritess, Farahnaz, Eileen. BS, U. Philippines, Quezon City, 1966; MD, Southwestern U., Philippines, 1973. Contract med. worker Gov. of Iran, 1976—79; founder Fabunan Med. Clin., San Marcelino, 1975; ind. med. rschr. Gen. Medicine, 1975—; chmn. Fil-Am Tech Inc, 2001—. Recipient First Place award in Biotechnology Poison Antidote, Invention Convention, Calif., 1997; named Most Outstanding Southwestern U. Alumnus in Medicine, Cebu City, Philippines, 2002. Mem.: Nat. Inventors Hall of Fame, Am. Soc. of Patent Holders (life), Philippine Med. Assn. (life). Achievements include patents for Fabunan injection viral treatment for HIV/AIDS, influenza, and dengue fever; envenomation antidote for snake bites, catfish stings, and other animal poisons; HIV Treatment. Office Fax: 213-381-2502. Personal E-mail: farahfabunan@yahoo.com.

FADDIS, MITCHELL N., cardiac electrophysiologist, educator; BS, Kans. State U., 1985; MD, Wash. U., 1995. Diplomate Am. Bd. Internal Medicine-clin. cardiac electrophysiology, 2000, Am. Bd. Internal Medicine, 2006, Am. Bd. Internal Medicine-cardiovasc. disease, 2009. Resident internal medicine Barnes Jewish Hosp., 1993—95, fellow cardiovasc. disease, 1998, fellow clin. cardiac electrophysiology; assoc. prof. medicine Wash. Univ., sect. head cardiac electrophysiology. Co-author: (articles) Intracellular injection of heparin and polyamines; effects on phototransduction in Limulus ventral photoreceptors., 1993, A decrease in approximate entropy predicts the onset of atrial fibrillation., 1998, Precise navigation of an endocardial ablation catheter by a novel magnetic guidance system., 1998, Magnetic guidance system for cardiac electrophysiology: A prospective trial of safety and efficacy in humans., 2003, numerous articles. Named one of The Best Doctors in America, 2005—06, 2008, 2010. Office: Barnes Jewish Hospital 216 S Kingshighway Ste 4402 Saint Louis MO 63110 Office Phone: 314-454-7834.

FADEN, ALAN IRA, neurology educator; b. Phila., Jan. 11, 1945; BA in Physics, U. Pa., 1966; postgrad., Ind. U., 1966-67; MD, U. Chgo., 1971. Resident in neurology U. Calif., San Francisco, 1972-75; research neurologist Walter Reed Army Inst. Research, Washington, 1975-80; assoc. prof. neurology and medicine Uniformed Services U. of Health Scis., Bethesda, Md., 1978-81, prof. neurology and physiology, 1981-84, vice chmn. neurology, 1980-82; chief neurobiol. research unit Uniformed Serviced U. of Health Scis., Bethesda, Md., 1982-84, prof. neurology, 1984-91; vice chmn. dept. U. Calif., San Francisco, 1984-90; chief neurology VA Med. Ctr., San Francisco, 1984-90; dir. Ctr. for Neural Injury, San Francisco, 1984-91, Georgetown Inst. Cognitive and Computational Scis., 1995—98; dean rsch., sci. dir. Sch. of Medicine Georgetown U., 1991—96, prof. neuroscience, neurology and pharmacology, 1996—; prof. anesthesiology U. Md. Sch. Medicine, 2009, dir., Shock Trauma Anesthesiology Oraganised Rsch. Ctr., 2009. Sci. dir. Nat. Research Inst. for Neural Injury, Washington, 1983—; vis. prof. Dept. Chem. and Biochem. James Cook U., Townsville, Australia, 1990-91. Editor-in-chief Neuro TherapeuticsRx; assoc. editor J. Neurotrauma; mem. editl. bd. Arch Neurol, Clin. Neuropharmacology and CNS Trauma; contbr. articles to profl. jours.; patentee in field. Named one of 100 Top Leaders of Washington, Washington mag., 1982. Fellow ACP, Am. Acad. Neurology, Molecular Med. Soc.; mem. Am. Soc. Pharmacolgy and Exptl. Therapeutics, Am. Soc. Clin. Investigation, Am. Physiol. Soc., Am. Neurol. Assn., Neurotrauma Soc. (pres.), Soc. Neural Spectroscopy (coun.), San Francisco Neurol. Soc. (sec., v.p., treas., pres.), Am. Soc. for Exptl. Neurotherapeutics (sec., treas, pres.). Avocations: jogging, history, art collecting. Home: 6624 Barnaby ST NW Washington DC 20015-2332 Business E-Mail: fadena@georgetown.edu.

FADL, HELENA, gynecologist; b. Lappträsk, Finland, Jan. 17, 1965; MD, Turku U., Finland, 1997. Maternal health care unit cons. Örebro Läns Landsting, 2006—. Office: Universitetssjukhuset Örebro Örebro 70185 Sweden E-mail: helena.fadl@orebroll.se.

FAGERBERG, JAN CHRISTER, medical researcher; b. Stockholm, Jan. 27, 1962; s. Bengt and Erna (Klingbeil) F.;1 child: Mikaela. MD, Karolinska Inst., Stockholm, 1988, PhD, 1995. Intern Motala Hosp., Sweden, 1988-90; registrar Karolinska Hosp., Stockholm, 1990-95, cons., 1995-98, chief physician, 1998-99; asst. med. dir. Roche AB, Stockholm, 1999-2000; clin. scientist oncology global drug devel. F. Hoffmann-LaRoche Ltd., Basel, Switzerland, 2000—02, clin. team leader, 2002—05, clin. sci. leader, 2002—05, therapeutic area expert, oncology, 2005—06; med. dir. TopoTarget A/S, Copenhagen, 2006—09; sr. v.p., chief med. officer Micromet Inc., Bethesda, Md., Munich, 2009—. Cons. in field. Contbr. articles to profl. jours. Mem. European Soc. Med. Oncology, Am. Soc. Clin. Oncology. Office: Micromet EU-Site Staffelseestr 2 Munich 81477 Germany also: 9201 Corporate Blvd Ste 400 Rockville MD 20850 Home: Stora Sodergatan 57 B SE Lund 222 23 Sweden Office Phone: 1-240 752 1437, 49-89 89 52 77301. Business E-Mail: jan.fagerberg@micromet-inc.com.

FAGIEN, STEVEN, ophthalmologist, consultant; b. Neptune, NJ, Mar. 7, 1957; s. Melvin Blumenthal and Sondra Parker; m. Debra L Rattner, Dec. 26, 1981; children: Samantha Michelle, Alyssa Nicole, Kayla Danielle. BS, U. Fla., 1979, MD, 1983. Cert. Am. Bd. Ophthalmology, Am. Soc. Ophthalmic Plastic and Reconstructive Surgery, Am. Acad. Facial Plastic and Reconstructive Surgeons. Internal medicine U. Fla., resident-ophthalmology, 1979—83; fellow-ophthalmic plastic surgery U. Ill., 1987—88; aesthetic eyelid plastic surgery pvt. practice, Boca Raton, Fla., 1988—. Founder Collagenesis, Inc., Beverly, Mass., 1975—2002; educator, instr. Am. Soc. Aesthetic Plastic Surgery, Los Alamitos, Calif.; founder and co-director SEE Internat., Santa Barbara, Calif., 1991—96; cons., med. advisor Allergan, Inc., Irvine, Calif., 1997—, Medicis, Inc, Scottsdale, Ariz., 2002—; founder, pres. Collagen Matrix Technologies, Boca Raton, Fla., 2002—; cons., med. advisor Dermik Aesthetics, Inc, Berwyn, Pa.; chief, dept. surgery Boca Raton Cmty. Hosp., Boca Raton, Fla.; co-dir. Internat. Plastic Surgery Edn. Initiative. Contbr. articles to profl. jours.; mem. editl. adv. bd. New Beauty. Bd. mem. Boca Raton Cmty. Hosp. Recipient Man of Yr., Cystic Fibrosis Found., 2001, Dr. of Yr., Boca Raton Women's Club, 2002; named one of World's Best Plastic Surgeons Specializing in Eyelids, W Mag. Fellow: Am. Soc. Ophthalmic Plastic and Reconstructive Surgery (co-dir.), Am. Acad. Ophthalmolgy; mem.: Allergan's Nat. Edn. Faculty, Am. Soc. Aesthetic Plastic Surgery (assoc.). Achievements include research in new techiques in blepharoplasty; advanced techniques for the use of botulinum toxin type A in facial enhancement; advanced techniques in injectable soft tissue augmentation agents; development of inectable human collagen matrix; research in soft tissue augmentation. Avocations: jazz, music. Office: 660 Glades Road Ste 210 Boca Raton FL 33431 Office Fax: 561-347-0772. E-mail: sfagien@aol.com.

FAGIN, CLAIRE MINTZER, nursing administrator, educator; b. NYC; d. Harry and Mae (Slatin) Mintzer; m. Samuel Fagin, Feb. 17, 1952; children: Joshua, Charles. BS, Wagner Coll., 1948; MA, Tchrs. Coll. Columbia, 1951; PhD, NYU, 1964; DSc (hon.), Lycoming Coll., 1983, Cedar Crest Coll., 1987, U. Rochester, 1987, Med. Coll. Pa., 1989, U. Md., 1993, Wagner Coll., 1993, Loyola U., 1996, Case Western Res. U., 2002; LLD (hon.), U. Pa., 1994, U. Toronto, 2004; DHL (hon.), Hunter Coll., 1993, Rush U., 1996, Johns Hopkins U., 2003, Syracuse U., 2010. Staff nurse, clin. instr. Sea View Hosp., SI, NY; clin. instr. Bellevue Hosp., NYC; psychiat. nurse cons. Nat. League for Nursing, NYC; asst. chief psychiat. nursing svc. clin. ctr. NIH; rsch. project coord. dept. psychiatry Children's Hosp., Washington; instr., assoc. prof. psychiat.-mental health nursing NYU, NYC, dir. grad. programs in psychiat. mental health nursing, 1965—69; chmn. nursing dept., prof. Herbert H. Lehman Coll., CUNY, NYC, 1969—77; dir. Health Professions Inst., Montefiore Hosp. and Med. Ctr., 1975—77; Margaret Bond Simon dean sch. of nursing U. Pa., Phila., 1977—92, Leadership chair prof., 1992—96, interim pres., 1993—94, dean emeritus, prof. emeritus, 1996—. Bd. dirs. Provident Mut. Ins. Co., 1988—96, chmn. audit com., 1985—96, exec. com., 1986—96, adv. com., 1996—2003; bd. dirs., mem. audit com. Salomon, Inc., 1994—97; bd. dirs., compensation Radian Inc., 1994—2002; bd. dirs. Vis. Nurse Soc., NY, Van Ameringen Found., 1996—2004, Nat. Sr. Citizens Law Ctr.; dir. program bldg. acad. geriatric nursing John A. Hartford Found., 2000—05; spkr., cons. in field. Contbr. articles to profl. jours.; movie, Mode of Honor, 2008. Recipient Achievement award, Wagner Coll., 1956, Tchrs. Coll., 1975, Disting. Alumna award, NYU, 1979, Founders award, Sigma Theta Tau, 1981, Hon. Recognition award, ANA, 1988, Woman of Courage award, Women's Way, 1990, Alumni Merit award, U. Pa., 1991, First Leadership award, Trustee Coun. Pa. Women, 1991, Caring award, Phila. Vis. Nurses Assn., 1994, Lillian Wald award,

N.Y. Vis. Nurses Assn., 1994, Hildegard Peplau award outstanding contbn. psych-nursing, 1994, Pres. medal, NYU, 1998, Nightingale Lamp award, Am. Nurses Found., 2002; named Disting. Dau. Pa., 1994; disting. scholar, Am. Nurses Found., 1984, hon. fellow, Royal Coll. Nursing, 2002, nursing bldg. at U. Pa. named Claire M. Fagin Hall in her honor, 2006. Mem.: Am. Nurses Assn. (Hall of Fame 2010), Nat. League for Nursing (pres. 1991—93), Am. Orthopsychiat. Assn. (bd. dirs. 1972—75, exec. com. bd. dirs. 1973—75, pres. 1985—86), Am. Acad. Nursing (governing coun. 1976—78, Living Legend award 1998, Civitas award 2005), Inst. Medicine of NAS (governing coun. 1981—83, chmn. bd. health promotion and disease prevention 1991—94, mem./chair Lienhard Com. 1999—2004). Address: 200 Central Park S Apt 12E New York NY 10019-1415 Personal E-mail: cfagin@att.net.

FAGIN, JAMES C., pediatrician, allergist, immunologist, educator; Attended, U. Brussels, 1976. Diplomate Am. Bd. Pediatrics, Am. Bd. Allergy & Immunology. Hosp. affiliations include Long Island Jewish Med. Ctr., Steven and Alexandra Cohen Childrens Med. Ctr. of NY; resident pediat. North Shore Univ. Hosp., 1977—79; fellow allergy and immunology Childrens Hosp. of Pitts., 1979—81; asst. prof. pediat. NY Univ. Sch. of Medicine. Office: Steven and Alexandra Cohen Childrens Medical Center of NY Ste 101 865 Northern Blvd Great Neck NY 11021-5303 Office Phone: 516-622-5070. Office Fax: 516-622-5060.

FAGNANI, ENELTON, chemist; b. Araraquara, Brazil, Jan. 19, 1978; Degree in Chemistry, UNESP, 1999; PhD, UNICAMP, 2009. Chemist UNICAMP, 2002—. Office: Albert Einstein 951 Campinas SP 13083852 Brazil Office Phone: 55-19-3521-2303. Business E-Mail: enelton@fec.unicamp.br.

FAHED, CHARBEL DAWOOD, ophthalmologist; b. Ashcout, Lebanon, Oct. 15, 1951; s. Dawood Tamer and Daad Yousef (Dariane) F.; m. Victoria Mary-Hala Chebaya, Oct. 4, 1981; children: Dawood, John, Joseph, Mariam, Anna, Grace. BS, Am. U., Beirut, 1976, MS, 1977, MD, 1980. Clin. instr. ophthalmology Am. U., Beirut, 1984-85, assoc., 1985-88; dir. ophthalmology Ctr. Hosp. St. Georges, Ajaltoun, Lebanon, 1984—; part time cons. Eye & Ear Hosp., Naccash, Lebanon, 1995—; co-founder Ophthalmic Cons. of Beirut, Laser Eye Ctr. of Beirut. Med. dir. Najjar Found., Beirut, 1986—; br. dir. ForeSight Found., Beirut, 1992—; moderator multiple local symposiae. Contbr. articles to profl. jours. Mem. Am. Acad. Ophthalmology, Soc. of Ophthalmology, Am. U. Beirut Alumni. Roman Catholic. Avocations: tennis, swimming, classical music. Office: Eye & Ear Hospital International Naccash Rd Dbayeh Lebanon also: St George Hosp Ajaltoun Lebanon Home Phone: 961 4 524938; Office Phone: 961 4725060. E-mail: Fahd@cyberia.net.lb.

FAHIEN, LEONARD AUGUST, physician, educator; b. St. Louis, July 26, 1934; s. John Henry and Alice Katherine Fahien; m. Rose Marian Burmeister, June 21, 1958; children: Catherine Fahien Reuter, Lisa Fahien Uldrich, James. AB, Washington U., St Louis, 1956; MD, Washington U., 1960. Intern U. Wis., Madison, 1960-61; surgeon NIH, Bethesda, Md., 1964-66; asst. prof. dept. pharmacology U. Wis. Med. Sch., Madison, 1966-69, asso. prof., 1969-71, prof., 1974—, asso. dean, 1979-83, advisor Children's Diabetes Ctr., 2002—; vis. prof. Inst. Protein Rsch. Osaka U., Japan, 1991; prof. El Julios U. Barcelona (Spain), 1997. Contbr. chapters to books, articles to profl. jours. With USPHS, 1964—66. Numerous NIH grants, 1966—. Mem.: Phi Beta Kappa, Sigma Xi. Lutheran. Home: 3212 Topping Rd Madison WI 53705-1435 Office: 426 S Charter St Madison WI 53715-1626 Home Phone: 608-231-2174; Office Phone: 608-262-9683. Business E-Mail: lafahien@facstaff.wisc.edu.

FAHLE, MANFRED, ophthalmology researcher; b. Duesseldorf, Germany, Dec. 10, 1950; s. Fritz and Helma (Westerfeld) F.; m. Sigrid Henke, Aug. 3, 1979; children: Nora Katharina, Till Patrick Jakob; m. Karoline Spang, Aug. 4, 2001; 1 child: Julia Patricia. Degree in Biology, U. Goettingen, Fed. Republic Germany, 1972; degree in Medicine, U. Giessen, Fed. Republic Germany, 1973; MA in biology, U. Mainz, Fed. Republic Germany, 1975; MD, U. Tuebingen, Fed. Republic Germany, 1977. Fellow Max-Planck Inst. for Biol. Cybernetics, Tuebingen, 1977-81; head electrophysiol. lab. Univ. Eye Clinic, Tuebingen, 1981-88; vis. scientist U. Calif., Berkeley, 1984, MIT, Cambridge, Mass., 1989-90; fellow German Rsch. Coun., Tuebingen, 1990-93; prof. ophthalmology, head sect. visual sci. Univ. Eye Hosp., Tuebingen, 1994-98; head Inst. Brain Rsch. IV, human-neurobiology U. Bremen, Germany, 2000—; dir. Ctr. Cognitive Rsch., U. Bremen, 2005—. Wiersma vis. prof. Calif. Inst. Tech., Pasadena, 1996; prof., head dept. optometry and visual sci. City U., London, 1998-99; prof. human neurobiology U. Bremen, Germany, 1999—; dir. Inst. for Brain Rsch., 2003—, Ctr. Cognitive Sci., 2005—; vis. prof. Univ. Coll., London, 1999-2002; part-time prof. Applied Vision Rsch. Ctr., City Univ., 2000-05, Henry Wellcome Labs. Vision Rsch., London, 2006-2011. Mem. editl. bd. German Jour. Ophthalmology, 1991-97, Neuroophthalmology, 1993-2003, Vision Rsch., 1994-2004, Pub. Libr. Sci. Biology, 2006—; Perception, 2009-; author: (with T. Poggio) Perceptual Learning, 2002, (with M. Greenlee) Visual Neuropsychology, 2003. Bd. dirs. Grad. Program Neurobiology, Tuebingen, 1986-91, Drug Rsch. Program, Tuebingen, 1996-99; academic senate, Bremen U., 2003-. Recipient Heisenberg award German Rsch. Coun., 1989, prize von Humboldt/Max-Planck Soc., 1992. Avocations: music, literature, sailing, windsurfing. Home: Graf-Moltkestr 56 D28211 Bremen Germany Office: Inst Human Neurobiology Hochschulring 18 D28359 Bremen Germany Office Fax: 49 421 218 63985. Business E-Mail: mfahle@uni-bremen.de.

FAHMIDA, UMI, research scientist, educator; b. Jakarta, DKI, Indonesia, Mar. 20, 1972; d. Ngadino Ahmad Khanan and Kemi Dwiasih; m. Mahdi Fahmida; children: Muhammad Qalbu Dary, A. Biruni Fikri. PhD, U. Indonesia, Salemba Raya, 2003. Rschr., lectr. SEAMEO-TROPMED RCCN, U. Indonesia, Ctrl. Jakarta, 1997—, head doctorate program, 2004. Cons. Asian Devel. Bank, Jakarta, 2005—06, 2005—06; cons., prin. investigator UNICEF, Jakarta, 2005—06; rschr., prin. investigator Otago U., New Zealand, 2004—06, SEAMEO-RCCN UI, Jakarta, 2004—06, assoc. investigator, 2007—, TIFN, Netherlands, 2007—. Contbr. articles to profl. publs. (UI award, 2007). Mem. Ind. Rsch. Review Panel NTB. Recipient Best Rschr. in Health Sci., 2008. Office: SEAMEO-TROPMED RCCN Univ Indonesia Salemba Raya DKI Jakarta 10430 Ctrl Jakarta Indonesia Office Phone: 62 21 3913932. Office Fax: 62 21 31902950. Business E-Mail: ufahmida@seameo-rccn.org.

FAHN, STANLEY, neurologist, educator; b. Sacramento, Nov. 6, 1933; s. Ernest and Sylvia F.; m. Charlotte, June 21, 1958; children: Paul N., James D. BA, U. Calif., Berkeley, 1955, MD, 1958. Diplomate Am. Bd. Neurology. Resident in neurology Neurol. Inst., NY, 1959-62; rsch. assoc. NIH, 1962-65; mem. faculty Columbia U., NYC, 1965-68, prof. neurology, 1973-78, H. Houston Merritt prof., 1978—, dir. Morris K. Udall Parkinson Disease Rsch. Ctr., 1999—2003; mem. faculty U. Pa., Phila., 1968-73. Dir. Dystonia Rsch. Ctr., 1981—97; sci. dir. Parkinson's Disease Found., 1979—; chmn. adv. com. peripheral and nervous sys. drugs FDA, 1987—89, 1991—96; organizer, chmn. World Parkinson Congresses, 2006—. Editor Movement Disorders, 1985-95; assoc. editor Neurology, 1977-87. With USPHS, 1962-65 Grantee NIH, 1974—77, 1980—82, 1984—91, 1994—97. Mem.: Inst. of Medicine, Dystonia Med. Rsch. Found. (bd. dirs. 1998—, hon. life), Movement Disorder Soc. (pres. 1988—91), Am. Neurol. Assn., Am. Acad. Neurology (chair edn. com. 1986—93, v.p. 1993—97, pres.-elect 1999—2001, pres. 2001—03, chair meeting mgmt. com. 2009—). Home: 155 Edgars Ln Hastings On Hudson NY 10706-1107 Office: 710 W 168th St New York NY 10032-2603 Business E-Mail: sf1@columbia.edu.

FAHR, ALFRED, pharmacist, educator; b. Meersburg, Baden-Württemberg, Germany, Nov. 17, 1949; s. Alfred and Maria Fahr; m. Sabine Tessmer. D, U. Constance, 1981. Prof. Philips U., Marburg, Hessen, Germany, 1996—2002, Friedrich Schiller U., Jena, Thueringen, Germany, 2002—. Dept. head Inst. Pharmacy, Jena, 2002—. Mem.: Rotary. Home: Heinrich-Heine-Str 27b Coelbe Hessen 35091 Germany Office: Friedrich-Schiller-Univ Lessingstrasse 8 Jena Thueringen 07743 Germany Office Fax: 49 3641 949902. Business E-Mail: alfred.fahr@uni-jena.de.

FAIMAN, CHARLES, endocrinologist; b. Winnipeg, Man., Can., Dec. 6, 1939; s. Max and Bessie (Freedman) F.; m. Carol Lee Fien, June 16, 1963; children— Barton Shale, Gregg Howard, Matthew Randall. B.Sc. in Medicine, U. Man., MD, 1962, M.Sc., 1966. Intern Winnipeg Gen. Hosp., 1962-63, resident, 1963-64; Med. Research Council Can. fellow U. Man., 1964-65, U. Ill. Coll. Medicine, 1965-67, Mayo Clinic, Rochester, Minn., 1967-68; asst. prof. physiology and medicine U. Man., 1968-71, assoc. prof., 1971-75, prof., 1975—92; dir. clin. investigation unit Winnipeg Gen. Hosp., 1971-74; head sect. endocrinology & metabolism dept. medicine U. Man & Health Scis. Ctr., Winnipeg, 1977—92. Chmn., dept. endocrinology, diabetes & metabolism Cleve. Clinic, 1992—2000, sr. staff, 2000—05, cons., 2005—. Bd. dirs. Winnipeg Hebrew Sch., 1969-76, 77-86, pres., 1982-83, bd. govs., chmn., 1986—92. Med. Research Council Can. scholar, 1968-73. Master Am. Coll. Endocrinology; fellow Royal Coll. Physicians Can.; mem. Endocrine Soc., Am. Soc. Clin. Investigation, Am. Soc. Clin. Endocrinologists, Can. Soc. Endocrinology and Metabolism (pres. 1979-80), Can. Fertility and Andrology Soc. (nat. dir. 1988-91). Office: Cleveland Clinic 9500 Euclid Ave Cleveland OH 44195 *

FAIRBANK, JOHN A., psychiatrist, educator; PhD, Auburn Meml. Hosp., 1980. Asst. prof. dept. psychology & neuroscience Duke U. Med. Ctr.; co-dir. Nat. Ctr. for Child Traumatic Stress. Office: Brightleaf Square 905 W Main St Ste 24-E Durham NC 27701 Office Phone: 919-682-1552 ext. 255. E-mail: jaf@psych.mc.duke.edu.

FAIRCHILD, ROBERT CHARLES, pediatrician; b. Kansas City, Mo., Dec. 22, 1921; s. Charles Clement and Ada Mae (Baker) F.; m. Patricia Louise Russell, May 20, 1961; children: Robert, Nancy, Rex Hartman, Dan Hartman Student, Kansas City Jr. Coll., 1938-40, BA, U. Kans., 1942, MD, 1950. Diplomate Am. Bd. Pediatrics. Intern Kansas City Gen. Hosp., 1950-51; resident in pediatrics U. Kans. Med. Ctr., 1951-53; practice medicine specializing in pediatrics Mission, Kans., 1953-70; dir. area clinics Children's Mercy Hosp., Kansas City, Mo., 1970-74, dir. outpatient services, 1974-88, ret., 1991. Prof. pediatrics emeritus U. Mo.-Kansas City Sch. Medicine; mem. adv. com. Assoc. Degree nursing program Johnson County Community Coll. Contbr. articles to med. jours. Served to maj. U.S. Army, 1942-46 Decorated Bronze Star; recipient Physician's Recognition award AMA, 1990; Porter scholar U. Kans. Sch. Medicine, 1950. Mem. AMA, Am. Acad. Pediatrics, Mo. State Med. Assn., Met. Med. Soc. of Kansas City, Greater Kansas City Pediatric Soc., Kansas City S.W. Clin. Soc., Alpha Omega Alpha, Nu Sigma Nu, Sigma Nu. Home: Claridge Ct 8101 Mission Rd Apt 233 Prairie Village KS 66208-5247

FAIRCHOK, MARY PATRICIA, pediatrician; b. Milw., Sept. 10, 1960; BA, Harvard U., 1982; MD, Tufts U., 1986. Gen. pediatrician 34th Gen. Hosp., Augsburg, Germany, 1989—92; pediatric infectious disease fellow Walter Reed Army Med. Ctr., 1992—94; chief peds ID, officer, dir. pediatric residency Madigan Army Med. Ctr., 1994—97, rsch. physician, pediatric infectious disease specialist, 2007; pediatric hospitalist, dir., WWAMI pediatric clerkship Mary Bridge Children's Hosp., 2007—. Clin. prof. pediat. U. WA, 1994; assoc. prof. pediat. USUHS, 1994. Decorated Bronze Star US Army, Humanitarian Svc. medal; recipient Excellence award, US Army M.C., Order of Mil. Med. Merit. Fellow: AAP; mem.: IDSA, Alpha Omega Alpha. Avocations: running, sailing, hiking. Home: 12816 135 Ave Cte Puyallup WA 98374 Personal E-mail: fairchokmp@hotmail.com.

FAIRMAN, RONALD MARC, thoracic surgeon; b. Phila., Mar. 8, 1951; MD, Jefferson Med. Coll., 1977. Prof. surgery, chief divsn. vascular surgery & endovascular therapy U. Pa., 1996—. Recipient Luigi Mastroianni Clin. Innovator award, U. Pa. Health Sys. Fellow: Eatern Vascular Soc., Southern Assn. Vascular Surgery, Soc. Vascular Surgery, Am. Surg. Assn., Clin. Soc. Vascular Surgery, Am. Coll. Surgeons. Avocation: fly fishing. Office: 3400 Spruce St Philadelphia PA 19104 Office Fax: 215-662-4871. Business E-Mail: ron.fairman@uphs.upenn.edu.

FAJANS, STEFAN STANISLAUS, retired internist; b. Munich, Mar. 15, 1918; arrived in U.S., 1936, naturalized, 1942; s. Kasimir M. and Salomea (Kaplan) Fajans; m. Ruth Stine, Sept. 6, 1947; children: Peter S., John S. BS, U. Mich., Ann Arbor, 1938, MD, 1942. Intern Mount Sinai Hosp., NYC, 1942—43; rsch. fellow U. Mich., 1946—47, 1949—51, resident, 1947—49; mem. faculty U. Mich. Med. Sch., 1950—, prof., 1961—88, active prof. emeritus, 1988—. Mem. endocrinology study sect. NIH, 1958—62, mem. diabetes and metabolism tng. grants com., 1966—70, mem. nat. diabetes adv. bd., 1987—91; chief divsn. endocrinology and metabolism Mich. Diabetes Rsch. and Tng. Ctr., 1973—87, dir., 1977—86; chmn. Am. zone internat. sci. adv. com. Congresses Internat. Diabetes Fedn., 1977—79; Banting meml. lectr., 1978. Contbr. articles med. publs. Mem. career devel. com. VA Med. Rsch. Svcs., 1987—91. Officer M.C. US Army, 1943—46. Fellow, Life Ins. Med. Inst., 1950—51; vis. scholar rsch. fellow in medicine, ACP, 1949—50. Master: ACP; mem.: NAS (sr. mem. inst. med.), Ctrl. Soc. Clin. Rsch., Assn. Am. Physicians, Am. Soc. Clin. Investigation, Am. Fedn. Clin. Rsch., Endocrine Soc. (v.p. 1970—71, coun. 1967—71, 1978—81), Am. Diabetes Assn. (pres. 1971—72, Banting medal 1972, Banting Meml. award 1978), Alpha Omega Alpha, Sigma Xi. Home: 827 Asa Gray Dr # 360 Ann Arbor MI 48105-3520 Office: PO Box 0354 Ann Arbor MI 48109-0354 Office Phone: 734-936-5039. Business E-Mail: sfajans@umich.edu.

FAKIHA, ZAKI ABDULRAHMAN, dental educator, dean; b. Makkah, Saudi Arabia, Sept. 26, 1958; BDS, King Saud U., Riyadh, Saudi Arabia, 1983. Clin. cert. prosthodontics Ala., 1987. Intern King Saud U., Coll. Dentistry, Riyadh, 1983—84, demonstrator, 1984—87, asst. dir. labs., 1988, lectr., 1988—91, dir. labs., 1988—92, asst. prof. dept. prosthetic dental scis., 1991—, asst. prof./cons. dept. restorative dental scis., 1991, chmn. dept. restorative dental scis., 1997—99, chmn. dept. prosthetic dental scis., 2000—02, dir. interns' tng. com., 2002—, vice dean for adminstrn. and clin. affairs, 2002—; cons., dir. Hail (Saudi Arabia) Dental Ctr., 1993—94, Bisha (Saudi Arabia) Dental Ctr., 1994—95; chmn. Saudi Prosthodontic Club, Riyadh, 1996—2001. Mem. implant team com. dept. prosthetic dental scis. King Saud U. Coll. Dentistry, Riyadh, 1999—, mem. postgrad. programs devel. com., 2002—, mem. coll. bd. coun., 2002—; coord. Exam. for the Saudi Health Coun. Licensure for Prosthodontics, Riyadh, 2001—; chmn. SDS Departmental Demonstrator Com., Riyadh, Saudi Arabia, 2001—. Chmn. Saudi Prosthodontic Club, Riyadh, Saudi Arabia, 1996. Achievements include research in rapid mixing of zinc phosphate cement for fixed prosthodontic procedure; preparation of a complete crown finish line when access is restricted and a core reconstruction is required; use of pins in fixed prosthodontics, part I; use of pins in fixed prosthodontics, part II; comparison in changes in vertical dimension of the upper and lower complete dentures processed using two investing methods; conditions of partially edentulous patients and clinicians awareness towards RPD designs; a technique for duplicating complete dentures; dental fluorosis in 12-15 year-old rural children exposed to fluorides from well drining water in the Hail region in Saudi Arabia; evaluation of retention of cast posts using different cementing techniques; rapid mixing of zinc phosphate cement for fixed prosthodontic procedure. Home: P O Box 60169 Riyadh 11545 Saudi Arabia Office: King Saud Univ Coll Dentistry POBox 60169 Riyadh 11545 Saudi Arabia Office Fax: 966 1 4678548; Home Fax: 966 1 4678548. Personal E mail: zfakiha@yahoo.com.

FALANGA, ANNA, hematologist; b. Naples, Italy, Apr. 18, 1953; m. Arrigo Schieppati; 1 child, Francesca Schieppati. MD, U. Naples, 1978. Cert. in international medicine Bd. U. Naples, 1983, in hematology U. Verona, Italy, 1988. Sr. investigator Mario Negri Inst., Milan, 1984—90; cons. Ospedali Riuniti Bergamo, Italy, 1984—90, clin. hematologist, 1990—2005, lab. dir., 2005—07, dir. hemostasis and thrombosis ctr., 2007— V.p. Med. Women Internat. Assn., Rome, 2006—08; pres. Soroptimist Internat.-Club Bergamo, 2005—07. Mem.: Soc. Italiana Ematologia Sperimentale, Soc. Italiana Ematologia, Am. Assn. Cancer Rsch., Società Italiana Studio dell'Emostasi e Trombosi, Am. Soc. Hematology, Internat. Soc. Thrombosis and Hemostasis (sec. sci. and standardization com. 2008—). Office: Ospedali Riuniti Bergamo Largo Giovanni Barozzi 1 24128 Bergamo BG Italy Office Fax: 39 035 266659

FALANGA, VINCENT, dermatologist, educator; MD, Harvard Coll., 1977. Diplomate Am. Bd. Internal Medicine, Am. Bd. Dermatology. Resident internal medicine Univ. Miami Med. Ctr., Miami, Fla., 1978—80; fellow dermatology Hosp. Univ. Pa., 1980—82; prof. Boston Univ. Sch. of Medicine, chmn. dermatology dept.; chmn. tng program Roger Williams Med. Ctr., Providence, hosp. affiliation include; cons. Nat. Inst. of Health; mem. adv. bd. NeoStem Inc. Author has over 200 publs., co-author four textbooks on wound healing. Mem.: Am. Coll. of Rheumatology, Am. Coll. of Physicians, Am. Acad. of Dermatology, Am. Fedn. of Clin. Rsch., Soc. of Investigative Dermatology, Am. Dermatol. Assn. Office: NeoStem Inc Ste 450 420 Lexington Ave New York NY 10170 Office Phone: 212-584-4180. Office Fax: 646-514-7787.

FALCONE, MARCO, internist; b. Cosenza, Italy, Jan. 26, 1978; MD, Sapienza U. Rome (formerly U. degli studi di Roma La Sapienz), 2002. Asst. physician Sapienza U. Rome, 2007—. Named Best Italian Young Rschr., Italian Soc. Internal Medicine, 2009. Mem.: European Soc. Clin. Microbiology and Infectious Diseases, Italian Nat. Group Nosocomial Infections and Bacterial Resistance, Italian Soc. Internal Medicine. Avocations: sports, winemaking. Home: Via della Giuliana 37 Rome 00195 Italy Business E-Mail: marcofalc@libero.it.

FALK, HENRY, pediatrician, epidemiologist, researcher; b. NYC, Feb. 7, 1943; m. 1971; 3 children. BA, Yeshiva Coll., 1964; MD, Albert Einstein Coll. Medicine, 1968; MPH, Harvard U., 1976. Intern Children's Hosp., Phila., 1968-69; resident Bronx Mcpl. Hosp. Ctr., NYC, 1969-72; med. epidemiologist Ctr. Disease Control, Atlanta, 1976—2010, disting. cons. on environ health issues, 2010—; dir. div. of environ. hazards and health effects Nat. Ctr. for Environ. Health, Centers for Disease Control, 1985—99, dir., 2003—10; asst. adminstr. Agency for Toxic Substance and Disease Registry (ATSDR), 1999—2003, acting dir. Mem. Am. Acad. Pediat. (liaison mem. com. environmental health 1978), Am. Coll. Epidemiology Rsch., Am. Pub. Health Assn., Soc. Pediatric Rsch. Epimediologi rsch. on etiology of cancer; environmental and occupational exposures; evaln. vinyl chloride exposed individuals and devel. hepatic tumors. Office: Centers Disease Control and Prevention 1600 Clifton Rd Atlanta GA 30333 *

FALK, LARS WILHELM, dermatologist venereologist; b. Lund, Mar. 13, 1954; MD, Umeå U., 1981; PhD, Linköping U., 2004. Tutor, cons. dept. dermatology and venereology and r & d dept. County Coun. Östergötland, 2006—. Recipient Frithiof Lennmalm prize, Swedish Soc. Medicine, 2005. Mem.: SSDV. Office: Landstinget i Östergötland Sankt Larsgatan 9D Linköping SE-581 85 Sweden Business E-Mail: lars.falk@lio.se.

FALK, RENA ELLEN, clinical geneticist, educator; B., UCLA, MD, 1971. Lic. Calif., 1972, diplomate Am. Bd. Pediatrics, 1976, cert. Am. Bd. Clin. Genetics-Med. Genetics, 1982, Am. Bd. Clin. Cytogenetics-Med. Genetics, 1984. Fellow UCLA, 1973—75, prof. pediat.; fellow

Ronald Raegan UCLA Med. Ctr., 1977; hosp. affiliation include Children's Hosp., La.; intern Cedars-Sinai Med. Ctr., 1972, resident pediat., 1971—73, dir. prenatal diagnosis ctr., med. dir. cytogenetics lab. Office: Cedars-Sinai Medical Center 8700 Beverly Hills Blvd Los Angeles CA 90048 Office Phone: 310-423-6451.

FALKOW, STANLEY, microbiologist, educator; b. Albany, NY, Jan. 24, 1934; s. Jacob and Mollie (Gingold) F.; children from previous marriage: Lynn Beth, Jill Stuart; m. Lucy Stuart Tompkins, Dec. 3, 1983. BS in Bacteriology cum laude, U. Maine, 1955, DSc (hon), 1979; MS in Biology, Brown U., 1960, PhD, 1961; MD (hon.), U. Umea, Sweden, 1989. Asst. chief dept. bacterial immunity Walter Reed Army Inst. Rsch., Washington, 1963-66; prof. microbiology Med. Sch. Georgetown U., 1966-72; prof. microbiology and medicine U. Wash., Seattle, 1972-81; prof., chmn. dept. med. microbiology Stanford U., Calif., 1981-85, prof. microbiology, immunology & medicine Calif., 1981—, Robert W. and Vivian K. Cahill prof. in cancer rsch. Calif. Karl H. Beyer vis. prof. U. Wis., 1978-79; Sommer lectr. U. Oreg. Sch. Medicine, 1979, Kinyoun lectr. NIH, 1980; Rubbro orator Australian Soc. Microbiology, 1981; Stanhope Bayne-Jones lectr. Johns Hopkins U., 1982; mem. Recombinant DNA Molecule Com, task force on antibiotics in animal feeds FDA, microbiology test com. Nat. Bd. Med. Examiners. Author: Infectious Multiple Drug Resistance, 1975; editor: Jour. Infection and Immunity, Jour. Infectious Agents and Diseases. Recipient Ehrlich prize, 1981, Altemeier medal Surg. Infectious Diseases Soc., 1990, Disting. Achievement in Infectious Disease Rsch. award Bristol-Myers Squibb, 1997, Lasker Koshland Spl. Achievement award in Med. Sci., Lasker Found., 2008; Bristol-Myers Squibb unrestricted infectious disease grantee. Fellow Am. Acad. Microbiology; mem. Inst. Medicine, AAAS, Infectious Disease Soc. Am. (Squibb award 1979), Am. Soc. Microbiology (Becton-Dickinson award in Clin. Microbiology, 1986, Abbott-ASM Lifetime Achievement award, 2003), Genetics Soc. Am., NAS, Royal Soc. UK (fgn.), Sigma Xi. Office: Stanford U Dept Microbiology and Immunology 299 Campus Dr Stanford CA 94305-5402 Office Phone: 650-723-9187, 650-723-2671. Office Fax: 650-725-7282. E-mail: falkow@stanford.edu. *

FALLETTA, JOHN MATTHEW, pediatrician, educator; b. Arma, Kans., Sept. 3, 1940; s. Matthew John and Norma (Luke) F.; m. Carolyn Ontjes, June 22, 1963; children: Elizabeth, Matthew. AB, U. Kans., 1962, MD, 1966. Diplomate Am. Bd. Pediat., Am. Bd. Hematology-Oncology. Intern in mixed medicine Kans. U. Med. Ctr., Kansas City, 1966-67; surgeon Epidemic Intelligence Svc., Tex. Children's Hosp. USPHS, Houston, 1967-69; asst. instr. pediat. Baylor Coll. Medicine, Houston, 1967-69, resident, 1969-71, chief resident Tex. Children's Hosp., 1971, postdoctoral fellow hematology-oncology, 1971-73, asst. prof. pediat., 1973-76; assoc. prof. Duke U., Durham, NC, 1976-83, prof., 1984—, chief divsn. hematology-oncology, 1976-94, dir. Clin. Pediat. Lab., 1976-95. Chmn. transfusion com. Duke U. Med. Ctr., 1978—, mem. exec. com. med. staff, 1978—, instl. rev. bd. human rsch., 1979—, chmn., 1994—; mem. instl. rev. bd. human rsch. Baylor Coll. Medicine, 1974-76; mem. acad. coun. Duke U., 1982-86, 87-96, 98-2000, exec. com., 1988, faculty compensation com., 1988—, faculty com. on univ. governance, 1988, trustee-faculty com. to rev. pres., 1989, search com. for pres., 1992; cons. pediat. hematologist-oncologist Charlotte Meml. Hosp., NC, 1978-94, mem. Copernicus Independent Rev. Bd., 2002—, vice-chair, 2004—; mem. med. adv. bd. Children's Cancer Rsch. Fund, 2001—; mem. coun. accreditation Assn. for Accreditation Human Rsch. Protection Programs, Inc., 2005— Contbr. more than 120 articles to Nature, Am. Jour. Ophthalmology, Pediat., New Eng. Jour. Medicine, Clin. Pediat. Oncology, others. Cons. pediat. hematologist-oncologist Project Hope, Pediatric Inst., Krakow, Poland, 1979—; prin. investigator Pediat. Oncology Group, 1981-95, chmn. epidemiology com., mem. prin. investigator's exec. com., new agts. and pharmacology com.; chmn. prophylactic penicillin study I Nat. Heart, Lung and Blood Inst., NIH, 1982-86, chmn. study II, 1987-95; active Cancer Ctr. Support Rev. Com. Nat. Cancer Inst. NIH, 1986-90, NIH Reviewers Res., 1990—, Cancer Clin. Investigation Rev. Com., 1991-96, chmn., 1995-96; trustee Ronald McDonald House Charities, 1986—. Mem. Am. Acad. Pediat., Am. Pediat. Soc., Am. Soc. Clin. Oncology, So. Soc. Pediat. Rsch. (pres. 1981-82), Soc. Pediat. Rsch., NC Pediat. Soc., NC Med. Soc., Phi Beta Kappa, Alpha Omega Alpha. Office: Duke U Med Ctr PO Box 2712 Durham NC 27705-3826

FALLON, JOHN A., insurance company executive, physician, educator; b. Mass. AB in Chemistry, Coll. Holy Cross; MD, Tufts U.; MBA, U. South Fla. Diplomate American Bd. of Internal Medicine. Chmn. physician network Ptnrs. Healthcare System; past CEO of Clin. Affairs SUNY Downstate Med. Ctr.; founder, CEO North Shore Health System; sr. v.p. Blue Cross Blue Shield Mass., Inc., chief physician exec. Clin. prof. preventive med. and cmty. health SUNY Downstate Med. Ctr. Coll. of Medicine, clin. prof. Sch. of Pub. Health; co-chair State of Mass. Patient Centered Med. Home Initiative Coordination Coun.; bd. dirs. New Eng. Healthcare Inst.; chair Blue Cross Blue Shield Assn. Nat. Coun. of Physician Execs. Bd. dirs. Nat. Com. for Quality Assurance Med. Stds., Neighborhood Health Plan, MASSPRO; bd. advisors Temple Univ. Sch. of Medicine. Fellow: ACP. Office: Blue Cross Blue Shield Massachusetts Inc Landmark Center 401 Park Dr Boston MA 02215 Office Phone: 617-246-5000. Office Fax: 617-832-4832. *

FALLON, JOSEPH JAMES, endocrinologist; MD, Finch U. Health Scis./Chgo. Med. Sch., 1979. Resident endocrinology, diabetes and metabolism Thomas Jefferson Univ. Hosp.; resident internal medicine Hahnemann Univ. Hosp.; endocrinologist Underwood Meml. Hosp. Office: Underwood- Memorial Hospital 509 North Broad St Woodbury NJ 08096 Office Phone: 856-853-2011.

FALLUCCO, ELISE, child, adolescent psychiatrist; b. Austin, Tex., Apr. 11, 1979; BA, Princeton U., 2000; MD, Vanderbilt Sch. Medicine, 2004. Instr. Wash. U. Sch. Medicine, 2009—11; psychiatrist Nemours Childrens Clinic, 2011—. Recipient Eli Robins award, Wash. U. Dept. Psychiatry; named one of Resident Tchr. of Yr.; Rsch. grant, Cmtys. Healing Adolescent Depression and Suicide, Coalition Mental Health, St. Louis Children's Hosp. Found. Mem.: Am. Acad. Child and Adolescent Psychiatry (Robinson-Cunningham award). Avocations: swimming, reading. Office: 807 Children's Way Jacksonville FL 32207

FALMAGNE, RACHEL JOFFE, psychologist, educator; PhD in Psychology, Univ. Brussels. Faculty Clark Univ., Worcester, Mass., 1973—, now prof., dept. psychology. Co-editor: Mind and Social Practice: Selected Writings by Sylvia Scribner, 1997, Representing Reason: Feminist Theory and Formal Logic, 2003; author: Language as a Constitutive Factor in Logical Knowledge, 1988. Mem.: Internat. Soc. Theoretical Psychology (pres. 2005—09). Office: Dept Psychology Clark Univ 950 Main St Worcester MA 01610-1477 Office Phone: 508-793-7262. Business E-Mail: rfalmagne@clark.edu.

FALSONE, JACK JOSEPH, physician; b. Queens, NY, Nov. 6, 1923; s. Joseph and Margaret (Cutelli) F.; m. Anna Mandracchia, Dec. 23, 1945; children: Margaret, Catherine. AB, Columbia Coll., 1944; MD, L.I. Coll. Medicine, 1947. Diplomate Am. Bd. Internal Medicine. Intern Bklyn. Hosp., 1947-48, resident in internal medicine, 1948-51; attending physician Norwalk (Conn.) Hosp., 1954—91, assoc. chief chest diseases, 1970-87; instr. coll. medicine Yale U., 1955-61, asst. clin. prof. medicine, 1961-69; sr. rsch. assoc. Beulah Hinds Ctr., Norwalk Hosp., 1991—; vol. physician AmeriCare Free Clinic, Norwalk, 1994—, vol. med. dir., 1999—. Served with AUS, 1943-46, USAF, 1951-53. Fellow ACP; mem. Norwalk Heart Assn. (pres. 1955), Norwalk Med. Soc. (pres. 1975), Am. Coll. Chest Physicians. Roman Catholic. Office: Beulah Hinds Ctr Norwalk Hosp Norwalk CT 06856 Home Phone: 203-227-8165; Office Phone: 203-855-3615. E-mail: jack.falsone@norwalkhealth.org.

FALTER, ROBERT GARY, real estate broker, realtor, educator; s. Lawrence Z. and Helen (Smith) F.; m. Kathleen Ann Burrill, July 9, 1982; children: John William Wright III, Jason Michael Wright. AA, St. John's U., 1965, BA, 1967; MA, Kean U., 1973; MBA, Cornell U., 1976; PhD, Walden U., 1993. Lic. real estate broker, cert. realtor Mass., real estate instr., seniors real estate specialist, e-Pro Internet profl., accredited buyer rep., Mass. Assn. Realtors grad. REALTOR Inst., Loss Mitigation, loss mitigation cert. Nat. Assn. Realtors, short sale foreclosure resource cert. Nat. Assn. Realtors, Real Estate Buyer's Agent Coun. Adminstrv. resident NY Hosp./Cornell Med. Ctr., NYC, summer 1975; mgr. ophthalmology Hahnemann Med. Coll. & Hosp., Phila., 1976-77; dir. out-patient clinic USPHS Ctr. for Disease Control, Atlanta, 1977—78; project officer ambulatory care data systems USPHS Divsn. Hosps. and Clinics, West Hyattsville, Md., 1978-80; assoc. dir. ambulatory care USPHS Hosp., Boston, 1980-81; adminstr. family medicine Sch. of Medicine U. Tenn., Memphis, 1981-82; asst. v.p. customer svc./instnl. benefits Blue Cross/Blue Shield of NY, NYC, 1982-86; assoc. v.p. ops. SI Hosp., 1986-87; assoc. dir. adminstrv. svcs. divsn. fed. employee occupl. health USPHS Region II, NYC, 1988-89; health/resources and svcs. adminstr. Rockville, Md., 1989; materiel mgmt. officer, dep. br. chief, 1989; health care adminstr. individual ready rsch. USPHS, Rockville, 1989-90, chief program liaison unit, 1990-91, chief budget officer BOP/HSD, 1991-93, chief br. budget and mgmt. support, 1993-99; chief health svcs. officer Office of the Surgeon Gen./Pub. Health Svc., 1995-99; adminstrv. officer Fed. Med. Ctr., Fed. Bur. Prisons, Devens, Ayer, Mass., 1999-2000, quality risk mgr., 2000; health care adminstr. correctional med. svcs. MCI-Shirley-Medium, Mass., 2000—02; adminstr.-in-tng. Clark Manor Healthcare Ctr., 2002; asst. adminstr. Tower Hill Ctr. for Health and Rehab., Canton, Mass., 2002—03, Harborlights Nursing and Rehab. Ctr., 2002; interim adminstr. Avery Manor Rehab. and Nursing Ctr., Needham, Mass., 2003; adminstr. Linda Manor Extended Care Facility, Leeds, Mass., 2003—04; realtor Coldwell Banker Residential Brokerage Park Ave., Worcester, Mass., 2004—07; broker assoc., trainer Weichert Realtors, Home & Land Ptnrs., Auburn, Mass., 2007—08, Keller Williams Realty, Worcester, 2008—09, Gold Triangle Realty, Shrewsbury, 2009—10, ERA Key Realty Svcs., Worcester, 2010—. Chmn. hosp. and med. care adminstrs. Health Care Profls. Adv. Com., 1989—91; co-chmn. centennial symposium planning com. Health Svcs. Officers, 1989; lectr. fiscal mgmt. Christian Bros. U., Memphis, 1982; lectr. health econs. grad. program in health svcs. adminstrn. Salve Regina Coll., Newport, RI, 1984; mem. assoc. grad. faculty, acad. advisor Ctrl. Mich. U. Coll. Extended Learning Health Svcs. Adminstrn., 1995—2004; adj. asst. prof. divsn. nursing rsch. Uniformed Svcs. U. Health Scis. Grad. Sch. Nursing, Bethesda, 1996—2001; adj. instr. Vanderbilt U. Sch. Nursing, Nashville, 1999—2005; sr. lectr. Western New Eng. Coll., Springfield, Mass., 2000—02; bd. dirs. Nat. Commn. on Correctional Health Care, 1991—94, mem. program com., 1991—92, mem. publs. com., 1991—94, mem. exec. com., 1992—94, mng. editor Jour. Correctional Health Care, 1994—97; adj. asst. prof. preventive medicine and biometrics, Health Svcs. Adminstrn., Uniformed Svcs. U. of Health Scis., Bethesda, 1999—2001; real estate instr., Mass., 2006—; instr. Ctr. for Real Estate Studies & Training, Worcester Regional Assn. of Realtors, 2007—; dean Grad. REALTOR Inst., Mass. Assn. Realtors, 2007—, instr., 2009, Real Estate Buyer's Agent Coun., Nat. Assn. Realtors, 2010—, North Ctrl. Mass. Assn. Realtors, 2010—, Berkshire County Bd. Realtors, 2011—; newsletter proofreader Mass. Rental Housing Assn., 2008; charter mem. Family Care Real Estate Network Nat. Caregivers Libr., 2011—. Bd. dirs. Vis. Nurse Assn. Memphis Inc., 1982; mem. cmty. adv. bd. Primary Health Care for Srs., Allston-Brighton Med. Care Coalition, Boston, 1981; usher coord. St. Michael's Cath. Ch., Poplar Springs, 1989-91; vol. U. Mass. Meml. Med. Ctr., Worcester, 2006-, Town of Shrewsbury, Mass., mem., Coun. Disabilties, 2010-; bd. dirs. Centro las Americas, Worcester, 2011-. With US Army, 1968—71, Commissioned Corps. O-6 US Pub. Health Svc., 1977—2001, ret. US Pub. Health Svc., 2001. Recipient Capt. Stanley J. Kissel, Jr. award USPHS/Health Svcs. Officer, 1994, Surgeon Gen.'s Exemplary Svc. medal USPHS, 1996, 99; 5 Year Service award, Worcester Regional Assn. of Realtors; Rookie of Yr., Worcester Regional Assn. Realtors, 2006, Educator of Yr., 2010. Fellow: Am. Acad. Med. Adminstrs. (hon.), Am. Coll. Healthcare Execs. (life; editl. bd. Healthcare Execs. 1986—88, book reviewer Hosp. and Health Svcs. Adminstrn.); mem.: Mil. Officers Assn. Am. (pres. Worcester (Mass.) county chpt. 2002—04, mem. exec. com. 2004—, personal affairs officer 2007—), Worcester Regional Assn. Realtors (mem. edn. com. 2005—08, profl. stds. com. 2008—, alt. dir., bd. dirs. 2009, membership com. mem. 2009—, mem. edn. com. 2010—, named Rookie of Yr. 2006, Educator of Yr. 2010), Mass. Assn. Realtors (mem. edn. and events com. 2006, mem. profl. standards com. 2007—, forms rev. com. 2008, dir., bd. dirs. 2009—10), Nat. Assn. Realtors, Real Estate Educators Assn., D.C.-Md.-Va. Hosp. Assn. (chmn. liaison com. 51st ann. conv. 1991), Commd. Officers Assn. USPHS (sec. Atlanta chpt. 1978), Assn. Mil. Surgeons U.S. (reviewer Mil. Medicine 1989—, cons.), Healthcare Mgmt. Assn. Mass., Assn. Health Care Adminstrs. Nat. Capital Area, Anchor and Caduceus Soc. (charter), Res. Officers Assn. U.S. (newsletter editor Montgomery County chpt. 1989), KC (warden St. Michael's of Poplar Springs coun. 1990—91, chancellor 1991—92, mem. mktg. com. 2005, Adelphi Coun. #4181, Shrewsbury). Independent. Roman Catholic. Avocations: travel, writing, consulting, teaching, coaching. Home: 50 Deerfield Rd Shrewsbury MA 01545-1571 Office Phone: 508-372-6445. Office Fax: 508-372-6445. Business E-Mail: rgf4@cornell.edu, bobfalter@erakey.com.

FALUDI, BÉLA, neurologist; b. Bonyhád, Hungary, June 24, 1966; MD, Med. U., Pécs, Hungary, 1991, PhD, 1996. Physician dept. neurology U. Pécs, 1996—. Mem.: European Sleep Rsch. Soc., Hungarian Sleep Soc. Office: Rét St 2 Pécs Baranya H-7623 Hungary Office Fax: 36 72 535911. Business E-Mail: bela.faludi@gmail.com.

FAN, DONGSHENG, hospital administrator; b. Jinan, Shandong, China, Aug. 29, 1963; PhD, Jichi Med. U., Japan, 1996. V.p. Peking U. Third Hosp., 2002—. Mem.: Chinese Med. Assn. Office: 49 North Garden Rd Haidian Dist Beijing 100191 China Office Fax: 62017700. Business E-Mail: dsfan@sina.com.

FAN, FENLING, physician; b. China, Nov. 15, 1971; D, Xi'an Jiaotong U., 2009. Attending physician 1st Hosp. Xi'an Jiaotong U., 2000—. Vis. postdoc. fellow Baker IDI Heart & Diabetes Inst., 2010—. Mem.: CSANZ. Office: 277 Wester Yanta Rd Xi'an Shaanxi 710061 China Business E-Mail: happyling@mail.xjtu.edu.cn.

FAN, HONGBIN, orthopedist, educator; b. China, Feb. 20, 1975; MD, Fourth Mil. Med. U., PhD, 1998. Prof., cons., dept. orthop. surgery Xijing Hosp. Fourth Mil. Med. U., 1998—. Recipient Yisu Zhao award, Chinese Med. Soc. Fellow: Nat. U. Singapore; mem.: Tissue Engring. and Regenerative Medicine Soc. Avocations: swimming, reading, travel. Office: Dept Orthop Surgery FMMU Xi'an Shaanxi 710032 China Personal E-mail: fanhb75@yahoo.com.cn.

FAN, TAI-SHEN LIU, dietician; b. Taichung, Taiwan, Nov. 15, 1950; came to the U.S., 1976; d. Chi-Pei and Ching-Lien Liu; m. Chien-Chung Fan, Feb. 22, 1975; 1 child, Caroline. BA in Social Edn., Nat. Taiwan Normal U., Taipei, 1972; AS in Med. Lab. Tech., Miami Dade CC, Fla., 1980; BS in Nutrition and Med. Dietetics, U. Ill., Chgo., 1986. Lic. dietitian State of Ill. Dept. Profl. Regulation. Counselor, tchr. Ta-Li Girls' Jr. H.S., Taipei, 1972-73, chief counselor, tchr., 1973-76; clin. dietitian Suburban Hosp. and Sanitarium, Hinsdale, Ill., 1986—87, St. Francis Hosp., Evanston, Ill., 1987—. Dean of acads. Chinese Lang. Sch., Chinese Cultural and Ednl. Assn., Skokie, Ill., 1993-95, rec. sec., 1995-96, asst. prin., dean acads., 1996-97; trustee Chinese Cultural and Ednl. Assn., 2000-02, mem. exec. com., 2003—. Cheng-Fu Hsieh Meml. scholar, Taipei, 1971, Yun-Wu Wang scholar, Taipei, 1971. Mem. Am. Dietetic Assn. (registered dietitian), Ill. Dietetic Assn., U. Ill. Alumni Assn., Phi Tau Phi, Phi Theta Kappa. Avocations: reading, cooking. Office: PO Box 4572 8141 Kedvale Ave Skokie IL 60076-4572 Personal E-mail: ts_fan@sbcglobal.net.

FAN, ZHUPING, physician, director; b. Jiangsu, China, Oct. 26, 1965; MS, Shanghai Second Med. U., 1989, PhD, 2004. Dir. Ren Ji Hosp., Health Care Ctr., 2008—. Assoc. prof. Shanghai Jiao Tong U., Sch. Medicine, 2006—. Office: 1630 Dong Fang Rd Shanghai 200127 China Business E-Mail: zhuping_fan@163.com.

FANCHER, EDWIN CRAWFORD, psychologist, educator; b. Middletown, NY, Aug. 29, 1923; s. Frank Dane and Elizabeth (McGarr) F.; m. Vivian Kramer, Nov. 8, 1969; children: Bruce Daniel, Emily Jill. BA, The New Sch. U., 1949, MA, 1951. Psychologist Linden (N.J.) Mental Hygiene Clinic, 1955-58; therapist Cmty. Guidance Svc., NYC, 1958-88; pvt. practice psychology, counseling NYC, 1958—; co-founder, dir. Washington Sq. Inst. Psychotherapy and Mental Health, NYC, 1960-70. Co-founder, pub. Village Voice, N.Y.C., 1955-74; dir. Orange County Telephone Co., Middletown, N.Y., 1946-60; cons. Plumsock Fund, Indpls., 1974-96, pres. 1985-96; founding pres. N.Y. Sch. for Psychoanalytic Psychotherapy and Psychoanalysis, 1978—. Founder, past chmn. N.Y. Neighborhoods Coun. on Narcotics Addiction. Served with U.S. Army, 1943-46. Decorated two Bronze stars. Mem. APA, Internat. Psychoanalytical Assn., Am. Inst. Psychotherapy and Psychoanalysis, Am. Orthopsychiat. Assn., N.Y. State Psychol. Assn., N.Y. Sch. for Psychoanalytic Psychotherapy and Psychoanlysis (pres. 1978—), N.Y. Freudian Soc. (mem. faculty tng. analyst 1985—), Am. Psychoanalytic Assn., Gipsy Trail. Democrat. Office: 33 Greenwich Ave New York NY 10014-2701 Home: 45 Gramercy Pk N 14 B New York NY 10010 Office Phone: 212-620-0514. Personal E-mail: edwinfancher@earthlink.net.

FANELLO, SERGE, public health service officer, educator; b. Le Havre, July 1, 1952; PhD, Angers U., 1978; D in Economics, U. Paris Dauphine, 1989. Pôle chief CHU Angers, 2008—. Prof. dept pub. health, 2000. Recipient Order of Academic Palms. Mem.: Soc. Françise De Santé Pub. Office: 4 Rue Larrey Angers Maine Et Loire 49933 France Office Fax: 0241353455. Business E-Mail: sefanello@chu-angers.fr.

FANG, HSIU-YU, cardiologist; b. Tainan, Taiwan, Dec. 7, 1978; Degree, Tzu Chi U., 2004. Physician divsn. cardiology Kaohsiung Chang Gung Meml. Hosp., 2004—. Office: 123 Ta Pei Rd Niao Sung Dist Kaohsiung 813 Taiwan E-mail: ast42aiu@hotmail.com.

FANG, I-MO, ophthalmologist, director; b. Tainan, Taiwan, Feb. 22, 1969; PhD, Nat. Taiwan U., 2009. Chief resident, clin. investigator, dept. ophthalmology Nat. Taiwan U. Hosp., 2000—02, asst. prof., 2009—; dir., dept. ophthalmology Taipei City Hosp., ZhonghXiao Br., 2002—. Recipient Best Internship prize, Nat. Taiwan U. Mem.: Laser and Photonics Medicine Soc. ROC, Am. Acad. Ophthalmology, Ophthal. Soc. Taiwan. Avocations: travel, reading. Office: 87 Tonde Rd Taipei 886 Taiwan E-mail: fimort@yahoo.com.tw.

FANG, TE-CHAO, nephrologist, educator; s. Wan-Chu Fang and Chin-Ho Tsai; m. Yen-E Cheng; children: Hsuan-Hsiang, Tsai-Hsuan. MD, Kaohsiung Med. U., Taiwan, 1990; MSc, Tzu Chi U., Hualien, Taiwan, 1997; PhD, U. London, 2006. Cert. Bd. Medicine, Taiwan Govt., 1990, Taiwan Soc. Internal Medicine, 1993, Taiwan Soc. Nephrology, 1994. Dir., divsn. nephrology & dialysis unit Tzu Chi Gen. Hosp., Hualien, Taiwan, 2005—; assoc. prof. Tzu Chi U., 2006—. Edn. com. mem. Taiwan Soc. Nephrology, Taipei; editor bd. Tzu Chi Med. Jour., 2007—, Acta Nephrologica, 2008—. Recipient Rsch. award, Taiwan Soc. Nephrology, 2000, Tzu Chi Gen. Hosp., 1998, 1999, 2008, Nat. Sci. Coun., 1997, 1998. Office: Buddhist Tzu Chi Gen Hosp 707 Chung Yang Rd Sect 3 Hualien 970 Taiwan Personal E-mail: fangtechao@gmail.com.

FANG, XIANG, neurologist; b. Changde, Oct. 30, 1963; MD, Hunan Med. U., 1985, PhD, 1993. Asst. prof. U. Tex. Med. Br., 2010—. Rsch. scientist U. Iowa, 1993—2006. Mem.: AMA, Am. Acad. Neurology. Office: 301 University Blvd Galveston TX 77555 Business E-Mail: xiang.fang01@gmail.com.

FAN-GIBSON, CHIANN, cosmetic dentist; m. Jim Gibson. Grad., Tufts Sch. Dental Medicine, Boston; grad. with honors, THombrook Ctr. Advacned Clin. Edn. Cert. Invisalign. Clin. instr. dep. restorative dentistry Tuft Sch. Dental Medicine; owner Smiles By Gibson & Assocs. Advanced tng. The Ctr. For Esthetic Excellence, Chgo.; lectr. Chgo. Dental Soc., Calif. Dental Soc., ADA. Contbr. columns in newspapers Naperville Sun Times; featured in Am. Assn. Women Dentists Mag., 2006. Named Official Dentist of Miss Universe, Miss Universe Inc., Wash.'s Jr. Miss, Miss Wash. USA, Mrs. US, 2005—06, 1 of only 66 Distinguished Delta Alumni, Tri-Delta Sorority, 2006. Mem.: Ill. State Dental Soc., Fox Valley Dental Soc., Chgo. Dental Soc., ADA, Am. Assn. Women Dentists, Acad. Gen. Dentistry, Am. Acad. Cosmetic Dentistry. Office: Smiles By Gibson & Associates The Promenade 55 S Main St Ste 290 Naperville IL 60540 Office Phone: 630-357-3333.

FANNING, FRED ELDRIDGE, public administrator; b. Valdosta, Ga., Dec. 8, 1956; s. Aden Eldridge and Glenda Jean Fanning; m. Tammy Lu Hanson, Apr. 22, 1978; children: Fred Eldridge Fanning II, Ted Aldridge. AS, Cloud County C.C., 1984; BS, Excelsior Coll., 1993; MEd, Nat. Louis U., 1996; MA, Webster U., 2005. Cert. safety profl. 2010. Safety specialist Safety Office, 1st Inf. Divsn., Ft. Riley, Kans., 1986—89, Safety Divsn., 8th Inf. Divsn. (Mech), Bad Kreuznach, Germany, 1989—90; safety mgr. Safety Office, US Army Berlin and Berlin Brigade, 1990—94; safety specialist Safety Divsn., US Army Europe, Heidelberg, Germany, 1994—95; safety dir. G-1, US Army V Corps, Heidelberg, 1995—98, US Army Maneuver Support Ctr., Fort Leonard Wood, Mo., 1999—2004; sr. safety mgr. Office of the Dir. of Army Safety, Arlington, Va., 2004—05; dir. office occupl. safety and health US Dept. Commerce, Washington, 2005—07, dir. for adminstrv svcs., appt. sr. exec. svc., 2007—09; dir., Office Program Integration & logistics Ops. US Dept. Energy, Washington, 2009—. Vice chmn. South Ctrl. Mo. Safety Coun., Lebanon, 2000, Greater St. Louis Safety Coun., 2002—04; instr. Pk. Univ., Ft. Leonard Wood, Mo., 2001—04; vice chairperson Fed. Adminstrv. Mgrs. Assn., 2007—08, chairperson, 2008—09; asst. adminstr. Am. Soc. Safety Engrs. Pub. Sector Practice Specialty, 2009—11, adminstrn., 2007—09. Author: (technical book) Basic Safety Administration: A Handbook for the New Safety Professional, (tech. chpt.) Safety Traning & Documentation Principles in Safety Professional Handbook; contbr. chapters to books, articles to jours. Sgt. US Army, 1975—78, Ft. Riley, Kansas. Decorated Good Conduct medal US Army, Achievement medal for Civilian Svc., Armed Forces Civilian Svc. medal, NATO medal for Svc. in the Former Yugoslavia, Commander's Award for Civilian Svc. US Army, Superior Civilian Svc. medal; recipient Bronze medal, US Dept. Commerce. Mem.: Am. Soc. Safety Engrs., Masonic Lodge. Conservative. Christian. Avocations: reading, writing. Home: 3 Chandler Ct Fredericksburg VA 22405

FANTINI, GARY A., vascular surgeon, educator; BA, Boston U., 1979; MD, Albert Einstein Coll. of Medicine, 1983. Diplomate Am. Bd. Surgery-gen. surgery, Am. Bd. Surgery-vascular surgery. Internship, residency gen. surgery The NY Hosp. Cornell Med. Ctr., 1988—89, fellowship; fellowship Moffitt Long hosps. Univ. of Calif., San Francisco, 1989—90; assoc. attending surgeon vascular Hosp. Spl. Surgery; clin. assoc. prof. surgery Weill Med. Coll. Cornell Univ.; assoc. attending surgeon The New York-Presbyterian hosp. Weill Cornell Ctr. Office: New York Physicians 635 Madison Ave New York NY 10022 Office Phone: 212-317-4550. Office Fax. 212-752-2454.

FANTONG, WILSON YETOH, geologist; b. Cameroon, Dec. 18, 1972; PhD with honors, U. Toyama, Japan, 2010. Asst. rschr. Inst. Rsch. Geology and Mining Yaounde, Cameroon, 2002—09, sr. rschr., 2009—; vis. lectr. U. Buea Cameroon, 2010—11. Monbushu scholarship, Ministry of Culture and Edn., Japan, Rsch. grant, Sasagawa Found. Japan. Mem.: Internat. Assn. Hydrogeologist. Avocations: tennis, gardening, reading. Office: PO Box 4110 Nlongkak Yaounde 4110 Cameroon Personal E-mail: fyyetoh@yahoo.com.

FARADAY, NAUDER, physician, educator; b. Buffalo, Nov. 3, 1962; BA, Columbia U., 1984; MD, Mt. Sinai Sch. Medicine, 1988. Assoc. prof. anesthesiology, critical care medicine, surgery Johns Hopkins U., 1993—. Mem.: Alpha Omega Alpha. Office: Johns Hopkins Hosp Dept Anesthesiology Critical Care Medici Baltimore MD 21287 Office Fax: 410-955-8978. Business E-Mail: nfaraday@jhmi.edu.

FARAH, TONY G., cardiologist; MD, Am. Univ. Beirut, Lebanon, 1984. Diplomate Am. Bd. Internal Medicine, 1987, Am. Bd. Internal Medicine-cardiovasc. disease, 1989, Am. Bd. Internal Medicine-interventional cardiology, 2009. Intern Allegheny Gen. Hosp., Pitts., resident internal medicine, 1984—87, fellow cardiovasc. disease, 1987—90, chief med. officer, med. dir. cardiac catheterization labs., interim quality officer; resident UPMC Magee Women's Hosp., fellow; physician Cardiology Assocs. Inc.; clin. asst. prof. medicine Drexel Univ. Office: Allegheny General Hospital Allegheny Professional Building 490 E N Ave Ste 307 Pittsburgh PA 15212 Office Phone: 412-359-5822. Office Fax: 412-359-6620.

FARAHAT, FAYSSAL, medical educator; b. Shibin el Kom, Menoufia, Egypt, Oct. 30, 1970; PhD, Menoufia U., 1994. Assoc. prof. pub. health Menoufia U., 2008—. Office: Menoufia University Shibin el Kom Menoufia Egypt Personal E-mail: fmfayssal@hotmail.com.

FARAHMAND, PARVIS, physician, researcher; b. Berlin, Jan. 16, 1972; s. Akbar and Ina (Caspereit) Farahmand. A-Levels, Kopernikus-Gymnasium, Niederkassel, Germany, 1991. Cert. medical bd. U. Cologne, 1999, Step I and II US med. lic. exam., 2000, emergency medicine Med. Chamber, Nordrhein, 2003, travel medicine German Acad. Aviation and Travel Medicine, German Soc. Aviation and Space Medicine, German Soc. Tropical Medicine and Internat. Health, 2005, aviation medicine German Acad. Aviation and Travel Medicine, 2005, diplomate Bd. Internal Medicine Med. Chamber Nordrhein, 2007. Intern med. Dept. Hematology and Oncology U. Cologne, Leverkusen, Germany, 2001, intern med. Dept. Cardiology and Emergency Medicine, 2001—02, resident internal medicine, rheumatology & osteology, 2002—05, dep. cons. physician internal medicine, rheumatology and osteology, 2005—. Project mgr. hosp. info. sys. ITB Informationstechnologie & Beratung, Cologne, 1995—2000; med. advisor pvt. health ins. cos. DKV Deutsche Krankenversicherung, Cologne, 2000—02; lectr. Sch. Nursing, Leverkusen, 2003—, German Soc. Nutrition, Bonn, Germany, 2006—; lectr. Sch. Paramedics and Firemen City of Leverkusen Fire Dept., 2004—. Contbr. articles to profl. jours. Emergency med. relief for tsunami victims with Deutsche Minenraumer, Pottuvil, Sri Lanka, 2005; emergency med. relief for earthquake victims with Deutsche Minenraumer and Order of Malta, Yogjakarta, Java, Indonesia, 2006. Recipient Best Poster prize, Dochverband Osteologie Berlin Germany, 2010, Pleuary Poster award, Am. Soc. Bone & Med. Rsch., San Diego, 2011. Mem.: German Soc. Aviation and Travel Medicine (mem. bd. dirs.), German Soc. Osteology, German Soc. Endocrinology, German Soc. Internal Medicine, Aviation Sports Club, German Aeroclub, Order of Malta. Achievements include research in metabolic bone diseases. Avocations: travel, hiking, glider flying. Office: West German Osteoporosis Ctr Klinikum Leverkusen Med Klinik IV Am Gesundheitspark 11 Leverkusen D-51375 Germany Office Fax: 0049214132294. Personal E-mail: parvis@farahmand.de. Business E-Mail: farahmand@klinikum-lev.de.

FARASYN, ANDRE DANIEL, osteopath, researcher; b. Ghent, Belgium, Feb. 17, 1951; s. Daniel Farasyn and Gilberte Schepens; life ptnr. Yvonne De Clercq. PhD, Vrye U., Brussels, 1974. Diplomate in osteopathy European Sch. Osteopathy, UK, 1983. Pvt. practice phys. therapist, Ghent, Belgium, 1974—83; pvt. practice osteopath, 1983—. Asst. prof. Vrije U., Brussels, 1984—. Lt. reserves Belgium Infantry, 1974—75. Master: De Zwijger GLB Belgium (assoc.); mem.: Internat. Myopain Soc. (assoc.). Liberal. Achievements include research in non-specific low back pain; tension headache, pressure pain thresholds (algometry) myopain, referred muscle pain back ache disability index. Home: Krijgslaan 195 Ghent BE 9000 Belgium Personal E-mail: andre.farasyn@telenet.be. Business E-Mail: andre.farasyn@vub.ac.be.

FARBER, ALIK, surgeon; b. Beltsy, Moldova, Apr. 29, 1965; BS, Brown U., 1987; MD, Harvard Med. Sch., 1992. Chief vascular surgery Boston U. Med. Ctr., 2008—. Fellow: ACS; mem.: Soc. Vascular Surgery. Office: 88 East Newton St Boston MA 02118 Business E-Mail: alik.farber@bmc.org.

FARBER, GEORGE ALLAN, dermatologist, educator; b. Miami, Fla., Jan. 4, 1934; s. Charles R. and Clara M. (Milman) F.; m. Nancy Graves, Dec. 26, 1955; children: George Allan, Michael G., Jeffrey N., Guy C., Scott Q. BS, La. State U., 1955, MD, 1959. Diplomate Am. Bd. Cosmetic Surgery., Am. Bd. Dermatology. Intern So. Bapt. Hosp., New Orleans, 1959-60; resident Charity Hosp. of New Orleans, 1963-66; commd. 2d lt. M.C. USAF, 1955, advanced through grades to lt. col., 1965; chief aviation medicine and mil. pub. health Luke AFB, Phoenix, 1960-63; flight surgeon, chief dermatology and syphilology 12th USAF Hosp., Cam Ranh Bay, Vietnam, 1966-67; chief dermatology svc., cons. to Surgeon Gen. S.E. region USAF Med. Referral Ctr., Keesler AFB, Miss., 1967-70; ret. USAF, 1970; asst. prof. medicine Tulane U. Sch. Medicine, New Orleans, 1970-75, assoc. prof., 1976-84; pvt. practice dermatology, 1970—; clin. assoc. prof. dermatology Tulane U. Sch. Medicine, New Orleans, 1975-84; mem. staff Kenner Regional Ctr. Hosp., 1994-2000. Past mem. staff Charity Hosp. New Orleans, East Jefferson Hosp., So. Bapt. Hosp., Kenner (La.) Regional Med. Ctr.; mem. courtesy staff LifeCare Hosp., Kenner; prof., med. dir. resident and postgrad. accredited tng. program Gulf South Med. and Surgery Inst., Kermer, La.; mem. profl. staff Kenner Dermatology Clinic; ret. dir. Fairground Corp., New Orleans; mem. courtesy staff Northshore Regional Med. Ctr., Slidell, La.; bd. dirs. La. Divsn. Am. Lukemia Soc. Decorated Bronze Star; named Physician of Yr., Nat. Rep. Congl. Com. Physicians' Adv. Bd., 2003, 2004; named one of Ams. Top Physicians, Consumer's Rsch. Coun. Am., 2006. Fellow Am. Acad. Oral and Maxillofacial Surgery; mem. Kenner Med. Soc. (founder, sec./treas. 1998), N.Am. Acad. Cosmetic and Reconstructive Surgery (founder, bd. dirs., pres. 1998-99), Am. Soc. Dermatologic Surgery (co-founder, past officer and dir.), Am. Acad. Cosmetic Surgery (co-founder, past officer and dir.), Am. Bd. Cosmetic Surgery (examiner, rev. course lectr., past officer and dir.), Leukemia and Lymphoma Soc. L.A. (sec. 2005, 06), Am. Acad. Dermatology (life), So. Med. Assn., Internat. Soc. Hair Restoration Surgery, La. State Med. Soc. (mem. pub. health com. and ins. com. 2003-06), St. Bernard Parish Med. Soc. Home: 3705 Florida Ave Kenner LA 70065-2473 Office: Gulf South Med Surg Inst 3705 Florida Ave Kenner LA 70065-2473 Office Phone: 504-471-3100. Personal E-mail: gsmi3705@yahoo.com.

FARBER, HAROLD F., dermatologist; BA in Gen. Arts and Sciences, Pa. State U. Diplomate Am. Bd. Dermatology. Med. tng. Albany Med. Coll.; internal medicine internship Albany Med. Ctr.; with Lankenau Med. Ctr., 1995—; with dermatology dept. Thomas Jefferson Univ. Hosp., resident dermatology dept., chief resident dermatology. Guest lectr. Phila. Dermatol. Soc., Pa. Acad. of Dermatology. Author numerous publs. regarding his work as dermatologist. Named one of Top Surgeons, Mainline Today, 2008. Mem.: AMA, Phila. Dermatology Soc., Pa. Acad. of Dermatology, Am. Acad. of Dermatology, Phila. County Med. Soc., Am. Soc. for Dermatologic Surgery, Pa. Med. Soc. Office: Harold F Farber MD and Associates Ste 100 822 Montgomery Ave Narberth PA 19072 Mailing: Suites 202 204 Moss Plz 9892 Bustleton Ave Philadelphia PA 19115 Office Phone: 610-664-4433, 215-676-2464.

FARBER, ISADORE E., psychologist, educator; b. St. Joseph, Mo., May 21, 1917; s. Jacob and Rose (Malkin) F.; m. Billie Frances Gulko, May 5, 1942, (dec.); children: Ronna Ellen (dec.), Deborah. Student, St. Joseph Jr. Coll., 1934-36; BA, U. Mo., 1939, MA, 1940; PhD, U. Iowa, 1946. Instr. psychology U. Rochester, 1946-47; asst. prof. to prof. psychology U. Iowa, 1947-64; vis. prof. U. Wis., 1955, Stanford, 1960; research cons. Med. Sch., U. of Okla., 1956-57; prof. psychology U. Ill., Chgo., 1964-84, prof. emeritus, 1984—, head dept. psychology, 1964-68, 76-81. Vis. prof., sr. Fulbright fellow Hebrew U., Jerusalem, 1971-72. Founding editor Jour. Exptl. Research in Personality, 1965-71; editor Psychology series, Dodd, Mead & Co., 1965-73; cons. editor Jour. Abnormal and Social Psychology, 1955-61, Jour. of Personality, 1955-61, Jour. Abnormal Psychology, 1973-79; contbr. articles to profl. jours. Served with Q.M.C. AUS, 1941-42; to 2d lt. USAAF, 1942-45. Fellow APA, Assoc. Psychol. Sci.; mem. Midwestern Psychol. Assn. (past pres.), Psychonomic Soc., Phi Beta Kappa, Sigma Xi. Jewish. Home: 2601 Chestnut Ave #1303 Glenview IL 60026

FARBER, MARK ADAM, medical association administrator; b. Dallas, June 12, 1964; MD, Tulane U., 1991. Dir. aortic ctr. UNC Divsn. Vascular Surgery, 1998—. Mem.: UNC Divsn. Vascular Surgery. Office: 3025 Burnett Womack CB#7212 Chapel Hill NC 27599 Business E-Mail: mark_farber@med.unc.edu.

FARBER, MARTHA J. (MARTY FARBER), ophthalmologist, medical association administrator; BS in Biology, Rensselaer Polytechnic Inst., 1972; MD, SUNY Downstate Medical Ctr. Coll., 1982. Prof., chief ophthalmology Albany Medical Coll.; assoc. chief of staff for edn. Albany VA, chief ophthalmology, 1993—. Mem.: American Assn. Ophthalmic Pathologists (sec. treas. 1999—2002, pres. 2008—09), American Bd. Ophthalmology (chair 2009).

FARBER, ROSANN ALEXANDER, geneticist, educator; b. Charlotte, NC, Nov. 21, 1944; d. J. Wilson Jr. and June Adell (Childs) Alexander; m. Gerald Lee Farber, July 28, 1966 (div. Jan. 1969); m. Thomas Douglas Petes, July 20, 1973; children: Laura Elizabeth Petes, Diana Christine Petes. AB in Biology, Oberlin Coll., 1966; postgrad., U. Pitts., 1967-68, Albert Einstein Coll. Medicine, 1969; PhD in Genetics, U. Wash., 1973. Diplomate in clin. cytogenetics and clin. molecular genetics Am. Bd. Med. Genetics. Postdoctoral fellow Nat. Inst. for Med. Rsch., London, 1973-75; rsch. assoc. Children's Hosp. Med. Ctr., Boston, 1975-77; from asst. prof. to assoc. prof. U. Chgo., 1977-88; assoc. prof. dept. pathology and lab. medicine, program molecular biology and biotechnology, curriculum genetics and molecular biology U. N.C., Chapel Hill, 1988-97, prof., 1997—, prof. dept. genetics, 2001—, assoc. chair dept. genetics, 2007—. Mem. U. N.C. Lineberger Comprehensive Cancer Ctr., 1996—. Contbr. articles to profl. jours. NIH grantee, 1978—. Mem. AAAS, Am. Soc. Human Genetics, Am. Coll. Med. Genetics. Achievements include research in human molecular genetics, somatic cell genetics, cancer genetics. Home: 612 Morgan Creek Rd Chapel Hill NC 27517-4928 Office: U NC CB 7525 Brinkhous-Bullitt Bldg Chapel Hill NC 27599 Office Phone: 919-966-6920. Business E-Mail: rfarber@med.unc.edu.

FARGEAUDOU, YANN ANTOINE, radiologist; b. Paris, Apr. 30, 1975; s. Evelyne Anne-Marie Fargeaudou-Dupont and Pierre Alain Fargeaudou; life ptnr. Claire Lafollet; 1 child, Yasmine Lafollet. MD, U. Paris VI, 2003; MSc in Med. Physics, U. Paris XI, 2003. Interventional radiologist Hôsp. Lariboisière - APHP, Paris, 2004—. _ _. Mem.: Cardiovasc. and Interventional Radiology, European Soc. Radiology, Soc. Française Radiologie. Home: 3 Allée Léon Gambetta Clichy 92110 France Office: Hôsp Lariboisière - APHP 2 Rd Ambroise Paré Paris 75475 Cedex 10 France Office Phone: 33 1 47 30 52 00. Office Fax: 01133149958270. Personal E-mail: yannfargeaudou4@hotmail.com. Business E-Mail: yann.fargeaudou@lrb.aphp.fr.

FARGHALI, HASSAN, pharmacologist, administrator, educator; b. Manfalot, Assiut, Egypt, June 6, 1943; arrived in Czech Republic, 1981; s. Hassan and Naima Abd El Shafi; m. Jana Brantova, Oct. 10, 1950; children: Omar, Hany. PhD, Charles U., Czech Republic, 1973; DSc, Charles U., 1996. Diplomate in pharmacology (med. scis.). Asst. prof. U. Basarh, Iraq, 1977-81; rschr. Acad. Sci. Czechoslovakia, 1981-86; postdoctoral fellow U. Medicine and Dentistry N.J., 1986-87; assoc. rsch. prof. U. Pitts., 1988-92; assoc. prof. Faculty of Medicine Charles U., Prague, 1994-97, chmn., prof., 1997—. Rsch. cons. Acad. Scis. of Czech Republic, 1997—. Co-editor: Basic and Applied Pharmacology, 2007; contbr. articles to profl. jours. Mem. Czech Pharmacol. Soc., N.Y. Acad. Scis. Avocations: jogging, reading, music. Home: Piscita 331 Jahodnice 19800 Prague 9 Czech Republic Office Phone: 420 224 968106. Business E-Mail: hfarg@1fl.cuni.cz.

FARIA, ELISANGELA JACINTO, medical geneticist; b. Campinas, Jan. 3, 1976; PhD, Unicamp, 2007. With, fibrose cística Unicamp, 2000. Home: Desembargador Campos Maia 194 Campinas São Paulo 13090100 Brazil Personal E-mail: elliiss@yahoo.com.br.

FARIAS, MYLENE CHRISTINE QUEIROZ DE, engineering educator, researcher; b. João Pessoa, Brazil, Oct. 26, 1971; d. Afonso Gutemberg de and Celia Melo de Queiroz Farias; m. Marcelo Menezes de Carvalho, Feb. 15, 1997. BSEE, U. Fed. Pernambuco, Recife, Brazil, 1994; MSEE, U. Estadual, Campinas, Brazil, 1997; PhD, U. Calif., Santa Barbara, 2004. Rsch. engr. Centro de Pesquisa e Desenvolvimento em Telecomunicações, Campinas, 1997—98; intern rsch. engr. Philips Rsch. Laboratories Nat. lab., Eindhoven, Netherlands, 2003; rschr. U. Calif., Santa Barbara, 2004—05; rschr. engr. Intel Corp., Chandler, Ariz., 2005—06; rschr., vis. prof. U. Fed. Campina Grande, Brazil, 2006—08, prof. Scholar, CAPES, 1998—2002; Rsch. grant, Centro de Pesquisa e Desenvolvimento em Telecomm., Brazil, 1991—94. Mem.: IEEE. Office: Univ de Brasília Instituto de Ciências Exatas Dept de Ciência da Computação Asa Norte 70910 900 Brasilia DF Brazil Office Phone: (061) 3072785 Ext 237. Personal E-mail: mylenefarias@yahoo.com.

FARIES, PETER L., vascular surgeon; b. Phila., Dec. 22, 1964; m. Lisa Faries; children: Christopher, Brendan, Catherine. MD, U. Pa., Phila., 1992. Diplomate Am. Bd. Surgery, with vascular qualification. Chief, vascular surgery Mt. Sinai Sch. Medicine, NYC, Franz W. Sichel prof., surrgery, asst. prof. surgery, 2000—02, Cornell U., Weill Med. Sch., NYC, 2002—, Columbia U., Coll. Physicians and Surgeons, NYC, 2002—; chief endovascular surgery N.Y. Presbyn. Hosp., NYC, 2002—; dir. Vascular Surgery Residency & Fellowship Tng. Program. Contbr. articles to profl. jours., chapters to books. Recipient Career Devel. award, NIH, von Leibig Vascular Surgery Rsch. award, Transl. Scis. award. Fellow: ACS (Trauma Surgery Rsch. award 1996); mem.: NY Acad. of Sciences, N.Y. Surg. Soc., Peripheral Vascular Surgery Soc. (award), Soc. for Clin. Vascular Surgery, Soc. for Vascular Surgery (Lifeline Found. grantee). Avocations: tennis, travel, writing, bicycling. Office: Div Vascular Surgery Mt Sinai Sch Med 5 E 98th St Box 1273 New York NY 10029 Office Phone: 212-241-5386. Business E-Mail: peter.faries@mountsinai.org.

FARISS, BRUCE LINDSAY, endocrinologist, consultant; b. Allisonia, Va., July 22, 1934; s. Alven Pierce and Hetty Jo (Lindsay) Fariss; m. Cheryl Louise Tomasie, Jan. 18, 1975; children: Bruce Lindsay, Melissa, Margaret, Susan, Henry, Sarah Jane, Caroline, Adam. BS, Roanoke Coll., 1957; MD, U. Va., 1961. Diplomate Am. Bd. Internal Medicine, Am. Bd. Endocrinology. Med. intern U. Va. Hosp., Charlottesville, 1961-62; commd. capt. M.C. U.S. Army, 1962, advanced through grades to col., 1976; gen. med. officer Ft. Monroe, Va., 1962-63; resident in internal medicine Brooke Gen. Hosp., Ft. Sam

Houston, Tex., 1963-66; fellow in endocrinology U. Calif., San Francisco, 1966-68; chief endocrine service Madigan Gen. Hosp., Tacoma, 1968-71, chief clin. rsch. svc., 1968-76, asst. chief dept. medicine, 1972-73, dir. endocrine fellowship program, 1971-76, chief dept. clin. investigation, 1979-85, dir. endocrine-metabolism fellowship tng. program, 1979-85; cons. internal medicine MEDCOM Europe, 1976-79; cons. endocrinology to surgeon gen. U.S. Army, 1979-85; with dept. biology Va. Poly. Inst., Blacksburg, 1987-99; sec., treas. Radford Cmty. Hosp., 1998—2000, vice chrmn., 2000—02, chmn., 2002—04, chmn. dept. M & D, 2005—06; clin. assoc. prof. Va. Coll. Osteo. Medicine, Blacksburg, 2006—. Contbr. articles to profl. jours. Mem. bd. suprs. Pulaski County, Va., 1988—2004, mem. recreation com. Va., 1989—93, mem. planning commn. Va., 1992—94, vice chmn. Va., 2000—04. Decorated Legion of Merit with oak leaf cluster; recipient Meritorious Svc. award, Office Surgeon Gen. Army, 1977, Roanoke Coll. medal, 1982. Fellow: ACP, Am. Coll. Endocrinology; mem.: Am. Assn. Clin. Endocrinologists, NY Acad. Sci., So. Med. Assn., Am. Diabetes Assn. (trustee 1986—89), Endocrine Soc. (ednl. com. 1980—83), Am. Fedn. Clin. Rsch., S.W. Va. Med. Soc., Alpha Omega Alpha. Office Phone: 540-674-5900.

FARKAS, PAUL STEPHEN, gastroenterologist; b. NYC, 1952; s. Benjamin J. and Ellen (Tanner) F.; m. Esta Miriam Cantor, June 24, 1973; children: Melanie Sharon, Joshua David. AB magna cum laude with distinction in psychology, Brandeis U., 1972; MD, Tufts U., 1976. Diplomate Am. Bd. Internal Medicine, Am. Bd. Gastroenterology. Intern Baystate Med. Ctr., Sprinfield, Mass., 1976-77, resident in internal medicine, 1977-79; fellow in gastroenterology Albert Einstein Coll. Medicine, Bronx, N.Y., 1979-81; asst. clin. prof. medicine Tufts U., Boston, 1985—; med. advisor Med. Assist Program Springfield Tech. C.C., 1989—; pres. Pioneer Valley Surgictr., 2009—10; CEO Farkas Med. Corp., Longmeadow, Mass.; bd. dirs. temple Beth Ec Springfield, 2011—. Co-dir. med. edn. Mercy Hosp., Springfield, 1990-95, chmn. dept. gastroenterology, 1995—, dir. libr., 1988-97, mem. exec. com., 1995—, treas. med. staff, 1999—; mem. adv. bd. VNA, Springfield, 1984-88; adj. asst. prof. clin. pharmacology Mass. Coll. Pharmacy, Boston, 1982—; bd. dir., Temple Beth El Springfield, Mass., 2011-. Author: Diagnostic Diagrams Gastroenterology, 1985; contbr. book chpts., articles and revs. in field. Bd. dirs. B'nai Jacob Synagogue, Springfield, 1987-88, Com. for Longmeadow, Mass., 1989, Yeshiva, Longmeadow, 1994-99; trustee Mercy Hosp., 1997-98. Fellow ACP (cmty. based excellence in tchg. award 2000), Am. Gastroent. Assn., Am. Gastro. Assn.; mem. AMA, Am. Coll. Gastroenterology, Am. Soc. Gastrointestinal Endoscopy. Office: 299 Carew St Springfield MA 01104-2301 Office Phone: 413-737-7951. Personal E-mail: docpsf@aol.com.

FARKAS, TAMAS ANDRAS, orthopedist, surgeon; b. Budapest, Hungary, Dec. 30, 1936; s. Jozsef Farkas and Edit Khudy; m. Ildiko Daroczy, Apr. 19, 1969; children: Ildiko, Krisztina, Martina. MD, Semmelweis Med. U., 1962; PhD, Hungarian Acad. Sci., 1977; degree (hon.), Haynal Postgrad. Med. U., Budapest, 1993. Diplomate 1962. Mem. faculty SOTE Orthop. Hosp., Budapest, 1962—70; from asst. med. staff to dir. clin. studies Nat. Inst. Traumatology, Budapest, 1970—93, dir. clin. studies, 1993—. Mem. staff Royal Nat. Orthop. Hosp., Stanmore, England, 1967—68; rsch. fellow Mass. Gen. Hosp., Boston, 1975; sabbatical W.Va. U., Morgantown, W.Va., 1985; vis. prof. German Acad. Exch. Program, Heidelberg, Germany, 1991. Editor: Intramedullary Fixation, 1993, Ligamentous Injuries, 1994; author: Bone Circulation, 1984, Upper Extremity Arthroplasty, 1997, Tramatology, 2000 (Best Textbook of Yr. award, 2000). Lt. Hungarian Army Reserves, 1962—90. Recipient Excellent Work award, Ministry of Health, 1993, Lumniczer medal, 2010. Mem.: Seddon Soc., Austrian Trauma Soc. Roman Catholic. Avocations: music, gardening, wines. Office: 2045 Torokbalint 6 Hós Utca Hungary

FARLEY, THOMAS ALEXANDER, city health department administrator, epidemiologist, pediatrician; b. Summit, NJ, Apr. 5, 1956; BA, Haverford Coll., 1977; MD, Tulane Univ., 1981, MPH. Residency Northwestern Univ. Med. Ctr., Chgo., 1982—85; child health physician Haiti; epidemiologist Centers for Disease Control (CDC), La. Office Pub. Health, New Orleans; prof. & chmn. cmty. health services dept. chmn. Tulane Univ. Sch. Pub. Health & Tropical Med., New Orleans, 2000—09; commr. NYC Dept. Health & Mental Hygiene, 2009—. Sr. adv. to commr. NYC Dept. Health & Mental Hygiene, 2007—08. Contbr. articles to profl. jours.; co-author (with Deborah A. Cohen): Prescription for a Healthy Nation. Office: NYC Dept Health & Mental Hygiene 125 Worth St New York NY 10013

FARMAKI, KALLISTHENI, hematologist, director; b. Nicosia, Cyprus, Apr. 29, 1952; MD, Faculty Medicine Montpellier France, 1976, degree in Hematology, 1980. Cons. Gen. Hosp. Corinth, Greece, 1981—84, directress blood transfusion svc. & thalassemia ctr., 1984—, med. labs. dir., 1987—2002, pres. sci. coun., 2006—09, mem. bd. dirs., 2009—11. Expert Hellenic Accreditation Sys. SA, 2009—11; mem. exam. com. licensure haematology med. U. Patras Greece, 2010—11. Contbr. articles to profl. jours. Recipient Hon. award, Gen. Hosp. Corinth, Silver award, Pan-Hellenic Thalassemia Assn., Pan-Hellenic Blood Vols. Assn., Corinth's Thalassaemia Assn. Master: Hellenic Soc. Hematology; mem.: European Haematology Assn., Internat. Soc. Blood Transfusion, NY Acad. Sci., Am. Soc. Hematology. Avocation: martial arts. Home: 1 Dervenakion Corinth Corinthia 20100 Greece Home Fax: 30 2744062623. Business E-Mail: stheni@otenet.gr.

FARMAN, ALLAN GEORGE, radiologist, pathologist, educator; b. Birmingham, Eng., July 26, 1949; came to the U.S., 1980; s. George and Lily (Hewitt) F.; m. Taeko Takemori, May 21, 1994. B Dental Surgery, U. Birmingham, Eng., 1971; PhD, U. Stellenbosch, Cape Town, South Africa, 1977, DSc, 1996; EdS, U. Louisville, 1983, MBA with distinction, 1987. Diplomate Am. Bd. Oral and Maxillofacial Radiology, Japanese Bd. Oral and Maxillofacial Radiology; specialist registration in oral pathology South African Med. and Dental Coun.; lic. specialist Ky. Bd. Dentistry Oral and Maxillofacial Radiology, specialist in dental and maxillofacial radiology, Gen. Dental Coun., UK. Sr. lectr. oral pathology U. Stellenbosch, Cape Town, 1974-77; head dept. oral biology U. Riyadh, Saudi Arabia, 1978-79; prof., head divsn. radiology and imaging scis. Dental Sch., U. Louisville, 1980—; clin. prof. dept. diagnostic radiology Med. Sch., U. Louisville, 1990—; rep. to internat. dicom com. Am. Acad. Oral Maxillofac Radiol., 2010—. Cons. Joint Commn. for Dental Bd. Examination, Chgo., 1984—92, NIH, Bethesda, Md., 1990—; rep. to internat. Digital Imaging & Comm. Medicine Com. Am. Dental Assn., 2001—10; rep. to internat. DICOM com. Am. Acad. Oral Maxillofa-

cial Radiology, 2010—; co-chmn. DICOM Working Group 22, 2003—; voting mem. US Sub-Tag ISO-TC 106 (Dentistry) 2009; adj. prof. anatomical sci. and neurobiology U. Louisville, 1990—. Author: Oral and Maxillofacial Diagnostic Imaging, 1993, Panoramic Radiology-Seminars on Maxillofacial Imaging and Interpretation, 2007; editor: Advances in Maxillofacial Imaging, 1997, (oral and maxillofacial radiology sect.) Oral Surgery, Oral Medicine, Oral Pathology, Oral Radiology and Endodontics, 1988-95, 2005—09; co-editor CARS Procs., Computer-Assisted Radiology and Surgery, 1998-; dep. editor Internat. Jour. Computer Assisted Radiology and Surgery, 2006—; mem. editl. bd. Cranio, Oral Radiology, Acta Stomatologica Croatia, Japan Dental Science Review, Inside Dentistry, eDentico; contbr. more than 400 articles to profl. jours. Recipient DSM, U. Louisville, 2006, MS Student Mentoring award, 2010. Mem. Am. Dental Assn., Japanese Soc. Oral and Maxillofacial Radiology, Internat. Assn. Dento Maxillofacial Radiology (pres. 1994-97, trust fund chmn. 1997—), Internat. Congress and Exposition on Computed Maxillofacial Imaging (initiator, founder, organizer 1995—), Am. Acad. Oral and Maxillofacial Radiology (editor 1988-95, 2005—09, pres. elect 2007-09, pres., 2009-11), Am. Assn. Dental Schs. (chmn. oral radiology sect. 1988-89). Office: U Louisville Sch Dentistry 501 S Preston St Louisville KY 40292-1701 Office Phone: 502-852-1241. Business E-Mail: agfarm01@louisville.edu.

FARMER, CHERYL CHRISTINE, internist, industrial hygienist; b. Detroit, Sept. 15, 1946; d. Donald Richard and Dorothy Ruth Farmer; m. Dennis Michael Mukai, Aug. 3, 1968 (div. Sept. 1977). BA in Edn., Mich. State U., 1968; BS in Biology, Wright State U., 1974; MS in Indsl. Hygiene, U. Mich., 1978; MD, Mich. State U., 1982. Tchr. art Five Points Elem. Sch., Fairborn, Ohio, 1968-70; real estate saleswoman Dawson Realty, 1970; sanitarian trainee Dayton Health Dept., Dayton, 1973; acting chief air pollution control southwest dist. Ohio EPA, 1975, data analyst ctrl. dist. Columbus, 1976; intern St. Joseph Mercy Hosp., Ann Arbor, Mich., 1982-83, resident medicine, 1983-85; internist Winton Hills Med. Ctr., Cin., 1985-87; pvt. practice Ann Arbor, Mich., 1988—. Internist, Elm St. Med. Ctr., Cin., 1987-88; mem. peer rev. com. Magnacare Health Maintenance Orgn., Cin., 1988; mem. membership com. St. Joseph Mercy Hosp., 1990-94; mem. bioethics com. Mich. State Med. Soc., 1994—; past com. mem. Washtenaw County Med. Soc., 1992-94, exec. com. mem., 2008-, mem. med. adv. bd. Mich. Sec. State's Office, 2009-10. Co-chmn. Citizens for Clean Air Com., Dayton, 1970-74, Miami Valley Citizens for Transfer, Fairborn, 1974; mayor of Ypsilanti, Mich., 1995-06; commr. City of Ypsilanti, 2010-. Recipient Athena award, Ypsilanti area C. of C., 1996, Liberty Bell award, Wash. County Bar Assn., 1998, Found. Cmty. Svc. award, Mich. State Med. Soc., 2009, Bill Steude award for ethics in govt., Mich. Assn. Municipal Atty.'s, 2002, Martin Luther King Jr. Humanitarian award, Eastern Mich. Univ., 2003; named Woman Physician of the Yr., Mich. State Med. Soc., 2002, one of Washtenaw County's Most Influential Women of 2003, Business Direct Weekly, 2003. Mem. AMA, ACP, LWV, NOW, Sierra Club, Phi Kappa Phi, Kappa Delta Pi, Alpha Kappa Delta (hon.).Washtenaw County Med. Assn.(pres., 2010). Democrat. Avocations: sailing, gardening, victorian home restoration. Office: 1950 Manchester Rd Ann Arbor MI 48104-4916 Office Phone: 734-973-4800.

FARMER, DIANA LEE, pediatric surgeon; b. Chgo., Nov. 28, 1955; married. BA in Biology, Wellesley Coll., Mass., 1977; premed., Harvard Coll., Coll. Idaho; MD, U. Wash. Sch. Medicine, Seattle, 1983. Cert. Am. Bd. Surgery, 2004, in pediatric surgery Am. Bd. Surgery, 2005. Internship in surgery U. Wash. Sch. Medicine, 1986—87; fellowship in surg. oncology U. Calif. Sch. Medicine, San Francisco, 1987—89, residency in gen. surgery, 1990—91, sr. resident, gen. surgery, 1991—92, chief resident, gen. surgery, 1992—93, assoc. prof. surgery to prof. clin. surgery, pediat., ob-gyn and reproductive sciences; fellowship Children's Hosp., Detroit, 1993—95, pediatric surgeon, 1995—98, Henry Ford Hosp., Detroit, 1995—98, St. John's Hosp., Detroit, 1995—98; asst. prof. surgery Wayne State U. Sch. Medicine, Detroit, 1995—98; hosp. appointment in pediatric surgery U. Calif. Med. Ctr., 1998, Calif. Pacific Med. Ctr., 1998—, Kaiser Permanente Med. Ctr., 1998; surgeon-in-chief U. Calif. Children's Hosp., San Francisco, vice-chair dept. surgery, divsn. chief pediatric surgery, co-dir. fetal treatment ctr., 2003—06. Rschr. Woods Hole Oceanographic Inst., Stanford, Calif., Bermuda; asst. med. dir. cancer immunology DuPont Pharm., Wilmington, Del. Contbr. articles to profl. jours. Rhodes Scholar finalist, Lucar Scholar, Nat. U., Singapore. Fellow: RCS. Office: Univ Calif San Francisco Sch Medicine Campus Box 0570 513 Parnassus Ave San Francisco CA 94143-0570 Office Phone: 415-476-2538. Office Fax: 415-476-2929. Business E-Mail: pedsurg@surgery.ucsf.edu.

FARMER, HARRY FRANK, JR., public health officer; b. Daytona Beach, Fla., Nov. 9, 1941; s. Harry Frank and Lottie (Ditson) F.; m. Peggy Hines, Oct. 26, 1973; children: Harry Frank III, Kevin. BA, Stetson U., 1964; MA in History, U. Ga., 1966, PhD in History, 1969; MD, Med. Coll. Ga., 1976. Asst. prof. history Ga. Southwestern Coll., Americus, 1968-69. 71-72; resident in family practice Halifax Hosp., Daytona Beach, Fla., 1976-77; resident in internal medicine Univ. Hosp., Jacksonville, Fla., 1977-80; pvt. practice, New Smyrna Beach, Fla., 1980-90; med. dir. for Medicare, Blue Cross/Blue Shield, Jacksonville, Fla., 1990-92; pvt. practice Ormond Beach, Fla., 1992—; surgeon gen. Fla. Dept. Health, Tallahassee, 2011—. Pres. Endeavors-Physicians Ind. Physicians Assn., Volusia County, Fla., 1993—. Capt. US Army, 1969-71, Vietnam. Decorated Bronze Star, Vietnamese Cross of Gallantry; recipient Disting. Cmty. Svc. award American Coll. Physicians Fla. chapter, 2002 Mem. AMA, American Soc. Internal Medicine, Fla. Soc. Internal Medicine, Fla. Med. Assn. (pres. 2001, editor hist. issue of Jour. 1988-95). Republican. Avocation: reading. Office: Florida Department Health 2585 Merchants Row Blvd Tallahassee FL 32399 Office Phone: 850-245-4321. Office Fax: 850-922-9453. *

FARMER, KEITHA, retired pediatrician; b. Taumarunui, New Zealand, Feb. 4, 1928; d. D'Arcy Alban Corlett and Constance Rose Tremain; m. Jon Brian Stapley Farmer, June 10, 1962. MB ChB, Otago, Dunedin, New Zealand, 1950; MRCP, Edinburgh, 1958; PhD, Inst. Child Health, London, 1963. Ho. physician Auckland Hosp., 1950—53; sr. ho. officer Selly Oak, Birmingham, 1955—56; ho. resp sick children London, 1958; ho. registrar Guys Hosp., London, 1959; tutor specialist Auckland Hosp., 1960; rsch. fellow Inst. Child Health, London, 1961—63; pediat. Starship Children's Hosp., Auckland, 1964—2000; rschr. Nat. Women's Hosp., Auckland, 1964—70, pediatrician, 1970—95. Contbr. scientific papers to nat. rsch. publs.

Mem.: Australasian Soc. Infectious Disease, Pediat. Soc. (past pres., mem. sub com. infections and immunizations 2003). Home: 88 Ngapuhi Road 1050 Auckland New Zealand

FARMER, KENNETH LLOYD, JR., health system administrator, retired military officer; b. Leeds, Ala., Apr. 13, 1950; married; 4 children. BS, Auburn U.; MD, U. Ala., 1975; grad., Army Command Gen. Staff Coll., Army War Coll. Diplomate Am. Bd. Family Practice. Commd. 2d lt. U.S. Army, advanced through grades to maj. gen., 2002, ret., 2006; early assignments include Madigan Army Med. Ctr., Ft. Lewis, Wash., 9th Med. Detachment and Health Clinic, Heilbronn, Germany, 1976-79; chief of family practice dept. Keller Army Hosp., West Pt., NY; divsn. surgeon 101st Airborne divsn., Ft. Campbell, Ky.; dep. comdr. clin. svcs. Ft. Campbell Hosp.; comdr. 85th Evacuation Hosp., Dhahran, Saudi Arabia, 22nd Support Group (provisional), 1990—91; dept. chief of family practice residency program Eisenhower Army Med. Ctr., Ft. Gordon, Ga.; comdr. Bayne-Jones Army Cmty. Hosp., Ft. Polk, Deatnl Army Cmty. Hosp. and U.S. Army Med. Dept. Activity, Ft. Hood, Tex.; command surgeon U.S. European Command, Stuttgart, Germany, 1994-97; dir. Healthcare Svcs. and surgeon 18th Airborne Corps. Ft. Bragg, NC; comdg. gen. 44th Med. Brigade, Ft. Bragg, NC, 1999-2000, Western Regional Med. Command, Tacoma, 2000—02, TRICARE NW Region, Ft. Lewis, 2000—02; dep. surg. gen., chief of staff US Army Med. Commd., 2002—04; commdg. gen. N. Atlantic Regional Med. Command & Walter Reed Army Med. Ctr., Washington, 2004—06; exec. v.p., COO TriWest Healthcare Alliance, Phoenix, 2006—. Decorated Disting. Svc. medal with oak leaf cluster, Def. Superior Svc. medal, Legion of Merit with 3 oak leaf clusters, Bronze Star, Meritorious Svc. medal with 4 oak leaf clusters, Order of Mil. Med. Merit. Fellow Am. Acad. Family Physicians (Robert Graham Physician Exec. award 2001). Office: TriWest Healthcare Alliance 16010 N 28th Ave Phoenix AZ 85053 Office Phone: 602-564-2038. Business E-Mail: kefarmer@triwest.com.

FARMER, PAUL EDWARD, medical anthropologist; b. Oct. 26, 1959; m. Didi Bertrand; 1 child, Catherine. MD, PhD, Harvard U., 1990. Co-founder, exec. v.p. Partners in Health, 1987—; Presley prof. med. anthropology dept. social medicine Harvard Med. Sch., Boston, 1995—; attending physician divsn. infectious disease Brigham and Women's Hosp., Boston; med. co-dir. Clinique Bon Sauveur, Haiti. Mem. internat. sci. com. ids; coord. berculosis; mem. DOTS-Plus working group for the global tuberculosis programme WHO, mem. sci. com. working group on DOTS-Plus for MDR-TB; chief advisor tuberculosis programs Open Soc. Inst.; chief med. cons. tuberculosis treatment project in prisons of Tomsk (Siberia) Pub. Health Rsch. Inst.; mem. Commonwealth of Mass. Bur. Communicable Disease Control; mem. sci. rev. bd. 10 internat. confs. on AIDS; dep. spl. envoy to Haiti UN, 2009—. Author: (book) AIDS and Accusation: Haiti and the Geography of Blame, 1992, The Uses of Haiti, 1994, Infections and Inequalities, 1998, Pathologies of Power, 2003; co-editor: Women, Poverty and AIDS, 1996, The Global Impact of Drug-Resistant Tuberculosis, 1999; contbr. articles to profl. jours. Recipient Margaret Mead award, Am. Anthrop. Assn., 1999, Humanitarian award, Duke U., Heinz Humanitarian award, 2003, Outstanding Internat. Physician award, AMA; named a MacArthur fellow, John D. and Catherine T. MacArthur Found., 1993. Mem.: Am. Acad. Arts & Sciences, Inst. of Medicine (life). Office: Harvard Med Sch Dept Social Medicine 25 Shattuck St Boston MA 02115

FARMER, RICHARD GILBERT, academic physician, foundation administrator; b. Kokomo, Ind., Sept. 29, 1931; s. Oscar Irvin and Elizabeth Jane (Gilbert) Farmer; m. Janice Mae Schrank, Nov. 29, 1958; children: Amy Lynn, David Richard. Student, Ind. U., 1949—52; MD, U. Md., 1956; MS in Medicine, U. Minn., 1960. Diplomate Am. Bd. Internal Medicine, Gastroenterology. Fellow in internal medicine Mayo Clinic, Rochester, Minn., 1957—60; mem. staff Cleve. Clinic Found., 1962—91, chmn. dept. gastroenterology, 1972—82, bd. govs., 1974—79, chmn. divsn. medicine, 1975—91, mem. med. exec. com., 1975—91, mem. exec. com. bd. trustees, 1975—77; sr. med. advisor Bur. for Europe Agy. for Internat. Devel. US Dept. State, Washington, 1992—94; cons. health care Ea. Europe and former Soviet Union, 1995—98; med. dir. Quality Health Internat., Boston, 1997—98; cons. Scandinavian Care, 1998—2003; prof. medicine, chief digestive and liver disease unit U. Rochester Med. Ctr., NY, 2004—09, prof., medicine, 2003—11; clin. prof. medicine (gastroenterology) Georgetown U. Med. Ctr., Washington, 1992—2004. Mem. nat. sci. adv. bd. Nat. Found. Ileitis and Colitis, 1973—91; mem. nat. adv. bd. Nat. Commn. Digestive Diseases, 1977—79; mem. Coun. Subsplty. Socs. in Internal Medicine, 1978—85; chmn. grants rev. com. Nat. Found. Ileitis and Colitis, 1981—85; mem. com. to assess quality care in Medicare program, GAO and ways and means com. U.S. Ho. of Reps., 1986—89; cons. Am. Medico-Legal Found., Phila., 1996—2003, Inst. for Health Policy Analysis, Washington, 1996—2004; med. dir. Eurasian Med. Edn. Program (Russian Fedn.), 1998—2004. Editor 6 books; contbr. over 275 articles to sci. jours., books. Lt. comdr. USNR, 1960—62. Recipient Jubilee medal, Charles U. Prague, 1998, Mentors Rsch. Scholars award, Amer Gastro Assn., 2007. Master: ACP (gov. Ohio 1980—84, health and pub. policy com. 1982—91, chmn. med. tech. assessment com. 1985—86, reprint 1985—91, chmn. health and pub. policy comm. 1986—88, chmn. clin. practice subcom. 1988—91, del. to AMA 1989—94, Spl. Presdl. citation 1984), Am. Coll. Gastroenterology (trustee, exec. com. 1975—80, pres. 1978—79, master 1991); mem.: Internat. Orgn. for Study Inflammatory Bowel Disease (dep. chmn. 1982—86), Interstate Postgrad. Med. Assn. (pres. 1983—84), Inst. Medicine of NAS (life; elec. mem. 1983), Am. Gastroent. Assn. (commn. on future 1973—74, tng. and edn. com. 1975—78, chmn. subcom. grad. edn. 1975—78), Assn. Program Dirs. in Internal Medicine (founding pres. 1977—79, Founder's award 1993). Democrat. Mem. Soc. Of Friends. Home: 9126 Town Gate Ln Bethesda MD 20817-4111 Office: U Rochester Med Ctr Box 646 Rochester NY 14642 Office Phone: 585-275-7432. Fax: 585-276-1911. Business E-Mail: Richard_Farmer@urmc.rochester.edu.

FARO, SCOTT H., radiologist, educator; BS, Rutgers Coll., New Brunswick, NJ, 1979; MD, Rutgers U., New Brunswick, NJ, 1986. Diplomate Am. Bd. Radiology, Am. Bd. Radiology-neuroradiology, Am. Bd. Radiology-diagnostic radiology. Hosp. affiliations include Jeanes Hosp., Hahnemann Univ. Hosp., Temple Univ. Hosp., prof. radiology, dir. functional brain imaging ctr. and clin. MRI. Co-author numerous sci. publs. Named one of America's Top Doctors, Castle

Connolly, 2011. Office: Temple University Hospital 3401 N Broad St Philadelphia PA 19140 Office Phone: 215-707-4263. Office Fax: 215-707-9389. E-mail: scott.faro@tuhs.temple.edu.

FAROUK, OSAMA AHMED, orthopedist, educator; b. Cairo, Nov. 21, 1964; s. Ahmed Abdel-Aal and Samiha Ahmed Abdel-Moneim; m. Zolfa Mohammad Doheim, Feb. 1, 1998; children: Sarah Osama, Mohammad Osama, Ahmed Osama. MB, Assiut U., Egypt, 1987, MSc in Orthops., 1991, MD in Orthops., 1998. Resident dr. orthpedics and traumatology Assiut U. Hosp., Egypt, 1989—93; fellow trauma surgery Hannover Med. Sch., Germany, 1994—96; asst. lectr. orthop. surgery Assiut U. Hosp., Egypt, 1997—98, lectr. orthop. surgery, 1999—2002, asst. prof. orthop. surgery, 2003—08, prof. orthop. surgery, 2009—, dir. trauma unit Egypt, 2008—. Co-dir trauma unit Assiut U. Hosp., Egypt, 2002—. Contbr. scientific papers to med. jours. Sec. Assiut Childhood and Devel. Assn., Egypt, 1997—2005. Mem.: Physician Syndicate of lower Saxon, Egyptian Orthopaedic Assn. (Best rsch. prize), Internat. Soc. Orthop. Surgery and Traumatology, Biomechanics Group Hannover Trauma Ctr. (hon.), The German Orgn. Sci. Exch. Achievements include research in field of minimal invasive plate osteosynthesis of long bone fractures. Avocations: travel, computers. Office: Assiut Univ Faculty Medicine Orthopedic Dept Assiut 71516 Egypt Office Phone: 0020882359282. Office Fax: 0020 88 2333327. Business E-Mail: osama_farouk@yahoo.com.

FARQUHAR, JOHN WILLIAM, physician, educator; b. Winnipeg, Man., Can., June 13, 1927; arrived in U.S., 1934; s. John Giles and Marjorie Victoria (Roberts) Farquhar; m. Christine Louise Johnson, July 14, 1968; children: Margaret F., John C.M.;children from previous marriage: Bruce E., Douglas G. AB, U. Calif., Berkeley, 1949; MD, U. Calif., San Francisco, 1952. Intern U. Calif. Hosp., San Francisco, 1952—53, resident, 1953—54, 1957—58, postdoctoral fellow, 1955—57; resident U. Minn., Mpls., 1954—55; rsch. assoc. Rockefeller U., NYC, 1958—62; asst. prof. medicine Stanford (Calif.) U., 1962—66, assoc. prof., 1966—73, prof., 1978—, C.F. Rehnborg prof. in disease prevention, 1989—2000; dir. Stanford Ctr. Rsch. in Disease Prevention, 1973—98; dir. collaborating ctr. for chronic disease prevention WHO, 1985—99; prof. health rsch. and policy, 1988—. Mem. staff Stanford U. Hosp.; chair Victoria Declaration Implementation com. Author: The American Way of Life Need Not Be Hazardous to Your Health, 1978, 1987; author: (with Gene Spiller) The Last Puff, 1990; author: The Victoria Declaration for Heart Health, 1992, How to Reduce Your Risk of Heart Disease, 1994, The Catalonia Declaration: Investing in Heart Health, 1996, Worldwide Efforts to Improve Heart Disease, 1997; author: (with Spiller) Diagnosis Heart Disease: Answers to Your Questions about Recovery and Lasting Health, 2001; contbr. articles to profl. jours. With US Army, 1944—46. Recipient James D. Bruce award, ACP, 1983, Myrdal prize, 1986, Dana award for Pioneering Achievement in Health, Dana Found., 1990, Nat. Cholesterol award for Pub. Edn., Nat. Cholesterol Edn. Program of NIH, 1991, Rsch. Achievement award, Am. Heart Assn., 1992, Order of St. George for Svc. to Autonomous Govt. of Catalonia, 1996, Joseph Stokes Preventive Cardiology award, Am. Soc. Preventive Cardiology, 1999, Ancel Keys Meml. lectureship, Am. Heart Assn., 2000, Fries prize Improving Pub. Health, 2005. Mem.: Internat. Heart Health Soc., Soc. Behavioral Medicine (pres. 1991—92), Am. Heart Assn. (coun. epidemiology and prevention), Am. Soc. Clin. Investigation, Inst. Medicine NAS, Gold Headed Cane Soc., Alpha Omega Alpha, Sigma Xi. Episcopalian. Office: Stanford U Sch of Medicine Stanford Prevention Rsch Ctr 251 Campus Dr Stanford CA 94305-5411 Business E-Mail: John.Farquhar@stanford.edu.

FARQUHAR, MARILYN GIST, cell biologist, pathologist, educator; b. Tulare, Calif. d. Brooks DeWitt and Alta (Green) Gist; m. John W. Farquhar, June 4, 1952; children: Bruce, Douglas (div. 1968); m. George Palade, June 7, 1970. AB, U. Calif., Berkeley, 1949, MA, 1952, PhD, 1955. Asst. rsch. pathologist Sch. Medicine U. Calif., San Francisco, 1956—58, assoc. rsch. pathologist, 1962—64, assoc. prof., 1964—68, prof. pathology, 1968—70; rsch. assoc. Rockefeller U., NYC, 1958—62, prof. cell biology, 1970—73, Sch. Medicine Yale U., New Haven, 1973—87, Sterling prof. cell biology and pathology, 1987—90; prof. cell molecular medicine pathology U. Calif., San Diego, 1990—, chair cellular and molecular medicine, 1991—99, disting. prof. cellular & molecular medicine, 1990—, chair dept. cellular & molecular medicine, 1999—2009. Mem. editorial bd. numerous sci. jours.; contbr. articles to profl. jours. Recipient Career Devel. award NIH, 1968-73, 2009-, Disting. Sci. medal Electron Microscope Soc., 1987, Gomori medal Histochem. Soc., 1999, A.N. Richards award Internat. Soc. Nephrology, 2003, FASAB Excellence Sci. award, 2006. Mem.: NAS, Internat. Soc. Nephrology (A.N. Richards award 2003), Am. Soc. Nephrology (Homer Smith award 1988, Gottschalk award 2002), Am. Assn. Investigative Pathology (Rous Whipple award 2001), Am. Soc. Cell Biology (pres. 1981—82, E.B. Wilson medal 1987), Am. Acad. Arts and Scis. Home and Office: U Calif San Diego Sch Med 12894 Via Latina Del Mar CA 92014-3730

FARRAR, JOHN THRUSTON, health facility administrator; b. St. Louis, June 26, 1920; s. Benedict and Ruth Elizabeth (Gregg) F.; m. Joan Hayward Niedringhaus, May 20, 1947 (div. Feb. 1964); children: John Hayward, Leslie Tweedy; m. Pamela Sedgwick Gibson, May 15, 1966 (div. Mar. 1994); children: Elizabeth Gregg, Anne Dandridge; m. Rowena Kay Bryan, Oct. 28, 1995. AB, Princeton U., NJ, 1942; MD, Washington U., St. Louis, 1945. Diplomate Am. Bd. Internal Medicine, Am. Bd. Gastroenterology. Intern St. Louis County Hosp., Clayton, Mo., 1945-46; asst. resident in pathology Boston City Hosp., 1948-49; intern in medicine Mass. Meml. Hosps., Boston, 1949-50, asst. resident in medicine, 1950-51, rsch. assoc. divsn. gastroenterology, 1951-54; instr. medicine Boston U. Sch. Medicine, 1954-55; asst. prof. clin. medicine Cornell U. Coll. Medicine, NYC, 1956-63; assoc. prof. medicine Med. Coll. Va., Richmond, 1963-65, chmn. divsn. gastroenterology, 1963-78, prof. medicine, 1965-92, assoc. dean vets. affairs, 1979-90, prof. emeritus, 1992—. Chief gastroenterology sect. med. svc. Vets. Hosp., N.Y.C., 1955-63; assoc. chief of staff rsch. devel. Vets. Affairs Med. Ctr., N.Y.C., 1956-63; cons. gastroenterology McGuire Vets. Affairs Med. Ctr., Richmond, 1963-78, chief of staff, 1979-90; nat. adv. panel nat. program rev. com. VA, 1965-69; adv. com. gastrointestinal drugs FDA, Washington, 1971-74, 77-82, cons., 1976-77; grants rev. com. Nat. Found. Ileitis Colitis, Inc., 1975-79, nat. scientific adv. com. 1975-79; chmn. long range planning com. Nat. digestive Diseases Edn. Info. Clearinghouse, 1983-85, chmn. scientific Evaluation subcom. 1983-85, chmn. exec. com. advisors, 1983-90; mem. steering com. Internat. Conf. Gastrointestinal Motility, 1975-81, chmn. steering com., 1977-79; chmn. Am. Bd. Gastroenterology, 1979-83; mem. bd. govs. Am. Bd. Internal Medicine, 1979-85; first vice-chmn. Coalition Digestive Desease Orgns., 1983-85; pres. Digestive Disease Nat. Coalition (formerly Coalition Digestive Disease Orgns.), 1986-91; rsch. com. Am. Fedn. Aging Rsch., 1983-89; assoc. dep. chief med. dir. Dept. Vets. Affairs, Vets. Affairs Ctrl. Office, Washington, 1990-91, dep. chief med. dir., 1991-93, acting under sec. health, 1993-94, dep. under sec. health, 1994-95; assoc. chief of staff extended care Vets. Affairs med. Ctr., Martinsburg, W.Va., 1995—. Author: (chpts.) Miniaturization, 1961, Modern Trends in Gastroenterology, 1961, Medicine, Essentials of Clinical Practice, 1970, Medical Engineering, 1974, Gastrointestinal Motility, 1971, Scientific Foundations of Gastroenterology, 1980, Tratado De Gastroenterologia Y Hepatologia, 1982, Clinics in Gastroenterology, 1982, Clinical Medicine, 1983, Social Security Practice Guide, 1986, Surgical Management of the Elderly Patient, 1992; editor: Practice of Medicine, Vol. Gastroenterology, 1973-78; mem. editl. bd. Am. Jour. Digestive Diseases, 1959-64, 88—, editor, 1968-76, Gastroenterology, 1964-68, Am. Jour. Med. Electronics, 1962-82; mem. editl. coun. Rendiconti Romani di Gastro-enterologia, 1969-89; contbr. over 55 articles to profl. jours. Bd. trustees Elk Hill Farm for Boys, 1974-80; pres. Goochland Family Svc. Soc., 1975-76, 79-81. Capt. U.S. Army Med. Corps., 1946-48. Mem.: ACP (coun. .subspecialty socs. 1985—88, chmn. gastroenterology com. 1985—88, chair Washington 1986, chair San Francisco 1987), Am. Liver Found. (bd. dirs. 1986—, chmn. 1990—94), Am. Clin. Climatol. Assn., Am. Gastroent. Assn. (rssch. com. 1968—71, nat. liaison com. 1971—73, 1977—80, treas. 1972—77, chmn. publs. com. 1977—80, gov. bd. 1972—77, 1980—89, v.p 1980—81, pres.-elect 1981—82, pres. 1982—83, chmn. com. pub. policy and govt. rels. 1986—89, historian, archivist 1989—98), Am. Fedn. Clin. Rsch. Home: 431 Dogleg DR Williamsburg VA 23188-7411 Personal E-mail: farrar8@cox.net.

FARRELL, CHRISTOPHER M., orthopedist; MD, Georgetown U., 1999. Diplomate Am. Bd. Orthopaedic Surgery. Resident Mayo Clinic, Rochester; hosp. affiliations include Shady Grove Adventist Hosp., Suburban Hosp.; surgeon Wash. Adventist Hosp., 2006—. Named one of the Top Doctors, Washingtonian Mag., 2011. Office: Washington Adventist Hospital Number 205 19847 Century Blvd Germantown MD 20874 Office Phone: 301-515-0900. Office Fax: 240-912-2210.

FARRELL, GREGORY ALAN, biomedical engineer; b. Bklyn., May 12, 1942, s. Edmond William and Edna Florence (Williams) F.; m. Mary Louise Lupiani, Sept. 3, 1966; children: Juliana Eden, Cristina Elizabeth. BSME, Cooper Union, 1964; MS in Biomed. Engring., Columbia U., 1972, postgrad., 1972—. Mech. engr. Gen. Dynamics, San Diego, 1964-65, Rochester, NY, 1965-67; rsch. asst. Columbia U. Med. Sch., NYC, 1968-69; instr. pathology N.Y. Med. Coll., 1969-72; rsch. engr. Technicon Instruments Corp., Tarrytown, NY, 1972-82; mgr. mech. engring. Baker Instruments Corp., Allentown, Pa., 1982-84, prin. mech. engr., 1984-86; prin. engr. Nat. Patent Devel. Corp., NYC, 1986-87; project engr. Bayer Diagnostics (divsn. Bayer Healthcare), Tarrytown, 1987—90, new product devel. mgr., 1990—99, prin. staff engr., 2000—, mgr. mech. engring., 2001—05; pres. Gregory A. Farrell & Assocs., LLC, 2006—. Patentee in field; contbr. articles to profl. jours. Winner med. design excellence award, Indsl. Designers Soc. Am., 1998. Democrat. Roman Catholic. Achievements include development of several automated clinical hematology, chemistry and immunology instruments. Home: 447 Hillcrest Rd Ridgewood NJ 07450-1520 Personal E-mail: gtkat@verizon.net.

FARRELL, MATTHEW M., physician, educator; Studied, Columbia U., 1980. Diplomate Am. Bd. Family Practice, cert. adolescent medicine, geriatric medicine, sports medicine. Intern Somerset Hosp., resident family medicine; asst. clin. prof. family medicine Univ. Conn.; physician Danbury Hosp. Office: Danbury Hospital Ste 2A 60 Old New Milford Rd Brookfield CT 06804 Office Phone: 203-775-6365. Office Fax: 203-740-3010.

FARRELL, PETER CRAIG, health care company executive; b. Sydney, New South Wales, June 9, 1942; s. Leslie Joseph and Thelma Marie (Harrison) F.; children: Catherine Ann, Paul Anthony, Michael James. BE, U. Sydney, 1964; SM, MIT, 1967; PhD, U. Wash., 1971; D of Sci., U. New South Wales, 1981. Research engr. Union Carbide Corp., Sydney, 1964-65, Montreal, 1965-66, Chevron Corp., San Francisco, 1967-68; indsl. liaison officer MIT, Cambridge, Mass., 1968-70; research asst. prof. U. Wash., Seattle, 1971-72; from lectr. to prof. U. New South Wales, Sydney, 1972-89, vis. prof., 1990—; v.p. Baxter World Trade Corp., Chgo., 1984-89, with exec. com., 1985-89; mng. dir. Baxter Ctr. for Med. Research, Sydney, 1985-89; chmn., CEO ResMed, Inc., Sydney, 1989—2008, exec. chmn., 2008—. Bd. dirs. Nurasive Inc (Nuva), QRx Pharma, chair exec. coun. Divsn. Sleep Medicine, Harvard Med. Sch. Author: In Search of Health and Fitness, 1985, also numerous revs. and articles to peer-reviewed jours. Pres. MCA San Diego. Fellow Australian Acad. Tech. Sci. and Engring., Instn. Engrs. Australia, Australian Inst. Co. Dirs., Australian Inst. Mgmt.; mem. Princeton Club N.Y., NSW Golf Club, La Jolla Country Club. Roman Catholic. Avocations: golf, bicycling, running, music, current affairs. Office: ResMed Inc 9001 Spectrum Ctr Blvd San Diego CA 92123

FARRELL, PHILIP M., pediatrician, medical educator, former dean; b. St. Louis, Nov. 26, 1943; m. Alice Yeakle; children: Michael Henry, David Sean, Bridget Mary. AB, St. Louis U., 1964, MD, PhD, St. Louis U., 1970. Diplomate Am. Bd. Pediatrics. Intern U. Wis. Hosps., 1970—71, resident in pediatrics, 1971—72; fellow pediatric metabolism br. Nat. Inst. Arthritis, Metabolism and Digestive Diseases, NIH, Bethesda, Md., 1972—74, sr. investigator pediatric metabolism br., 1974—75; chief Neonatal and Pediatric Medicine Br., Nat. Inst. Child Health and Human Devel., NIH, Bethesda, Md., 1975—77, Chief, Sect. Devel. Biology and Clin. Nutrition, 1975—77; Asst. prof. dept. child health George Washington U., Washington, 1975; asst. prof. pediatrics U. Wis., Madison, 1977-78, dir. Cystic Fibrosis Ctr., 1977—83, co-dir., 1983—88, affiliate scientist Wis. Regional Primate Research Ctr., 1978, affiliate faculty dept. nutrition scis., 1978, assoc. prof. pediatrics, 1978-82, dir. Pediatric Pulmonary Specialized Ctr. of Research, 1981-85, prof. pediatrics, 1982—, chmn. dept. pediatrics, 1985-95, med. dir. Children's Hosp., 1988—95, Alfred Dorrance Daniels prof. on diseases of children, 1990—; interim dean U. Wis. Sch. Medicine and Pub. Health, Madison, 1994—95, dean, 1995—2006, vice-chancellor med. affairs, 2001, prof. pediat. and population health scis. Editor: Lung Development: Biological and Clinical Perspectives, 1982. Recipient Heritage Found. Award, 2007; Avalon Found. scholar, 1965—67, Thurston Meml. scholar, 1966—70, Fogarty Internat. fellow, 1985. Mem. Am. Chem. Soc., Am. Acad. Pediatrics, Soc. Pediatric Rsch., Am. Thoracic Soc., Soc. Exptl. Biology and Medicine, Am. Inst. Nutrition, Am. Soc. Clin. Nutrition, Wis. Assn. Perinatal Care, Sigma Xi, Phi Beta Kappa, Alpha Omega Alpha. Office: U WIs Sch Medicine and Pub Health 785 Warf Office Bldg 610 Walnut St Madison WI 53726 Office Phone: 608-263-9094. E-mail: pmfarrell@wisc.edu.

FARRIA, DIONE MARIE, radiologist, educator; d. Guy Villa and Betty Session Farria; children: Emily Tigist children: Ethan Wondemu, Eva Almaz. BS, Xavier U., New Orleans, 1985; MPH, UCLA, 1997; MD, Harvard Med. Sch., Boston, 1989. Asst. prof. Thomas Jefferson U. Hosp., Phila., 1998—99; asst. prof. radiology Wash. U. Sch. Medicine, St. Louis, 1999—, assoc. prof, 2007—. Adj. asst. prof. St. Louis U. Sch. Pub. Health, 2002—; co-dir. Siteman Cancer Ctr., Program Elimination Cancer Disparities, St. Louis, 2003—06, dir., 2003—06. Author: (educational cd-rom) Interpretive Skills Assessment, Versions 1 and 2, (video) Between Friends: Dealing with the Diagnosis of Breast Cancer, (patient handbook) One Step at a Time: Dealing with the Diagnosis of Breast Cancer; contbr. articles to profl. jours. Recipient Career Devel. award, Dept. Def., 2000—03, Salute to Excellence in Health Care award, Mound City Med. Forum/St. Louis Am. Found., 2004, Clin. Trials Participation award, Am. Soc. Clin. Oncology, 2005, Disting. Com. Svc. award, Am. Coll. Radiology, 2005; grantee, Nat. Cancer Inst., 2005—, Avon Found., 2005—06; fellow, Am. Roentgen Ray Soc., 1997—98, Cancer, Culture and Literacy Inst., Tampa, Fla., 2005; scholar Robert Wood Johnson scholar, UCLA, 1995—97. Fellow: Am. Coll. Preventive Medicine (mem. com. 2004), Soc. Breast Imaging (breast imaging patterns ad hoc com. 2003); mem.: Am. Coll. Radiology (edn. com. appropriateness criteria expert panel 2002). Avocations: gardening, reading. Office: Washington U Sch Medicine 510 S Kingshighway Blvd Box 8131 Saint Louis MO 63110

FARRINGTON, BERTHA LOUISE, retired nursing administrator; b. Poteet, Tex., Jan. 20, 1937; d. Leonard Gilbert and Janie (Hernandez) Lozano; m. James Charles Farrington, Jan. 30, 1965; children: Mark Hiram, Robert Lee. BSN, Tex. Women's U., 1960; NP, U. Tex., 1984. RN, Tex. Charge nurse emergency rm. Parkland Meml. Hosp., Dallas; head nurse emergency rm./day surgery Bapt. Meml. Hosp., Pensacola, Fla.; asst. dir. health svcs. U. Tex. Southwestern Med. Ctr., Dallas, dir. student health svcs., ret., 2002. Cons. Student Health Com. E-mail: j.bfarrington@sbcglobal.net.

FARRIS, PATRICIA K., dermatologist, educator; MD, Tulane U. Cert. dermatologist. Resident Tulane U. Dept. Dermatology; clinical asst. prof. Tulane U. Sch. Med.; pvt. practice Old Metairie Dermatology, Ctr. for CosMedic Rejuvenation & Wellness, Manchester, Vt. Recipient Presdl. award, Am. Acad. Dermatology; named Best Dermatologist, New Orleans Gambit Mag.; named a Top Dermatologist, New Orleans Mag. Mem.: AADA, Internat. Soc. Cosmetic Dermatology, Am. Soc. Laser Med. & Surgery, Am. Dermatologic Assn., Am. Soc. Dermatologic Surgery. Office: 701 Metairie Rd Metairie LA 70005 Office Phone: 504-836-2050.

FARRON, ROBERT, family practice physician; b. NYC, May 17, 1947, s. Irving and Anne (Zavoznick) F.; m. Lorraine Herzberg, May 27, 1972; children: Cory, Eric, Jeffrey. BS, CCNY, 1968; DO, Kansas City Coll. Osteo. Med., 1972. Diplomate Am. Osteo. Bd. Family Practice. Intern Interboro Gen. Hosp., Bklyn., 1972—73; practice medicine specializing in family practice Far Rockaway, NY, 1973—, Valley Stream, NY, 1978—; attending physician St. John's Episcopal Hosp.-South Shore, Peninsula Hosp. Ctr., Far Rockaway, 1985—. Asst. prof. family practice N.Y. Coll. Osteopathic Medicine. Recipient Physicians Recognition award AMA, 1983, 86, 89, 92, 95, 98. Fellow Am. Acad. Family Physicians; mem. Am. Osteo. Assn., N.Y. Osteo. Soc., Am. Osteo. Coll. Family Practice, Mensa, N.Y. State Med. Soc., Nassau County Med. Soc. Avocation: boating. Office: 2240 Mott Ave Far Rockaway NY 11691-3070 also: 201 E Merrick Rd Valley Stream NY 11580-5952 Office Phone: 718-471-3159. Personal E-mail: bobf17@yahoo.com.

FARRONATO, GIAMPIETRO, orthodontist, department chairman; b. Bassano Del Grappa, Italy, Aug. 27, 1951; s. Vigilio Farronato and Letizia Brotto; m. Emanuela Gastaldello, July 26, 1955; children: Davide, Marco. MD, U. Padova, IT, 1976; DDS in odontostomatology, U. Milan, 1978; PhD in orthodontics, 1980. Prof. U. Bari, Italy, 1997—2001, U. Milan, 2001—, rschr., 1983—97, chmn. dept. orthodontics, 2001—, chmn. dept. dental hygiene, 2002—, chmn. dept. gnathology, 2006—, chmn. orthodontic sch., 2008—; chmn. Dental Hygienist Sch., 2002—; head Inst. Odontostomatology & Maxillofacial Surgery, Bari, 1997—98, Dept. Odontostomatology & Surgery, Bari, 1998—2001. Author: (book) Odontostomatology For Dental Hygienist. Mem.: European Orthodontic Fedn., Italian Soc. Straight Wire (chmn. 2002—04), Italian Soc. Maxillofacial Surgery, Iitalian Soc. Presurgical Orthodontics (chmn. 2005—07), Italian Soc. Pediatric Dentistry, World Fedn. Orthodontics, European Orthodontic Soc., Am. Assn. Orthodontics, Italian Orthodontic Soc., Italian Soc. Orthodontics (gen. sec. 1995—97). Achievements include research in periodontics & adult orthodontics, rapid palatal expansion & breathing function; enzimathic control bacterial plaque, electromyography & kinesiography, 3d cephalometry, rhinomanometry, stabilometry. Home: Vercelli 51 Milan 20144 Italy Office: Corso Europa 10 20122 Milan MI Italy Office Phone: 39276023582, 39276022598. Office Fax: 39276021299. Personal E-mail: giampietro.farronato@tin.it. Business E-Mail: giampietro.farronato@unimi.it.

FARSHIDI, ARDESHIR B., cardiologist, educator; b. Kerman, Iran, June 13, 1945; arrived in U.S., 1972, naturalized, 1977; s. Jamshid and Farangis Farshidi; m. Katayoon Kavoussi, Jan. 2, 1982. MD, Tehran U., 1969. Diplomate Am. Bd. Internal Medicine, Am. Bd. Cardiovasc. Disease, Am. Bd. Cardiac Electrophysiology. Intern, Washington, 1972—73; resident U. Pa., Phila., 1973—75, resident in cardiology, 1975—77, electrophysiologist, 1977—78; asst. prof., assoc. prof. medicine U. Conn., Farmington, 1978—84; dir. electrophysiology LA Heart Inst., 1984—90; dir. arrhythmia ctr. Los Robles Regional Med. Ctr., 1990—. Dir. electrophysiologist U. Conn., Farmington, 1982—84, attending cardiologist, 1982—84; co-dir. electrophysiology, asst. prof. medicine Yale U., 1979—82; attending cardiologist Yale U. Hosp., 1979—82; chief cardiology sect. VA Hosp., Newington, Conn., 1982—84. Rschr. Am. Heart Assn., 1981. Lt. Iranian

Army, 1969—72. Fellow: ACP, Am. Heart Assn., Am. Coll. Cardiology; mem.: Am. Electrophysiologic Soc., Am. Fedn. Clin. Rsch. Achievements include research in clin. cardiac electrophysiology and arrhythmia. Home: 3011 Grandoaks Dr Westlake Village CA 91361-5563 Office: 2100 Lynn Rd Ste 220 Thousand Oaks CA 91360-8036 Home Phone: 818-865-1286; Office Phone: 805-449-9990. Personal E-mail: drfarshidi@gmail.com.

FARSON, RICHARD EVANS, psychologist; b. Chgo., Nov. 16, 1926; s. Duke Mendenhall and Mary Gladys (Clark) F.; m. Elizabeth Lee Grimes, May 21, 1954 (div. 1962); children: Lisa Page, Clark Douglas; m. 2d Dawn Jackson Cooper, Jan. 4, 1964 (div. 1990); children: Joel Andrew, Ashley Dawn, Jeremy Richard. BA, Occidental Coll., LA, 1947, MA, 1951; postgrad., UCLA, 1948-50; PhD, U. Chgo., 1955. Faculty human rels. Harvard Bus. Sch., 1953—54; dean Sch. Design Calif. Inst. Arts, Valencia, 1969-73; pres. Esalen Inst., Big Sur and San Francisco, 1973-75; faculty Saybrook Inst., San Francisco, 1975-79; pres. Western Behavioral Scis. Inst., La Jolla, Calif., 1958-68, 1979—, chmn. bd., 1968-79. Dir. Internat. Design Conf. in Aspen, Colo., 1971-2001, pres. 1976-80, 94-97; pub. dir. AIA, 1999-2001. Editor: Science and Human Affairs, 1967; author: Birthrights: A Bill of Rights for Children, 1974, Management of the Absurd: Paradoxes in Leadership, 1996; (with others) The Future of the Family, 1969; (with Ralph Keyes) Whoever Makes the Most Mistakes Wins: The Paradox of Innovation, 2002, The Power of Design: A Force for Transforming Everything, 2008, Making The Invisible Visible, 2009, Will All Marriage Experts Please Leave The Room: Paradoxes of Matrimony, 2010, Will All Parenting Experts Please Leave The Room: Paradoxes of Parenthood, 2010. Served to lt. j.g. USNR, 1955-57. Fellow, World Acad. Art and Sci., Design Futures Coun. Mem.: APA. Home: 7520 Mar Ave La Jolla CA 92037 Office Phone: 858-454-2048. Personal E-mail: rfarson@wbsi.org.

FARUQUI, AZHAR MASOOD A., cardiologist, educator; b. Karachi, Sindh, Pakistan, June 10, 1948; s. G.N. and S.B. Faruqui; m. Shahida A. Ahmed, May 2, 1971; children: Najmus, Ainul, Raquib. MBBS, Dow Med. Coll., 1971. Diplomate Am. Bd. Internal Medicine, Am. Bd. Cardiovascular Disease. Resident, fellow Emory U. Sch. Medicine, Atlanta, 1972-76; tutor in cardiology Royal Postgrad. Med. Sch., London, 1976; asst. prof., dir. cath lab. Emory U. Sch. Medicine, Atlanta, 1977; from asst. prof. to prof. cardiology Nat. Inst. Cardiovascular Diseases, Karachi, 1978-96, exec. dir., chmn. acad. faculty, 1996—2008. Vis. prof. Aga Khan U., Karachi, 1995—, Cromwell Hosp., London, 1995—, Emory U. Sch. Medicine, 1994; dean faculty of cardiology Coll. Physicians and Surgeons, Karachi, 1995—. Editor Pakistan Heart Jour., 1978-98; former assoc. editor Asia Pace Newsletter, Jour. Pakistan Med. Assn.; contbr. over 200 articles to med. jours. Advisor in Cardiovascular Diseases WHO, Geneva, 1989—. Fellow Am. Heart Assn. (coun. mem.), Am. Coll. Cardiology, Pakistan Acad. Med. Scis., Nat. Acad. Med. Scis. Pakistan, Coll. Physicians and Surgeons Karachi (hon.), Royal Coll. Physicians and Surgeons Can.; mem. Pakistan Cardiac Soc. (mem. coun. 1978—, past pres.), Pakistan Hypertension League (founder, pres. 1996—). Avocations: travel, writing, think tanks. Office: The Heart Clinic Jinnah Hosp Rd 75350 Karachi Pakistan Office Phone: 92-213-522 1292. Personal E-mail: amafaruqui@hotmail.com.

FASSBENDER, HANS GEORG, pathologist, educator; b. Koblenz, Germany, Jan. 29, 1920; s. Klaus and Anne (Odenhausen) F.; m. Regine Kurth, Mar. 1957; children: Klaus, Manuel, Susanne. Grad., U. Cologne, Germany, 1945; Habilitation, U. Mainz, Germany, 1951, MD, 1945. Prof. gen. pathology and path. anatomy U. Mainz, Germany, 1957, rsch. asst. Inst. Pathology, 1946-51, asst. dir., 1951-57, vice-dir., 1960-64; assoc. dir. Inst. Path. U. Zurich, Switzerland, 1958-59; dir. German Armed Forces Inst. Pathology, Mainz, 1965-77, Ctr. for Rheuma-Pathology, WHO Ctr., Mainz, 1977—. Ann. chmn. Regensburg Bd. Med. Continuing Studies, 1975-76; vis. prof. pathology Rush U., Chgo., 1984—, vis. prof. biochemistry, 1989—; vis. prof. rheumatology Duke U., Durham, N.C., 1984—; vis. prof. pathology U. Zagreb, 1997—; adj. prof. medicine, dir. sect. pathology WHO Ctr., U. Ala., Birmingham, 1984—; hon. prof. Fed. U. Pernambuco, Brazil, 1980. Author: Pathology of Rheumatic Diseases, 1975 (Carol Nachman prize for rheumatology, 1976), Pathology and Pathobiology of Rheumatic Diseases, 2001; co-author: 8 textbooks; writer: 9 sci. films (internat. awards); contbr. articles 285 articles to profl. jours. Pres. Rheinland-Pfalz regional unit German League Against Rheumatism, Mainz, 1976-80. Capt. Med. Svc., German Navy, 1965-77. Decorated Bundesverdienstkreuz 1st class (Germany); recipient medal of honor U.S. Armed Force Inst. Path., Washington, 1968. Mem. German Soc. Pathology, German Soc. Rheumatology, Orthopaedic Rsch. Soc., also hon. mem. 13 internat. sci. socs. Roman Catholic. Avocation: literature. Office: Ctr for Rheuma-Pathology Breidenbacherstrasse 13 D-55116 Mainz Germany Office Phone: 49-6131-228638. Business E-Mail: mail@zrp.klinik.uni-mainz.de.

FASSLER, STEVEN A., colon and rectal surgeon, educator; BA in Philosophy and Biology, Brandeis U., Waltham, 1987—91; MD, Temple U., Phila., 1991—95. Diplomate Am. Bd. Surgery, Am. Bd. Colon and Rectal Surgery, lic. Pa., 2001. Resident in gen. surgery Univ. Conn., Farmington, 1995—2000; fellow in colon and rectal surgery Robert Wood Johnson sch. medicine Univ. Medicine and Dentistry of NJ, NB, 2000—01; clin. asst. prof. surgery sch. medicine Temple Univ., Pa., 2002—; clin. assoc. prof. surgery sch. medicine Drexel Univ., 2008—; asst. surgeon Abington Meml. Hosp., 2001—10, sr. surgeon, 2011—. Author: various publs. Recipient Chief Resident Med. Student Tchg. award, Univ. Conn., 1999, Thomas L. Dent Tchg. award, 2004; named one of Top Doctors, Phila Mag., 2011. Fellow: Phila. Acad. of Surgery, Pa. Soc. of Colon and Rectal Surgeons, ACS, Am. Soc. of Colon and Rectal Surgeons; mem.: Crohn's and Colitis Found. of America, UCONN Surgical Soc., AMA. Office: Abington Memorial Hospital 1200 Old York Rd Abington PA 19001 Office Phone: 215-517-1250.

FATELA CANTILLO, DANIEL, physician; b. Plasencia, July 1, 1977; PhD, Salamanca U., 2000, Sevilla U., 2007. Facultativo especialista en análisis clínicos, cons. Hosp. Alto Guadalquivir, 2006—. Office: Avenida Blas Infante Andújar Jaén 23740 Spain E-mail: danielfatela@yahoo.es.

FATHMAN, CHARLES GARRISON, medical educator; b. Mo., Aug. 30, 1942; MD, Washington U. Med. Sch., St. Louis, 1969. Clin. assoc. NIH, 1973—75; mem. Basel Inst. Immunology, 1975—77; assoc. prof. Mayo Clinic, 1977—81; prof. Stanford U. Med. Sch., 1981—. Assoc. editor Ann. Rev. Immunology, 1981—2005; sci. adv. bd. Bayhill Therapeutics, 2003—07, ICOS Corp., 2003—08, Lumen Therapeutics LLC, 2005—11; transplantation adv. bd. Novartis, 2005—07. Recipient Disting. Achievement award, Soc. Investigative Derematology. Master: Am. Coll. Rheumatology; mem.: Fedn. Clin. Immunological Socs. (pres.), Clin. Immunology Soc. (pres.), Am. Soc. Clin. Investigation (coun. mem.), Assn. Am. Physicians, Am. Assn. Immunologists. Office: CCSR Rm 2225 300 Pasteur Dr Stanford CA 94305 Office Fax: 650-725-1958. Business E-Mail: cfathman@stanford.edu.

FATTORUTTO, MAURIZIO, anesthesiologist; b. Haine-St. Pierre, Belgium, Aug. 2, 1971; s. Angelo Fattortutto and Lucia Nazzi; life ptnr. Severine Petrolo; children: Lisa, Hugo. Grad., U. Mons-Hainaut, Belgium, 1994, U. Paris, 2001, U. Libre de Bruxelles, Belgium, 2003. Contbr. articles to profl. jours. Achievements include research in effects of recombinant activated factor VII on a rabbit model of bleeding and thrombosis. Office: CHU Tivoli Avenue Max Buset 34 7100 La Louviere Belgium Office Phone: 0032 64 27 76 10. Business E-Mail: mfattorutto@coag.be.

FATUSIC, ZLATAN, gynecologist, educator, obstetrician; b. Lukavac, Bosnia, July 5, 1955; s. Latif and Kadrija Fatusic; m. Dusanka Vukovic, Apr. 26, 1980; children: Jasenko, Srebrenko. Degree, U. Sarajero, 1979. Head surgery dept. ob-gyn. Ob-Gyn. Clinic, Tuxla, Bosnia, 1996—98, head clinic, 1998—. Head clinic U. Clin. Ctr., Tuzla, 1998—; haed ob-gyn. med. faculty U. Tuzla, 1999—. Author: History of Gynecology, 2001; contbr. articles to profl. jours. Mem.: Assn. Perinatal MGB (pres. 2000—), World Assn. Perinatal Medicine (bd. dirs. 2000—). Avocations: classical music, handball, volleyball. Home: Slatina 3/28 Tuzla 75000 Bosnia-Herzegovina Office: Univ Clin Ctr Trnovac bb Tuzla 75000 Bosnia-Herzegovina Office Fax: 287-35251493. E-mail: jax@bih.net.ba.

FAU, DANIEL ROGER, biologist, researcher; b. Bois-Colombes, Paris, France, July 7, 1948; s. Paul F. and Odette (Boulanger) F.; 1 child, Anne-Cécile. M of Physiology, U. Paris, 1969, D of Univ., 1973, DSc, 1981. Cert. rsch. scientist. Rschr. Nat. Ctr. Sci. Rsch., Paris, 1973-81, 85-88; vis. prof. U. Calif., Davis, 1982-84; rschr. Nat. Inst. Sci. Rsch. Medicine, Clichy-Paris, 1989—. Cons. Elf, Paris, 1979-82, P. Fabre, France, 1995-97. Contbr. articles to profl. jours. Grantee NSF, 1982-84. Mem. Am. Soc. Nutritional Scis., N.Y. Acad. Scis., Sigma Xi. Office: CNRS FEMTO Inst 32 Ave Observatoire F25044 Besançon France Business E-Mail: daniel.fau@dr6.cnrs.fr.

FAUCHERON, JEAN-LUC OLIVIER, surgeon; b. Verzy, Marne, France, Jan. 17, 1959; s. Jean-Marie Maurice and Bernadette Marie-Paule (Gavroy) F.; m. Odile Marie-Louise Bosseaux, July 22, 1994; children: Olivier, Richard, Henri, Berengere, Alienor. MD, U. Paris, 1988, Manchester U., Eng., 1989; Diploma Advanced Rsch., U. Marseille, France, 1993. Chief resident in surgery U. Paris, 1988-94; cons. anatomy St. Antoine Hosp., Paris, 1990-94; cons. Michallon Hosp., Grenoble, 1994—; prof. U. Grenoble, 2001—, head colorectal unit, 2003. Author: Rob and Smith Operative Surgery, 1993. Capt. French Mil., 1980. Recipient Duval-Marjolin Price award, 1988, Laureat, French Nat. Soc. Gastroenterology, 1990; grantee British Coun., 1989. Avocations: skin diving, tennis, making champagne. Home: 2 D Chemin Maupertuis 38240 Meylan Isere France Office: Parc Albert Michallon 38000 Grenoble Isere France Office Phone: 33-4-76-76-53-71, 33476765526. Business E-Mail: jlfaucheron@chu-grenoble.fr.

FAUCI, ANTHONY STEPHEN, federal agency administrator, allergist, immunologist; b. Bklyn., Dec. 24, 1940; s. Stephen A. and Eugenia A. Fauci. AB, Coll. of Holy Cross, Worcester, Mass., 1962; MD, Cornell U. Med. Coll., NYC, 1966; DSc (hon.), Coll. Holy Cross, 1987, Georgetown U., 1990, Hahnemann U., 1990, Mt. Sinai Sch. Medicine, 1990, Universita di Roma, 1990, St. John's U., 1991, LI U., 1992, Med. Coll. Wis., 1993, Bard Coll., 1993, Bates Coll., 1993, SUNY, Farmingdale, 1994, U. Conn. Health Ctr, 1994, Duke U., 1995. Diplomate Am. Bd. Internal Medicine, Am. Bd. Allergy & Immunology, Am. Bd. Infectious Diseases. Intern NY Hosp.-Cornell Med. Ctr., 1966—67, asst. resident dept. medicine, 1967—68, chief resident dept. medicine, 1971—72; clin. assoc. Nat. Inst. Allergy & Infectious Diseases (NIAID), Bethesda, Md., 1968—70, chief immunoregulation lab., 1980—, dir., 1984—; sr. staff fellow NIH, 1970—71, sr. investigator, 1972—74, head clin. physiology sect., 1974—80, dep. clin. dir., 1977—80; assoc. dir. to dir. NIH Office AIDS Rsch., Bethesda, Md., 1988—94. Cons. Naval Med. Ctr., Bethesda, 1972—; lectr. in field. Editor: Harrison's Principles of Internal Medicine; contbr. numerous articles to profl. jours. Trustee Doris Duke Charitable Found. Recipient Meritorious Svc. award, USPHS, 1979, Arthur S. Fleming award, 1983, Clemons von Pirquet award, Georgetown U. Med. Ctr., 1986, Disting Clin. Educator award, NIH Clin. Ctr., 1988; Leadership award, Columbus Citizens Found., Inc., 1988, AIDS Rsch. award, Nat. Hemophilia Fedn., 1989, Lee P. Brown Nat. Pub. Svc. award, Nat. Acad. Pub. Adminstrn./Nat. Soc. Pub. Adminstrn., 1989, Helen Hayes award for med. rsch., 1989, Lifetime Sci. award, Inst. Advanced Studies Immunology & Aging, 1990, Internat. Chiron prize, 1990, Pres.'s award, NY Acad. Sci., 1990, Thomas H. Ham-Louis R. Wasserman award, Am. Soc. Hematology, 1992, Dr. Nathan Davis award, AMA, 1992, Outstanding Achievement award, Howard U., 1992, Humanitarian award, Tiro a Segno Fedn., 1993, Cartwright prize, Columbia U. Coll. Physicians & Surgeons, 1993, Theobald Smith award, Albany Med. Coll., 1995, David Rumbough Sci. award, Juvenile Diabetes Fedn. Internat., 1996, Ellen Browning Scripps medal, Scripps Fedn. Medicine & Rsch., 1996, Md. Gov.'s Citation, 1997, Thomas J. D'Alesandro Jr. award, Assoc. Italian Am. Charities, 1997, Frank Brown Berry prize, US Med. & Delta Dental Plan Calif., 1999, Frank Annunzio Humanitarian award, Christopher Columbus Fellowship Found., 2001, Ellis Island Family Heritage award, Statue of Liberty-Ellis Island Found., 2003, Nat. Sci. Medal, NSF, 2007, Mary Woodard Lasker award for pub. svc., Albert & Mary Lasker Found., 2007, Presdl. Medal of Freedom, The White House, 2008; named 13th most cited scientist amongst pub. jour. articles, Inst. for Sci. Info., 1983—2002, 9th most cited scientist in immunology, 1993—2003, 10th most-cited HIV/AIDS rschr., 1996—2006, America's Best in Sci. & Medicine, CNN/TIME Mag., 2001, Scientist of Yr., R&D Mag., 2005; named one of The Top 50 Sci. Leaders, Sci. America, 2003, America's Best Leaders, US News & World Report, 2008, The 25 Greatest Pub. Servants Over Past 25 Yrs., Coun. Excellence in Govt., 2008. Master: AAAS (Westinghouse award 1988); fellow: ACP (Richard & Hinda Rosenthal award 1995, John Phillips Meml. award 1997), Am. Acad. Microbiology, NY Acad. Medicine (hon. Extraordinary Accomplishments award 2004), Am. Acad. Arts & Scis., Am. Acad. Allergy Asthma & Immunology (hon.), Am. Med. Writers Assn. (hon. John P. McGovern award 1997); mem.: NAS, Am. Philos. Soc., Royal Acad. Medicine (Spain), Royal Danish Acad. Sci. & Letters, Inst. Medicine (coun. mem.), Assn. Am. Physicians (recorder 1988—93, councillor 1993—), Am. Soc. Clin. Investigation, Infectious Diseases Soc. America (Squibb award 1983), Internat. AIDS Soc., Am. Fedn. Clin. Rsch. (pres. 1980—81), Am. Soc. Cell Biology, Am. Soc. Virology, Am. Assn. Immunologists (prog. chmn. 1982—85, Kober lectr. 1988, Lifetime Achievement award 2005). Roman Catholic. Avocations: running, tennis. Office: Nat Inst Allergy & Infectious Diseases Bldg 31 Claude D Pepper Bldg 7A03 31 Center Dr MS 2520 Bethesda MD 20892 Office Phone: 301-496-2263. Office Fax: 301-496-4409. Business E-Mail: anthony.fauci@nih.gov. *

FAULCONER, ROBERT JAMIESON, pathologist, educator; b. Sedlescombe, Sussex, Eng., July 11, 1923; came to U.S., 1925, naturalized, 1932; s. Robert Hoffman and Gladys Alice (Jamieson) F.; m. Virginia Myrl Davis, Aug. 11, 1945; children: Anne Faulconer Hurley, Elizabeth Myrl, Mary Waite, John Edmund. BS, Coll. William and Mary, 1943; MD, Johns Hopkins U., 1947; DSc (hon.), Ea. Va. Med. Sch., 1998. Diplomate Am. Bd. Pathology. Intern Johns Hopkins Hosp., 1948, fellow, 1948-49; resident Presbyn.-U. Pa. Med. Ctr., Phila., 1949-52; pathologist DePaul Hosp., Norfolk, Va., 1954-78, pathologist, dir. labs., 1965-78; clin. prof. pathology Med. Coll. Va., 1972-79; prof. pathology Ea. Va. Med. Sch., 1974-94, chmn., 1978-93, prof. emeritus, 1994—. Cons. pathologist U.S. Naval Hosp., Portsmouth, Va., VA Hosp., Hampton, Va., Children;s Hosp., Norfolk, Va. Beach Gen. Hosp.; chmn. Health Svcs. Adv. Bd., Norfolk; mem. adv. com. Va. Cancer Registry. Med. editorial bd. Histology and Histopathology Jour.; contbr. articles on pathology to profl. publs. Pres. Va. div. Am. Cancer Soc., 1963-66, mem. nat. bd. dirs., exec. and sci. rev. coms.; bd. visitors Coll. William and Mary, 1972-76, 79-87, chmn. William and Mary Olde Guarde, 1997-98. With USNR, 1943-46, M.C., U.S. Army, 1952-54. Recipient J. Shelton Horsley award merit, Va. div. Am. Cancer Soc., 1966, Alumni medallion, Coll. William and Mary, 1985. Fellow AAAS; mem. AMA, Internat. Acad. Pathology, Am. Soc. Clin. Pathologists, Coll. Am. Pathologists, Am. Assn. Anatomists, Am. Soc. Clin. Oncology, Am. Assn. Phys. Anthropologists, Va. Soc. Pathology (pres. 1958-59), Norfolk Acad. Medicine (pres. 1964-65), Am. Assn. History of Medicine, Am. Assn. Pathologists, Assn. Pathology Chmn., Cypher Soc. (Coll. William and Mary), Norfolk Yacht and Country Club, Town Point Club (bd. govs.), Commonwealth Club (Richmond); Sigma Xi. Episcopalian. Home: 1507 Buckingham Ave Norfolk VA 23508-1354 Office: Ea Va Med Sch Med Coll of Hampton Roads PO Box 1980 Norfolk VA 23501-1980 Business E-Mail: crd@borg.evms.edu.

FAULKNER, JUDITH, private health services software company executive; M in Computer Sci., U. Wis. Taught computer sci. U. Wis., Madison; worked as healthcare software developer; founder, CEO Epic Systems Corp. (originally known as Human Services Computing, Inc.), Verona, Wis., 1979—. Named one of 100 Most Influential People in Healthcare, Modern Healthcare Mag., 2011. Office: Epic Systems Corporation 1979 Milky Way Verona WI 53593 Office Phone: 608-271-9000. Office Fax: 608-271-7237.

FAULKNER, LARRY R., medical association administrator, former dean, educator, researcher, writer; b. Walla Walla, Washington; m. Judy Faulkner; 1 child. MD, U. Washington, 1974. Diplomate Am. Bd. Psychiatry and Neurology, Nat. Bd. Med. Examiners. Resident U. Ark.; dir. edn. for med. students and residents U. Portland Oreg. Health Sciences Ctr.; prof. U. S.C. Sch. Medicine, chmn. Dept. Neuropsychiartry and Behavioral Sci., 1990—95, interim dean, 1994—95, dean, 1995—2006, v.p. med. affairs; exec. v.p. and CEO, now pres., CEO Am. Bd. Psychiatry and Neurology, Inc., Chgo., 2006—. Rschr., writer in field; dir. William S. Hall Psychiatric Inst.; dir. Divsn. Rsch. and Edn. SC Dept. Mental Health. Contbr. articles to profl. jours. Recipient Physician's Recognition award, AMA; fellow NIH. Mem.: Am. Psychiatric Assn. (disting. fellow 2003), Carolina Alumni Assn. (hon. life mem. 2004), Benjamin Rush Soc., Alpha Omega Alpha (faculty initiate 1996). Office: American Board of Psychiatry Neurology 2150 E Lake Cook Rd Ste 900 Buffalo Grove IL 60089-1875 *

FAUST, DOMINIK, gastroenterologist; b. Mainz am Rhein, Rheinland-Pfalz, Germany, Sept. 10, 1965; s. Wofgang Dietmar Faust and Gunhild Else Faust-Tinnefeldt; m. Antje Schneider. Degree, Gutenberg U., Mainz, Germany, 1992; PhD, Goethe-U., Frankfurt, Hessen, Germany, 2004. Lic. in medicine State Office Social Affairs/State Rheinland-Pfalz, 1993, cert. internal medicine specialist Med. Assn. Hessen, Germany, 2001, gastroenterology specialist 2006. Med. officer German Fed. Armed Forces, Wildflecken, Bayern, Germany, 1994; resident U. Hosp., Frankfurt, 1992—93, intern, asst. med. dir., 2004—07; dept. head Asklepios Clin. Ctr., Langen, Hessen, 2007—. Lt. col. med. corps, 2007. Fellow: European Bd. Gastroenterology; mem.: German Bd. Internal Medicine, German Bd. Gastroenterology. Office: Asklepios Clin Ctr Roentgenstrasse 20 Langen Hessen D-63225 Germany Office Fax: 49 6103 9121848. Business E-Mail: d.faust@asklepios.com.

FAVA, MAURIZIO, hospital administrator, researcher; b. Valdagno, Italy, May 8, 1956; came to U.S., 1985; s. Ezio Fava and Olga Danieli; m. Stefania Lamon, May 18, 1985; 1 child, Giovanni. Med. degree, U. Padua, Italy, 1982. Dir. depression rsch. program Mass. Gen. Hosp., Boston, 1990-94, dir. depression clin. and rsch. program, 1994—, assoc. chief psychiatry for clin. rsch., 2000—06, vice chair. dept. psychiatry, 2006—. Prof. psychiatry Harvard Med. Sch., Boston, 2002—. Co-editor: Research Designs and Methods in Psychiatry, 1992. DuPont-Warren fellow Mass. Gen. Hosp., 1988. Mem. Am. Psychiat. Assn., Am. Coll. Neuropsychopharmacology. Office: Mass Gen Hosp Bulfinch 351 55 Fruit St Boston MA 02114-3117 E-mail: mfava@partners.org. *

FAVARO, MARY KAYE ASPERHEIM, pediatrician & family practice, writer; b. Edgerton, Wis., Sept. 30, 1934; d. Harold Wilbur and Genevieve Catherine (Hyland) Asperheim; m. Biagino Philip Favaro, May 31, 1969; children: Justin Peter, Gina Sue. BS, U. Wis., 1956, MD, 1969; MS, St. Louis Coll. Pharmacy, 1965. Instr. pharmacology St. Louis U. and St. Mary's Hosp. Sch. Practical Nurses, 1959-64; staff pharmacist U. Hosps., Madison, Wis., 1964—69; intern Albany Med. Ctr., NY, 1969-70; resident, 1970-71; resident in pediatrics U. SC, Charleston, 1971-72, asst. prof. pediatrics, 1973-75;

pvt. practice pediatrics family practice, 1974-99; locumtenens physician, 2000—. Author: The Pharmacologic Basis of Patient Care, 1985, Introduction to Pharmacology, 2009. Mem.: AMA. Roman Catholic. Home: 1407 Southwood Dr Myrtle Beach SC 29575 Office Phone: 843-267-6879. Personal E-mail: maryfav@aol.com.

FAWCETT, JAMES WILLIAM, neuroscientist, educator; b. London, Eng., Mar. 13, 1950; s. Edward Charles Fawcett and Janet Carolin Hughes; m. Kay-Tee Khaw, Oct. 14, 1950; children: Nicola, Andrew. BA, Oxford U., Eng., 1972; MB BS, London U., 1975. Scientist Nat. Inst. Med. Rsch., London, 1978—82; asst. prof. Salk U., La Jolla, Calif., 1983—86; lectr. Cambridge (Eng.) U., 1987—2001, prof. Exptl. Neurology, dir. Brain Repair Ctr., 2001—. Sci. dir. Internat. Spinal Rsch. Trust, London, 1996—2004; mem. adv. bd. Acorda Therapeutics, Tarrytown, NY, 2002—. Co-author: Brain Damage, Brain Repair, 1981; contbr. articles to profl. jours. Fellow: Royal Coll. Physicians. Avocations: sailing, bagpipes. Office: Cambridge Univ Brain Repair Ctr Robinson Way Cambridge CB2 2PY England Office Phone: +44 1223 331160. Business E-Mail: jf108@cam.ac.uk.

FAWCETT, SHERWOOD LUTHER, lab administrator; b. Youngstown, Ohio, Dec. 25, 1919; s. Luther T. and Clara (Sherwood) F.; m. Martha L. Simcox, Feb. 28, 1953; children: Paul, Judith, Tom. BS, Ohio State U., 1941, PhD (hon.); MS, Case Inst. Tech., 1948, PhD, 1950; PhD (hon.), Gonzaga U., Whitman Coll., Otterbein Coll., Detroit Inst. Tech., Ohio Dominican Coll. Registered profl. engr., Ohio. Mem. staff Columbus (Ohio) Labs. Battelle Meml. Inst., 1950-64, mgr. physics dept., 1959-64; dir. Pacific Northwest Labs., Richland, Wash., 1964-67; trustee Battelle Meml. Inst., Columbus, 1968-92, exec. v.p., 1967-68, CEO, 1968-84, pres., 1968-80, chmn., 1981-84, chmn. bd. trustees, 1985-87, assoc. trustee, 1987-94. Emeritus chmn. bd. dirs. Transmet Corp. With USNR, 1941-46. Decorated Bronze Star; recipient Washington award Western Soc. Engrs., 1989. Mem. AIME, NSPE, Am. Phys. Soc., Am. Nuc. Soc., Am. Phys. Soc., Sigma Xi, Tau Beta Pi, Delta Chi, Sigma Pi Sigma. Home: 1800 Riverside Dr Apt 2314 Columbus OH 43212-1823 *

FAWCETT, WILLIAM JOHN, anesthesiologist, educator; b. Wiltshire, Eng., Mar. 23, 1962; s. Michael John and Angela Rosemary Fawcett; m. Helen Fiona Gledhill, May 31, 1986. Degree, Bradfield Coll., Berkshire, 1980; MBBS, U. London, 1985. Lectr. anaesthesia U. London, 1992—94; cons. anaesthesia and pain medicine Royal Surrey County Hosp., Guildford, England, 1994—2008; lectr. U. Surrey, Guildford, 1999—, sr. fellow Postgrad. Med. Sch., 2009. Contbr. articles to profl. med. jours. Recipient Nat. Clin. Excellence award, Dept. Health, 2007. Fellow: Faculty Pain Medicine, Royal Coll. Anesthetists. Business E-Mail: wfawcett@nhs.net.

FAXON, DAVID PARKER, cardiologist; b. Manchester, NH, 1944; BA, Hamilton Coll., Clinton. NY, 1967; MD, Boston U. Sch. Medicine, 1971. Cert. internal medicine, cardiology, interventional cardiology. Intern Mary Hitchcock Meml. Hosp., 1971—72, resident, 1972—74, fellowship, cardiol., 1974—76; resident, internal medicine Darmouth-Hitchcock Med. Ctr., 1974; fellowship, cardiology Boston U. Med. Ctr., 1976; assoc. prof., medicine Boston U. Sch. Medicine, prof. medicine, dir. interventional cardiol., acting chief cardiology, 1976—93; prof., medicine, chief divsn. cardiology U. So. Calif. Med. Ctr., 1993—2000, U. Chgo. Med. Ctr., 2000—06; prof. medicine, dir. strategic planning, dept. medicine Brigham and Women's Hosp., Boston, 2006—, vice chair, integrated clin. svcs., 2006. Contbr. articles various profl. jours., chapters to books; editl. bd. mem. Circulation, Am. Jour. Cardiology, Jour. Am. Coll. Cardiology. Chmn. Am. Heart Assn. Sci. Adv. and Coord. Com., edit. bd. mem. Circulation, The Am. Jour. of Cardiology, Jour. of the Am. Coll. of Cardiology. Mem.: Am. Heart Assn. (pres. 2001—02, bd. dirs.), Assn. U. Cardiologists, Soc. Cardiac Angiography and Interventions, Am. Coll. Cardiol. Achievements include first to angioplasty, a non-surgical technique for restoring blood flow through clogged arteries; research in methods to prevent renarrowing of vessels after angioplasty. Office: Brigham and Women's Hosp Cardiovascular Divsn 75 Francis St PBB-1 Boston MA 02115 Office Phone: 773-702-1919, 617-525-8358. Office Fax: 617-525-7752. Business E-Mail: dfaxon@partners.org.

FAYAD, GEORGE G., surgeon, consultant; s. George Fouad Fayad and Jeannette Alexander Joseph; m. Denise Elias Joseph, Oct. 31, 1994; children: Aida-Maria, Raissa Maria. MD, Brussels U., 1988, MBA, 1991, cert. in ENT surgery, 1996. Cons. surgeon Eye & Ear Hosp., Beirut, 1996—99, also bd. dirs.; cons. surgeon St. George's Hosp., London, 1999—2000, St. Mary's Hosp., London, 2000—02, Basildon Hosp., Essex, England, 2002—. Contbr. articles to profl. jours. Fellow: Internat. Coll. Surgeons; mem.: Lebanon Soc. Medicine, Knights of St. John. Avocations: reading, tennis, golf. Office: Basildon Hosp Nethermayne SS16 5NL Basildon England Office Fax: (01268) 598501. Business E-Mail: fayadent@doctors.net.uk.

FAYDA, MERDAN, oncologist, educator; b. Istanbul, Turkey, Nov. 26, 1976; s. Mustafa and Kevser Fayda; m. Sema Nur Altug, Aug. 21, 2001; 1 child, Müjgan Binnaz. MD, Istanbul U., 1999, degree in Radiation Oncology, 2004. Asst. prof., dept. radiation oncology Kocaeli U., Turkey, 2006—; radiation oncologist Istanbul U. Oncology Inst., 2009—. Mem.: ASTRO. Office: Istanbul Univ Oncology Inst Capa Istanbul 34390 Turkey

FAZEL, IRADJ, surgeon; b. Isfahan, Iran, 1939; MD, Tehran U., Iran, 1964. Prof. Shahid Beheshti Univ. of Med. Sciences, Tehran, Iran; chief vascular dept. and organ transplantation Taleghani Med. Ctr., Iran; prof. Nat. Univ. of Iran; min. Higher Edn., 1975, Health and Med. Edn., 1989. Mem.: Iranian Soc. for Organ Transplantation (pres.), Iranian Assn. of Surgeons (pres.), Iranian Acad. of Med. Sciences (founder and pres. 1991—2010). Office: Iranian Academy of Medical Sciences PO Box 19395-4655 Tehran Iran Office Phone: 98212930390. Office Fax: 98212932125. Business E-Mail: fazel@ams.ac.ir. *

FAZIO, RICHARD ANTHONY, gastroenterologist, educator; MD, U. Bologna, Italy, 1978. Diplomate Am. Bd. Internal Medicine, Am. Bd. Internal Medicine-gastroenterology. Intern Maimonides Med. Ctr., NY, resident internal medicine, 1979—81; fellow gastroenterology St. Vincent's Med. Ctr., SI, NY, 1981—83; prof. medicine SUNY Downstate Med. Ctr.; gastroenterology Richmond Univ. Med. Ctr., NY. Office: Richmond University Medical Center 78 Todt Hill Rd Staten Island NY 10314 Office Phone: 718-448-1122. Office Fax: 718-448-8318.

FEACHEM, RICHARD GEORGE ANDREW, medical educator; b. 1947; m. Neelam Sekhri Feachem. MD, U. London; PhD in Environ. Health, U. New South Wales; ED (hon.), U. Birmingham, 2007. Dean London Sch. Hygiene & Tropical Medicine, 1989—95; dir. health, nutrition & population World Bank, 1995—99; prof. global health U. Calif., San Francisco, Berkeley, founding dir. Inst. Global Health San Francisco, 1999—2002, exec. dir. Global Health Group, 2007—; exec. dir. Global Fund to Fight AIDS Tuberculosis & Malaria, 2002—07. Treas. Internat. AIDS Vaccine Initiative; vis. prof. London U.; hon. prof. U. Queensland. Author numerous books and articles on pub. health and health policy. Decorated Comdr. Order of British Empire, 1995. Fellow: Royal Acad. Engring., Royal Coll. Physicians Faculty Pub. Health Medicine (hon.), Am. Soc. Tropical Medicine & Hygiene (hon.). Office: UCSF Global Health Scis 3333 California St Ste 285 San Francisco CA 94143 Office Fax: 415-502-6045, 405-512-6052. *

FEARON, WILLIAM, cardiologist; m. Yvonne Louise Karanas, May 17, 1997. BA, Dartmouth Coll., 1990; MD, Columbia U., 1994. Cert. Cardiovascular Disease American Bd. Internal Medicine, 2001, Interventional Cardiology American Bd. Internal Medicine, 2002. Asst. prof. cardiovascular medicine Stanford U., 2004—. Co-principal investigator on the FAME (Fractional Flow Reserve Versus Angiography for Multivessel Evaluation) presented at the 20th annual Transcatheter Cardiovascular Therapeutics scientific symposium, 2008, published in New England Jour. Medicine, 2009. Grantee, NIH, 2004—. Office: Stanford U Med Ctr 300 Pasteur Dr Stanford CA 94305-5637 Office Phone: 650-725-2621. Fax: 650-725-6766.

FEASTER, BURNES LYNN, III, other: medicine; b. Memphis, Tenn. married; 4 children. BA cum laude, U. Fla., 1969—73, MD, 1973—77. Diplomate Am. Bd. Internal Medicine, 1980, Am. Bd. Internal Medicine- pulmonary disease, 1982, Am. Bd. Internal Medicine- critical care medicine, 1998. Instr. Advanced Trauma Life Support; course dir. instr. Advanced Cardiac Life Sipport; intern William Beaumont Army Med. Ctr., El Paso, Tex., 1977—78, resident in internal medicine, 1978—80, staff in pulmonary disease svc., 1982—84, dir. med. intensive care unit, 1982—84; fellow in pulmonary disease Walter Reed Army Med. Ctr., Washington, 1980—82; teaching fellow US Uniformed Health Sci. Med. Sch., Bethesda, Md., 1980—82; chief in pulmonary disease svc. Landstuhl Army Regional Med. Ctr., Germany, 1984—87; cons. in pulmonary disease to 7th med. command Heidelberg, Germany, 1984—87; med. staff St. Petersburg Med. Clinic, Fla., 1987—95; clin. asst. prof. Sch. Medicine Univ. South Fla., 1988—; med. dir. Vocat. tech. Inst. of St. Petersburg, Fla., 1988; nat. faculty mem. Am. Acad. of Allergy and Immunology, 1991—; med. dir. in critical care medicine St. Anthony's Hosp., 1996—; med. dir. Vencor Hosp., 1997—; hosp. affiliation includes Bayfront Med. Ctr. Chmn. spl. care com. Landstuhl Army Regional Med. Ctr., Germany, 1986—87; M.I.C.U. com. St. Anthony's Hosp., St. Petersburg, Fla., 1987—, respitory therapy com., 1987—; chmn. pharmacy and therapeutics com. St. Anthony Hosp., 1989—92, exec. com., 1989—92; chmn. spl. care com. St. Anthony's Hosp., 1996—; intensive care unit com. Edward H. White Meml. Hosp., St. Petersburg, Fla., 1987—90; critical care com. Bayfront Med. Ctr., 1990—, chmn. pharmacy and therapeutic com., 1994—, chmn. cardiac care com., 1997—; SICU com. All Children's Hosp., 1992—; chief of staff Vencor Hosp., 1997—. Office: Bayfront Medical Center 625 6th Ave Ste 475 Saint Petersburg FL 33701-2227 Office Phone: 727-822-6666.

FEDDER, WENDE, medical association administrator; b. Milw., Dec. 21, 1972; BSN, Marquette U., 1995; D in Nursing Practice, Rush U., 2011. Exec. dir. Alexian Bros. Health Sys., 2004—. Bd. dirs. Stroke Coords. Assn., 2009—; cons. NeuStrategy, 2009. Fellow: Am. Heart Assn.; mem.: Am. Coll. Healthcare Executives, Sigma Theta Tau. Home: 1255 Town Ctr Vernon Hills IL 60061 Personal E-mail: wendenf@aol.com.

FEDDERSEN STEWARD, MARYANN ODILIA, psychotherapist; b. Wilmington, Del., Nov. 17, 1945; d. Charles Martin Steward and Ann Catherine Feddersen; m. Fred A. Steward; children: Sarah Catherine, Anna Marie. BA, Duquesne U., 1967; MEd, U. Pitts., 1970, PhD, 1975. Counselor, group leader Neighborhood Youth Corps, Pitts., 1967—68; ednl. coord. Cmty. Action Pitts., 1968—71; ednl. facilitator Mon-Yough Coun. Drug Abuse, McKeesport, Pa., 1971—73; counselor cons. Allegheny Intermediate Unit Pitts., 1973—75; child and family therapist No. Communities Mental Health Program, Pitts., 1974—85; psychologist FosterGrandParents/Home Visitor Program, Pitts., 1976—80. Pvt. practice, 1977—; cons., trainer Washington Green County Head Start, Pa., 1979—82; trainer Title XX Programs, Pa., 1979—81; mem. adv. coun. North Side Pitts. Salvation Army, 1983—2000; bd. dirs. Pitts. Cancer Guidance Inst., 1988—93. Recipient recognition award, Foster Grandparent Program, 1980. Mem.: AAUW (Fox Chapel br. bd. mem. 2004—, br. pres. 2007—08), Assn. Counseling Assn., Western Pa. Family Ctr., US Internat. Fireball Assn. (dist. 4 commodore 1984—89), Moraine Sailing (sec. 1982—88). Home and Office: 309 N Pasadena Dr Pittsburgh PA 15215-1832

FEDELE, MONICA, research scientist, educator; b. Naples, Italy, Mar. 23, 1969; Degree in Biol. Scis., U. Naples Federico, 1993, PhD in Cellular and Molecular Biology & Pathology, 2000. Fellow rschr. Thomas Jefferson U., Kimmel Cancer Inst., Phila., 1998—99; postdoc. rschr. U. Naples Federico, Italy, 2000—01, adj prof. Sch. Biotech., 2007—; rschr. Nat. Rsch. Coun., Naples, 2001—05, sr. rschr., 2006—. Recipient Outstanding Sci. Publ. award, Fondazione Guido Berlucchi, 2008; Young Investigator grant, Regione Campania, 2002, grant, Italian Ministry Rsch., Programmi di Ricerca Sci. di Rilevante Interesse Nat., CNR. Mem.: European Assn. Cancer Rsch. (Highly Commended Young Rschr. award 2007), Italian Soc. Cancerology. Avocations: guitar, piano, singing. Home: Vico Acitillo 160 Naples 80127 Italy Office Phone: 0039-0817463054. Home Fax: 0039-081-7463749. Personal E-mail: mfedele@unina.it.

FEDER, BARNABY, reporter; BA, Williams Coll., 1972; JD, Univ. Calif., Berkeley, 1977. Writer World Bus. Weekly, Energy User News; reporter North Adams Transcript, Mass., New York Times, 1980—, bus. reporter London, 1982—85, bus. correspondent Chgo., 1992—98, now tech. & med. device reporter. Office: New York Times 620 8th Ave New York NY 10018 Office Phone: 212-556-7728. Office Fax: 212-556-1448. Business E-Mail: barnaby@nytimes.com.

FEDERER, DEBRA, physician; b. Wyo., Jan. 21, 1952; MD, U. d'Aix-Marseille, 1981. Physician Emergency Physician Hosp., 1986—. Home: PO 14580 Bradenton FL 34280 Business E-Mail: debra.federer@hcahealthcare.com.

FEDERICI, AUGUSTO B., medical educator; b. Milan, Jan. 16, 1952; MD, U. Milan, 1977; postdoc. in Hematology, U. Pavia, 1980. Rsch. fellow Scripps Clinic Rsch. Found., La Jolla, Calif., 1981—84; asst., assoc. dir. A. Bianchi Bonomi Hemophilia Thrombosis Ctr., Milan, 1980—2001, dir., lab. unit bleeding disorders, 1985—2009; assoc. prof., hematology U. Milan, 2001—. Head, divsn. hematology and transfusion medicine L. Sacco U. Hosp. U. Milan, Italy, 2009—11. Contbr. more than 150 articles to profl. jours. European Cmty. grant, Support Project Von Willebrand Disease, Support Project on Orphan Drugs VWD, Nato grant, Collaboration with Scripps Clinic Rsch. Found., Italian Ministry Health grant, Italian Registry on Von Willebrand Disease. Mem.: European Hematology Assn., Internat. Soc. Thrombosis and Haemostasis, Am. Soc. Hematology. Avocations: literature, music, tennis. Home: Via S Orsola 3 Milan 20123 Italy E-mail: augusto.federici@unimi.it.

FEDERLE, MICHAEL PETER, medical educator; b. Cin., Aug. 18, 1948; BS, Marquette U., 1970; MD, Georgetown U., 1974. Prof., chmn. U. Pitts. Med. Ctr., 1989—2008; prof. Stanford U., 2008—. Recipient Canon medal, Soc. Gastrointestinal Radiology. Fellow: Am. Coll. Radiology; mem.: Soc. Computed Tomography and MRI, Soc. Abdominal Imaging. Avocations: golf, reading. Office: Rm S-092 Stanford University Med Ctr Stanford CA 94305-5105 Office Fax: 650-725-7296. Business E-Mail: federle@stanford.edu.

FEDERMAN, DANIEL DAVID, academic administrator, endocrinologist, educator; b. NYC, Apr. 16, 1928; m. Elizabeth Buckley; children: Lise, Carolyn. BA, Harvard U., 1949, MD, 1953. Diplomate Am. Bd. Internal Medicine. Intern Mass. Gen. Hosp., Boston, 1953—54, resident in medicine, 1954—55, fellow in medicine, 1958—60; instr. to prof. Harvard Med. Sch., Boston, 1961—72, dean students and alumni, 1977—89, prof. medicine, 1977—92, dean med. edn., 1989—2000, Carl W. Walter prof. medicine and med. edn., 1992—, sr. dean alumni rels. & clin. tchg., 2000—05; chmn. medicine Stanford Med. Sch., Palo Alto, Calif., 1972—77. Author: (med. textbook) Abnormal Sexual Development, 1967; editor: Scientific American Medicine. Recipient Disting. Educator Award, Endocrine Soc., 1999, Abraham Flexner Award for Disting. Svc. to Med. Edn., Assn. Am. Med. Colleges, 2001. Master: ACP (pres. Phila. 1982—83, named Mass. Physician of Yr. 1994, Disting. Tchr. Award 1995); fellow: NY Acad. Medicine; mem.: Inst. Medicine. Office: Harvard Med Sch Office of Dean Bldg A-101 25 Shattuck St Boston MA 02115-6027

FEDERMAN, NOAH, pediatrician, educator; b. NY, June 1, 1975; BA, Williams Coll., 1997; MD, Mt. Sinai Sch. Medicine, 2002. Dir., UCLA's pediat. bone and soft tissue sarcoma program, asst. prof. pediat. UCLA David Geffen Sch. Medicine, 2008. Mem.: Connective Tissue Oncology Soc., Am. Soc. Pediat. Hematology, Oncology, Sarcoma Alliance Rsch. Through Collaboration. Office: A2-410 MDCC 10833 Le Conte Ave Los Angeles CA 90095 Business E-Mail: nfederman@mednet.ucla.edu.

FEDERSPIEL, JOHN C., hospital administrator; 3 children. BS, Ohio State U., 1975; MBA, Temple U., 1977. Mem. State Hosp. Rev. and Planning Council; chmn. Northern Met. Hosp. Assn.; chmn. nominating and corp. governance com. Hudson Valley Hosp. Ctr., dir., 2001—, CEO, pres. Recipient, Arthritis Found., Vis. Nurse Assn. of Westchester. Mem.: Am. Coll. of Health Care Execs. (diplomat status). Office: Hudson Valley Hospital Center 1980 Crompond Rd Cortlandt Manor NY 10567 Office Phone: 914-737-9000.

FEDERSPIL, PIERRE JEAN-PIERRE, ear, nose and throat specialist, educator; b. Bettembourg, Luxembourg, Nov. 7, 1936; arrived in Germany, 1963; s. Jean-Pierre Federspil and Anna Federspil-Weiler; m. Lieselotte Mletzko, Aug. 28, 1964; 1 child, Philippe André. Priv doz dr med attending, U. Strasbourg, 1957—63; MD, Commn., Luxembourg, 1962. Cert. ear, nose and throat specialist Ministry Health, 1968, Ministry Health, U. Saarland, 1978. Internship Hosp. Saverne, Hosp. Selestat, 1963; sci. asst. U. Munich, 1964—70; sr. sci. asst. U. Homburg, Germany, 1970—85; prof. ORL dept. U. Saarland, Homburg, 1975; pvt. dozent med. Vice dir. ORL dept. U. Homburg, 1985—2001; respiratory tract infections expert World Health Orgn., Germany, 1987—99; infectious diseases, oncology, immunology expert Commn. of Ministry of Health, Berlin, 1988—95. Author: Moderne HNO Therapie, 1984, 1986, Antibiotikaschäden des Ohres, 1979, Lehrbuch der Hals Nasen Ohren Heilkunde, 1993. Bd. mem. German ENT Soc., Bonn, Germany, 1991—99; head infectious diseases com. Internat. Fedn. ORL Soc., 1993—2002. Decorated Officier de l'Ordre de Mérite Luxembourg, Officier de l'Ordre Grand-Ducal de la Couronne de Chêne; recipient Commandeur de l'Ordre de Merite, 1998, Ernst von Bergmann Plakette award, German Med. Bd., 1994. Fellow: Am. Acad. ORL; mem.: German Soc. ORL, Head and Neck Surgery (Ludwig Haymann award 1995), European Acad. Facial Plastic Surgery (sr.). Achievements include research in new concepts of ototoxicity, 1975; CROS rehab. of unilateral deafness with bone-achored hearing aid, first effective case in the world, 1990; bilateral hearing rehab. with bone-anchored hearing aids Cordelle, first case in the world, 2001; development of Medicon ti-epiplating system for the bone-anchorage of prostheses and hearing aids, 2008; guidelines of the antibiotic treatment of the infections of the ENT, head & neck, consensus report on behalf of the presidency of the German society of ORL and H/N Sugery. Avocations: reading, badminton, politics. Home: Akazienweg 1 66424 Homburg Germany Office Phone: 0049684167566. Home Fax: 49684167566. Personal E-mail: P.Federspil@uniklinik-saarland.de. Business E-Mail: p.federspil@uks.eu.

FEDOROFF, NINA VSEVOLOD, research scientist, consultant, educator; b. Cleve., Apr. 9, 1942; d. Vsevolod N. Fedoroff and Olga S. (Snegireff) Stacy; children: Natasha, Kyr, James. BS, Syracuse U., NY, 1966; PhD, Rockefeller U., N.Y.C., 1972. Asst. mgr. transl. bur. Biol. Abstracts, Phila., 1962-63; flutist Syracuse Symphony Orch., 1964-66; acting asst. prof. UCLA, 1972-74; postdoctoral fellow UCLA and Carnegie Inst. Washington, Los Angeles and Balt., 1974-78; staff scientist Carnegie Inst. Washington, Balt., 1978-95; dir. Biotechnol. Inst., Pa. State U., 1995—, Willaman prof. of life scis., 1995—, Evan Pugh prof., 2002—; external prof. Santa Fe Inst., 2003—. Dir. Life Scis. Consortium, Pa. State U., 1996—2002; prof.

dept. biology John Hopkins U., 1979-95; mem. devel. biology panel NSF, Washington, 1979-80; sci. adv. panel Office of Tech. Assessment, Congress, Washington, 1979-80; recombinant DNA adv. com. NIH, Bethesda, Md., 1980-84; sci. adv. com. Japanese Human Frontier Sci., 1988; sci adv. com. Competitive Rsch. Grants Office, USDA; mem. commn. on life scis., basic biology bd. NRC, NAS, 1984-90; bd. dirs. Genetics Soc. Am.; mem. bd. overseers Harvard U., 1988-91; trustee BIOSIS, Phila., 1990-96; mem. NAS Coun., 1991-94; dir. Internat. Sci. Found., 1992-93; mem. adv. com. Directorate for Biol. Scis., 1994-97; bd. dirs. Sigma-Aldrich Corp.; mem. nat. sci. bd. NSF, 2000-06; sci. and tech. advisor to US Sec. of State Condoleezza Rice, 2007-. Editor: Gene, 1981—84, Perspectives in Biology and Medicine, 1991—2001, Procs. Nat. Acad. Sci., 1996—2000; editor, bd. rev. editors: Sci., 1985, mem. sci. adv. bd.: The Plant Jour., 1991—98, book editor: various publs.; contbr. chapters to books articles to profl. jours. Recipient Merit award, NIH, 1990, Howard Taylor Ricketts award, U. Chgo., 1990, Arents Pioneer award, Syracuse U., 2003, Nat. Medal Sci., NSF, 2006; grantee, NSF and USDA, 1979—84, NIH, 1984—99, NSF, 1992—, NASA, 1997—2000. Mem.: AAAS, NAS (editor procs. 1995—2000), AAAS (bd. dirs. 2000—03), European Acad. Scis., Am. Acad. Arts and Scis., Sigma Xi (McGovern Sci. and Soc. medal 1997), Phi Beta Kappa (vis. scholar 1984—85, vis. scholar 1984—85). Avocations: choral music, gardening, tango. Home: 700 New Hampshire Ave NW Apt 1416 Washington DC 20037 Office: STAS US Dept State Rm 3240 2201 CST NW Washington DC 20520 Office Phone: 202-647-8725. Office Fax: 202-647-5136. Business E-Mail: nvf1@psu.edu, fedoroffnv@state.gov.

FEDOROWSKI, ARTUR, internist; b. Wroclaw, Poland, July 9, 1965; MD, Wroclaw Med. U., 1990, PhD, 1999. Cert. gen. practice specialist Nat. Bd. of Health and Welfare, Sweden, internal medicine specialist Nat. Bd. of Health and Welfare, Sweden, Dept. of Health, Provincial Office, Wroclaw. Postgrad. resident Home Office Hosp., Wroclaw, 1990—91; gen. practitioner, rschr. Örebro (Sweden) County Coun., 2000—04; internal medicine specialist Scania Health Region, Ystad, Malmoe, Sweden, 2004—. Med. cons. Polish-German Soc. Electromagnetic Therapy, Poznan, Poland, 1992—94. Recipient 2d Grade prize, Nat. Chemistry Contest for High Schs., Poland, 1983—84, Best Student award, Wroclaw Med. U., 1990. Mem.: Polish Cardiac Soc. (assoc.), Polish Soc. Med. Physics (assoc.), Internat. Soc. Bioelectromagnetism (assoc.). Achievements include research in influence of low-frequency electromagnetic fields on biological processes (E G Experimental Tumor Growth). Avocations: travel, philosophy, yoga, meditation, geography. Office: Malmö Univ Hosp Dept Cardiology 205 02 Malmö Sweden Personal E-mail: artfed2002@yahoo.se. E-mail: artur.fedorowski@skane.se.

FEDORUK, LYNN, cardiologist; b. Can., June 10, 1964; BSc, U. Alta., 1986, MD; MHSc, U. BC, 1988. Chief, cardiac surgery Royal Jubilee Hosp., 2010—. Mem.: Soc. Thoracic Surgeons. Avocations: diving, golf, hockey. Office: 106 2020 Richmond Ave Victoria BC V8R 6R5 Canada Business E-Mail: lfedoruk@telus.net.

FEELY, MALACHY PIO, mental health services professional, researcher; b. Mullingar, Westmeath, Ireland, Nov. 3, 1959; arrived in Eng., 1987; s. Joseph John and Bridget Veronica (O'Callaghan) F.; m. Anne Mary McCormack, Sept. 20, 1985; 1 child, Stephen Noel. MA in Mental Health Studies, Portsmouth U., Eng., 1996; PhD, U. Ulster at Jordanstown, No. Ireland, 2007. Registered psychiat. nurse; cert. in counseling; diploma in nursing. Staff nurse Midland Health Bd., Ireland, 1985-87, Chichester Priority Care Svcs., Eng., 1987-89, charge nurse, 1989-91, clin. care coord., 1991-92, sr. charge nurse, 1992-94, sr. charge nurse comty., 1994-96; lectr., practitioner in mental health Chichester Priority Care, U. Surrey, 1996; deputy nursing officer Mental Health Louth Meath Mental Health Svc., 1996-98; resource officer mental health svcs. North Eastern Health Bd., Navan, Meath, Ireland, 1998-99; nursing officer Louth Meath Mental Health Svcs., 1999-2000; acting nursing practice devel. coord. North Eastern Health Bd., Mental Health Svcs., Ardee, Ireland, 2000; nursing practice development coord. Mental Health Svcs., 2000—05; coord. nurse practice devel. Dublin N.E. Mental Health Svcs., Ireland, 2005—07; nurse adv., mental health and intellectual disability Dept. Health and Children, Nursing Policy Divsn., Dublin, 2007—. Mem. strategic planning group Chichester Priority Care, 1992—93, chmn. crisis svc. working group, 1994—95; mem. regional forum comty. Inter Agy., England, 1995; mem. nurse edn. com., Ireland, 1996—2004; chair workshop Irish Commn. Nursing, 1997, clin. audit coord., 98; mem. steering group Regional Suicide Prevention, 1998—99, Tragedy Response Group, 1999; nat. resource officer, coord., founder No. Ireland Suicide Awareness, scope of practice facilitator, 2001—06, critical incident debriefing team mem., 2000—04, regional mental health nursing group, 2000—06, mem. svc. to quality steering group, 2000—06; mem. course bd. psychiat. nursing Dundalk Inst. Tech., 2001—06, mem. preregistration local joint working group, 2000—06, mem. postgrad. program devel. steering group, 2002, mem. northea. health bd. strategy devel. group, 2002—03, mem. NEHB mental health svcs. policy group, 2003—06, mem. nurse education and policy devel. group, 2004—06; chairperson evaluation bd. Health Svc. Exec. Area Awards, 2007—08; mem. steering grp. Health Care Assts. Mental Health Svcs. Contbr. articles to profl. and med. jours. Mem. Nat. Working Group Violence and Aggression Workplace, 2007—09; steering group mem. Nat. Nursing & Midwifery Practice Devel. Policy Devel., 2007—09, Nat. Nursing & Midwifery Role Expansion, 2009—10, Dublin West-SW Mental Health Nursing Recruitment & Retention, 2007—09, Post-Registration Psychiatric Nursing, 2007—09; sec. Louth Meath Mental Health Svcs. Drugs & Therapeutics Com., 2010, Louth Meath P.C.C.C. Drugs & Therapeutics Com., 2010. Roman Catholic. Achievements include development of psychiatric theory of connectivity in relation to depression. Avocations: Judo, guitar, suba diving, listening to music, Irish language and culture. Office: St Brigid's Campus Ardee Co Louth Ireland Office Phone: 00 353 86 6002 802. Business E-Mail: malachy.feely@hse.ie.

FEENEY, DON JOSEPH, JR., psychologist; b. Greenville, NC, Jan. 17, 1948; s. Don Joseph Sr. and Louise (Saieed) Feeney; 1 child, Kelly Lynn. BA, Colgate U., 1971; MA, Gov.'s State U., 1973; PhD, Loyola U., Chgo., 1979. Registered psychologist Ill., Ind., diplomate Am. Bd. Psychol. Specialties, Am. Bd. Psychology, cert. addictions counselor; profl. coach Grow Tng. Inst., Inc. Clin. dir. Champaign (Ill.) Coun. on Alcoholism, 1976-79; pvt. practice psychology, hypnotherapy, family svcs. Downers Grove, Ill., 1979—, Dangerous Drugs Com., Chgo., 1979-80; psychologist Tri-City Mental Health Ctr., East Chicago, Ind., 1980-82; psychologist alcohol treatment program Christ Hosp., Oak Lawn, Ill., 1982—; cons. Cons. Psychol. Svcs. PC, Downers Grove, 1985—, CEO, 1998—. Chmn. adv. coun. alcoholism Govs. State U., University Park, Ill., 1979—82; devel., presenter self-hypnosis and wellness programs on smoking, weight control and chem. abuse. Author: Entrancing Relationships: Exploring the Hypnotic Framework of Addictive Relationships, 1999, Motif: The Transformative Creation of Self, 2001, Creating Cultural Motifs in the War Against Terrorism, 2003, Motifs of Life Altering Experience; contbr. articles to profl. jours.; guest cons. (TV series) Oprah Winfrey, Jerry Springer, Jenny Jones, others. Loyola U. fellow, 1976. Fellow: Am. Coll. Forensic Examiners (diplomate); mem.: APA, Chgo. Coun. Fgn. Rels., Ill. Psychol. Assn. Roman Catholic. Avocations: chess, tennis, weightlifting, jogging, reading. Office: Cons Psychol Svcs PC 6900 Main St Ste 160 Downers Grove IL 60516-3455 Personal E-mail: drtc11@hotmail.com, drte@att.net.

FEENEY, MARY KATHERINE O'SHEA, retired public health nurse; b. Niagara Falls, NY, July 10, 1934; d. James T. and Mary Elizabeth (Woodside) O'Shea; m. Gerald E. Feeney, Apr. 27, 1957; children: Patricia, Elizabeth, Susan, Kathleen. BSN, Niagara U., 1956; MS in Mgmt., SUNY, Binghamton, 1981. RN, NY; cert. hypnotherapist; Assessment Modified Reflexology for Nurses. Staff nurse St. Mary's Hosp., Niagara Falls, 1956—57; part-time staff U. Ga. Med. Ctr., Augusta, 1957—58; pub. health nurse Herkimer County (NY) Pub. Health Nursing Svc., 1966—94; sci. educator Herkimer, 1998—. Coord. Herkimer County Long Term Health Care, 1987-89; bd. dirs. Oneida/Herkimer Coalition for Smoke Free Mohawk Valley. Mem.: Gen. Fedn. Women's Clubs, Wash. Home: 146 State Route 169 Little Falls NY 13365-5017

FEENSTRA, CHERYL JEAN, nursing educator; b. Holland, Mich., Jan. 8, 1950; BSN, U. Mich., 1972; PhD, Mich. State U., 1996. Prof., dept. chairperson Calvin Coll., 1989—. Mem.: ANA, Assn. Women's Health, Obstetric and Neonatal Nursing, Sigma Theta Tau Internat. Honor Soc. Nursing. Avocations: skiing, gardening. Office: Sci Bldg 231 1734 Knollcrest Ci Grand Rapids MI 49546 Business E-Mail: cfeenstr@calvin.edu.

FEERICK, JOHN PAUL, neurologist, researcher, military officer; b. NYC, Aug. 15, 1950; s. James Paul and Frances Teresa (Ugis) Feerick; children from previous marriage: John Paul, Meaghan Ann, Catherine Marie, Thomas Patrick. Diploma, U. Vienna, Austria, 1967; BS in Biology, Georgetown U., Washington, 1972, MD, 1978; grad., Naval Aerospace Med. Inst., 1980. Diplomate Am. Bd. Pain Mgmt., cert. neurorehabilitation Am. Soc. Neurorehabilitation. Intern dept. neurology med. ctr. Georgetown U., Washington, 1978—79, resident dept. neurology med. ctr., 1980—81, chief resident dept. neurology med. ctr., 1982; neurologist Geisinger Med. Group, Wilkes-Barre, Pa., 1982—87; neurologist, rschr. Zamesville, Ohio, 1987—2004; Force Surgeon II Marine Expeditionary Force, Camp Lejeune, NC, 2005; dir. field study team 1st marine divsn USMC, Iraq, 2006—. Dir. stroke & neurpharmacologic rsch. Pharmacotherapy Rsch. Assocs., Inc., Ohio, 1987—2004; dir. combat traumatic brain injury rsch. USMC, Iraq, 2006; dir., traumatic basic injury VATBI Comprehensive Care Ctr., WBPVAMC, 2007—; chief, neurology svc. Wilkes-Barre Pa., VA Med. Ctr., 2009—. Editor-in-chief: Neurorehabilitation News, 1992—2004, spl. issues editor: Neurorehabilitation and Neural Repair, 1997—2004. Bd. dir. Am. Soc. Neurorehab., 2002—08. Lt. USNR, 1979, capt. USNR, 1994. Recipient Academic Clin. Excellence in Neurology award, Georgetown U., Washington, 1978, DSM, Ohio State Legis., 2002; fellowship, AFIP, 1981, Training fellowship, Chiappa Lab., 1982—83. Fellow: Am. Heart Assn.; mem.: AMA, VFW, Am. Soc. Neurorehabilitation, Am. Acad. Neurology (chair, sect. neurorehab. 2008—), Am. Legion. Avocation: archaeology. Home: 11 Riverside Dr Wilkes Barre PA 18702-2316

FEICHTINGER, WILFRIED, endocrinologist, director; b. Vienna, Oct. 19, 1950; MD, U. Vienna, Med. Sch., 1975; degree in Ob-Gyn., II. U. Frauenklinik Wien, 1982. Asst. 2nd U. Women's Clinic, Vienna, 1977—82, Inst. Endocrinology Reprodn. and in Vitro Fertilization, Vienna, 1983—91; founder, mng. dir. Wunschbaby-Zentrum, Inst. Reproductive Medicine, Vienna, 1991—. Recipient Silver medal, Republic of Austria, Knight's cross, Hungarian Order of Merit; named Deemed Extraordinary U. Prof., Austrian Fed. Pres. Master: Internat. Assn. Pvt. Assisted Reproductive Tech. Clinics and Labs.; mem.: Fedn. Internat. Ob-Gyn. (expert adv. panel on reproductive medicine). Avocation: music. Office: Lainzer St 6 Vienna A-1130 Austria Office Fax: 0043 1 877 77 75-34. Business E-Mail: presse@wunschbaby.at.

FEIG, STEPHEN ARTHUR, pediatrician, hematologist, oncologist, educator; b. NYC, Dec. 24, 1937; s. Irving L. and Janet (Oppenheimer) F.; m. Judith Bergman, Aug. 28, 1960; children: Laura, Daniel, Andrew. AB in Biology, Princeton U., NJ, 1959; MD, Columbia U., NYC, 1963. Diplomate Am. Bd. Pediat., Am. Bd. Hematology-Oncology. Intern Mt. Sinai Hosp., NYC, 1963—64, resident in pediat., 1964—66; hematology fellow Children's Hosp. Med. Ctr., Boston, 1968—71, assoc. in medicine, 1971—72; asst. prof. pediat. UCLA, 1972—77, chief divsn. hematology and oncology Sch. Medicine, 1977—2005, assoc. prof., 1977—82, prof., 1982—2005, exec. vice chmn. dept. pediat. Sch. Medicine, 1994—2004, prof. emeritus, 2005—. Trustee LA chpt. Leukemia Soc. Am., 1978—2004, trustee, 1984—2004; chair exec. com. subsect. hemotology/oncology Am. Acad. Pediat., 2005-09; mem. Coun. Pediat. Subspltys., 2006-09, Reviewer Am. Jour. Pediatric Hematology/Oncology, Blood, Pediat., Pediatric Rsch., Jour. Pediat., editl. bd. mem. Jour. Pediat. Hematology & Oncology. Contbr. articles to profl. jours. Active numerous other pediatric hosps. and med. sch. coms. Served with USNR. Mem. Am. Soc. Hematology, Soc. Pediatric Rsch., Am. Pediatric Soc., Am. Soc. Pediatric Hematology, Oncology. Jewish. Avocations: native arts, opera, travel. Office: UCLA Sch Medicine Dept Pediatrics 10833 Le Conte Ave Los Angeles CA 90095-3075 Office Phone: 310-825-6708.

FEIGELSON, EUGENE B., academic administrator, educator, retired dean; Prof., chief psychiatry St. Lukes Hosp.; faculty mem. SUNY Downstate Med. Ctr. Coll. Medicine, Bklyn., 1978—, prof., chmn. dept. psychiatry, sr. v.p. biomed. edn. and rsch., dean, 1996—2005, interim pres. Health Sciences Ctr., 1997—99, dir. office internat. edn. and global health. Fellow: NY Acad. Medicine. Office: SUNY Downstate Med Ctr Coll Medicine 450 Clarkson Ave Brooklyn NY 11203 *

FEIGL, ERIC OTTO, physiology educator; s. Herbert and Maria Feigl; m. Polly Bartholomew, July 30, 1957; children: Kurt, Mark H. BA, BS, U. Minn., 1954, MD, 1958. Instr. Med. Sch. U. Pa., Phila., 1959-61; officer Nat. Heart Inst., Bethesda, Md., 1962-64; asst. prof. U. Pa., Phila., 1964—69; from assoc. prof. to prof. physiology U. Wash., Seattle, 1969—72. Assoc. editor Am. Jour. of Physiology, 1981—86, editl. bd., Circulation Rsch. Officer U.S. Pub. Health Svc., 1962—64; mem. com. Am. Physiol. Assn., Am. Heart Assn. Recipient Outstanding Rsch. award Internat. Soc. for Heart Rsch., 1985. Fellow Am. Physiolog. Soc. (chmn. CV sect. 1981-82), Am. Heart Assn. (Louis N. Katz Basic Sci. Rsch. Prize 1969). Home: 2360 43rd Ave E Apt 311 Seattle WA 98112-2701 Office: U Wash Med Sch 357290 Dept Physiology Seattle WA 98195-7290 Office Phone: 206-543-1496.

FEIGON, JUDITH TOVA, ophthalmologist, surgeon, educator; b. Galveston, Tex., Dec. 2, 1947; d. Louis and Ethel Feigon; m. Nathan C. Goldman; children: Michael G., Miriam G. AB, Barnard Coll., Columbia U., 1970; postgrad., Rice U., U. Houston, 1970-71; MD, U. Tex., San Antonio, 1976. Diplomate Am. Bd. Ophthalmology. Intern Mt. Auburn Hosp., Cambridge, Mass.; intern, clin. tchg. fellow Harvard U. Med. Sch., 1976-77; resident in ophthalmology Baylor Coll. Medicine, Houston, 1977-80, fellow in retina, 1980-82, clin. faculty, 1982-95; asst. prof. ophthalmology U. Tex. Med. Br., Galveston, 1982-85, clin. asst. prof., 1985-91, clin. assoc. prof., 1992—; pvt. practice medicine specializing ophthalmology, vitreoretinal diseases, surgery, Houston, 1983—. Physician advisor to Houston br. Tex. Soc. to Prevent Blindness, 1987-89, also bd. dirs., mem. staff Meth., St. Lukes, Tex. Children's Hosp. Contbr. articles to profl. publs. Mem. Am. Acad. Ophthalmology, Tex. Med. Assn. Houston Ophthal. Soc., Harris County Med. Soc., U. Tex. San Antonio Alumni Assn., Am. Soc. Retina Specialists, Tex. Ophthalmol. Assn., Houston Ophthal. Soc. (exec. bd. 2000-03). Office: 7515 Main St Ste 650 Houston TX 77030-4599

FEIN, LINDA ANN, nurse anesthetist, consultant; b. Cin., Dec. 10, 1949; d. Joseph and Elizabeth P. (Kannady) Stofle; m. Thomas Paul Fein, Dec. 11, 1971. Nursing diploma, Miami Vly. Hosp. Sch. Nursing, Dayton, Ohio, 1971, Wright State U., 1969; postgrad., U. Cin. Med. Ctr., 1978. Nursing asst. Miami Valley Hosp, 1969-71; staff nurse operating rm. Cin. Children's Hosp. and Med. Ctr., 1971, 73, Peninsula Hosp., Burlingame, Calif., 1972-73; staff nurse operating rm., emergency rm. Doctors Hosp., San Diego, 1972; staff nurse emergency rm. Ohio State U. Hosps., Columbus, 1973-75, head nurse operating rm., 1975-76; staff nurse anesthetist Bethesda Hosps., Cin., 1978-86, Mercy Hosp. Fairfield, Cin., 1986-95, 2010—; locum tenens anesthetist Fort Hamilton-Hughes Hosp., Hamilton, Ohio, 1994—95, staff anesthetist, 1995—2006, Butler County Surgery Ctr., Hamilton, 2000—06, Bethesda Hosp., Cin., 2006—10; clin. instructor U. Cin., Sch. Nurse Anesthesia, 2007—, Tex. Wesleyan U., Sch. Nurse Anesthesia, 2007—10, Mercy Hosp., Fairfield, 2010—. Childbirth educator psychoprophylactic method, 1975—; critical care nursing cons. Med. Communicators & Assocs., Salt Lake City, 1985-89; ind. nursing cons., 1989—; co-owner Exec. Shops, Cin., 1982-85; spkr. in field. Search com. Cin. Gen. Hosp. Sch. Anesthesia for Nurses, 1981-82; bd. dirs. YWCA, 1988-91, Children's Diagnostic Ctr., 1989-95, pres. bd. dirs., 1994, Planned Parenthood, 1992-95. Recipient recognition award for profl. excellence First Nurse Anesthesia Faculty Assocs., 1982, Florence Nightingale awards, 1995. Mem. Miami Vly. Hosp. Sch. Nursing Alumni Assn., Cin. Gen. Hosp. Sch. Anesthesia for Nurses Alumni Assn., Nurse Anesthetists Greater Cin., Ohio Assn. Nurse Anesthetists, Am. Assn. Nurse Anesthetists, Am. Assn. Critical Care Nurses, Nat. Registry Cert. Nurses in Advanced Practice (cert.), Ohio Coalition Nurses with Specialty Cert., Am. Soc. Critical Care Medicine, Am. Trauma Soc., NAFE, Altrusa Internat. (officer 1985-92), Order Eastern Star. Republican. Methodist. Avocations: antiques, swimming, cooking. Home: 650 History Bridge Ln Hamilton OH 45013-3659 *

FEIN, WILLIAM, ophthalmologist; b. NYC, Nov. 27, 1933; s. Samuel and Beatrice (Lipschitz) F.; m. Bonnie Fern Aaronson, Dec. 15, 1963; children: Stephanie Paula, Adam Irving, Gregory Andrew. BS, CCNY, 1954; MD, U. Calif., Irvine, 1962. Diplomate Am. Bd. Ophthalmology. Intern L.A. County Gen. Hosp., 1962-63, resident in ophthalmology, 1963-66; instr. U. Calif. Med. Sch., Irvine, 1966-69; faculty U. So. Calif. Med. Sch., 1969—, assoc. clin. prof. ophthalmology, 1979—; attending physician Cedars-Sinai Med. Ctr., LA, 1966—, chief ophthalmology clinic svc., 1979-81, chmn. divsn. ophthalmology, 1981-85; attending physician L.A. County-U. So. Calif. Med. Ctr., 1969—; chmn. dept. ophthalmology Midway Hosp., 1975-78; dir. Ellis Eye Ctr., LA, 1984—2006. Mem. editorial bd. CATARACT, Internat. Jour. of Cataract and Ocular Surgery, 1992—2000; contbr. articles to profl. jours. Chmn. ophthalmology adv. com. Jewish Home for Aging of Greater L.A., 1993-2006. Fellow Internat. Coll. Surgeons, Am. Coll. Surgeons; mem. Am. Acad. Ophthalmology, Am. Soc. Ophthalmic Plastic and Reconstructive Surgery, Royal Soc. Medicine, AMA, Calif. Med. Assn., L.A. Med. Assn. Home: 718 N Camden Dr Beverly Hills CA 90210-3205 Office Phone: 310-859-0760.

FEINBERG, ANDREW P., medical geneticist, oncologist, educator; BA, Johns Hopkins U., 1973, MD, 1976, MPH, 1981. King Fahd prof. molecular medicine, oncology, and molecular biology and genetics Johns Hopkins U. Sch. Medicine, Balt. Contbr. articles to profl. jours. Recipient MERIT award, NIH, 2001, Tovi Comet-Walerstein prize, Bar-Ilan U., 2004. Mem.: Am. Acad. Arts & Sciences, Inst. Medicine, Assn. Am. Physicians, Am. Soc. Clin. Investigation.

FEINBERG, DAVID T., hospital administrator; BA cum laude in Econs., U. Calif., Berkeley; MD with distinction, U. Health Scis. / Chgo. Med. Sch.; MBA, Pepperdine U., 2002. Med. dir. Resnick Neuropsychiatric Hosp., UCLA; assoc. vice chancellor, CEO UCLA Hosp. Sys. Prof. clin. psychiatry David Geffen Sch. Medicine, UCLA; spkr. in field. Contbr. articles to profl. jours. Office: UCLA Med Ctr Box 957400, Ste 1320, 757 Westwood Plaza Ronald Reagan UCLA Med Ctr Los Angeles CA 90095-7400 Office Phone: 310-267-9315. Office Fax: 310-267-3516. E-mail: dfeinberg@mednet.ucla.edu. *

FEINBERG, DENNIS LOWELL, dermatologist; b. Bridgeport, Conn., June 10, 1951; AB, Cornell U., 1973; MD, SUNY, Syracuse, 1976. Diplomat Nat. Bd. Med. Examiners, Am. Bd. Internal Medicine, Am. Bd. Dermatology. Intern U. Miami (Fla.) Affiliated Hosps., 1976-77, resident, 1977-78, Johns Hopkins Med. Inst., Balt., 1978-80; dermatologist pvt. practice, Washington, 1981, Stratford, Conn.,

1981—. Sr. attending Bridgeport Hosp., 1981—; attending St. Vincent's Med. Ctr., Bridgeport, 1981—; cons. Milford (Conn.) Hosp., 1982-2000; asst. clin. prof. Yale U. Sch. Medicine, New Haven, 1985—. Fellow Am. Acad. Dermatology; mem. AMA, ACP, Atlantic Dermatol. Soc., New Eng. Dermatol. Soc., Conn. Dermatology and Dermatologic Surgery Soc. (pres., 2006-07), Conn. State Med. Soc., Fairfield County Med. Assn., Greater Bridgeport Med. Assn., Syracuse Med. Alumni Assn. Office: 2875 Main St Stratford CT 06614-4937

FEINBERG, RICHARD ALAN, psychologist; b. Oakland, Calif., Aug. 12, 1947; s. Jack and Raechel Sacks (Hoff) F. BA, Calif. State U., Hayward, 1969; MA in Clin. Psychology, Mich. State U., 1972, PhD, 1979. Cert. Nat. Register Health Svc. Providers in Psychology. Instr. Merritt Coll., Oakland, 1975-76; clin. psychology Highland Gen. Hosp., Oakland, 1976-79; assoc. Lafayette Ctr. Counseling and Edn., 1978-79; clin. psychology Tri-City Mental Health Ctr., Fremont, Calif., 1979-81, dir., 1981-86; pvt. practice, Fremont, 1976—. Participant profl. conf. USPHS fellow, 1969-71. Mem. APA, Calif. Psychol. Assn.

FEINBERG, SHELDON NORMAN, pediatrician, educator; b. NYC, Mar. 16, 1930; m. MaryEllen Wisker, Jan. 2, 1988; children: Lynn Ann, Bette Joan, Barbara Ellen, Paul Howard, John Joseph. MD, N.Y. Med. Coll., 1955. Diplomate Am. Bd. Pediat. Intern Bronx Mcpl. Hosp. Ctr., NYC, 1955-56; resident Met. Hosp., NYC, 1956-57; fellow pediatrics N.Y. Med. Coll., 1959-60; pediat. staff Passack Valley Hosp., Westwood, NJ, 1960-82; emergency physician various hosps., 1982-85; pediat. staff Hackensack (N.J.) U. Med. Ctr., 1985—; clin. asst. prof. pediat. U. Med. & Dentistry N.J., Newark, 1985—2010; chmn., emeritus com. Suffolk County Med. Soc., 2009—11. Inventor infant scale guard, simple stool stain. Maj. USAF med. corps., 1957-59. Honor award Bergen County Med. Soc., 1965. Fellow Am. Acad. Pediat.; mem. AMA, N.J. Pediat. Soc. (pres. 1989-91, Honor award 1991). Home: 125 N Country Rd Mount Sinai NY 11766-1503

FEINGOLD, ANAT, infectious disease pediatrician; MD, Washington U. Sch. of Medicine, 1983. Diplomate Am. Bd. of Pediatrics-pediatric infectious disease. Intern Montefiore Med. Ctr., Bronx, NY, resident; fellow St. Christopher Hosp. for Children; head divsn. of pediatric infectious disease Cooper Univ. Hosp., dir. inpatient pediatric unit; assoc. program dir. Pediatric Residency Program. Adj. asst. prof. Touro Univ. Nevada; asst. prof. pediatrics Cooper Univ. Hosp.; dir. Southern NJ Regional Family HIV Treatment Ctr. Recipient Robert Wood Johnson Medi. Sch. Faculty award for Superior Mentorship of Students, award for Distinguished Tchg.,Attending of the Yr Mem : Adv Bd for NJ, Infectious Disease Soc. of America, Am. Acad. of Pediatrics,Pediatric Infectious Disease. Office: Cooper University Hospital Three Cooper Plaza Ste 200 Camden NJ 08103 Office Phone: 856-342-2617. Office Fax: 856-968-8414.

FEINGOLD, DANIEL LEON, anesthesiologist, consultant; b. Boston, May 19, 1958; s. Macey Gerson and Helene Sultana (Benlolo) F. BS with distinction, U. Ill., Chgo., 1980; MD, U. Health Scis., Chgo. Med. Sch., 1984. Intern Weiss Meml. Hosp., Chgo., 1984-85; resident in anesthesiology U. Ill. Hosps. and Clinics, Chgo., 1986-89; anesthesiologist Hosp. Anesthesia Group, Chgo., 1989—. Contbr. articles to profl. publs. Mem. AMA, AAAS, Am. Soc. Anesthesiologists, Ill. State Med. Soc. Home: PO Box 577429 Chicago IL 60657-7429 Office: PO Box 25678 Chicago IL 60625-0678

FEINGOLD, DAVID SIDNEY, microbiology and biochemistry educator, researcher; b. Chelsea, Mass., Nov. 15, 1922; s. Louis Edward and Miriam F.; m. Batia Babette Haber, Nov. 15, 1949; children: Oded, Anat, Michele. BS, MIT, 1944; PhD, Hebrew U., Jerusalem, Israel, 1956. Chemist Lucidol Corp., Buffalo, 1944; jr. research biochemist U. Calif. at Berkeley, 1957-60; asst. prof. biology U. Pitts., 1960-62, asso. prof., 1962-65, prof., 1965—; prof. microbiology Sch. Medicine, 1966-93, prof. emeritus molecular genetics and biochemistry, 1993—. Contbr. articles to profl. jours. With USNR, 1944—46. Recipient State of Israel prize in natural sci., 1957, Career Devel. award NIH, 1965-75 Fellow Infectious Disease Soc. Am.; mem. Internat. Endotoxin Soc., Am. Soc. for Biochemistry and Molecular Biology. Home: 6420 Bartlett St Pittsburgh PA 15217-1832 Personal E-mail: udpglcdh@juno.com.

FEINS, RICHARD HARRY, thoracic surgeon; b. Greenville, SC, May 29, 1947; s. Ann N Feins; m. Mary L Norton, Dec. 9, 1972; children: Eric Norton, Jonathan Charles. MD, U. Vt., Burlington, 1973. Cert. Am. Bd. Thoracic Surgery, 1984. Assoc. prof. surgery U. Rochester, NY, 1987—2005; prof. of surgery U. NC, Chapel Hill, 2005—. Bd. dirs. Thoracic Surgery Found. Rsch. and Edn., Burlington, Mass., 2007—, Joint Coun. Thotacic Surg. Edn., Chgo., 2008—; chair Am. Bd. Thoracic Surgery, Chgo., 2007—. Founder Pittsford Crew, Pittsford, NY, 1997—2008. Lt. (j.g.) Pub. Health Svc., 1974—76, Gallop, N.Mex. Mem.: Soc. Thoracic Surgery (bd. dirs. 2005—), ACS, Am. Assn. Thoracic Surgery. Jewish. Avocation: golf. Home: 10424 Stone Chapel Hill NC 27517 Office: Univ NC 3040 Burnett-Womack CB 7065 Chapel Hill NC 27599-7065 Office Fax: 919-966-3475. Business E-Mail: rfeins@med.unc.edu.

FEINSILVER, DONALD LEE, psychiatry professor; b. Bklyn., July 24, 1947; s. Albert and Mildred (Weissman) Feinsilver. BA, Alfred U., 1968; MD, Autonomous U., Guadalajara, Mexico, 1974. Diplomate Am. Bd. Psychiatry and Neurology, Am. Bd. Forensic Psychiatry. Intern in medicine L.I. Coll. Hosp., Bklyn., 1975—76; resident in psychiatry SUNY-Bklyn., 1977—78, chief resident, 1979; asst. prof. psychiatry and surgery Med. Coll. Wis., Milw., 1980—85, assoc. prof., 1985—; dir. psychiat. emergency svc. Milw. County Mental Health and Med. Complexes, 1980—88; dir. med.-psychiat. unit Milw. Psychiat. Hosp./West Allis Meml. Hosp., 1988—. Contbr. articles to profl. jours.; editor: Crisis Psychiatry: Pros and Cons, 1982; mem. editl. bd.: Psychiat. Medicine Jour., 1983—. Mem.: AAAS, AMA, Acad. Psychosomatic Medicine, Am. Acad. Psychiatry and the Law, Am. Psychiat. Assn. Office: West Allis Psychiat Assocs 2424 S 90th St Milwaukee WI 53227-2455 Office Phone: 414-328-8690.

FEINSTEIN, ROBERT P., dermatologist; b. NYC, July 31, 1941; s. Jerome and May (Wolpin) F.; m. Diane Marla Gutstein, Oct. 25, 1969; children: Steven, Michelle, Suzanne, Gary, Lori. AB in Biology, NYU, 1963, MD, 1967. Diplomate Am. Bd. Dermatology. Intern Kings County Hosp. Ctr., Bklyn., 1967-68; resident in dermatology Columbia U., NYC, 1968-71, assoc. clin. prof. dept. dermatology; chief of dermatology, innoculations and phys. exams. Navy Regional Med. Clinic, Washington, 1971-73; pvt. practice in dermatology Mineola, NY, 1973-99, Smithtown, NY, 1983-2000. Author: (book) Dermatology, 1975, (monograph) Rosacea, 1998, Androgenetic Alopecia, Farre Racouchot Syndrome; contbr. articles to profl. jours. Lt comdr. USNR, 1971-73. Fellow Am. Acad. Dermatology (mem. managed care com., 1995-99, mem. com. physician practice, professionalism study group program for dermatology in 21st cent., vice chmn. adv. bd. 2001-04), Am. Soc. for Dermatologic Surgery, Noah Worcester Dermatology Soc. (mem. bd. trustees 2008-11); mem. AMA, NY State Soc. of Dermatology (pres. 1997-99), L.I. Dermatology Soc. (pres. 1996-98), Suffolk County Dermatology Soc. (pres. 1982-84), Atlantic Dermatology Soc. (bd. dirs. 1995), NY State Med. Soc. (health care delivery sys.). Avocation: golf. Office Fax: 631-824-9393.

FEIT, BARBERI PAULL, psychotherapist, writer, composer; b. NYC, July 27, 1949; d. S. Paull and Alyce (Togniere) Platt; m. Glenn M. Feit, May 24, 1975. Diploma, Juilliard Sch. Music, NYC, 1972; BS, NYU, 1979, MS, 1980. Dir. Barberi Paull Musical Theatre, 1969-75; pvt. practice psychotherapy NYC, 1980—. Studied with Pulitzer prize winning composers Charles Wuorinen and Jacob Druckman; gen. asst. to Mme. Koussevitzky at Tanglewood and asst. condr. to Leonard Bernstein, 1972—74; founder Illumina, Inc.; creator Illumina, Inc. Imprint; co-founder Barberi Paull Feit and Glenn Martin Feit Charitable Trust; spkr. in field; music educator. Composer: The American Dream, I Have a Dream, Believe, America I Hear You Singing, Celebration, Angel Music, electronic ballets, music for films, (chorus) A Christmas Carol and Close to the Sky, others; author: Le Petit Foret, 1999, The Angel Chronicles, 2002, Love and Dreams, 2005, Hidden Wealth, 2007, Love Dreams and Everyday Miracles: an Internet Publ., 2008; pub.: newsletter The Loveletter, 1990—, eNewsletter, 1998—. Recipient Lehman Engles BMI Musical Theatre Workshop fellow, 1972—73, Dellus award, 1979, Emmy award, 2000, 2001, Smoke Free Campaign, Am. Cancer Soc., award, 2002; named honoree, Meet the Composer, 1972—80; fellow, NEA, 1982. Mem.: ASCAP (awards 1980—), Internat. League Women Composers (bd. dir.), The Century Assn., The Soc. Meml. Sloan-Kettering Cancer Ctr., The Met. Opera Club, Mus. City of N.Y. (vice-chmn.), Hort. Soc. N.Y. (vice-chmn.), The Doubles Club. Avocations: interior decorating, yachting, French, landscape and floral design. Home: PO Box 1906 Bridgehampton NY 11932-1906 Office: One Lincoln Plz # 33K New York NY 10023 Personal E-mail: barberi27@aol.com.

FEJERSKOV, OLE, medical researcher, science foundation director; b. Skive, Denmark, Apr. 4, 1943; s. Peter Ingeman and Karen Fejerskov; children: Jesper, Mikkel, Rasmus, Jakob Malte. DDS, Aarhus U., Denmark, 1967, PhD, 1970, D in Odontology, 1973; D in Odontology (hon.), U. Göteborg, Sweden, 1994, U. Oslo, 2005. Prof., chmn. Royal Dental Coll., Aarhus, 1973—93, dean, 1979—87; hon. prof. Beijing Hosp., 1987; rector Danish Rsch. Acad., 1993—98, dir. Nat. Rsch. Found., Copenhagen, 1999—2000, prof., head Inst. Anatomy, Faculty Health Sci. U. Aarhus, 2007—. Mem. Med. Rsch. Coun., Denmark, 1977—84; mem. expert panel WHO, 1982—; vice chmn. Nordic Rsch. Acad., Norway, 1993—99; pro vice-chancellor Danish Ministry SCi. and Tech and Innovation; exec. dir. Sino-Danish Ctr. Edn. & Rsch., Grad. U. Chinese Acad. Scis., Beijing, 2008—. Author: Dental Fluorosis, 1988; editor: Dental Caries, 2003; contbr. articles to profl. jours. Recipient Friendship award, Peoples Rep. of China, 2005; named Knight of Dannebrog, Queen of Denmark. Mem.: European Orgn. Caries Rsch. (Orca prize 1988), European Rsch. Group Oral Biology (sec. gen. 1978—99), Internat. Assn. Dental Rsch. (bd. dirs. 1991—96, Basic Rsch. prize 1979). Home: Bakkedraget 14 DK 8270 Højbjerg Denmark Office: Aarhus Univ Inst Anatomy Faculty Health Scis Denmark Office Phone: 4582423017. Business E-Mail: of@ana.au.dk.

FELDERMAN, LENORA I., physician; b. NYC, July 17, 1952; d. Ephraim Jacob and Sylvia (Farber) F.; children: Alexandra Danielle, Johnathan Reed. MD, NY Med. Coll., 1981. Diplomate Am. Bd. Dermatology. Resident in dermatology Albert Einstein Med. Ctr., Bronx, 1982-85; resident in internal medicine Montefiore Hosp., Bronx, N.Y., 1981-82, assoc. attending dermatologist, 1985-97, Lenox Hill Hosp., NYC, 1985—; asst. prof. medicine/dermatology Albert Einstein Coll. Medicine, NYC, 1985-97, Cornell U. Med. Coll., 1998—; physician NY Hosp.-Presby. Hosp. Spkr. in field; cons. in field to media, print, web and TV. Contbr. articles to profl. jours. Bd. dirs. Variety Children's Charity. Recipient Am. Women's Med. Assn. award, 1985, Pathology award N.Y. Med. Coll., 1985, named Best Dr. in NY & US. Fellow Am. Acad. Dermatology, Am. Soc. Dermatology Surgery, Internat. Soc. Dermatology, Soc. Pediatric Dermatology, Am. Soc. Dermatol. Surgeons, Am. BD. Dermatology; mem. AMA, Dermatology Soc. Greater NY, Med. Soc. State NY, New York County Med. Soc., Alpha Omega Alpha. Avocations: reading, skiing, dance, bicycling. Office: 1317 3rd Ave New York NY 10021-2995 Office Phone: 212-734-0091.

FELDMAN, ARTHUR M., cardiologist; m. Susan Boochever; children: Emily Kate, Elizabeth Willa. BA, Gettysburg Coll., Pa., 1970; MS, U. Md., 1973, PhD, 1974; MD, La. State U., 1981. Diplomate Nat. Bd. Med. Examiners; diplomate in internal medicine and in cardiovasc. disease Am. Bd. Internal Medicine. Intern, resident, fellow in cardiology Johns Hopkins Hosp., Balt., 1981-86, from asst. prof. to assoc. prof. medicine, 1986-94; Harry S. Tack prof. medicine, prof. cell biology/physiology U. Pitts., 1994—2002, chief divsn. cardiology, dir. Cardiovasc. Inst., 1998—2002; Magee prof., chmn. dept. medicine Jefferson Med. Coll., Phila., 2002—. Chief sci. advisor, bd. dirs., co-founder Cardioline, Inc. Editor-in-chief Clin. and Translational Sci.; mem. editl. bd. Heart Failure, Jour. Cardivasc. Pharmacology and Therapeutics, Jour. Cardiovasc. Pharmacology, Clin. Cardiology, Cardiac Failure, others. Trustee Gettysburg Coll., 1996-2002. Grantee, NIH, 1989—94, 1999—. Fellow: ACP, Am. Coll. Cardiology, Coun. Clin. Cardiology (exec. com. 1996—2000, basic rsch. coun.), Am. Heart Assn.; mem.: Assn. Univ. Cardiologists (councilor 1999—2001), Heart Failure Soc. Am. (founding mem. 1995, sec. 1996—98, pres. 1998—2000), Assn. Profs. Cardiology (treas. 2000—01, pres. 2002—03), Assn. Subsplty. Profs., Internat. Soc. Heart Rsch., Assn. Am. Physicians, Am. Soc. Clin. Investigation. Home: 136 Knightsbridge Wynnewood PA 19096 Office: Jefferson Med Coll Coll Bldg Rm 822 1025 Walnut St Philadelphia PA 19096 Office Phone: 215-955-6946. Business E-Mail: arthur.feldman@jefferson.edu.

FELDMAN, BRUCE ALLEN, otolaryngologist; b. Washington, Mar. 22, 1941; s. Irvin and Miriam Thelma (Rothstein) F.; m. Sharon Lee Pearlman, Dec. 25, 1966; children: Kathryn Ellen, Michael Aaron. AB, Dartmouth Coll., 1962, B Med. Sci., 1963; MD, Harvard U., 1965. Diplomate Am. Bd. Otolaryngology. Intern Hosp. of U. Pa., Phila., 1965-66, resident in surgery, 1966-67; resident in otolaryngology Mass. Eye and Ear Infirmary-Harvard U., Boston, 1967-70; pvt. practice Washington, 1972—; clin. prof. surgery (otolaryngology), pediatrics George Washington U., Washington, 1990—; clin. prof. otolaryngology Georgetown U. Sch. Medicine, Washington, 1995—. Pres. med. staff Children's Hosp. DC Nat. Med. Ctr., Washington, 1994-96; vice chmn. bd. Children's Hosp. DC, Washington, 1994-1996, bd. dirs., 1994-2004; pres. Feldman ENT Group, PC. Contbr. articles to med. jours., chpt. to book. Lt. comdr. M.C., USNR, 1970-72. Mosby scholar, 1963; recipient Physician's Recognition award Children's Hosp. Washington, 1991, Best Doctors in Am., 1992-; Named Best Dr., Washington, 2010, Mag. Wash. Census Checkboard, 2011, Best Dr. Northern Va. Fellow ACS, Am. Laryngol., Rhinol. and Otol. Soc. (Mosher award 1981), Am. Acad. Pediatrics, Am. Acad. Otolaryngology; mem. AMA, Acad. Medicine Washington, Med. Soc. D.C., Jacobi Med. Soc. (pres. 1986-87), Washington Met. Ear, Nose and Throat Soc. (pres. 1978-79), Woodmont Country Club (Rockville, Md.), Phi Beta Kappa, Alpha Omega Alpha, Phi Delta Epsilon (pres. grad. club 1979-80). Jewish. Office: 5454 Wisconsin Ave Chevy Chase MD 20815 Office Phone: 301-652-8847.

FELDMAN, DAVID, orthopedist, surgeon, educator; Attended, Albert Einstein Coll. of Medicine, 1988. Diplomate Am. Bd. of Orthopaedic Surgery. Intern NY Univ. Med. Ctr., 1988—89; resident tng. Hosp. For Joint Diseases, 1989—93; clin. fellow Hosp. For Sick Children, 1993—94; assoc. prof. NY Univ. Sch. of Medicine, chief NY Univ. Hosp. for Joint Diseases; chief pediatric orthopedic surgery NY Univ. Langone Med. Ctr., chief pediat. dept. Co-author: (publs.) Clinical efficacy of aspirin and dextran for thromboprophylaxis in geriatric hip fracture patients, 1993, Results of complete soft tissue clubfoot release combined with calcaneocuboid fusion in the 4-year to 8-year age group following failed clubfoot release, 1998, Correction of tibia vara with six-axis deformity analysis and the taylor spatial frame, 2003, and numerous other publications. Office: New York University Langone Medical Center 8th Fl 67 Irving Pl New York NY 10003 Office Phone: 212-533-5310.

FELDMAN, ELAINE BOSSAK, medical nutritionist, educator; b. NYC, Dec. 9, 1926; d. Solomon and Frances Helen (Fania) Nevler Bossak; m. Herman Black, Dec. 23, 1951 (div. 1957); 1 child, Mitchell Evan; m. Daniel S. Feldman, July 19, 1957 (dec. June 2005); children: Susan, Daniel S. Jr. AB magna cum laude, NYU, 1945, MS, 1948, MD, 1951. Diplomate Am. Bd. Internal Medicine, Nat. Bd. Med. Examiners; cert. in Clin. Nutrition. Rotating intern Mt. Sinai Hosp., NYC, 1951-52, resident in pathology, 1952, asst. resident, 1953, fellow in medicine, resident in metabolism, 1954-55, rsch. asst. in medicine, 1955-58, clin. asst. physician Diabetes Clinic, 1957; asst. vis. physician Kings County Hosp., Bklyn., 1958-66, assoc. vis. physician, 1966-72; asst. attending physician Maimonides Hosp., Bklyn., 1960-68; spl. fellow USPHS Dept. of Physiol. Chemistry U. of Lund, Sweden, 1964-65; attending physician Eugene Talmadge Meml. Hosp., Augusta, Ga., 1972-92, Univ. Hosp., Augusta, 1972-92, cons., 1973; prof. medicine Ga. Health Scis. U., Augusta, 1972-92; prof. emeritus Med. Coll. Ga., Augusta, 1992—, chief sect. of nutrition, 1977-92, chief emeritus, 1992—, acting chief sect. of metabolic/endocrine disease, 1980-81, prof. physiology and endocrinology, 1988-92, prof. emeritus physiology and endocrinology, 1992—; instr. medicine SUNY Downstate Med. Ctr., 1957-59, asst. prof. medicine, 1959-68, assoc. prof. medicine, 1968-72. Tchg. fellow dept. zoology U. Wis. Grad. Sch., 1945-46, dept. biology NYU Grad. Sch., 1946-47; cons. N.Y.-N.J. Regional Ctr. for Clin. Nutrition Edn., 1983-92; vis. prof. and Harvey lectr. Northeastern Ohio Sch. Medicine, Youngstown, 1985; cons., vis. prof. U. Nev. Sch. Medicine (NCI grant), 1989-94; mem. nat. adv. com. nutrition fellowship program Nat. Med. Fellowship Inc., 1988-95; dir. Ga. Inst. Human Nutrition, 1978-92, dir. emeritus, 1992—; dir. Clin. Nutrition Rsch. Unit, 1980-86; mem. med. nutrition curriculum initiative adv. bd. U. N.C., Chapel Hill, 1992-2001; advisor ednl. materials Am. Inst. Cancer Rsch., 1997—, mem. adv. com., Kraft Foods Nutrition Update, 1997-. Author: Essentials of Clinical Nutrition, 1988; (with others) Conference on Biological Activities of Steroids in Relation to Cancer, 1969, Nicotinic Acid, 1964, The Menopausal Syndrome, 1974, Hyperlipidemia, Medcom Special Studies, 1974, Medcom Famous Teaching in Modern Medicine, 1979, Harrison's Principles of Internal Medicine, 1980, Health Promotion: Principles and Clinical Applications, 1982, The Encyclopedic Handbook of Alcoholism, 1982, The Climacteric in Perspective, 1986, Selenium in Biology and Medicine, Part A., 1987, Medicine for the Practicing Physician, 1988, Clinical Chemistry of Laboratory Animals, 1989, Ency. Human Biology, 1991, Laboratory Medicine: The Selection and Interpretation of Clinical Laboratory Studies, 1993, Modern Nutrition in Health and Diseases, 1994, Nutrition Assessment-A Comprehensive Guide for Planning Intervention, 1995, The Women's Complete Healthbook, 1995, The American Medical Women's Association's Guide to Nutrition and Wellness, 1996, Normal Nutrition and Therapeutics, 1996, Handbook of Nutrition and Food, 2001; editor: Nutrition and Cardiovascular Disease, 1976, Nutrition in the Middle and Later Years, 1983 (paperback edit. 1986), Nutrition and Heart Disease, 1983, Handbook of Nutrition and Food, 2001, 2d edit., 2007, Human Nutrient Needs in the Life Cycle, 2001; mem. editl. adv. bd. Contemporary Issues in Clin. Nutrition, 1980-92; mem. edit. bd. Am. Jour. Clin. Nutrition, 1983-91, 92-98, Jour. Clin. Endocrinology and Metabolism, 1984-88, MidPoint: Counseling Women through Menopause, 1984-85, Jour. Nutrition, 1985-89; cons. editor Jour. Am. Coll. Nutrition, 1982-94; mem. edit. bd. Complementary Med. for the Physician, 1996-2000; contbg. editor Nutrition Rev., 1997-2002; mem. editl. bd. Nutrition Today, 1999—; reviewer Jour. Lipid Rsch., Biochm. Pharmacology, Sci., The Physiologist, Jour. Am. Acad. Dermatology, Israel Jour. Med. Scis., N.Y. State Jour. Medicine, Jour. of Nutrition Edn., Jour. Am. Dietetic Assn., Am. Jour. Medicine, Am. Jour. Med. Sci., So. Med. Jour., Jour. AMA, Jour. NCI; contbr. more than 175 articles to profl. jours; presenter in field. Mem. tech. adv. com. for sci. and edn. Rsch. Grants Program, Human Nutrition Grants Peer Panel, USDA, 1982, mem. bd. sci. counselors human nutrition; Community Svc. Block Grant Discretionary Program Panel; vice chmn. Urban and Rural Econ. Devel. Panel, Dept. HHS, 1982, grant reviewer, 1983; mem ad hoc and spl. rev. coms. and groups NIH, 1979-93, mem. nutrition study sect., 1976-80; mem. Rev. Panel Nat. Nutrition Objectives, Life Scis. Rev. Office, Fed. Am. Socs. Exptl. Biology, 1985-86; mem. subcom. Women's

Health Trial Nat. Cancer Inst., 1987, mem. bd. sci. counselors cancer prevention and control program, 1990-94; mem. adv. com. Clin. Nutrition Rsch. Unit, U. Ala., 1986-94, Ga. Nutrition Steering Com., 1974-75, Ctrl. Savannah River Area Nutrition Project Coun. 1974-75, ednl. adv. com. Health Central, 1980; mem. geriatrics and gerontology rev. com. Nat. Inst. on Aging, 1986-90; breast cancer initiative peer rev. Dept. of Def., 1997, 98. N.Y. Heart Assn. rsch. fellow, 1955—57. Fellow Am. Heart Assn. Coun. on Atherosclerosis (nominating com. 1978, chmn. nominating com., mem. exec. com. 1979-80, Spl. Recognition award 1995), Am. Inst. Nutrition (grad. nutrition edn. com. 1980-83, 89-93); mem. Am. Coll. Nutrition (chmn. com. pub. affairs), Am. Soc. for Clin. Nutrition (com. on nutrition edn. 1982, chmn. subcom. on nutrition edn. in med. schs. 1983-84, chmn. com. on med./dental residency edn., 1985-87, com. on subsplty. tng. 1988-92, nominating com. 1982, 90, chair nominating com. 1994, com. on clin. practice issues in health and disease 1989-92, Nat. Dairy Coun. award 1991, rep. coun. acad. socs. 1990-96, membership com. 1996-2005, chair 1999, 2000), Fedn. Am. Socs. Exptl. Biology. Am. Oil Chemists Soc., Am. Physiol. Soc., Endocrine Soc., Soc. Exptl. Biology and Medicine, So. Soc. Clin. Investigation, Am. Diabetes Assn., Am. Fedn. Clin. Rsch., Am. Gastroent. Assn., AMA (Joseph B. Goldberger award 1990), Am. Med. Women's Assn. (profl. resources com. 1975-76, med. edn. and rsch. fund com. 1976-79, chmn. 1978-90, chmn. student liaison subcom. of membership com. 1981-84, pres. Br. 51, Augusta 1977-80, treas. 1980-97, Calcium Nutrition Edn. award 1991, CSRA Girl Scout Women of Excellence award 1994), Am. Soc. Parenteral and Enteral Nutrition, Am. Heart Assn. (Ga. affiliate, nutrition com., chmn. sci. session for nutritionists, 1978, chmn. nutrition com. 1979-90, mem. long range planning com. 1980-81, rsch. com. 1980-83, bd. dirs. 1987-90, profl. edn. task force, 1988-89), Richmond County Med. Assn., Augusta Opera Assn. (bd. dirs. 1973-2002, 06-09, rec. sec. 1973-74, pres. 1974-75, coord. audience devel. 1975-77, at-large exec. com. 2006—09, chair nominating com. 1994-96, 07—09, corr. sec. 1998-99, 1st v.p. 1999-2000, chair search com., gen. dir. 2002), Augusta Symphony League, 2005—, Augusta Sailing Club (women's com. 1973), Greater Augusta Arts Coun. (Arts Festival Collage 1982 chmn. promotion and publicity com., Festival coms. 1983-86, 89-93, 95, 96, 98, 99, bd. dirs. 1984-94, Vol. of the Yr., 2001), Gertrude Herbert Inst. Art (bd. dirs. 1987-92), Med. Coll. Ga., Augusta Arts Coun., Authors Club Augusta, Philomathic Club (sec. 1999-2001), Phi Beta Kappa, Sigma Xi (chpt. sec. 1982-83, pres. elect 1983-84, pres. 1984-85), Alpha Omega Alpha. Avocations: opera, wine tasting, travel. Home: 4275 Owens Rd Apt 1222 Evans GA 30809 Personal E-mail: efeldman17@comcast.net.

FELDMAN, EVA LUCILLE, neurology educator; b. NYC, Mar. 30, 1952; d. George Franklin and Margherita Enriceta (Cafiero) F.; children: Laurel, Scott, John Jr. BA in Biology and Chemistry, Earlham Coll., 1973; MS in Zoology, U. Notre Dame, 1975; PhD in Neurosci., U. Mich., 1979, MD, 1983. Diplomate Am. Bd. Neurology; lic. med. practitioner, Mich. Instr. dept. neurology U. Mich., Ann Arbor, 1987-88, asst. prof. neurology, 1988-94, mem. faculty Cancer Ctr., 1992-2000, assoc. prof. neurology, 1994-2000, prof., 2000—, Russell N. DeJong prof. neurology, 2004—. Mem. faculty neurosci. program U. Mich., Mich. Diabetes Rsch. and Tng., Ann Arbor, 1988—; dir. JDRF Ctr. for the Study of Complications in Diabetes. Contbr. chpts. to books, articles to profl. jours. Grantee, NIH, 1989, 1994, 1997, 1998, 2001, 2003, 2006, 2008, Juvenile Diabetes Rsch. Found., 1994, 1997, 1999, 2001, 2006, 2008, Am. Diabetes Assn., 2005, 2008. Achievements include research on the elucidation of the role of growth factors in the pathogenesis of human disease.

FELDMAN, GARY MARC, nutritionist, consultant; m. Debra Lynn. Diploma in Sci. of Nutritional Cons., Am. Nutrition Cons. Assn., 1986. Pres. Steps In Health, Ltd., Douglaston, NY, 1986-88, Margate, Fla., 1988-90, Lake Grove, NY, 1990—. Freelance health/nutrition writer; educator in sci. of food and nutritional supplementation; spkr., writer on genetically modified organisms related to food; initiative campaign to have mandated labeling of GMO food products, instr. adult program Great Neck Pub. Schs., Port Washington Public Schs. Continuing Edn., 2007, Scope Cmty. Edn. Programs, Smithtown, NY; lectr. Libr. & Orgns., Queensborough Cmty. Coll. Continuing Edn., 2010. Developer: Steps in Health Ltd.'s Catalogue of Vegetarian Name-Brand Nutritional Supplements and Health Products; author nutrition newsletter; contbr. health/nutrition articles to jour. Vol. listen to children program Mental Health Assn. and Vol. Program Broward County (Fla.) Pub. Schs., 1989; arbitration participant Better Bus. Bur. South Fla., 1989-90. Mem. Organic Consumers Assoc., Life Extension Found., Pub. Citizen Health Rsch. Group, People for Ethical Treatment of Animals, Doris Day Animal League, Humane Soc. Broward County, Ctr. for Sci. in the Pub. Interest, Internat. Platform Assn., N.Y. State Sheriffs Assn., L.I. Assn. Inc., Herb Rsch. Found., Vegetarian Resource Group, N.Am. Vegetarian Soc., Nutritionists Health Am. (nutrition edn. program com.), Ctr. Sci. Pub. Interest (edn. com.), Feingold Assn., U.S. Co-op Am. Bus. Network, N.Y. Acad. Scis. Avocations: reading and data collection in health field, bodybuilding. Office: PO Box 220123 Great Neck NY 11022-0123

FELDMAN, JEFFREY, internist; MD, Allegheny U. of Health Sciences, Pa, 1976. Diplomate Am. Bd. in Intrnal Medicine, Am. Bd. in Nephrology. Intern Bronx Lebanon Hosp. Ctr., NY, 1977, resident NY, 1979; fellow Kings County Hosp. Ctr., Bklyn., 1981; internist JFK Med. Ctr., Overlook Hosp., Trinitas Hosp., Union Plainfield Med. Assoc.; resident Albert Einstein Coll. of Medicine. Named Recognized Dr., HealthGrades. Office: Union Plainfield Medical Associate Ste 1 440 Chestnut Union NJ 07083-3100 Office Phone: 908-866-9330.

FELDMAN, JOEL J., plastic surgeon; b. 1943; BS with honors, Dartmouth Coll., 1965; MD cum laude, Harvard Med. Sch., 1969. Cert. Am. Bd. Plastic Surgery, Am. Bd. Surgery. Intern, surgery Mass. Gen. Hosp., Boston, 1969—70; resident Mass. Gen Hosp., Boston, 1970—74, Johns Hopkins Hosp., Balt., 1974—76; pvt. practice Cambridge, Mass. Assoc. clinical prof. surgery Harvard Med. Sch.; active staff Mt. Auburn Hosp., Cambridge; clinical assoc. Mass. Gen. Hosp.; emeritus cons. Boston Shriners Burns Inst. Contbr. articles to profl jours.; author: Neck Lift, 2006. Fellow: ACS; mem.: Am. Assn. Plastic Surgeons (Clinician of Yr. 2008), Am. Soc. Plastic Surgeons, American Soc. Aesthetic Plastic Surgery (bd. dirs.), Northeastern Soc. Plastic Surgeons (past pres.). Office: 300 Mt Auburn St Ste 304 Cambridge MA 02138 Office Phone: 617-661-5998. Office Fax: 617-661-6438. Business E-Mail: info@DrJoelFeldman.com.

FELDMAN, KENNETH W., pediatrician; b. Janesville, Wis., June 24, 1944; s. Julius and Ida May Feldman; m. Jane Ann Kroncke, May 5, 1944; children: George K., Katherine J. Brotzman. MD, U. Wis., Madison, 1970. Cert. Am. Bd. Pediats., Bd. Child Abuse Pediat., 2010. Med. dir. child protection program, Seattle, 1983—2010. Fellow: Am. Acad. Pediat. (child abuse exec. com. 2006, sect. child abuse exec. com. 2006—, AAP-Pediatric Practitioner Rsch. award 1983); mem.: Helfer Soc. (exec. com. 2004—06, 2011—). Home: 1218 17th Ave East Seattle WA 98112 Office: Children's Hosp & Regional Medical Ctr 2101 East Yesler Way Seattle WA 98122 Office Fax: 206-329-9764; Home Fax: 206-329-9764. Business E-Mail: kfeldman@u.washington.edu. *

FELDMAN, NANCY JANE, insurance company executive; b. Green Bay, Wis., July 6, 1946; d. Benjamin J. and Ellen M. Naze; m. Robert P. Feldman, Aug. 24, 1968 (dec. May 2006); 1 child, Sara J. BA, U. Wis., 1969, MS, 1974. Supr. EPSDT program Minn. Dept. Human Svcs., St. Paul, 1974-80, supr. healthcare programs, 1980-84; team leader human resources budget Minn. Dept. Fin., St. Paul, 1984-87; asst. commr. Minn. Dept. Health, St. Paul, 1987-91; team leader CORE program Minn. Dept. Adminstrn., St. Paul, 1991-93; dir. state pub. programs Medica, Allina Health Sys., Mpls., 1993-95; CEO UCare Minn., St. Paul, 1995—. Bd. mem. Minn. Coun. Health Plans, Mpls., 1995-, Stratis Health, 2000-, Nat. Inst. Health Policy, 2002-, Alliance Cmty. Health Plans, 2003-; Vols. Am. Nat. Svc., 2007-; bd. mem., 2007. Mem. Women's Health Leadership Trust. Avocations: distance swimming, bicycling, travel. Office: UCare Minn PO Box 52 Minneapolis MN 55440-0052 Home: 4822 Folwell Dr Minneapolis MN 55406 Business E-Mail: nfeldman@ucare.org.

FELDMAN, RONALD ARTHUR, sociologist, educator, social worker; b. Buffalo, Jan. 17, 1938; s. David Jacob and Clara (Spector) F.; m. Dina Cohen Feinstein, Dec. 23, 1962; children: Daniel, Deborah, Darrah. BA, U. Buffalo, 1960; MSW, U. Mich., 1963, PhD, 1966. Cert., Acad. Cert. Social Workers. Asst. prof. U. Calif., Berkeley, 1966-68; Fulbright lectr. Social Services Acad., Ankara, Turkey, 1968-69; assoc. prof. Washington U. Sch. Social Work, St. Louis, 1969-72, prof., 1972-86, acting dean, 1973-74; dir. Ctr. for Study of Youth Devel., Boys Town, Nebr., 1974-78, Ctr. for Adolescent Mental Health, St. Louis, 1983-87; assoc. dean Columbia U. Sch. Social Work, NYC, 1985-86, prof., dean, 1986—2001, Ruth Harris Ottman Centennial prof., 1995—, dir. Ctr. Study Social Work Practice, 2002—09, dean emeritus, 2001—. Cons. NIMH, Rockville, Md., 1980-91; bd. dirs. Ednl. Inst., Jewish Bd. Family and Children's Svcs., N.Y.C., 1986-2004, Bd. Behavior and Mental Disorders, Inst. Medicine. Sr. author: Contemporary Approaches to Group Treatment, 1975, The St. Louis Conundrum: The Effective Treatment of Antisocial Youths, 1983, Children at Risk: In the Web of Parental Mental Illness, 1987; sr. editor: Advances in Adolescent Mental Health, vols. 1-4, 1986—. Citizen leader Clayton (Mo.) Bd. Edn., 1981-82; mem. profl. rev. bd. Mo. Dept. Mental Health, Jefferson City, 1981-86; trustee Wm. T. Grant Found., 1993-2004 Recipient Disting. Faculty award Washington U., St. Louis, 1984; research grantee NIMH, Rockville, Md., 1970-75, 80-84, Office of Human Devel. Services, Washington, 1983-87. Fellow NASW, Soc. for Rsch. in Child Devel., Am. Acad. Social Work & Social Welfare; mem. Coun. on Social Work Edn. (bd. dirs. 1992-95), Am. Sociol. Assn., Internat. Assn. Child and Adolescent Psychiatry and Allied Professions (v.p. 1995-2005), Avocations: swimming, tennis. Office: Columbia U Sch Social Work 1255 Amsterdam Ave New York NY 10027 Office Phone: 212-851-2265. Business E-Mail: raf1@columbia.edu.

FELDMANN, EDWARD GEORGE, pharmaceutical chemist, pharmacologist, medical scientist; b. Chgo., Oct. 13, 1930; s. Edward Louis and Vera (Arnesen) F.; stepmother Helen E. Whitney; m. Mary J. Evans, Aug. 30, 1952; children: Ann Marie Whittington, Edward William, Robert George, Karen Lynn Zaragoza. BS in Chemistry, Loyola U., Chgo., 1952; MS in Pharmacy (research fellow Am. Found. Pharm. Edn. 1953-55), U. Wis., 1954, PhD in Pharm. Chemistry-Biochemistry, 1955; postgrad. in Med. Scis., Northwestern U., 1956; postgrad., U. Chgo., 1958. Tchg. asst. Loyola U., Chgo., 1951—52; rsch. asst. U. Wis., 1952—53; sr. chemist Am. Dental Assn., 1955—58, dir. divsn. chemistry, 1958—59; assoc. dir. sci. divsn. Am. Pharm. Assn., 1959—60, dir., 1960—85, assoc. editor sci. edit. assn. jour., 1959—60, editor, 1960—97, assoc. exec. dir. sci. affairs, 1970—83, v.p. sci. affairs, 1983—85, project dir. Handbook of Non-Prescription Drugs, 1985—89, mng. editor, 1989—90, project cons. Handbook on Non-Prescription Drugs, 1991—93, mem. adv. panel, 1994—95; exec. sec. Acad. Pharm. Scis., 1983—85; mem. adv. panel Am. Pharm. Assn., 1994—99; pvt. pharm. cons., 1985—; assoc. dir. revision Nat. Formulary, 1959—60; dir. revision Nat. Fomulary, 1960—70. Adv. panel dental drugs Nat. Formulary, 1955-60, Am. Pharm. Assn. Handbook of Non-Prescription Drugs, 1994-95; reviewer Internat. Pharmacopeia, WHO, 1958; spl. lectr., adj. prof. drug standards George Washington U., 1960-64; del. conf. on fellowships Nat. Health Council, 1960; mem. coordinating com. Nat. Conf. Antimicrobial Agts., Soc. Indsl. Microbiology, 1960-63; adv. panel pharm. nomenclature A.M.A.-Am. Pharm. Assn.-U.S. Pharmacopeia, 1961-66, nomenclature com., 1962-66; sec. U.S. Com. Internat. Drug Standards, 1964-65; adv. panel food chems. codex Nat. Acad. Scis.-NRC, 1961-71, liaison rep. to drug research bd., 1968-76; spl. liaison rep. to Commn. of Life Scis., NAS-NRC, 1973-85; lab. com. Am. Pharm. Assn. Found., 1961-75; mem. com. Ebert prize, 1961-75; judge Lunsford-Richardson Pharmacy Awards, 1962-69; cons. Council on Drugs, A.M.A., 1962; vis. scientist Am. Assn. Colls. of Pharmacy, NSF, 1963-66; expert adv. panel on internat. pharmacopeia and pharm. preparation World Health Orgn., 1963-75; mem. US President's Task Force on Hosp. Drug Coverage Under Medicare, 1963-64; drug abuse cons. to Office of US Pres., Lyndon B. Johnson, 1965, drug cons. Office Sec., U.S. Dept. Health, Edn. and Welfare, 1967-70; nomenclature cons. to Commr., U.S. Food and Drug Adminstrn., 1968-71; mem. expert working group Indsl. Devel. Orgn., UN, 1969; organizing com. 31st Internat. Congress Pharm. Scis., 1970-71; mem. NRC, 1971-85; del. U.S. Pharmacopeia, 1970-85, 90-95; mem. Nat. Council on Drugs, 1976-83; scientific adv. bd. Biodecision Labs., Inc., 1987-90; scientific cons. Am. Assn. Pharmaceutical Scientists, 1986-93; pharm. scis. cons. ERGO Sci. Inc., 1992—; steering com. Japan-U.S. Pharmaceutical Scis. Congress, 1987; expert witness congressional drug legis. hearings and civil litigation cases, Drug quality specifications, Fed. legal requirements, Clinical pharmacology and Toxicology, 1965-; lectr. in field. Assoc. editor Drug Standards, 1959-60, editor, 1960; chmn. (1960-70) Nat. Formulary Bd.; editor Jour. Pharm. Scis., 1961-75, cons. editor, 1975-85, 87-89, interim editor, 1991, editor in chief, 1991-94, emeritus editor 1994-95; editor APS Acad. Reporter, 1983-85; author more than 420 articles in field, editor or co-editor 24 ref. books; mem. editorial adv. bd. Index Chemicus, 1968-71; med. contbr. World Book Ency., 1986-88. Mem. membership com. Ravenwood Park Citizens Assn., Falls Church, Va., 1962, mem. nominating com., 1971-72; mem. Lake Barcroft Community Assn., 1975-97. Recipient Spl. Recognition award U.S. Pres. Lyndon Johnson, 1965, Man of Yr. award Nat. Assn. Pharm. Mfrs., 1970, Disting. citation U. Wis., 1971, Commr.'s citation FDA, 1975, G.A. Bergy Lectr. award U. W.Va., 1975, Pres. award Am. Assn. Pharm. Scis., 1993. Fellow Acad. Pharm. Scis.; mem. Am. Pharm. Assn. (life, Hon. Mem. award 2005), Am. Chem. Soc. (emeritus), Am. Assn. Pharm. Scis. (charter mem., fellow, fellows selection com. 1989, Pres.'s award 1993), N.Y. Acad. Scis., Nat. Soc. Med. Rsch. (coun. 1961-69), Am. Testing Materials, Coun. Biology Editors, AMA (affiliate), Fedn. Internat. Pharm., US Tennis Assn., Mid-Atlantic Tennis Assn. (chmn. rules com., 1991-96), Fla. Tennis Assn., Sarasota County Sr. Men's Tennis Assn. (team capt. 2003-07), Sleepy Hollow Bath and Racquet Club (Falls Church, Va.), Arlington Tennis and Squash Club, 4-Seasons Tennis Club, Fairfax Golden Racquets Club, Venice (Fla.) Golf and Country Club (bd. mem. tennis assn. 1998-05, pres. 2002-05, mem. sports and health com. 2002-05, mem. Disaster Preparedness Comm. 2006-11, mem. Glenridge on Palmer Ranch, 2010-, hurricane & disaster coord., 2010-, players prodr., 2011-), K.C., Sigma Xi, Rho Chi, Lambda Chi Sigma. Roman Catholic.

FELDMANN, MARC, immunologist, researcher; b. Lvov, Poland, Dec. 2, 1944; s. Elie and Cyla Feldmann; m. Tania Gudinski Feldmann; children: Robert, Pia Menzies. MBBS, U. Melbourne, 1967, BMedSci with honors, 1970, PhD, 1972; MD (hon.), Technische U., Munich, 2002. Lic. Registration Bd. Victoria, 1967, Gen. Med. Coun., London, 1986. Resident in internal medicine St. Vincent's Hosp., Melbourne, Australia, 1968; head Kennedy Inst. Rheumatology divsn. Imperial Coll., London, head Kennedy Inst. Rheumatology, head Dept. Cytokine and Cellular Immunology, 1992—; with tumour immunology unit Imperial Cancer Rsch. Found., London, 1972—77, spl. appt. grade, 1977—85; dep. dir., head immunology unit Charing Cross Sunley Rsch. Ctr., London, 1985—92. Spl. appointment Imperial Cancer Rsch. Fund., 1977—85; sci. adv. bd. Roche, Palo Alto, Calif., 1991—, Centocor, Malvern, 1992—2000, Wyeth Rsch., Cambridge, Mass., 1996—, Almirall Prodesforma, Barcelona, 1998—2003, Novo-Nordisk A/S, Denmark, 2002—, Receptor BioLogix, San Francisco, 2004—; cons. in field. Mem. editl. bd.: Med. Immunology, Jour. Autoimmunity, Cytokine and Growth Factor Revs., Cytokines, Jour. Ex Pathology, 1997—, trasmitting editor: Internat. Immunology, 2001—; contbr. articles to profl. jours. Recipient Carol-Nachman prize, City of Wiesbaden, 1999, Crafoord prize in Polyarthritis, Royal Swedish Acad. Sciences, 2000, Albert Lasken Clin. Med. Rsch. award, Lasker Found., 2003, Cameron prize therapeutics, U. Edinburgh, 2004, Internat. RA award, Japan Rheumatism Found., 2007, Curtin medal, Australian Nat. U., 2007, Dr. Paul Janssen award, NY, 2008; fellow, Acad. Med. Sci., 2001. Fellow: Royal Coll. Pathologists, Royal Coll. Physicians, Acad. Med. Scis., Internat. Cytokine Soc. (pres. 2002—03), Royal Soc.; mem.: NAS (fgn. assoc.), EMBC, Australian Acad. Scis. (corr.). Achievements include discovery of TNF as a therapeutic target for rheumatoid arthritis (basis of Crafoord Prize and Lasker Award) and patents for anti-TNF antibodies and Methotrexate in the treatment of autoimmune disease. Avocations: tennis, hiking. Office: Kennedy Inst Rheumatology Imperial Coll ARC Bldg 65 Aspenlea Rd London W6 8LH England Office Phone: 44 (0) 20 8383 4400. Business E-Mail: m.feldmann@imperial.ac.uk. *

FELDSTEIN, JULIE TERUYA, hematologist; b. Honolulu, Sept. 12, 1963; MD, John A. Burns Sch. Medicine, 1992. Dir. immunohistochemistry lab, hematopathology tng. program Meml. Sloan Kettering Cancer Ctr., 1999—. Mem.: Can. Acad. Pathology, Am. Soc. Hematology, US Acad. Pathology. Office: 1275 York Ave Rm C502 Box 36 New York NY 10162 Office Fax: 212-717-3203. Business E-Mail: feldstej@mskcc.org.

FELDSTEIN, MARTIN STUART, economics professor; b. NYC, Nov. 25, 1939; s. Meyer and Esther (Gevarter) Feldstein; m. Kathleen Foley, June 19, 1965; children: Margaret, Janet. AB summa cum laude, Harvard U., Cambridge, Mass., 1961; MA, Oxford U., 1964, DPhil, 1967; LLD (hon.), Rochester U., 1984, Marquette U., Milw., 1985, Dartmouth Coll., 2008. Rsch. fellow Nuffield Coll., Oxford U., 1964—65, ofcl. fellow, 1965—67, lectr. pub. fin., 1965—67; asst. prof. econs. Harvard U., 1967—68, assoc. prof., 1968—69, prof., 1969—84, George F. Baker prof. econs., 1984—. Pres. Nat. Bur. Econ. Rsch., Cambridge, 1977—82, 1984—2008, pres. emeritus, 2008—; chmn. Coun. Econ. Advs., Exec. Office of Pres., Washington, 1982—84; bd. dirs. Eli Lilly & Co., 2001—; mem. exec. com. Trilateral Commn., Washington, 1987—, Group of Thirty, Washington, 2003—; mem., pres. Fgn. Intelligence Adv. Bd., Washington, 2006—09, Econ. Recovery Adv. Bd., 2009—11; mem. internat. adv. coun. J.P. Morgan; trustee Coun. Fgn. Rels., 2000—. Bd. contbrs.: Wall St. Jour. Hon. fellow, Nuffield Coll. Fellow: European Econ. Assn., Am. Philos. Soc., Nat. Assn. Bus. Economists, Brit. Acad. (corr.), Am. Acad. Arts & Scis., Econometric Soc. (coun. 1977—82); mem.: Inst. Medicine NAS, Am. Enterprize Inst. (Irving Kristol award 2011), Nat. Tax Assn. (Daniel Holland medal 2003), Coun. Fgn. Rels. (bd. dirs. 1998—2006, 2009—), Austrian Acad. Scis. (fgn.), Am. Econ. Assn. (v.p. 1988, pres. 2004, exec. com. 1980 2005—, John Bates Clark medal 1977), Phi Beta Kappa. Office: Nat Bur Econ Rsch 1050 Massachusetts Ave Cambridge MA 02138-5317 Office Phone: 617-868-3905. Personal E-mail: msfeldst@gmail.com. Business E-Mail: mfeldstein@nber.org.

FELGAR, RAYMOND EUGENE, pathologist, educator; b. Mt. Pleasant, Pa., Mar. 2, 1963; s. Samuel Hurst and Anna June (Stull) Felgar. BS in Microbiology with honors, Pa. State U., University Park, 1985; PhD in Pathology, U. Pitts., 1990, MD, 1992. Diplomate Am. Bd. Pathology in Anatomic and Clin. Pathology, Am. Bd. Pathology, cert. subspecialty in Hemotology Am. Bd. Pathology, 2002, in anatomic & clin. pathology 1998, in hematology 2002. Resident in anatomic and clin. pathology U. Pa. Med. Ctr., Phila., 1992—96; fellow in hematopathology dept. pathology Vanderbilt U., Nashville, 1996—98; dir. hematopathology and clin. flow cytometry Hahnemann Hosp., Phila., 1998; asst. prof. dept. pathology and lab medicine MCP-Hahnemann Sch. Medicine, Drexel U. Coll. Medicine, Phila., 1998; dir. clin. flow cytometry lab., hematopathologist, dir. hematopathology Strong Meml. Hosp., Rochester, NY, 1998—2007; asst. prof. Dept. Pathology & Lab. Medicine U. Rochester Sch. Medicine

& Dentistry, 1998—2004, assoc. prof. Dept. Pathology & Lab Medicine, 2004—06; assoc. dir. hematopathology fellowship program U. Pitts. Med. Ctr., 2007—, dir. hematopathology fellowship program, 2010—, mem., grad. med. edn. com., 2007—, mem., cancer com., 2009—; assoc. prof. dept. pathology U. Pitts. Sch. Medicine, 2007—. Co-dir. Course on T-cell lymphomas, ASCP Nat. Meeting; former mem. sci. adv. bd. Bioreference Labs. Inc., Elmwood Park, N.J., 2003-08; exec. editl. bd. mem. Internat. Jour. Clin. and Exptl. Pathology, 2007-, mem., Grad. Med. Edn. Com., U. Pitts. Med. Ctr., 2007-, Cancer Com. U. Pitts. Med. Ctr., 2009-. Contbr. articles to profl. jours., chapters to books. NIH med. scientist tng. fellow, 1987-92. Fellow Coll. Am. Pathologists, Am. Soc. Clin. Pathologists (co-dir. course t-cell lymphomas nat. mtg., mem. resident in-svc. & fellows in-svc. exam. coms. 2011-, resident and Hematopathology fellow in svc., Exam. Com., 2011-), Am. Assn. Clin. Pathologists; mem. AMA, Am. Soc. Hematology, U.S. and Can. Acad. Pathology, Soc. for Hematopathology, European Assn. for Hematopathology, Pitts. Pathology Soc., Eastern Coop. Oncology Group (pathology com.), Southwestern Oncology Group, Children's Oncology Group, Pa. State U. Alumni Assn., Phi Beta Kappa, Am. Mensa, Mensa Internat., Western Pa. Mensa, Pa. Med. Soc. Business E-Mail: felgarre@upmc.edu.

FELICETTA, JAMES VINCENT, endocrinologist, educator; b. Seattle, Mar. 1, 1949; s. Vincent Frank and Alice Marie (Felton) F.; m. Susan Marie Roman, Aug. 3, 1985. BS, U. Wash., 1970, MD, 1974, postgrad., 1977-80. Intern U. Utah, Salt Lake City, 1974—75, resident, 1975—77; fellow in endocrinology and metabolism U. Wash., 1977—80; asst. prof. medicine U. Mich., Ann Arbor, 1980—84; chief endocrinology Wayne County Gen. Hosp., Westland, Mich., 1980—84; from asst. prof. medicine to vice chief endocrinology Wayne State U., Detroit, 1984—87; chief endocrinology VA Med. Ctr., Allen Park, Mich., 1985—87; chief medicine Phoenix VA Med. Ctr., 1987—; assoc. clin. prof. medicine U. Ariz., Tucson, 1988—95, prof. clin. medicine, 1995—. Adj. prof. Coll. of Liberal Arts, Ariz. State U., Tempe, 1991—; dir. Phoenix Citywide Endocrinology and Metabolism Fellowship Prog., 1994—. Contbr. many articles and abstracts to profl. jours. Fellow Am. Coll. Physicians; mem. Am. Fed. for Clin. Research, Am. Diabetes Assn., Am. Soc. Hypertension, The Endocrine Soc. Roman Catholic. Avocations: hiking, films. Home: 5543 E Sheena Dr Scottsdale AZ 85254-2961 Office: VA Med Ctr 7th St Phoenix AZ 85034 Office Phone: 602-277-5551 ext 7031, 602-222-6436. Business E-Mail: james.felicetta@med.va.gov, jfelicetta@aol.com.

FELICIANI, CLAUDIO, dermatologist, educator; b. Pescara, Italy, June 10, 1961; s. Silvio Feliciani and adopted s. Maria Pia Toffoli. MD, U. G.d'Annunzio, Chieti, Italy, 1988. Diplomate dermatology U. Chieti, 1992. Lectr. dermatology U. Chieti, Italy, 1988—93; asst. prof. U. of Chieti, 1993—2002; assoc. prof. Cath. U. Sacro Cuore, Rome, 2003—. With arty. Italian Army, 1979—80. Mem.: Italian Soc. Dermatology Med., Surg., Esthetical and Ssexually Transmitted Diseases (assoc.). Achievements include research in mechanisms of acantholysis in pemphigus; role of cytokines in skin immune system. Office: Univ Cattolica del Sacro Cuore Largo Gemelli Roma 00168 Italy Office Fax: +39-063016293. E mail: feliciani @rm.unicatt.it.

FELICIANO, LORENZO GONZALEZ, public health service officer; Attending physician Montefiore Med. Ctr., Bronx, NY, 1989—91, Bronx Mcpl. Hosp. Ctr. - Jacobi Hosp., NY, 1989—91, Morrisania Neighborhood Family Care Ctr., Bronx, NY, 1991—93, North Ctrl. Bronx Hosp., NY, 1991—93, Sharon Regional Health System, Pa., 1993—96; clin. instr. Western Pscyhiat. Inst., 1993—96; med. dir. specialized treatment unit II First Hosp. Panamericano, Cidra, PR, 1996—97; med. dir. behavioral health system NW Med. Ctr., Franklin Oil City, PR, 1997—2000; attending physician George Jr. Republic Residential Treatment Ctr., Grove City, Pa., 1997—; chief med. officer Danville State Hosp., Pa., 2001—03; med. dir. Mepsi Ctr., Bayamon, PR, 2003—05; sec. PR Dept. Health, San Juan, 2009—. Consultation liaison svc. chief fellow child and adolescent dept. Columbia Presbyn. Hosp., 1992—93; mem. hospitalization and continuum of care com. Am. Acad. of Child and Adolescent Psychiatry, 1996—2002. Mem.: American Acad. Child & Adolescent Psychiatry (mem. hospitalization and continuum of care com. 1996—2002), Pa. Med. Assn. Office: Puerto Rico Department of Health PO Box 70184 San Juan PR 00936-8184 Office Phone: 787-274-7874. Office Fax: 787-274-5739. *

FELICIO, JOANA D'ARC, research scientist; b. Igarapava, São Paulo, Brazil, Dec. 8, 1959; BS in Chemistry, IQ- UNESP, 1982; D in Organic Chemistry, IQ-USP, 1990. Rsch. scientist, mem. Inst. Biológico Govt., 1985. Contbr. articles to profl. jours., chapters to books. Home: Rua Francisco Marcondes Vieira 3 B5 Ap73 São Paulo 05639-090 Brazil Home Fax: 0551135017431. Business E-Mail: felicio@biologico.sp.gov.br.

FELIPE, LONICE, biology professor; b. Pocos de Caldas, Minas Gerais, Brazil, Nov. 22, 1945; Biologia, UFPr, 1967; D, Inst. de Biofisca, 1985. Prof. U. Estadual de Londrina, 1975—, adj. prof., 1975—. Mem.: Brazilian Soc. Immunology. Avocation: travel. Office: Campus Universitario Londrina Parana 86051-990 Brazil E-mail: ionice@uel.br.

FELIX, CAROLYN A., pediatric hematologist-oncologist educator; BS summa cum laude, Boston Coll., 1977; MD, Boston U., 1981. Diplomate Am. Bd. Pediatrics, Am. Bd. Pediatrics-hematology-oncology. Intern Children's Hosp., Pitts., resident; fellow pediatric br. Nat. Cancer Inst.; asst. prof. pediat. Univ. of Pa. Sch. of Medicine, 1991—2000, assoc. prof. pediat., 2000—06, prof. pediat., 2006—. Office: The Childrens Hospital of Philadelphia Colket Translational Research Bldg 3501 Civic Center Blvd Room 4006 Philadelphia PA 19104 Office Phone: 215-590-2831.

FELLNER, FRANZ A., radiologist; b. Passau, Germany, July 15, 1966; s. Franz and Franziska Fellner; m. Claudia M. Pruell. MD, U. Munich, 1991, U. Erlangen, Germany, 2001. Prof. radiology U. Erlangen, 2001; head dept. magnetic resonance, dep. chief inst. radiology Head Clinic Wagner Jauregg, Linz, Austria, 2002—05; head inst. radiology AKH, Linz, Austria, 2005—. Mem. supervisory bd. Ars Electronica, Linz, 2007—. Contbr. articles to profl. jours. R & d mem. Tech. Coll. Upper Austria, Linz, 2005—08, Wels, 2005—08, Steyr, 2005—08, Hagenberg, 2005—08. Recipient award, Med. Soc. Upper Austria, 2005. Mem.: Austrian X-ray Soc., German X-ray Soc. Office: AKH Linz Inst Radiology Krankenhausstr 9 Linz 4020 Austria Office Fax: 4373278062099. Business E-Mail: franz.fellner@akh.linz.at.

FELLUS, JONATHAN L., neurologist; b. London, Ont., Can., June 9, 1966; MD, U. Medicine and Dentistry N.J.-R.W. Johnson Med. Sch., 1992. Diplomate Am. Bd. Neurology. Intern Mountainside Hosp., Montclair, NJ, 1992; resident Pa. Hosp., Phila., 1992—93; fellow in neurorehab. Kernan Hosp.-U. Md. Med. Ctr., Balt., 1996—97; staff neurologist Kessler Inst. Rehab., West Orange, NJ, 1997—; dir. brian injury svcs., clin. asst. prof. neuroscis. U. Medicine and Dentistry N.J.-N.J. Med. Sch., 1997—. Named one of Top Drs. 2003 an 2005, N.J. Monthly Mag. Office: Kessler Institute 1199 Pleasant Valley Way West Orange NJ 07052-1424

FELSON, DAVID, epidemiologist, educator, rheumatologist; Chief Multidisciplinary Clinical Rsch. Ctr.; prin. investigator Multipurpose Arthritis & Musculoskeletal Disease Ctr.; prof. med. & epidemiology Boston U. Sch. Med.; assoc. dir. Clinical Translational Sci. Award Training Program. Recipient Henry J. Kunkel Young Investigator award, Am. Coll. Rheumatology. Mem.: Am. Soc. Clinical Investigation. Office: 650 Albany St Bldg X Ste 200 Boston MA 02118 Office Phone: 617-638-5180. E-mail: dfelson@bu.edu.

FELTHOUS, ALAN ROBERT, psychiatrist; b. San Francisco, Oct. 16, 1944; s. Robert Alan and Agnetta Wilhelmena (Blindheim) F.; m. Mary Louise Wilkins, Aug. 6, 1971; children: Erik Alan, Emily Anna, Elizabeth Ashley. BS, U. Wash., 1967; MD, U. Louisville, 1971. Diplomate Nat. Bd. Med. Examiners, Am. Bd. Psychiatry and Neurology added qualifications in forensic psychiatry, Am. Bd. Forensic Psychiatry (v.p. 1992-93, pres. 1993-94). Intern Roosevelt Hosp., NYC, 1971-72; resident in psychiatry McLean Hosp./Harvard Med. Sch., Belmont, Mass., 1972-75; staff psychiatrist Naval Regional Med. Ctr., Oakland, Calif., 1975-77; psychiatrist, sect. chief Menninger Found., Topeka, 1977-83, ch. adult divsn., 1993—; chief forensic svc. dept. psychiatry and behavioral scis. U. Tex. Med. Br., Galveston, 1984—, assoc. prof. dept. psychiatry and behavioral scis., 1984-89, prof. dept psychiatry and behavioral scis., 1989-98, Marie B. Gale centennial prof. psychiatry, 1994-98; prof. dept. psychiatry So. Ill. U. Sch. Medicine, Springfield, 1998—2006, dir. forensic psychiatry, 1998—2006; med. dir. Chester Mental Health Ctr., Ill., 1998—2006; prof. sch. law Carbondale, 2001—06; prof. psychiatry, dir. forensic psychiatry St. Louis U. Sch. Medicine, 2006—. Assn. dirs. Forensic Psychiatry Fellowship Programs, 2006—, sec., 2006—. Author: The Psychotherapist's Duty to Warn or Protect, 1989; newsletter editor: Am. Acad. Psychiatry and the Law, 1988-93; co-editor (forensic sect.) Current Opinion in Psychiatry, 1993-2001, Behavioral Sciences and the Law, 1997-2001, sr. editor, 2002-; co-editor The Internatnational Handbook on Psychopathic Disorders and Law, 2007; contbr. articles to profl. jours. and handbooks Pres. American Acad. Psychiatry and Law, 2006—07. Capt. USNR, 1969—99. Recipient Wood-Prince awards for sci. pubs., The Menninger Found., 1978—82, Outstanding Achievement award, Gulf Coast Mental Health and Mental Retardation, Galveston, 1991, Exemplary Psychiatrist award, Nat. Alliance for the Mentally Ill, 1993. Fellow Am. Acad. Forensic Scis. (sect. sec. psychiatry and behavioral sci., chmn. 1997-2000, dir. 2000-03, mem.-at-large exec. com. 2002-03, v.p. 2009-, Maier I. Tuchler award 2000), Am. Psychiat. Assn. (disting.); mem. Am. Acad. Psychiatry and the Law (pres.-elect 2005-06, pres. 2006-07, immediate past pres. 2007—08, Outstanding Svc. award 1994), German Soc. for Psychiatry, Psychotherapy and Neurology, Naval Res. Assn. (life). Achievements include research in abnormal aggressive behaviors. Office: St Louis U Sch Medicine Dept Neurol Psychiatry 1438 S Grand Blvd Saint Louis MO 63104 Personal E-mail: arfelt@aol.com. Business E-Mail: felthous@slu.edu.

FENCHEL, GERD HERMANN, psychoanalyst; b. Berlin, Mar. 29, 1926; arrived in U.S., 1940; s. Eric Otto and Rosa (Goldschmidt) F.; children: Karen Fenchel Spiler, Erich; m. Leslie Spitz, June 30, 1991. BSS, CCNY, 1949, MS in Edn., 1950; PhD, NYU, 1959; cert., Washington Sq. Inst., 1970. Cert. psychologist, N.Y., Pa. Pvt. practice psychoanalysis, NYC, 1949—; asst. dean Alfred Adler Inst., NYC, 1955-73; psychotherapist, supr. and dir. group psychotherapy L.I. Cons. Ctr., Forest Hills, N.Y., 1953-60; mem. faculty Inst. for Analytic Psychotherapy, N.J., 1960-71; exec. dir., dean Washington Sq. Inst., NYC, 1960—. Author: Psychoanalytic Reflections on Love and Sexuality, 2006; co-author: Development of Ego and Emergence of the Self in Group Psychotherapy, 1979; editor: Psychoanalysis at 100, 1994, The Mother-Daughter Relationship, 1998; contbr. articles to profl. jours. Fellow Coun. Psychoanalysts and Psychotherapists (pres. 1966-67), Am. Group Psychotherapy Assn., Pa. Psychol. Assn.; mem. APA. Avocations: travel, photography. Office: Washington Sq Inst 41 E 11th St Fl 4 New York NY 10003-4678 Office Phone: 212-477-2600. Personal E-mail: ghfenchel@hotmail.com.

FENDERSON, CAROLINE HOUSTON, psychotherapist; b. East Orange, NJ, June 17, 1932; d. George Cochran and Mary Bullard (Saunders) Houston; m. Kendrick Elwell Fenderson, Jr.; 1 child, Karen Sibley. BA, Vassar Coll., 1954; MA, U. So. Fla., 1973. Lic. mental health counselor, Fla.; diplomate Am. Bd. Cert. Managed Care Providers, Nat. Bd. for Cert. Clin. Hypnotherapists, Inc.; cert. trainer, devel. of human capacities Found. for Mind Rsch.; cert. Eye Movement Desensitization and Reprocessing therapist; cert. profl. counselor Com. Psychotherapy Assn. Bd.; ordained to ministry of edn. Unitarian Universalist; diplomate Am. Psychotherapy Assn. Dir. religious edn. Unitarian Universalist Ch., St. Petersburg, Fla., 1960—80, min. religious edn. Clearwater, Fla., 1981—83; cons. counselor and staff devel. Pinellas County Schs., Fla., 1973—83; pvt. practice Clearwater and Palm Harbor, 1983—. Author: Life Journey, 1988; (with Kendrick Fenderson Jr.) Magnets, 1961, Southern Shores, 1964; (with others) Man the Culture Builder, 1970, U.U. Identity, 1979; contbr. articles to profl. jours. Pub. affairs chmn. St. Petersburg Jr. League, 1960; founder Childbirth and Parent Edn. League of Pinellas County, 1960-70, pres., v.p., com. chair, tchr.; v.p. Child Guidance Clinic, St. Petersburg, 1960. Fellow; APA, Am. Psychotherapy Assn.; mem.: ACA, Eye Movement Desensitization and Reprocessing Internat. Assn., Liberal Religious Edn. Dirs. Assn. (v.p. 1980-81), Assn. Transpersonal Psychology, Assn. Humanistic Psychology, Internat. Transpersonal Assn., Unitarian Universalist Assn. (com. 1975-79), Phi Beta Kappa, Kappa Delta Pi. Home: 29 Freshwater Dr Palm Harbor FL 34684-1106 Office: 25 400 US 19 N Ste 112 Clearwater FL 33763 Office Phone: 727-797-7211.

FENG, BAOMIN, medical educator; b. Jian City, Jilin, China, Aug. 8, 1975; PhD, Shenyang Pharm. U., 2002. Prof. Dalian U., 2009—. Recipient 1st Class Sci. and Technol. award, Ministry Edn. of China. Office: Xuefu Rd Dalian Liaoning 116622 China Business E-Mail: fengbaomin@dlu.edu.cn.

FENG, LEI, medical researcher; arrived in U.S., 1989; s. Liesun Feng; m. Chen Zheng, Aug. 17, 1999. BS, Peking Union Med. Coll., 1989; MD, Columbia U., 1998; PhD, The Rockefeller U. Lic. NY, 1999, Calif., 2004, diplomate Am. Bd. Radiology, 2003. Assoc. rsch. scientist Columbia U., NYC, 1998—2003; clin. instr. UCLA, LA, 2004—05; asst. prof. Columbia U., 2004—05; dir. interventional neuroradiology Kaiser L.A. Med. Ctr., 2005—; asst. prof. UCLA, 2005—. Prin. investigator Am. Diabetes Assn., Alexandria, Va., 2004—, Juvenile Diabetes Rsch. Found., NYC, 2004—05; holman pathway rsch. resident Radiology Soc. N.Am., Chgo., 1999—2003. Contbr. articles to profl. jours., chpts. to books. Recipient Holman Rsch. Resident Seed award, Radiol. Soc. N.Am., 2000; grantee, Am. Diabetes Assn., 2004, Juvenile Diabetes Rsch. Found., 2004; fellow, Columbia U., 2003—04. Mem.: AMA, Am. Coll. Radiologist. Achievements include invention of Endothelial biopsy; research in MRI guided neurovascular intervention.

FENG, LIU, medical technician; b. Jiangxi, China, 1979; PhD, Huazhong U. Sci. and Tech., 2011. Supervising technician dept. blood transfusion Union Hosp. Tongji Med. Coll., 2001—. Office: 1277 Jiefang Ave Wuhan Hubei 430022 China Business E-Mail: liu_feng_email@126.com.

FENG, LU-JEAN, plastic surgeon, educator; BA in Molecular Biophysics and Biochemistry, Yale U., New Haven, MD. Diplomate Am. Bd. Plastic Surgery. Intern gen. surgery Univ. Calif. Hosp., resident gen. surgery; resident plastic surgery divsn. of plastic and reconstructive surgery Univ. NC; fellow microvascular surgery NYU Med. Ctr.; clin. instr. surgery (plastic surgery) sch. medicine NYU; clin. assoc. prof. surgery sch. medicine Case Western Res. Univ., Cleve., mem. internat. vis. com.; founder The Lu-Jean Feng Clinic, Ohio, med. dir. Ohio. Mem.: Ohio Valley Soc. of Plastic Surgeons, Am. Soc. for Reconstructive Microsurgery, AMA, Am. Soc. for Aesthetic Plastic Surgery, Am. Soc. of Plastic Surgeons. Achievements include being one of the first to use autogenous tissue for breast reconstruction, which gained national attention in the 80s; one of few surgeons to perform an all-natural breast enhancement using a patient's own regenerative stems cells and fat; introduced a "painless and drainless" abdominoplasty (tummy tuck). Office: The Lu-Jean Feng Clinic 31200 Pinetree Rd Pepper Pike OH 44124 Office Phone: 216-831-7007.

FENG, SHI LIANG, physician, medical researcher; b. China; s. Yuechen Feng; m. Shuying Bai; children: Xue Bai, Taichi. MD, China Med. U., Shenyang, 1982, Liaoning U. of Traditional Chinese Medicine, 1988, Pyongyang U., Korea, 1996. Cert. in Specialty and Tech. Liaoning Provincial Pers. Dept., 1997. Chief Liaoning Provincial Diabetes Med. Ctr. & Shenyang City Diabetes Inst., Liaoning, China, 1991—; chief dir. USA Diabetes Med. Ctr., LA, 1999—. Dir. Chinese Med. Assn., Beijing, 1994—; com. mem. Diabetes Expert Consultative Com. of MOH, Beijing, 1996—; mng. dir. Liaoning Provincial Med. Assn., Shenyang, Liaoning, China, 1996—; member-in-chief Shenyang Diabetes Assn., Liaoning, China, 1997—; profl. sect. mem. Am. Diabetes Assn., Alexandria, Va., 2000—. Translator: (medical books) Obesity and Diabetes Mellitus, Cecil Textbook of Medicine Endocrine and Metabolic Disease; author: (medical work) Clinical Acupuncture of Integrated Traditional and Western Medicine, (scientific paper) An Experimental and Clinical Study of Effect of Shiliang Powder on Reducing Plasma Glucose, An Experimental Study of the Effect of Decocted Chinese Medicinal Herbs Prescription on Diabetic Rats, Effect of Ligustrum Fruit Extract on Reproduction in Experimental Diabetic Rats; dir.: (scientific paper) An Experimental Study of the Preventive Effect of Decocted Chinese Medicinal Herbs Prescription on Diabetic Chronic Complication; author: (scientific paper) A Related Study of Shenyang HLA and TAP Gene Polymorphism To LADA. Com. mem. The Chinese People's Polit. Consultative Conf., Beijing, 1998—2003. Recipient the First Session Cup of Med. St. Nat. Ministry Health, Ministry Pub. Health China, 1994, Meritorious Model Worker Shenyang, Shenyang People's Govt., 1998, An Exemplary Party Mem. China Party for Pub. Interest in Province and City, The Party Ctrl. Com. China Party for Pub. Interest, 1995, Shenyang City Model Worker China, Shenyang People's Govt., 1996, Internat. Man of the Yr. 1995, The Am. Biog. Inst. and Its Bd. Internat. Rsch. (ABI), 1996, Medal of May 1, The People's Govt. of Liaoning Province, 1997, Golden medal, Liaoning Provincial Party Com., CPC, 1997, Provincial and City Award of Achievements in Sci. & Tech., Liaoning Provincial and Shenyang City Sci. & Tech. Found., 1997; grantee The State Coun. Govt. Spl. Subsidy in China, The State Coun. China, 1997; scholar, Russian Acad. Med. Sci., 1997. Mem.: Am. Diabetes Assn. (corr.). Office: Liaoning Prov Diabetes Med Ctr 1 48 No Quanyuan Rd Dongling Dis 110015 Shenyang Liaoning China Office Fax: 862424239287.

FENG, YIMIAO, dentist; b. Taizhou, Zhejiang Province, China, Sept. 9, 1976; MS, Shanghai Jiaotong U., 2000. Dentist Chinese Orthodontic Soc., 2001. Office: Jiefang Rd 88 Hangzhou Zhejiang Province 310009 China Business E-Mail: zjxfym@126.com.

FENG, ZIXIA, research scientist; b. Shanghai, July 6, 1947; PhD, U. Tenn., 1992. Prin. scientist Novartis Insts. Bio-Med. Rsch., 1994—. Mem.: Am. Chem. Soc. Avocations: music, ping pong/table tennis. Office: 6201 South Freeway Fort Worth TX 76134 Office Fax: 817-615-3396. Business E-Mail: zixia.feng@alconlabs.com.

FENNELL, GAIL M., internist; BA in Biology summa cum laude, Mercy Coll., NY, 1988; MD, U. Conn., Farmington, 1992. Diplomate A. Bd. Internal Medicine. Intern internal medicine Greenwich Hosp./Yale Univ., Conn., 1992—93, resident internal medicine Conn., 1993—95, chief resident Conn., 1994—95; active med. staff Greenwich Hosp. Recipient Patient's Choice award, 2008—09; named Best Dr. in America, 2007—09, Best Dr., NY Mag., 2008—09, Top Physician in America, 2009, Top Doctor, Castle Conolly, 2010—11; named one of 101 Top Doctors in Fairfield County, Conn., 2008—09. Mem.: AMA, ACP. Avocations: gardening, hiking, skiing, photography. Office: Greenwich Hospital 5 Perryridge Rd Greenwich CT 06830-4697 also: Greenwich Medical Group 75 Holly Hill Lane Greenwich CT 06830 Office Phone: 203-863-3000.

FENNER, DEE ELLEN, medical educator; b. Lexington, Mo., Dec. 28, 1957; MD, U. Mich., Columbia, 1985. Prof. U. Mich., 1991—. Fellow: Am. Coll. Ob-Gyn.; mem.: Am. Urogynecologic Soc. Office: 1500 E Medical Ctr Dr Ann Arbor MI 48109-5276 Business E-Mail: deef@umich.edu.

FENNESSEY, PAUL VINCENT, pediatrics and pharmacology educator, researcher; b. Oct. 3, 1942; m. Susan Blackwell; children: Shirley, Karl, Shaun. BS in Chemistry, U. Okla., 1964; PhD of Organic Analytical Chemistry, MIT, 1968. Rsch. asst. U. Okla., Norman, 1963-64; predoctoral fellow MIT, Cambridge, 1964-69; asst. prof. pediat. and pharmacology U. Colo. Health Sci. Ctr., Denver, 1975-81, co-dir. mass spectral ctr., 1980, assoc. prof. pediat. and pharmacology, 1981-90, prof. pediat. and pharmacology, 1990—, vice chair pediat., 1991—. Contbr. articles to profl. jours. Asst. program scientist Viking Project, Martin Marietta Corp., Denver, 1969-72, program scientist, 1972-74. Recipient NSF Undergrad. Rsch. award, 1963-64, Merck award in Organic Chemistry, 1963; fellow Woodrow Wilson, 1964-65, NIH, 1964-68. Mem. Am. Chem. Soc., Am. Soc. Mass Spectrometry, Nat. Acad. Clin. Biochemists, Soc. Inherited Metabolic Diseases, Am. Soc. Pharmacology and Exptl. Therapeutics, Internat. Soc. Study Xenobiotics, Sigma Xi. Home: 13009 S Parker Ave Pine CO 80470-9617 Office: Children's Hosp 13123 East 16th Ave B-065 Aurora CO 80045 Office Phone: 720-777-7286. Business E-Mail: paul.fennessey@ucdenver.edu.

FENSKE, TIMOTHY SEAN, medical educator; b. West Allis, Wis., Apr. 18, 1969; M.S., U. Wis., Madison, 1997, MD, 1999. Assoc. prof. medicine Med. Coll. Wis., 2005—. Mem. Eastern Coop. Oncology Group, 2005—. Rsch. grant, Takeda Pharms. Mem.: Am. Soc. Hematology. Achievements include research in improving the outcomes for patients with lymphoma (both Hodgkin lymphoma and non-Hodgkin lymphoma). Avocations: motorcycling, tennis, golf. Office: Froedtert Med Coll Medicine Clin Cancer Ctr Milwaukee WI 53226 Office Fax: 414-805-4606. Business E-Mail: tfenske@mcw.edu.

FENSTERSHEIB, MARTIN, city health department administrator; b. Pitts., 1949; MD, U. Autonoma de Guadalajara, 1975. Internist MC Pa. Hosp., Phila., 1975—77; resident, pediat. Milw. Children's Hosp., 1977—79; fellow, preventive medicine U. Calif., Berkeley, 1981—82; clin. practice Ira Greene Positive PACE Clinic; health officer, pub. health med. dir. Santa Clara Co. Pub. Health Dept., San Jose, Calif., 1994—. Chair, dept. cmty. health and preventive medicine Valley Med. Ctr. Mem.: Santa Clara Co. Med. Assn. (v.p., cmty. health), Calif. Conf. of Local Health Officers (past pres.). Office: Santa Clar County Pub Health 976 Lenzen Ave San Jose CA 95126 Office Phone: 408-792-5202. Office Fax: 408-792-5203.

FENTON, JOHN EUGENE, surgeon, educator, consultant; s. James Bernard and Mary Patricia Fenton; m. Lucy Mary Borthwick, Oct. 4, 1996; children: Isolde Marie, Seamus Michael, Saorla Patricia. MB, BChir, Royal Coll. Surgeons, Dublin, Ireland, 1984; BSc in Anatomy with honors, U. Coll., Dublin, Ireland, 1986. Cons. Mid Western Regional Hosp., Limerick, Ireland, 2001—; academic Nat. Inst. Health Sciences, Limerick, Ireland, 2001—03; med. liason dir. dept. clin. therapies U. Limerick, 2002—, adj. prof.; nat. advisor on evidence-based medicine Inst. OHNS, Dublin. Mem. editl. bd. Irish Jour. of Med. Sci., 2002—; contbr. articles to profl. jours. Recipient Best Presentation award, Royal Acad. Ireland, 1994. Fellow: Royal Coll Surgeons Ireland; mem.: Irish Otolaryngology Soc. Avocations: rugby, golf, travel. Office: Dept ENT/HNS MW Regional Hosp Dooradoyle Limerick Ky Ireland Office Fax: 353 61 482921; Home Fax: 353 61 482921. E-mail: jfenton@mwbh.ie.

FENTON, KEVIN ANDREW, epidemiologist, educator; b. Glasgow, Scotland, Dec. 19, 1966; s. Sydney and Carmen F. MBBS with honors, U. West Indies, Kingston, Jamaica, 1990; MSc in Pub. Health Medicine, London Sch. Hygiene & Tropical Med., 1993; diploma in genitourinary medicine, 1994. Lectr. epidemiology UCL Med. Sch., London, 1995-99; cons. epidemiologist PHLS Communicable Disease Surveillance Ctr., London, 1999; sr. lectr. epidemiology and pub. health Royal Free and Univ. Coll. Med. Sch., London, 1999—2004; dir. HIV & Sexually Transmitted Infections Surveillance Dept. Health Protection Agy., England; chief Nat. Syphilis Elimination Effort Centers for Disease Control, Atlanta, 2005, dir. Nat. Ctr. for HIV/AIDS, Viral Hepatitis, Sexually Transmitted Diseases and Tb Prevention, 2005—. Dir. Big Up, London, 1997-2000; 2d Nat. Survey of Sexual Attitudes and Lifestyles, MRC, 1999, Mayisha Study, AVERT, 1997. Author: Exploring Ethnicity and Sexual Health, 1999. Scholar London Sch. Hygiene and Tropical Medicine, 1992; Carreras post-grad. scholar, 1992; recipient medal in ob-gyn. U. West Indies, 1990, Allenbury prize in internal medicine, 1990. Mem. Faculty of Pub. Health Medicine, Brit. Med. Assn. Office: Nat Ctr for HIV STD TB Prevention Corp Square Bldg 8 Corp Square Blvd Rm 6171 Atlanta GA 30329 Office Phone: 404-639-8000. Office Fax: 404-639-8600. E-mail: kfenton@cdc.gov. *

FENTON, LAWRENCE JULES, medical educator; b. Chgo., June 1, 1940; s. Arthur S. Fenton and Dorothy (Schochet) Wade; m. Gayle Ann Yeager, Apr. 10, 1965; children: Lori Ann Novak, Scott L. BS, U. Mich., 1962; MD, U. Cin., 1966. Diplomate Am. Bd. Pediatrics, Sub-bd. Neonatal and Perinatal Medicine; cert. in hospice palliative medicine Am. Bd. Pediatries, 2010. Intern U. Cin. Med. Ctr., 1966-67, jr. and sr. resident, 1967-69, chief pediatric resident, 1969-70, fellow neonatal, perinatal medicine, 1972-74; asst. prof. pediatrics U. Ariz. Health Scis. Ctr., Tucson, 1974-78; assoc. prof. pediatrics U. S.D. Sch. Medicine, Sioux Falls, 1978-84, head sect. of neonatal, perinatal medicine, 1979-88, prof. pediatrics, 1984—2007, chmn. dept. pediatrics, 1988—2007, prof. emeritus, 2007—. Dir. newborn intensive care unit Sioux Valley Hosp., 1980-88; chmn. pharmacy and therapeutics com. Sioux Valley Hosp., 1982-97, bd. dirs., 1997—2002; v.p. children's med. svcs. Sioux Valley Hosp. and U. S.D. Med. Ctr., 2000-02; chief sect. Pediat. Palliative Care, 2008-. Author: (with others) Current Therapy in Neonatal and Perinatal Medicine, 1989, Conn's Current Therapy, 1989, 90; contbr. articles to profl. jours. Chmn. rsch. funding group Am. Heart Assn., Dakota Affiliate, 1986-88; mem. allocations com. Childrn's Miracle Network Telethon, Sioux Falls, 1986-87; bd. dirs. Childrens Miracle Network, 1996-99; chmn. Health Svcs. Adv. Com., State of S.D., 1991-93. Maj. U.S. Army, 1970-72. Rsch. grantee Nat. Inst. Child Health and Human Devel., Tucson, Sioux Falls, 1976-79, Am. Heart Assn., Sioux Falls, 1984, grant Wellmark Found., 2007-10; recipient Army Commendation medal, 1991-93, Pioneer award S.D. Perinatal Assn., 1993; inductee Hall of Honor Children's Hosp. U. Cin. MEd. Ctr., 1993. Fellow Am. Acad. Pediatrics; mem. Society for Pediatric Rsch., Midwest Soc. for Pediat. Rsch., SD States Med. Assn., Am. Soc. Clin. Hypnosis. Avocations: water-skiing, boating, hiking, scuba diving, classical music. Office: Sanford Children's Hosp 1600 W 22nd St Sioux Falls SD 57117-5039 Office Phone: 605-312-1040. Business E-Mail: lawrence.fenton@usd.edu.

FENTON, MONICA, retired biomedical researcher; b. Elizabeth, NJ, Mar. 2, 1944; d. Edward B. and Veronica (Kryszczuk) Zacharczyk; m. C. Gerald Bischoff (div. 1971); m. Roger A. Fenton, July 30, 1983 (dec. Jan. 1995). Student, Union Coll., Cranford, NJ, 1962-66. Sr. rsch. tech. Bristol-Myers Co., Hillside, N.J., 1963-75; tech. adminstr., electron microscopist Albert Einstein Coll. Medicine, Bronx, N.Y., 1975-88; asst. to dir. Ctr. Rsch. Occupational & Environ. Toxicology Oreg. Health Sci. U., 1988—2000; ret., 2000. Mng. editor Third World Med. Rsch. Found., N.Y.C., 1987-95, editorial cons., 1990—; corr. & devel. editor Experimental and Clinical Neurotoxicology, 1992-2000; copy editor (proc.) The Grass Pea: Threat and Promise, 1989, Nutrition, Neurotoxins and Lathyrism, 1994, (transcripts) Toxicity of Cycads, 1988; contbr. articles to profl. jours. Mem. Electron Microscopy Soc. Am. Avocations: skiing, biking, gourmet cooking. Home: PO Box 880321 Steamboat Springs CO 80488-0321

FENWICK, SHERIDAN MELLON, psychologist, director; d. Robert Thomas and Janet Mellon Fenwick; m. Worth V. Bruntjen, May 26 (dec.); 1 child, Ashley Fenwick Naditch stepchildren: Warner Bruntjen, Eric Bruntjen. BA, Goucher Coll., 1963; attended, Yale Law Sch., 1963—64; D in psychology, Cornell U., 1975. Dir. social policy planning City Chgo., 1965—70; asst. prof. Columbia U., NYC, 1975—77; dir. behavioral med. clinic Abbott-N.W. Hosp., Mpls., 1981—94; exec. officer Psy Bar, LLC, Edina, Minn., 1995—. Trustee, chmn. academic affairs com. Mpls. Coll. Art and Design, 1992—99; chmn. Ripley Meml. Found., 1993—95. Author: Getting It, 1976. Trustee Illusion Theater, 1990—96. Mem.: Jane Austen Soc. Avocations: tennis, bicycling. Office: Psy Bar LLC 5150 Edina Ind Blvd Edina MN

FENZL, VANJA, gynecologist; b. Zagreb, Croatia, Aug. 16, 1966; MD, Med. Sch., U. Zagreb, 1990; PhD, U. Zagreb, 2011. Specialist ob-gyn. U. Hosp. Merkur, 2000—11, specialist ob-gyn. dept. human reproduction, 2010—. Lectr. U. Applied Health Studies, Zagreb, 2010—11; ob-gyn. intern U. Vienna. Home: Bijenicka 52 Zagreb 10000 Croatia Business E-Mail: vanja.radic@inet.hr.

FERBER, RICHARD ALLEN, neurologist, educator; b. Mar. 11, 1944; MD, Harvard Med. Sch., 1970. Intern Children's Hosp. Boston, 1970—71, resident, 1973—74, fellow, 1974—79, sr. assoc. neurology, dir. Ctr. for Pediatric Sleep Disorders; staff assoc. in neurology Nat. Inst. Health, 1971—73; assoc. prof. neurology Harvard Med. Sch. Mem.: Nat. Sleep Found., Am. Bd. Sleep Medicine, Am. Acad. Pediatrics, Am. Acad. Sleep Medicine. Office: Children's Hospital Neurophysiology, Fegan 9 300 Longwood Avenue Boston MA 02115 also: Center for Pediatric Sleep Disorders 9 Hope Ave Waltham MA 02453 Office Phone: 617-355-6663, 781-216-2570. Office Fax: 617-730-0463, 781-216-2516.

FERBER, SARI GOLDSTEIN, psychologist; d. Jeny and Bruno Goldstein; m. Gidon Ferber, Apr. 17, 1986 (div.); children: Yaara, Timna, Lotem; life ptnr. Daniel Jaron. PhD, Bar Ilan U., Ramat Gan Israel, 1998; postgrad., Harvard Med. Sch., 2004. Cert. clinical psychologist Ministry Health, Israel, 1988, specialist Newborn Individualized Devel. Care and Assessment Program, 2004, Assessment of Pre-term Infant Behavior specialist Harvard Med. Sch., 2005. Lectr. Haifa U., Israel, 2001—06; lectr. program for security and diplomacy studies Tel Aviv U., 2007—. Chief scientist, Interdisciplinary Ctr. Technol. Analysis and Forecasting Tel Aviv U., 2004—05; vis. prof. divsn. neurodevel. sci., dept. psychiatry NY State Psychiatric Inst. Columbia U. Med. Sch.; dir. devel. core Wolfson Med. Ctr. Dept. Neonatology, Suckler Sch. Medicine-Tel Aviv U. Assoc.: Behavioral and Brain Sciences, 2006—. 1st sgt. Israeli mil., 1976—79. Decorated Mil. Svc. award Israeli Def. Forces Chief Staff; recipient Intelligence Dept. award, Israeli Intelligence Heritage and Co-memorial Center, Inbar Found., 2005; grantee, Pentagon Office of Net Assessment; Rsch. grant, Binational Am. Israeli Sci. Found., 2004—. Mem.: Newborn Individualized Devel. Care and Assessment Program Fedn. Internat. Achievements include first to adopt research methods such as microanalitic methods for analysis of verbal and visual data; research in developing the field of psychostrategy; strategic nuclear froliferation; first woman reporter from battlefield, Israeli Def. Forces, Lebanon. Avocations: running, travel, music, poetry, writing. Personal E-mail: ferbers@post.tau.ac.il.

FERENCZ, CHARLOTTE, retired pediatrician, epidemiologist; b. Budapest, Hungary, Oct. 28, 1921; came to U.S., 1954; d. Paul Ferencz and Livia deFekete. BSc, McGill U., 1944, MD, CM, 1945; MPH, Johns Hopkins U., 1970. Cert. pediatrics Royal Coll. Physicians and Surgeons, Can., pediatric cardiology Am. Bd. Pediatrics. Demonstrator McGill U., Montreal, 1952-54; asst. prof. pediatrics Johns Hopkins U., Balt., 1954-58, U. Cin., 1959-60; asst. prof. SUNY, Buffalo, 1960-66, assoc. prof., 1966-73; assoc. prof. epidemiology and preventive medicine U. Md. Sch. Medicine, Balt., 1973-74, prof., 1974-98, prof. pediatrics, 1985—2008, prof. emeritus, 1998—2008. Prin. investigator population based study Etiology of Congenital Heart Disease, 1981-89; mem. epidemiology and disease control study sect. NIH, 1984-88; pres. Delta Omega Alpha chpt. Pub. Health Soc., 1990-92. Recipient M.E.S. Abbott scholarship McGill U., 1943-45, M.E.R.I.T. award Nat. Heart, Lung & Blood Inst., 1987, Fogarty Internat. Ctr. Health Sci. Exchange award NIH, 1988, Helen B. Taussig award Am. Heart Assn. Md. Affiliate, 1991, Achievement award Univ. Ctr. Life Scis., Balt., 1993, Johns Hopkins U. Disting. Alumnus award, 2001, Health Sci. Libr., Theodore E Woodward award U. Md., 2008; named to Johns Hopkins Women's Med. Alumnae Assn. Hall of Fame, 2011. Fellow Am. Acad. Pediatrics (Spl. Achievement award Md. chpt. 1994), Am. Coll. Cardiology; mem. Teratology Soc. Democrat.

FERENTINO, SHEILA CONNOLLY, psychologist, consultant; d. John Francis Connolly and Mabel Rose McCabe; 1 child, James. BA, Hunter Coll. CUNY; MS in Spl. Edn., CUNY, 1963; profl. diploma in Psychology, St. John's U., 1973; PhD in Psychology, Hofstra U., 1991. Cert. tchr. blind and partially sighted NYS, 1962, braillist Libr. Congress, 1964, sch. psychologist NY, 1972, lic. psychologist NY, 1993. Tchr. elem. sch. Nassau County Sch. Dist., 1960—61; tchr. blind Nassau Bd. Cooperative Edn. Svcs. Spl. Edn., NY, 1961—72, psychologist, 1972—2004; child psychologist, children with disabilities pvt. practice, Freeport, NY, 2005—. Tchr. Summer Headstart, Hollis, NY, 1968—69, dir., 1970; adj. prof. Hunter Coll. CUNY, NYC, 1963—65; asst. dir. after sch. activities for blind Bd. Cooperative Edn. Svcs., 1965—70. Contbr. articles to profl. jours. Chmn. mus. trips com. Helen Keller Svcs. for Blind, Nassau County, 1961—70; contbr. Evaluation Measures for Handicapped Pre-Schoolers. Grantee, NY State Dept. Edn., 1980, 1989, Vanderbilt U., 1988. Mem.: APA, Nat. Assn. Prevention Blindness, Nassau Couny Psychol. Assn., NY State Psychol. Assn., Sigmund Freud Soc., Orton Soc. Avocations: classical music, opera, travel, wildlife conservation, maritime museums. Office: 110 Garfield St Freeport NY 11520 Office Phone: 917-655-5691. Personal E-mail: posone@verizon.net.

FERGUSON, AMANDA ELIZABETH, psychologist, writer; b. Sydney, May 10, 1962; d. David Arnold Keith and Anne Elizabeth Ferguson. BA in Social Anthropology with honors, U. Sydney; M in Orgnl. Psychology, Macquarie U., 2000. Registered clin. hypnotherapist. Tech. writer Westpac, 1987—88, Fujitsu, 1988; sr. book editor Reader's Digest, Sydney, 1988—92; policy oficer NSW Cancer Coun., 1993—95; mgr. Wild & Woolley Book Pub., Sydney, 1995—98; counsellor, registered psychologist pvt. practice, Sydney, 1994—. Author: Lifeworks: Rediscover Yourself, 2002, jour. articles in field. Mem.: APA, Australian Soc. Clin. Hypnotherapists, Australian Psychol. Soc., Australian Soc. Authors, Australian Psychologists Soc. Achievements include appearing regularly in print and on radio and TV in Australia. Avocations: running, swimming, meditation, sailing. Home: PO Box 921 Spit Junction 2088 Australia Office: SE 17 L I 3 Brady St 2088 Sydney NSW Australia Office Phone: 61 2 99600116. Office Fax: 61 02 9960 0144. Business E-Mail: amanda@lifethatworks.com.

FERGUSON, EARL WILSON, cardiologist, healthcare executive; b. Lebanon, Pa., Aug. 29, 1943; s. Warren Earl and Norma Laura (Wilson) F.; m. Sun Hye Paik, May 1, 1998; children: Steven Mark, Matthew Earl, Erin Lee. BA in Chemistry, Baylor U., 1965; MD, PhD in Physiology, U. Tex., Galveston, 1970. Diplomate Am. Bd. Internal Medicine, Cardiovasc. Disease, Am. Bd. Preventive Medicine. Grad. tchg. asst. dept. physiology U. Tex. Med. Br., Galveston, 1967-70, intern medicine, 1970-71; resident medicine, then fellow cardiology Duke U. Med. Ctr., Durham, NC, 1971-75, mem. assoc. faculty dept. medicine, 1974-75; research assoc. cardiology VA Hosp., Durham, 1974-75; commd. lt. USAF, 1966, advanced through grades to col., 1984-95; staff cardiologist, dir. coronary care Wilford Hall USAF Med. Ctr., Lackland AFB, Tex., 1975-76, chief cardiology, dir. cardiology tng. program, 1983-84; asst. prof. biochemistry, medicine and mil. medicine Uniformed Svcs. U. Health Scis., Bethesda, Md., 1976-80, assoc. prof. physiology, medicine and mil. medicine, 1980-84, asst. comdt., 1977-82, mem. faculty senate, 1979-80, adj. prof. physiology, 1984-93; dir. hosp. svcs. USAF Med. Ctr., Scott AFB, Ill., 1984-86; comdr. USAF Hosp., Little Rock AFB, Ark., 1986-88; dep. command surgeon Mil. Airlift Command, Scott AFB, 1988-90; comdr. USAF Med. Ctr., Wiesbaden, Germany, 1990-93; dir. Aerospace Medicine and Occupl. Health NASA, Washington, 1993-96; CEO Sun Biomed. Techs., 2000—. Cons. to surgeon gen. for cardiology, medicine and physiology USAF, 1980—95; cons. NJ State Police and NJ Atty. Gen.'s Office, 1984—90, Ind. Atty. Gen's Office, 1985—87, NASA, 1997—, life scis. subcom., 1989—93; adj. assoc. prof. preventive medicine Uniformed Svcs. U. Health Scis., Bethesda, Md., 1993—96; interagency working group on telemedicine NASA, 1994—96; advisor House/Senate Com. on telemedicine and health care, 1994—96; physician So. Sierra Med. Clinic, Ridgecrest, Calif., 1996—2007; corp. bd. Ridgecrest Regional Hosp., 1997—, chief of medicine, 2001—04; chair bd. dir. Calif. Telemedicine and eHealth Ctr., 2002—04, adv. com., 2004—05; clin. prof., health policy & mgmt. Health Sci. Ctr. Loma Linda U., 2005—; chief of staff Ridgecrest Regional Hosp., 2005—06; external adv. com. Nat. Space Biomed. Rsch. Inst., Houston, 2006—; dir., telemedicine outreach rural health care devel. Ridgecrest Regional Hosp., 2007—11; exec. dir. Southern Sierra Telehealth Network, 2004—, Calif. Telehealth Network Bd. Dir., 2008—, mem. exec. com., 2010—, Calif. Health & Human Svcs., 2010—. Mem. editl. bd.: Telemedicine and e-Health Jour., 1996—2003, 2007—; contbr. articles to profl. jours. Rsch. grantee VA, 1974-75, Dept. Def., 1976-82, NASA, 1982-84, Coop. R&D Agreements, Naval Air Warfare Ctr., China Lake, Calif., 2000—, Dept. Def. SBIRS, 2002-08, NSF, 2004-05, Ctr. Disease Control, 2006—10, Coop. R&D Agreement Naval Air Warfare Ctr., VA, Loma Linda, U. Sao Paulo, Naval Med. Rsch. Ctr., Walter Reed Army Med. Ctr., Walter Reed Army Inst. Rsch 2002-; Cardiovasc. Health fellow Health Forum/Am. Hosp. Assn., 1999-00; Ashbel Smith Disting. Grad., 1993-. Fellow ACP, Am. Coll. Cardiology (bd. govs. 1985-88), Am. Coll. Preventive Medicine, Calif. State Rural Healthcare Assn. (bd. dirs. 2006—, chair, Rural Tech. Advocacy. Com. 2008-, pres. elect. 209-10, pres. 2010-11, United Healthcare-PacifiCare grant, 2008-11, HRSA grant, 2008-11). Unitarian Universalist. Avocations: physical fitness activities, flying. Office: Ridgecrest Regional Hosp 1081 N China Lake Blvd Ridgecrest CA 93555 Business E-Mail: info@sunbmt.com.

FERGUSON, JOHN DUNCAN, medical research educator; b. Saskatoon, Sask., Can., Aug. 20, 1929; s. George Alexander and Urdine (LeValley) F.; m. Tamara van den Bergh, Sept. 12, 1958. MA, U. Toronto, Ont., Can., 1956; PhD, Columbia U., 1966. Project dir. Bur. Applied Social Rsch., Columbia U., NYC, 1958-64; asst. prof. Northeastern U., Boston, 1966-68; from assoc. prof. to prof. U. Windsor, Ont., 1968—; mem. assoc. med. staff Harper Hosp., Detroit, 1982-2000, rsch. cons., 2000—. Author reports in field. Grantee Ont. Cmty. and Social Svcs. Ministry, 1991-93. Presbyterian. Home: 1516 Iroquois Ave Detroit MI 48214-2747 Office: U Windsor Windsor ON Canada N9B 3P4 E-mail: tamjackferg@worldnet.att.net.

FERGUSON, JOHN PATRICK, health facility administrator; b. Weehawken, NJ, Jan. 22, 1949; s. Donald George and Margaret (Rienzo) F.; m. Gene Marie Promersperger, Jan. 16, 1971; children: Adam, David, Kate. BS in Econs., St. Peter's Coll., 1970; MBA in Hosp. Adminstrn., George Washington U., 1973; LHD (hon.), Felician Coll., 2005. Sr. v.p. St. Vincent's Hosp., NYC, 1972-81; v.p. ops. Hackensack U. Med. Ctr., NJ, 1981—85, sr. v.p., 1985, acting pres., chief exec. officer, 1985—86, pres., chief exec. officer, 1986—2009; chmn. bd., CEO & pres. Blue Horizon Internat. LLC, NYC. Pres. Met. Health Adminstrs., NYC, 1977—78; adj. faculty New Sch. for Social Rsch. Grad. Sch. Mgmt. and Urban Professions, NYC, 1978—84; chmn. bd. trustees Univ. Health Sys. (now NJ Coun. Tchg. Hosps.),

Trenton, 1999—2001, vice chmn., 2002—03; trustee UMDNJ, 2002—05, sec. bd. trustees, 2003—05. Trustee Garden State Arts Found., 2004—07; mem. jobs growth and econ. devel. commn. State of NJ, 2002; co-chmn. health transition team Gov.-elect Jim McGreevey, 2001; trustee Molly Found. for Diabetes Rsch., 1995—; commr. Econ. Devel. Commn. of City of Hackensack, 1996—2002; founding commr. Bergen County Econ. Devel. Corp., 1996—2007; mem., bd. govs. Greater NY Hosp. Assn., 2000—; trustee St. Peter's Coll., 2000—06; mem. bd. dirs. Martha's Vineyard Hosp., Inc., 2000—; chmn. bd. dirs. Martha's Vineyard Hosp., 2002—; mem. exec adv. com. State of NJ Commn. on Cancer Rsch., 2000. Recipient Man of Yr. award, Tomorrow's Children's Fund, 1989, Medallion award, Bergen CC, 1993, Disting. Cmty. Svc. award, Anti-Defamation League, 1995, Disting. Citizen award, Hackensack C. of C., 1995, Disting. Cmty. Health Svc. award, Bergen County Bd. of Chosen Freeholders, 1996, Pres.'s award, NJ State Nurses Assn., 1999, Med. Exec. award, Acad. Medicine NJ, 2000, Good Scout award, No. NJ Coun. Boy Scouts Am., 2000, Ellis Island medal of honor, 2002, Disting. Alumni award for profl. achievement, St. Peter's Coll., 2002, Humanitarian award, Nat. Conf. for Cmty. and Justice, 2003, Disting. Alumni award, George Washington U. Health Sci. Mgmt. and Policy, 2004, County of Bergen Significant Contbr. honor, Bergen Cath. HS, 2006, Achievement award, Modern Healthcare Mag., 2007, Leadership award, New England Healthcare Assembly Trustee, 2008; named One of Top 12 Up and Coming Healthcare Execs., Modern Healthcare mag., 1988, One of 50 Bus. People to Watch for the 1990's, NJ Bus. Jour., 1990, Citizen of Yr., Meadowlands Regional C. of C., 1993, Man of Yr., Nat. Burn Victim Found., 1994, Humanitarian of Yr., Make A Wish Found., 1996, Disting. Citizen of NJ, Ramapo Coll. Found., 1998, Humanitarian of Yr., Boys' Towns of Italy, 1999; named one of 100 Most Powerful People in Healthcare in US, Modern Healthcare Mag., 2004, 2005, 2006, NJ 50 Most Influential Players in Polit. Healthcare Arena, Healthsense, Inc., 2005, 400 People Who Make a Difference, Cape Cod Life Mag., 2007; named to, Found. for Free Enterprise Hall of Fame, 2002. Fellow: Am. Coll. Healthcare Execs. (regent, gov. dist. II 1994—99, Regents Recognition award 2004); mem.: Met. Health Adminstrn. Assn. (Distinction award 1997), Am. Fedn. for Aging Rsch. (bd. dirs. 1997—2000), Commerce and Industry Assn. NJ (bd. dirs. 1996—, chmn.'s award for Outstanding Leadership 1997), Am. Heart Assn. (pres. Mid-Bergen divsn. 1992—93, bd. dirs. 1993—94), Cath. Hosp. Assn., Am. Hosp. Assn. Office: Blue Horizon Internat LLC 300 West 14th St Ste 304 New York NY 10014 Business E-Mail: lgiani@humed.com, jferguson@bluehorizonhospital.com.

FERGUSON, THOMAS BRUCE, JR., cardiothoracic surgeon; b. St. Louis, Mo., June 22, 1953; MD, Wash. U., St. Louis, 1979. Cert. Am. Bd. Thoracic Surgery, Am. Bd. Surgery. Resident, gen. & thoracic surgery Duke U. med. Ctr., Durham, NC, 1979—88; hosp. appointment Barnes Hosp., St. Louis, assoc. prof. surgery, divsn. cardiothoracic surgery Wash. U.; staff physician East Carolina Heart Inst.; assoc. dir., cardiothoracic and vascular surgery East Carolina U. Contbr. articles to profl. jours. Office: East Carolina Heart Inst Brody Outpatient Ctr 600 Moye Blvd TA 340 Greenville NC 27834 Office Phone: 252-744-5232. Office Fax: 252-744-5233. E-mail: Fergusont@ecu.edu.

FERLINI, CRISTIANO, biomedical researcher; b. Rome, Nov. 25, 1965; MD, U. Florence, 1990; PhD, U. Rome, 1995. Dir. biomedical rsch. Danbury Hosp., 2009—. Clin. prof. U. Vt., 2010. Mem.: AACR. Office: 131 West St Danbury CT 06810 Office Fax: 203-739-8739. Business E-Mail: cristiano.ferlini@danhosp.org.

FERLINZ, JACK, cardiologist, educator; b. Marburg, Austria, Feb. 18, 1942; came to U.S., 1957. s. Anthony and Maria (Nachtigall) F. AB, Harvard U.; MBA, Northeastern U., 1965; MD, Boston U., 1969; doctorate (hon.), U. Maribor, Slovenia, 1990. Diplomate Am. Bd. Internal Medicine, Am. Bd. Cardiovascular Diseases. Intern. U. Hosp. Boston U., 1969-70; jr. resident M. Hitchcock Hosp. Dartmouth Med. Sch., Hanover, NH, 1970-71; sr. resident Jackson Meml. Hosp., U. Miami, 1971-72; NIH rsch. fellow cardiology P.B. Brigham Hosp., Harvard U., Boston, 1972-74; dir. cardiac cath. lab., asst. chief cardiology V.A.M.C., Long Beach, Calif., 1974-82; asst. prof. medicine U. Calif., Irvine, 1975-81, assoc. prof. medicine, 1981-82; chmn. adult cardiology Cook County Hosp., Chgo., 1982-88; prof. medicine Chgo. Med. Sch., North Chicago, Ill., 1984-88; chmn. dept. of internal medicine Providence Hosp., Southfield, Mich., 1988-92; clin. prof. medicine Wayne State U. Sch. Medicine, Detroit, 1989-92; dir. med. edn. & rsch., prof. medicine & cardiology Hamad Med. Ctr., Doha, Qatar, 1992-94; chief dept. medicine Aleda E. Lutz VA Med. Ctr., Saginaw, Mich., 1994—2006, assoc. chief staff, 2006—07; attending staff Mich. Cardiovasc. Inst., 2007—; clin. prof. medicine Mich. State U. Coll. Human Medicine, 1994—. Vis. prof. numerous U.S., Canadian and European med. schs., 1980—. Mem. editl. bds. Am. Jour. Cardiology, 1989—, Am. Jour. Noninvas Cardiology, 1987-2001, Jour. Am. Coll. Cardiology, 1984-88, 89-93; contbr. over 300 book chpts. and sci. papers. Named to Begg's Soc. Boston U. Sch. Medicine, 1969. Fellow Am. Coll. Cardiology, Am. Coll. Chest Physicians (chmn. coronary sect. 1983-85), Am. Heart Assn., Am. Coll. Physicians, Am. Coll. Angiology; mem. Am. Fedn. Clin. Rsch., Am. Soc. Clin. Pharm. Therapy. Avocations: mountain climbing, skiing, tennis, scuba diving. Office: 4039 Parsons Walk Saginaw MI 48603-7260 Home Phone: 989-792-6244; Office Phone: 989-276-0010. Business E-Mail: jcreplusw@ad.com.

FERNANDES, ANDRE, medical association administrator; b. Salvador, Bahia, Brazil, June 3, 1977; D, Fed. U. Medicine, 1996. Coord. Hosp. Ana Neri, 2008—. Fellow: Fed. U. Bahia. Office: Rua Saldanha Marinho S/N Hosp Ana Neri Salvador Bahia 40000 Brazil Personal E-mail: andremsf@hotmail.com.

FERNANDES, JANAINA, healthcare educator, researcher; b. Rio de Janeiro, Apr. 14, 1973; B, Fundação Técnico-educacional Souza Marques, 1994; M, U. Fed. do Rio de Janeiro, 2000; PhD, U. Ulm, Germany, 2004, U. Fed. do Rio de Janeiro, 2005. Postdoc. fellow U. Fed. do Rio de Janeiro, 2005—09, adj. prof., 2009—. Editl. bd. mem. Omics Pub. Group, 2009; ad hoc advisor Brazilian Ministry Health. Recipient Carlos Chagas Filho award, UFF Vasconcellos Torres award; grant, Programa Nacional de pós Doutorado, DAAD, Auxilio Instalação. Mem.: AAAS, Am. Chem. Soc. Avocations: piano, movies, history. Home: Rua da Tangerina 46 Curicica Rio de Janeiro 22780-630 Brazil

FERNANDEZ, JAMIE WINDERBAUM, physician, educator; b. NY, Oct. 14, 1976; MD, Cornell U., 2004. Asst. prof. U. South Fla., 2008—. Office: 3515 E Fletcher Ave MDC 14 Tampa FL 33613 Business E-Mail: jfernan1@health.usf.edu.

FERNANDEZ, JOHN J., orthopedist; m. Nicole Fernandez. BS magna cum laude, U. Akron, 1986; MD, N.E. Ohio U. Coll. Med., 1990. Lic. Ill., Ind., Fla., Penn., diplomate Nat. Bd. Med. Examiners, 1991, Am. Bd. Independent Med. Examiners, 1998, Am. Bd. Orthopaedic Surgery, 1998. V.p. Southern Fla. Microsurgical Assoc., 1997—98; dir. microsurgery Midwest Orthopaedics, Chgo., 1998—; asst. prof., orthopaedic dept. Rush Presbyn.-St. Luke's Hosp., 1998—. Intern, gen. surgery U. Pitts. Med. Ctr., 1990—91, residency, orthopaedic surgery, 1991—95; fell., hand and microvascular surgery Ind. Hand Ctr., Indianapolis, 1995—96. Contbr. articles to numerous profl. jours. Recipient award of Distinction, Ohio Regents Bd., 1984, Ann Schilling Scholar, 1988—89, Kopsch award, 1988—89. Mem.: Am. Coll. Occupational and Environ. Medicine, Am. Soc. Surgery of the Hand, Am. Acad. Orthopaedic Surgeons. Avocations: running, carpentry, target shooting. Office: Midwest Orthopaedics at Rush 1725 West Harrison St Ste 1042 Chicago IL 60612 Office Phone: 312-432-2300.

FERNANDEZ, JOVELLE B. LAOAG, obstetrician, gynecologist, medical researcher; b. Pangasinan, Philippines, Sept. 20, 1967; d. Juliana Bautista and Jovencio Collante Laoag; m. Alex Marcelo Fernandez, Sept. 9, 1966; children: Abel Jovince, Aebert Justin, Alexis Julian. BS in Biology, St. Louis U., 1987, MD, 1992; PhD, Kobe U., 2003. Bd. Cert. Bd. Of Medicine, 1993, Bd. Cert. Fellow Phil Bd. of Ob-Gyn, 2002. Resident physician St. Louis U. Hosp., Baguio, Philippines, 1994—98; vis. cons. Asian Med. Hosp., Manila, Philippines, 2002—; post-doc rschr. Kobe Univ Hosp., Japan, 2003—. Cons. Asian Med. Drs. Assn., Osaka, Japan, 1998—, Philippine Org., Osaka, 1999—; rschr. reproductive endocrinology, gynecologic oncology. Editor: (newletter) Baguio Benguet Med. Soc. Newsletter. Health adv. Dept. Edn., Culture and Sports, Philippines, 1993. Recipient Grand prize, Philippine Obstetrics and Gynecol. Soc., 1997, 2000, Japan Soc. of Obstetrics and Gynecology, 1999, Rsch. award, Dept. of Sci. and Tech., 1998; Japanese govt. scholar, Ministry of Edn. and Sci., 1998—2003. Fellow: Philippine Soc. Obstetrics and Gynecology; mem.: Internat. Soc. Endocrinology, Internat. Soc. Ultrasound in Obstetrics and Gynecology, Philippine Med. Assn. (life), Japan Soc. Obstetrics and Gynecology. Achievements include research in reproductive endocrinology, infertility and oncology. Personal E-mail: docjovelle@med.kobe-u.ac.jp.

FERNANDEZ-BOTRAN, RAFAEL, biology professor; b. Guatemala City, Aug. 13, 1957; BS in Biol. Chemistry, U. San Carlos, Guatemala, 1979; PhD in Immunology, U. Kans. Med. Ctr., 1985. Asst. prof. U. Louisville, 1992—2000, assoc. prof., 2000—. Mem. Inst. Molecular Diversity and Drug Design, 1999, Ctr. Genetics and Molecular Medicine, 2002; exec. coun. mem. Autumn Immunology Conf., 2000. Recipient Biomedical Scis. award, U. Kans. Alumni Assn., New Investigator Recognition award, Clin. Immunology Soc., Pres.'s Young Investigator award, U. Louisville. Mem.: Internat. Cytokine Soc. (ICS), Soc. for Leukocyte Biology (SLB), Am. Assn. of Immunologists (AAI), Internat. Network of Sci., Tech. and Innovation of Guatemala. Avocations: music, cooking, sports. Office: University Louisville 511 South Floyd St Louisville KY 40292 Office Fax: 502-852-1177. Business E-Mail: rafael@louisville.edu.

FERNANDEZ BREIS, JESUALDO TOMAS, biology professor; b. Archena, Murcia, Spain, May 20, 1976; PhD in Computer Sci., U. Murcia, 2003. Assoc. prof. U. Murcia, 2008—. Recipient Best Rsch. Paper, EKAW, 2010. Mem.: Internat. Assn. Ontology and its Applications, Internat. Soc. Computational Biology. Office: Facultad Informatica Campus Espinardo Murcia 30071 Spain Business E-Mail: jfernand@um.es.

FERNANDEZ-BUSSY, SEBASTIAN, medical educator; b. Argentina, Mar. 29, 1971; MD, U. Salvador, Argentina, 1997; degree in Pulmonary and Critical Care, U. Fla., 2007. Asst. prof. U. Fla., 2007—. Mem.: Am. Bronchology Assn. Home: 2725 SW 91st St Ste 110 Gainesville FL 32608 Business E-Mail: bussysf@medicine.ufl.edu.

FERNANDEZ-CASTILLO, ANTONIO, psychology professor; b. Granada, Spain, Feb. 4, 1967; PhD, U. Granada, 1998. Prof. U. Granada, 1995. Office: Faculty Educational Scis Campus Granada 10071 Spain Business E-Mail: afcastil@ugr.es.

FERNANDEZ-DEL CASTILLO, CARLOS, surgeon, director; b. Mexico City, Jan. 11, 1959; MD, Nat. Autonomous U. Mex., 1982. Dir., pancreas and biliary surgery program Mass. Gen. Hosp., 1991—. Prof., surgery Harvard Med. Sch. Recipient Tchg. award, Harvard Med. Sch. Fellow: ACS; mem.: Am. Pancreatic Assn., Am. Surg. Assn. Office: Mass Gen Hosp 15 Parkman St Boston MA 02114 Business E-Mail: cfernandez@partners.org.

FERNANDO, NEIL VERNON PATRICK, medical educator, academic administrator; b. Colombo, Sri Lanka, May 18, 1928; arrived in Malaysia, 1983; s. P. Nataniel and Rose Mabel (Wickramaratne) F.; m. Kalyani Gamage Haththotuwa, Oct. 22, 1957; children: Michael, Patrick, Kevin, Danny, Kenneth. B in Medicine and Surgery, U. Ceylon, Colombo, Sri Lanka, 1953; PhD in Pathology, U. Toronto, Ont., Can., 1963. Supernumeray pathologist Gen. Hosp. of Colombo, 1963-67; provincial pathologist Galle (Sri Lanka) Dept. of Health, 1967-69; pathologist U. Teaching Hosps., Kandy, Sri Lanka, 1970-76, Colombo, 1976-83; assoc. prof. Sch. of Med. Scis. U. Sains Malaysia, West Malaysia, 1983-93, head pathology dept., 1985-89; prof. pathology, internat. student advisor St. Georges U. Sch. Medicine, Grenada, West Indies, 1993—2002; prof. pathology Sch. Medicine U. Sint Eustatius, Netherlands Antilles, 2003—04; vol. social worker, 2005—. Vol. social worker, Scarborough, Canada, 2005. Personal E-mail: neilkaly@rogers.com.

FERNANDO, SUJATHA SAROJINI, pathologist, educator, researcher; b. Colombo, Sri Lanka, Dec. 14, 1944; m. Ranjan Lakdasa Fernando; children: Suran, Lakmalie Perera. MBBS (hon.), Faculty Medicine Colombo, Sri-Lanka, 1968; MSc (with distinction), U. London, 1975. Cons. histo/cyto pathologist S. Western Area Pathology Svcs. Liverpool, NSW, Australia, 1980—84; dir. pathology Bankstown Hosp., 1984—89; dir. anatomical pathology S. Western Area Pathology Svcs. Liverpool, 1989—97; sr. lectr. U. New South Wales, 1989—97; dir. anatomical pathology Quinn Pathology Svcs., 1997—2002; dir. lab. svcs., dir. anatomical cytopathology, sr. cons. Ctrl. West Pathology Svcs., Orange NSW, Australia; clin. assoc. prof. U. Sydney, 2002—. Fellow: Internat. Acad. Cytology, Royal Coll. Pathologists Australia. Home: 11/162 Burwood Rd 2137 Concord NSW Australia Office Phone: 0428121700.

FERNIANY, WILLIAM (ISAAC WILLIAM FERNIANY), health system administrator; b. Mobile, Ala., Mar. 15, 1951; s. Joe Michael and Vivian Elizabeth (Farah) F.; m. Dana Brownell Hardy, Apr. 19, 1978; children: Dylan Hardy, Glennie Brownell. BS, U. Ala., 1973; MS, U. Ala., Birmingham, 1975, PhD, 1984. Asst. adminstr. Bryce Hosp., Tuscaloosa, 1975—77; dir. resource devel. S.W. Health Systems Agy., Mobile, 1977—79; owner Mgmt. Resources, Birmingham, 1981—83; faculty U. Ala., Birmingham, 1982—83; v.p. devel. Health Care Services Am., Birmingham, 1983—87; CEO Hill Crest Hosp., Birmingham, 1987—88; exec. adminstr. U. Ala., Birmingham, 1988—90, assoc. adminstr. strategic planning and market devel., 1990—; sr. v.p. and chief adminstrv. officer U. Pa. Health System, Phila., 1992—2006; assoc. vice chancellor, CEO U. Miss. Med. Ctr. (UMMC), Jackson, 2006—08; CEO UAB Health Sys., 2008—. Mem. faculty U. Ala., Birmingham, 1987-92, lectr., 1993—; adj. faculty Wharton Sch. Bus., 1993—; sr. fellow Leonard Davis Inst., 1993—. Author: Bay Area Directory, 1979. Mem.: Am. Mktg. Soc. Episcopalian. Avocations: bike riding, walking, kayaking. Office: UAB Health Sys John N Whitaker Bldg 500 22nd St S, Ste 408 Birmingham AL 35233-3110 Office Phone: 205-975-5362. E-mail: wferniany@yahoo.com.

FERNICOLA, DANIEL JEROME, cardiologist, educator; MD, Georgetown U. Diplomate Am. Bd. Internal Medicine, Am. Bd. Internal Medicine-cardiovasc. disease. Resident internal medicine Thomas Jefferson Univ. Hosp.; fellow Nat. Heart, Lung and Blood Inst., 1991—93; fellow cardiology Georgetown Univ. Med. Ctr., 1993—96; asst. prof. medicine Georgetown Univ.; hosp. affiliations include Wash. Adventist Hosp., Shady Grove Adventist Hosp., Suburban Hosp.; dir. non-invasive vascular testing Cardiovasc. Consultants. Named one of Top Doctors, Washingtonian Mag., 2011. Office: Cardiovascular Consultants Ste 306 15215 Shady Grove Rd Rockville MD 20850 Office Phone: 301-990-0040. Office Fax: 301-990-0043.

FERRARA, NAPOLEONE M.A., molecular oncologist; b. Catania, Italy, July 26, 1956; arrived in US, 1983; MD cum laude, U. Catania Med. Sch., 1981. Resident dept. ob-gyn. U. Catania Med. Sch., 1981—85; rsch. fellow gynecology and reproductive scis. U. Calif. Reproductive Endocrinology Ctr., San Francisco, 1983—85; intern dept. ob-gyn. Oreg. Health Scis. U., Portland, 1985—86; rsch. fellow U. Calif. Cancer Rsch. Inst., San Francisco, 1986—88; scientist Genentech, South San Francisco, 1988—93, sr. scientist, 1993—97, staff scientist, 1997—2002, fellow dept. molecular oncology, 2002—. Mem. editl. bd.: Angiogenesis, Cardiac and Vascular Regneration, Endothelium, Jour. Cardiovasc. Pathobiology, Jour. Clin. Investigation, Vascular Pharmacology; contbr. articles to sci. jours. Recipient Prize for rsch. in opthalmic disorders, Italian Assn. Search & Cure Diseases of Eyes, 2004, Am.-Italian Cancer Found. prize, 2004, Discover Mag. award for medicine, 2004, Bruce F. Cain Meml. award, Am. Assn. Cancer Rsch., 2005, Passano award, 2006, GM Cancer Rsch. award, 2006, Soc. Medicines Rsch. award, 2006, C. Chester Stock award, Meml. Sloan-Kettering Cancer Ctr., NYC, 2007, Sci. of Oncology award, Am. Soc. Clin. Oncology, 2007, Arnall Patz award, Macula Soc., 2008, Internat. award, Pezcoller Found./Am. Assn. Cancer Rsch., 2009, Lasker-DeBakey Clin. Med. Rsch. award, Lasker Found., 2010. Mem.: NAS. Achievements include research leading to the creation of Avastin, an FDA-approved targeted therapy indicated for first-line treatment of patients with certain types of metastatic carcinoma; research in the regulation of angiogenesis (formation of new blood vessels); discovery of the gene for human VEGF as a major regulator of angiogenesis in a broad variety of circumstances, including embryonic development, reproductive functions and endochondral bone formation. Office: Genentech 1 DNA Way Mailstop 40 South San Francisco CA 94080-4990 *

FERRARI, GIULIO, ophthalmologist, researcher; b. Reggio Emilia, Italy, Mar. 16, 1980; MD, U. Parma, Italy, 2004. Clinician and scientist San Raffaele Hosp., 2009—; postdoc. fellow Schepens Eye Rsch. Inst., Harvard Med. Sch., 2009—10. Bietti Eye Found. fellowship, 2009—11. Mem.: Italian Med. Bd. (Parma), Am. Acad. Ophthalmology, Assn. Rsch. Vision and Ophthalmology (SILO travel grant). Avocations: swimming, reading, writing. Home: Via Bandini 5 Parma 43123 Italy Business E-Mail: giulio.ferrari@schepens.harvard.edu.

FERRARI, PIERRE ROBERT, psychiatrist; b. Paris, Jan. 13, 1935; s. Joseph Ferrari and Georgina Meriot; m. Brigida Cwancygier, Jan. 31, 1976; 2 children. MD, Faculty of Paris, 1962; Clin. Chief, Pitie Salpetriere Hosp., Paris, 1975; Prof. in Psychiatry, Med. Sch., Paris and Reims, 1976—. Cert. in child and adolescent psychiatry. Clin. chief Pitie-Salpetriere Hosp., Paris, 1972—75; med. chief La Roche Guyon Hosp., France, 1975—76; chief of the dept. of child psychiatry Reims Hosp., Marne, France, 1976—90, Fond. Vallee, Paris, 1990—2000, pres. of the med. commn., 1990—2000; prof. in child and adolescent psychiatry U. Paris XI, 1990—. Dir. rsch. networks on autism INSERM, Paris, 1988—96; v.p. Internat. Assn. of Child and Adolescent Psychiatry, New York, NY, 1994—2002; pres. European Assn. of Child and Adolescent Psychopathology, Paris, 1997—2007, French Soc. of Child and Adolescent Psychiatry, Paris, 2000—02; contracts in field Inserm, Paris. Editor: (novels) Actualites en psychiatrie de l'enfant et de l'adolescent, 2001; author L'autisme infantile, 2000; editor Traite de psychiatrie de l'enfant et de l'adolescent, 1992; editor, coord.: European Textbook of Child and Adolescent Psychiatry, 2005. Expert in psychiatry Justice Ct., Paris, 2000—02; mem. jury Lavoisier (French Min.), Paris, 1995—2002; mem. adminstrn. Med. Hosp. Found. Vallee, Paris, 1990—2000. Recipient rsch. contracts in field, INSERM, Paris. Mem.: Internat. Psychoanalytical Assn., France Psychanalytic Assn. (editl. bd. mem. 1985—2005). Roman Catholic. Home: 4 rue des Carmes F-75005 Paris France Office: 173 Blvd Pereire 75017 Paris France Office Phone: 0143257814. Personal E-mail: pierre.ferrari@wanadoo.fr.

FERRARO, RONALD LOUIS, health facility administrator; b. Washington, Pa., Apr. 14, 1943; s. Michael A. and Rose (Marino) F.; m. Lilyan McConomy, June 28, 1980; children: Suzanne Marie Claussen, Lynaia Lorraine Delgesso. BA, Juniata Coll., 1965; MSW, W.Va. U., 1967. Diplomate Am. Bd. Examiners in Clin. Social Work; LCSW Pa., quality certified social worker. Supr. social work Embreeville State Hosp., Coatesville, Pa., 1967-72; from chief social worker to dir. mental health The Consortium, Phila., 1972-88, dir. base svc. unit, 1988-91; asst. dir. Resources for Human Devel., Phila., 1991—2002; dir. quality mgmt. COMHAR Inc., 2002—. Bd. dirs. Big Bros./Big Sisters Bucks County, Doylestown, pa., 1986-91. Mem. NASW (cert., diplomate, bd. dirs. 1973-86). Home: 40 New Pond Ln Levittown PA 19054-3822 Office Phone: 215-203-3022. Office Fax: 215-203-3078.

FERRAZ, FRANCISCO MARCONI, neurological surgeon; b. Floresta, Pernambuco, Brazil, Aug. 14, 1951; arrived in U.S., 1976; Student, Colegio Nobrega, Recife-Brazil, 1967—69; MD, Faculdade de Medicine da Universidade Federal de Pernambuco-Brazil, 1975. Diplomate Am. Bd. Neurol. Surgery. Intern Jamaica Hosp., NYC, 1976—77; resident Georgetown U. Med. Ctr. and Affiliated Hosps., Washington, 1977—82; pvt. practice medicine specializing in neurol. surgery Washington, 1982—; mem. staff Georgetown U. Hosp., 2010—; faculty clin. instr. Georgetown U. Sch. Medicine, 1982—; faculty clin. assoc. prof. George Washington Sch. Medicine, 1994—; asst. prof. neurosurgery U. La., Ky., 2010—. Cons. in health care fin., internat. health care. Contbr. articles to profl. jours. Fellow: ACS, Internat. Coll. Surgeons; mem.: AMA, Congress of Neurol. Surgery, Washington Acad. Neurosurgery, Neurosurg. Soc. of D.C., Arlington Med. Soc., Am. Assn. Neurol. Surgeons. Office: 611 S Carlin Springs Rd Ste 105 Arlington VA 22204-1061 Business E-Mail: fferraz@cox.net.

FERRAZ-NETO, BEN-HUR, surgeon, educator; b. São Paulo, Brazil, Aug. 21, 1962; MD, Cath. U. São Paulo, 1987; PhD, U. Campinas, 1995. Chmn., prof. surgery Cath. U. São Paulo, 2001—; head abdominal transplantation Hosp. Israelita Albert Einstein, 2005—. Mem.: Brazilian Transplantation Soc. (pres. 2010—). Avocation: motorcycling. Home: Rua Guarara 500 apto 111 São Paulo 01425-000 Brazil Home Fax: 551121513388. Personal E-mail: ben-hur@einstein.br.

FERRAZZANO, GIANMARIA FABRIZIO, dentist; b. Milan, May 5, 1967; Degree in Dentistry, U. Naples Federico II, 1990, PhD, 1995. Cons. U. Hosp. Naples Federico II, 2005—. Contract prof. U. Naples Federico II, 2003. Named Best Internat. Dental Rschr., SIDOC, 2006. Mem.: IADR. Avocation: swimming. Office: via S Pansini 5 Naples Campania 80121 Italy E-mail: gianmariafabrizio@yahoo.it.

FERREIRA, ANA CARINA, nephrologist; b. Lisbon, Portugal, July 6, 1979; MD, Faculdade de Ciências Médicas, 2003. Physician Hosp. de Curry Cabral, 2005—. Recipient Roche award, 2009, Simbolic award, 2009. Mem.: European Soc. Organ Transplantation, European Dialysis Transplantation Assn., Portuguese Soc. Nephrology, Ordem dos Médicos. Avocation: reading. Office: Rua Beneficência n°8 Lisbon 1069-639 Portugal Personal E-mail: karinadacostafer@hotmail.com.

FERREIRA, ANTÓNIO GUILHERME, psychiatrist, psychology professor; b. Lisbon, Portugal, Mar. 27, 1937; s. Guilherme and Sara (Domingues) Ferreira; m. Maria do Rosário Vieira Coelho, Dec. 26, 1963; children: Guilherme Manuel, Antonio Artur, Luisa Isabel. MD, U. Lisbon, 1962; DSc in Psychiatry (hon.), Sciccuna Internat. U., Lavalleta, Malta, 1989. Resident in gen. practice Santa Maria Hosp., Lisbon, 1962-64, resident in psychiatry, 1964-67; cons. in psychiatry Lisbon Ctrl. Dispensary, 1968, Miguel Bombarda Hosp., 1969-78, head svc., 1978, head psychiat. dept., 1978-87, head tng. program dept., 1982—2002, dir. hosp., 1987-99, clin. dir., 1988-97. Prof. Superior Inst. for Applied Psychology, Lisbon, 1980—, Modern Univ., 1998-2008; temp. advisor WHO; standing com. pres. Internat. Non-govermental Organ. Concerned with Mental Health Issues, 1990-93. Co-author: Social Psychiatry and World Accords, 1992; mem. editl. bd. Social Psychiatry (Jour. World Assn. for Social Psychiatry), Mediterranean Jour. Social Psychiatry, Psicopatologia, dir. Grupanálise; also articles. Recipient Dr. Leonidas A. Finiffes award Pierides Found. Larnaca, Cyprus, 1981, Gold medal Portuguese Govt., 2005. Fellow World Assn. for Social Psychiatry (pres. 1988-92, plaque 1992), Portuguese Assn. for Social Psychiatry (gen. sec. 1973-75, pres. 1975-85, hon. pres. 1986—), Mediterranean Socio-Psychiat. Assn. (v.p. 1980-95, pres. 2000—); mem. Portuguese Assn. Group Analysis (pres. 1981-94), Group Analytic Soc. (London), Internat. Assn. Group Psychotherapy (bd. dirs. 1976-86, 95-2003), Portuguese Psychiat. Assn. (speaker pres. gen. assembly 1991), Portuguese Soc. of Psych. Epid. (pres. auditor's com. 1988-91), Portuguese Soc. of Epidemiology, Portuguese Br. of World Assn. for Psycho Soc. Rehab. (pres. auditor's com. 1997—99, 2005-07, pres. gen. assembly, 2001-05), NY Acad. Scis., Internat Govtl. Orgn. Avocations: history, philosophy, literature, music, opera. Personal E-mail: ag.ferreira@netcabo.pt.

FERREIRA, LESLIE PICCOLOTTO, medical educator; b. São Paulo, Aug. 18, 1949; D, U. Fed. De São Paulo, 1990. Prof. titular Pontificia U. Católica De São Paulo, 1973. Mem.: Sociedade Brasileira De Fonoaudiologia. Home: Rua Jesuino Bandeira 73 São Paulo 05048-080 Brazil Home Fax: 55-11-3875-2940. Personal E-mail: lesliepf@pucsp.br.

FERREIRA, MAÍRA PERES, pharmaceutical executive; b. São Sebastião do Paraíso, Brazil, Oct. 16, 1979; Degree, FMRP-USP, 2001, PhD in Med. Sci., 2010. Lab. tech. Faculty Pharm. Scis. Ribeirão Preto, 2004—. Office: Avenida do Café Monte Alegre Ribeirão Preto São Paulo 14040-903 Brazil Business E-Mail: maira@fcfrp.usp.br.

FERREIRA, RUI SEABRA, JR., toxicologist; b. Botucatu, São Paulo, Brazil, Sept. 17, 1973; Degree in Vet. Medicine, São Paulo State U., 1999, M in Tropical Diseases, 2004, PhD in Tropical Diseases, 2006. Toxinologist expert Ctr. Study Venoms And Venomous Animals, São Paulo State U., 2000, toxinologist, rsch. scientist, 2008—; venomous animals expert Medicine Sch., São Paulo State U., 2000—02, rschr. tropical diseases, 2005—06; mgmt. edn. expert Juiz De Fora Fed. U., 2003—04; postdoc. rschr. Butantan Inst., 2006—08; prof., advisor, coun. mem. São Paulo State U., mem. bd. Cevap; leader Toxicology Rsch. Group. Co-editor Jour. Venomous Animals And Toxins Including Tropical Diseases, 2008. Decorated Forest Ranger Std. award Mil. Police São Paulo - Brazil; recipient Best Sci. Work award, Tropical Diseases Brazilian Soc., Votes Congratulations award, Municipality Botucatu, Brazil; grant, São Paulo Rsch. Found. Master: Masonic Lodge; fellow: São Paulo Rsch. Found.; mem.: Brazilian Assn. Sci. Editors (bd. mem. 2008—10, Future Editor's award), Distance Edn. Brazilian Assn., Brazilian Toxinology Soc. Avocations: boating, mountain climbing, sports. Office: José Barbosa De Barros 1780 Fazenda Ex Botucatu São Paulo 18610-307 Brazil Office Phone: 55 14 38145555. Office Fax: 55 14 38145555. Business E-Mail: rseabra@cgvap.org.br.

FERREIRA-COELHO, JOSÉ MANUEL MARTINS, surgeon, urologist, educator; b. Lisbon, Portugal, May 7, 1943; s. Fernando Xavier and Maria Julieta Lopes Martins Ferreira-Coelho; m. Maria José Mayer Bleck da Silva Ferreira-Coelho, Nov. 4, 1967; children: Manuel Xavier, Ana Mafalda. MD, Classic Faculty Medicine U. Lisbon, Portugal, 1967, PhD, 2000; D Med. Sci. (hon.), Yorker Internat. U., Milan, Italy, 2008. Resident gen. surgery Hosp. Civis, Lisbon, Portugal, 1972—75, resident urology, 1976—79, hospitalar asst. urology, 1980, hospitalar asst. gen. surgery, 1982, specialist gen. surgery, 1982—89, graduation chief svc. gen. surgery, 1989; fellow gen. surgery coll. Ordem Médicos, 1975, fellow urology coll., 1982; graduation chief svc. gen. surgery Hosp. Desterro-Capuchos, 1991—2003; cons. gen. surgeon and urologist Hosp. Júlio de Matos, 2004—07. Free asst. pathology anatomy U. Lourenzo Marques, Mozambique, 1969; mem. profl. juries Human Anatomy U. Lisbon, 1972—84, Resident Specialties U. Lisbon, 1981, Gen. Surgery Residents St. Maria Hosp., 1986, Gen. Surgery Residents Svc. 6 Capuchos Hosp., 1993, Surg. Bd. Admission Gen. Surgery Svc. 5 Capuchos Hosp., Portugal, 1995, Gen. Surgery Residents Svc. 1 Desterro Hosp., Portugal, 1997; asst. prof. human anatomy Med. Sch. U. Lisbon, Portugal, 1972—84; asst. prof. gen. surgery and propedeutic Hosp. Desterro, 1975—76; hospitalar asst. gen. surgery emergency staff Hosp. St. José, 1982—91, chief emergency staff, 1998—2002, Hosp. Capuchos, Lisbon, Portugal, 1991—98; mem. profl. juries Gen. Surgery Residents Portugal Inst. Oncology, Portugal, 1977. Demonstrator (med. procedural videos); contbr. articles to profl. jours., numerous confs.; author: (book) Portugese History 13th 14th 15th Centuries Historical Reflexions, 2010. Recipient Honoree, Dir. Portuguese Health Svc. Navy, 1970, Commdr. Portuguese Navy, 1970, Dr. Bentes de Jesus prize, Hosp. St. José, 1977, medal, Order Internat. Assns.; named Hon. Nurse Prof. Physiology, U. Santa Maria, Lisbon, 1971—72, Hon. Nurse Prof. Anatomy, Red Cross Sch., Lisbon, 1973—76, Hon. Nurse Prof. Physiology, 1973—76, Hon. medal, Internat Biog. Ctr., Cambridge, Eng. Fellow: ACS; mem.: Geographic Soc. Lisbon Conf. (v.p., Corte-Real Commn.), Geographic Soc. Lisbon, Internat. Soc. Surgeons, Brazilian Soc. Urology, Internat. Urology Soc., European Assn. Endoscopic Surgery and Other Internat. Techniques (moderator sci. forum ACS rectal cancer XXX Portuguese Congress surgery 2010), Soc. Laproscopic Surgeons (mem. congress organizing com. 2003, VIP moderator 15th SLS Boston 2006, VIP moderator 16th SLS San Francisco 2007, VIP moderator 17th SLS Chgo. 2008, VIP moderator 18th SLS Boston 2009, VIP moderator 19th SLS, NY 2010), Portuguese Soc. Endoscopy and Laproscopic Surgery, Portugese Urology Soc., Pan Am. Soc. Anatomy, Soc. Luso Brasileira de Anatomia (internat. adv. bd.), Assn. Anatomists, Portugese Gastroent. Soc., Portugese Soc. Surgeons, Portugese Anatomical Soc., Lisbon Soc. Med. Scis., Nat. Geographic Soc., ELOS Club Tavira, Internat. Gastro-Surg. Club. Independent. Roman Catholic. Avocations: art, porcelain and pottery, classic cars, Portugese history, art, history. Home: Rua Bartolomeu Dias 2 4 Dto. 2685-187 Portela LRS Portugal Office: Euromedic Lisbon Ave Miguel Bombarda 37B Lisbon 1050-161 Portugal Office Phone: 00-351-213194130, 00-351-217928660. Office Fax: 213194149. Personal E-mail: jferreiracoelho@yahoo.com.

FERREIRA DA COSTA GOMES, MARCELO, research scientist; b. Porto Alegre, Brazil, Mar. 6, 1983; PhD, Inst. Física, U. Fed. Rio Grande do Sul, 2011. Rschr. Inst. Física, U. Fed. do Rio Grande do Sul, 2006—. Home: R Ivan Iglesias 136 Jardim Itú-Sabará Porto Alegre 91210-340 Brazil Personal E-mail: marfcg@gmail.com.

FERRELL, RICHARD BRADLEY, neuropsychiatrist; b. South Bend, Ind., Aug. 13, 1943; s. Rupert Tyler and Beatrice Bradley Ferrell; m. Melanie A. Ferrell; children: Catherine Lynn Ferrell de Correa, Elisabeth Jane Ferrell Horan, Anne Christine. AB, DePauw U., 1961—65; MD, Ind. U., 1965—69. Diplomate Am. Bd. of Psychiatry and Neurology, Inc., 1975, in Geriatric Psychiat. Am. Bd. of Psychiatry and Neurology, Inc., 2001, in Behavioral Neurology and Neuropsychiatry United Coun. Neurologic Subspecialties, 2006. Asst. prof. psychiatry Dartmouth Med. Sch., 1975—81, assoc. prof. psychiatry, 1981—. Contbr. articles to profl. jours. Girls basketball coach Hanover Recreation Dept., NH, 1982—2009; bd. mem. Opera North, Lebanon, NH, 1991—97. Recipient Alpha Omega Alpha Mem., Alpha Omega Alpha, 1969. Fellow: Am. Psychiatric Assn. (disting. life fellow); mem.: Am. Neuropsychiatric Assn. Office: Dartmouth-Hitchcock Med Ctr One Medical Ctr Dr Lebanon NH 03756 Business E-Mail: richard.ferrell@dartmouth.edu.

FERRENDELLI, JAMES ANTHONY, neurologist, educator; b. Trinidad, Colo., Dec. 5, 1936; s. Alex and Edna Ferrendelli; children: Elisabeth, Cynthia, Michael AB cum laude in Chemistry, U. Colo., Boulder, 1958; MD, U. Colo., Denver, 1962. Diplomate Am. Bd. Psychiatry and Neurology. Intern U. Ky. Med. Ctr., 1962-63; resident in neurology Cleve. Met. Gen. Hosp., 1965-68; research fellow in neurochemistry Washington U. Sch. Medicine, St. Louis, 1968-70, asst. prof. neurology and pharmacology, 1970-74, assoc. prof., 1974-77, prof., 1977-95, Seay prof. clin. neuropharmacology in neurology, 1977-95; chmn. dept. neurology U. Tex., Houston, 1995—2006, prof., 1995—, Kraft-Eidmann prof., 1995—. Contbr. numerous articles to profl. jours. Served to capt. M.C., U.S. Army, 1963-65 Recipient rsch. career devel. award USPHS, 1971-76, Founders Day award Washington U., 1981, Disting. Tchr. award, 1993, 94, Disting. Prof. of Yr. award, 1993, NIH grantee, 1971—. Fellow Am. Acad. Neurology; mem. Am. Neurol. Assn., Am. Soc. for Pharmacology and Exptl. Therapeutics (Epilepsy award 1981), Am. Epilepsy Soc. (Lennox lectr. 1991, pres. 1995, William G. Lennox award 2002), Assn. Univ. Prof. Neurology (pres. 2002-04). Avocations: fly fishing, numismatics. Office: U Tex-Houston Med Sch Dept Neurology 6431 Fannin St Ste 7102 Houston TX 77030-1501 Home Phone: 713-660-9753; Office Phone: 713-500-7080. Business E-Mail: james.a.ferrendelli@uth.edu.

FERRER, BARBARA, city health department executive director; MEd, Univ. Mass., Boston; MPH, Boston Univ., 1988; PhD, Brandeis Univ., 1994. Dir. health promotion & disease prevention and dir. maternal & child health div. Mass. Dept. Pub. Health, 1994—98; dep. dir. Boston Pub. Health Commn., 1998—2004; high sch. prin. Boston Pub. Schools, 2004—07; health commr. & exec. dir. Boston Pub. Health Commn., 2007—. Pew Scholar, 1988. Office: Boston Public Health Commn 1010 Massachusetts Ave Boston MA 02118 Office Phone: 617-534-5395, 617-554-5264. Office Fax: 617-534-5358.

FERRERAS, ANTONIO, ophthalmologist, researcher; b. León, Spain, Aug. 1, 1972; s. Antonio Ferreras and Begoña Amez; m. Ana Belen Pajarin, Sept. 10, 1999; children: Javier, Guillermo, Daniel. MD, U. Zaragoza, Spain, 1996, PhD in Medicine, 2003. Eye surgery training, ophthalmology residency Miguel Servet U. Hosp., Zaragoza, 1999—2003, cons. ophthalmologist, opthalmic surgeon, 2003—. Assoc. prof. ophthalmology U. Zaragoza, 2007, assoc. prof. optics and optometry, 2007—. Contbr. articles to profl. jours. Second lt. med. unit, 1997, Zaragoza. Grantee, Carlos III Health Inst., Aragon Inst. Health Sci. Mem.: European Glaucoma Soc., Am. Acad. Ophthalmology, European Assn. Vision and Eye Rsch. (assoc.), Spanish Soc. Glaucoma (assoc.), Spanish Soc. Ophthalmology (assoc.), Internacional Soc. Dacryology and Dry Eye (assoc.), Assn. Rsch. Vision and Ophthalmology (assoc.). Achievements include research in all aspects of glaucoma diagnosis and treatment with a particular focus on early glaucoma diagnosis techniques. Avocations: travel, golf, hunting, fishing, photography. Office: Miguel Servet Univ Hosp Isabel la Catolica 1-3 Zaragoza 50009 Spain Home: Breton 12 3A 50005 Zaragoza Spain Office Phone: 34976765558. Office Fax: 0034976566234. Personal E-mail: aferreras@msn.com.

FERRERI, ANTHONY C., hospital administrator; b. Jan. 19, 1951; s. Joseph V. Ferreri and Lucy DiSerafino; m. Michele DeStasio; children: Toni Ann Spinella, Joseph. BA, Wagner Coll., SI, NY, 1972; MS in Human Resources and Indsl. Rels., Rutgers U., 1981. V.p. human resources St. Barnabas Med. Ctr., Livingston, NJ; asst. adminstr. Alexian Bros. Hosp., Elizabeth, NJ; dir. of personnel United Hosps. Med. Ctr., NJ, Hosp. Ctr., NJ; pres. Metrotemp Svcs. Co. Inc., 1986—2001; exec. v.p. SI Univ. Hosp., NY, 2001, pres. NY, 2003—, CEO NY, 2003—. Pres. NJ Assn. for Healthcare Human Resources Adminstrn., NJ Assn. of Hosp. Recruiters, NJ Assn. of Temporary Svcs., Moore Cath. High Sch. Family Assn., 1993—97; chairperson Am. heart walk Am. Heart Assn., 2000, bd. dirs., NY; chmn. March of Dimes Gourmet Gala, 2004; bd. dirs. SI Univ. Hosp. Sys. Inc., SI Univ. Hosp., North Shore-LIJ Health System Inc., Snug Harbor Cultural Ctr. Recipient Lewis R. Miller Award, SI C. of C., 2001; named New Dorp High Sch. Hall of Fame, 2005, Mgr. of the Yr., Internat. Mgmt. Coun. Mem.: Wagner Coll. DaVinci Soc. (charter mem.). Office: Staten Island University Hospital 475 Seaview Ave Staten Island NY 10305 Office Phone: 718-226-9000.

FERRERI, MICHAEL VICTOR, optometrist; b. Park Ridge, Ill., May 15, 1967; s. Samuel Joseph and Dolores Jean (Liebich) F.; m. Heather Elaine (Katz) F.; children: Christopher, Anthony, Brendon. BS in Biol. Scis., U. Calif., Irvine, 1989; OD, So. Calif. Coll. Optometry, 1993. Cert. therapeutic optometrist, Calif., Tex.; tng. cert. US Army Externship Program, 1992. Extern Ctr. for Partially Sighted, Santa Monica, Calif., 1992—93; pvt. practice Long Beach, Calif., 1993—2000; assoc. optometrist Antelope Mall Vision Ctr., Palmdale, Calif., 1995—99, So. Calif. Permanente Med. Group, Fontana, 2000—. Color vision analysis cons. Dept. Health and Human Svcs., Long Beach, 1994-97; participating doctor Vision USA, Long Beach, 1995-2000; optometry, orthoptics guest lectr., 2009-. Contbr. articles to profl. jours. Mem. Rep. Nat. Com., 1991—; v.p. congregation and elder Grace Luth. Ch., Long Beach, 1996-99, grp. leader, Crown of Life Luth. Ch., Corona, Calif., 2006-; Merit Award, U.S. Congress Recognition Eagle Scout Rank, BSA, 1985, Outstanding Coll. Students Am. Cert. of Recognition, 1989. Recipient Corning Low Vision award Corning Optics, Anaheim, Calif., 1993, Vision Therapy Enhancement cert. So. Calif. Coll. Optometry, Fullerton, 1993, appreciation cert. for outstanding contbns. to Save Your Vision Week, U.S. Senate, 1997, gov.'s letter of commendation for organizing coloring and essay contest for sch. children State of Calif., 1997, appreciation certificate Calif. Optometric Assn., 1998, Svc. award Kaiser Permanente Optometry Dept., 2003, Cert. of Recognition, Nat. Campaign for Tolerance, 2004.Leadership Award Pack 77, BSA, 2007. Mem. Am. Optometric Assn. (contact lens sect.), Calif. Optometric Assn., Fellowship of Christian Optometrists, Optometric Ext. Program (clin. assoc.), Rio Hondo Optometric Soc. (treas. 1997-99), Eisenhower Commn. Rep. Nat. Com., Reagan Congl. Comm., Rep. Nat. Comm., Patriots Club, Heritage Found. Avocations: camping, golf, water-sports. Office: So Calif Permanente Med Group Bldg 4 Mod 1 9985 Sierra Ave Fontana CA 92335 Office Phone: 888-750-0036.

FERRERO, ANNAMARIA, gynecologist, researcher; b. Turin, Italy, Oct. 19, 1964; d. Bartolomeo Ferrero and Maddalena Germanetto; m. Giuseppe Diano, June 29, 1996; 1 child, Matteo Diano. MD, U. Turin, 1990; PhD in Gynecologic Oncology, La Sapienza U., Rome, 2000. Bd. cert. in obstetrics and gynecology U. Turin, 1994. Resident U. Turin Sch. Obstetrics and Gynecology, Italy, 1991—94; vis. dr. dept. obstetrics and gynecology U. Milan, Monza, 1993; clin. asst. dept. gynecologic oncology Inst. Obstetrics and Gynecology, U. Turin, 1995—96; cons. dept. gynecologic oncology, obstetrics and gynecology U. Turin, Mauriziano Hosp., 1999—; cons. dept. gynecologic oncology U. Turin Inst. for Cancer Rsch. and Treatment, Candiolo, 2000—; vis. dr. dept. gynecology U. Leiden, Netherlands, 2002. Group leader gynecol. cancer rsch., dept. gynecologic oncology U. Turin Inst. for Cancer Rsch. and Treatment, Candiolo, 2000—; spkr. Nat. and Internat. Sci. Meeting. Contbr. articles to profl. jours., chapters to books. Grantee grant, S. Anna Hosp., 1996. Mem.: European Soc. Gynecol. Oncology, Italian Soc. Gynecol. Oncology, European Orgn. for Cancer Rsch. and Treatment. Home: Via Giosuè Carducci N20 Turin Pianezza 10044 Italy Office: Dept Gynecol Oncol University of Torino Largo Turati N62 Turin 10128 Italy Office Fax: +390115082683. Personal E-mail: a.ferrero@katamail.com.

FERRETTI, SILVIA, dean, osteopath; BS, Gannon U., Erie; DO, Phila. Coll. Osteo. Medicine. Cert. Nat. Bd. Osteopathic Physicians, in phys. medicine and rehab. American Osteopathic Assn., in geriatric medicine American Osteopathic Assn., American Osteopathic Bd. Family Practice, in lower limb prosthetics NYU Post Grad Med. Sch. Intern Phila. Coll. Osteo. Medicine Hosp.; residency in phys. medicine rehab. U. Pa. Hosp., Phila.; accupuncture tng. St. Agnes Pain Ctr.; burn mgmt. tng. St. Agnes Burn Ctr.; electromyography tng. U. Pa.; pediatric tng. Atlantic City Children's Seahorse House; faculty mem. Phila. Coll. Osteo. Medicine; chief of rehab. Great Lakes Rehab. Hosp., Erie; provost, sr. v.p., dean acad. affairs, clin. prof. internal/phys. medicine and rehab. Lake Erie Coll. Osteo. Medicine, Erie, Pa., 1992—. Past chair Pa. Dept. State Bur. Profl. and Occupl. Affairs, Pa. State Bd. Osteopathic Medicine. Mem.: American Osteopathic Assn., American Osteopathic Coll. Rehab. Medicine, American Congress Rehab., American Acad. Phys. Medicine and Rehab., Erie County Med. Soc., Pa. Osteopathic Med. Assn. (del., mem. bd. trustees). Office: Lake Erie Coll Osteopathic Medicine 1858 West Grandview Blvd Erie PA 16509-1025 Office Phone: 814-866-6641. *

FERRI, ANDREA, physician; b. Parma, Sept. 19, 1980; MD, Parma U., 2005. Physician U. Hosp. Parma, 2005—. Mem.: Italian Assn. Moebius Syndrome, Italian Assn. Maxillo-Facial Surgery, European Assn. Cranio-Maxillo-Facial Surgery. Office: Via Volturno 74 Parma 43125 Italy Office Fax: 390521703761. Business E-Mail: a.ferri@libero.it.

FERRINI, FAUSTO, endocrinologist; b. Montegranaro, Marche, Italy, Nov. 9, 1952; s. Guerrino Ferrini and Clelia Rossi. MD, Catholic U., Rome, 1977, post grad. specialization in Endocrinology, 1980; post grad. in Andrology, U. Florence, Italy, 1998. Master course in obesiology Italian Soc. Obesity, 1999. Gen. practitioner Nat. Health Svc., Montegranaro, Italy, 1981—; pvt. practice endocrinology Civitanova, 1981—, Macerata, 1984—86, Fermo, 1986—88; pvt. practice andrology Civitanova, 1998—. Labour physician Dist. Area Svc., Marche, Italy, 1982—92. Councillor responsible Municipality of Montegranaro, 1985; mem. com. environment, energy and ecology Nat. Assn. Municipalities, Rome, 1988; mem. found. Bank Fermo, Fermo, 1992. Named comdr., Order of Italian Republic, 1994. Mem.: Am. Thyroid Soc., Endocrine Soc., Internat. Soc. Sexual Medicine, European Soc. Sexual Medicine, European Soc. Reproductive Medicine, European Acad. Andrology, Am. Assn. Clin. Endocrinologists, Am. Diabetes Assn., Am. Soc. Bone and Mineral Rsch., N.Am. Assn. Study of Obesity, Am. Soc. Reproductive Medicine, N.Am. Soc. Andrology, Rotary. Avocations: sports cars, watches, literature. Office: Via Vittorio Veneto 152 Civitanova Marche Italy Home: Via Vecchia Fermana 79 63812 Montegranaro FM Italy Office Phone: 0039-0739-890033.

FERRUZZI, MARIO G., nutritionist, food scientist, educator; BS in Chemistry, Duke U., 1996; MS in Food Sci. & Nutrition, Ohio State U., 1998, PhD in Food Sci. & Nutrition, 2001. Asst. prof. foods & nutrition Purdue U. Office: Purdue University Food Science Bldg 745 Agriculture Mall Dr West Lafayette IN 47907-2009 Office Phone: 765-494-0625. E-mail: mferruzz@purdue.edu.

FERSIS, NIKOS, surgeon, researcher, physician; b. Sindelfingen, Germany, Oct. 13, 1961; m. Gritt Fersis; 1 child, Paul. MD, U. Heidelbeg, Heidelberg, Germany, 1987. Lic. Gynecologist Aerztekammer Freiburg Germany, 1995. Resident U. Heidelberg, Heidelberg, Germany, 1988—95, chief resident, 1995—98. Chief of the breast clinic U. Tuebingen, Germany, 1998—2003. Mem. Greece-Germany Academic Orgn., Schwetzingen, Germany, 1995—2003. Mem.: ASCO (assoc.). Orthodox. Home: Überrückweg6 Ubstadt 76698 Germany Office Fax: +49-7071-295381. Personal E-mail: niko.fersis@t-online.de. E-mail: nikos.fersis@med.uni-tuebingen.de.

FERSTENFELD, JULIAN ERWIN, internist, educator; b. Des Moines, Sept. 5, 1941; m. Sharon Rukas, Mar. 8, 1975; children: Megan Ann, Adam Justin. BA, U. Iowa, 1963, MD, 1966. Intern Milw. County Gen. Hosp., 1966—67, resident in internal medicine, 1969—71, fellow infectious diseases, 1972—73; instr. internal medicine Med. Coll. Wis., 1974—75, asst. prof. medicine, 1975—78, asst. clin. prof. medicine and family practice, 1978—83, assoc. clin. prof. family practice and medicine, 1983—; internal medicine dir. Waukesha family practice residency, 1978—; practice medicine specializing in infectious diseases Milw., 1974—. Mem. staff Waukesha Meml. Hosp., Wis., West Allis Meml. Hosp., Wis., Elmbrook Meml. Hosp., Brookfield, Wis., Froedtert Meml. Hosp., Milw. Contbr. articles to profl. jours. Served as capt. M.C. US Army, 1967—69, Korea. Fellow: ACP; mem.: Am. Fedn. Clin. Rsch., Wis. Thoracic Soc., Phi Beta Kappa.

FERTIG, ANGELA RICE, economics professor; b. Republic of Korea, Oct. 11, 1972; PhD, Brown U., 2001. Postdoc. fellow Princeton U., 2001—04; asst. prof. Ind. U., 2004—05, U. Ga., 2005—. Office: 203D Baldwin Hall University Ga Athens GA 30602 Business E-Mail: afertig@uga.edu.

FERZLI, GEORGE SALEM, surgeon; b. Lebanon, Jan. 10, 1955; came to US, 1979; s. Salem and Milia Ferzli; m. Berthe Ferzli, Aug. 25, 1983; children: Georgina, Christina, George Jr., Christopher. MD, St. Joseph U., Beirut, 1979. Lic. physician, France, NJ, NY; diplomate Am. Bd. Gen. Surgery, Am. Bd. Surg. Critical Care. Resident gen. surgery S.I. U. Hosp., NY, 1979-84, dir. surg. ICU, assoc. dir. surgery, 1984—90, dir. laparoendoscopic surgery, 1991—2003; prof. surgery SUNY Health Sci. Ctr., Bklyn., 1999—; dir. laparoendoscopic surgery Luth. Med. Ctr., Bklyn., 2004—, chmn. dept. surgery, 2005—. Vis. and oper. surgeon NYU, Cornell U., Columbia Presbyn. Hosp., Beth Israel Hosp., Maimonides Med. Ctr., Montefiore Hosp., L.I. Coll. Hosp., St. Mary's Hosp., Valley Hosp., St. Peter's Hosp., U. Medicine and Dentistry N.J. Children's Hosp., Newark, Overlook Hosp., L.I. Coll. Hosp.; vis. & oper. surgeon Tulane U., New Orleans, New Delhi; vis. and oper. surgeon China, South Africa, France, Russia, Bahrain, Kuwait, Kazakhstan, Greece, Egypt, Lebanon, Uzbekistan, Portugal, Belgium, Can., New Delhi, India, Japan, Singapore, Italy, Dominican Republic; vis. prof. Spain, Portugal, Norway, Singapore, Italy, Belgium, New Delhi, Turkey, Japan, France, Can., Scotland, Poland, Switzerland, Sweden, India. Reviewer Jour. ACS, Surg. Endoscopy, Am. Jour. Surgery, Archives of Surgery, Jour. Laparoendoscopic Surgery, Hernia, Ann. Surg. Oncology Bd., contbr. over 100 articles to profl. jours., chpts. to books; patentee in field. Fellow ACS, Am. Coll. Gastroenterologists; mem. AMA, Soc. for Surgery Alimentary Tract, Am. Soc. Bariatric Surgery, N.Y. Surg. Soc., Soc. Internat. de Chirurgie, Soc. Am. Gastrointestinal Endoscopic Surgeons, Assn. Francaise de Chirurgie, Soc. Critical Care Medicine, Am. Soc. Parenteral and Enteral Nutrition, Richmond County Med. Soc., Med. Soc. State N.Y., European Assn. Endoscopic Surgery, Internat. Fedn. Surg. Colls. Office: 65 Cromwell Ave Staten Island NY 10304-3933 Office Phone: 718-667-8100. Business E-Mail: info@drferzli.com, george@scferjk.com.

FESSEL, WALFORD JEFFREY, rheumatologist; b. London, June 20, 1932; came to U.S., 1957; s. Jack Isaac and Alma (Yarmolinski) F.; m. Nicole J. Noble, Sept. 11, 1957; 1 child, Jason N. MB, BS, U. London, 1955. Diplomate Am. Bd. Internal Medicine. Intern U. Coll. Hosp., London, 1955; resident Can. Red Cross Hosp., Taplow, England, 1956, U. Calif., San Francisco, 1963, 64; rheumatologist Kaiser-Permanente, San Francisco, 1965—, chief of medicine, 1979-89, dir. internal medicine residency tng. program, 1979-89, dir. HIV rsch. unit, 1989—; clin. prof. medicine U. Calif., San Francisco, 1983-97, mem. clin. faculty promotion com., 1986—, emeritus clin. prof. medicine, 1997—. Chmn. regional chiefs of medicine No. Calif. Permanente Med. Group, 1980-89. Contbr. articles to profl. jours. Fellow ACP, Royal Coll. Physicians, Am. Coll. Rheumatology (founder). Jewish. Avocations: gardening, art, music, travel, languages. Office: Kaiser Permanente 2238 Geary Blvd San Francisco CA 94115-3394 Office Phone: 415-833-2854. Business E-Mail: jeffrey.fessel@kp.org. E-mail: jeffrey.fessel@pacbell.net.

FETCHERO, JOHN ANTHONY, JR., otolaryngologist; b. Jeannette, Pa., June 4, 1951; s. John Anthony Sr. and Cleda (Byerly) F.; m. Wynona Ann Kestler, Feb. 26, 1982; children: John Anthony III, Christopher Jason, Dominic Vincent, Victor Thomas. BS in Biology, St. Vincent Coll., 1973; DO, Coll. Osteo. Medicine, Des Moines, 1976. Intern Des Moines Gen. Hosp., 1976-77; Flight surgeon Naval Aero. Med. Inst., Pensacola, Fla., 1977-78; resident Nat. Naval Med. Ctr., Bethesda, Md., 1980-84; otorhinolaryngologist, oro-facial plastic surgeon Am. Co. Osteo. Opthalmology and Otorhinolaryngology, 1986; otolaryngologist Am. Coll. Otolaryngology, 1988; pvt. practice, Orange Park, Fla., 1988—. Capt. USNR, 1973—2001, ret. Med. Sch. scholar USN, 1973-76. Mem. Fla. Osteo. Assn., Osteo. Acad. Otorhinolaryngology, Am. Acad. Otolaryngology, Am. Osteo. Assn., Fla. Med. Assn., Clay County Med. Soc. Republican. Roman Catholic. Avocations: running, photography, boating, bowling. Home: 2862 Country Club Blvd Orange Park FL 32073-5728 Office Phone: 904-278-3820.

FETNER, ROBERT HENRY, radiobiologist; b. Savannah, Ga., Feb. 22, 1922; s. William Westcott and Lucille Fedora (Goodrich) F., m. Mary Carolyn Guiney, July 8, 1972; 1 dau., Amber. BS, U. Miami, Fla., 1950, MS, 1952; PhD, Emory U., 1955. Mem. faculty Ga. Inst. Tech., Atlanta, 1955—, prof. radiation biology, 1963—, dir. Sch. Biology, 1964-70. Cons. in field. Contbr. articles in field to profl. jours.; patentee computer digitizer. Served with AUS, 1942-45. Decorated Combat Inf. badge. Mem. Ga. Acad. Sci. (editor bull. 1960-64), Sigma Xi, Phi Kappa Phi. Presbyterian. Address: 2219 Walker Dr Lawrenceville GA 30043-2473 Office Phone: 770-963-6118. Personal E-mail: roberthfetner308@bellsouth.net.

FETTER, LEE F., hospital administrator; Assoc. vice chancellor adminstrn. and fin., COO Faculty Practice Plan Wash. U. Sch. Medicine; pres. St. Louis Children's Hosp., 2002—; sr. exec. officer BJC HealthCare. Office: St Louis Children's Hosp One Children's Place Saint Louis MO 63110 Office Phone: 314-454-6000.

FETTER, TREVOR, healthcare industry executive; b. San Diego, Jan. 16, 1960; married; 2 children. BS in Econs., Stanford U., 1982; MBA, Harvard U., 1986. With investment banking divsn. Merrill Lynch Capital Mkts.; sr. v.p. MGM/UA Comm. Co., 1988; exec. v.p., CFO Metro-Goldwyn-Mayer, Inc.; exec. v.p. Tenet Healthcare Corp., Dallas, 1995—96, exec. v.p., CFO, 1996—2000; chmn., CEO Broad Ln., Inc., San Francisco, 2000—02; pres. Tenet Healthcare Corp., Dallas, 2002—03, pres., acting CEO, 2003, pres., CEO, 2003—. Bd. trustees Healthcare Leadership Coun. Chmn. bd. Santa Catalina Island Conservancy; trustee Santa Barbara Zool. Garden. Office: Tenet Healthcare Corp 13737 Noel Rd Dallas TX 75240 *

FETZER, APRIL M., orthopedist; BS in Bio., U. Ill., 1995; MD, Des Moines U., 1999. Diplomate Am. Bd. Phys. Medicine and Rehab., 2004, cert. subspecialty in pain medicine Am. Bd. Anesthesiology, 2004, Penn., 2001, Nat. Bd. Osteopathic Med. Exam., 2000. Tchg. asst., osteopathic manipulation Des Moines U., 1996—97; clin. instr. Temple U. Med. Sch., 2002—03; lectr., dept. phys. medicine and rehab. U. Mich., 2003—04; med. staff, dept. internal medicine Oak Park Hosp., 2004—; provisional staff, dept. internal medicine Ctrl. Dupage Hosp., 2004—; asst. prof., dept. orthopedic surgery RUSH U. Med. Ctr., 2004—, asst. prof., attending, dept. phys. medicine and rehab., 2004—; med. staff Weiss Meml. Hosp., 2005—. Spkr. in field. Contbr. articles to numerous profl. jours. Mem.: Am. Soc. Interventional Pain Physicians, Physiatric Assn. Spine, Sports and Occupational Rehab., Am. Acad. Phys. Medicine and Rehab., Internat. Spinal Injection Soc., No. Am. Spine Soc. Office: Rush Orthopaedics Ste M30 800 S Wells Chicago IL 60607 Office Phone: 312-243-4244. Business E-Mail: contact_rush@rush.edu.

FEUCHT, MATTHIAS, ophthalmologist, researcher, vitreoretinal and cataract surgeon; Cert. in medicine Govt. Oberbayern, 2001. Cons. U. Eye Hosp. Hamburg Eppendorf, Germany, 2005—07, Klinikum Stuttgart Augenklinik KH, Germany, 2007—. Office: Klinikum Stuttgart Augenklinik KH Kriegsbergstr 60 Stuttgart 70174 Germany

FEUERWERKER, ELIE, biologist, educator; b. Paris, Dec. 2, 1948; arrived in U.S., 1989, naturalized, 1999; s. David Feuerwerker and Antoinette Gluck; m. Anne Esther Ackermann, Dec. 28, 2004; 1 child, David. BSc in Biology, U. Montreal, Que., Can., 1971, MSc in Biology, 1976, PhD in Biology, 1983. Postdoctoral fellow Harvard U., Cambridge, Mass., 1985—87; rsch. assoc. Boston U., 1987—88; rsch. fellow McGill U., Montreal Neurol. Inst., 1987—89; mem. I-V team The Mount Sinai Med. Ctr., NYC, 1990—94; tchr. biology Lycee Français de N.Y., 1994—2000; tchr. N.Y.C. Bd. Edn., 2000—. Presenter in field. Contbr. articles to profl. jours. and newspapers. Grantee, The Hannah Inst. for the History of Medicine, NSF, The Rockefeller U. Mem.: N.Y. Acad. Scis. Jewish. Avocation: photography. Home: 1617 Cherry St Highland Park NJ 08904-3716

FEURLE, GERHARD ENGELBERT, medical educator, research scientist; b. Graz, Steiermark, Germany, July 15, 1938; s. Martin and Maria Agathe Therese (Seip) F.; m. Sabine Bassenge, Apr. 17, 1970; children: Juliane, Uta. MD, U. Munich, 1963. Resident Temple U., Phila., 1966; resident Medizinische Klinik U. Göttingen, 1967-71; sr. resident Medizinische Poliklinik U. Heidelberg, 1971-86; chief dept. medicine DRK-Krankenhaus Neuwied, 1986—2003; sci. coord. European Project on Whipples Disease, 2003—06. Discoverer xenin; contbr. articles to profl. jours. Mem. AAAS, Deutsche Gesellschaft Verdauungs U. Stoffwechselerkrankungen. Avocation: mountain climbing. Personal E-mail: g.e.feurle@t-online.de.

FEW, JULIUS WARREN, JR., surgeon; b. Detroit, Mich., June 12, 1967; m. Jennifer Lynn Coon, 1999. Harvard Coll. Collaboration, Biochemistry Rsch., 1988; BS in Biochemistry, Physiology, Mich. State U., 1988; MD with honors, Univ. Chgo. Pritzker Sch. Medicine, 1992. Cert. Am. Bd. Surgery, Am. Bd. Plastic Surgery. Intern gen. surgery U. Mich. Med. Ctr., 1992—93, resident gen. surgery, 1993—96, chief resident gen. surgery, 1996—97; resident plastic surgery Northwestern U., 1997—99, chief resident instr., plastic surgery, 1999—2000; ophthalmic plastic surgery tng. Flowers Clinic, Honolulu, NY Eye, Ear Infirmary, Manhattan Eye, Ear & Throat Hosp., Paces Surgery Ctr., Atlanta, 2000; plastic surgeon Northwestern Plastic Surgery Ctr., 2001—. Rsch. fell. Ingham Med. Ctr., 1987; vol. Ingham Med Ctr., 1987; asst. to dean of Minority Med. Student Affairs U. Chgo., 1989—90; lectr. in field. Contbr. articles to profl. jours., chapters to books; med. corr. NBC, 2001—02, med. corr., aesthetic topics CNN, 2002—, med. corr., breast surgery, aesthetic Univision/Telemundo, 2002, mem. adv. panel Good Morning America, 2001—. Recipient Hubbard Hall Scholastic award, 1986—87, Academic Excellence award, 1987—88, U. Chgo. Scholastic Scholarship, 1988, Resident Month, Ann Arbor Veterans Med. Ctr., 1993, Profl. Achievement award, Univ. Mich., 1994—95, Frederick A. Coller Tour award, 1996, Best Congenial Paper award, Plastic Surgery Sr. Resident Conf., 2000, Chgo. Plastic Surgery Presentation award, 2000; named to Crain's 40 Under 40, 2002. Mem.: ACS, AMA, Am Soc. Aesthetic Plastic Surgery (mem. media/pub. relations 2002—, future leadership 2003—), Frederick A. Coller Surgical Soc., Nat. Med. Assn., Am. Soc. Plastic and Reconstructive Surgery, Phi Kappa Phi. Office: Northwestern Plastic Surgery 675 N St Clair Ste 19 250 Chicago IL 60611 Office Phone: 312-695-6022. Office Fax: 312-695-5672. Business E-Mail: jfew@nmh.org.

FEWEL, JOHN GERRARD, government agency administrator, director; b. Chickasha, Okla., Aug. 20, 1944; s. Kenneth Jack and Cleo Brees Fewel; m. Vicki Ann Huber, May 27, 2000; children: Jeffrey Scott Pickens, Sean Allen, BA in Microbiology, U. Tex., Austin, 1966; MS in Mgmt., U. Tex., San Antonio, 1980. Rsch. asst. U. Ky. Med. Ctr., Lexington, 1966—69; rsch. assoc. NJ Coll. Medicine, Newark, 1969—75; dir. cardiothoracic rsch. lab VA Med. Ctr., San Antonio, 1975—82, adminstrv. officer trainee Memphis, 1982—83; adminstrv. officer rsch. VA Outpatient Clinic, Boston, 1983—84, VA Med. Ctr., Boston, 1984—84, Dallas, 1984—2003; exec. dir. Dallas VA Rsch. Corp., Dallas, 1990—2002; ret., 2003. Rsch. coord. U. Tex. Southwestern Med. Ctr., Dallas, 1984—90. Author: Reflections from the Shaman's Tear, Pursuing the Wings of Pegasus; contbr. articles to profl. jours. Pres., chmn. bd. dir. Miracle Wish Found., 2006; hon. chmn. Nat. Rep. Congressional Com. Bus. Adv. Coun., Tex., 2006—, House Rep. Trust, Rep. Bus. Summit, 2007. Recipient Congl. medal of distinction, 2006, 2008, Presdl. Commn., 2008, Nat. Leadership award, Nat. Rep. Congressional Com., Republican of Yr.; named Businessman of Yr., 2006—. Mem.: Soc. of Rsch. Adminstrs. (pres. govt. divsn. 1997—98). Achievements include development of quantitative analytical technique measuring variety of metabolites in tissue biopsies; research in underlying biochemistry of hemorrhagic/endotoxin shock and cardio pulmonary bypass. Avocations: sailing, creative writing, running. Home and Office: 1307 High Ridge Drive Duncanville TX 75137 E-mail: vickiern7@netzero.com.

FEWKES, JESSICA LYNN, dermatologist, educator; MD, U. Calif., 1978. Diplomate Am. Bd. Dermatology, 1982. Resident dermatology Mass Gen. Hosp., Boston, 1979—82, hosp. affiliation include; fellow chemosurgery Duke Univ. Med. Ctr., Durham, NC, 1982—83; asst. prof. dermatology dept. Harvard Med. Sch. Office: Massachusetts Eye and Ear Main Campus 243 Charles St Boston MA 02114 Office Phone: 617-573-3789. Office Fax: 617-573-3727.

FIBLA, JUAN JOSE, thoracic surgeon; b. Tortosa, Tarragona, Spain, Aug. 27, 1972; s. Juan Jose Fibla and Maria Josefa Alfara. MD, U. Navarra, Pamplona, Spain, 1996; rsch. degree, U. Autonoma Barcelona, Spain, 2001; PhD, U. Autonoma, Barcelona, Spain, 2004. Bd. certified thoracic surgery Spanish Ministry Health, 2003. Resident Hosp. De La Santa Creu I Sant Pau, Barcelona, 1999—2003; fellowship European Sch. Cardio-thoracic Surgery, Bergamo, Italy, 2003—. Cons. Red Respira, Barcelona, 2003—, endoscopic thoracic surgeon Hosp. De La Santa Creu I Sant Pau, Barcelona, 2003—. Author: (book chapter) Casos Clinicos Para Residentes De Cirugia Toracica (Editorial Luzan); contbr. articles to profl. jours. Recipient Best Paper, Nat. Surgery Meeting, 2002; grantee rsch. grant, Catalan Soc. Thoracic Surgeons, 2003. Mem.: Cardio-thoracic Surgery Network, European Assn. Cardio-thoracic Surgery, Nat. Group Sympathic Endoscopic Surgery, Acad. Med. Sci. Catalonia And Baleares, Spanish Soc. Pneumology And Thoracic Surgery, Catalan Soc. Thoracic Surgeons (pres. resident chpt. 2003). Avocations: golf, windsurfing, literature. Office: Hosp De La Santa Creu I Sant Pau St Antoni Maria Claret 167cirtorax 08025 Barcelona Spain

FICHELLE, JEAN MARC GABRIEL, thoracic surgeon; b. Clichy-Seine, France, June 27, 1949; BS, St. Marie De Monceau, 1967; PhD, U. Paris VII, 1980. Asst. Hosp. St. Louis, 1992—2011, Hosp. St. Joseph and Clinique Bizet, 1980—. Mem.: French Acad. Surgery, French Coll. Vascular Medicine, Peripheral Vascular Surgery, French Vascular Soc. Home: Ave du Ponant Villeneuve-la-Garenne Ile-de-France 92390 France Business E-Mail: jm.fichelle@wanadoo.fr.

FICHTER, MANFRED MAXIMILIAN, psychiatrist, researcher; b. Beilngries, Germany, Sept. 19, 1944; s. Max Alois and Friedolina K. (Brand) F.; m. Renate Flegler; children: Andreas, Alina, Julian. MD, U. Heidelberg, Germany, 1971; Dipl Psych, U. Heidelberg, 1975; Habil in Med, U. Munich, 1984. Diplomate in clin. psychology, specialist in psychiatry, neurology and psychotherapeutic medicine. Postdoctoral fellow UCLA, 1972-73; asst. prof. Max Planck Inst. Psychiatry, Munich, 1975-79; assoc. prof. dept. psychiatry U. Munich, 1979-84, prof. psychiatry, head divsn. epidemiology/evaluation, 1991—; med. dir. Klinik Roseneck/U. Munich, Prien, Germany, 1985—2009. Author: Magersucht und Bulimia, (Hermann Emminghaus award 1986), 1985, Verlauf Psychischer Erkrankungen in der Bevölkerung, (Hermann Simon award 1991), 1990, Bulimia Nervosa, 1990, Course of Eating Disorders, 1990 (Christina-Barz award 1991, Internat. Soc. Behavioral Med. award, 2004), Treatment and Course of Alcoholism, 1991, Magersucht und Bulimie, 2008; editor Verhaltenstherapie, 1998—2008; assoc. editor Internat. Jour. Eating Disorders, 2006—11 (Leadership award in Rsch., Acad. Eating Disorders, 2007). Mem. World Psychiat. Assn. (v.p. sect. eating disorders), German Assn. for Verhaltensmedizin (v.p. 1993-02), Eating Disorder Rsch. Soc. (pres. 1999-2000), German Soc. Eating Disorders, Deutsche Gesellschaft Essstoerungen (pres. 2006—10, treas. 2010-), Lions Club Prien (pres. 2011-). Avocations: skiing, sailing. Office: Klinik Roseneck-Hosp Behav Medicine Am Roseneck 6 83209 Prien Germany Office Phone: 49 8051 683001. Business E-Mail: mfichter@schoen-kliniken.de.

FIDA, NADIA MOHAMMED, pediatrician, educator, consultant; d. Mohammed Abdulsamid Fida and Khadija Mohammed Al Sharif; m. Tarek Mohammed Al Harthy, Nov. 2, 1981; children: Basma Al Harthy, Ahmad Al Harthy, Abdulelah Al Harthy, Abdulaziz Al Harthy. Degree in medicine, Cairo U., 1980. Ho. officer King Abdulaziz U. Hosp., Jeddah, Saudi Arabia, 1981—82, sr. ho. officer, 1982—86, registrar physician, 1986—92, sr. registrar physician, 1992, coord. ho. officer, 1992—94, pediat. cons., 1992—; assoc. prof. dept. pediats. King Abdulaziz U., 2004—. Mem. univ. edn. com. (female sect.) representing med. coll. Faculty Medicine and Allied Scis. King Abdulaziz U., 2000—03, mem. neonatology com., 2000—01, mem. cardiopulmonary resuscitation com., 2000—01. Contbr. articles to profl. jours. Mem.: Pediat. Assn., Thalassemia Soc., Assn. Med. Edn. in Europe (assoc.). Achievements include research in projects in evaluation of diagnostic value of Serum C-Reactive Protein and Il-16 as early diagnosis of meningitis and neonatal sepsis; optimizing theophylline use in management of bronchial asthma in children and neonatal apnea; prospective study of congenital malformations among live-born neonates; breastfeeding in Saudi Arabian community; Interleukin-1a, Interleukin-6 and tumor necrosis factor alpha levels in children with sepsis and meningitis; serum inflammatory mediators in neonatal sepsis and meningitis. Office: King Abdulaziz U Hosp Al Sulaimania Dist 80215 Jeddah Saudi Arabia Office Fax: (+966)26403975. Personal E-mail: nadiafida@hotmail.com.

FIDALGO, TATIANA KELLY DA SILVA, dental educator; b. Rio de Janeiro, Sept. 23, 1982; DDS, MDS, 2007; PhD student in Pediatric Dentistry, Fed. U. Rio de Janeiro. Prof., continuing edn. program pediatric dentistry Fed. U. Rio de Janeiro, 2009—. Home: Rua Joaquim Távora 244/202 Niterói Rio de Janeiro 24230541 Brazil

FIDEL, RAYA, information science educator; b. Tel Aviv, Jan. 18, 1945; came to U.S., 1977; BSc, Tel Aviv U., 1970; MLS, Hebrew U., Jerusalem, 1976; PhD, U. Md., 1982. Tchr. Adult Edn. Ctr., Jerusalem, 1971-72; br. libr. Hebrew U., Jerusalem, 1972-77; asst. prof. libr. sci. U. Wash., Seattle, 1982-87, assoc. prof. libr. sci., 1987-2000, prof. Info. Sch., 2000—, head Ctr. Human-Info. Interaction The Info. Sch., 2003—. Vis. libr. Duke U. Libr., Durham, N.C., 1992-93. Author: Database Design, 1987; editor Advances in Classification, 1991-94 (award 1992-94); contbr. articles to profl. publs. Recipient Research award Am. Society for Information Science, 1994 Mem. AAUP (chair U. Wash. chpt. 1990-92, pres. state conf. 1992-97), Assn. Computing Machinery, Am. Soc. Info. Sci. (dir.-at-large 2000-02). Home: 5801 Phinney Ave N Seattle WA 98103-5862

FIEL, STANLEY BRUCE, internist, pulmonologist, educator; b. Aug. 9, 1948; children: Jami Marissa, Seth Jordan, Marla Anne. BS, U. Conn., 1969; MD, Med. Coll. of Pa., 1973. Diplomate Am. Bd. Internal Medicine, Pulmonary Bd. Internal Medicine; lic. physician, Pa. Intern Temple U. Hosp., Phila., 1973-74, resident, 1974-76; pulmonary disease fellow Hosp. of U. Pa., Phila., 1976-78; attending physician Temple U. Sch. Medicine, Phila., 1978-91, Am. Oncologic Hosp., Phila., 1982-92, St. Christopher's Hosp. for Children, Phila., 1998—2003, Med. Coll. Pa., Phila., 1991—; asst. prof. medicine, assoc. prof. Temple U. Sch. Medicine, Phila., 1978-89, prof. medicine, 1990—, Med. Coll. Pa., Phila., 1991—, Allegheny U. Health Scis., Phila., 1994—; regional chmn. dept. medicine Atlantic Health Sus., 2004—; prof., chair dept. medicine Morristown (NJ) Meml. Hosp., 2004—; prof. medicine Drexel U. Coll. Medicine, 2004—, U. Medicine and Dentistry NJ Med. Sch., 2005—08, Mt. Sinai Sch. Medicine, 2008—. Chief pulmonary disease and critical care medicine sect. Drexel U. Coll. Medicine, 1991—2003, v.p. medicine, chief medicine, 2001; attending physician, chief pulmonary unit Drexel U. Coll. Medicine, 1991—2003, dir. fellowship tng. program, 1991—, dir. Adult Cystic Fibrosis Program, 1991—, dir. Respiratory Care Svcs., 1991—, exec. com. of faculty, 1992—, utilization com., 1992—, chmn. search com. Cmty. and Preventive Medicine, 1992-93, sec. Exec. Faculty Com., 1993—. Mem. editl. bd. Clin. Respiratory Medicine, 1993—, Jour. of Asthma, 1993—; assoc. editor New Insights into Cystic Fibrosis, 1993—; contbr. articles to profl. jours. and chpts. to books. Recipient Lange Book award in Medicine, 1973, Rittenhouse Book award, 1973, Mosby Book award, 1973, Golden Apple Teaching award, 1985, 88; named Finalist for Lindbach Teaching award, 1990; grantee NIH, 1978-83, 89-91, Maternal and Child Health Care, 1984-88, Cystic Fibrosis Found., 1987-89, 93, Rorer Pharms., 1991-92,Am. Lung Assn., 1989-90, Glaxo Pharm. Co., 1991-93, G.H. Besselaar Assocs., 1991-93, ICI Pharm. Group, 1991-2000, Cortech Pharm. Group, 1993-2000, Genentech, Inc., 1993. Mem. Am. Thoracic Soc., Am. Coll. Chest Physicians, Assn. Am. Med. Colls., Am. Coll. Physicians, Soc. Clin. Decision Making, Am. Fedn. Clin. Rsch., ASTE, Phila. County Med. Soc., Pa. Med. Soc., Pa. Thoracic Soc. Home: 9 S Gables Dr Chester NJ 07930 Office: Morristown Meml Hosp 100 Madison Ave Morristown NJ 07962 Office Phone: 973-971-5136. Business E-Mail: stanley.fiel@atlantichealth.org.

FIELD, JAMES BERNARD, internist, educator; b. Fort Wayne, Ind., May 28, 1926; s. Abraham and Clara (Ridner) F.; m. Dorothy Spivey, Sept. 25, 1954; children: Carolyn, Nancy, Douglas, Susan. Student, Harvard Coll., 1944, student, 1946—47; MD cum laude, Harvard Med. Sch., 1951. Diplomate: Am. Bd. Internal Medicine. Intern internal medicine Mass. Gen. Hosp., Boston, 1951-52, asst. resident internal medicine, 1952-53, resident internal medicine, 1953-54; practice medicine specializing in endocrinology Pitts., 1962-78, Houston, 1978-89. Med. officer USPHS, Nat. Inst. Arthritis and Metabolic Diseases, Bethesda, Md., 1954, sr. asst. surgeon, 1954-58, sr. investigator, 1958-60, surgeon, 1958-60, sr. surgeon, 1960-61; asst. in medicine diabetic dept. Kings Coll. Hosp., London, 1957-58; med. officer Nat. Inst. Metabolic Disease, Bethesda, Md., 1961-62; head divsn. endocrinology and metabolism U. Pitts. Sch. Medicine, 1962-78, assoc. prof. medicine, 1962-66, prof. medicine, 1966-78, dir. clin. research unit, 1962-78; Rutherford prof. medicine Baylor Coll. Medicine, Houston, 1978-89, head div. endocrinology and metabolism, 1978-87; vis. prof. dept. exptl. medicine Univ. Coll. Med. Sch., London, 1985-86; dir. Diabetes and Endocrinology Rsch. Ctr., Baylor Coll Medicine, 1980-89; med. adv. bd. Nat. Pituitary Agy., 1967-69; research collaborator Brookhaven Nat. Lab., 1972-85; mem. nat. diabetes adv. bd. HEW, 1977-85, chmn., 1982-85; mem. endocrinology study sect. USPHS, 1965-69, chmn., 1968-69, endocrinology and metabolism tng. grant com., 1970-74, gen. clin. rsch. ctr. rev. com., 1976-79; mem. panel clin. scis. com. study nat. needs biomed. and behavioral rsch. pers. Nat Rsch. Coun., 1976-80; mem. VA merit rev. com. on endocrinology and metabolism, 1982-85; lectr. medicine Harvard Med. Sch., 1992-2002; mem. honors com. Harvard Med. Sch., 1993-2001. Editor (assoc. editor): Metabolism, 1959—69; editor: (editor-in-chief), 1969—2010; editor: (contbg.) Clin.Thyroidology, 1988—2000; contbr. numerous research articles on endocrinology to profl. jours. Bd. dirs. Gen. Clin. Research Centers, 1977-79; physician, vols. Medicine Clin., Hilton Head, 2001—. Served with U.S. Army, 1944-45. Decorated Purple Heart, Bronze Star; recipient Van Meter prize award Am. Goiter Assn., 1961, Prize Boylston Soc., 1951. Mem. Assn. Am. Physicians, Endocrine Soc. (mem. coun. 1972-75, internat. liaison com. 1972-75, mem. pub. affairs com. 1972-75, mem. awards com. 1972-75, chmn. 1974-75, nominating com. 1982-84, chmn. 1984), Am. Diabetes Assn. (dir. 1968-74, vice chmn. com. on rsch. 1972-73, chmn. com. rsch. 1975-77, mem. established investigator rev. bd. 1975-77, Eli Lilly award 1958), Am. Fedn. Clin. Rsch., Am. Clin. and Climatol. Assn., Am. Physiology Soc., Am. Soc. Clin. Investigation, Mass. Med. Soc. (chmn. com. on ret, physicians 1993-2002, Prize 1951, Vol. of Yr. 2001), Harvard Med. Alumni Assn., (treas. 1997-2000), Sea Pines Country Club (Hilton Head), Alpha Omega Alpha. Home: 50 Stoney Creek Rd Hilton Head Island SC 29928

FIELD, STEVEN PHILIP, medical educator; b. Newark, Feb. 21, 1951; s. Irving and Florence (Engel) F. BA, Yale U., 1973; MD, NYU, 1977, cert. in Bioethics and Med. Humanities, 2003. Diplomate Am. Bd. Internal Medicine, Am. Bd. Gastroenterology; cert. psychodynamic psychotherapy NYU Psychoanalytic Inst., Bioethics, Montefiore, NYU. Intern in internal medicine Bellevue Hosp., NYC, 1977-78, resident in internal medicine, 1978-81; instr. in medicine Mt. Sinai Hosp., NYC, 1981-83, NYU Sch. of Medicine, NYC, 1983—, clin. asst. prof. medicine, 1991—. Contbr. articles to med. jours., chpts. to med. textbooks. Recipient John Addison Porter Prize Yale U., 1973. Mem.: ACP, Crohn's and Colitis Found. Am. (sci. adv. coun.), N.Y. State Med. Soc., N.Y. Acad. Gastroenterology (v.p. 1995—96), Am. Gastroent. Assn., Yale Club Ctrl. N.J. (alumni schs. com.), Alpha Omega Alpha. Office: 245 E 35th St New York NY 10016-4283 Office Phone: 212-686-9477. Business E-Mail: steven.field@med.nyu.edu.

FIELDING, ALLEN FRED, oral and maxillofacial surgeon, educator; b. Paterson, NJ, Jan. 22, 1943; s. Fred W. and Emily Claire (Boehm) F. BS, Fairleigh Dickinson U., 1961, DMD, 1963; postgrad. in oral surgery, N.Y. U., 1965-66; MD, U. Health Sci. Antigua, 2001; MBA, U. Phoenix, 2003. Diplomate Am. Bd. Oral and Maxillofacial Surgery (adv. bd. 1983-86), Am. Bd. Forensic Medicine, Dental Nat. Anesthesia Bd. Intern in oral surgery Roosevelt Hosp., NYC, 1966-67; resident in oral surgery Phila. Gen. Hosp., 1967-69; practice dentistry specializing in oral-maxillo facial surgery Phila., 1969—; prof., chmn. dept. oral and maxillofacial surgery Temple U., Phila., 1983-88, staff prof., chief dept. oral and maxillofacial surgery univ. hosp., 1982-87, prof. emeritus, Kornberg Sch Dentistry, 2006—, prof., sch. medicine; assoc. resident dir., dept. oral & maxillo facial surgery Temple U. Hosp., 2008—. Cons. VA Hosp., Wilmington, Del.; staff St. Christopher's Hosp. for Children, Phila., Northeatern Hosp.; staff, chief divsn. oral and Maxillofacial surgery Epics. Hosp.; sect. chief oral and maxillofacial surgery Quakertown (Pa.) Hosp., Lawndale Hosp., Phila.; cons. Gt. Lakes Naval Hosp., Ill., Brandywine Hosp.; lectr. in field. Contbr. articles to profl. jours. Mem. Chapel of Four Chaplains, Valley Forge, Pa.; amb. People To People, 2004. Served to capt. USAF, 1963-65. ICOI fellowship. Fellow Am. Dental Soc. Anesthesiology, Royal Soc. Health, Am. Soc. Oral and Maxillofacial Surgeons (Pa. del.), World Affairs Coun. (Phila. chpt.), Am. Coll. Dentistry (editor local chpt.), Internat. Coll. Dentists, Internat. Assn. Oral and Maxillofacial Surgeons, Am. Assn. Oral and Maxillofacial Surgeons (del. house OMFS 2000-), Am. Coll. Oral and Maxillofacial Surgeons, Internat. Assn. Oral Maxillofacial Surgery; mem. AAUP, ADEA, ADA, Pa. Dental Soc. (nat. bd. exam writer), Phila. County Dental Soc. (bd. govs. 2000-07), Liberty Dental Soc. (meeting coord. 2010), Assn. Mil. Surgeons, Am. Assn. Dental Schs., Del. Valley Soc. Oral Surgeons (com. resident tng. 1973-85, exec. com., pres. 1985), Am. Assn. Hosp. Dentists (sec.-treas. Del. County chpt. 1972-74, v.p. 1974, pres. 1976), Great Lakes Soc. Oral Maxillofacial Surgeons, Mid-Atlantic Soc. Oral Maxillofacial Surgeons, Temple U. Oral Surgery Honor Soc. (advisor), Pa. Soc. Oral and Maxillofacial Surgeons (exec. com., govt. affairs com., pres. 1995-96), Coll. Physicians and Surgeons Phila., Dental Assts. Nat. Bd. (adv. bd.), Internat. Assn. Oral Implantologists, Del. Valley Acad. Osseointegration, Pierre Fauchard Soc. (elected mem.), Omicron Kappa Upsilon (pres. 1985, CODA site visitor Temple chpt.), Internat. Assn. ADA Student Clinicians (assoc.). also: County Line Med Ctr 5279 Lincoln Hwy Gap PA 17527 Office: Temple U Episc Hosp Campus 100 E Lehigh Ave Philadelphia PA 19125 Home: Symphony House Ste 2308 440 Ave Arts Philadelphia PA 19146-4901 Office Phone: 215-707-3613, 215-707-2065. Personal E-mail: impactor@comcast.net. Business E-Mail: allen@dental.temple.edu. *

FIELDING, JONATHAN EVAN, county health department administrator, pediatrician; b. Oct. 4, 1942; BA, Williams Coll., 1964; MA, MD, Harvard Coll., 1969, MPH, 1971; MBA, U. Pa., 1977. Diplomate Am. Bd. Pediats., Am. Bd. Preventive Medicine. Josiah Macy fellow Harvard U., Cambridge, Mass., 1969; intern, resident Boston Children's Hosp., 1969-71; fellow Harvard U., Boston, 1971; resident in pediats. Georgetown U. Med. Ctr., Washington, 1971-72, prin. med. svcs. nat. officer Job Corps, 1971-73; commr. pub. health Commonwealth of Mass., 1975-79; prof. health svcs. & pediats. UCLA, 1979—; dir. pub. health L.A. County, 1997—. Spl. asst. to dir. Bur. Cmty. Health Svcs. Health Svcs. & Mental Health Adminstrn. HEW, 1971-73; co-dir. Ctr. Health Enhancement Edn. & Rsch., 1979-84; co-dir. Ctr. for Healthier Children, Families & Cmtys., 1995-2004; lectr. Harvard U., Boston, 1973-75, Boston U., 1975-79, Brandeis U., 1975-79, Northwestern U., 1975-79; vis. lectr. UCLA, 1977; rsch. assoc. Urban Rsch. Ctr. Hunter Coll. CUNY, 1978; vis. prof. Nordic Sch. Pub. Health, Sweden, 1980, 83, 93. Editor: Ann. Revs. Pub. Health, 1995—; asst. editor Mercy-Rosenau Pub. Health and Preventive Medicine 1992-98, 14th edit. Vice-chair Partnership for Prevention, 1997—2002, chmn., 2002—, U.S. Cmty. Preventive Svcs. Task Force, 1996—, chair, 2001—. Mem. Am. Legacy Found. (bd. dir. 2005-), Sec.'s adv. com. health objectives nation (chair 2008), Pub. Health Adv. Com., Calif.; Fellow Assn. Health Svcs.; mem. NAS Inst. Medicine, Am. Acad. Pediats., Am. Assn. Pub. Health Physicians, Am. Med. Peer Rev. Assn., Am. Pub. Health Assn., Assn. Health Svcs. Medicine, Am. Heart Assn., Am. Coll. Preventive Medicine (pres. 1997-99). Office: UCLA Sch Pub Health Ctr Health Sci 61 253A Los Angeles CA 90095-0001

FIELDS, ABBIE L., gynecologic oncologist; BA, Case Western Res. U., Cleveland, 1982; MD, Ohio State U., 1987. Diplomate Am. Bd. Ob-Gyn, 1994, Am. Bd. Ob-Gyn, 1996, Am. Bd. Ob-Gyn-gynecologic oncology, lic. NY, 1993. Resident ob-gyn. Northwestern Univ., Chgo., 1987—91; fellow gynecologic oncology Johns Hopkins Univ., Baltimore, 1991—93; assoc. prof. Albert Einstein Coll. Medicine/Montefiore Med. Ctr.; med. dir. Va. Gynecologic Oncology; hosp. affiliations include Georgetown Univ. Hosp., Wash. Hosp. Ctr. Mem.: AMA, ACOG, Am. Cancer Soc. (Clin.Oncology Fellowship award 1992—93), Med. Soc. Va., Richmond Ob-Gyn. Soc., Richmond Acad. of Medicine, NY Obstet. Soc., Bronx Gynecologic and Obstet. Soc., NY Med. Assn., Soc. of Gynecologic Oncologists, Am. Soc. Clin. Oncology, ACS, Am. Assn. for Cancer Rsch. Office: Washington Hospital Center Ste 420 2021 K St NW Washington DC 20006 Office Phone: 202-877-2391.

FIELDS, HOWARD LINCOLN, neurologist, physiologist, educator; b. Chgo., Dec. 12, 1939; s. Charles and Mae (Pinkert) Fields; m. Carol Margaret Felts, Dec. 31, 1966; children: Rima Margaret Johnson, Gabriel Charles. BS, U. Chgo., 1960; MD, Stanford U., 1965, PhD in Neuroscience, 1966. Research neurologist Walter Reed Research Inst., Washington, 1967-70; clin. fellow Harvard Med. Sch., Boston, 1970-72; asst. prof. U. Calif., San Francisco, 1973-78, assoc. prof., 1978-82, prof., 1982—, vice chmn. neurology, 1993—2010; dir. Wheeler Ctr. for Neurobiology of Addiction. Cons. NIH, Bethesda, 1979—84; vis. fellow Clare Hall Coll. Cambridge U., England, 1979; vis. prof. Royal Soc. Medicine, 1988. Editor: Recent Advances in Pain Research and Therapy, 1985, Core Curriculum for Professional Education in Pain, 1991, 2d edit., 1995; author: Pain, 1987, Pain Syndromes in Neurology, 1990, Pharmacotherapy of Pain, 1994; contbr. articles to profl. jours. Recipient Rsch. Career Devel. award, NIH, Merit award, Nat. Inst. Drug Abuse, Kerr award, Am. Pain Soc., 1997. Mem.: Am. Acad. Arts & Sci., Inst. Medicine of NAS, Soc. Neuroscience, Am. Neurol. Assn. (councillor 1991, mem. program com. 1991, R.D. Adams award 2006), Am. Acad. Neurology (Cotzias lectr. award 2000), Am. Soc. Clin. Investigation, Internat. Assn. Study Pain (program chmn. 1981—84, sec. 1990—93, editor-in-chief IASP Press 1993—2003). Office: U Calif Dept Neurology 5858 Horton St Ste 200 Emeryville CA 94608 Business E-Mail: hlf@phy.ucsf.edu.

FIELDS, JAMES PERRY, dermatologist, dermatopathologist, allergist, pharmacologist, pharmacist; b. Sherman, Tex., July 30, 1932; s. John Galloway and Alma (Goff) F.; m. Linda Hensley, May 30, 1958; children: Timothy Austin, Amy Elizabeth. BS, U. Tex., 1953, MS, 1957; MD, U. Tex., Galveston, 1958. Diplomate Am. Bd. Dermatology, Am. Bd. Allergy and Immunology, spl. competence cert. in dermatopathology. Dir. dept. dermatology USPHS, SI, N.Y., 1964-78; assoc. prof. medicine and pathology Vanderbilt U. Sch. of Medicine, Nashville, 1978-88; pvt. practice, Nashville, 1988—; dir. dermatopathology Lab. of the Mid-South, Nashville, 1988—. From instr. to assoc. clin. prof. dermatology and pathology Columbia-Presbyn. Hosp. and Coll. of Physicians and Surgeons, N.Y.C., 1968-88; assoc. clin. prof. medicine Vanderbilt U. Sch. Medicine, Nashville, 1988—. Author (with others): Mycobacterial Diseases, 1991, 2d edit., 2000; contbr. articles to profl. jours. Bd. dirs. Am. Leprosy Missions Internat., Greenville, S.C., 1974—2007, Med. Program cons., 07-, bd. dirs. Am. Registry Pathology, Washington, 80-; vol. med. missionary, United Meth. Vols. in Mission, 1984—2004. Capt. USPHS, 1958-79. Recipient citation for meritorious svcs. President's Com. on Employment of Handicapped, 1970, Meritorious Svc. medal USPHS, 1978, Good Samaritan award Nashville Acad. Medicine, 2002. Fellow ACP (Volunteerism and Cmty. Svc. award in Medicine, Tenn. chpt. 2000), Am. Acad. Allergy and Immunology, Am. Acad. Dermatology, Am. Coll. Allergy and Immunology, Am. Soc. Dermatopathology, Am. Soc. for Dermatologic Surgery, N.Y. Acad. Medicine (sec. 1976-77, chmn. sect. on dermatology 1977-78). Home: 411 Lynwood Blvd Nashville TN 37205-3434 Office: 4301 Hillsboro Rd # 222 Nashville TN 37215-3314 Home Phone: 615-298-1625. Personal E-mail: darmpathlab@earthlink.net.

FIELDS, JEREMY DAVID, neurologist, educator; b. Nairobi, Kenya, Dec. 21, 1970; BA, Yale U., 1993; MD, U. Calif., San Francisco, 2003. Asst. prof., interventional neuroradiology and neurocritical care Oreg. Health & Sci. U., 2009—. Dir. Neurocritical Care Fellowship, Oreg. Health & Sci. U., 2010. Rsch. grant, NIH. Mem.: Am. Stroke Assn., Am. Acad. Neurology, Am. Heart Assn., Neurocritical Care Soc., Soc. Neurointerventional Surgery. Office: OHSU 3181 SW Sam Jackson Pk Rd CR Portland OR 97239 Business E-Mail: fieldsje@ohsu.edu.

FIELDS, RONALD H., cardiologist; MD, Milton S. Hershey Coll. of Medicine. Diplomate Am. Bd. Internal Medicine, Am. Bd. Internal Medicine-cardiovasc. diseases and interventional cardiology. Resident Letterman Army Med. Ctr., Calif., fellow cardiology Calif.; interventional cardiology St Mary Medical Center. Maj. med. corps US Army. Recipient Maj. Gen. Kenyon Joyce Rsch. award, Meritorious Service medal, US Army; named one of Top Doctors, Phila. Mag., 2011. Fellow: Am. Coll. of Cardiology. Office: Saint Mary Medical Center Office Bldg Ste Number 320 1203 Langhorne-Newtown Rd Langhorne PA 19047 Office Phone: 215-750-7818. Office Fax: 215-752-0436.

FIETSAM, ROBERT, JR., physician; b. Columbus, Ohio, Dec. 15, 1956; s. Robert and Mary E. (Maccombie) F.; m. Jill Courtney Brach, Nov. 6, 1993; children: Dominique, Desiree, Alexandra, Robert Mac, Elle, Paris. BSChem., U. Mich., 1978; MD, Wayne State U., 1986. Diplomate Am. Bd. Surgery, Am. Bd. Thoracic Surgery. Cardiac surgeon Southeastern Cardiovasc. Assn., Dothan, Ala., 1995-96; asst. prof. surgery Duke U., Durham, NC, 1996-98; dir. cardiac surgery Village Surg. Assocs., 1998—2003; pres. Sandhills Heart Surgery P.A., Fayetteville, NC, 2003—07, Genesis Heart Inst., 2007—. Contbr. chpt. Cardiac Issues, 1992; contbr. artcles to profl. jours. Recipient Charles C. Guthrie award Vascular Surg. Soc., 1990, Charles Johnston award Detroit Surg. Assn., 1991. Mem. AMA, ACS, Soc. Thoracic Surgeons, Am. Athletic Med. Assn., Cumberland County Med. Soc., Scott County Med. Soc. Home Phone: 563-514-4163; Office Phone: 563-421-3990. Business E-Mail: fietsamr@genesishealth.com. E-mail: dellnewjet@aol.com.

FIG, LORRAINE MARILYN, nuclear medicine physician, director; b. Cape Town, South Africa, Nov. 9, 1949; MBChB, U. Cape Town, 1973; MPH, U. Mich., 1985. Lectr., asst. prof., assoc. prof. nuc. medicine dept. U. Mich., 1991—2004, prof. radiology dept., 2004; assoc. program dir., nuc. medicine radiation safety svc. Dept. Vet.

Affairs, 1991—. Bd. dirs. Intersocietal Commn. Accreditation Nuc. Labs., 2002; exec. bd., academic coun. Soc. Nuc. Medicine, 2007; bd. regents Am. Coll. Nuc. Medicine, 2007; mem., nuc. medicine residency rev. com. Accreditation Coun. Grad. Med. Edn., 2010; bd. dirs. Am. Bd. Sci. Nuc. Medicine, 2011. Contbr. articles to profl. publs. Recipient Disting. Achievement award, Divsn. Nuc. Medicine, U. Mich., Spl. Contbn. award, Dept. Vet. Affairs, Superior Performance award, Disting. Svc. award, Academic Coun., Soc. Nuc. Medicine. Fellow: Am. Coll. Nuc. Medicine; mem.: Am. Bd. Sci. Nuc. Medicine, South African Soc. Nuc. Medicine, Am. Coll. Radiology, Soc. Nuc. Medicine. Avocations: walking, reading, genealogy. Office: Nuclear Medicine 115 VA Ann Arbor Ann Arbor MI 48105 Address: 2215 Fuller Rd Ann Arbor MI 48105 Business E-Mail: lfig@umich.edu.

FIGL, ANDREA, plastic surgeon, consultant; b. Dolo, Italy, Apr. 27, 1966; s. Giuseppe Figl and Giordana Michieletto; m. Patricia Barbero, June 21, 2002; children: Alexandre, Chiara. MD (hon.), U. Pavia, Italy, 1991; diploma in hand surgery, U. Montpellier, France, 1997; diploma in breast surgery, U. Paris, 2003. Cert. specialist plastic and reconstructive surgery U. Pavia, 1997. Lab. asst. Bayer Ag, Leverkusen, Germany, 1989; asst. surgeon dept. plastic surgery U. Pavia, Milan, 1991—96; asst. surgeon dept. plastic and hand surgery Ctr. Hosp. U., Nice, France, 1996—97; fellow plastic surgery Clinica Ivo Pitanguy, Rio de Janeiro, 1997—97; sr. ho. officer dept. plastic surgery Addenbrooke's Hosp., Cambridge, England, 1998—2000; cons. breast surgeon Ctr. Antoine Lacassagne, Nice, France, 2000—; aesthetic surgeon Clinique St. Antoine, Nice, France, 2002—. Adv. bd. Unite De Concertation Multidisciplinaire En Pathologie Mammaire, Nice, France, 2000—. Author: Atti Della Xi-xii Riunione Medico Scientifica Del Dipartimento Di Chirurgia, Pavia, 1996, Atti Del Convegno Di Lovran, Tacchi Editore, 1997, Le Sein, Masson, 2002, 8 Cours Francophone Sur Le Cancer Du Sein, 2003. Lt. Health Svc., 1994—96, Como, Italy. Recipient Hon. Vis. Scholar, Internat. Fedn. Med. Students' Assn., 1990; Vis. Fellowship, Canniesburn Hosp. Bearsden Scotland, 1998. Mem.: Ordine Dei Medici E Chirurghi (assoc.), Ordre Des Medecins (assoc.). Avocations: tennis, piano, photography. E-mail: andrea.figl@nice.fnclcc.fr.

FIGLIN, ROBERT ALAN, hematologist, oncologist; b. Phila., June 22, 1949; s. Jack and Helen Figlin; Jonathan B., Zaclary H. BA in Chemistry, Temple U., Phila., 1970; postgrad. in inorganic chemistry, Temple U., 1972; MD, Med. Coll. Pa., 1976. Diplomate Am. Bd. Internal Medicine, Am. Bd. Med. Oncology, Nat. Bd. Med. Examiners; lic. physician, Calif. Med. intern, resident in medicine Cedars-Sinai Med. Ctr., LA, 1976-79, chief resident in medicine, 1979-80; fellow in hematology-oncology UCLA, 1980-82, dir., hematology-oncology fellowship program, divsn. hematology-oncology, dept. medicine, 1992—2003, co-dir., oncology program area divsn. hematology-oncology, dept. medicine, 1993—95; asst. prof. medicine, divsn. hematology-oncology, dept. medicine UCLA Sch. Medicine, 1982-88, assoc. prof., divsn. hematology-oncology, dept. medicine, 1988-94, med. dir., thoracic oncology program, dept. medicine and surgery, divsns. hematology-oncology and thoracic surgery, 1994—2006, med. dir., genitourinary oncology, dept. medicine and surgery, divsns. hematology-oncology and urology, 1995—2006, Henry Alvin and Carrie L. Meinhardt chair in urol. oncology, 2000—06; prof. medicine, divsn. hematology-oncology, dept. medicine UCLA David Geffen Sch. Medicine, 1994—2006, prof. clin urology, divsn. urologic oncology, dept. urology, 2000—06; emeritus prof. medicine & urology UCLA, 2006—, asst. dir., Bowyer Multi-disciplinary Oncology Clinic Jonsson Comprehensive Cancer Ctr., UCLA, 1985—90, dir. Bowyer Oncology Ctr., dir. outpatient clin. rsch. unit, 1990-92, dir. clin. rsch. unit, 1993-98, dir. hematology/oncology fellowship program, 1995—2003, assoc. program dir., solid tumor oncology, 1996—97, program dir., solid tumor oncology, 1997—98, program dir., solid tumor develop. therapeutics, 1998—2001, co-dir., genitourinary oncology, 2004—06, co-dir., lung cancer rsch. program, 2005; assoc. dir. clin. rsch., Comprehensive Cancer Ctr. City of Hope, Duarte, Calif., 2006—09, chair, dept. med. oncology & exptl. therapeutics rsch., 2006—10, Arthur and Rosalie Kaplan prof. med. oncology, 2006—10, acting dir., Comprehensive Cancer Ctr., 2008—09; dir. City Hope Comprehensive Cancer Ctr., 2009—10; prof., dir., divsn. hematology-oncology Cedars-Sinai Med. Ctr.; dir. academic programs Samuel Oschin Comprehensive Cancer Ctr., 2010—, David Geffen Sch Medicine UCLA, LA. Co-principal investigator, mem. exec. bd. Lung Cancer Study Group, UCLA, 1982—89; co-principal investigator, mem. genitourinary com., mem. kidney cancer subcommittee Eastern Cooperative Oncology Group, 1988—93; mem. exec. bd. UCLA Med./Surgical Oncology Ctr., 1989—95; FDA cons., 1990—92; prin. investigator UCLA S.W. Oncology Group, 1990—2000, mem. lung com., 1990—2003, bd. gov., 1990—2000, mem. genito-urinary com., 1990—2003; mem. med. adv. bd. Nat. Kidney Cancer Assn., 1993—; med. dir. U. Calif. Preferred Oncology Networks of Calif., 1994—95; sci. founder Agensys, 1996—2007; chmn. instl. rev. bd., mem. human rsch. policy bd. UCLA, 1998—2006; co-prin. investigator, clin. dir. NCI Specialized Program of Rsch. Excellence, Lung Cancer, 2000—06, NCI Bladder Cancer Prevention, 2003—06; co-dir. Lung Cancer Rsch. Program, 2003—06; chmn. scientific adv. bd. Phase One Found., 2005—; mem., bd. dirs. Lung Cancer Found. America. Editor: Interferons in cytokines, 1988—90, Kidney Cancer Jour., 1993—94, Current Clin. Trials, 1992—96; UCLA Cancer Trials Newsletter, 1990—96, Seminars on Oncology-Kidney Cancer, 1995, Cancer Therapeutics, 1997, Cancer Biotherapy and Radio Pharms., 1997; contbr. articles and revs.; editor: Renal & Adrenal Tumors, 2002, Kidney Cancer Jour., 2003—. Named one of Best Doctors in Am., 1994-, America's Top Doctors for Cancer 2006- Fellow ACP, Internat. Soc. for Biologic Therapy; mem. Am. Soc. Clin. Oncology, Am. Fedn. Clin. Rsch., Am. Assn. for Cancer Rsch., Soc. for Biologic Therapy (chmn. ann. scientific meeting 1997, pres. cancer panel 1997, S.W. Oncology Group, Assn. Subspecialty Profs., Am. Urological Assn., Internat. Assn. for Study of Lung Cancer. Office: Cedars Sinai Med Ctr Samuel Oschin Comprehensive Cancer Inst 700 Beverly Blvd AC 1042 B N Tower Los Angeles CA 90048 Office Phone: 310-248-6736. Business E-Mail: robert.figlin@cshs.org.

FIGUEIREDO, CLAUDIA REGINA, otolaryngologist; b. Sao Paulo, Brazil, Mar. 19, 1968; MD, U. ABC, 1993; PhD, U. Fed. de Sao Paulo, 2003. Physician Hosp. Sao Paulo, 2002—. Mem.: Brazilian Otorhinolaryngology Soc. Avocations: running, mountain climbing, reading. Office: Rua Fidencio Ramos 195 10 andar Sao Paulo 04551-010 Brazil Office Fax: 11 2198 3444. Business E-Mail: claufig@uol.com.br.

FIGUEIRÓ-FILHO, ERNESTO ANTONIO, obstetrician, gynecologist, researcher; b. Campo Grande, Mato Grosso do Sul, Brazil, Aug. 9, 1974; s. Ernesto Antonio and Maria Nai Coelho Figueiró; m. Tamara Lemos Maia Figueiró, July 24, 2004. PhD, Faculty Medicine FMRP, USP, Ribeirão Preto, São Paulo, 2003. Cert. in maternal fetal medicine FEBRASGO, 2004. Prof. medicine Fed. U. Mato Grosso do Sul, Campo Grande, 2004—. Achievements include research in pregnancy and infections; fetal medicine; high risk pregnancy; perinatology; ultrasounds in OB/GYN. Office: Faculty Medicine UFMS Av Mato Grosso 1421 Campo Grande Mato Grosso do Sul 79002231 Brazil Office Phone: 55-67-3042-5005. Business E-Mail: eafigueiro@uol.com.br.

FIGUERAS, JAUME B., cardiologist; b. Barcelona, Feb. 17, 1945; s. Andreu and Isabel Bellot (Pascual) Figueras; m. Cristina Coll, June 26, 1971; children: Guillem, Marc. PhD, U. Autonomous Barcelona, 1992. Diplomate Spain, 1969. Critical care fellow U. So. Calif., LA, 1973—75; cardiology fellow UCLA, 1975—77; assoc. & clin. chief cardiology H. U. Vall d'Hebron, Barcelona, 1978—88; dir. coronary care unit Hosp. U. Vell d'Hebron, Barcelona, 1989—; assoc. prof. medicine U. Autonomous Barcelona, 1991—. Mem.: European Soc. Cardiology (corr.). Achievements include research in mechanisms of unstable angina, acute pulmonary edema, cardiac rupture. Home: Rambla Jardi 104 Valldoreix Barcelona 08197 Spain

FIGUEREDO, CARLOS MARCELO, dental educator, researcher; b. Rio de Janeiro, June 26, 1969; Degree in Dentistry, U. Grande Rio, 1991; PhD, Karolinska Inst., 1999. Assoc. prof. Rio de Janeiro State U., 1999—. Guest rsch. Karolinska Inst., 1999. Avocations: swimming, motorcycling. Office: Ave Marechal Henrique Lott 180 bl 1 1904 Rio de Janeiro 22631370 Brazil Personal E-mail: cmfigueredo@hotmail.com.

FIGUEREDO, VINCENT M., cardiologist, educator; BA, Haverford Coll., 1979—83; MD, Columbia U., 1983—87. Diplomate Am. Bd. Internal Medicine, Am. Bd. Internal Medicine-cardiovasc. diseases, Am. Soc. of Nuclear Cardiology, cert. Nat. Bd. of Echocardiography, diplomate Am. Soc. of Hypertension. Resident internal medicine Columbia Presbyn. Med. Ctr., 1987—90; fellow cardiology Univ. of Calif., 1990—94, asst. prof. of medicine; chair cardiology and cardiothoracic surgery dept. Lovelace Health Sys.; clin. assoc. prof. Univ. of N.Mex Health Sciences Ctr.; dir. echocardiography lab. San Francisco Gen. Hosp.; assoc. prof. of medicine Jefferson Med. Coll.; dir. cardiovasc. diseases fellowship programs Albert Einstein Med. Ctr., 2007—. Coordinating editor Practical Reviews Cardiology; reviewer for several peer-reviewed publs. Named one of Top Doctors, Phila. Mag., 2011. Office: Albert Einstein Medical Center Ste 363 Klein Professional Bldg 5401 Old York Rd Philadelphia PA 19141 Office Phone: 215-456-5955. Office Fax: 215-456-7926.

FIGUEROA, JOHN G., medical products executive; BA, UCLA; MBA, Pepperdine Univ. Various sr. mgmt. positions Baxter Healthcare Corp.; v.p. sales Calif. to regional v.p. we. region McKesson Health Systems, 1997—2000; sr. v.p. nat. accounts McKesson Corp., 2000—02, sr. v.p. customer ops. southwest region to pres. nat. retail accounts, 2002—06, pres. US pharmaceutical, 2006—10; CEO Omnicare, Inc., Covington, Ky., 2011—. Mem. bd. gov. GS1 US; bd. dir. Reliance Steel & Aluminum Co. Bd. dir. Boys Hope Girls Hope; mem. bd. gov. exec. com. Pepperdine Univ. Sch. Bus. Served through capt. US Army. Office: Omnicare Inc 1600 Rivercenter II Covington KY 41011 Office Phone: 859-392-3300. *

FILA, JOHN CHARLES, psychoanalyst; b. Boston; s. John F. and Marion L. Fila. AB, Harvard U., Cambridge, Mass., 1992; PhD, U. Berkeley, Mich., 1995. Diplomate Am. Coll. Profl. Mental Health Practitioners. Pvt. practice, Wellesley, Mass., 1997—2000, Santa Monica, Calif., 2000—. Nat. bd. dirs. Internat. Acad. Philosophy, N. Hollywood, Calif. Contbr. articles to profl. jours. Vol. mentor for disadvantaged, 1995—; ombudsman, officer The Prometheus Soc. Internat., The Lewis Terman Soc.; mem. Nat. Com. on Am. Fgn. Policy, NYC, Nat. Campaign for Tolerance, Montgomery, Ala. Mem.: AAAS, Internat. Neuro-Psychoanalysis Soc., Royal Overseas Soc., NY Acad. Scis., Menninger Soc., Harvard Club (Boston, So. Calif., Palm Beach). Republican. Episcopalian. Achievements include research in post traumatic stress disorder and its comorbid relationship to a syndrome of mental health issues. Avocations: eclectic reading, sports, travel, theater, films. Home: Apt 40 2928 4th St Santa Monica CA 90405 Office: Ste 1215 5155 Rosecrans Ave Hawthorne CA 90250 Office Phone: 310-491-3680. Personal E-mail: psychdr721@hotmail.com.

FILDISSIS, GEORGE, medical educator, nursing educator; m. Anastasia Tsimogianni; children: Elena, Arianna. Degree in Medicine, U. Athens, Greece, 1980. Cert. in internal medicine Athens U., 1990, in critical care medicine Athens U., 1993. Physician Critical Care Unit, KAT Gen. Hosp., 1990—; asst. prof. Athens U., Faculty Nursing, 2004—, assoc. prof. crical care & hyperbaric medicine, 2009—. Vis. asst. prof. Duke U. Hyperbaric Ctr., Durham, NC, 1997—98. Fellow, Greek Govt., 1997. Office: Faculty Nursing ICU Athens Uni 2 Nikis St Kifisia Athens 14561 Greece Office Phone: 0030-6974-190499. Business E-Mail: fildiss@nurs.uoa.gr.

FILERMAN, GARY LEWIS, healthcare educator; b. Mpls., Nov. 16, 1936; s. Joseph H. and Bonnie (Kobrin) F.; m. Jane Harding, Sept. 15, 1962; children: Amy Beth, Joseph Harding, Suzanne Louise. BA, U. Minn., 1959, M.Health Adminstrn. (Phillips Found. fellow 1959-60), 1961, MA (W.K. Kellogg fellow 1961-64), 1963, PhD (Milbank travel grantee 1964, Orgn. Am. States fellow 1964), 1970. Adminstrv. resident Johns Hopkins Hosp., 1961-62; acting dir. Minn. Hosp. Assn., 1965; pres. Assn. Univ. Programs in Health Adminstrn., Washington, 1965-93; exec. sec. Accrediting Commn. Edn. Health Services Adminstrn., 1968-80; assoc. dir. PEW Health Professions Commn., Washington, 1993-95; dir. David A. Winston Fellowship, 1986—2007, pres., 1998—2003, Altas Health Found., 2011—. Mem. faculty George Washington U., chmn., prof. dept. health mgmt. and policy, 1998-2000, prof. health svc. adminstrn., chmn., prof. health sys., Georgetown U., 2000—09, sr. v.p., Atlas Rsch. LLC, 2009-; guest scholar Brookings Instn., 1962; sr. health advisor Acae. Ednl. Devel., 1998-2000; cons. in field, advisor Joint Com. Internat., 2006-. Author: A Future of Consequence, 1989;, editor Jour. Health Adminstrn. Edn., 1982-93; author articles in field.; mem. editl. bds. profl. jours. Mem. nat. health professions adv. coun. HHS, 1983-87, coun. agy for health care policy and rsch., 1990-92; bd. dirs. Am. Refugee Commn., 1982-2004, Fairfax Audubon, 1989-93, Am. Internat. Health Alliance, Companion Care Assn., 2005-; chmn. Planned Parenthood Metro Washington, 1990-91, bd. dirs. 1989-92; bd. dirs. Ctr. for Transformational Leadership, 2000-02; internat. adv. bd. Vols. of Am., 2003—07, bd. dir. 2008-; trustee Citizens Advocacy Ctr., 2006—, McLean Cmty. Found., 2007-, mem. Inst. Medicine Forum Drug Discovery, Devel. & Translation., 2009- Recipient Silver medal Leuven (Belgium) U., 1972, Disting. Contbn. award Assn. U. Programs Health Adminstrn., 1979, Outstanding Achievement award Regents of U. Minn., 1982, Outstanding Achievement award Ohio State U., 1992, Humanitarian award, Am. Refugee Com., 2005; Salzburg Seminar fellow, 2000. Fellow APHA, Am. Acad. Med. Adminstrn. (hon.), hon. alumni, Univ. Chgo.,1992, diplomate Am. Coll. of Health Care Execs., 1990—; mem. Royal Soc. Health, Assn. Am. Med. Colls., Cosmos Club (Washington), Phi Beta Kappa. Home: 1322 Banquo Ct Mc Lean VA 22102-2707 Office Phone: 202-687-8150.

FILES, DOUGLAS SCOTT, aerospace medicine specialist; b. Ithaca, NY, Mar. 15, 1966; s. Donald Howard and Barbara Distin Files. BA in Linguistics, Mich. State U., East Lansing, 1987; MD, Wayne State U., Detroit, 1994; MPH, U. Utah, Salt Lake City, 2003. Diplomate Am. Bd. Preventive Medicine, cert. aerospace medicine Am. Coll. Preventive Medicine. Rsch. asst. Mich. State U., 1984—87; English tutor Luth. Social Svcs., Lansing, Mich., 1987—90; resident in internal medicine Duke U. Med. Ctr., Durham, NC, 1994—97; internal medicine physician Omni Healthcare, Palm Bay, Fla., 1997—99; brigade surgeon 101st Airborne Divsn., Ft. Campbell, Fla., 1999—2002; resident in aerospace medicine Sch. Aerospace Medicine, Brooks City Base, Tex., 2003—05; chief aerospace medicine 47th Med. Group, Laughlin AFB, Tex., 2005—08; commd. USAF, 2002, advanced through grades to lt. col., 2007. Bd. govs. Hugh O'Brian Youth Leadership, Tex., 2005—08. Decorated Meritorious Svc. medal, Army Commendation medal. Mem.: Aerospace Medicine Assn., Alpha Omega Alpha, Phi Kappa Phi, Phi Beta Kappa. Avocations: travel, running, reading. Home: 3920 W 16th St Panama City FL 32401 Office: Flight Medicine 566F 325 th Med Group Tyndall AFB FL 32403

FILIACI, FRANCO, allergist, researcher; b. Arquata del Tronto, Italy, Aug. 4, 1944; s. Carlo Filiaci and Maria Vecchiotti; m. Piera Enza Settembrini; children: Fabio, Flavia, Fabrizia. MD, U. La Sapienza, Rome, 1970. Resident in ENT U. La Sapienza, 1973, ENT asst., 1974—79, audioloty asst., 1979—80, ENT asst., 1980—82, assoc. prof. pediat. ENT, 1982—86, assoc. prof. otolaringology, 1986—; resident in allergology and immunology U. Florence, 1976. Cons. Aeronautic Medicolegal Inst., Rome, 1972—80; dir. National Inst. Rsch., Rome, 1979—83; contbg. editor Internat. Jour. Clin. and Investigate Allergy, Madrid, 1996—; mem. sci. coun. cardiorespiratory Nat. Inst. Rsch., Rome, 1983—86; editor ENT sect. Italian Jour. Allergy and Clin. Immunology, 1991. Author: ENT Allergo-immunological Problems, 1983; contbr. articles to profl. jours. Recipient G. Ferreri award, ENT Italian Soc., 1972. Mem.: European Rhinologic Soc., Italian Soc. Allergy and Clin. Immunology (dir. rsch. group on rhinitis 1998—), Otolaryngological Italian Soc. Avocations: painting, swimming. Home: Nadir 10 00012 Guidonia Montecelio Italy Office: U Rome La Sapienza Policlinico 179 00161 Rome Italy Home Phone: 0390774 363712; Office Phone: 03906 44790521. Office Fax: 03906 4460378; Home Fax: 0390774 363712. Business E Mail: franco.filiaci@uniroma1.it.

FILIP, AGATA ANNA, geneticist, educator; b. Lublin, Poland, Jan. 16, 1966; DVM, U. Life Scis., Lublin, 1991; PhD, Med. U. Lublin, 1998. Asst. dept. med. genetics Med. U. Lublin, 1991—2001, asst. prof. dept. cancer genetics, 2001—. Recipient Achievements award, Rector Med. U. Lublin, award, Polish Soc. Human Genetics. Fellow: Polish Soc. Genetics; mem.: European Soc. Human Genetics, Polish Soc. Hematologists and Transfusionologists, Polish Soc. Human Genetics. Avocations: sailing, hiking. Office: 11 Radziwillowska St Lublin 20-950 Poland Office Fax: 48(81)5288410. Personal E-mail: aafilip@hotmail.com.

FILIPIAK, KRZYSZTOF J., cardiologist, educator; b. Poznan, Poland, Feb. 28, 1972; s. Jerzy Filipiak and Miroslawa Luczak-Filipiakowa. MD, Med. U. Sch., Warsaw, 1997, PhD, 2000. Lectr. clin. pharmacology Med. U. Sch., Warsaw, 1997—98, asst. prof. cardiology, 1998—2003, head biomarkers and cardiovasc. pharmacotherapy lab., 2003—, assoc. prof., 2005—. Editor (co-author): (textbook) Renin-Angiotensin System Drugs, Statins-The Basic Clinical Pharmacology, Acute Coronary Syndromes (Spl. Sci. Award of Polish Cardiac Soc., 2004); mng. editor: Kardiologia po Dyplomie, 2002—, sect. editor: Polish Jour. Cardiology, 1999—. Mem. MENSA Poland, Warsaw, 1996, Ministry of Health Expert Group on Health Tech. Assessment, Warsaw, 2004—05. Recipient Young Rschr. award, Jagiellonian Med. Rsch. Centre, Cracow, Poland, 2001, Sci. award, Ministry of Health, 2004. Mem.: European Soc. Cardiology (mem. working groups acute coronary care, mem. cardiovasc. pharmacology and drug therapy), Inst. Atherothrombosis (sec. sci. bd.), Polish Cardiac Soc. (dep. chmn. of club 30 - Polish top jr. cardiologists 2004—). Roman Catholic. Achievements include development of Banach risk score system, long-term Polish risk score for acute coronary syndrome patients. Avocations: travel, history. Office: Central Univ Hosp 1a Banach St Warsaw 02097 Poland Office Fax: +48 22 5991957. E-mail: krzysztof.filipiak@amwaw.edu.pl.

FILIPPOU, DIMITRIOS, surgeon, researcher; s. Konstantinos Filippou and Niki Delimichali-Filippou; m. Argyro Trigka, June 23, 2002; 2 children. Diploma in Medicine, U. Athens, Greece, 1995, PhD, 2002. Rsch. fellow dept. physiology Med. Sch., U. Athens, 1997—2002; register in surgery Agii Anargiri, Athens Anticancer Hosp., Kifissia, 1997—2000, Agia Olga, Athens Gen. Hosp., 2001—03, Piraeus (Greece) Gen. Hosp., 2003—05; vis. surgeon Hopital Cantonal, Fribourg, Switzerland, 2005—. Pres. Sci. Assn. Greek Med. Students, Athens, 1993—96; bd. mem. European Med. Students Assn., Hamburg, Germany, 1994—95; pres. Sci. Assn. Greek Young Doctors, Athens, 1997—2002; gen. sec. Med. Soc. Messinia, Kalamata, Greece, 1997—97; mem. sci. com. Agii Anargiri, Athens Anticancer Hosp., 1998—99, mem. ethical com., 1998—99, mem. edn. com., 1998—99; vis. prof. anatomy U. Athens, 2007. Author: Guide for Specialties in Greece, 1994, Guide to Pre-and Post-Graduate Grants for the Medical Students, 1995, Guidlines for First Aids, 1996, Synoptic Cellular Biology, 2002; co-author: Medicine and Medical Education in Europe, 1998, Laparoendoscopic Surgery, 2000, Laparoscopic Surgery, 2000, Intensive Care, 2006, Laparoscopic Surgical Oncology, 2006; author, editor Advances in Obstructive

Jaundice Diagnosis and Treatment, 2006; co-editor: Blood-Heart-Circulation, 1992, Theoretical and Practical Importance of Thrombosis and Fibrinolysis, 1993; assoc. editor: Jour. European Med. Students Assn. Med. and Sci. Affairs, 1994—95; translator: Exercise Physiology, 2000, Human Physiology, 2000, Atlas of Surgical Operations, 2001, Atlas of Surgical Techniques, 2001, Health and Fitness, 2003, Cecil's Internal Medicine, 2001—02, Gastroenterology, 2002, Gastroenterology-Hepatology, 2002, Secrets of Hypertension, 2002, Functional Histology, 2002, Research Methodology in Physical Activity, 2002;: Sports Medicine, 2002, General Practice and Family Medicine, 2002—03, Diet: Health, Healthness and Performance, 2003, Fight Fat After Forty, 2003, Textbook of General Surgery, 2005, Ophthalmology, 2004, Clinical Anatomy Netter's, 2006, A Plate to Plate Atlas for Netter's Human Anatomy, 2006, The Good Samaritan, 2006, Current on Surgical Diagnosis and Treatment, 2006, AAOS Emergency, 2006; contbr. chapters to books, articles to profl. jours. Sociomedical, blood donor Sci. Assn. Greek Med. Students, Greece, 1993—95, sociomedical, first aid tng., 1993—95; social and cultural com. Union of Mirofillo Imigrants, Athens, 1991—92. Scholar, Greek Gen. Sec. for Rsch. and Tech., 1999—2001. Mem.: Hellenic Soc. Gastrointestinal Oncology (assoc.), Hellenic Surg. Soc. (assoc.), Athens Med. Soc. (assoc.), Greek Anticancer Soc. (assoc.). Achievements include research in alterations of oxidants, nitricoxide products and antioxidants in the early and late phase of burned patients; development of modified capitonage in partial cystectomy performed for liver hydatid disease. Avocations: reading, writing, painting, music, technology. Home: 14 Agias Eirinis str 11146 Galatsi Athens Greece Home Fax: +30.210.2220892. Personal E-mail: d_filippou@hotmail.com, d_filippou@yahoo.gr.

FILIS, ANDREAS, neuroscientist; s. Konstantinos Filis and Dimitra Vlami-Fili. MD, Athens Nat. U. Kapodistriako, 2004. Lic. in practice medicine Prefecture Athens, 2004, cert. ECFMG, 2008. Predoc. rsch. lab. psychophysiolgy. dept. psychiatry, Athens Med. Sch., 1999—2000; predoc. rsch. dept. physiology Athens U., 2001—02; resident, dept. neurosurgery U. Hosp. Goettingen, Germany, 2004—06, U. Hosp. Erlangen, Germany, 2006—07; fellow Minimally Invasive Neurosurgery Lab., Cleveland, 2008—, tchg. residents, 2008—. Contbr. articles to profl. jours. Mem.: Kaplan Med.

FILLEY, CHRISTOPHER MARK, neurologist, researcher; b. Saranac Lake, NY, July 31, 1951; s. Giles Franklin and Mary Brown (Klinefelter) F. BA, Williams Coll., 1973; MD, Johns Hopkins U., 1979. Diplomate Am. Bd. Psychiatry and Neurology. Intern U. Conn., Farmington, 1979—80; resident in neurology U. Colo., Denver, 1980—83; behavioral neurology fellow Boston U., 1983—84; from instr. to asst. prof. neurology U. Colo. Sch. Medicine, Denver, 1984—91, assoc. prof. neurology, 1991—97, prof. neurology, 1997—; neurology svc. chief Denver Va. Med. Ctr., 2010—. Prin. investigator studies in Alzheimers Disease NIH, Bethesda, Md., 1991-94. Author: Neurobehavioral Anatomy, 1995, Neurobehavioral Anatomy, 2d edit., 2001, 3rd edit., 2011, The Behavioral Neurology of White Matter, 2001; contbr. articles to profl. jours. Health com. Denver Found., 1995-98. Fellow Am. Acad. Neurology; mem. Am. Neurol. Assn., Internat. Neuropsychol. Soc. (bd. govs. 2008-), Soc. for Behavioral and Cognitive Neurology, Colo. Soc. Clin. Neurologists. Home Phone: 303-355-2672; Office Phone: 303-724-2187. Business E-Mail: christopher.filley@uchsc.edu.

FILLEY, WARREN VERNON, allergist; b. Topeka, Kans., Oct. 27, 1950; MD, U. Kans. Sch. Medicine, 1976. Diplomate Am. Bd. Allergy and Immunology, Am. Bd. Internal Medicine. Intern U. Okla., 1976-77, resident in internal medicine, 1977-79; fellow allergy and immunology Mayo Clin., Rochester, Minn., 1979-81; with Presbyn. Hosp., Oklahoma City; clin. prof. medicine U. Okla. Mem. AMA, Am. Acad. Allergy, Asthma and Immunology, Am. Coll. Allergy, Asthma and Immunology, Okla. Med. Assn. Office: Okla Allergy and Asthma Clin 750 NE 13th St Oklahoma City OK 73104-5051 Home Phone: 405-340-3448; Office Phone: 405-235-0040. Business E-Mail: wfilley@oklahomaallergy.com.

FILLINGAME, ROBERT H., biochemistry professor department chairman; b. Washington, June 22, 1946; BS in Chemistry, Wash. State U., 1968; PhD in Biochemistry, U. Wash., 1973. Daymon Runyon postdoc. fellow Harvard Med. Sch., 1973—75; prof., chair, dept. biomolecular chemistry U. Wis. Med. Sch., 1975—. Recipient Med. Alumni Named Professorship award, Wis. Med. Alumni Assn., Disting. Tchg. award, Kellett Mid-Career Rsch. award, Wis. Alumni Rsch. Found., Dean's Tchg. award, Wis. Sch. Medicine & Pub. Health, NIH Merit award. Mem.: Am. Assn. Biochemistry & Molecular Biology. Avocation: boating. Home: 5046 Lake Mendota Dr Madison WI 53705 Home Fax: 608-262-5253. Business E-Mail: rhfillin@wisc.edu.

FILLIOS, LOUIS CHARLES, retired science educator; b. Boston, July 1, 1923; s. Charles Louis and Pagona (Kefalas) F.; m. Iphigenia Loomis, June 15, 1947; children: Despena Fillios Billings, Diana Fillios Downey, Hilary Fillios Grant. AB, Harvard, 1948, MS, 1953, ScD, 1956. Rsch. assoc., then assoc. Harvard U., 1956-60; rsch. assoc. in biochemistry, asst. prof. physiol. chemistry MIT, 1961-64, assoc. prof., 1964-66; rsch. prof. biochemistry and pathology Boston U. Sch. Medicine, 1966-68; prof. nutritional sci. Boston U., 1968-94; prof. biochemistry Boston U. Sch. Medicine, 1970-94; dir. divsn. basic sci. Boston U. Sch. Medicine (Sch. Grad. Dentistry), 1970-75, chmn. dept. nutritional scis., 1973-94; prof. biochemistry emeritus Boston U., 1994—; emeritus prof. Boston U. Sch. Medicine, 1955—. Chmn. Mass. Task Force Nutrition and Aging, 1970-71; cons. Mass. Office of Elder Affairs, 1971-73; co-chmn. nutrition sect. White House Conf. Aging, 1971-72; cons. VA, Bedford, Mass., 1982-87; mem. pres.'s adv. coun. Hellenic Coll., 1968-73. Author numerous research articles fields biochemistry, pathology and nutrition; contbr. sci. and profl. jours. 1st lt. USAAF, 1943-45. Decorated D.F.C., Air Medal with 3 oak leaf clusters (7 battle stars); recipient Outstanding Educator of Am. award Boston U., 1972, Spl. Honor, 1995. Fellow AAAS, Am. Heart Assn. (established investigator 1961-66); mem. Am. Inst. Nutrition (chmn. fellow award com. 1978-81), Sigma Xi (Harvard chpt.), Omicron Kappa Upsilon (hon.). Home: 19 Eliot Rd Lexington MA 02421-5630

FILLMORE, JOSEPH H., physiatrist; BS in Bio., St. Bonaventure Univ., 1976; MBA in Hosp. Admin., Univ. Chgo., 1982; MD, Univ. Ill., 1994. Diplomat in Pain Medicine Am. Bd. Phys. Medicine and Rehab., cert. US Med. Lic. Exam., Ill., Colo., Ind., Advanced Life Support Provider, Controlled Substance Registration. Environ. svcs. supervisor Crothall Hosp. Svcs., Newark, Del., 1976—77; middle school tchr. St. Barbara's Sch., Lackawanna, NY; high sch. tchr. Mission High Sch., Boston; mgr., health care planning and mktg. div. Herman Smith Assoc., Chgo., 1987—91; rsch. asst. Univ. Ill., 1991—92; ind. cons., 1994; physiatrist Midwest Orthopaedics at Rush, 2002, Advanced Pain and Anesthesia Consuls., Chgo., 2001, Colo. Comprehensive Spine Inst. Clinical adv. Am. Running Assn. Grantee Kaiser Found. Fell., Univ. Chgo., 1980—82, Scholl Found. Rsch. Fell., 1996. Avocations: running, sailing, acting, skiing. Office: Colo Comprehensive Spine Inst 3277 S Lincoln St Englewood CO 80113 Office Phone: 303-762-0808.

FILOSTO, MASSIMILIANO, neurologist, researcher; s. Aldo Filosto and Maria Di Pino; m. Marianna Rinaldi, Sept. 18, 2005; children: Lorenzo, Francesco. Degree in Medicine and Surgery, U. Catania, 1993; degree in Neurology, 1999, PhD in Neuroscis., 2003. Prof. neurology U. Brescia, Italy; neurologist U. Hosp., Brescia, 2000—. In-charge, sect. neuromuscular disease & neuropathies. Office: Univ Hosp Spedali Civili Piazzale Spedali Civili 1 25123 Brescia BS Italy Business E-Mail: filosto@med.unibs.it.

FILSOUFI, FARZAN, thoracic surgeon, educator; b. Iran, July 9, 1966; MD, U. Paris, 1997. Prof. Mt. Sinai Med. Ctr., 2002—. Mem.: Soc. Thoracic Surgeons, European Assn. Cardio-Thoracic Surgery, Am. Assn. Thoracic Surgery, Soc. Heart Valve Disease, Internat. Soc. Heart and Lung Transplantation. Office: 1190 5th Ave New York NY 10029 Office Fax: 212-659-6818. Business E-Mail: farzan.filsoufi@mountsinai.org.

FILTHUTH, HEINZ AUGUST ADOLF WILHELM, science association director; b. Goettingen, Niedersachsen, Germany, Dec. 29, 1925; s. August and Gertrud Filthuth; m. Elke Ursula Bergmann, Sept. 12, 1977; children: Michael, Andreas, Eckhard, Filthuth Isabelle. Abitur, Felix Klein Gymnasium, Goettingen, 1935—43; Dr.rer.nat, U. Heidelberg, 1954. Cert. prof. U. Heidelberg, 1964, Ecole Normale Superieure, Paris, 1996, Ecole Superieure Physique et Chimie Indutrielle, Paris, 1997; diplomate physician Cern, European Org. Nuc. Rsch., 1955. Chair physics U. Heidelberg, Germany, U. Muenchen, Germany, U. Wis., Madison, 1963—68, U. Mass., Amherst, 1963—68, SLAC Stanford U., Calif.; sci. dir. Lab. Radiation Measuring Instruments Industry, Sci. and Medicine, 1976—. Cons., mem. European Com. Future Accelerators, Geneva, 1964—75; mem., prof., physician European Com. Constn. Big European Hydrogen Bubble Chamber, Geneva, 1964—75; mem. adv. com., prof., physician Internat. Isotope Soc., Kans. City, Kans., 1964; prof., physician, sci. dir. Lab. Prof. Dr. Berthold, Bad Wildbad, Germany, 1976—95; dir., founder Inst. High Energy Physics, U. Heidelberg, 1964—75; dir. Lin Analyser, Dig Autoradiog, Microimager, Chem., Biol. and Med., 1976—96, Ctrl. European Divsn. CED Preis, 1996; mem. minerra com. Weizmann Inst., Israel; mem. MaxPlanck Inst. Nuc. Physics, Heidelberg. Gefreit Airforce, 1943—45, France, Poland, Germany. Mem.: Italian Phys. Soc., European Phys. Soc. (life; founder, adv. sci. com, Ettore Majorana, Internat. Sch. Subnuc. Physics). Achievements include research in measurement of sigma lamda parity Heisenberg theory, proves Gell Manns theory; cern accelerator with hydrogen bubble chamber; detectors for beta-radiation and light in chem istry, biology, medicin linear analyser, 2-dimensional wire chamber, microimager, novel radioactivity microsenso; cosmic rays at sea level and at 3600m altitude, elementary particle reactions of pi and k-mesons. Home: Hermann Frese St 79 Bremen 28355 Germany Office: MaxPlanck Inst Marine Microbiology Celsius St 1 Bremen 28359 Germany

FINBERG, LAURENCE, pediatrician, educator, dean; b. Chgo., May 20, 1923; s. Joseph and Anne (Malkow) F.; m. Harriet Levinson, June 17, 1945 (dec. Jan. 1994); children: Robert, Jeanne, James; m. Joann Quane, Mar. 17, 1995. BS, U. Chgo., 1944, MD, 1946. Diplomate: Am. Bd. Pediatrics (examiner 1969-94, bd. dirs. 1974-79, 82-88, pres. 1978, chmn. 1987). Intern U. Chgo. Clinics, 1946-47; asst. resident pediatrics Balt. City Hosps., 1949-50, resident in pediat., 1950-51; practice medicine specializing in pediat. Balt., 1951-63, NYC, 1963-94; asst. chief pediatrician Balt. City Hosps., 1951-61, dir. pediatric out-patient dept., 1951-63, dir. premature nursery, 1951-59, assoc. chief pediatrics, 1961-63; pediatrician Harriet Lane Home, 1951-63; chmn. dept. pediatrics Montefiore Hosp. and Med. Center, Bronx, NY, 1963-80, SUNY Health Sci. Ctr., Bklyn., 1982-95, prof. pediatrics, 1982-95, prof. emeritus, 1995—, dean, 1988-91; prof. clin. pediat. U. Calif., San Francisco, 1995—, Stanford U. Sch. Med., 1997—. Instr. pediatrics Johns Hopkins U., 1951-56; asst. prof., 1956-63; prof. pediatrics Albert Einstein Coll. Medicine, Yeshiva U., Bronx, 1963-82, chmn., 1968-80; cons. in field; pediatric adv. com. NYC Dept. Health, 1970-94 Mem. editl. bd. Jour. Pediat., 1973-83, Am. Jour. Diseases of Children, 1984-94, named changed to Archives of Pediat. and Adolescent Medicine, 1994-2002, editor nutrition sect., 1995-2002; editor Saunders Manual of Pediat. Practice, 1997, 2002 Served with USPHS, 1947-49. Recipient Bela Schick medal, 1992, Nutrition award Am. Acad. Pediatrics, 1992. Mem. AAAS, AMA (Goldberger Clin. Nutrition award 1993), Am. Pediatric Soc., Soc. Pediatric Research, Am. Acad. Pediatrics (com. on environ. hazards 1968-83, chmn. 1979-83, com. nutrition 1983-89—, chmn. 1984-89), Am. Coll. Nutrition, Am. Soc. for Nutritional Scis., Nat. Cholesterol Edn. Program Coordinating Com. (panel on children and adolescents 1989-93), Ambulatory Pediatric Assn., Am. Soc. Clin. Nutrition, Am. Fedn. Clin. Research, Sociedad Peruana de Pediatria, Sociedad Dominica De Peditria, Harvey Soc., N.Y. Acad. Medicine (past chmn. pediatric sec.), Phi Beta Kappa, Sigma Xi, Alpha Omega Alpha. Achievements include research in electrolyte physiology. Home: 152 Lombard St Apt 602 San Francisco CA 94111-1134 Home Phone: 415-398-6205; Office Phone: 415-398-6205. Business E-Mail: laurence.finberg@ucsf.edu.

FINCH, ALBERTA MAY, retired pediatrician; b. Port Jervis, NY, Jan. 27, 1926; d. Herbert LeRoy Finch and Bertha May Funnell; m. Otto Roy Weber, July 12, 1952; children: Lawrence, Charles, Kathy, Phillip, Jeffrey. BS, Pa. State U., 1946; MD, Temple U., 1950. Diplomate Am. Bd. Family Practice. Pvt. practice pediatrics, Linglestown, Pa., 1952—62; pvt. practice family medicine Stroudsburg, Pa., 1962—85; pediatrician United Meth. Ch., Zaire, 1985—90, Pocono Med. Ctr., East Stroudsburg, Pa., 1993—99; sch. physician East Stroudsburg U., 1990—93; ret., 1999. Mem. exec. bd. Pocono Med. Ctr., East Stroudsburg, 1971—75. Sec./treas. Torch, 1990—; bd. mem. Health Cmty. Alliance, 2001—, v.p., 2008—; bd. dirs. Children and Youth Svcs. Monroe County, Stroudsburg, 1971—77, 1980—86, 1996—2002; bd. dirs., treas., v.p., pres. Monroe County Planned Parenthood, Stroudsburg, 1965—74; child health physician Monroe County, 1962—85, 1991—92; mem. com. United Way of Monroe County, Tannersville, Pa., 1989—94; mem. PMC Cmty. Health Assessment Steering Com., East Stroudsburg, 1993—98, Ch. Women United, 2000—, pres., 2000—03; Sunday sch. tchr. Stroudsburg United Meth. Ch., 1963—70, 1972—85, 2002—; mem. Stroudsburg Coun. Chs., 1992—, pres., 2000—02; bd. dirs. Home Health Svcs. Monroe County, East Stroudsburg, 1971—78, Cmty. Coalition for Improvement of Maternal and Child Health, East Stroudsburg, 1982—98. Recipient Mission Recognition award, Stroudsburg United Meth. Ch., 1986, Liberty Bell award, Monroe County Law Assn., 1983, Health Promotion award, Monroe County C. of C., 1983, Svc. Above Self award, Rotary, 1999, Gold medal, Pocono Med. Ctr., 1999, Eugenia S. Eden award, Pocono Svcs. Family and Children, 2005, Margaret Wells award, Ch. Woman United, 2007; named Lady of Yr., Beta Sigma Phi, Stroudsburg, 1978, Alberta Finch Children's Endowment Fund in her honor, 1997, Paul Harris fellow, Rotary Found., 1999, Humanitarian of Yr., Pocono Mountains C. of C., 2000, Woman of Distinction, East Stroudsburg U., 2001. Mem.: DAR, Torch (pres. 1995—96, sec./treas. 1998—), Quiet Valley Hist. Assn. (bd. dirs. 1992—98). Republican. Avocations: camping, travel, medical antiques, doll collecting, dollhouses. Home: RD # 5 Box 5106 Stroudsburg PA 18360 E-mail: aoweber@ptd.net.

FINCHER, EDGAR FRANKLIN, dermatologic surgeon; b. Dallas, Apr. 23, 1966; s. Edgar Franklin Fincher, III and Elaine Allen Reinika; m. Helen Horn Fincher, July 13, 1991; children: Eden Montgomery, Avery Michele, Harrison Nichols. BS in Biology, Rhodes Coll., 1988; PhD in Physiology, U. Tenn., Memphis, 1997, MD, 1997. Bd. cert. dermatology Am. Bd. Dermatology, 2004. Postdoctoral rsch. fellow Stanford (Calif.) U., 1998—2001, dermatology resident, 2001—04; fellow Mohs micrographic surgery, laser and cosmetic surgery Ronald L. Moy, MD, LA, 2004—05; dermatologic surgeon Moy-Fincher Med. Group, LA, 2005—; clin. instr. David Geffen Sch. Medicine, UCLA, 2004—. Editor: (reference text) Advanced Facelift, 2006, Blepharoplasty; contbr. chapters to books, articles to profl. jours. Grantee, NIH, 1999—2001. Fellow: Am. Acad. Cosmetic Surgery, Am. Coll. Mohs Micrographic Surgery and Cutaneous Oncology, Am. Acad. Dermatology; mem.: Am. Acad. Dermatologic Surgery. Office: Moy-Fincher Medical Group 421 N Rodeo Dr Ste 1 Beverly Hills CA 90210-4514

FINCHER, RUTH MARIE EDLA, medical educator, dean; b. Hartford, Conn., Dec. 16, 1949; d. Wilber Roe and Hannah Camilla (Andersen) Griswold; m. Michael Edward Fincher, June 26, 1977. BA, Colby Coll., 1972; BMS, Dartmouth U., 1974; MD, Emory U., 1976. Diplomate Am. Bd. Internal Medicine. Intern then resident internal medicine Emory Hosps., Atlanta, 1976-79; practicing internist Pub. Health Svc., Ludowici, Ga., 1979-81; pvt. practice internal medicine Hinesville, Ga., 1981-82; staff physician Am. Lake VA Med. Ctr., Tacoma, Wash., 1982-84; asst. prof. medicine Med. Coll. Ga., Augusta, 1984-89, assoc. prof., 1989-94, prof. medicine, 1994—, vice dean acad. affairs, 1994—. Pres. Clerkship Dirs. in Internal Medicine, Washington, 1992—93; com. chair Nat. Bd. Med. Examiners, Phila., 1995—96, bd. dirs., 2005—; co-chair rsch. in med. edn. com. Assn. Am. Med. Colls., Washington, 1995—96, chair group on ednl. affairs, 1996—97. Co-editor: Clinical Medicine 2nd Edit., 1995; contbr. articles to profl. jours. Bd. dirs. Nat. Bd. Med. Examiners at Large, 2005—07, mem. exec. com., 2007—11. Recipient Edithe J. Levit Disting. Svc. award, Nat. Bd. Med. Examiners at Large, 2011. Master: Am. Coll. Physicians (governor Ga. chpt. 2003—07, bd. dirs. ACP Found. 2003—07, exec. comm. bd. of governors 2004, elected to mastership 2008, J. Willis Hurst Tchg. award 1994, Disting. Tchg. award 1996, Jane F. Des Forges Disting. Tchr. award 2011); mem.: Assn. Am. Med. Colls. (Ednl. Affairs Career scholarship So. Group 2006, Merrel Flair award 2006), Alpha Omega Alpha (bd. dirs. 2003—, Robert J. Glaser Disting. Tchg. award 1996, Daniel S. Tostesen award 2003, Inaugural inductee U. Sys. Ga. Hall of Fame 2004). Avocations: woodworking, gardening, running. Office: Med Coll Ga CB 1843 1457 Laney Walker Blvd Augusta GA 30912

FINDER, ROBERT ANDREW, healthcare company executive; b. Washington, Mo., Apr. 27, 1947; s. Richard Joseph and Jeanette Mary (Graser) Finder; m. Sheryl Jean Johnson, Feb. 6, 1971. B in Chem. Engring., U. Detroit, 1970. Process engr. Monsanto-J.F. Queeny Plant, St. Louis, 1970-71, prodn. supr., 1975-79, project mgr., 1980-81; engring. supt. Monsanto-Trenton (Mich.) Plant, 1981-82, gen. supt. mfg., 1982-85; mng. dir. Monsanto Chems. Thailand, Bangkok, 1985-89; chmn. bd., mng. dir. Rhone-Poulenc Thai Industries Ltd., Bangpoo Samutprakarn, Thailand, 1989-91; dir. mfg. Rhone-Poulenc Inc., Princeton, N.J., 1992-93; v.p. mfg. and process tech. Ecogen, Inc., Langhorne, Pa., 1993-95; v.p. ops. Purepac Pharm. (Faulding, Inc.), Elizabeth, N.J., 1995-99; COO, gen. mgr. Faulding China and Orals Pharms., Adelaide, Australia, 1999-2000; pres., COO Asia Pacific Faulding Pharm., Adelaide, 2000—01; pres., COO Asia Pacific/Americas, Mayne/Faulding Pharms., 2001—02; CEO, mng. dir. GroPep Ltd., Adelaide, 2002—06; CEO Novozymes GroPep, 2006—07; chmn. bd. LBT Innovations Ltd (formerly LabTech Sys. Ltd), 2007—; adelaide, chmn. bd. Reproductive Health Scis., 2008—09; bd. dir. Nat. Pharmacies, 2009—, Living Cell Techs., 2009—11. Mem. pres.'s cabinet U. Detroit, 1988—. Life mem. World Wildlife Fund, Bangkok, 1988. Lt. US Army, 1971—74. Mem.: AIChE, Australian Inst. Co. Dirs., Am. Philatelic Soc., Royal Bangkok Sports Club. Home: 37 Tennyson Heights Ct Tennyson SA 5022 Australia Office: LBT Innovations 300 Flinders St Adelaide SA 5000 Australia Home Fax: 61 882350085. Business E-Mail: bob@lbtinnovations.com.

FINDLAY, MICHAEL W., plastic surgeon; b. Melbourne, Australia, Jan. 1, 1973; BSc, U. Queensland, MBBS, 1997; PhD, Melbourne U., 2008. Plastic, reconstructive and hand surgeon Barwon Health, 2008, Peninsula Health, 2008, Austin Health, 2008, Western Health, Victoria, Australia, 2008, Peter MacCallum Cancer Ctr., 2010. Fellow Bernard O'Brien Inst. Microsurgery, St. Vincent's Hosp. Melbourne, 2002—04; rsch. fellow NYU, Sch. Medicine, 2003—04; instr., emergency mgmt. severe burns course ANZBA, 2008; adj. sr. lectr. Monash U., 2009. Recipient Young Investigator award, Surg. Rsch. Soc. Australasia, 2002, Victorian Plastic Surgery Trainee Presentation prize, Australian Soc. Plastic Surgeons, 2005. Fellow: Royal Australasian Coll. Surgeons (Victorian Regional Com. mem. 2011); mem.: Australian Med. Assn., Sect. Academic Surgery. Avocation: sports. Office: OBrien Inst 42 Fitzroy St Fitzroy Victoria 3065 Australia Business E-Mail: mifindlay@mac.com.

FINDLEY, JOHN SIDNEY, dentist; b. Bryan, Tex., Oct. 3, 1942; s. Sidney Albert and Leila Mae (Reading) Findley; m. Patricia Ann Reep, June 10, 1967 (div. 1977); children: John Brett, Sidney Alan; m. Judith Ann Smith, May 22, 1981. Student, USAF Acad., N. Tex. State U., So. Meth. U., Dallas; DDS, Baylor U. Coll. Dentistry, Waco, Tex., 1970. Pvt. practice gen. dentistry, Plano, Tex., 1970—. Councilman City of Cross Rds., Tex., 1988—89, mayor, 1992—94. Recipient Cert. of Recognition, Am. Acad. Dental Radiology, 1970, Disting. Alumni award, Baylor U. Coll. Dentistry, 1996. Fellow: Internat. Coll. Dentists, Am. Coll. Dentists; mem.: ADA (mem. task force on governance 2000—01, trustee 2003—07, pres.-elect 2007—08, pres. 2008—09), Acad. Gen. Dentistry, Dallas County Dental Soc. (pres.-elect 1992—93, pres. 1994, bd. dirs., editor DDS News, Dentist of Yr. 1995), Tex. Dental Assn. (pres.-elect 1996, pres. 1997—98, chmn. coun. legis. and regulatory affairs 1999—2003, Pres. award 1994, 1995, 1996, 1999, 2000, 2001, 2003), Rotary (bd. dirs., pres. 1977—78). Methodist. Office: 1410 14th St Plano TX 75074-6359 Mailing: ADA 211 E Chgo Ave Chicago IL 60611 Personal E-mail: john.findley@gte.net. *

FINDLING, ROBERT LAWRENCE, psychiatrist; MD, Med. Coll. Va., 1987. Dir. child/adolescent psychiatry Case Western Reserve U., Cleve., 1992—. Office: UHCMC Dept Psychiatry 10524 Euclid Ave Cleveland OH 44106 Office Phone: 216-844-1717.

FINE, DAVID JEFFREY, hospital administrator, educator; b. Flushing, NY, Oct. 10, 1950; s. Arnold and Phyllis F.; m. Susan Gory, Dec. 29, 1985; children: Jeffrey Jacob, Christopher Lee. BA, Tufts U., 1972; MHA, U. Minn., 1974; PhD (hon.), U. Southern Miss., 2007. Asst. to dir. U. Calif. Hosp. and Clinics, San Francisco, 1974—76, asst. dir., 1976—78; sr. assoc. dir. U. Nebr. Hosp. and Clinic, Omaha, 1978—83; adminstr. W.Va. Univ. Hosp., Morgantown, 1983—84; pres. W.Va. Univ. Hosps., Inc., Morgantown, 1984—87; pres., COO Health Net, Inc., Charleston, 1985—87; vice provost for health affairs, CEO U. Cin. Health Sys., 1987—90; pres. U. Cin. Med. Assocs., 1988—90; vice chancellor Tulane U. Med. Ctr., New Orleans, 1990—95, emeritus vice chancellor, 1995—; prof., chmn. dept. health sys. mgmt. Sch. Pub. Health and Tropical Medicine Tulane U., New Orleans, 1990—99; pres., CEO New Orleans Region Columbia/HCA Healthcare Corp., 1995—96; pres. Columbia Health Edn. and Rsch. Found., 1996—97, S.E. Med. Alliance, 1998—99; CEO U. Ala. Birmingham Health Sys., 1999—2004; pres., CEO St. Luke's Episcopal Health Sys., Houston, 2004—. Prof. med. econ. and pharmacy U. Cin., 1987-90; vice chair Nat. Ctr. Healthcare Leadership; vis. fellow King Fund Coll.; prof. Dept. Health Svcs. Adminstrn. Sch. Health Related Professions, UAB, 1999-2004, Dept. Health Care Org. and Policy Sch. Pub. Health, 2003-04; Regents prof. Dept. Health Sys. Mgmt., Tulane U. Sch. Pub. Health and Trop. Medicine, 1996-99; prof. mgmt. policy and cmty. health, U. Tex. Sch. Pub. Health, 2004-, Baylor Coll. Med., 2005-; sec.-treas., 2009-10, chair elect, 2010, vice chair Commn. Accreditation Healthcare Mgmt. Edn., Accreditation Coun. Grad. Med. Edn.; cons. in field. Mem. editl. bd. Hospital Formulary, 1982-87, Health Adminstrn. Press, 1991-94, Jour. Health Adminstrn. Edn., 1991-2001; contbr. jour. articles, book chpts. and films. Trustee Monongalia Arts Coun., 1984-86, Cin. Chamber Orch., 1987-91; sec.-treas. Internat. Found. for Pharmacy Edn. Recipient James A. Hamilton prize, U. Minn., 1974; Am. Coll. Healthcare Exec. award. Fellow Am. Coll. Healthcare Execs. (Robert S. Hudgens Young Adminstr. of Yr. award 1985, mem. com. on awards and testimonials, Regents, 2009-11), Royal Coll. Medicine, mem. Am. Hosp. Assn. (mem. regional policy bd., mem. ho. of dels., mem. governing coun. sect. on met. hosps.), Am. Assn. Med. Coll. (coun. tchg. hosps. administrv. bd, 2005), Assn. U. Programs in Health Adminstrn. (chmn. 2000-02), Coronado Club, Petroleum Club, Omicron Delta Epsilon, Delta Omega. Episcopalian. Office: St Luke's Episcopal Health Sys 6624 Fannin Ave Ste 1100 Houston TX 77030 Office Phone: 832-355-7661. Business E-Mail: dfine@slch.com.

FINE, HOWARD A., medical researcher; BA, U. Pa., Phila.; MD, Mt. Sinai Sch. Medicine, NYC. Intern and resident in internal medicine Hosp. of U. Pa.; fellow in med. oncology Dana-Farber Cancer Inst., Harvard Med. Sch., Boston, dir. Neuro-Oncology Disease Ctr.; dir. Neuro-Oncology Program Harvard Cancer Ctr.; chief Neuro-Oncology Br. Ctr. Cancer Rsch., Nat. Cancer Inst., NIH, Bethesda, Md., 2000—. Mem. editl. bd. Jour. Clin. Oncology, Neuro-Oncology, The Oncologist; mem. Brain Tumor Program Rev. Group, Am. Joint Com. on Cancer. Recipient Brain Tumor Soc. Rsch. Award, 1992, Emil Frei III Clin. Investigator Award, 1993, Clin. Investigator Award, Dana-Farber Harvard Cancer Ctr., 1999. Office: Neuro Oncology Br Ctr Cancer Rsch Bloch Bldg #82 Rm 235 9030 Old Georgetown Rd Bethesda MD 20892 Office Phone: 301-402-6383. Office Fax: 301-480-2246. E-mail: hfine@mail.nih.gov. *

FINE, IRWIN HOWARD, ophthalmologist, surgeon, educator; b. Syracuse, NY, Apr. 30, 1936; s. David William and Ann (Sobol) F.; m. Victoria Bond, June 16, 1963; children: William, Laura, Edward. BS, MIT, 1961; MD, Boston U., 1966. Diplomate Am. Bd. Ophthalmology. Intern St. Elizabeth's Hosp. of Boston, 1966-67; resident Boston U. Med. Ctr. & Affil. Hosps., 1967-70; pvt. practice Eugene, Oreg., 1970—; full clin. assoc. prof. ophthalmology Oreg. Health Scis. U., Portland, 1987—. Author, editor: Clear Corneal Cataract Surgery and Topical Anesthesia, 1993, Phacoemulsification: New Technology and Clinical Application, 1996; author, assoc. editor Cataract Surgery: Technique, Complications and Management, 1995; designer 20 surg. instruments. With US Army, 1959—60. Named one of Best Drs. in America, 25 Most Influential Ophthalmologists; recepient ASCRS Innovator's award, Am. Acad. Ophthalmology's Sr. Honor award, Kelman Lecture award, Maumenee award Baylor & Welsh Cataract and Refractive Surgery Congress, Rayner medal UK and Ireland Socs. Cataract and Refractive Surgery, Brazilian Phaco Club award, Disting. Alumnus award, Boston U. Sch. Medicine, Oreg. Health and Scis. U. Meritorious Achievement award, Golden Orchid award Nat. Healthcare Group Singapore, Ophthalmologist of Millennium award Internat. Acad. Advances Ophthalmology India, Strampelli medal Italian Soc. Ophthalmology, Charles Kelman medal Videocataracttarefrattiva, Milan, Charles Kelman medal Brazilian Soc. Cataract and Implantation Surgery, Binkhorst medal Am. Soc. Cataract and Refractive Surgery, Kelman award, 2011. Mem. AMA, Internat. Intraocular Implant Club (pres. 2008-10; medal 2011), Am. Acad. Ophthalmology (mem. quality care anterior segment panel 1995-96, Honor award 1994), Am. Soc. Cataract and Refractive Surgery (CFO 1997-, mem. sci. adv. bd. 1992-94, mem. govt. rels. com. 1991-, pres. 2001-02, Innovator's award 1994), Outpatient Ophthalmic Surgery Soc. (bd. dirs. 1990-), Am. Coll. Eye Surgeons (bd. dirs. 1993-96), Am. Bd. Eye Surgery (bd. dirs. 1996), Oreg. Acad. Ophthalmology (pres. 1980), Oreg. Med. Assn. (mem. med. peer review com.). Republican. Jewish. Achievements include research in surgical procedures including cortical cleaving hydrodissection, chip and flip, crack and flip, and choo-choo chop and flip phacoemulsification techniques and temporal self-sealing clear corneal incision; invention of 30 surgical techniques. Avocations: weightlifting, motorcycling. Office: I Howard Fine MD PC 1550 Oak St Ste 5 Eugene OR 97401-7701

FINE, JEFFREY LOUIS, psychologist, educator, writer; b. NYC, Mar. 2, 1941; s. Joseph Fine and Helen Bloomfield; m. Dalit Kamerman Fine, Apr. 5, 1998; 1 child, Kesem Joseph. BS in biology, NYU, NYC, 1966; MS in health edn., New Sch. for Social Rsch., 1968; PhD in psychology, U. London, 1974. Cert. eating disorder specialist (CEDS), bd. cert. diplomate Internat. Assn. Eating Disorders, 1993. Clinical assoc. Acad. Orthomolecular Psychiatry, Manhasset, NY, 1976—77; rsch. cons. in psychodietitrics Coun. Nutrition, Am. Chiropractice Assn., NYC, 1976—77; dir. Shangi-La Natural Health Inst., Bonita Springs, Fla., 1977—80; mng. dir. Bay Harbour Health Inst., Stuart, Fla., 1980—81; owner, clinical dir. Fineway House Clinic and Spa, Palm Beach, Fla., 1981—86; pvt. practice NYC, 1986—2001, Bal Harbour, Fla., 2001—. Spkr. in field for TV and radio, 1980—94; adv. bd. Birthing the Future, Bayfield, Colo., 2003—04; dir. Am. Found. for Conscious Parenting, Miami, 2004; pres. Carlebach Synagogue, NYC, 1991—94. Editor, writer (jour.) Alternatives mag., 1976—77; author: (jour.) Jour. Energy Medicine, 1980—82, (weekly column) "Ask Dr. Fine", 1995—97, The New Parenting, 2004. Recipient TV Emmy award for costume design, Nat. Acad. TV Arts and Scis., 1970, Rsch. award, Am. Holistic Health Sci. Assn., Milw., 1983. Achievements include identifying and naming the "Night Eating Disorder Syndrome" (NEDS), 1992; advancing the application and understanding the use of "consciousness itself" in the psychotherapeutic process, 1997; founder/dir. NYC chpt. "The Mankind Project" and "New Warrior Training Adventure", 1994. Avocations: music, scuba diving, bodybuilding, antiques, clothing design. Mailing: 49 Albert Schweitzer Rd 34995 Haifa Israel E-mail: drfine@the-beach.net.

FINE, MICHAEL DAVID, public health service officer, state official; b. NYC, Aug. 31, 1953; Grad., Haverford Coll., 1975, MD, Case Western Reserve Sch. Medicine, 1983. Founder, physician operating officer Hillside Ave Family & Cmty. Medicine, 1992—2008; mng. dir. HealthAccessRI, 2006—11; interim dir. RI Dept. Health, Providence, 2011, dir., 2011—. Office: Rhode Island Department of Health Cannon Bldg 3 Capitol Hill Providence RI 02908-5097 *

FINE, NEIL A., surgeon; b. Pasadena, Calif., May 12, 1961; BS with high distinction, Univ. Nevada, Reno, 1983; MD, UCLA, 1987. Diplomate Nat. Bd. Med. Examiners, 1988, Am. Bd. Surgery, 1993, Am. Bd. Plastic Surgery, 1996, cert. Advanced Trauma Life Support 1989, lic. Mass., 1991, Ill., 1994. Attending surgeon Northwestern Mem. Hosp., 1994; assoc. mem. Lurie Cancer Ctr., 1994; attending Evanston Northwestern Health Care, 1994, Shriner's Hosp., 1995, VA Chgo. Health Sys. Lakeside Divsn.; surgeon Northwestern Med., Chgo., Northwestern Med. Faculty Found. Clin. fell., surgery Harvard Univ., 1987—94; asst. prof. surgery Northwestern Univ., Chgo., 1994—. Contbr. articles to numerous profl. jours. Recipient Best Paper in Microsurgery, Sr. Resident's Meeting, Harvard, 1984; named Regents Scholar, UCLA, 1983—87. Fellow: Am. Coll. Plastic Surgeons; mem.: Am. Soc. Reconstructive Microsurgery, Chgo. Soc. Plastic Surgeons, Am. Soc. Plastic Surgeons, Midwestern Assn. Plastic Surgeons, Mass. Med. Soc. Office: Northwestern Med Faculty Found Galter Pavillion 675 N Clair St Ste 19-250 Chicago IL 60611 Office Phone: 312-695-6022. Office Fax: 312-695-5672.

FINE, PERRY G., anesthesiologist, educator; BA in Biology, U. Calif., Santa Cruz; grad. tng. in biophysics, Georgetown U., Washington; MD, Med. Coll. Va., Richmond, 1981. Cert. American Bd. Anesthesiology, 1985, in pain medicine American Bd. Anesthesiology, 2004, Nat. Bd. Med. Examiners, American Acad. Hospice and Palliative Medicine. Intern in family & cmty. medicine Cmty. Hosp., Santa Rosa, Calif.; resident in anesthesiology U. Utah Health Sciences Ctr., Salt Lake City, 1982—84; fellow in pain medicine U. Toronto Smythe Pain Clinic, Ontario, Canada, 1984—85; prof. anesthesiology U. Utah Sch. Medicine, Salt Lake City; physician U. Utah Health Care. Team physician, football U. Utah Utes; med. officer Winter Olympic Games, Salt Lake City, 2002. Mem.: American Acad. Pain Medicine (pres. 2011—). Office: University Utah Health Care Pain Mgmt Ctr 546 Chipeta Way Salt Lake City UT 84108 Office Phone: 801-518-7246. *

FINE, PETER S., health facility administrator; Bachelor's Degree, Ohio U.; Master's Degree in Healthcare Adminstrn., George Washington U. Asst. adminstr. Porter Meml. Hosp., Valparaiso, Ind.; pres., CEO Grant Hosp., Chgo.; sr. v.p. ops. Northwestern Meml. Hosp., Chgo.; pres. West Allis Meml. Hosp.; exec. v.p., COO Aurora Health Care, Milwaukee; pres., CEO Banner Health, Phoenix, 2000—. Bd. dirs. Premier, Inc. Mem. Health Mgmt. Acad., Greater Phoenix Leadership, Bus. Coalition Leadership Coun., Arizona Commission on Med. Edn. and Rsch., Citizen's Task Force on the Maricopa County Health Care System, Citizen's Fin. Review Commission for the State of Arizona; bd. dirs. Translational Genomics Rsch. Inst., Heard Mus. Recipient Heroes of Edn. award, Maricopa Cmty. Coll. Found., 2006, Nat. Healthcare award, B'nai B'rith Internat., 2007, 2010 CEO IT Achievement award, Phoenix Bus. Journal Most Admired CEO award, 2010, Healthcare Leadership award, Arizona Bus. Mag., 2010. Fellow: American Coll. of Healthcare Executives (mem. bd. governors); mem.: American Hosp. Assn. Office: Banner Health 1441 N 12th St Phoenix AZ 85006

FINE, RICHARD NISAN, pediatrician, educator, dean; b. Phila., Oct. 3, 1937; s. Eve Fine; children: Joanne, Michael; m. Shawney Wagner, Aug. 28, 1972. BS, Muhlenberg Coll., 1958; MD, Temple U., 1962. Intern Boston City Hosp., 1962-63, jr. asst. resident, 1963-64; sr., chief resident Children's Hosp. L.A., 1964-66; instr. pediatrics U. So. Calif., LA, 1966-68, asst. prof. pediatrics, 1968-72, assoc. prof. pediatrics, 1972-76, prof. pediatrics, 1976-80, U. Calif., LA, 1980-89, vice chmn. clin. affairs, 1985-90; prof., chmn. dept. pediatrics Sch. Medicine at Stony Brook U. Med. Ctr., SUNY, Stony Brook, 1991—, dean, 2005—. Recipient Nat. Med. award in Nephrology, Nat. Kidney Found. N.Y./N.J., 1992. Mem.: N.Am. Pediatric Transplant Coop. Study (v.p.-treas.), Internat. Pediatric Transplant Assn. (sec.-treas.), Am. Soc. Transplantation (pres.). Office: Stony Brook Sch Medicien Dean's Office Health Sciences Ctr Level 4 Stony Brook NY 11794-8430 Office Phone: 631-444-6130. Office Fax: 631-444-6266.

FINE, ROBERT LANCE, medical oncologist, educator; BS in Biochemistry and Philosophy, Richard Stockton Coll., Pomona, 1971—75; MD, U. Chgo., Ill., 1975—79. Diplomate Nat. Bd. Med. Examiners, 1980, Am. Bd. Internal Medicine Examiners, 1983, Am. Bd. Internal Medicine, 1985, Am. Bd. Internal Medicine-med. oncology, registered NY, 1996. Resident in internal medicine Stanford Univ. Hosp., Calif., 1979—82; lt. comdr. USPHS, 1982—88; fellow in oncology Nat. Cancer Inst., Bethesda, Md., 1982—88, attending for med. br., 1985—88, med. investigator clin. pharmacology br., 1986—88; medicine asst. prof. hematology/oncology divsn. Duke Univ., Durham, NC, 1988—95, Durham VA Med. Centers, 1988—95; dir. hematology/oncology clinic Durham VA Hosp., 1989—95; asst. prof. pharmacology medicine sch. Duke Univ., 1990—95; dir. Herbert Irving comprehensive cancer ctr. Columbia Univ., NY, 1997—, Herbert Irving asst. prof. med. oncology divsn. physicians and surgeons coll., 1997—; asst. prof. medicine physicians and surgeons coll. NY-Presbyn. Hosp./Columbia Univ. Med. Ctr., 1995—99, dir. exptl. therapeutics program, 1995—2006, dir. pancreas ctr. physicians and surgeons coll., 2006—. Co-author (Y. Li, P. M. Yao, Y. Mao): The Synergistic Induction of Apoptosis by Alternating Docetaxel-Gemcitabine/Capecitabine (T-GX) in Pancreatic Cancer Cells is Mediated by Selective Activation of p38 and c-JUN MAPK Pathways; co-author: (J. S. Rubin) Emerging Applications for Somatostatin Analogues in Oncology, 1998; co-author: (C. Balmaceda) Gliomas, 2000; co-author: (D. Fogelman) Metastatic Pancreatic Adenocarcinoma Treated with Gemcitabine/Docetaxel/Capecitabine, 2003; co-author: (A. Khorana) Pancreatic Cancer and Thromboembolic Disease, 2004; co-author: various others. Recipient Herbert Irving Translational Cancer award, 2001—02, S.G. Kaplansky award, 2004—07, Cordaro Found. award, 2005—08; named one of Best Oncologists, NY Mag., 2006—07, Best Doctors, Castle Connolly, 2006—07, numerous others. Mem.: PhD Thesis Com. in Biomedical Engrng. (columbia univ. 1998—), Sch. of Publ.Health PhD Thesis Com. (columbia univ. 1999—), Vet. Oncology Assn., Southwest Oncology Group (bd. dirs.), Children's Oncology Group, Am. Soc. Clin. Oncology, Am. Assn. Cancer Rsch. (bd. dirs.), AAAS. Office: New York-Presbyterian Hospital Columbia University Medical Center Black Bldg 650 W 168th St New York NY 10032 Office Phone: 212-305-1168. Office Fax: 212-305-7348.

FINEBERG, HARVEY VERNON, health science association administrator; b. Pitts., Sept. 15, 1945; s. Saul and Miriam (Pearl) Fineberg; m. Mary Elizabeth Wilson, May 16, 1975. BA in Psychology, magna cum laude, Harvard U., 1967, MD, Master of Pub. Policy, 1972, PhD in Pub. Policy, 1980; DSc (hon.), NY Med. Coll., 2004, U. Ark., 2007, George Washington U., 2007; MD (hon.), U. South Fla., 2006. Intern Beth Israel Hosp., Boston, 1972—73, clin. fellow medicine Harvard U., Boston, 1972—73, asst. prof., Sch. Pub. Health, 1973—78, assoc. prof., 1978—81, prof., 1982—2001, dean Sch. Pub. Health, 1984—97, provost Harvard U. Mass., 1997—2001, prof. emeritus, 2002—. Faculty Kennedy Sch. Govt., Harvard U., 1973—81; physician East Boston Health Ctr., 1974—76, Harvard St. Health Ctr., Boston, 1976—84; mem. Mass. Pub. Health Coun., 1974—79; Mellon fellow Aspen Inst. Humanistic Studies, Colo., 1975; cons. WHO, 1982—; v.p. Internat. Coun. Global Health Progress, 1993—; fellow Ctr. Advanced Study in Behavioral Scis., Palo Alto, Calif., 2002. Co-author: The Swine Flu Affair: Decision-Making on a Slippery Disease, 1978, Clinical Decision Analysis, 1980, The Epidemic That Never Was, 1983, Adverse Effects of Pertussis and Rubella Vaccines, 1991, Society's Choices: Social and Ethical Decision Making in Biomedicine, 1995, Innovators in Physician Education: The Process and Pattern of Reform in North American Medical Schools, 1996; mem. editl. bd. Med. Decision Making, 1981—85, Med. Care Rev., 1982—88, Health and Human Rights, 1993—97, Preventive Medicine, 1994—97; contbr. articles to profl. jours. Bd. trustees Carnegie Endowment Internat. Peace, 2009—; bd. dirs. Am. Found. AIDS Rsch., 1986—97, William & Flora Hewlett Found., 2003—. Recipient Stephen Smith award for lifetime achievement, NY Acad. Medicine, 2008, Harvard Medal, 2009. Fellow: AAAS, Am. Acad. Arts & Scis., NY Acad. Scis.; mem.: AMA, APHA, Am. Coll. Preventive Medicine, Nat. Acad. Medicine Mex., Soc. Med. Decision Making (trustee 1979—80, pres. 1980—81, John M. Eisenberg award 2003), Inst. Medicine (pres. 2002—). Jewish. Mailing: NAS Institute of Medicine 500 5th St NW Washington DC 20001-2721 Office: 2101 Constitution Ave Washington DC 20418 Office Phone: 202-334-3300. Office Fax: 202-334-3851. E-mail: fineberg@nas.edu.

FINEEBRG, MARC STEVEN, orthopedist; b. Buffalo, June 27, 1967; MD, Northwestern Med. Sch., 1993. Chief sports medicine, assoc. prof. orthop. surgery U. Buffalo Orthopaedics and Sports Medicine, 1999—. Team physician Buffalo Sabres-Nat. Hockey League, UB Bulls-NAAC. Office: 4949 Harlem Rd Amherst NY 14226 Business E-Mail: msf5@buffalo.edu.

FINEGOLD, DAVID NEAL, pediatric endocrinologist, medical educator; b. Pitts., Oct. 5, 1947; BS in Physics, U. Pitts., 1968; MD, U. Pitts. Sch. Medicine, 1972. Diplomate Am. Bd. Pediat., cert. in pediatric endocrinology, clin. biochemical genetics. Intern pediat. Children's Hosp. Pitts., 1972—73, resident endocrinology, 1973—75; postdoc. rsch. fellow George S. Cox Med. Rsch. Inst., Hosp. U. Pa., Phila., 1975-77; JDF fellow Children's Hosp. Phila., 1977-78; clin. assoc. dept. pediat. U. Pa., 1978—79, rsch. assoc. dept. biochemistry & biophyics, 1978-81, asst. prof. pediat., 1979-81; asst. prof. pediat. & medicine U. Pitts. Sch. Medicine, 1981-88, assoc. prof. pediat. & medicine, 1989-96, prof. pediat. & medicine, 1996—. Asst. physician dept. medicine, divsn. endocrinology & diabetes Children's Hosp. Phila., 1978—81; faculty mem., divsn. med. genetics Children's Hosp. Pitts., 1996—. Contbr. articles to profl. jours., chapters to books. Mem.: Soc. Inherited Metabolic Disorders, Am. Soc. Nephrology, Soc. Pediatric Rsch., Endocrine Soc., Am. Fedn. Clin. Rsch., Am. Diabetes Assn. (exec. bd. mem. western Pa. affiliate 1981—90, chmn. profl. edn. com. 1982—86, v.p. western Pa. affiliate 1987—88, pres. western Pa. affiliate 1988—91), Lawson Wilkins Pediatric Endocrine Soc., Am. Soc. Human Genetics. Office: U Pitts Sch Medicine Divsn Gen Academic Pediat 3414 Fifth Ave Ste Fl 3 Pittsburgh PA 15213-2524 Office Phone: 412-692-5070. Office Fax: 412-692-6472. Business E-Mail: david.finegold@chp.edu. *

FINEGOLD, SYDNEY MARTIN, infectious disease and microbiology researcher; b. NYC, Aug. 12, 1921; s. Samuel Joseph and Jennie (Stein) F.; m. Mary Louise Saunders, Feb. 8, 1947 (dec. June 1994); children: Joseph, Patricia, Michael; m. Gloria Weiss, Feb. 18, 1996. AB, UCLA, 1943; MD, U. Tex., 1949. Diplomate: Am. Bd. Med. Microbiology (mem. bd. 1979-85), Am. Bd. Internal Medicine. Intern USPHS, Galveston, Tex., 1949-50; fellow in medicine U. Minn. Med. Sch., 1950-52, research fellow, 1951-52; resident medicine Wadsworth Hosp., VA Ctr., Los Angeles, 1953-54; instr. medicine U. Calif. Med. Ctr., Los Angeles, 1955-57, asst. clin. prof., 1957-59, asst. prof., 1959-62, assoc. prof., 1962-68, prof., 1968—2000, emeritus, 2000—, prof. microbiology and immunology, 1983—2000, emeritus, 2000—; chief chest and infectious disease sect. Wadsworth Hosp., 1957-61, chief infectious disease sect., 1961-86, assoc. chief staff for research and devel., 1986-92; staff physician infectious disease sect. VA Med. Ctr., LA, 1992—. Mem. pulmonary disease rsch. program com. VA, 1961-62, infectious disease rsch. program com., 1961-65, merit rev. bd. (infectious diseases), 1972-74, med. rsch. program specialist, 1974-76, adv. com. on infectious disease, 1974-87; mem. NRC-Nat. Acad. Sci. Drug Efficacy Study Group, 1966-69; mem. subcom. on gram-negative anaerobic bacilli Internat. Com. on Nomenclature Bacteria, 1966—, chmn., 1972-78; mem. adv. panel U.S. Pharmacopoeia, 1970-75; chmn. working group on anaerobic susceptibility test methods Nat. Com. Clin. Lab. Standards, 1987-97, advisor, 1998-2002. Mem. editl. bd. Calif. Medicine, 1966-73, Applied Microbiology, 1973-74, Western Jour. Medicine, 1974-77, Am. Rev. Respiratory Disease, 1974-76, Jour. Clin. Microbiology, 1975-85, Infection, 1976—, Jour. Infectious Disease, 1979-82, 84-85, Antimicrobial Agts. Chemotherapy, 1980-89, Diagnostic Microbiology and Infectious Diseases, 1982-90; editor Revs. of Infectious Diseases, 1990-91, Clin. Infectious Diseases, 1992-2000; sect. editor: infectious diseases vols. Clin. Medicine, 1978-82, Microbiol. Ecology in Health and Disease, 1987-90; assoc. editor, consulting editor Anaerobe, 1994—. editor-in-chief, 1998—2009. Vice chmn. UCLA Acad. Senate, 1986-87, chair, 1987-88. Served with USMCR, with USNR, 1943-46, to 1st. lt. AUS, 1952-53. Co-recipient V.A. William S. Middleton award for biomed. rsch., 1984; recipient Profl. Achievement award UCLA, 1987, Mayo Soley award Western Soc. Clin. Investigation, 1988, Disting. Alumnus award U. Tex. Med. Br., 1988, UCLA Med. Alumni Assn. Med. Scis. award, 1990, Hoechst Roussel award Am. Soc. Microbiology, 1992, medal Helsinki U., Finland, 1996, Lifetime Achievement award Infectious Disease Assn. Calif., 1995, Wm. H. Oldendorf Lifetime Achievement awrd VA Med. Ctr., 1996, Lifetime Achievement award Internat. Soc. Anaerobic Bacteriology, 1998, Lifetime Achievement award, Anaerobic Soc. America, 2006, Becton Dickinson award in Clin. Microbiology, 1999; organism named Finegoldia magna, 1999; new species named Alistipes finegoldii, 2003; new species named Bacteroides Finegoldii, 2006; Dickson Emeritus professorship award, UCLA, 2007. Master ACP; fellow APHA, AAAS, Am. Acad. Microbiology, Infectious Diseases Soc. Am. (councilor 1976-79, pres.-elect 1980-81, pres. 1981-82, exec. com. 1980-83, Bristol award 1987, Soc. citation 1999); mem. Assn. Am. Physicians, Am. Soc. Microbiology (chmn. subcom. on taxonomy of Bacteroidaceae 1971-74, 1st annual Alex Sonnenwirth award 1986), Am. Thoracic Soc., Western Soc. Clin. Rsch., Western Assn. Physicians, Wadsworth Med. Alumni Assn. (past pres.), Anaerobe Soc. of the Ams. (interim pres. 1992-94, pres. 1994-96), Soc. Intestinal Microbiology Ecology and Disease (interim pres. 1982-83, pres. 1983-87), Va. Soc. Physician in Infectious Diseases (pres. 1986-88), Am. Fedn. Clin. Rsch., Sigma Xi, Alpha Omega Alpha. Democrat. Jewish. Office: Infectious Disease Sect VA Med Ctr Wilshire & Sawtelle Blvds Los Angeles CA 90073 Home: 13082 Mindanao Way #17 Marina Del Rey CA 90292 Office Phone: 310-268-3678. Personal E-mail: sidfinegol@aol.com.

FINIELS, PIERRE-JACQUES S, neurosurgeon; b. Nimes, France, Jan. 7, 1965; s. Jacques Constant F. and Renee Elizabeth Pailloux. MD, U. Montpellier I, Nimes, France, 1990, MSc. Resident dept. neurosurgery Ctr. Hosp. Universitaire Chauliac, Montpellier, France, 1991-94, Ctr. Hosp. Universitaire St. Marguerite, Marseille, France, 1994-95, asst. neurosurgeon Montpellier, France, 1995—99; pvt. practice Nimes, 1999—. Cons. rschr. exptl. morphology lab. U. Medicine Nimes, France, 1992—; jud. expert for med. affairs. Contbr. articles, abstracts to med. jours. Mem.: Teach Com. Assn. European Rsch. Groups for Spinal Osteosynthesis, French Speaking Spinal Neurosurg. Soc., N.Y. Acad. Scis., French Neurosurg. Soc., French Speaking Neurosurg. Soc. Roman Catholic. also: 49 Ave Jean Jaurès 30900 Nimes France Office Phone: 33 4 66 36 05 14. E-mail: dr.pjfiniels@club-internet.fr.

FINK, BERND, orthopedic surgeon; b. Bonn, Germany, Sept. 23, 1964; s. Wilfried and Hedwig (Jäntgen) F.; m. Claudia Olga Elfriede Hinze, July 29, 1994; children: Alexander Jürgen, Maximilian Benedikt. MD, U. Bonn, Germany, 1989; habilitation, 1999, prof., 2001. Resident in surgery Alfried Krupp von Bohlen and Halbach Hosp., Essen, Germany, 1990-91; resident in trauma surgery BG Trauma Hosp., Hamburg, 1991-93; resident in orthopedic surgery Heinrich-Heine U., Dusseldorf, 1993-96; fellow in orthopedic surgery Univ. Hosp. UKE, Hamburg, 1997—99; cons. Hamburg U. Hosp. UKE, 1999—2004; head dept. endoprosthetic orthop. and surgery of rheumatic diseases Clinic Markgroeningen, 2004—. Contbr. articles to profl. jours. Mem. Deutsche Gesellschaft fur Orthopeadic u. Traumatologie, Assn. for the Application of the Methods of Ilizarov, German Orthop. Rsch. Soc., Assn. Orthop. Rheumatology, European Rheumatoid Arthritis Surg. Soc. Avocations: tennis, skiing. Office: Orthop Clinic Markgroeningen Kurt Lindemann Weg 10 71706 Markgroeningen Germany Office Phone: 497145912201. Business E-Mail: b.fink@okm.de.

FINK, DANIEL L., hospital administrator; B in Biology, Baylor U., Waco, Tex.; MBA, Tulane U., New Oreleans; M in Pub. Health, Tulane U. Cert. Med. Practice Exec. Am. Coll. Med. Practice Executives. With Cook Children's Health Care System, Tex., Meth. Hospitals of Dallas; COO Riley Hosp. for Children, Indpls., 2005—09, pres., CEO, 2009—. Fellow: Am. Coll. Healthcare Executives; mem.: Ind. Healthcare Executives Network. Office: Riley Hosp for Children 702 Barnhill Rd Indianapolis IN 46202 Office Phone: 317-274-4071.

FINK, DAVID LEONARD, surgeon; b. St. Louis, June 6, 1936; s. Sidney Fink and Estelle Esses Goldstein; m. Frances Carole Bower, June 13, 1965 (dec. Oct. 20, 2008); children: Dana Lynne, Denise Lysette. BA, Columbia Coll., 1957; MD, Cornell U., NYC, 1961. Diplomate Am. Bd. Surgery. Resident in surgery St. Luke's Hosp. Med. Ctr., NYC, 1961-64, U. Wis. Med. Ctr., Madison, 1964-66; pvt. practice, Paterson, N.J., 1970—; chief exec. officer Gen. Surgeons North Jersey, P.A., Paterson, 1970—. Chief surgery Barnert Meml. Hosp., Paterson, 1982-86, 2003-08, pres. med. staff, 1988; assoc. clin. prof. surgery Seton Hall Postgrad. Sch. Medicine Maj. U.S. Army, 1966-70. Decorated Army Commendation medal; recipient Am. Top Surgeons. Fellow ACS, Soc. of Surgeons of N.J.; mem. Vascular Soc. N.J., Ea. Vascular Soc., Southeastern Surg. Soc., Cornell U. Med. Alumni Assn. (bd. dirs. 1986-89), Stuyvesant Yacht Club. Avocation: sailing. Office: Gen Surgeons North Jersey 707 Broadway Paterson NJ 07514-1425 Office Phone: 973-742-3371.

FINK, LEAH W.H., medical educator; b. Australia, Sept. 7, 1968; BSc with honors, Monash U., 1991, PhD, 1995. Rsch. asst. prof. W.Va. U., 2002—06, lectr., adj. asst. prof., 2006—08, assoc. prof., 2008—. Rsch. fellow RMIT U., Melbourne, Australia, 1995—97; med. rep. Wyeth Pharms., Australia, 1997—98; rsch. assoc. U. Miss. Med. Ctr., 1999—2000, instr., 2000—02. Postdoc. fellowship, Am. Heart Assn., grant, NIH. Mem.: Am. Physiology Soc. (Young Investigators Travel award), Internat. Assn. Med. Sch. Educators, Am. Soc. Pharmacology and Exptl. Therapeutics (Travel award). Avocations: gardening, reading. Office: Dept Physiology and Pharmacology WVa University 1 Morgantown WV 26508 Business E-Mail: lhammer@hsc.wvu.edu.

FINK, MATTHEW E., neurologist; b. Phila., Jan. 15, 1951; BA cum laude, U. Pa., 1972; MD cum laude, U. Pitts., 1976. Diplomate Am. Bd. Critical Care Medicine, Am. Bd. Psychiatry and Neurology, Am. Bd. Internal Medicine, Nat. Bd. Med. Examiners. Intern then asst. resident in medicine Boston City Hosp., 1976-78, chief resident in internal medicine, 1978; asst. resident then chief resident in neurology Columbia-Presbyn. Med. Ctr., NYC, 1978-82, chief neurology clin., 1982-84, dir. neurology ICU, 1983-93, co-investigator Coma Clin. Rsch. Ctr., 1986-90, dir. neurology and neurosurgery ICU, 1991-93; clin. fellow Coll. Physicians and Surgeons Columbia U., NYC, 1978-82, assoc. in clin. neurology Coll. Physicians and Surgeons, 1982-83, from. asst. prof. to assoc. prof. in clin. neurology Coll. Physicians and Surgeons, 1983-90, dir. divsn. critical care neurology, 1988-93, assoc. prof. clin. neurology depts. neurology and neurosurgery, 1990; asst. attending neurologist Presbyn. Hosp., NYC, 1982-90; chmn. dept. neurology and comprehensive stroke ctr. Beth Israel Med. Ctr., NYC, 1993-97, co-dir. Inst. Neurology & Neurosurgery, 1996—, pres., CEO, 1997—2002; prof. neurology & medicine Albert Einstein Coll. Medicine, 1994—; prof. clinical neurology, vice chmn. clinical services Weill Med. Coll., Cornell U.; chief divsn. stroke & critical care neurology NY Presbyterian Hosp./Weill Cornell Med. Ctr., interim chair, neurologist-in-chief, 2008—. Tchg. assoc. dept. medicine Sch. Medicine Boston U., 1979-80; emergency svcs. physician Health Ins. Plan N.Y., 1980-83; co-investigator Am. Critical Care, Inc., 1985, Nat. Inst. Neurol. and Communicative Disorders and Stroke, 1987-89, Nat. Inst. Neurol. Diseases and Stroke, 1991-95; sr. investigator Nat. Stroke Assn.; vis. prof. rounds Sch. Medicine Robert Wood Johnson U., New Brunswick, N.J., 1990, St. Vincent's Hosp. and Med. Ctr., N.Y.C., 1990, New Rochelle (N.Y.) Hosp., 1991, U. Med. and Dentistry NJ, Newark, 1992, Mt. Sinai Hosp., 1993, numerous others; vis. prof., grand rounds Yale-New Haven Med. Ctr., Sch. Medicine Yale U., 1990, Health Scis. Ctr. U. Oreg., Portland, 1991, Jersey Shore Med. Ctr., Neptune, 1993, others; course dir. neuro-critical care Child Neurology Soc., 1993, World Congress Neurology, Can., 1993, others; examiner Am. Bd. Psychiatry and Neurology, Inc., 1998; dir. Yarmen Stroke Ctr., 2003--; cons., lectr. and presenter in field. Ad hoc reviewer Archives Neurology, 1988—, Neurology, 1988—, Neurosurgery, 1988—, New England Jour. Medicine, 1988—; mem. editl. bd. Neurology Chronicles, 1991—; contbr. articles to profl. jours., chpts. to books. Nat. Inst. Neurol. Diseases and Stroke grantee, 1991-95; Nat. Stroke Assn. rsch. fellow, 1993-95. Mem. Am. Acad. Neurology (sec. sect. critical care and emergency medicine 1989, vice chmn. sect. critical care and emergency neurology 1991, chmn. sect. critical care and emergency medicine 1993), N.Y. County Med. Soc., World Fedn. Neurology (founding mem. rsch. group intensive mgmt. neurology 1989), Alpha Omega Alpha, Sigma Xi. Office: Weill Cornell Med Ctr 1300 York Ave Box 144 New York NY 10021 Office Phone: 212-746-4564. Business E-Mail: mfink@med.cornell.edu.

FINK, MICHAEL KARL, internist, hematologist, oncologist; b. Heidelberg, Germany, Aug. 29, 1945; s. Erwin and Maria Fink. MD, U. Heidelberg, 1971; D Med. Habilitation, U. Munich, 1990. Resident Klinikum Grosshadern, Munich, 1978-88; asst. med. dir. Klinikum Fürth, Germany, 1989—2008; privatdozent U. Erlangen, Germany, 1991. Author: Cancer Research, 1982; co-author: Internat. Jour. of Cancer, 1985 (Vincenz Czerny award German Soc. for Hematology and Oncology); contbr. articles to profl. jours. Recipient Internat. Proficiency badge for glider piloting Fedn. Aero. Internat., 1984. Avocation: gliding. Personal E-mail: fink-fuerth@t-online.de.

FINK, MITCHELL PHILLIP, surgeon, researcher; b. San Francisco, Calif., Dec. 27, 1948; s. Walter and Betty (Donnenfield) F.; children: Emily, Matthew. BS, U. Calif., Davis, 1970; MS, U. Calif., Irvine, 1971; MD, Washington U., St. Louis, 1976; MA, Harvard U., 1996. Diplomate Am. Bd. Surgery; cert., in Surgical Critical Care, Am. Bd. Surgery. Asst. prof. surgery Naval Rsch. Inst., Bethesda, Md., 1983—84; assoc. prof. surgery U. Mass. Med. Sch., Worcester, 1984—91, prof. surgery and anesthesia, 1990—91; dir. divsn. surgical critical care Mass. Gen. Hosp., Boston, 1992—93; chief divsn. surgical critical care Beth Israel Hosp., 1993—95; surgeon-in-chief Beth Israel Deaconess Med. Ctr., 1995—99; co-founder Critical Therapeutics Inc., Lexington, Mass., Logical Therapeutics, Inc., Waltham, Mass. Mem. defense sci. rsch. coun. Defense Advanced Rsch. Project Agency; mem. surgery, anesthesiology and trauma study sect. NIH. Mem. numerous editl. bds. in field; Assoc. Editor Jour. Pharmacology and Experimental Therapeutics; assoc. editor Jour. Leukocyte Biology; Scientific Editor Critical Care Medicine; Editor, co-editor 16 books in field; contbr. over 350 articles to peer-reviewed pubs., over 100 chpts. to books. Lt. comdr. USNR, 1970-84. Decorated Joint Svc. Commendation medal; recipient Kraft scholarship award, U. Calif. Berkley, 1966, Robert Carter Med. Sch. Prize, Wash. U. Med. Sch., 1974, 1977, Richard S. Brookings Med. Sch. Prize, 1975, Med. Alumni Scholarship award, 1976, Merck Manual award, 1977, Millennium Lectr. award, Soc. Critical Care Medicine, 2000, Presdl. Citation, 2002, Presdl. Citation Lecture award, Am. Coll. Chest Physicians, 2001; named Laerdal Meml. Lectr., Soc. Critical Care Medicine, 1994. Mem.: Alpha Omega Alpha (Book Prize 1977). E-mail: finkmp@gmail.com.

FINK, PAUL JAY, psychiatrist, educator; b. Pa., June 26, 1933; MD, Temple U., 1958. Adj. prof., dept. psychiatry Temple U. Sch. Medicine, 2000—. Mem.: ACP, APA, GAP. Avocation: opera. Office: 191 Presidential Blvd Ste C-132 Bala Cynwyd PA 19004 Office Fax: 610-664-5279. Business E-Mail: pjayfink@aol.com.

FINK, RAYMOND, medical educator; b. NYC, Apr. 21, 1927; s. William and Yetta (Rales) F.; m. Ruth Ursula Gebhard, May 28, 1961 (div. 1982); children: William D., David S.; m. Louise Berenson, Jan. 27, 1983. BBA, CCNY, 1947; MA, U. Denver, 1949; PhD, Cornell U., 1956. Statistician Opinion Rsch. Ctr. U. Denver, 1949; survey statistician U.S. Bur. Census, Suitland, Md., 1949-50, 56; rsch. assoc. human resources rsch. George Washington U., Washington, 1952-53; rsch. assoc. Bur. Social Sci. Rsch., Washington, 1957-60; assoc. dir. drinking practices study Calif. State Dept. Pub. Health, Berkeley, 1960-62; v.p. rsch. and stats. Health Ins. Plan Greater NY, NYC, 1962-78; prof. community and preventive medicine NY Med. Coll., Valhalla, 1978-2000, dir. health policy mgmt., 1982-90, dir. health svcs. rsch., 1990-2000; dir. rsch. Mid-Hudson Family Health Inst., New Paltz, NY, 1999—. Chmn. social sci. adv. com. Planned Parenthood Fedn. Am., NYC, 1966-71; chair task force on HMOs Nat. Inst. Mental Health, Rockville, Md., 1971-72. Contbr. articles to profl. jours. Trustee Health Svcs. Improvement Fund, NYC, 1986-2000; active United Hosp. Fund NY. Sgt. US Army, 1950-52. Grantee Nat. Inst. Mental Health, 1968-72, Nat. Cancer Inst., 1972-78, Social Sci. Rsch. Coun., 1982-83, Robert Wood Johnson Found., 1990-94. Mem. APHA, Am. Assn. Public Opinion Rsch. (co-editor 1968-69), Med. and Health Rsch. Assn. (chair 1975-2002), Assn. for Health Svcs. Rsch., Herman Biggs Soc. (pres. 1994-98, 2006—), NY Assn. Pub. Opinion Rsch.(councilor at large) Jewish.

FINK, ROBERT MICHAEL, pharmacist; b. Greeneville, Tenn., June 11, 1960; s. Ralph Rye and Thelma Gertrude Fink; m. Jonna Fink Fink. BS in Pharmacy, Mercer U., Atlanta, 1980—83, PharmD, 1983—84; MBA, E.Tenn. State U., Johnson City, Tenn., 1986—90. Cert. nutrition support pharmacist Bd. Pharm. Specialties, 1994, pharmacotherapy specialist Bd. Pharm. Specialties, 1995. Clin. pharmacy coord. Johnson City Med. Ctr., Tenn., 1984—97; assoc. dir. clin. pharmacy svcs. med. ctr. Baylor U., Dallas, 1997—98; dir. pharmacy svcs. Meth. Med. Ctr., Dallas, 1998—2001, sr. dir., chief pharmacy exe., Cmty. Health Sys., Franklin, Tenn., 2001—. Fellow: Am. Soc. Healthcare Exec., Am. Coll. Healthcare Exec., Am. Soc. Health Sys. Pharmacists; mem.: Tenn. Soc. Health Sys. Pharmacists (secretary-treasurer 1996—97, Tenn. Hosp. Pharmacist of Yr. award 1989), Am. Coll. Clin. Pharmacy, Am. Soc. Parenteral & Enteral Nutrition, Brentwood Rotary Club. R-Consevative. Meth. Avocations: golf, travel. Office: Cmty Health Sys 4000 Meridian Blvd Franklin TN 37068

FINK, YOEL, science educator, researcher; BSc in Chem. Engring., Israel Inst. Tech.(Technion), 1994, BA in Physics, 1995; PhD in Materials Science, Mass. Inst. Tech., 2000. Rsch. asst. Israel Inst. Tech. (Technion), 1991—95, part-time instr. physics advancement project, 1993—95, lab instr. chemistry and physics track project, 1993—95; postdoctoral assoc. dept. physics MIT, Cambridge, asst. prof., 2000—04, Thomas B. King assoc. prof. materials sci., dept. materials sci. and engring., 2004—. Co-founder, pres. OmniGuide Comm., 2000—; prin. invesitgator Rsch. Lab Electronics, MIT. Contbr. articles to profl. jours. Recipient NAS award for Initiatives in Rsch., 2004; named one of Top 100 Young Innovators under the age of 35, MIT Tec. Review, 1999. Achievements include research in optical materials synthesis, optical characterization, simulation and theory; design of novel optical structures and devices; development of processing method for photonic band gap fibers; created Omni directional dielectric mirror, which has become a life-saving surgery tool; patents in field. Office: MIT Rm 13-5013 77 Massachusetts Ave Cambridge MA 02139 Office Phone: 617-258-6113. Fax: 617-452-3432. Business E-Mail: yoel@mit.edu.

FINKEL, KEVIN, medical educator, director; b. Elizabeth, NJ, Oct. 18, 1960; MD, U. Tex., Houston, 1987. Prof., chief, internal medicine LBJ Gen. Hosp. Harris County Hosp. Dist., 2004—08; prof., medicine, renal divsn. dir. U. Tex. Med. Sch., Houston, 2008—. Fellow: ACP, Am. Soc. Nephrology, Am. Soc. Critical Care Medicine. Office: 6431 Fannin MSB 5134 Houston TX 77030 Business E-Mail: kevin.w.finkel@uth.tmc.edu.

FINKEL, MARION JUDITH, internist, pharmaceutical administrator; b. NYC, Nov. 2, 1929; d. Israel and Bella (Stillman) Finkel; m. Simon V. Manson, Sept. 12, 1954. Student, L.I. U., 1945-48; MD (Howard Sloan Meml. scholar), Chgo. Med. Sch., 1952. Intern Jersey City Med. Ctr., 1952-53; resident in internal medicine Bellevue Hosp., NYC, 1954-56; med. editor Merck and Co., 1957-61; pvt. practice specializing in internal medicine, NYC, 1956-57, NJ, 1961-63; with FDA, 1963-85, dir. divsn. metabolic and endocrine drugs, 1966-70, dep. dir. bur. drugs, 1970-71, 72-74, dir. office new drug evaluation, 1971-72, 74-82, dir. office orphan products devel., 1982-85; exec. dir. R&D Berlex Labs., Inc., 1985-88; v.p. drug registration and regulatory affairs Sandoz Pharms., Inc., 1988-94, v.p. corp. regulatory compliance, 1994-95, cons. regulatory affairs, clin. R&D, 1995—. Contbr. chpts. to books, numerous articles to profl. jours. Recipient award of merit FDA, 1972, Superior Svc. award USPHS, 1976, 84, Fed. Woman's award Fed. Govt., 1976, Meritorious Exec. award, 1980; named Disting. Alumnus, Chgo. Med. Sch., 1977, L.I. U., 1980. Office: 21 Squirrel Run Morristown NJ 07960-6411

FINKEL, TERRI HELMAN, pediatric rheumatologist; MD, Stanford U., 1982. Diplomate Am. Bd. Pediatrics, Am. Bd. Pediatrics-pediatric rheumatology, lic. Pa., 1999. Intern pediat. Children's Hosp., 1983; resident pediat. Univ. of Colo. Hosp., 1985; fellow pediatric rheumatology Nat. Jewish Health, 1990; hollander endowed chair pediatric rheumatology Children's Hospital of Philadelphia, chief rheumatology divsn., dir. rheumatology fellowship program. Recipient Arthritis Hero, Arthritis Found., Miracle Worker, Children's Hosp. Network, First Physician Scientist, Colo. Women's Hall of Fame; named one of Top Doctors, Phila Mag., 2010—11. Office: Children's Hospital of Philadelphia 34th St and Civic Center Blvd Philadelphia PA 19104 Office Phone: 215-590-1000.

FINKELSTEIN, JAMES DAVID, physician, educator; b. NYC, Oct. 16, 1933; s. Harry and Sylvia Z. (Bernstein) F.; m. Barbara Joan Eisenberg, Dec. 12, 1959; children: Donna Ilene, Laura Helene. AB, Harvard U., 1954; MD, Columbia U., 1958. Diplomate Am. Bd. Internal Medicine. Intern, resident in medicine Presbyn. Hosp., NYC,

1958—63; chief med. svc. VA Med. Ctr., Washington, 1979-99, chief gastroenterology, 1970-79, assoc. chief staff for rsch., 1975-79, med. investigator, 1970-75, clin. investigator, 1965-68, chief biochemistry rsch. lab., 1965—2005, sr. clinician, 1999—. Cons. Children's Hosp., Washington, 1968-85; prof. medicine George Washington U., 1969—; clin. prof. medicine Georgetown U., 1981-2001; prof. medicine Howard U., Washington, 1983-2001; mem. Nutrition Study sect. NIH, 1972-78; hon. pres. 2d Internat. Conf. on Homocysteine Metabolism, Nijmegen, Netherlands, 1998. Contbr. articles on biochemistry and nutrition of methionine to profl. jours. Served as surgeon USPHS, 1963-65. Recipient F.P. Gay Rsch. award Columbia U., NYC, 1956, Arthur S. Fleming award Jr. C. of C., Washington, 1971, Disting. Rschr. medal George Washington U., 1999; NIH grantee, 1966-95. Mem. Am. Soc. for Clin. Investigation, Am. Gastroent. Assn., Assn. of Am. Physicians, Am. Inst. Nutrition, Am. Soc. Clin. Nutrition (Robert H. Herman award 2001), Am. Fedn. Clin. Rsch., Harvard Club. Office: VA Med Ctr 50 Irving St NW Washington DC 20422-0001 Office Phone: 202-745-8373. E-mail: james.finkelstein@med.va.gov. *

FINKELSTEIN, WARREN, gastroenterologist, educator; b. Brooklyn, NY, Oct. 25, 1946; BS cum laude, Brooklyn Coll., NY, 1964—68; MD, Med. Coll. Va., 1968—72. Diplomate Am. Bd. Internal Medicine, 1975, cert. gastroenterology 1983. Med. intern Boston City Hosp., 1972—73, asst. med. resident, 1973—74; chief resident in medicine Boston Veterans Adminstrn. Hosp., 1974—75; fellow gastroenterology Mass. Gen. Hosp., Boston, 1975—77, clin. fellow in medicine gastroenterology, 1975—76; rsch. fellow in medicine gastroenterology Harvard Med. Sch., Boston, 1976—77; fellow Am. Coll. of Gastroenterology, 1984, Am. Coll. of Physicians, 1993; vis. facultu upper gastrointestinal diseases UCLA and Univ. of Conn., 1977; vis. faculty Annenberg Ctr. for Health Sciences Eisenhower Med. Ctr., Rancho Mirage, Calif., 1995—; clin. asst. prof. medicine Univ. of Medicine and Dentistry of NJ NJ Med. Sch., 2003—; attending in medicine gastroenterology Mountainside Hosp., Montclair, NJ, 1977—, chmn. nutrition care com., 1980—99, credentials com. mem. medicine dept., 1982—2001, oper. room com., 1990—2004, exec. com. medicine dept., 2000—. Author numerous articles. Named one of Top Doctors (Gastroenterology) NY Metro Area, Castle Connolly Guide, 2001—09, Top Doctors (Gastroenterology), NJ Monthly Mag., 2003—09, Best Doctors (Gastroenterology), NY Mag., 2003—09, Inside Jersey Mag., 2009. Mem.: AMA, ACP, Crohn's and Colitis Foun. of America (exec. com. NJ chpt. 1991—2002), Am. Soc. for Laser Medicine and Ssurgery, Am. Coll. of Gastroenterology (practice mgmt. com. 2001—02, pub. rels. com. 2001—04, nominating com. 2003, membership com. 2003—04, nominating com. 2005), The Acad. of Medicine of NJ, NY Gastroenterological Assn., Essex County Med. Soc., Orange Mountain Med. Soc., NY Endoscopic Soc., NJ Soc. for Gastrointestinal Endoscopy, NJ Gastroenterology Soc., Am. Soc. for Gastrointestinal Endoscopy, Associated Physicians of Montclair and Vicinity. Office: Mountainside Hospital 1 Bay Ave Montclair NJ 07042

FINLEY, SARA CREWS, medical geneticist, educator; b. Lineville, Ala., Feb. 26, 1930; m. Wayne H. Finley; children: Randall Wayne, Sara Jane. BS in Biology, U. Ala., 1951, MD, 1955. Diplomate Am. Bd. Med. Genetics; cert. clin. geneticist; cert. clin. cytogeneticist. Intern Lloyd Noland Hosp., Fairfield, Ala., 1955-56; NIH fellow in pediatrics U. Ala. Med. Sch., Birmingham, 1956-60; NIH trainee in med. genetics Inst. Med. Genetics, U. Uppsala, Sweden, 1961-62; mem. faculty U. Ala. Med. Sch., 1960-96, co-dir. lab. med. genetics, 1966-96, prof. pediatrics, 1975-96, occupant Wayne H. and Sara Crews Finley chair med. genetics, 1986-96, prof. emerita, 1996—; Disting. Faculty lectr. Med. Ctr. U. Ala. at Birmingham, 1983; mem. staff U. Ala. Hosp., Children's Hosp. Ala. Mem. ad hoc com. genetic counseling Children's Bur., HEW, 1966; mem. ad hoc rev. panel for genetic disease and sickle cell testing and counseling programs, 1980; mem. genetic diseases program objective rev. panel Bur. Maternal and Child Health and Resources Div., HHS, 1989, mem. adv. group on lab. quality assurance, 1989. Birmingham Author papers on clin. cytogenetics, human congenital malformations, human growth and devel. Mem. White House Conf. Health, 1965; mem. rsch. manpower rev. com. Nat. Cancer Inst., 1977-81; mem. Sickle Cell Disease Adv. Com., NIH, 1983-87; chairperson physician's campaign bd. dirs. United Way, 1993-95. Recipient Disting. Alumna award U. Ala. Sch. Med. Alumni Assn., 1989, Med. award Ala. Assn. for Retarded Children, 1969, Turlington award Planned Parenthood of Ala., 1982, Nat. Outstanding Alumnae award Zeta Tau Alpha, 1992, Disting. Alumna award U. Ala. Nat. Alumni Assn., 1994, Brother Bryan Prayer Point award Birmingham Women's Com. of 100, 2001, Gardner award Ala. Acad. Sci., 2002, Local Legend award Am. Med. Women's Assn. Nat. Libr. Medicine, 2004, Lifetime Achievement award Birmingham Bus. Jour., 2003, So. Women of Dist. award So. Women's Ctr., 2005, Martha Myers Role Model award U. Ala. Med, Alumni Assn., 2009; co-recipient Will Holmes award Children's Aid Soc. Birmingham, 1999; named Top Ten Women in Birmingham, 1989, Top 31 Most Outstanding Alumnae U. Ala., Tuscaloosa, 1993, Ala. Healthcare Hall of Fame, 2001; Finley-Compass Bank Genetics Conf. Ctr. with portrait opened, 2001. Fellow AMA (founding), Am. Coll. Med. Genetics; mem. Am. Soc. Human Genetics, Med. Assn. Ala. (Samuel Buford Word award 2003, Fifty Year Club 2005), Ala. Acad. Sci., Jefferson County Med. Soc. (pres. 1990), Jefferson County Pediatric Soc., So. Med. Assn., NY Acad. Sci., Caduceus Club, Rotary Club of Birmingham, Phi Beta Kappa, Sigma Xi, Alpha Omega Alpha, Alpha Epsilon Delta, Omicron Delta Kappa, Phi Kappa Phi, Zeta Tau Alpha. Office: U Ala Kaul Bldg 210E Birmingham AL 35294 E-mail: scfinley@webtv.net.

FINLEY, SARAH MAUDE MERRITT, retired social worker; b. Atlanta, Nov. 19, 1946; d. Genius and Willie Maude (Wright) Merritt; m. Craig Wayne Finley, Aug. 10, 1968; children: Craig Wayne Jr., Jarret Lee. BA, Spelman Coll., 1968; postgrad., Atlanta U., 1968-69. CSW, cert. GPS/MAPP leader 2001. Job placement advisor Marsh Draughton Bus. Coll., Atlanta, 1971-72; child attendant Fulton County Juvenile Ct., Atlanta, 1972; social worker Fulton County Dept. Family and Children Svcs., Atlanta, 1972-2000, casework supr., 1976-98, Title VI customer svc. coord. Ctrl. City/North Area office, 1990-98, ret., 1998; counselor/asst. to the project dir. Right Way Home Project N.W. Area Office, 1998-99; social svcs. case mgr. Placement Resource Devel. N.W. Area Office, 2000; social worker Dept. Family and Children Svcs. Clayton County, Jonesboro, Ga., 2000—05, ret., 2005. Supr. Count on Me video Ga. Dept. Human Resources, 1987; mem. Spelman's Team of Alumni Recruiters, Spelman Coll.; bd. dirs. E.D. Cubed, Inc., Ga., South Fulton County, 501(c)(3) Orgn. Vol. coord. family support program Family Support Group of Atlanta Detachment of 2d Army Maneuver Tng. Command.; vol. family support coun. 87th Maneuver Area Command (now 4th Brigade, 87th Divsn.), 1991-93; del. Ft. McPherson (Ga.) Army Family Symposium, 1992, 3d ann. worldwide USAR Family Support Conf., St. Louis, 1992 Mem.: Fulton County Ret. Employees Assn., Nat. Alumnae Assn. Spelman Coll., Womens Aux. Ga. VFW. Methodist. Avocations: poetry, reading, volunteer work, stress management, writing. Personal E-mail: maudngen@aol.com.

FINLEY, WAYNE HOUSE, medical educator; b. Goodwater, Ala., Apr. 7, 1927; s. Byron Bruce and Lucille (House) F.; m. Sara Will Crews, July 6, 1952; children: Randall Wayne, Sara Jane. BS, Jacksonville State U., 1948; MA, U. Ala., 1950, MS, 1955, PhD, 1958, MD, 1960; postgrad., U. Uppsala, Sweden, 1961-62. Cert. clin. cytogenetics Am. Bd. Med. Genetics, 1983. Sci. tchr. High Sch., Tuscaloosa, Ala., 1949-51; intern U. Ala. Hosps. and Clinics, 1960-61; from asst. prof. to assoc. prof. pediat. U. Ala. Sch. Medicine, 1962-70, prof., 1970-96, asst. prof. biochemistry, 1965-75, prof., 1975-96, asst. prof. physiology and biophysics, 1968-75, assoc. prof., 1975-96, chmn. med. student rsch. day, 1965-75, dir. Lab. Med. Genetics, 1966-96, prof. epidemiology, pub. health and epidmiology, 1975-96, prof. emeritus, 1996—, adj. prof. biology, 1980-96, chmn. faculty coun. Sch. Medicine, 1977-78, 84-87. Dir. med. genetics grad. program U. Ala. at Birmingham, 1983-96, dir. Am. Bd. Med. Genetics approved tng. program, 1978-96, dir. med. genetics residency program, 1995-98; chmn. Carey Phillips Travel Fellowship, 1972—; mem. com. on genetic counseling Children's Bur., Dept. HEW, 1966-67; nat. adv. rsch. resources coun. NIH and HEW, 1977-80; sr. scientist Comprehensive Cancer Ctr., Cystic Fibrosis Rsch. Ctr., Ctr. for Health Risk Assessment and Disease Prevention, 1982-96; bd. dirs. Southeastern Regional Genetics Group, 1982-2000, editor newsletter, 1997-2000; chmn. steering com. Reynolds Hist. Libr. Assocs., 1981-2007, Com. on Future Needs in Med. Genetics, Genetics Svc. Br., USPHS, 1987, Carmichael Fund for Grad. Students, 1989—2009; faculty rep. U. Ala. Sys. Bd. Trustees, 1995-96; senator U. Ala. at Birmingham Faculty Senate, 1995-96; mem. adv. and nominating com. Ala. Healthcare Hall of Fame, 1998—, chmn., 2007-. Author University of Alabama Medical Alumni Association, 1859-2003; contbr. articles on human malformations and clin. cytogenetics to tech. jours. Deacon Dawson Meml. Bapt. Ch., 1960-. With Infantry US Army, 1945—46, Germany, officer Chemical Corps US Army, 1951—53, with USAR, 1946—74, lt. col., ret. Recipient Med. award Ala. Assn. Retarded Children, 1969, Outstanding Educators of Am., 1971, Turlington award, 1982, Disting. Faculty Lectr. award U. Ala. Med. Ctr., 1983, Wayne H. and Sara C. Finley chair in med. genetics U. Ala., Birmingham, 1986, Alumnus of Yr. award Jacksonville State U., 1989, Portrait Reynolds Libr., 1991, Will Gaines Holmes award Childrens Aid Soc., 1999, Brother Bryan Humanitarian award, 2001, Gardner award Ala. Acad. Sci., Samuel Buford Word award Med. Assn. State of Ala., 2003, Lifetime Achievement award Birmingham Bus. Jour., 2003, named to Ala. Healthcare Hall of Fame, 2001; Finley-Compass Bank Genetics Conf. Ctr. established at U. Ala. Birmingham, 2001. Fellow Am. Coll. Med. Genetics (founder, edn. com. 1993-97, program dir. 1996), Royal Soc. Medicine; mem. AMA (Physicians Recognition award 1971, 75, 81, 84, 87, 90, 93, 96), AAAS, N.Y. Acad. Scis., Soc. Exptl. Biology and Medicine, Am. Inst. Chemists, Am. Fedn. Clin. Rsch., Am. Soc. Human Genetics, So. Med. Assn., So. Soc. Pediat. Rsch., Med. Assn. Ala. (counsellor 1990—), Jefferson County Med. Soc. (maternal and child health com. 1975-79, chmn. 1976-77, pres. 1983), Jefferson County Pediat. Soc., Ala. Acad. Sci. (trustee 1991—2001), Caduceus Club (pres. 1984-86), NIH Alumni Assn., U. Ala. Sch. Medicine Alumni Assn. (pres. 1974-75, Disting. Alumni award 1978, Disting. Svc. award 2005, Martha Myers Role Model award 2008), Greater Birmingham Area C. of C. (bd. dirs. 1983-86), Newcomen Soc., Kiwanis (pres. Shades Valley 1973-74), Rotary Club Birmingham, Am. Acad. Pediat. Della Robbia Club (gold mem. 2008), SAR (flag chmn.), ALSSAR, Wayne Finley Breakfast Club, Sigma Xi (pres. U. Ala. Birmingham chpt. 1972-73), Kappa Delta Pi, Phi Delta Kappa, Alpha Omega Alpha, Phi Beta Pi, Omicron Delta Kappa. Baptist. Avocations: reading, golf, genealogy, medical history. Home: 3412 Brookwood Rd Birmingham AL 35223-2023 Office: U Ala Birmingham Dept Genetics Kaul 210 1530 Third Ave S Birmingham AL 35294-0017 Home Phone: 205-969-1942; Office Phone: 205-934-4983. Personal E-mail: wfinley1942@charter.net.

FINNEY, ROY PELHAM, JR., urologist, surgeon, inventor; b. Gaffney, SC, Dec. 7, 1924; s. Roy P. Finney Sr. and Mary Frances (Cannon) Woodard; m. Kay Harkness, Apr. 5, 1963; children: Wright C., James L., Joella R., Gray, Kevin. MD, Med. U. S.C., 1952. Diplomate: Am. Bd. Urology. Resident in urology Johns Hopkins U., Balt., 1952-57; prof. surg. urology U. South Fla., Tampa, 1972-84, dir. div. urology, 1972-84; ret. Designer and inventor implantable prostheses incontinence device inflatable penile prostheses treatment impotence, Double J ureteral stent, developer new surg. procedures treatment impotence; patentee in field. Fellow ACS; mem. Am. Urology Assn., Soc. Internationale D'Urologie, Internat. Continenece Soc., Urodynamic Soc. Republican. Home: 4382 Cortez Blvd Weeki Wachee FL 34607-1209 Personal E-mail: royf@atlantic.net.

FINO, M. ELIZABETH, reproductive endocrimologist, gynecologist; b. Scranton, Pa., July 17, 1974; BA, Georgetown U., 1996; MD, Temple U. Sch. Medicine, 2002. Physician NYU Fertility Ctr., Greenwich Fertility Ctr., 2009—, resident ob-gyn., 2004, fellow reproductive endocrinology infertility, 2009. Asst. clin. prof. NYU Langone Med. Ctr., 2009—. Recipient Berlex Jr. Faculty Devel. award, Berlex Found., Barton's award, NYU Med. Ctr. Fellow: ACOG; mem.: AMA, Bellevue Obstet. & Gynecol. Soc., AOA, ASRM. Avocations: running, sailing. Office: 55 Holly Hill Ln Ste 270 Greenwich CT 06830 Personal E-mail: elizabethfino@yahoo.com.

FINOCCHI, VANINA, radiologist; b. Rome, Jan. 1, 1974; MD, U. Rome Sapienza, 2000, degree in Radiology, 2004. Radiologist St. Andrea Hosp., 2006—. Avocations: water-skiing, horseback riding. Office: via Di Grottarossa 1035 Rome 00189 Italy Business E-Mail: vaninafinocchi@libero.it.

FINS, JOSEPH JACK, medical ethicist; b. NYC, Nov. 16, 1959; s. Herman and Ruth (Lovett) Fins; m. Amy B. Ehrlich, July 2, 1989. BA with honors, Wesleyan U., Middletown, Conn., 1982; MD, Cornell U., NYC, 1986. Diplomate Am. Bd. Internal Medicine. Psychiatry intern Payne Whitney Psychiat. Clinic, NYC, 1986—87; resident in medicine NY Hosp./Cornell Med. Ctr., NYC, 1987—89, fellow in medicine, 1990—92; instr. Cornell U. Med. Coll., 1992—93, asst. prof. medicine, 1993—98; assoc. prof. medicine, assoc. prof. medicine in psychiatry Weill Cornell Med. Coll., NYC, 1998—2003, assoc. prof. pub. health, 2001—03, chief divsn. med. ethics, 2001—, prof. medicine, 2003—, prof. pub. health, 2003—, prof. medicine in psychiatry, 2003—10. Vis. assoc. in medicine Hastings Ctr., Briarcliff Manor, NY, 1990—92, Garrison, NY, 1992—2007, fellow, 2007—; asst. attending physician NY Hosp., 1992—98; dir. med. ethics NY Presbyn. Hosp./Weill Cornell Med. Ctr., 1994—, assoc. attending physician, 1998—2003, attending physician, 2003—; vis. prof. med. ethics Univ. Complutense, Madrid, 1993, 95, 96, Philipps U., Marburg, Germany, 2006; physician, ethicist in residence Healthcare Chaplaincy, NYC, 1994—2002; apptd. mem. NY Atty. Gen.'s Quality Care at End of Life Commn., 1997—98; apptd. commr. White House Commn. Complementary & Alternative Medicine Policy, 2000—02; adj. faculty Rockefeller U., NYC, 2003—; sr. attending physician Rockefeller U. Hosp.; sr. sci. cons. Advanced Rsch. Inst. Geriatric Psychiatry, Nat. Inst. Mental Health, 2003—08; fellow Richard W. Riley Inst. Govt., Politics & Pub. Leadership, Furman U., Greenville, SC, 2005; apptd. mem. NY State Task Force Life & the Law, 2007—. Author: A Palliative Ethic of Care: Clinical Wisdom at Life's End, 2006; mem. editl. bd. BioMed Ctrl. Med. Ethics, Neuroethics, Jour. Pain & Symptom Mgmt., Cambridge Quar. Healthcare Ethics, The Oncologist; contbr. articles to profl. jours. Mem. nat. adv. com. Woodrow Wilson Nat. Fellowship Found., 2003—06; hon. mem. adv. bd. Inst. Study of Humanities & Bioethics, U. PR, 1995—2000; bd. trustees Wesleyan U., 2004—07, Fund for Modern Courts; chair Wesleyan U. Alumni Assn., 2008—10; bd. dirs. NY Organ Donor Network, 2003—07. Recipient Faculty Scholars award, Soros Open Soc. Inst. Project Death in America, 1997—2000, Health Advocacy award, NY chpt. Soc. Patient Representatives, 1998, Tchg. Excellence award, Weill Cornell Med. Coll., 2000, 2006, Wholeness of Life award, HealthCare Chaplaincy, 2001, Sheldon Berrol Meml. Chautauqua, American Congress Rehabilitation Medicine/American Soc. Neurorehabilitation, 2002, John P. McGovern Ann. award, American Osler Soc., 2006, Robert Wood Johnson Found. Investigator award in health policy rsch., 2007—10; grantee vis. fellowship, Woodrow Wilson Nat. Fellowship Found., 1997—. Fellow: ACP (councilor at large 2003—06, vice chair, act ethics human rights com. 2007—09, gov. 2007—, trustee ACP Found.), NY Acad. Medicine; mem.: American Soc. Bioethics & Humanities (pres.-elect 2009—, bd. trustees), Inst. Medicine, American Geriat. Soc. (vice chair ethics com. 1994—96). Office: New York Presbyterian Hospital-Weill Cornell Ctr Divsn Med Ethics 435 E 70th St Ste 4J New York NY 10021 Office Phone: 212-746-9663. Office Fax: 212-746-4609. Business E-Mail: jjfins@med.cornell.edu. *

FINUCANE, KEVIN EUGENE, retired physician; b. Australia, July 25, 1933; MB, U. Western Australia; MS, MBBS, 1957. Sr. med. registrar, dept. cardiology Royal Perth Hosp. Western Australia, 1963—64; hon. assoc. physician, thoracic medicine Prince Henry Hosp., Sydney, 1965—67, Boehringer Ingelheim rsch. fellow thoracic medicine U. NSW, 1965—67; rsch. fellow, rsch. assoc., dept. physiology Harvard U. Sch. Pub. Health, 1967—71; head, dept. pulmonary physiology and sleep medicine, dir., respiratory high dependency unit Sir Charles Gairdner Hosp., Nedlands, 1972—98. Mem. to chmn., divsn. diagnostic medicine SCGH, 1980—93; mem. to chmn. Clin. Assn. Exec. Sir Charles Gairdner Hosp., 1984—87; dep. chair U. Notre Dam Australia Human Rsch. Ethics Com., 2010—. Recipient Laennec medal, TSANZ, 1991, Soc. medal, 1999, Fulbright fellowship, Australian & Am. Fulbright Commn., Milton Rsch. fellowship, Harvard U. Sch. Pub. Health. Fellow: Royal Australasian Coll. Physicians; mem.: Australian Lung Found., Australian Med. Assn., Australian Sleep Assn., Thoracic Soc. Australia & New Zealand (pres. 1975—77, 1989—91, chmn., profl. stds. com. 1992—94). Avocations: swimming, walking. Home: PO Box 352 Cottesloe Perth 6911 Australia Business E-Mail: finucane@cygnus.uwa.edu.au.

FIORENTINO, PAOLO, medical researcher; b. Italy, Dec. 1, 1969; MD, U. Palermo, 1994; PhD, U. Turin, 2005. Rsch. fellow U. Toronto, 1998—2003; clin. & rsch. fellow U. Rochester, 2004—08; clin. fellow U. Montreal, 2008—09, U. Palermo, 1994—97, 2009—. Adj. prof. U. Turin; pvt. practice. Grant, U. Turin, Hong Kong Fedn. grant. Mem.: Am. Assn. Orthodontics. Avocations: writing, history, mythology. Office: 345 Bloor St E Toronto ON M4W 3J6 Canada Personal E-mail: paolo05@yahoo.com.

FIORETTO, JOSE ROBERTO, medical educator; b. Botucatu, July 21, 1961; Degree, Botucatu Med. Sch., Sao Paulo State U., Brazil, 1985. Assoc. prof. Botucatu Med. Sch., Sao Paulo State U., 1985, adj. prof., 1989, assoc. prof., 2006—. Grant, FAPESP. Avocation: music. Office: University Estadual Paulista Júlio Mesquita Filho Faculy Medicina Botucatu Sao Paulo 18618-970 Brazil Office Fax: 55-14-38116274. Business E-Mail: jrf@fmb.unesp.br.

FIORI, ENRICO, surgeon, educator; b. Cagliari, Italy, Apr. 4, 1955; Grad. in Medicine, 1979, degree in Gen. Surgery, 1984. Prof. Sapienza U. Rome, 1982—. Surgeon Azienda Policlinic Umberto I, 1990. Contbr. articles to profl. publs. Grant, Italian Soc. Surgery. Fellow: U. Senate, Italian Soc. Digestive Endoscopy, Italian Soc. Surgery. Avocations: sports, music. Office: Sapienza University Rome viale del Policlinic 155 Rome 00161 Italy Office Fax: 390649972182.

FIRE, ANDREW ZACHARY, biologist, pathology professor; b. Palo Alto, Calif., Apr. 27, 1959; BA in Math., U. Calif., Berkeley, 1978; PhD in Biology, MIT, 1983. Postdoc. fellow Med. Rsch. Coun. Lab. Molecular Biology, Cambridge, England, 1983—86; staff mem. dept. embryology Carnegie Instn. of Washington, Balt., 1986—2003; prof. dept. pathology and genetics Stanford U. Sch. Medicine, Calif., 2003—. Adj. prof. biology Johns Hopkins U., Balt., 1989—2003; mem. bd. sci. counselors Nat. Ctr. Biotechnology, NIH. Contbr. articles in profl. jours. Recipient Md. Disting. Young Scientist award, 1997, Genetics Soc. of America medal, 2002, Meyenburg prize, Germany, 2002, Wiley prize, Rockefeller U., 2003, Dr. H.P. Heinken prize in biochemistry and biophysics, Netherlands Acad. Arts & Sci., 2004, Gairdner Found. Internat. award, 2005, Lewis S. Rosenstiel award, Brandeis U., 2005, Massry prize, 2005, Nobel prize in physiology/medicine, 2006, Paul Ehrlich & Ludwig Darmstaedter prize, Germany, 2006. Fellow: Am. Acad. Arts & Scis.; mem.: NAS (award in Molecular Biology 2003), Inst. Medicine. Achievements include discovery of process now known as RNAi (with Craig C. Mello), that double-stranded RNA can quash the activity of specific genes. Office: Dept Pathology and Genetics Stanford U Sch Medicine 300 Pasteur Dr L235 Stanford CA 94305-5324 Office Phone: 650-723-2885. Office Fax: 650-725-6902, 650-724-9070. Business E-Mail: afire@stanford.edu. *

FIREMAN, PHILIP, pediatrician, allergist, immunologist; b. Pitts., 1932; MD, U. Chgo., 1957. Diplomate Am. Bd. Allergy and Immunology (chmn. 1992-93). Intern Phila. Gen. Hosp., 1957-58; resident in pediatrics Children's Hosp., Pitts., 1958-60; fellow in allergy and immunology NIH, Bethesda, Md., 1960-62; fellow allergist, immunologist Harvard Children's Hosp., Boston, 1962-64; prof. pediatrics, internal medicine U. Pitts. Med. Sch. Chmn. Am. Bd. Allergy & Immunology, 1990—91. Recipient Disting. Alumni award, U. Chgo. Mem.: Am. Acad. Allergy, Asthma and Immunology (pres. 1997—98).

FIRMAN, JAMES P., medical association administrator; MBA, Columbia Univ., PhD in Edn. Sr. program officer Robert Wood Johnson Found., 1981—84; pres., CEO United Seniors Health Coop., 1985—95, Nat. Coun. on the Aging, Washington, 1995—. Co-founder Grantmakers in Aging; past chmn. Leadership Coun. of Aging Organizations (twice), Access to Benefits Coalition; bd. dir. Generations United, Nat. Human Svcs. Assembly. Office: Nat Council on Aging 1901 L St NW 4th Fl Washington DC 20036 Office Phone: 202-479-1200. Office Fax: 202-479-0735. Business E-Mail: james.firman@ncoa.org. *

FIRMIN, MICHAEL WAYNE, psychology professor; b. New Orleans, July 28, 1961; s. Lloyd John and Betty L. (Shepherd) F.; m. Karen Sue Tuttle, Aug. 4, 1984; children: Ruth, Sarah. BA, Calvary Bible Coll., 1983; MA, Calvary Theol. Sem., 1985; MS, Bob Jones U., 1987, PhD, 1988; MA, Marywood U., 1992; PhD, Syracuse U. Nat. cert. counselor; lic. psychologist, Ohio. Dir. counseling svcs. Bapt. Bible Coll. of Pa., Clarks Summit, 1988-98, assoc. prof., 1988-98, chmn. divsn. grad. studies, 1995-97; resident in psychology TCN: Behavioral Health Svcs., 2000—01; assoc. prof. psychology Cedarville U., Ohio, 1998—2004, prof. psychology, 2004—, chmn. dept. psychology, 2000—09. Cons. for psychol. svcs. Assn. Bapts. for World Evangelism, Harrisburg, Pa., 1991—94, 1999—2003; clin. assessment cons. Keystone City Residence, 1994—2000; pvt. practice Miami Valley Assessments, 2003—. Editor: Jour. Ethnographic & Qualitative Rsch., 2006—. Pastor Faith Fellowship Bapt. Ch., Danbury, Conn., 1991-94. Mem. Psi Chi. Republican. Home: 84 E Elm St Cedarville OH 45314-8513 Office: Cedarville Univ 251 N Main St Cedarville OH 45314-0601

FIROZVI, KASHIF, oncologist, hematologist; Grad., Johns Hopkins U.; MD, Georgetown U. Diplomate Am. Bd. Internal Medicine-hematology, Am. Bd. Internal Medicine-med. oncology. Resident internal medicine Sch. of Medicine Georgetown Univ.; fellow hematology and oncology Lombardi Cancer Ctr., Georgetown, fellow devel. therapeutics; physician Md. Oncology Hematology. Named one of the Top Doctors in Oncology/Hematology, Wash. Mag., 2010—11. Office: Capital Oncology and Hematology Associates 2101 Med Park Dr 200 Silver Spring MD 20902 Office Phone: 301-933-3216. Office Fax: 301-933-4941.

FIRST, LEWIS RICHARD, pediatrician; b. Phila., May 12, 1954; s. Howard M. and Barbara M. F.; m. Sandra L. First, June 9, 1985; children: David Louis, Rachel Tessa. BA in Biochemistry magna cum laude, Havard U., 1976; MD, Harvard Med. Sch., Boston, 1980; MS in Epidemiology, Harvard Sch. Public Health, Boston, 1985. Bd. Cert. Diplomate Am. Bd. Pediat. Intern, resident, pediat. Children's Hosp. Boston, Mass., 1980-83, chief resident, pediat. Mass., 1983-84, clin. fellow, ambulatory/emergency pediat. Mass., 1984-85, asst. in medicine Mass., 1985—90, acting med. dir., divsn. emergency medicine Mass., 1985—86, assoc. dir., divsn. emergency medicine Mass., 1986—88, dir., Pediat. Group Assocs. Mass., 1986—94, assoc. in medicine Mass., 1990—94, dir. edn., divsn. gen. pediat. Mass., 1990—94, dir., med. student edn., dept. medicine Mass., 1992—94; instr. pediat. Harvard Med. Sch., 1985—90, asst. prof. pediat., 1990-1994; prof., chmn., dept. pediat. U. Vt. Coll. Medicine, Burlington, 1994—, sr. assoc. dean, ednl. and curriculum affairs, 2003—09; chief, pediat. Med. Ctr. Hosp. Vt., 1994—95; attending physician Children's Health Care Svc., Fletcher Allen Health Care, 1994—2002, physician leader, 1995—2002; attending physician Vt. Children's Hosp. at Fletcher Allen Health Care, 2000—, chief, pediat., 2002—. Med. cons., pediat. edn., seminars in pediat. gastroenterology and nutrition, 1991—94; mem. Pediat. Test Develop. Com., 1995—2001; chair, pediat. test develop. com. Nat. Bd. Med. Examiners, 1997—2000, chair, Step II Com. US Med. Licensing Examination, 2001—; several vis. professorship; invited lectr. in field. Editor (and author): (novels) Pediatric Medicine, 1989—93; contbr. several articles to profl. jours.; mem. adv. bd. Harvard Family Health Letter, 1992—93, editl. bd. mem. Pediatrics, 1993—98, sr. consulting editor, 1999—, dep. editor, 2009, editor-in-chief, 2009—, co-editor in chief Am. Acad. Pediat. Grand Rounds (monthly newsletter), 1998—. Safety officer Burlington Little League, 1999—. Recipient Nat. Rsch. Svc. award in environ. epidemiology, 1985, Tchr. of Yr. award, Harvard Med. Sch., 1992, 1995, U. Vt. Sch. of Medicine, 1996-2000, 2001, vis. prof. award, 2001, Green Mountain Pediatric award, 2001, Miller-Sarkin Mentoring award, Ambulatory Pediat. Assn., 2007. Fellow: Am. Acad. Pediat. (mem. Vt. chpt., mem. future pediat. edn. II workforce subgroup 1996—, (Vt. chpt.) Green Mt. Pediat. award for Outstanding Pediatrician 2002, Nat. Edn. award 2007); mem.: Coun. on Med. Student Edn. in Pediat., Assn. of Med. Sch. Pediat. Dept. Chairs (exec. coun. mem. 2001), Vt. State Med. Soc., AMA, Ambulatory Pediat. Assn. (ex-officio, task force mem. for continuity clini spl. interest group 1987—), Am. Pediat. Soc., Alpha Omega Alpha (and Assn. Am. Med. Coll. Robert J. Glaser Disting. Tchr. award for Nat. Excellence in Med. Edn. 2002), Phi Beta Kappa. Office: Univ Vt Coll Med Dept Pediat E203 Given Bldg 89 Beaumont Ave Burlington VT 05405-0068 Office Phone: 802-656-0027, 802-656-2296. Office Fax: 802-656-2077. E-mail: lewis.first@vtmednet.org, lewis.first@uvm.edu.

FISCELLA, KEVIN A., physician, educator; BA in Psychology, Antioch Coll., Yellow Springs, Ohio, 1976; MD, Med. Coll. Va., Richmond, 1980; MPH, U. Rochester Sch. Medicine & Dentistry, 1996. Clin. and rsch. fellow Univ. and Eastman, 1975—76; resident, family medicine SUNY, Buffalo, 1983; fellow, dept. family medicine U. Rochester Sch. Medicine & Dentistry, 1992—95, asst. prof., dept. family medicine and cmty. and preventive medicine, 1996—99, assoc. prof., dept. family medicine and cmty. & preventative medicine, 1999—; family physician Geneva B. Scruggs Cmty. Health Ctr., Buffalo, 1983—92, med. dir., 1985—92; staff family physician Westside Cmty. Health Ctr., Rochester, NY, 1992—. Mem. study sect. Agy. for Healthcare Quality and Rsch., Health Care Quality and Effectiveness, 2001—03; mem. Inst. Medicine Com. on Design, Nat. Healthcare Disparities Report, 2002; assoc. dir. Rochester Ctr. to Improve Comm. in Health Care: Building Relationships, Eliminating Disparities, 2003—; mem. adv. com. for Physician Tng. to Reduce Racial/Ethnic Disparities AMA, 2002—03; mem. adv. com. for racial and ethnic disparities in healthcare Aetna, 2002—06; mem. expert roundtable on Robert Wood Johnson Foundation's Future Work in Racial and Ethnic Disparities, 2003—04; mem. Nat. Com. for Quality Assurance Expert Panel on Culturally & Linguistically Appropriate Services (CLAS) to Address Health Care Disparities in Managed Care, 2004—05; co-chair Ambulatory Care Project: Healthcare Disparities Technical Adv. Panel, Nat. Quality Form, 2006—; HIV clin. coord. Westside Cmty. Health Ctr.; mem. spl. emphasis panel for NIH/Nat. Ctr. for Minority Health & Health Disparities for applications for Establishing Comprehensive Rsch. Centers of Excellence, 2006. Contbr. articles to peer reviewed publs. Office: Dept Family Medicine 777 S Clinton Ave 1381 South Ave Rochester NY 14620 Office Phone: 585-506-9484, 585-436-3040. Business E-Mail: kevin_fiscella@urmc.rochester.edu.

FISCH, ROBERT OTTO, medical educator; b. Budapest, Hungary, June 12, 1925; came to U.S., 1957. s. Zoltan and Irene (Manheim) F.; 1 dau., Rebecca A. Med. diploma, U. Budapest, 1951; study art, Acad. Fine Arts, Budapest, 1943, Mpls. Coll. Arts and Design, 1970-76. Gen. practice medicine, Hungary, 1951-55; pub. health officer, 1955; pediatrician Hosp. for Premature Children, Budapest, 1956; intern Christ Hosp., Jersey City, 1957-58; intern pediatrics U. Minn. Hosps., 1958-59, researcher, 1959-60, research fellow, 1961; instr. U. Minn. Sch. Medicine, 1961-63, asst. prof., 1963-72, assoc. prof., 1972-79, prof., 1979—, dir. phenylketonuric clinic, 1961-97. Author: Respiratory Diseases; PKU, Child Development (Best Cover Minn. Med. 1975), Light from the Yellow Star: A Lesson of Love from the Holocaust, 1994, The Metamorphosis to Freedom, 2000, Dear Dr. Fisch: Children's Letters to a Holocaust Survivor, 2004, Fisch Stories Reflection in Life, Liberty, and the Pursuit of Happiness, 2009; contbr. articles to profl. jours.; exhibited art works in various one-man and group shows. Mem. Soc. Pediatric Rsch., Am. Physician Art Assn. (Best of Show award 2002, numerous others). Home: 1201 Yale Pl 2301 Minneapolis MN 55403 E-mail: fisch001@umn.edu.

FISCHBACH, GERALD D., science foundation director, neurobiology educator, former dean; b. New Rochelle, NY, Nov. 15, 1938; children: Elissa, Peter, Neal, Mark. AB, Colgate U., Hamilton, NY, 1960; MD, Weill Cornell Med. Coll., NYC, 1965; MA (hon.), Harvard U., 1978. Intern U. Wash. Hosp., Seattle, 1965-66; sr. surgeon lab. neurophysiology, Nat. Inst. Neurol. Diseases & Stroke (NINDS), NIH, Bethesda, Md., 1966-69, fellow behavioral biology br., Nat. Inst. Child Health, 1969-73, dir. NINDS, 1998—2001; assoc. prof. pharmacology Harvard Med. Sch., Boston, 1973—78, prof., 1978-81, Nathan Marsh Pusey prof. neurobiology, chair dept. neurobiology, 1990-98; Edison prof. neurobiology, chmn. dept. anatomy and neurobiology Washington U. Sch. Med., St. Louis, 1981-90; exec. v.p. health and biomed. sciences, dean faculty medicine Columbia U. Coll. Physicians & Surgeons, NYC, 2001—06; sci. dir. The Simons Found., NYC, 2006—. Mem. exec. com. Program in Cell and Devel. Biology, Harvard Med. Sch., 1974-81; nonresident tutor Leverett House, Harvard Coll., 1974-77; clk. of corp. Marine Biol. Lab., Woods Hole, Mass, 1978-81, trustee, 1982—, exec. com., 1984-89; master Fuller Albright Acad. Soc., Harvard Med. Sch., 1979-81, faculty coun., 1980-81; chmn. Gordon Conf. on Molecular Pharmacology, 1983; dir. Ctr. for Cellular and Molecular Neurobiology, Washington U. Sch. of Med., 1983-90, dir. Jacob Javits Ctr. for Excellence in Neurosci., 1985-90, dir. Ctr. for Higher Brain Function, 1988-90, mem. Med. Ctr. Bd., 1989-90; dir. Neurosci. Ctr., Mass. Gen. Hosp., 1990—; mem. adv. bd. Nat. Spinal Cord Injury Assn., 1978—, Neurology B Study Sect., NIH, 1978-80, Alfred P. Sloan Found., 1984-89, Dept. Biology Adv. Coun., Princeton U., 1984-88, Fidia Rsch. Found., 1986—, McKnight Neurosci. Rsch. Awards Rev. Com., 1986—, Howard Hughes Med. Inst., 1988—, SUNY Health Sci. Ctr. at Bklyn, 1988—, Helen Hay Whitney Found., 1991, Children's Hosp., Boston, 1991; vis. prof. Dept. Pharmacology U. Calif. at San Francisco, 1978; lectr. Disting. Lecture Series in Pharmacology, U. Md. Sch. Medicine, 1978, 25th Ann. Bishop Lecture, Washington U. Sch. Medicine, 1980, Disting. Lecture Series, Dept. Zoology, U. Tex., 1981; invited speaker 5th Ann. Meeting European Neurosci. Assn., 1981; Alden Spencer lectr. Coll. Physicians and Surgeons, Columbia, U., 1981, Stephen W. Kuffler lectr. Harvard Med. Sch., 1990, numerous others; assoc. Neurosci. Rsch. Program, 1981—. Editor Jour. Cell Biolog, 1985-86; assoc. editor Devel. Biology, 1974-78, Jour. Neurophysiology, 1975-81, 1989—, Jour. Neurobiology, 1986—; corr. editor Proc. Royal Soc., Series B, London, 1989—; contbr. articles to profl. jours. Recipient Polk award Cornell U., 1965, Mathilde Solowey award Found. for Advanced Edn. in the Scis., NIH, 1975, W. Alden Spencer award Coll. Physicians and Surgeons, Columbia U., 1981; N.Y.State Regents scholar, 1956-60, N.Y. State med. scholar, Cornell U., 1962-65; Salk Inst. non-resident fellow, 1990. Mem.: NAS (coun. mem. 2005—08), Am. Soc. Cell Biology, Soc. Gen. Physiologists, Soc. Neurosci. (pres. 1983—84), Phi Beta Kappa. Office: The Simons Found 160 5th Ave New York NY 10010-7003 Office Phone: 212-337-3036. Office Fax: 646-654-0220. E-mail: gf@simonsfoundation.org.

FISCHELL, ROBERT ELLENTUCH, physicist; b. NYC, Feb. 10, 1929; s. Philip and Julia (Ellentuch) Fischell; m. Marian Standard (dec. May 2005); children: David R., Tim A., Scott J.S.; m. Susan Rudolph, Sept. 3, 2006. BSMechE cum laude, Duke U., 1951; MS in Physics, U. Md., 1953, ScD (hon.), 1996; LHD (hon.), Johns Hopkins U., 2008. Physicist U.S. Naval Ordnance Lab., Silver Spring, Md., 1951—56; prin. staff engr. Emerson Rsch. Labs., Silver Spring, 1956—60; various staff positions Applied Physics Lab., Johns Hopkins U., Laurel, Md., 1959—97, prin. profl. physicist, 1962—, chief engr. space dept., 1972—80, chief tech. transfer space dept., 1978—88; pres., chmn. bd. MedInnovations, Inc., Dayton, Md., 1988—90; chmn. bd. MedInTec, Inc., Dayton, Md., 1990—; pres. Fischell Biomed. LLC, 2000—; prof. practice of engring. U. Md., 2003—. Chmn. bd., v.p. R & D Cathco, Inc., 1991—; pres., chmn. bd. IsoStent, Inc., Dayton, Md., 1993—; chmn. emeritus NeuroPace, Inc., Dayton, 1997—; cons. Cordis, a J&J Co., 1998—; expert witness Brown and Bain, Palo Alto, Calif., 1992—93; rsch. assoc. in medicine Johns Hopkins U. Sch. Medicine, 1983—95, Yale U. Sch. Medicine, 1988—95; mem. exec. panel Chief of Naval Ops., Washington DC, 1983—87; expert witness Fish and Neave, NYC, 1986—92; field reviewer for orphan products FDA, 1984—90; mem. rsch. com. Md. affiliate Am. Heart Assn., 1985—87; mem. tech. com. on space guidance and control AIAA, 1972—75, chmn. nat. conf., 1973; mem. space com. Internat. Fedn. Automatic Control, 1970—75; mem., chmn. photovoltaic specialities com. IEEE, 1959—72; chmn., pres. Neuralieve, Inc., 1998—2001; chmn. Angel Med. Sys., Inc., 2001—; dir. U. Sys. Md.; chmn. and CTO Svelte Med. Sys. Inc., 2008—. Author over 50 tech. publs.:, assoc. editor: AIAA Jour. Spacecraft and Rockets, 1972—75; holder 150 patents in field of biomed. engring., biomed. devices and spacecraft. Bd. visitors U. Md., 1997—; trustee U. Md. Found., 2000—. Recipient Tech. Achievement award, ASME, 1962, Outstanding Young Engr. award, Washington Capitol area, 1963, awards for most significant inventions, Indsl. Rsch. mag., 1967, 1970, 1973, Inventor of Yr. award, Intellectual Property Owners Assn., 1984, Gold medal for contbn. to aerospace sci. and tech., N.Y. Acad. Sci., 1987, Exceptional Engring. award for MAGSAT satellite, NASA, 1980, Individual Achievement award for human tissue stimulator, 1982, Exceptional Engring. medal, 1984, Space Act prize, 1984, Disting. Engring. Alumnus award, Duke U., 1992, Tech. for Humanity award, Discover Mag., 1993, TED prize, Tech., Entertainment, Design Conf., 2004, Woodrow Wilson award for pub. svc., 2007, Pres.'s Outstanding Alumnus award, U. Md., 2009; named Disting. Citizen of Yr., "M" Club U. Md., 1984; named to Space Tech. Hall of Fame, U.S. Space Found., 1988. Mem.: NAE, Internat. Soc. for Artificial Organs, Beta Omega Sigma, Pi Tau Sigma, Sigma Pi Sigma, Pi Mu Epsilon, Tau Beta Pi, Phi Beta Kappa. Avocations: tennis, sailing. Home and Office: Fischel Biomedical LLC 14600 Viburnum Dr Dayton MD 21036-1247 Home Phone: 410-988-9509; Office Phone: 301-854-0606, 301-854-0600. Personal E-mail: mfischell@aol.com.

FISCHELL, TIM ALEXANDER, cardiologist; b. Washington, Feb. 10, 1956; s. Robert Ellentuch and Marian (Standard) F.; m. Anne Elizabeth Arbetter, Sept. 23, 1984; children: Evan Daniel, Jonathan Morris, Emma Julia. AB, Cornell U., 1977, MD, 1981. Diplomate Am. Bd. Internal Medicine (subspeciality cardiovas. disease and interventional cardiology). Intern internal medicine Harvard/Mass. Gen. Hosp., Boston, 1981-82, resident, 1982-84; fellow cardiology Stanford U., Calif., 1984-87, asst. prof. medicine Calif., 1987-92; assoc. prof. medicine Vanderbilt U., Nashville, 1992-96; dir. cardiovascular rsch., Borgess Rsch. Inst. Mich. State U., Kalamazoo, 1996—, prof. medicine, 1996—; cardiologist Heart Ctr. for Excellence, Kalamazoo. Med. adv. bd. Scimed, Mpls., 1992—, Cardima, Inc., Fremont, Calif., 1993—, Isostent, Inc., San Carlos, Calif., 1995-; lectr. in field. Patentee in field; contbr. articles to profl. jours., chpts. to books. Recipient Fischbach Residency Scholarship, 1986, Nat.Rsch. Svc. award grant NIH, 1986-87, clin. investigator award NIH, 1987-92, biomed. rsch. support grant NIH/Stanford U., 1988-90; Inventor of Yr. prize Thoraxcenter Course on Intracoronary Stenting, Rotterdam, The Netherlands, 1996. Fellow Am. Coll. Cardiology, Soc. Cardiac Angiography and Interventions, Andreas Gruntzig Soc., Am. Heart Assn. (coun. on circulation, advanced fellowship award Calif. affiliate 1987, grant in aid award 1988-90), Phi Beta Kappa, Phi Kappa Phi, Alpha Omega Alpha. Achievements include patents pending in field; patents in field; pioneered the world's first radioisotope stent; co-inventor of the BX Velocity Stent for the Johnson & Johnson Company inserted for blocked arteriesin 2000; co-inventor of the cardiosaver system. Avocations: basketball, tennis, skiing, golf. Home: 1701 Embury Rd Kalamazoo MI 49008 Office: Borgess Health Heart Center for Excellence 1722 Shaffer St Suite 1 Kalamazoo MI 49048 Office Phone: 269-226-8374, 269-226-8362, 269-381-3963. E-mail: taf1@net-link.net.

FISCHER, ALFRED GEORGE, geology educator; b. Rothenburg, Germany, Dec. 10, 1920; arrived in US, 1935; s. George Erwin and Thea (Freise) F.; m. Winnifred Varney, Aug. 26, 1939; children: Joseph Fred, George William, Lenore Ruth. Student, Northwestern Coll., Watertown, Wis., 1935-37; BA, U. Wis., 1939, MA, 1941; PhD, Columbia U., 1950. Instr. Va. Poly. Inst. and State U., Blacksburg, 1941-43; geologist Stanolind Oil & Gas Co., Kans. and Fla., 1943-46; instr. U. Rochester, NY, 1947-48; from instr. to asst. prof. U. Kans., Lawrence, 1948-51; sr. geologist Internat. Petroleum, Peru, 1951-56; prof. geology Princeton (N.J.) U., 1956-84, U. So. Calif., LA, 1984, now prof. emeritus. Co-Author: Invertebrate Fossils, 1952, The Permian Reef Complex, 1953, Electron Micrographs of Limestone, 1967; editor: Petroleum and Global Tectonics, 1975. Recipient Verrill medal Yale U. Fellow Geol. Soc. Am. (Penrose medal 1993), Geol. Soc. London (hon., Lyell medal 1992), Soc. Econ. Paleontologists (hon., Twenhofel medal); mem. AAAS, NAS(Mary Clark Thompson medal, 2009), U.S. Nat. Acad. Sci., Am. Assn. Petroleum Geologists, Paleontol. Soc. (medal 1995), German Geol. Soc. (Leopold von Buch medal), Geol. Union (Gustav Steinmann medal 1992), Mainz Acad. Sci. Lit. (corr.), Lincei Acad. Rome (fgn.), U.S. Nat. Acad. Sci.(Thompson medal 2009), Sigma Xi. Office: U So Calif Dept Earth Scis Zumberge Hall of Sci 117 Univ Park Los Angeles CA 90089-0001 Home: 5500 Calle Real Apt C215 Santa Barbara CA 93111-3604

FISCHER, CARL ROBERT, retired health facility administrator; b. Rahway, NJ, Nov. 15, 1939; s. Robert Carlton and Elsie Marie (Wolfarth) F.; m. Lynn Elaine Ekstrand, Mar. 12, 1966; children: Kristen, Leslie, Meredith, Kelly. BSN, Wagner Coll., 1964; MS, SUNY-Buffalo, 1966; MPH, Yale U., 1968. With Yale-New Haven Hosp., 1968-77, assoc. dir., 1975-77; exec. assoc. adminstr. U. Cin. Med. Ctr., 1977-80; exec. dir. clin. programs U. Ark. for Med. Scis., Little Rock, 1980-86; assoc. v.p. health scis., CEO Med. Coll. of Va. Hosps., Richmond, 1986-99; exec. v.p. corp. functions VCU Health Sys., 1999—2002; ret., 2003. Bd. dirs. Univ. Health Systems Consortium, exec. com. 1994-2000, chmn. bd. dirs. 1997-98, chmn. supply and svcs. divsn., 1988-89, 95-96; mem. exec. com. Nat. Assn. Pub. Hosps., 1999-2002. Pres. Ctrl. Va. Health Planning Agy., 1991-93, mem.-at-large, 1997-2002, exec. com., 2000-2002; bd. dirs. Richmond Luth. Home, 2000-01. Mem. Am. Assn. Med. Colls., Am. Hosp. Assn., Va. Hosp. Assn. (bd. dirs. 1986-91, 99-2000, chmn. coun. on adminstrn. and health planning 1988, coun. on assn. devel. 1987-88, physician liaison com. 1989-90, chmn. ctrl. Va. regional planning coun. 1997-99). Personal E-mail: flyfischn@aol.com. *

FISCHER, CRAIG LELAND, physician; b. Bklyn., Feb. 17, 1937; s. Emil Carl and Ruth Barbara (Minarcik) F.; m. Sandra Lucile Canfield, Feb. 17, 1962; children: Craig L. Jr., Emil Lewis, Lisa Anne. BS, Kans. State U., 1958; MD, U. Kans., 1962. Diplomate Nat. Bd. Med. Examiners, Am. Bd. Family Practice; cert. anat. and clin. pathology, nuclear medicine. Intern in anatomic pathology Kansas U.

Med. Ctr., 1962—63, resident in anatomic pathology, 1963—64, rsch. fellow in pathology (pub. health svc.), nuc. medicine, 1962—64, rsch. fellow pathology, nuc. medicine, 1965—66; resident in clin. pathology, Meth. Hosp. Baylor U. Coll. Medicine, 1967—68; rsch. med. officer Manned Spacecraft Ctr., NASA, Houston, 1965—68, pathologist, chief clin. labs., 1968—71; chief med. ops. Johnson Space, NASA, Houston, 1980—82; assoc. dir. labs. to dir. labs. Eisenhower Med. Ctr., Rancho Mirage, Calif., 1971—72, pathologist, dir. clin. labs., 1972—78, assoc. dir. nuc. med., 1975—78, gen. practice medicine Palm Desert, 1978—80; pathologist, co-dir. Valley Clin. Labs., Palm Desert, 1978—80; gen. practice medicine Indio, Calif., 1982—99; dir. post grad. edn. J.F. Kennedy Hosp., 1982—92; lt. col. USAFR, 1983—97; dir. Fischer and Yao Cons. Pathologists, Indio, 1987—89; pres. Fischer Assocs., Cons. in Pathology, Indio, 1989—95; ptnr. Fischer and Starke Assocs., Indio, 1995—99; sr. aviation med. examiner FAA, 1991—99, 1999—2007; asst. dir. space medicine NASA Johnson Space Ctr., 1999—2001, assoc. dir. clin. lab., 1999—2007, chief, Space Medicine & health Care Sys. Office, 2001—03, asst. dir. internat. space medicine, 2003—07. Clin. prof. dept. preventive medicine and cmty. health U. Tex. Med. Br., Galveston, 2002-07; asst. clin. prof. U. Calif., Irvine, 1986-99; mem. sci. adv. bd. Dept. Air Force, Washington, 1986-90, NAE, NRC; mem. Air Force Studies Bd., Washington, 1987-93; mem. aerospace med. adv. com. Office Space Scis. and Applications, NASA Hdqrs., Washington, 1988-93, chmn. operational medicine discipline working group, Life Scis. Directorate, 1988-92, mem. Shuttle-Mir Joint Sci. Working Group, 1993-94, mem. Adv. Coun. Task Force on the Shuttle-Mir Rendezvous and Docking Missions, 1995; mem. Mir Sci. Program Rev. Panel, 1993-98; mem. Internat. Space Sta. Task Force (Stafford Commn.), 1995-2007; chmn. multinat. med. ops. panel, 2000-04, chmn. Space Medicine Ops. Team, 2000-04, co-chmn. Space Craft Integrated Investigation Team, 2004-07; cons. lab. medicine project tektite U.S. Dept. Interior, 1969-70. Contbr. numerous articles to profl. jours. Capt. USAR, 1964—66, commd., maj, MC USAFR, 1983, commd., lt. col., MC USAFR, 1983, lt. col. USAFR, 1986, with USAFR, 1997, with USAF, Washington. Recipient Group Achievement award NASA Manned Spacecraft Ctr., 1966, 69, 70, Group Achievement award Gemini support team NASA Manned Spacecraft Ctr., Apollo 7 Flight Ops. Team award NASA Manned Spacecraft Ctr., 1969, Sustained Superior Achievement award NASA Manned Spacecraft Ctr., 1969, Superior Achievement award, 1969, Skylab Group Achievement award NASA Johnson Space Ctr., 1974, Presdl. medal of Freedom Apollo 13 Mission Ops. Team, 1970, Group Achievement award NASA Space Shuttle Launch and Ops. Team NASA Manned Spacecraft Ctr., 1982, Meritorious Civilian Svc. award Dept. of Air Force, 1990, Outstanding Contbn. Medicine award, Riverside County Med. Assn., 1996, STS-107 Columbia Contingency Support Team, 2003, Russian Fedn. Space Agy. award for internat. coop. in space exploration, 2005, Exceptional Svc. medal NASA, 2006, Silver Snoopy award Shuttle Commdr. Robert Cabana, 2006, NASA Exceptional Achievement award, 2007, Melbourn W. Boyington award Am. Astronautical Soc., 2007, NASA Outstanding Leadership medal, 2009. Fellow Am. Coll. Preventive Medicine, Am. Coll. Nuc. Physicians, Coll. Am. Pathologists, Am. Soc. Clin. Pathologists (CCE Commr.'s medal 1989), Aerospace Med. Assn. Republican. Presbyterian. Avocations: sailing, tennis, flying. Home: 3134A NASA Rd 1 #113 Seabrook TX 77586 Personal E-mail: clfspacemed@aol.com.

FISCHER, CRAIG PETER, surgeon; b. Rochester, Minn., Jan. 26, 1968; s. Ronald Peter and Nancy Marie Fischer. BS, Tulane U., New Orleans, 1987; MPH, U. Tex. Sch. Pub. Health, Houston, 1991; MD, U. Tex. Health Sci. Ctr., Houston, 1992. Lic. surgeon Am. Bd. Surgery, 2000. Surgery resident Case Western Res. U., Cleve., 1992—94; surg. oncology rsch. fellow Mass. Gen. Hosp., Boston, 1994—96, sr., chief resident in surgery, 1997—98; resident in gen. surgery The Lahey Clinic, Burlington, Mass., 1996—97; registrar in surgery Royal Infirmary Edinburgh, 1999—2001; attending hepatobiliary surgeon Meth. Hosp., Houston, 2006—; asst. prof. surgery Cornell U. Weill Med. Coll. Lectr. in field. Mem. Mus. Fine Arts, Houston, 2005—. Recipient Dean's Tchg. Excellence award, U. Tex. Health Sci. Ctr., 2002—05; named Most Outstanding Faculty Mem., MD Anderson Cancer Ctr., Tex. Children's Hosp., Lyndon Banes Johnson Charity Hosp. and Meml. Hermann Hosp., 2002—05, Most Outstanding Tchr. in Surgery, U. Tex. Health Sci. Ctr., 2003. Fellow: ACS, Royal Coll. Surgeons (corr.); mem.: Am. Hepato-Pancreato-Biliary Assn., The Pancreas Club, Internat. Hepato-Pancreato-Biliary Assn., Soc. Am. Gastrointestinal Endoscopic Surgeons, Southwestern Surg. Congress, Assn. Surgeons Great Britain, Northern Ireland, Soc. Internat. de Chirurgie, Assn. Surg. Edn., Assn. Acad. Surgery, ACS South Tex. Chpt., Houston Surg. Soc., Harris County Med. Soc., Mass. Gen. Hosp. Surg. Alumni Assn., Assn. Surgeons in Tng. UK, Tex. Med. Assn., Am. Pub. Health Assn., Am. Med. Student Assn., Soc. Surgery the Alimentary Tract (sci. program com. 2006—), Phi Beta Kappa. Achievements include development of gene therapy vectors for pancreatic cancer; blood conserving techniques in surgery; new techniques in liver and pancreatic surgery; advanced imaging software for pancreatic and liver surgery planning; introducing laparoscopic appendectomy to the Texas Medical Center; first to use minimally invasive surgical techniques for advanced pancreatic surgery. Office Fax: 713-790-6470; Home Fax: 713-790-6470. Business E-Mail: cpfischer@tmhs.org.

FISCHER, EDMOND HENRI, biochemist; b. Shanghai, Apr. 6, 1920; arrived in US, 1953, naturalized; s. Oscar and Renée (Tapernoux) Fischer; m. Nelly Gagnaux, 1948 (dec. 1961); children: Francois, Henri; m. Beverley Bullock, 1963; 1 stepchild, Paula. Degree in biology, U. Geneva, 1944, PhD in Chemistry, 1947; D (hon.), U. Montpellier, France, 1985, U. Basel, Switzerland, 1988, Med. Coll. Ohio, 1993, Ind. U., 1993, U. Bochum, Germany, 1994. Rsch. fellow Rockefeller Found., NYC, 1950—53; rsch. assoc. biology Calif. Inst. Tech., Pasadena, 1953; asst. prof. biochemistry U. Wash., Seattle, 1953—56, assoc. prof., 1956—61, prof., 1961—90, prof. emeritus, 1990—. Mem. exec. com. Pacific Slope Biochem. Conf., 1958—59, pres., 1975; mem. biochemistry study sect. NIH, 1959—64; symposium co-chmn. Battelle Seattle Rsch. Ctr., 1970, 73, 78; mem. sci. adv. bd. Friedrich Miescher Inst., Basel, Switzerland, 1976—84, chmn., 1981—84; mem. sci. adv. bd. Muscular Dystrophy Assn., 1980—89, Basel Inst. Immunology, 1995—98, Scripps Rsch. Inst., La Jolla, Calif., 1995—2001, Principe Felipe Sci. Mus., Valencia, Spain, 1998—, Venetian Inst. Molecular Medicine, U. Padova, Italy, 2001—; mem. sci. adv. bd., bd. governors Weizmann Inst. Sci., Rehovot, Israel, 1998—; Bert & Kugie Vallee vis. prof. Harvard Med. Sch., 1998—. Mem. editl. adv. bd. Biochemistry, 1961—66, assoc. editor, 1966—92; contbr. numerous articles to sci. jours. Mem. sci. coun. Am. Heart Assn., 1977—80; bd. dirs. Washington Tech. Ctr., 1986—89. Recipient Werner medal, Swiss Chem. Soc., 1952, Lederle Med. Faculty award, 1956—59, Guggenheim Found. award, 1963—64, Disting. Lectr. award, U. Wash., 1983, Laureate Passano Found. award, 1988, Steven C. Beering award, 1991, Nobel prize in physiology/medicine, 1992, Internat. Union Biochemistry & Molecular Biology medal, 2009; named an Hon. Citizen, City of New Orleans, 2007. Fellow: Royal Soc. London (fgn. mem.), Am. Acad. Arts & Scis.; mem.: NAS, Spanish Royal Acad. Scis. (fgn. assoc.), European Acad. Scis. (hon.), Royal Acad. Medicine & Surgery (hon.), Venice Acad. Sci., Arts & Letters (assoc.; fgn.), Japanese Biochem. Soc. (hon.), Korean Acad. Sci. & Tech. (hon.), Am. Chem. Soc. (mem. exec. com., divsn. biology 1969—72, monograph adv. bd. 1971—73), Am. Soc. Biol. Chemists (coun. mem. 1989—93). Office: U Washington Dept Biochemistry 1705 NE Pacific St Box 357350 Seattle WA 98195-7350 E-mail: efischer@u.washington.edu. *

FISCHER, HARRY D., rheumatologist, educator; Studied, Mt. Sinai Sch Med, 1979. Diplomate Am. Bd. of Internal Medicine, 1983, Am. Bd. of Internal Medicine-rheumatology, 1990, Am. Bd. of Internal Medicine-rheumatology, 2000, Am. Bd. of Internal Medicine-rheumatology, 2010. Resident internal medicine Beth Israel Med. Ctr., NYC, 1980—83; fellow rheumatic diseases Hosp. for Joint Diseases, NYC, 1983—85; assoc. prof. of clin. medicine Albert Einstein Coll. of Medicine; chief divsn. of rheumatology dept. of medicine Beth Israel Med. Ctr. Named one of Top Doctors-NY Metro Area, Castle Connolly's, Best Doctors, NY Mag., 2008. Office: Beth Israel Medical Center Phillips Ambulatory Care Center 10 Union Sq E Rm 3D New York NY 10003 Office Phone: 212-844-8101. E-mail: hfischer@bethisraelny.org.

FISCHER, JOSEF E., surgeon, educator; b. NYC, May 7, 1937; s. Max and Molly (Ochs) F.; m. Karen Jean Down, Oct. 24, 1965; children: Erich, Alexandra. AB summa cum laude, Yeshiva Coll., 1957; MD magna cum laude, Harvard U., 1961; DM (hon.), Lund U., Sweden, 1990. Diplomate Am. Bd. Surgery, Nat. Bd. Med. Examiners. Surg. intern Mass. Gen. Hosp., Boston, 1961-62, 3d asst. surg. resident, 1962-63, 2d asst. surg. resident, 1965-66, asst. resident surgery, 1966-68, chief resident, 1969-70, asst. in surgery, 1970-73, chief surg. physiology lab., 1970-78, chief hyperalimentation unit, 1972-78, asst. surgeon, 1973-76, assoc. vis. surgeon, 1976-78; practice medicine, specializing in surgery Boston, 1970-78, Cin., 1978—; commd. med. officer USPHS, 1963; rsch. assoc. lab. clin. sci. NIMH, 1963-65; tchg. fellow in surgery Harvard U. Med. Sch., 1968-69, instr. surgery, 1970-72, asst. prof., 1972-75, assoc. prof., 1975-78; Christian R. Holmes prof., chmn. dept. surgery U. Cin. Med. Ctr., 1978—2001; surgeon-in-chief U. Cin. Hosp., Children's Hosp. Med. Ctr.; chiar surgery Beth Borad Deaconess Med. Ctr., 2001—08; prof. surgery Harvard Med. Sch., 2001—05, William V. McDermott prof. surgery. Bd. dirs. Weston Med. Labs., Inc., 1973, Ethics Inst. Editor: Total Parenteral Nutrition, 1978, 2nd edit., 1991, Surgical Nutrition, 1983, Hepatic Encephalopathy in Chronic Liver Failure, 1984, Surgical Basic Science, 1993, Nutrition and Metabolism in the Surgical Patient, 2nd edit., 1996, Mastery of Surgery, 3rd edit., 1996; editor Internat. Jour. Artificial Organs, 1977; mem. editl. bd. Jour. Surg. Rsch., 1976-84, AMA Archive of Surgery, Am. Jour. Surgery, Jour. Enteral and Parenteral Nutrition, Current Surgery; hepatology sect. editor Current Opinion in General Surgery; assoc. editor surg. gastroenterology Jour. ACS; contbr. articles to med. jours. Co-chmn. steering com. Seminarians; dept. Am. Decorative arts Boston Mus. Fine Arts, 1975-76; bd. dirs. Beacon Hill Nursery Sch., 1971-77, Maimonides Sch., 1973-78, Classical Music Hall of Fame, 1996—, chmn. bd. dirs. Cin. Chamber Orch., 1983-93. Recipient McCurdy-Rinkel award, 1971; James IV surg. fellow, 1974-75 Fellow Am. Surgery Bd. (bd. dirs. 1991—, vice-chmn. 1996—, chmn. 1997-98), ACS (vice chmn. exec. com., com. pre-op. and post-op. care 1987-89, vice chmn. surg. res. and edn. com. 1992-93, mem. exec. com. surg. res. and edn. 1991—, chmn. 1995—, gov. 1992-97, chmn. med. liability com. bd govs. 1993-97, mem. exec. com. bd. govs. 1993-97, 1st v.p. elect 1998, pres.-elect Ohio chpt. 1990-91, pres. 1991-92, 1st v.p.-elect 1997-98, mem. coun. 1987-90, Disting. Svc. award 1997); mem. Am. Assn. for Study Liver Disease, Am. Gastroent. Assn., Am. Soc. Clin. Investigation, So. Surg. Assn., Surg. Biology Club (sec. 1989-92), Assn. for Acad. Surgery (mem. exec. com. 1975, recorder 1976, mem. surg. res. subcom.), Internat. Soc. Parenteral Nutrition, Soc. for Parenteral Alimentation, Am. Surg. Assn., Ctrl. Surg. Assn. (mem. exec. coun. 1990—, treas. 1993-96, pres.-elect 1998), Ill. Surg. Soc. (hon.), Soc. Univ. Surgeons (chmn. com. social and legis. issues 1981-84, mem. exec. coun. 1981-84), Soc. Surgery of Alimentary Tract (chmn. membership com. 1985-89, treas. 1996—), Halsted Soc. (sec. 1991-93, pres. 1995), Ohio Surg. Panel (pres. 1992-96), Surg. Infection Soc. (treas. 1991-93, pres. 1995), Boston Inter-Hosp. Liver Group, Mass. Med. Soc., Boston Surg. Soc., N.Y. Acad. Scis., Chgo. Surg. Soc. (hon.), Ky. Surg. Soc. (hon.), Colombia Soc. Surgery (hon.), Cin. Surg. Soc., Acad. of Medicine of Cin., Soc. Surg. Chairmen, Med. Soc. Rome (hon.), Royal Coll. Surg. Edinburgh (Scotland, hon.). Home: 6 W Cedar St Boston MA 02108-3502 Office: Renaissance Building 1135 Tremont St Boston MA 02120 Business E-Mail: jfischel@bidmc.harvard.edu. *

FISCHER, JOSEPH L., pharmaceutical executive; BS in Acctg., Pa. State U., 1972. Former rschr. Fin. Acctg. Standards Bd.; various positions including group pres. of global personal care products, pres. J&J Canada, and corp. controller Johnson & Johnson, 1981—95; various mgmt. positions including sr. v.p. Dial Corp., 1995—2002; interim CEO ImClone Systems Inc., NYC, 2006. Bd. dirs. ImClone Systems Inc., 2003—06, mem. audit and compensation comt., 2003—06.

FISCHER, KURT WALTER, education educator; b. Balt., June 9, 1943; s. Kurt Wilhelm and Irmgaard Louise (Funke) Fischer; m. Sandra Pipp (div.); 1 child, Seth; m. Jane Haltiwanger, Dec. 7, 1986; children: Johanna, Lukas, Kara. BA in Psychology summa cum laude, Yale U., 1965; MA in Soc. Rels., Harvard U., 1968, PhD in Soc. Rels., 1971. Asst. prof. Univ. Denver, 1972-78, assoc. prof., 1978-85, prof., 1985-87; prof. edn. Harvard U., Cambridge, Mass., 1986—, Charles Bigelow prof., chair human devel., 1989—92, 1994—95, 1999—2000, dir. mind, brain and edn., 1999—. Vis. scholar Univ. Geneva, 1978—79; vis. prof. U. Pa., Phila., 1985—86; master lectr. U. Groningen, The Netherlands, 1996; vis. prof. Nanjing Normal U., China, 2000; resident scholar Ross Sch., NY, 2007—08. Author: Cognitive Development, 1981, Levels and Transitions in Cognitive Development, 1983; co-author: Psychology Today: An Introduction, 2d and 3d edits., 1972, 75, Human Development from Conception to Adolescence, 1984, Development in Context, 1993, Human Behavior and the Developing Brain, 1994, Self Conscious Emotions, 1995, Development and Vulnerability in Close Relationships, 1996, Socioemotional Development across Cultures, 1998, Mind, Brain, and Education in Reading Disorders, 2007, Human Behavior, Learning, and the Developing Brain, 2007; founding editor jour. Mind, Brain, and Edn., 2007, The Educated Brain, 2008; contbr. articles to profl. jours. Fellow James McKeen Cattell Fund, 1985-86, Ctr. for Advanced Study, Palo Alto, Calif., 1992-93; grantee Carnegie Found., Nat. Inst. Child Health and Devel., 1994—2004, Sloan Found., Spencer Found., Rose Found., 1995-2007, Nat. Leadership Coll., 2003—, Ross Inst., 2007-. Mem. Jean Piaget Soc. (pres. 1988-91), Internat. Mind Brain Edn. Soc. (founding pres. 2004-), Phi Beta Kappa, Sigma Xi (Transforming Edn. Through Neurosci. award, 2009). Home: 29 Vincent Ave Belmont MA 02478-4418 Office: Harvard U Grad Sch Edn Larsen 702 Cambridge MA 02138 Home Phone: 617-489-2212; Office Phone: 617-495-3446. E-mail: kurt_fischer@harvard.edu.

FISCHER, LINDA MARIE, nursing educator; b. Paterson, NJ, Sept. 26, 1959; d. William Jr. and Marie (Bilz) F. BSN cum laude, Coll. Misericordia, 1981; MSN magna cum laude, Bloomsburg U., 1996. Clin. nurse specialistin cardiovascular nursing, Bloomsburg U., 1996, RN, Pa. Staff nurse cardiac ICU Geisinger Med. Ctr., Danville, Pa., 1981-90, clin. nurse II cardiac ICU, 1987-90, clin. instr. cardiac ICU and cardiovasc. spl. care unit, 1990—, med. leave, 1990. Chair adv. group profl. pers. case record rev. subcom. Columbia-Montour Home Health/Vis. Nurses Assn., Inc.; mem. Harvard Nurses Health Study, 1986— Contbr. articles to profl. jours.; contbr. 2 photographs Internat. Libr. Photography. Active Montour-Riverside chpt. Am. Heart Assn., 1989-92. Mem. AACN, Sigma Theta Tau (nominating com. Theta Zeta chpt. 1995-2001)

FISCHER, MARKUS, otolaryngologist, educator; s. Rudolf Georg and Heike Emma Fischer; m. Anke Sabine Knauer-Fischer; children: Lukas Felix, Justus Benedikt. Cert. otorhinolaryngologist Med. Chamber North Rhine, 1996. Physician Inst. Hygiene U. Heidelberg, Germany, 1990—90; physician dept. oto-rhino-laryngology U. Essen, 1990—92; scientist German Cancer Rsch. Ctr., Heidelberg, 1992—94; physician dept. oto-rhino-laryngology U. Essen, 1994—97, cons. dept. oto-rhino-laryngology, 1997—2002, vice chair dept. oto-rhino-laryngology, 2003—07, assoc. prof. dept. oto-rhino-laryngology, 2003—07, ATOS Clinic Heidelberg, 2007—. Gen. co-ord. 4th European Congress Oto-Rhino-Laryngology, Head and Neck Surgery, Berlin, 1999—2000. Office: ATOS Clinic Heidelberg Bismarck Str 9-15 D 69115 Heidelberg Germany Office Phone: 49(0)6221 9832500. Office Fax: 49(0)6221 9832503. Personal E-mail: fischer@atos.de.

FISCHER, ROBERT A., infectious disease physician; MD, Harvard Med. Sch. Diplomate Am. Bd. Internal Medicine, Am. Bd. Internal Medicine-infectious disease. Intern USC LA Med. Ctr., resident, fellow Univ. of Mass. Med. Sch.; chmn. infectious disease dept. Albert Einstein Med. Ctr. Office: Albert Einstein Medical Center Klein Building Ste 331 5401 Old York Rd Philadelphia PA 19141 Office Phone: 215-456-6948. Office Fax: 215-455-1933.

FISCHER, SETH H.Z., pharmaceutical executive; b. Akron, OH; married, 2 children. BA, Ohio Univ. Joined as a sales rep, holding various positions of increasing responsibility in sales, mktg. and managed care Johnson & Johnson, NJ, 1983—98, v.p. sales & mktg. Ortho McNeil Pharm. Inc., 1998—2000, pres. Ortho-McNeil Pharm., Inc., 2000—04, group chmn. N.Am. pharm., 2004—. Editl. bd. Product Management Today. Bd. dir. Epilepsy Found. Served to capt. USAF. Recipient Martin House Humanitarian of Yr. award, 2001. Office: Johnson & Johnson One Johnson & Johnson Plz New Brunswick NJ 08933 *

FISCHER, TANYA ZAREMBA, physician, director; b. Aug. 28, 1972; PhD, Rutgers U., 2000; MD, UMDNJ-Robert Wood Johnson Med. Sch., 2002. Clin. instr. Yale U., 2006—08, VA dir.-VHA multiple sclerosis regional ctr., 2008, assoc. rsch. scientist, 2008—10, asst. prof., 2010—11, asst. clin. prof., 2011; dir. neurosci.-global clin. rsch. Bristol-Myers Squibb, 2011—. Career Devel. grant, VA. Mem.: Women Faculty Forum, Yale U., Internat. Assn. Study Pain, Am. Acad. Neurology. Home: 131 Westwood Rd New Haven CT 06515

FISCHER-RASMUSSEN, WIGGO, obstetrician, gynecologist; b. Naestved, Denmark, May 25, 1935; s. Ulrich and Bodil I. M. (Axel Jensen) Fischer-Rasmussen; m. Lieselotte Niemann; children: Torsten, Mads, Mikkel. MD, U. Copenhagen, 1961, DMS, 1972. Cert. specialist obs.-gyn. Danish Nat. Health Bd., 1973. Registrar Hosps., Copenhagen, 1961-68; rsch. fellow, resident, sr. registrar obs.-gyn. U. Copenhagen, 1968-76, sr. cons. Hvidovre Hosp., 1976-97, sr. cons. urogynecology Rigs Hosp., 1997—2002, sr. lectr. ob-gyn., 1989-97; pvt. practice ob-gyn. Copenhagen, 2002—. Chief ob-gyn. dept. KFCH, Gizan, Saudi Arabia, 1983. Author: (textbook) Gynaekologi og obstetrik, vol. I, 1982, vol. II, 1986, Obstetrik & Gynaekologi, 1996; co-author: Kirurgisk Kompendium, 1988, 2003, 2005, Gynaekologi, 1990, 2003, Obstetrik, 1993; assoc. editor: Acta Obstetricia et Gynecologica Scandinavica, 1992—94, 1999—2000, chief editor:, 1994—98; contbr. articles to profl. jours. Mem. patient injury appeals bd. Danish Min. of Health, 1997—2003. Lt. surgeon Royal Danish Navy, 1962—64. Mem.: Fedn. Scandinavian Socs. Ob-Gyn. (bd. dirs. 1992—98), Danish Soc. Ob-Gyn. (pres. 1992—94, 1994—96). Home: Fagerbo 19 DK-2950 Vedbaek Denmark Office: Copenhagen Fertility Ctr Lygten 2C 4th Fl DK 2400 Copenhagen Denmark Home Phone: 45 4589 2160; Office Phone: 45 3325 7000. E-mail: wiggo.fischer@dadlnet.dk.

FISCHHOFF, BARUCH, psychologist, educator; b. Detroit, Apr. 21, 1946; s. Henry and Shirley (Levine) F.; m. Andrea Marks, Dec. 22, 1968; children: Maya, Ilya, Noam. BS in Math., Wayne State U., 1967; MA in Psychology, Hebrew U., Jerusalem, 1972, PhD in Psychology, 1975. Rsch. assoc. Oreg. Rsch. Inst., Eugene, 1974-76, Decision Rsch., Eugene, 1976-85, Applied Psychology Unit Med. Rsch. Coun., Cambridge, England, 1981-82, Eugene Rsch. Inst., 1985-87; prof. Carnegie-Mellon U., Pitts., 1987—, Univ. prof., 1998—, Howard Heinz prof., 2002—. Vis. prof. U. Stockholm, 1982-83; mem. panels NRC; mem. sci. adv. bd. EPA; cons. in field. Author: Acceptable Risk, 1981, Mental Models, 2001; mem. editl. bd. Jour. Risk Uncertainty, Decision Analysis, Risk Analysis, also others; contbr. numerous articles to profl. jours. Mem. Eugene Commn. on Rights of Women, 1975-81; pres. Eugene Human Rights Coun.,

1979-81; mem. sci. adv. bd. EPA, 2003—; mem. sci. tech. adv. com. Dept. Homeland Security, 2004-; Chair FDA risk comm. adv. com., 2007. Fellow APA (Disting. Sci. award 1981, psychology in Pub. Interest award 1991), Soc. for Risk Analysis (pres. 2004, Disting. Achievement award 1991), Soc. Judgment and Decision-Making (mem. coun. 1988-91, pres. 1990-91), Inst. Medicine, Phi Beta Kappa. Home: 1437 Denniston Ave Pittsburgh PA 15217-1332 Office: Carnegie Mellon U Dept Engring and Pub Policy Pittsburgh PA 15213-3890 Home Phone: 412-421-2298; Office Phone: 412-268-3246. Business E-Mail: baruch@cmu.edu.

FISER, DEBRA H., pediatrician, educator, dean; Grad., U. Ark., Fayetteville; MD, U. Ark., 1977. Intern, resident pediat. U. Ky. Sch. Medicine; critical care fellowship U. Fla. Coll. Medicine; joined faculty U. Ark. for Med. Scis., 1981, prof., chair Dept. Pediat., 1995—, dean Coll. Medicine, vice chancellor, 2006—; founder Pediat. Critical Care Medicine Sect. and Pediatric Intensive Care Unit Ark. Children's Hosp., chief pediat., 1995. Recipient Women in Medicine Silver Achievement Award, Assn. Am. Medical Colls. Fellow: Am. Coll. Chest Physicians, Am. Coll. Critical Care Medicine, Am. Acad. Pediat.; mem.: Am. Pediat. Soc., Soc. Pediat. Rsch., Am. Bd. Pediat., Soc. Critical Care Medicine, Assn. Med. Sch. Pediat. Dept. Chairs (past pres.). Office: U Ark for Med Sci Coll Medicine 4301 W Markham St Little Rock AR 72205 Office Phone: 501-296-1100.

FISH, FALK, microbiologist, consultant, immunologist, researcher, inventor; b. Rehovoth, Israel, July 10, 1946; s. Aharon and Rivka (Halperin) F.; m. Tamar David, Aug. 18, 1975; children: Shlomi, Michal, No'a. MSc, Tel Aviv U., 1974, PhD, 1979. Faculty assoc. U. Tex. Health Sci. Ctr., Dallas, 1979-81; vis. fellow Bur. Biologics, FDA, Bethesda, Md., 1981-82; asst. prof. Tel Aviv U., 1982-88; co-founder, dir. R & D Orgenics Ltd., Yavne, Israel, 1985-89, v.p. tech., 1989—; sr. v.p. Self Help (Israel) Ltd., 1994-95; mng. dir., founder Orgenics Biosensors Ltd., Yavne, Israel, 1997—2000; rsch. and devel. counsel Unipath Ltd., 2002—. Gen. counsel Inverness Med. Ltd., England, 1995—2000; founder Episight, Ltd., 1998—2010; exec. v.p. CTO Orgenics Ltd Alere Inc. Co., 2005—. Contbr. articles to profl. jours. Mem. Am. Soc. for Microbiology, Israel Microbiol. Soc. Achievements include patents in method for non-radioactive DNA labeling and its use in diagnosis; in isolation of specific DNAs; in enhanced enzyme immunoassay format and kit; in rapid method and kit for detection of metabolic toxicity; in novel molded strip format for blood tests; in novel design for electrochemical blood glucose sensors; in novel blood coagulation sensing; research in novel approaches for painless blood glucose determination in rapid blood typing test strip in lateral flow rapid tests for infections Diseases. Home: 4 Hakim St Apt 12 Tel Aviv 69120 Israel Office: Orgenics Ltd North Industrial Zone Yavne 70650 Israel Home Phone: 972-3-6424668; Office Phone: 972-8-9429227. Fax: 972-3-6414319. Business E-Mail: falk.fish@alere.com. E-mail: falkfish@gmail.com.

FISH, MARK, insurance company executive; Grad., Assn. Health Ins. Plan's Exec. Leadership Program; BBA in Actuarial Sci., U. Wis., BS in Math. With Aetna, Inc., Hartford, Conn.; consulting actuary Milliman, Inc., Milw.; mem. sr. mgmt. team MVP Health Care, 1999—, v.p. fin., chief actuary, exec. v.p. network mgmt., exec. v.p., CFO. Fellow: Soc. of Actuaries; mem.: American Cancer Soc. (bd. dirs., Capital Region), American Acad. of Actuaries. Office: MVP Health Care 625 State St PO Box 2207 Schenectady NY 12301-2207 Office Phone: 518-370-4793. Office Fax: 518-370-0830. *

FISH, ROBERT H., healthcare company executive; BA in Sociology, Whittier Coll.; MPH, U. Calif., Berkeley; postgrad., Ethel Percy Andrus Sch. Gerontology, U. So. Calif., LA. CEO ValleyCare Health Sys., Calif.; pres., CEO St. Joseph Health Sys., Calif.; mng. prtnr. Sonoma-Seacrest, LLC, Calif.; interim CEO Genesis Health Ventures, Inc., Kennett Square, Pa., 2002, chmn., CEO; chmn. Coram, Inc. Office: Genesis HealthCare Corp 101 E State St Kennett Square PA 19348 Office Phone: 610-444-6350. Office Fax: 610-925-4000. Business E-Mail: rfish@genesishcc.com.

FISHER, ARON BAER, physiology educator; b. Phila., Apr. 20, 1936; m. Joan C. Fisher, 1957; children: Marc L., Steven A., Eric R., Mara E. BS in Chemistry summa cum laude, Dickinson Coll., 1956; MD, U. Pa., 1960. Diplomate Am. Bd. Internal Medicine; diplomate Nat. Bd. Med. Examiners. Intern and resident in medicine U. Hosps., Cleve., 1960-61, 64-65; resident in pulmonary medicine Hosp. U. Pa., 1965-66; fellow dept. physiology U. Pa., 1966-68, assoc. in medicine, assoc. in physiology, 1968-70, from asst. prof. to assoc. prof. medicine, 1970-80, prof. medicine, 1980—, from asst. prof. to assoc. prof. physiology, 1970-1980, prof. physiology, 1980—, prof. environmental medicine, 1986—; staff physician VA Hosp., Phila., 1968-73, clin. investigator, 1973-76, cons. in pulmonary medicine, 1976-82; mem. med. staff Hosp. U. Pa., 1976—, dir. hyperbaric medicine clin. practice, 1985—; dir. Inst. Environ. Medicine U. Pa., 1985—. Mem. Am. Heart Assn. student rsch. fellowship adv. com. U. Pa., 1983-97, mem. diabetes ctr. adv. com., 1985—, mem. teaching awards com., 1989-92, chmn. animal care com. 1982-84, 87-89, chmn. com. for animal facility planning, 1985-86, chmn. transgenic mouse facility com., 1989, chmn. instnl. animal care and use com., 1989-92, mem. bioengring. grad. group, 1988—, chmn. biochemistry grad. group rev. com., 1989-90, others, supr. grad. students; fellow dept. biophysics and phys. chemistry U. Pa., 1971-72; mem. study sect. Pa. Coal Worker's Respiratory Disease Program, 1976-78; mem. cardiovascular study sect. A NIH, 1979-81, mem. respiratory and applied physiology sect., 1981-83; mem. adv. panel U.S. Army Med. R&D Command, 1980-85; mem. VA Merit rev. com. for respiration, 1998—. Editor: (with others) Handbook of Physiology: The Respiratory System (Section 3), vol. 1, 1980-85; mem. editorial bd. Exptl. Lung Rsch. 1979-88, Am. Rev. Respiratory Diseases, 1981-87, Jour. Applied Physiology, 1984-87, Am. Jour. Physiology, 1988—; guest editor Symposium on Lung Surfactant Apoproteins, 1984; contbr. numerous articles and revs. to profl. jours., chpts. to books. With USPHS, 1958, 59-61; capt. MC USAR, 1961-65. Grantee NIH, 1986-91, 1988—; recipient Clin. Investigator award VA Res. Svc., 1973-76, Established Investigator award Am. Heart Assn., 1977-82, Christian R. and Mary F. Lindback Found. award for Disting. Teaching, 1984. Mem. AAAS, ACP, Am. Physiol. Soc. (chmn. respiration dinner 1991, councillor respiratory sect. 1991-95), Am. Thoracic Soc. (sec. assembly on structure, function and metabolism 1973-74, chmn. 1981, sec. sect. on pulmonary circulation 1979, councillor ea. sect. 1973-77, chmn. ann. meeting program com. 1976, pres. 1983), Am. Fedn. Clin. Rsch., Am. Soc. Clin. Investigation, Am. Heart Assn. (cardiopulmonary coun.), Am. Soc. Cell Biology, Undersea and Hyperbaric Med. Soc., Oxygen Soc., Aerospace Med. Assn., John Morgan Soc. U. Pa., Laennec Soc. Phila., Pa. Thoracic Soc. (chmn. rsch. com. 1985-87), Phi Beta Kappa, Alpha Omega Alpha. Home: 239 E Gowen Ave Philadelphia PA 19119-1021 Office: U Pa Inst Environ Medicine One John Morgan Bldg 36th St and Hamilton Walk Philadelphia PA 19104-6068 Business E-Mail: abf@mail.med.upenn.edu.

FISHER, BERNARD, surgeon, educator; b. Pitts., Aug. 23, 1918; BS, U. Pitts., 1940, MD, 1943, DSc (hon.), 2009, Mt. Sinai Sch. Medicine, CUNY, 1986; HHD (hon.), Carlow Coll., Pitts., 2003; DMS (hon.), Yale U., 2004. Diplomate Am. Bd. Surgery. Intern Mercy Hosp., Pitts., 1943—44, resident in surgery, 1944—48; fellow in surg. research, resident in gen. surgery Harrison Dept. Dept. Surg. Research U. Pa., Phila., 1950—52; fellow London Postgrad. Med. Sch. Hammersmith Hosp., 1955—56; tchg. fellow in pathology U. Pitts., 1944—45, 1945—47, assoc. prof., 1956—59, prof. surgery, 1959—86, Disting. Svc. prof., 1986—; Fulbright Commn. award appointee to Peru, 1965; med. surg. staff Presbyn.-Univ. Hosp., 1953—98. Past mem. cons. staff Children's Hosp., Pitts.; mem. cons. staff Magee-Women's Hosp., VA Hosp., Pitts.; chmn. Nat. Surg. Adjuvant Breast and Bowel Project, 1967—94, sci. dir., 1995—2005; chmn. Adjuvant Therapy Ctr., 1973—94, Breast Care and Diagnostic Ctr., 1980—93, Pitts. Cancer Inst., 1985—, Comprehensive Breast Care Ctr., 1992—98; mem. spl. del. to China, 1977; mem. President's Cancer Panel, 1979—82, Nat. Cancer Adv. Bd., 1986—92, Inst. Medicine of NAS. Mem. editl. bd.: Transplantation, 1966—71, Cancer, 1970—88, 1975, Year Book of Cancer, 1973—85, Internat. Jour. Radiation Oncology Biology Physics, 1975—78, Cancer Clin. Trials, 1977, Invasion and Metastis, 1981—85, Cancer Metastasis Revs., 1981—85, Jour. Clin. Oncology, 1982—87, Internat. Jour. Breast and Mammary Pathology, 1982—84, Cancer Rsch., 1976, Seminars in Oncology, 1979, Breast Cancer Rsch. and Treatment, 1980, 1992—, Clin. and Exptl. Metastasis, 1980—94, Breast Diseases: Yr. Book Quar., 1989—95, Annals Surg. Oncology, 1993—94, Internat. Jour. Oncology, 1993—94, Advances in Oncology, 1992—96, Breast Disease: Internat. Jour., 1993—96, Cancer Jour., 1994—, Internat. Jour. Cancer, 1993—94, European Jour. Cancer, 1995—97; contbr. more than 585 articles to med. jours. Recipient Man of Yr. award in medicine, Pitts. Jr. C. of C., 1966, Philip Hench Disting. Alumnus award, U. Pitts. Sch. Medicine, 1976, McGraw medal, Detroit Surg. Assn., 1978, Lucy Wortham James Clin. Rsch. award, 1981, Heath Meml. award, 1982, Joseph H. Morton Meml. award, 1983, Julia Hudson Freund Meml. award, 1983, Albert Lasker Med. rsch. award, 1985, Hammer Cancer prize, 1988, Am. Cancer Soc. Medal of Honor, 1986, Susan Komen Found. Sci. Distinction award, 1988, Milken Med. Found. Ctr. Rsch. award, 1989, Assn. Commn. Cancer Ctrs. award, 1990, Chancellors Dist. Rsch. award U. Pitts., 1992, Nat. Health Couns. Med. Rsch. award, 1992, Brinker Internat. Breast Cancer award, 1992, Durham N.C. City of Medicine award, 1992, Dr. Josef Steiner Cancer Rsch. prize, 1992, GM Cancer Rsch. Found. Kettering prize, 1993, Bristol-Myers Squib award, 1993, James Ewing Lectr. award SSO, 1993, Gottlieb Meml. award, 1993, Sheen award, 1993, Claude Jacquillet award, 1995, Lifetime Achievement award in Breast Cancer Rsch., Senologic Internat. Soc., 1996, Health Care Lifetime Achievement award, Pitts. Bus. Times, 1998, Potamkin Found. award for breast cancer rsch., Pa. Breast Cancer Coalition, 1999, Celebrating Survival: A Century of Advancements in Early Breast Cancer award, 2000, Am. Surg. Assn. Medallion for Sci. Achievement, 2000, Flance-Karl award for contbns. to sci. of clin. surgery, 2001, St. Gallen Internat. Breast Cancer award, 2003, AstraZeneca Hist. Milestone Excellence Clin. Rsch. award, 2003, Jill Rose award, Breast Cancer Rsch. Fond., 2003, Internat. Spirit of Life Rsch. award, 2003, C. Chester Stock award, Meml. Sloan Kettering Cancer Ctr., 2004, Breast Cancer Awareness Month award, 2004, Disting. Med. Svc. award, Friends of Nat. Libr. Medicine, 2007, Pathfinder award, Am. Soc. Breast Disease, 2008; named Bernard Fisher prof. surgery lectureship established in his honor, U. Pitts., 2006, Bernard Fisher chair surgery established in his honor, 2006; Markle scholar in med. sci., John and Mary Markle Found., 1953—58, Fisher Breast Cancer lectureship established in his honor, U. Pitts., 1989. Fellow: AAAS, Royal Coll. Physicians and Surgeons Can. (hon.), Am. Med. Writers Assn. (hon.), Am. Coll. Radiology (hon.); mem.: ACS, AAUP, Am. Italian Fedn. Cancer Rsch., Internat. Assn. Breast Cancer Rsch., Assn. Italiana per la Divulgaxione Sci. della Cancerologia Clinica, Italian Surg. Rsch. Assn., Pitts. Surg. Soc. (pres. 1979), Pitts. Acad. Medicine, Allegheny County Med. Soc. (Man of Yr. award 1983), Pa. Med. Soc., Am. Socs. for Exptl. Biology, Soc. Univ. Surgeons, Soc. Surg. Oncology, N.Y. Acad. Scis., Am. Surg. Assn. (v.p. 1996), Cell Kinetic Soc., Assn. Am. Med. Colls., Am. Physiol. Soc., Am. Soc. Clin. Oncology (pres. 1992-93, bd. dirs., Karnofsky award 1980, Disting. Svc. award for sci. achievement 1999), Am. Assn. Cancer Rsch. (bd. dirs., 3d Jos. H. Burchenal Clin. Rsch. award 1998, Lifetime Achievement award 2006), Oncology Nursing Soc. (hon.), Peruvian Acad. Surgery (hon.), Am. Soc. Therapeutic Radiology and Oncology (hon.), Phi Beta Kappa, Alpha Omega Alpha. Office: U Pitts Dept Surgery 200 Lothrop St Ste 7098 Pittsburgh PA 15213

FISHER, COLLEEN L., medical researcher; b. Key West, Fla., Oct. 10, 1968; Diploma, Florin HS, 1986; degree, Western Career Coll., 2005. Clin. rsch. coord. No. Calif. Rsch., 2005—09; site dir., clin. rsch. coord. Capital Nephrology Med. Group, 2009—. Recipient Deans Honor Role, Florin HS, Western Career Coll. Avocations: cooking, gardening. Office: 77 Cadillac Dr Ste 130 Sacramento CA 95825 Office Fax: 916-929-4529. E-mail: colleen.fisher@cnmgonline.com.

FISHER, DALE DUNBAR, animal scientist, dairy nutritionist; b. Lewisburg, Pa., Feb. 13, 1945; s. Glenn Murray and Elsie May (Bryson) F.; divorced; children: Elsie Maria, Maria Vanessa. BS Animal Sci., Pa. State U., 1967, MS Animal Industry, 1978, PhD Animal Industry, 1980. Vol. animal husbandry Peace Corps, Ciudad Quesada, Costa Rica, 1967—71; area animal husbandry-pasture specialist Costa Rican Ministry Agr., Ciudad Quesada, 1971—73; vis. scientist Internat. Ctr. for Tropical Agr., Cali, Colombia, 1973—75; animal nutritionist Co-op. Feed Dealers, Inc., Chenango Bridge, NY, 1981—. Contbr. articles to profl. jours. Eva B. and G. Weidman Groff Meml. scholar Pa. State U., 1979. Mem. Am. Soc. Animal Sci., Am. Dairy Sci. Assn., Am. Soc. Agronomy, Am. Acad. Vet. Nutrition, N.Y. Acad. Scis., Am. Coll. Nutrition, Sigma Xi, Phi Kappa Phi, Gamma Sigma Delta. Democrat. Avocations: jogging, reading. Home Phone: 607-724-3384. Business E-Mail: nutrition@co-opfeed.com.

FISHER, DELBERT ARTHUR, pediatric endocrinologist, educator, retired health facility administrator; b. Placerville, Calif., Aug. 12, 1928; s. Arthur Lloyd and Thelma (Johnson) Fisher; m. Beverly Carne Fisher, Jan. 28, 1951; children: David Arthur(dec.), Thomas Martin, Mary Kathryn. BA, U. Calif., Berkeley, 1950; MD, U. Calif., San Francisco, 1953. Diplomate Am. Bd. Pediat., Sub Bd. Pediatric Endocrinology. Intern, resident in pediat. U. Calif. Med. Ctr., San Francisco, 1953—55; resident in pediat. U. Oreg. Hosp., Portland, 1957—58; Irwin Meml. fellow in pediatric endocrinology, 1958—60; from asst. prof. to prof. pediat. Med. Sch. U. Ark., Little Rock, 1960—68; prof. pediat. UCLA Med. Sch., LA, 1968—73, prof. pediat. and internal medicine, 1973—91, prof. pediat. and internal medicine emeritus, 1991—; chief, pediat. endocrinology Harbor-UCLA Med. Ctr., 1968—75, rsch. prof. devel. and perinatal biology, 1975—85, chmn. pediat., 1985—89, sr. scientist Rsch. and Edn. Inst., 1991—, chmn. bd. Rsch. and Edn. Inst., 2001—02; dir. Walter Martin Rsch. Ctr., 1986—91; pres. Nichols Inst. Reference Labs, San Juan Capistrano, Calif., 1991—93; pres. acad. assocs., chief sci. officer Nichols Inst., San Juan Capistrano, Calif., 1993—94, Quest Diagnostics-Nichols Inst., San Juan Capistrano, Calif., 1994—97, sr. sci. officer, 1997—98, chief sci. officer, 1998—99; v.p. sci. and innovation Quest Diagnostics Inc., 1999—2005, sr. sci. officer, 2005—07, acad. assoc., 2007—. Cons. genetic disease sect. Calif. Dept. Health Svcs., 1978—98; mem. organizing com. Internat. Conf. Newborn Thyroid Screening, 1977—88; examiner Am. Bd. Pediat., 1971—80, mem. subcom. on pediat. endocrinology, 1976—79. Co-editor: Pediatric Thyroidology, 1985, 10 other books; editor-in-chief: Jour. Clin. Endocrinology and Metabolism, 1978—83, Pediat. Rsch., 1984—89; contbr. over 450 articles to profl. jours., over 100 chpts. to books. Capt. M.C. USAF, 1955—57. Recipient Career Devel. award, NIH, 1964—68; named to Hall of Honor, NICHHD, NIH, 2003. Master: Am. Coll. Endocrinology; mem.: Am. Assn. Clin. Chemistry (So. Calif. sect., Albert L. Nichols award 2004), Clin. Ligand Assay Soc. (Disting. Scientist award 2001), Western Soc. Pediat. Rsch. (pres. 1982—83), Lawson Wilkins Pediatric Endocrine Soc. (pres. 1982—83, Van Wyk award 2008), Assn. Am. Physicians, Am. Soc. Clin. Investigation, Am. Thyroid Assn. (pres. 1988—89, Disting. Lectr. 1982), Endocrine Soc. (pres. 1983—84, Leadership award 1998), Am. Pediat. Soc. (pres. 1992—93, John Howland medal 2001), Soc. Pediat. Rsch. (v.p. 1973—74), Am. Acad. Pediat. (Borden award 1981), Nat. Acad. Clin. Biochemistry, Inst. Medicine of NAS, Alpha Omega Alpha, Phi Beta Kappa. Home: 24582 Santa Clara Ave Dana Point CA 92629-3031 Personal E-mail: fisherd1@cox.net.

FISHER, DIERDRE DENISE, mental health nurse, administrator, educator; b. NYC, Mar. 13, 1945; d. Horace Anderton and Alma (Ames) Taylor; m. Robert Fisher, Oct. 29, 1962 (dec. 1978); children: Sevareid, Pheon (dec.). AAS, Mercer County Coll., 1972; BS, Coll. NJ, 1979; MSN, U. Pa., 1982. Cert. clin. nurse specialist, nursing adminstr. Supr. Nursing Svcs. Trenton Psychiat. Hosp., NJ, 1979—81, program coord., 1981—84; cons. Pub. Health NJ State Dept. Health, Trenton, 1984—87; psychiat. nurse cons. Div. Mental Health and Hosps., Princeton, NJ, 1987—89; asst. complex adminstr. Trenton Psychiat. Hosp., 1989-91; dir. edn. and practice NJ State Nurses Assn., Trenton, 1991-96; dir. continuing edn. U. Tex. Health Sci. Ctr., San Antonio, 1996-98; owner, pres. Ames High, 1997—. Educator Ocean County Coll., Toms River, NJ, 1985-96; clin. instr. nursing Burlington County Coll., Pemberton, NJ, 1988-91; cons., educator Lake Area Health Edn. Ctr., Erie, Pa., 1988-96; site vis., appraiser Am. Nurses Credentialing Ctr., 1996—; advanced practice nurse Vericare, 2001-. Author nursing publs. Bd. dirs. Trenton YWCA, 1989-95; advisor Concord Home Health, San Antonio, Tex., 2007-. Recipient Care Givers award Delta Sigma Theta, 1991. Mem. Tex. Nurses Assn. (bd. dirs. Dist. 8, 1997-99), Sigma Theta Tau, Delta Sigma Theta. Home: 1918 Enero Park San Antonio TX 78230-0934 Office Phone: 210-694-0625. Personal E-mail: dfisher@ameshigh.com.

FISHER, DONALD WAYNE, medical association administrator; b. Pitts., Mar. 2, 1946; s. David H.W. and Jean K. F.; children by previous marriage: Kimberly Elizabeth, Jeffrey Wayne. AA, Hinds Jr. Coll., 1966; BS in Biology and Chemistry, Millsaps Coll., 1968; MS in Anatomy, U. Miss., 1970, PhD in Anatomy, 1973; postgrad. in assn. mgmt., U. Md., 1977-79. Cert. assn. exec. Instr. dept. chemistry and biology Hinds Jr. Coll., Raymond, Miss., 1968-74; instr. dept. anatomy U. Miss. Sch. Medicine, Jackson, 1973-74, co-dir. and exec. officer physician asst. program, 1972-74; asst. professorial lectr. George Washington U. Sch. Medicine, 1974—80; exec. dir. Assn. Physician Asst. Programs, Arlington, Va., 1974-80, Am. Acad. Physician Assts., Arlington, 1974-80; pres., CEO Am. Med. Group Assn., Alexandria, Va., 1980—; chmn. Am. Med. Group Corp., Inc., Anceta, 2001—; chmn. bd. Anceta; treas. polit. action com. Am. Med. Group, 1980—. Mem. Nat. Commn. on Allied Health Edn., 1977-80; mem. adv. com. for tng., devel. and utilization of physician extenders Systems Scis., Inc., 1975-80; pres. Am. Acad. Physician Assts. Ednl. and Rsch. Found., 1977-80; sec., treas. Am. Med. Group Found., 1980—; mem. Am. Express Health Care Faculty, 1985-88; mem. bd. dirs. Alliance Bank Va., 2009-. Robert Wood Johnson Found. grantee, 1973-80 Mem. Am. Soc. Assn. Execs. (govt. rels. com. 1980—), Assn. Am. Med. Colls., AAAS, Am. Internat. Health Alliance (bd. dirs. 1992—, treas. 1995-2003, chair 2004-08), Disease Mgmt. Assn. Am. (bd. dirs. 2004-09), Greater Washington Soc. Assn. Execs., Fairfax County Hosp. Assn., Arlington (Va.) C. of C, Am. Internat. Alliance (chair, 2004—08), Alliance Bank of Va. (bd. dirs. 2009-, chmn. 2011-). Home: 3814 Ivanhoe Ln Alexandria VA 22310-2170 Office: Am Med Group Assn 1422 Duke St Alexandria VA 22314-3430

FISHER, EDWARD ABRAHAM, cardiologist, educator; b. Honolulu, Apr. 30, 1958; s. Hyman Wendell and Rosalie (Joseph) F.; m. Vivian Degenszejn, Mar. 27, 1993; children: Rebecca, Alexander, Oliver. BA in Econs., U. Va., 1980; MD, Ea. Va. Med. Sch., 1984. Diplomate Nat. Bd. Med. Examiners, Am. Bd. Internal Medicine, Am. Bd. Cardiovascular Disease; lic. physician, N.Y. Intern Lenox Hill Hosp., NYC, 1984-85, resident, 1985-87, adj. attending physician dept. medicine, 1987—; cardiology fellow Mt. Sinai Med. Ctr., NYC, 1987-89, cardiology rsch. fellow, 1989-90, clin. asst. dept. medicine, 1990, asst. dir. echocardiography dept. medicine divsn. cardiology, 1990-98; asst. attending Mt. Sinai Sch. Medicine, NYC, 1990-92, asst. clin. prof., 1992-97, assoc. clin. prof., assoc. attending, 1997—. Co-author: Effects of Estrogen and Progesterone on Blood Vessels, 1991, Restrictive Cardiomyopathy, 2002, Native Aortic Valve Endocarditis, 2003; author numerous articles concerning transthoracic, transesophageal echocardiography and coronary CT angiography. Fellow ACP, Am. Coll. Cardiology, Am. Heart Assn. Avocation: marathon running. Office: 45 East 85th St New York NY 10028 Office Phone: 212-472-7370. *

FISHER, (DONALD) GARTH, plastic surgeon; b. Sacto, MS, May 24, 1958; s. Donald Fisher; m. Brooke Burke, 2001 (div. 2005); children Neriah, Sierra Sky; m. Jessica Canseco, 2007. BA in Biology, U. Miss., Oxford, 1980; MD, U. Miss., Jackson, 1984. Diplomate Am. Bd. Plastic Surgery, Am. Bd. Surgery. Intern in gen. surgery U. Calif., Irvine, 1984-85, resident in gen. surgery, 1985-89, resident in plastic surgery, 1989-91; fellow in aesthetic plastic surgery Santa Ana, Calif., 1991; pvt. practice Beverly Hills, Calif., 1991—. Instr. dept. surgery U. Miss. Sch. Medicine, 1980, dept. anatomy, 1980; lectr. in field; consulted extensively for many TV, news and magazine interviews. Author: (5 part ednl. video series) The Naked Truth About Plastic Surgery, The Informed Patient; contbr. articles to sci. and profl. jours.; appeared in: (TV series) Extreme Makeover; guest appearances Good Morning America, Oprah, Today Show, CBS Evening News, NBC Evening News, CNN, Entertainment Tonight, Access Hollywood, EXTRA, E!, and the Discovery Channel, featured in Elle, Allure, GQ, People, Details, In Touch, LA Mag., Town & Country, TV Guide, Wall Street Journal, US Weekly, Parade, LA Times, and USA Today. Fellow ACS; mem. AMA, Calif. Med. Assn., Los Angeles County Med. Assn., L.A. Soc. Plastic Surgeons. Achievements include first plastic surgeon selected to appear on ABC's hit show "Extreme Makeover". Office: 120 S Spalding Dr Ste 222 Beverly Hills CA 90212-1840 Office Phone: 310-273-5995. Office Fax: 310-273-9079. Personal E-mail: garthmd@earthlink.net.

FISHER, GEORGE ALBERT, JR., internist, oncologist; b. Worcester, Mass., Mar. 9, 1954; PhD, Stanford U. Sch. Medicine, MD, 1987. Cert. Med. Oncology. Intern, internal medicine Stanford U. Sch. Med., Calif., 1988, resident, med. oncology Calif., 1989, fellow Calif., 1993, assoc. prof. medicine Calif. Dir. Cancer Clin. Trial Office, Standford; program leader GI Oncology, Standford. Contbr. several articles to profl. jours. Mem.: Am. Cancer Soc. (pres. Calif. divsn. 2009). Office: Stanford Comprehensive Cancer Ctr MC 5826 875 Blake Wilbur Dr Stanford CA 94305 Office Phone: 650-725-9057. Business E-Mail: georgeaf@stanford.edu.

FISHER, GEORGE ROSS, III, physician, educator; b. Erie, Pa., May 8, 1925; s. George Ross and Margaret (Schwitay) F.; m. Mary Stuart Blakely (dec. April 24, 2006); children: George Ross IV, Miriam Schaefer, Margaret Fisher-Rosenthal, Stuart Blakely. BS, Yale U., 1945; MD, Columbia U., 1948. Diplomate Am. Bd. Internal Medicine. Intern Pa. Hosp., Phila., 1948-50, med. resident, 1953-54, dir. house staff, 1954-56; fellow in endocrinology Jefferson Hosp., Phila., 1950-51; surgeon endocrinology br. Nat. Cancer Inst., NIH, Bethesda, Md., 1951-53; from instr. to asst. prof. clin. medicine Jefferson U., Phila., 1955— ; asst. prof. clin. medicine U. Pa., Phila., 1960—. Pres. Phila. Profl. Standards Rev. Orgn., 1981-84; med. dir. Heritage Health Systems, King of Prussia, Pa., 1986—; chmn. Ross and Perry, Inc. Book Pubs., Haddonfield, NJ; cons. in field. Author: The Hospital That Ate Chicago, 1980; contbr. articles on endocrinology and med. econs. to profl. jours. Served as sr. asst. surgeon USPHS, 1951-53. Fellow ACP, Phila. Coll. Physicians; mem. AMA (ho. of dels. 1978—), Pa. Med. Soc. (ho. of dels. 1969-89, chmn. coun. of med. econs. 1985-88, trustee 1989—), Phila. County Med. Soc. (bd. dirs. 1969-81), Pa. Soc. Internal Medicine (pres. 1980), Am. Soc. Internal Medicine (ho. of dels. 1974—), Union League (life), Right Angle Club Phila. (pres. 2007—). Republican. Mem. Soc. Of Friends. Avocations: computer science, Phila. history. Home: 203 Chews Landing Rd Haddonfield NJ 08033-3837 Office: 3 South Haddon Ave Haddonfield NJ 08033-1882 Office Phone: 856-427-6135. Personal E-mail: grfisheriii@gmail.com. Business E-Mail: gfisher@rossperry.com.

FISHER, HANS, nutritional biochemistry educator; b. Breslau, Silesia, Germany, Mar. 4, 1928; s. George and Johanna (Gottheiner) F.; m. Ruth Hirschberg, July 24, 1950; children: Deborah M. Joseph, David E. Fisher, Daniel Z. Fisher. MS, U. Conn., 1952; PhD, U. Ill., 1954. Cert. Am. Bd. Nutrition. Asst. prof. Rutgers U., New Brunswick, NJ, 1954—57, assoc. prof., 1957—62, prof., 1962—72, dept. chair, 1966—88, assoc. provost, 1988—90, disting. prof., 1972—2007, prof. emeritus, 2007—. Cons. food and pharm. industries, 1955—. Author: Rutgers Guide to Lowering Your Cholesterol, 1986, Prolonging Healthful Living with a Fiber-rich Diet, 2010; trans.: (with Ruth H. Fisher) Mendel Rosenbusch, Tales for Jewish Children (from German into English), 1991; contbr. articles to profl. jours. Pres. Highland Park (N.J.) Temple Ctr., 1975-77; v.p. YMHA, Highland Park, 1958-70. Fellow AAAS, Am. Soc. Nutritional Scis., N.Y. Acad. Scis.; mem. Brit. Nutrition Soc., Rsch. Soc. on Alcoholism, Soc. for Exptl. Biology and Medicine. Jewish. Achievements include research in fiber lowering cholesterol, Tryptophan ameliorates neuroleptic side effects and supresses voluntary alcohol consumption. Discoverer novel treatment for alcohol withdrawal and craving, high intake of vitamin E exacerbates alcoholic fatty liver in rats, histamine and carnosine in wound healing and trauma amelioration, dietary treatments for alcoholic fatty liver. Home: 216 N 3rd Ave Highland Park NJ 08904-2412 Office: Rutgers U 96 Lipman Dr New Brunswick NJ 08901-8525 Office Phone: 732-932-9825. Business E-Mail: fisher@aesop.rutgers.edu.

FISHER, JACK, medical educator, plastic surgeon; b. Mar. 10, 1947; BCS, U. Ill., 1969; MD, Emory U., Atlanta, 1973. Cert. Am. Bd. Plastic Surgery. Intern George Washington U. Med. Ctr., Washington, 1973-74, resident in gen. surgery, 1974-77, chief resident in gen. surgery, 1977-78; resident in plastic surgery Emory U. Hosp., 1978-80; staff, attending plastic surgeon Mayo Clinic, Rochester, Minn., 1981—86; assoc. clin. prof. dept. plastic surgery Vanderbilt U., Nashville, 1986—. Contbr. articles to profl. jours. Named one of Castle Connolly's America's Top Doctors, 2001—06. Fellow: ACS; mem.: Plastic Surgery Rsch. Coun., Am. Soc. Plastic Surgeons, Am. Soc. Aesthetic Plastic Surgery. Office: 310 23rd Ave N Ste 101 Nashville TN 37203-1525 Office Phone: 615-329-4227. Office Fax: 316-329-8931. Business E-Mail: info@drjackfisher.com.

FISHER, JAMES WILLIAM, pharmacologist, medical educator; b. Tucapau, SC, May 22, 1925; s. Ernest Amaziah and Mamie V. (Turner) F.; m. Carol Barbara Brodarick, June 5, 1947 (dec.), Maryann Hillyer Annis; children: Candis Loreen Fisher Rush Smith, Patricia Eileen Fisher Valladares, Richard W., William E., John C., Elaine Marie Fisher Spurr; m. Maryann Hillyer Annis, Sept. 30, 2006. BS, U. S.C., 1947; PhD in Pharmacology (USPHS fellow), U. Louisville, 1958. Devel. chemist Armour Pharm. Rsch. Labs., Chgo., 1950-53, Ayerst Pharm. Labs., Rouses Point, NY, 1953—54; pharmacologist Lloyd Bros. Pharm. Co., Cin., 1954-56; instr. pharmacology U. Tenn., 1958-60, asst. prof., 1960-62, assoc. prof., 1962-66, prof., 1966-68; prof., chmn. dept. pharmacology Med. Sch., Tulane U., 1968-96; Regents prof. Tulane U., 1996—99, Regents prof. emeritus, chmn., 1999—. Vis. prof. U. Zambia, Lusaka, 1987, Keio U., Tokyo, 1987, U. Nairobi, 1993; external examiner U. W.I., Trinidad, 1992; vis. scientist Christie Hosp. and Holt Radium Inst., Manchester, Eng., 1963-64; dir. Tulane-Universidad Nacional del Nordeste, Corrientes, Argentina, Pan Am. Health Orgn. Physiol. Scis. Tng. Program, 1972-77; lectr. in field; mem. Nat. Heart, Lung and Blood Inst. (erythropoietin com. 1971-74), mem. NIH hematology tng. grants com., 1977; mem. Cooley's Anemia Nat. Rsch. Com., 1974; pres. So. Blood Club, 1975-77; mem. Wellcome Professorships Com., 1976, 93, 94, 95; mem. pharmacology com. Nat. Bd. Med. Examiners, 1988-92; mem. ad hoc group med. rsch. funding AAMC, 1990-93. Author: Readings on the History of Pharmacology, 1970, History of Pharmacology at Tulane, 2004; editor: Kidney Hormones, Vol. I, 1971, Vol. II, 1977, Vol. III, 1986, Renal Pharmacology, 1971, Handbook of Pharmacology: Blood and Blood Forming Organs, 1992, History of Pharmacology at Tulane, 1834-2004; co-editor: Erythropoiesis, 1975, Erythropoietin and Erythropoiesis, 1981; cons. editor: Erythropoietin, 1968; mem. editl. bd. Proc. Soc. Exptl. Biology and Medicine, 1971-86; contbr. articles to profl. jours. Served to lt. (j.g.) USNR, 1943-46, PTO. Recipient rsch. career devel. award USPHS, 1960-65, Purkinje medal Czechoslovakia Med. Soc., 1975, Golden Sovereign award, 1976, Aspet Exptl. Therapeutics award, 1992, U. Louisville Med. Sch. Alumni award, 1999; named Disting. faculty AOA Honor Med. Soc., 1993; Ann. Tulane Fisher Lectureship established in his honor, 1992. Mem. AAAS, AAUP, Am. Soc. Pharmacology and Exptl. Therapeutics (Sollman awards com. 1981, exptl. therapeutics award com. 1982, 94, alerting network 1986-90, ednl. affairs com. 1986-89, Krayer awards com. 1990, Exptl. Therapeutics award 1992, nominating com. 1997), Soc. Exptl. Biology and Medicine, Am. Soc. Nephrology, Am. Soc. Hematology (sci. affairs com. 1973-74, chmn. erythropoietin subcom. 1973), Assn. Med. Sch. Pharmacology (exec. com. 1979-82, nominating com. 1975, 86, 94, 96, 99, chmn. essential knowledge base in pharmacology com. 1984-95, pres. 1990-92), N.Y. Acad. Scis., Sigma Xi. Home: 67 Grand Canyon Dr New Orleans LA 70131 Business E-Mail: jfisher@tulane.edu.

FISHER, JOHN E, research scientist; b. Brookline, Mass., Sept. 14, 1947; s. Philip Edward and Mimi M Fisher; 1 child, Benjamin David. BSc magna cum laude, U. Mass., 1981; PhD, Drexel U., 2000. Rsch. assoc. Merck Rsch. Labs., West Point, Pa., 1997—2000, rsch. fellow, 2000—. Contbr. articles to profl. jours. Bd. dirs. Jenkintown Libr., Pa., 1996—2002. Mem.: Endocrine Soc., Am. Soc. for Bone and Mineral Rsch. Achievements include contributions to understanding of molecular mechanism of action of N-bisphosphonates, role of cell adhesion molecules in osteoclast biology and biological activity of PTHrP. Avocations: hiking, music, literature. Office: Merck Rsch Labs 26A-1000 West Point PA 19486 Home: 7716 Lycoming Ave Elkins Park PA 19027 Business E-Mail: john_fisher@merck.com.

FISHER, JOHN FREMONT, medical educator; b. Dayton, Ohio, May 13, 1943; BA, U. Notre Dame, 1965; MD, Va. Commonwealth U., 1969. Prof., medicine and infectious diseases Ga. Health Scis. U. Med. Coll. Ga., 1977—, program dir., infectious disease, 2004. Named one of 18 Educator of Yr., Med. Coll. Ga. Fellow: ACP, Infectious Diseases Soc. America (Clin. Tchr. award); mem.: Am. Soc. Microbiology, Alpha Omega Alpha Honor Med. Soc. Avocations: golf, music. Office: Ga Health Scis University Med Coll Ga Augusta GA 30912 Office Fax: 706-721-7244. Business E-Mail: jfisher@georgiahealth.edu.

FISHER, KAREN A., physician, educator; b. London, Apr. 2, 1964; d. John Anthony and Pixie Ann Fisher; children: Natalia K., Amanda C., Patrick P., James J. BA, U. Sydney, LLB, 1987, MBBS, 2001. Cert. NSW Med. Bd., 2001. Physician Manly Hosp., NSW, Australia, 2003—04, CDAM, Nepean Hosp., Penrith, 2004—. Educator Nepean Clin. Sch., Penrith, NSW, 2004—. Mentor med. students U. Sydney Med. Soc., 2004—08. Recipient Tchr. of Yr., Nepean Clin. Sch., 2006—08. Achievements include establishment of new integrated clinic for co-morbid patients. Office: CDAM Nepean Hosp Somerset St 2074 Penrith NSW Australia Office Fax: 0247341341. Business E-Mail: karenf@gmp.usyd.edu.au, fisherk@wahs.nsw.gov.au.

FISHER, LAURA LANI, physician, educator; b. East Orange, NJ, July 13, 1959; d. Hyman Wendell and Rosalie Jane (Joseph) F.; m. Adi Raviv; children: Micaela Sara, Jessica Alana, Gabriella Noa. BA in Biology and Biomed. Ethics, Brown U., 1981, MD, 1984. Intern in internal medicine N.Y. Hosp., 1984-85, resident in internal medicine, 1985-87, chief resident in medicine, 1989-90, dir. Lyme Disease Ctr., 1990—; from clin. to rsch. fellow in infectious diseases Mass. Gen. Hosp., Boston, 1987-89; dir. student health svc. Cornell Med. Coll., NYC, 1990-93, asst. prof. medicine, 1990—. Contbr. articles to profl. jours. Mem. nat. cabinet Israel Bonds-Young Leadership, U.S., 1992-94, mem. city bd. dirs., 1993-94; mem. Anti-Defamation League, N.Y.C., 1993-94. Recipient Rsch. Scientist award NIH, 1988-89. Fellow ACP; mem. AMA, N.Y. Med. Soc., Mass. Med. Soc., Brown Med. Soc., Infectious Disease Soc. Am. Republican. Jewish. Avocations: painting, sports, sculpture, reading, travel. Office: 1385 York Ave New York NY 10021-3904 Office Phone: 212-717-5920.

FISHER, MARK JAY, neurologist, neuroscientist, educator; b. Bklyn., Aug. 23, 1949; s. Ralph Aaron and Dorothy Ann (Weissman) F.; m. Janeth Godeau, Aug. 5, 1994. BA in Polit. Sci., UCLA, 1970; MA in Polit. Sci., U. S.D., 1972; MD, U. Cin., 1975; JD, Loyola U., 1997. Diplomate Am. Bd. Psychiatry and Neurology. Intern UCLA Sepulveda VA Hosp., 1975-76; resident UCLA Wadsworth VA Med. Ctr., 1976-79, chief resident, 1979-80; faculty mem., dir. stroke rsch. program U. So. Calif. Sch. of Medicine, LA, 1980-98, prof. neurology, 1995-98; dir. residency tng. program U. So. Calif. Sch. Medicine, LA, 1992-96; chmn. dept. neurology U. Calif. at Irvine, Orange, 1998—2006, prof. neurology and anatomy and neurobiology, 1998—, prof. polit. sci., 2003—. Editor: Medical Therapy of Acute Stroke, 1989. Recipient Tchr. Investigator award NIH, Bethesda, Md., 1984-89, Program Project grantee, 1994-99. Mem.: Internat. Soc. Polit. Psychology, Am. Polit. Sci. Assn., State Bar Calif., Internat. Soc. for Thrombosis and Haemostasis, Am. Polit. Sci. Assn., Am. Heart Assn. (stroke coun.), Am. Neurol. Assn., Am. Acad. Neurology. Office: U Calif Irvine Dept Neurology 101 The City Dr S Orange CA 92868-3201

FISHER, NANCY LOUISE, pediatrician, geneticist, retired nurse; b. Cleve., July 4, 1944; d. Nelson Leopold and Catherine (Harris) F.; m. Larry William Larson, May 30, 1976 (div. Oct. 2000); 1 child, Jonathan Raymond. Student, Notre Dame Coll., Cleve., 1962-64; BSN, Wayne State U., 1967; postgrad., Calif. State U., Hayward, 1971-72; MD, Baylor Coll. of Medicine, 1976; M in Pub. Health, U. Wash., 1982, certificate in ethics, 1993. Diplomate Am. Bd. Pediatrics, Am. Bd. Med. Genetics. RN coronary care unit and med. intensive care unit Highland Gen. Hosp., Oakland, Calif., 1970-72; RN coronary care unit Alameda (Calif.) Hosp., 1972-73; intern in pediatrics Baylor Coll. of Medicine, Houston, 1976-77, resident in pediatrics, 1977-78; attending physician, pediatric clinic Harborview Med. Ctr., Seattle, 1980-81; staff physician children and adolescent health care clinic Columbia Health Ctr., Seattle, 1981-87, founder, dir. of med. genetics clinic, 1984-89; maternal child health policy cons. King County div. Seattle King County Dept Pub. Health, 1983-85; dir. genetic svcs. Va. Mason Clinic, 1986-89; dir. med. genetic svcs. Swedish Hosp., 1989-94; pvt. practice Seattle, 1994-97; med. cons. supr. office of managed care Wash. State Dept. Social and Health Svcs., Olympia, 1996-97; med. dir. Medicaid Dept. of Social and Health Svcs., Wash., 1997-99; assoc. med. dir. Govt. Programs Regence Blue Shield, 1999; med. dir. Regence Blue Shield, 2000—02; chief med. officer Wash. State Health Care Authority, 2003—; pediat. family practise Swedish Hosp. MC, 1989—94. Nurses aide psychiatry Sinai Hosp., Detroit, 1966—67; charge nurse Women's Hosp., Cleve., 1967; rsch. asst. to Dr. Shelly Liss, 76; with Baylor Housestaff Assn., Baylor Coll. Medicine, 1980—81; clin. asst. prof. grad. sch. nursing U. Wash., Seattle, 1981—85, clin. asst. prof. dept. pediat., 1982—92, clin. assoc. prof. dept. pediat., 1992—; com. appointments include Seattle CCS Cleft Palate Panel, 1984—97; bd. dirs., first v.p. King County Assn. Sickle Cell Disease, 1985—86, acting pres., 1986, pres., 1986—87; hosp. affiliation include Childrens Orthopedic Hosp. and Med. Ctr., Seattle, 1981—, Virginia Mason Hosp., Seattle, 1985—89, Harborview Hosp., Seattle, 1986—89; mem. Wash. State Steering Coun. Stroke and Heart Disease, 2006—, Wash. State Vaccine Adv. Com., 2006—; with Wash. State Health Tech. Assessment Work Group, 2006—, Advanced Imaging Work Group, Wash., 2009—10; co-chair Nat. Quality Forum, Child Health Steering Com., CDC, Evaluation Genomic Application Practice & Prevention, 2010—. Contbr. articles to profl. jours. Active Seattle Urban League, 1982-96, 101 Black Women, 1986-94; bd. dirs. Seattle Sickle Cell Affected Family Assn., 1984-85, Am. Heart Assn., 2001—, March of Dimes 2002—; mem. People to People Citizen Ambassador Group; sec. Health and Human Svcs. Com. on Infant Mortality, 1993—2003; mem. Twins Com. Inst. of Medicine, 1995-2000; Evaluation, Rsch. and Planning Group Ethical Legal and Social Implications Nat. Human Gerome Project, 1997-2000. Served to lt. USN Nurse Corps, 1966-70; active State Steering Com. on Heart Disease and Stroke, 2005-, Washington State Govs. Coun. on Disparities, 2006—, pres. Am. Heart Assoc. Pacific Mountain Affliate Bd., 2009 , Baylor Coll. Medicine Exec. Alumni Assoc., 2009-10, CDC com. EGAPP, 2010-; v.p. Wash. Health Found., 2009-. Fellow Am. Coll. Medicine Genetics (founder); mem. AMA, APHA, Am. Heart Assn. (bd. dirs. King County 2001—, Pacific NW affiliate bd. 2006—, pres. 2009-, Physician of Yr.), Am. Acad. Physician Execs., Student Governing Body and Graduating Policy Com. Baylor Coll. Medicine (founding mem. 1973-76, exec. alumni com. pres. 2008-09), Loans and Scholarship Com. Baylor Coll. Medicine (voting mem. 1973-76), Am. Med. Student Assn., Student Nat. Med. Assn., Admission Com. Baylor Coll. Medicine (voting mem. 1974-76), Am. Med. Women's Assn., Am. Acad. Pediatrics, Am. Soc. Human Genetics, Nat. Spkrs. Assn., Nat. Quality Found. (steering com.), Wash. State Assn. Black Providers of Health Care, Soc. Health and Human Values, Wash. State Soc. Pediatrics, Wash. State Med. Assn. (women in medicine com., intersplty. coun., fin. com.), Seattle C. of C. (mem. Leadership Tomorrow 1988—89), Sigma Gamma Rho, Phi Delta Epsilon. Office: Wash State HCA 676 Woodland Sq Loop SE MS-42701 Olympia WA 98504-2701 Office Phone: 360-923-2709. Business E-Mail: nancy.fisher@hca.wa.gov.

FISHER, PIERRE JAMES, JR., physician; b. Chgo., Oct. 29, 1931; s. Pierre James and Evelyn F.; m. Carol Ann Walton, Mar. 16, 1951; children: James Walton, David Alan, Steven Edward, Teresa Ann. Student, Taylor U., 1949-51, Ball State U., 1951-52; MD, Ind. U., 1956. Diplomate Am. Bd. Surgery. Intern U.S. Naval Hosp., San Diego, 1956-57, resident in surgery, 1957-61; pvt. practice specializing in surgery Surgeons Inc., Marion, Ind., 1965—, pres., 1977—; mem. staff Marion Gen. Hosp., chief staff, 1970; bd. dirs. Cultural Ctr. Charlohe County. Trustee Meth. Hosp., Indpls., 1972-94; bd. dirs. Charlotte County Cultural Ctr., 2005—. Served with USN, 1956-65. Recipient Physicians Recognition award AMA, 1974, 77, 80, 83, 89; named to Marion HS Hall of Distinction, Ind., 2011. Fellow ACS; mem. AMA, Grant County Med. Soc. (pres. 1980), Marion Area C. of C. (v.p. 1979-81), N.Am. Med. Golf Assn. (v.p. 1989-90, pres. 1991-93), Rotary (pres. Marion 1983-84, Dist. 656 Disting. Svc. award 1989), Kingsway Country Club (bd. dirs., pres. 1997-99), Royal Order of Ponce de Leon Conquistadors (Ponce), Kingsway Golf Villas (bd. dirs. 2011). Methodist. Home: 11250 SW Essex Dr Lake Suzy FL 34269 Office: Surgeons Inc 330 N Wabash Ave Ste 450 Marion IN 46952-2600 *

FISHER, RANDALL G., pediatrician, educator; s. Arnold Garth and Geraldine Fisher; m. Melody Ann Cameron, June 29, 1991; children: Garrett Alexander, Grayson Clark. MD, Tulane U. Sch. Medicine, 1988. Cert. in pediatrics Am. Bd. Pediat., 1991. Asst. prof. pediat. Duke U. Sch. Medicine, Durham, NC, 1997—2000, attending faculty, pediatric infectious diseases, 1997—2000; asst. prof. pediat. Ea. Va. Med. Sch., Norfolk, Va., 2000—04, assoc. prof. pediat., 2004—. Attending physician Children's Hosp. King's Daughters, Norfolk, 2000—, dir., infectious diseases clin. divsn., 2001—. Co-author: (textbook) Moffet's Textbook Pediat. Infectious Diseases, 4th edit. Lippincott Williams and Wilkins. News reader for blind Triangle Radio Reading Svc., Durham, 1998—2000; cons. Hampton Rds. Pub. Schs., Va., 2002. Maj. US Army, 1988—94. Decorated Meritorous Svc. medal US Army; recipient Faculty Tchg. award, Ea. Va. Med. Sch. Children's Hosp. King's Daughters, Norfolk, Va., 2005—06, Physician Recognition award, AMA, 1997, 2004, 2007. Fellow: Am. Acad. Pediat.; mem.: AAP, Sect. Infectious Diseases, Va. Chpt., Am. Acad. Pediat., Infectious Diseases Soc. Am., Pediat. Infectious Diseases Soc. Avocation: music. Office: Children's Hosp King's Daughters 601 Children's Ln Norfolk VA 23507 Office Fax: 757-668-8275. Business E-Mail: randall.fisher@chkd.org.

FISHER, ROBERT, gastroenterologist, health facility administrator; b. Bklyn., July 28, 1939; married. BSE, Princeton U., 1960; MD, U. Pa., 1964. Intern Chgo. Wesley Meml. Hosp., 1964-65; resident in internal meedicine Temple U. Hosp., Phila., 1967-70; fellow in gastroenterology Hosp. U. Pa., 1970-72; from asst. prof. to assoc. prof. Temple U. Sch. Medicine, 1972-80, prof. medicine, 1980—; dir. Functional Gastrointestinal Disease Ctr. Temple U. Hosp., Phila., 1984—, chief gastroenterology sect., 1985—. Mem. Am. Coll. Gastroenterology, Am. Gastroent. Assn., Am. Soc. Gastrointestinal Endoscopy, Am. Fedn. Clin. Rsch., Rsch. Soc. Alcoholism. Office: Temple Univ 3400 N Broad St Philadelphia PA 19140-5104 Office Phone: 215-707-3433. Business E-Mail: robert.fisher@temple.edu.

FISHER, SEYMOUR, psychologist, educator; b. NYC, Nov. 4, 1925; s. George and Fannie (Hesselson) F.; m. Carmen Eldridge, June 20, 1959; children: Mark, Andrew. BA, NYU, 1948; PhD, U. N.C., 1952; postgrad., Washington Sch. Psychiatry, 1954-55. Diplomate Am. Bd. Examiners in Psychol. Hypnosis. Clin. psychologist trainee VA Hosp., Roanoke, 1950, psychology trainee, 1952; intern Psychol. Clinic, U. N.C., Chapel Hill, 1950-51; supervising clin. psychologist Walter Reed Army Inst. Rsch., Washington, 1952-58; rsch. psychologist Psychopharmacology Svc. Ctr., NIMH, Bethesda, Md., 1958-60; chief spl. studies unit Psychopharmacology Rsch Br., NIMH, Bethesda, 1960-63; prof. psychiatry (psychology), dir. rsch. tng., dir. psychopharmacology lab., divsn. psychiatry Boston U. Sch. Medicine, 1963-78; prof. dept. psychiatry and behavioral scis., U. Tex. Med. Br., Galveston, 1978—, prof. emeritus, 2000—, assoc. chmn. for rsch., 1978-80, rsch. advisor to chmn. dept., 1980-91, dir. Ctr. for Medication Monitoring, 1987-2000. Vis. prof. Harvard U., Boston U., May to Nov., 1988; cons. NIMH, Chevy Chase, Md., 1964-66, mem. clin. psychopharmacology rsch. rev. com., 1973-77, mem. treatment devel. and assessment rsch. rev. com., 1979-83; cons. Office Naval Rsch., Washington, 1964-66, Mass. Dept. Mental Health, 1969-78, FDA, 1973-77; pres. Boston Mental Health Found., Inc., 1970-72; mem. Commn. on Cmty. Care of Mentally Ill, chmn. tech. com. Hogg Found., 1987-90, planning com. for 50th anniversary rsch. conf., 1988-89 Mem. editl. bd. Psychopharmacology Svc. Ctr. Bull., 1959-63; assoc. editor Psychol. Record, 1960-66; sr. editor vol. on clin. and biobehavioral aspects of cocaine, Oxford U. Press, 1987; mem. adv. bd. Internat. Jour. Methods Psychiatry, 1998-2000; contbr. numerous articles to profl. jours., chpts. in books. Recipient Disting. Alumnus award U. N.C., 1981, Donald E. Francke award for best paper Drug Info. Jour., 1987. Fellow APA (mem. exec. coun. divsn. psychopharmacology 1979-82), Am. Coll. Neuropsychcopharmacology (life, pres. 1984, asst. sec.-treas. 1974-77, chmn. hon. awards com. 1985-87, mem. other coms. 1973-87, emeritus), Soc. Clin. and Exptl. Hypnosis, Internat. Coll. Psychosomatic Medicine, Collegium Internat. Neuro-Psychopharmacologicum (emeritus); mem. Am. Psychopathol. Assn. (exec. coun. 1970-72), Psi Chi, Sigma Xi, Beta Lambda Sigma. Office Phone: 409-539-0155. Business E-Mail: sfisher@utmb.edu.

FISHER-HOCH, SUSAN P., epidemiologist, educator; b. Eng., 1940; m. Joseph McCormick, 1992. MB, BS First Class with honors in Pathology, U. London, 1975; MB, BS, LRCP, MRCS, Royal Free Hosp. Sch. Medicine, 1976; MSc in Med. Microbiology, London Sch. Hygiene and Tropical Medicine, U. London, 1978; MRCPath, Royal Coll. Pathologists, Virology, 1981; MD in Epidemiology, U. London, 1981. Lic. Royal Coll. Physicians, 1975. House surgeon St. Luke's Hosp., Guildford, 1975—76; house physician to Dame Sheila Sherlock Med. Unit, Royal Free Hosp., 1975—76; trainee med. microbiologist Oxford Regional Pub. Health Lab., Radcliffe Hosp., 1976—77; sr. registrar, dept. virology St. George's Hosp. Med. Sch., 1979—82, hon. lectr., 1982—; sr. registrar, dept. microbiology Kingston Hosp., 1979—82; Wellcome Trust Fellowship Wellcome Trust Unit, Bangkok and Spl. Pathogens Ref. Lab., Porton Down, 1982—85; cons. med. microbiologist, dir. Viral Zoonoses Lab., Ctrl. Pub. Health Lab., 1985—86; assoc. prof. Emory Sch. Pub. Health, 1991—; dep. br. chief Spl. Pathogens Br., Divsn. Viral and Rickettisial Diseases, Ctrs. for Disease Control and Prevention, Atlanta, 1986—90, acting br. chief, 1988; sr. med. epidemiologist, mycotic diseases br., divsn. baterial and mycotic diseases Ctrs. for Disease Control and Prevention, Atlanta, 1990—93; rsch. prof., dept. pathology Aga Khan U. Med. Sch., Karachi, Pakistan, 1993—97; dir. Laboratoire Jean Mérieux, BSL4, Fondation Marcel Mérieux, Lyon, France, 1993—97; prof. U. Tex. Houston Sch. Pub. Health, Brownsville, 2000—; faculty, grad. sch. biomedical scis. U. Tex. Health Scis. Ctr., Houston, 2001. Invited spkr. in field. Contbr. several articles to profl. jours., chapters to books, scientific papers; writer of invited editls. Lancet, provided expert advice to the lay press and TV, featured in both media and books about hemmorrhagic fever; co-author (with husband): Level 4: Virus Hunters of the CDC. Recipient Chevalier de la Légion d'Honneur, Pres. French Republic, Jacques Chirac, 1999, Medal de la Ville de Lyon, by mayor and former Prime Minister of France, Raymond Barre, 2000, Priz Scientique du Groupe Paris-Lyon, 2000; named one of Women In Technology Internat. Hall of Fame, 2008. Mem.: Royal Coll. Pathologists, Royal Coll. Surgeons. Avocations: skiing, running, backpacking, music, literature, languages, history, art, cooking. Office: U Houston Health Sci Ctr Sch Pub Health U Tex Brownsville 80 Fort Brown Set B Rm 1 334 Brownsville TX 78520 Office Phone: 956-882-5167. Office Fax: 956-882-5152. Business E-Mail: susan.p.fisher-hoch@utb.edu.

FISHMAN, DANIEL B., clinical psychology professor; b. NYC, July 1, 1938; BA, Princeton U., 1960; PhD, Harvard U., 1965. Asst. prof., clin. psychology U. Colo. Med. Sch., 1967—71; dir., adminstrn. and evaluation Adams County Mental Health Ctr., 1972—76; dir., psychol. svcs. Grad. Sch. Applied & Profl. Psychology, Rutgers U., 1976—87, assoc. prof., clin. psychology, 1976—82, prof., clin. psychology, 1982—. Editl. bd. mem., evaluation and program planning Elsevier Publs., 1992; editor-in-chief pragmatic case studies psychotherapy Rutgers U. Librs., 2005. Author: (book) The Case for Pragmatic Psychology, 1999. Fellow: APA; mem.: Internat. Soc. Psychotherapy Rsch. Avocations: computers, politics, reading. Home: 57 Jaffray Ct Irvington NY 10533 Personal E-mail: dfish96198@aol.com.

FISHMAN, DAVID, gynecologic oncologist, educator; MD, U. Tex., 1988. Diplomate Am. Bd. Ob-Gyn, 2009. Prof. ob-gyn. NY Univ. Medical Sch., prof. reproductive sci.; resident ob-gyn. Yale Univ. Sch. Medicine, 1988—92, fellow gynecology oncology, 1992—94; prof. pb-gyn. Mt. Sinai Sch. Medicine. Invited lectr. Am. Coll. Obstetricians and Gynecologists, 2005, Oncology World Congress, 2005, Am. Gynecol. and Obstet. Soc., 2005; Susan Teck lectr. George Wash. Univ., 2005; keynote lectr. Univ. Wis., 2005, Soc. of Gynecologic Oncologists, Canada, 2005; dir. Nat. Ovarian Cancer Early Detection Program, prin. investigator. Co-author: (publs.) The Activity of Medroxyprogesterone Acetate, an Androgenic Ligand, in Ovarian Cancer Cell Invasion, 2008, S1P induced changes in epithelial ovarian cancer proteolysis, invasion, and attachment are mediated by Gi and Rac, 2008, Contrast-enhanced transvaginal sonography of benign versus malignant ovarian masses: preliminary findings, 2008, Silencing of VEGFR-2 by RNA Interference Inhibits LPA-induced Invasion, 2009, LPA receptor 2 mediates LPA-induced endometrial cancer invasion, 2009, various others. Recipient Honorary Chmn., Presidents Physician Adv. Bd., 2006, NIH Nat. Cancer Inst. Early Detection Rsch. Network award, 2007; named one of Best Doctors, NY Mag., 2009. Mem.: Nat. Ovarian Cancer Coalition, Soc. Gynecologic Oncologists, Soc. Gynecologic Investigation, Am. Gynecologic and. Obstet. Soc., AOA. Office: Mount Sinai Medical Center 1176 5th Ave New York NY 10029 Office Phone: 212-241-5995.

FISHMAN, HENRY JAMES, allergist, immunologist, educator; MD, U. Rochester, 1979. Diplomate Am. Bd. Internal Medicine, 1982, Am. Bd. Allergy and Immunology, 1985. Resident internal medicine George Wash. Med. Ctr., 1980—82; fellow allergy & immunology Georgetown Univ. Hosp., 1982—84, former chief allergy; asst. clin. prof. medicine Georgetown Univ.; owner Fishman Allergy & Asthma. Writer and reporter Associated Press Radio Network. Office: Fishman Allergy and Asthma NW Ste 206 2141 K St Washington DC 20037 Office Phone: 202-833-3500. Office Fax: 202-833-3503.

FISHMAN, KENNETH Y., dentist, educator; Grad., Nobel Biocare Implant Residency Sch., Temple U.; grad. Pankey Inst. of Advanced Restorative Seminar, grad. Strupp All Porcelain Restorative Program, grad. Frank Spear Advanced Occlusion Workshop; completed the Ctr. Profl. Devel. Excellence program, Scottsdale, Ariz.; completed Blatchford Advanced Dental and Patient Mgmt. Tng. Co-founder FishmanRothChase and Assocs.; educator ACT Dental Advancement Program. Mem.: NY Dentofacial Study Club, Occlusal Concepts Study Group Club. Office: SmilesNY Cosmetic & Implant Dentistry Lobby F 220 East 63rd St New York NY 10065 Office Phone: 888-757-7645. Office Fax: 212-421-0410. Business E-Mail: drfishman@smilesny.com.

FISHMAN, MARVIN ALLEN, pediatric neurologist, educator; b. Chgo., Feb. 16, 1937; s. Joseph and Mary (Schneider) F.; m. Gloria Brenda Greenberg, Dec. 20, 1959; children: Bradley Steven, Patricia Ann. BS, U. Ill., 1959, MD, 1961. Diplomate Am. Bd. Pediatrics, Am. Psychiatry and Neurology. Intern, then resident in pediat. Michael Reese Hosp. and Med. Center, Chgo., 1961—64; resident in neurology Mass. Gen. Hosp., Boston, 1966—67; fellow in pediat. neurology St. Louis Children's Hosp., 1967—70, dir. Birth Defects Ctr., 1971—79; prof. pediat., neurology and preventive medicine Washington U. Med. Sch., St. Louis, 1970—79, dir. Irene Walter Johnson Inst. Rehab., 1974—79; prof. pediat. and neurology Baylor Coll. Medicine, Houston, 1979—2007, prof. emeritus pediat. and neurology, 2007—, dir. pediat. neurology tng. program, 1979—2004, vice chmn. dept. pediat., 1992—2007; chief neurology svc. Tex. Children's Hosp., Houston, 1979—2004, chief Blue Bird Clinic for Child Neurology, 2003—05. Mem. residency rev. com. for neurology Accreditation Coun. for Grad. Med. Edn., 1991-96, chmn., 1995-96; bd. dirs. Am. Bd. Psychiatry and Neurology, 1991-97, exec. com., 1995-97, v.p., 1996, pres., 1997, cons., 1999-05; cons. Am. Bd. Pediat., 1999-05. Conbr. articles in field, chpts. in books; mem. editl. bd. Jour. Pediat., 1980-87, Jour. Child Neurology, Pediat. Neurology, Annals of Neurology; editor textbook. With USAR, 1964-66. Grantee HEW, Grant Found., Ga. Warm Springs Found., Nat. Found.-March of Dimes. Mem. Am. Soc. Neurochemistry (councilor 1977-79), Child Neurology Soc. (exec. com., councillor 1980-82, sec.-treas. 1984-86, pres.-elect 1986-87, pres. 1987-89, past pres. 1989-90, John B. Hower award 1999), Houston Neurol. Soc. (pres.-elect 1989-90, pres. 1990-91), Am. Acad. Pediat., Am. Acad. Neurology, Am. Neurol. Assn., Am. Pediat. Soc., Soc. Pediat. Rsch., Soc. Neuroscis., Tex. Neurol. Soc. (Lifetime Achievement award 2009). Home: 1523-B Potomac Dr Houston TX 77057-1925 Personal E-mail: mfishman@comcast.net.

FISHMAN, ROBERT ALLEN, retired neurologist, educator, department chair; b. NYC, May 30, 1924; s. Samuel Benjamin and Miriam (Brinkin) F.; m. Margery Ann Satz, Jan. 29, 1956 (dec. May 29, 1980); children: Mary Beth, Alice Ellen, Elizabeth Ann.; m. Mary Craig Wilson, Jan. 7, 1983. AB, Columbia U., 1944; MD, U. Pa., 1947. Mem. faculty Columbia Coll. Physicians and Surgeons, 1954-66, asso. prof. neurology, 1962-66; asst. attending neurologist N.Y. State Psychiat. Inst., 1955-66, Neurol. Inst. Presbyn. Hosp., NYC, 1955-61, asso., 1961-66; co-dir. Neurol. Clin. Research Center, Neurol. Inst., Columbia-Presbyn. Med. Ctr., 1961-66; prof. neurology U. Calif. Med. Ctr., San Francisco, 1966-94, chmn. dept. neurology, 1966-92, prof. emeritus, 1994—; ret., 2005. Cons. neurologist San Francisco Gen. Hosp., San Francisco VA Hosp., Letterman Gen. Hosp.; dir. Am. Bd. Psychiatry and Neurology, 1981-88, v.p., 1986, pres., 1987 Author: Cerebrospinal Fluid in Diseases of the Nervous System, 1992; chief editor Annals of Neurology, 1993-97; contbr. articles to profl. jours. Nat. Multiple Sclerosis Soc. fellow, 1956-57; John and Mary R. Markle scholar in med. sci., 1960-65; recipient Disting. Alumnus award U. Pa. 1996. Mem. Am. Neurol. Assn. (pres. 1983-84), Am. Fedn. for Clin. Research, Assn. for Research in Nervous and Mental Diseases, Am. Acad. Neurology (v.p. 1971-73, pres. 1975-77), Am. Assn. Physicians, Am. Soc. for Neurochemistry, Soc. for Neurosci., N.Y. Neurol. Soc., Am. Assn. Univ. Profs. Neurology (pres. 1972-73), AAAS, Am. Epilepsy Soc., N.Y. Acad. Scis., AMA (sec. sect. on nervous and mental diseases 1964-67, v.p. 1967-68, pres. 1968-69), Alpha Omega Alpha (hon. faculty mem.), NAS Insts. Medicine. Home: 205 Paradise Dr Belvedere Tiburon CA 94920-2534 Personal E-mail: raf530@comcast.net.

FISHMAN, SCOTT M., anesthesiologist, educator; MD, Univ. Mass. Cert. internal medicine Am. Bd. Internal Medicine, psychiatry Am. Bd. Neurology and Psychiatry, pain medicine Am. Bd. Pain Medicine. Med. dir. Mass. Gen. Hosp. Pain Ctr. at Harvard Med. Sch.; prof. anesthesiology, pain mgmt., chief, divsn. pain mgmt. Univ. Calif., Davis. Cons. pain expert Discoveryhealth.com. Author: The War on Pain, 2000; co-author: Massachusetts General Hospital Handbook of Pain Management, 2002; co-editor: Essentials of Pain Medicine and Regional Anesthesia, 2005; editor (forensic pain sect.): Pain Medicine jour.; columnist Pain Monitor Newsletter, Am. Pain Found. Mem.: Am. Pain Found. (past. bd. dir.), Am. Pain Soc. (bd. dir., John and Emma Bonica award for Pub. Svc.), Am. Acad. Pain Medicine (pres. 2005). Office: Divsn Pain Medicine UC Davis ACC/UCMC One Shields Ave Davis CA 95616 Office Phone: 916-734-6824.

FISHMAN, STEVEN J., surgeon, educator; b. Chgo., Dec. 21, 1961; BS, Northwestern U., 1984, MD, 1986. Pediatric surgeon Children's Hosp. Boston, 1992—. Assoc. prof. surgery Harvard U., 2006—11. Fellow: ACS, Am. Acad. Pediat.; mem.: New Eng. Surg. Soc., Am. Pediatric Surg. Assn., Am. Surg. Assn., Alpha Omega Alpha. Office: 300 Longwood Ave Boston MA 02115 Office Fax: 617-730-0752. Business E-Mail: steven.fishman@childrens.harvard.edu.

FISSEHA, SENAIT, physician, educator; b. Addis Ababa, Ethiopia, July 10, 1970; BA, Rosary Coll., 1999; MD, Southern Ill. U., JD, 1999. Asst. prof. U. Mich., 2006—, med. dir. Ctr. Reproductive Medicine, 2008, resident, ob-gyn. Recipient Promising Investigators award, Trans Atlantic Reproductive Tech. Network; named Best Doctors in Am., Best Doctors Inc.; Faculty Devel. award, Berlex Found., grant, NIH, Blue Cross Blue Shield Mich., fellowship, U. Mich. Fellow: Am. Coll. Legal Medicine, Am. Coll. Obstetrics and Gynecology; mem.: European Soc. Human Reproduction and Embryology, Am. Soc. Reproductive Medicine. Avocations: travel, reading. Office: University Mich L4100 Women's Hosp 1500 E Med Ctr Dr Ann Arbor MI 48109 Office Fax: 734-763-7682. Business E-Mail: sfisseha@umich.edu.

FITCH, DIANE K., human services administrator; b. Afton, Okla., Oct. 18, 1954; d. Everett Leroy Gray and Patricia Dean Bailey; 1 child, Christopher Michael. AS, Butler County C.C., Eldorado, Kans., 1988; BS, Friends U., 1991. Advanced dispute resolution State of Kans., 2000. Intake counselor Salvation Army, Wichita, Kans., 1989—92, youth counselor, 1989—91, Sedgwich County, Wichita, 1990—91; human svc. specialist Social and Rehab. Services, Wichita, 1991—. Equal employment officer Social and Rehab. Svcs., Wichita, 1991—2000. Rep. United Way of the Plains, Wichita, 1989—2005; v.p. Social and Rehab. Kans., Wichita; treas. Lunch Bunch, Wichita, 1998—2005. Recipient Outstanding Recognition in Philosophy and Religion, Nat. Collegiate Awards Acad., 1988, Kans. Quality Mgmt. Award of Excellence, State of Kans., 1998; named Legal Eagle, 1992; scholar, Friends U., 1989—91. Mem.: Gen. Fedn. of Women's Clubs Internat. (Delta Hypatia chpt.) (assoc.). Democrat. Avocations: gardening, landscaping. Office: Social and Rehabilitation Services PO Box 1620 320 East William Wichita KS 67201 Office Phone: 316-337-6387. Business E-Mail: dkf@srskansas.org, dkf@srs.ks.gov.

FITCH, FRANK WESLEY, pathologist, immunologist, educator; b. Bushnell, Ill., May 30, 1929; s. Harold Wayne and Mary Gladys (Frank) F.; m. Shirley Dobbins, Dec. 23, 1951; children— Mary Margaret, Mark Howard. MD, U. Chgo., 1953, S.M., 1957, PhD, 1960; MD (hon.), U. Lausanne, Switzerland, 1990. Postdoctoral research fellow USPHS, 1954-55, 57-58; faculty U. Chgo., 1957—, prof. pathology, 1967—, Albert D. Lasker prof. med. sci., 1976—, emeritus prof., 1996, assoc. dean med. and grad. edn. div. biol. scis., 1976-85, dean acad. affairs, 1985-86, dir. Ben May Inst., 1986-95. Vis. prof. Swiss Inst. Exptl. Cancer Research, Lausanne, Switzerland, 1974-75. Editor-in-chief The Jour. of Immunology, 1997-2002; contbr. chpts. to books, articles to profl. jours. Recipient Borden Undergrad. Research award, 1953, Lederle Med. Faculty award, 1958-61; Markle Found. scholar, 1961-66; Commonwealth Fund fellow U. Lausanne (Switzerland) Institut de Biochimie, 1965-66; Guggenheim fellow, 1974-75 Mem. Fedn. Am. Socs. for Exptl. Biology (pres. 1993-94), Am. Assn. Immunologists (pres. 1992-93), Am. Soc. for Investigative Pathology, Am. Assn. for Cancer Rsch., Chgo. Path. Soc., Transplantation Soc., Sigma Xi, Alpha Omega Alpha. Business E-Mail: fwfitch@uchicago.edu.

FITCH, RACHEL FARR, health policy analyst; b. July 27, 1933; d. Allen Edward and Rosie Leola (Jones) Farr; m. Coy Dean Fitch, Mar. 31, 1956; children: Julia Anne, Jaquelyn Kay. Student, Little Rock U., 1965-67; BS, St. Louis U., 1974, MS, 1976, PhD, 1983. RN, Mo. Psychiat. staff nurse VA Ft. Root Hosp., North Little Rock, Ark., 1954-57; surg.-med. staff nurse St. Vincent Infirmary, Little Rock, Ark., 1957-65; acute care nurse Georgetown U. Hosp., Washington, 1968-69; pub. health nurse to adminstr. South office Vis. Nurse Assn. Greater St. Louis, 1970-73; cons. in edn. St. Louis City Health Dept., 1977-80; rsch. specialist Sen. John C. Danforth, St. Louis, 1980; owner RFF Assocs., 1983-86. Project dir. study of infant mortality in city of St. Louis, 1978. Mem. community health edn. com. Am. Heart Assn., 1977-87; bd. dirs. LWV of Mo., 1984-2001, 2003—, dir. health issues, 1987-99, 1st v.p. 1999-2001, 2003-07, bd. dirs. 2007-; chmn. Mo. Consumer Health Care WATCH, 1996-2002; mem. adv. com. Mo. Medicaid Consumer, 1996-97; mem. Mo. Welfare Coord. Com., 1997-99; mem. healthcare mgmt. and policy adv. com. Maryville U., 2002-04; mem. Mo. Found. for Health Advocates steering com., 2003-04; sec. St. Louis U. Hosp. Aux. Mem. APHA, Acad. Polit. Sci., Grand Jury Assn. St. Louis (bd. dirs.), Woman's Club St. Louis U. Sch. Medicine (past pres., bd. dirs. 2004—), St. Louis Vol. Assn., Jr. League St. Louis, Sigma Theta Tau. Address: 23 Lenox Pl Saint Louis MO 63108-1901 Office Phone: 314-961-6869. Personal E-mail: rachel.farr.fitch@sbcglobal.net.

FITCH, ROBERT D., orthopedic surgeon; MD, Duke U. Sch. Medicine, NC, 1976. Orthopedic residency Duke U. Sch. Medicine, 1978—82; pediatric orthopedic surgery fellowship Scottish Rite, Tex., 1982—83; chief, pediatric orthopedics Duke U. Med. Ctr. Contbr. articles to profl. publs. Achievements include research in limb lengthening and external fixation; the effects of non steroidal anti-inflammatories on the quality of bone regenerate formed with distraction osteogenesis. Office: Duke U Med Ctr Duke Med Ctr Box 2911 Durham NC 27710 Office Phone: 919-684-3104. Office Fax: 919-681-8703.

FITZ, J. GREGORY, dean, gastroenterologist, educator; BS, U. NC, Chapel Hill, 1975; MD, Duke U., Durham, NC, 1979. Cert. in internal medicine 1982, in gastroenterology 1986. Residency in internal medicine U. Calif., San Francisco, 1979—83, fellowship in gastroenterology, 1983—84; head divsn. gastroenterology and hepatology U. Colo. Health Sciences Ctr.; prof. medicine, dir. gastroenterology fellowship program Duke U. Med. Ctr.; joined U. Tex. SW Med. Ctr., Dallas, 2003, prof., Donald W. Seldin disting. chmn. in internal medicine, Atticus James Gill, MD chair in med. sci., Nadine and Tom Craddick disting. chair in med. sci., dean sch. medicine, exec. v.p. academic affairs, provost, 2009—. Recipient MERIT award, NIH, 2002. Mem.: Assn. American Physicians, American Fedn. Clin. Rsch., American Assn. for Study Liver Rsch., American Gastroenterol. Assn., American Soc. Clin. Investigation (Best Doctors in America 2001—03). Office: University Tex SW Med Ctr at Dallas Office of Dean 5323 Harry Hines Blvd Dallas TX 75390 Office Phone: 214-648-2509. Business E-Mail: greg.fitz@utsouthwestern.edu. *

FITZGERALD, BRENDA, public health service officer, state official; BS in Microbiology, Ga. State U.; MD, Emory U. Diplomate Am. Bd. Ob-Gyn. Resident Emory-Grady Hospitals, Atlanta; asst. clin. prof. Emory Med. Ctr.; dir. Divsn. Pub. Health Ga. Dept. Cmty Health (DCH), 2011—. Served at Wurtsmith Air Force Strategic Air Command Base, Mich., Andrews Air Force Base, Washington; chmn. bd. Ga. Pub. Policy Found., sr. fellow; 7th dist. rep. Ga. State Sch. Bd. Maj. USAF. Mem.: Ga. OB-GYN Soc. (bd. mem., former pres.). Office: Georgia Department of Public Health Two Peachtree St NW Atlanta GA 30303-3186 Office Phone: 404-657-2700.

FITZGERALD, BRIAN JOSEPH, pharmacist; b. Omaha, Nebr., Apr. 6, 1964; MS, Creighton U., 1989; PharmD, U. Nebr., 1995. Pharmacist Bartell, 1996—2011. Assoc. clin. prof. U. Wash. Coll. Pharmacy, 1996—2011. Contbr. articles to profl. publs. Recipient Pharmacology award, U. Nebr. Sch. Medicine, award, Lemmon Pharm. Co. Avocations: bicycling, photography. Office: 843 198th Pl SE Sammamish WA 98075 Personal E-mail: bfitz6@yahoo.com.

FITZGERALD, DESMOND JOSEPH, biomedical researcher; MD, Univ. Coll. Dublin. Assoc. prof. medicine & pharmacology Vanderbilt U., Nashville, 1989—91; cons. lectr. medicine Univ. Coll. Dublin (UCD), 1991—94; clin. prof. pharmacology Royal Coll. Surgeons, Ireland, 1994—2004, dir. Inst. Biopharm. Scis., 2003—04; prof. molecular medicine, v.p. rsch. UCD Conway Inst. Biomolecular & Biomed. Rsch., 2004—, dir. Conway Inst., 2009—10, chmn. bd. mgmt. Conway Inst. Contbr. articles to profl. jours. Office: UCD Conway Inst Biomolecular & Biomed Rsch Office VP Rsch Belfield Dublin Ireland Office Phone: 353 1 7164031. Business E-Mail: des.fitzgerald@ucd.ie. *

FITZGERALD, JOSEPH FRANCIS, pediatric gastroenterologist; b. Chgo., Nov. 8, 1935; BS in Biology, St. Joseph Coll.; MD, Ind. U., 1965. Cert. in pediat. 1971, in pediatric gastroenterology Am. Bd. Pediat., 1990. Pediat. intern Ind. U. Med. Ctr., 1965—66, internal medicine resident, 1966—67, fellow, 1967—69; dir. divsn. gastroenterology/hepatology/nutrition James Whitcomb Riley Hosp. for Children. Prof. pediat. Ind. U. Sch. Medicine, adj. prof. nutrition and dietetics, Sch. Allied Health Scis.; past chmn. Children's Digestive Health and Nutrition Found.; lectr. in field. Co-author: Manual of Pediatric Gastroenterology; mem. editl. bd.: Pediat., Jour. Pediatric Gastroenterology and Nutrition; contbr. chapters to books, articles to profl. publs. Recipient Disting. Svc. award, N.Am. Soc. Pediatric Gastroenterology, Hepatology, and Nutrition, Salute of Excellence award, Am. Liver Found.; named a Master Endoscopist, Am. Soc. Gastrointestinal Endoscopy. Master: Am. Coll. Gastroenterology (midwest regional councillor, Ind. gov.); fellow: Am. Acad. Pediat.; mem.: Am. Gastroenterology Assn. (Disting. Clinician award), Crohn's and Colitis Found. America (Man of Yr.). Office: JW Riley Hosp Children Ind U Med Ctr 702 Barnhill Dr Indianapolis IN 46202 Office Phone: 317-274-3774. Office Fax: 317 274 8521.

FITZGERALD, REBECCA, dermatologist, educator; MD, La. State U. Med. Ctr., 1985—89. Diplomate Am. Bd. Dermatology, lic. Hawaii, 2010, Fla., 2010, La., 2010, Mass., 2010, Nev, 2010, Calif., 1990. Intern internal medicine UCLA/Cedars Sinai Med. Ctr., 1989—90, resident internal medicine, 1990—92; resident dermatology La. State Univ. Med. Ctr., New Orleans, 1992—95; dermatologist and acting chief Stanocola Med. Ctr., Baton Rouge, 1995—97; dermatologist NE Dermatology Assocs., Boston, 1997—98, Southern Calif. Kaiser Permanente, Panorama, 1998—2007; dermatologist pvt. practice LA, 2005—; dermatologist and clin. instr. medicine Olive View UCLA Med. Ctr., Calif., 2006—; med. edn. faculty Allergan, 2007—, Bioform Med., 2007—, Merz Pharm.; owner Rebecca Fitzgerald Dermatology. Med. adv. bd. Sanofi-Aventis, 2005—; steering com. advances in beauty Medscape, 2008—. Asst. editor Jour. of Drugs in Dermatology, 2008—; co-author: Sweet's Syndrome, 1996, CTCL in Patients Under Twenty Years of Age: A Series of Five reports, 1997, Dermatologic Implications of Skeletal Aging: A focus on Aesthetic Correction of the Lower Face, 2008—, Poly-L-Lactic Acid Injection for HIV-Associated Facial Lipoatrophy: Treatment Principles, Case Studies, and Literature Review, 2008—, Facial Dermal Fillers, 2008—, various publs. Fellow: Am. Acad. of Dermatology; mem.: AMA, Calif. Soc. of Dermatology and Dermatologic Surgery, Am. Soc. of Dermatologic Surgery, LA Metro Dermatology Soc., Leaders Soc. Office: Rebecca Fitzgerald Dermatology Ste 906 321 N Larchmont Blvd Los Angeles CA 90004 Office Phone: 323-464-8046.

FITZGERALD, TIMOTHY L., surgeon, educator; b. Pontiac, Mich., Nov. 21, 1966; s. Arthur Michael and Mary Ann Fitzgerald; 1 child, Liam Russell. BS magna cum laude, Wayne State U., 1990; MD, U. Mich., 1994. Diplomate Am. Bd. Surgery. Surg. resident, chief adminstrv. resident Washington Hosp. Ctr., 2000; fellow in surg. oncology U. Toronto, Canada, 2002—04; dir. surg. oncology Lacks Cancer Ctr., Grand Rapids, Mich., 2002—08; chief gen. surgery St. Mary's Health Care, Grand Rapids, Mich., 2004—08; assoc. prof. surg. oncology divsn. East Carolina U., 2009—. Clin. asst. prof. Mich. State U., Grand Rapids, 2003—08; mem. med. adv. bd. Molina Health Care, Mich., 2004—08. Contbr. articles to profl. jours. Fellow: ACS (assoc.); mem.: Soc. Surg. Oncology, Midwest Surg. Assn. Business E-Mail: fitzgerl@trinity-health.org, fitzgeraldt@ecu.edu.

FITZMAURICE, GERARD JAMES, surgeon; b. Ireland, Dec. 15, 1978; MB BCh BAO, Queens U. Belfast, 2007. Surgeon NHS, 2007—. Mem.: Royal Coll. Surgeons Ireland. Office: Royal Victoria Hosp Grosvenor R Belfast Antrim BT12 6BA Ireland E-mail: f1502102@qub.ac.uk.

FITZMAURICE, KERRY CLARE, orthoptist, educator; b. Melbourne, Victoria, Australia, Dec. 7, 1951; d. John Wraith Fitzmaurice and Ailsa Gladys Gardiner; m. Alan Leslie Pearce, Mar. 25, 1984. Diploma in secondary tchg., Secondary Tchrs. Coll., Melbourne, Australia, 1973; diploma in Orthoptics, Lincoln Inst. Health Sci., Melbourne, 1982; PhD, U. Melbourne, 1998. Diploma Orthoptic Bd. Australia; cert. secondary tchr. Victoria Registration Bd., tech. tchr. Victoria Registration Bd. Tchr. Victorian Edn. Dept., Warragul, Australia, 1974—80; first yr. coord. Sch. Orthoptics, Lincoln Inst. Health Scis., Victoria, 1983—87; coord. vision rehab., rsch., cons. Sch. of Orthoptics, Lincoln Inst. Health Scis., Victoria, 1988—95; head sch. Sch. Orthoptics, La Trobe U., Victoria, 1997—2005, assoc. prof. Victoria, 2003—, head dept. clin. vision scis., 2005—. Sr. orthoptist Royal Victorian Inst. for Blind, Melbourne, Australia, 1983—87. Sec., pub. officer Plenty Hist. Soc., Victoria, Australia, 2001—04. Grantee Commonwealth Govt. Rsch. & Develop. grant, Dept. Cmty. Svcs. and Health, 1990, 1991, 1992, ARC Large grant, Australian Rsch. Coun., 2000, 2001, 2002. Fellow: Orthoptic Assn. Australia (pres. 1998—2000, chair, Internat. Orthoptic Congress Organizing Com. 2000—04, Mary Wesson award 1992); mem.: Australian Orthoptic Bd. (chmn. 2000—), Internat. Orthoptic Assn. (Australian rep., Internat. Orthoptic Coun. 1996—2004), Royal Australian and New Zealand Coll. Ophthalmologists, Internat. Soc. Low Vision Rsch. and Rehab. Avocations: bushwalking, travel. Office Fax: 61-3-9479-3692; Home Fax: 61-3-9479-3692. Personal E-mail: kerlan@vicnet.net.au. Business E-Mail: k.fitzmaurice@latrobe.edu.au.

FITZPATRICK, RICHARD E., dermatologist, educator; MD, Emory U., 1970; BA, Princeton U. Diplomate Am. Bd. Dermatology, 2003. Resident dermatology UCLA Med. Ctr., LA, 1975—78; assoc. clin. prof. Univ. of Calif. San Diego; dir. La Jolla Cosmetic Surgery Centre; hosp. affiliation include Scripps La Jolla Hosps. and Clinics. Mem.: Am. Soc. for Laser Medicine and Surgery (past pres.), Am. Soc. of Dermatologic Surgery, Am. Acad. of Dermatology. Office: La Jolla Cosmetic Surgery Centre Ste 130 9850 Genesee Ave San Diego CA 92121 Office Phone: 858-452-2066.

FIUMARA, ETTORE, neurosurgeon; b. Alcamo, Sicily, Italy, May 20, 1954; s. Gabriele Fiumara and Maria Calamia; m. Maria Impellizzeri, Dec. 30, 1978; children: Roberta, Gabriele. Med. diploma, Palermo U., 1978; postgrad., Cath. U. Rome, 1983. Asst. to top neurosurgeon Hosp. Niguarda, Milan, 1979-90; vice-head neurosurgeon Casa Sollievo della Sofferenza Hosp. S. Giovanni, Rotondo, Italy, 1990-98, Villa Sofia Hosp., Palermo, Italy, 1998—. Univ. tchr. spl. svc. sch. neurosurgery, Catania, Italy, 1998—2002. Contbr. articles to profl. jours. Fellow: Italian Neurosurgical Soc. Achievements include research in intracranial vascular maliformations. Office: Villa Sofia Hosp Dept Neuro piazzetta Salerno 1 Sicily Palermo Italy Office Phone: 39917808269, 00390917808268. Personal E-mail: ettorefiumara@virgilio.it.

FIUMERA, CHARLES CHRISTOPHER, psychologist; b. Walton, NY, Nov. 18, 1951; BS, Ind. State U., 1974; PhD, Ohio State U., 1993. Diplomate Am. Coll. Forensic Examiners, Am. Bd. Psychol. Specialties. Owner Fiumera & Assocs., 1995—. Mem. exec. bd. Knox County Mental Health Assn., 1980—84, cons. Riverside Pub. Co., 1993—95; mem. exec. bd., chair Kno Ho Co Head Start, 1995—2001; rsch. rev. bd. mem. Kenyon Coll., 1996—98; mem. supt. adv. bd. Mt. Vernon City Schs., 2008—. Recipient Eugenia Boggus Leadership award, Head Start Assn., Spkr. Recognition award, Be The Piece. Fellow: Am. Coll. Forensic Examiners; mem.: APA, Am. Bd. Psychol. Specialties, Ohio Psychol. Assn. Avocation: kayaking. Office: 202 S Gay St Mount Vernon OH 43050 Office Fax: 740-392-3399. E-mail: fiumera@aol.com

FIVUSH, ROBYN, psychology professor, department chairman; BA in Psychology, SUNY, Stony Brook, 1975; MA in Psychology, New Sch. U. Social Rsch., NYC, 1977; PhD in Devel. Psychology, CUNY Grad. Ctr., NYC, 1983. Instr. CUNY Baruch Coll., NYC, 1980—82; rsch. coord. NICHD tng. program, devel. psychology program CUNY, 1981—82; post doctoral fellow, ctr. human processing U. Calif., San Diego, 1982—84; asst. prof. psychology Emory U., Atlanta, 1984—90, assoc. prof. psychology, 1990—96, dir., inst. women's studies, 1996—99, prof. psychology, 1996—, associated faculty, inst. women's studies, 1996—, Samuel Candler Dobbs prof. psychology, 2001—, chair, dept. psychology, 2006—. Vis. prof., dept. psychology U. Otago, Dunedin, New Zealand, 1992; cons. in field. Co-editor (with J.A. Hudson): Knowing and Remembering in Young Children, 1990; co-editor: (with S. Golombok) Gender Development, 1994; co-editor: (with U. Neisser) The Remembering Self: Construction and Accuracy in the Life Narrative, 1994; co-editor: (with E. Winograd and W. Hirst) Ecological Approaches to Cognition and Perception: Essays in Honor of Ulric Neisser, 1999; co-editor: (with C. Haden) Autobiographical Memory and the Construction of a Narrative Self: Developmental and Cultural Perspectives, 2003; co-editor: (with J. Lucariello, J.A. Hudson, and P.A. Bauer) The Mediated Mind: Essays in Honor of Katherine Nelson, 2004; mem. editl. bd.: Memory, 1991—2001, Applied Cognitive Psychology, 1993—2002, Cognitive Devel., 1993—99, Devel. Psychology, 1993—95, 2003—, Discourse Processes, 1994—2001, Jour. Cognition and Devel., 1999—; contbr. articles to profl. jours., chapters to books. Fellow: Am. Psychol. Soc.; mem.: APA (divsn. 7 rep. to coun. 2003—07), Soc. Rsch. in Child Devel., Cognitive Devel. Soc. (program com. 1999, bd. dirs. 1999—2004), Soc. Applied Rsch. in Memory and Cognition, Internat. Soc. Traumatic Stress Studies, Jean Piaget Soc. (mem. governing bd. 1998—2001). Office: Dept Psychology Emory Univ Atlanta GA 30322 Office Phone: 404-727-4124. Office Fax: 404-727-0372. Business E-Mail: psyrf@emory.edu.

FLACKE, JOAN WAREHAM, physician, anesthesiologist, educator; b. Evanston, Ill., Dec. 16, 1931; d. Loyal Delbert and Alice (Cummings) Wareham; m. Werner E. Flacke, Aug. 7, 1957; children: Christopher, Gary, Timothy. BA, Scripps Coll., Claremont, Calif., 1953; MD, Harvard U., Cambridge, Mass., 1959. Rsch. fellow Med. Sch., Harvard U., Boston, 1964-67, rsch. assoc., 1967-69, instr., 1969-70; asst. prof. med. sci. U. Ark., 1972-75, assoc. prof. med. sci., 1975-76; adj. assoc. prof. UCLA, 1977-82, adj. prof., 1982-89, prof.-in-residence, 1989-95, prof. emeritus, 1995—. Cons. to FDA, 1989-93; assoc. examiner Am. Bd. Anesthesiology, L.A., 1974-76; program chmn. Anesthesia Ednl. Found., La.A., 1986-91; dir. cardiovascular anesthesiology UCLA Hosp., 1990-91. Contbr. numerous articles to profl. jours. Mem. Am. Soc. Anesthesiologists, Assn. Univ. Anesthesiologists, Internat. Anesthesia Rsch. Soc., Soc. Cardiovascular Anesthesiologists, Calif. Soc. Anesthesiologists, Mass. Med. Soc. Roman Catholic. Avocations: reading, skiing, needlecrafts, horseback riding. Home and Office: PO Box 308 Wolcott CO 81655-0308 E-mail: flacke@colorado.net.

FLAD, THOMAS, pharmacist; b. Boettingen, Germany, Nov. 16, 1967; s. Dieter and Margot Flad; m. Ursula Flad, Nov. 16, 1995; children: Anna, Lena. PharmD, U. Tuebingen, Germany, 1995, PhD, 1998. Rsch. scientist U. Tuebingen, 1998—2004; chief sci. officer PANATecs GmbH, Tuebingen, 2004—. Gefreiter Rocketa arty., 1987—88, Pfullendorf, Germany. Grant, German Ministry Rsch. and Edn., 1998—2004. Mem.: Deutscher Apothekerverband. Achievements include patents pending for verfahren zur Detektion von modifikationen in einem protein oder peptid. Office: PANATecs GmbH Vor dem Kreuzberg 17 Tuebingen 72070 Germany Personal E-mail: thomas.flad@gmx.de. Business E-Mail: tflad@panatecs.com.

FLAHERTY, ALICE WEAVER, neurologist; b. June 21, 1963; AB, Harvard Coll.; MD, Harvard Med. Sch., 1994; PhD in neuroscience, MIT, 1992. Cert. Neurology, 1999. Asst. prof. neurology Harvard Med. Sch., Boston; neurologist Mass. Gen. Hosp., Boston, dir. Brain Stimulator Unit, dir. movement disorders fellowship. Author: The Midnight Disease: The Drive to Write, Writer's Block, and the Creative Brain, 2004; co-author: Luck of the Loch Ness Monster: A Tale of Picky Eating, 2007, The Massachusetts General Hospital Handbook of Neurology. Office: Mass Gen Hosp VBK 905B 55 Fruit St Boston MA 02114

FLAHERTY, JOSEPH H., geriatrician, educator; BA, U. Dallas, 1986; MD, St. Louis U., 1990. Diplomate Am. Bd. Internal Medicine, 1993, Am. Bd. Internal Medicine-geriatrics, 1996. Resident internal medicine Univ. Kans., 1990—93; fellow geriatric medicine St. Louis Univ., 1993—95, assoc. prof. medicine, asst. program dir. divsn. of geriatric medicine, 2006—; hosp. affiliations include Des Peres Hosp., St. Louis Univ. Hosp., St. Louis VA Med. Ctr.; med. dir. Nursing Home and Hospice Agency; co-med. dir. Home Care Program; with dept. of internal medicine divsn. of geriat. St. Louis Univ. Sch. of Medicine & Geriatric Rsch., 1995—. Named one of Best Doctors in St. Louis, 2004, 2005, 2006, 2007, 2008, 2009, Best Doctors in America, 2006, 2009—10. Office: Saint Louis University Hospital 3635 Vista at Grand Blvd Saint Louis MO 63110 Office Phone: 314-577-8000. Office Fax: 314-577-8003.

FLAHERTY, KAREN, career military officer, nurse; b. Winsted, Conn. B, Skidmore Coll., Saratoga Springs, NY; grad., Officer Indoctrination Sch., Newport, RI; MS, U. Pa., Phila. From nurse corps candidate through the grades to rear admiral US Navy, 1973—; staff nurse, nurse-in-charge on the surg. ward, orthopedic ward and the maximum care unit Quantico Naval Hosp.; charge nurse gen. surgery unit and ob-gyn. clinic Phila. Naval Med. Ctr., 1977—79; officers program officer Naval Recruiting Command, Navy Recruiting Dist. NJ, 1979—82; joined US Navy Res., 1982, various positions including commdg. officer Fleet Hosp., Ft. Dix., exec. officer, dir. nursing services, officer-in-charge and tng. officer; joined Fleet Hosp. 15, Al Jubail, Saudi Arabia, 1991; dep. comdr. force integration Nat. Capitol Area; dep. chief health care ops. US Navy Bur. Medicine and Surgery, dir. nurse corps then chief wounded, ill and injured, dep. surgeon gen. Navy medicine, vice chief, 2010—. Sr. exec. leadership positions Thomas Jefferson U. Hosp., Phila., St. Francis Hosp., Wilmington, Del., Phila. Veterans Affairs Med. Ctr. Decorated Legion of Merit, Meritorious Svc. medal, Marine Corps Commendation medal, Navy and Marine Corps Achievement medal, Meritorious Unit Citation, Nat. Def. Svc. medal, Humanitarian Svc. medal, Armed Forces Res. medal, Marine Corps Overseas Svc. Ribbon, Saudi Arabia Liberation medal, Kuwait Liberation medal. Office: US Navy Bur Medicine and Surgery 2300 E St NW Washington DC 20372-5300 *

FLAHERTY, TIMOTHY THOMAS, radiologist; b. Fond du Lac, Wis., 1933; m. Joan Flaherty; 4 children. MD, Marquette U., 1959. Diplomate Am. Bd. Radiology. Intern St. Marys Hosp., Milw., 1959—60; resident in radiology, chief resident U. Wis., Madison, 1963—66, fellowship U. Wis. Hosps., Madison, 1964—65; pvt. practice, 1965—. Bd. dirs., sec. Nat. Patient Safety Found.; founding dir. Physicians Ins. Co.-Wis., exec. com. and underwriting com., chair investment com., chmn. bd. dirs.; mem. Govs. task force on health reform, Wis.; founding dir. SMS Svcs., Inc.; bd. dirs. Bank One of Appleton, N.A.; chair Profl. Svcs. Network, Inc.; trustee Novus Health Group Inc., Appleton, Wis., 1988-94; mem. med. exec. com., bd. trustees dept. radiology Theda Clark Regional Med. Ctr., Neenah, Wis., chmn. dept. radiology, 1980-95; clin. prof. dept. radiology U. Wis. Ctr. for Health Scis., Madison, Med. Coll. of Wis., Milw. Maj. gen. USAF, ret. Fellow Am. Coll. Radiology (councilor); mem. AMA (exec. com. 1995—, chair fin. com., chair com. on membership 1996-97, chair com. on orgn. and operation, mem. compensation com., commr. to joint commn. on accreditation of healthcare orgns. 1994, dir. Commn. on Office Lab. Assessment, 1996—, bd. trustees 1994—, chair bd. trustees, 2001-02, sec.-treas. exec. com.), AMPAC (bd. dirs.), State Med. Soc. of Wis. (vice chair bd. dirs., commn. chair), Wis. Radiol. Soc. (past pres.), Radiol. Soc. of N.Am. (counselor 1991-97), Soc. of Med. Cons. of the Armed Forces, Aerospace Med. Assn., Assn. of Mil. Surgeons, Soc. of Air Force Flight Surgeons. Office: AMA 515 N State St Chicago IL 60610-4325 Address: Radiology Assoc Fox Valley 547 E Wisconsin Neenah WI 54956-2966 *

FLAITZ, CATHERINE M., former dean, dental educator; BA in Psychology, Creighton U., 1974, DDS, 1978; MS in Pediat. Dentistry, U. Iowa, 1981. Bd. cert. oral and maxillofacial pathology. With Creighton U., U. Iowa, U. Colo.; pvt. practice pediat. dentistry Denver; prof., chair diagnostic sci. Dental Branch, U. Tex., Houston, dir. oral and maxillofacial pathology residency program, 2001—02, interim dean, 2002—04, dean, 2004—09; prof. oral & maxillofacial pathology art pediat. dentistry Dental Branch U. Tex., 1990—. Mem. editl. bd. Pediat. Dentistry, Jour. Dentistry Children, Am. Jour. Dentistry; cons. commn. dental accreditation advanced specialty edn. programs ADA; bd. mem. Friends of the Nat. Inst. of Dental and Craniofacial Rsch., 2005—. Mem. editl. bd.: Archives of Pathology and Laboratory Medicine. Recipient George W. Teuscher Silver Pen award, Jour. Dentistry Children, 2001, William N. Finnegan III Professorship in Dental Scis., U. Tex. Health Sci. Ctr.-Houston, 2005, Pres.'s Scholar award for excellence in tchg., 2004, Jack Harris award, Greater Houston Dental Soc. Alliance, 2009; named Tex. Dentist of Yr., Tex. Acad. Gen. Dentistry, 2005. Fellow: Am. Acad. Pediat. Dentistry (mem. grants and fellowship com., mem. pres. circle); mem.: ADA, Internat. Coll. Dentists, Omicron Kappa Upsilon, Tex. Dental Assn. (Presdl. Svc. award 2010), Internat. Assn. Dental Rsch., Am. Assn. Dental Rsch., Am. Acad. Oral Medicine (mem. clinical investigation and abstract com., Svc. Recognition award 2010), Greater Houston Dental Soc., Am. Acad. Oral and Maxillofacial

Pathology (exec. coun.), Am. Dental Edn. Assn., Am. Coll. Dentists. Office: Univ Tex Health Sci Ctr Dental Branch 6516 MD Anderson Blvd Rm 3 0944 Houston TX 77030 Office Phone: 713-500-4420. Office Fax: 713-500-4416. Business E-Mail: catherine.m.flaitz@uth.tmc.edu.

FLAKE, ALAN WAYNE, pediatric surgeon; BS, U. Ark., 1973—77, MD, 1981. Diplomate Am. Bd. Surgery-pediatric surgery, lic. Pa., 1996. Intern gen. surgery Univ. of Calif. San Francisco Med. Ctr., 1982, resident gen. surgery, 1988, active clin. staff, 1990—94; fellow pediatric surgery Children's Hospital Med. Ctr., 1990; asst. prof. surgery and pediat. divsn. Univ. of Calif., 1990—94; active clin. staff. Calif. Pacific Med. Ctr., 1990—94; courtesy staff Kaiser Permanente Hosp., 1990—94; active clin. staff Children's Hosp. of Mich., 1994—96, dir. fetal surgery, 1994—96; active clin. staff Henry Ford Hosp., 1994—96, Hutzel Hosp., 1994—96, St. John's Hosp., 1994—96, Children's Hosp. of Phila., 1996—, prof. pediatric surgery, 1996—, pediatric surgery fellowship tng. dir., 1997—; assoc. prof. surgery and ob-gyn. Univ. of Pa., 1996—2002, 2000—, full mem. inst. of human gene therapy, 1997—; dir. Children's Inst. of Surg. Sci., 1996—; active clin. staff Hosp. of the Univ. of Pa., 1997—; courtesy staff surgery dept. Pa. Hosp., 1997—; consulting staff dept. surgery Chester County Hosp., 1997—, Abington Meml. Hosp., 1999—. Co-author: (publs.) Renal effects of partial bladder outlet obstruction in the fetal lamb, 1997, Fetal tracheal occlusion in the rat model of nitrofen induced congenital diaphragmatic hernia, 1999, Does a Myelomeningocele Sac Compared to No Sac Result in Decreased Postnatal Leg Function following Maternal Fetal Surgery for Spina Bifida Aperta?, 2007, Molecular Clinical Genetics and Gene Therapy, 2011, and other numerous publications. Named one of Top Doctors, Phila. Mag., 2007, 2010—11. Fellow: ACS; mem.: Am. Soc. for Blood and Marrow Transplantation, Internat. Soc. of Exptl. Hematology, Am. Soc. of Hematology, Am. Soc. of Gene and Cellular Therapy, Internat. Soc. for Prenatal Diagnosis, Am. Acad. of Pediat., Am. Pediatric Surg. Assn., Cell Transplant Soc., Councilman Assn. for Acad. Surgery, Assoc. for Acad. Surgery, Am. Assn. for the Advancement of Sci., Extracorporeal Life Support Orgn., Internat. Fetal Medicine and Surgery Soc. Office: Children's Hospital of Philadelphia 34th St and Civic Center Blvd Philadelphia PA 19104 Office Phone: 215-590-3671.

FLAMINI, RODRIGO DE CARVALHO, radiologist; b. Rio de Janeiro, Dec. 13, 1979; MD, Fed. U. Juiz de Fora, 2005. Cert. nuc. medicine specialist Brazilian Coll. Radiology, 2009. Nuc. medicine resident Nat. Cancer Inst. Brazil, 2006—09; fellow PET/CT Albert Einstein Hosp., 2009—10; radiology resident Fed. U. Pernambuco, 2010—. Avocations: movies, music, running. Home: Rua Nestor Silva 70/103 Recife Pernambuco 52060410 Brazil Personal E-mail: rcflamini@yahoo.com.br.

FLAMM, MELVIN DANIEL, JR., cardiologist; b. LA, Jan. 29, 1934; s. Melvin Daniel and Mary (Peterek) F.; m. Carla Baker, June 24, 1955; children: Scott Daniel, Bradley John, Jason Andrew, Amanda Paige. BA, UCLA, 1956; MD, Stanford U., 1960. Diplomate Am. Bd. Internal Medicine, Am. Bd. Cardiovascular Disease and Interventional Cardiology. Rotating intern Walter Reed Gen. Hosp., Washington, 1960-61; med. resident Stanford U., 1964-66, fellow in cardiology, 1966-68; cardiologist in pvt. practice No. Calif. Cardiology Assocs., Sacramento; clin. prof. medicine U. Calif., Davis, mem. admissions com., 2003—; med. dir. Cardiac Catheterization Labs. Sutter Meml. Hosp., Sacramento, 1976-92. Chmn. instl. rev. com. Sutter Comty. Hosps., 1987-93; examiner Subspecialty Bd. of Cardiovasc. Diseases of Am. Bd. Internal Medicine, 1971-75; vis. prof. cardiology Nat. Def. Med. Sch. and Vets. Gen. Hosp., Taiwan U. Sch. Medicine, 1978, Queen Mary Hosp. of Hong Kong, U. Sch. Medicine and Hong Kong Cardiologic Soc., 1978. Contbr. numerous articles to profl. jours. Trustee Sutter Hosps. Found., 1987-89. Col. M.C., USAF, 1959-74, active res., 1974-84. Fellow ACP, Am. Coll. Cardiology, Coun. on Clin. Cardiology of Am. Heart Assn. (chmn. and mem. rsch. com. and rsch. allocation com. Golden Empire chpt.); mem. AMA, Am. Fedn. Clin. Rsch., Sacramento-El Dorado Med. Assn., Calif. Med. Assn. Avocations: gardening, travel, music. Office: Sutter Medical Center Sacramento CA 95819

FLANAGAN, CLYDE HARVEY, JR., psychiatrist, psychoanalyst, educator; b. Louellen, Ky., Aug. 21, 1939; s. Clyde H. Sr. and Ruby M. Flanagan; m. Gloria Kay Glymph, June 1, 1961 (div. Feb. 1974); children: Clyde H. III, Christopher Shane; m. Carol Anne Ross, Apr. 13, 1974; children: Patrick Ross, Colleen Helen. BS, Maryville Coll., 1962; MD, U. Tenn. Med. Unit, Memphis, 1966. Cert. Am. Bd. Psychiatry and Neurology in Adult, Child, Adolescent Psychiatry; diplomate Nat. Bd. Med. Examiners. Commd. 2d lt. U.S. Army, 1965, advanced through grades to col. MC, 1980; rotating med. intern U.S. Army Tripler Gen. Hosp., Honolulu, 1966-67; gen. psychiatry resident U.S. Army Walter Reed Gen. Hosp, Washington, 1967-69; child psychiatry resident Walter Reed Hosp., Washington, 1969-71; asst. chief child guidance svc. Walter Reed Army Med. Ctr., Washington, 1971-80; chief Cmty. Mental Health Activity, Ft. Belvoir, Va., 1980-86; asst. head tri-svc. alcohol rehab. dept. Nat. Navy Hosp., Bethesda, Md., 1986-88; dir. gen. psychiat. residency program W.S. Hall Psychiat. Inst., Columbia, SC, 1988-92; mem. clin. faculty, dept. psychiatry, behavioral sci. U. SC Sch. Medicine, Columbia, 1988—, dir. divsn. psychoanalysis dept. psychiat., behavioral sci., 1992—. Candidate in psychoanalysis Washington Psychoanalytic Inst., 1978-88; tng. and supervising analyst, UNC-Duke PSA Inst., 1991-, asst. dir. PSA Inst. Carolinas, Chapel Hill, 1999-2007. Contbr. chapters to books. Recipient Tchr. Yr. award Resident's Gen. Psychiat. Rsch. Program William S. Hall Psychiat. Inst., 1995, Spl. Alumni citation Maryville Coll., 2000. Fellow: Am. Acad. Child and Adolescent Psychiatry (Franklin Robinson award 1975, Disting. fellow), Am. Coll. Psychoanalysts (com. pub. edn. 1998—99, Laughlin fellow selection com. 2000—03, membership devel. com. 2003—05), Am. Psychiat. Assn. (disting. life fellow); mem.: Am. Assn. Child Psychoanalysis, Internat. Psychoanalytic Assn., Am. Group Psychotherapy Assn. (founder, cert. group psychotherapist), SC Psychiat. Soc. (chair membership com. 1991—), NC Psychoanalytic Soc., Am. Psychoanalytic Assn. (councilor 1989—2004, cert. in adult, adolescent, and child psychoanalysis 1991). Avocations: fishing, boating. Office: U SC Sch Medicine Dept Neuropsychiatry 3555 Harden St Ext Ste 301 Columbia SC 29203-6894 Office Phone: 803-434-4250. Business E-Mail: clyde.flanagan@uscmed.sc.edu.

FLANAGAN, STEVEN, physiatrist; BS, Fairfield U.; MD, U. Medicine and Dentistry - NJ Medical Sch., 1988. Chief resident Mt. Sinai Sch. Medicine, 1992, led Traumatic Brain Injury program, 1992—2008, vice chair rehab. medicine; prof., chmn. dept. rehab. NYU Sch. Medicine, 2008—; medical dir. Rusk Inst. Rehab. Medicine NYU, 2008—. Peer reviewer American Jour. Physical Medicine and Rehab. Medicine, Archives Physical Medicine and Rehab.; examiner American Bd. Physical Medicine and Rehab. Office: Rusk Inst Rehab Medicine 400 E 34th St New York NY 10016

FLANDERS, ADAM E., radiologist, educator; MD, Rush Med. Coll., 1983. Diplomate Am. Bd. Radiology, Am. Bd. Radiology-neuroradiology. Resident diagnostic radiology Univ. of Ill., 1987; fellow neuroradiology Thomas Jefferson Univ. Hosp., 1989, prof. radiology and rehab. medicine, co-dir. divsn. of neuroradiology, dir. radiology informatics rsch. Author/co-author over 70 sci. papers, 9 rev. articles, 1 text book and 3 book chptrs., reviewer Am. Jour. of Neuroradiology. Named one of Top Docs, Phila. Mag., 2010. Mem.: Am. Spinal Injury Assn. (ASIA), Am. Med. Informatics Assn. (AMIA), Soc. for Computer Applications In Radiology (SCAR), Cervical Spine Rsch. Soc. (CSRS), Internat. Soc. of Magnetic Resonance Imaging in Medicine (ISMRM), Radiolog. Soc. of N.Am. (RSNA) (electronics comm. com., scholars grant 1992), Soc. of Magnetic Imaging in Medicine (sr.), Soc. of MRI (sr.), Am. Soc. of Neuroradiology (ASNR) (sr.). Office: 1072 Main Bldg 132 S 10th St Philadelphia PA 19107 Office Phone: 215-955-2430. Office Fax: 215-955-8741. E-mail: Adam.Flanders@jefferson.edu.

FLANIGAN, ROBERT CHARLES, urologist, educator; b. Lima, Ohio, May 2, 1946; children: Nancy, Charles. BA in Chemistry, Coll. of Wooster, 1968; MD, Case Western Res. U., 1972. Resident in surgery and urology Case Western Res. U., 1972-78; vol. asst. prof. urology U. Nebr., 1978-80; asst. prof. surgery U. Ky. Med. Ctr., Lexington, 1980-84, assoc. prof. surgery, 1984-86; prof. urology, chmn. dept. Loyola U. Med. Ctr., Maywood, Ill., 1986—. Chief urology Hines VA Hosp., 1986—; trustee Am. Bd. Urology. Officer M.C., USAF, 1978-80. Recipient Cardinal's Medallion, Archdiocese of Chgo., 1995. Fellow ACS; mem. Am. Bd. Urol. (pres. 2005-), Am. Urol. Assn., Am. Assn. Genito-Urinary Surgeons, Soc. Pelvic Surgeons, Am. Soc. Transplant Surgeons, Chgo. Urol. Soc. (past pres.), Soc. Univ. Urologists (sec.-treas.), Soc. Urologic Oncology (sec.), Loyola U. Physicians Found. (v.p. 1995—). Office: Loyola U Med Ctr Bldg 54 Room 237A 2160 S 1st Ave Maywood IL 60153-3304 E-mail: rflanig@luc.edu.

FLANZ, BRUCE J., hospital administrator; B, SUNY; MBA in Health Care Adminstrn., Baruch Coll.; MD, Mt. Sinai Sch. Medicine. Served coverage and access task force Am. Hosp. Assn.; exec. v.p. Medisys Health Network Inc., CEO, 2011—, pres., 2011—; exec. v.p. Jamaica Hosp. Med. Ctr., 1975, COO, 1980—, CEO, 2011—, pres., 2011—. Recipient Disting. Svc. award, Hosp. Assn. of NY State. Office: Jamaica Hospital Medical Center 8900 Van Wyck Expy. Richmond Hill NY 11418 Office Phone: 718-206-6000. Office Fax: 718-206-8673.

FLATT, ADRIAN EDE, surgeon; b. Frinton, Eng., Aug. 26, 1921; came to U.S., 1956, naturalized, 1960; s. Leslie Neeve and Barbara F.; m. Judith Johnson. BA, Cambridge U., 1942, MA, 1945, MBBchir., 1946, MD, 1953, M. chir., 1972. Diplomate: Am. Bd. Orthopedic Surgery. Rotating intern, then resident in gen., plastic and orthopaedic surgery London (Eng.) Hosp., 1946-54, 55-56; mem. faculty U. Iowa Med. Sch., 1956-79; prof. orthopaedic surgery and anatomy, dir. div. hand surgery, chmn. dept. surgery Norwalk (Conn.) Hosp., 1979-82; clin. prof. Yale U. Med. Sch., 1979-82; chief dept. orthopaedics Baylor U. Med. Ctr., Dallas, 1982-92, coord. rsch. Tom Landry Sports Medicine Ctr., 1992-94, dir. edn. dept. orthopaedics, 1995—. Hunterian prof. Royal Coll. Surgeons, 1962; McIlrath guest prof. Royal Prince Alfred Hosp., Sydney, Australia, 1972; Sir R. Watson-Jones lectr. Brit. Orthopaedic Assn., 1986; cons. in hand surgery to surg. gen. U.S. Air Force, 1962— Editor in chief Jour. Hand Surgery, 1981-91; author textbooks, papers in field; patentee artificial wrist and finger joints. Served as officer RAF, 1948-50. Recipient Kappa Delta award Am. Acad. Orthopaedic Surgeons, 1976 Mem. Am. Soc. Surgery Hand(pres.), Brit. Hand Soc.(founder mem.), Brit. Assn. Plastic Surgery (hon.), Group Etude de la Main, Am. Orthopaedic Assn., Am. Acad. Orthopaedic Surgeons, Am. Soc. Plastic and Reconstructive Surgery, British Assn. Orthopaedic Surgeons Office: Baylor U Med Ctr George Truett James Orthopedic Inst 3500 Gaston Ave Dallas TX 75246-2096 Office Phone: 214-820-1989. Business E-Mail: adrianf@baylorhealth.edu.

FLAX, HERSCHEL, surgeon; b. Capetown, South Africa, Feb. 9, 1941; came to U.S., 1974; s. Alexander Elliah and Mary Freda (Pasvolsky) F.; m. Elana Yehudith Matzkin; children: Joshua, Daniel, Rachel, Alexander. MB ChB, U. Capetown, 1964; ChM, U. Capetown Med. Sch., 1974; MA, NYU, 1978. Diplomate Am. Bd. Surgery. Intern Groote Schuur Hosp., Cape Town, South Africa, 1965-66; surg. registrar U. Cambridge, London, Birmingham, Eng. and Cape Town, 1966-72; chief resident Albert Einstein Coll. of Medicine, Bronx, NY, 1974-75, attending surgeon, asst. clin. prof., 1975—, attending surgeon, 1975—, assoc. clin. prof. surgery, 1989-97, prof. clin. surgery, 1997—2010; attending surgeon, specializing in diseases of the breast Mt. Sinai Hosp., NYC, 1999—, prof. anatomy, 2010—. Vis. prof. surgery Mt. Sinai Med. Sch., NYC. Contbr. articles to profl. jours. Recipient Frank Forman prize, Moffat Meml. prize, Sir Abe Bailey Travel Bursar, Paul Martini European prize, Bronte-Stewart Rsch. prize. Fellow ACS, Royal Coll. Surgeons (Eng.); mem. Med. Soc. State N.Y., N.Y. Surg. Soc., N.Y. Met. Breast Cancer Soc. Avocations: piano, photography, politics, travel, skiing. Office: 9 E 63rd St New York NY 10065 Home Phone: 516-487-3185; Office Phone: 212-755-3833. E-mail: hflax@hotmail.com.

FLAX, MARTIN HOWARD, pathologist, retired educator; b. NYC, Jan. 19, 1928; s. Abraham and Sadie (Finkel) F.; m. Ann E. Brockway, June 26, 1955; children: Adam, Jonathan, Elizabeth. AB, Cornell U., 1946; AM, Columbia U., 1948, PhD, 1951; MD, U. Chgo., 1955; MS in Health Mgmt., MIT, 1979. Intern Mt. Sinai Hosp., NYC, 1955-56; fellow pathology U. Chgo., 1956-57; chief biophysics br. Armed Forces Inst. Pathology, Washington, 1957-59; clin. fellow Mass. Gen. Hosp., Boston, 1959-61, asst. pathologist, 1961-66; fellow pathology Harvard U. Med. Sch., 1959-61, instr. pathology, 1961-63, assoc. pathology, 1961-66, asst. prof., 1966-69; prof., chmn. pathology dept. Tufts U. Sch. Medicine, 1970-97; chmn. pathology dept. Tufts U. Sch. Vet. Medicine, 1985-96; pathologist-in-chief New Eng. Med. Ctr. Hosp., Boston, 1970-97; emeritus prof. pathology Tufts U., 1998—. Cons. pathology B study sect. NIH, 1970-74. Vol. Peabody Mus. Anthropology and Ethnology, Cambridge, Mass., 1998—2005, George Eastman House, Rochester, NY, 2001—05. Capt. M.C. USAF, 1957—59. Recipient Rsch. Career Devel. award NIH, 1966-69; Nat. Cancer Inst. fellow, 1959-61, Med. Found. fellow, 1963-65, Sloan fellow MIT, 1979. Mem.: Sigma Xi, Phi Beta Kappa. Home: 32 Gate House Rd Chestnut Hill MA 02467 Personal E-mail: martinflax@earthlink.net.

FLECHTNER-MORS, MARION M., nutritionist, researcher; d. Leopold Flechtner; m. Karl-Hermann Mors; children: Mona Mors, Mira Mors. PhD, U. Ulm, Germany, 1995, U. Hohenheim, 2005. Cert. nutritionist U. Hohenheim, Germany, 1990. Head obesity rsch. U. Ulm, 1998—. Rschr. UCLA, Ctr. Human Nutrition, 1996—98. Contbr. articles to profl. jours. Office: University Ulm Albert Einstein Allee 47 Ulm 89081 Germany Business E-Mail: marion.flechtner-mors@uni-ulm.de. E-mail: marion.mors@uniklinik-ulm.de.

FLECK, CHRISTIAN, pharmacologist, educator; b. Berlin, Feb. 2, 1952; s. Franz and Margarete (Jentsch) F.; m. Marlies Radtke, Nov. 27, 1976; children: Constanze, Susanne. Diploma in medicine, U. Jena, Germany, 1977, Dr.med., 1979, Dr.med.habil., 1989. Asst. med. faculty U. Jena, 1978-90, sr. dr., 1990-93, prof., 1993—. Head dept. Inst. Pharmacology and Toxicology, Friedrich Schiller U., Jena. Mem. editl. bd. Arzneim Fursch/Drug Res, Exptl. Toxicol. Pathology, editor procs., 1996, 99; editor procs. Nova Acta Leopoldina, 1998 Capt. German Med. Svc., 1970-72. Recipient Virchow prize Health Ministry Berlin, 1990. Mem. German Soc. Pharmacol. Toxicology, European Soc. Biochem. Pharmacology (sec. 1994—), German Soc. Pharmacy, ISSX, DAC. Avocation: painting. Home: Erfurter Strasse 60 D-07743 Jena Germany Office: U Jena Inst Pharmacology Nonnenplan 4 D-07740 Jena Germany Home Phone: 49-3641-447799; Office Phone: 49-3641-938720. E-mail: Christian.Fleck@mti.uni-jena.de.

FLEEKOP, PHILIP, allergist, immunologist; MD, Emory U. Diplomate Am. Bd. Internal Medicine, Am. Bd. Allergy and Immunology, lic. Pa., Ga. Resident Emory Univ. Hosp.; fellow Hosp. of Univ. Pa.; hosp. affiliation includes Abington Meml. Hosp., Pa.; profl. staff Allergy, Asthma & Clinical Immunology Assocs., P.C. Fellow: ACP, Coll. of Physicians of Phila., Am. Coll. of Allergy, Asthma and Immunology, Am. Acad. of Allergy, Asthma and Immunology; mem.: European Acad. of Allergology and Immunology, Pa. Allergy and Asthma Assn. Office: Allergy, Asthma & Clinical Immunology Associates, P.C. Ste M-66 2300 Computer Ave Willow Grove PA 19090 Office Phone: 215-659-5480. Office Fax: 215-659-5482.

FLEET, JAMES C., medical educator, researcher; b. St. Louis, Feb. 19, 1959; BS, Cornell U., 1981, PhD, 1988. Scientist ii Tufts U. Human Nutrition Rsch. Ctr. Aging, 1988—97; asst. prof. U. NC, Greensboro, 1997—2000; prof. Purdue U., 2000—, dir. grad. studies interdept. nutrition program, 2003—. Freelance sci. writer, 1988—2011. Recipient Mead Johnson award, Am. Soc. Nutrition; Rsch. grant, NIH. Mem.: AAAS, Am. Assn. Cancer Rsch., Am. Soc. Bone and Mineral Rsch., Am. Soc. Nutrition, Am. Gastroent. Assn. Avocations: music, art, baseball. Office: 700 West State St Rm G1B Stone Hall West Lafayette IN 47906-2059 Office Fax: 1-765-494-0906. Business E-Mail: fleet@purdue.edu.

FLEISCHAKER, GORDON HENRY, JR., pediatrician; b. Louisville, July 1, 1928; s. Gordon H. and Agnes Rose (Shatzen) F.; m. Barbara Lorraine Draeger, Aug. 15, 1954 (dec. 1998); children: Rachel, Judith, James. BA in Zoology, U. Louisville, 1949, MD, 1953. Diplomate Am. Bd. Pediatrics, 1960. Intern Univ. Hosp., Madison, Wis., 1953-54; resident in pediat. The Children's Hosps., Denver, 1956-58; fellow in pediatric rheumatology State U. Iowa, Iowa City, 1958-60; practice medicine specializing in pediat. Denver, 1960—. Assoc. clin. prof. pediat. U. Colo. Sch. Medicine, Denver, 1960—; mem. active med. staff The Children's Hosp. Colo. Served to capt. MC, USAF, 1953-56. Fellow Am. Acad. Pediat.; mem. AMA, AAAS, Colo. Med. Soc., Clear Creek Valley Med. Soc. (pres. 2002-03). Office: G H Fleischaker MD 4485 Wadsworth Blvd Wheat Ridge CO 80033-3318 Office Phone: 303-421-0194. Personal E-mail: PeeDaTrx@aol.com.

FLEISCHER, ARTHUR C., medical educator, radiologist; b. Miami, Fla., May 15, 1952; s. Eugene and Lucille Fleischer; m. Leona Fleischer, May 25, 1975; children: Braden, Jared, Amy. BS in Biology, Emory U., 1973; MD, Med. Coll. Ga., 1976. Diplomate Am. Bd. Radiology. Prof. radiology Vanderbilt U. Med. Ctr., Nashville, 1987—, prof. ob-gyn., 1988—. Author: Principles and Practice of Ultrasonography in Ob/Gyn, 2004, 20 books on diagnostic sonography. Named Disting. Alumnus award, Med. Coll. Ga., 2007. Fellow: Am. Inst. Ultrasound in Medicine (bd. govs. 1989—91, William Fry award 1999), Am. Coll. Radiology, Soc. Radiologists in Ultrasound (Larry Mack award 1999, Frank H. Boehm award for continuing med. edn. 2005, C.A.N.D.L.E. award for med. student tchg. 2005, Disting. Alumnus award, Med. Coll. Georgia 2007). Office: Vanderbilt Univ Med Ctr 1161 21st Ave S Nashville TN 37232

FLEISCHMAN, ALAN ROBERT, medical educator, administrator; b. NYC, Mar. 8, 1946; BS cum laude, CCNY, 1966; MD with honors, Albert Einstein Coll. Medicine, 1970. Studied pediatrics John Hopkins Hosp., Balt.; joined Albert Einstein Coll. Medicine, NYC, 1974, Montefiore Med. Ctr., NYC, 1975, prof. pediatrics, prof. epidemiology and social medicine, dir. divsn. neonatology, 1981-94; clin. prof. pediatrics, clin. prof. epidemiology and population health Albert Einstein Coll. Medicine, NYC, 1986—; acting chair to chmn., Fed. Adv. Com., ethics advisor, Nat. Children's Study Nat. Inst. Child Health and Human Develop., NIH, 2004—; sr. v.p. NY Acad. Medicine, 1994—2004, sr. advisor, 2004—07; sr. v.p., med. dir. March of Dimes Found., NY, 2007—. Mem. adv. com. Human Rsch. Protections, Office for Human Rsch. Protections, US Dept. HHS; mem. sec. adv. com. on human rsch. protections' subcommittee on rsch. involving children Dept. HHS. Co-editor (with Robert C. Cassidy) Pediatric Ethics-From Principles to Practice, 1996; contbr. numerous articles to profl. jours. Mem. N.Y. State Gov. Task Force on Life and the Law. Fellow, perinatal physiology, NIH; Royal Soc. Medicine Found. Scholar Oxford U., UK. Mem.: Am. Pub. Health Assn., Ambulatory Pediatrics Assn., Am. Pediatric Soc., Soc. for Pediatric Rsch., Inst. Medicine (expert advisor, com. on clin. rsch. involving children, com. on ethical issues on housing-related health hazard rsch.), Am. Acad. Pediatrics Bioethics, Pediatric AIDS Com., Alpha Omega Alpha, Phi Beta Kappa. Office: March of Dimes 1275 Mamaroneck Ave White Plains NY 10605

FLEISCHMAN, GARY FRANKLIN, acupuncturist; s. Edward Norman and Lillian Ruth Fleischman; 1 child, Wayne. MD in Podiatry, Ohio Coll. of Podiatric Medicine, 1966; OMD, China Inst. of Acupuncture, 1998. Bd. cert. acupuncturist Conn. Resident St. Lukes Hosp. and Children's Med. Ctr., Phila., 1966—67; position in pathology Mt. Sinai Hosp., Hartford, Conn., 1967—68; pvt.practice podiatric medicine and surgery, 1968—72; instr. So. Conn. State U., New Haven, 1985—, Quinnipiac U., Hamden, Conn., 1996—97; clin. tng. Guangdong Provincial Hosp. of Traditional Chinese Medicine, 1998. Author: Acupuncture: Everything You Ever Wanted To Know, 1998. Recipient Cert. of Appreciation award, Conn. Student Nurses Assn., 1999. Mem.: Am. Med. Writers Assn., Connection for Health Network (pres. 1997—2000). Office: Acupuncture Health Svcs New Haven 188 Fountain St New Haven CT 06515-1902

FLEISHER, ARTHUR A., II, physician; b. Phila., Sept. 7, 1932; s. Oscar Teller and Beatrice Naomi (Rosenzweig) F.; m. Francine Queenth, June 26, 1955; children: Rebecca, Martin Q., Arthur III, Carolyn B. BS, U. Miami, Fla., 1954; MD, U. Miami, 1958. Diplomate Am. Bd. Obstetrics and Gynecology. Resident in obstetrics and gynecology Jackson Meml. Hosp., Miami, Fla., 1959-62; obstetrician/gynecologist So. Calif. Permanente Med. Group, Panorama City, Calif., 1962—, chief dept. ob-gyn, 1975-81; assoc. clin. prof. ob-gyn L.A. County/U. So. Calif. Med. Ctr., Los Angeles, 1972—; clin. prof.; assoc. clin. prof. ob-gyn UCLA, 1964-83. Fellow Am. Coll. Ob-Gyn, ACS, Los Angeles Ob-Gyn Soc. (pres. 1997-98). *

FLEISHER, GARY ROBERT, pediatrician, educator; b. Atlantic City; MD, Jefferson Med. Coll., 1973. Pediat. intern Children's Hosp. Phila., 1973—74, pediat. resident, 1974—76, infectious disease resident, 1976—77, emergency medicine fellow, 1977—79; chief, pediat. divsn. Children's Hosp. Boston, 1986—2001, physician-in-chief, 2001—, chmn. Assoc. prof. Harvard Med. Sch., Boston, 1986—97, Egan Family Found. prof. pediat., 1997—. Fellow: Am. Coll. Emergency Physicians, Am. Acad. Pediat.; mem.: Inst. Medicine. Office: Childrens Hosp Hunnewell 2 Rm HU-260-2 300 Longwood Ave Boston MA 02115 Office Phone: 617-355-5022. Office Fax: 617-730-0469. Business E-Mail: gary.fleisher@childrens.harvard.edu.

FLEISHER, LEE ALAN, anesthesiologist, educator; b. Phila., July 22, 1960; s. Louis and Lois (Solowey) F.; m. Renee Lee Cohen, Dec. 28, 1991; 2 children. BA, U. Pa., 1981; MD, SUNY, Stony Brook, 1986. Asst. prof. anesthesiology Yale U. Sch. Medicine, New Haven, 1990-92, Johns Hopkins Sch. Medicine, Balt., 1992-96, assoc. prof. anesthesiology, 1996—2002, prof. anesthesiology, 2002—04, joint appts. in medicine, health policy and mgmt. and health scis. informatics, 1996—2004, vice chair for clin. investigation, anesthesiology, 2001—04; clin. dir. oper. rms. Johns Hopkins Hosp., Balt., 2000—04; Robert D. Dripps prof., chair anesthesia U. Pa., Phila., 2004—. Founder Investigators in Heart Rate Variability, 1991-96; dir. Found. for Effectiveness, Ctr. for Innovations Johns Hopkins Medicine, 2002-2004; co-med. dir. Global Perioperative Rsch. Orgn., 2002—; assoc. scholar Ctr. for Clin. Epidemiology and Biostatis.; sr. fellow Leonard Davis Inst. Editor: Evidence-based textbook of Anesthesia, 2005, Anesthesia and Uncommon Diseases, 5th edit.; co-editor: Myocardial Ischemia and Infraction, 1992, Essence of Anesthesia Practice, 1996, 2002, Problems in Anesthesia, 1997-2001; assoc. editor Anesthesiology, 2001—, Anesthesia, 5th edit.; sect. editor Jour. Cardiovasc. Anesthesia; cons. editor Anesthesia Clinics NA, 2002—. Burroughs Wellcome scholar Found. Anesthesia Edn. & Rsch., 1989; recipient Young Investigator award Am. Soc. Critical Care Anesthesiologists, 1990, Outcomes award Soc. Ambulatory Anesthesia, 2000. Fellow Am. Coll. Cardiology, Internat. Soc. Ambulatory Monitoring (founding fellow); mem. Inst. Medicine, Internat. Anesthesia Rsch. Soc., Am. Soc. Anesthesiologists, Am. Heart Assn. (mem. task force 1994-2002, study sect. 1997—, chair 2003—), Soc. Cardiovascular Anesthesiologists (rsch. com. 1993—, chmn. 1997-2003, bd. dirs. 1995-2001). Office: Univ Pennsylvania School Medicine 3400 Spruce St Dulles 680 Philadelphia PA 19104 Office Phone: 215-662-3738. Office Fax: 215-349-5341. Business E-Mail: fleishel@uphs.upenn.edu.

FLEISHER, THOMAS ARTHUR, physician; b. Rochester, Minn. s. Gerard and Gisela Fleisher; m. Mary Fleisher; children: Jeffrey, Jeremy, Matthew. BS, U. Minn., 1969, MD, 1971. Diplomate Am. Bd. Pediats., Am. Bd. Allergy and Immunology. Staff physician bone marrow transplant svc. Naval Med. Rsch. Inst., Bethesda, Md., 1975—77; commd. lt.comdr. USNR, 1975—77; commd. USPHS, 1977—80, advanced through grades to capt., 1983—2001; ret., 2001; clin. assoc. metabolism br. Nat. Cancer Inst., NIH, Bethesda, 1977—80; asst. chief allergy clin. immunology svc. Walter Reed Army Med. Ctr., Washington, 1980—83; chief immunology svc. Warren G. Magnuson Clin. Ctr., NIH, Bethesda, 1983—, chief dept. lab. medicine, 1998—. Tng. program dir. clin. lab. immunology NIH, Bethesda, 1992—; bd. dirs. Am. Bd. Allergy and Immunology, Phila., 1991—2001, chair, 1996. Editor Clin. Immunology, 1985—89, 1993—, Immunology, 1983—86, Clin. Diag. Lab. Immunology, 1993—, Cytometry, 1996—, contbr. numerous articles to sci. jours., —. House capt. Christmas in April, Montgomery County, Md., 1991—2000; deacon, elder St. Mark Presbyn. Ch., Rockville, Md., 1983—88; bd. dirs. Bethesda Soccer Club, 1987—95. Fellow: Am. Acad. Allergy, Asthma and Immunology (bd. dirs. 2003—); mem.: Clin. Immunology Soc. (pres. 2004—), Clin. Cytometry Soc., Soc. for Pediat. Rsch., Am. Assn. Immunologists. Avocations: travel, skiing, woodworking. Office: National Institute of Health 10 Center Dr MSC 1508 Bethesda MD 20892 E-mail: tfleisher@mail.nih.gov.

FLEISHMAN, PHILIP ROBERT, internist; b. Hartford, Conn., Apr. 17, 1935; s. Morris and Anna Lillian (Farber) Fleishman; m. Anita Rose Coopersmith, Oct. 18, 1964; children: David, Beth, Rachael. BS, Trinity Coll., Phi Beta Kappa, Hartford, 1957; MD, SUNY, Bklyn., 1961. Diplomate Am. Bd. Internal Medicine. Med. intern Bklyn. Jewish Hosp., 1961—62, med. resident, 1962—65; practice specializing in internal medicine East Islip, NYC, 1967—; attending physician, dir. medicine Southside Hosp., Bay Shore, NY, 1993—; attending physician Good Samaritan Hosp., W. Islip, NY; v.p. med. bd. Southside Hosp., 1986-89; pres., 1989—; clin. asst. prof. SUNY Med. Sch., Stony Brook, 1967—; asst. dir. medicine, 1988—; dir. med. sch., 1993—; founder, co-dir. diabetic clinic Southside Hosp.; also bd. dirs., 1999—. Bd. dir. Southside Hosp. Contbr. articles to profl. jours. Co-author, chmn. constn. and bylaws Pro-Arts Group Islips, 1979; asst. basketball coach Police Athletic League, 1979; v.p., trustee Bay Shore Jewish Ctr., 1979—, pres., 1988—90. Capt. M.C. US Army, 1965—67. Fellow: ACP; mem.: AMA, Suffolk County Med. Soc., N.Y. State Soc. Internal Medicine (past chpt. pres.), N.Y. State Med. Soc., Am. Diabetes Assn. Office Phone: 631-968-7373.

FLEMING, CONSTANCE M., nurse; b. Springfield, Mass., Apr. 14, 1955; BSN, Northern Mich. U., 1977; MSN, Madonna U., 1991. Adminstr. outpatient women's health Hutzel Hosp., 1990—91; dept. head maternal child Carson Tahoe Hosp., 1991—92; RN Botsford Hosp., 1992—. Adv. bd. mem. Region 2 North Health Care Coalition, 2008; commr. emergency preparedness, Farmington Hills, 10; nursing program adv. com. Henry Ford CC, 2011. Mem.: Emergency Nurses Assn., Mich. Orgn. Nurse Executives, Sigma Theta Tau. Avocations: dog breeding, gardening. Office: 28050 Grand River Ave Farmington Hills MI 48336 Office Fax: 248-615-7214. Business E-Mail: cfleming@botsford.org.

FLEMING, DAVID W., city health department director; BS, SUNY, Albany; MD, SUNY Upstate Med. Ctr., Syracuse. Cert. internal med. State epidemiologist State of Oreg.; dep. dir. Centers for Disease Control & Prevention, 2000—03, acting dir., 2002; dir. global health strategies prog. Bill & Melinda Gates Found., 2003—06; dir. & health officer Seattle & King County Pub. Health, 2006—. Faculty mem. pub. health Univ. Wash., Oreg. Health Sciences Univ.; bd. mem. Global Alliance for Vaccines & Immunizations, Global Alliance for Improved Nutrition; pres. Coun. of State & Territorial Epidemiologists. Office: Pub Health Seattle & King County Ste 1300 401 5th Ave Seattle WA 98104 Office Phone: 206-296-4600.

FLEMING, GEORGE ROBERT, psychologist; 1 child, Maisha Amira. BA, Hillsdale Coll., 1969; MA in Clin. Psychology, Mich. State U., 1972, PhD in Clin. Psychology, 1975. Lic. psychologist Mich., Am. Bd. Profl. Disability Cons., Psychol. Am. Coll. Forensic Examiners, Emergency Crisis Response, Am. Acad. Experts in Traumatic Stress, cert. Profl. Qualification in Psychology, Assn. State and Provincial Bd. Staff mem. Allied Health-Detroit Med. Ctr.; staff dept. psychiatry and behavioral neuroscis. Harper Hosp. and Detroit Receiving Hosp., 1990—; ind. psychiatric examiner mental divsn. Wayne County Probate Ct., 1991—; psychologist risk mgmt. divsn. Detroit Police Dept., 1997—; allied health staff mem. Geropsychiatry Dept. Botsford Gen. Hosp., 2008—; clin. dir. Wayne County Juvenile Assessment Ctr., Mich., 2000—03. Cons. Sacred Heart Rehab. Ctr., Inc., Detroit, 1981-84, Detroit Pub. Schs., 1981, 1986, Southgate Regional Ctr. for Devel. Disabilities, Mich. Dept. Mental Health, 1989-90, 1995; cons., facilitator Morehouse Rsch. Inst., Morehouse Coll., Atlanta, 1990-92; advisor African Am. Males at Risk, Rockefeller Found., NYC, 1989-90; workshop panelist Congl. Black Caucus Found., Washington, 1988 Bd. trustees Optometric Inst. and Clinic of Detroit, 1995—; clin. asst. prof. dept. psychiatry and behavioral neuroscis. Wayne State U., 1991—. Recipient Spirit of Detroit award, 1986; named one of Outstanding Young Men in Am., U.S. Jaycees, 1982; fellow Nat. Inst. Mental Health, Mich. State U., 1974—75. Mem. Am. Psychol. Assn., Assn. Black Psychologists (past pres. Mich. chpt., 1981-82), Nat. Register Health Svc. Providers in Psychology, Am. Bd. Profl. Disability Cons., Am. Coll. Forensic Examiners (diplomate 1997—), Nat. Black Child Devel. Inst., Am. Acad. of Experts in Traumatic Stress (diplomate 1999-), Soc. Cmty. Rsch. and Action. Office: 243 W Congress Blvd Ste 350 Detroit MI 48226 Personal E-mail: gpsychdet@sbcglobal.net. Business E-Mail: gpsychdet@comcast.net.

FLEMING, SAMUEL CROZIER, JR., healthcare executive; b. Phila., Sept. 30, 1940; s. Samuel Crozier Sr. and Josephine Coverdale (Plowman) F.; m. Nancy Elizabeth McAdam, Sept. 7, 1963; children: David McAdam, Timothy Crozier. BChemE, Cornell U., 1963; MBA, Harvard U., 1967. Rsch. engr. DuPont Co., 1963; mgmt. cons. Arthur D. Little, Inc., 1967-90, v.p., 1977-83, sr. v.p., 1983-90; pres., CEO ADL Impact Svcs., 1976-79, Arthur D. Little Decision Resources, 1979-83, chmn. bd. dirs., 1983-90; CEO Decision Resources, Inc., Waltham, Mass., 1990—2003, chmn. emeritus, 2004—; CEO Briland LLC, Waltham, 2004—. Mem. chem. engring. adv. coun. Cornell U., Ithaca, NY, 1989—96, mem. engring. coll. adv. coun., 1996—, univ. trustee, 1997—2009, vice chmn. bd. trustees, 2002—09; bd. dirs. Picker Inst., Boston, 2000—, Charlesbridge Pub., Watertown, Mass., 1977—, Commonwealth Fund, NYC, 2003—; chmn. bd. dirs. Opinion Rsch. Corp., Princeton, NJ, 1984—88; trustee BNY Mellon Instl. Funds, Boston, 1986—2008, Mass. Eye and Ear Infirmary, Boston, 2006—; overseer Weill Cornell Medical College, NYC, 2008—. Mem. Vestry Trinity Ch., Boston, 1980-84; chmn. bd. dirs. New Eng. Bapt. Hosp., Boston, 1984-90, New Eng. Bapt. Health Care Corp., 1985-91; bd. dirs. CareGroup Inc., 1996-2007, Pathway Health Network Inc., Boston, 1994-96. 1st lt. US Army, 1963—65. Mem. The Country Club (Brookline, Mass.), Baker Hill Golf Club, Cornell Club of N.Y. Avocation: investments. Home: 61 Meadowbrook Rd Weston MA 02493-2407 Business E-Mail: sfleming@brilandllc.com.

FLEMING, WILLIAM HARE, surgeon; b. Columbus, Ohio, May 1, 1935; s. William Bush and Charlotte (Hare) F.; m. Carolyn Etta Swift, June 25, 1959 (div. May 1978); children: Alice Fleming Guzick, William Swift, Edgar Hare; m. Pamela Anderton, Jan. 21, 1995. BA, Yale U., 1957; MD, Columbia U., 1961. Diplomate Am. Bd. Surgery, Am. Bd. Thoracic Surgery. Intern in surgery Presbyn. Hosp., NYC, 1961-62, resident in surgery, 1962-66; resident in thoracic surgery Manhattan VA Hosp., NYC, 1967, Harlem Hosp., NYC, 1967, Presbyn. Hosp., NYC, 1968; asst. prof. Emory U., Atlanta, 1971-76; chief thoracic surgery VA Hosp., Atlanta, 1971-76; adj. sr. research scientist Ga. Inst. Tech., Atlanta, 1974-76; assoc. prof. surgery U. Nebr. Med. Ctr., Omaha, 1976-80, prof. surgery, 1980-96, chief thoracic surgery, 1980-92; bd. chmn. Pharma Techs. Inc., Omaha. Pres. bd. dirs. Profl. Fees Office Nebr. Clinicians Group, Omaha, 1985-91. Contbr. over 100 articles to profl. jours. Served to maj. U.S. Army, 1969-70, Vietnam. Decorated Bronze Star. Fellow ACS, Am. Coll. Cardiology; mem. AMA (Physicians Recognition award 1988), Am. Assn. Thoracic Surgery, Happy Hollow Club, Champions Club. Republican. Presbyterian. Avocations: tennis, sailing, boating. Home: 17850 S Reflection Ave Bennington NE 68007-5727 Home Phone: 402-315-9089. E-mail: stowaways@cox.net. *

FLEMING, WILLIAM WRIGHT, JR., retired pharmacology professor; b. Washington, Jan. 30, 1932; s. William Wright and Esme (Reeder) F.; m. Dolores D. Atchison, Sept. 1, 1952; children: Lisa Marie, Jennifer Amelia, David William. AB cum laude, Harvard U., 1954; PhD (Procter fellow), Princeton U., 1957. Mem. faculty W.Va. U. Med. Ctr., Morgantown, 1960—, prof. pharmacology, 1966—, chmn. dept., 1966-86, Mylan Chmn. of Pharmacology and Toxicology, 1986-99, prof. emeritus, 1999—. Vis. prof. U. Melbourne, Australia, 1969, St. George's Hosp. Med. Sch. U. London, 1978, Flinders U., Adelaide, Australia, 1985, 87, U. Adelaide, 1987; adj. prof. pharmacology U. Pitts. Sch. Medicine, 2005-; cons. Mead Johnson Rsch. Ctr., Evansville, Ind., 1970-77, Spriggs & Hollingsworth Law Firm, Washington, 2004-06; mem. pharmacology-toxicology rsch. program. Nat. Inst. Gen. Med. Scis., NIH, 1973-77, chmn., 1975-77; mem. drug abuse rsch. rev. com. Nat. Inst. Drug Abuse, 1985-89; mem. pharmacology study sect., div. rsch. grants NIH, 1990-94. Mem. editl. bd. Jour. Pharmacology and Exptl. Therapeutics, 1966-85, Life Scis., 1978-90; contbr. articles to profl. jours. USPHS postdoctoral fellow Harvard U., 1957-60; Fogarty sr. internat. fellow, 1978; recipient P.L. MacLachlan award W.Va. U. Med. Sch., 1964, 67, 78, 89, 92, 97, 99; named Outstanding Tchr., W.Va. U. Found., 1978. Mem. AAAS, Am. Soc. Pharmacology and Exptl. Therapeutics (councilor 1975-78, pres. 1981-82, chmn. bd publs. trustees 1984-90, Otto Krayer award 1986, Croker Meml. lectr. 1988, Torald Sollman award 1999), Assn. Med. Sch. Pharmacology (councilor 1977-79, treas. 1977-78, pres. 1986-88), Fedn. Am. Socs. for Exptl. Biology (dir. 1980-83), Internat. Union Pharmacology (del. 1980-83, 91-94, mem. internat. adv. com. for Congress of Pharmacology 1987, exec. com. 1994-98, 2002—06, pres. 1998-2002). Office: WVa U Health Scis Ctr Dept Physiology & Pharmacology Morgantown WV 26506 Home: 1586 Hunter Station Rd Tionesta PA 16353 Personal E-mail: wfle216184@aol.com.

FLEMMING, DAVID PAUL, biologist; b. Kittanning, Pa., Oct. 23, 1953; s. Paul Ross and Jeanne Marie (Seaton) F.; m. Diane Frances MacKenzie, Sept. 17, 1983; children: Daniel Robert, Peter David. BS in Biology, Grove City Coll., 1975; MS in Biology, Bowling Green State U., 1977. Child care worker George Jr. Rep., Grove City, Pa., 1978-79; park naturalist State of Pa.-McConnell's Mill State Park, Portersville, 1979; biologist sect. 7 U.S. Fish & Wildlife Svc., Washington, 1979-80, Atlanta, 1980-83, recovery coord. Denver, 1983-87, biologist endangered species Vero Beach, Fla., 1987-88, chief divsn. endangered species Atlanta, 1988-96, chief ecol. svcs., 1997-98, ecol. svcs. supr., 1998—. Contbg. author: Conservation and Resource Management, 1993. Asst. coach T-ball and soccer YMCA, Lawrenceville, Ga., 1991—92, premier soccer coach Snellville, Ga., 1995—2001; USS Ofcl., 1996—2003. Business E-Mail: dave_flemming@fws.gov.

FLESHMAN, JAMES W., medical association administrator; b. New Orleans, Aug. 2, 1954; BA summa cum laude, Wash. U., 1975; MD, Wash. U., St. Louis, 1980. Surgery residency Jewish Hosp., St. Louis, 1980—86; fellowship colon & rectal surgery U. Toronto, 1986—87; now prof. surgery Wash. U. Sch. of Medicine, St. Louis; chief colon & rectal surgery. Mem.: Am. Soc. Colon and Rectal Surgeons (sec.), Am. Bd. Surgery. Office: Wash U Sch of Medicine Box 8109 660 S Euclid Campus Saint Louis MO 63110 Home Phone: 314-878-9030; Office Phone: 314-454-7204.

FLETCHER, JAMES, radiologist, educator; b. Belleville, Ill., Sept. 6, 1943; MD, St. Louis U., 1968. Prof. radiology Ind. U. Sch. Medicine, 2000—. Fellow: Am. Coll. Radiology; mem.: SNM, Am. Bd. Nuc. Medicine (life). Avocations: skiing, motorcycling, sailing. Office: University Hosp Rm 0655 550 N University Blvd Indianapolis IN 46202 Business E-Mail: jwfletch@iupui.edu.

FLETCHER, ROBERT HILLMAN, medical educator; b. Abington, Pa., Mar. 26, 1940; s. Stevenson Whitcomb and Wanda (Moss) F.; m. Suzanne Wright, June 15, 1963; children: John Wright, Grant Selmer BA, Wesleyan U., Middletown, Conn., 1962; MD, Harvard U., 1966; MSc, Johns Hopkins U., 1973. Diplomate Am. Bd. Internal Medicine. Intern, resident in medicine Stanford U. Hosp., Palo Alto, Calif., 1967-68; resident in medicine Balt. City Hosp., 1971-73, asst. prof. faculty of medicine McGill U., Montreal, Que., Canada, 1973-78; assoc. prof. medicine Sch. Medicine U. N.C., Chapel Hill, 1978-83, prof. medicine, clin. prof. epidemiology, 1983-90, dir. Robert Wood Johnson Clin. Scholars Program, 1983-90, co-dir. Clin. Epidemiology Resource and Tng. Ctr., Internat. Clin. Epidemiology Network, 1986-90; assoc. exec. v.p. ACP, Phila., 1990-92, sr. v.p., 1992-93; prof. Harvard Med. Sch., Boston, 1994—; assoc. med. dir. clin. edn. Harvard Pilgrim Health Care, Boston, 1998, dir. tchg. ctr., dept. ambulatory care and prevention, 1992—2002. Bd. dirs. INCLEN Inc., chmn., 1993-97. Sr. author: Clinical Epidemiology, The Essentials, 1982, 2d edit., 1988, 3d edit., 1996; co-editor: Jour. Gen. Internal Medicine, 1984-89, Annals of Internal Medicine, 1990-93; primary care editor UpToDate, 1997-. Served to maj. M.C., U. S. Army, 1968-71. Master ACP; mem. Am. Pub. Health Assn., Soc. Gen. Internal Medicine (pres. 1991-92), Phi Beta Kappa, Sigma Xi. Democrat. Mem. Soc. Of Friends. Home: 208 Boulder Bluff Chapel Hill NC 27516 Office: Dept Ambulatory Care/Prevention 133 Brookline Ave 6th Fl Boston MA 02215-3920 E-mail: robert_fletcher@hms.harvard.edn.

FLETCHER, RONALD DARLING, microbiologist educator; b. Foxboro, Mass., Jan. 18, 1933; s. Howard Wendel and Ada Louise (Darling) F.; m. Barbara Gundersen, Jan. 30, 1954; children: Deborah, Mark Ronald, Christopher Gary. BS, U. Conn., 1954, MS, 1959, PhD, 1963. Dog trainer AKC Obedience Trials, Slater Pk. Animal Rescue Facility, Pawtucket, RI, 1947—50; mule skinner U.S. Forest Svc., St. Maries, Idaho, 1952; instr. U. Conn., Storrs, 1959-63; rschr. Am. Cyanamid Co., Pearl River, N.Y., 1964-67; dir. microbiology McKeesport Hosp., Pa., 1971-79; prof., assoc. chair dept. microbiology U. Pitts., 1967—86, prof. microbiology dept. clin. lab. scis., 1989—; assoc. dir. Armed Forces Med. Intelligence Ctr. Dept. Def., Frederick, Md., 1984—85, sr. analyst Armed Forces Med. Intelligence Ctr., 1986—89; v.p. Affordable Tech., Inc., Pitts., 1990—91; exec. v.p. ATI Bioremediation, Inc., Pitts., 1991—92; cons. pathobiology U. Conn., 2008—. Biotech. steering com. U.S. Dept. Def., 1987-89; cons. U.S. Army, Frederick, 1978-82, Mellon Inst., Pitts., 1981, Cons.'s Brokerage, Mountain View, Calif., 1981, Battelle Meml. Inst., Columbus, Ohio, 1989-90. Contbr. articles to profl. jours. Judge Internat. Sci. and Engring. Fair, Mpls., 1980, Milw., 1981, Dallas, 1982, Nat. Jr. Sci. and Humanities Symposium, West Point, N.Y., 1983, 85; dept. state lectr. med. schs. in Ankara and Istanbul, Turkey, 1982. Col. USA & USAR, 1954-85. USPHS fellow U. Zurich, Switzerland, 1963-64; grantee U.S. Army, Am. Cancer Soc., NIH; Postdoctoral fellow U. Saskatchewan, Can., 1965, Harvard Med. Sch., 1966, cert. of achievement in microbiology Surgeon Gen. U.S. Army, 1973, Disting. Alumni award, U. Conn., Storrs, 2008. Fellow AAAS, Am. Acad. Microbiology (registered microbiologist, specialist microbiologist); mem. Internat. Assn. Dental Research (pres. Pitts. 1979-80), ADA, Assn. Mil. Surgeons, Am. Soc. Microbiologists, N.Y. Acad. Scis., Am. Soc. for Cell Biology, Nat. Mil. Intelligence Assn., Internat. Assn. Chiefs of Police, Am. Legion Personal E-mail: fletchuconn@yahoo.com.

FLETCHER, SUZANNE WRIGHT, epidemiologist, medical educator, editor; b. Jacksonville, Fla., Nov. 14, 1940; d. Robert Dean and Helen (Selmer) Wright; m. Robert H. Fletcher; children: John Wright, Grant Selmer. BA, Swarthmore Coll., 1962; MD, Harvard Med. Sch., 1966; MSc, Johns Hopkins U., 1973. Diplomate Nat. Bd. Med. Examiners, Am. Bd. Internal Medicine. Intern Stanford (Calif.) U. Med. Ctr., 1966—67, resident, 1967—68; physician 22nd med. detachment U.S. Army, New Ulm, Germany, 1969—70; asst. prof. epidemiology and health Mc Gill U., Montreal, Canada, 1974—77, assoc. prof., 1977—78, asst. prof. medicine, 1973—78; dir. med. clinic dept. medicine NC Meml. Hosp., 1978—82; assoc. prof. medicine U. NC, 1978—83, co-chief divsn. gen. medicine and clin. epidemiology dept. medicine, 1978—86, rsch. assoc. health svcs. rsch. ctr., 1978—90, vice chmn. clin. svcs., 1981—90, prof. medicine, clin. prof. epidemiology, 1983—90, program dir. faculty devel. gen. medicine and gen. pediatrics, 1985—90, co-dir. internat. clin. epidemiology network program Rockefeller Found., 1986—90; prof. ambulatory care and prevention Harvard Med. Sch., 1994, prof. emerita ambulatory care and prevention. Adj. prof. medicine U. Pa., Phila., 1990—93, Jefferson Med. Coll., 1991—93, U. NC, 1994—; physician internal medicine; chmn. NIH Tech. Assessment Conf., 1992, Nat. Cancer Inst. Internat. Workshop, 1993; faculty World Bank Seminar on Preventive Strategies in Med. Edn., Hangzhou, China, 1986; active Ad Hoc NCI Com. on Breast Cancer Detection Rsch., 1986; chair Macy Conf. on Continuing Edn. of Health Profls., 2007. Author: Clinical Epidemiology—The Essentials, 1982, 4t edit., 2005; editor: Annals of Internal Medicine, 1990—93; contbr. chapters to books, articles to profl. jours. Recipient Can. Nat. Health Rsch. Scholar award, Can. Govt., 1975—78; named rsch. grantee, Conseil de la Recherche en Sante du Quebec, 1975—77; grantee, Health and Welfare Can., 1976—78, Robert Wood Johnson Teaching Hosp. Gen. Medicine Group Practice Program, 1980—84, Nat. Ctr. Health Scis. Rsch. and Health Tech., 1985—89, Rockefeller Found. Clin. Epidemiology Resource and Tng. Ctr., 1986—90, NIH, 1987—90, 1997—. Master: ACP (med. knowledge self assessment program 1984—85, clin. practice subcom. 1987, pub. policy subcom. 1988—89); fellow: Coll. Physicians Phila., Am. Coll. Epidemiology (bd. dirs. 1990—93, chmn. pub. com. 1992—94); mem.: APHA, Am. Bd. Internal Medicine (bd. govs. 1981—87), NCI Bd. Sci. Advisors, World Assn. Med. Editors (v.p. 1997—2001), Internat. Clin. Epidemiology Network (bd. dirs.), Inst. Medicine (coun. 1993—96, exec. com. 1993—96), Soc. Gen. Internal Medicine (counsellor 1978—81, pres.-elect 1982—83, pres. 1983—84, co-editor Jour. Gen. Internal Medicine 1984—89, mem. publs. com. 1990—, chmn. Glaser award com. 1991). Unitarian Universalist. Home: 208 Boulder Bluff Trail Chapel Hill NC 27516-9652

FLETCHER, THOMAS B., physician; b. Houston, Dec. 2, 1953; BA, Vanderbilt U., 1976; MD, UT Southwestern, 1983. Sr. ptnr. Austin Radiol. Assn., 1989—. Past v.p., pres., bd. dirs. Tex. Radiol. Soc., 2003—09. Recipient Gold medal, Tex. Radiol. Soc. Fellow: Am. Coll. Radiology; mem.: Phi Beta Kappa, Alpha Omega Alpha. Avocations: bicycling, rock climbing. Home: 2206 E Windsor Rd Austin TX 78703 Home Fax: 512-771-6783. Personal E-mail: fletchertmd@gmail.com.

FLICK, FERDINAND HERMAN, surgeon, preventive medicine physician; b. Bklyn., Feb. 19, 1925; s. Paul Albert and Elizebeth Kath (Herz) F.; m. Marie T. Flick, Apr. 7, 1945; children: Paul, Ferdinand, Annette Flick Riddle. BS, MS, Fordham U.; MD, Yale U., 1951. Diplomate Am. Bd. Preventive Medicine. Intern SUNY Downstate, 1951-52; resident in ob-gyn Coll. Physicians & Surgeons Columbia U., NYC, 1952; asst. prof. Columbia U. Coll. Physicians & Surgeons, NYC, 1959-62; surgeon 77th Divsn. USAR, NYC, 1962-76; chief plant physician Fort Motor Co., Mahwah, N.J., 1976-80, Edison, N.J., 1980—. Asst. prof. U. Calif., Berkeley, 1946-47; trauma lectr. Middlesex C.C., 1984-85. Contbr. articles to profl. jours. including Nature and Am. Jour. Ob-gyn. Mem. smoking intervention team Am. Cancer Soc., New Brunswick, N.J., 1993-95. Col. USAR, 1946-76. Decorated Meritorious Svc. medal. Mem. Am. Coll. Occupl. and Environ. Medicine, Am. Coll. Preventive Medicine, Am. Soc. Abdominal Surgeons, Sigma Xi (Yale chpt.). Avocations: hunting, skiing. Home: 233 Evans Ave Piscataway NJ 08854-2937 *

FLICKINGER, JOHN C., radiation oncologist; Attended, U. Chgo., Chgo. Cert. therapeutic radiology. Resident Mass. Gen. Hosp., Boston; with radiation oncology dept. Univ. of Pitts. Med. Ctr. Office: University of Pittsburgh Physicians Department of Radiation Oncology 5230 Centre Ave Pittsburgh PA 15232 Office Phone: 412-623-6720.

FLIER, JEFFREY S., dean, endocrinologist, educator; b. NYC, 1948; BS in Biology, CCNY, 1968; MD, Mt. Sinai Sch. Medicine, 1972; MD (hon.), U. Athens, 1997. Diplomate Am. Bd. Internal Medicine. Intern Mt. Sinai Hosp., NYC, 1972—73, resident in internal medicine, 1973—74; fellow in endocrinology NIH, Bethesda, Md., 1974—77; asst. prof. medicine Harvard Med. Sch., Boston, 1978—82, assoc. prof. medicine, 1982—93, prof. medicine, 1993—, George C. Reisman prof. medicine, 1999, dean, 2007—, Caroline Shields Walker prof. medicine; chief diabetes unit Beth Israel Hosp., Boston, 1978—90, chief divsn. endocrinology, 1990—2000; vice chair for rsch. dept. medicine Beth Israel Deaconess Med. Ctr., Boston, 1998—2002, chair rsch. strategy com., 1999, Harvard faculty dean academic programs, 2000, chief acad. officer, 2002. Vis. scientist Whitehead Inst., MIT, Cambridge, Mass., 1985—86; lectr. in field; Smith Kline Beecham vis. prof. U. Cambridge, 1998. Contbr. articles to profl. jours. Recipient Eli Lilly award for outstanding sci. achievement, Am. Diabetes Assn., 1991, Transatlantic medal, Brit. Endocrine Soc., 2004. Fellow: Am. Acad. Arts and Scis., AAAS; mem.: Assn. of Am. Physicians, Inst. Medicine (life; pres. 2001), Inter Urban Clin. Club. Avocations: golf, skiing. Office: Flier Lab Research North 390 99 Brookline Ave Boston MA 02215 also: Harvard Medicial School Gordon Hall 25 Shattuck St Boston MA 02115 Office Phone: 617-667-8575. Office Fax: 617-667-2927. E-mail: jflier@bidmc.harvard.edu. *

FLOARES, ALEXANDRU GEORGE, neurologist, researcher; b. Iasi, Moldova, Romania, Apr. 15, 1961; s. Gheorghe and Valeria Floares; m. Carmen Elena Ganea, Aug. 17, 2002. MD, U. Medicine and Pharmacy, Iasi, Romania, 1986. Neurology Specialist U. of Medicine and Pharmacy, Iasi, Romania, 1986; Certificate of attendance Neural Networks in Classification, Regression & Data Mining, Portugal, 2002, Participation Certificate Internat. Sch. on Neural Nets E.R.Caianiello, Italy, 2002, Math. Seminar Al. Myller, Iasi, Romania, 1984. Head dept. Artificial Intelligence Dept., Romanian Soc. Surg. Oncology, Cluj-Napoca, Transilvania, Romania, 2000—05; pres. S.A.I.A. Solutions of Artificial Intelligence Applications, Cluj-Napoca, Transilvania, Romania, 2003—. Coord. Artificial Intelligence Dept.-Oncological Inst. Cluj - Napoca, Transilvania, Romania, 2005—. Mem.: IEEE Computational Intelligence Soc., Assn. Computing Machinery, Romanian Soc. Med. Oncology, Romanian Soc. Med. Informatics, Internat. Neural Networks Soc. Eastern Orthodox. Achievements include research in intelligent systems for medical diagnostic, prognostic, optimization and individualization of therapeutic strategies; developing methods for automatic mathematical modeling of complex biomedical data; founding knowledge based medicine; developing biomarker, oncologist concepts, and the first complete intelligent system for clinical decision support in bladder cancer-diagnostics, prognosis, recurrence and survival. Avocations: swimming, travel, computer games. Home: G-ral Eremia Grigorescu Transilvania Cluj-Napoca 400299 Romania Office: Oncolog Inst Cluj-Napoca Republicii Nr 34-36 400015 Cluj-Napoca 400015 Romania Office Fax: 40 264 580177; Home Fax: 40 264 420621. Personal E-mail: alexandru_floares@ieee.org. Business E-Mail: alexandru.floares@iocn.ro, alexandru.floares@oncopredict.com.

FLOCH, MARTIN HERBERT, physician; b. NYC, July 24, 1928; s. Samuel and Jean (Scheinman) F.; m. Gladys Wisser, Nov. 24, 1954; children: Jeffrey Aaron, Craig Lawrence, Lisa Suzanne, Neil Robert. BA, NYU, 1949; MS, U. N.H., 1950; MD, N.Y. Med. Coll., 1956. Diplomate: Am. Bd. Internal Medicine, Am. Bd. Gastroenterology Am. Bd. Nutrition. Intern Beth Israel Hosp., NYC, 1956-57, resident in medicine, 1957-59; fellow in gastroenterology Seton Hall Coll. Medicine, South Orange, NJ, 1959-60; instr. medicine U. P.R., 1960-62; asst. attending physician Montefiore Hosp., NYC, 1962-64; mem. staff Norwalk Hosp., 1964—, chmn. dept. medicine, 1970-94, chief gastroenterology and nutrition, 1970-98; clin. prof. medicine Yale U., New Haven, 1976—, dir. ambulatory gastroenterology svcs., 2005—11, clin. conf. coord., 2011—. Bd. dirs. Norwalk Bank, 1987. Editor Am. Jour. Gastroenterology, 1985-91, The Gastroenterologist, 1992-98; asst. editor Am. Jour. Clin. Nutrition; editor-in-chief Jour. of Clin. Gastroenterology, 1998—; contbr. articles in field to profl. jours. Trustee Aspetuck Valley Health Dist., 1974-76, Norwalk Hosp., 1972-78. Served with M.C. U.S. Army, 1960-62. Grantee, Conn. Digestive Disease Soc., 1974—76, NIH, 1975—78, Leslie Found., 1980, Ednl. Found. Am., 1989—92, 2001—03; U.S. Army Med. Rsch. grantee, 1964—67. Fellow ACP, Master Am. Coll. Gastroenterology (bd. trustees 1985-90), Am. Soc. Gastroendoscopy, Am. Coll. Nutrition; mem. Am. Soc. Clin. Nutrition, Am. Inst. Nurtition, Am. Gastroenterology Assn. (clin. counselor governing bd. 1997-2000), Am. Fedn. Clin. Rsch., Fairfield County Med. Soc., Conn. Med. Soc. (pres. gastroenterology sect. 1972-74), Assn. Am. Med. Coll., Conn. Digestive Disease Soc. (pres. 1972-74), Am. Gastro. Assn. Home: 32 Woody Ln Westport CT 06880-2259 Office: Digestive Disease Sect Yale U Sch Medicine 40 Temple St Ste1A New Haven CT 06510 Home Phone: 203-227-3646; Office Phone: 203-785-4138. Business E-Mail: martin.floch@yale.edu.

FLOCH-BAILLET, DANIELE LUCE, ophthalmologist; b. Brest, France, Jan. 9, 1948; d. Herve Alexandre and Lucie (Henry) Floch; m. Gilles Pierre Baillet, Dec. 6, 1980; 1 child, Victoire-Amelie. MD, Med. U. Brest, 1972. Cert. in ophthalmology, 1975. Med. cons. ophthalmology Brest Hosp., 1976-85; gen. practice ophthalmology Landivisiau, France, 1977—. Researcher ophthalmic bacteriology, 1985—. Author: (with P. Francois) Nosological Outlines from Coats, 1975, Exsudation from Coats, 1976. Mem. French Ophthalmologist Soc., European Contact Lenses Soc. Ophthalmologists, Nat. Syndicat French Ophthalmology, Contact Lens Assn. Ophthalmologists, Assn. Ophthalmologic Improvement from East-Paris. Roman Catholic. Home: 11 Rue Creach Joly 29600 Morlaix France Office: 7 Rue Georges Pompidou 29400 Landivisiau France Home Phone: 0298621658; Office Phone: 0298680673.

FLOMENBERG, NEAL, oncologist, educator; BS, Pa. State U., 1974; MD, Thomas Jefferson U., 1976. Diplomate Am. Bd. Internal Medicine, Am. Bd. Internal Medicine-med. oncology, Am. Bd. Internal Medicine-hematology. Intern Albert Einstein Coll. of Medicine, NY, resident NY; intern Bronx Mcpl. Hosp., Bronx, NY; fellow Meml. Sloan Kettering Med. Ctr., NY, rsch. fellow NY, 1980—81, rsch. assoc. NY, 1981—84; instr. medicine Cornell Univ. Med. Coll., 1981—82, assoc. prof. medicine, 1990—91; asst. attending physician Meml. Hosp. for Cancer and Allied Diseases, NY, 1982—90, clin. asst. physician NY; prof. medicine and microbiology Wis. Med. Coll.; dir. hematologic malignancies and hematopoietic stem cell transplant program Thomas Jefferson Univ. Hosp., 1994—; acting dir. Jefferson Med. Coll., 2001—03, dir. divsn. med. oncology, 2003—06, prof. med. oncology and microbiology and immunology, interim chair, dept. med. oncology, 2006—; hosp. affiliations include Thomas Jefferson Univ. Hosp., Methodist Hosp. Divsn. of Thomas Jefferson Univ. Hosp.; clin. dep. dir. Kimmel Cancer Ctr. Recipient Svc. to Mankind award, Leukemia and Lymphoma Soc., 2006, Gratz award, Thomas Jefferson Univ.; named Man of the Year for Eastern Pa., Leukemia and Lymphoma Soc., 2003, outstanding alumnus, Pa. State Univ., 2006; named one of Top Docs, Phila. Mag, 2010. Office: Thomas Jefferson University Hospital Ste 220A 925 Chestnut St Philadelphia PA 19107 Office Phone: 215-955-8874. Office Fax: 215-503-7697.

FLOOD, DOROTHY GARNETT, neuroscientist; m. Paul David Coleman, Feb. 26, 1983 (div. 2006). BA cum laude, Lawrence U., 1973; student, U. Ill., 1972-73; MS, PhD, U. Rochester, NYC, 1980. Sr. instr. in anatomy U. Rochester, 1980-83, asst. prof. neurology, neurobiology and anatomy, 1984-90, assoc. prof. neurology, neurobiology and anatomy, 1990-94; sr. sci. Cephalon, Inc., West Chester, Pa., 1994—. Contbr. to book chpts. and articles in field; mem. editl. bd. Neurobiology of Aging, 1997—. Recipient Fenn award U. Rochester, 1980; grantee NSF, NIH, Office of Naval Rsch., 1979-94. Mem. Soc. Neurosci. Office: Cephalon Inc 145 Brandywine Pkwy West Chester PA 19380-4249 Business E-Mail: dflood@cephalon.com.

FLOR, HERTA, psychology professor; BA, U. Würzburg, Germany, 1977; diploma, U. Tübingen, Germany, 1981, PhD, 1984. Postdoctoral fellow Yale U., New Haven, 1983-84; asst. prof. U. Bonn, Germany, 1984-85; vis. asst. prof. U. Pitts., 1985—87; asst. prof. U. Tübingen, 1987—90; vis. prof. U. Marburg, Germany, 1990-91; Heisenberg fellowship U. Tübingen, 1991-93; assoc. prof. Humboldt U., Berlin, 1993-94, prof., 1995—2000; prof. neurosci. U. Heidelberg Ctrl. Inst. Mental Health, Mannheim, Germany, 2000—. Author: Psychobiology of Pain, 1991. Recipient Pain Rsch. prize German Pain Soc., 1992, 2000, prize for clin. rsch., Smithkline Beecham Found., 1996, Sertürner award for pain rsch., 1999, Max-Planck Rsch. prize, 2000, Muscle Pain Rsch. award, 2001, German Psychology prize, 2002, Basic Rsch. award German Fed. State Baden-Württemberg, 2004; fellow Deutsche Forschungsgemeinschaft, 1987-90. Mem. AAAS, Internat. Assn. Study of Pain, Soc. for Psychophysiol. Rsch., Soc. for Neurosci. Achievements include research in psychophysiology and behavioral treatments of chronic pain; role of cortical reorganiztion in chronic pain, especially phantom limb pain; emotional learning; psychophysiology and therapy of anxiety disorders, tinnitus, drug addiction; brain computer interfaces. Office: U Heidelberg/Ctrl Inst Mental Health J5 Dept Clin & Cognitive Neuroscience 68159 Mannheim Germany Business E-Mail: herta.flor@zi-mannheim.de.

FLORENTIN, MATILDA, internist; b. Greece, Sept. 9, 1981; MD, U. Ioannina, 2005. Officer, dept. internal medicine U. Hosp. Ioannina, 2010. Office: University Hosp Ioannina Ioannina 45221 Greece Personal E-mail: matildaflorentin@yahoo.com.

FLORES, ROSEANNE L., psychology professor; b. Kings County, Calif., July 3, 1959; PhD, Grad. Sch. and U. Ctr., CUNY, 1993. Asst. prof. Hunter Coll., CUNY, 1994—2007, assoc. prof., 2007—. Nat. Head Start fellowship, Office of Head Start, Adminstrn. Children and Families. Mem.: APA (mem., children, youth and families com., mem., Leadership Inst. Women Psychology 2011), Eastern Psychol. Assn. Avocations: reading, hiking. Office: Hunter Coll 695 Park Ave New York NY 10065 Office Fax: 212-772-5620. Business E-Mail: rflores@hunter.cuny.edu.

FLÓREZ, ÁNGELES, dermatologist, consultant; b. Oviedo, Spain, Apr. 4, 1972; MD, Oviedo U., Spain, 1996; PhD in Dermatology, Santiago de Compostela U., Spain, 2000. Resident in dermatology-physician Santiago de Compostela Hosp., 1996—2000; cons. dermatologist Pontevedra Hosp. -CHOP, Spain, 2000—. Dermatoblog webmaster Ferrer, 2010—11. Mem.: Spanish Acad. Dermatology and Venereology. Avocations: swimming, reading, travel. Office: Hosp Provincial Loureiro Crespo 2 Pontevedra 36001 Spain Office Fax: 34986807029. Business E-Mail: angeles.florez@telefonica.net.

FLORI, ANNA MARIE DIBLASI, health facility administrator, nurse, anesthesiologist; b. Amsterdam, NY, Oct. 29, 1940; d. Tony Flori and Maria (Macario) DiBlasi Flori; m. Gilberto Flori Flori, May 24, 1986; children: Tammy, Tina, Toni. Degree, Albany Med. Ctr. Sch. Nursing, 1962, Fairfax Hosp. Sch. Nurse Anesthetists, Va., 1972; BS in Anesthesia, George Washington U., 1979; M in Bus. & Pub. Adminstrn., Southeastern U., Washington, 1982; PhD, Columbia Pacific U., 1983. Cert. anesthetist; RN. Staff nurse West Seattle Gen. Hosp., 1962—64; nurse Filmore Buckner, Md., Seattle, 1964—66; staff nurse anesthetist Fairfax Hosp., 1972—73, Potomac Hosp., Woodbridge, Va., 1973; chief nurse anesthetist, 1973—; dir. Potomac Hosp. Sch. for Nurse Anesthetists & Sch. for Nurse Anesthesia; faculty mem. Columbia Pacific U., 1973—90; chief nurse anesthetist No. Va. Anesthesia Assn., 1988—; guest lectr No. Va. CC; guest lectr. Inservice Potomac Hosp., George Washington U. Contbr. articles to profl. jours. Mem.: Nat. Italian Am. Found., Va. Nurse Anesthesia Assn., Am. Assn. Nurse Anesthetists. Home: 12954 Pintail Rd Woodbridge VA 22192-3831 Office Phone: 703-490-5496. Personal E-mail: crnhamf@aol.com.

FLORIAN-LACY, DOROTHY, psychologist, educator; b. Dearborn, Mich., Oct. 27, 1958; d. Raymond Joseph and Dorothy Mae Florian; m. Bill George Lacy, July 25, 1981; children: Jason M., Miles, Anderson. BS in Psychology and Edn., Ea. Mich. U., Ypsilanti, 1978, MA in Guidance and Counseling, 1979; EdD in Counselor Edn., Tex. Southeastern U., 1998. Lic. profl. counselor, Tex. Realtor Century 21, Ann Arbor, Mich., 1978—79; tchr. Adult Exception Ctr., Compton, Calif., 1979—81; owner, dir. Village Learning & Play Ctr., Houston, 1982—94; dept. chair spl. edn. Milby Sr. H.S., Houston, 1994—2000; therapist Houston Achievement Place, 1998—; speicalist in sch. psychology Spring Branch Independent Sch. District, 2010—. Author: Fundamentals of Mathematics I, Fundamentals of Mathematics II, Consumer Math; co-author: Reference Manual for Special Education Department Chairpersons. Vol. Child Abuse Prevention, Houston, 1989-91, vol. coach YMCA, Houston, 1987-90. Recipient Adaptor grant Impact II, 1997, Study Group grant Impact II, 1998. Mem. ACA, Children's Mus Avocation: golf coach. Office: Houston Achievement Place 236 W 17th St Houston TX 77008-4002 Office Phone: 713-868-2909 ext. 272. Personal E-mail: dflorian@houstonisd.org. Business E-Mail: dlacy@hapkids.org.

FLOTTE, TERENCE ROBIN, dean, researcher, medical educator; b. New Orleans, Dec. 4, 1961; s. Arthur Victor and Marie Therese (Indest) F.; children: David Edward, Lindsay Hanna, Jesse Cole. BS summa cum laude, U. New Orleans, 1982; MD, La. State U., 1986. Diplomate Am. Bd. Pediatrics, subspecialty in pulmonary pediatrics. Pediatric resident Johns Hopkins Hosp., Balt., 1986-89; pediatric pulmonary fellow Johns Hopkins U., Balt., 1989-92, instr., 1992-93, asst. prof., 1993-96; postdoctoral rsch. fellow NIH, Bethesda, Md., 1989-92; asst. prof. pediats. and molecular genetics U. Fla. Coll. Medicine, Gainesville, 1996—98, co-dir. Powell Gene Therapy Ctr., 1996—2000, dir. Powell Gene Therapy Ctr., 2000—02, dir. Genetics Inst., 2000—02, prof., chmn. pediat., 2002—07; dean Sch. Med., provost, exec. dep. chancellor U. Mass. Med. Sch., Worcester, 2007—. Contbr. articles to profl. jours. Recipient Leroy Mathews Physician Scientist award Cystic Fibrosis Found., 1991, Chancellor's award La. State U. Sch. Medicine, 1986, E. Mead Johnson award, 2005; NIH CF Gene Therapy Ctr. Rsch. grantee, 1993; Nemours Eminent scholar. Mem. AMA, Am. Thoracic Soc., Alpha Omega Alpha. Roman Catholic. Achievements include research on first NIH recombinant DNA advisory committee - approved gene therapy protocol using an adeno-associated virus vector in humans; inventor 5 patents of AAV-Vectors for cystic fibrosis gene therapy and production process for these vectors. Office: Office of Dean U Mass Med Sch 55 Lake Ave N Worcester MA 01655 Office Phone: 508-856-2107, 508-856-8000. Business E-Mail: terry.flotte@umassmed.edu. *

FLOWER, DAVID JOHN COLIN, physician; b. London, June 7, 1956; s. Ernest Alfred and Mary Rosina Flower; m. Harriett Ann Sinclair, June 6, 1987; children: Alice Elizabeth Caroline, Edward George Hugo. BSc in Engring., U. Coll., London, 1974—77, MB, BS, 1977—82; MD, United Med. and Dental Schs. Guy's and St Thomas' Hosps., London, 1993—96. Diplomate Royal Coll. Obstetricians and Gynecologists, 1986, in aviation medicine 1999, accredited specialist in occupl. medicine Tng. Authority Med. Royal Colls., 1997. Ho. physician St. Charles Hosp., London, 1982—83; ho. surgeon U. Coll. Hosp., London, 1983—83; resident med. officer The London Clinic, 1983—84; trainee Gen. Practice Vocat. Tng. Program, Cheltenham and Gloucester, England, 1984—88; prin. in gen. practice Newbury St. Practice, Wantage, Oxfordshire, England, 1988—91; sr. registrar in occupl. medicine U.K. Atomic Energy Authority, Harwell, Oxfordshire, England, 1991—94, Brit. Airways plc, London, 1994—96, cons. in occupl. medicine, 1996—2000, sr. cons. in occupl. medicine, 2000—02; group head occupl. health Centrica plc, Windsor, Berkshire, England, 2002—06; sr. health dir. BP plc, Sunbury, England, 2006—. Vis. lectr. U. Birmingham, England, 1992—94; mem. Assn. European Airlines European Commn. Task Force on Flight Time Limitations, Brussels, 1996—98; mem. Assn. European Airlines Reps. Joint Aviation Authorities Med. Sub-committee, Hoofddorp, Netherlands, 1996—2002; mem. U.K. Cosmic Radiation Adv. Group, London, 1998—2002; chmn., cosmic radiation group Assn. European Airlines, Brussels, 1998—2002, chmn., med. advisers group, 2000—02; mem., exercise physiology steering group Brit. Olympic Assn., London, 1998—2004; mem. sci. adv. bd. on alertness mgmt. Air Transport Assn. Am., Washington, 2000—02; chmn., med. adv. group Internat. Air Transport Assn., Geneva, 2001—02; steering com. mem. Flight Safety Found., Boeing, Airbus Industrie Ultra Long Range Ops. Workshop, Washington, Paris, Kuala Lumpur, 2001—03; mem. of the coun. of healthcare advisers Gerson Lehrman Group, NYC, 2003—09; cons. advisor U.K. Sport, London, 2004—08; mem. Am. Petroleum Inst. Fatigue Risk Mgmt. Com., Am. Coll. Occpl. & Environ. Medicine Pres. Task Force, Fatigue, 2010—11, Health Com. Internat. Assn. Oil & Gas Producers & Internat. Petroleum Industry Environ. Cons. Assn., 2011—. Contbr. chapters to books, articles to profl. jours. Fellow: Royal Coll. Physicians (faculty occupl. medicine), Royal Soc. Medicine (mem. coun. 2003, pres. sect. occupl. medicine 2005—06, v.p. sect. occupl. medicine 2006—), Am. Coll. Occupl. and Environ. Medicine; mem.: Royal Coll. Gen. Practitioners, Internat. Assn. Physicians of Overseas Svcs., Soc. Occupl. Medicine. Achievements include development of an alertness management program for flight and cabin crew for British Airways, plc and a fatigue risk management program for BP. Office: BP plc Chertsey Rd Sunbury-on-Thames TW16 7LN England Business E-Mail: david.flower@uk.bp.com.

FLOWERS, FRANKLIN P., dermatologist, educator; MD, U. Fla., 1971. Diplomate Am. Bd. Dermatology, 1976, Am. Bd. Pathology-dermatopathology, 1981. Intern Univ. Ky. Med. Ctr., 1971—72; resident dermatology Ohio State Univ., Columbus, Ohio, 1972—75; fellow mohs micrographic surgery and cutaneous oncology Univ. Ala., Birmingham, Ala., 1992—93; fellow Am. Coll. of Mohs Micrographic Surgery and Cutaneous Oncology, 1997, dir. dermatol. surg. tng. Univ. of Fla., med. dir. Dermatology and Skin Cancer Ctr., chief dermatology and cutaneous surgery divsn., prof. medicine, hosp. affiliation include Shands. Mailing: University FL Dermatology & Skin Cancer Clinic Park Ave 1014 NW 57th St Gainesville FL 32605 Office: Division of Dermatology & Cutaneous Surgery PO Box 100277 Gainesville FL 32610-0277 Office Phone: 352-265-8001, 352-392-4984 Office Fax: 352-392-5376.

FLOWERS, ROBERT SWAIM, medical educator, surgeon; b. Greenville, Ala., Sept. 13, 1934; m. Susan Flowers; children: Swaim, Rob, Christian, Jonathan. BS in Chemistry and Biology, U. Ala., 1955, MD, 1960. Diplomate Am. Bd. Plastic Surgery. Intern U.S. Army Tripler Med. Ctr., 1960-61; battle group surgeon U.S. Army, 1961-63; resident gen. surgery Cleve. Clinic, Ohio, 1963-66, resident plastic surgery Ohio, 1966-68; chmn. plastic surgery sect. Straub Clinic, Honolulu, 1968-72; chmn. dept. plastic surgery Queen's Med. Ctr., Honolulu, 1972-74; asst. clinical prof. plastic surgery U. Hawaii, 1971—; dir., prin. surgeon Plastic Surgery Ctr. of the Pacific Inc., Honolulu, 1975—2009; surgeon, dir. Flowers Clinic, Honolulu, 1993—. Chief, dir. Hawaii Postgrad. Fellowship Prog. Aesthetic & Asian Plastic Surgery; co-founder Gender Identity Clinic, Hawaii U.; vis. prof., lectr. Stanford U., U. Miami, U. Calif., Emory U., U. Zagreb, Yugoslavia, U. Munich, Germany, Columbia Presbyn. U., 1983, Duke U., 1985—86, Cleve. Clinic, 1985, UCLA, 1987, U. Louisville, U. Ala., Saarland U., Germany, 1993, U. Colo., 1994, U. Toronto, U. Manitoba. Contbr. articles to profl. jours., chapters to books. Pres. congregation, choir dir. Calvary By The Sea Luth. Ch., Honolulu, liturgist, lay minister, 1969—2004; bd. dirs. Honolulu Symphony, 2007. Recipient Renaissonce Plastic Surgeon of 20th Century award, Am. Soc. Ophthal. Plastic Surgery; named Top Plastic Surgeon in World, Japanese Soc., Best Aesthetic Surgeon, North America Soc. Austhetic Surgeons, Japanese Soc. Aesthetic Surgeons, 2001. Fellow: Am. Coll. Surgeons; mem.: AMA, Med. Assn. Ala., Pan-Pacific Surgical Assn., Internat. Soc. Clinical Plastic Surgeons, Internat. Soc. Aesthetic Plastic Surgeons, Honolulu County Med. Soc. (bd. govs. 1990—94), Hawaii Plastic Surgical Socs., Southeastern Soc. Plastic Surgeons (hon.), Australasian Soc. Aesthetics Plastic Surgery (hon.), Northwest Soc. Plastic Surgeons (hon.), Hawaii Med. Assn., Can. Soc. Aesthetic Plastic Surgeons, Calif. Soc. Plastic Surgeons, Oriental Soc. of Aesthetics, Am. Soc. Plastic Surgeons, Am. Assn. Plastic Surgeons, Honolulu Club, Waikiki Yacht Club, Outrigger Canoe Club. Avocations: drawing, painting, writing, sailing, singing, writing, sculpting. Office: Flowers Clinic 4627 Dolly Ridge Rd Birmingham AL 35243-2205 Home: 4627 Dolly Ridge Rd Birmingham AL 35243

FLOYD, CANDACE L., medical educator; b. Va., Feb. 29, 1968; PhD, Med. Coll. Va., Va. Commonwealth U., 2000. Postdoc. rsch. fellow U. Calif., Davis, 2001—04, asst. prof., 2004—06, U. Ala., Birmingham, 2006—. Cons. InQ Biosys., 2010. Various grants, Dept. Def. Congressionally Directed Med. Rsch. Programs, grant, NIH. Mem.: AAAS, Soc. Neurosci., Internat. Brain Injury Assn., Am. Spinal Injury Assn., Nat. Neurotrauma Soc. Avocations: bicycling, golf, kickboxing. Office: Spain Rehab Ctr 546 1717 6th Ave S Birmingham AL 35249-7330 Office Fax: 205-934-5086.

FLYE, M. WAYNE, surgeon, immunologist, educator, writer; b. Tarboro, NC, June 23, 1942; s. Charlie A. and Martha E. (Bullock) F.; m. Phyllis Webb, June 7, 1964; children: Christopher Warren, Brandon Reid. BS, U. N.C., 1964, MD, 1967; MA in Immunology, Duke U., 1972, PhD in Immunology, 1980; MA (hon.), Yale U., 1985. Diplomate Am. Bd. Surgery, Am. Bd. Thoracic Surgery, Am. Bd. Vascular Surgery. Intern. surg. Case-We. Res. U., Cleve., 1967-68, res. gen. and cardio-thoracic surgery, 1968-75; instr., teaching scholar, vascular and transplantation surgery Duke U. Med. Ctr., Durham, NC, 1975-76; sr. investigator, chief thoracic surg. svc. NIH, Bethesda, Md., 1977-79; chief vascular surgery U. Tex. Med. Br., Galveston, 1979-82, assoc. prof. surgery and microbiology, 1980-82; dir. div. organ transplantation and immunology, prof. transplantation, dir. sect. gen. surgery Yale U. Sch. Medicine, New Haven, 1983-85; prof. surgery, molecular microbiology and immunology Washington U. Med. Sch., St. Louis, 1985—, prof. radiology, 2000—, mem. admissions com., 2000—. Trustee New Eng. Organ Bank, Boston, 1984-85; com. mem. United Network Orgn. Sharing, Richmond, Va., 1986-89; mem. anesthesiology and trauma study sect. NIH Surgery, 1991-95; merit rev. com. for surgery VA, 1994-96, chmn., 1996—; merit rev. com. Am. Heart Assn. study sect., 2001--; chief of surgery St. Louis Regional Hosp., 1996; chief thoracic surgery St. Louis VA Hosp., 1996—. Editor: Principles of Organ Transplantation, 1989, The Thymus: Regulator of Cellular Immunity, 1993, Atlas of Organ Transplantation, 1994; mem. editl. bd. Clin. Transplantation, 1986—, Prospectives in Gen. Surgery, 1988-94, Transplantation, 1989-2000, Xanthus Intelligence Unit Reports, 1990—, Shock: Molecular, Cellular and Systemic Pathobiology of Injury, 1993-99, Transplantation Sci., 1993—, Jour. Surg. Rsch., 1995-2000, Surgery, 1997—, Graft, Jour. Organ and Cellular Transplantation, 1998—, New Surgery, 2000—; assoc. editor Jour. Immunology, 1996-99, Hepatology, 2003—. Lt. col. U.S. Army, 1976-78. Recipient James W. McLaughlin medal U. Tex.-Galveston, 1982. Fellow ACP, So. Thoracic Surg. Assn. (Best Sci. Paper award 1980); mem. Am. Assn. Immunologists, Internat. Cardiovascular Soc., N.Y. Acad. Sci., Soc. Thoracic Surgeons, Am. Soc. Transplant Physicians, Am. Soc. Transplant Surgeons (program com. 1984-86, Ethics Com. 1994-95), Brit. Soc. Immunology, Transplantation Soc., Mid-Am. Transplant Assn. (bd. dirs. 1986-89), Am. Fedn. Clin. Rsch., Royal Soc. Medicine, AAAS, Surg. Infection Soc. (edn. and fellowship com. 1998-2002), Reticuloendothelial Soc., Soc. Univ. Surgeons, Soc. Clin. Vascular Surgery, Brit. Transplantation Soc., So. Assn. Vascular Surgery, Am. Coll. Chest Physicians, Soc. Surg. Oncology, Am. Assn. Thoracic Surgery, Surg. Biology Club I, Am. Assn. Study Liver Diseases, Am. Surg. Assn., So. Surg. Assn., Cen. Surg. Assn., Soc. Internat. de Chirurgie, Midwestern Vascular Surg. Soc., Soc. Vascular Surg., World Ann. Hepato Pancreato-Bilary Surg., Soc. Surgery of Alimentary Tract, Shock Soc., Gen. Thoracic Surgery Club, Soc. Thoracic Surg., St. Louis Surg. Soc. (v.p. 2002-03, treas. 2003—), Sigma Xi, Alpha Omega Alpha., Chi Psi, Young Republicans N.C. Episcopalian. Avocations: sports, genealogy, medical history, scuba diving, beekeeping. Home: 385 Coeur De Royale Dr Apt 402 Saint Louis MO 63141-6915 Business E-Mail: flyew@wustl.edu.

FLYNN, JOANNA MARY, physician; b. Melbourne, Australia, Dec. 10, 1952; d. Daniel Mannix Flynn and Olive Monica O'Dwyer; life ptnr. Joan Lorraine Bruton. MBBS, U. Melbourne, 1975; MPH, Monash U., Melbourne, 1993. Diplomate RANZCOG, 1981. Gen. practitioner Grantham St. Gen. Practice, Brunswick West, Vic, Australia, 1991— Pres. Med. Practitioners Bd. Victoria, Melbourne, 2000—08, Australian Med. Coun., Canberra, 2003—08. Bd. mem. Star Sea Coll., Brighton, Vic, 2003—09; eastern health chair Med. Bd. Australia, 2009—. Recipient Ryan prize Surgery, U. Melbourne, 1975, Jacobson prize, 1975, Order of Australia, 2011. Fellow: Royal Australian Coll. Gen. Practitioners (state dir. 1989—98); mem.: Australian Med. Assn. Office: 69 Grantham St Victoria West Brunswick 3055 Australia Office Phone: 61-3-9380-1384. Business E-Mail: joanna.flynn@gsgp.com.au.

FLYNN, PATRICK ALEX, pediatric cardiologist; BS, Villanova U., Pa., 1982; MD, U. Md. Sch. Medicine, 1986. Cert. Am. Bd. Pediat., 1990, in pediatric cardiology 2006. Pediat. intern NY Presbyn. Weill Med. Coll., Cornell U., 1986—87, pediat. resident, 1987—89, pediat. chief resident, 1989—90, pediatric cardiology fellow, 1990—93, assoc. attending pediatrician. Assoc. prof. clin. pediat. Weill Cornell Med. Coll. Contbr. articles to profl. jours. Recipient Claire Lucille Pace Humanitarian award for participation in healing children, Guatemalan Heart Team, 1995, Outstanding Tchr. award, 1996, Excellence in Tchg. award, Weill Cornell Med. Coll., 2000. Mem.: Alpha Omega Alpha. Office: NY Presbyn Weill Med Coll Cornell U 525 E 68th St Ste F-677 New York NY 10065 Office Phone: 212-746-3561. Office Fax: 212-746-8373. Business E-Mail: paflynn@med.cornell.edu.

FOA, EDNA, psychologist, educator; b. 1937; BA in Psychology & Lit., Bar Ilan U., 1962; MA in Clinical Psychology, U. Ill., 1970; PhD in Clinical Psychology & Personality, U. Mo., 1970. Prof. clinical psychology U. Pa., dir. Ctr. for Treatment & Study of Anxiety. Recipient Disting. Scientific Contributions to Clinical Psychology award, American Psychological Assn., Disting. Scientist award, Soc. for Sci. Clinical Psychology, Lifetime Achievement award, Internat. Soc. for Traumatic Stress Studies; named one of The 100 Most Influential People in the World, TIME mag., 2010. Mem.: Internat. Soc. for Traumatic Stress Disorders (chmn. Treatment Guidelines Task Force). Office: University of Pennsylvania Dept of Psychology 3720 Walnut St Solomon Lab Bldg Philadelphia PA 19104-6241 Office Phone: 215-746-3327. Office Fax: 215-898-7301. E-mail: foa@mail.med.upenn.edu.

FODOR, LUCIAN, plastic surgeon; s. Marian and Rodica Fodor; m. Adriana Gelu, Oct. 8, 2000. MD, PhD, Med. Sch., Cluj Napoca, 1998, Romania, 2005. Plastic surgery specialist Romania, 2006. Physician Emergency Distric Hosp., Cluj Napoca, 1998—2008, chief plastic surgery and burn unit, 2006—; sr. plastic surgeon Rambam Med. Health Care Campus, Haifa, Israel, 2006—. Prin. investigator-internat. grant Emergency Dist. Hosp., Cluj Napoca, 2008—. Contbr. scientific papers to med. rsch. jours. (Kaplan award, 2005), 32 articles. Grant, Pain-Out, 2008—, Plastic Surgery fellowship, Israel, 2001—06. Mem.: Romanian Soc. Hand Surgery and Microsurgery. Achievements include research in plastic and reconstructive surgery, annals of plastic surgery and trauma, burns, dermatologic surgery. Office: Emergency Dist Hosp Clinicilor 3-5 Cluj Napoca Cluj 3400 Romania Home: Alee Meziad 23 400546 Cluj - Napoca Romania

FODOR, PETER BELA, plastic surgeon, educator; b. Cluj, Romania, May 14, 1942; MD, U. Wis. Med. Sch., 1966. Cert. Am. Bd. Surgery, Am. Bd. Plastic Surgery, lic. Colo., Conn., Mich., NY, Calif., Wis. Intern, gen. surgery Parkland Meml. Hosp., Dallas, 1966—67; resident, plastic surgery Columbia-Presbyn. Med. Ctr., 1967—68; resident St. Luke's Hosp., NYC, 1974—76; faculty, plastic surgery St. Luke's-Roosevelt Hosp.; faculty, reconstructive plastic surgery and gen. surgery Columbia U. Coll. Physicians and Surgeons; assoc. clin. prof. plastic surgery UCLA Med. Ctr., LA; practicing plastic surgeon, dir. Century Aesthetics, LA. Hosp. appointment Santa Monica/UCLA Med. Ctr.; staff mem., plastic surgery Century City Doctors Hosp., LA, Olympia Hosp., LA, St. John's Hosp., Santa Monica, Calif.; mem. adv. bd., exec. editl. cons., round table moderator Consumer Guide to Plastic Surgery. Contbr. scientific papers to peer-reviewed jours., chapters to books; medical editor Be Your Best: A Comprehensive Guide to Aesthetic Plastic Surgery, 2006. Bd. mem., patron Coun. of Children's Burn Found., Helen Keller Manhattan League for the Blind, Music Ctr. LA, Sonance-House Ear Inst., LA Wild Beat Soc., Music Ctr.-Fraternity of Friends, Peterson Auto Mus. Checker 200, Thalians-President's Club, Bel Air Navy League, Calif. Hwy. Patrol Found. Capt. USAF. Recipient Ellis Island Medal of Honor. Fellow: Internat. Coll. Surgeons Plastic Surgery, ACS; mem.: Semmelweiss Scientific Soc. (past pres.), Royal Soc. Medicine, Northeastern Soc. Plastic Surgeons (founding mem.), NY Acad. Medicine, NY County Med. Soc., NY Regional Soc. Plastic and Reconstructive Surgeons, LA Soc. Plastic Surgeons, Lipoplasty Soc. N.Am. (immediate past pres., past treas.), Internat. Soc. Aesthetic Plastic Surgery, Conn. Soc. Plastic and Reconstructive Surgeons (founding mem.), Conn. State Med. Soc., Calif. Soc. Plastic Surgeons (past sec.), Bay Surgical Soc., Am. Soc. Plastic Surgeons, Am. Soc. for Aesthetic Plastic Surgery (past pres., past v.p., past treas., past clin. investigator), Am. Assn. Plastic Surgeons. Office: Century Aesthetics 2080 Century Park E Ste 710 Los Angeles CA 90067 Office Phone: 866-370-9042. Office Fax: 310-203-9798. Business E-Mail: pbfodor@centurysurgery.com.

FOEGE, WILLIAM HERBERT, public health administrator, educator; b. Decorah, Iowa, Mar. 12, 1936; s. William August and Anne Erika (Ermisch) F.; m. Paula S. Ristad, Dec. 23, 1958; children: David, Michael, Robert. BA, Pacific Luth. U., 1957; MD, U. Wash., 1961; MPH, Harvard U., 1965. Intern USPHS Hosp., SI, NY, 1961-62; epidemic intelligence svc. officer Communicable Disease Ctr., Atlanta, 1962-64; med. officer Immanuel Med. Ctr., Yahe, Nigeria, 1965-66; epidemiologist smallpox eradication/measles control program Nigeria, 1969-70; dir. smallpox eradication program Ctr. Disease Control, Atlanta, 1970-73, dir., 1977-83; med. epidemiologist smallpox program Southeast Asia Regional Office WHO, New Delhi, 1973-75; exec. dir. Carter Ctr., Atlanta, 1987-92; Presdl. Disting. prof. internat. health Rollins Sch. Pub. Health Emory U., Atlanta, 1997—2001, emeritus Presdl. Disting. prof. internat. health, 2001—; exec. dir. Task Force for Child Survival and Devel., 1984—99; sr. medical advisor Bill and Melinda Gates Found., 1999—2001, sr. fellow. Cons. WHO, Bangkok, Thailand, 1967, Kinshasha, Zaire, 1968; dep. field coord. Internat. Red Cross Joint Relief Action, Nigeria. Trustee Rockefeller Found. Recipient Public Welfare medal, Nat. Acad. Sci., 2005; named one of America's Best Leaders, US News & World Report, 2007. Office: Emory U Rollins Sch Pub Health 1518 Clifton Rd NE Atlanta GA 30322-4201

FOFT, JOHN WILLIAM, physician, educator; b. LA, May 13, 1928; s. Wilford L. and Mary E. (McMahon) F.; m. Marianne T. Deibler, Mar. 12, 1957; children— John, Christine. BS, U. Nebr., 1951; MD, 1954. Intern Mpls. Gen. Hosp., 1954-55; asst. prof. pathology, dep. dir. clin. chemistry U. Chgo., 1965-67, asso. prof. clin. pathology U. Ala., 1968-70, dir. pediatric-clin. pathology lab., 1968-70, dep. chmn. research clin. pathology, 1969-70, prof., chmn. dept. clin. pathology, 1970-77, clin. prof. dept. pathology, 1977-91; ret., 1991. Chmn. dept. pathology Carraway Meth. Med. Center, 1977-91, Norwood Clinic, 1977-91. Served as capt. AUS, 1955-57,capt. USAF, 1961-64. Nat. Heart Inst. fellow U. Minn. Hosps., 1959-61; Am. Cancer Soc. scholar Argonne Cancer Research Hosp., 1968 Mem. Am. Assn. Pathologists, Ala. Assn. Pathologists, Sigma Xi, Alpha Omega Alpha. Research on clin. lab. systems in developing countries. Home: 3529 Spring Valley Ct Birmingham AL 35223-1467 *

FOGARTY, CHARLES MICHAEL, pulmonologist, researcher; b. Sioux City, Iowa, Sept. 18, 1944; s. Charles F. and Wilma M. Fogarty; m. Jane C. McNerney, June 24, 1968; children: Charles D., Thomas F., John W. BS, Providence Coll., 1966; MD, U. Rochester, NYC, 1970. Diplomate Am. Bd. Internal Medicine, 1978. Intern internal medicine Strong Meml. Hosp., Rochester, NY, 1970—71, resident internal medicine, 1973—75; resident pulmonary diseases Hosp. U. Pa., Phila., 1975—78; ptnr. Lung & Chest Med. Assoc., 1978—; med. dir. Spartanburg Med. Rsch., 1994—. Chmn. dept. internal medicine Spartanburg Regional Med. Ctr., 1994—2000; med. dir. respiratory therapy Spartanburg Tech. Coll., 1990—. Capt. US Army, 1971—73. Mem.: European Respiratory Soc., Am. Thoracic Soc., Internat. Soc. Clin. Densitometry, Acad. Pharm. Physicians and Investigators, Am. Coll. Physicians. Catholic. Avocation: travel. Home: 450 Mudd Creek Rd Inman SC 29349 also: 485 Simuel Rd Spartanburg SC 29303-4755 E-mail: cmf@medresearch.com.

FOGARTY, STEPHEN JAMES, retired medical association administrator; b. Melbourne, Australia, Oct. 17, 1940; s. Tom and Barbara Emily (Campbell) F.; m. Patricia Ann Darbyshire, Nov. 24, 1962; children: Sarah, David, James, Simon. Secondary edn., Melbourne Grammar Sch., Australia, 1950-58. Sr. rep. Nestle Co., Melbourne, Australia, 1965-73; regional sales mgr. Baxter Healthcare, Melbourne, Australia, 1973-81; mkt. R & D mgr. Terumo Corp., Melbourne, Australia, 1981-85, nat. sales mgr., 1985-92, gen. mgr. Sydney, Australia, 1992—2002, corp. historian, 2002—. Vis. lectr. Coll. of Pharmacy, Melbourne, Australia, 1978—81; vice chmn. Monash U. Ctr. for Biomed Engring., Melbourne, 1994—2005, chmn., 2005—09, also bd. dirs.; chmn. Med. Industry Assn. Australia, Sydney, 1996—2001; hon. rsch. assoc. Monash U., 2006—; chmn., exec. com. LMA Pacmed. Pty., Ltd, Australasia, 2007—10. Fellow Australian Inst. Co. Dirs., Australian Inst. of Mgmt.; mem. Melbourne Cricket Club, Melbourne Club. Avocations: swimming, reading, gardening. Home: 20 Bass St Flinders Victoria 3929 Australia

FOGARTY, THOMAS JAMES, surgery educator; b. Cin., Feb. 25, 1934; s. William Henry and Anna Isabella (Ruthemeyer) F.; m. Rosalee Mae Brennan, Aug. 28, 1965; children: Thomas James Jr., Heather Brennan, Patrick Erin, Jonathan David. BS in Biology, Xavier

U., 1956; MD, U. Cin., 1960; D (hon.), Xavier U., 1987. Intern U. Oreg. Med. Sch., Portland, 1960-61, resident, 1962-65, instr. surgery, 1967-68; chief resident, instr. surgery divsn. cardiovascular surgery Stanford (Calif.) U. Med. Ctr., 1969-70, asst. prof. surgery, 1970-71, asst. clin. prof. surgery, 1971-73; cardiovascular surgeon pvt. practice, Stanford, 1973-78; pres. med. staff Stanford U. Med. Ctr., 1977-79; cardiovascular surgeon pvt. practice, Redwood City, Calif., 1978-93; dir. cardiovascular surgery Sequoia Hosp., Redwood City, Calif., 1980-93; clin. prof. surgery Stanford U. Med. Ctr., 1993—. Bd. dirs. Acorn Cardiovascular Inc., Satellite Dialysis Ctrs., Inc.; co-founder, bd. dirs. AneuRx, Inc., Biopsys Med., Inc., Cardiac Pathways, Inc., Emergency Med. Sys., Windy Hill Tech., Inc., Gen. Surg. Innovations, Inc., LocalMed, Inc., Vital Insite, Inc., Raytel Med. Corp., Cardiovascular Imaging Sys., Inc., Devices for Vascular Intervention, Inc., Hancock Labs., Imagyn Med., Inc., Physiometrix, Inc., Ventritex, Inc., Xenotech; mem. scientific adv. bd. Autogenics, BioLink Corp., Cardio Thoracic Sys., Inc., bd. dirs.; pres., founder Fogarty Engring., Inc.; co-founder, sr. ptnr. Three Arch Ptnrs., Baccitus Vascular, Novare Surg., Vascular Archs. Safety; founder, proprietor Thomas Fogarty Winery, 1981-. Portrait included in Bay Area Hon. Mus., 1998; contbr. articles to profl. jours.; patentee in field. Fellow U. Cin. Coll. Medicine, Good Samaritan Hosp., 1961-62, Nat. Heart Inst. Surgery br., Bethesda, Md., 1965-67, rsch. fellow divsn. cardiovascular surgery Stanford Med. Ctr., 1968-69; recipient AstroLobe award Roger Bacon High Sch., 1974, Disting. Alumnus award U. Cin. Med. Sch., 1989, Lifetime Achievement award Phoenix Hall of Fame, 1997, No. Calif. 1998 Entrepreneur of Yr. award Ernst & Young, 1998, Lemelson-MIT $500, 000 Prize invention and innovation, 2000, Assn. Advancement Med. Instrumentation's Found.'s Ann. Laufman-Greatbatch prize, 2000, Sci. Leadership award Nat. Breast Cancer Coalition, 2000, Internat. Soc. award Excellence in Endovascular Innovation Internat. Soc. Endovascular Specialists, 2001, Jacobson Innovation award Am. coll. Surgeons, 2001; named Inventor of Yr., San Francisco Patent and Trademark Assn., 1980; inducted into the Nat. Inventors Hall of Fame, 2001. Mem. AMA, ACS, Am. Assn. Thoracic Surgery, Am. Bd. Thoracic Surgery, Am. Coll. Physican Inventors, Am. Heart Assn. (grantee), Am. Inst. Med. and Biol. Engring., Assn. for Advancement Med. Instrumentation, Med. Device Mfrs. Assn., Am. Med. Polit. Action Com., Am. Surg. Assn., Internat. Soc. Specialists Surgery, Western Thoracic Surg. Soc., Calif. Med. Soc., Pacific Coast Surg. Assn., San Francisco Surg. Soc., San Mateo County Med. Assn., Santa Clara County Med. Assn. (Achievement award in medicine), Internat. Soc. Cardiovascular Surg. (N.Am. chpt.), Soc. Clin. Vascular Surgery, Soc. Vascular Tech., Soc. Thoracic Surgeons, Soc. Vascular Surgery (past pres. 1995), Copco Lake Sportsmen Assn., Santa Cruz Mountain Winegrowers Assn., South Skyline Assn., Sports Car Club Am., Rapley Trail Improvement Assn., Soc. Med. Friends of Wine. Republican. Achievements include invention of balloon embolectomy catheter. Avocations: hunting, fishing, pond gardening, woodworking, genealogy. Office: 3274 Alpine Rd Portola Valley CA 94028 also: Thomas Fogarty Winery 3270 Alpine Rd Portola Valley CA 94028

FOGT, FRANZ, pathologist, educator; MD, Ludwig Maximilian Universitat, Germany, 1988; PhD magna cum laude, Technische U., Germany, 1989; MBA, Eastern U., 1999. Diplomate Am. Bd. Pathology-anat. and clin. pathology, 1995, cert. European Assn. of Pathology, 1998. Rsch. fellow Cancer Rsch. Inst., 1989—90; resident pathology Univ. of Ulm, Germany, 1990—91; resident anatomic pathology New Eng. Deaconess Hosp., 1991—93, resident clin. pathology, 1993—94, chief resident clin. pathology, 1994—95, fellow gastrointestinal pathology, 1995—96; assoc. prof. pathology and lab. medicine Hosp. of the Univ. of Pa., Presbyn. Med. Ctr.; interim chmn. ophthalmic pathology Scheie Eye Inst.; dir. custer lab. Penn Presbyn. Med. Ctr. Co-author: (publs.) Uveal Melanocytomas: Genetic Comparison With Uveal and Dermal Melanomas Arch, 2005, Expression of hepatocyte growth factor and its receptor c-met, correlates with severity of pathological injury in experimental alcoholic liver disease, 2005, Applications of Laser Capture Microdissection: Use in DNA-Based Parentage Testing and Platform Validation, 2005, and other numerous publications. Named one of America's Top Doctors, 2008, 2010, Top Doctors, Phila. Mag., 2008—11. Fellow: Royal Coll. of Pathology; mem.: Coll. of Am. Pathologists, Am. Soc. of Clin. Pathologists, Royal Coll. of Pathology. Office: Penn Presbyterian Medical Center Department of Pathology 551 Wright Saunders Bldg Philadelphia PA 19104 Office Phone: 215-662-8077. E-mail: franz.fogt@uphs.upenn.edu.

FOHLMEISTER, JURGEN FRITZ, biology professor; b. Germany, Nov. 18, 1941; BS in Physics, U. Minn., MS, 1965, PhD, 1970. Assoc. prof. U. Minn., 1971—. Recipient Writer's award, Minn. Aviation Hall of Fame. Office: University Minn Integrative Biology and Physiology Dept Minneapolis MN 55455 Office Fax: 612-625-5149. E-mail: jurgen@umn.edu.

FOK, AGNES KWAN, retired cell biologist, educator; b. Hong Kong, China, Dec. 11, 1940; came to US, 1962; d. Sun and Yau (Ng) Kwan; m. Fok, June 8, 1965; children: Licie Chiu-Jane, Edna Chiu-Joan. BA in Chemistry, U. Great Falls, 1965; MS in Plant Nutrition and Biochemistry, Utah State U., 1966; PhD in Biochemistry, U. Tex., 1971. Asst. rsch. prof. pathology U. Hawaii, Honolulu, 1973-74, Ford Found. postdoctoral fellow, anatomy dept., 1975, asst. rsch. prof., 1975-82, assoc. rsch. prof., 1982—88, rsch. prof. Pacific Biomed. Rsch. Ctr., 1988-96, grad. faculty, dept. microbiology, 1977—2003, dir., 1994-96, dir., prof. biology program, 1996—2003, prof. emeritus, 2003—. Contbr. articles to profl. jours. Mem. Soc. for Protozoologists, Sigma Xi (treas. Hawaii chpt. 1979-2002). Avocations: reading, gardening, hiking, sewing. Office: U Hawaii Biology Program Honolulu HI 96822 Business E-Mail: fok@hawaii.edu.

FOLB, HENRY ALLEN, physician, internist; MD, Northwestern U., Evanston, 1980. Diplomate Am. Bd. Internal Medicine, Am. Bd. Internal Medicine-geriatric medicine, cert. Pa., 1992. Intern Evanston Hosp., 1981, resident, 1983; physician Washington Hosp. Group mem. Washington Physicians Svcs. Named one of the Top Doctors, Pitts. Mag., 2011. Office: Washington Hospital Ste 208 2001 Waterdam Plz Canonsburg PA 15317 Office Phone: 724-942-6480.

FOLCH-SERRANO, KAREN D., psychologist, consultant; b. Mayagüez, PR, Feb. 20, 1969; d. José Folch and Digna J. Serrano. BA in Psychology, U. P.R., Mayaguez, 1991; MS in Clin. Psychology, Carlos Albizu U., San Juan, 1994, PhD in Clin. Psychology, 1998. Cert. forensic psychologist Carlos Albizu U., P.R., 1999, in gerontology U. P.R., San Juan, 2006. Asst. to dir. clin. tng. program Carlos Albizu U., San Juan, 1997—98; dir. Ctr. Clinico Roig, Lucy Lopez Roig and Assocs., San Juan, 1999; clin. psychologist Ramsay Youth Svcs. of P.R., San Juan, 1999—2000, Inst. Psychol. Treatment, San Juan, 2000—02, Clin. Support Group, Inc., San Juan, 2002—08; pvt. practice San Juan, 2002—, Support Therapy Ctr., Inc., Caguas, PR, 2004—05. Cons. in field; lectr. in field; presenter in field. Named Outstanding Student Counselor of Yr., U. PR, 1990, Outstanding Student Gerontology Program, Med. Scis. Campus U. PR, 2006. Mem.: APA. Roman Catholic. Avocations: reading, travel, collecting barbies. Office: 611 Calle Dr Pavia Fernandez Ste 213 San Juan PR 00909-2244 Office Phone: 787-722-3944. Office Fax: 787-722-2170. Personal E-mail: kdfolch@yahoo.com, dr.karendfolch@gmail.com.

FOLDY, SETH LEONARD, public health service officer, physician, educator; b. Cleve., Sept. 3, 1955; s. Leslie Lawrance and Roma (Bisgyer) F; m. Joan Marie Bedinghaus, June 7, 1986; children: Benjamin, Eva. BA in Human Biology with distinction, Stanford U., 1977; MD, Case Western Res. U., 1982; M in Pub. Health, Medical Coll. Wis., Milw., 2005. Dilomate American Bd. Family Practice, American Bd. Preventive Medicine, Nat. Bd. Med. Examiners. Intern in family practice Cleve. Met. Gen. Hosp., 1982-83, resident in family practice, 1983-85, chief resident in family practice, 1984-85; family physician Great Brook Valley Health Ctr., Worcester, Mass., 1985-87; med. dir. MetroHealth Family Practice, Cleve., 1987-94, dir. cmty. health svcs., 1994-96; med. dir. City of Milw. Health Dept., 1996-98, health commr., 1998—2004; prin. health.e.volution Consulting, 2004—09; med. dir. Healthcare for the Homeless, Milw., 2005—09; adminstr. & state health officer divsn. pub. health Wis. Dept. Health Services, Madison, 2009—11; dir. pub. health informatics & tech. program office Centers for Disease Control & Prevention (CDC), Atlanta, 2011—. Asst. prof. family medicine Case Western Res. U., Cleve., 1987-96; assoc. clin. prof. family and cmty. medicine and Population Health, Med. Coll. Wis., Milw., 1996—, clin. prof. health adminstrn. and informatics, U. Wis., Milw., 2001-, adj. prof. dept. population health scis., Sch. Medicine & Pub. Health, U. Wis., Madison, 2009-; pub. health systems cons., Ctr. Internat. Health, 2005-09, sr. pub. health cons., e Health Initiative, 2005-08; spl. term appointee Argonne Nat. Lab., Ill., 2004-09 Co-author: Health Information Exchange: From Start-Up to Sustainability, 2007; asst. editor: Urban Family Practice: A Resource Monograph, 1994; editor (newsletter) Urban Health News, 1990-96; assoc. editor Advances in Disease Surveillance, 2006-09. Co-founder, chief med. officer Wis. Health Info. Exch., 2004-09; trustee Friends Sch. in Cleve., 1972-74; nat. com. War Resisters League, NYC, 1970-74; mem. Nat. Health Policy Leadership Coun., Washington, 1991-92, Ohio legis. adv. com. on environ. lead abatement, Columbus, 1994-95, Wis. Turning Point Transformation Team, 1998—, Wis. pub. health system terrorism and pub. health emergencies legis. coun. com., 2002; mem. info. coun. US CDC, 2000-04, steering com. Rand Inst. Summits on Info. Tech. Infrastructure for Bioterrorism, 2001, Operation Combined Assistance, US Navy Project Hope Tsunami Task Force, 2005; Inst. Medicine, Nat. Rsch. Coun. Com. Biosurveillance Sys., 2008-09, founder Milw. Pub. Health Found. and Health Champion Award, 2002; bd. dirs. eHealth Initiative & eHealth Inititative Found., 2002-07, Greater Milw. Bus. Group on Health, 2002-, Southeast Wis. Bioterrorism Prepardness Group, Inc., 2003-07, Benedict Ctr., 2007-09, Planning Coun. Health and Human Svcs., 2007-09, Wis. State Lab. Hygiene, 2009-, Nat. Health Collaborative, 2010-, Nat. Gov.'s Assn. State Alliance eHealth, 2010-; mem. Wis. Homeland Security Coun., 2009-. Recipient award for Excellence in Info. Tech., Nat. Assn. County & City Health Officers, 1999, Milton & Ruth Roemer Prize for Creative Local Pub. Health Work Pres.'s Vol. Svc. award, 2005, 2007. Fellow American Acad. Family Physicians; mem. AMA, APHA (gov. coun. 1992-94, 96-98, Milton & Ruth Roemer Prize for Creative Local Pub. Health award, 2002), Nat. Assn. City and County Health Officers (various coms.), Assn. State and Territorial Health Officials, Pub. Health Leadership Soc., Wis. Med. Soc., Milw. Acad. Medicine (pres. 2009), Milw. County Med. Soc. (chair pub. health com. 1996—, Cmty. Svc. award 1997), Phi Beta Kappa. Achievements include participated in detecting and elimination of monkeypox virus outbreak from Western Hemisphere. Avocations: fly fishing, hiking, birding. Office: CDC 2500 Century Parkway Mailstop E-78 Atlanta GA 30333 Personal E-mail: sfoldy@sbcglobal.net. *

FOLEY, CARMEL A., child and adolescent psychiatrist; MD, Nat. U. of Ireland, 1972. Lic. NY, diplomate Am. Bd. Psychiatry, Am. Bd. Psychiatry and Neurology-child and adolescent psychiatry, Am. Bd. Psychiatry and Neurology-forensic psychiatry. Resident in psychiatry St. Patrick's Hosp., Dublin, 1973—76, Lafayette Clinic, Detroit, 1976—77, fellow in child and adolescent psychiatry, 1977—79; assoc. prof. psychiatry Yeshiva Univ.; chief child and adolescent psychiatrist Long Island Jewish Med. Ctr., NY. Author: (publ.) Effects Of Late-afternoon Methylphenidate Administration On Behavior And Sleep In Attention-deficit Hyperactivity Disorder, 1995, Can Antidepressants Be Used To Treat The Schizophrenia Prodrome? Results Of A Prospective, Naturalistic Treatment Study Of Adolescents, 2007. Office: Long Island Jewish Medical Center 270-05 76th Ave. New Hyde Park NY 11040 Office Phone: 718-470-7000. Office Fax: 718-470-9402.

FOLEY, EUGENE F., colon and rectal surgeon, educator; MD, Harvard U., 1985. Diplomate Am. Bd. Surgery, Am. Bd. Colon and Rectal Surgery. Intern New England Deaconess Hosp., resident; fellow in surgical endoscopy Mass. Gen. Hosp., Boston, 1989; fellow in colon and rectal surgery Lahey Clinic Med. Ctr., Burlington, 1992—93; faculty mem. sch. medicine and pub. health Univ. Wis.; hosp. affiliations include Meriter Hosp., William S. Middleton Meml. Veterans Hosp., Univ. Wis. Hosp. and Clinics. Co-author: (articles) Cyclical increase in diverticulitis during the summer months, 2011, Optimizing surgical care of colon cancer in the older adult population, 2011, Short-term outcomes after laparoscopic-assisted proctectomy for rectal cancer: results from the ACS NSQIP, 2011, Visceral obesity is associated with outcomes of total mesorectal excision for rectal adenocarcinoma, 2011, Preoperative chemoradiation for rectal cancer using capecitabine and celecoxib correlated with posttreatment assessment of thymidylate synthase and thymidine phosphorylase expression, 2011, various others. Office: University of Wisconsin Hospital 600 Highland Ave Madison WI 53792 Office Phone: 608-263-6400.

FOLEY, MIKE, diversified financial services company executive; b. 1962; B in Math and Economics, Fairfield U., Conn.; MBA in Mktg. and Fin., Northwestern U., Evanston, Ill. Fin. mgmt. trainee Armtek Corp.; from assoc. to v.p. Deerpath Group, 1989—93; pres. Electrocal, Inc., Conn., 1993—96; prin. McKinsey & Co., Chgo., 1996—2006; COO N.Am. comml. bus. divsn. Zurich Fin. Services Group, 2006—08, CEO N.Am. comml. bus. divsn., regional chmn. of Americas, 2008—. Bd. dirs. Friends of Lucerne; mem. civic com. The Comml. Club, Chgo. Office: Zurich North America 1400 American Ln Schaumburg IL 60196 *

FOLEY, RAYMOND J., critical care specialist; MD, NY Coll. of Osteopathic Medicine, 1993. Diplomate Am. Bd. Internal Medicine-pulmonary disease, 1999, Am. Bd. Internal Medicine- critical care medicine, 2000, Am. Bd. Internal Medicine, 2006. Resident in internal medicine Univ. Conn., Farmington, Conn., 1994—97, fellow in pulmonary disease, 1997—2000; hosp. affiliation includes Univ. Conn. Health Ctr.- John Dempsey Hosp. Office: University of Connecticut Health Center John Dempsey Hospital 263 Farmington Ave Farmington CT 06032-1956 Office Phone: 860-679-3343.

FOLEY, WILLIAM T., healthcare company executive; B in Sociology, St. Louis U.; M in Hosp. and Health Adminstrn., Xavier U., Cin. Group pres. Cath. Health Initiatives, Phila.; pres., CEO Cath. Healthcare-West, Ariz., Provena Health, Ill., Ind., 2001—06; mng. dir. Wellspring Partners; interim CEO Natividad Med. Ctr., Salinas, Calif.; CEO Cook County Health & Hospitals Sys., Ill., 2009—11; pres. Chgo. market Vanguard Health Systems, 2011—. Mem.: American Coll. Healthcare Executives. Office: Vanguard Health Systems 20 Burton Hills Blvd Ste 100 Nashville TN 37215 Office Phone: 615-665-6000. *

FOLK, FRANK ANTON, surgeon, educator; b. Chgo., Dec. 15, 1925; s. Frank A. and Anna (Pilisauer) F.; m. Lorna C. Hill, June 18, 1949; children: Laura, Lawrence, Patricia, Elizabeth, Thomas, James, Mary, Tracy Ann, William. BS, Northwestern U., 1945; postgrad., U. Wis., 1945-46; MD, U. Ill., 1949. Diplomate Am. Bd. Surgery, Nat. Bd. Med. Examiners; lic. Ill., Wis. Rotating intern Cook County Hosp., Chgo., 1949-51; resident in gen. surgery Cook County/Columbus Hosp., Chgo., 1951, Cook County Hosp., Chgo., 1954-57, surgeon, 1958-69, dir. of surgery, 1969-72; mem. faculty Stritch Sch. Medicine Loyola U., Maywood, Ill., 1958—, prof. surgery Stritch Sch. Medicine, 1972-96; prof. emeritus, 1997—; rsch. fellow Hektoen Inst., Chgo., 1959-64; asst. chief surgery VA Hosp., Hines, Ill., 1972-95, chief surg. svc., 1995-96. Mem. editl. bd.: The Am. Surgeon, 1984-92; contbr. articles to med. jours. including Am. Jour. Physiology, Jour. Occupl. Medicine, Annals of Surgery, Archives of Surgery, Jour. Trauma, Surg. Clinics of N.Am. Unit pres., exec. bd. Am. Cancer Soc., Chgo., 1972-89; mem. pres.'s adv. com. Benedictine U., Lisle, Ill., 1965-90. Lt. USN, 1951-53, Korea. Decorated Bronze Star, 1953. Fellow ACS (gov., chmn. gen. surgery Chgo. com. on trauma 1975-83, pres. met. chpt. 1977-78, mem. SESAP com. II and III, instr. ACS advanced trauma life support course 1980-87); mem. Am. Surg. Assn., Am. Assn. for Surgery of Trauma, Assn. Mil. Surgeons of U.S., Assn. for Acad. Surgery, Soc. for Surgery of Alimentary Tract, Assn. VA Surgeons, Internat. Soc. Digestive Surgry, Ctrl. Surg. Assn., Midwest Surg. Assn. (pres. 1974-75), Western Surg. Assn., Ill. Surg. Soc. (pres. 1971-72), Chgo. Surg. Soc. (pres. 1989-90), Inst. Medicine of Chgo. Roman Catholic. Avocation: history. Home: 446 S Columbia St Naperville IL 60540-5418 Home Phone: 630-355-1762. Personal E-mail: fafolk@aol.com.

FOLLANSBEE, WILLIAM P., cardiologist, nuclear cardiologist; MD, U. Pa. Sch. of Medicine, Phila., Pa. Diplomate Am. Bd. Internal Medicine, cert. cardiovasc. disease, nuc. cardiology, lic. to practice Pa., 1975. Intern Hosp. of the Univ. of Pa., Phila., 1975, fellow, 1978, resident; hosp. affiliations include Magee-Womens Hosp. of Univ. of Pitts. Med. Ctr. (UPMC), UPMC Presbyn. Office: Magee-Womens Hospital University of Pittsburgh Medical Center 300 Halket St Pittsburgh PA 15213 Office Phone: 412-641-1000.

FOLLENZI, ANTONIA, medical educator; b. Cerignola, Foggia, Italy, July 10, 1966; MD, U. Torino, 1992, PhD, 2001. Asst. prof. U. Piemonte Orientale, 2006—. Vis. asst. prof. Albert Einstein Coll. Medicine, 2003—11. Recipient Young Investigator award, European Soc. Gene and Cell Therapy. Mem.: ISTH. Avocations: reading, swimming, bicycling, travel. Home: 10 Kraft Ave Bronxville NY 10708 Business E-Mail: afollenz@aecom.yu.edu.

FOLLET, HELENE, medical researcher; b. France, Aug. 28, 1972; PhD, INSA Lyon, 2002. Rschr., biomechanics INSERM U1033, 2005—. Office: 7-11 Rue G Paradin Faculty Medicine Lyon 69372 France Business E-Mail: helene.follet@inserm.fr.

FOLLICK, EDWIN DUANE, law educator, dean, chiropractor; b. Glendale, Calif., Feb. 4, 1935; s. Edwin Fulfford and Esther Agnes (Catherwood) Follick; m. Marilyn K. Sherk, Mar. 24, 1986. BA in Social Sci., Calif. State U., LA, 1956, MA in Edn., 1961; MA in Social Sci., Pepperdine U., 1957, MPA, 1977; PhD in Social Sci., Sem. Free Prot. Episc. Ch., London, 1958, DTh, 1958; MS in LS, U. So. Calif., 1963, MEd in Instrnl. Materials, 1964, AdvMEd in Edn. Adminstrn., 1969; postgrad., Calif. Coll. Law, 1965; LLB, Blackstone Law Sch., 1966, JD, 1967; DC, Cleve. Chiropractic Coll., LA, 1972; PhD in Eccles. Law, Academia Theatina, Pescara, 1978; MA in Orgnl. Mgmt., Antioch U., LA, 1990. Tchr., libr. adminstr. L.A. City Schs., 1957-68; law libr. Glendale U. Coll. Law, 1968-69; coll. libr. Cleve. Chiropractic Coll., LA, 1969-74, dir. edn. and admissions, 1974-84, prof. jurisprudence, 1975—2003, dean student affairs, 1976-92, coll. chaplain, 1985—2003, dean of edn., 1989—2003, rector, 2003—04, rector emeritus, 2004—11; assoc. prof. Newport U., 1982; extern prof. St. Andrews Theol. Coll., London, 1961; dir. West Valley Chiropractic Health Ctr., 1972-2000, West Valley Chiropractic Consulting, 2001—04; cons. instnl. chaplain, 2004—; libr. dir. South Baylo U., 2004—, u. chaplain, 2004—; libr. dir. Calif. U. Mgmt. and Sci., 2004—. Adj. prof. law Calif. U. Mgmt. and Sci., 2004—, univ. chaplain, 2004—. Contbr. articles to profl. jours. Chaplain's asst. US Army, 1958—60. Decorated cavaliere Internat. Order Legion of Honor of Immaculata (Italy); Knight of Malta, Sovereign Order of St. John of Jerusalem; Knight Grand Prelate, comdr. with star, Order of Signum Fidei; comdr. chevalier Byzantine Imperial Order of Constantine the Gt.; comdr. ritter Order St. Gereon; chevalier Mil. and Hospitaller Order of St. Lazarus of Jerusalem (Malta), Chaplain to the Order of St. Stanislas; numerous others. Mem. ALA, NEA, Am. Assn. Sch. Librarians, LA Sch. Libr. Assn., Calif. Sch. Libr. Assn., Assn. Coll. and Rsch. Librarians, Am. Assn. Law Librarians, Am. Chiropractic Assn., Internat. Chiropractors Assn., Nat. Geog. Soc., Internat. Platform Assn., Phi Delta Kappa, Sigma Chi Psi, Delta Tau Alpha. Democrat. Episcopalian. Home: 6435 Jumilla Ave Woodland Hills CA

91367-2833 also: 7022 Owensmouth Ave Canoga Park CA 91303-2005 Address: 1126 N Brookhurst St Anaheim CA 92801 Office Phone: 714-533-6077. Business E-Mail: edfollick@southbaylo.edu.

FOLMSBEE, MARTHA, medical researcher; b. Hudson, NY, Apr. 2, 1962; PhD, U. Okla., 2004. Staff scientist Pall Corp., 2007—. Postdoc. fellow Ctrs. Disease Control, 2005—07. Postdoc. fellowship, Am. Soc. Microbiology, Nat. Ctrs. Infectious Disease. Mem.: Parenteral Drug Assn. Office: 25 Harbor Park Dr Port Washington NY 11050 Business E-Mail: martha_folmsbee@pall.com.

FOLTRAN, FRANCESCA, epidemiologist; b. Vittorio Veneto, Italy, Oct. 31, 1975; Degree in Medicine and Surgery, U. Padua, 2002; PhD, U. Pisa. Postdoc. fellow U. Padua, 2010—. Home: Via Mussato 12 c/o Broch Abano Terme 35031 Italy Personal E-mail: francescafoltran@libero.it.

FOMIN, VICTOR V., occupational therapist, educator; b. Moscow, Sept. 17, 1978; MD, I.M. Sechenov Moscow Med. Acad., PhD, 2001. Asst. prof., therapy and occupl. diseases chair Moscow Med. Acad. n.a. I.M. Sechenov, 2003—07, assoc. prof., vice-dir. Sci. Rsch. Ctr., 2007—10; prof. internal and occupl. diseases chair; dean pre-univ. faculty First Moscow State Med. U. n.a. I.M. Sechenov, 2010—. Vice editor-in-chief Clin. Nephrology Med. Jour., 2008; editor-in-chief Pharmateca Med. Jour., 2009. Master: Russian Sci. Soc. Nephrology, Russian Med. Soc. Arterial Hypertension, Russian Sci. Internists Soc. Office: Trubetskaya 8 Moscow 119991 Russia Office Fax: (499)248-41-55. Business E-Mail: fomin_vic@mail.ru.

FOMMEI, ENZA, cardiologist, researcher; b. Grosseto, Italy, Oct. 7, 1951; MD, U. Pisa, 1976. Co-responsible cardiovasc. medicine clin. dept. CNR-CREAS Hosp. and Rsch. Inst., 2000—04; head dept. cardiovasc. day hosp. unit CNR-Regione Toscana Found. G. Monasterio, U. Pisa, 2003—. Med. asst. Inst. Patologia Speciale Medica, U. Pisa., 1976—82; med. rschr. CNR Inst. Clin. Physiology, Pisa, 1982—87, Dept. Internal Medicine, U. Pisa, 1987—2011. Mem.: European Soc. Hypertension. Avocation: walking. Home: via del Capanone 9 Pisa 56122 Italy Personal E-mail: fommei@ifc.cnr.it.

FONAROW, GREGG CURTIS, cardiologist, educator; b. LA, Calif., Aug. 23, 1962; BS in Biomedical Sci., U. Calif., Riverside, 1983; MD, UCLA, 1987. Cert. Am. Bd. Internal Medicine, Am. Bd. Internal Medicine, Cardiovascular Disease. Intern, internal medicine U. Calif., LA Ctr. for Health Scis. (also called UCLA Sch. Medicine), Calif., 1987—88, resident Calif., 1988—90, fellow, cardiology Calif., 1990—93; fellow, cardiomyopathy Ahmanson-UCLA Cardiomyopathy Ctr., U. Calif., Calif., 1990—91; assoc. dir. Ahmanson-UCLA Cardiomyopathy Ctr., Calif., 1993—96, dir. Calif., 1997—; asst. prof., medicine, divsn. cardiology UCLA, Calif., 1993—99, assoc. prof., medicine, divsn. cardiology Calif., 1999—2003, prof. medicine, divsn. cardiology Calif., 2003—, assoc. dir., cardiology fellowship tng. program Calif., 1994—96, dir., cardiology fellowship tng. program Calif., 1997—, co-dir., preventative cardiology program Calif., 2000—, Eliot Corday Chair, cardiovascular medicine and sci. Calif., 2003—; physician, cardiology, heart transplatation UCLA Med. Ctr. Co-dir., CHAMP (Cardiovascular Hospitalization Atherosclerosis Mgmt. Program) UCLA Med. Ctr. Contbr. several articles to peer-reviewed jours.; reviewer for several cardiovascular jours., mem. editl. bd. of several cardiovascular jours. Recipient Carl Fugie Meml award for Outstanding Med. Student, 1984, Bristol Myers Travel award, Am. Coll. Cardiology, 1993, W. Proctor Harvey, MD, Young Tchr. award, 1998; UCLA Dept. Medicine Fellowship Tchg. award, 1992. Mem.: Am. Heart Assn. (mem. steering com., Get With the Guidelines Program, mem. steering com., ADHERE Registries and OPTIMIZE-HF, Laverna Titus Young Investigator award 1993, Get With the Guidelines-Coronary Artery Disease Nat. Champion Recognition award 2001, Meritorious Achievement 2004), Alpha Omega Alpha. Office: Ahmanson-UCLA Cardiomyopathy Ctr UCLA Med Ctr 10833 Le Conte Ave Los Angeles CA 90095 Mailing: UCLA Med Ctr Divsn Cardiology Office 67-130A CHS 10833 Le Conte Ave Los Angeles CA 90095-1679 Office Phone: 310-206-9112. Office Fax: 310-825-8811. Business E-Mail: gfonarow@mednet.ucla.edu.

FONDEUR, FERNANDO, chemist; b. Dominican Republic, June 26, 1963; PhD, Tulane U., 1998, Case Western Res. U., 1994. Rsch. scientist Savannah River Nat. Lab., 1998—. Mem.: AIChE, Am. Chem. Soc. Office: 773a B124 Aiken SC 29808 Business E-Mail: fernando.fondeur@srnl.doe.gov.

FONDILLER, SHIRLEY HOPE ALPERIN, nursing educator, journalist, historian; b. Holyoke, Mass. d. Samuel and Rose (Sobiloff) Alperin; m. Harvey V. Fondiller, Dec. 27, 1957 (div. June 1984); 1 child, David Stewart. BS, Columbia U., 1962, MA, 1963, MEd, 1971, EdD, 1980. Editor Am. Nurse, Kansas City, Mo., 1975-78; assoc. prof., asst. to dean for spl. projects Rush-Presbyn.-St. Luke's Med. Ctr., 1979-86; exec. dir. Mid-Atlantic Regional Nursing Assn., NYC, 1986-89; adj. assoc. prof. Columbia U., 1986—99; founder, prin. Pub. for Health Dimensions, phd, 1990—. Author of books; contbr. articles to profl. jours. Fellow Am. Acad. Nursing; mem. Kappa Delta Pi, Sigma Theta Tau. Office Phone: 212-663-4557. E-mail: sfondiller@att.net.

FONG, BERNARD W.D., physician, educator; b. Honolulu, May 18, 1926; s. Leonard K. and Francis C. Fong; m. Roberta Wat, Aug. 14, 1950; children: Phyllis K., Jeffrey S., Camille K., Allison K. BS, Bucknell U., 1948; MD, Jefferson Med. Coll., 1952. Diplomate Am. Bd. Internal Medicine. Intern Germantown Hosp., Phila., 1952-53, chief med. resident, 1953-55; teaching fellow cardiology Jefferson Med. Coll. Hosp., Phila., 1955-56; attending physician Queen's Med. Ctr., Honolulu, 1956—2002, St. Francis Hosp., Honolulu, 1956-89; clin. prof. medicine U. Hawaii, Honolulu, 1982—2004; med. dir. medicare part B Aetna Ins. Co., Hawaii, Guam, 1988-97, Transamerica Occidental Life Ins. Co., Hawaii and Guam, 1997-2000, Noridian Adminstrv. Svcs., Hawaii and Guam, 2000—04; ret., 2004. Adv. coun. Nat. Heart, Lung and Blood Inst., NIH, Bethesda, Md., 1976-80, chmn. 3d forum on cardiovascular risk factors, 1985; adv. com. cardiovascular risk factors in minorities NIH, 1976-89; pres. Triple C, 1996-2001. Pres. Hawaii Heart Assn., Honolulu, 1962-63; bd. dirs. Am. Heart. Assn., N.Y.C., 1963-66; pres. Chung Shan Assn., Honolulu, 1969-70, United Chinese Soc. Hawaii, Honolulu, 1973-74; 1st v.p. Wong Leong Doo Benevolent Soc., Honolulu, 1973-2003; 1st v.p. Ocean View Cemetery, Honolulu, 1973-2003; bd. dirs. Palolo Home, 2004—. With USNR, 1944-46, PTO. Named Modelfather of Yr., United Chinese Soc., 2009. Fellow ACP (bd. govs. 1972-76, inaugural laureate internal medicine Hawaii chpt. 1986), Am. Coll. Cardiology (bd. govs. 1992-96, chair 1995-96, trustee 1997-2002), Am. Coll. Chest Physicians, Am. Heart Assn; mem. Am. Soc. Internal Medicine (pres. Hawaii chpt. 1980-82). Republican. Roman Catholic. Home: 97 Dowsett Ave Honolulu HI 96817-1107 Personal E-mail: bernard4568@aol.com, bernardfong@msn.com.

FONG, DANIEL YEE-TAK, research scientist, consultant; BSc, U. Hong Kong, 1991, MPhil, 1993; PhD, U. Waterloo, Can., 1997. Asst. prof. Nanyang Technol. U., Singapore, 1997—98; rsch. asst. prof. Clin. Trials Ctr. Hong Kong U., 1998—2003, hon. asst. prof. Dept. Orthop. Surgery, 2003—. Sr. med. statistician Clin. Trials Ctr. Hong Kong U., 1998—; assoc. fellow Cancer Rsch. Centre, Hong Kong U., 2001—; internat. advisor WellnessOptions mag., Toronto, Ont., 2000; vis. scientist Oreg. Health and Sci. U., Portland, 2000—01. Contbr. articles to profl. jours. Grantee Health Care Promotion Fund, Hong Kong SAR Govt., 2002; scholar, Am. Women's Assn. Hong Kong, 1987, Croucher Found., 1993—96; Sir Edward Youde Meml. fellow, Hong Kong SAR Govt., 1991. Fellow: The Hong Kong Jockey Club Ctr. Suicide Rsch. and Prevention (hon.); mem.: Am. Statis. Assn., Biometrics, Soc. Clin. Trials, Drug Info. Assn., Ctr. Suicides Studies. Office: Clin Trials Ctr Hong Kong U Pokfulam Rd Hong Kong Hong Kong E-mail: dytfong@hku.hk.

FONKALSRUD, ERIC WALTER, pediatric surgeon, educator; b. Balt., Aug. 31, 1932; s. George and Ella F.; m. Margaret Ann Zimmermann, June 6, 1959; children: Eric Walter Jr., Margaret Lynn, David Loren, Robert Warren. BA, U. Wash., 1953; MD, Johns Hopkins U., 1957. Diplomate Am. Bd. Surgery, Am. Bd. Pediatric Surgery, Am. Bd. Thoracic Surgery. Intern Johns Hopkins Hosp., Balt., 1957-58, asst. resident, 1958-59, U. Calif. Med. Ctr., Los Angeles, 1959-62, chief resident surgery, 1962-63, asst. prof. surgery, chief pediatric surgery, 1965-68, assoc. prof., 1968-71, prof. LA, 1971—2001, emeritus prof., 2001—, vice chmn. dept. surgery, 1981-89; resident pediatric surgery Columbus (Ohio) Childrens Hosp. and Ohio State U., 1963-65; practice medicine specializing in pediatric surgery LA, 1965—. Mem. surg. study sect. NIH; James IV surg. traveller to, Gt. Britain, 1971, pres. UCLA Emeriti Assn. Exec. Bd., 2011- Mem. editl. bd. Jour. Surg. Rsch., Archives Surgery, Am. Jour. Surgery, Annals Surgery, Surgery, Current Problems in Surgery, Jour. Pediat. Surgery, World Jour. Surgery, Japanese Jour. Surgery, Turkish Jour. Pediat. Surgery, Med. Video Jour. Surgery; contbr. over 650 articles to profl. jours., chpts. to books; co-author: The Undescended Testis, 1981, Infections and Immunologic Disorders in Pediatric Surgery, 1993, Essentials of Pediatric Surgery, 1995, Gastroesophageal Reflux in Childhood; Current Problems in Surgery, 1996, Pediatric Surgery, 1998, 5th edit., 2006, Principles of Pediatric Surgery, 2003, 6th edit., 2006. Recipient Golden Apple award UCLA Sch. Medicine, 1968; John and Mary R. Markle scholar, 1963-68; named Nat. Champion Rowing Crew, U. Wash., 1950, 53, Tree Farmer of Yr. Western Wash., 1998; Johns Hopkins U. Soc. of Scholars, 2003; Profl. Achievement Award, UCLA Sch. of Medicine, 2003, Longmire Legacy award, UCLA Dept. Surg., 2010. Fellow ACS (surg. forum com., bd. govs. 1978-84, pres. So. Calif. chpt. 1995-96, hon. award, 2011, Mead Johnson award 1963), Am. Acad. Pediat. (exec. bd., chmn. surg. sect. 1986-87, Salzberg award 2000, William E. Ladd medal 2006), German Assn. for Surgery (hon.), Polish Assn. Pediat. Surgery (hon.), Japanese Pediat. Surgery Assn. (hon.), John Hopkins Soc. Scholars (hon., pres. UCLA emeritus exec. bd. 2011-); mem. AMA, Am. Thoracic Surg. Assn., Am. Acad. Sci., Am. Assn. Acad. Surgery (pres. 1972), Soc. Univ. Surgeons (pres. 1976, sec. 1972-76), Calif. Med. Assn., Crohns and Colitis Found. of So. Calif. (Man of Yr. 1999), Internat. Surg. Group (treas. 1993-2003), Lilliputian Surg. Soc. (chmn. 1989), L.A. County Med. Assn., Am. Surg. Assn., Pan Pacific Surg. Assn., Pacific Coast Surg. Assn. (recorder 1979-85, pres. 1989), Am. Pediat. Surg. Assn. (bd. govs. 1975-78, pres. 1989), Pacific Assn. Pediat. Surgeons (pres. 1983-84, Coe medal 1998), S.W. Pediatric Soc., L.A. Pediat. Soc., Soc. for Clin. Surgery, Transplantation Soc., Pediat. Surgery Biology Club, Bay Surg. Soc., L.A. Surg. Soc. (sec. 1988-90, pres. 1991, pres. emeriti exec. bd. 2011-), Town Hall (L.A.), Pithotomy Club (pres. 1956-57), Sigma Xi, Alpha Omega Alpha. Methodist. Home: 428 24th St Santa Monica CA 90402-3102 Office: U Calif Med Ctr Dept Surgery Los Angeles CA 90095

FONSECA, ANTÓNIO PEDRO, immunologist, educator; b. Angola, June 5, 1967; s. António Augusto and Maria Luz Fonseca; life ptnr. Clara Isabel Extremina; 1 child, João Pedro. BSc in Biology, U. Porto, Portugal, 1991, BSc, 1999, MSc in Biomed. Engring., 1999, PhD in Human Biology, 2007. Tchr. Pub. and Pvt. HS, Porto, 1989—98; rschr. INEB, Inst. Biomed. Engring., Porto, 2000—01; asst. prof., faculty medicine U. Porto, 2000—07, rschr., Ipatimup, Inst. molecular pathology and immunology, 2002—, asst. prof., faculty medicine, 2007—. Contbr. articles to profl. jours. Mem.: Coll. Biotech. Ordem Dos Biólogos, Ordem dos Biologos.

FONSECA, VIVIAN ANDREW, physician; b. Nov. 29, 1952; m. Sarita Fonseca; children: Adam, Neil. MBBS, Armed Forces Medical Coll., Poona, India, 1974; MD, Bombay Univ., 1978; MRCP, Royal Coll. Physicians, London, 1980. Diplomate Am. Bd. Internal Medicine, Am. Bd. Endocrinology, Metabolism and Diabetes. Internship King Edward Meml. Hosp., Bombay, 1975-76; sr. house officer internal medicine Bombay Hosp., St. George's Hosp., J.J. Hosp., Bombay, 1976-77; registrar in gen. medicine King Edward Meml. Hosp., 1977-78; rsch. fellow Indian Coun. Medical Rsch. King Edward Meml. Hosp., Bombay, 1978-79; sr. house officer rotation internal medicine Oldchurch Hosp., Romford Essex, U.K., 1979-80; registrar in medicine and diabetes Queen Elizabeth Hosp., Welwyn Garden City, U.K., 1981-82; asst. prof. medicine & Endocrinology Riyadh Univ., Saudi Arabia, 1982-83; rsch. fellow Royal Free Hosp., London, 1983-85; sr. registrar medicine, diabetes, endcrinology Royal Free Hosp, London, 1985-92; assoc. prof. medicine divsns. endocrinology, staff physician Univ. Ark., Little Rock, 1992—; prof. Dept. Endocrinology Tulane U., New Orleans, La. Dir. Univ. Hosp. Diabetes Program, Diabetes Edn. Program; mem. promotions com. U. Ark. Med. Scis.; mem. outpatient clin. parctice com. Univ. Hosp. Contbr. numerous articles to profl. jours.; book chpts. Mem., bd. dirs. Am. Diabetes Assn. Recipient Bombay Univ. scholarship, 1976, Medical Edn. award Univ. Ark., 1995, rsch. grant Ednl. Trust Fund Delhi, 1979. Mem. The Endocrine Soc., Royal Soc. Medicine, British Diabetic Assn., European Assn. Study of Diabetes, Internat. Diabetes Fedn., Am. Assn. Clinical Endocrinologists, Am. Coll. Physicians. Home: 1505 Soniat St New Orleans LA 70115-4033 *

FONTAINE, GUY HUGUES, cardiologist, researcher; b. Corbeil-Essonnes, Ile de France, France, Dec. 24, 1936; s. Andre and Gisele (Maisonneuve) F.; m. Ilfat Masri; children: Nadia, Marc, Florence, Corinne. MD with high distinction, U. Paris, 1966; PhD with high distinction, U. Paris XI, Orsay, France, 1991. Attache cons. Paris Hosp., 1979—2002; co-dir. dept. clin. electrophysiology Hosp. Jean Rostand, Ivry sur Seine, France, 1979—2002. Vis. prof. U. Ariz. Health Scis. Ctr., Tucson, 1986; U. Shanghai, 1990; frequent cons. in ARVD and electrophysiol. treatment for patients internationally; organizer chmn. Internat. Symposium on Fulguration and Laser in Cardiac Arrhythmias, Paris, 1985, Arrhythmogenic Right Ventricular dysplasia/cardiomyopathy, 1996; rsch. dir. U. Paris, 1993; co-chmn. World Congress on Catheter Ablation, 1986; mem. sci. bd. World Congress on Cardiac Arrhythmias, 1996—. Author: (with others) The Essential of Cardiac Pacing, 1976, rev. 3d edit., 1985; co-editor: L'essentiel sur L'enregistrement de l'Holter de l'ECG, 1983, Cardiac Pacemakers, 1985, Ablation in Cardiac Arrhythmias, 1987, Cardiac Arrhythmias, Recent Progress in Investigation and Management, 1988, Les Troubles du Rythme Cardiaque, 1993, Arrhythmogenic Right Ventricular Cardiomyopathy and Related Disorders, 2000; contbr. 826 papers to profl. jours., sci. confs. etc., large number of which were written in English; mem. editl bd. Cardiovascular Reports (Germany), Heart and Vessels (Japan), Jour. Cardiovascular Electrophysiology (U.S.), Circulation (US), Annales Cardiol. Angéiol. (France), Rhythmology, (Can.), Revista Latina de Cardiologia (Argentina), Hertz (Germany), Stimucoeur (France); reviewer for 114 internat. med. jours.; lectr. in France and abroad on cardiac treatment especially treatment of cardiac arrhythmias and arrhythmogenic Right Ventricular Cardiomyopathies; about 12 lectrs. yearly 1968—; patentee in field. Mem. pioneer Pacing and Electrophysiology, Heart Rhythm Soc., 2005, Prix de Found. Lucien Dreifus, 2008. Named 4th Murray Kornfeld Meml. Lectr., Am. Coll. Chest Physicians, Boston, 1989; recipient Master Tchr. award Cardiovascular Revs. and Reports, 1990, prix Electicité-Santé, Paris, 1992; co-recipient Found. Pr. Pierre Rijlant prize, Belgian Royal Acad. Medicine, 1995, Golden Caduceus, Assistance Pub. des Hopitaux de Paris, 1997. Fellow European Soc. Cardiology, Am. Coll. Cardiology, Am. Heart Assn. (coun. clin. cardiology); Heart Rhythm Soc., mem. French Soc. Cardiology (Medtronic prize 1994), Internat. Soc. and Fedn. of Cardiology (co-chmn. working group on cardiomyopathy/dysplasia 1991—2003.

FONTAINE, JEAN-FRANÇOIS, allergist; b. Reims, France, Feb. 12, 1964; s. Robert Fontaine and Ginette Jacquin-Romary; m. Sylvie Boucher, Sept. 12, 1987; children: Alexandra, Jean-Baptiste. MD, U. Reims, 1991. Pvt. practice, Reims, 1993—; allergist U. Hosp., Reims, 1994—; mgr. Eassafe Co., 2009. Contbr. articles to profl. jours. Mem.: Nat. Assn. Postgrad. Formation Allergy (gen. sec. 2003—), European Acad. Allergy Clin. Immunology, French Soc. Allergy Clin. Immunology. Office: Cabinet d'allergologie 113 rue de Vesle Reims 51100 France Office Phone: (33)326406675. Business E-Mail: drjffontaine.allergovesle@orange.fr.

FONTANA, LUIGI, internist, educator; b. Rome, Sept. 29, 1939; MD, U. La Sapienza, Rome, 1963, degree in Internal Medicine and Hematology, 1967. Assoc. prof. U. Rome, Tor Vergata, 1989—99, internal medicine prof., 1999—. Pres. Italian Soc. Aallergy and Clin Immunology, 2008—11. Mem.: SIMI, SIAIC, EAACI, WAO. Home: Via del Casaletto 64 Rome 00151 Italy Personal E-mail: luigi.fontana@uniroma2.it.

FONTANGES, ROBERT, microbiologist, immunologist, consultant; b. Belleville, France, Nov. 22, 1928; s. Louis and Fernande (Bouquin) F.; m. Josette Crotte, July 18, 1952 (dec.); children: Guillemette, Thierry, Arnaud. MD, U. Lyon, France, 1953, D es Scis., 1965; Diploma, Inst. Pasteur, Paris, 1961. Cert. serologist, microbiologist, immunologist, cellular physiologist. Head chem. microbiology divsn. Svc. Santé Armées, Lyon, 1963—86; maitre de confs. U. Grenoble and Lyon, France, 1965—71; dean physiology and psychophysiology U. Lyon, 1971—77, prof., 1971—93; dir. rsch. ctr., lt. gen. medicine inspector Svc. Santé Armées, Paris, 1986—88; hon. prof. scis. Cellular Physiology Lab. U. Lyon, Villeurbanne, France, 1993—; pres. Centre de Bioexperimentation Valbex U. Lyon I, expert pharmacologue toxicology bacteriology. Cons. aerosols, immunomodulators, vaccinations; cons. fermentation, bacteria, viruses, sterilization, solid/liquid plants for the pharma. and biotech industry. Contbr. over 300 articles to profl. jours. Decorated officer Legion of Honor, Mil. Merit Cross, Comdr. Order Nat. Merit (France), comdr. Order Acad. Palmes (France); comdr. Nat. Order Niger; recipient vermeil medal Svc. Santé des Armées, Tricentenaire Silver medal; Paul Harris fellow Rotary Internat., 1999, with Sapphire, 2005. Mem. N.Y. Acad. Scis., Rotary (pres. 1998-99). Avocations: movies, travel. Office: Univ Lyon I Ctr Bioexperimentation Valbex A Bat 76 69622 Villeurbanne France Home: 24 Rue du Commandant Faurax 69006 Lyon France Office Phone: 33 04 72 69 20 41. Home Fax: 33 04 78 94 02 79.

FONTENOT, TERI GRAYSON, hospital administrator; b. Biloxi, Miss., June 16, 1953; d. Robert Dowell and Mildred Louise (Coshatt) Grayson; m. Jimmy Dale Whitworth, June 26, 1971 (div. Dec. 1978); 1 child, Stephanie; m. Gerald Fontenot, Oct. 30, 1981; 1 child, Rachel Fontenot. BBA with honors, U. Miss., 1979; MBA, Northeast La. U., 1988. CPA, La. Instr. La. State U., Eunice, 1991; chief fin. officer St. Francis Med. Ctr., Monroe, La., 1982-87; v.p., chief fin. officer S.W. Fla. Regl. Med. Ctr., Ft. Myers, Fla., 1987-88; chief fin. officer Opelousas Gen. Hosp., La., 1988-91; sr. v.p., chief fin. officer, treas. Woman's Hosp., Baton Rouge, 1992—94, exec. v.p., COO, 1994—96, pres., CEO, 1996—; exec. v.p. Woman's Health Found., Baton Rouge, 1994, treas. Bd. dirs. Sixth Dist. Fed. Reserve Bank, chair audit com.; bd. mem. HBCS, 2000—10, chair; mem. adv. com. Rsch. on Women's Health for NIH; ind. dir. Capital One Mutual Funds, chair audit com. Cabinet mem. United Way, Baton Rouge, 1994; treas. Safety Coun., Baton Rouge, 1990-95; leadership Greater Baton Rouge C. of C., 1993-94, chair, 2002; mem. La. State U. Sys. Rsch. and Tech. Found. Exec. Com.; bd. mem. Baton Rouge Water Co. Recipient Baton Rouge Women of Achievement award; named one of Top 25 Women in Healthcare, 2005, 25 Most Influential Women in Baton Rouge; named to La. State U. E.J. Ourso Coll. of Bus. Hall of Distinction, 2011. Fellow American Coll. of Healthcare Executives (chair CEO Com., bd. and officer nominating com., Service award, 2009); mem. Coun. Women's and Infants' Specialty Hosps. (pres. 1994-95), Health Care Fin. Adminstrn. (v.p. 1991-92), La. Health Care Alliance (bd. dirs. 1993—), La. Healthcare Data Coun. (chmn. 1993—), Hosp. Fin. Mgrs. Assn. (v.p. 1991), American Hosp. Assn. (pres.-elect, Baton Rouge chpt. 1994, chair-elect, 2010, bd. trustee and co-chairs HRET Com. Rsch.), La. Hosp. Assn. (mem. Profl. and Gen. Liability Trust Fund., bd. dirs. 2002, Golden Pelican President's award, 2010) Office: Womens Hosp 9050 Airline Highway Baton Rouge LA 70815 *

FONTOURA, DENISE REN, speech pathology/audiology services professional, researcher; b. Porto Alegre, Brazil, June 16, 1977; MS, Pontifícia U. Católica Rio Grande do Sul, 2005; PhD student, U. Nova Lisboa, Portugal. Cert. in speech-lang. pathology and therapy Inst. Metodista Educação E Cultura, IPA-IMEC, Brazil, 1999. Speech-lang. therapist, 1999—; speech-lang. therapist rschr. Hosp. Clínicas de Porto Alegre, 2009; gest lectr., neuropsychology Projecto-Ctr. Cultural E De Formação, 2011. Vis. lectr. U. Fed. Rio Grande Do Sul, 2009. Mem.: Soc. Brasileira Fonoaudiologia. Avocations: swimming, singing. Home: Rua Estácio de Sá 895 ap 602 Porto Alegre Rio Grande do Sul 91330-430 Brazil Personal E-mail: denisedafontoura@yahoo.com.

FONTOURA, PAULO PACHECO DA, neurologist, researcher; b. Lisbon, Portugal, Feb. 22, 1970; s. Luis de Oliveira Fontoura and Anabela Palma Mestre Pacheco da Fontoura; m. Monica Marta Neves Santos. MD, Faculty Med. Scis., Lisbon, 1994. Intern Hosp. St. Antonio Capuchos, Lisbon, 1995—96; asst. prof. anatomy Faculty Med. Scis., Lisbon, 1997—2000; neurology resident Hosp. Egas Moniz, Lisbon, 1997—2000; postdoctoral fellow Stanford (Calif.) U., 2000—03; neurologist Hosp. South Bernardo Setubal, 2004—08; asst. prof. immunology Faculty Med. Scis., Lisbon, 2004—09, faculty PhD, 2007; translational medicine leader CNS Roche Pharms., Basel, 2008—10; head CNS Translational Medicine Roche Pharms., Basel, 2010—. Contbr. articles to profl. jours. Recipient Rsch. award, Luso Am. Devel. Found., 2000—02, Student Rsch. Abroad Award, Fulbright Found., 2001, Rsch. award, Christopher Reeve Paralysis Found., 2001, Young Investigator award, European Charcot Found., 2004, award, Found. Salud, 2000, 2004; grantee, Gulbenkian Found., 2000—02. Mem.: Portuguese Immunological Soc., Portuguese Neurol. Soc., Am. Acad. Neurology. Roman Catholic. Avocations: reading, sports, computers, music, politics. Office: F Hoffman La Roche Grenzacherstrasse BS 4070 Basel Switzerland Business E-Mail: paulo.fontoura@roche.com.

FONT RIOS ETXEANDIA UNANUE ASPIAZU, CECILIO RAFAEL, retired biology educator, physician; b. San Sebastian, PR, Sept. 25, 1947; s. Cecilio Rafael Font and Juana N. Rios; m. Mercedes Garcia Campos, Nov. 24, 1977 (div. July 3, 1995); 1 child, Santi; m. Elisa Maria Baez, Apr. 2, 1998 (div. Feb. 9, 2005); children: Rafael Font, César Font; m. Maria Elsa Duarte, 2005; 1 child, Diego. BS, Mayagüez A&M U., PR, 1968; MD, U. Valencia, Spain, 1977; diploma in labor medicine, Nat. Sch. Labor Medicine, Madrid, 1980; postgrad., U. PR, San Juan, 1986—89. Asst. prof. physiology Ctrl. U. Caribbean, Bayamon, PR, 1978—79; gen. practice Nat. Health Sys., Castellon, Spain, 1979—81, Bilbao, Spain, 1981—82, Valencia, Spain, 1982—86; assoc. prof. physiology San Juan Bautista Sch. Medicine, 1986—2002; prof. biology Coll. Philosophy and Edn., Bronx, NY, 1998—99; ret., 2002. Vis. fellow in physiology U. Copenhagen, 1980, King's Coll., London, 1983, Inst. Sur La Nutrition, Paris; adj. prof. biology Mercy Coll., NY, 1994—95; editor in fields. Author: 30 books in field; editor: Blood Fluxes & Membranes, Cronopios, Latin Jazz, Medical Anthropology; contbr. over 60 articles to profl. jours.; author: El Barrio News. Recipient Hostos prize, Regular Dem. Club, Bronx, N.Y., 2003. Mem.: Drs. Without Borders, Amnesty Internat., Children Internat., Blood Brain Barrier Club. Democrat. Achievements include discovery of a carrier for inositol, an allosteric carrier the INOGJFON Carrier. Avocations: photography, jogging, writing, music, poetry, reading. Mailing: Hub Station Rios Etxeandia PO Box 668 Bronx NY 10455-0668 Personal E-mail: font-membrane@juno.com.

FOO, EDWARD CHEE BOON, physician, consultant; b. Singapore, July 1959; s. Alan Hee Fong and Betty Swee Yin Foo; m. Corinne Gek Kim Chia, Oct. 18, 1986; children: Lesley Xianglin Fu, Elliot Xiangyao Fu, Ellery Xiangyao Fu, Zachary Xiangchu Fu. MB, BChir, Nat. U. Singapore, 1983. Diplomate Am. Coll. Surgery. Med. officer Singapore Armed Forces, 1984—86, Singapore Gen. Hosp., 1987—88; resident Maimonides Med. Ctr., NYC, 1989—94; cons. Alexandra Hosp., Singapore, 1995—2003, Mt. Elizabeth Hosp., Singapore, 2004—. Mem. exec. com. The Cancer Inst., Singapore, 2000—03, Singapore Vascular Soc., 2000—03. Mem. Japan Airlines Scholars Alumni, Singapore, 1982—2005. Capt. Singapore mil., 1985—86. Named Best Tchr. of Yr., SUNY, 1994; acad. scholar, Singapore Pub. Svc. Commn., 1979, Cultural Appreciation scholar, Japan Airlines, 1981, rsch. grantee, Singapore Med. Rsch. Coun., 2003. Fellow: Royal Coll. Physicians and Surgeons (Glasgow); mem.: Singapore Vascular Soc. (treas. 2000—03). Achievements include development of surgical technique for performing circular stapled hemorrhoidectomy under local anesthesia; novel technique for pain control after laparoscopic hernia repair using a continuous bupivicaine infusion. Avocations: golf, travel. Office: Mt Elizabeth Hospl 3 Mt Elizabeth Rd Singapore 228510 Singapore Home: 26 Elite Park Avenue 458847 Singapore Singapore Fax: (65) 62423530. E-mail: foo_edward@yahoo.com.sg.

FOODY, JOANNE MICALE, physician, educator; married. AB, Princeton U., NJ, 1986; MD, U. Chgo., 1990. Staff physician Brigham and Women's Hosp., Boston, 2007; assoc. prof. Harvard Med. Sch., Boston, 2007—. Office: Brigham and Women's Hosp 75 Francis St Boston MA 02110

FOOTE, WARREN EDGAR, neuroscientist, psychologist, educator; b. Boston, Nov. 5, 1935; s. Warren Edgar and Edith Irene Foote; m. Cynthia Sue Hall, July 21, 1973; children: Pamela Fowler, Sarah Canby, Julia Landry, Christopher Warren. BA, Hamilton Coll., 1958; MA, Boston U., 1960; PhD, Tufts U., Medford, Mass., 1965. Rsch. assoc. Harvard U. Med. Sch., 1966—67, vis. asst. prof. psychology, 1970—73, asst. prof., 1974—83, assoc. prof., 1983—. USPHS postdoctoral fellow Yale U., 1967—69; rsch. scientist Norwich State Hosp., Conn., 1969—70; sr. Fulbright scholar Max-Planck Inst., Munich, 1973—74; assoc. pscyologist Mass. Gen. Hosp., Boston, 1974—, psychologist, 1984—95, sr. psychologist, 1995—; cons. Gen. Foods Corp., 1970—74, Neurotech Corp., 1987—88; advisor Wayland Pub. Sch. Found., 1982—. Contbr. articles and revs. to profl. jours. With M.C. US Army, 1959—60. Recipient McCurdy prize, Mass. Soc. Rsch. in Psychiatry, 1962; grantee, Nat. Inst. Neurol. Disease and Stroke, 1974—77, NIMH, 1970—73, Nat. Eye Inst., 1979—, Nat. Inst. Communicative Disorders and Stroke, 1983—; Sr. Fulbright fellow, 1973—74. Mem.: AAAS, APA, Soc. Neurosci., NY Acad. Sci., Harvard Club (Boston), Sigma Xi. Office: Mass Gen Hosp PO Box 70 Boston MA 02114 Home: 165 Pleasant St #208 Cambridge MA 02139 Office Phone: 617-726-3832. Business E-Mail: wfoote@partners.org.

FORBES, HELEN, nursing educator, director; b. Bacchus Marsh Victoria, Nov. 21, 1949; BSN, La Trobe U., 1991; PhD, U. Sydney, 2007. Dir. tchg. & learning Deakin U., 2007—. Mem.: Royal Coll. Nursing. Office: Deakin Univerity Burwood Hwy Burwood Victoria 3125 Australia Business E-Mail: helen.forbes@deakin.edu.au.

FORBES, JOSEPHINE MAREE, endocrinologist, researcher; b. Melbourne, Australia, Aug. 20, 1970; BSc, U. Melbourne, 1991, PhD, 2000. Head, glycation and diabetes Baker IDI Heart and Diabetes Inst., 2002—. Prof. Monash U., 2004—11; prin. rsch. fellow U. Melbourne, 2007—11. Recipient Commonwealth Health Min's. award, Govt. of Australia, Excellence award, NHMRC Australia; Sr. Rsch. fellowship. Office: 75 Commercial Rd Melbourne Victoria 3004 Australia Office Fax: 61 3 8532 1480. Business E-Mail: josephine.forbes@bakeridi.edu.au.

FORBES, KENNETH ALBERT FAUCHER, retired urological surgeon; b. Waterford, NY, Apr. 28, 1922; s. Joseph Frederick (dec.) and Adelle Frances (Robitaille) Faucher (dec.); adopted s. James Peter Forbes; m. Jeanne Ann Bonacci, June 18, 1947 (dec.); 1 child: Michael; m. Eileen Ruth Gibbons, Aug. 4, 1956; children: Diane, Kenneth E., Thomas, Maureen, Daniel. BS cum laude, U. Notre Dame, Ind., 1944; MD, St. Louis U., 1947. Diplomate Am. Bd. Urology. Intern St. Louis U. Hosp., 1947-48; resident in urol. surgery Barnes Hosp., VA Hosp., Washington U., St. Louis U. schs. medicine, St. Louis, 1948-52; asst. chief urology Letterman Army Hosp., San Francisco, 1952-54; fellow West Roxbury (Harvard) VA Hosp., Boston, 1955; asst. chief urology VA Hosp., East Orange, N.J., 1955-58; practice medicine specializing in urology Green Bay, Wis., 1958-78, Long Beach, Calif., 1978-85; ret., 1999. Cons. staff Fairview State Hosp. U. Calif. Med. Ctr., Irvine, VA Hosp., Long Beach; commr. State Med. Soc. Wisc., 1975—77, chmn. legal def. com., 1976—77; pres. Wis. Urological Soc., 1977—78; asst. clin. prof. surgery U. Calif., Irvine, 1978—85; cons. in field. Contbr. articles to profl. jours. Served with USNR, 1944-46, ensign 1947-51; capt. US Army, 1952-54. Named Outstanding Faculty Mem. by students, 1981. Fellow ACS, Royal Soc. Medicine (emeritus), Internat. Coll. Surgeons; mem. AMA, AAAS, Calif. Med. Assn., Am. Urol. Assn. (exec. com. North Ctrl. sect. 1972-75, Western sect. 1980—), NY Acad. Scis., Surg. Alumni Assn. U. Calif.-Irvine, Justin J. Cordonnier Soc. Washington U., Urologists Corr. Club, Notre Dame Club (Man of Yr. award 1965), Miles City Club (Mont.), Phi Beta Pi. Republican. Roman Catholic. Home: 9571 Oakham Way Elk Grove CA 95757-5122

FORBES, MICHAEL L., pediatrician; b. Kingston, Jamaica, Feb. 7, 1964; BS in Chemistry, U. Pitts. Sch. Medicine, 1986, MD, 1990. Dir., PICU clin. rsch. & outcomes analysis Akron Children's Hosp., 2007—. Office: Akron Children's Hosp One Perkins S Akron OH 44308 Business E-Mail: mforbes@chmca.org.

FORBES, SARAH ELIZABETH, gynecologist, real estate company officer; b. Currituck, NC, May 4, 1928; d. Dexter and Mary (Brock) Forbes. BA, U. Rochester, 1949; MD, Med. Coll. of Va., 1954. Diplomate Am. Bd. Ob-Gyn. Intern Norfolk (Va.) Gen. Hosp., 1954-55; resident ob-gyn Johnston-Willis Hosp., 1955-56, Norfolk Gen. Hosp., 1956-57, chief resident, 1957-58; pvt. practice gynecologist Newport News, Va., 1958—; pres., real estate investor Mary B. Forbes Land Corp., Newport News, 1972—; pres. Sebrof Corp., Newport News, 1978—, Haras, Inc., Newport News, 1984—, S.S. U.S., Inc., Newport News, 1984—. Bd. dirs. Family Planning Coun.; mem. teaching staff ob-gyn dept. Riverside Hosp. Pres. Peninisula Soc. for Prevention Cruelty to Animals, 1966—; mem. adv. bd. Peninisula chpt. Parents without Ptnrs.; bd. dirs. Newport News chpt. Am. Cancer Soc., pres., 2d v.p., 1971-72, 1st v.p., 1972-73, pres., 1973-74, chmn. rsch., 1961-69; candidate for Newport News City Coun., 1986; bd. dirs. Va. Peninsula Boys and Girls Club, 1991-99, 1st v.p., pres. Va. Peninsula Boys and Girls Club, 2000—. Recipient AMA Physicians Recognition award for Continuing Edn., 1973-76, Twin award Va. Peninsula YWCA, 1987, Medallion award Peninsula Boys and Girls Club, 1993; named Woman of Yr. for Peninsula Area, 1975. Mem. Va. Peninsula Acad. Medicine (pres. 1973-74, v.p. 1972-73, sec., treas. 1971-72); fellow AMA, Va. Med. Soc., Newport News Med. Soc. Am. Coll. Ob-Gyn, Tidewater Ob-Gyn Soc. Office: 12420 Warwick Blvd Newport News VA 23606-3001

FORCIOLI, PASCAL, hospital administrator; b. Paris, June 29, 1955; s. Andre Forcioli and Genevieve Jeanningros; m. Marion Van Wonterghem; children: Maxime, Margot, Cesar. Student Scis. PO, Paris, 1978; student, ENSP, Rennes, France, 1982. Dir. gen. hosp., Beauvais, France, 1982—88; advisor Ministry of Health, Paris, 1988—91; gen. dir. Gen. Hosp., Senlis, 1991—97, Simone Veil Hosp., Eaubonne-Montmorency, 1997—2005; dir. Picardie Regional Agy. for Health, Amiens, France, 2005—. Cons. expert Anaes, Paris, 1998. Editor: (book) Hospital Budget, 1999, Health Accreditation, 2002. Mem.: Hosp. Dirs. Assn. (nat. sec. 1995—98). Office: ARH de Picardie 6 Rue des Hautes Cornes 80 000 Amiens France Office Phone: 03 22223331. Business E-Mail: pascal.forcioli@arhpicardie.net.

FORD, ANN SUTER, retired family practice nurse practitioner; b. Mineola, NY, Oct. 31, 1943; d. Robert M. and Jennette (Van Derzee) Suter; m. W. Scott Ford, 1964; children: Tracey, Karin, Stuart. RN White Plains Hosp., Sch. Nursing, NY, 1964; BS in Nursing with high distinction, U. Ky., 1967; MS in Health Planning, Fla. State U., 1971, PhD, 1975, MSN, 1992. Nurse U. Ky. Med. Ctr., 1964-65, Tallahassee Meml. Hosp., 1968-69; guest lectr. health planning dept. urban/regional planning Fla. State U., Tallahassee, 1973-76, health planner and research assoc., 1974-76, vis. asst. prof., 1976-77, asst. prof. and dir. health planning splty., 1977-83, assoc. prof., 1982-83, health care analyst and policy cons., 1983-86; med., health program analyst Aging and Adult Svcs. for State of Fla., 1986-90; coordinator Fla. Alzheimer's Disease Initiative, 1986-90; family nurse practitioner Capital Area Physicians' Svcs., 1993-94; assoc. prof. nursing Fla. A&M U., 1994—2002; clin. nurse Tallahassee Meml. Regional Ctr., 1990—2010. Bd. dirs. Regional Fla. Lung Assn., 1986-91; mem. exec. com. human services and social planning tech. dept. Am. Inst. Planners, 1977-83. Author: The Physician's Assistant: A National and Local Analysis, 1975; contbr. articles to profl. jours., chapters to books. USPHS grantee, 1965-67; HEW grantee, 1978; Univ. fellow Fla. State U., 1971-72; recipient Am. Inst. Planners' Student award, 1975. Mem. Am. Planning Assn. (charter mem. human services and social planning tech. dept. 1976-83, chmn. health planning session Oct. 1978, 79, health policy liaison 1979-83, author assn. health policy statement), Am. Health Planning Assn., Fla. Nurses Assn., Phi Kappa Phi, Sigma Theta Tau. Address: 2602 Cline St Tallahassee FL 32308-0810 Personal E-mail: annscott64@comcast.net. *

FORD, CHARLES NATHANIEL, otolaryngologist, educator; b. NYC, June 25, 1940; s. Charles Nathaniel and Marie (Casa) F.; children: C. David, Brian C.; m. Sharon L. James, Feb. 3, 1990; stepchildren: Scott James, Julie James. BA, SUNY, Binghamton, 1961; MD, U. Louisville, 1965. Intern and resident Henry Ford Hosp., Detroit, 1965-70; with Gundersen Clinic, LaCrosse, Wis., 1973-81; chief otolaryngology Middleton VA Hosp., Madison, Wis., 1982-94; prof. otolaryngol. divsn. dept. surgery U. Wis., Madison, 1981-93, chmn. otolaryngol. divsn. dept. surgery, 1993—2008. Med. bd. U. Wis. Ctr. for Health Scis., 1989-91, sec., 1992-93, v.p., 1994-95, pres. med. staff, chair med. bd. 1996-98, numerous eponymous lectr.; keynote lectr. Brit. Voice Assn., 2000, Voice Symposium Australia, 2002, Voice Found., Phila., 2003, Internat. Fedn. Otolaryn. Socs., 2009. Author, editor: Phonosurgery: Assessment and Surgical Management of Voice Disorders, 1991; mem. editl. bd.: Jour. Voice, Otolaryngol. Head and Neck Surgery, Laryngoscope, Microsurgery; author over 100 peer reviewed papers. Maj. USAF, 1971-73. Avalon Found. scholar, 1962-63; named to Best Drs. in Am., Woodward/White, Inc., 1991—. Fellow ACS, Am. Laryngol., Rhinol. and Otolog. Soc., Am. BronchoEsophagological Assn. (past pres.), Am. Laryngol. Assn. (Presdl. Citation 2005, Newcomb award, 2006), Am. Soc. for Head and Neck Surgery, Am. Acad. Otolaryngology, Head and Neck Surgery (honor award 1992); mem. AMA, Soc. Univ. Otolaryngologists-Head and Neck Surgeons (past pres.), Internat. Assn. Phonosurgeons, Am. Speech-Lang.-Hearing Assn. Democrat. Unitarian Universalist. Avocations: tennis, golf, theater, art, music. Office: U Wis Ctr Health Sci 600 Highland Ave Madison WI 53792-0001 Office Phone: 608-263-0192. Business E-Mail: ford@surgery.wisc.edu.

FORD, CHARLES WILLARD, medical educator; b. Bloomsburg, Pa., Oct. 28, 1938; s. John Willard and Pauline Teresa Ford; m. Barbara Marie Hanawalt, June 6, 1959; children: Lane(dec.), Lori, Lanae, Lanette. BA, Taylor U., Upland, Ind., 1960; BS, Pa. State U., 1961, MEd, 1962; PhD, SUNY, Buffalo, 1970; postgrad., U. Mich., 1976—77. HS tchr., 1961-64; faculty Erie CC, 1965-70; fgn. svc. officer Peace Corps, Ghana, 1970-72; various positions Sch. Health Related Professions, SUNY, Buffalo, 1972-75, 77-79, assoc. dean Sch. Health Related Professions, 1978—79; with Grand Rapids Med. Edn. Ctr., Mich., 1975-77; dean U. Health Scis./Chgo. Med. Sch., 1979—80; dean undergrad. colls. U. New Eng., Biddeford, Maine, 1982-84, pres., 1984-91, prof. health sci., 1983—. Active in accreditation and curriculum program devel. in 40 states and 8 countries; vis. prof. Israel, Tel Aviv, Jerusalem, Haifa, spring, 1999—2010. Author (with M. K. Morgan): (book) Teaching in the Health Professions, Clinical Education for the Allied Health Professions; contbr. articles to profl jours. Pres. Maine Higher Edn. Coun., 1987—88, Maine Ind. Coll. Assn., 1988—89; bd. govs. Am. Assn. Coll. Osteo. Medicine, 1984—91. Recipient Study Exch., Rotary, Germany and Turkey, 1995. Mem.: NEA (life), Assn. Schs. Allied Health Profls. (life), Am. Assn. Higher Edn. (life). Office: University New Eng Coll Health Portland ME 04101

FORD, DONALD HERBERT, psychologist, educator; b. Sioux City, Iowa, Aug. 15, 1926; s. Herbert Owen and Esther (Sanow) F.; m. Carol Clark, May 30, 1948; children— Russell, Martin, Douglas, Cameron. BS, Kans. State U., 1948; MS, 1951; PhD, Pa. State U., 1955. Counselor Kans. State U., 1948-52; asst. prof. psychology Pa. State U., University Park, 1955-64, assoc. prof., 1964-67, assoc. prof human devel., 1967-72, prof. human. devel., 1972—, prof. biobehavioral health, 1992—. Asst. dir. div. counseling, 1956-59, dir., 1959-67; dean Coll. Human Devel., 1967-77, head dept. Communications Disorders, 1988-89, head biobehavioral health, 1992. Author: Systems of Psychotherapy; A Comparative Study, 1963, Humans as Self-Constructing Living Systems, 1987, 2d edit., 1992, Developmental Systems Theory, 1992, Contemporary Models of Psychotherapy, 1998. Served with USAAF, 1944-45. Mem. AAAS, Am. Psychol. Assn., Am. Psychol. Soc., Ea. Psychol. Assn. Home: 130 Slab Cabin Rd State College PA 16801-6971 Office: Penn State U Coll Health & Human Devel University Park PA 16802 E-mail: dhf6@psu.edu. *

FORD, LORETTA C., retired dean, educator, consultant, nurse; b. NYC, Dec. 28, 1920; d. Joseph F. and Nellie A. (Williams) Pfingstel; m. William J. Ford, May 2, 1947; 1 child, Valerie. BSN, U. Colo., Boulder, 1949, MS, 1951, EdD, 1961; DSc (hon.), Ohio State Med. Coll., Columbus, 1997, Simmons Coll., Boston, 1997, U. Colo., Boulder, 1997; LLD (hon.), U. Md., College Park, 1990; DSc (hon.), U. Rochester, NY, 2000, Ind. State U., Terre Haute, 2007; LHD (hon.), Binghamton U., NY, 2001. RN N.J. Staff nurse New Brunswick Vis. Nurse Svc., 1941—42; supr., dir. Boulder County (Colo.) Health Dept., 1947—58; from asst. prof. to prof. U. Colo. Sch. Nursing, 1960—72; dean Sch. Nursing, DON, prof. U. Rochester, NY, 1972—86, acting dean Grad. Sch. Edn. and Human Devel. NY, 1988—89; vis. prof. U. Fla., 1968, U. Wash., Seattle, 1974, St. Lukes Coll. Nursing, Tokyo, 1987. Mem. educators adv. panel GAO; dir. Security Trust Co., Rochester, Rochester Telephone Co.; internat. cons. in field. Contbr. chapters to books, articles to profl. jours. Mem. adv. com. Commonwealth Fund Exec. Nurse Fellowship PRogram; bd. dirs. Threshold Alt. Youth Svcs., Easter Seal Soc., ARC, Monroe Cmty. Hosp. With Nurse Corps USAF, 1942—46. Recipient N.Y. State Gov.'s award for women in sci., medicine and nursing, Modern Healthcare Hall of Fame award, Modern Health Care Jour., 1994, Lillian D. Wald Spirit of Nursing award, N.Y. Vis. Nurse Svc., 1994, Lifetime Achievement award, Nat. Conf. Nurse Practitioners, 1999, Trailblazer award, Am. Coll. Nurse Practitioners, 2003, Elizabeth Blackwell award, Hobart and William Smith Colls., 2003, Amazing Exemplar award, Friends of Nat. Inst. Nursing, 2005, Second Century Excellence in Health Care award, Columbia U., 2006, The Princess Srin Garinde award, 2010; named Colo. Nurse of Yr, Colo. Nurses Assn., Alumni of Century, U. Colo. Sch. Nursing Alumni Assn., 1998; named to Nat. Womens Hall Of Fame, Seneca Falls, NY, 2011. Fellow: Nat. League Nursing (Linda Richards award), Am. Acad. Nursing (Living Legend award 1999); mem.: NAS Inst. Medicine (Gustav O. Leinhard award 1990), ANA, APHA (Ruth B. Freeman award), Am. Coll. Nurse Practitioners (Crystal Trailblazers award 2003), Am. Coll. Health Assn. (Boynton award), Sigma Theta Tau, Alpha Omega Alpha (hon.). Personal E-mail: lorettaford@cfl.rr.com.

FORD, NEVILLE F., clinical pharmacologist; b. Greenock, Scotland, Nov. 30, 1934; m. Branka P. Ford, May 19, 1978. BSc, U. Bristol, England, 1955, PhD, 1958, DSc, 1975; MD, Washington U., St. Louis, 1985. Sr. chemist Ciba Pharm., Summit, NJ, 1960—68, dir. chem. rsch., 1969—71; exec. dir. pharm. divsn. Ciba-Geigy, Summit, 1971—81; assoc. dir. clin. pharm. Bristol-Myers Squibb, Princeton, NJ, 1988—90, dir. clin. pharmacology, 1991—97, exec. dir. clin. pharmacology, 1998—2000; pres. Woodfield Clin. Cons., Lawrenceville, NJ, 2000—05, Green Valley, Ariz., 2005—. Cln. assoc. prof. medicine U. Medicine and Dentistry NJ, New Brunswick, 2000—. Recipient Vol. Faculty Tchg. award, U. Medicine and Dentistry NJ, 2005. Fellow: ACP, Am. Coll. Clin. Pharmacology. Presbyterian. Office: Woodfield Clin Cons LLC 5481 S Acacia Creek Dr Green Valley AZ 85622 Office Phone: 520-648-2713. Business E-Mail: neville@woodfieldclinical.com.

FORD, SANDRA ELIZABETH, public health service officer, state agency administrator; m. Dominic Conrad Bouchelion. BS in Psychology, Stanford U.; MD, Howard U., MBA in Health Services Adminstrn. Cert. pediatrician. Dep. state health officer, dep. sec. Children's Med. Services Fla. Dept. Health, Tallahassee, 2003—05; dist. health dir. Dekalb County Ga. Dept. Cmty. Health, 2005—; interim dir. Divsn. Pub. Health Ga. Dept. Human Resources, Atlanta, 2008—09. Recipient Robinson/Dickens award; grantee Nat. Med. Fellowship; fellow, Commonwealth Fund. Office: Georgia Department Community Health 455 Winn Way, Room 536 PO Box 987 Decatur GA 30031-1701 Office Phone: 404-294-3789. Office Fax: 404-492-3715. *

FORDHAM, LYNN ANSLEY, pediatric radiologist; b. Corning, NY, Mar. 23, 1963; MD, Tufts U., 1989. Cert. in diagnostic radiology 1993, in pediatric radiology 1998. Pediatric radiology resident U. NC Hosp., 1989—93, sect. chief, pediatric imaging Chapel Hill; fellow Children's Hops. Boston, 1993—94; assoc. prof. radiology U. NC Sch. Medicine. Contbr. articles to profl. publs. Mem.: Soc. for Pediatric Radiology, Radiol. Soc. North America, Am. Roentgen Ray Soc., Am. Inst. of Ultrasound in Medicine, Am. Coll. Radiology, Am. Assn. of Women in Radiology. Office: U NC Dept Radiology Chapel Hill NC 27599 Office Phone: 919-966-3084. Office Fax: 919-966-1994. Business E-Mail: fdh@med.unc.edu.

FORDTRAN, JOHN SATTERFIELD, physician; b. San Antonio, Nov. 15, 1931; s. William M. and Josephine (Bell) F.; m. Jewel Evans, July 25, 1953; children: William, Bess, Josephine, Amy. Student, U. Tex., 1949-52; MD, Tulane U., 1956; DSc (hon.), Med. Coll. Wis., 1988; MD (hon.), Karl Franzens U., Graz, Austria, 1995. Internal medicine intern Parkland Meml. Hosp., Dallas, 1956-57, asst. resident internal medicine, 1957-58; research fellow gastroenterology Mass. Meml. Hosp., Boston, 1960-62; instr. internal medicine U. Tex. Southwestern Med. Sch., Dallas, 1962-63, asst. prof. internal medicine, 1963-67, assoc. prof. internal medicine, 1967-69, prof., 1969-79, chief sect. gastroenterology, 1963-79; chief dept. internal medicine Baylor U. Med. Center, Dallas, 1979-96; pres. Baylor Rsch. Inst., Baylor U. Med. Ctr., Dallas, 1991-2000. Mem. attending staff Parkland Meml. Hosp., Dallas, 1963-79; cons. gastroenterology Dallas VA Hosp., 1963-79. Contbr. articles to profl. jours.; editorial bd. Jour. Clin. Investigation, 1968-73; editor Gastroenterology, 1977-81; co-editor: Gastrointestinal Disease, 5th edit., 1993. Served with USPHS, 1958-60. Recipient King Faisal prize in medicine Saudi Arabia, 1984 Fellow Royal Coll. Physicians Eng.; mem. ACP, Am. Soc. Clin. Investigation (past pres.), Am. Gastroent. Assn. (Disting. Achievement award 1971, Kirsner prize 1990, Disting. Educator award 1991, Friedenwald medal 1993), Am. Gastroenterology Assn. (Lifetime Achievement in Digestive Sci. award, 1999). Office: Baylor U Med Ctr 3500 Gaston Ave Dallas TX 75246-2096 Home: 3408 Hanover St Dallas TX 75225-7643 Office Phone: 214-820-2672. E-mail: johnfo@baylorhealth.edu.

FORDYCE, JAMES GEORGE, physician; b. Detroit, Jan. 9, 1945; s. James Alexander and Stella Marie (Pakron) F.; m. Kathleen Marie Ray, June 17, 1967; children: James A., Jonathan A., Jared A. BS, Mich. State U., 1966, DVM, 1968; MD, Wayne State U., 1974. Diplomate Am. Bd. Pediats., Am. Bd. Allergy and Immunology. Intern, resident Children's Hosp. Mich., Detroit, 1973-76; fellow allergy and clin. immunology Henry Ford Hosp., Detroit, 1976-78; physician Dearborn (Mich.) Allergy and Asthma Clinic, PC, 1978—. Cons. Metro Med. Group, Detroit, 1979-95. Author: Asthma in Clinical Pulmonary Medicine, 1992. Bd. trustees Oakwood Healthcare, Inc., 1996-2000. Fellow Am. Acad. Pediats., Am. Acad. Allergy, Asthma and Immunology, Am. Coll. Allergy, Asthma and Immunology; mem. Mich. Allergy and Asthma Soc. (pres. 1991-92). Avocations: fishing, flying, sailing. Office: Dearborn Allergy & Asthma Clinic PC 20200 Outer Dr Dearborn MI 48124-2634 Office Phone: 313-565-3565. Personal E-mail: jgfordyce@comcast.net.

FORDYCE, MICHAEL, rehabilitation hospital administrator; m. Terri Fordyce; children: Betsy, Chris. Student, U. Cin. V.p. human resources Sisters of Charity Health Care Systems of Cin.; sr. v.p. human resources Catholic Health Initiatives, 1996—99, chief adminstrv. officer, 1999—2008; pres. Craig Hosp., Englewood, Colo., 2008—. Bd. dirs. Craig Hosp., Englewood, Colo., 1998—2005, chmn., 2003—04. Office: Craig Hospital 3425 S Clarkson St Englewood CO 80113 Office Phone: 303-789-8000.

FOREMAN, JOHN WILLIAM, pediatrician, educator; b. Washington, June 23, 1947; s. William Roy and Elizabeth Roberts (McLean) F.; m. Linda Poffenberger, May 27 1973; children: Matthew John, Jennifer Lynne. BS, Duke U., 1969; MD, U. Md., 1973. Diplomate Nat. Bd. Med. Examiners, Pa., Va., N.C., Am. Bd. Pediatrics, subbd. pediatric nephrology. Intern, resident Montreal (Que., Can.) Children's Hosp., 1973-75; asst. chief resident pediatrics Children's Hosp. Phila., 1975-76, fellow pediatric nephrology, 1976-79, staff physician, 1979-86; instr. pediatrics U. Pa. Sch. Medicine, Phila., 1976-79, clin. asst. prof., asst. prof., 1979-85, assoc. prof., 1985-86; assoc. prof. pediatrics Med. Coll. Va., Va. Commonwealth U., Richmond, 1986-90, prof., 1990-93; prof., chief divsn. pediatric nephrology Duke U. Med. Ctr., Durham, NC, 1993—. Cons. WHO, 1984; chmn. med. adv. bd. Nat. Kidney Found. Va., 1989-92, mem. exec. com. pediatric urology and nephrology coun.; mem. pediatric delegation to Chinese Med. Assn. of People's Republic of China. Contbr. articles to profl. jours., chpts. to books. Bd. dirs. Transplant Found., Richmond, 1991. Daland fellow Am. Philos. Soc., Phila., 1980-81; grantee Am. Heart Assn., 1984-88, NIH, 1988-91. Fellow Am. Acad. Pediat.; mem. Soc. Pediatric Rsch., Am. Pediatric Soc., So. Soc. Pediatric Rsch. (councillor 1989-91), Internat. Pediatric Nephrology Soc. (councillor 1993-98), Am. Soc. Pediatric Nephrology (coun. mem. 2002-06), Am. Soc. Nephrology, chair exec. com. Sect. on Nephrology 2004-10), Am. Acad. Pediat., Am. Bd. Pediat. (bd. mem. pediat. nephrology, 2008-). Avocation: reading. Home: 9 Streamley Ct Durham NC 27705-5396 Office: Duke U Med Ctr PO Box 3959 Durham NC 27710-0001 Office Phone: 919-684-4246. Business E-Mail: forem001@mc.duke.edu.

FOREMAN, SPENCER (SPIKE FOREMAN), retired hospital administrator, pulmonologist; b. Phila., Nov. 10, 1935; s. Samuel and Freda F.; m. Sandra Lee Finkelstein, June 10, 1961; children: Corinne, Todd, Cheryl, Andrea. BS, Ursinus Coll., 1957; MD, U. Pa., 1961. Diplomate in internal medicine and pulmonary disease Am. Bd. Internal Medicine. Intern Henry Ford Hosp., Detroit, 1961-62; med. officer USPHS, San Pedro, Calif., 1962-63; resident in internal medicine USPHS Hosp., New Orleans, 1963-65; fellow in pulmonary diseases Tulane U., 1965-67; asst. chief dept. internal medicine USPHS Hosp., Balt., 1967-68, chief dept. internal medicine, 1968-73, hosp. dir., 1971-73; CEO Sinai Hosp., Balt., 1973-86; pres. Montefiore Med. Ctr., Bronx, NY, 1986—2008, pres. emeritus, 2008—. Prof. medicine, prof. social medicine and epidemiology Albert Einstein Coll. Medicine, Bronx; mem. Accreditation Coun. on Med. Edn., 1981-87, ProPAC (Prospective Payment Assessment Commn.) 1996. Contbr. articles to med. jours. Commr. Md. Health Resources Commn., 1982-86, Liaison Com. for Med. Edn., 1989-91; bd. dirs. Am. Jewish Joint Distbn. Com., Inc., Ursinus Coll., Collegeville, Pa.; chmn. Biomed. Rsch. Alliance N.Y., 1998-2000, chmn., 2000-; vice chmn. Ursinus Coll., 2002-04, chmn., 2004-. Capt. USPHS, 1962-73. Fellow ACP, N.Y. Acad. Medicine; mem. Inst. Medicine Nat. Acad. Scis., Assn. Am. Med. Colls. (rep. assembly, chmn. 1986, adminstrv. bd. Coun. Tchg. Hosps., chmn.-elect assembly 1991-92, chmn. 1992-93), Am. Hosp. Assn. (bd. dirs. 1995-98), Health Forum (bd. dirs. 1998-99), Greater N.Y. Hosp. Assn. (bd. dirs., vice chmn., chmn.), League Vol. Hosps. (bd. dirs., sec.-treas., chmn.), N.Y. Bot Garden (bd. mgrs. 2007-), Soc. Med. Adminstrs. (pres. 2000-02). *

FOREMAN, THOMAS ALEXANDER, dentist; b. Tionesta, Pa., Oct. 24, 1930; s. James Aura and May Lanson Foreman; m. Dorothy Jean Wolf, June 12, 1953; children: Bonnie Jean, Julie Marie, Mary Aleta, Lloyd George. Student, Grove City Coll., 1948—50; BS, Allegheny Coll., 1952; DDS cum laude, U. Pitts., 1957, DMD, 1970. Gen. practice dentistry, Clarion, Pa., 1961—. Active Clarion Hosp. Assn., 1965—; exec. bd. Colonel Drake coun. Boy Scouts Am., 1969-72, mem.-at-large French Creek coun., 1972-73, vice-chmn. Indian Trails dist., 1971-73; governing coun. Alpha Christian Acad. Sch., 1977-81. Capt. with Dental Corps., strategic air command USAF, 1957—61. Fellow, Pierre Fauchard Acad.; fellowship, Royal Soc. Health, 1973—2008. Fellow Acad. Dentistry Internat., Am. Coll. Dentists, Internat. Coll. Dentists; mem. ADA, Pa. Dental Assn. (dir. 8th dist. 1964-87, 91-2009, pres. 1974-76, 2006-08, trustee 1987-91), Acad. Gen. Dentistry (master), AMA (affiliate), Clarion County Dental Soc. (pres. 1983-87), SAR (pres. Capt. Samuel Brady chpt. 1970-71, 77-80), Soc. Mayflower Descs., Pilgrim Edward Doty Soc., Fedn. Denture Internat., Pa. Soc., We. Pa. Conservancy, Cook Forest Ctr. for Arts, Clarion County Hist. Soc., Masons, Shriners, Phi Beta Phi, Omicron Kappa Upsilon, Delta Sigma Delta, Theta Chi, The Am. Legion. Presbyn. (pres. bd. trustees 1966-67, supt. Sunday sch. 1966-67, chmn. endowment trust fund dirs. 1980-84, 2006-08, elder 2001—). Home: 147 S 7th Ave Clarion PA 16214-2006 Office: 832 E Main St Clarion PA 16214-1168

FORERO, DIEGO A., biomedical researcher, educator; b. Bogotá, Colombia, Nov. 27, 1980; MD, Nat. U. Colombia, 2003; PhD, U. Antwerp, 2009. Rschr. Nat. U. Colombia, 2003—05, Flanders Inst. Biotech., 2006—09; asst. prof. Antonio Nariño U., 2009—. Editor hum-molgen.org, 2008—11. Contbr. articles to numerous sci. profl. publs. Travel fellowship, Internat. Brain Rsch. Orgn., fellowship, Flanders Inst. Biotech. Mem.: Colombian Assn. Human Genetics, Colombian Assn. Neurosci. Avocations: history, photography. Home: Av 19 # 125-65 Apt 104 Bogotá Cundinamarca Colombia Personal E-mail: daforerog@gmail.com.

FORESE, LAURA LEE, hospital administrator, orthopedist; b. Suffern, NY, Aug. 17, 1961; m. Robert J. Downey; 3 children. BSE in civil engring. and ops. rsch. (summa cum laude), Princeton U., 1983; MD, Columbia U. Coll. Physicians and Surgeons, 1987; M in Health Svc. Mgmt., Columbia Sch. Pub. Health (now called Mailman Sch. Pub. Health), 1995. Intern, orthop. surgery NY Presbyterian Hosp., NYC, NJ, 1987—88, asst. attending orthop. physician, 1994, v.p. med. affairs, 2003—05; asst. attending physician Helen Hayes Hosp., West Haverstraw, NY, 1993—97, chief surgical and anesthesia services, 1994—97; resident, orthop. surgery Columbia U., 1988—93, vice chair, dept. orthopaedic surgery, 1998—2002; sr. v.p., chief med. officer NY Presbyterian Hosp./Weill Cornell Med. Ctr., NYC, 2005—, COO, 2006—. Faculty mem. specializing in pediatric orthopaedic surgery, assoc. clin. prof. Columbia U., 1993—; teaches physician-patient comm. to orthopaedic surgeons in the US; lectr. in field. Mem.: Am. Coll. Physician Executives, NY Acad. Medicine, Am. Acad. Orthopaedic Surgeons (editor-in-chief, Orthopedic Medical Legal Advisor, comm. skills mentor), Assn. Am. Med. Coll., Health Mgmt. Acad., Alpha Omega Alpha, Phi Beta Kappa. Office: NY Presbyterian Hosp/Weill Cornell Med Ctr M-106 525 E 68th St New York NY 10021 *

FORGHANI-ABKENARI, BAGHER, virologist, researcher; b. Bandar-Anzali, Iran, Mar. 10, 1936; U.S.A., 1969; s. Baba Forghani-Abkenari and Jahan Rahimi; m. Nikoo Alavi Forghani; children: Niki, Nikta. MS, Justus Liebig U., 1961, PhD, 1965. Postdoctoral fellow Utah State U., Logan, 1965—67, rsch. assoc., 1969—70; asst. prof. Nat. U. Iran, Tehran, 1967—69; various positions State of Calif. Dept. Pub. Health, Richmond, 1970—82; chief viral immunoserology sec. State of Calif. Dept. Health Svc., Richmond, 1982—2007. Cons. Nat. Registry Microbiologists, Washington, 1976—; mem. sci. adv. bd. Varicella-Zoster Virus Rsch. Found., NYC, 1991. Contbr. chapters to books, more than 80 articles to profl. jours. Mem.: Am. Soc. Microbiology, Am. Soc. Clin. Pathology (assoc.; cert. specialist in microbiology 2005). Office: 850 Marina Bay Parkway Richmond CA 94804 Office Phone: 510-307-8617. Business E-Mail: bagher.forghani@cdph.ca.gov.

FORGIONE, DANA ANTHONY, accounting educator; BBA, U. Mass., Amherst, 1975; MBA, 1977, MS in Acctg., 1980, PhD, 1987; cert. in Christian Leadership with high honors, Heritage Bapt. Inst., Springfield, Mass., 1979, cert. in Ch. Ministries, 1983. CPA Md., Tex., Fla., CMA, cert. fraud examiner. Asst. prof. C.W. Post Ctr. Sch. Profl. Accountancy LI U., Greenvale, NY, 1981-83; asst. prof. Sch. Bus. We. New Eng. Coll., Springfield, Mass., 1983-87; asst. prof. Coll. Bus. Adminstrn., Grad. Sch. Bus. Tex. A&M U., College Station, 1987-93; assoc. prof. Merrick Sch. Bus. U. Balt., 1993-2000, prof., 2000-2001, dir. profl. MBA program Merrick Sch. Bus., 1993-2000, advisor MBA specialization in healthcare mgmt., 1993-2001; affilliate assoc. prof. Sch. Pharmacy U. Md., Balt., 1996-2000, affiliate prof., 2000-2001; dir., prof. Sch. Acctg. Fla. Internat. U., Miami, 2001—05, prof., dir. Ctr. for Acctg., Auditing and Tax Studies, Sch. Acctg., 2006; Janey S. Briscoe endowed chair in bus. health, dept. acctg. U. Tex. Coll. Bus., San Antonio, 2006—; adj. prof., Sch. Pub. Health U. Tex., 2007—, adj. prof., dept. pediat., Sch. Medicine, 2008—, adj. prof., dept. cardiothoracic surgery, Sch. Medicine, 2011—. Prin. Global Anti-Fraud Cons., Inc., Balt., 1998—2001; cons. U.S. Dept. Vets Affairs, 1997; cons in field. Author: Costly Reflections in a Midas Mirror, 1994, Costly Reflections in a Midas Mirror, 2d edit., 1999; co-author: Pet Polygon Mfg. Company Management Accounting Case, 1992, Pet Polygon Mfg. Company Management Accounting Case, 3d edit., Laser Logos, Inc., 1994, Laser Logos, Inc., 2d edit., 1997; sr. editor Rsch. in Healthcare Fin. Mgmt., 1994—2000; sr. editor: mng. editor Rsch. in Healthcare Fin. Mgmt., 2000—09,: chmn. editl. rev. bd. The White Paper, 1996—99, columnist Jour. Health Care Finance, reviewer Internat. Jour. Pub. Adminstrn., Govt. Accts. Jour., reviewer: reviewer Govtl. and Non Profit Acctg., 1992—2009,: mem. editl. bd. Today's CPA, 1992—93, Jour. Econ. and Fin., 1992—95, Pub. Budgeting, Acctg. and Fin. Mgmt., 1994—, mem. editl. bd.: mem. editl. bd. Jour. Health Care Fin., 1996—2009, Rsch. in Govt. and Nonprofit Acctg., 1996—2009, rev. Issues in Acctg. Edn., 1997—2007,: mem. editl. bd., 1998—, Fin. Accountability and Mgmt., 1994—, assoc. editor N.Am., 1998—; contbr. articles to profl. jours.; rev.: Internat. Jour. Pub. Adminstrn., 2001—. Litig. support, expert testimony, cons. Tex. Atty. Gen., 1992—93. Symposium fellow Office for Govt. Acctg. Rsch. and Edn. U. Ill. Chgo., 1984; recipient Chancellor's Citation for Undergrad. Instrs., U. Mass., 1973, Hon. Mention Manuscript award Mass. Soc. CPAs, 1976, Outstanding Fac. Mem. award, Beta Alpha Psi (acctg. Hon. Fraternity), 1992, Incentive Grant for Tchg., Ctr. for Tchg. Excellence, Tex. A&M U., 1992, Curriculum Funds Development Awd., Merrick Sch. Bus., 1994, Manuscript award Nat. Assn. Accts., Black and Decker Rsch. Awd., Merrick Sch. Bus., U. Balt., 1995, 99, Top 10 List, Merrick Sch. of Bus., 1995, Diploma of Honor, U. San Marcos, Peru, 2004, Best Faculty award Fla. Internat. U. Acctg. Assoc., 2004, Outstanding Rsch. Paper award Am. Acctg. Assoc. Govt. and Non-Profit Sect., 2008; Rsch. fellowship Ctr. Acctg., Audit and Tax Rsch., Fla. Internat. U., 2005-2006; named hon. prof. Ricardo Palma U., Peru, 2004—. Mem.: Inst. Pub. Sector Acctg. Rsch. U. Edinburgh (internat. assoc.), Assn. Cert. Fraud Examiners (bd. regents 1999—2000, regent emeritus 2001—), Internat. Soc. Rsch. in Healthcare Fin. Mgmt. (dir. 1994—2011, founder), Internat. Assn. Mgmt. (Internat. Regional Publ. award 1996, sr. editor jour. 1996—98, chmn. healthcare mgmt. divsn. 1997—98, Divsn. award 1998), Am. Acctg. Assn. (mem. exec. com. Mid-Atlantic region 1994—2001, pres. Mid-Atlantic region 1996—97, mem. nat. coun. 1996—97, sec., treas. govt. and nonprofit sect. 2003—04, pres. govt. and nonprofit sect. 2005—06, mem. nat. coun. 2005—06). Baptist. Avocations: computers, biblical chronology, woodworking. Office: U Texas at San Antonio One UTSA Circle San Antonio TX 78249-0632 Business E-Mail: dana.forgione@utsa.edu.

FORLENZA, VINCENT A., medical products executive; BS in Chem. Engring., Lehigh U.; MBA, Wharton Grad. Sch., U. Penn., 1980. Various positions including product mgr., pres. diagnostic systems, pres. microbiology systems Becton, Dickinson & Co., Franklin Lakes, NJ, 1980—98, sr. v.p. strategy and devel., 1999—2003, pres. BD Biosciences San Jose, Calif., 2003—06, exec. v.p. Franklin Lakes, NJ, 2006—08, pres., 2009—10, pres., COO, 2010—11, pres., CEO, 2011—. Mem. U. Md. Balt. County Bd. of Visitors; trustee Valley Hospital. Office: Becton Dickinson and Co 1 Becton Dr Franklin Lakes NJ 07417-1880 *

FORLEO, ROMANO C., gynecologist, journalist, novelist; b. Bologna, Italy, Nov. 12, 1933; m. Giulia Pagliai, Sept. 24, 1959; children: Patrizia, Pier Francesco. MD, U. Florence, 1958, PhD in Ob-gyn., 1965, PhD in Endocrine Gynecology, 1968. Resident U. Florence, 1958—62; rsch. fellow in ovarian endocrinology Chelsea Hosp., London, 1962-63; asst. prof. U. Florence, 1965-68, U. La Sapienza, Rome, 1968-72; prof. Sch. Midwifery Tor Vergata U., 1998—. Prof. postgrad. sch. ob-gyn. I Univ., Rome, 1968—72, prof. sexology faculty psychology, 1975—78, 2000—; prof. postgrad. ob-gyn. Cath. U., 1972—80, II Univ. Rome, 1980—, prof. history medicine, faculty medicine, 1996—2001, Sch. Midwifery, 2001—; head dept. ob-gyn. Fatebenefratelli Hosp., 1972—97; cons. gyn. dept. Citta di Roma and Aurelian Hosp., 2001—; mem. Nat. Com. on Bioethics, 1999—. Contbr. numerous scientific publications including books on physiopathology of reproduction, gynecological surgery, medical care in childbirth, sex education, childbirth care and educational books for adolescents; also contbr. numerous articles to newspapers. Senator Italian Republic, 1992—94; mem. Nat. Com. Christian-Social Movement, 1994—2000. Decorated Order of Merit of Italian Republic. Mem.: ACOG, Internat. Soc. History Medicine (italian del.), Nat. Com. Bioethics, Order of Journalists, Acad. Sanitaria Art and Sci., Italian Soc. Sterility and Fertility (v.p. 1987—89), Adolescent Gynecology Soc. (gen. sec. 1991—99), World Assn. Sexology (past pres.), Italian Soc. Ob-Gyn., Movement Italian Cath. Adult Scouts. Office: Villa Citla di Roma 200152 Via Maidalchini Italy Home: Via della Lungarina 65 153 Rome RM Italy Office Phone: 39-06-5881137. Business E-Mail: rcforleo@mclink.it.

FORMAN, SARA F., pediatrician, adolescent medicine, educator; MD, Harvard U., 1988. Diplomate Am. Bd. Pediatrics-adolescent medicine, 2005. Resident pediat. Children's Hosp., Phila., 1989—91, fellow adolescent Boston, 1991—92, dir. resident and med. student tng. in adolescent medicine, dir. outpatient eating disorders program; asst. prof. pediat. Harvard Med. Sch. Office: Children's Hospital Boston 333 Longwood Ave Fl 5th Boston MA 02115-5724 Office Phone: 617-355-7181. Office Fax: 617-730-0184.

FORMENTO, ENRIQUE ALONSO, emergency physician; b. Zaragoza, Spain, Nov. 17, 1971; m. Blanca Envid Lazaro; children: Ines Alonso Envid, Pablo Alonso Envid. PhD, U. Zaragoza, 1995. Lic. Hosp. Miguel Servet Zaragoza, 2000. Emergency physician Hosp. Obispo Polanco, Teruel, Spain, 2000—05. Tchr. Nursing Sch., Teruel, 2000—05. Mem.: SEMES. Office: Hosp Obispo Polanco Teruel Avda Ruiz Jarabo S/n Teruel Spain Home: Plaza Playa de Aro 3 44002 Teruel Spain E-mail: ealonsof@papps.org.

FORNAGE, BRUNO DENIS, radiologist, educator; b. Reims, France, July 2, 1949; came to U.S., 1987; s. Louis and Genevieve (Mercier) F.; m. Brigitte Wittmer, Oct. 18, 1991; 1 child, Louis Bruno. MD, Med. Sch. Reims, 1974. Diplomate French Bd. Radiology, French Bd. Oncology. Resident in oncology Inst. Jean-Godinot Regional Cancer Ctr., Reims, 1974-76, resident in radiology, 1976-79, asst. dept. biophysics and nuc. medicine, 1976-82, dir. dept. radiology, 1982-87; assoc. prof. radiology U. Reims, 1986-87; assoc. prof. radiology, chief sect. ultrasound U. Tex. M.D. Anderson Cancer Ctr., Houston, 1987-2000, prof. radiology, 1990—, prof. surg. oncology, 1999—. Author 5 textbooks; editor 2 textbooks; mem. editl. bd. various jours.; editor-in-chief Jour. of Clin. Ultrasound, 1997—; reviewer jours.; contbr. chpts. to books, articles to profl. jours.; patentee in field. Fellow Am. Inst. Ultrasound in Medicine, Soc. Radiologists in Ultrasound, Soc. Breast Imaging; mem. Am. Roentgen Ray Soc., Radiol. Soc. N.Am., Am. Coll. Radiology, Am. Soc. Breast Disease, Internat. Skeletal Soc., numerous others. Office: U Tex MD Anderson Canc Ctr 1515 Holcombe Blvd Houston TX 77030-4009 Personal E-mail: fornage@swbell.net. Business E-Mail: bfornage@di.mdacc.tmc.edu.

FORNARA, FERDINANDO, psychologist, researcher; b. Rome, Aug. 26, 1969; s. Marco Fornara and Ines Narducci. MSc in Environ. Psychology, U. Surrey, Guildford, UK; PhD in Social Psychology, Sapienza U. Rome, degree in Psychology. Rsch. fellow environ. psychology Sapienza U. Rome, 2000—02, Inst. Cognitive Scis. and Techs., Italian NRC Rome, 2003; rschr. social and environ. psychology U. Cagliari, Italy, 2005—, lectr. social and environ. psychology, 2005—. Social worker children, adolescents and elderly Coop. Meta, Rome, 1996—99. Recipient award, Italian Assn. Psychology, 2003, Assn. Psychologists, 2003; Rsch. fellowship, Sapienza U. Rome, 2000—02, Inst. Cognitive Scis. and Techs., Italian NRC Rome, 2003. Office: Psychology Dept Univ Cagliari Via Is Mirrionis 1 9123 Cagliari CA Italy Office Phone: 0039 070 6757516. Business E-Mail: ffornara@unica.it.

FORNARI, VICTOR M., psychiatrist; b. NYC, June 20; s. Ermanno and Alice (Notrica) F.; m. Alice Johnson, Mar. 27, 1977; children: Eric, Amy, Marci. BS in Biology, Cornell U., 1974; MS in Human Nutrition, Columbia U., 1975; MD, SUNY-Downstate Med. Ctr., Bklyn., 1979. Diplomate Am. Bd. Psychiatry and Neurology, Am. Bd. Child and Adolescent Psychiatry and Neurology. Intern LI Coll. Hosp., Bklyn., 1979-80; resident in psychiatry Hosp. U. Pa., Phila., 1980-82; fellow in child and adolescent psychiatry LI Jewish Med. Ctr., New Hyde Park, 1982-84; staff child psychiatrist Schneider's Children's Hosp./LI Jewish Med. Ctr., 1984-85; physician-in-charge Child Psychiatry Inpatient Unit/LI Jewish Med. Ctr., 1985-86; physician-in-charge, child psychiatry cons. liaison svc., eating disorders program North Shore-Cornell U. Hosp., Manhasset, NY, 1986-91, dir. tng./clin. svcs. div. child and adolescent psychiatry, 1991—98; assoc. chmn. edn. and tng. North Shore U. Hosp./NYU Sch. Medicine, 1998—2006; acting dir. divsn. child and adolescent psychiatry Zucker Hillside Hosp. North Shore-LI Jewish Health Sys., 2006—; dir. divsn. child and adolescent psychiatry North Shore LI Jewish Health Sys., 2007. Assoc. prof. psychiatry and pediatrics Cornell U. Med. Coll., NYC, 1991—; assoc. prof. NYU Sch. Medicine, 1993-2006, prof. psychiatry, 2006-; clin. dir. dept. psychiatry North Shore U. Hosp., 2007-2008. Fellow Am. Psychiat. Assn. (disting.), Am. Acad. Child and Adolescent Psychiatry; mem. Greater LI Psychiat. Soc. (pres.), Am. Assn. Dirs. of Psychiat. Resident Tng., Soc. Profs. of Child and Adolescent Psychiatry. Office Phone: 718-470-3510.

FORNESS, STEVEN ROBERT, educational psychologist; b. Denver, May 13, 1939; s. Robert E. and Rejeana C. (Houck) F. BA in English, U. No. Colo., 1963, MA in Ednl. Psychology, 1964; EdD in Spl. Edn., UCLA, 1968. Tchr. Santa Maria (Calif.) H.S., 1964—66; counselor Sch. Edn. UCLA, 1966—68; spl. educator Neuropsychiat. Inst., 1968—2003, chief ednl. psychology child outpatient dept., 1970—2003, mem. mental retardation rsch. ctr., 1970—2003, prof. dept. psychiatry, 1972—2003, prin. inpatient sch., 1976—2003, dir. mental retardation and devel. disabilities tng. program, 1985—92, disting. prof. emeritus, 2003—. Grant rev. panelist U.S. Dept. Edn., 1974-2000; cons. Nat. Assn. Exceptional Children, Venezuela, 1974-2000; commn. ednl. psychology Calif. State Bd. Behavioral Scis. Examiners, 1977-99. Author: (with Frank Hewett) Education of Exceptional Learners, 3d edit., 1984, (with K. Kavale) Science of Learning Disabilities, 1985, (with Kavale and Bender) Handbook of Learning Disabilities, vols. I, II and III, 1987, 88; (with K. Kavale) Nature of Learning Disabilities, 1995, Efficacy of Special Education, 1999, (with E. Sinclair) Learning Disabilites and Related Disorders, 2002, (with L. Serna) Social Skills in Picture, Stories, and Songs, 2007; cons. editor various jours. Sr. scholar Shaklee Inst. on Spl. Edn., 1996-2001. Recipient Disting. Alumni award U. No. Colo., 2006; Fulbright scholar Ministry of Edn., Portugal, 1976. Fellow Internat. Acad. Rsch. in Learning Disabilties, Am. Assn. Mental Retardation; mem. Tchr. Educators of Children with Behavior Disorders (pres. 1985-86), Coun. Children with Behavior Disorders (pres. 1987-88, Leadership award 1995, Forness Regional Scholarship 2003), Am. Assn. Univ. Affiliated Programs in Developmental Disabilities (interdisciplinary coun. 1972-89), Internat. Coun. for Exceptional Children (del. Assembly 1988-91, Wallin award 1992, Excellence in Tchr. Edn. award 1995, honors com. 1999-2002), Acad. on Mental Retardation (exec. com. 1989-91), Nat. Mental Health and Spl. Edn. Coalition (co-chair of Definition Task Force 1987-2000), Am. Psychiat. Assn. (DSM IV subcom. on learning disorders 1988-94), Profl. Group for Attention and Related Disorders (com. profl. advisors 1990-91), Midwest Symposium on Behavioral Disorders (Leadership award 1993), Am. Acad. Child and Adolescent Psychiatry (co-chmn. practice parameters on learning disabilities 1996-98, Sidney Berman award on learning disorders 2000), Knights of Malta (Order of St. John 1994). Home: 11901 W Sunset Blvd Los Angeles CA 90049-4240

FORNI, PATRICIA ROSE, nursing educator; b. St. Louis, Feb. 14, 1932; d. Harold and Glenda M. (Keay) Brown. BSN, Washington U., St. Louis, 1955, MS (USPHS trainee), 1957; PhD (USPHS fellow), St. Louis U., 1965; postgrad. (USPHS scholar), U. Minn., summers 1968, 70. Staff nurse McMillan EENT Hosp., St. Louis, summer 1955, Renard Psychiat. Hosp., St. Louis, part-time 1955-57; rsch. asst. Washington U. Sch. Nursing, St. Louis, 1957-59, rsch. assoc., 1959-61, asst. prof., 1964-66, assoc. dean in charge grad. edn., assoc. prof. gen. nursing sci., 1966-68; assoc. prof. pub. health nursing Wayne State U., Detroit, 1968-69; asst. dir. for manpower and edn. Ill. Regional Med. Program, Chgo., 1969-71; project dir. Midwest Continuing Profl. Edn. for Nurses, St. Louis U., 1971-75; dean, prof. nursing So. Ill. U., Edwardsville, 1975-88; dean Coll. Nursing U. Okla., Oklahoma City, 1988—2004, prof. Coll. Nursing, 1988—, dean emeritus, Coll. Nursing, 2008—. Grant proposal reviewer Divsn. Nursing, USPHS, 1972-79, 88, 91, NSF, 1978, U.S. Dept. Edn., 1980; mem. Ill. Implementation Commn. on Nursing, 1975-77, Okla. State Health Plan Adv. Com., 1994—. Mem. peer rev. panel Nursing Outlook, 1987-91; mem. editl. bd. Health Care for Women Internat., 1984—, Jour. Profl. Nursing, 1988-90. Chairwoman articulation of nursing programs task force Okla. State Regents for Higher Edn., 1990-91; bd. dirs. Greater St. Louis Health Sys. Agy., 1976-81, Adult Edn. Coun. Greater St. Louis, 1973-76, Edwardsville unit Am. Cancer Soc., 1981-88. Fellow WHO, Sweden, Finland, 1985. Mem. Nat. League for Nursing (accreditation site visitor 1979—, nominating com. Coun. Baccalaureate and Higher Degree Programs 1979-82, pub. policy and legis. com. 1981-85, bd. dirs. 1991-93, treas. 1991-93, fin. com. 1991-95), Nat. League for Health Care (trustee 1991-93), Nat. League for Nursing Accrediting Commn. (peer review panel, baccalaureate and higher degree programs 1997-2000, 06, commr. 2000-06, chmn. 2001-06), Am. Nurses Assn. (chmn. continuing edn. publs. com. 1975-76), Mo. Nurses Assn. (chmn. edn. com. 1973-77), Greater St. Louis Soc. Health Manpower Edn. and Tng. (chmn. legis. com. 1974-75), Midwest Alliance in Nursing (1st governing bd. 1979-80, 93-96, chmn. nominations com. 1980-81, fin. com. 1993-94, chair fin. com. 1994-96, treas. 1994-96, pres. 1998-2000), Am. Assn. Colls. Nursing (hon., program com. 1978-82, mem.-at-large, bd. dirs. 1990-92, chair rsch. com. 1990-92), Ill. Coun. Deans/Dirs. Baccalaureate and Higher Degree Programs in Nursing (chmn. 1979-81), Am. Acad. Nursing (treas., chair fin. com., gov. coun. 1989-93, editor Newsletter 1982-87), Ill. Nurses Assn. (commn. on adminstrn. 1983-87, commn. on edn. 1987-89), Okla. Nurses Found. (pres. bd. trustees 1990-93), Sigma Theta Tau Internat. (charter mem. Epsilon Eta chpt. 1980). Office: Univ Okla Coll Nursing PO Box 26901 Oklahoma City OK 73216-0901

FORREST, DAVID VICKERS, psychiatrist, educator; b. NYC, July 8, 1938; s. Melbourne Arthur and Cleo Florence (Garello) Forrest; m. Lynne Putnam Stetson; children: Daniel Stetson, Susannah Forrest Karajannis. AB summa cum laude, Princeton U., 1960; MD, Columbia U., 1964, cert. in psychoanalysis, 1974. Cert. in psychiatry Am. Bd. Psychiatry and Neurology. Intern in medicine St. Luke's Hosp., NYC, 1964-65; resident in psychiatry N.Y. State Psychiat. Inst., Columbia Presbyn. Med. Ctr., NYC, 1965-68; chief psychiatric clinic 935th Med. Det. (KO) 93d Evacuation Hosp., Long Binh, Vietnam, 1968-69; chief psychiatric consultation Letterman Army Med. Ctr., San Francisco, 1969-70; pvt. practice psychiatry NYC, 1970—; mem. psychiatry faculty Columbia U., NYC, 1970—; dir. edn. ednl. rsch. dept. N.Y. State Psychiat. Inst., 1970-77; assoc. prof. clin. psychiatry Columbia U., Coll. Physicians and Surgeons, NYC, 1984—, faculty psychoanalytic ctr., 1974—, consultation-liaison psychiatrist neurology (movement disorders), 1977—, clin. prof. of psychiatry NYC, 2000—. Lectr. psychiatry U. Saigon Med. Sch., Vietnam, 1968-69; lectr. abnormal psychology Far East div. U. Md., Long Binh, Vietnam, 1969. Author: Selected American Expressions, 1974, 76, 82; co-author: Treating Schizophrenic Patients, 1983, (video cassette series) Electronic Textbook of Psychiatry, 1972-77; co-author, pub: The Ballet Company Game, 1973; founding editor, pub. Spring: The Jour. of the E. E. Cummings Soc., N.Y.C., 1980—; editor: Neural Net News, N.Y. State Psychiat. Inst., 1989-91; technical cons. Star Trek TV series, 1997—; contbr. articles to profl. jours., textbooks. Psychiat. cons. N.Y.C. Ballet Co., 1973; first aid instr. Boy Scouts Am., 1983—. Capt. USAF, 1968-70, Vietnam. Decorated Bronze Star; Gen. Motors nat. scholar; recipient Excellence award APA, 2007-08, Nancy CA Roeske MD award, APA, 2007. Fellow Am. Psychiat. Assn., Am. Coll. Psychiatrists, Am. Acad. Psychoanalysis (program chair), Am. Coll. Psychoanalysts (program chair 1987-89, bd. regents 1989-92, v.p. 1993, pres.-elect 1994, pres. 1995), Explorers Club; mem. Am. Acad. Neurology (assoc.), NY Clin. Soc. (v.p. 1995, pres. 1996), Med. Strollers (v.p. 2007, pres. 2008-10), Soc. Illustrators. Episcopalian. Avocations: invention, discovery, magic. also: 155 W 68th St Apt 1219 New York NY 10023-5818 Office: 115 E 61st St Ste 8E New York NY 10065-8185 Office Phone: 212-319-5929.

FORREST, JOHN BENNETT, urologist; b. Tulsa, Okla., Oct. 20, 1951; BA, U. Tulsa, 1972; MD, U. Okla., 1976. Resident gen. surgery, urology U. Va., 1976—82; fellow Meml. Sloan Kettering Cancer Inst., 1982—83; staff physician Urologic Specialists Okla., Inc., 1983—. Trustee, pres. elect Am. Bd. Urology, 2007—; chmn. Practice Guidelines Com. Am. Urol. Assn., 2008—; past pres. South Ctrl. Sect. Am. Urol. Assn., 2009—10. Recipient Disting. Alumni award, U. Tulsa, 2005. Fellow: ACS. Avocations: horseback riding, tennis. Office: 10901 E 48th St Tulsa OK 74146 Office Fax: 918-392-2255. Business E-Mail: jforrest@sjmc.org.

FORRESTER, ALFRED WHITFIELD, psychiatrist, educator; b. Springfield, Mass., May 15, 1953; s. Wallace Lomax and Alma Mae (Brooks) F. BA magna cum laude, Yale U., 1975; MD, Johns Hopkins U., 1979. Diplomate Nat. Bd. Med. Examiners, Am. Bd. Psychiatry and Neurology. Med. resident dept. medicine Mt. Auburn Hosp., Cambridge, Mass., 1979-82; psychiatry resident dept. psychiatry and behavioral scis. Johns Hopkins Med. Insts., Balt., 1982-85, research fellow, 1985-86, instr., 1986-93; clin. asst. prof. dept. psychiatry U. Md., Balt., 1987—; pvt. psychiat. practice, 1988—. Staff psychiatrist Cann Health Resources, Fallston, Md., 1987-88, The Sheppard and Enoch Pratt Hosp., 1988-97, QCI Behavioral Health, Largo, Md., 2009-; dir. psychiat. svcs. Chase-Brexton Health Svcs., Balt., 1988-90, staff psychiatrist, 1985-2000; med. dir. Behavioral Sci. Assocs., Lutherville, Md., 1993-97, Nicotine Addiction Treatment Ctrs., Lutherville, 1997-2002; med. cons. Bon Secours Hosp., Balt., 1983-90; psychiat. cons. Shock-Trauma Ctr. U. Md. Hosp., 1987-90. Contbr. articles to profl. jours. Active Groton (Mass.) Sch. Bd. Govs., 1983-85, AIDS com., Med. and Chirurgical Faculty State of Md., 1988-91. Nat. Achievement scholar, 1971—75. Fellow APA; mem. AMA, ACP, Med. and Chirurgical Faculty State Md., Md. Psychiat. Soc., Md. Psychiat. Liaison Assn., Yale Alumni Assn. (fundraiser 1975-2003), Greater Balt. Bus. Profl. Assn., Mory's Assn. (New Haven), Yale Club (Md.), Johns Hopkins Club. Democrat. Episcopalian. Avocations: classical music, theater. Home: 115 Saint Dunstans Rd Baltimore MD 21212-3311 Office: 9515 Deereco Rd Ste 1001 Timonium MD 21093 Office Phone: 410-453-0901. Business E-Mail: a.w.forrester@att.net.

FORRESTER, JAMES STUART, cardiologist, medical educator; b. Phila., July 13, 1937; s. James S. and Mildred W. (Smith) F.; m. Deborah MacAdam, 1963 (div. 1974); children: Jeffrey Lance, Brent Worth; m. Barbara Ann Bick, May 27, 1975; 1 child, Justin Bick. BA, Swarthmore Coll., 1959; MD, U. Pa., 1963. Diplomate Am. Bd. Internal Medicine; bd. cert. cardiovascular disease. Intern U. Pa. Hosp.; resident Harbor Gen. Hosp.; fellow Peter Bent Brigham Hosp.; prof. medicine, David Geffen Sch. Medicine UCLA, 1986—; dir. divsn. cardiology Cedars-Sinai Med. Ctr., LA, 1989-95, dir. cardiovascular rsch. inst., 1993—, George Burns and Gracie Allen prof. cardiology, 1989—. Recipient Goldman award for laser rsch. SPIE, 1990, Kellerman award for prevention cardiology rsch. Internat. Soc. Heart Failure, 1996; named Best Doctors in Am., 1994, 95, 96, 97, 98, Best Heart Doctors in Am., Good Housekeeping, 1996. Mem. Am. Coll. Cardiology (bd. trustees 1993-98), Am. Heart Assn. (bd. dirs. 1993—2003, Disting. Sci. Achievement award 1990, Lifetime Achievement award 2009). Office: Cedars Sinai Med Ctr 8700 Beverly Blvd Los Angeles CA 90048-1865 also: David Geffen Sch Medicine SINAI-5347 UCLA Los Angeles CA 90095 Office Phone: 310-423-3977.

FORSLEFF, LOUISE STEWART, psychologist, educator; b. Portland, Maine, Oct. 7, 1933; d. Roland and Gertrude (More) Peterson; m. Elmer Andrew Forsleff Dec. 24, 1965 (dec. June 4, 1993); children: Mary Anne, John Clark. AB, Lake Erie Coll., 1959; MA, Western Mich. U., 1962; PhD, Mich. State U., 1967. Lic. psychologist, Mich.; diplomate Am. Bd. Sexology. Testing, rsch. Kalamazoo Pub. Schs., 1962; counselor Western Mich. U., U. Counseling Ctr., Kalamazoo, 1962-68, dir., 1968-85; assoc. v.p. student svcs. Western Mich. U., Kalamazoo, 1985-90, prof. Sch. Cmty. Health Svcs., 1990-98, prof. emerita, 1998—. Coord. Profl. Exchg. Clearing House, 1977-79. Contbr. editor: An Outline of Sexology, 1993. Loaned exec. United Way, 1988; bd. dirs. Homestead, Inc., 1990-97, West Main Hill Neighorhood Assn., 1993-97. Faculty Rsch. grant, Western Mich. U., 1992. Mem. Internat. Assn. Counseling Svcs. (bd. dirs. 1976-79, pres.-elect 1983-84, pres. 1984-85), Soc. Human Ecology, Inst. Noetic Scis. (del. Threads to the Future Conf. New Zealand 1996). Mem. Soc. Of Friends. Avocations: gardening, travel, sailing. Personal E-mail: lforsleff@yahoo.com. *

FORSLOFF, CAROL MARIE, human services and communication professional, retired counselor, editor, journalist; b. La Grande, Oreg., Mar. 31, 1941; d. Ted Eugene and Faye Marie Matthews; m. Delbert Raymond Forsloff, Feb. 14, 1984. BA, U. Wash., Seattle, 1967; MA, SUNY, Albany, 1969. Cert. rehab. counselor, hypnotherapist. Edn. dir. Assoc. Children Learning Disabilities, 1969—74; adj. instr. Penn State U., 1971—73, Allegheny CC, 1974—77, Hawaii Pacific Coll., 1978—79, Northwestern State U., 2007—; evaluation coord., cons. Goodwill Industries, Honolulu, 1984—98; pres. Heritage Valley Pub., Honolulu, 1998—; owner, mgr., pres. Forsloff and Assoc., Honolulu, 1998—2005; owner, mgr. La Maison de Aloha, Natchitoches, La., 2005—; pub. Green Heritage News, Portland, Oreg., Natchitoches, La. Supr. Crawford Healthcare Mgmt., Las Vegas, 1984—92; v.p., gen. mgr. Heritage Cons., Honolulu, 1993—2005; cons. in field. Author: Vocational Profiling: Workplace Solutions, 1987; co-editor, co-pub. The Real Views Newspaper and News mag., 2006—; contbr. articles to profl. jours. Pres. Orton Soc., Pitts., 1976—77, Rehab. Assn. Hawaii, 1996, Punahou Gardens, Honolulu, 1979—83; Katrina vol. counselor Red Cross, Natchitoches, 2005. Recipient Elizabeth Ducey award, Portland State U., 1960, Honor, Women U. Washington, 1964; named Outstanding Spl. Edn. Tchr., Saddle River (NJ) Schs., 1969, Disting. Prof. in Rehab., Crawford Healthcare, Honolulu, 1985, 1989; named one of Outstanding Tchrs. Spl. Edn. academic therapy, 1975. Mem.: Internat. Assn. Life Care Planners, Nat. Rehab. Assn., Am. Counseling Assn., Kiwanis. Avocations: writing, singing. Office: 242 B Keyser Ave #122 Natchitoches LA 71457

FORSLUND, THOMAS ODELL (TOM FORSLUND), state official, former city manager; b. Forest City, Iowa, Aug. 23, 1951; s. Cyrus Odell and Alice Marie (Michelson) F.; m. Barbara Jean Hime, Mar. 1, 1975; children: Eric, Elizabeth. AA, Waldorf Coll., 1971; BA, U. Iowa, 1973; MPA, U. Mo., 1977. Adminstr. City of Richland, Mo., 1977-80, City of Beatrice, Nebr., 1980-86; asst. city mgr. City of Casper, Wyo., 1986-88, city mgr. Wyo., 1988—2011; dir. Wyo. Dept. Health, 2011—. Mem. American Soc. Pub. Adminstrn., American Mgmt. Assn., Internat. City Mgmt. Assn., Rotary. Lutheran. Office: Wyoming Dept Health 401 Hathaway Bldg Cheyenne WY 82002 Office Phone: 307-777-7656. Office Fax: 307-777-7439. *

FORSTER, TAMAS, cardiologist; b. Szekesfehervar, Hungary, Nov. 19, 1954; MD, U. Szeged, 1979. Dir. 2nd Dept. Medicine and Cardiology Ctr., 2002—. Prof., cardiology U. Szeged, 2002. Master: Hungarian Soc. Cardiology; fellow: Am. Coll. Cardiology, European Soc. Cardiology; mem.: Am. Heart Assn. Avocations: photography, ping pong/table tennis, reading. Office: Koranyi Fasor 6 Szeged Csongrad 6720 Hungary Office Fax: 36-62-544568. E-mail: tforster54@gmail.com.

FORSTOT, STEPHAN LANCE, ophthalmologist; b. NYC, Aug. 19, 1943; s. Shepard and Edith Forstot; m. Lynne Rochelle Bitton, June 15, 1945; children: Michele, Jordan. AB, Princeton U., 1965; MD, Johns Hopkins U., 1969. Diplomate Am. Bd. Ophthalmology. Ophthalmologist Corneal Cons. of Colo., Denver, 1982—, U. Colo. Sch. of Medicine, Denver, 1976-82, clin. prof., 1982—. Contbr. articles to profl. jours. Recipient Honor award Am. Acad. Ophthalmology, Sr. Honor award Am. Acad. Ophthalmology. Mem. Contact Lens Assn. Ophthalmology (bd. dirs. 1985-87, 2004-, pres.-elect 2006, pres. 2007-09), Internat. Soc. Refractive Surgery (bd. dirs. 1995-96). Avocation: tennis. Office: Corneal Cons Colo 8381 Southpark Ln Littleton CO 80120-4508 Office Phone: 303-730-0404. Personal E-mail: SL4STOT@aol.com.

FORSTROM, LEE ARTHUR, physician; b. Alpha, Minn., Oct. 4, 1936; s. Elmer Leroy and Ione Grace (Simpson) F.; m. Nancy Mulcahy, June 17, 1964; children: Michael, Jennifer, Kerstin, Eric. BA, U. Minn., 1957; MD, Yale U., 1962; PhD, Cambridge U., Eng., 1977. Diplomate Am. Bd. Internal Medicine, Am. Bd. Nuclear Medicine. Asst. prof. Simm Fraser U., Burnaby, B.C., Canada,

1965—66; resident U. Minn., Mpls., 1968-72, fellow in nuclear medicine, 1972-73; grad. rsch. asst. Cambridge (Eng.) U., 1974-75; asst. prof., physician U. Minn., Mpls., 1976-84; nuclear medicine cons., assoc. prof. Mayo Clin., Rochester, Minn., 1984—. Contbr. articles to profl. jours. including Jour. Nuclear Medicine, Radiology, among others. Pres. Am.-Swedish Inst. Ch., Mpls., 1978-80; bd. dirs. Luth. Ch. Good Shepherd, Mpls., 1980-82. Fellow Am. Scandinavian Found., 1959-60, NIH, 1975, HSF, 1963-65; grantee Am. Cancer Soc., 1958. Mem. AMA, Am. Coll. Nuclear Physicians, Soc. Nuclear Medicine, Brit. Soc. Philosophy Sci., European Assn. Nuclear Medicine, Am. Soc. Nuclear Cardiology. Lutheran. Avocations: music, photography, travel. Office: Mayo Clin 200 1st St NW Rochester MN 55901 Business E-Mail: lforstrom@mayo.edu.

FORSYTH, KIRSTY ANNE, occupational therapist, researcher; d. William B and Anne Forsyth. BSc in Occupl. Therapy, Queen Margaret U., Edinburgh, 1989; MSc in Occupl. Therapy, U. Ill., Chgo., 1996; PhD in Pub. Health, U. Ill., 2000. Occupl. therapist Dundee Healthcare Trust, Scotland, 1989—91, sr. occupl. therapist, 1992—94, 1996; rsch. asst. prof. U. Ill., Chgo., 1996—2000, rsch. specialist, 2000—08; occupl. therapy cons. NHS Lothian, England, 2000; lectr. Queen Margaret U., 2000—03, sr. lectr., 2003—08, prof., 2008—. Recipient Lillian B. award, Torrance award; fellowship, U. Ill., 2000—02. Mem.: Phi Kappa Phi. Office: Queen Margaret Univ Queen Margaret Univ Dr Edinburgh EH20 9NX Scotland Office Fax: 44 (0) 131 474 0001.

FORT, PATRICE ELIE, ophthalmologist, educator; b. Oyonnax, France, Dec. 26, 1978; PhD, Louis Pasteur U., 2005. Asst. prof. U. Mich., 2011—. Recipient Outstanding Postdoc. award, Penn State Hershey, 2009—10. Mem.: Assn. Rsch. Vision and Ophthalmology, Am. Diabetes Assn. Office: 1000 Wall St Ann Arbor MI 48105 Business E-Mail: patricef@umich.edu.

FORTENBERRY, J. DENNIS, pediatrician, educator, internist; MD, U. Okla., Norman, 1979. Diplomate Am. Bd. Internal Medicine, Am. Bd. Internal Medicine-adolescent medicine, 2004. Resident internal medicine Univ. Okla. Hosp. Ctr., 1980—81, fellow adolescent medicine, 1982—83; with Ind. Univ. health; prof. pediat. Ind. Univ. Mem.: Cancer Prevention and Control. Office: Indiana University Department of Pediatrics 575 N W Dr Room 070 XE070 Indianapolis IN 46202 Office Phone: 317-274-8812. Office Fax: 317-274-0133.

FORTIN, THOMAS, dental educator; b. Dijon, France, June 26, 1966; m. Nadege Boisnard; children: Eloise, Arsene, Come, Nine. DDS, PhD. Cert. dental surgeon U. Lyon, France, 1990. Assoc. prof. dept. oral surgery dental U. Lyon, prof., 1991—. Mem. TIMC Lab. Achievements include invention of image guided surgery for oral implant placement. Home: 18 Rue Joseph Cugnot Bourgoin Jallieu 38300 France Office: Dental Sch 11 Rue Guillaume Paradin Lyon 69007 France Office Phone: 33474934141, 33684015160. Home Fax: 33474280784. Business E-Mail: thomas.fortin@univ-lyon1.fr.

FORTINA, ANTONIO FORMIA, orthopedic surgeon; b. Novara, Italy, July 29, 1952; s. Mario Boschi and Renata Vittonatto (Formia) Fortina; m. Michela Pesce Genta, June 3, 1978; children: Elisabetta, Giorgio. MD, U. Torino, Italy, 1977, degree in orthopedics, 1981, degree in physiotherapy, 1984. Prof. orthopedic diseases Regional Sch. Physiotherapy, Novara, 1988-89, 91-92, 94-95; asst. orthopedist Hosp. Novara, 1978-88, sub-chief orthopedics dept., 1989-95; in charge Integrated Orthopedic Activities Orgn., 1995-2000; prof. orthopedic diseases U. Ea. Piedmont, 1998-2000; in charge outpatient dept. orthopedic diseases ASL Novara, 2000—. Tutor U. Torino, 1996—98, U. Eastern Piedmont, 1998—2003; prof. orthop. diseases U. Novara, 1998—99; lectr. in field. Contbr. articles to profl. jours. including Encyclopedia Medica Italiana. Chief med. staff Iris Oleggio Football Club, 1982—95. Recipient medal, Nobile Collegio Caccia, 1977. Mem.: Italy Study Group for Severe Osteoporosis & Orthop., Study Group Scoliosis and Spinal Diseases, Fedn. Medico-Sportiva Italiana, Italian Soc. Ankle and Foot Surgery, Italian Soc. Phys. and Rehab. Medicine, Italian Soc. Orthop. and Traumatology. Roman Catholic. Avocations: bicycling, history. Home: Viale Camillo Pasquali 15 28100 Novara NO Italy

FORTON, FABIENNE MARCELLE NICOLE, dermatologist, consultant, researcher; b. Brussels, July 7, 1960; children: Sophie Pascale Pierrette Seys, Bernard Pascal Benoît Seys, François Marc Antoine Seys. MD, Cath. U. Louvain, 1985; degree in dermatology, Free U. Brussels, 1989. Pvt. practice, Brussels, 1989—; mgr. dermatologic svc. Hosp. New Paul Brien, Brussels, 1993—99. Cons. Ctr. Hosp. Etterbeek-Ixelles, Brussels, 1989—92, Hosp. New Paul Brien, Brussels, 1989—93, Polyclinic Oasis, Brussels, 1989—2003. Contbr. articles to profl. jours. Mem.: European Acad. Dermatology and Venereology, Société Royale Belge de Dermatologie et Vénérologie. Achievements include invention of standardized skin surface biopsy to measure the Demodex folliculorum density in the human skin; research in proving demodicoses are frequent and occur among immunocompetent patients, and papulopustular rosacea with normal Demodex density are rare; discovery of Demodex folliculorum density is higher in the skin of patients with papulopustular rosacea than in normal skin, where it is lower or equal to 5/cm^2; presence of perifollicular infiltrate and presence of Demodex inside the follicles are statistically related; research in acaricidal activity of benzyl benzoate and crotamiton on Demodex folliculorum in vivo; discovery of false negative results can occur with the standardized skin surface biopsy. Office: Rue Frans Binjé 8 Brussels 1030 Belgium Business E-Mail: fabienne.forton@skynet.be.

FORTUNATO, ELIZABETH ANN, biology professor; b. NYC, Aug. 8, 1964; BS, MIT, 1986; PhD, U. Calif., San Diego, 1995. Assoc. prof. U. Idaho, 2000—. Office: University Idaho Dept Biological Scis Moscow ID 83844-3051 Business E-Mail: lfort@uidaho.edu.

FORTUNATO, JOSEPH, retail executive; Controller Motor Coils Mfg. Co.; pres. Fortunato & Assocs. Fin. Consulting Group; joined General Nutrition Centers, Inc. (GNC), Pitts., 1990, dir. fin. ops., 1990—97, v.p. fin. ops., 1997—98, sr. v.p. store devel. and ops., 1998—2000, exec. v.p. store ops. and devel., 2000—01, exec. v.p., COO, 2001—05, sr. exec. v.p., COO, 2005, pres., CEO, 2005—. Office: GNC 300 Sixth Ave Pittsburgh PA 15222 *

FORTUNY, ALBERT, retired gynecologist; b. Reus, Dec. 19, 1934; MD, PhD, U. Barcelona, 1959. Resident physician, rsch. fellow Columbia Hosp. Women, 1963—67. Prof., head. ob-gyn. Hosp. Clinic. U. Barcelona Med. Sch., 1970—2005. Rsch. fellow, Rsch. Found. Columbia Hosp., Washington. Fellow: Am. Coll. Obstetricians and Gynecologists. Home: Compte Urgell 264 Barcelona 08036 Spain Business E-Mail: afortunye@ub.edu.

FORZLEY, GREGORY, physician, medical association administrator; m. Kathy M. Forzley. MD, Wayne State U. Sch. Medicine, 1974—78; residency tng., family practice, Grand Rapids Family Practice Residency, 1978—81. Bd. cert., family practice 1981, 1987, 1993, 1999, 2006. Faculty Grand Rapids Family Practice Residency Program, Grand Rapids, Mich., 1984—92; pvt. office med. practice Specialists in Family Medicine, Grand Rapids, Mich., 1981—93; med. dir., sys. devel. Priority Health, Grand Rapids, Mich., 1993—98, Advantage Health, Grand Rapids, Mich., 1998—2003; chief med. info. officer Saint Mary's Health Care, Grand Rapids, 2003—. Dist. bd. mem. Mich. State Med. Soc., chair bd., 2002—; bd. mem. Mich. Health and Safety Coalition, 2001—; chair Mich. Health Info. Technology Commn., 2006—; exec. com. mem. Mich. Ctr. Effective IT Adoption, 2009—11. Author: (six reference chpts.) Procedures in Primary Care, 1992, 2d edit., 2003. Chair, leadership coun. First United Meth. Church, Grand Rapids, 1997—2000; steering com. mem. Healthy Kent 2010, Grand Rapids, 1994—2003; com. mem. Tobacco Free Partners, Grand Rapids, 2000—. Fellow: Am. Acad. Family Practice; mem.: Kent County Med. Soc. (pres. 2011—), Mich. State Med. Soc. (vice chmn. bd. dirs. 2006—07, chair bd. dirs. 2007—11), Am. Med. Informatics Assn. Methodist. Home: PO Box 6303 Grand Rapids MI 49516 Office: Saint Mary's Health Care 200 Jefferson St Grand Rapids MI 49503 Office Phone: 616-685-6477.

FOSTER, CAROL MARVEL, pediatric endocrinologist; b. Detroit, Sept. 12, 1952; d. Howard and Margaret (Paulson) Marvel; m. Norman L. Foster, Nov. 19, 1977; children: Daniel, Sarah. BS, Purdue U., 1974; MD, Washington U., St. Louis, 1978. Lic. physician Md., Mich., cert. Am. Bd. Pediat., 1983, in pediatric endocrinology 1983. Pediat. intern U. Utah, Salt Lake City, 1978—79, pediatric endocrinology resident, 1979—81; NIH fellow U. Mich., Ann Arbor, 1981—84, asst. prof. pediatric endocrinology, 1985—93, assoc. prof. pediatric endocrinology, 1993—99, prof. pediatric endocrinology, 1999, dir., divsn. endocrinology, assoc. dir. pediat. programs, Cin. Rsch. Ctr.; prof. pediat., divsn. pediat. endocrinology Utah Diabetes Ctr. Prof. U. Utah Health Scis. Ctr. and Primary Children's Med. Ctr. Contbr. articles to profl. jours. Recipient Am. Diabetes Assn. rsch. award, 1987; NIH grantee, 1991. Mem. Endocrine Soc., Soc. Pediatric Rsch., Am. Fedn. for Clin. Rsch., Lawson Wilkins Pediatric Endocrine Soc., Phi Beta Kappa, Phi Kappa Phi. Achievements include research on mechanisms involved in initiation of puberty, mechansims of action of growth hormone, nature of steroid hormone receptors in transformed cells. Office: Utah Diabetes Ctr 615 Arapeen Dr Ste 100 Salt Lake City UT 84108 Office Phone: 801-581-7761. Office Fax: 801-587-3920. Business E-Mail: carol.foster@hsc.utah.edu.

FOSTER, CAROLE LYNN, medical association administrator; b. Spartanburg, SC, Sept. 29, 1956; Degree, USC-Upstate, 1976. Adminstr. Palmetto Hematology Oncology, P.C., 1980—2009; dir. med. oncology, infusion svcs. Spartanburg Regional Med. Ctr., Gibbs Cancer Ctr., 2009—. Mem.: SC Oncology Mgrs., ACCC, MGMA. Avocations: reading, cooking, singing. Office: 380 Serpentine Dr Spartanburg SC 29303 Office Fax: 864-560-0824 E-mail: lynnfoster@srhs.com.

FOSTER, CRAIG ALLEN, plastic surgeon; b. Mpls., Aug. 31, 1948; m. Blake Paddock Foster, 1990. MD, U. Minn., 1974. Diplomate Am. Bd. Plastic Surgery, Am. Bd. Otolaryngology. Intern U. Minn., Mpls.; resident in gen. surgery U. Minn. Hosps., resident in otolaryngology; resident in plastic surgery NYU, NYC; pvt. practice plastic surgery NYC; plastic surgeon Manhattan EE Hosp., NYC, with Lenox Hill Hosp. Mem.: Am. Soc. for Aesthetic Plastic Surgery. Office: 850 Park Ave Ste 1A New York NY 10075-1857 Office Phone: 212-744-5746. Business E-Mail: drcraigfoster11@aol.com.

FOSTER, EARL JAMES, orthopedist; b. Brocklyn, Iowa, Jan. 4, 1948; s. Lawrence Franklyn and Lila Irene Foster; m. Carol Marie Blanchord, May 29, 1951; children: Taryn, Kyle. BS in Gen. Sci., U. Iowa, 1970, MD, 1974. Intern U. Ind., Indpls., 1975; orthopedic resident U. Syracuse, NY, 1979; hand surgery fellow New Orleans, 1979—80; physician Scott Orthopedic Ctr., Huntington, W.Va., 1980—, pres., 1996—; chmn. of bd. Three Gable Surgery Ctr. Chief orthopedics Cabell Hosp. and St. Mary Hosp., Huntington, 1988—90; pres. med. staff Cabell Huntington Hosp., 1994—96. Fellow: ACS, Am. Acad. Orthopedic Surgery; mem.: Am. Soc. Surgery Hand. Avocations: fitness, golf, reading. Home: 85 Camelot Dr Huntington WV 25701 Office: Scott Orthopedic Ctr 2828 1st Ave Huntington WV 25702 Office Phone: 304-525-6905. Personal E-mail: earlfoster@hushmail.com.

FOSTER, ELYSE, cardiologist, educator; b. Bklyn., Mar. 4, 1952; MD, Tufts U. Sch. Medicine, 1977. Cert. Internal Medicine, Cardiovascular Disease. Intern, internal medicine Boston U. Hosp., Mass., 1977—78, resident, internal medicine Mass., 1978—79; resident, cardiology Boston Med. Ctr., Mass., 1979—80, fellow, cardiovascular disease Mass., 1983, hosp. appointment Mass.; asst. prof. Boston U. Sch. Medicine, Mass.; prof., medicine, divsn. cardiology U. Calif., San Francisco, dir., adult echocardiography lab., dir., adult congenital heart disease svc. Mem.: Am. Coll. Cardiology (mem., women in cardiology com.), Internat. Soc. Adult Congenital Heart Diseases (mem. exec. com.). Office: U Calif San Francisco Divsn Cardiology 505 Parnassus Ave San Francisco CA 94143-0214 Office Phone: 415-353-9156. Office Fax: 415-353-8687.

FOSTER, GARY D., psychologist; BA in Psychology, Duquesne U.; MS in Psychology, U. Pa.; PhD in Clinical Psychology, Temple U. Intern Med. Coll. Pa., Hahnemann U.; dir. Ctr. for Obesity Rsch. & End. Temple U. Sch. Medicine, prof. medicine & pub. health. Office: Temple U Med Education & Research Bldg 3500 N Broad St Philadelphia PA 19140 Office Phone: 215-707-8632. Office Fax: 215-707-6475. E-mail: gary.foster@temple.edu.

FOSTER, HARRIS E., urologist, educator; MD, U. of Miami, 1987. Diplomate Am. Bd. Urology, 2003. Resident surgery Univ. Michigan Med. Ctr., Ann Arbor, Mich., 1987—89, resident urology, 1989—92; urologist Yale Med. Group Adminstrv. Office, New Haven. Prof. urology Yale Univ. Mem.: Soc. of Univ. Urologists, Nat. Assn. for Continence, Conn. Chpt. Multiple Sclerosis Soc. Adv. Com., Urodynamics Soc., Am. Urological Assn. Office: Yale Urology Group 800 Howard Ave Fl 3 New Haven CT 06520-8062 Office Phone: 203-785-2815.

FOSTER, JILL, infectious disease pediatrician; MD, Med. Coll. Pa., 1990. Diplomate Am. Bd. of Peadiatrics-pediatric infectious disease. Intern St. Christopher's Hosp. for Children, 1991, resident, 1993, chief immunology sect., dir. Dorothy Mann ctr. for pediatric and adolescent HIV, attending immunologist; fellow Children's Hosp. of Phila., 1994. Assoc. prof. pediatrics Drexel Univ. Coll. of Medicine. Office: St Christophers Hospital for Children 3601 A St Philadelphia PA 19134 Office Phone: 215-427-5000. Office Fax: 215-427-5555.

FOSTER, RICHARD SCOTT, urologist, educator; AB cum laude, Miami U., Oxford, Ohio, 1976; MD, Ind. U. Med. Sch., Indpls., 1980. Lic. Ind., cert. Am. Bd. Urology. Surgical intern, resident Ind. U. Hospitals, 1980—82, urology resident, 1982—86; asst. prof., dept. urology Ind. U. Sch. Medicine, Indpls., 1986—92, assoc. prof., dept. urology, 1992—98, prof. dept. urology, 1998—. Mem. WHO Com. on Biomedical & Nonsurgical Alternative Treatments of BPH. Contbr. several articles to profl. jours.; reviewer for several profl. jours. Mem.: Am. Soc. Clin. Oncology (mem. GU cancer subcommittee), European Assn. Urology (corr. mem.), Soc. Surgical Oncology, Societe Internationale d'Urologie, Soc. Urologic Oncology, Hoosier Oncology Group (co-chmn. GU/GYN com.), ACS, Soc. U. Urologists, Am. Urological Assn. (mem. north ctrl. sect.), Eastern Cooperative Oncology Group (chmn., Testis Cancer Subcommittee), Phi Beta Kappa, Phi Eta Sigma. Office: Ind Cancer Pavillion 535 Barnhill Dr RT 420 Indianapolis IN 46202 Office Phone: 317-274-3458. Business E-Mail: rsfoster@iupni.edu.

FOSTER, RICHARD SHAW, actuary; s. Walter Dean and Elizabeth Shaw Foster; m. Nancy Warfield Allen, June 10, 1971. BA, Coll. Wooster, Ohio, 1971; MS, U. Md., Catonsville, 1973. Actuary Social Security Adminstrn., Balt., 1973—75, spl. asst. to chief actuary, 1975—77, supervisory actuary, 1978—81, acting dep. chief actuary, 1981—84, dep. chief actuary, 1985—94; chief actuary Ctrs. for Medicare & Medicaid Svcs., 1995—. Seminar instr. Ga. State U., Atlanta, 1981—92; mem. Nat. Acad. Social Ins., Washington, 1985—; bus. instr. Soc. of Actuaries, Iowa City, 1994—96; bd. dirs. Am. Acad. Actuaries, Washington, 1999—2001. Author: (fiction short story) A Nice Morning Drive; contbr. articles to profl. pubs. Recipient Presdl. Meritorious Exec. award, Fed. Govt., 1998, Presdl. Disting. Exec. award, 2001, Sec.'s Disting. Svc. award, HHS, 2004, Disting. Alumni award, Coll. Wooster, 2006, Robert J. Myers Pub. Svc. award, Am. Acad. Actuaries, 2006; named Outstanding Alumnus of Yr., U. Md., 1997; named one of Top 100 Most Influential People in Healthcare, Modern Healthcare Mag., 2007—08. Fellow: Soc. Actuaries (mem. of numerous soa committees 1981—96); mem.: Nat. Health Policy Forum Steering Com., Sr. Executives Assn., Nat. Acad. Social Ins., Am. Econ. Assn., Am. Statis. Assn., Am. Acad. Actuaries (bd. of directors 1999—2001, Robert J. Myers Pub. Svc. Award 2006), Mid. Atlantic Actuarial Club, Balt. Actuaries Club (pres. 1991—92). Presbyterian. Achievements include research in economic assumptions affecting Social Security and Medicare; the analysis of trust fund assets needed for Social Security and Medicare contingency reserves; social insurance. Avocations: photography, writing, motorcycling, graphics, guitar. Office: Ctrs for Medicare & Medicaid Services 7500 Security Blvd Baltimore MD 21244 Office Fax: 410-786-1295. Business E-Mail: richard.foster@cms.hhs.gov *

FOSTER, ROGER SHERMAN, JR., surgeon, educator, health facility administrator; b. Washington, Jan. 8, 1936; s. Roger Sherman and Genevieve Wakeman (Bartlett) F.; m. Joan Crile, June 25, 1960 (dec. Feb. 2000); children: Roger Sherman III, Charles Bartlett, Elizabeth Crile, Halle Crile Foster Moore; m. Barba J. Grube, July 3, 2004. AB, Haverford Coll., 1957, MD, Case Western Res. U., 1961. Diplomate Am. Bd. Surgey, Nat. Bd. Med. Examiners. Intern then resident in surgery Univ. Hosps., Cleve., 1961-66; research fellow Roswell Park Meml. Inst., Buffalo, 1966-68; asst. prof. surgery U. Vt., Burlington, 1970-73, assoc. prof. surgery, 1973-80, prof. surgery, 1980-92, dir. comprehensive cancer ctr., 1984-92; attending surgeon Med. Ctr. Hosp. of Vt., 1970-92; Wadley Glenn prof. surgery Emory U., Atlanta, 1992-99; chief surgical svcs. Crawford Long Hosp. of Emory U., 1992-99. Mem. cancer clin. investigation rev. com. NIH, 1987-92, chmn., 1991-92, chmn. various coms.; cons. Am. Internat. Health Alliance for Tblisi, Georgia Hosp., 1992-96. Assoc. editor: Clinical Surgery, 1987; co-editor: Essentials of Clinical Surgery, 1991; editor-in-chief: Breast Surgery: Index and Reviews, 1993-95; assoc. editor: Surgery: Problem-Solving Approach, 2d edit., 1995; co-editor: Q & A Review for Surgery, 1995; manuscript reviewer: Jour. AMA, Jour. Trauma, others; contbr. more than 100 articles to profl. jours. Trustee Univ. Health Ctr., Burlington, 1986-89, Vt. Ethics Network, 2001—06. Served to maj. U.S. Army, 1968-69. Grantee NIH, 1971-92; summer rsch. fellow Josiah Macy Jr, Found., 1958-59. Fellow ACS (bd. regents 1991-2000, bd. govs. 1981-87, adv. coun. for gen. surgery 1989-92, 95-2000, sec./treas. Vt. chpt. 1979-80, v.p. 1980-81, pres. 1981-82), Am. Surg. Assn.; mem. AMA, AAAS, New Eng. Surg. Soc. (treas. 1986-89, exec. com. 1981-92, 2001-03, pres. 2001-02), Soc. Univ. Surgeons, So. Surg. Assn., Southeastern Surg. Congress, Soc. Surg. Oncology, Ea. Surg. Soc. (pres. 1994), Am. Endocrine Surg. Soc. (coun. 1992-95), Am. Soc. Clin. Oncology (pub. rels. 1989-91 and pub. issues coms. 1989-94), Transplantation Soc., New Eng. Cancer Soc. (treas. 1983-87, v.p. 1988-89, pres. 1989-90), Assn. Acad. Surgery, Newfoundland Club Am. (bd. dirs. 1976-78, 1st v.p. 1979), Nat. Surg. Adjuvant Breast Project, 1971-92 (exec. com. 1978-81). Avocations: white water canoeing, breeding newfoundland dogs, wilderness travel, chamber music, cellist. Home: 395 Stevenson Rd New Haven CT 06515 E-mail: halirock@aol.com.

FOSTER-BARBER, AUDREY ELIZABETH, neurologist, educator; BS in Biology with high honors, Harvard College; MD in Biochemistry, U. Calif. Sch. Medicine, San Francisco, 1999. Cert. in neurology, in child neurology 2006. Pediat. resident U. Calif., San Francisco, 2002, child neurology resident, 2005, from clin. instr. neurology to asst. prof.; chief neurology resident U. Calif. Med. Ctr., San Francisco. Recipient Exceptional Physician award, U. Calif. San Fransisco Med. Ctr., 2005, Pediat. Dept. Fellow Tchg. award; grantee, Acad. Med. Educators, 2006—; A. P. Giannini Med. Rsch. fellowship, Bank of America. Mem.: Am. Acad. Pediat., Child Neurology Soc., Am. Acad. Neurology. Office: U Calif Box 0137 350 Parnassus Ave #609 609 San Francisco CA 94143 Office Phone: 415-353-4149. Office Fax: 415-353-2400. Business E-Mail: fostera@neuropeds.ucsf.edu.

FOTI, MARGARET, medical association administrator, editor, consultant; b. Phila., Dec. 15, 1944; d. Samuel A. and Margaret M. (DiBiase) F. BA, Temple U., 1975, MA in Comm., 1985, PhD in

Comm., 1995; MD (hon.), U. Rome, La Sapienza, 2003, U. Catania, Sicily, 2008, CEU-SAN Pablo U., Madrid, 2009. Tech. editor U. Pa., Phila., 1962—64, asst. to bus. adminstr., 1964—65; sr. editl. asst. Cancer Rsch. Jour., Phila., 1965—69, mng. editor, 1969—; CEO Am. Assn. Cancer Rsch., Phila., 1982—; sec.-treas., CEO Am. Assn. Cancer Rsch. Found. for the Prevention and Cure of Cancer. Adminstrn., pub. edn., devel., editl. and pub. cons., lectr. in field. Contbr. articles to profl. jours. Pres. Nat. Coalition Cancer Rsch., 1994-96, bd. dirs. 2004. Recipient Cert. Appreciation, Am. Assn. Cancer Rsch., 1975, 1985, 1990, 1999, Margaret Kripke Legend award, 2009, Women of Distinction award, 1999, Cino del Duca award, 2000, Ville de Paris award, 2000, award, City of Trento, Italy, 2002, Solemn Encomium recognition, U. Palermo, Italy, 2003, Cmty. Caring award, William S. Graham Found. for Melanoma Rsch., Am. Soc. Clin. Oncology Spl. Recognition award, Disting. Svc. award, Assn. Am. Cancer Insts., Margaret Kripke Legend award, 2009, European Cancer Orgn. Life Time Achievement award, 2009, Lifetime Achievement award, European Cancer Orgn., 2009, Phila. Pinnacle award, 2010. Mem.: NCCR (bd. dirs.), AAAS, Coun. Engrs. and Sci. Soc. Execs., Coun. Biology Editors (pres. 1980—81), Soc. Scholarly Publs. (pres. 1996—97), Internat. Fedn. Sci. Editors, European Assn. Sci. Editors, Am. Assn. Cancer Rsch., Am. Soc. Assn. Execs., Japanese Cancer Assn. (hon.), European Assn. Cancer Rsch. (hon.; disting.). Democrat. Roman Catholic. Office: Am Assn Cancer Rsch 615 Chestnut St 17th Fl Philadelphia PA 19106-4404 Office Fax: 215-440-9322. E-mail: margaret.foti@aacr.org.

FOTIADES, GEORGE L., investment company executive; BA in Econ., Amherst Coll.; MBA, Northwestern U. Sr. mgmt. Procter & Gamble and Richardson-Vicks; pres. Bristol-Meyers Squibb's Consumer Products Group, Japan, Warner Welcome Consumer Healthcare, Warner Lambert Co.; group pres., Americas and Asia/Pacific R.P. Scherer, pres. and COO; exec. v.p., group pres. Cardinal Health Inc., Dublin, Ohio, 1998—2000, pres., CEO life sci. products & svc., 2000—04, pres., COO, 2004—06; chmn., healthcare investments Diamond Castle, NYC, 2007—; non-exec. chmn. Catalent Pharma Solutions, Somerset, NJ, interim pres. & CEO, 2008—09. Trustee ProLogis, 2001—; bd. dir. Alberto-Culver Co., Cantel Med. Corp. Office: Diamond Castle Holdings 280 Park Ave 25th Fl E Tower New York NY 10017 Office Phone: 212-300-1953. Business E-Mail: gfotiades@dchold.com.

FOTTLER, MYRON DAVID, health services educator; b. Boston, Sept. 5, 1939; s. Myron Dustin and Anna Eileen Fottler; m. Carol Ann Fottler, Aug. 11, 1972. BS, Northeastern U., 1962; MBA, Boston U., 1963; PhD, Columbia U., 1970. Asst. prof. SUNY, Buffalo, 1967—75; from assoc. prof. to prof. U. Ala., Tuscaloosa, 1976—83, prof., PhD program dir. Birmingham, 1983—99; prof., program dir. U. Ctrl. Fla., Orlando, 1999—. Cons. numerous legal firms and corps. Author 21 books; contbr. over 40 chpts. to books and over 140 articles to profl. jours. Recipient Hayhew award, Am. Coll. Health Care Execs., 1997, Outstanding Svc. award, Acad. Mgmt.-Healthcare Mgmt. Divsn., 1999, Faculty Pub. of Yr., Am. Acad. Med. Adminstrs., 2001. Episcopalian. Avocation: tennis. Office: Univ Ctrl Fla Coll Health and Pub Affairs 210A HPA2 Orlando FL 32816-0001 Home: 4670 Links Village Dr Unit A 502 Ponce Inlet FL 32127-2008 Home Phone: 386-788-9924; Office Phone: 407-823-5531. *

FOUAD, YASSER M., gastroenterologist, educator; b. Minia, Egypt, Feb. 14, 1967; MBBCh, Minia Med. Sch., 1990, MD, 2002. Prof. Minia coll. Medicine Minia U., 2007—, dir. endoscopy unit, 2008—10. Named Ideal Dr., Egyptian Med. Syndicate. Mem.: Egyptian Soc. Tropical Medicine, Egyptian Soc. Gastroenterology and Hepatology, Am. Coll. Gastroenterology. Office: Horryia St Minia 19111 Egypt Personal E-mail: yasserfouad10@yahoo.com.

FOULKES, HELENA B., pharmaceutical executive; b. 1964; married; 4 children. BA, Harvard Univ., 1986, MBA, 1991. Fin. mgmt. positions Goldman Sachs; mgmt. positions Tiffany & Co.; mktg. mgmt. positions through v.p. CVS Pharmacy Inc., 1992—2002, sr. v.p. advt. & mktg., 2002—07, sr. v.p. mktg. & ops. services, 2007, sr. v.p. health services, 2007—09; exec. v.p., chief mktg. officer CVS Caremark Corp., 2009—11, exec. v.p., chief mktg. officer, chief health care strategy officer, 2011—. Office: CVS Caremark Corp 1 CVS Dr Woonsocket RI 02895 *

FOULKES, WILLIAM DAVID, psychologist, educator; b. East Orange, NJ, May 29, 1935; s. Paul Bergen and Alice (Hinson) F.; m. Nancy Helen Kerr, Apr. 19, 1978. BA, Swarthmore Coll., 1957; PhD, U. Chgo., 1960; MD (hon.), U. Ferrara, 1992. Instr. Lawrence Coll., Appleton, Wis., 1960-63; rsch. assoc. U. Chgo., 1963-64; from asst. prof. to prof. U. Wyo., Laramie, 1964-77; prof. psychiatry Emory U., Atlanta, 1977-97, ret., 1997. Author: The Psychology of Sleep, 1966, A Grammar of Dreams, 1978, Children's Dreams, 1982, Dreaming: A Cognitive Psychological Analysis, 1985; co-editor: Dreaming as Cognition, 1993, Children's Dreaming and the Development of Consciousness, 1999. Fellow Ctr. for Advanced Study in Behavioral Scis., 1974-75; recipient Disting. Scientist award Sleep Rsch. Soc.

FOULKS, GARY NEAL, ophthalmologist, educator; b. Salt Lake City, June 7, 1944; s. James N. and Ruth E. Foulks; m. Sims B. Brockenbrough, May 25, 1968; children: Guy B., Beverley N., Heather Ainslie. AB, Columbia U., NYC, 1966, MD, 1970. Diplomate Am. Bd. Ophthalmology, 1977. Intern U. Calif. San Diego, 1970—71; with USPHS, 1971—73; resident ophthalmology Duke U. Eye Ctr., 1973—76; clin. and rsch. fellow Harvard U., Boston, 1976—78; prof. ophthalmology Duke U., Durham, NC, 1978—96, U. Pitts., 1996—2003; Keeney prof. ophthalmology U. Louisville, 2003—. Cons. in field; lectr. in field. Editor: The Ocular Surface, —; mem. editl. bd.: Cornea, 1990—, Ocular Surface, 1990—, Eye and Contact Lens, 1996—. Exec. sec. gen. Internat. Med. Contact Lens Coun., Denver, 2004—; treas. Sjogren's Syndrome Found., Bethesda, Md., 2004—06. Lt. comdr. USPHS, 1971—73. Fellow: ACS, Am. Acad. Ophthalmology (Sr. Honor award 1998); mem.: Assn. Vision and Ophthalmology (chmn. program com. 1990—92), The Cornea Soc. (pres. 1997—99, Castroviejo medal 2005), Contact Lens Assn. Ophthalmologists (pres. 2001—02, chmn. bd. trustees ophthalmologists edn. and rsch. found. 2001—06, Whitney Sampson award 2003). Independent. Achievements include invention of temporary keratoprosthesis; research in corneal transplantation; clinical trial design in ocular surface disease. Avocations: fly fishing, gardening, travel. Office: University of Louisville 301 E Muhammad Ali Blvd Louisville KY 40202 Office Fax: 502-852-4102. Business E-Mail: gnfoul01@louisville.edu.

FOUNTAIN, ANDRE FERCHAUD, academic program director; b. Oklahoma City, Nov. 12, 1951; s. J. E. and Neaumatta Abilene (Edwards) F.; m. Linda K. Young. BS in Nursing, U. Okla., Norman, 1978. RN, Okla; cert. master hyrdotherapist, Kniepp Inst., Germany, massage therapist. Exec. dir. New Life Programs, Oklahoma City, 1981-87; dir. Praxis Coll. Health, Arts and Scis., Oklahoma City, 1988—. Speaker in field. Author: A Psychoprophylactic Workbook, 1981; co-author: Psychological Reports, 1977. Found. Caucus for Men in Nursing, Norman, 1976. Recipient 1st Pl. award Internat. Sci. Fair Balt., 1970; honored for Oklahoma City bombing vol. work, U.S. Dept. Justice. Mem. Internat. Childbirth Edn. Assn. (state coord. 1982-84), Am. Soc. Psychoprophylaxis in Obstetrics, Body Workers and Wellness Therapies Assn., Okla. Sports Massage Assn., Masons. Office Phone: 405-879-0224. E-mail: afountain@praxiscollege.com.

FOUNTAIN, KAREN SCHUELER, retired physician; b. Aberdeen, SD, Oct. 14, 1947; BA, No. State Coll., Aberdeen, SD, 1968; MD, U. Md., Balt., 1972. Diplomate Nat. Bd. Med. Examiners, Am. Bd. Radiology in Therapeutic Radiology. Intern Md. Gen. Hosp., Balt., 1972-73, resident in radiation oncology, 1973-74; fellow in radiation oncology Mayo Clinic, Rochester, Minn., 1974-76, cons. in oncology, 1976-81; clin. asst. prof. Columbia U., NYC, 1981-83, residency program dir. dept. radiation oncology, 1981—93, clin. assoc. prof., 1983—2001, ret., 2004. Mem. med. bd. Presbyn. Hosp., N.Y.C., 1983-86, Med. Res. Corps., 2004-; faculty coun. mem. Columbia U., 1982-89; del. N.Y. State Radiological Soc., N.Y.C., 1987-2004. Fellow Am. Coll. Radiology (councilor 1999-04), Am. Radium Soc. (exec. com. 2004-06), N.Y. Acad. Medicine; mem. Am. Soc. Therapeutic Radiology and Oncology, Radiol. Soc. N.Am., Am. Soc. Clin. Oncology, Am. Assn. for Women Radiologists (bd. dirs. 1995-96), So. Med. Assn., N.Y. Roentgen Soc. (sect. chmn. 1989-90), N.Y. State Radiol. Soc. (bd. dirs. 1996-02), N.Y. Acad. Scis.

FOUNTAIN, LINDA KATHLEEN, health science association executive; b. Fowler, Kans., Apr. 30, 1954; d. Ralph Edward and Ruth Evelyn (Cornelson) Young; m. Andre Fountain. BS in Nursing, Cen. State U., Edmond, Okla., 1976. RN, Okla. Staff nurse med./surg. and coronary care unit Presbyn. Hosp., Oklahoma City, 1976-79; mgr. nursing Hillcrest Osteo. Hosp., Oklahoma City, 1979-80; staff nurse, mgr. Oklahoma U. Teaching Hosp., Oklahoma City, 1981-82; pres. New Life Programs, Oklahoma City, 1981-88, Nursing Entrepreneurs, Ltd., Oklahoma City, 1988—; mgr. Internat. Health Supply, Oklahoma City, 1988—. Coord. lactation cons. program State of Okla., 1981-98, new life car seat rental program at various hosps., 1983-92, also speaker Success Co., Oklahoma City, 1984—; owner Rainbows Overhead Graphic Media, Oklahoma City, 1984-91; speaker in field. Founder Praxis Coll., Oklahoma City, 1988. Named Mentor of Yr., Okla. Metroplex Childbirth Network, Oklahoma City, 1984; honored for vol. work with families and rescue after Oklahoma City bombing, U.S. Dept. Justice, 1995. Mem. Am. Nurses Assn., Internat. Lactation Cons. Assn., Internat. Platform Assn., Bodyworkers and Wellness Therapies Assn. Avocations: gemology, travel. Office Phone: 405-879-0224. Business E-Mail: Lfountain@praxiscollege.com.

FOURNIER, CHRISTOPHE, international medical association executive, physician, surgeon; MD, U. Clermont-Ferrand, France. Degree in Tropical Medicine, Epidemiology, Biostatistics. Med. dr., head of mission in projects, Burundi, Uganda, Honduras, Chile; ops. mgr. Médecins Sans Frontières (Doctors Without Borders), NYC, 2000—06, internat. pres. Geneva, 2006—. Office: Medecins Sans Frontieres rue de Lausanne 78 Cp 116 1211 Geneva Switzerland Office Phone: 41 (22) 849.84.00. Office Fax: 41 (22) 849.84.04.

FOURNIER, DUDLEY JOHN, surgeon; b. Capreol, Ont., Can., June 23, 1923; arrived in USA, 1925, naturalized, 1936; s. Dudley Thomas and Margaret Mary (Conway) Fournier; m. Barbara Jane Arnold, Dec. 2, 1950; children: Dudley John Jr., Michele Fournier McLellan. BSc, Northwestern U., Evanston, Ill., 1945, MB, 1947, MD, 1948. Served with USN, Chgo., 1943—45; intern Queen of Angels Hosp., LA, 1947—48; med. officer USN, 1949—51; resident in surgery St. Mary's Hosp., San Francisco, 1953—55; fellow in cancer rsch. U. Calif. Med. Sch., San Francisco, 1955—56, mem. surg. faculty, 1956—63; pvt. practice surgeon San Francisco, 1956—2007. Surgeon emergency hosps. San Francisco Health Dept., 1956—78; team physician San Francisco Warriors (now Golden State Warriors), 1962—66. With USN, 1943—45, lt. comdr. USN, 1949—51. Recipient Man and Youth award, San Francisco Boys and Girls Club, 1990. Mem.: Olympic Club (San Francisco), Bohemian Club (San Francisco), The Guardsmen (San Francisco) (life). Republican. Roman Catholic. Avocations: golf, skiing. Personal E-mail: dfournier948@md.northwestern.edu.

FOURNIER, ERIC, internist, pulmonologist; b. Lille, France, June 23, 1950; MD, U. Lille, 1980; postgrad., U. Minn., 1983; DEA, U. Paris, 1984, diploma in Physiopathology and Sleep Cardio-Respiration, 1991. Intern Ctr. Hospitalier Universitaire Lille, 1975-80, asst. to hosp., asst. to univ., 1980-85; dept. head Polyclinique de Henin Beaumont, France, 1985—. Recipient medal of Honor Nat. Com. Against Tb and Respiratory Diseases, 1983. Fellow Am. Coll. Chest Physicians; mem. Société Pneumologie de Langue Français, Société Française d'Allergologie, N.Y. Acad. Scis., Société Pathologie Thoralique der Nord (pres. 2003—), Regional Coun. Nord (pres. 2005-06). Home: 30 bis rue General de Gaulle F59139 Wattignies France Office: Polyclin de Henin Beaumont 62256 Hénin Beaumont France

FOURNIER, JEAN GUY, biologist, researcher; b. Arnouville, Val D'Oise, France, May 26, 1947; s. Jean Fournier and Marguerite Lopez; m. Dominique Madeleine Le Meur, May 27, 1981; children: Marc-Alexandre, Guy-Awen, Carine Olivier, Gregory Olivier. BS, Lycee Honoré de Balzac, Paris, 1967; superior technician grad., Ecole Superieure Du Laboratoire, Paris, 1969; PhD in Cytology, U. Paris VI, 1978. Cert. social asst. Mairie Sarcelles, 1973. Predoctoral fellow Med. Rsch. Found., Paris, Paris, 1979—81; attaché de recherche Nat. Inst. Health and Med. Rsch. (INSERM), Paris, France, 1981—85, chargé de recherche Paris, 1985. Cons. Prion Com., Paris, 1996. Author: Molecular Histology, 1994; guest editor: Microscopy Rsch. and Technique (jour.); editor (spl. issue), 2000. 1st class French Infantry, 1972—73. Mem.: European Acad. Scis., French Soc. Neuropathology, French Microscopy Soc. (paris 1976). Achievements include research in 1)-Demonstration of the persistence of measles virus RNA in lymphocytes of normal subjects and patients with subacute sclerosing panencephalitis. 2)-Location of the normal prion protein at the synapse. Office Fax: 33146547726. Business E-Mail: fournier@dsvidf.cea.fr.

FOWLER, BRUCE ANDREW, toxicologist, researcher, public health service official; b. Seattle, Dec. 28, 1945; s. Andrew and Dolores Yvonne F.; children from previous marriage: Glenn Andrew, Randall Bruce. BS in Fisheries, U. Wash., 1968; PhD in Pathology, U. Oreg., 1972. From staff fellow to head metal toxicology Nat. Inst. Environ. Health Scis., Research Triangle Park, NC, 1972—86, head metal toxicology, 1986—87; dir. toxicology program U. Md., 1987—2001; sr. rsch. advisor Agy. for Toxic Substances and Disease Registry, Atlanta, 2002—03, assoc. dir., sci. divsn. toxicology and environ. medicine, 2003—11; scientist environ. health Sr. Biomed. Rsch. Svc. USPHS, 2003—07, disting. cons., 2008—11; Pres.'s rotating prof. U. Alaska, 2006—; adj. prof. Rollins Sch. Pub. Health, Emory U., 2009—; sr. fellow ICF Internat., 2011—. Prof. pathology U. Md. Med. Sch., 1987—2001, prof. epidemiology and toxicology, 2001—03, dir. lab. of cellular and molecular toxicology dept. of epidemiology and preventive medicine, 2001—03; dir. office collaborative studies on adaptive responses estuarine species U. Md., 1988—2001; Meyer Bodansky lectr. Dept. Pathology, U. Tex. Med. Br., Galveston; adj. assoc. prof. U. NC, NC; temporary adv. WHO; work group mem. Internat. Agy. Rsch. Against Cancer; mem., chmn. Sci. Com. on Toxicology of Metals; mem. Md. Gov.'s Coun. on Toxic Substances, 1988—93, chmn., 1990—93, Dahlem Workshop on Mechanisms of Cell Injury: Implications for Human Health, Berlin, 1985; mem. toxicology info. program com. on toxicology; chmn. com. on measuring lead in critical populations; mem. com. on women in sci. and engring., com. on biologic markers in urologic toxicology NAS/NRC, 1989—93, com. on evaluation on viability of augmenting potable water supplies with reclaimed water, 1996—97, subcom. on arsenic in drinking water, 1997—99; co-chmn. NY Acad. Scis. Conf. on Mechanisms of Chem.-Induced Porphyrinopathies, Rye, NY; fellow Japan Soc. for Promotion Sci., 1990; Swedish Med. Rsch. Coun. vis. prof. Karolinska Inst., 1994—95; Colgate-Palmolive vis. prof. U. Wash., 1998—99; mem. Fulbright scholarship rev. com., Scandinavia, 1999—2001, chair, Scandinavia, 2000—01; mem. nat. metals assessment panel sci. adv. bd. U.S. EPA, 2002—03, mem. nat. metals risk assessment framework review panel sci. advisory bd., 2004—05, mem. all ages lead model review panel sci. adv. bd., 2005—06, mem. clean air sci. adv. lead review panel sci. adv. bd., 2006—08; mem. Particular Matter Rsch. Program Adv. Panel Sci. Adv. Bd., 2008—; mem. expert panel Ctr. Evaluation of Risks to Human Reproduction Nat. Toxicology Program, 2003—; mem. Nat. Toxicology Program Inter Agy. Comm. Chemical Evaluation & Coord., 2008—, Nat. Toxicology Program Interagency Sci. Review Group, 2008—, US Pharmacopeia Toxicology Expert Com., 2010—, NCEH/ATSDR Lisison to NAS/NRC Com. on Emerging Sci. for Environmental Health Decisions, 2010—11. Editor: Biological and Environmental Effects of Arsenic, 1983, Mechamisms of Cell Injury: Implications for Human Health; co-editor: Mechanisms of Chemical Induced Porphyrinopathies, Handbook on the Toxicology of Metals, 3d edit.; mem. editl. bd. Chemico-Biol. Interacctions, 1980—85, Environ. Health Perspectives, 1981—97, Toxicology and Applied Pharmacology, 1985—96, Internat. Archives of Environ. Health, 1986—, Renal Failure, 1988—, Internat. Jour. Occupl. and Environ. Health, 1994—96, Jour. Biochem. and Molecular Toxicology, 2000—, Open Toxicology Revs., 2006—, Chemistry Ctrl. Jour., 2007—; assoc. editor: Environ. Health Perspectives, 2007—, Open Proteomics Jour, —, Toxicology and Applied Pharmacology, 2011—; contbr. articles to profl. jours., chapters to books. Rsch. fellow Japanese Soc. Promotion of Sci., 1990; Fulbright scholar Karolinska Inst., 1994; finalist Charles C. Shepard award CDC, 2007, 11, Individual Leadership Honor award, NCEH/ATSDR, 2010, CDC-ATSDR, 2011, finalist award PBPK Modelling Group, 2010, Group award Deepwater Horizon Oil Spill Response Team, 2010, Group Honor award, 2011. Fellow Acad. Toxicol. Scis. (bd. dirs. 2006-09); mem. AAAS (recruitment and screening panel ct. apptd. sci. experts project 2000—), Soc. Toxicology (councilor mechanisms of toxicity sect., pres. metals splty. sect. 1996, councilor nat. capitol area regional chpt. 1994-95, v.p. in-vitro splty. sect. 2001-02, pres. in-vitro splty. sect. 2003-04, councilor 2005-07), Am. Coll. Toxicology (councilor 1995-98, councilor, SOT Mixtures Splty. Sect.), Soc. Occupl. and Environ. Health (councilor 1988, v.p. 1993), Fulbright Assn. (Ga. Chpt.) (bd. dirs. 2010-11), NY Acad. Sci., Internat. Commn. Occupl. Health (chmn. sci. com. toxicology of metals 1996-2002), Profl. Assn. Diving Instrs., Sigma Xi. Home: 5225 Pooks Hill Rd Unit 207 S Bethesda MD 20814 Office: ICF Internat 9300 Lee Hwy Fairfax VA 22031 Personal E-mail: drtox@earthlink.net. Business E-Mail: bfowler@icfi.com.

FOWLER, ELIZABETH J. (LIZ FOWLER), federal official, former legislative staff member; b. Taipei, Taiwan, 1967; BA, U. Pa., Phila.; PhD, Johns Hopkins Sch. Pub. Health, Balt.; JD, U. Minn. Bar: DC, Md. Payment policy rschr. Health Care Financing Adminstrn.; health services rschr. HealthSystem Minn.; atty. Hogan & Hartson LLP, Washington; policy analyst to Rep. Pete Stark US Joint Econ. Com., Washington; chief health & entitlements counsel US Senate Fin. Com., Washington, 2001—05; sr. counsel, chief health counsel US Senate Finance Com., 2008—10; v.p. pub. policy & external affairs WellPoint., Inc., 2006—08; dep. dir. Office Consumer Info. & Ins. Oversight (OCIIO), US Dept. Health & Human Services, Washington, 2010—11; spl. asst. to Pres. for health care & econ. policy Nat. Econ. Coun., The White House, Washington, 2011—. Named one of The 100 Most Powerful Women in DC, Washingtonian mag., 2009, The Most Influential Lawyers, The Nat. Law Jour., 2011. Democrat. Office: National Economic Council The White House 1600 Pennsylvania Ave Washington DC 20500 *

FOWLER, JOHN DALE, JR., biotechnologist, consultant, investment banker; b. Norfolk, Va., May 15, 1957; s. John Dale and Margaret (Kimmel) F.; m. Corey Keane Phillips, Aug. 2, 1980; children: John Dale III, Douglas Houghton, Grace Phillips. BA, U. Va., 1979, MBA, JD, 1986. Asst. v.p. Jefferson Nat. Bank, Charlottesville, Va., 1979-82; fin. analyst Marine Midland Bank, NYC, 1983; assoc. law Hawkins, Delafield & Wood, NYC, 1984; assoc. Merrill Lynch Capital Markets, NYC, 1985; v.p. Salomon Bros. Inc., NYC, 1986-92; mng. dir. Wheat First Butcher & Singer Capital Markets, Richmond, Va., 1992; mng. dir. Health Care Group Salomon Bros. Inc., NYC, 1992—98; mng. dir. J.P. Morgan, 1998—2001; pres. Large Scale Biology, 2001—03; mng. ptnr. Baycrest Capital LLC, 2003—; mng. dir. Bio-Strategic Dirs. LLC, 2004; vice chmn., health care banking Deutsche Bank Securities, Inc., NYC, 2004—06; vice chmn., head health care investment banking Deutsche Bank AG London, London, 2006—. Bd. dirs. Beverley Enterprises Inc., 2002—06. Mem. NY Bar Assn. Office: Deutsche Bank in Europe 1 Great Winchester St London EC2N 2DB England Personal E-mail: john_fowlerjr@yahoo.com.

FOWLER, LINDA MCKEEVER, health facility administrator, educator; b. Greensburg, Pa., Aug. 7, 1948; d. Clay and Florence Elizabeth (Smith) McKeever; m. Timothy L. Fowler, Sept. 13, 1969 (div. July 1985). Nursing diploma, Presbyn. U. Hosp., Pitts., 1969; BSN, U. Pitts., 1976, M in Nursing Adminstrn., 1980; D in Pub. Adminstrn., Nova U., 1985. Supr., head nurse Presbyn. Univ. Hosp., Pitts., 1969-76; mem. faculty Western Pa. Hosp. Sch. Nursing, Pitts., 1976-79; acute care coord. Mercy Hosp., Miami, 1980-81; asst. adminstr. nursing North Shore Med. Ctr., Miami, 1981-84, v.p. patient care, 1984-88, Golden Glades Regional Med. Ctr., Miami, 1988-89, Humana Hosp.-South Broward, Hollywood, Fla., 1989-91, assoc. exec. dir. nursing; v.p., chief nursing officer Columbia Regional Med. Ctr., Bayonet Point, 1991-96; COO, chief nursing officer Greenbrier Valley Med. Ctr., 1996-97; quality mgmt. coord. Greenbrier Valley Hospice, 1997-98; pvt. practice healthcare cons., 1998-99; chief nursing officer Marlboro Park Hosp., 1999—2002; pvt. practice healthcare cons., 2002—; chief clin. officer Intermedical Hosp. of S.C., 2003—. Mem. adj. faculty Barry U., Miami, 1984-97, Broward C.C., Ft. Lauderdale, 1984-85, Nova U., 1986-87; cons. Strategic Health Devel. Inc., Miami Shores, Fla., 1986-90, So. Coll., Cleveland, Tenn., 1995-96. Dept. HEW trainee, 1976, 79-80; bd. dirs. Pasco County Am. Cancer Soc., 1992-95. Mem. Am. Orgn. Nurse Execs. (legis. com. 1988-90), Fla. Orgn. Nurse Execs. (bd. dirs. 1986-88), S.C. Orgn. Nurse Execs., South Fla. Nurse Adminstrs. Assn. (sec. 1983-84, bd. dirs. 1984-86), U. Pitts. Alumni Assn., Presbyn. U. Alumni Assn., Portuguese Water Dog Club Am. (bd. dirs. 1988-89), Ft. Lauderdale Dog Club (bd. dirs. 1981-82, 83-85, v.p. 1982-83), Am. Kennel Club (dog judge), Moore County Kennel Club, Sigma Theta Tau. Lutheran. Office: Taylor at Marion Sts Columbia SC 29220 E-mail: lfowler@intermedical.us.

FOWLER, W. CRAIG, ophthalmologist, educator; MD, Med. Coll. Va, 1985. Resident George Washington U. Med. Ctr., 1989; fellow U. Okla. Health Sciences Ctr. Dean A. McGee Eye Inst., 1990—91; assoc. med. dir. Duke U. Med. Ctr. FEL Laser Lab.; asst. prof. ophthalmology Duke U. Eye Ctr., 1992—2000, assoc. prof. ophthalmology; med. dir. NC Eye Bank. Recipient US Top Ophthalmologists award, Rsch. Coun. Am., 2002, 2004; named Best Drs., 2000—08. Office: Ambulatory Care Center 130 Mason Farm Rd Chapel Hill NC 27599 also: UNC School of Medicine Dept Ophthalmology 5151 Bioinformatics Bldg CB #7040 Chapel Hill NC 27599-7040 Office Phone: 919-966-2061, 919-966-5296. Office Fax: 919-966-1908.

FOX, ADAM TOBIAS, pediatrician; b. London, Apr. 10, 1972; s. Danny and Shirley Fox; m. Tanya Lisa Meltzer, Mar. 14, 1999; 1 child, Ethan Benjamin. MA with honors, Cambridge U., Eng., 1993; MSc, Inst. of Child Health, London, 2002; MB,BS, U. Coll. London, 1996. Diplomate Royal Coll. of Pediats., 2000. Specialist registrar in pediat. Luton & Dunstable Hosp., Bedfordshire, England, 2000—02; specialist registrar in pediat. allergy St Mary's Hosp., London, 2002—03; specialist registrar in pediat. gastroenterology Royal Free Hosp., London, 2003—. Dir Pediat. Edn. Solutions, London, 2003—; web tng. dir. Doctorsworld.com, London, 2000—01. Editor: (editor in chief) InternetJour. of Pediats. and Neonatology (Golden Web Award, 2003). Recipient Vincent Wigglesworth prize, 2001. Master: Royal Coll. of Paediatrics & Child Health; mem.: European Acad. Allergy and Clin. Immunology, Am. Acad. Asthma, Allergy and Clin. Immunology, Brit. Soc. of Allergy and Clin. Immunology. Jewish. Achievements include internat. authority on origins and usage of med. slang; research in pediatric allergy. Avocations: travel, parapsychology. Home: 48 Lansdowne Rd Middlesex Stanmore HA7 2SA England Business E-Mail: adam_fox@btinternet.com.

FOX, ARTHUR CHARLES, cardiologist, educator; b. Newark, Sept. 16, 1926; s. Jacob and Mae (Bonda) F. Student, Harvard U., Cambridge, Mass., 1943-44; MD, NYU, 1948. Cert. Am. Bd. Internal Medicine, 1956, in internal medicine Am. Bd. Internal Medicine, 1974, in cardiovascular disease Am. Bd. Internal Medicine, 1975. Intern, asst. resident, chief resident medicine Bellevue Hosp., NYC, 1948—52; from asst. to full prof. medicine NYU Sch. Medicine, NYC, 1954—, chief cardiology sect., 1968—2001. Cons. Manhattan VA Hosp.; attending physician, NYU Hosp., Bellevue Hosp. Contbr. articles to profl. jours. 1st lt. to capt. M C USAF, 1952—54, prof. asst., 1953—54, Divsn. Med. Scis., Nat. Rsch. Coun. NIH fellow, 1954-56; grantee, 1956-80; recipient Great Tchr. award NYU, 1992. Master ACP (gov. region 1981-86, Laureate award NY Chpt.); fellow Am. Coll. Cardiology, Am. Heart Assn.; mem. AAAS, Am. Fedn. Clin. Rsch., NY Heart Assn. (pres. 1987-89), NY Cardiologic Soc. (pres. 1992-93), Alpha Omega Alpha, Sigma Xi. Home: 330 E 33rd St Apt 20-L New York NY 10016-9466 Office: 550 1st Ave New York NY 10016-6402 Business E-Mail: arthur.fox@med.nyu.edu.

FOX, DANIEL MICHAEL, author, advisor; b. NYC, Aug. 20, 1938; s. Alexander E. and Rose (Leitner) F.; m. Carol Anne Kemps, Sept. 8, 1963 (div. 1985); children: Aaron, Miriam, Joshua, Benjamin; m. Louise O. Vasvari, Dec. 26, 1988 (div. 2003). AB, Harvard U., Cambridge, Mass., 1959, AM, 1961, PhD, 1964. Instr. Harvard U., Cambridge, Mass., 1964—65, asst. prof., 1967—72; dir. field ops. Applachian Vols., Berea, Ky., 1965—66; assoc. dir. Commonwealth of Mass. Svc. Corps, 1965—67; prof., v.p. SUNY, Stony Brook, 1972—89. Assoc. dir. Nat. Ctr. for Health Svcs. Rsch., Rockville, Md., 1975-78; pres. Milbank Meml. Fund, NYC, 1990-2007, pres. emeritus, 2007-; faculty U. Sydney, Columbia U., 2007-; cons. in field. Author: Engines of Culture, 1963, rev. edit., 1995, The Discovery of Abundance, 1967, electronic edit., 2002, Economists and Health Care, 1979, Health Policies, Health Politics, 1986, Photographing Medicine, 1988, AIDS: The Burdens of History, 1989, AIDS: The Making of a Chronic Disease, 1992, Power and Illness: The Failure and Future of American Health Policy, 1993, 2nd edit., 1995, The Convergence of Science and Governance: Research, Health Policy, and American States, 2010. Bd. dir. Village Care NY Inc., vice chmn., 1996—; treas. Employee Benefit Rsch. Inst., 2003—04; bd. dir. ECRI, The Health Tech. Ctr., 2001—09, Health Quality Coun. Sask., 2002—. Shaw traveling fellow Harvard U., 1959-60, Sheldon traveling fellow, 1962; also numerous grants. Mem.: APHA, NY Acad. Medicine, Am. Assn. for the History of Medicine, Nat. Acad. Social Ins., Am. Hist. Assn. (Beveridge prize 1965), Coun. on Fgn. Rels., Inst. Medicine of NAS, Century Assn. Jewish. Business E-Mail: dmfox@milbank.org.

FOX, DAVID ALAN, rheumatologist, immunologist; b. Montreal, July 5, 1953; s. Lester L. and Zelda L. (Rothbart) F.; m. Paula L. Bockenstedt, July 10, 1977; children: Sharon Elizabeth, Michelle Caroline, Jonathan William. BS, MIT, 1974; MD, Harvard U., 1978. Diplomate Am. Bd. Internal Medicine, Am. Bd. Rheumatology. Intern, then resident Brigham and Women's Hosp., Boston, 1978-81; fellow in rheumatology and immunology Harvard U. Med. Sch., Boston, 1981-85; asst. prof. U. Mich., Ann Arbor, 1985-90, assoc. prof., 1990-95, prof., 1995—, acting chief divsn. rheumatology, 1990-91, chief divsn., 1991—. Dir. U. Mich. Multipurpose Arthritis Ctr., Ann Arbor, 1990—2001, U. Mich. Rheumatic Disease Core Ctr., 2001—; trustee Arthritis Found., 1992—2008. Assoc. editor Jour. Clin. Investigation, 1997-2002; contbr. chpts. to books, articles to profl. jours. Mem.: Assn. Am. Physicians, Am. Soc. Clin. Investigation, Am. Assn. Immunologists, Am. Coll. Rheumatology (pres. 2007—08). Achievements include discovery of T lymphocyte surface molecules and development of various monoclonal antibodies. Office: U MichMed Ctr Rackham Arthritis Rsch Unit 3918 Taubman Ctr Ann Arbor MI 48109 Business E-Mail: dfox@umich.edu.

FOX, DAVID S., hospital administrator; MBA, U. of Chgo.; BA, Haverford Coll. Pres., CEO Advocate Good Samaritan Hosp., 2003—; bd. dirs. Lincoln Found. for Performance Excellence, Downers Grove Econ. Devel. Corp. Mem. strategic planning com. Ill. Hosp. Assn., chair polit. action com.; immediate past chair Glen Ellyn Children's Chorus. Recipient Downers Grove Area C. of C. Enterprise award, 2008, Excellence in Advocacy award, Ill. Hosp. Assn., 2010; named CEO of the Yr., Becker's Hosp. Rev. Mag., 2009; named to Fire Starter Hall of Fame, The Studer Group, 2009. Mem.: Am. Heart Assn., Am. Coll. of Healthcare Execs. Office: Advocate Good Samaritan Hospital 3815 Highland Ave Downers Grove IL 60515 Office Phone: 630-275-5900.

FOX, EMILE, physician; b. Luxembourg, Jan. 4, 1953; s. Nicolas and Lucie (Waltzing) Fox. MD, U. Nancy, France, 1980, diploma in pub. health, 1982; MS in Tropical Medicine, London Sch. Hygiene, 1983. Registrar Ctrl. Hosp., Luxembourg, 1980-83; specialist physician Nat. Health Lab., Luxembourg, 1983-84; sr. med. officer Internat. Ctr. Med. Rsch., Lahore, Pakistan, 1984-85; lectr. medicine U. Papua New Guinea, 1985-86; staff epidemiologist USN Med. Rsch. Unit #3, Cairo, 1986-90; med. officer WHO, Kigali, Rwanda, 1990-92, cons., 1993-94; med. officer, team leader WHO/GPA, Beijing, 1994-95; country program advisor UNAIDS, Beijing, 1996—2003. Rsch. asst. prof. internat. health U. Md., Balt., 1984—90; hon. cons. Port Moresby Gen. Hosp., Papua New Guinea, 1985—86; team leader epidemiol. rsch. expdns. NAMRU-3, Djibouti, 1987—90. Author (with others): Tuberculosis in the Tropics, 1991; contbr. articles to profl. jours. Recipient Frederic Murgatroyd award, London Sch. Hygiene, 1983. Fellow: Royal Soc. Tropical Medicine; mem.: APHA, Am. Soc. Tropical Medicine and Hygiene, Am. Soc. Microbiology. Home: 16 Rue Nicolas van Werveke 2725 Luxembourg Luxembourg Home Phone: 359-443678. E-mail: emilefox@hotmail.com.

FOX, ERVIN R., medical educator, researcher; b. Clarksdale, Miss., Dec. 21, 1966; BS in Biol. Engring., Miss. State U., 1989; MD, U. Miss. Med. Ctr., 1993. Assoc. prof. medicine U. Miss. Med. Ctr., 2001—. Dir. echocardiography and nuc. labs. Divsn. Cardiovasc. Diseases, U. Miss. Med. Ctr., 2001; co-investigator Jackson Heart Study, 2001. Recipient Excellence Rsch. award, Dept. Medicine, U. Miss. Med. Ctr., Nat. Role Model Faculty award, Minority Access, Inc. Fellow: Am. Heart Assn., Am. Coll. Cardiology; mem.: Am. Soc. Echocardiography, Am. Soc. Human Genetics, Assn. Black Cardiologists. Avocations: tennis, walking, travel. Office: University Miss Medical Ctr Jackson MS 39216 Business E-Mail: efox@umc.edu.

FOX, HAROLD EDWARD, obstetrician, researcher, gynecologist, educator; b. East Orange, NJ, Feb. 19, 1945; s. Willis Edward and Elizabeth (Strathearn) F.; m. Rhea Keller, June 18, 1966; children: Alison, Michael Antaniate. BA, U. Rochester, 1967, MS, MD with honors, 1972. Diplomate Am. Bd. Ob-Gyn., Am. Bd. Maternal-Fetal Medicine. Intern, resident Strong Meml. Hosp., Rochester, NY, 1972-75; dir. Regional Perinatal Program, Rochester, NY, 1975-79; dir. obstetrics and maternal fetal medicine U. Rochester, 1977-79; dir. maternal fetal medicine Columbia U., NYC, 1979-95, dir. obstetrics, 1985-88, vice-chmn. ob-gyn., 1988-91, chmn. protem dept. ob-gyn., 1991-95; Oscar I. and Mildred S. Dodek prof., chmn. ob-gyn. George Washington U., Washington, 1995-96, exec. dir. Ctr. Excellence for Women's Health, 1995-96; ob-gyn. in-chief Johns Hopkins Medicine, Balt., 1996—, Dr. Dorothy Edwards prof. ob-gyn., 1996—, chair women's health ctr. oversight com., 1997—, chmn., dir. ob-gyn. Trustee Johns Hopkins Med. Svc. Corp., Johns Hopkins Home Care Group, 1996—, Kennedy Kreige Inst., 1996—2003; bd. dirs. JH Cmty. Physicians, JH Health Care; vice chair med. bd. Johns Hopkins Hosp., 1999-2002, chmn. med. bd., 2002-05, 11-, bd. dirs., 2002-05, vice chair, 2009-11, chmn. med. bd., JHH, 2011-; mem. adv. bd. Johns Hopkins Medicine, bd. govs., chmn. govt. affairs com.; mem. Gov.'s Commn. on Infant Mortality, State of Md., 2000—; chmn. women and infant transmission study NIH, 1988-93; mem. pediat. com. AIDS clin. trials group, 1988-91; organizing mem. women's com.; mem. obstet. adv. com. N.Y.C. Dept. Health; bd. midwifery N.Y. State Edn. Dept., 1994-95; chmn. N.Y. Acad. Medicine Ob-gyn. sect., 1993-94; mem. Gov.'s Commn. on Infant Mortality, State Md., 1999—; co-chair innovations in patient care; chair med. adv. bd. United Premier Med. Group, Johns Hopkins Internat., 2003—; mem. med. adv. bd. Bridgtech Asia, 2004-, Barnev Inc., Israel, 2000-09; chair MCICI Vt. Safety Com., 2002-08; mem. CME Adv. Bd., 1997-. Editor Pediatric AIDS, 1991-95, Practical Revs. in Ob-Gyn., 2001—; contbr. articles to profl. jours. Grantee NIH, 1988-95, USPHS, 1991-95, March of Dimes. Fellow Soc. Gynecologic Investigation, Am. Coll. Ob-Gyn.; mem. Internat. AIDS Soc., Am. Gynecol. and Obstet. Soc., Am. Inst. Ultrasound in Medicine, ACMB JHIT (chmn. 2009-11), Perinatal Rsch. Soc., Washington Acad. Medicine, Washington Gynecol. Soc., N.Y. Obstet. Soc., Med. Soc. State of Md. (chair maternal mortality com. 2003—), Johns Hopkins HealthCare LLC (bd. trustees 1996-, chair), UHCP (bd. trustees 1996-), Johns Hopkins Home Care Group (bd. trustees 1996-), John Hopkins Cmty. Physicians (chair), SCDC (chair), Alpha Omega Alpha, Phi Beta Delta. Avocations: boating, art, exercise. Office: Johns Hopkins Medicine Dept Gyn-Ob 600 N Wolfe St Rm 264 Baltimore MD 21287-0005 Home: PO Box 9 Gibson Island MD 21056-0009 Office Phone: 410-614-0178. Business E-Mail: hfox@jhmi.edu.

FOX, JAMES GAHAN, veterinarian, educator, researcher; b. Reno, Mar. 8, 1943; married; 2 children DVM, Colo. State U., 1968; MS, Stanford U., 1972. Resident veterinarian Biol. Lab. Animal Div. U.S. Army Vet. Corps, Ft. Detrick, 1968-70; asst. prof., staff veterinarian Med. Ctr. U. Colo., 1973-74; inst. veterinarian, dir. animal care facility MIT, Cambridge, 1974-75, inst. veterinarian, assoc. prof., dir. div. comparative medicine, 1975-82, dir., prof. comparative medicine, 1983—. Adj. prof. U. Pa. Sch. of Vet. Med., 1989; faculty affiliate dept. clinics and surgery Colo. State U., 1973-74; adj. assoc. prof. dept. comparative medicine Tufts U. Sch. Vet. Medicine, 1981-82, adj. prof., 1983—; prin. investigator NIH Diagnostic Investigative Lab. grant, 1975—1990, NIH/Nat. Cancer Inst. Campylobacter and Helicobacter Infections in Animals and Man, 1983—, NIH postdoctoral tng. grant in comparative animal medicine, 1989—; chmn. com. lab. animal usage NAS, 1986—; mem. NIH/DRR/ARB Study Sect., 1981-85, chmn., 1985; cons. in field, 1976-78; mem. editl. bd. Lab Animal Science, 1983-86, Am. Jour. Vet. Rsch., 1990-92, Helicobacter, 1995—, Jour. Clin. Microbiology, 1995—., edtl. bd. mem. Zoonos PS & Pub. Health, 2008- NIH fellow in lab. animal medicine and med. microbiology Stanford U., 1970-72; grantee Animal Rsch. Ctr., Nat. Cancer Inst., 1977-80, 83—, Nat. Cancer Inst./NIH, 1988—, Sci. Achivement award, AUMA ASLP, 2000, AALAS Griffin award, 2008, Nat Brewer Sci. Achievement award, 2001, Sci. Achievement award, Am. Coll. Lab Animal med., 2007 Fellow Soc. Infectious Diseases Am.; mem. AVMA (Charles River award 1990), Am. Assn. Accreditation Lab. Animal Care (chmn. animal medicine 1983-85), Am. Coll. Toxicology, Am. Assn. Lab. Animal Sci., Am. Coll. Lab. Animal Medicine (pres. 1990), Mass. Soc. Med. Rsch. (exec. com. 1984—1992, pres. 1990-93), Am. Lab. Animal Diseases (exec. com. 1984—, pres. 1990-92, exec com., 2007-10), Inst. Medicine, ILAR Coun., NAS, AAVMC(pres., 2008-09), BOD-One Health Commn-(vice chmn., 2009-), NAS Home: 349 Littleton Rd Harvard MA 01451-1236 Office: MIT Dept Biol Engring Divsn Comparative Medicine 16-825C 77 Mass Ave Cambridge MA 02139-4307 Office Phone: 617-253-1757. Office Fax: 617-252-1877. E-mail: jgfox@mit.edu.

FOX, JAMES W., plastic surgeon; Grad., Jefferson Med. Coll., 1970. Diplomate Am. Bd. of Facial Plastic and Reconstructive Surgery. Intern Thomas Jefferson Univ. Hosp., resident; fellow Univ. Va. Med. Ctr. Named one of Top Docs, Phila. Mag., 2010. Office: Jefferson University Hospital 840 Walnut St 15th Fl Philadelphia PA 19107 Office Phone: 215-625-6630. Office Fax: 215-625-6640.

FOX, JOHN T., interventional cardiologist, educator; MD, NY Med. Coll., 1989. Diplomate Am. Bd. Internal Medicine-cardiovascular disease, Am. Bd. Internal Medicine-interventional cardiology. Asst. prof. in medicine Yeshiva Univ.; resident in internal medicine Beth Israel Med. Ctr., NY, 1990—93, fellow in cardiovascular disease, 1993—96, fellow in interventional cardiology, 1996—97, cardiologist. Office: Beth israel Medical Center 1st Ave at 16th St, 11 Dazian New York NY 10003 Office Phone: 212-420-2416.

FOX, KEITH A.A., cardiology researcher, consultant, professor; b. Aug. 27, 1949; s. Arthur A. and Magdalen C. (Henning) F.; m. Aileen E.M. Fox; children: Natalie, Alastair. BS with honors, Edinburgh U., Scotland, 1972, MB, BChir, 1974. Fellow in cardiology Washington U. Sch. Medicine, St. Louis, 1981-83, asst. prof. internal medicine, 1983-85; sr. lectr. cardiology, hon. cons. cardiologist U. Wales Coll. Medicine, Cardiff, 1985-89, Duke of Edinburgh prof. cardiology, cons. cardiologist U. Edinburgh, Scotland, 1989—. Prof. cardiology Cardiovascular Rsch. Unit, Edinburgh, 1989; cons. cardiologist Royal Infirmary, Edinburgh. Internat. editor European Heart Jour., Heart, 1989; contbr. 310 articles on basic and clin. cardiovas. rsch. to profl. jours. Recipient numerous awards and grants for cardiovascular rsch. Fellow RCS (bd. mem.), Acad. Med. Scis., European Soc. Cardiology (bd. mem.); mem. Brit. Cardiovasc. Soc. (pres., 2009-). Office: U Edinburgh Chancellor's Bldg 49 Little France Crescent Edinburgh Scotland EH16 4SB Business E-Mail: k.a.a.fox@ed.ac.uk.

FOX, KEVIN R., oncologist, educator; AB magna cum laude, Princeton U., 1977; MD, Johns Hopkins U., 1981. Diplomate Am. Bd. Internal Medicine, 1985, Am. Bd. Internal Medicine-med. oncology, 1985. Intern medicine Johns Hopkins Hosp., Baltimore, Md., 1981—82, asst. resident medicine, 1982—83, resident medicine, 1983—84; fellow hematology-oncology sect., dept. medicine Hosp. of Univ. Pa., 1984—87; med. dir. Rena Rowan breast ctr., Abramson cancer ctr. Univ. Pa., Marianne T. and Robert J. MacDonald prof., breast cancer care excellence, 2007—; hosp. affiliation includes Hosp. of Univ. Pa. (UPHS). Co-author: (publs.) A phase I/II dose escalating trial of liposomal doxorubicin (TLC D-99, Myocet) in combination with paclitaxel (Taxol, T) for patients (pts) wit metastatic breast cancer (MBC), 2002, Fifteen-year results of breast-conserving surgery and definitive irradiation for stage I and II breast cancer: the University of Pennsylvania experience, 2002, Buffering effects for family and friend support on associations between partner unsupportive behaviors and coping among women with breast cancer, 2002, Fifteen year results of breast conserving surgery and definitive irradiation for stage I and II breast carcinoma, 2003, Hypereosinophilia associated with Cardiac Rhabdomyosarcoma, 2003, and numerous other publs. Recipient Donald B. Martin Teaching Svc. award, Univ. Pa. Sch.of Medicine, 1997, Donna McCurdy Housestaff Tchg. award, 2001; named I.S. Ravdin Master Clinician, Univ. Pa. Health System, 2002; named one of Top Docs, Phila. Mag., 1993, America's Best Doctors for Cancer. Office: University of Pennsylvania Perelman Ctr for Advanced Medicine 3 W Pavilion 3400 Civic Ctr Blvd Philadelphia PA 19104 Office Phone: 215-662-7469. Office Fax: 215-662-7352. E-mail: krfox2@mail.med.upenn.edu.

FOX, MAURICE SANFORD, retired molecular biologist, educator; b. NYC, Oct. 11, 1924, s. Albert and Ray F.; m. Sally Cherniavsky, Apr. 1, 1955; children: Jonathan, Gregory, Michael. BS in Meteorology, U. Chgo., 1944, MS in Chemistry, 1951, PhD, 1951; Docteur honoris causa, Université Paul Sabatier, Toulouse, France, 1994. Instr. U. Chgo., 1951-53; asst. Rockefeller Inst., 1953-55, asst. prof., 1955-58, assoc. prof., 1958-62, MIT, Cambridge, 1962-66, prof., 1966-79, Lester Wolfe prof. molecular biology, 1979-96, head dept. biology, 1985-89; ret., 1997. Mem. Radiation Effects Rsch. Found., Hiroshima, 1997—2000. Mem. Internat. Bioethics Com. UN Ednl., Sci. and Cultural Orgn., 1997-2003. Served with USAAF, 1943-46. USPHS fellow, 1952-53; Nuffield Rsch. fellow, 1957; Fogarty scholar, 1991. Fellow: AAAS; mem.: NAS, Am. Acad. Arts and Scis., Inst. Medicine. Office: MIT Dept Biology 77 Massachusetts Ave Cambridge MA 02139-4307 Office Phone: 617-253-4728. Business E-Mail: msfox@mit.edu.

FOX, NATHAN S., physician; b. Chgo., June 11, 1974; BA, Columbia U., 1997; MD, Mt. Sinai Sch. Medicine, 2001. Asst. clin. prof. Mt. Sinai Sch. Medicine, 2008—. Office: 70 E 90th St New York NY 10128 Office Fax: 212-722-7185. Business E-Mail: nfox@mfmnyc.com.

FOX, RENÉE CLAIRE, sociology educator; b. NYC, Feb. 15, 1928; d. Paul Fred and Henrietta (Gold) F. AB summa cum laude, Smith Coll., 1949, LHD, 1975, Harvard U., 1954; MA (hon.), U. Pa., 1971, D (hon.) in Social Sci., DSc (hon.), 2011; MA (hon.), U. Oxford, 1996; ScD (hon.), Med. Coll. Pa., 1974, St. Joseph's Coll., Phila., 1978; D (hon.), Katholieke U., Leuven, 1978; LHD (hon.), La Salle U., Phila., 1988; DSc (hon.), Hahnemann U., 1991, U. Nottingham, Eng., 2002, U. Pa., 2011; LLD (hon.), Harvard U., 2010; PhD (hon.), Kings Coll., London, 2010. Rsch. asst. Bur. Applied Social Rsch., Columbia U., 1953-55, rsch. assoc., 1955-58; lectr. dept. sociology Barnard Coll., 1955-58, asst. prof., 1958-64, assoc. prof., 1964-66; lectr. sociology Harvard U., 1967-69; rsch. fellow Ctr. Internat. Affairs, 1967-68, rsch. assoc. program tech. and soc., 1968-71; prof. sociology, psychiatry and medicine U. Pa., Phila., 1969-98, Annenberg prof. social scis., 1978-98, chmn. dept. sociology, 1972-78, Annenberg prof. social scis. emerita, 1998—, sr. fellow Ctr. for Bioethics, 1999—2002, sr. fellow emeritus Ctr. for Bioethics, 2005—, affiliated faculty Solomon Asch Ctr. for the Study of Ethnopolit. Conflict, 2001—07. Rsch. assoc. Refugee Studies Centre, Queen Elizabeth House, U. Oxford, 1998-2006; sci. advisor Centre de Recherches Sociologiques, Kinshasa, Zaïre, 1963-67; vis. prof. sociology U. Officielle du Congo, Lubumbashi, 1965; vis. prof. Sir George Williams U., Montreal, summer 1968; Phi Beta Kappa vis. scholar, 1973-75; dir. humanities seminar med. practitioners NEH, 1975-76; maitre de cours U. Liège, Belgium, 1976-77; vis. prof. Katholieke U., Leuven, Belgium, 1976-77; Wm. Allen Neilson prof. Smith Coll., Mass., 1980; dir. d'Etudes Associè, Ecole des Hautes Etudes en Sciences Sociales, Paris, summer 1989; George Eastman vis. prof. Oxford U., 1996-97; vis. scholar Tokyo Med. and Dental U., 2001; mem. bd. clin. scholars program Robert Wood Johnson Found., 1974-80; mem. Pres.'s Commn. on Study of Ethical Problems in Medicine, Biomed. and Behavioral Rsch., 1979-81; dir. human qualities of medicine program James Picker Found., 1980-83; Fae Golden Kass lectr. Harvard U. Sch. Medicine and Radcliffe Coll., 1983, Kate Hurd Mead lectr. Med. Coll. Pa./Coll. Physicians Phila., 1990, Lori Ann Roscetti Meml. lectr. Rush-Presbyn.-St. Luke's Med. Ctr., Chgo., 1990; vis. scholar Women's Ctr., U. Mo., Kansas City, 1990, vis. scholar Case Western Res. Sch. of Med., 1992; opening address 13th Internat. Conf. on Social Scis. and Medicine, Hungary, 1994, vis. prof. U. Calif., San Francisco Sch. of Medicine, 1994; lectr. founds. of medicine Faculty of Medicine McGill U., Montreal, 1995; Supernumerary fellow Balliol Coll. Oxford U., 1996-97; WHR Rivers disting. lectr. dept. social medicine Harvard Med. Sch., 1998; assembly series lectr. Washington U., St. Louis, 1998; William J. Rashkind Meml. lectr, Am. Heart Assn., 1998, Salinger-Forlang lectr. U. Tex. Health Scis. Ctr. at San Antonio, 1999, Frances H. Schlitz lectr. U. Kans., Wichita, 2002; Stambaugh lectr. U. Louisville Sch. Medicine, 2004; mem. editl. adv. bd., Clin. Ethics, 2008- Author: Experiment Perilous, 1959; author: (with Willy De Craemer) The Emerging Physician, 1968; author: (with Judith P. Swazey) The Courage to Fall, 1974, rev. edit., 1978, 2002; author: Essays in Medical Sociology, 1979, 2d edit., 1988, L'Incertitude Medicale, 1988, The Sociology of Medicine: A Participant Observer's View, 1989; author: (with Judith P. Swazey) Spare Parts: Organ Replacement in American Society, 1992; author: In the Belgian Château: The Spirit and Culture of European Society in an Age of Change, 1994, French lang. edit., 1997, Organ Transplantation: Meanings and Realities (edited with Stuart Youngner and Laurence O'Connell), 1996; author: (in Japanese) Looking Intimately at Bioethics: Fifty Years as a Medical Sociologist, 2003; editor (with Victor N. Lidz and Harold J. Bershady): After Parsons: A Theory of Social Action for the Twenty-First Century, 2005; editor: (With Judith P. Swazey) Observing Bioethics, 2008; assoc. editor Am. Sociol. Rev., 1963—1196, Social Sci. and Medicine, Jour. Health and Social Behavior, 1985—87, Perspectives in Biology and Medicine, 1996—, mem. editl. com. Ann. Rev. Sociology, 1975—79, mem. editl. adv. bd. Tech. in Soc., Sci., 1982—83, mem. editl. bd. Bibliography of Bioethics, 1979—, Culture, Medicine and Psychiatry, 1980—86, Jour. of AMA, 1981—94, Am. Scholar, 1994—99, Current Revs. in Publs., 1994—, Am. Jour. Bioethics, 1999—, vice chair adv. bd. Am. Jour. Ethics and Medicine, A Festschrift published in her honor Society and Medicine: Essays in Honor of Renée Fox, 2003; contbr. articles to profl. jours.; editor: In the Field: A Sociological Journey, 2010; author: In The Field: A Sociologist's Journey, 2010. Bd. dir. Medicine in Pub. Interest, 1979-94; mem. tech. bd. Milbank Meml. Fund, 1979-85; mem. overseers com. to visit univ. health svcs. Harvard Coll., 1979-86; trustee Russell Sage Found., 1981-87; vice chmn. bd. dir. Acadia Inst., 1990-97; mem. adv. com. Sch. Nursing LaSalle U., 1998—; mem. advancement com. King Baudouin Found. US Inc., 1998—, mem., sec. bd. dir. Acadia Inst., 2002—; mem. info. sci. adv. coun. Innovia Found., Netherlands, 2002—; mem. external bd. Ctr. Bioethics, Columbia U., 2002—; mem. Internat. and Sci. Adv. Coun., 2002—, adv. bd. MS in bioethics program, Columbia U., 2009-. Recipient E. Harris Harbison Gifted Tchg. award Danforth Found., 1970, Radcliffe Grad. Soc. medal, 1977, Lindback Found. award for tchg. U. Pa., 1989, Centennial medal Grad. Sch. Arts and Scis. Harvard U., 1993, Chevalier de l'Ordre de Leopold II (Belgium), 1995, M. Powell Lawton Quality of Life award Phila. Corp. Aging, 2006, Lifetime Achievement award Am. Soc. for Bioethics and Humanities, 2007; Wilson Ctr., Smithsonian Instn. fellow, 1987-88, Guggenheim fellow, 1962, Andrew W. Mellon Emeritus fellowship, 2004-05; Fulbright Short-Term Sr. scholar to Australia, 1994; 1st W.H.R. Rivers Disting. lectr. Harvard Med. Sch., 1998. Fellow African Studies Assn., AAAS (dir. 1977-80, chmn. sect. K 1986-87), Am. Sociol. Assn. (coun. 1970-73, 79-81, v.p. 1980-81), Am. Acad. Arts and Scis. (co-chair Class III section I membership com., 1994-96), Inst. Medicine of NAS (coun. 1979-82), Inst. Soc., Ethics and Life Scis. (founder, gov.); mem. AAUP, AAUW, Assn. Am. Med. Colls., Social Sci. Rsch. Coun. (v.p., dir.), Ea. Sociol. Soc. (pres. 1976-77, Merit award 1993), NY Acad. Scis., Soc. Sci. Study Religion, Inst. Intercultural Studies, 1969-93, (asst. sec. 1969-78, sec. 1978-81, 89-92, v.p. 1987-89), Am. Bd. Med. Specialists, Coll. of Physicians of Phila. (coun. 1993-98), Phi Beta Kappa (senate 1982-87, Ralph Waldo Emerson book award com. 1998-2001), Alpha Omega Alpha (hon.). Home and Office: The Wellington 135 S 19th St 1104 Philadelphia PA 19103-4912 Business E-Mail: rcfox@ssc.upenn.edu.

FOX, SHELDON, retired radiologist, medical educator; b. NYC, May 11, 1919; s. Max and Sara (Lefcowitz) Fuchs; m. Anitta Ruth Boyko, 1948; children: Serena, Daniel, Judith. BA, Johns Hopkins U., 1938, MD, 1942. Diplomate Am. Bd. Radiology, Am. Bd. Nuclear Medicine. Intern in Pediatrics Yale U., 1942; pediatric fellow Vanderbilt U., 1945-46; fellow med. mycology Duke U.; resident in diagnostic radiology N.Y.U.- Bellevue Med. Ctr., 1947; radiology postgrad. fellow Columbia Presbyn. Hosp.; NCI fellow in radiation Therapy Bellevue; attending radiologist Meml. Hosp.-Sloan Kettering Inst., 1951-54; radiologist Elizabeth (N.J.) Gen. Hosp. and Wuester Cancer Clinic; pvt. practice Elizabeth, N.J., 1956-70; dir. radiology dept. Alexian Brothers Hosp., 1960-83, attending radiologist, 1983-90, ret., 1990. Asst. clin. vis. prof. radiology N.Y.U.-Bellevue. Avocations: tennis, music, reading, swimming, skiing. Home: 936 Westminster Ave Hillside NJ 07205-2923 *

FOX, STUART IRA, physiologist; b. Bklyn., June 21, 1945; s. Sam and Bess Fox; m. Ellen Diane Berley; 1 child, Laura Elizabeth. BA, UCLA, 1967; MA, Calif. State U., LA, 1967; postgrad., U. Calif., Santa Barbara, 1969; PhD, U. So. Calif., 1978. Rsch. assoc. Children's Hosp., LA, 1972; prof. physiology LA City Coll., 1972-85, Calif. State U., Northridge, 1979-84, Pierce Coll., 1986—. Cons. McGraw-Hill, 1976—. Author: Computer-Assisted Instruction in Human Physiology, 1979, Laboratory Guide to Human Physiology, 10th edit., 2003, 14th edit., 2011, Textbook of Human Physiology, 1986, 12th edit., 2011, Human Anatomy and Physiology, 1986, Perspectives on Human Biology, 1991, Laboratory Manual for Anatomy and Physiology, 1986;: 5th edit., 1999, Fundamentals of Human Physiology, 2008; co-author: Biology, 5th edit., 1999, Synopsis of Anatomy and Physiology, 1997. Mem.: AAAS, Am. Anatomy and Physiology Soc., Am. Physiol. Soc., Sigma Xi. Home: 5556 Forest Cove Ln Agoura Hills CA 91301-4047 Office Phone: 818-710-2832. Business E-Mail: Foxsi@piercecollege.edu.

FOY, HUGH M., critical care surgeon, educator; MD, U. Nebr., 1978. Diplomate Am. Bd. of Surgery, 1985, Am. Bd. of Surgery-surg. critical care, 1993. Intern internal medicine divsn. Univ. Wash. Med. Ctr., 1979, resident internal medicine divsn., 1979—83, fellow Burn, 1983—84, hosp. affiliations include, Va. Puget Sound health care System, Seattle, Swedish Med. Ctr., Harborview Med. Ctr.; prof. suregery dept. Univ. Wash. Co-author: Patterns Of Errors Contributing To Trauma Mortality: Lessons Learned From 2,594 Deaths, 2006, Bilateral Anterior Abdominal Bipedicle Flap With Permanent Prosthesis For The Massive Abdominal Skin-grafted Hernia, 2007, A Salvage Procedure With A steep Learning Curve, 2008, Laboratory-Based Instruction For Skin Closure And Bowel Anastomosis For Surgical Residents, 2008, Acquiring Basic Surgical Skills: Is A Faculty Mentor Really Needed?, 2009, various pubs. Office: Harborview Medical Center 7th Fl Maleng Bldg PO Box 359866 325 9th Ave Seattle WA 98104 Office Phone: 206-744-3241, 877-744-9700.

FOYOUZI-YOUSSEFI, REYHANEH, pharmacologist; b. Tehran, Iran, Dec. 6, 1964; arrived in Switzerland, 1983. d. Amin and Seyedeh (Salimi-Eshkevari); m. Hamid R. Mostafavi, 2001; 1 child, Mahan Ali. Diploma of Asst. Pharmacist, Sch. Pharmacy, Geneva, Switzerland, 1988, Diploma of Pharmacy, 1991; PhD in Pharmacy, U. Geneva, Geneva, Switzerland, 1999. Pharmacist, Geneva, 1991—; sr. scientist Estee Lauder Cos., Inc., 2000—04. Contbr. articles to profl. jours.

FRAENKEL, EMIL, physician, consultant; b. Kosice, Slovak Republic, June 23, 1976; s. Emil Fraenkel and Valeria Fekete Fraenkelova. Degree, Safarik U., Kosice, 2001; PhD, 2008. Cert. in internal medicine Semmelweis U. Budapest, Hungary, 2007. Secondary physician, resident Ter. Hosp., Sahy, Slovakia, 2002—04; secondary physician Balcsy-Zsilinszky Hosp., Budapest, 2005—07; cons. L. Pasteur U. Hosp., Kosice, 2008—, Internat. Contact Club MedPrev.s.r.o., 2008—. Contbr. articles to profl. jours. Mem. New Jerusalem Cmty., 2007—, Sanct Egidio Cmty., Budapest, 2007—; adv. bd. mem. Providentia Found., Kosice, 2000—03. Recipient award, Kosice Med. Assn., 2000, Selye Javos Coll. Komarno, 1998—, Young Specialist award, Internal Medicine, Czech Republic & Slovakia, 2007, award, Dean Med. Faculty, 2008. Mem.: Hungarian Assoc. Internal Medicine, Hungarian Assoc. Liver Diseases. Avocations: travel, swimming, skiing. Office: Safarik Univ Hosp I-stDepIntMed TrSNP 1 Kosice Slovakia Home: Maria utca 56 VII/4 Budapest 1085 Hungary Home Phone: 00421 0904 320 536; Office Phone: 00-421-556403100. Personal E-mail: emil.fraenkel@hotmail.com.

FRAGA, JOSE CARLOS, pediatrician, educator; b. Porto Alegre, Rio Grande do Sul, Brazil, Apr. 4, 1959; MD in Medicine, Fed. U. Rio Grande do Sul, 1983, PhD in Medicine, 1996. Assoc. prof. Sch. Medicine, Fed. U. Rio Grande do Sul, 1998—. Cons. in pediat. surgery Hosp. Moinhos Vento, Brazil, 1988, Hosp. Mãe de Deus, Brazil, 1990; cons., chief pediat. surgery svc. Hosp. Clínicas Porto Alegre, Brazil, 1994; assoc. prof. postgrad. course in surgery Sch. Medicine, Fed. U. Rio Grande do Sul, 1998; hon. prof. in pediat. Hosp. Clinicas Porto Alegre, 2000, hon. prof. in gen. surgery, Brazil, 11. Fellow: Sect. Surgery, Am. Assn. Pediat.; mem.: Brazilian Soc. Pediat., Brazilian Pediat. Surgery Assn. Avocations: running, reading, travel. Office: Rua Ramiro Barcelo 2350 Sala 600 Porto Alegre Rio Grande do Sul 90035-903 Brazil Office Fax: 55 51 3334 0146. Business E-Mail: jc.fraga@terra.com.br.

FRAGULIDIS, GEORGIOS PANAGIOTIS, surgeon, educator; b. Russia, Mar. 12, 1959; MD, U. Athens, 1985. Rsch. fellow dept. surgery, U. Miami Med. Sch., Jackson Meml. Hosp., Divsn. Liver-GI Transplantation, 1994—98; clin. transplant fellow dept. surgery Carolina's Med. Ctr., Divsn. Transplantation, 2000—02; asst. prof. surgery dept. surgery U. Athens Med. Sch., 2003—. Home: 23 ElVenizelos Str Glyfada Attica 16675 Greece Home Fax: 30 210 9690184. Personal E-mail: gfragulidis@aretaieio.uoa.gr.

FRAIMOW, HENRY S., infectious disease physician, educator; MD, U. PA. Diplomate Am. Bd. Internal Medicine, Am. Bd. Internal Medicine-infectious disease. Intern Mt. Sinai Med. Ctr., NY, resident; fellow Montefiore Med. Ctr.; assoc. prof. medicine UMDNJ-Robert Wood Johnson Med. Sch., Camden, NJ; sr. med. cons. Southern NJ Regional Splty. Chest Clinic. Office: Cooper University Hospital Three Cooper Plaza Ste 513 Camden NJ 08103 Office Phone: 856-963-3715. Office Fax: 856-635-1052.

FRAIZER, A. LINDSAY, medical educator, researcher; MD, Dartmouth Med. Sch., 1984; ScM, Harvard Sch. Pub. Health, 1993. Resident pediat. Boston Children's Hosp.; fellow, pediat.-hematology-oncology Dana-Farber Cancer Inst., Mass.; asst. prof. pediat. Harvard Med. Sch., 1990—. Contbr. articles to jours. Office: Dana-Farber Cancer Inst Shields-Warren G350 44 Binney St Boston MA 02115 Office Phone: 617-632-2273. Office Fax: 617-525-2008. Business E-Mail: lindsay_fraizer@dfci.harvard.edu.

FRAKER, THEODORE D'ESTON, JR., cardiologist, educator; b. Delaware, Ohio, Jan. 16, 1947; MD, Ohio State U. Coll. Medicine and Pub. Health, 1973. Cert. Internal Medicine, Cardiovascular Disease. Intern, cardiovascular disease Ohio State U. Med. Ctr., Columbus, 1973—74, resident, 1974—76; fellow Duke U. Med. Ctr., Durham, NC, 1976—79; dir., fellowship tng. program Med. Coll. Ohio, Toledo, assoc. dean, clin. affairs, dir., echocardiography lab., dir., cardiac catheterization lab., dir., managed care coll.; prof., internal medicine Ohio State U. Med. Ctr., assoc. divsn. dir., clin. affairs & ops., divsn. cardiovascular medicine; med. dir. Ohio State U. Heart Ctr. at Gahanna; practicing medicine, 1976—; tchg., 1979—. Spkr. in field. Contbr. several articles to peer-reviewed jours. Named to Best Doctors Listings. Mem.: Am. Heart Assn. (past pres., Ohio chpt.), Am. Coll. Cardiology, Alpha Omega Alphs, Phi Eta Sigma. Office: Ohio State U Med Ctr 248 Davis Heart and Lung Inst 473 W 12th Ave Columbus OH 43210 Business E-Mail: ted.fraker@osumc.edu.

FRALEY, ROBERT T., biotechnologist; b. Danville, Ill. m. Laura Fraley; children: Steven, Devin, Katherine. BS in Biology, U. Ill., 1974, PhD in Microbiology/Biochemistry, 1978; postgrad., Northwestern U., 1991. Postdoctoral fellow U. Calif., San Francisco, 1979—80; co-pres. agrl. sector Monsanto Co., St. Louis, 1980—2000, exec. v.p., chief tech. officer, 2000—. Past mem. adv. com. Agriculture Biotechnology Rsch.; past mem. health molecular cytology study sect. NIH; tech. advisor to US Dept. Agriculture, NSF, Office of Technology Assessment, CAST, Agency for Internat. Develop., NAS and Internat. Svc. for the Acquisition of Agri-Biotech Applications. Contbr. articles to profl. jours.; mem. editl. bds. of several scientific jours. Recipient Nat. Award for Agrl. Excellence in Sci., Nat. Agri-Mktg. Assn., 1995, Kenneth A. Spencer award for Outstanding Achievement in Agrl. and Food Chemistry, 1995, Nat. Medal Tech., 1998, award for indsl. application of sci., NAS, 2008; named Man of the Year, Progressive Farming mag., 1995. Fellow: AAAS. Achievements include development of part of the team that developed the world's first practical system to introduce foreign genes into crop plants and development of insect-and-herbicide-resistant plants. Avocations: skiing, gardening, tennis. Office: Monsanto Co 800 N Lindbergh Blvd Saint Louis MO 63167-0001

FRALIX GOLD, CAROLYN M., medical/surgical nurse, educator, consultant; b. Pulaski, Tenn., Oct. 12, 1951; d. Gardner and Louetta (Miller) Fralix; children: Sean Adams, Amber Holcomb-Keene; m. Ronald David Gold, Jan. 1, 2000. ADN, San Antonio Coll., 1982; BSN, U. Tex. Health Sci. Ctr., San Antonio, 1988; MSN, U. Tex., San Antonio, 1995. RN; cert. EMT, BLS, CPR instr. Tchr., rsch. assoc. U. Tex. Health Sci. Ctr., San Antonio; staff devel. coord. St. Rose and Villa Rosa Hosp., San Antonio; neonatal ICU Santa Rosa Hosp., San Antonio, 1982; cons. for ednl. resources, med. surg. staff nurse Santa Rosa Health Care Corp., San Antonio, 1984-88; med.-surg. pool nurse Meth. Hosp., San Antonio, 1994-95; vocat. nursing instr. St. Philip's Coll., San Antonio, 1991-95; nursing instr. U. Tex. Health Sci. Ctr., San Antonio, 1995-98, rsch. nurse coord., 1999, asst. prof., 2006—; assoc. prof. Dept. Nursing San Antonio Coll., 1998-99; intake coord. SNU Methodist Hosp., 1999—2001. Adj. faculty dept. nursing U. Tex. Health Sci. Ctr., San Antonio, 2002, S.W. Tex. Meth. Women's Ctr., 2002-05; founder, owner Hearts Alive Inc., 2003—; cons. in field. Asst. clinical prof. UTHSCSA Sch. Nursing, 2006—07; asst. prof. course coord. BSN nursing program Wayland Baptist U., 2007—; founder, first aid ministry Oak Hills Ch., San Antonio, 2004—, dir., first aid ministry, 2004—. Recipient various scholarships. Mem. ANA, Holistic Nurses Assn., Am. Urol. Assn. Allied, Tex. Nurses Assn., U. Tex. Nursing Alumni Assn. (past treas.), Tex. Jr. Coll. Tchrs. Assn., Rotary, Sigma Theta Tau.

FRAMPTON, MARK W., medical educator, director; b. Omaha, Feb. 6, 1947; Degree, Calif. State U., Long Beach, 1969; MD, NYU, 1973. Prof. medicine & environ. medicine Sch. Medicine U. Rochester, 1988—, assoc. dir., clin. rsch. ctr., 2010—. Assoc. editor Inhalation Toxicology, 2008—; bd. dirs. Am. Lung Assn. NY State, 1998—2001. Grantee Multidisciplinary Tng. Pulmonary Rsch. grant, NIH; Pulmonary Rsch. Tng. fellowship, grant, Health Effects Inst. Fellow: ACP; mem.: NY State Thoracic Soc., Am. Thoracic Soc. (chair environ. and occupl. health assembly 2001—03, chair sect. terrorism and inhalation disasters 2003—05). Avocations: tennis, golf. Office: 601 Elmwood Ave PO Box 692 Rochester NY 14642-8692 Office Fax: 585-273-1114. Business E-Mail: mark_frampton@urmc.rochester.edu.

FRANASZCZUK, PIOTR JULIAN, medical educator; b. Warsaw, Aug. 26, 1954; MSc, U. Warsaw, 1978, PhD, 1988. Rsch. assoc. U. Warsaw, 1978—88, asst. prof., 1988—96, U. Md. Sch. Medicine, 1993—99; assoc. prof. Johns Hopkins U. Sch. Medicine, 1999—. Grant proposals reviewer NIH, 2005, Med. Rsch. Coun., England, 2010; cons. Merck Inc, 2007; cons., grant proposals reviewer Ministry of Sci. & Higher Edn., Poland, 2009; editl. bd. mem. Computational Intelligence & Neurosci., 2011. Recipient Jr. Investigator award, Am. Epilepsy Soc., 1st prize Nat. Competition, Polish Soc. Nuc. Medicine; Bennet fellowship, U. Md., Rsch. grant, NIH. Mem.: IEEE Engring. Medicine & Biology Soc., IEEE Computer Soc., IEEE Signal Processing Soc., Am. Epilepsy Soc. Office: 600 N Wolfe St Meyer 2-147 Baltimore MD 21287 Business E-Mail: pfranasz@jhmi.edu.

FRANÇA, SUZELEI CASTRO, research scientist; b. Araçatuba, Apr. 9, 1948; PhD, U. London, 1998. Rsch. scientist U. Ribeirão Preto, 1981—, bd. dirs., 1985—, coord., post-graduation program, 2001—. Recipient Sci. Merit medal, Governo Estado São Paulo, Arvore Da Vida award, Fundação Amparo A Pesquisa, Sci. Merit award, Fundação Jose Pedro Araujo, 2004; Produtividade fellowship, Conselho Nat. Pesquisa, grant, Ministerio Saude Do Brasil. Mem.: Soc. Brasileira Bioquímica, Soc. Brasileira Para Progresso Sci. Avocations: tennis, running, travel. Office: Av Costabile Romano 2201 Ribeirão Preto São Paulo 14096-900 Brazil Office Fax: 55 16 36037030. Business E-Mail: sfranca@unaerp.br.

FRANCE, NEWELL EDWIN, retired health facility administrator; b. Massillon, Ohio, Sept. 30, 1927; s. Lawrence Joel and Marcella Ruth (Nelson) F.; m. Eve Elisabeth Voluter, 1953; children: Philip J., Corinne E., Anne-Claire I., Stephen C., Louise A. BS, Northwestern

U., 1953, MS in Hosp. Adminstrn, 1955. Adminstrv. resident Herrick Meml. Hosp., Berkeley, Calif., 1954-55; evening supt. Chgo. Wesley Meml. Hosp., 1955-56; asst. adminstr. St. Lukes Episcopal and Tex. Children's hosps., Houston, 1956-58, assoc. adminstr., 1958-64, adminstr., 1964-73, exec. dir., 1973-83; pres. emeritus Tampa Gen. Hosp., Fla., 1983-91, 91—; pres. Patrick Philbin & Assocs., Austin, 1993—; cons. Hok Architecture, 1995—. Assoc. adminstr. Tex. Heart Inst., Houston, 1958-64, adminstr., 1964-73, exec. dir., 1973-83; cons. adv. council HEW and NIH; staff cons. AID, 1969—; cons. program projects rev. com. Nat. Inst. Neurol. and Communicative Disorders and Stroke; mem. com. pediatrics NRC-Nat. Acad. Scis., 1975—; chmn. Greater Houston Hosp. Coun., Children's Hosps. Execs. Council, 1972-73; dir. Child Care Center, Tex. Med. Ctr., 1967—; adj. assoc. prof. Sch. Architecture, Rice U.; prof. health scis. Tex. Women's U. Bd. dirs. Met. Houston chpt. Nat. Found. March of Dimes, First City Bank Med. Center; trustee Pin Oaks Charity Horse Show Assn., Houston Bot. Soc.; mem. exec. bd. South Main Center Assn., Inc.; active Houston/Baku Sister City Assn. Served with USNR, 1946-48, 51-52. Fellow Am. Coll. Hosp. Adminstrs.; mem. Am. Hosp. Assn., Tex. Hosp. Assn. (chmn. coun. hosp. auxs. 1969-73, trustee 1972—, adviser, chmn. coun. on profl. svc. 1976—), Houston Area Hosp. Assn. (pres. 1968-69), Nat. Assn. Childrens Hosps. and Related Instns. (pres. 1969-70, conf. chmn. 1969, trustee 1971—, chmn. coun. past pres.'s 1973-74), Am. Assn. Hosp. Planning, Statutory Teaching Hosps. Coun. (Fla.) (chmn. 1988-91). Clubs: Rotary Internat; Doctors (Houston). Methodist. Home: 6609 Coolglen Dr Dallas TX 75248-2902

FRANCESCHI, DINKO, radiologist, educator; b. Split, Croatia, Oct. 10, 1953; MD, Med. Sch., U. Zagreb, 1977. Assoc. scientist Brookhaven Nat. Lab., 1997—2000; assoc. clin. prof., dept. radiology SUNY, Stony Brook, 2000—. Mem.: EANM, SNM. Avocations: gardening, soccer, tennis. Office: Nicolls Rd Stony Brook NY 11794 Business E-Mail: dfranceschi@notes.cc.sunysb.edu.

FRANCESCHINI, NORA, medical researcher; MD, Fed. Univ. Rio Grande do Sul (UFRGS), Brazil, 1986; MPH, U. NC, Chapel Hill, 2004. Diplomate Am. Bd. Internal Medicine, cert. in nephrology. Internal medicine/nephrology residency HCPA (Hospital das Clinicas de Porto Alegre), Brazil, 1987—90; nephrology rsch. fellowship Oreg. Health Sci. U., Portland, 1993—95; internal medicine residency U. Utah Med. Ctr., Salt Lake City, 1995—98; nephrology fellowship Duke U. Med. Ctr., Durham, NC, 1998—2000; instr. medicine, divsn. nephrology & hypertension, Sch. Medicine U. NC, Chapel Hill, 2001—05, posdoc. fellow epidemiology, Sch. Pub. Health, 2005—07, rsch. asst. prof., dept. epidemiology, 2007—. Mem. editl. bd. Clin. Nephrology, 2003—; contbr. articles to profl. jours. Recipient Young Investigator award, Nat. Kidney Found., 2002—03; fellow, Internat. Soc. Nephrology, 1993—95. Mem.: Internat. Genetic Epidemiology Soc., Soc. Epidemiology Rsch., Am. Soc. Nephrology, Internat. Soc. Nephrology. Achievements include research in cardiovascular disease, nephrology and hypertension & genetic epidemiology. Office: Univ NC Dept Epidemiology 137 E Franklin Ste 306 CB #8050 Chapel Hill NC 27514 Office Phone: 919 966-1305. Office Fax: 919-966-9800. E-mail: noraf@unc.edu. *

FRANCETIC, OLIVERA, research scientist; b. Belgrade, Serbia, Oct. 1, 1959; PhD, U. Belgrade, Yugoslavia, 1990. Rsch. scientist Inst. Molecular Genetics and Genetic Engrng., Belgrade, 1987—90; postdoc. scientist Tufts U., 1990—94, Inst. Pasteur, 1995—2000, rsch. assoc., 2001—. Office: 25 rue du Dr Roux Paris 75724 France Business E-Mail: ofrancet@pasteur.fr.

FRANCIA, ADA, medical association administrator; b. Terni, Italy, May 7, 1951; Degree in medicine, La Sapienza U. Rome, 1976, specialization in Neurology, 1980. 3rd chair neurol. clinic U. Rome, La Sapienza, 1994—; head ctr. reference clin. neuroimmunology Policlinico Umberto I, Rome, 2006—. Pres. SCAN onlus, 1999—. Office: Viale dell Università 30 Rome 00185 Italy E-mail: ada.francia@uniroma1.it.

FRANCIOSA, JOSEPH ANTHONY, pharmaceutical consultant; b. Easton, Pa., Apr. 24, 1936; s. Joseph and Letitia Beatrice (Cascioli) F.; m. Antonietta Battistoni, Feb. 8, 1964 (div. 1972); m. Barbara Ann Neilan, Aug. 3, 1973 (div. 1989); 1 child, Christopher David; m. Robin J. McGarry, Oct. 4, 1998. BA, U. Pa., 1958; MD, U. Rome, 1963. Diplomate Am. Bd. Internal Medicine; lic. in Pa., Md., Ark. Intern USPHS Hosp., SI, N.Y., 1964-65; resident Washington Hosp. Ctr., 1967-69; cardiology fellow VA Hosp.-Georgetown U., Washington, 1969-71; chief ICU Va. Hosp., Washington, 1971-73; asst. prof. medicine Georgetown U. Med. Sch., 1971-73, assoc. dir. cardiovascular tng. program, 1974-75; dir. CCU Va. Hosp., Mpls., 1974-76; asst. prof. medicine U. Minn., Mpls., 1977-79; chief cardiology VA Hosp., Phila., 1979-82; assoc. prof. U. Pa., Phila., 1979-82. Adj. prof. 1987-98; adj. prof. medicine Mt. Sinai Med. Sch., N.Y.C., 1989—, Cornell U. Weill Coll. Med., N.Y.C., 1999-, SUNY Downstate Med. Sch., 2008-; dir. cardiology div. U. Ark., Little Rock, 1982-86; prof., 1982-86; dir. cardio-renal drugs ICI Americas Inc., Wilmington, Del., 1986-88; v.p. R&D Zambon Corp., East Rutherford, N.J., 1988-90; exec. dir. med. affairs Ciba-Geigy Pharm., Summit, N.J., 1990-91; exec. dir. med. svcs. Ciba-Geigy, 1992-95; health care/pharm. cons., N.Y.C., 1995—. Contbr. numerous articles to med. jours. Mem. med. rsch. com. Am. Heart Assn., Mpls., 1976-79, Phila., 1981-82. Lt. comdr. US Pub. Health Svc., 1965—67. VA grantee, 1974-84, U. Ark. grantee, 1982-83, NIH grantee 1985-86. Fellow ACP, Am. Coll. Cardiology, Am. Coll. Chest Physicians (chmn. hypertension com. 1981-83, gov. Ark. 1984-86), Am. Heart Assn. (circulation coun. 1978—, coun. high blood pressure rsch. 1982—, clin. cardiology coun. 1984, bd. dirs. N.J. affiliate 1994-98); mem. Am. Soc. Clin. Pharmacology and Therapeutics (vice chmn. cardiopulmonary com. 1981-89), Assn. Univ. Cardiologists, Am. Acad. of Pharm. Physicians (charter mem. v.p. publs. com. 2002-2004), Heart Failure Soc. Am. Avocations: computers, physical fitness. Office: 300 East 77th St Apt 28C New York NY 10075 Office Phone: 212-879-2366. Personal E-mail: josephafranciosa@gmail.com.

FRANCIS, DAVID HULET, medical educator; b. Murray, Utah, June 18, 1947; BS, Brigham Young U., 1971; PhD, U. Mo., 1978. Prof. SD State U., 1978—. Indsl. cons. numerous orgn. Office: Dept Veterinary & Biomedical Sci Brookings SD 57007 Office Fax: 605-688-6003. Business E-Mail: david.francis@sdstate.edu.

FRANCIS, LESLIE JOHN, theology educator, psychology researcher; b. Colchester, Eng., Sept. 10, 1947; s. Ronald Arthur and Joan Irene (Swann) F. BA in Theology, U. Oxford, Eng., 1970; BD in Theology, U. Oxford, 1990, DD in Theology, 2001; PhD in Edn., U. Cambridge, Eng., 1976; ScD in Edn., U. Cambridge, 1997; MTh, U. Nottingham, Eng., 1976; MSc in Psychology, U. London, 1977; Dlitt in Religious Studies, U. Wales, 2007. Leverhulme rsch. fellow London Ctrl. YMCA, 1977-82; rsch. officer Culham Coll. Inst., Abingdon, Eng., 1982-88; Mansel Jones fellow Trinity Coll., Carmarthen, Wales, 1989-99; D.J. James prof. pastoral theology U. Wales, Lampeter, 1992-99; dir. Welsh Nat. Ctr. Religion Edn., prof. practical theology U Wales, Bangor, 1999—2007; prof. religions and edn. U. Warwick, 2007—, Canon Theological, Bangor, Cathedral, 2006—. Curate Haverhill, Suffolk, Eng., 1973-77; priest-in-charge Little Wratting and Great Bradley, Suffolk, Eng., 1977-82, North Cerney and Bagendon, Gloucestershire, Eng., 1982-85; dean of chapel Trinity Coll., Carmarthen, 1994-99. Author: Teenage Religion and Values, 1995, Drift from the Churches: Attitudes toward Christianity during Childhood and Adolescence, 1996, Church Watch: Christianity in the Countryside, 1996, Personality Type and Scripture: Exploring Mark's Gospel, 1997, Gone But Not Forgotten: Church Leaving and Retaining, 1998, The Long Diaconate, 1999, Rural Ministry, Rural Visitors, Rural Youth and other numerous books. Fellow Brit. Psychol. Soc., Coll. Preceptors. Anglican. Avocations: music, walking, countryside, architecture, public service vehicles. Office: Univ Warwick Coventry CV4 7AL England E-mail: leslie.francis@warwick.ac.uk.

FRANCIS, WARREN WILLIAM, retired surgeon, educator; b. NYC, Sept. 10, 1924; Grad., Princeton U., 1944; MD, Columbia U., 1948. Diplomate Am. Bd. Surgery. Intern Lenox Hill Hosp., NYC, 1948-50; resident surgery R.I. Hosp., Providence, 1952-56, surgeon, 1956-97; surg. cons. Women & Infants Hosp., 1986-97; clin. assoc. prof. surgery Brown U., 1983-97, ret., 1997. Med. officer USNR, 1950-52. Fellow ACS; mem. EVS, New Eng. Surg. Soc., NESVS.

FRANCISCO, EDITH GABA, medical/surgical nurse; b. Gattaran, Cagayan, The Philippines, Sept. 16, 1939; came to U.S., 1963; d. Leon and Maria (Manuel) Gaba; m. Pedro R. Francisco, June 27, 1965; children: Perry, Pierre, Eugene. BSN, Philippine Union Coll., 1961. RN, Calif., Ill., Pa. Staff nurse Children's Hosp. Phila., Michael Reese Hosp. & Med. Ctr., Chgo., U. Hosp., San Diego, Community Hosp. Chula Vista (Calif.), Paradise Valley Hosp., National City, Calif. Home: 1036 Dearborn Dr San Diego CA 92154-2156 Home Phone: 619-429-7289.

FRANCISCO, PRISCILA M. S. BERGAMO, medical researcher, educator; b. Piraju, São Paulo, Brazil, Jan. 1, 1973; B in Stats., UNICAMP, 1997, PhD, 2006. Epidemiology rschr. U. Estadual de Campinas - UNICAMP, 2000—06, 2008—, tchr., rsch. collaborator, 2009—. Fellow: Fundação de Amparo à Pesquisa do Estado de São Paulo. Avocations: reading, running. Office: DMPS/FCM/UNICAMP Caixa Postal 6111 Campinas São Paulo 13.083-970 Brazil Office Fax: 55 19 3521 8035. Business E-Mail: primaria@fcm.unicamp.br.

FRANCK, ARDATH AMOND, psychologist, educator; d. Arthur and Helen Lucille (Sharp) Amond; m. Frederick M. Franck, Mar. 18, 1945; children: Sheldon, Candace. BS in Edn., Kent State U., 1946, MA, 1947; PhD, Western Res. U., 1956. Cert. high sch. tchr., elem. supr., sch. psychologist, speech and hearing therapist. Instr. Western Res. U., Cleve., 1953, U. Akron, 1947—50; sch. psychologist Summit County Schs., Ohio, 1950—60; cons. psychologist Wadsworth Pub. Schs., Ohio, 1946—86, dir. Akron Edn. Campus, Ohio, 1950—, Pres. Twirling Unlimited, 1982—; cons., dir. Hobbitts Pre-Sch., 1973—88. Author: Your Child Learns, 1976. Mem.: Ohio Psychol. Assn., Internat. Reading Assn., Mensa. Home: 631 Ghent Rd Akron OH 44333 2629 Office: Akron Edn Ctr 700 Ghent Rd Akron OH 44333-2698 Office Phone: 330-666-1161.

FRANCK-LARSSON, KARIN, physician, director; m. Kent Larsson, Oct. 18, 1986; children: Hanna, Simon Larsson, Lukas Larsson. BA, Gymnastik-och Idrottshögskolan, Stockholm, 1980; MD, U. Uppsala, Sweden, 1991; PhD, U. Uppsala, 2010. Internship Jämtlands Läns Landsting, Östersund, 1991—95, physician, 1995—98; cons. Uppsala U. Hosp., 1998—2007; med. advisor, mgr. Wyeth AB, Stockholm, 2007—09; European therapeutic area dir. Wyeth, Maidenhead, England, 2009—10; dir. med. affairs Pfizer, Stockholm, 2010—.

FRANCO, DOMINIQUE JEAN, surgeon, educator; b. Vannes, Jan. 20, 1944; s. Léonce Marie and Jeanne Franco; m. Anna Mikke, Jan. 27, 1979; 1 child, Timothée Jérémie. Baccalauréat, Coll. St.-François Xavier, Vannes, 1959. Cert. Surgeon France, 1974. Asst. prof. Hôpital Paul Brousse, Villejuif, France, 1973—; surgeon Hôpital Louis-Michel, Evry, France, 1983—90; chief surg. dept. Hôpital Antoine-Béclère, Clamart, France, 1990—. Recipient prize, Acad. Médecine, 1970. Achievements include research in laparoscopic liver surgery; transplantation of hepatocytes. Avocations: sailing, travel. Home: 33 allée de la Pitancerie Hôpital Cachan 94230 France Office: Hôpital Antoine-Béclère 157 Rue de la Porte-de-Trivaux Clamart 92141 France Office Fax: 33 1 45 37 49 78. Business E-Mail: dominique.franco@abc.aphp.fr.

FRANCO, MANUEL ANTONIO, research scientist; b. Bogotá, Colombia, Apr. 2, 1962; MD, Colegio Mayor de Nuestra Señora del Rosario, 1986; PhD, U. Paris, 1990. Prof. Pontificia U. Javeriana, 1998—2009, dir. postgraduate programs sch. of sci., 2009—. Recipient Poste vert, INSERM, Fellowship, Walter and Idun Berry Found.; ECLAIR Fellowship, EEC. Mem.: AAAS, Colombian Soc. Allergy, Asthma, Immunology, Editl. comittee of the Jour. of Virology. Office: Carrera 7 43-82 Edificio 50 3er piso Bogotá Colombia Office Phone: 57-1-3208320 ext. 4077.

FRANCO, SHARONE ELIZABETH, psychiatrist; b. Cambridge, Eng., Sept. 11, 1959; arrived in South Africa, 1978; came to US, 1994; d. Nissim Haim and Betty Irene (Martin) Franco; m. John Allan Barwise, Feb. 24, 1990; children: Oliver Allan Barwise, Alexander Abraham Barwise. MD, U. Cape Town, 1983, M in Chem. Pathology, 1992. Cons. chem. pathology U. Cape Town, South Africa, 1992-94; resident psychiatry Vanderbilt U., Nashville, 1994-98; staff psychiatrist Western Mental Health Inst., Bolivar, Tenn., 1999—2002; pvt. practice Psychiatry and Outpatient Mental Health Clinic, 2002—05; attending psychiatrist outpatient mental health clinic VA Med. Ctr., Nashville. Contbr. articles to profl. jours. Mem. AMA, Am. Psychiat. Assn., Tenn. Psychiat. Assn.

FRANCOIS, M. RONY, public health service officer; b. Port-au-Prince, Haiti; arrived in US, 1979; m. Joelle Francois; children: Rony Andre, Patrick George, Joelle Anne. MD, Univ. So. Fla., 1979; MA, Univ. Ctrl. Fla.; MSPH, Univ. So. Fla., PhD in toxicology. Asst. prof., dir. public health practice program Coll. Public Health, Univ. So. Fla.; sec. Fla. Dept. Health, Tallahassee, 2005—07; asst. sec., Office Pub. Health Louisiana Dept. Health and Hospitals, 2008—. Office: La Dept Health & Hospitals 628 N 4th St PO Box 629 Baton Rouge LA 70821-0629 Office Phone: 225-342-9500. Office Fax: 225-342-5568.

FRANK, ANDREW OLIVER, consultant rheumatologist and rehabilitation medicine physician, educator; b. Cuckfield, Eng., Sept. 4, 1944; s. Ernest Oliver and Doris Helen (McBean) Frank; m. Cynthia Mary Siviter, June 30, 1974; children: Anthony David, Christina Ann, Julia Linda. MBBS, Middlesex Hosp., London, 1968; DSc (hon.), Brunel U., Uxbridge, Eng., 2003. Cons. in rehab. medicine and rheumatology Northwick Pk. Hosp., Harrow, England, 1980—, clin. dir., 1990—95; cons. in rehab. medicine, stanmore specialist Wheelchair Svc., Harrow, 1997—; prof. assoc. Brunel U., Sch. Health Studies and Social Care, 1997—. Clin. chair NHS Modernisation Agy. Wheelchair Collaborative, London, 2002—04; chair profl. adv. bd. Kynixa Ltd. Editor: Disabling Diseases, 1989, Low Back Pain, 2002, Vocational Rehabilitation, 2003; author: Improving Services for Wheelchair Users and Caregivers: Good Practice Guide. Pres. Middlesex br. Nat. Osteoporosis Soc., Harrow, 1998—2005. Fellow: Royal Coll. Physicians (London) (regional splty. advisor 1997—2005); mem.: Vocat. Rehab. Assn. (trustee), Brit. Soc. Rehab. Medicine (pres. 2000—02). Home Phone: +44 1923 285362; Office Phone: +44 208 869 2102. Office Fax: +44 208 4264358. Personal E-mail: andrew.frank1@btinternet.com.

FRANK, BARBARA BALIS, gastroenterologist, educator; b. Reading, Pa., Jan. 11, 1937; d. Irvin and Ruth Helen (Knoblauch) B.; m. Leonard Arnold Frank, Aug. 17, 1958; children: Michael Scott, Bradford Allan. BA magna cum laude, Smith Coll., 1958; MD, U. Pa., 1962. Diplomate Am. Bd. Internal Medicine and Gastroenterology. Intern and fellow in gastroenterology Hosp. U. Pa., Phila., 1962—64, instr. internal medicine, 1966—69; resident internal medicine Bryn Mawr (Pa.) Hosp., 1964-66; dir. divsn. gastroenterology Crozer-Chester Med. Ctr., Chester, 1968—89, attending gastroenterologist, 1968—94; clin. asst. prof. medicine Hahnemann U., Phila., 1973-75, clin. assoc. prof., 1975—85; clin. prof. Drexel U. Coll. Medicine, Phila., 1985—. Cons. Sacred Heart Hosp., Chester, Pa., 1974-94; mem. sci. adv. com. Nat. Found. Ileitis and Colitis, Phila., 1980-85; mem. gastroenterology-urology devices panel, FDA, 1988-90, chmn., 1990-92, cons. 1993-94; mem. gastrointestinal drugs adv. com. FDA, 1995-99, cons., 2000—; mem. Physician Payment Rev. Commn., Consensus Panel for Evaluation and Mgmt. Svcs., 1990; rep. for gastroenterology carrier adv. com. Pa. Medicare, 1993-2005; v.p. N Am. Congresso Panamericano de Endoscopia, 1993-95, 99-2001. Assoc. editor MKSAP in gastroenterology and hepatology 2; contbr. articles to profl. jours. Honoree Barbara D. Frank Endoscopic Learning Ctr. Drexel U. Coll. Medicine, Phila., 2007. Named Outstanding AGA Women Sci., 2008, Outstanding Women Sci., Am. Gastroenterological Assn., 2008; recipient History of Medicine prize U. Pa. Sch. Medicine, 1962, Legion of Honor award Chapel of Four Chaplains, Phila., 1978, Achievement award, Pa. Soc. Gastroenterology, rsch. grantee U. Pa., 1961-62. Fellow ACP, Coll. Physicians Phila., Am. Coll. Gastroenterology (ad hoc com. on women in gastroenterology 1989—, gov. ea. Pa. 1992-96, 2003—, regional councillor, bd. govs. 1994-96, chmn. com. for ICD-9-CM revision 1986-89, mem. govt. rels. com. 1987-88, sci. exhibits com. 1985-86, ann. sci. selection com. 1984-85, 90-91, nominating com. 1988-89, ednl. affairs com. 1992-2001, Sr. Govs. award 2006), Am. Soc. Gastrointestinal Endoscopy (councillor, governing bd. dirs. 1986-90, 92-94, pres. 1991-92, Disting. Educator award 2005); mem. AMA, Am. Gastroenterol. Assn. (patient care com. 1986-88, tng. adn edn. com. 1989-90, abstract selection com. 199, nominating com. 1986-87, program evaluation com. 1981-85, mem. pub. policy com. 1992-93, mem. clin. svcs. task force 1994-95, chmn. nominating com. 1995-96, others, Disting. Educator award 2005) Am. Assn. Study Liver Disease, Am. Liver Found., Internat. Assn. for Study of the Liver, Pa. Med. Soc., Phila. GI Tng. Group (pres. 1987-93), Phila. Gastrointestinal Rsch. Forum, Delaware County Med. Soc., Delaware Valley Soc. Gastrointestinal Endoscopy (pres. 1984-86, councillor, governing bd. dirs. 1986-88), Pa. Soc. Gastroenterology councillor for Phila. 1982-84, 87-91, 2001—, governing bd. dirs.), Israel Med. Assn., Bockus Internat. Soc. of Gastroenterology (pres. 2009-11), Alpha Omega Alpha, Sigma Xi, Alpha Phi, Kappa Psi, Phi Beta Kappa Del. Valley (gov. coun. 1991-93, 98— v.p. 1993-95, pres. 1995-97, 98—, gov. coun. 2000—; Recognition award 2006). Democrat. Jewish. Avocations: sketching, dance. Office: Fl 5 MS 913 219 N Broad St Philadelphia PA 19107

FRANK, EMILY, anthropologist; b. Glen Ellyn, Ill., May 8, 1967; PhD, Ind. U., 2006. Sr. strategist, humanistics team In-sync Consumer Strategy, 2008—. Rsch. assoc. Ind. U., 2006; bd. mem. AIDS and Anthropology Rsch. Group, 2009. Mem.: Soc. Africanist Anthropology, Soc. Med. Anthropology. Home: 375 Windermere Beaconsfield QC H9W1W8 Canada Business E-Mail: efrank@indiana.edu.

FRANK, LILLIAN GORMAN, human resources executive, management consultant; b. NYC, July 4, 1953; d. Helmuth H. and Ida (Malitsch) Degen; m. Stephen E. Frank, Feb. 10, 2001. BA in Psychology, Lehman Coll., CUNY, 1975; MA in Indsl. Psychology, Case Western Res. U., 1978, PhD in indsl. Psychology, 1979; MBA in Corp. Fin., U. So. Calif., 1986. Econ. benefits asst. Girl Scouts U.S.A., NYC, 1971—75; psychologist Pers. Rsch. Svcs., Cleve., 1975—79; cons. psychologist Pers. Rsch. & Devel. Corp., Cleve., 1977—78; mgr. pers. rsch. 1st Interstate Bank, LA, 1979—82, v.p., mgr. human resource planning and devel., 1982—85; v.p., mgr. human resource planning and exec. devel. 1st Interstate Bancorp, LA, 1985—86; exec. v.p., human resources dir. First Interstate Bank of Calif., 1986—90; exec. v.p. human resources First Interstate Bancorp, 1990—96; sr. v.p. human resources Edison Internat., Rosemead, Calif., 1996—2000; prin. Frank Insights, LA, 2000—. Trustee Autry Mus. Western Heritage, 2001—05; bd. dirs. INROADS/So. Calif., 1986—2005, YMCA of Met. L.A., 2002—05, Nev. Women's Fund, 2005—, Reno Chamber Orchestra, 2007—, Renown Health Found., 2007—. Mem. APA, Soc. for Psychologists in Mgmt. (bd. dirs. 1993-97), Soc. for Human Resources Mgmt. Home and Office: 5865 Strasbourg Ct Reno NV 89511 Business E-Mail: lillian@avantwireless.com.

FRANK, MARTIN, physiologist, educator, medical association administrator; b. Chgo., Oct. 22, 1947; s. Edward D. and Ann (Horwitz) F.; m. Cheryl Lynn Motel, Aug. 19, 1970; children: Beth Susan, Eric Lawrence. AB (Evans scholar), U. Ill., 1969, MS, 1971, PhD, 1973. USPHS predoctoral research trainee U. Ill., 1971-73; research assoc. Mich. Cancer Found., Detroit, 1973-74; dept. pharmacology Mich. State U., 1974-75; assoc. prof. physiology George Washington U., 1980—. Exec. sec. physiology study sect. divsn. rsch. grants NIH, Bethesda, Md., 1978—85; exec. dir. Am. Physiol. Soc., Bethesda, 1985—; pres., treas., bd. dirs. Commn. on Profls. in Sci. and Tech., 1986—2000; mem. internat. adv. panel Galileo Found., 1990—93; mem. life scis. subcom. NASA Space Sci. and Applications Adv. Com., 1991—94; coord. Washington Prins. Coalition for Free Access to Sci., 2004—. Editor Physiologist, 1985—; contbr. articles to profl. jours. Vice pres., bd. dirs. Bennington Community Assn., Gaithersburg, Md., 1976-78, 80-81, mem. Gaithersburg City Planning Commn., 1982-85. Recipient Disting. Alumni award dept. molecular and integrative physiology U. Ill., Urbana, 2001, Presdl. award 2003; grantee Nations' Capitol Affiliate Am. Heart Assn.,1975-78, NIH, NSF. Mem. AAAS, Am. Physiol. Soc., Am. Soc. Assn. Execs., Coalition Engring Scientific Soc. Execs. Office: Am Physiol Soc 9650 Rockville Pike Bethesda MD 20814-3998 Office Phone: 301-634-7118. E-mail: mfrank@the-aps.org. *

FRANK, MARY LOU BRYANT, psychologist, educator; b. Denver, Nov. 27, 1952; d. W. D. and Blanche (Dean) Bryant; m. Kenneth Kerry Frank, Sept. 9, 1973; children: Kari Lou, Kendra Leah. BA, Colo. State U., 1974, MEd, 1983, MS, 1986, PhD, 1989. Tchr. Cherry Creek Schs., Littleton, Colo., 1974—80; grad. dir. career devel. Colo. State U., Ft. Collins, 1980—86; intern U. Del., Newark, 1987—88; psychologist Ariz. State U., Tempe, 1988—93; assoc., lead prof. psychology Clinch Valley Coll. U. Va., Wise, 1992—96, asst. acad. dean, 1993—95; head psychology dept., prof. North Ga. Coll. and State U., Dahlonega, 1996—2001; dean undergrad. and univ. studies, dean univ. coll., prof. psychology Kennesaw (Ga.) State U., 2001—06; assoc. v.p. for acad. affairs, prof. psychology Gainesville State Coll., Ga., 2006—10; fel. Inst. Higher Educ., U. Ga., 2010—; chief exec. officer Athens Community Career Acad., 2010—11; v.p. academic affairs prof. psychology Middle Ga. Coll., Cochran, Ga., 2011—. Chmn. bd. regents adv. com. Psychology, 2000—01; instr. Colo. State U., Ft. Collins, 1981—82, counselor, 1984—85, Ft. Collins, 1986—87; spkr. in field; cons. Nat. Resource Ctr. for 1st Coll. Yr. Author: (program manual) Career Development, 1986; contbr. chapters to books; reviewer: Buros Mental Measurements Yearbook. Founding bd. mem. Wind Found Women; pres. elect South Hall Kiwanis, 2010; bd. dirs. Ct. Apptd. Spl. Advocates, 2000—08, Enotah Legis. Dist., Helping Teens Succeed, 2004—07; mem. Youth Adv. Coun. Lumpkin County, 2000—02; adv. bd. mem. Chatahoochee Tech. Coll., 2004—07; v.p., founding bd. Ga. Women's Inst., 2006—; v.p. Turknett Leadership Character Edn.; bd. dirs. Possible Woman Found., 2006—, co-chair, 2008—10, adv. bd., 2010—; founding bd. Wind Found. Woman, 2010—. Recipient Commendation award; named annual award in honor of Mary Lou Frank, Ga. Women's Inst., 2007—. Mem.: ACA, AAUP, APA, Internat. Acad. Dispute Resolution (bd. mem. 2010—), Ga. Osteoporosis Initiative (bd. dirs. 2009—, bd. mem.), Atlanta Women's Network (adv. bd. 2004—06), Atlanta Women's Alliance (mem. exec. com. 2004—06), Ga. ACE Network (mem. exec. com. 2001—06), Ga. Assn. Women Higher Edn. (pres. 2001—04), Am. Assn. State Colls. and Univs., Southeastern Psychol. Assn. (chair undergrad. rsch. 1996—2000), Am. Assn. Higher Edn., Am. Counselor Edn. and Supv., Am. Assn. Counseling and Devel., Odeka, Phi Beta Kappa, Psi Chi (Ga. Woman of Yr. com. 1999—, vice chair 2003—, v.p. Woman of Yr. com. 2004—, documentary project), Pi Kappa Delta, Phi Kappa Phi (Internat. Woman's Day program com. 2003, planning com. so. women in pub. svc. conf. 2003—04, Promotion of Excellence grantee 2002—03). Avocations: music, hiking, reading. Office: Gainesville State Coll Office Academic Affairs PO Box 1358 Gainesville GA 30503 also: Athens Community Career Academy 490 Dearing Extension Athens GA 30606 Office Phone: 478-934-3019. Personal E-mail: maryloufrank@gmail.com. Business E-Mail: mlfrank@gsc.edu, mlfrank@mgc.edu.

FRANK, MICHAEL M., physician; b. Bklyn., Feb. 28, 1937; s. Robert and Helen (Prakin) F.; m. Ruth Sybil Pudolsky, Nov. 5, 1961; children: Robert E., Abigail B., Brice S.H. AB, U. Wis., 1956; MD, Harvard U., 1960. Intern Boston City Hosp., 1960-61; resident in pediatrics Johns Hopkins Hosp., 1961-62, 64-65; vis. scientist Nat. Inst. Med. Research, London, 1965-66; with NIH, 1967-90; chief lab. of clin. investigation, clin. dir. Nat. Inst. Allergy and Infectious Diseases, Bethesda, Md., 1977-90; prof. Duke U. Med. Ctr., Durham, NC, 1990—, chmn.Ddept. Pediatrics, 1990—2004. Mem. ACP, Assn. Am. Physicians, Am. Soc. Clin. Investigation, Soc. Pediatric Rsch., Am. Pediatric Soc., Infectious Diseases Soc., Am. Acad. Allergy, Am. Acad. Pediatrics. Office: Duke U Med Ctr PO Box 3556 Durham NC 27710 Home Phone: 919-489-1964. Business E-Mail: frank007@mc.duke.edu.

FRANK, RICHARD G., healthcare educator; b. Boston, Apr. 27, 1952; BA in Econs., Bard Coll., 1974; PhD in Econs., Boston U., 1982. Prof. dept. health econs. Harvard Med. Sch., Boston, 1994-99, Margaret T. Morris prof. health econs., 1999—. Rsch. assoc. Nat. Bur. Econ. Rsch., Cambridge, Mass. and N.Y.C., 1987—. Office: Harvard Med Sch Dept Health Care Policy 180 Longwood Ave Boston MA 02115-5821 Office Phone: 617-432-0178. Business E-Mail: frank@hcp.med.harvard.edu.

FRANKEL, ARTHUR E., oncologist, educator; AB, Harvard Coll., 1969; MD, Harvard Med. Sch., 1973. Cert. oncology & hematology Am. Bd. Internal Medicine. Intern Yale U., 1974; rsch. scientist Nat. Inst. Health, 1978; resident Stanford U., 1980, fellow, 1982; dir. Cancer Ctr. Scott & White Hosp., dir. Divsn. Hematology & Oncology, dir. Cancer Rsch. Inst.; prof. medicine Texas A&M Health Sci. Ctr. Coll. Medicine. Editor-in-chief Dovepress Clinical Pharmacology Jour. Mem.: Am. Soc. Clinical Oncology, Am. Soc. Hematology, Am. Assn. Cancer Rsch. Office: 2401 S 31st St Temple TX 76508 Office Phone: 254-724-2111.

FRANKEL, LORRY ROBERT, pediatrician; b. LA, Jan. 5, 1950; BA, UCLA, 1972; MD, U. Antwerp, 1978. Prof. pediat. critical care Stanford U., 1983—2010; chair pediat. Sutter Physician Med. Found., CPMC, 2010—. Co-dir. PICU Stanford U. Hosp., 1983—91; dir. pediat. critical care svcs. Lucile Packard Children's Hosp., Stanford, 1991—2010. Recipient Humanitarian award, Am. Coll. Chest Physicians, Rambar-Mark award, Stanford U. Med. Ctr. Fellow: Am. Acad. Pediat., Am. Coll. Critical Care Medicine. Avocations: reading, golf, hiking. Office: 3700 California St San Francisco CA 94118 Office Fax: 415-600-0741. Business E-Mail: frankel@sutterhealth.org.

FRANK-KAMENETSKII, MAXIM D., biomedical engineer; b. Nizhniy Novgorod, Russia, Aug. 7, 1941; arrived in US, 1993; s. David A. and Elena E. (Fridman) F.; m. Alla D. Voskoboinik, Jan. 7, 1961 (dec. 1985); 1 child, Michael. MS, Moscow Phys. & Tech. Inst., 1964, PhD, 1967; DSc, Inst. Chem. Physics Moscow, 1972. Jr. scientist Kurchatov Inst. Atomic Engery, Moscow, 1967-72, sr. scientist, 1972-78; head lab. Inst. Molecular Genetics, Moscow, 1979-89, head. dept., 1989-93; prof. Boston U., 1993—. Disting. vis. prof. U. Ala., Birmingham, 1989, Ohio State U., Columbus, 1991-92. Author: Unraveling DNA, 1993, 97. Fellow: Am. Inst. Med. & Biol. Engr. Avocation: tennis. Office: Boston U Dept Advanced Biotechnology 36 Cummington St Boston MA 02215-2427 Office Phone: 617-353-8498. Business E-Mail: mfk@bu.edu.

FRANKL, WILLIAM STEWART, cardiologist, educator; b. Phila., July 15, 1928; s. Louis and Vera (Simkin) Frankl; m. Razelle Sherr, June 17, 1951; children: Victor S.(dec.), Brian A. BA in Biology, Temple U., 1951, MD, 1955, MS in Medicine, 1961. Diplomate Am. Bd. Internal Medicine, Am. Bd. Cardiovasc. Disease. Intern Buffalo Gen. Hosp., 1955—56; resident in medicine Temple U., Phila., 1956—57, 1959—61; faculty Temple U. Sch. Medicine, 1962—68, dir. EKG sect. dept. cardiology, 1966—68, dir. cardiac care unit, 1967—68; prof. medicine, dir. divsn. cardiology Med. Coll. Pa., Phila., 1970—79; prof. medicine, assoc. dir. cardiology divsn. Thomas Jefferson U., Phila., 1979—84; physician-in-chief Springfield Hosp., Mass., 1968—70; prof. medicine, co-dir. William Likoff Cardiovasc. Inst. Hahnemann U., Phila., 1984—86, dir. William Likoff Cardiovasc. Inst., dir. divsn. cardiology, 1986—92, Thomas J. Vischer Prof. medicine, chmn. dept. medicine, 1987—92; prof. medicine, dir. cardiovasc. regional programs Allegheny U. of Health Scis., 1992—98; dir. cardiovasc. regional programs Allegheny U. Hosps., 1992—98; v.p. cardiovasc. program devel. Allegheny U. Hosps. Sys., 1995—98; prof. medicine cardiology divsn. dept. medicine Temple U. Sch. Medicine, 1998—2000. Cons. cardiology Phila. VA Hosp., 1970—79; Fogarty Sr. Internat. fellow Cardiothoracic Inst., U. London, 1978—79; clin. prof. medicine Temple U. Sch. Medicine, 2000—. Contbr. articles to profl. jours. Capt. M.C. US Army, 1957—59. Recipient Golden Apple award, Temple U. Sch. Medicine, 1967, award, Med. Coll. Pa., 1972, Lindback award for Disting. Tchg., 1975; Cardiovasc. Rsch. fellow, U. Pa., 1961—62. Fellow: ACP, Coun. Clin. Cardiology of Am. Heart Assn. (coun. arteriosclerosis), Am. Coll. Clin. Pharmacology (regent 1980—85, 1993—98), Phila. Coll. Physicians, Am. Coll. Cardiology (gov. eastern Pa. 1986—89); mem.: AAAS, AAUP, Philadelphia County Med. Soc. (pres. 1993—94, 1st dist. trustee to Pa. Med. Soc. bd. trustees 1998—2001), Am. Soc. Clin. Pharmacology and Exptl. Therapeutics, Am. Heart Assn. (bd. govs. S.E. Pa. chpt. 1972—84, pres. 1976, Pa. affiliate pres. 1984—85), Assn. Am. Med. Colls., Am. Fedn. Clin. Rsch., N.Y. Acad. Scis. Home and Office: 536 Moreno Rd Wynnewood PA 19096-1121 Office Phone: 610-649-5947. Business E-Mail: bfrankl@comcast.net.

FRANKLIN, CRAIG L., laboratory animal pathologist, educator; b. Danville, Pa., Feb. 5, 1962; DVM, U. Mo., 1987, PhD, 1992. Prof. U. Mo., 1992—. Office: N128 RADIL 4011 Discovery Dr Columbia MO 65201 Office Phone: 573-882-6623. Office Fax: 573-884-7521. Business E-Mail: franklinc@missouri.edu.

FRANKLIN, PAULA ANNE, artist, writer, psychologist; b. Wheaton, Ill., Feb. 2, 1928; d. Paul Spangler and Ella Creighton (Daniels) Fowler; m. Richard Clarence Franklin, Aug. 13, 1950; children: Jan Franklin BenDor, Timothy Vickery, Edward Lee. Student, Manchester U., Eng., 1946-47; BSc in History, Northwestern U., 1949, postgrad., 1975, So. Ill. U., 1959-61; MA, W.Va. U., 1970; PhD, Union Inst., 1980; BA with honors in Art, Towson U., Md., 2003. Lic. psychologist, Md. Pres., dir. Franklinc Behavioral Sci. Cons., Balt., 1969—; human resource and orgnl. devel. faculty Johns Hopkins U., Balt., 1972—92; rsch. project dir. Social Security Adminstrn., Balt., 1973—99. Adj. faculty dept. psychology U. Balt., 1989-91. Author: (with R. Franklin) Tomorrow's Track, 1976, (with others) Disability in the U.S., 1990; editor: The Maryland Psychologist, 1994-98; contbr. articles to profl. jours. Com. mem. LWV, 1950-75; active Girl Scouts U.S., Boy Scouts Am., 1950-70. Mem. Am. Psychol. Assn., Md. Psychol. Assn. (Cert. of Recognition 1981), Internat. Assn. for Study Dreams. Unitarian Universalist. Avocations: music, theater, gardening, photography, travel. Home and Office: Unit B 23 500 E Marylyn Ave State College PA 16801 Office Phone: 814-237-0028. Personal E-mail: franklin@charm.net.

FRANKLIN, REY, emergency physician; b. Aug. 8, 1953; s. Susan and George Franklin; m. Samantha Franklin; 1 adopted child, Alison children: Paul, Kim. AB, Colgate Univ., 1975; MS, Georgetown Univ., 1976, MD, 1980. Intern Emory Univ., 1983—86, resident, 1986—90; physician Meriks Clinic, Sandy Springs, Ga., 1991—99, ER dept. chief, 2000—05, pres., physician, 2006—. Football team physician Sandy Springs Sch. Dist., 2003—, bd. dir., 2007—. Liberal. Avocations: Aikido, racquetball. Office: Meriks Clinic 6065 Roswell Rd NE #2227 Sandy Springs GA 30328-4044

FRANKLIN, ROOSEVELT, minister; b. Chattanooga, Aug. 30, 1933; s. James R. and Cora Ann (Ponds) F.; m. Darnell Pinkston, Sept. 30, 1972; children: Sophia, Siemoran Dellazar. BS, Northeastern U., 1958; MA (hon.), Savannah State Coll., 1962; M. of Cybernetics, Grad. Sch. Wicca, St. Charles, Mo. Lic. metaphysician. Pastor Free For All Bapt. Ch., Greenwood, SC, 1959-61; radio min. Spiritual Ch., Aiken, SC, 1961-63; nat. lectr. United Coun. Spiritual Ch., Raleigh, NC, 1963-66; min. Holy Trinity House of God, Macon, Ga., 1966—. Youth dir. Holy Trinity Ch., Macon, 1966-72, talent coord., 1966-73; dir. Spiritual Singers, 1966—; lectr. in field; world renown authority on witchcraft and transcendental meditation; expert in clairvoyance, spiritual meditation; supporter Macon County Little League Baseball; internat. tour Prosperity Way of Living Teachings. Editor: Prosperity Way of Living. Organizer voters registration, Macon, 1977; pub. relations vol. Nat. Dem. Party, Atlanta, 1984; bd. dirs. Retired Persons Assn., 1980—. Capt. U.S. Army, 1951-54, Korea. Named extrovert promoter Music Workshop, 1979; recipient Proclamation and Key to City, Roanoke, Va., 1977, Afro Am. Heritage award Afro Am. Heritage Mus., 1987, Golden Eagle award Macon Courier, 1988, Nat. Achievers award Nat. Black Secs. Assn., 1990, Ednl. award Ptnrs. Youth Club, 1991, Golden Eagle award 500 Black Men of Am. Club, 1992, Black Achievement award Nat. Negro Achievers Assn., 1993, Humanitarian award. Gov. of Ga., 1993, Nat. Rschrs. Occult award United Spiritual Coun. Chs., 1994, Hon. Citizens award, Tuskegee, Ala., 1994, Mahogany Triumph award Am. Black Affluent Assn. Am., 1995, Cert. Recognition City of Memphis, 1995, Concerned Citizens award People in Action Club, 1996, Good Samaritan award United Youth Fellowship Club, 1997, Model Citizen's award Office of the Gov. Ga., 1997, Registered Spiritual award, Registered Psychic award and Mystic award United Spiritual Coun. Assn., 1998, Self Awareness Lecture award, Howard U., 1998, Appreciation award for continuous contbns. UNCF, 1998, Commemorative award Ga. Farmer's Assn., 1998, Activist award Boys Clubs Am., 1998, Outstanding Activities award United Fraternities Am., 1998, Presdl. Acknowledgement, Nat. Assn. Disabled Persons, 1999, Dr. of Metaphysics award, Dr. of Biblical Counseling award and Dr. of Religion award, 1999, Outstanding Citizenship award, Pilot Club, 1999, Contemporary Spkr. award, Chgo., 2000, Lectr. of Yr. award Nat. Bible Soc., Silver Raven award, 2002, Ea. Mysteries award for excellence, 2002, Order of Nostradamus, Cert. Seminar of Appreciation, 2002, Spkr. of Yr. award Spiritism, 2002, others. Mem. NAACP (life), SCLC (life), Nat. Assn. Pastoral Counselors (career specialist advisor 2000, dir. conf. on prosperity), Ednl. Media Assn. (founder 2002, counseling tax force 2001, Pursuit of Excellence award 2002), Inner Circle Congl. Aides, C. of C., Ministers Alliance (v.p. 1966—, Citizens award 1979), Ga. Black Am. Pageant (coord. 1980—, Leadership award 1982), Direct Sellers League, Smooth Ashlar (dist. dep. 1970—), Rolls-Royce Club, Woodsmen of Am., Pioneer Club, Shriners (nat. amb.), Masons (33 deg., sovereign grand gen. inspector, Grand Orator 33 deg. Scottish Rite 2002), Optimists, Kiwanis, Civitan, Elks, Nat. Lodge (treas. 1987—), Potentate of the Rosicruscians, Sertoma, Lions, VFW (life), DAV (life), Am. Legion (life). Democrat. Avocations: martial arts, billiards. Office: Holy Trinity House of God 280 Straight St Macon GA 31204-6100

FRANKLIN-GRIFFIN, CATHY LOU HINSON, nursing educator; b. Newton, NC, Nov. 8, 1950; d. Willie A. and Evelyn Irene (Thornton) Hinson; 1 child, John Eric; m. Harry Griffin. ADN, Western Piedmont Comm. Coll., 1971; BSN, East Carolina U.; postgrad., Med. U. SC; MA, Appalachian State U., 1990; PhD, U. NC, Greensboro, 2004. RN, N.C., S.C., Ga., Ala., N.D., Calif., Va. Patient educator Wayne County Meml. Hosp., Goldsboro, N.C., developer cardiac rehab. & permanent pacemaker implantation programs, 1980-81; infection control nurse Charleston (S.C.) Meml. Hosp., 1981-83; instr. nursing United Health Careers, Inc., San Bernardino, Calif., 1986-88, Caldwell C.C., CCC & TI, Hudson, NC, 1988—91; rsch. coord. weekend/evening nursing program CCC and TI, Boone, N.C., 1991-93; dean nursing & allied health Rockingham C.C., Wentworth, N.C., 1993-2000; freelance contract nurse edn. Rowan-Cabarrus C.C., 2000—04; dir. program svcs. NC C.C. Sys., 2004—05. Cons., contract grant writer, 2000—; spkrs. bur. Rockingham C.C.; bd. dirs. Rockingham Mental Health Ctr., Free Clinic Reidsville; legis. chair NC ADN Coun., 1997-99, pres. NC Conf. Dirs. ADN Programs, 1999-2000; nurse educator NC Bd. Nursing, 2000-02, bd. dirs.; spkr. in field. Author (with others): Fundamentals of Nursing, Nursing the Whole Person; author: Survival Guide for Directors of Nursing Programs in Community Colleges in North Carolina, 2002; pub.: CCC & TI Skillbook, editorial cons. and contbr.: Mosby Nursing Texts, ind. contractor: NCCCS manual. Capt. fundraising for Civic Ctr.; mem. faculty dept. Chairs Inst. Named one of Outstanding Young Women of Am., 1987. Mem. ADN (pres., bd. dirs., chmn. legis. adv. coun., liaison NC. PN educators), Phi Theta Kappa, Phi Kappa Phi, Sigma Theta Tau.

FRANKS, JEFRI ANN, public health service officer, consultant; b. Salina, Kans., Feb. 2, 1957; BGS, U. Kans., 1979, MS, 1985. Spkr., cons., life coach, author jeftifranks.com, 2008—. Past pres., Cancer Ctr. Bd. Children's Mercy Hosp., 2004—05, parent cons, Pediat. Advanced Comfort Team, 2005—, parent to parent end life vol., 2005—; parent cons. Initiative Pediat. Palliative Care, 2005—. Author: (book) Heather's Journey: A Mother's Accidental Guide Through Loss to Hope. Vol. Hope Faith Ministries. Mem.: Nat. Spkrs. Assn. (Kans. City chpt.), Heartland Coaches Assn. Home: 11115 NW 55th St Kansas City MO 64152 Personal E-mail: jefri@kcnet.com.

FRANKS, RONALD DWYER, dean, psychiatrist, educator; b. Balt., Jan. 15, 1946; s. Wylie and H. Jeanette (Dwyer) F.; m. Vicky Ruth Vicklund; children: Aaron Matthew, Alexis Linda. Student, Albion Coll., 1964-67; MD with distinction, U. Mich., 1971. Intern Virginia Mason Hosp., Seattle, 1971-72; resident in psychiatry U. Colo. Med. Ctr., Denver, 1972-76; instr. psychiatry U. Colo. Sch. Medicine, Denver, 1976-77, asst. prof. psychiatry, 1977-83, assoc. prof., 1983-88, asst. dean student affairs, 1982-84, asst. dean student and curricular affairs, dir. inpatient svcs. dept. psychiatry, 1986-88; dean, prof. psychiatry U. Minn. Sch. Medicine, Duluth, 1988-97; v.p. health affairs East Tenn. State U., Johnson City, 1997—2007, dean James H. Quillen Coll. Medicine, 1997—2006, prof. psychiatry and behavioral scis., 1997—2007; v.p. health scis. U. South Ala., 2007—. Bd. dirs. Bank of Tenn., 2004—07; chmn. State Health Planning and Adv. Bd., Tenn. Contbr. numerous articles to profl. jours. Mem. Med. Assn. State Ala., Am. Psychiat. Assn., Alpha Omega Alpha. Office: VP for Health Sciences Univ of S Alabama 307 N University Blvd CSAB 170 Mobile AL 36688-0002 Office Phone: 251-460-7189. Office Fax: 251-460-6073. Business E-Mail: rfranks@usouthal.edu. *

FRANOLIC, MARIO DRAGUTIN, emergency medicine physician; b. Sarajevo, Bosnia-Herzegowina, Jan. 30, 1960; arrived in Croatia, 1991; s. Dragutin Petar and Zora Miloš (Kontić) von F. MD, U. Belgrade, 1986; Acupuncture Dr., Acad. Trad. Chinese Medicine, Beijing, 1991. Mil. rescue team med. physician former Yugoslav Peoples Army, Divulye, Croatia, 1986-87; physician Med. Ctr., Hvar, 1988-91; exper sec./asst. prof./physician Internat. Inst. Traditional Chinese Medicine of European Ctr, Belgrade, 1991; pvt. practice Belgrade and Wien, Austria, 1992-97; chief of emergency svc. Med. Ctr. Rab, Croatia, 1997; physician emergency svc. Med. Ctr., Rovinj, Croatia, 1997; physician, dir. Polyclinic for Baromedicine "Oxy", Pula, Croatia, 1997—. Expert sec. Internat. Inst. for Traditional Chinese Medicine of European Ctr. for Peace and Devel., Belgrade, 1991; cons. physician Labor Dostal, Vienna, 1992—96, Weisser Hoff, Klosterneuberg, 1994—95, Hera Sanatorium, Vienna, 1996; physician Croatian Mountain Rescue Soc., 2001—. Mem. Croatian Med. Assn., Croatian Soc. Emergency Medicine, Croatian Soc. Acupuncture, Croatian Soc. for Nautical, Underwater and Hyperbaric Medicine.

Avocations: nature and science photography, nature conservation, diving, mountain climbing, speleology. Office: Poliklinika Baromedicine Oxy Kochova Bb Po Box 47 52-100 Pula Croatia E-mail: oxy@gradpula.com.

FRANTZ, DEAN LESLIE, psychotherapist; b. Beatrice, Nebr., Mar. 27, 1919; s. Oscar C. and Flora Mae (Gish) F.; m. Marie Flory, Aug. 31, 1940; children: Marilyn, Shirley, Paul. BA, Manchester Coll., Ind., 1942; MDiv, Bethany Theol. Sem., Oak Brook, Ill., 1945; diploma, C.G. Jung Inst. Zurich, 1977. Assoc. prof. Bethany Theol. Sem., 1957-64; dir. ch. rels. Manchester Coll., North Manchester, Ind., 1964-72; pvt. practice Ft. Wayne, Ind., 1977—. Author: Meaning for Modern Man in the Paintings of Peter Birkhauser, 1977; editor: Barbara Hannah: The Cat, Dog, and Horse Lectures, and the Beyond, 1992, Barbara Hannah: The Inner Journey, 1999, The Ten Oxherding Pictures, 2003. Mem. Internat. Assn. Analytical Psychology, Assn. Grad Analytical Psychologists. Home: 3320 E State Blvd Fort Wayne IN 46805

FRANTZ, ELMAN G., pediatric cardiologist, surgeon; b. Lebanon, Pa., Jan. 17, 1956; MD, Pa. State U., Hershey, 1981. Diplomate Am. Bd. Pediat., Am. Bd. Pediat. Cardiology, lic. NC. Intern pediat. U. NC Meml. Hosp., Chapel Hill, 1981—82, resident pediat., 1982—84, fellowship pediat. cardiology, 1984—85, staff divsn. cardiology; fellowship pediat. cardiology Cardiovasc. Rsch. Inst., San Francisco, 1985—87; assoc. prof. pediat. U. NC Sch. Medicine. Coord. pediat. cardiothoracic transplant team U. NC Meml. Hosp. Contbr. articles to profl. jours. Mem.: Am. Acad. Pediat. Office: U NC Sch Medicine CB 7220 Bldg 311 Burnett Womack Chapel Hill NC 27599 Office Phone: 919-966-4601. Office Fax: 919-966-6894.

FRANTZ, RITA, dean, nursing educator; BSN, Marycrest Coll.; MA in Med./Surg. Nursing, U. Iowa, Iowa City, PhD in Ednl. Psychology. Instr. U. Iowa Coll. Nursing, 1972—78, asst. prof., 1978—96, area chair, systems and practice, 1995—2007, prof., 1996—, Kelting dean and prof., 2007—. Clin. assoc. in nursing Iowa Veteran's Home, Marshalltown. Contbr. articles to profl. jours. Recipient Collegiate Tchg. award, U. Iowa, Sharon Baranoski Founder's award, Regent's award, Michael J. Brody award; grantee, Nat. Inst. Nursing Rsch., NIH. Fellow: Am. Acad. Nursing; mem.: Coun. for the Advancement Nursing Sci., Am. Geriatric Soc. Office: Univ Iowa Coll Nursing 101F Nursing Bldg 50 Newton Rd Iowa City IA 52242-1121 Office Phone: 319-335-7009. Business E-Mail: rita-frantz@uiowa.edu.

FRANTZVE, JERRI LYN, psychologist, educator, consultant; d. Rolland and Marjorie Weiland. Student, Purdue U.; BA in Psychology and History, Marian Coll.; MS in Organizational Psychology, George Williams Coll.; PhD in Indsl. and Organizational Psychology, U. Ga. Sr. mktg. rsch. analyst Quaker Oats Co., Barrington, Ill., 1971-75; asst. prof. sch. of mgmt. SUNY, Binghamton, 1979—83; dir. human resources Conoco/DuPont, Ponca City, Okla., 1983—88; cons. psychologist Mass., 1988-89; assoc. prof. psychology Radford U., Va., 1989—94; mgmt. cons. J.L. Frantzve & Assocs., Placitas, N.Mex., 1994—; divsn. head human svcs. Coll. New Rochelle, NY, 1994—99; affiliate prof. Milano Grad. Sch. of Mgmt. New Sch. U., NYC, 1999—2008; sr. cons. Lead Life Inst., New Hope, Pa., 2004—; cons. Gen Quest Inc., 2007—; adj. prof. Anderson Schs. Mgmt. U. N.Mex, Albuquerque, 2008—; adj. prof. exec. MBA program Helsinki Sch. Economics, 2009—; ptnr. The Luminarias Group, 2009—. Instrn. cons. USAF, Rome, N.Y., 1979-83; dir. Israel Overseas Rsch. Program, Ginozar, Israel, 1982, Japanese Overseas Rsch. Program, Tokyo, 1983; dir. rsch. Ctr. Gender Studies, Radford U., 1989-94, adj. prof. dept. psychology Bklyn. Coll., 2000-05. Author: Behaving in Organizations: Tales from the Trenches, 1983, Guide to Behavior in Organizations, 1983; contbr. articles to profl. jours. Bd. dirs. Broome County Alcoholism Clinic, Binghamton, N.Y., 1980-83, bd. dirs. Broome County Mental Health Clinic, Binghamton, 1981-83; del. Dem. Caucus, Okla., 1985. Mem. APA (com. on women in psychology 1986-88), AAUW, Acad. Mgmt., Internat. Pers. Mgmt. Assn., Assn. for Women in Psychology. Avocations: ceramics, jazz, murder mysteries. Home and Office: 2 Windmill Ct Placitas NM 87043 Office Phone: 505-771-8862.

FRANZEN, THOMAS U. E., surgeon; b. Linköping, Sweden, Apr. 12, 1955; s. Inge Lennart and ulla Margaretha (Hjalmarsson) F.; m. Lena Marie Larsson, Apr. 30, 1983; children: Erika, Sofia, Johanna. Student, Karolinska Inst., Stockholm, 1975, U. Uppsala, Sweden, 1977-79; MD, U. Linköping, 1983, med. diploma, 1984, PhD, 2003. Resident in surgery Ctrl. Hosp., Norrköping, Sweden, 1983-89, fellow in surgery, 1989-92; cons. surgeon U. Hosp., Linköping, 1992—, head Esophageal Labs., 2000—, head, upper GI surgery, 2002—05. Formal lectr. med. students, tutor PBL Med. Sch, U. Health, Linköping, 1992-, instr, tchr. disaster medicine drs. nurses & students, 1994-; vis. prof. U. Pa. Med. Ctr., Phila., 1999. Mem. SSAT, Soc. Surgery Alimentary Tract, Rotary (clubmaster Linköping 1995-2008), Swedish Med. Soc., Swedish Surg. Soc., Swedish Soc. Upper GI Surgery, Swedish Trauma Assn., Scandinavian Assn. Gastrointestinal Motility, Swedish Soc. Gastroenlerology. Avocations: horseback riding, wine tasting, boule. Office: Univ Hosp Dept Surgery S-58185 Linköping Sweden Office Phone: 46 10 1030000. Fax: 46 13 22 3570. Personal E-mail: thomas.franzen@lio.se. E-mail: thomas.franzen@swipnet.se.

FRANZINI, LUISA, healthcare educator, director; b. Rome, Mar. 26, 1955; PhD, London Sch. Economics, 1983. Prof., divsn. dir. U. Tex. Sch. Pub. Health, 2000—. Office: 1200 Pressler Dr Houston TX 77030 Business E-Mail: luisa.franzini@uth.tmc.edu.

FRAS, CHRISTIAN IVAN, orthopedist; b. Binghamton, NY, Aug. 24, 1969; s. Ivan and Inge Fras; m. Khiet Quach, Apr. 27, 2002; children: Sebastian Ivan, Christian, Torsten Ivan. MD, Columbia U., NYC, 1994. Attending surgeon St. Luke's-Roosevelt Hosp., NYC, 2000—03, Lenox Hill Hosp., NYC, 2002—03, Meml. Hermann Hosp., Woodlands, Tex., 2003—04, Conroe Regional Med. Ctr., Tex., 2003—04, Lankenau Hosp., Wynnewood, Pa., 2007—; attending, asst. prof. U. Pa., Phila., 2004—07. Reviewer U. Pa. Orthop. Jour., 2004—07, Spine Jour., 2006—, adv. editl. bd., 2006—; abstract reviewer Am. Acad. Orthop. Surgeons Ann. Meeting, 2007—; editl. bd. & reviewer Jour. Orthop. History, 2008—. Recipient Louis Goldstein award, Scoliosis Rsch. Soc., 1999; named one of Best Doctors, Del. Valley Consumers' Checkbook, 2007, Top Surgeons — Orthop. Surgery, Main Line Today, 2008. Fellow: ACS, Royal Soc. Medicine, Am. Acad. Orthop. Surgeons; mem.: North Am. Spine Soc. Avocations: photography, history, travel, antiques. Office: 2000 Sproul Rd Ste 320A Broomall PA 19008 Office Fax: 484-427-8103.

FRASCINO, LUIZ FERNANDO, plastic surgeon; b. São Paulo, Brazil, Jan. 11, 1959; MD, U. São Paulo, Ribeirão Preto, 1983; PhD, Faculdade de Medicina de São José do Rio Preto, 2009. Dept. head Hosp. do Coração IMC São José do Rio Preto, 1997—. Recipient George Arie prize, Brazilian Soc. Plastic Surgery. Office: Rua Antonio de Godoy 3945 São José do Rio Preto São Paulo 15015-100 Brazil Business E-Mail: zeroplastia@terra.com.br.

FRASER, DAVID WILLIAM, epidemiologist; b. Abington, Pa., May 10, 1944; s. Grant Clippinger and Ella Finlaw (Ayars) F.; m. Barbara Josephine Gaines, June 25, 1966; children: Evan Grant, Leigh Robertson. BA, Haverford Coll., Pa., 1965, DSc (hon.), 1991; MD, Harvard U., 1969; ScD (hon.), Moravian Coll., 1987. Diplomate Am. Bd. Internal Medicine. Intern in internal medicine U. Pa. Hosp., Phila., 1969-70, resident, 1970-71, chief resident in internal medicine, 1973-74, fellow in infectious diseases, 1974-75; commd. officer USPHS, 1971-73, 75-82; chief spl. pathogens br., bacterial diseases divsn. Bur. Epidemiology, Ctr. Disease Control, USPHS, Atlanta, 1975-80, med. epidemiologist, asst. dir. bacterial diseases divsn., 1981-82; pres. Swarthmore (Pa.) Coll., 1982-91; head dept. social welfare Secretariat of His Highness Aga Khan, Gouvieux, France, 1991-95; cons. in internat. health and edn., 1996, 2000—; exec. dir. INCLEN, Inc., 1996-2000; rsch. assoc. Asian sect. U. Pa. Mus. Archaeology and Anthropology, 1999—2009; cons. scholar Asian Sect. U. Pa. Mus. Archaeology & Anthology, 2009—; rsch. assoc. The Textile Mus., Washington, 2004—. Adj. prof. medicine U. Pa. Sch. Medicine, 1983-91, adj. prof. epidemiology, 1997—. Author: A Guide to Weft Twining and Related Structures with Interacting Wefts, 1989, (with Barbara G. Fraser) Mantles of Merit: Chin Textiles from Myanmar, India and Bangladesh, 2005, editl. bd. Annals of Internal Medicine, 1991-94; contbr. articles to profl. med. and textile jours. Bd. mgrs. Haverford Coll., 1980-83; bd. advisors Educators for Social Responsibility, 1986-91; chmn. bd. Consortium on Financing Higher Edn., 1986-87; trustee The Textile Mus., Washington, 1986-2003, v.p., 1990-91, 96, pres., 1997-2003; bd. dirs. Albert G. Oliver Found., 1985-91; sci. adv. bd. Ctr. Infectious Diseases, 1989-91; mem. immunization practices adv. com. Ctrs. Disease Control, 1988-92; mem. com. to visit med. sch. and sch. dental medicine Harvard U., 1988-94; costume and textile com. Phila. Mus. Art, 1988-91, 2009-. Recipient Meritorious Svc. medal USPHS, 1978, John Scott award City of Phila., 1986, R.L. Shep Book award Textile Soc. Am., 2006; co-recipient Ancient and Modern prize Hali, Cornucopia, and Oriental Art, 2005, Millia Davenport Publ. award Costume Soc. Am., 2006, Juried Status, Fiber, Pa. Guild Craftsmen, 2008; Clementine Cope fellow Haverford Coll., 1965, Daland fellow Am. Philos. Soc., 1974. Fellow ACP (Richard and Hinda Rosenthal Found. award 1979), Infectious Diseases Soc. Am., Am. Coll. Epidemiology; mem. Am. Epidemiol. Soc., Aesculapian Club, Founders Club (Haverford Coll.). Home and Office: 907 N Pennsylvania Ave Yardley PA 19067-2023 Home Phone: 215-295-2016; Office Phone: 215-295-2016. Personal E-mail: dwffraser@comcast.net.

FRASER, ELEANOR RUTH, retired radiologist, administrator; b. Woodlake, Calif., May 31, 1927; d. Morton William and Dorothy Jean (Harding) F. BA magna cum laude, Pomona Coll., Claremont, Calif., 1949; MD, Stanford U., Calif., 1954. Diplomate Am. Bd. Radiology. Resident in radiology Los Angeles County Hosp., 1957; radiologist St. Joseph Hosp., Orange, Calif., 1957—61; pvt. practice Anaheim, Calif., 1961—78; radiologist Radiology Nuc. Med. Group, Bakersfield, Calif., 1978—85; dir. radiology Kern Valley Hosp., Lake Isabella, Calif., 1985—2009, chief of staff, 1992—99; ret. Mem. AMA, Calif. Med. Assn., Kern County Med. Assn., Kern Valley Exch. Club (sec. 1992-94), Phi Beta Kappa. Methodist. Avocations: music, writing. Home and Office: PO Box 1657 Lake Isabella CA 93240-1657 Personal E-mail: erufray@aol.com.

FRASER, JOSEPH ROBERT EMMOTT, physician, consultant; b. Inglewood, Victoria, Australia, Sept. 27, 1927; s. William Wilfred and Alphina Deborah (Emmott) F.; m. Muriel Ruth McKain, Jan. 20, 1951; children: Gail, Peter, Ian, David, Martin. MB, BS, U. Melbourne, Australia, 1949, MD, 1954; Hon. MD, Uppsala U., Sweden, 1988. Medical diplomate. Cons. physician Prince Henry's Hosp., Melbourne, 1960-66, mem. exec. sr. med. staff, 1961-65; cons. physician Royal Melbourne Hosp., 1966-92, chmn. bd. med. rsch., 1984-92, head of unit, 1989-92, hon. cons. physician, 1993—; asst. dir. dept. medicine U. Melbourne, 1966-78, dep. chmn., 1978-92, hon. sr. rsch. assoc. lab. for fetal and neonatal immunology, 1993—. Vis. scientist Inst. Med. and Physiol. Chemistry, Uppsala U., 1980-92; vis. assessor tertiary health and med. edn. Papua New Guinea, 1981; advisor fed. and state govts. on arbovirus disease. Contbr. chpts. to books and articles to profl. and sci. jours. Named Fgn. mem. Royal Soc. Sci., Uppsala, 1985, Order of Australia, Gov.-Gen. of Australia, 1990. Fellow Royal Australasian Coll. Physicians, Royal Coll. Physicians (London); mem. Royal Swedish Acad. Sci. (fgn. mem.), Soc. In Vitro Biol. (USA), Matrix Biology Assn. Australia and New Zealand (pres. 1978-80), Cardiac Soc. Australia and New Zealand, Australian Rheumatology Assn. Avocations: natural history, literature, snow sports. Home: 131 Manning Rd East Malvern VIC 3145 Australia

FRASER, ROBIN, pathology educator; b. Melbourne, Australia, Dec. 20, 1933; arrived in N.Z. 1974; s. Malcolm and Kathleen Elizabeth (Gault) F.; m. Isabel Emily Gidney, Aug. 14, 1957 (div. 1976); children: Elizabeth Jean, Jane Caroline, Simon Hugh, Sarah Anne; m. Linda Marjorie Bowler, May 5, 1979; children: Kate Victoria, Rachel Lucille. BSc, U. Sydney, NSW, Australia, 1956, MB, 1958; PhD, Australian Nat. U., 1968; MD, U. Otago, 1987. Registered med. practitioner, N.Z. Resident Royal Prince Alfred Hosp., Sydney, 1958-59, sr. resident, 1959-60, registrar, 1960-61; gen. practice medicine Coonabarabran, Australia, 1961-66; postgrad. scholar John Curtin Sch. Med. Rsch., Canberra, Australia, 1966-68; USPHS fellow in pathology U. Chgo., 1969-70; sr. lectr. pathology U. Sydney, 1970-74; assoc. prof. pathology Christchurch Sch. Medicine, New Zealand, 1974-96, assoc. dean rsch., 1988-91, prof. pathology, head of dept., 1997—2000, emeritus prof., 2000—. Dir. project grants N.Z. Health Rsch. Coun., 1974—; elected inaugural patron of med. students Christchurch Sch. Med.; pres. 9th Internat. Symposium on Cells of the Hepatic Sinusoids, Christchurch, 1998; med. dir. Canterbury Med. Rsch. Found., 2006-. Contbr. articles to internat. jours. Recipient Royal Hon., Officer New Zealand Order Merit, 2006. Fellow Royal Coll. Pathologists Australia; mem. Sigma Xi. Achievements include research in the "Liver Sieve," which separates the circulation from the hepatocytes. Its ultrafiltration of lipoproteins, viruses, and artificial vectors which transport lipids, DNA, siRNA, mRNA-HDL, influences cholesterol metabolism, atherogenesis, viral diseases and epigenetics. Office: Christchurch Hosp U Otago Christchurch New Zealand Home: 45 Kidson Terrace 8022 Christchurch New Zealand Office Phone: 64-3-3640585. Personal E-mail: phaser@xtra.co.nz. Business E-Mail: robin.fraser@otago.ac.nz.

FRATER, ROBERT WILLIAM MAYO, surgeon, educator; b. Cape Town, South Africa, Nov. 12, 1928; came to U.S., 1964, naturalized, 1974; s. Kenneth and Ethel (Barrow) F.; m. Elaine Glynn Nagle, Aug. 27, 1954; children: Hugh R., Dirk A., Phillipa. M.B., B.Chir. (Jagger Scholar, Medalist, Anatomy, Surgery, Pathology), U. Cape Town Med. Sch., 1952; MS in Surgery (Minn. Heart Assn. fellow), U. Minn., 1961. Intern medicine and surgery Groote Schuur Hosp., Cape Town, 1953; resident casualty officer Lewisham Hosp., London, 1955; fellow in gen. and thoracic surgery Mayo Clinic, Rochester, Minn., 1955-61; sr. lectr. cardiothoracic surgery U. Cape Town, 1962-64; asst. prof. surgery Albert Einstein Coll. Medicine, NYC, 1964-68, assoc. prof., 1968-72, prof. surgery, 1972—, chief cardiothoracic surgery, 1968—, acting chmn. dept. surgery, 1971-75; mem. Albert Einstein Coll. Medicine (Senate Council), 1971-74; chief cardiothoracic surgery Montefiore Hosp. and Med. Center, 1975-92; mem. staff, exec. council Bronx Mcpl. Hosp. Center, Albert Einstein Coll. Hosp., 1969—; mem. staff Lawrence Hosp., Bronxville, NY; pres. Glycar, Inc., Bronxville. Mem. organizing and sci. coms. Internat. Symposium on Cardiac Bioprosthesis, 1982, 95, 88, 91, 94, honored guest, 1985; pres. Glycar Inc.; med. dir. St. Jude Med. Inc., 2000—. Editor: Jour. Valvular Heart Disease, Replacement Cardiac Valves, New Horizons and the Future of Heart Valve Bioprostheses, 1994; mem. editl. bd. Cardiac Chronicle, Jour. Cardiac Surgery, 1987—, Mem. Concern for Dying Coun., 1982-88. Recipient award Noble Found., 1961, Bronx Coun. of the Arts Humanitarian award, 1989, Disting. Alumnus award Mayo Found, 2001; grantee NIH, 1965-70, 68-70, 74-78, 79-81, 82-84, Am. Heart Assn., 1966, 71. Fellow ACS, Royal Coll. Surgeons, Am. Coll. Cardiology, Am. Heart Assn. (exec. com. coun. on Cardiovasculary Surgery 1979-84, program com. 1979-82); mem. Am. Assn. Thoracic Surgery, Soc. Thoracic Surgeons (postgrad. edn. com. 1978, chmn. postgrad. program 1981), N.Y. Soc. Thoracic Surgery (pres. 1978), N.Y. Surg. Soc. (mem. coun. 1975-80), Thoracic Surgery Dirs. Assn. (exec. coun. 1982-85), Assn. Acad. Surgeons, Soc. Cardiothoracic Surgeon Great Britain and Ireland (hon. guest and mem. 1989), Soc. Heart Valve Disease (founder, chmn. membership com. 2001-, honored guest biennial Vancouver meeting, 2005), Bronxville Field Club (squash capt., bd. govs. 1987-90). Home: 17 Gladwin Pl Bronxville NY 10708-2201 Office: 1575 Blondell Ave Bronx NY 10461-2660 Personal E-mail: rwmfglycar@aol.com.

FRAUMENI, JOSEPH FRANCIS, JR., federal agency administrator, epidemiologist; b. Boston, Apr. 1, 1933; s. Joseph Francis and Pauline (Malta) Fraumeni; m. Patricia Welch D'Arcy, Apr. 23, 1977. AB, Harvard U., 1954; MD, Duke, 1958, MSc in epidemiology, Harvard U., 1965. Diplomate Am. Bd. Internal Medicine. Commd. lt. USPHS, 1962, advanced through grades to rear admiral (asst. surgeon gen.), 1997; med. intern, resident Johns Hopkins Hosp., Balt., 1958-60; med. resident, chief resident Meml. Sloan Kettering Cancer Ctr., NYC, 1960-62; staff assoc. Nat. Cancer Inst., NIH, Bethesda, Md., 1962-65, head ecology studies sect., 1966-75, chief environ. epidemiology br., 1975-82, dir. epidemiology & biostats. program, 1979-95, dir. divsn. cancer epidemiology and genetics, 1995—. Attending physician Clin. Ctr. NIH, Bethesda, Md., 1966—, adj. prof. epidemiology Uniformed Svcs. U., Bethesda, 1985—, Harvard U. Sch. Pub. Health, Boston, 1993—, George Washington U. Med. Ctr., 1997—. Mem. editl. bd.: more than a dozen med. and sci. jours.; contbr. chpts. to books, 750 articles to profl. jours. Recipient DSM, USPHS, 1983, Gorgas medal, Assn. Mil. Surgeons U.S., 1989, W.W. Sutow award, U. Tex. M.D. Anderson Cancer Ctr., 1992, Disting. Alumnus award, Duke U. Med. Ctr., 1992, Alumni Award of Merit, Harvard Sch. Pub. Health, 1993, Wick Williams Meml. award, Fox Chase Cancer Ctr., 1993, Dir.'s award, NIH, 1994, Charles Mott prize, GM Cancer Rsch. Found., 1995, John Snow award, APHA, 1995, Selikoff award, Ramazinni Inst., 1996, Robert S. Gordon award, NIH, 1996, Dr. Nathan Davis award, AMA, 2002, Alton Ochsner award relating smoking and health, Am. Coll. Chest Physicians, 2002. Fellow: ACP (James D. Bruce Meml. award 1997), AAAS, Am. Coll. Preventive Medicine, Am. Coll. Epidemiology (bd. dirs. 1985—89, Abraham Lilienfeld award 1993, hon. fellow 1998); mem.: NAS, Assn. Am. Physicians, Am. Assn. Cancer Rsch. (bd. dirs. 1983—87, Am. Cancer Soc. award rsch. excellence epidemiology, prevention 1993), Am. Soc. Preventive Oncology (pres. 1981—83, Disting. Achievement award 1993), Inst. Medicine. Office: Nat Cancer Inst Divsn Cancer Epidemiology and Genetics 6120 Executive Blvd Bethesda MD 20892-7335 Office Phone: 301-496-1611. Office Fax: 301-402-3256. E-mail: fraumeni@nih.gov. *

FRAUNFELDER, FREDERICK THEODORE, ophthalmologist, educator; b. Pasadena, Calif., Aug. 16, 1934; s. Reinhart and Freida Fraunfelder; m. Yvonne Marie Halliday, June 21, 1959; children—Yvette Marie, Helene, Nina, Frederick, Nicholas. BS, U. Oreg., 1956, MD, 1960, postgrad. (NIH postdoctoral fellow), 1962. Diplomate Am. Bd. Ophthalmology (bd. dirs. 1982-90). Intern U. Chgo., 1961; resident U. Oreg. Med. Sch., 1964-66; NIH postdoctoral fellow Wilmer Eye Inst., Johns Hopkins U., 1967; chmn. dept. ophthalmology U. Ark. Health Scis. Ctr., 78-98, prof., 1978—; prof., chmn. dept. ophthalmology Oreg. Health Scis. U. Dir. Casey Eye Inst., 1992-98, Nat. Registry Drug-Induced Ocular Side Effects, 1976—; vis. prof. ophthalmology Moorfields Eye Hosp., London, 1974. Author: Drug-Induced Ocular Side Effects and Drug Interactions, 1976, 6th edit., 2008, Current Ocular Therapy, 1985, 6th edit., 2008, Recent Advances in Ophthalmology, 8th edit., 1985; assoc. editor: Retirement Rx, 2008, Clin. Ocular Toxicology, 2008, Retire Right, 2009, Jour. Toxicology: Cutaneous and Ocular, 1984-2002; mem. editl. bd. Am. Jour. Ophthalmology, 1982-92, Ophthalmic Forum, 1983-90, Ophthalmology, 1984-89; contbr. over 200 articles on ocular toxicology or ocular cancer to med. jours. Served with U.S. Army, 1962-64. FDA grantee, 1976-86; Nat. Eye Inst. grantee, 1970-87; named Best Doc. in Am., 2005 Mem. AMA, ACS, Am. Acad. Ophthalmology, Assn. Univ. Profs. in Ophthalmology (pres. 1976), Am. Ophthalmol. Soc., Am. Coll. Cryosurgery (pres. 1977), Assn. Research in Ophthalmology. Clubs: Lions, Elks. Home: 13 Cellini Ct Lake Oswego OR 97035-1307 Office: Casey Eye Inst 3375 SW Terwilliger Blvd Portland OR 97239-4197 Home Phone: 503-636-7229; Office Phone: 503-494-5686. Business E-Mail: fraunfel@ohsu.edu.

FRAUNFELDER, FREDERICK WEB, ophthalmologist, educator; b. Balt., Sept. 29, 1967; BA in Economics, Baylor U., 1990; MD, Oreg. Health & Sci. U., 1994, MBA. Prof. ophthalmology, dir. cornea, refractive surgery Casey Eye Inst., Oreg. Health & Sci. U., 2001—. Master: Internat. Soc. Ocular Toxicology; mem.: Internat. Soc. Ocular Pharmacology & Toxicology, Cornea Soc., Am. Acad. Ophthalmology (Achievement award), Am. Ophthal. Soc. Avocations: tennis, piano, music. Office: 3375 SW Terwilliger Blvd Portland OR 97239 Home Phone: 503-636-2930; Office Phone: 503-494-3941. Business E-Mail: fraunfer@ohsu.edu.

FRAZIER, THOMAS G., surgeon, educator; MD, U. Pa. Diplomate Am. Bd. Surgery. Resident Hosp. of the Univ. of Pa.; hosp. affiliations include Lankenau Med. Ctr., Paoli Hosp., Bryn Mawr Hosp., med. dir. comprehensive breast ctr., sr. attending surgeon; clin. prof. surgery Thomas Jefferson Univ. Principal investigator Nat. Surg. Adjuvant Project (NSABP), 1976, bd. dir. Mem.: ACS (commn. on cancer, past pres. Phila. met. chpt.), Phila. Acad. of Surgery (pres.). Office: Bryn Mawr Hospital 414 Paoli Pike Malvern PA 19355 Office Phone: 484-596-5400.

FRAZIER, THOMAS WILLIAM, psychologist; b. Geneva, Ohio, July 24, 1975; PhD, Case Western Res. U., 2004. Staff, rsch. dir. Ctr. Autism Cleve. Clinic, 2006—. Grant, NIH, Brain and Behavior Rsch. Found., NIMH. Mem.: APA, Internat. Soc. Autism Rsch. Avocations: running, basketball, weightlifting. Office: 2801 Martin Luther King Jr Dr Cleveland OH 44104 Office Phone: 216-448-6440. Office Fax: 216-448-6445. Business E-Mail: fraziet2@ccf.org.

FRECHETTE, PETER LOREN, medical products executive; b. Janesville, Wis., Aug. 15, 1937; s. Francis Michael and Gladys Jean F.; m. Patricia Jean O'Brien, June 24, 1961; children: Kathleen and Kristen (twins). BS in Econs., U. Wis., 1960; MBA, Northwestern U., 1980. Pres. Sci. Products, McGaw Park, Ill., 1975-82, Patterson Dental Co., Mpls., 1982—2003, CEO, 1982—2005; chmn. Patterson Companies, Inc. Served with U.S. Army, 1961-63. Mem. Am. Dental Trade Assn. Office: Patterson Companies Inc 1031 Mendota Heights Rd Mendota Heights MN 55120-1401 Office Phone: 651-686-1700. E-mail: pete.frechette@pattersondental.com.

FREDERICK, BARBARA, health science association administrator; b. Charleston, W.Va., Nov. 30, 1953; BS, U. Tenn., 1975; MPA, U. Memphis, 1985. Asst. bus. mgr. U. Tenn. Med. Group, 1979—96; practice administr. Met. Anesthesia Alliance, 1996—2004; bus. mgr. U. Tenn. Health Sci. Ctr., 2004—. Mem.: Nat. Coun. Rsch. Adminstr. Avocation: music. Office: 930 Madison Memphis TN 38173 Business E-Mail: bfrederick@uthsc.edu.

FREDERICK-MAIRS, T(HYRA) JULIE, administrative health services official; b. Bayshore, NY, Jan. 4, 1941; d. Manuel and Thyra C. (Thorsen) Cajiao. BA, Adelphi U., 1961; MSW, U. So. Calif., 1972, MPA, 1991. Social worker L.A. County Dept. Social Svcs., 1966-67, social work supr., 1967-70, planning cons., 1972-76; dep. to supr. 4th dist. L.A. County, 1976-80; asst. dir. L.A. County Office Alcohol Programs, 1980-90; assoc. adminstr. ELACO Health Ctrs., 1990—2003; CEO East Country Health Ctrs.; health care process improvement and change mgmt. cons., 2003—; chair Project Five-O-LA: Policy Summit- Violence Against Women, 2008. Fellow U. So. Calif., 1988-90. Author: (with others) Youth Program Planning, 1975. Trustee LEARNS, 1992; active L.A. Child Sexual Abuse Project, Commn. for Sexual Equality, L.A. Unified Sch. Dist., Harbor Policy Cmty. Adv. Coun., L.A.; mem. Perinatal Substance Abuse Coun. L.A.; mem. ops. com. Interagy. Coun. Child Abuse and Neglect; adv. com. UCLA Alcohol Rsch. Ctr. Mem. Los Amigos de la Humanidad, DHS Latino Mgrs., Alpha Epsilon Delta, Sigma Kappa Soc., Beta Beta Beta, Bus. and Profl. Women's Club, Soroptimist Internat. (pres. L.A. Club, dir. Found. of L.A. 1986-88, 2006-2008). Office Phone: 818-512-0083.

FREDERICSON, MICHAEL, physiatrist; BA, U. Redlands, 1982; MD, NY Medical Coll., Vahalla, NY, 1988. Cert. Physical Medicine and Rehab. American Bd. Physical Medicine and Rehab, 1993, Sports Medicine American Bd. Physical Medicine and Rehab, 2007. Intern Mt. Zion, 1989; assoc. prof. Stanford Medical Coll., 1992—; dir. physical medicine and rehab. sports medicine service Stanford Hosp. & Clinics, 1994—. Sr. assoc. editor PM&R The Journal of Injury, function and Rehabilitation, 2007—; scientific advisory bd. Runner's World mag., 2001—. Office: Stanford Medical Ctr 450 Broadway St Pavilion A 2nd Floor MC 6120 Redwood City CA 94063 Office Phone: 650-723-5643. Office Fax: 650-721-3422.

FREDERIKSEN, MARILYNN C., physician; b. Chgo., Sept. 12, 1949; d. Paul H. and Susanne (Ostergren) Conners; m. James W. Frederiksen, July 11, 1971; children: John K., Paul S., Britt L. BA, Cornell Coll., 1970; MD, Boston U., 1974; grad. Exec. Leadership in Acad. Medicine, Allegheny U. Health Scis., 1998. Diplomate Am. Bd. Ob-Gyn., Am. Bd. Maternal-Fetal Medicine, Am. Bd. Clin. Pharmacology. Pediat. intern U. Md. Hosp., 1974-75, resident in pediat., 1975-76; resident in ob-gyn. Boston Hosp. for women, 1976-79; fellow in maternal fetal medicine Northwestern U., 1979-81, fellow clin. pharmacology, 1981-83, instr. ob-gyn. Chgo., 1981-83, asst. prof. ob-gyn., assoc. clin. pharmacology, 1983-91, assoc. prof. ob-gyn., 1991—, sect. chief gen. ob-gyn., 1993—2001. Mem. gen. faculty com. Northwestern U., Chgo., 1994—97, mem. ob-gyn. adv. panel, 1985—2000, chair ob-gyn. adv. panel, 2000—05; mem. U.S. Pharm. Com. Revision, Rockville, Md., 1986—2005; del. U.S. Pharm. conv. Northwestern U. Med. Sch., 1990, 95, 2000; mem. gen. clinic rsch. ctr. com. NIH, 1989—93, chairperson, 1992—93; mem. Task Force Writing Group on Asthma in Pregnancy, Nat. Heart, Lung and Blood Inst., 1991—92; examiner Am. Bd. Ob-Gyn., 1997—98; mem. Task Force Working Group, Nat. Bd. Med. Examiners, 1997—98, mem. acute care com., 1999—2001. Mem. editorial bd. Clin. Pharmacology & Therapeutics, 1993; contbr. numerous articles to profl. jours. Bd. dirs. Cornell Coll. Alumni Assn., Mt. Vernon, Iowa, 1986—90, PRCH, 1997—2005, Planned Parenthood of Chgo. Area, 1999—2005, Northwestern Med. Faculty Found., 1995—98. Recipient Pharm. Mfrs. Assn. Found. Faculty Devel. award, 1984-86, Civil Liberties award ACLU, 1991. Fellow Am. Coll. Ob-Gyn.; mem. Soc. Maternal Fetal Medicine, Ctrl. Assn. Obstetricians and Gynecologists (bd. dirs. 1997-99), Am. Soc. Clin. Pharmacology and Therapeutics (bd. dirs. 1994-97), Chgo. Gynecologic Soc. (treas. 1994-97), Phi Beta Kappa. Episcopalian. Avocations: gardening, needlecrafts. Office: Northwestern Perinatal Assocs 680 N Lake Shore Dr Ste 1428 Chicago IL 60611 Office Phone: 312-981-4350. Personal E-mail: frederiksen.marilynn@gmail.com. Business E-Mail: mcf810@northwestern.edu.

FREDRICK, DOUGLAS ROBERT, pediatric ophthalmologist; b. San Jose, Calif., Oct. 6, 1960; MD, Baylor Coll. Medicine, Houston, 1986. Cert. Am. Bd. Ophthalmology, 1991. Internship in ophthalmology St. Mary's Hosp. Med. Ctr., San Francisco, 1986—87; residency in pediatric ophthalmology U. Calif., San Francisco, 1987—90, assoc. prof. ophthalmology; fellowship in pediatric ophthalmology Children's Hosp., Boston, 1990—91; hosp. appointment U. Calif. Med. Ctr., San Francisco; clin. prof., vice chair clin. affairs, dept. ophthalmology Stanford U. Sch. Medicine, Calif. Office: Stanford Sch Medicine Dept Ophthalmology 300 Pasteur Dr A157 MC 5308 Stanford CA 94305 Office Phone: 650-498-1984. Office Fax: 650-725-0288.

FREE, HELEN MURRAY, retired chemist consultant; b. Pitts., Feb. 20, 1923; d. James Summerville and Daisy (Piper) Murray; m. Alfred H. Free, Oct. 18, 1947 (dec. May 2000); children: Eric, Penny, Kurt, Jake, Bonnie, Nina. BA in Chemistry, Coll. of Wooster, Ohio, 1944, DSc (hon.), 1992; MA in Clin. Lab. Mgmt., Ctrl. Mich. U., 1978, DSc (hon.), 1993. Cert. clin. chemist Nat. Registry Cert. Chemists. Chemist Miles Labs., Elkhart, Ind., 1944—78, dir. mktg. svcs. rsch. products divsn., 1978-82; chemist, mgr., cons. Bayer HealthCare Diabetes Care, Elkhart, 1982—2008. Mem. adj. faculty Ind. U., South Bend, 1975—96; keynote spkr. Pres. Awards Excellence for Math. and Sci. Tchrs., 2007; spkr. in field. Author (with others): (books) Urodynamics and Urinalysis in Clinical Laboratory Practice, 1972, 1976; contbr. articles to encys. and profl. jours. Bd. dirs. Nat. Inventors Hall of Fame Found.; women's chmn. Centennial of Elkhart, 1958; mem. adv. bd. Intellectual Property Sch. Law, Akron U.; indsl. adv. bd. chemistry/chem. engring. Trine U., Angola, Ind. Recipient Disting. Alumni award, Coll. of Wooster, 1980, Medi Econ. Press award, 1986, Nat. Leadership award, Lab. Pub. Svc., 1994, Nat. Medal Tech. and Innovation, The White House, 2010; named Woman of Yr., YWCA, 1993, Kilby Found. Laureate, 1996; named to Hall of Excellence, Ohio Found. Ind. Colls., 1992, Engring. and Sci. Hall of Fame, 1996, Nat. Inventors Hall of Fame, 2000. Fellow: AAAS, Assn. Women in Sci., Royal Soc. Chemistry, Am. Inst. Chemists (co-recipient Chgo. award 1967); mem.: Nat. Com. Clin. Lab. Stds. (bd. dir.), Am. Soc. Clin. Lab. Sci. (chmn. assembly, Achievement award 1976), Soc. Chem. Industry (hon.), Assn. Clin. Scientists (diploma of honor 1992), Am. Assn. Clin. Chemistry (pres. 1990, coun., bd. dir., nominating com. and pub. rels. com., nat. membership com., coord. profl. affairs, Outstanding Contbn. award 2006), Am. Chem. Soc. (pres. 1993, bd. dir., chmn. Chemistry Week task force, bd. com. pub. affairs and pub. rels., chmn. women chemists com., internat. activities com., grants and awards com., prof. and mem. rels. com., nominating com., coun. policy pub. affairs and budget, councilor, chair Progress project, with nat. historic chem. landmark 2010, Garvan medal 1980, Svc. award local chpt. 1981, co-recipient Mosher award 1983, 1st recipient Helen M. Free Pub. Outreach award 1995, Helen M. Free award named in her honor 1995), Altrusa (pres. 1982—83, bd. dir.), Sigma Delta Epsilon (hon.), Iota Sigma Pi (hon.). Presbyterian. Achievements include patents in field. Home: 3752 E Jackson Blvd Elkhart IN 46516-5205 Personal E-mail: hmfree23@aol.com.

FREEDLAND, STEPHEN JAY, urologist; b. Sacramento, Feb. 15, 1972; s. Richard Allan and Beverly Jane Freedland; m. Inna Shapiro. MD, U. Calif., Davis, 1997. Diplomate Am. Bd. Urology. Resident in urology UCLA Sch. Medicine, 1997—2003; fellow urologic oncology Johns Hopkins Sch. Medicine, Balt., 2003—05; asst. prof. urology and pathology Duke U. Med. Ctr., Durham, 2005—08, assoc. prof., 2008—. Vice chmn. Western Student Med. Rsch. Forum, Reno, 1995—96, chmn., 1996—97, sr. advisor, 1997—98. Contbr. articles to profl. jours. Asst. scout master Boy Scouts America, Davis, 1990—97. Recipient E. E. Osgood award, Western Student Med. Rsch. Forum, 1995, Abe Zarem Rsch. award, UCLA Dept. Urology, 2000, Physician Tng. award, US Dept. Def., 2005, Johns Hopkins Young Investigators award, 2005, Merit award, ASCO Found., 2005, Rising Star in Urology award, Am. Urol. Assn. Found., 2006; Rsch. scholar, US Dept. Def., 2003—10, Am. Found. Urol. Disease/Am. Urol. Assn. Edn. & Rsch., 2004. Mem.: Am. Urol. Assn. (1st prize Miley B. Wesson resident essay competition 2001), Golden Key, Phi Beta Kappa. Jewish. Avocations: travel, basketball. Office: Duke U Dept Surgery / Divsn Urology DUMC 2626 Durham NC 27710 Office Phone: 919-668-8361. Business E-Mail: steve.freedland@duke.edu.

FREEDMAN, AARON DAVID, retired medicine and biochemistry educator, dean; b. Albany, NY, Jan. 4, 1922; s. Jacob Abraham and Pauline Rebecca (Hoffman) F.; m. Alice Maurer, Sept. 10, 1948, dec. 2001; children: Abigail, Jonathan, Jeremy; m. Virginia Weliky, Apr. 14, 2005. AB, Cornell U., 1942; MD, Albany Med. Coll., 1945; PhD, Columbia U., 1958; MA, U. Pa., 1972. Diplomate Am. Bd. Internal Medicine. Asst. prof. medicine and biochemistry Columbia U., NYC, 1958-65; clin. prof. U. Kans., Kansas City, 1965-69, chmn. dept. medicine Menorah Med. Ctr., 1965-69; prof., assoc. dean U. Pa., Phila., 1969-75, exec. dir. Grad. Hosp., 1972-75; prof. medicine Med. Sch. CUNY, 1975—2006, acting dean, 1978-79, dep. dean acad. affairs, 1990-92, emeritus prof., 2006—. Examiner N.Y. State Bd. Med. Examiners, Albany, 1962-65; cons. Touro Coll., N.Y.C., 1980; career investigator N.Y. Pub. Health Rsch. Coun., 1963-65; dir. Danciger Med. Inst., Kansas City, Mo., 1966-69. Mem. Ardsley (N.Y.) Bd. of Edn., 1962-65. Libman Fund fellow, 1951-54, USPHS fellow, 1958-60. Mem. Am. Soc. for Cell Biology, Am. Soc. Biochemistry and Molecular Biology. Jewish. Home Phone: 970-586-9216. Personal E-mail: anv@beyondbb.com.

FREEDMAN, GARY M., radiation oncologist educator; Attended, Temple U. Diplomate Am. Bd. Radiology-radiation oncology. Intern Abington Meml. Hosp.; resident Fox Chase Cancer Ctr., fellow, assoc. dir. breast evaluation ctr., program dir. radiation oncology residency; with breast cancer radiation oncology team Abramson Cancer Ctr.; assoc. prof. radiation oncology Univ. of Pa. Health System. Recipient Assn. of Residents in Radiation Oncology Educator of the Yr. award; named America's Top Doctors for Cancer; named one of Top Docs, Phila. Mag., 2011. Mem.: Am. Radium Soc., Radiation Therapy Oncology Group, Am. Soc. for Therapeutic Radiology and Oncology, Am. Soc. of Clin. Oncology. Office: Perelman Center for Advanced Medicine 3400 Civic Center Blvd Philadelphia PA 19104 Office Phone: 800-789-7366.

FREEDMAN, GORDON M., pain medicine physician, educator; MD, Tel-Aviv U., Israel, 1985. Diplomate Am. Bd. Anesthesiology, Am. Bd. Anesthesiology-pain medicine. Resident anesthesiology Mt. Sinai Hosp., NY, 1988—91, fellow pain medicine NY, 1991; assoc. clin. prof. anesthesiology and pain mgmt. Mt. Sina Sch. of Medicine. Co-author: (publs.) Geriatric Pain Management: The Anesthesiologist's Perspective, 2000. Office: Mount Sinai Medical Center One Gustave L. Levy Pl New York NY 10029 Office Fax: 212-241-6500.

FREEDMAN, JAMIE, oncologist, medical researcher; MD, PhD, Tufts U. Rschr., Beth Israel Deaconess Med. Ctr. Harvard University; various positions, clin. pharmacology, clin. oncology, and exptl. medicine Merck Rsch. Labs; pres., CEO Locus Pharmaceuticals; exec. v.p., R&D, bus. devel. OPKO Health, Inc., 2009—. Adj. asst. prof., medicine U. Pa. Med. Ctr. Office: OPKO Health Inc Ste 1180 4400 Biscayne Blvd Miami FL 33137 Office Phone: 305-575-4138. Business E-Mail: jfreedman@opko.com. *

FREEDMAN, JESSICA, physician, medical association administrator; d. Jeffrey and Marian Freedman; m. Randy Katzke, Sept. 1, 2002; children: Talia Katzke, Mariel Katzke. BS, Haverford Coll., Pa., 1990; MD, Temple U., Phila., 1995. Diplomate Am. Bd. Emergency Medicine, 2000. Rsch. asst. Scripps Rsch. Inst., La Jolla, 1990—91; resident physician Cook County Hosp., Chgo., 1995—99; asst. prof. Mt. Sinai Sch. Medicine, NYC, 1999—2008; staff physician Valley Hosp., Ridgewood, NJ, 2008—; pres. MedEdits Med. Admissions, Demarest, NJ, 2008—. Course dir., intro. to emergency medicine Mt. Sinai Sch. Medicine, NYC, asst. residency dir. dept. emergency medicine, 2001—02; assoc. residency dir. Mt. Sinai Dept. Emergency Medicine, NYC, 2002—05; medscape med students editl. adv. bd. WebMD LLC, New York, NY, 2009—. Editor: (book) Good Housekeeping First Aid Book, 2nd edit.; contbr. articles to profl. jours., chapters to books. Mem.: Assn. Internat. Grad. Admissions Consultants, Coun. Emergency Medicine Dir., Soc. Academic Emergency Medicine. Office: PO Box 234 Demarest NJ 07627 Office Phone: 201-244-6142. Business E-Mail: info@mededits.com.

FREEDMAN, LOUIS MARTIN, dentist; b. Newark, Mar. 19, 1947; s. Morris and Sylvia (Swimmer) F.; m. Elizabeth Norine Palmer, June 17, 1978; children: Steven, Julie, Brian. Student, Emory U., 1963—66, DDS, 1970. Dentist Freedman, Freedman & Weitman DDS, P.C., Atlanta, 1970—; clin. instr. Emory U. Dental Sch., Atlanta, 1970—77. Team dentist Atlanta Hawks Basketball Team, 1971—, Atlanta Flames Hockey Team, 1979-80, Atlanta Knights Hockey Team, 1992-96, Atlanta Fire Ants Roller Hockey Team, 1994-96. Mgr. Sandy Springs Youth Sports Little League Baseball, 1979-96; head coach Sandy Springs United Meth. Ch. basketball program, 1991-96. Mem. Acad. Osseointegration, Internat. Congress Oral Implantologists, Alpha Epsilon Delta, Omicron Kappa Upsilon. Jewish. Avocations: softball, little league managing, gardening, skiing, water-skiing, swimming. Office: Freedman Freedman & Weitman 3111 Piedmont Rd NE Atlanta GA 30305-2507 Office Phone: 404-261-5388.

FREEDMAN, PHILIP, internist, educator; b. London, June 25, 1926; came to U.S., 1963, naturalized, 1970; s. Myer and Mildred (Frankel) F.; m. Jean Kennis Cunningham, Dec. 21, 1954; children: Simon John, Marion Rose, Mark Alexander, Paul Daniel, Adam James. MB, BS with honors, Univ. Coll. Hosp. Med. Sch., London, 1948, MD, 1951. House surgeon Univ. Coll. Hosp., 1948, med. registrar, 1953-56, rsch. asst. professorial med. unit, 1956-57, Bilton Pollard fellow, 1957-59; sr. house physician Chase Farm Hosp., 1949; 1st asst. physician St. George's Hosp., London, 1959-60; cons. Woolwich Hosp. Group, London, Redhill Hosp. Group, Surrey, Eng., 1960-63; chief Chgo. Med. Sch. Divsn., Dept. Medicine Cook County Hosp., 1963-66; prof., chmn. dept. medicine Chgo. Med. Sch., 1967-74; dir. renal unit Cook County Hosp., Chgo., 1963-66; chmn. dept. medicine Mt. Sinai Hosp. Med. Ctr., Chgo., 1966-79; prof., sr. attending physician Rush Med. Coll., Rush-Presbyn.-St. Luke's Med. Ctr., Chgo., 1975-96; clin. prof. medicine U. Ill. Coll. Medicine, Urbana-Champaign, 1999—. Contbr. articles to profl. jours. With M.C. Brit. Army, 1951-53. Fellow ACP, Royal Coll. Physicians; mem. Ctrl. Soc. Clin. Investigation, Med. Rsch. Soc. London, Alpha Omega Alpha (faculty mem.). Home: 101 W Windsor Rd Urbana IL 61802-6663 Business E-Mail: pfreedmn@uiuc.edu.

FREEDMAN, RALPH STUART, obstetrician, gynecologist, educator; b. Capetown, South Africa, Feb. 6, 1941; came to U.S., 1975; s. Barry and Hilda (Dick) F.; m. Jennifer M. Goldin, Mar. 7, 1972; children: Paul, Lara. MB, ChirB, Witwatersrand U., Johannesburg, South Africa, 1965, PhD, 1975. Asst. prof. U. Tex. M. D. Anderson Cancer Ctr., Houston, 1977-81, assoc. prof., 1981-87, prof., 1987—. Dir. lab. immunology and molecular biology U. Tex. M. D. Anderson Cancer Ctr., Houston, 1988—. Contbr. articles to profl. jours.; patentee tumor cell surface binding monoclonal antibody, 1995. Mem. Nat. Cancer Adv. Bd. appointed by Pres. Clinton, 2000—06. Eli Lilly fellow, 1976; grantee NCI, 1992, 94, Am. Cancer Soc. Fellow Royal Coll. Ob-gyn.; mem. Felix Rutledge Soc., Am. Assn. Cancer Rsch., Am. Radium Soc., Am. Assn. Immunologists, Am. Coll. Ob-gyn. Avocations: fishing, travel. Home: 215 Electra Dr Houston TX 77079-7336 Office: U Tex MD Anderson Cancer Ctr 1515 Holcombe Blvd # 67 Houston TX 77030-4009 Business E-Mail: rfreedman@mdanderson.org. *

FREEDMAN, ROBERT J., cardiologist, educator; MD, Tulane U. Sch. Med.; grad., USAF Sch. Aerospace Med. & Cardiology. Resident Baylor Coll. Med.; founder Life Recovery Sys.; founder & mng. ptnr. Freedman Meml. Cardiology; clinical asst. prof. Tulane U. Flight surgeon USAF. Fellow: Am. Coll. Cardiology (bd. govs.). Office: 3311 Prescott Rd Ste 112 Alexandria LA 71301

FREEDMAN, SHARON FRIDOVICH, opthalmologist; b. Durham, NC, May 2, 1959; m. Neil J. Freedman, June 26, 1983. BS, Duke U., 1981; MD, Harvard U., 1985. Diplomate Am. Bd. Opthalmology. Residency in ophthalmology Mass. Eye and Ear, Boston, 1986-89; fellow in pediat. opthalmology Children's Hosp., Boston, 1989-90; fellow in glaucoma Duke Eye Ctr., Durham, 1990-92, asst. prof. to prof. ophthalmology and pediat., 1995—; asst. prof. U. NC, Chapel Hill, 1992-94. Contbr. articles to profl. jours. Office: Duke Med Ctr Box 3802 2351 Erwin Rd Durham NC 27710

FREEMAN, ARTHUR MERRIMON, III, psychiatry professor, dean; b. Birmingham, Ala., Oct. 10, 1942; s. Arthur Merrimon II and Katherine (Lide) F.; m. Linda Poynter; children: Arthur M. IV, Katherin Leigh, Edward Todd. AB in Philosophy, Harvard U., Cambridge, Mass., 1963; MD, Vanderbilt U., Nashville, Tenn., 1967.

Diplomate Am. Bd. Psychiatry and Neurology; lic. psychiatrist, Ala., NC, La. Asst. prof. dept. psychiatry and behavioral scis. Stanford U., Calif., 1974—77; prof., vice chmn. dept. psychiatry U. Ala., Birmingham, 1977—90; med. dir. Appalachian Hall Hosp., Asheville, NC, 1990—91; prof., chmn. dept. psychiatry La. State U. Med. Ctr., Shreveport, 1991—2003, dean, 1993—96; prof., chmn. dept. psychiatry Health Sci. Ctr. U. Tenn., Memphis, 2003—05; clin. prof. psychiatry U. Ala., Birmingham, 2006—. Regional med. dir. divsn. mental health La. Dept. Health and Hosps., 1992-94. Author: Psychiatry for the Primary Care Physician, 1979. Bd. dirs. Vols. of Am., Shreveport, 1993-96, Shreveport Symphony, C. of C., 1993-96. Lt. comdr. M.C., USN, 1972-74. Nat. Merit scholar Harvard U., 1959-63; Biochemistry fellow Karolinska Inst., Stockholm, 1965, fellow in hepatic disease Royal Free Hosp., London, 1966, Disting. Paul Harris fellow Rotary Club. Fellow APA (Disting. life fellow, vice-chmn. fin. oversight com.), Am. Coll. Psychiatrists (Laughlin fellow 1971, bd. regents), Acad. Psychosomatic Medicine, So. Psychiat. Assn. (mem. fin. com.); mem. So. Psychiatry Assn., Am. Acad. Psychosomatic Medicine, Royal Coll. Psychiatrists, Collegium Internat. Neuropsychopharmacologia. Home: 3536 Brookwood Rd Birmingham AL 35223 Business E-Mail: amfreeman@utmem.edu.

FREEMAN, BOB A., retired microbiology educator, retired dean; b. Eastland, Tex., May 7, 1926; s. Oswald Ledbetter and Osielee (Wilcox) F.; m. Rosemary David, June 4, 1960; children: Susan A., Robert D., Katherine E., Andrew W. BA, U. Tex., 1949, MA, 1950, PhD, 1954. Instr. biology Tex. A & M U., College Station, 1950-51; rsch. scientist I U. Tex., Austin, 1951-54; instr., asst. prof. U. Chgo., 1954-64; assoc. prof. U. Tenn., Memphis, 1964-66, prof., 1966 88, chmn. microbiology dept., 1970-83, vice chancellor, 1982-88, Disting. Svc. prof., 1988-96, interim dean Coll. Grad. Health Scis., 1993-96, dean, prof. emeritus, 1997—. Cons. WHO, Calcutta, India, 1968. Author: Burrows Textbook of Microbiology, 21st edit., 1979, 22d edit., 1984; mem. edit. bd. Jour. Dental Edn., 1980-83, U. Tenn. Press., 1983-2001; contbr. articles to profl. jours. Bd. dirs. Memphis Heart Gala, 1984-90. With USN, 1944-46, PTO. Grantee U.S. Army Rsch. and Devel. Command, USPHS, U.S. Dept. Agr. Mem. AAAS, Am. Soc. for Microbiology (br. councillor 1969-71), Imhotep Soc., Sigma Xi (chpt. pres. 1974-75). Republican. Methodist. Avocation: woodworking. Home: 1319 E Crestwood Dr Memphis TN 38119-5000

FREEMAN, CAROLYN RUTH, oncologist; b. Kettering, Eng., Jan. 2, 1950; emigrated to Can., 1974, naturalized, '78; d. Ivor Thomas and Winifred Mary (Scotney) F.; m. J.C. Negrete, July 25, 1981. Student, King's Coll. London U., 1967-69; MB, BS, Westminster Med. Sch. London U., 1972. Prof., chmn. dept. radiation oncology, faculty medicine McGill U., Montreal, 1979—; radiation oncologist-in-chief McGill U. Hosps., Montreal, 1979—. Contbr. articles to med. publs. Fellow Royal Coll. Physicians (Can.); mem. Can. Assn. Radiol. Oncologists (pres. 1991-93), Am. Soc. Therapeutic Radiology and Oncology. Office: 1650 Cedar Ave Montreal PQ Canada H3G 1A4 Home: 4270 Boul de Maisonneuve O Montreal PQ Canada H3Z 1K6 Office Phone: 514-934-8040. Business E-Mail: carolyn.freeman@muhc.mcgill.ca.

FREEMAN, CORINNE, financial analyst, retired mayor; b. NYC, Nov. 9, 1926; d. Bernard J. Hirschfeld and Sidonie (Daxe) Lichtenstein; m. Michael S. Freeman, Mar. 14, 1948; children: Michael L., Stephan J. Student, Adelphi Coll. Sch. Nursing, 1944—47. RN, N.Y., Mass. Nurse numerous hosps. in N.Y. and Mass., 1948-64; mayor St. Petersburg, Fla., 1977-85; mem. Pinellas County Sch. Bd., St. Petersburg, Fla., 1989-98, chmn., 1996-98; bd. trustees Palms of Pasadena Hosp., St. Petersburg, 1998—, dir., 1998—2004. Fin. advisor Prudential Securities, Stephan J. atty wells fargo advisors; bd. dirs. Creativity in Child Care. Chmn. Social Svc. Allocations Com., St. Petersburg, 1972-76, City Budget Rev. Com., 1973-76, Youth Svc. System, Pinellas County, 1975-76, West Coast Regional Water Supply Authority; past mem. community redevel. com. U.S. Conf. of Mayors; past pres. Fla. League Cities; past mem. Pinellas County Mayors Coun.; past mem. Nat. League of Cities Revenue and Fin. Task Force; pres. LWV, St. Petersburg, 1970-72, 75-76; trustee Fire Pension Bd., St. Petersburg, 1989-92, Bayfront Med. Ctr.; dir. Palms of Pasadena Hosp., 1999-2003 Recipient Disting. Alumni award Adelphi U. Mem. Fla. Nursing Assn. Mem.: Treasure Island Yacht and Tennis Club (bd. dirs. 2004—). Republican. Home: 2101 Pelham Rd N Saint Petersburg FL 33710-3659 Office: 700 Ctrl Ave Ste 100 Saint Petersburg FL 33701 Office Phone: 727-551-2303. Business E-Mail: corinne_freeman@wachoviasec.com, corinne_freeman@wfadvisors.com.

FREEMAN, HAROLD PAUL, oncologist, educator, director; b. Washington, Mar. 2, 1933; s. Clyde and Lucille Freeman; m. Arti Artholian Palmer, 1957; children: Harold P. Jr., Neale P. AB in Biology, Cath. U. Am., 1954; MD, Howard U., 1958; DSc (hon.), Albany Med. Sch., 1989, Niagara U., 1989; DS (hon.), Adelphi U., 1989, Cath. U., 1990. Diplomate Am. Bd. Surgery; lic. oncologist, N.Y., Md. Rotating intern Howard U. Hosp., Washington, 1958-59, resident in gen. surgery, 1959-62, chief resident in surgery, 1963-64; resident in surgery Meml. Sloan Kettering Hosp., NYC, 1962-63, sr. resident, 1964-67; fellow in surgery Cornell U. Med. Ctr., NYC, 1965-66; asst. in surgery Columbia U., 1967-70, instr. surgery, 1970-73; attending Presbyterian Hosp., 1974—99; asst. clin. prof. Columbia U., 1973-74, dir. surgery, 1974—99, Harlem Hospital Ctr., 1974—99; prof. Columbia U., 1989—; chair President's Cancer Panel, Bethesda, 1991—2002; pres., CEO, dir. surgery North General Hospital, NYC, 1999—2001; dir. Ralph Lauren Ctr. for Cancer Care and Prevention, NYC, 2003—, Ctr. Reduce Cancer Health Disparities, Nat. Cancer Inst., 2000—, founding dir., 2005. Asst. attending surgeon N.Y. Infirmary, N.Y.C., 1969-82, St. Luke's/Roosevelt Med. Ctr., N.Y.C., 1983—, Harlem Hosp. Ctr., N.Y.C., 1967-73, chmn. cancer com., 1968-73, attending surgeon, dir. surgery, 1974—; adj. attending surgeon Bklyn. Jewish Hosp., 1970-74, Meml. Sloan Kettering Hosp., 1981—; assoc. attending surgeon Presbyn. Hosp., N.Y.C., 1974—; attending surgeons Columbia Presbyn., 1998; chmn. eastern region Black Leadership Initiative on Cancer, NY State Commn. for Healthy NY. Contbr. articles to profl. jours.; presentations in field. Nat. pres. Am. Cancer Soc., 1988-89, chmn. nat. adv. com. on cancer in the socio-economically disadvantaged, 1987-88, chmn. med. and sci. exec. com., 1986-87, chmn. med. and sci. com., 1985-86, chmn. nat. adv. com. on cancer in minorities, 1984-87, pres. Harlem unit, 1983-88, med. dir.-at-large bd. dirs. 1977—, bd. dirs. N.Y.C. div., 1977—; mem. Columbia U. Comprehensive Cancer Ctr., 1987—; bd. trustees Howard U., 1994—; chmn. Pres. Cancer Panel, 1991—. Recipient Howard U. Women's Club award, 1977, Profl. award Nat. Pres. Am. Cancer Soc., 1988-89, Disting. Lectr. award Manhattan Cen. Med. Soc., 1988, Disting. Cmty. Svc. award Mut. of Am., 1989, Susan G. Komen Breast Cancer Found. Betty Ford award, 1999, Mary Lasker Pub. Svc. award, 2000, Time, Inc. Health Lifetime Achievement award, 2000, CDC Champion of Prevention award, 2001, Jill Rose award, Breast Cancer Rsch. Found., 2002, Am. Soc. Clin. Oncology Spl. Recognition award, 2003, Susan B. Komen Breast Cancer Found. Champion of Change award, 2003, Assn. Cmty. Cancer Center's annual Achievement award, 2004, Rudin Prize award, NY Acad. Medicine, 2004; honored Susan G. Komen for the Cure Capitol Hill Champions, 2007. Fellow N.Y. Acad. Medicine, Am. Surgical Assn.; mem. ACS (exec. com. 1989—, gov. 1988—, com. on cancer, 1981—, sr. mem. commn. on cancer 1987—, chmn. pres. cancer panel 1991—, Medal of Honor), NIH (breast cancer task force 1979-84), Nat. Cancer Inst. (subcom. on cancer detection rsch. and applications 1987 -90), Soc. Surg. Oncology (exec. coun. 1987—), Nat. Med. Assn. (chmn. surg. sect. 1984-86), Inst. Medicine Nat. Acad. Sci. (elected 1997), Internat. Soc. Surgeons, N.Y. Acad. Scis., Am. Surg. Assn., Inst. of Medicine Nat. Acad. of Sci., County Med. Soc. N.Y., Alpha Omega Alpha, Nat. Am. Calif. Soc.(bd. dirs., 1979-2009), Inst. Medicine. Office: Ralph Lauren Ctr for Cancer Care & Prevention 1919 Madison Ave New York NY 10035

FREEMAN, JOHN MARK, pediatric neurologist; b. Bklyn., Jan. 11, 1933; s. Leon Lucas and Florence (Kann) F.; m. Elaine Kaplan, Aug. 26, 1956; children: Andrew David, Jennifer Beth, Joshua Leon. BA, Amherst Coll., 1954; MD, Johns Hopkins U., 1958. Internship Harriet Lane Home, Johns Hopkins U., Balt., 1958-59, residency in pediat., 1959-61; fellow in neurology Columbia Presbyn. Hosp., NYC, 1961-64; rsch. physician Walter Reed Army Inst. Rsch., Washington, 1964—66; asst. prof. pediat. and neurology Stanford U., Calif., 1966-69; assoc. prof. neurology and pediat. Johns Hopkins U., 1969-82, prof. neurology and pediat., 1982—, Lederer prof. pediatric epilepsy, 1991—2003, dir. pediatric neurology, 1969-90, dir. pediatric epilepsy ctr., 1973—2002, dir. birth defects treatment center, 1969-90; active staff Johns Hopkins Hosp. Pres. Epilepsy Assn. Md., 1977-82; mem. profl. adv. bd. Epilepsy Found. Am., 1975-82, sec., 1977, v.p., 1982—, hon. life dir., 1991—. Author: The Practical Management of Meningomyelocele, 1974, editor: Prenatal and Perinatal Factors Associated with Brain Disorders, 1985; co-author: Tough Decisions: A Casebook in Medical Ethics, 1987, 2nd edit., 2000, The Epilepsy Diet Treatment: An Introduction to the Ketogenic Diet, 1994, 3rd. edit, 2000, Seizures and Epilepsy in Childhood: A Guide for Parents, 1990 (Nat. Book award, 1991), 3rd edit., 2002; contbr. articles to profl. jours. Served with AUS, 1964-66. Recipient Lucy Moses prize, Columbia Presbyn. Med. Ctr., 1966, Frank Ford Tchg. award, Johns Hopkins U., 1983, Disting. Alumni award, 2007, Cmty. Leadership award, Epilepsy Assn. Md., 1991, Spl. Friend award, Upton Sch., Balt. City Sch. Sys., 1992; named Physician of Yr., Gov.'s Com. on Employment Handicapped, 1979, Health Care Profl. of Yr., Gov.'s Com. on Employment of Persons with Disabilities, 1990. Fellow: Am. Acad. Pediats. (chmn. neurology sect. 1978—80), Am. Acad. Neurology; mem.: Am. Neurol. Assn., Am. Epilepsy Soc. (Lennox award 1993, Penry award 2001), Am. Fedn. Clin. Rsch., Am. Pediat. Soc., Child Neurology Soc. (exec. com. 1979—81, Hower award 2004), Profs. of Child Neurology (pres. 1980—82). Home: 1026 Rolandvue Rd Baltimore MD 21204-6815 Home Phone: 410-825-1767. Business E-Mail: jfreeman@jhmi.edu.

FREEMAN, KENNETH W., dean, retired health facility administrator; b. 1950; m. Janice W. Freeman. BS, Bucknell U., 1972; MBA, Harvard U., 1976. Various positions Corning Inc., Corning, NY, 1972—95, v.p., corp. controller, 1985—87, named sr. v.p., 1987, gen. mgr. sci. products divsn., 1989—90, pres., CEO Corning Asahi Video Products Co., 1990—93, exec. v.p., 1993—95, pres., CEO Corning Clin. Labs., 1995—97; chmn., CEO Quest Diagnostics, Inc. (formerly Corning Clin. Labs.), Teterboro, NJ, 1997—2004, Massonite Internat., 2005—07, chmn., 2007—09; mng. dir. Kohlberg Kravis & Co., L.P., NYC, 2005—10, gen. ptnr., 2007—10, sr. adv., 2010—; gen. ptnr. KKR & Co. L.L.P., NYC, 2009—10, mem. KKR Mgmt. LLC, 2009—10; dean, Allen Questrom prof. Boston U. Sch. Mgmt., 2010—; chmn. Masonite, Inc., Mississauga, Canada, 2009—10; exec. chmn. Accellent, Inc., Wilmington, Mass., 2007—. Bd. dirs. Quest Diagnostics, Inc., 1995—2004, Accellent, Inc., 2005—, Masonite Inc., 2009—, HCA, Inc., 2009—. Chmn. bd. trustees Bucknell U. Office: Boston University School of Management 595 Commonwealth Ave Boston MA 02215 Office Phone: 617-353-9720.

FREEMAN, LAURA GOMEZ, ophthalmologist; b. Cali, Sept. 21, 1968; MD, Rosario U., 1989. Cert. ophthalmologist Barraquer Inst. America, 1994. Cornea and refractive surgeon Codet Aris Vision Inst., Tijuana, Mexico, 1998—2002; ophthalmologist anterior segment ISEU AC Inst., Tijuana, 2002—; rschr. masters of advanced studies clin. rsch. U. Calif. San Diego, 2003—05, ophthalmic specialist JRC, 2008—. Fellow Castroviejo Ophthalmic Rsch. Ctr., Complutense U., Madrid, 1995—96; fellow cornea and refractive surgery Moorfields Eye Hosp., London, 1996—97; pres. MLG Consulting, 2007—; mem. internat. bd. La Salle U. Mem.: Am. Soc. Optometry and Ophthalmology, Internat. Soc. Refractive Surgery, Am. Soc. Cataract and Refractive Surgery, Assn. Rsch. in Vision and Ophthalmology, Am. Acad. Ophthalmology. Avocations: ballet, languages, yoga. Home: 4752 Vista De La Tierra Del Mar CA 92014 Personal E-mail: laurafreemanmd@gmail.com.

FREEMAN, LEONARD MURRAY, radiologist, nuclear medicine physician, educator; b. NYC, Apr. 20, 1937; s. Joseph and Tillie (Krutman) F.; m. Marlene Carolyn Held, Apr. 28, 1967; children: Eric Lawrence, David Robert, Joy Esther. BA, N.Y. U., 1957; MD, Chgo. Med. Sch., 1961. Diplomate: Am. Bd. Radiology, Am. Bd. Nuclear Medicine. Intern Beth Israel Hosp. and Med. Center, NYC, 1961-62; resident in radiology Bronx Municipal Hosp. Center, 1962-65; mem. staff Albert Einstein Coll. Medicine, NYC, 1965—; co-dir. div. nuclear medicine Jacobi Med. Ctr., NYC, 1965-83; dir. nuclear medicine Montefiore Med. Center, NYC, 1976—, attending radiologist, 1977—; cons. nuclear medicine USPHS Hosp., SI, NY, 1967-82, St. Barnabas Hosp., Bronx, 1967—, Beth Israel Hosp. and Med. Center, 1974—, Maimonides Hosp. and Med. Center, 1974-99, Bklyn. VA Hosp., 1984—2001; asst. instr. radiology Albert Einstein Coll. Medicine, Bronx, 1964-65, instr., 1965-67, asst. prof., 1967-72, assoc. prof., 1972-77, prof., 1977—, prof. nuclear medicine, 1983—, vice chmn. dept. nuclear medicine, 1987—. Mem. adv. com. nuclear medicine program Brookhaven Nat. Labs., Upton, NY, 1972-82; examiner nuclear medicine Am. Bd. Radiology; spkr. in field. Author: Clinical Scintillation Scanning, 1969, Clinical Scintillation Imaging, 1975, Freeman and Johnson's Clinical Radionuclide Imaging, 1984; co-editor Seminars in Nuclear Medicine, 1970—, Physicians Desk Reference for Radiology and Nuclear Medicine, 1971-80, Clinical Nuclear Medicine, 2007; reviewer Jour. Nuclear Medicine, 1972—; editor Nuclear Medicine Ann., 1980-2004, Current Concepts in Diagnostic Nuclear Medicine, 1983-87, Advances in Functional Neuroimaging, 1988-90; mem. editl. bd. European Jour. Nuclear Medicine, 1979—, Jour. Nuclear Medicine and Allied Scis., 1982-96, Nuclear Medicine Communications, 1986-2002, Quar. Jour. Nuclear Medicine, 1996—; contbr. over 30 chapters to books, and over 140 articles to profl. jours. Recipient Disting. Educator award, Soc. Nuclear Medicine, 1993, Berson-Yalow award, Greater NY Chpt., Soc. Nuclear Medicine, 1997, Disting. Alumnus award, Chgo. Med. Sch., 1978; named one of Best Doctors in Am., 1992—, Top Doctors in NY Metro Area, 1999—, Best Doctors in NY, NY Mag., 1998, 2001—03, 2007—09. Fellow Am. Coll. Radiology, Am. Coll. Nuclear Physicians, NY Acad. Medicine (chmn. sect. nuc. medicine 2000-02); mem. Soc. Nuclear Medicine (gov. local chpt. 1973—, nat. trustee 1973-77, nat. v.p. 1977-78, nat. pres. 1979-80, chmn. pub. rels. com. 1981-91, chmn. correlative imaging coun. 1982-84, chmn. awards com. 1983-86, Disting. Edn. award 1993, Berson-Yallow award Greater NY chpt. 1997), Radiol. Soc. N.Am., Soc. Gastrointestinal Radiologists, NY State Med. Soc., New York County Med. Soc., Pan Am. Med. Assn. (hon. life), European Assn. Nuclear Medicine, LI Soc. Nuclear Med. Technologists (hon. life), Alpha Omega Alpha (hon.). Avocations: travel, golf, theater. Home: 50 Sutton Pl S New York NY 10022-4167 Office: 111 E 210th St Bronx NY 10467-2401 Home Phone: 212-688-9395; Office Phone: 718-920-6060. Business E-Mail: lfreeman@montefiore.org.

FREEMAN, LYNETTA J., medical educator; b. Tex., Jan. 6, 1955; DVM, Okla. State U., 1981; MS, Wash. State U., 1986. Assoc. prof. Purdue U., 2006—. Office: 625 Harrison St West Lafayette IN 47907 Business E-Mail: ljfreema@purdue.edu.

FREEMAN, MICHAEL JEARLAN, nuclear medicine supervisor; b. Fort Sill, Okla., May 8, 1956; s. Jerry (Jearlan) and Alta Joyce Freeman; m. Suzanne Elizabeth Steele, Mar. 20, 1976; children: Amy Elizabeth, Sarah Michele. AA, Univ. Ctrl. Ark., Conway, Ark., 1980. Cert. ARRT, NMTCB, ASCP, LTL, RTL. Tech. RT UAMS Ark. Child Hosp., Ark., 1979—84; sr. tech. UAMS, Ark., 1982—84; nuc. med. supr. St. Joseph's Mercy Med. Ctr., Hot Springs, Ark., 1984—. Cons. in field. Co-author: (manual) Nuclear Medicine Laboratory Technology, 1979. Mem.: Ark. Soc. Nuc. Cardiology, Am. Soc. Clin. Pathology, Nuc. Med. Tech. Cert. Bd., Am. Registry Radiologic Tech., Ark. Soc. Radiological Tech., Ark. Soc. Nuc. Tech., Soc. Nuclear Medicine Tech., Young Rep., Elks Club. Meth. Avocations: fishing, hunting, guitar, camping, travel. Home: 102 Meadow Hill Pl Hot Springs AR 71913 Office: St J MMC 300 Werner St Hot Springs AR 71901 Office Phone: 501-622-1940.

FREEMAN, PHILLIP, psychiatrist; b. Norfolk, Va., Jan. 16, 1954; BA, Princeton U., 1975; MS, U. Calif., Berkeley, 1977; DMH, U. Calif., San Francisco, 1980; MD, Columbia U., 1984. Lic. Mass., 1985, diplomate Am. Bd. Psychiatry, 1989, cert. Am. Psychoanalytic Assn., 1996. Intern St. Vincents Hosp., NYC, 1984-85; resident, clin. fellow psychiatry McLean Hosp., Harvard U. Dept. Psychiatry, Belmont, Mass., 1985-88; pvt. practice in psychiatry and psychoanalysis Mass., 1986—; clin. instr. psychiatry Harvard Med. Sch., Boston, 1988—; asst. prof. psychiatry Boston U. Med. Sch., 1988—, assoc. dir. med. student program in psychiatry, 1988—98, assoc. vice chmn. edn. and tng., dept. psychiatry, 1998—2000; clin. instr. Boston Psychoanalytic Soc. & Inst., 1988—, tng. and supervising psychoanalyst, 2001—. Asst. attending psychiatrist McLean Hosp., Belmont, 1988 ; asst. vis. physician Univ. Hosp., Boston, 1988—; theater and film cons. Am. Repertory Theater, Am. Repertory Theater Inst., Actors' Shakespeare Project, Mud/Bone Co. Contbr. articles to profl. jours. including Jour. Nervous and Mental Disease, Psychiat. Annals; script cons.: (films) Almost You. Recipient Jacob O. Swartz Tchg. award, Boston U. Sch. Medicine, 1991, 2001. Mem. Am. Psychoanalytic Assn., Am. Psychiat. Assn. (Nancy C.A. Roeske, M.D. Cert. Recognition), Mass. Psychiat. Assn., Boston Psychoanalytic Assn. Office Phone: 617-978-0287. Business E-Mail: psfreeman@comcast.net.

FREEMAN, THEODORE MONROE, physician; b. Orlando, Fla., Jan. 3, 1955; s. Fred Monroe and Mary Ann (Ridgeway) F.; m. Karen Bonaccorso, Aug. 11, 1978; children: Kathryn Maria, Michelle Terese, Jeannine Nicole, Jason Monroe. BS in Chemistry, Duke U., 1977; MD, U. So. Fla., 1980. Diplomate Am. Bd. Internal Medicine, Am. Bd. Allergy and Immunology. Intern Jacksonville (Fla.) U. Hosp., 1980-81; commd. capt. USAF, 1981, advanced through grades to col., resident internal medicine Keesler AFB Biloxi, Miss., 1981-83, staff physician Dyess AFB Abilene, Tex., 1983-84, fellow allergy and immunology Wilford Hall Med. Ctr., Lackland AFB San Antonio, 1984-86, fellow diagnostic lab. immunology Mass. Gen. Hosp. Boston, 1986-87, staff allergist and immunology Wilford Hall Med. Ctr., 1987-89, chmn. dept. allergy and immunology, program dir., 1989—2001. Med. dir. transplants Wilford Hall Med. Ctr., 1989-2002. Contbr. articles to profl. jours. Fellow ACP, Am. Coll. Allergy and Immunology, Am. Acad. Allergy and Immunology; mem. AMA, Soc. Air Force Physicians. Roman Catholic. Office Phone: 210-614-3923. Personal E-mail: tfree95900@aol.com. Business E-Mail: docfreeman@sanantonioallergydoc.com.

FREIRE, MARIA C., medical association administrator; b. Lima, Peru; PhD in biophysics, U. Va. Founder, dir. Office of Tech. Devel. U. Md., Balt.; dir. Office of Tech. Transfer NIH, 1995—2001; CEO Global Alliance for TB Drug Devel. (TB Alliance), NYC, 2001—08; pres. Albert and Mary Lasker Found., NYC, 2008—. Recipient Sec.'s award for Disting. Svc., DHHS, Arthur S. Flemming award, 1999, Bayh-Dole award, 2002; fellow Fulbright Found.; US Congl. Sci. fellow. Mem.: Inst. Medicine. Office: Albert and Mary Lasker Found Ste 1300 110 E 42nd St New York NY 10017 Office Phone: 212-286-0222. E-mail: mfreire@laskerfoundation.org.

FREIRE, SONIA MARIA DE FARIAS, medical educator, researcher; b. Ouricuri, Brazil, Sept. 29, 1944; D, U. Fed. Maranhão, 2010. Cert. physician Faculdade Medicina, UFPe, 1969. Dept. head U. Fed. Maranhão, 2008—10. Adj. prof. U. Fed. Maranhão, 2001—11. Home: Rua das Figueiras Q 6 N 1 São Luis Maranhão 65076-150 Brazil Personal E-mail: soniafreire@ufma.br.

FREIREICH, EMIL J, hematologist, educator; b. Chgo., Mar. 16, 1927; s. David and Mary (Klein) F.; m. Haroldine Lee Cunningham, Mar. 13, 1953; children: Debra Ann, David Alan, Lindsay Gail, Thomas Jon. BS, U. Ill., 1947, MD with honors, 1949, D.Sc. (hon.), 1982. Diplomate Am. Bd. Internal Medicine. Intern Cook County (Ill.) Hosp., Chgo., 1949-50; resident in internal medicine Presbyn. Hosp., Chgo., 1950-53; rsch. assoc. in hematology Mass. Meml. Hosp., Boston, 1953-55; sr. investigator, head Leukemia Svc. USPHS, Nat. Cancer Inst., Bethesda, Md., 1955-65; prof. medicine U. Tex. System Cancer Ctr., Houston, 1965—, chief rsch. in hematology, 1965-85, head dept. devel. therapeutics, 1972-83, chmn. dept. hematology, 1983-85, dir. Adult Leukemia Rsch. Program, 1985—; prof. medicine U. Tex. Health Sci. Ctr. (Sch. Medicine), 1973—, chief divsn. oncology, 1973-81; mem. faculty Grad. Sch. Med., Health Scis. Ctr., 1965—, dir. Spl. Medical Edn. Programs, 2000—. Mem. rev. com. drug. devel. div. cancer treatment Nat. Carsin Inst., 1975-80; Ruth Harriet Ainsworth chair in devel. therapeutics, 1980—; spl. asst. dir. Nat. Cancer Inst., 1990-91. Assoc. editor Cancer, 1976—, Cancer Research, 1977-86; mem. editorial bd. Oncology News, 1975-90, Cancer Treatment Reports, 1976-80, Leukemia Research, 1976-87, Med. and Pediatric Oncology, 1974—, Leukemia 1987—; contbr. numerous articles on research in hematology and oncology to profl. jours. Recipient Albert Lasker Med. rsch. award, 1972, Charles F. Kettering prize Gen. Motors Cancer Rsch. Found., 1983, Outstanding Investigator award Nat. Cancer Inst., NIH, 1985-92, Alumnus award NIH, 1990; named Alumnus of Yr., U. Ill. Alumni Assn., 1974, Alumni Achievement award, 2000, Pollin prize Columbia U., 2003. Fellow ACP, AAAS; mem. Internat. Soc. Hematology, Am. Soc. Hematology, Am. Fedn. Clin. Research, Am. Soc. Clin. Pharmacology and Therapeutics, Am. Soc. Clin. Oncology (David A. Karnofsky award 1976, pres. 1980-81), Am. Soc. Clin. Investigators, Am. Assn. Cancer Research, Leukemia Soc. Am. (pres. Gulf Coast chpt. 1968-70, trustee 1968-70, Robert Roesler DeVilliers award 1979, grant rev. subcom. 1986-89), Tex. Med. Assn., AMA (editorial bd. jour. 1973-83), Assn. Am. Physicians, Alpha Omega Alpha. Achievements include research in therapy of human acute leukemia and leukocyte physiology. Co-developer of combination chemotherapy and the cureative therapy for childhood acute lymphoblastic leukemia. Developed the first successful platelet replacement therapy. Inventor of continuous-flow cell separator. Home: 810 Monte Cello St Houston TX 77024-4515 Office: M D Anderson Cancer Ctr 1515 Holcombe Blvd Houston TX 77030-4009 Home Phone: 713-468-3728; Office Phone: 713-792-2660. Business E-Mail: efreirei@mdanderson.org.

FREITAG, FREDERICK GERALD, osteopathic physician; b. Milw., Feb. 12, 1952; s. Frederick August and Shirley June (Siewert) F.; m. Lynn Nadene Stegner, Sept. 10, 1977; children: Crescentia Adella, Abigail Amadea, Genevieve Angelica. BS in Biochemistry, U. Wis., 1974; DO, Chgo. Coll. Osteo. Medicine, 1979. Cert. in headache mgmt., specialities cert. in headache medicine United Coun. for Neurologic. Intern Brentwood Hosp., Warrensville Heights, Ohio, 1979-80, resident in family practice, 1980-81, certified headache medicine, 2007—; dir., physician Twinsburg (Ohio) Family Clinic, 1981-83; assoc. prof. family medicine Coll. Osteo. Medicine, Ohio U., Warrensville Heights, 1982-83; staff Diamond Headache Clinic, Chgo., 1983-86, assoc. dir., 1986—2008, co-dir., 2008—10; attending staff mem. Louis A. Weiss Meml. Hosp., Chgo., 1983-93; attending staff Columbus Hosp., 1993—2000, St. Joseph's Hosp., 2000—10; clin. assoc. prof. family medicine Chgo. Med. Sch. Rosalind Franklin U. Health and Sci., 1999—2007; clin. asst. prof. family medicine Clin. Model Sch. Rosaland Franklin U. Medicine Scis., 2007—; med. dir. Comprehensive Headache Ctr., Baylor U. Med. Ctr., Dallas, 2010—; dir., headache medicine rsch. Baylor Rsch. Inst., Dallas, 2010—; attending staff, neurology, family medicine Baylor U. Med. Ctr., Dallas, 2010—. Clin. assoc. family medicine Midwestern U./Chgo. Coll. Osteo. Medicine, 1999-2010; vis. lectr. dept. family medicine Chgo. Coll. Osteo. Medicine, 1984-99; clin. assoc. dept. medicine Pritzker Sch. Medicine U. Chgo., 1989-93; mem. editl. bd. Headache Quar., 1991-2003; chmn. instnl. rev. bd. Louis A. Weiss Meml. Hosp., 1991-93; mem. migraine adv. coun. Abbott, 1995-2003, mem. primary care adv. coun., 1997—2008; mem. adv. group Glaxo Wellcome, 1996-2005; mem. migraine adv. coun. Zeneca, 1996—2008; mem. U.S Headache Consortium guidelines project; bd. dirs. Nat. Bd. for Cert. in Headache Mgmt., 2000—, sec.-treas., 2000-2002, v.p., 2002—; mem. Allergan Botox Internat. Adv. Com., 2002-09; co-chair Primary Care Migraine Partnership, 2002—07; mem. Ortho-McNeil headache specialists adv. bd., 2003-08. Coord. editor Headache Quar.; mem. editl. bd. Headache and Pain, 2003-08; contbr. articles to profl. jours., chpts. to books. Bd. dirs. Nat. Headache Found.; v.p. bd. dir. Nat. Headache Found., 2010-; liaison stds. care com. to Am. Acad. Neurology; mem. pres. adv. bd. Concordia U., Chgo., 2006-10. Fellow Am. Assn. for Study of Headache; mem. AMA, Am. Coll. Gen. Practioners in Osteo. Medicine, Am. Osteo. Assn. (chair headache coun. 2000—), Am. Soc. Clin. Pharmacology and Therapeutics (vice chmn. headache sect. 1995-96), Ill. Assn. Osteo. Physicians and Surgeons, Am. Headache Soc. (chair primary care spl. interest sect. 1999-2004, mem. ethics com. 2002-04, mem. edn. com. 2002-04, co-chair practice com. 2006—08), Nat. Headache Found., German Wine Soc. (past pres. Chgo. chpt.), U. Wis. Alumni Assn., Tex. Med. Soc., Dallas Med. Soc., Tex. Asteopathic Med. Assn. Lutheran. Avocations: german oenophile, gardening, model railroading, home carpentry. Home: 931 Clinton Pl River Forest IL 60305-1503 Office: Baylor Headache Ctr Ste 400 9101 N Central Expy Dallas TX 75231 Home Phone: 708-771-3214; Office Phone: 214-820-9272. Personal E-mail: dhcdoc@gmail.com.

FREITAS JUNIOR, AMILCAR CHAGAS, dentist; b. Ceara, Fortaleza, Aug. 10, 1981; DDS, Fed. U. Ceara, 2004; PhD, Sao Paulo State U., 2011. Rsch. scientist NY U. Coll. Dentistry, 2010—. Mem.: Grupo Brasileiro Materiais Dentarios, Soc. Brasileira Pesquisa Odontologica, Acad. Osseointegration, Internat. Assn. Dental Rsch. Office: José Bonfácio 1193 Aracatuba Sao Paulo 16015-050 Brazil

FRELICK, ROBERT WESTSCOTT, physician, consultant; b. Potsdam, NY, Feb. 27, 1920; s. H. Victor and Ruth (Scott) F.; m. Jane Hayden, Jan. 22, 1944; children: Susan, Alcy, Sally, William, Scott. AB, Union Coll., Schenectady, NY, 1941; MD, Yale U., New Haven, Conn., 1944. Diplomate Am. Bd. Internal Medicine, Am. Bd. Medical Onocology, Am. Bd. Nuc. Medicine. Intern New Haven Hosp., 1944—45; resident Meml. Hosp., Wilmington, Del., 1947—49, Meml. Hosp. Ctr., NYC, 1949—50; pvt. practice Wilmington, 1950—82; program dir. Nat. Cancer Inst., Bethesda, Md., 1982—87; cons. Del. Divsn. Pub. Health, Wilmington, 1987—96; med. dir. South Jersey Cancer Ctr., 1995—97, cons., 1998—. Chief medicine Wilmington Med. Ctr., Del., 1965-72. Contbr. to profl. jours. Bd. CARE coun. bd. alumni, NYC then Atlanta, 1980-97; pres. Assn. Cmty. Cancer Ctrs., Rockville, Md., 1979-80. Capt. (Med. Svc. Corps.) US Army, 1944-47. Recipient Disting. Svc. award Del. Med. Soc., 1977, Outstanding Svc. to Cmty. award Assn. Cmty. Cancer Ctrs., 1987, St. George's medal Am. Cancer Soc., 1990. Fellow ACP (laureate, gov.); mem. AMA, APHA, ACS (surveyor hosp. cancer programs 1988-97), Med. Soc. Del. (chair com. ethics, pres. 1980-81), Soc. Surg. Oncology, Am. Soc. Internal Medicine, Am. Soc. Clin. Oncology, Am. Sch. Health Assns. Home: 1018 Overbrook Rd Wilmington DE 19807-2236 Personal E-mail: rfrelick@comcast.net.

FRENCH, DOUGLAS DEWITT, medical facility administrator; b. Augusta, Ga., Jan. 14, 1954; married. BS, Trevecca Nazarene Coll., 1976; M Health Adminstrn., Xavier U., 1979. Adminstrv. resident St. Thomas Hosp., Nashville, 1978-79, dir. ambulatory svcs. and planning, 1979, dir. mgmt. svcs., 1980, adminstrv. asst., 1980-82, asst. adminstr., 1982-85, v.p., 1985-86; exec. v.p., COO St. Mary's Med. Ctr., Evansville, Ind., 1986-89, pres., CEO, 1979-94; CEO St. Vincent's Hosp., Indpls., 1994; pres., CEO Ctrl. Ind. Health Sys., 1998; exec. v.p., COO Daughters of Charity Nat. Health Sys., 1998—99; COO Ascension Health, 1999—2001, pres., CEO, 2000—04; mng. dir. Sante Health Ventures, 2007—. Bd.dirs. Herman Miller, Inc., 2002—. Fellow: Am. Coll. Health Care Execs. Office: Sante Health Ventures Frost Bank Tower Ste 2950 401 Congress Ave Austin TX 78701 Office Phone: 512-721-1200. Business E-Mail: Douglas_French@hermanmiller.com.

FRENCH, ELIZABETH IRENE, retired biology professor, musician, violin teacher; b. Knoxville, Tenn., Sept. 20, 1938; d. Junius Butler and Irene Rankin (Johnston) F. MusB, U. Tenn., 1959, MS, 1962; PhD, U. Miss., 1973. Tchr. music Kingsport (Tenn.) Symphony Assn., 1962-64, Birmingham (Ala.) Schs., 1964-66; NASA trainee in biology U. Miss., Oxford, 1969-73; asst. prof. Mobile (Ala.) Coll. (name now U. Mobile), 1973-83, assoc. prof., 1983-94, prof., 1994—2008. Orch. contractor Am. Fedn. Musicians, 1983—; 1st violin Kingsport Symphony Orch., 1962-64, Birmingham Symphony Orch., 1964-66, Knoxville Symphony Orch., 1955-62, 66-68, Memphis Symphony Orch., 1970-73, Mobile Symphony Orch., 1974—, Pensacola Symphony Orch., Gulf Coast Symphony Orch., Mobile Symphony Players Com., 2001—; concertmaster Riviera Symphony Orch. and Chorus, Ala., 2005—. Violin recitalist Ala. Artists Series, 1978-81, Fairhope (Ala.) Concert Series, 1998. Mem. project Choctaw Nat. Wildlife Refuge, 1997-98. Named Career Woman of Yr., Gayfer's, Inc., 1985. Mem. Assn. Southeastern Biologists, Human Anatomy and Physiology Soc. (nat. com. to construct standardized test on anatomy and physiology), Wilderness Soc., Ala. Acad. Scis. (presenter 1996), Ala. Ornithol. Soc., Mobile Bay Audubon Soc. (bd. dirs. 1997—), Costal Birding Assn., Am. Fedn. Musicians, Ala. Fedn. Music Clubs (chmn. composition contest 1986-90, historian 1991-94), Schumann Music Club (pres. 1977-79, 85-87, 94-97, 2000-03, 2008-11, adv. bd. 2005—). Republican. Roman Catholic. Avocations: camping, photography, birdwatching. Home: 6609 Hounds Run S Mobile AL 36608-5419

FRENCH, JAMES, pediatrician; b. Petersburg, Va., Dec. 2, 1959; BS, Randolph-Macon Coll., 1982; MD, Med. Coll. Va., 1990. Pediatric, hematologist, oncologist Dayton Childrens Med. Ctr., 2000—. Med. dir. West Ctrl. Ohio Hemophilia Ctr., 2000—11. Mem.: COG, ISTH, HTRS, ASH. Office: 1 Childrens Plz Dept Hematology Oncology Dayton OH 45404 Business E-Mail: frenchj@childrensdayton.org.

FRENCH, LARS E., dermatologist, educator; b. Geneva, Mar. 8, 1963; s. Bernard and Rita French; life ptnr. Katrin Kerl; children: Sophie Kerl, Ines, Lorenzo Bullani, Oliviero Bullani. Internat. Baccalaureat, Geneva Internat. Sch., 1981; MD, Geneva U., 1988. Resident Geneva U. Hosp., 1988—96, asst. prof., 1996—2003, Louis Jeantet prof. medicine, 2003—06; rsch. fellow Geneva U. Med. Ctr., 1990—93; vis. prof. U. Pa., Phila., 1999—2000; prof., dept. dermatology Zurich U. Hosp., Switzerland, 2006—, chmn., dept. dermatology, 2006—. Chmn. bd., founder Apoxis SA, 2001—07. Recipient Roche prize Dermatol. Rsch., 1995, Claude Perrier prize, Found. Promotion l'Enseignement Recherche Pharmacotherapie, 1998, Leenaards Found. prize, 1999, Pfizer prize Clin. Rsch. Immunology, Rheumatology, 2000. Mem.: Apotech SA (bd. mem. 1999—), European Soc. Dermatol. Rsch., European Dermatology Forum. Office: Zurich Univ Hosp Derm Dept Gloriastrasse 31 8006 Zurich Switzerland Business E-Mail: lars.french@usz.ch.

FRENCH, LAURENCE ARMAND, social sciences educator; b. Manchester, NH, Mar. 24, 1941; s. Gerald Everett and Juliette Teresa (Boucher) F.; m. Nancy Picthall, Feb. 13, 1971. BA cum laude, U. NH, 1968, MA, 1970, PhD, 1975; postdoctorate, SUNY, Albany, 1978; PhD, U. Nebr., 1981; MA, Western N.M. U., 1994. Diplomate Am. Bd. Forensic Medicine, Am. Bd. Forensic Examiners, Am. Bd. Psychol. Specialties in Forensic Psychology & Neuropsychology, Am. Coll. Advanced Practice Psychologists; lic. psychologist, Ariz. Instr. U. So. Maine, Portland and Gorham, 1971-72; asst. prof. Western Carolina U., Cullowhee, NC, 1972-77, U. Nebr., Lincoln, 1977-80; psychologist I NH Hosp., Concord, 1980-81; psychologist II Laconia State Sch., NH, 1981-88; sr. psychologist NH Divsn. for Children & Youth Svcs., Concord, 1988-89; prof., chair dept. social scis. Western N.Mex. U., Silver City, 1989—2003, prof. emeritus of psychology, 2003—; sr. rsch. assoc. justiceworks U. NH Inst. for Policy and Social Sci. Rsch., 2002—; prof., head dept. psychology Coll. Juvenile Justice and Psychology, Prairie View A&M U., 2003—04. Profl. adv. bd. Internat. Coll. Prescribing Psychologists; cons. NC Dept. Mental Health, 1972—77, Cherokee Indian Mental Health Program, NC, 1974—77, Nebr. Indian Commn., Lincoln, 1977—80; cons. alcohol program Lincoln Indian Ctr., 1977—80; adj. assoc. prof. U. So. Maine, 1980—84; faculty adviser Psi Chi Nat. Honor Soc. in psychology Western N.Mex. U., 1995—2003; mem. Psi Chi Rocky Mountain Regional Steering Com., 2001—02; faculty adviser Psi Chi Nat. Honor Soc. in psychology Prairie View A&M U., 2003—; vis. prof. criminal justice Grambling State U., 2006. Author: The Selective Process of Criminal Justice, 1976; author: (with Richard Crowe) Wee Wish Tree: Special Qualla Cherokee Issue, 1976; author: (with Hornbuckle) Cherokee Perspective, 1981; author: (with Letman et al.) Contemporary Issues in Corrections, 1981; author: Indians and Criminal Justice, 1982, Psychocultural Change and the American Indian, 1987, The Winds of Injustice, 1994, Counseling American Indians, 1997, The Qualla Cherokee Surviving in Two Worlds, 1998, Addictions and Native Americans, 2000, Native American Justice, 2003; author: (with Manzanarez) NAFTA & Neocolonialism, 2004; author: Legislating Indian Country. Peter Lang, 2007; spl. issue editor Quar. Jour. Ideology, Vol. II, 1987, mem. editl. bd. Jour. Police and Criminal Psychology; author: (book) An Oral History of Southern Appalachia, 2008; contbr. articles to profl. jours.; author: (book) Running the Border Gauntlet, 2010. Commr. Pilsbury Lake Village Dist., Webster, NH, 1985-90. With USMC, 1959-63, Badge of Honor, Republic of China, 1998, vis. endowned chair criminology, criminal justice, St Thomas U. Fredricton, New Brunswick, Can., 2010 Recipient Hon. medal Rep. China, 1998, Nat. Int. Drug Abuse 1st Leadership in Rsch. award, 1999, Lifetime Achievement award N.Mex. Assn. for Addiction Profls., 2004; Dissertation Yr. fellow U. NH 1971-72, Nebr. U. System grad. faculty fellow, 1978, Sr. Fulbright scholar U. Sarajero, Bosnia-Herzegovina, 2009-10. Fellow: APA, Am. Coll. Forensic Examiners (diplomate), Soc. Psychol. Study Social Issues, Prescribing Psychologists Register (diplomate); mem.: VFW (life), N.Mex. Alcohol and Drug Abuse Counselors Assn. (Educator of Yr. 1997), Am. Soc. Criminology (life), Nat. Assn. Alcohol and Drug Abuse Counselors (clin. issue com. 1996—98, nat. chmn.), Internat. Coll. Prescribing Psychologists Inc. (profl. adv. bd.), Nat. Assn. Sch. Psychologists, 3rd Marine Divsn. Assn. (life), Psi Chi (steering com. Rocky Mountain region 1999—2003, Regional Faculty Advisor award 2002—03), Phi Delta Kappa (treas. Rocky Mountain region 1990—91, pres. 1991—92). Office Phone: 603-862-1493. Personal E-mail: frogwnmu@yahoo.com. E-mail: Laurence_French@unh.edu.

FRENCH, MICHAEL FRANCIS, medical educator; b. La Crosse, Wis., July 25, 1948; s. Albert Frank Jr. and Kathryn Patricia (MacKoske) F.; m. Janet Alan Streeter Head, Nov. 26, 1991. BS in Edn., U. Wis., 1972. Cert. emergency med. technician. Tng. coord. emergency med. svcs. Wis. Dept. Health and Social Svcs., Madison, 1975-80, tng. dir. emergency med. svcs., 1980-84, chief emergency med. svcs., 1984-90; co-dir. Area Health Edn. Ctrs. office Kirksville (Mo.) Coll. Osteo. Medicine, 1990—, adj. instr. family medicine and cmty. health, 1990—. Emergency med. svcs. cons., Kirksville, 1984—; founding mem. Continuing Edn. Coordinating Bd. for Emergency Med. Svcs., Inc., Kirksville, 1992. Author: (tng. curriculum) EMS Instructor Training Course-U.S. Dept. Transportation, 1985; editor newsletter, editor-in-chief publs. Nat. Assn. Emergency Med. Technicians, 1983-91; author book chpts. V.p., pres. bd. dirs. Adair County Ret. Sr. Vol. Program, Kirksville, 1992-95; com. chair, bd. dirs. Mo. Rural Opportunities Coun., 2000—. Recipient Lunda Trauma award Am. Trauma Soc., 1982, Svc. awards Nat. Coun. State EMS Tng. Coords., 1982, 83, A. Roger Fox Founders award Nat. Assn. Emergency Med. Technicians, 1989, others. Mem. ASTM, ASCD, ASTD, APHA, Nat. Rural Health Assn. (rural health policy bd. 1998, gov. affairs com. 2000—, sec. 2005—09, trustee 2005—), Mo. Rural Health Assn. (bd. dirs. 1995-96, 99—, pres.-elect 1996-97, pres. 1997-99, exec. com. 1999-2010, v.p. 2006-2008), Mo. PEW Health Professions Partnership (chair exec. com. 1994-95), Mo. Pub. Health Assn. (awards chair 1996), Wis. Emergency Med. Tech. Assn., Am. Coll. Healthcare Execs. (assoc.), Nat. Orgn. Area Health Edn. Ctr. Program Dirs. (nominations com. 1996), Nat. Area Health Edn. Ctrs. Orgn. (pub. policy com. 2001—, chair reauthorization task force, 2006-2010), Mensa, Missouri Coalition Oral Health(bd. mem., 2006-, v.p., 2009-) Avocations: bicycling, reading, computer games. Office: KCOM AHEC Program 800 W Jefferson St Kirksville MO 63501-1443

FRENCK, ROBERT W., JR., pediatrician, educator, epidemiologist; BA magna cum laude, U. Calif., San Diego, 1977; MD, U. Tex. Med. Sch., Houston, 1981. Cert. pediatrics, infectious diseases. Intern & resident US Naval Hosp., Bethesda, Md., 1981—84; fellow U. Tex. Med. Sch., Houston, 1987—90; clinical asst. prof. pediatrics U. Calif., San Francisco, 1991—93; asst. prof. pediatrics Eastern Va. Med. Sch., 1994—96, U. Health Sciences Uniformed Svcs., 1994—97, assoc. prof. pediatrics, 1997—; dir. UCLA Ctr. for Vaccine Rsch., 2004—06, prof. pediatrics, 2004—06, Cin. Children's Hosp. Chmn. US Naval Hosp. Dept. Pediatrics, Oakland, 1992—93; head infectious diseases Naval Med. Ctr. Dept. Pediatrics, Portsmouth, 1993—96; head clinical investigations branch in Cairo Naval Med. Rsch. Unit 3, Egypt, 1996—99, head enteric disease rsch. program, 1999—2004. Recipient Delmer J. Pascoe award, US Naval Hosp., 1991, Staff Physicians Rsch. award, 1993. Mem.: Am. Acad. Pediatrics. Office: Cincinnati Children's Hospital Medical Center 3333 Burnet Ave Cincinnati OH 45229-3039 Office Phone: 513-636-4509. Office Fax: 513-636-3959. E-mail: robert.frenck@cchmc.org.

FRENK, JULIO JOSE, dean, medical educator; b. Mexico City, Mex., Dec. 20, 1953; s. Silvestre and Alicia (Mora) Frenk; m. Josefina Quezada (div. 1955); children: Esteban Frenk Quezada, Emilio Jose Frenk Quezada; m. Felicia Marie Knaul, Nov. 11, 1995; 1 child, Hannah Sofia Frenk Knaul. MD, Nat. Autonomous U. of Mexico, 1979; MPH, U. Mich., Ann Arbor, 1981, MA in Sociology, 1982, PhD in Med. Orgn. and Sociology, 1983. Asst. prof. Sch. Pub. Health U. Mich., Ann Arbor, 1982—84; founding dir. Ctr. for Pub. Health Rsch. Min. Health, Mexico, 1984—87; founding dir. gen. Nat. Inst. Pub. Health, Cuernavaca, Mexico, 1987—92; vis. prof. Ctr. for Population and Devel. Studies Harvard U., Cambridge, 1992—93; dir. Project of Health and Economy Mexican Health Found., Mexico, 1993—94; exec. v.p. Mexican Health Found., Mexico, 1995—98; exec. dir. evidence info. policy WHO, Geneva, 1998—; min. of health Govt. of Mexico, 2000—06; dean, T & G Angelopoulos prof. pub. health and internat. devel. Harvard Sch. Pub. Health, 2009—. Adj. prof. doctoral program Nat. Inst. Pub. Health, Cuernavaca, 1994—; part time adv. World Bank, Washington, 1995—96; regional editor for L.Am. and Caribbean Health Policy Jour., Leuven, Belgium, 1993—, mem., 1987—. Author 8 books, 1976, 1978, 1988, 1992, 1993, 1994; contbr. chapters to books; editor 7 books, 1985, 1990, 1991, 1995, 1997; contbr. articles to profl. jours. Mem. adv. group on reconstrn. of health svcs., Mexico City, 1985—86; mem. Adv. Scientific Coun. Sci. Mus. Nat. U. Mex., Mexico City, 1995—. Recipient Cecilio A. Robelo award for scientific rsch., State Govt. Morelos, Mex., Cuernavaca, 1993; named Nat. Rschr., Nat. Rschrs. Sys., Mex., 1984—. Mem.: APHA, Inst. Medicine NAS, Nat. Acad. Medicine. Avocations: classical music, opera, kaleidoscopes. Office: Office of Dean / Harvard School of Public Health Kresge Building, Room 1005 677 Huntington Ave Boston MA 02115 Office Phone: 617-495-2936. E-mail: jfrenk@hsph.harvard.edu. *

FRENKEL, EUGENE PHILLIP, physician; b. Detroit, Aug. 27, 1929; s. David Eugene and Eva (Antin) Frenkel; m. Rhoda Beth Smilay, Dec. 21, 1958; children: Lisa Michelle, Peter Alan. BS, Wayne State U., 1949; MD, U. Mich., 1953. Diplomate Am. Bd.

Internal Medicine (bd. govs. 1980-87, chmn. subspecialty com. hematology 1980-85), Am. Bd. Hematology, Am. Bd. Med. Oncology. Intern Wayne County Gen. Hosp., Eloise, Mich., 1953-54; resident in internal medicine Boston City Hosp., 1954-55; resident in internal medicine, then instr. U. Mich. Med. Center, 1957-62; mem. faculty U. Tex. Southwestern Med. Ctr., Dallas, 1962—, prof. internal medicine and radiology, 1969—, chief divsn. hematology-oncology, 1962-91, Patsy R. and Raymond D. Nasher Disting. chair in cancer rsch., 1990—, A. Kenneth Pye prof. in cancer rsch., 1994—; chief nuclear medicine, cons. hematology-oncology VA Med. Center, Dallas, 1962-80; Sydney and J.L. Huffines, Jr. disting. chair U. Tex. Southwestern Med. Ctr., 1998—, Elaine Dewey Sammons Disting. chair cancer rsch. in honor of Eugene P. Frenkel, MD, 2003—. Cons. com. evaluation rsch. hematology, nutrtion Nat. Inst. Arthritis and Metabolic Diseases, 1979—82; active Am. Joint Commn. Cancer, 1986—95; interim dir. divsn. hematology-oncology VA Med. Ctr., Dallas, 1995—97; dir. The Boone Pickens Fund for Cancer Rsch. and Treatment Honoring Dr. Eugene P. Frenkel, 2004—. Contbr. rsch. papers in field. Dir. The Boone Pickens Fund, 2004. Officer M.C. USAF, 1955—57. Recipient 2008, ACP, 2008. Master: ACP (coun. subspecialty secs. 1992—2006), Internat. Soc. Hematology; mem.: Internat. Assn. Study Lung Cancer, Internat. Soc. Hematology (councillor 1992—97), Am. Fedn. Clin. Rsch., Soc. Nuc. Medicine, Am. Urol. Assn., So. Soc. Clin. Investigation, Am. Soc. Clin. Investigation, Am. Soc. Biol. Chemists, Am. Assn. Cancer Edn., Am. Assn. Cancer Rsch., Assn. Am. Physicians, Am. Cancer Soc. (pres. Dallas unit 1970—71, mem. sci. adv. com. clin. investigations II-chemotherapy and hematolog 1978—82, mem. nat. clin. fellowship com. 1978—87, dir. Tex. divsn. 1978—, Emma Freeman prof. 1981—91, mem. internat. rsch. grants com. 1988—90, mem. sci. adv. coun. 1991—97), Am. Soc. Clin. Oncology (chmn. membership com. 1982—85), Am. Soc. Hematology (treas. 1976—84), Alpha Omega Alpha. Office: U Tex Southwestern Med Ctr Dallas TX 75390-8852

FRESHWATER, SHAWNA MARIE, neuropsychologist, clinical psychologist, cognitive neuroscientist; b. Roseau, Minn., Aug. 10, 1964; d. Robert D. and Andrea K. Porter; children: Michaël, David. BA (magna cum laude), U. Miami, 1995; MS in Clin. Psychology, Nova Southeastern U., Ft. Lauderdale, 1996, PhD, 2000. Lic. Psychology Fla., 2001. Behavioral medicine/health psychology trainee Behavioral Medicine Clin. Rsch. Ctr., U. Miami, 1993—95; psychology intern Cmty. Mental Health Ctr., Nova Southeastern U., Ft. Lauderdale, 1995—96, psychology intern child and adolescent traumatic stress program, 1995—96, psychology intern program for seriously emotionally disturbed, 1995—96; intern Brain Injury Rehab. Program, Ft. Lauderdale, 1996—97, Brief Psychotherapy Program, Ft. Lauderdale, 1997—98, V.A. Hosp., Miami, 1997—99, neuropsychology resident East Orange, NJ, 2000; resident Cornell Med. Ctr., NYC, 2000, N.Y. Presbyn. Hosp., NYC, 2000; dir., pres. Neuropsychological Inst., P.A., Miami, 2002—, postdoc. fellow, faculty rschr dept. neurology U. Fla., Gainesville, 2000—02, postdoc. fellow, coll. medicine Mcknight Biain Inst, 2002. Contbr. articles to jours. including Jour. Clin. Geropsychology, Clin. Neuropsychologist, Archives Clin. Neuropsychology, others. Mem.: Fla. Soc. Neurology, Internat. Neuropsychological Soc., Nat. Acad. Neuropschology, APA, Phi Theta Kappa, Phi Kappa Phi, Phi Beta Kappa. Office: Neuropsychological Inst 801 Brickell Ave Ste 900 Miami FL 33131 Office Phone: 305-371-4446, 305-350-5659. Personal E-mail: neuropsychologymiami@gmail.com.

FRESSINAUD MASDEFEIX, CATHERINE, neurologist, researcher; b. Angers, France, Dec. 16, 1959; d. Louis Marie Henry and Lucienne Simonne (Loudenot) F.-M.; 1 child, Clara. MD with distinction, U. Limoges, France, 1988; postgrad., U. Limoges, 1990; PhD in Molecular and Cellular Biology, U. Strasbourg, 1989, Habil in Rsch. in Molecular & Cell. Bio., 1993. Intern Univ. Hosp., Limoges, 1982-86; with Neurochemistry Ctr., Strasbourg, 1986-87; intern Nat. Inst. for Sci. and Med. Rsch., Strasbourg, 1987-89; asst. chief neurology dept. Univ. Hosp., Limoges, 1990-93; mem. staff neurology dept. Médecin des Hôpitaux U. Hosp., Angers, 1994—. Contbr. numerous articles on neurology and neurochemistry to Devel. Biology, Jour. Neurochemistry, Muscle and Nerve, Neurology, Jour. Cellular Physiology, Glia, others; reviewer articles internat. jours. and application grants French Assn. for Muscle Diseases. Recipient prize Ligue Francaise contre la Sclérose en Plaques, 1993; Nat. Inst. for Sci. and Med. Rsch. grantee Found. for Med. Rsch., 1990, Assn. Rsch. la Sclérose en Plaques, 1991, 93, others. Mem. French Soc. Neurology, French Neuropathology Soc., French Neurosci. Soc., European Soc. for Neurochemistry, Am. Soc. for Neurochemistry (corr.), Internat. Soc. Neurochemistry. Avocations: painting, tennis, golf, horseback riding. Office: Univ Hosp Neurology Dept 4 Rue Larrey 49933 Angers France Fax: 33-0-2-41-35-35-94. E-mail: Catherine.fressinaud@univ-angers.fr.

FRETTS, RUTH CECILIA, obstetrician, gynecologist, educator; b. Cold Lake, Alta., Can. BS, U. Ottawa, Can., 1983; MD, Queen's U., Can., 1987; MPH, Harvard Sch. Pub. Health, 1994. Bd. registration in medicine Commonwealth of Mass., 1992, specialist cert. in ob-gyn., practice medicine Corp. Profl. des Medecins du Que., 1992, diplomate Am. Bd. Ob-gyn., 1994, Am. Bd. Ob-gyn., 2003. Instr. in ob-gyn. and reproductive biology Harvard Med. Sch., 1992—97, asst. prof. ob-gyn. and reproductive biology, 1998—. Obstetrician-gynecologist Roxbury Comprehensive Cmty. Health Ctr., 1992—94, Brigham and Women's Hosp., Boston, 2001—, Harvard Vanguard Med. Assocs. Wellesley Office, 2002—, Newton Wellesley Hosp., Mass., 2003—; chairperson, Ob-Gyn. Peer Rev. Harvard Pilgrim Healthcare, 1995—2007, mem. appeals com., 1997—2003; physician, leader ob-gyn. Harvard Vanguard Med. Assocs. Wellesley Practice, 2001—10; chair Stillbirth Rev. Com. BWH, 2003—; co-chair Harvard Vanguard Ob-gyn. Rsch. Devel. Com., 2005—; reviewer Am. Jour. Ob-Gyn., Internat. Jour. Quality in Health Care, Am. Jour. Pub. Health, Jour. Am. Med. Assn. Contbr. chapters to books, articles to numerous profl. jours. Mem. Can. Med. Assn., 1985—98, Am. Coll. Ob-gyn., 1988—2008, Am. Assn. Pub. Health, 1996—97; vol. Brookline Med. Res. Corp., 2006—; med. dir. Kicks Count Adv. Bd. 1st Candle, 2009—. Recipient Aesculapian award, Queens U., 1985—87, Solomon Peer Recognition award, Harvard Vanguard Med. Assocs., 2006; NSERC grant, U. Ottawa, 1982. Fellow: Royal Coll. Physicians and Surgeons (Can.) (mem., divsn. ob-gyn. & surgery); mem.: Mass. Med. Soc. Office: Harvard Vanguard Med Assocs 230 Worcester St Wellesley MA 02481 Home: 1100 W Roxbury Pky Chestnut Hill MA 02467 Office Fax: 781-481-5548. Business E-Mail: ruth_fretts@vmed.orq, rfretts@partners.orq.

FREUDENREICH, CATHERINE H., biology professor; b. Charleston, SC, June 30, 1966; BA, Rice U., 1988; PhD, Duke U., 1994. Assoc. prof. Tufts U., 1999—. Grant, NIH, Gen. Med. Scis. Mem.: Genetics Soc. Am. Office: Dept Biology Dana 120 Sandisfield MA 01255 Business E-Mail: catherine.freudenreich@tufts.edu.

FREY, DALE FRANKLIN, financial investment company executive, manufacturing company executive; b. Lancaster, Pa., Aug. 14, 1932; s. Franklin W. and Mary A. (Strickler) F.; m. Betty Ann Heistand, Aug. 22, 1953; children— Scott, Philip, Kyle, Susan BS in Econs., Franklin and Marshall Coll., 1954; MBA, NYU, 1957. With GE, Fairfield, Conn., 1957-97, mgr. group fin. ops., 1975-77, internat. and Can. group staff exec., internat. sector, 1977-80, v.p., treas., 1980—97; chmn. bd., pres. GE Investment Corp., Stamford, Conn., 1984-97, dir., 1997. Bd. dirs. Praxair Inc., Danbury, Damon Runyon-Walter Winchell Cancer Rsch. Fund, Roadway Express, Akron, After Market Tech., Chgo., Cmty. Health Sys., Go Co-op, Maitland, Fla., Yankee Candle, South Deerfield, Mass., McLeod USA, Cedar Rapids, Iowa; mem. adv. bd. NYU Stern Sch. Trustee Franklin and Marshall Coll., chair 2004-. Capt. USAF, 1955—57. Mem.: Bent Creek Golf Club (Lititz, Pa.), Bald Peak Golf Club (Melvin Village, N.H.), Medalist Golf Club (Hobe Sound, Fla.), Old Marsh Golf Club (Palm Beach Gardens, Fla.), Aspetuck Valley Country Club (Weston, Conn.). Address: Damon Runyon Cancer Rsch Fund 675 Third Ave New York NY 10017 Office: Michael Allen Company 9 Old Kings Hwy S Darien CT 06820-4505

FREY, HOWARD, urologist; Grad. magna cum laude in Biology, Harvard Coll.; MD, Johns Hopkins U., 1977. Diplomate Am. Bd. Urology. Resident surgery Johns Hopkins Hosp., Balt., 1978—79; resident urology UCLA Med. Ctr., LA, 1979—83; dir. dept. of urology Valley Hosp., Ridgewood, NJ, chmn. urology tumor bd.; urologist Urology Group Pa, Midland Pk. Named one of Best Doctors- NY Metro Area, Castle-Connolly Guide, 1998, 1999, featured Top Doctors, Consumer's Checkbook. Fellow: ACS. Office: Urology Group Pa 4 Godwin Ave Midland Park NJ 07432 Office Phone: 201-444-7070. Office Fax: 201-444-7228.

FREY, SHARON ELIZABETH, internist, adult infectious disease physician; b. Bethlehem, Pa., Sept. 30, 1952; MD, Marshall U. Sch. Medicine, Huntington, W.Va., 1985. Cert. internal medicine, adult infectious diseases. Resident, internal medicine SUNY Upstate Med. Univ., Syracuse, 1985—88, fellow, 1988—89; fellow, infectious diseases St. Louis Univ. Hosp., Mo., 1989—90, hosp. appt. Mo.; prof. internal medicine, divsn. infectious diseases St. Louis Univ. Sch. Medicine, Mo. Prin. investigator vaccice clin. trial, evaluation vaccines to counter bioterrorism/biowarfare including smallpox vaccine trials St. Louis Univ. Sch. Medicine; clin. dir. Ctr. Vaccine Devel. Office: St Louis University Sch Medicine 1110 S Grand Blvd DRC 8 Saint Louis MO 63104 Office Phone: 314-977-6333.

FREYD, JENNIFER JOY, psychology professor; b. Providence, Oct. 16, 1957; d. Peter John and Pamela (Parker) F.; m. John Q. Johnson, June 9, 1984; children: Theodore, Philip, Alexandra. BA in Anthropology magna cum laude, U. Pa., Phila., 1979; PhD in Psychology, Stanford U., Calif., 1983. Asst. prof. psychology Cornell U., 1983-87, mem. faculty coun. reps., 1986-87; assoc. prof. psychology U. Oreg., Eugene, 1987-92, mem. exec. com. Inst. Cognitive and Decision Scis., 1991—94, prof., 1992—, mem. dean's adv. com., 1990-91, 92-93, 2009—10, mem. exec. com. Ctr. for the Study of Women in Soc., 1991-93, mem. child care com., 1987-89, 90-91, mem. instnl. rev. bd., 2002—05, dir. undergrad. studies dept. psychology, 2004—08, mem. exec. com. dept. psychology, 2006—08. Author: Betrayal Trauma: The Logic of Forgetting Childhood Abuse, 1996 (Disting. Publ. award Assn. of Women in Psychology 1997, Pierre Janet award Internat. Soc. for Study Dissociation 1997), Spanish edit., 2003; co-editor: (with A.P. De Prince) Trauma and Cognitive Science: A Meeting of Minds, Science, and Human Experience, 2001; mem. editl. bd. Jour. Exptl. Psychology: Learning, Memory, and Cognition, 1989-91, Gestalt Theory, 1985—, Jour. of Aggression, Maltreatment, and Trauma, 1997—, Jour. of Psychopathology and Behavioral Assessment, 2001-03, Jour. Psychological Trauma, 2003—, Jour. of Trauma and Dissociation, 1999-2005, assoc. editor, 2004, editor, 2005—; guest reviewer Am. Jour. Psychology, Am. Psychologist, others; contbr. over 150 articles to profl. jours. including Sci. Mag. Grad. fellowship NSF, 1979-82, Univ. fellowship Stanford U., 1982-83, Erskine fellowship, U. Canterbury, 2009, Presdl. Young Investigator award NSF, 1985-90, IBM Faculty Devel. award, 1985-87, fellowship Ctr. for Advanced Study in the Behavioral Scis., 1989-90, John Simon Meml. fellowship Guggenheim Found., 1989-90, Rsch. Scientist Devel. award NIMH, 1989-94, Pierre Janet award Internat. Soc. Study of Dissociation, 1997, 05, Psychologist-Scientist of Yr. award Lane County Psychologists Assn., 2006, Rsch. Innovation award, U. Oreg. 2009 Fellow AAAS, APA (liaison divsn. 35 to sci. directorate 1998-2000, liaison divsn. 56 to sci. dir. 2006-09, chair sci. com. trauma psychology divsn. 2006-09, Outstanding Contbns. award, 2011), Am. Psychol. Soc., Psychonomic Soc., Internat. Soc. Study Trauma & Dissociation; mem. Internat. Soc. Study of Traumatic Stress, Cannon Inst. (rsch. com. mem.), Brisbane. Office: Dept Psychology 1227 U Oreg Eugene OR 97403-1227 Office Phone: 541-346-4950. Business E-Mail: jjf@dynamic.uoregon.edu.

FREZZA, ELDO E., surgeon, educator; s. Giovanni and Rosa Frezza; m. Patrizia Costa; children: Edoardo, Gianmarco. MD, Padua U., Italy, 1989. Diplomate Am. Bd. Surgery, 2003. Asst. prof. U. Pitts., 2002—03; prof. Tex. Tech U. Health Scis. Ctr., Lubbock, Tex., 2003—, chief gen. surgery, 2003—. Recipient Neely Treadwell Cancer Investigator award, S.W. Cancer Ctr., Lubbock, Tex., 2004, Rsch. Presdl. ward, Tex. Tech U. Health Scis. Ctr., 2006; named to Guide to America's Top Surgeons, Consumer's Rsch. Coun. Am., 2006; fellow, SAGES, 2003. Mem.: AMA, ACS, Italian Bd. Surgery, Southeastern Soc. Surgery, Soc. Am. Gastrointestinal Endoscopic Surgeons, Assn. Academic Surgery, Am. Soc. Bariatric Surgery (life). Avocations: journalism, basketball. Office: Tex Tech Univ Health Sciences Ct 3601 4th St MS 8312 Lubbock TX 79430 Office Fax: 806-743-4670. Business E-Mail: eldo.frezza@ttuhsc.edu.

FREZZOTTI, RENATO, ophthalmologist; b. Imperia, Italy, Dec. 19, 1924; s. Giuseppe and Rosa (Pirani) F.; m. Angela Tabanelli, Feb. 6, 1961; children: Maria Luce, Paolo, Guido. Laureate in Medicine and Surgery, U. Perugia, 1949. Asst. and clin. oculist U. Siena, 1950-67, full prof. ophthalmology, 1967-2000, prof. emeritus, 2001—. Author: Oftalmologia Essenziale, 1982, 2d edit., 2006, Patologia, Clinica e Terapia delle Malattie dell'Orbita, 1985; contbr. 460 articles to sci. jours. Decorated grande ufficiale della Rep. Italiana; recipient Mangia d'Oro prize, Gold medal Italian Ministry Edn. and Culture, Gold medal Maestri della Oftalmologia, others. Mem. Italian Soc. Ophthalmology (pres. 1994-97), Yacht Club. Office: U Siena Viale Mazzini 37 53100 Siena Italy Home: Via Ventiquattro Maggio 23 53100 Siena SI Italy Business E-Mail: frezzotti@unisi.it.

FRIANT, SYLVIE, biologist; b. Strasbourg, Alsace, France, Mar. 2, 1970; d. Aloyse and Anne-Marie Friant; m. Fabrice Michel, Aug. 28, 1999; children: Chloé Michel, Thibault Michel. MS in Biochemistry and Molecular Biology, U. Louis Pasteur, Strasbourg, France, 1993, PhD in Cellular Biology, 1997. Postdoctoral rschr. Biozentrum of U. Basel, Switzerland, 1997—2000; head lab. Ctr. Nat. Rsch. Sci., Strasbourg, 2005—. Contbr. articles to profl. publs. Recipient ATIP in Cellular Biology, French Govt., 2005—, Bronze medal, Ctr. Nat. Rsch. Sci., 2005; grantee, Agy. Nat. Recherche, 2008; fellow, European Molecular Biology Orgn., 1998, Human Frontier Sci. Program, 1998—2000; scholar, French Govt., 1995—97; Rsch. grantee, Assn. Cancer Rsch., 2001—04, Sidaction, 2005—. Mem.: Club Exo-Endocytose (assoc.), French Soc. Molecular Biology (assoc.), French Soc. Biochemistry and Molecular Biology (assoc.). Achievements include research in initiation of Ty1 transposition; identification of the role of sphingolipids in membrane trafficking and in cellular stress response; determination of the cellular function of Epsin proteins Ent3 and Ent5 in yeast. Office: Umr7156 Cnrs-University de Stranboung 21 Rue Rene Descartes Strasbourg 67084 France Business E-Mail: s.friant@ibmc.u-strasbg.fr.

FRIAS, JAIME LUIS, retired pediatrician, clinical geneticist, educator; b. Concepcion, Chile, Mar. 20, 1933; came to U.S., 1970; s. Luis Humberto and Olga Ana (Fernandez) F.; m. Jacqueline May Steel, Apr. 8, 1961; children: Jaime Arturo, Juan Pablo, Patricio Andres, Maria Josefina. MD, U. Chile, 1959. Diplomate Am. Bd. Pediatrics, Am. Bd. Human Genetics. Intern Hospital Regional, Concepcion, 1958-59; resident in pediatrics Calvo Mackenna Hosp., Santiago, Chile, 1960-62; clin. genetics and dysmorphology fellow U. Wis., Madison, 1965-66, U. Wash., Seattle, 1966-67; asst. prof. pediatrics U. Concepcion, 1967-69, U. Fla. Coll. Medicine, Gainesville, 1970-74, assoc. prof., 1974-77, prof., 1977-86, chief divsn. genetics, 1977-86, chmn. med. sch. admissions com., 1983-86; prof., chmn. dept. pediatrics U. Nebr. Med. Ctr., 1986—91; prof. pediatrics U. South Fla. Coll. Medicine, Tampa, 1991—2004, chmn. dept. pediatrics, 1991-99, dir. Birth Defects Ctr., 1999—2004, emeritus prof., 2004—; vis. scientist Nat. Ctr. for Birth Defects and Devel. Disabilities, CDC, Atlanta, 2004—. Chmn. Com. for Protection of Human Subjects, 1975-78; chmn. Fla. Com. on Prevention Devel. Disabilities, 1979-82, chmn. infant hearing screening adv. coun., 1982-86; cons. Spanish Collaborative Project on Congenital Malformation, Madrid, 1983—. Contbr. chpts. to books, articles to profl. jours. Trustee All Children's Hosp., 1991-99, Ronald McDonald Charities Tampa Bay, 1999-2001; exec. com. Assn. Med. Sch. Pediat. Dept. Chmn., 1993-96; steering com. Nat. Folic Acid Coun., 1999-2003. Named Tchr. of Yr., U. Fla. Coll. Medicine, 1978-79, Lewis A. Barness Endowed Chair Pediatrics, 1994-99. Mem. ACP (affiliate; W.K. Kellogg fellow 1965-67), Am. Acad. Pediatrics (com. genetics 1995-2002), Am. Pediatric Soc., Am. Soc. Human Genetics, Assn. Clin. Scientists, Smoke Rise Golf and Country Club. Democrat. Roman Catholic. Office: MS E-86 1600 Clifton Rd Atlanta GA 30333 Business E-Mail: jfrias@cdc.gov.

FRIBERG, THOMAS R., ophthalmologist, educator; MS, Stanford U. Sch. of Medicine, MD, U. Minn. Med. Sch., Mpls. Minn., 1973. Diplomate Am. Bd. Ophthalmology, lic. to practice Pa., 1985. Intern Hennepin County Med. Ctr., 1974; resident Stanford Univ. Med. Ctr., Stanford, Calif., 1977; fellow Duke Univ. Sch. of Medicine, Durham, NC, 1979, Mass. Eye and Ear Infirmary, Boston, 1978; dir. med. and surg. retinal diseases; hosp. affiliations include Inst. on Aging, Univ. of Pitts. Med. Ctr. (UMPC) Presbyn., Children's Hosp. of Pitts. of UPMC, Magee-Womens Hosp. of UPMC, UPMC Mercy, UPMC St. Margaret. Prof. ophthalmology. Office: University of Pittsburgh Eye Center Mercy 1400 Locust St Ste 3103 Pittsburgh PA 15219 Office Phone: 412-647-2200.

FRICK, OSCAR LIONEL, pediatrician, educator; b. NYC, Mar. 12, 1923; s. Oscar and Elizabeth (Ringger) F.; m. Mary Hubbard, Sept. 2, 1954. AB, Cornell U., 1944, MD, 1946; M.Med. Sci., U. Pa., 1960; PhD, Stanford U., 1964. Diplomate: Am. Bd. Allergy and Immunology (chmn. 1967-72). Intern Babies Hosp., Columbia Coll. Physicians and Surgeons, NYC, 1946-47; resident Children's Hosp., Buffalo, 1950-51; pvt. practice medicine specializing in pediatrics Huntington, NY, 1951-58; fellow in allergy and immunology Royal Victoria Hosp., Montreal, Que., Canada, 1958-59; fellow in allergy U. Calif.-San Francisco, 1959-60, asst. prof. pediatrics, 1964-67, assoc. prof., 1967-72, prof., 1972—, dir. allergy tng. program, 1964—; fellow immunology Inst. d'Immunobiologie, Hosp. Broussais, Paris, 1960-62. Contbr. articles papers to profl. publs. Served with M.C., USNR, 1947-49. Mem. Am. Assn. Immunologists, Am. Acad. Pediatrics (chmn. allergy sect. 1971-72, Bret Ratner award 1982), Am. Acad. Allergy (exec. com. 1972—, pres. 1977-78), Internat. Assn. Allergology and Clin. Immunology (exec. com. 1970-73, sec. gen. 1985—), Am. Pediatric Soc. Clubs: Masons. Home: 370 Parnassus Ave San Francisco CA 94117-3609

FRICKE, REINHARD W. H. K., rheumatologist; b. Bremen, Germany, June 22, 1931; s. Herbert J W and Irmgard V Fricke; m. Waldtraut C M Fricke, May 27, 1955; children: Cornelia, Juliane, Leonhard. MD, U. Göttingen, Germany, 1957; Privatdozent, Medizinische Hochschule, Hannover, Germany, 1970, Prof., 1974, D (hon.) of Rheumatology, 2006. Rsch. fellow Mass. Gen. Hosp./Harvard Med. Sch., Boston, 1962-64; head phys. medicine U. Ulm, Germany, 1975; head dept. internal medicine Weserberglandklinik, Höxter, 1975-80; head dept. rheumatology St. Joseph Stift, Sendenhorst, 1980-96; head dept. rsch. Weserlandklinik, Bad Seebruch, 1996—. Editor (with F Hartmann): (book) Connective Tissues, 1974; editor: Zukunft der Rehabilitation in Deutschland, 1999; author, ed: book Rheumafunktions-Training, Grundkurs, 2001, editor (jour in field). Decorated Cross Honor and Ribbon Fed. Republic Germany; recipient Golden Honor Needle award, German League Against Rheumatism. Mem.: German Soc. Phys. Med. and Rehab. (pres. 1985—87), Indian Soc Physical Med and Rehab, German Soc Rheumatology, German Soc Internal Med, Polish Soc Rheumatology (hon.), Austrian Soc Physical Med and Rehab (hon.), Soc Physiotherapy (hon.), Polish Soc Balneology (hon.), Polish Soc Kryotherapy (hon.), Rotary (pres.

2005—06, gov. 2006—07). Achievements include development of cold air chamber treatment in Europe for treatment of autoimmune and rheumatic diseases and for activation and stimulation in sport. Home: Nienkamp Str 25 D-48324 Sendenhorst Germany Office: Weserland Klin Bad Seebruch Seebruch Str 33 32602 Vlotho Germany Office Fax: +49 5733925944. E-mail: Fricke-Sendenhorst@t-online.de.

FRID, ANDERS, physician; b. Hidinge, Sweden, Apr. 12, 1951; MD, Med. Sch., Gothenburg, 1977; DMS, Karolinska Inst., Stockholm, 1992. Sr. cons. U. Hosp. SUS, Malmo, Sweden, 2001—. Mem.: Am. Diabetes Assn., European Assn. Study Diabetes. Home: Cykelvagen 6 Dalby 24750 Sweden Personal E-mail: anders.frid@skane.se.

FRIDELL, JONATHAN AARON, transplant surgeon; b. Montreal, Quebec, Canada, Jan. 2, 1970; s. Joe and Betty Fridell; m. Jennifer Ellen Schwartz, Nov. 9, 1997. MDCM in Gen. Surgery, McGill U., Montreal, Quebec, Canada; MSc, McGill U., Montreal, Quebec. Lic. Am. Bd. of Surgery, 2002, Royal Coll. of Physicians and Surgeons of Can., 2000. Transplant surgeon Ind. U. Sch. of Medicine, Indpls., 2002—. Dir. of pancreas transplantation Ind. U. Sch. of Medicine, Indpls., 2003—. Office: Ind U Sch Medicine Room 4258 550 N University Blvd Indianapolis IN 46202 Office Fax: 317-278-3268. E-mail: jfridell@iupui.edu.

FRIDMAN, GERARDO ABRAHAM, pharmacist, educator; b. Corrientes, Argentina, Dec. 6, 1969; s. Julio Fridman and Beatriz Titiosky; m. Cynthia Andrea Zimerman. D in Pharmacy, U. Buenos Aires, 1993, PhD, 2008. Pharmacy sch. tchr. U. Misiones, 1993—94, U. Buenos Aires, 2001—. Cons. Regional Coll. Neutopsychopharmacology, Corrientes, 1999—; creator and mem. sci. dept. Corrientes Pharm. Assn., 1999—; mem. sci. dept. Argentinian Pharm. Assn., Buenos Aires, 2002—06; mem. Argentina Pharmacopoeia Commn., Buenos Aires, 2002—, Argentinian Bd. Pharm. Cert., Buenos Aires, 2003—; pharmacy master tchr. U. Sucre, Bolivia, 2004; sec. Corrientes Pharmacists Assn., 2007—. Editor: (book) Psychiatric Pharmacy. Pres. Corrientes Hebrew Club, 2006—08; chief, youth dept. Israeli Cultural Assn. Scholem Aleijem, Corrientes, 2006—08. Mem.: EPPN, Litoral Coll. Neuropsychopharmacology, CPNP. Office: Farmacia Corrientes Calle Santa Fe 1204 W3400CHT Corrientes Argentina Office Phone: 54 3783 462609. Office Fax: 54 3783 462609. Business E-Mail: gfridman@arnet.com.ar.

FRIED, CHARLES, law educator; b. Prague, Czechoslovakia, Apr. 15, 1935; arrived in US, 1941, naturalized, 1948; s. Anthony and Marta (Winterstein) F.; m. Anne Sumerscale, June 13, 1959; children: Gregory, Antonia. AB, Princeton U., 1956; BA, Oxford U., Eng., 1958, MA, 1961; LLB, Columbia U., 1960; LLD (hon.), New Eng. Sch. of Law, 1987, Pepperdine U., 1994, Suffolk U., 1996. Bar: DC 1961, Mass. 1966. Law clk. to Hon. John M. Harlan U.S. Supreme Ct., Washington, 1960; from asst. prof. to prof. law Harvard U., Cambridge, Mass., 1961-85, Carter prof. gen. jurisprudence, 1981-85, 89-95, Carter prof. emeritus, disting. lectr. Law Sch., 1995-99, Beneficial prof. law, 1999—; assoc. justice Supreme Jud. Ct. Mass., Boston, 1995-99; Fensterstock vis. prof. law Columbia Law Sch., 2008—09. Spl. cons. US Dept. Treasury, 1961—62; cons. White House Office Policy Devel., Washington, 1982, US Dept. Transp., Washington, 1981—82, US Dept. Justice, 1983, solicitor gen., 1985—89. Author: An Anatomy of Values, 1970, Medical Experimentation: Personal Integrity and Social Policy, 1974, Right and Wrong, 1978, Contract as Promise: A Theory of Contractual Obligation, 1981, Order and Law: Arguing the Reagan Revolution, 1991, (with David Rosenberg) Making Tort Law: What Should Be Done and Who Should Do It, 2003, Saying What The Law Is: The Constitution in The Supreme Court, 2004, Modern Liberty, 2006; co-author (with Gregery Fried) Because It Is Wrong: Torture Privacy and Presidential Power in the Age of Terror, 2010; contbr. legal and philos. jours. Guggenheim fellow, 1971—72. Fellow Am. Acad. Arts and Scis.; mem. Inst. Medicine, Am. Law Inst., Phi Beta Kappa. Office: Harvard Law Sch 333 Areeda Hall Cambridge MA 02138 Office Phone: 617-495-4636. Business E-Mail: fried@law.harvard.edu.

FRIED, GUY W., physiatrist, educator; Studied in Chemistry, Biology and Economic, Hofstra U., NYC, 1981, BA in Psychology; MD, Yale Med. Sch., 1985. Diplomate Am. Bd. Physical Medicine and Rehab., cert. pain medicine, spinal cord injury medicine, electrodiagnostic medicine. Resident Thomas Jefferson Univ. Hosp., assoc. prof. clin. and ednl. scholarship track of rehab.; staff Magee Rehab. Hosp., 1989, med. dir. spinal cord injury unit, med. dir. outpatient svcs., chief med. officer. Recipient Jefferson Rehab. Residency Attending of the Year award for tchg., Robert H. Condon Tchg. award, 2003, Gerald J. Herbison MD award for Mentorship, 2007; named one of the Top Doctors in America, 2007—08, the Best Doctors, Phila. Mag., 2011. Office: Magee Rehabilitation Hospital 1513 Race St Philadelphia PA 19102-1177 Office Phone: 215-587-3000. Office Fax: 215-568-3736.

FRIED, LINDA PHYLLIS, dean, medical educator; b. NYC, 1949; MD, Rush Med. Coll., 1979; MPH, Johns Hopkins U., Balt., 1985; BA in Polit. Sci., Colgate U. Diplomate Am. Bd. Internal Medicine. Intern Rush Presbyn. St. Luke's Med. Ctr., Chgo., 1979—80, resident in internal medicine, 1980—82; fellow in internal medicine Johns Hopkins Med. Inst., Balt., 1982—85, fellow in epidemiology, 1983—85, fellow in geriatrics, 1985—86, prof. medicine, epidemiology & health policy, dir. geriatric medicine & gerontology div., 2003—08; legis. dir. Congresswoman Connie Morella, Washington, 1987—98; staff Johns Hopkins Hosp.; dean, DeLamar prof. pub. health practice Mailman Sch. Pub. Health, Columbia U., NYC, 2008—; sr. v.p. Columbia U. Med. Ctr., 2008—; prof. epidemiology and medicine Columbia U., 2008—. Geriatrician and dir. Johns Hopkins Ctr. on Aging and Health; vice chair clin. epidemiology and health svcs. rsch. Johns Hopkins Dept. Medicine, mem. pres.'s coun.; advisor Paul Beeson Faculty Scholars in Aging Rsch., Health and Retirement Survey; staff liaison Congl. Caucus for Women's Issues, 104th Congress. Contbr. articles to profl. jours.; mem. editl. bd. Jour. Gerontology, Am. Jour. of Medicine. Pres. Women's Policy, Inc., 1999—; co-founder Experience Corps, Balt., 2002—. Recipient Archstone award, APHA, 2000, Marion Spenser Fay award for the 2000 Disting. Woman Physician/Scientist, Herbert R. DeVries Disting. Rsch. award, Coun. on Aging and Adult Devel., 2000, Merit award, Nat. Inst. Aging; named one of Md.'s Top 100 Women, (Md.) Daily Record, 2003; fellow Exec. Leadership in Acad. Medicine Program fellow; scholar Kaiser Found. scholar in gen. internal medicine. Fellow: Am. Heart Assn. (Coun. on Epidemiology and Prevention); mem.: ACP, SGIM, SER, AGS, Inst. of Medicine of NAS. Office: Mailman Sch Pub Health Dean's Office / Rosenfield Bldg 722 W 168th St, 14th Fl New York NY 10032 Office Phone: 212-305-9300. Office Fax: 212-305-9342. E-mail: lpfried@columbia.edu.

FRIEDBERG, JOSEPH STEWART, surgeon; b. Phila., May 7, 1959; s. Milton Joseph and Jane (Kauffman) F.; m. Jo Buyske, Sept. 22, 1990; children: David, Emilia. BA Sci. summa cum laude, U. Pa., Phila., 1981; MD cum laude, Harvard U., 1986. Markley scholar surg. rsch. dept. Harvard Med. Sch. Children's Hosp., Boston, 1985; Claude Welch rsch. fellow Mass. Gen. Hosp., Boston, 1989-91, surg. resident, 1986-94; cardiothoracic surg. fellow Brigham and Women's Hosp., Boston, 1994-96; cardiothoracic surgeon Hosp. of U. Pa., Phila., 1996—. Med. reviewer Mosby Books, Chgo., 1990-91. Contbr. articles to profl. jours. Achievements include 1st to demonstrate transplantability and function of human fetal intestine, 1st to demonstrate effective and selective killing of bacteria using monoclonal antibody targeted photolysis. Home: 2109 Lombard St Philadelphia PA 19146-1216 Office: Penn-Presbyterian Med Ctr Dept Thoracic Surgery 51 N 39th St Philadelphia PA 19104

FRIEDEL, ROBERT OLIVER, physician; b. Corona, NY, Aug. 4, 1936; s. August W. and Denise G. (D'Aoust) F.; m. Susanne Weber, June 30, 1961; children: Christine, Scott, Karin, Linda. BS, Duke U., 1958, MD, 1964. Diplomate: Am. Bd. Psychiatry and Neurology. Intern Duke U. Med. Ctr., Durham, NC, 1964-65, resident in psychiatry, 1967-70, asst. prof. psychiatry and pharmacology dept. psychiatry, 1970-73, assoc. prof. psychiatry and asst. prof. pharmacology, 1973-74; assoc. prof. psychiatry and pharmacology U. Wash. Sch. Medicine, Seattle, 1974-77, dir. div. psychopharmacology, 1974-77, vice chmn., dir. clin. services dept. psychiatry and behavioral scis., 1975-77; prof., chmn. dept. psychiatry Med. Coll. Va.-Va. Commonwealth U., Richmond, 1977-84; prof., chmn. dept. psychiatry, exec. dir. Mental Health Rsch. Inst. U. Mich., Ann Arbor, 1984-85; v.p. psychiat. medicine and rsch. Charter Med. Corp., Macon, Ga., 1985-90, psychiatrist in chief, 1987-90, sr. v.p. clin. svcs. and rsch., 1990, physician in chief, 1990, also bd. dirs.; prof., chmn. dept. psychiatry U. Ala., Birmingham, 1992-2001; disting. clin. prof., dept. psychiatry Va. Commonwealth U., Richmond, 2001—. Mem. sci. adv. bd. Nat. Edn. Alliance for Borderline Personality Disorder. Author: Borderline Personality Disorder Demystified, 2004, www.bpdemystified.com, 2007, (with others) Behavioral Science: A Selective View, 1972; editor (with L.R. Baxter) Current Psychiatric Diagnosis and Treatment, 1999, (with D. Evans) Current Psychiatry Reports and Current Psychosis and Therapeutic Reports; mem. editl. bd. Jour. Clin. Psychopharmacology, Hosp. and Cmty. Psychiatry, 1986-92; contbr. book chpts. and articles. Bd. dirs. Nat. Mental Health Assn., 1987-92. Served to lt. comdr. USPHS, 1965-67. Fellow Am. Psychiat. Assn. (disting. life); mem. AMA, Am. Coll. Psychiatrists, Soc. Biol. Psychiatry, Med. Soc. Va., Am. Coll. Neuropsychopharmacology (life), Alpha Omega Alpha. Home: 13722 Hickory Nut Point Midlothian VA 23112 Office Phone: 804-744-5261.

FRIEDEMANN, MIRIAM, epidemiologist, microbiologist, hygienist; b. Berlin, Jan. 1, 1962; MD in Medicine, Humboldt-U., Berlin, 1988; MD in Hygiene, Epidemiology & Pub. Health, Sechenov Inst., Moscow, 1988; PhD in Microbiology, Humboldt-U., Berlin, 1999; MS in Epidemiology and Stats., Tech. U., Berlin, 2005. De juro specialist / Facharzt Arztekammer Berlin in microbiology and epidemiology of infectious diseases 1996; approbation Berlin, 1988. With Inst. Med. Microbiology and Hygiene, 1989—95, Urban Hosp. Vivantes Clin. Ctr., Berlin, 1996—2002, Fed. Inst. Risk Assessment, 2002—. Office: Fed Inst Risk Assessment BfR Diedersdorfer Weg 1 Berlin 12277 Germany Office Phone: 493084122384. Business E-Mail: m.friedemann@bfr.bund.de.

FRIEDEN, ILONA JOSEPHINE, pediatric dermatologist; b. Oakland, Calif., Oct. 12, 1949; d. Michael and Evelyn Judith (Fargo) F.; m. Mark Andrew Jacobson, Apr. 17, 1987; children: Michael, Sarai. AB, Boston U., 1973; MD, U. Calif., San Francisco, 1977. Diplomate Am. Bd. Pediats., Am. Bd. Dermatology. Residency in pediat. U. Calif., San Francisco, residency in dermatology, asst. prof., 1990-93, assoc. prof., 1993-97, prof. clin. dermatology, dept. dermatology and pediat., 1997—; staff dermatologist Kaiser Permanent, Oakland, Calif., 1983-89. Founder, dir. U. Calif. Vascular Anomalies Clinic, San Francisco, 1991—; founder Hemangioma Investigator Group; bd. dirs. Am. Bd. Dermatology, past pres. Author: (with others) Pediatric Dermatology, 1995, Rudolph's Textbook of Pediatrics, 1995, Textbook of Dermatology, 1996; mem. editl. bd. Current Problems in Dermatology, 1994—, Pediat. Dermatology, 1998—; editor-in-chief, co-editor Neonatal Dermatology; contbr. over 75 articles to profl. jours. Recipient Chancellor's award, Women of Distinction, U. Calif. San Francisco, Mentor of Yr. award, Women's Dermatologic Soc.; named Nancy B. Esterly Lectr., Wis. Dermatology Soc., Williams Moores Lectr., Ind. Dermatology Soc., Cawley Lectr., U. Va., Harold Perry Lectr., Mayo Clinic, Tchr. of Yr., U. Calif. San Francisco; named to Best Doctors, Bay Area, Best Doctors, USA. Mem. Am. Acad. Dermatology (mem. editl. bd. 1998—), Soc. Pediat. Dermatology (Founders Lectr., bd. dirs. 1990-93, past pres.). Office: Univ Calif PO Box 316 San Francisco CA 94143-0001 Office Phone: 415-353-7883, 415-353-7800.

FRIEDEN, THOMAS R., federal agency administrator; b. NYC, Dec. 7, 1960; BA, Oberlin Coll., Ohio, 1982; MD, Columbia U. Coll. Physicians & Surgeons, NYC, 1986; MPH, Columbia U. Mailman Sch. Pub. Health, 1986. Med. intern, resident Columbia Presbyn. Hosp., 1986-89; fellow in infectious disease Yale U., New Haven, 1989-90; EIS (epidemiologic intelligence svc.) officer NYC Dept. Health & Mental Hygiene, 1990-92, dir. Bur. Tuberculosis Control, asst. commr., 1992-96, commr., 2002—09; med. officer WHO, New Delhi, 1996—2001; dir. Centers Disease Control & Prevention (CDC), US Dept. Health & Human Services, 2009—, adminstr. Agy. Toxic Substances & Disease Registry (ATSDR), 2009—. Office: CDC 1600 Clifton Rd Atlanta GA 30333 Office Phone: 800-232-4636. Business E-Mail: Tomfrieden@cdc.gov. *

FRIEDENBERG, RICHARD MYRON, radiologist, physician, educator; b. NYC, May 6, 1926; s. Charles and Dorothy (Steg) F.; m. Gloria Geshwind, Jan. 22, 1950; children: Lisa, Peter, Amy. AB, Columbia, 1946; MD, L.I. Coll. Medicine, 1949. Diplomate: Am. Bd. Radiology. Intern in medicine Maimonides Hosp., Bklyn., 1949-50; resident in radiology Bellevue Hosp., NYC, 1950-51, Nat. Cancer fellow, 1951-52; fellow radiology Columbia-Presbyn. Hosp., 1952-53; cons. radiologist 3d Air Force, London, Eng., 1953-55; asst. prof. radiology Albert Einstein Coll. Medicine, 1955-66, assoc. clin. prof. radiology, 1966-68; dir., chmn. dept. radiology Bronx Lebanon Hosp. Center, 1957-68; prof., chmn. dept. radiology N.Y. Med. Coll., 1968-80; prof., chmn. dept. radiol. scis. U. Calif., Irvine, 1980—92, emeritus prof. radiol. scis., 1992—. Dir. radiology Flower Fifth Ave. Hosp., Met. Hosp. Ctr., Bird S. Coler Hosp., NYC, Westchester County Med. Ctr., 1968—80. Author: (with Charles Ney) Radiographic Atlas of the Genitourinary System, 1966, 2d edit., 1981; Contbr. (with Charles Ney) articles to profl. jours. Fellow Am. Coll. Radiology, N.Y. Acad. Medicine; mem. Assn. Univ. Radiologists, Radiol. Soc. N.Am., Am. Roentgen Ray Soc., N.Y. Acad. Scis., Assn. Am. Med. Colls., AMA, Soc. Chairmen Acad. Radiology Depts. (past pres.), N.Y. Roentgen Soc. (past pres.), Orange CTY Radiology Soc. (past pres.). Home: 18961 Castlegate Ln Santa Ana CA 92705-2801 Office: U Calif Dept Radiology Irvine CA 92697-0001 Office Phone: 714-456-5303.

FRIEDLAENDER, GARY ELLIOTT, orthopedist, educator; b. Detroit, May 15, 1945; s. Alex Seymour and Eileen Adrianne (Berman) Friedlaender; m. Linda Beth Krohner, Mar. 16, 1969; children: Eron Yael, Ari Seth. BS, U. Mich., 1967, MD, 1969; MA (hon.), Yale U., 1984. Diplomate Am. Bd. Orthop. Surgery. Intern, then resident in surgery U. Mich., Ann Arbor, 1969-71; resident in orthop. Yale New Haven Hosp., 1971-74; fellow in musculoskeletal oncology Mass. Gen. Hosp., Boston, 1983; dir. tissue bank Naval Med. Rsch. Inst., Bethesda, Md., 1974-76; instr. surgery Yale U., New Haven, 1974, asst. prof., 1976-79, assoc. prof., 1979-84, prof., chief orthop., 1984-86, prof. chmn. dept. orthop. and rehab., 1986—, Wayne O. Southwick prof. of orthop. and rehab., 1997—. Mem. orthop. and musculoskeletal study sect. NIH, 1986—89, mem. nat. adv. bd. arthritis and musculoskeletal and skin diseases, 1991—95, chmn., 1993—95; mem. blood products adv. com. FDA, 1995—97; mem. adv. coun. Nat. Inst. Arthritis and Musculoskeletal and Skin Diseases, 1998—2001. Mem. bd. cons. editors: Jour. Bone and Joint Surgery, 1981—89, mem. bd. assoc. editors: Clin. Orthop. and Related Rsch., 1986—97, dep. editor:, 1997—, mem. bd. assoc. editors: Modern Medicine, 1988—; editor: Rheumatology Digest, 1986—95; mem. editl. bd.: Transplantation Scis., 1991—, Jour. Cancer, 1994—; contbr. articles to profl. jours. Served to lt. comdr. USN, 1974—76. Recipient Outstanding Rsch. award, Kappa Delta, 1982, Nicholas Andry award for Outstanding Orthoped. Rsch., 1995. Fellow: ACS, Am. Acad. Orthop. Surgeons (chmn. com. biol. implants 1987—93, chmn. com. rsch. 1999—2002, bd. dir. 1999—2002, chmn. com. academic advocacy 2001—, chair musculoskeletal splty. soc. 2001—02); mem.: NIH (orthop. and musculoskeletal study sect. 1986—89, mem. nat. adv. bd. arthritis and musculoskeletal and skin diseases 1991—95, chmn. 1993—95), AMA, Acad. Orthop. Soc. (pres. 1995—96, chmn. com. rsch. 1999—2002), Assn. Bone and Joint Surgeons (pres. 2001—02), Am. Orthop. Assn., Am. Soc. Transplant Surgeons, Soc. for Surg. Oncology, Am. Coun. on Transplantation (pres. 1983—85), Musculoskeletal Tumor Soc., Transplantation Soc., Orthop. Rsch. Soc. (pres. 1994—95), Am. Assn. Tissue Banks (pres. 1983—85, Disting. Svc. award 1996), Alpha Omega Alpha. Jewish. Home: 15 Old Still Rd Woodbridge CT 06525-1101 Office: Yale U Dept Orthopedics and Rehab PO Box 208071 New Haven CT 06520-8071 Office Phone: 203-737-5660. Business E-Mail: gary.friedlaender@yale.edu.

FRIEDLAND, JACK ARTHUR, plastic surgeon; b. East Chicago, Ind., Feb. 10, 1940; s. Peter and Bettye (Manfield) Friedland; m. Harriet Anita Simensky, July 1, 1962; children: Margo Lynn, Jonathan Elliot, Julie I. BA, U. Wis., Madison, 1961; BS, Northwestern U. Med. Sch., 1962, MD, 1965. Diplomate Am. Bd. Surgery, Am. Bd. Plastic Surgery, Nat. Bd. Med. Examiners, lic. NY, NJ, Calif., Ariz., Idaho. Intern, surgery NYU, Bellevue Med. Ctr., 1965-66, surg. resident, chief resident, 1966-70; resident in plastic surgery and chief resident Inst. Reconstructive Plastic Surgery NYU Med. Ctr., NYC, 1972-74; attending physician Phoenix Plastic Surgery Fellowship Prog., 1985—; pvt. practice Phoenix, 1974—. Clinical instr. surgery NYU Sch. Medicine, 1966—70, clinical instr. plastic surgery, 1972—74; chief dept. plastic surgery Maricopa Med. Ctr., 1975—82; chief dept. surgery Phoenix Children's Hosp., 1983—88, chief staff, Children's Rehabilitative Svcs., 1984—86, chief dept. plastic surgery, 1988—; asst. dir. Phoenix Plastic Surgery Residency Prog., 1974—84; assoc. prof. plastic surgery Extramural Faculty Mayo Med. Sch., 1996—; other hosp. appointments include St. Joseph's Hosp. & Med. Ctr., Good Samaritan Regional Med. Ctr., Scottsdale Healthcare-Osborn, Shea, Thompson Peak Med. Ctrs., Biltmore Outpatient Surgical Facility and Phoenix Surgicenter; examiner, oral examinations Am. Bd. Plastic Surgery, 1994—, dir., 2004—; lectr. in field; traveling prof. for several universities. Contbr. articles to profl. jours.; cons. editor Ariz. Medicine (sect. surgery), 1976—86, article and book reviewer Plastic and Reconstructive Surgery, 1990—, assoc. editor, 2002—, reviewer editor, 2004—, mem. of several editl. bds. Bd. dirs. men's arts coun. Phoenix Art Mus., 1975—; vol. MADD, Phoenix, 1985—86. Maj. USAF, 1970—72, USAF Hosp., Luke AFB, Ariz., chief hosp. svcs. and chief surgery. Recipient Nat. Svc. award, Ariz. Med. Assn., 1999. Fellow: ACS (gov. 2006—); mem.: AMA, Maricopa County Med. Soc., Maricopa County Plastic Surgeons Soc., Rhinoplasty Society, Inc. (pres. 2007—08), Internat. Soc. Aesthetic Plastic Surgery, Am. Burn Assn., U. Club Phoenix (bd. dirs. 1974—84, past pres.), Ariz. Soc. Plastic & Reconstructive Surgeons, Maricopa County Med. Assn., Ariz. Med. Assn., Am. Cleft-Palate-Craniofacial Assn., Am. Assn. Plastic Surgeons, Am. Soc. Plastic Reconstructive Surgeons, Am. Soc. Aesthetic Plastic Surgery (pres. 1990—91, bd. trustees), 100 Club (bd. dirs. 2002—), Alpha Omega Alpha. Avocations: running, flying, scuba diving, travel, tennis. Office: Aesthetic Surgeons Ariz 7425 E Shea Blvd Ste 103 Scottsdale AZ 85260 Office Phone: 480-905-1700. Office Fax: 480-905-6941. Business E-Mail: jaf@jackafriedlandmd.com.

FRIEDLAND, MICHAEL LAWRENCE, dean, medical educator; b. Aug. 30, 1942; BS, Bklyn. Coll., 1963; MD, SUNY, Bklyn., 1967. Asst. prof. medicine, dir. hematology/oncology Brown U./Miriam Hosp., Providence, 1973-81; assoc. prof. medicine Med. Coll. Pa., 1981-82; prof. clin. medicine, sr. assoc. dean clin. affairs NY Med. Coll., 1982-87, chmn. dept. medicine, prof. clin. medicine, 1987-92; dean Binghamton Clin. Campus SUNY, Syracuse, 1992-97; v.p. affiliated programs SUNY Health Sci. Ctr., Syracuse, 1993-95; interim exec. v.p. for acad. affairs/dean medicine Tex. A&M U. Sys. Health Sci. Ctr., College Station, Tex., 1997-99; dean of medicine U. Mo. Kansas City, 1999—2001; dean ea. divsn. W.Va. U. Health Scis Ctr., Martinsburg, 2001—04; prof. biomed. sci., v.p. med. programs Fla. Atlantic U., Boca Raton, 2004—, dean Charles E. Schmidt Coll.

Biomed. Sci., 2006—. Mem. Medicare Coverage Adv. Com.; v.p. med. programs, founding dean Charles & Schimet Coll. Medicine-,FAU, 2011- Co-author: (abstract) IME 21st Ann. Session, 1996, (sect. of book) The Chemotherapy Source Book, 1996; contbr. over 50 articles to profl. jours. Bd. dirs. Brazos Valley chpt. Am. Lung Assn., Bryan, Tex., 1998. Mem. AMA (governing coun. sect. on med. schs., chair sect. on med. schs. 2002-04), Mo. State Med. Assn. (coun. on med. edn.). Office: Florida Atlantic Univ Biomed Sci 777 Glades Road PO Box 3091 Boca Raton FL 33431-0991 Home Phone: 561-964-4477; Office Phone: 561-297-2219. Business E-Mail: michael.friedland@fau.edu.

FRIEDLER, ELI, psychiatrist; MD, Johns Hopkins U., Balt., 1981; MPH, UCLA, 1986. Lic. Calif., 1983, diplomate Am. Bd. Psychiatry and Neurology-psychiatry, 1988, Am. Bd. Psychiatry and Neurology-child and adolescent psychiatry, 1990, Am. Bd. Psychiatry and Neurology-geriatric psychiatry. Resident psychiatry UCLA/Sepulveda VA, 1982—86; fellow child and adolescent psychiatry Cedars-Sinai Med. Ctr., LA, 1986—88; hospital affiliations includes Kaiser Permanente LA Med. Ctr. Office: Kaiser Mental Health Center 765 W College St. Los Angeles CA 90012 Office Phone: 213-580-7230.

FRIEDMAN, AARON L., dean, pediatrician, educator; b. Bad Reichenhal, Germany, Oct. 29, 1948; came to U.S., 1949; s. Reuben and Sylvia (Zysman) F.; m. Sarah Seay Jones, June 17, 1971; children: Rebeccah, Robbin. BS, Cornell U., 1970; MD, SUNY, Syracuse, 1974. Resident pediatrics U. Wis., Madison, 1974-76, fellow pediatric nephrology, 1976-80, chief resident pediatrics, 1978-79; asst. prof. Duke U., Durham, N.C., 1980-81, U. Wis., Madison, 1981-86, assoc. prof., 1986-91, prof., 1991—2004, chair dept. pediatrics, 1996—2004; prof., chmn. dept. pediatrics Brown U., RI Hosp., Providence, 2004—08; prof. pediat. U. Minn. Med. Sch., Mpls., 2008—, Ruben-Bentson chmn. in pediat., 2008—10, v.p. health sciences, dean, 2011—; pediatrician-in-chief U. Minn. Amplatz Children's Hosp., Mpls., 2008—10. Bd. dirs., sec.-treas. Am. Bd. Pediatrics. Contbr. articles to profl. jours. Named Best Doctor in Am. Am. Healthcare Mag., 1996. Fellow Am. Acad. Pediatrics; mem. Am. Soc. Pediatric Nephrology (pres.), Am. Acad. Pediatrics, Soc. for Pediatric Rsch., Am. Bd. Pediatrics (bd. dirs.), Internat. Pediatric Nephrology Assn. Achievements include research in amino acid and renal transport; in angiotensin converting enzyme inhibition in children; in growth of chronic renal disease; in medical management of chronic renal failure; in water and electrolyte physiology in children. Office: University Minn Med Sch Office of Dean Mayo Mail Code 293 420 Delaware St SE Minneapolis MN 55455 Office Phone: 612-626-4949. Office Fax: 612-626-4911. Business E-Mail: alfried@umn.edu. *

FRIEDMAN, ALAN H., pediatric cardiologist, educator; b. Detroit, Michigan; m. Jennifer Friedman; children: Sydney, Jake, Tess, Dylan. MD, Wayne State U., Detroit, 1987; studied, U. Mich., Ann Arbor. Cert. Pediatric Cardiovascular Disease, 2011, diplomate Am. Bd. Pediatrics pediatric cardiology, 2004. Intern Children's Meml. Hosp., Chgo., 1988, resident pediat., 1988—91, chief resident, 1991; fellow pediatric cardiology Yale-New Haven Hosp., Conn., 1991—94, prof. pediat. cardiology Yale Univ.; assoc. chair edn. Yale Med. Group, dir. pediatric residency program, chief interim pediatric cardiology, dir. pediatric echocardiography lab. Office: Yale New Haven Hospital 20 York St New Haven CT 06510 Office Phone: 203-688-4242.

FRIEDMAN, ALLAN HOWARD, neurosurgeon; b. Chgo., Feb. 15, 1949; BS, Purdue U., West Lafayette, Ind., 1970; MD, U. Ill. Coll. Medicine, Chgo., 1974. Cert. in neurol. surgery 1983. Gen. surg. resident Duke U. Med. Ctr., Durham, NC, 1974—75, neurosurg. resident, 1975—78, neurosurg. chief resident, 1978—80, asst. prof., 1981—90, assoc. prof., 1990—93, Guy L. Odom prof. neurol. surgery, 1993—, chief divsn. neurosurgery, 1996—, co-dir., brain tumor ctr., 1998, co-dir. clin. oncology program, 1998, co-dir. collegiate athlete premed. experience, 2004; vascular fellow U. Western Ontario, London, Canada, 1980—81; chief. divsn. neurosurgery Durham Vets. Adminstrn. Hosp., 1981—89. Co-dir. Rev. and Update in Neurobiology for Neurosurgeons, 1999, Advanced Skull Base Microanatomy and Hands on Dissection Workshop, 2000, 3rd Pan Pacific Neurosurg. Congress, 2000; dir. Rsch. Update in Neurosci. for Neurosurgeons, 2004. Contbr. articles to profl. jours. Recipient David Mortimer Olkon award, U. Ill.; James Scholar of Medicine. Fellow: Am. Coll. Surgeons; mem.: AMA, AMA Stroke Coun., Am. Acad. Neurol. Surgery, Southern Neurosurg. Soc. (chmn. program com. 1985, pres. 1997—98), Am. Assn. Neurol. Surgeons, Neurosurg. Soc. America (chmn. program com. 1985, v.p. 1996—97, chmn., long range planning com. 1999—2000, treas. 2000—03, pres. elect 2005), NC Neurosurg. Soc. (sec. tres. 1995—97, pres. 1997—99), Durham-Orange County Med. Soc., NC Med. Soc., Southern Med. Assn., Congress Neurol. Surgeons (scientific program chmn., upper extremity course 1999), Joint Sect. on Disorders Spine and Peripheral Nerves the Am. Assn. Neurol. Surgeons and the Congress Neurol. Surgeons (course dir. 2000), Joint Sect. on Cerebrovascular Surgery the Am. Assn. Neurol. Surgeons and the Congress Neurol. Surgeons, Omicron Delta Kappa, Sigma Delta Chi, Sigma Pi Sigma. Office: Duke Univ Hosp Box 3807 Durham NC 27710 Office Phone: 919-681-6421. Office Fax: 919-681-7872. Business E-Mail: fried010@mc.duke.edu.

FRIEDMAN, ELI A., nephrologist, educator; b. NYC, Apr. 9, 1933; s. Israel and Ida (Gutman) F.; widowed; children: Amy Louise, Rebecca Alicia, Sara Jo. BS, Bklyn. Coll., 1953; MD, SUNY Downstate Med. Center, 1957; DSc (hon.), Maduri Kamaraj U., India, 1985, L.I. U., 1991. Intern in medicine Harvard Med. Sch., 1957-58; resident in medicine Peter Bent Brigham Hosp., Boston, 1960-61; Am. Heart Assn. rsch. fellow Harvard U., 1958-60; mem. faculty, chief divsn. renal disease Downstate Med. Ctr., Bklyn., 1963—; prof. Health Sci. Ctr. SUNY, Bklyn., 1972—, Disting. Tchg. prof., 1992—, dep. chair dept. medicine, 2003—, chair instnl. rev. bd., 2002—. Bd. dirs. Am. Bur. Med. Aid to China, 1979—, Cleve. Found., 1979—, Bklyn. Nephrology Found., 1978—; Kasperzak lectr. Cleve. Clinic, 1998; Alpha Omega Alpha lectr. SUNY Health Sci. Ctr., Bklyn., 1999; Conrad Pirani lectr. Columbia Coll. Physician and Surgeons, 2000; Helen and Payne Whitney lectr. N. Shore Univ. Hosp., 2001; excellence in dialysis participant, Karachi, Pakistan, 00; mem. faculty masters in nephrology U. Naples, Italy, 2001; rsch. grants coun. reviewer Nat. Natural Sci. Found. of China, 2001; George E. Schreiner lectr. Canisus Coll., Buffalo, 2003; vis. prof. Vanderbilt U., 2002. Author: Acute Renal Failure, 1973, Strategy in Renal Failure, 1978, Diabetic Renal-retinal Syndrome, 1980, Diabetic Renal-retinal Syndrome 3 Therapy, 1986, Diabetic Nephropathy, 1986, Diabetic Renal-retinal Syndrome 4: Management Strategy, 1987; editor: Journal of Diabetic Complications, 1986—. Adv. bd. Nat. Kidney Found. Singapore, 1999. Lt. comdr. USPHS, 1961-63. Recipient Hoenig award, Nat. Kidney Found., 1986, Silver medal, U. Bologna, 1988, Disting. Svc. to Black Kidney patients award, Howard U., 1989, Physicians award, Am. Assn. Kidney Patients, 1989, Alumni medal, SUNY Downstate Med. Coll., William Dock Master Tchr. award, Alumni Assn. SUNY Health Scis. Ctr., 1992, Recognition award, N.Y. Regional Transplant Program, 1994, Nat. Torchbearer award, Am. Kidney Fund, 1995, Excellence medal, 1996, award, Juvenile Diabetes Found., Bklyn., 1995, Medal of Excellence award, 1996, Torchbearer award, Organ Transplantation and Kidney Disease, 1998, Internat. Torchbearer award, India, 1998, Samuel L. Kountz award, Howard U., 1999, Peter Lundin award, Am. Assn. Kidney Patients, 2001, alumni award in nephrology, Downstate Med. Ctr., 2002, Excellence in Postgrad. Tchg., 2002, Pres.'s award, 2010, Lifetime Achievement award, Internat. Soc. Hemodialysis, 2005, Alumni Assn. Downstate Med. Ctr., 2007—08, Belding Scribner Lifetime Achievement award, Internat. Soc. Hemodialysis, 2006, Sesquicentennial Hon. award, Downstate Med. Ctr., 2010, Gibbs award, NY Acad. Ctr., 2010; named NY Super Drs., 2004, 2009—10; named one of Best Drs. in N.Y., N.Y. Mag., 2000—02, 2004, Am.'s Top Drs., 2001, 2002, Best Doctors in America, 2003—04, 2008—09, Top Drs. in America, 2005, 2009—10; grantee, NIH, Am. Kidney Fund, N.Y. State Kidney Disease Inst., USPHS, N.Y. Kidney Found. Fellow Explorers Club (1st prize photo competition 1995), Royal Coll. Physicians (hon. 2004); mem. ACP (Master 1996), Am. Soc. Nephrology, Internat. Soc. Nephrology, Am. Soc. Artificial Internal Organs (pres. 1987—, editor Transactions 1985-2003, Barney Clark award 2010), Am. Soc. Immunology, Transplantation Soc., Assn. Am. Physicians, Internat. Soc. Artificial Organs (pres. 1986), Italian Soc. Nephrology (hon.), Royal Soc. Medicine Belgium (corrs. mem.), German Soc. Clin. Nephrology (hon., Nils Alwall medal 2003), Internat. Soc. Geriatric Nephrology and Urology (pres. 2003-07). Home: 1049 E 17th St Brooklyn NY 11230-4412 Office: 450 Clarkson Ave Brooklyn NY 11203-2056 Office Phone: 718-270-1584. Personal E-mail: elifriedmn@aol.com.

FRIEDMAN, GARY, plastic surgeon; BS, MD, Ohio State U. Diplomate Am. Bd. Plastic Surgery, cert. Advanced Edn. Cosmetic Surgery Am. Soc. Aesthetic Plastic Surgery. Intern Mt. Zion Hosp., San Francisco; gen. surgery resident Marquette U., Milw.; plastic surgery resident St. Francis Hosp., San Francisco; pvt. practice San Francisco, 1973—. Chief plastic surgery Calif. Pacific Med. Ctr.; clinical instr. St. Francis Hosp., 1973—98. Contbr. articles to profl. jours., chapters to books. Recipient Physician Recognition award, Continuing Medical Edn., Am. Med Assn. Mem.: AMA (Physician Recognition award in Continuing Med. Edn.), San Francisco Med. Soc., Calif. Soc. Plastic Surgeons, Calif. Med. Assn., Am. Soc. Aesthetic Plastic Surgery, Am. Soc. Plastic & Reconstructive Surgeons. Office: 6052 Shelter Bay Ave Mill Valley CA 94941-3040 Office Phone: 866-677-8587. E-mail: gdf@sf-plasticsurgeon.com.

FRIEDMAN, GARY DAVID, epidemiologist; b. Cleve., Mar. 8, 1934; s. Howard N. and Cema C. F.; m. Ruth Helen Schleien, June 22, 1958; children: Emily, Justin, Richard. Student, Antioch Coll., 1951-53; BS in Biol. Sci., U. Chgo., 1956, MD with honors, 1959; MS in Biostats., Harvard Sch. Pub. Health, 1965. Diplomate Am. Bd. Internal Medicine. Intern, resident Harvard Med. Svcs., Boston City Hosp., 1959-61; 2d yr. resident Univ. Hosps. Cleve., 1961-62; med. officer heart disease epidemiology study Nat. Heart Inst., Framingham, Mass., 1962-66; chief epidemiology unit, field and tng. stn., heart disease ctrl. program USPHS, San Francisco, 1966-68; sr. epidemiologist divsn. rsch. Kaiser Permanente Med. Care Program, Oakland, Calif., 1968-76, asst. dir. epidemiology and biostats., 1976-91, dir., 1991-98, sr. investigator, 1998-99, adj. investigator, 1999—; cons. prof. Dept. Health Rsch. and Policy Stanford U. Sch. Medicine, 1998—. Rsch. fellow, then rsch. assoc. preventive medicine Harvard Med. Sch., 1962-66; lectr. dept. biomed. and environ. health scis., sch. pub. health U. Calif. Berkeley, 1968-95; lectr. epidemiology and biostats. U. Calif. Sch. Medicine, San Francisco, 1980-2000, asst. clin. prof. 1967-75, assoc. clin. prof., 1975-92 depts. medicine and family and cmty. medicine; US-USSR working group sudden cardiac death NHLBI, 1975-82, com. on epidemiology and veterans follow-up studies Nat. Rsch. Coun., 1980-85, subcom. on twins, 1980-94, epidemiology and disease ctrl. study sect. NIH, 1982-86, US Preventive Svcs. Task Force, 1984-88, scientific rev. panel on toxic air contaminants State of Calif., 1988-2010, adv. com. Merck Found./Soc. Epidemiol. Rsch., Clin. Epidemiology Fellowships, 1990-94; sr. advisor expert panel on preventive svcs. USPHS, 1991-96; mem. instl. rev. bd. Kaiser Permamente, 1997—. Author: Primer of Epidemiology, 1974, 5th edit. 2004; assoc. editor, then editor Am. Jour. Epidemiology, 1988-96, 99—; mem. editl. bd. HMO Practice, 1991-98, Jour. Med. Screening, 1997—; contbr. over 300 articles to profl. jours., chpts. to books; composer: Autumn for oboe and piano (First prize Composers Today Competition Music Tchrs. Assn. Calif. 1999), Fugue for Four Winds (Second prize Music Tchrs. Assn. Calif. 2000). Oboist San Francisco Civic Symphony, 1990—, Symphony Parnassus, 1994-2004, Bohemian Club Band, 1994—, Coll. Marin Orch., 2004—; bd. dirs. Chamber Musicians No. Calif., Oakland, 1991-98. Sr. surgeon USPHS, 1962-68. Recipient Roche award for Outstanding Performance as Med. Student; Merit grantee Nat. Cancer Inst., 1987, Outstanding Investigator grantee, 1989, 94; named to Disting. Alumni Hall of Fame Cleve. Heights High Sch., 1991. Fellow Am. Heart Assn. (chmn. com. on criteria and methods 1969-71, chmn. program com. 1973-76, coun. epidemiol.), Am. Coll. Physicians; mem. APHA, Am. Epidemiol. Soc. (mem. com. 1982-86, pres. 1999-2000), Am. Soc. Preventive Oncology, Internat. Epidemiol. Assn., Soc. Epidemiologic Rsch. (exec. com. 1998-2001), Med. Biol. Alumni Assn. U. Chgo. (Disting. Svc. award 2000), Phi Beta Kappa, Alpha Omega Alpha, Delta Omega. Achievements include research on cancer, cardiovascular disease, gallbladder disease, effects of smoking, alcohol and medicinal drugs, evaluation of health screening tests. Office: Stanford U Sch Medicine Dept Health Rsch and Policy Redwood Bldg Rm T210 Stanford CA 94305-5405 E-mail: gdf@stanford.edu.

FRIEDMAN, HARVEY MICHAEL, infectious diseases educator; b. Montreal, May 29, 1944; came to U.S., 1971; s. Sidney and Sybil (Garfinkle) F.; m. Cynthia Diane Mickey, Apr. 12, 1980; children: Lisa, Steven, Julie. BS, McGill U., 1965, MD, 1969. Cert. in internal medicine 1975, in infectious diseases 1976. Intern, resident Jewish Gen. Hosp., Montreal, 1969-71; fellow in virology Wistar Inst., Phila., 1971-73; fellow in infectious disease U. Pa. Hosp., Phila., 1973-75; asst. prof., assoc. prof. Med. Sch. U. Pa., Phila., 1975-91, prof. Med. Sch., 1991—. Med. dir. Clin. Virology Lab. Children's Hosp., Phila., 1975—96; chief infectious diseases U. Pa., 1990—, dir. Penn-Botswana Program, 2001—. Contbr. numerous papers and book chpts. Grantee NIH, Found., 1978—. Fellow: Infectious Disease Soc. Am.; mem.: AAAS, Am. Clin. and Climatological Assn., Assn. Am. Physicians, Am. Soc. Clin. Investigation. Achievements include description of novel mechanisms used by herpes simplex virus glycoproteins that favor virus escape from immune attack. Office: U Pa Med Sch 502 Johnson Pavilion Philadelphia PA 19104-6073

FRIEDMAN, IRA HUGH, surgeon; b. NYC, July 17, 1933; s. Leonard Seymour and Ruth (Binder) F.; m. Erika Berger, Oct. 22, 1961; children: Richard Lawrence, Joanne Beth BA, NYU, 1953, MD, 1957. Diplomate Am. Bd. Surgery, Nat. Bd. Med. Examiners. Intern, resident in surgery Beth Isreal Med. Ctr., NYC, 1957-59, 61-63; surg. resident Bellevue Hosp., NYC, 1959-60; practice medicine specializing in surgery NYC, 1963—. Attending surgeon Beth Isrel Med. Ctr., pres. med. bd., 1981-82; assoc. clin. prof. surgery Albert Einstein Coll. Medicine; med. adv. to N.Y.C. dir. SSS, 1968. Contbr. articles to profl. jours. Bd. dirs. Union Orthodox Jewish Congregations Am., Am. Com. for Shaare Zedek Hosp. of Jerusalem, Yeshiva Sha-alvim, Israel; pres. P'Tach; co-chmn. bd. dirs. Yeshiva Chofetz Chaim, N.Y.C. Recipient Koach award Israel Bond Orgn., 1977; N.Y. Heart Assn. fellow, 1960-61 Fellow ACS (elected gov. 1996), Am. Coll. Gastroenterology, Am. Soc. Colon and Rectal Surgeons, Royal Soc. Medicine; mem. AMA, N.Y. Acad. Medicine, N.Y. Surg. Soc., Soc. Surgery of Alimentary Tract, Soc. Am. Gastrointestinal Endoscopic Surgeons, Am. Gastroent. Assn., Am. Soc. Gen. Surgeons, Am. Hernia Soc., Am. Soc. Breast Surgeons, N.Y. Gastroent. Assn., N.Y. Cancer Soc., N.Y. Soc. Colon and Rectal Surgeons, Collegium Internationale Chirugiae Digestive, N.Y. State Med. Assn., N.Y. County Med. Assn. Home: 1175 Park Ave New York NY 10128-1211

FRIEDMAN, JEFFREY M., molecular geneticist, educator; b. Orlando, Fla., June 20, 1954; BS in Biology, Rensselaer Poly. Inst., Troy, NY; MD, Albany Med. Coll., Union U., 1977; PhD in Molecular Biology, Rockefeller U., NYC, 1986. Resident Albany Med. Ctr. Hosp.; gastroenterology fellowship Cornell U. Med. Coll.; asst. to assoc. prof Rockefeller U., 1986—95, prof., 1995—99, founding dir. Starr Ctr. Human Genetics NYC, 1995—, Marilyn M. Simpson prof., 1999—. Asst. investigator Howard Hughes Med. Inst., 1986—96, investigator, 1996—; co-founder, mem. sci. adv. bd. Envoy Therapeutics, Inc., Jupiter, Fla. Contbr. articles to profl. jours. Recipient Bristol-Myers Squibb award for disting. achievement in metabolic rsch., 2001, Passano Found. award, 2004, Gairdner Found. Internat. award, 2004, Danone Internat. prize for nutrition, 2007, Keio Med. Sci. prize, Tokyo, 2009, Albert Lasker Basic Med. Rsch. award, Lasker Found., 2010; co-recipient Shaw award in life sci. & medicine, 2009. Mem.: NAS (Jessie Stevenson Kovalenko medal 2007), Royal Swedish Acad. Scis. (fgn.), Inst. Medicine. Achievements include discovery of Leptin, a hormone derived from fat cells; research in the causes and treatment options for obesity. Office: Rockefeller U Lab Molecular Genetics 1230 York Ave New York NY 10021 Office Phone: 212-327-8086. E-mail: Jeffrey.Friedman@rockefeller.edu. *

FRIEDMAN, JEFFREY ROBERT, psychiatrist, educator; b. Mpls., May 26, 1956; s. Harry Samuel and Gertrude (Rotenberg) F.; m. Laura Jean Weisblatt, July 14, 1985; children: Gabrielle Eve, Daniel Adam. BA, Yale U., 1978; MD, U. Chgo., 1982. Diplomate Am. Bd. Psychiatry and Neurology. Intern in medicine Mt. Auburn Hosp., Cambridge, Mass., 1982-83, attending physician, dept. psychiatry, 2004—; intern in neurology Mass. Gen. Hosp., Boston, 1982-83; resident in psychiatry McLean Hosp., Belmont, Mass., 1983-86, asst. psychiatrist, 1986-88, asst. clin. psychiatrist, 1988—; instr. psychiatry Harvard U. Med. Sch., Boston, 1986-88, clin. instr., 1988—99, asst. clin. prof. psychiatry, 2000—, psychiatrist Harvard Community Health Plan, 1988-96; assoc. residency dir. Harvard Longwood Psychiatry Residency, Boston, 1995-99; psychiatrist Harvard Pilgrim Health Care, Boston, 1996-97, Harvard Vanguard Med. Assoc., Boston, 1997—2000, faculty Boston Psychoanalytic Soc. and Inst., 2005—, Boston Inst. Psychotherapy, 2005—; physician, divsn. psychiatry Va. Hosp. Candidate Boston Psychoanalytic Soc. and Inst., 1986-97; grad. analyst Boston Psychoanalytic Soc. and Inst. Recipient Paul Howard award McLean Hosp., 1986; Group for Advancement Psychiatry Ginsburg fellow, 1984-86. Mem. Am. Psychiat. Assn. (disting. fellow, 2009), Boston Psychoanalytic Soc. and Inst., Am. Bd. Geriatric Psychiatry, Am. Bd. Forensic Psychiatry, Am. Psychoanlytic Assn., Am. Acad. Psychiatry and Law. Avocations: tennis, cross country skiing. Office: 875 Massachusetts Ave Ste 51 Cambridge MA 02139-3015

FRIEDMAN, KENNI, health facility administrator, councilman; BA, UCLA, 1963, MBA, 1964. Councilwoman City of Modesto, Calif., 1991-99, vice mayor, 2000—; mem. bd. Sutter-affiliated Meml. Hosps. Assn., Sacramento, chmn. bd., 1993-95; bd. dirs. Sutter Health Inc., Sacramento. Bd. dirs. Sutter Gould Med. Found., Modesto; active League Calif. Cities, United Way Sanislaus County, Modesto Symphony Assn.; former mem. state bd. dirs. and nat. bd. dirs. LWV; mem. policy bd. San Juaquin Valley Unified Air Pollution Control Dist. Mem. Modesto C. of C. (bd. dirs.). *

FRIEDMAN, LAWRENCE B., pediatrician, adolescent medicine, educator; BA/MD in Biology and Medicine, U. Mo., Kansas City, 1980. Diplomate Am. Bd. Pediatrics-adolescent medicine. Resident pediat. Univ. of Miami Jackson Meml. Hosp., 1980—83, fellow adolescent medicine, 1983—85, hosp. affiliations includes, Mt. Sinai Med. Ctr.; prof. of pediat. Univ. of Miami Miller Sch. of Medicine, 1985—, dir. divsn. adolescent medicine dept. of pediat., 1997—. Expert in adolescent health care and transitional svcs. Fla. Dept. of Health; adolescent human immunodeficiency virus expert Fla.-Caribbean AIDS Edn. and Tng. Ctr.; prin. investigator Nat. Inst. of Child Health and Human Devel. (NICHD), 1994—2001; mem. Adolescent Medicine Trials Network for HIV/AIDS Interventions, 2001—11; investigator Pediatric AIDS Clin. Trials Group, 1999—. Recipient Vis. Professorship to University of Mo., Pfizer, 2003, Friends award, Ctr. for Ethics and Public svc., 2005, Flowers award for Innovative Leadership in Pub. Health, Dade County Health Dept., 2009; named one of the Best Doctors in America, 2007, the Best Doctors, 2008. Office: University of Miami Medical Center 1601 NW 12th Ave Rm 1055 Miami FL 33136-1005 Office Phone: 305-243-5880.

FRIEDMAN, LYNN S., obstetrician, gynecologist, educator; MD, NYU. Diplomate Am. Bd. Ob-Gyn. Resident ob-gyn. Mt. Sinai Hosp., physician ob-gyn.; asst. clin. prof. ob-gyn. Mt. Sinai Sch. of Medicine.

Co-author: (publs.) Sclerosing Stromal Tumor of the Ovary, 1990, A Woman Doctor's Guide to Miscarriage, 1996, Pregnancy for Dummies, 1998, The Morning Sickness Companion, 2003. Named one of Top Doctors NY Metro Area, Castle Connolly, 1998—2008, Top Doctors, NY Mag. Office: Mount Sinai Medical Center One Gustave L Levy Pl New York NY 10029 Office Phone: 212-241-6500.

FRIEDMAN, MERTON HIRSCH, retired psychologist, educator; b. Boston, Apr. 12, 1925; s. Isadore and Frances (Ponack) F.; m. Judith Lee Freeman, Nov. 27, 1955; 1 child, Eric Lund. BS, Coll. William and Mary, 1945; MA, U. Pa., 1947; PhD, U. Ill., 1952. Lic. psychologist, N.J., Mass. Psychology intern Conn. Valley Hosp., Middletown, 1947—48; postdoctoral intern Dept. VA Mental Health Clinic, Phila., 1952—53; staff psychologist Dept. VA Med. Ctr., Boston, 1953—59, chief psychology svc. Providence, 1959—62; chief psychologist Cmty. Mental Health Ctr., Brookline, Mass., 1962—64; dir. clin. svcs. Jewish Vocat. Svc., Milw., 1966—67; clin. assoc. prof. psychiatry U. Medicine and Dentistry N.J., 1968—92; chief psychology svc. Dept. VA Med. Ctr., East Orange, NJ, 1967—96; ret., 1996. Vis. lectr. Fulbright program Lund U., Sweden, 1964-66. Contbr. articles to profl. jours. USPHS Rsch. fellow, NIMH, U. Ill., 1951—52. Fellow Am. Orthopsychiat. Assn.; mem. APA, Mass. Psychol. Assn., N.J. Psychol. Assn., Sigma Xi (U. Ill. chpt.). Democrat. Jewish. Avocations: piano, hiking, stamp collecting/philately, classical music. Home: 79 Falcon Rd Livingston NJ 07039-4414 Home Phone: 973-994-1935.

FRIEDMAN, MICHAEL, surgeon; BA, Yeshiva U., NY, 1968; MD, U. Ill. Chicago Sch. of Medicine, 1972. Cert. Am. Bd. of Otolaryngology, 1977. Intern Ill. Masonic Med. Ctr., 1972—73; surgery residency U. Ill., Chicago, 1973—74, otolaryngology-head and neck surgery residency, 1974—77; otolaryngologist-head and neck surgeon Ill. Masonic Med. Ctr., 1977—; dir. head and neck training U. Ill., 1980—95; med. dir. Advanced Ctr. for Specialty Care, Ill. Masonic Med. Ctr., 1980—; otolaryngologist-head and neck surgeon Rush-Presbyterian-St. Luke's Med. Ctr., 1991—, Grant Hosp., 1991—. Editor-in-chief Operative Techniques in Otolaryngology—Head & Neck Surgery; assoc. prof., chmn. head and neck surgery, dept. of otolaryngology and bronchoesophagology Rush Med. Coll., 1991—95, prof., chmn. head and neck surgery, dept. of otolaryngology and bronchoesophagology, 1995—. Published more than 150 scientific articles; co-author 28 book chapters or textbooks. Recipient Edmund Prince Fowler award for Excellence in Basic Rsch., Am. Laryngological, Rhinological and Otological Soc., 1986; named a Top Doctor, Chicago Mag., 2001—06; named one of Top Doctors, Castle Connolly Med. Guide, 2001. Mem.: AMA, Am. Rhinologic Soc., Internat. Assn. of Phonosurgeons, Am. Broncho-Esophagological Assn., Am. Soc. for Head and Neck Surgery, Am. Coll. of Surgeons, Chicago Laryngological and Otological Soc., Am. Acad. of Otolaryngology-Head and Neck Surgery, Chicago Med. Soc., Am. Sleep Disorders Assn., Clinical Sleep Soc. Office: 30 N Michigan Ave Chicago IL 60602 Office Phone: 312-236-3642. Office Fax: 312-236-5162.

FRIEDMAN, MONROE, psychologist, educator, consultant, editor, writer; s. Isadore and Pearl Friedman; m. Rita Joyce Shaffer, Sept. 2, 1956; children: Ethan, Mark, Jordan. BS, Bklyn. Coll., 1956; PhD, U. Tenn., 1959. Human factors scientist Sys. Devel. Corp., Santa Monica, Calif., 1959—64; prof. Ea. Mich. U., Ypsilanti, 1964—, dir. Contemporary Issues Ctr., 1970—79; editl. cons. Greenwood Press, 1991—92, Prentice Hall, 1991—92. Vis. prof. Tilburg (The Netherlands) U., 1982—83, U. Leuven, Belgium, 1990—91; cons. Pres.'s Com. on Consumer Interests, Washington, 1966, Consumer Interests Found., Washington, 1972—73, NSF, Washington, 1973—74, U.S. Gen. Acctg. Office, Washington, 1973—74, FTC, Washington, 1976—77, ACLU Found., NY, 2001—02; bd. dirs. Consumer Interest Rsch. Inst., Washington; reviewer consumer edn. lit. Fed. Res. Bd., Washington, 2004—; sr. peer counselor Ctr. Healthy Aging, Santa Monica, Calif., 2007—08; mem. insight panel NY Times, 2006—; mem. bd. dirs. FAME Santa Monica Redevel. Corp., 2010—; presenter in field; issue co-editor Jour. Am. Culture, 2011. Author: A Brand New Language, 1991, Consumer Boycotts, 1999 (Outstanding Academic Title of Yr., Assn. for Coll. and Rsch. Librs. 2000); editor: Jour. Consumer Affairs, 1980-84; co-editor: Frontier of Research in the Consumer Interest, 1988; issue editor Jour. Social Issues, 1991, Jour. Am. Culture, 2007; mem. editl. bd. Jour. Consumer Affairs, 1984-93, 98—, Jour. Consumer Rsch., 1973-77, 1982-85, Jour. Am. Culture, 2004—, Jour. Popular Culture, 2005-, Jour. Interdisciplinary 20th Century Studies, 2005-, Jour. Consumer Policy, 1976—, Jour. Pub. Policy and Mktg., 2006—, Jour. Personal Fin., 2011-; contbr. over 100 articles to profl. jours. Pres. Am. Coun. Consumer Interests, 1989—90; mem. & sec. treas. Santa Monica Commn. Sr. Cmty., 2008—10; mem. exec. coun. Emeritus Coll., Santa Monica, Calif., 2005—. Rsch. grantee AARP Andrus Found., 1990, 92, Mich. Coun. for Humanities, 1975; Congl. fellow Am. Polit. Sci. Assn., 1966-67; Nat. Inst. Aging postdoc. fellow U. Mich., 1988-89; recipient Disting. Faculty award Mich. Bd. Regents, 1983, Bronze prize for ednl. films Internat. Film Festival Berlin, 1975. Fellow APA (divsn. Population and Environ. Psychology, divsn. Tchg. Psychology, divsn. Internat. Psychology, mem. program rev. com. 2007, 2008, 2009, divsn. Media Psychology, divsn. Adult Devel. and Aging, Soc. Psychol. Study Social Issues, mem. fellows selection com. 2010-), Am. Psychol. Soc. (charter), Am. Assn. Applied and Preventive Psychology (charter), Am. Coun. on Consumer Interests (disting., Applied Consumer Econs. award, 1991, 97), Soc. for Consumer Psychology, Soc. for the Psychol. Study Social Issues, Soc. for Psychology Aesthetics, Creativity, and the Arts, and Soc. for the Study Peace, Conflict and Violence (mem. program rev. com. 2008); mem. Internat. Assn. for Rsch. in Econ. Psychology (US rep. bd. trustees 1982—2005, sci. com., 2001, 02,), Internat. Assn. Applied Psychology (US rep. bd. trustees econ. psychology divsn. 1988—2005, sci. com., 1998), Found. Soc. Consumer Affairs Profls. (chair rsch. agenda com. 1984-87, trustee), Am. Psychol. Assn. (mem., media referral panel, 2008-, spkrs.' bur. 2009-, judge, Divsn. 1 Grad. Student award 2011) Home and Office: 855 10th St Ste 301 Santa Monica CA 90403 Office Phone: 310-656-4943. Business E-Mail: mfriedman@emich.edu.

FRIEDMAN, NEIL J., medical educator; b. NY, Dec. 21, 1965; AB, Dartmouth Coll., 1988; MD, Harvard Med. Sch., 1992. Physician MPOMG, 2000—. Office: 900 Welch Rd Palo Alto CA 94304 Office Phone: 650-324-0056.

FRIEDMAN, PAUL JAY, retired radiologist; b. NYC, Jan. 20, 1937; s. Louis Alexander and Rose (Solomon) Friedman; m. Elisabeth Clare Richardson, June 18, 1960; children: Elizabeth Ruth Coley, Deborah Anne Yeager, Matthew Alexander Xu-Friedman, Rachel Clare Lentz. BS, U. Wis., 1955; postgrad., Oxford U., Eng., 1957—58; MD, Yale U., 1960. Diplomate Am. Bd Radiology. Fellow academic radiology Picker Found., Yale U. Sch. Medicine, 1966—68; Markle scholar academic medicine, 1969—74; Picker scholar radiology, 1968—69; intern Einstein Med. Sch., NYC, 1960-61; resident in radiology Columbia-Presbyn. Hosp., NYC, 1961-64; from asst. prof. to assoc. prof. U. Calif. San Diego Med. Sch., 1968-75, prof. radiology, 1975-2001, prof. emeritus, 2001—, from assoc. dean to dean acad. affairs, 1982-95; Hans Kende lectr. Mich. State U., 2008; cons. Nat. U. Singapore, 2007; sec.-treas Emeriti Assn., UCSD, 2007—10. Cons. VA Hosp., 1971—2001; vis. scholar Inst. Med./NAS, AAMC, 1988—89; mem. adv. com. rsch. integrity HHS, 1991—93; cons. 26th, 27th, and 28th edit. Stedman's Med. Dictionary; specialist in chest radiology, rsch. ethics CT of COPD; bd. dirs. Am. Coun. Edn., 1996—97. Mem. editl. bd. Investigative Radiology, 1976—87, Am. Jour. Roentgenology, 1986—88; contbr. over 100 original articles to various jours. Lt. cmdr. MC USNR, 1964—66. Fellow: Am. Coll. Radiology, Am. Coll. Chest Physicians; mem.: Physicians Nat. Health Plan (chair SD chpt. PNHP Calif.), San Diego County Med. Soc., Roentgen Ray Soc. (emeritus), Radiol. Soc. N.Am. (emeritus), Assn. Univ. Radiologists (emeritus), Internat. Soc. Magnetic Resonance Medicine (emeritus), Assn. Am. Med. Colls. (disting. svc. mem.), Fleischner Soc. (sr.; pres. 1994—95), Phi Beta Kappa, Alpha Omega Alpha. Avocations: singing, computers, gardening. Home: 5644 Soledad Rd La Jolla CA 92037-7048 Office: University Calif Sch Medicine Dept Radiology 410 Dickinson St San Diego CA 92103-8749 Office Phone: 619-543-5206. Personal E-mail: paulfriedman2@gmail.com. Business E-Mail: pfriedman@ucsd.edu.

FRIEDMAN, RICHARD ALAN, psychiatrist; b. NYC, Sept. 11, 1956; s. Jerome G. and Frances B. F. BA, Duke U., Durham, NC, 1978; MD, Robert Wood Johnson Med. Sch., NJ, 1982. Cert. Am. Bd. Psychiatry, 1989. Intern in psychiatry Mt. Sinai Hosp., NYC, 1982—83, resident, 1983—87; prof. clin. psychiatry Weill Cornell U. Med. Coll., NYC, 1987—, dir. psychopharmacology clinic. Frequent contbr. to sci. sect. NY Times. Fellow Am. Psychiat. Assn. (disting. fellow). Avocations: piano, swimming, music. Office: The New York Hosp Payne Whitney Clinic 535 E 68th St New York NY 10021-4870 Office Phone: 212-746-5775. Business E-Mail: rafriedm@med.cornell.edu.

FRIEDMAN, RICHARD CHARLES, psychiatrist, educator; b. NYC, Jan. 20, 1941; s. William and Henrietta Friedman; m. Susan Matorin, Nov. 24, 1979; 1 child, Jeremiah Simon. BA, Bard Coll., Annandale-on-Hudson, NY, 1961; MD, U. Rochester, NY, 1966; grad., Columbia U., NYC, 1978. Diplomate Am. Bd. Psychiatry and Neurology, NY, 1973. Chief resident, dept. psychiatry Columbia Presbyn. Med. Ctr., NYC, 1969—70, resident, psychiatry, 1967—69, NY State Psychiat. Inst., 1967—69, chief resident, 1969—70; capt., US army, chief, in-patient psychiatry William Beaumont Gen. Hosp., El Paso, Tex., 1970—71, maj.; asst. psychiatrist Presbyn. Hosp., NYC, 1972—76, assoc. psychiatrist, 1976—81; instr., clin. psychiatry, Coll. Physicians and Surgeons Columbia U., 1973—76, adj. asst. prof., Sch. Pub. Health, 1977—79, assoc. clin. prof., psychiatry, 1986—94, lectr., psychiatry, 1994—, asst. prof., clin. psychiatry, 1977, Cornell U. Med. Coll., NYC, 1977—81, assoc. prof., clin. psychiatry, 1981—83, clin. assoc. prof., psychiatry, 1983—86, clin. prof., 1996—; assoc. psychiatrist St. Luke's-Roosevelt Hosp. Ctr., NYC, 1986—94, NY Hosp.-Cornell Med. Ctr., White Plains, 1981—86; adj. rsch. prof., psychology Derner Inst. Advanced Psychol. Studies, Adelphi U., NYC, 1989—; psychiatrist NY Hosp., 1996—. Asst. editor Jour. Am. Acad. Psychoanalysis, NYC, 1989—2002; chmn. rsch. com., chmn. program com. Am. Acad. Psychoanalysis, Bloomfield, Conn., 1993—96, cons., 1997—, assoc. editor, NYC, 2003—, mem., cons., Joint Com. Am. Psychoanalytic Assn., NYC; pres. Am. Coll. Psychoanalysts, Dallas, 1997—98; editl. bd. mem. Jour. Am. Acad. Psychoanalysis and Psychodynamic Psychiatry, Internat. Jour. Sex Rsch., Archives Sexual Behavior, NYC, 1998—; co-leader, Group Advancement Psychiatry, Dallas, 2004—. Author: (book) Male Homosexuality: A Contemporary Psychoanalytic Perspective; editor: Behavior and the Menstrual Cycle; co-author (with Downey): Sexual Orientation and Psychoanalysis: Sexual Science and Clinical Practice; co-editor: Masculinity and Sexuality: Selected Topics in the Psychology of Men, Sexuality: New Perspectives, Sex Differences in Behavior; spkr., invited lectr. Psychoanalysis, Psychotherapy and Sexual Orientation, Gender Role Behavior, Homosexuality: Historical Issues, Homophobia, A Psychoanalytic Perspective; contbr. articles to numerous profl. jours. Maj. M.C. US Army, 1970—72, El Paso. Recipient Laughlin award, Columbia U., 1970, Henry P. Laughlin award, Am. Coll. Psychoanalysts, 2002, Henry and M. Page Laughlin Disting. Tchg. award, 2002, Best Drs. Am. award, Castle Connolly Med. Ltd., 2006—, Mary S. Sigourney award, Internat. Psychoanalytic Assn. and The Sigourney Trust, 2009, Presdl. award, Am. Acad. Psychoanalysis and Dynamic Psychiatry, 2009, John and Samuel Bard award, Bard Coll., 2011; named Tchr. of Yr., Cornell U. Med. Coll., 1998. Fellow: Am. Psychiat. Assn.; mem.: Internat. Psychoanalytic Assn., Group Advancement Psychiatry, Am. Psychoanalytic Assn., Assn. Psychoanalytic Medicine, Am. Assn. Advancement Sci., Internat. Acad. Sex Rsch. Avocations: piano, Scrabble, walking, history, literature, reading. Office: Richard C Friedman MD 225 Ctrl Pk W Apt 103 New York NY 10024 Office Fax: 212-595-8164. Business E-Mail: rcf2@columbia.edu.

FRIEDMAN, ROBERT, ophthalmologist, educator; MD, Albert Einstein Coll. of Med. Lic. NY. Intern St. Luke's Roosevelt Hosp. Ctr., 1984; resident Lenox Hill Hosp., 1987, with; fellow Retina & Vitreous Manhattan Eye, Ear & Throat Hosp., 1988; asst. clin. prof. ophthalmology Mt. Sinai Med. Ctr. Office: The Mount Sinai Medical Center One Gustave L Levy Place New York NY 10029-6574 Office Phone: 212-241-6500.

FRIEDMAN, ROBERT BARRY, neurosurgeon; b. Bklyn., Dec. 28, 1953; s. Roy and Bernice (Berger) Friedman. BA, SUNY, Stony Brook, 1975; MD, SUNY Health Sci. Ctr., Bklyn., 1980. Diplomate Am. Bd. Neurol. Surgery. Gen. med. officer Indian Health Svc. USPHS, Sacaton, Ariz., 1981—82; neurosurgeon USAF, Wright Patterson AFB, Ohio, 1989—91, South Broward Neurosurg. Assn., Pembroke Pines, Fla., 1991—95, Cleve. Clinic Fla., Ft. Lauderdale, 1995—97, Spectrum Neurosurg. Specialists, Marietta, Ga., 1997—98, Henry Neurosurg. Specialists, P.C., Stockbridge, Ga., 1998—. Med. staff fellow NIH, Bethesda, Md., 1986—88. Contbr. articles to profl. jours. Maj. USAF, 1988—91. Recipient Neuroscience award, U. Pitts., 1989. Fellow: ACS; mem.: AMA, Fla. Med. Assn., So. Med. Assn., Congress Neurol. Surgeons, Am. Assn. Neurol. Surgeons. Libertarian. Avocations: private pilot, computers, photography. Home: 602 Redbud Ln Stockbridge GA 30281 Office: care Henry Neurosurg Specialists 150 Eagle Spring Ct Stockbridge GA 30281-7350 Office Phone: 770-506-3303. Personal E-mail: robert3018@msn.com.

FRIEDMAN, SANFORD J., cardiologist, educator; MD, Tuft U. Sch. Medicine, 1971. Diplomate Am. Bd. Internal Medicine, Am. Bd. Cardiology-cardiovascular disease. Assoc. clin. prof. medicine Mt. Sinai Sch. Medicine; resident in internal medicine Mt. Sinai Med. Ctr., NY, 1972—74, fellow in cardiovascular disease, 1974—76, cardiologist. Office: Mount Sinai Medical Center 941 Pk Ave New York NY 10028 Office Phone: 212-988-3772. Office Fax: 212-861-4672.

FRIEDMAN, STEVEN C., urologist; BS magna cum laude in Chemistry and Psychology, American U., 1974—78; grad. studies in Biology, NYU Grad. Sch., 1978—79; MD, State U. of NY, Bklyn, 1979—83. Lic. no. 159850 State of NY, 1984, diplomate Am. Bd. Urology, 1991, Am. Bd. Urology-recertification, 2000, urologic laser cert. Univ. of Pa., 1987, microsurgical tng. course NYU Postgraduate Med. Sch., 1989, laparoscopy cert. NYU Postgraduate Med. Sch., 1992, robotic surgery cert. DaVinci Surg. Sys., 2001. Resident urology Maimonides Med. Ctr., Bklyn., 1985—88, chief padiatric, assoc. attending urology, 1988—; fellow pediatric urology Children's Hosp. of Mich., Detroit, 1990—91; resident gen. surgery Beth Israel Med. Ctr., NY, 1983—85; attending urology Luth. Med. Ctr., Bklyn., 1994—, Meth. Hosp., Bklyn., 1994—, North Shore Univ. Hosp., Manhasset, NY, 1998—; assoc. attending urology Schneider Children's Hosp., 1997—, LI Jewish Med. Ctr., New Hyde Pk., NY, 1997—; sec. bd. dirs. Bklyn. Sch. for Spl. Children, 2002. Surg. adv. com. Maimonides Med. Ctr., 1994, perioperative svcs. com., 98, exec. med. com., 1999—2002, com. on mut. respect, 2007. Co-author: (publs.) Acute Scrotal Wall Edema as the initial Manifestation of Nephrotic Syndrome, 1991, A Review of Pharmacological Treatment of Enuresis, 1997, Laparoscopic Fowler-Stephens Orchiopexy for the High Abdominal Testis, 1999, Biofeedback Therapy expedites the resolution of Reflux in Older Children, 2002, and numerous others. Recipient Outstanding Svce. as Tchg. Attending, Maimonides Med. Ctr. - Urology, 1990; named one of Best Doctors in NY, NY Mag., 2000, 2003, 2005, 2008. Fellow: ACS; mem.: AMA, Am. Acad. of Pediat., Am. Urologic Assn., Soc. of Pediatric Urology, Soc. of Fetal Urology, Bklyn. LI Urologic Soc., Bklyn. Pediatric Soc. Office: Pediatric Urology Associates 909 49th St Brooklyn NY 11219 Office Phone: 718-283-7743. Office Fax: 718-283-6603. Personal E-mail: Scccf@aol.com.

FRIEDMAN, STUART ANDREW, allergist, immunologist; MD, Universidad de Zaragoza, Spain, 1976. Diplomate Am. Bd. Internal Medicine, 1980, Am. Bd. Allergy and Immunology, 1983, lic. Fla., 1981. Resident internal medicine Winthrop Univ. Hosp., 1978—80; fellow immunology Univ. Cin., 1980—82; hosp. affiliations include Delray Med. Ctr., Boca Raton Cmty. Hosp. Named one of Top Doctors, Gulf Stream Mag., 2009. Office: Boca Raton Community Hospital 800 Meadows Rd Boca Raton FL 33486-2368 Office Phone: 561-955-7100.

FRIEDMAN, SUZANNE, holistic medical practitioner; BA in Japanese Language and Lit., Univ. Mich., Ann Arbor, Mich., 1990; JD, Univ. Colo., Boulder, Colo., 1993; DMQ in Med. Qigong Oncology, Beijing Western Dist. Qigong Sci. and TCM Rsch. Ctr., 2003. Cert. acupuncturist, herbalist. Founder San Francisco Inst. Med. Qigong (now Breath of the Dao). Chair, Medical Qigong Sci. Dept. Acupuncture and Integrative Medicine Coll., Berkeley, Calif.; asst. instr. Internat. Inst. Med. Qigong, Pacific Grove, Calif., 2004; instr. Qiqong San Francisco Sch. Massage, 2003. Contbr. articles to numerous profl. jours.; co-editor: (medical texts) Chinese Medical Qigong Therapy: A Comprehensive Clinical Text, 2005; writer, narrator, instr.: (excercise video) Guigen Qigong Video, 2003. Office: Breath of the Dao Holistic Medicine Clinic 650 Chenery St San Francisco CA 94131 Office Phone: 415-505-8855. E-mail: suzannefriedman@earthlink.net.

FRIEDMAN, SYDNEY M., anatomist, educator, medical researcher; b. Montreal, Que., Can., Feb. 17, 1916; s. Jacob and Minnie (Signer) F.; m. Constance Livingstone, Sept. 23, 1940. B.Sc., McGill U., Montreal, Can., 1938, MD, C.M., 1940, M.Sc., 1941, PhD, 1946. Med. licentiate, Que. Teaching fellow anatomy McGill U., Montreal, Que., Can., 1940-42, asst. prof. anatomy, 1944-48, assoc. prof. anatomy, 1948-50; prof., head dept. anatomy U. B.C., Vancouver, Can., 1950-81, prof. anatomy, 1981-85, prof. emeritus, 1985—. Mem. panel on shock Def. Research Bd., Ottawa, Can., 1955-57; sci. subcom. Can. Heart Found., 1962-66, Am. Heart Assn., 1966-68, B.C. Heart Found., Vancouver, founding mem. Author: Visual Anatomy, 1950, 2d edit., 1970; contbr. more than 200 articles to profl. publs. Served as flight lt. RCAF, 1943-44. Recipient Premier award for rsch. in aging CIBA Found., 1955, Outstanding Svc. award Heart Found. Can., 1981, Disting. Achievement award Can. Hypertension Soc., 1987; Commemorative medal 125th Anniversary Can. Confedn.; Pfizer travel fellow Clin. Rsch. Inst., Montreal, 1971. Fellow AAAS, Royal Soc. Can., Coun. High Blood Pressure Rsch.; mem. Am. Anatomical Assn. (exec. com. 1970-74), Can. Assn. Anatomists (pres. 1965-66, J.C.B. Grant award 1982), Internat. Soc. Hypertension, Am. Physiol. Soc., Royal Vancouver Yacht Club, Alpha Omega Alpha. Avocation: painting. Home: 4916 Chancellor Blvd Vancouver BC Canada V6T 1E1

FRIEDMANN, PAUL, surgeon, educator, research and development company executive; b. Vienna, Dec. 2, 1933; immigrated, 1938; naturalized, 1944. s. Erich and Rochelle (Behar) F.; m. Janee Armstrong, Apr. 24, 1962; children: Pamela, Cynthia. BA, U. Pa., 1955; MD, Harvard U., 1959; MBA, U. Mass., 2000. Diplomate, Am. Bd. Surgery (Vascular Surgery). Chmn. dept. surgery Baystate Med. Ctr., Springfield, Mass., 1971-98, sr. v.p. acad. affairs, 1996—2005; exec. dir. Pioneer Valley Life Scis. Rsch. Inst., Springfield, 2005—. Prof. surgery Tufts U. Sch. Medicine, Boston, 1985—, chmn. ad interim dept. surgery, 1996-2001; mem. residency rev. com., 1985-91, chmn., 1989-91; chmn. RRC Coun., Accreditation Coun. for Grad. Med. Edn., 1989-91, mem., 1994-2000, dean's prof. in biomed. innovation Isenberg Sch. Mgmt., U. Mass., Amherst, 2006-. Contbr. articles to profl. jours. Pres. Springfield Symphony Orch., 1999—2001, bd. chmn., 2001—03. Capt. USAF, 1961—63. Fellow ACS (bd. govs. 1978-84, 94—, vice chmn., 1998-99, pres. Mass. chpt.

1987, exec. com. bd. govs. 1996-99, adv. coun. for gen. surgery 1996-2003, chmn. 2001-03), Am. coll. Surgeons (2nd v.p. 2007-08); mem. Am. Surg. Assn., Assn. Program Dirs. in Surgery (sec. 1985-87, pres. 1987-89), Coun. Med. Specialty Socs. (bd. dirs., sec. 1995-96, pres. elect 1996-97, pres. 1997-98), New Eng. Soc. Vascular Surgery (recorder 1989-90, pres.-elect 1990-91, pres. 1991-92), New Eng. Surg. Soc. (treas. 1991-95, pres.-elect 1995-96, pres. 1996-97), Accreditation Coun. for Grad. Med. Edn. (exec. com. 1995—, chmn. designate 1997-98, chmn. 1998-2000, John C. Gienapp award Contbns. Grad. Med. Edn. 2003). Office: PVLSI 3601 Main St Springfield MA 01199-1001 Personal E-mail: p.friedmann@comcast.net, paul.friedmann@bhs.org.

FRIEDRICH, MICHAEL, gynecologist; s. Helmut and Edith Friedrich; m. Monika Kremer, May 23, 1998; children: Dominique, Cecile, Pascal, Benedict. MD, U. Freiburg, Germany, 1991. Sr. registrar dept. ob-gyn. U. Hosp. Homburg, Germany, 1992—2003, Saar, 1992—2003; vice dir. dept. ob-gyn. U. Lübeck Hosp., Germany, 2003—07. Dir. dept. ob-gyn. Tchg. Hosp., Krefeld, Germany, 2007. Contbr. articles to profl. jour. Recipient Mittelrheinische, DGGG. Office: Dept Ob-Gyn Lutherplatz 40 47805 Krefeld Germany Office Fax: 00492151322220. Personal E-mail: friedrichmichael@hotmail.com. Business E-Mail: michael.friedrich@helios-kliniken.de.

FRIELINGSDORF, JÜRGEN, physician, consultant; s. Paul Frielingsdorf and Helga Von Zeppelin. MD, U. Zürich, Switzerland, 1983. Cons. Stadtspital Triemli, Zürich, 2000—09. Contbr. articles in profl. jours. including Circulation and Jour. Am. Coll. Cardiology. Recipient Hypertension award, Swiss Soc. Hypertension, 2000; nominee Prof., U. Zurich, 2010. Avocations: sports, reading, history. Office: Kantonsspital Brauerstrasse 15 8400 Winterthur Switzerland Business E-Mail: juergen.frielingsdorf@ksw.ch.

FRIEMAN, BARBARA G., orthopaedic surgeon; BA, Skidmore Coll., Saratoga Springs, NY; MD, Thomas Jefferson U., Phila., Pa., 1980. Lic. Pa., 1981, NJ, 1993, diplomate Am. Bd. Orthopaedic Surgery. Intern Main Line Hosp.; resident gen. surgery Thomas Jefferson Univ. Hosp., 1981, fellow orthop. surgery, 1985. Author: (jours.) Effusion criteria and clinical importance of glenohumeral joint fluid: MR imaging evaluation, 1995, Rotator cuff disorders: interobserver and intraobserver variation in diagnosis with MR imaging, 1995, Anterior acromioplasty: effect of litigation and workers' compensation, 1995, Indications, technique, and results of total shoulder arthroplasty in osteoarthritis, 1998, Tuberoplasty: creation of an acromiohumeral articulation-a treatment option for massive, irreparable rotator cuff tears, 2002. Named one of the Top Doctors, Phila. Mag., 2011. Mem.: Am. Acad. Orthop. Surgeons, Am. Shoulder & Elbow Surgeons, Pa. Orthop. Soc., Phila. Orthop. Soc., Ruth Jackson Women's Orthop. Assn. Office: Jefferson University Hospital Rothman institute 925 Chestnut St 5th Fl Philadelphia PA 19107 Office Phone: 000-321-2222. Office Fax: 215 503 0568.

FRIEND, HAROLD CHARLES, neurologist; b. Chgo., Nov. 28, 1946; s. Leonard Nathan and Sharlee (Friedman) F.; children: Reed, Chad. BA, U. Tex., 1968, MD, 1972. Diplomate Am. Bd. Neurology. Resident Upstate Med. Ctr., Syracuse, NY, 1972-73, Albert Einstein Coll. Medicine, Bronx, NY, 1973-75; mem. staff Boca Raton Cmty. Hosp., Fla., 1975—; pres. Neurosci. Ctr., Boca Raton, Fla., 1984—2007, Boca Neurology, Boca Raton, Fla., 2006—; rsch. prof. dept. brain sci. Fla. Atlantic U., Boca Raton, 2002—05, clin. prof. biomed. scis., 2004, co-dir. neurosci. and neurobehavior, 2004—07, clin. dir. neurosci. and neurobehavior, 2007—08, adj. clin. prof. biomed. scis., 2007—; affilate rsch. prof. Ctr. Complex Sys. Brain Scis., 2008—. Spl. expert witness Fla. Agy. for Health Care Adminstrn.; expert med. advisor divsn. workers compensation Fla. Dept. Labor and Employment Security, 1994-2003; pres. Puget Sound Yellow Taxi, Inc., 1994-95. Author: Territorial Marking, 1968, Bell's Palsy, 1975, Transient Global Amnesia, 1977. Exec. bd., v.p. Gulfstream coun. Boy Scouts Am., 1988—93, pres. coun., area IV v.p., 1993—95, area I v.p., 1990—92, area IV pres., 1995—98, so. region exec. bd., 1993—, internat. scouting com., 1998—, chmn. direct svc. com., 1999—2004, nat. adv. coun., 2000—; treas. Interam. Scout Found., 2001—07, pres., 2003—05; exec. bd. Palm Beach County agy. rels. com. United Way, 1992—95, allocation com., 1990—92; chmn. direct svc. com. Boy Scouts Am., 2010—; bd. dirs. Raton Children's Mus., 1989—92. Recipient Order of Arrow Vigil Honor award Boy Scouts Am., 1983, Dist. Merit award, 1987, Silver Beaver award, 1990, Disting. Commr. award, 1991, Disting. Eagle Scout, 1997, Silver Antelope award, 1997, Silver Buffalo award, 2008, Youth in America's award, 2010; James West fellow, 1993, 1910 Soc., 1998, Baden Powell fellow, 2000. Fellow: Am. Acad. Neurology; mem.: Am. Headache Soc., Fla. Med. Assn., Fla. Soc. Neurology, NY Acad. Sci. (life), So. Clin. Neurol. Soc., Am. Soc. Neuroimaging (cert.), Internat. Fellowship Wellness & Fitness Rotarians (internat. chair 2010—), Internat. Fellowship Scouting Rotarians (N.Am. sect. chmn. 1995—96, internat. sec. 1996—98, internat. vice chair 1998—99, internat. chair 1999—2002, internat. commr. 2002—05, internat. v.p. human resources 2007—08, nominating com. chair 2008—, Silver Wheel award 2002), Rotary Internat. Fellowship Running and Fitness Rotarians (internat. chmn. 1992—98, internat. treas. 1998—99, internat. sec. 1999—2001, internat. chair 2003—06, 2008—10), Boca Raton Road Runners Club (pres. 1992—93), Rotary (bd. dir., pres. Boca Raton Club dist. world fellowship chmn. 1992—94, dist. found. chmn. 1994, gov.'s rep. 1994—95, chmn. dist. conf. 1995, gov.'s rep. 1996—97, dist. gov. 1998—99, chmn. coll. gov. 1999—2000, zone coord. Children at Risk 2000—01, cmty. svc. task force 2001—02, fellowship com. 2004—05, chair (polio), District Found. 2009—, Dist. Found. Svc. award 1992, Pres. Salute Commendation 1993, featured on cover of The Rotarian 2003, Paul Harris fellow), Sierra Club (life), Phi Beta Kappa, Alpha Phi Omega, Theta Xi, Phi Kappa Phi. Avocation: marathons. Office: 1500 NW 10th Ave Ste 101 Boca Raton FL 33486

FRIES, JAMES FRANKLIN, internal medicine educator; b. Normal, Ill., Aug. 25, 1938; s. Albert Charles and Orpha (Hair) F.; m. Sarah Elizabeth Tilton, Aug. 27, 1960; children: Elizabeth Ann, Gregory James. AB, Stanford U., 1960; MD, Johns Hopkins U., 1964. Diplomate Am. Bd. Internal Medicine. Intern Johns Hopkins Hosp., Balt., 1964-65, resident in medicine, 1965-66, fellow connective tissue disease divsn., 1966-68; resident in medicine Stanford (Calif.) U. Sch. Medicine, 1968-69, instr. in medicine, 1969-71, asst. prof. medicine, 1971-77, assoc. prof. medicine, 1978-93, prof. medicine, 1993—. Dir. Arthritis, Rheumatism, Aging Med. Info. Sys., Stanford, 1975—; chmn. bd. dirs. Fries Found., Menlo Park, Calif.; chmn. Healthtrac, Inc., 1984-2001; exec. com. The Health Project, 1992—. Author: Take Care of Yourself, 1975, 2004, 2009, Prognosis, 1981, Living Well, 1997, 1999, 2004, Taking Care of Your Child, 2009, The Arthritis Helpbook, 2005, Arthritis, 2005; mem. editl. bd. Jour. Rheumatology, Jour. Clin. Rheumatology. Recipient C. Everett Koop Nat. Health award, 1994; named Best Med. Specialist in U.S., Town and Country mag., 1984, Best Dr. in U.S., Good Housekeeping mag., 1991, Rsch. Hero, Arthritis Found., 2001, Highly Cited Rschr., ISI, 2008, Disting. Alumnus, Johns Hopkin's U., 2010; named one of Best Drs. in Am., Woodward-White, 1995. Master Am. Coll. Rheumatology (Clin. Rsch. award 2005); fellow ACP, Am. Coll. Med. Info. Avocations: skiing, running. Home: 135 Farm Rd Woodside CA 94062-1210 Office: Stanford U Sch Medicine 1000 Welch Rd Ste 203 Palo Alto CA 94304-1808 Office Phone: 650-723-6003. Business E-Mail: jff@stanford.edu.

FRIESECKE, RAYMOND FRANCIS, health company executive, president; b. Mar. 12, 1937; s. Bernhard P. K. and Josephine (De Tomi) F. BS in Chemistry, Boston Coll., 1959; MSCE, MIT, 1961. Product specialist Dewey & Almy Chem. divsn. W. R. Grace & Co., Inc., Cambridge, Mass., 1963-66; market planning specialist USM Corp., Boston, 1966-71; mgmt. cons. Boston, 1971-74; dir. planning and devel. Schweitzer divsn. Kimberly-Clark Corp., Lee, Mass., 1974-78; v.p. corp. planning Butler Automatic, Inc., Canton, Mass., 1978-80; pres. Butler-Europe Inc. Greenwich Conn. & Munich, Germany, 1980; v.p. mktg. and planning Butler Greenwich Inc., 1980-81; pres. Strategic Mgmt. Assocs., San Rafael, Calif., 1981-96; chmn. Beyond Health Corp., 1994—2009, Health-E-America Found., 2000—; pres. TPED Found., 2008, Beyond Health Internat., 2009—. Bd. dirs. Better Physiology, Ltd., 2000-05; corp. clk., v.p. Bldg. R&D, Inc., Cambridge, 1966-68. Host, prodr. Beyond Health Show, Sta. KEST, San Francisco, 1994—98, WWNN, 1995—2009, Sta. KBZS, 1998—2001, Stas. WRPT and WSRO, 1999—2001; host, prodr. KYCY, 2001—05; host, prodr. KRLA, KSBN, KFNX, 2003—05, KNTS, 2005—09, KKNT, 2006—09; pub.: Beyond Health News, 1995—; author: Management by Relative Product Quality, 1982, The New Way to Manage, 1983, Never Be Sick Again, 2002, Never Be Fat Again, 2007, Never Fear Cancer Again, 2011; contbr. articles to profl. jours. State chmn. Citizens for Fair Taxation, 1972-73; state co-chmn. Mass. Young Reps., 1967-69; chmn. Ward 7 Rep. Com., Cambridge, 1968-70; vice-chmn. Cambridge Rep. City Com., 1966-68; bd. dirs. Kentfield Rehab. Hosp. Found., 1986-88, chmn., 1988-91; Rep. candidate Mass. Ho. of Reps., 1964, 66; pres. Marin Rep. Coun., 1986-91; chmn. Calif. Acad., 1986-88; sec. Navy League Marin Coun., 1984-91, v.p., 1994-2000; bd. dirs. The Marin Ballet, 1996-98; bd. dirs. Insts. for Behavioral Physiology, Seattle, 1999-2000; nat. chmn. Project to End Disease, 2005—. 1st lt. U.S. Army, 1961-63. Recipient Green Sch. Green Difference award, 2010; named Businessman of Yr., Bus. Adv. Coun., 2006. Mem. NRA, Nat. Health Fedn., Am. Chem. Soc., Physicians Com. for Responsible Medicine, Marin Philos. Soc. (v.p. 1991-92), Ctr. for Sci. in Pub. Interest, Health Medicine Forum, Assn. of Am. Physicians and Surgeons, Orthomolecular Health Medicine Soc., The World Affairs Coun., Am. Holistic Health Assn., Naval Inst., Milt. Officers Assn. Am., Am. Legion. Office: 6555 Powerline Rd Ste 108 Fort Lauderdale FL 33309 Business E-Mail: raymond@beyondhealth.com.

FRIESEN, HENRY GEORGE, endocrinologist, educator; b. Morden, Man., Can., July 31, 1934; s. Frank Henry and Agnes (Unger) F.; m. Joyce Marylin Mackinnon, Oct. 12, 1967, children: Mark Henry, Janet Elizabeth. BSc, MD, U. Man., 1958. Diplomate Am. Bd. Internal Medicine. Intern Winnipeg (Man.) Gen. Hosp., 1958-60; resident Royal Victoria Hosp., Montreal, Que., 1961-62; rsch. assoc. New Eng. Centre Hosp., Boston, 1962-65; prof. exptl. medicine McGill U., Montreal, 1965-73; prof. physiology and medicine U. Man., 1973-92, head dept. physiology, 1973-92; pres. Med. Rsch. Coun. Can., 1991-2000; former founding chmn. Genome Can., Winnipeg; disting. prof. emeritus U. Man. Chmn. exec. com. Med. Rsch. Coun. Can., mem. exec. com., 1981-87; pres. Nat. Cancer Inst. Can., 1990-92. Contbr. numerous articles to profl. jours. Decorated Companion Order of Can.; recipient Gairdner Found. Internat. award, 1977, Gairdner Found. Wightman award, 2001; named to, Can. Med. Hall of Fame, 2001. Fellow Royal Soc. Can. (McLaughlin medal 1987), Royal Coll. Physicians and Surgeons; mem. AAAS, Am. Physiol. Soc., Endocrine Soc. (Koch award 1987), Can. Soc. Clin. Investigation (pres. 1974, G. Malcolm Meml. award 1982, Disting. Sci. award 1987), Nat. Acad. Scis. (fgn. assoc.), Can. Physiol. Soc., Am. Fedn. Clin. Research, Am. Soc. Clin. Investigation, Can. Soc. Endocrinology and Metabolism (past pres.), Internat. Soc. Neuroendocrinology, U.S. Nat. Acad. Sci. (fgn. assoc.). Mennonite. Office: U Man Ctr Advancement Medicine 753 Mcdermot Ave Winnipeg MB Canada R3E 0T6 Personal E-mail: hfriesen2@shaw.ca. E-mail: Henry_Friesen@umanitoba.ca. *

FRIESENECKER, BARBARA, physician; b. München, Germany, Oct. 23, 1961; d. Friedrich and Elisabeth Friesenecker. MD, Innsbruck Med. Sch., Austria, 1991. Attending U. Hosp. Gen. and Surg. Intensive Care Medicine, Innsbruck, 2001—. Recipient Young Investigators award, Blood Substitute Meeting, 1993; grantee Jubiläumsfonds, Österreichischen Nationalbank, 1995; fellow, Austrian Sci. Found., 1993—94. Avocations: skiing, hiking, travel, horseback riding, piano. Office: Med Univ Innsbruck Anichstr 35 Innsbruck A-6020 Austria Office Fax: 43 512 504 25832. Business E-Mail: barbara.friesenecker@uki.at.

FRIGER, MICHAEL, statistician, educator; b. Khabarovsk, Russia, Oct. 31, 1950; MA, Tomsk State U., Russia, 1972; PhD, Moskow State Pedagogical Inst., Russia, 1986. Assoc. prof. dept. epidemiology and health svcs. evaluation Ben-Gurion U. Negev, 2005—09, prof., dep. chair dept. epidemiology and health svcs. evaluation, 2009—. Statis. cons. Soroka U. Hosp., Beer-Sheva, 1993—2011. Mem.: Israel Statis. Assn. Home: 22 Zarchin Alexander Beer-Sheva Negev 84837 Israel Personal E-mail: friger.m1@gmail.com.

FRIGOLETTO, FREDRIC DAVID, JR., physician; b. Fitchburg, Mass., Feb. 20, 1933; s. Fredric David and Alba (Merlino) F.; m. Martha McKay, June 4, 1966; children: Susan, Laurie Anne. AB, Brown U., 1954; MA, Boston U., 1955, MD, 1962. Diplomate Nat. Bd. Med. Examiners, Am. Bd. Ob-Gyn. Intern in surgery Boston City Hosp., 1962-63, jr. asst. resident in surgery, 1963-64; resident in ob-gyn Boston Hosp. for Women, 1964-67, med. dir. ambulatory svcs., 1969-72, dir. ednl. svcs., 1973-80, dir. obstetrics, 1974-80; chief maternal-fetal medicine Brigham and Women's Hosp., Boston, 1980-89, med. dir. obstetrics, 1985-89, dir. antenatal diagnostic ctr., 1985-93, chief obstetrics, vice chmn. dept. obstetrics, 1989-93; chief Vincent Meml. Obstetrics divsn. Mass. Gen. Hosp., Boston, 1993—. William Lambert Richardson prof. obstetrics Harvard Med. Sch., 1986-93, Charles Montraville Green and Robert Montraville Green prof. ob-gyn., 1993—. Contbr. over 100 articles to profl. jours, chpts. 2 books; editor 2 books. Recipient award NIH. Fellow ACOG (chmn. com. on obstetrics 1982-85, chmn. com. on profl. stds. 1991—, pres.-elect 1995, pres. 1996); mem. Soc. Perinatal Obstetricians, Am. Gynecol. and Obstet. Soc., Am. Gynecologic Club. Office: Massachusetts Gen Hosp Dept Ob/Gyn 32 Fruit St Boston MA 02114-2620 Office Phone: 617-724-3775.

FRISÉN, JONAS, biomedical researcher; MD, Karolinska Inst., 1986—91, PhD, 1991—93. Lic. 1995. Fellow in molecular biology Bristol-Myers Squibb, Princeton, NJ, 1995—97; asst. prof. cell and molecular biology, Med. Nobel Inst. Karolinska Inst., Stockholm, 1997—2000, assoc. prof., 2000—01, prof. stem cell rsch., 2001—; sci. founder Neuronova AB, Sweden, 1998—. Office: Frisén Lab Box 285 Karolinska Inst CMB SE-171 77 Stockholm Sweden Office Phone: +46-8-524 87562. Office Fax: +46-8-32 49 27. E-mail: jonas.frisen@ki.se.

FRISHBERG, DAVID P., pathologist, director; married. AB, Bowdoin Coll., Brunswick, Maine, 1979; MD, George Washington U., Washington, 1984. Diplomate dermatopathology Am. Bd. Pathology and Dermatology, 1993, anatomic and clin. pathology Am. Bd. Pathology, 1989. Lt. col. USMC, 1984—96; staff dermatopathologist Armed Forces Inst. Pathology, Washington, 1995—96; chief, anatomic pathology Walter Reed Army Med. Ctr., Washington, 1993—96; dir. surg. pathology St. Agnes Hosp., Balt., 1996—2000; chief pathology Sinai Hosp. Balt., 2000—06; dir. surg. pathology Cedars-Sinai Med. Ctr., LA, 2006—10, dir. anat. pathology, 2010—. Vice chair, surg. pathology com. Coll. Am. Pathologists, Evanston, Ill., mem., cancer com., 1997—2005; mem. Am. Joint Com. Cancer, Chgo., 2008—; pres. LA Soc. Pathologists, LA, 2009. Musician: SMC symphonic band. Trustee Barrie Sch., Silver Spring, Md., 1993—96. Decorated Meritorious Svc. medal US Army; named LA Top Doctors, LA Times, 2009. Fellow: Am. Soc.Dermatopathology, Coll. Am. Pathologists; mem.: US and Can. Acad. Pathology. Office: Cedars-Sinai Med Ctr 8700 Beverly Blvd Room 8709 Los Angeles CA 90048 Business E-Mail: frishbergd@cshs.org.

FRISHMAN, WILLIAM HOWARD, cardiologist, educator, department chairman, cardiovascular pharmacologist, gerontologist; b. NYC, Nov. 9, 1946; s. Aaron and Frances (Fishel) F.; m. Esther Rose Sandowsky, Mar. 11, 1971; children: Sheryl Renée, Amy Helene, Michael Aaron. BA, MD, Boston U., 1969. Diplomate Am. Bd. Internal Medicine, Am. Bd. Cardiovascular Medicine, Am. Bd. Critical Care Medicine, Am. Bd. Clin. Pharmacology, Am. Bd. Geriatrics, Am. Bd. Med. Mgmt. Intern Montefiore Hosp., Bronx, NY, 1969—70, resident in medicine, 1970—71, Bronx Mcpl. and Einstein Hosps., 1971—72; fellow in cardiology N.Y. Hosp.-Cornell U. Med. Coll., NYC, 1972—74, instr., 1974—76; dir. noninvasive cardiac labs. Einstein Hosp. and Montefiore Hosp., 1976—80, dir. cardiology svc., 1980—82, chief medicine, 1982—91; prof. medicine and epidemiology, assoc. chmn. dept. medicine Albert Einstein Coll. Medicine Yeshiva U., Bronx, 1991—97; prof. medicine and pharmacology, chmn. dept. medicine N.Y. Med. Coll., Valhalla, 1997—; chief of medicine Westchester Med. Ctr., Valhalla, NY, 1997—. Expert cons. cardiorenal divsn. FDA, Bethesda, Md., 1987-97; panel mem. US Pharmacopeia Conv., Rockville, Md., 1990-2000. Author: (med. book) Clinical Pharmacology of the Beta Blocking Drugs, 1980, 2nd edit., 1984, Management of Lipid Disorders, 1992, co-author: Calcium Channel Antagonists in Cardiovascular Disease, 1984, Therapy of Angina Pectoris, 1986, Current Cardiovascular Drugs, 1994, 4th edit., 2005, Beta-3 Adrenergic Agonism, 1995, Cardiovascular Pharmacotherapeutics, 1997, 2nd edit., 2003, 3rd edit., 2011, Manual of Cardiovascular Pharmacotherapeutics, 1998, 2nd edit., 2004, Hypertension: A Clinical Guide, 2001, Complementary and Integrative Therapies for Cardiovascular Disease, 2005, Cardiovascular Regeneration and Stem Cell Therapy, 2007, Hypertension - A Clinical Guide, 2007; editor: Year Book of Medicine: Heart Disease, 1998—2003, Cardiology in Rev., Am. Jour. Medicine (supplements); contbr. chapters to books and articles to profl. jours. Mem. fiscal affairs com. Village of Scarsdale, N.Y., 1991—. Lt. col. M.C., U.S. Army, 1969-90. Named to Boston Collegium of Disting. Alumni, Boston U., 1988, Disting. Alumnus sch. medicine, 1994; teaching scholar Am. Heart Assn., 1979-82; preventive cardiology acad. award Nat. Heart, Lung and Blood Inst., 1980-85; recipient Disting. Tchr. award AAMC-AOA, 1997, Med. Humanism award AAMC, 2001. Master: ACP; fellow: Am. Coll. Chest Physicians, Am. Coll. Cardiology (bd. govs. 1987—91, pres. N.Y. State chpt. 1991); mem.: N.Y. Cardiology Soc. (pres. 1996—97), Assn. Profs. Medicine, Am. Soc. for Clin. Rsch., Am. Soc. for Clin. Pharmacology and Therapeutics (McKeen Cattell award 1990), Scarsdale Town and Village Club, Alpha Omega Alpha (regional councilor, bd. dirs.). Jewish. Avocation: reading. Home: 7 White Birch Ln Scarsdale NY 10583-7634 Office: Munger Pavilion NY Med Coll Valhalla NY 10595 Home Phone: 914-723-1030; Office Phone: 914-594-4383.

FRISINA, ROBERT DANA, neuroscientist, educator; b. Evanston, Ill., Sept. 11, 1955; s. Robert and Louise (Boaz) Frisina; m. Susan Taylor Frisina, July 31, 1982; children: Laurin Taylor, Taylor Robert. AB in Exptl. Psychology summa cum laude, Hamilton Coll., 1977; PhD in Neurosci., Syracuse U., 1983. Rsch. asst. Hamilton Coll., Clinton, NY, 1977; Root fellow in sci. Inst. Sensory Rsch., Syracuse (NY) U., 1977-78, NSF grad. fellow, 1978-81, grad. rsch. assoc., 1981-83; NIH rsch. fellow Ctr. Brain Rsch. U. Rochester, 1983-85; asst. prof. physiology and otolaryngology U. Rochester, 1985-91, assoc. prof. surgery, neurobiology and anatomy, 1991-99, prof. surgery, neurobiology, anatomy, and biomed. engring., 1999—, dir. rsch. otolaryngology, 1988-92, assoc. chmn. otolaryngology, 1992—; v.p. and founder Auditory Sys. Technologies, Inc., Pittsford, 1989-98. Charter mem. adv. bd. Internat. Ctr. Hearing, Speech Rsch., 1988—2002, assoc. dir., 2002—; chmn. study sect. NIH, 2000—02; adj. assoc. prof. comm. sci. Nat. Tech. Inst. Deaf, Rochester, NY, 1993—2004, prof. comm. scis., 2004—; adj. prof. comm. scis. U. Buffalo, 1998—; disting. rsch. prof. Rochester Inst. Tech., NY, 2003—10. Dir. vols. Hamilton Coll. Aspect Marcy Psychiat. Ctr., NY, 1974—77. Recipient 1st award in Communicative Disorders, NIH, 1988—94. Fellow: Acoustical Soc. Am. (assoc. editor jour. 1996—99), Am. Acad. Otolaryngology, Head, Neck Surgery; mem.: Acoustical Soc. Found. (charter, bd. dirs. 1996—2009, gen. sec., chief fin. officer 1998—2006), Soc. Neurosci., Assn. Rsch. Otolaryngology, Psi Chi, Sigma Xi, Phi Beta Kappa. Roman Cath. Achievements include patents for for a noise suppression electronic circuit for enhancing speech in the presence of background noise; a hearing aid circuit which can be custom fit to a patients's hearing loss using laser trimming. Office: U Rochester Med Ctr Otolaryngology Dept Rochester NY 14642-8629 Office Phone: 585-275-8130. Personal E-mail: rdjfz@aol.com. Business E-Mail: robert_frisina@urmc.rochester.edu.

FRISINGHELLI, ANNA, cardiologist; b. Biella, Italy, Aug. 18, 1964; MD, U. Milan, Italy, 1989, MSc in Sci. Comm., 2003. Cert. in cardiology U. Milan, 1993, in echocardiography Italian Soc. Cardiovasc. Echocardiography, 2003. Cardiologist Dpt Cardiologic Rehab., Passirana Hosp., Garbagnate, Italy, 1992—; del., ANMCO lombardia Assn. Nazionale Med. Cardiologi Ospedalieri, Milan, 2006—; del. Heart Care Found. Lombardia Ovest, Florence, Italy, 2008. Contbr. articles to sci. jours. Recipient Young Investigator award, Italian Soc. Cardiology, 1990, Investigator award, Italian Soc. Internal Medicine, 1991. Fellow: European Soc. Cardiology, Italian Assn. Hosp. Cardiologists; mem.: Italian Fedn. Cardiology, Italian Group Cardiac Prevention, Rehab., Italian Soc. Cardiovasc. Echocardiography. Home: Via FOPPA 45 Milano 20144 Italy Office: Passirana Hosp AO G SALVINI Viale Forlanini 121 20020 Garbagnate M.se Italy Office Phone: 3902994304471. Office Fax: 3902994304526. Personal E-mail: annafris@tin.it. Business E-Mail: afrisinghelli@aogarbagnate.lombardia.it.

FRISK, MAX HARRY DANILO, psychiatrist, medical educator; b. Lovisa, Finland, Apr. 24, 1928; m. Anja-Riitta Okkonen; children: Kjell, Måns, Dan. Med. lic., U. Helsinki, Finland, 1955; D in Medicine, U. Helsinki, 1968. Head doc. Adolescent Clinic, Helsinki; prof. Uppsala U., Sweden, 1972-93; pensioner U. Hosp., Uppsala, Sweden, 1993—. Chmn., dir. child and adolescent psychiatry SW Med. Rsch., 1987-97. Achievements include research in psychosocial, performing, physic and school problems in children and adolescents regarding different background factors such as social and family problems but with special focus on CNS-dysfunctions; dyslexia and slow cognitive processing noted as great problems in the world of today. Office: Univ Hosp Dept Child-Adol Psychiatry 750 17 Uppsala Sweden

FRIST, BILL (WILLIAM HARRISON FRIST), investment company executive, Former United States Senator from Tennessee, thoracic surgeon; b. Nashville, Feb. 22, 1952; m. Karyn McLaughlin Frist, 1982; children: Harrison, Jonathan, Bryan. AB in health care policy, Princeton U. Woodrow Wilson Sch. Pub. and Internat. Affairs, 1974; MD, Harvard U., 1978. Resident Mass. Gen. Hosp. Stanford U., 1978-83, rsch. fellow in surgery, 1983—84; chief registrar CT Surgery Southampton Gen. Hosp., Eng., 1983; chief resident CT Surgery Mass. Gen. Hosp. Stanford U., 1984-85; chief resident CT Surgery, sr. fellow cardiac transplant svc. Stanford U. Med. Ctr., 1985-86; founder, surgeon Vanderbilt Transplant Med. Ctr., 1986—, asst. prof. surgery, 1986-93, dir. heart and lung transplantation, 1986-93; founder, surgical dir. Vanderbilt Multi-Organ Transplant Ctr., 1989-93; US Senator from Tenn., 1995—2007; majority leader, 2003—07; ptnr. Cressey & Co. LP, Chgo., 2007—; Frederick H. Schultz prof. internat. econ. policy Woodrow Wilson Sch. Pub. & Internat. Affairs, Princeton U., 2007—08; Univ. Disting. prof. Owen Grad. Sch. Mgmt., Vanderbilt U., Nashville, 2008—. Mem. fin. com., health, edn., labor & pensions com., rules & adminstrn. com.; mem. Nat. Bipartisan Comm. on Future of Medicaire, 1998-99; vice chair Alliance for Health Reform, 1995; Chmn. Tenn. Medicaid Task Force, 1992-93 Author: Transplant: A Heart Surgeon's Account of the Life-and-death Dramas of the New Medicine, 1989, When Every Moment Counts: What You Need to Know About Bio-terrorism from the Senate's Only Doctor, 2002; co-author (with J. Lee Annis): Tennessee Senators, 1911-2001: Portraits of Leadership in a Century of Change, 1999; co-author: (with Shirley Wilson) Good People Beget Good People: A Genealogy of the Frist Family, 2003; editor (with J. Harold Helderman): Grand Rounds in Transplantation, 1995. Bd. regents Smithsonian Inst., Washington; bd. trustees Princeton U.; bd. dirs. Sergeant York Hist. Assn., YMCA Found. Met. Nashville. Recipient Taxpayer's Hero award, Coun. for Citizens Against Govt. Waste, 1997, Taxpayer's Friend award, Nat. Taxpayer's Union, 1998, Champion of Sci. award, Sci. Coalition, 1999, Hero of the Taxpayer, Americans for Tax Reform, 2000, Disting. Bd. Dir. award, Healthcare Fin. Mgmt. Assn., 2002, Nat. Leadership award, The Nat. Ctr. for Leadership, 2002, Excellence in Immunization award, Nat. Partnership for Immunization, 2002, Congl. Champion award, YMCA, 2003, IRI Freedom award, Internat. Rep. Inst., 2003, James Madison award, Am. Whig-Cliosophic Soc., 2003, Woodrow Wilson award, Princeton U., 2003, Lifetime Achievement award, Nat. Minority Health Month, 2003; named one of most influential people, TIME mag., 2005. Mem. Alpha Omega Alpha, Am. Coll. Chest Physicians, Am. Coll. Surgeons, AMA, Tenn. Med. Assn., Am. Soc. Transplant Surgeons, Assn. Acad. Surgery, Internat. Soc. Heart & Lung Transplantation, Middle Tenn. Heart Assn. (pres.), Soc. Thoracic Surgeons, So. Thoracic Surgical Assn., Tenn. Transplant Soc., United Way De Tocqueville Soc. Republican. Presbyn. Office: Owen Graduate School Management Vanderbilt University 401 21st Ave S Nashville TN 37203 Office Phone: 615-322-2534. E-mail: bill.frist@owen.vanderbilt.edu.

FRISTAD, MARY ANTONETTE, psychology professor; b. Mandan, ND, Oct. 22, 1959; d. C. Gus and Helen R. (Minette) F.; m. Joseph F. Fiala, June 18, 1988; children: Elise M. Fiala, Peter J. Fiala. BA, Coll. of St. Catherine, 1981; MA, U. Kans., 1983, PhD, 1986. Lic. psychologist Ohio, cert. in clin. psychology, in clin. child and adolescent psychology. Intern clin. child psychology Brown U., Providence, 1985-86; mem. psychology staff, rsch. coord. children's program Ohio State U. Divsn. Child/Adolescent Psychiatry, Columbus, 1986—; clin. child psychologist, divsn. child and adolescent psychiatry Ohio State U., Columbus, 1987—, dir. child psychiatry outpatient program, 1989-90, asst. prof. dept. psychiatry, 1986-92, asst. prof. dept. psychology, 1987-91, dir. rsch., child and adolescent psychiatry, 1990—, assoc. prof. dept. psychiatry to prof. psychiatry and psychology, 1992—, dir. child psychometric lab., 1992—. Presenter in field; mem. human subjects com. Coll. Medicine Ohio State U., Columbus, 1993—, mem. faculty recruitment subcoms. depts. pediatrics and family rels. and human devel., 1989, mem. child/adolescent faculty recruitment subcom. dept. psychiatry, 1987-88, mem. med. records subcom. dept. psychiatry, 1986—, mem. clin. psychology internship tng. com. dept. psychiatry, 1986-89, mem. child and adolescent psychiatry edn. com., 1986—. Occasional reviewer Jour. Abnormal Child Psychology, Jour. Cons. and Clin. Psychology, Children's Hosp. Rsch. Found. Grant Proposals; co-author: (with others) Current Perspectives on Major Depressive Disorders in Children, 1984, Psychoeducational Psychotherpy (PEP): Treatment Manual for Children with mood Disorders, A Clinical Manual for the Management of Bipolar Disorder in Children and Adolescents, Childhood Mental Health Disorders: Evidence Base and contextuyal Factors for Psychosocial, Psychopharmacological, and Combined Interventions; contbr. articles to profl. jours., book chapters. Nat. Merit scholar, 1977-81; recipient Mother Antonio McHugh award, 1981, 6th Annual Clin. Rsch. award Am. Acad. Clin. Psychiatrists, 10th Annual Clin. Rsch. award Amm. Acad. Clin. Psychiatrists, 1988, NIMH Traineeship, 1981-82; grantee NIMH, 1989-90, 90-95, 91-95, Ohio State U. Seed grantee, 1986, 90-91, Ohio State U. Bremer grantee, 1986, 89-90, Ohio Dept. Mental Health grantee, 1987, Nat. Rsch. and Info. grantee, 1985. Mem. APA (divsn. 12 clin. psychology sect. I clin. child psychology, divsn. 37 child and youth and family svcs., divsn. 43 family psychology, pres. divsn. 53 Soc. Clin. Child and Adolescent Psychology, 2009), Ohio Psychol. Assn., Mental Health Assn. Ohio, Soc. Rsch. in Child and Adolescent Psychopathology, Thomas More Soc., Psi Chi, Phi Beta Kappa, Pi Gamma Mu, Kappa Gamma Pi. Roman Catholic. Avocation: music. Office: Dept Psychology Ohio State Univ 1670 Upham Dr Ste 460G Columbus OH 43210 Office Phone: 614-293-4572. Office Fax: 614-293-4949. Business E-Mail: fristad.1@osu.edu. *

FRITSCH, MICHAEL H., surgeon, educator; b. Jan. 01; MD, U. Nebr., 1980. Physician, prof., 1987—. Mem.: Am. Acad. Otolaryngology-Head and Neck Surgery. Office: 9002 N Meridian Str Ste 204 Indianapolis IN 46260 Office Fax: 317-848-3623. Personal E-mail: mfritschmd@gmail.com.

FRITTS, HARRY WASHINGTON, JR., retired internist, educator; b. Rockwood, Tenn., Oct. 4, 1921; s. Harry Washington and Hyder (Smith) F.; m. Helen Dyer Goodwin, Aug. 25, 1949; children: John Goodwin, Benjamin Carroll, Patricia Louise. Student, Vanderbilt U., 1941; BS, Mass. Inst. Tech., 1943; MD, Boston U., 1951. Diplomate: Am. Bd. Internal Medicine (mem.). Mem. research staff MIT, 1946-47; intern, then resident Univ. Hosp., Boston, 1951-53; vis. fellow Columbia Coll. Physicians and Surgeons, 1953-56, mem. faculty, 1956-73, prof. medicine, 1967-73, Dickinson W. Richards prof. medicine, 1972-73; prof., chmn. dept. medicine Sch. Medicine, State U. N.Y. at Stony Brook, 1973-87, Edmund D. Pellegrino prof. medicine, 1986-87. William Harris vis. prof. Nat. Med. Sch. Taiwan, 1987-88; vis. physician Bellevue Hosp., 1957-68, Presbyn. Hosp., N.Y.C., 1961-73; vis. physician, cons. Manhattan VA Hosp., 1957-68; vis. prof. U. London, 1982; bd. dirs., adv. council research N.Y. Heart Assn.; mem. sci. council Parker Francis Found.; mem. physiology study sect., mem. cardiovascular tng. com. USPHS; mem. council Nat. Heart, Lung and Blood Inst. Author: On Leading a Clinical Department, 1997; assoc. editor: Jour. Clin. Investigation; mem. editl. bd.: Am. Rev. Respiratory Diseases; contbr. articles to profl. jours. Served to lt. (j.g.) USNR, 1943-46. Guggenheim fellow, 1959-60 Fellow ACP; mem. Am. Physiol. Soc., Am. Soc. Clin. Investigation, Assn. Am. Physicians, Am. Clin. and Climatol. Soc., Alpha Omega Alpha. Home: 79 Bevin Rd Northport NY 11768-1133 Office: SUNY at Stony Brook Dept Medicine Stony Brook NY 11794-0001

FRITZ, BARBARA JEAN, occupational health nurse; b. Helena, Mont., Sept. 16, 1936; d. Marion Caldwell and Clara K. (Bernard) Heffern; m. Bernard John Fritz Sept. 2, 1961; children: Cathleen, Stephen, Elizabeth. Diploma in nursing, Sacred Heart Sch. Nursing, 1957; BS in Nursing, St. Louis U., 1959; postgrad., Oreg. State U., Portland State U., Oreg. Health Scis. U. Cert. occupl. health nurse. Occupl. health nurse Chloride Western Battery, Portland, Oreg., 1984-85; occupl. health nurse unit mgr. Pub. Health Dept. Fed. Occupl. Health, Portland, 1985-86; occupl. health relief nurse James River Corp., Portland, 1986-88; occupl. health nurse Harder Mech./James River Site, Camas, Wash., 1988; health and safety mgr. Armour Foods, Portland, 1988-90; occupl. health cons. Pacific Rim Occupl. Health & Safety Svcs., Portland, 1990—2009; occupl. health nurse mgr. Toyota Vehicle Processing, Inc., Portland, 1992-95; med. case mgr. Gates McDonald, Beaverton, Oreg., 1995-96; temp. occupl. health mgr. L.S.I. Logic, Gresham, Oreg., 1997; parish nurse St. Charles Cath. Ch., 2005—; relief nurse Gen. Motors, 2000—06. Relief occupl. health cons. Atlas, Copco, Wagner Mining, Portland, 1986-99, 2011; instr. in field. Chmn. northeast citizen's adv. Portland Planning Commn., 1988, com. historic landmarks, 1988; mem. Urban Tour Group, Portland; leadership group Mid-County Sewer Project, 1992-2011; vol. Portland Ctr. Performing Arts. Recipient Cert. of Appreciation, 25th Anniversary of Urban Tour Group, 1995. Mem. Am. Assn. Occupl. Health Nurses, Oreg. State Assn. Occupl. Health Nurses (registered lobbyist, historian 1992-96, govtl. affairs co-chair 1995-96, chair 1996-97, Nat. Govtl. Affairs award 1996, 98). Democrat. Roman Catholic. Avocation: floral arranging. Home and Office: 4705 NE Ainsworth St Portland OR 97218-1818 Office Phone: 503-288-1027. Personal E-mail: prohealthme@msn.com.

FRITZ, EDWARD LANE, dentist; b. Evansville, Ind., Dec. 15, 1932; s. Edward E. and Virginia B. (Lane) F.; m. Bettye J. Samples, July 31, 1954; children: Mary Ann, Sarah Jane. AB, Ind. U., 1954, DDS, 1957; BS, U. Evansville, 1975, MBA, 1978. Pvt. practice dentistry, Evansville, 1959-99; ret.; pres., chmn. bd. Health Resources, Inc., 1986-99, chmn. bd., 1986—2007. Corp. bd. dirs. Va. Corp., Evansville, 1962-72, Dynatron, Inc., 1980-87; bd. dir. S.W. Ind. Oral Health Found. Editor: The Bulletin of the Am. Assn. of Dental Examiners, 1981-85. Capt. U.S. Army, 1957-59. Named Disting. Alumnus Ind. U. Sch. Dentistry, 1991. Fellow Am. Coll. Dentists (ethics achievement award 2004), Acad. Gen. Dentistry, Acad. Dentistry Internat., Internat. Coll. Dentists; mem. ADA (continuing edn. com. 1981-83, cons./evaluator 1980), Ind. Dental Assn. (trustee 1983-91, Disting. Svc. award 1996), Vanderburgh County Dental Soc. (pres. 1967, various offices), First Dist. Dental Soc. (pres. 1976-77, various offices), Am. Assn. Dental Examiners (pres. 1989, various offices), Ind. Bd. Dental Examiners (pres. 1982-83, sec. 1980-82), Acad. Operative Dentistry, Internat./Am. Assn. Dental Rsch., Am. Assn. Dental Editors, Acad. Gen. Dentistry, Pierre Fauchard Acad., Sagamores of the Wabash, Ky. Col., Phi Kappa Phi. Home: 12200 Edgewater Dr Evansville IN 47720-8169

FRITZ, JUERGEN, orthopedist, consultant; married. MD, U. Tuebingen, Germany, 1995. CEO Tetec Ag, Reutlingen, Germany, 2000—09. Cons. orthopaedic surgeon Winghofer Medicum, Rottenburg, Germany, 2004—. Contbr. surgical manuals. Mem.: Internat. Cartilage Repair Soc. (Zürich), DGU(Berlin). Achievements include patents for surgical instruments and implants for cartilage repair. Office: Winghofer Medicum Roentgenstrasse 38 Rottenburg 72108 Germany Office Phone: 49. 7472. 926-0. Business E-Mail: fritz@tetec-ag.de, j.fritz@winghofer-medicum.de.

FRITZ, JULIE M., physical therapist, educator; b. Valparaiso, Ind., Feb. 28, 1968; MS in Phys. Therapy, U. Indpls., 1992; PhD, U. Pitts., 1998. Assoc. prof. U. Utah, 2004—. Clin. outcomes rsch. scientist Intermountain Healthcare, 2004. Office: 520 Wakara Way Salt Lake City UT 84108 Office Fax: 801-585-5629. Personal E-mail: julie.fritz1@comcast.net.

FRITZHAND, IRVIN DICK, psychologist; b. Bklyn., Aug. 2, 1936; s. Philip and Hannah Frances (Arbeit) Fritzhand; m. Sheila Wynn Block, June 23, 1963; children: Alan, Aaron, Jason. BS, CUNY, Bklyn., 1959; MS, CUNY, NYC, 1962; PhD, Hofstra U., 1974. Lic. psychologist NY, state cert. sch. psychologist NY; workers compensation bd. cert. authorization. Psychol. examiner NYU, NYC, 1963; grad. tchg. asst. La. State U., Baton Rouge, 1963-64; psychologist children's unit Kings Park Psychiat. Ctr., NY, 1964-71, supervising psychologist children's unit, 1971-73, treatment team leader, 1973-76, treatment svc. chief, 1983-95; pvt. practice psychology Smithtown, NY, 1975—2003; chief treatment svc. Central Islip Psychiat. Ctr., NY, 1976-83. Cons. psychologist Advanced Ctr. Psychotherapy, Hempstead, NY, 1966—72; panel psychologist NY Bur. Disability Determination, 1977—2003; adj. supr. grad. psychology dept. Hofstra U., Hempstead, 1971—75. Mem. editl. bd. Jour. Psychiat. Treatment and Evaluation, 1980—81. Mem.: APA, Am. Acad. Behavioral Medicine (diplomate in behavioral medicine 1980), Internat. Acad. Profl. Counseling and Psychotherapy (diplomate in psychotherapy 1983), Obsessive-Compulsive Found., Am. Profl. Soc. Abuse Children, Coun. Nat. Register Health Svc. Providers Psychology, Assn. Advancement Behavior Therapy, Suffolk County Psychol. Assn., NY State Psychol. Assn., Ea. Psychol. Assn. Jewish. Avocations: swimming, bicycling, gardening, travel, chess. Personal E-mail: dfritzphd@aol.com.

FROEHLICH, FLORIAN EMANUEL, gastroenterologist, educator; b. Zurich, Switzerland, Dec. 17, 1959; s. Rudolf and Annemarie Froehlich; m. Isabelle Duthé, May 0, 1989; children: Lorin, Auréliane, Naël, Anaïs. MD, U. Zurich, 1986. Registered Swiss Med. Assn., 1995. Surg. resident Wattwil Hosp., Switzerland, 1987—88; med. resident Moutier Hosp., Switzerland, 1988—89; gastroent. resident U. Lausanne, Switzerland, 1989—90, med. resident, 1990—91, gastroent. registrar, 1992—95, gastroent. resident, 1993, asst. prof. gastroenterology, 1997—2005; rsch. fellow RAND, UCLA, 1995; head, gastroenterology Porrentruy Regional Hosp., Switzerland, 1995—; asst. prof. gastroenterology U. Basle, Switzerland, 2005—. Mem. editl. bd. Jour. Endoscopy, 2005—; reviewer European Jour. Gastroenterology & Hepatology, Scandinavian, Jour. Gastroenterology, Social & Preventive Medicine. Contbr. articles over 100 original peer review jours. 1st lt. Arty. Recipient Peter Reizenstein prize, Internat. Soc. Quality in Health Care, 2000, prize, Lausanne Inst. Social & Preventive Medicine, 2006. Fellow: Am. Coll. Gastroenterology; mem.: Gastromed Suisse, Swiss Ultrasound Soc., Swiss Soc. Internal Medicine (Oral Presentation prize 1997), IBD. Net, Am. Soc. Gastrointestinal Endoscopy, Am. Gastroent. Assn., Swiss Soc. Gastroenterology & Hepatology (Rsch. prize 1993, 1995, 1997, poster prize 2003). Office: Rue Achille-Merguiin 44 Porrentruy Jura CH-2900 Switzerland Office Fax: 41324662955. Business E-Mail: florian.froehlich@bluewin.ch.

FROESCHER, WALTER EBERHARD, retired neurologist; b. Biberach, Germany, Mar. 14, 1941; s. Julius Karl Georg and Emma Emilie (Wanner) F.; m. Mathilde Gertraud Huerkamp, Aug. 25, 1967; children: Rolf, Hans-Joerg, Felix. MD, U. Tuebingen, Germany, 1967; Habilitation, U. Bonn, Germany, 1978. Lic. neurologist and psychiatrist. With dept. internal medicine U. Tuebingen Gen. Hosp., Laupheim, 1967—69; resident, asst. med. dir., prof. dept. neurology, epileptology and psychiatry U. Bonn, 1969-85; med. supt. dept. neurology and epileptology Ravensburg-Weissenau U. Ulm, Germany, 1985—2005; pvt. practice Markdorf, Germany, 2005—. Vis. assoc. prof. dept. neurology Johns Hopkins Hosp., Balt., 1984. Author: Treatment of Status Epilepticus, 1979; editor: Tolerance to Beneficial and Adverse Effects of Antiepileptic Drugs, 1986, Neurology, 1991, Mental Disturbance in Epilepsy, 1992, The Epilepsies, 1993, The Treatment of Epilepsy, 2000, Neurology, reprint, 2001, The Epilepsies, 2nd edit., 2004, Med. Treatment Epilepsies, 4th edit., 2008. With German Army, 1960—61. Grantee Fed. Sec. for Youth, Family and Health, 1975, Deutsche Forschungsgemeinschaft, 1977, 94. Mem. German & Polish League Against Epilepsy (hon.), Royal Soc. Medicine. Office Phone: 07515579585. Personal E-mail: w.froescher@arcor.de.

FROHLICH, EDWARD DAVID, medical educator; b. NYC, Sept. 10, 1931; s. William and May (Zneimer) F.; m. Sherry Linda Fine, Nov. 1, 1959; children: Marjorie, Bruce, Lara. BA, Washington and Jefferson Coll., 1952; MD, U. Md., 1956; MS, Northwestern U., 1963; DSc (hon.), U. Buenos Aires, 2001. Diplomate Am. Bd. Internal Medicine. Intern, resident D.C. Gen. Hosp., 1956-58; resident Georgetown U. Hosp., Washington, 1958—60; clin. investigator VA Rsch. Hosp., Chgo., 1962-64; assoc. in medicine Northwestern U., 1963-64; staff mem. rsch. divsn. Cleve. Clinic, 1964-69; prof. medicine, physiology and biophysics U. Okla., Oklahoma City, 1969-76, George Lynn Cross rsch. prof., 1975-76; prof. medicine and physiology La. State U., 1976—; clin. prof. medicine, adj. prof. pharmacology Tulane U., 1976—; mem. staff, v.p. edn. and rsch. Alton Ochsner Med. Found., 1976—86, v.p. acad. affairs, 1986—89, disting. scientist, 1986—. Cons. in field. Editor: Pathophysiology-Altered Regulatory Mechanisms in Disease, 1972, 1976, 1984, Rypins' Medical Licensure Examinations, 13th - 18th edits., 1981—2001, Rypins' Intensive Revs., 13 vols., 1996, Take Heart, 1990, Hypertension: Evaluation and Treatment, 1998, Hypertension Atlas, 2009; editor-in-chief: Jour. Lab. and Clin. Medicine, 1973—76, Hypertension, 1994—2002; mem. editl. bd. (jours.) Am. Jour. Cardiology, 1982—91; actor(mem. editl. bd.): (jours.) Am. Jour. Cardiology, 2002—05; consulting editor (jours.) Am. Jour. Cardiology, 2006—, mem. editl. bd. Circulation, 1978—91, Archives of Internal Medicine, 1978—88, Modern Medicine, 1980—2000, Jour. Hypertension, 1994—2003; assoc. editor: Am. Jour. Physiology, Heart Circulation; contbr. chapters to books, articles to profl. jours. Capt. U.S. Army, 1960-62. Recipient Honors Achievement award, Angiology Rsch. Found., 1964, Ann. award, So. Med. Assn., 1971, Janice M. Pfeffer Disting. Lectureship, Internat. Soc. Heart Rsch., 2005, William Harvey award, Am. Soc. Hypertension, 2007; rsch. fellow, Georgetown U. Hosp., 1958—59. Master: ACP (laureate 1996); fellow: AAAS, Coun. High Blood Pressure Rsch. (exec. com. 1972—75, 1981—85, vice chmn. 1986—88, chmn. 1989—91), Am. Coll. Cardiology (gov. La. chpt. 1988—91, bd. trustees La. chpt. 1991—92, 1996—2000, Disting. Scientist award 2005), Royal Coll. Physicians and Surgeons Glasgow (hon.); mem.: Am. Soc. Hypertension (William Harvey award 2007), Polish Acad. Arts Sci. (faculty medicine), Columbian Soc. Cardiology, Peruvian Soc. Cardiology, Assn. Am. Physicians, Am. Soc. Clin. Investigations, So. Soc. Clin. Rsch., Ctrl. Soc. Clin. Rsch., Am. Soc. Nephrology, Am. Physiol. Soc., Am. Soc. Clin. Pharmacology and Therapeutics (past pres.), Am. Soc. Pharmacology and Exptl. Therapeutics, Am. Soc. Clin. Investigation, Soc. Geriat. Cardiology (pres. 2000—01), Inter-Am. Soc. Hypertension (Lifetime Achievement award 1999), Am. Heart Assn. (dir. La. chpt. 1979—83, chmn. Coun. High Blood Pressure Rsch. 1988—91, award of merit 1986, Lifetime Achievement award 1994, Okamoto Internat. award 1994), Internat. Soc. Hypertension (sci. coun. 1974—84, treas. 1980—82, v.p. 1982—84, Astra award 2000), Alpha Kappa Alpha, Phi Sigma, Chi Epsilon Mu. Office: Ochsner Clinic Found 1516 Jefferson Hwy New Orleans LA 70121-2429 Office Phone: 504-842-3700. Business E-Mail: efrohlich@ochsner.org.

FROHMAN, LAWRENCE ASHER, endocrinology educator, scientist; b. Detroit, Jan. 26, 1935; s. Dan and Rebecca (Katzman) F.; m. Barbara Hecht, June 9, 1957; children: Michael, Marc, Erica, Rena. MD, U. Mich., 1958. Diplomate: Am. Bd. Internal Medicine. Intern Yale-New Haven Med. Ctr., 1958—59, resident in internal medicine, 1959—61; asst. prof. medicine SUNY, Buffalo, 1965—69, assoc. prof., 1969—73; prof. medicine U. Chgo., 1973—81; dir. endocrinology Michael Reese Hosp., Chgo., 1973—81; prof., dir. div. endocrinology and metabolism U. Cin., 1981—92; prof. medicine U. Ill., Chgo., 1992—, chmn. Dept. Medicine, 1992—2001; dir. Med. Svcs. U. Ill. Hosp., Chgo., 1992—2001. Dir. Gen. Clin. Rsch. Ctr., 1986-90; mem. sci. rev. com. NIH, Bethesda, Md., 1972-76; mem. sci. rev. bd. VA, Washington, 1979-82; mem. endocrine adv. bd. FDA, Washington, 1982-86; mem. adv. com. Nat. Inst. Diabetes, Digestive and Kidney Diseases, NIH, 1983-94, chmn., 1991-93; mem. sci. adv. bd. Edison Biotech. Inst., Ohio U. Editor: (with others) Endocrinology and Metabolism, 2001; editl. bd. 7 med. and sci. jours., 1970—; contbr. articles to profl. jours. NIH research grantee, 1967-98, Endocrine Soc. Rorer Clin. Investigator award, 1991. Mem.: ACP, Ctrl. Soc. Clin. Rsch. (pres. 2004), Am. Clin. Climatological Assn., Pituitary Soc., Internat. Soc. Neuroendocrinology, Am. Diabetes Assn., Am. Soc. Clin. Investigation, Assn. Am. Physicians, Endocrine Soc. Office: U Ill at Chgo Sect Endocrinology M/C 275 1747 W Roosevelt Rd Rm 517 Chicago IL 60608-7333 Office Phone: 312-996-7525. Business E-Mail: frohman@uic.edu.

FROLIK, LAWRENCE ANTON, lawyer, educator, consultant; b. Lincoln, Nebr., Jan. 10, 1944; s. Elvin F. and Rita K. (Haley) F.; m. Ellen M. Doyle, Sept. 25, 1973; children: Winnefred, Cornelius. BA with distinction, U. Nebr., 1966; JD cum laude, Harvard U., 1969, LLM cum laude, 1972. Asst. prof. U. Pitts., 1975-78, assoc. prof., 1978-81, prof., 1981—. Bd. dirs. Kendal Corp., 2000-10. Author: Loss and Damage, 1987, Fed. Tax Aspects of Injury, 1993; co-author: Pa. Elder Law Manual, 1988, Advising the Elderly and Disabled Client, 1991, 4th edit., 2007, Elderly and the Law: Cases and Materials, 5th edit., 2011, Elder Law in a Nutshell, 1995, 5th edit., 2010, Aging and the Law: An Interdisciplinary Reader, 1999, Law of Employer Pension and Welfare Benefits, 2nd edit., 2008, The Law of Later-Life Health Care and Decision Making, 2006, Residence Options For Older and Disabled, 2008, Everyday Law for Seniors, 2010; editor -in-chief NAELA Journal, 2006—08. Exec. com. Gruter Inst. Law and Behavioral Rsch., Pa. AARP exec. coun., 2002-08, Pa. Coun. on Aging, 2003-05. Capt. U.S. Army, 1969-71. Capt. US Army, 1969—71. Named Disting. Faculty scholar. Fellow Am. Bar Found., Am. Coll. Trust and Estate Counsel; mem. Phi Beta Kappa. Office: U Pitts Sch Law 3900 Forbes Ave. Pittsburgh PA 15260 Home: 154 N Bellefield Ave Apt 96 Pittsburgh PA 15213-2691 Office Phone: 412-648-1363. Business E-Mail: frolik@pitt.edu.

FROMM, ERWIN FREDERICK, retired insurance company executive; b. Kalamazoo, Oct. 24, 1933; s. Erwin Carl and Charlotte Elizabeth (Wilson) F. Student, U. Mich., 1951-52, Flint Jr. Coll., 1952-53; BA, Kalamazoo Coll., 1959; postgrad., Ill. State U., 1970-72. CPCU, CLU; cert. nursing home adminstr. Underwriter State Farm Ins., 1959-72; cons. Met. Property & Liability Ins. Co., Warwick, R.I., 1972-73, dir. underwriting and policyholders svcs., 1973, asst. v.p., 1973-74, v.p., 1974—. Sr. v.p. Royal Ins. Co., Charlotte, N.C., 1979-90; ret., 1990; nursing home exec. Royal Crest Health Care Ctr., Inc., 1990-92; pres. Royal Monarch Cons., Inc., 1990—; past chmn. All Industry Ins. Com. for Arson Control; chmn. Nat. Coun. on Compensation Ins.; past chmn. Comml. Lines Com. Ins. Svc. Office; past mem. adv. com. underwriting program Ins. Inst. Am.; cert. long term care ombudsman, 1998—. Past mem. adv. coun. Bus. Sch., U. R.I.; past bd. dirs. Charlotte Symphony; bd. dirs. N.C. Ins. Edn.; mem. Calif. Sr. Legisature, 2000—, mem. adv. coun. on aging; bd. dirs. Calif. Found. on Aging; past mem., bd. dirs. Compulsive Gambling Inst. Mem. CPCU Assn. (Calif. chpt.), CLU Assn. (Calif. chpt.), Masons, Shriners. Lutheran. Home and Office: 73 Colgate Drive Rancho Mirage CA 92270 E-mail: pssstca@aol.com.

FRONTERA, WALTER R., dean, physiatrist, educator; b. Coamo, PR; MD, U. PR, 1979; PhD, Boston U., 1986. Cert. Physical Medicine and Rehab., 1985. Intern in physical medicine and rehab. U. Dist. Hosp., Rio Piedras, PR, 1979—80; resident U. PR, San Juan, 1980—83; Earl P. and Ida S. Charlton prof. and chair physical medicine and rehab. Harvard Med. Sch., Boston; chmn. of physical medicine and rehab. Spaulding Rehab. Hosp., Boston; chief of svc. Mass. Gen. Hosp., Boston, Brigham and Women's Hosp., Boston; dean, Sch. Medicine U. PR, San Juan, 2006—, prof. physical medicine and physiology, 2006—. Editor-in-chief Am. Jour. of Physical Medicine and Rehab. Fellow: Am. Coll. Sports Medicine, Am. Acad. Physical Medicine and Rehab., Assn. Academic Physiatrists; mem.: Inst. Medicine, Internat. Fedn. Sports Medicine, Internat. Soc. Physical Medicine and Rehab., Kottke Soc. Office: U PR Sch Medicine Office A-880 PO Box 365067 San Juan PR 00936-5067 E-mail: wfrontera@rcm.upr.edu.

FRONZA, LEO F., JR., retired hospital administrator; B, Pa. State U.; M, George Wash. U. Assoc. dir. Elmhurst Meml. Healthcare, 1978, COO, pres., CEO, 1992. Recipient Career Achievement award, Chgo. Health Execs. Forum. Office: c/o Elmhurst Memorial Healthcare 155 E Brush Hill Rd Elmhurst IL 60126 Office Phone: 331-221-1000.

FROSI, ALBERTO RICCIOTTI, internist; b. Milan, Dec. 8, 1947; s. Paolo Frosi and Elvezia Barattini; m. Rosa Lucia Babbini, June 26, 1976; 1 child, Giacomo. MD, U. Pavia, Italy, 1972, postgrad., 1979, U. Parma, 1982. Asst. physician Inst. Ospitalieri, Cremona, Italy, 1973—86; vice-chief internal medicine Ospedale Sesto S. Giovanni, Milan, 1991—98, chief liver and gastroenterology, 1994—. Mem. adv. bd. Found. for Rsch. into Biol. Therapies of Cancer, Milan, 2000; tchr. nursing sch. and continuing med. edn. for practitioners. Contbr. articles to profl. jours. Counselor Alcoholics Anonymous, Milan, 1980—. Mem.: Italian Soc. Amyloidosis, Italian Soc. Internal Medicine, European Assn. for Study of Liver Disease. Avocations: sailing, canoeing. Office: Ospedale Sesto S Giovanni Viale Matteotti 83 20099 Sesto San Giovanni Italy Home: Via Giacomo Boni 45 20144 Milan MI Italy

FROST, BRANDY L., pediatrician; b. Kans. City, Mo., Dec. 2, 1973; BA, U. Kans., 1996, MD, 2004. Physician North Shore U. Health Sys., 2007—. Mem.: Am. Acad. Pediat. Office: Dept Pediatrics 2650 Ridge Ave Evanston IL 60201 Business E-Mail: bfrost@northshore.org.

FROST, DAVID, retired biology professor, science editor, consultant; b. Bklyn., Dec. 19, 1925; s. Charles and Regina (Sad) Feivlowitz; m. Ruthann Steinberg, Dec. 24, 1946; children: Michael Joseph, Jane Alice. BS, CCNY, 1945, MED, 1949; MS, NYU, 1952, PhD, 1960. Instr. in biology CCNY, 1946-49; instr. in sci. Rhodes Sch., NYC, 1949-52; asst. prof. biology Rutgers U., Newark, 1952-59, adj. prof. biology New Brunswick, 1960-78; sci. editor Squibb Inst. for Med. Rsch., Princeton, 1959-75; pvt. practice Plainfield, NJ, 1975—2002, Olmstedville, NY, 1975—2002; ret., 2002. Pres. N.J. SANE, 1964-65; co-chmn. Plainfield Joint Def. Com., 1970-85; newsletter editor Cen. Jersey/Masaya, Nicaragua Friendship Cities Project, 1985-97. Mem. Coun. Sci. Editors (pres. 1982-83), Schroon Lake Assn. (v.p., 1980—, pres. 1997-2007), Plainfield Shade Tree Commn. Home: 1229 E Seventh St Plainfield NJ 07062-1907 Office Phone: 908-755-3286.

FROST, ELIZABETH ANN MCARTHUR, physician; b. Glasgow, Scotland, Oct. 29, 1938; arrived in US, 1963; d. Robert Thomas and Annie M. (Ross) F.; m. Wallace Capobianco, Sept. 4, 1965 (dec. May 1988); children: Garrett, Ross, Christopher, Neil. MBChB, U. Glasgow, 1961. Diplomate Am. Bd. Anesthesiology, Royal Coll. Ob-Gyn., London. Intern in surgery Royal Infirmary, Glasgow, 1961-62; intern in medicine Victoria Infirmary, Glasgow, 1962; intern in obstetrics Royal Maternity Hosp., Glasgow, 1962-63; resident in internal medicine Englewood (N.J.) Hosp., 1963-64; resident in anesthesiology N.Y. Hosp., NYC, 1964-66; instr. in anesthesiology Albert Einstein Coll. Medicine, Bronx, NY, 1966-68, asst. prof. to assoc. prof., 1968-81, prof. anesthesiology, 1981-91, mem. dept. history of medicine, 1973-91; prof. dept. anesthesiology N.Y. Med. Coll., Valhalla, 1992-99; clin. prof. dept. anesthesiology Mt. Sinai Med. Ctr., NYC, 2000—; attending anesthesiology VA Bronx, 2000-04. Book reviewer New Eng. Jour. of Medicine, 1983—; editor Preanesthetic Assessment, Anesthesiology News, 1984—, Gen. Surgery News, 1991; author/contbr. books; contbr. articles to profl. jours. Mem. NY State Soc. Anesthesiologists, Am. Soc. Anesthesiologists, Assn. Univ. Anesthesiologists, Soc. Neurosurg. Anesthesia and Neurologic Supportive Care, Am. Assn. Neurol. Surgeons, Anesthesia History Assn., NY Acad. Medicine. Home: 2 Pondview West Purchase NY 10577 Personal E-mail: elzfrost@aol.com.

FROST, ELLEN ELIZABETH, psychologist; b. NYC; d. John Joseph and Josephine Mary (Cornell) F., m. Jerry Melnick, Jan. 8, 1982; children: Mariel Frost, Matt James. BA magna cum laude, St. John's U., 1969; MA, Fordham U., 1971, PhD, 1982; candidate NYU Postdoctoral Program for Psychotherapy and Psychoanalysis, 1982—84. Cert. Eye Movement Desensitization Reprocessing tng., 2000. Clin. psychology intern Columbia-Presbyn. Psychiat. Inst., NYC, 1972-73; asst. team leader staff psychologist Bensonhurst inpatient unit South Beach Psychiat. Ctr., Bklyn., 1973-75, sr. psychologist, Bensonhurst outpatient dept., 1975-81, assoc. psychologist, supr., 1982-89; dir. Phobia Svc., 1982-89; pvt. practice, 1983—; clin. supr. New Hope Guild, Bklyn., 1983—2000. Faculty L.I. Inst. Mental Health, 1990-97, supr., 1993-97. N.Y. State regents fellow, 1969-72; USPHS fellow, 1969-72. Mem. Am. Psychol. Assn., EMDR Internat. Assoc., Sigma Xi. Office: 200 E 33rd St Apt 25J New York NY 10016-4831 Office Phone: 212-725-0543. Office Fax: 212-725-0543. Personal E-mail: efrostphd@aol.com.

FROST, GAVIN W., preventive medicine physician; b. Sydney, Apr. 8, 1946; MBBS, U. Sydney, 1973, MPH, 1990. Exec. dean medicine U. Notre Dame, Australia, 2008—. Hon. fellow, Hong Kong Coll. Cmty. Medicine. Fellow: Royal Australasian Coll. Physicians, Royal Australasian Coll. Med. Adminstrs. Office: 47 Henry St Fremantle Western Australia 6959 Australia Business E-Mail: gavin.frost@nd.edu.au.

FROST, KEVIN ROBERT, foundation administrator; Rsch. asst. NYU Med. Ctr., NYC; inpatient care coord., AIDS program Bellevue Hosp., NYC; joined Am. Found. AIDS Rsch., NYC, 1994, CEO, 2007—. Mem. adv. panels FDA; mem. internat. adv. com. XIV Internat. AIDS Conf., Barcelona; mem. sci. com. XVI Internat. AIDS Conf., Toronto, Canada, 2006. Contbr. articles to profl. jours. Office: Am Found AIDS Rsch 120 Wall St 13th Fl New York NY 10005-3908 Office Phone: 212-806-1600. Office Fax: 212-806-1601. *

FROST, PHILLIP, pharmaceutical executive, dermatologist; BA, Univ. Pa., 1957; MD, Albert Einstein Coll., Bronx, NY, 1961. Chmn. dept. of dermatology Mt. Sinai Med. Center, Miami, Fla., 1972—90; chmn. Key Pharms., Miami, Fla., 1972—86; pres. Ivax Corp., Miami, Fla., 1991—95, founder, chmn., CEO, 1987—2006; interim CEO ImClone Systems Inc., NYC, 2005—06, exec. v.p., chief scientific officer, 2006; vice-chmn. Teva Pharmaceuticals Industries, Ltd., 2006—10, chmn., 2010—, Ladenburg Thalmann Fin. Services, Inc., 2006—; chmn., CEO OPKO Health, Inc., 2007—. Bd. dir. Ladenburg Thalmann Fin. Svcs., 2001—02; chmn. IVAX Diagnostics, Inc.; bd. dir. Northrop Grumman Corp., Continucare Corp., Cellular Tech. Svcs.; co-vice-chmn. bd. governors Am. Stock Exchange; chmn. Ladenburg Thalmann Fin. Svcs., 2006—; bd. dirs. Kidville Inc. (formerly Longfoot Comm. Corp.), Prolor Biotech Inc (formerly Modigene Inc.), Ideation Acquisition Corp.; vice chmn. Teva; bd. dir. Castle Brands Inc., 2005—07, bd. dirs., 2008—. Mem. bd. regents Smithsonian Inst.; trustee Scripps Rsch. Inst.; trustee, past chmn. Univ. of Miami. Named one of Forbes 400: Richest Americans, 2006—. Office: OPKO Health Inc 4400 Biscayne Blvd Miami FL 33137 Office Phone: 305-575-6015. Business E-Mail: pfrost@ladenburg.com. *

FROTHINGHAM, THOMAS ELIOT, pediatrician; b. Boston, June 21, 1926; s. Channing and Clara Morgan (Rotch) F.; m. Phyllis Mary Steiner, June 12, 1954 (div. 1983); children: Phyllis Eliot, Thomas Dean, Benjamin Rotch, David Griffith; m. Barbara Mathis, Dec. 28, 1987 (div. 2002). Student, Harvard U., Cambridge, Mass., 1944-46, MD, 1951. Intern Bellevue Hosp., NYC, 1951-52; resident, rsch. fellow in infectious diseases Children's Hosp., Boston, 1955-59; asst. prof. epidemiology Tulane U. Med. Sch., 1959—60; assoc. mem. Pub. Health Rsch. Inst., City of N.Y., 1960-61; asst. prof., then assoc. prof. tropical pub. health Sch. Pub. Health Harvard U., 1961-69; pediatrician Corvallis Clinic, Oreg., 1969-73; prof. pediat., family and cmty. medicine Duke U. Med. Ctr., 1973-94, prof. emeritus, 1994—. Contbr. articles to profl. jours. Co-founder Ctr. for Child and Family Health, N.C., 1996—. With USNR, 1944-46, 52-55. Mem. Am. Soc. Tropical Medicine and Hygiene, Am. Acad. Pediatrics. Home: 2701 Pickett Rd Apt #129 Durham NC 27705 Personal E-mail: tefro@mindspring.com.

FROTSCHER, MICHAEL, physician, researcher; b. Dresden, Saxony, Germany, July 3, 1947; s. Karl and Emmy (Gabriel) F.; m. Maria Magdalena Faber, Aug. 27, 1976; children: Max, Martha. MD, Humboldt U., 1974; Habilitation, J.W. Goethe U., 1982. Sci. asst. Inst. Anatomy Humboldt U., Berlin, 1973-79; prof. Inst. Anatomy U. Heidelberg, Fed. Republic of Germany, 1982, J.W. Goethe U., Frankfurt, Fed. Republic of Germany, 1983-89, U. Freiburg, Fed. Republic of Germany, 1989—. Contbr. articles to profl. jours. Recipient Leibniz prize German Rsch. Found., 1993; grantee German Rsch. Found., 1983—. Mem. AAAS, Soc. for Neurosci., European Neurosci. Assn., Anatomische Gesellschaft, Neurowissenschaftliche Gesellschaft. Avocations: classical music, sports. Office: U Freiburg Inst Anatomy Postfach 111 79001 Freiburg Germany Business E-Mail: michael.frotscher@anat.uni-freiburg.de.

FRUEHAUF, STEFAN, physician, clinician; b. Herborn, Hessen, Germany, Aug. 9, 1964; s. Peter and Marianne (Mohr) F.; m. Esther Willmann, May 8, 1992 (div., Feb. 18, 2005), m. Daniela Mijatovic, Aug. 16, 2008, children: Maximilian, Leopold, Julius. MD summa cum laude, U. Heidelberg, Germany, 1992, PhD Habilitation in Internal Medicine, 1999, Prof., 2005. Cert. internal medicine specialist, hematologist/medical oncologist, in palliative medicine, 2010. Clin. asst. Med. U. Hosp., Heidelberg, 1990-94, 95-99; rsch. fellow Johns Hopkins Hosp., Balt., 1991, U. Leiden, Netherlands, 1994—95; attending physician Oberarzt Med. U. Hosp., Heidelberg, 1999—2006, prof., 2005; leading physician Ctr. Tumor Diagnostics and Therapy, Osnabrueck, Germany, 2006—. Cons. German Cancer Rsch. Ctr., Heidelberg, 1992—; sci. reviewer/expert European Commn., 2005—; leader Onkologisches Zentrum, 2010, Ctr. Integrative Oncology and Palliative Care, 2010. Mem. editl. bd., Gene Vaccines and Therapy, 2003, Onkologie Internat. Jour. for Cancer Rsch. and Treatment, 2003; contbr. articles to books and profl. jours. Scholar Studienstiftung des Deutschen Volkes, German Nat. Merit Found., Bonn, Germany, 1985-90; recipient Scientific award for medical rsch. of Otto-Weber-Found., U. Heidelberg, 2000, Promotion award, Cancer Soc. Lower Saxony, 2009, Ann. Cancer award, Niedersächsische Krebsgesellschaft, 2009. Mem. Am. Soc. for Hematology, Internat. Soc. for Cellular Therapy (European v.p. 2006-08, European v.p. elect 2011-), European Soc. Med. Oncology, Deutsche Gesellschaft fuer Gentherapie, Deutsche Gesellschaft fuer Haematologie und Onkologie (mem. adv. bd. 2007—). Avocation: genealogy. Office: Ctr Tumor Diagnostic and Therapy Paracelsus Klinik Am Natruper Holz 69 Osnabrück 49076 Germany Office Phone: 49-541-966-3040. Office Fax: 49-541-966-3046. Personal E-mail: prof.stefan.fruehauf@pk-mx.de.

FRUMKIN, WILLIAM IRA, cardiologist; b. Israel, July 21, 1962; MD, SUNY Downstate, 1986. Cert. Internal Medicine. Resident, internal medicine Lenox Hill Hosp., NY, 1986—89, fellow, cardiology NY, 1989—91, Hosp. appointment NY; fellow Deborah Heart & Lung Ctr., 1991—92. Contbr. several articles to profl. jours. Office: 130 E 77th St 9th Fl New York NY 10021 Office Phone: 212-535-1550.

FRY, DONALD LEWIS, physiologist, educator; b. Des Moines, Dec. 29, 1924; s. Clair V. and Maudie (Long) F.; children: Donald Stewart, Ronald Sinclair, Heather Elise, Laurel Virginia. MD, Harvard U., 1949. Rsch. fellow Univ Minn Hosp., Mpls., 1952-53; sr. asst. surgeon gen. NIH, Bethesda, Md., 1953-56, surgeon, 1956-57, sr. surgeon, 1957-61, med. dir., 1961-80; prof. Ohio State U., Columbus, 1980—2004, prof. emeritus, 2004. Contbr. numerous articles and papers on physiology and biophysics of pulmonary mechanics, blood vascular interface, transvascular mass transport and the genesis of atherosclerosis to profl. jours., books. Mem. Am. Soc. Clin. Investigation. Mailing: PO Box 340187 Columbus OH 43234-0187 Business E-Mail: fry.1@osu.edu.

FRY, LIONEL, dermatologist; b. London, Mar. 19, 1933; s. Ansel Fry and Basia Mintzman; m. Minne Zidel, Nov. 27, 1955; children: Michael, Tessa, Katherine. BSc, Kings Coll., London, 1954; MD, BS, Kings Coll., 1957, MD, 1965. House physician Kings Coll. Hosp., London, 1958, med. registrar, 1959-61; sr. registrar dept. dermatology The London Hosp., 1965-66, rsch. fellow, 1966-69; prof. dermatology Faculty Medicine Imperial Coll., London, 1969—98; emeritus prof., 1999—. Author: Dermatology, 1973, 3d edit., 1983, Atlas of Dermatology, 1997, 5th edit., 2005, Atlas of Atopic Ecsema, 2004, Atlas of Psoriasis, 2004, Atlas of Bullous Diseases, 2006; contbr. articles to profl. jours. Recipient Archibald Gray medal, 2005. Mem. Royal Coll. Physicians (lectr.) Home: 16 Caroline Pl London W2 4AN England Office: Imperial Coll Norfolk Pl London W2 1PG England Office Phone: 44-207-935 2421. Business E-Mail: l.fry@imperial.ac.uk.

FRY, PATRICK E., insurance company executive; b. Berwin, Ill. BA in Pub. Health Adminstrn., U. Calif., Davis, 1979; MA in Health Svcs. Adminstrn., George Wash. U., 1982. Adminstrv. intern Univ. of Calif. Davis Med. Ctr., Sacramento, 1977; dir. Calif. Pacific Med. Ctr.; rsch. asst. Ryan Advisors, Gaithersburg, Md., 1981; adminstrv. resident Sutter Gen. Hosp., 1982, adminstrv. asst., 1983, asst. adminstr. for ops., 1985—90; asst. adminstr. Sutter Solano Med. Ctr., 1983—85; adminstr., v.p. Sutter Davis Hosp., 1990—93; COO Sutter Gen./Meml. Hosps., 1993—95; CEO Sutter Cmty. Hosps., 1995—97; regional pres. Sutter Health Ctrl., 1995—96; with Sutter Health, 1982—, pres., eastern divsn., 1996—99, exec. v.p. western divsn., 1999—2000, exec. v.p., COO, 2000—05, pres., CEO, 2005—; dir. VHA Inc., 2009—, chmn., 2011—; dir. St. Luke's Hosp. Bd. mem. Imaging Centers of Sacramento, 1988—90, Northern Calif. PET Imaging Ctr., 1994—98, bd. chair, 1997; bd. mem. Sutter Connect (MSO), 1995—, bd. chair, 1996; bd. v.p. Sutter PRIDE Back Inst., 1989—93; pres. Sacramento Sierra Hosp. Coun., 1993, 94; bd. mem. Hosp. Coun. of Northern Calif., 1994. Leadership Sacramento, 1986; bd. dirs. Diogenes Youth Services, 1986—88, treas., 1988; bd. dirs. United Way, 1994, United Way Adv. Bd., 1996, Make-A-Wish-Found., 1996; bd. mem. People Reaching Out, 1996; bd. chair health care team Sacramento Metro C. of C., 1996—97; bd. chair Health Cmty. Forum, 1996, 1997; bd. mem. Novation, 2002; mem. Econ. Develop. Commission, City of Davis, 1991; football coach Davis Blue Devils. Nominee Emerging Leader award, Health Care Forum, Young Adminstr. of the Yr. award, American Health Care Execs. Mem.: Hosp. Trade Assn., Calif. Hosp. Assn. (chair bd. trustees 2010—, bd. mem. 2005), Med. Group Mgmt. Assn., Leadership Inst., Sacramento Health Mgmt. Assn. (exec. com. 1992), American Coll. of Healthcare Execs., Davis Rotary. Office: Sutter Health 2200 River Plz Dr Sacramento CA 95833 Office Phone: 916-733-8800, 415-296-1866. Office Fax: 415-296-8290. E-mail: FryP@sutterhealth.org. *

FRY, ROBERT ANDREW, anesthesiologist; b. Cape Town, South Africa, Dec. 2, 1958; s. Dennis James and Alison Claire (Hopley) F.; m. Andrea Shelley Moses, Dec. 19, 1987; children: Lewis Ellerton, Emily Anne. MB, BChb, U. Cape Town, South Africa, 1984. Intern Groote Schuur Hosp., Cape Town, South Africa, 1983; house surgeon Victoria Hosp., Cape Town, South Africa, 1984, house physician, 1985; sr. house officer Addington Hosp., Durban, South Africa, 1985, Red Cross War Meml. Hosp., Cape Town, 1985, Palmerston North Hosp., 1986, registrar, 1987, Middlemore Hosp., Auckland, New Zealand, 1987, Nat. Women's Hosp., Auckland, New Zealand, 1987, Greenlane Hosp., Auckland, New Zealand, 1988, Northland Base Hosp, Whangarei, New Zealand, 1988, Bristol Maternity Hosp., England, 1988-89, Bristol Royal Infirmary, England, 1989, Bristol Childrens Hosp., England, 1989, Frenchay Hosp., Bristol, 1989; S.H.O. Bristol Maternity Hosp., 1989; registrar Middlemore Hosp., 1990, 91, Auckland Hosp., 1991, provisional fellow, 1992, specialist anesthetist, Epsom Anaesthetic Group; specialist North Shore Hosp., 1993. Presenter and rschr. in field. Contbr. articles to profl. jours. Med. asst. with Zimbabwe mil., 1977-78. Fellow Australian Coll. Anesthesiologists; mem. Am. Soc. Regional Anesthesiologists, New Zealand Soc. Anesthesiologists Avocations: running, oncology, windsurfing, canoeing. Office: Auckland Hosp Park Rd Auckland New Zealand

FRY, SIRPA-RAIJA, psychoanalyst, researcher; b. Helsinki, Finland, May 19, 1946; d. Jalmari and Aili (Lipsonen) Raatikainen; m. Pekka Juhani Korpela, June 13, 1970 (div. Apr. 1996); 1 child, Hanna Marjaana; m. Douglas Pottenger Fry, July 31, 1998 (div.). BA in Psychology, Helsinki U., 1972, MA in Psychology, 1974; diploma in psychoanalysis, Therapeia Found./IFPS, 1987; lic. in psychology, Åbo Akademi U., Finland, 1997. Vocat. psychologist State Employment Agy., Lahti, Helsinki and Vantaa, Finland, 1975-81; psychologist Kellokoski Psychiat. Hosp., Tuusula, Finland, 1981-85; pvt. practice as psychotherapist, psychoanalyst, supr. Helsinki, 1986—; rschr. Abo Akademi U., Dept. Psychology, 1991—. Supr. mental health dist. Päijät Häme Ctrl. Hosp., Lahti, Finland, 1986—91, Mental Health Offices, Helsinki, 1987—91, Psychiat. Clinics, Helsinki, 2007; supr. in advanced level psychotherapist tng., Turku, 2001—03, Oulu, 2007—, Helsinki, 2009—, Psychiat. Clinic Helsinki, 2008—; tng. psycho analyst Therapeia Found., 2004—. Contbr. articles to profl. jours., including Aggressive Behavior Jour. Co-founder artistic theater group Therapeia Found., 1987, bd. dirs., 1992—95, mem. tng. psychoanalysts and therapists bd., 2005, sec. tng. psychoanalysts and therapists bd., 2005—, chair psychoanalysts meetings, 2004—, mem. trainer's collegium, 2004—, sec. trainer's collegium bd., 2004—05. Rsch. grantee State Edn. Bd., 1991-96. Mem.: Internat. Soc. Rsch. on Aggression, Internat. Fedn. Psychoanalytic Socs., Sigma Xi (assoc.). Avocations: music, visual arts, travel, languages, summer cottage. Office Phone: 358-9-710481. Personal E-mail: sirpa.fry@abo.fi.

FRYBACK, DENNIS G., health services research educator; BA in Psychology and Math., UCLA, 1969; MA in Math., U. Mich., 1973, PhD in Math. and Psychology, 1974. Mem. faculty U. Wis., Madison, 1974—, prof. population health sciences & ind. engring., 1984—. Chmn. Bd. Scientific Counselors Nat. Lib. Medicine, 1992—94, spl. expert, Lister Hill Nat. Ctr. Biomedical Comm., 1995; chair, Health Care Tech. Study Sec. US Agy. Health Care Policy & Rsch., 1992—96; mem. Com. on Summarizing Population Health Inst. Medicine, 1997—98; founding mem. Soc. Med. Decision Making, 1978—. Contbr. articles to profl. jours. Mem. US Preventive Svcs. Task Force, 1990—96; mem. Panel on Cost Effectiveness in Health & Medicine US Dept. HHS, 1993—96; apptd. to Nat. Adv. Coun. for Health Care Policy, Rsch, & Evaluation, 1997. Fellow: Assn. of Health Svcs. Rsch.; mem.: Soc. for Med. Decision Making (pres. 1982—83, Eugene L. Saenger award for career svc. 1994, Career Achievement award 1999), Inst. of Medicine/NAS. Office: Univ Wisc 685 Warf Office Bldg 610 Walnut St Madison WI 53726-2397

FRYE, RAYMOND, dentist; b. Las Vegas, Nevada; married; children: Ciera, Paris, Christian, Holden. DMD with honors, Oreg. Health Scis. U., 1998. Founder Bling Dental, Portland, Oreg., 2009, owner, pres., 2009—. Office: Bling Dental 926 NW 13th Ave Ste 150 Portland OR 97209 Office Phone: 503-227-2444.

FRYE, ROBERT LEO, medical educator, cardiologist; b. Okla. City, Jan. 30, 1932; BA in biology, Vanderbilt U., Nashville; MD, Vanderbilt U., 1956. Cert. internal medicine and cardiovasc. disease Am. Bd. Internal Medicine. Intern Johns Hopkins Hosp., Balt., 1956—57, resident, 1957—58, 1960—61; fellow Nat. Heart Inst., Bethesda, Md., 1958—60; prof. medicine cardiovasc. diseases dept. Mayo Clinic, Rochester, Minn. Chair Bypass Angioplasty Revascularization Investigation in Type 2 Diabetes Steering Com. Recipient Mayo Clinic Disting. Alumni award, Mayo Found., 2007. Mem.: Gottlieb C. Friesinger Soc. Office: Mayo Clinic Dept Cardiovasc Diseases 200 1st St SW Rochester MN 55905 Office Phone: 507-284-2511.

FRYXELL, GRETA ALBRECHT, marine botany educator, oceanographer; b. Princeton, Ill., Nov. 21, 1926; d. Arthur Joseph and Esther (Andreen) Albrecht; m. Paul A. Fryxell, Aug. 23, 1947; children: Karl Joseph, Joan Esther, Glen Edward. BA, Augustana Coll., 1948; MEd, Tex. A&M U., 1969, PhD, 1975. Tchr. math and sci. jr. high schs., Iowa, 1948-52; research asst. Tex. A&M U., College Station, 1968-71, research scientist, 1971-80, asst. prof. oceanography, 1980-83, assoc. prof., 1983-86, prof., 1986-94, prof. emeritus, 1994—; adj. prof. botany U. Tex., Austin, 1993—. Vis. scientist U. Oslo, 1971; chmn. adv. commn. Provasoli-Guillard Ctr. for Culture Marine Phytoplankton, Bigelow Lab, Maine, 1985-87; hon. curator NY Bot. Garden, 1992-2000; courtesy prof. U. Oreg., 1994-2000; sr. rsch. scientist U. Tex. Marine Sci. Inst., 1996-2003. Editor: Survival Strategies of the Algae, 1983; contbr. articles to profl. jours. Recipient Outstanding Woman award Brazos County, College Station, 1979, Outstanding Achievement award Augustana Coll., Rock Island, Ill., 1980; Faculty Disting. Achievement award in rsch. Tex. A&M U., 1991, Geoscis. and Earth Resources Adv. Coun. medal, 1993; grantee NSF. Fellow: AAAS; mem.: ACLU, Oceanographic Soc., Tex. Assn. Coll. Tchrs., Internat. Diatom Soc. (coun. 1986—92), Am. Soc. Plant Taxonomists, Internat. Phycol. Soc., Brit. Phycol. Soc., Phycol. Soc. Am. (editl. bd. 1976—79, 1982—85, chair Prescott award com. 1991, award of Excellence in Phycology 1996). Democrat. Unitarian-Universalist. Office: U Tex Sch Biol Scis Sect Integrative Biology Austin TX 78712 Mailing: 650 Harrison Ave Claremont CA 91711

FU, JUNG-CHUNG, physician; b. Kaohsiung, Taiwan, Jan. 25, 1957; PhD, U. SC, 2009. Attending physician Kaohsiung Mcpl. United Hosp., 1989—2011. Recipient Excellent Rsch. award, Kaohsiung Mcpl. United Hosp. Mem.: Kaohsiung Med. Assn. Home: 11-12 Chien Kuo 1st Rd Linya Kaohsiung 802 Taiwan Personal E-mail: ufifuh@yahoo.com.tw.

FU, LIN-SHIEN, immunologist, nephrologist; b. Taipei, Taiwan, Feb. 3, 1962; d. Yung-hsi Fu and Kuei-yu Hsueh; m. Chiu-yang Wu, Sept. 17, 1956; children: Kung-ta Daniel Wu, Ming-ta David Wu, Ming-tzu Amanda Wu. MD, Yang-min U., 1986. Chief ped. immunology & nephrology sect. Veterans Gen. Hosp., Taichung, Taiwan, 1988—; asst. prof. Ji-nan U., Pu-li, 2003—. Councillor Taiwan Asthma Edn. Soc., Taichung, 1999—, Taiwan Pediatric Immunology and Allergy Soc., Taipei, 2002—, Com. New Drug Clin. Trial Ctr., VGH, Taichung, 2002—, Com. Med. Investigation, VGH, 2004—. Contbr. articles to profl. jours. Recipient MedJohn's Travellor's award, 1995. Achievements include research in Principle investigator for clinical trial:Staloral:oral hyposensitization for allergic rhinitis. Result: get the marketing liscence of Staloral: in Taiwan, approved by Health Administration. Office: Veterans General Hospital Taichung Sec 3 Chung-kang Rd Taiwan Taichung 407 Taiwan Office Fax: 886-4-23741359; Home Fax: 886-4-24630870. Personal E-mail: linshienfu@yahoo.com.tw.

FU, PING, nephrologist, educator; b. Sichuan, China, Jan. 7, 1967; MD, West China Coll. Medicine Sichuan U., 1990, PhD, 2005. Prof., dir., nephrology dept. West China Hosp. Sichuan U., 2005—. Recipient Sci. and Tech. award, Chinese Med. Assn., Sichuan, Academic Pacemaker award, Sichuan Provincial Dept. Health; fellowship, Internat. Soc. Nephrology, grant, Nat. Natural Sci. Found. China. Master: Sichuan Br. Chinese Soc. Nephrology; mem.: Nephrology Sub-Assn. China Assn. Chinese Medicine, Nephrology Sub-Assn. Chinese MD Assn., Standing Com. Chinese Soc. Blood Purification Adminstrn., 8th Standing Com. Chinese Soc. Nephrology. Avocations: swimming, ping pong/table tennis. Office: 37 Guo Xue Alley Chengdu Sichuan 610041 China Office Fax: 86 28 85422335. Business E-Mail: fupinghx@163.com.

FUCHS, ELAINE V., molecular biologist, educator; b. Hinsdale, Ill., May 5, 1950; m. David T. Hansen, Sept. 10, 1988. BS in Chemistry with highest distinction, U. Ill., Champaign-Urbana, 1972; PhD in Biochemistry, Princeton U., 1977; DSc (hon.), Mt. Sinai U., 2003, U. Ill., 2006. Postdoctoral fellow dept. biology MIT, 1977-80; asst. prof. U. Chgo., Dept. Molecular Genetics & Cell Biology, 1980—85, assoc. prof., 1985—88; Amgen Prof. Basic Sciences U. Chgo., 1988—2002; investigator Howard Hughes Med. Inst., 1988—; Rebecca C. Lancefield prof. mammalian cell biology and devel. Rockefeller U., NYC, 2002—. Mem. review bd. chair Searle Scholar, 1996—98; mem. review bd. Burroughs Welcome, 1998—2005; mem. adv. coun. to NIH dir., 1996—2000; mem. scientific adv. bd. RIKEN Develop. Biology Inst., Kobe, Japan, 2001—, Whitehead Inst., 2003—, Sirna Pharm. Co., 2005—07, MIT, 2009—; bd. dirs. Damon Runyon Cancer Rsch. Found., 2004—; mem. scientific review bd. Weizmann Inst., 2005—, Life Sciences, European Rsch. Coun., 2009—; mem. scientific bd., CBRI Inst. for Biomedical Rsch. Harvard Med., 2006—; mem. selection com. Pezcoller Found. award, 2007; Nat. Cancer Inst. RFA panel stem cells, 08; disting. vis. scientist, Singapore, 04; invited lectr. in field; spkr. in field. Assoc. editor Jour. Cell Biology, 1993-, scientific review bd.; mem. editl. bd. Genes & Development 2001-, Developmental Cell, 2001-, Cell, 2001-, Cell Stem Cell, 2007-; contr. articles to profl. jours. Recipient Bensely award Am. Assn. Anatomists, 1988, Searle Scholar award Chgo. Cmty. Trust, 1981-84, Presdl. Young Investigator award NSF, 1984-89, NIH Merit award, 1993, 98, Wm. Montagna award Soc. Investigative Dermatology, 1995, Keith Porter Lecture award Am. Soc. Cell Biology, 1996, Sr. Woman Achievement award, 1997, Cartwright award 2001, Richard Lounsbery award, 2001, Dickson prize in Medicine, 2004, Fedn. Am. Societies for Exptl. Biology award for scientific excellence, 2006, Beering award, 2006, NIH Merit award, 2009-, Nat. Medal Sci., NSF, 2009, L'Oréal-UNESCO award in the Life Sciences, 2010; co-recipient Novartis award in biomedical rsch., 2003, Fellow NY Acad. Sciences, Am. Philos. Soc., AAAA; mem. Am. Acad. Arts and Scis., Am. Acad. Microbiology, IOM, Am. Soc. Cell Biology (pres., 2001), Harvey Soc.(pres.-elect 2007-08), NAS (coun. mem. 2001-04, chair selection com., Richard Lounsbery award 2005-,class II membership com., 2005-), German Soc. Dermatology, Internat. Soc. for Stem Cell Rsch. (mem. bd. scientific dirs. 2007, v.p. 2008, pres.-elect 2010), Rosalind Franklin Soc. (founding bd. mem.), Phi Beta Kappa. Office: Rockefeller U Lab Mammalian Cell Biology and Devel 1230 York Ave Box 300 New York NY 10021 Office Phone: 212-327-7953. Office Fax: 212-327-7954. Business E-Mail: fuchslb@rockefeller.edu.

FUCHS, ROBYN, medical educator; PhD, Oreg. State U., 2002. Asst. prof., adj. prof., dept. anatomy and cell biology Ind. U., 2008—. Career Devel. grant, NIH. Mem.: Am. Coll. Sports Medicine, Am. Soc. Bone and Mineral Rsch. Office: Ind University 1140 W Michigan St Indianapolis IN 46239 Business E-Mail: rfuchs@iupui.edu.

FUCHS, ROLAND JOHN, geography educator, academic administrator; b. Yonkers, NY, Jan. 15, 1933; s. Alois L. and Elizabeth (Weigand) F.; m. Gaynell Ruth McAuliffe, June 15, 1957; children: Peter K., Christopher K., Andrew K. BA, Columbia U., 1954, postgrad., 1956—57, Moscow State U., 1960—61; MA, Clark U., 1957, PhD, 1959, DSc (hon.), 1995. Asst. prof. to prof. emeritus U. Hawaii, Honolulu, 1958—, chmn. dept. geography, 1964-86, asst. dean to assoc. dean Coll. Arts and Scis., 1965-67, dir. Asian Studies Lang. and Area Ctr., 1965-67, adj. rsch. assoc. East West Ctr., 1980—, spl. asst. to pres., 1986; vice rector UN U., Tokyo, 1987-94; dir. Internat. Start Secretariat, 1994—2008; sr. fellow East West Ctr., 2008—. Vis. prof. Clark U., 1963-64, Nat. Taiwan U., 1974; bd. internat. orgns. and programs NAS, 1976-81, chmn., 1980-81, bd. sci. and tech. in devel., 1980-85; mem. U.S. Nat. Commn. for Pacific Basin Econ. Coop., 1985-87; sr. advisor UN U., 1986; chmn. adv. com. UN U. Inst. for Environ. and Human Security. Author, editor: Geographical Perspectives on the Soviet Union, 1974, Theoretical Problems of Geography, 1977, Population Distribution Policies in Development Planning, 1981, Urbanization and Urban Policies in the Pacific-Asia Region, 1987, Megacities: The Challenge of the Urban Future, 1994, Global-Regional Linkages in the Earth System, 2002; asst. editor Econ. Geography, 1963-64; mem. editl. adv. com. Soviet Geography: Rev. and Translation, 1966-85, Geoforum, 1988-96, African Urban Quar., 1987, Global Environ. Change, 1990-2000, Asian Geographer, 1991-98, Internat. Jour. Environmental Pollution, 1994—. Ford Found. fellow, 1956-57; Fulbright Rsch. scholar, 1966-67. Mem. Assn. Am. Geographers, Am. Geophys. Union, Internat. Geog. Union (v.p. 1980-84, 1st v.p. 1984-88, pres. 1988-92, past pres. 1992-96), Assn. Am. Geographers (Hon. award 1982), Am. Assn. Advancement of Slavic Studies (bd. dirs. 1976-81), Pacific Sci. Assn. (mem. coun. 1978—, mem. exec. com. 1986-99, sec. gen-treas. 1991-99), Acad. Europaea (elected fgn. mem.). Home: 1200 N Nash St Arlington VA 22209-3616 Office Phone: 808-944-7518. Business E-Mail: rfuchs@agu.org.

FUCHS, VICTOR ROBERT, economist, educator; b. NYC, Jan. 31, 1924; s. Alfred and Frances Sarah (Scheiber) Fuchs; m. Beverly (Beck), Aug. 29, 1948; children: Nancy, Frederic, Paula, Kenneth. BS, N.Y. Univ., 1947; MA, Columbia Univ., 1951, PhD, 1955. Internat. fur broker, 1946—50; lectr. Columbia Univ., NYC, 1953—54, instr., 1954—55, asst. prof. econ., 1955—59; assoc. prof. econ. N.Y. Univ., NYC, 1959—60; program assoc. Ford Found. Program in econ., devel., and adminstrn., 1960—62; mem. sr. rsch staff Nat. Bur. Econ. Rsch., 1962—; prof. econ. Grad. Ctr. City Univ. of N.Y., NYC, 1968—74; prof. cmty. medicine Mt. Sinai Sch. Medicine, 1968-74; v.p. rsch. Nat. Bur. Econ. Rsch., 1968—78; prof. econ. Stanford U., Stanford Med. Sch., 1974—95; Henry J. Kaiser Jr. prof. Stanford U., Stanford Med. Sch., 1988—95, prof. emeritus, 1995—. Author: The Economics of the Fur Industry, 1957; co-author (with Aaron Warner): Concepts and Cases in Econ. Analysis, 1958; author: Changes in the Location of Mfg. in the U.S. Since 1929, 1962, The Svc. Economy, 1968, Prodn. and Productivity in the Svc. Industries, 1969, Policy Issues and Rsch. Opportunities in Indsl. Orgn., 1972, Essays on the Economics of Health and Med. Care, 1972, Who Shall Live? Health, Economics, and Social Choice, 1975; co-author (with Joseph Newhouse): The Economics of Physician and Patient Behavior, 1978; author: Economic Aspects of Health, 1982, How We Live, 1983, The Health Economy, 1986, Women's Quest for Econ. Equality, 1988, The Future of Health Policy, 1993, Individual and Social Responsibility: Child Care Edn., Med. Care, and Long-term Care in Am., 1996, Who Shall Live? Health, Economics and Social Choice, expanded edit., 1998; contbr. articles to profl. jour. Served in USAF, 1943—46. Fellow: Am. Econ. Assn. (disting., pres. 1995), Am. Acad. Arts and Sci.; mem.: Am. Philos. Soc. (John R. Commons award), Am. Inst. Medicine of NAS, Beta Gamma Sigma, Sigma Xi. Home: 796 Cedro Way Stanford CA 94305-1032 Office: NBER 30 Alta Rd Stanford CA 94305-8006 Office Phone: 650-326-7639.

FUDDY, LORETTA JEAN, public health service officer; b. 1948; Grad., Sacred Hearts Acad.; Grad. in Sociology, Social Work & Public Health, U. Hawaii; Grad. in Sociology, Social Work, & Public Health, Johns Hopkins U., Baltimore. Chief family health services divsn. Hawaii Dept. Health, acting dir., 2011, dir., 2011—. Chmn. Hawai'i Public Health Assn.; pres. Assn. of State and Territorial Public Health Social Workers; treas. and sec. Assn. of Maternal and Child Health Programs. Recipient Sustained Superior and Exemplary Performance award, Hawaii Dept. Health. Office: Hawaii Department of Health 1250 Punchbowl St Honolulu HI 96813 Office Phone: 808-586-4410. Office Fax: 808-586-4444. *

FUDENBERG, HUGH, neuroimmunologist, educator; b. NYC, Oct. 24, 1928; s. Nathan and Frances (Chackowitz) F.; m. Betty Roof, June 1956 (div.); children: Drew, Brooks, David, Haskell. AB, UCLA, 1949; MD, U. Chgo., 1953; MA, Boston U., 1958. Diplomate Am. Bd. Med. Lab. Immunology. Intern U. Utah Hosp., 1953—54; trainee in hematology New Eng. Ctr. Hosp., Tufts U., Boston, 1954—56; resident Mt. Sinai Hosp., NYC, 1956—57, Peter Bent Brigham Hosp., Harvard U., Boston, 1957—58; rsch. assoc. Rockefeller Inst., NYC, 1958—60; asst. prof. medicine U. Calif. Sch. Medicine, San Francisco, 1960—62, assoc. prof. medicine, 1962—66, prof., 1966—75; assoc. prof. immunology U. Calif., Berkeley, 1965—66, prof. bacteriology and immunology, 1966—75; prof., chmn. dept. basic and clin. immunology and microbiology Med. U. SC, Charleston, 1974—85, prof. medicine, immunology, 1974—88; dir. rsch. NeuroImmuno-Therapeutic Rsch. Found., Spartanburg, SC, 1988—. Adj. prof. pub. health U. Calif., Berkeley, 1966-75; adj. prof. epidemiology U. NC, Chapel Hill, 1977—; vis. prof. univs. and rsch. insts. in US and Europe, including Karolinska Inst., Sweden, Middlesex Hosp., Eng., Harvard U., Yale U., Princeton U., NYU, U. Ala., Wayne State U., U. So. Calif., U. Amsterdam, U. Leiden, U. Paris, U. Glasgow, U. Edinburgh, U. PR, U. Medellin, Colombia, Caracas, Venezuela, U. Innsbruck, Weismann Inst., Israel, Weifang Med. Sch., China, U. Norway, U. Helsinki, also Cancer Rsch. Inst., France, Italy, Russia, and The Netherlands; spkr. in field; mem. nat. adv. coun. Nat. Inst. Allergy and Infectious Diseases, 1981-85; mem. expert adv. panel on immunology WHO, 1962-82; mem. panel biomed. manpower NRC, 1974-78, mem. com. on immunization, 1978-80; mem. nat. task force on multiple myeloma and chronic leukemia NIH, 1966-71; chmn. external evaluation sci. com. U. Merida, Venezuela, 1982-86; mem. sci. adv. bd. UNESCO Internat. Ctr. for Immunology, Lyon, France, 1982-88; chmn. sci. adv. bd. Integra Inst., 1988-92; chmn. bd. sci. direction Inst. Immunology, Weifang Med. Coll., Changdong, China, 1988—; v.p. rsch. Neuro Immunology Therapeutic Rsch. Found., editl. bd. mem., Internat. Jour. Clin. Investigation, 2005, co-editor chief Internat. Jours. Clin. Invest. Author: (with others) Basic Immunogenetics, 1972, 3d edit., 1984, Basic and Clinical Immunology, 1974, 4th edit., 1982 (transl. into 12 lang.), Introduction to Medical Immunology, 1986, 2d edit., 1990; editor: (with others) Phagocytic Mechanisms in Health and Disease, 1972, Biomedical Scientists and Public Policy, 1978; editor: Biomedical Institutions, Biomedical Funding, and Public Policy, 1983; past mem. 35 editl. bds. including African Jour. Clin. and Exptl. Immunology, Annals Allergy, Biomedicine and Pharmacotherapy, Clin. and Exptl. Immunology, Folia Allergologica et Immunologica Clinica, Alzheimer's Longevity and Aging, Hosp. Practice, Jour. Irreproducible Results; co-editor in chief Internat. Jour. Clin. Investigation; contbr. 850 articles to sci. jour.; patentee in field. Mem. nat. adv. coun. Nat. Inst. Allergy and Infectious Diseases, 1981-85; mem. expert adv. panel immunology WHO, 1962-82; mem. panel biomed. manpower Nat. Rsch. Coun., 1974-78, mem. com. on immunization, 1978-80; mem. nat. task force on multiple myeloma and chronic leukemia NIH, 1966-71; chmn. external evaluation sci. com. U. Merida, Venezuela, 1982-86; mem. sci. adv. bd. UNESCO Internat. Ctr. for Immunology, Lyon, France, 1982-88; chmn. sci. adv. bd. Integra Inst., 1988—; chmn. bd. sci. dir. Inst. Immunology, Weifang Med. Coll., Shandong, People's Republic of China, 1988—; v.p. rsch. Neuro Immunology Therapeutic Rsch. Found.; mem. adv. bd. Cambridge Internat. Biog. Centre, 1992; numerous others. Recipient Pasteur medal Inst. Pasteur, 1962, Robert A. Cook medal Am. Acad. Allergy, 1966, Berman medal Am. Acad. Dermatology, 1973, Disting. Svc. award U. Chgo. Med. Alumni, 1973, Petrov Cancer medal Govt. USSR, 1976, Carl Neuberg medal Virchow-Pirquet Med. Soc., 1980, Koch medal German Soc. Microbiology, 1980, von Behringer medal, 1981, Semmelweis medal Hungarian Soc. Immunology, 1981, Metchnikoff Centennial, 1983, Phagocytosis medal Italian Soc. Immunology, 1983, Danish Cancer Soc., 1988, Castelloa di Pietrarossa award, Italy, 1991, Internat. First Prize, Frontiers in Medicine, Italy, 1992, 1st prize Biomed. Rsch. Italian Acad. Arts and Sci., 1992, 20th Century award rsch. sci. med. rsch. and edn., 1993; decorated Order of San Ciriaco, Italy, 1993, Internat. 1st prize in Exptl. Medicine, Italian Govt., 2000; named hon. prof. U. Kuopio, Finland, 1982, U. Claude Bernard, France, 1985, Free Sci. U., Bologna, Italy, 1985, Weifang Med. Coll. Fellow AAAS, Am. Acad. Microbiology; mem. Am. Assn. for Cancer Rsch., Am. Assn. Immunologists (com. for congl. liaison for HEW appropriations, long range planning com.), Am. Rheumatism Assn., Am. Soc. for Clin. Investigation (chmn. com. on pub. info. 1971-74), Am. Soc. Hematology (pres. subdivsn. immunohematology and immunogenetics 1970, subcom. mem., 1974, rsch tchg. methods 1961-65), Am. Soc. Human Genetics (exec. coun. 1969-72), Assn. Am. Med. Sch. Microbiology (chmn., pub. affairs com.), Assn. Am. Physicians, Genetics Soc, Am. Internat. Soc. Blood Transfusion (exec. councillor 1965-71), Internat. Soc. Environment Toxicology and Cancer (bd. councilors), Internat. Soc. Hematology, Internat. Union Immunology Soc. (immunoglobin subcom. mem. 1977), Internat. Platform Assn., Midwinter Conf. Immunologists (founder, past pres.), Royal Soc. Medicine (assoc.), Soc. Clin. Immunology, Am. Soc. Med. Labs., Med. Immunology, Sigma Xi. Personal E-mail: nitrf@hotmail.com. Business E-Mail: nitrf@charter.net.

FUENTES, JUAN CARLOS, plastic surgeon; MD, Universidad de Guanajuato, 1982—86. Cert. Mexican Bd. Plastic, Aesthetic and Reconstructive Surgery, 1996. Intern Instituto Nacional de la Nutrición, 1987; resident gen. surgery Hosp. Gen. Regional, 1990—91; resident plastic surgery Hosp. de Especialidades, 1991—94, chief resident plastic and reconstructive surgery, 1993—94; fellow aesthetic surgery Connell Aesthetic Surgery Network, 1995—96; plastic surgeon, 1996—. Recipient A.H. Robins award, 1988. Office: 1527 Mision de San Diego Suite 301 Zona Rio 22460 Tijuana Mexico Office Phone: 6194284803. Office Fax: 6195912777.

FUENTES-AFFLICK, ELENA, pediatrician, epidemiologist, educator; BS in Biomedical Sci., U. Mich., Ann Arbor, 1984; MD, U. Mich. Med. Sch., 1986; MPH, U. Calif., Berkeley, 1991. Pediatric intern, resident U. Calif., San Francisco, 1986—90, fellow in health policy, 1991—93, faculty, 1993—, prof. pediat., epidemiology & biostatistics. Chief pediat. San Francisco Gen. Hosp. Mem. nat. adv. com. Robert Wood Johnson Found. Clin. Scholars Program; past mem. nat. adv. coun. Eunice Kennedy Shriver Nat. Inst. Child Health & Human Devel., Agy. Healthcare Rsch. & Quality. Generalist Physician Faculty Scholar, Robert Wood Johnson Found., 1998—2003. Mem.: Soc. Pediatric & Perinatal Epidemiologic Rsch., Soc. Pediatric Rsch. (pres. 2008—09), Soc. Epidemiologic Rsch., Inst. Medicine, American Acad. Pediat., Ambulatory Pediatric Assn. Achievements include research in perinatal outcomes among Latina women, with a focus on the role of ethnicity, acculturation and immigration status. Office: Univ Calif MS 6E SFGH 1001 Potrero Ave San Francisco CA 94110 Office Phone: 415-206-4196. Office Fax: 415-206-3686. E-mail: efuentes@sfghpeds.ucsf.edu. *

FUHRMAN, CARL R., radiologist, educator; grad., MD, U. Pitts. Diplomate Am. Bd. Radiology-diagnostic radiology. Resident Univ. Pitts. Med. Sch.; chief of thoracic radiology Univ. Pitts. Med. Ctr. Presbyterian, dir. undergraduate med. edn., prof. radiology; hosp. affiliations include Magee-Womens Hospital of UPMC, UPMC McKeesport, UPMC Passavant, UPMC Shadyside, UPMC Mercy, UPMC St. Margaret. Vis. prof. Boston Univ., Emory Univ., La. State Univ., Univ. Mass., Univ. Va., W.Va. Univ. Office: University of Pittsburgh Medical Center Presbyterian 200 Lothrop St PUH E-177 Pittsburgh PA 15213 Office Phone: 412-647-7288. E-mail: fuhrmancr@upmc.edu.

FUJIHARA, HISAKO, oral surgeon, educator; b. Tokyo, Dec. 22, 1972; MDS, Kyushu Dental Coll., 1998; PhD in Medicine, U. Tokyo, 2003. Bd. cert oral surgeon Japanese Soc. Oral and Maxillofacial Surgeons, 2010. Resident dept. oral and maxillofacial surgery Kyushu Dental Coll., 1998—99; clin. fellow dept. oral and maxillofacial surgery U. Tokyo, 2003—09; asst. prof. dept. oral and maxillofacial surgery Tsurumi U., 2009—. Fellow: Japanese Soc. Oral and Maxillofacial Surgeons; mem.: Asian Soc. Oral and Maxillofacial Surgeons, Japanese Cancer Assn., Internat. Assn. Dental Rsch. Avocations: yoga, piano. Office: 2-1-3 Tsurumi Tsurumi-ku Yokohama Kanagawa 2308501 Japan Office Phone: 81-45-581-1001. Office Fax: 81-45-573-9599. Business E-Mail: fujihara-h@tsurumi-u.ac.jp.

FUJII, KEISUKE, anesthesiologist, educator; b. Japan, Oct. 21, 1974; MD, Wakayama Med. U., 2000, PhD, 2009. Staff anesthesiologist Japanese Red Cross Soc., Wakayama Med. Ctr., 2002—10; asst. prof. Wakayama Med. U., 2011—. Office: Kimiidera 811-1 Wakayama 641-8509 Japan Business E-Mail: fujiik@topaz.ocn.ne.jp.

FUJII, TAKAHIRO, endoscopist; b. Mikuni-cho, Fukui, Japan, Dec. 15, 1957; s. Kazuo and Kazuko Fujii; m. Mari Katsurashima, Dec. 15, 1985; children: Ryuta, Takashi, Takaki. MD, Kanazawa Med. U., 1983; PhD, Toho Med. U., Tokyo, 1998. Med. staff Kanazawa (Japan) Med. U., Kanazawa, 1983—86; resident Nat. Cancer Ctr. Hosp., Chuo-ku, Tokyo, Japan, 1986—90, dir. endoscopy, 1998—2003; dir. Fujii Takahiro Clinic, Chuo-ku, Tokyo, Japan, 2003—. Dir. polyp study Japanese Ministry of Health Labor & Welfare, Chiyoda-ku, Tokyo, 2000—03. Contbr. articles. Recipient Best Endoscopic picture, Olympus, 1994. Mem.: Japanse Gastric Cancer Assn., Japanese cancer assn., JSGE (diplomate), JGES (sci. program committiee 2003, diplomate). Avocations: golf, swimming. Office: Fujii Takahiro Clinic 7F Ginza M&S Bldg 4-13-11 Ginza Chuo-ku 104-0061 Japan Office Fax: +81-3-3544-6267. E-mail: tfclinic@khaki.plala.or.jp.

FUJII, TAKASHI, neurosurgeon; b. Numata, Japan, July 23, 1947; MD, Shinsyu U., 1973; DSc, Gunma U., 1982. Chief exec. Fujii Neurosurg. Hosp., Utsunomiya, Japan, 1989—. Office: Fujii Neurosurg Hosp 461 Nakaokamoto Utsunomiya 329-1105 Japan

FUJII, YOICHI ROBERTUS, virologist, veterinarian; b. Sapporo, Japan, Jan. 23, 1957; s. Shizuya and Kakuko Fujii; m. Hisae Fujii, Feb. 11, 1984; children: Asuka, Ryoma, Takara. DVM, Hokkaido U., Japan, 1981, PhD, 1987. Asst. prof. Yamagata U., Japan, 1983—86; scientific officer Oxford U., England, 1986—88; lectr. Nagoya U., Japan, 1995—98; assoc. prof. Nagoya City U., 1998—. Mailing: Molecular Biol and Retroviral Genetics Grad Sch Pharm Sci Nagoya City U Nagoya 4678603 Japan Office: Nagoya City U Tanabe-Dori 3-1 Nagoya 467 8603 Japan Home: Kawada-cho 106-6 Nagoya 456 0062 Japan Home Phone: 852 682 7003; Office Phone: 09091778015. Personal E-mail: fatfuji@hotmail.com.

FUJIKAWA-YAMAMOTO, KOHZABURO, cell biologist, educator; b. Shimizu, Shizuoka, Japan, Apr. 6, 1947; s. Soutaro and Yasu (Shibata) Yamamoto; m. Yoshiko Fujikawa, Oct. 10, 1977; children: Takumasa, Mika. BS, Hokkaido U., Sapporo, Japan, 1970, MS, 1972, PhD, 1977. Clk. Rikho Trading Corp., Tokyo, 1978-80; asst. Kanazawa Med. U., Ishikawa, Japan, 1980-85, lectr., 1985-89, assoc. prof. cell biology, 1989—, prof. cell biology, 1996—. Contbr. articles to profl. jours. Mem. Internat. Soc. Analytical Cytology, Japan Soc. Cell Biology, Japan Cytometry Soc., Japan Chem. Soc. Avocations: social dancing, shooting, reading. Office: Kanazawa Med U Daigaku 1-1 Uchinada 920-0293 Japan Business E-Mail: fujikawa@kanazawa-med.ac.jp.

FUJIMORI, HIROYUKI, pharmacist, educator; b. Japan, Mar. 3, 1949; PhD, Sci. U. Tokyo, 1982. Prof., faculty pharm. scis. Setsunan U., 2008. Office: 45-1 Nagaotoge-cho Hirakata Osaka 573-0101 Japan Business E-Mail: fujihiro@pharm.setsunan.ac.jp.

FUJIMORI, SHUNJI, internist, educator; s. Takeshi and Harue Fujimori; married. MD, Nippon Med. Sch., Tokyo, 1989, PhD, 1999. Physician 3rd internal medicine Nippon Med. Sch., 1989—95, physician Chiba-Hokusou Hosp. Japan, 1995—2003, lectr. dept. internal medicine, divsn. gastroenterology, 2003—. Contbr. articles to med. jours. Office: Gastroenterology Nippon Med Sch 1-1-5 Sendagi Bunkyo-ku Tokyo 113-8603 Japan Business E-Mail: s-fujimori@nms.ac.jp.

FUJIMOTO, NAOHIRO, urologist, educator; b. Kumamoto, Japan, June 17, 1958; MD, Shimane Med. U., 1984. Assoc. prof. dept. Urology U. Occupl. and Environ. Health, 2001—. Mem.: European Urol. Assn., Am. Urol. Assn., Japanse Urol. Assn. Office: 1-1 Iseigaoka Yahatanishi Kitakyushu Fukuoka 807-8555 Japan Office Fax: 81-93-603-8724. Business E-Mail: n-fuji@med.uoeh-u.ac.jp.

FUJIMOTO, TAKAHIRO, finance educator; MD (hon.), Shinsyu U., Nagano, 1995; PhD (hon.), Tokyo U., 2004; MBA (hon.), Wales U., 2006. Clin. assoc. U. Tokyo Sch. Medicine; assoc. prof. U. Wales Validated MBA Programme, Tokyo, 2004—. Clin. staff Kanagawa Children's Med. Ctr., Yokohama, Japan, 1997—98, Tokyo Met. Geriatric Hosp., Itabashi-ward, Tokyo, 1998—2000; rsch. asst. Hosp. U. Tokyo, Bunkyo-ward, 2003—04; clin. assoc. Instn. Med. Rsch. U. Tokyo, Minato-ward, 2004—05. Fellow: Am. Laser Soc. Medicine Surgery; mem.: Europe Assn. Dermatology and Venerology (internat. 2007). Office: Clinic F 4F 6-6-1 Koujimachi Chiyoda Tokyo 102-0083 Japan Business E-Mail: fujimoto@clinic-f.com.

FUJIMOTO, YASUSHI, otolaryngologist; b. Gifu, June 21, 1965; MD, Nagoya U., PhD, 1990. Otolaryngology Nagoya U., 1992—. Asst. prof., 1995. Office: 65 Tsurumai-Cho Showa Nagoya Aichi 466-8550 Japan Office Fax: 81-52-744-2325. Business E-Mail: yasushif@med.nagoya-u.ac.jp.

FUJIMURA, MASAKI, medical educator; b. Kanazawa, Ishikawa, Japan, Apr. 12, 1953; s. Masayoshi and Chiyoko Fujimura; m. Keiko Tanaka; children: Natsuki, Chihiro. DMS, Kanazawa U., Japan, 1984. Assoc. prof. Kanazawa U., 2000—06; clin. prof. Kanazawa U. Hosp., 2006—. Contbr. articles to profl. med. jours. Recipient Young Investigator award, Japanese Respiratory Soc., 1991. Fellow: Am. Coll. Chest Physicians. Achievements include discovery of atopic cough as a cause of chronic cough. Office: Kanazawa Univ Hosp 13-1 Takaramachi Kanazawa Ishikawa 920-8641 Japan

FUJIOKA, SHIGEKAZU, cardiologist; b. Kobe, Hyogo, Japan, Oct. 11, 1960; s. Yoshio and Shiomi Fujioka. MD, Osaka Med. Coll., Takatsuki City, Japan, 1988; DSc, Osaka Med. Coll., Takatsuki City, 1996. Lic. physician, cardiologist. With 3d divsn. internal medicine Osaka Med. Coll., Takatsuki City, 1988—98, asst. prof. Ctrl. Clin. Lab., 1999—, jr. assoc. prof. Ctrl. Clin. Lab., 2008—; prof., dept. rehab. sci. Osaka Health Sci. U., 2011—. Contbr. articles to profl. jours. Recipient rsch. grant, Japanese Ministry Edn., Sci., and Culture, 1999. Fellow: Japanese Circulation Soc.; mem.: Am. Heart Assn., Internat. Soc. for Heart Rsch. Office: Dept Rehabilitation Sci Osaka Health Sci University 1-9-27 Temma Kita-ku Osaka 530-0043 Japan Office Phone: 81-6-6352-0093.

FUJISHIMA, MASAHIRO, biology educator; b. Morioka, Japan, Apr. 13, 1950; BS, Hirosaki U., Japan, 1973; MS, Tohoku U., Sendai, Miyagi Prefecture, Japan, 1975, DSc, 1978. Asst. Biol. Inst. Faculty of Sci. Yamaguchi (Japan) U., 1979-83, assoc. prof., 1984-91, prof., 1995—. Rsch. fellow Alexander von Humboldt Found., Münster, Germany, 1980-81; vis. rsch. fellow Hong Kong U., 1988. E-mail: fujishim@yamaguchi-u.ac.jp.

FUJISHIRO, MITSUHIRO, gastroenterologist, educator; s. Akito and Kazuyo Fujishiro; m. Midori Tajiri, Aug. 31, 1997; children: Mitsuki, Masaki. MD, U. Tokyo, 1995, PhD, 2004. Diplomate Ministry Health & Welfare, 1995. Resident U. Tokyo Hosp., 1995—96, Hitachi Gen. Hosp., Ibaraki, Japan, 1996—97, Nat. Cancer Ctr. Hosp., Tokyo, 1997—2000; med. staff U. Tokyo Hosp., 2000—05, asst. prof. medicine, 2005—09, assoc. prof. medicine, 2009—; dir., endoscopy & endoscopic surgery U. Tokyo, 2009—. Fellow: Japan Gastroent. Endoscopy Soc., Japanese Soc. Gastroenterology, Japanese Soc. Internal Medicine. Office: Univ Tokyo Dept Gastroenterology 7-3-1 Hongo Bunkyo-ku Tokyo 113-8655 Japan Office Fax: 81 3 5800 8806. Business E-Mail: mtfujish-kkr@umin.ac.jp.

FUJITA, FUMIKO, medical association administrator, researcher, pharmacist; b. MitoyoGun, Kagawa, Japan, Sept. 7, 1940; d. Noboru and Masako Sone; m. Masahide Fujita; children: Masako Koike, Hisako, Tetsuichi. MD, Osaka U., Suita, Osaka, Japan, 1988. Rschr. Shionogi Rswch. Labs., Osaka, 1963—67; rschr. dept. surgery rsch. Inst. for Microbial Diseases Osaka U., Suita, 1981—90; rschr. Rabiton Inst. Inc., Nishiwaki, Hyago, Japan, 1988—89; pres. Exptl. Cancer Chemotheraphy Rsch. Lab. Co. Ltd., Minoh, Japan, 1990—. Contbr. articles to profl. jours., chapters to books. Recipient award, Found. for Promotion Contemporary Therapy of Cancer, Tokyo, 1986. Mem.: Japan Soc. for Biol. Therapy, Japan Soc. Clin. Oncology, Japanese Cancer Assn., Assn. for Anticancer Drug Search (rschr. 1990—). Avocations: classical music, reading. Office: Exptl Cancer Chemotherapy Rsch Lab Co Lt Hakunoshima 3-13-1 Minoh 562-0012 Japan Office Phone: 82 072-724-9949.

FUJITA, MASANORI, cardiovascular surgeon; b. Tokyo, Jan. 16, 1966; s. Akio and Sumie Fujita; m. Kazue Takanokura, Dec. 18, 1973. MD, Nat. Def. Med. Coll., Tokorozawa, Japan, 1992. Resident Nat. Def. Med. Coll., Tokorozawa, Saitama, Japan, 1992—94, sr. resident, 1997—99, postgrad. rschr., 2000—; flight surgeon Fifth Air Wing, Japan Air Self-Def. Force, Shintomi, Miyazaki, Japan, 1994—97; lt. col. Japan Air Self-Def. Force, 2000—. Mem.: Japanese Assn. for Thoracic Surgery (licentiate; tokyo, japan), Japan Surg. Soc. (licentiate; tokyo, japan), Aerospace Med. Assn. (life; us). Office: Nat Def Med Coll Dept Med Engring Namiki 3-2 Saitama Tokorozawa 359-8513 Japan Office Fax: +81-4-2996-5199. Personal E-mail: BXB01424@nifty.ne.jp.

FUJITA, MASAYUKI, biologist, educator; b. Takamatsu, Kagawa, Japan, Aug. 15, 1956; s. Hiroshi and Matsuko Fujita; m. Tomoko Fukuoka, Nov. 30, 1959; 1 child, Sorachi. DAgr, Nagoya U., Japan. Assoc. prof. Kagawa U., Miki-cho, Japan, 1991—99, prof., 1999—. Rschr. Inst. Biol. Chemistry, Wash. State U., 1996—97. Fellow Co-operative rsch. programme: Biol. resource mgmt. for sustainable agrl. systems, Orgn. for Econ. Co-operation and devel. (OECD), 1996. Mem.: Am. Chem. Soc., Phytochemical Soc. N.Am., Am. Soc. Plant Biologists. Achievements include research in plant molecular biology and phytochemistry. Home: 1379-22 Mure Mure-cho Takamatsu Kagawa 761-0121 Japan Office: Kagawa Univ 2393 Ikenobe Miki-cho Kagawa 761-0795 Japan Office Fax: 81-87-891-3021. Business E-Mail: fujita@ag.kagawa-u.ac.jp.

FUJITA, SHIGEKIYO, neurologist, director; PhD, Kobe U., 1959. Asst. prof. Kobe U., Japan, 1972—79, assoc. prof., 1979—80. Dir. to v.p. Hyogo Brain & Heart Ctr., Himeji, Japan, 1980—99; dir. Inst. Advanced Neurol. Medicine and Computed Imaging Ishikawa Hosp., Himeji, Japan, 1999—. Contbr. articles to rsch. jours. Achievements include research in diseases like migraine, vertigo and dementia related to platelet hyperaggregability and its correction reads to prevention. Office: Rsch Inst Ishikawa Hosp 2-150 Bessho Bessho-Cho Himeji 671-0221 Japan Office Phone: 81-79-252-5235.

FUJITA, TAKAYUKI, nephrologist, educator; b. Tokyo, Dec. 21, 1952; MD, Nihin U. Sch. Medicine, 1978, PhD, 1982. Assoc. prof. Nihon U. Sch. Medicine, 2008—. Vice dir., dept. nephrology, hypertension, endocrinology Nihon U. Itabashi Hosp., 2008. Recipient Academic Incentive award, Nihon U. Alumni Assn. Fellow: Japanese Soc. Nephrology; mem.: Japan Coll. Rheumatology, Japan Diabetes Soc. Office: 30-1 Oyaguchi-kamimachi Itabashiku Tokyo 173-8610 Japan Office Fax: 81-3-3972-1098. E-mail: tfujita@med.nihon-u.ac.jp.

FUJIWARA, PETER EDWARD, urologist; s. Edward John and Cora Yosho Fujiwara; m. Ann Marie Badding, Dec. 6, 1975; children: Mary Elizabeth, Sarah Ann, Martha Arlene. BA, U. Mich., 1966, MD, 1970. Bd. cert. Am. Bd. Urology. Intern Ohio State U. Hosp., 1970—71; active staff Bay Regional Med. Ctr., Bay City, Mich., 1977—, chmn. dept. surgery, 1991—; urology resident SUNY, Buffalo, 1973—77. Capt. US Army, 1971—73, Vietnam. Fellow: ACS. Roman Catholic. Avocations: photography, skeet shooting. Office: East Medical Bldg 2110 16th St Bay City MI 48708

FUJIWARA, YOSHINORI, research scientist; b. Kyoto, June 10, 1962; MD, Hokkaido U., 1993; PhD, Kyoto U., 2000. Sub-leader Tokyo Met. Inst. Gerontology, 2007—. Recipient award, Japan Pub. Health Assn. Office: TMIG 35-2 Sakae-cho Itabashi-ku Tokyo 173-0015 Japan Office Fax: 81-3-3579-4776. Business E-Mail: fujiwayo@tmig.or.jp.

FUJIWARA, YOSHIYUKI, gastroenterologist, educator; b. Okayama, Japan, Feb. 3, 1962; MD, Osaka U., PhD, 1987. Assoc. prof., dept. gastroent. surgery Osaka U., 2009—; chief Osaka Med. Ctr. Cancer & Cardiovasc. Diseases, 2011—. Avocations: sports, music. Office: 1-3-3 Nakamichi Higashinariku Osaka 537-8511 Japan Office Fax: 81-6-6981-8055. Business E-Mail: fujiwara-yo@mc.pref.osaka.jp.

FUKAO, KENJIRO, psychiatrist, educator; b. Osaka, Japan, Jan. 12, 1966; MD, Kyoto U., 1991, PhD, 2009. Lectr. Kyoto U. Grad. Sch. Medicine, 2011—. Fellow: Japanese Soc. Epileptology, Japanese Soc.

Psychopathology and Psychotherapy; mem.: Japanese Soc. Psychiatry and Neurology. Office: 54 Shogoin-kawahara-cho Sakyo-ku Kyoto 606-8517 Japan Office Fax: 81-751-4212. Business E-Mail: fukao@kuhp.kyoto-u.ac.jp.

FUKATA, MASAYUKI, gastroenterologist, hematologist; b. Kawagoeshi, Saitamaken, Japan, Jan. 23, 1969; s. Hiroji and Kyoko Fukata; m. Yuko Mitsuboshi, Oct. 23; children: Yuki, Mai, Masahiro. BS, Jikei Pre-Med. Sch., Tokyo, 1987; MD, Jikei U. Sch. Medicine, Tokyo, 1994, PhD, 2003. Cert. internal medicine specialist Japanese Soc. Internal Medicine, 1997. Intern, resident in internal medicine Jikei U. Hosp., Nishishinbashi, Tokyo, 1994—96; gastroenterology fellow Jikei U. Daisan Hosp., Komae, Tokyo, 1996—98; clin. instr. divsn. gastroenterology and hepatology Jikei U. Hosp., 1998—2003; post doctoral fellow Cedars-Sinai Med. Ctr., LA, 2003—04, Mt. Sinai Sch. Medicine, NYC, 2003—06, asst. prof. medicine divsn. gastoenterology, 2007—08, U. Miami, Miller Sch. Medicine, 2008—. Contbr. articles to profl. jours., chapters to books. Recipient Young Investigator award, Japan Soc. Histochemistry and Cytochemistry, 2002, Career Devel. award, Crohn's and Colitis Found. Am., 2006; Rsch. grant, Japanese Ednl. Ministry, 2003, Astrazeneca, 2003, Rsch. fellow, Uehara Meml. Found., 2005. Avocations: camping, fishing, music, movies, travel. Office: U Miami Miller Sch Medicine PO Box 016960 D-49 Miami FL 33101 Home: 13120 SW 92nd Ave Apt 307 Miami FL 33176-5783 Business E-Mail: mfukata@med.miami.edu.

FUKAYA, HIDEHIRA, medical educator; b. Japan, Jan. 27, 1977; MD, Kitasato U., 2001, PhD, 2008. Asst. prof. dept. cardioangiology Sch. Medicine, Kitasato U., 2008—. Mem.: Japanese Coll. Cardiology, Japanese Soc. Electrocardiology, Japanese Heart Rhythm Soc., Japanese Circulation Soc., Japanese Soc. Internal Medicine. Avocation: golf. Office: 1-15-1 Kitasato Minami-ku Sagamihara Kanagawa 252-0374 Japan Business E-Mail: hidehira@med.kitasato-u.ac.jp.

FUKAYA, YASUKO, nursing educator; b. Japan, Mar. 14, 1949; Degree, St. Lukes Coll. Nursing, 1989; PhD, U. Tokyo. Prof. Sch. Health Scis., Tokai U., 2001—. Office: 143 Shimokasuya Isehara Kanagawa 259-1193 Japan Home Phone: 0467-43-3198; Office Phone: 0463-90-2055. Business E-Mail: yfukaya@is.icc.u-tokai.ac.jp.

FUKAZAWA, HAJIME, oral maxillofacial surgeon, educator; b. Mito-Shi, Japan, May 25, 1947; s. Izumi Kudoh and Chizuko Fukazawa; m. Noriko Nitanai, May 2, 1975; children: Hanae, Yuhshi. DDS, Iwate Med. U., Morioka, Japan, 1975; D Med. Sci., Iwate Med. U., 1980. Chmn. Hachinohe (Japan) Red Cross Hosp., 1982—83; asst. prof. Iwate Med. U., 1981—92; vice chmn. Niigata Rohsai Hosp., Johetsu, Japan, 1993—94; asst. prof. Niigata U., 1992—2000; chmn. Yuri Nokyo Gen. Hosp., Honjoh, Japan, 1994—2000, Ookubo Hosp., Mito, Japan, 2000—; asst. prof. Meikai U., 2006—. Dir. dept. Iwate Med. U., 1980-88, 89-92; lectr. Akita Ministry of Welfare, 1994. Contbr. articles to profl. jours. Recipient spl. award of invention Iwate Med. U., 1991, Thanksgiving award Japan Soc. for Cancer Therapy Sapporo, 1995, Ranking award Japan Cancer Hosp. by Media Works: Best Doctor of head and neck cancer, N. Japan, 1999, Indian Med. Cultural award, 2004-2008; named one of the Best Dr. Japanese Surgeons, 2008. Active Fellow Am. Soc. for Head and Neck Surgery (active); mem. Internat. Physicians for the Prevention of Nuclear War, Japan Soc. Oral Tumors (coun.). Avocations: golf, skiing, baseball, travel. Home: Morioka-shi Yamagishi 6-39-12 Morioka Iwate ken Japan Office: 4-4040-32 Ishikawa Mito-shi Ibaraki 310-0905 Japan Office Phone: 0292544555. Personal E-mail: hajimefuma3justnetnejp@msn.com.

FUKS, ZVI YECHIEL, radiation oncologist; b. Tel Aviv, Apr. 7, 1936; arrived in US, 1984; MD, Hebrew U. Hadassah Med. Sch., Jerusalem, 1960. Diplomate American Bd. Radiology, cert. in therapeutic radiology. Intern Hadassah U. Hosp., Jerusalem, 1961—64, resident radiation therapy and med. oncology Tel Aviv, 1964-69, prof., head radiation oncology Jerusalem, 1976-78, prof., chmn. dept. radiation oncology, 1978-84; asst. prof. radiology Stanford U., Calif., 1969-76; attending radiation oncologist Meml. Sloan-Kettering Cancer Ctr., NYC, 1984—, chmn. dept. radiation oncology, 1984-98, prof. molecular pharmacology and chemistry. Mem.: American Assn. Cancer Rsch., Radiation Rsch. Soc., NY Cancer Soc., Inst. Medicine, European Soc. Therapeutic Radiol. Oncologists, American Coll. Radiology, American Soc. Clin. Oncology, American Soc. Therapeutic Radiology & Oncology. Achievements include recognition as one of the principal developers of 3-D conformal radiation therapy, a system for delivering radiation that permits precise shaping and targeting of radiation beams. Office: Meml Sloan-Kettering Ctr 1275 York Ave New York NY 10021-6094 Office Phone: 212-639-5868. Office Fax: 212-714-3988. E-mail: fuksz@mskcc.org. *

FUKUDA, KEIJI, international organization administrator, epidemiologist; b. Japan, Aug. 22, 1955; BA, Oberlin Coll., Ohio; MD, U. Vermont Coll. Medicine, Burlington, 1984; MPH in Epidemiology, U. Calif. Berkeley, 1989. Resident, internal medicine Mt. Zion Hosp., San Francisco, 1984—87, chief resident, internal medicine, 1987—88; clin. instructor U. Calif., San Francisco, 1989—90; with Nat. Ctr. Infectious Disease, Divsn. Viral Rickettsial Disease, 1990; clin. asst. prof., dept. cmty. and preventive medicine Emory U. Sch. Medicine, Atlanta, 1993; joined as epidemic intelligence officer Ctr. for Disease Control and Prevention, 1990, epidemiology sect. chief, influenza branch, 1996; global influenza program coord., dept. epidemic and pandemic alert and response WHO, Geneva, 2006—08, dir. global influenza program, dept. epidemic and pandemic alert and response, 2008—, interim asst. dir. gen. health security and environment, 2009—. Vis. prof., dept. pub. health Osaka City U. Contbr. to numerous published research studies, book chapters and reviews on infectious diseases. Comdr. US Pub. Health Svc., Commd. Corps. Mem.: Commn. Corps Officers Assn., Am. Coll. Physicians. Achievements include being responsible for national influenza surveillance in the US; and led the CDC field teams that investigated the outbreak of avian influenza A (H5N1) in 1997 and influenza A (H9N2) in 1999 cases in Hong Kong; worked in China and Hong Kong in 2003 on SARS; worked in Vietnam in 2004 to assist the WHO efforts to investigate and control H5N1. Office: WHO avenue Appia 20 1211 Geneva Switzerland *

FUKUDA, MASAHIKO, ophthalmologist, educator; b. Kyoto, June 19, 1957; adopted s. Hajime and Yoko Fukuda, s. Hajime Ueda; m. Satori Ikami, Dec. 9, 1984; children: Hitomi, Tatsuya, Saya. MD, Kinki U., Osaka-Sayama City, Japan, 1983, PhD, 1989. PhD Kinki U. Sch. of Medicine, 1989. Asst. prof. Kinki U., Sch. Medicine, 1989—, faculty dept. ophthalmology, 1989—91. Dir. cornea svc., dept. ophthalmology KInki U., Sch. Medicine, 1999—; rsch. fellow cornea and contact lens rsch. unit U. NSW, Sydney, 1992—93. Recipient Med. award, Kinki U., 2003. Mem.: Assn. Rsch. Vision and Ophthalmology (assoc.), Internat. K-pro Soc. (assoc.), Ocular Surface Soc. (assoc.), Japanese Soc. Virology (assoc.), Japanese Soc. Ocular Infection (assoc.), Japanese Soc. Ophthalmic Surgeons (assoc.), Japan Cornea Soc. (assoc.), Japanese Ophthal. Soc. (assoc.). Achievements include first to first osteo-odonto-keratoprosthesis surgeon in Japan. Office: Dept Ophthalmol Kinki Univ 377-2 Ohno-Higashi Osakasayama City 589-8511 Japan Office Fax: 81-723-68-2559. E-mail: fukuda@ganka.med.kindai.ac.jp.

FUKUDA, MITSUNORI, cell biologist; b. Tokyo; s. Atsuo and Kyoko Fukuda; m. Hiroko Fukuda; children: Shunya, Yuto. BSc, Tohoku U., 1990, MSc, 1992; PhD, U. Tokyo, 1996. Rschr. Japan Soc. Prom. Sci., Tokyo, 1996—98; rsch. scientist Brain Sci. Inst., Inst. Phys. Chem. Res., Wako, Saitama, Japan, 1998—2002; unit leader Initiative Res. Unit, Inst. Phys. Chem. Res., Wako, 2002—07; prof. Tohoku U. Grad. Sch. Life Sci., Sendai, Miyagi, Japan, 2006—. Adv. bd. mem. Jour. Biochemistry, 2008—; assoc. editor Cell Structure Functions, 2011—. Recipient Young Scientist award, Japanese Biochemical Soc., 2004, Kao Found. Arts Sci., 2006, Molecular Biology Soc. Japan, 2007. Mem.: Molecular Biology Soc. Japan, Japan Soc. Cell Biology, Japan Neuroscience Soc., Japanese Biochemical Soc., Am. Soc. Biochemistry Molecular Biology. Achievements include research in cell biology field. Avocations: birdwatching, badminton. Office: Tohoku Univ Grad Sch Life Sci Aobayama Aoba-ku Sendai 980-8578 Japan Office Fax: 81-22-795-7733.

FUKUDA, TAEKO, medical educator; b. Japan, July 2, 1958; MD, Tsukuba U., PhD, 1983. Assoc. prof. Tsukuba U., 1990—. Mem.: Am. Soc. Anesthesiologists. Office: Tenno-dai 1-1-1 Tsukuba Ibaraki 305-8575 Japan Business E-Mail: taekof@md.tsukuba.ac.jp.

FUKUI, HIROYUKI, medical educator; b. Kaizuka, Sept. 8, 1948; MD, Osaka U., PhD, 1973. Prof. Tokushima U., 1998—. Office: 1-78-1 Shomachi Tokushima 7708505 Japan Business E-Mail: hfukui@ph.tokushima-u.ac.jp.

FUKUI, MELANIE, radiologist; b. Phila., Sept. 8, 1961; AB, Bryn Mawr Coll., 1982; MD, U. Pitts., 1987. Vice chmn. Allegheny Radiology Assocs., 2001—. Office: Allegheny Gen Hosp 320 E North Ave Pittsburgh PA 15212 Business E-Mail: mfukui@wpahs.org.

FUKUI, MICHIAKI, physician; b. Hikone, Japan, Oct. 26, 1964; m. Akemi Nakagawa, Mar. 26, 1967; children: Saya, Rina. MD, Kyoto Prefectural U. Medicine, 1990, PhD, 1998. Med. staff internal medicine Meiji Acupuncture Hosp., Kyoto, 1992—94, Ayabe Mcpl. Hosp., Kyoto, 1998—2000, Osaka Gen. Hosp. West Japan Railway Co., Osaka, 2000—04, Kyoto Prefectural U. Medicine, 2004—. Contbr. articles to profl. jours. Achievements include first to hormonal role for atherosclerosis in men. Home: Ikenosato 12-9 Otsu 520-0827 Japan Office: Kyoto Prefectural U Medicine Kamigyo-ku Kawaramachi Hirokoji Kajii-cho 465 Kyoto 602-8566 Japan Office Fax: +81-75-252-3721. E-mail: sayarinapm@hotmail.com.

FUKUTA, HIDEKATSU, medical educator; b. Japan, Sept. 23, 1969; MD, Nagoya City U., Grad. Sch. Med. Scis., 1995, PhD, 2004. Asst. prof. Nagoya City U., Grad. Sch. Med. Scis., 1995—. Office: 1 Kawasumi Mizuho-cho Mizuho-ku Nagoya Aichi 467-8601 Japan Office Fax: 81-52-852-3796. Business E-Mail: fukuta-h@med.nagoya-cu.ac.jp.

FUKUTOMI, YASUSHI, gastroenterologist; b. Gifu, Japan, July 19, 1958; m. Naoko Saito, Mar. 21, 1985; children: Keisuke, Yoshihiro. MD, Aichi Med. U., Nagoya, Japan, 1983; PhD, Gifu U., Japan, 1991. Physician in chief Gifu Prefectural Hosp., Gifu, 1999—. Mem.: Japanese Soc. Gastrointestinal Endoscopy (cert. 1989, councilor 2004—), Japanese Soc. Gastroent. (cert. 1989, councilor 2003—), Am. Gastroent. Assn., Am. Soc. Gastrointestinal Endoscopy. Achievements include research in clinical diagnostic and therapeutic procedure of gastroenterological endoscopy. Home: 2492-1 Nagara Fukumitsu Gifu 5020817 Japan Office: Gifu Prefectural Hosp Gastroenterol 4-6-1 Noissiki Gifu 5008717 Japan Office Fax: 81-58-246-1111; Home Fax: 81-58-294-6954. Personal E-mail: fyash@jasmine.ocn.ne.jp.

FUKUYAMA, YUKIO, child neurologist, pediatrics educator; b. Takachiho-machi, Miyazaki, Japan, May 28, 1928; s. Masaharu and Kiku Fukuyama; m. Ayako Arai, Nov. 6, 1954. MD, U. Tokyo, 1952, postgrad., 1953-56, PhD, 1959. Intern U. Tokyo Hosp., 1952-53; asst. prof. pediat. U. Tokyo Faculty Medicine, 1960—64, assoc. prof., 1964—65; dir. divsn. neurology Nat. Children's Hosp., Tokyo, 1965—67; prof. pediat. Tokyo Women's Med. Coll, 1967-94, chmn. dept., 1967-94, prof. emeritus, 1994—; prof. pediat. Saitama Med. Sch., 1994-99; dir. Child Neurology Inst., 1994—. Editor (monographs): Epilepsy Bibliography Online, 11th edit., 2011, Child Neurology Atlas, 1986, EEG and Evoked Potentials in Children, 1990, Modern Perspectives of Child Neurology, 1991, Fetal and Neonatal Neurology, 1992, Crossroads of Child Neurology, 1995, Congenital Muscular Dystrophies, 1997; editor-in-chief No to Hattatsu, 1969—87, Brain and Devel., 1979—96. Recipient Hughling Jackson's prize, Japan Found. Epilepsy Rsch., 1993, Grand award, Japan Med. Assn., 1999, Duchenne-Erb prize, Gesellschaft fur Muskelkranke, 1999, Lifetime Achievement award, World Fedn. of Neurology, 2003, Henri Gastaut prize, Ligue Francaise Contre Epilepsie, 2003, William G. Lennox award, Am. Epilepsy Soc., 2004, Amb. for Epilepsy award, Internat. League Against Epilepsy, 2007, Asahi award, Asahi Shimbun Cultural Found., 2008, Achievement Grand award, Japan Pediat. Soc., 2008, Spl. Recognition award, Japanese Soc. Child Neurology, 2008, The Order of Sacred Treas., Cabinet Office, Japanese Govt., 2008, Outstanding Achievement award, Japan Epilepsy Soc., 2010. Mem.: Japanese Soc. Child Neurology (chmn. bd. trustees 1968—93, hon. chmn. 1993—), Philippine Child Neurology Soc. (hon.), European Pediat. Neurology Soc. (hon.), Japanese Soc. Human Genetics (hon. Grand award 1999), Japan Soc. Clin. Neurophysiology (hon.), Japan Teratology Soc. (hon.), Japan Epilepsy Soc. (hon. Outstanding Achievement award 2010), Japan Pediat. Soc. (hon. Grand award 2008), Czechoslovakian Neurol. Soc. (hon.), Can. Child Neurology Soc. (hon.), Am. Acad. Neurology (hon.), Child Neurology Soc. (hon.), Am. Neurol. Assn. (hon.), Asian and Oceanian Child Neurology Assn. (hon.; pres. 1983—90, hon. pres. 1993—), Internat. Child Neurology Assn. (hon.; pres. 1982—86, v.p. 1986—90, mem. presdl. adv. com. 2004—10, Frank Ford Lectr. award 1992). Avocation: stamp collecting/philately. Home: 6-12-16 Minami-Shinagawa Shinagawa-ku Tokyo 140-0004 Japan Office: Child Neurology Inst 6-12-17-201 Minami-Shinagawa Shinagawa-ku Tokyo 140-0004 Japan Home Phone: 03-3474-8677; Office Phone: 03 5781 7680. Business E-Mail: yfukuyam@sc4.so-net.ne.jp.

FULCHER, CLAIRE E, psychotherapist, organization consultant; b. LA, Aug. 8, 1925; d. James H. and Eleanor (Davis) F. BA, Pomona Coll., 1946; MA, Stanford U., 1950; EdD, Columbia U., 1955. Cert. counselor, clin. mental health counselor. Asst. dir. Stanford U., Palo Alto, Calif., 1947-49; asst. dean, biology instr. Palos Verdes Coll., Rolling Hills, Calif., 1949-52; dean of women, assoc. dean of students, prof. U. Bridgeport, Conn., 1954-72; dir. Women's Resource Ctr. Nat. YWCA, NYC, 1972-74; prin., psychotherapist, pres. Team Assocs., NYC, 1974—. Author: Residence Hall, A Human Relations Laboratory, 1955, Techniques for Effective Action and Management, 1973, 2d rev. edit., 1978; co-editor (pamphlet) Project: Re-Entry, 1968; creator pictorial exhibit Women Hold Up Half the Sky, 1986. Del., mem. planning com. UN Conf. on Women, Copenhagen, 1980, Nairobi, 1985, Beijing, 1995; co-founder, chair non-govtl. orgns. com. UN Devel. Fund for Women, 1988—; bd. dirs. Virginia Gildersleeve Internat. Fund for Women, 1983—, global network convenor, 1991—, 2d v.p., 1993—; co-founder, non-govtl. orgns. com. Mental Health, 1986. Recipient Tchr. of Yr. award U. Bridgeport, 1958, 65, UNA-USA Citation, 1969. Mem. APA, AAUW (life, endowed named internat. fellowships, 1984—, recipient State Named Gifts award Conn. State, 1968, Br. Named Gifts award Bridgeport Br., 1977, 2001, Woman of Achievement award N.Y.C. Br., 1984-, Veteran Feminists of America (medal 1998), former nat. v.p., mem. leadercorps, 1988—), ACA, Assn. Group Specialists, Nat. Assn. Women in Edn., Internat. Fedn. Univ. Women (UN rep. 1979-83, v.p. 1980-83), Internat. Fedn. Bus. and Profl. Women Permanent (UN rep. 1983—), Assn. Psychol. Types, Women Grad. US (charter mem. 2008-), Jungian Inst., YWCA (bd. dirs. Bridgeport chpt.), Delta Kappa Gamma (mortar bd. mem., Pomona Coll. 1945-). Democrat. Mem. United Ch. of Christ. Avocations: travel, photography, reading, music, climbing mountains. Office Phone: 520-885-2485. Personal E-mail: clairefulcher@rcn.com, fulokerclaire@gmail.com. Business E-Mail: clairefulcher@rcu.com.

FULKERSON, JOHN P., surgeon; b. NY, Dec. 9, 1946; MD, Yale U., 1972. Orthop. surgeon Orthop. Assocs. Hartford, 1995—; clin. prof. orthop. surgery U. Conn. Pres. Patellofemoral Found.; past resident Herodicus Soc.; founder Internat. Patellofemoral Study Group. Recipient Lifetime Achievement award, San Francisco Bay Area Knee Soc. Office: 499 Farmington Ave Farmington CT 06032 E-mail: jpfulkersonmd@aol.com.

FULKERSON, WILLIAM, hospital administrator, pulmonologist; b. Charlotte, NC, Sept. 8, 1951; Grad., U. N.C., Chapel Hill, 1973; MD, U. N.C., 1977; grad., Duke U. Intern Vanderbilt U. Hosp., Nashville, 1977—78, resident internal medicine, 1978—81, fellow pulmonary disease, 1981—83; asst. prof. medicine Duke U. Sch. Medicine, 1983—90, assoc. prof., 1990—95, prof., 1995—, vice chmn. dept. medicine, 1997—98, chief pulmonary and critical care medicine, 1997—99, exec. med. officer Private Diagnostic Clinic PLLC, 1997—99; chief med. officer Duke U. Hosp., 2000—02, CEO, 2002; sr. v.p. clin. affairs Duke U. Health Sys., exec. v.p. Contbr. articles to profl. jours., chapters to books. Fellow: Soc. Critical Care Medicine, Am. Coll. Chest Physicians; mem.: Am. Thoracic Soc., ACP. Office: Duke Univ 14209 Hosp S Box 3708 Med Ctr Durham NC 27710 *

FULLER, DAVID A., orthopaedic surgeon, educator; Attended, U. Pa. Diplomate Am. Bd. Orthopaedic Surgery, Am. Bd. Orthopaedic Surgery-hand surgery. Intern Univ. Hosps., Cleve., resident; fellow Thomas Jefferson Univ. Hosp., Albert Einstein Med. Ctr.; asst. prof. orthop. surgery Cooper Univ. Hosp., dir. hand and upper extremity surgery. Named one of the Top Doctors, Phila. Mag., 2011. Office: Cooper University Hospital Bldg 2 Ste 203 300 Centennial Blvd Voorhees NJ 08043 Office Phone: 856-325-6677. Office Fax: 856-325-6678.

FULLER, MARGARET JANE, medical technologist, priest; b. Park Rapids, Minn., Jan. 29, 1947; d. Rudolph Kenneth and Jean Ellen (Klenk) Haas; m. Phillip Fuller, Aug. 7, 1970; 1 child, Sharon Dawn. BS in Chemistry, Muhlenberg Coll., 1969; diploma in med. tech., Allentown Hosp., Pa., 1972; MPA, Angelo State U., 1988; MS in Microbiology, Tex. Tech. U., 1992; MDiv, Episcopal Theol. Sem. of the S.W., 2006. Ordained deacon Episcopal Ch., 2005, ordained priest Episcopal Ch., 2006. Lab. dir. San Angelo-Tom Green County Health Dept., 1984-89; outpatient lab. supr. Meth. Hosp., Plainview, Tex., 1995-96; lab. mgr. Highland Med. Ctr., Lubbock, Tex., 1996-98; instr. microbiology Great Basin Coll., Ely, Nev., 1998—2002. Mem. med. adv. bd. Planned Parenthood West Tex., San Angelo, 1987-89; scientist-by-mail, assoc. Children's Mus. Houston, 1991-92; direct patient vol. Hospice of Lubbock, 1993-98. Bd. dirs. El Camino coun. Girl Scouts U.S.A.; sec. Big. Bros.-Big Sisters Ely, 2002-03; sec., treas. White Pine Ministerial Assn., 2009-; chaplain, White Pine County Sheriff's Office, 2009-. Recipient Thanks Badge, El Camino coun. Girl Scouts U.S.A., 1986. Mem. Am. Soc. Microbiology, Am. Soc. Clin. Lab. Sci., Am. Soc. Clin. Pathologists (assoc., cert. med. technologist), Mensa, Beta Beta Beta, Sigma Theta Tau, Internat. Conf. Police Chaplains Episcopalian. Personal E-mail: pegfuller@yahoo.com.

FULLWOOD, MICHAEL DAVID, lawyer; b. Hereford, Tex., Jan. 7, 1947; s. Edward Fenton and Helen Edith (Watson) F. BA with honors, U. Wis., 1969; JD, Harvard U., 1972. Bar: N.Y. 1973, U.S. Supreme Ct. 1977. Atty. Arabian American Oil Co., NYC, 1972-73, Dhahran, Saudi Arabia, 1973-74, The Hague, Netherlands, 1975-81; sr. atty. Caltex Petroleum Co., NYC, 1981—83, Scallop Corp. of Royal Dutch Shell Group, NYC, 1983—87; atty. then as group v.p. for fin. and adminstrn., and later as exec. v.p., CFO Witco Corp., NYC, 1987—96; sr. v.p., chief financial and adminstrv. officer, sec. and gen. counsel Commodore Environmental Services, Commodore Applied Technologies, and Commodore Separation Technologies, 1997—98; exec. v.p., CFO EmblemHealth, Inc. (parent co. of HIP Health Plan (HIP) and Group Health, Inc. (GHI)), 1998—. Pres. West 15 Block Assn., N.Y.C., 1984-86, West 15 Townhouse Corp., N.Y.C., 1984—. Mem. Internat. Bar Assn., ABA, NY State Bar Assn., Assn. Bar of NYC (mem. Health Law Com.), Am. Soc. Internat. Law, Internat. Law Assn., NY Geneal. and Biog. Soc. Clubs: Travelers Century LA, bd. dirs. NY Chpt. Fin. Exec. Inst. Roman Catholic. Avocations: travel, genealogy. Office: EmblemHealth Inc 55 Water St New York NY 10041 Office Phone: 212-630-8220. Office Fax: 212-216-7050. Business E-Mail: mfullwood@hipusa.com. *

FULMER, HUGH SCOTT, physician, educator; b. Syracuse, NY, June 18, 1928; s. Herbert C. and Emily (Price) F.; m. Zola M. Jones, July 12, 1952; children: James, Kim, Scott. AB, Syracuse U., 1948; MD, SUNY-Syracuse, 1951; M.P.H., Harvard U., 1961. Intern R.I. Hosp., 1951-52; resident internal medicine SUNY-Syracuse, 1954-57; fellow pulmonary medicine SUNY, Syracuse, 1957-58; asst. dir., rsch. assoc. Navajo-Cornell Field Health Research Project, 1958-60; instr. pub. health and preventive medicine Cornell U. Coll. Medicine, 1958-60; asst. prof. community medicine U. Ky. Coll. Medicine, 1960-64, assoc. prof., 1964-66, prof., 1966-68, dir. sr. med. student internat. cross-cultural program, 1964-68, dir. preventive medicine residency program, 1964-68; tech. cons. health Peace Corps, Malaysia, 1968-69; prof., chmn. dept. community and family medicine U. Mass. Med. Sch., 1969-77, assoc. dean clin. edn. and primary care, 1975-79, chief sect. gen. medicine, dept. medicine, 1979—83; dir. ambulatory and community svcs. Carney Hosp., Boston, 1983-88, dir. community-oriented primary care program, 1988-93, dir. preventive medicine residency, 1988-93; exec. dir. Ctr. for Cmty. Responsive Care, Boston, 1992—2000, dir. preventive medicine residency & COPC fellowship program, 1992—2002. Adj. prof. socio-med. scis., cmty. medicine and pub. health Boston U. Sch. Medicine and Pub. Health, 1983—96; adj. prof. family and internal medicine SUNY, Syracuse, 2005—. Served with M.C., USAF, 1952-54. Mem. APHA, Mass. Med. Soc., Assn. Tchrs. Preventive Medicine (past pres., Outstanding Tchr. award 1993), Am. Assn. Pub. Health Physician, Am. Coll. Preventive Medicine (bd. regents 1988-94), Harvard Sch. Pub. Health Alumni Assn. (pres. 1974-76, Alumni Award of Merit, 2011). Achievements include educational initiatives to merge medicine and public health in response to community needs. Home: 61 Cherlyn Dr Northborough MA 01532-1135 Business E-Mail: hsfulmer@massmed.org.

FULMER, TERRY T., nursing educator, geriatric nurse practitioner; BSN, Skidmore Coll., Saratoga Springs, NY, 1975; MSN, Boston Coll., 1977, PhD, 1983. Geriatric nurse practitioner post-master's cert. NYU; RN. Staff nurse Beth Israel Deaconess Med. Ctr.; asst. then assoc. prof. Boston Coll. Sch. Nursing; rsch. scientist, assoc. prof. gerontological nursing Yale Sch. Nursing, New Haven, 1987—91; assoc. dean rsch., Anna C. Maxwell prof. nursing Columbia U. Sch. Nursing, NYC, 1991—94; faculty NYU, 1994—, head divsn. nursing, 2002—, dean Coll. Nursing, 2005—, Erline Perkins McGriff prof. Assoc. dir. Harvard Geriatric Edn. Ctr., 1983—87; clin. nurse specialist geriatrics Yale New Haven Hosp., 1987—91; co-dir. Consortium NY Geriatric Edn. Centers, John A. Hartford Found. Inst. Geriatric Nursing; attending in nursing NYU Langone Med. Ctr. Co-author (numerous editions): Critical Care Nursing of the Elderly, The Encyclopedia of Elder Care: The Comprehensive Resource on Geriatric and Social Care; co-author: others, contbr. articles to profl. Jours. Bd. trustees Skidmore Coll., 2007—, Bassett Hosp., Cooperstown, NY. Brookdale Nat. Fellowship, 1992. Fellow: NY Acad. Medicine (bd. trustees), Gerontological Soc. America (past pres.), American Acad. Nursing (Nurse Leader in Aging award 2010); mem.: Nat. Academies Practice (disting. practitioner), American Geriatrics Soc. (bd. dirs.), Inst. Medicine. Office: NYU Coll Nursing 1096 726 Broadway New York NY 10003 Office Phone: 212-998-5303. Office Fax: 212-995-3143. E-mail: tf1@nyu.edu. *

FUMIHITO, HIRAI, medical educator; b. Kumamoto, Japan, Mar. 4, 1966; Degree in Medicine, Fukuoka U., 1991. Asst. prof. Fukuoka U. Chikushi Hosp., Japan, 1991. Office: 1-1-1 Zokumyoin Chikushino Fukuoka 818-8501 Japan Business E-Mail: fuhirai@cis.fukuoka-u.ac.jp.

FUMINORI, TANABE, medical educator; b. Japan, Mar. 25, 1959; MD, Fukushima Med. Coll., PhD, 1988. Prof. U. Yamanashi, 2002—. Office: University Yamanashi 1110 Shimokato Chuo Yamanashi 4093898 Japan Business E-Mail: ftanabe@yamanashi.ac.jp.

FUNA, KEIKO, molecular cell biologist, physician; b. Ashiya, Hyogo, Japan, Jan. 3, 1949; arrived in Sweden, 1974; d. Yasuo and Sadako (Uesugi) F.; m. Hans Erik Agren; children: Nina, Nils. MD, Kyoto U., Japan, 1974, Uppsala U., Sweden, 1978, PhD, 1984. Diplomate Japan, Sweden. Intern Uppsala U. Hosp., 1975-78, resident, 1978-84; rschr. NIH-NCI, Bethesda, Md., 1984-85, Ludwig Inst., Uppsala, 1986-97; prof. med. cell biology U. Gothenburg, Sweden, 1997—. Contbr. articles to profl. jours. Fogarty fellow NIH, 1984-85; named Best Presenter of Yr., Swedish Oncology Radiology Assn., 1985. Mem. Swedish Med. Assn., Am. Cancer Rsch. Assn., Am. Soc. Microbiology. Avocation: travel. Office: Sahlgrenska Cancer Ctr Acad University Gothenburg PO Box 425 Gothenburg SE 405 30 Sweden Office Phone: 46 31 7863360. Business E-Mail: keiko.funa@gu.se.

FUNABASHI, NOBUSADA, cardiologist, educator; s. Shigeru and Hiromi Funabashi. M.D., Chiba U., 1989, PhD, 1998. Rsch. scholar Stanford U., Palo Alto, Calif., 1996—99; chief cardiovascular surgery dept. Nat. Ctr. Neurology and Psychiatry, 1999—2000; instr. Chiba U. Grad. Sch. Medicine, 2001—. Contbr. articles to profl. jours. Achievements include research in coronary angiography by EBT; myocardial fibrosis by multislice CT; patents for stent graft. Office: Chiba Univ 1-8-1 Inohana Chuo-ku Chiba 260-8670 Japan

FUNARI, ROBERT GLENN, healthcare services company executive; b. Pitts., Sept. 20, 1947; s. Mario Ronald and Virginia Alice Funari; m. Marilyn Romcea, July 18, 1970; children: Carla Marie, Michael Anthony. BS in Mech. Engring., Cornell U., 1969; MBA, Harvard U., 1975. Various positions Baxter International, Inc., Deerfield, Ill., 1975—77, dir. distbn., 1977—79, v.p. materials mgmt., 1979—83, pres. Medcom, Inc. (subs.) Garden Grove, Calif., 1983—86, pres. Paramax Sys. divsn. Irvine, Calif., 1986—89, corp. v.p., pres. Pharmaseal divsn. Valencia, Calif., 1989—93; exec. v.p., COO Syncor Internat., Woodland Hills, Calif., 1993—96, pres., CEO, 1996—2002; chmn., CEO Crescent Healthcare, Inc., 2004—. Bd. dirs. Pope & Talbot, 2001—, First Consulting Group, 2004—, Beckman Coulter Inc., 2005—. Recipient Entrepreneur of Yr. award, Ernst & Young LLP, 2010; Baker scholar, 1975. Office: Crescent Healthcare Inc 11980 Telegraph Rd Ste 10 Santa Fe Springs CA 90670-3797 Home: 1400 E Ocean Blvd Unit 14 D1 Long Beach CA 90802 Office Phone: 562-347-2800. Business E-Mail: rfunari@beckmancoulter.com, robert_funari@poptal.com.

FUNG, CHIN-PING, science educator; b. Taipei, Taiwan, May 8, 1962; s. Ju-Bo Fung and A-Bau Lin; m. Huey-Ju Yen, July 1, 1989; children: Huai-Ji, Shin-Ji. BSc, Chung Cheng Inst. Tech., Tao-Yuan, Taiwan, 1984; MSc, Nat. Ctrl. U., Chung-Li, Taiwan, 1988; PhD, U. Manchester, England, 1995. Lectr. Chung Cheng Inst. Tech., 1988—91, assoc. prof., 1997—2004, prof., 2004—. Home: 4F No 83 San-Ming Rd Sect 1 Tao-Yuan 33049 Taiwan Office: Oriental Inst Tech No 58 Sec 2 Sih-Chuan Rd Pan-Chiao City Taipei 22061 Taiwan Office Fax: 886-2-77386648. Personal E-mail: cpfung@mail2000.com.tw. Business E-Mail: cpfung@mail.oit.edu.tw.

FUNG, WYE POH, gastroenterologist, consultant, physician; b. Telok-Anson, Malaysia, Jan. 9, 1937; s. Kwok Chan and Swee Lin (Man) F.; m. Saw Lin Ong, Nov. 1961; children: Li-May, Chee-Ming. MBBS, U. Malaya, 1961; MD, U. Singapore, 1972. Cert. Med. Bd. West Australia, New South Wales, South Australia. Sr. lectr. medicine U. Singapore, 1965—74, assoc. prof. medicine, 1975; sr. lectr. medicine U. We. Australia, Perth, 1976—85; cons. physician Royal Perth Hosp., 1976—85; vis. assoc. prof. U. Calif. at San Francisco Med. Ctr., 1981—82; gastroenterologist St. John of God Hosp., Perth, 1985—; pvt. practice West Perth, 1985—; gastroenterologist Swan Dist. Hosp., Perth, 1985—, Osborne Pk. Hosp., Perth, 1986—, Armadale Kelmscott Hosp., Perth, 1987—. Cons. physician Royal Perth Hosp., 1976-85. Contbr. articles to profl. jours. Fellow Royal Australasian Coll. Physicians, Am. Coll. Gastroenterology, Acad. Medicine Singapore; mem. Gastroent. Soc. Singapore (co-founder, sec. treas. 1967-75). Avocation: golf.

FUNK, CARLA JEAN, library association director; b. Wheeling, W.Va., Sept. 21, 1946; d. David H. and Jean (Duffy) Belt. BA in Psychology, Northwestern U., 1968; MLS, Ind. U., 1973; MBA, U. Chgo., 1985. Libr. adult svcs. Northbrook (Ill.) Pub. Libr., 1973-77; dir. Warren-Newport Pub. Libr. Dist., Gurnee, Ill., 1977-80; cons. Suburban Libr. Sys., Burr Ridge, Ill., 1980-83; dir. automation and tech. svcs., med. student svcs. AMA, Chgo., 1983-92; exec. dir. Med. Libr. Assn., Chgo., 1992—. Adj. faculty Dominican U., 1986—2000, mem. GSLIS adv. commn. Contbr. articles to profl. jours. Fellow: Chartered Inst. Libr. & Info. Profl. (hon.); mem. Internat. Fedn. Libr. Assns. and Insts., Am. Soc. Assn. Execs. (cert. assn. exec.), Assn. Forum of Chicagoland, Beta Phi Mu, Delta Zeta, Med. Libr. Assn. (hon.), Friends Nat. Libr. Medicine (bd. mem.), U. Chgo. Women's Alliance (bd. mem.). Office: 65 E Wacker Pl Ste 1900 Chicago IL 60601-7246 Business E-Mail: funk@mlahq.org.

FUNK, MARK EUGENE, medical librarian; b. Waynesville, Mo., July 20, 1949; s. Harry C. and Jean Funk; m. Carolyn Anne Reid. BA in Zoology, U. Mo., Columbia, 1971, BS in Edn., 1973, MA in Libr. Sci., 1976. Clin. med. libr. U. Mo., Kansas City, 1977—80; head, collection devel. U. Nebr. Med. Coll., Omaha, 1980—87; head, resource mgmt. collections Weill Cornell Med. Libr., NYC, 1987—2009, assoc. dir. resources and edn., 2010—. Mem.: Med. Libr. Assn. (bd. dirs. 2000—03, treas. 2001—03, pres. 2007—08). Office: Weill Cornell Med Coll 1300 York Ave New York NY 10065

FUNKHOUSER, WILLIAM KEITH, JR., pathologist, educator; b. Piqua, Ohio, July 10, 1953; MD, Vanderbilt U., 1979; PhD, Caltech, 1992. Prof., dir. anatomic and pathology U. NC, 1996—, dir. anatomic and surg. pathology. Mem.: CAP, AMP, ADASP, USCAP, ASCP. Office: University NC CB # 7525 Brinkhous Bullitt Bldg Chapel Hill NC 27599-7525 Business E-Mail: bill_funkhouser@med.unc.edu.

FURER, MANUEL, psychotherapist; b. NYC, Apr. 13, 1923; AB, Cornell U., 1944; MD, Cornell Med. Coll., 1948. Physician NY Psychoanalytic Inst., 1958—. Tng. & supervising analyst, Brill and Freud meml. hon. lectr. Home and Office: 166 E 93rd St New York NY 10128 Office Fax: 212-987-8133. Personal E-mail: bmdpc@yahoo.com.

FURLAN, ANTHONY, neurologist, department chairman; b. Chgo., Dec. 16, 1947; MD magna cum laude, Loyola Stritch, 1973. Chmn., dept. neurology Case Western Res. U., 2008—. Co-dir. Neurol. Inst. U. Hosps., 2008. Recipient Feinberg award, Am. Stroke Assn., Codman award, Joint Commn. Hosp. Accreditation. Fellow: Am. Heart Assn., Am. Acad. Neurology. Office: 11100 Euclid Ave Mail Stop HAN5040 Cleveland OH 44106 Business E-Mail: anthony.furlan@uhhospitals.org.

FURLAN, DANIELA, biologist, educator; b. Varese, Italy, Sept. 30, 1967; Degree in Biol. Scis., U. Pavia, Italy, 1990. Fellow Nat. Cancer Ins., Milan, 1991—93; technician U. Insubria, Italy, 1993—2000, asst. prof., 2001—. Biologist mgr. Varese Hosp., Italy, 2002—11. Mem.: Italian Soc. Genetics, Italian Soc. Oncology. Avocations: reading, painting, gardening. Home: Brianza 18 Saronno Varese 21047 Italy Personal E-mail: daniela.furlan@uninsubria.it.

FURLAUD, RICHARD MORTIMER, pharmaceutical executive; b. NYC, Apr. 15, 1923; s. Maxime Hubert and Eleanor (Mortimer) F.; children: Richard Mortimer, Eleanor Jay, Elizabeth Tamsin; m. Isabel Phelps Furlaud. Student, Institut Sillig, Villars, Switzerland; AB, Princeton U., 1944; LLB, Harvard U., 1947. Bar: NY 1949. Assoc. Root, Ballantine, Harlan, Bushby & Palmer, 1947-51; with legal dept. Olin Mathieson Chem. Corp., 1955-56, asst. to exec. v.p. for finance, 1956-57, asst. pres., 1957-59, v.p., 1959-64, gen. counsel, 1957-60, gen. mgr., v.p. internat. div., 1960-64, exec. v.p., 1964-66, now dir., 1964-94; pres., dir. E. R. Squibb & Sons, Inc., 1966-68; pres., chief exec., dir. Squibb Beech-Nut, Inc. (renamed Squibb Corp. 1971), Princeton, NJ, 1968-74; chmn., chief exec., dir. Squibb Corp. (merged with Bristol-Myers Co.), NYC, 1974-89; pres., bd. dirs. Bristol-Myers Co. (renamed Bristol-Myers Squibb Co.), NYC, 1989-91. Mem. profl. staff Ho. of Reps. Com. Ways and Means, 1954; chmn. emeritus Rockefeller U. 1st lt. JAGC U.S. Army, 1951-53. Mem. Assn. Bar City of N.Y., Coun. on Fgn. Rels., River Club. Home: 745 HiMount Rd Palm Beach FL 33480 Office: 8th Fl West 777 S Flagler Dr West Palm Beach FL 33401 Home Phone: 561-848-2267; Office Phone: 561-515-6016. Personal E-mail: ternaboutx@aol.com.

FURLONG, NATALIE VACCARI, physician; MD, U. New England Coll. of Osteopathic Medicine, 1994. Diplomate Am. Bd. Family Medicine, lic. to practice Pa., 1995. Tng. South Hills Family Medicine; hospital affiliation includes Jefferson Regional Med. Ctr. Office: Jefferson Regional Medical Center PO Box 18119 Pittsburgh PA 15236 Office Phone: 412-469-5000.

FURMAN, LYDIA M., pediatrician, educator; b. Cleve., Nov. 9, 1957; BA, Princeton U., NJ, 1979; MD, Case Western Reserve U. Sch. Medicine, Cleve., Ohio, 1983. Cert. Am. Bd. Pediat. Intern and resident, pediat. Children's Hosp. Boston, 1983—86; clin. fellow, pediat. Harvard U., 1983—86; clin. instr., pediat. Harvard Med. Sch., 1988—90, Case Western Reserve U. Sch. Medicine, 1990—95, asst. clin. prof., 1995—98, asst. prof., 1988—2004, assoc. prof., 2004—; pediatrician Centre Pediat., Brookline, Mass., 1986—88; staff mem. Rainbow Babies and Children's Hosp., Cleve. Mem. edn. com. Rainbow Babies and Children's Hosp., 1999—. Contbr. several articles to profl. jours. Recipient Pediat. Residents Pearls Day Tchg. award, 2001—02, 2009. Fellow: Am. Acad. Pediat.; mem.: Acad. for Breastfeeding Medicine, No. Ohio Pediat. Soc., Alpha Omega Alpha. Office: Univ Hosp Rainbow Babies and Childrens Hosp 11100 Euclid Ave Cleveland OH 44106 Office Phone: 216-844-8260. Office Fax: 216-844-8444. Business E-Mail: lydia.forman@uhhosptitals.org.

FURMAN, MARK EVAN, neuroscientist; b. Bronx, NY, Mar. 14, 1962; s. Edward and Charlotte F.;m. Monica J. Michalski; children: Lauren Ashley, Jonathan Cyle. BA in Behavioral Scis./Psychology, Coll. of SI, 1984. Cert. practitioner of neuro-linguistic programming. Dir. edn. and rsch. Assoc. Schs. Music, Inc., Cooper City, Fla., 1988-97; spkr., author, human performance cons., 1990—; founder, exec. dir. Furman Rsch. Assocs., Boca Raton, Fla., 1987—; dir. edn. and rsch. The Keys to Success, Inc., Coral Springs, Fla., 1992—2000, Ozone Park, NY, 1992—2000; human performance cons. Interactive Response Techs., 2001—04; dir. behavioral scis. Burton Tng. Group, Inc., 2004—; pres. Mind Imaging Techologies, Inc., 2006—. Lectr. in field of neurosci.; founder, exec. dir. Furman Rsch. Assocs.; designer comm. program Jewish Ednl. Found. of Am., theoretical tng. model Syntonics Ednls., Switzerland; cons. Keys to Success Music Sch., NY, Century 21, Fla.; founder Internat. Soc. for Edn. Neurosci.; developer Intelligent Learning Systems, Mind Imaging, Neuroprint, Human Performance Modeling & Engineering, Decernomics; numerous others application models. Author: Mind in Motion, The Human Performance Technology for the Next Millenum, 1996; author: Jour. for the Soc. of Neuro-Linguistic Programming, 1995-2002, The Neurophysics of Human Behavior: Explorations at the Interface of Brain, Mind, Behavior and Information, 1999, (audio CD) Escaping the Mind Prison, 2006; contbg. author: Energy Psychology in Psychotherapy, 2002; contbr. articles to profl. jours. Mem.: APA (affiliate, divsn. 48, divsn. peace psychology), AAAS, Soc. for Study of Peace, Conflict and Violence, Internat. Soc. for Cognitive Neurophysics (founder). Achievements include developing intelligent learning systems (ILS); neuroprint; mind imaging; decernomics and human performance modeling and engineering; currently pioneering coordinated research and development efforts in the field of education neuroscience, studying the neurophysics of human information processing and its application to the field of human education, psychotherapy, marketing, crisis negotiation and the management sciences; advanced standard theory: Pattern-Entropy dynamics of matter and energy interaction; formerly established the interdisciplinary branch of science known as cognitive neurophysics. Office: 20423 State Rd 7 Ste F6-114 Boca Raton FL 33498 Personal E-mail: neuroprint@yahoo.com.

FURNAS, DAVID WILLIAM, plastic surgeon, educator; b. Caldwell, Idaho, Apr. 1, 1931; s. John Doan and Esther Bradbury (Hare) F.; m. Mary Lou Heatherly, Feb. 11, 1956; children: Heather Jean, Brent David, Craig Jonathan. AB, U. Calif., Berkeley, 1952, MS, 1957, MD, 1955. Diplomate Am. Bd. Plastic Surgery, Royal Coll. Surgeons. Intern U. Calif. Hosp., San Francisco, 1955-56, asst. resident in surgery, 1956-57; asst. resident in psychiatry, NIMH fellow Langley Porter Neuropsychiat. Inst. U. Calif., San Francisco, 1959-60; resident in gen. surgery Gorgas Hosp., Panama Canal Zone, 1960-61, asst. resident in plastic surgery N.Y. Hosp., Cornell Med. Center, NYC, 1961-62; chief resident in plastic surgery Cornell U. Svc., VA Hosp., Bronx, NY, 1962-63; registrar Royal Infirmary and Affiliated Hosps., Glasgow, Scotland, 1963-64; assoc. in hand surgery U. Iowa, 1964-68, sr. resident, faculty assoc. in surgery, 1964-65, asst. prof. surgery, 1966-68, assoc. prof., 1968-69; assoc. prof. surgery, chief div. plastic surgery U. Calif., Irvine, 1969-74, prof., chief div. plastic surgery, 1974-80, clin. prof., chief div. plastic surgery, 1980-99, clin. prof. plastic surgery, 1999—2002, emeritus prof. plastic surgery, 2002—. Surgeon East Africa Flying Drs. Svc., African Med. and Rsch. Found., Nairobi, Kenya, 1972-73; plastic surgeon S.S. Hope, Nicaragua, 1966, Sri Lanka, 1968; mem. Balabkayan med. mission Mindanao and Sulu, The Philippines, 1980-82; overseas vis. prof. plastic surgery Ednl. Found., 1994; Godrej vis. prof. Assn. Plastic Surgeons of India, 2000; keynote spkr. Pan African Assn. Plastic Surgeons, 2000; dir. Am. Bd. Plastic Surgeons, 1979-85; trustee Royal Coll. Surgeons Found., 1995-2002. Contbr. chpts. to textbooks, articles to profl. jours.; author, editor 5 textbooks; mem. editl. bd. Jour. Hand Surgery, Annals of Plastic Surgery, Jour. Craniofacial Surgery; reviewer Plastic and Reconstructive Surgery. Expedition leader Flag 171 Skull Surgeons of the Kisii Tribe Explorer's Club, Kenya, expedition leader Flag 44 Skull Surgeons of the Marakwet Tribe, 1987; bd. govs. Bowers Mus. Cultural Art, 2000—02. Capt. M.C. USAF, 1957—59, col. M.C. USAR, 1989—92. Recipient Golden Apple award U. Calif.-Irvine Sch. Medicine, 1980, Kaiser-Permanente award U. Calif.-Irvine Sch. Medicine, 1981, Humanitarian Svc. award Black Med. Students, U. Calif. Irvine, 1987, Sr. Rsch. award Plastic Surgery Ednl. Found., 1987, Cert. of Spl. Recognition, U.S. Congress, 1998; named Orange County Press Club Headliner of Yr., 1982, Physician of the Year, Orange County Med. Assn., 1998, Alumnus of Yr. U. Calif. San Francisco Alumni Assn., 2005. Fellow ACS, Royal Coll. Surgeons Can., Royal Soc. Medicine, Explorers Club (chmn. So. Calif. chpt. 2001-02), Royal Geog. Soc.; mem. AMA (Disting. Svc. award 2002), Calif. Med. Assn., Orange County Med. Assn. (Physician of Yr. 1998), Am. Soc. Plastic Surgery (bd. dirs. 1970-73), Am. Soc. Reconstructive Microsurgery, Soc. Head and Neck Surgery, Am. Cleft Palate Assn., Am. Soc. Surgery of Hand, Soc. Univ. Surgeons, Am. Assn. Plastic Surgeons (trustee 1983-86, treas. 1988-91, v.p. 1993-94, pres.-elect 1994, pres. 1995, Godrej vis. prof. 2000), British Assn. Plastic Surgeons (hon.), Am. Soc. Craniofacial Surgery, Am. Soc. Aesthetic Plastic Surgery, Am. Soc. Maxillofacial Surgeons, Assn. Acad. Chairmen Plastic Surgery (bd. dirs. 1986-89), Assn. Surgeons East Africa, Assn. Plastic and Reconstructive Surgeons So. Africa (hon.), Pacific Coast Surg. Assn., Internat. Soc. Aesthetic Plastic Surgery, Internat. Soc. Reconstructive Microsurgery, Internat. Soc. Craniomaxillofacial Surgery, Pan African Assn. Neurol. Sci., African Med. and Rsch. Found. (bd. dirs. U.S.A. 1987-2002, team leader Reconstruct! mission for victims of Am. Embassy bombing, Nairobi, Kenya, 1999), Muthaiga Club, Ctr. Club, Club 33, Univ. Club, Phi Beta Kappa, Alpha Omega Alpha. Personal E-mail: daktari1@cox.net.

FURST, ALEX JULIAN, thoracic and cardiovascular surgeon; b. Augusta, Ga., Aug. 21, 1938; m. George Alex and Ann (Segall) F.; m. Elayne Kobrin, Aug. 11, 1962; children: James Andrew, Jeffrey Michael, Joseph Robert. Student, U. Fla., 1963; MD, U. Miami, 1967. Intern U. Miami Hosp., 1967-68, resident, 1968-72, clin. instr. dept. surgery, 1974-91; chief resident in thoracic and cardiovascular surgery Emory U. Hosp., Atlanta, 1972-73, sr. surg. registrar of thoracic unit, 1972-73, Hosp. for Sick Children, London, 1973-74; practice medicine specializing in thoracic and cardiovascular surgery Miami, Fla.; clin. assoc. prof. surgery and cardiology, chief surg. svc. Miami VA Med. Ctr., 1991—2003, clin. prof., surgery and medicine, chief of surgery; chief surgeon West Palm Beach Med. Ctr., Va., 2000—02; sr. cons. dept. surgery Miami Va Med. Ctr., 2005—. Chief thoracic surgery, pres. med. staff Mercy Hosp.; mem. staff Bapt. Hosp., South Miami Hosp., Doctor's Hosp. (all Miami), North Ridge Gen. Hosp., Ft. Lauderdale; program dir. cardiothoracic surgery U. Miami Sch. of Medicine, 1998-2000. Fellow ACS, Am. Coll. Cardiology, Am. Coll. Chest Physicians; mem. Dade County Med. Assn., Fla. Med. Assn., Heart Assn. Greater Miami, Soc. Thoracic Surgeons, So. Thoracic Surg. Assn. Home: 8802 Arvida Dr Miami FL 33156-2302 Office Phone: 305-575-3157.

FURTH, JOHN JACOB, molecular biologist, educator, pathologist; b. Phila., Jan. 25, 1929; s. Jacob and Olga (Berthauer) F.; m. Mary Autry, June 24, 1959; children: Karen, Susan, Robin. BA, Cornell U., 1950; student, Yale Law Sch., 1950-51; MD, Duke U., 1958; MA, U. Pa., 1972. Intern Bellevue Hosp., NYC, 1958-59; resident in pathology NYU Sch. Medicine, NYC, 1959-60, postdoctoral fellow dept. microbiology, 1960-62; mem. faculty dept. pathology U. Pa. Med. Sch., Phila., 1962—, prof., 1978—2001, emeritus prof., 2001—. Mem. sci. com. Sharpe-Strumim Found. Limr. Contbr. articles to profl. jours. Bd. dirs., chmn. hist. sites com. Darby Creek Valley Assn., 1984-96, 1st v.p. 1997—; bd. dirs., founder Friends of the Swedish Cabin (constructed circa 1654), Upper Darby, Pa., 1987, pres. 2002-03; bd. dirs. Fair Housing Coun. of Suburban Phila., 1995-97, 2d dist. leader Upper Darby Democratic Party, 1994-2002, chmn., 2002-06; candidate for Congress, 7th Dist. Pa. 2d lt. Q.M.C., US Army, 1951-53. Recipient Hoffman LaRoche award, 1958; Eleanor Roosevelt fellow, 1977-78. Mem. AAAS, Am. Soc. Biol. Chemists and Molecular Biologists, Am. Assn. Cancer Rsch., Am. Assn. Pathologists, Sharpe-Strumia Rsch. Found. (bd. dir. 2006-). Democrat. Mem. Soc. Of Friends. Achievements include codiscovery of RNA polymerase. Home: 43 Roselawn Ave Lansdowne PA 19050-2317 Office: U Pa Sch Medicine Dept Pathology and Lab Med Philadelphia PA 19104-6082 E-mail: jjfurth@mail.med.upenn.edu.

FURUKAWA, KYOJI, research scientist; b. Hiroshima, Japan, Sept. 18, 1968; PhD, Iowa State U., 2004. Assoc. sr. scientist Radiation Effects Rsch. Found., 2004—. Office: 5-2 Hijiyama Pk Minami Hiroshima 732-0815 Japan Business E-Mail: furukawa@rerf.or.jp.

FURUKAWA, SATOSHI, surgeon; b. Nagoya, Japan, Apr. 4, 1958; naturalized, US; s. Toru and Kiyo Furukawa; m. Lynn Boeth, Oct. 1, 1986; children: Alyssa, Jesse, Luke, Anne. BSE in Chem. Engring., U. Pa., 1980, MD, 1984. Cert. Am. Bd. Surgery, Am. Bd. Thoracic Surgery, diplomate Nat. Bd. Med. Examiners. Intern Hosp. U. Pa., 1984—85; resident, gen. surgery U. Pa., 1985—87, surg. rsch. fellow, 1987—89, surgery resident, 1989—90, chief resident, surgery, 1990—91, resident, cardiothoracic surgery, 1991—93, clin. instr. surgery, 1989—93; fellow, lung transplantation Hosp. U. Pa., 1991—93, Temple U. Hosp., Phila., 1993—96; asst. prof. surgery Temple U., Phila., 1993—99, assoc. prof. surgery, 1999—; attending surgeon Temple U. Hosp., Phila., 1993—, surg. dir., lung transplantation program, 1993—, chief sect. cardiothoracic surgery, 2001—. Tchg. attending cardiothoracic surgery, 1993—; lectr., surg. pathophysiology, 1995—; faculty, Minimally Invasive Vein Harvest; presenter in field various profl. meetings, symposia, and internat. confs. Contbr. articles to profl. jours., chpt. to book. Grantee rsch., NHLBI, 1993—. Mem.: Soc. Thoracic Surgery. Avocations: baseball, bowling, music, travel. Office: Cardiac and Thoracic Surgery Ste 300 Parkinson Pavilion 3401 N Broad St Philadelphia PA 19140 Office Phone: 215-707-3601. *

FURUKAWA, YOSHIAKI, neuroscientist, educator; b. Osaka, Japan, Oct. 4, 1974; PhD, Kyoto U., Japan, 2002. Assoc. prof. Keio U., 2010—. Mem.: Chem. Soc. Japan, Soc. Neurosci., Japan Neurosci. Soc., Protein Sci. Soc. Japan, Biophys. Soc. Japan (award). Office: 3-14-1 Hiyoshi Kohoku Yokohama Kanagawa 223-8522 Japan Office Fax: 81-45-566-1697. Business E-Mail: furukawa@chem.keio.ac.jp.

FURUNO, NOBUAKI, biologist, researcher; b. Miyawaka City, Fukuoka, Japan, Jan. 3, 1959; s. Furuno Shigeru and Furuno Nobue; m. Furuno Koura, Mar. 10, 1991; children: Furuno Takayuki, Furuno Masayuki, Furuno Tomoyuki. BS, Kyushu U., Fukuoka, 1982, MS, 1984, PhD, 1990. Asst. prof. Kurume U., Fukuoka, Japan, 1989—93, Kyushu U., Fukuoka, Japan, 1994—2002; assoc. prof. Hiroshima U., Higashihiroshima, Japan, 2002—. Grantee, Ministry Edn., Sci. and Culture Japan, 1992—95, 1995, 2001—03, 2001—02, 2003—04; fellow, U. Cambridge, England, 1997—99; scholar, Royal Soc. and Sci. Coun. Japan, 1997—99, Novartis Found., 1997. Buddhist. Achievements include research in analysis of the mos function during oocyte maturation; analysis the cyclin A function in mitosis; effects of hypergravity and strong magnetic field on early frog development and oocyte maturation. Avocations: mountain climbing, star watching, reading. Home: 531-3 Mizuwara Miyawaka 822-0151 Japan Office: Hiroshima University Inst Amphibian Biology Grad Sch Sci 1-3-1 Kagamiyama Hiroshima 739-8526 Japan Office Fax: 81-82-424-0739; Home Fax: 81-949-55-3025. Business E-Mail: nfuruno@hiroshima-u.ac.jp.

FURUTA, MASARU, molecular biologist; Rsch. fellow Nat. Inst. Neuroscience, Kodaira, Tokyo, Japan, 2000—02; asst. mgr. Shimadzu Corp., Kyoto, 2002—, mgr., 2009—. Contbr. articles to profl. jours. Office: Shimadzu Corp 1 Nishinokyo-Kuwabaracho Nakagyo-ku Kyoto 604-8511 Japan Office Fax: 81-75-841-9326. Business E-Mail: furu@shimadzu.co.jp.

FURUYA, KENICHI, reproductive endocrinologist, gynecologic surgeon; b. Tokyo, Sept. 18, 1953; s. Hiroshi and Setsue Furuya. MD, Juntendo U., Tokyo, 1979, PhD, 1986. Clin. asst. Nat. Def. Med. Coll., Saitama, Japan, 1979-88; post-doctoral fellow Inst. Hormone and Fertility Rsch. Hamburg U., Germany, 1988-90; asst. prof. Nat. Def. Med. Coll., Saitama, Japan, 1992—2005, prof., chair dept. ob-gyn, 2005, dir. divsn. maternal and fetal medicine, 2005—08, dir. ctrl. surgery ctr., 2006—08, prin., Nurse Acad., 2009—11, dir., Med. Oncology Ctr., 2011—, pres., 2008—, Med. Assn. Nat. Def. Med. Coll. Charles Darwin, 2005—. Fellow: Japan Coll. Surgeons, Internat. Coll. Surgeons; mem.: Saitama Soc. Ob-gyn. (pres. 2011—), Japan Soc. Gynecologic and Obstetric Breast Cancer (dir. 2010—), Japan Soc. Minimally-Invasive and Endoscopic Surgery (dir. 2009—), NY Acad. Scis., Japan Soc. Ob-gyn. (councillor 2006—), Japan Soc. Reproductive Medicine (councillor 2006—, dir. 2010—), Japan Soc. for Study of Hypertension in Pregnancy (dir. 2008), Japan Soc. Obstetric and Gynecologic Nutrition and Metabolism (dir. 2006—), Japan Soc. Study of Kidney and Pregnancy (dir. 2007—, pres. 2011—), Japan Soc. Gynecologic Oncology (councilor 2005—), Japan Soc. Fertility and Implantation (councillor 1994—, dir. 2010—), Japanese Soc. Female Pelvic Floor Medicine (dir. 2005—, pres. 2009—), Japanese Soc. Maternal Health (councillor 2005—, dir. 2010—), Japan Soc. Gynecologic and Obstetric Surgery (councillor 2004—, dir. 2005—), Japan Soc. Reproductive Immunology (councillor 2005—, dir. 2006—), Japan Soc. Endometriosis (dir. 2006—), Japan Soc. Psychosomatic Ob-gyn. (dir. 2005—, pres. 2009—), NY Acad. Scis. (Charles Darwin Assocs. 2005—), Japan Soc. Reproductive Endocrinology (councillor 2000—), Japan Soc. Adolescent Medicine (councillor 2001—), Japan Soc. Reproductive Surgery (councillor 1990—), Japan Soc. Gynecologic Endoscopic Surgery (councillor 1995—, dir. 2005—), Japan Soc. Fertility and Sterility (councillor 1995—), Japan Soc. Endocrinology (councillor 1992—). Avocations: classical music, tennis, photography, Judo, Japanese chess. Office: NDMC Dept Ob-gyn 3-2 Namiki Tokorozawa Saitama 359-8513 Japan Office Phone: 81-4-2995-1687, 81429951687, 81429965213. Business E-Mail: furuyakn@ndmc.ac.jp.

FUSARO, RAMON MICHAEL, dermatologist, preventive medicine physician, researcher; b. Bklyn., Mar. 6, 1927; s. Angelo and Ida (Pucci) F.; m. Lavonne Johnsen, Nov. 6, 1971; children: Lisa Ann, Toni Ann; stepsons: Jeff, Scott. BA, U. Minn., 1949, BS, 1951, MD, 1953, MS, 1958, PhD, 1965. Diplomate Am. Bd. Dermatology. Intern Mpls. Gen. Hosp., 1953-54, resident in dermatology, 1954—57; from instr. to assoc. prof. U. Minn., 1957-70, dir. outpatient dermatology clinic, 1962-70; prof., chmn. dept. dermatology U. Nebr. Med. Center, Omaha, 1970-82; prof. dermatology sect. dept. internal medicine U. Nebr. Med. Ctr., Omaha, 1982—2008, acting chief sect. dermatology, 1991-94; prof., chmn. dept. dermatology Creighton U., Omaha, 1975-87; prof. dermatology dept. internal medicine Creighton U. Sch. Medicine, Omaha, 1983-89; prof. Creighton U., Omaha, 1989—2008; dir. dermatology residency program Creighton/Nebr. Univs. Health Found., 1975-83; prof. dept. pub. health and preventive medicine Hereditary Cancer Inst., Creighton U., 1984—. Adj. prof. coll. pharmacy dept. pharmacy scis. Creighton U., 2007—. Contbr. more than 300 articles to profl. publs., chpts. to books. With USN, 1944-46. Mem. Am. Acad. Dermatology, Sigma Xi. Home: 908 Beaver Lake Blvd Plattsmouth NE 68048-4500 Office: Creighton University Pharmacy & Health Profs Nixon-Lied Bldg Dept Pharmacy Sci 2500 California Plz Omaha NE 68178-0403 Office Phone: 402-280-2893, 402-280-2942. Business E-Mail: rmfusaro@creighton.edu, rfusaro@unmc.edu.

FUSELIER, HAROLD ANTHONY, JR., urologist, director, educator; b. Abbeville, La., Dec. 1, 1942; s. Harold Anthony and May Elizabeth (Fowler) F.; m. Ann Valentino, May 17, 1968; children: Harold Anthony III, F. Scott, J. Prentice, Mims Michael. BS, La. State U., Baton Rouge, 1964; MD, La. State U., New Orleans, 1967. Diplomate Am. Bd. Urology. Internship Charity Hosp., New Orleans, 1967-68; residency urology Alton Ochsner Medical Found., 1970-74; mem. dept. urology Ochsner Clinic Found., New Orleans, 1974—2008, chmn. dept. urology, 1989—2002; med. dir. surgery Ochsner Found. Hosp., New Orleans, 1990—2006; clin. prof. urology Tulane U. Med. Ctr., New Orleans, 1988—, La. State U. Med. Ctr., New Orleans, 1990—2008; prof., urology La. State U. Health Sci. Ctr., 2008—. Program dir. La. State U./Ochsner Urology Tng. Program, 1991-2005. Contbr. articles to profl. jours. Capt. USAF, 1968-70. Fellow ACS; mem. Am. Urol. Assn., Soc. Internat. d'Urologie, Soc. for Study of Impotence, Soc. Univ. Urologists. Roman Catholic. Avocations: golf, hunting, fishing. Office: La State Univ Health Sci Ctr 1542 Tulane Ave Rm 547 New Orleans LA 70112 Office Phone: 504-568-2207. Business E-Mail: hfusel@lsuhsc.edu.

FUSHIH, PAN, surgeon; MD, U. Chgo., PhD in Chem; B in Chemistry, Nat. Taiwan U. Cert. Surgeon Am. Bd. of Plastic Surgeon. Dr. plastic & reconstructive surgery Univ. of Pa. Hosp., Univ. of Chgo. Hosp., dr. gen. surgery; dr. plastic & reconstructive surgery Ren-Ai Hosp., Taichung, Taiwan; supt. China Med. Ctr., Taipei, Taiwan; dr. plastic & reconstructive surgery Kang-Ning Hosp., Taipei, Taiwan; supt. Mutabor Clinic, Taipei. Instr. divsn. of plastic surgery Univ. Pa.; fellow craniofacial surgery Children's Hosp. of Phila. Mem.: Am. Soc. of Plastic Surgeons. Office: Bionet Aesthetic Clinic 34 L 270 Sec 1 Tun-Hwa S Rd Taipei Taiwan Office Phone: 886227213069. *

FUSHIKI, HIROAKI, neuroscientist, neurotologist; b. Himi-city, Japan, Apr. 27, 1965; s. Atsuko Fushiki; m. Yukari Obayashi, Sept. 4, 1967; 1 child, Rino. MD, Toyama Med. and Pharm. U., 1990, PhD, 1994. Instr. U. Toyama, Toyama, Toyama, 1994—. Office: Toyama Univ 2630 Sugitani Toyama 930-0194 Japan Office Fax: 81-76-434-5038. Business E-Mail: hfushiki@med.u-toyama.ac.jp.

FUSHIMI, MASAHITO, psychiatrist, director; s. Toshinobu and Eiko Fushimi; m. Hiromi Sato. MD, Akita U., Japan, 1990, PhD, 1997. Med. staff Dept. Psychiatry Sch. Medicine Akita (Japan) U., 2000—03; dir. Akita (Japan) Prefectural Mental Health and Welfare Ctr., Daisen City, 2003—. Mem.: Japanese Soc. Clin. Neurophysiology (licentiate), Japanese Soc. Psychiatry and Neurology (licentiate). Avocation: travel. Office: Akita Pref Mental Health and Welfare C 2-1-51 Nakadori Akita City 010 0001 Japan Office Phone: 81-188-313946. Office Fax: 81-188-312306. Personal E-mail: fushimi@sings.jp. Business E-Mail: fushimi@pref.akita.lg.jp, fushimi-jscn@umin.ac.jp.

FUSTER, VALENTIN, cardiologist, educator; b. Barcelona, Jan. 20, 1943; s. Joaquin and Pilar Fuster; m. Angela-Maria Guals, Sept. 3, 1968; children: Pablo, Silvia. Baccaluarate, Colegio Jesuitas, Barcelona, 1961; MD, Barcelona U., 1967; granted several honorary degrees. Diplomate Am. Bd. Internal Medicine (mem. com. subsplty. bd. cardiovas. disease), Am. Bd. Cardiology. Intern Hosp. Clinico, Barcelona, 1967-68; rsch. fellow, cardiology U. Edinburgh, Scotland, 1968-71; resident, medicine and cardiovasc. diseases Mayo Grad. Sch. Medicine, Rochester, Minn., 1971-74; asst. prof. medicine Mayo Med. Sch., Rochester, 1974-77, assoc. prof. medicine, 1978-81, assoc. prof. pediat., 1980—, prof. medicine and cardiovasc. diseases, 1981-82; Mallinckrodt prof. medicine Harvard Med. Sch., 1991—94; chief cardiology unit Mass. Gen. Hosp., 1991—94; chief, divsn. cardiology, Mt. Sinai Sch. Medicine, NY, 1981—91, Arthur A. and Hilda M. Master prof. medicine NY, 1982—91, dir., Zena & Michael A. Wiener Cardiovasc. Inst. and Marie-Josée & Henry R. Kravis Ctr, for Cardiovascular Health NY, 1994—, Richard Gorlin, MD/Heart Rsch. Found. prof. NY. Mem. cardiology adv. com. NIH; mem. com. Am. Bd. Cardiology; hon. lectr. numerous orgns.; mem. adv. coun. Nat. Heart, Lung and Blood Insts., 1997, strategic planning com. Stanley J. Sanroff Endowment for Cardiovasc. Sci., 2002-04; former chmn., Fellowship Tng. Directors Program, Am. Coll. Cardiology; mem. scientific adv. bd. Vasogen, Inc. Mem. editl. bd. Am. Jour. Cardiology, 1982, Arteriosclerosis, 1982, Jour. The Am. Coll. Cardiology, 1987, Circulation, 1988, consulting editor, 1992, circulation rsch. consulting editor, 1997; editor-in-chief Nature Clinical Practice Cardiovascular Medicine, 2004-; lead editor (textbook) The Heart, Atherothrombosis and Coronary Artery Disease; contbr. several articles to profl. jours. Recipient 30 rsch. and tchg. awards including Andres Gruntzig Scientific award European Soc. Cardiology, 1992, Disting. Scientist award Am. Coll. Cardiology, 1993, Disting. Conner Lectr. award Am. Heart Assn., 1993, Principe de Asturias award for sci. and tech. U. Asturias in conjunction with Royal Family of Spain, 1996, Andreas Gruntzig award Internat. Soc. Interventionalists, 2002, Disting. Researcher award, Interamerican Soc. Cardiology, 2005, Kurt Polzer Cardiovascular award, European Acad. Sci. Arts, 2008; named Disting. Scientist, AHA/ASA, 2003; named to European Acad. Yuste; named one of Medical Marvels, New York Mag., 2006. Fellow Am. Coll. Cardiology (chair tng. dirs. com. 1997, Disting. Scientist award, Disting. Bishop Lectr. award 1994, Disting. Svc. award 2000, chair cardiology tng. and workforce com., 2000-03), Royal Coll. Physicians; mem. Am. Heart Assn. (chmn. pub. com., bd. dirs. 1994, pres.-elect 1997, pres. 1998-99, Disting. Achievement award 1997, James B. Herrick Achievement award, Coun. Clin. Cardiology, 2001, Lewis A. Connor Meml. award, Gold Heart award, 2003, Disting. Scientist award), Am. Soc. Clin. Investigations, Assn. Am. Physicians, European Soc. Clin. Investigation, Brit. Cardiac Soc. (corr.), European Soc. Cardiology (U.S. bd. dirs. and Industry, Gold medal, 2007), World Heart Fedn. (pres-elect 2003-04, pres. 2005-06), Fundacion Centro Nacional de Investigaciones Cardiovasculares Carlos III (pres. scientific adv. and external evaluation com.), Inst. Medicine. Achievements include contributing first hand to the launching of the new forum for young investigators of the AMA. Office: Mt Sinai Med Ctr 1 Gustave L Levy Pl # 1030 New York NY 10029-6500 also: Cardiovascular Medicine Assocs 5 E 98th St 3rd Fl New York NY 10029 Office Phone: 212-241-7911. Office Fax: 212-423-9488. Business E-Mail: valentin.fuster@mssm.edu.

FYE, W. BRUCE, III, cardiologist; b. Meadville, Pa., Sept. 25, 1946; s. W. Bruce Jr. and Anne Elizabeth (Schreck) F.; m. Lois Eileen Baker, May 10, 1969; children: Katherine Anne, Elizabeth Jane. AB, Johns Hopkins U., 1968, MD, 1972, MA in Med. History, 1978. Diplomate Am. Bd. Internal Medicine, Am. Bd. Cardiovascular Diseases. Intern N.Y. Hosp.—Cornell Med. Ctr., NYC, 1972-73, asst. resident, 1973-74, sr. asst. resident, 1974-75, fellow cardiology, 1975; fellow in cardiology Johns Hopkins U. Sch. Medicine, Balt., 1975-77, postdoctoral fellow in med. history, 1976-78, instr. in medicine, 1977-78; dir. cardiographics lab. Marshfield (Wis.) Clinic, 1978-99, chmn. dept. cardiology, 1981-99, dir. noninvasive cardiology, 1999; assoc. prof. medicine Med. Coll. Wis., Milw., 1988-99; prof. medicine and history medicine Mayo Clin. Coll. of Medicine, Rochester, Minn., 2000—. Vice chief of staff St. Joseph's Hosp., Marshfield, 1989-99, exec. com., bd. dirs., 1994-97; clin. prof. medicine, adj. prof. history medicine U. Wis., Madison, 1990—; sr. assoc. cons. Mayo Clinic, Rochester, 2000, cons., 2001—; dir. Mayo Clinic Ctr. for the History of Medicine, 2006—. Author: The Development of American Physiology, 1987; editor: William Osler's Collected Papers on the Cardiovascular System, 1985, Classic Papers on Coronary Thrombosis and Myocardial Infarction, 1991; editor-in-chief: Classics of Cardiology Library, 1985—; author: American Cardiology; The History of a Specialty and Its College, 1996; mem. editl. bd. Marshfield Med. Bull., 1985-95, Am. Jour. Cardiology, 1990—, Clin. Cardiology, 1994—; co-editor (with J. Willis Hurst, Richard Conti, W. Bruce Fye): Profiles in Cardiology, 2003. Recipient Lifetime Achievement award, Am. Osler Soc., 2009; named to Soc. Scholars, Johns Hopkins U., 2005. Fellow Am. Coll. Cardiology (chmn. libr. com. 1991, historian 1991—, gov. Wis. chpt. 1993-96, steering com. bd. govs., 1994—, nominating com., 1994-96, chair govt. rels. com. 1996-99, trustee 1997—, v.p. 1999—, pres. 2002—); mem. State Med. Soc. Wis. (alt. del. 1990-94), Am. Hist. Assn., Am. Osler Soc. (pres. 1988-89), Am. Heart Assn. (exec. com. coun. on clin. cardiology 1991-97, chmn. membership com. coun. on clin. cardiology 1994-97, chair credentials com. coun. on clin. cardiology 1994-97), Inst. for Study of Cardiovasc. Medicine (bd. dirs. 1994—), Am. Assn. History Medicine (program chair 1987, v.p. 2006-, pres., 2008-), Found. Advances in Medicine and Sci., Johns Hopkins Soc. Scholars, Phi Beta Kappa, Alpha Omega Alpha, Grolier Club. Presbyterian. Avocation: collecting and selling antiquarian medical books. Home: 1533 Seasons Ln SW Rochester MN 55902 Office: Mayo Clinic Coll of Medicine 200 1st St SW Rochester MN 55905-0002 Office Phone: 507-266-4130. Business E-Mail: fye.bruce@mayo.edu.

FYFE, ALISTAIR IAN, cardiologist, scientist, educator; b. Hobart, Tasmania, Australia, Sept. 5, 1960; came to U.S., 1991; s. Ian John and Merrill Millicent (Faragher) F.; married Michelle Lee Fenner; children: Alexander Jonathan, Calista Madison, Ethan Alexander. B of Med. Sci., U. Tasmania, 1980, B of Med. Sci. with honors, 1981, MBBS, 1984; PhD in Molecular Biology, UCLA, 1995. Diplomate Am. Bd. Internal Medicine and Cardiovasc. Disease. Intern Royal Hobart Hosp., 1985-86; resident in internal medicine U. B.C., Vancouver, Can., 1986-89; cardiology fellow U. Toronto, Ont., Can., 1989-91; cardiac rsch. fellow UCLA, 1991-95, asst. prof. medicine and cardiology, 1995-99, dir. Ctr. for Cholesterol and Lipid Mgmt., 1995-98, assoc. mem. Molecular Biology Inst., 1996-98; cardiologist Heart Place, Dallas, 1999—2000, Dallas Heart Group, 2000—04; founder Cardiac Assocs. Dallas, 2004—; dir. primary and secondary cardiac prevention Med. City, Dallas, 2004—. Author: (with others) Progress in Pediatric Cardiology, 1993; contbr. articles to profl. jours. Recipient Fellowship Clinician Scientist award Med. Rsch. Coun., Can., 1992. Fellow Royal Coll. Physicians Can., Am. Coll. Cardiology, Coun. Arterial Sclerosis; mem. Internat. Heart Transplant Soc., Am. Heart Assn. (fellow arteriosclerosis coun., reviewer 1993—,

Young Investigator award, 1993, 95), Am. Soc. Clin. Investigation, Am. Diabetes Assn. Achievements include first demonstration of genetic modification of solid organ transplants, cardiac services to Christmas Island Kiribati. Office: Cardiac Assocs Dallas 7777 Forest Ln Ste C 655 Dallas TX 75230-2500 Office Phone: 972-566-8474. Business E-Mail: afyfe@cadmd.com.

GAAB, MICHAEL ROBERT, neurosurgery educator, consultant; b. Landau, Germany, Mar. 11, 1947; s. Erich and Margarete (Hollinger) G.; m. Hannelore Sommer (div. 1972); 1 child, Marcus; m. Katharina Maria Weller, Sept. 28, 1974; children: Oliver, Jasmin, Florian. BS, U. Würzburg, Germany, 1972, U. Kiel, 1972; MD, PhD, U. Würzburg, Germany, 1973; MD, U. Vienna., Austria, 1982; PhD, U. Vienna, Austria, 1983. House officer Knappschafts Hosp., Bochum, Germany, 1973; registrar, asst. neurosurgeon U. Hosp. Würzburg, 1974—79, sr. neurosurgeon, 1979—81, assoc. prof. neurosurgery, 1981—82; assoc. prof., head dept. pediatric neurosurgery U. Hosp. Vienna, Austria, 1982—84; assoc. prof. Med. Sch., U. Hannover, Germany, 1984—87, prof., 1987-92; full prof., head dept. neurosurgery Ernst Moritz Arndt U., U. Hosp. Greifswald, 1992—2003; med. dir. U. Hosp., Greifswald, 1997-2000; head Hannover Nordstalt Hosp. Neurosurgery, Hannover, 2003—. Cons. neurosurgeon City Hosp. Braunschweig, Germany, 1984-92. Author: Registration of Intracranial Pressure, 1981 (E.K. Frey award 1981), Telemedicine, 1999; mem. editl. adv. bd. Brit. Jour. Neurosurgery, 1987-93; editl. bd. Neurosurg. Rev., 1995-2006, Pan Arab Jour. Neurosurgery, 1998—; reviewer Neurosurgery, 2003—, World Neurosurgery, 2009-; patentee device for intracranial pressure monitoring, in spondylodesis, devices for neuroendoscopy. Mem. Christian Dem. Union, Hannover, 1973—. German Rsch. Comty. grantee, 1981, 83, 95, German Ministry Rsch. and Tech. grantee, 1981, 82, German Cen. Nervous Sys. bd. trustees grantee, 1991, 92. Mem. Am. Assn. Neurosurgeons, German Neurosurg. Soc., European Assn. for Pediatric Neurosurgery (sec. congress 1984), World Fedn. Neurosurg. Socs. (asst. treas. congress 1981), German Soc. Neuroendoscopy (pres. 1997-2002). Roman Cath. Avocations: tennis, flying, flight instructor. Home: Senator-Bauer-Strasse 36 D-30625 Hannover Germany Office: Neurosurgical Hospital Nordstadt Haltenhoffstrasse 47 D-30167 Hannover Germany Office Phone: 49-511-970-1245. Business E-Mail: michael.gaab@krh.eu.

GABAY, ERAN, medical researcher, educator; b. Haifa, Israel, Sept. 29, 1975; DMD, Hebrew U., Jerusalem, 2004, PhD, 2006. Rschr., lectr. RAMBAM, Health Care Campus, Sch. Grad. Dentistry & Dept. Periodontology, 2007—. Instr. human anatomy and neuroanatomy course Hebrew U., 1999—2001. Recipient B.Sc.Med. with distinction, Hebrew U. Jerusalem. Mem.: Am. Pain Soc. (Young Investigator award 2005), Israeli Dental Assn., Israeli Periodontal and Osseointegration Soc., European Fedn. Periodontology, IADR (Israel br. and global mem.). Avocations: music, travel, sports, soccer. Home: Oren 19 Haifa 34736 Israel Home Fax: 972-4-8733377. Personal E-mail: eran.gabay@mail.huji.ac.il.

GABBAI, ALBERTO ALAIN, neurology educator, researcher; b. Cairo, May 19, 1953; arrived in Brazil, 1958; s. Maurizio and Farida (Sasson) G.; m. Miriam Benasayag Birmann, Sept. 21, 1978; children: Carolina, Lisa. Physician, Paulista Sch. Medicine, Sao Paulo, Brazil, 1976, MS, 1981, D in Medicine, 1986. Med. diplomate. Intern Paulista Sch. Medicine, 1977, resident in clin. neurology, 1978-80; rsch. fellow Tufts-New Eng. Med. Ctr., Boston, 1981-82; clin. and rsch. fellow Mass. Gen. Hosp. Harvard U., Boston, 1987-89; asst. prof. Paulista Sch. Medicine, 1982-86, assoc. prof. medicine, 1989-97, prof., chmn. dept. neurology, 1997—. Cons. Rsch. Found. State of Sao Paulo, 1991—. Contbr. articles on AIDS, HTLV and neuro-oncology, and neuroimmunology to med. jours. Fellow Brazilian Acad. Neurology; mem. Am. Acad. Neurology (clin. assoc.), Brazilian Soc. Progress of Sci. Office: Paulista Sch of Medicine Dept of Neurology Rua Botucatu 740 04023-900 Sao Paulo SP Brazil Office Phone: 5511 55755240. Business E-Mail: gabbai@unifesp.br.

GABBARD, GLEN OWENS, psychiatrist, psychotherapist; b. Charleston, Ill., Aug. 8, 1949; s. Earnest Glendon and Lucina Mildred (Paquet) G.; children: Matthew, Abigail, Amanda, Allison; m. Joyce Eileen Davidson, June 14, 1985. BS, Eastern Ill. U., 1972; MD, Rush Med. Coll., 1975; degree in psychoanalytic tng., Topeka Inst. for Psychoanalysis, 1984. Diplomate Am. Bd. Psychiatry and Neurology. Resident in psychiatry Menninger Sch. Psychiatry, Topeka, 1975-78, mem. faculty, 1978—; staff psychiatrist C.F. Menninger Hosp., Topeka, 1978-83, sect. chief, 1984-89. Med. dir., 1989-94; tng. analyst Topeka Inst. for Psychoanalysis, 1989-2001, dir., 1996-2001; v.p. for adult svcs. Menninger Clinic, 1991-94; clin. prof. psychiatry U. Kans. Med. Sch., 1991-2001; Callaway Disting. prof. Menninger Clinic and Karl Menninger Sch. Psychiatry, 1994-2001; prof. psychiatry Baylor Coll. Medicine, 2001—, Brown Found. chair psychoanalysis, 2003—. Author: With the Eyes of the Mind, 1984, Psychiatry and the Cinema, 1987, 2d edit., 1999, Medical Marriages, 1988, Sexual Exploitation in Professional Relationships, 1989, Psychodynamic Psychiatry in Clinical Practice, 1990, Portuguese transl., 1992, Italian transl., 1992, 2d edit., 1994, Korean transl., 1996, Japanese transl., 1997, 4th edit., 2005, Treatments of Psychiatric Disorders: the DSM-IV Edition, 1995; meml. editl. bd. Am. Jour. Psychiatry, Am. Psychiat. Press; joint editor-in-chief Internat. Jour. Psychoanalysis; contbr. articles to profl. jours. V.p. Topeka Civic Theatre, 1981-82, pres. 1982-83, bd. dirs. 1981-83. Named one of Outstanding Young Men in Am. U.S. Jaycees, 1984. Mem. AAAS, Am. Psychoanalytic Assn. (assoc. editor jour., mem. editl. bd.), Am. Psychiat. Assn. (Falk fellow 1976, Edward A. Strecker award 1994, Disting. Psychiatrist lectr. 1995, C. Charles Burlingame award 1997, Mary S. Sigourney award 2000, Disting. Svc. award 2002, Adolf Meyer award 2004), Sch. Psychotherapy Rsch., Menninger Sch. Psychiatry Alumni Assn. (pres. 1982-83), Alpha Omega Alpha. Avocations: theater, music. Home: 1290 Jimmy Phillips Blvd Angleton TX 77515 Office: Dept Psychiatry Baylor Coll Medicine One Baylor Plz MS 350 Houston TX 77030 Office Phone: 713-798-6397. Business E-Mail: ggabbard@bcm.tmc.edu.

GABBASOV, ZUFAR AKHNAFOVICH, cell biologist, researcher; b. Ufa, Russia, Feb. 8, 1957; s. Akhnaf Gabbasovich Gabbasov and Klara Khalimovna Usmanova; m. Natalia Teplyakova, Mar. 16, 1983; 1 child, Anastasia Gabbasova. MSc, Moscow Inst. Physics and Tech., Dolgoprudnyi, 1980; PhD, Inst. Exptl. Cardiology, Cardiology Rsch. Ctr., USSR Acad. Scis., Moscow, 1985. Jr. rsch. scientist Cardiology Rsch. Ctr., 1980—83, rsch. worker, 1983—99, sr. rschr., 1999—2004, leading rschr., 2004—. Mem.: European Platel Group (assoc.; bd. mem. 1991—97). Achievements include research in a close relationship between the presence and progression of stenotic atherosclerosis and appearance in peripheral blood of bone marrow stromal stem/progenitor cells; patents for a highly sensitive method and device for analysis of platelet aggregation; a new method and device for human sperm evaluation; a method and device for blood cell count measurement; development of a portable hematological analyzer for hospitals and point-of-care and mobile automobile-based laboratories. Office: Cardiology Rsch Ctr 3d Cherepkovskaya St 15A Moscow 121 552 Russia Office Fax: 7 495 4146923. Personal E-mail: zufargabbasov@yandex.ru. Business E-Mail: gabbasov@cardio.ru.

GABBE, STEVEN GLENN, dean, obstetrician, gynecologist, educator; b. Newark, Dec. 1, 1944; s. Charles Paul and Marcia May Gabbe; m. Jessica Gabbe, June 26, 1966 (div. 1980); children: Amanda, Daniel; m. Patricia Temple, July 26, 1981. BA, Princeton U., 1965; MD, Cornell U., 1969; MA (hon.), U. Pa., 1983. Diplomate Am. Bd. Ob-Gyn (examiner 1980-01), Am. Bd. Maternal-Fetal Medicine (examiner 1979-01). Intern in medicine NY Hosp., NYC, 1969-70; rsch. fellow reproductive medicine Boston Hosp. for Women, 1970-71, resident in ob-gyn, 1972-74; rsch. fellow in biol. chemistry Harvard Med. Sch., Boston, 1970-71, clin. fellow ob-gyn., 1972-74; asst. prof. ob-gyn U. So. Calif., LA, 1975-77; assoc. prof. U. Colo. Sch. Medicine, Denver, 1977-78; assoc. prof. ob-gyn. and pediatrics U. Pa. Sch. Medicine, Phila., 1978-87, prof. radiology, 1987; mem. staff Hosp. of U. Pa., Phila., 1978-87, dir. Jerrold R. Golding divsn. fetal medicine, 1978-87, mem. med. bd. and numerous coms., 1984-87; prof. U. Pa. Sch. Nursing, Phila., 1982-87; prof., chmn. dept. ob-gyn Ohio State U. Coll. Medicine, Columbus, 1987-96; prof., chmn. dept. ob/gyn. U. Wash. Sch. Medicine, Seattle, 1996—2001; dir. Jerrold R. Golding divsn. fetal medicine Hosp. of U. Pa., Phila., 1978-87, mem. med. bd. and numerous coms., 1984-87; dean Sch. of Medicine Vanderbilt U., Nashville, 2001—07; sr. v.p. health scis. Ohio State U., 2007—; CEO Ohio State U. Med. Ctr., 2007—. Vis. prof. ob-gyn King's Coll. Hosp., London, 1985-86; dir. maternal and infant care program Phila. Dept. Health, Disease Prevention and Health Promotion, 1982-87; mem. maternal and infant care adv. coun. Dept. Pub. Health, Phila., 1983-87; mem. subcom. on pregnancy and weight gain NRC, NAS, 1981; mem. internat. sci. bd. Reproductive Toxicology Ctr., 1984—; bd. dirs., med. adv. bd. Diabetes Treatment Ctrs. Am., 1984, others; mem. Coun. Univ Chairs of Ob-Gyn., 1996—; chair Maternal Fetal Medicine Rsch. Network Nat. Inst. Child and Human Devel. Author: Clinical Obstetrics and Gynecology: Diabetes and Pregnancy, 1985, Clinical Obstetrics and Gynecology: Obstetric Ultrasound Update, 1988; (with J.R. Niebyl and J.L. Simpson) Obstetrics: Normal and Problem Pregnancies, 1986, 4th edit., 2002; contbr. numerous articles to profl. jours. and chpts. to books; editor in chief Am. Jour. Perinatology, 1983—87; mem. numerous editl. bds. Mem. Pa. Diabetes Task Force, 1981-87, Ohio Diabetes Task Force, 1987—; bd. dirs. UNITE, Jeanes Hosp., 1980-87. Recipient Sr. Resident's award for Excellence in Tng., L.A. County Women's Hosp., 1976, Disting. Tchr. award from Graduating Class, U. Wash., 1999; grantee Juvenile Diabetes Found., 1981, HHS, 1984, 1985, Diabetes Treatment Ctrs. Am., 1986. Fellow Am. Coll. Obstetricians and Gynecologists (mem. Prolog self assessment program task force 1981-82, chmn. 1986, mem. Prolog subcom. 1986—); mem. Am. Gynecol. and Obstet. Soc., Am. Inst. Ultrasound in Medicine, Perinatal Rsch. Soc., Soc. Gynecologic Investigation, Soc. Perinatal Obstetricians (v.p. 1986, pres. 1987-88, bd. dirs. 1983-88, chmn. credentials, constn. and by-laws com. 1983-87), Am. Diabetes Assn. (mem. nat. rsch. bd. 1981-83, chmn. coun. on diabetes in pregnancy 1985, com. on food and nutrition 1976-80), Juvenile Diabetes Found. (mem. med. sci. rev. com., med. sci. adv. bd. 1981-83), Phila. Neonatal Soc., Obstet. Soc. Phila. (program chmn. 1986-87), Phila. Perinatal Soc. (pres. 1982-84), Columbus Ob-Gyn Soc., Pa. Diabetes Acad. (acad. steering com. 1986—, editl. rev. com. 1986—), Union League (Phila.), Phi Beta Kappa, Alpha Omega Alpha. Avocations: sports, running. Office: Ohio State U Med Ctr 410 W 10th Ave Columbus OH 43210

GABELNICK, HENRY LEWIS, medical research administrator; b. Boston, May 10, 1940; s. Murray and Lillian G.; m. Faith Schectman, June 17, 1962; children: Deborah Anne, Tamar Miriam; m. Judith Andai, Mar. 15, 2003. BS, MIT, 1961, MS, 1962; PhD, Princeton U., 1966. Sr. chem. engr. Monsanto Co., Springfield, Mass., 1966-68; biomed. engr. NIH, Bethesda, Md., 1968-1986; dir. extramural rsch. CONRAD Program Ea. Va. Med. Sch., Arlington, 1986-89, dep. dir. CONRAD Program, 1989-90, dir. CONRAD Program, 1990—. Tech. expert UN Devel. Program, Haifa, Israel, 1973; tech. advisor WHO, Geneva, 1977—; pres. Reprodn. Rsch. Inst., 1997—2001; mem. adv. panel on contraception Internat. Fedn. Ob-gyns., 1998—; mem. adv. coun. dept. chem. engring. Princeton U., 2004—09; bd. dirs. Alliance for Microbicide Devel.; founding bd. mem. Internat. Partnership for Microbicides, sec., 2002—06; v.p., bd. trustees Egon and Ann Diczfalusy Found., 2008—. Editor: Rheology of Biological Systems, 1973, Drug Delivery Systems, 1976, Heterosexual Transmission of AIDS, 1990, Barrier Contraceptives, 1993, Biology, Pharmacology, and Clinical Applications of Androgens, 1996. Recipient Lifetime Achievement award, 5th Internat. Symposium on AIDS, India, 2005, Internat. Microbicides Conf., Pitts., 2010, Microbicides Internat. Symposium, 2010. Fellow Textile Resch. Inst.; mem. APHA (chair population, reproduction & sexual health sect. 2010-11), N.Y. Acad. Scis., Am. Chem. Soc., European Soc. Contraception, Controlled Release Soc., Soc. Reproductive Care (bd. dirs. 2000—08, v.p. 2001-02, pres. 2002-08), Assn. Reproductive Health Profls., Indian Soc. Study Reprodn. and Fertility (life), Global Health Coun., Cosmos Club, Sigma Xi, Egon and Ann Diczfalusy Found. (v.p., bd. trustee, 2008-). Avocation: nature photography. Home: 6315 Swords Way Bethesda MD 20817 Office: 1911 Ft Myer Dr Ste 900 Arlington VA 22209-1607 Office Phone: 703-276-3904. Personal E-mail: hgabelnick@alum.mit.edu. Business E-Mail: hgabelnick@conrad.org.

GABER, WALTER, physician, director; b. Langen, Germany, Feb. 12, 1955; s. Alois and Ingeborg Gaber; m. Jaqueline Kainar, Jan. 19, 1984; children: Janine, Laureen. MD, U. Frankfurt, Frankfurt am Main, Germany, 1984. Cert. physician Germany, Hessen, 1984. Pub. health officer Pub. Health Orgn., Frankfurt am Main, 1984—; emergency physician Fraport AG, Frankfurt am Main, 1985—, sports physician, 1988, occupl. physician, 1989—, med. dir., rep. med. affairs, 1996—, environ. physician, 1997—; med. adviser ACI World, Geneva, 2003—; med. adviser adv. ADV Germany, Berlin, 2003—. Dir., bd. mem. Com. Work Nat. Level Various Orgns. Contbr. articles to publs. Bd. mem. EAGOSH, Frankfurt am Main, 2000—, Emergency Medicine Frankfurt, Frankfurt am Main, 2000—; active German Aviation Medicine, Germany, 1999—. Capt. M.C., 1984—85, Walldürn. Recipient Silver Prin. award, 1995, Superior Svc. award, US Force, 2004. Mem.: Aerospace Medicine Assn. Office: Fraport AG Frankfurt Airport 60547 Frankfurt Germany Office Phone: 00496969066031. Office Fax: 00496969059642. Business E-Mail: w.gaber@fraport.de.

GABILAN, YEDA PEREIRA LIMA, physical therapist, educator; b. Brazil, Aug. 23, 1957; Degree in Physiotherapy, UNICID, 1995; PhD, U. Fed. São Paulo, 2010. Adj. tchr. UNICID, 1997—2009, coord., 2005—. Home: 622 Aliança Liberal Sao Paulo 05088-000 Brazil Business E-Mail: ygabilan@uol.com.br.

GABOW, PATRICIA ANNE, internist, health facility executive; b. Starke, Fla., Jan. 8, 1944; m. Harold N. Gabow, June 21, 1971; children: Tenaya Louise, Aaron Patrick. BA in Biology, Seton Hill Coll., 1965; MD, U. Pa. Sch. Medicine, 1969. Diplomate Am. Bd. Internal Medicine, Am. Bd. Nephrology, Nat. Bd. Med. Examiners; lic. Colo. Internship in medicine Hosp. of U. of Pa., 1969-70; residency in internal medicine Harbor Gen. Hosp., 1970-71; renal fellowship San Francisco Gen. Hosp. and Hosp. of U. Pa., 1971-72, 72-73; instr. medicine divsn. renal diseases, asst. prof. U. Colo. Health Scis. Ctr., 1973-74, 74-79, assoc. prof. medicine divsn. renal diseases, prof., 1979-87; chief renal disease, clin. dir. dept. medicine Denver Gen. Hosp., 1973-81, 76-81, dir. med. svcs., 1981-91; CEO, med. dir. Denver Health and Hosps., 1992—2008; CEO Denver Health, 2008—. Intensive care com. Denver Gen. Hosp., 1976-81, med. records com., 1979-80, ind. rev. com., 1978-81, continuing med. edn. com., 1981-83, animal care com., 1979-83; student adv. com. U. Colo. Health Scis. Ctr., 1982-87, faculty senate, 1985, 86, internship adv. com., 1977-92; exec. com. Denver Gen. Hosp., 1981—, chmn. health resources com., 1988-90, chmn. pathology search com., 1989, chmn. faculty practice plan steering com., 1990-92. Mem. editorial bd. EMERGINDEX, 1983-93, Am. Jour. of Kidney Disease, 1984-96, Western Jour. of Medicine, 1987-98, Annals of Internal Medicine, 1988-91, Jour. of the Am. Soc. of Nephrology, 1990-97; contbr. numerous articles, revs. and editorials to profl. publs., chpts. to books. Mem. Mayor's Safe City Task Force, 1993; mem. sci. adv. bd. Polycystic Kidney Rsch. Found., 1984-96, chmn., 1991; mem. sci. adv. bd. Nat. Kidney Found., 1991-94; mem. Nat. Pub. Health and Hosps. Inst. Bd., 1993-2001, 03—. Recipient Sullivan award for Highest Acad. Average in Graduating Class, Seton Hill Coll., 1965, Pa. State Senatorial scholarship, 1961-65, Kaiser Permanente award for Excellence in Tchg., 1976, Ann. award to Outstanding Woman Physician, 1982, Kaiser Permanente Nominee for Excellence in Tchg. award, 1983, Seton Hill Coll. Disting. Alumna Leadership award, 1990, Florence Rena Sabin award U. Colo., 2000, Nathan Davis award AMA, 2000, Good Housekeeping Women in Govt. award, 2002, Nat. Ctr. Healthcare Leadership award, 2008, Lifetime Achievement award, Denver Bus. Jour., Champions in Healthcare, 2009, Bonfils Sta. Found. Lifetime Achievement award, 2010; named to Colo. Women's Hall of Fame, 2004, One of the Best Drs. in America, 1994-95, 2002-09, Top 25 Women in Healthcare, 2005, 09, 100 Most Influential People in Healthcare in Modern Healthcare, 2005, 09, Women Who Make a Difference International Women's Forum, 2005, Unique Woman Colo., 2007; grantee Bonfils Found., 1985-86, NIH, 1985-90, 91-96, 96-00, W.K. Kellogg Found., 1997—, AHRQ, 2000-03. Mem. Denver Med. Soc., Colo. Med. Soc., Polycystic Kidney Disease Rsch. Found. (sci. advisor 1984-96), Nat. Kidney Found. (sci. adv. bd. 1987-91), Women's Forum of Colo., Inc., Assn. Am. Physicians. Roman Catholic. Office: Denver Health 777 Bannock St Denver CO 80204-4506 Address: Denver Health 777 Bannock St Denver CO 80204 Office Phone: 303-436-6611.

GABRIEL, MICHAEL, psychology professor; b. Phila., May 5, 1940; s. Michael and Josephine (Alesio) G.; m. Linda Prinz, June, 1967 (div.); 1 child, Joseph Michael; m. Sonda S. Walsh, 1984. AB in Psychology, St. Joseph's Coll., 1962; MA, U. Wis., 1965, PhD, 1967. Asst. prof. Pomona Coll., Claremont, Calif., 1967—70; staff psychologist Pacific State Hosp., Pomona, Calif., 1968-70; NIMH sr. postdoctoral fellow U. Calif.-Irvine, 1970-72; asst. prof. U. Tex.-Austin, 1973-77, assoc. prof., 1977-82; prof. psychology U. Ill., Urbana, 1982—2004, appointee Ctr. for Advanced Study, 1990-91, prof. dept. psychology and Beckman Inst., 2004. Area chmn. Biol. Psychology Program, U. Tex., Austin, 1979-82; mem. rev. panel in behavioral and neural scis. NSF, 1988-91, prin. investigator database system for neuronal pattern analysis project NSF, 1992—, ad hoc mem. biopsychology rev. panel, NIMH, 1997-98; faculty Beckman Inst., U. Ill., Urbana, 1989—; chmn. Neuronal Pattern Analysis Group, Beckman Inst., mem. neuroinformatics rev. panel, NIH, 2000-. Co-editor: (with J. Moore) Learning and Computational Neuroscience: Foundations of Adaptive Networks, 1989, (with B. Vogt) Neurobiology of Cingulate Cortex and Limbic Thalamus, 1993; mem. editl. bd. Neural Plasticity, Neurobiology of Learning and Memory. Grantee NIMH, 1978-88, 1998-2002, NIH, 1988-2003, Air Force Office Sci. Rsch., 1988-91, NSF, 1992-2003, NIDA, 1996-2001. Fellow Am. Psychol. Soc., Internat. Behavioral Neurosci. Soc.; mem. Sigma Chi. pioneered methods for simultaneous multi-site recording and analysis of neuron activity during active avoidance learning in behaving animals; performed presently the only neurologic analysis of the neural substrates of active avoidance learning in animals; provided the first documentation of neuron activity in multiple learning-relevant brain areas throughout the course of active avoidance learning; pioneered simultaneous use of de-afferenting lesions and recording of neuron activity in key brain areas to document learning-relevant interactions among involved brain regions; first demonstrated learning-relevant activity (discrimination and reversal of brief-latency neuron activity) in the medial geniculate nucleus (MGM), a region previously believed to be involved in sensory processing but not learning; first demonstration that neurons in the basolateral nucleus of the amygdala play an essential role in the development of discriminative (learning-relevant) neuron activity in the MGm and cingulate cortex; first demonstration in various cytoarchitectural areas of cingulate cortex and anterior thalamus, of early, intermediate and late-developing discriminative neuron activity during learning; first demonstration of training-induced pre-avoidance neuron activity in cingulate cortex; first hypothesized that medial temporal lobe (MTL) and cingulate cortical interactions promote context-based retrieval of learned behavior and memory; first use of dual task strategy to demonstrate context-specific and context-independent neuronal activity in various MTL and cingulate cortical areas; first demonstration that MTL and cingulate cortical interactions are necessary for context-based concurrent learning of two (avoidance and approach) discrimination tasks; first demonstration of latent inhibition (LI) at the neuron level, and dependence of the neural and behavioral LI effect on contextual stimuli; documentation of specific anterior cingulate cortical brain changes resulting from exposure to cocaine in-utero. Office: Beckman Inst Univ Ill Urbana IL 61801-2325 Office Phone: 904-540-9955. Business E-Mail: mgabriel@uiuc.edu, mgabriel@illinois.edu.

GABRIEL, RONALD SAMUEL, child neurologist; b. Monterey, Calif., Mar. 19, 1937; s. Philip Louis and Theresa Shaheen Gabriel; children: Philip Louis III, Paula Shaheen, Matthew William. BA with honors, Yale U., 1959; MD, Boston U., 1963. Diplomate Am. Bd. Psychiatry and Neurology (examiner 1978-88), Am. Bd. Pediatrics. Intern, resident in pediatrics Los Angeles County Gen. Hosp., 1963-66; fellow in neurology and pediatric neurology UCLA med. ctr., 1966-68, 70-71; head physician, cons. Calif. Children's Svcs., 1970—; clin. prof. neurology/pediatrics UCLA Sch. Medicine, 1971—, dir. pediat. neurology/outpatient, 1971-76. Cons. Regional Ctr.-Calif., 1971—; vis. prof. Prince of Wales, Royal Children's Hosp., Sydney and Melbourne, Australia, 1978; mem. expert panel L.A. Superior Ct., 1992—; founding and mng. gen. ptnr. Med. Imaging of So. Calif., L.A., 1980-94; mng. dir. GFA Cattle and Farm Co. Author: The 410 Shotgun, 2000, Diary of a Mountain Hunter, 2000; contbr.: Textbook of Child Neurology, 1974, 4 edits., 1990, Difficult Diagnoses in Pediatrics, 1990, Founders of Child Neurology, 1990. Mng. dir. GFF Natural History Mus. Maj. U.S. Army, 1968-70. Spl. fellow Nat. Inst. Neurol. Disease/Stroke, 1966-68, 70-71. Fellow Am. Acad. Pediatrics, Am. Acad. Neurology; mem. Calif. Med. Assn. (mem. sci. adv. panel 1987-94, chmn. sci. adv. com. 1989-90). Roman Catholic. Avocations: writing, mountain climbing, hunting. Office: Neurology-Pediat Neurology Assocs 2080 Century Park E Ste 203 Los Angeles CA 90067-2005 Fax: (310) 277-9285.

GABRILOVE, JACQUES LESTER, physician; b. NYC, Sept. 21, 1917; s. Benjamin and Pauline (Levine) G.; m. Hilda R. Weiss, May 19, 1946 (dec.); children: Sandra Leslie Saltzman, Janice Lynn Gabrilove Dirzulaitis. BS magna cum laude, CCNY, 1936; MD Alpha Omega Alpha prize, NYU, 1940. Diplomate Am. Bd. Internal Medicine. Intern Mt. Sinai Hosp., NYC, 1940-41, rotating intern, 1941-43, vol. radiology, 1943, resident medicine, 1943-44, Blumenthal fellow medicine, 1946-48, research asst. medicine, 1949-51, asst. attending physician, 1952-60, assoc. attending physician, 1960-68, attending physician, 1969—. Clin. prof. medicine Mt. Sinai Sch. Medicine, 1969-82, chief endocrine clinic, 1969-92, Baumritter prof., 1982-90, Baumritter prof. emeritus, 1990—, prof., 1995—, cting dir. divsn. endocrinology, 1985, assoc. dir. divsn., 1986-2005, dir. endocrine fellowship program, 1986—2005; Libman fellow in medicine Yale U., 1945; clin. asst. prof. SUNY Coll. Medicine, N.Y.C., 1957-59, clin. assoc. prof., 1959-66, clin. prof., 1966-69, professorial lectr., 1969—; cons. endocrinology VA Hosp., East Orange, N.J., 1958-66, Elizabeth A. Horton Hosp., Middletown, N.Y., 1961—, VA Hosp., Bronx, N.Y., 1969—, Norwalk (Conn.) Hosp., 1974—, Elmhurst (N.Y.) City Hosp., St. Francis Hosp., Port Jervis, N.Y.; mem. panel on metabolic and rheumatoid diseases U.S. Pharmacopeia, 1956; mem. spl. com. on rsch. tng. grants in diabetes, endocrinology and metabolism NIH, 1976-79, mem. com. on diabetes rsch. and tng. ctrs., 1977-79; Saltzman lectr. Mt. Sinai Hosp., Cleve., 1974; cons. Jour. Urology, 1984-89. Mem. editl. bd. Mt. Sinai Jour.; contbr. chpts. to books, articles to profl. jours. Trustee, v.p. area Jewish synagogue. Recipient Globus prize Mt. Sinai Jour., Townsend Harris medal CCNY Alumni Assn., 1998; J. Lester Gabrilove award established in his honor, 1988; Hilda and J. Lester Gabrilove MD Divsn. Endocrinology, Diabetes and Bone Disease named in his honor, 2007; named to Hall of Fame Alumni Assn. Townsend Harris H.S. Fellow ACP, Am. Coll. Endocrinology (Disting. Clin. Endocrinologist award 1996, Festschrift in his honor on 80th birthday, Hilda and J. Lester Gabrilove MD divsn. endocrinology, diabetes and bone disease named in his honor 2007, Ann. J. Lester Gabrilove MD lectureship named in his honor 2007), N.Y. Acad. Medicine, Phi Beta Kappa; mem. AMA, AAAS, Am. Assn. Clin. Endocrinologists (Disting. Clin. Endocrinologist award 1996), Am. Diabetes Assn., Harvey Soc., Endocrine Soc., Royal Soc. Medicine, Pan Am. Med. Assn. (v.p. N.Am. endocrinology), Peruvian Endocrine Soc. (hon.), N.Y. Acad. Scis., N.Y. County Med. Soc., N.Y. Diabetes Assn., Mt. Sinai Alumni Assn. (pres. 1970, Jacobi medallion 1973), Lotos Club (bd. dirs.), Alpha Omega Alpha, Phi Beta Kappa. Achievements include research in delineaton of hyperfunctioning and hypofunctioning endocrine disorders of the adrenal cortex and gonads; mechanism of gynecomastia; medical treatment of thyrotoxicosis; medical treatment of benign prostatic hyperplasia; pathogenesis of the polycystic ovary syndrome. Home: 25 E 86th St New York NY 10028-0553 Business E-Mail: lester.gabrilove@mssm.edu.

GADAG, JAYANTNARAIN RAVINDRA, biochemist, educator; b. Belgaum, India, Nov. 1, 1949; s. Ravindra Narayen and Radha Ravindra Gadag; m. Chhaya Jayantnarain Hombali, July 3, 1979; children: Srirang Bhushan Jayantnarain, Manjiri Jayantnarain. BSc with honors, Bombay U., 1970, MSc in Biochemistry, 1972, PhD in Biochemistry, 1976. Cert. in Radio Immuno Assay Bhabha Atomic Rsch. Ctr., Bombay. Lectr. univ. grants commn. Karnatak U., Dharwad, India, 1977—89, reader in biochemistry, 1989—98, prof. biochemistry, 1998—, chmn. dept. biochemistry, 2006—. Bd. of examiners biochemistry, microbiology, biotech. and applied genetics Karnataka U., 2001—, bd. of studies in biochemistry, microbiology and applied genetics, 2001—; presenter in field. Contbr. articles to profl. jours. Chief contact person, tech. trustee Rotary Club Dharwad Midtown and, blood bank at Our Lady Of Lourdes Hosp., 2000—; mgr. pulse polio nat. immunization day programs, coord. health checkup camps Rotary Club Dharwad Midtown, 1997—, spkr. on blood donation, transfusion medicine and AIDS awareness, coord. animal health check up camps, 1997—2005. Recipient Gov.'s Outstanding award, Rotary, 2001; named Paul Harris fellow, Rotary Internat., 2004; grantee, R.D.Birla Smark Kosh, Bombay Hosp. Rsch. Ctr., 1996—98; scholar, Imperial Chem. Industries (ICI), 1966—70; jr. and sr. rsch. fellow, Univ. Grants Commn., 1972—76. Mem.: Soc. Biol. Chemists (India), Sci. Acad. (Dharwad) (life), Assn. Hosp. and Practicing Biochemists and Med. Technologists (life), Soc. Polymer Sci. (India) (life), Nat. Magnetic Resonance Soc. (life), Assn. Clin. Biochemists India (life), Freemasons (worshipful master 1992—93, 25 Yr. Jewel award 2005). Avocations: trekking, dramatics, poetry, debating, conducting quiz programs. Office: Dept Biochemistry Karnatak U Dharwad 580003 India Home: Srirang' Sbi Colony Keshavnagar 580 007 Dharwad India Office Fax: 9108362747884. E-mail: jayantgadag@gmail.com.

GADALLAH, WAFAA, physician, educator; b. Assiut, Egypt, July 20, 1969; MD, Assiut U., 1992. Asst. prof. Faculty Medicine, 2009—. Adj. prof. Assiut U. Mem.: ERS, AACR. Office: 85 Elhelaly St Assiut 70001 Egypt Personal E-mail: wafaagadallah@yahoo.com.

GADELRAB, RITA, anesthesiologist, consultant; MBBCh, Cairo U., 1982. Register Addenbrooke's Hosp., Cambridge, England, 1990—91; sr. register Freeman Hosp., Newcastle upon Tyne, England, 1991—95; cons. anesthetist Royal Nat. Orthopaedic Hosp., London, 1996—. Fellow: Faculty Anaesthetists, Royal Coll. Surgeons Ireland; mem.: Brit. Soc. Orthopaedic Anaesthetists (pres. 2007—, sec. 1996—2002). Office: Royal Nat Orthopaedic Hosp Brockley Hill Stanmore HA7 4LP England Office Phone: 02089542300. Personal E-mail: ritagadelrab@hotmail.com.

GAEDE, JAMES ERNEST, physician, educator; b. Calgary, Alta., Can., July 2, 1953; s. John Ernest and Florence Eleanor (Hilmer) G.; married, Dec. 23, 1994; children: Graham, Jason, Nikki, Mary Frances, Sydney, Camille. BA, Augustana Coll., 1975, MA, 1976; MD, U. S.D., 1980. Diplomate Am. Bd. Family Practice. Staff physician Queen of Peace, Mitchell, SD, 1983—2001, chief of staff, 1988, med. dir., 1988-89, St. Joe's Med. Assn., Howard, SD, 1988—2000, Women's Health Clinic, Mitchell, SD, 1983—2000; assoc. prof. U. S.D. Sch. Medicine; 2005med. dir. Desert Regional Med. Ctr., Palm Springs, Calif., 2001—05; med. dir. Tenet Home Health, 2005; CEO Physiogard LLC, 2005—. Presenter U.S. Senate, Washington, 1991; med. dir. Cave South Home Health, 2005, Sleep Disorders of Palm Springs, 2005 Contbr. articles to profl. jours. Bd. dirs. Dakota Weslayan U., Mitchell, 1986-89, Dakota Mental Health, Mitchell, 1988-90; mem. Commn. 2000 S.D., Sioux Falls, 1988-00; pub. health officer City of Mitchell, 1983-01. Recipient Edward J. Batt meml. award, 1996—97; named one of Top 100 Family Physicians in U.S., Consumer Rsch. Coun., Washington, Top 70 Drs. in 35 Specialties, Caste Connolly Med. Ltd. Fellow Am. Acad. Family Practice (Active Tchrs. award 1984—); mem. AMA, Calif. Acad. Family Practice, S.D. Assn. Family Practice, S.D. State Med. Assn. (del. 1983-2000, sec. 1998-99, v.p. 1999, pres. 2000), Calif. State Med. Assn., Mitchell C. of C., Mayo Alumni Assn., Doctors Mayo Soc. Achievements include patents in field. Avocations: sailing, music, auto restoration. Home: 31240 Calle Cayuga Cathedral City CA 92234-0100 *

GAENGLER, PETER WOLFGANG, dentist, researcher; b. Meissen, Saxony, Germany, Oct. 30, 1941; s. Wolfgang Ernst-Otto and Dorothea Friedericke (Moebius) G.; m. Sabine Gertrud Ahlborn, Nov. 6, 1970; children: Felix Peter, Beate Petra. Stomatology Diploma, Faculty of Dental Medicine, Leningrad, Russia, 1965; DrMedDent, Sch. Dental Medicine, Dresden, Germany, 1967, PhD, 1974; DHC (hon.), Semmelweis U., Budapest, 2004. Diplomate in dentistry. Dentistry Community Hosp., Wittenberge, Germany, 1965-66; asst. prof. Sch. Dental Medicine, Dresden, 1966-75, prof., chmn. Erfurt, Germany, 1975-92, Internat. Rsch. Exch. Program, 1979, Faculty of Dental Medicine, Witten/Herdecke, Germany, 1992—, dean, 1992—2006; bd. dirs. U. Witten/Herdecke, 1995—2002, mem. exec. bd., 2002—06. Mem. joint working group FDI/WHO, Geneva, 1979, 2005; v.p. for rsch. U. Witten/Herdecke, 2003—05, CEO, ORMED Inst. Oral Medicine, 2009—. Author: Lehrbuch der Konservierenden Zahnheilkunde, 5th edit., 2010; editor Medizin aktuell, 1975-90; mem. editl. bd. European Jour. Dental Edn., 2000—, Jour. Oral Rehab., 2001-05, Ceska Stomatologie, 2005— Recipient Humboldt medal Ministry Higher Edn., Berlin, 1978; grantee in field. Mem.: Biomedicine Soc. Dortmund (exec. com. 1998—2009), Internat. Assn. for Dental Rsch. (com. on membership and recruitment 1989—93, mem. publs. com. 2002—05), Assn. Dental Edn. Europe (exec. com. 1997—2001), Assn. Stomatology (v.p. 1988—90, Philipp-Pfaff medal 1988), Assn. Conservative Dentistry (pres. 1978—87), Hungarian Assn. Dentistry (hon. Semmelweis medal 1993), Polish Assn. Dentistry (hon.). Avocations: literature, sailing, skiing. Home: Waldweg 9 D-58313 Herdecke Germany Office: U Witten/Herdecke Faculty Health, Dept Dental Medicine Alfred-Herrhausen-Str. 50 58448 Witten Germany Office Phone: 0049-2302-926-664. E-mail: peter.gaengler@uni-wh.de.

GAETA, GIOVANNI, cardiologist; b. Capua, Caserta, Italy, Mar. 27, 1955; s. Alfonso Gaeta and Lucia Pesticcio; m. Silvana Berardesca, Sept. 28, 1985; 1 child, Lucia. MD, Federico II U., Napoli, Italy, 1979. Dirigente medico Antonio Cardarelli Hosp., Napoli, 1989—2006, dirigente medico, responsabile di struttura semplice, 2006—. Contbr. scientific papers to profl. jours. Fellow: Am. Coll. Cardiology, Assn. Nat. Medici Cardiologi Ospedalieri, European Soc. Cardiology, Am. Heart Assn. Avocation: travel. Office: Antonio Cardarelli Hosp 9 Antonio Cardarelli Naples 80131 Italy Office Phone: 00390817472143. Personal E-mail: giovanni.gaeta@tin.it. Business E-Mail: giovanni.gaeta@ancardarelli.it.

GAETA, ROSEMARIE, psychotherapist; b. Bklyn., Apr. 15, 1947; d. James and Rose (Scorcia) G. BS, Fordham U., 1968, MSW, 1970. Diplomate NASW; lic. clin. social worker, NY; bd. cert. clin. social worker, Am. Bd. Examiners, 1988, bd. cert. clin. social work psychoanalysis, 2004. Pvt. clin. practice, SI, 1973—. Co-founder Psychoanalytic Consortium, 1991. Bd. mem. Accreditation Council for Psychoanalytic Edn., 2004—08. Recipient Disting. Practitioner, Nat. Acad. Practice in Social Work. Mem. NY State Soc. Clin. Social Work Psychotherapists (diplomate, chair state com. on psychoanalysis 1987-91), Inst. Psychoanalytic Tng. and Rsch., Internat. Psychoanalytical Assn., Am. Assn. Psychoanalysis Clin. Social Work (1st pres. 1991-93). Office: 416 Crown Ave Staten Island NY 10312-2828 Office Phone: 718-356-8881. Personal E-mail: rosemariegaeta@aol.com.

GAETANO, CARLO, oncologist; b. Rome, May 5, 1961; Degree in Medicine, U. Rome La Sapienza, 1986. Postdoc. Fogarty fellow Nat. Cancer Inst., 1989—92; vis. scientist NIH, 1995—96; vis. assoc. prof. McMaster U., 1999—2000; sr. scientist Istituto Dermopatico dell'Immacolata, 1996—. Recipient Inst. Pasteur award, Cenci Bolognetti Found.; fellowship, Anna Villa Rusconi found., Internat. Exch. Scientist fellowship, Internat. Union Against Cancer. Fellow: Am. Heart Assn. Avocations: music, martial arts, cooking. Office: Via Monti di Creta 104 Rome Lazio 00167 Italy Office Fax: 0039 6 66462430. Business E-Mail: gaetano@idi.it.

GAFFNEY, MARGARET MARY, dermatologist, educator; b. St. Louis, Feb. 12, 1953; d. Raymond Aloysius Gaffney and Lorraine Elizabeth Rich; m. Matthew Reppert Galvin; children: Sarah, Joseph; m. Charles Eugene Greer (div. 1998); 1 child, Erin E. Greer. BA in English, Ind. U., Bloomington, 1975; MD, Ind. U., Indpls., 1981. Diplomate Am. Bd. Of Dermatology. Pvt. practice, Indpls., 1985—88; asst. clin. prof., dermatology Ill. Sch. Med., 1988—99, assoc. clin. prof., med., 1999—. Dir. Ind. U. Conscience Project, 1998—; chair Wishard Hosp. Ethics Com., 1998—. Contbr. scientific papers. With Deans Coun., JO Ritchery Soc., 1999—; commr. Ind. Dept. Environ. Mgmt., 1992—98; dir. Ind. Health Care Ethics Network, 1995—2003; with The Pres. Cir., Ind. U., Bloomington, 2008. Recipient Tchg. award, AMWA, 2003, Gender Equity award, 2003, Ann. Faculty Tchg. award, Ind. U. Sch. Medicine, 2010. Fellow: Am. Acad. Dermatology; mem.: Ind. State Med. Assn., Ind. Acad. Dermatology, Alpha Omega Alpha. Avocations: literature, gardening, hiking, bicycling. Office: Dept Medicine 1001 W 10thSt Wop m200 Indianapolis IN 46202 Office Phone: 317-630-6721.

GAFFNEY, THOMAS EDWARD, physician; b. East St. Louis, Ill., Nov. 5, 1930; s. John V. and Leola (Heisner) G.; m. Edith Ann Heitholt, June 12, 1954; children— John, David, Michael. AB, U. Mo., 1951, MS, 1953; MD, U. Cin., 1957. Intern Harvard Med. Service of Boston City Hosp., 1957-58; resident medicine Mass. Gen. Hosp., 1958-59; instr. pharmacology, asst. medicine U. Cin., 1959-60; clin. assoc. Nat. Heart Inst., 1960-62; assoc. prof. pharmacology U. Cin., 1962-67, asst. prof. medicine, 1962, dir. div. clin. pharmacology, 1962-72, prof. pharmacology, 1967-72, prof. medicine, 1969-72; prof., chmn. dept. pharmacology, prof. medicine Med. U. S.C., 1972-90, disting. prof., 1986-90; vis. scientist Merck Sharp & Dohme Rsch. Labs., Rahway, NJ, 1989-93; vol. clinician Buncombe County Health Ctr., 1998—2004; prof. medicine U. S.C. Sch. Medicine, Columbia, 2004—; surveillance council Diabetes Initiative SC, 2008—. Cardiovascular panel NAS Drug Efficacy Study, 1967-70; pharmacology and exptl. therapeutics study sect. Nat. Heart Inst., 1967-69; med. adv. bd. Coun. High Blood Pressure Rsch., 1969—; mem. Coun. on Basic Scis. of Am. Heart Assn., 1969—, cardiovascular A study sect., 1972; program rev. com. pharmacology and toxicology Nat. Inst. Gen. Med. Scis., 1971-75, chmn. 1973-75; mem. tech. adv. bd. S.C. Rsch. Authority, 1986-89 Mem. editorial bd. Jour. Pharmacology and Exptl. Therapeutics, 1965-77, Ann. Rev. Pharmacology and Toxicology, 1986-91. Served with USPHS, 1960-62. Recipient Rsch. Career devel. award Nat. Heart Inst., 1962, 67, 72; Myrtle Wreath award for research Hadassah, 1980; Sr. Rsch. fellow NIH, 1989. Mem. Am. Fedn. Clin. Rsch., Am. Soc. Pharmacology and Exptl. Therapeutics, Ctrl. Soc. Clin. Rsch., Am. Soc. Clin. Investigation, Alpha Omega Alpha. Home: 1342 Sanford Dr Columbia SC 29206 Personal E-mail: tegaff@att.net.

GAGE, DEBORAH, health products executive; BA in Economics, U. Mich., 1979, MBA, 1984—86. Pers. adminstr. Johnson Controls, 1976—79, corp. adminstr. employee benefits, 1979—80, corp. adminstr. casualty ins., 1980—82, corp. mgr. risk mgmt., 1982—84, corp. dir. strategic planning, 1984—86; bus. analyst Deloitte & Touche Mgmt. Consulting, 1986—87; dir. nat. accts. and new markets The MEDSTAT Group, 1987—88, dir. marketscan svcs., 1988—90, v.p. marketscan svcs., 1988—90; v.p., gen. mgr. systemetrics divsn., 1992—94; sr. v.p., gen. mgr. FoxMeyer Corp., 1995—96; pres., CEO Solution Point, 1996—99; cons., CEO Gage Assocs., 1999—2000, cons., 2009—11; pres., CEO Rosettamed (acquired by Kryptiq Corp.), 2000—22, GTESS Corp., 2002—08, MEDecision. Office: MEDecision Chesterbrook Corp Ctr 601 Lee Rd Wayne PA 19087 Office Phone: 610-540-0202. Office Fax: 610-540-0270.

GAGE, L. PATRICK (LEONARD PATRICK GAGE), biotechnology & pharmaceutical industry consultant; b. Endicott, NY, May 4, 1942; s. Leonard Augustine and Mary Margaret (O'Brien) G.; m. Nancy Virginia Graffius, Aug. 7, 1965 (div. Mar. 1985); children: Darren, Cynthia; m. Evelyn Anne Devine, June 29, 1985 (div. Apr. 2009); children: Christopher, Devin. BS, MIT, 1964; PhD, U. Chgo., 1969. NIH postdoctoral fellow Carnegie Inst., Washington, 1969—71; mem. dept. cell biology Roche Inst. Molecular Biology, 1971—80, dir. dept. molecular genetics Nutley, NJ, 1981—83, v.p. biol. R&D, 1983—84; v.p. exploratory rsch. Hoffmann-La Roche Inc., Nutley, NJ, 1984—89; exec. v.p. Genetics Inst., Inc., Cambridge, Mass., 1989—93, COO, 1993—97, pres., 1997—98, Wyeth Rsch., Collegeville, Pa., 1998—2002; founder En. Gage Biotech. Cons., 2009—. Chmn. Dublin Molecular Medicine Ctr., 2002—04, Adnexus Therapeutics (also known as Compound Therapeutics), 2003—07, Acceleron Pharma, 2004—06, Neose Tech., Inc., 2006—09, PDL BioPharma, 2007, CEO, 2007—08; bd. dirs. Functional Genetics, Alvine Pharm., Corridor Pharm., Inc.; exec. chmn. Virdante Pharm., 2009—; venture ptnr. Flagship Venture, Cambridge, Mass., 2003—07. Mem. vis. com., Pritzker Sch. Medicine U. Chgo., 2007—10; trustee Marine Biol. Labs., 2008—; bd. dirs. Phila. Orch., 1999—2009. Avocations: skiing, golf. Home and Office: 820 Dearfield Hane Bryn Mawr PA 19010 Home Phone: 610-667-3107; Office Phone: 617-460-4020. Business E-Mail: pat@engagebc.com.

GAGE, MIRIAM BETTS, retired nutritionist; b. Nelsonville, Ohio, Jan. 9, 1928; d. Charles Donald and Lillian Mary (Linscott) B.; m. Robert Averill Gowdy, Oct. 12, 1950 (div. 1977); children: Carol Jo, Robert Jr., Bruce; m. George Joel Gage, Aug. 16, 1997. BA in Home Econs., Ohio Wesleyan U., 1949; postgrad., Duke U., 1949-50, Calif. State U., LA, 1975-76. Registered dietitian. Pvt. practice dietitian, LA, 1977-91; cons. Nat.-in-Home Health, Van Nuys, Calif., 1984-87; clin. dietitian Lake Mead Hosp., 1991-94; pvt. practice Las Vegas, Nev., 1994-97; contract dietitian Pulse Health Svcs., Las Vegas, 1995-97; ret., 1997. Mem. Am. Diabetes Assn. (con. San Fernando Valley unit 1976-80, bd. dirs. N.W. chpt. 1977-82), Nev. Dietetic Assn. (nominating com. 1995-97), So. Nev. Dietetic Assn. (mem. chmn. 1991-92, pres. 1993-94), Cons. Nutritionists (chmn.-elect So. Calif. chpt. 1979-81), Calif. Dietetic Assn. (chmn. diabetes care practice 1979-81), Am. Heart Assn. (governing bd. N.W. chpt. 1988-89). Republican. Methodist. Home: 10813 Brinkwood Ave Las Vegas NV 89134-5248

GAGLIARDI, RAYMOND ALFRED, physician; b. New Haven, Nov. 20, 1922; s. Carl Albert and Carmela (Esposito) G.; m. Patricia DeTuncq, Apr. 6, 1946; children: Laura E. Quigley, John Bell. BS, Yale U., 1943, MD, 1945. Pvt. practice radiology, Pontiac, Mich., 1951-92; chmn. dept. radiology St. Joseph Mercy Hosp., Pontiac, 1976-91, chmn. emeritus, 1991—. Clin. faculty radiology Wayne Univ. Sch. of Medicine, 1951—92. Author: The Golf Story: An Anecdotal History of Golf, 1999, Reflections and Recollections, 2000; editor-in-chief History of the Radiological Sciences, 1995; contbr. articles to profl. jours. Capt. U.S. Army, 1946-48; PTO. Fellow Am. Coll Radiology; mem. Am. Roentgen Ray Soc. (pres. 1987-88, Gold Medal award 1989, Hartman medal 1995, Centennial lectr. 2000), Mich. Radiol. Soc. (pres. 1972), Mich. Med. Soc. (Disting. Svc. award 1988), Oakland Hills Country Club, Royal Palm Yacht and Country Club (past commodore 1994), Heathers Club. Independent. Avocation: golf. Home: 789 Upper Scotsborough Way Bloomfield Hills MI 48304-3827 Address: 2100 Queen Palm Rd Boca Raton FL 33432 Home Phone: 248-792-6946. Personal E-mail: raygagliardi@bellsouth.net.

GAGLIO, PAUL J., medical educator; b. Bronx, NY, Mar. 26, 1962; BA, Rutgers Coll., 1984; MD, UMDNJ NJ Med. Sch., 1988. Asst. prof. medicine UMDNJ NJ Med., 1993—96; assoc. prof. medicine Tulane U. Med. Sch., 1996—2001; assoc. prof. clin. medicine Columbia U. Coll. Physicians and Surgeons, 2001—07; prof. clin. medicine Albert Einstein Coll. Medicine, 2007—. Fellow: ACP, Am. Gastroenterology Assn.; mem.: Alpha Omega Alpha, Phi Beta Kappa. Office: Albert Einstein Coll Medicine 111 East 210th St Bronx NY 10467 Office Phone: 718-920-6240.

GAGNER, MICHEL, surgeon, educator; b. Montreal, Que., Can., Apr. 28, 1960; s. Raymond Gagner and Louise Duchaine; m. France LaPointe, Dec. 31, 1984; children: Xavier, Guillaume, Maxime. DEC, Seminaire de Sherbrooke, 1978; MD, U. Sherbrooke, 1982. Gen. surgery resident McGill U., 1988; asst. prof. surgery U. Montreal, 1990-95; assoc. prof. surgery Cleve. Clinic, 1997-98, attending staff surgeon, 1995—98; prof. surgery Mt. Sinai Sch. Medicine, NYC, 1998—, chmn., Franz W. Sichel prof. surgery. Chief laparoscopic surgery, Cleve. Clinic Found., 1995-98, Mt. Sinai Hosp., NYC, 1998-2003, prof. surgery, chief laparoscopic and bariatric surgery Cornell U., NYC, 2003—07; chief surgery Mt. Sinai Med. Ctr., Miami Beach, 2008-09. Author: First World Laparoscopic Adrenalectomy, 1992, First World Laparoscopic Pancreatic Resection, First World Endoscopic Parathyroidectomy, 1995, Biliopancreatic Diversion with Duodenal Switch for Morbid Obesity, 1999, Laparoscopic Sleeve Gastrectomy For Morbid Obesity, 2000, First World Transatlantic Telesurgery, 2001, First World Transoral Cholecystectomy, 1997, iLeal Interposition, 2005, First Laparoscopic Pancreatic Resection; patentee in field. Recipient medal, French Nat. Assembly, 2010—11. Fellow: ACS, Royal Coll. Surgeons; mem.: Can. Soc. Laparoscopic Surgery, Assn. Francaise de Chirurgie (hon.), French Soc. Endocrinology (hon.), Soc. Mex. Laparoscopy (hon.), Peruvian Surg. Soc. (hon.). Office Phone: 514-757-9199. Business E-Mail: gagner.michel@gmail.com.

GAHAGAN, THOMAS GAIL, obstetrician, gynecologist; b. Brush Valley, Pa., Apr. 14, 1938; s. Ben D. and Zula C. (Brown) G.; m. Mary A. Miller, Dec. 23, 1960; children: David, Diane, Kevin, Keith. BA, Washington and Jefferson Coll., 1960; MD, U. Pa., Phila., 1964. Diplomate Am. Bd. Ob/Gyn. Intern U. Ky., Lexington, 1964-65, resident in ob/gyn., 1965-68; group practice Dr. Jones and Kelch P.A., Newark, Ohio, 1970-71, Naples (Fla.) Ob/Gyn., 1971-85; pvt. practice Naples, 1985-99; ret., 1999. Capt. USAF, 1968-70. Fellow ACOG, Fla. Ob-Gyn. Soc.; mem. AMA, Am. Cancer Soc. (life, bd. dirs. Collier unit 1973-93, bd. dirs. Fla. div. 1976-91, pres. 1986-87, St. George medal 1990), Fla. Med. Assn., Collier County Med. Soc. (exec. com. 1989-94, pres.-elect 1991-92, pres. 1992-93). Republican. Presbyterian. Avocations: scuba diving, flying, golf, skiing, fishing.

GAHALAUT, PRATIK, medical educator; b. Moradabad, Uttar Pradesh, India, Sept. 5, 1977; MBBS, Kasturba Med. Coll., Manipal, 1999; MD in Dermatology, Kasturba Med. Coll., Mangalore, India, 2004. Lectr. Christian Med. Coll., Ludhiana, 2005—06; assoc. prof. Sri Ram Murti Smarak Inst. Med. Scis., Bareilly, Uttar Pradesh, 2007—. Grant, Ministry of Health and Family Welfare, Govt. of India. Fellow: Acad. Gen. Edn.; mem.: Cosmetology Soc. India, Indian Assn. Dermatologists, Venereologists and Leprologists. Avocations: travel, music. Home: Silver Estate Bareilly Uttar Pardesh 243006 India Personal E-mail: drpratikg@rediffmail.com.

GAHERY, YVES, retired neuroscientist; b. Masserac, France, Aug. 18, 1940; s. Jean Gahery and Eugénie Bougouin. BS in Chem. Physiology, Faculty Scis., Rennes, 1962, DSc, U. Paris VI, 1972. Cert. diploma in higher edn. Faculty Scis., Rennes, 1964. Chargé rschr. Ctr. Nat. Rsch. Sci., Paris, 1966—81, dir. rschr. Marseilles, France, 1982—2003. Contbr. scientific papers to profl. publs. Recipient Acad. Scis. prize, 1988. Mem.: Groupement Retraités Educateurs Sans Frontières, Paris (edn. expert 2003—09). Achievements include patents for ambulatory computer device for gait rehabilitation. Home: Bâtiment B5 83 Blvd du Redon Marseilles 13009 France Personal E-mail: gahery.yves@yahoo.fr.

GAHRTON, GÖSTA CARL ARNOLD, internist, hematologist, educator; b. Malmö, Sweden, Dec. 20, 1932; s. Arnold Harald Valdemar and Asta Jula Rosette (de Shàrengrad) G.; m. Birgitta Irene Nilsson, Apr. 1959 (div. 1976); children: Måns, Charlotte; m. Astrid Elisabet Toresson, Sept. 27, 1976; children: Elisabeth, Caroline. MD, U. Lund, Sweden, 1959; PhD, Karolinska Inst., Stockholm, 1966. Cert. specialist in internal medicine and hematology. Resident dept. medicine U. Lund, 1959-61; rsch. assoc. Inst. Med. Cell Rsch. Karolinska Inst., 1961-67, mem. Nobel com., 1988-97, vice chmn. Nobel com., 1994-96, chmn., 1997; resident dept. medicine Karolinska Hosp., 1967-73; assoc. prof. Karolinska Inst. Huddinge (Sweden) U. Hosp., 1973-85; prof. Karolinska Inst. Huddinge (Sweden) Hosp., 1985-97, head dept. medicine, 1985-97; prof. Karolinska Inst., 1998—; cons. hematology and medicine, dept. medicine Huddinge U. Hosp., 1998—. Vis. rsch. assoc. Children's Cancer Rsch. Found., Harvard U. Med. Sch., Boston, 1963-64, 68-69. Editor: Blood Diseases, 1983, 2d edit., 1994, 3d edit., 1997, Multiple Myeloma, 1996, Multiple Myeloma and Related Disorders, 2004; chmn. editl. bd. Jour. Internal Medicine, 1993—; mem. editl. or adv. bd. several sci. jours.; contbr. over 400 articles on hematology and oncology to internat. sci. jours. Recipient Trafvenfelt diploma Swedish Soc. Med. Scis. 1976, A.F. Regnells prize, 1990; Malthes Legat award Norwegian Med. Soc., 1981. Mem. Swedish Soc. Hematology (pres. 1985-86), European Group for Blood and Marrow Transplantation (pres. 1988-90), Internat. Soc. Hematology (councillor 1985—, v.p. 1995-2000), Austrian Soc. for Transplantation, Transfusion and Genetics (hon.), World Marrow Donor Assn. (pres. 2001-02), Swedish Soc. Gene Therapy (pres. 2002-04). Avocations: classical music, tennis, mountain climbing, hunting, ice skating. Home: Hallingsbacken 8 16767 Bromma Sweden Office: Karolinska U Hosp Huddinge Dept Medicine SE-14186 Stockholm Sweden Home Phone: 46 8267969; Office Phone: +46 8 58582439, 46 706655284. Business E-Mail: gosta.gahrton@ki.se.

GAIESKY, VERA LÚCIA VALENTE, biologist, educator; b. Pelotas, Rio Grande do Sul, Brazil, Dec. 6, 1947; d. Clóvis Rodrigues and Zilda da Silva Valente; m. Adalberto Gaiesky, Oct. 3, 1981; children: Luciana Valente, Elisa Valente. PhD in Genetics, UFRGS, Porto Alegre, Brazil, 1984. Prof. UFRGS, 1999—; titular mem. Acad. Brasileira de Ciencias, Rio de Janeiro, 2008. Fellow CNPq, Brasilia, Brazil, 2003—. Contbr. scientific papers. Mem.: Soc. Brasileira de Genetica. Avocation: travel. Office: UFRGS Inst Biosci Dept Genetica Ave Bento Gonçalves 9500 Bl 3 Porto Alegre Rio Grande do Sul 91501-970 Brazil Personal E-mail: vera.valente@bol.com.br.

GAIHA, VISHNU DAS, cardiologist; b. New Delhi, May 2, 1945; arrived in U.S., 1969; MBBS, All India Inst. Med. Scis., 1968. Diplomate Am. Bd. Internal Medicine, Am. Bd. Cardiology, bd. cert. Am. Bd. Interventional Cardiology, 2002. Intern Albert Einstein Med. Ctr., Phila., 1969-70; resident internal medicine Northwestern U. Med. Ctr., Chgo., 1970-72; fellow cardiologist U. Mich. Hosps., Ann Arbor, 1972-74; attending physician active cons. St. Francis Hosp., Evanston, Ill., 1974—. Attending physician, cons. Swedish Covenant Hosp., Rush N. Shore Hosp., 1974—. Fellow Am. Coll. Cardiologists (cert.), Am. Coll. Chest Physicians, Soc. Internat. Cardiology. Office: 800 Austin St Ste 602 Evanston IL 60202-3446 Office Phone: 847-491-1977. Office Fax: 847-491-0949.

GAINES, BARBARA A., pediatric surgeon; MD, U. Va., 1990. Diplomate Am. Bd. Surgery, Am. Bd. Surgery-pediatric surgery, Am. Bd. Surgery-surgical critical care. Resident Vanderbilt Univ., 1998, Children's Hosp. of Pitts., 2000; fellow Univ. of Pitts, 1995. Mem. Pa. Trauma Sys. Found. Recipient Alfred E. Blalock award, Vanderbilt Univ., Travel award, Tolerance Symposium, Young Investigator award, Am. Motility Soc.; named Outstanding Surgeon, Children's Hosp. of Pitts. Fellow: ACS, Am. Acad. of Pediatrics; mem.: Hosp. and Healthsystem Assn. of Pa., Assn. of Women Surgeons, Soc. of Critical Care Medicine (SCCM), Southeastern Surgical Congress, Assn. for Academic Surgery, Surgical Infection Soc., Eastern Assn. for the Surgery of Trauma, Am. Pediatric Surgical Assn. (APSA), Assn. for Surgical Edn., Am. Assn. for the Surgery of Trauma. Office: Childrens Hospital of Pittsburgh of UPMC 1 Childrens Hospital Drive 4401 Penn Ave Pittsburgh PA 15224 Office Phone: 412-692-7280.

GAJARSKI, ROBERT J., cardiologist, educator; b. Plainfield, NJ, Jan. 29, 1962; BS, Wash. U., 1980; MD, U. Okla., 1988. Dir. cardiac intensive care medicine and transplantation U. Mich., 2000, prof. pediat. cardiology, 2000—. Fellow: Am. Coll. Cardiology; mem.: Internat. Soc. Heart and Lung Transplantation, Alpha Omega Alpha. Avocations: hiking, woodworking, piano. Office: L1242 Women's Box 0204 1500 E Med Ctr Dr Ann Arbor MI 48109 Office Fax: 734-936-9470. Business E-Mail: rjgaj@umich.edu.

GAJEWSKI, JAN, engineering educator; b. Warsaw, Oct. 18, 1958; MSc in Engring., Warsaw U. Tech., 1982; PhD, Polish Acad. Sci., 1997. Asst. Józef Pilsudski U. Phys. Edn., 1994—97, asst. prof., 1997—2009, prof., 2009—. Rschr. Inst. Sport, 1983—; sci. cons. Coaching Acad., 2009—. Recipient Sci. Achievement award, Min. Sci. & Higher Edn. Fellow: Polish Soc. Biomechanics; mem.: Polish Soc. Biomed. Engring. Avocations: rock climbing, reading. Office: Marymoncka 34 Warsaw 02-640 Poland Business E-Mail: jan.gajewski@awf.edu.pl.

GALAMBOS, JOHN THOMAS, internist, medical educator; b. Budapest, Hungary, Oct. 29, 1921; came to U.S., 1947; m. Eva G. Cohn; children: Sharon Tobae Galambos McDuff, John Douglas, Michael Robert. BS, U. Ga., 1948; MD, Emory U., 1952. Diplomate Nat. Bd. Med. Examiners, Am. Bd. Internal Medicine, Am. Bd. Gastroenterology. Intern Barnes Hosp., St. Louis, 1952-53; resident U. Chgo. Clinics, 1953-55; dir. gastroenterology teaching program Emory U. Sch. Medicine, Atlanta, 1957-92, dir. gastroenterology labs., 1958-92, dir. div. digestive diseases, 1966-92. Dir. Gastroenterology Clinic Grady Hosp., Atlanta, 1957-92; mem. adv. bd. Nat. Inst. Digestive Diseases, NIH, Washington, 1985-88. Author: Cirrhosis, 1979, Digestive Diseases, 1983; author or co-author 36 book chpts.; contbr. 165 articles to profl. jours. Fellow ACP, Am. Coll. Gastroenterology (pres. 1975), Am. Gastroenterol. Assn., Am. Assn. for Study Liver Diseases, Internat. Assn. for Study Liver Diseases, Alpha Omega Alpha. Republican. Jewish. Avocation: sailing. Office: 95 Collier Rd NW Ste 4075 Atlanta GA 30309-1751 Office Phone: 770-804-0492. Personal E-mail: jgalambos@myway.com.

GALANDIUK, SUSAN, colon and rectal surgeon, educator; b. NYC, Mar. 6, 1957; d. Joseph and Dora (Neu) G.; m. Hiram C. Polk Jr., Dec. 22, 1991. BS cum laude, SUNY, Albany, 1976; MD summa cum laude, Julius Maximilians U., Wuerzburg, Germany, 1982. Diplomate Am. Bd. Surgery, Am. Bd. Colon and Rectal Surgery. Surg. intern Chirurgische Univ. Klinik, Julius Maximilians U., Wuerzburg, Germany, 1982-83, Cleve. Clinic Found., 1983-84, surg. resident, 1984-88; Price fellow in surg. rsch., dept. surgery U. Louisville, 1988-89, colon and rectal surgery fellow dept. surgery, 1989-90, instr. dept. surgery, 1990-91, asst. prof. dept. surgery, 1991-96, assoc. prof., 1996, program dir. sect. colon and rectal surgery, 1999—, prof., 2001—; dir. Price Inst. Surg. Rsch., 2001—; hon. prof. translational surg. rsch. Blizard Inst. Cell & Molecular Sci., 2009—. Presenter in field. Editl. bd. Digestive Surgery, Mayo Clin. Procs., Diseases Colon Rectum, Archives of Surgery; contbr. chpts. to books, articles to profl. jours. Chmn. fund raising com. ARC, Louisville, 1993, 1995—97, bd. dirs., 1997—2000, chmn. bd., 2001—03; bd. mem. Fund for the Arts, 1996—2009; chair med. adv. com. Ky. chpt. Crohn's and Colitis Found. Am., Louisville, 1993—97, 1999—2003. William E. Lower Fellow Thesis prize, Clinic Found., Cleve., 1986. Fellow ACS, AAUP, Am. Soc. Colon and Rectal Surgeons (mem. chmn. rsch. found. young rschrs. com. 1996—, mem. program com. 1994-96, trustee rsch. found., 2001—, membership com., 2000—); mem. AMA, Am. Med. Women's Assn., Am. Soc. Microbiology, Assn. Acad. Surgery, Assn. Women Surgeons, Collegium Internat. Chirurgiae Digestivae, Jefferson County Med. Soc., Ky. Med. Assn. (mem. cancer com.), Louisville Surg. Soc. (pres. 2005), Hiram C. Polk Jr. Surg. Soc., Ohio Valley Soc. Colon and Rectal Surgeons, Priestly Soc., Soc. Surgery of Alimentary Tract, Soc. Am. Gastrointestinal Endoscopic Surgeons, Soc. Surg. Oncology (mem. corp. rels. and issues, govt. affairs coms.), Southea. Surg. Congress (councillor 1997-99), Surg. Infection Soc., Soc. Univ. Surgeons, Am. Soc. Gastrointestinal Endoscopists, Ctrl. Surg. Assn., Western Surg. Assn., Am. Gastroent. Assn., So. Surg. Assn., Am. Gastroenterol. Assn., Am. Soc. Human Genetics, Am. Soc. Clin. Oncology, Assn. Program Dir. in Colon & Rectal Surgery, Surg. Biol. Club, Soc. Pelvic Surgeons (pres. elect, 2010-), Am. Surg. Assn. Greek Catholic. Office: U Louisville Dept Surgery 550 S Jackson St Louisville KY 40202-1622 Office Phone: 502-583-8303.

GALANTE, GUSTAVO E., plastic surgeon; b. Buenos Aires, Apr. 23, 1959; BA summa cum laude, Wabash Coll., 1981; MD, Ind. U. Sch. Medicine, 1985. Cert. Nat. Bd. Med. Examiners, Am. Bd. Plastic Surgery. Internship gen. surgery Loyola U. Med. Ctr., Maywood, Ill., 1985—86, resident plastic surgery, 1986—91; fellow Inst. for Aesthetic & Reconstructive Surgery, Nashville, 1991; pvt. practice Schererville and Valparaiso, Ind., 1992—. Active staff Cmty. Hosp., Munster, Ind., 1992, St. Anthony Med. Ctr., Crown Point, Ind., 1993, Ill. Surg. & Med. Ctr., Munster, 1994; with St. Margaret Mercy Health Care Ctr. Recipient Physicians Recognition award in continuing med. edn., AMA, 1995—2001. Fellow: ACS, Ohio Valley Soc. Plastic and Reconstructive Surgery, Am. Soc. Laser Medicine and Surgery; mem.: Am. Soc. Plastic Surgeons, Phi Beta Kappa, Alpha Omega Alpha. Avocations: music, reading, running, swimming, bicycling. Office: 322 Indianapolis Blvd Ste 103 Schererville IN 46375 also: 1700 Pointe Dr Valparaiso IN 46384 Office Phone: 219-322-3131, 800-721-3244.

GALANTER, EUGENE, psychologist, educator; b. Phila., Oct. 27, 1924; s. Max and Sarah (Honigman) G.; m. Patricia Anderson, Dec. 22, 1962; children: Alicia, Gabrielle, Michelle. AB, Swarthmore Coll., 1950; A.M., U. Pa., 1951, PhD, 1953. From instr. to prof. psychology U. Pa., 1952—59; sr. rsch. fellow Harvard U., 1956—58, Ctr. Advanced Study Behavioral Scis., 1958-59; chmn. dept. psychology U. Wash., 1962-64, prof., 1964-66; Joseph Klingenstein vis. prof. social psychology Columbia U., NYC, 1966-67, prof. psychology, 1967—2007, prof. emeritus, 2007—. Cons. NIH, NSF, also to industry; mem. Coun. for Biology in Human Affairs; chmn. commn. on biology, learning and behavior Salk Inst.; founder Children's Computer Sch., 1980, sold to CompuServe, 1984; founder, chmn. bd. dirs. Children's Progress Inc., 1999—. Author: Plans and Structure of Behavior, 1960, 2d edit., 1986, CD edit., 2005, New Directions in Psychology, 1962, Textbook of Elementary Psychology, 1966, Kids & Computers: The Parents' Microcomputer Handbook, 1983, Kids & Computers: Elementary Programming for Kids in BASIC, 1983, Kids & Computers: Advanced Programming Handbook, 1984; editor: Handbook of Mathematical Psychology, 3 vols., 1963-64, Readings in Mathematical Psychology, 2 vols., 1963-65, Psych Tech Notes, 1988, version 2.1, 1994, 2004, version 2.2 CD, 2004, People, Preferences & Prices, Bentham Sci. Publs., Ltd., Oak Pk., 2010. Served with AUS, 1943-46. Decorated Legion of Merit, Bronze Star Valor, Croix de Guerre with Palm France. Fellow AAAS, APA, Acoustical Soc. Am., NY Acad. Scis.; mem. Eastern Psychol. Assn., Assn. Aviation Psychologists (pres. 1970-71), Human Factors Soc., Internat. Soc. for Psychophysics, Sigma Xi (past chpt. pres.). Achievements include patent in field. Office: Children's Progress Inc 108 W 39th St #1300 New York NY 10018 Office Phone: 212-280-4382, 570-470-1213. Business E-Mail: eg@childrensprogress.com.

GALANTER, MARC, psychiatrist, educator; b. NYC, Sept. 17, 1941; s. Jacob and Ada (Simms) G. BA, Columbia U., 1963; MD, Albert Einstein Coll. Medicine, 1967. Diplomate Am. Bd. Psychiatry and Neurology with added qualifications in addiction psychiatry; cert. Am. Soc. Addiction Medicine. Intern UCLA Hosp., 1967-68; resident in psychiatry Albert Einstein Coll. Medicine-Bronx Mcpl. Hosp. Ctr., 1968-71, fellow in community psychiatry, 1972-73, clin. instr., 1972-74, dir. Drug and Alcohol Cons. Service, 1972-75, career tchr. drug abuse and alcoholism Nat. Inst. on Alcohol Abuse and Alcoholism, Nat. Inst. Drug Abuse, 1973-76, asst. prof., 1974-78, dir. div. alcoholism and drug abuse, 1975-87, assoc. prof., 1978-83, prof. dept. psychiatry, 1983-87; prof. psychiatry, dir. div. alcoholism and drug abuse NYU Sch. Med., 1987—; dir. addiction divsn., rsch. scientist Collaborating Ctr. WHO, 1987-98, dep. dir. Collaborating Ctr., 1998—. Clin. assoc. Lab. Clin. Psychopharmacology, NIMH, Washington, 1970-72; instr. psychiatry residency program St. Elizabeth's Hosp.; presenter at profl. confs. U.S., Can., Thailand, Germany, Japan, India, Kenya and Italy; chmn. Nat. Conf. on Alcohol and Drug Abuse Edn., 1977; program chmn. Internat. Conf. Med. Edn. in Alcohol and Drug Abuse, WHO and Assn. Med. Edn. and Rsch. in Substance Abuse, 1982, founder, pres., 1976-77; dir. Lab. Alcoholism and Drug Abuse WHO. Editor: Ofcl. Sci. Procs. of Nat. Coun. on Alcoholism, 1978-80, Alcohol and Drug Abuse in Medical Education, 1980, (book series) Currents in Alcoholism, 1979, 80, 81, Recent Developments in Alcoholism; mem. editl. bd. Am. Jour. Drug and Alcohol Abuse, 1978—; assoc. editor jour. Alcoholism Clin. and Exptl. Rsch., Am. Jour. of Addictions, 1979, Jour. Substance Abuse Treatment, 1995—; co-editor: Advances in the Psychosocial Treatment of Alcoholism, 1984; editor-in-chief Substance Abuse Jour., 1978—; author: Cults: Faith, Health and Coercion, 1989, 2nd edit., 1999, Network Therapy for Alcohol and Drug and Abuse, 1993, 2nd edit., 1999, Spirituality and the Healthy Mind, 2005. Recipient Psychopharmacology award Am. Psychol. Assn., 1972; Career Tchr. award in drug abuse and alcoholism NIMN, 1973-77, Organon Tchg. awad Am. Psychiat. Assn., 1999; ann. Book award Commonwealth Fund, 1978-82, Macarthur medal Assn. Med. Edn. and Rsch., 1994. Fellow Am. Psychiat. Assn. (life, chmn. panel on alcoholism, nat. task force on psychiat. treatment 1983—, mem. task force on cults 1977-80, mem. com. on alcoholism, chmn. com. on addiction edn. 1992—, chmn. com. on religion 1985-90, Gold Achievement award 1993, bd. dirs. pub. group 1998--, Seymour Vastermark Edn. awrd 2002), Am. Soc. on Addiction Medicine (bd. dirs. 1986—, 2002—, sec. 1995-97, pres. elect 1997-99, pres. 1999-2001); mem. AAAS, Internat. Soc. Addiction Medicine (bd. dirs. 1999—), Am. Bd. Psychiatry and Neurology (vice chair com. on added qualifications in addiction psychiatry 1992-98), Rsch. Soc. on Alcoholism (sec. 1983-85), N.Y. State Task Force on Dual Psychiat. and Addictive Disorders (task force chmn. 1986-89, 93), N.Y. Psychiat. Soc., Am. Acad. Addiction Psychiatrists (v.p. 1987-89, pres. 1991-93, bd. dirs. 1986—, Founders award 2004), Nat. Inst. Alcohol Abuse and Alcoholism (Nat. Adv. Coun. 1997—). Office: Div Alcoholism & Drug Abuse NYU School of Medicine 550 First Avenue New York NY 10016 Office Phone: 212-887-4093, 212-263-6960. Business E-Mail: marcgalanter@nyu.edu.

GALARNYK, IHOR ANTON MICHAEL, psychiatrist, educator; MD, McGill U., Montreal, Quebec, 1982. Lic. Calif., 1988, diplomate Am. Bd. Psychiatry and Neurology-psychiatry, 1990, Am. Bd. Psychiatry and Neurology-child and adolescent psychiatry, 1991, Am. Bd. Psychiatry and Neurology-addiction psychiatry, 2003, Am. Bd. Psychiatry and Neurology-geriatric psychiatry, 2006. Intern Univ. Hawaii, resident psychiatry, 1983—85; fellow child and adolescent psychiatry McLean Hosp., Boston, 1985—87; assoc. clin. prof. psychiatry Loma Linda Univ.; hosp. affiliations include Eisenhower

Med. Ctr., Ronald Reagan UCLA Med. Ctr. Office: Eisenhower Medical Center Ste 308 42700 Bob Hope Dr Rancho Mirage CA 92270 Office Phone: 760-341-8341.

GALASKO, GAIL T., pharmacologist, educator; d. David I. Galasko and Rose Shames. BSc with honors, U. Witwatersrand, Johannesburg, 1963, MSc, 1965; PhD, Queen Mary Coll., U. London, 1970. Lectr., sr. lectr., assoc. chair U. Witwatersrand, 1972—89; rsch. assoc. prof. U. Va., Charlottesville, 1989—94; assoc. prof., sect. head pharmacology SIU Sch. Dental Medicine, Alton, Ill., 1994—2005; prof. Fla. State U. Coll. Medicine, Tallahassee, 2005—, yr. 2 dir., 2008—. Vis. scientist Weizman Inst. Sci., Rehovot, Israel, 1981; vis. prof. W.Va. U., Morgantown, 1972—73. Contbr. articles to profl. publs. Chmn. women, scis. South African Women's Bur., South Africa, 1980—89; chair Zonta Club Alton Wood River, Ill., 2004—05. Fellow: Gemmological Assn. Gt. Britain; mem.: ITC (pres. coun. number 1 South Africa region 1979—80), Johannesburg Toastmistress Club (pres. 1976), Zonta, Hadassah (life). Achievements include patents for insulin mediator. Avocations: reading, travel. Office: Fla State University Coll Medicine 1115 W Call St Tallahassee FL 32306 Business E-Mail: gail.galasko@med.fsu.edu.

GALBO, HENRIK, medical educator; b. Copenhagen, May 5, 1946; s. Hans and Else Galbo; m. Benedicte Fritzbøger, June 21, 1985; children: Julie, Christoffer, Thomas. MD, U. Copenhagen, Copenhagen, 1971. Cert. specialist internal medicine & rheumatology Ministry Health, 1993. Rsch. asst. Inst. Exptl. Immunology, U. Copenhagen, 1971—72; asst. prof. Dept. Med. Physiology, U. Copenhagen, 1972—76, assoc. prof., 1976—86, chmn., 1984—86; various clin. positions U. Hosps., Copenhagen, 1985—95; chief dr. Dept. Rheumatology,Copenhagen U. Hosp., 1996—; prof. human pathophysiology Med. Faculty, 1995—2002; head human biology edn. Faculty Health Scis. U. Copenhagen, 1995—2005, prof. internal medicine & rheumatology, 2002—. Vice chmn. Internat. Rsch. Group on the Biochemistry of Exercise, 1985—2000; cons. Diabetes Rsch. Inst., Novo Nordic A/S, Copenhagen, 1987—93; vice chmn. The Copenhagen Muscle Rsch. Ctr., 1995—2001, chmn., 2004—09; panel mem. Nato's Advanced Study Institute, Brussels, 1997—98, Nato's Life Sci. Tech. Panel, 1999—2002. Recipient Silver medal, U. Helsinki, 1991, Citation award, Am. Coll. Sports Medicine, 2003, Honour award, Internat. Rsch. Group on the Biochemistry of Exercise, 2003. Home: Prins Valdemars Vej 44 Gentofte 2820 Denmark Office: Rigshospitalet Blegdamsvej Copenhagen 2100 Denmark Office Phone: (45) 40466267. Office Fax: (45) 35457568. Business E-Mail: hga@sund.ku.dk.

GALBRAITH, WILLIAM BRUCE, internist, educator; b. Romeo, Mich., Oct. 21, 1930; s. Bruce McKenzie and Helen Athelene (Stringham) G.; m. Jo Anne Fetterly Ames, June 27, 1953; children: Elise, Susan, Scott. BS, Ariz. State U., 1953; MD, George Washington U., 1957. Diplomate Am. Bd. Internal Medicine. Internship Good Samaritan Hosp., Phoenix, 1957-58; residency U. Iowa Hosps. and Clinics, Iowa City, 1958-61; instr. internal medicine U. Iowa Coll. Medicine, Iowa City, 1961-63, asst. prof., 1963-65, dir. gen. medicine tng. program, 1994-96, assoc. internal medicine, 1994-95; prof. clin. internal medicine U. Iowa, Iowa City, 1995—98, prof. emeritus, 1998—; owner Internists P.C., Cedar Rapids, Iowa, 1965-93, pres., 1986-93, Henrys Fork Vill. Water Co., 2003—. Bd. dirs. Am. Bd. Internal Medicine, Phila., 1992-96. Trustee Mercy Med. Ctr., Cedar Rapids, 1997—2009, Meth-Wick Cmty., 1998-2008, chair, 2005-2007, trustee, Mercy Med. Ctr. Found., 2011-; founding chmn. Cmty. Health Free Clinic, Cedar Rapids, 2002-06. Fellow ACP/ASIM (gov. for Iowa 1979-83, Laureate award 1988, Master 1997). Avocation: fly fishing. Personal E-mail: WGalbra66@aol.com.

GALDAMES, IVAN SUAZO, biology professor; b. Rancagua, Oct. 31, 1973; PhD, UNIFESP, 2009. Assoc. prof. U. De Talca, 2003—. Assoc. prof. and head dept. basic & biomedical scis., 2008—11. Grant, CONICYT. Mem.: Panamerican Assn. Anatomy. Office: Avda Lircay S/N Talca Talca Maule 3480981 Chile

GALDURÓZ, JOSÉ CARLOS FERNANDES, psychiatrist, researcher; b. Sorocaba, São Paulo, Brazil, Feb. 6, 1958; s. José Fernandes and Anna Rosa Maiello Galduróz; m. Ruth Ferreira Santos; 1 child, Rodrigo Martins. PhD, UNIFESP, São Paulo, 1996. Psychiatrist Hosp. Servidor Público Estadual, 1988. Head dimesad, discipline medicine and sociology drug abuse UNIFESP, São Paulo, 2006—, Assoc. prof. psychobiology, 2006—. Achievements include research in studies on the effects of polyunsaturated fatty acids (PUFAs). Office: UNIFESP Napoleão Barros 925 São Paulo 04024-002 Brazil Office Fax: 55 11 5084-2793. Business E-Mail: galduroz@psicobio.epm.br.

GALE, ARNOLD DAVID, pediatric neurologist, consultant; b. Chgo., Nov. 2, 1949; s. Benjamin and Revelle Frances (Steinman) G.; m. Sharon Ann Stone, 1997. AB summa cum laude, Stanford U., 1971; MD, Johns Hopkins U., 1976. Diplomate Am. Bd. Pediat., Nat. Bd. Med. Examiners; med. lic., Calif. Resident in pediat. Mass. Gen. Hosp., Boston, 1976-78; postdoctoral fellow Johns Hopkins Hosp., Balt., 1978-79, resident in neurology, 1979-82; asst. prof. pediat. and neurology George Washington U. Sch. Medicine, Washington, 1982-89; dir. neurology tng. program Children's Hosp. Nat. Med. Ctr., Washington, 1982-89; clin. assoc. prof. neurology, neurological scis. and pediat. Sch. of Med. Stanford U., Stanford, Calif., 1989—; med. info. officer Muscular Dystrophy Assn., Tucson, 1992—. Cons. neurologist Vaccine Injury Program U.S. Dept. HHS, Rockville, Md., 1989—, Inst. Vaccine Saftey, Bloomberg Sch. Pub. Health Johns Hopkins U., Balt., 1998—, Anthrax Vaccine Expert Com., 1999—; mem. adv. panel FDA, Rockville, 1983—89; vis. lectr. U. Pitts. Sch. Medicine, 1981—89; cons. Office Human Rsch. Protection U.S. Dept. Health and Human Svcs., 2003—; cons. Brighton Collaboration, Ctrs. for Disease Control, Atlanta, 2003—; mem. Clin. Expert Immunization Com. US Dept. Health and Human Svcs., Rockville, Md., 2003—; cons. Federal Trade commn., Washington, 2008—. Author: Pediatric Emergency Medicine, 1989; contbr. articles to profl. jours. Support group coord. Muscular Dystrophy Assn., San Jose, Calif., 1989—; mem. Pres.'s Com. Employment of People Disabilities, Washington, 1992—; med. adv. bd. Multiple Sclerosis Soc., Santa Clara, Calif., 1990—; v.p. Muscular Dystrophy Assn., Tucson, 1992-94, bd. dirs., 1993-96; med. vol. disaster preparedness, Dept Pub. health, Santa Clara County, Calif., 2005-. Recipient Nat. Rehab. award, Allied Svcs., Scranton, Pa., 1994, Exceptional Civilian Svc. award, US Dept. Defense, 2004, Adminstrs. citation, Health Resources and Svcs. Adminstrn., 2004, Heritage award, Johns Hopkins U., 2005. Fellow Am. Acad. Pediat.; mem. Am. Acad. Neurology, Am. Soc. Neurol. Investigation (founding mem.), Am. Acad. Immunotherapy, Child Neurology Soc., Calif. Children's Lobby, Nat. Alumni Coun. (Johns Hopkins U.), Phi Beta Kappa, Alpha Omega Alpha. Jewish. Avocations: writing, travel. Office Fax: 408-261-9969.

GALGUT, PETER NEIL, periodontist; b. Pretoria, Transvaal, South Africa, Dec. 30, 1946; s. Harry and Pondy (Kusner) G.; m. Harriet Batami Sher, Aug. 19, 1971; children: Resa, Saul. BDS, U. Witwatersrand, South Africa, 1971; MSc, U. London, 1982, MPhil, 1993, MFGDP, 1993, MRD.RCS, 1994, Diploma in Dental Homeopathy, 1998; PhD, U. Leeds, 2002. Cert. witness expert Cardiff U., 2006. Gen. practice dental surgeon, London, 1971-81; dir. Sch. Dental Hygiene Univ. Coll. Hosp., London, 1983-90, rsch. fellow, 1992—2001; sr. rsch. fellow Eastmans Dental Inst., London, 1993—2005; lectr. U. London, 1993—; pvt. practice periodontist London, 1993—. Del. to nat. coun. Gen. Dental Practitioners Assn., UK, 1974-82; European coord. clin. trials, cons. in trial validation for clin. trials in oral hygiene products and regulatory approval for internat. pharm. cos., 1994-97. Author: (with others) Periodontics: Current Concepts and Treatment Strategies, 2001; contbr. numerous articles to profl. publs. Mem. coun., hon. sec., chmn. NWRS, London, 1988-96. Named UK Nat. Dentist of Yr., 2010; fellow, Higher Edn. Authority, 2007. Mem. Royal Coll. Surgeons (restorative dentristry), Brit. Dental Assn. (meetings sec. Middlesex and Hertfordshire br. 1986-90, chmn. Hendon sect. 1992-93), Brit. Soc. Periodontology, Am. Acad. Periodontology, Internat. Acad. Periodontology, Western Soc. Periodontology, Inst. Tchg. and Learning. Jewish. Avocations: photography, music, walking. Office: 26 Pembroke Hall Mulberry Close NW4 1QW London England Office Phone: 0208 2028360, 4402082030949. Business E-Mail: png@periodontal.co.uk, peter@periodontal.co.uk, admin@periodental.co.uk.

GALINSKY, DAVID E., physician, internist; MD, Temple U., Phila. Diplomate Am. Bd. Internal Medicine, 1998, cert. geriat. 2005. Intern Upstate Med. Ctr., Syracuse; resident Med. Coll. Pa.; cons. geropsychiatric unit Belmont Ctr., phil.; med. dir. Simpson House, Main Line Health Ctr., Shannondell; staff Lankenau Med. Ctr., 1993—, attending physician main line healthcare ctr. Bd. dir. sr. svcs. Simpson House; med. dir. Heal Program. Co-author: (publ.) Pneumonia following influenza in an elderly population, 1980, Digoxin Levels as predictors of toxic arrhythmias in the aged, 1981, Incidence of previously unsuspected tuberculosis discovered by mandated screenings of potential long term care facility employee, 1981, Vascular Medicine, 1985, Study of a Decision Tool for Chemotherapy in the Aging Population, 2008. Named one of the Top Doctors in Geriatric Medicine, Main Line Today, Phila. Mag., the Top Doctors, 2002, 2004, 2011. Mem.: ACP, Del. Valley Geriatric Soc., Am. Geriatric Assn. Office: Lankenau Medical Center Main Line Health Center 10000 Shannondell Dr Eagleville PA 19408 Office Phone: 866-225-5654.

GALL, CAROLIN, psychologist, researcher; b. 1982; Diploma in Psychology, Humboldt U., Berlin, 2004; PhD in Neurovisual Rehab., U. Magdeburg, 2010. Rschr. NovaVision AG, Ctr. Excellence Vision Therapy, Magdeburg, 2003—05, InnoMed, Network Neuromedical Engring., Magdeburg, Saxony-Anhalt, Germany, 2005—07; head group applied neuropsychology Inst. Med. Psychology, U. Magdeburg, Germany, 2007—. Achievements include research in neurovisual rehabilitation opportunities for cerebrally damaged patients with partial visual field loss and estimation of quality of life in patients with neuroopthalmologic disorders. Office: Inst Med Psychology Leipziger Str 44 Magdeburg Saxony-Anhalt 39120 Germany Business E-Mail: carolin.gall@med.ovgu.de.

GALL, ERIC PAPINEAU, internist, educator; b. Boston, May 24, 1940; s. Edward Alfred and Phyllis Hortense (Rivard) Gall; m. Katherine Theiss, Apr. 20, 1968; children: Gretchen Theiss, Michael Edward. AB, U. Pa., 1962, MD, 1966. Diplomate Am. Bd. Internal Medicine, 1972, Am. Bd. Rheumatology, 1974. Asst. instr. U. Pa., Phila., 1970-71, post doctoral trainee, fellow, 1971-73; from asst. prof. to prof. internal medicine U. Ariz., Tucson, 1973—94, prof. surgery, 1983-94, prof. family/community medicine, 1983-94, chief rheumatology allergy and immunology, 1983—94, dr. arthritis ctr., 1986-94, prof. clin. medicine, 2010—; interim dir. Ariz. Arthritis Ctr., 2010—; prof. medicine Rosalind Franklin Univ. Medicine & Sci., The Chgo. Med. Sch., North Chicago, Ill., 1994—2009, emeritus prof. medicine, 2010—, prof. microbiology and immunology, 1994—2009, chmn. dept. medicine, 1994—2009, chief rheumatology divsn., 1994-98, 2005—09, assoc. dean clin. affairs, 1996-97, dir. metabolic bone unit, 1998—2007; prof. medicine Scholl Coll. Podiatric Medicine, 2007—09. Author, editor: Rheumatoid Arthritis: Illustrated Guide to Path DX and Management of Rheumatoid Arthritis, 1988, Rheumatic Disease: Rehabilitation and Management, 1984, Primary Care, 1984; editor: Clinical Care in the Rhematic Diseases, 1996; contbr. articles to profl. jours. Chmn. med. and sci. com. Arthritis Found., Tucson, 1979—81; mem. Ill. Partnership Arthritis; chair profl. edn. task force Ill. Dept. Pub. Health, 2001—08. Major M.C. US Army, 1968—70. Decorated Bronze Star medal, Army Commendation medal. Master: ACP (coun. Ill. chpt. 1995—, Laureate award 2002), Chgo. Inst. Medicine, Am. Coll. Rheumatology (founding fellow 1986, founding chair ednl. materials com. 1986—96, edn. coun. 1991—96, bd. dirs. 1992—95, chmn. rehab. sect. 1992—95, master 2005); mem.: AMA (rep. sect. on med. schs. 1995—2002), Lake County Med. Soc. (treas. 1998—99, sec. 2000—01, pres. 2002—03), Ill. Med. Soc. (del. 2002—09), Assn. Profs. Medicine, Arthritis Found. (nat. vice chmn. 1982—83, chmn. profl. edn. com. 1996—2001, trustee Greater Chgo. chpt. 1997—, bd. dirs. 1997—, exec. com. 1998—, treas. 2003—06, sr. vice chmn. 2006—07, chmn. 2008—09, blue ribbon com. on quality of life, pub. health com. 2010—, chair 2011—), Ctrl. Soc. Clin. Investigation, Inst. Medicine Chgo., Am. Fedn. Clin. Rsch., Am. Assn. Med. Colls., Arthritis Health Professions Assn. (nat. pres. 1982—83, Addie Thomas Disting. Svc. award 1988, Star award 2005), Alpha Epsilon Delta, Alpha Omega Alpha (counselor Chgo. Med. Sch. chpt. 1995—2009, regional counselor 1998—2004, nat. bd. dirs. 2006—09), Sigma Xi. Roman Catholic. Avocation: photography. Office: 7671 E Knollwood Cir Tucson AZ 85750 also: Arthritis Ctr University Az 1501 N Campbell Ave Tucson AZ 85724 Office Phone: 520-626-3618. Business E-Mail: egall@mail.arizona.edu, egall@aol.com.

GALL, JOSEPH GRAFTON, biologist, researcher, educator; b. Washington, Apr. 14, 1928; s. John Christian and Elsie (Rosenberger) G.; m. Dolores Marie Hogge, Sept. 17, 1955 (div. 1982); children: Lawrence, Barbara.; m. Diane Marie Dwyer, July 17, 1982. BS in Zoology, Yale U., 1949, PhD, 1952. Faculty U. Minn., 1952-63, prof., 1963; prof. biology and molecular biophysics Yale, 1963-83; staff dept. embryology Carnegie Instn., Balt., 1983—, Am. Cancer Soc. prof. developmental genetics, 1984—. Mem. cell biology study sect. NIH, 1963-67, chmn., 1972-75; chmn. bd. sci. counselors Nat. Inst. Child Health and Human Devel., NIH, 1986-90; mem. Yale Corp., 1989-95. Contbr. articles profl. jours. Recipient E.B. Wilson award Am. Soc. Cell Biology, 1983, Wilbur Cross medal Yale U., 1988, V.D. Mattia award Roche Inst. Molecular Biology, 1989, Purkinje medal Czech Acad. Scis., 1999, Lasker-Koshland Spl. Achievement award in Med. Sci., Lasker Found., 2006, Louisa Gross Horwitz prize, Columbia U., 2007. Mem. AAAS (Mentor award for lifetime achievement 1996), Am. Soc. Cell Biology (pres. 1967-68), Genetics Soc. Am., Nat. Acad. Scis., Am. Acad. Arts and Scis., Am. Philos. Soc., Accademia Nazionale dei Lincei, Soc. Developmental Biology (pres. 1984-85, Lifetime Achievement award 2004). Home: 107 Bellemore Rd Baltimore MD 21210-1314 Office: Carnegie Instn Dept Embryology 3520 San Martin Dr Baltimore MD 21218 Office Phone: 410-246-3017. E-mail: gall@ciwemb.edu. *

GALL, STANLEY ADOLPH, immunologist, researcher; b. Bismarck, ND, May 31, 1936; s. Adolph and Wilma Thelma (Nickisch) G.; m. Florence Marie Ketterling, Aug. 17, 1958; children: Stanley, Kathryn Louise, Mark Allan, Thomas Andrew. BA, U. Minn., 1958, MD, 1962. Diplomate Am. Bd. Ob-Gyn. Intern U. Oreg. Hosp., Portland, 1962-63; resident in ob-gyn U. Minn. Hosp., Mpls., 1963-66; asst. prof. ob-gyn U. Miami, Fla., 1968-73; assoc. prof. ob-gyn Duke U. Med. Ctr., Durham, NC, 1973-78, prof., 1968—, dir. divsn. perinatal medicine; prof. ob-gyn, assoc. head dept. ob-gyn U. Ill. Coll. Medicine, 1985-89; prof. U. Louisville, 1989—, chmn. dept. ob-gyn., 1989—2000. Contbr. articles to profl. jours. Capt. M.C., U.S. Army, 1966-68. Fellow ACOG (liaison to Adv. Com. for Immunization Practice); mem. Soc. Gynecol. Oncology, Soc. Gynecol. Investigations, Infectious Diseases Soc. Ob-Gyn, Soc. Maternal Fetal Medicine. Episcopalian. Office: U Louisville Dept Ob-Gyn 550 S Jackson St Louisville KY 40202-1622 Office Phone: 502-561-7447. Business E-Mail: sagall@louisville.edu.

GALLAGHER, J. CHRISTOPHER, medical educator; Cert. English Bd. Internal Medicine, 1969, Am. Bd. Internal Medicine. Intern, medicine and surgery Manchester Royal Infirmary, England, 1965—68; intern Manchester Hosp., England, 1966—68; resident, gen. medicine Leeds U. Hosp., England, 1968—70; endocrine rsch. fellow Mayo Clinic, Rochester, Minn., 1975—77; prof. medicine and chief bone metabolism sect. Creighton U. Med. Ctr. Office: Bone Metabolism Section Creighton U Med Ctr 601 N 30th St Omaha NE 68131-2197 Office Phone: 402-280-4518. Office Fax: 402-280-4517.

GALLAGHER, J. P., hospital administrator; Grad., Princeton U.; MBA, U. Pa. Sr. v.p. Glenbrook Hosp.; joined NorthShore Univ. Health Sys., 2002; sr. v.p. Evanston Hosp., 2004; adminstrv. position Adv. Christ Med. Ctr.; pres. Evanston Hosp. Office: Evanston Hospital 2650 Ridge Ave Evanston IL 60201 Office Phone: 847-570-2000.

GALLAGHER, J. PATRICK, JR., insurance company executive; b. Chgo., 1952; BA in Govt., Cornell U., 1974. From v.p. ops. to pres. Arthur J. Gallagher & Co., Itasca, Ill., 1985—90, pres., 1990—95, pres., CEO, 1995—2006, chmn., pres., CEO, 2006—. Trustee Am. Inst. CPCU; bd. founding dirs. Internat. Ins. Found. Mem. adv. coun. Boys Hope / Girls Hope, Chgo.; mem. bd. adv. Catholic Charities, Chgo. Mem.: Comml. Club Chgo., Executives Club Chgo., Econ. Club Chgo. Office: Arthur J Gallagher & Co Two Pierce Place Itasca IL 60143 *

GALLAGHER, JASON C., medical educator; b. Phila., Apr. 5, 1977; PharmD, Rutgers U., 2001. Clin. assoc. prof. Temple U. Sch. Pharmacy, 2004—. Adj. prof. Drexel U. Sch. Medicine, 2004—. Recipient Golden Apple award, Drexel U. Sch. Medicine. Office: Temple University Sch Pharmacy 33 Philadelphia PA 19140 Business E-Mail: jason.gallagher@temple.edu.

GALLAGHER, MARTIN JOSEPH, neurologist, neuroscientist; s. George Vincent and Gertrude Mary Gallagher; m. Nancy Gail Henis, June 11, 1995. BS in Chemistry, U. Notre Dame, 1989; MD, Wash. U., St. Louis, 1997, PhD in Molecular Biophysics, 1997. Cert. Am. Bd. Psychiatry and Neurology (specialty in clin. neurophysiology), epilepsy monitoring Am. Bd. Clin. Neurophysiology. Vis. scholar Harvard U. Sch. Medicine, Boston, 1992—96; intern in internal medicine Wash. U. Sch. Medicine, St. Louis, 1997—98, resident in neurology, 1998—2001, epilepsy fellow, 2001—02, instr. dept. neurology; asst. prof. dept. neurology, divsn. epilepsy Vanderbilt U. Sch. Medicine, Nashville, 2002—10, assoc. prof. with tenure, 2010—. Recipient Young Investigator award, Am. Epilepsy Soc., 2003, Early Career Physician Scientist award, Am. Epilepsy Soc., Milken Family Found., 2005. Mem.: AMA, Soc. for Neurosci., Am. Acad. Neurology (Dreifuss-Penry Epilepsy award 2010), Am. Epilepsy Soc., Am. Neurol. Assn. Office: Vanderbilt U Med Ctr 465 21st Ave S 6140 MRBIII Nashville TN 37232 Office Fax: 615-322-5517.

GALLAGHER, MARY PATRICIA, pediatric endocrinologist, researcher; b. Nov. 25, 1969; MD, U. Medicine & Dentistry NJ, Newark, 1995. Diplomate Am. Bd. Pediat., Am. Bd. Pediat. Endocrinology. Resident pediat. NY Presbyn. Hosp.-Columbia U. Med. Ctr., 1996—99, clin. fellowship pediat. endocrinology, 1999—2002, attending physician, dir. pediat. endocrine testing. Adv. virtual preceptor dept. pediat. NY Presbyn. Hosp.-Columbia U. Med. Ctr. Achievements include research in assessing changes in bone markers, body composition, and growth parameters in children with congenital adrenal hyperplasia who are treated with growth hormone and GnRH agonists. Office: Columbia Presbyn Med Ctr Divsn Pediat Endocrinology 622 W 168th St PHSE 519 New York NY 10032 Office Phone: 212-305-6559. Office Fax: 212-305-4778.

GALLAGHER, ROLLIN M., psychiatrist, anesthesiologist; b. Boston, 1943; BA, Harvard U.; MD, Boston U., 1970; MPH, Columbia U. Cert. Psychiatry, 1978, Pain Medicine, 2000. Intern in psychiatry Presbyn. Med. Ctr., Denver, 1970—71; resident in epidemiology Dartmouth U., 1973—76; NIH epidemiology fellow Columbia U., 1987—88; assoc. prof. psychiatry and family medicine SUNY, Stony Brook, 1990, founder, dir. clin. pain tchg. prog., U. Vt.; dir. pain medicine prog. Drexel U. Coll. Medicine, Phila.; dir. pain mgmt. Phila. VA Med. Ctr., 2004—; clin. prof. psychiatry, anesthesiology and critical care U. Pa. Sch. Medicine, Phila., 2004—, co-founder, dir. Ctr. for Pain Medicine, Rsch. and Policy, 2005—. Named one of Best

Doctors in America, 2008. Mem.: Am. Pain Found., Am. Acad. Pain Medicine (editor-in-chief Pain Medicine 1998—, pres. 2009—10, Disting. Svc. award 2005), Am. Bd. Pain Medicine (bd. dirs. 2008—11), Nat. Pain Found. (founding bd. mem. 2000—07). Office: Phila VA Med Ctr 3900 Woodland Ave Philadelphia PA 19104 also: Am Acad Pain Medicine 4700 W Lake Glenview IL 60025 *

GALLAGHER, SCOTT FARRELL, surgeon, researcher; s. Farrell John and Mary Jean Gallagher; m. Linda S. Boyer, Sept. 19, 1998; 1 child, Mitchell Scott. BA, Ohio Wesleyan U., 1993; MD, Ohio State U., 1997. Diplomate Am. Bd. Surgery, 2004. Intern U. South Fla. Health, Tampa, 1997—98, resident, 1998—2001, chief resident, 2001—02, asst. prof. surgery, 2004—, jr. faculty fellow in surg. endocrinology, 2005; advanced GI and Bariatric Surgery Fellow U. South Fla. Coll. Medicine, Tampa, 2002—04. Assoc. dir. bariatric surgery divsn. gen. surgery U. South Fla., Tampa, 2005—. Contbr. chapters to books, articles to profl. jours. Eagle Scout; pres. Epsilon Chpt. Housing Corp., Delaware, Ohio, 2004—06; bd. dirs. Delaware, Ohio, 2004—06. Recipient Chrysler Leadership award, Army Reserve Scholar-Athlete award. Mem.: AMA, Assn. for Acad. Surgery, Soc. for Surgery of the Alimentary Tract, Soc. for Am. Gastrointestinal and Endoscopic Surgery, Am. Soc. Bariatric Surgery, Tampa Bay Surg. Soc., Soc. for Laparoendoscopic Surgeons, ACS Candidate & Assoc. Soc. (assoc.), The Pancreas Club, Ohio State Alumni Assn., Alpha Sigma Phi Frat. (life Delta Beta Xi award 2001). Roman Catholic. Avocations: travel, piano. Office: Tampa General Hospital 1 Tampa General Cir Tampa FL 33606-3571 Office Fax: 813-844-1920. Business E-Mail: sgallagh@health.usf.edu.

GALLANT, GREGORY G., orthopedist; Attended, Fairfield U.; MD, U. Conn. Cert. orthopaedic surgery, hand surgery. Resident Univ. Conn. Health Ctr.; fellow in hand surgery Univ. Pa., Pa.; med. staff pres. Doylestown Hosp., Pa., 2009—11, hosp. affiliations include, Abington Meml. Hosp. Named one of Top Doctors, Phila. Mag., 2011. Mem.: Pa. Med. Soc. (interspecialty bd. rep.), Pa. Orthopaedic Soc. (treas.), Bucks County Med. Soc. Avocation: exercise. Office: Doylestown Hospital Orthopaedic Specialty Center 599 W State St Ste 205 Doylestown PA 18901 Office Phone: 215-230-3555.

GALLEGO, LUCIA, medical educator, microbiologist; b. Abejera, Zamora, Spain, Jan. 26; m. Jose Ignacio Duran; children: Almudena Duran, Marina Duran. MD in Medicine and Surgery, Leioa, Bizkaia, Spain, PhD in Medicine and Surgery, 1987. Cert. dr. in medicine Pub. Health, magister in recombinant DNA tech. Prof. microbiology and immunology U. Basque Country, Leioa, 1992—. With cooperation project U. Nat. San Simon, Cochabamba, Bolivia, 2006—; reviewer Internat. Jours. Microbiology & Chemotherapy. Grant, Brit. Coun., 1989—92, Basque Govt., 1997, U. Basque Country, 1999, Ministry Edn. & Univs., 2007. Achievements include research in new carbapenemases and plasmids in Acinetobacter baumannii. Home: Avda Madariaga 5 5° F Bilbao Bizkaia 48014 Spain Office: Univ Basque Country Fac Medicine and Dentistry barrio Sarriena 48940 Leioa Spain Office Phone: 690016388. Office Fax: 34 946013495. Business E-Mail: lucia.gallego@ehu.es.

GALLEHER, GAY, clinical psychologist, artist; b. Delaware, Ohio, Nov. 3, 1946; d. Richard Adair Galleher and Ellen Jean Huntsberger; m. Charles Frost Gould III (div.). MS in Learning Disabilities, Med. Sci. Sch. U. Pacific, San Francisco, 1976; MS in Psychology, Pacific Grad. Sch. Profl. Psychology, Palo Alto, 1983, PhD in Psychology, 1987. Bd. cert. clin. psychologist, bd. cert. diplomate in clin. psychology Am. Bd. Profl. Psychology, lic. psychologist Maine, Calif. Pvt. practice clin. psychologist Gay Galleher PhD, West Bath, Maine, 1990—2000; clin. psychologist USAF, Lakenheath, England, 2001, Maine Gen. Med. Ctr., Waterville, 2002—04; pvt. practice clin. psychologist Gay Galleher PhD, ABPP, Bath, 2004—11. Contbr. articles to profl. jours. Mem.: Am. Bd. Profl. Psychology, Nat. Register Health Svc. Providers, San Francisco Psychotherapy Rsch. Group. Democrat. Congregationalist. Avocations: painting, gardening, interior decorating, old house renovation. Home: 10 State Rd Ste 9 PMB266 Bath ME 04530 Office: Dr Gay Galleher 10 State Rd Ste 9 Bath ME 04530-6020 Office Phone: 207-443-1016. Business E-Mail: gaygalleher@comcast.net.

GALLERY, EILEEN DM, nephrologist; d. Terence and Ellen Gallery; m. Kevin Burrows, Dec. 7, 2008. MBBS, NSW U., Sydney, 1969; MD, Sydney U., 1979. Sr. staff specialist, nephrology Royal North Shore Hosp., Sydney, 1984—, cons. physician, 1984—2009; co-dir., perinatal rsch. group Kolling Inst. Sydney U. RNHS, 2002—09. Contbr. scientific papers to profl. publs. Fellow: Royal Australian Coll. Physicians. Office: Sydney Univ Royal North Shore Hosp Pacific Hwy Saint Leonards NSW 2065 Australia Office Fax: 612 94363719. Business E-Mail: eileeng@med.usyd.edu.au.

GALLI, STEPHEN JOSEPH, pathologist, biomedical researcher; b. Somerville, Mass., Feb. 15, 1947; s. Joseph Marcello and Beatrice Vita Galli; m. Anne Blakeslee Stuart, Mar. 16, 1974; 1 child, David Blakeslee. BA, Harvard Coll., Cambridge, Mass., 1968; BMS, Dartmouth Med. Sch., Hanover, NH, 1970; MD, Harvard Med. Sch., 1973. Diploma Nat. Bd. Med. Examiners. Intern, resident Mass. Gen. Hosp., 1973—77, fellowship, 1977—79; instr. to full prof. pathology Harvard Med. Sch., 1979—99; Mary Hewitt Loveless, MD prof., chair dept. pathology Stanford U. Sch. Medicine, Calif., 1999—, prof. pathology, microbiology and immunology, 1999—. Paul Kallos meml. lectr. Collegium Internationale Allergologicum, Austria, 1996. Contbr. articles to profl. jours., chapters to books. Bd. trustees Cambridge Sch., Weston, Mass., 1995—2003. Recipient Merit award, NIH, 1995, Sci. Achievement award, Internat. Assn. Allergy & Clin. Immunology, 1996; fellow, Karin Gruenbaum Cancer Rsch. Found., 1971—72, Med. Found. Boston, 1977—78. Fellow: Coll. American Pathologists (hon.); mem.: AAAS, Investigation Am. Soc., Accademia Nazionale dei Lincei, Assn. American Physicians, Assn. Univ. Pathologists, Inst. Medicine, American Soc. Clin. Investigative Pathology (pres. 2005—06), American Assn. Immunologists. Achievements include patents in field. Office: Stanford Univ Sch Medicine Dept Pathology 300 Pasteur Dr L235 MC 5324 Stanford CA 94305-5324 Office Phone: 650-723-7975. Office Fax: 650-725-6902. *

GALLIAN, DANTE MARCELLO, healthcare educator; b. Sao Paulo, Brazil, Mar. 28, 1966; Grad., U. Sao Paulo, 1988, PhD, 1992. Dir., prof. U. Fed. São Paulo, 2003—11. Dir. Ctr. Philosophy and History Health Scis. Office: Botucatu 720 Sao Paulo 04023-900 Brazil Business E-Mail: dante.cehfi@epm.br.

GALLICANO, G. IAN, biology professor; b. Wilmington, Del., June 1, 1966; BS, Ariz. State U., 1988, PhD, 1994. Postdoc. fellow U. Chgo., 1995—2000; assoc. prof. Georgetown U. Med. Ctr., 2000—, dir. transgenic shared resource, 2002—10. Sr. editl. bd. mem. Am. Jour. Stem Cells; editl. bd. mem. Jour. Stem Cells. Del. Am. Leading Scientists Office Sci. and Tech., Embassy of France. Recipient Donna Garff Mariott Rsch. award, Am. Heart Assn.; grant, NIH. Mem.: Ctr. Study Sex Differentiation, Soc. Devel. Biology, Am. Soc. Cell Biology (Novel and Newsworthy award). Avocations: baseball, model building. Office: Georgetown University Med Ctr Washington DC 20057 Business E-Mail: gig@georgetown.edu.

GALLIN, JOHN I., federal agency administrator, medical researcher; b. NYC, Mar. 25, 1943; s. Nathaniel Mitchel and Helen (Cohen) Gallin; m. Elaine Barbara Klimerman, June 23, 1966; children: Alice Jennifer, Michael Louis. BA cum laude, Amherst Coll., Mass., 1965, DSc (hon.), 1988; MD, Cornell U. Med. Coll., 1969. Diplomate Nat. Bd. Med. Examiners. Intern medicine NYU Bellevue Hosp. Med. Ctr., NYC, 1969-70, asst. resident, 1970-71; tchg. asst., instr. medicine NYU Sch. Medicine, 1970—81; assoc. lab. clin. investigation Nat. Inst. Allergy & Infectious Diseases (NIAID), NIH, Bethesda, Md., 1971-74, sr. investigator, 1975-91, dir. NIAID divsn. intramural rsch., 1985-94, chief Lab. Host Defenses, 1991—2003, dir. NIH Clin. Ctr., 1994—, assoc. dir. clin. rsch., 1994—2005. Ret. asst. surgeon gen., rear adm. USPHS. Editor: (textbooks) Inflammation, Basic Principles and Clinical Correlates, 1999, Principles of Clinical Research, 2002, 2nd edit., 2007; contbr. articles to profl. jours., chapters to books. Recipient Lifetime Achievement award, Jeffrey Modell Found., 1990, Disting. Svc. medal, USPHS, 1992, Surgeon Gen.'s Exemplary Svc. medal, 1993, Sec.'s award for disting. svc., HHS, 2006; named Physician Exec. of Yr., USPHS, 2001. Master: ACP (Richard & Hinda Rosenthal Found. award 2006); mem.: Inst. Medicine, Soc. Leukocyte Biology (Marie T. Bonazinga Lifetime Achievement award 2002), Am. Assn. Immunologists, Am. Fedn. Med. Rsch., Am. Soc. Clin. Investigation, Assn. Am. Physicians, Infectious Diseases Soc. of America (Squibb award 1987), Am. Clin. & Climatological Assn. Office: NIH Clin Ctr Mark O Hatfield Clin Rsch Ctr 6-2551 10 Center Dr Bethesda MD 20892-1504 Office Phone: 301-496-4114. Office Fax: 301-402-0244. Business E-Mail: john.gallin@nih.gov. *

GALLIN, PAMELA FRANCES, pediatric ophthalmologist; b. NYC, Sept. 26, 1952; d. Martin and Saara (Lang) Gallin; children: Laura, Abigail, Hilary, Peter; m. Leonard Yablon, Aug. 1997. AB in Biology, Wash. U., St. Louis, 1974, BS in Computers, 1974, MD, 1978. Diplomate Nat. Bd. Med. Examiners, Am. Bd. Ophthalmology. Intern NYU Med. Ctr., NYC, 1978—79; ophthalmology resident Mt. Sinai Med. Ctr., NYC, 1979—82; clin. prof. ophthalmology Columbia U. Coll. Physicians & Surgeons, NYC, 1983—86, instr. clin. ophthalmology, 1986—89, assoc. clin. ophthalmology, 1989—90, asst. prof. clin. ophthalmology, 1990—93, dir. pediatric ophthalmology, 1991—2010, asst. prof. clin. pediatric ophthalmology, 1994—97, assoc. clin. prof. pediatric ophthalmology, 1997—2005, clin. prof. ophthalmology, 2005—, clin. prof. pediat., 2005—. Fellow pediatric ophthalmology Children's Nat. Med. Ctr., Washington, 1982, vis. fellow pediatric ophthalmology Johns Hopkins Med. Ctr., Balt., 1982; fellow pediatric ophthalmology and oncology Columbia Presbyn. Med. Ctr., NYC, 1983; asst. ophthalmologist Beth Israel Med. Ctr., 1983—85, NY Presbyn. Hosp., 1983—86, assoc. ophthalmologist, 1989—90, asst. attending ophthalmologist, 1990—97, assoc. attending ophthalmologist, 1997—; med. staff Wash. Heights-Inwood Ambulatory Care Network, 1990—92, dir. pediatric ophthalmology Fight for Sight Children's Eye Clinic, NYC, 1991—2002, bd. dirs., 1999—2005; examiner Am. Bd. Ophthalmology, 1991—2003; mem. White House Health Care Task Force, 1993. Author: How to Survive Your Doctors Care, 2003; co-author: The Savvy Mom's Guide to Medical Care, 1999; editor: Practical Pediatric Ophthalmology, 2000; contbr. articles to profl. jours., chapters to books. Vol. NYC Eye Care Project, 2004; bd. dirs. Fight for Sight, 1999—2004, Nat. Ctr. Policy Rsch. for Women & Families, 2004—. Recipient Lange award for med. excellence, Wash. U., 1978; named one of Best Doctors in NY Metro Area, Castle Connolly Med. Ltd., 1997—, Best Doctors in America, 2001—, America's Top Ophthalmologists, 2002—, Best Doctors in NY, NY mag.; fellow Heed Ophthalmic Found., 1982—83. Fellow: ACS, Am. Acad. Pediat.; mem.: National Assn. Visually Handicapped (bd. dirs. 1983—), Nat. Soc. Prevent Blindness in America (bd. dirs. 2005—), Manhattan Ophthalmological Soc., Costenbader Soc., Am. Assn. Pediatric Ophthalmology & Strabismus, Am. Acad. Ophthalmology, Tau Beta Pi, Phi Beta Kappa. Office: Edward Harkness Eye Inst Columbia Presbyn Med Ctr 635 W 165th St New York NY 10032-3701 Office Phone: 212-305-5407. Office Fax: 212-305-8082. Business E-Mail: pgallin@columbia.edu.

GALLO, ROBERT CHARLES, research scientist; b. Waterbury, Conn., Mar. 23, 1937; s. Francis Anton Gallo, Louise Mary (Ciancuilli) Gallo; m. Mary Jane Hayes, July 1, 1961; children: Robert, Marcus, Caroline. BA in biology, Providence Coll., 1959, DSc (hon.), 1974; MD, Jefferson Med. Coll., 1963; 28 hon. degrees, Ireland, Peru, Argentina, Germany, Mex. Intern, resident medicine U. Chgo., 1963-65; clin. assoc. med. br. Nat. Cancer Inst. NIH, Bethesda, Md., 1965-68, sr. investigator human tumor cell biology br., 1968-69, head sect. cellular control mechanisms, 1969-72, chief lab. tumor cell biology, 1972—95; founder, dir. Inst. Human Virology, U. Md., Balt., 1996—, dir. Basic Sciences Divsn.; prof. Medicine, Microbiology and Immunology, Sch. Medicine U. Md., Balt. Adj. prof. genetics George Washington U.; adj. prof. biology Johns Hopkins U., Balt., hon. prof. biology, 1985—; hon. prof. medicine Karolinska Inst., Stockholm, 1998—; US rep. to world com. Internat. Comparative Leukemia and Lymphoma Assn., 1981—95; mem. bd. govs. Franco Am. AIDS Found., 1987, World AIDS Found., 1987; sr. cons. HIV/AIDS China CDC, 2005—. Author: (book) Virus Hunting, 1991; author: (or co-author) more than 1,200 sci. papers. With USPHS, 1965—68. Recipient Dameshek award, Am. Hematol. Soc., 1974, CIBA-GIEGY award in biomed. sci., 1977, 1988, Superior Svc. award, USPHS, 1978, Meritorious Svc. medal, 1983, DSM, 1984, First F. Stohlman lecture award, Am. Soc. Hematol., 1979, Albert Lasker award for basic biomed. rsch., 1982, 1986, Abraham White award in biochem., George Washington U., 1983, First Otto Herz award for cancer rsch., Tel Aviv U., 1982, Griffuel prize, Assn. for Cancer Rsch., France, 1983, GM award in cancer rsch., 1984, Gruber prize, Am. Soc. Investigative Dermatology, 1984, Lucy Wortham prize in cancer rsch., Am. Soc. for Surg. Oncology, 1984, Gold medal, Am. Cancer Soc., 1984, Berla Internat Sci. prize, India, 1985, Hammer prize for cancer rsch., 1985, Gairdner prize for biomed. rsch., Can., 1987, spl. award, Am. Soc. Infectious Disease, 1986, Gold Plate award, Am. Acad. Achievement, 1987, Lions Humanitarian award, 1987, Japan prize in sci. and tech., 1988, Ciba Corning award, 1993, 1st Dale McFarlin award for rsch., Internat. Soc. Human Retrovirology, 1994, 1st Gustav Embden award, U. Frankfurt, 1996, Pomesa award, 1996, 1st award, Internat. Soc. Blood Transfusion, 1997, Nomura prize for AIDS and Cancer Rsch, Japan, 1998, Warren Alpert prize, Harvard U., 1998, Paul Erlich award, Germany, 1999, Hero in Medicine award, Can, 2000, Frank Annunzio sci. award, Washington, 2000, Prince Asturias prize, Spain, 2000, 1st award, Ireland C. of C. and USA, 2001, Seminal contbrns. to field of Human Retrovirology award, Internat. Soc. HTLV, 2001, award, Internat. Retrovirology Assn., 2001, World Health award, Pres. M. Gorbachev Found., 2001, Austria, 2001, Archimedes prize in sci., Italy, 2003, Lifetiime Achievement award, Sons of Italy, 2004, Ellis Island Medal of Honor, 2005, Tevi Comet-Wallerstein prize, Bar-Ilan U., Israel, 2005, Servero Ochoa award, 2006, Gold Mercury award, 2006, award, Abbott Labs., 2008, James Joyce award, U. Coll. Dublin, 2009, Dan David prize, Tel Aviv U., 2009; named to Inventor's Hall of Fame, 2004. Mem.: AAAS, NAS, Fedn. for Advanced Edn. in Scis., Am. Fedn. Clin. Rsch., Am. Soc. Microbiology, Am. Assn. Cancer Rsch., Biochem. Soc., Am. Microbiology Soc., Am. Soc. Biol. Chemists, Am. Soc. Clin.Investigation, Internat Soc. Hematology, Inst. Medicine, Royal Acad. Medicine of Spain (hon.), Royal Soc. Medicine (hon.), Royal Soc. Physicians of Scotland (hon.), Royal Soc. Medicine Belgium (sr.), Alpha Omega Alpha. Achievements include being the co-discoverer of the AIDS virus, 1984; discovery of the first and second human retroviruses(1980,82) and Interleukin-2 (IL-2)(1976); development of HIV blood test, 1984; discovery of human herpes virus-6, 1986. Office: 725 W Lombard St Ste S307 Baltimore MD 21201-1009

GALSON, STEVEN KENNETH, pharmaceutical executive, former Surgeon General of the United States; b. Syracuse, NY, July 5, 1956; s. Edgar Leon and Eva Charlotte Galson; m. Jessie Wolfe; three children. BS, Stony Brook U., 1978; MD, Mt. Sinai Sch. Medicine, 1983; MPH, Harvard Sch. Pub. Health, 1990. Diplomate Am. Bd. Preventive Medicine and Pub. Health, Occupl. Medicine. Supr. med. officer Nat. Inst. Occpl. Safety & Health/Ctrs. Disease Ctrl., Cin., 1990-91, dep. dir. divsn. studies devel. & tech. transfer, 1993-94, chief med. sect., 1991-93; chief med. officer office environ., safety & health US Dept. Energy, Washington, 1994-96, chief med. office, counselor office sec., 1996-97; sci. dir., advisor to the adminstr. US EPA, Washington, 1997-98, dir. Office of Sci. Coord. & Policy, 1998—2001; dep. dir. Ctr. Drug Evaluation & Rsch., US FDA, Washington, 2001—05, dir., 2005—07; acting surgeon gen. US Dept. Health & Human Services, Rockville, Md., 2007—09; sr. v.p. Sci. Applications Internat. Corp., 2010; v.p. global regulatory affairs Amgen, Inc., Calif., 2010—. Reviewer Jour. Am. Med. Assn., 1994 ; liaison mem. bd. health sci. policy Inst. of Medicine, mem. forum on Drug Discovery, Develop. and Translation; mem. com. environ. health policy U.S. Dept. Health & Human Services; former mem. Nat. Bd. Med. Examiners. Contbr. article to Lancet.; peer reviewer for med. jours. Capt. USPHS. Recipient Achievement award Pub. Health Svc., 1991, unit commendation award, 1991, foreign duty svc. ribbon, 1993, Sec. Energy Gold awards (three). Office: Amgen Inc One Amgen Center Dr Thousand Oaks CA 91320-1799 *

GALTON, VALERIE ANNE, endocrinologist, educator; b. Louth, Eng., May 6, 1934; came to U.S., 1959; d. Wilfrid and Eileen (Watson) Hamilton; m. Michael Galton, Aug. 26, 1956 (dec. 1968); children: Ian Andrew, Kenneth Anthony. BSc with honors, U. London, 1955, PhD, 1958., 1967-75; Research assoc. Nat. Inst. Med. Research, Mill Hill, London, 1955-58; research assoc. Med. Sch., Harvard U., Boston, 1959-61; instr., then asst. prof. Dartmouth Med. Sch., Hanover, N.H., 1961-66, assoc. prof., 1968-75, prof., 1975—. Cons. NIH, Bethesda, Md., 1973-98. Mem. editl. bd. Endocrinology, 1982-85, Am. Jour. Physiology, 1982-85, 95—; contbr. articles to profl. jours. NIH grantee, 1962— Mem. Am. Thyroid Assn., Endocrine Soc. Home: 57 Jenkins Rd Lebanon NH 03766-2002 Office: Dartmouth Med Sch Lebanon NH 03756 Office Phone: 603-650-7735. Business E-Mail: val.galton@dartmouth.edu.

GALUN, ESRA AMIEL, plant genetics educator; b. Leipzig, Germany, Apr. 7, 1927; arrived in Israel, 1933; s. David Mendel and Erna (Markus) G.; m. Margalith Katz, May 3, 1953; children: Eithan, Ehud. MSc, Hebrew U., Jerusalem, 1954, PhD, 1959; postdoctoral study, Calif. Inst. Tech., 1962. Rsch. asst./rsch. assoc. Weizmann Inst. Sci., Rehorot, Israel, 1953-60, acting head dept. plant genetics, 1956-70, sr. scientist, 1963, assoc. prof., 1968, head dept. plant genetics, 1970-88, prof. biology, 1972, dean Feinberg Grad. Sch., 1974-75, head postdoctoral fellowship program, 1976-80, dean faculty biology, 1988-91, Irene and David Schwartz prof. plant genetics; prof. plant genetics Weizmann Inst. Scis., Rehovot, Israel. Chmn. tchg. com. for life scis. Feinberg Grad. Sch., Weizmann Inst. Sci., 1972-73; mem. Nat. Coun. R & D, 1986-89, chmn., 1982-84; disting. vis. scientist Roche Inst. Molecular Biology, Nutley, N.J., 1985; Fulbright rsch. fellow divsn. biology Calif. Inst. Tech., Pasadena, 1960-62; lectr./presenter profl. confs.; cons. in field; mem. sci. adv. bd. DNA Plant Tech. Corp., N.J., 1982-89; mem. planning com. Internat. Potato Ctr., Lima, Peru, 1990. Author: Pollination Mechanism, Reproduction and Plant Breeding, 1977, Transgenic Plants, 1997, Manufacture of Medical and Health Products by Transgline Plants, 2001, Transposable Elements, 2003, RNA Silencing, 2005, Plant Patterning, 2007, Phytohormone and Plant Patterning, 2010; contbr. numerous articles to sci. publs.; patentee method for removal of heavy elements from indsl. effluents by hyphal fungi biomass, process for producing arrested cells, prodn. of cucumber seeds; holder several breeder's rights certs. Maj. Israel Def. Army, 1974-80. Recipient Armando Kaminitz award for Achievements in Agrl. Rsch., 1984; rsch. grantee various orgns., most recently U.S. AID, Peru, 1984-87, 87-89, Germany-Israel/Nat. Coun. R & D, 1987-90, EEC/Nat. Coun. R & D, 1987-90, Nat. Coun. Vegetable Growers in mex. and ZERAIM Seed Co., Gedera, Israel, annually, 1987—2001. Mem. Am. Soc. Plant Physiologists, Internat. Assn. Plant Tissue Culture, Internat. Soc. Plant Molecular Biology (bd. dirs. 1987-91), Botany Soc. Israel, Genetics Soc. Israel (hon. life mem. founding com. 1958-65, chmn. 1966-67), Israel Soc. Plant Tissue Culture and Molecular Biology (hon., chmn. 1988-90). Jewish. Avocations: music, history, israeli archaeology. Office: Weizmann Inst Sci Dept Plant Scis 76100 Rehovot Israel Home Phone: 97289468103; Office Phone: 97289342637. E-mail: esra.galun@weizmann.ac.il.

GALVIN, MATTHEW REPPERT, psychiatry educator; b. Seattle, July 24, 1950; s. Ralph B. and Virginia (Reppert) G.; children: Joseph, Sarah, Erin; m. Margaret Gaffney. AB with honors, Ind. U., 1975, MD, 1979. Diplomate Am. Bd. Adolescent Psychiatry, Am. Bd. Psychiatry and Neurology. Asst. prof. Ind. U. Med. Ctr., Indpls., 1984-95, clin. assoc. prof., 1995—. Staff psychiatrist Larue Carter Meml. Hosp., Indpls., 1984-88, assoc. dir. youth svcs., 1988, acting dir., 1988-90; child psychiatrist Riley Child Psychiatry Svcs., Indpls., 1990-98, Pleasant Run Children's Home, 1998-2001, St. Vincent Stress Ctr., 2001-06, Children's Bur. Inc., 2001—, Ind. Sch. for the Blind, 2003—; vol. faculty Riley Child Psychiatry and Ind. U. Med. Ethics Program. Author: Ignatius Finds Help, A Story about Psychotherapy, 1988, Otto Learns About Medicine, 1988, 3d edit., 2001, A Story About Grown-ups Helping Children, 1988, Clouds and Clocks, A Story for Children Who Soil, 1989, 2 edit., 2007, The Otters of Conscience-Berg, 2005, Carlotta Learns About Her Medicine, 2005, 2d edit., 2007, Grandma Grady's Grade-A Gray Day, 2007, The Lyric of Lafracoth, 2008; co-author: Sometimes Y, A Story for Families with Gender Identity Issues, 1993, The Conscience Celebration, 1998, Right vs. Wrong: Raising a Child with a Conscience, 2000, Rachel and the Seven Bridges of Conscience-Berg, 2002, A Guide to Conscience, 2007; editorial staff Conscience Works; contbr. articles to profl. jours. With M.C., U.S. Army, 1970-73, Vietnam. Fellow Am. Psychiat. Assn.; mem. Am. Acad. Child Adolescent Psychiatry, Am. Soc. Adolescent Psychiatry, Nat. Alliance Against Mental Illness (affiliate), Ind. Coun. Child and Adolescent Psychiatry (treas. Indpls. chpt. 1986-89, pres. elect 1989-90, pres. 1990-91). Office Phone: 317-844-0055.

GALVIN, ROBERT STEVEN, healthcare services executive; b. Cleve., July 28, 1950; BA, U. Pa., 1972, MD, 1981; MBA, Boston U. Sch. Mgmt., 1995. Diplomate American Bd. Internal Medicine. Intern, resident internal medicine Boston Med. Ctr., 1981—84; various positions GE, 1990—96, exec. dir. health services, chief med.officer, 1996—2010; CEO Equity Healthcare, Blackstone Group LP, 2010—. Co-founder Leapfrog Group, 1998, chmn. bd. dirs., 2003—05; vice-chair Washington Bus. Group on Health, 2001—04; founder Bridges to Excellence Diabetes Care Link, 2003; adj. prof. medicine Yale U. Sch. Medicine, New Haven. Contbr. articles to profl. jours. Mem. nat. adv. bd. Commonwealth Fund Commn. on Highly Effective Healthcare Sys., Agy. Healthcare Rsch. & Quality, US Dept. Def. Task Force Future of Mil. Health Care; dir. health policy seminar series Robert Wood Johnson Clin. Scholar Program; bd. mem. health care solutions group Vanderbilt U. Med. Ctr., Nashville; past chmn. Mass. Bus. Roundtable Health Care Task Force; bd. dirs. Nat. Commn. Quality Assurance, Nashville Heath Care Coun. Fellow: ACP; mem.: Soc. Med. Administrators, Inst. Medicine. Office: Blackstone Group 345 Park Ave New York NY 10154 Office Phone: 212-583-5000. *

GAMA, PAULO DINIZ DA, neurologist, educator; b. Sorocaba, Brazil, Mar. 25, 1965; Degree, Escola La Salle, 1982; MD in Medicine (hon.), Pontifical Cath. U. São Paulo, Sorocaba, 1990; PhD in Neurology (hon.), U. Sao Paulo, 2009. Specialist in neurology and neurosurgery Sch. Medicine Pontifical Cath. U. Sao Paulo, specialist in neurophysiology Sch. Medicine UNESP Botucatu. With Reference Ctr. for Treatment of Multiple Sclerosis Conjunto Hospitalar Sorocaba; asst. prof. neurology Pontifical Cath. U. Sao Paulo, 2008. Clin. dir. Inst. Cerebro Sorocaba. Mem.: Brazilian Com. Treatment and Rsch. Multiple Sclerosis (bd. mem.), Brazilian Acad. Neurology. Office: R Conde Francisco Matarazzo 58 Sorocaba SP 18030-010 Brazil Office Phone: 55-1532338591. Office Fax: 55-1532110387. Personal E-mail: inst.cerebro@globo.com.

GAMBADAURO, PIETRO, gynecologist, researcher; b. Barcellona Pozzo Gotto, Italy, Nov. 5, 1973; s. Giampiero Gambadauro and Lina La Vena; life ptnr. Malin Ylander. MD in Medicine and Surgery, U. Cattolica del Sacro Cuore, Rome, 1998, degree in Ob-Gyn., 2003. Lic. Italy, 1999, registered Gen. Med. Coun., UK, 2005. Specialist registrar Dept. Ob-Gyn., U. Cattolica Sacro Cuore, 1998—2003, rsch. fellow, 2003—07; clin. rsch. fellow Minimally Invasive Therapy & Endoscopic Tng. Ctr., U. Dept. Ob-Gyn., Royal Free Hosp., London, 2005—06; gynecologist IVI Inst. Valenciano Infertilidad, Barcelona, 2007—. Vis. gynecologist U. Hosp. Puerto Real, Cadiz, Spain, 2001, U. Hosp. Bellvitge, Hospitalet de Llobregat, Barcelona, 2002. Contbr. articles to numerous profl. jours. Specialist Tng. grant, Italian Ministry U., 1998—2003, Leonardo da Vinci fellowship, European Union, 2001, rsch. grant, Italian Ministry U., 2004—07. Master: Italian Assn. Jr. Ob-Gyns. (co-founder to pres. 2003—05); mem.: Brit. Soc. Gynecol. Endoscopy, European Network Trainees Ob-Gyn. Achievements include invention of PC based system for affordable telementoring in gynecological surgery. Avocations: reading, travel, music, fishing, cooking. Office: IVI-Inst Valenciano Infertilidad Ronda General Mitre 14 Barcelona 08017 Spain Personal E-mail: gambadauro@gmail.com. Business E-Mail: pgambadauro@ivi.es.

GAMBHIR, SANJIV SAM, nuclear medicine physician, educator; BS, Ariz. State U., 1983; MD, PhD, UCLA, 1993. Cert. Nuclear Medicine, 1996. Intern UCLA Med. Ctr., 1994, resident, 1995, fellow, 1996; prof. radiology and Bio-X prog. Stanford U., 2003—, chief nuclear medicine divsn., 2003—, dir. molecular imaging prog., 2003—, prof. bioengineering, 2005—. Recipient Taplin award, Western Regional Soc. Nuclear Medicine, 2002, Holst medal, 2003, Disting. Clin. Sci. award, Doris Duke Charitable Found., 2004, Hounsfield medal, Imperial Coll., London, 2006, Tesla medal, UK Royal Coll. Radiologists. Mem.: Inst. Medicine, Am. Soc. Clin. Investigation, Soc. Nuclear Medicine (Paul C. Aebersold award 2006), Soc. Molecular Imaging (Achievement award 2004), Acad. Molecular Imaging (Disting. Basic Sci. award 2004). Office: Stanford U Molecular Imaging Prog E Wing 1st Fl 318 Campus Dr Stanford CA 94305-5427 Office Phone: 650-725-2309. Office Fax: 650-724-4948. E-mail: sgambhir@stanford.edu.

GAMBINO, S(ALVATORE) RAYMOND, lab administrator, educator; b. NYC, Oct. 13, 1926; s. Salvatore Benedict and Rose (Ragona) G.; m. Madeline Russo, Apr. 5, 1953; children: Catherine Rose Garroni, Stephen Raymond. BS, Antioch Coll., 1948; MD, U. Rochester, 1952. Diplomate Am. Bd. Pathology. Dir. labs. Englewood Hosp., NJ, 1961—68; prof. pathology Columbia U., NYC, 1968—82; dir. chemistry labs. Presbyn. Hosp., NYC, 1968—77; dir. labs. St. Luke's-Roosevelt Hosp., 1978—82; chief med. officer, exec. v.p. MetPath, Inc., Teterboro, NJ, 1983—94, exec. v.p., chief med. officer emeritus, 1994—. Adj. prof. pathology Columbia U., N.Y.C., 1983—; mem. Corning (N.Y.) Mgmt. Group, 1984-94; bd. dirs. Ciba-Corning, 1988-94. Co-author: Beyond Normality, 1975; editor: (newsletter) Lab Report for Physicians, 1979-98. Mem. Englewood Cliffs (N.J.) Sch. Bd., 1966-69. Served with USN, 1945-46. Mem. Am. Soc. Clin. Pathologists (editor check sample program 1968-93), Alpha Omega Alpha. Roman Catholic. Avocations: exercise, writing, travel. *

GAMBLE, VANESSA NORTHINGTON, historian, healthcare educator, bioethicist; b. May 20, 1953; BA, Hampshire Coll., 1974; MD, U. Pa., 1983, PhD, 1987. Resident U. Mass. Med. Ctr.; visiting scholar Harvard U. Sch. Pub. Health; assoc. prof. family & comty. medicine U. Mass.; asst. prof. history of medicine, science and family medicine U. Wis., Madison, 1989-93, assoc. prof., 1994—2000; dir. Ctr. for the Study of Race and Ethnicity in Medicine U. Wis. Sch. of Medicine, Madison, 1996—2000; v.p. Div. Comty. & Minority Programs Assn. Am. Med. Colleges, 2000—02; assoc. prof. health policy & mgmt. Johns Hopkins Bloomberg Sch. Pub. Health, 2002—04; dir. Nat. Ctr. Bioethics in Rsch. & Health Care Tuskegee U., 2004—, prof. bioethics & health care, 2004—; prof. med. humanities The George Washington U., 2007—. Adv. bd. Nat. Ctr. Primary Care Morehouse Sch. Medicine; adv. bd. Ctr. Study of Health Disparities Tex. A&M U.; adv. com. Soros Reproductive Health & Rights Fellowship; bd. trustees Ctr. for the Advancement of Health. Health commentator The Tavis Smiley Show, NPR; author: The Black Community Hospital: Contemporary Dilemmas in Historical Perspective, 1989, Germs Have No Color Line: Blacks & American Medicine 1900-1940, 1989, Making a Place for Ourselves: The Black Hospital Movement, 1920-1945, 1995 (Choice mag. Outstanding Academic Book). Chairwoman Tuskegee Syphilis Study Legacy Com., 1996—97. Mem.: Inst. Medicine. Office: c/o George Washington U Sch Medicine & Health Sci 2300 Eye St NW Washington DC 20037 Office Phone: 202-994-0978. Business E-Mail: vngamble@gwu.edu.

GAMBOA, LUCITO G., pathologist; b. Pampanga, Philippines, Jan. 7, 1929; came to U.S., 1952; s. Serapion M. and Jacinta L. Gamboa; m. Sylvia V. Roque, Sept. 18, 1953; children: Richard, Virginia Majer, Debra Jorgensen. MD, U. Santo Tomas, Manila, 1952; MS, U. Colo., 1955. Diplomate Am. Bd. Pathology. Dir. pathology and clin. labs. Edgewater Hosp., Chgo., 1958-69, 80-90; dir. blood bank and sr. pathologist Little Co. of Mary Hosp., Evergreen Park, Ill., 1969-80; mem. staff Ctrl. Valley Gen. Hosp., Hanford, Calif., 1990—. Contbr. numerous articles to profl. jours. Bd. dirs. Chgo. Dist. Tennis Assn., 1973-76. Recipient Disting. Physician award Philippine Med. Soc. Chgo., 1966. Mem. Assn. Philippine Physicians in Am. (pres., founder 1972-74, Disting. Svc. award 1975), Assn. Philippine Pathologists in Am. (pres., founder 1970-72), Dove Canyon Country Club. Avocations: golf, tennis, photography, travel. Office: Ctrl Valley Gen Hosp 1025 N Douty St Hanford CA 93230-3722 Personal E-mail: lgamboamd@aol.com.

GAMBONE, VICTOR, JR., internist, geriatrician; b. Phila., Aug. 28, 1949; s. Victor Emmanuel and Eleanor Joyce (Porambo) G. BS, Pa. State U., 1971, MD, 1975. Diplomate Am. Bd. Quality Assurance and Utilization Rev. Physicians, Am. Bd. Internal and Geriatric Medicine; cert. med. dir. in long term care. Intern, resident in internal medicine U. South Fla., Tampa, 1975-78; pvt. practice medicine internal medicine and geriatrics Dunedin, Fla., 1978—2010; med. dir. Evercare (United Health Group), Oldsmar, Fla., 1996—2010; project coord. Fla. Med. Quality Assurance, Inc., Tampa, 2000—07; chief med. officer Traditions Mgmt., Dunedin, Fla., 2007—10; med. dir. AmeriChoice UnitedHealthcare, Laguna Beach, Calif., 2010—11, Nat. Clin. United Health Care Medicare and Retirement, Santa Ana, 2011—. Med. dir. Hospice Care, Inc., Pinellas County, 1982—86; chmn. dept. internal medicine Mease Health Care, Dunedin, Fla., 1989; med. dir. Stratford Ct. Health Ctr., Palm Harbor, Fla., 1991—2010, St. Mark Village, 1993—2010, Mease Continuing Care, Dunedin, Fla., 1993—2007, Largo Health Care Ctr., 1999—2007, Spanish Gardens Nursing Ctr., Dunedin, Fla., 1994—98, East Bay Nursing Ctr., 1996—2005, Sylvan Health Ctr., 1996—2002, Manor Care Nursing Ctr., Dunedin, Fla., 1996—2001, Bayview Nursing Pavillion, Clearwater, 1996—99, Arbors of Safety Harbor, 1997—98, Mariner Health Belleair, 1997—98, Sabal Palms Health Care Ctr., Largo, Fla., 1997—99, Morton Plant Rehab. Ctr., 1998—2000, Drew Village Rehab. and Nursing Ctr., Clearwater, Fla., 1998—99, Oak Manor Village, Largo, Fla., 1999, Encore Sr. Village, Clearwater, Fla., 1999—2004. Author: Post Operative Recall of Intra-Operative Events, 1975 (rsch. award U. Miami Med. Sch.). Fellow: ACP; mem.: AMA, Calif. Longterm Care Medicine, Fla. Med. Dirs. Assn. (pres. 2003—05, chmn. bd. dirs. 2006—09), Am. Geriatrics Soc., Am. Med. Dirs. Assn. Home: 1504 Skyline Dr Laguna Beach CA 92651

GAME, DAVID AYLWARD, physician; b. Adelaide, Australia, Mar. 31, 1926; s. Tasman Aylward and Clarice Mary (Turner) G.; m. Patricia Jean Hamilton, Dec. 8, 1949; children: Ann, Philip, Timothy, Ruth. MB, BS, U. Adelaide, 1949. Resident Royal Adelaide Hosp., 1950, Outpatient Registrar, 1951; gen. practice medicine Adelaide, 1953-96. Chmn. Eastern Region Geriatric and Rehab. Adv. Com., 1976-83; chmn. Cen. Ea. Health Adv. Com., 1983-86. Mem., chmn. social welfare coun. Diocese of Adelaide; chmn. Anglican Cmty. Svcs. Coun., 1989-95; mem. standing com. Synod Diocese Adelaide, Ch. of Eng., 1966-79, 81-84. Decorated officer Order of Australia, knight of grace Sovereign Order St. John of Jerusalem. Fellow Australian Med. Assn., Royal Australian Coll. Gen. Practitioners (chmn. fed. coun. 1969-72, pres. elec. 1972-74, pres. 1974-76, censor in chief, 1976-80), Royal Coll. Gen. Practitioners (fellow ad eudem), Hong Kong Coll. Gen. Pracitioners, Australian Postgrad. Fedn. in Medicine (life, gov., patron); mem. Coll. Family Physicians of Can., World Orgn. Nat. Colls. and Acads. and Academic Assns. Gen. Practitioners/Family Physicians (hon. sec. treas. 1972-80, pres. 1983-86), Australian Postgrad. Fedn. Medicine (coun.), Australian Med. Assn., Australian Geriatric Soc., Lorna Laffer Med. Dir. of South Australian, Postgrad. Mech. Edn. Assn., Adelaide Club. Home and Office: 12 Oaklands Ave Royston Park SA 5070 Australia Home Phone: 61 8 8362 1933. Business E-Mail: dgame@accessdigital.com.au.

GAMELLI, RICHARD LOUIS, academic administrator, surgeon, educator; b. Springfield, Mass., Jan. 18, 1949; married; 3 children. AB in Chemistry magna cum laude, St. Michael's Coll., Colchester, Vt., 1970; MD, U. Vt., 1974. Diplomate Nat. Bd. Med. Examiners, Am. Bd. Surgery (dir. 1993); lic. surgeon, Ill. Straight surg. intern. Med. Ctr. Hosp. Vt., 1974-75, surg. resident PG-II, PG-III, PG-IV, 1975-79; asst. prof. surgery U. Vt. Coll. Medicine, 1979-85, assoc. prof., 1985-89, prof., 1989-90, dir. surg. rsch. labs. dept. surgery, 1985-90, dir. house staff tng. program., 1985-89, vice chmn. dept. surgery, 1985-90, chmn. sect. gen. surgery, 1989; attending surgeon Med. Ctr. Hosp. Vt., 1979-90, dir., founder burn program, 1980-90, dir. nutritional support svcs., 1980-88, dir. resident teaching conf., 1983-90, assoc. surgeon-in-chief, 1985-89; prof. depts. surgery and pediatrics Strich Sch. Medicine, dir. Shock-Trauma Inst., chief burn ctr., dir. surg. rsch. Foster G. McGaw Hosp. Loyola U. Med. Ctr., Maywood, Ill., 1990—, chmn, prof., dept. of surgery, dean Stritch Sch. Medicine, 2009—11, sr. v.p. & provost health services Stritch Sch. Medicine, 2011—. Chmn. quailty assurance com. burn ctr. Loyola U. Med. Ctr., 1990—, infection control com., 1990—, rsch. com. coun., 1990—, surg. rsch. com., 1991—, intensive care unit com., 1991—, EMS bldg. com., 1991—, med. chmn. nutrition com., 1992—, managed care task force, 1993—, commitment to teaching task force, 1993—, OR/PAR com., 1995—, MD/PhD steering com., 1998—, med. exec. com., 1998-2000; Dr John C. Hartnett lectr. St. Michael's Coll., 1983; mem. spl. study sect. NIH, 1991. Co-author: Trauma 2000, 1992, A Compendium of Slides on Surgical Infections, 1992; co-editor: Clinical Surgery, 1987, Early Care of the Injured Patient, 1990, Essentials of Clinical Surgery, 1991; mem. editorial bd., reivewer Jour. Trauma, 1984—, Essentials Clin. Surgery, 1988—, Clin. Surgery, 1990—, Shock, 1993—; reviewer Circulatory Shock, Surgery, Jour. Surg. Rsch.; contbr. 172 articles to profl. jours., 16 chpts. to books. Recipient Dr. James E. DeMeules 1st Annual Rsch. award U. Vt. Dept. Surgery, 1990, Disting. Acad. Achievement award U. Vt., 2000; grantee NIH, 1981-84, 89-93, Ethicon, Inc., 1988-90, Genetech., Inc., 1988-89, Amgen, Inc., 1989-90, U. Ill., Chgo., 1991. Fellow ACS (vice chmn. Vt. state com. on trauma 1984-86, chmn. Vt. state com. on trauma 1986-91, sec.-treas. Vt. state chpt. 1987-90, subcom. on publs. 1987-90, exec. com. 1991-93, reviewer com. on trauma verification/consultaion program for hosps., 1991, 92, 93 chmn. audit com. 1992, 93, bd. dirs. 1992, cons., beta test site NTRACS, 1993); mem. Am. Burn Assn. (instr., dir. advanced burn life suuport course 1988—, regionalization com. 1992—, chair region V. 1992—, beta test site registry 1993, 1st v.p.), N.Am. Burn Soc. (pres. 1991), Shock Soc., Soc. for Leukocyte Biology, Soc. Univ. Surgeons (chmn. com. on social and legis. issues 1990-93, exec. com. 1990-93), Surg. Infection Soc. (edn. com. 1988—, chmn. fellowhsip com. 1990—), Surg. Biology Club III, Ea. Assn. for Surgery Trauma (exec. com. 1991-93, bd. dirs. 1992, chmn. audit com. 1992, 93), Internat. Soc. for Burn Injuries, John H. Davis Soc. (founding., bd. dirs. 1988—, coun. 1988-90, sec.-treas. 1990-92, pres. 1993—), New England Surg. Soc. Office: Loyola U Med Ctr 2160 S 1st Ave Maywood IL 60153-3304 *

GAMMON, SALLY (SARA T. GAMMON), hospital administrator, physical therapist; BS in Physical Therapy, U. Conn., Storrs, Ct.; MBA, Rivier Coll., Nashua, NH. Physical therapist State of Conn., Easter Seal Rehab. Ctr., Manchester, NH, dir. physical therapy; adminstr. Easter Seal Rehab. Ctr. of Southern NH; v.p. fiscal affairs Easter Seal Society/Goodwill Industries of New Hampshire/Vermont, Inc., CFO, v.p. fiscal affairs; divsn. dir. oncology, rehab. and orthopedics Health Northeast/Elliot Hosp., Manchester, NH; pres., CEO Rehab. Ctr. Fairfield County, Bridgeport, Conn., 1990—97, Good Shepherd Rehab., Allentown, 1997—. Office: Good Shepeherd Rehab 850 S Fifth St Allentown PA 18103 Office Phone: 610-776-3100.

GAMPEL, ERIC, philosopher, educator; b. NYC, Apr. 28, 1959; BA, U. Mass., Amherst, 1981; PhD, U. Mich., Ann Arbor, 1991. Prof. Calif. State U., Chico, 1991—. Newcombe Nat. fellowship. Mem.: Am. Philos. Assn. Office: 115 Trinity Calif State University Chico CA 95926 Business E-Mail: egampel@csuchico.edu.

GAN, HWA-WOOI, cardiologist; b. Penang, Malaysia, Nov. 19, 1972; MBBS, U. Malaya, 1998. Cons. Changi Gen. Hosp., 2007—. Recipient Gold Reviewer award, Annals Acad. Medicine, Singapore, Best Case award, Cardiovasc. Rsch. Found., 2009, Bronze award, Nat. Heart Ctr., Singapore, Productivity award. Fellow: FAMS, Asia Pacific Soc. Interventional Cardiology, Acad. Medicine Singapore; mem.: RCP, ACSM CES, European Assn. Percutaneous Cardiovasc. Interventions, European Soc. Cardiology, Acad. Medicine Malaysia. Office: 2 Simei St 3 Singapore City 529889 Singapore E-mail: hwawooi@yahoo.com.

GANAI, SABHA, surgeon, researcher; b. Royal Oak, Mich., Apr. 23, 1976; d. Zulqarnain Ganai and Mussarat Abidi. BS in Biomed. Engring., U. So. Calif., LA, 1997, MD, 2001; PhD in Molecular and Cellular Biology, U. Mass., Amherst, 2007. Lic. Mass. Bd. of Registration in Medicine, 2004, cert. advanced trauma life support instr. ACS, 2003, lic. Ill., 2010. Surg. resident Baystate Med. Ctr., Springfield, Mass., 2001—; surg. oncology fellow U. Chgo., 2010—. Contbr. articles to profl. jours. Recipient Significance in Rsch. award, Baystate Med. Ctr., 2006, 2007. Mem.: AAAS, ACS (assoc.), Soc. Surgery of Alimentary Tract, Assn. for Acad. Surgery, USC Salerni Collegium, Am. Med. Soc., Soc. of Am. Gastrointestinal Endoscopic Surgeons (assoc.), Airplane Owners and Pilots Assn., Tau Beta Pi Engring. Honor Soc. Islam. Avocations: aviation, writing, guitar, art. Office: Baystate Med Ctr 759 Chestnut St Springfield MA 01199 E-mail: sabha.ganai@bhs.org. *

GANAWAY, GEORGE KENNETH, psychiatrist, psychoanalyst, educator, researcher; b. Davenport, Iowa, Mar. 22, 1946; s. Kenneth Joseph and Elizabeth Earl Ganaway; m. Elzada Lawson, Dec. 27, 1969; children: Heather, Erin. BS in Clin. Psychology, Duke U., 1968; MD, Emory U., 1973; grad., Emory Psychoanalytic Inst., 2001. Diplomate Am. Bd. Psychiatry and Neurology; lic. physician, Ga. Resident in psychiatry Emory Affiliated Hosps., Atlanta, 1973-76; pvt. practice in gen. adult and adolescent psychiatry Atlanta, 1976—; regional med. advisor Social Security Disability Program, 1997—; pvt. practice psychoanalysis, 2001—; founder, program dir. Ridgeview Ctr. for Dissociative Disorders, Smyrna, Ga., 1987-96; med. cons. dissociative disorders Ridgeview Inst., 1996—2006; asst. prof. psychiatry Emory U. Sch. Medicine, Atlanta, 1976-80, clin. asst. prof. psychiatry, 1981—, Morehouse Sch. Medicine, Atlanta, 1990—; tchg. faculty Emory Psychoanalytic Inst., 1997—, assoc. tchg. analyst, 2002—. Psychiat. cons. Disability Adjudication br. Social Security Adminstrn., Atlanta, part-time, 1980-87, Douglas County Mental Health Clinic, Douglasville, 1977-81, South Cobb Mental Health Ctr., Austell, Ga., 1978-80, Atlanta Depression Clinic of Ctr. Metabolic Studies, 1976-77, others; ann. chmn. S.E. Regional Conf. Dissociative Disorders, 1987-96; med. staff Ridgeview Inst., 1976-98, courtesy staff, 1999-2006. Asst. editor Dissociation: Progress in Dissociative Disorders, 1988-98; assoc. editor Internat. Jour. Clin. and Exptl. Hypnosis, 1995-96; mem. editl. adv. bd. Insight mag.; editl. reviewer Am. Jour. Psychiatry, Child Abuse and Neglect: The Internat. Jour., Jour. Psychology and Theology, Jour. Nervous and Mental Disease,

Dissociation: Progress in the Dissociative Disorders; contbr. articles to profl. jours., chpts. to textbooks of psychiatry. Sci. adv. bd. False Memory Syndrome Found., 1992—. Fellow: Internat. Soc. for Study of Dissociation (task force on stds. of practice 1991—96), Am. Psychiat. Assn. (life); mem.: Internat. Psychoanalytical Assn., Atlanta Psychoanalytic Soc. (chair sci. program com. 2001—03, pres.-elect 2003—05, pres. 2005—07), Ga. Psychiat. Physicians Assn., So. Med. Assn., Am. Psychoanalytic Assn. Avocation: collecting maritime antiques. Office: D-201 5064 Roswell Rd NE Ste 201D Atlanta GA 30342-2266 Office Phone: 404-252-4525. Business E-Mail: gganawa@emory.edu.

GANDHI, ALOK D., surgeon; b. NY, Dec. 1, 1977; BS, NY Inst. Tech., 1999; D, NY Coll. Osteo. Medicine, 2002. Bariatric & gen. surgeon Rochester Gen. Hosp., 2008—; fellow Bariatric Surgery U. Med. Ctr. Pricerton, NJ, 2007—09; bd. trustee NY chpt. surgeon Am. Soc. Metabolics Bariatric. Bd. trustees NY chpt. Am. Soc. Metabolic and Bariatric Surgeons, 2010—11. Fellow: Am. Coll. Osteo. Surgeons; mem.: NY State Med. Soc., Am. Osteo. Assn. Office: 1415 Portland Ave Ste 225 Rochester NY 14621 Personal E-mail: dr.agandhi@gmail.com.

GANDHI, NOSHIR, surgeon, orthopedist, consultant; arrived in UK, 1994, naturalized, 2007; s. Jamshedji and Soona Gandhi; m. Lily Gandhi, Feb. 7, 1977; children: Jamshid, Tinaz. MBBS, GS Med. Coll. and King Edward Meml. Hosp. U. Bombay, 1957; MCh Orth, U. Liverpool, England, 1965; MSurg, King Edward Meml. Hosp. U. Bombay, India, 1965; MD in Complementary Medicine (hon.), Medicina Alternativa The Open Internat. U. Complementary Medicine, Columbo, Sri Lanka, 1986; PhD in Complementary Medicine (hon.), Medicina Alternativa The Open Internat. U. Complementary Medicine, Copenhagen, Denmark, 1987, DSc (hon.) in Complimentary Medicine, 1987. Hon. prof. in orthop. Grant Med. Coll., U. of Bombay, 1970—93; cons. orthop. surgeon J J Group of Hospitals, Bombay, 1970—93; med. expert Medicolegal Reporting, County Durham and County Tyne and Wear, 1994—; med. expert witness panel Crown Solicitors; on register UK Med. Expert Witnesses, 1994—; cons. orthop. surgeon U. Hosp. of North Durham and Shotley Bridge, 1994—98, Bishop Auckland Gen. Hosp., 1999—2003, Darlington Meml. Hosp., 1999—2003, Woodlands Hosp., Darlington, 2000—; sr. cons. orthop. surgeon BUPA Hosp., 1996—2003; med. expert witness panel Crown Solicitors. Cons. and tchr. U. of Newcastle upon Tyne Hospitals, 1994—; rep. cons. U. of Durham, Festival of Sci., 1997—98. Contbr. articles to profl. pubs.; presenter sci. papers in internat. confs. Justice of Peace Govt. of Maharashtra, Bombay, 1973—74, Spl. Exec. Magistrate, 1977—94, Govt. Gazetted Officer, class 1, 1970—93. Recipient Gold Medal for Surgery, 1954, Dag Hammerskjold award for Profl. Excellence, Open U., 1986, Academie Merit, Academie Diplomatique de la Paix, 1987, Knight Comdr., Royal Order of the Grand Cross of Peace and Justice, 1989, Seva Shree award, Maharastra State; fellow in Gen. Surgery, Royal Coll. Surgeons, 1962, Internat. Coll. Surgeons, 1989. Master: Royal Arch Chpt. Strict Benevelonce, Mason United Grand Lodge Eng. Companion, Worshipful Master Vedra Lodge (United Grand Lodge Eng.); fellow: Internat. Coll. Surgeons, Royal Coll. Surgeons Edinburgh; mem.: Brit. Med. Assn., Indian Orthopaedic Assn. (life), Assn. Study and Application of Methodology of Illzharov (life), Indian Med. Assn. (life), Global Alliance for Internat. Advancement, UN Orgn. (nominated mem. 2008), Med. Protection Soc. GB, Soc. Internat. Coll. Orthop. Surgery and Traumatology Belgium, Lions Club Internat. (chmn. medicine and health com., Bombay chpt. 1970—81), 3137 United GRand Lodge Eng. Achievements include first to sucessful re-implantation of severed upper limb surgery; introduction of sucessful surgical leg lengthening procedure in India; research in Gandhi's Pinch Test; clinical sign in diagnosis of impending septic arthritis of the hip; development of direct foraminal injection as successful treatment of acute and recurrent sciatica. Avocations: classical music, reading, Reiki. Home Fax: 00 44 191 3779773. Personal E-mail: noshir.gandhi@gmail.com.

GANDHI, RAJINDER, pediatric surgery, educator; Attended, Inst. Of Medicine, Burma, 1966. Diplomate Am. Bd. Surgery, Am. Bd. Surgery-pediatric surgery. Resident Lutheran Hosp., Bronx Lebanon Hosp. Ctr.; fellow Columbia-Presbyn. Med. Ctr., 1974—75; assoc clin. prof. Columbia Univ.; affiliation Valley Hosp. Home: Valley Hospital Ste 235 30 W Century Rd Paramus NJ 07652 Office Phone: 201-225-9440.

GANDJBAKHCH, IRADJ, thoracic surgeon, consultant; b. Tehran, Iran, Nov. 6, 1941; s. Hossein Gandjbakhch and Ehtechamzadeh; children: Christian, Emmanuelle, Frédérique, Estelle. MD, U. Pierre Marie Curie, Paris, 1976. Diplomate U. Paris, 1970. Prof. U. Pierre Marie Curie, 1976—; dir. cardiothoracic surgery dept. Groupe Hosp. Pitié Salpêtrière, Paris, 1990—. Cons. Air France Co., Paris, Svc. Santé Des Armées, Paris. Contbr. articles to profl. jours., chapters to books. Mem. Conseil Nat. U., Paris, 1994, Acad. Nat. Chirurgie, Paris, 1996, Acad. Nat. Médecine, 2001; pres. Sect. 51 Conseil Nat. Chirurgie, 2006. Recipient, Chevalier l'Ordre Nat. Mérite, 1988, Médaille d'honneur Svcs. Santés Armées, 1990, Chevalier dans l'Ordre Palmes Acads., 2003, Officier dans l'Ordre Nat. érite, 2004. Master: ADICARE, ADETEC, Assn. Pour Recherche Sur Cancer; mem.: Mediteraneen Soc. Cardiology and Cardiac Surgery, European Soc. Cardio Thoracic Surgery, Internat. Soc. Heart and Lung Transplantation, European Soc. Transplantation, Soc. Française Transplantation, Soc. Chirurgie Thoracique Lan. Française, Soc. Française Cardiologie. Achievements include first to heart transplantation and circulatory assistance; minimally invasive coronary artery bypass. Home: 12 Rue Galliéni Le Perreux-sur-Marne Paris 94170 France Office: Groupe Hosp Pitié-Salpêtrière 47-83 bd de l' Hosp Paris 75013 France Office Fax: 0142165684. Business E-Mail: iradj.gandjbakhch@psl.aphp.fr.

GANDY, GERALD LARMON, rehabilitation counseling educator, psychologist, writer; b. Thomasville, Ga., Feb. 9, 1941; s. Larmon Brinkley and Ruby Wylene (Vickers) G.; m. Patricia Kay Haltiwanger, Jan. 22, 1966. BA, Fla. State U., 1963; MA, U. S.C., 1968, PhD, 1971. Lic. profl. counselor, Va.; lic. clin. psychologist, Va.; nat. cert. rehab. counselor; nat. cert. counselor; cert. profl. qualification in psychology Assn. of State and Provincial Psychology Bds. Profl. counselor U. S.C. Counseling Ctr., Columbia, 1968-70; counseling psychologist VA Regional Office, Columbia, 1970-75, chief counseling psychologist, 1974-75; ind. cons., prof. emeritus Med. Coll. Va., Va. Commonwealth U., Richmond, 1996—, prof., program dir., 1975-95. Chair nat. com. on undergrad. rehab. edn. Nat. Coun. on Rehab. Edn., 1984-89; mem. numerous state and govt. adv. coms., 1970—; cons. in field. Author: Mental Health Rehabilitation, 1995; co-author: Rehabilitation and Disability, 1990; co-author/editor: Rehabilitation Counseling and Services, 1987, Counseling in the Rehabilitation Process, 1999; co-editor: International Rehabilitation, 1980, 89; contbr. numerous articles to profl. jours. Faculty pres. Sch. of Cmty. and Pub. Affairs, VA Commonwealth U., 1989-93. Capt. US Army, 1963-66. Recipient Disting. Svc. award Sch. Cmty. and Pub. Affairs, 1988, School and U. Leadership award, 1993. Fellow Internat. Acad. of Behavioral Medicine, Counseling and Psychotherapy (diplomate); mem. APA, ACA, World Fedn. for Mental Health, Phi Kappa Phi, Sigma Alpha Epsilon. Home and Office: Highland Springs 300 Southern Ct Richmond VA 23075-1519 Office Phone: 804-737-6089. Business E-Mail: ggandy@vcu.org.

GANDY, SAM, neurologist, neuroscientist, educator; b. Chesterfield, SC, Nov. 3, 1956; s. Sam Evans Gandy and Millie Frances King; m. Michelle E. Ehrlich, Feb. 7, 1987. BS in Chemistry summa cum laude, Charleston So. U., SC, 1976; MD, PhD in Molecular and Cellular Biology, Med. U. SC, 1982. Diplomate Am. Bd. Psychiatry and Neurology. Intern dept. medicine Presbyn. Hosp., NYC, 1982—83; vis. clin. fellow Coll. Physicians and Surgeons Columbia U., Columbia-Presbyn. Med. Ctr., NYC, 1982—83; resident and clin. assoc. neurology NY Hosp.-Cornell Med. Ctr., NYC, 1983—86; rsch. assoc. lab. molecular and cellular neuroscience Rockefeller U., NYC, 1986—91, asst. prof. lab. molecular and cellular neuroscience, 1991—92; asst. prof., lab. dir., asst. attending neurologist dept. neurology and neuroscience NY Hosp.-Cornell Med. Ctr., NYC, 1992—93, assoc. prof., lab. dir., assoc. attending neurologist dept. neurology and neuroscience, 1993—97, rsch. scientist Nathan S. Kline Rsch. Inst. Psychiat. Rsch. and prof. psychiatry and cell biology NYU Sch. Medicine, Orangeburg and NYC, 1997—2001; dir. Farber Inst. Neurosciences and prof. dept. neurology dept. biochemistry and molecular biology Thomas Jefferson U., Phila., 2001—07; prof. neurology and psychiatry Mt. Sinai Sch. Medicine, NYC, 2007—, Sinai prof. Alzheimer's rsch., 2007—. Ad hoc site visit mem. Nat. Inst. Neurol. Diseases and Stroke, 1993; dir. molecular basis of human neurol. diseases Cold Spring Harbor Labs, 1996—; adj. prof. Rockefeller U., NYC, 1997—; vis. disting. prof. U. We. Australia, Perth, 1999—2000; eminent scholar Ga. Rsch. Alliance, 2007—. Assoc. editor Alzheimer's Disease and Associated Disorders, 2003, cons. editor Jour. Clin. Investigation, 2003, mem. editl. adv. bd. Alzheimer's Disease and Associated Disorders, 1992—, Neurodegenerative Diseases, 2003; contbr. articles to numerous profl. jours.; reviewer in field, investigator in field. Recipient Arthur Cherkin Meml. award in geriatric medicine, 2008; fellow, Huntington's Disease Found., 1986—87; Glorney-Raisbeck fellow, NY Acad. Medicine, 1986—87. Mem.: Am. Fedn. Aging Rsch. (mem. nat. sci. adv. coun. 1995, mem. rsch. com. 1996—2001), Fisher Found. Alzheimer's (chair sci. adv. bd. 2001—03), Alzheimer's Assn. (chair nat. med. and sci. adv. coun. 2005—), Rotary (chair CART grant award com. 2000—05). Office: Dept Neurology Mt Sinai Sch Medicine Annenberg Bldg Rm 14 60 1 Gustave L Levy Pl Box 1137 New York NY 10029 Office Phone: 212-241-4215. Personal E-mail: samgandy@gmail.com. Business E-Mail: samuel.gandy@mssm.edu.

GANDY, WINSTON H., JR., cardiologist; MD, Howard U., Washington, DC, 1986. Diplomate Am. Bd. Internal Medicine, 1989, Am. Bd. Internal Medicine-cardiovasc. disease, 2002, cert. echocardiography Nat. Bd. of Echocardiography. Resident internal medicine Emory Univ. Affiliation Hosp., Atlanta, 1986—89; fellow cardiovasc. disease Univ. Ala., Birmingham, 1989—92; gen. cardiologist Piedmont Heart Inst. Fellow: Am. Coll. of Cardiology. Office: Piedmont Heart Institute-Perimeter Ste 385 1140 Hammond Dr Atlanta GA 30328

GANELLIN, CHARON ROBIN, medical educator, chemist, researcher; b. London, Jan. 25, 1934; s. Leon and Beila (Cluer) G.; m. Tamara Greene, Dec. 27, 1956 (dec. Nov. 1997); children Nicole Joanne, Mark David; m. Monique Lehmann Garbarg, July 2003. BSc in Chemistry, Queen Mary Coll., London, 1955, PhD, 1958; DSc, London U., 1986; DSc (hon.), Aston U., 1995. Rsch. chemist Smith, Kline & French, London, 1958-61, head medicinal chemistry Welwyn Garden City, 1962-75, dir. histamine rsch., 1975-80, v.p. rsch., 1980-84, v.p. chemistry, 1984-86; Smith, Kline & French prof. medicinal chemistry Univ. Coll., London, 1986—2003, emeritus prof. medicinal chemistry, 2003—. Editor, author: Pharmacology of Histamine Receptors, 1982, Frontiers in Histamine Research, 1985, Dictionary of Drugs, 1990, Medicinal Chemistry, 1993, Dictionary of Pharmacological Agents, 1996, Analogue-based Drug Discovery, 2006, Analogue-based Drug Discovery II, 2010. Recipient Prix Charles Mentzer, Soc. de Chimie Therapeutique, France, 1978, Nauta award for pharmacochemistry, European Fedn. Medicinal Chemistry, 2004, Pratesi medal Med. Chem. Divsn. Soc. Chimica ITaliano, 2006; inductee Nat. Inventors Hall of Fame, Akron, Ohio, 1990. Fellow Royal Soc., Royal Soc. Chemistry (medicinal chemistry medallion 1977, Tilden medal 1982, Adrian Albert medal 1999), Queen Mary Westfield Coll.; mem. Am. Chem. Soc. (Medicinal Chemistry award 1980, Hall of Fame Divsn. Medicinal Chemistry 2007), Soc. for Chem. Industry (Messel medal 1988), Soc. for Drug Rsch. (Drug Discovery award 1989), British Pharm. Soc., Soc. Española Chim. Therapeutica (hon.), Spanish Royal Acad. Pharmacy (fgn. corr. adacemician 2006). Office: U Coll London Dept Chem 20 Gordon St WCIH OAJ London England Business E-Mail: c.r.ganellin@ucl.ac.uk.

GANEM, DONALD E., immunologist; AB, MA, Harvard U., 1972, MD, 1977. Asst. prof. microbiollogy, immunology and medicine U. Calif., San Francisco, 1982—88, assoc. prof. microbiology and medicine, 1988—90, prof. microbiology and medicine, 1990—, vice-chair, Dept. Microbiology & Immunology, 1995—; assoc. investigator Howard Hughes Med. Inst., San Francisco, 1991—94, investigator, 1995—. Recipient Soma Weiss award for med. student rsch., Harvard Med. Sch., 1975, Leon Resnick prize for rsch., 1977, Kaiser award for excellence in basic sci. tchr., 1986, Acad. Senate Tchg. award, U. Calif., 1986, 2d Yr. Students' Tchg. award for small group tchg., 1986, 2d Yr. Students' Tchg. award for excellence in lecturing, 1987, 1989, 1991; scholar Harkness scholar, Harvard Med. Sch., 1972. Fellow: Am. Acad. Arts and Scis.; mem.: NAS, Am. Soc. Clin. Investigation (v.p. 1997), Assn. Am. Physicians, Inst. of Medicine (life), Am. Acad. Microbiology, Alpha Omega Alpha. Office: UCSF Box 0552 San Francisco CA 94143-0552 Office Phone: 415-476-2826. Office Fax: 415-476-0939. E-mail: ganem@cgl.ucsf.edu.

GANG, ELI S., cardiac electrophysiologist, educator; MD, Columbia U., 1975. Diplomate Am. Bd. Internal Medicine, 1978, Am. Bd. Internal Medicine-cardiovasc. disease, 1981. Resident internal medicine Roosevelt Hosp., 1976—78; fellow cardiovasc. disease Columbia Presbyn. Hosp., 1978—79; clin. prof. medicine UCLA; co-dir. clin. electrophysiology Cedars-Sinai Med. Ctr. Author publs. more than 100 peer-reviewed abstracts and articles. Recipient numerous rsch. grant awards. Office: Cardiovascular Medical Group 414 N Camden Dr Ste 1100 Beverly Hills CA 90210 Office Phone: 310-278-3400.

GANG, WANG, surgeon; b. Harbin, China, Aug. 12, 1979; D, Harbin Med. U., 2009. Pancreatic dept. Hosp. Harbin Med. U., 2009—. Office: You Zheng St Harbin Hei Long Jiang 150001 China Business E-Mail: wgilu79@yahoo.com.cn.

GANLEY, CHARLES JAMES, federal agency administrator, internist; b. Oct. 25, 1954; BS in Chemistry, U. Pitts.; MD, Hahnemann U. Med. Coll., Phila., 1981. Cert. Internal Medicine, 1984. Resident tng., internal medicine Hahnemann Hosp.; fulfilled Pub. Health Svc. obligation; fellowship, clin. pharmacology Cornell U. Med. Ctr.; med. reviewer, divsn. cardio-renal drug products FDA, Md., 1989, med. team leader, Divsn. Cardio-Renal Drug Products Md., dir., Over-the-Counter Drug Products (reorganized into the Office of Nonprescription Drug Products) Md., 1999—2005, dir., Office of Nonprescription Drug Products Md., 2005—. Office: Office Nonprescription Products Ctr for Drug Evaluation and Rsch FDA 10903 New Hampshire Ave WO22 Silver Spring MD 20903

GANLEY, JAMES POWELL, retired ophthalmologist; b. Altadena, Calif., Apr. 25, 1937, s. Joseph Harrington and Ruth Alice (Carr) G., m. Anne Hay Hunter, Aug. 7, 1965; children: Anne Hay, Susan Powell, Katherine Carr, Elizabeth Pearson. BS in Biology, Mt. St. Mary's U., 1959; MD, Georgetown U., 1963; MPH, Johns Hopkins U., 1969, DPH, 1972. Diplomate Am. Bd. Med. Examiners, Am. Bd. Preventive Medicine (fellow), Am. Bd. Ophthalmology (fellow). Intern Washington Hosp. Ctr., 1963-64; resident in ophthalmology SUNY Upstate Med. Ctr., Syracuse, 1965-68; resident in preventive medicine Johns Hopkins U., Balt., 1969-71; sr. staff fellow Nat. Eye Inst., NIH, Bethesda, Md., 1971-74; asst. prof. ophthalmology U. Ariz. Med. Ctr., Tucson, 1974 80; assoc. prof., dept. head La. State U. Med. Ctr., Shreveport, 1980-82, asst. dean clin. affairs, 1981-87, prof., head dept., 1982-97, prof., 1998—2004. Sci. adv. panel Onchocerciasis Control Program, WHO, Geneva, Switzerland, 1974-79; med. adv. bd. Internat. Eye Found., Bethesda, 1974-77, bd. dirs., 2004—, med. dir., 2006—07, chmn. 2008-09; ophthalmic drugs adv. com. FDA, HEW, Rockville, Md., 1976-82; epidemiol. and disease control study sect. NIH, 1982-86. Author: book chpts., procs.; founding editor Ophthalmic Epidemiology, 1993—2006, emeritus editor, 2007—, editl. bd. Sightsaver, Nat. Soc. to Prevent Blindness, 1982—86, Evidence-Based Eye Care, 1999—2004. Bd. dirs. Northwest Lions Eye Bank, Shreveport, 1987. Lt. USN, 1964-65. Recipient Promotion of Peace and Vision award, Internat. Eye Found. Mem. Am. Coll. Preventive Medicine, Am. Acad. Ophthalmology (com. rsch. regulatory agys. and fed. sys. 1986-91, chmn. 1990-91), Internat. Soc. Geog. Ophthalmology (pres. 1982-88, treas. 1988-, exec. bd. 1988-), Am. Coll. Epidemiology, La. Assn. Blind (bd. dirs. 1980-96, 1st vice chmn., sec. exec. bd. 1989-91, chmn. bd. 1992-93), Shreveport Med. Soc. (bd. dirs. 1990-96, 2d v.p. 1993, 1st v.p. 1994, pres. 1995), Gibson Island Corp. (bd. dirs. 2006-08, chair, pest eradication com.), Assn. Rsch. in Vision and Ophthalmology (program planning com. 1993-96, internat. mems. com. 2001-04), Revs. Rsch. NIH, Monsignor Tierney Honor Soc., Alpha Omega Alpha Med. Honor Soc. Democrat. Roman Catholic. Avocations: swimming, sailing.

GANNON, MARC JAY, optometrist; b. Cleve., Sept. 22, 1951; s. Leonard Justin and Norma S. (Falcovich) Goldstein; m. Cheryl Denise Congress, Aug. 4, 1974; children: Jennifer, Joshua. Student, Miami U., Oxford, Ohio, 1972; OD magna cum laude, Ill. Coll. Optometry, Chgo., 1976. Cert. optometrist, Fla. Intern, then resident Naval Regional Med. Ctr., Portsmouth, Va., 1976-78; pvt. practice Ft. Lauderdale, Fla., 1978—. Pres. Oculon Vison Enhancement, Inc., Boca Raton, Fla., 1984-89, Gannon Ctr. for Low Vision, Low Vision Inst.; dir. Gannon Ctr. Low Vision. Patentee in field. Dist. exec. Lighthouse dist. Boy Scouts Am., 1980-82; pres. Kiwanis, Pompano Beach, Fla., 1981-82, Bus. Forum, Pompano Beach, 1982-83. Lt. comdre. USN, 1976-78. Fellow Am. Acad. Optometry, Internat. Acad. Low Vision Specialists; mem. Am. Optometric Assn., Fla. Optometric Assn., Nat. Eye Rsch.Found., Broward County Optometric Assn., Tomb and Key Honor Soc, Renewview Sys. Low Vision Rehabilitation (founder, creator). Avocations: sailing, scuba diving, photography. Office: 2021 E Comml Blvd Ste 301 Fort Lauderdale FL 33308 Office Phone: 954-776-5223. Personal E-mail: gannonlvi@aol.com.

GANS, BRUCE MERRILL, physiatrist, educator, health facility administrator; b. NYC, Jan. 15, 1947; s. Murray and Bessie Jean (Schnitzer) G.; m. Linda Sharon Aberbach, June 22, 1969; children: Rebecca, Jeremy. BSEE, Union Coll., Schenectady, 1968; MS, BMEE, MD, U. Pa., 1972; MS, U. Wash., 1976. Diplomate Am. Bd. Phys. Medicine and Rehab. (bd. dirs.). Intern Phila. Gen. Hosp., 1972-73; resident in phys. medicine and rehab. U. Wash., 1973-76, instr. Seattle, 1976-78; from asst. prof. to prof., chair dept. phys. medicine/rehab. Tufts U. Sch. Medicine, Boston, 1978-88; physiatrist-in-chief New Eng. Med. Ctr., Boston, 1978-88; pres. Rehab. Inst. Mich., Detroit, 1989-99; chair dept. phys. medicine and rehab. Wayne State U. Sch. Medicine, Detroit, 1989-99; sr. v.p. Detroit Med. Ctr., 1989-99, North Shore-Long Island Jewish Health Sys., 1999—2001; chair dept. phys. medicine and rehab. L.I. Jewish Med. Ctr., Parker Jewish Inst., North Shore U. Hosp., 1999—2001; exec. v.p., chief med. officer Kessler Rehab. Corp., West Orange, 2001—03; chief med. officer Kessler Inst. for Rehab., West Orange. Bd. dirs. Greenery Rehab. Group, Inc., Newton, Mass., 1988-93. Editor: Principles and Practice of Rehabilitation Medicine, 4th edit., 2004; editl. bd.: Jour. Head Trauma Rehab., 1988—92. Trustee Met. Ctr. for High Tech., Detroit, 1989-94; bd. dirs. Health and Retirement Properties Trust, 1995-99, Five Star Quality Care, Inc., 2002-, Hospitality Properties Trust, 2009-. Fellow Am. Acad. Phys. Medicine and Rehab. (bd. dirs., pres. 2004); mem. Am. Hosp. Assn. (chair governing coun. sect. for rehab. 1992), Assn. Acad. Physiatrists (pres. 1993), Am. Rehab. Assn. (bd. dirs. 1995-97), Am. Med. Rehab. Providers Assn. (bd. dirs. 1997—, chmn. bd. dirs. 2009-). Avocations: computers, reading, video. Office: Kessler Inst Rehab 1199 Pleasant Valley Way West Orange NJ 07052 Home Phone: 973-665-0885; Office Phone: 973-324-3658. E-mail: bgans@kessler-rehab.com.

GANS, EUGENE HOWARD, dermatological and pharmaceutical company executive, consultant; b. Dec. 17, 1929; married, 1953; 2 children. BS, Columbia U., 1951, MS, 1953; PhD, U. Wis., 1956. Lab. asst. Columbia U., 1951—53; sr. scientist group leader Hoffman-LaRoche, Inc., NJ, 1956—60; head new product devel. sect. Vick Div. R&D Labs. Richardson-Merrell, NY, 1960—64, asst. dir. devel. NY, 1964—67, dir. NY, 1967—71; dir. rsch. Vicks Personal Care div. Richardson-Vicks div. Proctor-Gamble, Shelton, Conn., 1972—76, v.p., dir. R&D, 1976—87; pres. Hastings Assocs., Westport, Conn., 1987—, Lincoln Techs., Westport, 1989—. Chmn. proprietary drug task group FDA, 1976—86; chmn. sci. adv. com. Cosmetic, Toiletry and Fragrance Assn., Washington, 1984—86; chmn. Consumer Health Products Assn. task group FDA, 1996—2003; chmn. ctrl. rsch. Medicis Pharm. Co., Phoenix, 1992—2002, sr. advisor, 2002—. Mem.: Soc. Investigative Dermatology, Am. Acad. Dermatology, Am. Chem. Soc., Am. Pharm. Assn., Sigma Xi. Home and Office: Hastings Sr Associates 514 Harvest Commons Westport CT 06880-3450 Office Phone: 203-216-1055. Personal E-mail: egans48845@aol.com. Business E-Mail: ggans@medicis.com.

GANS, JEROME SAMUEL, psychiatrist; b. Rochester, NY, Aug. 15, 1940; BA, Harvard Coll., 1962; MD, U. Rochester Sch. Medicine, 1967. Pvt. practice, 1971—. Fellow: Am. Psychiat. Assn. (life named Disting. Fellow), Am. Group Psychotherapy Assn. (life named Disting. Fellow). Avocations: tennis, reading. Office: 55 Cleveland Rd Wellesley Hills MA 02481 Office Fax: 781-239-0353. Personal E-mail: jsgans@comcast.net.

GANS, JOHN A., pharmacist, educator; BS in Pharmacy, Phila. Coll. Pharmacy and Sci., 1966, PharmD, 1969. Pharmacist, Broomall, Pa., 1966—67; resident Hosp. of Univ. Pa., 1967—68, asst. dir. pharmacy, 1968—70; mng. dir., Pharmservices, 1974—85; faculty Phila. Coll. Pharmacy and Sci., 1980—88, dean sch. pharmacy, 1988—89; exec. v.p., CEO Am. Pharmacists Assn., Washington, 1989—2008; prof. pharmacy and healthcare & pharm. bus., assoc. dean profl. programs U. of Sciences, Phila., 2009—. Chmn. Del. Valley Regional Poison Control Program; sec. gen. Pan Am. Fedn. Pharmacy, 1991—94, v.p., N. Am., 1994—. Recipient PCP&S Alumni award, 1997, Harvey A.K. Whitney Lecture award, Am. Soc. Health-sys. Pharmacists, 1998. Mem.: Am. Soc. Hosp. Pharmacists (pres. 1986—87). Office: University of Sciences in Phila 600 S 43d St Philadelphia PA 19104 Office Phone: 215-596-7471. Office Fax: 215-596-8598. Business E-Mail: j.gans@usciences.edu. *

GANSKE, GREG (JOHN GREG GANSKE), plastic surgeon, former United States Representative from Iowa; b. New Hampton, Iowa, Mar. 31, 1949; s. Victor Wilber and Mary Jo (O'Donnell) G.; m. Corrine Mikkelson, 1976; children: Ingrid, Briget, Karl. BA, U. Iowa, 1972, MD, 1976. Diplomate Am. Bd. Plastic Surgery, Am. Bd. Surgery. Intern U. Colo. Med. Ctr., Denver, 1976-78; resident in gen. surgery U. Oreg. Health Sci. Ctr., Portland, 1978-81, chief resident in gen. surgery, 1981-82; resident in plastic surgery Harvard Med. Sch., Boston, 1982-84; chief resident plastic surgery Brigham and Women's Hosp. and Children's Hosp., 1983-84; mem. US Congress from 4th Iowa dist., Washington, 1995—2003; pvt. practice Des Moines, 1984-94, 2003—. Staff Iowa Luth. Hosp., Iowa Meth. Med. Ctr., Mercy Hosp. Med. Ctr. Lt. col. M.C., USAR, 1984—. Fellow ACS, Am. Soc. Plastic and Reconstructive Surgeons; mem. AMA, Am. Assn. Plastic Surgeons, Iowa Med. Soc., Iowa Soc. Plastic and Reconstructive Surgeons, Am. Assn. Hand Surgery, Am. Soc. Surgery Hand, Am. Cleft Palate-Craniofacial Assn. Republican. Roman Catholic. Office: Lakeview Medical Center 6000 University Ave Ste 400 West Des Moines IA 50266 Office Phone: 515-265-4414. E-mail: gregganskemd@gmail.com.

GANT, NORMAN FERRELL, JR., obstetrician, gynecologist, educator; b. Wichita Falls, Tex., Feb. 16, 1939; s. Norman Ferrell and Eleanor (Taylor) Gant. BA, North Tex. State U., Denton, 1962; MD, U. Tex., 1964. Diplomate Am. Bd. Ob-Gyn. (exec. dir.). Intern Parkland Meml. Hosp., Dallas, 1964—65, resident, 1965—68; mem. faculty U. Tex. Southwestern Med. Sch., Dallas, 1968—, prof. obstetrics and gynecology, 1976—, chmn. dept., 1977—83. Bd. dirs. Am. Bd. Ob-Gyn., Inc., 1993—; v.p. Internat. Soc. for Study of Hypertension in Pregnancy, 1992—94. Co-author: Williams Obstetrics; editor, sec./treas. Clin. Jour. of Hypertension; contbr. articles to med. jours. Recipient Outstanding Alumnus award, U. North Tex., 1998. Fellow: Am. Coll. Ob-Gyn., Royal Coll. Ob-Gyn.; mem.: Inst. Medicine, Southwestern Gyn. Assembly (pres. 1993), Am. Bd. Ob-Gyn. (maternal-fetal medicine, examiner for ob-gyn. and maternal-fetal medicine bds., mem. exec. com., credentials com.), Dallas-Ft. Worth Obstet. and Gynecol. Soc., Tex. Assn. Ob-Gyns., Dallas County Med. Assns., Soc. Gynecol. Investigation (pres. 1991). Address: Am Bd Ob-Gyn 2915 Vine St Dallas TX 75204-1045 Office: UT Southwestern Medical Ctr 5323 Harry Hines Blvd Dallas TX 75390-9032 Office Phone: 214-871-1619. Business E-Mail: ccash@abog.org.

GANTZ, BRUCE JAY, otolaryngologist, educator; b. NYC, May 18, 1946; m. Mary Katherine DeJong; children: Ellen Katherine, Jessica Rose, Jay Alexander. BS in Gen. Sci., U. Iowa, 1968, MD, 1974, MS in Otolaryngology, 1980; fellow neurotology, U. Zürich, Zurich, 1981-82. Asst. prof. dept otolaryngology U. Iowa Coll. Medicine, Iowa City, 1980-84, assoc. prof., 1984-87, prof., 1987—, interim head dept. otolaryngology head & neck surgery, 1993-95, head dept. otolaryngology head & neck surgery, 1995—, Brian F. McCabe Disting. chair in otolaryngology, 1998—. Mem. adv. bd. Deafness Research Found. Sci., 1988—. Mem. editl. bd. Am. Jour. Otology, Laryngoscope, Skull Base Surgery, Operative Techniques in Otolaryngology-Head and Neck Surgery, Anales De Otolarnolaringologica Mexicana, Annals Otolaryngology, Rhinology and Laryngology; contbr. articles to profl. jours. Recipient Tchr.-Investigator Devel. award Pub. Health Svc., 1981-86, Program Project award NIH, 1985—; clin. rsch. ctr. grantee NIDCD, 1990, 95. Mem.: AMA, NAS Inst. Medicine, Collegium Oto-Rhino-Laryngologicum Amictuae Sacrum, Am. Otological Soc. (pres. 2009—10), Am. Neurotology Soc. (v.p. 1994—96, pres.-elect 1996—97, pres. 1997—98), Soc. Univ. Otolaryngologists, Am. Acad. Otolaryngology-Head and Neck Surgery, Deafness Rsch. Found. (state chmn. 1985—), Assn. Rsch. in otolaryngology (pres. 1995). Office: U Iowa Hosps & Clinics 200 Hawkins Dr Iowa City IA 52242-1078 Office Phone: 319-356-2173. *

GANTZER, MARY LOU, medical products executive; d. Richard John and Mary Jane (Capistrant) G. B in Chemistry, U. Minn., 1972, MS, 1976; PhD in Chemistry, U. Va., 1980. Instr., postdoctoral fellow dept. chemistry U. Va., Charlottesville, 1980—81; rsch. scientist diagnostics divsn. Miles, Inc., Elkhart, Ind., 1981—84, sr. rsch. scientist, 1984—86, staff scientist, 1986—87, supr. R&D, 1987—91, project mgr., 1991—98, coord. clin. and outcomes rsch., 1996—98; dir. clin. and sci. affairs Siemens Healthcare Diagnostics, Newark, Del., 1998—2004, v.p., clin. and sci. affairs, 2004—. Mem. Women in Mgmt. del. to People's Republic of China, 1988; bd. dirs. Clin. and Lab. Stds. Inst. (formerly Nat. Comm. for Clin. Lab. Stds.), 2003-, sec. 2007—. Contbr. articles to chemistry jours.; patentee in field. Mem. Am. Assn. Clin. Chemistry (chmn. Chgo. sect. 1988, chair long range planning com. 1993-95, bd. editors Clin. Chem. News 1993-95, pres. 2002, Chmn.'s award 1988), Am. Heart Assn. (profl. mem.). Roman Catholic. Avocation: needlecrafts. Office: Siemens Healthcare Diagnostics Inc PO Box 6101 Newark DE 19714-6101

GANZ, PATRICIA ANNE, medical educator, physician; b. LA, Mar. 23, 1948; d. Raymond W. and Ida (Shrier) Conn; m. Tomas Ganz, Aug. 16, 1970; children: David, Rebecca. BA magna cum laude, Harvard-Radcliffe, 1969; MD, UCLA, 1973. Diplomate Am. Bd. Internal Medicine, Am. Bd. Med. Oncology. Post doctoral tng., internal medicine and med. oncology UCLA Med. Ctr.; chief resident in medicine med. ctr. UCLA Sch. Medicine, 1977-78, from asst. to assoc. prof. medicine San Fernando Valley program, 1978-90, prof., 1990-92, prof. health svcs. and medicine, schs. medicine and pub. health, 1990—. Dir. divsn. cancer prevention and control rsch. Jonsson Comprehensive Cancer Ctr., LA, 1993—; clin. rsch. prof., Am. Cancer Soc., 1999—, researcher, Breast Cancer Rsch. Found.; mem. bd. scientific advisors Nat. Cancer Inst.; onvolvement of clin. trials, with leadership roles in Southwest Oncology Group and Nat. Surgical Adjuvant Breast and Bowel Project; founding mem. Nat. Coalition for Cancer Surviorship. Assoc. editor Journal Clin. Oncology, Journal of National Cancer Inst., mem. editl. group Cochrane Breast Cancer Group; contbr. articles to profl. jours. Named Susan G. Komen Prof. of Surviorship. Mem.: Inst. Medicine. A medical oncologist who has spent the past 20 years doing systematic research on the health-related quality of life impact of cancer and its treatment; has contributed to the understanding of how women adjust to the diagnosis of breast cancer, including its effects on their physical, emotional, social, and sexual well-being. Office: UCLA Divsn Cancer Prevention PO Box 951772 Los Angeles CA 90095-1772 Office Phone: 310-206-1404. Office Fax: 310-206-3566. Business E-Mail: pganz@ucla.edu.

GAO, FEN-FEI, medical educator; b. Jiangxi, China, Oct. 17, 1971; D, Shantou U., 2008. Asst. rschr. Shantou U. Med. Coll., 2003—08, assoc. prof., 2009—. Physician Hosp. Hongcheng Prison, Nanchang, Jiangxi, 1994—2000. Recipient 2nd prize, People's Govt. Guangdong Province, 1st prize, People's Govt. Shantou City. Mem.: Guangdong Pharmacological Soc., Chinese Pharmacological Soc. Avocations: Go, reading, swimming. Office: 22 Xinling Rd Shantou Guangdong 515041 China

GAO, JINGCHUN, medical educator; b. Shandong, China, Nov. 13, 1964; MD, Gifu U., Japan, PhD, 2005. Assoc. prof. Zhongshan Hosp. Xiamen U., 2010—. Mem.: AACR. Office: Hubin Nan Rd 201-209 Xiamen Fujian 361004 China Personal E-mail: jingchun_gao@yahoo.com.

GAO, LEI, ophthalmologist; b. Yantai, Shandong, China, Apr. 18, 1963; B, Shandong U., 1985; M, Qingdao U., 2001. Vice dir. dept. Ophthalmology, 2002—; prof. Qingdao U., 2005—11. Fellowship, Chinese U. Hongkong, Li Ka Shing Found. Mem.: Chinese Medicine Assn. Avocations: running, mountain climbing, music. Office: Yuhuangding Donglu 20 Yantai Shandong 264000 China Personal E-mail: gl6365@yahoo.com.cn.

GAO, NAIPING, engineering educator; b. Jiangsu, China, Oct. 8, 1978; PhD, Hong Kong Poly. U., 2006. Assoc. prof. Tongji U., 2008—. Recipient Bronze award, 35th Internat. Exhbn. Inventions, New Techniques & Products, Geneva. Mem.: ASHRAE. Home: Rm 401 Bldg 37 Zhengli Rd 508 Shanghai 200433 China Office Phone: 86-21-65983867. Home Fax: 86-21-65983867. Personal E-mail: gaonaiping@tongji.edu.cn.

GARAT, JOSÉ MARÍA, urologist; b. Uruguay, Oct. 20, 1941; MD, 1968. Cert. urologist 1973. Jefe unidad uropediatría Fundación Puigvert, 1977—. Cons. Facultad de Medicina, 1978—2010. Recipient medal, Sociedad Iberoamericana de Urología Pediatrica. Mem.: Asociación Española de Urología, Sociedad Iberoamericana de Urología Pediátrica. Avocations: gardening, tennis, movies. Home: Paseo Miramar 2 Castelldefels Barcelona 08860 Spain Home Fax: 934169730. Personal E-mail: garatjm@hotmail.com.

GARAVAGLIA, JAN C., forensic pathologist, chief medical examiner; married; 2 children. AB magna cum laude, St. Louis U. Sch. Medicine, 1978, MD, 1982. Cert. Am. Bd. Pathology in combined anatomic and clin. pathology, Am. Bd. Pathology in forensic pathology. Fellowship, forensic pathology Dade County Med. Examiner's Office, Miami, Fla.; intern, internal medicine St. Louis U. Hosp., 1982, resident, anatomic/clin. pathology dept., 1983—87; assoc. med. examiner Duval County, Jacksonville, Fla., 1988—91, Ga., 1991—93; med. examiner Bexar County Forensic Sci. Ctr., San Antonio, 1993—2003; dep. chief med. officer Med. Examiner's Office, Orlando, Fla., 2003—04; chief med. examiner Orange-Osceola Med. Examiner's Office, Dist. 9, Orlando, Fla., 2004—. Clin. asst. prof., dept. pathology U. Tex. Health Sci. Ctr., San Antonio, 2000, mem. grad. faculty coun., grad. sch. biomedical sci.; given numerous presentations and lectures at various institutions. Published media Jour. of Forensic Sciences, Am. Jour. Forensic Medicine and Pathology, host Dr. G: Chief Medical Examiner (Discovery Channel), 2004—; author: How Not to Die, 2008. Recipient Hidalgo award, Bexar County Commrs. Ct., Tex., 2000. Mem.: Am. Acad. Forensic Scis., Nat. Assn. Med. Examiners. Office: Dist Nine Medical Examiner's Office 2350 E Michigan St Orlando FL 32806-4939

GARBARINI, WILLIAM NICHOLAS, pharmaceutical executive; b. Somerville, NJ, Oct. 24, 1969; s. William Nicholas and Janet L. Garbarini; m. Maureen Elizabeth Murphy, June 10, 1995; children: Dana Marie, William Nicholas. BS in Econs., Coll. N.J., 1992; MBA in Pharm. Studies, Fairleigh Dickinson U., 2002. Profl. sales rep. Glaxo SmithKline, Research Triangle Park, NC, 1993—96; account supr. Lowe Healthcare Worldwide, NYC, 1996—98; product mgr. Key Pharmaceuticals Schering-Plough Corp., Kenilworth, NJ, 1998—2000; dir. client svcs. Caresoft, Inc., Sunnyvale, Calif., 2000—01; exec. dir. sales and mktg. Ferring Pharms. Inc., Suffern, NY, 2001—. Recipient Dir. Leading Change award, Burroughs Wellcome Co., 1995; named Premier Performer, 1994—95; named to Ferring Excellence Club, 2003, 2005, 2006. Mem.: Delta Mu Delta, Phi Kappa Psi (chpt. pres. 1991—92). Roman Catholic. Avocations: music, baseball, golf, woodworking. Home: 421 Manor Ave Cranford NJ 07016 Office: Ferring Pharmaceuticals Inc 4 Gatehall Dr 3rd Fl Parsippany NJ 07054 Office Fax: 973-796-1711. Business E-Mail: william.garbarini@ferring.com.

GARBARINO, SERGIO, neurologist, educator; b. Genova, Italy, Aug. 30, 1960; s. Maria Caterina Magalotti and Giuseppe Garbarino; m. Maria Elisabetta Bonetti, May 5, 1995; children: Federica, Emanuela. Degree in Medicina, U. Genova, 1988. Cert. neurophysiologist Italy, 1993, neurologist Italy, 1998. Health svc. state police Dept. Interior, Genoa, Italy, 1993—; prof. Dept. Health Scis. and Preventive Medicine, Genoa, 1999—. Pres. Sci. Working Com. Rd. Accidents and Sleepiness Italian Sleep Medicine Assn., 2004—. Contbr. articles to profl. jours. (Internat. "Edward Schaeffer award", 2004). Prevention sleep related accidents Nat. And Internat., Genoa, 1998—2008. Col. State Police, 2001—08, Italy. Liberal. Roman Catholic. Avocations: music, skiing, history. Business E-Mail: uffsanitpol.ge@libero.it.

GARBAY, JEAN-REMI, surgeon; b. Paris, Mar. 8, 1959; MD, U. Paris, 1986. Sr. asst. Inst. Gustave Roussy, Villejuif, France, 1999—. Office: 114 rue E Vaillant Villejuif 94805 France Business E-Mail: garbay@igr.fr.

GARBER, ALAN MICHAEL, internist, educator, economist; s. Harry Garber; m. Anne Yahanda, Oct. 9, 1988. AB in Econs. summa cum laude, Harvard Coll., 1976, AM in Econs., 1977, PhD (hon.) in Econs., 1982; MD, Stanford U., 1983. Diplomate Am. Bd. Internal Medicine. Cons. Inst. Medicine, Washington, 1979-80; clin. fellow Med. Sch. Harvard U., Boston, 1983-86, rsch. fellow John F. Kennedy Sch. Govt. Cambridge, Mass., 1986; staff physician VA Palo Alto Health Care System, Calif., 1986—; rsch. assoc. Nat. Bur. Econ. Rsch., Palo Alto, Calif., 1986—, dir. health care program Cambridge, 1990—; asst. prof. Stanford U., Calif., 1986-93, assoc. prof., 1993-98, dir. Ctr. Health Policy/Ctr. Primary Care and Outcomes Rsch., 1997—, prof. medicine, 1998—, Henry J. Kaiser jr. prof., endowed chair; contractor Office Tech. Assessment, Washington, 1987-88, 89-92. Chair Medicare Coverage Adv. Com., 2005—07; mem. Nat. Adv. Coun. Aging, 2004—07. Grad. fellow NSF, 1976, Henry J. Kaiser faculty fellow Kaiser Found., 1989-92. Fellow ACP, Acad. Health; mem. Inst. Medicine of NAS, Soc. Med. Decision Making (trustee 1989-91), Am. Econ. Assn., Am. Fedn. Clin. Rsch. (nat. councillor 1991-96), Soc. Gen. Internal Medicine, Am. Soc. for Clin. Investigation, Assn. Am. Physicians, Internat. Health Econs. Assn. Office: Primary Care Outcomes Rsch Ctr Health Policy 117 Encina Commons Stanford CA 94305-6019 Office Phone: 650-723-0920.

GARBER, DAVID ALEXANDER, dentist, educator; b. Johannesburg; Grad., U. Witwatersrand, South Africa, 1970; postgrad in Periodontics, U. Pa., Phila., 1977, postgrad in Periodontal Prosthesis (Fixed Prosthodontics), 1978, DMD, 1981. Lic. Great Britain, 1970, South Africa, 1970, Nat. Bd. USA, 1976, Pa., 1977, Ga., 1981. Lectr. and clin. instr. Univ. Witwatersrand, South Africa, 1973—74; tchg. fellow form and function of the masticatory system sch. of dental medicine Univ. Pa., 1977—78; editor Fixed Prosthodontics, Clark's Clin. Dentistry, 1985; asst. prof. form and function of the masticatory system sch. of dental medicine Univ. Pa., dir. group clin. practice sch. of medicine, 1978—82, dir. fixed prosthodontics didactic program, 1981—82, dir. fixed prosthodontics (crown and bridge) sch. of medicine, 1981—82, dir. diagnosis and treatment planning seminars, 1978—82, ast. prof. restorative dentistry sch. of dental medicine, 1978—82, asst. clin. prof. periodontics, 1983; spl. letr. esthetic dentistry sch. of medicine Emory Univ., 1984—91; clin. prof. dept. of prosthodontics La. State Univ., 1996—; clin. prof. of periodontics sch. of dental medicine Med. Coll. of Ga., 1987—, clin. prof. of oral rehab. sch. of dental medicine, 1988—; adj. prof. dept. of restorative dentistry Univ. Tex. Health Sci. Ctr., San Antonio, 1999—; dentist Goldstein, Garber and Salama. Editl. bd. Clin. Implant Dentistry and Related Rsch., 2000; sci. cons. Revista Dental Press de Estética, 2006; editor Functional Esthetics and Restorative Dentistry Adv. Bd., 2007—. Co-author: (publ.) Porcelain Laminate Veneers, Bleaching Teeth, orcelain & Composite Inlays and Onlay, Complete Dental Bleaching, (jour.) A Method of Registering Centric Relation, Temp. Stblzn. of Periodontally Involved Teeth, Adjunctive Orthodontics in Oral Rehab., 1977, A Temp. Permanent Splint, 1979, An Alternative to Cast Bridgework in Selected, 1979, various jours. including Loss of Arch Integrity Due to Interproximal Caries, Repair of a Bony Defect Using a Intraoral Exostosis as the Donor Site and Treatment of Posterior Bite Collapse-Occlusal Therapy. Recipient The Sauk Schulger Meml. award for Excellence in Diagnosis and Treatment Planning, Gordon J. Christensen Lectr. Recognition award, The Northeastern Periodontal Soc. Isador Hirschfield award for Clin. Excellence, Prof. of the Year award, Univ. Pa. Fellow: Internat. Coll. of Dentists; mem.: Am. Prosthodontic Soc., Am. Acad. of Periodontics, Am. Acad. of Fized Prosthodontics, Acad. of Osseointegrations, Am. Acad. of Esthetic Dentistry. Office: Goldstein, Garber and Salama LLC Ste 800 600 Galleria Parkway SE Atlanta GA 30339 Office Phone: 404-261-4941. Office Fax: 404-261-4946.

GARBER, JEFFREY RICHARD, endocrinologist; b. Bklyn., Nov. 25, 1949; s. Aaron and Mae Garber; m. Sheri Leiman, May 30, 1974; children: Benjamin, Solomon. AB, Cornell U., Ithaca, NY, 1971; MD, SUNY, Stony Brook, 1974. Diplomate Am. Bd. Internal Medicine, Am. Bd. Endocrinology. Chief endocrinology Harvard Vanguard Med. Assocs., Boston, 1981—; assoc. prof. medicine Harvard Med. Sch. Author: The Harvard Medical School Guide to Overcoming Thyroid Problems, 2005. Mem. med. adv. coun. Thyroid Found. Am., Boston. Recipient physician recognition award, Harvard Cmty. Health Plan, 1985, 1988, Disting. Alumnus award, Stony Brook U. Sch. Medicine, 2009; Peabody Clin. fellow, Harvard Med. Sch., 1981—84. Fellow: ACP, Am. Thyroid Assn. (mem. exec. coun. 2000—04), Am. Assn. Clin. Endocrinology (bd. dirs. 1999—2005, sec./treas. 2005—06, v.p. 2007—08, pres. elect 2008—09, pres. 2009—10), Am. Coll. Endocrinology (trustee 2003—06, chancellor 2010, pres. elect 2011). Office: Harvard Vanguard Med Assoc 133 Brookline Ave Boston MA 02215

GARBHAPU, ASUNTHA, physician, educator; b. India, Aug. 15, 1970; PharmM, AU coll. Pharm. Scis., 1995; PhD in Pharmacology, SP Women's U., Tirupati, 2009. Assoc. prof., physician S P W Poly., 2000—. Mem.: Indian Pharm. Assn. Office: S P W Polytech Tirupati Andhra Pradesh 517502 India Personal E-mail: yasuntharaj@yahoo.co.in.

GARCEZ, AGUINALDO SILVA, dental educator, researcher; b. Trremembé, Brazil, Nov. 5, 1973; Degree in Dentistry, Taubaté U., 1995; PhD, IPEN, São Paulo, 2007. Asst. prof. Dental Rsch. Ctr. São Leopoldo Mandic, 2009—. Rschr. Nat. Inst. Nuc. and Energetic Rsch., 2007. Grant, Nat. Coun. Rsch., CNPq. Office: Rua Nossa Senhora da Lapa 671 sala 53 São Paulo 05072-000 Brazil Office Fax: 55 11 3645 1985. Personal E-mail: garcez.segundo@gmail.com.

GARCHA, VIKRAM, dentist, educator; b. Ferozepur, Punjab, Aug. 19, 1977; BDS, Bharati Vidyapeeth Deemned U., Pune, India, 2002; MDS in Pub. Health Dentistry, Dr. D.Y. Patil Dental Coll. and Hosp., Pimpri, Pune, 2008. Sr. lectr. Singhad Dental Coll. and Hosp., Pune, 2010—. Mem.: Indian Assn. Pub. Health Dentistry, Indian Dental Assn. Avocations: sports, mountain climbing. Home: A-4/302 Ganga Satellite Wanowrie Pune Maharashtra 411040 India Personal E-mail: garchavikram@rediffmail.com.

GARCÍA, ELBA, dentist, former city councilwoman; b. Mexico City; m. Domingo García; 2 children. Degree in Odontology, U. Autonoma Metropolitana, Mexico City; DDS, Baylor Coll. Dentistry, Coll. Station, Tex. Pvt. practice García-Ibancovichi Dental, Dallas, 1990—; councilwoman, Dist. 1 Dallas City Coun., 2001—09, mayor pro tempore, 2007—09, chair pub. safety com., mem. fin., audit & accountability com., housing com., vice-chair Trinity River Project. Chair City of Dallas Domestic Violence Task Force. Recipient Motherhood Lifetime Achievement award, Dallas Can! Acad., 2006, Advocacy in Film award, Dallas Film Commn., 2006, Aspen Inst.-Rodel Fellowship in Pub. Leadership, 2007, 100 Women of Distinction award, Am. Assn. Univ. Women, 2008, Women of Spirit award, Am. Jewish Congress, 2008, OHTLI award, Inst. of Mexicans Abroad, 2008, Presdl. Citation, Tex. Animal Control Assn., 2008; named Best City Coun. Mem., Dallas Observer, 2002, Citizen of Yr., Oak Cliff Tribune, 2005; named a Most Outstanding Cmty. Leader, Dallas Can! Acad., 2003. Mem.: Oak Cliff C. of C. (Pub. Servant award 2008), Lake Cliff Neighborhood Assn., Greater Hispanic C. of C. (Leadership award 2008). Mailing: Dallas City Hall 1500 Marilla St Rm 5EN Dallas TX 75201-6390 Office Phone: 214-670-4052. Fax: 214-670-3409. E-mail: egarcia@mail.ci.dallas.tx.us. *

GARCIA, ISABEL (ANA ISABEL GARCIA), federal agency administrator, dentist, medical researcher; BS in Chemistry, U. Mary Washington; MD in Dental Surgery, Med. Coll. of Va.; MPH, U. Mich. Diplomate Am. Bd. Dental Public Health. Health sci. adminstr. Agency for Healthcare Rsch. and Quality; spl. asst. for sci. transfer Nat. Inst. of Dental and Craniofacial Rsch., NIH, Bethesda, Md., 1995, dir. Office of Sci. Policy and Analysis, dep. dir., 2007—, acting dir., 2010—. Recipient Spl. Assignment Award, Hazardous Duty Award, Fgn. Award. Mem.: Am. Pub. Health Assn., Am. Assn. Pub. Health Dentistry (exec. coun., mem. Oral Health Sect.). Office: National Institute of Dental and Craniofacial Research NIH 31 Center Dr Bethesda MD 20892-2190 Office Phone: 301-496-9469. E-mail: isabel.garcia@nih.gov. *

GARCIA, JEAN-MICHEL, research scientist; b. Toulouse, France, Sept. 17, 1974; Degree in Chem. Engring., ENSCL, 1998; PhD, U. Law and Health, Lille, 2003. Translational rsch. group leader HKU-Pasteur Rsch. Ctr., 2003—. Recipient Young Investigator awards, IX & X Internat. Symposium Respiratory Viral Infections. Mem.: AAAS, Asia Pacific Soc. Med. Virology. Office: Dexter HC Man Bldg 8 Sassoon Rd Hong Kong Hong Kong Business E-Mail: jmgarcia@hku.hk.

GARCIA, JOSE MANUEL, endocrinologist, educator; b. Argentina, Mar. 23, 1974; MD, U. Catolica De Cordoba, 1997; PhD, Baylor Coll. Medicine, 2011. Asst. prof., dept. vets. affairs Baylor Coll. Medicine, 2005—. Mem.: Endocrine Soc. Office: 2002 Holcombe Blvd Houston TX 77030 Business E-Mail: jgarcia1@bcm.edu.

GARCIA, JOXEL, dean, former federal agency administrator; b. Arecibo, PR, Feb. 21, 1962; m. Ingrid Grafals; children: Joshua, Kristen. B in pre-med, U. Puerto Rico, 1984; MD, Ponce Sch. Medicine, PR, 1988; MBA, U. Hartford, Conn., 1999; cert. in advanced pelvic endoscopy laser, U. Fla. (Gainesville) Sch. Me., 1991; cert. in advanced hysteroscopic surgery, St. Francis Hosp. Med. Ctr., Hartford, 1993; cert. laparoscopic vaginal hysterectomy, St. Raphael's Hosp., 1993; cert. colposcopic, laparoscopic, and hysteroscopic surgery, The Grad. Sch., Philadelphia, Pena., 1994. Diplomate Am. Bd. Ob-Gyn. Resident in ob-gyn Mt. Sinai Hosp, Hartford, Conn., 1988-91, chief resident in ob-gyn, 1991-92; asst. dir. St. Francis Hosp. Med. Ctr., Hartford, Conn., 1995-99; resident site dir. in ob-gyn Mt. Sinai Hosp., Hartford, Conn., 1995-96; asst. attending physician St. Francis Hosp. and Med. Ctr., Hartford, Conn., 1995-96; asst. clin. prof. U. Conn. Sch. Med., Farmington, Conn., 1996—; dir. gynecol. endoscopy edn. St. Francis Hosp. Med. Ctr., Hartford, Conn., 1997-99; commr. Conn. Dept. Pub. Health, Hartford, Conn., 1999—2003; dep. dir. Pan Am. Health Org. (PAHO); sr. v.p., sr. medical adv. Maximus Federal Services; asst. sec. for health US Dept. Health & Human Services, Washington, 2008—09; pres., dean Ponce Sch. Medicine and Health Sciences, PR, 2009—. Contbr. articles to profl. jours.; inventor laparoscopic trocar port filter. Bd. dirs. Cath. Families Svcs. Capital Region; mem. Cath. Charities. Fellow Am. Coll. Ob-Gyn; mem. AMA, Hartford County Med. Soc., Greater Hartford Ob-Gyn Soc., Am. Soc. Reproductive Med., Internat. Pelvic Pain Soc., Am. Inst. Ultrasound in Med., Soc. Pelvic Reconstructive Surgeons, Am. Assn. Gynecol. Laparoscopists, Soc. Laparoscopic and Endoscopic Surgeons. Avocations: tennis, skiing, music. Office: Ponce Sch Medicine & Health Sciences PO Box 7004 Ponce PR 00732 *

GARCIA, MARIA LUISA, biochemist, researcher; b. Valladolid, Spain, Oct. 9, 1953; came to U.S., 1979; d. Baldomero and Dolores (Garcia) G.; m. Gregory Kaczorowski, June 21, 1982. PhD, Autonoma U., Madrid, 1979. Sr. rsch. biochemist Merck & Co., Rahway, NJ, 1985—87, rsch. fellow, 1987—91, sr. rsch. fellow, 1991—97, sr. investigator, 1997—2003, disting. sr. investigator, 2003—09, Kanalis Consulting, LLC, 2009—, v.p. Invited speaker, presenter papers in field. Contbr. numerous articles and revs. to profl. jours.; patentee in field. Mem. AAAS, Am. Soc. Biol. Chemists, Biophys. Soc. Home: 5 Ashbrook Dr Edison NJ 08820-4318 Personal E-mail: mlgarciagarcia@optonlinc.net.

GARCIA, ROBERT, lawyer; b. Guatemala, Aug. 4, 1952; BA, Stanford U., 1974; JD, Stanford Law Sch., 1978. Exec. dir. Ctr. Law In Pub. Interest, 2003—06; exec. dir., counsel, founder The City Project, 2000—. Chair Citizens' Sch. Bond Oversight Com., 2000—05. Recipient Pres.'s award, APHA. Mem.: Latino Coalition Healthy Calif. Avocations: reading, camping, bicycling. Office: 1055 Wilshire Blvd Ste 1660 Los Angeles CA 90017 Office Fax: 213-977-5457. Business E-Mail: rgarcia@cityprojectca.org.

GARCIA, YERKA, pharmacist, consultant; b. Antofagasta, Feb. 20, 1940; Degree in Pharmaceutical Chemistry, U. Chile, 1963; MSc in Clinical Pharmacy, 2008. Diplomate pharmaceutical U. Chile, 2001; cert. in lab. specialist U. Chile, 1969. Chief clinical lab Cardiovascular Ctr. Luis Calvo Mackenna Hosp., 1964—2001; chief pharmacy and clinical lab Pediatric Cardiology Inst., 1994—2005; pharmacy cons Pasteur Ophtalmological Clinic, 2010—. Adj. prof. Lab Clin. Pathology Faculty Chemistry and Pharmacy., U.Chile, 1970—71; instr. Pediatric Dept. Sch.Medicine. U. Chil, 1979—80; sup. prof. clin. lab training Sch. Biochemistry. U. Chile, 1982—89. Mem.: Soc. Chilena de Quimica Clinica (founder mem. 1988), ConFedn. LatinoAm.a de Bioquimica Clinica, Internat. Fedn.Clin. Chemistry, Soc. Quimicos Farmaceuticos y Bioquimicos Lab. (dir. 1964). Avocations: bicycling, gymnastics, bridge. Home: Helsby 8796 Casa g la reina Santiago Chile Home Fax: 33028207152.

GARCIA-BUÑUEL, LUIS, neurologist; b. Madrid, Feb. 24, 1931; came to U.S., 1955; s. Pedro Garcia and Concepcion Buñuel; m. Virginia May Hile, June 30, 1960. BA, BS, U. Zaragoza, Spain, 1949; MD, U. Zaragoza, 1955. Diplomate Am. Bd. Psychiatry and Neurology. Resident neurology Georgetown U., Washington, 1955-59; postdoctoral fellow Washington U., St. Louis, 1959-61; asst. prof. neurology Thomas Jefferson U., Phila., 1961-67; assoc. prof. U. N.Mex., Albuquerque, 1967-72, U. Oreg. Health Scis. Ctr., Portland, 1972-84; chief neurology svc. Portland VA Med. Ctr., 1972-84; pvt. practice, Phoenix, 1984—; chief staff Carl T. Hayden VA Med. Ctr., Phoenix, 1984-96. Contbr. articles to sci. jours., including Nature, Sci., Neurology, Jour. Neurol. Sci. Lt. Spanish Air Force, 1952 55. Fellow Am. Acad. Neurology (sr. mem.), Sigma Xi. Unitarian Universalist. Avocations: painting, computer art, steel-welded sculpture. Home and Office: 128 N French Dr Prescott AZ 86303 Personal E-mail: lgbunuel@gmail.com.

GARCIA FRANCO, CARLOS ENRIQUE, thoracic surgeon; b. Madrid, June 26, 1974; s. Francisco Garcia Aguilera and Mercedes Franco Frias. MD, Complutense U. Med. Sch., 1998. Cert. Ednl. Commn. Br. Fgn. Med. Grads., 2005. Resident gen. thoracic surgery Fundacion Jimenez Diaz, Madrid, 2000—05; clin. fellow gen. thoracic surgery Mayo Clinic, Rochester, Minn., 2005—, fellow, 2005—06. Contbr. articles to profl. jours. Mem.: Spanish Soc. Pulmunology and Thoracic Surgey, European Soc. Thoracic Surgeons (assoc.). Christian. Avocations: reading, trekking, golf, skiing. Office: Mayo Clinic 200 First Street SW Rochester MN 55905 Home Fax: +34915439891. Personal E-mail: cgarciafranco@terra.es. Business E-Mail: garciafranco.carlos@mayo.edu.

GARCIA-GERMAN VAZQUEZ, DIEGO, orthopedist; b. Madrid, Jan. 7, 1977; MD, U. Complutense, Madrid, 2011. Orthop. surgeon, 2002; tchr. orthop. U. San Pablo Ceu, 2009. Recipient Miguel Cabanela award, Secot-Mayo Clinic. Fellow: European Bd. Orthop.; mem.: AEA, SOMACOT, SECOT. Office: Reina Victoria 24 Madrid 28003 Spain E-mail: doctorgarciagerman@gmail.com.

GARCIA-LAVIN, SILVIA, podiatrist; b. Sept. 4, 1968; DPM, NY Coll. Podiatric medicine, 2000. Podiatrist C&GL Podiatry Assocs., PC, 2010—. Office: 1324 Bergen St Brooklyn NY 11213 Personal E-mail: silugl@yahoo.com.

GARCIA-MEDINA, JOSE, physician, department chairman; b. Murcia, Spain, Feb. 19, 1957; MD, Facultad de Medicina de Murcia, 1982. Chmn. Interventional Radiology Dept., 2005—. Office: Avda Intendente Jorge Palacios 1 Murcia 30003 Spain Office Fax: 0034968359949. Business E-Mail: josegmedina@seram.org.

GARCÍA-MENAYA, JESÚS MIGUEL, allergist; b. Badajoz, Spain, Aug. 12, 1967; s. Rafael García and Concepción Menaya; m. Concepción Cordobes-Durán, June 10, 2006; 1 child, Nicolás García-Cordobés. Allergy specialist Hosp. Infanta Cristina, Badajoz, 2000—. Author: (book) Polymorphism NAT2 and Human Pathology, Allergy Diagnosis. Mem.: Spanish Soc. Allergy and Clin. Immunology, European Acad. Allergy and Clin. Immunology. Office: Hosp Infanta Cristina Ave De Portugal S/N Badajoz 06080 Spain Personal E-mail: susmi1@hotmail.com.

GARCÍA MENDIETA, JORGE SAÚL, cardiologist, educator; b. Tuluá, Valle del Cauca, Colombia, Dec. 4, 1949; s. Saulo Antonio Mendieta and Josefina García; m. Aura Vásquez Palacios; 1 child, Jorge Saúl García Vásquez. Diplomate U. Nacional, Colombia, 1977, cert. gen. and digestive surgery U. Autonoma, Spain, 1983, cardiovascular surgery ASCOFAME, Colombia, 1986. Tchr. cardiovasc. surgery U. Nacional, Bogotá DC, Cundinamarca, Colombia, 1985—; surgeon congenital cardiac anomalies pediatry U. Materno-Insular Hosp., Las Palmas de GC, Las Palmas, Spain, 2001—; illustrator Surg. Techs. Surgery Congenital Heart Diseases. Founder U. Nacional, Bogotá, Cundinamarca, Colombia, 1988, consultor, 1985—2000; prof. U. Las Palmas de Gran Canaria, Las Palmas, Spain, 2008—, prof. master's degree (cooperacion y desarrollo internacional), 2008—, prof. master's degree(atencion primaria en salud), 2010—; surgery prof. U. Alcalá de Henares, Alcalá de Henares, Madrid, Spain, 2000—10; internat. coord. Between U. Nacional, U. Ctrl. del Valle del Cauca and U. Alcalá de Henares, Bogotá-Las Palmas, Colombia, 1995—; sci. adviser European Union, Las Palmas, 2002—; prof. ad honorem U. Ctrl. del Valle del Cauca, Tulua, Valle del Cauca, Colombia, 2001—; hon. chmn. Expociencia, Tuluá, 2005—; hon. prof. U. Alcalá de Henares, Madrid, 2007—; ten yr. plan for edn. adviser Secretaría de Educación, Tuluá, Valle del Cauca, Colombia, 2008—; sci. dir. II Congreso Sociedad Española de Cardiología Pediatrica y Cardiopatias Congenitas, San Bartolomé de Tirajana, Maspalomas, Las Palmas, Spain, 2004; adviser sci. innovation corpen U. Las Palmas de Gran Canaria, Las Palmas de GC, Las Palmas, 2008—. Contbr. articles to profl. jours. Gestor Granja Autosostenible, Barragan Tuluá, Valle del Cauca, Colombia, 2009—10. Recipient Premio Norma award, Norma Editl., 1968, Internat. Academic Award Winner (Med. Specialties), Spanish Govt., 1979, Facultad de Ciencias de la Salud Jorge Saul Garcia Mendieta, U. Ctrl. del Valle del Cauca Tulua Colombia, Distincion Saul Garcia a la investigacion en salud, U. Ctrl. del Valle del Cauca, Tuluá, Colombia, 1997, Condecoracion, U. Ctrl. del Valle del Cauca, 1997, Mejor residente del Hosp. (Departamento de Cirugia Gen.) y mejor residente del servicio de todos los tiempos (Cirugia Cardiaca Pediatrica), Comision de Docencia Hosp. Ramon y Cajal, 1998, Embajador Tulueño: Maxima distincion, Cámara de Comercio: FENALCO:Tuluá/Colombia, 2002, Personaje del Mural-Homenaje:, Concejo Mcpl. de Tuluá, Colombia, 2002, Homenaje al talento Vallecaucano en el exterior, Gobernación Valle del Cauca, Colombia, 2003, Orden Independencia Vallecaucana en el grado de, Asamblea Departamental del Valle del Cauca, Colombia, 2003, Condecoración, Alcaldia Tulua Colombia, 2006, award, Cámara de Representantes del Hon. Congreso de la República de Colombia, 2007, Excellence medal, U. Ctrl. Valle Colombia, 1997, Dr. Manuel Quero Jimenez award, Spanish Soc. Pediat. Cardiology Maspalomas Congress, 2004, Order as Honorific Disting. award, Tulua, 2004, Outstanding Sci. Character award, El Tabloide Newspaper, Tulua, 2010, Nina Martinez de Gonzalez medal, City Hall fair Tulua Valle, 2010. Mem.: Jorge Saul Garcia Mendieta Sci. Club, UNESCO (hon.; chair human rights & democracy 2011), Asociación de especialistas Medicos. Tuluá (hon.; tulua 2009—10, Hon. Mem. 2009). Avocations: investigation, reading.

GARCIA-VALDECASAS, JUAN, JR., physician, consultant; b. Granada, Jan. 17, 1977; MD, Granada Sch. Medicine, 2001, MD, 2007. Med. cons. Hosp. U. S. Cecilio Granada, 2007—. Prof. Granada Sch. Medicine, 2007—. Mem.: Soc. Española ORL y PCF. Avocations: skiing, travel. Office: Av Dr Oloriz Granada 18012 Spain E-mail: orlvaldecasas@gmail.com.

GARD, GUNVOR ELISABET, physical therapist, educator; b. Orebro, July 11, 1950; Degree in Psychology, Uppsala U., 1972. Registered physiotherapist Karoiinska Inst. Stockhoj, 1977. Asst. prof. Lund U., 1987, mem. ethical bd. med. faculty, 1997; prof. physical therapy Lulea U., 2004—. Grantee, Social Insurance company and Vardai Found. Sweden. Mem.: Stress Mgmt. Orgn. Avocation: music. Home: Skallavangsvagen 18 Sodra Sandby 24733 Sweden

GARDEN, OLIVIER JAMES, surgeon, educator; b. Carluke, Scotland, Nov. 13, 1953; s. James Garden and Marguerite Jeanne Vourc'h; m. Amanda Gillian Merrills; children: Stephen, Katherine. BSc, U. Edinburgh, Scotland, 1974, MB, BChir, 1977, MD, 1987. Lectr. U. Glasgow, Scotland, 1985—88; sr. lectr. U. Edinburgh, 1988—97, prof. hepatobiliary surgery, 1997—2000, Regius prof. clinical surgery, 2000—, head Sch. Clin. Scis. and Cmty. Health, 2002—06. Dir. Scottish Liver Transplant Unit, Edinburgh, 1992—2004; cons. surgeon Royal Infirmary, Edinburgh, 1988—; co. sec. British Jour. Surgery Soc., Ltd., 2003—; surgeon to the Queen, Scotland, 2004—. Contbr. articles to profl. jours., editor: numerous undergrad. and postgrad. textbooks. Fellow: Royal Coll. Surgeons Edinburgh, Royal Coll. Physicians and Surgeons Glasgow, Royal Coll. Physicians and Surgeons Can. (hon.), Royal Coll. Surgeons Edinburgh, Royal Australian Coll. Surgeons (hon.); mem.: Internat. Hepato-Pancreato-Biliary Assn. (pres. elect 2010—), Assn. Upper GI Surgeons Great Britain and Ireland (pres. 2002—04), Am. Surg. Assn. (hon.), New Club, Craigielaw Golf Club. Home: 22 Moston Terrace Edinburgh EH9 2DE Scotland Office: Clinical & Surg Scis Royal Infirmary 51 Little France Crescent Edinburgh EH16 4SA Scotland Home Phone: 44 131 667 3715; Office Phone: 44 131 242 3614. Office Fax: 44 131 242 3617. Business E-Mail: ojgarden@ed.ac.uk.

GARDIN, JULIUS MARKUS, cardiologist, educator; b. Detroit, Jan. 14, 1949; s. Abram and Fania (Toba) G.; children: Adam Lev, Tova Michal, Margot Anne; m. Stacey M. Berman Teaneck, Aug. 23, 2010. BS with high distinction, U. Mich., 1968, MD cum laude, 1972. Diplomate Am. Bd. Internal Medicine; cert. cardiovascular diseases. Intern then resident in medicine U. Mich., Ann Arbor, 1972-75; fellow in cardiology Georgetown U., Washington, 1975-77; dir. cardiology noninvasive lab., staff cardiologist Lakeside VA Med. Ctr., Chgo., 1977-79; staff cardiologist Northwestern U., Chgo., 1977—79, asst. prof. Med. Sch., 1978—79; dir. cardiology noninvasive lab. Irvine Med. Ctr. U. Calif., Orange, 1979-2000, from asst. prof. to assoc. prof. Irvine Med. Ctr., 1979—89, prof., 1989-2000, chief cardiology Irvine, 1994-99; acting chief cardiology Long Beach (Calif.) VA Med. Ctr., 1982—84; prof. Wayne State U., Detroit, 2000—; St. John Guild disting. chair, cardiovascular diseases St. John Hosp. and Med. Ctr., Detroit, 2000—, chief div. cardiology, 2000—07, vice chmn. rsch. dept. medicine, 2007—; prof., founding chmn. dept. internal medicine Touro U. Coll. Medicine, NJ, 2008—09; chmn. dept. internal medicine Hackensack U. Med. Ctr., NJ, 2008—; prof. dept. internal medicine U. Medicine and Dentistry, NJ Med. Sch., 2008—. Co-editor: Textbook of Two-Dimensional Echocardiography, 1983, assoc. editor Preventive Cardiology: A Practical Approach, 2000, 05; assoc. editor (jour.) Update on Cardiovascular Diagnostics, 1982, Am. Jour. Cardiac Imaging, 1985-97, Jour. Am. Soc. Echocardiography, 2007—; mem. editl. bd. Archives of Internal Medicine and Chest, 1978-88, Am. Jour. Noninvasive Cardiology, 1985-95, Am. Jour. Cardiology, 1987-94, 97—, Cardiovascular Imaging, 1988, Echocardiography, 1985—, Jour. Am. Coll. Cardiology, 1990-94, 2001-05, Am. Jour. Geriatric Cardiology, 1992-2008, Am. Jour. Sports Medicine, 1998-2004, Jour. Am. Soc. Echocardiography, 1992-, Preventive Cardiology, 2010; cardiovasc. area editor Jour. Clin. Ultrasound, 1989-94; contbr. articles to profl. jours. Maj. Med. Svc. Corps USAR. Grantee Am. Heart Assn., 1980-84, 99-02, Nat. Heart Lung and Blood Inst., 1988-2008; named one of Best Drs. in Am. Woodward White Publs., 1994-, Am.'s Top Drs. Castle Connolly Publs., 2002-. Fellow ACP, Am. Coll. Cardiology (physician workforce adv., health care reform and echocardiography coms., 1993-99, publs. com. 2007-08, ACC/AHA/ACP-ASIM task force to update guidelines for mgmt. of patients with chronic stable angina 1998-99, 01-02, co-chair 2007—), Am. Heart Assn. (coun. clin. cardiology, coun. epidemiology and prevention, coun. cardiovascular radiology, Seymour Gordon Disting. Achievement Award AHA Detroit chpt. 2006), Soc. Geriat. Cardiology (v.p. 1990-92, pres. 1992-93); mem. Internat. Cardiac Doppler Soc. (bd. dirs., chmn. Pan-Am. sect. 1984—, v.p. 1988-90, pres. 1990-92, exec. sec. 2006-), Am. Soc. Echocardiography (bd. dirs., treas. 1989-91, v.p. 1991-93, pres. 1993-95, chmn. nomenclature and stds. 1991-95, chmn. task force on standardized echo report 1999-02, co-chmn. writing group on vascular imaging 2001—07, assoc. editor Jour. 2007—, extramural rsch. com. 2010-), U. Mich. Med. Ctr.

Alumni Assn. (bd. govs. 1979-81), Phi Beta Kappa, Alpha Omega Alpha, Phi Delta Epsilon. Jewish. Office: Hackensack U Med Ctr 30 Prospect Ave Hackensack NJ 07601 Office Phone: 201-996-3500. Personal E-mail: gardindoc@aol.com.

GARDNER, BERNARD, surgeon, educator; b. Bklyn., Oct. 1, 1931; s. Charles and Selma (Lovenberg) G.; m. Joan E. Mann., Dec. 18, 1954; children: Karen A., Pamela D., Robert A. AB cum laude, NYU, 1952, MD, 1956. Intern Bellevue Hosp. Ctr., NYC, 1956-57; resident Mt. Sinai Hosp., NYC, 1957-58, U. Calif. Med. Ctr., San Francisco, 1961-65; asst. prof. surgery SUNY Downstate Med. Ctr., Bklyn., 1965-68, assoc. prof., 1968-72, prof., 1972; prof. surgery, dir. Bklyn. Cancer Ctr., 1973—; prof., dir. divsn. surg. edn. U. Medicine and Dentistry of N.J., 1983—; dir. dept. surgery Hackensack Med. Ctr., 1983-92. Cons. VA Hosp., Luth. Med. Ctr., Swedish Hosp., Meth. Hosp., Kingsbrook Med. Ctr., all Bklyn., VA Hosp., Newark, N.J. Univ. Hosp., Newark; dir. divsn. surg. oncology Kings County Hosp., 1971; mem. study sect. on cancer edn. Nat. Cancer Inst., 1981-83. Author: (book) Emergency Surgery, 1974, 2d edit., 1986, Basic Surgery: Patient Oriented Text, 1978, 5th edit., 1995, Principles of Cancer Surgery, 1981, 2000, The Value of Corruption in a Democratic Society, prodr.: (plays) Two Mystery Plays, 2008, 5 Plays, 2010. Capt. USAF, 1958-60. Fellow Am. Cancer Soc., 1965-68; Markle fellow, 1968-73; recipient numerous grants, 1962— Fellow Soc. Surg. Oncology (pres. 1994—); mem. Am. Surg. Assn., Soc. Univ. Surgeons, Assn. Acad. Surgery (chmn. com. on issues 1971—), N.Y. Surg. Soc., N.Y. Cancer Soc., Soc. Exptl. Medicine and Biology. Achievements include research on mechanisms of cancer, mechanism of gall stone dissolution. Personal E-mail: mdbg10012@comcast.net.

GARDNER, CLYDE EDWARD, healthcare executive, consultant, educator; b. Steubenville, Ohio, Oct. 8, 1931; s. Peter D. and Louella Mary (Gillespie) G.; m. Patricia Jackson, Oct. 4, 1953 (div. Dec. 1977); 1 child, Bruce Stephen. BA, San Francisco State U., 1969, MS, 1971. Adminstr. Gardner Convalescent Hosp., Napa, Calif., 1955-68; exec. dir. Haight Ashbury Free Med. Clinic, San Francisco, 1970-71; lectr. San Francisco State U., 1969-71; dir. planning and rsch. divsn. N. Country Com. on Area Wide Health Planning, Canton, NY, 1971-77; prof. Gov.'s State U., University Park, Ill., 1977-83; sr. ptnr. Health Care Cons., Park Forest, Ill., 1983-86; exec. dir. Mahoning Shenango Area Health Edn. Network, Youngstown, Ohio, 1986-90; pres., CEO Mahoning Edn. and Tng. Network, Youngstown, Ohio, 1990-92, Health Sci. Assocs., Tucson, 1992—. Adj. prof. SUNY, Canton, 1975-76, Youngstown State U., 1987-90; bus. rep. Apollo Coll., 1994-95; rschr. FMR Rsch.; artist in residence Gardner Studio, 1994-2008; lectr. San Francisco State U., 1969-71. Author: Data Book for Health and Institutional Planning, 1981; author of numerous pub. health planning, health edn. studies and funded pvt., state and fed. health care grants, 1971-90. Pres. Found. I Ctr. for Human Devel., Harvey, Ill., 1978-83, U. Profls. of Ill., Chgo., 1982-83; bd. dirs. Blue Cross/Blue Shield Drug and Alcohol Benefit Study, Chgo., 1980-83; coord. pub. rels. and resource devel. VISTA; vol. Habitat for Humanity, Vista Leadership Corp, Tucson, 1997-98 Recipient Recognition award Ill. Dangerous Drugs Commn., 1980, 81, Outstanding Svc. award U. Profls. Ill., 1983-84, Outstanding Svc. award Ill. Fedn. Tchrs., 1983. Mem. Disabled Artist Assn. (bd. dirs., chair resource devel. com. 1992-93). Democrat. Avocations: painting, writing.

GARDNER, HOWARD EARL, psychologist, educator, writer; b. Scranton, Pa., July 11, 1943; s. Ralph and Hilde (Weilheimer) G.; m. Ellen Winner; children: Kerith, Jay, Andrew, Benjamin. AB summa cum laude, Harvard U., Cambridge, Mass., 1965, PhD, 1971; degree (hon.), Wheaton Coll., Mass., 2002, Curry Coll., Milton, Mass., 1992, New Eng. Conservatory Music, 1993, Ind. U., 1995, Moravian Coll., 1996, Cleve. Inst. Music, 1996, Salem State Coll., 1996, LI U., 1997, Macalester Coll., St. Paul, Minn., 1997, Tel-Aviv U., 1998, Princeton U., NJ, 1998, Pa. State U., State Coll., 1998, Ithaca Coll., NYC, 1999, Conn. Coll., New London, 1999, McGill U., Montreal, Quebec, Can., 1999, U. Hartford, Conn., 2000, Mass. Sch. Profl. Psychology, 2000, Nat. U. Ireland, 2001, U. Toronto, 2001, U. Urbino, Italy, 2003, East China Normal Univ., 2004, U. Valparaiso, Chile, 2006, Hanyang U., Republic of Korea, 2007, Wheelock Coll., 2009, U. Aegean, 2009, Nat. U. Athens, 2009, U. Rhodes, Greece, 2009, U. Athens, 2009, U. Sofia, Bulgaria, 2009. Lectr. edn. Harvard U., Cambridge, Mass., 1971-86, co-dir. Project Zero, 1972-2000, prof. edn., 1986-98—, affiliated prof. psychology, 1987—, Hobbs prof. cognition and edn., 1998—. Prof. neurology Boston U. Sch. Medicine, 1984-87, adj. prof. neurology, 1987-05; rsch. psychologist Boston VA Med. Ctr., 1978-93; hon. prof. East China Normal U., 2004. Author: The Shattered Mind, 1975, Art, Mind and Brain, 1982, Frames of Mind, 1983 (Best Book award APA 1984), The Mind's New Science, 1985 (William James award 1988), To Open Minds, 1989, The Unschooled Mind, 1991, Creating Minds, 1993, Leading Minds, 1995, Extraordinary Minds, 1997, The Disciplined Mind, 1999, Intelligence Reframed, 1999, (with M. Csikszentmihalyi and W. Damon) Good Work, 2001, (with W. Fischman, B. Solomon and D. Greenspan) Making Good, 2004, Changing Minds, 2004, The Development and Education of the Mind, 2006, Multiple Intelligences: New Horizons, 2006, Howard Gardner Under Fire, 2006, Five Minds for the Future, 2007, Responsibility at Work, 2007, Multiple Intelligences Around the World, 2009, Goodwork: Theory & Practice, 2010. Bd. mem. Amherst Coll., 2009—; bd. dir. Mus Modern Art, 2005—, Spencer Found., 2001—. Recipient Grawemeyer award in edn., 1990, Disting. Svc. medal Columbia U. Tchr.'s Coll., 1994, Pa. Gov.'s award in humanities, 1994, McGovern award Smithsonian Inst., 1998, Walker prize Boston Mus. of Sci., 1999, Samuel T. Orton award Internat. Dyslexia Assn., 1999, medal of the Pres. of Italy, 2001, Commonsense Media award, 2010; MacArthur Prize fellow, 1981, Guggenheim Found. fellow, 2000; rsch. grantee numerous govtl. and pvt. founds. Fellow AAAS, Am. Edn. Rsch. Assn.; mem. Am. Acad. Arts and Scis., Am. Philos. Soc., Royal Soc. Arts (Eng.), Phi Beta Kappa. Office: Harvard U Grad Sch Edn Larsen Hall Cambridge MA 02138 Business E-Mail: hgasst@pz.harvard.edu.

GARDNER, HOWARD GARRY, pediatrician, educator; b. Gary, Ind., Oct. 5, 1943; s. Oscar and Anita (Arenson) G.; m. Judith (Geen), June 21, 1986; children: Molly, Joseph. BA, Ind. U., 1965, MD, 1968. Intern, resident St. Louis U., 1969-73; pvt. practice Hinsdale (Ill.) Pediatrics, 1973-79, DuPage Pediatrics, Darien, Ill., 1979—; attending staff Hinsdale Hosp., 1973—, chmn. dept. pediatrics, 2000—02; courtesy staff Childrens Meml. Hosp., Chgo., 1988—. Clin. prof. dept. pediatrics Loyola U. Sch. of Medicine, Maywood, 1983-2002; chmn. dept. pediatrics Hinsdale Hosp., 1983-85, 2000-02; prof. clin. pediatrics Northwestern U. Med. Sch.; med. adv. bd. YMCA of the USA, Chgo., 1989-2006. Mem. editl. bd. Pediatric News, 1990—; contbr. articles to profl. jours. Co-chmn. med. adv. bd. DuPage Easter Seal Ctr., Villa Park, Ill.; past, founding mem. bd. dirs. Loyola Ronald McDonald House; co-founder, past pres. Ill. Child Passenger Safety Assn.; mem. med. adv. bd. Pathways Awareness Found.; officer, steering com. DuPage Interagy. Coun. on Early Intervention. Lt. USN, 1969-71. Recipient Outstanding Clin. Tchr. award Loyola Med. Sch., 1978, Tchr. of Yr. award Hinsdale Hosp. Family Practice Residency, 1981, Chgo. Caring Physician's award Met. Chgo. Health Care Coun., 1987, Buckle Up Am.! award Ill. Coalition for Safety Belt Use, 1991, Parent and Child Edn. Soc. 20th Anniversary Achievement award, 1992, Outstanding Vol. award West Suburban United Way, 1999, Carol Sanicki Crystal Heart award Easter Seals, DuPage, 2002, Dean's Tchg. Excellence award Northwestern U. Feinberg Sch. Medicine, 2007, Pioneer award Pathways Awareness Found., 2007. Fellow Am. Acad. Pediat. (past pres. Ill. chpt., past mem. nat. nominating com., instnl. rev. bd., chmn. com. on injury and poison prevention 2007-, Pisani Pediatrician of Yr. award 1986); mem. Chgo. Pediat. Soc. (past pres., Archibald Hoyne Pediatrician of Yr. 1994), Ill. Maternal and Child Health Coalition (bd. dirs., pres., 2000-2002, Advocacy award 1996), DuPage County Med. Soc. Democrat. Jewish. Avocations: reading, skiing, photography. Office: DuPage Pediatrics 1306 Plainfield Rd Darien IL 60561-5038 E-mail: ggard4922@aol.com.

GARDNER, JOHN HOWLAND, III, neurologist; b. New Haven, Oct. 1, 1931; s. John Howland Jr. and Ruth (Huntley) G.; m. Anne Kates Larkin, Apr. 23, 1960 (dec. Apr., 2006); children: Elizabeth Larkin Gardner Milgram, Helen Douglass Gardner. Student, Harvard U., 1949-52; MD, Yale, 1956. Diplomate Am. Bd. Psychiatry and Neurology. Intern Stanford, 1956-57; asst. to assoc. resident in medicine Strong Mem. Hosp., Rochester, NY, 1957-59; resident in neurology Boston City Hosp., 1959-61; resident in neuropathology Strong Mem. Hosp., Rochester, NY, 1961-62; officer in charge in neurology USAF Hosp. Keesler AFB, Biloxi, Miss., 1962-64; asst. prof. Case Western Res. U. Sch. Med., Cleve., 1965-67; asst. clin. prof. Case Western Res. U. Sch. Medicine, Cleve., 1967-83, assoc. clin. prof., 1983-98, emeritus assoc. prof. neurology, 1998—; chief of neurology St. Luke's Hosp., Cleve., 1967-85; neurologist U. Suburban Health Care Ctr., Cleve., 1975-96. Pres. Greater Cleve. Chpt. Epilepsy Fdn. America, 1973-75; chmn. Mediation Comm. Acad. Med. Cleve., 1982-84. Vestryman, St. Paul's Episcopal Church, Cleveland Hts., 1980-82. Capt. USAF, 1962-64. Decorated Commendation Medal, USAF. Fellow Am. Acad. Neurology; mem. AMA, Acad. Med. Cleveland, Ohio State Med. Assn., Yale Alumni Assn. (v.p. Cleve. 1988—). Avocations: skeet shooting, photography, hunting, music, sailing. Business E-Mail: jhgardner@earthlink.net.

GARDNER, SHERYL PAIGE, gynecologist; b. Bremerton, Wash., Jan. 24, 1945; d. Edwin Gerald and Dorothy Elizabeth (Herman) G.; m. James Alva Beat, June 20, 1986. BA in Biology, U. Oreg., 1967, MD cum laude, 1971. Diplomate Am. Bd. Ob-Gyn. Intern L.A. County Harbor Gen. Hosp., Torrance, Calif., 1971-72, resident in ob-gyn., 1972-75; physician Group Health Assn., Washington, 1975-87; pvt. practice Mililani, Hawaii, 1987—; chmn. dept. ob-gyn. Wahiawa Gen. Hosp., 1996—2007. Med. staff sec. Wahiawa (Hawaii) Gen. Hosp., 1994-95. Mem. Am. Coll. Ob-Gyn., Am. Soc. Colposcopy and Cervical Pathology, N.Am. Menopause Soc., Sigma Kappa, Alpha Omega Alpha, Hawaii Med. Assn. Democrat. Office: 95-1249 Meheula Pkwy Ste 127 Mililani HI 96789-1763 Office Phone: 808-625-5277. Business E-Mail: sgardner@my.teampraxis.com.

GARDNER, TIMOTHY JOSEPH, surgeon, educator; b. Phila., Dec. 6, 1938; s. Joseph Thomas and Elva (Flynn) G.; m. Nina Hooton, July 4, 1964; children: Julie, Joseph, Emily, Nicholas. BA, Georgetown Coll., 1962; MD, Georgetown U., 1966. Intern Johns Hopkins Hosp., Balt., 1966-67, asst. resident in surgery, 1967-68, 71-74, rsch. fellow cardiac surg. lab., 1970-71, chief resident, 1974-75, chief resident in cardiac surgery, 1975-76, asst. prof., 1976-80, assoc. prof., 1980-86, cardiac surgeon, 1976—93; prof. Johns Hopkins U. Sch. Medicine, 1986-93; clin. prof. surgery, divsn. cardiothoracic surgery and former William M. Measey prof. surgery U. Pa. Sch. Medicine, Phila., 1993—2003; chief divsn. cardiothoracic surgery U. Pa. Health Sys., 1993—2003; with Christiana Care Health Sys., Newark, Del., 2005—; med. dir. Christiana CareCtr. for Heart & Vascular Health, Newark, Del., 2007—. Speaker in field; vis. prof. Royal Australasian Coll. Surgeons, Hobart, Tasmania, 1994, Royal Prince Alfred Hosp., Sydney, 1989, U. Kans. Sch. Medicine, 1984, Children's Hosp. Phila., 1981. Contbr. articles to profl. jours.; guest editl. reviewer: Jour. Thoracic and Cardiovascular Surgery, 1981-83, Circulation, 1983-91; book reviewer: Annals Thoracic Surgery, 1985-89. With U.S. Army, 1968-70. Fellow ACS, Am. Coll. Cardiology; mem. Am. Surg. Assn., Assn. for Acad. Surgery, Balt. City Med. Soc., Med. and Chirurgical Faculty Md., So. Thoracic Surg. Assn., Soc. Thoracic Surgeons, Soc. Univ. Surgeons, Am. Assn. for Thoracic Surgery (councillor, v.p. thrn pres., 1999-2002), So. Surg. Assn., Am. Surg. Assn., Am. Heart Assn. (mem. coun. on cardiovasc. surgery, nat. pres. 2008-09, chief vol. sci. and med. officer, mem. sci. adv. and coordinating com., nat. bd. dirs.), Am. Bd. Med. Specialists Thoracic Surgery (dir., 1995-2005, vice-chair, 2001-2003, chair, 2003-2005). Office: Christiana Care Health Sys 4755 Ogletown-Stanton Rd Newark DE 19718 Office Phone: 302-733-1241.

GARDNER, WILLIAM ALBERT, JR., pathologist, medical products executive; b. Sumter, SC, Aug. 2, 1939; s. William A. and Betty Lee (Kennedy) G.; m. Kathryn Ann Medlin, June 30, 1960; children: Mary Elizabeth, Kathryn Lee, William Dylan. BS, Wofford Coll., Spartanburg, SC, 1960; MS in Anatomy, Med. Coll. SC, Charleston, 1963, MD, 1965. Diplomate Am. Bd. Pathology, 1965, 67, 76, 81. Intern dept. pathology The Johns Hopkins Hosp., Balt., 1965-66, fellow in pathology, 1965-67, asst. resident dept. pathology, 1966—67; asst. resident dept. pathology Med. Ctr. Duke U., Durham, NC, 1967-68, instr. pathology, chief resident, 1968-69; career resident lab. svcs. VA Med. Ctr., Durham, 1967—69, chief lab. svc. Charleston, SC, 1969—76, Nashville, 1976-81; rsch. asst. in anatomy Med. U. SC, Charleston, 1961—63, tchg. asst. in anatomy, 1962—63, asst. prof. pathology, 1969-72, assoc. prof. pathology, 1972-76, vis. prof. pathology, 1976—81; prof. pathology, vice chmn. dept. pathology Sch. Medicine Vanderbilt U., Nashville, 1976-81; prof., chair dept. pathology Coll. Medicine U. South Ala., Mobile, 1981—2002, pres. health svc. found., 1988—91, Locke disting. prof. pathology Coll. Medicine, 1994—2002, assoc. dean clin. affairs, 1997—, interim dean, v.p. med. affairs Coll. Medicine, 1997—99, emeritus prof. Coll. Medicine, 2002—, asst. v.p. risk adminstrn. Coll. Medicine, 2001. Exec. dir. Am. Registry Pathology, Washington, 2002-; pres., CEO Internat. Registry Pathology, 2003-. Contbr. articles on oncology, urology, parasitology and pathology to profl. jours. Recipient Outstanding Teaching award Med. U. S.C., 1975, Disting. Alumnus award Med. U. S.C., 1988; named to Alumni Assn. Centennial Recognition list, 1992; Fulbright scholar, 1996. Fellow Am. Soc. Clin. Pathologists, Coll. Am. Pathologists (del. for govtl. pathology); mem. AMA, Internat. Acad. Pathology (v.p., chair fin. com. 1994—, internat. councillor 1994—), U.S.-Can. Acad. Pathology (v.p., pres.-elect 1993-95, pres. 1995-96, mem. fin. com. 1996—), Acad. Clin. Lab. Physicians and Scientists, Ala. Med. Assn., Assn. Pathology Chmn. (coun., pres. 1992-94), Armed Forces Inst. of Pathology (mem. sci. adv. bd. 1996—, chair sci. adv. bd., 1997—), Alpha Omega Alpha. Methodist. Office: Am Registry Pathology 14th St at Alaska Ave Washington DC 20306-6000 Business E-Mail: gardnerw@afip.osd.mil.

GARG, GARIMA, periodontist, educator; b. Gwalior, India, May 6, 1982; BS in Dental Surgery, Govt. Dental Coll. and Hosp., Bangalore, 2004; MS in Dental Surgery, Periodontics, Govt. Dental Coll. and Rsch. Inst., Bangalore, 2010. Lectr. Yerala Med. Trust's Dental Coll. and Hosp., Kharghar, Navi-Mumbai, 2010—. Assoc. editor Archives Oral Scis., Dental Jour., 2011. Recipient Gold medal, Bangalore Acad. Periodontology and RGUHS, Karnataka; Rsch. grant, Colgate. Avocations: painting, music. Office: Yerala Med Trust's Dental Coll and Hosp Dept Peridontics Navi-Mumbai Maharashtra 410210 India Personal E-mail: garg_gg@yahoo.co.in.

GARG, PANKAJ, colon and rectal surgeon, educator; b. India, Dec. 27, 1972; MB, All India Inst. Med. Scis., New Delhi, BChir, 1995, CM, 1999. Sr. cons. Fortis Super Splty. Hosp., Mohali, India, 2004—. Chmn., minimal invasive surgery dept. PPSSJ Charitable Hosp., SriGurusarmodia, Rajasthan, India, 2000—03; founder & dir. Assn. Breast Cancer Death Eradication, 2006—; cons. & internat. mem. Asia Pacific Pioneers Cir., 2007—10; asst. prof. MM Inst. Med. Scis. & Rsch. Ctr., Haryana, India, 2008—; assoc. editor World Jour. Gastroenterology, 2010—. Recipient Rotary Internat. award, 2003, Nat. Youth award, Nat. Youth Sabha, India, 2003. Mem.: Indian Assn. Gastro-Intestinal & Endoscopic Surgeons, Assn. Minimal Access Surgeons India, Internat. Soc. U. Colon & Rectal Surgeons, Endoscopic & Laparoscopic Surgeons Asia, Soc. Am. Soc. Gastrointestinal Surgeons. Avocations: travel, tennis, badminton, golf. Home: 1042 Sector 15 Panchkula Haryana 134113 India Personal E-mail: drgargpankaj@yahoo.com.

GARG, SUKANT KUMAR, medical educator; b. Chandigarh, India, May 7, 1975; MBBS, Govt. Med. Coll. and Hosp., Chandigarh, 1998, MD in Pathology, 2004. Reader, assoc. prof., dept. pathology Dr. Harvansh Singh Judge Inst. Dental Scis. and Hosp., Panjab U., Chandigarh, 2007—. Recipient award, Indian Acad. Paediat., 1997. Mem.: Indian Assn. Pathologist and Microbiologist, Indian Med. Assn. Avocations: reading, travel, music. Home: House 3273 Sector 35-D Chandigarh 160022 India Personal E-mail: sukantgarg@rediffmail.com.

GARIBALDI, LUIGI R., pediatric endocrinologist, educator; MD, U. Genoa, Italy, 1973. Diplomate Am. Bd. Pediatrics, Am. Bd. Pediatrics-pediatric endocrinology. Resident pediatrics Gaslini Inst. and Children's Hosp., Genoa, Italy, 1978, Mott Children's Hosp., 1985; fellow pediatric endocrinology and metabolic disorders St. Christopher's Hosp. for Children and Temple Univ., Phila., 1982; hosp. affliation include/s Magee-Womens Hosp. of UPMC, Children's Hosp. of Pitts. of UPMC. Rsch. assoc. pediatric endocrinology Wyler Children's Hosp., 1987. Mem.: Soc. for Pediatric Rsch., Lawson Wilkins Pediatric Endocrine Soc., Endocrine Soc. Office: Childrens Hospital of Pittsburgh of UPMC 1 Childrens Hospital Drive 4401 Penn Ave Pittsburgh PA 15224 Office Phone: 412-692-5170. Office Fax: 412-692-5834. E-mail: luigi.garibaldi@chp.edu.

GARLAND, DOUGLAS EDWARD, physician, director; b. Boone, Iowa, Apr. 12, 1944; MD, Creighton U., 1969; degree in Orthop. Surgery, Tulane U., 1976. Chief, joint replacement ctr. Long Beach Meml. Med. Ctr., 2011—. Bd. mem. Los Amigos Rsch. & Edn. Inst., 1995—2011. Mem.: OOAS. Avocation: gardening. Office: 2760 Atlantic Ave Long Beach CA 90806 Office Fax: 562-987-0027. Business E-Mail: dougarland@msn.com.

GARLAND, LARETTA MATTHEWS, psychologist, nursing educator; b. Jacksonville, Fla. d. Wilburn L. and Clyde-Marian (Chamberlin) Matthews; m. John B. Garland, Mar. 2, 1946; children: John Barnard, Brien Freeling, Amy-Gwin. Diploma, Fla. State Sch. Nursing, 1942; BSN, Emory U., 1950, MA, 1953; BA in Edn., U. Fla., 1951; cert. cardiovascular nurse specialty, Tex. Med. Ctr., 1965; EdD, U. Ga., 1975; postgrad. in counseling and guidance, Ga. State U., 1969; grad. cert. in gerontology, 1981. Cert. nat. counselor. Office and staff nurse, Lakeland, Fla., 1942, 45; nurse ARC, Buffalo, 1956; asst. prof. nursing Med. Coll. Ga., 1965-67; instr. Emory U., 1952-54, assoc. prof., 1967-71, prof., 1972-86, asst. to dean, prof. emeritus, 1987—. Ednl. psychologist, dir. gerontol. nurse practitioner program, 1978-80, asst. to dean, 1983-86. Author: (with Carol Bush) Coping Behavior and Nursing, 1982; contbr. articles to profl. jours. With Nurse Corps, U.S. Army, 1942-45. Decorated 2 Bronze Stars; recipient Outstanding Tchg. award Emory U. Sch. Nursing Grad. Srs., 1977, Appreciation award So. Region Constituent Leagues, Nat. League for Nursing award, 1987, Mabel Korsell award of appreciation Ga. League Nursing, 1987, Spl. Recognition award Ga. Nurses Assn., 1988, 90, Nurse of Yr. award, 1992, Appreciation award Ga. Assn. Nursing Students, 1990, Van de Vrede award Ga. League Nursing, 1993; HEW fellow, 1967-68. Mem. APA, AACD, ANA, Ga. Assn. Nursing Students (hon.), Nat. League Nursing, Bs. and Profl. Women, China Burma India VA Assn. (mem. nat. bd. 1993—), 14th Air Force Asssn. (Flying Tigers), Hump Pilots Assn., Ormond Beach Womens Club, Ormond Beach Hist. Trust, Nat. Assn. Women Vet. (steering com.), Women in Mil. Svc. Meml. Found. (charter), ARC Nurses, Panhellenic Assn., Hist. Trust, Alpha Chi Omega, Sigma Theta Tau, Kappa Delta Pi, Alpha Kappa Delta, Omicron Delta Kappa. Office: Emory U Nell Hodgson Woodruff Sch Atlanta GA 30322-0001 Home: 611 SW 7TH PL Cape Coral FL 33991-1972 Office Phone: 386-677-9466.

GARMAN, RAY FILLMORE, occupational physician, director; s. Wynona Hudson Garman; m. Eugenie (Gigi) Virginia Moravec, Aug. 16, 1958; children: Ray Fillmore III, Scott Clayton, Andrew Seitz.

AB, Johns Hopkins U., Balt., 1957; MD, George Wash. U., Washington, DC, 1961; MPH, Med Coll. Wis., Milw., 1995. Cert. in internal medicine U. Penna Grad. Sch. Medicine, Phila., 1962, Am. Bd. Internal Medicine, 1968, in pulmonary diseasese Am. Bd. Internal Medicine, 1974, in occupl. medicine Am. Bd. Preventive Medicine, 1996. Pulmonary medicine physician Guthrie Clinc/Robert Packer Hosp., Sayre, Pa., 1972—81, chief pulmonary medicine, 1981—90, med. dir., 1991—95; chief occupl. medicine and environ. health Lexington Clinic, Ky., 1995—99; med. dir. Gen. Electric Appliance Divsn., Bloomington, Ind., 1999—2000; clin. med. dir. Toyota Motor Mfg., Georgetown, Ky., 2000—04; assoc. prof., dir. occupl. med. training U. Ky., Lexington, 2004—, vice chair, dept. preventive medicine & environ. health, dir., Occupl. Medicine Residency Program, 2004—; survey chair Lexington Forum, 1997—2005, bd. dirs., 2009—. Sr. aviation med. examiner FAA, Lexington, 1977—; pres. Bradford County Med. Soc., Sayre, Pa., 1979—80; instr. quality process Quality Coll. (Crosby), Winter Park, Fla., 1989—90. Active Lexington Children's Mus., 1995—99; treas. Lex-Fayette Urban County Airport Bd., Lexington, 2003, sec., 2002, chmn., 2004—05; vice chair-med. Lexington Arts & Cultural Coun., 2000—04; pres. Lexington Opera Soc., 2005—07, bd. dirs.; pres. Lexington Kennel Club, 2002—05; chmn. Flight 5191 Meml. Commn., 2006—; bd. dirs. Planned Parenthood of the Bluegrass, 2005—07, Aviation Mus. Ky., 2006—, chair bd., 2007—. Capt. USAF, 1963—66, Brig Gen. Res., mobilization asst. to surgeon AF Material Command USAF, chief flight surgeon. Decorated Golden Cross of Royal Order of Phoenix King of Greece, Legion of Merit USAF. Mem.: Ky. Occupl. Med. and Environ. Health Assn. (v.p. 2007, pres. 2008), Ky. Dept. Aviation, Lexington Club, Delta Omega (Disting. Alumni Membership, MCW). Home: 1214 Richmond Rd Lexington KY 40502-1614 Office: Univ Ky Coll Pub Health 200 Washington Ave Lexington KY 40536 Business E-Mail: ray.garman@uky.edu.

GARN, HOLGER, biologist, researcher; b. Leipzig, Germany, Aug. 1, 1964; MSc, U. Leipzig, 1989, PhD, 1992. Postdoc. fellow, group leader Philips U. Marburg, Inst. Immunology, Marburg, Germany, 2004—; head rsch. Philipps U. Marburg, Dept. Clin. Chemistry and Molecular Diagnostics, Marburg, 2004; mng. dir. Sterna Biols. GmbH & Co. KG Biomed. Rsch. Ctr., Marburg, 2009—. Office: Sterna Biols GmbH & Co KG Biomed Rsch Ctr Hans Meerwein Str 2 Marburg D 35043 Germany also: Philipps Univ Marburg Hans-Meerwein-Str. 2 35043 Marburg Germany Office Phone: 49 6421 9830050, 49 6421 2866048. Business E-Mail: garn@staff.uni-marburg.de, h.garn@sterna biologicals.com.

GARN, STANLEY MARION, physical anthropologist, educator; b. 1922; AB, Harvard U., 1942, AM, 1947, PhD, 1948. Rsch. assoc. chem. engring. Chem. Warfare Svc. Devel. Lab. MIT, 1942-44; tech. editor Polaroid Co., 1944-46; cons. applied anthropology, 1946-47; rsch. fellow cardiology Mass. Gen. Hosp., Boston, 1946-52; instr. anthropology Harvard U., 1940-52, anthropologist Forsyth Dental Infirmary, Boston, 1947-52; dir. Forsyth face size project Army Chem. Corps, 1950-52; chmn. dept. growth and genetics Fels Rsch. Inst., Yellow Springs, Ohio, 1952-68; fellow Ctr. Human Growth and Devel. U. Mich., Ann Arbor, also prof. nutrition and anthropology, 1968-92, prof. emeritus, 1993—. Raymond Pearl lectr. Human Biol. Coun., 1992—; E.D.D. Neuhauser lectr. Soc. Pediatric Radiology, 1981. Author: Human Races, 1970, Gain and Loss of Cortical Bone, 1970; also contbr. over 1000 articles to profl. jours.; editorial bds. numerous jours. Recipient Disting. Svc. award, U. Mich., Charles Darwin Lifetime Achievement award, Am. Assn. Phys. Anthropologists, 1994, Franz Boas award, Human Biol. Coun., 2002. Fellow AAAS, Am. Acad. Pediatrics (hon. assoc.), Am. Anthropol. Assn., Am. Acad. Arts and Scis., Human Biology Coun., Am. Soc. Clin. Nutrition, Am. Soc. Nutrition Scis.; mem. NAS, Am. Assn. Phys. Anthropologists, Internat. Assn. Dental Rsch., Internat. Orgn. Study Human Devel., Am. Soc. Naturalists, Internat. Assn. Human Biologists (coun.).

GARNAVI, RAHIL, engineer, researcher; b. Iran, May 15, 1980; MS in Engring., U. Isfahan, 2005; PhD, U. Melbourne, 2011. Rschr. U. Isfahan, 2003—05; software engr. Caspian Co., 2006—07; rschr. U. Melbourne, 2007—11; rsch. fellow IBM, 2011—. Avocations: meditation, photography, literature. Home: 1703/570 Lygon St Carlton Melbourne Victoria 3053 Australia Business E-Mail: r.garnavi@ee.unimelb.edu.au.

GARNAVOS, CHRISTOS, orthopedic surgeon; b. Piraeus, Greece, Apr. 28, 1959; s. Spiridon Thomas and Fotini (Marouda) G.; m. Satmatia Tina Xirou, Feb. 17, 1985; 1 child, Christina. MD, U. Patras, Greece, 1983. Gen. practice medicine, Greece, 1984-86; sr. house officer gen. surgery Kavala (Greece) Gen. Hosp., 1986-87; trainee in orthopedic surgery Asklipiion Gen. Hosp., Athens, 1987-91, Derbyshire Royal Infirmary NHS Trust, Derby, Eng., 1991-94; staff orthopedic surgeon Telford, Eng., 1994-97; cons. orthopedic surgeon Evangelismos Gen. Hosp., Athens, 1997-99, Princess Royal Hosp., Telford, 1999—. Tchr. nursing sch., Kavala, 1986-87; rep. non-cons. career grade drs., Telford, 1996-97. Patentee orthopedic implant intramedullary nail; contbr. articles to profl. jours. Fellow Greek Orthopedic Assn., Brit. Orthopedic Assn. Avocations: computing, stamp collecting/philately, photography. Home: 8 Londou 16675 Glyfada Greece Office: Evangelismos Hosp Athens Greece

GARNE, ESTER, pediatrician; b. Nibe, Denmark, June 26, 1957; MD, U. Southern Denmark, 1983. Paediatric epidemiologist EUROCAT, 2002. Office: Kolding Hosp Paediatric Dept Skovvangen 2-6 Kolding 6000 Denmark Business E-Mail: egarne@dadlnet.dk, ester.garne@sib.regionsyddanmartz.dk.

GARNER, ALGEAN, II, healthcare company administrator, consultant; s. Algean and Charmaine Garner. BA in Psychology summa cum laude, Shaw U., 1993; PsyD, Ill. Sch. Profl. Psychology, 2001. Lic. clin. psychologist Ill. Psychology intern Houston Ind. Sch. Dist., 1997—98; assessment coord. Shelia Jenkins and Assocs., Houston, 1998—2000; postdoc. fellow ADAPT Counseling, Houston, 2000—02; dir. comprehensive svcs. Near North Health Svc. Corp., Chgo., 2002—06; asst. dir. health and human svcs. Village of Hoffman Estates, Ill., 2006—, dir. tng. Ill., 2006—. Bd. dirs. Houston Assn. Marriage and Family Therapists, 2001—02; presenter in field; bd. mem. CEDA Northwest, 2007—, bd. pres., 2009—; dir. health & human svcs. Vill. Hoffmon Estates, 2007—; adj. prof. Adlec Sch. profl. Psychology, 2011—; bd. mem. WINGS, 2011—. Mem. aux. bd. Childrens Place Assn., 2005—. Mem.: APA. Avocations: cooking, health and fitness. Office: Vill Hoffman Estate Dept Health Human Svcs 1900 Hussell rd Hoffman Estates IL 60169 Office Fax: 847-781-4869. Personal E-mail: agarnerii@sbcglobal.net.

GARNER, JULIE LOWREY, occupational therapist; b. Paris, Tex., Aug. 6, 1953; d. John Robert and Rachel (Garner) Lowrey; BS, U. Tex., Galveston, 1975; MS, Tex. Woman's U., 1982; MEd, Tex. A&M U., Commerce, 2001. Cert. occupational therapist, Tex.; cert. to administer and interpret So. Calif. Sensory Integration Tests Sensory Integration Internat., neurodevel. treatment approach to cerebral palsy. Occupl. therapist Presbyn. Hosp. Dallas, 1976—77, Duncanville Ind. Sch. Dist., Tex., 1977-81, 89-90, Grand Prairie Ind. Sch. Dist., Tex., 1978—81, U. Tex., Dallas, 1981—83, Lewisville Ind. Sch. Dist., Tex., 1983—85, Collin County Coop. Spl. Svcs., Wylie, Tex., 1983—89, Commerce Ind. Sch. Dist., Tex., 1990—97, M.J. Care, Gunter, Tex., 1997—99, Gentina Health Svcs., 2006—, Gentiva Home Health, Tex., 2006—08, Home Health Paris, 2008—; occupl. therapist region X Ednl. Svc. Ctr., Richardson, Tex., 1977; rehab. mgr. Parkview Convalescent Ctr., Paris, Tex., 2005—07, Occupl Therapist, Gentiva Home, Paris, Tex., 2006—08, Mays Home Health, Paris, Tex., 2008; occupl. therapist Paris Regional Med. Ctr., 2008—11, County Home Care, Clarkville, Tex., 2008—09. Bd. dirs. United Cerebral Palsy Assn. Dallas, 1980-84. Recipient Hurdle Cert. of Honor Soroptomist Internat., Dallas, 1976. Methodist. Avocations: sewing, arts and crafts, computers. Home: 360 9th SE Paris TX 75460

GARNER, MABLE TECOLA, health facility administrator; b. Sharon, Miss., June 11, 1931; d. Annie B. (Johnson) Garner; 1 child, Wendell Orson Siggers. BA, Fisk U., 1953; MD, Meharry Med. Coll., 1959; MTH, Springhill Coll., Mobile, Ala., 1996. Diplomate Am. Bd. Clin. Pathology, 1967, Am. Bd. Anatomical Pathology, 1968. Intern Meharry Med. Coll., Nashville, asst. prof. pathology, 1968; resident in pathology Hubbard Hosp./Meharry Med. Coll., Nashville, 1963—66; sr. resident palatomic clin. and pathology VA Hosp., Nashville, 1966—67, resident, anatomic and clin. pathology, 1967—68; USPHS spl. postdoctoral fellow dept. biochem. hypertension rsch. Case Western Res. U., Cleve., 1969—70; dir. health cons. Fayette St. Clinic Ltd., Shaw, Miss., 1979—. Mem.: Alpha Omega Alpha. Home and Office: PO Box 798 Shaw MS 38773-0798 Office Phone: 662-754-2314.

GARNER, STEVEN C., radiologist, emergency physician; m. Anne Garner; children: Hope Garner Stephens, Eve. Grad., Chgo. Med. Sch. Diplomate Am. Bd. Radiology, Am. Bd. Emergency Physicians, cert. aviation med. examiner, diplomate Am. Coll. Healthcare Executives. Chief med. officer St. Vincent Hosp. & Med. Ctr., NY; sr. v.p. St. Vincent Cath. Med. Ctrs.; intern Brookdale Med. Ctr., Bklyn.; resident Mt. Sinai Hosp.; asst. prof. radiology N.Y. Med. Coll.; chmn radiology NY Methodist Hosp. Cons. N.Y.P.D; cons. U.S. customs dept. N.Y. JFK Internat. Airport, pres. med. ctr. Host (NETNY TV series) Ask The Doctor; contbr. Fox News Channel, columns in newspapers. Capt. USAF, major USAR. Recipient Castle Connolly Top Doctor award. Fellow: Am. Acad. Emergency Physicians; mem.: Am. Coll. of Radiology (nat. emergency radiology com.), Am. Heart Assn. (edn. com., cert. fed. aviation med. examiner). Avocations: piano, Organ, cello, Broadway shows.

GARRATT, KIRK NOEL, cardiologist; b. LA, Feb. 26, 1955; MSc, U. Calif., Irvine, 1979, MD, 1983. Chair, divsn. cardiology Franciscan-Skemp Med. Ctr. Mayo Clinic, 1990—2005; assoc. dir., divsn. cardiac intervention, clin. dir. interventional cardiovasc. rsch. Lenox Hill Heart and Vascular Inst. NY, 2005—, dir. interventional cardiovasc. quality, 2010—. Mem. exec. com., edn. and rsch. com. Nat. Cardiovasc. Data Registry (CathPCI), 2010—. Recipient Tchg. award, Mayo Clinic Cardiology Fellows. Fellow: Soc. Cardiovasc. Angiography & Intervention (emeritus bd. trustees), Am. Coll. Cardiology; mem.: AMA, Am. Heart Assn. Avocations: music, travel, cooking. Office: 130 E 77th St 9th Fl New York NY 10075 Office Fax: 212-434-2205. Business E-Mail: kgarratt@lenoxhill.net.

GARRETT, ALGIN B., dermatologist, educator; MD, Pa. State U., 1978. Diplomate Am. Bd. Dermatology, 1983. Intern internal medicine Washington VA Med. Ctr. Georgetown Univ. Sch. of Medicine, 1978—79; resident internal medicine Washington VA Med. Ctr., 1979—80; resident dermatology Va. Commonwealth Univ. Med. Ctr., 1980—83, prof., chmn. dermatology dept.; fellow mohs surgery Cleve. Clinic, 1987—88. Office: VA Commonwealth University Department of Dermatology 9000 Stony Point Pky Richmond VA 23235 Office Phone: 804-560-8991.

GARRETT, KEVIN O., surgeon, educator; b. Pitts., Jan. 6, 1962; BS, CMU, 1983; MD, U. Pitts., 1987. Surgeon UPP Dept. Surgery, 1995—. Clin. prof. surgery UPMC, 1995—2011. Fellow: ACS; mem.: AMA. Home: 2112 Legendary Ln Allison Park PA 15101 Business E-Mail: garrettko@upmc.edu.

GARRETT, MARSHALL LEE, anesthesiologist, educator; b. Sacramento, 1951; m. Carol E. Kolbo, June 21, 1986; children: Mackenzie Lee, Lane Christian, William James. BA cum laude, U. of the South, 1972; MD, Creighton U., 1978. Diplomate Am. Bd. Anesthesiology. Intern St. Mary Med. Ctr., Long Beach, Calif., 1978—79; resident in anesthesiology U. Fla., Gainesville, 1979—81; chief fellow cardiothoracic anesthesiology Clevel. Clin. Found., 1988-89; anesthesiologist Cypress Fairbanks Med. Ctr., Houston, 1993—. Assoc. prof. U. Calif. Med. Ctr., Davis, 1983—85, Thomas Jefferson U., Phila., 1985—86. Bible Study fellow. Mem.: Harris County Med. Assn., Tex. Med. Assn., Soc. Cardiothoracic Anesthesiologists, Am. Soc. Anesthesiologists, Phi Beta Kappa.

GARRETT, ROBERT C., hospital administrator; m. Laura Garrett; children: Jonathan, David. B, Binghamton U.; M in Health Adminstrn., Wash. U. Joined Hackensack Univ. Med. Ctr., 1981, exec. v.p and COO, 1986—2011, acting pres., 2011, pres. and CEO, 2011—; bd. chmn. NJ Coun. of Tchg. Hosps., 2010—. Recipient Modern Healthcare's Up and Comers award, 1996, Distinguished Citizen award, Greater Hackensack C. of C., 2001, Assn. of Healthcare Execs. Distinguished Svc. award, 2004. Mem.: Am. Diabetes Assn. (former sec., former treas., chmn. bd. devel. com.). Office: Hackensack University Medical Center 30 Prospect Ave Hackensack NJ 07601 Office Phone: 201-996-2000.

GARRETT, SCOTT T., investment company executive; BS in Mech. Engring., Valparaiso U.; MBA, Lake Forest Grad. Sch. Mgmt. Various positions Baxter Internat., Am. Hosp. Supply Corp.; chmn. Dade Behring, 1994—97; interim CEO Kendro Lab. Products, L.P., 2000; CEO Garrett Capital Advisors; pres., clin. diagnostic divsn. Beckman Coulter, Inc., Fullerton, Calif., 2002—03, pres., COO, 2003—05, pres., CEO, 2005—09, chmn., pres., CEO, 2009—10; operating ptnr. Water Street Healthcare Partners, Brea, Calif., 2011—. Chmn. LifeStream Internat.; vice chmn. Kendro Lab. Products; dir. Inovision Holdings, Sunol Molecular Corp., Biotrin Holdings plc, Ability One Corp., Lake Forest Hosp. Found.; mem., adv. bd. Radius Ventures. Office: Water Street Healthcare Partners 250 S Kraemer Blvd Brea CA 92821 *

GARRO-BISSETTE, SUSAN ANN, adult nurse practitioner; b. Lynchburg, Va., May 12, 1944; children: Lisa, Tony, Pilar. BSN, Cath. U. Am., 1984, MSN, 1995. RN, S.C.; cert. adult nurse practitioner. Adult nurse practitioner Dr. R.D. Gibbs, Moncks Corner, S.C., 1996-98, Ralph H. Johnson VA Med. Ctr., Charleston, S.C., 1998—; clin. faculty adult nurse practitioner program Med. U. S.C. Sch. Nursing, Charleston, 1997-2000. Guardian ad litem State of S.C. Office of Gov., Charleston, 1996-2002. Mem.: ANA, Am. Coll. Nurse Practitioners, S.C. Nurses Assn. and Advanced Practice Coun. (mem.-at-large 2001—03), Am. Acad. Nurse Practitioners, Low Country Advanced Practice Nurses (pres. 1998—2001), Sigma Theta Tau. Home: 22 Short St Charleston SC 29401-1908 Office: VA Med Ctr Trident Clinic 9279 University Blvd North Charleston SC 29406 Office Phone: 843-789-6683. E-mail: susangarro@bellsouth.net.

GARROD, KENNETH J., orthopedist, surgeon; b. Newark, May 11, 1950; s. Roslyn Garrod; m. Beth L. Rosenthal, May 17, 1981; children: Evan, Scott. BS, U. Wis., 1972; MD, U. Medicine and Dentistry NJ, 1977. Cert. in orthopedic surgery and surgery of the hand Am. Bd. Orthopedic Surgery. Attending physician Orthop. Surgery Assocs., Boca Raton, Fla., 1984—95; mem. faculty Miller Sch. Medicine, U. Miami. Physician, pres. South Fla. Hand and Orthop. Ctr., Boca Raton, 2001—. Contbr. articles to profl. jours. Fellow, Tufts U. Med. Sch., Boston, 1983—84. Fellow: ACS, Am. Acad. Orthop. Surgeons; mem.: AMA, Fla. Orthop. Soc., Am. Soc. Surgery of Hand. Avocations: skiing, golf, travel. Office: 1905 Clint Moore Rd Ste 105 Boca Raton FL 33496 Office Fax: 561-998-4246. E-mail: southfloridahand@bellsouth.net.

GARRUTO, RALPH MICHAEL, biomedical anthropologist, biologist, educator; b. Binghamton, NY, Nov. 20, 1943, s. Ralph Anthony and Josephine Janet (DiMartino) G.; children: Jessica Anne, Jason Michael, John Ralph. BS, Pa. State U., 1966, MA, 1969, PhD, 1973. Postdoctoral fellow NIH, Bethesda, Md., 1972-73, staff, then sr. staff fellow, 1973-78, from rsch. biologist to supervisory rsch. biologist, 1978—2003; adj. prof. med. genetics Coll. Medicine U. South Ala., Mobile, 1982—; adj. sr. scientist biol. anthropology Pa. State U., University Park, 1985—95; prof. biomedical anthropology neuroscis. SUNY, Binghamton, 1997—, assoc. dir. Inst. Biomed. Tech., 2000—, dir. grad. program biomed. anthropology, 2003—10; adj. clin. prof. pathology Upstate Med. U., Syracuse, 1998—; dir. Binghamton U. Biol. Specimen Archive Facility, 2010—. Participant anthropol. and biomed. fieldwork, Cambodia, China, Mariana Islands, Papua New Guinea, Peru, Philippine Islands, Vanuatu, Western Caroline Islands, 1969—; mem., NIH rep. US Nat. Com. US Man and the Biosphere Program, 1993 95; founding mem. bd. trustees Nat. Mus. Health and Medicine Found., Washington, 1989-91; exec. sec. Commn. on Aging and the Aged, Zagreb, Yugoslavia, 1985-89; cons. WHO, 1987; chair selection com. Paul T. Baker Disting. lectr. in human biology and anthropology Pa. State U., 1986-98; Wellcome Found. lectr., vis. prof. U. Mich., Dearborn, 2001. Co-editor: Biological Anthropology and Aging: Perspectives on Human Variation over the Lifespan, 1994, Dermatoglyphics: Science in Transition, 1991, contbr. articles on neurodegenerative disorders, neurosci. and aging, biomed. anthropology, food chain disorders and genetics to profl. jours.; patentee bil. agts. Recipient Commendation for Rsch., Guam Legislature, 1987, Spl. Achievement award, 1990, Merit award NIH, 1991, Dir.'s award, 1993; Wenner-Gren Found. leadership grantee, 1986, grantee, 1993-95, NIH grants, 2003—; Alumni fellow Pa. State U., 1987. Fellow AAAS, Am. Coll. Epidemiology, Am. Dermatoglyphics Assn. (sec.-treas. 1981-82, pres. 1987-89, disting. achievement award 1995), Human Biology Assn. (pres./pres.-elect 1993-96, exec. com. 1991-93), Internat. Assn. of Human Biologists (pres. 1999-2002, Gorjanović-Krambergeri medal 1999-2000, Franz Boas Disting. Achievement award 2005), Internat. Genetic Epidemiology Soc. (founding fellow), NAS, Acad. Sci. for the Developing World, TWAS; mem. Soc. for Neurosci., World Fedn. Neurology (rsch. com. on neurepidemiology) Avocations: field trialing, environmental projects. Business E-Mail: rgarruto@binghamton.edu.

GARSON, ARTHUR, JR., academic administrator, medical educator; b. NYC; m. Suzan Garson; 2 children. Grad., Princeton U., 1970; MD, Duke U., 1974; MPH, U. Tex., Houston, 1992. V.p. Tex. Children's Hosp.; fellow in pediat. cardiology Baylor Coll. Medicine, 1979, chief pediat. cardiology, 1988, sr. v.p., dean acad. ops., 1995; assoc. vice chancellor health affairs Duke U., 1992; dean, v.p. U. Va. Sch. Medicine, 2002—07, provost, 2007—. Mem. White House Adv. Panel on Health Sys. Improvement; chair quality nat. adv. coun. Agy. Healthcare Rsch. Mem.: Inst. Medicine, Assn. Acad. Health Ctrs., U. Hosps. Consortium, Assn. Am. Med. Colls. (adv. panel on healthcare delivery), Am. Coll. Cardiology (pres. 2000—01, trustee, mem. govt. rels. com., mem. quality of care com.). Office: U Va Health Sys PO Box 800793 Charlottesville VA 22908 Office Phone: 434-924-5118. E-mail: garson@virginia.edu.

GARSON, SEBASTIEN, plastic surgeon; b. Toulouse, Haute Garonne, France, Jan. 24, 1972; s. Jean Paul Garson and Jacqueline Castet; life ptnr. MD, Amiens Med. Sch., 2001. Lic. Plastic Surgeon Amiens Med. Sch., 2004, European Plastic Surgeon European Bd. Plastic Surgery, 2004. Assoc. Morphology And Cognitive Lab., Lyon, Rhone, France, 2002—; pvt. practice Senlis, France, 2005—. Contbr. articles to profl. jours. in field. Recipient Gold medal, Univ. Hosp. Amiens, 2001. Mem.: Plastic and Reconstructive Surgery Soc. (assoc.), French Plastic Surgery Soc. (assoc.). Roman Catholic. Achievements include research in surfacic 3D development in medical use. Office: SELARL Dr Garson 7 impasse de la Passerelle Oise 60300 Senlis France Office Fax: 00-33-3-44-27-87-02; Home Fax: 00-33-3-44-27-87-02. Personal E-mail: garson.md@free.fr, info@drgarson.fr.

GARSTEN, JOEL JAY, gastroenterologist; b. NYC, Jan. 10, 1948; s. Richard Maxwell and Gertrude Ann (Perlberg) G.; m. Marion Susan Moscovitz, July 10, 1971; children: Bryan David, Lauren Roberta. BA in Biology, CUNY, 1968; MD, Georgetown U., 1973. Resident in internal medicine Cornell-Coop. Hosps. Program, NYC, 1973-76;

fellow gastroenterology Yale Affiliated Gastroenterology Program, New Haven and Waterbury, Conn., 1976-78; gastroenterologist Gastroenterology Assocs. of Waterbury, 1978-90; physican, mng. ptnr. Digestive Disease Ctr. of Conn., 1990—; dir. sect. of gastroenterology Waterbury Hosp. Health Ctr., 1990—; assoc. dir. Yale Affiliated GI fellowship program Waterbury Hosp. and Hosp. of St. Raphael, New Haven and Waterbury, 1990-2000; clin. instr. internal medicine Yale U. Sch. Medicine, New Haven, 1978, asst. clin. prof., 1981, assoc. clin. prof., 1987—. Med. dir. Liberty Health Plan, Naugatuck, Conn., 1987-89, Physicians Health Plan, Trumbull, Conn., 1989-90, med. adv. bd., 1990-92, Am. Lion Found., 2005-. Contbr. articles to profl. jours. Med. adv. chmn. Crohn's and Colitis Found., WTBY Satelite, Waterbury, 1990—; resource speaker Waterbury Celiac Group, Thomaston, Conn., 1990—, Am. Cancer Soc., 1991—; prin. investigator multiple drug trials. Fellow ACP, Am. Coll. Gastroenterology; mem. Am. Soc. for Liver Disease, Conn. Soc. Internal Medicine (pres. sect. gastroenterology 1996-98), Am. Soc. Internal Medicine, Am. Gastroenterology Assn., Am. Soc. Parenteral and Enteral Nutrition, others. Achievements include introduction of home parenteral nutrition of sclerotherapy, esophageal stenting, percutaneous gastrostomy, other endoscopic techniques to Waterbury; prin. investigator in drug rsch. trials (chosen for Best Drs. in the Am.). Home: 47 Harvest Ct Cheshire CT 06410-1844 Office: Digestive Disease Ctr Conn 60 Westwood Ave Waterbury CT 06708-2460 Office Phone: 203-574-3007. Business E-Mail: jgarsten@ddcct.com.

GARTHWAITE, THOMAS LEONARD, medical officer; b. Port Allegany, Pa., July 8, 1947; 2 children. AB, Cornell U.; MD, Temple U., 1973. Intern Med. Coll. Wis. Affiliated Hosp., 1973—74, resident, 1974—76; with Veterans Health Adminstrn., 1976—87, chief of staff, 1987—95, dep. under sec. for health, 1995—2000, undersec. for health, 2000—02; assoc. prof., medicine Med. Coll. Wis., 1985—95, assoc. dean, 1987—95; dir., chief med. officer L.A. Co. Dept. Health Svcs., 2002—05; chief med. officer Catholic Health East, Newton Square, 2006—. Office: Catholic Health East 3805 West Chester Pike # 100 Newtown Square PA 19073-2304

GARTNER, LAWRENCE MITCHELL, pediatrician, medical educator; b. Bklyn., Apr. 24, 1933; s. Samuel and Bertha (Brimberg) G.; m. Carol Sue Blicker, Aug. 12, 1956; children— Alex David, Madeline Hallie. AB, Columbia U., 1954; MD, Johns Hopkins U., 1958. Intern pediatrics Johns Hopkins Hosp., 1958-59; resident pediatrics Albert Einstein Coll. Medicine, 1959-60, chief resident, 1960-61, instr. pediatrics, 1962-64, asst. prof., 1964-69, assoc. prof., 1969-74, prof., 1974-80, dir. divsn. neonatology, 1967-80, dir. divsn. pediatric hepatology, 1967-80; dir. clin. research unit Rose F. Kennedy Ctr., 1972-80; attending physician Hosp. of Albert Einstein Coll. Medicine, 1967-80; prof. dept. pediatrics U. Chgo. Pritzker Sch. Medicine, 1980-98, prof. dept. obstetrics and gynecology, 1995-98, prof. emeritus pediatrics and obstetrics and gynecology, 1998—; chmn. dept. pediatrics, med. dir. Wyler Children's Hosp., U. Chgo. Med. Ctr., 1980-93. Chmn. Physicians Breastfeeding Network of Ill., 1993-98. Contbr. articles to med. jours. and textbooks. Pediatrician-of-the-Yr. award Ill. chpt. Am. Acad. Pediatrics, 1995; recipient award NIH, 1967-74; Appleton Century Crofts prize, 1956; Mosby book award, 1958. Mem. AAAS, Am. Pediatric Soc. (chmn. coun. 1989-90), Soc. Pediatric Rsch., Perinatal Rsch. Soc., Am. Assn. Study Liver Disease, Chgo. Pediatric Soc. (editor 1990-91, treas. 1992-93, sec. 1993-94, v.p. 1994-95, pres. 1995-96), Am. Acad. Pediatrics (chair breastfeeding workgroup 1994-2000, chair exec. com. sect. on breastfeeding 2000-06), N.Am. Soc. Pediatric Gastroenterology (pres. 1974-75), The Milk Club (chmn. 1994-96), Acad. Breastfeeding Medicine (founding bd. dirs. 1994-95, editor newsletter 1995-2000, v.p. 1997-98, pres., 1998-99, adv. coun. 2006—), LaLeche League Internat., Phi Beta Kappa, Alpha Omega Alpha. Personal E-mail: gart@midway.uchicago.edu.

GARVEY, PATRICK BRYAN, plastic surgeon, educator; b. La., Oct. 3, 1974; BA, U. Tex., Austin, 1997; MD, La. State U., New Orleans, 2001. Diplomate Am. Bd. Plastic Surgery, 2011, Am. Bd. Surgery, 2011. Gen. surgery resident Mayo Clinic, 2001—06; plastic surgery resident U. Va. Health Sys., 2006—08; microvascular and reconstructive surgery fellow U. Tex. Md. Anderson Cancer Ctr., 2008—09, asst. prof. plastic surgery, 2009—. Mem.: ACS, Houston Soc. Plastic Surgeons, Am. Soc. Reconstructive Microsurgery, Am. Soc. Maxillofacial Surgeons, Am. Soc. Plastic Surgeons. Office: 1400 Pressler Unit 443 Houston TX 77030 Business E-Mail: pbgarvey@mdanderson.org.

GARZIONE, JOHN EDWARD, physical therapist; b. Newburgh, NY, Jan. 3, 1950; s. John Edward and Della Elizabeth (Gentila) G.; m. Anita Louise Hirschman, Sept. 21, 1974; children: Adriana, Katrina. AAS, Orange County C.C., Middletown, NY, 1970; BS, Ithaca Coll., NY, 1973; D in Physical Therapy, Boston U., 2005. Mem. staff phys. therapy Chenango Meml. Hosp., Norwich, NY, 1973-74; sr. phys. therapist N.Y. State Vets. Home, Oxford, NY, 1974-86; CEO Chenango Therapeutics, Norwich, 1975—; lic. examiner NY State, 1976-86; cons. phys. therapy Broome Devel. Ctr., Binghamton, NY, 1985—, Upstate Home for Children, Milford, NY, 1986-88, Hospice Chenango County, Norwich, 1991—; cons. DJO Global Electrotherapy, 2009—. Adj. instr. Czenovia Coll., 1982-87; guest lectr. Ithaca Coll., 1993-94; clin. instr. EMPI Corp., 1996—; cons. BlueCross/Blue Shield, Utica, 1998-2001, YMCA, Norwich, NY, 2000; guest lectr. electrotherapy Utica Coll., 2000; presenter in field. Contbr. articles to profl. jours. Bd. dirs. STRIDE, 2000-04. Mem. Am. Phys. Therapy Assn. (sec. pain mgmt. spl. interest group 1996-01, v.p. 2001-06, pres. 2007—), Am. Coll. Sports Medicine, Am. Acad. Pain Mgmt. (diplomate; clin. assoc., Continuing Edn. Excellence award 1996, 99, 00, 01, 02, 03, 05, 06, 07, 08, 09), NY Acad. Scis., Lions (v.p. 1990). Congregationalist. Avocation: politics. Home: PO Box 451 Sherburne NY 13460-0451 Office: Chenango Therapeutics Country Club Rd Norwich NY 13815-1613 Office Phone: 607-334-6273. E-mail: jgarzione@frontiernet.net.

GARZO, GARZO, medical association administrator; b. Valparaiso, Chile, June 25, 1949; MD, U. Chile, 1975; degree in Infertility, UCSD, 1986. Med. dir. Reproductive Ptnrs., UCSD Regional Fertility Ctr., 1978—. Clin. asst. prof., reproductive medicine UCSD, 1987. Fellow: Am. Coll. ob-gyn. Avocation: music. Office: 9850 Genesee Ave La Jolla CA 92037 Office Fax: 858-4552-9188. Personal E-mail: drgarzo@gmail.com.

GARZON, MARIA C., pediatric dermatologist; b. 1959; Grad., Harvard U.; MD, Columbia U. Coll. Physicians & Surgeons, NY. Diplomate Am. Bd. Pediat. Dermatology. Resident pediat. Babies Hosp., Columbia Presbyn. Med. Ctr.; resident dermatology Collumbia U. Coll. Physicians & Surgeons, assoc. prof. clin. dermatology & pediat., 1995—; fellowship pediat. dermatology Children's Meml. Hosp., Chgo.; staff Morgan Stanley Children's Hosp. NY-Presbyn., 1995—. Founder divsn. pediat. dermatology Morgan Stanley Children's Hosp. NY-Presbyn. Contbr. articles to profl. jours. Fellow: Am. Acad. Pediat., Am. Acad. Dermatology. Office: Columbia U Med Ctr Irving Pavilion 161 Ft Wash Ave New York NY 10032 Office Phone: 212-305-5293. Office Fax: 212-795-1859. Business E-Mail: mcg2@columbia.edu.

GASPERINI, CLAUDIO, neurologist; b. Rome, Feb. 2, 1962; MD, U. La Sapienza Rome, 1989. Cons., dept. neuroscis., 1999—. Grant, AISM, MS. Mem.: SNO. Avocation: football. Home: Circonvallazione Gianicolense 87 Rome 00152 Italy Home Fax: 00390658704650. Personal E-mail: c.gasperini@libero.it.

GASS, MARGERY STOOPS, obstetrician, gynecologist; b. Cin., Oct. 7, 1944; d. Jean Todd and Margaret Elizabeth Stoops; m. Frederick Stuart Gass, June 19, 1966; children: Molly Margaret, David Frederick. BA, DePauw U., 1966; MA, Miami U., Oxford, Ohio, 1969; MD, U. Cin., 1980. Diplomate Am. Coll. Ob-Gyn. Assoc. prof. clin. ob-gyn U. Cin. Coll. Medicine, 1984—, dir. Univ. Hosp. Menopause and Osteoporosis Ctr. Cin., 1990—. Part-time faculty Talladega (Ala.) Coll., 1969-70; lectr. Miami U., Oxford, 1972; apptd. advisory coun. Nat. Ctr. Complementary and Alternative Medicine, NIH, 2007-. Vol. United Appeal, Am. Cancer Soc., Planned Parenthood, YWCA, Oxford, 1972-75. Named one of Best Doctors in America, Woodward White Inc., 1998, 2004, Best Specialists in the Tri-State, Cincinnati Mag., 2003, 2004. Fellow Am. Coll. Ob-Gyn; mem. AMA, Mortar Bd., Alpha Lambda Delta, Alpha Omega Alpha, Phi Beta Kapp. Office: Univ Cin/Dept Ob-Gyn 231 Bethesda Ave Cincinnati OH 45229-2827 also: Univ Ob Gyn Assocs 222 Piedmont Ave Ste 51 Cincinnati OH 45219-4231

GASSNER, HOLGER GUENTHER, surgeon, consultant; b. Erlangen, Germany, Feb. 6, 1972; s. Dieter Siegmund and Anneliese Gassner; m. Jordana Rae Knecht, Sept. 17, 2005; children: Jonathan Patric Knecht, Daniel Johann. MD, U. Erlangen, 1998. Diplomate Am. Bd. Otorhinolaryngology, 2007, German Acad. Otorhinolaryngology. Rsch. fellow Mayo Clinic, Rochester, Minn., 1998—99, resident physician, 2001—06, U. Erlangen, 2000—01; fellow Am. Acad. Facial Plastic Surgery, Seattle, 2006—07; staff cons. U. Regensburg, Germany, 2007—, head divsn. facial plastic surgery, 2007—. Contbr. scientific papers to profl. pubs. Fellow: Am. Acad. Facial Plastic Surgery (Ben Schuster award 2000, Sir Howard Delf Gillies award 2007, Ben Schuster award 2006); mem.: European Acad. Facial Plastic Surgery (internet com. mem. 2008—), Am. Acad. Otorhinolaryngology, Head and Neck Surgery. Achievements include patents for new method to improve the appearance of cutaneous scars; use of Botulinum toxin to immobilize skin wounds in order to improve scarring and description of simultaneous use of Botulinum toxin with local anaesthetic agent in order to improve predictability of Botulinum toxin injections; first to desribe previously unknown anatomic structures in the face, including sublevator space and sublevator extension of buccal fat pad. Office: Univ Washington Dept Otorhinolaryngology Seattle WA 98195-6515 Office Fax: 206-386-3553; Home Fax: +49-941-6083437. Business E-Mail: info@drgassner.eu.

GASSON, JUDITH C., molecular biologist, research scientist; m. David Kronemyer; children: Andrew, Lauren. BS in Microbiology, Colo. State Coll., 1973; PhD in Physiology, U. Colo., 1979. Postdoc. rschr. Salk Inst., La Jolla, Calif., 1979—82; with UCLA Jonsson Comprehensive Cancer Ctr., 1983—, dir., 1995—; and co-dir. UCLA Inst. Stem Cell Biology and Medicine, 2005—; prof. medicine & biol. chemistry UCLA Sch. Medicine. Pres. Jonsson Cancer Ctr. Found., 1995—; bd. dirs. Am. Assn. Cancer Rsch. Recipient Scholar award, Leukemia Soc. Am., 1988, Stohlman Scholar award, 1991, Women of Sci. award, UCLA, 1991, Am. Soc. Clin. Investigation award, 1994. Office: Jonsson Comprehensive Cancer Found UCLA 8-950 Louis Factor Bldg Box 951780 Los Angeles CA 90095-1781 Office Phone: 310-206-0675. Office Fax: 310-267-0102. *

GASTPAR, MARKUS T., psychiatrist, educator; b. Rheinfelden, Switzerland, June 17, 1941; arrived in Germany, 1987; s. Max Gastpar and Emma Heiniger; m. Gabrielle F. Frei, Aug. 18, 1972; children: Désirée, Raphael, Alexandra. Diploma in Med. Studies, U. Basel, Switzerland, 1967. Chief depression rsch. unit dept. psychiatry U. Basel, 1976—86; chmn. dept. psychiatry U. Duisburg-Essen, Germany, 1987—2006; med. dir. Fliedner Klinik, Berlin, 2007—. Mem. adv. bd. Janssen-Cilag Germany, Neuss, 1999—2006, Wyeth Germany, Muenster, 1998—2007, Lab. Servier, Munich, 2006—. Maj. Swiss Army. Mem.: German Coll. Neuropsychopharmaco (pres. 1997—98), Swiss Assn. Psychiatry (pres. 1986—87), German Assn. Psychiatry (pres. 1994—95), Swiss Med. Acad. Sci. (corr.), Lions (pres. 2003—04). Office: Fliedner Klinik Berlin Markgrafenstrasse 34 10117 Berlin Germany

GASTWIRTH, GLENN BARRY, medical association administrator; b. NYC, Sept. 18, 1946; s. Milton and Janette (Wasserman) Gastwirth; m. Joy Ann Binstock, Nov. 29, 1969; children: Sara Beth, Bradley Aaron. BA, Ohio State U., 1968; DPM magna cum laude, NY Coll. Podiatric Medicine, NYC, 1974; LHD (hon.), Ohio Coll. Podiatric Medicine, 2004. Diplomate Am. Bd. Podiatric Surgery, cert. foot and ankle surgeon. Surg. residency Kern Hosp., Detroit; predoc. fellow preventive medicine NYU Sch. Medicine; pvt. practice podiatry Southgate, Mich., 1975-86, Tri-County Family Podiatrists, Pontiac, Mich., 1979-86; dir. sci. affairs Am. Podiatric Med. Assn., Bethesda, Md., 1986-92, dep. exec. dir., 1992—98, exec. dir., 1998—. Pres. Mich. Podiatric Med. Assn., 1981—82. Editor-in-chief Jour. Am. Podiatric Med. Assn., 1989—91, exec. editor, 1991—. Pres. Cold Spring Sch. PTA, Potomac, Md., 1988—90; bd. dirs. Nat. Coun. Aging, Washington, 1996—. Recipient Appreciation cert., NY Coll. Podiatric Medicine, 1998, Lifetime Achievement award, NY State Podiatric Med. Assn., 2006, Podiatry Mgmt. Mag., 2006, Disting. Svc. medallion, Fedn. Internat. Podiatrists, 2007; named Ky. Colonel, 1998; named a Disting. Practitioner, Nat. Acads. Practice, 1994; named to, Podiatry Mgmt. Hall of Fame, 2005; fellow, NIH, 1968—69, NYC Dept. Pub. Health, 1970. Fellow: Am. Soc. Pediat. Surgeons, Am. Assn. Hosp. Podiatrists, Am. Coll. Foot & Ankle Surgeons, UK Soc. Chiropodists & Podiatrists (hon.), Am. Coll. Foot Surgeons; mem.: Am. Soc. Podiatric Execs., Am. Acad. Podiatric Practice Mgmt. (hon.), Am. Soc. Assn. Execs., Am. Podiatric Med. Assn. (house of dels. 1973—74, 1980—86, Disting. Svc. citation 1996), Am. Diabetes Assn., Am. Pub. Health Assn. (sect. coun. mem. 1972—74). Avocations: running, writing. Office: Am Podiatric Med Assn 9312 Old Georgetown Rd Bethesda MD 20814-1646 Office Phone: 301-581-9200. Business E-Mail: gbgastwirth@apma.org. *

GATELL, JOSE MARIA, physician; b. Brafim, Tarragona, Spain, Jan. 14, 1951; s. Jose and Maria (Artigas) G.; m. Rosa Gatell, Sept. 29; children: Mariano, Griselda, Violeta. MD, Med. Sch., Barcelona, 1976, PhD, 1981. From intern to resident Hosp. Clinic, Barcelona, 1976-80; rsch. fellow Mass. Gen. Hosp., Boston, 1982; chief infectious disease unit Hosp. Clinic, Barcelona, 1990—; prof. medicine Faculty of Medicine, Barcelona, 1982—. Author and editor of numerous books and articles on infectious diseases, AIDS. Mem. Am. Soc. Microbiology, Infectious Diseases Soc. Am.., Spanish Infectious Diseases Soc. (pres. 1998-2000), Nat. Geographic Soc., Spanish AIDS Soc. (vice-chmn. 1990-94), Catalan Soc. Infectious Diseases (pres. 1992-94). European AIDS Soc. (chmn. 2004-). Avocations: tennis, skiing, sailing. Office: Hosp Clinic Villarroel 170 Barcelona 08036 Spain Home: Calle Santapau 62 8016 Barcelona Spain Home Phone: 34-93-3497698; Office Phone: 34 932275430. Personal E-mail: gateel0@attglobal.net. Business E-Mail: jmgatell@clinic.ub.es.

GATENBY, PAUL ALLAN, physician, immunologist, dean; s. Harald Bowers and Jean Thorburn Gatenby; m. Lindsay Margaret Gray, Apr. 27, 1980; children: Sophie, Alice. MBBS with honors, U. Tasmania, Hobart, Australia, 1966—71; PhD, U. Sydney, Australia, 1977—81. Cert. Royal Australasian Coll. Physicians, 1979, Royal Coll. Pathologists Australasia, 1979, Royal Australasian Coll. Med. Adminstrs., 1997. Staff immunologist Royal Prince Alfred Hosp., Sydney, 1979—80, 1982—94; postdoctoral rschr. Stanford U., Palo Alto, Calif., 1980—82; assoc. dean Canberra Clin. Sch., U. Sydney, Australia, 1994—2002; prof. prof., dir. ACT Pathology, Canberra, Australia, 2000—02; found. dean Australian Nat. U. Med. Sch., Canberra, 2002—08; dir. rsch., prof. immunology Canberra Hosp., Australian Nat. U., 2008—. Co-dir. Australian Postgraduate Fedn. in Medicine, Canberra, 1995—2002; bd. mem. Nat. Health Scis. Ctr., Canberra, Australia, 1995—2005; mem. ACT Health and Cmty. Care Svc. Bd., Canberra, Australia, 2000—02; bd. mem. Menzies Sch. Health Rsch., Darwin, Australia, 1999—2002. Contbr. chapters to books, articles to profl. jours. Recipient Disting. Alumni award, U. Tasmania, 1999, award, Am. Order Austrailia, 2008; grantee, Nat. Health & Med. Rsch. Coun., Canberra Region Med. Found. Mem.: Australian Soc. for Clin. Immunology and Allergy, Internat. Soc. Reproductive Immunology, Australian Rheumatology Assn., Australia Soc. for Immunology, Clare Hall (life). Office: ACT Health Dir Rsch PO Box 11 Woden ACT 2606 Australia Office Fax: 612 6244 3092. Business E-Mail: paul.gatenby@anu.edu.au.

GATES, JONATHAN DEAN, surgeon, educator; b. Boston, Mar. 27, 1957; MD, Cornell U., 1983. Cert. in surgery, subspecialty in gen. vascular surgery, subspecialty in surg. critical care. Intern Beth Israel Hosp., Boston, 1983-84, resident in gen. surgery, 1984-89, fellow in cardiac surgery, 1989-90; fellow in vascular surgery Brigham-Women's Hosp., Boston, 1990-91, vascular assoc. surgeon, dir. trauma ctr.; asst. prof. surgery Harvard Med. Sch., 1995—. Mass. Med. Soc. Office: Brigham and Womens Hosp Division of Trauma Burns & Critical Care 75 Francis St Dept Surgery Boston MA 02115-6106 Office Phone: 617-732-7715. Business E-Mail: jgates@partners.org.

GATES, ROBERTA PECORARO, nursing educator; b. Elmira, NY, May 22, 1948; d. Patrick George and Verle Elizabeth (Warriner) Pecoraro; m. William Franklin Gates III, May 20, 1972; 1 child, William Franklin IV. BSN, U. Ariz., 1970; MSN in Family Nursing, U. Ala., Huntsville, 1981. Cert. clin. specialist in med.-surg. nursing; bd. cert. Advanced practice nurse; cert. lactation counselor. Charge nurse St. Mary's Hosp. and Mental Health Ctr., Tucson, 1970-72; asst. head nurse Torrance (Calif.) Meml. Hosp., 1973-74; dist. nurse Sierra Sands Sch. Dist., Ridgecrest, Calif., 1974-76; instr. Albany (Ga.) Jr. Coll., 1978-80, John C. Calhoun Coll., Decatur, Ala., 1981-83; learning resources coord. Albany State Coll., 1984-85; asst. prof. Sinclair C.C., Dayton, Ohio, 1990-91, Darton Coll., Albany, 1986-89, 92—. Bd. dirs. Network Trust, Albany; cons. Cmty. Health Inst., Albany, 1993, Early County Bd. Edn., Blakely, Ga., 1994, Ga. State U., 1996—, Ga. Interagy. Coordinating Coun., 1997—; mem. Dist. Health Perinatal Bd., 2002-05; mem. Breastfeeding Task Force, 2002; cons. Project SCEIs, Ga. State U., 1996—. Author: A Model for Adolescent Health Promotion in the Dougherty County Community, 1993. Mem. Ga. Coun. Prevention of Child Abuse, Albany, 1988, 93; mem. Albany Mus. Art, 1993—; mem. Cmty. Ptnrs. Health Care Initiative, Dayton, 1990-91; bd. dirs. March of Dimes, Albany, 1986-89; mem. Albany-Dougherty 2000, DOCO Alternative Adv. Bd., State Consortium Early Intervention, Babies Can't Wait, 1995. Recipient NISOD award tchg. excellence, 2002; Named to Outstanding Young Women of Am., 1983. Mem. Ga. Higher Edn. Consortium, Sigma Theta Tau, Phi Kappa Phi. Avocations: gardening, walking, boating, reading. Office: Darton Coll 2400 Gillionville Rd Albany GA 31707-3023 E-mail: roberta.gates@darton.edu.

GATES, STEVEN LEON, physician; b. Newton, Kans., Aug. 13, 1954; s. Leon Martin and Mary Lorine (Adams) G.; m. Paula Ellen Banwart, Jan. 1, 1977; children: Stephanie, Scott, Jeffrey. PharmD summa cum laude, SW Okla. State U., 1976; DO, Okla. State U., 1986. Diplomate internal medicine and geriatrics Am. Bd. Internal Medicine. Intern Osteopathic Med. Ctr. Tex., Ft. Worth, 1986-87; resident in internal medicine Dallas/Ft. Worth Med. Ctr., Grand Prairie, Tex., 1987-90; pharmacist M & D Star Drug Store, Okmulgee, Okla., 1976-80; pharmacist, mgr. Wal-Mart Pharmacy Divsn., Okmulgee, Okla., 1980-82; chief med. resident Ready Care Minor Emergency Ctr., Bedford, Tex., 1987-90; jail physician Tarrant County Sheriff's Dept., Ft. Worth, 1989-90; pvt. practice internal medicine Grand Prairie, Tex., 1990-97, Cleburne, Tex., 1997—2006; dir. med. edn. Bay Area Corpus Christi Med. Ctr., Tex., 2007—. Internal medicine physician and minor emergency physician Ready Care Med. Clinic, Bedford, Tex., 1990-91; dir. med. edn. Dallas/Ft. Worth Med. Ctr.-Grand Prairie, 1991-96; clin. asst. prof. dept. medicine U. North Tex., Tex. Coll. Osteopathic Medicine, Ft. Worth, 1990— Fellow Am. Bd. Internal Medicine: mem. Am. Coll. Osteo. Internists (bd. cert. with added qualification in geriatrics), Am. Osteo. Assn., Tex. Osteo.

Med. Assn. (trustee 2004—), Assn. Osteo. Dirs. & Med. Educators (nat. bd. trustees), Sigma Sigma Phi. Republican. Avocations: reading, exercise, travel, theater. Office Phone: 361-761-3280. Personal E-mail: sgates5160@aol.com.

GATMAITAN, LUIS P., medical physician, writer, consultant; MD. Med. cons., Doctors On Line DZAS, Philippines, host, children's storytelling program, Wan Dey, Isang Araw; chmn. Kuwentista ng mga Tsikiting (KUTING); sectoral rep. Philippine Bd. on Books for Young People. Author: Sandosenang Sapatos (Bologna Internat. Children's Book Fair, 2005, 2005 Outstanding Book for Young People with Disabilities, IBBY, listed on Internat. Bd. on Books for Young People (IBBY), (book series) Mga Kuwento ni Tito Dok (several storybooks for children tackling issues such as disability, senility, coping with death, coping with cancer, childhood diseases, and children's rights). Recipient Cath. Mass Media Awards, Salanga Writers Prize, Philippine Bd. on Books for Young People; named one of The Ten Pillars of the Philippine Health Care Industry, HealthToday Philippines Mag., The Ten Outstanding Young Men of the Philippines, 2003; named to Palanca Hall of Fame, 2005; finalist Ten Outstanding Young Persons of the World, 2004. Office: Philippine Board on Books for Young People 2nd Fl FSS Bldg 20 Scout Tuason St 1103 Quezon Philippines Office Phone: 3723548. *

GATSOULIS, NIKOLAOS IOANNIS, physician, surgeon; b. Lefkimmi, Corfu, Greece, Oct. 8, 1951; s. Ioannis Alexandros and Constantina Dimitrios (Monastirioti) G.; m. Grammatiki Odysseas Hana; 1 child, Ioannis. MD, U. Thessaloniki, 1978; PhD, U. Athens, 2000. Physician Greek Army, 1978-79, trainee in gen. surgery 401 Army Gen. Hosp. Athens, 1979-80; physician Prefecture of Corfu, 1980-81; trainee in gen. surgery Gen. Hosp. Pireus, 1982-85; cons. gen. surgeon Gen. Hosp. Corfu, 1986—. V.p. Corfu Med. Coun., 1999-2001; sec. sci. com. Gen. Hosp. Corfu, 1986-89, 95-98; vis. cons. U. Hosp. St. Mary's, London, 1997, U. Hosp. Louis A. Weiss, Chgo., 1999. Author: Laparoscopic and Interventional Techniques in the Early 21st Century, 2000; contbr. articles to profl. jours. including Obesity Surgery, Internat. Jour. Quality in Health Care, Prehosp. Immediate Care, among others. Prefectural councillor Prefecture of Corfu, 1998—. Mem. Hellenic Surg. Soc., European Assn. for Endoscopic Surgery (The Netherlands), Soc. Laparoendoscopic Surgeons. Mem. Christian Orthodox Ch. Avocations: general and underwater photography, scuba diving, sailing, painting, music. Office: Gen Hosp Corfu Ioulias Andreadi 1 49100 Corfu Greece E-mail: gats@otenet.gr.

GATTI, EUGENE ANTHONY, adult & pediatric allergist & immunologist; b. Camden, NJ, June 14, 1955; MD, Georgetown U., 1982. Diplomate Am. Bd. Allergy & Immunology, Am. Bd. Pediatrics. Resident pediatrics Thomas Jefferson U. Hosp., Phila., 1982-85, fellow allergy & immunology, 1985-87; immunologist West Jersey Hosp., Voorhees, NJ, 1987—, Cooper Hosp., Camden, 1987—. Mem. AMA, Am. Acad. Allergy and Immunology, Am. Acad. Pediatrics, Am. Coll. Allergy & Immunology. Home: 1135 Washington Ave Haddonfield NJ 08033 Address: 54 E Main St Marlton NJ 08053 2180 Office Phone: 856-988-0570.

GATTI, MARIA SILVIA, medical educator; b. Altinópolis, Dec. 8, 1954; BS in Biomedicine, 1976; D, UNIFESP, 1994. Prof. U. Campinas, 1983—, coord., 1998—2002. Office: Charles Darwin Campinas São Paulo 13083-970 Brazil Business E-Mail: msvgatti@unicamp.br.

GATTI, RITA, pharmacist, educator; b. Riolo Terme, Ravenna, Italy, Jan. 31, 1950; PharmD, 1974. Prof. pharm. scis. U. Bologna, 1986—. Mem.: Italian Chem. Soc. Avocations: travel, skiing. Office: Via Belmeloro 6 Bologna 40126 Italy Office Fax: 390512099734. Business E-Mail: rita.gatti2@unibo.it.

GATZ, MARGARET, psychology professor, department chairman; PhD. Faculty mem. U. So. Calif., LA, 1985—, prof. psychology, gerontology and preventive medicine, chair dept. psychology. Faculty athletic rep. to the NCAA and Pacific-10 Conf. U. So. Calif., 1986—91; mem. rsch. com. NCAA, 1991—98; fgn. adj. prof. Karolinska Institutet, Sweden, 2000—. Author: Emerging Issues in Mental Health and Aging, 1995; co-author (with M.A. Messner and S.J. Ball-Rokeach): Paradoxes of Youth and Sport, 2002; co-author: (with M.J. Karel, S. Ogland-Hand and J. Unützer) Assessing and Treating Late-Life Depression: A Casebook and Research Guide, 2002; contbr. articles to profl. jours. Recipient Disting. Mentorship award, Gerontol. Soc. Am., 1997, Donald F. Kent award, 2006, Master Mentor award, Retirement Rsch. Found., APA, 1999, Raubenheimer Outstanding Sr. Faculty award, USC, 2001, Disting. Rsch. Achievement award, APA Divsn. 20, 2005, Award the Advancement of Psychology and Aging, APA Com. on Aging, 2005; Zenith fellow, Alzheimer's Assn., 2003—04. Office: Dept Psychology Univ So Calif SGM 520 3620 S McClintock Ave Los Angeles CA 90089-1061 Office Phone: 213-740-2212. Business E-Mail: gatz@usc.edu.

GATZIOUFAS, ZISIS, medical researcher; MD, Aristotle U. Sch. Medicine, Thessaloniki, Greece. Rsch. assoc. Muenster U. Sch. Medicine, Nordrhein-Westfalen, Germany, 2004—06; sr. rsch. assoc. Saarland U. Sch. Medicine, Homburg, Germany, 2006—. Recipient Rsch. award, Saarland Found. Rsch. Ophthalmology, 2008. Mem.: European Assn. Vision and Eye Rsch., Assn. Rsch. Vision and Ophthalmology, German Soc. Ophthalmology. Office Fax: 4968411622488. Business E-Mail: zisis.gatzioufas@uniklinikum-saarland.de.

GÀUCAN, IOAN, neurologist; b. Sfantul Gheorghe, Covasna, Romania, June 21, 1933; s. Ioan and Elena C.; m. Adriana Maria Niculescu, May 13, 1961; children: Ioan, Mihaela. MD, Med. U. IASI, 1958. Resident neurologist U. Timisoara, Romania, 1958-63; neurologist Mcpl. Hosp., Ploiesti, Romania, 1964-77; head neurology dept. Mcpl. Hosp. Schüller, Ploiesti, 1978—2003; pvt. practice Ploiesti. Author: Neuropatia Diabetica, 1987, Natural History of Diabetic Neuropathy, 1988; contbr. articles to profl. jours. Named honoured med. man, Ministry Pub. Health, 1977. Mem. Internat. Psychogeriatric Assn., Internat. League Against Epilepsy, N.Y. Acad. Scis. Avocations: mountain trips, flower gardening. Office: Mcpl Hosp Schuller Ana Ipatescu St 59 2000 Ploiesti Romania Home: Strada Ionescu Toma 11 100169 Ploiesti Romania

GAUDET, TRACY W., federal agency administrator; BA, MD, Duke U. Founding exec. dir. program in integrated medicine Univ. Ariz.; joined faculty Duke Univ., 2000; asst. prof. ob-gyn. dept. Duke Univ. Med. Ctr., Durham, exec. dir. Ctr. for Integrated Medicine, 2001, chair membership. com., 2002—04, mem. steering, exec. endn. and policy com.; dir. patient centered care and cultural transformation program US Dept. Veterans Affairs, 2011—. Author: (books) Consciously Female, 2004, Body, Soul and Baby, 2007; columnist Body+Soul Mag.; contbr. numerous publs. Named one of the 11 Women Who Shape the World, Shape, 2008, the Top 25 Women in Health Care, Modern Healthcare Mag., 2011. Office: United States Department of Veterans Affairs 820 Vermont Ave Washington DC 20420 Office Phone: 800-827-1000.

GAUR, AMAR CHAND, microbiologist; b. Pidhwal, Mau, India, July 20, 1933; s. D. N. and Dhanpati G.; m. Chhaya, Feb. 20, 1943; children: Anupam, Amitabh. BS, Agra U., India, 1952, MS, 1954; DPhil, U. Allahabad, India, 1957; DS, U. Paris, 1962. Soil microbiologist I.A.R.I., New Delhi, 1964-70, sr. microbiologist, 1971-78, prof., 1978-82, prin. scientist, 1983-85, prof. head, 1986-93; prof. A.M.U., Aligarh, India, 1995-96; emeritus scientist Dept. Sci. and Tech., New Delhi, 1998-2000; FAO cons. Soil Microbiology Western Samoa, 1990. Advisor (tech.) for setting up & operation of organo-phos compost plant, Delhi, 2001-02; FAO/ICAR regional coords. composting FAO/ Asian Network on Bio and Organic Biofertilizers, 1983-93; advisor, Human Devel. Soc., New Delhi, 2006-; vis. scientist Inst. Agrl. Microbiology, St. Petersburg, Russia, 1976; cons. biofertilizers, improved compost techs. and biopesticides; rschr. in field. Author: A Practical Manual of Rural Compositing, 1982, Organic Manures, 1984, Phosphorus Solubilising Microorganisms as Biofertilizers, 1990, Microbial Technology for Composting of Agricultural Residues by Improved Methods, 1999, Handbook of Organic Farming and Biofertilizers, 2006, Biofertilizers in Sustainable Agriculture, 2006. Fellow Nat. Acad. Agrl. Sci.; mem. Nat. Acad. Scis., Assn. Microbiologist India. Avocations: photography, stamp collecting/philately, gardening. Home: E-7 Sector XV Pusa Apts 110 089 New Delhi India Office Phone: 099680-73957. E-mail: acgaur2007@rediffmail.com.

GAUSAS, ROBERTA ELISABETH, oculoplastic and orbital surgeon; b. Chgo., Jan. 6, 1964; m. Allen J. Model, Jan. 11, 2003. MD, Northwestern U., Chgo., 1989. Diplomate Am. Bd. Ophthalmology. Fellow in oculoplastic surgery U. Wis., Madison, 1993—94; fellow in orbital surgery Moorfields Eye Hosp., London, 1994—95; intern McGaw Hosp., Chgo., 1989—90; resident U. Wis. Hosp. and Clinic, Madison, 1990—93; instr. U. Wis.-Madison Hosp. and Clinics, 1995—96; dir. oculoplastic and orbital surgery svc., assoc. prof. dept. ophthalmology U. Pa. Med. Sch., Phila., 1996—. Recipient Top Doc award, Phila. Mag., 2000, 2002; scholar, DAAD, German Academic Exch. Svc., 1985. Fellow: Am. Soc. Ophthalmic Plastic and Reconstructive Surgery (program chmn. ann. sci. symposium 2002, mem. exec. com. 2002—04, program chmn. ann. spring sci. symposium 2003, Merril Reeh Pathology award 1999), Am. Acad. Ophthalmology (Achievement award 2001). Avocations: travel, conservation, art. Office: Scheie Eye Inst U Pa 51 North 39th St Philadelphia PA 19104

GAUTAM, PENNATHUR, biotechnologist, educator; b. Chennai, India, May 22, 1959; MSc, Vivekananda Coll., 1981; PhD, Indian Inst. Sci., 1989. Rsch. assoc. U. Chgo., 1989—92; prof. Anna U., Chennai, 1993—, chmn., faculty tech., 2008. Office: Anna University Ctr Biotech Chennai Tamilnadu 600025 India Office Fax: 914422350299. Personal E-mail: pennathurpersonal@gmail.com.

GAUTAM, UJJAL K., chemistry professor; b. Jorhat, Assam, India, Oct. 28, 1976; PhD in Chemistry, Indian Inst. Sci., 2006. ICYS rschr. Nat. Inst. Materials Sci., 2006—11; prof., new chemistry unit JN Ctr. Advance Sci. Rsch., 2011—. ICYS fellowship, MEXT, Japan (NIMS). Avocations: badminton, photography. Office: JN Ctr Advanced Sci Rsch Jakkur Bangalore 560064 India Office Fax: 918022082627. Business E-Mail: gautam.ujjal@nims.go.jp.

GAUTAM, VIKAS, physician, consultant; s. Sat Prakash and Madhu Gautam; m. Shabnam Sharma, Nov. 5, 2003. MD in Microbiology, Rohtak, 2001. Demonstrator Pandit Bhagwat Dayal Sharma Postgrad. Inst. Med. Scis., Rohtak, India, 2001—01, Govt. Med. Coll. & Hosp., Chandigarh, India, 2001—04; lectr. Maharaja Agrasen Med. Coll., Hisar, India, 2004—04; asst. prof. Postgrad. Inst. Med. Edn. & Rsch., Chandigarh, 2004—. Cons. Gerson Lehrman Group, 2004—, Sci. Adv. Bd., 2005—; technical assessor Nat. Accreditation Bd. Ltd., 2006—. Contbr. articles to jour., chapters to books. Adminstr. MBBS Colleagues, Rewari, India, 1993; supr. Nat. Pulse Polio Program, Chandigarh, India, 2003. Mem.: Indian Assn. Mycoplasmalogists, Indian Med. Assn., Biotechnology Soc. India, Indian Assn. Med. Microbiologists, Internat. Soc. Infectious Diseases, Am. Soc. Microbiology. Avocations: travel, science & spirituality, history of medicine, complementary and alternative medicine. Home: Sector 21 D H No 3243 Chandigarh 160022 India Office: Pgimer Sector 12 Chandigarh 160012 India Office Fax: +91 172 2744401, 2745078. Personal E-mail: r_vg@yahoo.co.uk. Business E-Mail: vgautam72@rediffmail.com.

GAUTHIER, ANDRE PIERRE, retired gastroenterologist, educator; b. Brioude, France, Aug. 4, 1933; s. Marcel Antoine and Odette (Soulier) G.; m. Claude Marie Caire, Sept. 22, 1962; children: Pascale Michele, Pierre-Andre. MD, Med. Sch. Marseilles, 1960, Prof. Medicine, 1966. Intern, resident Marseilles Pub. Assistance, 1956-60, hosp. asst., 1960-62; chief of clinic Med. Sch. Marseilles, 1962-66, aggregation, 1966-76, prof., 1976-80, prof. 1st class, 1980—; chief of dept. Sainte Marguerite Hosp., Marseilles, 1973-82, La Conception Hosp., Marseilles, 1982-98, med. cons., 1998-2000; ret., 2001. Adminstr. Marseilles Hosp., 1984-88, Observatoire Regional de la Sante, Marseilles, 1985-2003. Author: Digestive Allergy, 1960, Intensive Care in Hepatology, 1984; contbr. numerous articles to profl. jours. Regional councillor Provence, France, 1992-98; city councillor, Marseilles; mil. affairs and vets. attaché, 1995-2001; greater marseilles councillor, 1995-2001. With French Army, 1957—58. Decorated knight Ordre Nat. du Merite, knight Ordre Nat. de la Légion d'honneur. Roman Catholic. Home: 302 Rue Paradis Marseille France 13008 Personal E-mail: andre.gauthier0819@orange.fr.

GAUTHIER, JEAN MARIUS, cardiologist, consultant; b. Arles, France, Feb. 15, 1947; s. Victorin Gauthier and Jeanne Pignatel; m. Marie Françoise Gauthier, July 12, 1971; children: Christophe, Benjamin. MD, Faculty of Medicine, Montpellier, France, 1972; cert. in Ultrasound, U. Montpellier, 1976, cert. in Sports Medicine, 1976. Head dept. cardiovascular disease Paoli Ctr., France, 1972—; faculty sports physiology Montpellier U., 1985—; head med. ctr. Paul Ricard Circuit, Toulon, 2000—. Clin. expert med. rsch. French Health Govt., 1983—; med. advisor Fedn. Internat. de Football, 1984—; cons. in sports medicine, 1994—. Co-author: (book) Sports Traumas Among Adults, 1997, Child and Sport, 1998, Sports Cardiology, 2000. Mem.: French Cardiology Soc., World Acad. for Biomed. Tech. Home: Chemin de Cazeneuve Mas Pt St Jean 13200 Arles France Office: Cardiology Dept 21 Blvd Georges Clemenceau 13200 Arles France Home Phone: 0033490968269; Office Phone: 0033607719516. E-mail: gauthierfife@wanadoo.fr.

GAVENCAK, JOHN RICHARD, pediatrician, allergist; b. Bklyn, June 21, 1949; m. Madeline Gavncak Aug. 12, 1972. BA, NYU, 1970; MD, N.Y. Med. Coll., Valhalla, 1974. Diplomate Am. Bd. Pediatrics, Am. Bd. Allergy and Immunology. Resident in pediats. Met. Hosp., NYC, 1974-76, fellow in allergy and immunology, 1976-78; pvt. practice allergist East Rockaway, N.Y., 1976—. Fellow Am. Coll. Pediatrics, Am. Coll. Allergy and Immunology.; mem. N.Y. Allergy Soc., Long Island Allergy Soc. Avocations: fishing, gardening, boating. Office: John R Gavencak MD 53-42 Francis Lewis Blvd Bayside NY 11364 also: 400 E Atlantic Ave East Rockaway NY 11518

GAVIN, MARY JANE, retired medical/surgical nurse; b. Prairie Du Chien, Wis., Sept. 1, 1941; d. Frank Grant and Mary Elizabeth Wolf; m. Alfred William Gavin, Nov. 9, 1963; children: Catherine Heidi Elizabeth, Carl Alfred Eric. Student, North Cen. Coll., Naperville, Ill., 1959-61; BS, RN, U. Wis., 1964; postgrad., Deepmuscle Tng. Ltd., 1980; postgrad. in Deep Muscle Therapy. RN, Wis. Staff nurse U. Wis. Hosps., Madison; nurse home response VA, Milw.; ret., 2006. Unit chair Badger Girls State, 1991-2005; active Wis. Am. Legion Aux.; task force for handicapped Eastside Wis. Evang. Luth. Ch., Madison, 1993 U. Wis. scholar. Mem.: DAV Auxiliary (life), Monona Grove Am. Legion Aux. (pres. Unit 429 1990—2005). Achievements include writer material that made a federal law null and void.

GAVINO, ALDE CARLO PATDU, dermatologist; b. Manila, Nov. 3, 1977; s. Cesar Jamandron and Lucia Patdu Gavino. MD, U. Philippines Coll. Medicine, Manila, 2001. Intern, internal medicine Cleve. Clinic, 2002—03; postdoc. rsch. fellow, immuno dermatology U. Tex. Southwestern Med. Ctr., Dallas, 2003—05; resident, anatomic and clin. pathology U. Okla. Health Scis. Ctr., Oklahoma City, 2005—06, U. Tex. Southwestern Med. Ctr., 2006—08, chief resident, 2008—09, resident dermatology Austin, 2010—; fellow, dermatopathology U. Ala. Birmingham, 2009—10. Recipient Nancy K. Hall award, 2006; rsch. fellowship, Dermatology Found., 2004, grant, Children's Med. Ctr. Dallas Clin. Rsch. Adv. Com., 2004. Mem.: Travis County Med. Soc., Tex. Med. Assn., Am. Soc. Dermatologic Surgery, Am. Acad. Dermatology, Coll. Am. Pathologists. Conservative. Roman Catholic. Home: 2505 Shupe Ct Irving TX 75060 Office: 601 E 15th St Austin TX 78701 Personal E-mail: carlogavino.md@gmail.com.

GAVITA, OANA ALEXANDRA, medical researcher; b. Beius, Oct. 21, 1981; MA, Oradea U., 2007; PhD, Babes-Bolyai U., 2011. Clin. psychologist Ctr. Child and Parent Counseling, 2005—08; psychologist HILL Internat., 2007—08; HR specialist Intesa Sanpaolo Bank, 2008—; exec. dir., Internat. Coaching Inst. Babes-Bolyai U., 2009, postdoc. rschr., 2009—. Recipient award, Nat. Coun. Rsch. Higher Edn.; Rsch. fellowship, Harvard Med. Sch., Found. Dinu Patriciu, Clin. fellowship, King's Coll. London. Mem.: European Found. Psychology, Albert Ellis Inst. (NY) (Young Rschrs. award). Avocations: swimming. Office: 37 Republicii Cluj-Napoca Cluj 400015 Romania Office Fax: 40264434141. E-mail: gavita.oana@gmail.com.

GAW, JAMES RICHARD, retired corporate executive; b. Bklyn., Sept. 2, 1943; s. James A. and Catharine (Clough) G.; m. Lorraine Osenbruk, July 21, 1973; children: Sean James, Joshua Timothy, Desiree Ann. BA, L.I. U., 1965, MA, St. John's U., 1967. Cert. health cons. Underwriter Royal-Globe Ins. Co., NYC, 1969-70; rep. Blue Cross/Greater N.Y., NYC, 1970-75; mktg. specialist Community Health Plan, Albany, N.Y., 1975-78; dir., mktg. support Blue Cross/Northeastern N.Y., Albany, 1978-82, sr. advisor to pres., 1982-84; dir. program svcs. Empire Blue Cross/Shield, NYC, 1984-89, dir. records mgmt., 1989-90; dir. adminstrn. and facilities svcs., 1990-99; dir. corp. devel. Support Svcs. Alliance, Schoharie, N.Y., 1999-2001; v.p. ins. svcs., corp. compliance officer Support Svcs. Alliance, Inc., 2001—. N.Y. state project dir. Blue Cross Assn., Chgo., 1979-83; preceptor Union U., Schenectady, N.Y., 1980-82. V.p. Cath. Charities, Albany, 1983-88; gov. Adirondack Mountain Club, Inc., Glen Falls, N.Y., 1980-83; mem. Nat. Com. on Alcohol & Drugs, Chgo., Washington, 1980-82; pres. Schoharie Family & Community Svcs., Cobleskill, N.Y., 1976-78; coord. Health Info. Sharing Project, Albany, 1979-81. With USMC, 1967-69, Vietnam. Recipient Svc. Award Recognition Schoharie Family and Cmty. Svcs., 1988, Energy Conservation awrd Silverlight/Am. Energy Care, 1994; grantee Nat. Inst. Drug Abuse, 1981-83. Mem. Internat. Facilities Mgmt. Assn., Assn. Records Mgmt. and Administr., Bldg. Owners and Mgrs. Assn., Am. Inst. Arch. (affiliate), Nat. Assn. Health Underwriters, Schoharie County C. of C. (bd. dirs., treas. 2000-2005, pres. 2005—07) Roman Catholic. Avocations: hiking, camping, photography, furniture design, bagpiping.

GAWADE, SHIVAJI PRATAP, principal, medical educator; b. Khatav, Maharashtra, India, May 1, 1952; s. Vijayalaxmi Pratap Gawade; m. Nandini Shivaji Gawade, June 1, 1976. B in Pharmacy, Govt. Coll. Engring. Karad, Maharashtra, 1974; PharmM, Haffkine Inst., Parel, Mumbai, 1977, PhD in Pharmacology, 1981. Prof. dept. pharmacology Al-Ameen Coll. Pharmacy, Bangalore, Karnataka, India, 2001—06; prin., prof. pharmacology Coll. Pharmacy, Pandharpur, Maharashtra, 2006—09. Rsch.-in-charge Inst. Pasteur, Paris, 1982—83. Named Outstanding Scientist 20th Century, Internat. Biog. Ctr., Eng., 2000; grantee, All India Coun. Tech. Edn., New Delhi, 1996—2001. Mem.: Indian Pharmacological Soc. Achievements include discovery of presynaptic nicotinic facilitatory type of autoreceptors expression following toxin antivenin treatment on mammalian n-m preparation subjected to high frequency stimulation. Home and Office: Ges Satara Coll Pharmacy 1539 New Additional MIDC Deguan Satara MS 415 004 India Personal E-mail: sneskw@gmail.com.

GAWANDE, ATUL A., surgeon, writer; b. Bklyn., Nov. 5, 1965; s. Atmaram S. Gawande, Sushila Goswami Gawande; m. Kathleen Hunter Hobson; children: Walker, Hattie, Hunter. BS in Applied Sci., Stanford U., Calif., 1987; degree in Philosophy, Politics and Economics, Balliol Coll., Oxford, Eng., 1989; MD, Harvard Med. Sch., 1995;

MPH, Harvard Sch. Pub. Health, 1999. Chief social policy advisor Clinton/Gore 1992 Campaign, Little Rock, 1992—92; deputy dir. health policy Clinton/Gore Presdl. Transition Team, Washington, 1992—93; intern, resident Brigham & Women's Hosp., Boston, 1995—2003, assoc. surgeon, gen. & endocrine surgery, 2003—, asst. dir., Ctr. Surgery & Pub. Health, 2004—; asst. prof. dept. surgery Harvard Med. Sch., Boston, 2003—; asst. prof. dept. health policy & mgmt. Harvard Sch. Pub. Health, Boston, 2004—. Author: Complications: A Surgeon's Notes on an Imperfect Science, 2002, Better: A Surgeon's Notes on Performance, 2007, The Checklist Manifesto: How to Get Things Right, 2009; staff writer The New Yorker, 1998— (AAAS Sci. Journalism award for mag. reporting, 2005); contbr. articles to peer-reviewed jours. Recipient Nat. Mag. award for Pub. Interest Writing, Am. Soc. Mag. Editors, 2010; named a MacArthur Fellow, John D. & Catherine T. MacArthur Found., 2006; named one of The 20 Most Influential South Asians, Newsweek mag., 2004, The 100 Most Influential People in the World, TIME mag., 2010; grantee Rhodes scholarship, 1987—89. Office: Brigham & Womens Hosp Dept Surgery 75 Francis St Boston MA 02115 also: Ctr Surgery & Pub Health One Brigham Cir 1620 Tremont St 4th Fl Ste 0 20 Boston MA 02115 Office Phone: 617-732-6830. Business E-Mail: agawande@hsph.harvard.edu, gawande@gawande.com. *

GAY, DOUGLAS MACKENZIE, pharmacologist; b. Ilion, NY, May 7, 1959; s. Raymond Edward and Alice (Fean) G.; m. Carol Ann Houser Gay, June 2, 1984; children: Elizabeth Ann, Stephanie Marie, Rebecca Danielle. BS in Pharmacy, Albany Coll. Pharmacy, NY, 1982. Grad. intern Fay's Inc., Liverpool, NY, 1982-83, staff pharmacist Dewitt, NY, 1983, Mohawk Valley Gen. Hosp., Ilion, NY, 1983-85, Fay's Inc. # 127, Utica, NY, 1985-87, supervising pharmacist, 1987—93, Fay's Inc. # 35, Ilion, NY, 1993—96, Eckerd Inc. # 5081, Ilion, NY, 1996—2006, Eckerd Inc. # 5872, Utica, 2006—07, Rite Aid #10782, Utica, 2007—08, Rite Aid #10771, Herkimer, 2008—11, Rite Aid Floating Pharmacist, 2011—. Fay's Drugs Spkrs. group, Fay's Inc., Ilion, N.Y., 1992-96; peer rev. cons. Eckerd Drugs, 1999—; judge Eckerd Drugs Quiz Show, 1993—2005, Rite Aid Drug Quiz Show Judge 2006-10. Exec. bd. Gen. Herkimer coun. Boy Scouts Am., Revolutionary Trails coun., 2002—11. Mem. Am. Pharm. Assn., Elks (chaplain Ilion lodge 1995-96, esquire 1996-97, loyal knight 1997-98, leading knight, 1998-99, exalted ruler 1999-2000, trustee 2000-06, chmn. drug awareness N.Y. State ctrl. dist. 1995—2011). Avocations: camping, travel, snowmobiling, reading, photography. Home: PO Box 326 Ilion NY 13357-0326 Office: Rite Aid #10771 323 East Albany St Herkimer NY 13350

GAY, PETER, physician; b. NYC, May 22, 1954; BA, Middlebury Coll., 1976; MD, U. Hawaii, 1981. Cons., pulmonary, critical care, and sleep medicine Mayo Clinic, 1981—, prof., medicine, 2009. Recipient H. Frederic Helmholz, Jr., M.D. Sci. Lecture award, North Regional Respiratory Care Soc., 2008, Sepracor Achievement award, Am. Respiratory Care Found., 2009. Fellow: Am. Acad. Sleep Medicine, Am. Coll. Chest Physicians. Office: 200 1st St SW Rochester MN 55905 Business E-Mail: pgay@mayo.edu.

GAY, WILLIAM ARTHUR, JR., thoracic surgeon; b. Richmond, Va., Jan. 16, 1936; s. William Arthur and Marion Harriette (Taylor) G.; m. Frances Louise Adkins, Dec. 17, 1960; children— William Taylor, Mason Arthur. BA, Va. Mil. Inst., 1957; MD, Duke U. Med. Sch., 1961. Diplomate American Bd. Surgery, American Bd. Thoracic Surgery. Resident, general surgery Duke U. Med. Ctr., Durham, NC, 1961—63, 1965—69, resident, thoracic surgery, 1969—71; clin. assoc. Nat. Heart, Lung, and Blood Inst., 1963—65; asst. prof. surgery Cornell U. Med. Coll., NYC, 1971—74, assoc., prof., 1974—78; cardiothoracic surgeon-in-chief N.Y. Hosp., 1976—84; prof., chmn. dept. surgery U. Utah Sch. Medicine, 1984—92; v.p. for health scis. U. Utah, 1990—91; thoracic surgeon Washington U. Sch. Medicine, St. Louis. Prof. surgery Sch. Medicine Washington U., St. Louis; exec. dir. Am. Bd. Thoracic Surgery, 2001—08. Contbr. articles to profl. jours. With USPHS, 1963—65. Recipient Career Scientist award, Irma T. Hirschl Charitable Trust, 1972. Mem.: ACS, Soc. Univ. Surgeons (treas. 1977—80), Am. Surg. Assn., Am. Assn. Thoracic Surgery (treas. 1989—94, sec., treas. 2000), Soc. Thoracic Surgery, Soc. Vascular Surgery, Am. Bd. Thoracic Surgery (bd. dirs. 1988—97, chmn. 1995—97, exec. dir. 2006—08), Am. Bd. Surgery (bd. dirs. 1989—95). Office: Washington Univ Sch Medicine 3180 Queeny Tower 1 Barnes Jewish Hospital Plz Saint Louis MO 63110-1013 Office Phone: 312-202-5900. Office Fax: 312-202-5960. E-mail: gayw@wustl.edu. *

GAYDOS, JOEL CARL, physician; b. Edenborn, Pa., 1942; AB, W.Va. U., 1964, MD, 1968; MPH in Epidemiology, U. Pitts., 1972. Diplomate Nat. Bd. Med. Examiners, Am. Bd. Preventive Medicine. Intern Walter Reed Gen. Hosp., Washington, 1968-69, resident in gen. preventive medicine, 1972-74; commd. 2d lt. U.S. Army, 1964, advanced through grades to col.; mil. physician Med. Corps, 1968-97; dir. occupl. and environ. health U.S. Army Environ. Hygiene Agy., Aberdeen Proving Ground, Md., 1983-85; occupl. health cons., chief preventive medicine cons. divsn. Dept. of the Army Office of the Surgeon Gen., Falls Church, Va., 1985-89; assoc. prof., assoc. dean acting Uniformed Svcs. U. of the Health Scis., Bethesda, Md., 1989-93; dir. clin. preventive medicine U.S. Army Ctr. for Health Promotion and Preventive Medicine, Aberdeen Proving Ground, Md., 1994-97; dir. pub. health practices Dept. of Def. Global Emerging Infections Surveillance & Response Sys., 1997—2008; sr. scientist Henry M. Jackson Found., Rockville, Md., 1997—2010. Adj. prof. Uniformed Svcs. U. Health Scis., 1999—, adj. prof., professorial lectr. George Washington U., Washington, 2000—2010, sci. adv. Armed Forces Health Surveillance Ctr., 2008- Contbr. chapters to books, articles to profl. jours. Decorated Def. Superior Svc. medal, Legion of Merit. Fellow: Am. Coll. Occupl. and Environ. Medicine, Am. Coll. Preventive Medicine, Infectious Diseases Soc. Am.; mem.: AMA, Assn. Mil. Surgeons US, Am. Soc. Tropical Medicine and Hygiene. Office: Armed Forces Health Surveillance Ctr 11800 Tech rd Ste 220 Silver Spring MD 20904 Business E-Mail: joel.gaydos@us.army.mil.

GAYLE, HELENE D., humanitarian organization administrator, pediatrician; b. Buffalo; BS in Psychology cum laude, Columbia U. Barnard Coll., 1976; MD, U. Pa., 1981; MPH, John Hopkins U., 1981. Diplomate American Bd. Pediatricians. Intern then resident in pediats. Children's Hosp. Nat. Med. Ctr., Washington, 1981-84; epidemic intelligence svc. officer br. epidemiology divsn. nutrition Ctr. Health Promotion and Edn., 1984-86; preventive medicine resident divsn. evaluation and rsch. office internat. health program Ctrs. Disease Control Ga. State Dept. Health, 1986-87; med. epidemiologist pediatricians and family studies sect., AIDS program Centers for Disease Control (CDC), US Dept. Health & Human Services, 1987-89, acting spl. asst. minority HIV policy coordination office dep. dir. (HIV), 1988-89, asst. chief sci., 1989-90, chief internat. activity divsn. HIV/AIDS Atlanta, 1990-92; assoc. dir. Centers forDisease Control, US Dept. Health & Human Services, Washington, 1994-96; agy. AIDS coord., chief divsn. HIV-AIDS US Agy. for Internat. Devel. (USAID), Washington, 1992-94; dir. Nat. Ctr. HIV, Sexually Transmitted Diseases and Tb Prevention Ctrs. Disease Control (CDC), US Dept. Health & Human Services, Atlanta, 1995—2001; dir. HIV, Tb, reproductive health The Bill & Melinda Gates Found., Seattle, 2001—06; pres., CEO Cooperative for Assistance & Relief Everywhere, Inc. (Care USA), Atlanta, 2006—. Lectr. Sch. Medicine Morehouse U., 1987—92; lectr. masters in pub. health program Emory U., Atlanta, 1989, 90, clin. asst. prof. cmty. medicine, 1996—; bd. dirs. Colgate-Palmolive Co., 2010—, Cox Enterprises, 2011—, Africa American Inst. Global Health Coun., Internat. Ctr. Rsch. in Women, Inst. Medicine, Coun. Fgn. Rels.; adj. assoc. prof. Sch. Pub. Health U. Wash. Contbr. articles to profl. jours. Adm. USPHS. Merit scholar, 1981; recipient Henrietta and Jacob Lowenburg prize, 1981, Model Excellence award Colgate-Palmolive Co., 1992, Medal of Excellence Columbia U., 1996, Sec. Award Disting. Svc. US Dept. Health & Human Services, 1999, Disting. Svc. Award Nat. Med. Fellowships, 2003, Disting. Alumnus Award, John Hopkins U. Sch. Pub. Health; named a Barnard Woman of Achievement Barnard Coll., 2001; named one of 50 Women to Watch, The Wall St. Jour., 2006. Mem. AAS, AMA, APHA, Am. Coll. Epidemiology, Internat. AIDS Soc. (pres.), Soc. Against AIDS in Africa, Inst. Med. (coun. mem.). Office: CARE USA 151 Ellis St NE Atlanta GA 30303 *

GAYLE, LLOYD BRUCE, plastic surgeon, educator; MD, NYU. Diplomate Am. Bd. Plastic Surgery, Nat. Bd. Medical Examiners. Resident Booth Meml. Med. Ctr., NY Hosp-Cornell Univ. Med. Ctr.; fellow Ralph K. Davies Med. Ctr.; assoc. prof clin. surgery Weill Cornell Med. Coll., former site chief of plastic surgery divsn.; faculty Maimonides Med. Ctr., co-dir. of plastic surgery, vice chair of surgery; clin. dir. of plastic surgery Hosp. for Spl. Surgery. Fellow: Royal Soc. of Medicine, ACS; mem.: Am. Soc. for Reconstructive Microsurgery, Am. Assn. of Plastic Surgeons, Am. Soc. for Aesthetic Plastic Surgery, Am. Soc. of Plastic Surgeons. Office: Maimonides Medical Center 4902 Tenth Ave Brooklyn NY 11219 Office Fax: 718-283-6000.

GAYLIN, WILLARD, physician, educator; b. Cleve., Feb. 23, 1925; s. Harry C. and Fay (Baumgard) Gaylin; m. Betty Schofer, June 15, 1947; children: Ellen Andrea, Jody. AB, Harvard U., 1947; MD, Western Res. U., 1951. Lic. psychiatrist N.Y. Intern Cleve. City Hosp., 1951—52; resident psychiatry Bronx VA Hosp., 1952—54; faculty Columbia Psychoanalytic Sch., 1956—, clin. prof. psychiatry, 1972—; adj. prof. psychiatry Union Theol. Sem.; adj. prof. psychiatry and law Columbia Sch. Law, 1970; founder The Hastings Ctr., Briarcliff Manor, NY, 1970—, chmn. bd., 1970—96. Author: The Meaning of Despair, 1968, In The Service of Their Country: War Resisters in Prison, 1970, Partial Justice: A Study of Bias in Sentencing, 1974, Caring, 1976; author: (with others) Doing Good: The Limits of Benevolence, 1978; author: Feelings: Our Vital Signs, 1979, The Killing of Bonnie Garland: A Question of Justice, 1982, The Rage Within: Anger in Modern Life, 1984, Rediscovering Love, 1986, Adam and Eve and Pinocchio, 1990, The Male Ego, 1992, The Perversion of Autonomy, 1996, Talk Is Not Enough: How Psychotherapy Really Works, 2000, Hatred: The Psychological Descent into Violence, 2003; contbr. articles to profl. jours. Bd. dirs. Helsinki Watch., Nat. Bd. Planned Parenthood. With USNR, 1943—45. Recipient George E. Daniels medal of Merit for contbns. to psychoanalytic medicine, 1973, Elizabeth Cutter Morrow lectureship, Smith Coll., 1970; fellow Chubb, Yale U., 1972. Fellow: Am. Psychiat. Assn.; mem.: N.Y. Psychiat. Soc., Am. Psychoanalytic Assn., Inst. Medicine NAS. Office Phone: 914-478-2712. Personal E-mail: willgaylin@gmail.com.

GAYLOR, DONALD HUGHES, surgeon, educator; b. Bklyn., Apr. 17, 1926; s. Norman Hunter and Frances (Hughes) G.; m. Joan Winifred Power, Apr. 3, 1948; children: David (dec.), Christopher, Steven, Susan, Timothy. AB, U. Rochester, 1946, MD, 1949. Diplomate Am. Bd. Surgery, Am. Bd. Thoracic Surgery. Commd. lt. (j.g.) USN, 1949, advanced through grades to capt. M.C., 1966; intern U.S. Naval Hosp., Phila., 1949-50; student flight surgeon Sch. Aviation Medicine, Pensacola, Fla., 1950-51; flight surgeon U.S. Naval Sta., Trinidad, B.W.I., 1951-53; resident gen. surgery U.S. Naval Hosp., St. Albans, NY, 1953-57; postgrad. fellow surgery Royal Victoria Hosp., McGill U., Montreal, Canada, 1957; resident thoracic surgery U.S. Naval Hosp., St. Albans, NY, 1957-59; resident cardiovascular surgery St. Francis Hosp., Roslyn, NY, 1958; staff thoracic surgeon U.S. Naval Hosp., Portsmouth, Va., 1959-64; surgeon U.S.S. Enterprise, 1964; staff thoracic surgeon U.S. Naval Hosp., Nat. Naval Med. Ctr., Bethesda, Md., 1964-65, chief thoracic and cardiovascular surgery, 1965-68; chief surgery, exec. officer U.S.S. Repose, 1968-69; exec. officer Naval Med. Sch., Bethesda, Md., 1969-72; ret., 1972; clin. assoc. surgery U. Pa. Sch. Medicine, 1976-90; prof. clin. surgery Hahnemann U. Sch. Medicine, 1986-96. Chief surgery Allentown (Pa.) Hosp., 1972-90, Sacred Heart Hosp., 1973-76, Lehigh Valley Hosp. Ctr., 1974-90. Contbr. articles to profl. jours. Fellow ACS; mem. AMA, Am. Thoracic Soc., Am. Trauma Soc. (pres. Pa. divsn. 1979-83, treas. 1985-91), Soc. Thoracic Surgeons (founding), Pa. Assn. for Thoracic Surgery, Assn. Mil. Surgeons U.S., Am. Trauma Soc. (founding mem.). Roman Catholic. Home and Office: 3761 Devonshire Rd Allentown PA 18103-9628 Personal E-mail: capdonjo@earthlink.net.

GAYLOR, JAMES LEROY, biomedical research educator; b. Waterloo, Iowa, Oct. 1, 1934; s. David P. and Lena (Livingston) G.; m. Marilyn Louise Gibson, Mar. 25, 1956; children: Douglas, Ann, Robert, Kenneth. BS, Iowa State U., 1956; MS, U. Wis., 1958, PhD, 1960. From asst. prof. to prof. biochemistry Cornell U., Ithaca, NY, 1960—77, chmn. biochemistry, molecular and cell biology sect., 1970—76; prof., head dept. biochemistry U. Mo., Columbia, 1977—80; assoc. dir. life scis. rsch. E.I. duPont Cen. Rsch., Wilmington, Del., 1981—83, dir. health sci. rsch., 1984—85; dir. biol. rsch. E.I. duPont Pharms., Wilmington, Del., 1986—87; v.p. sci. and technology Johnson & Johnson, New Brunswick, NJ, 1987—97; adj. prof. biochemistry Emory U. Sch. Medicine, 1997—2001, ret., 2001. Vis. prof. U. Ill., summer, 1964-65; sabbatical leave U. Oreg. Sch. Medicine, 1966-67, U. Osaka, Japan, 1973-74; vis. lectr. La Molina, Peru, summer 1962; nutrition cons. Pew Found., Phila., 1986-92; mem. bd. sci. counselors div. cancer prevention Nat. Cancer Inst., NIH, Bethesda, Md., 1987-91. Contbr. over 150 rsch. articles to profl. jours.; mem. editl. bd.: Jour. Biol. Chemistry, 1970-76, Biochimica Biophysica Acta, 1971-81, Jour. of Lipid Rsch., 1972-87, assoc. editor, 1983-87. NIH fellow, 1958-60, Spl. fellow, 1966-67, Guggenheim fellow, 1973-74. Fellow: Am. Heart Assn. (emeritus); mem.: Am. Chem. Soc. Achievements include patents for specific synthetic inhibitors of cholesterol synthesis; research on biosynthesis of cholesterol and other membrane-bound enzymes including inborn errors of cholesterol synthesis. Home: 1950 W Jester Park Dr Polk City IA 50226-1158 Personal E-mail: mljlgaylor@aol.com.

GAYNOR, MITCHELL, oncologist, consultant; b. Plainview, Tex. MD, U. Tex. Southwestern Med. Sch., Dallas. Cert. med. oncology, internal medicine, hematology. Fellow in molecular biology Rockefeller U.; founder Gaynor Integrative Oncology; clinical prof. Cornell U. Weill-Med. Coll.; dir. med. oncology Weill-Cornell Ctr. for Integrative Medicine; cons. & former dir. med. oncology Strang Cancer Prevention Ctr. Adv. bd. Healthy Living Mag., Sass Med. Found.; ed. bd. Integrative Cancer Therapies. Author: Dr. Gaynor's Cancer Prevention Program, 1999, Healing Essence, 2000, The Healing Power of Sound, 2002. Mem.: NY Acad. Sciences, Am. Coll. Physicians, Am. Soc. Clin. Oncology. Office: 215 E 72nd St New York NY 10021 Office Phone: 212-472-2828.

GAZELLE, G. SCOTT, radiologist, researcher; b. Cleve., July 12, 1959; s. Harry Gazelle, Donna Tabar Gazelle; m. Ayca Gazelle; children: Gokce, Orhan. BA, Dartmouth Coll., 1981; MD, Case Western Res. U., 1985; MPH in Health Care Mgmt., Harvard U., 1996, PhD in Health Policy, 1999. Diplomate Am. Bd. Radiology. Chief resident Univ. Hosps. Cleve.; fellowship in abdominal imaging and interventional radiology Mass. Gen. Hosp., assoc. dir., Ctr. Imaging and Pharm. Rsch. Charlestown, Mass., 1993—98, founding dir., DATA Group Boston, 1997—, dir., Clin. Rsch. Support Office, 2001—, dir., Inst. Tech. Assessment, co-dir., assoc. vice-chair rsch., Dept. Radiology; dir. Partners Radiology, Boston, Dana-Farber/Harvard Cancer Ctr. Program in Cancer Outcomes Rsch. Tng. Founding co-dir. BWH-Mass. Gen. Hosp. Ctr. Clin. Trials in Radiology, Boston, 1995—99; founding dir. CIMIT Tech. Assessment and Outcomes Analysis Program, Boston, 1998—; assoc. prof. radiology Harvard Med. Sch., Boston, 1998—; assoc. prof. health policy and mgmt. Harvard Sch. Pub. Health, Boston, 1999—; sr. scientist Partners Inst. Health Policy. Contbr. more than 180 sci. articles to profl. jours. Chmn. Am. Coll. Radiology Commn. on Rsch. and Tech. Assessment, RSNA Rsch. Devel. Com.; past pres. Assn. Univ. Radiologists, Radiology Rsch. Alliance, New Eng. Roentgen Ray Soc. Office: Partners Radiology 101 Merrimac St Ste 334 F Boston MA 02114 Business E-Mail: scott@mgh-ita.org.

GAZIANO, J. MICHAEL, cardiovascular epidemiologist, cardiologist, educator; MD, Yale Med. Sch.; MPH, Harvard Sch. Pub. Health. Dir. Mass. Veteran's Epidemiology Rsch. & Info. Ctr., Boston Geriatric Rsch. Edn. & Clinical Ctr.; dir. preventive cardiology Boson VA Healthcare Sys.; chief div. aging Brigham & Women's Hosp., dir. cardiovascular epidemiology; prof. med. Harvard Med. Sch. Prin. investigator Physicians Health Study II. Office: Brigham and Women's Hospital One Brigham Cir 1620 Tremont St Boston MA 02120 Office Phone: 617-278-0785. Office Fax: 617-525-7740. E-mail: jmgaziano@partners.org.

GAZZANIGA, MICHAEL S., neuroscientist, psychologist; married; 6 children. AB, Dartmouth Coll., 1961; PhD, Calif. Inst. Tech., 1964; MA (hon.), Dartmouth Coll., 2000. Post-grad. fellow Calif. Inst. Tech., 1964—66, Inst. Physiology, Pisa, Italy, 1966; asst. prof. dept. psychology, U. Calif. Santa Barbara, 1967—68, assoc. prof., chmn., 1968—69; assoc. prof. NYU Grad. Sch., 1969—72, prof., 1973—78, SUNY Stony Brook, 1973—78, Cornell U. Med. Coll., 1977—88, dir. cognitive neuroscience div., neurology dept., 1977—88; pres. Cognitive Neuroscience Inst., 1982—; Andrew W. Thomson Jr. prof. psychiatry Dartmouth Med. Sch., 1988—92, dir. program in cognitive neuroscience, 1988—92; prof. U. Calif. at Davis, 1992—96, dir. Ctr. for Neuroscience, 1992—96; David T. McLaughlin Disting. Prof. Dartmouth Coll., 1996—, dir. Ctr. for Cognitive Neuroscience, 1996—, dean of faculty, 2002—04; dir. Sage Ctr. for Study of Mind, U. Calif., Santa Barbara, 2006—. Adv. bd. Cortex Pharmaceuticals, 1988—, Children's Television Workshop, 3-2-1 Contact Extra, NYC; Mind/Body planning com. MacArthur Found.; dir. McDonnell Summer Inst. in Cognitive Neuroscience, 1989—; cons. WGBH History of Sci. program, 1996—; founding fellow Genisis, San Francisco, 1999—. Editor-in-chief emeritus: Jour. Cognitive Neuroscience; editor: Monographs in Cognitive Neuroscience; assoc. editor: Cerebral Cortex, 1990—; author: numerous books on neuroscience & psychology; contbr. scientific papers, articles to scientific journals. Adv. NAS com. on Brain & cognition, 1988, WHO, Beijing; Office of Tech. Assessment adv. bd. US Congress, 1991; founder, bd. govs. Cognitive Neuroscience Soc., 1993—; mem. President's Bioethics Coun., Washington. Recipient John Simon Guggenheim Meml. Fellowship, 1982—83, Javits Neuroscience Investigator award, 1985—92, C.U. Ariens Kappers Medal for Neuroscience, Royal Netherlands Acad. Arts & Sciences. Fellow: Am. Acad. Neurology, AAAS, Am. Physiological Soc., APA; mem.: NAS, Am. Acad. Arts & Sciences, Inst. Medicine, Am. Neurol. Assoc., Internat. Neuropsychology Group, Psychonomics Soc., Soc. for Neuroscience (elected counselor 1992—96), Soc. Exptl. Psychologists, Sigma Xi. Office: Sage Ctr for Study of Mind U Calif Santa Barbara Santa Barbara CA 93106-9660 Office Phone: 603-646-1182, 805-893-5448. Office Fax: 805-893-4330. Business E-Mail: m.gazzanigo@psych.ucsb.edu. E-mail: michael.s.gazzaniga@dartmouth.edu. *

GE, NORMAN N., plastic surgeon; b. Shanghai, Aug. 27, 1964; MD, Baylor Coll. Medicine, 1998. Med. dir. OC Ctr. Aesthetic Surgery, 2007—. Prof. U. Calif., Irvine, 2003. Recipient Excellence award, Orange County Med. Soc., 2008—. Fellow: ACS. Office: 16300 Sand Canyon Ave Ste 201 Irvine CA 92618 Office Phone: 949-727-1818. Personal E-mail: dctrnorman@yahoo.com.

GEALT, MICHAEL A., environmental microbiologist, educator; b. Phila., Nov. 27, 1948; s. Edward Leonard Gealt and Lillian Rose Brenner; m. Maryjanet McNamara, Jan. 2, 1981; 1 child; m. Antonia Malandrucco, May 12, 1967 (div. 1977); 2 children. BA, Temple U., 1970; PhD, Rutgers U., 1974. Rsch. assoc. Med. Sch. Rutgers U., Piscataway, NJ, 1974-76; postdoct. assoc. Inst. Cancer Rsch., Phila., 1976-78; asst. prof. biol. scis. Drexel U., Phila., 1978-84, assoc. prof., 1984-90, prof., 1990-2000, dir. Sch. Environ. Sci., Engring. and Policy, 1994-2000; dean Sch. Engring., Math. and Sci. Purdue U.

Calumet, Hammond, Ind., 2000—05, prof. biology, 2000—05, U. Ark., Little Rock, 2006—, dean Coll. Sci. and Math., 2006—. Contbr. articles to profl. jours. Grantee EPA, 1983, 85, 89, NSF, 1981, 94, 97, USAF, 2002. Mem. AAAS, Am. Soc. Microbiology (chair environ. and applied micro divsn. 1995), Am. Soc. Cell Biology, Assn. Environ. Engrs. & Science Profs., Am. Soc. Engring. Educ., Sigma Chi. Avocations: motorcycles, photography. Office: Univ Ark Little Rock 2801 S University Ave Little Rock AR 72204 Office Phone: 501-569-3247. Business E-Mail: magealt@ualr.edu.

GEARHART, JOHN D., obstetrician, gynecologist, medical educator, developmental geneticist; BSc in Biology, Pa. State U., 1964; MSc in Plant Genetics, U. NH, 1966; PhD in Genetics and Devel., Cornell U., 1970. Fellow Fox Chase Cancer Ctr.; with John Hopkins Sch. Medicine, Balt., 1979—, C. Michael Armstrong prof. medicine, dir., stem cell program, Inst. Cell Engring.; prof., gynecology and obstetrics, physiology and comparative medicine John Hopkins U. Sch. Medicine; prof., biochemistry and molecular biology John Hopkins Bloomberg Sch. Pub. Health; dir., Inst. for Regenerative Medicine U. Pa., 2008—, Penn Integrates Knowledge Prof., 2008—, James W. Effron U. Prof., Dept. Cell and Develop. Biology Sch. Medicine and Dept. Animal Biology Sch. Medicine, 2008—. Co-dir., Stem Cell Biology and Ethics Program (SCoPE) John Hopkins Berman Ethics Inst.; serves on several adv. bds. and coms. of founds., insts. and profl. socs. involved with stem cell rsch. and policy; cons. or expert witness for many govtl. agencies, in states, at the nat. level and to fgn. govts. Contbr. several articles to profl. jours. Named to Acad. Achievement, 1999. Mem.: Internat. Soc. for Stem Cell Rsch. (founding mem.). Achievements include being the leader in the development and use of human reproductive technologies, embryo and germ cell manipulations and in the genetic engineering of cells; in 1998, published with research team at John Hopkins the first report on the derivation of pluripotent stem cells from germ cells of the human embryo. Office: Biomedical Research Bldg 421 Curie Blvd 1151 Philadelphia PA 19104 Office Phone: 410-614-3444, 215-898-9871. Office Fax: 410-614-3976, 410-955-7427. Business E-Mail: gearhart@jhmi.edu, gearhart@upenn.edu. *

GEARHART, JOHN PHILLIP, urologist; b. Lexington, Ky., May 24, 1949; s. J. Edwin and B. Jane (Underwood) G. BS with high distinction, Morehead State U., Ky., 1972; MD with honors, U. Louisville Sch. Med., Ky., 1976. Diplomate Am. Bd. Urology. Intern, surgery Med. Coll. Ga., Augusta, 1975—76, resident, surgery, 1976—77, resident, urology, 1977—79, chief resident, urology, 1979—80; fellow, pediatric urology Alder Hey Children's Hosp., U. Liverpool Sch. Medicine, 1980—81; urologist St. Mary's Hosp., Huntington, W.Va., 1982—84; fellow, pediatric urology John Hopkins Hosp., Balt., 1984—85; instr. Johns Hopkins Sch. Medicine, Balt., 1984-86, asst. prof., 1986-91, assoc. prof., 1991-95, prof., 1995—; dir. pediatric urology Johns Hopkins Hosp. and Children's Ctr., Balt., 1993—. Invited lectr. in field. Contbr. articles to profl. jours. Recipient Outstanding Alumnus, Morehead State U., 1987. Fellow ACS, Am. Acad. Pediatrics (urology sect.)(co-recipient Rsch. award, San Antonio, Tex., 1987); mem. Am. Urol. Soc., Brit. Urol. Soc., Soc. Pediatric Urology, British Ass. Urol. Surgeons, Soc. Reconstructive Genitourinary Surgeons (founding), Md. Urol. Assn., European Soc. Pediatric Urology (invited mem.), Royal Soc. Medicine (Anglo-Am. vis. prof. tchg. scholarship and medal, London, 1995); Masons. Methodist. Avocations: fly fishing, travel. Office: Johns Hopkins Medicine 149 Marburg 600 N Wolfe St Baltimore MD 21287-0005 Office Phone: 410 955 5358. Office Fax: 410-955-0033. Business E-Mail: jgearhart@jhmi.edu

GEBBIE, KRISTINE MOORE, medical educator; b. Sioux City, Iowa, June 26, 1943; d. Thomas Carson and Gladys Irene (Stewart) Moore; m. Lester N. Wright; children: Anna, Sharon, Eric. BSN, St. Olaf Coll., 1965; MSN, UCLA, 1968; DPH, U. Mich., 1995. Project dir. USPHS Tng. Grant, St. Louis, 1972—77, coord. nursing St. Louis U., 1974—76, asst. dir. nursing, 1976—78, clin. prof., 1977—78; adminstr. Oreg. Health Div., Portland, 1978—89; sec. Wash. State Dept. Health, Olympia, 1989—93; coord. Nat. AIDS Policy, Washington, 1993—94; assoc. prof. Sch. Nursing Columbia U., 1994—2007, prof., 2007—; assoc. prof. Oreg. Health Scis. U. Portland, 1980—90. Chair secretarial panel on evaluation of epidemiologic rsch. activities U.S. Dept. Energy, 1989—90; mem. Presdl. Commn. on Human Imunodeficiency Virus Epidemic, 1987—88. Author (with Deloughery and Neuman): Consultation and Community Orgn., 1971; author: (with Deloughery) Political Dynamics: Impact on Nurses, 1975; author: (with Scheer) Creative Teaching in Clinical Nursing, 1976. Bd. dirs. Lusth. Family Svcs. Oreg. and S.W. Wash., 1979—84, Oreg. Psychoanalytic Found.1, 1983—87. Recipient Disting. Alumna award, St. Olaf Coll., 1979; scholar Disting. scholar, Am. Nurses Found., 1989. Fellow: Am. Acad. Nursing; mem.: Am. Soc. Pub. Adminstrn. (Adminstrn. award II 1983), N.Am. Nursing Diagnosis Assn. (treas. 1983—84), Inst. Medicine, Am. Pub. Health Assn. (exec. bd.), Assn. State and Territorial Health Ofcls. (pres. 1984—85, exec. com. 1980—87, McCormick award 1988). Office: Columbia U Sch Nursing 630 W 168th St New York NY 10032-3702 Business E-Mail: KMG24@columbia.edu.

GEBO, SUSAN CLAIRE, consulting nutritionist; b. Bristol, Conn., June 22, 1954; d. Ernest Edward and Lena Clara (Julian) G.; m. Joseph Louis Vasile, Oct. 10, 1987. BS, Cornell U., 1976; MPH, U. Mich., 1980. Registered dietitian. Pub. health nutritionist Navajo & Apache County Health Dept., Holbrook and St. Johns, Ariz., 1976-77; coord., WIC nutritionist Miss. State Bd. Health, Tupelo, 1977-78; asst. state WIC nutrition coord. Conn. Dept. Health Svcs., Hartford, 1978-79; nutritionist Cmty. Health Svcs., Hartford, 1981-84; pvt. practice West Hartford, Conn., 1983—; nutritionist Wesleyan U., Student Health Svcs., Middletown, Conn., 1988—, U. Conn. Family Medicine Residency Program, Hartford, 1985—, faculty, 1985—, asst. clin. prof., 2007—. Adj. faculty U. Hartford, West Hartford, 1981-88, So. Conn. State U., New Haven, 1985-2002, Albertus Magnus Coll., 1991-2000, St. Joseph Coll., West Hartford, 1992—, Manchester C.C., 1994—2008; fellow Nat. Nutrition Consortium, Washington, 1980. Author: What's Left to Eat?, 1992; writer (video) The Diet Interview: A Guide for Paraprofessionals, 1980, featured in video Culinary Hearts Kitchen Course, Am. Heart Assn., 1988, panelist (PBS-TV spl.) Women's Hearts at Risk, 1996, featured nutrition expert (PBS-TV series) 3 episodes America's Walking, 2003; featured nutrition expert: Women's Health Series (Conn. Pub. TV), 2005. Bd. dirs. Am. Heart Assn., Hartford, chmn. program com. greater Hartford br., 1989-91; mem. com. State Communications, 1991-94, media spokesperson, 1991— (Outstanding program award 1990, Outstanding HeartGuide Spokeswoman 1990, Time, Feeling, and Focus award, 1992). Mem. AAUP, Am. Pub. Health Assn., Am. Dietetic Assn., Conn. Dietetic Assn. (co-chmn. pub. rels. com. 1991-93, mem. media spokesperson com. 1993-98, Registered Dietitian of Yr., 1994, del. 1996-99). Avocations: walking, photography, gardening. Office: 854 Farmington Ave West Hartford CT 06119-1587 Office Phone: 860-232-5415. Personal E-mail: suegebo@sbcglobal.net.

GECELTER, GARY RAYMOND, gastrointestinal surgeon, researcher; b. Johannesburg, S. Afica, Aug. 18, 1958; came to U.S., 1993; s. Louis and Sybil (Win) G.; m. Jacqueline Naomi Gittleson, Jan. 29, 1986; children: Ryan J., Rachel C., Amy M. MBBCh, U. Witwatersrand, Johannesburg. Intern Johannesburg Hosp., 1982, attending surgeon, 1992-93; surg. resident U. Witwatersrand, Johannesburg, 1985-90, fellow in gastroenterology, 1990-92; asst. prof. surgery SUNY, Stony Brook, 1993-98; chief gen. surgery L.I. Jewish Hosp., New Hyde Park, NY, 1998—. Oper. rm. dir. Stony Brook U. Hosp., 1994-98, chmn. med. exec. bd., 1998 Mem. editl. bd. S. African Jour. Surgery, 1989-90; contbr. articles to profl. jours. Lt. S. African Med. Corps, 1983-84. Fellow ACS, Coll. Surgeons; mem. Soc. Gastrointestinal Endoscopic Surgeons. Jewish. Avocations: golf, tennis, jogging, piano. Office: LI Jewish Med Ctr 270-05 70th Ave New Hyde Park NY 11040

GEDALIA, ABRAHAM, pediatrician, educator; b. Israel, June 15, 1943; MD, Hebrew U., Jerusalem, 1970. Prof. pediat., head, divsn. pediat. rheumatology Children's Hosp. La. State U. Health Scis. Ctr., 1992—. Fellow: Am. Acad. Pediat., Am. Coll. Rheumatology. Avocation: travel. Office: Children's Hosp 200 Henry Clay Ave New Orleans LA 70118 Office Fax: 504-896-9410. Business E-Mail: a61543@pol.net.

GEDERS, JANE M., gastroenterologist, educator; Attended, Fla. State U., 1972, MS in Nutrition, 1974; PhD in Human Nutrition, Va. Polytechnic Inst. and State U., 1978; MD, U. South Fla., 1987. Diplomate Am. Bd. Internal Medicine, 1990, 2001, diplomate Am. Bd. Internal Medicine-gastroenterology, 1993, 2003. Intern internal medicine North Shore Univ. Hosp., Manhasset, NY, resident internal medicine, 1988—90, Meml. Sloan-Kettering Cancer Ctr., NYC, 1987—88; fellow gastroenterology Mt. Sinai Med. Ctr., NYC, 1990—92, fellow hepatology, 1992—93; asst. prof. medicine NYU Sch. of Medicine; gastroenterology Northern Westchester Hops. Office: Mount Kisco Medical Group Southeast Executive Pk 185 Rte 312 Brewster NY 10509-2338 also: Mount Kisco Medical Group 90 South Bedford Rd Mount Kisco NY 10549-3412 Office Phone: 845-278-7000, 914-241-1050.

GEDIK, RÜSTÜ, dentist; b. Jan. 11, 1950; s. Resit and Naime Gedik; m. Saadet Müftüoğlu-Gedik; children: Aziz Resit Alp, Tugce Naime. Asst. Hacettepe U., Ankara, Turkey, 1986—93; dr. asst. Dicle U., Diyarbakir, Turkey, 1994—96; head dr. Cumhuriyet U., Sivas, 1996—97, chief dept., 1997—2006. Cons. in field. Contbr. articles to profl. jours. Mem.: Turkish Dentomaxillofacial Radiology, European Dentomaxillofacial Radiology. Avocations: tool repair, cooking. Office: Cumhuriyet Univ Faculty Dentistry 58140 Sivas Turkey Business E-Mail: rgedik@cumhuriyet.edu.tr.

GEENEN, VINCENT GASTON MARCEL JEAN, internist; b. Verviers, Belgium, Feb. 6, 1958; s. Marcel and Claire (Fontaine) Geenen; m. Anne Boubeyran; children: Jerome, Pierre-François. MD, U. Liege, 1982, PhD, 1987; degree in internal medicine, Liege Med. Sch., 1988; biotech. cert., U. Paris VII, 1988. Intern U. Hosp. Liege, 1982—89, sr. clin. head in endocrinology and internal medicine, 1989—; rsch. fellow Nat. Fund Sci. Rsch., Liege, 1982—86, rsch. asst., 1986—88, rsch. assoc., 1988—96, sr. rsch. assoc., 1997—2001, rsch. prof., 2001—; dir. Liege Ctr. Immunology, 2001—04, chmn., 2004—. Mem. steering com. Europe Sci. Found., Network Neuro Immuno Modul, 1988—92, mem. steering com. grad. sch. immunology, 2006—; mem. rsch. coun. U. Liege, 1989—93, prof. embryology and devel. biology, 1994—; chmn 3d Gordon Conf. on Neuroendocrine-Immunology; rschr. thymus physiology, endocrine autoimmunity and tolerogenic therapy of type 1 diabetes; coord. FP6 Integrated Project Euro-Thymaide; mem. Belgian Com. Bioethics, 2011—. Editor: (book) Regulatory Peptides, 1993, Current Opinion in Pharmacology, Immunomodulation Issue, 2010; co-editor: (book) Horizons in Endocrinology, 1991, Thymus, 1993, In Vivo Immunology, 1994, Immunoendocrinology in Health and Disease, 2004; author: Cryptocrine Signaling in the Thymus and the Central T-Cell Self Tolerance of Neuroendocrine Principles, 1995; contbg. author: Encyclopedia Neuroscience, 2d edit., 1997, 3d edit., 2004; mem. editl. bd. Jour. Endocrinology, 2001—, NeuroImmuno Modulation; contbr. over 130 sci. papers to profl. publs.; contbg. author: Thymus and T cells, 2003. Pres. St. Benoit-St. Servais Alumni; sec. Fund Leon Fredericq Biomed. Rsch. Recipient Masius prize, Medico-Surg. Soc., 1985, Semper prize, Nat. Fund Sci. Rsch., 1988, Smith Kline-Beecham prize, Royal Acad. Medicine, 1992, Alumni prize, Belgium U. Found., 1993; Travel grantee, State of Belgium, 1984. Mem.: NY Acad. Scis., Immunology Diabetes Soc., Am. Assn. Immunologists, Eurosci., European Assn. Study of Diabetes, Am. Diabetes Assn., Juvenile Diabetes Found., Internat. Soc. NeuroImmuno Modulation, Endocrine Soc. Roman Catholic. Achievements include patents for thymus-based tolerogenic approaches against type 1 diabetes; creation of spin-off ThymUP. Office: U Liege Ctr Immunology Inst Pathology CHU-B23 B-4000 Liège Sart Tilman Belgium Home: Pl des Deportes 5 Liège B 4000 Belgium Home Phone: 32477469095; Office Phone: 3243662550. Office Fax: 3243669859. Business E-Mail: vgeenen@ulg.ac.be.

GEER, JACK CHARLES, retired pathology educator; b. Galesburg, Ill., Sept. 19, 1927; s. John Charles and Ruth Helen (McGee) G.; m. Sara Kathleen Williamson, Feb. 16, 1951; children: Charles Robert, Richard John, John Michael, Cynthia Jane, Michael James. BS, La. State U., 1950, MD, 1956. Rsch. asst. prof. La. State U., Baton Rouge, 1954-66; prof. U. Tex., San Antonio, 1966-67; prof., chmn. Ohio State U., Columbus, 1967-72; assoc. pathologist Davidson Labs., Columbus, 1972-75; prof. pathology U. Ala., Birmingham, 1975-90, prof. emeritus, 1990—, chmn. dept., 1975-88. Cons. nutrition study sect. Nat. Heart, Lung and Blood Inst., Bethesda, Md., 1965-69, cons., chmn. pathology study sect., 1976-80; mem. rsch. com. Am. Heart Assn., 1968-82, pres. Ala. affiliate, 1983-84. Author: Smooth Muscle Cells in Atherosclerosis, 1972; mem. editorial bd.: Jour. Exptl. and Molecular Pathology, 1967—, Am. Jour. Pathology, 1969-80; contbr. articles to profl. jours. Mem. Ala. region ARC Blood Svcs., 1979-90. With USN, 1945-47, ATO. USPHS research career devel. award, 1959-66; recipient Disitng. Faculty citation La. State U., 1964, Disting. Service award Am. Heart Assn., 1972-75, Outstanding Vol. Achievement award ARC, 1981; named to ALumni Hall of Distinction La. State U., 1982. Fellow Coll. Am. Pathologists; mem. AMA, Am. Registry Pathology (exec. mem., pres. 1985-87). Home: 2223 Hemingway Dr Nashville TN 37215-4111 E-mail: jackgreen@aol.com.

GEFEN, AMIT, biomedical engineer; b. Ramat-Gan, Israel, Feb. 8, 1971; BSME, Tel Aviv U., 1994, MSc in Biomed. Engring. with honors, 1997, PhD in Biomed. Engring., 2001. Assoc. prof., dept. biomed. engring. Tel Aviv U., 2001—. Contbr. articles to profl. jours. including Jour. Biomech. Engring., Annals Biomed. Engring., Jour. Biomech. Achievements include research on experimental and computational analysis of the mechanical behavior of hard and soft biological tissues; role of the mechanical stress distribution within tissues in development of pathologies. Office: Dept Biomed Engring Tel Aviv University Ramat Aviv Faculty Engineering 69978 Tel Aviv Israel Home Phone: 972-3-5356950; Office Phone: 972-3-6408093. Fax: 972-3-6405845. E-mail: gefen@eng.tau.ac.il.

GEFFNER, DONNA SUE, speech pathology/audiology services professional, audiologist, educator; d. Louis and Sally (Weiner) Geffner. BA magna cum laude, Bklyn. Coll., 1967; MA, NYU, 1968, PhD (NDEA fellow), 1970; postgrad., Advanced Inst. Analytic Psychology, 1973—75; EdD (hon.), Providence Coll., 2003. Asst. prof. Lehman Coll., 1971-76; assoc. prof. dept. speech St. John's U., 1976-81, prof., 1982—. Dir. Speech and Hearing Ctr., 1976—, chmn. dept. speech comm. scis. and theater, 1983—92, developer M.A. program in speech pathology and audiology, 1984, developer Au.D audiology and doctoral consortia, 2004, dir. grad. program in speech-lang. pathology and audiology, 1992—; pvt. practice, 1980—; cons. to corp. execs.; TV prodr. and hostess NBC, 1977—78, CBS, 1978—79; mem. N.Y. State Licensure Bd., 1993—97. Issue editor: Jour. Topics Lang. Disorders, 1980; editor: ASHA monograph, 1987, Auditory Processing Disorders, 2007—; author: What Professionals Need to Know About Attention Deficit Hyperactivity Disorder, 2005, The Listening Inventory, 2005, Geffmer-Goldman Auditoy Skills Assesments(ASA), Pearson Assesments, 2010; contbr. articles to profl. jours., chapters to books. Recipient Emmy nomination for outstanding instrnl. program, 1978, award, Pres.'s Com. Employment Handicapped, Disting. Achievement award, N.Y.C. Speech-Lang.-Hearing Assn., 1994, Honors, L.I. Speech-Lang.-Hearing Assn., 1998; grantee, CUNY Rsch. Found., 1972, N.Y. State Dept. Edn., 1976—78. Fellow: Am. Speech, Lang. and Hearing Assn. (legis. councillor 1978—87, 1988—90, 1990—94, v.p. acad. affairs 1995—97, pres.-elect 1998, pres. 1999, past pres. 2000, ednl. standards bd. 1992—94); mem.: Coll. Bd. Com. on Literacy, Pearson Assessments (mem. bd. advisors), N.Y. State Speech and Hearing Assn. (pres. 1978—80, honors). Office: St John's University Speech and Hearing Ctr 1025 Northern Blvd Roslyn NY 11576

GEHA, ALEXANDER SALIM, cardiothoracic surgeon, educator; b. Beirut, June 18, 1936; arrived in US, 1963; s. Salim M. and Alice I. (Hayek) G.; m. Diane L. Redalen, Nov. 25, 1967; children— Samia, Rula, Nada BS in Biology, Am. U. Beirut, 1955, MD, 1959; MS in Surgery and Physiology, U. Minn.-Rochester, 1967; MS (privatum), Yale U., 1978. Asst. prof. U. Vt., Burlington, 1967-69; asst. prof. Washington U., St. Louis, 1969-73, assoc. prof., 1973-75, Yale U., New Haven, 1975-78, prof., chief cardiothoracic surgery, 1978-86, Case Western Res. U. and Univ. Hosp. of Cleve., 1986-98; Jay L. Ankeney prof. cardiothoracic surgery Case Western Res. U., 1994-98; pres. Univ. Cardiothoracic Surgeons, Inc., Cleve., 1986—2000; prof., chief cardiothoracic surgery U. Ill. Med. Ctr., Chgo., 1998—2007, prof. chief emeritus cardiothoracic surgery, 2007—; chief cardiothoracic surgery Mt. Sinai Hosp. Med. Ctr., Chgo., 2000—07; prof. cardiothoracic surgery U. Calif., San Diego Med. Ctr., 2008—; attending cardiothoracic surgeon La Jolla VA Hosp., San Diego, 2009—. Cons. VA Hosp., West Haven, Conn., 1975-86, VA Hosp., Cleve., 1986-98, Westside VA Hosp., Chgo., 1998-2007, Cleve. Met. Health Med. Ctr., 1986-98, Mt. Sinai Med. Ctr., Cleve., 1990-98, Waterbury Hosp., 1976-86, Sharon Hosp., 1981-86, Michael Reese Hosp., 2002-06; mem. study sect. Nat. Heart Lung and Blood Inst., 1981-85. Editor: Glenn's Thoracic and Cardio-vascular Surgery, 4th edit. 1983, 5th edit. 1991, 6th edit. 1996; editor Basic Surgery, 1984, House Officer Guild to ICU Care, 1994, 2nd edit., 1996, 3rd edit., 2010 Bd. dirs. New Haven Heart Assn., 1981-85; trustee Am. U. Beirut. Mem. AMA, Assn. Clin. Cardiac Surgery (chmn. membership com. 1978-80, sec.-treas. 1980-83, pres. 1988), Am. Heart Assn. (bd. dirs. 1981-85. councils on basic sci., cardiovascular surgery), Am. Coll. Chest Physicians (steering com. 1980-84), Am. Assn. Thoracic Surgery, Am. Coll. Cardiology, ACS (mem. coordinating com. on edn. in thoracic surgery 1980-95, chmn. 1992-95), Am. Lung Assn., Am. Physiol. Soc., Am. Surg. Assn., Assn. Acad. Surgery, Central Surg. Assn., Chgo. Inst. Medicine, European Assn. Cardiothoracic Surgery, Internat. Soc. Heart and Lung Transplantation, Internat. Soc. Cardiovascular Surgery, Lebanese Order Physicians, New Eng. Surg. Soc., Pan Am. Med. Assn., Halsted Soc., Soc. Thoracic Surgeons (govt. rels. com., manpower com., program com., edn. and resources com.), Soc. for Vascular Surgery, Soc. Univ. Surgeons, Chgo. Surg. Soc., also others. Office Phone: 858-642-3808, 312-996-4942. Business E-Mail: ageha@ucsd.edu. E-mail: ageha@uic.edu.

GEHLERT, SALLY OYLER, clinical aroma therapist, healing touch practitioner; b. Cin., Feb. 12, 1949; d. Ralph Thomas and Inez R. (Morgan) Oyler; m. Robert Gehlert; 1 child, Chloe. AS, U. Cin., 1971, M in Ednl. Adminstrn., 1976; BS in Allied Health Edn., U. Ky., 1974. Cert. dental hygienist Ohio, healing touch practitioner, clin. aromatherapist; practitioner Healing Touch Internat., 2005, clin. aromatherapist Nat. Assn. Holistic Aromatherapy, 2007. Dental hygienist, Cin., 1971—; dental cons. Proctor & Gamble Corp., Cin., 1985-95, John O. Butler Co., Chgo., 1990—; pvt. practice Cin., 1985—2000. Adv. bd. John O. Butler Co., Chgo.; cons. in field. Edit. adv. Journal of Dental Hygiene, 1993; author ednl. programs for dental profls. Mem. Am. Dental Hygienist Assn., Ohio Dental Hygienist Assn., Cin. Dental Hygienist Assn., Healing Touch Internat. (practitioner), Healing Touch Profl. Assn. Home: 2476 Walnutview Ct Cincinnati OH 45230-2455 Office Phone: 513-231-9783. Personal E-mail: sallygehlert@fuse.net.

GEHRIG, LEO JOSEPH, retired surgeon; b. Mapleton, Minn., Apr. 25, 1918; s. Paul P. and Marcella (Hund) G.; m. Marillyn May Nelson, June 10, 1944; children: Gregory Paul, Mark Nelson. BS, U. Minn.,

1942, MB, 1944, MD, 1945. Diplomate Am. Bd. Surgery, Am. Bd. Thoracic Surgery. Intern Salt Lake County Gen. Hosp., Salt Lake City, 1944—45; resident New Eng. Deaconness Hosp., Boston, 1947—50; with USPHS, 1945—70, advanced through grades to rear adm., ret., 1970, chief chest surgery unit SI, NY, 1950—52, resident, 1952—55, chief thoracic surgery Seattle, 1955—57, asst. chief divsn. hosps. Washington, 1957—59, dep. chief, 1959—60, program officer bur. med. svcs. Washington, 1960—61; med. dir. Peace Corps, Washington, 1961—62; asst. surgeon gen., dep. chief Bur. Med. Svcs., 1962—64, chief bur., 1964—65, dep. surgeon gen., 1965—68; dir. office internat. health HEW, 1968—70; assoc. dir. Washington svc. bur. Am. Hosp. Assn., 1970—72, v.p., 1972—75, sr. v.p., dir. Washington office, 1978—80. Dir. rsch. Health Rsch. Edn. Trust, 1985—89. Bd. dirs. St. Lukes Inst., Silver Spring, Md., 1988—2002. Recipient U.S. Disting. Svc. medal. Fellow ACS, Am. Coll. Thoracic Surgery; mem. AMA, APHA, Am. Heart Assn., Assn. Mil. Surgeons, USPHS Clin. Soc., Mil. Officer Assn. Am. (bd. dirs. Alexandria, Va. 1990-97), Alpha Omega Alpha. Home: 5919 Centerville rd Apt 330 North Oaks MN 55127

GEHRING, DAVID AUSTIN, cardiologist, physician, health facility administrator; b. Bryn Mawr, Pa., Dec. 6, 1930; s. Harry Rittenhouse and Anne Gardiner (Bozarth) G.; m. Joan Helen Lotz, June 7, 1953 (div. Aug. 1982); children: David, Paul, Peter, Sue, Barbara, Eric; m. Victoria Marie Damiano, Sept. 2, 1982 (dec. May 2000); children: Theresa, Judy Lynne, Michael Austin; m. Rose Y. Barron, May 5, 2001. BA magna cum laude, U. Pitts., 1952, MD, 1956; grad., Naples Sch. Real Estate, 2000. Diplomate Am. Bd. Internal Medicine; cert. geriatric medicine. Commd. USN, 1956, advanced through grades to lt. comdr., intern, then resident in internal medicine U.S. Naval Hosp. Phila., 1956—60, mem. staff internal medicine U.S. Naval Hosp., 1960—61, chief internal medicine heart sta. U.S. Naval Hosp. Annapolis, Md., 1961—63, resigned, 1963; cardiologist K.G.E. Med. Group, Woodbury, NJ, 1963—82; cardiologist, pres. Hobbs Cardiology, P.A., N.Mex., 1982—86; med. dir. Polk Ctr., Pa., 1986—91; physician, chief grade VA Med. Ctr., Coatesville, Pa., 1991—97, assoc. chief of staff for ambulatory care, 1993—96, chief med. svc., 1995—96, chief primary care and chief of staff, 1995—96, chief of staff, 1995—96, cardiologist, 1996—97; assoc. med. dir. for correctional med. svcs. South Jersey, 1997—98; med. dir. site South Woodstate Prison, 1997—98; clin. dir. Del. Hosp. Chronically Ill, 1998—99; clin. dir. long term care pub. health divsn. State of Del., 1998—99; physician VA Clinic, Naples, Fla., 2002—10. Clin. dir. Del. Hosp. for Cronically Ill, Smyrna, 1998—99; v.p. Regent Park Villas II Assoc., Inc., Naples, Fla., 1999—2000, pres., 2000—01; realtor VIP Lodge McKee Realtors, 2000—01, VIP Lodge McKee, 2000—01; sect. chief VA Med. Ctr., Salisbury, NC, 2001—02, occupl. health physician, 2002, mem. ethics com., 2001—02, mem. hosp. disaster com., 2002, chair small pox com., 02; testing cardiologist Anthropometrics United Med. Group, Cherry Hill, NJ, 1974—82; clin. asst. prof. medicine Temple U. Hosp., Phila., 1975—82; adj. asst. prof. medicine Jefferson Meml. Coll., 1981—82; chief cardiac rehab. unit Lea Regional Hosp., Hobbs, 1982—86; chief med. svcs. 829th Sta. Hosp., USAR, Lubbock, Tex., 1984—86; cons. cardiology, Oil City, Pa., 1986—91; staff Franklin (Pa.) Regional Med. Ctr., 1986—90, Oil City Area Health Ctr., 1986—91; teaching staff St. Joseph Hosp., Lancaster, Pa., 1991—97; clin. preceptor U. Pa. Sch. Nursing, 1993—96; cons. Southeastern Vets. Ctr., Spring City, Pa., 1997—98, Providence Med. Ctr., Media, 1997—98; others; assoc. med. dir. Correctional Med. Svcs. South Jersey, 1997—98; mem. adult protective svcs. coun. State of Del., 1998—99; mem. profl. devel. com. Naples Area Bd. Realtors, 2000—01, mem. complaint rev. com., 2000—01; chair pharmacy and therapeutics com. Dept. Health and Social Svcs., State of Del., 1998—99; mem. pharmacy and therapeutics com. for VISN 6 dept. Vet. Affairs, 2001—02, sec.; cons. in field. Author: EKG Workbook, 1972, EKG Workbook I, 1978; contbr. articles to profl. jours. Project dir. 23 Greater Del. Valley Reg. Med. Program, Pa., 1971—75; mem. ACLS Inst. and affiliated faculty Pa. Heart Assn., 1986—98, bd. dirs. N.W. chpt., 1988—90; bd. dirs. Inst. Christianna Hosp., Del., 1998—99; bd. dirs. adv. com., chmn. personnel com. med. health, rehab., drugs and alcohol Venango County, Franklin Parl, Pa., 1986—90, pres., 1988—89; mem. Health Care Adv. Com. to Congressman William F. Clinger, Jr., 23d Dist., 1989—91, Naples Mus. Art, 2000—10; patron Philharmonic Ctr. for Arts, 1998—2010, Carolina Opera, 2001—03; lector St. Joseph Ch., Oil City, 1987—91, eucharistic min., 1990—92, Swedesboro, NJ, 1992—93, Sacred Heart Ch., Mt. Ephraim, 1994—99, lector, 1998—99. Lt. col. USAR, 1983—90, lt. comdr. USN, 1955—63. Recipient Outstanding Svc. award Am. Cancer Soc. NJ, 1967, Benjamin Berkowitz award NJ Heart Assn., 1975, Nat. Def. Svc. medal, 1975, USAR Components Achievement medal, 1988, Letter of Commendation USAR, 1988, 90, Pres.'s medal of Merit, Rep. Task Force, 1984, Letter of Commendation Sec. of Vets. Affairs, 1994, Robert Wicarey award, 2009; Cert. of Appreciation, Sec. of State N.Mex., 1982, Venango County Commrs., 1987, 88, 89, 90, Polk Ctr. award of Merit, 1991, Spl. Contbn. award and Mgr. of Yr. award VAMC Coatesville, 1996, Spl. Contbn. award VA Med. Ctr., Salisbury, NC, 2002, Named Am. Top Physician Consumers Rsch. Coun. America, 2008-09, Robert Carey award. Fellow ACP (life, Recognition awards 1967-70), Am. Coll. Cardiology, Am. Coll. Chest Physicians, Coll. Physicians Phila., Am. Coll. Clin. Pharmacology; mem. AMA, Am. Geriat. Soc., St. Jude Soc., Holy Name Soc., Assn. Miraculous Medal (promoter 1987—), Venango County Med. Soc. (pres. 1989-91), Assn. Mil. Surgeons, Mil. Officers Assn. Am. (life), Am. Coll. Physician Execs., Mil. Officers Club Collier County Fla., Am. Legion (chmn. Cable Com., Saturnia Lakes, Naples, Fla.), Mil. Officers Assn. SW Fla., KC. Republican. Roman Catholic. Avocations: stamp collecting/philately, reading, walking, swimming, opera. Home: 2347 Butterfly Palm Dr Naples FL 34119 Personal E-mail: david34119@yahoo.com.

GEHRING, WALTER JAKOB, retired biology professor, geneticist; b. Zurich, Switzerland, Mar. 20, 1939; s. Jakob and Marcelle (Rebmann) G.; m. Elisabeth Lott, Jan. 31, 1964; children: Stephan, Thomas. Diploma in Zoology, U. Zurich, 1963, PhD, 1965; PhD (hon.), U. Torino, Italy, 2003, U. Nuevo Léon, Mex., 2003, U. Pierre et Marie Curie, France, 2007, U. Barcelona, 2009, U. Salento, Italy, 2008, Bundesverdienstkreuz, Germany, 2010. Rsch. assoc. U. Zurich, 1963-67; postdoctoral fellow Yale U., New Haven, 1967-69, assoc. prof., 1969-72; prof. U. Basel, Switzerland, 1972—2011. Assoc. editor: Jour. Exptl. Zoology, Mechanisms of Devel., Growth & Differentiation. Recipient Otto Nägeli prize Zurich, 1982, Warren Triennial prize Harvard Med. Sch., Cambridge, Mass., 1986, Dr. Albert Wander prize, Bern, Switzerland, 1986, Charles Léopold Mayer prize Inst. of France, Paris, 1986, Louis Jeantet prize for medicine City of Geneva, 1987, Prix d'Honneur, Moet Hennessy Louis Vuitton, 1993, Newcomb Cleve. prize AAAS, 1994-1995, Otto Warburg-medaille, 1996, Paul Wintrebert prize U. Pierre and Marie Curie, 1996, March of Dimes prize Devel. Biology, 1997, Karl von Frisch prize German Zool. Soc., 2000, Kyoto prize Inamori Found., 2000, Preis der Alfred Vogt Stiftung zur Förderung der Augenheilkunde, Zürich, 2001, Premio Balzan, Fondazione Internat. Premio E. Balzan, 2003. Mem. AAAS, NAS, European Molecular Biology Orgn., European Devel. Biology Orgn., Deutsche Akademie der Naturforscher Leopoldina, Academia Europaea, Genetics Soc. Am., Internat. Soc. for Developmental Biology, Swiss Soc. for Cell Biology, Molecular Biology and Genetics, Am. Soc. for Developmental Biology, Human Genome Orgn., Royal Soc. London (fgn.), Acad. Scis. Paris (fgn. mem.), Sigma Xi. Avocations: birdwatching, photography. Home: Hochfeldstrasse 32 CH-4106 Therwil Switzerland

GEIER, C. DAVID, JR., orthopaedic surgeon; b. May 10, 1973; m. Christian Smith; 1 child, Marshall Conrad. BA in Economics (magna cum laude), Wake Forest U., 1995; MD, Med. U. SC, 1999. Intern, gen. surgery U. Tenn., 1999—2000; resident U. Tenn.,Campbell Clinic, 2000—04; dir. Med. U. SC (MUSC) Sports Medicine; asst. prof., orthop. surgery Med. U. SC (MUSC). Orthop. surgeon James Island Soccer Club; head team physician and orthop. surgeon West Ashley HS; team physician Burke HS, Garrett Acad., North Charleston HS, Academic Magnet HS, Baptist Hill HS, Wash. U., St. Louis, 2004—05, St. Louis Rams, 2004—05, St. Louis Cardinals, 2004—05; provided orthop. coverage Rhodes Coll. Football and Basketball Teams, 2000—04, Memphis Marathon, 2002, Kroger St. Jude Tennis Racquetball Champions, 2003, Cellular South Cup, 2003, US Open Racquetball Championships, 2003; invited presenter in field. Reviewer Am. Jour. Sports Medicine; contbr. chapters to books. Literacy tutot and worked in food shelters in Charleston area MUSC Gives Back, 1996—99. Sports Medicine, Wash. U., St. Louis, 2004—05. Mem.: Omicron Delta Epsilon, Charleston County Med. Soc., Am. Acad. Orthop. Surgeons (cand. mem.), Am. Orthop. Soc. for Sports Medicine (cand. mem.), Phi Beta Kappa, Alpha Omega Alpha. Avocations: weightlifting, reading, politics. Office: Medical University South Carolina 96 Jonathan Lucas St CSB 708 PO Box 250622 Charleston SC 29425 Office Phone: 843-792-4088. Office Fax: 843-792-3843. Business E-Mail: geiercd@musc.edu.

GEIJO MARTÍNEZ, MARÍA PALOMA, epidemiologist; b. Madrid, Feb. 21, 1958; d. Manuel Geijo Rodriguez and Antonia Martínez Alonso; m. Angel García Imbroda, Oct. 2, 1983; children: Rocío García Geijo, Juan Jose García Geijo. BS in Medicine and Surgery, Complutense U., Madrid, 1981; MS in Internal Medicine, U. Clin. Hosp., Madrid, 1986; MD, Complutense U., Madrid, 1998. Cert. med. titulars corps Health Nat. Sch. Spain, 1985, med.epidemiology Med. Coll. Cuenca., Spain, 1982. Internal medicine resident U. Clin. Hosp., Madrid, 1982—86; phisician med. internal medicine Virgen Luz Hosp., Cuenca, 1986—95; specialist phisician in infectious disease Ramon y Cajal Hosp., Madrid, 1988—89; dr. med. responsible for internal medicine-infectious disease Virgen Luz Hosp., Cuenca, 1995—. Assoc. tchr. gen. patology med. student Complutense U., Madrid, 1982—86; assoc. tchr. microbiology and infectious disease U. Sch. Nurse, Cuenca, 1986—90; dir. projects sci. rsch. Autonoma U., Madrid, 2002—, dir. doctoral theses, 2003—; tchr. internal medicine family medicine and internal medicine residents Virgen Luz Hosp., 1987—. Contbr. articles to numerous profl. jours. Mem. Atacama Desert, Chile, 1996, Dolomia Club, Cuenca, 1981—2008, Medicos sin fronteras, Madrid, 2006—08. Recipient award, Faculty Medicine. Complutense U. Madrid, 1981, Investigation Biomedical award, Med. Coll. Cuenca, 2002, Better Exptl. Med. Work award, Faculty of Medicine. Castilla-La Mancha, 2005; grantee grantee, VACH., 2002—05; garatee, GESIDA, 1998—99, grantee, 2000—02, Inst. Salud Carlos III. Madrid, 1995—97, Conserjería Sanidad. Castilla-la Mancha., 1996—98, 1998—2001. Master: Assn. Médica VACH Estudios Multicéntricos, Infectious Work Group; fellow: Grupo Trabajo SIDA, Internal Medicine Spanish Soc.; mem.: Sociedad Española Interdisciplinaria Del SIDA, Sociedad Española Enfermedades Infecciosas Microbiologia clin. Achievements include research in therapy Knowledge Hiv and Ensayo early access of Mk-0518. Office: Hosp Virgen de la Luz Hermandad de donantes de sangre 1 Cuenca 16002 Spain Business E-Mail: mgeijo@sescam.jccm.es.

GEISLER, DANIEL P., colon and rectal surgeon; MD, St. Louis U. Diplomate Am. Bd. Colon and Rectal, Am. Bd. Surgery. Resident Univ. Okla.; fellow St. Vincent Health Ctr.; practice ctr. for colon and rectal surgery Allegheny Gen. Hosp., physician. Named one of Top Doctors, Pitts. mag., 2011. Office: Allegheny General Hospital 320 E N Ave Pittsburgh PA 15212 Office Phone: 412-359-3131. Office Fax: 412-359-4108.

GEISS, ROGER WILLIAM, pathologist, medical educator; b. Jersey City, Sept. 13, 1947; s. Robert William and Eleanor Gladys Rich; m. Agnes Josephine Meadows, Aug. 5, 1972 (dec.); m. Dianne Louise Welch, Sept. 13, 1980; children: Kevin James Easter, Kenneth David Geiss. BSc in Biology, Georgetown U., 1969; MD, Cornell U., 1975. State med. license, W. Va., Iowa, Miss.; Am. Bd. Pathology; cert. in anatomic pathology, clin. pathology, cytopathology. Intern in pathology Meml. Hosp. Med. Ctr., Long Beach, Calif., 1975-76; resident in anatomic pathology U. Chgo. Hosps. and Clinics, Chgo., 1976-78; resident in clin. pathology U. Ariz. Health Sci. Ctr., Tucson, 1978-80, fellow in anatomic pathology, 1980-81; assoc. pathologist Clin. Pathologists, Inc., Colorado Springs, 1981-82, Morgantown Pathology Con., W.Va., 1982-84; clin. asst. prof. W.Va. U. Med. Ctr., Morgantown, 1982—84, asst. prof. pathology, 1984—89, Creighton U. Med. Ctr., Omaha, 1989—95; assoc. prof. pathology U. Miss. Med. Ctr., Jackson, 1995—2004; prof., chair pathology U. Ill. Coll. Medicine, Peoria, 2004—. Dep. coroner El Paso County, Colorado, 1981-82; dep. med. examiner Monongalia County, W.Va., 1984-89; consulting pathologist Mercy Hosp., Corning, Iowa, 1989-92, designated forensic pathologist State of Miss., Jackson, 2000-04. Contbr. articles to profl. jours. including Am. Jour. Otology, 1991, Bulletin of Pathology Edn., 1994, So. Med. Jour., 1996, Modern Pathology, 1999, Pathology Education, 2001, Archives of Pathology and Laboratory Medicine, 2002, 04, Cancer Rsch., 2008, Molecular Cancer Therapeutics, 2008. Recipient Golden Apple award Creighton U., Omaha, 1993, Best Instr. U. Ill. Peoria, 2004-11, Faculty Outstanding Tchg. award, 2006-07, Faculty Outstanding Svc. award, 2010-11, Alpha Omega Alpha Creighton U., 1994. Fellow Coll. Am. Pathologists, Am. Soc. Clin. Pathologists; mem. W.Va. Assn. Pathologists (sec./treas. 1988-89), Group Rsch. Pathology Edn. (pres. 1999-2001, chair, learning objectives com., 1998-), Assn. Pathology Chairs, Internat. Acad. Pathology, Internat. Assn. Med. Sci. Educators, Pulmonary Pathology Soc., Ill. Soc. Pathologists, Ill. State Med. Soc., Peoria Med. Soc. Avocations: photography, travel. Office: Dept Pathology U Ill Coll Medicine 1 Illini Dr Box 1649 Peoria IL 61656-1649 Home: 6637 N Toronado Ct Peoria IL 61614 Office Phone: 309-671-8440. Business E-Mail: rgeiss@uic.edu.

GEISTFELD, RONALD ELWOOD, retired dental educator; b. St. James, Minn., Nov. 9, 1933; s. Victor E. and Viola (Becker) G.; m. Lois N. Tolzman Wilkens, June 15, 1955 (div. June 1974); m. Annette L. Swenson, Jan. 14, 1977; children: Shari, Mark, Steven, Ann, Leah, Erik. AA, Bethany Jr. Coll., 1952; BS, U. Minn., 1954, DDS, 1957. Pvt. practice dentistry, Northfield, Minn., 1959-72; clin. asst. prof. dentistry U. Minn. Sch. Dentistry, Mpls., 1969-72, assoc. prof., 1972-82, chmn. dept. operative dentistry, 1978-87, prof., 1982-97, prof. emeritus, 1997; dir. quality programs Pentegra Dental Group, Inc., 1998-2000. Dental cons. Hennepin County Med. Ctr., Mpls., 1975-96, VA Hosp., Mpls., 1977-96, VA Hosp., St. Cloud, Minn., 1978-96, Human Performance and Informatics Inst., Atama, Japan, 1990-95, K-9 Dental Sys. Quidnunc Australia Pty. Ltd., 1994-95, Metro Dental Group, Mpls., 1995-2000, The Dentists Ins. Co., 1995-99, VGM Expert Systems, 1996-98, Met. Life Ins. Co., 1996—, Pentegra Ltd., 1997-2000; mem. resource faculty for Bush faculty devel. program on excellence and diversity in teaching U. Minn., 1993-94; founder Global Network for Systematic Healthcare, 2003. Pres. PTA, Northfield, 1965, Arts Guild, Northfield, 1968; bd. dirs., chairperson Rice County Health and Sanitation Bd., Faribault, Minn., 1966-74; bd. dirs. Northfield Bd. Edn., 1969-74; pres. Roseville Luth. Ch., 1987-88. Capt. U.S. Army, 1957-59. Am. Coll. Dentists fellow, 1972; recipient Prof. of Yr. award Century Club, 1996-97. Mem. Am. Dental Assn. (chairperson operative dentistry sect. 1979-80, curriculum cons. 1981-88, grants and spl. projects request evaluator 1988-92, Am. fund for Dental Health, edit. review bd. JADA 1992-96), Minn. Dental Assn. (ethics com. 1969-76, chairperson sci. and ann. sessions com. 1984-86, spkr. house del. 1992-96, del. to ADA 1992-96, bd. dirs. 1992-96), Mpls. Dist. Dental Soc. (program chairperson 1978-79, peer rev. com. 1988-92, bd. dirs. 1979-80, 87-89, MDA del. 1989-92), Minn. Acad. Restorative Dentistry (pres. 1979-80), Minn. Acad. Gnathological Rsch. (pres. 1986-87), Am. Assn. Dental Schs. (chairperson operative dentistry sect. 1984-85, edit. rev. bd. 1984-88), Acad. Operative Dentistry (exec. council 1978-81, rsch. com. 1987-89), Am. Acad. Gold Foil Operators, Northfield C. of C. (treas. and chairperson 1968-70), Delta Sigma Delta, Omicron Kappa Upsilon (Theta chpt.). Lodges: Rotary (pres. Northfield 1972-73). Personal E-mail: RAGeist@comcast.net.

GEJERMAN, GLEN, radiation oncologist, educator; MD, U. Medicine and Dentistry of NJ-Sch. Health Related Prof. Asst. clin. prof. of radiation oncology Albert Eistein Coll. of Med.; med. intern Long Island Jewish Med. Ctr., 1991; resident in radiation oncology Montefiore Med. Ctr., Bronx, NY, 1991—95; radiation oncologist Hackensack Univ. Med. Ctr. Office: Hackensack University Medical Center 30 Prospect Ave Hackensack NJ 07601

GEKELMAN, DIANA, dentist, educator, medical researcher; d. Edward and Margareta Gekelman; m. Jean-Sebastien El Kaim; children: David Gekelman El Kaim, Daniel Gekelman El Kaim. DDS, U. Sao Paulo, Brazil, 1993; specialization in endodontics, U. Sao Paulo, 1997, MS, 2000. Post-doctoral fellow lasers in dentistry U. Calif., San Francisco, 2000—02, asst. prof. clin. endodontics, 2002—. Presenter in field; spkr. nat. and internat. confs. Sci. reviewer (articles); contbr. articles to profl. jours. Grantee, Sao Paulo Found. Rsch., 1999—2000, Found. Sci. and Technol. Devel. Dentistry, 2000, Lares Rsch., 2001—02, Parnassus Funding, U. Calif., San Francisco Sch. Dentistry, 2004—05. Mem.: ADA, Am. Dental Edn. Assn., San Francisco Dental Soc., Calif. Dental Assn., Am. Assn. Endodontists, Am. Assn. Dental Rsch., Soc. Photo-Optical Instrumentation Engrs., Acad. Laser Dentistry, Internat. Assn. Dental Rsch. Office: Univ Calif San Francisco Sch Dentistry 707 Parnassus Ave San Francisco CA 94143-0758 E-mail: gekelmand@dentistry.ucsf.edu.

GELB, ADRIAN W., anesthesiologist, educator; b. Paarl, South Africa, Oct. 28, 1948; MBChB, U. Cape Town, 1972. Assoc. prof., dept. anesthesia U. Western Ont., 1986—2004, prof., chair, 1991—2004, prof., clin. neurol. sci., 1994—2004; prof. U. Calif., San Francisco, 2004—. Bd. dirs., pres. Soc. Neuroanesthesia and Critical Care, 1986—97; bd. dirs., bd. chair Internat. Anesthesia Rsch. Soc., 1995—2006; internat. organizing com. mem. EuroNeuro, 1999—2011; sect. editor Anesthesia & Analgesia, 2006—10; exec. com. mem. Calif. Soc. Anesthesiologists, 2009—11; hon. prof. Benares Hindu U., India. Recipient Faculty Mentoring award, U. Calif., 2009, Devel. Contbns. award, Chinese Soc. Anesthesiology. Fellow: RCP (Can.); mem.: Can. Anesthesiologists Soc., Internat. Soc. Anesthetic Pharmacology, Soc. Neurosci. Anesthesia & Critical Care (Disting. Svc. award 2010, named Disting. Tchr. 2003), Calif. Soc. Anesthesiology, Am. Soc. Anesthesiology. Avocation: travel. Office: University Calif Dept Anesthesia C450 521 Parnassus Ave San Francisco CA 94143-0648 Office Fax: 415-476-9516. Business E-Mail: gelba@anesthesia.ucsf.edu.

GELB, BRUCE DAVID, pediatrician, medical educator, researcher; b. Bklyn., Dec. 16, 1958; m. Lisa Beth Belkin, Nov. 8, 1987. Grad., Amherst Coll., Mass.; MD, U. Rochester Med. Sch., NY, 1984. Diplomate American Bd. Pediat., cert. in pediatric cardiology. Pediatric residency Babies Hosp., Columbia-Presbyn. Med. Ctr., NYC, 1984—87; pediatric cardiology fellowship Tex. Children's Hosp., Baylor Coll. Medicine, Houston; faculty dept. pediat. Mt. Sinai Sch. Medicine, NYC, 1991—, faculty dept. genetics and genomic sciences, 1993—, dir. Ctr. Molecular Cardiology, 2006—, dir. Child Health & Devel. Inst., 2010—, Gogel Family prof. child health & devel., 2010—. Mem. Nat. Children's Study Fed. Adv. Com., NIH. Contbr. articles to profl. jours. Mem.: American Soc. Clin. Investigation, Inst. Medicine, American Pediatric Soc. (Norman J. Siegel New Mem. Outstanding Sci. award), Soc. Pediatric Rsch. (E. Mead Johnson award 2004). Achievements include research in genetics of congenital heart defects; discovery of the first gene for a relatively common Mendelian trait, Noonan syndrome, proving the gene an important oncogene for childhood leukemias; a new disease class, the so-called RASopathies, which comprises several genetic traits. Office: Mt Sinai Sch Medicine Atran Berg Lab Bldg Fl 3 Rm 3 02 1428 Madison Ave New York NY 10029 Office Phone: 212-241-3302. Office Fax: 212-241-3310. Business E-Mail: bruce.gelb@mssm.edu.

GELEHRTER, THOMAS DAVID, medical educator, geneticist; b. Liberec, Czechoslovakia, Mar. 11, 1936; arrived in U.S., 1939; married 1959; 2 children. BA, Oberlin Coll., 1957; MA, U. Oxford, Eng., 1959; MD, Harvard U., 1963. Intern, then asst. resident in internal medicine Mass. Gen. Hosp., Boston, 1963—65; rsch. assoc. in molecular biology NIAMD NIH, Bethesda, Md., 1965—69; fellow in med. genetics U. Wash., 1969—70; asst. prof. human genetics, internal medicine and pediatrics Sch. Medicine Yale U., 1970—73, assoc. prof., 1973—74, U. Mich., Ann Arbor, 1974—76, prof. internal medicine and human genetics, 1976—87, dir. divsn. med. genetics, 1977—87, chmn. dept. human genetics, 1987—2004, prof. human genetics and internal medicine, 1987—2007, prof. emeritus, 2007—. Josiah Macy, Jr. Found. faculty scholar and vis. scientist Imperial Cancer Rsch. Fund Labs., London, 1979-80; vis. fellow Inst. Molecular Medicine; Keeley vis. fellow Wadham Coll., U. Oxford, Wellcome Rsch. Travel grantee, 1995. Mem. editl. bd. Jour. Biol. Chemistry, 1995-2000. Trustee Oberlin Coll., 1970-75; mem. NIH Recombinant DNA Adv. Com., 2002-05. Rhodes scholar, 1957-59. Fellow AAAS, Am. Coll. Med. Genetics; mem. Am. Soc. Human Genetics (bd. dir. 1994-96), Am. Soc. Clin. Investigation, Am. Soc. Biochemistry and Molecular Biology, Assn. Am. Physicians. Office: Univ Mich Med Sch Dept Human Genetics SPC 5618 1241 Catherine St Ann Arbor MI 48109-5618 Office Phone: 734-936-2860. Business E-Mail: tdgum@umich.edu.

GELENBE, SAMI EROL, computer scientist, engineering educator; b. Istanbul, Turkey, Aug. 22, 1945; arrived in France, 1972; s. Ali Yusuf and Maria (Sacchet) G.; m. Deniz Arman, June 8, 1968; 1 child, Pamir. BSEE, Mid. East Tech. U., Turkey, 1966; MSEE, Poly. Inst. Bklyn., 1968, PhD, 1969; DSc, U. Paris, 1973; D of Engring. (hon.), U. Rome, 1996; PhD (hon.), Boğaziçi U., Istanbul, 2004; DSc (hon.), U. Liege, 2006. Asst. prof. U. Mich., Ann Arbor, 1970-72; prof. U. Liege, Belgium, 1972-79, U. Paris, 1979—. Sci. dir. Inria, Rocquencourt, France, 1973—82; sci. advisor Sec. State, Paris, 1984—86; chaired prof. Duke U., 1993—98; assoc. dean engring. U. Ctrl. Fla., 1998—2003, univ. chaired prof., 2001—03; chair tech. adv. bd. US Army Simulation and Tng. Command, 1999—2003; Dennis Gabor chair Imperial Coll., London, 2003, head of intelligent sys. and networks, chaired prof., 2003—; mem. sci. and tech. bd. Def. Tech. Ctr. on Data and Info. Fusion, Ministry of Def. U.K., 2003—09. Author: (books transl. into Japanese and Korean) Analysis and Synthesis of Computer Systems, 1980, 2010, Introduction aux reseaux de files d' attente, 1982, Multiprocessor Performance, 1988, Concurrency Control in Distributed Databases, 1989, Introduction to Networks of Queues, 1999; mem. editl. bd.: Acta Info., 1978—, Performance Evaluation, 1979—, IEEE Transactions on Software Engring, 1979—92, Computer Comms., 1999—, Telecomm Systems, 1993—, Simulation Practice and Theory, 1996—, Annales des Telecommunications, 2002—, Computational Mgmt. Sci., 2002—, Recherche Opérationnelle, 1994—, editor-in-chief: Computer Jour., 2008—; contbr. articles to profl. jours. Adv. com. elec. US Army, 1995, mem. tech. adv. bd. army simulation and tng. command, 1999—2003. Decorated chevalier and officer Order of Merit France, chevalier Palmes Académiques, France, Comdr. Order of Merit Italy, Knight Comdr. Order Star Italy; recipient Silver Core award, IFIP, 1980, Sci. award, Parlar Found., Turkey, 1994, French Acad. Sci. award, Grand Prix France Telecom, 1996, Disting. Alumnus award, Poly. Inst. NY, 2010; fellow, Fulbright Found., 1966, Gordon McKay fellow, Harvard U., 1974. Fellow: IEE, ACM (Signetrics award), IEEE (rev. bd. France 1974—82, mem. editl. bd. 1985—93, Meritorious Svc. award 1989, 1992); mem.: Hungarian Acad. Scis. (fgn. mem.), French Nat. Acad. Engring., Turkish Acad. Sci., Academia Europaea, Eta Kappa Nu, Epsilon Pi Upsilon, Sigma Xi. Achievements include numerous patents in field; invention of first finite state models to predict the performance of memory paging algorithms, concurrently with W.F. King of IBM; the random neural network and the G-network queuing model and obtained their analytical solutions; the cognitive packet network routing algorithms for computer networks; proved that the FIFO paging algorithm is strictly equivalent to a random page replacement policy for the independent memory references establishing a hierarchy of memory management policies; going from random to optimal and deriving their page fault ratios in explicit form; derived first diffusion approximation for queuing systems using holding times at the boundries; thus providing for better accuracy than conventional "reflecting boundary" diffusions at light traffic, and good accuracy at heavy traffic; later applying it to the analysis of Asynchronous Transfer Mode cell traffic, leading to a patented call admission control protocol for ATM networks; published the first performance analyses of window protocols in computer networks; introduced new queueing network models with product form solutions called Gelenbe Networks; developed the theory and application of Random Neural Networks; designed and invented a Cognitive Packet Routing Algorithm for computer networks; development of the application of 6 networks to gene regulatory networks. Avocations: history, bicycling. Office: Imperial College SW7 2AZ London England Office Phone: 44-207 594 6342. E-mail: e.gelenbe@imperial.ac.uk.

GELFAND, MICHAEL JOSEPH, radiologist, educator; b. Detroit, Mar. 4, 1945; s. Jacob and Mildred (Weine) G.; m. Janelle Ann Magnuson, Mar. 24, 1973; children: Rebecca Ann, Karin Janelle. BA, U. Mich., 1966; MD, Stanford U., 1971. Diplomate Am. Bd. Pediat., Am. Bd. Nuc. Medicine. Intern Children's Hosp., Cin., 1973-74, resident in pediat., 1974-75; resident in nuc. medicine U. Cin., 1975-77, asst. prof. pediat., 1978-90, assoc. prof. pediat., 1990-95, prof. pediat., 1995—, asst. prof. radiology, 1977-83, assoc. prof. radiology, 1983-90, prof. radiology, 1990—. Asst. attending radiologist Children's Hosp. Cin., 1978-79, attending radiologist, 1979—. Editor: Effective Use of Computers in Nuclear Medicine (Gelfand M.J., Thomas S.R.), 1998, Pediatric Nuclear Imaging, 1994 (Miller J.H., Gelfand M.J.); contbr. chpts. to books, articles to med. jours. Served with USPHS, 1971-73. Mem. Soc. Nuc. Medicine (treas. 1993-96, fin. chmn. 1996-2000, v.p. 2001-02, pres. 2002-03, bd. dirs. 1993-2004), Soc. Pediatric Radiology, Radiologic Soc. N.Am, Am. Coll. Radiology, Am. Coll. Nuc. Physicians. Office: Childrens Hosp Cincinnati OH 45229-3039

GELHAUS, HERBERT CARL, biomedical researcher; b. Cin., Aug. 25, 1976; BS, U. Cin., 1998; PhD, U. Colo., 2004. Prin. rsch. scientist Battelle Biomed. Rsch. Ctr., 2008—. Office: Battelle Biomed Research Ctr 505 King Ave JM-7-007A Columbus OH 43201 Business E-Mail: gelhaush@battelle.org. E-mail: carlgelhaus@yahoo.com.

GELLER, DAVID A., surgeon, educator; b. Ohio, Jan. 20, 1963; BS, Northwestern U. Med. Sch., 1984, MD, 1988. Richard L. Simmons prof. surgery U. Pitts. Med. Ctr., 1998—. Recipient Outstanding Svc. award, Am. Liver Found., Allegheny chpt., 2011. Fellow: ACS. Avocation: tennis. Office: University Pitts Med Ctr Liver Cancer Ctr 3459 5th Ave Pittsburgh PA 15213 Business E-Mail: gellerda@upmc.edu.

GELLER, KENNETH ALLEN, otolaryngologist; b. Bklyn., Feb. 5, 1948; MD, U. So. Calif., 1972. Cert. in otolaryngology. Intern L.A. County-U. So. Calif. Med. Ctr., LA, 1972-73; resident in gen. surgery Wadsworth VA Hosp., LA, 1973-75; resident in otolaryngology UCLA Health Scis. Ctr., LA, 1975-78; fellow Pediat. Otolaryngology Children's Hosp., LA, 1978—79; active Childrens Hosp., LA, 1978—; courtesy Huntington Meml. Hosp., 1993—. Assoc. clin. prof. U. So. Calif. Mem. ACS, Am. Acad. Otolaryngology-Head and Neck Surgery, Am. Acad. Pediatrics, Am. Bronco-Esophagological Assn., Am. Soc. Pediat. Otolaryngology. Office: Childrens Hosp Divsn Otolaryngology # 58 4650 Sunset Blvd Los Angeles CA 90027-6062 Address: 435 Bedford Dr Ste 203 Beverly Hills CA 90210 Office Phone: 323-361-2145. E-mail: kgeller@chla.usc.edu.

GELLER, STEPHEN ARTHUR, pathologist, educator; b. Bklyn., Apr. 26, 1939; s. Sam John and Alice (Podber) G.; m. Kate Eleanor DeJong, June 24, 1962; children: David Phillip, Jennifer Lee. BA, Bklyn. Coll., 1959; MD, Howard U., 1964. Diplomate Am. Bd. Pathology, Nat. Bd. Med. Examiners. Intern Lenox Hill Hosp., NYC, 1964-65; resident in pathology Mt. Sinai Hosp., NYC, 1965-69; chief lab. Naval Hosp., Beaufort, SC, 1969-71; asst. prof. pathology Mt. Sinai Med. Ctr., NYC, 1971-75, assoc. prof., 1975-78, prof., 1978-84; chmn. dept. pathology Cedars-Sinai Med. Ctr., LA, 1984—2006, chmn. emeritus Dept. Pathology, 2006—; prof. pathology UCLA, 1984—. Co-author: Histopathology, 1989, Biopsy Interpretation of the Liver, 2004, Biopsy Interpretetion of the Liver, 2nd edit., 2009; contbr. articles to profl. jours. Recipient Excellence in Teaching award CUNY, 1974, Golden Apple tchg. award Cedars-Sinai Med. Ctr., 1986, 2000, 02, 04, 05. Fellow Coll. Am. Pathologists, Am. Soc. Clin. Pathologists; mem. Am. Assn. Study of Liver Diseases, Hans Popper Hepatopathology Soc., Calif. Soc. Pathologists (sec. 1989-91, v.p. 1991-93, pres. 1994-96), L.A. Soc. Pathologists (v.p. 1989-91, pres. 1992), N.Y. Pathol. Soc., Alpha Omega Alpha. Democrat. Jewish. Avocations: music, photography, writing fiction. Office: Cedars Sinai Med Ctr 8700 Beverly Blvd Los Angeles CA 90048-1865 Office Phone: 310-423-6632. Business E-Mail: geller@cshs.org.

GELLERT, JAY M., health and medical products executive; b. Mar. 13, 1954; BA, Stanford U., 1975. Dir. health services, County of San Mateo Calif. Dept. of Health Services; sr. v.p., COO Calif. Healthcare System, 1985-88; pres., CEO Bay Pacific Health Corp., 1988-91; dir. strategic advisory engagements Shattuck Hammond Ptnrs. Inc.; pres., COO Health Systems Internat. Inc. (merged with Found. Health. Corp. in 1996), 1996—97, Health Net, Inc. (formerly Found. Health Systems), 1997—98; pres., CEO Health Net, Inc., 1998—, bd. dirs., 1999—. Chmn., admin. simplification com. Coun. Affordable Quality Healthcare; bd. dirs. Am. Assoc. Health Plans, MedUnite, Inc., Miavita, Inc. Office: Health Net Life Insurance Co 21281 Burbank Blvd Woodland Hills CA 91367-6607 *

GELLIS, STEPHEN E., dermatologist, educator; MD, Harvard Coll., 1973. Diplomate Am. Bd. Pediatrics, 1978, Am. Bd. Dermatology, 1979, Am. Bd. Dermatology-pediatric dermatology, 2006. Intern Children's Hosp., Boston, 1973—74, resident pediat., 1974—76, program dir. dermatology, resident dermatology Mass. Gen. Hosp., Boston, 1976—78; asst. prof. dermatology Harvard Med. Sch. Office: Childrens Hospital Boston 300 Longwood Ave Boston MA 02115 Office Phone: 617-355-6117. Office Fax: 617-730-0308.

GELMAN, SIMON, anesthesiologist, educator; b. St. Petersburg, Russia, May 26, 1936; arrived in US, 1976, naturalized, 1982; s. Isaac Gelman and Raisa Mekler; m. Maria Gelman, July 7, 1959; children: Alex, Dan Samuel. MD, First Leningrad Med. Inst., USSR, 1959; PhD, Kirov Advanced Inst. Doctors, Leningrad, USSR, 1965. Lic. specialist in anesthesiology Israel Med. Assn., 1975, diplomate Am. Bd. Anesthesiologists, 1981. Head surg. office Polyclinic, Siktivkar, Russia, 1959—61; physician, resuscitationist Ctr. Treatment Patients with Myocardial Infarction, Leningrad, 1964—65; assoc. prof. anesthesiology Kirov Advanced Tng. Inst. Doctors, 1965—73; sr. anesthesiology Eilnson Med. Ctr. Tel Aviv U., Petah Tikva, Israel, 1974—75; from assoc. prof. to prof. Sch. Medicine U. Ala., Birmingham, Ala., 1978—81, prof. Sch. Medicine, 1981—92, dir. clin. rsch. anesthesiology Sch. Medicine, 1979—84, vice chmn. rsch. in anesthesiology Sch. Medicine, 1984—89, chmn. Dept. Anesthesiology Sch. Medicine, 1989—92; chmn. Dept. Anesthesiology Brigham and Women's Hosp., Boston, 1992—2002, prof. anesthesiology, 2002—. Mem. numerous coms. U. Ala., 1985—92, Brigham and Women's Hosp., 1992—, Partners Cmty. Healthcare, Inc., Boston, 1994—2003; mem. search com. chief of anesthesia Mass. Gen. Hosp., 1993—93; mem. Am. Medico-Legal Found., 1994—; dir. Found. Anesthesia Edn. and Rsch., 1996—; chair, grant rev. com. Found. for anesthesia Edn. and Rsch., 2001—; Leroy D. Vandam and Benjamin G. Covino prof. anaesthesia Harvard U., Boston, 1992—2002, Leroy D. Vandam and Benjamin G. Covino disting. prof. anaesthesia, 2002—; Jobson vis. prof. Royal Prince Alfred Hosp. U. Sydney, 2002; lectr. in field. Editor: Anesthesia and Organ Transplantation, Anaesthesia for Major Vascular Surgery. Recipient Rsch. award, Am. Soc. Anesthesiology, 1979. Master: Alpha Omega Alpha; fellow: Australian and New Zealand Coll. Anesthesia; mem.: Acad. Anesthesia Mentors, Acad. Anesthesia Mentors (pres. 2006), Israel Soc. Anesthesiologists (hon.), Found. Anesthesia Edn. and Rsch. (chmn. grant rev. com., bd. dirs.). Jewish. Office: Brigham and Womens Hospital 75 Francis Street Boston MA 02115 Office Fax: 617-264-5230. Business E-Mail: sgelman@partners.org.

GELMANN, EDWARD PAUL, oncologist, educator; b. NYC, May 31, 1950; m. Connie Sommers; children: Lauren R., Elyssa R., Emily B, Jonathan S. BS magna cum laude, Yale U., 1972; MD, Stanford U., 1976. Diplomate Nat. Bd. Med. Examiners, Am. Bd. Internal Medicine. Intern then resident U. Chgo. Hosps., 1976—78; med. staf fellow Nat. Cancer Inst., Bethesda, Md., 1979—83, sr. investigator, 1983—88; adj. assoc. prof. microbiology Georgetown U., Washington, 1986—88, prof. medicine and cell biology, 1988—2007, chief med. oncology divsn., 1988—93, chief hematology/oncology divsn., 1993—95, vice chair Dept. Medicine, 1997—98; prof. Columbia U., NYC, 2007—, chief divsn. hematology/oncology, 2007—; dep. dir. Herbert Irving Comprehensive Cancer Ctr., 2007—. Dir. urologic oncology program Lombardi Cancer Rsch. Ctr., 1990-93, dir. prostate cancer program, 1993-2007, dir. program in growth regulation of cancer, 2001-07, William M. Scholl Professorship in Oncology, 2002. Mem. editl. bd. jour. Blood, 1985-90, Cancer Rsch., 2004—, Clin. Oncol, 2009-; ad hoc reviewer jours.; contbr. 180 articles to profl. jours Sr. surgeon USPHS, 1978-88. Grantee Nat. Cancer Inst., 1990—. Fellow ACP; mem. AAAS, Am. Soc. Clin. Investigation, Am. Assn. Cancer Rsch., Am. Soc. Clin. Oncology. Office Phone: 212-305-8602. Business E-Mail: gelmanne@columbia.edu.

GELMI, OTTAVIO, retired urologist; b. Ambivere, Bergamo, Italy, Nov. 30, 1921; s. Gino Giovanni Gelmi and Valentina Wedenissow; 1 child, Alessandra. Diploma, Liceo-Ginnasio, Bergamo, 1940; MD, U. Milan Med. Sch., 1952. Diplomate Urology Bd., 1969. Internship U. Va. Med. Sch., Charlottesville, 1952—53; residence, urology Georgetown U. Med. Coll., Washington, 1953—58, instr. urology, 1959—84; pvt. practice Washington, 1959—84; staff mem. Prince George's Hosp. & Med. Ctr., Cheverly, 1959—84, chmn., dept. urology, 1971—82; dir., urology Castelli Clinic, Bergamo, 1984—92. Home: Passaggio Pierantonio Cividini 4 24122 Bergamo BG Italy

GEMBRUCH, ULRICH, obstetrician, gynecologist, educator; b. Frankfurt, Germany, Sept. 19, 1954; s. Werner and Waltraud (Gutberlet) G.; m. Gabi Rothe, 1982; children: Janina, Christoph, Oliver. Abitur, Gymnasium Frankfurt, 1973; MD, U. Frankfurt, 1980; PhD, U. Bonn, 1992. Resident in cardiology Rotenburg (Germany), 1980; neonatology, pediatric cardiology resident U. Bonn (Germany), 1981-82; resident ob.-gyn. U. Bonn., 1982-87, attending physician dept. ob.-gyn., 1987-90, attending physician dept. prenatal diagnosis and therapy, 1990-93; prof. divsn. of prenatal medicine dept. ob.- gyn. U. Lübeck (Germany), 1993—2002; prof., dir. clinic of obstet. and prenatal medicine U. Bonn, 2002—. Mem. editl. bd. Ultrasound in Obstetrics and Gynecology, Archives of Perinatal Medicine; contbr. chpts. to sci. books, articles to profl. jours. Capt. Med. Branch German Mil., 1982. Rsch. grantee Dres Haackert Found., 1989. Fellow German Soc. Gynecology and Obstetrics; mem. Internat. Soc. Ultrasound in Ob.-Gyn., German Soc. Prenatal and Obstetrical Medicine. Evangelical. Office: Univ Bonn Dept Obstet Prenatal Medicine Sigmund-Freud Str 25 Bonn D-53105 Germany Business E-Mail: ulrich.gembruch@ukb.uni-bonn.de.

GEMMA, MARCO, anesthesiologist; b. Milan, May 3, 1962; Degree in Medicine & Surgery, U. Milan, 1987, degree in Anesthesia and Intensive Care Splty., 1991. Asst. dir. neuroanesthesia & intensive care Sci. Inst. S. Raffaele Hosp., Milan, 1993—2002, clin. rsch. coord., 2000, quality assessment and improvement coord., head & neck dept., 2009, coord. neuroanesthesia & intensive care, 2002—. Mem.: Rianimazione e Terapia Intensiva, Società Italiana di Anestesia, Analgesia, European Soc. Intensive Care. Avocations: martial arts, mountain climbing. Office: Via Olgettina 60 Milan 20132 Italy Office Fax: 0039 03 2643 7862. Business E-Mail: gemma.marco@hsr.it.

GEMMATI, DONATO, geneticist; b. Rome, Jan. 12, 1963; s. Trifone Gemmati and Maria Teresa Bovio. Degree in Biology, U. Ferrara, Italy, 1987, PhD in Biomed. Sci., 2010. Cert. in med. genetics U. Ferrara, 2006. Grad. technician U. Ferrara, 1991—2002, rschr., 2002—, dir., ctr. hemostasis & thrombosis, 2009—. Fellow: Italian Soc. Haemostasis & Thrombosis; mem.: Sci. Com. Orphanet-Italy Onco-Hematology (Rome) (mem., CSS-mendel inst.), Pharmacology & Molecular Oncology Doctorate. Achievements include research in gene environment interaction in the establishment of multifactorial disorder; patents for genetic markers of wound healing. Office: University Ferrara Via Girolamo Savonarola 44121 Ferrara FE Italy Office Fax: 39 0532 209 010. Business E-Mail: d.gemmati@unife.it.

GEMMELL-AKALIS, BONNI JEAN, psychotherapist; b. Lansing, Mich., Mar. 11, 1950; d. James Stewart Gemmell and Alpha Alice (Hackenberg) Vanden Bosch; m. Gary Alfred Eddy, Jan. 1, 2001; 1 stepchild, Patrick Eddy; children: Scott Aaron, Ty Alexander, Zachary Alan. BS, Ctrl. Mich. U., 1972, MA, 1974. Ltd. lic. psychologist, Mich.; lic. social worker, Mich. Clin. psychologist, sr. mental health therapist Lincoln Ctr. for Emotionally Disturbed Children & Youth, Lansing, 1974-77; outpatient psychologist Grand Rapids (Mich.) Child Guidance Clinic, 1978-81; pvt. practice Grand Rapids Psychiat. Svcs., 1981-88, 96—, Associated Therapists, Inc., Grand Rapids, 1988-96, pres., 1989-90. Grad. fellow Ctrl. Mich. U., 1972-73. Mem. Mich. Psychoanalytic Coun., Mich. Women Psychologists, Mich. Assn. Profl. Psychologists, Am. Group Psychotherapy Assn. (founder nat. registry 1996), Psi Chi. Home: 632 Duxbury Ct SE Ada MI 49301 Office: 1025 Spaulding Ave SE Ste B Grand Rapids MI 49546-3703 Office Phone: 616-285-9141.

GEMMRICH, ARMIN RICHARD, biologist, educator; b. Gronau, Germany, June 18, 1944; s. Richard and Ingeborg (Burda) Gemmrich; m. Dagmar Agthe Gemmrich, 1969; children: Silene, Gwendolin, Moritz, Ronja. Diploma in biology, U. Gießen, Germany, 1971, D in Natural Scis., 1973. Asst. Justus Liebig U., Giessen, 1971-73; rsch. asst. in botany U. Ulm, Germany, 1973-80, asst. in botany, 1980-84, prof., 1984-88, Fachhochschule Heilbronn, Germany, 1988—2009; exec. German Inst. Sustainable Devel. Author: (book) Umweltschutz im Weinbau, 1991, Nachhaltige Weinwirtschaft, 1998; contbr. articles to profl jours. Mem.: Vereinigung Allgemeine und Angewandte Mikrobiologie, German Botany Assn. Office: Hochschule Heilbronn Max Planck Str 39 D-74081 Heilbronn Germany

GEMOU-ENGESAETH, VASILIKI (VASSO), pediatric immunologist, educator, writer, allergist, researcher; d. Athanasios Gemos and Maria Gemou, m. Leif Rafael Engesaeth, Dec. 15, 1984; children: Athanasios Edvard Engesaeth, Maria Athena Beatric Engesaeth. Diploma in Medicine, Nat. U. Athens, Greece, 1975; med. degree with full honors (hon.), Nat. U. Athens, 1983; med. degree, U. Oslo, 1989, PhD in molecular immunopathology childhood asthma, 2003. Cert. specialized in pediat. allery and pulmonology Ulleval and Rikshospitalet U. Hosp., 1986. Sr. ho. officer dept. tuberculosis Sanatorium Hosp. in Provinces, Lamia, Greece, 1975—76; sr. ho. officer dept. internal medicine Palace of Health Hosp., Athens, 1976—77; full-time clin. and rsch. fellow dept. immunology, internal medicine Athens U., 1977—78; sr. ho. officer 1st Pediatric Clinic, Athens U. Aghia Sophia Children's Hosp., 1978—80; clin. and rsch. fellow 1st Pediatric Clinic, Athens U., 1980—81, sr. pediatrician, 1981—83; hon. registrar dept. children's allergy Ullevål U. Hosp., Oslo, 1983—86, hon. cons., clin. rschr. dept pediat. allergy and pulmonology, 1988—90, hon. rsch.

fellow dept. pediat., 1993—94; sr. cons. pediatrician, sr. rschr. Ulleval U. Hosp., Oslo, 1994—95, assoc. prof. dept. pediat., 1995—; clin. ednl. fellow Voksentoppen Allergy Inst., Rikshospitalet, Nat. U. Hosp., Oslo, 1986—88; hon. clin. rsch. fellow dept. pediat. respiratory medicine and allergy Nat. Heart and Lung Inst., Royal Brompton Hosp., London, 1990—91, hon. clin. rsch. fellow, hon. ped. respiratory registrar, 1991—93; locum cons. pediatric allergist, pulmonologist Royal Nat. Throat Nose Ear Hosp., London, 1991—92; hon. cons. pediatrician, sr. lectr. dept. respiratory medicine and allergy Kings Coll., Guys, Kings and St. Thomas Sch. of Medicine, London, 2001. Tchr. dept. pediat. Ulleval U. Hosp., Norway, 1984—, cons. dept. pediat., 1988—90, rotating lectr. dept. immunology and transfusion medicine, 1994—2003, mem. rsch. coun., 2003—04; sr. pediatrician 1st Pediatric Clinic, Athens U., Greece, 1981—83; tchr. thoracic medicine Royal Brompton Hosp., Nat. Heart and Lung Inst., London U., London, 1990—93; cons., lectr. depts. pediatric respiratory and allergy and clin. immunology Royal Brompton Hosp., Nat. Heart and Lung Inst., London, 1990—93; vis. prof. dept. respiratory medicine and allergy Kings Coll., Guys, Kings and St. Thomas Sch. Medicine, 2005—. Author: (booklet) Atopic Eczema: What you need to know to help your child; contbr. several orginal articles to profl. jours. and books; main organizer numerous classical concerts. Sec. bd. dirs. Greek Orthodox Ch. Evagelismos tis Theotokou and Greek Orthodox Soc. in Norway, Oslo, 1999—2003; bd. dirs. Greek Orthodox Ch. Evagelismos tis Theotokou, and Greek Orthodox Soc. in Norway, Oslo, 1997—; bd. dirs. patients com. Norwegian Assn. for Asthma and Allergy, Oslo, 2001—02; bd. dirs., exec. com. for rsch. lab. Coll. Akershus, Bekkestua, Norway, 1999—2001; bd. dirs. Coun. Greek Parents and Guardians in Oslo, 1994—99, Greek Sch., Kingston, London, 1990—93; hon. mem. Mcpl. Mixed Choir of Paleo Faliro, Athens, 1996—. Recipient Rsch. award, Dir. of Ulleval Univ. Hosp., 2003; named one of Top 10 Most Successful Internat. Women in Norway, 2004; grantee, Greek Ministry Social Welfare, 1980—81, Norwegian Asthma & Allergy Assn., 1994, Glaxo, 1994, Norwegian Assn. for Health and Rehab., 2000, GlaxoSmithKline, 2001, 2002; scholar, Norwegian State, 1983—86, U. Oslo, Internat. Summer Sch., 1984, U. Oslo, 1995. Mem.: AAAS (corr.), European Soc. Pediatric Allergy and Clin. Immunology (licentiate), Brit. Soc. Allergy and Clin. Immunology (licentiate), Greek Soc. Immunology (licentiate), Greek Soc. Allergy (licentiate), Norwegian Soc. Allergology and Immunopathology (licentiate), Norwegian Pediatric Soc. (licentiate), European Pediatric Respiratory Soc. (licentiate), European Acad. Allergology and Clin. Immunology (licentiate), Brit. Med. Assn. (licentiate), Brit. Med. Coun. (licentiate), Norwegian Med. Assn. (licentiate cert. in child health 1994, cert. in adminstrn.and leadership in health svcs. 1995, cert. in leadership, mgmt. and adminstrn. 2000, cert. in drs. responsibility in hosp. 1999), Greek Pediatric Soc. (licentiate). Greek Christian Orthodox. Avocations: skiing, swimming, painting, dance, singing. Office Fax: +47-22118663; Home Fax: +47-22734590. Personal E-mail: vasiliki@online.no. E-mail: vasiliki.gemou-engesaeth@medisin.uio.no.

GENC, ARZU, physical therapist; b. Turkey, May 16, 1974; PhD, Hacettepe U., 1995. Phys. therapist Dokuz Eylul U., Sch. Physiotherapy, 1995—. Office: Mithatpasa Dokuz Eylul University Sch Physiotherapy Izmir Inciralti 35340 Turkey Office Fax: 90 2324124946. Business E-Mail: arzu.genc@deu.edu.tr.

GENDEN, ERIC MICHAEL, otolaryngologist; b. June 6, 1964; BA, Columbia U., Columbia Coll., 1987; MD with Distinction in Rsch., Mt. Sinai Sch. Medicine, 1992. Cert. Am. Bd. Otolaryngology, Head and Neck Surgery. Intern surgery Barnes Hosp., Wash. U., St. Louis, 1992—93, resident, otolaryngology-head and neck surgery, 1993—98; emergency room physician Regional Hosp., St. Louis, 1993—97; cardiothoracic surgery Mo. Baptist Hosp., 1996—98; attending, ototlaryngology-head and neck surgery Elmhurst Hosp., NY, 1996—98, Bronx VA Med. Ctr., NY, Elmhurst Hosp.; fellow microvascular reconstruction of the head and neck Mt. Sinai Med. Ctr., 1998—99; asst. prof. otolaryngology-head and neck surgery Mt. Sinai Sch. Medicine, 1999—2003, assoc. prof. otolaryngology-head and neck surgery, 2003—07, prof. otolaryngology, 2007—, chief divsn. head and neck oncology, dept. otolaryngology, 2002—, assoc. prof. Immunobiology Ctr., 2003—, prof. neurosurgery, 2007—, interim chmn. dept. otolaryngology-head and neck surgery, 2004—05, chmn. dept. otolaryngology-head and neck surgery, 2005—; surgical dir. Multidisciplinary Program for Head and Neck Cancer. Contbr. chapters to books, several articles to peer-reviewed journals. Recipient Am. Acad. Otolaryngic Allergy award, 1996, Combined Plastic Surgery Ednl. Found. and Am. Acad. Otolaryngology Head and Neck Surgery Found. Rsch. award, 1996, Am. Soc. for Peripheral Nerve Rsch. award, 1996, Award for Outstanding Resident Rsch. in Basic Sci., Washington U., 1997, Excellence in Tchg., Wash. U., 1998, Best Clin. Innovations award-the use of osseointegrated implants in Maxillary Reconstruction, Acad. Osseointegration, 2003, Am. Acad. Otolaryngology Head and Neck Surgery's Honor award, 2003; named Physician of Yr., Mt. Sinai Med. Ctr., 2002, Educator of Yr. Dept. Otolaryncology-Head and Neck Surgery, Mt. Sinai Sch. Medicine, 2003. Fellow: ACS; mem.: Am. Soc. Clin. Oncologists, Am. Head and Neck Soc., Soc. U. Otolaryngologists Assn., Am. Broncho-Esophagological Assn., Am. Acad. Sleep Medicine, NY Head and Neck Soc., Am. Soc. Transplantation, Am. Fedn. Clin. Med. Rsch., Am. Acad. Otolaryngic Allergy, Am. Bd. Facial Plastic and Reconstructive Surgery, Am. Bd. Otolaryngology-Head and Neck Surgery, AMA, Ear, Nose and Throat Club of St. Louis, Alpha Omega Alpha. Achievements include performing the first composite tracheal transplant in 2003; being the leader of a team of 19 specialists who performed the first total jaw transplant in 2006. Office: 5 E 98th St 8th Fl New York NY 10029 Office Phone: 212-241-9410. Office Fax: 212-831-3700. Business E-Mail: eric.genden@mountsinai.org.

GENDLER, ELLEN, dermatologist; b. Bklyn., Feb. 15, 1956; m. James Salik; 2 children. BA, Wesleyan Univ.; MD, Columbia U., 1981. Diplomate Am. Bd. Dermatology. Internal med. intern Lenox Hill Hospital, NYC; resident in dermatology NYU Med. Ctr., NYC, 1982—85; pvt. practice dermatology NYC, 1985—. Clin. assoc. prof. dept. dermatology NYU Sch. Medicine, NYC, 1990—; trustee Dermatology Found.; consul., med. advisor to numerous cosmetics and health-care companies; spkr. in field. Contbr. articles to numerous profl. jours. Mem.: Am. Acad. Dermatology (assoc.; dir. cosmetics symposium). Office: 1035 Fifth Ave New York NY 10028

GENDZWILL, JOYCE ANNETTE, retired health officer; b. Milw., Aug. 8, 1927; d. Felix Vincent and Antoinette Marie (Borske) G.; m. Lauren E. Trombley, June 13, 1952 (div. Jan. 1960); children: Regan Eve Trombley Kovacich, Eugene Vincent, Paul Quentin. BS, U. Mich., 1949, MD, 1952, MPH, 1961. Cert. pub. mgr., Ala. Internship USPHS, Detroit, Cleve., 1952-53; dir. extern edn. Beyer Meml. Hosp., Ypsilanti, Mich., 1953-54; resident in radiology St. Luke's Hosp., Denver, 1954-55; health officer Dickinson-Iron Dist. Health Dept., Stambaugh, Mich., 1959-76; dir. bur. local health svc. Ala. Dept. Pub. Health, Montgomery, Ala., 1976-81, asst. state health officer, 1981-91; ret., 1991. Mem. AMA, So. Med. Assn., Mensa, Phi Beta Kappa, Delta Omega, Phi Kappa Phi. Home: 6580 Thorman Rd Port Charlotte FL 33981-5579

GENÉ-BADIA, JOAN, physician, director; b. Sta Coloma Gramanet, Barcelona, Spain, May 27, 1955; s. Joan Gené-Roigé and Conxa Badia-Mutlló; m. Dolors Camps- Surroca, Mar. 18, 1981; children: Marta Gené-Camps, Gemma Gené-Camps. MD, Barcelona U., Spain, 1978. Dir. Castelldefels Health Ctr. Catalan Health Inst., Barcelona, 1990—99, dir. Primary Care Divsn., 2000—. Cons. Nicare - Tacis, Moscow, 1993—2003. Editor: (jour.) Atención Primaria (indexed ni Medline, 1989), Cuadernos de Gestión para le profesioal de Atención Primaria, (book) Gestión en Atención Primaria. Recipient Quality in Mgmt. award, Catalan Govt., 1998. Mem.: Med. Coll. Barcelona, Catalan Soc. Family Medicine (founder and pres. 1987—90), Spanish Soc. Family Medicine (founder and mem. of the exec. 1985—88), World Orgn. Nat. Colls. Acads. Europe (sec. European region and founder 1990—94). Home: Emancipació 20-22 3 1 Barcelona 08022 Spain Office: Institut Català de la Salut Gran Via de les Corts Catalanes 587 Barcelona 08022 Spain Office Fax: +34934824522. Personal E-mail: joangene@daem-bcn.com.

GENEL, MYRON, pediatrician, educator; b. York, Pa., Jan. 6, 1936; s. Victor and Florence (Mowitz) G.; m. Phyllis Norma Berkman, Aug. 25, 1968; children: Elizabeth, Jennifer, Abby. BS (hon.), Moravian Coll., Bethlehem, Pa., 1957, DSc (hon.), 1995; MD, U. Pa., Phila., 1961; MA (hon.), Yale U., New Haven, Conn., 1983. Diplomate Am. Bd. Pediat. Intern Mt. Sinai Hosp., NYC, 1961—62; resident in pediat. Children's Hosp. Phila., 1962—64; trainee pediat. endocrinology Johns Hopkins Hosp., Balt., 1966—67; instr. pediat. U. Pa. Sch. Medicine, 1967—69, assoc. in pediat., 1969—71; trainee in genetics, inherited metabolic diseases Children's Hosp. Phila., 1967—69, assoc. physician, 1969—71; attending physician Yale-New Haven Hosp., 1971—; faculty Yale U. Sch. Medicine, New Haven, 1971—, dir. pediat. endocrinology, 1971—85, program dir. Children's Clin. Rsch. Ctr., 1971—86, prof., 1981—2004, prof. emeritus, sr. rsch. scientist, 2004—, assoc. dean, 1985—2004, dir. Office Govt. and Cmty. Affairs, 1985—2004. Mem. genetic adv. bd. State of Conn., 1979—82, 1994—, mem. stem cell adv. com., 2005—; cons. subcom. investigations, oversight com. sci. and tech. US Ho. of Reps., 1982—84; mem. adv. bd. New Eng. Congenital Hypothyroidism Collaborative; cons. Hosp. St. Raphael, Milford Hosp., Norwalk Hosp., Greenwich Hosp.; chmn. transplant adv. com. Office of Commr. Conn. Dept. Income Maintenance, 1984—92; health policy fellowship bd. Inst. Medicine, 1989—95; clin. rsch. roundtable Inst. Medicine NRC, 2000—04; mem. fed. adv. com. nat. children's study Nat. Inst. Child Health and Devel./NIH, 2005—09; mem. Sec.'s Adv. Com. on Human Rsch. Protections, 2006—09. Contbr. articles to profl. jours. Bd. dirs. Rsch. America!, 1997—2000. Capt. USAR, 1964—66. Robert Wood Johnson Health Policy fellow Inst. Medicine NAS, Washington, 1982-83; recipient ann. award Conn. Campaign Against Cooley's Anemia, 1979, Ann. Comenius Alumni award Moravian Coll., 1990, Abraham Jacobi Meml. award Am. Acad. Pediat. and AMA, 1999, Joseph W. St. Geme Leadership award Fedn. Pediat. Orgns., 2004,, Pres. award American Acad. Pediatrics, 2011 Fellow: AAAS; mem.: AMA (med. schs. sec. 1985—, coun. on sci. affairs 1994—2001, task force on fin. grad. med. edn. 1995, alt. del. governing coun., med. schs. sec. 1995—98, task force on privacy and confidentiality 1998—99, del. 1998—2002, chair 2003—04), APHA, Soc. Clin. and Transnational Scis., Assn. Patient Oriented Rsch., NY Acad. Medicine, Conn. Acad. Sci. and Engring. (coun. 2000—, v.p./pres.-elect 2006—08, pres. 2008—10), Soc. Pediat. Rsch. (Disting. Svc. award 2003), Endocrine Soc. (rsch. initiative com. 1995—99, govt. affairs com. 2002—05), Conn. United for Rsch. Excellence (chmn. steering com. 1989—90, pres. 1990—93, chmn. bd. dirs. 1993—94), Conn. Endocrine Soc., Nat. Assn. Biomed. Rsch. (bd. dirs. 1990—93, exec. com. 1991—93), Assn. Program Dirs. GCRC (pres.-elect 1980—81, pres. 1981—82), New Haven County Med. Assn. (bd. govs. 1990—2002, 2004—11), Assn. Am. Med. Colls. (adminstrv. bd. coun. acad. socs. 1987—92, chmn.-elect coun. acad. socs. 1989—91, exec. coun. 1989—92, adv. panel on rsch. 1999—2003, Disting. Svc. mem. 2005), Am. Pediat. Soc., Am. Fedn. Med. Rsch., Am. Diabetes Assn. (co-recipient Jonathan May award 1979), Am. Coll. Preventive Medicine, Am. Coll. Nutrition, Am. Assn. Clin. Endocrinologists, Am. Acad. Pediat. (task force organ transplants, com. on fed. govt. affairs, Pres.'s Outstanding Svc. award 2011), Sigma Xi. Jewish. Avocation: running. Office: Yale Sch Med Child Health Rsch Ctr PO Box 208081 New Haven CT 06520-8081 Office Phone: 203-785-6019. Business E-Mail: myron.genel@yale.edu.

GENEST, JACQUES, nephrologist, clinical scientist, science administrator; b. Montreal, Que., Can., May 29, 1919; s. Rosario and Annette (Girouard) G.; m. Estelle Deschamps, Oct. 3, 1953; children: Paul, Suzanne, Jacques, Marie, Helene. BA, Coll. Jean de Brebeuf, Montreal, 1937; postgrad. in Anatomy, Harvard U., 1937, postgrad. in Physiology, 1938, postgrad. in Chemistry, 1948; MD, U. Montreal, 1942; LLD (hon.), Queen's U., 1966, U. Toronto, Can., 1970; DSc (hon.), Laval U., Can., 1973, Sherbrooke U., 1974, Meml. U. Nfld., 1978, McGill U., Can., 1979, U. Ottawa, 1980, St. Francis Xavier U., 1983, SUNY, Buffalo, 1984, Rockefeller U., 1986, Concordia U., Montreal, 1986, Chinese Acad. Med. Scis., 1987, U. Montpelier, France, 1989. Resident in medicine and pathology Hôtel-Dieu Hosp., Montreal, 1942-45, cons. physician in nephrology, endocrinology and internal medicine, 1952-91; rsch. fellow Johns Hopkins Hosp., Balt., 1945—48, Harvard Sch. Chemistry, Boston, 1948, Rockefeller Hosp. Med. Rsch., NYC, 1948-51; chmn. dept. medicine U. Montreal, 1962—65, prof. medicine, 1965-96; prof. exptl. medicine McGill U., Montreal, 1960-98; founder, 1st dir. Clin. Rsch. Inst. Montreal, 1965-84, adviser, 1984-94. Editor: (with Erich Koiw) Hypertension, 1972; (with Erich Koiw and Otto Kuchel) Hypertension: Physiopathology and Treatment, 1977, 83; (with Marc Cantin, Otto Kuchel, Pavel Hamet) 2d edit., 1983; author: One Ideal, One Life, 1998, L'Homme Seul, 2005, 2008. Decorated companion Order of Can., grand officer Ordre Nat. du Que.; recipient award Gairdner Found., 1963, Archambault medal Can. Assn. for Advancement Sci., 1965, Stouffer prize, 1969, Marie-Victorin Sci. prize Govt. of Que., 1977, Royal Bank award, 1980, Isaac Walton Killam award, 1986, Armand Frappier prize Govt. of Que., 1996, Patronat du Quebec prize, 1998, Grand Montrealais award, 2000, FCAR award Govt. Que., 2001, Purkynje medal Czech Acad. Sci., 2002; named to Can. Med. Hall of Fame, 1994. Master ACP; fellow Royal Coll. Physicians and Surgeons Can. (James H. Graham award of merit 1993), Royal Soc. Can. (Flavelle medal and award 1968); mem. Assn. Am. Physicians, Am. Clin. and Climatol. Assn., Am. Heart Assn. (Disting. Scientist award 2003), Peripatetic Club. Roman Catholic. Office: Inst de Recherches Cliniques 120 Pine Ave Montreal PQ Canada H2W 1R7 Home: 5955 Av Wilderton Montreal PQ Canada H3S 2V1 Business E-Mail: jacgensr@sympatico.ca.

GENIESER, NANCY BRANOM, radiologist; MD, Med. Coll. Pa., 1962. Diplomate Am. Bd. Radiology, Am. Bd. Diagnostic Radiololgy, Am. Bd. Pediat. Radiology. Intern Phila. Gen. Hosp., 1962—63; resident radiology NYU Hosps., NYC, 1963—65; prof. radiology NYU Med. Ctr.; staff Bellevue Hosp., NYC; cons. Manhattan VA; assoc. dean, admissions and fin. aid NYU Sch. Medicine, 2004—. Fellow Am. Coll. Radiology; mem. NYC Med. Soc., NY Radiol. Soc., NY State Radiol. Soc., Radiol. Soc. N.Am., Soc. Pediat. Rsch Office Fax: 212-263-7666.

GENIESER-DEROSA, ANYA, psychologist; m. Darren J. DeRosa, Apr. 23, 1994; 1 child, Emma S. DeRosa. BA in Econs., Gettysburg Coll., Pa., 1991; MS in Counseling Psychology, Chestnut Hill Coll., Pa., 1995; D in Psychology, Phila. Coll. Osteo. Medicine, 2002. Lic. psychologist Pa. State Bd. Psychology, 2004. Psychologist Ctr. Mental Health Reading Hosp., West Reading, Pa., 2002—06, DGR Mgmt. Comprehensive Behavioral Health Svc., 2006—. Adj. prof. Phila. Coll. Osteo. Medicine, 2000—06, Chestnut Hill Coll., 2005. Mem.: APA, Berks Area Psychol. Assn., Assn. Behavioral and Cognitive Therapies, Pa. Psychol. Assn. Office: 2201 Ridgewood Rd Ste 400 Wyomissing PA 19610 Personal E-mail: dranyaderosa@hotmail.com.

GENKINS, GABRIEL, physician; b. Berlin, Mar. 20, 1928; came to U.S., 1940, naturalized, 1945; s. Arkady and Tamara (Schlesinger) G.; children: Karen Lee Genkins Fairbank, Steven M., Amy E. BS, NYU, 1949, MD, 1952. Diplomate Am. Bd. Internal Medicine, Am. Bd. Cardiology. Intern, resident Mt. Sinai Hosp., NYC, 1952-57; practice medicine specializing cardiology NYC; chief myasthenia gravis clinic rsch. labs. Mt. Sinai Med. Ctr., NYC, 1972—, clin. prof. medicine, 1973—2009, clin. prof. medicine emeritus, 2009; attending physician cardiology Mt. Sinai Hosp., NYC, 1973—; mem. nat. med. adv. bd. Myasthenia Gravis Found., 1956—, v.p. bd. dirs., 1973—. Contbr. articles to profl. jours., chpts. to books. Served with airborne inf., U.S. Army, 1945-46. Democrat. Home Phone: 718-268-5412; Office Phone: 718-268-5412. Office Fax: 718-268-5412. Business E-Mail: ggenkins@nyc.rr.com.

GENNARELLI, THOMAS A., neurosurgeon, consultant; b. Berwyn, Ill., Apr. 20, 1943; s. Thomas and Matilda Racich Gennarelli; m. Alice Kay Doddridge, Aug. 27, 1965; children: Laura Michelle, Thomas Andrew, Gregory Scott, Philip Alexander. MD cum laude, Loyola U. Stritch Sch. Medicine, Maywood, Ill., 1968; MA (hon.), U. Pa., Phila., 1999. Diplomate NBMS, 1978. Fellow neurology Harvard U., Boston, 1969—70; clin. assoc. Nat. Insts. Health, USPHS, Bethesda, Md., 1970—72; resident neurosurgery Georgetown U., Washington, 1972—76; prof. neurosurgery U. Pa., Phila., 1976—95, Allegheney U., Phila., 1995—99, chair; prof. neurosurgery Med. Coll. Wis., Milw., 1999—2009, chair. Chmn. Internat. Com. Injury Scaling (AIS), Des Plaines, Ill., 1980—2005, Joint Sect. Neurotrauma (AANS-CNS), Chgo., 1988—90; coun. bd. mem. Internation Coun. on Biomechanics Impact, Lyon, France, 1990—; pres. Internation Neurotrauma Soc., Glasgow, Scotland, 1998—2002. Contbr. scientific papers. Surgeon USPHA, 1970—72, Bethesda, Md. Recipient Merit award, Assn. Advancement Automotive Medicine; named Best Doctor's Am., 1987—. Fellow: Assn. Advancement Automotive Medicine (pres. 1992—93), ACS, Am. Assoc. Surgery of Trauma. Achievements include research in diffuse axonal injury and discovered it's causation. Home and Office: 822 Grist Mill Ln West Chester PA 19380 Personal E-mail: tgennarelli@att.net. Business E-Mail: tgenn@mcw.edu.

GENNARI, F. JOHN, nephrologist, educator; b. Jersey City, May 18, 1937; s. Frank and Amelia (Sargia) G.; m. Emily Hewson Michie, Sept. 15, 1958; children: John Hewson, Jennifer Meade, Amelia Sargia. BS with Cum Laude, Yale U, New Haven, 1959; MD, Yale U, New Haven CT, 1959—63. Diplomate Am. Bd. Internal Medicine, Am. Bd. Nephrology. Resident medicine U. Va. Hosp., Charlottesville, 1963—66; fellow nephrology Tufts New Eng. Med. Ctr, Boston, 1968—71; asst. prof. medicine Tufts U Sch. Medicine, Boston, 1971—75, assoc. prof. medicine, 1975—79; prof. medicine U. Vt. Coll. Medicine, Burlington, 1979—, dir., nephrology divsn., 1979—2002, assoc. chair, dept. medicine, 1987—92, acting chair, dept. medicine, 1993—93. Mem. Nephrology bd. Am. Bd. Internal Medicine, 1994-2000. Co-author: Acid-Base, 1981, Acid-Base Disorders, 1987; editor Medical Mgmt. of Kidney and Electrolyte Disorders, 2001; sr. editor Acid-Base Disorders and Their Treatments, 2005; contbr. articles to profl. publs., chpts. to books. Mem. exec. com. Vt. Heart Assn., 1982-85; mem. exec. com. Vt. Kidney Assn., 1980—, pres., 1984-86; mem. merit rev. bd. VA, Washington, 1989-92. Capt. Med. Corps, USAF, 1966-68. Capt. USAF, 1966—68, Tachikawa, Japan. Grantee NIH, 1971-91, Fogarty Internat., 1991. Fellow ACP; mem. Am. Fedn. Clin. Rsch., Am. Soc. Clin. Investigation, Am. Soc. Nephrology, Am. Physiol. Soc., Internat. Soc. Nephrology. Democrat. Avocations: skiing, hiking.

GENNARO, ANTONIO L., biology professor; b. Raton, N.Mex., Mar. 18, 1934; s. Paul and Mary Lou (Gasperetti) G.; m. Virginia Marie Sullivan, May 15, 1955 (div. 1979); children: Theresa Ann, Carrie Marie, Janelle Elizabeth; m. Marjorie Lou Cox, Sept. 27, 1980. BS, N.Mex. State U., 1957, MS, 1961, PhD, 1965. Tchr. biology Las Cruces (N.Mex.) H.S., 1957-58; asst. prof. biology St. John's U., Collegeville, Minn., 1964-65; prof. biology Eastern N.Mex. U., Portales, 1965—. Bd. trustees N.Mex. Mus. Natural History, 1996—. Served to capt. U.S. Army, 1958-59; USAR, 1959-66. Recipient presdl. faculty award Eastern N.Mex. U., 1970, pres.'s faculty award for excellence in rsch., 1988, spirit of east award, 1995, outstanding sci. award N.Mex. Acad. Sci., 1975, disting. faculty emeritus, 1998. Mem. Southwestern Naturalists (treas. 1974-78), Am. Soc. Mammalogists, Herpetologists League, Sigma Xi, Phi Kappa Phi (pres. 1970-74). E-mail: tonygennaro_08@msn.com.

GENNARO, KAREN ELISE GLOWACKI, psychiatrist; b. Detroit, Oct. 29, 1954; MD, Case Western Reserve U., 1995. Intern psychiatry U. Hosp., Cleve., 1996—97; resident psychiatry Cornell Med. Ctr., White Plains, NY, 1997—2000; psychiatrist St. Vincents Hosp., Harrison, NY, 2000—10. Pres. Psychiat. Soc. Westchester County, 2007—08; sec. Westchester County Med. Soc., 2009—10; pres. Westchester Acad. Medicine, 2010—. Recipient Leadership award (Young Physician), AMA Found., 2006. Office: St Vincents Hosp 275 North St Harrison NY 10528 Office Phone: 914-925-5443. Office Fax: 914-925-5150.

GENNARO, VALERIO, physician; b. Vicenza, June 25, 1952; MD, Genoa U., 1979, degree in Oncology, 1984, PhD in Pub. Health, 2007. Physician Nat. Cancer Rsch. Inst. (IST), 1980—. Postdoc. felowship, Johns Hopkins U., Balt. Mem.: Delta Omega. Office: Largo Rbenzi 10 Genoa 16132 Italy Office Fax: 39.010.5737336. Business E-Mail: valerio.gennaro@istge.it.

GENOV, KRASIMIR ROZENOV, neurologist, consultant; b. Nicopol, Bulgaria, Nov. 24, 1958; s. Rozen Genov Nicolov and Rusca Asenova Nicolova; m. Neli Petrova Genova, Nov. 5, 1980; 1 child, Rosen Krasimirov Rozenov. Student, Med. U., Varna, Bulgaria, 1981—87; PhD, Med. U., Sofia, 2005. Resident Mil. Med. Acad., Sofia, 1987—88, mil. physician Mil. Unit Varna, 1988—91, clin. intern, 1991—93, head of neurol. cons. rm., 1993—98, departmental chief, 1998—2002, clinic of neurology chief, 2002—03, dept. chief, 2003—05, clinic of neurology chief, 2005—. Cons. neurologist Mil. Med. Acad., 1998—; expert Nat. Health Ins. Fund, Sofia, Bulgaria, 2005—. Author: (book) Multiple Sclerosis, 2002; co-author: Multiple Sclerosis and Emotions, 1997, Memory, Mind and Multiple Sclerosis, 1997. Cons. Multiple Sclerosis Soc., Sofia, 2003—05. Lt. col. Mil. Med. Acad., 1988—2005, Sofia. Recipient Award for Young Neurologists, Prof. Chalamanov, 1993. Mem.: Bulgarian Headache Soc., Balcanic Soc. of Alzheimer, Bulgarian Soc. Neurology. Avocations: music, travel. Home: Drugba 2 B 302 enG Apt 17 Sofia 1582 Bulgaria Office: Mil Med Acad 3 Georgi Sofiyski Str Sofia 1606 Bulgaria Personal E-mail: kr_genov@abv.bg.

GENSABELLA FURNARI, MARIANNA, social sciences educator; b. Messina, Italy, Nov. 5, 1950; d. Salvatore Gensabella and Vincenza Bruno; m. Salvatore Furnari, June 8, 1977; children: Santi Furnari, Maria Teresa Furnari. Degree in Philosophy, U. Messina, 1972; postgrad. studies in philosophy, Rome, 1977. Rsch. fellow U. Messina, Italy, 1974—80, rschr., 1980—2000, assoc. prof. bioethics, 2000—. Mem. Affiliates Global Bioethics, 2000—, Ethics Com. Hosp. Piemonte, Messina, 2002—. Author: (books) L'oggetto perduto. Desiderio e verità in Lacan, Giannini, Napoli 1984, I sentieri della libertà. Saggio su Luigi Pareyson, Guerini, Milano 1994, Tra autonomia e responsabilità Percorsi oli Bioetica, Rubbettino, Soveria 2000., (essays in books) in Itinerari dell'idealismo, Le radici della bioetica, Women's Health Issues, Il filo(sofare) di Arianna, Spostando mattoni a mani nude; editor: (books) Alle frontiere della vita. Eutanasia ed etica del morire, Rubbettino, voll. 2, Soveria 2001-2003, (book) V.R. Potter, Bioetica. Ponte verso il futuro, traduzione italiana, Sicania, Messina 2000; author: (essays) in Criterio, Rivista Rosminiana, Itinerarium, Segni e comprensione Medicina e Morale, Perspectives in Biology and Medicine. Mem. Centro Italiano Femminile, Rome, 1997—2004, Soroptmist Club, Messina, 1997—2004. Home: Viale Liberta' N251 Messina 98121 Italy Office: Dipartimento Scienze Cognitive Via XXIV Maggio n21 Messina 98100 Italy Home Fax: 3990364721. Personal E-mail: marianna.gensabella@unime.it.

GENTILE, RONALD C., ophthalmologist, educator; BS in (Biochemistry), magna cum laude, SUNY, 1983—87; MD summa cum laude, SUNY Health Sci. Ctr., Bklyn., NY, 1987—91. Diplomate Am. Bd. of Opthalmology, 1997. Intern Columbia Presbyn. Med. Ctr., 1991—92; fellow Wayne State Univ., Kresge Eye Inst., 1996—98, The NY Eye & Ear Infirmary, 1995—96, resident, 1992—95, chief resident, 1994—95, with residency selection com., 1998, co-dir. ocular trauma svc. dept of ophthalmology, 2000, with rsch. coun.; asst. clin. prof. dept. of ophthalmology NY Med. Coll., Valhalla, NY, 1998. Contributor (publs.) Diagnosis of traumatic cyclodialysis by ultrasound biomicroscopy, Imaging congenital optic disc pits and associated maculopathy using optical coherence tomography, Ultrasound biomicroscopic features of iris retraction syndrome, Risk factors for ciliochoroidal effusion following panretinal photocoagulation, and numerous other publs. Recipient Alumni Fund award, SUNY HSCAB, 1988, NIH Summer Rsch. Fellowship award, 1988, Upjohn achievement award, 1991, 1856 award (highest award for academic excellence), 1991, Louis J. Girard Resident Rsch. award, 1995, Britan F. Payne Ophthalmic Pathology award, 1996; scholar, SUNY HSCAB, 1991. Mem.: AMA, Nassau County Med. Soc., Med. Soc. of the State of NY, NY State of Ophthalmologic Soc., Am. Uvetis Soc., Assn. Rsch. in Vision and Ophthalmology, Am. Acad. of Ophthalmology. Office: The New York Eye and Ear Infirmary 310 East 14th St 2nd Ave New York NY 10003 Office Phone: 212-979-4000, 212-979-4120. Office Fax: 212-979-4512.

GENTILE, TOM (THOMAS C. GENTILE III), medical products executive; b. 1964; Gen. course degree in Internat. Rels., London U.; BA in Econ. magna cum laude, Harvard U., 1986, MBA, 1988. Joined McKinsey & Co., worked, automotive clients, London office England, Switzerland, Germany; trade analyst, Motors Trading Corp. General Motors Co., 1986—88; sr. v.p., strategy GE Global Consumer Fin., 1998; six sigma quality leader GE Global Consumer Finance, 1998—2000, pres., CEO France, 2000—02, GE Money, Australia, 2002—06, chief mktg. officer, 2006—08; v.p., gen. mgr., services GE Aviation, 2008—11; pres., CEO GE Healthcare Systems, 2011—. Former bd. mem., Asia Pacific MasterCard Internat. Fellow: Australian Banking & Finance Inst. Office: GE Healthcare Systems 3000 N Grandview Blvd Waukesha WI 53188 *

GENTILESCHI, PAOLO, surgeon, educator; b. Rome, May 21, 1967; MD, U. Rome Tor Vergata, 1991. Cert. specialist in digestive surgery U. Rome Tor Vergata, 1996. Aggregate prof. surgery U. Rome Tor Vergata, 1996—, prof. surgery, 2006, chief polyclinic. Prof. Bariatric Surgery Unit Baratric Surgery. Mem.: Italian Soc. Surgery. Office: Viale Oxford 81 Rome 00133 Italy Office Fax: 39-06-20902926. E-mail: gentilp@yahoo.com.

GENTRY, MARILYN, medical association administrator; Pres., CEO Am. Inst. Cancer Rsch., World Cancer Rsch. Fund Internat. Office: Am Inst Cancer Rsch 1759 R St NW Washington DC 20009 also: World Cancer Rsch Fund Internat 19 Harley Street W1G 9QJ London England Office Phone: 4420 73434200. Office Fax: 4420 73434220. *

GENTZLER, MARC DOUGLAS, psychologist, educator; b. Montclair, Calif., Aug. 4, 1981; BA in Psychology, U. Ky., 2003; MA in Psychology, Claremont Grad. U., 2007. Grad. assoc. U. Ctrl. Fla., 2005—, rsch. asst., cons., 2005, adj. instr., 2007. Mem.: Nat. Dean's List, Golden Key Honor's Soc., Human Factors and Ergonomics Soc., Psi Chi Honor's Soc. Avocations: drawing, bicycling, aviation. Office: Dept Psychology 4000 Central Florida Blvd Orlando FL 32816 Business E-Mail: mgentzler@knights.ucf.edu.

GEOCADIN, ROMERGRYKO G., medical educator; b. Philippines, Mar. 30, 1966; MD, U. East Ramon Magsaysay Coll. Medicine, 1991. Assoc. prof. neurology, anesthesiology-critical care medicine and neurosurgery Johns Hopkins U. Sch. Medicine, 2008—. Sec. Neurocritical Care Soc., 2009—11. Recipient Clin. Roundtable award, Am. Acad. Neurology. Fellow: Am. Acad. Neurology; mem.: Am. Heart Assn., Am. Neurol. Assn. Avocation: motorcycling. Office: Johns Hopkins Hosp 600 N Wolfe St Baltimore MD 21287 Business E-Mail: rgeocad1@jhmi.edu.

GEORGE, GLADYS, hospital administrator; b. 1946; With Lenox Hill Hosp., NYC, 1973—, pres., 1989—. Named one of The 100 Most Influential Women in NYC Bus., Crain's NY Bus., 2007. Office: Lenox Hill Hosp 100 E 77th St New York NY 10021-1850

GEORGE, JAMES NOEL, hematologist, oncologist, educator; b. Columbus, Ohio, Sept. 23, 1938; BA, Ohio State U., MD, 1962. Diplomate Am. Bd. Internal Medicine, cert. in hematology, lic. Okla., Tex., Ohio. Intern, resident dept. medicine Vanderbilt U. Sch. Medicine, Nashville, 1962—63, 1966—67; rsch. hematologist Walter Reed Army Inst. Rsch., Washington, 1963—66; resident in medicine, hematology fellow, chief resident Strong Meml. Hosp., U. Rochester Sch. Medicine, NY, 1967—70; asst. prof., assoc. prof. then prof. dept. med. divsn. hematology U. Tex. Health Sci. Ctr., San Antonio, 1970—90; prof. dept. medicine, chief hematology-oncology sect. U. Okla. Health Sci. Ctr., Oklahoma City, 1990—, George Lynn Cross prof., dept. medicine, 2005—. Mem. transfusion com. Bexar County Hosp., San Antonio, 1970—87; rsch. assoc. Theodor Kocher Inst., Berne, Switzerland, 1975—76; chmn. hematology peer rev. panel Life Scis. Space Flight Experiment prog. NASA, 1978; mem. hematology study sect. I NIH, 1986—94; vis. prof. dept. physiol. chemistry U. Wis., Madison, 1987—88; assoc. prof. Hosp. Lariboisiere, U. Paris, 1988—89; mem. adv. bd. Gladstone Found. Labs. Cardiovasc. Rsch., U. Calif., San Francisco, 1991; bd. trustees Gorgas Sci. Found., Inc., Brownsville, Tex., 1992—; staff physician Okla. Blood Inst., Oklahoma City, 1994—; mem. oncology task force Midwest City Regional Hosp., Okla., 1995—. Mem.editl. bd.: Blood Jour., 1985—90; contbr. articles to profl. jours. Capt. M.C. US Army, 1963—66. Fellow: ACP; mem.: So. Soc. Clin. Investigation, Ctrl. Soc. Clin. Rsch., Am. Soc. Hematology (com. on ednl. affairs/tng. 1986—89, sci. subcom. on platelets 1986—89, com. on publs. 1991—, chmn. edn. prog. on platelets 1993—96, ad hoc com. on practice guidelines 1994—, nominating com. 1995, pres. 2005), Am. Soc. Clin. Investigation, Am. Heart Assn. (thrombosis coun., 1st Ann. Lyndon B. Johnson award 1976), Am. Fedn. Clin. Rsch., Alpha Omega Alpha (councilor Tex. Epsilon chpt. 1978—81). Achievements include research in epidemiology, clinical course, and long-term outcomes of platelet disorders. Office: U Okla Health Scis Ctr 801 NE 13th St Rm 335 PO Box 26901 Oklahoma City OK 73190-0001 Office Phone: 405-271-2330 x48387. Business E-Mail: James_George@ouhsc.edu.

GEORGE, JEFF, pharmaceutical executive; BA in Internat. Rels., Carleton Coll.; M, Johns Hopkins U.; MBA, Harvard U. Engagement mgr. McKinsey and Co., 2001—04; sr. dir. strategic planning and bus. devel. Gap, Inc., 2004—08; head comml. ops. western and eastern Europe vaccines and diagnostics divsn. and head Asia, Middle East, Africa, CIS at Novartis Pharma Novartis AG, 2007—08, divsn. head Sandoz, mem. exec. com., 2008—. Office: Novartis Internat AG 4002 Basel Switzerland *

GEORGE, KURUVILLA, psychiatrist, consultant; b. Singapore, Jan. 10, 1950; came to Australia, 1995; s. K. K. and A. George; m. Margaret Powell, Apr., 1977; children: George, Elizabeth, Amy, Lydia. MB BS, Kasturba Med. Coll., 1974; MPhil, U. Edinburgh, 1980; DPM, U. London, 1978. Intern Kasturba Med. Coll. Hosp., Manipal, India, 1973—74, resident psychiatry, 1974—75; ships med. officer M.V. Logos, 1975—76; sr. house officer psychiatry Royal Edinburgh Hosp., registrar psychiatry, 1977—79; sr. registrar psychiatry Newcastle Gen. Hosp., England, 1979—81; cons. psychiatrist Newcastle, 1981—86; gen. sec. E.M.F.I., India, 1988—95; cons. psychiatrist North-We. Health, Melbourne, Australia, 1995—2000, clin. dir. aged psychiatry, 1997—99; dir. aged psychiatry Peter James Ctr., Melbourne, 2000—; dep. chief psychiatrist Victoria, 2002—; dir. med. svcs. Peter James Ctr. Wantirna Health, 2009—; adj. assoc. prof. U. Notara Dame, Australia, 2007—; clin. assoc. prof Monash U., Australia, 2008—. Adj. prof. Deakin U., Melbourne, 2002-; internat. faculty mem. Haggai Inst., 1996— Contbr. articles to profl. jours. Bd. dirs. Ashirwad Child Devel. Rsch. Ctr., India, 1988—95, Emmanuel Hosp. Assn., India, 1988—95, Emmanuel Blind Relief Soc., India, 1988—95, Asha Kiran Hosp., India, 1988—95, Christian Fellowship Hosp. and Cmty. Health Ctr., India, 1988—95. Fellow Royal Coll. Psychiatrists, Royal Australian and New Zealand Coll. Psychiatrists. Achievements include research in service developments and depression in aged psychiatry. Office: Peter James Ctr Forest Hill Melbourne VIC 3131 Australia Office Phone: 61 3 98811749. Personal E-mail: kuruvilla.george@easternhealth.org.au. Business E-Mail: kuruvilla.george@peterjames.org.au.

GEORGE, LIZIAMMA, pulmonologist, educator; Attended, Trivandum Med. Coll., India, 1980. Diplomate Am. Bd. Internal Medicine, Am. Bd. Internal Medicine-critical care medicine, Am. Bd. Internal Medicine-pulmonary disease, Am. Bd. Internal Medicine-sleep medicine. Intern Trivadum Med. Coll., India; resident in internal medicine St. Joseph Med. Ctr., Yonkers, NY, 1985—87, fellow in pulmonary disease, 1987—89; assoc. clin. prof. medicine Cornell Univ.-Weill Med. Coll.; pulmonologist NY Methodist Hosp. Office: New York Methodist Hospital 506 6th St Brooklyn NY 11215 Office Phone: 718-780-5835.

GEORGE, OLIVIER, research scientist; b. Laval, France, Feb. 21, 1978; PhD, U. Bordeaux, 2004. Staff scientist Scripps Rsch. Inst., 2006—, lab. dir., 2008. Mem.: Rsch. Soc. on Alcohol, Soc. Rsch. on Nicotine and Tobacco, Soc. Neurosci. Office: 10550 N Torrey Pines RF La Jolla CA 92037 Business E-Mail: ogeorge@scripps.edu.

GEORGE, SANJU, medical educator, consultant; b. Feb. 9, 1973; MBBS, St. John's Med. Coll., Bangalore, India, 1996. Cons. addiction psychiatrist & sr. rsch. fellow Birmingham and Solihull Mental Health NHS Trust, England, 2005—. Contbr. scientific papers. Recipient Hosp. Dr. award, 2007. Master: RCP, London (editl. bd. mem. jour.); mem.: General Med. Coun. (case examiner & supr.). Home: 339 Monmouth Dr Saxton Coldfield West Midlands B73 63X England Office: Birmigham Solihull Mental Hlth Tr Chelmsley Wood The Bridge B15 2QZ Birmingham England Office Phone: 0044-0121-6784900. Office Fax: 0121-6784901. Business E-Mail: sanju.george@bsmhft.nhs.uk.

GEORGE, SUZANNE, medical association administrator; b. Boston, Apr. 16, 1968; AB, Harvard U., 1990; MD, U. Mass. Med. Sch., 1995. Clin. dir. Ctr. Sarcoma and Bone Oncology Dana-Farber Cancer Inst., 2004—. Mem.: Mass. Med. Soc., Connective Tissue Oncology Soc., Am. Soc. Clin. Oncology. Avocations: music, skiing. Office: 450 Brookline Ave D1212 Boston MA 02215 Office Fax: 617-632-3408. Business E-Mail: sgeorge2@partners.org.

GEORGE, THOMAS, cardiologist, consultant; s. George Mangalathil Thomas and Aleyamma George; m. Blessie Varghese, Apr. 10, 1980; children: Sharon Elizabeth Thomas, George Thomas, Shalom Mary Thomas. MD, Lokmanya Tilak Med. Coll., Mumbai, India, 1983. Sr. cons. Indira Gandhi Coop. Hosp., Kochi, India, 1994—. Life mem. YMCA, Kochi, India, 1994. Fellow Fellow, Cardiol. Soc. of India, 2005, Indian Acad. of Echocardiography, 2006. Mem.: Indian Acad. Echocardiography, Cardiol. Soc. India (life; convener echocardiography sub-speciality coun. 2003—05), YMCA (life). Achievements include development of classification and nomenclature for coronary artery disease; clinical classification of hypertension; first to organize doppler diastology; debunk tissue doppler echocardiography. Avocations: travel, music, swimming. Office: I Indira Gandhi Coop Hosp Gandhi Nagar Kerala Kochi 682 020 India Home: C-13 682 020 Kochi 682 020 India Personal E-mail: gthomas@doctor.com.

GEORGESCU, EUGEN FLORIN, medical educator; b. Craiova, May 23, 1964; MD, U. Medicine & Pharmacy Craiova, 1988, PhD, 2000. Prof. internal medicine U. Medicine & Pharmacy Craiova, 1991—. Mem.: European Soc. Digestive Oncology, European Soc. Clin. Investigation, European Assn. Study Liver, Am. Gastroent. Assn. Avocations: literature, philosophy, computers. Office: Constantin Brancusi nr 3 Craiova Dolj 200136 Romania Office Fax: 40351813110.

GEORGHIOU, GEORGIOS PANAYI, cardiothoracic surgeon; b. Pafos, Cyprus, Mar. 31, 1972; s. Panayis and Maroulla Georghiou; m. Efrosini Flourenzou Georghiou, Oct. 3, 1998; children: Amalia, Panos, Christos. MD, Albert Szent Gyorgyi Med. U., Szeged, Hungary, 1997; diploma in thoracic and cardiovascular surgery, Sackler Faculty of Medicine, Tel Aviv U., 2005. Intern Pafos Gen. Hosp., Pafos, Cyprus, 1997—98, Larnaca Gen. Hosp., Larnaca, Cyprus, 1998; resident in cardiothoracic surgery Rabin Med. Ctr., Petah Tiqva, Israel, 1999—2005. Guest reviewer European Jour. Cardiothoracic Surgery, Interactive Cardiovascular and Thoracic Surgery, Heart, Chest, Annals of Thoracic Surgery, Internat. Rev. Panel of Med. Sci. Monitor, Switzerland, 2004—. Contbr. articles to profl. jours. Sgt. Mil. Police, 1989—91, Cyprus. Mem.: Soc. Thoracic Surgeons, European Soc. Thoracic Surgeons, European Assn. Cardiothoracic Surgery, Israel Med. Assn., Cyprus Med. Assn. Greek Orthodox. Avocations: reading, travel, swimming. Home: Dafnis 17 Aradippou 7100 Larnaka Cyprus Office: American Heart Inst P.O. Box 25610 1311 Nicosia Cyprus Home Phone: 357-2482-3523; Office Phone: 357-2281-9666. E-mail: georgios@ahi.com.cy.

GEORGIEV, PLAMEN TZVETANOV, neurologist, consultant; b. Vidin, Bulgaria, Oct. 20, 1964; s. Tzvetan Georgiev Nikolov and Tzenka Slavcheva Nikolova; life ptnr. Gergana Svetoslavova Atanasova. MD, U. Pleven, 1989. Cert. Neurologist Bulgarian State Bd. of Neurology, 1994. Asst.-in-chief Neurology dept. U. Pleven Hosp., Bulgaria, 1990—. Cons. U. Pleven Hosp., 1995—. Mem.: Bulgarian Soc. Neurology. Achievements include research in Clinical Neurophysiology, Stroke, Neuroimmunology. Home: Rousse Blvd # 43 app 8 5800 Pleven Bulgaria Office: Univ Pleven Hospital Neurology Dept G Kochev 8A St 5800 Pleven Bulgaria Personal E-mail: tzvetanovplamen@hotmail.com.

GEORGIEV, TCHAVDAR NIKOLOV, pathologist, educator; b. Sofia, Bulgaria, Dec. 19, 1945; s. Nikola Todorov and Ema Konstantinova (Bosadjieva) Georgiev; m. Lylia Dimitrova Arnaudova, Feb. 10, 1980; children: Tchavdar, Ana Georgieva. MD, U. Sofia, Bulgaria, 1971; PhD, U. Sofia, 1977, MSc, 1978, DSc, 1988. Asst. prof. dept. pathology U.Sofia, Bulgaria, 1971—74, rsch. asst. dept. pathology, 1974—77, asst. prof. dept. pathology, 1977—79, sr. asst. prof., 1979—81, head asst. prof., 1981—97, assoc. prof., 1997—2003. Cons. in endocrine pathology Inst. Endocrinology, Sofia, Bulgaria, 1979—92; cons. in neonatal and pediatric pathology Dept. Pahology, Sofia, 1979—81; head dept. infectious diseases and AIDS, Sofia, 1991—. Author: (book) Clinical Endocrinology, 1981, Pituitary Adenomas, 1987 (Nat. Book award, 1988), Prolactinomas, 1985, Lung Cancer, 1996; contbr. articles to profl. jours., 1978. Lt. Anti-aircraft Bulgarian Mil. Force, 1972—73. Mem.: Bulgarian Sci. Soc., N.Y. Acad. Scis., European Soc. Pathology. Eastern Orthodox. Avocations: history, literature, music, sports. Office: Med Faculty Pathology U Sofia blv g Sofiisky No 1 1431 Sofia Bulgaria Home: Sredna Gora 9 1320 Sofia Bulgaria Office Phone: 9230845. Home Fax: 997 8315. Personal E-mail: chavdar_georgiev@hotmail.com.

GEORGIEV, VIDEN, physiologist, educator; b. Gintsi, Bulgaria, Feb. 1, 1925; s. Ivan Georgiev Markov and Zorka Lozeva Peneva; m. Elena Vasileva Kisselkova, Jan. 8, 1956; children: Vassia, Ivan. MD, Med. U. Sofia, 1954; PhD, Inst. Exptl. Medicine, St. Petersburg, Russia, 1962. Diplomate. Asst. Nat. Sports Acad., Sofia, Bulgaria, 1955—58, sr. asst., 1959—63; rsch. fellow Sorbonne, Paris, 1964—66; assoc. prof. Nat. Sports Acad., 1967—75, prof. physiology, 1975—. Head lab. neurophys. Nat. Sport's Acad., 1967—91. Author: Proprioreceptors and Circulation, 1965, Vascular Reactions in Sportsmen after Physical Efforts, 1973, Nervous System and Sport, 1975, Peripheral and Brain Circulation at Physical Efforts, 1991. Co-founder

Civil Soc. Protection of Sci. & Edn., Sofia, 2001. Mem.: N.Y. Acad. Sci., Bulgarian Soc. Sports Medicine, Bulgarian Soc. Physiological Sci. Orthodox. Avocation: swimming. Home: 14 Tzar Petar St 1463 Sofia Bulgaria Address: Nat Sports Acad Dept Physiology and Biochemistry 1710 Sofia Bulgaria Home Phone: 8523965. Business E-Mail: vidivger@abv.bg.

GEORGIOS, STAMATIOU, otolaryngologist; b. Thessaloniki, Greece, June 20, 1975; MD, U. Bucharest, Romania, 2000. Resident, internship in gen. surgery Agrinio Gen. Hosp., 2004—05; sr. resident, dept. otology and laryngology Hippokration Gen. Hosp., U. Athens, Greece, 2008—. Avocations: chess, basketball, reading. Office: 114 Vassilisis Sofias St Athens 15121 Greece Personal E-mail: georgiosstamatiou@gmail.com.

GEPFORD, BARBARA BEEBE, retired nutrition educator; b. Buffalo, Sept. 2, 1930; d. Kenneth Hildreth and Martha Bell (Griswold) Beebe; m. William George Gepford, Dec. 28, 1952; children: David, Scott, Joanna, Andrea. BS in Home Econs. Edn., Iowa State U., 1952. Nutrition instr. Sidon Girl's Sch., Lebanon, 1953-56; instr. textiles and clothing Beirut Univ. Coll., Lebanon, 1955-56, 62-63; nutrition cons. Hong Kong Coun. of Social Svcs., 1967-71; commd. fraternal worker Presbyn. U.S.A., Lebanon, Hong Kong, 1953-71; mgr. Lila's Fabric Store, Cambridge, Ohio, 1973-74. Overseas missionary advisor to Assembly Coun. of Presbyn. Ch., U.S.A., 1971-72. Elder Presbyn. Ch., New Concord, Ohio, 1974-79, mem. com. on Ministry, Detroit, 1987-94; pres. Presbyn. Women of Littlefield Ch., 1987-89, vice-moderator Presbyn. Women of Presbytery of Detroit, 1996-97, moderator, 1997-99; synod of covenant women's rep. Churchwide Coordinating Team of Presbyn. Women, 1999-2002; chair Presbyn. Women Triann. Global Exch. to Africa, 2002-03; elder, Littlefield Presbyn. Ch., Dearborn, Mich., 2006—08, session mem., 2010-; advisor YWCA Head Start Program, Dearborn, Mich., 1988-91; bd. dirs. YWCA, 1985-96, pres., 1993-95. Named Ohio Mother of the Yr., Am. Mothers Com., New Concord, 1978. Mem., AAUW (bd. dirs. 1987-89, internat. rels. area rep.). Democrat. Avocations: reading, gardening, sewing, knitting. Home: 9421 Westwind Dr Livonia MI 48150-4530 Personal E-mail: barbbgepford@msn.com, wiamfrd@msn.com.

GEPNER, BRUNO ALBERT, psychiatrist; b. Paris, May 5, 1962; s. Armand Aaron and Jacqueline Rachel Gepner. MD Psychiatry, U. Medicine, Marseille, France, 1992; PhD Neuroscis., U. Mediterranée, Marseille, 1997. Med. dir. Montperrin Hosp., Aix-en-Provence, France, 1996—2008; prof. child & adolescent psychiatry U. Hosp, Liege, Belgium, 2008—09. Assoc. prof. U. Psychology, Aix en Provence, Paris, 1999—; assoc. rschr. Speech and Lang. Lab., UMR-CNRS, Aix en Provence; specialist in Autism; pres. Fedn. Autism vie Entiere. Contbr. articles to profl. jours. Recipient prize, U. Marseille, 1994. Avocation: violin. Office: Ctr Studies Assessment and Care Persons with Autism Spectrum Disorders Aix-en-Provence France Home Phone: 0033 491351432; Office Phone: 0033 442164965. Business E-Mail: bruno.gepner@univ-provence.fr.

GERA, TARUN, pediatrician; b. Delhi, Sept. 13, 1972; MBBS, Maulana Azad Med. Coll., 1996, MD, 1999. Cons. SL Jain Hosp., 2002—10, Fortis Hosp., 2010—. Sec. nutrition chpt. Indian Acad. Pediat., 2007—11. Mem.: IMA, IAP. Avocations: poetry, reading, literature, music. Home: B-256 Derawala Nagar Delhi 110009 India Personal E-mail: tarun256@yahoo.com.

GERACI, GIROLAMO, surgeon, researcher; b. Palermo, Italy, Dec. 5, 1973; s. Domenico Geraci and Maria Grazia Romano; m. Mariangela Mortillaro, May 13, 2005; 1 child, Enrico. Specialized in gen. surgery U. Palermo, 2004, cert. rsch. dr. 2007. Rschr. U. Palermo, 2008—. Achievements include research in biliary operative endoscopy. Office Fax: 0916552720. Personal E-mail: girgera@tin.it.

GERACI, GIUSEPPE FEDERICO ELIO, molecular biologist, educator; b. Naples, Italy, Mar. 18, 1933; s. Arturo and Pia (Spezzaferro) G.; m. Rosa Alberti, Mar. 27, 1960. D in Chemistry, U. Naples, Italy, 1956. Rschr. Pharm. Industry, Naples, Italy, 1958-62, Italian Nat. Rsch. Coun., Naples, Italy, 1962-71; assoc. rschr. Cornell U., Ithaca, NY, 1966-67, Harvard Med. Sch., Boston, 1967-68, assoc. staff in medicine, 1968-69; dir. rsch. Lab. of Molecular Embryology, Naples, 1971—; prof. molecular biology U. Naples, 1981—; vis. prof. Harvard Med. Sch., Boston, 1991. Sci. adv. bd. CNR Ctr. for Molecular Biology, Rome, 1971-80, Ctr. for Genetic Engring., Naples, 1985—; dir. Inst. Gen. Biology and Genetics, U. Naples, 1981-85, pres. U. Coun. on Biol. Sci., dir. dept. gen. and molecular biology, 1996-98. Editor, author: (book) Le Nuove Frontiere della Biologia, 1991; contbr. papers to Jour. Biol. Chemistry, Biochemistry, Jour. Molecular Biology and other profl. jours. Recipient award Italian Soc. Biochemistry, 1988. Mem. Italian Soc. Biophys. and Moleculary Biology (cons. 1966-68), Italian Soc. Biochemistry, Italian Nat. Acad. Letters, Scis. and Arts (pres. 1997-99), Internat. Lions Club. Roman Catholic. Achievements include the distinction of being the first to demonstrate Allosteric Regulation in mammalian enzyme; first to prepare human hemoglobin chains with different functional properties; demonstration of evidence of pre-determinative events in sea urchin embryo development. Home: Via Botteghelle 212 80046 San Giorgio a Cremano Italy Office: U Naples Dept Genetics Via Mezzocannone 8 80134 Naples Italy Business E-Mail: geraci@unina.it.

GERACI, MICHAEL CHARLES, JR., sports medicine physician; b. Buffalo, Sept. 4, 1953; BS in Phys. Therapy, Daemen Coll., 1979; MD, U. Autonoma de Guadalajara, 1983. Dir., fellowship program and sports medicine Buffalo Spine and Sports Inst., 1991—. Clin. assoc. prof. SUNY, Buffalo, Mich. State U., 1984—2011. Fellow: Am. Acad. Phys. Medicine and Rehab. (Disting. Clinician award 2006). Avocations: skiing, tennis, golf. Home: 57 Darwin Dr Snyder NY 14226 Home Fax: 716-626-9193. Personal E-mail: mgeraci@pol.net.

GERALD, BARRY, retired radiology educator, neuroscientist; b. Greenville, Miss., Feb. 10, 1934; s. Louis Elmo and Eula (Mitchell) G.; m. Marjorie Brown, Aug. 6, 1955; children: Lucy Gerald Cook, Lee, Paul. Student, U. Miss., Oxford, 1951-54; MD, U. Miss., Jackson, 1958. Diplomate Am. Bd. Radiology. Intern Hermann Hosp., Houston, 1958-59, resident in radiology, 1959-62; fellow in pediatric radiology Children's Hosp. Med. Ctr., Cin., 1962-64; mem. faculty dept. radiology U. Ark., Little Rock, 1964-65, 67-69; dir. radiology dept. Children's Hosp. Med. Ctr., Oakland, Calif., 1965-66; mem. faculty dept. radiology U. Tenn. Coll. Medicine, Memphis, 1969—2004, prof., chmn. dept., 1979-95; fellow in neuroradiology Tufts-New Eng. Med. Ctr., Boston, 1971-72, interim chair dept. radiology, 2004—09, emeritus prof. radiology, 2009. Dir. radiology dept. Le Bonheur Children's Hosp., Memphis, 1983-88, 1991-2002; acting dir. radiology dept. St. Jude Children's Rsch. Hosp., Memphis, 1985-87; trainee Nat. Cancer Inst., 1960-62. Contbr. articles to med. jours., chpts. to books. Fellow Am. Coll. Radiology; mem. Am. Soc. Neuroradiology, Soc. for Pediatric Radiology, Radiol. Soc. N.Am. (councillor 1980-85), Am. Roentgen Ray Soc., Southeastern Neuroradiologic Soc. (founder, pres. 1977-78), So. Radiologic Conf. (pres. 1975-76). Avocations: tennis, history. Home: 694 Clanlo Dr Memphis TN 38104-5067 Personal E-mail: barrygerald@gmail.com.

GERALD, MICHAEL CHARLES, pharmacy educator; b. NYC, Nov. 20, 1939; s. Tobias Gerson and Ruby Rose (Weinstock) Gerald; m. Gloria Elaine Gruber, Jan. 31, 1965; children: Marc Jonathan, Melissa Suzanne. BS in Pharmacy, Fordham U., 1961; PhD, Ind. U., 1968. Registered pharmacist NY. Postdoc. fellow USPHS, U. Chgo., 1968—69; asst. prof. Coll. Pharmacy Ohio State U., Columbus, 1969—74, assoc. prof., 1974—80, prof., 1980—93, prof. and assoc. dean, 1984—93; dean, prof. Sch. Pharmacy U. Conn., Storrs, 1993—2002, prof., 2002—; cons. WHO, Geneva, 1983—84; Gustavus A. Pfeiffer Meml. rsch. fellow Am. Found. Pharm. Edn., 1983—84; mem. adv. panel US Pharmacopeia Com. Revision, Washington, 1980—85; bd. dirs. Patient Access Network Found., 2006—. Author: Pharmacology: An Introduction to Drugs, 1981, Nursing Pharmacology and Therapeutics, 1988, The Poisonous Pen of Agatha Christie, 1993, Complete Idiot's Guide to Prescription Drugs, 2006; co-author: The Nurse's Guide to Drug Therapy: Drug Profiles for Patient Care, 1984; editor: Instruction in Pharmacology: New Approaches and New Faces, 1979. Mem. FDA Drug Abuse Adv. Com., 1993—96. 1st lt. USAF, 1963—65. Fellow: Acad. Pharm. Scis. (sect. sec. 1975—77, sect. v.p. 1978—79); mem.: Am. Soc. Pharmacology and Exptl., Am. Assn. Colls. Pharmacy (bd. dirs. 1980—82). Avocations: photography, reading, music, walking. Office: University Conn Sch Pharmacy 69 North Eagleville Rd Storrs Mansfield CT 06269-3092 Home Phone: 860-487-4675; Office Phone: 860-486-5416. Business E-Mail: michael.gerald@ucomn.edu.

GERARD, GARY, neurologist; b. NYC, Apr. 16, 1949; s. Victor and Sylvia G.; m. Pauline Judd; 1 child, Michael. BA, NYU, 1971; MD, Hahnemann U., 1975. Diplomate Am. Bd. Neurology and Psychiatry. Intern medicine Brookdale Med. Ctr., Bklyn., 1975-76; resident in diagnostic radiology Mt. Sinai Med. Ctr., NYC, 1976-78; resident in neurology L.I. Jewish Med. Ctr., New Hyde Park, NY, 1978-81; chief of neurology Winthrop U. Hosp., Mineola, NY, 1984-89; assoc. prof. neurology and radiology, dir. cerebrovascular lab. Med. Coll. Ohio, Toledo, 1990-94, vice chmn. neurology, 1991-94; med. dir. Neurology Ctr. Ohio, Toledo, 1994—, dir., 1994-96. Contbr. chpts. to books; guest editor jour. Seminars in Neurology, 1986. Bd. dirs. Ohio Rsch. Ctr., Toledo, 1994-97. Recipient Robert J. Tidrick award Med. Coll. Ohio, 1991. Mem. Am. Soc. Neuroimaging (bd. dirs. 1984-90).

GÉRARD, JEAN-PIERRE, oncologist; b. Lyon, France, Jan. 10, 1944; MD, U. Claude Bernard Lyon, 1972. Dept. radiotherapy oncology head CHU Lyon-Sud, 1980—2001; dean Faculté de Médecine Lyon-Sud, 1994—99; directeur général, CEO Ctr. Anti-cancéreux Antoine Lacassagne, Nice, 2001—09. Pres. ESTRO European Soc. Therapeutic Radiation Oncology, 1999—2001. Mem.: ASCO, ASTRO, ESTRO, SFRO. Office: 33 av de Valombrose Nice Alpes-Maritimes 06189 France Business E-Mail: jean-pierre.gerard@nice.fnclcc.fr.

GERARD, PERRY, nuclear medicine physician, educator, radiologist; Attended, Ross. U., Rouseau, Dominica. Diplomate Am. Bd. of Radiology, cert. nuclear cardiology, level 2 cardiovascular ct angiography. Intern Lutheran Med. Ctr., Brooklyn, NY; resident Maimonides Med. Ctr.; assoc. prof. radiology MY Med. Coll., Valhalla, NY, vice chmn. nuclear medicine & radiology. Recipient Radiology Attending of the Year award, Maimonides Med. Ctr., 2005, Tchg. Recognition award, Westchester Med. Ctr., 2010; named one of Top Doctors, Castle Connolly, 1999—2010, Best Doctors, MY Mags., 2003—04, 2006—10. Office: Westchester Medical Center 100 Woods Rd Valhalla NY 10595 Office Phone: 914-493-7000.

GERARDI, PAUL, cardiologist, educator; b. Bklyn., Apr. 26, 1949; BS, Fordham U., 1981; MD, Tufts U., 1985. Cert. Internal Medicine, 1988, Cardiovascular Disease, 1991. Intern internal medicine North Shore U. Hosp., Manhasset, NY, 1985—86, resident cardiology, 1986—88, fellowship cardiology, 1988—90; acting staff mem. Sound Shore Med. Ctr., New Rochelle, NY, 1990; asst. attending cardiology Westchester County Med. Ctr., Valhalla, NY, 1990, NY Presbyn. Hosp., 2000—; staff mem. Greenwich Hosp., Conn., 2003—; cardiologist Sound Shore Cardiology, P.C., New Rochelle, NY. Adj. asst. clin. prof. Weill Med. Coll., Cornell U., 2000, now clin. asst. prof. medicine. Office: Sound Shore Cardiology PC 175 Memorial Hwy New Rochelle NY 10801 also: 933 Mamaroneck Ave Mamaroneck NY 10543 Office Phone: 914-235-3535, 914-698-2056. Office Fax: 914-235-4108, 914-698-2417.

GERBER, DIANE, plastic surgeon; BA, Vassar Coll., 1973; MD, Columbia U. Coll. of Physicians & Surgeons, 1977. Cert. Am. Bd. of Plastic Surgery, 1984. Residency in gen. surgery Northwestern U., 1977—80, residency in plastic surgery, 1980—83; pvt. practice. Named one of Top Cosmetic Surgeons, Town & Country mag., Top Doctors, Chicago mag. Mem.: AMA, Lipoplasty Soc. of N. Am., Am. Assn. for Accreditation of Ambulatory Surgery Facilities, Chicago Soc. of Plastic Surgery, Chicago Med. Soc., Ill. State Medical Soc., Am. Coll. of Surgeons, Am. Soc. for Aesthetic Plastic Surgery, Am. Soc. of Plastic Surgeons (chmn. young plastic surgeons comm.). Office: 680 N Lake Shore Dr Ste 930 Chicago IL 60611

GERBER, GWENDOLYN LORETTA, psychologist, educator; b. Calgary, Alta., Can. came to U.S., 1958; d. Ernest and Alma (Tesky) G. AB, UCLA, 1961, MA, 1964, PhD, 1967; cert. in psychoanalysis, NYU, 1970. Lic. psychologist, N.Y. Clin. psychologist Hillside Hosp., Glen Oaks, N.Y., 1970-73; asst. prof. psychology John Jay Coll. of Criminal Justice CUNY, NYC, 1973-77, assoc. prof. psychology, 1977-90, prof., 1991—; pvt. practice in psychotherapy NYC, 1970—. Contbr. chapters to books, articles to profl. jours. USPHS fellow, 1962-63, 66-67, NIMH fellow, 1967-69; CUNY grantee, 1989-92, 99-2000, 2002-05, 45 Found. grantee, 1991-96. Fellow: APA (bd. dirs. sect. III 1988—92, liaison divsn. 35 1989—, bd. dirs. sect. III 1994—95, bd. dirs. divsn. 39 1997—2005), N.Y. Acad. Scis. (chair psychology com. 1992—2010, mem. steering com.); mem.: N.Y. State Psychol. Assn. (pres. acad. divsn. 1989—90, coun. rep. 1991—96, 2003—05, pres. acad. divsn. 2007, coun. rep. 2009—, William Wundt award 1993, Disting. svc. award 1996, Kurt Lewin award 1999), Phi Beta Kappa, Psi Chi, Chi Delta Pi. Office: John Jay Coll CUNY 445 W 59th St New York NY 10019-1104

GERBER, MINJA, research scientist; b. Johannesburg, Mar. 10, 1979; B in Pharmacy, Potchefstroom U. Christian Higher Edn., 2001; PhD, NW U., South Africa, 2007. Rschr. NW U., 2008—. Mem.: Pharm. Soc. South Africa, CosChem Cosmetic Soc., South African Pharmacy Coun. Avocations: singing, bicycling. Office: 11 Hoffman St Potchefstroom North West 2531 South Africa Office Fax: 2718 293 5219. Business E-Mail: minja.gerber@nwu.ac.za.

GERBER, NANCY, art educator, director; b. Phila., Mar. 24, 1946; MS, Hahnemann U., 1977; PhD, Union Inst. & U., 2004. Dir., grad. art therapy edn. MA program Drexel U., 1996—2010, dir., PhD program creative arts therapies, 2010—. Sr. lectr. U. Arts, 1997—2011. Mem.: Assoc. Psychoanalytic therapy, Phila. Psychoanalytic Ctr., Del. Valley Art Therapy Assn. (hon. mem.), Am. Art Therapy Assn. (Disting. Educator award). Avocations: drawing, painting, music. Office: 1505 Race St MS 905 Philadelphia PA 19102 Office Fax: 215-762-6933. Business E-Mail: ng27@drexel.edu.

GERBER, NAOMI LYNN HURWIRTZ, physiatrist, educator; AB magna cum laude, Smith Coll., 1965; MA, Harvard U., 1966; MA, MD, Tufts U., 1971. Lic. Md., 1974, DC, 1988, Va., 2006, diplomate Nat. Bd. Med. Examiners, 1971, Am. Bd. Internal Medicine, 1975, Am. Bd. Physical Medicine and Rehab., 1979. Intern in medicine New England Med. Ctr., Boston, 1971—72, resident in medicine, 1972—73; clin. assoc. arthritis and rheumatism br. NIH, Bethesda, Md., 1973—75, chief rehab medicine, 1976—2005, panel chief orthopedic surgery, 1984—99; resident in physical medicine and rehab. George Washington U., Washington, 1975—77, adj. prof. internal medicine, 1975—98; clin. prof. physical medicine and rehab. Georgetown U., Washington, 1988—90, clin. prof. internal medicine, 1992—; med. staff Nat. Rehab. Hosp., Washington, 1995—; dir. Ctr. for the study of Chronic Illness and Disability George Mason U., Fairfield, Va., 2006—, prof. rehab. sci., 2006—, prof. biostatistics, 2007—. Recipient Commendation medal, USPHS, 1980, Exemplary Svc. plaque, 1989, Women in Sci. and Engring. award, 1986, GEICO Pub. Svc. award, 1990, Dir.'s award for Outstanding Leadership, NIH, 1992, Health Advocate award, Am. Occupational Therapy Assn., 1996, Debbra Flomenhoft Humanitarian award, Am. Physical Therapy Assn., 2001, Disting. Academician award, Assn. Academic Physiatrists, 2003, Goldenson award, United Cerebral Palsy Found., 2003, Disting. Svc. award, Am. Acad. Physical Medicine and Rehab., 2006, Disting. Alumna award, Smith Coll., 2008. Mem.: Inst. Medicine, Am. Acad. Physical Medicine and Rehab. Office: Ctr Study of Chronic Illness and Disability George Mason U 4400 Univ Dr 5B7 Fairfax VA 22030

GERBER, STEVEN L., internist; MD, Temple U. Diplomate Am. Bd. Internal Medicine. Intern Overlook Hosp., Summit, NJ, resident; fellow Cleveland Clinic, Ohio, Univ. of Med. & Dentistry of NJ; hosp. affiliations include Virtua Hosp. Berlin, Virtua Hosp. Marlton, Virtua Hosp. Voorhees. Named one of the Top Doctor, Phila. Mag., 2011. Office: Virtua Main Corporate Office Lake Ctr Bldg 50 Ste 401 401 Route 73 N Marlton NJ 08053 Office Phone: 856-355-6000.

GERBER, SUSAN I., public health service officer; b. 1961; married; 1 child. BA in Biochemistry, U. Ill. Urbana-Champaign, 1983; MD, Loyola U. Stritch Sch. Medicine, 1987. Chief resident dept. pediat. U. Chgo., 1987—90, fellow dept. pediat. and infectious diseases, 1991—94, attending physician dept. pediat. and infectious diseases, 1994—96; post-doctoral rschr. dept. microbiology and immunization Northwestern Meml. Hosp., 1996—98; med. dir. dept. communicable disease Chgo. Dept. Pub. Health, 1998—2007, chief med. officer, 2007—. Contbr. articles to profl. jours.

GERBERDING, JULIE LOUISE, pharmaceutical company executive, former federal agency administrator; b. Estelline, SD, Aug. 26, 1955; m. David Rose; 1 stepchild, Renada. BA in Chemistry & Biology, Case Western Reserve U., Cleve., 1971, MD, 1981; MPH, U. Calif., Berkeley, 1990. Intern and resident, internal medicine U. Calif., San Francisco, chief med. resident, fellow in clin. pharmacology and infectious diseases, assoc. prof. medicine, epidemiology and biostatistics; clin. prof. medicine (infectious disease) Emory U.; founder, dir., Epidemiology Prevention and Interventions Ctr. San Francisco Gen. Hosp., 1987—98; dir., divsn. healthcare quality promotion Centers for Disease Control & Prevention (CDC), US Dept. Health & Human Services, Atlanta, 1998—2001, acting dep. dir. sci., 2001—02, dir., 2002—09; adminstr. Agy. for Toxic Substances and Disease Registry (ATSDR), 2002—09; pres. Merck Vaccines Merck & Co., Inc., Whitehouse Station, NJ, 2010—. Mem. Mayor's AIDS Task Force City of San Francisco, 1985—87; dir., Prevention Epicenter U. Calif., San Francisco; mem., scientific program com. Nat. Conf. on Retroviruses CDC, mem., HIV adv. com., mem., scientific program com., Nat. Ctr. for Infectious Diseases; cons. NIH, AMA, Occupational Safety and Health Adminstrn., Nat. AIDS Commn., U.S. Congress, Congl. Office Tech. Assessment, and WHO.; invited spkr. in field. Edtl. bd. Annals Internal Medicine, assoc. editor Am. Jour. Medicine, peer-reveiwer for numerous types of jours. in the field, contbr. to profl. publs. and textbooks. Recipient Disting. Svc. award, US Dept. Health & Human Services (HHS), 2001, Case Med. Alumni Assn. Disting. Alumnus/a award, Case Western Reserve U., 2003, President's award for Disting. Alumni, 2004; named one of The 100 Most Powerful Women, Forbes mag., 2005—08, The 100 Most Influential People in the World, TIME mag., 2004. Fellow: Infectious Diseases Soc. Am. (chair and co-chair com. profl. devel. and diversity, mem. nominations com., co-chair. annual program com.); mem.: ACP, Nat. Acad. Pub. Adminstrn., Inst. Medicine, Am. Epidemiology Soc., Soc. for Healthcare Epidemiology Am. (mem. AIDS/Tuberculosis com., bd. acad. counselor), Am. Soc. Clin. Investigation, Alpha Omega Alpha, Phi Beta Kappa. Achievements include being the first female director for the CDC. Avocations: scuba diving, reading, gardening. Office: Merck & Co Inc 1 Merck Dr Whitehouse Station NJ 08889 *

GERBES, ALEXANDER L., medical educator; Degree, U. Munich, 1981, cert. in internal medicine, 1991, cert. in gastroenterology, 1993. Staff physician Klinikum Munich-Grosshadern, Munich, 1983—90, asst. prof., 1992—2000, vice dir. dept. med., 2001—; head Liver Ctr. Munich, 2008—; invited rschr. lab molecular genetics Clin. Rsch.

Inst., Montreal, 1991—92. Prof. internal medicine U. Munich, 1995—. Assoc. editor: Gut, 2007; dep. editor Gut, 2010—; contbr. articles to profl. jours. Grantee, Deutsche Forschungsgemeinschaft, 1989—94, 1996—99, 1999—2001, 2001—, Friedrich-Baur-Stifung, 1994, Gesellschaft Gastroentrologie Bayern, 1998. Fellow: Am. Gastroent. Assn.; mem.: German Transplant Assn., German Soc. Verdauungs and Stoffwechselkrnkheiten, European Assn. Study Liver, German Assn. Medicine, Am. Fedn. Clin. Rsch., Am. Assn. Study Liver Disease. Office: Klinikum U Munich-Grosshadern Marchioninistr 15 Munich 81377 Germany Office Fax: +49-89-7095-2392. E-mail: gerbes@med.uni-muenchen.de.

GERDES, HANS, gastroenterologist; MD, Cornell U., 1983. Diplomate Am. Bd. Internal Medicine, Am. Bd. Internal Medicine-gastroenterology. Resident internal medicine NY Hosp., NYC, 1983—86; fellow gastroenterology Meml. Sloan-Kettering Cancer Ctr., NYC, 1986—89, gastroenterology and nutrition svc. Office: Memorial Sloan-Kettering Cancer Center 1275 York Ave New York NY 10065 Office Phone: 212-639-7108.

GERDING, DALE NICHOLAS, internist, medical educator; b. Belgrade, Minn., May 16, 1940; s. Eugene and Lorraine Gerding; m. Mary Borgerding; 3 children. BS in Physics and Math., St. John's U., Minn., 1962; MD, U. Minn., Mpls., 1968. Diplomate Am. Bd. Internal Medicine, cert. in infectious diseases. Space sys. analyst Hughes Aircraft Co., El Segundo, Calif., 1962-64; intern internal medicine Peter Bent Brigham Hosp., Boston, 1968-69; rsch. assoc. NIH, Bethesda, Md., 1969-71; resident internal medicine U. Minn. Hosp., 1971-73; fellow infectious disease VA Med Ctr., Mpls., 1973—75; asst. prof. medicine U. Minn., 1975—79, assoc. prof., 1979—86, prof. medicine, 1986—92; prof. medicine, assoc. chmn. Feinberg Sch. Medicine, Northwestern U., Chgo., 1992—2003; prof. medicine Loyola U. Chgo. Stritch Sch. Medicine, Maywood, Ill., 2003—. Med. cons. MSI Ins., St. Paul, 1973—92; staff physician VA Med Ctr., Mpls., 1974—80, chief infectious diseases, 1980—92; chief medicine Va. Lakeside Med. Ctr., Chgo., 1992—2003; assoc. chief of staff, rsch. & devel. Edward Hines, Jr. VA Hosp., Ill., 2003—. Contbr. articles to profl. jours., chapters to books. Surgeon USPHS, 1969—71. Fellow: Infectious Disease Soc. America (bd. dirs. 2005—08); mem.: Am. Soc. Microbiology, Soc. Hosp. Epidemiologists America (sec. 1993, pres. 2000), VA Soc. Infectious Diseases (pres. 1990—92), Alpha Omega Alpha. Roman Catholic. Avocations: fishing, antique collecting. Office: Loyola U Med Ctr Dept Medicine 2160 S First Ave Maywood IL 60153 Business E-Mail: dale.gerding2@va.gov. *

GERE, GÉZA, biologist, ecologist, educator, researcher; b. Budapest, Hungary, Aug. 19, 1927; s. Géza and Anna (Szöke) G.; m. Maria Pogány, Oct. 5, 1928; m. Maria Wagner, Mar. 20, 1939; children: Tibor, Zsolt, Dénes, Tamás, Laszló, Pál. Student, Eötvös Loránd U., Budapest, 1945-50, PhD, 1960; DSc, Hungarian Acad. Scis., Budapest, 1981. From asst. prof. to prof. Eötvös Lorand U., Budapest, 1950-88, prof., 1988—. Leader zool. rsch. Kis-Balaton Area, Hungary, 1984—; dir. PhD program zool. Etvös Loránd U., Budapest, 1995—. Co-author: Hungarian Encyclopaedia, 1990; contbr. over 100 articles to profl. jours. Mem. Corp. Body Hungarian Acad. Scis. (zool. com. 1990-96, 99—, ecol. com. 1996-99, hydrobiol. com. 1996-2002), N.Y. Acad. Sci. Office: Eötvös Loránd U Pázmány Péter Sétány 1/c H 1117 Budapest Hungary Home: Bereck Utca 5 1118 Budapest Hungary E-mail: gere27@freemail.hu.

GERECITANO, JOHN FRANK, oncologist, educator; b. NY, June 25, 1969; BS, Cornell U., 1992; MD, NYU, 2000, PhD. Asst. attending physician Meml. Sloan-Kettering Cancer Ctr., 2006—. Clin. educator Weil Cornell Sch. Medicine, 2006—. Recipient Tchg. award, Meml. Sloan-Kettering Cancer Ctr. Mem.: Am. Soc. Clin. Oncology, Am. Soc. Hematology. Avocations: photography, cooking. Office: Dept Medicine 1275 York Ave New York NY 10065 Office Fax: 646 422 2285. Business E Mail: gerecitj@mskcc.org.

GERETY, ROBERT JOHN, microbiologist, researcher, pediatrician, pharmaceutical executive, drug developer; b. Jersey City, Oct. 16, 1939; s. James Leo and Helen (Beck) G.; m. Joan Imelda Grant, Feb. 3, 1967; children: Andrew, Kathleen, Nancy. BA with spl. honors, Rutgers U., 1962; MA, Stanford U., 1966, PhD, 1971; MD, George Washington U., 1970. Diplomate Nat. Bd. Med. Examiners. Rsch. assoc. dept. med. microbiology Stanford (Calif.) U. Med. Sch., 1969-70; intern in pediatrics Stanford U. Hosp., 1970-71, resident, 1974-75; staff assoc. Lab. Viral Immunology, NIH, Bethesda, Md., 1971-72; staff assoc. Bur. Biologics, FDA, Bethesda, 1972-73, dir. hepatitis br., 1973-84, assoc. dir. medicine and sci., chief infectious diseases br., 1984-85; exec. dir. virus & cell biology Merck Rsch. Labs., West Point, Pa., 1985-89, chief clin. evaluation of vaccines and antiviral drugs, 1985-89; v.p. devel. ops. Biogen, Inc., Cambridge, Mass., 1989-93; v.p. pharm. ops. Immulogic Pharm. Corp., Waltham, Mass., 1993-94, CEO, pres. and dir., 1994-96; v.p. devel. and regulatory affairs ORAVAX, Cambridge, Mass., 1997-99; exec. v.p. corp. devel. Cell Gate Inc., Sunnyvale, Calif., 1999-2000; v.p. regulatory affairs and clin. ops. Inhale Therapeutic Sys., San Carlos, Calif., 2000—02; v.p., head proprietary products, prin. devel. fellow Nektar Therapeutics, San Carlos, 2002—07; chief devel. officer Medicine in Need, Cambridge, Mass., 2007—. Mem. exec. com. Nektar Bus. Rev., chmn. product develop. team; adj. prof. medicine Jefferson Med. Sch., Phila., 1985; Plenary lectr. Internat. Symposium on Viral Hepatitis and Liver Disease, London, 1987; mem. U.S. Army Med. R&D Adv. Bd., 1987; mem. AIDS subcom. Nat. Inst. Allergy and Infectious Diseases, 1988; mem. Nat. Vaccine Adv. Com., 1990-92, sci. bd. Oravax, Cambridge, Mass., 1991-94; cons. Max-Cyte, 2000-, Visterra Inc., 2007-, Scidose, 2007-, numerous others; chief devel. officer Medicine in Need, 2007-; participant confs., symposia and workshops. Editor: Non-A, Non-B Hepatitis, 1981, Hepatitis A, 1984, Hepatitis B, 1985; mem. editl. bd. Biols., 1990-94; contbr. over 200 articles to sci. jours. Med. dir. USPHS, 1970-85. Recipient commendation medal USPHS, 1975, Outstanding Svc. medal, 1982, Disting. Svc. medal, 1985; Patriotic Svc. award U.S. Dept. Treasury, 1983; Henry Rutgers fellow, 1961-62, fellow NIH, 1962-65, Calif. Tb and Health Assn., 1964-67, U.S. Health Professions scholar and microbiology fellow, 1966-70. Fellow Infectious Disease Soc. Am.; mem. AMA, Am. Soc. for Microbiology, Am. Acad. Pediatrics, Am. Assn. Immunologists, William Beaumont Soc., Henry Rutgers Soc., Internat. assn. for Biol. Standards, Internat. Soc. Interferon Rsch. Achievements include major contribution to development and/or approval of vaccine against Hepatitis A and Hepatitis B, pediatric vaccines including Hemophilus Influenza B and varicella, Biogen's beta interferon product to treat multiple sclerosis (Avonex) Medicines Company's product (Angiomax) direct thrombin inhibitor); patents for Inactivation of Non-A, Non-B Hepatitis Agent; Hepatitis B Immune Globulin used to Inactivate Hepatitis B Virus in Injectable Biological Products; Detection of Non-A, Non-B Hepatitis Associated Antigen; Heat Treatment of a Non-A, Non-B Hepatitis Agent to Prepare a Vaccine; Hepatitis B Core Antigen Vaccine; Hepatitis B Core Antigen Vaccine Made by Recombinant DNA; Purified Antigen from Non-A, Non-B Hepatitis Causing Factor: Screening Test for Reverse Transcriptase Containing Viruses in human blood. Home: 103 Livingston Rd Wellesley MA 02482 E-mail: yteregb@yahoo.com.

GERHARD, H. JOHN, orthopaedic surgeon, retired military officer; b. Portsmouth, Va., Oct. 29, 1955; s. Harry E. and Barbara M. Gerhard; m. Dianne Heath, Aug. 17, 1990; children: Christopher Ansley, Katherine Leigh, J. Stephen, Ian Jonas. BS, US Naval Acad., 1977; MD, Harvard U., Boston, 1981; MS, Indsl. Coll. Armed Forces, 1998. Diplomate Am. Bd. Orthopaedic Surgery, cert. naval flight surgeon Naval Aerospace Med. Inst. Commd. Ens. USN, 1977, advanced through grades to capt.; intern Naval Regional Med. Ctr. San Diego, 1981—82; flight surgeon Carrier Air Wing Two, NAS Miramar, Calif., 1982—84; orthopaedic surgery resident Duke U. Med. Ctr., Durham, NC, 1984—89, fellow hand and upper extremity surgery, 1992—93; staff orthopaedic surgeon Naval Hosp., Camp Lejeune, NC, 1989—92, dir. clin. svcs.; chief orthopaedics, staff orthopaedic surgeon, 1993—96; staff orthopaedic surgeon Brigade Svc. Support Group 4, Ops. Desert Shield/Storm, Iraq, 1990—91, USNS Comfort, Operation Uphold Democracy, Haiti, 1994; physician adviser to pres. Nat. Def. U., Ft McNair, DC, 1996—97; force surgeon USMC Forces, Atlantic, Europe, South, Norfolk, Va., 1998—2001; staff orthopaedic hand surgeon Naval Med. Ctr., Portsmouth, Va., 2001—02; exec. officer/COO Naval Hosp., Beaufort, SC, 2002—05, commdg. officer/CEO Lemoore, Calif., 2005—07. Presenter in field. Decorated various campaign and svc. medals/ribbons Dept. Navy, Ground Combat Action ribbon, Navy And Marine Corps Commendation medal, Meritorious Svc. medal, Legion Of Merit,; recipient USN Surgeon Gen.'s award, Naval Aerospace Med. Inst., Pensacola, Fl, 1980; Trident scholar, US Naval Acad. Fellow: Am. Acad. Orthopaedic Surgeons; mem.: Piedmont Orthopaedic Soc. Office: James A Haley Veterans Hosp Tampa FL 33612 Home: 21031 Picasso Ct # 4202 Land O Lakes FL 34639 Personal E-mail: d89f04@aol.com. Business E-Mail: h.john.gerhard@va.gov.

GERHART, GLENNA LEE, pharmacist; b. Houston, June 11, 1954; d. Henry Edwin and Gloria Mae (Mrnustik) G. BS in Pharmacy, U. Houston, 1977. Registered pharmacist, Tex. Staff pharmacist Meml. City Med. Ctr., Houston, 1977—84; asst. dir. pharmacy Meml. Hosp.-Meml. City Med. Ctr., Houston, 1984-98; pharmacy supr. Meml. Hermann-Meml. City Hosp. Pharmacy, Houston, 1998—; investigational drug pharmacist Meml. City Med. Ctr., Houston, 2000—; staff pharmacist Christus St. Catherine Health and Wellness Ctr., 2000—02. Active Humane Soc. US. Mem.: AARP, Tex. Czech Heritage Soc., Pharm. and Therapeutics Soc., Houston-Galveston Area Soc. Hosp. Pharmacists, Tex. Soc. Health-Sys. Pharmacists, Tex. Pharm. Assn., Am. Soc. Hosp. Pharmacists, Am. Pharm. Assn., Nat. Birman Fanciers, U. Houston Alumni Orgn. (life), Houston SPCA, Humane Soc. U.S., Nat. Cougar Club, Houston Cat Club, 100 CLub (life), Slavonic Benevolent Order of Tex. SPJST Lodge #88, Kappa Epsilon. Methodist. Avocations: reading, gardening, walking, raising cats. Home: 25527 Winston Hollow Katy TX 77494 Office: Memorial Hermann-Memorial City Hosp 929 Gessner Houston TX 77024-2312 Personal E-mail: glennacat@aol.com. Business E-Mail: glenna.gerhart@memorialhermann.org

GERL, ROBERT RAYMOND, psychologist, priest; b. Milw., Feb. 10, 1951; s. Evelyn Pauline (Sobocinski) and Clarence William Gerl. BA in Theology and Psychology, St. Francis DeSales Coll., Milw., 1973; MA in Psychology, Radford U., Va., 1974; MTS in Theology and Behavioral Sci., St. Francis Sem., Milw., 1977; D in Min., St. Mary's Sem. and U., Balt., 1986; ABD, Mich. State U., East Lansing, 1990; PhD in Psychology, Capella U., Mnpls., 2005. Cert. Criminal Justice Specialist Endorsement Nat. Bd. Addiction Examiners, 1997, Approved Supr. Am. Assn. for Marriage and Family Therapy, 1997, Substance Abuse Profl. US Dept. Transp., 2001. Faculty Cardinal Stritch Coll., Milw., 1974—77; deacon St. Patrick Parish, Brighton, Mich., 1978—79; priest Ch. of the Resurrection, Lansing, Mich., 1979—82, St. Gerard Parish, Lansing, 1982—85; faculty Nazareth Coll., Kalamazoo, 1986—91; v.p. for academic affairs, COO St. Catharine Coll., Ky., 1991—97; campus min. St. Thomas More Cath. Student Parish, Kalamazoo, 1997—2000; therapist, counselor, psychologist Cath. Family Svcs., Kalamazoo, 1998—, 1998—; sch. psychologist Allegan Area Edn. Svcs. Agy., Mich., 2000—06; faculty Davenport U., Kalamazoo, 2001—06, U. Phoenix. West Mich., Grand Rapids, 2005—; therapist, counselor, psychologist Desert Streams Group Practice, Kalamazoo, 2006—; faculty Spring Arbor U., Mich., 2006—, U. Phoenix. West Mich., Grand Rapids. Fellow Ky. Ednl. Reform Act Program, Louisville, 1992—94; cons., adult educator Archdiocese of Louisville, 1992—95; bd. mem. Coun. for Human Svc. Edn., Fitchburg, Mass., 1988—91; MA intern supr. Cath. Family Svcs., Kalamazoo, 1998—2006; adult edn. cons. Diocese of Kalamazoo, 1998—2006. Mem. Rotary Club, Springfield, Ky., 1992—95; adult edn. Parishes of Diocese of Kalamazoo, 1987—2006; bd. mem. Pretty Lake Adventure Camp, Kalamazoo, 2000—01. Title III planning Grant, US Dept. Edn., 1992, Endowment Challenge Grant, 1994, Grant, Gheens Found., 1993, Alliant Health, 1994, Renovation grant for Nursing program, James Graham Brown Found., 1994. Mem.: NASP, APA, Mich. Psychol. Assn., Mich. Assn. for Marriage and Family Therapy (election com. 2003—06), Am. Counseling Assn., Am. Assn. for Marriage and Family Therapy. Achievements include research in the effect of religious education on socialization of children; design of a weekend model for discovering adult transitions; research in the effect of parental stress on the development of emotional competence of adolescents. Home: 1538 Evanston Ave Kalamazoo MI 49008 Office: Allegan Area Edn Svcs Agy 212 Grove St Allegan MI 49010 Office Phone: 269-760-3318. Personal E-mail: robert1051@aol.com. Business E-Mail: rgerl@alleganaesa.org.

GERMAIN, PAMELA, health facility administrator, educator; b. Buffalo, Feb. 17, 1952; d. Philip William and Alma Thering Germain; children: Constantine Skagias, Amelia Katerina Skagias. BA in Econs., LeMoyne Coll., Syracuse, NY, 1973; MBA, Harvard U., Boston, 1985. Dist. mgr. comml. lines casualty property The Travelers, Worcester, Mass., 1981—83; assoc. dir. external rels. Harvard Bus. Sch., Boston, 1985—87; dir. corp. strategy and bus. diversification group The Travelers, Hartford, Conn., 1987—88; divsn. v.p. managed care and employee benefits ops. divsn. The Travelers Corp., Hartford, 1988—93; dir. network devel. and ops., COO MFHS Managed Care, Inc. Millard Fillmore Health Sys., Buffalo, 1995—97; v.p. managed care and outreach Roswell Pk. Cancer Inst., Buffalo, 1998—. Lectr. mgmt. devel. programs Harvard Bus. Sch. Club, Buffalo, 1995—; adj. faculty D'Youville Coll., Buffalo, 2004—05; products and svcs. com. mem. Nat. Comprehensive Cancer Network, Phila., 1997—; presenter in field. Bd. mem. Mid-Erie Treatment and Counseling Svcs., Buffalo, 1996—, pres., 2005—07. Roman Catholic. Avocations: travel, cultural arts, walking. Home: 59 Round Trail Rd West Seneca NY 14218-3723 Office: Roswell Park Cancer Institute Elm & Carlton Sts Buffalo NY 14263 Home (Summer): 29 Gen Lawrence Rd South Yarmouth MA 02664 Office Fax: 716-845-1610; Home Fax: 716-677-5515. Personal E-mail: pgermainsk@aol.com. Business E-Mail: pamela.germain@roswellpark.org.

GERMAN, DONALD FREDERICK, physician; b. San Francisco, Oct. 2, 1935; m. Marilyn Sue King; children: Susan, Charles, Donald. BS, U. San Francisco, 1956; MD, U. Calif., San Francisco, 1960. Diplomate Am. Bd. Pediats., Am. Bd. Allergy and Immunology. Intern Kaiser Found. Hosp., San Francisco, 1960-61, resident in pediats., 1963-65, fellow in allergy, 1966-68; staff pediatrician Kaiser Med. Ctr., Santa Clara, Calif., 1965-66, staff allergist, 1968-69; chief dept. allergy Kaiser Permanente Med. Ctr., San Francisco, 1969-99, allergy staff physician, 1999—. Clin. prof. pediatrics U. Calif. Med. Sch., San Francisco, 1991—; bd. dirs. Asthma, Allergy and Immunology Found. No. Calif. Capt. USAF, 1961-63. Fellow Am. Acad. Pediats., Am. Coll. Allergy and Immunology, Am. Acad. Allergy and Immunology; mem. Calif. Soc. Allergy and Immunology (past pres.). Avocations: running, hiking, fly fishing, travel. Address: 1030 Sir Francis Drake Blvd Ste 110 Kentfield CA 94904 Office Phone: 415-460-6686. Personal E-mail: dfgerman2@yahoo.com.

GERMENI, EVI, medical researcher; b. Athens, Nov. 28, 1979; BSc, U. Ioannina, 2002; PhD, Sch. Medicine, U. Crete, 2010. Rsch. scientist dept. hygiene, epidemiology and med. stats. Athens U. Med. Sch., 2006—. Mem.: Hellenic Soc. Social Pediat. and Health Promotion. Home: 15 Epigenous St Athens Attica 11143 Greece Personal E-mail: evigerm@yahoo.gr.

GERNER, EDWARD WILLIAM, medical educator; b. NYC, Nov. 8, 1940; s. David and Anne (Robbins) G.; m. Judith E. Delbaum, June 5, 1983; 1 child, Danielle. BA magna cum laude, Clark U., 1961; MD, NYU, 1965. Diplomate Am. Bd. Ophthalmology, Am. Bd. Neurology. Intern Presbyn. U. Pitts. Hosp., 1965-66; resident Hosp. U. Pa., Phila., 1967-69; instr. dept. neurology U. Pa. Sch. Medicine, Phila., 1967-69, instr. dept. ophthalmology, 1972-74; attending neurologist Tulane U. Sch. Medicine, New Orleans, 1969-71; asst. surgeon Wills Eye Hosp., Phila., 1981-88, assoc. surgeon, 1988—; asst. prof. dept. neurology T. Jefferson U. Sch. Medicine, Phila., 1978-88, asst. prof. dept. ophthalmology, 1982-88, assoc. prof., 1988—. Bd. dirs. Pa. Physicians Healthcare Plan, Harrisburg. Contbr. chpts. to books and articles to profl. jours. Lt. comdr. USPHS, 1969-72. N.Y. State Regent scholar N.Y. State Bd. Regents, 1957-61; Jones fellow Mayo Clinic, Rochester, Minn., 1965. Fellow Am. Acad. Ophthalmology, Am. Acad. Neurology; mem. Royal Soc. Medicine (affiliate), Phi Beta Kappa. Avocations: photography, gardening. Office: 1015 Chestnut St # 1125 Philadelphia PA 19107-5127 Office Phone: 215-928-1212.

GERRITSEN, MARY ELLEN, vascular and cell biologist; b. Calgary, Alta., Can., Sept. 20, 1953; arrived in US, 1978; d. Thomas Clayton and Alice Irene (Minton) Cooper; m. Paul William Gerritsen, May 24, 1975 (div. 1977); m. Thomas Patrick Parks, Oct. 11, 1980; children: Kristen, Madelene. BSc summa cum laude, U. Calgary, 1975, PhD, 1978. Postdoctoral fellow U. Calif., San Diego, 1978-80; asst. prof. N.Y. Med. Coll., Valhalla, 1981-86, assoc. prof., 1986-90, sr. staff scientist Pharm. divsn. Bayer Corp., West Haven, Conn., 1990-93, head inflammation exploratory rsch., 1990-96, prin. staff scientist, 1993-97; vis. scientist Harvard U., 1996; assoc. dir. cardiovasc. rsch. Genentech, South San Francisco, 1997—2001; sr. dir. Millennium Pharms., South San Francisco, 2003—04; v.p. Molecular and Cellular Pharm., Exelixis Inc., South San Francisco, 2004—09, Med. Coll. Pharm., 2009—. Cons. Insite Vision, Alameda, Calif., 1987-89, Boehringer Ingelheim Pharms., Ridgefield, Conn., 1985-88, Xoma, Berkeley, Calif, 2003-04, Frazier Health Care Ventures, Palo Alto, Calif, 2003—, Macusight, Union City, Calif., 2004—10, Interim Corp., 2010-; adj. assoc. prof. N.Y. Med. Coll., 1990-99. Co-author: Masdevallias: Gems of the Orchid World, 2005, Calochortus, Mariposa Lilies and Their Relatives, 2007, Targeting Protein Kinases for Cancer Therapy, 2010; mem. editl. bd. Am. Jour. Physiology, 1983—90, Am. Jour. Cardiovasc. Pathology, 1996—98, Circulation Rsch., 1997—99, Endothelium, 1999—, editor-in-chief Microcirculation, 1993—98, cons. editor, 1998—2010; contbr. articles to profl. jours. Fellow I. W. Killam Found. 1976, Med. Rsch. Coun. Can. 1978-80; scholar Province Alb., Sinsheimer Scholar; recipient Kurt Weiderman award, Rsch. Career Devel. award NIH. Mem. Am. Soc. for Pharmacology and Exptl. Therapeutics, Am. Physiol. Soc., Am. Soc. Investigational Pathology, Microcirculatory Soc. (mem. coun. 1989-92, chairperson publs. com. 1991-93, Mary Weideman award 1985, Young Investigator award 1984), N.Am. Vascular Biology Orgn. (mem. steering com. 1993, mem. coun. 1994-97, editor-in-chief newsletter 1994-97, sec.-treas. 1997-99, pres. 1999, chair devel. com., 2004-05), Peninsula Orchid Soc. (bd. dirs. 2001, 09, 10, v.p. 2005-07, 10, pres. 2008), Am. Orchid Soc., San Francisco Orchid Soc., Pleurothallid Alliance, Orchid Digest. Avocations: orchids, horticulture, photography. Personal E-mail: meg570@comcast.net.

GERSON, MYRON CRAIG, cardiologist, researcher; b. Cleve., Oct. 27, 1947; s. Gerald and Estelle Anita Gerson; m. Joanne Steiner, June 21, 1969; children: Craig Alan, Linda Deborah. BA in Med. Scis., U. Wis., 1969; MD, Ind. U., Indpls., 1972. Diplomate Am. Bd. Internal Medicine. Cardiovasc. disease intern internal medicine Ind. U. Sch. Medicine, Indpls., 1972-73; resident Ind. U. Hosp., 1972-75, fellow in cardiology, 1977-79; prof. medicine and radiology, dir. cardiac exercise lab. U. Cin., 1979—. Acting dir. divsn. cardiology U. Cin., 2004—06. Editor: Cardiac Nuc. Medicine, 3d edit., 1997; editl. adv. bd. Jour. Nuc. Cardiology, 1993-95, editl. bd., 1996—; editl. bd. Am. Heart Jour., 1997—; contbr. articles to profl. jours. V.p. Ohio Cardiac Coun., Columbus, 1987-90. Maj. USAF, 1975-77. NIH grantee, 1989-92. Fellow Am. Coll. Cardiology (trustee Ohio chpt. 1994-96), Am. Heart Assn. (coun. clin. cardiology, coun. rep. Ohio 1989-92, grantee 1980-87, 92-94, 97-99); mem. Am. Soc. Nuclear

Cardiology (pres. 2006, founder, mem. exec. coun.). Avocation: bicycling. Office: U Cin Divsn Cardiology PO Box 670542 Cincinnati OH 45267-0542 Office Phone: 513-475-8521, 513-558-3074. *

GERSON, WILLIAM THOMAS, pediatrician; b. New Haven, Conn., June 22, 1956; AB, Harvard Coll., 1978; MD, John Hopkins U. Sch. Medicine, 1982. Cert. Pediat., lic. Mass., Vt. Intern and resident, pediat. Children's Hosp. Boston, Mass., 1982—85, chief resident, pediat. Mass., 1985—86, fellow, pediat. pulmonolgy Mass., 1986—88, asst. in medicine Mass., 1986—88, asst. dir., cystic fibrosis program Mass., 1986—88, attending physician, Pediat. Group Assoc. Mass., 1986—88; clin. fellow, pediat. Harvard Med. Sch., 1982—86, instr., pediat., 1986—88; assoc., pediat. Beth Israel Hosp., Boston, 1986—88; attending, pediat. Fletcher Allen Health Care, Burlington, Vt., 1988—, attending physician, pediat. intensive care unit, 1991—; clin. prof. U. Vt. Coll. Med., 1988—95, clin. assoc. prof., 1995—. Contbr. articles to profl. jours. Recipient Physician's Recognition award, AMA, 1993; named one of Best Doctors in America, 1996—97, 2002—03, 2005—06, 2007—08. Mem.: Alpha Omega Alpha, Phi Beta Kappa. Office: 52 Timber Ln South Burlington VT 05403 Office Phone: 802-658-2320. Office Fax: 802-863-6933.

GERSONY, WELTON MARK, pediatrician, cardiologist, educator; b. Syracuse, NY, Nov. 19, 1931; s. Irving and Ann (Cohen) Gersony; m. Susan Gersony; children: Neal, Anne, Richard, Deborah. AB, Syracuse U., 1954; MD, SUNY, Syracuse, 1958. Diplomate Am. Bd. Pediatrics, Am. Bd. Pediatric Cardiology. Intern Cleve. Met. Gen. Hosp., 1958-59, resident in pediat., 1959-61; resident in pediatrics Babies and Childrens Hosp., Cleve., 1959-61; fellow in cardiology Harvard U., 1963-65; asst. prof. pediat. U. Tex., Dallas, 1965-68; from asst. prof. to assoc. prof. Columbia U., 1968—74, prof., 1974—, Alexander S. Nadas prof., 2000—. Dir. divsn. pediatric cardiology Columbia-Presbyn. Med. Ctr., 1971—2005; prof. Cornell U., 1997—; dir. divsn. pediatric cardiology Columbia-Cornell Pediatric Cardiovasc. Ctr., 1999—2005, ped card fellowship dir., 1971—95; mem. Sub.-Bd. Pediatric Cardiology, 1976—83, chmn., 1981—83; vis. prof., named lectureships multiple US and Fgn. Med. Ctrs., mem. com. ofcl. examiners, 1983—90; vis. dir. pediatric cardiology Gt. Ormond St. Hosp. Sick Children, London, 1984—85; organizer 2d World Congress Pediatric Cardiology, NYC, 1985; cons. Extramural Affairs divsn. Nat. Heart Lung and Blood Inst., 1988—; steering com. chmn. World Congress Pediatric Cardiology and Cardiac Surgery, 1989—97, plenary lectr., 2001, plenary chair, 05; pres. faculty practice orgn. Coll. Physicians and Surgeons Columbia U., 2003—05; mem. adv. bd. Congress Pediat. Cardiology Internat., 1998—; steering com. mem. Vision 2020, Adult Congenital Heart Disease Assn., 2008—, bd. dirs., 2009—; chmn. publ. com. Pediat. Heart Network; lectr. in field. Author: Nelson's Textbook of Pediatrics, 1983, 3d edit., 1991, Congenital Heart Disease in the Adult, 2002; assoc. editor: The American Heart Association Consultant, 2001, 2d edit., 2006; assoc. editor 3rd edit., 2010, mem. editl. bd. Pediatric Cardiology, 1978—90, Jour. Pediat., 1986—93, Jour. Am. Coll. Cardiology, 1990—94, Cardiology in Young, 1990, Progress in Pediatric Cardiology, 1991—, Criculation, 1993—96; cons. editor: Criculation, 1996—2001; internat. adv. bd. Japanese Circulation Jour., 1996—2002, Cardiology, 2006—, World Jour. Pediat. Congenital Heart Surgery, 2010—; contbr. revs. to profl. jours., chapters to books. Mem. internat. com., bd. dirs. Internat. Cardiology Found., 1993—; mem. program com. Internat. Kawasaki Disease Chmn. Cardiology Symposium, 1989, 1992, 1995, 1998, 2001, 2007, hon. chmn., 2011. Capt. M.C. US Army, 1961—63. Recipient Disting. Practitioner award, Columbia U., 2005, NY Presbyn. Hosp., 2005, Disting. Alumnus award, SUNY, Syracuse, 2008, NY Presbyn. Columbia Soc. Alumni, 2010, NY Presbyn. Alumnus award, 2010, Disting. Tchg. award, 2011; grantee, Pediat. Heart Network, 2002—, Nat. Heart Lung and Blood Inst., 2006—; NIH grantee, 1977, 1983, 1993, 2002, Falkner fellow, U. Sydney, 1983. Master: Am. Contract Bridge League (life); fellow: Am. Acad. Pediat. (Cardiology Sect. Founders award 2007, Founders Lecture 2008), Am. Coll. Cardiology (named Disting. Tchr. 2011); mem.: AMA (cons. 1985—, accreditation coun. grad. med. edn. 1994—), Internat. Soc. Adult Congenital Heart Disease, Harvey Soc., Am. Fedn. Clin. Rsch., Assn. European Paediatric Cardiologists (corr.), Am. Heart Assn. (pres. coun. cardiovasc. disease in young 1989—90, T. Duckett Jones lectr. 1998, Disting. Achievement award 2003), Am. Pediatric Soc., Soc. Pediatric Rsch. Achievements include research in cardiovascular disease in infants, children and adults; natural history congenital heart disease in children; ductus arteriosus in premature infants; persistence of the fetal circulation; congenital coronary artery malformations. Office: Columbia U 630 W 168th St New York NY 10032-3795

GERST, PAUL HOWARD, physician; b. Sept. 24, 1927; s. David and Hilde (Werbel) G.; m. Elizabeth Carlsen, Aug. 3, 1957; children—Steven R., Jeffrey C., Andrew L. AB, Columbia U., 1948, MD, 1952. Diplomate: Am. Bd. Surgery, Am. Bd. Thoracic Surgery. Intern Columbia Presbyn. Med. Center, NYC, 1952-53, resident, 1956-62, mem. staff, 1962—; instr. physiology U. Pa., 1955-56; practice medicine specializing in surgery NYC, 1962—; asst. clin. prof. surgery Columbia U., 1964-72; prof. surgery Albert Einstein Coll. Medicine, 1972—2003. Dir. surgery Bronx-Lebanon Hosp. Ctr., NYC, 1964—2003 Contbr. articles to profl. jours. Served 1st lt. U.S. Army, 1953-55. USPHS postdoctoral fellow, 1955-56; recipient Rsch. Career Devel. award, 1964-65. Fellow ACS; mem. Am. Physiol. Soc., N.Y. Soc. for Thoracic Surgery, N.Y. Surg. Soc., N.Y. Soc. for Cardiovasc. Surgery, Am. Heart Assn. Home: 141 Tekening Dr Tenafly NJ 07670-1218 Fax: 201-569-5198. Personal E-mail: pgerst@msn.com.

GERSTENBERGER, PATRICK D., gastroenterologist; b. Vallejo, Calif., Dec. 13, 1953; AB, U. Calif., Berkeley, 1976; MD, Wash. U., St. Louis, 1980. Gastroenterologist Digestive Health Assocs., PC, 1985—. Bd. dirs. Am. Assn. Ambulatory Surgery Ctrs., 2001—05, Clin. Outcomes Rsch. Initiative, 2002—05. Fellow: Am. Gastroenterology Assn., Am. Soc. Gastrointestinal Endoscopy, Am. Coll. Gastroenterology; mem.: European Soc. Gastrointestinal Endoscopy. Avocations: kayaking, skiing, bicycling. Office: 2 Burnett Ct Durango CO 81301 Office Fax: 970-385-4337. Business E-Mail: pgerstenberger@digestivehealth.net.

GERSTENBLITH, GARY, medical educator, cardiologist; b. 1946; BA, NYU; JD, U. Md.; MD, U. Pa., Phila., 1971. Cert. cardiovasc. disease Md. Resident U. Pa. Hosp., Phila.; fellow Nat. Inst. on Aging, Jackson Meml. Hosp.; prof. medicine, dir. clinical rsch., divsn. cardiology Johns Hopkins Hosp., Balt., dir. Reynolds Ctr. Cardiovasc. Clinical Rsch. Tng. Program. Mem.: ABA. Avocations: boating, skiing. Office: Johns Hopkins Hosp Carnegie 591 600 N Wolfe St Baltimore MD 21287 Home: 12413 Knollcrest Rd Reisterstown MD 21136 Office Phone: 410-955-6835. Business E-Mail: gblith@mail.jhmi.edu.

GERTLER, MENARD M., physician, educator; b. Saskatoon, Sask., Can., May 21, 1919; arrived in U.S., 1947, naturalized, 1953; s. Frank and Clara (Handelman) G.; m. Anna Paull, Sept. 4, 1943; children: Barbara Lynn, Stephanie Jocelyn, Jonathan Paull. BA, U. Sask., Saskatoon, 1940; MD, McGill U., Montreal, 1943, MS, 1946, DSc (hon.), 2003, U. Sask., 2006; DSc, NYU, 1960. Intern Royal Victoria Hosp., Montreal, Que., Canada, 1943—44; resident Mass. Gen. Hosp., Boston, 1947—50; rsch. fellow in medicine Mass. Gen. Hosp., Harvard Med. Sch., 1947—50; dir. cardiology Francis Delafield divsn. Columbia Presbyn. Med. Ctr., NYC, 1950—54; spl. rsch. fellow NIH, NYU Dept. Biochemistry, 1954—56; prof. Sch. Medicine, dir. cardiovascular rsch. Rusk Inst. NYU Med. Ctr., 1958—71; sr. med. examiner FAA, 1975; dir. Washington Fed. Savs. & Loan Assn., 1972—83; adj. prof. medicine McGill U., 1996—; clin. prof. medicine N.Y. Hosp.-Cornell Med. Ctr., attending physician. Prof. medicine Weill Med. Sch., Cornell U.; attending physician N.Y. Hosp./Presbyn. Hosp., 1998—; med. dir. Sinclair Oil Corp., 1958-68; internat. cons. cardiovascular diseases, social and rehab. svcs. HEW, Washington, 1968-92. Author: Coronary Heart Disease in Young Adults, 1954, Coronary Heart Disease, 1974; Contbr. articles to profl. jours. Pres. Friends of McGill U., 1983-2001; mem. dean's com. McGill U. Med. Sch. With M.C., Royal Can. Army, 1940-43. Recipient Founders Day award NYU, 1959, medal of honor McGill U., 1993, award of merit McGill U., 1993, Yoda Meml. Gold medal, Rsch. Soc. of Grant, M Coll. and J.J. Hosp., Bombay, 1997. Mem. Gallatin Assocs. NYU, Cosmos Club (Washington), Harvard Club (Boston), Univ. Club. Home: 1385 York Ave Apt 16F New York NY 10021-3938

GERTZBEIN, STANLEY DAVID, orthopedic surgeon; b. Toronto, Can., Sept. 25, 1941; MD, U. Toronto, Can., 1966. Cert. Am. Bd. Orthop. Surgeons, Am. Bd. Spine Surgery. Fellow, orthop. surgery Royal Coll. Physicians and Surgeons (Can.), 1971; rsch. and clin. fellow Sunnybrook Med. Ctr., Toronto, 1972; spinal tng. London and Hong Kong, 1973; prof. U. Toronto, U. Tex. Med. Sch.; active staff mem. Christus St. Joseph Hosp., Houston; staff mem. Methodist Hosp., Houston; full prof., dept. orthop. surgery Baylor Coll. Medicine, Houston. Vis. prof. and guest lectr. at Colleges, Universities and symposia throughout the world; presenter in field. Adv. editor Spine, Spine Jour.; contbr. article to peer-reviewed jours., chapters to books; guest appearance Miracle Workers (ABC), 2006. Trustee AO Found.; chmn. AO Spine Courses. Mem.: Tex. Orthop. Assn., Tex. Med. Assn., Harris County Med. Soc., Canadian Orthop. Assn., AMA, Am. Acad. Orthop. Surgeons, Internat. Soc. for Study of the Lumbar Spine (exec. bd. dir., Volvo award for the best Basic Sci. Rsch. study 1984), N.Am. Spine Soc. (mem. exec. com.). Office: Baylor Coll Medicine Dept Orthopedic Surgery 6620 Main St 13th Fl Houston TX 77030 Address: Inst for Spinal Disorders 6560 Fannin St Houston TX 77030 also: Christus St Joseph Hosp 1401 St Joseph Pkwy Houston TX 77002 Office Fax: 713-986-5711. E-mail: bkdoctor@aol.com.

GERVAIS, SISTER GENEROSE, hospital consultant; b. Currie, Minn., Sept. 18, 1919; d. Philip Frederick and Elizabeth Eleanor (Sandgathe) Gervais. BS, Stout State U., Menomonie, Wis., 1945; M. Hosp. Adminstrn., U. Minn., 1954. Joined Sisters of St. Francis, Roman Catholic Ch., 1938; adminstrv. dietitian St. Marys Hosp., Rochester, Minn., 1948-50, adminstrv. asst., 1951-52, asst. adminstr., 1954-63, assoc. adminstr., 1963-71, hosp. adminstr., 1971-81, exec. dir., 1981-85, bd. trustees, 1968-86; hosp. cons., 1985-90. Cons. dietitian Mercy Hosp., Portsmouth, Ohio, 1950-51; v.p., sec. Family Health Ctr. LaCrosse, Inc., 1985-91, pres., 1991-93; residency adv. bd. St. Francis-Mayo Family Practice, 1993-95; v.p. Caledonia Health Care Ctr., 1986-90; treas. Franciscan Cmty. Programs 1985-94. Bd. dirs. United Way of Olmstead County, 1968-73, Sr. Citizens Svcs. Inc., Rochester, Minn., 1988-94, Diocese of Winona Found., 1991-2000; bd. dirs. Madonna Towers, Rochester, 1987—2006, 08, chair, 1991-97, 2003-05; bd. dirs. Olmstead County Hist. Soc., 1994-97, 2008-, Regina Med. Ctr., Hastings, Minn., 1996-02, Madonna Meadows, 2002—06, 08-; pres. Poverello Found., Rochester, 1983—; bd. adv. Winona State U. Rochester Ctr., 1985-93; fin. coun. Diocese of Winona, 1986-91; mem. Franciscan Skemp Healthcare Cmty. Bd., LaCrosse, 1995—. Decorated Lady of Equestrian Order of Holy Sepulchre, 1989; recipient Alumni Disting. Service award U. Wis.-Stout, 1978, Teresa of Avila award Coll. of St. Teresa, 1980, Outstanding Achievement award Rochester chpt. U. Minn. Alumni Assn., 1981, Women of Achievement in Area of Bus. award YWCA, 1985, Pro Ecclesiae et Pontifice medal, 1985, Service to Mankind award Sertoma 700 Club, 1987, Mayor's Medal of Honor City of Rochester, 1990, The Athena award, 1994, Outstanding Alumni award Coll. Human Devel., U. Wis.-Stout, 2001; named Boss of Yr., Rochester Jaycees, 1980, named in her honor Sister Generose Gervais Bldg. St. Marys Hosp., 1991; Paul Harris fellow Nat. Rotary Club, 1998, Benedictine Health Sys. Trustee of Yr., 2008. Mem. Cath. Health Assn. U.S. (trustee 1979, vice chair 1981-82, chair 1982-83, speaker membership assembly 1983-84, Lifetime Achievement award 2011), Am. Coll. Hosp. Adminstrs., Am. Hosp. Assn., Minn. Hosp. Assn., Minn. Conf. Cath. Health Facilities (past dir.), Rochester Area C. of C. Republican. Address: 1216 2nd St SW Rochester MN 55902-1906 Office Phone: 507-255-5158. Business E-Mail: hanson.sandra@mayo.edu.

GERVOIS, PHILIPPE, biomedical researcher, educator; Lic. in biochemistry, U. Scis. and Techs. of Lille, France, 1993, MS in Biochemistry, 1995, MS in Life Scis. and Health, 1996; PhD in Pharm. Scis., U. Lille II, 2000, HDR, 2006. European advisor Inst. Prevention and Health TNO, Leiden, Netherlands, 2000—01; biomed. rschr. Pasteur Inst., Lille, 2001—02; asst. prof. U. Lille II, 2001—02, prof., 2002—. Scientist French Inst. Health and Med. Rsch., Lille. Contbr. articles to profl. jours. Recipient Ednl. award, Internat. Symposium on Atherosclerosis, 2003, Nouvelle Soc. Francaise d'Athérosclérose, 2006; grantee, Found. Med. Rsch., 1999, Keystone Symposium, 2001; PhD grant, Région Nord Pas de Calais, Pasteur Inst. Lille, 1997, Congress grant, Groupe Lillois pour la Recherche en Pathologie, Vasculaire, France, 1998, European Cmty. Rsch. Tng. grant, Marie Curie Fellowship Assn., 2000—01. Achievements include research in the mechanisms of action of nuclear receptors in the modulation of molecular risk of cardiovascular disease; the pharmacology of nuclear receptors and engineeringof pre-clinical models designed at evaluating new drugs in the attenuation of atherosclerosis and associated diseasees. Office: Faculte Pharmacy Lab Biochemie 3 Rue Laguesse 59006 Lille France

GERZELI, GIUSEPPE, biologist, educator; b. Milan, Apr. 1, 1931; m. Gabriella Pedrazzi, Apr. 25, 1960; children: Daniele, Elena, Simone. MD, U. Pavia, 1954. Asst. U. Pavia, Italy, 1959-70, asst. prof., 1961-70, prof. comparative anatomy, 1970—2006, prof. emeritus, 2006; ret., 2006. Dir. inst. comparative anatomy U. Pavia, 1967-82, dean faculty scis., 1982-97, dir. dept. animal biology, 1997-2000. Contbr. articles to profl. jours. Recipient Premio G.B. Grassi Accademia Nazionale dei Lincei, 1962, first class diploma with gold medal for achievements in sci. and culture Pres. of the Republic, 1996. Mem. Inst. Lombardo Accademia Sci. Lett., Royal Microscopical Soc., Am. Soc. Cell Biology, Histochem. Soc., N.Y. Acad. Scis., Societa Italiana di Istochimica (v.p. 1970-73, pres. 1990-93), European Jour. Histochemistry (mem. editl. bd. 1979), Cellular and Molecular Biology (mem. editl. bd. 1977), Kiwanis Club Pavia (pres. 1992-93). Business E-Mail: gerzeli@unipv.it.

GESCHWIND, DANIEL H., psychology and neurology professor; b. Summit, NJ, Dec. 21, 1960; s. Stanley and Dena (Schur) Geschwind; m. Sandy Avol, Dec. 28, 1986. AB in Chemistry and Psychology, Dartmouth Coll., Hanover, NH, 1982; MD, PhD in Medicine and Neurobiology, Yale U., New Haven, 1991. Diplomate Am. Bd. Psychiatry & Neurology, cert. in adult neurology. Intern internal medicine UCLA Sch. Medicine, 1991—92, resident neurology, 1992—95, fellow neurogenetics, clin. instr. neurology, 1995—97, asst. prof. neurology, 1997—2003, dir. neurogentics prog, 1997—, assoc. prof. neurology, 2003—05, dir., Ctr. Autism Rsch. & Treatment, 2003—, prof. neurology, psychiatry and obehavioral scis., 2005—, Gordon & Virginia MacDonald disting. chair in human genetics, 2005—. Oral bd. examiner Am. Bd. Neurology & Psychiatry, 1998—; chmn. steering com. Autism Genetic Resource Exch., 1999—2004; neurogenetics sect. head Faculty of 1000 Medicine, 2005—; mem. nat. adv. metal health coun. Nat. Inst. Mental Health, 2007—; mem. sci. adv. bd. Cure Autism Now. Mem. editl. bd. Lancet Neurology, 2002—05, assoc. editor Neurobiology of Disease, 2004—06, dep. editor Biological Psychiatry, 2006—; contbr. articles to profl. jours. Recipient Young Investigator award, Nat. Alliance for Rsch. Schizophrenia & Depression, 1999—2001, Derek Denny-Brown Neurological Scholar award, Am. Neurological Assn., 2004, Harold Brenner Pepinsky award in Behavioral Neurosci., Ohio State U., 2006, MERIT award, Nat. Inst. Mental Health, 2006, Sci. Svc. award, Autism Speaks, 2008. Mem.: Am. Acad. Neurology, Soc. Neurosci. (chmn. edn. com. 2003—06), Alpha Phi Omega. Office: 2309 The Gonda Neurosci and Genetics Rsch Ctr 695 Charles E Young Dr S Los Angeles CA 90095 Office Phone: 310-794-7537. Office Fax: 310-267-2401. Business E-Mail: dhg@ucla.edu. *

GETER, RODNEY KEITH, plastic surgeon; b. Baton Rouge, Nov. 13, 1946; s. Argless William and Jewel Alma (Rudolph) G. BA in Chemistry with honors, U. Mo., 1975, MD, 1979. Resident in gen. surgery U. Mo., Columbia, 1979-83, fellow in microvascular surgery, 1983-84, resident in plastic surgery, 1984-86; pvt. practice Springfield (Mo.) Clinic, 1986—. Chmn. dept. surgery St. John's Regional Health Ctr., Springfield, 1992-94, chmn. two hosp. coms., 1994-97; v.p. med. staff St. John's Hosp., 1996-97, chmn. plastic surgery dept., 2000-02. Contbr. articles to profl. jours. Pres. Springfield Music Found., 1989—; leader troop 210 Boy Scouts Am., Springfield, 1995-98. Sgt. Spl. Forces, U.S. Army, 1968-71, Vietnam. Mem. Am. Soc. Plastic Surgeons, Greene County Med. Soc., Mo. State Med. Assn., Phi Beta Kappa, Phi Lambda Upsilon. Avocations: playing keyboard in band, fishing, backpacking. Office: St Johns Clinic Plastic Surgery 1229 E Seminole Ste 340 Springfield MO 65804 Office Phone: 417-820-9330. Business E-Mail: rodney.geter@mercy.net.

GETTYS, THOMAS WIGINGTON, medical researcher; BS in Biology, Lander Coll., 1978; PhD in Nutrition, Clemson U., 1984. Grad. rsch. asst. animal sci. dept. Coll. Agr. Clemson U., SC, 1979—84; rsch. assoc. Howard Hughes Med. Inst., Dept. Molecular Physiology and Biophysics Vanderbilt U. Sch. of Medicine, Nashville, 1985—87; rsch. assoc. divsn. gastroenterology, dept. medicine Duke U. Med. Ctr., Durham, NC, 1987—90, rsch. asst. prof. divsn. gastroenterology, dept. medicine, 1990—, rsch. asst. prof. dept. cell biology, 1992—93; assoc. prof. medicine Med. U. SC, Charleston, 1993—, assoc. prof. biochemistry and molecular biology, 1995—, prof. medicine, 2000—; prof., chief exptl. obesity divsn. Pennington Biomed. Rsch. Ctr., Baton Rouge. Contbr. articles to profl. jours., chapters to books. Grantee, NIH, 1990, 1994, 1996, 1998, 2003, 2005, 2006, 2007, USDA, 1997, 2000, Am. Diabetes Assn., 2006; fellow predoctoral rsch., Clemson U., 1981—82. Mem.: Am. Diabetes Assn. (grant review panel 2006, Rsch. award 1996, 2003—05), Am. Soc. Biochemistry and Molecular Biology, Sigma Xi. Office: Pennington Biomed Rsch Ctr 6400 Perkins Rd Baton Rouge LA 70808 Office Phone: 225-763-3165. Business E-Mail: gettystw@pbrc.edu.

GEUDER, JAMES W., vascular surgeon; Grad., Med. Coll. Wis., 1981. Diplomate Am. Bd. Surgery-gen. surgery, Am. Bd. Surgery-vascular surgery. Residency Univ. of Medicine and Dentistry of NJ, Newark, 1986; fellowship NY Univ. Med. Ctr., NYC, 1988; with Hackensack Univ. Med. Ctr., Hackensack, NJ. Office: Hackensack University Medical Center 30 Prospect Ave Hackensack NJ 07601 Office Phone: 201-996-2000.

GEWERTZ, BRUCE LABE, surgeon, educator; b. Phila., Aug. 27, 1949; s. Milton and Shirley (Charen) G.; children: Samantha, Barton, Alexis; m. Diane Weiss, Aug. 31, 1997. BS, Pa. State U., State Coll., 1968; MD, Jefferson Med. Coll., Phila., 1972. Diplomate Am. Bd. Surgery. Surg. resident U. Mich., Ann Arbor, 1972-77; asst. prof. U. Tex., Dallas, 1977-81; assoc. prof. U. Chgo., 1981-87, prof. surgery, 1988—, faculty dean med. edn., 1989-92, Dallas Phemister prof., chmn. dept. surgery, 1992—2006; chmn. dept. surgery, surgeon-in-chief, v.p. Cedars-Sinai Med. Ctr., LA, 2006—. Tchg. scholar Am. Heart Assn., Dallas, 1980-83; pres. Assn. Surg. Edn., 1983-84; dir. vascular surgery bd. Am. Bd. Surgery, 2001-07. Author: Atlas of Vascular Surgery, 1989, 2005, Surgery of the Aorta and its Branches, 2000; editor Jour. Surg. Rsch., 1987-2002; patentee removable vascular filter. Recipient Coller award Mich. chpt. Am. Coll. Surgeons, 1975, Outstanding Sci. Alumnus award Pa. State U., 2003; Alumni fellowship, Pa. State U., 2009. Mem. Soc. Vascular Surgery, Midwestern Vascular Soc. (pres. 1994-95), Soc. Clin. Surgery, Soc. Univ. Surgeons, Chgo. Surg. Soc. (pres. 2005), Western Surg. Assn. (pres.

2007-08), Am. Surg. Assn., Pacific Coast Surg. Soc. Office: Cedars-Sinai Med Ctr 8700 Beverly Blvd Suite 8215 Los Angeles CA 90048 Office Fax: 310-423-0231. Business E-Mail: bruce.gewertz@cshs.org. *

GEWITZ, MICHAEL HAROLD, pediatric cardiologist; b. Jan. 20, 1949; m. Judith Lipshutz, May 12, 1973; children: Emily, Andrew. BA, Yale U., 1970; MD, Hahnemann U., 1974. Intern Children's Hosp. Phila., Phila., 1974—75, resident, 1975—76, Hosp. Sick Children, London, 1976—77; fellow Yale New Haven Hosp., 1977—79; dir. noninvasive cardiology Children's Hosp. Phila., 1979—83; asst. prof. pediat. Sch. Medicine U. Pa., Phila., 1979—83; chief pediat. cardiology N.Y. Med. Coll. and Westchester Med. Ctr., 1983—; dir. dept. pediat., chief pediat. cardiology Children's Hosp. Westchester, Valhalla, NY, 1991—; prof., vice chair dept. pediat. N.Y. Med. Coll., Valhalla, NY, 1992—; pres. med. staff Westch Med. Ctr., 1998—2002; chief pediat. cardiology Maria Fareri Children's Hosp., 1983—, physician in chief, 2004—, exec. dir., 2004—. Editor: (book) Primary Pediatric Cardiology, 1995; assoc. editor; (journal) Heart Diseases, 1999-2004; section editor (jour,) Cardiovasc Reviews, 2004—. Fellow Am. Acad. Pediat., Am. Coll. Cardiology, N.Y. Acad. Medicine, Am. Heart Assn. (exec. com. cardiovasc. disease in young 1999—, chmn., 2010-, com. Rheumatic fever, endocarditis and Kawasaki disease 1995—, vice chmn. 2001-04, 2008—, chmn. 2004—09), Am. Coll. Physician Execs.; mem. Pediat. Acad. Soc. Office Phone: 914-493-6160.

GEWURZ, ANITA TARTELL, physician, medical educator; b. Buffalo, July 30, 1946; MD, Albany Med. Coll., 1970. Resident in pediat. U. Ill., Chgo., 1971—73; resident in allergy and immunology Rush-Presbyn.-St. Luke's Hosp., Chgo., 1974—76; fellow allergy and immunology Max Samter Inst., Grant Hosp., Chgo., 1976—77, Northwestern U. Med. Coll., Chgo., 1983—85; assoc. prof. immunology/microbiology, pediat. and internal med. Rush U. Med. Coll., Chgo., 1993—2003, prof. immunology/microbiology, pediat. and internal med., 2003—; physician Rush U. Med. Ctr., Chgo., 1974—. Chair, Tng. Program Dirs. Com. Am. Acad. Allergy, Asthma & Immunology, 2000—02; chair Am. Bd. Allergy and Immunology, 2004—05; initial cert. task force Am. Bd. Med. Specialties, 2001—06, sub com. chair, 2001—05; vol. physician pediatc. Stroger Hosp., Cook County, Ill., 1997—. Office: Rush Univ Med Ctr 1725 W Harrison St Ste 117 Chicago IL 60612 Office Phone: 312-942-6296. Business E-Mail: agewurz@rush.edu.

GEYER, CHARLES E., oncologist, educator; MD, Tex. Tech. Univ. Diplomate Am. Bd. Oncology-med. oncology. Resident Baylor Coll. of Medicine Affiliated Hosp., Tex., fellow in oncology; assoc. prof. human oncology Drexel Univ.; dir. med. affairs for nat. surgical adjuvant breast and bowel project Allegheny Gen. Hosp., dir. breast med. oncology, vice chmn. dept. human oncology. Named one of Top Doctors, Pitts. mag., 2011. Fellow: ACP. Office: Allegheny General Hospital 320 E N Ave Pittsburgh PA 15212 Office Phone: 412-359-3131. Office Fax: 412-359-4108.

GEYMAN, JOHN PAYNE, physician, educator; b. Santa Barbara, Calif., Feb. 9, 1931; s. Milton John and Betsy (Payne) Geyman; m. Eugenia Clark Deichler, June 9, 1956; children: John Matthew, James Caleb, William Sabin. AB in Geology, Princeton U., 1952; MD, U. Calif., San Francisco, 1960. Diplomate Am. Bd. Family Practice. Intern L.A. County Gen. Hosp., 1960—61; resident in gen. practice Sonoma County Hosp., Santa Rosa, Calif., 1961—63; pvt. practice specializing in family practice Mt. Shasta, Calif., 1963—69; dir. family practice residency program Cmty. Hosp. Sonoma County, Santa Rosa, 1969—71; assoc. prof. family practice, chmn. divsn. family practice U. Utah, 1971—72; prof., vice chmn. dept. family practice U. Calif., Davis, 1972—77; prof., chmn. dept. family medicine U. Wash., 1977—90, prof. family medicine, 1990—93, prof. family medicine emeritus, 1993—. Author: The Modern Family Doctor and Changing Medical Practice, 1971, Family Practice: Foundation of Changing Health Care, 1980, 2d edit., 1985, Flight as a Lifetime Passion: Adventures, Misadventures and Lessons, 2000, Falling Through the Safety Net: Americans Without Health Insurance, 2005; editor: Content of Family Practice, 1976, Family Practice in the Medical School, 1977, Research in Family Practice, 1978, Preventive Medicine in Family Practice, 1979, Profile of the Residency Trained Family Physician in the U.S, 1970—79, Funding of Patient Care, Education and Research in Family Practice, 1981, The Content of Family Practice: Current Status and Future Trends, 1982, Archives of Family Practice, 1980—82, Family Practice: An International Perspective in Developed Countries, 1983, Jour. Am. Bd. Family Practice, 1990—2003; founding editor Jour. Family Practice, 1973—90; co-editor: Behavioral Science in Family Practice, 1980, Evidence-Based Clinical Practice: Concepts and Approaches, 2000, Textbook of Rural Medicine, 2000, Health Care in America: Can Our Ailing System Be Healed?, 2002, The Corporate Transformation of Health Care: Can the Public Interest Still be Served?, 2004, Shredding of the Social Contract: The Privatization of Medicare, 2006, An Open Cockpit Biplane Dream: Honey Bee III, 2005, The Corrosion of Medicine: Can the Profession Reclaim Its moral Legacy, 2008, Do Not Resuscitate Why the Health Insurance Industry is Dying and How We Must Replace It, 2008, The Cancer Generation: Baby Boomers Facing a Perfect Storm. Pres. Physicians for Nat. Health Program, 2005—07. Served to lt. (j.g.) USN, 1952—55, PTO. Recipient Gold-Headed Cane award, U. Calif. Sch. Medicine, 1960, Alumnus of Yr. award, 1998. Mem.: Inst. Medicine NAS, Soc. Tchrs. Family Medicine, Am. Acad. Family Physicians. Unitarian Universalist. Home: 615 Harrison St Apt D Friday Harbor WA 98250-7301 Business E-Mail: jgeyman@u.washington.edu.

GHAEMI, S. NASSIR, psychiatrist, educator; b. Tehran, Iran, 1966; s. Kamal and Guity Kamali Ghaemi. BA in History, George Mason U., 1986; MD, Med. Coll. Va., 1990; MA in Philosophy, Tufts U., 2001; MPH, Harvard Sch. Pub. Health, 2004. Intern Mass. Gen. Hosp., 1991, fellow in psychopharmacology, 1995; resident in adult psychiatry McLean Hosp., 1994; prof. psychiatry Tufts Med. Ctr., dir. Mood Disorders & Psychopharmacology Program. Editorial bd. numerous psychiatric jours. Author: The Concepts of Psychiatry: A Pluralistic Approach to the Mind and Mental Illness. Fellow: Am. Psychiatric Assn.; mem.: Assn. for Advancement Philosophy & Psychiatry (exec. com.), Internat. Soc. Bipolar Disorders (chmn. Diagnostic Guidelines Task Force). Office: 800 Washington St #1007 Boston MA 02111 E-mail: nghaemi@tuftsmedicalcenter.org.

GHALI, ANWAR YOUSSEF, psychiatrist, educator; b. Cairo, May 30, 1944; arrived in U.S.A., 1974, naturalized, 1980; s. Youssef and Insaf Wahba (Soliman) G.; m. Violette Fouad Saleh, May 23, 1968; 1 child, Susie MD, Cairo U., 1966, DPM, 1970, DM, 1971; MPA, NYU, 1999. Diplomate Am. Bd. Psychiatry and Neurology; cert. adminstrv. psychiatry. Registrar in psychiatry Woodilee Hosp., Glasgow, Scotland, 1973-74; resident in psychiatry N.J. Med. Sch., Newark, 1974-77, instr., 1977-78, clin. asst. prof., 1978-79, asst. prof., 1979-83, clin. assoc. prof., 1983—; chief Outpatient Dept.-Community Mental Health Ctr., N.J. Med. Sch., Newark, 1978-86; dir. Emergency Psychiat. Svcs. Univ. Hosp., U. Medicine and Dentistry of N.J., Newark, 1986-87; med. dir. Profl. Counsel Ctr., Westfield, NJ, 1984-87; med. chief ambulatory psychiat. svcs. Elizabeth (N.J.) Gen. Hosp., 1987-89; dir. psychiat. tng. VA Med. Ctr., East Orange, NJ, 1989—2001, asst. chief psychiatry, 1990—91, assoc. chief psychiatry, 1991—2001; chmn. psychiatry Trinitas Hosp., Elizabeth, NJ, 2001—. Contbr. articles to profl. jours. Recipient Exceptional Merit award Coll. Medicine & Dentistry, Newark, 1981 Mem. AMA, Christian Med. Soc., Am. Psychiat. Assn., N.J. Psychiat. Assn., N.Y. Acad. Scis. Republican. Presbyterian. Home: 22 Benvenue Ave West Orange NJ 07052-3202

GHANEM, MAHA KAMEL, pulmonologist, educator; b. Assiut, Egypt, June 16, 1964; MBBCh, Faculty Medicine, 1987; MSc, Assiut U., MD, 1999. Resident, asst. lectr., chest diseases Faculty Medicine, Assiut U. Hosps., 1989—96, cons. pulmonologist, intensivist and sleep disorders specialist, 1999—, lectr., chest diseases and tuberculosis, 1999—2005, asst. prof., 2005—10, prof., 2010—; clin. rsch. fellow, resident, chest diseases Respiratory Medicine Unit, Royal Infirmary, Edinburgh, 1996—98. Com. mem. Quality Assurance Unit Assiut Faculty Medicine, 2008—; reviewer Med. Jours., 2009. Recipient Young Investigators award, Pan Arab Soc. Cardiovasc. Surgery, 1998, Best Rschrs. award, Egyptian Soc. Bronchology, 2003, 2006; Rsch. fellowship, Mission Authority, Egyptian Govt. Fellow: Am. Coll. Chest Physicians; mem.: Gerson Lehrman Group Couns. (cons. 2011), Internat. Union Against Chest Diseases and Tuberculosis, European Respiratory Soc. (Silver medal 2009), Am. Thoracic Soc. (Travel award 2004). Avocations: reading, travel, cooking. Office: Dept Chest Diseases Assiut University Assiut 71111 Egypt Office Fax: 2 088 2333327.

GHANEM, VINICIUS CORAL, ophthalmologist; s. Emir Amin Ghanem and Cleusa Coral-Ghanem. MD, U. Fed. Do Paraná, Curitiba, 1999; PhD, U. São Paulo, Brazil, 2007. Observer Moorfields Eye Hosp., London, 1997—97, Bochner Eye Inst., Toronto, Canada, 1998—98; med. resident U. Campinas, São Paulo, 1999—2002; ophthalmologist Sadalla Amin Ghanem Eye Hosp., Joinville, Santa Catarina, Brazil, 2002—, pres. infection control com., 2003—. Cmty. campaigns, Joinville, 1995—2008. Decorated Waring medal, recipient Best Ophthalmologic Resident, U Campinas, 1999—2002; Fellowship, U. Calif., 2002. Mem.: Internat. Soc. Refractive Surgery, Conselho Brasileiro de Oftalmologia, Am. Soc. Cataract & Refractive Surgery. Achievements include development of surgical technique on iridectomy of anterior iris STROMA in patients with iridoschisis; research in advanced surface ablation; corneal transplantation; phacoemulsification in patients with marfan syndrome. Office: Sadalla Amin Ghanem Rua Abdon Batista 172 Joinville Santa Catarina 89201010 Brazil Personal E-mail: vcghanem@hotmail.com.

GHANTOUS, VICTOR E., nephrologist; MD, St. Joseph U., Beirut; attended, Am. U. of Beirut. Diplomate Am. Bd. of Internal Medicine-nephrology, Am. Bd. of Internal Medicine. Fellow nephrology Hosp. of St. Raphael. Named Top Docs, Phila. Mag., 2011. Office: Abington Memorial Hospital 1200 Old York Rd Abington PA 19001 Office Phone: 215-481-2000.

GHARABAWI GARIBALDI, GEORGE MILAD, psychiatrist, neuroscientist; arrived in US, 1996, naturalized, 2005; s. Milad Hanna Gharabawi and Ragaa Mitri Armand; m. Sonia Sami Boulos, Oct. 8, 1985; 1 child, Jesse Milad Gharabawi. BcH, Cairo U., 1983; degree in Psychopharmacology, U. Pitie Salpetriere, Paris, 1991; D in Psychiatry, U. Rene Descartes, Paris, 1992. Cert. France, 1993. Primary care physician internship, residency Behman Hosp., Cairo, 1983—88; cons. child psychiatry Bobigny Med. Sch., France, 1989—93; med. expert Sandoz Pharmaceuticals, Basel, Switzerland, 1992—97; exec. dir. Novartis Pharmaceuticals, East Hanover, NJ, 1997—2001; lead therapeutic area Janssen Pharmaceuticals, Titusville, NJ, 2001—06; v.p. global clin. neurosciences Hoffman-La Roche, Nutley, NJ, 2006—. Contbr. chapters to books, articles to profl. jours. Master: Internat. Soc. Ctrl. Nervous Sys. Clin. Trial Methodology (pres. 2007—); mem.: Collegium Internationale Neuropsychopharmacologicum, Am. Acad. Child and Adolescent Psychiatry. Achievements include development of a treatment for the management of symptoms of Alzheimer's disease.

GHARIBO, CHRISTOPHER, pain medicine physician, educator; MD, U. Medicine and Dentistry of NJ-Sch., 1992. Diplomate Am. Bd. Anesthesiology, Am. Bd. Anesthesiology-pain medicine. Intern in internal medicine Robert Wood Johnson Univ. Hosp., 1992—93; resident anesthesiology NYU Med. Ctr., 1993—96; fellow pain mgmt. Thomas Jefferson Univ. hosp., 1996—97; asst. prof. of anesthesiology Sch. of Med. NYU; med. dir. of pain medicine dept. of anesthesiology NYU Hosp. Author: (publs.) Desirable attributes of a pain clinic in caring for the patient with complex regional pain syndrome, 1998, Spinal injections in diagnosis and treatment of low back pain, 1999; co-author: Succesful treatment of phantom radiculopathy with fluoroscopic epidural steroid injections, 2005. Mem.: NYU Anesthesia Assocs. Office: NYU Langone Medical Center Hospital for Joint Diseases 301 East 17th St 10th Fl Suite 1001 New York NY 10003 Office Phone: 212-598-6342. Office Fax: 212-598-6342.

GHAZARYAN, SEDRAK HAMAYAKI, chemist, researcher; b. Aghin Village, Armenia, Feb. 19, 1942; s. Hamayak Khachaturi and Zvart Avetisi (Margaryan) Ghazaryan; m. Hranush Azati Sahakyan, Sept. 4, 1942; children: Hamazasp Sedraki, Araqsia Sedraki. MA, Yerevan State U., 1965; PhD in Biorganic Chemistry, Moscow U., 1971. Lab. asst. Inst. Fine Organic Chemistry NAS, Yerevan, Armenia, 1959—63, chemist, 1963—65, jr. rschr., 1965—75, chief rschr., 1976—. Author: sci. papers in field. Recipient award, The Armenian Nat. Fund Sci. and Advanced Techs., The U.S. Civilian R&D Fund; grantee, Internat. Sci. and Tech. Ctr., 2001. Avocation: collecting pictures. Home: Mamikonyants Ave 47/16 Yerevan 375051 Armenia Office: Inst Fine Organic Chemistry NAS Azatutyan 26 Yerevan 375014 Armenia Personal E-mail: sedrham@yahoo.com.

GHAZLE, HAMAD, medical educator, director; m. Afifa H. Ghazle; children: Zayneb H., Zahra'a H., Batool H. BS, Rochester Inst. Tech., NY, 1988; MS, U. Rochester, NY, 1991, EdD, 2008. Cert. in diagnostic medical sonography Am. Registry Diagnostic Med. Sonography, 1992. Sonographer U. Iowa Hosp. and Clinics, Iowa City, 1991—94, U. Rochester, Strong Meml. Hosp., 1994—2008; prof. Rochester Inst. Tech., 1994—, dir. Pres. Rochester Ultrasound Soc., 1996—. Contbr. articles to profl. jours.; keynote spkr. of numerous orgns. Site visitor Joint Rev. Com. Diagnostic Med. Sonography, St. Paul, 1995—2008. Recipient RIT Eisenhart award, 2002, Student Affairs award, 2002; finalist RIT Provost's Excellence Tchg. award. Mem.: Soc. Diagnostic Med. Sonography (state rep. 1997—2003, edn. com. 2003—04). Home: 7 Chamber Valley Estate Spencerport NY 14559 Office: Rochester Inst Tech 153 Lomb Memorial Dr Rochester NY 14623 Business E-Mail: hhgscl@rit.edu.

GHEBREMEDHIN, BINIAM, physician, consultant; s. G. Medhin Ghebremedhin. MSc in Biochemistry, U. Hannover, Germany, 1996; MD, Med. Sch. Hannover, 1999; PhD. Physician MHH, Hannover, 2000—02; consulting physician & prin. investigator U. Clinic OVG U., Magdeburg, Germany, 2003—, adj. prof., 2010—. Contbr. articles to sci. jours. Mem., musician Traditional & Cultural Group, Germany, 1988—91. Recipient Study award, German Govt., 1990—96, Post-doc. award, ICAAC, 2009, ASM award, 2011; Travel grants, OVG U., 2004—, ISID, 2006, German Rsch. Found., 2008, Rsch. Fund grant, Fed. State SA, 2008—, German African Mut. Rsch. & Tchg. grant, Fed. Ministry Economical Cooperation & Devel., 2009—, German African Project grant, Fed. Ministry Econ. Cooperation & Devel., 2009—. Mem.: Eritrean Med. Assn. (bd. mem. 1994—98), ASM (Wash.). Home Phone: 00491731547242; Office Phone: 00493916713328. Business E-Mail: beniam.ghebremedhin@med.ovgu.de.

GHEDIN, ELODIE, parasitologist, virologist, biomedical researcher, educator; b. 1967; BS, McGill U., 1989, PhD, 1998; MS, U. Quebec, Montreal, 1993. Postdoctoral fellow Nat. Inst. Allergy and Infectious Diseases, 1998—2000; asst. investigator, head Viral Genomics Group Inst. Genomic Rsch., 2000—06; asst. prof. Dept. Computational and Systems Biology U. Pitts. Sch. Medicine, 2006—, mem. Ctr. Vaccine Rsch. Assoc. investigator J. Craig Venter Inst. Contbr. articles to med. jours. Named a MacArthur Fellow, John D. & Catherine T. MacArthur Found., 2011. Office: University of Pittsburgh Center for Vaccine Research BST3, Room 9043b 3501 5th Ave Pittsburgh PA 15261 Office Phone: 412-383-5850. Office Fax: 412-383-5851. E-mail: elg21@pitt.edu. *

GHERARDI, GIORGIO, pathologist, researcher; b. Musoma, Tanzania, Mar. 3, 1952; s. Sergio and Bianca Maria; life ptnr. Stefania Francesca Rossi; m. Margherita Gabriotti, Aug. 19, 1978 (div. Jan. 4, 1998); children: Dario, Andrea, Sergio. Laurea in medicine and surgery, U. La Sapienza, Rome, 1977, specialty degree in anaiomic pathology, 1980, specialty degree in clin. oncology, 1985. Prof. in pathology Postgrad. Sch. Gastroenterology U. Pisa, Italy, 1986—91; dir. anatomic pathology Ospedale Civile, Sondrio, Italy, 1987—98, Ospedale Fatebenefratelli e Oftalmico, Milan, 1999—; prof. cytopathology Postgrad. Sch. Anaiomic Pathology U. Milan, Milan, 1999—. Fellow, Ospedale Civile, 1980—86. Roman Catholic. Avocations: bicycling, skiing, travel. Office: Ospedale Fatebenefratelli e Oftalmico Corso di Porta Nuova 23 Milano I-20121 Italy Office Fax: 390263632742. Personal E-mail: ggherard@tiscali.it. E-mail: giorgio.gherardi@fbf.milano.it.

GHETTI, BERNARDINO FRANCESCO, neuropathologist, educator; b. Pisa, Italy, Mar. 28, 1941; s. Getulio and Iris (Mugnetti) G.; m. Caterina Genovese, Oct. 8, 1966; children: Chiara, Simone. MD cum laude, U. Pisa, 1966, specialist in mental and nervous diseases, 1969; laureate (hon.), U. Siena, 2005. Lic. physician, Italy; cert. Edn. Coun. for Fgn. Med. Grads.; diplomate Am. Bd. Pathology. Postdoctoral fellow U. Pisa, 1966-70; rsch. fellow in neuropathology Albert Einstein Coll. Medicine, Bronx, NY, 1970-73, resident, clin. fellow in pathology, 1973-75, resident in neuropathology, 1975-76; asst. prof. pathology Ind. U., Indpls., 1976-77, asst. prof. pathology and psychiatry, 1977—78, assoc. prof. pathology and psychiatry, 1978—83, prof. pathology and psychiatry, 1983—91, assoc. dir. program in med. neurobiology, 1983—2000, assoc. dir. divsn. neuropathology, 1989-93, prof. pathology, psychiatry, med. and molecular genetics, 1991—97, dir. Alzheimer Disease Ctr., 1991—, dir. divsn. neuropathology, 1993—, Disting. prof. pathology and lab. medicine, psychiatry, med. and molecular genetics, neurology, 1997—, chancellor's prof., 2007—. Mem. Nat. Inst. Neurol. Disorders and Stroke rev. com. NIH, 1985-89; mem. NIH Reviewers Res., 1989-93, pres., Internat. Conf. Frontotemporal Dementias, 2010. Contbr. articles to profl. jours. Alzheimer's disease rsch. sci. rev. com. Am. Health Assistance Found., 1998—2002. Recipient Potamkin prize, 1999. Mem. Internat. Soc. Neuropathology (v.p. 2000-03, pres.-elect 2005, pres. 2006—10), Am. Acad. Neurology, Am. Neurol. Assn., Am. Assn. Neuropathologists (pres. 1996-97), Soc. Neurosci., Assn. Rsch. in Nervous and Mental Diseases, Internat. Brain Rsch. Orgn., Am. Soc. Cell Biology, Italian Soc. Psychiatry, Italian Soc. Neurology, Sigma Xi. Roman Catholic. Home: 1124 Frederick Dr S Indianapolis IN 46260-3421 Office: Ind U 635 Barnhill Dr Rm 138 Indianapolis IN 46202-5126 Office Phone: 317-274-7818. Business E-Mail: bghetti@iupui.edu.

GHICA, MIHAELA VIOLETA AL., medical educator; b. Cimpina, Romania, May 15, 1976; d. Alecsandru St. and Fiorentina Gh. Galoiu; m. Florin Viorel M. Ghica, Apr. 28, 2001. Degree in Pharmacy, U. Medicine and Pharmacy, Bucharest, Romania, 2000; MS in Phys. Chemistry and Applied Radiochemistry, U. Bucharest, 2004; degree in Gen. Pharmacy, U. Medicine and Pharmacy Carol Davila, Bucharest, 2004, PhD in Pharmacy cum laude, 2008. Jr. asst. Faculty Pharmacy, U. Medicine and Pharmacy, 2002—04, asst., 2004—07; lectr. Faculty Pharmacy, U. Medicine and Pharmacy Carol Davila, 2007—. Achievements include patents pending for hydrogel with indomethacin and manufacturing method. Home: 26-28 Calcrangasi Bl48-49 Sc A Ap4 Bucharest 060339 Romania Office: Univ Medicine and Pharmacy Carol Davila Faculty Pharmacy 6 Traian Vuia Bucharest 020956 Romania Office Fax: 40213180750. Personal E-mail: mihaelaghica@yahoo.com.

GHO, YONG SONG, research scientist, science educator; b. Cheju, Republic of Korea, Mar. 17, 1964; s. Duho Gho and Jungsook Kang; m. Youngjoo Park, Nov. 11, 1990; 1 child, Junsoo. BA, Seoul Nat. U., 1987, MS, 1989; PhD, U. N.C., Chapel Hill, 1997. Post doctoral

POSTECH, Pohang, Republic of Korea, 1997—98; vis. fellow NIH, Bethesda, Md., 1998—2000; asst. prof. Kyung Hee U., Yong In, Kyunggi Do, Republic of Korea, 2000—04; asst. prof. dept. life sci. POSTECH, Pohang, Republic of Korea, 2004—. Contbr. articles to profl. jours. Mem.: Biochemical Soc. of the Republic of Korea (assoc.). Achievements include patents for Beta-Amyloid Binding Factors and Inhibitors. Office: Dept Life Sci POSTECH San 31 Hyoja-Dong Pohang 790-784 Republic of Korea E-mail: ysgho@postech.ac.kr.

GHONEIM, ASSER IBRAHIM, pharmacologist, educator; b. Egypt, 1974; PhD in Pharmacy, 2006. Asst. prof., pharmacology & toxicology, faculty pharmacy Ain Shams U., Egypt, 2006—10, Damanhour U., 2010—. Adj. prof., faculty pharmacy Misr Internat. U., 2006—10. Recipient Internat. Publ. award, Ain Shams U., 2009; Rsch. grant, German Rsch. Found. & Acad. Sci. Rsch. and Tech., 2009, 2011. Office: Faculty Pharmacy El Gomhouria St Damanhour El Behera 22514 Egypt Business E-Mail: asser@asu-pharmacy.edu.eg.

GHOSH, CHINMOY, research scientist; b. Burdwan, West Bengal, India, Dec. 23, 1978; MSc, Maulana Azad Coll. Sci., Aurangabad, Maharashtra, India, 2000; attending, Jiwaji U., Gwalior, Madhya Pradesh. Quality control chemist Aristo Pharmaceuticals Ltd., Mandideep, Bhopal, Madhya Pradesh, 2003—05; rsch. scientist-II Cadila Pharmaceuticals Ltd., Dholka, Gujarat, 2005—. Editl. bd. mem. Global Jour. Analytical Chemistry, Bioanalysis. Home: A-204 Sanatan Residency Vejalpur Ahmadabad Gujarat 380051 India Personal E-mail: chinmoy_ghosh@yahoo.com.

GHOSH, PARTHA S., pediatrician; b. Kolkata, India, Jan. 25, 1975; MD, Calcutta Med. Coll., Kolkata India, 2000; DM, Post Grad. Inst. Med. Edn. & Rsch., Chandigarh, India, 2006. Resident physician dept. gen. pediat. Cleve. Clinic, 2007—09, fellow rschr., pediatric neurology, 2009—. Contbr. scientific papers to profl. publs. Recipient First prize, Pediat. Dept., Cleve. Clinic, Gold medal, Calcutta Med. Coll., Shailendra Nath Sen Meml. prize; fellowship, Mayo Clinic. Mem.: Child Neurology Soc., Am. Assn. Neurology. Avocation: travel. Office: 9500 Euclid Ave Desk S60 Cleveland OH 44195 Business E-Mail: ghoshp3@ccf.org.

GHOSH, RICHIK NILOY, cytologist; b. India, June 21, 1963; BS, Cornell U., 1984, PhD, 1991. Assoc. rsch. scientist pathology dept. Columbia U. Coll. Physicians & Surgeons, 1995—96; asst. prof. biochemistry dept. Weill Cornell U. Med. Coll., 1997—98; project mgr., prin. scientist, dir. assay feasibility Cellomics, 1998—2005; dir. high content reagent devel., pierce biotechnology Thermo Fisher Sci., 2006—10, dir. rsch. & applications, cellomics bus. unit, 2010—. Mem.: Soc. Lab. Automation & Screening, Internat. Soc. Analytical Cytology, Am. Soc. Cell Biology. Office: Thermo Fisher Scientific 100 Technology Dr Pittsburgh PA 15219 Business E-Mail: richik.ghosh@thermofisher.com.

GHOSH, SANJOY, engineering educator; b. Kolkata, West Bengal, India, Aug. 19, 1966; PhD, Indian Inst. Tech. Chennai, 2002. Prof., dept. biotechnology Indian Inst. Tech. Roorkee, India, 2006—. Fellow: Internat. Soc. Biotech.; mem.: Biotech. Rsch. Soc. India, Indian Inst. Chem. Engrs. Office: Indian Inst Tech Roorkee Dept Biotechnology Roorkee Uttarakhand 247667 India Office Fax: 91-1332-273560. Business E-Mail: ghoshfbs@iitr.ernet.in.

GHOSH, SHANTANU, research scientist, educator; b. Dhanbad, India, May 12, 1974; BA with honors, St. Xavier's Coll. Ranchi, 1996; PhD, Ctr. Linguistics, 2006. Asst. prof. Indian Inst. Tech. Delhi, 2007—. Vis. prof. Heinrich-Heine U. Duesseldorf, Germany, 2011. Grant, Dept. Sci. and Tech., Govt of India, UNESCO-IAEA Travel fellowship, Abdus Salam ICTP, Trieste, Italy. Mem.: Soc. Neurochemistry India, EU-India Grid, IEEE-INNS, Internat. Soc. Cerebral Blood Flow and Metabolism (Gordon Travel fellowship). Achievements include research in FMRI, calcium signaling in neuron-glia interactions, modeling auditory perception. Avocations: photography, mountain climbing. Home: 44 Vaishali Apt IIT Delhi Campus New Delhi Delhi 110016 India Personal E-mail: sghosh.neu@gmail.com.

GHOSH, SOUMEN, engineering educator; b. West Bengal, India, Jan. 10, 1970; PhD, 1991. Asst. prof. Jadavpur U., 2001—. Fellowship, Govt. of India, FCT, Portugal. Mem.: Indian Soc. Surface Sci. & Tech. Office: Raja S C Mullick Rd Jadavpur Kolkata West Bengal 700032 India Personal E-mail: gsoumen70@hotmail.com.

GHOSHAL, NUPUR, neurologist, educator, medical researcher; d. Nani Gopal and Chhanda Ghoshal. BS, Iowa State U., Ames, 1995; MD, Northwestern U. Feinberg Sch. Medicine, 2003; PhD, Northwestern U.-Grad. Sch., Evanston, Ill., 2001. Diplomate in neurology ABPN, 2008. Internal medicine intern Barnes-Jewish Hosp., St. Louis, 2003—04, neurology resident, 2004—07, adminstrv. chief resident neurology, 2006—07; dementia fellow Wash. U., St. Louis, 2007—09, instr. neurology, 2009—11, asst. prof. neurology, 2011—. Mem.: Soc. Neurosci., AMA, Am. Acad. Neurology, Phi Kappa Phi, Gamma Sigma Delta, Alpha Omega Alpha, Sigma Xi. Office: Washington University 660 S Euclid Ave Campus Box 8111 Saint Louis MO 63110 Office Fax: 314-286-1985. Business E-Mail: ghoshaln@neuro.wustl.edu.

GHOSSAINI, SOHA NADIM, medical educator; d. Nadim and Noha (Kaasamany) Ghossaini. MD, Am. U., Lebanon, 1994, degree in otolaryngology head and neck surgery, 2000. Internship, residency in otolaryngology-head and neck surgery Am. U. of Beirut, Lebanon, 1995—2000; otology-neurotology clin. fellowship Columbia U., Coll. Physicians and Surgeons, NYC, 2000—02, cilincal instr., 2002—03; asst. prof. Columbia U. Med. Ctr., NYC, 2003—08; assoc. prof. otolaryngology; dir. otology; dir. cochlear Implant Program Penn State U., Hershey Med. Ctr., Pa., 2008—. Practice site med. dir. Audiology Clinic Hershey Med. Ctr., 2008—; adj. assoc. rsch. scientist Columbia U., Coll. Physicians and Surgeons, 2008—. Recipient Tchg. award, Columbia U., Coll. Physicians and Surgeons, 2005. Fellow: ACS; mem.: Am. Acad. Otolaryngology Head and Neck Surgery Found. (grantee 2005, scholar 2004—05). Achievements include research in Baha; tinnitus; sudden hearing loss; cochlear implants; otosclerosis. Office: Penn State Hershey Med Ctr Coll Medicine H&N Surgery H091 500 University Dr PO Box 850 Hershey PA 17033 Office Phone: 717-531-6718. Office Fax: 717-531-6160. Personal E-mail: sghossaini@gmail.com. Business E-Mail: sghossaini@hmc.psu.edu.

GHOSSEIN, CYBELE, nephrologist; b. Beirut, June 27, 1963; MD, Albert Einstein Coll. Medicine, 1990. Assoc. prof. Northwestern U. Feinberg Sch. Medicine, 1998—. Office: 675 North St Clair Ste 18-275 Chicago IL 60657 Business E-Mail: c-ghossein@northwestern.edu.

GHOUSIA, S., dental educator; b. Bangalore, Karnataka, India, May 5, 1981; BDS, Ambedker Dental Coll., 2004; MDS, Coll. Dental Scis., 2010. Asst. prof. AECS Maaruti Coll. Dental Scis. & Rsch. Ctr., 2010—. Asst. prof., cons. pediatric dentist. Home: Door 85 Kothanda Rama Layout Anna S Bangalore Karnataka 560042 India Office Phone: 9880775708. Personal E-mail: drghousia786@gmail.com.

GHUMAN, JASWINDER KAUR, medical educator; b. Dakha, Punjab, India, Mar. 27, 1950; MD, Christian Med. Coll., Ludhiana, Punjab, 1972. Assoc. prof., psychiatry and pediat. with tenure U. Ariz. Coll. Medicine, 2003—. Asst. prof., psychiatry and behavioral scis. Johns Hopkins U. Sch. Medicine, 1988—2003. Career Devel. grant, NIMH. Mem.: Nat. Inst. Mental Health (study sect. review panel mem. intervention com.), Am. Acad. Child and Adolescent Psychiatry. Avocations: travel, reading. Office: 1501 N Campbell Ave Tucson AZ 85724 Business E-Mail: jkghuman@email.arizona.edu.

GIACCONE, GIUSEPPE, oncologist, researcher; MD cum laude, U. Torino Med. Sch., Italy, 1980; PhD, Free Univ. Med. Ctr., Amsterdam, 1990. Clin. oncology and internal medicine training U. Torino, 1980—88; sr. oncologist Free Univ. Med. Ctr., 1990—2000, prof. med. oncology, 2000—07, head dept. med. oncology, 2003—07; chief Med. Oncology Br. and Affiliates, head thoracic oncology sect. Ctr. Cancer Rsch., Nat. Cancer Inst., NIH, Bethesda, Md., 2007—. Mem. European Orgn. Rsch. and Treatment of Cancer Lung Cancer Cooperative Group, 1982—, chair, 1993—2000. Contbr. articles to profl. jours. Office: Nat Cancer Inst Bldg 10 - Magnuson CC, Rm 12N226 10 Center Dr Bethesda MD 20892 Office Phone: 301-496-4916. Office Fax: 301-402-0172. E-mail: giacconeg@mail.nih.gov. *

GIAMBRA, BARBARA K., pediatrics nurse; b. Milw., May 16, 1964; BSN, Vanderbilt U., 1986; MS, U. Buffalo, 1999. Evidence-based practice mentor, advanced practice nurse Cin. Children's Hosp. Med. Ctr., 2000—. Grant, Am. Nephrology Nurses Assn. Mem.: Nat. Assn. Pediat. Nurse Practitioners, Soc. Pediat. Nurses, Sigma Theta Tau Internat. Office: 3333 Burnet Ave MLC 8006 Cincinnati OH 45229-3039 Office Fax: 513-636-8893. Business E-Mail: barbara.giambra@cchmc.org.

GIANNASI-MARSON, LILIAN CHRYSTIANE, dentist, educator; b. Santos, July 4, 1968; Degree in Odontology, U. Taubaté, 1992; PhD, U. Vale do Paraíba, 2008. Assoc. prof., rschr. U. Nove Julho, 2009. Mem.: Sleep Brazilian Assn., Am. Acad. Dental Sleep Medicine (Clin. Rsch. award). Home: R Esperança 265 sl 31 São José dos Campos São Paulo 12243-710 Brazil Home Fax: 55 12 39510800.

GIANNATTASIO, CRISTINA, cardiologist, educator; b. Milan, Aug. 3, 1960; MD, U. Milan, PhD, 1985, degree in Cardiology, 1989. Full prof., head, hypertension unit U. Milan, Bicocca and Azienda Ospedaliera S. Gerardo Monza, 2005. Office: Ospedale S Gerardo Via Pergolesi 33 Monza MB 20100 Italy Business E-Mail: cristina.giannattasio@unimib.it.

GIANNELLA, LUCA, medical researcher; b. Italy, June 20, 1976; D, U. Modena and Reggio Emilia, Italy, 2001. Rschr. AUSL Reggio Emilia - Cesare Magati Hosp., Scandiano, 2008. Office: Viale Martiri della Libertà 6 Scandiano Reggio Emilia 42020 Italy

GIANNINI, A. JAMES, psychiatrist, educator, researcher, author; b. Youngstown, Ohio, June 11, 1947; s. Matthew and Grace Carla (Nistri) G.; children: Juliette Nicole, Jocelyn Danielle. BS, Youngstown State U., Ohio, 1970; MD, U. Pitts., 1974; postgrad., Yale U., 1974-78, U. London, 1996-97. Diplomate Nat. Bd. Med. Examiners. Intern St. Elizabeth Med. Ctr., Youngstown, 1974, assoc. dir. family medicine, psychiatry, 1978-80; resident in psychiatry Yale U., New Haven, 1975-78, chief resident, 1977-78; assoc. psychiatrist Elmcrest Psychiat. Inst., Portland, Conn., 1976-78; acting ward chief Conn. Mental Health Ctr., New Haven, 1977; assoc. dir. family medicine, psychiatry St. Elizabeth Med. Ctr., Youngstown, 1978-80; from asst. prof. to assoc. prof. dept. psychiatry N.E. Ohio Med. Coll., 1978-84, program dir., 1980-88, prof., 1984-90, vice-chmn., 1985-89; assoc. clin. prof. dept psychiatry Ohio State U., 1983-89, clin. prof., 1989-96; chmn. depts. psychiatry and toxicology Western Res. Care System Hosp., 1985-87, med. dir. toxicology, 1987; acting dir. dual diagnosis unit Youngstown Osteo. Hosp., 1987—2000; pres., corp. med. dir. Chem. Abuse Ctrs., Inc., Ohio and Mich., 1987—2004; med. dir. substance abuse svcs. Cmty. Mental Health Ctr. of Mid. Ga., Dublin, 2004—; lt. col. M.C., U.S. Army, 2004—05. Dir. alumni schs. com. Yale U., New Haven, 1997-2005; vis. prof. Inst. for Scis. Comm. and Sci. Edn., Columbia Coll., Chgo., U. Naples, Italy, 1990, U. Zagreb, Croatia, 1990; examiner in psychology LaTrobe U., Bundoora, Australia, 1988-89; sr. mentor U. Pitts., 2001—05, U. Pitts. Alumni Recruitment Team, 2005-; sr. cons. Fair Oaks Hosp., Summit, N.J., 1979, Regent Hosp., N.Y.C., 1981-96, chmn. Nat. Adv. Council Prevention and Control of Rape, NIMH, Rockville, Md., 1983-86, spl. reviewer mood disorders com., 1995-97; mem. drug abuse clin., behavioral and rsch. rev. com. Nat. Inst. Drug Abuse, Rockville, Md., 1987-88; chief forensic psychiatrist Mahoning County Prosecutor, 1989-97; Am. Participant USIA Drug Abuse program to Cyprus, Italy, Can., Barbados, St. Lucia and Yugoslavia, 1990-94; panelist, moderator Renaissance Weekend, Hilton Head and Charleston, S.C., 1997—; cons. Smith-Kline Labs., McNeil Labs., Excerpta Medica Pubs., Amino Labs., Fund for Am. Renaissance; dir. clin. rsch. Princeton Diagnostic Labs., South Plainfield, N.J., 1987-89; med. dir. med. adv. bd. Neurodata Inc., 1987-89, pres., 1989-2004, med. dir. Chem. Abuse Ctrs. Inc., 1987, corp. med. dir., 1987-97; spl. reviewer initial review group, 1995-97, health, behavior and prevention review com. NIH, Rockville, Md.; ethics com. Mahoning County Mental Retardation Bd., Youngstown, Ohio, 1995-98, treas. 1996-97, vice-chmn., bd. treas., 1997-98; psychiatrist emeritus Stony Lodge Hosp., Briar Cliff Manor, NY; book reviewer Psychiat. Times, 2000—. Author: (with Henry Black) Psychiatric, Psychogenic, Somatopsychic Disorders, 1978; (with Robert Gilliland) Neurologic and Neuropsychiatric Disorders, 1983; (with Andrew Slaby) Overdose and Detoxification Emergencies, 1983; Biological Foundation of Clinical Psychiatry, 1988, (with Andrew Slaby) Drugs of Abuse, 1989, 2d edit., 1996, Comprehensive Laboratory Services in Psychiatry, 1986; (with Philip Jose Farmer) Red Orc's Rage, 1991; (with Andrew Slaby) The Eating Disorders, 1993, 2d edit., 1997, Drugs of Abuse, 2d edit., 1998, Drug Abuse: A Family Guide to Recognition and Treatment, 1999; contbr. numerous articles to profl. jours. Vice chmn. Mahoning County (Ohio) Mental Health Bd., 1982-84, chmn., 1984-86; councilor Nat. Italian Am. Found. Named Ky. Col., 2007; recipient Physician's Recognition award, 1978—, rsch. award Fair Oaks Hosp., 1979, bronze award Brit. Med. Assn., 1983, Outstanding Leadership award Mahoning County Mental Health Bd., 1986, Silver Rose award Assn. Italiano Donati d'Organo, Milan, 1990, Excellence award Yale U. Admissions Com., 2002, Rschr. of Yr. award Western Res. Behavioral Medicine Inst., 2006. Fellow: APA (disting. fellow 2003—11, disting. life fellow 2011—), Royal Soc. Medicine (sub-dean 2005—), Am. Coll. Clin. Pharmacology (sec.-treas. Ohio chpt. 1990—97, nat. govt. affairs com. 1990—2003, steering coun., exec. com. Ohio chpt. 1990—, pres. 1997—2004, nat. edn. com. 2003—04), N.J. Acad. Medicine, Acad. Medicine, Royal Acad. Medicine (Eng.); mem.: Pub. Diplomacy Alumni Assn., Ga. Psychiat. Assn., Acad. Clin. Psychiatry, N.Y. Acad. Scis., Royal Coll. Medicine, European Neurosci., Brit. Brain Soc., Soc. Neurosci., Am. Psychiat. Assn. (fellow 1989—2003, disting. fellow 2003—), Dublin C. of C., Youngstown C. of C. (vice-chmn. health com. 1986—89, chmn. 1989—96), Athletic Club (Atlanta), Atrium Club (Warren, Ohio), Yale Club (Cleve., Pitts., Atlanta), Youngstown Club, Domus (London), Dublin Country Club, Swim and Racquet Club (Poland, Ohio), Morey's (New Haven), Cercola di Corso (Florence, Italy), Sigma Xi. Republican. Roman Catholic. Office: 463 Deer Creek Trail Dublin GA 31021-3248 Office Phone: 478-272-1190.

GIANNONE, PETER JOHN, pediatrician; b. Bronx, NY, May 9, 1970; BS, Siena Coll., 1992; MD, SUNY Health Sci. Ctr., Syracuse, 1996. Dir., neonatal-perinatal medicine Ohio State U. Med. Ctr., 2011—. Novel Therapuetic Target Necrotizing Enterocolitis grant, NIH. Fellow: Acad. Pediat.; mem.: Soc. Pediatric Rsch. Office: 700 Childrens Dr Columbus OH 43205 Business E-Mail: peter.giannone@nationwidechildrens.org.

GIANNOTTA, STEVEN LOUIS, neurosurgery educator; b. Detroit, Apr. 4, 1947; s. Louis D. and Betty Jane (Root) G.; m. Sharon Danielak, June 13, 1970; children: Brent, Nicole, Robyn. Student, U. Detroit, 1965-68; MD, U. Mich., 1972. Diplomate Am. Bd. Neurol. Surgeons. Surg. intern U. Mich., Ann Arbor, 1972-73, neurosurg. resident, 1973-78; asst. prof. neurosurgery UCLA, 1978-80; asst. prof. neurosurgery Sch. Medicine U. So. Calif., LA, 1980-83, assoc. prof. neurosurgery Sch. Medicine, 1983-89, prof. neurosurgery Sch. Medicine, 1989—, chmn. dept. neurosurgery, 2004—. Bd. dirs. Am. Bd. Neurol. Surgery, 1995—2001, sec., 1999—2000, chmn., 2000—01. Fellow ACS, Am. Heart Assn. (stroke coun., rsch. grantee 1980, 84), So. Calif. Neurol. Soc. (pres. 1993-94), Congress Neurol. Surgeons (sec. 1986-89, v.p. 1993) Soc. Clin. Neuroscis. (L.A. pres. 1992-93), Am. Assn. Neurol. Surgeons (bd. dirs. 2001-). Democrat. Roman Catholic. Avocations: golf, skiing, sports cars. Office: Dept Neurosurgery Ste 5046 1200 N State St Los Angeles CA 90033-1029 Office Phone: 323-442-5720.

GIANNOULIS, MANTHOS GEORGIOS, endocrinologist, researcher; s. Georgios Giannoulis and Anna Giannouli; m. Sabine Klocker Giannouli, Aug. 3, 2001; 1 child, Georgios Albert. MBBS; MD, U. Medicine and Pharmacy, Timisoara, Romania, 1988, U. London, 2006. Resident in internal medicine Papanikolaou Hosp., Thessaloniki, 1992—94; rsch. fellow in endocrinology St. Bartholomew's Hosp., London, 1995—96; clin. fellow in endocrinology Ippokratio Hosp., Thessaloniki, Greece, 1997—98; clin. rsch. fellow, lectr. diabetes and endocrinology King's Coll., St.Thomas's Hosp., London, 1999—2003, hon. rsch. fellow in diabetes and endocrinology, 2004—. Consulting St. Thomas' Hosp., GKT Sch. Medicine, King's Coll., London, 1999—2003; cons., 2004—. Grantee, Spl. Trustees for St. Thomas's & Guy's Hosp. London, 1999. Mem.: The Endocrine Soc., European Soc. Endocrinology, Hellenic Med. Assn. Achievements include research in efects of growth hormone and/or testosterone in healthy elderly men. Office: Private praxis 20 Mitropolitou Iosif Thessaloniki 54622 Greece E-mail: manosgiannoulis@hotmail.com.

GIANOPOULOS, JOHN GEORGE, obstetrician; b. 1952; MD, Loyola U., Stritch Sch. Medicine, Maywood, Ill., 1977. Cert. Am. Bd. Obstetrics and Gynecology, 1984, in Maternal and Fetal Medicine 1985. Resident, ob-gyn. Loyola U. Med. Ctr., Maywood, Ill., 1977—81, fellow, maternal fetal medicine, 1981—83; Mary Isabelle Caestecker prof., chmn. dept., ob-gyn. Loyola U., Stritch Sch. Medicine, Maywood, Ill., 1997—. Office: Loyola Univ Sch Medicine 2160 First Ave Maywood IL 60153 Office Phone: 708-216-5923.

GIARDINA, ELSA GRACE VONNA, cardiologist, educator; b. Newark, Aug. 1, 1941; d. John and Elsa (Freda) G.; m. Alan L. Saroff, June 1, 1974; 1 child, John Saroff. AB, Bryn Mawr Coll., 1961; MD, NY Med. Coll., 1965. Diplomate Am. Bd. Internal Medicine, Am. Bd. Cardiology; cert. internal medicine, cardiovascular disease. Resident Roosevelt Hosp., NYC, 1965-69; cardiology resident Columbia Presbyn. Med. Ctr., NYC, 1969-71, NIH cardiovascular pharmacology fellow, 1971-72; asst. prof. medicine Columbia U., NYC, 1972-79, assoc. prof. medicne, 1980-87, prof. medicine, 1987—. Mem. cardiorenal adv. com. Food & Drug Adminstrn., Rockville, Md., 1984-88; mem. pharmacology study sect. NIH, Bethesda, Md., 1989-93; dir. Ctr. for Women's Health, Columbia-Presbyn. Med. Ctr., N.Y.C., 1994—. Contbr. articles to profl. jours. Sec., bd. dirs. Sarnoff Rsch. Found., 2004—; bd. dirs. Sarnoff Endowment for Cardiovascular Sci., 2000—. Fellow: ACP, Heart Rhythm Soc., Am. Heart Assn., Am. Coll. Cardiology; mem.: NY Acad. Medicine (trustee 2008, bd. dir.). Office: Columbia U 630 W 168th St New York NY 10032-3795 Office Phone: 212-305-6154. Business E-Mail: evg1@columbia.edu.

GIARDINA, EMILIANO, medical researcher, educator; b. Rome, Apr. 16, 1976; PhD in Med. Genetics, Tor Vergata U., Rome, 2004. Rschr., med. genetics Tor Vergata U., 2004—, prof., forensic genetics, prof., ocular genetics, prof., med. genetics, U. Urbino, Italy, 2006—; forensic geneticist, many Italian ct. rm. Author: (monography) Genetica Medica Pratica; contbr. articles to numerous sci. publs. Office: Tor Vergata Univ Rome Via Montpellier 1 Rome 00133 Italy Office Fax: +390620427313. Business E-Mail: emiliano.giardina@uniroma2.it.

GIARDINA, PATRICIA-JANE VONNA, pediatrician, hematologist, oncologist; BS, Vassar Coll., 1964; MD, NY Med. Coll., 1968. Diplomate Am. Bd. of Pediatrics, cert. pediatric hematology-oncology. Intern Lenox Hill Hosp.; resident Weill Cornell med. Ctr.

NY-Presbyn. Hosp., fellow Weill Cornell med. ctr., dir. Thalassemia program Weill Cornell med. coll., 1978, chief pediatric divsn. hematology-oncology; prof. clin. pediat. Weill Cornell Medical Coll.; with Meml. Sloan-Kettering Cancer Ctr., 1983. Recipient Cooley's Anemia Found. Recognition award, 1992, DeWitt-Clinton Masonic award for Cmty. Svc., 1993, Eagle and Rose Medal, Anemia Found. award, 2003; named Best Dr., 2007. Office: Weill Cornell Medical College 525 E 68th St Paysin Pavilion 695 New York NY 10065 Office Phone: 212-746-3400. Office Fax: 212-746-8609.

GIARDINO, ANGELO PETER, pediatrician, director; m. Eileen Giardino. MD, U. Pa., Phila., 1987; PhD, U. of Pa. Grad. Sch. of Edn., 1999. Lic. pediatrician Am. Bd. Pediat., 1991, dr. Pa., 1993, Tex., 2005, cert. patient safety officer Quality Colloquium, 2007, physician exec. Certifyilng Commn. Med. Mgmt., 2007. Assoc. physician, med. dir. cmty. edn. dept., chair quality improvement com. Children's Hosp. Phila., 1993—2002; v.p. clin. affairs St. Christopher's Hosp. Children, Phila., 2002—05; med. dir., chair med. adv. com. Tex. Children's Health Plan, Inc., Houston, 2005—; clin. assoc. physician Baylor Coll. Medicine, Houston, 2005—; attending physician Child Protection Team, Tex. Children's Hosp., Houston, 2005—. Lectr. U. Tex. Sch. Nursing, Houston, 2006—. Author: (book) Helping Children Affected by Abuse: A Parent's and Teacher's Handbook for Increasing Awareness; editor: (books) Child Safety: A Pediatric Guide for Parents, Teachers, Nurses, and Caregivers, Intimate Partner Violence/Domestic Violence, to profl. jours. articles. Bd. mem. US Conf. Cath. Bishops' Nat. Rev. Bd. for Protection of Children, DC, 2004; bd. dirs. Justice for Children, Houston, 2005. Recipient Ronald Reagan award, Nat. Rep. Caucus, 2005, Disting. Child Adv. award, Support Ctr. Child Advocates, 2005, Physician's Recognition award, AMA, 2006—08. Mem.: Am. Coll. Med. Quality, Am. Coll. Physician Execs., Ambulatory Pediatric Assn., Am. Acad. Pediat., Suspected Child Abuse and Neglect, Inst. Safe Families. Office: Tex Children's Health Plan Inc 2450 Holcombe Blvd Ste 34L Houston TX 77021 Home Fax: 832-825-8765. Business E-Mail: apgiardi@texaschildrens.org.

GIBBONS, GARY HUGH, cardiologist, educator; b. Oct. 4, 1956; married; 3 children. B, Princeton U.; MD magna cum laude, Harvard Med. Sch., 1984. Cert. Internal Medicine, 1987, Cardiovascular Disease, 1989. Resident Brigham & Women's Hosp., Boston, fellow in cardiology; faculty Stanford U., 1990—96, Harvard Med. Sch., 1996—99; dir. Cardiovascular Rsch. Inst. Morehouse Sch. Medicine, Atlanta, 1999—, prof. medicine, 1999—, attending cardiologist, 1999—. Scholar PEW Found. Mem.: Inst. Medicine. Office: Cardiovascular Rsch Inst Morehouse Sch Medicine 720 Westview Dr SW Atlanta GA 30310-1495 Office Phone: 404-752-1545. Office Fax: 404-752-1042. E-mail: ggibbons@msm.edu.

GIBBONS, RAYMOND JOHN, cardiologist; b. NYC, Sept. 4, 1949; BSE in Aerospace and Mechanical Sciences, Princeton U.; MS, MSc in Math., U. Oxford, Eng.; MD, Harvard Med. Sch., 1976. Intern Mass. Gen. Hosp., Boston, 1976-77, resident, internal medicine, 1977-78; fellow, cardiovascular divsn., dept. medicine Duke U. Med. Ctr., Durham, 1978-81; prof. medicine Mayo Med. Sch., 1992—. Contbr. articles to profl. jours.; mem. editl. bd. Circulation, Jour. Am. Heart Assn., Jour. Am. Coll. of Cardiology and others. Fellow Am. Coll. Cardiology; Am. Heart Assn. (pres. 2006-07). Office: Mayo Clinic 200 1st St SW Rochester MN 55905-0002 Office Phone: 507-284-2541. Business E-Mail: gibbons.raymond@mayo.edu.

GIBBONS, VINCENT PAUL, pediatric neurologist, educator; b. Cambridge, Mass., Apr. 21, 1949; m. Marcellina Murphy; 3 children. Grad., Harvard Coll., Boston; MD, Georgetown U., Washington, DC, 1975. Diplomate Am. Bd. Pediat., Am. Bd. Psychiatry & Neurology. Intern pediat. Children's Nat. Med. Ctr, Washington, 1975—76, resident pediat., 1976—77; resident child neurology George Wash. U. Med. Ctr., 1977—78; fellowship neurophysiology Children's Hosp. Boston, 1978—82; attending physician SSM Cardinal Glennon Children's Hosp., St. Louis, 1987—97, Methodist Med. Ctr., Ill., 1997—99, St. John's Hosp., Springfield, Ill., 1999—2000, U. San Francisco, 2000; asst. prof. neurology St. Louis U. Med. Sch., 1987—97, U. Ill., Peoria, 1997—99; assoc. prof. neurology So. Ill. U., Springfield, 1999—2000; assoc. clin. prof. pediat. & neurology U. Calif. Sch. Medicine, San Francisco, 2001—07; head divsn. pediat. neurology Albany Med. Ctr., NY, 2007—. Contbr. articles to profl. jours. Mem.: Am. Epilepsy Soc., Am. Acad. Clin. Neurophysiology, Am. Clin. Neurophysiology Soc., Am. Acad. Neurology. Office: AMC Neurology Group Physicians Pavilion 1st Fl 47 New Scotland Ave MC 70 Albany NY 12208 Office Phone: 518-262-5226. Office Fax: 518-262-5041.

GIBBONS, WILLIAM, reproductive endocrinologist; MD, Baylor Coll. Med., Houston. Cert. reproductive endocrinology & infertility, obstetrics & gynecology. Resident & fellow Baylor Coll. Med., dir. div. reproductive endocrinology & infertility; faculty U. Southern Calif. Sch. Med., 1979—82; with Jones Inst. Reproductive Med.; chmn. dept. obstetrics & gynecology Eastern Va. Med. Sch.; reproductive endocrinologist fertility specialist A Woman's Ctr. Reproductive Med. Mem.: Wimberley Soc., Am. Assn. Obstetrics & Gynecology, Soc. Reproductive Surgeons, Am. Soc. Reproductive Med., Soc. Gynecologic Investigators, Endocrine Soc., Soc. Assisted Reproductive Technologies (bd. mem.), Soc. Reproductive Endocrinology & Infertility (former pres.). Achievements include being part of team responsible for the nation's second In Vitro Fertilization baby. Office: Woman's Hospital Physician Tower I 9000 Airline Hwy Ste 670 Baton Rouge LA 70815-4114 Office Phone: 225-926-6886.

GIBBS, DENIS LAUREL, radiologist; b. Wayne, Mich., Mar. 6, 1945; s. Laurel Pierce and Alwyn Marie (Larson) G.; m. Paula Kay Lynn, Sept. 6, 1974 (div. Aug. 1988); children: Jeremy Paul, Matthew Ryan, Kevin Christopher, Denis Patrick; m. Kathleen Marie DeLaFuente, July 9, 1989; 1 child, Andrew Zachery. BS, Andrews U., Berrien Springs, Mich., 1967, postgrad., 1967-69; DO, Kansas City Coll. Osteopathic Medicine, 1974. Diplomate Am. Bd. Radiology. Intern, radiology resident Doctors' Hosps., Columbus, Ohio, 1974-78, staff radiologist, 1978; chmn. dept. radiology Rocky Mountain Hosp., Denver, 1978-88, vice chief of staff, 1982, chief of staff, 1983, 84; chmn. dept. radiology Colo. Plain Med. Ctr. Regional Trauma Ctr., Ft. Morgan, 1988—2002, vice chief of staff, 1992—93; staff radiologist, vice chmn. dept. Lakeland Med. Ctr., Niles, Mich., 2002—, radiologist, vice chair of dept., 2002—; ptnr., CFO Radiology Assn. Berrien County, Mich., 2005—; radiologist Lakeland Hosp. Systems, St. Joseph, Mich., 2005—; site chief Lakeland Hosp., Niles, 2005—. Med., legal cons., Colo., 1979—, Calif., 1979—, Fla., 1979—; consulting radiologist East Morgan Hosp., Luth. Health Sys., Brush, Colo., 1988—2002; CEO IRS Radiology Cons., P.C., Ft. Morgan, 1988—2002, Interstate Radiology Services, Henderson, Nev., 2002—; v.p. Niles Imaging Physicians, Mich., 2002—. Med. reviewer Post Grad. Medicine. Mem. Am. Osteopathic Assn., Am. Osteopathic Coll. Radiology, Am. Roentgen Ray Soc., Radiology Soc. N.Am., Soc. Nuc. Medicine, Mich. Radiologic Soc., Mich. Osteopathic Assn., Nat. Assn. Seventh-Day Adventist Osteopaths, Colo. Med. Soc., Soc. Nuclear Medicine Physicians. Republican. Avocations: snorkeling, skin diving, racquetball, sports car enthusiast and owner, travel. Office: PO Box 820 Niles MI 49120

GIBBS, JEWELLE TAYLOR, retired educator and clinical psychologist; b. Stratford, Conn., Nov. 4, 1933; d. Julian Augustus and Margaret Pauline (Morris) Taylor; m. James Lowell Jr. Gibbs, Aug. 25, 1956; children: Geoffrey Taylor, Lowell Dabney. AB cum laude, Radcliffe Coll., 1955; postgrad. in Bus. Adminstrn., Harvard-Radcliffe Program, 1959; MSW, U. Calif., Berkeley, 1970, PhD, 1980. Jr. mgmt. asst. U.S. Dept. Labor, Washington, 1955—56; market rsch. coord. Pillsbury Co., Mpls., 1959—61; clin. social worker Stanford (Calif.) U. Student Health Svc., 1970—74, 1978—79, rsch. assoc. dept. psychiatry, 1971—73; asst. prof. Sch. Social Welfare U. Calif., Berkeley, 1979—83, acting assoc. prof., 1983—86, assoc. prof., 1986—92, Zellerbach prof. social policy, 1992—2000; chair faculty Sch. Social Welfare, 1993—94, ret., 2000; pvt. practice as clin. psychologist, 1983—91; ret.; fellow Bunting Inst., Radcliffe Coll., Spring, 1985. Bd. regents U. Santa Clara (Calif.), 1980—84; mem. Minn. State Commn. Status Women, 1963—65; co-chairperson Minn. Women's Com. Civil Rights, 1963—65; mem. adv. coun. Nat. Ctr. Children Poverty, 1987—95; bd. dirs. Ctr. Populations Options, 1989—93; trustee Radcliffe Coll., 1991—95; v.p. Van Leoben Sels Rembe Rock, Rembe Rock Found., 2000—06; vis. fellow Rsch. Inst. Ctr. Comparative Study Race & Ethnicity, Stanford U., 2001—02; v.p. bd. dirs. Mus. African Diaspora, 2006—; mem. editl. bd. Am. Jour. Orthopsychiatry, 1980—84. Author: Children of Color: Psychological Interventions with Minority Youth, 1989, Race and Justice: Rodney King and O.J. Simpson in a House Divided, 1996; co-author: Preserving Privilege: California Proposition Politics, and People of Color, 2001; editor: Contbr. Young, Black and Male in America, 1988; contbr. chapters to books, articles to profl. jours. Disting. scholar, Joint Ctr. Pol. & Econ. Studies, Washington, DC, 1991—92, Vis. scholar, U. London, 1993, U. Toronto, 1994, NIMH fellow, 1979, Soroptimist Internat. grantee, 1978—79, Vis. fellow, Rsch. Inst. Ctr. Comparative Studies in Race and Ethinicity, Stanford U., 2001—02. Fellow: Am. Orthopsychiat. Assn. (bd. dirs. 1985—86); mem.: Am. Assn. Suicidology (McCormick award 1987), Western Psychol. Assn., Nat. Assn. Social Workers, Am. Psychol. Assn. (Black Leadership Forum award 2002, Berkeley Citation 2000), Phi Beta Kappa (hon.). Democrat. Home: 100 Bay Pl Apt 1204 Oakland CA 94610

GIBBS, LINDA I., city official; b. Menands, NY, July 17, 1959; m. Tom McMahon. BA, Queens Coll.; JD, SUNY, Buffalo, 1985. With NYC Dept. Employment; spl. advisor to dir. fin. divsn. NYC Coun.; dep. dir. social services, Office Mgmt. & Budget NYC, NYC, dep. commr. mgmt. & planning Adminstrn. for Children's Services, commr. Dept. Homeless Services, 2002—06, dep. mayor for health & human services, 2006—. Office: City Hall 52 Chambers St New York NY 10007

GIBBS, PATRICIA HELLMAN, physician; b. Boston, Oct. 22, 1958; d. Frederick Warren and Patricia Christina (Sander) H.; m. Richard D. Gibbs, Dec. 22, 1984; children: Ruth, Samuel, Matthew, Kate, Frank. BA summa cum laude, Williams Coll., 1982; MD, Yale U., 1987. Diplomate Am. Bd. Family Practice. Intern, resident in family practice U. Wash., Seattle, 1987-90; ptnr. Tricia Gibbs, MD and Richard Gibbs, MD, San Francisco, 1990-95; co-founder, med. dir. San Francisco Free Clinic, 1993—. Supervising physician San Francisco Ballet, 1990-95. Co-author: Medical and Orthopedic Issues of Active and Athletic Women-Skiing, 1993, Spine Care-Dance, 1993, Medical and Orthopedic Issues for Women, 1993; contbr. articles to profl. jours. Mem. US Alpine ski team, 1976-78; founder Sugar Bowl Acad., 1999. Women's scholar Williams Coll., 1982, Class of '25 Athlete scholar, 1982; named Family Physician of Yr., Calif. Acad. Family Physicians, 1998; recipient Pub. Health Heroes Institutional award Berkeley Sch. Pub. Health U. Calif., 2006, Positive Coaching Alliance Honoring the Game award, Sugar Bowl Ski Team Found., Williams Coll. Bicentennial award 2002. Mem. AMA, Am. Acad. Family Physicians, Am. Assn. Intercollegiate Athletics for Women (All-Am. Athlete 1979, 1981), Phi Beta Kappa, Sigma Xi. Jewish. Avocations: distance running, ski racing, computers. Office: San Francisco Free Clinic 4900 California St San Francisco CA 94118-1115 Office Phone: 415-750-9894. Business E-Mail: pgibbs@sffc.org. *

GIBBS, TERRELL T., pharmacologist, educator; b. Houston, Nov. 16, 1950; BS, MIT, 1973; PhD, Harvard Med. Sch., 1980. Rsch. assoc. SUNY Downstate Health Sci. Ctr., Bklyn., 1980—85, rsch. asst. prof. anatomy & cell biology, 1987—90; substitute asst. prof. biology CUNY Coll. Staten Island, 1986—89; asst. prof. pharmacology & exptl. therapeutics Boston U. Sch. Medicine, 1990—2002, assoc. prof. pharmacology & exptl. therapeutics, 2002—. Mem.: Soc. Neurosci. Avocation: Aikido. Office: Boston University Sch Medicine Dept Pharmacology 72 E Concord St Boston MA 02118 Business E-Mail: tgibbs@bu.edu.

GIBBY-SMITH, BARBARA, psychologist, nurse; b. Woodburn, Oreg., Dec. 13, 1938; d. Chester Clifton and Marvel Elizabeth (Hill) Gibby; m. Roy Milton Smith, June 2, 1957 (div. June 1990); children: Thomas Clifton, Jeffery Shawn, Mark Anderson. ADN, Chemeketa C.C., Salem, Oreg., 1972; BS, SUNY, Albany, 1980; MS, Western Oreg. State Coll., 1982; D of Psychology, Pacific U., Forest Grove, Oreg., 1993. Diplomate Am. Bd. Profl. Disability Cons., Am. Bd. Specialist, Am. Bd. Forensics Medicine; cert. addiction examiner. Adminstr. Birch St. Manor, Dallas, Oreg., 1973—81; disability determination specialist State of Oreg. Workers' Compensation Dept., Salem, 1983—85; counselor Women's Crisis Ctr., Salem, 1986—88; rehab. counselor Employer Rehab. Svcs., Portland, Oreg., 1985—87; therapist, counselor Pacific U., Hillsboro, Oreg., 1988—89, Forest Grove, 1989—91; intern psychology Portland State U., 1991—92, Kaiser-Permanente, Salem, 1991—92; resident psychology Tillamook Counseling Ctr., Oreg., 1993—95; hosp. privileges psychology and medicine Quality Healthcare, Forest Grove, 1996—; pvt. practice clin. psychology Mountain View Counseling Ctr., Forest Grove, Oreg., 1993—. Group therapy counselor Women's Crisis Ctr., Dallas, 1982-83; eating disorders group therapy facilitator, Salem, 1986-88; nat. register Doctoral Addiction Examiner. Author: William G. Hill: Pioneer of Oregon, 2004, Ted's Story: WWI, 2008, Let us Wait: Uganda, East Africa, 2010. Active Women's Coalition Orgn., Salem, 1988—; active missionary work schs. Bless Children, Salem, Oreg., 2004—11; sec. sponsor Eagles Adult Choir; active missionary work schs. DBA Matsiko Children's Network, associated with Gospel Messengers, KGANDA, Uganda, 2004—11; exec. dir. Matsiko Children's Choir TM, 2010—11; bd. mem. Imani Milele Children Non Profit Orgn., 2011—. Mem. APA, Am. Coll. Forensic Examiners (diplomate, 2008), Nat. Bd. Addiction Examiners (diplomate), Oreg. Psychol. Assn., Prescribing Psychologist Assn. (diplomate), Am. Mental Health Alliance (Oreg.). Democrat. Avocations: golf, bicycling, travel, genealogy, walking. Office: Mountain View Counseling Ctr 1911 Mountain View Ln Ste 500 Forest Grove OR 97116-2248 Office Phone: 503-357-0206. Personal E-mail: barbpg@juno.com.

GIBERT, CYNTHIA LIVINGSTONE, infectious diseases physician; b. Washington, Oct. 25, 1941; d. Kenneth Mackay and Anna Champion (Taliaferro) L.; m. Stephen Pierre Gibert; children: Christopher, Jennifer. BA in French, Sweet Briar Coll., 1963; MS in Phys. Chemistry, Cath. U. Am., 1974; MD, Howard U., 1984. Diplomate Am. Bd. Internal Medicine with subspecialty infectious diseases, Nat. Bd. Med. Examiners; lic. physician Va. Intern in medicine Washington Hosp. Ctr., 1984-85, resident in medicine, 1985-87, fellow in infectious diseases, 1988-89, Dept. Vets. Affairs Med. Ctr., Washington, 1987-88, infectious diseases clin. dir., 1992—2001, asst. chief sect. infectious diseases, 1992—2004, dir. spl. projects med. svc., 2004—; acting dep. chief cons. Pub. Health Strategic Health Care Group, Dept. Vets. Affairs, Washington, 2011. Asst. prof. medicine Georgetown U., Washington, 1990—99, assoc. prof. medicine, 1999-2009, prof. medicine, 2009-, faculty mem. HIV/AIDS Inst., 2007-; pres. Vets. Affairs Soc. Practitioners Infectious Diseases, 2008-10, Nat. Cathedral Sch., Alumnae Assn., 2002-04; mem. Nat. Cathedral Sch., Gov. Bd., 2002-04; v.p. Nat. Assn. Va. Physicians & Dentists, 2010-; lectr. in field. Contbr. numerous articles and abstracts to profl. jours. Mem. ACP, Greater Washington Infectious Diseases Soc. (pres. 2004-05), Internat. AIDS Soc., Am. Soc. Microbiology, Am. Med. Women's Assn. (pres. D.C. chpt. 1995-96); fellow Infectious Diseases Soc. America. Episcopalian. Avocations: gardening, swimming, skiing, travel. Home: 6530 Sunny Hill Ct Mc Lean VA 22101-1639 Office: VA Medical Ctr Sect Infectious diseases 50 Irving St NW Washington DC 20422-0001 Office Phone: 202-745-8695.

GIBLIN, NAN J., psychologist, educator; b. Kankakee, Ill., Sept. 18, 1946; d. Kenneth Theodore Johnson and Rose Marie Pocock; m. Walter Patrick Giblin, Oct. 5, 1968; 1 child, Daniel. BS in English Lit., Loyola U. Chgo., 1968, PhD of Ednl. Counseling, 1984; MA in Ednl. counseling, Northeastern Ill. U. Chgo., 1978. Registered psychologist Ill. Tchr. Sacred Heart Acad., Chgo., 1968—70; asst. prof. Northeastern Ill. U., Chgo., 1985—90; pvt. practice psychology Park Ridge, Ill., 1986—95; assoc. prof., prof. Northeastern Ill. U., Chgo., 1990—. Chair counseling edn. Northeastern Ill. U., Chgo., 1987—92, 2005—, assoc. dean Coll. Edn., 1992—98, dean Coll. Edn., 1998—; mem. Ill. State Cert. Bd., Springfield, 2001—05. Co-author: Finding Help: A Resource Guide to Personal Concerns, Individual Counseling: Skills and Techniques; co-editor: Family Counseling in School Settings. Mem.: ACA, Am. Assn. Coll. Tchr. Educators. Office: Northeastern Ill Univ 5500 N Saint Louis Chicago IL 60025 Office Phone: 773-442-5552.

GIBSON, EDGAR THOMAS, retired surgeon, educator; b. Phila., Mar. 23, 1915; s. Albert and Mabel (Cave) G.; m. Helen Tomlinson, Nov. 7, 1943; children: Ann Peluso, Barbara, Jeanne, Helen Tucker. BS, Villanova U., 1938; MD, Jefferson Med. Coll., 1942; postgrad., U. Pa., 1947-48. Resident surgery Cleve. Clinic, 1943-44, West Jersey Hosp., Camden, NJ, 1948—51; resident thoracic surgery Phila. Gen. Hosp., 1952-54; pres. staff Camden County Chest Hosp., 1950-88; chmn. dept. surgery West Jersey Hosp. Group, 1975-78; staff mem. Our Lady of Lourdes Hosp., Camden, NJ, 1950-88; instr. surgery Jefferson U., Phila., 1950-88, U. Penna Med. Sch., 1947—48. Pres. Camden County Heart Soc., 1960. Capt. U.S. Army, 1944-46, ETO. Fellow AMA, ACS, Am. Bd. Surgery, N.J. Soc. Surgeons; mem. Camden County Med. Soc. (pres.). Republican. Avocations: sailing, skiing, photography. Home: 8 Pond Head Rd Southport ME 04576-3343

GIBSON, FRANCES, nurse; b. Junction, Tex., Sept. 28, 1936; d. August and Juanita (Corpus-Garcia) Rehwoldt; m. Richard Gibson, July 4, 1954 (dec. July 25, 1962); children; Kenneth, René, Allison. AA, East Los Angeles Coll. Lic. vocat. nurse, Calif.; RN, Calif.; cert. oper. rm. technician, Calif.; cert. adult edn. tchr.; paralegal. Instr., profl. expert East LA Coll., Monterey Park, Calif., 1971-74; hostess talk show (in Spanish) Sta. KMEX-TV, LA, 1970-76; tchr. adult edn. Garvey Sch. Bd., Rosemead, Calif., 1976-77; case mgr. AIDS Healthcare Found., LA, 1991-93; clin. nurse Los Angeles County/U. So. Calif. Med. Ctr., 1981-89, AIDS clinician, 1993. Vol. nurse Lung Assn., L.A., 1970-76, ARC, L.A., 1969—; instr. health classes ARC, also instr. Spanish to ARC pers., mgr. info. booths at health fairs and convs., provider first aid at various gatherings, immunization clinics, chmn. adv. bd., 1971-72, bd. dirs., 1972-75, 79-82; med. editor, legal asst. Ivie & McNeill, L.A., 1986-96. Author: Spanish for English-Speaking Personnel, 1972. Recipient Spotlight award ARC, 1972, Clara Barton award ARC, 1976, 30-Yr. Vol. award ARC, 1999, Associate Womens Students award East L.A. Coll., 1969; named one of Ten Prettiest Chicanas in East Los Angeles, East L.A. Merchants, 1970. Mem. Nat. Assn. Chicano Nurses, AFL-CIO, Alpha Gamma Sigma. Democrat. Baptist. Avocations: gardening, crafts. Home: 1388 N Monroe Blvd Ogden UT 84404 Personal E-mail: fgrnbaby@aol.com.

GIBSON, MILTON EUGENE, cardiologist; b. Laporte, Ind., July 11, 1939; s. Maurice Wayne and Mary Leola Gibson; m. Gloria Jean Birky, Aug. 12, 1961; children: Kevin Scott, Bradley Mark. BA, Valparaiso U., 1961; MD, Ind. U., 1965. Diplomate Am. Bd. Internal Medicine, Am. Bd. Cardiovasc. Disease, Am. Bd. Interventional Cardiology. Rotating intern Meml. Hosp. of South Bend, 1965—66; resident in internal medicine Meth. Hosp. Grad. Med. Ctr., 1968—70, fellow in cardiology, 1970—72; cardiologist Cardiology Assocs., Inc., South Bend, Ind., 1972-88, pres., 1984-88; cardiologist, pres. Heart Group, South Bend, 1988—2004; cardiologist South Bend Clinic, 2004—05. Chmn. cardiac cath com. Meml. Hosp., South Bend, 1973-90, St. Joseph's Med. Ctr., South Bend, 1999-2001; chmn. dept.

medicine Meml. Hosp., South Bend, 1976-79; asst. clin. prof. medicine Ind. U., Indpls., 1980—. Author: Heart Sounds and Murmurs, 1973; contbr. articles to profl. jours. Pres. Am. Heart Assn., Indpls., 1977, pres. St. Joseph County chpt., 1975; bd. dirs. Vis. Nurse Assn., South Bend, 1984; mem. adv. bd. South Bend Pops Orch., 1978. Capt. U.S. Army, 1966-68, Vietnam. Decorated Bronze Star; recipient Man of Yr. award St. Joseph County Heart Assn., 1976. Fellow Am. Coll. Cardiology, Am. Coll. Chest Physicians, Coun. Critical Cardiology, Am. Heart Assn., Soc. Cardiac Angiography and Interventions; mem. ACP. Personal E-mail: megibso@comcast.net.

GIDDA, MAHESWARUDU, biologist; b. Andhra Pradesh, India, July 9, 1957; s. Krishnamurthy and Saraswathi Gidda; m. Lakshmi Janardhani Posina; 1 child, Saraswathi. PhD, Andhra U., Visakhapatnam, India, 1986. Sr. scientist, Mandapam camp CMFRI, Tamil Nadu, India, 1986—2000, sr. prin. scientist Visakhapatnam, Andhra Pradesh, 2000—09, scientist-in-charge, Visakhapatnam Regional Ctr., 2009—. Mem.: Forum Fisheries Profls., Marine Biol. Assn. India. Home: 4-69-11/1 Lawsons Bay Colony Visakhapatnam Andhra Pradesh530017 India Office: CMFRI Pandurangapuram Visakhapatnam Andhra Pradesh 530003 India Home Phone: 91-891-2591728; Office Phone: 918912543793. Personal E-mail: maheswarudu@yahoo.com.

GIDDON, DONALD B(ERNARD), psychologist, educator; b. Newark, May 1, 1930; s. William and Ruth (Franklin) G.; m. Phoebe L. Rothman, Aug. 28, 1955; children: David, Kenneth, Joanna, James. AB, Brown U., 1952; MA, Boston U., 1953; DMD, Harvard U., 1959; PhD in Psychology, Brandeis U., 1961. Lectr. psychology Brandeis U., 1954-71, 82-84, lectr. phys. edn., 1985-89; prof., chmn. dental ecology Harvard U., 1972-75, vis. prof., 1976-89, lectr., 1989-98, clin. prof. growth and devel., 1999—2005, clin. prof. devel. bio, 2005—, lectr. health svcs. adminstrn. Sch. Pub. Health, 1972-75, asst. dean adminstrn. Sch. Dental Medicine, 1973-75; assoc. staff New Eng. Med. Center, 1964-73; assoc. prof., chmn. dept. social dentistry Tufts U., Boston, 1964-67, prof., chmn. dept. social dentistry, 1967-72, asst. dean, 1967-69, assoc. dean, 1969-71; dean NYU Dental Ctr., 1975-78, prof. epidemiology and health promotion, 1976—; prof. psychology Grad. Sch. Arts and Scis., prof. anesthesiology NYU Med. Center, 1976-80; prof. Faculty of Medicine, U. Groningen, The Netherlands, 1980-81. Cons. Astra Pharm. Products, Inc., 1960—, dept. medicine and surgery VA, 1966-69, med. rsch. cons., 1988-90, Peter Bent Brigham Hosp., 1975-76, Meml. Sloan-Kettering Cancer Ctr., 1976-78, psychologist dept. anesthesiology Brigham and Women's Hosp., 1979—; vis. prof. U. Gothenburg, Sweden, 1971, Royal Dental Coll., Aarhus, Denmark, 1972, U. Pa., 1972, medicine McGill Med. U., 1981-83, psychology Mass. Coll. Pharmacy and Allied Health Scis., 1984-89; mem. exec. com. Goldwater Meml. Hosp., 1976-78; vis. staff physician NYU Med. Ctr., 1976-2006, hon. staff mem., 2006-; mem. med. staff Brookdale Hosp., 1977-2006, hon. staff mem., 2006-; clin. prof. Brown U., 1989-2006, emeritus, 2007—; clin. prof. U. Ill., Chgo., 1994—, Health Scis. Ctr. Stony Brook U., 2004—; founding dir. Rsch. Inst., Royal Victoria Hosp., Montreal, 1981-82. Contbr. articles to profl. jours. Bd. dirs. Mass. Health Coun., 1965-70, pres., 1968-69; pres. Hamilton sch. PTA, Newton Lower Falls, Mass., 1963-64; trustee Emerson Coll., 1991-2000, Berkshire Opera, 1996—2009, Colonial Theatre, 2006; mem. Com. on Univ. Resources, bd. overseers Harvard U., 1991—, NIH study sect., 2000—. Named Fulbright scholar, 1971. Fellow AAAS, APA, Acad. Behavioral Med. Rsch., Am. Pub. Health Assn., Am. Coll. Dentists, Internat. Coll. Dentists, Internat. Coll. Psychosomatic Medicine, Royal Soc. Medicine; mem. AAUP, Am. Statis. Assn., Internat. Assn. Study Pain, Am. Psychosomatic Soc., Am. Coll. Sports Medicine, Am. Dental Soc. Anesthesiology (assoc. editor 1965-72, chmn. ethics com. 1979-81), Behavioral Sci. in Dental Rsch. (pres. 1976-77), Internat. Assn. Dental Rsch. (pres. Boston sect. 1965-66), Am. Pain Soc. (dir. 1977-79), Soc. Behavioral Med., Soc. Psychophys. Rsch., Soc. Clin. and Experimental Hypnosis, Sigma Xi. Office: 277 Linden St Wellesley MA 02482-5900 Business E-Mail: donald_giddon@hms.harvard.edu. *

GIDIRI, MUCHABAYIWA FRANCIS, gynecologist; b. Harare, Zimbabwe, Jan. 11, 1967; s. Abraham and Virginia Gidiri; m. Fadziso Fiona Java; children: Tatenda, Chido. MBChB, Godfrey Huggins Sch. Medicine, Zimbabwe, 1992. Specialist registrar, Hull, Yorkshire, England, 2004—06, York, Scarborough; sr. specialist registrar Women and Children's Hosp., Kingston Upon Hull, East Yorkshire, 2007—. Contbr. scientific papers. Master: RCOG. Independent Thinkers. Avocations: football, music, sports. Home Fax: 441482641924. Personal E-mail: fmgidiri@doctors.org.uk.

GIESE, SHARON Y., plastic surgeon, educator; b. Dec. 20, 1964; AB in Biochemistry, Vassar Coll., 1983—87; grad. in Gen. Studies, Columbia U., 1987—88; MD, Northwestern U., 1989—93. Lic. Calif., 1995, NY, 1998, DC, 1998, diplomate Am. Bd. Plastic Surgery, 2000. Resident gen. surgery Stanford Univ., 1993—96, resident plastic and reconstructive surgery, 1995—98; fellow breast and aesthetic surgery Georgetown Univ., 1999; clin. asst. prof. Georgetown Univ. Med. Ctr., 1999; clin. asst. prof. Health Sci. Ctr. SUNY, 2000—01; founder Arete Medical Found. Inc.; cons. Misonix Inc. Author: (publs.) Safety Considerations in Large Volume Lipoplasty, 2001; co-author: Improvements in cardiovascular risk profile after large volume Lipoplasty: a 1 year follow-up study, 2001, Critical mass of subcutaneous fat in the pathogenesis of insulin resistance, 2003, numerous publs. Recipient Baxter Rsch. award, Northwestern Univ., 1990, Cert. of Excellence, 24th Annual Am. Soc. for Aesthetic Plastic Surgery, 1991; scholar Clin. Rsch. award, Plastic Surgery Educ., 2000. Mem.: Zedplast, AMA Women Physician Congress, Northeastern Soc. of Plastic Surgery, Am. Soc. of Aesthetic Plastic Surgery, Am. Soc. of Plastic Surgery, Phi Rho Sigma. Office: 114 East 61st St New York NY 10021 Office Phone: 212-421-3400. Office Fax: 212-421-3435.

GIESEL, ANN E., pediatrician, adolescent medicine, educator; MD, U. Louisville, 1985. Diplomate Am. Bd. Pediatrics, 2005, Am. Bd. Pediatrics-adolescent medicine, 2009. Resident pediat. Children's Hosp. & Med. Ctr., Seattle, 1986—88; fellow adolescent medicine Univ. Washington Med. Ctr., Seattle, 1989—91; assoc. clin. prof. pediat. Univ. Washington Sch. of Medicine, clin. prof. divsn. adolescent medicine; med. dir. Country Doctor FreeTeen Clinic for Homeless Youth, King County Juvenile Detention Center Health Clinic; dir. pediatric and adolescent gynecology Seattle Children's Hosp., clinic chief gynecology. Office: Seattle Children's Hospital 4800 Sand Point Way NE Seattle WA 98105

GIFFORD, DAVID RALSTON, health care association administrator, geriatrician; b. 1962; BA in Biology, Kenyon Coll., 1984; MD, Case Western Res. Sch. Medicine, Cleve., 1989; MPH, UCLA, 1994. Geriatric fellowship UCLA, 1994—95; med. dir. Steere House Nursing & Rehabilitation, 1995—2002; asst. prof. medicine & cmty. health Brown U., Providence, 1995—2005; med. dir. St. Elizabeth Home, 1998—2005; chief med. officer Quality Ptnrs. RI, 2000—05; dir. RI Dept. Health, Providence, 2005—11; sr. v.p. quality & regulatory affairs American Health Care Assn. (AHCA)/ Nat. Ctr. for Assisted Living (NCAL), Washington, 2011—. Dir. hospital & nursing home quality improvement projects RI Peer Rev. Org.; bd. dirs. RI Quality Inst. Contbr. articles to profl. jours. Office: American Health Care Association 1201 L St NW Washington DC 20005 Office Phone: 202-842-4444. Office Fax: 202-842-3860. *

GIFFORD, GERALD FREDERIC, retired science educator; b. Chanute, Kans., Oct. 24, 1939; s. Gerald Leo and Marion Lou (Browne) Gifford; m. Cinda Jean Lowman, June 26, 1982. Student, Kans. U., 1957-60; BS in Range Mgmt., Utah State U., 1962, MS in Watershed Mgmt., 1964, PhD in Watershed Sci., 1968. Asst. prof. watershed sci. Utah State U., Logan, 1967-72, assoc. prof., 1972-80, prof., 1980-84, chmn. watershed sci. unit, 1967-84, dir. Inst. Land Reclamation, 1982-84; head range, wildlife and forestry U. Nev., Reno, 1984-92, chmn. environ. and resource sci. dept., 1992—94, prof. hydrology and natural resource mgmt., 1994—2000, ret., 2000. Exch. scientist NSF, Canberra, Australia, 1974; cons. in field. Author: (book) Rangeland Hydrology, 1981; assoc. editor: Jour. Range Mgmt., 1982—87, 1991—95, Arid Soil Rsch. and Rehab., 1985—90; contbr. scientific papers to profl. pubs. Mem.: Soil and Water Conservation Soc., Am. Water Resources Assn. Avocations: racquetball, antiques, garage sales. Home: 3880 Squaw Valley Cir Reno NV 89509-5663 Office Phone: 775-826-7932. Personal E-mail: fredandcinda@sbcglobal.net.

GIFT, JAMES JOSEPH, aquatic toxicologist; BA in Biology, Harvard U, 1964; MA in Environ. Sci., Rutgers U., 1968, PhD in Environ. Sci., 1970. Lab. rsch. dir. Ichthyological Assocs., Brigantine, NJ, 1970-75; sr. v.p., dir. sci. and tech. EA Engring., Sci. & Tech. Inc., Md., 1975-97; owner Quail's Roost Environ. Svcs., 1997—, Quail's Roost Photography, 1997—. Mem.: Am. Fisheries Soc. Achievements include direction of a multimedia assessment contrasting ocean disposal of sewage sludge with various land-based waste management options; direction of ocean site designation studies for New York City and other municipalities; preparation of the first Special Permit Application for ocean disposal of sewage sludge; direction of a wide variety of ecological and human health risk assessments; conducting of research on the physiological effects of thermal gradients of numerous marine, estuarine and freshwater fish species; award-winning nature photographer. Personal E-mail: jgift42@msn.com.

GIGLER, VISHAKHA VORA, dermatologist, educator; BA in Psychology, U. Calif., San Diego, 1993, MD, 2000. Bd. cert. dermatologist Am. Bd. Dermatology. Dermatologist, dermatologic surgeon Dermatologist Med. Group, San Diego, 2003—08; surgeon Comprehensive Dermatology Group, 2008—. Recipient award, Achievement Rewards for Coll. Scientists, 1999, 2000, Top Doctor award, San Diego County Med. Soc., 2007—10. Mem.: San Diego Dermatological Surgery Soc. (sec.-treas.), Calif. Dermatology Soc., Am. Soc. Dermatological Surgery, Am. Acad. Dermatology, Phi Beta Kappa. Office: Comprehensive Dermatology Group 477 N El Camino Real C204 Encinitas CA 92024

GIGLI, IRMA, dermatologist, academic administrator, educator, immunologist; b. Cordoba, Argentina, Dec. 22, 1931; d. Irineo and Esperanza Francisca (Pons de Gigli) Gigli; m. Hans J. Muller-Eberhard. BA, Liceo Nacional Manuel Belgrano, Cordoba, 1950; MD, Universidad Nacional de Cordoba, 1957. Intern Cook County Hosp., Chgo., 1957—58, resident in dermatology, 1958—60; fellow in dermatology NYU, 1960—61; mem. faculty Harvard Med. Sch., 1967—75, asso. prof. dermatology, 1972—75; chief dermatology service Peter Bent Brigham Hosp., Robert B. Brigham Hosp., 1971—75; prof. dermatology and exptl. medicine N.Y. U. Med. Center, NYC, 1976—82, mem. faculty N.Y. Grad. Sch. Med. Scis., dir. Asthma and Allergic Disease Center for Immunodermatology Studies, 1980—91; prof. medicine, chief div. dermatology U. Calif.-San Diego, 1983—95; prof. medicine and dermatology U. Tex. Health Sci. Ctr., Houston, 1995—2003; assoc. dir. Inst. Molecular Medicine for Prevention Human Diseases U. Tex., Houston, 1998—2003, dep. dir., emerita, 2003—09, Walter and Mary Mischer prof. molecular medicine Houston, 1998—2009, Hous J Miller Eber Hard chair; dir. Rsch. Ctr. Immunology and Autoimmune Diseases, 1995—2009; prof. emeritus U. tex. Health Sci. Mem. Nat. Inst. of Allergy and Infectious Diseases Coun., 1978—79, bd. sci. counselors, 1997—; chmn. study sect. Allergy and Immunology Inst., NIH, 1978—83; mem. Guggenheim Found. Western Hemisphere and Phillippines Com. of Selection; adv. bd. NIH Fogarty Internat. Ctr., 1984—97. Bd. dirs. U.S. Civilian R&D Found. Recipient Rsch. award, Am. Cancer Soc., 1970—72, NIH, 1972—76, Disting. Profl. Woman of Yr. award, U. Tex. Health Sci. Ctr. at Houston, 2003, David Martin Carter Mentor award, Am. Skin Assn., 2005; grantee, Guggenheim Found., 1974—75. Mem.: Acad. Medicine, Engring, & Sci. Tex. (bd. dirs.), Am. Acad. Arts and Scis., Henry Kunkel Soc. (councilor 1999—), PEW Latin Am. Fellows Program in Biomed. Scis. (nat. adv. com. 1998—2005), Inst. Medicine/NAS, Am. Dermatol. Assn., Assn. Am. Physicians, Am. Acad. Allergy, Am. Acad. Dermatology, Am. Assn. Immunologists, Am. Soc. Clin. Investigation, Soc. Investigative Dermatology (hon.; pres. 1990—91, Stephen Rothman Meml. award 1996). Home Phone: 858-454-6396. Business E-Mail: irma.gigli@uth.tmc.edu.

GIKAS, PAUL WILLIAM, medical educator; b. Lansing, Mich., July 23, 1928; s. John and Minnie (Neumann) G.; m. Lois Suzanne Haglund, Dec. 27, 1952; children— Sandra Jane, Sarah Elizabeth, Paula Suzanne. AB, U. Mich., 1950, MD, 1954. Diplomate: Am. Bd. Pathology. Chief lab. service VA Hosp., Ann Arbor, Mich., 1960-68; mem. faculty U. Mich. Med. Sch., Ann Arbor, 1959—, assoc. prof. pathology, 1966-69, prof., 1969-95, prof. emeritus, 1995—, faculty rep. to Big Ten Intercollegiate Conf., Nat. Collegiate Athletic Assn., 1982-88, asst. dean for admissions, 1990-97. Cons. Armed Forces Inst. Pathology, 1966-74 Author: The Accident Problem, 1976, Uropathology, 1976, Forensic Aspects of the Highway Crash, 1983; co-editor: The Prevention of Highway Injury, 1967. Mem. adv. com. traffic safety HEW, 1966-68; mem. Gov. Mich. Spl. Commn. Traffic Safety Mich., 1964; chmn. bd. dirs. Pub. Citizen, Inc., 1971-2002; co-trustee Center Study Responsive Law, Washington, 1969-71. Served to capt. M.C. AUS, 1956-58. Recipient Auto Safety award Med. Tribune, 1966-67, Distinguished Service award U. Mich., 1965, Disting. Svc. award U. Mich. Med. Ctr. Alumni Soc., 1998. Fellow Coll. Am. Pathologists, U.S. and Can. Acad. Pathology, Alpha Omega Alpha, Nu Sigma Nu. Lutheran. Achievements include research with preservation of blood for transfusion by freezing and rsch. in pathogenesis of injury in highway crashes. Home: 1900 Mershon Dr Ann Arbor MI 48103-5939

GIL, KAREN M., dean, psychology professor; b. Bklyn., Aug. 8, 1956; BA in Psychology, SUNY, Stony Brook, 1974—78; MA in Clin. Psychology, West Va. U., 1980—82, PhD in Clin. Psychology, 1982—85. Lic. practicing psychologist NC. Internship Duke U. Med. Ctr., 1984—85, clin. assoc., 1985—86, asst. prof. med. psychology, 1986—92; asst. prof. psychology-social and health sciences Duke U., 1991—93, assoc. prof. psychology-social and health sciences, 1994—95, assoc. prof. med. psychology, 1992—95; assoc. prof. dept. psychology U. NC, Chapel Hill, 1995—2000, prof. dept. psychology, 2000—, sr. assoc. dean undergrad. edn., 2001—04, chair dept. psychology, 2004—07, Gillian T. Cell disting. term prof., dept. psychology, 2005—, sr. assoc. dean social sciences, coll. arts and sciences, 2007—. Prof. dept. psychiatry U. NC Sch. Medicine; adj. assoc. prof. dept. psychiatry and behavioral sciences Duke U. Med. Ctr. Contbr. articles to profl. jours. Fellow, Ctr. Creative Leadership, 2006; Academic Leadership fellow, Inst. Arts and Humanities, 2006—. Fellow: APA (Logan Wright Disting. Rsch. award 2003, Outstanding Contbn. to Health Psychology award 1996), Soc. Behavioral Medicine; mem.: Sigma Xi. Office: UNC-CH Dept Psychology 201 Davie Hall Chapel Hill NC 27599-3270 Office Phone: 919-962-3088. Office Fax: 919-962-2537. Business E-Mail: kgil@email.unc.edu.

GILBERT, DANIEL TODD, psychology professor; BA summa cum laude in Psych., U. Colo., Denver, 1981; PhD in Social Psych., Princeton U., NJ, 1985. Asst. prof. U. Tex., Austin, 1985—90, assoc. prof., 1990—95, prof., 1995—96, Harvard U., Cambridge, Mass., 1996—2005, Harvard Coll. prof., 2005—. Fellow Ctr. Advanced Study in Behavioral Scis., 1991—92; Ford vis. prof. behavioral sci. U. Chgo. Sch. Bus., 2003. Contbr. articles to profl. jours., to popular media; co-editor: Handbook of Social Psych., 4th edit., 1998; editor: Selected Works of Edward E. Jones, 2003; author: Stumbling on Happiness, 2006 (Royal Soc. gen. book prize, 2007). Recipient Rsch. Scientist Devel. award, NIMH, 1991—96, James McKeen Cattell award, 1999, Phi Beta Kappa Teaching prize, Harvard U., 1999, Diener award, Found. Personality and Social Psychology, 2008; grantee John Simon Guggenheim Meml. Found. fellowship, 1999, Am. Philos. Soc. fellowship, 1999. Fellow: Am. Acad. Arts and Scis., Soc. Exptl. Social Psych., APA (Disting. Sci. award, Early Career Contbn. to Psych. 1992), Soc. Personality and Social Psych. Office: Dept Psych Harvard U Cambridge MA 02138 E-mail: gilbert@wjh.harvard.edu.

GILBERT, DENNIS A., pharmaceutical executive; BS in Biochemistry, cell biology, Univ. Calif., San Diego; PhD in Genetics, Johns Hopkins Univ.; postdoctoral study in Population Genetics, Nat. Cancer Inst. Program mgr., genetics W.R. Grace; joined as rsch. scientist Applera/Applied Biosystems, Foster City, Calif., from v.p., gene discovery to v.p. genomics applications, v.p. adv. rsch. and tech.; chief science officer, v.p. rsch. Applied Biosystems, Foster City, Calif., 2004—07; v.p. Applera Corp., Foster City, Calif., 2004—07; founder, chief sci. officer VitePath Genetics, 2008—. Office: VitaPath Genetics 348 Hatch Dr Foster City CA 94404

GILBERT, FRED, clinical geneticist, educator; BS in Biology, Mass. Inst. Tech., 1962; MD, Albert Einstein Coll. of Medicine of Yeshiva U., 1966. Cert. clin. genetics. Residency in interal medicine Barnes Hosp., St. Louis, Miss., 1967—68; clin. assoc. Nat. Insts. of Health, 1968—71, residency in interal medicine Bethesda, Md., 1968—71; fellowship clin. human genetics Yale Univ. Sch. Medicine, 1971—74; assoc. prof. pediat. Weill Cornell Med. Coll.; assoc. attending pediatrician NY-Presbyterian Hosp.; dept. head genetics divsn. Bklyn. Hosp. Ctr. Founding editor (journal) Genetic Testing. Mem.: Alpha Omega Alpha. Office: Weill Cornell Medical College 1300 York Ave New York NY 10065 Mailing: The Brooklyn Hospital Center 121 Dekalb Ave Brooklyn NY 11201 Office Phone: 646-962-2205. Office Fax: 646-962-0273.

GILBERT, GORDON JOEL, neurologist, electroencelographer; b. NYC, Mar. 24, 1933; s. Benjamin Leon Henry and Lunny (Zalenko) Gilbert; m. Adele Schwartz, July 10, 1960; children: Benette Lisabeth Rosen, Stefanie Celeste, Benjamin Leon. AB, Harvard U., 1953; MD, NYU, 1957. Diplomate Am. Bd. Psychiatry and Neurology; diplomate Am. Electroencephalographic Soc. Intern Johns Hopkins Hosp., Balt., 1957-58; fellow in neurology Yale U. Sch. Medicine, New Haven, 1958-59, 60-61, Boston City Hosp., 1959-60; asst. prof. neurology Yale U. Sch. Medicine, New Haven, 1965; chief neurology St. Anthony's Hosp., Tampa, Fla., 1965-92; clin. prof. physiology and biophysics U. South Fla., Tampa, 1977—2006, clin. prof. molecular pharmacology and physiology, 1977—; chief of staff Humana Hosp., St. Petersburg, Fla., 1991-92, chmn. bd. trustees, 1996-97. Chmn. Med. Adv. Bd. MDA, St. Petersburg, 1966-81; expert witness Fla. Dept. Health, 2004-11. Contbr. chpts. to books; Neurological Complications of Therapy, 1982, Spinocerebellar Degenerations, 1991; articles to jours: JAMA, Neurology, Lancet, New Eng. Jour. Medicine. Mem. collections com. Harvard Art Mus., 1996—; (paintings and sculpture subcom.); bd. govs. NYU Sch. Medicine, 1994—; trustee Mus. Fine Arts, St. Petersburg, 2000-06, 07-, chair accessions com., 2001-. Capt. USAF, 1961—63. Fellow Am. Acad. Neurology; mem. Pinellas County Med. Soc. (bd. govs. 1997-2004), Harvard Club (pres. Fla. west coast 1986-88), Harvard Alumni Assn. (bd. dir. 1991-94, regional dir. West Coast of Fla.), Phi Beta Kappa, Alpha Omega Alpha. Republican. Jewish. Achievements include discovery of effective treatment for spasmodic toricollis and for hemiballismus; description of spinocerebellar diseases, first descripton of turtle headache, quinidine dementia, pseudohemiparetic parkinsonism; first to describe the relationship of herpes zoster ophthalmicus to granulomatous angiitis of the central nervous system. Avocations: collection and study of 16th and 17 century Dutch and Flemish paintings.

GILBERT, JANE H., health science association administrator; BA in Comm. and Speech, So. Meth. U., Dallas; MBA, U. Nebr., Omaha. Dir. devel. Boys & Girls Clubs, Omaha; dep. dir. mktg. & devel. Heartland chpt. Am. Red Cross, Omaha, 1995—99, CEO Charter Oak chpt. Hartford, Conn., 1999—2003, CEO Mid-Atlantic svc. area Raleigh, NC, 2003—05, sr. v.p. chpt. ops. Washington, 2005—08; pres., CEO ALS Assn., Calabasas Hills, Calif., 2009—. Recipient Disting. Alumni Achievement award, U. Nebr., 2008. Office: ALS Assn 27001 Agoura Rd Ste 250 Agoura Hills CA 91301 Office Phone: 818-880-9007. *

GILBERT, MARK R., neuro-oncologist, educator; s. Norman and Gloria Gilbert; 1 child, Tess A. MD, Johns Hopkins U., Balt., 1982. Diplomate Johns Hopkins, Md., 1982, cert. Am. Bd. Internal Medicine, 1985, Am. Bd. Neurology and Psychiatry, 1990. Resident/fellow, dept. internal medicine John Hopkins Hops., Balt., 1982—85, resident/fellow, dept. neurology, 1984—88, Keck Found. neuro-oncology fellow, 1986—87; instr. Johns Hopkins Sch. Medicine, Balt., 1988—90; asst. prof. U. Pitts., 1990—96; assoc. prof. Emory U., Atlanta, 1996—2000, M.D. Anderson Cancer Ctr., Houston, 2000—. Contbr. articles to profl. publs. Mem.: Soc. Neuro-Oncology, Am. Soc. Clin. Oncology, Am. Acad. Neurology, Am. Assn. for Cancer Rsch., Alpha Omega Alpha. Office: MD Anderson Cancer Ctr Dept Neuro-Oncology 1515 Holcombe Blvd Box 431 Houston TX 77030

GILBERT, MARTIN N., pediatric gastroenterologist; MBA, UCLA; MD, Wayne State U., Detroit; Advanced Mgmt. Program, Harvard U.; Advanced Leadership Program, U. NC. Fellowship, pediatric gastroenterology University of California; pediatric gastroenterologist Southern Calif. Permanente Med. Group; area med. dir., chief of staff, chief of pediat., asst. area dir., Bellflower Med. Ctr. Kaiser Permanente; exec. med. dir. Kaiser Permanente Ins. Co.; assoc. exec. dir., ops. strategy, nat. The Permanente Fedn. LLC. Former bd. dirs. Broadlane Inc. Bd. visitors UC Davis Health System; mem. adv. bd., Healthcare Initiative Harvard Bus. Sch. Office: Kaiser Permanente 1 Kaiser Plz Oakland CA 94612 Office Phone: 510-271-5800. Office Fax: 510-267-7524. Business E-Mail: martin.gilbert@kp.org. *

GILBERT, SCOTT FREDERICK, biologist, educator, author; b. NYC, Apr. 13, 1949; s. Marvin Marshall and Elaine (Caplan) G.; m. Anne Marie Raunio, Dec. 30, 1971; children: Daniel, Sarah, David. BA, Wesleyan U., 1971; MA, PhD, Johns Hopkins U., 1976; PhD (hon.), U. Helsinki. Postdoctoral assoc. U. Wis., Madison, 1976-78, 1978-80; asst. prof. Swarthmore (Pa.) Coll., 1980-86, assoc. prof., 1986-92, prof., 1992—. Author: Developmental Biology, 1985, 88, 91, 94, 97, 2000, 03, 06, 10, Embryology, 1997, Ecological Development Biology, 2009; zoology editor Jour. Irreproducible Results, 1979-93, Com. de Patronage, Annales Hist. Philosophie Sci.; mem. editl. bd. Embryo, Jour. Exptl. Zoology, Internat. Jour. Devel. Biol., Evolution and Devolution; contbr. articles to sci. jours. Recipient Dwight J. Ingle award Perspectives in Biology and Medicine, 1984, medal of Francois I, Coll. de France, 1996; Guggenheim fellow, 1999. Fellow AAAS; mem. Soc. Devel. Biology (Viktor Hamburger prize 2002), Soc. Integrative Comparative Biology, Internat. Soc. for Differentiation (exec. bd.), Soc. Human Genetics, Hist. Sci. Soc., St. Petersburg Soc. Naturalists (hon. fellow 2001, Kowalevsky prize 2004, Finnish Disting. Prof. award 2010), Internat. Soc. Hist., Philos. Soc. Studies Biology, Phi Beta Kappa, Sigma Xi. Democrat. Jewish. Home: 224 Cornell Ave Swarthmore PA 19081-1932 Office: Swarthmore Coll Dept Biology 500 College Ave Swarthmore PA 19081-1306 Office Phone: 610-328-8049 Business E-Mail: sgilber1@swarthmore.edu

GILBERT BARNESS, ENID F., pathologist, educator; b. Sydney, May 31, 1927; arrived in U.S., 1952, naturalized, 1975; d. Christian Henry and Mabel (Milne) Fischer; m. James Bryson Gilbert, Aug. 12, 1954; children: Mary M., Elizabeth A., James C. (dec.), Jennifer E., Rebecca D.; m. Lewis Barness, July 5, 1987. MBBS, U. Sydney, 1950, MD, 1983, MD (hon.), 1999; DSc (hon.), U. Wis., 1999, U. Southern Fla.; MD (hon.), U. Sydney, 2004. Diplomate Am. Bd. Pediat., Am. Bd. Clin. Pathology, Am. Bd. Anatomical Pathology, Am. Bd. Pediat. Pathology. Resident Children's Hosp., Boston, Phila., Washington, Brackenridge Hosp., Austin, Tex.; from asst. prof. to assoc. prof. U. W.Va., 1963-70; from assoc. prof. pathology and pediats. to prof. U. Wis., Madison, 1970-93, Disting. Med. Alumni prof., 1986-93, dir. pediat. pathology, 1970-93, prof. emeritus pathology and pediat., 1993—, Disting. Med. Alumni prof. emeritus, 1993—; prof. pathology, pediats. and ob-gyn. U. So. Fla., 1993—. Mem. editl. bds. Pediat. and Devel. Path. Med. jours., 1986—. Author: Introduction to Pathology, 1978, Genetic Aspects Developmental Pathology, 1987, Potters Pathology of the Fetus and Infant, 1997, Atlas Infant and Fetal Pathology, 1998, Metabolic Diseases, 2000, Atlas Embryo Fetal Pathology, 2004, Clinical Use of Pediatric Diagnostic Tests, 2003, Pediatric Autopsy Pathology, 2004; also numerous chpts., articles. Decorated Order of Australia; recipient Disting. Pathologist award, Royal Coll. Pathologists (Australia), 2002; grantee, NIH, 1972—92. Mem. Am. Soc. Clin. Pathology, Soc. Pediat. Pathology (pres. 1986-87), Internat. Acad. Pathology, Internat. Pediat. Pathology Assn. (pres. 1990-92), Teratology Soc., Cardiovasc. Soc. S.Am. (hon.), Am. Pediat. Soc., Am. Acad. Pediat., U.S. Can. Acad. Pathology, Arthur Purdy Stout Soc. Surg. Pathology, N.Y. Acad. Sci., Alpha Omega Alpha. Democrat. Avocation: writing. Home: 3301 Bayshore Blvd #403 Tampa FL 33629 Office: Tampa Gen Hosp Dept Pathology Tampa FL 33601 Office Phone: 813-844-7565. Business E-Mail: egilbert@tgh.org.

GILBERTSON, DOROTHY L., medical educator, director; b. Jan. 12, 1968; MS, CSUF, 1995; MD, Albany Med. Coll., 2000. Asst. prof. U. Ariz., 2006—. Med. dir., pediatric radiology, 2010—. Mem.: NASCI, AUR, ACR, SPR. Office: 1501 N Campbell Ave PO Box 245067 Tucson AZ 85718 Business E-Mail: dgilbertson@radiology.arizona.edu.

GILBOA, YAFIT, medical educator; b. Israel, Dec. 25, 1977; BOT in Occupl. Therapy, 2003, MA in Spl. Edn., 2005; student, U. Haifa, Occupl. therapist Machon Achiya, 2004; rsch. fellow U. Haifa, 2007, lectr., 2010. Office: Mount Carmel Haifa 31905 Israel Personal E-mail: yafitlaytman@yahoo.com.

GILCHRIST, GERALD SEYMOUR, pediatric hematologist, oncologist, educator; b. Springs, Transvaal, South Africa, May 25, 1935; arrived in U.S.A., 1962; s. David and Anne (Lipschitz) G.; m. Antoinette E. Besset, May 7, 1967; children: Daniel J., Michael A., Lauren D. MB BCh, U. Witwatersrand Med. Sch., Johannesburg, South Africa, 1957; Diploma in Child Health, Royal Coll. Physicians and Surgeons, London, 1961. Diplomate Am. Bd. Pediat. Intern Johannesburg Gen. Hosp., 1958-59; resident Transvaal Meml. Hosp. for Children and Baragwanath Hosp., Johannesburg, 1959-60; resident in pediatrics Hosp. for Sick Children, London, 1961; resident in pediat. Children's Hosp., Cin., 1962-63; fellow pediat., hematology/oncology Children's Hosp. of L.A., 1963-65, cons. hematology and blood banking, 1965-71, attending physician, 1968-71; asst. prof. pediat. U. So. Calif., LA, 1966-71; assoc. prof. pediat. Mayo Med. Sch., Rochester, Minn., 1972-78, chmn. dept. pediat., 1984-96; cons. pediatric hematology/oncology Mayo Clinic and Found., Rochester, 1971-2000; prof. pediat. Mayo Med. Sch., Mayo Clinic and Found., Rochester, 1978-2000; Helen C. Levitt prof. Mayo Clinic and Found., Rochester, 1987-2000; prof. emeritus Mayo Found. and Med. Sch., 2000—. Mem. Commn. on Cancer ACS, 1982—85; bd. dirs. Hemophilia Ctr., Dept. Maternal and Child Health, Rockville, Md., 1978—2000; prin. investigator Children's Cancer Study Group Nat. Cancer Inst., Bethesda, 1981—99; mem. Accreditation Coun. Grad. Med. Edn. Residency Rev. Com. Pediat., 1997—2002. Co-author: You and Leukemia, 1976; contbr. chpts. to books, numerous articles to profl. jours. Med. advisor Northland Childrens Oncology Svcs., Rochester, Minn., 1978-80; bd. dirs. Minn. chpt. Nat. Hemophilia Found. Found., Mpls., 1981-84; chpt sec. Physicians for Social Responsibility, Rochester, 1982-85; bd. dirs. Nat. Childhood Cancer Found., 1990-97; chair med. and sci. adv. bd. Nat. Children's Cancer Found., 1995-97; mem. adv. com. Reach Out and Read MN, 2005—. Recipient Joseph D. Early award, Nat. Hemophilia Found., 1997, Lifetime Achievement award, Minn., Dakotas Chpt. Nat. Hemophilia Found., 2000, Abraham Jacobi Meml. award, Am. Acad. Pediat., AMA, 2001; named to Children's Med. Ctr. Hall of Honor, Cin., 1994. Fellow: Am. Acad. Pediat. (chmn. sect. on pediat. hematology-oncology 1988—90, chair coun. on sects. 1999—2002, com. on pediat. edn. 1999—2005, com. on pediat. workforce 2003—05); mem.: European and Am. Osteosarcoma Study Group (ind. data monitoring com. 2005—), Children's Oncology Group (data monitoring and safety comm. 2000—), Am. Soc. Pediat. Hematology/Oncology (trustee 1996—98), Soc. Pediat. Rsch. Accrediation Coun. Grad. Med. Edn. (residency rev. com. pediat. 1997—2002), Am. Bd. Pediat. (chmn. sub-bd. pediat. hematology-oncology 1989—91, bd. dirs. 1990—91), Am. Pediat. Soc., Am. Soc. Hematology, Am. Soc. Clin. Oncology, Reach Out and Read (mem. adv. com. 2005—). Democrat. Jewish. Avocations: sailing, bicycling, kayaking.

GILCHRIST, JOHN MARK, otolaryngologist; b. Dallas, Dec. 10, 1959; s. Ronald Wallace Jr. and Patricia Gene G.; m. Melissa Paige LaBoon, Jan. 4, 1986; children: Sarah, Claire, Michael. BS, Wheaton Coll., Ill., 1982; MD, U. Okla., Oklahoma City, 1986. Diplomate Am. Bd. Otolaryngology. Intern U. Okla. Med. Ctr., 1986-87, resident otolaryngology, head and neck surgery, 1987-91; mem. staff Mercy Health Ctr., Oklahoma City, 1991—, Bapt. Med. Ctr., Oklahoma City, 1991—2006, Deaconess Hosp., Oklahoma City, 1991—2006; head, otolaryngology sect., dept. of surgery Mercy Health Ctr., Oklahoma City, 1995-2000; pvt. practice Okla. Otolaryngology Assocs., Inc., Oklahoma City, 1991—, Pres. Okla. Acad. of Otolaryngology, 1996-97. Mem. com. Young Life, Oklahoma City, 1987-97. Mem. AMA, Am. Acad. Otolaryngology-Head and Neck Surgery, Okla. Med. Assn., Okla. Acad. Otolaryngology (pres. 1995-). Office: Okla Otolaryngology Assocs 4200 W Memorial Rd Ste 606 Oklahoma City OK 73120-8359 Office Phone: 405-755-1930. Business E-Mail: jmgilchristmd@okoa.org. *

GILES, CONRAD LESLIE, ophthalmic surgeon; b. NYC, July 14, 1934; s. Irving Samuel Giles and Victoria Ampole; m. Marilyn Toby Schwartz, June 20, 1955 (div. 1978); children: Keith Martin, Suzanne Speer, Kevin William, Brian Alan; m. Lynda Fern Schenk, Nov. 26, 1978; stepchildren: Jared Schenk, Jamie Schenk Dewitt. MD, U. Mich., 1957, MS, 1961. Diplomate Am. Bd. Ophthalmology. Clin. assoc. NIH, Bethesda, Md., 1961-63; clin. asst. prof. Wayne State U. Sch. Medicine, Detroit, 1965-72, clin. assoc. prof. ophthalmology, 1973-89, clin. prof. ophthalmology, 1989—; chief ophthalmologist Children's Hosp. Mich., 1985-99, emeritus chief, 1999—, chief emeritus, 2000—. Contbr. articles to profl. jours. Active Jewish Welfare Fedn., Detroit, 1981-86, pres., 1986-89; bd. govs. Jewish Agy. for Israel, 1995-2000; vice-chair United Jewish Cmty., 2000-2002; vice chair Jewish Coun. Pub. Affairs, 2005-09; chair JCPA, 2009-. Fellow: Am. Acad. Ophthalmology; mem.: AMA, Mich. State Ophthalmol. Soc., Jewish Coun. Pub. Affairs (vice chair 2005—08, chair 2010—), United Jewish Cmtys. (vice chair 2000—02), Mich. Jewish Conf. (pres. 1992—95), United Jewish Appeal Fedns. N.Am. (co-pres. 1997—99), Coun. Jewish Fedns. (v.p. 1992—95, treas. 1995—96, pres. 1996—99). Avocation: golf. Home: 6300 Westmoor Rd Bloomfield Hills MI 48301-1359 Office: 31500 Telegraph Rd Bingham Farms MI 48025 Office Phone: 248-594-6702. Personal E-mail: clgilesmd@gmail.com.

GILES, LYNTON GILLESPIE FISHER, former health facility administrator, consultant; b. Johannesburg, South Africa, Feb. 7, 1941; arrived in Australia, 1972; s. Ronald Harry Fisher and Margaret Elizabeth (Gillespie) G.; m. Jennifer Irene Lowry, Oct. 19, 1974; 1 child, Elizabeth Irene. DC, Can. Meml. Chiropractic Coll., Toronto, 1970; MSc, U. Western Australia, Perth, 1983, PhD, 1987. Lic. chiropractor/scientist. Dir. Claremont Chiropractic Clinic, Perth, 1972-83; sr. rsch. fellow Griffith U., Brisbane, Queensland, Australia, 1989-92; assoc. prof. James Cook U. North Queensland, Townsville, Australia, 1994-98; clin. dir. spinal pain unit Townsville Gen. Hosp., 1997—2002; medico-legal cons. in spinal injuries, 1994—. Hon. clin. scientist Townsville Gen. Hosp., 1995-02; adj. prof. divsn. health scis. Murdoch U., Perth; adj. assoc. prof. faculty medicine, health and molecular scis. Sch. Pub. Health, Tropical Medicine and Rehab. Scis., James Cook U., Townsville, Queensland, Australia. Author: Anatomical Basis of Low Back Pain, 1989; co-editor: Clinical Anatomy and Management of Low Back Pain, 1997, Clinical Anatomy and Management of Cervical Spine Pain, 1998, Clinical Anatomy and Management of Thoracic Spine Pain, 2000, 50 Challenging Spinal Pain Syndrome Cases, 2003, 100 Challenging Spinal Pain Syndrome Cases, 2009; contbr. articles to profl. jours. Mem. Brit. Assn. Clin. Anatomists, Spine Soc. Australia. Presbyterian. Avocations: reading, photography, travel, walking. Address: PO Box 1335 Townsville Queensland 4810 Australia

GILFILLAN, RICHARD, health services organization executive; Grad., MD, Georgetown U.; MBA, U. Pa. Family practice physician, Mass.; med. dir Medigroup Ctrl. HMO; held several positions with Independence Blue Cross, 1989—2000, chief med. officer, 1992—95; sr. v.p. for nat. network mgmt. Coventry Health Care, 2001—05; pres., CEO Geisinger Health Plan, 2005—09; exec. v.p. ins. ops. Geisinger Health System, 2005—09; cons. Geisinger Consulting Services, 2009—10; acting dir. Ctr. for Medicine and Medicaid Innovation (CMI or Innovation Ctr.), Ctr. for Medicare and Medicaid Services (CMS), 2010—. Serves on numerous cmty. and corp. boards. Named one of 100 Most Influential People in Healthcare, Modern Healthcare Mag., 2011. Office: Centers for Medicare and Medicaid Services 7500 Security Blvd Baltimore MD 21244 *

GILKES, CATHERINE ELIZABETH, neurosurgeon; b. Liverpool, Eng., July 17, 1975; d. Donald Gordon and Elizabeth Kay Gilkes. MA Cantab, U. Cambridge, Eng., 1997; MBChB, U. Edinburgh, 2000. House officer Royal Infirmary, Edinburgh, 2000—01; sr. house officer Kings Coll. Hosp., London, 2001—02, Nat. Hosp. Neurology and Neurosurgery Queens Sq., London, 2002, Gen. Surgery and Orthop. Royal Free Hosp., London, 2002—04; registrar, neurosurgery Frenchay Hosp., Bristol, England, 2004—10, Derriford Hosp., Plymouth, England, 2005—07; fellow Nat. Hosp. Neurology & Nuesurgey, 2010—11; skull base fellow Salford Royal Hosp., Manchester. Chmn. Brit. Neurosurgical Trainees Assn., 2008—10. Contbr. articles and sci. papers. Master: Royal Coll. Surgeons; mem.: Soc. Brit. Neurosurgeons (trainees rep. coun. 2008—, Best Poster Presentation award 2006). Avocations: music, swimming, running, art. Office: Nat Hosp Neurology and Neurosurgery Queen Square London WCINBG England also: 22 Coll Rd N Crosby CROSB9 Liverpool L238UT England also: Salford Royal Hosp Manchester M68HD England

GILL, ANGELA SUE, clinical psychologist; b. Springfield, Mo., Mar. 8, 1972; d. Ronald Eugene and Connie Sue Gill. BS in Polit. Sci., S.W. Mo. State U., 1994, BS in Psychology, 1994; MA in Clin. Psychology, SW Mo. State U., 1999; PsyD in Psychology, Forest Inst. Profl. Psychology, 2002. Lic. clin. psychologist Mo., cert. pain mgmt.; EMDR, 2011. Intern Family Svc. and Guidance Ctr., Topeka, 2001—02, postdoctoral trainee, 2002—03, coord. ADHD program, 2002—04, supr., 2002—04; clin. psychologist St. John's Hosp., Springfield, Mo., 2004—; clin. chair, 2011. Mem.: APA. Office: St Johns Springfield MO 65804 Business E-Mail: angela.gill@mercy.net.

GILL, HARCHARAN, medical educator; b. Kenya, Apr. 5, 1955; MD, U. Nairobi, 1977. Prof. Stanford U. Sch. Medicine, 1991—. Mem.. Am. Urologic Assn. Avocation: running. Office: 875 Blake Wilbur Stanford CA 94305 Business E-Mail: hgill@stanford.edu.

GILL, JANE ROBERTS, retired psychotherapist, clinical social worker; b. Boston, Dec. 6, 1923; d. Penfield Hitchcock and Cecilia (Washburn) Roberts; m. P.L. Gill Gill, Dec. 1943 (div. 1973); children: Jonathan Penfield, Dorcas Pearson, Nicholas Brinton(dec.), Timothy Roberts. Student, Wellesley Coll., 1941—43; BA, Boston U., 1954, MSW, 1956. Bd. cert. diplomate Acad. Cert. Social Workers, BCD. Social worker obstet, pediat. svc. Beth Israel Hosp., Boston, 1956—57; social worker S. End Family Program, Boston, 1957—58, Margaret Gifford Sch., Cambridge, Mass., 1963—75, Adams House Psychiat. Clinic, Boston, 1967—76; with John R. Graham Headache Rsch. Found., 1970—94; pvt. practice psychotherapy Brookline, 1970—95; clin. instr. Smith Coll. Sch. Social Work, 1971—79, Simmons Sch. Social Work, 1971—87; supr. sr. clin. social work, coord. outpatient clinic Faulkner Hosp., Boston, 1975—87, John R. Graham Headache Ctr., 1987—94; rsch. interviewer Stone Ctr. Women's Studies, Wellesley Coll., 1989—90; ret., 1995; instr. family program NAMI, Springfield, Vt., 2000. Contbr. chapters to books, articles to profl. jours. on effects of emotions on physiology. Mem. Dem. Town Com., Newton Wellesley, 1959—64; program chmn. Mass. Mental Health Ctr. Aux. Bd., 1969—71; mem. social svc. com. Am. Heart Assn., 1979—83; bd. dirs. Rutland Corner House, 1982—96; poster Internat. Headache Soc., London, 1994, 2002, 2004; invited spkr. Brazilian Headach Soc., 1996; bd. dirs. Town Putney Libr., 1996—2006; cons. to bd. dirs. Putney Cares, 1998—2006. Mem.: NASW, Putney Sch. Alumni Assn., Peacham Hist. Assn. (Vt.), Internat. Stress and Tension Control Soc., Internat. Headache Soc., Acad. Psychosomatic Medicine. Home: 30 W Hill Rd Putney VT 05346 Personal E-mail: jrobertsgill@myfairpoint.net.

GILL, THOMAS JAMES, III, pathologist, educator; b. Malden, Mass., July 2, 1932; s. Thomas James and Marguerite (Capobianco) G.; m. Faith Libbie Etoll, July 8, 1961; children: Elizabeth Ruth, Thomas James IV, Christopher Gregory. AB summa cum laude, Harvard U., 1953, AM in Chemistry, 1957, MD, 1957. Diplomate Am. Bd. Pathology. Asst. in pathology Peter Bent Brigham Hosp., Boston, 1957-58; intern N.Y. Hosp.-Cornell Med. Center, 1958-59; jr. fellow Soc. Fellows Harvard U., 1959-62; mem. faculty Harvard U. Med Sch., 1962-71, asso. prof. pathology, 1970-71; prof. pathology, chmn. dept. U. Pitts. Med. Sch., 1971-90; pathologist-in-chief Univ. Health Ctr. Pitts., 1971-90, Maud L. Menten prof. exptl. pathology, 1988—98, prof. human genetics, 1988-98, prof. emeritus human genetics and exptl. pathology, 1999—; prof. clin. immunology post-grad. studies U. Rijeka, Croatia, 1996—2008; fellow U. Pitts. Ctr. for Philosophy Sci., 1996—98, assoc., 1999—2001; vis. scholar in biology Harvard U., 1998-2001; lectr. orthop. surgery Harvard Med. Sch., 2004—. Affiliate of Eliot House, Harvard Coll., 1998—; cons. to govt. and industry; mem. sci. adv. bd. St. Jude Children's Rsch. Hosp., Memphis, 1969-77, chmn., 1974-76; mem. allergy and immunology rsch. com. Nat. Inst. Allergy and Infectious Diseases, 1973-76; mem. med. rsch. svc. merit rev. bd. in immunology VA, 1976-79, chmn., 1977-79; mem. sci. adv. com. Damon Runyon-Walter Winchell Cancer Fund, 1978-81; mem. com. on animal models and genetic stocks NRC, 1978-86, chmn. com., 1983-86, mem. com. on rabbit genetic resources, 1979-80, mem. coun. Inst. Lab. Animal Resources, 1986-92, mem. com. on preservation of lab. animal resources, 1985-90, com. on transgenic animals, 1991-92; mem. surgery, anesthesiology and trauma study sect. NIH, 1983-84; sci. adv. com. on immunology and immunotherapy Am. Cancer Soc., 1986-88; mem. Armed Forces Epidemiol. Bd., 1966-72; adj. prof. U. Milan, 1990-92; nutrition found. Italy lectr. U. Milan, 1986-97; trustee Am. Bd. Pathology, 1981-92, life trustee, 1992—, pres., 1992; mem. Maternal and Child Health com. Nat. Inst. Child Health and Human Devel., 1992-96; chmn., 1995-96; mem. immunology task force Nat. Inst. Allergy and Infectious Diseases, 1996-98; mem. adv. com. for the Rat Genome Project and Rat EST Project, Nat. Heart, Lung, and Blood Inst., 1998; rsch. scientist, dir. rsch. in sports medicine Mass. Gen. Hosp., 2004—; instr. orthop. surgery Harvard Med. Sch., 2004-07; lectr. orthop. surgery, 2008. Mem. editl. bd. several sci. and med. jours.; contbr. articles to profl. jours. Bd. dirs. Easter Seal Soc., Allegheny County, 1972-77, Univs. Assn. for Rsch. and Edn. in Pathology, 1979-90. Recipient Lederle med. faculty award, 1962-65, rsch. career devel. award NIH, 1965-71, MERIT award NIH, 1992-2002, cert. of appreciation for patriotic civilian svc. Dept. Army, 1973, Spl. Qualification in Pathology: Immunopathology, 1983, Disting. Scientist award in genetics S.W. Found. for Biomed. Rsch., 1986, Charter with medal U. Rijeka, 1990, medal U. Pitts., 1990; named George H. Fetterman lectr. U. Pitts., 1981, George Hoyt Whipple lectr. U. Rochester, N.Y., 1984, Aron E. Szulman lectr. U. Pitts., 1993, Raymond O. Berry Meml. lectr. Tex. A&M U., 1995, Mühlblock lectr. Internat. Coun. for Lab. Scis., 1995, Spiridion Brusina award Croatian Soc. Natural Scis., 1997. Fellow Assn. Pathology Chairmen (pres. 1978); mem. AMA, Am. Assn. Immunologists, Am. Assn. Pathologists, Am. Soc. Molecular Biology and Biochemistry, Am. Soc. Human Genetics, Transplantation Soc. (v.p. 1982-84), Am. Soc. for Immunology of Reprodn. (v.p. 1988-89, Disting. Investigator award 1991, pres. 1995-96), Genetics Soc. Am., Internat. Acad. Pathology, Internat. Soc. Immunology of Reprodn. (pres. 1992-95, hon. pres. 1995—), Alps Adria Soc. for Immunology of Reprodn. (hon. pres. 1994-07), European Soc. Reproductive Immunology, Mass. Med. Soc., Harvard Club (Boston), Harvard Varsity Club. Business E-Mail: gilliii@massmed.org.

GILLAN, JAMES W., public health service officer; m. Teresita S. Fejarang; children: Todd, Amalia, Emma, Mary Catherine. Cons. Nichido Ins. Co. Pacific, PMC Isla Health System; COO GMHP Health Ins. Ltd.; dir. Guam Dept. Pub. Health & Social Services, 2011—. Office: Guam Department of Public Health and Social Services 123 Chalan Kareta Mangilao GU 96913-6304 Office Phone: 671-735-7173. Office Fax: 671-734-5910. *

GILLARD, MONTGOMERY, dermatologist; b. Des Moines, Iowa, Feb. 3, 1967; m. Gabrielle Allegra Tuchow, June 15, 1996; children: Isabelle Rose children: Benjamin Joel. MD, U. Mich. Diplomate Am. Bd. Dermatology. Lectr. U. Mich. Med. Ctr., Ann Arbor, 2002—04; dir. Ctr. for Skin Cancer Surgery, Clinton Township, Mich., 2004—07; co-dir. The Boyd Gillard Inst. Aesthetic and Dermatol. Surgery, Ypsilanti, Mich., 2007—. Contbr. articles to profl. jours. Mem.: AMA, Am. Soc. Dermatol. Surgery, Am. Coll. Mohs Micrographic Surgery and Cutaneous Oncology, Am. Acad. Dermatology. Office: Boyd Gillard Inst Aesthetic and Dermatol Surgery 4990 W Lark Rd Bldg A Ste 200 Ypsilanti MI 48197 Home: 1101 Martin Pl Ann Arbor MI 48104-3512 Office Fax: 734-572-7777. Personal E-mail: montgomery_gillard@ihacares.com.

GILLESPIE, DEIRDRE Y., pharmaceutical company executive; b. 1956; BSc, London U., 1976, MD, 1980; MBA, London Bus. Sch., 1990. Positions in bus. develop. 3 Dimensional Pharm.; positions in clin. devel. Sandoz (now Novartis), 1986—90; various positions including v.p. mktg. DuPont Merck Pharm. Co., 1990—96; sr. med. cons. Communications Strategy Group, 1996—98; exec. v.p., chief bus. officer Vical, Inc., 1998—2000, exec. v.p., COO, 2000—01; pres., CEO Oxxon Therapeutics, Inc., 2001—05, La Jolla Pharmaceutical Co., San Diego, 2006—. Bd. dirs. La Jolla Pharmaceutical Co., 2004—, NexMed, Inc., 2010—. Office: La Jolla Pharmaceutical Co 4365 Executive Dr Ste 300 San Diego CA 92121

GILLESPIE, GARY DON, physician; b. Jackson, Mich., Apr. 23, 1943; s. Harold Don and Marion Estella (Diemer) G.; m. Nancy Bliven Hinkle, June 29, 1969 (div. July 1980; children: Brian James, Julie Elizabeth; m. Elaine Marie Beard, July 25, 1984. BS, U. Mich., 1966, D of Medicine, 1971. Diplomate Am. Bd. Family Practice. Intern Edward W. Sparrow Hosp., Lansing, Mich., 1971-72, resident in family practice, 1971-74; physician Dept. Family Practice, USN Med. Corps., Orlando, Fla., 1974-76; pvt. practice Okemos, Mich., 1976—2001; ret., 2001. Chmn. continuing edn., dept. family practice Edward W. Sparrow Hosp., 1976-91; asst. clin. prof. dept. family practice Mich. State U. Coll. Medicine, East Lansing, 1981-2001. Lt. comdr. med. corps USN, 1974—76. Mem. AMA, Am. Acad. Family Physicians, Am. Bd. Family Practice, Mich. Acad. Family Physicians (treas. Capitol chpt. 1982-92). Republican. Avocations: reading, music, photography, travel, golf.

GILLESPIE, WILLIAM ALLEN, pediatrician, insurance company executive; b. Morgantown, West Virginia, Sept. 22, 1951; MD, U. Va., 1976. Diplomate American Bd. of Pediatrics. Intern, pediatrics U. Va. Hosp., Charlottesville, 1976—77, resident, 1977—79; pediatrician and general practioner; pres. Kaiser Health Plan; CEO Permanente Med. Group, Southwest Divsn., Kasier Permanente, OptumHealth; exec. v.p., chief med. officer Ovations (Divsn. of United Health Group); chief med. officer EmblemHealth, Inc. (parent co. of HIP Health Plan (HIP) and Group Health, Inc. (GHI)), 2009—. Office: EmblemHealth Inc 55 Water St New York NY 10041 *

GILLETT, JAMES WALTER, minister, missionary; b. Waterloo, Iowa, Feb. 19, 1949; arrived in Ireland, 1970; s. James L. and Mabel M. (Hersey) G.; m. Jean Nancy Brewster, Mar. 29, 1969; children: Jonathan, Julie. Student, McPherson Coll., Kans., 1967-68, Missionary Tng. Ctr., 1968-69. Founder and dir. Aids for Bible Edn., Dublin, 1970—, Emmaus Corres. Sch., Ireland, 1972—, Overseas Assistance Teams, Dublin, 1980—; founder and pres. Ireland Outreach Internat., Dublin, 1972—, Waterloo, 1980—; dir. Source of Light Assoc. Sch., Dublin, 1978—. Asst. leader Lit. Crusades Team, Lyon, France, 1969; founder regional dir. Emmaus Corr. Sch., Dublin, 1972—; founder, dir. Emmaus Bible Ctr., Nigeria, 1994; distbr. Emmaus Bible Ctr. method, English-speaking Africa, 1994; founder, internat. coord. Emmaus Bible Ctrs., Ghana, 1997; founder Haven of Hope, Kwang Village, Nigeria, 2002, Hope Med. Clinic, Nigeria, 2004; established Emmaus Bible Ctrs. Zambia, 2004, mem. European Emmaus Com., 1993—, mem. Congress for Itinerant Evangelists, Amsterdam, 1983. Actor screening for Pilgrims Progress, 1977; film rschr.; Patmos, 1981. Participant Lausanne Congress on Evangelism, 1974, Internat. Prayer Assembly, Seoul, 1984, Lausanne II Congress for World Evangelism, Manila, 1989. Mem. Christian European Visual Media Assn. Republican. Plymouth Brethren. Avocations: swimming, travel. Office: Ireland Outreach Internat Charleville Harbour Rd Dalkey County Dublin Ireland

GILLHAM, NICHOLAS WRIGHT, geneticist, educator; b. NYC, May 14, 1932; s. Robert Marty and Elizabeth (Enright) G.; m. Carol Lenore Collins, June 2, 1956. BA, Harvard, 1954, MA, 1955, PhD (USPHS fellow), 1962. From instr. to asst. prof. Harvard U., 1963-68; assoc. prof. zoology Duke U., 1968-72, prof., 1973-82, James B. Duke prof. biology, 1982—2002, chmn. dept. zoology, 1986—89, profl. emeritus, 2002—. Mem. biochemistry, molecular genetics and cell biology interdisciplinary cluster Pres.'s Biomed. Rsch. Panel, 1975; mem. study sect. in genetics NIH, 1976-80; mem. N.C. Gov.'s Bd. Sci. and Tech., N.C. Gov.'s Task Force on Sci. and Tech., chmn., bd. dirs. Am. Type Culture Collection, 1993-96. Author: (with R. Krueger and J. Coggin) Introduction to Microbiology, 1973, Organelle Heredity, 1978, Organelle Genes and Genomes, 1994, A Life Sir Francis Galton: From African Exploration to the Birth of Eugenics, 2001, Genes, Chromosomes, and Disease, 2011; mem. editl. bd. Genetics, 1975-78, Jour. Cell Biology, 1977-79, Intl. Review of Cytology, 1987-97; sr. editor Plasmid, 1977-86. Served to 1st lt. Med. Service Corps USAF, 1955-58. Postdoctoral fellow USPHS, 1962-63 Spl. fellow, 1967-68; Rsch. Career Devel. grant USPHS, 1972-77; Guggenheim fellow, 1984-85. Mem. Genetics Soc. Am., Sigma Xi. Office: Duke Univ Dept Biology PO Box 90338 Durham NC 27708-1000 Business E-Mail: gillham@duke.edu.

GILLIG, PAULETTE MARIE, psychiatry clinician educator, author, researcher; b. Boston, Mar. 24, 1949; d. Franklin Joseph and Marie Robichaud (Collins) G.; m. Douglas K. Fairobent, June 13, 1981. BA cum laude hons. psychology, SUNY, Buffalo; MA, Ohio State U., Columbus; PhD in Social Psychology, Ohio State U., 1973; MD, Med. Coll. Ohio, 1977. Diplomate Am. Bd. Psychiatry and Neurology, Am. Bd. Geriat. Psychiatry. Resident in neurology Med. Coll. Ohio, 1978-79, U. Mich., Ann Arbor, 1979-81; resident in psychiatry Ohio State U., Columbus, 1981-83, clin. asst. prof., 1983-85; asst. prof. U. Cin., 1985-90; assoc. prof. Wright State U., Dayton, 1990-2000, prof. psychiatry, 2000—. Prof. pub. psychiatry Ohio Dept. Mental Health, 1997—. Sect. editor Psychiatry, 2004—08; editor (co-author): Clinical Guide to the Treatment of the Mentally Ill Homeless Person, 2006, Incorporating Psychotherapy Into Community Psychiatry Appointments, 2009; editor: (co-author with R.D. Sanders) Psychiatry and Neurology, 2010; contbr. articles to profl. sci. jours., chapters to books. Founding Bd. Domestic Abuse and Violence Inst. of Dayton, 2000—; patron Cin. Ballet Co., Dayton Ballet Co., Xavier U., Humane Soc. U.S., Dayton Opera Co., Cin. Symphony Orch., Balletech Ohio, Warren County Animal Shelter, Nat, Wildlife Fedn., Middfest Internat., Xavier U. Classical Piano and Guitar Svc.; chair Domestic Violence Rsch. Group, 1999-2002. Recipient Clin. Neuroscis. award, Med. Coll. Ohio, Nancy Roeske award, Am. Psychiat. Assn., 2007, Faculty Mentor award, Wright State U., 2008, Sr. Clin. Neuroscientist award, Acad. Medicine, Dayton, Ohio, 2009, Faculty Mentor award, Burnshoft Sch. Medicine; named Sr. Tchr. & Rschr. of Yr., Acad. Medicine, Dayton, Ohio, 2009; named one of Best Dr. in America, Bestdoctors.com, 2005—, Top Psychiatrists, Consumers Rsch., 2007—; grantee Pruitt Found., 1992, Ohio Dept. Mental Health, 1995—. Fellow Am. Psychiat. Assn. (disting. fellow, com. on poverty, homelessness, and psychiatric disorders 1999-2006); mem. Am. Assn. Women Psychiatrists, Am. Assn. Cmty. Psychiatrists (Midwestern rep. 2002—, chair tng. com., Moffic award 1999), Ohio Psychiat. Assn. (chmn. com. on minorities 1999-2002, Pres.'s award 2001), WHO (contbr. internat. classification diseases 9), Alpha Omega Alpha. Avocations: ballet, opera, piano. Office: Wright State U Dept Psychiatry PO Box 927 Dayton OH 45401-0927 E-mail: paulette.gillig@wright.edu.

GILLIGAN, WILLIAM J., orthopedist; MD, Northwestern Univ. Med. Sch., Chgo. Cert. Am. Bd. Orthopaedic Surgery Examiners. Examiner Am. Bd. Orthopaedic Surgeons; orthopaedic consul. Malcolm Grow US Airforce Hosp.; assoc. prof., orthopaedic surgery Northwestern Univ. Med. Sch., Loyola Univ. Med. Sch., George Washington Univ. Med. Sch., Rush Presbyterian St. Luke's Med. Ctr.; ptnr. Hinsdale Orthopaedic Assoc., S.C. Intern Wesley Hosp., Chgo.; resident Northwestern Univ. Med. Sch.; fell., hand surgery LA Orthopaedic Hosp. Mem.: Clin. Orthopaedic Soc., Am. Assn. Hip and Knee Surgeons, Mid-Am. Orthopaedic Soc., Mid-America Orthopaedic Soc., Ill. Orthopaedic Soc., Chgo. Orthopaedic Soc., Am. Acad. Orthopaedic Surgeons. Office: Hinsdale Orthopaedic Assoc 550 W Ogden Ave Hinsdale IL 60521

GILLILAND, GARY, oncologist, researcher; BS in Bacteriology, U. Calif., Davis; PhD in Microbiology, U. Calif., Los Angeles, 1980; MD, U. Calif., San Francisco, 1984. Chief med. resident Brigham & Women's Hosp., fellow in hematology, sr. attending physician; fellow in med. oncology Dana Farber Cancer Inst., sr. attending physician; investigator Howard Hughes Med. Inst.; prof. medicine Harvard Med. Sch.; prof. Stem Cell & Regenerative Biology Harvard U.; sr. v.p. oncology Merck Rsch. Lab. Assoc. bd. mem. Harvard Med. Sch., MIT; dir. Leukemia Program Dana-Farber Harvard Cancer Ctr.; dir. Cancer Stem Cell Program Harvard Stem Cell Inst. Recipient Gold-Headed Cane award, U. Calif., Stephen Birnbaum Scholar award, Leukima & Lymphoma Soc. Mem.: WHO (clincial adv. com.), Am. Assn. Physicians, Am. Soc. Clinical Investigation (Stanley J. Korsmeyer award), Am. Soc. Hematology (William Dameshek award). Office: Brigham & Women's Hospital 1 Blackfan Cir Rm 05-210 Boston MA 02115 Office Phone: 617-355-9092. Office Fax: 617-355-9093. E-mail: ggilliland@rics.bwh.harvard.edu.

GILLILAND, ROBERT, gastroenterologist; b. Lisburn, Northern Ireland, Mar. 11, 1960; MB BCh BAO, Queen's U. Belfast, 1983, MD, 1997. Cons. gen., colorectal surgeon Western Health and Social Care Trust, 1997—2008, South Eastern Health and Social Care Trust, 2008—. Basic surg. tng. program dir. Northern Ireland Med. and Dental Tng. Agy., 2002—08, dep. head, sch. surgery NI, 2008—11; hon. clin. sr. lectr surgery Queen's U. Belfast, 2004. Fellow: Royal Coll. Surgeons Edinburgh; mem.: Ulster Soc. Gastroenterology, Irish Assn. Coloproctology (sec. 2000—05), Assn. Surgeons Gt. Brit. & Ireland, Assn. Coloproctology Gt. Brit. & Ireland. Office: Ulster Hosp Dundonald Upper Newtown Dundonald BT16 1RH Northern Ireland Business E-Mail: robert.gilliland@setrust.hscni.net.

GILLISS, CATHERINE LYNCH, academic administrator, dean, nursing educator; b. New Britain, Conn., Apr. 18, 1949; d. James A. and Lorraine Lynch; m. Thomas P. Gilliss, June 6, 1970. BS in Nursing, Duke U., 1971; MS in Nursing, Cath. U. Am., Washington, 1974; D of Nursing Sci., U. Calif., San Francisco, 1983; cert. adult nurse practitioner, U. Rochester, 1979; D (hon.), U. Portland, Oreg., 2007; MA (hon.), Yale; DHL (hon.), Portland. Chmn. dept. family health care U. Calif., San Francisco, 1984-98, prof. emeritus, 1999—; prof. Sch. Nursing, Yale U., New Haven, 1998—2004, dean Sch. Nursing, 1998—2004; dean Sch. Nursing Duke U., 2004—; prof. Helene Fuld Health Trust Duke U. Sch. Nursing, 2009—; vice chancellor nursing affairs, 2004—; gov. appointed mem. NC Inst. Medicine, 2010—. Chair NIH, Nat. Inst. Nursing Rsch. Study Sect., 1997-2000; founding dir. DJNI. Co-author: Toward a Science of Family Nursing, 1989, The Nursing of Families, 1993; Jour. Family Nursing, Jour. Nat. Assn. Hispanic Nurses, Jour. Nat. Black Nurses Assn.; contbr. articles to profl. jours. Bd. dirs. Nat. Coun. Family Relations, 1986-88, Am. Acad. Nursing, 2000-04, Soc. Primary Care Policy Fellows, 1996-99, Nat. Orgn. Nurse Practitioner Faculties, 1994-97. Recipient Disting. Alumna award Duke U. Sch. Nursing, 1991; Pres.'s Fellowship award U. Calif., 1983; Sr. fellow Ctr. for Health Professions, 1996-99, Primary Health Care Policy fellow USPHS, 1993; Regent U. Portland, Oreg., 1994-2000; named to Wall of 100 Disting. Alumni, U. Calif. San Francisco Sch. Nursing, 2007, Lifetime Achievement award in Rsch. Internat. Family Nursing Soc., 2007 Fellow Am. Acad. Nursing (co-chair task force on health disparities 2001-04, co-chair program planning com. 2002, co-chair raise voice campaign 2007-, pres. 2009-, chair strategies planning com. 2009-10); mem. ANA, Nat. Orgn. Nurse Practitioner Faculties (v.p. 1994-95, pres. 1995-96, past pres. 1996-97, mem. adv. bd. nat. coun. state bds. nursing, FNP project, 1995-97), Soc. Primary Care Policy Fellows (bd. dirs., pres. 1996-99), Am. Assn. Colls. Nursing (fin. com., 2006—07.) Office: Duke Univ Sch of Nursing DUMC 3322 Durham NC 27710

GILMAN, ALFRED GOODMAN, pharmacologist, educator; b. New Haven, July 1, 1941; s. Alfred and Mabel (Schmidt) Gilman; m. Kathryn Hedlund, Sept. 21, 1963; children: Amy, Anne, Edward. BS, Yale U., New Haven, 1962; MD, PhD, Case Western Res. U., Cleve., 1969, DSc (hon.), 1995, U. Chgo., 1991, U. Miami, 1999; DMS (hon.), Yale U., 1997. Pharmacology rsch. assoc. NIH, Bethesda, Md., 1969—71; asst. prof., then assoc. prof. pharmacology U. Va., Charlottesville, 1971—77, prof., 1977—81, dir. med. sci. tng. program, 1979—81; prof. pharmacology, chmn. dept. U. Tex. Southwestern Med. Ctr., Dallas, 1981—2005, Raymond & Ellen Willie disting. chmn. molecular neuropharmacology, 1987—2009, regental prof. pharmacology emeritus, 1994—, interim dean Southwestern Med. Sch., 2004—05, dir. Cecil H. & Ida Green Comprehensive Ctr. Molecular Computational and Sys. Biol., 2004—09, provost, exec. v.p. acad. affairs, dean Southwestern Med. Sch., 2005—09; chief scientific officer Cancer Prevention Inst. Tex., 2009—. Mem. pharmacology study sect. NIH, 1977—81, mem. nat. adv. gen. med. scis. coun., 1992—95; bd. sci. counselors Nat. Heart, Lung Blood & Inst., 1982—86; mem. sci. adv. com. Am. Cancer Soc., NYC, 1982—86; mem. sci. adv. bd. Huntsman Cancer Inst., U. Utah, 1995—2000, Ernest Gallo Clinic & Rsch. Ctr., U. Calif., San Francisco, 1996—2001, Lucille P. Markey Charitable Trust, Miami, 1984—96; mem. sci. rev. bd. Howard Hughes Med. Inst., Bethesda, 1986—93; dir. Regeneron Pharmaceutics, 1989—, Eli Lilly and Co., Inc., 1995—; mem. vis. com. Case Western Res. U. Sch. Medicine, 1995—99; chmn. steering com. Alliance Cellular Signaling, 2000—08. Editor The Pharmacological Basis of Therapeutics; contbr. articles to profl. jours. Recipient Poul Edvard Poulsson award, Norwegian Pharmacology Soc., 1982, Gairdner Found. Internat. award, 1984, Albert Lasker award for basic med. rsch., 1989, Passano Sr. award, Passano Found., 1990, Waterford Biomed. Sci. award, Scripps Clinic & Rsch. Found., 1990, Basic Sci. Rsch. prize, Am. Heart Assn., 1990, City of Medicine award, Durham, NC, 1991, Ciba-Geigy Drew award, 1991, Nobel prize in physiology/medicine, 1994, Disting. Alumnus award, Case Western Res. U., 1995, Am. Acad. Achievement award, 1995, Med. Honor Basic Rsch. award, Am. Cancer Soc., 1995; named to Tex. Hall of Fame, 2001. Mem.: NAS (Richard Lounsbery award 1987), Tex. Acad. Sci. Engring. & Medicine, Am. Acad. Arts & Scis., Inst. Medicine, Am. Soc. Biol. Chemistry, Am. Soc. Pharmacology & Exptl. Therapeutics (John J. Abel award in pharmacology 1975, Louis S. Goodman and Alfred Gilman award 1990, Torald Sollman award 1997). Office: Cancer Prevention & Rsch Inst Tex 5323 Harry Hines Blvd Dallas TX 75390-8520 Office Phone: 214-648-0558. E-mail: agilman@cprit.state.tx.us. *

GILMAN, PAUL B., oncologist, educator; MD, Thomas Jefferson U. Diplomate Am. Bd. Internal Medicine, 1982, Am. Bd. Internal Medicine-internal medicine, 1979, Am. Bd. Internal Medicine-oncology, 1995. Intern New Eng. Deaconess Hosp., Boston, resident; fellow Thomas Jefferson Univ. Hosp., Phila.; asst. prof. medicine Thomas Jefferson Univ., Phila., 1983—; hosp. affiliations include Lankenau Med. Ctr., 1986—; med. dir. Lankenau Hosp. Cancer Ctr.; main line oncology hematology assocs. chief divsn. hematology/oncology Lankenau Hosp., sect. chief med. oncology for main line health; hosp. affiliations include Bryn Mawr Hosp., 1997—, Paoli Hosp., 1997—. Co-author: (publs.) Breast Cancer Risk Perceptions Among Affected Probands, 2005, Bin1 and P-Cadherin as Prognostic Markers for Survival in Early Stage Breast Cancer, 2006, Dose Escalation with Organ Sparing using Conformal Avoidance Intensity Modulated Radiation Therapy for Rectal Cancer: A Dosimetric Evaluation, 2007, Seroma Formation During Mammosite Brachytherapy Can Influence Presribed Treatment Doses, 2007, Cytotoxic Chemotherapy in Clinical Treatment of Cancer, 2007, Cancer Gentics Evaluation: Barriers to and Improvement for Referral, 2008. Mem.: Pa. Soc. of Hematology/Oncology, Pa. Med. Soc., Phila. County Med. Soc., Am. Fedn. for Med. Rsch., Am. Soc.of Hematology, Am. Soc. of Clin. Oncology. Office: Lankenau Cancer Center 100 Lancaster Ave Wynnewood PA 19096 Office Phone: 610-645-2494. Office Fax: 610-645-4456.

GILMAN, SID, neurologist; b. LA, Oct. 19, 1932; s. Morris and Sarah Rose (Cooper) G.; m. Carol G. Barbour. BA, UCLA, 1954; MD, 1957, FRCP, 2001. Intern UCLA Hosp., 1957-58; resident in neurology Boston City Hosp., 1960-63; from instr. to assoc. in neurology Harvard Med. Sch., 1965-68; from asst. prof. to prof. neurology Columbia U., NYC, 1968-76, H. Houston Merritt prof. neurology, 1976-77; prof., chair dept. neurology U. Mich., Ann Arbor, 1977—2004, William J. Herdman prof. neurology, 1997—2005, William J. Herdman disting. univ. prof. neurology, 2005—. Cons. VA Hosp., Ann Arbor, 1977—; mem. peripheral and ctrl. nervous sys. drugs adv. com. FDA, 1983-85, 86-87, 90-94, chmn., 1996-2000, cons., 2000—; adj. attending neurologist Henry Ford Hosp., Detroit; mem. chronic disease adv. com. Mich. Dept. Pub. Health, 1988-94; mem. neurol. sci. rsch. and tng. com. NIH, 1971-73, mem. neurol. disorders program project B com., 1976-80, mem. sci. programs adv. com. Nat. Inst. Neurol. Diseases, Communicative Disorders and Stroke, 1982-84, mem. nat. adv. neurol. disorders and stroke coun., 1994-97; mem. clin. trials subcom. Nat. Adv. Neurol. Disorders and Stroke Coun., 2001-04; dir. Mich. Alzheimer's Disease Rsch. Ctr., 1991—; mem. rsch. adv. coun. United Cerebral Palsy Found.; mem. sci. adv. coun. Nat. Ataxia Found., Nat. Amyotrophic Lateral Sclerosis Found., Inc.; mem. profl. adv. bd. Epilepsy Found. Am.; mem. rsch. adv. com. Nat. Multiple Sclerosis Soc., 1986-90; mem. exec. bd. Nat.

Coalition for Rsch., 1989-95, Nat. Found. for Brain Rsch., 1989-95; mem. rsch. adv. com. Dana Alliance; mem. sci. adv. bd. Merck, Inc., 2000-04, PPD Devel., 1999—, INC Rsch., 2000—; Henry Russel lectr. U. Mich., 2001. Author: (with J.R. Bloedel and R. Lechtenberg) Disorders of the Cerebellum, 1981, (with S.W. Newman) Manter and Gatz's Essentials of Clinical Neuroanatomy and Neurophysiology, 10th edit., 2003, (with J.C. Mazziotta) Clinical Brain Imaging: Principles and Applications, 1992, Clinical Examination of the Nervous System, 2000; editor: Neurobiology of Disease, 2007, Oxford Am. Handbook of Neurology, 2010; sect. editor editl. bd. Exptl. Neurology, Current Opinion in Neurology and Neurosurgery, Neurology, Annals Neurology, Jour. Neuropathology and Exptl. Neurology, Neurobase Arbor Pub. Co.; editor-in-chief MedLink Neurology, 1992—, Contemporary Neurology Series, 1995—, Neurology Network Commentary, 1996-2000, Lancet Neurology Network, 2000-02, Exptl. Neurology, 2003—, Neurolobiology of Disease, 2005-10; contbr. articles to profl. jours. Dir. Mich. Dem. Program, 1994-2000. With USPHS, 1958-60. Recipient Lucy G. Moses prize Columbia U., 1973, Weinstein Goldenson award United Cerebral Palsy Assn., 1981, UCLA Alumni Profl. Achievement award, 1992, UCLA Med. Alumni Profl. Achievement award, 1992. Fellow AAAS, Royal Soc. of Medicine, Royal Coll. Physicians, Am. Acad. Arts and Scis.; mem. Am. Neurol. Assn. (hon.; 1st v.p. 1985-86, pres.-elect 1987-88, pres. 1988-89), Mich. Neurol. Assn. (pres. 1987-88), Soc. Clin. Investigation, Am. Physiol. Soc., Am. Assn. Neuropathologists, Soc. Neurosci., Am. Acad. Neurology (vice chmn. geriatric neurology subcom. 1992-94, chmn. 1994-96, chmn. Decade of Brain com. 1990-95, AB Baker award 2004), Am. Epilepsy Soc., Assn. Rsch. in Nervous and Mental Disease, Assn. Am. Physicians, Inst. Medicine, Nat. Acad. Scis., The Nat. Acads. (nat. assoc.), Phi Beta Kappa, Alpha Omega Alpha. Home: 3411 Geddes Rd Ann Arbor MI 48105-2518 Office: University Mich Dept Neurology Mich House 2301 Commonwealth Blvd Ann Arbor MI 48105 Office Phone: 734-936-1808. Business E-Mail: sgilman@umich.edu.

GILMARTIN, RAYMOND VINCENT, management educator, former pharmaceutical company executive; b. Washington, Mar. 6, 1941; m. Gladys Higham; 3 children. BS in Elect. Engring., Union Coll., 1963; MBA, Harvard U., 1968. Sr. cons. Arthur D. Little Inc., 1968-76; v.p. corp. planning Becton Dickinson & Co., Paramus, NJ, 1976-79, pres. Becton Dickinson divsn., 1979-87, group pres., 1982-83, sr. v.p., 1983-86, exec. v.p., 1986-87, pres. Franklin Lakes, NJ, 1987-94, CEO, 1989-94; chmn., pres., CEO Merck & Co. Inc., Whitehouse Station, NJ, 1994—2005, spl. adviser to the bd. exec. com. Whitehouse, NJ, 2005—06. Bd. dirs. Merck & Co. Inc., 1994—2005, Microsoft Corp., 2001—, Gen. Mills, Inc.; prof. mgmt. practice Harvard Bus. Sch., Boston, 2006—, mem. bd. dean's advisors. Trustee Healthcare Leadership Coun., Healthcare Inst. NJ; bd. dirs. Alliance for Healthcare Reform, Am. Enterprise Inst.; Pharm. Rsch. and Mfrs. Am.; chmn. United Negro Coll. Fund; active Bus. Coun., Bus. Roundtable, Pres. Export Coun.; mem. exec. com. Coun. on Competitiveness, Transatlantic Bus. Dialogue, Trade and Poverty Forum. Mem.: Internat. Fed. Pharm. Mfrs. Assn. (chmn.). Office: Harvard Bus Sch Morgan Hall 15 Harvard Way Boston MA 02163 Office Phone: 617-495-5492, 617-496-4059. E-mail: rgilmartin@hbs.edu. *

GILMOUR, DAVID JAMES, psychologist; b. Phila., July 10, 1947; s. James William and Florence Elizabeth (Weinbrod) Gilmour; m. Deborah Anne Kaufold, July 2, 1977. BS, Muhlenberg Coll., 1969; MS in Adminstrn., George Washington U., 1974, MBA, Temple U., 1981, MEd, 2005; MS, U. Pa., 1995, MPhil, 1998; PhD, Temple U., 2008. Analyst Nat. Security Agy., Ft. Meade, Md., 1970-74; programmer, analyst Rohm & Haas Co., Phila., 1974-77; staff economist Sun Oil Co., Radnor, Pa., 1977-85; project leader Arco Chem. Corp., Phila., 1985-87; asst. v.p. Corestates Fin. Corp., Phila., 1987-98, cons., 1998—; adj. prof. Temple U., 2005—; advisor Ivy Advisory, 2007—. Hon. amb. Cu. Orgnl. Dynamics U. Pa., Phila. Author: (book) An Economic Model of Core States Financial Corporation, 1994, How to Write Term Papers Real Good, 1996, The Corestates/University of Pennsylvania Strategic Planning Model, 1997, The Philadelphia Ethos, 1998, 1776 and All That: A Memorable History of Philadelphia, 2002, Effective Use Of Technology In Classroom, 2008. With USN, 1970—74. Mem.: APA, NRA, Clan Morrison Soc., Mensa, Beta Gamma Sigma, Alpha Tau Omega (exchequer 1965—69, Thomas Arkle Clark award 1969). Republican. Anglican. Achievements include co-inventor semi-automatic pistol. Home and Office: 15 Keats Rd Yardley PA 19067-3219 Home Phone: 215-295-1188; Office Phone: 610-888-9107, 215-204-6197. Business E-Mail: jgilmour@jgilmourphd.com.

GILSTRAP, LARRY COWAN, III, medical association administrator, obstetrician gynecologist; b. Jacksonville, Fla., Nov. 26, 1944; s. Larry Cowan Gilstrap and Clara Wilford; m. Jo Ellen Reed, Aug. 21, 1965; children: Lori Caroline Monk, Lisa Christine Campbell, Jennifer Erin Bagwell. BA, Fla. State U., 1965; MD, U. of Miami, 1970. Diplomate Am. Bd. of Ob-Gyn. Dir. of obstetrics Wilford Hall USAF Med. Ctr., San Antonio, 1980—86; prof. of ob-gyn. U. Tex. Southwestern Med. Sch., Dallas, 1987—96; Emma Sue Hightower prof. and chmn. ob-gyn. and reproductive sciences dept. U. Tex. Houston Med. Sch., 1996—2006, chair emeritus, 2006—; dir. evaluation American Bd. Ob-Gyn., Dallas, 2006—07, pres., CEO, 2007—. Cons. to air force surgeon gen. USAF, San Antonio, 1982—86; assoc. editor Am. Jour. of Perinatology, NYC, 1992—; obstetric mem. Neonatal Network Adv. Bd., NIH, Washington, 1997—; expert cons. Tex. State Bd. of Med. Examiners, Austin, 1991—; editl. bd. Infectious Diseases in Ob-Gyn., NYC, 1993—; update editor Primary Care Update for Ob/GYN, Washington, 1995—; bd. of directors Soc. for Maternal Fetal Medicine, Washington, 1987—89; editl. bd. Obstetrics and Gynecology, 1984—87; bd. examiner Am. Bd. Ob-Gyn., Dallas, 1984—, bd. examiner divsn. maternal-fetal medicine, 1987—2001, sci. program chmn., Washington, 1995, bd. dirs., Dallas, former treas. Author: (medical textbook) Williams Obstetrics, 19th, 20th, and 21st edits., Study Guide for Williams Obstetrics, 19th, 20th, 21st edits.; editor: Operative Obstetrics, 1st and 2nd edits.; author: Operative Obstetrics 2nd edit. Study Guide, Case Files Obstetrics & Gynecology, Drugs and Pregnancy, 1st and 2nd edits., Infections in Pregnancy, 1st and 2d edits.; editor: (med. book) Guidelines for Perinatal Care, 5th edit.; guest editor (medical jour.) Operative Obstetrics. Bd. dirs. Meml. Hermann Healthnet Providers, Houston, 1999—2002. Col. USAF, 1966—86. Decorated Legion of Merit USAF; recipient Outstanding Svc. award, Soc. of Perinatal Obstetricians, 1998; named one of Best Drs. for Women, Good Housekeeping Mag., 1997, Best Drs. in Am., Am. Health Mag., 1996. Fellow: Am. Coll. of Obstetricians and Gynecologists (Outstanding Prof. award Armed dist. 1986); mem.: Houston Gynecol. and Obstet. Soc., Harris County Med. Soc., Am. Gynecologic and Obstetric Soc., Soc. of Gynecologic Investigation, Soc. of Maternal-Fetal-Medicine (bd. dirs. 1987—89, pres. 1993—93), Infectious Disease Soc. of Obstetrics and Gynecology (coun. mem. 1996—99), Tex. Assn. of Obstetricians and Gynecologists. Liberal. Methodist. Office: American Bd Ob-Gyn 2915 Vine St Dallas TX 75204 Office Phone: 214-871-1619. Office Fax: 214-871-1943. *

GIMBEL, HERVEY WILLIS, public health physician, medical administrator; b. Calgary, Alta., Can., Nov. 25, 1926; s. Jacob Allen Gimbel and Ruth Helen Johnson; m. Ann Matterand Gimbel, Dec. 23, 1951; children: Shirley Tetz, Denise Job, Kenneth, Marlin, Beverly Kramer. BA, Walla Walla U., 1950; MD, Loma Linda U., 1955, MPH, 1978. Diplomate Nat. Bd. Medicine; cert. Am. Bd. Preventive Medicine. Med. dir. North Hill Med. Clinic, Calgary, 1957-82; assoc. prof. Loma Linda U., Calif., 1982-84; area med. dir. Calif. Indsl. Med. Clinics, Irvine, Calif.; med. dir. Parkview Ctr. for Occupl. Medicine, Riverside, Calif., 1985-91, Rancho Canyon Occupl. Medicine, Temecula, Calif., 1991-2001, Steck Meml. Medica Ctr., Centralia, Wash., 2002—06. Founder, dir. Health Edn. Ctr., Calgary, 1969-82; dir. China-USA Health Project, Loma Linda, Calif., 1991—; cons. China Nat. Health Edn. Inst., Beijing, 1992—; guest prof. Huazhong U., Wuhan, China, 2002-04. Contbr. articles to profl. jours. Flight lt. Royal Can. Air Force Res., 1958—60. Recipient China Tobacco Control award Chinese Assn. Smoking and Health, 2000; named an Honored Alumus, Loma Linda U., 2005, Canadian U. Coll., 2006; named one of Am.'s Top Physicians, Consumers' Rsch. Coun. Am., 2004. Fellow Am. Coll. Preventive Medicine; mem. Am. Coll. Environ. and Occupl. Medicine, Med. Coll. Can. (licentiate), Delta Omega. Avocations: travel, photography, history. Home: 911 Landing Way Centralia WA 98531 Office Phone: 951-316-4945. Personal E-mail: hwgimbel@comcast.net.

GIMBRONE, MICHAEL ANTHONY, JR., research scientist, pathologist, educator; b. Buffalo, Nov. 16, 1943; married, 1971; 3 children. AB, Cornell U., 1965; MD, Harvard U., 1970. Intern, resident fellow Mass. Gen. Hosp., Boston, 1970-72; staff assoc. Nat. Cancer Inst., Bethesda, Md., 1972-74; resch. assoc. Harvard Med. Sch., Boston, 1974-76, from asst. prof. to assoc. prof., 1979-85, Elsie T. Friedman prof. pathology, 1985—; chmn. dept. pathology Brigham and Women's Hosp., Boston, 2001—. Cons. Nat. Heart, Lung and Blood Inst., NIH, 1976—; established investigator Am. Heart Assn., 1977-82; head Vascular Pathophysiol. Rsch. Lab., 1977-85; dir. vascular rsch. div. Brigham and Women's Hosp., 1985—, dir. Ctr. for Excellence in Vascular Biology. Recipient Achievement award in cardiovascular scis. Bristol-Myers Squibb, 2001, King Faisal prize (medicine), King Faisal Found., 2006. Fellow NIH, AAAS, Nat. Acad. of Scis., Am. Acad. Arts and Scis.; mem. Inst. of Medicine, Am. Heart Assn. (Basic Rsch. prize 1993), Am. Soc. Cell Biologists, Tissue Culture Assn., Am. Soc. Hematology, Am. Assn. Pathologists (v.p. 1991-92), Am. Soc. Invest. Pathology (pres. 1992-93), Am. Assn. Physicians, Fedn. Am. Socs. for Exptl. Biology (Exptl. Pathologist award 1982, bd. dirs. 1990-94), N.Am. Vascular Biology Orgn. (founding pres. 1994—, J. Allyn Taylor Internat. prize in medicine). Achievements include research in cardiovascular pathophysiology, especially atherosclerosis, thrombosis and inflammation, vascular cell biology. Office: Brigham and Womens Hosp Dept Pathology 75 Francis St Boston MA 02115 E-mail: mgimbrone@rics.bwh.harvard.edu.

GIMENES, SONIA REGINA ROSENDO, family therapist, psychologist; b. São Paulo, Brazil, Jan. 25, 1953; arrived in U.S., 1996; married; 2 children. BA in Psychology, U. Mogi Cruzes, São Paulo, 1980; M in Sci. Psychology with honors, U. Americas, Mexico City, 1988; postgrad. in psychology; cert. in clin. psychology, U. Paulista, São Paulo, 1994. Registered family therapist intern Fla., lic. clin. psychologist Brazil. Family therapist intern Clinica Oira, Mexico City, 1987—88; psychologist intern Clinica Psicologia Objetivo, São Paulo, Brazil, 1994, Pontificia U. Cath., São Paulo, 1995; clin. psychologist Human Inst., São Paulo, 1995—96; family therapist Counseling and Hypnosis Inc., Miami, Fla., 1999—. Clin. psychologist C. of C., Cross Cultural L.Am. Families. Author: Domestic Violence, 2001; contbr. monography project Child Abuse, 1988, articles to profl. jours. Established Internat. C. of C. Nonprofit Bus. Network. Mem.: ACA, Rotary Internat., AAMFT, Assn. Bi-Nat. C. of C. Fla., Am. Bd. Hypnotherapy, Am. Coll. Forensic Examiners, Am. Psychotherapy Assn., Rotary Internat. (Paul Harris medal of honor 1976). Avocations: music, dance, piano, arts and crafts.

GIMENEZ, LUIS FERNANDO, physician, educator; b. Antofagasta, Chile, Mar. 3, 1952; came to U.S., 1979; s. Luis Sr. and Nelly (Basulto) G.; m. Diane Marie Salazar, Sept. 20, 1957; children: Luis Andres, Pilar Elizabeth, Nicholas Miguel, Catherine Anne. MD, U. Chile, Valparaiso, 1976. Diplomate Am. Bd. Internal Medicine, Am. Bd. Nephrology. Intern U. Chile Sch. Medicine, Valparaiso, 1975-76; resident U. Concepcion Sch. Medicine, Chile, 1976-77, U. Chile Sch. Medicine, Valparaiso, 1977-79; research fellow in nephrology Johns Hopkins U. Sch. Medicine, Balt., 1979-81; intern Johns Hopkins Hosp., Balt., 1981-82, resident, 1982-84, clin. fellow nephrology div., 1984-85; instr. Johns Hopkins U. Sch. Medicine, Balt., 1985-86, asst. prof. medicine, 1986—. Dir. dialysis unit The Good Samaritan Hosp., Balt., 1985—, chief renal div., 1990; med. cons. to Social Security Adminstrn., 1985-93; mem. med. adv. bd. Am. Kidney Found., Balt., 1987-95. Contbr. articles to profl. jours. Recipient Outstanding Civic Svc. award Chilean Med. Assn., Valparaiso, 1974. Mem. Am. Fedn. for Clin. Research., Am. Soc. Nephrology, Am. Coll. Physicians, Internat. Soc. Nephrology, Internat. Soc. Peritoneal Dialysis, Md. Kidney Comn. Avocation: philatelist. Office: Johns Hopkins Hosp Renal Divsn 1830 Bldg Baltimore MD 21205-2109 Home: 5601 Loch Raven Blvd Ste 3N Baltimore MD 21239 Office Phone: 410-532-3775. Personal E-mail: lgimene@yahoo.com.

GIMENO-ORNA, JOSE A., physician; b. Zaragoza, Spain, Nov. 19, 1965; MD, Zaragoza U., 1989. Physician, diabetes HCU Lozano Blesa, 1994—2011. Home: Bielsa 27 Zaragoza 50014 Spain Home Phone: 685803437. Personal E-mail: jagimeno@salud.aragon.es.

GIMSING, STEEN, otolaryngologist; b. Copenhagen, Aug. 2, 1948; MD, U. Copenhagen, 1976. Intern Eksjö Hosp., Sweden, 1976—78; resident ENT dept. Linköping U. Hosp., Sweden, 1978—83; registrar audiology dept. Odense U. Hosp., Denmark, 1983—85; head audiology ENT dept. Esbjerg Hosp., Denmark, 1985—2002, Vejle Hosp., Denmark, 2002—. Adj. lectr. U. Southern Denmark, Odense, 2003. Avocation: horseback riding. Home: Möllekrogen 23 Esbjerg DK-6705 Denmark Personal E-mail: steen.gimsing@slb.regionsyddanmark.dk.

GIMSON, WILLIAM H., III, (BILL GIMSON), health facility administrator; b. 1951; BA, U. Wis., 1973; MBA, Duke U., 2002. Pub. health advisor, Chgo. & NYC Dept. Health Centers for Disease Control & Prevention (CDC), US Dept. Health & Human Services, 1974—81, dir., immunization program, Commonwealth Puerto Rico to acting asst. sect. health Pakistan, 1981—88, dir, fin. mgmt. office, 1996—2003, understudy for the position of dir. financial mgmt. office to assoc. dir. policy coordination, 1988—95, dir., financial mgmt. office, 1995—2003, COO, 2003—09, interim dir., 2009; exec. dir. Cancer Prevention & Rsch. Inst. Tex. (CPRIT), Austin, 2009—. Recipient Presdl. Meritorious Rank award, Presdl. Disting. Rank award, 2005. Fellow: Nat. Acad. Pub. Adminstrn. Office: Cancer Prevention & Rsch Inst Tex (CPRIT) PO Box 12097 Austin TX 78711 Office Phone: 512-463-3190. Office Fax: 512-475-2563. E-mail: cprit@cprit.state.tx.us.

GINAITT, PETER THADDEUS, state legislator; b. Warwick, RI, Dec. 28, 1960; m. Sharon Ann Snyzyk, Apr. 12, 1986; children: Bradford Thomas, Taylor Anne. BA in Resource Develop. and Plant Sci., U. RI, 1983; AS, CC RI, 1987, ADN (Assoc. Degree in Nursing), 1995. With Ginaitt's Landscape Svc.; firefighter Warwick Fire Dept., 1984—; mem., 22nd dist. RI Ho. of Reps., 1992—2007; dir., emergency mgmt. and preparedness RI Hosp., 2003—; coord., emergency responsiveness Lifespan Hosp. Network (which includes RI Hosp., Miriam Hosp., Newport Hosp. and Bradley Hosp.), 2007—. Sec., vice-chmn. com. health, edn. and welfare, chmn. com. environment and natural resources, RI Ho. of Reps. Mem. RI Long-Term Care Coord. Coun.; bd. dirs. RI Alzheimer's Found.; mem. State Conservation Com.; commr. Narragansett Bay Commn. Recipient Nathan Davis award for Outstanding Govt. Svc., AMA, 2008. Mem. Warwick Elks, Nathaniel Greene Masonic Lodge, Oakland Beach Vol. Fire Club, Conservation Law Found. Office: RI Hosp 593 Eddy St Providence RI 02903

GINEL RODRÍGUEZ, JOSÉ, dean, physician, educator; MD. Joined as asst. prof. pediat. Universidad Ctrl. del Caribe, Bayamon, PR, 1986, dir. clin skills devel., dean medicine, 2004—, pres., 2007—; treas. Ramon Ruiz Arnau U. Hosp., dir. residency program in pediat. Office: Universidad Ctrl del Caribe Office of Dean / Pres Avenida Laurel Santa Juanita Bayamon PR 00960-6032 Office Phone: 787-269-4510. Office Fax: 787-798-4990. Business E-Mail: jose.ginel@uccaribe.edu. *

GINGERICH, NAOMI R., emergency room nurse; b. Linwood, Mich., Sept. 18, 1945; d. Leroy and Mary Alice (Driver) G. Diploma in Nursing, Kansas City (Mo.) Gen. Hosp., 1967. RN, Pa., Md., Fla., Mo.; cert. ACLS, BLS, PALS, TNCC, advanced trauma life support. Charge nurse emergency rm. Kansas City Gen. Hosp. and Med. Ctr., Mo., 1967-70, oper. rm. nurse, 1971-74; charge nurse emergency rm. Univ. Med. Ctr., Kansas City, Kans., 1970-73; oper. room charge nurse Lancaster Gen. Hosp., Pa., 1974-79, charge nurse emergency rm., 1979-88, staff nurse emergency room Preferred Nursing Pool, Balt., 1988-90; with home health care, emergency room Norrell Health Care, Sarasota, Fla., 1990-91; office nurse Landisville Family Practice, 1991-92; on-call night nurse Hospice of Lancaster County, 1992-98, pvt. duty nurse, 1998—2000; emergency rm. nurse Bothwell Regional Health Ctr., Sedalia, Mo., 2001—06, Heart of Lancaster Regional Med. Ctr., 2006—. Office: 1500 Highlands Dr Lititz PA 17543 Personal E-mail: nginger@earthlink.net

GINGHER, MERLENE C., occupational therapist, educator; b. Buffalo; d. Earl George and Merna Bethene Gingher. BS, SUNY, Buffalo, NY, 1970, MS, 1975, EdD, 1989. Physical therapist Erie Co. Home Infirmary, Buffalo, 1970—75; instr. SUNY, Buffalo, 1975—76; occupl. therapist, dir. Indendent. Living Project, Buffalo, 1976—80; asst. prof. SUNY, Buffalo, 1980—91, D'Youville Coll., Buffalo, 1991—, chairperson occupl. therapy, 1997—2008. Mem.: Program Dirs.Edn. Coun. (vice chmn. 2002—06), Am. Occupl. Therapy Assn. Avocations: singing, reading. Office: D'Youville Coll 320 Porter Ave Buffalo NY 14201 Office Phone: 716-829-7830.

GINGRASS, MARY KATHERINE, plastic surgeon; b. Milw., Mar. 31, 1963; m. Christopher Stark. BS cum laude, Boston Coll., 1985; MD, Medical Coll. Wis., Milw., 1989. Diplomate Am. Bd. Plastic Surgery, Nat. Bd. Med. Examiners, Am. Soc. Aesthetic Plastic Surgeons, cert. Advanced Edn. Cosmetic Surgery Am. Soc. Aesthetic Plastic Surgery. Resident gen. surgery So. Ill. U. Sch. Med., 1989—92, resident plastic surgery, burn, 1992—94; fellowship aesthetic surgery, breast reconstruction Nashville Plastic Surgery, 1994—95; plastic, cosmetic surgeon Plastic Surgery Ctr., Nashville, 1995—. Bd. mem. Tenn. Breast Cancer Coalition; chief dept. plastic surgery Baptist Hosp., Nashville; med. staff Baptist Plaza Surgicare Outpatient Surgery Ctr., Nashville, Centennial Med. Ctr., Nashville. Spkr. (in field). Fellow: ACS; mem.: Tenn. Women Med., Tenn. Med. Assn., Am. Med. Assn., Am. Soc. Aesthetic Plastic Surgery, Nashville Acad. Med., Am. Soc. Plastic Surgeons. Office: Plastic Surgery Ctr 1915 State St Nashville TN 37203 Office Phone: 866-433-6066. Office Fax: 615-467-6778.

GINN, KAREN A., medical educator; b. Sydney, June 8, 1950; BSc, U. NSW, 1972, PhD, 2001. Sr. lectr. U. Sydney, 1990—2009, head discipline biomed. sci., 2006—11, assoc. prof., 2010—. MPA Rsch. grant, Physiotherapy Rsch. Found. Mem.: Australian & New Zealand Assn. Clin. Anatomists (bd. dirs. 1997—99), Shoulder & Elbow Physiotherapists Australasia (pres. 2004—10), Australian Physiotherapy Assn. Office: PO Box 170 Lidcombe NSW 1825 Australia Office Fax: 61 2 9351 9520. Business E-Mail: karen.ginn@sydney.edu.au.

GINSBERG, BARRY GAVRILLE, psychologist, marriage and family therapist; b. Bklyn., July 25, 1936; s. Elias Ginsberg and Leah Schwartz Ginsberg Epstein; m. Mindi Silverberg, Feb. 22, 1962; children: Joshua, Neil Daniel, Jeremy Marc. BS in Pharmacy, Columbia U., NYC, 1958; MS in Edn./Clin. Sch. Psychology, CCNY, 1969; PhD in Human Devel. and Family Studies, Pa. State U., 1971. Diplomate Am. Bd. Profl. Psychology, Am. Family Therapy Acad.; lic. pharmacist, NY, NJ, Calif., Fla.; cert. tchr., NY; lic. psychologist, Pa., Mass.; cert. in tchrs. of family therapy, Phila. Child Guidance Clinic, Children's Hosp. Phila., tchr., NYC; play therapist/supvr., supr. marriage and family therapy, AAMFT, family life educator, NCFR;

nat. cert. sch. psychologist. Pharmacist, mgr. Ginsberg Pharmacy, Bronx, N.Y., 1958-63; tchr. jr. and sr. h.s. N.Y.C. Bd. Edn., 1963-69; psychologist Bucks County Psychiat. Ctr., Chalfont, Pa., 1971-73; dir. child and family unit Lenape Valley Found., Chalfont, 1973-75, dir. cmty. svcs., 1975-78; psychologist dir. Ginsberg Assocs., Doylestown, Pa., 1978—; cons. and trainer, dir. Ctr. Relationship Enhancement, Doylestown, 1981—. Adj. assoc. prof. Temple U., 1975-85, adj. prof., play therapy, Postgrad. Cert. Program, 2011; cons. Bucks County Area Coun. Aging, 1988—, Bucks County Children and Youth, Doylestown, 1989—, Bucks County Head Start, Bucks County Assn. Retarded Citizens, Doylestown, 1982—; cons. Doylestown Hosp. Hospice Program, 2007—09; adj. prof. psychology Phila. Coll. Osteo. Medicine, 1997-99; adj. prof. clin. psychology Chestnut Hill Coll., 1999-2001; adj. faculty Rutgers U. Grad. Sch. Applied & Profl. Psychology, 1976-78, field supr., 1989-92, Rutgers U. Grad. Sch. Profl. Social Work, 1977-78, internship supr., 1975-76. Author: Relationship Enhancement Family Therapy, 1997, 50 Wonderful Ways to Be a Single Parent Family, 2002; columnist Parenting, 1988-89; co-host (cable TV) Parenting, 1994—; host (cable TV) Parent Connection. Bd. dirs. Big Bros./Big Sisters of Bucks County, 1972—, Bucks County Drug and Alcohol Commn., 1981-87, Network of Victims Asistance, 1990-95. Recipient Sterling Vol. award Ctrl. Bucks C. of C., 1996, Meritorious award Am. Bd. Profl. Psychology, 1992, Meritorious award Bucks County Drug and Alcohol Commn., 1987, Rsch. Practitioner award Internat. Assn. Marriage and Family Counselors, 2011, Bernard & Louise Guerney Outstanding Contbn. award, Assn. Filial and Relationship Enhancement Methods, 2011, Rsch. Practitioner award, Internat. Assn. Minnase Family Counselors Am. Counseling Assn., 2011, Benard Louise Germany award, 2011. Fellow APA (bd. dirs. divsn. family psychology, Meritorious awards divsn. family psychology 1986, 87, 88, 89), Pa. Psychol. Assn. (bd. dirs., pres. cmty. divsn.), Am. Assn. Marriage and Family Therapists (clin. mem., approved supr.), Ctrl. Bucks C. of C. (v.p., bd. dirs. 1975-89, chmn. parenting and family com. 1990—). Avocations: racquetball, folk dancing, ballet. Office: Ctr Relationship Enhancement 70 W Oakland St Ste 205 Doylestown PA 18901 Home Phone: 215-345-7543; Office Phone: 215-348-2424. Personal E-mail: enhancerelations@aol.com. Business E-Mail: barry@relationshipenhancement.com.

GINSBERG, BARRY HOWARD, endocrinologist, educator; b. Bklyn., May 9, 1945; s. Emanuel and Ruth (Friedman) G.; m. Marjorie Ellen Kanef, Aug. 20, 1967; children: Susan, David. BA, SUNY, Binghamton, 1965; PhD, Yeshiva U., NYC, 1971, MD, 1972. Intern Beth Israel Hosp., Boston, 1972-73, resident in internal medicine, 1973-74; fellow in endocrinology NIH, 1974-77; asst. prof. U. Iowa, Iowa City, 1977-82, assoc. prof. medicine and biochemistry, 1982—87, prof., 1988-90, assoc. dir. Diabetes-Endocrinology Rsch. Ctr., 1982-84, dir., 1984-86, co-dir. diabetes control and complications trial, 1984—86, dir., 1986-90; med. dir. worldwide diabetes healthcare Becton Dickenson and Co., Franklin Lakes, NJ, 1990—98; v.p. med. affairs BD Consumer Healthcare, 1999—2007; pres. Diabetes Tech. Cons., Wyckoff, NJ, 2007—; consulting med. dir. Agamatrix & Facet Techs., 2009—. Bd. dirs. Biodel Inc., 2008-, D-Med., 2010-; adj. prof. medicine Robert Wood Johnson Coll. Medicine, 1990-2005. Contbr. chpts. to med. books. Comdr. USPHS, 1974-77. Mem. Am. Diabetes Assn. (pres. Iowa chpt. 1982-84, bd. dirs. 1982-85, bd. dirs. N.E. chpt. 1989—2009). Office Phone: 201-665-9467. Personal E-mail: diabetes_consultants@yahoo.com.

GINSBERG, GREGORY G., gastroenterologist, educator; BS in Biology, Lafayette Coll., 1982; MS, Villanova U., 1983; MD, Thomas Jefferson Med. Coll., 1987. Diplomate Am. Bd. Internal Medicine, 1991, Am. Bd. Internal Medicine, 2001, Am. Bd. Internal Medicine-gastrointestinal medicine, 1993, Am. Bd. Internal Medicine-gastrointestinal medicine, 2001. Resident Georgetown Univ. Hosp., fellow; prof. Medicine Hosp. Univ. Pa., exec. dir. Endoscopic svcs. Parelman Sch. Medicine, physician. Co-author: Practice Patterns and Attitudes Towards theRrole of EUS In Staging of Gastrointestinal Malignancies: A Survey of Physicians and Surgeons, 2005, Neoadjuvant Therapy With Imatinib Mesylate For Locally Advanced Gastrointestinal Stromal Tumor, 2005, Bare Fiber Photodynamic Therapy Using Porfimer Sodium For Esophageal Disease, 2006, Multicenter Comparative Trial of the V-Scope System For Therapeutic ERCP, 2006, Diagnostic Endoscopy 2020 Vision, 2006, Esophageal Stents: Findings On Radiography In 46 Patients, 2006, Excellence In Endoscopy: Toward Practical Metrics, 2006, Comparison of Pelican Single-Use Multi-bite Biopsy Forceps Versus Traditional Double-bite Forceps: Evaluation In A Porcine Model, 2006, Ectopic Pancreatic Rest In The Proximal Stomach Mimicking Gastric Neoplasms, 2007, Gastrostomy Port Assisted Full Thickness Gastric Resection Using Per-Oral SurgASSISTTM Introductied Via An Oro-Esophageal Overtube In A Porcine Model, 2007. Named recognized, Best Doctors in America, 2005—06, 2007—08, 2009—10; named one of the Top Doctors, Phila. Mag., 2007—11, the Top Doctors in America, 2007—08, 2010. Mem.: Am. Soc. for Gastrointestinal Endoscopy, Am. Coll.of Gastroenterology, Am.Gastroenterology Assn. Office: Hospital of the University of Pennsylvania 3 Ravdin 3400 Spruce St Philadelphia PA 19104 Office Phone: 215-662-4279. Office Fax: 215-662-6530. Business E-Mail: gregory.ginsberg@uphs.upenn.edu.

GINSBERG, LAWRENCE DAVID, psychiatrist, researcher; married. MD, U. Miami, Fla., 1981. CEO Red Oak Psychiatry Assoc., Houston, 1991—. Office: Red Oak Psychiatry Assoc 17115 Red Oak Dr Houston TX 77090

GINSBERG-FELLNER, FREDDA, retired pediatric endocrinologist, researcher; b. NYC, Apr. 21, 1937; d. Nathaniel and Bertha (Jagendorf) Ginsberg; m. Michael J. Fellner, Aug. 27, 1961; children: Jonathan R., Melinda F. Bramwit. AB, Cornell U., 1957; MD, NYU, 1961. Diplomate Am. Bd. Pediatrics, Am. Bd. Pediatric Endocrinology. Intern Albert Einstein Coll. Medicine, NYC, 1961-62, fellow in pediatrics, 1962-63, 64-65, 66-67, resident in pediatrics, 1963-64, 65-66, clin. instr. pediatrics, 1967; assoc. in pediatrics Mt. Sinai Sch. Medicine, NYC, 1967-69, asst. prof., 1969-75, assoc. prof., 1975-81, dir. div. pediatric endocrinology, 1987—96, prof. pediatrics, 1981-96; ret., 1996. Med. scis. rev. com. Juvenile Diabetes Found., 1985-88, scis. adv. bd., 1991-; mem. N.Y. State Coun. on Diabetes, Albany, 1988-89; chmn. Camp NYDA for Diabetic Children, Burlingham, 1977-1995. Recipient Humanitarian award Juvenile Diabetes Found., 1994; grantee NIH, 1977-93, Am. Diabetes Assn., 1978, March of Dimes, 1983-87, Juvenile Diabetes Found., 1982-88, 93-95, Wm. T. Grant Found., 1985-89. Fellow Am. Acad. Pediatrics; mem. Am. Diabetes Assn. (chmn. council diabetes in youth 1992-94, Outstanding Contbns. award 1991, Svc. award 1994), Soc. Pediatric Rsch., Am. Pediatric Soc., Endocrine Soc., Lawson Wilkins Pediatric Endocrine Soc., N.Y. Diabetes Assn. (pres.-elect 1985-87, pres. 1987-89, Svc. award Camp NYDA 1989, Max Ellenberg Profl. Svc. award 1993). Personal E-mail: freddagf@aol.com.

GINSBURG, DAVID, genetics educator, researcher; b. Newburgh, NY, Aug. 11, 1952; s. Leonard and Ruth Helena Henrietta (Falkson) Ginsburg; m. Maureen Rose Kushinsky, June 7, 1981; children: Daniel William, Leah Beth. BA in Molecular Biophysics and Biochemistry, magna cum laude, Yale U., New Haven, 1974; MD, Duke U. Sch. Medicine, Durham, NC, 1977. Diplomate Am. Bd. Internal Medicine, cert. Am. Bd. Med. Genetics, in hematology and med. oncology. Pathology resident Presbyn. Hosp., San Francisco, 1977-78; intern, resident internal medicine Peter Bent Brigham Hosp., Boston, 1978-81; tng. program fellow hematology and med. oncology Brigham & Women's Hosp./Dana-Farber Cancer Inst., Boston, 1981-84; instr. medicine Harvard Med. Sch., 1984-85; asst. prof. human genetics U. Mich., Ann Arbor, 1985-89, assoc. prof., 1989-93, dir. divsn. med. genetics, 1993—2002, prof. internal medicine and human genetics, 1993—2003, Warner-Lambert/Parke Davis prof. medicine, 1994—, rsch. prof., Life Sci. Inst., 2003—, James V. Neel disting. Univ. prof. internal medicine and human genetics, 2003—. Asst. investigator Howard Hughes Med. Inst., 1985—89, assoc. investigator, 1989—93, investigator, 1993—; bd. dirs. Shire PLC, 2010—. Contbr. articles to profl. jours. Recipient Jerome W. Conn award, U. Mich., 1987—88, Disting. Faculty Achievement award, 2000, Frank E. Trobaugh Hematology Young Investigator award, Midwest Blood Club, 1988, Internat. Soc. Fibrinolysis & Proteolysis prize, 2002, Basic Rsch. prize, Am. Heart Assn., 2003, Jeanette Piperno Meml. award, Temple U., Phila., 2005, Cotlove award, Acad. Clin. Lab. Physicians & Scientists, 2006, Pasarow Cardiovasc. Rsch. award, Robert J. & Claire Pasarow Found., 2010. Fellow: AAAS; mem.: ACP, NAS (coun. mem. 2009—), Am. Soc. Hematology (E. Donnall Thomas prize 2000), Am. Soc. Human Genetics, Am. Acad. Arts & Scis., Inst. Medicine (coun. mem.), Am. Soc. Clin. Investigation (pres. 2002, Stanley J. Korsmeyer award 2004), Assn. Am. Physicians, Alpha Omega Alpha. Jewish. Office: Life Scis Inst Rm 5028 210 Washtenaw Ave Ann Arbor MI 48109 Office Phone: 734-647-4808. Office Fax: 734-936-2888. Business E-Mail: ginsburg@umich.edu.

GINSBURG, FRANCES W., reproductive endocrinologist, educator; MD, NYU, 1980. Diplomate Am. Bd. Ob-Gyn, cert. reproductive endocrinology. Resident Bellevue hosp. NYU Med. Ctr., 1981—84, fellow Bellevue hosp., 1984—86; asst. prof. ob-gyn. Columbia U.; with Stamford Hosp. Office: Stamford Hospital PO Box 9317 30 Shelburne Ave Stamford CT 06904-9317 Office Phone: 203-276-7559. Office Fax: 203-276-7259.

GINSBURG, HOWARD B., pediatric surgery, educator; Attended, U. Cin., 1968—72. Diplomate Am. Bd. Surgery-pediatric surgery, 2001. Resident gen. surgery NY Univ. Sch. of Medicine, 1972—77, founder pediatric surgery divsn., 1980—, assoc. prof. pediatric surgery; resident pediatric surgery Columbia-Presbyn. Med. Ctr., 1977—79; clin. fellow pediatric urology Mass. Gen. Hosp., 1979—80; with Bellevue Hosp. Ctr., NY Univ. Langone Medical Center. Co-author: (publs.) Management and outcomes for children with pyloric stenosis stratified by hospital type, 2010, An unusual form of duplicate bladder exstrophy, 2010, Complicated Peptic Ulcer Disease in Three Patients With Familial Dysautonomia, 2010, and numerous other publications. Mem.: Brit. Pediatric Surgical Assn., Am. Pediatric Surgical Assn. Office: New York University Langone Medical Center Ste 10W 530 First Ave New York NY 10016-6402 Office Phone: 212-263-7391.

GINSBURG, IONA HOROWITZ, psychiatrist; b. NYC, Dec. 2, 1931; d. A. Eugene and Gertrude (Seidman) Horowitz; m. Selig M. Ginsburg, Aug. 15, 1954 (div. 1984); children: Elizabeth, Jessica. AB, Vassar Coll., 1953; MD, Columbia U., 1957. Diplomate Am. Bd. Psychiatry and Neurology. Pvt. practice, NYC, 1961—; instr. psychiatry Columbia U., NYC, 1961-81, asst. clin. prof. psychiatry, 1981-95, assoc. clin. prof. psychiatry, 1995—; psychiatrist student health svc. NYU, NYC, 1978—2000. Cons.-liaison psychiatrist N.Y. Presbyn. Med. Ctr., N.Y.C., 1982—. Contbr. articles to profl. jours. Med. adv. bd. Nat. Psoriasis Found. 1990-95. Recipient Josie Bradbury Travel award, Psoriasis Assn. Gt. Britain. Mem. Am. Soc. Adolescent Psychiatry, N.Y. Soc. Adolescent Psychiatry (pres. 1986, cert. of appreciation 1986), Am. Psychiat. Assn., Am. Psychosomatic Soc., Met. Coll. Mental Health Assn. (pres. 1980), Assn. Psychocutaneous Medicine N.Am. (sec.-treas. 1994-95, v.p. 1995-98, pres. 1998-2000). Office Phone: 212-289-5050.

GINSBURG, KENNETH R., pediatrician, writer; b. Dec. 21, 1961; MD, Albert Einstein Coll. Medicine, 1987. Cert. Pediat., Adolescent Medicine. Pediatrician Children's Hosp. Phila., 1987—; assoc. prof. pediat. U. Pa. Sch. Medicine. Spkr. in field. Co-author: Less Stress, More Success: A New Approach to Guiding Your Teen Through College Admissions and Beyond, 2006; author: But I'm Almost 13!: An Action Plan for Raising a Responsible Adolescent, 2001, A Parent's Guide to Building Resilience in Children and Teens, 2006. Dir. health svcs. Covenant House, Pa. Named Top Docs, Phila. Mag. Office: Childrens Hosp Philadelphia Ste 10 324 S 34th St and Civic Ctr Blvd Philadelphia PA 19104-4399 Office Phone: 215-590-6864.

GINSBURG, PAUL B., health facility administrator; Degree, Binghamton U.; PhD in Econs., Harvard U. Dep. asst. dir. Congl. Budget Office, Washington, 1978—84; sr. economist RAND, 1984—86; founding exec. dir. Physician Payment Rev. Commn., 1986—95; pres. Ctr. for Studying Health Sys. Change, Washington, 1995—. Mem. adv. bd. Nat. Inst. for Health Care Mgmt. Rsch. and Ednl. Found., Washington, 2003—. Office: Ctr for Studying Health Sys Change 600 Maryland Ave SW Ste 550 Washington DC 20024 Business E-Mail: pginsburg@hschange.org.

GINTAUTAS, JONAS, physician, scientist, administrator; b. Justinava, Lithuania, Oct. 3, 1938; came to U.S., 1967; s. Jonas and Elena (Zavadzkyte) Sinsinas; m. Kristina Zebrauskaite, June 13, 1970 (div. June 1992); children: Stasys, Pasaka, Vadas; m. Lilija Isodaite, July 13, 2002; 1 child, Justinas. PhD, Northwestern U., 1976; MD, U. Juarez, Mex., 1984; MBA, Century U., 1996. Assoc. prof. Tex. Tech. U., Lubbock, 1975-77; assoc. prof. and dir. rsch. Tex. Tech. U. Health Scis. Ctr., Lubbock, 1979-82; dir. basic and clin. rsch., prof. neurology The Brookdlae U. Hosp. Med. Ctr., NYC, 1985—2002; dir. clin. rsch., prof. neurology MediaSys Corp., 2002—. Cons. Amtorg Corp., N.Y.C., 1987-94, Ralex Internat. Co., Boston, 1988-91, Arrow Biomed Inc., Metuchen, N.J., 1988—. Editorial cons. Jour. Aphasia Agnosia Apraxia, 1979—; contbr. articles on pharmacology, anesthesia and surgery to profl. jours. Charter mem. Rep. Presdl. Task Force, Washington, 1982—, Platinum mem., 2002—; mem. Nat. Rep. Senatorial Com., Washington, 1984—, U.S. Senatorial Club, Washington, 1984—; nat. campaign advisor Nat. Rep. Senatorial Com., Washington, 1995-96. Recipient medal of honor Rep. Presdl. Task Force, 1982; rsch. grantee various pvt. and govtl. agys. Fellow Internat. Coll. Physicians and Surgeons (hon.); mem. U.S. Senatorial Club (preferred). Avocations: woodworking, camping, scuba diving, fishing, reading. Home: RR 1 Box 42 Frametown WV 26623-9724 Home Phone: 718-850-0505. E-mail: jgintautas@jhmc.org.

GINZLER, ELLEN M., rheumatologist, educator; b. NYC, Mar. 24, 1944; MD, Case Western Res. U., 1969; MPH, Yale U., 1983. Prof., chief, rheumatology SUNY Downstate Med. Ctr., 1989—. SLE fellowship, Kirkland Found. Lupus Rsch. Office: Downstate Med Ctr 450 Clarkson Ave Brooklyn NY 11203 Office Fax: 718-270-1562. Business E-Mail: ellen.ginzler@downstate.edu.

GIORDANO, BILL A., psychotherapist; b. Newark, June 15, 1957; s. John and Marie Giordano. BA in Polit. Sci. cum laude, Fairleigh Dickinson U., Rutherford, NJ, 1979; postgrad. cert. in clin. social wk., NYU, 1982, MSW, 1992, postgrad., 2003—. LCSW N.Y. Case worker Cath. Charities, NYC, 1982; social worker Bklyn. Bur. C.C., 1986—89; primary therapist South Beach Psychiat. Ctr., SI, 1989—93; sr. therapist day tx. coord. H.S.S. Cmty. Cons. Ctr., NYC, 1993—. Cons., Think Tank mem. On Step Inst., NYC, 1998—; presenter in field. Mem. Dem. Nat. Com., 1976—; bd. trustees On Step Inst. Mental Health Rsch. Mem.: NASW, Phi Omega Epsilon. Achievements include research in paternal instinct; symptoms of parental alienation and its implications for clinicians and patients; coordination of multicultural day treatment program; depression in men. Home: 98 Ann St Newark NJ 07105-3110 Office: On Step Inst 169 E 74th St New York NY 10021 E-mail: bgeo15@aol.com.

GIORDANO, GABRIELE, physician, director; b. Santa Maria Capua Vetere, Italy, Jan. 29, 1963; Degree in Medicine, U. Federico II Naples, 1991; degree in Angiology. Dir. Divsn. Angiology, 2000—. Home: Via Santella Santa Maria Capua Vetere Caserta 81055 Italy Personal E-mail: ggiord@libero.it.

GIORDANO, JAMES JOSEPH, neuroscientist, neuroethicist, pain specialist; b. Staten Island, NY, Sept. 22, 1959; s. James and Gloria (Timpone) G.; m. Sherry (nee Loveless). BS, St. Peter's Coll., Jersey City, 1981; MA, Norwich U., 1982; MPhil, CUNY, 1985, MS, PhD cum laude, 1986. Diplomate Am. Acad. Pain Mgmt., Am. Soc. Behavioral Medicine. Rsch. asst. Einstein Med. Coll., Bronx, N.Y., 1983-86; rsch. fellow Johns Hopkins U., Balt., 1986-88; asst. prof. neurosci. Drake U., Des Moines, 1988-92; dir. pain rsch. Iowa Meth. Hosp., Des Moines, 1990-92; commd. lt. USN, 1992, divsn. officer Pensacola, Fla., 1992-93, dept. head aerospace physiology Cherry Point, NC, 1993—96; neurology prof. Lamar U., Tex., 1996—2000; dir. pain program, behavioral medicine HealthSouth Rehab. Hosp., 1996—2000; prof. neurosci., philosophy, ethics U. Oxford, 2009—, sr. rsch. assoc., Oxford Ctr. Neuroethics; dir., Ctr. Neurotech. Studies Potomac Inst., Va., 2009—. Textbook author; contbr. articles to profl. jours. Recipient Presdl. Point of Light award Pres. George Bush, 1991; Fulbright fellowship, Ludwig-Maximilians U. Munich, 2011-. Fellow Eur Acad. Scis. & Arts, Internat. Aerospace Med. Assn., Soc. USN Flight Surgeons, Aeromed. Engring. Soc. Avocations: weightlifting, Judo, piano, aviation. Office: University Oxford Oxford Ctr Neuroethics Oxford OX1 1PT England Business E-Mail: jgiordano@potomacinstitute.org.

GIORGADZE, TAMAR ALFRED, pathologist, physician; b. Tbilisi, Georgia, Apr. 6, 1960; d. Alfred G. Giorgadze and Venera O. Iosava; m. Archil G. Tsuladze, May 26, 1991. MD, Tbilisi State Med. Inst., 1982, PhD, 1987. Diplomate Am. Bd. of Pathology, 2002, in cytopathology Am. Bd. of Pathology, 2004, lic. physician Mich., 2002, Tenn., 2005. Resident in oncology Tbilisi State Med. Inst., Chair of Oncology, Tbilisi, Georgia, sr. lab. asst., 1985—94; staff oncologist Rep. Cancer Ctr., Dept. of Pediatric Oncology, Tbilisi, Georgia, 1984—85; rsch. fellow Patho Lab Ltd, Sci. Pk., Kiryat-Weizmann, Rechovot, Israel, 1995—96; pathology resident East Tenn. State U., Dept. Pathology, James H. Quillen Coll. Med., Johnson City, Tenn., 1998—2001, chief resident, 2001—02, asst. prof., 2004—; surg. pathology fellow Dept. Pathology and Lab. Medicine Hosp. U. Pa., Phila., 2002—03, cytopathology fellow Dept. Pathology and Lab. Medicine Hosp., 2003—04. Sr. lab. asst. editl. bd. chair of oncology Tbilisi State Med. Inst., Tbilisi, Georgia, 1987—89; manuscript reviewer Hosp. U. Pa., Phila., 2003—04, East Tenn. State U., 2006—. Contbr. chapters to books, articles to profl. jours. Grantee, East Tenn. State U., 2005. Fellow: Coll. Am. Pathologists; mem.: Internat. Acad. Cytology, Internat. Acad. Pathology, Am. Soc. Cytopathology, US and Can. Acad. Pathology. Orthodox Christian. Achievements include patents for Method of forming of the high oncoproctological risk groups; first to Innovative methodologies in cytopathology and endocrine pathology. Avocations: opera, art, reading, swimming, tennis. Office: East Tenn State Univ Dept Pathology PO Box 70568 Johnson City TN 37614

GIORGIO, ANTONIO, hospital administrator; b. S.Andrea di Conza, Avellino, Italy, Nov. 28, 1948; s. Giuseppe Giorgio and Maria Concetta Potuto; m. Teresa Aloisio, Oct. 11, 1975; children: Giuditta, Valentina, Azzurra. Degree in Medicine and Surgery, U. Naples, Italy, 1973. Dir. Infectious Disease and Interventional Ultrasound Unit D.Cotugno Hosp., Naples, 1999—. Contbr. numerous sci. articles. Mem.: Italian Assn. Study Liver Disese, Italian Soc. Infectious Disease, Italian Soc. Ultrasound Medicine and Biology. Office: D Cotugno Hosp Via Quagliariello 54 Naples Italy Home: Via Francesco Petrarca 129 N 80122 Naples NA Italy Office Fax: 39 081 5908278. Personal E-mail: assanui1@virgilio.it.

GIOURGOS, GEORGIOS, physician; b. Athens, Greece, Aug. 11, 1975; MD, U. Pavia, 2003, degree in Otorhinolaryngology Specialization, 2009, PhD in Exptl. Surgery & Microsurgery, 2011. Rsch. fellow Clinic Otorhinolaryngology S. Matteo Hosp., Pavia, 2010—. Recipient Clin. Work award, Nat. Congress Greek Rhinologic Soc., 2011. Mem.: European Soc. Rhinology. Avocations: swimming, snorkeling. Home: Via G Frank 9 Pavia Lombardia 27100 Italy Personal E-mail: ggdoc1@yahoo.com.

GIPS, CHRISTIAAN HENDRIK, medical educator; b. The Hague, The Netherlands, Feb. 18, 1932; s. Pieter and Françoise Hendrika (Van Wort) G.; m. Barbara Frey Meihuizen, Nov. 17, 1957 (dec. Apr. 1987); m. Johanna Barones Van Asbeck, July 8, 1988; children: Ariane Yvonne, Paul Jan, Cornelie Ernestine. MD, Leiden U., Netherlands, 1957, Copenhagen U., 1962; PhD cum laude, Groningen U., 1968. Resident, chief resident Odense (Denmark) Herning Hosps., 1959-63; asst., assoc. prof. U. Groningen, Netherlands, 1963-79, prof. medicine, 1979-93, prof. emeritus, 1993—; head divsn. hepatology U. Hosp., Groningen, 1980-93; dir. Prof. Gips Internat. Sch. Hepatology & Tropical Med. Groningen U., 1993—2007. Cons. Talma-Huis, Veenwouden, The Netherlands, 1969-97; co-founder, coord. Netherlands Liver Transplant Program, 1977-85. Author: Diagnostic Ammonia Tests, 1968; co-author: Atlas of Liver Disease Mortality, 1994; editor: Progress in Liver Transplantation, 1985, Software Techniques - Design for Quality, 2006; editor Netherlands Jour. Medicine, 1970-81; assoc. editor Jour. Liver, 1985-92, Jour. Alcohol and Drugs (Netherlands), 1974-95; steering com. Jour. Hepatology, 1984-90. Co-founder, vice chmn. Netherlands Alcohol Found., The Hague, 1975-80; co-founder, sec., chmn. Netherlands Assn. Study Liver, Rotterdam, 1977-83; co-founder, chmn., adviser Netherlands Digestive Diseases Found., Nieuwe Gein, 1981-2001; co-founder, chmn., adviser Groningen Liver Found., 1985-2004; mem. Project Mgmt. Group consecutive European Union projects on informatics in liver disease, 1990-98; active Cochrane Hepato-Biliary Group, 1995—2007; coord. multictr. liver cell cancer project Groningen-Indonesia Kanker Hati, Indonesia, 1995-98, Groningen-Indonesia Liver Disease, 1997-2000. 1st lt. M.C. Royal Netherlands Army, 1957-59. Decorated officer Order of Oranje Nassau; recipient Three Lights Found. Jubilee prize, 2000, Distinction award, Netherlands Digestive Diseases Found., 2006; nominee Nat. Network award; hon. fellow, Internat. Students Congress of Med. Scis., 2007. Mem. Internat. Assn. Study of Liver, European Assn. Study of Liver (past pres.), Netherlands Assn. Study of Liver (hon.), Netherlands Assn. Internists (past bd. dirs.), Netherlands Assn. Liver Patients (hon.), Danish Assn. Study of Liver, North Netherlands Golf and Country Club, Chris Gips Found.(initiator, advisor, prof., 2008-). Avocations: golf, walking, mountain climbing. Home: Parallelweg 59 9756 CC Glimmen Netherlands

GIRALT, SERGIO ANDRES, oncologist, hematologist; b. La Habana, Cuba, Feb. 4, 1959; s. Emilio Giralt and Maria Teresa Perez Abren; m. Rosa Gabriela Rondon, Feb. 21, 1987; children: Cesar Emilio, Elena Sofia, Sergio Miguel. Degree in Med. Cirujano, U. Ctrl. Venezuela, 1984. Diplomate American Bd. Internal Medicine, 1989, in oncology American Bd. Internal Medicine, 1994, in hematology American Bd. Internal Medicine, 1994. Prof. medicine U. Tex. MD Anderson Cancer Ctr., Houston, 1994—2011; chief adult bone marrow cancer svc. Meml. Sloan-Kettering Cancer Ctr., NYC, 2010—. Achievements include research in pioneered reduced intensity transplant. Office: Memorial Sloan-Kettering Cancer Ctr 1275 York Ave Box 235 New York NY 10065 Office Phone: 212-639-6009.

GIRARD, LOUIS JOSEPH, retired ophthalmologist, educator; b. Spokane, Wash., Mar. 29, 1919; s. Harry and Agnes (Cain) G.; m. Bonita Crossnay, Mar. 31, 1945, children: Hilaire Michelle Bryan, Suzanne Christina Ann, Michael Sanford (dec.), Hugh Ashley, Gabrielle Inez; m. Loraine McMurrey, June 30, 1967; 1 son, Louis McMurrey; m. Louise Bell, June 14, 1975. BA, Rice U., 1941; MD, U. Tex., 1944; postgrad., NYU, Med. Sch., 1947-48. Diplomate. Am. Bd. Ophthalmology. Intern Jersey City Med. Ctr., 1944-45; assoc. Dr. Conrad Berens, NYC, 1947—49; asst. attending St. Clare's Hosp., 1948—53; resident ophthalmology NY Eye and Ear Infirmary, 1949-51; asst. attending Willard Parker Hosp., 1949-53; dir. chronic infection project, 1949-52; asst. attending N. Country Community Hosp., 1951-53; assoc. Dr. Conrad Berens, 1951—53; asst. attending Nassau Hosp., 1951-53, asst. surgeon, 1951-53; assoc. dir. dept. rsch. NY Eye and Ear Infirmary, 1953—57, founder dept. rsch., 1956; cons. ophthalmologist Southside Hosp., 1951-53; attending ophthalmologist Jefferson Davis Hosp., 1953-59, VA Hosp., Houston, 1954—98, Tex. Children's Hosp., 1954—98, St. Luke's Episcopal Hosp., 1954—98, Meth. Hosp., 1955—98; cons. Montgomery County Hosp., 1955—98, Tex. Children's Hosp., 1953—57; assoc. prof., assoc. chmn. dept. ophthalmology Baylor Coll. Medicine, Houston, 1957—70, prof., chmn. dept., 1953—70; cons. VA Hosp., Houston, 1958—98; sr. attending Ben Taub Gen. Hosp., 1959—98, Meth. Hosp., 1959—98; cons. St. Luke's Episcopal Hosp., 1961—98, St. Joseph's Hosp., 1965—98; chief ophthalmology, co-chief surgery Ctr. Pavilion Hosp., 1970-76; clin. prof. Baylor Coll. Medicine, Houston, 1971—. Coord. grad. course ophthalmology NYU Postgrad. Med. Sch., 1948-49, instr., 1951-53; clin. asst. prof. U. Tex. Postgrad. Sch. Medicine, 1953-57, lectr., 1946; assoc. mng. dir. Ophthal. Found., N.Y., 1951-55, cons., 1957; founder Tex. Med. Ctr.-Lions Eye Bank, 1953; exec. dir. Girard Ophthal. Found., 1971—; cons. Meth. Hosp., St. Luke's Hosp.; founder, exec. dir. Inst. Ophthalmology, Tex. Med. Ctr., 1958—70; founder opthal. tissue culture lab. Baylor U., 1954; mem. Am. Orthoptic Coun., 1962-72; pres. Internat. Eye Film Library, 1967-71; med. adv. bd. Internat. Eye Bank, 1965-70; Pres. IX Pan Am Congress Ophthalmology, 1972; presenter in field. Author: Advanced Techniques in Ophthalmic Microsurgery, Vol. I: Ultrasonic Fragmentation for Intraocular Surgery, 1979, Vol. II: Corneal Surgery, 1981; author, editor 11 books; prodr. 70 films.; editor: Corneal Contact Lenses, 1964, 2d edit., 1971, Corneal Scleral Contact Lenses, 1967, Procs. of XI Pan Am Congress of Ophthalmology, 1974; mem. editl. bd. Ophthalmologia, 1965-72, Annals of Ophthalmology, 1968-74; contbr. articles to profl. jours.; cons. Highlights Ophthalmology, 1972; founded the Lions Ey Bank; founded the first Tissue laboratory devoted to ophthalmology in the world, 1959; established the first inst. of ophthalmology in southwestern USA at Baylor Coll. Medicine, 1961. Recipient Alfred H. Bond award for rsch. in ophthalmology, 1950, Prof. Ignacio Barraquer Meml. award Inst. Barraquer, 1965, 2d prize Internat. Eye Film Festival, 1966, 1st prize, 1970, 1st prize, 1972, Golden Eagle award Internat. Film Festival Nantes, France, 1970, 71, Alumnus award Baylor U., 1984, First Disting. Alumnus award NY Eye and Ear Infirmary, 1984, Disting. Alumnus award Rice U., 1985, Disting. Alumnus award U. Tex. Med. Br. at Galveston, 1991; named to Hall of Fame, Alcon Labs., 1990. Fellow ACS (bd. gov. 1966-72); mem. Am. Acad. Ophthalmology (2d pl. award sci. exhibits 1960, Honor award, Sr. Honor award), Pan Am. Assn. Ophthalmology (1st pl. award sci. exhibits 1960, 62, vis. prof. 1967, v.p. 1972), Assn. Research Ophthalmology, N.Y. Acad. Medicine, NY Acad. Sci., Nassau, Houston ophthal. socs., French Soc. Ophthalmology, Houston Neurol. Soc., Jules Gonin Club, Tex. Opthal. Assn., Alumni Assn. NY Eye and Ear Infirmary, AMA (certificate of merit sci. exhibit 1961), So. Med. Assn., Nat. Med. Found. Eye Care, Assn. Am. Physicians and Surgeons, Am. Assn. Ophthalomologists, Nat. Med. Found. Eye Care, Tex. Rehab. Assn., Harris County Med. Soc., Am. U. Prof. Ophthalmologists (founder, chmn. com. on ophthalmic asst.), Med. Rsch. Found. Tex., Contact Lens Soc. Ophthalmologists (Exceptional Merit award 1968), Inst. Horacio Ferrer (corr., lectr. 1959), Am. Eye Study Club (pres.) Achievements include inventing several instruments; originator numerous surg. techniques. Home: 5318 Del Monte Dr Houston TX 77056-4210 Personal E-mail: manalay@sbcqlobal.net.

GIRARDI, LEONARD NICK, thoracic surgeon, educator; children: Nicholas, Henry, Edward, Anthony. BA in Biochemistry, Harvard U., 1985; MD, Weill Cornell Med. Coll., NY, 1989. Diplomate Am. Bd. Surgery, Am. Bd. Thoracic Surgery, registered NY, 1990, lic. Tex., 1996. Intern NY Hosp. Med. Ctr. of Queens, 1990, resident in cardiothoracic surgery, 1994, fellow, 1996; fellow in aortic surgery Baylor Coll. of Medicine, Tex., 1997; assoc. attending surgeon Meml. Sloan Kettering Cancer Ctr.; intern NY Presbyn. Hosp./Weill Cornell Med. Ctr., resident in gen. surgery, O. Wayne Isom prof. cardiothoracic surgery, attending cardiothoracic surgeon. Co-author (with J. S. Coselli): (jour. article) Inflammatory aneurysm of the ascending aorta and aortic arch, 1997; author: (book chapters) Surgical approaches when aortic regurgitation is associated with aortic root disease, 2001, 2002, Valve repair versus replacement when regurgitation is caused by aortic root aneurysms: relative advantages and disadvantages and impact of decision on surgical indications, 2003, Primary repair of bicuspid aortic valve. Is it viable? Advances in Cardiology, 2004, various others. Named one of Top Doctors, Castle Connolly, Best Doctors, NY Mag. Fellow: ACS, mem.: DeBakey Internat. Surgical Soc., Soc. of Thoracic Surgery, Am. Assn. of Thoracic Surgery. Office: New York Presbyterian Hospital Weill Cornell Medical Center 525 E 68th St M-404 New York NY 10065 Office Phone: 212-746-5194. Office Fax: 212-746-8426.

GIRARDIS, MASSIMO, anesthesiologist, educator; b. Udine, Italy, July 6, 1967; MD, U. Udine, 1993. Assoc. prof. anesthesiology and intensive care U. Modena and Reggio Emilia, 2006—. Cons. U. Hosp. Modena, 2000—11. Mem.: Italian Soc. Anesthesia and Intensive Care, European Soc. Intensive Care Medicine. Home: Lgo del Pozzo 71 Modena 41100 Italy Business E-Mail: girardis.massimo@unimo.it.

GIRGIS, SUZETTE, clinical pharmacologist, researcher; d. Fawzy and Narges Tawfeek Rashed; m. Ihab Girgis, June 4, 1995; children: Abigail Mary, Sarah Marie. BSc in Pharmacy with honors, Cairo U., 1992; MSc in Applied Pharm. Scis., U. R.I., 1997, PhD in Pharm. Scis., 1999. Postdoctoral fellow in clin. pharmacokinetics Janssen Rsch. Found. Johnson & Johnson, Titusville, NJ, 2000; sr. scientist in pharmacokinetics Schering-Plough Corp., Kenilworth, NJ, 2000—03, assoc. prin. scientist in pharmacokinetics, 2003; sr. rsch. investigator in clin. discovery/oncology-immunology Bristol-Myers Squibb Co., Princeton, NJ, 2003—05, assoc. dir. clin. discovery, 2005—08; dir. Global Clin. Pharmacology, 2008—, Johnson & Johnson PRD, Titusville, NJ. Sunday sch. tchr. St. Mary and St. Mena Coptic Orthodox Ch., Cranston, RI, 1996—2000, St. Mary Coptic Orthodox Ch., East Brunswick, 2000—. Mem.: Am. Coll. Clin. Pharmacology, Am. Soc. Clin. Pharmacology and Therapeutics. Avocations: reading, drawing, painting, crafts. Home: 21 Brookside Dr Princeton NJ 08540 Office: 1125 Trenton Harbourton Rd Titusville NJ 08560 Office Phone: 609-730-2757. Business E-Mail: sgirgis@its.jnj.com.

GIRCUS, JOAN STERN, psychologist, educator, director; b. Albany, NY, Mar. 21, 1942; d. William Barnet and Louise (Mayer) Stern; m. Alan Chimacoff, Jan. 2, 1981; 1 child, Katherine-Louise Chimacoff Dickens. BA, Sarah Lawrence Coll., 1963; MA, The Grad. Faculty New Sch. for Social Research, 1965, PhD, 1969. Asst. prof. dept. psychology CCNY, NYC, 1969-72, assoc. prof., 1972-77, assoc. dean div. social sci., 1972-75, dean, 1975-77; prof. psychology Princeton U., 1977—, dir. Pew Sci. Program Undergrad. Edn., 1987—2002, chair dept. psychology, 1996—2002, spl. asst. to dean of faculty, 2003—. Contbr. articles and chpts. to profl. jours. and books. NSF fellow, NIH fellow; Research grantee CUNY, 1971-74; Nat. Inst. Child Health and Human Devel. research grantee, 1972-74; NSF grantee, 1975-79; NIMH grantee, 1985-91. Fellow APA, Am. Psychol. Soc.; mem. Eastern Psychol. Assn., Soc. Rsch. in Child Devel. Home: 306 Ridgeview Rd Princeton NJ 08540 Office: Princeton U Green Hall Princeton NJ 08544

GIRIBELA, CASSIANA ROSA GALVÃO, gynecologist, educator; b. São Paulo, Brazil, Jan. 22, 1976; Degree in Medicine, U. São Paulo, 1999, MD, 2007, PhD student, 2008—. Postdoc. fellow dept. gynecology Clinics Hosp., U. São Paulo, 2008—. Achievements include research in influence of oral contraceptives on endothelial function and cardiovascular disease. Avocation: mountain climbing. Office: Rua Matilde Paizer 36 Vila Yara São Paulo 06020030 Brazil Office Fax: 55 11 36820805. Business E-Mail: cgiribela@uol.com.br.

GIROLAMI, ANTONIO, internist, educator; b. Fanna, Pordenone, Italy, Sept. 23, 1931; MD, U. Padua Med. Sch., 1956. Prof. internal medicine U. Padua Med. Sch., 1981—2006, emeritus prof. internal medicine, 2006—. Fulbright scholarship, USA Govt. Office: Via Ospedale Civile 105 Padua Veneto 35128 Italy Office Fax: 0039 049 657391. Business E-Mail: antonio.girolami@unipd.it.

GISMONDO, MARIA RITA, microbiologist, educator; b. Catania, Italy, Feb. 18, 1954; d. Gaetano Gismondo and Paola Cosentino; children: Cecilia, Beatrice. Degree in biology, U. Catania, 1976, degree in medicine, 1984, postgrad. specialization in microbiology. Assoc. prof. clin. microbiology Inst. Med. Microbiology of Med. Sch. Dentistry Faculty, 1987—, Clin. Microbiology Polo U. L. Sacco Tchg. Hosp., Faculty Medicine and Surgery, U. Milan, 1996—, head clin. microbiology lab. Gen. secretariat Resistance of Antimicrobial Agents Internat. Biennal Symposium, 1991—; mem. internat. adv. bd. alzheimers disease IFE. Author: Meccanismi di Virulenza Batterica, 1994; contbr. over 237 articles to sci. pubs.; editor: Microbiologia del Cavo Orale, 1987; author, editor: Terapia Antibiotica: Un Boomerang?, 1991. Mem.: Internat. Soc. Chemotherapy, Assn. Prudent Use Antibiotics, European Soc. Clin. Microbiology and Infectious Diseases, Years Green Accad., Soc. Italiana Chemioterapie, NY Acad. Sci., European Soc. Clin. Microbiology, Rotary Manzoni Studium Milan (pres.). Achievements include research in activity and mechanisms of resistance of antimicrobial agents, probiotics, bioterrorism, and SARS. Avocations: tennis, writing. Office: L Sacco Tchg Hosp via GB Grassi 74 20133 Milan Italy Home Phone: 39 335 5935588; Office Phone: 39 0239042239. Business E-Mail: mariarita.gismondo@unimi.it.

GISTEREK, IWONA JOLANTA, physician; b. Wroclaw, Oct. 11, 1958; MD, PhD, Wroclaw Med. U., 1982. Physician Wroclaw Med. U., 1993—. Grant, Ministry of Poland. Mem.: FCI, PTO. Home: Nowa 8 Psary Wroclaw Lower Silesia 51-180 Poland Home Fax: 0071 3619111. Business E-Mail: gisti@op.pl.

GITLER, BERNARD, cardiologist, critical care specialist; b. Munich, Aug. 14, 1950; arrived in U.S., 1953, naturalized, 1957; s. Abe and Lola (Greenberg) G.; m. Ellen Spielman, Aug. 4, 1974; children: Stefanie, Cynthia, Bryan. BS in Chemistry, MIT, 1972, BS in Life Scis., 1972; MD, Cornell U., 1976. Diplomate Nat. Bd. Med. Examiners; diplomate in internal medicine, cardiovasc. diseases, critical care medicine Am. Bd. Internal Medicine; cert. Nat. Bd. Echocardiography; cert. Bd. Nuclear Cardiology. Resident in internal medicine Bronx Mcpl. Hosp. Ctr., Albert Einstein Coll. Medicine, Bronx, NY, 1976—79; cardiology fellow Montefiore Med. Ctr., Albert Einstein Coll. Medicine, 1979—81, chief fellow, 1980—81; clin. instr. Albert Einstein Coll. Medicine, 1981—84, asst. clin. prof. medicine, 1984—92, assoc. clin. prof. medicine, 1992—; attending cardiologist Sound Shore Med Ctr. Westchester, New Rochelle, 1981—; chief divsn. cardiology Sound Shore Med. Ctr. Westchester, 2002—, dir. Chest Pain Ctr., 2005—, dir. cardiology fellowship program, 2005—; assoc. attending cardiologist Montefiore Med. Ctr., Bronx, 1981—; pvt. practice cardiology Westchester Heart Specialists, New Rochelle, 1981—; asst. attending cardiologist Columbia-New York. Presbyn. Med. Ctr., NYC, 1992—; asst. prof. clin. medicine Columbia U., 1992—; attending cardiologist Westchester Med. Ctr., 2002—. Adj. assoc. prof. medicine N.Y. Med. Coll., 2006—; physician cons. Island Peer Rev. Orgn., N.Y., 1985-88; faculty senator Albert Einstein Coll. Medicine, 1987-89, co-dir. cardiology curriculum New Rochelle Hosp. Med. Housestaff, 1985-92; attending cardiologist dept. electrocardiography Montefiore Med. Ctr., Bronx, 1983—; pres. med. staff Sound Shore Med. Ctr. Westchester, 1996-99, bd. govs., 1993-99, clin. cardiology rschr., 1985—. Referee Am. Heart Jour., 1983-95, Jour. Am. Coll. Cardiology, 1987-89, N.Y. State Jour. of Medicine, 1990-91, Chest, 1998—; contbr. articles to profl. jours. Recipient Attending of the Yr. award Montefiore Hosp. Med. House Staff, 1985, Tchr. of the Yr. award New Rochelle Hosp. and Med. Ctr., 1986, William C. Schraft Jr. Meml. Tchg. award New Rochelle Hosp., 1996, Robert D. Brandstetter Meml. Tchg. award Sound Shore Med. Ctr. Westchester, 2006. Fellow: ACP (Outstanding Tchg. Preceptorship award 1996, Cmty. Based Excellence Tchg. award 2004), Am. Soc. Nuclear Cardiol., NY Cardiol. Soc., Am. Heart Assn. (pres. westchester divsn. 2008—11), Am. Coll. Cardiology, Am. Soc. Echocardiography, Am. Coll. Chest Physicians; mem.: AMA, NY Acad. Scis., Am. Coll. Sports Medicine, NY State Med. Soc., Soc. Chest Pain Ctrs., Am. Assn. Med. Rsch., Am. Med. Athletic Assn., Soc. Critical Care Medicine, Nat. Strength and Conditioning Assn., Mensa, Phi Beta Kappa, Phi Lamba Upsilon. Democrat. Jewish. Achievements include completion of ten marathons. Avocations: Okinowan Goju-ryu karate (black belt), marathon running. Office: Westchester Heart Specialists 150 Lockwood Ave New Rochelle NY 10801 4916 Office Phone: 914 633 7870. Personal E-mail: bgmd@aol.com.

GITONGA, ROBERT MURAGURI, statistician; b. Kenya, July 15, 1961; PhD, U. Reading, Eng., 2001. Clin. Rsch. scientist, biostatistician Health Decisions, Inc, 2004—. Named Outstanding Scientist, DFTX. Mem.: ISPOR. Avocations: reading, writing, travel. Home: 4339 Mantua Way Raleigh NC 27604 Personal E-mail: grmuraguri@yahoo.com.

GITTERMAN, ALEX, social work educator; b. Kolomea, Poland; came to U.S., 1948; s. Paul and Fay (Hirsch) G.; m. Naomi Janet Pines, Sept. 1963; children: Daniel Paul, Sharon Lynn. BA, Rutgers U., 1960; MSW, Hunter Coll., 1962; EdD, Columbia U., 1972. Div. dir. Bronx River Settlement, 1962-65; dir. East Side House Millbrook Ctr., Bronx, 1965-66; mem. faculty Columbia U., NYC, 1966—, prof., 1972—, assoc. dean, 1981-85; mem. faculty U. Conn. Sch. Social Work, 2000—. Cons. Manhattan VA, N.Y.C., 1974-80, Family Service of Westchester (White Plains), N.Y., 1978-80, Bur. Child Welfare, 1977-80, Drug Abuse Prevention Program, Archdiocese of N.Y., 1985—, Keio Acad.; vis. prof. U. Conn. Sch. Social Work, 2000--. Author: (with C.B. Germain) The Life Model of Social Work Practice, 1980, (with L. Shulman) Mutual Aid Groups and The Life Cycle, 1986, Handbook of Social Work Practice with Vulnerable Populations, 1991, Mutual Aid Groups, Vulnerable Populations and the Life Cycle, 1994, (with C.B. Germain) The Life Model of Social Work Practice: Advances in Theory and Practice, 1996, Handbook of Social Work Practice with Vulnerable and Resilient Populations, 2001, Mutual Aid Groups, Vulnerable and Resilient Populations and the Life Cycle, 2005, The Life Model of Social Health Practice Advices in Theory of Practice, 2008, Encyclopedia of Social Work With Groups, 2010; contbr. articles to profl. jours. Recipient Hexter award Hunter Coll., 1981, Hunter Coll. Hall Fame, 2008, Significant Life Time Achievement award Council Social Work Edn., 2009 Mem. Con. on Social Work Edn., Nat. Assn. Social Workers Democrat. Jewish. Office: U Conn Sch Social Work 1798 Asylum Ave West Hartford CT 06117-2001 Office Phone: 860-570-9016. Business E-Mail: Alex.Gitterman@uconn.edu.

GITTES, ELISSA B., pediatrician, adolescent medicine specialist, educator; MD, Harvard U., 1987. Diplomate Am. Bd. Pediatrics, 2005, Am. Bd. Pediatrics-adolescent medicine, 2005. Resident pediat. Calif. Pacific Med. Ctr., 1988—89, Univ. of Calif. San Francisco (UCSF) Med. Ctr., 1989—90, fellow adolescent medicine, 1990—92; asst. prof. pediat. Univ. Pitts.; pediatrician Children's Hosp. Pitts. Univ. of Pitts. Med. Ctr. Office: Childrens Hospital Pittsburgh 3420 5th Ave Pittsburgh PA 15213 Office Phone: 412-692-6677.

GITTES, GEORGE K., pediatric surgeon, educator; MD, Harvard Med. Sch., 1987. Diplomate Am. Bd. Surgery, Am. Bd. Surgery-pediatric surgery. Resident Univ. of Calif., San Francisco, 1994, fellow hormone rsch. inst. gastrointestinal rsch. labs., 1994; fellow Children's Mercy Hosp., Kansas, Mo., 1996; hosp. affliation include/s Magee-Womens Hosp. of UPMC, Children's Hosp. of Pitts. of UPMC, UPMC Children's Surgery Ctrs.; dir. pediatric surgical rsch. Childrens Hosp. of Pitts. of UPMC; prof. surgery dept. Univ. of Pitts. Co-author of numerous publications. Fellow: ACS, Am. Acad. of

Pediatrics; mem.: Pacific Assn. of Pediatric Surgeons, Am. Soc. of Cell Biology, Am. Diabetes Assn., British Assn. of Pediatric Surgeons, Plastic Surgery Rsch. Coun., Am. Pediatric Surgical Assn., Am. Surgical Assn., Am. Soc. of Clin. Investigators. Office: Childrens Hospital of Pittsburgh of UPMC 1 Childrens Hospital Drive 4401 Penn Ave Pittsburgh PA 15224 Office Phone: 412-692-7280.

GITTLER, MICHELLE S., physiatrist; BSE, U. Mich., 1984; MD, U. Ill., Chgo. Diplomate Am. Bd. Phys. Medicine and Rehab. Residency Northwestern U. Med. Sch., Rehab. Inst. Chgo.; physiatrist, residency program dir. Schwab Rehab. Hosp., Chgo.; physiatrist Mount Sinai Hosp., Chgo., Weiss Meml. Hosp., Chgo., Cook County Hosp.; physiatrist, assoc. prof. surgery U. Chgo. Med. dir. spinal cord injury program. Mem.: Am. Acad. Phys. Medicine and Rehab., Assn. Acad. Physiatrists. Office: Schwab Rehab Hosp 1401 S California Blvd Chicago IL 60608 Office Phone: 773-522-5853.

GIUDICE, AMERIGO, surgeon, educator; b. Polla, Salerno, Italy, Jan. 21, 1977; s. Mario Giudice and Maria Falcone; life ptnr. Mariella Ippolito. Diploma in Medicine and Surgery, Seconda Universita' Napoli, 2001. Diplomate Seconda Universita' Napoli, 2001. Fellow in maxillofacial surgery Seconda Universita' Napoli, Italy, 2001—; prof. Universita' Magna Graecia Catanzaro, Italy, 2005—. Cons. Universita' Magna Graecia Catanzaro, 2004—05. Contbr. articles to profl. jours. Named Best Fellow of Yr., Seconda Universita' Napoli Maxillofacial Surgery Inst., 2001—05; fellow, 2001—. Mem.: European Assn. Aestetic And Plastic Surgery (assoc.), Italian Assn. Pediatric Dentistry (assoc.), Italian Assn. Oral Pathology and Medicine (assoc.), Italian Assn. Oral and Maxillofacial Surgeons (assoc.). Home: Via Pozzillo Salerno Sala Consilina 84036 Italy Office: I Policlinico Piazza Miraglia Napoli 80138 Italy Office Fax: 00390815665294. Personal E-mail: amerigogiudice@hotmail.com. Business E-Mail: amerigo.giudice@unina2.it.

GIUDICE, LINDA CARMEN, obstetrician, gynecologist, biochemist, reproductive endocrinologist; b. NY, Sept. 7, 1949; m. Sakis Theologis; 2 children. BS in Engring, Columbia U., 1969; MSc, Wash. U., St. Louis, 1971; PhD in Biochemistry, U. Calif., Los Angeles, 1976; MD, Stanford U., 1982. Intern, ob-gyn. Kaiser Permanente Hosp., Santa Clara, Calif., 1982—83; resident, ob-gyn. Stanford U. Med. Ctr., 1983—84, fellow, 1986—87; resident, reproductive endocrinology and infertility Barnes-Jewish Hosp., 1984—86; assoc. chair rsch., ob-gyn. Stanford U. Sch. Medicine, 1998—2005, Stanley McCormick Endowed professorship, 2001—05; Robert B. Jaffe, MD endowed prof. & chmn dept. ob-gyn. and reproductive sciences U. Calif., San Francisco, 2005—. Dir., reproductive endocrinology & infertility lab. Stanford U. Med. Ctr., 1987—2005; dir., reproductive endocrinology & infertility fellowship Stanford U. Sch. Medicine, 1994—2005, dir., divsn. of reproductive endocrinology & infertility, dept. ob-gyn., 1995—2005, dir., Ctr. for Rsch. on Reproduction and Women's Health and Genomic Medicine, 1996—2005, dir., women's health@Stanford, 2001—05, dir., women's health scholarly concentration, 2003—05; chair FDA Reproductive Health Drugs Adv. Com.; mem. of study sections NIH and March of Dimes; chair NIH Reproductive Medicine Network, Gordon Rsch. Conf. on Reproductive Tract Biology; coun. mem. Gordon Rsch. Conf.; v.p. World Endometriosis Rsch. Found., 2006—; mem. NIH Adv. Com. on Rsch. on Women's Health, 2008—; lectr. and cons. in field. Co-editor: (textbook) The Endometrium; contbr. several articles to jours.; mem. of several editl. bd., assoc. editor of several profl. jours. Recipient Academia Nazionale dei Lincei Arnaldo Bruno Internat. prize, Italian Acad. Sciences, 2006; named Best Doctors in America, San Francisco Mag., 2004—05. Mem.: World Endometriosis Soc. (pres. 2008—), Soc. for Women's Health Rsch. (bd. dirs. 2002—07), Am. Soc. for Reproductive Medicine (bd. dirs. 2004—07, Disting. Researcher award 2008), Am. Fertility Soc. (Illuminations award 2008), Am. Med. Women's Assn. (Woman in Sci. award 2008), Inst. Medicine Nat. Academies, Soc. for Gynecologic Investigation (pres. 2006—07, mem. exec. coun., President's Achievement award 1998, Disting. Scientist award 2008). Avocations: running, reading, listening to classical guitar. Office: 505 Parnassus Ave M-1496 San Francisco CA 94143-0132 Office Phone: 415-885-7788, 415-476-2564. Office Fax: 415-476-1811. E-mail: giudice@obgyn.ucsf.edu.

GIUFFRIDA, REGINA, obstetrician, gynecologist; Attended, Columbia U., 1976, NY Med. Coll., 1980. Diplomate Am. Bd. Ob-Gyn, 1987, Am. Bd. Ob-Gyn, 1995. Intern Univ. of Calif., 1981, resident, 1983, chief resident, 1984; asst. clin. prof. ob-gyn. and reproductive sci. Mt. Sinai Sch. of Medicine; with Northern Westchester Hosp., Ambulatory Surgery Ctr., Mt. Kisco Med. Group. Office: Mount Kisco Medical Group 90 S Bedford Rd Mount Kisco NY 10549-3412 Office Phone: 914-241-1050.

GIULIANO, ROBERT PAUL, pharmacist; b. NYC, Mar. 7, 1943; s. Salvatore Anthony and Marie Rita (LoScalzo) G.; m. Maja Hreljanovic, July 2, 1966; children: Christopher Robert, Kenneth Paul. BS in Pharmacy, Fordham U., 1965; MS in Hosp. Pharmacy Adminstrn., L.I. U., 1970. Diplomate Am. Bd. Pharmacy, Nat. Registy Emergency Med. Technicians. Clin. pharmacist Columbia-Presbyn. Med. Ctr., NYC, 1965—70; dir. pharmacy dept. St. Barnabas Hosp., NYC, 1970—71; dir. dept. pharm. scis. Misericordia Hosp. Med. Ctr., NYC, 1971—78, adminstrv. dir. material mgmt., 1978—79, asst. adminstrv. dir., 1979—81; pres. Apotheke Assos. Ltd., NYC, 1980—81; pres., dir., CEO U.S. Home Health Care Corp. and Steri-Pharm subs., 1981—91; also chmn. bd.; mem. Tech. Adv. Svc. for Attys., 1988—. Pres. RPG Assoc., 1991—, pres. dir.; chmn. bd. Bryce Rx Labs Inc., 1995—; pres., dir. Red Rock Labs, Inc., 1997-99; v.p. Red Rock Rsch., 2001-06, Scarguard Labs, LLC, 2006—; affil. clin. instr. St. John's U., 1971-81; cons. Weleda Internat., 1991-92, Healix Health Care, 1992-96, Rye Beach Pharmacy, 1992-96, Champlain Valley Physicians Hosp., 1993-94, Columbia Presbyn. Med. Ctr., 1984-97, Transworld Home Health Corp., 1991-93, NY Med. Coll., 1992-95, ROR Group, 1992-93, Geneva Gen. Regional Hosp., 1994-95; home health care cons. Alternative Care Svcs., Inc., 1988-90, Robert Wood Johnson Found., 1985; clin. pharmacy adv. bd., 1971-81; exec. com. Bronx Emergency Med. Svcs. Coun., 1975-80; sr. emergency med. technician instr./coord. NY State Dept. Health, Bur. Emergency Med. Svcs., 1975-81; spkr.'s bur., CPR instr. AHA, 1975-81; CPR instr. Westchester Heart Assn., 1977-80; mem. spkrs. bur. Misericordia Hosp. Med. Ctr., Westchester County Soc. Hosp. Pharmacists; cons., surveyor Pharmacy Compunding Accreditation Bd., 2006—. Author: (with others) RX Technician Manual, 1994; editor: Misericordia Hosp. Pharmacy Newsletter, 1971-78, 2009-. Asst. cubmaster Boy Scouts Am., Eastchester, NY, 1976-78; coach youth baseball T.Y.A., Eastchester, 1975-83. Mem. Am. Pharm. Assn., Italian Pharm Assn., Am. Soc. Cons. Pharmacists, Am. Soc. Healthcare Pharmacists, N.Y. State Coun. Hosp. Pharmacists, Nat. Assn. Sr. Emergency Med. Technician Instrs., Nat. Assn. Emergency Technicians (founding), Am. Soc. Parenteral-Enteral Nutrition, League IV Therapists, Nat. IV Therapy Assn., Nat. Assn. Retail Druggists, Pharmacy Compounding Ctrs. Am., Internat. Acad. Compounding Pharmacists, Fordham U. Pharmacy Alumni Assn. (dir. 1982-98, 1st v.p. 1990-91, pres. 1992-95), N.Y. Athletic Club. Republican. Roman Catholic. Home: 157 Oakland Ave Eastchester NY 10709-5403 Office: PO Box 1 Eastchester NY 10709-1403 Office Phone: 800-798-7279, 203-359-6323. Business E-Mail: bob@brycerx.com, bob@scarguard.com.

GIURESCU, MARINA ELENA, radiologist; b. Bucharest, Romania, Mar. 16, 1962; MD, Mt. Sinai, NY, 1992. Staff radiologist Mayo Clinic Ariz., 2000, sect. head breast imaging, 2007. Avocations: travel, reading, classical music. Office: Mayo Clinic Ariz 13400 E Shea Blvd Scottsdale AZ 85259 Office Fax: 480-301-4303. Business E-Mail: giurescu.marina@mayo.edu.

GIUSEPPE, AMICI, surgeon, educator; b. Porto San Giorgio, Dec. 13, 1940; MD, Faculty Medicine Modena, 1966. Cons., prof. pediat. surgery U. Ancona, Italy, 1986—2011, prof., 1989—. Pres. Italian Soc. Pediat. Urology. Mem.: Italian Soc. Pediat. Surgery. Avocation: painting. Home: via Andrea Costa 233 Porto San Giorgio Fermo 63017 Italy Home Fax: 07136281. Personal E-mail: giusamici@tiscali.it.

GIUSTI, KATHY (KATHRYN ELLEN GIUSTI), foundation administrator; b. 1958; m. Paul Giusti; children: Nicole, David. BS in Biol. Sci., U. Vt., 1980; MBA in Gen. Mgmt., Harvard Bus. Sch., 1985. Asst. products mgr. Gilette Comp., Boston, 1985—88, sr. products mgr., 1988—93; assoc. dir., product mgmt. G.D. Searle & Co., 1993—94, dir., product mgmt., 1994—95, exe. dir., arthritis franchise worldwide, 1995—96; founder, CEO Multiple Myeloma Research Foundation, New Canaan, Conn., 1998—. Bd. dir. IMS Health. Recipient Women of Yr. award, Healthcare Businesswomen's Assn., 1998, Entrepreneurial award, Harvard Bus. Sch., 2001, Humanitarian award, McCarty Cancer Found., 2002, Joseph Michaeli award, Weill Med. Coll. of Cornell U., 2002, Angel award, Goldman Philanthropic Ptnrs., 2003, Alumni Achievement award, Harvard Bus. Sch., 2009. Mem.: Cancer Leadership Coun.

GIVEN, KENNA SIDNEY, surgeon, educator; b. Charleston, W.Va., Nov. 22, 1938; s. Virgil and Chessie Given; m. Charlene K. Given; children: Kari, Patrick, Amy. BA, W.Va. U., 1960; MD, Duke U., 1964. Diplomate Am. Bd. Surgery, Am. Bd. Plastic Surgery (chairperson-elect 1996-97, bd. dirs. 1992—). Intern Ind. U. Med. Ctr., Indpls., 1964-65; resident, then chief resident gen. surgery Grady Meml. Hosp./Emory U. Hosp., Atlanta, 1965-69; asst. resident, then chief resident plastic surgery Duke U. Med. Ctr., Durham, NC, 1975-77; clin. instr. surgery Emory U., Atlanta, 1972-74; chief surgery Lanier Meml. Hosp., Langdale, Ala., 1974; prof., chief divsn. plastic surgery Med. Coll. Ga., Augusta, 1977—2001, med. dir. oper. rm., 1989-90. Assoc. dir. burn unit Med. Coll. Ga. Hosp.; cons. Augusta Correctional and Med. Instrn.; plastic surgery dir. Children's Med. Svc., 1981—; mem. Residency Rev. Commn. for Plastic Surgery, 1991-2001, chmn., 1994-96; chair Am. Bd. Plastic Surgery, Inc., 1997-99; chmn. residency rev. com. Accreditation Coun. for Grad. Med. Edn., 1994-96; lectr. in field. Contbr. articles to profl. jours. Pres. Med. Rsch. Found. Ga., 1985-88; trustee Plastic Surgery Edn. Found., 1994-97, pres.-elect, 1997; bd. dirs. Augusta Country Day Sch.; bd. dirs. Augusta Prep. Day Sch., 1988, trustee, 1989-90. Fellow ACS; mem. AMA, Am. Assn. Plastic Surgeons (trustee 1994-97), Assn. Acad. Chmn. in Plastic Surgery (pres. 1996-97, bd. dirs. 1985-88, 93—), Southeastern Plastic and Reconstructive Surgery (chmn. continuing med. edn. com. 1987, bd. dirs. 1992-95), Am. Soc. Plastic and Reconstructive Surgery (bd. dirs. 1988), Am. Assn. Hand Surgery, Am. Cleft Palate Assn., Am. Soc. Aesthetic Plastic Surgeons, Internat. Soc. Clin. Plastic Surgeons, Ga. Plastic Surgery Soc. (pres. 1985), Med. Assn. Ga., Richmond County Med. Soc., Southeastern Surg. Congress., So. Med. Assn., Southeastern Soc. Plastic and Reconstructive Surgeons (pres. 1997), So. Surg. Soc. Baptist. Home: 748 Tripps Ct Augusta GA 30909 Office: Med Coll Ga Divsn Plastic Surgery HB-5049 Augusta GA 30912-4080 Office Phone: 706-721-6945. Business E-Mail: kgiven@mcg.edu.

GIZA, CHRISTOPHER CONRAD, neuroscientist, educator; b. Ind., May 17, 1965; AB, Dartmouth Coll., 1986; MD, W.Va. U., 1990. Postgrad. rschr. UCLA Brain Injury Rsch. Ctr., 1998—2000, asst. rschr., 2000—01, asst. prof., Mattel Children's Hosp. UCLA, 2001—07, assoc. prof., 2007—. Recipient Young Investigator award, UCLA Brain Injury Rsch. Ctr., 2002—03, Grand prize, Today's and Tomorrow's Children Fund, 2010; named Profl. of Yr., Brain Injury Assn. Calif., 2011; Shields fellowship, Winokur Family Found., Child Neurology Found., 2007—09. Avocations: hiking, climbing. Office: Rm 22-474 MDCC UCLA Pediatrics Neurology 1083 Los Angeles CA 90095 Office Fax: 310-825-5834. Business E-Mail: cgiza@mednet.ucla.edu.

GIZURARSON, SVEINBJÖRN, biopharmacist, vaccinologist; b. Reykjavik, Iceland, May 17, 1962; s. Gizur I. Helgason and María Sveinbjörnsdóttir; m. Kristín Linda Ragnarsdóttir, Aug. 21, 1982; children: Davíd Örn, Benjamín Ragnar, Gudlaug María. MSc, Royal Danish Sch. Pharmacy, Copenhagen, 1986, PhD, 1990. Cert. specialist in biopharmacy Ministry of Health Iceland, 1993. Project leader Novo Nordisk, Copenhagen, 1987-90; postdoctoral rschr. Nat. Inst. Health, Tokyo, 1990-91; assoc. prof. U. Iceland, Reykjavik, 1991-99, prof., 1999—; rsch. dir. Lyfjathroun, Reykjavik, 1991-99, CEO, 1999—2005. Cons. State Serum Inst., Copenhagen, 1995-97 FDA, CBER, U.S.A.; mem. adv. bd. Ministry of Industry, Reykjavik, 1998-99, Intranasal Therapeutics Inc., Kurve Tech. Inc.; specialist Supreme Ct., Reykjavik, 2000. Mem. editl. bd. Scandinavian Jour. Animal Scis.; contbr. some 150 articles to sci. publs. Mem. patent appeal com. Ministry of Industry, Iceland, 1994-2000; bd. dirs. U. Iceland, Reykjavik, 1998-99. Recipient Young Investigators award Nat. Rsch. Coun. Iceland, 1996, Innovation award Trade Coun. Iceland, 2004. Mem. Controlled Release Soc., Mucosal Immunology Soc., N.Y. Acad. Scis., Gideons Christian Pharmacists Fellowship Internat. Achievements include 16 patents in field, including nasal vaccine delivery system that is in clinical trials, delivery system to bypass the blood-brain barrier. Home: Aflagrandi 7 107 Reykjavik Iceland Office: U Iceland Hofsvallagata 53 107 Reykjavik Iceland E-mail: sveinbj@hi.is.

GIZZI, MARTIN SHERMAN, neurologist, neurophysiologist; b. Yonkers, NY, Jan. 1, 1957; s. Vincent George and Laura (Cronkhite) G.; m. Barbara Buono, Mar. 15, 2002; children Sarah, Allegra, Lance, Tessa, Ariella, Sofia. PhD, NYU, 1983; MD, U. Miami, Fla., 1985. Diplomate Am. Bd. Psychiatry and Neurology. Med. intern New Rochelle Hosp., NY, 1985-86; resident in neurology Mt. Sinai Hosp., NYC, 1986-89; asst. prof. neurology Mt. Sinai Sch. Medicine, NYC, 1989-92; assoc. prof. neurosci. Seton Hall U. Sch. Grad. Med. Edn., 1992-96, prof., assoc. chair, 1996—2002, chair, 2002—, assoc. dean, 2005—. Mem. editl. bd. Vision Rsch., 1998—2007; bd. examiner Am. Bd. Psychiatry Neurology; sci. cons., co-investigator Microgravity Vestibular Investigations Group, NASA, Johnson Space Ctr., 1990—99; program dir. neurology residency Seton Hall U., JFK Med. Ctr., 1995—99. Author: The Analysis of Moving Visual Patterns, 1995; contbr. articles to profl. jours. Pres. med. adv. bd. Music for all Seasons, NJ; grants officer JFK Med. Ctr., 2004—08; bd. dirs. DeVry U. Recipient Physician Scientist award, Nat. Eye Inst., 1989, Joint Legis. Resolution award, NJ Senate and Gen. Assembly, 2004; named Best Dr. in NY, NY mag., 1990, 2002—11, Best Dr. in NY Met., Castle-Connoly Med. Ltd., 1994—2011, Best Drs. in NJ, Inside Jersey Mag., 2009—11, Physician of Yr., Am. Heart Assn., 2009; named to Am. Top Drs., Castle-Connoly Med., 2002—11. Fellow ACP, Am. Acad. Neurology, N.Am. Neuro-Ophthalmol. Soc., Barany Soc., Am. Neurotology Soc., Am. Heart Assn. (Physician of Yr., 2009). Democrat. Avocations: music, exercise. Office: JFK Med Ctr PO Box 3059 Edison NJ 08818-3059 Office Phone: 732-632-1624. Business E-Mail: mgizzi@solarishs.org.

GJEDDE, ALBERT HELLMUT, neurology educator, neurobiology researcher; b. Gentofte, Denmark, Jan. 10, 1946; s. Albert and Elisabeth (Gjedde) Stoll; m. Susanne Borum Andersen, May 5, 1972 (div. 1981); 1 child, Nanna Louise; m. Suzan Eva Dyve, June 4, 1983; children: Laura Sophie, Nikolaj Kristian. MD, Copenhagen U., 1973, DSc, 1983. Rsch. assoc. dept. neurology NY Hosp., 1973-76; resident surgeon dept. neurosurgery Rigshospitalet, Copenhagen, 1976-79; asst. prof. med. physiology U. Copenhagen, 1979-81, assoc. prof. med. physiology, 1981-86; assoc. prof. neurology and neurosurgery McGill U., Can., 1986-89, prof. neurology and neurosurgery, 1989—. Dir., trustee Am. Field Svc. Inc., NYC, 1973-78; dir. Soc. Cerebral Blood Flow and Metabolism, 1984-88; MRC prof. brain rsch. Aarhus U. Hosps., Denmark, 1994-99, prof. med. neurobiology, 2000-08, prof. chair dept. neurosci. and pharm. U. Copenhagen, 2008-; mem. exec. coun. European Dana Alliance for the Brain, 1997—; mem. adv. bd. Arvid Carlsson Inst., U. Gothenburg, Sweden, 2004-06; mem. MRC Denmark, 2005—10; mem. sci. misconduct com. Ministry of Sci. and Tech., Denmark, 2006—; chmn. rsch. adv. bd. Royal Libr. of Denmark, 2006-09; ofcl. Danish del. European Union, 7th Framework Program Com. Health, 2007-. Contbr. over 475 articles to profl. jours. Trustee Steno Mus. Natural Scis., Aarhus, 1996—2004; mem. health scis. think tank Social Dem. Party, Aarhus, 1996-2005. With Denmark Royal Household Guards Regiment, 1965-67. Recipient Lederle award Am. Cyanamid Corp., 1971, Leo Dannin award for excellence in sci., Copenhagen, 1982, Christenson-Ceson award for sci. Danish Med. Assn., 1995, Grand Rsch. award Internat. Order Odd Fellows, Denmark, 2000, Erhoff prize, Denmark, 2010, Orr E. Reynolds award, APS, 2011, other awards. Fellow: AAAS, Am. Coll. Neuropsychopharmacology, Royal Soc. Can.; mem.: Am. Physiol. Soc., Internat. Soc. Cerebral Blood Flow Metabolism, Soc. Neurosci., Acad. Europe, Sclerosis Soc. Denmark (chmn. rsch. com. 1999—2004), Danish Soc. Neurosci. (founding mem. 1984, coun. 1984—86, 1997—2001), European Soc. Clin. Investigation (coun. 1996—2002), Univ. Club Montreal. Avocations: rare books, political history, bicycling, skiing. Home: 673 Silkeborgvej DK 8220 Brabrand Denmark Office: University Copenhagen Panum Inst 3 Blegdamsvej DK 2200 Copenhagen Denmark Home Phone: 45 86260803; Office Phone: 45 35327601, 45-30104961. Business E-Mail: gjedde@sund.ku.dk.

GJERRIS, FLEMMING OTT, neurosurgeon, educator; b. Copenhagen, July 1, 1936; s. Jens Christian and Erna (Petersen) G.; m. Annette Jensen, Mar. 9, 1963; children: Christine, Helene, Casper. MD, U. Copenhagen, 1963, specialist in neurosurgery, 1973, DSc, 1979. Cons. neurosurgeon U. Clinic Neurosurgery, Rigshospitalet, Copenhagen, 1976-83, prof., dir., 1985—2006; dir. dept. neurosurgery Copenhagen County Hosp., Glostrup, 1983-85; prof., dir. Lab. Clin. Skills and Competence, U. Copenhagen, 2002—04. Pres. Danish Neurol. Soc., 1980-83; councillor Scandinavian Neurosurg. Soc., 1985-92; v.p., pres. Academia Eurasiana Neurochirurgica, 1990-94. Contbr. chpts. to books and articles to profl. jours. Mem. European Assn. Neurosurg. Socs. (v.p. 1987-91, pres. 1995-99). Avocations: sailing, fishing. Office: Univ Clin Neurosurgery Rigshospitalet DK-2100 Copenhagen Denmark Home Phone: 4540105481. E-mail: flemming@g-jerris.dk.

GLADDEN, GARNETT LEE, psychologist, healthcare consultant, educator; b. May 8, 1922; s. Martin L. and Beatrice G. (Palmer) Gladden; m. Vivianne C. Gladden, 1958; children: Mark L., Jeanne Sue. AB, U. Calif., Berkeley, 1943; MA, Claremont Coll., Calif., 1948; PhD, Honolulu U., 1989. Prof. Riverside Cmty. Coll., Calif., 1946—77, prof. emeritus, 1976—, adj. prof., 2006; dir. Anza Human Relations Ctr., Riverside, 1950—77; dir. rsch. William R. Parker Found. Behavioral Rsch., Arrowhead Springs, Calif., 1960—62; v.p. Golden State U., LA, 1978—82; dean Grad. Studies and provost Honolulu U., 1982—98; healthcare cons. Japan Life Ltd., LA & Tokyo, 1986—98; adj. prof. San Bernardino Valley Coll., 2002; adj. prof. campus abroad program Oxford U., England, 2008; healthcare cons., 1989—2009. Faculty Osher Lifelong Learning Inst. U. Calif., Riverside, 2003—06. Author (with Vivianne Cervantes Gladden): How to Win the Aging Game, 1958. Fellow, Internat. Acad. Edn., 1983. Home: 6148 Turnberry Dr Banning CA 92220 Personal E-mail: gordont24@roadrunner.com.

GLADDEN, VIVIANNE CERVANTES, healthcare consultant, writer; b. Brookhaven, Miss., Oct. 8, 1927; d. Thomas James Guillory and Edna Beatrice Torry; m. Garnett Lee Gladden; children: Mark Lee, Jeanne Sue Wood. Grad., Edwin Lester Sch. Musical Theater, 1976; LittD (hon.), Union U., 1979; BA, Golden State U., 1980, PhD, DHL, Honolulu U., 1993. Ordained to ministry Cmty. Ch. of the Bay, 1985. Stage, film and TV actress, NYC, Hollywood, 1950—64; model Harry Conover, NYC, 1951; mannequin Jacques Heim, Paris, 1951; featured singer La Vien Rose, NYC, 1951—52, Copa City, Fla., 1951—52, Govt. House, Bermuda, 1953; nutritional cons. Ctr. Holistic Health Cedars-Sinai Hosp., LA, 1975—77; health and lifestyle counselor Beverly Hills and Newport, Calif., 1977—; lectr., cons. health sci. and products All Natural Products, Honolulu, Japan Life

Inc., Tokyo. Radio ministry Sta. KIEV, Glendale, Calif., 1985—86; mem. adv. bd. Nat. Acad. Sports Medicine, Chgo., 1993—2002; guest lectr. Oriel Coll., Oxford, England, 2008, Calif. State U., Northridge, 2009. Author (with Lee Gladden): (book) Heirs of the Gods, 1978 (Bronze Halo award So. Calif. Motion Picture Coun., 1982); author: (with Lee Gladden and Gary Couture) How to Win the Aging Game, 1979; author: Archeolinguistics, 1984. Chmn. Eco World, Hollywood, Calif., 1971; master of ceremonies Opening Ahmanson Theatre, LA, 1976. Recipient Gold award of merit, Martin Luther King Jr. Campaign Ctr., Port Arthur, Tex., 1988; named to Hall of Fame, Oakwood Coll., Huntsville, Ala., 1956. Avocations: singing, piano, yoga, running. Office Phone: 951-769-0392. Personal E-mail: gordont24@roadrunner.com.

GLADSTEIN, GINA F., ophthalmologist; Attended, Albert Einstein Coll. of Medicine, 1983. Diplomate Am. Bd. of Ophthalmology. Internship berkshire Med. Ctr.; resident Manhattan EEN&T Hosp., 1984—87, fellow, 1987—88. Office: Greenwich Hospital 5 Perryridge Rd Greenwich CT 06830 Office Phone: 203-863-3000.

GLAHN, KLAUS P. E., medical association administrator; b. Denmark, June 8, 1960; MD, Copenhagen U., 1986. Cheff cons. Danish Malignant Hypethermia Ctr., 2000—. Office: 75 Herlev Ringvej Herlev Copenhagen DK-2730 Denmark E-mail: kpeg@heh.regionh.dk.

GLANTZOUNIS, GEORGIOS K., surgeon, researcher; b. Lamia, Greece, May 28, 1967; s. Constantinos Glantzounis and Garyphalia Glantzouni; m. Ioanna Papaefstathiou, Feb. 10, 1996; children: Constantinos, Katerina, Filia. MD, U. Ioannina, Greece, 1991, PhD, 2004, U. London, 2007. Resident, surgery G. Hatzikosta Hosp., Ioannina, 1995—2001; rsch. fellow HPB and liver transplant unit dept. surgery Royal Free Hosp., London, 2001—04, sr. registrar HPB and liver transplant unit dept. surgery, 2004—08; asst. prof., surgery and transplantation Ioannina Med. Sch., 2008—. Med. coord. IFO refugee camp MSF (Doctors Without Borders), Dadaab, Kenya, 1994—95. Mem.: Internat. Soc. Free Radicals and Oxidative Stress, Internat. Soc. HPB Surgery. Achievements include pioneer work in the pathophysiology of pneumoperitoneum in laparoscopic surgery; original and innovative work in the pathophysiology of liver ischemia-reperfusion injury and pharmacological modulation of detrimental effects of reperfusion injury. Office: Dept Surgery Ioannina Univ Sch Medicine Ioannina 45110 Greece Personal E-mail: gglantzounis@gmail.com.

GLANVILLE, ALLAN ROBERT, medical educator; b. Sydney, Aug. 3, 1953; s. Claude Atholstone and Thalia Alice Glanville; m. Ann Freda Robinson, Nov. 30, 1974; children: Elsa Jane, Christopher James. MBBS, U. Sydney, 1977, MD, 1990. Dir. thoracic medicine St. Vincent's Hosp., Darlinghurst, 1995—; conjoint prof. medicine U. NSW, 2009—. Chair pulmonary coun. ISHLT, Addison, Tex., 2005—08; med. dir. Lung Transplant Unit, St. Vincent's Hosp., Darlinghurst, Nsw, Australia, 1998—; chair European and Australian Investigators Lung Transplantation, Sydney, 2004—; found. mem. Sharelife Australia, Sydney, 2005—, editl. bd. Am. Jour. Respiratory And Critical Care Medicine, NYC, 2005—; found. bd. mem. Outcomes Australia Pty. Ltd., 2006—, LAM Australia Rsch. Assn., Sydney, 2006—; chair liaison com. Lam Treatment Alliance, Boston, 2008—; editl. bd. Seminars In Respiratory And Critical Care Medicine, NYC, 2008—; dir. Internat. Soc. Heart and Lung Transplantation, Addison, Tex., 2009—; sr. editl. bd. cons. Jour. Heart And Lung Transplantation, Addison, Tex., 2009—. Contbr. articles to profl. jours., chapters to books. Chair Bilgola Beach Preservation Soc., NSW, 1990—98; donor Medicins sans Frontiers, 1998—. Fellow: RACP; mem.: European Respiratory Soc., Am. Thoracic Soc., Transplantation Soc. Australia And New Zealand, Thoracic Soc. Australia And New Zealand, Art Gallery Soc. NSW, Nat. Gallery Australia, Nat. Trust, Australian Club, State Libr. Found. NSW, Sydney Cricket Ground Trust. Avocations: cricket, bushwalking, skiing. Office: St Vincent's Hosp Victoria St Darlinghurst NSW 2010 Australia Home Fax: 61299185982. Personal E-mail: glanvilles@bigpond.com. Business E-Mail: aglanville@stvincents.com.au.

GLANZ, JASON, epidemiologist, researcher; BS in Biology, Boston U., 1993; MS in Biostatistics, U. Mass., Amherst, 1998; PhD in Epidemiology, U. Colo, 2005. Biostatistician Dept. Pharmacology U. Colo. Health Sciences Ctr., 2000—03; asst. prof. Dept. Preventive Medicine & Biometrics U. Colo Health Sciences Ctr., 2007—; sr. analyst & epidemiologist Kaiser Permanente Colo., 2001—06, rsch. investigator, 2007—. Co-principal investigator CDC Vaccine Safety Datalink. Office: PO Box 378066 Denver CO 80237-8066 E-mail: jason.m.glanz@kp.org.

GLASBERG, H(ERBERT) MARK, psychiatrist, educator; b. NYC, Oct. 11, 1939; s. Joesph and Elsa (Haber) G.; m. Paula Drillman, June 19, 1960; children: Scot Bradley, Hilary Jennifer. BA, Yeshiva U., 1953; MS, Columbia U., 1954; MD, SUNY, 1958. Diplomate Am. Bd. Psychiatry and Neurology. Intern Maimonides Hosp., NYC, 1958-59; resident in psychiatry Kings County Hosp., NYC, 1959-60; resident in internal medicine Kingbridge VA Hosp. of Columbia U. Coll. Med. Program, NYC, 1960-61; resident Payne Whitney Psychiat. Clin., N.Y. Hosp., 1963-65; psychiatrist pvt. practice, NYC, 1968—; attending physician dept. psychiatry Columbia U. Coll. Physicians & Surgeons; instr. Cornell U. Med. Sch., 1966-68; assoc. prof. psychiatry Mt. Sinai Sch. Medicine, 1968-80; dir. psychiat. outpatient svcs. Beth Israel Hosp., NYC, 1968-74, assoc. attending physician, 1968-74, chief psychiat. emergency & cons. svcs., 1974-75; attending psychiatrist & clin. prof. psychiatry Coll. Physicians & Surgeons, Columbia U., 1986—; neurosurgery Coll. Physicians & Surgeons, N.Y. Presbyn. Med. Ctr., 1982, clin. prof. neurosurgery, 1995; clin. prof. neurosurgery, attending neurosurgeon N.Y. Presbyn. Med. Ctr., 1995. Examiner Am. Bd. Psychiatry & Neurology, 1988—; cons. mem. panel of ind. psychiatrists N.Y.C. Mental Health Info. Svc., 1968—. Mem. Manhattan physicians com. United Jewish Appeal, 1970—; mem. com. admission sel. Cornell U. Med. Coll., Ctr. Alumni Assn. N.Y. Hosp. Col. M.C. AUS, 1961-63. Fellow N.Y. Hosp., 1965-66, spl. rsch. fellow Nat. Inst. Mental Health, 1966-68, Cornell U. Med. Sch. Fellow ACP, Am. Soc. Neurosurgeons, Am. Psychiat. Assn. (internat. platform com. 1980—); mem. APA, AAAS, Am. Psychosomatic Soc., N.Y. Acad. Scis., N.Y. Acad. Medicine, Soc. Adolescent Psychiatry, Internat. Platform Assn. Office: 14 E 73rd St New York NY 10021-4128 Office Phone: 212-744-6600.

GLASBERG, SCOT BRADLEY, plastic surgeon; b. NYC, June 30, 1964; s. H. Mark and Paula (Drillman) G.; m. Alisa Goldman, Oct. 17, 1999; children: Alexander Zachary, Evan Blake, Chloe Samantha. BA cum laude, Columbia U., 1986; MD with honors, NYU, 1990. Diplomate Am. Bd. Plastic Surgery, Am. Bd. Surgery, Nat. Bd. Med. Examiners. Resident in surgery U. Conn./Hartford Hosp., 1990-95, chief resident, 1995-96; craniofacial rsch. fellow Inst. Reconstructive Plastic Surgery, NYU Med. Ctr., NYC, 1992-93; fellow SUNY Health Sci. Ctr., Bklyn., 1996-98, program dir., dir. plastic surgery edn., 1998—2001. Attending staff Lenox Hill Hosp., Manhattan Eye Ear Throat Hosp., Beth Israel Med. Ctr.; assoc. chief plastic surgery Englewood Med. Ctr., 2004—. Contbr. articles to profl. jours.; featured on shows such as The East Show (CBS) Today show (NBC), Good Morning America (ABC), the Paula Zahn show (CNN) and the Morning show (WB)., guest appearances on nat. and local networks of NBC, CBS, ABC, WB and CNN. NY State Regents scholar, 1982-86; recipient first prize for presentation at the annual meeting, Soc. of Former Residents and Associates of Plastic Surgery, 1998. Fellow ACS; mem. AMA (del. resident physician sect. 1990-93, 96—98, plastic surgery caucus 1996-97, 99—, del. young physicians sect. 1999-2004, young physicians sect. governing coun. 2002-2004), Am. Soc. Plastic Surgeons (v.p. fin. 2009-, bd. dirs. 2008-, chmn. govt. rels. com., chmn. govt. rels. com. 2005—, plastypac bd. govs. 2001—, chair 2009-, Maliniac cir., parliamentarian bd. dirs. 2005-06, chair coun. state affairs surgery 2007-, chair 2009-10, Presdl. award, 2008), Northeastern Soc. Plastic Surgery (Resident/Fellows award 1997), Med. Soc. State NY (del. AMA resident physician sect. 1996-98, young physician sect. 1999-2006, mem. med. liability task force, legis./advocacy steering com., Outstanding Svc. award 1990), NY County Med. Soc.(litigation com., managed care task force, chair, gov. affairs 2008-), NY Regional Soc. Plastic Surgeons (pres.-elect 2010, exec. bd. 2006-, winner clin. paper competition 1997, treas. 2008, v.p. 2009-). Avocations: tennis, golf, swimming, card collecting. Office: Cosmetic & Reconstructive Plastic Surg 42A E 74th St New York NY 10021-2735 Address: 900 Park Ave Apt 19AB New York NY 10075 Office Phone: 212-717-8550. Business E-Mail: info@DrGlasberg.com. E-mail: scotbg@juno.com.

GLASER, BENJAMIN, endocrinologist, educator; b. Apr. 16, 1950; MD, U. Md., 1975. Prof., head endocrinology and metabolism svc. Hadassah-Hebrew U. Med. Ctr., 1991—. Mem.: Israel Endocrine Soc., Am. Diabetes Assn., Am. Endocrine Soc. Office: Endocrinology and Metabolism Dept Jerusalem 91120 Israel Office Fax: 972 2 6437940. Business E-Mail: beng@cc.huji.ac.il.

GLASER, RONALD, virologist, educator; b. NYC, Feb. 27, 1939; s. Irving and Pauline G.; m. Janice Kiecolt, Jan. 17, 1980; children: Andrew, Erik. BA, U. Bridgeport, 1962; MS, U. R.I., 1964; PhD, U. Conn., 1968. NIH postdoc. fellow Baylor Coll. Medicine, 1969; asst. prof. microbiology Ind. State U., 1969—70, Pa. State U., Hershey, 1970-73, asst. prof., 1973-77, assoc. prof., 1977-78; prof. chmn. dept. med. microbiology and immunology Coll. Medicine Ohio State U., Columbus, 1978—92; assoc. dean for rsch. and grad. edn. Med. Ctr. Ohio State U., Columbus, 1992-94, assoc. v.p. health sci. rsch. Med. Ctr., 1994-2001, assoc. v.p. rsch., 2001—03. Dir. Inst. for Behavioral Med. Rsch., 1996—. Editor: (with T. Gottleib-Stematsky) Human Herpes Virus Infections: Clinical Aspects, 1982; (with others) Epstein-Barr Virus and Human Disease, 1987; (with J. Jones) Human Herpes Virus Infections, 1994; (with J. Kiecolt-Glaser) Handbook of Human Stress, 1994. Franco-Am. Exch. Program; Fogarty Internat. Ctr., NIH and INSRM fellow, Paris, 1975, Ryon France 77; Leukemia Soc. Am. scholar, 1974-79. Fellow: AAAS (pres. 2007), Acad. Behavioral Medicine Rsch. (pres. psychoneuroimmunology rsch. soc. 2003); mem.: AACR, Am. Soc. Microbiology. Office: Ohio State University Med Ctr 460 Medical Center Dr Columbus OH 43210 Office Phone: 614-293-0178. Business E-Mail: ronald.glaser@osumc.edu.

GLASGOLD, ALVIN IRWIN, physician; b. NY, Apr. 28, 1936; m. Joyce Padrusch; children: Mark, Ellen, Robert. MD, N.Y. Med. Coll., 1961. Diplomate Am. Bd. Facial Plasitc and Reconstructive Surgery, Am. Bd. cosmetic Surgery, Am. Bd. Otolaryngology-Head and Neck Surgery. Intern Beth Israel Hosp., NYC, 1961-62; resident Bronx Vet.'s Hosp. and Columbia U. Coll. Physicians and Surgeons, 1962-66; chief dept. otolaryngology-head and neck surgery St. Peter's Med. Ctr., New Brunswick, N.J., Robert Wood Johnson Univ. Hosp. and Med. Sch., New Brunswick, 1995; attending physician Manhattan Eye, Ear and Throat Hosp., NYC; clin. prof. surgery, chief divsn. otolaryngology Robert Wood Johnson Med. Sch., New Brunswick, NJ; chmn. Facial Plastic sect. N.J. Acad. Ophthalmology and Otolaryngology, 1980-88. Chmn. ann. facial plastic symposium N.J. Acad. Ophthalmology and Otolaryngology, 1983-88; co-chmn. external rhinoplasty course Manhattan Eye, Ear and Throat Hosp., AAFPRS, 1989, 90; instr. rhinoplasty Mt. Sinai Hosp., 1986-88; mem. bd. govs. Am. Acad. Ophthalmomogy and Otolaryngology, 1981-84. Author: (book) Application of Biomaterials in Facial Plastic Surgery, 1991. Fellow Am. Acad. Facial Plastic and Reconstructive Surgery, Am. Acad. Cosmetic Surgery (pres., bd. dirs. Facial Plastic Surgery Info. Svc., Inc., credentials com.), Am. Coll. Surgeons, Am. Acad. Otolaryngology-Head and Neck Surgery (instr. revision rhinoplasty-external approach 1990, bd. govs. 1981-84, Honor award 1997), Am. Soc. Head and Neck Surgery, Am. Soc. Liposuction Surgery, Facial Plastic Surgury Fellowship(dir.). Office: 31 River Rd Highland Park NJ 08904-1731

GLASGOW, CONSTANCE LENORE, pediatrician; b. NYC, Jan. 31, 1934; d. Lester and Octavia Louisa Glasgow; m. Twitty Junius Styles, Aug. 11, 1962; children: Scott Peterson, Auria Octavia. BS, Hunter Coll., 1955; MD, SUNY Downstate, Bklyn., 1960. Intern Syracuse Upstate Med. Ctr., NY, 1960—61; resident Albert Einstein Bronx Mcpl. Hosp. Ctr., NY, 1961—63; rotating intern Upstate Med. Ctr., Syracuse; pediat. resident Jacobi Hosp./Bronx Mcpl. Hosp. Ctr., Albert Einstein U., Bronx; pvt. practice physician Clifton Park, NY, 1966—. Mem. ethics com. Ellis Hosp., Schenectady, NY, 1993—. Fellow: Am. Acad. Pediat.; mem.: Capital Dist. Links (co-chair nat. trends com. 1999—). Meth. Avocations: travel, music, walking. Office: Capital Care Pediat Clifton Park 942A Route 146 Clifton Park NY 12065 Office Phone: 518-371-8000.

GLASHOW, JONATHAN L., orthopedist, surgeon, educator; MD, Cornell U., 1984. Diplomate Am. Bd. Orthopaedic Surgery. Intern surgery Mt. Sinai Hosp.; physician Mt. Sinai Med. Ctr.; resident orthopaedic surgery Lenox Hill Hosp., 1985—89, physician; resident pediatric ortho Children's Hosp. Boston; fellow surgery Univ. Tex. Med. Ctr., 1990; assoc. clin. prof. Mt. Sinai Sch. of Medicine; chief sports medicine. Office: Mount Sinai Medical Center 159 E 74th St New York NY 10021 Office Phone: 212-794-5096. Office Fax: 212-570-1507. E-mail: jonathan.glashow@mountsinai.org.

GLASS, DAVID CARTER, psychologist, educator; b. NYC, Sept. 17, 1930; s. Samuel and Dorothy (Braunstein) Glass; m. Kathleen Kehoe, May 15, 1982. AB, NYU, 1952, MA, 1954, PhD, 1959, postdoctoral fellow, 1959—62. Mem. staff social psychologist Russell Sage Found., NYC, 1963—71; assoc. prof. psychology Rockefeller U., NYC, 1966—68; prof. psychology NYU, NYC, 1968—72; chmn., prof. dept. psychology U. Tex., Austin, Tex., 1972—75; vis. scholar Russell Sage Found., 1975—76; prof. psychology, dir. Lab. Biobehavior CUNY Grad. Ctr., NYC, 1976—82; prof. psychology and psychiatry SUNY, Stony Brook, 1982—94, vice provost for rsch. and grad. studies, 1982—86, spl. advisor to provost, 1987—89, v.p. for rsch., 1990—93, prof. emeritus psychology, 1994—. Vis. prof. psychology Inst. Health Rutgers U., New Brunswick, NJ, 1994—96; interim dir. rsch. Kessler Inst., West Orange, NJ, 1997—98; cons. in field. Author: Behavior Patterns, Stress and Coronary Disease, 1977; co-author (with J.E. Singer): Urban Stress: Experiments in Noise and Social Stressors, 1972 (AAAS prize, 71); contbr. articles to profl. jours. Fellow: AAAS, APA, Assn. Psychol. Sci.; mem.: Acad. Behavioral Medicine Rsch. (pres. 1981—82), Soc. Expl. Social Psychology, Soc. Psychophysiol. Rsch., Am. Psychosomatic Soc., Phi Kappa Phi, Sigma Xi. Home: 3333 Henry Hudson Pky Apt 21A Riverdale NY 10463 Personal E-mail: profdcglass@gmail.com.

GLASS, DONALD DAVID, anesthesiologist; b. Johnston, Pa., May 1, 1942; s. Donald S. and Meriel L. Glass; m. Bonnell W. Glass, Sept. 5, 1965 (div. Nov. 1992); children: David J., Jennifer J.; m. Alice M. Goldwine, June 27, 1998. Student, U. Pitts., 1960-62; MD, W.Va. U., 1966. Diplomate Am. Bd. Anesthesiology (chmn. CCM examination com. 1988—, asst. sec.-treas. 1991-94, chair com. on Americans and Disabilities Act 1991, chair credentials com. 1992, sec.-treas. 1994-96, pres. 1996-97); cert. spl. qualifications in critical care medicine, cert. continued demonstration of qualifications; lic. anethesiologist Miss., N.H. Rsch. assoc. dept. surgery W.Va. U., 1965-66; intern in surgery U. Pitts., 1966-67, resident in surgery, 1969-70; asst. resident in anesthesia Mass. Gen. Hosp., Boston, 1970-71, chief resident in anesthesiology, 1971-72; clin. fellow Harvard U., 1972; dir. edn. dept. anesthesiology, dir. cardiovascu. anesthesia U. Miss. Med. Ctr., Jackson, 1972-77, asst. dir. inhalation therapy, 1972-77, asst. prof. anesthesia, 1972-76, med. dir. ICU, 1975-77, assoc. prof. anesthesiology and surgery, 1976-77; assoc. prof. surgery and medicine Med. Sch., Dartmouth Coll., Hanover, NH, 1977-84, prof. surgery and medicine, 1984-88, prof. anesthesiology and medicine, 1988—93, chair, 1983—2008; med. dir. adult unit ICU Dartmouth-Hitchcock Med. Ctr., Hanover, 1977-87, chief sect. anesthesiology, 1983-89, chmn. dept. anesthesiology, 1989; chair Dartmouth-Hitchcock Med. Ctr., Dartmouth Med. Sch., 2008—. Mem nat. com. Accreditation Coun. for Grad. Med. edn., 1997—. Co-editor. (with M.P. Yeager) Anesthetic Management of the Vascular Surgical Patient, 1990, contbr. chpts. to books including Rhoads Textbook of Surgery, 1976, Intensive Care Therapeutics, 1980, Cardiac Anesthesia, 1987, Anesthesia in Vascular Surgery, 1989; contbr. numerous articles to med. jours. Elected rep. to ACGME Coun. Am. Bd. Med. Specialists. Recipient Lange Med. Publs. award, 1966. Fellow Am. Coll. Anesthesiology, Am. Coll. Chest Physicians, Faculty of Anesthesiologists of Royal Australian Coll. Surgeons, mem. Am. Soc. Anesthesiologists (U. Miss. preceptorship com. liaison 1974, coord. ICU workshop 1976, chmn. com. on sci. papers 1986, vice chmn. ann. meeting 1987, chmn. ann. meeting 1988, chair ABA ASA joint select com. on recertification 1988), Internat. Anesthesia Rsch. Soc., Soc. Critical Care Medicine, Assn. Cardiac Anesthesiologists (elected), Assn. Univ. Anesthesiologists, Assn. Critical Care Anesthesiologists, N.H./Vt. Soc. Anesthsiologists, Soc. Acad. Anesthesia Chairmen, Alpha Omega Alpha, Found. Anesthesia Edn. & Rsch. (bd. chmn. 2006-). Office: Dartmouth Hitchock Med Ctr Dept Anesthesiology Medical Center Dr Lebanon NH 03756 Home: PO Box 688 438 Rd Round The Lake Grantham NH 03753

GLASS, DOROTHEA DANIELS, physiatrist, educator; b. NYC; d. Maurice B. and Anna S. (Kleegman) Daniels; m. Robert E. Glass, June 23, 1940; children: Anne Glass Roth, Deborah, Catherine Glass Barrett, Eugene. BA, Cornell U., 1940; MD, Woman's Med. Coll. Pa., 1954; postgrad., U. Pa., 1960—61; DMS (hon.), Med. Coll. Pa., 1987. Diplomate Am. Bd. Phys. Medicine and Rehab. (guest bd. examiner 1978, 89). Intern Albert Einstein Med. Ctr., Phila., 1954-55, clin. asst. dept. medicine, 1956-59, attending phys. medicine and rehab., 1968-70, chmn. dept. phys. medicine and rehab., sr. attending, 1971-85; chief rehab. medicine VA Med. Ctr., Miami, Fla., 1985-95; clin. prof. dept. orthop. and rehab. U. Miami Sch. Medicine, 1985—. Lois Mattox Miller fellow preventive medicine Woman's Med. Coll. Pa., 1955-56, instr. preventive medicine, 1956-59, instr. medicine, 1960-62; resident phys. medicine and rehab. VA Hosp., Phila., 1959-62, chief phys. medicine and rehab., 1966-68, cons., 1968-82; asst. clin. dir. Jefferson Med. Coll. Hosp., Phila., 1963-66, Camden County Stroke Program, Cooper Hosp., Camden, N.J., 1963-66; gen. practice medicine, Phila., 1956-59; asst. med. dir., chief phys. medicine and rehab. Moss Rehab. Hosp., Phila., 1968-70, med. dir., 1971-82, sr. cons., 1982-; mem. active staff Temple U., Phila., 1968-, asso. prof. rehab. medicine, 1968-73, prof., 1973-, dir. residency tng. rehab. medicine, 1968-82; program dir. Rehab. Rsch. and Tng. Ctr., 1977-80, chmn. dept. rehab. medicine, 1977-82; staff physician Hosp. Med. Coll. Pa., Phila., 1955-59, vis. assoc. prof. neurology, 1973-79, clin. prof., 1977-82, vis. prof., 1982-96; mem. cons. staff Frankford Hosp., Phila., 1968-82, Phila. Geriatric Center, 1975-82; mem. active staff Willowcrest-Bamberger Hosp., Phila., 1980-82; asso. phys. medicine and rehab. U. Pa. Sch. Medicine, Phila., 1962-66; asst. prof. clin. phys. medicine and rehab., 1966-68; asst. clin. dir. dept. phys. medicine and rehab. Jefferson Med. Coll., Phila., 1963-66; cons. Vols. in Medicine Clinic, Stuart, Fla., 1996—. Contbr. articles to profl. jours. Mem. profl. adv. com. Easter Seal Soc. Crippled Children and Adults Pa., 1975-82; active Goodwill Industries Phila., 1973-82, Cmty. Home Health Svcs. Phila., 1974-82, Ea. Pa. chpt. Arthritis Found., 1968-82. Recipient Humanitarian Svc. cert. Gov.'s Com. on Employment Handicapped, 1974, Outstanding Alumnae award Commonwealth of Pa. Bd., Hosp. Med. Coll. Pa., 1975, Humanitarian award Pa. Easter Seal Soc., 1981, John Eiselie Davis award Am. Kinesiotherapy Assn., 1988, Carl Haven Young Svc. award, 1994, Disting. Career award Moss Rehab. Hosp., 1997, 2009, award, 2009, Outstanding Svc. and Accomplishments award Fla. Soc. Phys. Medicine and Rehab., 2001, Susan B. Anthony award LWV of Martin

County, 2002. Fellow Am. Congress Rehab. Medicine; mem. AMA, Am. Acad. Med. Dirs., Am. Acad. Phys. Medicine and Rehab. (Disting. Clinician award 1995, Krusen award 2000), Am. Assn. Electromyography and Electrodiagnosis (assoc.), Am. Assn. Sex Educators, Counselors and Therapists, Am. Burn Assn., Am. Coll. Angiology, Am. Coll. Utilization Rev., Am. Congress Rehab. Medicine (bd. govs. 1979-85, pres. 1986-87, gold Key award 1989), Am. Heart Assn. (coun. on cerebrovascular disease), Am. Lung Assn. Phila. and Montgomery County (bd. dirs. 1977-79), Am. Med. Women's Assn., Assn. Acad. Physiatrists, Assn. Med. Rehab. Dirs. and Coords., Coll. Physicians Phila., Emergency Care Rsch. Inst., Gerontol. Soc., Internat. Assn. Rehab. Facilities, Internat. Rehab. Medicine Assn., Pan Am. Med. Assn., Fla. Med. Assn., Fla. Soc. Phys. Medicine and Rehab. (pres. 1975-77, Award for Outstanding Svc. in Rehab. Medicine 2001), Pa. Med. Soc. (phys. medicine and rehab. adv. com. 1975-82), Pa. Thoracic Soc., Delaware Valley Hosp. Coun. Forum, Phila. Med. Soc., Phila. PSRO (bd. dirs. 1975-82), Phila. Soc. Phys. Medicine and Rehab. (pres. 1968-69), Laennec Soc. Phila., Royal Soc. Health, Alpha Omega Alpha. E-mail: glassrd@earthlink.net.

GLASS, JON, neurologist, oncologist; MD, SUNY, Brooklyn, 1986. Diplomate Am. Bd. Psychiatry and Neurology. Intern Kings County Hosp., Brooklyn, 1987; resident Boston Univ. Med. Ctr. Hosp., 1990; fellow Mass. Gen. Hosp., Boston, 1992; hosp. affiliations include Thomas Jefferson Univ. Hosp., Methodist Hosp. divsn. Named one of Top Docs, Phila. Mag., 2010. Office: Jefferson University Hospital 900 Walnut St Ste 200 Philadelphia PA 19107 Office Phone: 215-955-7000. Office Fax: 215-503-9170.

GLASS, JONATHAN DAVID, neurologist, educator; b. Patchogue, NY, Jan. 15, 1957; MD, U. Vt. Coll. Medicine, 1985. Cert. Am. Bd. Psychiatry and Neurology, Am. Bd. Psychology and Neurology, added qualifications in Clin. Neurophysiology, Am. Bd. Pathology (Neuropathology). Intern, neurology U. Md. Hosp., Balt., 1985—86; resident, neurological pathology & neurology John Hopkins Hosp., Balt., 1986—89; fellow John Hopkins U., Balt., 1989—91, attending neurologist, 1991—96, attending pathologist, 1991—96; attending neurologist Emory U., 1996, with, 1996—, prof. neurology and pathology Atlanta, dir. neuromuscular divsn., dir., ALS Ctr.; dir. Emory Neuromuscular Lab. Contbr. several articles to peer-reviewed publs. Named one of America's Top Doctors, 2001—08. Mem.: Soc. Neuroscience, Am. Neurological Assn., Am. Acad. Neurology. Achievements include being one of the first to focus on the role of nerve fiber degeneration as an early feature of motor neuron disease (ALS). Office: Whitehead Biomedical Research Bldg 615 Michael St 5th Fl Atlanta GA 30322 Office Phone: 404-727-3507. Office Fax: 404-727-3728. Business E-Mail: jglas03@emory.edu.

GLASS, PETER STANLEY ABRAHAM, anesthesiologist, educator; s. Erwin and Sophie Glass; m. Sabrina Glass; children: Sean, Ryan. MBChB, U. Witwatersrand, Johannesburg, 1976. Diplomate Am. Bd. Anesthesiology, 1990, cert. physician NY State, 1999. Intern Natalspruit Hosp., U. Witwatersrand, 1977; resident Johannesburg Hosp., U. Witwatersrand, 1980—81, sr. resident, 1981—83, cons., 1984; assoc. anesthesia Duke U. Med. Ctr., Durham, NC, 1984—85, asst. prof., 1985—94, rsch. fellow, 1987—88, assoc. prof., 1994—99, prof. with tenure, 1999; prof. and chmn., anesthesiology Stony Brook U. Med. Ctr., NY, 1999—, chmn., bd. dirs., clin. practice mgmt. plan, 2005—11. Chmn., sect. anesthesiology Southern Med. Soc., 1990; mem. Am. Soc. U. Anesthesiologists, 1992—, USP DI Sect. Anesthesia, 1993—, Best Drs. America, 2007—08; program chmn. SIVA Ann. Meeting, 1998—99; chmn. VA Merit Review Subcom. Alcoholism, Drug Dependence, Anesthesia and Clin. Pharmacology. Contbr. chapters to books, more than 100 articles to various med. jours. Numerous rsch. grants, 1992—2008. Mem.: AMA, Soc. Ambulatory Surgery (pres. elect. 2010), SCOR Task Force (SAMBA clin. outcomes registry), Soc. Intravenous Anesthesia (bd. mem. 1992—96, v.p. 1994, pres. 1996—97), Am. Soc. Regional Anesthesia, NC Soc. Anesthesiologists, NC Med. Soc., NY State Soc. Anesthesiologists (mem. com. clin. chairs 2002—, mem. program com. 2003—06), Am. Soc. Anesthesiologists, Assn. U. Anesthesiologists (mem. sci. adv. bd. 1997—99), Soc. Academic Anesthesiology Chairs, Assn. Anesthesiology Program Dirs., Soc. Ambulatory Anesthesia (chair com. on awards 1996—97, mem. com. on edn. 1996—98, mem. com. on rsch 1996—98, chmn. edn. com. 1999—2000, bd. dirs. 2004—, chmn. com. ann. meeting 2008—, mem. numerous coms., SAMBA clin. outcomes registry task force 2010, elected pres. SAMBA 2010, sec.), European Soc. Intravenous Anesthesia, South African Coll. Medicine, Internat. Anesthesia Rsch. Soc. Office: Stony Brook Univ Med Ctr Dept Anesthesiology HSC Level 4-060 Stony Brook NY 11794-8480 Office Fax: 631-444-2306. Business E-Mail: peter.glass@stonybrook.edu.

GLASS, RICHARD MCLEAN, psychiatry educator, medical editor; b. Phoenix, Sept. 25, 1943; s. Richard Kirkpatrick and Harriet Margaret (Bradshaw) G.; m. Rita Mae Catherine Denk, Mar. 4, 1967; children: Kathryn, Brendan Neil. BA, Northwestern U., 1965, MD, 1968. Diplomate Am. Bd. Psychiatry and Neurology. Asst. prof. psychiatry U. Chgo., 1975—82, assoc. prof., 1982—95, clin. prof., 1995—. Dir. adult psychiatry clinic U. Chgo., 1985-89. Mem. editl. bd. Archives of Gen. Psychiatry, 1984-2003; cons. editor JAMA, 1987-89, dep. editor, 1989-2010, contbg. editor, 2011-; contbr. articles to profl. jours. Served to major U.S. Army, 1970-72. Mem. Am. Psychiat. Assn. (Disting. fellow), AAAS, AMA, Am. Coll. Psychiatrists. Presbyterian. Avocations: tennis, music, trombone. Office: JAMA 515 N State St Chicago IL 60654 Home Phone: 773-924-4956; Office Phone: 312-464-2413. Business E-Mail: richard.glass@jama-archives.org.

GLASS, ROGER I., federal agency administrator, research scientist; m. Barbara Stoll; 3 children. BA, Harvard Coll., 1967; MD, Harvard Med. Sch., 1972; MPH, Harvard Sch. Pub. Health, 1972; PhD, U. Goteborg, Sweden, 1984. Med. officer environ. hazards br. Ctr.'s Disease Control & Prevention, Atlanta, 1977, chief viral gastroenteritis unit, Nat. Ctr. Infectious Diseases, 1986—2006; with Lab. Infectious Diseases NIH, Bethesda, Md., 1984—86, assoc. dir. internat. rsch., 2006—, dir. Fogarty Internat. Ctr. (FIC), 2006—. Contbr. articles to profl. jours., chapters to books. Recipient Charles C. Shepard Lifetime Sci. Achievement award, Ctr.'s Disease Control & Prevention, 2007, Dr. Charles Merieux award, Nat. Found. Infectious Diseases, 2008. Mem.: Inst. Medicine (life). Office: FIC 31 Ctr Dr MSC 2220 Bethesda MD 20892-2220 Business E-Mail: roger.glass@nih.hhs.gov. *

GLASS, RONALD BERNHARD JACOB, radiologist; b. Salisbury, Rhodesia, Dec. 20, 1952; arrived in U.S., 1984; s. Joseph and Inge Selma Glass. MB BCh, U. Witwatersrand, 1976. Diplomate Am. Bd. Radiology. Fellow pediat. radiology Northwestern U., Chgo., 1984—86; radiologist U. Chgo., 1986—87, Loyola U., Maywood, Ill., 1987—88, Children's Nat. Med. Ctr., Washington, 1988—92, R.I. Hosp., Providence, 1992—93, U. Tex., Houston, 1993—95, Mt. Sinai Hosp. Med. Ctr., NYC, 1995—2005, Beth Israel Med. Ctr., NYC, 2005—06, Children's Meml. Hosp., Chgo., 2006—07. Reviewer Am. Jour. of Roentgenology, Radiology, Radiographics. Contbr. numerous articles to profl. jours.; editor (assoc. editor): Radiology, Examiner Am. Bd. of Radiology. Fellow: ACR, Am. Coll. Radiology. Jewish. Office: Mt Sinai Med Ctr Elmhurst Hosp 1 Gustave L Levy Pl New York NY 10028

GLASSBERG, KENNETH I., urologist, educator; MD, State Univ. of NY Downstate, 1968. Diplomate Am. Bd. Urology. Resident surgery Montefiore Hosp. Med. Ctr., Bronx, NY, 1971—72; resident urology Univ. Hosp., Bklyn., 1972—75; fellow pediatric urology Adler Hey Children,s Hosp., Liverpool, England, 1975—76, Gt. Ormand Streat Hosp. for Sick Children, London, 1976; dir. divsn. of pediatric urology Morgan Stanley Children's Hosp. of NY-Presbyn.; dir. pediatric urology State Univ. of NY Downstate. Prof. urology Columbia Univ. Coll. of Physicians and Surgeons. Fellow: ACS, Am. Acad. of Pediats. Office: NewYork-Presbyterian Morgan Stanley Children's Hospital 622 W 168th St New York NY 10032 Office Phone: 212-305-2500.

GLASSBURN, JOHN R., radiation oncologist educator; Attended, MCP Hahnemann U. Diplomate Am. Bd. Radiology. Intern Montefiore Hosp., Pitts.; resident Hahnemann Univ. Hosp.; clin. prof. radiation oncology Univ. of Pa. Health System. Named one of Best Doctors in America, 2003—10, Top Docs, Phila. Mag., 2005—09, 2011, America's Top Doctors, 2008, 2010. Office: Kennedy Cancer Center Ste 100 900 Medical Center Dr Sewell NJ 08080 Office Phone: 856-582-3008. Office Fax: 856-582-3009.

GLASSCOCK, LARRY CLAYBORN, retired health insurance company executive; b. Cullman, Ala., Apr. 4, 1948; s. Oscar Claborn and Betty Lou (Norman) Glasscock; m. Lee Ann Roden, Sept. 13, 1969; children: Michael, Carrie BBA, Cleve. State U., 1970; postgraduate student, Columbia U. Am. Inst. Banking. V.p. pers. and orgn. AmeriTrust Co., Cleve., 1974-75, v.p. nat. divsn., 1976-78, v.p., mgr. credit card ctr., 1978-79, sr. v.p. consumer fin., 1980-81, sr. v.p. nat. divsn., 1981-83, exec. v.p. corp. banking adminstr., 1983-87; group exec. v.p. AmeriTrust Corp. and AmeriTrust Co., Cleve., 1987-92; pres., CEO Essex Holdings, Inc.; pres., COO First Am. Bank, N.A.; pres., CEO Blue Cross and Blue Shield of the Nat. Capital Area; COO CareFirst, Inc.; senior exec. v.p., COO Anthem Ins., Indpls., 1998—99, pres., CEO, 1999—2004, chmn., 2003—04; pres., CEO WellPoint, Inc. (formerly Anthem Ins.), Indpls., 2004—07, chmn., 2005—10. Chmn. Coun. Affordable Quality Healthcare, Washington, 2002-03; bd. dirs. Zimmer Holdings Inc., 2001-, WellPoint, Inc., 2004-10, Sprint Nextel Corp., 2007- Past trustee Cleve. State U. Devel. Found.; campaign chmn. Geauga County United Way, 1989. Served in USMC, 1970—76. Co-recipient Ind. Entrepreneur of Yr. award, Ernst & Young, 2003. Mem. Am. Inst. Banking, Am. Bankers Assn., Assn. Res. City Bankers, Greater Cleve. Growth Assn., Cleve. State U. Alumni Assn. (pres. 1987). Clubs: Union (Cleve.); Hillbrook (Chagrin Falls, Ohio); The Country (Pepper Pike, Ohio).

GLASSHEIM, JEFFREY WAYNE, allergist, immunologist, pediatrician; b. Far Rockaway, NY, Sept. 16, 1958; s. Ronald Alan and Glenda (Deitch) G.; m. Paulette Renèe, Apr. 16, 1989; children: Elyssa Gwen, Brenna Chase. BA cum laude, Temple U., 1980; DO in Osteo. Medicine (hon.), U. New. Eng., 1984. Diplomate Am. Bd. Pediatrics, 1989, Am. Bd. Allergy and Clin. Immunology, 1995. Commd. 2d lt. U.S. Army, 1980, advanced through grades to maj., 1989; intern pediat. Winthrop-Univ. Hosp., Mineola, NY, 1984-85; resident pediat. Madigan Army Med. Ctr., Tacoma, 1985-87; fellow allergy/immunology Fitzsimons Army Med. Ctr. and Nat. Jewish Med. Ctr., Denver, 1990—92, chief fellow allergy-clin. immunology, 1990—92; chief allergy-clin. immunology and immunizations svcs. Silas B. Hays Army Community Hosp., Fort Ord, Calif., 1992—93; resigned commn. USAR, 1993; dir. allergy-immunology Pediatric Med. Group of Fresno, Calif., 1994-95, Northwest Med. Group, Fresno, 1995-97; pvt. practice allergy and immunology Fresno, Calif., 1997—2005, Oshkosh, Wis., 2005—06; dir. allergy, asthma and immunology Theda Care Physicians, Inc., Oshkosh, 2006—08; dir. allergy, asthama and clin. immunology Childrens Hosp., Wis., 2008—11; asst. prof. dept. pediat. Med. Coll. Wis., 2008—; assoc. Ctr. for Asthma & Allergy Inc., 2011—. Cons. numerous pharm. companies. Contbr. articles to profl. jours.; mem. editl. adv. bd. Unique Opportunites, 1998—, contbg. editor, 2004—. Bd. dirs. Am. Lung Assn. Ctrl. Calif., 1999—2002. Fellow Am. Acad. Allergy Asthma and Immunology, Am. Coll. Allergy, Asthma and Immunology; mem. AMA, Am. Osteo. Assn., Am. Physicians Fellowship for Medicine in Israel, Wis. Med. Soc., Winnebago County Med. Soc., Wis. Asthma Coalition, Wis. Assn. for Osteopathic Physicians and Surgeons, Wis. Allergy Soc. Republican. Jewish. Avocations: meteorology, sports, reading, gardening, walking. Home Phone: 920-385-0028; Office Phone: 920-436-3840. Personal E-mail: glasjw@juno.com.

GLASSMAN, ALEXANDER HOWARD, psychiatrist, researcher; b. Chgo., Feb. 4, 1934; children: Steven, Laura Glassman Hercher. BS, U. Ill., Chgo., 1956, MD, 1958. Diplomate Am. Bd. Neurology and Psychiatry. Resident in psychiatry Albert Einstein Med. Coll. Medicine, Yeshiva U., NY, 1954-62; USPH fellow, 1963-64; asst. prof. psychiatry Albert Einstein Coll. Medicine, Bronx, NY, 1964-65, cons. psychopharmacologist, 1972-78; dir. residency tng. Letterman Gen. Hosp., San Francisco, 1967-68, chief psychiatry svc., 1968-69; dir. affective diseases N.Y. State Psychiat. Inst., NYC, 1973-78, chief clin. psychopharmacology, 1978—; prof. clin. psychiatry Coll. Physicians and Surgeons, Columbia U., NYC, 1980—. Mem. merit rev. bd. VA, Washington, 1987-90. Editor: Treatment Strategies in Refractory Depression, 1990, also 5 other books; contbr. articles to jours. in field; patentee in field. Lt. col. U.S. Army, 1967-69. Recipient Anna-Monika Found. Prize for Rsch. in Psychiatry, Established Investigator award Nat. Assn. for Rsch. Affective Diseases and Schizophrenia, 1990, also Disting. Investigator award, 2005, N.Y. State Psychiat. Rsch. award, 1994; invited spkr. Nobel Com. Conf. of Depression, Stockholm, 1983; Plenery spkr. German Psychiat. Assn., Fed. Republic Germany, 1990, Plenery spkr. Japanese Neurosci. Soc., Nagoya, 1994. Fellow Am. Coll. Neuropsychopharmacology, Am. Psychiat. Assn. (Lifetime achievement prize 1989); mem. AAAS, Am. Psychopath. Assn. (trustee), N.Y. Acad. Sci. Achievements include patent for clonidine in smoking cessation; first to recognize unique treatment response of delusionally depressed patients, to demonstrate relationship between antidepressant drug treatment outcome and individual differences in drug metabolism, to describe the cardiac antiarrhythmic effects of antidepressant drugs, to describe relationship between depression and cigarette smoking. Office: Columbia U Dept Psychiatry 1051 Riverside Dr New York NY 10032-2695 Business E-Mail: ahg1@columbia.edu.

GLASSMAN, ARMAND BARRY, physician, educator, scientist, administrator, pathologist; b. Paterson, NJ, Sept. 9, 1938; s. Paul and Rosa (Ackerman) G.; m. Alberta C. Macri, Aug. 30, 1958; children: Armand P., Steven B., Brian A. BA, Rutgers U., 1960; MD magna cum laude, Georgetown U., DC, 1964. Diplomate in anatomic, clinical pathology & tranfusion medicine Am. Bd. Pathology, Am. Bd. Nuc. Medicine. Intern Georgetown U. Hosp., Washington, 1964-65; resident Yale-New Haven Hosp., West Haven VA Hosp., 1965-69; asst. prof. pathology, Coll. Medicine U. Fla.; chief radioimmunoassay lab. Gainesville VA Hosp., Fla.; practice lab. and nuc. medicine, 1969-71; dir. clin. labs., assoc. prof., prof. pathology, cellular, molecular biology Med. Coll. Ga., Augusta, 1971-76; med. dir. clin. labs. Med. U. SC Hosp., Charleston, 1976-87; attending physician in lab. and nuc. medicine Med. U. SC, 1976-87, assoc. med. dir. Med. U. Hosp. and Clinics, 1982-86, prof., chmn. dept. lab. medicine, 1976-87, med. dir. MT and MLT programs, 1976-87, clin. prof. pathology, lab. medicine, and radiology, 1987—94, acting chmn. dept. immunology and microbiology, 1985-87, assoc. dean Coll. Medicine, 1979-85, asst. and assoc. dean Coll. Allied Health Sci., 1984-87, chmn. hosp. exec. com., 1985-86, acting med. dir. Univ. Hosp. and Clinics, 1985-86; med. dir. clin. labs. Charleston Meml. Hosp., 1976-87; sr. v.p. med. affairs, prof. lab. medicine and nuc. medicine Montefiore Med. Ctr. and Albert Einstein Coll. Medicine, Bronx, NY, 1987-89; v.p., lab. dir. Nat. Reference Lab., Nashville, 1989-92; from clin. prof. to prof. dept. pathology Vanderbilt U., Nashville, 1990-94; dir. Vanderbilt Pathology Lab. Svcs., 1992-94; dir. clin. labs. Vanderbilt U. Med. Ctr., 1993-94, O. Stribling chair, prof., 1994—2006; head and chair divsn./dept. lab. medicine, med. dir. med. tech. and cytogenetic tech. programs U. Tex., M.D. Anderson Cancer Ctr., Houston, 1994—96, med. dir. Med. Tech. & Cytogenetic Tech. programs, 1994—96, 2001—06, dir. sect. cytogenetics, 1994—2005, chair ops. and improvement mgmt. com. dept. hematopathology, 1998—2002; prof. Grad. Sch. Biol. Scis. U. Tex., 1994—2006; prof. emeritus Med. U. SC, 2006—. Adj. prof. Grad. Sch. Biol. Scis. and U. Tex. Health Scis. Med. Sch., 1994-; adv. coun. Trident Tech. Coll., 1976-87; bd. dirs. Fetter Family Health Ctr.; steering com. pathology and lab medicine U. Tex. M.D. Anderson Cancer Ctr., 1998-2000, radiation safety com., 1998-2005, pharmacy and therapeutics com., 2000-06, vice chmn., 2004-06, credentials com., 2002-06, radiation drug rsch. com., 2003-06, chmn. task force on antiemetic drugs, 2003-06, chmn. medication process com., 2004-06, faculty senate rep., 2004-06; founding dir. Sealite, Inc., 1987-99, chmn. bd. dirs., 1995-99; founding dir., bd. dirs. SynthRx, Inc., 2003-07; med. adv. com. Nashville Red Cross Blood Ctr., 1991-94, acting med. dir., 1991-92; v.p., bd. sci. advisors Nat. Health Labs./Nat. Reference Lab., 1992-94; trustee, bd. dirs. Gulf Coast Cmty. Blood Ctr., 1994-2006; cons. in field. Editor, co-editor 4 books; bd. editors Annals of Clin. and Lab. Scis., 1981—, book editor, 2005—; contbr. articles to profl. jours., chpts. to books. Trustee Coll. Prep. Sch., 1979-84, chmn. bd., 1983-84; trustee, bd. dirs., v.p. Mason Prep. Sch., 1984-87; bd. dirs. United Way, 1983-87, Am. Cancer Soc., 1984-87; co-founder, bd. dirs. Glassman Family Fund, 1998-; bd. mem., sec., vice-chmn. Kiawah Island Cmty. Assn., 2007-; mem. comm. com. Town of Kiawah Island, SC, 2006-07; donor M.D. Anderson Cancer Ctr., U. Tex., 1994-, Charleston Breast Cancer, 2006-; founder, chmn. Glassman Family Fund/Fidelity Charitable Gift Fund, 1996-. With USMCR, 1956—64. Johnson and Avalon Found. scholar Georgetown U., 1961-64, State scholar Rutgers U., 1956-60; Recipient Jacobi award in pediatrics, Washington, 1964; named Young Investigator of Yr. Soc. Nuclear Medicine 1971, Outstanding Tchr. Med. Coll. Ga., 1974, Olla Stribling Disting. Chair Cancer Rsch. U. Tex., M.D. Anderson Cancer Ctr., 1994-2006. Fellow ACP, Coll. Am. Pathologists (numerous coms. 1971-2005), Assn. Clin. Scientists (mem. numerous coms. 1969-, pres. 1990-91, exec. com. 1990-95, C.P. Brown lectr, 1995, editor 2006-, Diploma of Honor 1987, Clin. Scientist of Yr. 1993, book editor Annals Clin. and Lab. Scis., 2006-), Am. Soc. Clin. Pathology (coun. immunohematology and blood banking 1983-89, coun. grad. med. edn. and rsch. 1998—2004, Commr.'s award for Continuing Edn. 1989, nat. contbg. editor to Resident In-Svc. Exam. 2000-04), Coll. Nuc. Medicine, NY Acad. Medicine; mem. Am. Bd. Pathology (transfusion medicine/blood bank test com. 1984-88), Internat. Acad. Pathology, Am. Assn. Pathologists, Soc. Nuc. Medicine (chmn. edn. com. 1973-77, acad. coun. 1979-92), AMA (Physician's Recognition award, instnl. rep. to sect. on med. schs., 1987-94, 2003—), So. Med. Assn., Am. Geriat. Soc. (founding fellow So. divsn.), Am. Soc. Microbiology, Am. Assn. Blood Banks (chmn. cryobiology com. 1974-83, edn. com. 1978-85, sci. program com. 1981-84, autologous transfusion com. 1979-83, bd. dirs. 1984-87, transfusion practices com. 1992-96), Assn. Schs. Allied Health Professions (bd. editors jour. 1979-83), Soc. Cryobiology (treas., bd. dirs. 1978-80), AAAS, NY Acad. Scis., Acad. Clin. Lab. Physicians and Scientists (exec. coun. 1978-85, pres. 1982-83), S.E. Area Blood Bankers (pres. 1979-81, exec. coun. 1980-85), Tenn. Assn. Blood Banks (treas. 1993-94), Am. Coll. Physician Execs., Kiawah Island Cmty. Assn. (bd. sec., mem. various coms. 2007—), Sigma Xi, Alpha Eta, Alpha Omega Alpha. Avocations: tennis, community service. Office: Med Univ SC Dept Microbiology Immunology BSB201 173 Ashley Ave Charleston SC 29425 Personal E-mail: abglassmn@yahoo.com. Business E-Mail: glassma@musc.edu.

GLASSMAN, LEONARD M., radiologist; BS, Pa. State U., 1967; MD, Jefferson Med. Coll., 1969. Cert. Nat. Bd. Med. Examiners, 1970, Am. Bd. Radiology, 1974. Intern Temple U. Health Sciences Ctr., 1969—70; resident Thomas Jefferson U. Hosp., 1970—73; radiologist Washington Radiology Associates, DC; chief radiology Columbia Hosp. Women Med. Ctr.; breast imaging scientist Armed Forces Inst. Pathology. Former chmn. radiological devices panel US FDA Ctr. Devices & Radiological Health. Mem.: Soc. Breast Imaging, Soc. Radiologists Ultrasound, Am. Roentgen Ray Soc., Am. Inst. Ultrasound in Med., Radiological Soc. North America, Am. Coll. Radiology. Office: 2141 K St NW Washington DC 20037 Office Phone: 202-223-9722. Office Fax: 202-659-2819.

GLASSMANN, MARVIN JEAN, marriage and family therapist; b. NYC, June 13, 1935; s. Edward and Frances Blanche (Frankel) G.; m. Deanna Moskowitz, Dec. 27, 1959; children: Leonard, Steven, David. BA, Bklyn. Coll., 1957; MA, George Washington U., 1959; EdD, Columbia U., 1975. Diplomate Am. Bd. Family Psychology; lic. psychologist N.J.; cert. sch. psychologist N.Y.; nat. cert. sch. psychologist; Nat. Health Svc. provider psychology; lic. mental health counselor, N.Y.; lic. marriage and family therapist, N.Y. Rehab. counselor Jewish Guild for the Blind, NYC, 1959-62; sr. clin. psychologist Creedmoor State Hosp., Queens Village, N.Y., 1962-66; fellow L.I. Mental Health Ctr. (formerly L.I. Cons. Ctr.), Forest Hills, N.Y., 1963-65, psychotherapist and supr., 1965-85; sch. psychologist N.Y.C. Bd. Edn., Queens, N.Y., 1966-95; pvt. practice Huntington, Forest Hills, N.Y., 1966—; supr., dir. family therapy program L. Armstrong Mid. Sch., East Elmhurst, NY, 1999—2009; grad. student advisor, dept. marriage and family therapy Hofstra U., Hempstead, N.Y., 2000-01; family therapist Family Focused Grief Therapy At Sloan-Kettering, 2009—11. Externship program Ackerman Inst. for Family Therapy, 1994-96, mem., Huntington Greenway Trails Citizens Adv. Com. Co-author: Family Therapy, 1992; book reviewer Am. Jour. Family Therapy. Steward Town of Huntington, 1995—; disaster mental health worker ARC, 2001. Fellow: Acad. Family Psychology; mem.: APA, N.Y. Senate (mental health adv. com. 2000—05), N.Y. Mental Health Counselors Assn., Nassau-Suffolk Horsemens Assn. (mem. exec. bd. 1994—, 1st v.p.), Ea. Group Psychotherapy Soc., L.I. Assn. Marriage and Family Therapy (membership chmn. 1980—98, pres.-elect 1997—98, pres. 1999—2000, past pres. 2001, mem.-at-large 2002, bd. dirs., referral chmn., Disting. Svc. award, Presdl. award), N.Y. Assn. Marriage and Family Therapy (mem. exec. bd. 1990—2000, nominating chmn.), Am. Assoc. Marriage and Family Therapy (clin. mem., approved supr.), Psi Chi. Democrat. Jewish. Avocations: horseback riding, scuba diving, photography, cross country skiing, history. Home and Office: 91 Chichester Rd Huntington NY 11743-6340 Office: 71-36 110th St Forest Hills NY 11375 Home Phone: 631-423-0290; Office Phone: 718-268-1760, 681-423-0290. Personal E-mail: marvg13@aol.com, marvg13@yahoo.com.

GLASSROTH, JEFFREY, medical foundation administrator, internist, educator; b. NYC, Oct. 28, 1948; s. Murray and Marie (Cheynoweth) G.; m. Carol Holton, July 22, 1972; children: Marley, Drew. AB, Columbia U., 1969; MD, U. Cin., 1973. Diplomate American Bd. Internal Medicine, Subspecialty Bd. Pulmonary Medicine. Intern U. Cin. Med. Ctr., 1973-74, intern, resident, 1973-75, 77-78, resident, 1974-75, 77-78; fellow in pulmonary and critical care medicine Boston U., 1978-81, instr. medicine, 1979-81; from asst. to assoc. prof. medicine Northwestern U., Evanston, Ill., 1981-90, prof. medicine, 1990—95; prof. medicine, chair dept. Allegheny U. Health Scis., Phila., 1995—98; pres. American Thoracic Soc., NYC, 1999—2000; chmn., dept. of med. U. Wisconsin, 1998—2005; vice dean, prof. medicine Tufts U. Sch. Medicine, 2005—07; vice dean Feinberg Sch. Medicine, Northwestern U., 2007—09, chief acad. officer, 2007—09, interim dean, 2011—, pres., CEO Northwestern Medical Faculty Found., 2010—. Cons. Astra North America, Westboro, Mass., 1993-99, Genentech/Novartis, San Francisco, 2000-02, mem. adv. coun. for elimination of Tb, CDC, Atlanta, 1993-97; mem. ad hoc study sect. NIH, Bethesda, Md., 1993, 97, 2005. Editor: Scientific Basis Respiratory Infection, 1993; co-editor: Baum's Textbook of Pulmonary Diseases, 7th edit., 2003; assoc. editor American Jour. Respiratory Critical Care Medicine, 1994-99; mem. editl. bd. Chest, 1988-93. Surgeon, USPHS, 1975-77, Atlanta. Rsch. grantee NIH, 1987-97; recipient Pulmonary Acad. awards, 1983-89. Master ACP, fellow American Coll. Chest Physicians; mem. AAAS, American Thoracic Soc. (sec. 1996-97, v.p. 1997-98, pres.-elect 1998, pres. 1999-2000), Ctrl. Soc. for Clin. Rsch. (pres. 2002-03), European Respiratory Soc., Internat. Union Against TB and Lung Disease, Assn. Profs. Medicine (pres.-elect 2003, pres. 2004-05). Avocations: skiing, running. Office: Northwestern Sch of Medicine 303 E Chicago Ave Ward 4-009 Chicago IL 60611 also: Northwestern Medical Faculty Foundation 680 N Lake Shore Dr Ste 1118 Chicago IL 60611 *

GLAZEBROOK, RITA SUSAN, nursing educator; b. St. Paul, Apr. 26, 1948; d. David L. and Beverly Ruth (Penhiter) Beccue; m. Harold L. Glazebrook, Dec. 20, 1986; children: Julie, Robert J., Scott, Robert M., Katherine. Diploma, RN, Abbott Hosp. Sch. Nursing, Mpls., 1970; BS in Nursing, Augsburg Coll., Mpls., 1979; MS in Nursing, U. Minn., 1981, PhD in Edn. Adminstrn., 1987. Mem. staff, asst. head nurse United Hosps., Inc., St. Paul, 1970-78; mem. staff Med. Pers. Pool, St. Paul, 1978-81; prof. nursing, chmn. dept. St. Olaf Coll., Northfield, Minn., 1981—. Contbr. articles to profl. jours. Faculty devel. grant Evan. Luth. Ch. Am. Mem. ANA, Minn. Nurses Assn., Assn. of Women's Health Obstetric and Neonatal Nurses, Sigma Theta Tau. Home: 8941 Jasmine Ln S Cottage Grove MN 55016-3422 Office Phone: 507-786-3265, 507-786-3430. Business E-Mail: glazebro@stolaf.edu.

GLAZER, HOWARD IRWIN, psychologist, educator; b. Toronto, Ont., Can., May 8, 1946; BA with honor, U. Toronto, 1969; PhD, U. Tex., Austin, 1972. Clin. assoc. prof. psychology psychiatry & ob-gyn. Weill Coll. Medicine, Cornell U., 1974—; Found. Fund Rsch. Psychiatry fellow Rockefeller U., 1975—77; attending assoc. psychologist NY Presbyn. Hosp., 1977—2011. Pvt. practicce, 1975—2011. Fellowship, Woodrow Wilson Found. Fellow: NY Acad. Sci., Am. Acad. Pain Mgmt., Am. Bd. Sexology, Internat. Soc. Study Vulvovaginal Diseases; mem.: APA. Achievements include research in use of intrapelvic surface electromyography in the diagnosis and treatment of urological, gastrointestinal, and Pelvic, genital pain disorders, particularly dyspareunia. Avocations: scuba diving, skydiving, skiing. Office: 2166 Broadway Apt #6D New York NY 10024 Office Fax: 646-719-8659. Business E-Mail: drglazer@nyc.rr.com

GLEASON, CAROL ANN, retired mental health nurse; b. Fairfield, Iowa, Mar. 6, 1945; d. Maurice Alvin and Geraldine (Cook) Crist; m. Michael Gleason Jr., Nov. 26, 1966 (div. Nov. 1980); children: Daniel Lee, Raymond Joe, Christopher John, Crystal Dawn. ADN, Indian Hills Coll., 1977; AS in Adminstrn., Des Moines Area Coll., 1982; BSPA in Health Care, St. Joseph's, 1985; cert. nurses aides edn., U. Iowa, 1989; BSN, Drake U., 1997; grad., Nat. Inst. Paralegal Arts Sci., 2002. Lic. nursing home adminstr., Iowa; cert. psychiat. and mental health, gerontology ANA. Staff night charge nurse Mahaska Manor Nursing Home, Oskaloosa, Iowa, 1977; dir. nursing Tower Park Nursing Home, Oskaloosa, 1977—78, Pleasant Park Nursing Home, Oskaloosa, 1978—85, adminstr., 1985—86; staff nurse ICU-CCU Ottumwa Regional Hosp., Iowa, 1986; palative care and chronic psychiat. nurse Knoxville Vets. Hosp., Iowa, 1986—2009; with Heart Land Home Care, 2009; ret., 2009. Coord., instr. Iowa Ednl. Inst., Oskaloosa, 1987—; cons. Tower Park Nursing Home, Oskaloosa, 1985-87, Siesta Park Nursing Home, 1985-87, Mahaska Manor, 1993-95; nurse North Mahaska Nursing and Rehab. Ctr., Oskaloosa, 2004—, No. Mahaska Nursing and Rehab. Ctr., Iowa. Mem.: NAFE, Am. Fedn. Govt. Employers. Democrat. Roman Catholic. Avocations: football, walking, boating. Home: 220 Keomah Vlg Oskaloosa IA 52577-9671 Business E-Mail: cgleason@mahaska.org.

GLEASON, CHRISTINE ANNE, pediatrician, educator; b. Long Beach, Calif., Mar. 12, 1953; MD, U. Rochester Sch. Medicine & Dentistry, 1979. Asst., assoc. prof. pediat. Johns Hopkins Medicine, 1985—97; prof. pediat. & head, divsn. neonatology U. Wash. & Seattle Children's Hosp., 1997—. Office: 1959 NE Pacific St Seattle WA 98195 Office Fax: 206-543-8926. Business E-Mail: cgleason@uw.edu.

GLEESON, TADHG, radiologist, researcher; b. Limerick, Ireland, Apr. 25, 1977; s. Timothy and Noreen Gleeson; m. Petrina Nason, Dec. 30, 2004; children: Eoin, Charlie. BAO, RCSI, Dublin, 2001, BCh; MD, Faculty Radiology RCSI, 2006. Med. intern James Connolly Meml. Hosp., Blanchardstown, Dublin, 2001—02; med. sr. house officer Beaumont Hosp., Dublin, 2002—03; radiology specialist registrar Mater Misericordiae U. Hosp., Dublin, 2003—07; thoracic imaging fellow Vancouver Gen. Hosp., Bc, Canada, 2007—08; body imaging and intervention fellow St. Paul's Hosp., Vancouver, 2008—09; cons. radiologist Wexford Gen. Hosp., 2009—. Actor: (theatre production) Wild Harvest, Decadent Theatre Company, Galway; contbr. scientific papers. Fellow: RCS (Ireland); mem.: RCP (Ireland), Irish Faculty Radiologists, European Congress Radiology, Am. Coll. Radiology, European Soc. Gastrointestinal and Abdominal Radiology. Avocations: music, theatre, hockey, hurling. Office: Wexford Gen Hosp Wexford Ireland

GLEICH, GERALD JOSEPH, immunologist, researcher, educator; b. Escanaba, Mich., May 14, 1931; s. Gordon Joseph and Agnes (Ederer) G.; m. Elizabeth Louise Hearn, Aug. 16, 1955 (div. 1976); children: Elizabeth Genevieve, Martin Christopher (dec.), Julia Katherine; m. Kristin Marie Leiferman, Sept. 25, 1976; children: Stephen Joseph, David Francis, Caroline Louise, William Gerald. BA, U. Mich., 1953, MD, 1956. Diplomate Am. Bd. Internal Medicine, Am. Bd. Allergy and Immunology. Intern Phila. Gen. Hosp., 1956-57; resident Jackson Meml. Hosp., Miami, Fla., 1959-61; instr. in medicine and microbiology U. Rochester, NY, 1961—65; cons. in medicine, prof. immunology and medicine Mayo Clinic-Med. Sch., Rochester, Minn., 1965—2001; chmn. dept. immunology Mayo Clinic, Rochester, Minn., 1982-90, George M. Eisenberg prof., 1995—2001; disting. investigator Mayo Found., Rochester, 1988—2001; prof. medicine & dermatology U. Utah, Salt Lake City, 2001—, prof. pediats., 2008. Mem. bd. sci. counselors Nat. Inst. Allergy and Infectious Disease, 1981-83; chmn. subcom. on standardization allergens WHO, Geneva, 1974-75; lectr. Am. Acad. Allergy, 1976, 82; mem., chmn. immunological scis. study sect. NIH, 1984-87; John M. Sheldon Meml. lectr., 1976, 82, 88; Steve Lang Meml. Lectureship, 1980, Stoll-Stunkard lectr. Am. Soc. Parasitologists, 1986, David Talmage Meml. lectureship, 1987, Disting. lectr. Med. Scis. Mayo Clinic, 1988; original mem. Highly Cited Rschrs. Database, 2002. Contbr. articles on eosinophilic leukocyte to profl. jours. Served to capt. USAF, 1957-59. Recipient Landmark in Allergy award, 1990; grantee Nat. Inst. Allergy and Infectious Disease, 1970—; AAAS fellow for studies of structure, biol. properties and role in pathogenesis of disease of basic proteins present in cytoplasmic granules of eosinophilic leukocytes, 1993. Fellow ACP, Am. Acad. Allergy and Immunology (hon. fellow award 1992), AAAS; mem. Am. Soc. Clin. Investigation, Am. Assn. Immunologists, Assn. Am. Physicians, Phi Beta Kappa, Phi Kappa Phi, Alpha Omega Alpha. Office: University of Utah Dept Dermatology 4A330 SOM 30 North 1900 East Salt Lake City UT 84132-2409 Office Phone: 801-581-6465. Office Fax: 801-581-6484.

GLEIS, LINDA HOOD, physician; b. Louisville, Jan. 28, 1952; d. Edgar Pete Hood and Joan Ray (Brenner) Hulsey; m. Gregory Eric Gleis, Aug. 18, 1973; children: Eric, Matthew, Kevin, Anna. BA cum laude, Bellarmine Coll., 1974; MD, U. Louisville, 1978. Diplomate Am. Bd. Phys. Medicine and Rehab.; lic. physician Ky. Resident Frazier Rehab. Ctr., Louisville, 1978-81, chief resident, 1981, med. staff, 1982—96, dir. residency tng., 1985-95; asst. clin. prof. medicine U. Louisville, Louisville, 1985—; chief phys. medicine and rehab. VA Med. Ctr., Louisville, 1985—, med. staff, 1985—, acting chief of staff, 1999-2000; founding ptnr. Rehab. Assoc.-PSC, Louisville, 1985—2003. Spkr. in field. Health care task force Louisville C. of C., 1991—92; dir. JCMS Outreach Program, Inc., 1991-98, 1991—98; mem. cabinet Metro United Way, 1992—94; marriage sponsor Archdiocese of Louisville Holy Spirit Parish Couple to Couple Program, 1991—99; mem. Salute to Cath. Alumni Steering Com., 1991—97, chair, 1993—97; mem. U. Louisville Med. Alumni Bd., 1986—91, v.p., 1989—90, pres., 1990—91; mem. bd. overseers Bellarmine Coll., 1989—95; adv. bd. Jefferson County Office for Women, 1990—94; trustee Spalding U., 1992—2000, vice-chair, 1994—98, chair com. Acad. and Student Affairs, 1995—2000, Spalding U./Presentation Acad. Com., 1995—97, Devel. Com., 1994—95; adv. panel The Physicians Inc., 1993—95; bd. dirs. mem.-at-large U. Louisville Alumni Assn., 1993—2002; bd. dirs. Louisville Cmty. Found., 1992—99, 2001—; med. adv. group Home of the Innocents Pediatric Convalescent Ctr., 1993—95; adv. coun. Louisville Forum, 1995—99; pres. U. Louisville Med. Alumni Bd., 2008—; mem. Leadership Louisville Class of 1992, hon. chair scholarship campaign, 1994; judge exec. Jefferson County Small Bus. Growth Coun., 1992—93, Ky Spinal Cord & Head Injury Rsch. Bd., 2008—. Recipient 1st Ann. Salute to Cath. Schs. Disting. Alumni award Archdiocese Louisville, 1990, Disting. Alumni Svc. award U. Louisville, 1991, Bellarmine Coll. Outstanding Alumnus of Yr., 1991, Assumption H.S. Outstanding Alumna award, Louisville, 1993, Order of Merit U. Louisville Alumni Assn., 1993, Recognition award Ho. of Reps. Commonwealth Ky., 1998; honored with Tribute to Linda Gleis, M.D. Modern Day Heroine Congl. Record, 1992. Fellow: Am. Acad. Phys. Medicine and Rehab.; mem.: AMA, Cath. Edn. Found. (bd. dirs. 2002—), Jefferson County Med. Soc. (treas. 1990—91, physicians Metro United Way campaign chair 1990—94, found. bd. dirs. 1990—96, 1st woman pres. 1991—92, chmn. bd. dirs. 1992—93, bd. dirs. outreach program 1993—99, del. to Ky. Med. Assn. 1993—, 1st v.p. bd. dirs. 1994—96, found. bd. dirs. 1998—), Ky. Acad. Phys. Medicine and Rehab. (sec.-treas. 1988—), Ky. Med. Assn. (com. sch. health, phys. edn. and med. aspects of sports 1988—96, com. on domestic violence 1992—2002, physician orgn. study com. 1993—96, sec.-treas. 1999—), Assn. Acad. Physiatrists (v.p. 1994—95, pres. 1995—96, mem. grad. med. edn. com. 1995—97, sec./program chmn. residency program dirs. coun.), Am. Assn. Electrodiagnostic Medicine. Roman Catholic. Avocations: reading, tennis, golf, sailing. Office: VAMC 117 800 Zorn Ave Louisville KY 40206 Office Phone: 502-287-5105.

GLENDENING, TERRY SKY, psychologist; b. Cin., Apr. 19, 1961; BA, Cornell U., 1983; MA, U. Cin., 1986, PhD, 1995. Lic. psychologist Ohio, Ky., cert. corrective thinking practitioner 1999. Dir. recreation Indian Hill Cmty. Edn., Cin., 1986—92; pvt. practice in clin. psychologist, psychotherapist, 1982—. Tchg. asst. Cornell U., Ithaca, NY, 1982—83; cons. IHHS Peer Counseling Program, Indian Hill, Ohio, 1987—96; lectr. in field. Author: (book) Thought Patterns in Depression and Somatization, 1986, Cognitive Specificity in Non-Clinical Depressive Manifestations of Distress, 1995, Timeless Parenting Techniques: Fair, Firm and Functional, 2002, Pathways to Positive Thought, 2009, Your Life By Design, 2010, Journeys to Self Discovery, 2011, (workshop series) Beating Anxiety: A Structured Approach for Children, 2006, Coping Skills for a New Millenium, 2000. Vol. recreation for disabled Camp Stepping Stones, Cin., 1997—98; vol. Spl. Olympics, Cin., 1997—98. Recipient Sons and Daughters Am. Revolution award, 1974; named Outstanding Young Woman of Am., 1986, Diplomate, Nat. Inst. Sports, 2004—. Mem.: APA, Nat. Inst. Sports (diplomate 2004), Ohio Psychol. Assn., Psi Chi. Avocations: hiking, camping, art, sports, rock collecting. Office Phone: 513-688-7555.

GLENN, GUY CHARLES, pathologist; b. Parma, Ohio, May 13, 1930; s. Joseph Frank and Helen (Rupple) G.; m. Lucia Ann Howarth, June 13, 1953; children: Kathryn Holly, Carolyn Helen, Cynthia Marie. BS, Denison U., 1953; MD, U. Cin., 1957. Diplomate Am. Bd. Pathology, Am. Bd. Radioisotopic Pathology. Intern Walter Reed Army Med. Ctr., Washington, 1957-58; resident in pathology Fitzsimons Army Med. Ctr., Denver, 1959-63; commd. 2d lt. U.S. Army, 1956; advanced through grades to col., 1972; demonstrator pathology Royal Army Med. Coll., London, 1970-72; chief dept. pathology Fitzsimons Army Med. Ctr., Denver, 1972-77. Past pres. med. staff St. Vincent Hosp., Billings, Mont.; past mem. governing bd. Mont. Health Sys. Agy. Contbr. articles to profl. jours. Fellow: Coll. Am. Pathologists (chmn. chemistry resources com., chmn. commn. sci. resources, mem. budget com., coun. on quality assurance, chmn. practice guidelines com., bd. govs., chmn. nominating com.); mem.: Midland Empire Health Assn. (past pres.), Soc. Med. Cons. to Armed Forces, Am. Registry Pathology (bd. dirs., exec. com., search com., planning com.), Am. Soc. Clin. Pathology, Rotary (bd. dirs. emeritus local chpt.). Home: 3225 Jack Burke Ln Billings MT 59106-1113 Personal E-mail: guyglenn@bresnan.net.

GLENN, MEL B., physiatrist; b. Ft. Worth, Feb. 15, 1949; BA, Sarah Lawrence Coll., 1972; MD, NYU Sch. Medicine, 1978. Chief, chmn., dept rehab. medicine Boston U. Med. Ctr., 1993—97; staff physiatrist Spaulding Rehab. Hosp., 1998—. Assoc. prof. Harvard Med. Sch., 1998. Recipient Merit award, Brain Injury Assn. Mass., 1993. Mem.: Am. Congress Rehab. Medicine, Am. Acad. Phys. Medicine and Rehab. Avocations: birdwatching, swimming, travel. Office: Spaulding Rehab Hosp Boston MA 02114 Office Fax: 617-573-2769. Business E-Mail: mglenn@partners.org.

GLENN, MORTON BERNARD, retired internist; b. NYC, Mar. 21, 1922; s. Harold and Mimi (Steinberg) Glenn; m. Justine Manheim, July 21, 1963 (dec. Dec. 29, 2004); stepchildren: Adrienne Harkavy, Marcia Stamberg;children from previous marriage: Wendy, Valerie Jorgensen, John. AB, U. Pa., Phila., 1942; MD, NYU Sch. Medicine, NYC, 1946. Intern Bellevue Hosp., NYC, 1946, resident, 1949—52, chief obesity clinic, Knickerbocker Hosp., NYC; asst. attending physican U. Hosp., NYC; pvt. practice specializing nutrition and internal medicine; physician-in-charge Kips Bay and Morrishnia Obesity Clincs. Med. cons. UN, 1954—56; asst. clin. prof. medicine NYU Sch. Medicine, NYC, 1952—2005; pres. Food and Nutrition Coun. Greater NY, 1962—64; cons. NYC Dept. Health Bur. Nutrition; asst. vis. physician Bellevue Hosp., chief obesity clinic. Lt. USNR, 1943—45, lt. USNR, 1947—49. Fellow: NY Acad. Medicine, Am. Coll. Nutrition (past pres.); mem.: AMA, NYC and NY State Med. Soc., Am. Inst. Nutrition (Travel award 1962), Bellevue Alumni Soc. (pres.), Obesity Soc., Food and Nutrition Coun. Greater NY.

GLENNER, RICHARD ALLEN, dentist, educator, writer; b. Chgo., Apr. 14, 1934; s. Robert Joseph and Vivian (Prosk) G.; m. Dorothy Chapman, July 13, 1957; children: Mark Steven, Alison, Scott Jay. BS, Roosevelt U., 1955; BS in Dentistry, U. Ill., 1958, DDS, 1959; student, Army Med. Svc. Sch., 1960. Pvt. practice, Chgo., 1962—. Cons. on dental history to Smithsonian Instn., ADA, various corps., librs., univs., museums, dental jours, Dr. Samuel D. Harris Nat. Mus. Dentistry; dental and anthropol. rschr. Nat. Park Svc., Nat. Mus. Health and Medicine, 1993—; lectr. to various orgns., titanic rschr. & author, 2000-. Author: The Dental Office: A Pictorial History, 1984, How it Evolved: Dentistry's Pursuit for Excellence, 1997, How It Evolued-Dentistry's Pursuit for Exellence, 2002; co-author: The American Dentist, 1990, A Visit to the Dentist: Then & Now, 1996; appeared in PBS video Sci. Am. Frontiers: The Wild West, 1995; cons. editor A Bicentennial Salute to Am. Dentistry, 1976; contbr. articles to profl. and popular jours., 62 articles pub.; film maker The Dental Office, 1994; reviewer Jour. ADA, 1999—. Served to capt. AUS, 1960—68, medicine svc. officer basic course US Army, 1960. Mem. ADA (life), Ill. Dental Assn., Chgo. Dental Soc., Acad. Gen. Dentistry, Assn. Mil. Surgeons U.S., Am. Acad. History of Dentistry (historian 1984, chmn. smithsonian Instn. adv. group 1987, participated in symposium, 1987, Hayden-Harris award 1983, columnist Jour. History of Dentistry 1989—, mem. editl. bd. 1993—, hist. display com. 1993—, pub. com. 1993—, Hayden-Harris award com. 1995-99), Fedn. Dentaire Internat., Lindsay Soc. G.B., Ill. Dental Soc. (history com.), Pierre Fauchard Acad. (life), Am. Med. Writers Assn., Am. Dental Assn., Ill. State Dental Soc., Crown & Anchor Soc., Sci. Instrument Soc., Jewish War Vets. U.S., Westerners, Titanic Hist. Soc., Titanic Internat. Soc. (rschr.), Alpha Omega. Home: 6715 N Lawndale Ave Lincolnwood IL 60712-3711 *

GLENTHOJ, BIRTE YDING, psychiatrist; b. Odder, Denmark, June 19, 1951; d. Frank Pedersen and Ulla Yding; m. Anders Glenthøj, Dec. 20, 1975; children: Rasmus, Andreas. MD, U. Copenhagen, 1977, DMSc, 1994. Jr. resident Inst. Medicine, Surgery, Pediat., Psychiatry, Neurology, Ålborg, Hillerod and, Roskilde, Denmark,

1977-83, 85-86; sr. resident Univ. Hosps., Kommune Hosp. and Rigshosp., Copenhagen, 1984-85, 86-87; rsch. fellow Rigshospitale, Copenhagen, 1987—91; sr. resident, chief psychiatrist U. Hosp. Bispebjerg and Hillerod Hosp., Denmark, 1991-96; chief psychiatrist Univ. Hosp., Bispebjerg, 1996—2006; assoc. prof. U. Copenhagen, 1996—2006, prof. neuropsychiatry faculty health scis., 2006—; chair Lundbeck Found. Ctr. Excecllence Clin. Intervention & Neuropsychiat., Schizophenia Rsch., Psychiat. Ctr. Glostrup, 2009—; dir. rsch., Ctr. Neuropsychiat. Schizophrenia Rsch. Psychiat. Ctr. Glostrand Copenhagen U. Hosp., 2006—. Contbr. articles to profl. jours. Recipient The Rafaelsen award, Copenhagen, 1991. Mem. AAAS, Internat. Brain Rsch. Orgn., Scandinavian Coll. Neuropsychopharmacology (bd. mem. 2004—, pres. 2005-07), Danish Soc. Biol. Psychiatry (pres. 1993-97), Danish Psychiat. Assn. (chair com. biol. treatments in psychiatry), World Fedn. Socs. Biol. Psychiatry (v.p. 1997-2001, mem. sci. com. 2001—), Collegium Internat. Neuropsychopharmacology, European Soc., Neuropsychopharmacology, Soc. Biol. Psychiatry. Office: U Copenhagen Psychiat Ctr Glostrup NDR Ringvej DK-2600 Glostrup Denmark

GLESBY, MARSHALL JAY, physician, educator; b. Winnipeg, Manitoba, Canada, Sept. 27, 1963; U.S., 1985; MD, Johns Hopkins U., 1989, PhD, 1997; BSc, McGill U., 1985. Diplomate Am. Bd. Internal Medicine, Am. Bd. Infectious Diseases. Intern, resident Johns Hopkins Hosp., 1989—92, post-doctoral fellow divsn. infectious diseases, 1992—96; med. dir. Cmty. Rsch. Initiative on AIDS, NYC, 1996—99; asst. prof. medicine Weill Med. Coll. Cornell U., 1999—2005; assoc. prof. medicine and pub. health Weill Med. Coll. Cornell U., NYC, 2005—. Office: Weill Medical College of Cornell Univ 525 E 68th St Box 566 New York NY 10065 *

GLEZEN, WILLIAM PAUL, pediatrician, virologist, educator; b. Oblong, Ill., Mar. 15, 1931; s. Ward Anderson and Mary Elizabeth (Brown) Glezen; m. Dorothy Lou Luhman, Aug. 22, 1953; children: Laurie S., Paul L. BS in Biological Scis., Purdue U., Ind., 1953; MD, U. Ill. Coll. Medicine, Chgo., 1956. Diplomate Am. Bd. Pediat. Intern pediat. Wayne County Gen. Hosp., Eloise, Mich., 1956-57; resident pediat. Hurley Hosp., Flint, Mich., 1959-60, NC Meml. Hosp., Chapel Hill, 1960-61, chief resident, 1961-62; chief enteric and respiratory virus unit Kansas City Field Station Ctr. Disease Control, 1962-65; assoc. prof. pediat. U. NC Sch. Medicine, 1965-75; assoc. prof. microbiology and immunology/pediat. Baylor Coll. Medicine, Houston, 1975—77, prof. medicine, microbiology and immunology, 1977—89, prof. dept. molecular virology and microbiology, prof. and head preventive medicine sect., dept. pediat., 1989—. Assoc. attending pediatrician Harris County Hosp. Dist., Houston, 1976—2007; adj. prof., rschr. U. Tex. Ctr. Infectious Diseases, Houston, 1982—; mem. epidemiology and disease control study sect. NIH, 1985—89, mem. adv. com. immunization practices, 1987—90; med. expert Childhood Vaccine Injury Prog., USHHS, 1990—; mem. tnfluenza tech. adv. group Health Care Fin. Adminstrn., 1990—93; mem. task force on adult and maternal immunization Am. Coll. Obstetricians & Gynecologists, 2005—06. Contbr. articles to profl. jours., chapters to books. Comdr. USPHS, 1957—65. Recipient Commr.'s Spl. Citation, FDA, 1997, Disting. Physician award, Pediatric Infectious Disease Soc., 2004, Disting. Sci. Alumni award, Purdue U., 2006. Mem.: Tex. Pediatric Soc., Soc. Pediatric Rsch., Infectious Diseases Soc. America, Am. Pediatric Soc., Am. Acad. Pediat., Am. Epidemiological Soc. Presbyterian. Office: Baylor Coll Medicine Mail Stop BCM280 One Baylor Plz Houston TX 77030 Office Phone: 713-798-5249. Business E-Mail: wglezen@bcm.edu. *

GLICK, JOHN H., oncologist, medical educator; b. NYC, May 9, 1943; s. Arthur W. and Sybil (Goldman) Glick; m. Jane Mills, May 25, 1968; children: Katherine, Sarah. AB magna cum laude, Princeton U., 1965; MD, Columbia U., 1969. Diplomate Am. Bd. Med. Oncology, (sec. subsplty. com. med. oncology 1976-83, mem. subsplty. bd. med. oncology 1983-87, chmn. 1987-89, cert. exam. com. 1986-88, mem. bd. govs. 1987-89) Am. Bd. Internal Medicine. Intern in medicine Presbyn. Hosp., NYC, 1969-70, asst. resident in medicine, 1970-71; commd. surgeon, clin. assoc. medicine br. Nat. Cancer Inst., USPHS, Bethesda, Md., 1971-73; postdoctoral fellow in med. oncology Stanford (Calif.) U., 1973-74; asst. prof. medicine U. Pa., Phila., 1974-79, Ann B. Young asst. prof. cancer rsch., 1974, assoc. prof., 1979-83, prof., 1983—, Madlyn and Leonard Abramson prof. clin. oncology, 1988—; dir. clin. trials U. Pa. Cancer Ctr., Phila., 1977-79, assoc. dir. for clin. rsch., 1980-85, dir. Cancer Ctr., 1985—2006, mem. numerous acad. coms., dept. medicine coms., hosp. coms., 1974—; pres. Abramson Family Cancer Rsch. Inst., Phila., 1998—; v.p. U. Pa. Health Sys., 2006—; assoc. dean U. Pa. Sch. Medicine, 2006—. Attending physician Hosp. U. Pa., 1974—, dir. Hematology-Oncology Clinic, 1974—76; cons. Phila. VA Hosp., 1974—; mem. clin. trials rev. com. NIH, Bethesda, Md., 1980—83, mem. radiosensitizer /radioprotector working group, radiotheraphy devel. br., 1980—85, chmn. consensus devel. panel conf. adjuvant therapy for breast cancer, 1985; mem. com. accreditation med. oncology tng. programs Accreditation Coun. Grad. Med. Edn., Phila., 1983—, mem. appeals panel, 1984—94; prin. investigator Ea. Coop. Oncology Group U. Pa.; pres., dir. Abramson Family Cancer Rsch. Inst. U. Pa., Phila., 1987—; dir. Pa. Cancer Ctr. U. Pa., Phila., 1985—. Mem. editl. bd.: Am. Jour. Clin. Oncology, 1983—89, Blood, 1983—86, Jour. Clin. Oncology, 1987—93, Internat. Jour. Radiation Oncology, Biology and Physics; editor (assoc. editor): Cancer Rsch., 1984—88; contbr. articles to profl. jours. Recipient Faculty Rsch. award, Am. Cancer Soc., 1982—86; Rsch. grantee, Nat. Cancer Inst., Ea. Coop. Oncology Group, Am. Cancer Soc., others. Master: ACP (mem. various splty. coms. 1983—84); fellow: Coll. Physicians and Surgeons; mem.: John Morgan Soc. U. Pa., Am. Fedn. Clin. Rsch., Am. Soc. Hematology, Am. Radium Soc. (mem. exec. com. 1986—87), Am. Assn. Cancer Rsch., Am. Assn. Cancer Edn., Am. Soc. Clin. Oncology (chmn. program com. 1983—84, nominating com. 1983—84, mem. pub. issue com. 1984—85, bd. dirs., pres. 1995—96), Alpha Omega Alpha, Phi Beta Kappa. Office: Abramson Cancer Ctr of Univ Pa 3400 Spruce St Philadelphia PA 19104-4283 Office Phone: 215-662-6065. Business E-Mail: glickjh@mail.med.upenn.edu.

GLICK, NANCY LYNN, lobbyist; b. NYC, Aug. 23, 1948; d. Robert Lehman Burnstine and Lynn Phillips Manulis; m. Louis Gerstley Hecht, June 21, 1977; m. Michael Raymond Leaveck, Nov. 27, 1987. BS in Journalism, Boston U., 1970. Pub. rels. specialist Nat. Paint & Coatings Assn., Washington, 1971-72; dep. press sec. US Office Consumer Affairs, Washington, 1972-76; press officer FDA, Washington, 1976-79; account exec., dir., v.p., sr. v.p. Hill & Knowlton, Washington, 1979-89, sr. v.p., practice dir., 1991—2000; sr. v.p. Porter/Novelli, Inc., Washington, 1989-91; exec. v.p., practice dir health & nutrition affairs Ruder Finn, Washington, 2000—09; sr. v.p., head health & nutrition affairs practice MS&L Worldwide, Washington, 2009—. Mem. adv. com. Nat. Rehab. Hosp., Washington, 1993—; bd. mem. Nat. Women's Health Resource Coun., The Food Inst.; prin. Coun. for Excellence in Govt. Bd. dirs. U.S. World Food Programme. Named Pub. Rels. All Star, Pub. Rels. Jour., 1992; recipient Award of Excellence Pub. Rels. Soc. America, 1995. Office: MS&L Worldwide 1133 21st St #300 Washington DC 20036 Office Phone: 202-467-6600.

GLICK, RICHARD STEPHEN, internist, rheumatologist; b. Pitts., May 18, 1947; s. William and Ruthe (Scher) Glick; m. Joan Marie Skaf, Nov. 2, 1986; children: William Spencer, Michael Andrew. BA cum laude, U. Pa., 1969, MD, 1973. Diplomate Am. Bd. Internal Medicine (also subsplty. bd. rheumatology). Intern U. Mich. Hosp., Ann Arbor, 1973-74, resident, 1974-77; fellow in rheumatology U. Pa., 1977-78, Albany Med. Coll. Hosp., 1978-79; practice medicine specializing in rheumatology and internal medicine Ft. Lauderdale, Fla., 1979—. Contbr. articles to profl. jours. Mem. Am. Coll. Rheumatology, So. Med. Assn., Fla. Soc. Rheumatology. Office: 6405 N Federal Hwy Ste 105 Fort Lauderdale FL 33308-1414 Office Phone: 954-772-3660. Personal E-mail: rglick98@yahoo.com.

GLICK, SHIMON MICHAEL, medical educator; b. Paterson, NJ, June 30, 1932; arrived in Israel, 1974; m. Oct. 1956; six children. AB magna cum laude, NYU, 1951; MD, SUNY, Bklyn., 1955. Diplomate Nat. Bd. Med. Examiners, Am. Bd. Internal Medicine, Am. Bd. Internal Medicine Subspeciality Endocrinology Bd.; cert. specialist internal medicine, Israel, cert. specialist endocrinology, Israel; lic. N.Y., Conn., Pa., Israel. Intern Maimonides Hosp., Bklyn., 1955-56; asst. resident internal medicine Yale U., Grace New Haven (Conn.) Hosp., 1956-57; chief outpatient dept. and med. clinic USAR Army and Navy Hosp., Hot Springs, Ark., 1957-59; asst. resident internal medicine Mt. Sinai Hosp., NYC, 1959-60; trainee in diabetes and metabolic disorders USPHS Jewish Chronic Disease Hosp., Bklyn., 1960-61; spl. rsch. fellowship USPHS VA Hosp., Bronx, 1961-63, clin. investigator, 1963-64; assoc. dir. divsn. metabolism and endocrinology Maimonides Med. Ctr., 1964-74; prof. medicine Ben-Gurion U. of the Negev, Faculty of Health Scis., Beer-Sheva, Israel, 1974-97, dean, 1986-90; head internal medicine Soroka U. Hosp., 1974—. Chief div. metabolism and endocrinology Coney Island Hosp. of Maimonides Med. Ctr., 1964-69, chief med. svcs., 1967-74, vis. physician, 1967-74; clin. asst. prof. medicine SUNY, Downstate Med. Ctr., 1965-68, clin. assoc. prof., 1968-72, clin. prof., 1972-74; attending physician Maimonides Med. Ctr., 1967-74; chmn. divsn. medicine Ben-Gurion U. of the Negev and Soroka U. Hosp., 1974-83; established investigator Israel Ministry of Health, 1978-81, mem. nat. health coun., 1996—, nat. ombudsman, 1998-2009; vis. scientist NIH, 1983-84; chmn. faculty of health scis. Ctr. for Med. Edn., Ben-Gurion U. of the Negev, 1990—. Editorial bd.: Jour. Clin. Endocrinology and Metabolism, 1971-74; assoc. editor: Israel Jour. Med. Scis., 1978-98. Mem. nat. adv. com. on human experimentation Ministry of Health, Israel, 1985—90; head health svcs. Negev region, Kupat Holim (Sick Fund) of Gen. Fedn. of Labor, 1986-90, chmn. med. coun., 1986-90; ombudsman Israel Nat. Health Svcs., 1998—2009. Fellow ACP; mem. Israeli Soc. for Med. Ethics (coun. 1989—99), Endocrine Soc., Assn. Orthodox Jewish Scientists (pres. 1965-67), Israel Soc. Internal Medicine, Israel Diabetes Assn., Soc. Urban Physicians (pres. 1969), Am. Soc. for Clin. Investigation, Com. of Concerned Scientists (co-chmn. med. sci. sect. 1973-74), Israel Endocrine Soc. (pres. 1979-82), Inst. Medicine, NAS, Phi Beta Kappa, Alpha Omega Alpha (pres. sch. chpt. 1954-55). Office: Ben Gurion U Negev 84100 Be'er Sheva Israel Home Phone: 972 08 6230306; Office Phone: 972 8 6477415. Business E-Mail: gshimon@bgu.ac.il.

GLICKENHAUS, SARAH BRODY, speech therapist; b. Mpls., Mar. 8, 1919; d. Morris and Ethel (Silin) Brody; m. Seth Morton Glickenhaus, Oct. 23, 1944; children: James Morris, Nancy Pier. BS, U. Minn., Mpls., 1940, MS, 1945. Therapist Davison Sch. Speech Correction, Atlanta, 1940—42; speech pathologist U. Minn., 1945—46; speech therapist Queens Coll., 1946—48, VA, NYC, 1949—50, Abbott Sch. United Free Sch. Dist. 13, Irvington, NY, 1971—79; pvt. practice New Rochelle, NY, 1950—71, Scarsdale, NY, 1979—. Tutor learning disabled children New Rochelle Pub. Sch., 1968—71. Mem.: AAAS, Westchester Speech & Hearing Assn., NY State Speech &Hearing Assn., Am. Speech Hearing & Lang. Assn., Harvard Club (NYC). Jewish. Home and Office: 100 Dorchester Rd Scarsdale NY 10583-6051 Office Phone: 212-953-7855.

GLICKMAN, FRANKLIN SHELDON, dermatologist, educator; b. Bklyn., Dec. 14, 1929; s. Arthur Zachary and Hilda (Kurtz) G.; m. Leatrice Sallie Alter, Mar. 29, 1953; children: Todd Scott, Jeff Bret. BA cum laude, Hofstra Coll., 1950; MD, SUNY-Bklyn., 1954; MS in Health Care Mgmt., NYU, 1990. Diplomate: Am. Bd. Dermatology. Intern Flushing (N.Y.) Hosp., 1954-55; resident in dermatology Kings County Hosp., Bklyn., 1957-58, Bronx VA Hosp., 1958-60; practice medicine specializing in dermatology Bklyn., 1960-94; mem. faculty dermatology dept. SUNY-Bklyn., 1960—82, clin. prof., 1982-93, adj. clin. prof., 1993—96; dir. med. edn. Wyckoff Heights Med. Ctr., Bklyn., 1990-96, chmn. dept. grad. med. edn., 1992-96. Author: General Dermatology, 1978, Fundamentals of Dermatology: A Study Guide, 1990; contbr. articles to profl. jours. Served to capt. M.C. USAF, 1955-57. Fellow N.Y. Acad. Medicine, ACP; mem. Am. Acad. Dermatology, Bklyn. Dermatol. Soc. (pres. 1970-72), N.Y. State Med. Soc., Kings County Med. Soc., AMA, N.Y. State Soc. Dermatology (pres. 1983-85), Phi Beta Kappa. Home: 6841 Treves Way Boynton Beach FL 33437-6485 Personal E-mail: fsglickman@comcast.net.

GLICKMAN, HAROLD BRUCE, podiatrist, educator; b. Ft. Meade, Md., Sept. 15, 1945; s. Murray and Martha (Ratner) Glickman; m. Sherill Ann Turner, June 4, 1977; children: Erica Rachel, Meredith Ann. BA, Emory U., Atlanta, 1967; DPM, Pa. Coll. Podiatric Medicine, 1971. Chief resident Guiffré Med. Ctr., Phila., 1972-73; chief of podiatric medicine Group Health Assn., Washington, 1973-75; pvt. practice podiatrist Washington, 1975—. Prof. orthopedic surgery George Washington U. Med. Ctr. Fellow: Am. Assn. Hosp. Podiatrists; mem.: Am. Podiatric Med. Assn. (treas. 2002, v.p. 2003, pres.-elect 2004, pres. 2005), Am. Coll. Podiatric Sports Medicine, Am. Coll. Sports Medicine. Avocations: sports, golf, skiing. Office: 1145 19th St NW Ste 508 Washington DC 20036-3715

GLICKMAN, JOEL DAVID, nephrologist, educator; MD, State U. NY. Diplomate Am. Bd. of Internal Medicine, 1985, Am. Bd. of Internal Medicine-renal/nephrology, 1988. Intern Montefiore Hosp., resident; fellow Hosp. of the Univ. of Pa., assoc. prof. clin. medicine, dir. home dialysis programs. Named Top Docs, Phila. Mags., 2011. Mem.: Internat. Soc. for Peritoneal Dialysis, Internat. Soc. of Nephrology, Nat. Kidney Found., Am. Soc. of Nephrology, Internat. Soc. for Hemodialysis. Office: Hospital of the University of Pennsylvania 3400 Spruce St. Philadelphia PA 19104 Office Phone: 215-622-4000.

GLICKMAN, MARK, psychologist; s. Henry and Nora Glickman; m. Elana Glickman. BA in Spanish and Psychology magna cum laude, Washington U., St. Louis, 1998; PhD, U. Tex. Southwestern Med. Ctr., Dallas, 2002; student, Machon Shlomo, Jerusalem, 2002—04. Lic. psychologist Israel, Dept. Health. Rsch. fellow Ateres Yisroel Rabbinical Sem., Jerusalem, 2004—05; psychologist Psychol. Svcs. Bet Shemesh, Israel, 2006—08, Darchei Shalom Residential Treatment Ctr. Adolescents, Moshav Givat Yearim, Jerusalem, 2008—, Psychol. Svcs. Modiin Elite, 2008—. Psychol. and ednl. evaluator, cons. Sch. Dist. Bet Shemesh, 2006—; pvt. practice psychotherapy, Ramat Bet Shemesh, Israel, 2006—07. Scholar, Dept. Health, 2006—07. Mem.: APA. Achievements include research in depression and ADHD in children, cognitive behavior therapy. Home Phone: 11 972-2-992-5024; Office Phone: 11 972543035262. Personal E-mail: meirglickman@gmail.com.

GLICKMAN, ROBERT MORRIS, medical educator, former dean; b. Bklyn., June 23, 1939; s. David B. and Sally G.; m. Mary Holahan, June 20, 1961; children; Jonathan, Michael. BA magna cum laude, Amherst Coll., 1960; MD cum laude, Harvard U., 1964. Diplomate Am. Bd. Internal Medicine. Resident in medicine Harvard U. Med. Services, Boston City Hosp., 1965-66; research fellow in medicine Med. Sch., Harvard U., Boston, 1966-68; from instr. medicine to assoc. prof. Harvard U. Med. Sch., Boston, 1970-77; clin. and rsch. fellow in medicine Mass. Gen. Hosp., Boston, 1966-68, asst. in medicine, 1970-74, asst. physician, 1974-75; intern Harvard U. Med. Services, Boston City Hosp., 1964-65; chief divsn. gastroenterology, asst. physician Beth Israel Hosp., Boston, 1975-77, physician-in-chief, 1990—96; from assoc. prof. to prof. Coll. Physicians and Surgeons, Columbia U., NYC, 1977-82, Samuel Bard prof. medicine, chmn. dept. medicine, 1982-90, chief divsn. gastroenterology, 1977-84, chmn. gastrointestinal sect. abnormal biology, 1978-84; attending physician Presbyn. Hosp., NYC, 1981—90, dir. med. svc., 1982—90; Herrman L. Blumgart prof. medicine Harvard Med. Sch., Boston, 1990—98, chmn. exec. com. dept. medicine, 1996—98; physician-in-chief Beth Israel Deaconess Med. Ctr., 1996—98, sr. v.p. acad. and clin. strategies, 1996; dean NYU Sch. Medicine, NYC, 1998—2007, Robert M. and Mary H. Glickman prof. medicine and gastroenterology, 2007—; dean, CEO NYU Med. Ctr., NYC, 1998—2007. Mem. Nat. Digestive Diseases Adv. Bd., 1985—. Mem. editorial bd. Jour. Lipid Research, 1978-79, Jour. Clin. Investigation, 1979-84, Am. Jour. Medicine, 1981—; contbr. articles to med. jours. Maj. M.C. U.S. Army, 1968-70. Fellow ACP; mem. AMA (pres. 1997-98), Am. Fedn. Clin. Rsch. (councillor Eastern sect. 1975-79, sec.-treas. 1976-79), Am. Gastroent. Assn. (v.p. 1985-87, pres. elect 1987, pres. 1988), Nat. Acad. Medicine, Inst. Medicine NAS, Harvey Soc., Interurban Clin. Club, Assn. Am. Physicians (v.p. 1997, pres.), Nat. Found. Ileitis and Colitis (mem. sci. adv. bd. 1978), Am. Soc. Clin. Investigation (councillor 1981-84, pres. elect 1983, pres. 1984-85), Assn. Profs. Medicine (councillor 1989-94, pres. 1992-93), Am. Bd. Internal Medicine (sub-splty. bd. on gastroenterology 1988-93), Harvard Soc., Phi Beta Kappa, Sigma Xi, Alpha Omega Alpha. Office: NYU Sch Med 550 First Ave New York NY 10016 Office Phone: 212-263-5372. Business E-Mail: Robert.Glickman@nyumc.org.

GLICKSTEIN, JULIE SUE, pediatric cardiologist; b. Bklyn., May 24, 1960; d. Solomon and Lorraine (Layton) G.; m. Rick Ruvkun, Nov. 12, 1988; children: Carolyn Anne, Andrew. AB, Smith Coll., Northampton, Mass., 1982; MD, Chgo. Med. Sch., 1986. Cert. in pediat. 2006, in pediatric cardiology 2002. Internship and resident in pediat. NYU Med. Ctr. Bellevue Hosp., NYC, 1986-89, fellow pediatric cardiology, 1989-92; asst. prof. pediatric cardiology Albert Einstein Coll. Medicine/Montefiore Med. Ctr., Bronx, NY; assoc. prof. clin. pediat. Columbia U. Med. Ctr., NYC; adj. asst. prof. pediat., asst. attending pediatrician Weill Med. Coll. Cornell U., NYC. Recipient Young Investigator award Ea. Soc. Pediatric Rsch., 1991. Avocations: tennis, piano. Office: NY Presbyn Hosp Columbia U Med Ctr 3959 Broadway CHN 2 New York NY 10032 Office Phone: 212-305-8509. Office Fax: 212-305-4429.

GLIED, SHERRY A., federal agency administrator; b. 1961; BA in Economics, Yale U., New Haven, 1982; MA in Economics, U. Toronto, Can., 1985; PhD in Economics, Harvard U., 1990. Sr. economist health care & labor market policy Coun. Econ. Advisers, Exec. Office of the Pres., 1992—93; prof., chair dept. health policy & mgmt. Columbia U. Mailman Sch. Pub. Health, NYC; asst. sec. for planning & evaluation US Dept. Health & Human Services, Washington, 2010—. Vis. asst. prof. health care policy Harvard Med. Sch., 1996—97; faculty rsch. assoc. Nat. Bur. Econ. Rsch., Cambridge, Mass., 2000. Author: Chronic Condition, 1998; co-author: Better But Not Well: Mental Health Policy in the US Since 1950, 2006; mem. editl. bd. Jour. Health Politics, Policy & Law, Health Svcs. Rsch., Milbank Quarterly; contbr. articles to profl. jours. Recipient Health Policy Investigator award, Robert Wood Johnson Found., 1996, Eugene Garfield Econ. Impact of Med. & Health Rsch. award, Research!America, 2004, Charles E. Gibbs Leadership prize, Jacobs Inst. Women's Health, 2008. Mem.: Inst. Medicine. Office: US Department Healt & Human Services 200 Independence Ave SW Washington DC 20201 Office Phone: 202-690-7858. E-mail: sherry.glied@hhs.gov. *

GLIEDMAN, PAUL, radiation oncologist, educator; MD Coll. of Physicians and Surgeons, Columbia U. Resident in radiation oncology NYU Med. Ctr., 1984—87; assoc. dir. Continuum Cancer Centers, NY; dir. of radiation oncology Hackensack Univ. Med. Ctr., Beth Israel Med. Ctr., sr. attending physician in dept. of radiation oncology, St. Luke's- Roosevelt Hosp. Named a Top Doctors-New York Metro Area, Castle Connollys, 2009. Office: St. Luke's - Roosevelt Hospital Center 1000 10th Ave New York NY 10019

GLIJANSKY, ALEX, psychiatrist, psychoanalyst; b. Caracas, Venezuela, Oct. 6, 1948; arrived in US, 1975; s. Natalio and Ghenea (Rechtman) G.; m. Belinda Matyas, Aug. 12, 1973; children: Ghena, Avi. MD, Universidad Cen. de Venezuela, 1971, MS, 1974. Bd. cert.

in psychiatry Am. Bd. Psychiatry and Neurology. Resident in psychiatry Hahnemann U., Phila., 1978; med. dir. Fishtown/Lower Kensington Mental Health Ctr., Phila., 1978—82; assoc. psychiatrist dept. psychiatry Abington Meml. Hosp., Pa., 1982—. Clin. asst. prof. psychiatry Drexel U. Sch. Medicine, Phila., 1978. Fellow Am. Psychiat. Assn. (Disting. fellow); mem. Pa. Psychiat. Soc., Phila. Psychiat. Soc., Psychoanalytic Ctr. Phila., Am. Psychoanalytic Assn. Avocation: golf. Office: 1579 Old York Rd Abington PA 19001 Business E-Mail: alex@aglijanskymd.com.

GLIKLICH, JERRY, physician, educator; b. Jelenia Góra, Poland, May 6, 1948; came to U.S., 1958; s. Henry and Henia (Gotajner) G.; m. Jane Salmon, Sept. 12, 1976; children: David, Benjamin. AB, Columbia U., 1969, MD, 1975. Intern N.Y. Hosp., NYC, 1975-76, resident, 1977-78; fellow in cardiology Presbyn. Hosp., NYC, 1978-81, attending physician, 1981—; asst. prof. medicine Columbia U., NYC, 1981-91; assoc. clin. prof. Presbyn. Hosp., NYC, 1991-97, clin. prof., 1997—2001, David A. Gardner prof. medicine, 2001—. Cons. in field. Contbr. articles to profl. jours. Mem. ACP, Am. Coll. Cardiology, Phi Beta Kappa. Office: NY Presbyn Hosp 161 Fort Washington Ave New York NY 10032-3713

GLIKLICH, JERRY I., cardiologist, educator; Attended, Columbia U. Coll. Physicians & Surgeons, 1975. Diplomate Am. Bd. Internal Medicine-cardiovascular disease. Intern NY Hosp. Cornell Med. Ctr., resident in internal medicine, 1976—78; fellow in cardiovascular disease Columbia Presbyn. Med. Ctr., NY, 1978—81; clin. prof. medicine Columbia Physicians & Surgeons; cardiologist NY Presbyn. Med. Ctr. Office: New York Presbyterian 161 Ft WA Ave New York NY 10032 Office Phone: 212-305-5588. Office Fax: 212-342-5584.

GLIMCHER, LAURIE HOLLIS, immunologist, educator; b. Rochester, NY, Apr. 17, 1951; BA, Harvard U., Cambridge, Mass., 1972; MD, Harvard U. Med. Sch., 1976. Intern. Mass. Gen. Hosp., Boston, 1976—77, resident, 1977—78, fellow, 1982—83; post-doctoral tng. Harvard U.; post-doctoral tng. in the lab. immunology Inst Allergy and Infectious Diseases, Bethesda, Md.; sr. rheumatologist Brigham and Women's Hosp., Boston; prof. medicine Harvard Med. Sch., 1990—, head immunology program; Irene Heinz Given prof. immunology Harvard Sch. Pub. Health, Boston, 1990—, dir. divsn. biol. sciences program. Bd. dirs. Bristol-Meyers Squibb, 1997—, Waters Corp., 1998—, Pharmaceutical Corp.; assoc. mem. Broad Inst.; team leader Ragon Inst. of MGH, MIT and Harvard. Contbr. articles to profl. jours. Mem. fellowship com. Cancer Rsch. Inst.; mem. adv. bd. American Asthma Found., Immune Diseases Inst., Health Care Ventures, Burroughs-Wellcome Fund, Meml. Sloan Kettering Cancer Ctr. Recipient Soma Weiss award, Stohlman Meml. Scholar award, Leukemia Soc., Lee S. Howley award, Arthritis Found., Excellence in Sci award, FASEB, 2000, Klemper award, NY Acad. Sciences, 2003, Sr. Scholar award, AAUW, 2006, Disting. Investigator award, American Coll. Rheumatology, 2006. Fellow: American Acad. Arts and Sciences; mem.: NAS, AAAS, Health Care Ventures, Immune Disease Inst., American Asthma Found., American Assn. Advancement Sci., Inst. Medicine of NAS, American Assn. Immunologists (past pres., Huang Meritorious Career award 2006, Excellence in Mentoring award 2008), American Soc. Clin. Investigation (Outstanding Investigator award 2001), American Assn. Physicians. Office: Harvard Sch Pub Health Mailstop FXB Bldg Rm 205 651 Huntington Ave Boston MA 02115-6009 Office Phone: 617-432-0622. Office Fax: 617-432-0084. Business E-Mail: glimche@hsph.harvard.edu. *

GLIMCHER, MELVIN JACOB, orthopedic surgeon; b. Brookline, Mass., June 2, 1925; s. Aaron and Clara (Fink) Glimcher; m. Karin Wetmore, Mar. 8, 2000; children from previous marriage: Susan Deborah, Laurie Hollis, Nancy Blair. Student, Duke U., 1943-44; BS in Mech. Engring. with highest distinction; BS in Physics with highest distinction, Purdue U., 1946; MD magna cum laude, Harvard, 1950; postgrad., Mass. Inst. Tech., 1956-59; PhD in Engring. (hon.), Purdue U., 2004. Intern surgery Strong Meml. Hosp., Rochester, NY, 1950-51; 3d asst. resident surgery Mass. Gen. Hosp., Boston, 1951-52, 2d asst. resident, 1952-53, asst. resident orthopedic surgery, 1954-55, chief resident, 1956, chief orthopedic service, 1965-71, chmn. dept. orthopedic surgery, 1968-71; asst. resident orthopedic surgery Children's Med. Center, Boston, 1953-54, jr. resident, 1955-56; mem. faculty Harvard Med. Sch., 1956—, Edith M. Ashley prof. orphopedic surgery, 1965-71, Harriet M. Peabody prof., 1971—2009, Peabody disting. prof., 2009—; also chmn. dept.; orthopedic surgeon-in-chief Children's Hosp. Med. Center, Boston, 1971-81, dir. Lab. for Study of Skeletal Disorders and Rehab., 1980—2009. Trustee Forsyth Dental Inst., Hosp. Spl. Surgery, NYC, New Eng. Sinai Hosp. With USMCR, World War II. Recipient Soma Weiss award Harvard Med. Sch., 1950, Borden Research award, 1950; Kappa Delta award, 1959; Internat. Assn. Dental Research award, 1964; Ralph Pemberton award Am. Rheumatism Soc., 1969; Bristol-Meyers/Zimmer instl. grant for excellence; Disting. Achievement in Orthopaedic Research award Orthopaedic Research Edn. Found.; William Neuman award Am. Soc. Bone and Mineral Rsch., 1996; Physician Achievement award Arthritis Found., 1996. Fellow Am. Acad. Arts and Scis., Am. Acad. Orthopaedic Surgeons (Silver anniversary Kappa Delta prize 1974, Alfred Shands award jointly awarded with Orthop. Rsch. Soc 1997), Am. Orthopedic Assn.; mem. Orthopedic Research Soc. (past pres.), Assn. Bone and Joint Surgeons (Nicholas Andry award 1978), Internat. Soc. for Study Lumbar Spine (Volvo award 1983), Societe Internationale de Chirurgie Orthopedique et de Traumatologie. Office: 300 Longwood Ave Boston MA 02115-5724

GLIMCHER, PAUL W., neuroscientist, educator; b. Boston, Nov. 3, 1961; AB magna cum laude, Princeton U., 1983; PhD in Neuroscience, U. Pa., 1989. Rsch. assoc. Dept. Psychology U. Pa., 1989—90, NRSA postdoctoral rsch. fellow, 1990—93; asst. prof. Ctr. Neural Sci, NYU, 1994—98, asst. prof. neural sci., dir. undergraduate studies, 1998—2000, assoc. prof. neural sci. and psychology, 2001—; dir. Ctr. Neuroeconomics NYU, 2005—, assoc. prof. economics, 2006—, prof. neural sci., economics, and psychology, 2007—. Author: Decisions, Uncertainty, and the Brain: The Science of Neuroeconomics, 2004, Neuroeconomics: Decision Making and the Brain, 2008. Whitehall Found. Fellow, 1994—97, McKnight Scholar, 1996—99, Klingenstein Found. Fellow, 2000—03. Mem.: AAAS, American Econ. Assn., Soc. for Neuroscience, Soc. for Neuroeconomics (founding pres. 2004—05, past-pres. 2005—06, councilor 2006—07). Office: Center for Neural Science New York University 4 Washington Place, Room 809 New York NY 10003 Office Phone: 212-998-3904. Office Fax: 212-995-4011. E-mail: glimcher@cns.nyu.edu. *

GLINKA, ELENA, biologist, researcher; b. Tumen, Russia, Sept. 27, 1958; d. Maxim Rasskazov and Ludmila (Mileeva) Rasskazova; children: Peter, Vadim. Degree in biology, Lomonosov Moscow State U., 1981. Sr. scientist A.N. Bach Inst. Biochemistry RAS, Moscow, 1996—2001, Shemyakin and Ovchinnikovn Inst. Bioorganic Chemistry RAS, Moscow, 2002—. Recipient Memory of 850 Yrs. of Moscow award, Pres. Russian Fedn., 1997. Achievements include research in before 2002-investigation of polygalacturonase inhibiting proteins of plants; after 2002-designing of cancer gene therapy eukaryotic vectors. Office: Inst Bioorganic Chemistry RAS Miklukho-Maklaya 16/10 Moscow 117997 Russia Office Fax: 7-495-335-71-03. Personal E-mail: em_glinka@mail.ru.

GLOGAU, RICHARD G., dermatologist; b. Camden, NJ, Dec. 28, 1947; m. Pamela Ann Baj, June 11, 1977; 1 child, Gordon. AB, Dartmouth Coll., Hanover, NH, 1969; BMS, Dartmouth Med. Sch., Hanover, NH, 1971; MD, Harvard U., 1973. Diplomate Am. Bd. Dermatology, cert. in Dermatopathology, Am. Bds. Dermatology & Pathology. Intern, medicine Pa. Hosp., Phila., 1973-74; resident, dermatology U. Calif., San Francisco, 1974-77, chief resident, dept. dermatology, 1977-78, fellow, dermatologic surgery, 1978-79; active med. staff U. Calif. Hosps., 1979—2006; pvt. practice, 1979—. Departmental clin. adv. bd. mem., dept. dermatology, U. Calif., San Francisco, 1980-1998, mem. utilization review com., 1982-2000, mem. alternate dept. rep. clin. faculty assn., 1984-98, co-dir., dermatologic surgery fellowship, 1988-, Chancellor's Assocs., 1990-2006, clin. assoc. prof. dermatology, attending physician, 1988-94, clin. prof. dermatology, 1994-; cons. for Allergan Corp., Revance Therapeutics, Bioformis-Genzyme, Fibrogen, Inammed Corp., Medicis Corp., Neutrogena Corp., Liposonix, Inc.; commr., bd. examiner, Calif. State Bd. Med. Quality Assurance, 1989-95; lectr. in field. Co-author: Basics of Dermatologic Surgery, 1982, Flaps and Grafts, 1988, Cosmetic Dermatologic Surgery, 2d edit., 1989; co-editor: Dermatologic Surgery Year Book, 1991, 92, 93, 94; sect. editor Cosmetic Surgery, 1997-2004; mem. editl. bd. Archives of Dermatology, 1999-; contbg. editor Dermatologic Surgery, 2004-; featured on ABC's 20/20; contbr. chpts. to books and articles to profl. jours.; featured in several mag. articles. Pub. svc. U. Calif., San Francisco Med. Ctr. Glogau Teddy Bear Rescue Fund for Pediatrics, 2000—. Named one of "Top Docs", San Francisco Mag., 2001, 2003, 2004, 2005. Fellow Am. Acad. Dermatology (founder & chmn., DermPAC-Dermatology Polit. Action Com., 1994-2000, mem sect. on health policy, practice & rsch., 1996-2002, chmn., 1998-2002, bd. dir. SkinPAC-Dermatology Polit. Action Com., 2000-03), Am. Dermatol. Assn., Am. Acad. Facial Plastic and Reconstructive Surgery, Am. Coll. Mohs' Micrographic Surgery and Cutaneous Oncology (bd. dirs. 1989-92, chmn. bylaws com., 1989-92, mem. task force on CPT Coding, 1991-92), Am. Soc. for Dermatol. Surgery (chmn., practice support & liability com., 1985-87, chmn. task force on surgery & AIDS, 1989-93, mem. quality assurance com., 1994-97, dermatologic surgery fellowship task force, 1994-96, bd. dir. 1991-94, prog. dir. annual mtg. Rancho Mirage, Calif., 1986, Scottsdale, Ariz., 1992), Am. Soc. for Dermatopathology, Am. Acad. Cosmetic Surgery (bd. dir. 1993-98, chmn. exhibitos com., 1993-95), Am. Soc. Liposuction Surgery (charter fellow), N.Am. Soc. Phlebology (charter fellow), mem. Dermatology Found. Leaders Soc. (Calif. State chmn. (North), 1990-95, bd. trustee 1993-98), Calif. Dermatology Soc.(At-Large mem., bd. dir., 1993-2002, mem. legis. task force on AB 595 and AB1841, 1993-94, legis. task force on cosmetic surgery, 1997-98), San Francisco Dermatol. Soc., San Francisco Med. Soc., San Mateo County Med. Soc. Office: Dermatology 350 Parnassus Ave Ste 400 San Francisco CA 94117-3608 Office Phone: 415-564-1261.

GLORIA, FULVIA, medical educator, researcher; b. Manoppello, Italy, Sept. 27, 1946; d. Giacomo Gloria and Giacinta Di Pietrantonio; m. Egidio Bottini, Oct. 16, 1971; children: Nunzio, Massimo. PhD in Math., U. Rome, La Sapienza, 1971; MD, U. Rome, Tor Vergata, 1996. Fellow Inst. Genetics, U. Rome, 1972—78; asst. prof. Inst. Child Health, U. Rome, 1979—; lectr. med. stats. U. Rome, 1996—2006, temporary prof. med. stats., 2006—, chief, divsn. med. stats., 2001—. Rsch. asst. Ctr. Evolutionary Genetics, Rome, 1971—72; cons. Lincei Nat. Acad. Ctr. for Applied Math., Rome, 1979—85. Contbr. chapters to books. Grantee, Ministry Sci. Rsch., 2001—02. Mem.: Med. Genetics Assn. Avocations: gardening, music, travel. Office: Univ Rome Tor Vergata Via Montpellier 1 00133 Rome Italy Home: Largo Dell Olgiata 15 Lotto G ISOLA67 123 Rome RM Italy Home Phone: 39 6 30889514; Office Phone: 39 6 72596030. Business E-Mail: gloria@med.uniroma2.it.

GLOVER, DOUGLAS DENNIS, obstetrics, gynecology and pharmacology educator; b. Rowlesburg, W.Va., Feb. 7, 1929; s. Douglas and Iva (Hughes) G.; m. Barbara Anne Brady, Sept. 6, 1958; children: Joseph, William, Donald, Geoffrey, Robert. BS in Pharmacy, W.Va. U., Morgantown, 1951, BS in Medicine, 1959; MD, Emory U., Atlanta, 1961. Diplomate Am. Bd. Ob-gyn. Intern Grady Meml. Hosp., Atlanta, 1961-62, resident, 1962-65; pvt. practice, Marietta, 1965-82; prof. ob/gyn. Marshall U. Sch. Medicine, Huntington, W.Va., 1982-87, W.Va. U. Sch. Med., Morgantown, 1987—2004; prof. Sch. Pharmacy W.Va. U., 1987—. Vis. prof. Zhejiang Med. U., Hangzhou, People's Republic of China, 1993; past operator of 4 rural outreach clinics for disadvantaged pregnant women. Author: From the Everyday to the Extraordinary: West Virginia Pharmacists' Stories, 2009, The Evolution of Pharmacy Education in West Virginia: A History of the School of Pharmacy at West Virginia University 1914-2014, 2011; editor: Current Therapy in Obstetrics, 1988; contbr. articles to profl. jours. Mem. U.S. Pharmacopeial Conv., Inc., 1990—, gen. com. of revision, 1990-2000, chmn. ob-gyn adv. panel, 1990-2000, expert com. on nomenclature and labeling, 1990-2005. Served to 1st lt. AUS, 1952-53, 45th Inf. Divsn., Korea. Decorated Bronze Star, Purple Heart; recipient Outstanding Svc. award W.Va. U., 1972, 87, Outstanding Alumnus award W.Va. U. Sch. Pharmacy, 1982, Disting. Alumnus award, 1999, Dr. James H. Beal award W.Va. Pharmacists Assn., 1989, Sch. Medicine Faculty Recognition award, 1997, 2002, 2005, W.Va.Gov.'s Meritorious Svc. award, 2004, W.Va. U. Most Loyal Mountaineer, 2004, W.Va. U. Sch. Medicine award Excellence Svc. to Sch., 2005, Fellow Am. Coll. Ob-Gyn., Am. Soc. Reproductive Medicine (co-chair sessions mgmt. com. 1990—, chair registrations com. 1992-98), Internat. Infectious Diseases Soc. for Ob-Gyn. (mem. nat. steering com.), Masons (32d deg.), Sigma Xi, Phi Delta Theta (chpt. advisor 1988-2000), Phi Chi, Phi Lambda Sigma. Republican. Presbyterian. Achievements include patents in field; research in placental metabolism and pharmacokinetics of drugs during pregnancy. Avocation: military history. Home: 5 Maple Ave Morgantown WV 26501-6542 Office: WVa Univ 1136 Health Sci Ctr N Morgantown WV 26506 Office Phone: 304-293-4198. Business E-Mail: dglover@hsc.wvu.edu, dglover2@hsc.wvu.edu.

GLOVSKY, MYRON MICHAEL, medical educator; b. Boston, Aug. 15, 1936; divorced; five children. BS magna cum laude, Tufts U., 1957, MD, 1962. Bd. cert. Nat. Bd. Med. Examiners, Am. Bd. Allergy & Immunology, Am. Bd. Diagnostic Lab. Immunology. Intern Balt. (Md.) City Hosp., 1962-63; resident New Eng. Med. Ctr., Boston, 1965-66; spl. NIH fellow allergy and immunology Walter Reed Army Inst. Rsch., Washington, 1966-68; fellow hematology and immunology U. Calif., San Francisco, 1968-69; staff physician dept. internal medicine So. Calif. Permanente Med. Group, LA, 1969-72, dir. allergy & immunology lab., 1970-84, chief dept. allergy and clin. immunology, co-dir. residency program in allergy & clin. immunology, 1974-84, dir. pheresis unit, 1978-80; dir. L.A. County Gen. Hosp./U. So. Calif. Asthma Clinic; prof. medicine, head allergy and immunology labs. pulmonary divsn., head allergy and clin. immunology divsn. pulmonary medicine. U. So. Calif., Sch. Medicine, 1984-89, prof. pathology, 1986-89; clin. prof. medicine, clin. prof. pathology U. So. Calif., 1989—2003; dir. asthma and allergy referral ctr. Huntington Meml. Hosp., Pasadena, 1989—2003. Head fellowship and career devel. program Nat. Heart Inst., NIH, Bethesda, Md., 1963-65, fellowship bd. mem., 1964-65; vis. assoc. in chemistry Calif. Inst. Tech., Pasadena, 1977—; acad. assoc. complement and allergy Nichols Inst., San Juan Capistrano, Calif., 1980-2003, med. dir. immunology, 1980-89, 2003-06; clin. prof. medicine UCLA, 1983-84; vis. prof. clin. scholars program Eli Lilly & Co., Indpls., 1988; mem. steering com. Aspen Allergy Conf., 1988—. With USPHS, 1963-65. Fellow Am. Acad. Allergy; mem. AAAS, Am. Assn. Immunologists, Am. Thoracic Soc., Am. Fedn. for Clin. Rsch., Am. Coll. Allergy, L.A. Soc. Allergy and Clin. Immunology (pres. 1979-80), Collegium Internat. Allergolicum. Office: Huntington Asthma & Allergy Ctr 960 E Green St Pasadena CA 91106 Home: 951 S Fair Oaks Ave Pasadena CA 91105-2631 Home Phone: 626-755-7783; Office Phone: 626-793-6680. Business E-Mail: yksvolg@caltech.edu. *

GLOWINSKI, STANISLAW, surgeon, consultant; b. Szczuczyn, Poland, Jan. 31, 1932; s. Henryk and Czeslawa (Truszkowska) G.; m. Lidia Dubinska, July 1, 1967; children: Jerzy, Barbara. MD, U. Bialystok, Poland, 1957, PhD, 1969. Asst. dept. surgery U. Bialystok, 1957-64, asst. dept. thoracic, cardiac and vascular surgery, 1964-82, asst. prof., 1982-87, head dept. vascular surgery and transplantology, 1987—. Dist. cons. for vascular surgery, Poland, 1993—. Author: 300 articles to med. jours., including Jour. Cardiovasc. Surgery, Jour. Vascular Surgery, Jour. Haemostasis, Jour. Atherosclerosis. Mem.: European Soc. for Organ Transplantation (pres. 1995), Internat. Union Angiology (pres. 1984), European Soc. for Vascular Surgery (sec. 1993), European Soc. for Surg. Rsch. (pres. 1988). Avocations: opera, sailing. Office: U Bialystok Dept Vasc Surg Ul. Marii Sklodowskiej-Curie 24A 15-276 Bialystok Poland Home Phone: 48602491622. E mail: sglowinski@mediclub.pl.

GLUCKMAN, PETER, endocrinologist, fetal physiologist; b. New Zealand; s. Laurie and Ann Gluckman. With U. Auckland, New Zealand, 1974—, prof. pediat. & perinatal biology, dean, faculty med. & health scis., 1992—2001, founding dir. Liggin's Inst., 2001—; chief scientific officer Neuren Pharmaceuticals; founding dir. Nat. Rsch. Ctr. Growth & Development, New Zealand. Chmn. pregnancy nutrition com. WHO, NIH. Recipient Rutherford medal for sci. & tech., New Zealand Royal Soc., 2001, World Class New Zealand award, 2006, Companion of New Zealand Order of Merit, 1997; named New Zealander of Yr., NZ Herald, 2004, U. Disting. Prof., U. Auckland, 2001. Fellow: London Royal Soc.; mem.: Inst. Medicine (fgn. assoc.). Office: Neuren Pharmaceuticals Ltd Level 3 2-6 Park Ave Grafton Auckland New Zealand Office Phone: 64 9 373 7599 ext. 86476. Office Fax: 64 9 373 7497. E mail: director@liggins.auckland.ac.nz.

GLUECK-RAMBALDI, MARY AUDREY, retired psychiatric and mental health nurse; b. Bridgetown, Barbados; arrived in U.S., 1952; d. Hubert and Christina Cumming; m. Stephen G. Glueck (dec.); m. Robert Rambaldi, May 15, 2005. Grad. sch. nursing, St. Joseph's Mercy Hosp., Georgetown, Guyana; paralegal diploma, Profl. Career Devel. Inst., 2000. RN, Calif. Asst. nursing educator in new employee orientation San Mateo County Gen. Hosp., San Mateo, Calif., also facilitator video insvcs. for nursing staff, tchr. safety and emergency response procedures to staff, ret., 1998. Vol. emergency room U. Physicians Health Care-Kino Campus, Tucson. Mem. Mid. Mgrs. Assn., Am. Psychiat. Nurses Assn. Home: 3692 S Desert Cache Rd Tucson AZ 85735-5078 Personal E-mail: mary_glueck@yahoo.com.

GLYNN, KELLY JEAN, medical association administrator; b. Winchester, Mass., Feb. 10, 1964; BS, Salem State Coll., 1987. Proposal document coord., sales-acct. rep. Harvard Pilgrim Health Care, 1989—2000; contract adminstr. Alliance Imaging, Inc., 2002—03; supr. credentialing Harvard Vanguard Med. Assocs., 2003—06, physician recruiter, 2006—08, mgr. credentialing, physician recruiter, 2008—. Recipient Diamond medal, Harvard Pilgrim and Harvard Vanguard Med. Assocs. Mem.: Assn. Staff Physician Recruiters, NE Physician Recruiter Assn. Avocations: interior decorating, motorcycling, travel. Office: Harvard Vanguard Med Assocs 275 Grove St Ste 3300 Newton MA 02466 Office Fax: 617-559-8255. Business E-Mail: kelly_glynn@atriushealth.org.

GNANALINGHAM, MUHUNTHA GIRITHARALINGHAM, pediatric intensive care consultant; b. Colombo, Sri Lanka, Feb. 1, 1971; s. Sivagurunathar and Rajeswari Gnanalingham. MBChB with honors, U. Manchester, Eng., 1995; PhD in Devel. Physiol., U. Nottingham, Eng., 2005. Cert. FRCPCH London, NLP Eng. Specialist registrar in paediatrics Warrington Gen. Hosp., England, 1999—2000; specialist registrar in paediatric intensive care Alder Hey Children's Hosp., Liverpool, Merseyside, England, 2000—01; specialist registrar in neonatology Liverpool Women's Hosp., Liverpool, 2001; clin. lectr. in child health academic divsn. child health, U. Nottingham, 2001—05; specialist registrar in cmty. paediatrics Strelley Health Ctr., Nottingham, 2004—05; paediatric intensive care grid-trainee Alder Hey Children's Hosp., 2000—01, Liverpool, 2005—06, 2007—08; anaesthetic sr. house officer, dept. anaesthetics Glan Clwyd Hosp., Rhyl, England, 2006—07; fellow Royal Melbourne Children's Hosp., Australia, 2008—09. Recipient Rsch. and Devel. award, Warrington Gen. Hosp., 2000, Best Oral Presentation award, Paediatric Intensive Care Soc., 2005, Young Investigator award, Neonatal Soc., 2006; grantee Spl. Trustees grant., Nottingham U. Hosp., 2002, 2004.

Fellow: Royal Coll. Paediatrics and Child Health (vice-chair trainees com. 2007—08). Office: Paediat Intensive Care Unit Royal Manchester Children's Hosp Oxford Rd Manchester M13 9WH England Office Phone: 4401617018040, 4401617018041. Personal E-mail: molingham@doctors.org.uk. Business E-Mail: mo.gnanalingham@cmft.nhs.uk.

GNANT, MICHAEL, surgeon, educator; s. Rupert and Ingeborg Gnant; children: Lisa Gant, Anna. MD, Kollegium Kalksburg, Vienna, 1988. Prof. surgery Med. U. Vienna, 2004—. Achievements include research in breast cancer. Office: Med Univ Vienna Wahringer Guertel 18-20 Vienna A-1090 Austria

GNEPP, DOUGLAS ROBBIN, pathologist; b. Phila., Oct. 23, 1946; BSME, Drexel U., Phila., 1969; MS, MD, Duke U., 1974; MA (hon.), Brown U., 1993. Diplomate Am. Bd. Pathology. Intern and residency Barnes Hosp.-Washington U., St. Louis, 1974-77; from instr. to asst. prof. pathology W.Va. U. Sch. Medicine, Morgantown, 1977-81; asst. prof. to prof. St. Louis U. Sch. Medicine, 1981—91; prof. pathology R.I. Hosp./Brown U. Sch. Medicine, Providence, 1991—. Editor: Pathology of the Head and Neck, 1988, Surgical Pathology of the Salivary Glands, 1991, Diagnostic Surgical Pathology of Head and Neck, 2001, 2009. Office: Rhode Island Hosp Dept Pathology APC 12 593 Eddy St Providence RI 02903-4923 Office Phone: 401-444-8513, 401-444-5151.

GOAN, YIH-GANG, surgeon, researcher; b. Kaohsiung, Taiwan, Oct. 24, 1962; married. PhD, Nat. Sun Yat-sen U., Kaohsiung, 2006. Cert. Bd. Surgery, Taiwan Surg. Assn., 1992, Bd. Digestive Surgery, Taiwan Surg. Soc. Gastroenterology, 1992, Bd. Cardiovasc. Surgery, Taiwan Assn. Thoracic & Cardiovasc. Surgery, 1992, Bd. Chest Medicine, Taiwan Soc. Pulmonary and Critical Care Medicine, 1993, Bd. Emergency, Taiwan Soc. Emergency Medicine, 1999. Vis. staff, dept. emergency Kaohsiung Vets. Gen. Hosp., Kaohsiung, 1995—98; rsch. fellow, dept. med. oncology City Hope Comprehensive Cancer Ctr., Duarte, LA, Taiwan, 1998—99; vis. staff, divsn. thoracic surgery Vets. Gen. Hosp., Taiwan, 1999—2005; dir., divsn. thoracic surgery Kaohsiung Vets. Gen. Hosp., Taiwan, 2006—. Maj. NAVY, 1993—94. Recipient Outstanding Doctoral Dissertation award, Nat. Sun Yat-sen U., 2006. Office: Kaohsiung Veterans Gen Hosp 386 Ta-Chung 1st Rd Kaohsiung 813 Taiwan Business E-Mail: goan@seed.net.tw.

GÖBEL, KATJA, ophthalmologist; b. Cottbus, Germany, Mar. 3, 1975; d. Hartmut and Loretta Göbel. Asst. U. Eye Clinic, Rostock, Germany, 2001—05; cons. Schlosspark-Klinik, Berlin, 2006—. Mem.: ARVO. Office: Schlosspark-Klinik Heubnerweg 2 Berlin Germany Business E-Mail: katja.goebel@schlosspark-klinik.de.

GOBIN, Y. PIERRE, interventional neuroradiologist; b. Paris, Aug. 8, 1957; s. Yves Edouard and Marie Antoinette Gobin; m. Jovana Cvoric, Apr. 30, 1986; children: Anna Flore, Antoine Paul, Juliette Alice. MD, U. Paris 6, 1984. Bd. cert. radiologist France, 1988. Chef de clinique universitaire Hopital Lariboisiere, Paris, 1990—92; asst. prof. UCLA Sch. Medicine, 1995—99, assoc. prof., 1999—2001; prof. radiology neurosurgery and neurology Weill Cornell Med. Coll., NYC, 2001—; dir. interventional neuroradiology NY Presbyn., Weill Cornell. Co-founder, dir. Concentric Med., Inc, Mountain View, Calif., 1999—2005; vis. asst. prof. UCLA Sch. Medicine, 1992—95. Contbr. scientific papers. Recipient Innovation and Rsch. prize, French Coll. Interventional Radiology, 1992. Mem.: Nat. Stroke Assn., Am. Heart Assn. (stroke coun., program com. 2003—), World Soc. Interventional Neuroradiology, Soc. Neuro Interventional Surgery. Achievements include patents for clot capture coil; component mixing catheter; indwelling heat exchange catheter. Office: NY Presbyn-Weill Cornell 525 East 68th St New York NY 10021 Office Fax: 212-746-6653.

GOCHFIELD, MICHAEL, environmental and occupational health educator; MD, Albert Einstein Coll. of Medicine, NY, USA, 1965; PhD, City U. of NY, 1975. Diplomate Am. Bd. of Preventive Medicine, 1983. Resident Univ. Colo. Med. Ctr., 1965—66; fellow Rockefeller Univ., 1975—77; prof. environ. & occupl. medicine Robert Wood Johnson Med. Sch., dir. emviron. & occupl. residency program prof. Office: Robert Wood Johnson University Hospital One Robert Wood Johnson Place New Brunswick NJ 08901 Office Phone: 732-828-3000.

GODA, SEIJI, periodontist; PhD, DDS, Osaka Dental U., Japan, 1999. Cert. periodontitis Japanese Soc., 2007. Postdoc. fellow U. Minn., Mpls., 1999—2002; asst. prof. Osaka Dental U., 2002—. Grant, Japan Soc. Promotion Sci., 2005—07, 2008—10. Achievements include research in period ontology. Office: Osaka Dental Univ 8-1 Kuzuha Hanazono cho Osaka 573-1121 Japan Office Fax: 81 72 864 3179.

GÖDDE, GÜNTER HELMUT, psychotherapist; b. Munich, May 15, 1946; s. Franz Josef and Maria Gödde; m. Hilde Käthe Kronberg. Diploma in Psychology, Free U., Berlin, 1976, PhD in Psychology, 1980. Lectr. Berlin Acad. Psychotherapie, 1992—, supr., edn. therapist, 1992—, schwerpunktleitung, 1997—. Author: (scientific books) Traditionslinien des Unbewussten, Schopenhauer, Nietzsche, Freud, 1999, 2009, Mathilde Freud. Die älteste Tochter Sigmund Freuds in Briefen und Selbstzeugnissen, 2003, (pocket book), 2005; co-author (with M.B. Buchholz): Unbewusstes, 2011; co-editor: Das Unbewusste I-III, 2005—06; co-editor: (with J. Zirfas) Takt und Taktlosiskeit, 2011. Collaborator Forum History Psychoanalysis, Berlin, 1990—2008. Sentinal Party. Home and Office: Kuno-Fischer St 20 Berlin 14057 Germany Office Fax: 0303216386. Business E-Mail: g.goedde@t-online.de.

GODENNE, GHISLAINE DUDLEY, retired physician, psychotherapist, educator; b. Brussels; came to U.S., 1951; d. Pierre and Olive Dudley (Short) G. BS, Universite Catholique de Louvain, Belgium, 1948, MD, 1952. Intern Providence Hosp., Washington, 1951-52; resident in pediatrics, 1952-54; fellow in pediatrics Mayo Clinic, Rochester, Minn., 1954-57; fellow in pediatric research Johns Hopkins U., 1957-58, assoc. prof. mental hygiene, 1966-82, assoc. prof. psychiatry and pediatrics, 1966-82, psychoanalyst, 1972—94, prof. psychology, 1973-90, prof. psychiatry, pediatrics, and mental hygiene, 1982—94; resident in psychiatry Johns Hopkins Hosp., Balt., 1958-62, chief adolescent psychiat. service, 1964-73, dir. counseling and psychiat. services, 1973-90, dir. health svcs., 1978-88, dir. emeritus, 1990—; mem. staff various hosps. Balt., 1978-88; clin. prof. psychiatry U. Md., Balt., 1986—. Cons. psychiatrist Cylburn Children's Home, Balt., 1960-81, Catonsville (Md.) C.C., 1968-75, Good Shepherd Ctr., Balt., 1970-74, Assoc. Cath. Charity, Balt., 1970-77, Jewish Family of Children's Svcs., Balt., 1972-77, Mt. Washington Pediat. Hosp., Balt., 1974-81, Sheppard and Enoch Pratt Hosp., Balt., 1973-80, Loyola Coll., Balt., 1990-92. Mem. editorial bd.: Adolescent Psychiatry, 1978-83, Clinical Update Adolescent Psychiatry, 1982-85; contbr. articles to profl. jours. Bd. dirs. Balt. Girl Scouts Assn., 1958-60, 81-82, Met. Balt. Assn. Mental Health, 1965-69, Florence Crittendon Home, 1966-68; trustee McDonough Sch., 1975-83; pres. bd. Trustees Richmond Fellowship Md., 1975-77. Decorated Knight and Officer Order of Leopold (Belgium); recipient Christophe Plantin prize, Belgium, 1989; awarded Nobility Concession with the title of Baroness (Belgium) 1991; recipient Career Teaching award NIMH, 1963-65, Schonfeld award Am. Soc. Adolescent Psychiatry, 1995; grantee Fulbright Found., 1951-52, Parke Davis Co., 1957-58, NIMH, 1961-63. Fellow ACP, Am. Psychiat. Assn. (life), APHA (life), Am. Orthopsychiat. Assn. (life), Am. Soc. Adolescent Psychiatry (life, pres. 1981-82); mem. AAUP, Am. Psychoanalytic Soc., Md. Soc. Adolescent Psychiatry (pres. 1968-69), Md. Psychiat. Soc. (past chmn. program com., co-chmn. women's com. 1991-96), Md. State Conf. Social Welfare (past mem. child welfare com.), Am. Soc. Adolescent Medicine (charter), Am. U. and Coll. Counseling Ctr. Dirs., Internat. Soc. Adolescent Psychiatry (v.p. 1989-92, sec.-gen. 1992-95, v.p. 1995-99, co-editor monograph 2000-05), Women's Club of Johns Hopkins U. (pres. 1999-2000). Home: 15 Edgevale Rd Baltimore MD 21210-2215 Personal E-mail: g_godenne@msn.com, g_godenne@comcast.net. Business E-Mail: gigodenn@jhmi.edu. *

GODFRAIND, THEOPHILE JOSEPH, pharmacologist, educator; b. Bande, Belgium, Feb. 18, 1931; m. De Becker Anne, Dec. 4, 1957; children: Pierre, Catherine. MB, U. Libre de Bruxelles, Belgium, 1951; MD, U. Catholique de Louvain, Belgium, 1955, PhD, 1958; Cert., Inst. de Med. Tropicale, Anvers, Belgium, 1958; Doctor honoris causa, U. Louis Pasteur, Strasbourg, 1984, U. Henri Poincaré, Nancy, France, 2000, U. Comenius, Bratislava, Slovakia, 2006. Prof. U. Lovanium, Leopoldville, Congo, 1958-65, Université Catholique de Louvain, Brussels, 1965—; fellow Royal Acad. Medicine, Brussels, 1974-88, v.p., 1988-91, pres., 1991—; sec. gen. Internat. Union Pharmacology, 1987-94, pres., 1994-99, Belgian Coll. Pharm. Medicine, 2001—. Editor-in-chief Frontiers in Pharmacology, 2010—. Recipient Lauréat du Concours des Bourses de Voyage, 1955, Lauréat du Prix Spécia, 1955, Lauréat du Priz J.F. Heymans, 1967, Lauréat du prix Quinquennal des Sciences Thérapeutiques, 1973, Lauréat du Prix Smith Kline, 1982, Peter Debye prize U. Limburg, 1987, Lauréat du Prix de la Fondation de Physiopathologie Prof. Lucien Dautrebande, 1988, ASPET award, 1991, Europe and Medicine prize, 1997, Golden medal Slovak Acad. Sci., 1997. Fellow Am. Heart Assn., Coun. for High Blood Pressure Rsch.; mem .Acad. Royale de Médecine de Belgique, Acad. Nat. de Médecine de France, Acad. Nat. de Pharmacie de France, Acad. Europaea, Assn. des Physiologist, Deutsche Pharmakologische Gesellschaft, Biochem. Soc., Brit. Pharmacol. Soc., Physiol. Soc., N.Y. Acad. Scis., Am. Soc. for Pharmacology and Exptl. Therapeutics, Brit. Pharmacol. Soc. (hon.), Italian Pharmacol. Soc. (hon.), Slovak Pharmacol. Soc. (hon.). Achievements include pioneering work in the pharmacology of calcium channel blockers. Offices: Lab de Pharmacologie UCL 5410 Av Hippocrate 54 B-1200 Brussels Belgium Home: Rue du Bemel 19 1150 Brussels Belgium Business E-Mail: godfraind@farl.ucl.ac.be, theophile.godfraind@uclouvain.be.

GODFREY, KEITH A., gynecologist, director; b. Batley, Yorkshire, Eng., Mar. 31, 1949; s. Bertie George and Mary Vera Godfrey; m. Diane Collier, Aug. 29, 2003; children: Cathryn Helen, Stephen Richard, Louisa Cannell, Ellis. MBChB, Batley Grammar Sch., 1968. Cons., obstetrician & gynaecologist City Hosps., Sunderland, Tyne & Wear, England, 1985—2001; divisional dir., surg. svcs. Gateshead Health NHS Found. Trust, Tyne & Wear, 2001—; chair, gynecol. oncology site specific group North Eng. Cancer Network, NE England, 2006—. Dir. Northern Gynecol. Oncology Ctr., Gateshead, Tyne & Wear, 2001—; chair trustees Northern Cancer Care & Rsch. Soc., Gateshead, 2005—. Contbr. scientific papers. Coun. mem. Brit. Gynecol. Cancer Soc., 2007—. Fellow: Royal Coll. Ob-Gyn. (program dir. 2002—08). Achievements include development of comprehensive multidisciplinary model of patient care. Office: Northern Gynecol Oncology Ctr Queen Elizabeth Hosp Sheriff Hill Gateshead Tyne & Wear NE9 6SX England Office Fax: 00 44 191 445 6192. Business E-Mail: keith.godfrey@ghnt.nhs.uk.

GODFREY, MAURICE, biomedical scientist; b. Addis Ababa, Ethiopia, June 11, 1956; s. Robert and Liliana (Gandolfi) G.; m. Matilde Elena Almeida, July 5, 1985; children: C. Maximilian, R. Alessandro, D. Guillermo. BS, Monmouth Coll., 1977; MS, Columbia U., 1980, M in Philosophy, 1983, PhD, 1986. Postdoctoral fellow Oreg. Health Sci. U., Shrine Hosp., Portland, 1986-89; assoc. prof. pediatrics, dir. connective tissue lab. U. Nebr. Med. Ctr., Omaha, 1990—. Author: (with others) McKusick's Heritable Disorders of Connective Tissue, 1993, The Metabolic Basis of Inherited Disease, 1995; contbr. articles to profl. jours. Recipient grant-in-aid Am. Heart Assn., 1989, 93; Basil O'Connor scholar March of Dimes, 1991; established investigator Am. Heart Assn., 1995. Mem. AAAS, Am. Soc. of Human Genetics, Am. Fedn. for Clin. Rsch., Basic Sci. Coun. of the Am. Heart Assn. Achievements include co-discovery of fibrillin gene the cause of the Marfan syndrome. Office: UNMC Dept Pediatrics 982168 Nebr Med Ctr Omaha NE 68198-0001 also: National Marfan Foundation 22 Manhasset Ave Port Washington NY 11050-2023

GODFREY, NORMAN V., plastic surgeon; BS, Yale U., 1979; MD, Harvard U., 1973. Lic. physician N.Y., diplomate Am. Bd. Plastic Surgery. Resident in gen. surgery NYU-Bellevue Hosp. Med. Ctr., 1973—78, resident in plastic surgery, 1978—80; fellow in microvascular surgery Bellevue Hosp., 1978—80; pvt. practice plastic surgery NYC, 1980—. Chief divsn. plastic surgery NY VA Hosp., 1980—81; clin. instr. plastic surgery NYU-Bellevue Med. Ctr., 1980; attending surgeon NY Hosp. Med. Ctr. of Queens, 1982—, St. Vincent's Hosp. Med. Ctr., 1982—, Manhattan Eye, Ear and Throat Hosp., 1982—, NY Flushing Hosp., 1997; asst. clin. prof. surgery NY Med. Coll., 1995—98, Cornell U. Weill Med. Coll., 1998—; co-dir. divsn. plastic surgery NY Hosp. Med. Ctr. of Queens, 1982—. Contbr. articles to profl. jours. Mem.: AMA, Am. Soc. Plastic and Reconstructive Surgeons, N.Y. State Med. Soc. Office: 9 E 93rd St New York NY 10128

GODFREY, PHILIP M., plastic surgeon; BS, Yale U., 1974; MD, Med. Coll. Pa., 1981; DDS, U. Pa., 1981. Lic. physician N.Y., diplomate Am. Bd. Plastic Surgery. Resident in surgery Hartford Hosp., Conn.; resident in plastic surgery NY Hosp./Cornell Med. Ctr.; fellow in plastic surgery of the breast Meml. Sloan-Kettering Cancer Ctr.; pvt. practice plastic surgery Fresh Meadows, NY. Co-dir. divsn. plastic surgery NY Hosp. Med. Ctr. of Queens, 1982—, attending surgeon, 1986—, St. Vincent's Hosp. and Med. Ctr., 1987—, Manhattan Eye, Ear and Throat Hosp., 1994, NY Flushing Hosp., 1997; asst. clin. prof. surgery NY Med. Coll., 1995—98, Cornell U. Med. Coll., 1998—; contbr. Found. Reconstructive Plastic Surgery; spkr. in field. Contbr. articles to profl. jours. Named to Castle-Connolly Guide to Best Drs. in area. Mem.: AMA, Am. Soc. Plastic and Reconstructive Surgeons, N.Y. State Med. Soc. Office: 16303 Horace Harding Hwy Fresh Meadows NY 11365

GODIN, MICHAEL S., plastic surgeon; B, Rice U.; grad. with honors, Tulane U. Diplomate Am. Bd. Facial Plastic and Reconstructive Surgery, Am. Bd. Otolaryngology. Intern head and neck surgery Univ. of Calif.; advanced fellow cosmetic and reconstructive surgery Tulane Univ.; fellow dir. facial plastic surgery Am. Acad. of Facial Plastic and Reconstructive Surgery, 2004. Named one of Best Plastic Surgeon, Style Mag., 1999, Best Rhinoplasty Surgeon for Women, Richmond Mag., 2001—09, Top 40 under 40, Inside Bus. Mag. Office: Michael S Godin 410 Libbie Ave Richmond VA 23226 Office Phone: 804-285-8578.

GODINEZ, MARYE H., anesthesiologist; b. Louisville, Aug. 19, 1945; d. Jerome and Hilda Marie Durbin; m. Rodolfo I. Godinez, June 28, 1969; children: Lucas, Peter, Paul, Adela, Sarah, Ruth. BS, Gonzaga U., Spokane, Wash., 1967; MD, St. Louis U. Sch. Medicine, 1971. Diplomate Am. Coll. Anesthesiologists, 1974. Dir. ENT, neuro and opthalmology anesthesia Barnes Hosp., St. Louis, 1974—77; dir. obstet. anesthesia Temple U. Hosp., Phila., 1978—79; rsch. assoc. Dept. Anesthesiology and Critical Care Children's Hosp., Phila., 1985—2011. Contbr. articles to sci. jours. Home: 1036 Sproul Rd Bryn Mawr PA 19010

GODRON, MICHEL, biologist, professor; b. Isdes, Loiret, France, Aug. 26, 1931; s. Jacques and Marcelle (Langlois) G.; m. Catherine de Maintenant, June 2, 1956; children: Jacques, Béatrice, Francois, Antoine, Sylvie, Valérie, Guillaume. Civil Engr., des Eaux et Forêts, Nancy, France, 1953; Dr. Engring., U. Montpellier, France, 1966, ScD, 1972. Engr. Centre National de la Recherche Scientifique, Montpellier, 1957-73; prof. U. Montpellier II, 1974-93; assoc. prof. U. Laval, Québec, 1969; sec. Comité Ctrl. Agricole de Sologne, 1993—; prof. honorarius. Author: Ecologie de la Végétation Terrestre, 1984; co-author: Notice et Cartes Ecologiques de Sologne, 1964, Code Pour le Relevé Méthodique de la Végétation et du Milieu, 1968, (with Daget) Analyse Fréquentielle de l'Ecologie des Espèces, 1981, (with R. Forman) Landscape Ecology, 1986, (with H. Joly) Dictionaire des Paysages, 2006, Ecologie et Evolution du monde Vivant, 2011. Capt. French Navy. Decorated Mérite Militaire, Order Nat. du Mérite; recipien 1st award Internat. Assn.Landscape Ecology. Home: la Graineterie 18410 Brinon France

GODSON, GODFREY NIGEL, molecular geneticist, educator; b. London, June 20, 1936; s. Godfrey Edward and Elsie Louise (Harrington) G.; m. Barbara Cohen, Aug. 9, 1969; children: Rebecca Charlotte, Vanessa Alexandra. BS, London U., 1957, PhD, 1961, D.Sc. (hon.), 1984. Research fellow Calif. Inst. Tech., 1964-67; staff scientist Nat. Insts. Med. Research, Med. Research Council, Mill Hill, London, 1968-69; asst. prof., assoc. prof. radiobiology Yale Med. Sch., New Haven, 1969-74, 1974-80; prof. dept. biochemistry NYU Med. Sch., NYC, 1980—2006, chmn. dept. biochemistry, 1980—2006, prof. emeritus biochemistry, 2006—. Mem. biochemistry sect. Nat. Bd. Med. Examiners, 1985-89; mem. tropical medicine and parasitology study sect. NIAID, 1985-90. Editor: Gene jour., 1984-96, Jour. Cell and Molecular Biology, 1984-86; contbr. chpts. to books, articles to profl. jours. Mem. Am. Soc. for Biochemistry and Molecular Biology, N.Y. Acad. Scis. Office: NYU Med Sch 550 1st Ave New York NY 10016-6402 Business E-Mail: gnigelgodson@nyumc.org.

GODWIN, HAROLD NORMAN, pharmacist, educator; b. Ransom, Kans., Oct. 9, 1941; s. Harold Joseph and Nora Elva (Welsh) G.; m. Judy Rae Ricketts, June 9, 1963; children: Paula Lynn, Jennifer Joy. BS in Pharmacy, U. Kans., 1964; MS in Hosp. Pharmacy, Ohio State U., 1966. Lic. pharmacist, Kans., Ohio. Instr. Ohio State U. Coll. Pharmacy, Columbus, 1966-69; asst. dir. pharmacy Ohio State U., Columbus, 1966-69; dir. pharmacy U. Kans. Med. Ctr., Kansas City, 1969—2004; asst. prof. U. Kans. Sch. Pharmacy, Kansas City, 1969-74, assoc. prof., 1974-80, prof. pharmacy, 1980—, asst. dean pharmacy, 1975-89, assoc. dean pharmacy, 1989—, chmn. pharmacy practice, 1984—2006. John W. Webb lectr., vis. prof. Northeastern U., 1999; chmn. pharmacy exec. com. U. HealthSys. Consortium, 2001-04, exec. com., 2004-07; mem. exec. com. Novation Pharmacy, 2003-05. Author: Implementation Guide to IV Admixtures, 1977; (with others) Remington's Pharmaceutical Sciences, 1980, 85, 90, 95, 2000; contbr. over 100 articles to profl. jours. Recipient Clifton J. Latiolais award Ohio State U. Residents Alumni, 1986, Disting. Alumni award Ohio State U. Coll. Pharmacy, 1995; named Tchr. of the Yr., U. Kans. Sch. Pharmacy, 2001, Harold N. Godwin Leadership Legacy award U. Kans. Med. Ctr., 2004. Fellow: Am. Pharm. Assn. (bd. trustees 2006—, pres. 2010—, Disting. Achievement award 2000), Am. Soc. Health-Sys. Pharmacists (bd. dir. 1978—84, pres. 1982—83, bd. dir. rsch. and edn. found. 2002—06, Harvey A.K. Whitney award 1991); mem.: Kans. Pharmacy Found. (v.p. 2004—), Accredation Coun. Pharm. Edn. (bd. dir. 1988—2000, pres. 1992—96), Greater Kansas City Soc. Hosp. Pharmacists (pres. 1972), Kans. Soc. Hosp. Pharmacists (Kans. Hosp. Pharmacist of Yr. 1982, Harold N. Godwin award 1984), Kans. Pharmacists Assn. (pres 1977, v.p. 2005—09, bd. pharmacy specialties 2011, Kans. Pharmacist of Yr. 1982, 2010). Republican. Methodist. Avocations: walking, bicycling, cooking, wine tasting. Home: 10112 W 98th St Shawnee Mission KS 66212-5238 Office: U Kans Med Ctr MS4047 Rainbow Blvd At 39th St Kansas City KS 66106-7231 Office Phone: 913-588-2399. Business E-Mail: hgodwin@kumc.edu.

GODWIN, JOHN E., hematologist, oncologist; b. Mobile, Ala., Dec. 28, 1951; married; 3 children. BS summa cum laude, U. Montevallo, Ala., 1970—74; MD, U. Ala. Sch. Medicine, Birmingham, 1974—78; MS in Epidemiology, U. Tex. Sch. Pub. Health, Houston, 1981—83. Cert. Nat. Bd. Med. Examiners, 1979, Am. Bd. Internal Medicine,

1981, in Hematology 1986. Intern, internal medicine Baylor Coll. Medicine, Houston, 1978—79, resident, internal medicine, 1979—81, fellow, internal medicine, 1981—82, fellow, hematology and oncology, 1982—83; instr., dept. medicine Ben Taub Hosp., Houston, 1981—83; fellow, hematology and oncology U. N.C., Chapel Hill, 1983—85; instr., dept. medicine N.C. Meml. Hosp., Chapel Hill, 1983—85; cons. Hines Veterans Hosp., Ill., 1985—96; attending physician Foster G. McGaw Hosp., Maywood, 1985—2006, assoc. dir., spl. hematology clin. coagulation lab., dept. pathology, 1996—2006; asst. prof., dept. medicine and pathology Loyola U., Maywood, 1985—96, assoc. prof., dept. medicine and pathology, 1996—2006, prof., dept. medicine and pathology, 2002—06; prof. dept. medicine So. Ill. U. Sch. Medicine, Springfield, 2006—, chief divsn. hematology/oncology, 2006—. Chmn., blood utilization com. Loyola U. Med. Ctr., Maywood, 1990—2006, dir., dept. medicine, bone marrow lab., 1993—2006, asst. dir., hematology and oncology fellowship program, 1995—98, mem., pharmacy and therapeutics com., 2001—06; mem. Ctr. for Excellence in Molecular Hematology; assoc. dir. Simmons Cooper Cancer Inst., Springfield, 2006—. Reviewer for various jours. Fellow, Coun. on Arteriosclerosis, Thrombosis and Vascular Biology, 1997. Fellow: Am. Heart Assn.; mem.: AAAS, Am. Soc. Hematology. Achievements include research in leukemia, its biology and treatment, and in clinical thrombosis and clinical trials in various solid tumors. Office: Div Hematology/Oncology Southern Ill U Sch Medicine PO Box 19678 Springfield IL 62794-9678 Office Phone: 217-545-8124. Office Fax: 217-545-7021.

GOEAU-BRISSONNIERE, OLIVIER ARMAND, vascular surgeon; b. Paris, Jan. 6, 1952; s. Jean-Yves Armand Goeau-Brissonniere and Liliane Rozenfeld; m. Catherine Goulon, Mar. 1980; children: Fabien, Marc. MD, René Descartes U., Paris, 1981; PhD, Compiègne (France) U., 1987. Vascular surgeon Hopital Ambroise Paré, Boulogne, France, 1982—, head dept. vascular surgery, 1998—; dir. exptl. surgery Faculté de Médecine Paris-Ouest, 1987, prof. vascular surgery, 1990—. Mem. sci. com. on medicinal drugs and med. devices European Commn., Brussels, 2000-2004; cons., expert French Agy. for Security of Health Products, 1997—, mem. sci. coun., 2004-; expert and mem. couns., French High Authority Health, 2005- Editor: Les Urgences, 1997, Infections Artérielles, 1998, sr. editor Annuals of Vascular Surgery, 2007- Mem. Société de Chirurgie Vasculaire de Langue Francaise (bd. dirs.), European Soc. Vascular Surgery, Internat. Soc. Cardiovascular Surgery, Soc. for Vascular Surgery, French Fedn. Med. Specialties (pres. 2007-). Achievements include evaluation and development of biomaterials and new technologies; prevention and treatment of vascular graft infections and organization of medical specialties in France. Office: Hopital Ambroise Par 9 avenue Charles de Gaulle 92100 Boulogne France also: Land Fed Des Specialities Med 54 Bd Rodin Issg Les Roulineaux 92130 France Office Phone: 33 1 4909 5585. Business E-Mail: olivier.goeau-brissonniere@apr.aphp.fr.

GOEL, AMITABH, surgeon; b. India, Nov. 18, 1959; MBBS, Maulana Azad Med. Coll., 1982; MS in Orthop., Royal Coll. Surgeons, Edinburgh, 1988. Cert. Am. Bd. Phys. Medicine and Rehab., 1997, Am. Bd. Electrodiagnostic Medicine, 1999, subspecialty cert. in pain medicine 2001, subspecialty cert. in neuromuscular medicine 2009. Physician Wichita Clinic, 2002—. Clin. instr., dept. family practice Kans. U. Med. Sch., 2009. Recipient New Venture award, Wichita Clinic, Best Resident Rsch. award, Ctrl. Soc. Rehab. Medicine; named one of Americas Top Physicians, 2004—10. Fellow: RCS (Edinburg); mem.: Internat. Spinal Injection Soc., Am. Acad. Phys. Medicine and Rehab. Avocations: chess, walking, reading. Office: 1947 Founders Cir Wichita KS 67206 Office Fax: 316-613-4726. Personal E-mail: amitgoel@pol.net, amitgoel555@gmail.com.

GOEL, APUL, urologist; b. Mathura, Uttar Pradesh, India, June 23, 1966; MBBS, King George's Med. Coll., Lucknow, Utter Pradesh, MS in Surgery, 1989; MCh, All India Inst. Med. Scis., New Delhi, DNB, 2001. Prof. Chhatrapati Shahuji Maharaj Med. U., Lucknow, 2002—. Recipient Honor Cert., King George's Med. Coll.; Hargovind Meml. Travel fellowship, Urol. Soc. India, North Zone Chpt., Travel fellowship, Urol. Soc. India. Mem.: Nat. Acad. Med. Scis. (New Delhi). Avocations: reading, music, travel. Home: 2/107 Vijay Khand Gomti Nagar Lucknow Uttar Pradesh 226010 India Personal E-mail: goelapul1@rediffmail.com.

GOEL, BHIM SAIN, ophthalmologist; b. Nabha, Panjab, India, Dec. 12, 1939; s. Mohan Lal and Parma Devi Dewan; m. Renu Goel, May 17, 1967; children: Ashish, Ruchika. Student, Coll. Patiala, India, 1957; MB, BChir, Med. Coll., Patiala, 1962; MS in Ophthalmology, All India Inst. Med. Scis., New Delhi, 1965; PhD in Ophthalmology, Aligarh Muslim U., India, 1987. Tchg. fellow All India Inst. Med. Scis., 1964-65; surgeon Gandhi Eye Hosp., Aligarh, 1966, Oil and Natural Gas Commn., Dehradun, India, 1967; registrar Inst. Ophthalmology, 1967-68; lectr. Aligarh Muslim U., 1968-81, reader, 1981-86, prof., 1986—2001; dir. Inst. Ophthalmology Aligarh Muslim U., 1995—98; ret., 2002. Coord. Internat. Test in Ophthalmology, India; mem. Faculty of Medicine, Aligarh Muslim U.; mem. Acad. Coun. Aligarh Muslim U., mem. univ. ct.; examiner various ednl. instns.; commonwealth scholar, 1972-74; commonwealth fellow, RCS, Royal Eye Hosp. and Inst. Ophthalmology U. London, 1972-1974; sr. DAAD fellow, Germany, 1992; dir. Goel Eye and SQUINT Ctr., Aligarh; advisor Union Pub. Svc. Commn. Contbr. chpts. to 3 books, numerous articles to rsch. publs. Sr. DAAD fellow, Germany, 1992, Commonwealth fellow, Royal Coll. Surgeons, Royal Eye Hosp. and Inst. Ophthalmology U. London, 1972—74, fellow, Internat. Coun. Ophthal., 2010. Mem. All India Ophthal. Soc. (mem. mgmt. com.), Indian Med. Assn. Aligarh (past pres.), Strabismological Soc. India (past v.p., past pres.), Glaucoma Soc. India (past pres.), Uttar Pradesh Ophthal. Soc. (past pres.), Pvt. Drs. Assoc. (past pres.), Internat. Coun. Opthalmology (hon. fellow 2010). Achievements include research in amblyopia and strabismology. Avocations: travel, music, television. Office: Goel Eye and Sq Ctr Ramaghat Rd Uttar Pr Aligarh 202001 India Home: HIG 29 ADA Ramghat Rd Colony 241 301 Aligarh India Personal E-mail: drbsgoel@yahoo.com.

GOERRES, HANS-PETER, psychotherapist; b. Berlin, Dec. 13, 1940; s. Peter Willi and Liselotte Mathilde Goerres; m. Gerda Christine Hofmann, July 3, 1967; 1 child, Andrea Ingeborg. Diploma in psychology, U. Munich, Bavaria-Munich, Germany; 1st Lt., Sch. Engrs., Bavaria-Munich, Germany. Clin. psychologist Inst. Aviation Medicine, Fuerstenfeldbruck, Germany, 1969—2002; head psychologist German Air Force, Inst. Aviation Medicine, Fuerstenfeldbruck, Germany, 2002—. Author: (book) Selbstentfaltung, 1992. Lt. col. German Corps Engrs., 1962—67. Mem.: European Assn. Av. Psychologists. Christlich Soziale Union. Roman Catholic. Avocations: surfing, tennis, jogging, chess. Home: Meisenbach St 7 Emmering D-82275 Germany Office: Flugmed Inst LW Postfach 1264 KFL Fuestenfeldbruck D-82242 Germany E-mail: hanspetergoerres@t-online.de.

GOETZ, KENNETH LEE, cardiovascular physiologist, research consultant, writer; b. Java, SD, Jan. 7, 1932; m. Shirley Anne Caldwell, July 14, 1962 (div. 2003); children: Gregory Earl, Anne Katherine. PhD, U. Wis., 1963; MD, U. Kans., 1967. Instr., asst. prof. dept. physiology U. Kans. Med. Ctr., Kansas City, 1963-69; med. intern St. Luke's Hosp., Kansas City, 1969, head, div. of exptl. medicine, 1970-91, dir. rsch., 1980-91. Adj. prof. dept. physiology U. Kans. Med. Ctr., 1976-92; vis. prof. U. Kuopio, Finland, 1985, 91, U. Munich, 1992; vis. scientist German Inst. Aerospace Medicine, Cologne, 1993-94. Author (memoir): Bending the Twig, 2002. Recipient Alexander von Humboldt award, 1992. Fellow Am. Phys. Soc. (circulation sect.); mem. Am. Physiol. Soc., Alexander von Humboldt Assn. of Am. Achievements include research in Neurohumoral control of body fluid balance; influence of vasoctive peptides on hemodynamics; Vasopressin, atriopeptin, renal natriuretic peptide, endothelin; reflex control of the circulation. Home: 9535 Ash St # 211 Overland Park KS 66207 Personal E-mail: klg101@sbcglobal.net.

GOETZ, MATTHEW P., oncologist, educator; BA in Music, Wheaton Coll.; MD, U. ND Sch. Med. Cert. hematolgoy & oncology Am. Bd. Internal Med. Intern & resident U. Mich. Dept. Internal Med.; fellow Mayo Grad. Sch. Med.; breast cancer oncologist Mayo Clinic, asst. prof. pharmacology & oncology, assoc. prof., oncology & pharmacology. Office: Mayo Clinic Cancer Center 200 First St SW Rochester MN 55905 E-mail: goetz.matthew@mayo.edu.

GOETZ, RAYMOND RICHARD, medical researcher; b. Yonkers, NY, Dec. 15, 1951; BA, CUNY, 1976; PhD, Yeshiva U., 1983. Rsch. scientist Rsch. Found. Mental Hygiene (NYSPI), 1984—2004; asst. prof. med. psychology Columbia U. Coll. Physicians and Surgeons, 1987—; data mgr., analyst, rsch. design and statis. cons. NY State Psychiat. Inst., 1987—, rsch. scientist, 2007—, Mt. Sinai Sch. Medicine, 2004—06. Mem.: NY Acad. Sci. Avocation: music. Office: 1051 Riverside Dr New York NY 10032 Office Fax: 212-543-5386. Business E-Mail: rrg1@columbia.edu.

GOETZL, EDWARD JOSEPH, allergist, immunologist, educator; b. NYC, Nov. 6, 1941; MD, Harvard U., 1966. Diplomate Am. Bd. Allergy and Immunology. Intern Peter Bent Brigham Hosp., Boston, 1966-67, resident in medicine, 1967-68, 70-71; fellow in immunology Harvard U., Boston, 1971-73; dir. allergy and immunology, prof. med. micro-immunology U. Calif., San Francisco, 1982—, Robert L. Kroc prof. rheumatic diseases, 1985—. Attending physician Moffitt Long Hosps., U. Calif., San Francisco, 1982—; sr. clin. investigator Nat. Inst. on Aging, 2008-. Fellow ACP, AAAS; mem. Am. Acad. Allergy, Asthma and Immunology, Am. Assn. Immunology, Assn. Am. Physicians, Am. Soc. Clin. Investigation, Am. Soc. Biochemistry and Molecular Biology. Office: UCSF Geriat Research Ctr 302 Silver Ave San Francisco CA 94112

GOFF, STEPHEN PAYNE, molecular biologist, educator; b. Providence, Oct. 22, 1951; s. Godfrey and Virginia (Ross) G.; m. Marian B. Carlson, Oct. 15, 1977; children: Sarah Carlson Goff, Thomas Carlson Goff. AB, Amherst Coll., 1973; PhD, Stanford U., 1978; DSc (hon.), Amherst Coll., 1996. Postdoctoral fellow MIT, Cambridge, 1978-81; asst. prof. biochemistry Columbia U., NYC, 1981-85, assoc. prof., 1985-86, prof., 1986—90, Higgins prof. biochemistry and molecular biophysics, 1990—; investigator Howard Hughes Med. Inst., 1993—. Mem. NIH study sect., 1984-88, virology sci. adv. bd. Progenics Pharms., 1988-, chmn. 1991-. Mem. edit. bd. Jour. Virology, Molecular Cell Biology; editor Jour. Virology; contbr. articles to profl. jours. Recipient Irma T. Hirschl Career Devel. award Hirschl Found., 1982-1986, Searle Scholarship award G.D. Searl, Chgo., 1982-1985, Merit award NIH, 1990, 2004, Retrovirology prize 2005. Fellow Am. Acad. Arts Scis., Am. Acad. Microbiol.; mem. NAS. Office: Columbia U Coll of Physicians and Surgeons 701 W 168th St HHSC 1310 New York NY 10032

GOFFMAN, THOMAS EDWARD, radiation oncologist; b. Chgo., Apr. 16, 1953; s. E. and A. (Choate) G.; divorced; 1 child, James Edward. BA, Yale U., 1975; MD, Hahnemann U., 1979. Diplomate Am. Bd. Radiology, Am. Bd. Internal Medicine, Am. Coll. Radiation Oncology. Intern, resident Georgetown U. Hosp., Washington, 1979-82; med. staff fellow, epidemiology tng. program Nat. Cancer Inst., NIH, Bethesda, Md., 1982-83; resident in radiotherapy, Joint Ctr. for Radiation Therapy Harvard U. Med. Sch., Boston, 1983-86; instr. in radiation oncology Columbia U., NYC, 1986-87, asst. prof. of radiation oncology, 1987; attending in radiation oncology Washington Hosp. Ctr., 1987-89, vice chmn. dept. radiation oncology, 1988-89; asst. dir. radiation oncology Sibley Meml. Hosp., 1989; asst. clin. prof. radiation medicine Georgetown U., 1989—; assoc. prof. dept. radiation oncology/biophysics, med. dir. Sentora Norfolk Gen. Hosp., Va., 1997—, chief radiation oncology, 1997—99. Head clin. therapy sect., radiation oncology br. Nat. Cancer Inst., Bethesda, 1989—; asst. prof. radiology USUHS, Bethesda, 1989-91, dir. radiation oncology tng., 1989-92, assoc. prof. radiology, 1991-92; dir. radiation oncology tng. Nat. Cancer Inst. USUHS, Bethesda, 1990-92; dir. radiation oncology St. Agnes Hosp., Balt., 1992-93; rschr. internat. epidemiology nat. radiation NIH, 1983-84; med. dir. radiol. oncology Sentara Norfolk Gen. Hosp., 1999-2000, adj. prof. microbiology and molecular cell biology, Eastern Va. Med. Sch.; dir. Cancer Intelligence and Rsch., PC, 2005-; pres. Premier Avian Bird Flu Newsletter. Contbr. articles to numerous profl. jours. Bd. dirs. Lee's Friends, 2000—. Recipient Excellence in Medicine award, 1979, Blue Ribbon award, 1979; Mosby scholar, 1979, Nat. Rsch. Svc. award, 1983, Epidemiology Tng. fellow Nat. Cancer Inst.-NIH, 1983; named one of Top Physicians in Am., 2003, Americas Top Oncologists, Americas Top Radiologists, Am; Internat. Healthcare Profl. of Yr. (Gt. Britain), 2006; Best Am. Top Oncologists, 2008. Fellow ACP; mem. AAAS, ACS (oncology com. 2001—, bd. dirs.), Am. Soc. Clin. Oncology, Am. Soc. Therapeutic Radiology and Oncology (CMS com. 2003—), NY Acad. Scis., Com. on Physicians Assn., DC Med. Soc. (legis. com.), Nat. Cancer Inst. (internal rev. bd. 1989-90, biol. operating com. 1991-), Va. Med. Soc. (dir. cancer intelligence and rsch. com. 2005-, grant reviewer several jours. including CBRN work & internat. epidemiology, Named Top Oncologist, 2008, 09). Office Phone: 757-363-9885. Personal E-mail: tetomtg@yahoo.com.

GOFORTH, GARY ALAN, physician, educator; b. Honolulu, Apr. 20, 1955; MD, Vanderbilt Sch. Medicine, 1980; M in Tropical Medicine & Hygiene, Uniformed Svcs U. Health Scis., 1990. Family physician US Army, 1980—93; dir. med. edn., family medicine residency program dir., prof. Self Regional Healthcare, 1994—. Decorated Bronze star US Army; recipient Halford award, SC Area Health Edn. Consortium; named SC Acad. Family Physicians of Yr., 2008. Fellow: Am. Acad. Family Physicians; mem.: Volunteers Med. Missions, Christian Med. and Dental Assn., SC Med. Assn., Lakelands Rural Health Network. Avocations: horseback riding, scuba diving, computers. Office: 155 Academy Ave Greenwood SC 29646 Office Fax: 864-725-4883. Business E-Mail: ggoforth@selfregional.org.

GOGBASHIAN, ANDREW, surgeon, researcher; b. Welwyn Garden City, Eng., Oct. 31, 1977; s. Charles Andrew and Hilda Gogbashian; m. Lisa Suzanne Rogers, Dec. 23, 2000; 1 child, Luke Andrew. MD, Imperial Coll., London, 2001. Hon. rsch. fellow Royal Coll. Surgeons Eng., London, 2003—04; rsch. fellow Brigham & Women's Hosp., Boston, 2004—05, Beth Israel Deaconess Med. Ctr., Boston, 2004—05, Harvard Med. Sch., Boston, 2004—05; resident in surgery Hammersmith Hosp., London, 2005—06, resident in radiology, 2006—. Coord. endovascular aneurysm rsch. trial Charing Cross Hosp., London, 2001—02; anatomy instr. Imperial Coll. Sch. Medicine, London, 2002—03; spkr. in field. Contbr. articles to profl. jours. Recipient Burns prize, Imperial Coll. Sch. Medicine, 1996, Cert. of Merit in anatomy, 1995, Cert. of Merit in biochemistry, 1997, Rheumatology prize, Arthritis Rsch. Coun. United Kingdom, 2001; Rsch. fellow, Brigham & Women's Hosp., 2004. Mem.: Royal Coll. Surgeons Edinburgh, Royal Coll. Surgeons Eng. (George Quist Anatomy prize 1996). Evangelical. Achievements include development of novel device for treatment of aortic regurgitation secondary to aortic root dilatation; risk stratification scoring system to predict risk of atrial fibrillation in cardiac surgery utilizing nationwide US data; first to create meta-analysis of a risk scoring system within cardiac surgery. Avocations: computers, tennis. Personal E-mail: andrew@cardiacforum.com.

GOGINENI, RAMA RAO, physiatrist; MD, Kakatiya U., 1973. Diplomate Am. Bd. Psychiatry and Neurology-child and adolescent psychiatry. Intern Osmania Gen. Hosp., India; resident in psychiatry Univ. Pa. Hosp.; fellow Pa. Univ.; assoc. prof. Copper Univ. Hosp., head divsn. of child and adolescent psychiatry. Office: Copper University Hospital One Copper Plz Camden NJ 08103 Office Phone: 856-342-2000.

GOH, EUI-KYUNG, surgeon, educator; b. Jeju, Korea, July 16, 1953; s. Taek-gu and Junghee Hong Goh; m. Mie Lee, Apr. 19, 1981; children: Jinyoung, Taesik. MD, Pusan Nat. U., Busan, Korea, 1978; PhD, Pusan Nat. U., 1989. Asst., assoc. prof. Busan Nat. U. Med. Sch., Busan, Republic of Korea, 1986—97; prof. Pusan Nat. U. Med. Sch., Busan, Republic of Korea, 1998—2010, vice dean, 1999—2001, chmn. dept., 2001—07. Author: Equilibrium and Disequilibrium, 2005, Textbook of Otolaynology, 2002; editor: Tinnitus, 1999. Cons. Korean Health Ins. Review Agy., Seoul, 2003—06; pres. Korean Balance Soc., Seoul, 2007—09. Capt. Medicine, 1983—86, Republic of Korea. Mem.: Barany Soc., Politzer Soc., Am. Acad. Otolaryngology, Korean Otolaryngology Soc. Avocations: sports, golf. Office: Nat U Hosp 1-10 Ami-Dong Busan Republic of Korea 602 -739 Business E-Mail: gohek@pusan.ac.kr.

GOH, PAUL SOO CHYE, physician, director and senior consultant; MBBS, BChir, Nat. U. Singapore, 1987, M in Medicine, 1994. Registered Singapore Med. Coun. Regional head East Zone Polyclinics, Singapore, 1996—97; dep. dir. Family Health Svc., Singapore, 1998—2000; CEO Sing Health Polyclinics, Singapore, 2000—02, chmn., instl. rev. bd., 2002—; head Tampines Polyclinic, Singapore, 1997—99, dir., 2002—. Examiner, grad. sch. medicine Nat. U. Singapore, 1999—, clin. tchr., family medicine undergrad. programme, 1994—, supr. and trainer postgrad. family medicine programme, 1994—. Contbr. articles to profl. jours. Decorated SAF Good Svc. Medal, SAF Long Svc. and Good Conduct Medal; recipient Long Svc. award, Ministry Health, Sing Health Polyclinics, Excellent Svc. Gold award, Spring Singapore, 2008; Health Manpower Devel. Programme fellowship, Ministry Health, Singapore, Examiner fellowship, Coll. Family Physicians (Singapore), 2005—. Fellow: Coll. Family Physicians(Singapore). Office: Tampines Polyclinic 1 Tampines St 41 Singapore 529203 Singapore Home: 220 Wolskel Road Serangoon Park 358005 Singapore Singapore Personal E-mail: paul.goh@singhealth.com.sg.

GOIN, MARCIA KRAFT, physician; b. Portsmouth, NH, June 27, 1932; d. Wendell Everett and Dorothy (Spurr) Kraft; m. John Morehead Goin, Mar. 5, 1960 (dec. May 1995); children: Suzanne J., Jessica M. BA, Middlebury Coll., 1954; MD, Yale U., 1958; PhD, So. Calif. Psycho-Analytic Inst., 1972; DSc (hon.), Middlebury Coll., 2004. Intern in medicine U. Calif., San Francisco, 1958-59; resident in psychiatry U. So. Calif. Med. Sch., LA, 1959-62; pvt. practice psychiatry and psychoanalysis LA, 1962—; dir. residency edn. psychiat. outpatient dept. L.A. County/U. So. Calif. Med. Ctr., 1980—; clin. prof. psychiatry and behavioral scis. U. So. Calif. Sch. Medicine, 1980—. Co-author: Changing the Body: Psychological Effects of Plastic Surgery, 1981; author (med. jour. column) Practical Psychiatry and Behavioral Health, 1998—; contbr. articles to profl. jours. Mem. L.A. Coun. World Affairs. Recipient Humanitarian Svc. award AMA, 1964, Cert. of Merit, Am. Soc. Plastic Surgeons, 1985, Exemplary Psychiatrist award Nat. Alliance Mentally, Ill. chpt., 2005, Exceptional Mentoring award U. So. Calif., 2005. Fellow Am. Psychiat. Assn. (cons. commn. on psychotherapy 1993—, cons. steering com. practice guidelines 1993—, com. on grad. edn. 1997-99, elected trustee-at-large bd. trustees 1997-2000, v.p. 2000-2002, pres.-elect 2002-2003, pres. 2003-2004), Am. Coll. Psychiatrists; mem. Am. Soc. Aesthetic Surgery (assoc.), So. Calif. Psychoanalytic Inst. (faculty), So. Calif. Psychiat. Soc. (Disting. Svc. award 1991, 2005). Episcopalian. Avocations: tennis, travel, international politics. Office: 1127 Wilshire Blvd Ste 1115 Los Angeles CA 90017-4002 Home Phone: 323-469-5267; Office Phone: 213-977-1129. Business E-Mail: mgoin@usc.edu.

GOITZ, ROBERT J., orthopedist, educator; Grad. in Biomedical Engring., Boston U.; MD, Johns Hopkins U. Diplomate Am. Bd. Orthopaedic Surgery, Am. Bd. Orthopaedic Surgery-hand surgery. Fellow Ind. Univ. Hosps.; resident Univ. of Pitts. Med. Sch., assoc. prof orthopaedic surgery and plastic and reconstructive surgery; chief divsn, hand and upper extremity surgery Univ. of Pitts. Med. Ctr. Presbyterian; med. cons. athletics dept. Univ. of Pitts.; hosp. affiliations include UPMC Presbyterian South Surgery Ctr., Children's Hosp. of Pitts. of UPMC, UPMC Children's Surgery Centers; assoc. prof. bioengineering Pitt's Swanson Sch. of Engring. Vol. Nat. Disability Sport Alliance. Named one of Best Doctors in America, 2005—. Mem.: Pa. Orthopaedic Soc., Am. Soc. for Surgery of the Hand, Am. Orthopaedic Assn. Office: University of Pittsburgh Medical Center Department of Orthopaedic Surgery Ste 1010 3471 Fifth Ave Pittsburgh PA 15213 Office Phone: 412-687-3900.

GÖKÇE, AHMET, medical educator; b. Afyon, Turkey, Jan. 1, 1974; Degree, Ege U., 1998. Asst. prof. Mustafa Kemal U., 2008—. Office: Hatay Antakya 31030 Turkey Personal E-mail: aagokce@yahoo.com.

GOKHALE, PARAG ANANT, ophthalmologist; b. Olympia, Wash., Oct. 9, 1969; s. Anant Vaman and Kumud Anant Gokhale; m. Anuradha M. Limaye. BS, U. Utah, Salt Lake City, 1991, MD, 1995. Diplomate Am. Bd. Ophthalmology, 2000. Glaucoma fellow Shiley Eye Ctr., U. Calif. San Diego, La Jolla, 1999—2000; faculty physician Med. Coll. Ga., Augusta, 2000—06; eye physician, surgeon Va. Mason Med. Ctr., Seattle, 2006—. Named one of Ams. Top Ophthalmologists, Consumers Rsch. Coun., 2002—03, Best Dr. America, 2005—06, 2009—. Mem.: Am. Acad. Ophthalmology. Achievements include research in sleep apnea and glaucoma. Office: Va Mason Med Ctr 1100 Ninth Ave Seattle WA 98101

GOKHALE, SANJAY, pediatrician, consultant; b. Pune, Maharashtra, India, Jan. 2, 1956; s. Gajanan Sakharam and Neelakshi Gajanan Gokhale; m. Samruddhi Sanjay Bavdekar, Jan. 24, 1980; 1 child, Sankalp Sanjay. MD in Pediats., U. Mumbai, 1981; diploma in Child Health, Coll. Physicians and Surgeons, Mumbai. Jr. resident, registrar B.J. Wadia Hosp. Children, Wadia Inst. Child Health, Mumbai, 1979—81; cons., dept. pediat. & neonatology Rajhans Hosp. Saphale, Mumbai, 1981—, pediatrician, 1981—. Mem. internat. editl. bd. New Iraq Jour. Medicine; reviewer Brit. Med. Jour., England, Internat. Jour. Cardiology, Australia, Iran Jour. Pediat., Indian Jour. Clin. Medicine, Autism Insight, New Zealand. Contbr. scientific papers to profl. pubs.; reviewer: Brit. Med. Jour., Internat. Jour. Cardiology, Jour. Pediat., Jour. Medicine. Recipient Rashtriya Gourav award, India Internat. Friendship Soc. Med. Work, 2007. Mem.: Healthcare Adv. Bd. (Can.), Internat. Bio-Pharm. Assn., Assn. Clin. Rsch. Profls., Am. Acad. Pediats., Heart Valve Soc. America (corr.; sci. adv. bd. mem.), Indian Med. Assn. (life), Indian Acad. Pediat. (life), Indian Med. Assn. (life). Achievements include research in congenital malformations; postulated new hypothesis to explain associated malformations like Vacterl, Holt-Oram's Syndrome, others, on the basis of Darwinian evolution and genetic control of embryological morphogenesis; organized health and vaccination camps and helped various organizations in rehabilitaion programs for victims of flood and cyclone hit areas. Avocations: classical music, flute. Office: Rajhans Hosp Dept Pediatrics Station Rd Saphale Mumbai 401102 India Office Phone: 02525 636441. Personal E-mail: rajhanssanjay@yahoo.com.

GOKSEL, TAMER, oral surgeon, director; b. Istanbul, Turkey, Aug. 6, 1960; s. Ruhan Etem and Sevgi Ayse Goksel; m. Gloria Rincon; children: Will, Kate. BA, U. Va., Charlottesville, 1987; DDS, U. Tenn., Memphis, 1992; MD, U. Tex., San Antonio, 1999. Lic. Oral and Maxillofacial Surgery San Antonio Uniformed Svcs. Health Edn. Consortium, Tex., 2002, diplomate Am. Bd. Oral and Maxillofacial Surgery, Ill., 2004, Am. Bd. Cosmetic Surgery, 2007. Fellow gen. cosmetic surgery Am. Acad. Cosmetic Surgery, Little Rock, 2002—03; chief oral and maxillofacial surgery 31st Combat Support Hosp., Baghdad, 2004; chief program dir. Oral and Maxillofacial Surgery Residency, Brooke Army Med. Ctr., Ft. Sam Houston, Tex., 2006—07; chief, program dir. Eisenhower Army Med. Ctr., 2007—. Col. US Army, 1995. Decorated Meritorious Svc. medal Pres. US, Bronze Star medal, Combat Action Badge US Army, Order of Mil. Med. merit; named Surgeon Gen. A Proficiency Designator. Fellow: ACS, Am. Coll. Oral and Maxillofacial Surgeons; mem.: AMA, ADA, Am. Acad. Cosmetic Surgery, Am. Assn. Oral and Maxillofacial Surgeons. Conservative. Home: 519 Fort Augusta St Evans GA 30809-7217 Office: Eisenhower Army Med Ctr 300 E Hospital Rd Fort Gordon GA 30905 Home Phone: 706-364-7427; Office Phone: 706-787-5322. Home Fax: 706-787-1904. Business E-Mail: tamer.goksel@amedd.army.mil.

GÖL, MERT, medical educator; b. Edirne, Turkey, Dec. 1, 1971; Degree, Dokuz Eylul U. Sch. Medicine, 1996. Assoc. prof., dept. ob-gyn. Canakkale Onsekiz Mart U. Sch. Medicine, 2007—. Dept. head. TUBITAK grant, Charite U. Mem.: Turkish Gynecology and Obstetrics. Office: Terzioglu Campus Canakkale Marmara 17100 Turkey Personal E-mail: drgyno@hotmail.com.

GOLBAHAR, JAMAL, medical educator; b. Shiraz, Apr. 19, 1960; BSc, MSc, Leeds U., PhD, 1997. Assoc. prof. molecular medicine Coll. Medicine and Med. Scis., Bahrain, 2005—. Mng. dir. diagnostic svcs. Al-Jawhara Ctr. Molecular Medicine and Inherited Disorders, 2005—. Mem.: Am. Soc. Human Genetics. Office: Oman Rd PO Box 22979 Manama Salmania Bahrain Business E-Mail: jamalgo@agu.edu.bh.

GOLBE, LAWRENCE INGRAM, neurologist; b. NYC, Oct. 1, 1952; s. Alvin Victor and Cynthia (Boyars) G.; m. Devra Lifshitz; children: Jonathan, Susan. AB, Brown U., 1974; MD, NYU Sch. Medicine, 1978. Diplomate Am. Bd. Psychiatry and Neurology. Resident, then chief resident in neurology NYU-Bellevue Med. Ctr., NYC, 1980-83; instr. neurology Robert Wood Johnson Med. Sch., New Brunswick, NJ, 1983-89, assoc. prof., 1989-97, prof., 1997—; dir. Neurology Residency, NB, 2000—; mem. bd. dirs. Dwight Morraw HS Alumni Ednl. Alliance, 2004—; chmn. Dwight Morrow HS Alumni Ednl. Alliance, 2009—. Mem. editl. bd. Movement Disorders, 1997-2000, mem. bd. dirs., Peebler PSP Rsch. Found., 2004-2011. Mem. Am. Neurol. Assn., Soc. for Progressive Supranuclear Palsy (dir. rsch. & clin. affairs 1990-). Office: Robert Wood Johnson Med Sch Dept Neurology 125 Paterson St New Brunswick NJ 08901-2160 Office Phone: 732-235-7729. Business E-Mail: golbe@umdnj.edu.

GOLD, ALAN H., plastic surgeon; b. Bronx, NY, 1946; MD, SUNY-Downstate Med. Ctr., 1971. Diplomate Am. Bd. Plastic Surgery. Intern North Shore U. Hosp., Manhasset, NY, 1971—72, resident in gen. surgery, 1972—75; resident in plastic surgery Kings County-SUNY Med. Ctr., Bklyn., 1976—78; fellow in hand surgery Nassau County Med. Ctr., East Meadow, NY, 1975—76; pvt. practice plastic surgery Great Neck, NY, 1979—. Attending plastic surgeon North Shore U. Hosp., Manhassett. Mem.: Am. Soc. Plastic Surgeons, Am. Soc. for Aesthetic Plastic Surgery. Office: 833 Northern Blvd Ste 240 Great Neck NY 11021-5308 Home Phone: 516-496-9229; Office Phone: 516-498-2800.

GOLD, ARNOLD P., neurologist; b. NYC, Aug. 8, 1925; s. Michael and Rebecca (Perlman) Gold; m. Sandra Orenberg, Nov. 17, 1969; children: Jeffrey, Stephen, Jennifer, Amelia, Margaret. BA, U. Tex., 1947; MS, U. Fla., 1949; MD, U. Lausanne, 1954; D (hon.), U. Medicine & Dentistry N.J., 2001; DSc (hon.), Sacred Heart U., 2003, Mt. Sinai Med. Sch., 2008. Diplomate Am. Bd. Pediatrics, in child neurology Am. Bd. Psychiatry and Neurology. Intern Charity Hosp of La., New Orleans, 1954—55; resident, chief resident in pediat. Children's Hosp., Cin., 1955—58; NIH fellow in pediatric neurology Columbia Presbyn. Med. Ctr., NYC, 1958—61; prof. clin. neurology Columbia U., NYC, 1976—, prof. clin. pediat., 1976—, attending neurologist, 1958—, attending pediatrician, 1958—; advisory bd. Winston Sch., Short Hills, NJ, 2004—09. Cons. Cmty. Sch., Teaneck, NJ, 1975—; mem. interdisciplinary coun. Devel. and Learning Disabilities, Bethesda, Md., 1997—; attending neurologist and pediatrician N.Y. Presbyn. Hosp., 1999—; attending pediatrician Stanley Morgan Children's Hosp., NYC, 1999—. Editor, author: Neurology of Infancy and Childhood, 1974, Pediatric Therapy, 1963—80, Pediatrics, 1968, 1996; author: Merritt's Textbook of Neurology, 1984—2008. Chmn. Arnold P. Gold Found., 2005—07, bd. dirs., 1984—2010, Homes for Developmentally Disabled, NJ, 1984—; pres. Myoclonus Rsch. Found., 1992—2004; trustee, sec. AMA Found., 1999—2004; adv. coun. Naomi Berrie Diabetes Ctr., NYC, 1997—; adv. bd. Winston Sch., Short Hills, NJ; pres. Arnold P. Gold Found., Engelwood Cliffs, NJ, 1983—99, pres. bd. dirs., 1983—99, chmn. bd., 1983—2005; bd. dirs. N.J. Med. Sch., 1983—2007; admissions com. Ben Guron U., Beer-Sheeva, Israel, 1997—98; trustee, bd. advisors N.J. Med. Sch., 2001—. Recipient Brennerman award in pediat., 1968, Man of Yr. award, Assn. Brain Injured Children, 1968, Disting. Svc. award, Speech-Lang.-Hearing Assn., 1993, Miracle Maker of N.Y., Children's Miracle Network, 1994, Practitioner of Yr. award, Columbia Presbn. Med. Ctr., 1992, Disting. Svc. award, Columbia U., 1999, Lifetime Cmty. Svc. award, Autism Soc. Am., 2000, Humanitarian award, Sinai Inst., 2002, Humanitarian award multiple sclerosis rsch., U. Medicine and Dentistry N.J., 2003, Humanitarian award, N.J. Coun. for the Humanities, 2004, Disting. Citizen award, NJ Med. Sch., 2005, Pres.'s award, AMA Found., 2006, Edward J. Ill Excellence in Medicine award, 2007, award, Presbyn. Hosp. Alumni Assn., 2009, Leonard Tow Humanism Medicine award, 2009, Disting. Alumnus, Alumnus Soc. NY Presbyn. Hosp., Picker prize, 2010; named Best Dr. in Am., Am. Health Mar. issue, 1996, Best Dr. in N.Y., 1997, 1998, 1999, 2000, 2001. Fellow: Internat. Child Neurology Soc., Child Neurology Soc. (Lifetime Achievement award 2005), Am. Acad. Neurology, Am. Pediatric Soc., Am. Acad. Pediat. Avocations: gardening, stamp collecting/philately, travel, reading. Office: Neurol Inst NY 710 W 168th St New York NY 10032-2603 Office Phone: 212-305-5483. Business E-Mail: apg1@columbia.edu.

GOLD, AVRAM R., pulmonologist, educator; b. Highland Pk., NJ, Feb. 18, 1954; BA, NYU, 1975; MD, SUNY Downstate, 1979. Assoc. prof., Sch. Medicine Stony Brook U., 1988—, program dir., polysomnographic tech. program, Sch. Health Tech. and Mgmt., 2004—, program dir., sleep medicine fellowship, Sch. Medicine, 2007—, med. dir., Sleep Disorders Ctr., 2010—. Fellow: Am. Acad. Sleep Medicine; mem.: Am. Thoracic Soc. Office: DVA Med Ctr (111D) 79 Middlevile Rd Northport NY 11768 Office Fax: 631-266-6016. Business E-Mail: avram.gold@va.gov.

GOLD, JEFFREY PHILIP, cardiothoracic surgeon, dean, academic administrator; b. Bklyn., Aug. 16, 1952; BSE in Theoretical & Applied Mechanics, Cornell U., 1974, MD, 1978. Intern in gen. surgey The N.Y. Hosp., NYC, 1978-79, resident, 1979-82, adminstrv. chief resident, 1982-83, attending cardiothoracic surgeon, attending pediatrician, 1993-96; resident cardiothoracic surgery Brigham & Womnen's Hosp., Boston, 1983-84; resident pediatric cardiothoracic surgey Boston Children's Hosp., 1984-85; asst. prof. surgery cardiothoracic surgery Hosp. Spl. Surgery, 1983-91, asst. prof. pediatrics cardiothoracic surgery, 1983-91, assoc. prof., 1991-94; cardiothoracic surgeon-in-chief Albert Einstein Coll. Medicine, 1987—, Montefiore Med. Ctr., 1996—; prof. cardiothoracic surgery Med. Coll. Columbia U., 1993-96; prof. pediat. cardiothoracic surgery, chmn. Unified Dept. Cardiothoracic Surgery Albert Einstein Coll. Medicine, 1996—2005; dean Coll. Medicine U. Toledo, Ohio, 2005—, prof. surgery and pub. health, 2005—, sr. v.p. med. affairs, 2005—10, chancellor, exec. v.p. biosciences and health affairs, 2010—. Instr. surgery Cornell Med. Coll., biology Cornell Arts Coll., physics, grad. bioengring. Cornell Engring. Coll., undergrad. bioengring; clin. fellow surgery Harvard Med. Sch.; clin. instr. Cornell U. Coll. Medicine Surgery; instr., prosecutor Cornell U. Coll. Medicine Anatomy; program lectr. Surgeon's Asst. Program Cornell U.; dir. Montefiore Thoracic Surgery Tng. Program; co-dir. Montefiore-Einstein Cardiovascular Ctr. Assn. Abstract editor Surgery Gynecology & Obs.; editor: Internat. Dictionary of Biology & Medicine in Pediatric & General Surgery; sr. dept. editor Infections in Surgery; contbr. articles to profl. jours. Com. advisor N.Y. State Cardiac Adv. Com. John T. Hirschl scholar; recipient Degenshein award Greater N.Y. Breast Cancer Group, 1983, Excellence in Profl. & Scholarly Pubs. award Assn. Am. Pub., 1993, Acad. Excellence in Medicine award Merck Sharp & Dohme, Med. Scholarship award Lange Pubs.; named The Best Drs. in Am. Am. Health Mag., Best Drs. in N.Y. N.Y. Mag.; #1 rated cardiac surgeon N.Y. State Dept. Health. 1991, 92, 93; ann. endowed lectureship Jeffrey P. Gold Professordhip in Cardiothoracic Surgery, 1996. Fellow AMA, NIH, Am. Assn. Thoracic Surgeons (young profs. com.), Am. Coll. Angiology, Am. Coll. Cardiology, Am. Coll. Chest Physicians (surg. liaison com., program com. 1995, 96, surg. forum chmn. 1995), Am. Coll. Surgeons, Am. Heart Assn. (bd. dirs. 1995—, devel. com. 1995—, gala planning com. 1995, 96, 97), Assn. Acad. Surgery, Assn. Advancement Med. Instrumentation, N.Y. Acad. Medicine (adv. com., bioengring. com.), Internat. Soc. Cardiac Transplantation, Mass. Med. Soc., Nat. Assn. Advancement Sci., Am. Surg. Assn., N.Y. Cardiol. Soc., N.Y. Pediat. Soc., N.Y. Soc. Thoracic Surgery (pres. 1994-95, v.p. 1993-94, sec.-treas. 1988-93, chmn. post-grad. edn. 1999—), N.Y. Soc. Cardiology (bd. dirs.), N.Y. State Soc. Surgeons, Royal Soc. Medicine, Soc. Thoracic Surgeons, Soc. Univ. Surgeons, Tau Beta Pi (Eminent Engr. award 1983), Thoracic Surgery Dirs. Assn. (curriculum implementation task force, prerequisite edn. task force). Office: Univ Toledo Health Sci Campus Mulford Library Rm 213 MS 1018 3000 Arlington Ave Toledo OH 43614 Office Phone: 419-383-4243. Office Fax: 419-383-6100. Business E-Mail: jeffrey.gold@utoledo.edu. *

GOLD, JOSEPH, medical researcher; b. Binghamton, NY, Jan. 17, 1930; s. Leon and Gertrude J. G.; m. Judith Barbara Taylor, June 12, 1955; children: Shannon Gabriel, Skye Raphael. AB, Cornell U., 1952; MD, Upstate Med. Univ., Syracuse, 1956. Diplomate Nat. Bd. Med. Examiners. USPHS postdoctoral rsch. fellow U. Calif. Sch. Medicine, 1956—58; fellow dept. pharmacology Upstate Med. Univ., Syracuse, 1961—62, rsch. asst. prof., 1962—64, asst. prof. pathology, 1964—65; dir. Syracuse Cancer Rsch. Inst., 1965—, trustee, 1965—. Editor: Monsters and Madonnas, The Roots of Christian Antisemitism, 1999; contbr. numerous articles on cancer rsch. and therapy; contbr. chpts. to books. Served with USAF, 1958-61. Recipient Presdl. citation for work in Mercury Astronaut Selection Program, 1960; named Disting. Grad. Binghamton Sch. Dist., 1994. Mem. Am. Assn. Cancer Rsch., Am. Assn. for Lab. Animal Sci., NY Acad. Scis., Onondaga County Med. Soc., Med. Soc. State NY. Achievements include pioneering work in proposing gluconeogenesis as a biochemical mechanism of cancer cachexia, 1968; development of hydrazine sulfate, 1st specific anti-cachexia drug to be used in human cancer; invention of process for the synthesis and prodn. of DL-Glyceraldehyde-3-phosphate in a pure and stable form; patentee in field. Home: 127 Edgemont Dr Syracuse NY 13214-2010 Office: 600 E Genesee St Syracuse NY 13202-3111 Office Phone: 315-472-6616.

GOLD, JUDITH HAMMERLING, psychiatrist; b. NYC, June 24, 1941; d. James S. and Anne (Linder) Hammerling; m. Edgar Gold, June 27, 1965. MD, Dalhousie U., 1965; DHumL (hon.), Mt. St. Vincent U., 2002. Intern Victoria Gen. Hosp., Halifax, N.S., Canada, 1964-65; resident Dalhousie U., Halifax, 1967-71; practice medicine specializing in psychiatry Halifax, 1971—2002; staff psychiatrist Dalhousie U. Student Health Clinic, 1971-73; vis. colleague U. Wales Med. Sch., 1973-75; asst. prof. dept. psychiatry Dalhousie U., Halifax, 1975-78, assoc. prof., 1978-80, part-time, 1980-87; pvt. practice Brisbane, 1998—2007. Vis. prof., reader in psychotherapy studies dept. psychiatry U. Queensland, Brisbane, 1998-99. Editor: Clinical Practice Series, 1987-2001, 6 books; contbr. articles to profl. jours. Bd. govs. Mt. St. Vincent U., 1981-87, chmn., 1986-87. Med. Research Council Can. fellow, 1973-75; Health and Welfare Bd. Can. grantee, 1976-78 Fellow Am. Psychiat. Assn., Am. Coll. Psychiatrists (1st v.p. 1990-91, pres.-elect 1991-92, pres. 1992-93); mem. Can. Psychiat. Assn. (pres. 1981-82), Royal Coll. Phys. Surgeons Can. (exec. mem. 1992-94, coun. 1991-98), Order Can., Alpha Omega Alpha.

GOLD, MICHAEL ROBERT, cardiologist; b. NYC, Nov. 9, 1953; MD, U. Colo., 1985; PhD, U. Va., 1979. Chief cardiology MUSC, 2002—. Fellow: ACC, HRS. Office: MUSC 25 Courtenay Dr ART 7031 Charleston SC 29425 Office Fax: 843-876-4990. Business E-Mail: goldmr@musc.edu.

GOLD, PHIL, immunologist, educator, researcher; b. Montreal, Sept. 17, 1936; m. Evelyn Katz; 3 children. BSc in Physiology with honors, McGill U., Montreal, 1957, MSc, MD, 1961, PhD in Physiology, 1965; DSc (hon.), McMaster U., 1986. Licentiate Med. Coun. Can. Jr. rotating intern Montreal Gen. Hosp., 1961—62, jr. asst. resident in medicine, 1962—63, sr. resident in medicine, 1965—66, jr. asst. physician, asst. and assoc. physician, 1967—73, sr. physician, 1973—2003, physician-in-chief, 1980-95, dir. divsn. clin. immunology and allergy, 1977—80, dir. McGill U. Med. Clinic, 1980—95, also sr. investigator Research Inst.; faculty dept. physiology McGill U., 1964—, mem. faculty of medicine, 1965—, prof. medicine and clin. medicine, 1973—, chmn. dept. medicine and clin. medicine, 1985—90, prof. physiology, 1974—, prof. oncology, 1989—, mem. faculty of medicine exec. com. representing clin. depts., 1985—, D. G. Cameron prof. medicine (inaugural), 1987—; exec. dir. Clin. Rsch. Ctr. Mont. Gen. Hosp. and McGill U. Hosp. Ctr., 1995—. Vis. scientist Pub. Health Research Inst. N.Y.C., 1967-68; Chester M. Jones Meml. lectr. Mass. Gen. Hosp., 1974; vis. prof. U. Caracas, Venezuela, 1974; Squires Club vis. prof. Wellesley Hosp., Toronto, 1983; Cecil H. and Ida Green vis. prof., 1984 autumn lectures U. Brit. Columbia; cons. in allergy and immunology Mt. Sinai Hosp., St. Agathe des Monts, Quebec, 1975—; hon. cons. dept. medicine Royal Victoria Hosp., Montreal; cons. dept. internal medicine Douglas Hosp. Ctr., Montreal; vice chmn. med. adv. com. Council of Physicians, Dentists and Pharmacists, 1985-90; mem. Conseil d'Adminstrn., Found. Quebecoise du Cancer, 1986-88, adv. com. Burroughs Wellcome fellowship fund, 1998—; health com. mem. Centre d'Entreprises et d'Innovation de Montreal, 1996—; Sir Arthur Sims travelling prof., 1998; inaugurator Phil Gold chair medicine cGill U. Health Ctr, 2006. Mem. editorial bd. Clin. Immunology and Immunopathology, 1972—, Immunopharmacology, 1978—, Diagnostic Gynecology and Obstetrics, 1978-83, Oncodevelopmental Biology and Medicine, 1979—, Modern Medicine of Can., 1984-90, Jour. Internal Medicine, 1988—, Canadians for Health Rsch., 1989—, Current Therapeutic Rsch., 1992—, Nutrition Quar., 1992—; editorial cons. Jour. Chronic Diseases, 1981-84; mem. editorial adv. bd. Cancer Research, 1971-73, assoc. editor 1973-80; contbg. editor Practical Allergy and Immunology, 1991—; editl. bd. Can. Jour. Allergy & Clin. Immunology, 1996—; contbr. over 140 articles to med. jours. External referee Can. Red Cross Soc. Decorated companion Order of Can., officer L'ordre nat. du Quebec, Great Montrealer, knight comdr. Sovereign Order St. John Jerusalem, Knights of Malta; recipient Hiram Mills Gold medal, Mosby Scholarship Book award, Wood Gold medal, E.W.R. Steacie prize, Nat. Rsch. Coun. Can., 1973, Can. Silver Jubilee medal, 1977, Johann-Georg-Zemmerman prize for cancer rsch., Medizinische Hochschule, Hannover, Germany, 1978, Gold medal award of merit, Internat. award, Gardner Found., Ernest C. Manning prize, F.N.G. Starr award Izzak Walton Killam prize, Can. Coun., 1985, Tower of Hope award, Israel Cancer Rsch. Fund, 1985, Sci. Achievement medal, Govt. of Italy, 1990, Agora trophy, Ambassador's Club, 1991, Internat. Soc. Oncodevel. Biol. Medicine Internat. Abbott award, 1992, Commemorative medal 125th Anniversary of Can. Confedn., Govt. of Can., 1992, Carl Goresky Meml. award, 1999, Christie award, Can. Assn. of Profs. of Medicine, 1999, 20th Anniversary of L'Actualité Medicale award for outstanding contbns.

to medicine, 2000, Queen Elizabeth II Golden Jubilee medal, 2002, Edwin F. Ullman award, Am. Assn. for Clin. Chemistry, 2004, Alpha Omega Achievement medal, 2005, Exception Merit award, Can. Soc. Immunology, 2004; named Most Outstanding Can. Med. Personality of the past 25 years, MacLean's Mag., 1986, Establishment of Phil Gold Chair Medicine award, McGill U., 2006; MacDonald scholar, J. Francis Williams scholar, Univ. scholar. Fellow: AAAS; mem.: Internat. Assn. Health Profls. (chmn. 1998). Achievements include discovery of carcinoembryonic antigen. Office: Clin Rsch Ctr Montreal Gen Hosp 1650 Cedar Ave Montreal PQ Canada H3G 1A4 Office Phone: 514-934-8339. Business E-Mail: phil.gold@mcgill.ca.

GOLD, ROBERT LOUIS, cardiologist; MD, U. Md., 1978. Diplomate Am. Bd. Internal Medicine, Am. Bd. Internal Medicine-cardiovasc. disease, Am. Bd. Internal Medicine-clin. cardiac electrophysiology. Fellow cardiology George Wash. Univ. Hosp., 1983; former dir. electrophysiologic lab. Univ. of Mass.; dir. electrophysiologic lab. Shady Grove Adventist Hosp. Named one of Top Doctors, Washingtonian Mag., 2011. Fellow: Am. Coll. of Cardiology. Office: Shady Grove Adventist Hospital 9901 Medical Center Dr Rockville MD 20850 Office Phone: 240-826-6000.

GOLD, SCOTT D., otolaryngologist, educator; MD, Mt. Sinai Sch. Medicine, 1979. Diplomate Am. Bd. Otolaryngology. Attending physician St. Vincent's Med. Ctr.; resident in otolaryngology Mt. Sinai Med. Ctr., NYC, 1980—83, resident in gen. surgery, asst. clin. prof. otolaryngology, attending physician; chief of otolaryngology Beth Israel Med. Ctr., attending physician. Mem.: Am. Acad. of Otolaryngology. Office: Beth Israel MEdical Center 36A E 36th St Ste 200 New York NY 10016 3401 Office Phone: 212 889 8575.

GOLD, STEVEN NEAL, psychology educator; b. Jackson Heights, NY, Nov. 9, 1953; s. Leonard Carl and Shirley Lee (Bernstein) G.; m. Margaret Marie Angelici, Sept. 4, 1983 (div.); children: Andrea Lauren, Lylah Raquel, Adam Jacob. BA in Psychology, Washington U., St. Louis, 1975; MA in Psychology, Mich. State U., 1977, PhD in Psychology, 1981. Lic. psychologist, Fla.; cert. clin. hypnosis, Am. Soc. Clin. Hypnosis. Instr. Ctrl. Mich. U., Mt. Pleasant, 1980-81, asst. prof., 1981-82, Nova Southeastern U., Ft. Lauderdale, Fla., 1982-86, assoc. prof., 1986—, prof., 1997—; pvt. practice psychology Plantation, Fla., 1983—. Clin. supr. Cmty. Mental Health Clinic, Nova Southea. U., 1982-83, clin. dir., 1983-87, dir. sexual abuse survivors program, 1990—, dir. trauma resolution integration program, 1997—; cons. Elaine Gordon Treatment Ctr., Pembroke Pines, Fla., 1986-89. Bd. dirs. Ramat Shalom Synagogue, Plantation, 1985-86, Sidran Found., 2007-. NIMH fellow 1976, 77, 79; recipient grad. scholar award Mich State U., 1980. Mem. APA (divsn. psychotherapy, divsn. hypnosis, divsn. addictions), Am. Soc. Clin. Hypnosis, Internat. Soc. Study of Trauma and Dissociation, Internat. Soc. Traumatic Stress Studies. Democrat. Jewish. Office: Nova Southea Univ 3301 College Ave Fort Lauderdale FL 33314-7721

GOLD, STUART HARRISON, pediatrician; b. Atlanta, June 22, 1955; MD, Vanderbilt U., Nashville, 1981. Cert. in pediat. 1986, in pediatric hematology-oncology 1987. Internship in pediat. U. Colo. Health Sci. Ctr., Denver, 1981—83, residency in pediatric hematol. oncology, 1982—84, chief residency in pediat., 1984—85, fellowship in pediatric hematology oncology, 1985—89; hosp. appointment Meml. Hosp., Chapel Hill, NC; asst. prof. U. NC Sch. Medicine, Chapel Hill, assoc. prof. pediat., clin. rsch. & outpatient clinic dir., Lineberger Comprehensive Cancer Ctr., prof. pediatric hematology oncology divsn., chief pediatric hematology oncology divsn., 2008—. Com. mem. Children's Cancer Group. Contbr. articles to profl. jours. Bd. officer Ronald McDonald House, Chapel Hill. Office: U NC Sch Medicine 407 Macnider Bldg CB 7236 Chapel Hill NC 27599 Office Phone: 919-966-0985. Office Fax: 919-966-7629. Business E-Mail: stuart_gold@med.unc.edu.

GOLD, WILLIAM ELLIOTT, health care management consultant, educator; b. Bklyn., Oct. 21, 1948; s. Theodore David and Debra (Fridovich) Gold; m. Nili Rachel Scharf, June 1, 1972; children: Avitai, Doria Michelle. BA, SUNY, Stony Brook, 1970; MSS, Hebrew U. Jerusalem, Israel, 1972; PhD, U. Minn., 1982. Rsch. asst. Hebrew U. Jerusalem, 1971—72; rschr. Mt. Sinai Hosp., Mpls., 1973—74; instr. hosp. adminstrn. U. Minn., Mpls., 1974—75; coord., dir. Blue Cross/Blue Shield Greater N.Y. HMO, NYC, 1975—85; v.p. Rush-Presbyn. St. Luke's Med. Ctr., Chgo., 1985—88; pres. Gold Health Strategies Inc., NYC, 1988—. Cons. Dept. Health, Mpls., 1973—74; pres. ANCHOR, Chgo.; bd. dirs. NY Bus. Group Health, chmn. managed care task force, 1989—; vice chmn. The HMO Group, 1987—88; mem. steering com. U. Mo-Kansas City Nat. Ctr. Managed Care Adminstrn., 1986—98; asst. adj. prof. Columbia U., NYC, 1989—99, clin. prof., 1999—. Founding editor: Managing Employee Health Benefits. Mem. task force pub. health and managed care PEW Charitable Trust, 1995—96; mem. task force improving cardiovasc. health Am. Heart Assn., NYC, 1995—96. Fellow, Caldwell B. Esselstyn Found., 1991—92. Avocations: clarinet, music, sports, photography. Home: 322 W 72nd St # 14B New York NY 10023-2676 Office: Gold Health Strategies Inc 250 Park Ave Ste 2020 New York NY 10177-0001 Home Phone: 212-724-1148; Office Phone: 212-953-1504. Personal E-mail: billgold@att.net. Business E-Mail: bgold@goldhealthstrategies.com.

GOLDBERG, AMY J., surgeon; BA, U. Pa., 1983; MD, Mt. Sinai Sch. of Medicine, NYC, NY, 1987. Diplomate Am. Bd. Surgery, 1994, re-certification, 2003, cert. surg. critical care 1995, 2004. Fellow in traumatology and critical care Md. Inst. for Emergency Med. Svcs. Sys., Baltimore, Md., 1992—93; resident gen surgery Temple Univ. Hosp., 1987—92, chief trauma and surg. critical care, program dir., 2003—, dir. trauma regional resource trauma ctr., 2004—. With leadership devel. for physicians in academic health centers Harvard Sch. of Pub. Health, Boston., Mass., 2002; with exec. leadership in academic medicine Drexel Univ. Coll. of Medicine, Phila., 2004—05. Recipient Golden Apple award, Temple Univ. Sch. of Medicine, 1995, 1998, 2000, 2002, 2006, Russell C. Moses Meml. award for Excellence in Clin. Tng., 1996, 2006, The Coll. of Physicians of Phila. Exemplar of Humanism in Medicine award, 2006, Russell C. Moses Meml. award for Excellence in Clin. Tng., 2002, E. Emory Burnett award for Tchg. Excellence, Temple Univ. Hosp., 1995, 1997, 2000, Wallace P. Ritchie, Jr., MD, PhD award for Excellence in the Clin. and Scientific Practice of Surgery, 1995, 1997, 2000, Christian R. and Mary F. Lindback Found. award for Disting. Tchg., 2006; named Top Docs, Phila. Mag., 2011. Mem.: ACS (fellow 1994—, mem. at large for met. Phila. chapter 2001—04, mem. Pa. dist. 5 com. on appicants 2004—), Assn. of Surg. Edn., Am. Assn. of the Surgery of Trauma (mem. outcomes com. 2004—, with Pa. trauma sys. found. 2006—), Coll. of Physicians of Phila. (fellow 2003—05), Phila Acad. of Surgery (program chair 2001—), Ea. Assn. for Surgery of Trauma, Assn. Program dirs. in Surgery, Am. Soc. of Breast Surgeons, Assn. of Women Surgeons, Soc. of Critical Care Medicine. Office: Temple University Hospital 3401 North Broad St Philadelphia PA 19140 Office Phone: 215-707-2000.

GOLDBERG, ANNE CAROL, physician, educator; b. Balt., June 12, 1951; d. Stanley Barry and Selma Ray G.; m. Ronald M. Levin, July 29, 1989. AB, Harvard U., 1973; MD, U. Md., 1977. Diplomate Am. Bd. Internal Medicine, Am. Bd. Endocrinolgy and Metabolism. Intern in medicine Michael Reese Hosp., Chgo., 1977-78, resident in medicine, 1978-80; fellow in endocrinology Washington U., St. Louis, 1980-83, instr. medicine, 1983-85, asst. prof. medicine, 1985-94, assoc. prof. medicine, 1994—. Fellow ACP, Am. Heart Assn.; mem. AMA, Am. Diabetes Assn., Am. Med. Women's Assn., Endocrine Soc., Nat. Lipid Assn. (pres. 2007-08), Alpha Omega Alpha. Democrat. Jewish. Avocation: needlepoint. Office: Washington U Med Sch Box 8127 660 S Euclid Ave Saint Louis MO 63110-1010

GOLDBERG, ARNOLD IRVING, psychoanalyst, educator; b. Chgo., May 21, 1929; s. Morris Henry and Rose (Auerbach) Goldberg; m. Constance Obenhaus; children: Andrew, Sarah. BS, U. Ill., Chgo., 1949, MD, 1953. Diplomate Am. Bd. Psychiatry and Neurology, cert. psychoanalyst. Intern Cin. Gen. Hosp., 1954-55; psychiat. resident Michael Reese Hosp., Chgo., 1957-59; tng. and supervising analyst Chgo. Inst. for Psychoanalysis, 1970—, dir., 1990-92; assoc. psychiatrist Rush Presbyn. St. Luke's Hosp., Chgo., 1982 ; prof. psychiatry Rush Med. Coll., Chgo., 1982-97, Cynthia Oudejans Harris MD prof. psychiatry, 1997—. Author: (book) Models of the Mind, 1973, A Fresh Look at Psychoanalysis, 1988, The Prisonhouse of Psychoanalysis, 1990, The Problem of Perversion, 1995, Being of Two Minds, 1999, Misunderstanding Freud, 2004, Moral Stealth, 2006; editor: Future of Psychoanalysis: Progress in Self Psychology, Vols. 1-16, 1976—99, Errant Selves, 2000, The Analysis of Failure, 2011; contbr. articles to profl. jours. Capt. US Army, 1955—57. Recipient Mary S. Sigourney award, 2006. Fellow: Am. Psychiat. Assn. (life); mem.: Am. Psychoanalytic Assn. Home: 844 W Chalmers Pl Chicago IL 60614-3223 Office: Inst for Psychoanalysis Chgo 122 S Michigan Ave Ste 1305 Chicago IL 60603-6107 Home Phone: 773-348-0771; Office Phone: 312-922-6797. Personal E-mail: docaig@aol.com.

GOLDBERG, DANIEL JOSEPH, cardiologist; Attended, George Wash. U.; MD, NY Med. Coll., 1976. Diplomate Am. Bd. Internal Medicine, Am. Bd. Internal Medicine-cardiovasc. disease. Intern Wash. Hosp. Ctr., 1977, resident, 1979, chief med. resident; fellow cardiology Univ. of Louisville Hosp., 1981; former chmn. cardiology Shady Grove Adventist Hosp.; with med. staff exec. com. Montgomery Gen. Hosp., chief medicine, chief cardiology. Named one of Top Doctors, Washingtonian Mag., 2011. Fellow: Am. Coll. of Cardiology. Office: Montgomery General Hospital 18101 Prince Philip Dr Olney MD 20832 Office Phone: 301-774-8882.

GOLDBERG, EDWIN, rehabilitation specialist; D in Chiropractic, Columbia Inst. Chiropractic, 1960; grad. in cdn. of blind, Columbia U. Tchrs. Coll., NYC, 1967—68; postgrad., C.G. Jung Found., NYC, 1972—73; postgrad. in edn. of blind, NYU, NYC, 1973—74, postgrad. in tng. and devel., 1972; postgrad., Am. Inst. Psychoanalysis, Moreno Inst. Psychodrama; postgrad. in spl. edn., Fordham U., NYC, 1971; cert. of study, Alfred Adler Inst., 1970; MA in Edn., Hebrew Union Coll., 1971; cert. rehab. mgmt., Cornell U., 1973; student in Optics, Camden County Coll. Cert. citizenship in the community American Legion Nat., 1958, cert. med. rehab. coord., rehab. therapist in mobility tng. of the blind Am. Assn. Med. Rehab. Therapists and Specialists, rehab. counselor, master therapeutic recreation specialist, Nat. Bd. Cert. Counselor' registered therapeutic recreation adminstr., NJ; cert. mobility instr., rehab. tchr., NY; nat. cert. profl. rehab. tchr. the blind AER.; lic. rehab. counselor State of NJ; profl. cert. in crisis mgmt. Cornell U., 1972, rehab. mgmt., 1973; cert. assessment in aging U. Pa., 1987; cert. in microcounseling U. Buffalo, 1999; cert. in cane mobility tng. blind Joseph Kohn Rehab. Ctr., 1992; cert. in low vision, 1995; cert. in drug and alcohol counseling, Mercer Coun. Coll., NJ, 1997; qualified mental retardation profl., NJ; lic. in group rels. workshop, NYC, 1973, health edn. tchr. NJ Dept. Edn. State Bd. Examiners, drug and alcoholism treatment Resource CASAC Group, 2005-07. Mem. Dr. Samuel Losner staff coagulation lab. Isaac Albert Rsch. Inst., Bklyn., 1957-60; tech. eye bank and clin. lab. Bklyn. Eye & Ear Hosp., 1958-59; exec. Greater NY couns. Boy Scouts Am., 1961—63; supr. blood products divsn. Knickerbocker Biologicals, Charles Pfizer & Co., NYC, 1963-64; assoc. dir. Western Mediterranean ops. St. Jean Cap Ferrat A.M. USO, Nice, France, Naples, Italy, 1964-65; coord. rehab. skills Jewish Guild Blind, NYC, 1965-68, asst. dir., 1968-77; sect. chief Trenton Psychiat. Hosp., 1977-78; mobility cons. Elm & Maple Halls, Ancora Hosp., 1977-82; dir. Work Adjustment Ctr. Jewish Employment and Vocat. Svc., Phila., 1979-80; dir. Mary Campbell Ellis Vocat. Rehab. Ctr. S.I. (N.Y.) Aid for Retarded Children, 1980-86; sr. rehab. counselor/acting dir. Vocat. Rehab. dept. Ancora Hosp., Hammonton, NJ, 1982-87; rehab. cons. Dominican Coll. of Blauvet; program chmn. NY Fed. of Workers for the Blind, 1972; rehab. cons. Shield Inst., Flushing and Manhattan, NY, 2003—04, FEGS, NYC, 2003—04; dir. Seamark Ctr. Goodwill Industries NY and No. NJ, Bklyn., 2003—04; counselor Inter-Care Substance Abuse Treatment Ctr., NYC, 2004—06; counselor for blind children early intervention and transition program NY State Commn. for Blind, Exchange Place, 2006—; rehab. counselor NY State Commn. Blind Harlem, NYC, 2003—; cons. NY Eye & Ear Hosp., NYC, 1968—77, Manhatta Eye Hosp., Willis Eye Hosp., Phila. Cons. in mobility and occupational therapy Willowbrook State Sch. SI, NY, 1980-81; habilitation plan coord. State of NJ Div. Devel. Disabilities, Hammonton, 1988-91, New Lisbon Devel. Ctr., 1991-93; sr. rehab. counselor NJ State Commn. for the Blind, 1992-2002; rehab. cons. Beth Israel Hosp., NYC, Goldwater Meml. Hosp., NYC, Montefirore Med. Ctr., Bronx, NY, Harlem Med. Ctr., Bklyn., Jewish Home and Hosp. for Aged, NYC, Inst. Rehab. Medicine, NYU, Hillside Med. Ctr., Bklyn. Devel. Ctr., Manhattan Psychiat. Hosp., Keener Unit of Gov. Hosp., Albert Einstein Coll. Medicine, Bronx, Downstate Med. Ctr., Bklyn., Manhattanville Coll., Westchester, NY, LI U., Bklyn., Yonkers Home for the Aged Blind, Trenton State Coll., Bank Street Coll. of Edn., Staten Island CC, Kingsbrook CC, Exxon Homes, Morris Hall Rehab. Ctr., Jewish Geriatric Ctr., Phila., Nat. Rehab. Assocs.; mobility specialist for severely disabled blind State of NY, 1968-2003; coord. corrective therapy, internship program rehab dept. Manhattan Vets. Hosp., 1970-77; rehab. tng. specialist multiple disabled blind in NY area, 1970-77; instr. group rels. ongoing workshops; sr. vocat. counselor, summer camp. coord. for blind adolescents program Joseph Kohn Rehab. Ctr., New Brunswick, NJ, 2000-04; vocat. sr. counselor Bus. Enterprise Program State of NJ, Trenton, 1998-2002, sr. counselor coll. edn. unit NJ Commn. for Blind and Visually Impaired, Newark, 2002—2003; cons. rehab. Shield Inst., NY, 2002-03; adj. asst. prof. health and phys. edn. and adapted phys. edn. Hunter Coll., NYC, 1971-76; lectr. in field, 1970—, Zeman Ctr. Instrn., NYC, 1965-78; mobility cons. Yonkers Home for Aged Blind, 1968-71; contbr. to developing tchr. tng. on phys. edn. of physically disabled with prof. Paul J., Republic of China, 1973-77; cons. devel. disabled Keener Unit Goodwater Meml. Hosp. NYC, 1968-1970, Blind Vocational Rehab. Inst. Rehab. Medicine, 1966-1969; cons. on brain damage and visual loss JFK Rehab. Ctr., Edison, NJ, 1996-2000; presenter in field. Author: Mobilitiy Training Manual for Teachers of Visually Impaired Children, 1969, Isolation From the Human Scene: The Meaning and Direction of Loneness, 1972, Adapted and Corrective Physical Education Curriculum Handicapped, 1972, Rehabilitation Assessment in Psychiatric Facilities, 1984, Overcoming Feelings of Inferiority: The Role of Mobility Training for the Blind An Adlerian Viewpoint, 1986; TV appearances include Am. Speaks, 1960-62. Cons. on rehabilitation for the blind Rusk Inst., 1965-69, Roosevelt Hosp. NYC, 1965-77; legis rep. NY State Fedn. Workers Blind, 1973-76, program chmn., 1974; cons. legis. US Senate and Congl. Subcoms., 1972-77; lectr. mobility tng. the blind, Rusk Inst., 1965—1969, rehab. skills tng. vision impaired Geriatrics Ctr. Instrn., 1968-77; program chmn. NY Fedn. Blind, 1976. Recipient Silver award Nat. Coun. Boy Scouts Am., 1958, Recognition citation Rotary Club NYC, 1959, Dr. Frank E. Dean Meml. award for outstanding contbns. to sci. edn., 1976, Thomas E. Watson Silver citation Citizenship in Action medal SAR, Lydia Hayes Disting. Svc. award NJ Commn. for Blind and Visually Impaired, 2000. Fellow: World Med. Assn., Am. Inst. Sci., World Assn. Social Psychiatry, Royal Soc. Promotion Health, N.Y. Acad. Scis.; mem.: APA, Individual Psychology Assn., Am. Assn. Workers for the Blind, Am. Orthopsychia. Assn., Am. Public Health Assn., Royal Inst. Pub. Health and Hygiene London, Assn. Med. Rehab. Dirs. Coords., Am. Assn. Rehab. Therapy, Royal Inst. Pub. Health and Hygiene, Royal Soc. Health, Am. Congress Rehab. Medicine, Assn. Edn. and Visually Handicapped and Blind, Royal Soc. Medicine (London), Am. Assn. Med. Rehab. Specialists and Therapists, Nat. Therapeutic Recreation Assn., Am. Orthopsychiat. Assn. for Applied Psychoanalysis, N.Y. Counseling Assn., N.Am. Soc. Adlerian Psychology, Am. Rehab. Counseling Assn., John Burroughs Meml. Assn. (life). Office Phone: 212-961-5843. Personal E-mail: edgoldbergnewyork@yahoo.com.

GOLDBERG, HERB, psychologist, educator; b. Berlin, July 14, 1937; arrived in US, 1941; s. Jacob and Ella (Nagler) Goldberg; 1 child, Amy Elisabeth. BA cum laude, CUNY, 1958; PhD, Adelphi U., Garden City, NY, 1963. Lic. psychologist Calif. Pvt. practice, LA, 1965—. Prof. psychology Calif. State U., LA. Author: Creative Aggression, 1972, The Hazards of Being Male, 1976, Money Madness, 1978, The New Male, 1979, The Inner Male, 1986, The New Male/Female Relationship, 1982, What Men Really Want, 1991, What Men Still Don't Know About Women, Relationships and Love, 2007. Mem.: APA, Phi Beta Kappa. Office: 3739 Mayfair Dr Los Angeles CA 90065-3208 Office Phone: 323-225-4649, 323-225-7770. Personal E-mail: drherbgoldberg@aol.com.

GOLDBERG, IRA JAY, internist, educator; b. Elizabeth, NJ, Mar. 11, 1949; m. Ina N. Cholst; children: Sarah Cholst and Jacob Cholst (twins). BS, MIT, 1971; MD, Harvard U., Boston, 1975. Diplomate Am. Bd. Internal Medicine, Am. Bd. Endocrinology and Metabolism. Intern NYU-Bellevue Hosp. Med. Ctr., NYC, 1975-76, jr. and sr. resident in medicine, 1976-78; fellow in endocrinology and metabolism Mt. Sinai Sch. Medicine, NYC, 1978-79, fellow in arteriosclerosis and metabolism, 1979-81, instr. medicine, 1981-83; asst. prof. medicine Columbia U. Coll. Physicians and Surgeons, NYC, 1983-90, assoc. prof., 1990-96, prof., 1996—, acting dir. Inst. Human Nutrition, 1995, chief division preventative medicine and nutrition, 2000—, Dickinson Richards Professor of Medicine, 2005—. Asst. attending physician dept. medicine Columbia-Presbyn. Med. Ctr., 1983-90, assoc. attending physician, 1990—, assoc. dir. Arteriosclerosis Rsch. Ctr., 1985—; tchr. Lipid Clinic, Overlook Hosp., 1987-91; vis. prof. U. Rennes, France, 1993; Merck Frosst-McGill lectr. lipid metabolism McGill U., Montreal, Que., Can., 1993; spkr. Gordon Conf. on Lipoprotein Metabolism, 1992, spkr., session chmn., 1996, 98; spkr. Lofland Conf. on Atherosclerosis, 1993, Gordon Conf. on Atherosclerosis, 1995; spkr. Internat. Arteriosclerosis Soc., 1994, 97, session chmn., 1997; spkr. Baker Symposium on Cardiovasc. Disease, Melbourne, Australia, 1997; also others; editl. reviewer Jour. Clin. Investigation, Jour. Biol. Chemistry, Jour. Lipid Rsch., Am. Jour. Physiology, Arteriosclerosis and Thrombosis, New Eng. Jour. Medicine; mem. editl. bd. Jour. Clin. Endocrinology and Metabolism; ad hoc reviewer grant revs. metabolism study section Nat. Heart, Lung and Blood Inst., 1992-93, 96, 97, mem. spl. rev. com. for clin. investigator and physician scientist awards, 1987, 92, 94; cons. ong rant revs. to VA Health Svcs. and Rsch. Adminstrn., 1997, also others. Contbr. over 75 articles and revs. to med. jours., also numerous chpts. to books. Recipient established scientist award N.Y. Heart Assn., 1980-94; grantee NIH-Nat. Heart, Blood and Lung Inst., 1990-95, 96—, Schering Pharm. Corp., 1990-94, Coun. for Tobacco Rsch., 1991-94, Am. Heart Assn., 1990-93. Mem. ACP, AAAS, Am. Fedn. for Clin. Rsch., Am. Soc. for Clin. Investigation, Am. Heart Assn. (fellow coun. on arteriosclerosis, nutrition com. 1997—, nat. program com. 1997—, session chmn. ann. sci. sessions 1988, 90, 91, 93, 95-97, chmn. com. on cholesterol edn. N.Y.C. affiliate, mem. coun. profl. edn. com., bd. dirs. 1993-99, chmn. peer rev. com. 1995-97, bd. dirs. heritage entity 1998—, Clinician-Scientist award 1981-86), N.Y. Lipid Club (pres. 1992-93). Office: Columbia U Coll Phys & Surg Divsn Prev Med-Nutrition 630 W 168th St New York NY 10032-3702 Fax: 212-305-5384. E-mail: IJG3@columbia.edu.

GOLDBERG, IRVING HYMAN, molecular pharmacology and biochemistry educator; b. Hartford, Conn., Sept. 2, 1926; s. Morris Wolfe and Rose (Krechevsky) Goldberg; m. Margaret Field Ziskin, Apr. 15, 1956; children: Daniel Eliot, Nancy Elizabeth. BS, Trinity Coll., 1949; MD, Yale U., 1953; PhD, Rockefeller U., 1960; AM (hon.), Harvard U., 1964. Intern Columbia-Presbyn. Med. Ctr., NYC, 1953—54; asst. resident, chief resident, instr. medicine Columbia-Presbyn. Med. Ctr. (Coll. Phys. and Surgs.), 1954—57; asst. prof. medicine, biochemistry U. Chgo., 1960—64, assoc. prof., 1964;

assoc. prof. medicine Med. Sch. Harvard, 1964—68; prof. medicine Med. Sch. Harvard U., 1968—, chmn. divsn. med. scis. Faculty Arts and Scis., 1968—70, Gustavus Adolphus Pfeiffer prof. pharmacology, 1972—83, chmn. dept. pharm., 1972—86, Otto Krayer prof. pharmacology, 1983—86, Otto Krayer prof. biol. chemistry and molecular pharmacology, 1986—2007, rsch. prof. biol. chemistry, molecular pharmacology, 2008—; chief endocrinology-metabolism unit Beth Israel Hosp., 1964—68, physician, 1964—72, mem. bd. consultation in medicine, 1972—; cons. in pharmacology Dana-Farber Cancer Inst., Boston, 1980—87. Mem. rev. panel internat. program Howard Hughes Med. Inst., 1994; cons. in clin. pharmacology Children's Hosp. Med. Ctr., Boston, 1972—91; mem. rsch. com. Med. Found., Boston, 1968—77; mem. exptl. therapeutics study sect. NIH, 1974—77; mem. com. proposed legis. to restructure FDA Assembly Life Scis. NAS-NRC, Inst. Medicine, 1976; mem. sci. adv. com. Rite Allen Found., 1976—2006, Damon Runyon-Walter Winchell Cancer Fund, 1982—86; mem. life scis. panel NRC, 1992—93. Mem. editl. bd. Endocrinology, 1964—68, Antimicrobial Agents and Chemotherapy, 1974—88, Jour. Biochem. Pharmacology, 1973—84, Biochemistry, 1986—97. Rev. panel Internat. Program Howard Hughes Med. Inst., 1994; sci. adv. com. Rita Allen Found., 1976—2006. With USNR, 1945—46. Recipient Faculty Rsch. award, Am. Cancer Soc., 1960—71; fellow Guggenheim, dept. genetics, Oxford (Eng.) U., 1970—71, sr., Trinity Coll., 1974—76. Mem.: Brit. Pharm. Soc., Am. Soc. Microbiology, Am. Soc. Pharmacology and Therapeutics (Otto Krayer award 1994), Am. Chem. Soc., Assn. Am. Physicians, Am. Acad. Arts and Scis., Am. Soc. Clin. Investigation, Am. Soc. Biochemistry and Molecular Biology, Inst. Medicine NAS, Alpha Omega Alpha, Sigma Xi, Phi Beta Kappa. Home: 987 Memorial Dr Apt 472 Cambridge MA 02138-5737 Office: Harvard U Med Sch 45 Shattuck St Boston MA 02115-6091 Home Phone: 617-864-3111; Office Phone: 617-432-1787. Business E-Mail: irving_goldberg@hms.harvard.edu.

GOLDBERG, LARRY M., hospital administrator; BA, U. NC; M in health adminstrn., Duke U. Past position with Deloitte & Touche, NY, Ernst & Young, NY; v.p. hosp. ops. Northwestern Meml. Hosp., Chgo., 1998—2005; CEO, exec. dir. Vanderbilt U. Hosp., Tenn., 2005—. Office: Vanderbilt U Hosp 1161 21st Ave Nashville TN 37232 Office Phone: 615-343-4501. Office Fax: 615-343-7317. E-mail: larry.goldberg@Vanderbilt.Edu. *

GOLDBERG, LOIS D., health facility administrator, disability analyst; b. Mar. 30, 1940; m. Gerald Allen Goldberg, Dec. 18, 1960; children: Sheri Goldberg Smith, Nancy Cozart, Karen Galinkin. BS in Elem. Edn., U. Wis., Milw., 1961, MS in Spl. Edn., 1977. Cert. Am. Inst. Hypnotherapy and Psychotherapy, 1986, disability analyst 2000; in reading & learning disabilities 1980, mental health counselor Dept. Health and Social Svcs. Wis., 1985, Wis. Alcohol and Drug Abuse Cert. Bd., 1985, nat. acupuncture detoxification specialist NY, 1992. Tchr. elem. edn. Fox Point Sch., 1961—63; tchr. spl. edn. Juneau Acad., 1977—79; edn. dir. Commando Acad., 1979—81; counselor, tchr. Counseling Ctr. Milw., 1984—85, St. Charles Boys Home, 1981—87; health svcs. adminstr. Eastside Clinic, Milw., 1985—; acupuncture detox specialist, 1992-98. Pres. Eastside Youth and Family Clinic, 1981—87; weight therapist, 1984—85. Pres. Fox Point PTA, Milw., 1980; bd. dirs. Close Encounters Chamber Music. Recipient Fighting Back Initiative Cert. Recognition award, Milw. County for Reduction of Substance Abuse and Improvement of Life of Milw. County Residents, 2000. Mem.: Pi Lambda Theta (assoc. v.p. 1982). Avocations: music, swimming, tennis. Personal E-mail: goldberg.lois@gmail.com.

GOLDBERG, MARK ARTHUR, neurologist; b. NYC, Sept. 4, 1934; s. Jacob and Bertha (Grushlawska) G.; 1 child, Jonathan. BS, Columbia U., 1955; PhD, U. Chgo., 1959, MD, 1962. Resident neurology NY Neurol. Inst., NYC, 1963-66; asst. prof. neurology Columbia U. Coll. Phys. and Surgs., NYC, 1968-71; assoc. prof. neurology and pharmacology UCLA, 1971-77, prof. neurology and pharmacology, 1977—2004, emeritus prof., 2004—; chair dept. neurology Harbor UCLA Med. Ctr., Torrance, 1977—2005. Contbr. articles to profl. jours., chpts. to books. Capt. US Army, 1966-68. Fellow Am. Neurol. Assn., Am. Acad. Neurology; mem. L.A. Neurol. Soc., Palos Verdes Land Conservancy. Avocation: oriental cusine. E-mail: mrkgldbrg@yahoo.com.

GOLDBERG, MARTIN, internist, educator; b. Phila., Sept. 15, 1930; s. Samuel and Esther (Shreibman) Goldberg; m. Lynn Taksey, June 17, 1951 (dec. Aug. 31, 1976); children: Meryl I, Karen L, Dara S; m. Marion Lindblad, May 26, 1978; 1 child, David S. BA, Temple U., 1951, MD, 1955; MA (hon.), U. Pa., 1971. Diplomate Am. Bd. Internal Medicine, Nat. Bd. Med. Examiners. Intern Phila. Gen. Hosp., 1955-56, resident, 1957-59, sr. attending physician, 1970-76; resident Cleve. Clinic, 1956-57; fellow nephrology Hosp. U. Pa., Phila., 1959-61, sr. attending physician, 1962-79; mem. faculty U. Pa. Sch. Medicine, 1960-79, prof. medicine, 1970-79, chief renal electrolyte sect., 1966-79, acting chmn. dept. medicine, 1975-76; sr. attending physician Phila. VA Hosp., 1968-79; Gordon and Helen Hughes Taylor prof. medicine U. Cin., 1979-86; chmn. internal medicine U. Cin. Coll. Med. and Hosp., 1979-86; prof. medicine Temple U. Sch. Medicine, Phila., 1986-96, dean, vice pres., 1986-89, prof. emeritus, 1997—, asst. to dean for computer assisted instrn., 1997-2000; chmn. sci. adv. com. Gen. Clin. Rsch. Ctr. Temple U. Hosp., 1993—. Bd. mgrs. St. Christopher's Hosp. for Children, 1986—89; chmn. nephrology com. Am. Bd. Internal Medicine, 1976—79, bd. govs., 1976—79. Mem. editl. bd.: Jour Clin Investigation, 1969—70, Kidney Internat., 1972—74, Jour. Mineral and Electrolyte Metabolism, 1977—91, Am. Jour. Hypertension, 1990—97, First Consult, 2000—08, mem. editl. adv. bd.: others. Recipient Alumni prize, Temple U. Sch. Medicine, 1955, Rsch. Career Devel. award, NIH, 1963—70, Lindback award for disting. tchg., U. Pa., 1972, Disting. Med Scientist of Yr. award, Med. Alumni Temple U. Sch. Medicine, 1985, Honoree of the Yr. award, Greater Delaware Valley Kidney Found., 1997, A.N. Richards award, U. Pa., 1998, Centennial award, Assn. Chmn. Depts. Physiology, 1989; rsch. grantee, NIH, 1962—89, John Hartford Found., 1970—73. Master: ACP (nat. sci. program com. 1976—81); fellow: Royal Soc. Medicine, Am. Coll. Clin. Pharmacology; mem.: Physicians for Social Responsibility (adv. bd. Phila. chpt. 1988—98), Coll. Physicians Phila., Am. Med. Informatics Assn., Internat. Soc. Nephrology (coun. 1975—84), Am. Soc. Nephrology (sec.-treas. 1975—78), Am. Fedn. Clin. Rsch. (chmn. eastern sect. 1967), Am. Physiol. Soc., Am. Soc. Clin. Investigation, Assn. Am. Physicians, Assn. Am. Med. Colls. (coun. deans 1986—89), Interurban Clin. Club, Alpha Omega Alpha. Achievements include research in renal physiology and disease; electrolyte and acid-base metabolism, computer assisted instruction and diagnosis.

GOLDBERG, MICHAEL IRA, obstetrician, gynecologist; b. Bklyn., June 8, 1944; MD, U. Rome, 1970. Diplomate Am. Bd. Ob-Gyn., Am. Bd. Gynecol. Oncology. Intern Maimonedes Med. Ctr., Bklyn., 1971, resident in ob-gyn., 1972-75; fellow in gynecol. oncology Miami (Fla.)-Jackson Meml. Hosp., 1975-77; pvt. practice New Brunswick, NJ. Mem. staff RW Johnson U. Hosp., New Brunswick; clin. prof. ob-gyn. U. Medicine and Dentistry of N.J., RW Johnson Med. Sch.; chief gynecol. oncology St. Peter's U. Hosp., New Brunswick. Fellow ACS, ACOG; mem. Soc. Gynecol. Oncology. Office: 78 Easton Ave New Brunswick NJ 08901-1865 Office Phone: 732-828-3300. Fax: 723-937-5739.

GOLDBERG, MORTON EDWARD, pharmacologist; b. Phila., July 11, 1932; s. Herman and Ethel (Shill) G.; m. Janet Louise Werlin, Aug. 15, 1954; children— Shellie, Ellen, David. BS, Phila. Coll. Pharmacy and Sci., 1954, MS in Pharmacology, 1955, DSc in Pharmacology, 1958. Sr. pharmacologist Abbott Labs., North Chgo., 1958-60; asst. dir. pharmacology Union Carbide Corp., Tuxedo, NY, 1960-69; dir. pharmacodynamics Warner Lambert Research Inst., Morris Plains, NJ, 1969-73; dir. pharmacology Squibb Inst. Med. Research, Princeton, NJ, 1973-77; v.p. biomed. research Stuart Pharms. div. ICI Americas, Wilmington, Del., 1977-84; v.p. rsch., devel., and regulatory affairs ICI Pharm. Group divsn. ICI Ams. (now Astra Zeneca Pharm.), Wilmington, 1984-92; clin. prof. pharmacology and exptl. therapeutics Dept. Pharmacology U. Pa. Sch. Medicine, Phila., 1992-96; advisor, cons. several pharm. cos., 1996—. Vis. prof. toxicology Phila. Coll. Pharmacy and Sci.; vis. prof. pharmacology, Allegheny U. Med. Sch., Phila., 1978-2001, U. Pa. Sch. Med., Phila., 1996-2001; cons. to pharm. industry in drug discovery and devel., 1992—; mem. extramural sci. adv. bd. NIDA, 1993-95, mem. nat. adv. bd. 1996-2000. Editor-in-chief: series Pharmacological and Biochemical Properties of Drug Substances; contbr. articles to profl. jours. Asst. scoutmaster Boy Scouts Am., Glen Rock, N.J., 1968-72. NIH grantee, 1961-64 Fellow Acad. Pharm. Sci., AAAS, N.Y. Acad. Sci.; mem. Am. Soc. Pharmacology and Exptl. Therapeutics, Behavioral Pharmacology Soc., Internat. Soc. Biochem. Pharmacology, Soc. Toxicology (charter), Sigma Xi, Rho Chi. Home: 411 Meadowlark Ter Glen Mills PA 19342-3340 Office Phone: 302-598-7195. Home Fax: 302-478-7195.

GOLDBERG, MORTON FALK, ophthalmologist, educator; b. Lawrence, Mass., June 8, 1937; s. Maurice and Helen Janet (Falk) G.; m. Myrna Davidov, Apr. 6, 1968; children— Matthew Falk, Michael Falk AB magna cum laude, Harvard U., 1958, MD cum laude, 1962; Doctoris honoris causa, U. Coimbra, Portugal, 1995. Diplomate Am. Bd. Ophthalmology. Intern Peter Bent Brigham Hosp., Boston, 1962-63; resident Wilmer Inst. Johns Hopkins Hosp., Balt., 1963—67, head dept., dir. Wilmer Inst., 1989—2003; prof. and head ophthalmology Eye and Ear Infirmary U. Ill. Hosp., Chgo., 1970-89; Joseph Green prof. ophthalmology Johns Hopkins Med. Sch., 2003—. Author: (with D. Paton) Injuries of the Eye, the Lids and the Orbit: Diagnosis and Management, 1968, Management of Ocular Injuries, 1976, (with H. Tabandeh) The Retinia in System Disease, 2009; editor: Genetic and Metabolic Eye Disease, 1974, (with G.A. Peyman and D.R. Sanders) Principles and Practice of Ophthalmology (3 vols.), 1980; editor-in-chief Archives of Ophthalmology, Chgo., 1984-94; contbr. articles to profl. jours. Lt. comdr. USPHS, 1967-69 Recipient award for outstanding contbns. in the field of vision rsch. Alcon Research Inst., 1987, Univ. Scholar award U. Ill.-Chgo., 1986, Michaelson medal Israel Acad. Scis. and Humanities, 2000, Greatest Living Ophthalmologists award Ophthalmology Times, 1999, Mildred Weisenfeld Lifetime Achievement award Fight for Sight, Inc., 2001, Pryor award Am. Soc. Retinal Specialists, 2004, Heritage award Johns Hopkins U., 2007. Fellow: Am. Acad. Ophthalmology (Inaugural Helen Keller lectr. 2007, sr. honor award 1985), Royal Australian Coll. Ophthalmologists (hon.); mem.: Internat. Academia Ophthalmologia, Academia Ophthalmologica Internationalis, Macula Soc. (pres. 1980—82, Patz medal, Baylor Coll. Medicine 1999, David Paton medal 2002), Assn. Univ. Profs. Ophthalmology (trustee 1985—91, pres. 1990—91), Assn. Rsch. in Vision and Ophthalmology (trustee 1985—90, pres. 1989—90, Weisenfeld award 2000, Inaugural Silver medal), Chgo. Ophthal. Soc. (pres. 1985—86), Am. Ophthal. Soc., Inst. Medicine-NAS. Avocation: snorkelling. Office: Johns Hopkins Med Insts Wilmer Eye Inst 600 N Wolfe St Baltimore MD 21287-0005 E-mail: mgoldbrg@jhmi.edu.

GOLDBERG, MYRON D., gastroenterologist; MD, Albert Einstein Coll. Medicine, 1971. Diplomate Am. Bd. Internal Medicine, Am. Bd. Gastroenterology. Intern Maimonides Hosp., Bklyn., 1971-72; resident Montefiore Hosp., Bronx, 1972-73; fellow in gastroenterology Columbia Presbyn. Hosp., NYC, 1976-77; resident Lenox Hill Hosp., NYC, 1973-74, fellow in gastroenterology, 1977-78, attending physician, 1978—, assoc. chief gastroenterology, 1991—. Author: The Inside Tract: The Complete Guide to Digestive Disorders, 1982. Mem. health care adv. bd. Med. Leadership Coun., 1995—. Maj. USAF, 1974-76. Fellow ACP, Am. Coll. Gastroenterology; mem. AMA, Am. Assn. Study Liver Disease, Am. Gastroent. Assn., Am. Soc. for Gastrointestinal Endoscopy, AMA, N.Y. State and County Med. Soc. Office: 110 E 59th St Ste 10B New York NY 10022-1304 Office Phone: 212-583-2900.

GOLDBERG, NIECA, cardiologist, educator; b. Bkyln., Oct. 21, 1957; BA, Barnard Coll., 1979; MD, SUNY, Bklyn., 1984. Diplomate Am. Bd. Internal Medicine. Resident in internal medicine St. Lukes-Roosevelt Hosp., NYC, 1985-87; fellow in cardiology SUNY Health Sci. Ctr., Bklyn.; clin. assoc. prof. of medicine NYU Sch. Medicine, NYC; and co-med. dir. 92nd St. YMCA Cardiac Rehabilitation Ctr., NYC; dir. womans heart program NYU Langone Med. Ctr. Nat. spokesperson Am. Heart Assn. Go Red campaign; adv. bd. Woman's Day mag. Author: Women Are Not Small Men: Life-Saving Strategies for Preventing and Healing Heart Disease in Women, 2003, The Women's Health Heart Program: Life-saving Strategies for Preventing and Healing Heart Disease in Women, 2006, Dr. Nieca Goldberg's Complete Guide to Women's Health, 2008. Recipient Dr. with Heart award, Am. Heart Assn., Red Dress award, Woman's Day mag., Women to Watch award, Jewish Women Internat.; named to NY mag. Best Doctors issue, 1999, 2000, 2001, 2004—07. Mem. ACP, Am. Coll. Cardiology, Am. Heart. Assn., Am. Soc. Echocardiography, Am. Coll. Physicians. Office: Total Heart Care PC 177 E 87th St #503 New York NY 10128 Office Phone: 212-289-2045. Office Fax: 212-289-2473.

GOLDBERG, PAUL BERNARD, gastroenterologist, clinical researcher; b. Bklyn., Apr. 11, 1950; s. Samuel and Eva (Turkenitz) G.; m. Harriet Ruth Ferrer, July 8, 1973 (div. 1987); children: Deborah Lynn, Susan Michelle; m. Mary Alice Denaro, June 23, 1990(div. 2007); 1 child, Laura Alicia. BA in Chemistry summa cum laude, Cornell U., 1967-71, MD, 1971-75. Diplomate Am. Bd. Internal Medicine, Am. Bd. Gastroenterology. Intern in medicine Hosp. of U. of Pa., Phila., 1975-76, resident in medicine, 1976-78, fellow in gastroenterology, 1978-80, fellow in nutritional support svc., 1979-80; med. coord. and founder nutritional support svc. Lakeland (Fla.) Gen. Hosp., 1980-81; attending physician Halifax Med. Ctr., 1980—, Ormond Meml. Hosp., 1980—, Atlantic Med. Ctr., 1980-2000, Fish Meml. Hosp., New Smyrna Beach, Fla., 1989-99, Peninsula Med. Ctr., 1989-94. Pres. Sunshine Health Care Plan, Inc., 1983-86, v.p., 1986-87; chief staff Humana Hosp., Daytona Beach, 1986-88, trustee, 1986-89, mem. exec. com., 1984-91; mem. rev. bd. Coastal Instnl. Rev., 1990-93, chmn. rev. bd., 1993-96; expert reviewer Fla. Dept. Profl. Regulation, 1990—; pres. med. staff Halifax Hosp., 1996-97; clin. asst. prof. medicine dept. family medicine U. South Fla., 1987-2007. Rschr. and author in field. Physician adv. Daytona chpt. Crohn's and Colitis Found., 1991-95. Recipient Nat. award Ford Future Scientists of Am., 1967, Westinghouse Sci. Talent Search finalist, 1967. Fellow ACP, Am. Coll. Gastroenterology, Am. Gastroent. Soc.; mem. Am. Soc. Gastrointestinal Endoscopy, Am. Soc. for Parenteral and Enteral Nutrition (pres. Fla. chpt. 1991-92), Volusia County Med. Soc. (exec. com. 1991-94, co-chmn. mini internship program 1992-94, 2000-01), Fla. Gastrointestinal Soc., Fla. Med. Assn. (alt. del. to ho. of dels. 1990-95), Fla. Assn. Nutritional Support (1st pres.), Rotary, Phi Beta Kappa, Alpha Omega Alpha. Office: 1070 N Stone St Ste D Deland FL 32720 Office Phone: 386-822-9410. Personal E-mail: pbgoldberg@aol.com.

GOLDBERG, VICTOR M., orthopedist; b. NYC, June 11, 1939; m. Harriet Goldberg; children: Rebecca, Jonathan, Eden. MD, SUNY Downstate Med. Ctr., 1964. Diplomate Am. Bd. Orthop. Surgeons, 1973. Prof. Case Med. Ctr., Cleve., 1983—; Charles H. Herndon prof. Dept. Orthop., Case Western Res. U., Cleve., 1989—2002, chmn., 1989—2002. Contbr. articles to profl. jour. Vice chair to chair Orthop. Rsch. and Edn. Found., Chgo., 2003—05, chair bd. trustees, 2005—07. Capt. USAF, 1966—68, Walker Air Force Base. Recipient Shands award, Orthop. Rsch. Soc. & AOA, 2003. Mem.: Am. Acad. Orthop. Surgeons (Kappa Delta award 2003, Disting. Investor award 2008). Achievements include research in tissue engineering. Office: Case Medical Ctr 11100 Euclid Ave Cleveland OH 44106 Office Fax: 216-844-5970. Business E-Mail: victor.goldberg@uhhospitals.org.

GOLDBERG-BERMAN, JUDITH, endocrinologist; MD, Cornell U., 1987. Diplomate Am. Bd. of Internal Medicine-endocrinology, Am. Bd. of Internal Medicine-diabetes & metabolism, Am. Bd. of Internal Medicine. Intern NY Univ. Med. Ctr., resident, 1988—90; fellow NY Hosp., 1990—93; with Greenwich Hosp. Office: Greenwich Hospital 5 Perryridge Rd Greenwich CT 06830 Office Phone: 203-863-3000.

GOLDBLATT, PHILLIP B., psychiatrist; b. Phila., Dec. 6, 1939; s. Samuel and Ida Goldblatt; children: Lisa, Dana. BA, U. Pa., 1961, MD, 1965. Intern Michael Reese Hosp., Chgo., 1965—66; resident in psychiatry Med. Sch. Yale U., New Haven, 1966—71, rsch. assoc. dept. psychiatry, 1970—73, asst. clin. prof. psychiatry Sch. Medicine, 1973—; chief Hosp. W. Haven, New Haven, 1973—77; pvt. practice New Haven, 1970—; attending psychiatrist St. Raphael's Hosp., New Haven, 1977—; cons. psychiatrist Bridgeport Cmty. Mental Health Corp., Conn., 1993—97, Conn. Mental Health Ctr., New Haven, 1997—2006. Bd. dirs. New Haven Pvt. Practice Com., 1996—. Bd. dirs. Jewish Family Svc., New Haven, 1985—91. Mem.: APA, AMA, Phi Beta Kappa. Office: 79 Trumbull St New Haven CT 06511 Office Phone: 203-624-1624.

GOLDBLOOM, VICTOR CHARLES, pediatrician; b. Montreal, Que., Can., July 31, 1923; s. Alton and Annie (Ballon) G.; m. Sheila Barshay, June 15, 1948; children: Susan, Michael, Jonathan. MD, McGill U., Montreal, 1945; LLD (hon.), U. Toronto, Ont., Can., 1980, Concordia U., Montreal, 1993, St. Anne's U., NS, Can., 1996; LittD, McGill U., Montreal, 1992; Dr. of Univ., U. Ottawa, Ont., 1994. Intern Montreal Children's Hosp., 1945-47, 1949-50; resident Babies Hosp., NYC, 1947-48; pvt. practice, 1950-80; min. environment and mcpl. affairs Govt. of Province Que., Quebec, 1970-76; pres., CEO Can. Coun. Christians and Jews, Toronto, 1979-87; pres. Internat. Coun. Christians and Jews, 1982-90, Environ. Pub. Hearings Bd., Quebec, 1987-90; exec. dir. Fonds de la recherche en santé du Qué., Montreal, 1990-91; commr. Official Langs. of Can., 1991—99. Can. del. UN Environment Conf., Stockholm, 1972, UN Habitat, Vancouver, B.C., 1976; tchr. McGill U., 1950—66; chair Montreal Regional Health and Social Svc. Bd., 2002—. Mem. Canadian Inst. Child Health, 2000—, chair adv. coun., 2010—; pres. (hon.) Jules and Paul-Emile Léger Found., Montreal; pres. Temple Emanu-El-Beth Sholom, Montreal, 2000—04, Jewish Immigrant Aid Svcs. of Montreal, 2005—08. Decorated Companion Order of Can., officier Ordre Nat. du Que.; recipient Govt. of Can. award, 1990, James H. Graham award, Royal Coll. Physicians and Surgeons of Can., 1996, Centennial medal, Assn. médecins langue française du Can., Sheila & Victor Goldbloom award, Quebec Cmty. Groups Network, 2009, Speirs medal, Selwyn House Sch., 1996, award, Jewish Cmty. Found. Montreal, 2006, Non Nobis Solum award, Lower Can. Coll., 2009; named hon. co-chair, McGill U., 1998. Mem.: Canadian Inst. Child Health (chair adv. coun. 2009—), Can. Jewish Congress (chair Quebec region 2007—09, Samuel Bronfman medal 2004), Allied Jewish Cmty. Svcs. Montreal (Samuel Bronfman medal 1989), Alliance Israelite Universelle (René Cassin medal 1980). Avocations: opera, singing. Home: 1455 Rue Sherbrooke O # 701 Montreal PQ Canada H3G 1L2 Office Phone: 514-949-5043. E-mail: sgoldbloom@sympatico.ca.

GOLDEN, GERALD SAMUEL, retired national medical board executive; b. Newark, June 8, 1935; s. Clement Harold and Jeanette (Bellat) G.; m. Deborah Ann Berlatsky, March 22, 1959 (dec. 1984); children: Leah Rachel, Ruth Naomi; m. Constance Reisa Abramson, Jan. 26, 1985. AB, Princeton U., 1957; MD, Columbia U., 1961. Diplomate Am. Bd. Pediat., Am. Bd. Psychiatry and Neurology. Asst. prof. of neurology and pediatrics Albert Einstein Coll. of Medicine,

Bronx, NY, 1967-73, assoc. prof., 1973-77; prof. pediatrics and neurology U. Tex., Galveston, 1977-84; prof. pediatrics and neurology, dir. ctr. for devel. disabl. U. Tenn., Memphis, 1984-92; v.p. Nat. Bd. Med. Examiners, Phila., 1993—2002, con., 2002—. Adj. prof. neurology U. Pa., 1993—98. Author: Textbook of Pediatric Neurology; assoc. editor: Pediatric Neurology Jour., 1987-92, Jour. of Devel. and Behavioral Pediatrics, 1987-2000, Jour. Epilepsy, 1987-92; contbr. numerous articles to profl. jours. Bd. dirs. Harwood Day Tng. Ctr., Memphis, 1987-92 Memphis-Shelby County Assn. for Retarded Citizens, 1987-92, Memphis Oral Sch. for Deaf, 1987-92, Temple Israel Memphis, 1989-92. Recipient fed. grant Adminstrn. on Devel. Disabilities, 1990, Dept. of Human Svcs., 1990. Fellow Am. Acad. Pediat. (neurology sect. head 1981-83), Am. Assn. Mental Deficiency (v.p. for medicine, 1984-86); mem. Am. Assn. U. Affiliated Programs (bd. dirs. 1987-92, pres. elect 1988-89, pres. 1989-90), Accrediation Coun., United Coun. Neurologic Subspecialties. Democrat. Jewish. Avocations: amateur radio, travel, birdwatching. Personal E-mail: doc.gsg@cox.net.

GOLDEN, MATTHEW, epidemiologist; BA in history, Grinnell Coll., 1985; MPH, Johns Hopkins U., 1993, MD, 1994. Assoc. prof. medicine U. Wash., Seattle, adj. assoc. prof. epidemiology; dir. Sexually Transmitted Disease Control Prog. for Pub. Health in Seattle County and King County, Wash. Recipient Honor award for Excellence in Innovation, CDC Nat. Ctr. HIV/AIDS, Viral Hepatitis, STD and TB Prevention, 2006. Office: Harborview Med Ctr Box 359777 325 9th Ave GEC 38 Seattle WA 98104 Office Phone: 206-731-6829. Office Fax: 206-731-4151. E-mail: golden@u.washington.edu.

GOLDEN, RICHARD LAURENCE, retired internist; b. New York, Apr. 8, 1929; s. Nathaniel and Bertha Golden; m. Arlene Alvira Stickel, Feb. 3, 1957; children: John Theodore, Allision Laurie Scrittorale, Adam Bruce, Nancy Heather. BS cum laude, St. Johns U., NY, 1949; BMS, U. Geneva, 1953, MD, 1956. Lic. NY, Ohio, Ariz., 1960. Intern Jersey City Med. Ctr., 1957—58; resident Roosevelt Hosp., NYC, 1958—60; fellow Meml. Sloan Kettering Ctr. Cancer, NYC, 1960—61; physician-scientist Brookhaven Nat. Lab., Upton, NY, 1961—62; pvt. practice, internal medicine East Northport, NY, 1962—94. Asst. prof. clin. medicine SUNY, Stony Brook, 1973—; trustee Suffolk Acad. Medicine, Hauppauge, NY, 1982—96, chmn., history medicine and med. mus., 1982—96; curator Osler Libr. History Medicine, McGill U., Montreal, Quebec, Canada, 1989—; guest co-editor, supplement 1, Jour. Med. Biography Royal Soc. Medicine, London, 2007. Author: (book) Osler and Oriental Medicine, Oslerian Verse: An Annotated Anthology, The Works of Egerton Yorrick Davis, M.D.: Sir William Osler's Alter Ego, A History of William Osler's The Principles and Practice of Medicine, William Osler's The Beginnings of Modern Medicine: A Historiographic Study; co-author (with Charles G. Roland): Sir William Osler: An Annotated Bibliography with Illustrations; co-author: (with Charles S. Bryan & JT Golden) William Osler's The Transatlantic Voice: A Philological Study; contbr. articles to profl. jours. Recipient Guy Potter Lit. award, Royal Can. Numis. Assn., 1991. Fellow: Am. Geriat. Soc., Royal Micros. Soc., Royal Soc. Medicine; mem.: AAAS, ACP, AMA, Am. Assn. History Medicine, Am. Osler Soc. (pres. 1989—90, historian 2010, Lifetime Achievement award 2008), Japanese Osler Soc. (hon.), Am. Numis.Assn., Royal Can. Numis. Soc., Japanese Art Soc. America, Osler Club London. Avocations: history, art. Home: 56 Laurel Hill Rd Centerport NY 11721

GOLDEN, ROBERT NEAL, psychiatrist, researcher, dean, medical educator; b. Phila., Aug. 27, 1953; s. Maxwell Solomon and Rosalie (Shragowitz) G.; m. Shannon Celeste Kenney, May 27, 1979; children: Troy, Blair, Sean, Max. BA cum laude, Yale U., 1975; MD, Boston U., 1979. Diplomate Am. Bd. Psychiatry and Neurology. Resident in psychiatry U. NC, Chapel Hill, 1979-83, chief resident, 1982-83, asst. prof. psychiatry, 1985-89, assoc. prof. psychiatry, 1989-94; prof., chair Dept. Psychiatry U. NC Sch. Medicine, Chapel Hill, 1994—2005, vice dean; dean U. Wis. Sch. Medicine and Pub. Health, 2006—; vice chancellor med. affairs U. Wis., Madison, 2006—, Robert Turell prof. in med. leadership. Med. staff fellow clin. pharmacology sect. Nat. Inst. Mental Health Intramural Rsch. Program, 1983—85. Contbr. articles to profl. jours. Ginsburg fellow Group Advancement Psychiatry, 1981-82, Laughlin fellow Am. Coll. Psychiatry, 1983. Mem. AAAS, Am. Coll. Neuropsychopharmacology, Am. Coll. Psychiatry, Am. Psychiat. Assn., Soc. Biol. Psychiatry. Office Phone: 608-263-4910. E-mail: rngolden@wisc.edu. *

GOLDENBERG, DAVID MILTON, experimental pathologist, oncologist; b. NYC, Aug. 2, 1938; s. Leo and Lillie (Spivak) G.; m. Hildegard Gruenbaum, Apr. 28, 1961 (div. 1996); children: Eva, Deborah, Marc, Denis, Neil, Lee; m. Cynthia Sullivan, Aug. 13, 1997. Student, Shimer Coll., 1954-56; BS, U. Chgo., 1958; ScD, U. Erlangen-Nuremberg, Fed. Republic of Germany, 1965; MD, U. Heidelberg, Fed. Republic of Germany, 1966. Assoc. rsch. prof. pathology U. Pitts. Med. Sch., 1968-70; assoc. prof. pathology Temple U. Med. Sch., Phila., 1970-72, U. Ky. Med. Ctr., Lexington, 1972-73; prof., dir. div. exptl. pathology U. Ky., Lexington, 1973-83; pres. Ctr. for Molecular Medicine and Immunology, Belleville, NJ, 1983—; founder, pres. Garden State Cancer Ctr., Belleville, NJ, 1992—; adj. prof. surgery NJ Med. Sch., U. Medicine and Dentistry NJ, Newark, 1983—93. Adj. prof. microbiology immunology NY Med. Coll., Valhalla, 1993-2000; mem. VA Merit Rev. Bd. for Oncology, Washington, 1974-77; exec. dir. Ephraim McDowell Cmty. Cancer Network, Lexington, 1975-80; pres. Ephraim McDowell Cancer Rsch. Foun., 1978-80; sec., treas. Ky. Cancer Commn., Frankfort, 1978-80; mem. sci. adv. bd. German Fund for Cancer Rsch., Bonn, 1980-90; mem. exptl. immunology study sect. NIH, Bethesda, Md., 1980-83; chmn bd. Immunomedics inc., Morris Plains, NJ, 1983-; bd. trustees, Ctr. Molecular Medicine and immunology, Belleville, NJ, 1983-. Author more than 1600 articles, book chpts., abstracts, 1962—; mem. editl. bd. Tumor Biology, Antibody, Immunoconjugates and Radiopharms., Jour. Nuclear Medicine, Qtly. Jour. Nuclear Medicine, Tumor Targeting. Outstanding Investigator grantee Nat. Cancer Inst., 1985, 92; recipient Rsch. Found. award U. Ky., 1978, NJ Pride award in sci. and tech. NJ Monthly, 1986, Excellence in Cancer Rsch. award NJ Legis., 1986, Herz Meml. lectureship Tel Aviv U., 1991, 3M/Mayneord Meml. lectureship Brit. Inst. Radiology, 1991, Abbott prize Internat. Soc. Oncodevelopmental Biol. Medicine, 1994, Vikram Sarabhai Meml. Oration award, Soc. Nuclear Medicine, India, 1994, Ted Bloch Meml. lectr. Southwestern chpt. Soc. Nuc. Medicine, 1999, Elis Bervin lecture and medal, Swedish Oncology Soc., 2002, Garden State Cancer Ctr. Special Sci. award, 2003, Dist. Scientist award, Clinical Ligand Assay Soc., 2004, Paul Aebersold award, Soc. Nuclear Medicine, 2005; named Inventor of Yr., NJ Rsch. Devel. Coun., 2005. Hon. mem. Argentine Cancer Assn. Jewish. Achievements include more than 300 US and fgn. patents in field; Pioneered the development of radiolabeled antibodies for various applications in the detection, diagnosis and therapy of cancer. Under his leadership, the scientists and clinicians at the Garden State Cancer Center have developed antibodies for the diagnosis, detection and treatment of solid tumors such as colorectal, pancreatic, lung, breast and ovarian cancers, as well as certain hematologic cancers such as lymphoma and multiple myeloma. He has overseen the in-house clinic as well as clinical outreach at affiliated institutions in the United States and Europe for treatment of cancer patients with radiolabeled antibodies. He also helped develop two diagnostic radiopharmaceuticals marketed by Immunomedics Inc., which he established in 1982. Office: Immunomedics Inc 300 American Rd Morris Plains NJ 07950 also: CMMI 520 Belleville Ave Belleville NJ 07109 Personal E-mail: dmg.gscancer@att.net.

GOLDENBERG, GEORGE, retired pharmaceutical executive; b. NYC, Mar. 12, 1929; s. Gersh and Rose (Kolpacci) G.; m. Arlene Sandra Yudell, May 22, 1955; children: Steven Alan, Heidi Michele Goldenberg Handelsman, Jeffrey Evan. Student, Bklyn. Coll., 1946-47; BS, Bklyn. Coll. Pharmacy L.I. U., 1951. Pharmacist Dolcorts Pharmacy, NYC, 1951-56; export mgr. Chem. Specialties Co., Inc., NYC, 1956-58; sales mgr. Syntex Chem. Co., Inc., NYC, 1958-60; asst. to pres. Syntex Labs., Inc., NYC, 1960-61; gen. sales mgr. Panray-Parlam Corp., Englewood, NJ, 1961-63; v.p. Ormont Drug & Chem. Co., Inc., Englewood, 1963-64, exec. v.p., dir., 1964-66, pres., dir., 1966-81; sec., dir. Goldleaf Pharmacal Co., Inc., Englewood, 1966-81; pres., dir. Moleculon, Inc., 1982-88; pres., CEO, dir. Argus Pharms. Inc., The Woodlands, Tex., 1988-92. Bd. dirs. Fed. Pharmacal Co., Ft. Lauderdale, Fla., Bedford Acme Surg. Co., Inc., Bklyn., Lawton Labs., Inc., Englewood, Ormont Diagnostics Ltd., London. Trustee L.I. U., Bklyn. Coll. Pharmacy. Mem. Bklyn. Coll. Pharmacy Alumni Assn. (pres.), Fedn. Alumni Assns. L.I. U. (pres.), Am. Pharm. Assn., Englewood Jr. C. of C., Young Pres. Orgn., Am. Mgmt. Assn., Drug and Allied Trades Assn., Delta Sigma Theta. Clubs: B'nai B'rith, The Polo Club of Boca Raton (past pres. bd. govs.), Jewish Fedn. of S. Palm Beach County (mem., bd. dirs.), Delray Med. Ctr. (bd. dirs.). Home: 10672 Fawn River Trail Boynton Beach FL 33437 Personal E-mail: aggpolo@aol.com.

GOLDENBERG, KIM, retired academic administrator, internist, consultant; BS, SUNY, Stonybrook, 1968; MS, Polytech. Inst. N.Y., 1972; MD, Albany Med. Coll., NY, 1979. Test engr. lunar lander and naval jets, Grumman, NY, 1968—75; resident internal medicine Western Res. Care Sys., Youngstown, Ohio, 1979—82; dir. gen. internal medicine Wright State U. Sch. Medicine, Dayton, Ohio, 1983—89, vice chair medicine, 1988—89, assoc. dean for students and curriculum, 1989—90, dean, 1990—98; pres. Wright State U., Dayton, Ohio, 1998—2007.

GOLDFARB, JOEL PETER, internist, gastroenterologist; b. Fitchburg, Mass., Jan. 17, 1949; s. Abraham and Eunice (Caplan) G.; m. Elizabeth Weinshel, Dec. 5, 1954. BA, Yale U., 1971; MD, NYU, 1975. Diplomate Am. Bd. Internal Medicine, Am. Bd. Gastroenterology. Resident NYU Bellevue, NYC, 1975-78; fellow (liver) Yale, New Haven, 1978-79; fellow (G.I.) Columbia, NYC, 1979-81; asst. prof. medicine Yeshiva U., Bronx, NY, 1981-84; ptnr. D. Penn MD, J. Patrowitz MD, J. Goldfarb MD, PA., Fort Lee, NJ, 1984—; chief divsn. gastroenterology Holy Name Hosp., Teaneck, NJ, 2006—09. Asst. clin. prof. medicine Mt. Sinai. Named one of Best Doctors of NJ, NJ Monthly Mag., 1996, 2001, NY Mag., 2001, 2002, NJ Life Mag., 2005. Fellow Am. Coll. Physicians, Am. Coll. Gastroenterology. Avocations: cross country skiing, swimming, hiking, scuba diving, opera. Home: 2621 Palisade Ave Apt 5B Bronx NY 10463-6108 Office: 1086 Teaneck Rd Teaneck NJ 07666 E-mail: jpgoldfarb@cs.com.

GOLDFARB, ROBERT PAUL, neurological surgeon; b. St. Paul, July 17, 1936; s. Jack and Frances S. (Singer) G.; m. Lesley G. Zatz, Aug. 11, 1963; children: Jill, Pam. BA with distinction, U. Ariz., 1958; MD, Tulane U., 1962. Diplomate Am. Bd. Neurol. Surgery. Intern Michael Reese Hosp., Chgo., 1962-63; resident gen. surgery Presbyn. St. Luke's Hosp., Chgo., 1963-64; resident neurol. surgery U. Ill. Rsch. Hosp., Chgo., 1963-67; pres. med. staff Crippled Children's Svc. So. Ariz., Tucson, 1973-75; chief staff Tucson Med. Ctr., 1978-80; neurol. surgeon Western Neurosurgery, Ltd., Tucson, 1980—2009. Bd. disr. S.W. Physician Network; neurosurg. cons. U. Ariz. athletic teams, Tucson, 1980—; trustee El Dorado Hosp., 1999—2005; mem. Ariz. Bd. Med. Examiners, 2002-09, bd. sec., 2003-04, chmn. bd., 2006, chmn. Carondelet Neurol. Inst., 2009- Maj. USAFR, 1962-70. Baird scholar U. Ariz., 1958. Fellow ACS; mem. Am. Assn. Neurol. Surgeons, Congress Neurol. Surgeons, Rocky Mountain Neurosurg. Soc. (v.p. 1979). Office: Western Neurosurgery Ltd 6567 E Carondelet Dr Ste 305 Tucson AZ 85710

GOLDFINGER, LAWRENCE E., medical educator; b. Silver Spring, Md., Oct. 20, 1973; BS, Carnegie Mellon U., 1995; PhD, Northwestern U. Sch. Medicine, 1999. Asst. prof. Temple U. Sch. Medicine, 2008—. Rsch. grant, NIH Nat. Heart, Lung and Blood Inst. Mem.: North Am. Vascular Biology Orgn., Am. Soc. Cell Biology. Avocations: clarinet, piano, music. Office: 3400 N Broad St OMS 415 Philadelphia PA 19140 Business E-Mail: goldfinger@temple.edu.

GOLDFISCHER, MINDY, radiologist; MD, NYU, 1982. Diplomate Am. Bd. Medical Examiners, 1983, Am. Bd. Radiology, 1986. Intern Beth Israel Med. Ctr., NYC; resident diagnostic radiology Montefiore Hosp. and Med. Ctr., NYC, 1983—86, Newark Beth Israel Med. Ctr., Newark; fellow diagnostic radiology Thomas Jefferson Univ. Hosp., Phila., 1986—87; assoc. med. dir. Englewood Hosp. & Med. Ctr., NJ, chief breast imaging. Office: Englewood Hospital and Medical Center 350 Engle St Englewood NJ 07631 Office Phone: 201-894-3530.

GOLDFRANK, LEWIS ROBERT, physician; b. NYC, Sept. 8, 1941; s. Herbert John and Helen (Colodny) G.; m. Susan M. Harrington, Aug. 29, 1964; children: Michelle, Andrew, Jennifer, Rebecca. BA, Clark U., 1963; MD, U. Brussels, Belgium, 1970. Diplomate Am. Bd. Med. Toxicology (dir., chmn. 1985-90), Am. Bd. Internal Medicine, 1973, Am. Bd. Emergency Medicine, 1979. Resident Montefiore Hosp., Bronx, NY, 1971-73; dir. emergency medicine Morrisania Hosp., Bronx, 1973-76, North Cen. Bronx Hosp., 1976-79, Montefiore Hosp., 1976-79, Bellevue Hosp., NYC, 1979—, NYU Med. Ctr., NYC, 1979—; dir. N.Y.C. Poison Ctr., 1979—; prof. and chmn. dept. emergency medicine Sch. Medicine NYU, NYC, 2003—. Author, editor: Goldfrank's Toxicologic Emergencies, 1978, 9th edit., 2010, Emergency Doctor, 1987, Diagnostic Testing in the Emergency Department, 1984, 2d edit., 1995; editor: Preparing for Terrorism, 2002, Preparing for Psychological Consequences of Terrorism, 2003. Recipient hon. mention Am. Med. Writers Assn., 1988, Disting. Tchr. award NYU, 2003; faculty scholar NYU, 1999. Fellow: ACP, Am. Acad. Clin. Toxicology, Am. Coll. Emergency Physician; mem.: NAS (Inst. Medicine), Soc. for Acad. Emergency Medicine (Hal Jayne Acad. Excellence award 1990, Leadership award 1999). Avocation: gardening. Home: 55 Grace Ln Ossining NY 10562-2129 Office: Bellevue Hosp Ctr 1st Ave and 27th St New York NY 10016 Office Phone: 212-562-3346. Fax: 212-562-3001. Business E-Mail: lewis.goldfrank@nyumc.org.

GOLDFRIED, MARVIN ROBERT, psychology professor; b. Bklyn., Jan. 24, 1936; s. Samuel and Ann (Ozer) G.; m. Anita Powers, Dec. 23, 1967; children: Daniel, Michael. BA, Bklyn. Coll., 1957; PhD, SUNY, Buffalo, 1961. Diplomate Am. Bd. Profl. Psychology, Am. Bd. Clin. Psychology. Instr. dept. psychology SUNY, Buffalo, 1960-61; asst. prof. U. Rochester (N.Y.), 1961-64; from asst. prof. to prof. SUNY, Stony Brook, 1964—, Disting. prof. psychology, 2006—. Vis. prof. Bar-Ilan U., Ramat-Gan, Ilsrael, 1970-71, U. Calif., Berkeley, 1977-78, NYU, 1991-92; mem. rsch. study sect. NIMH. Author: (with G. Stricker and I.B. Weiner) Rorschach Handbook of Clinican and Research Application, 1971, (with G.C. Davison) Clinical Behavior Therapy, 1976; editor: Converging Themes in Psychotherapy: Trends in Psychodynamic, Humanistic, and Behavioral Practice, 1982, (with M. Merbaum) Behavior Change Through Self-Control, 1973, (with J.C. Norcross) Handbook of Psychotherapy Integration, 1992, 2d edit., 2005, From Cognitive-behavior Therapy to Psychotherapy, 1995, (with G.C. Davison) Clinical Behavior Therapy, How Therapists Change, 2001. NIMH grantee, 1964, 66-68, 67-71, 73-85, 85-97. Fellow APA (pres.-elect, psychology divsn., Disting. Contbns. award 1998, 2001, 02, 04, 05, 09, Disting. Psychologist award 2000); mem. Assn. Advancement Behavior Therapy (Outstanding Clin. Contbns. award 2003), Soc. Exploration Psychotherapy Integration (co-founder, mem. steering com.), Soc. Psychotherapy Rsch. (past pres.; Disting. Career award), AFFIRM: Psychologists Affirming Their Lesbian, Gay, Bisexual, and Transgender Family (founder, dir.), Soc. Clin. Psychology (pres. 2010). Avocations: skiing, tennis, pottery, fly fishing. Office: Psychology Dept State Univ NY Stony Brook NY 11794-2500 Office Phone: 516-632-7823. Business E-Mail: marvin.goldfried@sunysb.edu. *

GOLDHABER, SAMUEL ZACHARY, cardiologist, educator; b. NYC, Nov. 25, 1950; s. Paul and Ethel Renée (Gurland) G.; m. Reeve Lipworth, June 18, 1978; children: Alissa Beth, Benjamin Saul. AB cum laude, Harvard Coll., 1972, MD, 1976. Diplomate Am. Bd. Internal Medicine, Am. Bd. Cardiology. Intern Peter Bent Brigham Hosp., Boston, 1976-77, resident, 1977-79; chief resident West Roxbury VA Med. Ctr., Mass., 1979—80; cardiologist, sr. staff mem. Brigham and Women's Hosp., Boston, 1980—, dir. venous thromboembolism rsch. group, dir. anticoagulation svc. Cardiac Ctr.; assoc. prof. medicine Harvard Med. Sch., Boston, 1989—. Chmn. Venous Disease Coalition, Lakewood, Colo.; mem. editl. bd. Am. Jour. Cardiology, Circulation. Editor: Pulmonary Embolism and Deep Venous Thrombosis, 1985, Prevention of Venous Thromboembolism, 1993, Atlas of Heart Disease, Cardiopulmonary Diseases and Cardiac Tumors, 1995, Pulmonary Embolism, 1999. Recipient Clin. Leadership award, Brigham and Women's Hosp. Physicians Org., 2001; named Eberhard Mammen Lectr. in Clin. Coagulation Sci., 2004. Fellow Am. Coll. Chest Physicians; mem. AAAS, Am. Heart Assn., Am. Coll. Cardiology, Internat. Soc. on Thrombosis and Haemostasis (mem. program organizing com.), Coun. Thrombosis, World Fedn. Cardiology. Office: Brigham and Womens Hosp Cardiovascular Divsn Tower 3B 75 Francis St Boston MA 02115-6106

GOLDHAGEN, JEFFREY LEE, city health department administrator; m. Diana Goldhagen; children: Mia, Alanna, Tess, Eva, Julian. MD, U. Pitts.; MPH, U. Minn. Dir., med. programs for surg. aid Children of the World; co-dir., med. anthropology program Case Western Reserve U., Cleve.; med. dir. Cleve. Pub. Health Dept.; assoc. prof., pediat. U. Fla.; dir. Duval Co. Health Dept., Jacksonville, Fla., 1993—. Fellow: Am. Acad. Pediat. Office: Duval County Pub Health 515 W Sixth St MC #24 Jacksonville FL 32206

GOLDIE, SUE J., public health professor, medical researcher; b. Washington, Dec. 14, 1961; m. Aaron Bradley Waxman, Apr. 17, 1986; children: Jacob Benjamin, Matthew Ariel. BS, Union Coll., 1984; MD, Albany Med. Coll., 1988; MPH, Harvard U., 1997. Cert. Nat. Bd. Examiners, diplomate Am. Bd. Internal Medicine. Intern internal medicine Yale New Haven Hosp., Yale U. Sch. Medicine, 1988—89, resident internal medicine, 1989—91; fellow AHCPR policy award Harvard Sch. Pub. Health, Boston, 1996—98; attending physician Yale New Haven Hosp., 1990, Brigham and Women's Hosp., 1998; clin. asst. prof. medicine Yale U. Sch. Medicine, 1994—98; instr. medicine Harvard Med. Sch., Boston, 1998; asst. prof. health policy and health decision sci. Harvard Sch. Pub. Health, Boston, 1998, Roger Irving Lee prof. pub. health, dir. Ctr. Health Decision Sci.; co-dir. exec. com. Harvard Inst. Global Health (HIGH), Cambridge, Mass., 2007—10, dir., 2010—. Presenter in field. Contbr. articles to med. jour. Recipient Everett Mendelsohn Excellence in Mentoring Award, Harvard U.; Dana scholar, Charles A. Dana Found., 1981, Dana fellow, 1982—84, Charles P. Drumm and Harold C. Wiggers merit scholar, 1984—88, MacArthur Fellow, John T. and Catherine MacArthur Found., 2005, prin. investigator, NIH, CDC, Bill & Melinda Gates Found., Doris Duke Found. Mem.: Inst. Medicine (mem. Bd. Global Health), Soc. Med. Decision Making (editl. bd.), Am. Program Dirs. Internal Medicine (Original Investigation Competition award for innovative programs in med. edn. 1995), Soc. Gen. Internal Medicine (Larry Lynn award 1998), ACP, Alpha Omega Alpha. Avocations: Tae Kwon Do, skiing, climbing. Office: Harvard School Public Health 718 Huntington Ave, 2nd Fl Boston MA 02115-5924 also: Harvard Institute for Global Health 104 Mt Auburn St, 3rd Fl Cambridge MA 02138 Office Phone: 617-432-2019, 617-495-8222. Office Fax: 617-432-0190, 617-495-8231. E-mail: sgoldie@hsph.harvard.edu.

GOLDIN, STEVEN BRADLEY, surgeon, educator; b. Chgo., May 21, 1963; s. Elliot George and Sylvia Goldin; m. Pamela Anne Roach, Sept. 1, 1991; children: Jessica Megan, Ryan Michael. BA, Kalamazoo Coll., Mich., 1985; MD, U. Ill., Chgo., 1994. Residency in surgery Johns Hopkins Hosp., Balt., 1994—2001; asst. prof. surgery

U. South Fla., Tampa, 2001—06, assoc. prof. surgery, 2007—. Office: Univ S Fla Tampa Gen Hosp Rm F145 Tampa FL 33601 Office Fax: 813-844-7396. Business E-Mail: sgoldin@health.usf.edu.

GOLDING, ALLAN PETER, family physician; b. Jamestown, Australia, Mar. 26, 1960; s. Lawrence Edward and Annette Marie Golding; m. Dymphna Cynthia Jane Macintosh, Dec. 4, 1982; children: Vaughn Peter, Alexandra Jayne, Callum Asher. MBBS, U. Adelaide, Australia, 1984; diploma in Obstet., Gynecology and Neonatal Care, Royal Australian and New Zealand Coll. Ob-Gyn., 1987. Registered Med. Bd. South Australia, cert. Civil Aviation Medicine Australia, 2001. Intern Royal Adelaide Hosp., Adelaide, 1984, Lyell McEwin Health Svc., Elizabeth Vale, South Australia, 1985, resident med. officer, 1986; resident med. officer, obstet. Modbury Hosp., Modbury, South Australia, 1987; rural gen. practice Port Pirie, South Australia, 1988—; med. dir. Port Pirie Regional Health Svc., Inc., 2000—02; designated aviation med. examiner Civil Aviation Safety Authority, 2000—06. Clin. lectr., gen. practice U. Adelaide, 1993—; locum registrar in obstet. Queen Elizabeth Hosp., Woodville, South Australia, 2000; steering com. Mid-North Rural South Australia Divsn. Gen. Practice, 1994—; chmn., drug and therapeutics com. Port Pirie Regional Health Svc., Inc., 1994—2000, resource/house com., 1996—, continuum of care com., 2000—01, patient care com., 2000; mental health adv. com. Mid-North Regional Health Svc., Inc., 1996—2000, bd. dirs. Chmn. Heartbeat, Inc., 1990; mem. Port Pirie Asthma Support Group, 1992—; med. officer Port Pirie Abattoir, 1991—; club surgeon Port Pirie Racing and Harness Racing Club, 1993—95; club dr. Port Pirie Power Boat Club, 1990—2003. Fellow: Australian Coll. Rural and Remote Medicine, Royal Australian Coll. Gen. Practitioners; mem.: Rural Drs. Assn. Australia, Arthritis Found. Australia, Sports Medicine Australia, Australian Med. Assn., Port Pirie Med. Practitioners Soc. (sec. 1989, chmn. 1990, chmn. 1993—2000), Lord Baden-Powell Soc. (leader mem. 1990), Port Pirie Diabetics Assn. (patron 1991—), Asthma Found. (life). Avocations: bushwalking, Star Trek. Office: Central Clinic 101 Florence St Port Pirie SA 5540 Australia Office Phone: 08 8632 2144. E-mail: supadocs@westnet.com.au.

GOLDMAN, GEORGE DAVID, psychologist; b. NYC, Jan. 8, 1923; s. Irving Israel and Hattie Anna (Bennett) G.; m. Belle Hans, Sept. 11, 1948; children: Ira Stephen, Carol Marcia Goldman Reife, Deborah Sue Goldman Cohen. BS in Social Sci., CCNY, NYC, 1943; MA, NYU, NYC, 1946, PhD, 1950; cert. in psychoanalysis, William A. White Inst., NYC, 1958. Diplomate Am. Bd. Profl. Psychology, Am. Bd. Psychoanalysis in Psychology. Fellow CCNY, 1946-47, instr. psychology, 1947-53, NYU, 1948-51; pvt. practice psychology NYC, 1952—; pvt. practice Jericho, NY, 1956-95; clin. psychologist Bronx Va. Hosp., 1947—50, Montrose Va. Hosp., 1950—53; staff psychotherapist Low Cost Psychoanalytic Svc. William Alanson White Inst., NYC, 1952-58; clin. prof., supr., dir. clin. svcs. Postdoctoral Psychotherapy Ctr., Derner Inst., Adelphi U., Garden City, NY, 1958-94; supr. psychotherapy grad. div. Ferkauf Sch., Yeshiva U., Bronx, 1976-80. Cons. to supt. Manhasset Pub. Schs., NY, 1956-61; cons. psychotherapy VA, NY area, 1959-79; mem. arbitration panel on marital conflicts Am. Arbitration Assn., 1968—94. Co-editor: (with D.S. Milman) Modern Woman: Her Psychology and Sexuality, 1969, Psychoanalytic Contributions to Community Psychology, 1970, Innovations in Psychotherapy, 1971, The Neurosis of Our Time: Acting Out, 1973, Group Process Today, 1974, Man and Woman in Transition, 1978, Psychoanalytic Perspectives on Aggression, 1978, Modern Man: The Psychology and Sexuality of the Contemporary Male, 1979, Parameters in Psychoanalytic Psychotherapy, 1979, Therapists at Work: A Demonstration of Theory and Technique, 1979, Addiction—Theory and Treatment, 1980, Techniques of Working with Resistance, 1987; (with G. Stricker) Practical Problems of a Private Psychotherapy Practice, 1972, 2d edit., 1981; (with L. Saretsky) Integrating Ego Psychology and Object Relations Theory: Psychoanalytic Perspectives on Psychopathology, 1979; contbr. articles to profl. jours. Mem. profl. adv. bd. Nassau County chpt. Parents Without Ptnrs., 1970-95; pres. psychology divsn., bd. dirs. Am. Friends of Hebrew U. of Jerusalem, NYC, 1975-2002. With US Army, 1943-45. Decorated Bronze Star, Purple Heart with oak leaf cluster; named Disting. Practitioner in Psychology, Nat. Acads. of Practice, 1983; recipient Outstanding Contbn. to Psychology award CCNY, 1989, Disting. Svc. to Profession of Psychology award Am. Bd. Profl. Psychology, Inc., 1999. Fellow APA (divsn. 12, 29, 39, 42, 52, pres. psychologists in ind. practice 1987, pres. divsn. psychoanalysis, 1982, Disting. Contbn. award 1988, Disting. Psychologist award divsn. 42 1989, divsn. 39 award 1990, Disting. Lifetime Svc. award divsn. 39 2000), NY State Psychol. Assn. (past bd. dirs. clin. div.), Nassau County Psychol. Assn. (past bd. dirs.), NY Soc. Clin. Psychologists (pres. 1979), Am. Acad. Psychotherapists (past bd. dirs. and sec.), Am. Bd. Psychoanalysis in Psychology (bd. dirs. 1983-2007), Am. Bd. Profl. Psychology (trustee 2000-07). Democrat. Jewish. Avocations: swimming, travel. Office Phone: 212-722-6515. Personal E-mail: drgdgoldman@aol.com.

GOLDMAN, H. WARREN, neurosurgeon, director; MD, NY Med. Coll., 1973. Diplomate Am. Bd. Neurol. Surgery, lic. NJ, 2004. Intern NY Med. Coll., resident in gen. surgery, 1974; resident in neurosurgery Albert Einstein coll. medicine Yeshiva Univ.; resident in neurosurgery Montefiore Med. Ctr., Mcpl. Hosp., Jacobi Med. Ctr., Bronx, 1978; prof. surgery Cooper Univ. Hosp., NJ, dir. Cooper neurol. inst., chief neurosurgery dept. Fellow: ACS; mem.: Am. Assn. of Neurol. Surgeons. Office: Cooper University Hospital Three Cooper Plz Ste 104 Camden NJ 08103 Office Phone: 856-968-7965. Office Fax: 856-968-8697.

GOLDMAN, IRA STEVEN, gastroenterologist; b. Bronx, NY, May 19, 1951; s. George David and Belle (Hans) G.; children: Zachary, Joshua. BA, U. Rochester, 1973; student, Oxford U., 1972; MD, Columbia U., 1977. Diplomate Am. Bd. Internal Medicine, Am. Bd. Gastroenterology. Intern Columbia Presbyn. Med. Ctr., NYC, 1977-78, resident in internal medicine, 1978-80; fellow in gastroenterology and liver diseases U. Calif. Sch. Medicine, San Francisco, 1980-83; instr. in anatomy Columbia U., NYC, 1978; asst. prof. medicine U. Calif., San Francisco, 1983-85, Cornell U. Med. Coll., NYC, 1985-91, assoc. prof. clin. medicine, 1991-96; attending physician North Shore Univ. Hosp., Manhasset, N.Y., 1985—; assoc. prof. clin. medicine NYU Sch. Medicine, 1996—2011, Hofstra North Shore-LIJ Sch. Medicine, 2011—. Attending physician St. Francis Hosp., Roslyn, N.Y.; physicians adv. bd. Am. Liver Found., Greater N.Y. chpt., 1985—; sci. adv. commn. L.I. chpt. Nat. Found. for Ileitis and Colitis, 1985-91; vice chair clin. practice sec. Am. Gastroent. Assn., 1995-97, chmn., 1997-2000. Reviewer jours. Gastroenterology; contbr. articles to profl. jours., chpts. to books. Rsch. fellow Am. Liver Found., 1982, Clin. Investigator award NIH, 1983. Fellow ACP, Am. Coll. Gastroenterology, Am. Gastroenterol. Assn.; mem. Am. Assn. for Study of Liver Diseases, Med. Soc. State of N.Y., Nassau County Med. Soc., Nassau County. Acad. Medicine, N.Y. Soc. for Gastrointestinal Endoscopy (pres. 1996-97), Alpha Omega Alpha. Avocations: sailing, tennis. Office: North Shore-LIJ Ste 206 310 E Shore Rd Great Neck NY 11023-2432 Office Phone: 516-487-7677.

GOLDMAN, JANICE GOLDIN, psychologist, educator; b. Phila., Feb. 15, 1938; d. Samuel and Dorothea (Berenson) Goldin; m. Arthur S. Goldman, Aug. 31, 1958; children: Jill Ann Goldman-Callahan, Joshua N., Jennifer S. BA, U. Pa., 1960, MA, 1962; MS, Hahnemann Med. Coll., 1972, D in Psychology, 1975. Lic. psychologist, Pa. Chief psychologist Charles Peberdy Child Psychiatry Ctr. Hahnemann U., Phila., 1975-87, from clin. asst. to assoc. prof., 1985-87; pvt. practice Jenkintown, Pa., 1977—. Cons. Haverford (Pa.) State Hosp., 1982, Assn. for Mental Health Affiliates with Israel, 1984, 86; mem. profl. adv. bd. Pub. Radio Sta WHYY, Phila., 1984-86; workshop leader Women's Ctr. of Montgomery County, Jenkintown, 1982—. Contbr. articles to profl. jours. Board dirs. Assn. for Mental Health Affiliate with Israel, nationwide, 1984-88, Or Hadash Synogogue, Ft. Wash., Pa., 1989, 96-2000. Mem. APA, Am. Family Therapy Acad., Nat. Register Health Svc. Providers, Phila. Soc. Clin. Psychology (sec. 1977-79), Am. Amnesty Internat., Internat. Soc. for Study of Trauma and Dissociation, Greater Phila. Soc. Clin. Hypnosis, Phi Beta Kappa. Democrat. Avocations: tennis, bicycling, cooking, reading, writing. Office: The Plaza 1250 Greenwood Ave Jenkintown PA 19046-2901 Home Phone: 215-635-1693; Office Phone: 215-572-1355. Personal E-mail: jgold1332@comcast.net.

GOLDMAN, JERI JOAN, psychologist; b. Oklahoma City, Apr. 11, 1934; d. Clarence William and Opal Louise (Leach) Richards; div.; children: Susan, Lisa, Eric. BA, Trinity U., 1955; MA, So. Meth. U., 1956; PhD, Stanford U., 1961; MEd, Temple U., 1982. Cert. sch. psychologist, sch. adminstrn; Lic. psychologist, PA & NJ. Chief psychologist, asst. dir. West River Mental Health Ctr., Rapid City, SD, 1961—65; chief psychologist Woods Schs. and Residential Treatment Ctr., Langhorne, Pa., 1965-66, 74-89, health and clin. services adminstr., 1985-87, dir. clin. services, 1987-88; dir. Devel. Evaluation Ctr., Langhorne, 1971-72; supr. spl. edn. Camden City Pub. Schs., NJ, 1989—2000; adminstr. spl. edn., pupil personnel Chester Upland Sch. Dist., Pa., 2000—07. Cons. schs., clinics in Pa., NJ, 1966-71; adj. prof. Sch. Psychol, Temple U. Phila., 1977-. Contbr. numerous articles to profl. jours. and books. Fellow Am. Orthopsychiat. Assn. (life), Pa. Psychol. Assn.; mem. APA, Am. Assn. Intellectual & Developmental Disabilities, Pa. Tourette Syndrome Assn. Personal E-mail: jerigoldman@comcast.net.

GOLDMAN, JOHN MICHAEL, physician, consultant hematologist, educator; b. London, United Kingdom, Nov. 30, 1938; s. Carl Heinz and Bertha (Brandt) G. BM BCh, Oxford U., 1963, DM, 1981. Medicine Gen. Med. Coun., 1963. Dir. LRF Ctr. Adult Leukaemia Imperial Coll. London Hammersmith Hosp., London, 1989—2004; chmn. dept. haematology Imperial Coll. London Sch. Medicine Hammersmith Hosp., 1994—2004; med. dir. Anthony Nolan Bone Marrow Trust, London, 1989—2010; chair Internat. Chronic Myeloid Leukemia Found., 2009—. Editor Bone Marrow Transplantation, 1985—. Recipient Hon MD Poitiers, U. of Poitiers; Fogarty scholar, Hematology Br., Nat. Inst. Health, 2005—06. Fellow Royal Coll. Physicians, Acad. Med. Scis., European Group for Bone Marrow Transplantation (pres. 1990-94); European Hematology Assn. (pres. 1996-98). Achievements include research in Scientific papers on haematology, leukaemia, bone marrow transplantation, molecular biology. Office: Imperial Coll London Hammersmith Hosp Du Cane Rd London W12 0NN England Business E-Mail: jgoldman@imperial.ac.uk.

GOLDMAN, LEE, dean, cardiologist, educator; b. Phila., Jan. 6, 1948; s. Marvin and Kathryn (Schwartz) G.; m. Jill Steinhardt, Mar. 21, 1971; children: Jeff, Daniel, Robyn Sue. BA, Yale U., 1969, MD, MPH, Yale U., 1973. Diplomate Am. Bd. Internal Medicine (bd. dirs. 1996—), Am. Bd. Cardiovasc. Disease. Intern U. Calif., San Francisco, 1973-74, resident in medicine, 1974-75, Mass. Gen. Hosp., Boston, 1975-76; fellow in cardiology Yale-New Haven Hosp., 1976-78; asst. prof. medicine Harvard Med. Sch., 1978-83, assoc. prof., 1983-89, prof., 1989-95; prof., assoc. dean U. Calif., San Francisco, chair Dept. Medicine, 1995—2006; exec. v.p. health and biomedical scis., Harold & Margaret Hatch prof., dean Faculties of Health Scis. and Medicine Columbia U. Coll. of Physicians and Surgeons, NYC, 2006—. Mem. operating com. Ptnrs. Health Care Inc., 1993-95; Inst. Medicine, 1995—, Assn. Prof. Medicine, 1995—2006, pres. 2002, bd. dirs., 1998—2000; bd. dirs. UCSF Stanford Health Care, 1997—2000. Editor-in-chief Am. Jour. medicine, 1997—2005; assoc. editor New Eng. Jour. Medicine, 1989-95; contbr. numerous articles to profl. jours. Bd. dirs. Temple Shir Tikva, Wayland, Mass., pres., 1986-88. Henry J. Kaiser Family Found. scholar, 1982-87, Robert Williams award 2009. Fellow ACP (tchg. and rsch. scholar 1980-83, John Phillips award 2007), Am. Coll. Cardiology; mem. Am. Soc. Clin. Investigation, Soc. Gen. Medicine (pres. 1990; Glaser award 2002), Assn. Am. Physicians (pres. 2001; Blake award 2002). Office: Columbia U Coll of Physicians & Surgeons 630 W 168th St, P&S 2-401 New York NY 10032 Office Phone: 212-305-3671.

GOLDMAN, LYNN ROSE, dean, epidemiologist, pediatrician; b. Galveston, Tex., Apr. 24, 1951; d. Armond Samuel and Barbara Jean (Bangert) Goldman; m. Douglas George Hayward. BS, U. Calif., 1976; MPH, Johns Hopkins U., 1981; MS, U. Calif., Berkeley, 1979; MD, U. Calif., San Francisco, 1981. Diplomate Am. Bd. Pediatrics. Resident in pediatrics Children's Hosp. Med. Ctr., Oakland, Calif., 1985; resident in preventive medicine U. Calif., Berkeley, 1985; pub. health med. officer Calif. Dept. Health Svcs., Berkeley, 1985-91, pub. health med. adminstr., 1991-93; asst. adminstr. Office of Prevention, Pesticides and Toxic Substances, EPA, Washington, 1993-98; prof. Sch. Hygiene and Pub. Health Johns Hopkins U., Balt., 1999, prof. Environ. Health Sci., Occupational and Environ. Health, chair Interdepartmental Prog. in Applied Pub. Health; dean Sch. Pub. Health & Health Services George Washington U., Washington, 2010—. Prin. investigator Johns Hopkins Nat. Children's Study Ctr., Nat. Ctr. of Excellence for Study of Preparedness and Catastrophic Event Response. Recipient Woodrow Wilson award disting. govt. svc., John Hopkins U. Alumni Assn., 1999; named Alumna of Yr., U. Calif. Berkeley Sch. Pub. Health, 2002. Mem.: Inst. Medicine (acting chair Roundtable on Environ. Health Scis.). Democrat. Office: George Washington University School of Public Health Ross Hall 2300 Eye St, NW Washington DC 20037 Office Phone: 202-994-2160. Office Fax: 202-994-1850. E-mail: goldmanl@gwu.edu.

GOLDMAN, MARTIN ELLIOT, cardiologist; b. NYC, May 24, 1954; s. Hirsh Jacob and Shirley Goldman; m. Shera Stern; children: Sarah, Avi, Miriyam, Yehuda. MD, Albert Einstein Coll. Medicine, NYC, 1976. Diplomate Am. Bd. Internal Medicine, cert. in cardiovasc. disease. Med. intern Brigham & Women's Hosp., Boston, 1976—77, cardiology resident, 1977—78; cardiology fellowship Mt. Sinai Med. Ctr., NYC, 1978—80; prof. medicine & cardiology Mt. Sinai Sch. Medicine, 1981—, dir. Heart Echocardiography Lab., Dr. Arthur Master prof. medicine (cardiology). Author: Handbook Heart Drugs, 1992, Clinical Atlas of Echocardiography, 1996; reviewer: for numerous peer review jours. in cardiology and medicine. Mem. med. adv. bd. Living Heart Found. Fellow: Am. Coll. Cardiology; mem.: ACP, Am. Soc. Echocardiography (bd. dirs. 2000—), NY Soc. Echocardiography (pres. 2002). Achievements include first to utilize intra-operative transesophageal color-flow Doppler echocardiography to guide the hand of the cardiac surgeon in the operating room, allowing moment-to-moment decisions during heart valve repair and replacement. Office: Mt Sinai Med Ctr Cardiovasc Inst Guggenheim Pavilion Fl 6th Rm 6 250D 1190 Fifth Ave New York NY 10029 also: 5 E 98th St 3rd Fl New York NY 10029 Office Phone: 212-241-5586. Office Fax: 212-426-7196. Business E-Mail: martin.goldman@mssm.edu. *

GOLDMAN, MAURICE, retired physicist, consultant; b. Paris, Mar. 1, 1933; m. Micheline Dina Levy, Dec. 4, 1959; children: Frédéric, Didier Laurent. Chem. Engr., Ecole Supérieure de Physique et Chimie, Paris, 1955; D in Physics, U. Paris, 1967. Physicist Commissariat à l'Energie Atomique, Saclay, France, 1955—69, Commissariat à l'Energie Atomique, Saclay, France, 1984—89, rsch. dir., 1989—93; sous directeur de laboratoire Collège de France, Paris, 1969—83; ret. Cons. GE Healthcare, Malmö, Sweden, 1999—2006. Mem.: Academie des Sciences (Grand prix 1970). Achievements include research in theory and experiments on spin temperature; nuclear magnetic ordering; fundamental magnetic resonance physics; design of new contrast agents for MRI.

GOLDMAN, PHYLLIS E., psychology educator; BA, Rutgers U., 1966; MA, Seton Hall U., 1969; MS, Stevens Inst. Tech., 1978; EdD, Seton Hall U., 1983. Rsch. asst. Rutgers Univ., Newark, 1965-66; counselor N.J. Dept. of Labor and Industry, Newark, 1967-69; prof., psychology County Coll. of Morris, Randolph, N.J., 1969—; pvt. practice cons., 1978—. Author: The Role of Locus Control and Collective Barganing Attitudes, 1983, Academic Self-Concept, 1992; editor: Dimensions of Work and Human Behavior, 1980, 85, (jour.) Morris Manager, 1988, 89, 90; contbr. articles to profl. jours. Speakers bur. County Coll. Morris, Randolph, 1976—2005; bd. adv. Cath. Cmty. Svcs., Newark, 1978—80; adv. coun. US Postal Svc., 2003—04. Mem. Am. Psychological Assn., Psi Chi, Kappa Delta Pi, Phi Delta Kappa. Avocation: reading.

GOLDMAN, RALPH FREDERICK, research physiologist, educator; b. Boston, Mar. 3, 1928; s. Harry and May (Field) G.; m. Joan R. Krinsky, May 27, 1956; children: Harry, Ellen. BS in Chemistry, U. Denver, 1949; MA in Physiology, Boston U., 1951, PhD in Physiology, 1954; MS in Engring., Northeastern U., Boston, 1962. Lic. bldg. contractor 1980, stock broker 1970. Rsch. physiologist Natick Labs. U.S. Army, Mass., 1955—61; dir. div. environ. medicine U.S. Army Rsch. Inst., Natick, 1961—82; prin. cons. Dept. of Army for Environ. Physiology, Natick, 1971—82; chief scientist Multi-Tech Corp., Natick, 1982—88; chief scientist, R&D, clothing and human comfort Comfort Tech., Inc., Plymouth, Mass., 1989—2011; sr. cons. tech. and product devel. Arthur D. Little, Inc., Cambridge, Mass., 1993—97; mgr. Krinsky Realty Co. Inc., 1980—. Adj. prof. Boston U., 1970—2005, N.C. State U., 1989—2005; lectr. MIT, Cambridge, 1974-94; vis. scientist Peoples Rep. of China, 1981—2007; vis. scholar lectr. Springfield (Mass.) Coll., 1977, Ohio State U., 1977, 88; Rohles lectr., Kans. State U., 2008; chmn. rsch. group biomed. effects of clothing, NATO, 1981-86, located copper mem., 1965, real estate mem., 1960-1986. Author: 4 books; contbr. 26 chpts. to books, over 500 articles, abstracts and tech. reports to profl. jours. Scoutmaster Boy Scouts Am., Framingham, Mass., 1956-90, exec. bd., 1991-2002; mem. town meeting Town of Framingham, 1983-88, founder, Mil. Ergonomics, dir., Seweeting. Recipient Meritorious Civilian Svc. award U.S. Army R&D Command, 1963, Exceptional Civilian Svc. award Sec. of Army, 1976, Sr. Exec. Svc. award U.S. Civil Svc., 1979, Silver Beaver award Boy Scouts Am., 1981. Fellow: ASHRAE (life; bd. dirs. 1982—85, assoc. editor HVAC&R Rsch. 1995—2001, Disting. Fellow award 1992), Am. Coll. Sports Medicine (editl. bd. 1979—85), Ergonomics Soc. (hon.); mem.: ASTM, IEEE (life; AEMB Coun. 1978—84), Assn. Mil. Surgeons U.S., Am. Physiol. Soc. (editl. bd. 1972—78), Framingham Amateur Radio Assn. (treas. 1970—84), Tarpon Cove Yacht and Racquet Club, Naples, Fla. Jewish. Avocations: piano, gardening, walking. Home: 425 Cove Tower Dr Apt 704 Naples FL 34110-6505

GOLDMAN, STANFORD MILTON, medical educator; b. Salt Lake City, Nov. 28, 1940; s. Osher and Miriam (Solomon) G.; m. Harriet Kaplow, Apr. 2, 1965; children: Etan, Nava. BA, BRE, Yeshiva U., 1961; MD, Einstein Coll. Medicine, 1965. Intern Jefferson U. Sch. Medicine, Phila., 1965-66; resident Einstein Coll. Medicine, Bronx, 1966-69; chmn. dept. radiology USPHS Phoenix Indian Med. Ctr., 1969-71; asst. prof. radiology Einstein Coll. Medicine, Bronx, 1971-72; from instr. to asst. prof. radiology Johns Hopkins U. Sch. Medicine, Balt., 1972-79; from asst. prof. to assoc. prof. U. Md., Balt., 1975-81; assoc. prof. Johns Hopkins U., 1979-86; clin. prof. Uniformed Svcs. U., Bethesda, Md., 1981-94; prof. radiology Johns Hopkins U., 1986-94, prof. urology, 1988-93; prof., chmn. radiology U. Tex. Med. Sch., Houston, 1993—2000, prof. urology, 1995—, prof. radiology, 1993—. Adj. prof. radiology and urology Baylor Coll. Medicine, Houston, 1994—; med. dir. radiol. sch. tech. Houston C.C., 1994, ultrasound sch. tech., 1999-2001; prof. radiology M.D. Anderson Cancer Ctr., Houston, 1995-2003, adj. prof., 2007—. Editor: Computed Tomography of Kidneys & Adrenals, 1983, CT & MRI of the Genitourinary Tract, 1990, Tc E Rm Del Trattos Genito-Urinario, 1994; assoc. editor: Urologic Radiology, 1982-85, Radiology, 1986-94, European Urology, 1993-2004; cons. editor Urology, 1998—, editl. bd. Emergency Radiology, 2006-. Chair bd. edn. Beren Acad. Houston, 2005—08; mem. Radiation Control

Adv. Bd., Md., 1989—93. Lt. comdr. USPHS, 1969—71. Grantee, Royal Coll. Physicians, 2006—. Fellow: Soc. Uroradiology (bd. dirs. 1992—98, med. equipment com. 2000—01, ethics com. 2003, Lifetime Achievement award 2008), Radiol. Soc. N.Am. (chmn. sci. exhibits awards com. 1988—90, chmn. program coms. subcom. on gu radiology 1996—99), Am. Coll. Radiology (counselor from Tex. 1996—2002, mem. com. on coding and nomenclature of commn. on econs. 1996—2002, nominating com. 1999, co-chmn. nominating comm. 2000—01, alt. counselor 2002—, liason to com. on trauma ACS 2004—, com. emergency radiol. 2006—, mem. com. emergency radiology 2006—, 2006—, subcom. on radiation in pregnancy com. on safety 2007—08, liaison to publ. subcom., liaison to performance improvement and patient safety subcom.), Am. Soc. Emergency Radiology (indsl. com. 1994—98, bd. dirs. 1994—, abstract com. 1995—97, chmn. audit com. 1995—99, chmn. sci. program com. 1996—97, vice chair program com. 1996—97, fin. com. 1996—98, site com. 1996—98, sec.-treas. 1998—2000, exec. com. 1998—, sec.-treas. 2001, pres. 2002—04, chair site selection com. 2002—04, nominating com. 2002—04, chmn. bylaws com. 2004—08, alt. counselor to ACR 2007—09, counselor to ACR 2009—, jt. mem. bylaws com. SUR-SGR 2009—, jt. bylaws com. SUR SGR 2009—, Gold medal 2006); mem.: ACS, AMA, Johns Hopkins Med. and Surg. Assn., Assn. Univ. Radiologists (ethics com. 1997, nominating com. 1997—98), European Soc. Urogenital Radiology, Royal Belgian Radiol. Soc. (hon.), Houston Radiol. Soc. (treas. 2000—, pres. 2002), Houston Med. Soc., Tex. Radiol. Soc. (program com. 1994—96, chmn. long range planning com. 1996—97, bd. dirs. 1996—, fellowship nominating com. 1998—2000, 2d v.p. 2001, 1st v.p. 2002, chmn. program com. 2002—03, exec. com. 2002—, chmn. legis. com. 2003—04, pres. 2004—05, chair orgnl. structure coun. 2005—06, bd. govs. 2005—06, chair jud. affairs com. 2005—06, chair nominating soc. 2005—06, chmn. bylaws com. 2005—06, trustee 2005—06, chair bd. trustees 2005—06, mem. bd. trustees 2005—, Gold medal 2010), Tex. Med. Soc., Am. Urol. Assn. (hematuria guidelines panel 1998—99), Am. Roentgen Ray Soc., U.S.-Israel Bi-Nat. Sci. Found., Albert Einstein Alumni Assn. (bd. dirs. 1991—2002, 2003—, Disting. Alumni award 1996), U. Md. Alumni Assn. (assoc.). Jewish. Avocations: swimming, music. Office: U Tex Med Sch Dept Radiology 6431 Fannin St Ste 2100 Houston TX 77030-1501 Business E-Mail: stanford.m.goldman@uth.timc.edu.

GOLDMAN, STEVEN ANDREW, plastic surgeon, educator; s. John and Margaret Goldman; m. Jodie Lynn Goldman, June 11, 1995; children: Max, Mollie, Eli, Jacob. BA in Chemistry with honors, Dartmouth Coll., 1989; MD, U. Pitts., 1993. Cert. Am. Bd. Plastic Surgery. Intern in surgery U. Pitts. Sch. Medicine, 1993—94; resident in otolaryngology U. Pitts. Med. Ctr., 1994—98; resident in plastic surgery U. Hosps. Cleve., 1998—2000; asst. prof. plastic surgery Case Western Res. U. Sch Medicine, U. Hosps. Cleve., 2000—. Contbr. articles to profl. jours., chapters to books. Named Top Doc in Reconstructive Surgery, No. Ohio Live Mag., 2005; named to Who's Who in Execs. and Profls., Nat. Register, 2004. Fellow: ACS, Am. Acad. Facial Plastic and Reconstructive Surgery; mem.: Am. Acad. Otolaryngology/Head and Neck Surgery (cert.), Am. Rhinologic Soc., Am. Soc. Plastic Surgeons, Alpha Omega Alpha. Home: 2490 Blossom Ln Beachwood OH 44122 Office: Case Sch Medicine 11100 Euclid Ave Cleveland OH 44106 Office Phone: 216-514-8899. Office Fax: 216-884-8667. E-mail: info@drgoldman.com.

GOLDMANN, JAMES ALLEN, healthcare consultant, author; b. Milw., Feb. 26, 1952; s. Allen Abraham and Ruth Lois (Kolbur) G.; m. Pamela Anne McCole, June 6, 1980; children: Michael, Elissa, Kerry. AB, Harvard Coll., 1974; MHA, Washington U., St. Louis, 1979. V.p. Riverside Meth. Hosp., Columbus, Ohio, 1980—85; COO Children's Med. Ctr., Dallas, 1986—92; cons. APM, Inc., NYC, 1993—96; ptnr. Arthur Andersen, Dallas, 1996—2000, IBM, Dallas, 2001—03, JHD Group, Dallas, 2004—09, Ethos Ptnrs., 2009—, Navigant, 2011—. Bd. dirs. Hope Cottage, Dallas, 1989-93; scout leader Boy Scouts Am., Columbus and Grapevine, Tex., 1980-84, 92, 93. Fellow Am. Coll. Healthcare Execs.

GOLDNER, WHITNEY SEARS, endocrinologist; b. Omaha, Aug. 10, 1972; BA, Augustana Coll., Rock Island, Ill., 1994; MD, U. Nebr. Med. Ctr., 1998. Endocrinologist U. Nebr. Med. Ctr., 2004—, assoc. prof. Mem.: Am. Thyroid Assn., Am. Diabetes Assn., Endocrine Soc. Office: 983020 Nebr Med Ctr Omaha NE 68198-3020 Office Fax: 402-559-9504. Business E-Mail: wgoldner@unmc.edu.

GOLDSCHLAGER, NORA FOX, internist, cardiologist, educator; b. NYC, 1939; MD, NYU, 1965. Diplomate Am. Bd. Internal Medicine, Am. Bd. Cardiovasc. Medicine. Intern Montefiore Hosp., NYC, 1965-66, resident, 1966-67, Henry Ford Hosp., Detroit, 1967-68; fellow in cardiology Wayne State U., Detroit, 1968-69, Pacific Med. Ctr., Calif., 1969-70; prof. clin. medicine U. Calif., San Francisco, 1983—. Mem. staff San Francisco Gen. Hosp., 1978—. Master ACP; Fellow Am. Coll. Cardiology, Heart Rhythm Soc., Am. Heart Assn. Office: San Francisco Gen Hosp Dept Cardiology San Francisco CA 94110-2897

GOLDSCHMID, STEVE, dean, gastroenterologist, educator; MD, Wayne State U., Detroit, 1980. Cert. in internal medicine and gastroenterology American Bd. Internal Medicine. Residency in internal medicine and gastroenterology U. South Fla. Coll. Medicine; dir. clin. services Emory U. Sch. Medicine, Atlanta; assoc. prof. U. Ariz. Coll. Medicine, Tucson, 2000—, chief gastroenterology sect., 2000—06, chmn. dept. medicine, chief gastroenterology, dir. endoscopy/bronchoscopy lab., 2007—08, interim dean, 2008—09, dean, 2009—. Named one of Best Doctors in America, 2008—11. Fellow: American Coll. Physicians, American Coll. Gastroenterology; mem.: American Soc. Gastrointestinal Endoscopy, American Gastroenterology Assn. Office: University Ariz Coll Medicine Office of Dean 1501 N Campbell Ave Tucson AZ 85724 Office Phone: 520-626-6119. Office Fax: 520-874-7133. Business E-Mail: sgoldsch@email.arizona.edu. *

GOLDSCHMIDT-CLERMONT, PASCAL J., medical educator, cardiologist, dean; b. Brussels, Apr. 12, 1954; m. Emily Ann Boches. BS, Univ. Libre de Brussels, 1976, MD, 1980. Lic. physician Md., NC, Fla., Belgium. Intern and resident in medicine/cardiology Erasme Acad. Hosp./U. Libre de Brussels, 1980-83; rsch. fellow dept. immunology and microbiology Med. U. SC, Charleston, 1983-86; resident in medicine Union Meml. Hosp., Balt., 1986-88; clin. and rsch. fellow cardiology/cell biology/anatomy Johns Hopkins U., Balt., 1988-91, assoc. prof. dept. medicine/cardiology divsn., 1991-96, dir. Bernard Lab. Vascular Biology, 1991—97; attending CCU Johns Hopkins Hosp., Balt., 1991—97, co-dir. Thrombosis Ctr., 1994-96; co-dir. Henry Ciccarone Ctr. for Prevention Heart Disease, Balt., 1991—97; prof. medicine, dir. Heart and Lung Inst. Ohio State U., Columbus, dir. divsn. cardiology, 1998—2000; joined faculty Duke U., 2000; chief Divsn. Cardiology Duke U. Med. Ctr., chmn. Dept. Medicine; sr. v.p. med. affairs, dean U. Miami Leonard M. Miller Sch. Medicine, 2006—; CEO U. Miami Health Sys., 2007—. Lectr. in field. Contbr. numerous articles and abstracts to profl. jours., chpts. to books; reviewer New Eng. Jour. Medicine, Annals of Internal Medicine, Biochemistry, Blood, Cell, Cell Adhesion and Comm., Circulation Rsch., Jour. Cell Biology, Molecular Biology of the Cell, Am. Heart Assn., NIH. Recipient NATO Sci. award, 1983, 84; grantee Clinician Scientist Award, 1991-93, Syntex Scholars Program, 1992-95, Am. Heart Assn., 1992-94, 95—, NIH, 1992-96, 94-96, 95—; Am. Heart Assn. fellow, 1990, Med. U. S.C., 1984, 85., Jay & Jeasie Schotlenstein prize, Ohio State U., 2009 Mem. AAAS, Am. Heart Assn., Am. Soc. Clin. Investigators. Office: Univ Miami Miller Sch Medicine Med Campus R-699 1600 NW 10 Ave Miami FL 33136 Office Phone: 305-243-6545. Office Fax: 305-243-4888. E-mail: pgoldschmidt@med.miami.edu. *

GOLDSMITH, ARI J., pediatric otolaryngologist, educator; MD, Yeshiva U., 1988. Diplomate Am. Bd. Otolaryngology. Resident otolaryngology LI Jewish Hosp., 1989—93; fellow pediatric otolaryngology Children's Hosp., Boston, 1993—94, Harvard Med. Sch.; assoc. prof. otolaryngology SUNY Downstate Med. Ctr., 1994; pediatric otolaryngology Univ. Hosp. of Brooklyn at LI Coll. Hosp. Author articles and chapters on various topics of otolaryngology. Fellow: Am. Acad. of Pediat.; mem.: Am. Soc. of Pediatric Otolaryngology. Office: University Hospital of Brooklyn at Long Island College Hospital 339 Hicks St Brooklyn NY 11201

GOLDSMITH, DAVID JULIAN ALEXANDER, physician, nephrologist, consultant, director; b. Salford, Eng., Aug. 29, 1959; s. Michael and Wendy G.; m. Deborah Gillatt, July 14, 1990; children: Daniel, Rebecca. MA MB BChir, U. Cambridge, 1980. Intern St. Thomas' Hosp., London, 1977—83; resident Manchester (Eng.) Royal Infirmary, 1991—95; cons. physician, nephrologist Royal Sussex County Hosp., Brighton, 1995-98, Guy's Hosp., London, 1998—; dir. R & D Guy's & St. Thomas Hosps. NHS Found. Trust; clin. dir. London South, 2010—. Clin. tutor for medicine Guy's Hosp., London, 2000—05; sec. UK Renal Assn., 2004-08 Contbr. chapters to books, over 300 articles to profl. jours.; author: Color Handbook Renal Medicine, ABC of Kidney Diseases, 2007. Coun. mem. ERA, 2004—07. Fellow: RCP (London, Edinburg), Am. Soc. Nephrology. Achievements include research into ion transport in hypertension, ambulatory blood pressure, and arterial structure and function in renal failure. Office: Guy's Hosp Renal Unit St Thomas St SE1 9RT London England Fax: 020-7955-4909. Business E-Mail: david.goldsmith@gstt.nhs.uk.

GOLDSMITH, DONALD P., pediatric rheumatologist, educator; MD, U. Vt., 1967. Diplomate Am. Bd. Allergy and Immunology, Am. Bd. Pediatrics, Am. Bd. Pediatrics-pediatric rheumatology, lic. Pa., 1970, NJ, 1979. Intern pediat. Jefferson Hosp., 1968; resident pediat. St. Christopher's Hosp. for Children, 1973, fellow allergy and immunology, 1975, attending rheumatologist, chief sect. of rheumatology; prof. pediat. Drexel Univ. Coll. of Medicine; hosp. affiliations include Faxton St. Luke's Healthcare, Lehigh Valley Hosp. Muhlenberg, St. Luke's Hosp. Bethlehem. Named one of Top Doctors, Phila. Mag., 2011. Office: Saint Christopher's Hospital for Children 3601 A St Philadelphia PA 19134 Office Phone: 215-427-5000. Office Fax: 215-427-5555.

GOLDSMITH, ELEANOR JEAN, retired hospital administrator; b. Mount Vernon, NY, Aug. 16, 1929; d. Elias Benjamin Jacobson and Rose Millicent Liebowitz; m. Myles Robert Goldsmith, Mar. 8, 1981 (dec.); m. Marshall H. Numark (div.); 3 children. BS in commerce, Coll. of New Rochelle, NYC, 1949; MA in Edn., NYU, 1950, EdD, 1979. Cert. tchr. NY, 1950, lic. nursing home adminstr. Tex., 1983. Tchr. Mount Vernon Sch. Bus., Mount Vernon, 1949—50, Northport HS, NY, 1950—51; supr. recreation Greystone Park Psychiatric Hosp., Morris Plains, NY, 1969—80; dir. activities therapy Bellevue Psychiatric Hosp., NYC, 1980—82; adminstr. Mesquite Tree Nursing Home, Tex., 1983—84; edn. coord. dept. ophthalmology U. Tex. Southwestern Med. Ctr., Dallas, 1984—92; ret., 1992. Author several mag. articles. Elected mem. Bd. Edn., Fair Lawn, NJ, 1957—59. Mem.: Women's Am. Orgn. for Rehab. and Tng., Bridgeport Upper Merion Lions Club (past pres.). Avocations: travel, reading, bridge, skiing, ice skating. Home: 3000 W Valley Forge Cir #941 King Of Prussia PA 19406 Personal E-mail: elgoldsmith@comcast.net.

GOLDSMITH, HARRY SAWYER, surgeon, educator; b. Newton, Mass., Sept. 30, 1929; s. Leo and Dorothy Amy (Appleton) G.; m. Linda Perry, Dec. 8, 1961; children: John, Robert, Lynne. AB, Dartmouth, 1952; MD, Boston U., 1956; degree in medicine (hon.), Shanghai Second Med. U., 1988, Xuzhou Med. Coll., China, 1995. Intern Boston (Mass.) City Hosp., 1956-57, resident surgery, 1957-61, Meml. Sloan Kettering Inst., NYC, 1963-65, chief gastric, mixed tumor svc., 1965-70; Samuel D. Gross prof. surgery, chmn. dept. Jefferson Med. Coll., Phila., 1970-77, disting. prof. surgery, 1977; surgeon in chief Jefferson U. Hosp., Phila., 1970-77; prof. surgery Dartmouth Coll. Med. Sch., Hanover, NH, 1977-83; prof. surgery, adj. prof. neurosurgery Boston (Mass.) U. Sch. Medicine, 1983-95; clin. prof. surgery U. Nev., Reno, 1996—2005, cons. surgery, 2006—; clin. prof. neurosurgery U. Calif., Davis, 2009—. Author: A Conspiracy of Silence: The Health and Death of Franklin D. Roosevelt, 2007; editor-in-chief: Goldsmith's Practice of Surgery, 1976-89; editor: The Omentum: Research and Clinical Applications, 1990, The Omentum: Application to Brain and Spinal Cord, 2000, The Omentum: Basic Research and Clinical Applications, 2010; contbr. articles to profl. jours. Capt. U.S. Army, 1961-63. Mem. ACS, Soc. Vascular Surgery, Brit. Assn. Surg. Oncology, Soc. for Surgery Alimentary Tract, Internat. Surg. Soc., Ctrl. Surg. Assn., New England Surg. Soc. Address: PO Box 493 Glenbrook NV 89413-0493 Office Phone: 775-749-5801. Office Fax: 775-749-5861. Personal E-mail: hlgldsmith@aol.com.

GOLDSMITH, JANET JANE, pediatric nurse practitioner; b. Creston, Iowa, Mar. 3, 1942; d. Paul William and Mary Lucille (Crow) Schafroth; m. Olin Russel Goldsmith, Aug. 31, 1963; children: Rodney, Scott, Kristen. Diploma, Iowa Meth. Hosp. Sch. Nursing, Des Moines, 1963; PNP, U. Iowa, 1982; BSN, Graceland U., Lamoni, Iowa, 1984. Cert. pediatric nurse practitioner. Staff nurse Rosary Hosp., Corning, Iowa, 1963-66, 71-72; sch. nurse Corning Commun. Schs., 1966-67; area adminstr., occupant protection program adminstr. Iowa Gov.'s Traffic Safety Bur., Des Moines, 1985—2002; ret., 2002; sch. nurse West Des Moines Sch. Sys., 2004—; clin. study coord. Heartland Med. Rsch., 2004—; hwy. safety cons., 2002—. Clin. instr. Southwestern C.C., Creston, Iowa, 1970, adj. faculty, 1985—86; health/handicap coord. Matura-Head Start, Creston, 1973—81; pediat. devel. nurse Child Diagnostic and Planning Svc., Creston, 1975—81; pediat. nurse practitioner physician's office, Lenox, Iowa, 1982—84, Otologic Med. Svcs., Iowa City, 1982—87, Taylor County Pub. Health, Bedford, Iowa, 1982—87, Heart and Hands, Des Moines, 2003—04; cons. Hwy. Safety Area, adv. bd. Iowa Ctr. for Agrl. Safety and Health, Rural Rd. Way Safety Project; sexual assault nurse investigator, 2002; presenter, cons. in field. Author booklets, tng. video, articles, tng. curricula. Recipient Recognition of Accomplishment award Gov. of Iowa, 1989, award Commns. Spl. award, 2010; named to Agr. Hall of Fame I-CASH, 2009. Mem. Internat. Assn. Forensic Nurses and Iowa Chpt. (bd. mem., treas.), Iowa Pub. Health Assn. (exec. bd., legis. com.) Nat. Assn. Pediatric Nurse Assocs. and Practitioners (pub. rels. com.), Iowa Nurses Assn. (local treas., state policy com.), Iowa Assn. Nurse Practitioners (constn. and by-laws chmn., pres.), Iowa Traffic Control and Safety Assn. (bd. dirs., treas., sec., v.p., pres.). Methodist. Home: 1675 Walnut Woods Dr West Des Moines IA 50265-8511 Office Phone: 515-669-0641.

GOLDSMITH, JAY PAUL, pediatrician, neonatalogist, educator; s. Jerome and Fannie Goldsmith; m. Terri Lynn Buller, June 28, 1981; children: Lauren Faye, Leighton Elizabeth, Aaron Geoffrey. MD, Albert Einstein Coll. Medicine, Bronx, NY, 1970. Diplomate in neonatal-perinatal medicine Am. Bd. Pediat., 1981. Chmn. dept. pediat. Ochsner Med. Instns., New Orleans, 1978—2000; prof. pediat. Tulane U., New Orleans, 1990—. Cons. So. Gov.'s Task Force on Infant Mortality. Co-editor: (book) Assisted Ventilation of the Neonate, 1981, 1988, 1996, 2003, 2010; contbr. chapters to books. Adv. for children fin. com., sec. treas. Agenda for Children, New Orleans, 1998—. Maj. USAF, 1973—75, George AFB. Fellow: Am. Acad. Pediat. (co-chair, neonatal resuscitation program 2000—09); mem.: Com. on Med. Liability and Risk Mgmt. Independent. Jewish. Achievements include creator of the Oxygen With Love program to prevent retinopathy of prematurity. Avocations: tennis, skiing, piano. Office Phone: 504-236-3566. Office Fax: 504-895-8023. Personal E-mail: goldsmith.jay@gmail.com. *

GOLDSMITH, JEFF CHARLES, management consultant; b. Portland, Oreg., Oct. 31, 1948; BA, Reed Coll., 1970; PhD, U. Chgo., 1973. Dir. health planning, regulatory affairs U. Chgo. Med. Ctr., 1975-82; nat. advisor Ernst & Young, 1982-94; pres. Health Futures, Inc., 1982—; dir. Cerner Corp., 1999—2005, Onfocus Healthcare, 2008—; assoc. prof., pub. health sciences Sch. Medicine U. Va., 2007—. Lectr. U. Chgo. Grad. Sch. Bus., 1979—90, Wharton Sch., U. Pa., 1994—; adv. Burrill Biotech. Capital Fund. Author: Can Hospitals Survive?, 1981, Digital Medicine, 2003, The Long Baby Boom, 2008, The Sorcerer's Apprentice, 2010; mem. editl. bd. Health Affairs, 1990--; contbr. articles to profl. jours. including Harvard Bus. Rev., Jour. AMA, Health Affairs, NEJM. Recipient Woodrow Wilson Nat. Fellowship, 1971. Avocations: skiing, audiophile, native american art, whitewater. Personal E-mail: hfutures@healthfutures.net.

GOLDSMITH, LOWELL ALAN, medical educator; b. Bklyn., Mar. 29, 1938; s. Isidore Alexander and Ida (Kaplan) G.; m. Carol Amreich, June 11, 1960; children: Meredith, Eileen. AB, Columbia Coll., 1959; MD, SUNY, Bklyn., 1963; MPH, U. Rochester Sch. Medicine & Dentistry, 2002. Diplomate Am. Bd. Dermatology. Intern, then resident in medicine UCLA Med. Ctr., 1963-65; resident in dermatology Harvard U. Med. Sch., Boston, 1967-69, asst. prof. dermatology, 1970-73; asst. in dermatology Mass. Gen. Hosp., Boston, 1970-71, asst. dermatologist, 1971-73; assoc. prof. medicine Duke U. Med. Ctr., Durham, NC, 1973-78, prof., 1978-81; James H. Sterner prof. dermatology Sch. Medicine and Dentistry, U. Rochester (NY), 1981-96, chief dermatology unit, 1981-87, acting chmn. dept. medicine, 1985-87, chmn. dept. dermatology, 1987-96; dean Sch. Medicine and Dentistry U. Rochester, 1996-2000, dean emeritus, 2000—; prof. dermatology U. NC, Chapel Hill, 2002—, clin. prof. epidemiology Sch. Pub. Health, 2002—07. Mem. dermatology adv. com. FDA, 1983-87; chmn. Gordon Rsch. Cong. on Epithelial Differentiation and Keratiniazation, 1987, AAD-CDC Conf. on skin cancer prevention and edn., Washington, 1995; mem. gen. medicine A study sect. USPHS, NIH, 1988-92, chmn., 1990-92; mem. coun. NIAMS, NIH, 1996-99; chmn. med. adv. bd. Nat. Alopecia Areata Found., 1981-87, 90-2002, bd. dirs.; bd. dirs. Monroe Cmty. Hosp., Rochester, Ctr. for Alternatives in Animal Testing, Balt.; chmn. NIH Consensus Conf. on Diagnosis and Treatment of Early Melanoma, Bethesda, Md., 1992. Author, editor: Biochemistry and Physiology of the Skin, 1983, 2d edit., 1991, Physiology, Biochemistry and Molecular Biology of the Skin, 1991, Differential Diagnosis of Skin Disease, 2d edit., 1996; mem. editl. bd. Archives Dermatology, 1981-92, Clinics in Dermatology, 1982-96, Seminars in Dermatology, 1991-96, Jour. Dermatological Sci., 1994-2002; mem. editl. bd. Jour. Investigative Dermatology, 1987-95, editor, 2002-07; editor in chief Journal Watch Dermatology 2006—10, assoc. editor, Visualised Essential Eliminate Dermatology, 2010, Visual Essential Adult Dermatology, 2010, Visual Dx: Essential Dermatology in Pigmentation Stain, 2011, also numerous articles. With USPHS, 1965-67. Recipient Rsch. Career Devel. award USPHS, 1975-80; Macy Found. fellow, 1978-79. Mem. Assn. Am. Physicians, Am. Soc. Clin. Investigation, Am. Acad. Dermatology (bd. dirs., Presdl. citation 2003), Soc. Investigative Dermatology (bd. dirs., pres. 1994-95, Rothman Gold medal), Nat. Ichthyosis Found. (chmn. adv. bd. 1981-85), Assn. Profs. Dermatology (bd. dirs. 1984-87, pres. 1992-94), Am. Bd. Dermatology (bd. dirs. 1993-96), NY State Soc. Dermatology (pres. 1985-89), Am. Dermatol. Assn. (bd. dirs. 1996-2001, pres. 2002—03, Buffalo-Rochester Dermatology Soc. (pres. 1987), Rochester Dermatology Soc., Rochester Acad. Medicine, Polish Dermatol. Assn. (hon.), Brit. Dermatology Assn. (hon.), Japanese Dermatology Assn. (hon., DOHI lectr. 2003), Am. Skin Assn. (Martin Carter Mentorship award 2006), Berlin Dermatology Soc. (hon.), Deutsche Dermatologische Gesellschaft (hon.), Alpha Omega Alpha. Office: University NC Dept Dermatology 3100 Thurston-Bowles Bldg CB #7287 Chapel Hill NC 27599 Home Phone: 919-942-9263; Office Phone: 919-929-1572. Business E-Mail: lag1959@gmail.com.

GOLDSMITH, MICHAEL ALLEN, oncologist, educator; b. Bronx, NY, Jan. 28, 1946; s. Walter and Bertha (Tannenberg) G.; m. Judith Harriet Plaut, June 6, 1971; children: Sharon, Esther, Eva, Steven. BA, Yeshiva U., 1967; MD, Albert Einstein Coll. Medicine, 1971. Diplomate Am. Bd. Internal Medicine. Intern Bronx Mcpl. Hosp. Ctr., 1971-72; staff assoc. Nat. Cancer Inst., Bethesda, Md., 1972-74; resident in medicine Mt. Sinai Hosp., NYC, 1974-75, fellow in neoplastic diseases, 1975-77, asst. clin. prof. medicine and neoplastic diseases, 1977—2008; attending physician Oncology Consultants, P.C., NYC, 1977—2008; pres. NY Cancer Soc., 2008—09. Assoc. editor Cancer Investigation, 2001—07, reviewer Jour. AMA, 1988—90, New Eng. Jour. Medicine, 1995—98; contbr. articles to med. jours. Vice-pres. Congregation Orach Chaim, N.Y.C., 1978-83. Lt. comdr. USPHS, 1972-74. Fellow ACP; mem. Am. Soc. Clin. Oncology Achievements include research in new anticancer drugs.

GOLDSMITH, STANLEY JOSEPH, nuclear medicine physician, educator; b. Bklyn., Aug. 17, 1937; s. Jack and Mae (Greenzweig) G.; m. Miriam Schulman, June 6, 1959; children: Ira, Arthur, Beth, Mark. BA, Columbia U., 1958; MD, SUNY, Bklyn., 1962. Diplomate Am. Bd. Internal Medicine, Am. Bd. Nuclear Medicine bd. dirs. 1990-96, treas. 1995-96, Am. Bd. Internal Medicine Subspecialty Endocrinology & Metabolism. Intern SUNY-Kings County Med. Ctr., Bklyn., 1962-63, resident, 1965-66, chief resident, 1966-67; fellow in endocrinology Mt. Sinai Hosp., NYC, 1967-68, dir. physics nuclear medicine, 1973-92; clin. dir. nuclear medicine Meml. Sloan-Kettering Cancer Ctr., NYC, 1992-95; dir. nuclear medicine NY Hosp.-Cornell Med. Ctr., NYC, 1995—. Rsch. assoc. radioisotope svc. Bronx VA Hosp., NY, 1968-69; dir. nuc. medicine, asst. dir. endocrine dept. Nassau County Med. Ctr., East Meadow, NY, 1969-73; asst. prof. medicine radiology SUNY-Stony Brook Health Sci. Ctr., 1971-73; asst. prof. medicine Mt. Sinai Sch. Medicine, 1973-76, assoc. prof., 1976-84, prof. clin. medicine, 1985-91, prof. radiology and medicine, 1991-92, Cornell U. Med. Coll., 1993—, prof. radiology, medicine; bd. dirs. Capintec, Inc., Ramsey, NJ; rsch. collaborator Brookhaven Nat. Labs., Upton, NY, 1971-75; cons. nuclear medicine; cons. dept. health State of NY, 1973-77, Health Svcs. Adminstrn., NYC, 1976; radiopharm. adv. com. FDA, 1987-90, low level radioactive waste disposal site commn., NY, 1987-95, vis. lectr., U. Belgrade Sch. Medicine, 2005, Inst. Oncology, Novi Sad, Serbia, 2008. Assoc. editor Newline, 1984-93, Jour. Nuclear Medicine, editor-in-chief, 1993-98; mem. editl. bd. Am. Jour. Cardiology, 1978-82, European Jour. Nuclear Medicine, 1993-98, Cancer Biotherapy and Radiopharm., 1998—, Jour. Nuc. Medicine, 1999—, Archive of Oncology (Serbia), 2010-; reviewer Israeli Jour. Med. Scis., 1979, JAMA, 1983-92, Jour. Am. Coll. Cardiology, 1984-94, Jour. Nuclear Medicine, 1989-93, 99—, Cancer, 2003—, Jour. Clin. Oncology, 2002—, Kidney Internat., 2004—, American Journal of Roentgenology, 2008-; editor, Nuclear Oncology, Lippincott Williams & Wilkens, 2001; Hybrid SPECT/CT Imaging in Clinical Practice, Taylor & Francis, 2006. Mem., NY State Low Level Radioactive Waste Siting Commn., 1987-1995, Adv. Com. Med. Imaging Drugs, Food & Drug Adminstrn., 1988-91. Capt. US Army, 1963-65. Recipient Harry Z. Mellino Master Tchr. in Radiology award, SUNY Downstate Alumni, 2000, Frank A. Babbott Disting. Svc. award, 2007, DeWitt Clinton award for cmty. svc., NY State Masons, 2006, Distinguished Educator award, Soc. Nuclear Medicine, 1998. Fellow ACP, Am. Coll. Cardiology, Am. Coll. Nuclear Physicians (chmn. nuclear med. tech. affairs, chmn. Washington oversight com.), NY Acad. Sci.; mem. AAAS, Am. Fedn. Clin. Rsch., Am. Coll. Radiology, Endocrine Soc., NY Acad. Medicine (pres sect. on nuclear medicine 2004-2006), Radiol. Soc. N.Am. (program com. 2002-06), Soc. Nuclear Medicine (trustee 1982-84, pres.-elect 1984-85, prse. 1985-86, chmn. govt. rels. com. 1991-93, sec. Greater NY chpt. 1975-78, pres. 1979-80, pres. therapy coun. 2001-2003). Office: NY Presbyn Hosp Weill Cornell Med Ctr 525 E 68th St New York NY 10065-4885 Office Phone: 212-746-4588. Business E-Mail: sjg2002@med.cornell.edu.

GOLDSTEIN, ALLAN LEONARD, biochemist, educator; b. Bronx, NY, Nov. 8, 1937; s. Morris and Miriam (Siegel) G.; m. Linda Jo Tish, Dec. 23, 1975; children: Jennifer Joy, Dawn Eden, Adam Lee. BS, Wagner Coll., 1959, DSc (hon.), 1997; MS, Rutgers U., 1961, PhD, 1964. Tchg. asst. Rutgers U., New Brunswick, NJ, 1959-61, asst. instr. biology, 1961-63, instr. physiology, 1963-64; rsch. fellow Albert Einstein Coll. Medicine, 1964-66, instr. biochemistry, 1966-67, asst. prof., 1967-71, asso. prof., 1971-72; prof., dir. divsn. biochemistry U. Tex. Med. Br., Galveston, 1972-78, acting dir. multidisciplinary rsch. program in mental health, 1973-78; chmn. dept. biochemistry and molecular biology George Washington U. Sch. Medicine, 1978—2009, prof., dept. biochemistry and molecular biology, 1978—, pres., sci. dir. Inst. for Advanced Studies in Immunology and Aging, 1985-95; chmn. bd. Alpha 1 Biomeds., 1982-2000, RegeneRX Biopharms Inc., 2000—. Cons. Syntex Rsch., 1972-74, Hoffmann-LaRoche, 1974-82; spl. cons. bd. sci. counselors Nat. Inst. Allergy and Infectious Diseases, 1975; mem. med. rsch. svc. rev. bd. in oncology VA, 1977-80; cons. decisive network com. Biol. Response Modifiers program Divsn. Cancer Treatment, Nat. Cancer Inst., 1982-84; sci. adv. com. to pres. Papanicolaou Cancer Rsch. Inst. Miami, Inc., 1981-84; mem. AIDS task force adv. com. Nat. Cancer Inst., 1983-84; sci. bd. Alliance for Aging Rsch., 1986-96; trustee Albert Sabin Vaccine Inst., 2000-; bd. dirs. Richard B. and Lynne Chaney Cardiovascular Inst., 2006-. Discoverer (with Abraham White) Thymosins, hormones of thymus gland and HGP-30 a "core" based p17 AIDS Vaccine. Decorated chevalier des Palmes Academiques (France), comdr. Order Vasco Nuñez de Balboa; recipient Career Scientist award NYC Health Rsch. Coun., 1967, Alumni Achievement award Wagner Coll., 1974, Gordon Wilson medal Am. Clin. and Climatol Soc., 1976, Disting. Faculty Rsch. award U. Tex. Sch. Biomed. Scis., 1976, Van Dyke award in pharmacology Columbia Coll. Physicians and Surgeons, 1984, award Burroughs Wellcome Found., FASEB, 1986, Fernandez-Cruz award, 1989, Martin Rubin award Am. Coll. Advancement in Medicine, 1990, Michele Fodera Internat. prize for Biomed. Rsch., Italy, 1990, Disting. Rsch. award George Washington U. Med. Sch., 2003, Catherine Birch McCormick medal George Washington U. Med. Sch., 2005. Mem. AAAS, Am. Soc. Biol. Chemists and Molecular Biologists, Am. Assn. Immunologists, Internat. Soc. Immunopharmacology (coun. mem. 1985-94), Assn. Med. Sch. Chm. of Depts. Biochemistry, Acad. Medicine of Washington, Toastmasters Internat. (pres. NY chpt. 1971), Sigma Xi, Alpha Omega Alpha. Home: 800 25th St NW Apt 1005 Washington DC 20037-2207 Office: George Washington U Med Ctr Dept Biochemistry/Molecular Biology 2300 I St NW Washington DC 20037-2336 Business E-Mail: bcmalg@gwumc.edu.

GOLDSTEIN, AVRAM, pharmacology educator; b. NYC, July 3, 1919; s. Israel and Bertha (Markowitz) Goldstein; m. Dora Benedict, Aug. 29, 1947; children: Margaret, Daniel, Joshua, Michael. AB, Harvard, 1940, MD, 1943. Intern Mt. Sinai Hosp., NYC, 1944; successively instr., assoc., asst. prof. pharmacology Harvard U., 1947—55; prof. dept. pharmacology Stanford U., Palo Alto, Calif., 1955—89, exec. head dept., 1955—70, prof. emeritus, 1989—. Dir. Addiction Rsch. Found., Palo Alto, Calif., 1973—87. Author: Biostatistics, Principles of Drug Action, 1965, ADDICTION: From Biology to Drug Policy, 2001. Served from 1st lt. to capt., Med. Corps US Army, 1944—46. Mem.: AAAS, Am. Soc. Biol. Chemists, Am. Soc. Pharmacology and Exptl. Therapeutics, Am. Acad. Arts and Scis., Inst. Medicine NAS. *

GOLDSTEIN, BERNARD DAVID, environmental scientist, educator; b. Bronx, NY, Feb. 28, 1939; m. Russellyn Carruth, May 6, 1995; children: Lara, Ross, Casey. BS, U. Wis., 1958; MD, NYU, 1962. Diplomate Am. Bd. Toxicology, Am. Bd. Internal Medicine, Am. Bd. Hematology. Faculty depts. environ. medicine and medicine NYU Med. Ctr., NYC, 1968—80; prof., chmn. dept. environ. and cmty. medicine U. Medicine and Dentistry, NJ-Robert Wood Johnson Med. Sch., Piscataway, 1980—2001, dir. grad. program in pub. health, 1982—89, dir. environ. and occupl. health scis. inst., 1985—2000; asst. adminstr. for R & D EPA, Washington, 1983—85; acting dean Sch. Pub. Health NJ, Piscataway, 1998—99; dir. Nat. Inst. Environ. Health Scis. Ctr. Excellence, 1988—94; prof. environ. and occupl. health Sch. Pub. Health, U. Pitts., 2001—, dean, 2001—05. Chmn. clean air sci. adv. com. EPA, 1982—83; toxicology study sect. NIH, 1980—84, chmn., 1982—84; bd. sci. dirs. Risk Sci. Inst., 1986—2005, nat. adv. environ. health effects coun., 1987—91; chmn. ad hoc com. on dioxin EPA, 1988—89, vice-chmn., chmn. sci. group on methodology for sci. evaluation chems., 1989—, chmn. working group on Air Quality Guidelines for Major Urban Air Pollutants, 1985; health rev. com., chmn. health rsch. com. Health Effects Inst., 1987—2000; pres. Soc. Risk Analysis, 2002; pres., chair Nat. Bd. Pub. Health Examiners, 2005—. Recipient Solomon Berson Med. Alumni Achievement award, NYU, 1989, Kehoe award, Am. Coll. Occupl. Environ. Medicine, 1993, Sturgis award, Am. Coll. Preventive Medicine, 1995, Sullivan award, N.J. Pub. Health Assn., 1998, Disting. Achievement award, Soc. for Risk Analysis, 1999, Sen. Frank Lautenberg award, UMDNJ Sch. Pub. Health, 2005, Disting. Svc. award, Am. Coll. Toxicology, 2005. Mem.: Am. Soc. Clin. Investigation, Inst. Medicine NAS. Achievements include research in in concept of biological markers in the field of risk assessment. Office: U Pitts Grad Sch Pub Health 130 Desoto St Rm A710 Pittsburgh PA 15261 Business E-Mail: bdgold@pitt.edu.

GOLDSTEIN, BURTON JACK, psychiatrist; b. Balt., Sept. 23, 1930; s. Hyman and Roz (Levin) C.; m. Linda Feuer, June 16, 1989; children: Howard, Herbert, Brian, Esther, Leonard, Mark. BS in Pharmacy, U. Md., 1953, MD, 1960. Diplomate Am. Bd. Psychiatry and Neurology (bd. examiner). Intern Jackson Meml. Hosp., Miami, Fla., 1960-61, NIMH fellow in psychiatry, 1961-63, chief resident, 1963; dir. div. clin. psychopharmacology, dept. psychiatry U. Miami, 1964-92, chief div. research, 1964-71, prof. pharmacology, 1973—, prof. psychiatry, 1973—, acting chmn. dept. psychiatry, 1983-85, prof. epidemiology, pub. health Sch. Medicine, 1999; sr. cons. in psychopharmacology Mt. Sinai Med. Ctr., Miami Beach, 1993—; dir. psychiat. consultation liaison svc. Mt. Sinai Hosp., Miami Beach, 1993—; med. dir. behavioral health U. Miami, Miller Sch. Medicine, 2005—. Mem. bd. advisors Fla. Mental Health Inst., U. South Fla.; cons. in psychiat. rsch. South Fla. State Hosp., West Hollywood; cons. indsl. security program Dept. Def.; cons. VA Psychiatry Svc., Miami; chmn. panel on neuropharmacologic drugs U.S. Pharmacopeial Conv., Inc., 1990-2000, mem. exec. com.; mem. faculty Health Svcs. Ctr., U. Miami, 1996; med. rev. officer dept. athletics U. Miami, 1996—. Mem. editorial bd. Miami Medicine, Clin. Advancement in Treatment of Depression; contbr. chpts. to books, articles to profl. publs. Served to maj. AUS, 1953-62. Fellow Am. Psychiat. Assn. (life), Am. Coll. Psychiatrists, Am. Coll. Clin. Pharmacology, Am. Coll. Neuropsychopharmacology (life); mem. Royal Soc. Health, Am. Assn. Clin. Pharmacology and Chemotherapy, Am. Soc. Addiction Medicine, Collegium Internationale Neuropsychopharmacologium. Personal E-mail: bhls@earthlink.net. Business E-Mail: bgoldste@med.miami.edu.

GOLDSTEIN, CAROLYN S., pediatrician, adolescent medicine; MD, SUNY, 1971. Diplomate Am. Bd. Pediatrics, 1977, Am. Bd. Pediatrics-adolescent medicine, 2005. Intern Upstate Med. Ctr., 1972; resident pediat. University Hosp., Jacksonville, 1972—74; physician Baystate Med. Ctr. Office: Baystate Medical Center 140 High St C Level Springfield MA 01199 Office Phone: 413-794-2515. Office Fax: 413-794-5673.

GOLDSTEIN, DANIEL J., thoracic surgeon, medical educator; b. Caracas, Venezuela; BA, Brandeis U., Waltham, Mass., 1987; MD, Mt. Sinai Sch. Medicine, NYC, 1991. Diplomate Nat. Bd. Med. Examiners, Am. Bd. Surgery, Am. Bd. Thoracic Surgery. Intern, resident gen. surgery Columbia-Presbyn. Med. Ctr., NYC, 1991—97; rsch. fellow divsn. cardiothoracic surgery Columbia U., NYC, 1994—95, electrophysiology fellow, 1997, cardiothoracic fellow, 1998—99; cardiothoracic fellow divsn. thoracic surgery Meml. Sloan Kettering Hosp., NYC, 1998; attending asst. cardiothoracic surgery Columbia U. Coll. Physicians & Surgeons, 2000; attending staff dept. cardiothoracic surgery Newark Beth Israel Med. Ctr., 2002—05, surg. dir. cardiac transplantation/mechanical assistance, 2002—05; assoc. prof. Albert Einstein Coll. Medicine, Bronx, NY, 2005—; attending staff dept. cardiothoracic surgery Montefiore Med. Ctr., Bronx, 2005—, surg. dir. cardiac transplantation & mechanical assistance progs., 2005—. Co-editor: Contemporary Cardiology: Minimally Invasive Cardiac Surgery, 1999, Cardiac Assist Devices, 2000, Minimally Invasive Cardiac Surgery, 2003; reviewer Annals of Thoracic Surgery, Jour. Thoracic & Cardiovasc. Surgery, New Eng. Jour. Medicine, Jour. Heart & Lung Transplantation; contbr. articles to profl. jours., chapters to books. Recipient Claire Lucille Pace Humanitarian award, Guatemala Heart Team, 1995, Arnold P. Gold Tchg. Resident award, 1997, Harvey E. Nussbaum, MD award for disting. svc., Am. Heart Assn., 2001; named Surgeon of Yr., Montefiore Med. Ctr., 2007. Fellow: ACS, Am. Coll. Cardiology; mem.: AMA, Internat. Soc. Heart & Lung Transplantation, Soc. Thoracic Surgeons. Office: Montefiore Einstein Med Ctr 3400 Bainbridge Ave Bronx NY 10467 Office Phone: 718-920-2144. Business E-Mail: dgoldste@montefiore.org.

GOLDSTEIN, DAVID ARTHUR, biophysicist, educator; b. Rochester, NY, Nov. 8, 1934; s. Jacob David and Elizabeth Maude (Brown) G.; m. Marie Elaine Nardone, May 25, 1969; 1 child, David James. AB in Physics, Harvard U., 1956, MD, 1960. Rsch. fellow biophys. lab Harvard Med. Sch., Cambridge, Mass., 1960-62, rsch. assoc. biophys. lab., 1964-65; asst. prof. radiation biology and biophysics Rochester Sch. Med. and Dentistry, 1965-68, assoc. prof. biophysics, 1968—, assoc. prof. biomath., 1969-74, assoc. prof. med. informatics, 1988—98, prof. emeritus med. informatics, 1999—. Dir. Med. Ctr. Computing, U. Rochester Med. Sch., 1975-77, assoc. chmn. dept. radiation biology and biophysics, 1980-85, dir. divsn. med. informatics, 1988-98; cons. mathematician NIMH, Bethesda, Md., 1963-64. Contbr. articles to profl. jours. Treas. Stormers Soccer Club, Rochester, 1983-93; bd. dirs. Monroe County Girls Soccer League, Rochester, 1988-93. Surgeon, USPHS, 1963-64. Grantee AEC, NIH, NSF, ERDA, DOE, 1965-96. Mem. Biophys. Soc., N.Y. Acad. Scis. Home: 75 Deer Creek Rd Pittsford NY 14534-4147 E-mail: dgoldst2@frontiernet.net.

GOLDSTEIN, JEROME CHARLES, retired professional society administrator, otolaryngologist, surgeon; b. Glens Falls, NY, Nov. 4, 1935; s. Morris and Estelle (Ginsburg) G.; m. Rochelle Jacobs; children: Harry Glenn, Bradley John, Brian Louis. AB, U. Rochester, 1957; MD, SUNY, Syracuse, 1963. Diplomate Am. Bd. Otolaryngology (bd. dirs. 1982-2000). Intern Phila. Gen. Hosp., 1963-64; resident in gen. surgery Bronx Mcpl. Hosp. Ctr., NYC, 1964-65; resident in otolaryngology SUNY, Syracuse, 1965-68; asst. prof. Northwestern U. Med. Sch., Chgo., 1968-71; pvt. practice Glens Falls, NY, 1971-74; prof. surgery, head divsn. otolaryngology Albany (N.Y.) Med. Coll., 1974-83; exec. v.p. Am. Acad. Otolaryngology-Head and Neck Surgery, Washington, 1984-94, sr. exec. v.p., 1995-96, exec. v.p. emeritus, 1997-99. Otolaryngologist-in-chief Albany Med. Ctr. Hosp., 1974-83; prof. dept. otolaryngology, head and neck surgery Johns Hopkins Med. Sch., 1986—, Georgetown Med. Sch., 1990; chair sec. com. Combined Otolaryngology Spring Meeting., 1985—; pres. Centurions of Deafness Rsch. Found., N.Y.C., 1987-88. With USAFR, 1965-70. Fellow ACS, Royal Coll. Surgeons Edinburgh, Am. Acad. Facial, Plastic and Reconstructive Surgery, Triologic Soc., Am. Laryngol. Assn., Am. Soc. for Head and Neck Surgery (pres. 1982-83), Soc. Head and Neck Surgeons, Am. Neurotol. Soc. (hon.), Am. Bronchoesoph. Soc., Am. Head and Neck Soc., Nat. Assn. Physicians for the Environment (founding pres. 1993-95, pres. 1999-2000); mem. AMA, Am. Otol. Soc. (hon.), Internat. Fedn. Otorhino-Laryngol. Socs. (regional sec. for N.Am. 1985-2000), Coun. of Med. Splty. Socs. (pres. 1996), Pan Pacific Surg. Assn. (pres. 2004—06), Am. Soc. Geriatric Otolaryngology (founding pres. 2007—).

GOLDSTEIN, JONATHAN K., medical association administrator; b. Bklyn., Apr. 4, 1967; MBA, U. Wis., Madison, 1992. Dir., healthcare adv. group Lion & Co. CPAs, LLP, 2006; exec. dir. Beacon IPA, LLC, 2010—. Office: 75 Jackson Ave Ste 204 Syosset NY 11791 Personal E-mail: goldyjk@gmail.com.

GOLDSTEIN, JOSEPH LEONARD, biochemist, educator, geneticist, educator; b. Sumter, SC, Apr. 18, 1940; s. Isadore E. and Fannie A. Goldstein. BS, Washington & Lee U., Lexington, Va., 1962; MD, U. Tex. Health Sci. Ctr., Dallas, 1966; DSc (hon.), U. Chgo., 1982, Rensselaer Poly. Inst., 1982, U. Paris, 1988, U. Buenos Aires, 1990, So. Meth. U., 1993, U. Miami, 1996, Rockefeller U., 2001. Diplomate Am. Bd. Internal Medicine. Intern, resident in medicine Mass. Gen. Hosp., Boston, 1966—68; clin. assoc. biochemical genetics NIH, 1968—70; fellow med. genetics U. Wash. Sch. Medicine, Seattle, 1970—72; faculty U. Tex. Southwestern Med. Ctr., Dallas, 1972—, Paul J. Thomas chair in medicine, Julie and Louis A. Beecherl disting. chair in biomed. sci., 1977—, regental prof., 1985—. Mem. sci. rev. bd. Howard Hughes Med. Inst., 1978—84, mem. med. adv. bd., 1985—90, chmn. med. adv. bd., 1995—2002; non-resident fellow Salk Inst., La Jolla, Calif., 1983—94; chmn. awards jury Albert Lasker Med. Rsch. prizes, 1996—. Co-author: The Metabolic Basis of Inherited Disease, 5th edit., 1983; mem. editl. bd. Jour. Clin. Investigation, 1977—82, Ann. Rev. Genetics, 1980—85, Arteriosclerosis, 1981—87, Jour. Biol. Chemistry, 1981—95, Cell, 1983—, Sci., 1985—98; contbr. articles to profl. jours. Bd. trustees Rockefeller U., 1994—, Howard Hughes Med. Inst., 2002—. Recipient Heinrich-Wieland prize, 1974, Pfizer award in enzyme chemistry, Am. Chem. Soc., 1976, Passano award, Johns Hopkins U., 1978, Gairdner Found. award, 1981, NY Acad. Scis.award in biol. and med. scis., 1981, Lita Annenberg Hazen award, 1982, Rsch. Achievement award, Am. Heart Assn., 1984, Louisa Gross Horwitz award, Columbia U., 1984, Albert Lasker award in basic med. rsch., 1985, Nobel Prize in physiology/medicine, 1985, Trustees medal, Mass. Gen. Hosp., 1986, Nat. Medal Sci., 1988, Warren Alpert Found. prize, 2000, Albany Med. Ctr. prize in medicine and biomed. rsch., 2003, Woodrow Wilson award for pub. svc., 2005, Builder of Sci. award, Research!America, 2007. Mem.: ACP (award 1986), NAS (coun. 1991—94, Lounsbery award 1979), Tex. Philos. Soc., Royal Soc. London (fgn. mem.), Inst. Medicine, Am. Philos. Soc., Am. Fedn. Clin. Rsch., Am. Soc. Biol. Chemists, Am. Acad. Arts & Scis., Am. Soc. Human Genetics (William Allan award 1985), Am. Soc. Clin. Investigation (pres. 1985—86), Assn. Am. Physicians, Alpha Omega Alpha, Phi Beta Kappa. Office: U Tex Southwestern Med Ctr 5323 Harry Hines Blvd Dallas TX 75390-9046 E-mail: joe.goldstein@utsouthwestern.edu. *

GOLDSTEIN, JUDITH, pediatrician, educator; Attended, SUNY Downstate Health Sciences Ctr., 1972. Diplomate Am. Bd. Pediatrics. Intern Lenox Hill Hosp., NY, resident in pediat., 1973—75, with; asst. clin. prof. pediat. Cornell Univ.-Weill Med. Coll.; pediatrician NY Presbyn. Hosp. / Weill Cornell. Office: NewYork-Presbyterian 1559 York Ave New York NY 10028 Office Phone: 212-585-3329.

GOLDSTEIN, JULIUS LESTER, biomedical engineer, consultant; b. Bklyn., July 9, 1935; s. Benjamin and Dorothy (Steinberg) G.; m. Batya Abramson, June 17, 1962; children: Hillel N., Miriam D., Naama L., Avi D. BEE, Cooper Union, 1957; MEE, Poly. Inst. Bklyn., 1960; PhD, U. Rochester, 1965. Postdoctoral fellow Inst. for Perception Rsch., Eindhoven, Netherlands, 1965-66; rsch. assoc., Lab. Psychophysics Harvard U., Cambridge, Mass., 1966-68; asst. prof. elec. engring. MIT, Cambridge, Mass., 1968-71, assoc. prof. elec. engring., 1971-73; dir. biomed. engring. Tel Aviv U., Israel, 1973-76, chmn. dept. electronics, 1976-78, assoc. prof., 1973-82, prof. elec. engring., 1982-90; vis. prof. Johns Hopkins U., Balt., 1986-88; rsch. prof. Ctrl. Inst. for the Deaf, St. Louis, 1988-96; adj. prof. elec. engring. Washington U., St. Louis, 1996—, adj. prof. biomed.

engring., 2001—. Pres. Israel Soc. for Med. and Biomed. Engrs., Tel Aviv, 1975-77; dir. biomed. engring. program Tel Aviv U., 1973-76; cons. Digital Speech Systems, Tel Aviv, 1984-86, Models of Human Hearing, AT&T Bell Labs., Murray Hill, NJ, 1991-96; co-founder, pres. Hearing Emulations, LLC, 2000. Contrb. articles profl. jour. Organizer, symposium chmn. Assn. for Rsch. in Otolaryngology 17th Midwinter meeting, 1994. NIH grantee MIT, 1972, Johns Hopkins U., 1986-88, U.S./Israel Binational Fund grantee, 1977-80, NIH-NIDCD grantee Ctrl. Inst. for the Deaf, 1990-95, NSF-IBN grantee Washington U., 1998-00, NIH-NIDCD SBIR grantee BECS Tech., 1999-2004. Fellow Acoustical Soc. Am., Collegium Oto-Rhino-Laryngologicum Amicitae Sacrum, 1980; mem. IEEE (life). Achievements include research in principles of auditory signal processing; experimental research on properties of auditory uonlinearity was oasis for mterd-istiplinary studies (wifu Nelson Kiang) of neural correlates, clinical application (with M.Valente) of compressive amplification, and for supervised student research on pitch of complex tones; research in sound attenuation by the acoustic reflex, and central modification of cochlear response. Integrative models inphide nonlinear cochlear sound analysis, detection of signal peaks and intervals, central processing in pitch perception; sound compression by the cochlea and acoustic reflex is normal and irnpaired loudness perception, and hearing aids based -on auditory models; invention of hearing aids with instantaneous gain compression and adaptive nonlinear waveform compression; recognition of the potential for bearing conservation of quantified knowledge of cochlear and middle ear sound compression. Office Phone: 314-373-5869. Personal E-mail: julius@hearem.com.

GOLDSTEIN, LARRY BRUCE, neurologist, educator; b. NYC, May 27, 1955; s. Daniel and Sharon Goldstein; children: Sarah, Daniel. AB magna cum laude, Brandeis U., 1977; MD, Mt. Sinai Med. Sch., 1981. Intern Mt. Sinai Hosp., NYC, 1981-82, resident neurology, 1981—85, chief resident, 1985; fellow cereb rsch. Duke U. Med. Ctr., Durham, NC, 1985—87; assoc. Duke U., 1986—88, asst. prof., 1989—95, assoc. prof., 1995—2002, prof., 2002—; dir. Duke Stroke Ctr., NC. Contbr. articles to profl. jours. Recipient Saul Horowitz Jr. award, Mt. Sinai Sch. Medicine, 2004, Chmn.'s award, Am. Heart Assn., 2004; named Nat. Advocate of Yr., 2005. Fellow: Am. Acad. Neurology (G. Milton Shy award 1979); mem.: Am. Neurol. Assn., Am. Stroke Assn. (chair adv. com. 2002—04), Am. Heart Assn. (nat. bd. dirs. 2002—04, chair stroke coun. 2005—07, chair advocacy coord. com. 2008—10, nat. bd. dirs. 2008—11, Meritorious Achievement award 2007, William Feinberg award 2009), Alpha Omega Alpha. Office: Duke Stroke Ctr Duke Univ Medl Ctr PO Box 3651 Durham NC 27710 Office Phone: 919-684-3801. E-mail: golds004@mc.duke.edu.

GOLDSTEIN, LAWRENCE STEVEN, medical professor and investigator; b. 1956; BA in Biology and Genetics, U. Calif., San Diego, 1976; PhD in Genetics, U. Wash., Seattle, 1980. Postdoctoral rschr. U. Colo., Boulder, 1980—83, MIT, 1983—84; prof. dept. cellular and devel. biology, ind. rsch. Harvard U., 1984—93; prof. cellular and molecular medicine U. Calif., San Diego, 1993—, investigator Howard Hughes Med. Inst., 1993—. Co-founder, cons. Cytokinetics, Inc., San Francisco, 1997—. Contbr. articles to profl jours.; spkr. in field. Recipient Faculty Rsch. award, Am. Cancer Soc., Sr. Scholar award in aging rsch., Ellison Med. Found.; named Loeb Chair in Natural Scis., Harvard U. Fellow: Am. Acad. Arts & Scis.; mem.: Am. Soc. Cell Biology (chair pub. policy com.), Genetics Soc. America. Achievements include written contribution for the California proposition that created a $3 billion funding organization to support human stem cell research in the state. Office: Howard Hughes Med Inst 4000 Jones Bridge Rd Chevy Chase MD 20815 also: U Calif Med Ctr 3855 Health Scis Dr La Jolla CA 92093 Office Phone: 301-215-8500. Business E-Mail: lgoldstein@ucsd.edu.

GOLDSTEIN, LEONARD BARRY, dentist; b. Seaford, NY, Feb. 6, 1944; s. Jacob Martin and Adele (Pelzner) G.; m. Phyllis Lynn Kerwin, June 25, 1967; children: Marcie Ilene, Sherri Elysse. Student, Ind. U., 1961-63; DDS, Case Western Reserve U., 1967; Cert. in Orthodontics, Dewey Sch. Orthodontics, NYC, 1969; PhD in Electro-Medicine, City U., LA, 1988. Diplomate Am. Acad. of Pain Mgmt., Am. Bd. Forensic Medicine, Am. Bd. Forensic Dentistry. Gen. practice dentistry, Smithtown, 1969—; attending orthodontist Abe Stark Philanthropies Dental Clinic, Bklyn., 1970-77; med. dir. TMJ Facial Pain Ctr. Southside Hosp., Bay Shore. Guest prof. dept. phys. edn. Queens Coll., NY, 1979—; guest lectr. dept. phys. edn. Queensboro CC, NY, 1980—; dir. dental svcs. Good Samaritan Profl. Svcs., St. James, NY, 1979—, v.p. med. bd., 1979—; attending dental staff St. John's Episc. Hosp., 1980—, Cmty. Hosp. Western Suffolk, 1980—; bd. dirs. L.I. Ctr. for Cranio-Facial Pain, Smithtown; med. dir. TMJ/Facial Pain Ctr., Southside Hosp.; dir. grad. program in forensic exam. Touro Coll. Sch. Health Scis., Bay Shore; chmn. Instnl. Rev. Bd., Touro Coll.; vice chmn. com. on scholarly rsch., Touro Coll. Sch. Health Scis., asst. dean grad. program devel.; dir. clerkship edn. NY Coll. Osteo. Medicine, assoc. prof. Dept. Family Medicine. Contbr. articles to profl. jours. Served to capt. Dental Corps, US Army, 1967-69. Fellowship in removeable prosthetics, U.S. Army Dental Corps, 1967. Fellow Acad. Stress and Chronic Disease, Acad. Gen. Dentistry, Am. Endodontic Soc., Internat. Coll. Dentists; mem. Am. Equilibration Soc., Am. Coll. Sports Medicine, Internat. Acad. Preventive Medicine, Cranial Acad. of Am. Osteopathic Soc., Am. Orthodontic Soc., Internat. Soc. Orthodontists, Am. Dental Soc., NY Coll. Osteo. Medicine (dir. clerkship edn.), Cronio-Mandibular Study Club of NY, L.I. Gnathological Study Club, Northeastern Gnathological Soc. Personal E-mail: ddsphd@aol.com. Business E-Mail: lbgoldst@nyit.edu.

GOLDSTEIN, LORI J., oncologist, educator; MD, SUNY. Diplomate Am. Bd. Internal Medicine-med. oncology. Intern internal medicine Univ. Pitts., resident internal medicine; fellow oncology Nat. Cancer Inst., Bethesda, Md.; assoc. prof. Rsch. at Fox Chase; dir., breast evaluation ctr. Fox Chase Ctr. Editl. adv. bd. Jour. of the Nat. Cancer Inst., Jour. of Clin. Oncology. Named one of The Best Doctors in America. Mem.: ACP, Women in Cancer Rsch., Am. Assn. for the Advancement of Sci., Am. Soc. of Clin. Oncology, Am. Assn. for Cancer Rsch. Office: Fox Chase Center 333 Cottman Ave Philadelphia PA 19111 Office Phone: 215-726-6900.

GOLDSTEIN, MARC, surgeon, urologist, health facility administrator, educator; b. NYC, Mar. 22, 1948; BS cum laude, CUNY, Bklyn., 1968; MD summa cum laude, SUNY, Bklyn., 1972; DSc (hon.), SUNY Downstate Med. Ctr., 2008. Diplomate Nat. Bd. Med. Examiners, Am. Bd. Urology. Surgical intern Columbia-Presbyn. Med. Ctr., NYC, 1972-73, surgical resident, 1973-74; asst. instr., resident, chief resident dept. urology Downstate Med. Ctr. SUNY, Bklyn., 1977-80, asst. prof. urology dept. urology Downstate Med. Ctr., 1980-82; asst. attending surgeon U. Hosp., SUNY Downstate Med. Ctr., and Kings County Hosp. Ctr., Bklyn., 1980-82; fellow-in-residence Population Coun. Rockefeller U., NYC, 1980-82, rsch. assoc., 1980-83; assoc. physician Rockefeller U. Hosp., NYC, 1980-86, vis. assoc. physician, 1986-87; asst. attending surgeon urology NY Hosp., NYC, 1982-88; asst. prof. surgery Cornell U. Med. Ctr., NYC, 1982-88; staff scientist Population Coun. Ctr. Biomed. Rsch., NYC, 1982—2002, sr. scientist, 2002—; dir. divsn. male reproductive medicine and microsurgery, dept. urology NY Hops.-Cornell Med. Ctr., NYC, 1982—; assoc. attending surgeon NY Hosp., NYC, 1988-94; assoc. prof. surgery Cornell U. Med. Coll., NYC, 1988-94; attending surgeon NY Hosp., 1994—; prof. urology Cornell U. Med. Coll., NYC, 1994—, prof. urology and reproductive medicine, 1999—, dir. ctr. for male reproductive medicine and microsurgery, 1982—, co-exec. dir. Cornell Inst. Reproductive Medicine, 1999—; surgeon-in-chief Inst. Reproductive Medicine Cornell Ctr., 2001—. Mem. adv. com. Assn. Voluntary Surg. Contraception, 1984—; participant concept clearance meeting NIH, 1989; mem. editl. bd. Microsugery, 1983—, Jour. Andrology, 1991-93, Andrology Report, 1992—. Author: (with M. Feldberg) The Vasectomy Book: A Complete Guide to Decision Making, 1982, 2nd edit., 1985, (with G. Berger, M. Fuerst) The Couples Guide to Fertility, 1989, 2nd edit., 1995, 3rd edit., 2001, (with Doubleday Co.) Surgery of Male Infertility, 1995, Atlas of the Urology Clinics: Surgery for Male Infertility, 1999, (with Z. Kopenmak, M. Fuerit) A Bagt at Last, 2010; contbr. chpts. to books, articles to profl. jours.; patentee in field. Maj. USAF, 1974—77, maj. USAFR, 1977—90. Honor scholar Downstate Med. Ctr., 1969; Summer Rsch. fellow Downstate Med. Ctr., 1969-70, Ferdinand C. Valentine fellow NY Acad. Medicine, 1980-82; recipient Ferdinand C. Valentine Urology prize NY Acad. Medicine and NY sect. Am. Urological Assn., 1981, Best Movie award Am. Fertility Soc. and Can. Fertility and Andrology Soc., 1986, 96, Excellence in Video Prodn. award Video Urology, 1987, 90, SUNY Coll. Medicine, Downstate Med. Ctr. Master Urology Tchr. award SUNY Downstate, 1997, Tribute award, 2009-, Outstanding Dedication and Commitment to Family Bldg. award, 1997, RESOLVE, The Nat. Fertility Assn. and Am. Infertility Assn., Howard and Georgeanna Lifetime Achievement award Am. Fertility Assn., 2007, commd. Ky. Col., Commonwealth of Ky., 1988. Fellow ACS; mem. AMA, Am. Soc. Andrology (mem. various coms.), Am. Fertility Soc., Am. Urological Assn. (scholar 1980-82, mem. various coms., Best Movie award vasectomy reversal 2004), NY County Med. Soc., Internat. Microsurgical Soc., Soc. Study Reproduction, Soc. Reproductive Surgeons (fellowship com. 1989—), Soc. for Male Reproduction and Urology (pres. 1996), Alpha Omega Alpha, NY Rd. Runners Club (completed 20 NYC marathons), Brit. Mountaineering Coun. Office: Ctr Male Reproductive Medicine and Microsurgery 525 E 68th St Box 580 New York NY 10065-4885 Office Phone: 212-746-5470. Business E-Mail: mgoldst@med.cornell.edu.

GOLDSTEIN, MICHAEL L., neurologist; b. Chgo., June 14, 1945; s. Charles and Dorothy (Mack) G.; m. Barbara Joan Kaplan, June 18, 1967; children: Rachel, Elizabeth, Adam. AB, Princeton, 1966; MD, U. Chgo., 1970. Cert. Am. Bd. Neurology and Psychiatry with spl. comptence in child neurology. Intern Stanford U., 1970-71; resident in neurology Beth Israel Hosp., Boston, 1971-74; fellow in neurology Harvard U. Med. Sch., 1971-74; chief resident in neurology Children's Hosp., Boston, 1973-74; with Western Neurol. Assoc., Salt Lake City. Cons. Soc. Sec., Balt., 1990-91; bd. dirs., edn. comm chmn. Rowland Hall, St. Marks Sch., Salt Lake City, 1986-92; examiner Am. Bd. Psychiatry and Neurology, 1987—; clin. assoc. prof. U. Utah Med. Sch., Salt Lake City, 1977—. Co-author: Managing Attention Disorders, 1990, Parent's Guide to ADD, 1993; co-producer: Educating Inattentive Children, 1992, It's Just Attention Disorder, 1993; acad. officer, Neurology. Pres. synagogue, Salt Lake City, 1985-86. Fellow Am. Acad. Pediat., Am. Acad. Neurology (chair practice com., 1995-2000, treas. 2001, v.p. 2007-). Office: Western Neurol Associates PC 1151 E 3900 S Ste B150 Salt Lake City UT 84124 Office Phone: 801-262-3441. Office Fax: 801-269-9005.

GOLDSTEIN, MURRAY, medical epidemiologist and research administrator; b. NYC, Oct. 13, 1925; s. Israel and Yetta (Zeigen) G.; m. Sue Mary Michael, June 13, 1957; children: Patricia Sue Robertson, Barbara Jean Warner. BA, NYU, 1947; DO, Des Moines U., 1950; MPH, U. Calif., 1959; DSc (hon.), Kirksville Coll. Osteo. Medicine, 1970, U. New Eng., 1984, Ohio U., 1986, U. Osteo. Medicine and Health Scis., 1990, Mich. State U., 2000; LLD (hon.), NY Inst. Tech., 1982; Dr. honoris causa, Med. Univ. Pecs, Hungary, 1985; LHD (hon.), Coll. Osteo. Medicine Pacific, 1988; Dr. honoris causa, Med. Sch. U. Lund, Sweden, 1994. Diplomate Am. Osteo. Bd. Preventive Medicine (sec.-treas. 1987-88, vice chmn. 1988-92). Rotating intern Still Coll. Osteo. Hosp., Des Moines, 1950-51, resident internal medicine, 1951-53; commd. corps USPHS, 1953, advanced through grades to asst. surgeon gen., 1980, ret., 1993; asst. to chief, then asst. chief, grants and tng. br., Nat. Heart Inst. NIH, Bethesda, Md., 1953-58, dir. epidemiology and biometry tng. grant program, divsn. rsch. grants, 1956-58, asst. chief rsch. grants rev. br., divsn. rsch. grants, 1959-60; exec. sec. joint coun. subcom. cerebrovascular disease Nat. Inst. Neurol. Diseases and Stroke and Nat. Heart and Lung Inst., NIH, Bethesda, Md., 1961-67, 69-75; dir. extramural programs Nat. Inst. Neurol. and Communicative Disorders and Stroke, NIH, Bethesda, Md., 1961-76, dir. stroke and trauma program, 1976-78, dep. dir., 1978-81, acting dir., 1981-82, dir., 1982-93; pub. health trainee epidemiology Calif. State Dept. Pub. Health, Berkeley, 1958, acting chief sect. virus diseases ctrl. nervous system, Bur. Acute Communicable Disease, 1958; bd. dirs. United Cerebral Palsy Rsch. and Edn. Found., Washington, 1972-93, 2005—, med. dir., COO, 1993—2005, chmn. sci. adv. coun., 2005—; clin. prof. neurol. medicine NY Coll. Osteo. Medicine, 1977—; sr. lectr. dept. neurology Uniformed Svcs. U. Health Scis., 1986—; osteo. pioneer Des Moines U., 2000; chair Middle East Rsch. Cerebral Palsy Collaborative Project State Dept., 2005—09; chmn. sci. adv. coun. Fed. Policy Internat. Rsch. Found., 2006—. Bd. dirs. Nat. Stroke Assn., Burke Rsch. Inst., Robarts Rsch. Inst., Soc. Supranuclear Palsy; adj. prof. pub. health Nova-Southeastern U., 1995—; chmn. Commd. Corps Adv. Com. to NIH dir., 1990-93, WHO Task Force on stroke and other vascular cerebral disorders, 1986-89; dir. WHO Neurosci. Collaborating Ctr., Bethesda, 1981-93; liaison, mem. sci. adv. bd. Kent Waldrep Nat. Paralysis Found., 1989-94; vis. prof. med. rsch. Semmelweis Med. U., Budapest, Hungary, 1975; vis. sci. sect. neurology Mayo Clinic and grad. sch., Rochester, Minn., 1967-68; vis. scholar Henry Ford Hosp., 1979-80; v.p. Eisenhower Inst. Stroke Rsch., 1975-88; cons. bur. rsch. Am. Osteo. Assn., 1990-99; mem. nat. adv. coun. Nat. Ctr. Complimentary and Alternative Medicine/NIH, 2000-06; pres. Acad. Medicine, Washington, DC, 2004-06; mem. nat. adv. bd. rehab. rsch. NICHD/NIH, 2004—08; chmn. UCP Sci. Adv. Coun., 2005—; chmn. MERC Sci. Adv. Coun. on CP, 2006-09; lectr., cons. in field. Assoc. editor Stroke: A Journal of Cerebral Circulation, 1976-91, consulting editor, 1992—; mem. editl. bd. Osteo. Annals, 1973-85, 87-88, Internat. Jour. Neurology, 1980-04, Jour. Neuroepidemiology, 1981-90, Hosp. and Community Psychiatry, 1980—95, Alzheimer Disease: An Internat. Jour., 1985-93, Cerebralvascular and Brain Metabolism Revs., 1985-93; contbr. articles to profl. jours. Bd. dirs. Bapt. Home for Children and Adults, 1999-2001. With U.S. Army, 1943-45. Decorated DSM, Silver Star, Purple Heart; recipient USPHS Disting. Svc. medal with oak leaf cluster, Surgeon Gen.'s Exemplary Svc. medal, Surgeon Gen.'s medallion, Founders Day medal U. Osteo. Medicine and Health Scis., 1983, Patenge Pub. Svc. medal Mich. State U., 1987, Marjorie Guthrie award The Huntington's Disease Soc. Am., 1988, Burke award Buke Found., 1988, Spl. Leadership award United Cerebral Palsy Rsch. & Ednl. Found., 1989, Phillips Pubs. Svc. medal Ohio U., 1990, others; named Pioneer in Osteo. Medicine, Des Moines U., 2000. Fellow: Am. Acad. Neurology (mem. long range planning com. 1972—75, mem. manpower com. 1979—85, mem. neurology in govtl. svcs. and insts. com. 1979—85, chmn. 1981—83, 1981—83, mem. internat. affairs com. 1981—90, mem. com. govt. rels. 1983—85, ANA-AAN del. to World Fedn. Neurology 1983—85, mem. AAN com. on pub. comm. and legislation 1983—85, mem. ad hoc com. for soc. neurology liaison 1987—89, sr. advisor uniformed svcs. orgn. neurologists com. 1987—93, chmn. 1993—95, bd. dirs. 1993—95); mem.: Drumaldky House Owners Assn. (bd. dir. 2007—), Soc. Supranuclear Palsy (bd. dirs. 2006—), Acad. of Medicine of Washington DC 1998 (pres. 2004—06), NIH Alumni Assn. (v.p. bd. dirs. 1999—2004), Am. Acad. Cerebral Palsy and Devel. Medicine (liaison mem., bd. dirs. 1993—2005), United Cerebral Palsy Assn. (interim dir. 1998). Avocations: gardening, golf, swimming. Home: 6210 Swords Way Bethesda MD 20817-3349 Personal E-mail: goldtstein5@verizon.net.

GOLDSTEIN, RISE BELLE, medical researcher; AB cum laude, Wash. U., Coll. Arts and Scis., St. Louis, 1982; MSW, U. Wash., Sch. Social Work, Seattle, 1985; MPH, U. Pitts., Grad. Sch. Pub. Health, Pitts., 1986; PhD, U. Mass., Sch. Pub. Health and Health Scis., Amherst, 1994. Project dir. Office Health Policy, RI Dept. Health, Providence, 1991—92; rsch. scientist Clin. and Genetic Epidemiology Unit, NY State Psychiat. Inst., NYC, 1992—97; assoc. rsch. scientist Divsn. Clin.-Genetic Epidemiology, Dept. Psychiatry, Coll. Physicians and Surgeons Columbia U., NYC, 1994—95, asst. prof., 1995—97, asst. prof. dept. preventive medicine and cmty. health and dept. psychiatry Va. Commonwealth U., Richmond, 1998—99; rsch. dir., project mgr. ROW Scis., Inc., Rockville, Md., 1999—2001; sr. rsch. scientist, prin. adminstrv. analyst II Ctr. Cmty. Health, Divsn. Social and Cmty. Psychiatry, Dept. Psychiatry, U. Calif., LA, 2001—04, staff scientist Lab. Epidemiology and Biometry, Divsn. Intramural Clin. and Biol. Rsch., Nat. Inst. on Alcohol Abuse and Alcoholism, NIH, Bethesda, Md., 2004—. Mem., bd. dirs. Kemp Mill Synagogue, Silver Spring, Md., 2008—10. Recipient Young Investigator award, Nat. Alliance Rsch. Schizophrenia and Depression, 1997—98; fellow, Aaron Diamond Found., NYC, 1995—98. Mem.: APHA, Soc. Epidemiologic Rsch., Phi Beta Kappa. Office: LEB/DICBR NIAAA/NIH 5635 Fishers Ln Rm 3071 MS 9304 Bethesda MD 20892-9304 Personal E-mail: goldsteinrb@verizon.net.

GOLDSTEIN, SCOTT D., colon and rectal surgeon, director; MD, SUNY, Buffalo, 1978. Diplomate Am. Bd. Surgery, Am. Bd. Colon and Rectal Surgery, lic. Pa., 1984. Intern in gen. surgery Lenox Hill Hosp., NY, 1979, resident in gen. surgery, 1983; resident in colon and rectal surgery Univ. Medicine and Dentistry NJ, 1984; fellow John F. Kennedy Meml. Hosp., Muhlenberg Regional Med. Ctr.; dir. colon and rectal surgery divsn. Thomas Jefferson Univ. Hosp., Pa. Named one of Top Doctors, Phila. Mag., 2010. Fellow: ACS; mem.: Am. Soc. of Colon and Rectal Surgeons. Office: Thomas Jefferson University Hospital 5th Fl 1100 Walnut St Philadelphia PA 19107 Office Phone: 215-955-5869. Office Fax: 215-923-1881.

GOLDSTEIN, SIDNEY, pharmacist; b. Phila., Mar. 27, 1932; s. Israel and Gertrude (Stein) G.; m. Janice Levy, June 19, 1955; children: Rhonda, David, Nina. BSc in Pharmacy, Phila. Coll. Pharmacy & Sci., 1954, MSc in Pharmacy, 1955, DSc in Pharmacy, 1958. Cardiovascular unit head Eaton Labs, Norwich, NY, 1958—59; anti-inflammatory unit head Lederle Labs, Pearl River, NY, 1959-61; with Merrell Dow Rsch. Inst., Cin., 1961-93; v.p. global pharm. and analytical scis. Marion Merrell Dow Inc., Kansas City, Mo., 1991-93; v.p. sci. and tech. Duramed Pharm., Inc., Cin., 1994-98, v.p. bus. devel., sci. and tech., 1998—2002; chief sci. officer Prasco, Cin., 2002—. Adj. assoc. prof. U. Cin. Coll. Pharmacy, 1984-98, dean's adv. coun., 1998—; lectr. pharmacology Phila. Coll. Pharmacy, 1967-70, chair PQRI-drug product tech. com., 1997-2004, mem. steering com., 2003-05; mem. So. Ohio Life Sci. Task Force, 1999-2001, GPhA sci. com., 2001—; mem. tech. validation adv. bd. Cinn. Children's Hosp., 2003—. Contbr. articles to profl. jours. Bd. trustees Glen Manor Home for Aged, Cin., 1983-89. Recipient Award for Nicoderm, R&D Mag., 1992. Mem. Am. Assn. Pharm. Scientists, Am. Soc. Clin. Pharmacology and Therapeutics, Soc. Exptl. Biology and Medicine, Am. Soc. Pharmacology and Exptl. Therapeutics, B'nai B'rith (chpt. v.p. 1978). Home: 1125 Fort View Pl Cincinnati OH 45202-1713 Office: Prasco 6125 Commerce Ct Mason OH 45040-6723 Home Phone: 513-651-5575; Office Phone: 513-618-3333. E-mail: s.goldstein@prasco.com.

GOLDWATER, MARILYN, state legislator; b. Boston, Mass., Jan. 29, 1927; m. William H. Goldwater, 1948; children: Charles A., Diane L. Mem. Women's Suburban Dem. Club, Bethesda, Md., 1962—, bd. mem., 1966, pres., 1971—73; v. chairwoman Montgomery Cuntry Dem. Com., Md., 1965—66, chairwoman, 1966—68; Md. state del. Dist. 16, 1975—86, 1995—; dep. majority whip, 1984—86, 1995—; mem. Econ. Matters Com., 1995—, Joint Advisor Com. on Legislature Data Syst., 1999—, Joint Com. on Health Care Delivery & Financing, 1999—, Health & Govt. Ops. Com., 2003; dir. office fed. rels Md. State Dept. Health & Mental Hygiene, 1987—91; exec. asst. for health Gov.'s Office, Md., 1991—94; mem. exec. com. Nat. Conf. State Legislatures, 1997—; chairwoman Long Term Care Subcom., 2003; faculty assoc. U. Md. Sc. Nursing, Johns Hopkins Sch. Nursing, George Mason U. Sch. Nursing; bd. mem. Ctr. Health Policy Rsch., U. Md. Contbr. articles to profl. jours.; co-author: (book) Prescription for

Nurses: Effective Polit. Action, 1990. Recipient Ann London Scott award for Legislature Excellence, Md. Nat. Orgn. Women, 1979, Upjohn award for Legislature Contbn. to Home Health Care, Hon. Recognition award, Am. Nurses Assn., 1980, Am. Jour. Nursing Book of Yr. award, 1990; named Legislator of Yr. award, Md. Pub. Health Assn.; named one of Md. Top 100 women, Daily Record, 2002. Fellow: Am. Acad. Nursing (hon.); mem.: Am. Nurses Assn. (bd. mem. 1984), Mt. Sinai Sch. Nursing Alumnae, Red Cross, Order of Women Legislators, League Women Voters. Democrat. Mailing: Lowe House Off Bldg 84 College Ave, Rm 221 Annapolis MD 21401-1991 Home Phone: 301-656-1226; Office Phone: 410-841-3019. Office Fax: 410-841-3850. Business E-Mail: marilyn_goldwater@house.state.md.us.

GOLDWURM, GIAN FRANCO, psychiatrist, psychologist, psychotherapist; b. Trento, Italy, June 17, 1929; s. Corrado and Olga (Casagranda) G.; m. Giovanna Negrin, Aug. 3, 1957 (div. 1988); children: Massimiliano, Andrea, Giuliano, Stefano; m. Concepción Monserrat Gomez Ocaña, July 7, 1991. MD, U. Milan, 1954; specialist in psychiatry, U. Psychiat. Sch. Milan, 1959. Med. rschr. Pharmacological Inst., U. Sch. Medicine, Milan, 1956-59; psychiat. asst. Psychiat. Clinic, U. Milan, 1959-68, psychiat. chief, 1968-72; psychiat. dir. Psychiat. Hosp. Trento, Italy, 1972-74, Psychiat. Hosp., Pavia, Italy, 1974-77, Psychiat. Hosp. (Paolo Pini) of Milan, 1977-81; psychiat. chief Psychiat. Oper. Unit 38 Niguarda Hosp., Milan, 1981-92; dir. Cognitive Behavioral Psychotherapy Sch. Milan, 1993—. Author: Psichiatria e Riforma Sanitaria, 1979; co-author: Dal Manicomio al Territorio, 1978, Le Tecniche di Rilassamento Nelle Terapie Comportamentali, 1986, I Disordini Schizofrenici, 1987; editor, co-author: Medicina Comportamentale, 1994, Qualitá della Vita e Benessere Psicologico. Aspetti Comportamentali e Cognitivi del Vivere Felice, 2004; co-editor Terapia del Comportamento; co-worker Psicoterapia Cognitiva e Comportamentale. Lt. Italy Army Med. Svc., 1955—56. Mem. Italian Psychol. Assn., Italian Psychiat. Assn., Italian Soc. Positive Psychology (pres. 2004-06), Italian Assn. Anal. Modification of Behavior (pres. 1981-92, mem. dir. comm. 1992—), Collegium Internat. Activitatis Nervosae Superioris (pres. 1999-2001, 06-), European Assn. Behavior Cognitive Therapy, NY Acad. Scis. Office: Scuola ASIPSE Cognitive Behav Psych Sch via Settembrini 2 20124 Milan Lombardy Italy Home: Via Luigi Vanvitelli 50 20129 Milan MI Italy Office Phone: 0039-02-2043880. Business E-Mail: gianfranco.goldwurm@fastwebnet.it.

GOLETIC, TEUFIK, virologist, educator; b. Tuzla, July 19, 1968; married; 3 children. BSc, Sarajevo Vet. Faculty, Bosnia-Herzegovina, 1999, DVM, MS in Vet. Sci., 2006, PhD, 2009. Cert. BiH Fed. Vet. Bd. Rschr. Nat. Reference Lab. Avian Influenza and Newcastle Disease, 1999—, asst. & sr. asst., 1999—2009; asst. prof. Sarajevo Vet. Faculty, 2010—, chief avian virology lab., 2010—. Expert Avian Influenza - cons. BiH Fed. Civil Protection and BiH State Vet. Office. Recipient Silver medal, U. Sarajevo; Doc. grant, FAO. Achievements include research in Bosnia and Herzegovina avian influenza virus strain. Avocations: hiking, martial arts, gardening. Office: Zmaja od Bosne 90 Sarajevo Canton Sarajevo 71000 Bosnia-Herzegovina Office Phone: 387 61 108 093, 387 33 618 832. Home Fax: 387 33 659041. Personal E-mail: teufikg@gmail.com.

GOLFIERI, RITA, radiologist, educator; b. Bologna, Italy, Jan. 28, 1955; MD, U. Bologna, 1979. Prof., head radiology unit, 2003—. Mem.: Italian Soc. Med. Radiology, Radiol. Soc. N.Am. Office: Policlinico S Orsola-Malpighi Via Albertoni 15 Bologna 40138 Italy Office Fax: 39051-6362699. Business E-Mail: rita.golfieri@aosp.bo.it.

GOLITZ, LOREN EUGENE, dermatologist, pathologist, medical association administrator; b. Apr. 7, 1941; s. Ross Winston and Helen Francis (Schupp) G.; m. Deborah Burd Frazier, June 18, 1966; children: Carrie Campbell, Matthew Ross. MD, U. Mo., 1966. Diplomate Am. Bd. Dermatology, Nat. Bd. Med. Examiners. Intern USPHS Hosp., San Francisco, 1966—67, med. resident, 1967—69, resident in dermatology SI, 1969—71, dep. chief dermatology, 1972—73; vis. fellow dermatology Columbia-Presbyn. Med. Ctr., NYC, 1971—72; asst. in dermatology Coll. Physicians Surgeons, Columbia, 1972—73; vice-chmn. Residency Rev. Com. for Dermatology, 1983—85; assoc. prof. dermatology, pathology Med. Sch. U. Colo., Denver, 1974—88, prof., 1988—97, clin. prof. pathology, dermatology, 1997—. Chief dermatology Denver Gen. Hosp., 1974-97; med. dir. Ambulatory Care Ctr., Denver Gen. Hosp., 1991-97. Mem. editl. bd. Jour. Cutaneous Pathology, Jour. Am. Acad. Dermatology, Advances in Dermatology (editl. bd. Current Opinion in Dermatology); contbr. articles to med. jours. Fellow Royal Soc. Medicine; mem. AMA (residency rev. com. for dermatology 1982-89, dermatopathology test com. 1979-85), AAAS, Am. Soc. Dermatopathology (sec., treas. 1985-89, pres.-elect 1989, pres. 1990), Am. Acad. Dermatology (chmn. coun. on clin. and lab. svcs., coun. sci. assembly 1987-91, bd. dirs. 1987-91, chmn. joint dermatopathology com.), Soc. Pediat. Dermatology (pres. 1981), Soc. Investigative Dermatology, Pacific Dermatol. Assn. (exec. com. 1979-89, sec.-treas. 1984-87, pres. 1988), Noah Worcester Dermatol. Soc. (publs. com. 1980, membership com. 1989-90), Colo. Dermatol. Soc. (pres. 1978), Am. Bd. Dermatology Inc. (chmn. part II test com. 1989—, exec. com. 1993—, v.p. 1994, pres.-elect 1995, pres. 1996, dir. Emeritus, cons. to bd. 1997—), Colo. Med. Soc., Denver Med. Soc., Denver Soc. Dermatopathology, Am. Dermatol. Assn., Women's Dermatologic Soc., So. Med. Assn., Internat. Soc. Pediat. Dermatology, Am. Contact Dermatitis Soc., Am. Soc. Dermatologic Surgery, Physicians Who Care, Am. Bd. Med. Specialties (del.), N.Y. Acad. Scis., Brit. Assn. Dermatologists (hon.), Brazilian Soc. Dermatology (hon.), U. Mo. Med. Alumni Orgn. (bd. govs. 1993—). Office: Dermatopathology Svc PO Box 6218 Denver CO 80206-0218

GOLLAN, JOHN LACHLAN, dean, medical educator; b. Australia; m. Roseanne Gollan; children: Jackie, Tim, Jenny. MD, U. Adelaide, 1971; PhD in biochemistry, U. London, 1977. Faculty U. Calif., San Francisco, 1977—81, Brigham and Women's Hosp., Harvard Med. Sch., Boston, 1981—99, dir. div. gastroenterology and hepatology, 1989—99; head dept. medicine U. Adelaide, Australia, 1999—2001; dir. internal medicine service Royal Adelaide Hosp., U. Adelaide, 1999—2001, dir. Hanson Inst., 2000—01; Henry L. Lenhoff Prof. & chmn. dept. internal medicine U. Nebr. Coll. Medicine, 2001—03, dean, 2003—, Stokes-Shackleford prof. medicine, 2003—. Mem. editl. bd. Hepatology Watch. Author more than 80 articles and 45 book chpt. in sci. jours. Fellow: ACP, Royal Australasian Coll. Physicians, Royal Coll. Physicians, London; mem.: Assn. Am. Physicians, Am. Soc. Clin. Investigation, Am. Gastroent. Assn., Internat. Assn. for Study of the Liver (past pres.), Am. Assn. for Study of Liver Diseases (past pres.). Office: U Nebr Coll Medicine 986585 Nebr Med Ctr Omaha NE 68198-6585 Office Phone: 402-559-2259. *

GOLLANCE, ROBERT BARNETT, ophthalmologist; b. NYC, Oct. 25, 1937; s. Harvey and Sarah (Chinitz) G.; m. Carmen Cote Gollance, Nov. 8, 1969; 1 child, Stephen Andrew. BA cum laude, Harvard Coll., 1958; MD, Columbia Coll., 1962. Diplomate Am. Bd. Ophthalmology, Nat. Bd. Med. Examiners. Intern in medicine NYU-Bellevue, 1962-63, resident and chief resident in ophthalmology, 1963-66; fellowship NIH, 1964-69; sec.-treas. Ophthalmology Assocs., Wayne, NJ, 1970-93; pres. Eye Assocs. of Wayne, 1993—; lectr. in ophthalmology Columbia U., NYC, 1998-2001; adv. bd. for devel. UMDNJ, 2002—. Chmn. ophthalmology Chilton Meml. Hosp., Pompton Plains, NJ, 1987-89, pres. med. staff, 1991; great hands adv. com. Becton Dickinson Corp., Franklin Lakes, NJ, 1990—; adv. com. Bausch & Lomb Corp., Rochester, NY, 1980-83; found. bd. Eye Inst. NJ Med.-Dental Sch., faculty cataract surgery and lens implantation; cons. Pharmacia Corp. Clin. Rsch. Glaucoma Medications, 2002—. Contbr. articles to profl. jours. Chmn. parents fund raising Loomis Chaffee Sch., Windsor, Conn., 1989-90. Capt. U.S. Army, 1966-68. Recipient Letter of Appreciation Korean Opthalomology Soc., 1967, Cath. Med. Ctr., 1967. Fellow ACS, Am. Soc. Cataract and Refractive Surgery, Am. Acad. Ophthalmology, European Soc. Cataract and Refractice Surgery. Office: Eye Assocs Wayne 968 Hamburg Tpke Wayne NJ 07470 also: Eye Inst North 5677 Berkshire Valley Rd Oak Ridge NJ 07438 Home Phone: 973-872-1710; Office Phone: 973-696-0300, 973-208-0600. E-mail: rbgollance@yahoo.com, rbgollance@njeyeinstitute.com.

GOLLIN, SUSANNE MERLE, cell biologist, cancer researcher, geneticist; b. Chgo., Sept. 22, 1953; d. Harvey A. and Pearl (Reiffel) G.; m. Lazar M. Palnick; 1 child, Jacob Hillel. BA in Biology, Northwestern U., 1974, MS, 1975, PhD, 1980. Diplomate Am. Bd. Med. Genetics with cert. in clin. cytogenetics; cert. food protection specialist. Postdoctoral fellow U. Rochester (N.Y.) Med. Ctr., 1979-81; rsch. assoc. in cell biology Baylor Coll. Medicine, Houston, 1981-83, rsch. assoc. in genetics, 1983-84; asst. prof. dept. pathology and pediat. U. Ark. for Med. Sci., Little Rock, 1984-87; dir. cytogenetics lab. Ark. Children's Hosp., Little Rock, 1984-87; assoc. mem. Pitts. Cancer Inst., 1987-95, mem., 1995—; dir. U. Pitts., Cancer Inst. Cell Culture and Cytogenetics Facility, 1989—; asst. prof. human genetics U. Pitts., Grad. Sch. Pub. Health, 1987-95, dir. clin. cytogenetics lab., 1988-99, assoc. prof., 1995—2003, prof., 2003—, prof. human genetics, otolaryngology, pathology, 2003—; dir. rsch., clin. cons. Pitts. Cytogenetics Lab., 1999—. Pediat. oncology group, exec. com. Ark. Genetics Program, 1984-87; organizing com. Am. Cytogenetics Conf., 1990-2002; mem. Allegheny County Bd. Health, 1992-2004, vice chmn., 1997, 2000-04; bd. dirs. Tobacco-Free Allegheny, 2002-08; founding fellow Indian Assn. Molecular Pathologists 2009-; clin. lab. improvement adv. com. Ctrs. Disease Control and Prevention, HHS, 1994-2000, mem. genetic testing subcom., 1997-2000; founding fellow, Internat. Acad. Oral Oncology, 2005-; vis. sci. German Cancer Rsch. Ctr., Heidelberg, 1995; cons. med. devices adv. com. FDA, 1996—; mem. oral biol. med. I study sect. NIH, 1997; master gardener, 2000; spl. emphasis panel Nat. Cancer Inst., 2000; genetics spl. emphasis panel ZRG1-GEN-01S, NIH Ctr. for Sci. Rev., 2000, spl. emphasis panel Nat. Cancer Inst., Minority Instn./Cancer Ctr. Partnerships, 2000, 05, 11, mammalian genetics study sect., 2002; NIH Spl. emphasis panel ZRG ONC-HO2 M, Chromosomal Instability and Cancer, 2007, NIDCR Spl. Grants Review com., 2009; lectr. U.S.-Japanese Cancer Rsch. Collaborative Conf., Tokyo, 2001; lectr. 1st Dhirubhai Ambani Life Scis. Symposium, Mumbai, 2006; lectr. 4th Dhirubhai Ambani Life Sci. Symposium, Mumbai, 2009; immunol. devices panel FDA, 2004-08; mem. Clin. Rsch. & Epidemiology Review Group, Am. Cancer Soc., 2010-, Pa. Cancer Prevention Control & Rsch. Bd., 2010-; mentor girls, math. & sci. partnership, 2010-, mem. The Carnegie Sci. Ctr.; lectr. in field. Contbr. articles to profl. jours., chpts. to books; mem. editl. bd. Cytogenetics and Genome Rsch., 2005—, Genes, Chromosomes, & Cancer, 2007—, The Open Otorhinolaryngology Jour., 2008-, Int. J. Hum Genet, 2009-. Mem. deans' adv. com. Pa. Sch. Excellence for Healthcare Profls., 1991-95; v.p. faculty senate U. Pitts. Grad. Sch. Pub. Health, 1994-95, senate anti-discriminatory policies com., 1999-2002, faculty senate athletics com., 2004-2007, 11-, mem., search com. dean Grad. Sch. Pub. Health, chair human genetics, 2004-06, faculty adv. promotion tenure com., 2005-08, chair epidemiology search com., 2008-2010; mem. U. Pitts. Grad. Sch. Pub. Health Task Force on Smoking, 2007-08; vol. Lighthouse for Blind, Houston, 1983; vol. hort. dept. Pitts. Zoo, 2000-01; chmn. med. ethics and civil liberties com. ACLU, Pitts., 1989-91; alt. del. Dem. Nat. Conv., 1992, 96, 2000, mem. rules com., 2004. Fellow Am. Coll. Med. Genetics (founder); mem AAAS, Internat. Acad. Oral Oncology, Am. Assn. Cancer Rsch., Am. Soc. Human Genetics (info. and edn. com. 2004-05, mem. program com. 2005-08), Am. Soc. Cell Biology, Soc. Analytical Cytology, Pitts. Cancer Inst., Pitts. Cytogenetics Club (founder, coord. 1989-95), Soc. Exec. Leadership in Academic Medicine Internat., Phipps/Pitts. Garden Place, Western Pa. Conservancy, Rivers Club, Carnegie Museums, Pitts. Zoo, Orchid Soc. Western Pa., Sigma Xi (sec., treas, U. Pitts. chpt. 2009-10, pres. 2010-2011), Soc. Exec. Leadership in Acad. Medicine Internat. Avocations: mountain dulcimer, gardening, photography, embroidery, crocheting, knitting. Office: U Pitts Dept Human Genetics Grad Sch Pub Health 130 Desoto St Pittsburgh PA 15213-2535 Home Phone: 412-661-3633; Office Phone: 412-624-5390. Business E-Mail: gollin@pitt.edu.

GOLOGAN, RADU BUCUR, clinical physician, researcher; b. Bucharest, Romania, Feb. 27, 1944; s. Ion and Ana Maria Gologan; m. Irinel Caprini Gologan, July 26, 1969; 1 child, Serban Ion. Diploma, U. Medicine and Pharmacy, Bucharest, 1967. Doctoral tng. Inst. Virology, Bucharest, 1969—72, physician rsch., 1972—75, rschr., 1972—75; resident physician, rschr. Clinic Hematology, Fundeni Clin. Inst., Bucharest, 1976—80, lab. chief, immunohematology, 1976—90, attending physician, internal medicine rschr., 1980—93, sr. attending physician and sr. rschr., 1994—. Contbr. scientific papers. Grantee, Myelodysplastic Syndrome, 2000—02, 2006—08. Office: Fundeni Clin Inst Sos Fundeni Nr 258 Sector 2 Bucharest 022328 Romania Office Fax: 40 21 3180423. Personal E-mail: mds.fundeni@yahoo.com. Business E-Mail: rgologan@rdslink.ro.

GOLOGORSKY, EDWARD, anesthesiologist, educator; b. Kishinev, Moldova, Russia, Sept. 30, 1961; MD, Kishinev Med. Inst., 1984. Intern, resident U. Medicine and Dentistry NJ, 1989—91; resident, fellow U. Pitts. Med. Ctr., 1991—94; physician Miami Heart Inst., 1994—2000; dir. cardiac anesthesia Meml. Regional Hosp., Hollywood, Fla., 2000—08; assoc. prof. clin. anesthesiology U. Miami Miller Sch. Medicine, 2009—. Fellow: Am. Soc. Echocardiography; mem.: Soc. Cardiovasc. Anesthesiologists, Am. Soc. Anesthesiologists. Office: 1611 NW 12th Ave C 300 Miami FL 33140 Office Phone: 305-585-7169. Business E-Mail: egologorsky@med.miami.edu.

GOLOMB, BEATRICE ALEXANDRA, physician, medical researcher; b. Pasadena, Calif., May 16, 1959; d. Solomon W. Golomb; m. Terrence Joseph Sejnowski, Mar. 24, 1990. BS in Physics, U. So. Calif., 1979; PhD in Biology, U. Calif. at San Diego, 1988, MD, 1989. Lic. Calif., 1991, cert. Am. Bd. Internal Medicine, 1993. Technical aide A Jet Propulsion Lab., 1978, engr. I, 1979; postdoctoral fellow, computational neurobiology lab. Salk Inst., 1989—90; resident West LA VA Med. Ctr., 1990-93, chief med. resident, 1993-94, attending physician, emergency room, 1993—94; attending physician, divsn. gen. internal medicine VA San Diego Healthcare Sys., 1996—; Robert Wood Johnson clin. scholar UCLA, 1994—96; rsch. asst. prof. psychology U. So. Calif., 1995—98, rsch. assoc. prof., dept. psychology, Social Sci. Rsch. Inst., 1998—; asst. prof. medicine U. Calif., San Diego, 1998—2004, asst. prof. psychology, 2001—04, asst. prof. family and preventive medicine, 2002—04, assoc. prof. family and preventive medicine, 2004—, assoc. prof. medicine, divsn. gen. medicine, 2004—, dir. statin study rsch. group, 1999—. Health cons. RAND, Santa Monica, Calif., 1996—; mem. Stein Inst. for Rsch. on Aging, 2001—; scientific dir. Dept. VA Rsch. Adv. Com. on Gulf War Veterans Illnesses, 2002—03, chief scientist, 2003—05, mem., 2005—; mem. pharmacy and therapeutics com. West LA VA Med. Ctr., 1993—94, VA San Diego Med. Ctr., 2001—05, Robert Wood Johnson generalist phys. faculty scholar, 2003—07; mem. adv. bd. The Science Network, 2004—; expert panel participation in field; mem. briefings to govt. agencies; lectr. and presenter in field. Contbr. articles to profl. jours.; peer reviewer for numerous jours. Mem. Am. Soc. for Preventive Cardiology, Phi Kappa Phi.; fellow Am. Heart Assn. (assoc. fellow, Coun. on Epidemiology and Prevention, 1999, fellow 2000-) Office: U Calif San Diego Dept Medicine 0995 9500 Gilman Dr #0995 La Jolla CA 92093-0995

GOLOMB, FREDERICK MARTIN, surgeon, educator; b. NYC, Dec. 18, 1924; s. Jacob J. and Hannah (Loewy) G.; m. Joan E. Schneider, Nov. 28, 1954; children: James Bradley, Susan Lynn. BS, Yale U., 1945; MD, U. Rochester, 1949. Diplomate: Am. Bd. Surgery. Intern Johns Hopkins Hosp., 1949-50; resident NYU Hosp., 1950-56; mem. staff NYU Med. Ctr., 1950—, dir. chemoimmunotherapy divsn. tumor svc. dept. surgery, 1967-96; attending surgeon Tisch Hosp.; mem. faculty NYU Sch. Medicine, 1956—, prof., clin. surgery, 1977—. Mem. clin. trials rev. com. Nat. Cancer Inst., 1976-79; chmn. melanoma com. Eastern Coop. Oncology Group, 1978-80; prin. investigator Central Oncology Group, 1969-77, exec. com., 1976-77; co-prin. investigator Ea. Coop. Oncology Group NYU, 1978-95. Contbr. articles to profl. jours. Served with M.C. AUS, 1953-54, Korea. Fellow ACS; mem. AMA, Am. Assn. Cancer Rsch., Am. Soc. Clin. Oncology, N.Y. Cancer Soc. (pres. 1974-75), N.Y. Surg. Soc., N.Y. State Med. Soc., N.Y. County Med. Soc., Soc. Surg. Oncology, George Hoyt Whipple Soc., Brit. Assn. Surg. Oncology (editl. adv. panel 1980-85), Am. Alpine Club, Explorers Club, Sigma Xi. Office: Frederick M Golomb MD 59 Churchill Rd Tenafly NJ 07670-3123 Home Phone: 201-567-3680. Business E-Mail: frederick.golomb@med.nyu.edu.

GOLOMB, HARVEY MORRIS, hematologist, oncologist, educator; b. Pitts., Feb. 13, 1943; s. Russell Austin and Dorothy (Simon) G.; m. Lynne Rooth, Dec. 28, 1965; children: Adam, Sara. BA, U. Chgo., 1964; MD, U. Pitts., 1968. Diplomate Am. Bd. Internal Medicine, Am. Bd. Med. Oncology. Intern Boston City Hosp., 1968-69; resident Johns Hopkins U., Balt., 1971-72, fellow, 1972-73, U. Chgo., 1973-75, asst. prof. dept. medicine, 1975-79, assoc. prof., 1979-83, prof., 1983—, chief sect. hematology/oncology, 1981-98, chmn. dept. medicine, 1998—2005, dean clin. affairs divsn. biol. scis., 2005—09; chief med. officer U. Chgo. Med. Ctr., 2007—11. Chmn. subspecialty bd. med. oncology Am. Bd. Internal Medicine, 1991-95. Contbr. over 350 articles, papers to profl. publs.; co-editor: Lung Cancer, 1988, Oncologic Therapies, 1999, 2003. Capt. U.S. Army, 1971-73. Mem. Am. Soc. Hematology (bd. dirs. 1987-91), Am. Soc. Oncology (pres. elect 1989-90, pres. 1990-91). Office: U Chgo MC 1000 5841 S Maryland Ave Chicago IL 60637-1463 Business E-Mail: hgolomb@medicine.bsd.uchicago.edu.

GOLOMB, HERBERT STANLEY, dermatologist; b. Sept. 6, 1933; m. Suzanne Nazer, Dec. 20, 1964; children: Meredith, Valerie. AB, U. Pa., 1955; MD, SUNY, Bklyn., 1960. Diplomate Am. Bd. Dermatology. Intern Ohio State U. Hosp., Columbus, 1960—61; resident in dermatology SUNY-Kings County Med. Ctr., 1961—62, NYU Skin and Cancer Unit and Bellevue Hosp., NYC, 1962—64; pres. Falls Church (Va.) Med. Ctr., 1963—64; practice medicine specializing in dermatology Falls Church, 1964—66, 1968—; mem. staff George Washington U. Hosp., Fairfax (Va.) Hosp., Arlington (Va.) Hosp. Instr., then clin. assoc. prof. dermatology George Washington U. Sch. Medicine, 1964—; cons. USPHS Dermatology Clinic, 1964—66; chmn. Atlantic Dermatol. Conf., 1978. Fellow: Am. Acad. Dermatology; mem.: AMA, Va. Dermatol. Soc., DC Dermatol. Soc., Fairfax County Med. Soc., DC Med. Soc., Med. Soc. Va., Internat. Soc. Tropical Dermatology, Soc. Investigative Dermatology, Tuckahoe Swim and Tennis Club. Home: 1910 Woodgate Ln Mc Lean VA 22101-5441 Office: 6060 Arlington Blvd Falls Church VA 22044-2943 Home Phone: 705-556-9527; Office Phone: 703-533-2222. Personal E-mail: hgolomb@cox.net.

GOLOMBEK, SERGIO GUSTAVO, pediatrician, educator, neonatologist; b. Buenos Aires, May 14, 1959; s. Jaime Y. Golombek and Luisa R. Grunin; m. Karin Friederwitzer, Jan. 11, 1991; children: Gabriel David, Alexander. MD, U. Buenos Aires, 1983; MPH, N.Y. Med. Coll., 2004. Tng. in peds., Argentina; intern R. Blank Meml. Hosp. for Children, Des Moines, 1991—92, resident in pediatrics, 1992—93; fellow in neonatal perinatal medicine Children's Mercy Hosp., Kansas City, Mo., 1993-96; asst. prof. pediatrics SUNY, Stony Brook, 1996-99, N.Y. Med. Coll., Valhalla, 1999—2003, assoc. prof. pediatrics, 2003—; attending neonatologist Maria Fareri Children's Hosp., at Westchester Med. Ctr.; mem. faculty Sch. Pub. Health N.Y. Med. Coll., 2005—, prof. pediat. clin. pub. health, 2009—. Jewish. Avocation: tennis. Office: Regional Neonatal Ctr Children's Hosp at

Westchester Med Ctr Valhalla NY 10595 Office Phone: 914-493-8488. Fax: 914-493-1005. Personal E-mail: sgolombek@pol.net. Business E-Mail: sergio_golombek@nymc.edu.

GOLOVCENCU, LOREDANA, orthodontist, educator; b. Iasi, Romania, June 7, 1970; Degree in Dentistry, U. Medicine and Pharmacy Gr T Popa Iasi, 1993, degree in Orthodontistry, 1997. Lectr. U. Medicine and Pharmacy Gr T Popa Iasi, 1999—. Mem.: Romanian Soc. Human Genetics, Romanian Dental Assn. Edn., Romanian Soc. Oral Rehab., Romanian Nat. Orgn. Orthodontics. Avocations: reading, languages, travel. Home: Anastasie Panu 50 Iasi 7300019 Romania

GOLSBY, STEPHEN W., pharmaceutical executive; b. London; B in Bus., Strathclyde U., Glasgow, Scotland. With Unilever; sr. v.p., gen. mgr. Mead Johnson and Clariol Mead Johnson, 1997, pres. Mead Johnson Internat., 2000—04; pres. Mean Johnson Nutrition, 2004—08, pres., CEO, 2008—. Office: Mead Johnson Nutrition 4th Fl 2701 Patriot Blvd Glenview IL 60026 *

GOLTZ, ROBERT WILLIAM, retired dermatologist; b. St. Paul, Sept. 21, 1923; s. Edward Victor and Clare (O'Neill) G.; m. Patricia Ann Sweeney, Sept. 27, 1945; children: Leni, Paul Robert. BS, U. Minn., 1943, MD, 1945. Diplomate: Am. Bd. Dermatology (pres. 1975-76). Intern Ancker Hosp., St. Paul, 1944-45; resident in dermatology Mpls. Gen. Hosp., 1945-46, 48-49, U. Minn. Hosp., 1949-50; practice medicine specializing in dermatology Mpls., 1950-65; clin. instr. U. Minn. Grad. Sch., 1950-58, clin. asst. prof., 1958-60, clin. assoc. prof., 1960-65, prof., head dept. dermatology, 1971-85; prof. medicine and dermatology U. Calif., San Diego, 1985—2004, emeritus prof., 2004—, acting chair divsn. dermatology, 1995-97; prof. dermatology, head div. dermatology U. Colo. Med. Sch., Denver, 1965-71; ret. Former mem. editl. bd. Archives of Dermatology; editor Dermatology Digest. Served from 1st lt. to capt., M.C. U.S. Army, 1946-48. Mem. Assn. Am. Physicians, Am. Dermatol. Assn. (dir. 1976-79, pres. 1985-86, Hon. 2009), Am. Soc. Dermatopathology (hon; pres. 1981), Am. Dermatologic Soc. Allergy and Immunology (pres. 1981), AMA (chmn. sect. on dermatology 1973-75), Dermatology Found. (past dir.), Minn. Dermatol. Soc., Soc. Investigative Dermatology (pres. 1972-73, hon. 1988), Histochem. Soc., Am. Acad. Dermatology (pres. 1978-79, past dir.) (hon.), Brit. Assn. Dermatology (hon.), Chilean Dermatology Soc. (hon.), Colombian Dermatol Soc. (corr. mem.), Can. Dermatol. Soc. (hon. mem.), German Dermatol. Soc. (hon.), Pacific Dermatol. Soc. (hon.-mem.), S. African Dermatol. Soc. (hon. mem.), N.Am. Clin. Dermatol. Soc., Assn. Profs. Dermatology (sec.-treas. 1970-72, pres. 1973-74), West Assn. Physicians. Home: 400 Prospect St Apt 233 La Jolla CA 92037-4708 Home Phone: 858-456-4087. Personal E-mail: rwgoltz@san.rr.com.

GOLTZMAN, DAVID, endocrinologist, educator, researcher; s. Jack and Lily (Roth) G.; m. Naomi Lyon, Dec. 29, 1968; children: Jonathan, Rebecca, Daniel. BSc, McGill U., 1966, MD, 1968. Diplomate Am. Bd. Internal Medicine, Am. Bd. Endocrinology and Metabolism. Med. intern Royal Victoria Hosp., Montreal, 1968-69; med. resident Columbia U. Coll. Physicians and Surgeons, NYC, 1969-71; clin. and rsch. fellow in endocrinology Mass. Gen. Hosp., Boston, 1971-75; instr. medicine Harvard Med. Sch., Boston, 1974-75; asst. prof. medicine McGill U., Montreal, 1976-78, assoc. prof., 1978-83, prof., 1983—, chmn. physiology, 1988-93, dir. calcium rsch. lab., 1981—, hosmer prof. physiology, 1992-93, Massabki prof. medicine, 1994—, chmn. medicine, 1994—2004; dir. Ctr. Bone and Periodontal Rsch., 2002—. Sr. physician dept. medicine Royal Victoria Hosp., 1987—, physician-in-chief, 1994-98, physician-in chief, McGill U. Hlth. Ctr., 1998-2004; chmn. exptl. medicine com. Med. Rsch. Coun. Can., Ottawa, Ont., 1984-88; mem. gen. medicine B study sect., NIH, Bethesda, Md., 1987-91; active Exec. Med. Rsch. Coun. Can., 1993-99; hon. prof. Nanjing Med. U., China, 2006—. Author: (with others) Principles of Bone Biology, 2001, Primer of Metabolic Bone Disease and Disorders of Mineral Metabolism, 1996, 1989, 2009, Primer of Osteoporosis, 2000, Primer of Metabolic Bone Disease and Disorders of Mineral Metabolism, 2009, Principles and Practice of Endocrinology and Metabolism, 2001, Vitamin-D Physiology, Molecular Biology and Clinical Applications, 2010; editl. bd. Endocrinology Jour., 1985-90, Jour. Bone Mineral rsch., 1985-90, Bone and Mineral, 1991-94, Osteoporosis Internat., 1991-94, Assoc. Edn. Bone, 1989-94; assoc. editor: Jur. Bone Mineral research, 1995-2002; contbr. numerous articles to profl. jours. Recipient Chercheur Boursier award Que. Med. Rsch. Coun., 1980-83, Scientist award Med. Rsch. Coun. Can., 1983-88, Andre Lichtwitz prize Nat. Inst. for Med. Rsch., France, 1987; named officer Order of Can., 2000—, John G. Haddad Meml. Lectr. Penn. U, 2004, Gerald D. Aurbach Meml. Lectr. US Endocrine Soc., 2009 Fellow Royal Coll. Physicians and Surgeons, Royal Soc. Can., Can. Acad. Health Scis.; mem. Can. Soc. Endocrinology and Metabolism (pres. 1990-92), Am. Soc. for Bone and Mineral Rsch. (chmn. program com. 1989-90, pres. 1999-2000, Lawrence G. Raisz award 2010), Am. Assn. Physicians, Endocrine Soc. (program com. 1989-91, G.D. Aurbach award, 2009), Can. Soc. Clin. Investigation (councillor 1986-89, pres. 1998-99, G. Malcom Brownlectr., 2003) Am. Soc. Clin. Investigation, Can. Assn. Profs. of Medicine (pres. 1998-99, Ronald V. Christie award, 2010). Avocations: classical music, gardening, tennis. Office: Royal Victoria Hosp 687 Pine Ave W Montreal PQ Canada H3A 1A1

GOLUB, RICHARD W., colon and rectal surgeon, director, educator; MD, Yeshiva U., NY, 1984. Diplomate Am. Bd. Surgery, Am. Bd. Colon and Rectal Surgery, lic. Fla., NY, Ohio. Intern SUNY, Stony Brook, resident; fellow in colorectal surgery Grant Med. Ctr., Columbus, Ohio; asst. clin. instr. SUNY Downstate Med. Ctr., asst. prof. surgery, assoc. prof. clin. surgery, chief colon and rectal surgery dept., dir. anorectal physiology lab., dir. surgical endoscopy svc.; hosp. affiliations include Doctor's Hosp., Sarasota Meml. Hosp., Fla. Named one of Top 100 Minimally Invasive Surgeons, NY Mag., Best Doctors, America's Top Doctors, Castle Connolly. Fellow: NY Soc. Colon and Rectal Surgeons, Am. Soc. Colon and Rectal Surgeons, ACS; mem.: NY Surgical Soc., Sarasota/LI Chpt. of the Am. Coll. of Surgeons, NY Soc. Gastrointestinal Endoscopy, Soc. for Surgery of the Alimentary Tract, Am. Soc. Gen. Surgeons, Sarasota Surgical Soc., Assn. for Acad. Surgery, Soc. Am. Gastrointestinal Endoscopy, Am. Coll. Gastroenterology. Office: Sarasota Memorial Hospital 3333 Cattlemen Rd Ste 206 Sarasota FL 34232 Office Phone: 941-341-0042.

GOLUB, SHARON BRAMSON, retired psychologist, educator; b. NYC, Mar. 25, 1937; m. Leon M. Golub, June 1, 1958; children: Lawrence E., David B. Diploma, Mt. Sinai Hosp. Sch. Nursing, 1957; BS, Columbia U., 1959, MA, 1966; PhD, Fordham U., 1974. Head nurse Mt. Sinai Hosp., NYC, 1957—59; contbg. editor RN Mag., Oradell, NJ, 1967—74; asst. prof. psychology Coll. New Rochelle, NY, 1974—79, assoc. prof., 1979—86, prof., 1986—98, prof. emeritus, 1998—; ret. Pvt. practice individual and group psychotherapy, 1976—2005; dir. women's studies Coll. New Rochelle, 1978—79, chmn. dept. psychology, 1979—82; adj. prof. psychiatry N.Y. Med. Coll., Valhalla, 1980—94. Editor: Menarche, 1983 (Assn. Women in Psychology Disting. Pub. award 1984, Book of Yr. award Am. Jour. Nursing 1984), Lifting the Curse of Menstruation, 1983, Health Care of the Female Adolescent, 1984, Health Needs of Women as They Age, 1984, PERIODS from Menarche to Menopause, 1992; (with Rita Jackaway Freedman) Psychology of Women: Resources for a Core Curriculum, 1987; editor Women and Health, 1982-86, mem. editorial bd., 1986—; mem. editorial bd. Psychology of Women Quar., 1989-2000. Grantee Nat. Libr. Medicine, 1983-84; NIH rsch. fellow, 1971-74. Fellow Am. Psychol. Assn. (chmn. task force on teaching psychology of women 1980-83), Am. Psychol. Soc.; mem. Soc. for Menstrual Cycle Rsch. (pres. 1981-83, bd. dirs. 1981-93), Assn. Women in Psychology, Westchester County Psychol. Assn. (pres. acad. divsn., Disting. Svc. award 2003), Phi Beta Kappa, Sigma Xi, Psi Chi. Home Phone: 212-879-0560.

GOLUMBECK, CARL TIMOTHY, psychoanalytic psychotherapist, forensic psychiatrist; b. Chgo., Mar. 12, 1947; s. Carl A. and Ivy (Hannam) G.; m. Karyn Ingrid Kramer, Dec. 4, 1971; 1 child, Elizabeth. BA, Johns Hopkins U., 1968, MD, 1971. Diplomate Am. Bd. Psychiatry and Neurology in Gen. and Forensic Psychiatry, Am. Bd. Forensic Psychiatry; cert. mental health adminstr. APA. Asst. prof. psychiatry Emory U., Atlanta, 1977-80; supt. Ga. Regional Hosp., Savannah, 1977-80; dir. tng., asst. prof. SUNY, Buffalo, 1981-83; asst. prof. psychiatry and psychology Johns Hopkins U., Balt., 1983-85; chief psychiatry Wyman Park Health System, 1983-85; psychiatrist pvt. practice Kailua-Kona, Hawaii, 1985-87; asst. prof. psychiatry UCLA, 1987-93; dir. forensic psychiatry Alascadero (Calif.) Forensic Ctr., 1987-93; cons. psychiatrist Rosanna Forensic Psychiatry Ctr., Rosanna, Victoria, Australia, 1994-96; pvt. practice of psychiatry Delmont Pvt. Hosp., Burwood, Victoria, Australia, 1994-97. Chmn. med. adv. bd. Delmont Pvt. Hosp., 1995-97; cons. psychiatrist, Melbourne Clinic, Australia, 1997-. Maj. USAR-MC, 1975-77. Fellow Royal Australian and New Zealand Coll. Psychiatrists, Australian Coll. Legal Med., Am. Soc. for Psychical Rsch.; mem. Am. Psychiat. Assn., Australian Med. Assn., Am. Acad. Psychoanal & Dyn Psychiatry. Avocation: fountain pen repair and collecting. Home: 3 Victoria Ave Canterbury VIC 3126 Australia Office Phone: 61-3-9830-2208. E-mail: drctg@iprimus.com.au.

GOLUSIN, MILLARD R., obstetrician, gynecologist; b. Detroit, Feb. 14, 1947; s. Raddie and Joan (Lalich) Golusin; m. Yvonne Marie Cronovich, Sept. 29, 1974 (dec.); m. Cvetana Cindy Pavlovich, June 4, 2005. BS with honors, Wayne State U., 1968, MS, 1970, MD, 1975. Diplomate Am. Bd. Ob Gyn. Intern, then resident William Beaumont Hosp., Royal Oak, Mich., 1975-78; practice medicine specializing in obstetrics and gynecology Village Gynecologic and Obstetric Assocs., P.C., Southfield and Troy, Mich., 1978-92; pvt. practice specializing in obstetrics and gynecology Troy, Mich., 1992-98; assoc. Wilshire Obstetrics-Gynecol. Assocs. PC, Troy, 1998—; asst. prof. Oakland U. William Beaumont Sch. Medicine, 2011. Mem. quality assurance com. William Beaumont Hosp., Royal Oak, Mich., 1979—, mem. gynecol. quality assurance com., 1993—; charter mem., pres. Preferred Ob-Gyn. Mgmt. Group, LLC, bd. dirs., pun. Unasource Health, Troy, 2000—; trustee, mem. credentials com. Preferred Provider Network, 2000; trustee United Beaumont Physicians Group, 1993—. With US Army, 1969—71. Fellow: ACOG; mem.: Am. Inst. Ultrasound Medicine, Mich. State Med. Soc., Am. Soc. Reproductive Medicine, Serbian Singing Soc., Ravanica (musical dir. 1967—, pres. 1981—82). Republican. Serbian Eastern Orthodox. Avocations: music, golf. Office: Wilshire Obstetrics-Gynecol Assocs PC 4550 Investment Dr Ste 200 Troy MI 48098-6369 Office Phone: 248-267-5040. Business E-Mail: dr.golusin@wilshircobgyn.com.

GOMATHY, SETHURAMAN, dermatologist, educator; b. Madurai, India, Dec. 12, 1967; s. Gomathy Krishnan and Sundarammal Mahalingam; m. Revathy Agnihothri Varadaraj, Feb. 1, 1998; 1 child, Sethuraman Sanchana. BS in Medicine and Surgery, Madurai Med. Coll., India, 1991; MD, Postgraduate Inst. Med. Edn. & Rsch., India, 1996. Cert. Nat. Acad. Med. Scis., India, 2005. Resident dermatology Postgrad. Inst. Med. Edn. & Rsch., Chasndigarh, India, 1993—98, Jawaharlal Inst. Postgrad. Med. Edn. & Rsch., Pondicherry, India, 1999—2000; asst. prof. dermatology PSG Hosp., Coimbatore, India, 2000—01, All India Inst. Med. Scis., New Delhi, 2001—. Reviewer Brit. Jour. Dermatology, 2003—, Clin. Exptl. Dermatolgy, London, 2003—, Indian Jour. of Dermatology Venereology Leprology, Mumbai, India, 2004—, assoc. editor Indian Jour. Pediatric Dermatology, 2005—. Vis. scholar Scholarship award, Internat. Soc. Dermatology, 2004;, Am. Acad. Dermatology, 2005. Mem.: Nat. Acad. Med. Scis., Dermatopathology Soc. India (life), Indian Assn. Dermatologists, Venereologists and Leprologists (life). Home: F 73 Ansari Nagar All India Inst Med Sci New Delhi 110029 India Office: All India Inst Med Scis Ansari Nagar New Delhi 110029 India Office Fax: 91 11 26588641. Personal E-mail: kgsethu@yahoo.com.

GOMBERG, JONATHAN D., cardiologist, educator; BS in Biology, Trinity Coll., 1976; MD, Med. Coll. of Pa., 1979. Diplomate Am. Bd. Internal Medicine, 1985, Am. Bd. Internal Medicine-cardiovasc. medicine, 1987. Resident Med. Coll. of Pa.; fellow Penn Presbyn. Med. Ctr.; asst. prof. clin. medicine Univ. of Pa.; physician cardiology Penn Heart and Vascular Ctr., Penn Medicine. Named one of Top Doctors, Phila. Mag., 2011. Mem.: Phila. Acad. of Cardiology, Coun. on Clin. Cardiology, Am. Coll. of Cardiology, ACP, Am. Heart Assn. Office: Penn Medicine 250 King of Prussia Rd Radnor PA 19087 Mailing: c/o Ruth and Raymond Perelman Center for Advanced Medicine 2nd Fl E Pavilion 3400 Civic Center Blvd Philadelphia PA 19104-4283 Office Phone: 215-662-7700. Office Fax: 215-312-0053. E-mail: gombergj@uphs.upenn.edu.

GOMES, ANTOINETTE SUSAN, physician, educator; b. New Bedford, Mass., Aug. 28, 1942; MD, Woman's Med. Coll. Pa., 1969. Prof. radiology and medicine David Geffen UCLA Sch. Medicine, 1978—. Recipient Best Drs., Castle Connolly. Fellow: SIR; mem.: AHA. Office: 757 Westwood Plz Ste 2125D Los Angeles CA 90095-7437 Office Fax: 310-267-3631. Business E-Mail: agomes@mednet.ucla.edu.

GOMES, GECYNALDA SOARES DA SILVA, science educator; b. Rio Branco, Acre, May 29, 1974; MS, Fed. U. Pernambuco, 2005, PhD, 2010. Adj. prof. Fed. U. Bahia, 2009. Office: Av Adhemar de Barros-Campus de Ondina Salvador Bahia 40.170-110 Brazil E-mail: gecynalda@yahoo.com.

GOMES, JOSEPH A., cardiac electrophysiologist; MD, GOA Med. Coll. Diplomate Am. Bd. of Internal Medicine-cardiovasc. disease. Resident City Hosp. Ctr.; fellow Veterans Adminstrn. Med. Ctr. Named one of Best Doctors, New York Mag., 2009. Office: Cardiovascular Medicine Associates Guggenheim Pavilion 1190 5th Ave-1 South New York NY 10029 Office Phone: 212-427-1540. Office Fax: 212-241-9701.

GOMEZ, WILLIAM, orthopedist; b. NYC, Apr. 29, 1955; Degree, NYU, 1976; MD, Columbia U., NYC, 1982. Diplomate Am. Bd. Orthop. Surgeons. Intern in gen. surgery St. Vincent's Hosp., NYC, 1982—84; resident in orthop. Columbia-Presbyn. Med. Ctr., NYC, 1984—87; fellow in sports medicine U. Pitts., 1987—88; pvt. practice Trenton, NJ. Orthop. team physician Trenton Titans, Trenton Thunder, NY; affiliated physician St. Francis Med. Ctr., Trenton, Robert Wood Johnson Univ. Hosp., Hamilton, NJ, Capital Health Sys., Trenton; team physician Trenton Devils, NJ, 2008—. Named one of Top Drs. NY Metro Area, Castle Connolly, 2001—10, Top Drs., NJ Monthly Mag., 2003—05, Team Physician, NY Yankers Doubu AA Affilate, 2003—10. Fellow: Am. Acad. Orthop. Surgeons; mem.: NJ Orthop. Soc., Mercer County Med. Soc., NJ Med. Soc., Am. Orthop. Soc. Sports Medicine. Office: Orthop Surgery Bldg D Ste 220 1225 Whitehorse Mercerville Rd Trenton NJ 08619-3882 Office Phone: 609-581-2200.

GOMEZ BRAVO TOPETE, ENRIQUE, obstetrician, gynecologist, educator, secretary, health institute administrator; b. Toluca, Mex., Nov. 29, 1960; s. Enrique and Maria Magdalena (Topete) Gomez Bravo; m. Adelina Manzo Garcia; children: Enrique Gomez Bravo Manzo, Lorena Gomez Bravo Manzo, Adelina Gomez Bravo Manzo. Diploma, ACOG, Orlando, Fla., 1993, L.Am. Fedn. Gynecology and Obstetricians Socs., Republic Panama, 1996, Mexican Fedn. Ob-gyn., Distrito Fed., 1996. Cert. Mex. Com. Ob-gyn., 2001. Med. surgeon Medicine Faculty, Toluca, 1978—82; ob-gyn. Hosp. Issemym Toluca, 1986—89, Sanatorium Florencia, Toluca, 1992—; head external attention Hosp. Ob-gyn., Toluca, 1990—92, head edn. and rsch. dept., 1992, dir., 1993—99; med. attention chief Integral Devel. Family Sys. State Mex., Toluca, 1993, health svcs. mgr., 1999—2000; chief main directorate Health Inst. State Mex., 2002—05; health sec. Gov. State Mex., Toluca, 2002—05. Sci. moderator Internat. Congress Laparoendoscopist Surgeons, Toluca, 2001, 02. Contbr. articles to popular mags. Pres. Ob-gyn. Assn., Toluca, 1996—97; founding ptnr. Assn. State Climaterio Studies, Toluca, 1997. Honored, U. State Mex., 1993, Shriners Hosp. Children, Galveston, Tex., 2005, Mexiquense Acad. Sci., Toluca, 2005. Fellow: ACOG; mem.: Mexican Fedn. Ob-gyn., L.Am. Fed. Gynecology and Obstetrician Socs., Mexican Com. Ob-Gyn., Mexican Acad. Surgery (acad. mem. 2005). Office: Sanatorium Florencia Paseo Vicente Guerrero 213 50120 Toluca Mexico

GÓMEZ-JIMÉNEZ, CARLOS, science educator, microbiologist, geneticist; s. Carlos Gómez-Vázquez, Sr. and Emma Jiménez-Gómez. BS in Biology with honors, U. PR, Mayagüez, 1986, MS in Microbiology and Genetics, 1992; postgrad., Alliance Theol. Sem. Tchr. asst. U. PR, Mayagüez, 1986-88, 91, biochemistry lab. technician, 1988, full prof. Aguadilla, 1992—; quality assurance analyst Microbiology and Cell Culture Lab. Ortho Biologics, Inc., Manati, PR, 1989-90; prof. Inter Am. U., Aguadilla, PR, 1991-92, San Germán, 1992—; MCAT, PCAT, and DAT invited prof. Kaplan PR Ctr., 1997—; prof. Pontifica Cath. U. PR, 2000—. Acad. counselor sci. rsch. acad. tchrs. and gifted students Internat. Am. U. PR, San Germán, PR, 1992-, sci. advisor Young Scholars Program-NSF, San Germán, 1992-; cons. drugs, alcohol, violence and HIV/AIDS Prevention programs U. PR, Aguadilla, 1992-; curriculum and course dir., U. PR-Aguadilla, 1992-; mem. over 40 coms. U. PR pres. office & U. PR-Aguadilla, 1992-; dir. honor program, 1996-98, mem. exec. com. Superior Edn. Coun., 1996, 2001; mem. Nat. Collegiate Honors Coun., 1996-; bd. dirs. Assn. Hon. Programs; mentor prof. NSF and U. PR Program, 2001-08; academic senator, mem. adminstrv. bd. U. PR Aguadilla, 2002-08. Editor (newsletters) The Probe-Caribbean Soc. Biotech., Inc., 1994-, Biosfera-U. PR-Aguadilla, 1994-; contbr. articles to profl. jours.; author acad. manuals and modules in Microbiology, Genetics, Human Genetic, and General Biology Co-founder Leguísamo First Baptist Ch., Mayagüez, 1977-; first tenor Mayagüez Municipal Choir, 1994-, ROMANTIEZER Interdenominational Singing Ministry, 1996-; judge,advisor HS and Undergrad. Sci. Competitions, 1987-; liaison U. PR-Aguadilla & Am. Red Cross Assn. Communitarian Svc., 1994-. Mem.: AAAS, PR Soc. Microbiologists (bd. dirs. 1995—97, 2006—, pres. 2008—), Assn. U. Honor Programs (bd. dirs. 1997—), Biostudy I (counselor, bd. dirs. 1997—), Assn. Food Sci. Tech. PR, PR Sci. Tchr. Assn., Puertorrican Soc. Mycology (bd. dirs. 2002—08, pres. 2003—04), Caribbean Soc. Biotech. (bd. dirs. 1995—99), Am. Soc. Microbiology, Bapt. Student Union, Beta Beta Beta. Baptist. Avocations: singing, book collecting, French cooking. Office: U PR Aguadilla Dept Nat Scis PO Box 6150 61 Aguadilla PR 00604-6150 Office Phone: 787-890-2681 ext. 230, 787-890-2681 ext. 226. Office Fax: 787-890-0198. Business E-Mail: cgj_upra@yahoo.com.

GOMEZ-OLVERA, FRANCISCO JAVIER, sales manager; b. Mexico City, Mex., Mar. 17, 1970; m. Gabriela Gonzalez, Apr. 18, 1998. BA, MBA, U. Anahuac, Mexico City, 1994; attended, IPADE Bus. Sch., Mexico City, 2002. Salesman Metales Dentales Olver, Mexico, 1984—88; project specialist Nacional Financiera, Mexico, 1993—95; mktg. advisor Schering Plough, Mexico, 1995—97; jr. product mgr. biotech area Baxter Healthcare, Mexico, 1997—98; sr. product mgr. respiratory area Boehringer Ingelheim, Mexico, 1998—99; global mktg. mgr. intercontinental region ZLB Behring, King of Prussia, Pa., 1999—2004; sales mgr. Mex. and Ctrl. Am. Bayer Healthcare, Mexico, 2005—. Recipient Olympus Latinamerica Sales award, 1995. Mem.: Med. Mktg. Assn. (assoc.). Office: Bayer Healthcare Diagnostics Division AvCoyoacan 1553 Mexico City 03100 Mexico Business E-Mail: javier.gomez.jg@bayer.com.mx.

GÓMEZ-SÁEZ, JOSÉ-MANUEL, endocrinologist; b. Vitoria, Apr. 28, 1948; MD, Zaragoza, 1948; PhD, Barcelona, 1981. Chief clinician endocrinology Hosp. U. Bellvitge, 1981—. Adj. prof. U. Barcelona,

1981—2011. Recipient medal, Endocrine Spanish Soc. Mem.: Endocrine Soc. Avocations: movies, art. Home: c/Sabino de Arana 40 3° 2a Barcelona 08028 Spain Home Fax: 34 932604876. Business E-Mail: jmgs@bellvitgehospital.cat.

GÓMEZ TELLO, VICENTE, emergency physician, department chairman; b. Guadalajara, Spain, Apr. 21, 1962; MD, U. Alcalá de Henares, 1986; PhD, U. Autónoma de Madrid, 1999. Icu staff Hosp. Moncloa, 1994—. Chmn. internet work group Spanish Soc. Critical Care Medicine, 2002—06, chmn. work group elaborate stds. clin. info. sys., 2008—. Mem.: European Soc. Intensive Care Medicine. Avocations: mountain climbing, history, travel. Office: AvValladolid 83 Madrid 28290 Spain Business E-Mail: vgtello@vgt.e.telefonica.net.

GOMMEL, MICHAEL, consultant, trainer, coach, lecturer medical, organisational and research ethics; b. Heidenheim an der Brenz, Germany, Jan. 3, 1965; MSc in Biology, U. Ulm, 1993, DSc in Human Biology, 2005. Asst. Ambulante Dienste, Berlin, 1993—95; tchg. asst. Abteilung Psychosomatische Medizin und Psychotherapie U. Ulm, Germany, 1997—2001, sci. coord. AK Ethik in der Medizin, 2002—07. Tchr. adult edn. Georg-von-Vollmar-Akademie, Kochel, Germany, 2005—. Scholar, German Nat. Academic Found., 1986—92, 1995—97. Office: Inst Systemische Medizin- und Organisationsethik Weserstr 10 Berlin 10247 Germany Office Phone: 49 30 26076103, 49 30 26076103. Business E-Mail: info@michaelgommel.de.

GOMOLL, ALLEN WARREN, cardiovascular pharmacologist; b. Chgo., July 10, 1933; s. Herbert Fredrick and Sara Evelyn (Cowan) G.; m. Elaine L. Kirkpatrick, Sept. 17, 1955; children: Gary A., Lisa E. BS in Pharmacy, U. Ill., Chgo., 1955, MS, 1958, PhD, 1961. Instr. U. Ill. Coll. Medicine, Chgo., 1960—61, asst. prof., 1961—66; group leader Mead Johnson, Evansville, Ind., 1966—70, sect. leader, mgr., 1970—81; prin. rsch. scientist Bristol-Myers, Evansville, 1981—84, rsch. fellow Wallingford, Conn., 1984—90; sr. rsch. fellow Bristol-Myers Squibb, Princeton, 1990—2001. Reviewer Life Scis., 1973-2001, Jour. Med. Chemistry, 1975-2001, Circulation, 1989-2001; contbr. sci. articles to profl. jours. Fellow Am. Coll. Cardiology, Am. Heart Assn. Coun. Circulation and Basic Sci. Coun.; mem. Am. Soc. Pharmacology and Exptl. Therapy, Internat. Soc. Heart Rsch., Sigma Xi. Personal E-mail: gomolla@verizon.net.

GOMZHIN, ANDREY, urologist; b. Yakutskaya, Russia, Apr. 9, 1962; MD, Ural State Med. Acad., 1987, PhD in Medicine, 2010. Physician, urology dept. City Clin. Hosp. Nr. 40, Yekaterinburg, Russian Fedn., 2002—. Mem.: Russian Soc. Urology. Office: Volgogradskaya 189 Yekaterinburg Sverdlovskaya 620102 Russia Business E-Mail: agomzhin@list.ru.

GONÇALVES, GISELE MARA SILVA, medical educator, researcher; b. São Paulo, Brazil, Dec. 9, 1973; Degree in Pharmacy, U. Sao Paulo, 1995, PhD in Pharm. Scis., 2003. Adj. prof., rsch. scientist Pontifícia U. Católica de Campinas, 2003—. Bolsa De Doutorado fellow, FAPESP, Bolsa De Mestrado fellow, Bolsa De Iniciação Científica fellow, PIBIC/CNPq, Bolsas De Iniciação Científica Para Orientados fellow. Mem.: Brazilian Soc. Pharmacognosy, Brazilian Cosmetology Assn. Avocations: movies, reading, music. Office: Ave John Boyd Dunlop S/N JD Ipaussur Campinas SP 13060-904 Brazil Business E-Mail: gmsg@puc-campinas.edu.br.

GONÇALVES, MARIA ALICE GUIMARÃES, gynecologist, epidemiologist; b. Rio de Janeiro, Mar. 10, 1963; Degree in Medicine, U. Gama Filho, 1987; MS in Gynecology, U. de São Paulo, PhD in Epidemiology, 2004. With med. info. VIDAL, 2011—, postdoc. in immunology & vaccinology; cons. vaccinology phase III, IV. Avocation: travel. Home: 1A rue du Prè Saint Germer Gouvieux Picardie 60270 France Personal E-mail: epigin@hotmail.com.

GONÇALVES CARRASQUINHO, SARA CRISTINA DE SOUSA TEIXEIRA, ophthalmologist; b. Lisbon, Portugal, Dec. 14, 1974; d. David Teixeira and Arminda Maria de Sousa Gonçalves; m. José Eduardo Neto Carrasquinho, May 19, 2002. Degree in Nutrition, Nutrition and Alimentation Scis. Inst., Oporto U., 1995; degree in Medicine, Abel Salazar Biomed. Scis. Inst., Oporto U., 2001. Diploma Oporto U., 2001, Portuguese Med. Assn., 2001, cert. ophthalmology splty. Portuguese Coll. Ophthalmology, 2008. Gen. resident Civil Hosps., Lisbon, 2002—03; ophthalmology resident Fernando Fonseca Hosp., Lisbon, 2004—07; ophthalmology hosp. asst. med. surg. dept. Hosp. Espírito Santo Évora, 2008—; vol. intern, surg. retina dept. Moorfield Eye Hosp., London, 2007. Contbr. scientific papers, articles to profl. sci. jours. Recipient Best Sci. Paper Presentation award, Abel Salazar Biomed. Scis. Inst., Oporto U., 1999, Portuguese Ophthalmology Soc., 2007, Hon. Sci. Poster award, 2005, Best Sci. Photogs. award, 2005, Hon. Sci. Paper award, Fernando Fonseca Hosp., 2007. Mem.: Assn. Rsch. Vision and Ophthalmology, European Soc. Retina Specialists, Portuguese Coll. Ophthalmology, Portuguese Ophthalmology Soc., Portuguese Med. Assn. Personal E-mail: sgcarrasquinho@netcabo.pt.

GONCHAR, OLGA, physiologist; b. Rovenky, Lugansk Region, Ukraine, Oct. 14, 1960; MSc in Biology and Chemistry, Lugansk Pedagogical Inst., Ukraine, 1983; PhD in Biology, Human and Animals Physiology, Bogomoletz Inst. Physiology NAS Ukraine, 1996. Sr. sci. rschr. Bogomoletz Inst. Physiology NAS Ukraine, 1997—, head, sci. group, dept. hypoxic states, 2000—. Grant, Sachsischen Acad. der Wissenchaften zu Leipzig an der Friedrich-Schille Germany, 2002. Mem.: Ukrainian Pathophysiol. Soc., Ukrainian Physiol. Soc. Avocation: travel. Office: Bogomoletz 4 Kiev 01024 Ukraine Office Fax: 380 44 256-20-00. Business E-Mail: ogonchar@yandex.ru.

GONDHOWIARDJO, SOEHARTATI ARGADIKOESOEMA, oncologist, educator; b. Jakarta, Sept. 4, 1955; d. Abdullah and Soekaemi Argadikoesoema; m. Tjahjono Darminto Gondhowiardjo; children: Argadita, Aryateja, Arunaya. Degree in Radiation Oncology, Strahlentherapie Abteilung Wilhelm-Waestfaelichen U. Muenster, Germany, 1989; PhD, U. Indonesia, Jakarta, 1998. Prof., radiation oncology Cipto Mangunkusumo Hosp., Jakarta, head, radiotherapy dept., 2003—. Founder & pres. Indonesian Radiation Oncology Soc., 2000—; coun. mem. Asian Clin. Oncology Soc., 2000—; exec. com. mem. Asia and Pacific Fedn. Orgn. Cancer Rsch. and Control, 2002—; pres. Indonesian Soc. Oncology, 2006—10; founder, v.p. South East Asian Radiation Oncology Group, 2007—, pres., 2011—; nat. project coord., RCA-RAS/6/048 Internat. Atomic Energy Agy., 2007—09, nat. project coord., RCA-RAS/6/059, 2009—. Contbr. more than 38 sci. papers to profl. jours. Recipient Govt. Satyalancana Karya Satya award. Mem.: Asean Oceanian Clin. Oncology Assn., European Soc. Therapeutic Radiology and Oncology. Muslim. Achievements include research in radiotherapy in treatment of patients with stage III cervical cancers and optimisation of radiotherapy in low resource settings paediatric cancer patients. Office: Dept Radiotherapy RSCM Jl Diponegoro 71 10430 Jakarta Indonesia Office Phone: 62213147534, 62213103090. Office Fax: 62213147534. Personal E-mail: gondhow@gmail.com.

GONG, KAIZHENG, cardiologist, researcher; MD, Dalian Med. U., China; PhD, Peking U., China. Asst. prof. Dept. Internal Medicine Dali Med. Coll., China, 1999—2003; attending physician Dept. Cardiology First People's Hosp. Yangzhou, China, 2003—; attending physician 2d Clinic Sch. Med. Coll. Yangzhou U., China, 2003—. Contbr. articles to profl. jours. Committeeman Chinese Med. Assn., Yangzhou, Jiangsu, China. Grantee Social Devel. Project, Sci. and Tech. Office of Jiangsu, 2003. Mem.: Chinese Med. Assn. (cardiology com.). Achievements include research in immune activation mechanism of congestive heart failure; health-related quality of life (SF-36 and MHFQ) and influencing factors in Chinese patients with chronic heart failure; demonstration of ROS-mediated ERK activation in delayed protection from anoxic preconditioning in neonatal rat cardiomyocytes. Avocation: sport (badminton). Office: First People's Hosp of Yangzhou No 45 Taizhou Rd Jiangsu Yangzhou 225001 China Personal E-mail: yungkzh@126.com.

GONICK, DENISE V., insurance company executive; BA in Creative Studies, Hofstra U.; JD, Albany Law Sch.; completed the America's Health Ins. Plans Exec. Leadership Program. Cert. Managed Care Exec. (CMCE). Several years practicing pub. sector labor law State of NY at the Governor's Office Employee Relations; mem. legal dept. Empire Blue Cross Blue Shield; joined MVP Health Care, 1995, various positions in legal dept., exec. v.p. adminstrv. services, chief legal officer, 2005—. Trustee Schenectady Mus., 2003—, bd. co-pres.; bd. dirs. Union Grad. Coll., 2011—; vol. Junior Achievement; taught elementary sch. classes for introducing bus. concepts to sch. children for six years. Named one of Bus. Review's 40 Under 40 Up and Coming Bus. Leaders, 2006. Mem.: American Health Lawyers Assn., NY State Bar Assn. Office: MVP Health Care 625 State St PO Box 2207 Schenectady NY 12301-2207 *

GONICK, HARVEY CRAIG, nephrologist, educator; b. Winnipeg, Man., Can., Apr. 10, 1930; s. Joseph Wolfe and Rose (Chernick) G.; m. Gloria Granz, Dec. 16, 1967; children: Stefan, Teri, Julie, Suzanne. BS in Chemistry, UCLA, 1951; MD, U. Calif., San Francisco, 1955. Diplomate Am. Bd. Internal Medicine, Am. Bd. Nephrology. Intern Peter Bent Brigham Hosp., 1955-56; fellow in nephrology Mass. Meml. Hosp., 1956-57; fellow in nephrology, resident in internal medicine Wadsworth VA Hosp., Los Angeles, 1959-61, clin. investigator, 1961-64, chief metabolic balance unit, 1964-67, rsch. assoc. LA, 2002—; instr. medicine Sch. Medicine, UCLA, 1961-64, asst. prof., 1964-69, assoc. prof., 1969-72, adj. assoc. prof., 1972-76, adj. prof., 1976—2003, clin. prof., 2003—, assoc. chief div. nephrology, 1965-72, co-dir. Bone and Stone Clinic, 1972-76, coordinator postgrad. nephrology edn., 1975-78; mem. staff St. John's Hosp., Santa Monica, Calif., Century City Hosp., LA, med. dir. dialysis unit, 1972-79, chief medicine, 1978-79; mem. staff Cedars-Sinai Med. Ctr., LA, dir. trace element lab., 1979-96, clin. chief nephrology, 1983-85, coord. renal tng., dir. hypertension rsch., 1996—2003; practice medicine specializing in nephrology Los Angeles, 1972-94. Co-founder, med. dir. Berkeley East Dialysis Unit, Santa Monica, 1971-75; co-founder, cons. Kidney Dialysis Care Units Inc., Lynwood, Calif., 1971-78; co-dir. Osteoporosis Prevention and Treatment Ctr., Santa Monica, 1987-93; mem. numerous adv. coms. to state and fed. agys., 1969-83, cons. EPA Lead Studies, 2005-06, 10-11. Contbr. articles to profl. jours.; editor: Current Nephrology, 1977-96. Cons. Environ. Protection Agency, 2005-06, 2010-11Served to capt. M.C., USAF, 1957-59. Fellow Charles Nelson Fund, Kaiser Found., NIH; recipient Oliver P. Douglas Meml. award Los Angeles County Heart Assn., 1959, Vis. Scientist award Deutscher Academischer Austauschendienst, 1978. Fellow ACP; mem. AMA, AAAS, Internat. Soc. Nephrology (organizing com. internat. cong. 1984), Am. Soc. Nephrology, European Dialysis and Transplant Assn., Soc. Exptl. Biology and Medicine, Calif. Med. Assn., Los Angeles County Med. Assn., Nat. Kidney Found. (active ann. conf. 1963-65, sec. nat. med. adv. coun. 1969-70, regional rep. and legis. com. nat. med. adv. coun. 1970-73, grantee 1963), So. Calif. Kidney Found. (chmn. sci. adv. coun. 1968-70, co-chmn. legis. com. 1970-73, bd. dirs. 1974-83, honoree 1979), Am. Soc. Bone and Mineral Rsch., Am. Coll. Toxicology, Soc. Toxicology, Am. Heart Assn. (renal sect. of coun. on circulation), Am. Fedn. Clin. Rsch., Western Soc. Clin. Rsch., Western Assn. Physicians, Phi Beta Kappa, Sigma Xi, Alpha Omega Alpha, Phi Eta Sigma, Alpha Mu Gamma, Phi Lambda Upsilon. Avocation: tennis. Business E-Mail: hgonick@ucla.edu.

GONLACHANVIT, SUTEP, gastroenterologist, researcher; s. Seng Saetang and Prapai Tangsakhonnamwin; m. Nathaya Suwanpatra, June 19, 1999; children: Teton, Passawish, Chawisa. MD, Chulalongkorn U., Bangkok. Bd. cert. gastroenterologist Med. Coun., Thailand, 1997. Asst. prof. Chulalongkorn U. Divsn. Gastroenterology, Faculty Medicine, 2003—05, assoc. prof., 2006—. Dir. of prompiram dist. hosp. Ministry Pub. Health, Pisanulok, Thailand, 1989—92; dir. of gastrointestinal motility rsch. unit Chulalongkorn U., Bangkok, 2006—. Recipient Alvarez Award, Internat. Electrogastrography Soc., 2000, Simon Komarov prize, Phila. Gastroenterology Rsch. Forum, 2000, Young Clinician award, World Congress Gastroenterology, 2002; Gastrointestinal fellow, Temple U., Phila., 2000, Rsch. fellow, U. Mich., 2002. Mem.: Am. Gastroenterology Assn., Am. Motility Soc. (The Young Investigator Award 2000 and 2002). Achievements include research in effects of ginger on stabilizing electrical activities of the stomach during hyperglycemia in humans; characterizing the anorectal pressure events during flatus passages and gas induced abdominal pain in humans; effect of clonidine, an alpha-2 agonist, on rectal and anal sphincter functions; causes of idiopathic constipation in Thai constipated patients; factors that associated with failure of biofeedback therapy in patients with chronic constipation caused by pelvic floor dyssynergia; exploring the effect of high dose proton pump inhibitor on larlyngopharyngeal reflux disease; effects of acute acoustic stress on rectal perception in humans; effects of chili on rectal perception and its mechanism of actions in humans; effects of modulations of gastric emptying on postprandial plasma glucose in type II diabetes mellitus; relationships of proximal stomach functions and upper gastrointestinal symptoms in patients with functional dyspepsia; roles of 5HT3 receptors on chocolate induced gastroesophageal refluxes in patients with gastroesophageal reflux disease; effects of high fiber diet on intestinal gas transit in humans; effects of physical properties of meals on intestinal gas transit in humans; relationship of small bowel motor activities and intestinal gas transit. Avocations: travel, reading. Office: Chulalongkorn U Faculty of Medicine Rama 4 Rd Patumwan Bangkok 10330 Thailand Office Fax: 66 2 252 7839. Personal E-mail: gsutep@hotmail.com.

GONNERING, RUSSELL STEPHEN, ophthalmic plastic surgeon; b. Milw., Nov. 21, 1949; s. Russell Richard and Virginia Mary (Mlinar) G.; m. Sandra Lynne Brubaker, Aug. 6, 1971; children: Julie Kathleen, Stephen Russell, Scott Duncan. Student, U. Vienna, Austria, 1969—70; AB in History cum laude, Boston Coll., 1971; MD, Med. Coll. Wis., 1975; M of Med. Mgmt., U. So. Calif., LA, 2007. Diplomate Am. Bd. Ophthalmology; lic. physician, Wis.; cert. profl. in healthcare quality. Intern St. Luke's Hosp., Milw., 1975-76; resident in ophthalmology Med. Coll. Wis., Milw., 1977-80, asst. clin. prof. dept. ophthalmology, 1985-2000, prof. ophthalmology, 2000—05, clin. prof. ophthalmology, 2006—; fellow in ophthalmic plastic and reconstructive surgery U. Wis., Madison, 1980-81, asst. clin. prof. dept. ophthalmology, 1981-92, assoc. clin. prof. dept. ophthalmology, 1992-96, clin. prof. dept. ophthalmology, 1996—, Kambara lectr., 1997; ophthalmologist St. Luke's Hosp., Milw., chief ophthalmologist, 1983-94, 97-99, vice chief staff, 2000; pvt. practice Ophthalmic Plastic and Reconstructive Surgery, 1981-2000, 2006—. Full-time acad. practice, 2000-05; rsch. assoc. in corneal physiology Med. Coll. Wis., 1976-77; rsch. advisor to fellowship in ophthalmic plastic and reconstructive surgery U. Wis., Madison, 1983-2002; presenter in field. Author: (with others) Infections of the Eye and Ocular Adnexa, 1986, Oculoplastic, Orbital and Reconstructive Surgery, 1988, Oculoplastic and Orbital Emergencies, 1990, Ophthalmic Plastic, reconstructive and Orbital Surgery, 1997, Ophthalmic Surgery: Principles and Techniques, 1999; sect. editor: Principles and Practice of Ophthalmic Plastic and Reconstructive Surgery, 1995; contbr. numerous articles to profl. jours. Recipient Wisdom Soc. Honor award, 1999. Fellow: ACS (coun. Wis. chpt. 1996—2000), Am. Soc. Ophthalmic Plastic and Reconstructive Surgery (editl. bd. 1987—99, edn. com. 1988—99, vice chmn. edn. com. 1995—97, chmn. edn. com. 1997—99, Marvin H. Quickert award 1982, Rsch. award 1982, Reeh Pathology award 1999), Am. Acad. Ophthalmology (basic and clin. sci. course com. 1986—92, chmn. 1988—92, Honor award 1990, Ruedemann lectr. 1994, Sr. Achievement award 2001); mem.: Am. Coll. Physician Execs., Nat. Assn. for Healthcare Quality (cert. profl.), Project Mgmt. Inst., Christian Med. and Dental Assn., Am. Soc. Quality, Milw. Surg. Soc., Nat. Soc. to Prevent Blindness (mem. adv. bd. Wis. chpt. 1987—88), Am. Soc. Ocularists (med. adv. bd. 1987—2001), Milw. Ophthalmol. Soc. (treas. 1989—90, sec. 1990—91, v.p. 1991—92, pres. 1992—93), Milw. Acad. Surgery, Milw. Acad. Medicine, Milwaukee County Med. Soc. (del. to state med. soc. 1987—90, bd. dirs. 1989—94, Dirs. citation 1994), Med. Soc. Wis., Assn. for Rsch. in Vision and Ophthalmology, Internat. Dacryology Soc., European Soc. Ophthalmic Plastic and Reconstructive Surgery, Internat. Soc. Orbital Disorders, Black Belt Six Sigma (Villanova Univ.), Mensa. Avocations: sailing, skiing, tai kwon do, bicycling. Office Phone: 262-754-9921. Personal E-mail: rsgonnering@hotmail.com. Business E-Mail: info@rsgonnering.com.

GONSHAK, ISABELLE LEE, nurse, volunteer; b. Newark, Apr. 4, 1932; d. Robert John and Clara Kate (Cooperman) McClelland Barrold; m. David M. Gonshak, Aug. 8, 1953; children: Evan J., Brett A., Kathryn Susan. RN, N.J., Fla. Nurse Newark City Hosp., 1953; tchr. Ideal Sch. for Nurse's Aides, Miami, Fla., 1972-74. Vocal soloist numerous TV and social affairs; photographer multiple media, multi-faceted subjects. Bd. dirs. Miami Beach Symphony, 1971—, pres., 1978-79; bd. dirs. South Fla. Symphony; life mem. Opera Guild Soc. Ft. Lauderdale; active Statue of Liberty Refinishing Com; vol. Sarah Westman Davidson Tower at Hadassah Med. Ctr., Israel. Mem. Greater Miami Opera Assn., Hadassah (life) (sr. idol contestant). Jewish. Home: 1700 SW 72d Ave Plantation FL 33317-5037 *

GONZALEZ, ALVARO JOSE, pediatrician, educator; b. Santiago, Chile, Apr. 16, 1962; MD, Pontificia U. Catolica Chile, 1987, Magister in Pediat., 1990. Cert. ECMO specialist U. Wash. Childrens Nat. Med, Ctr., 2001. Dir. divsn. neonatology Faculty Medicine, Pontificia U. Catolica Chile, 1997—2010, assoc. prof., chmn. dept. pediat., 2010—. Dir. neonatology brach Chilean Soc. Pediat., 2004—09; chief neonatology svc., nicu Hosp. Clinico U. Catolica de Chile, Santiago, 1997—2010. Recipient Young Investigator award, So. Soc. Pediat. Rsch., New Orleans, 1994, Clin. Excellence award, Faculty Medicine, U. Catolica de Chile, 2010; named Best Pediat. Resident, Faculty Medicine U. Catolica de Chile; Neonatal Perinatal Medicine fellow, U. Miami, 1992—95. Mem.: Soc. Chilena Pediatria. Office: Lira 85 5° Piso Region Metropolitana Santiago 8330074 Chile Business E-Mail: alvgonza@med.puc.cl.

GONZÁLEZ, CLARA ISABEL, bacteriologist, educator; b. Colombia, Mar. 27, 1957; PhD cum laude, U. Granada, Spain, 1998. Cert. bacteriologist U. Indsl. Santander, 1979. Assoc. prof. U. Indsl. Santander, 1998—2005, titular prof., 2005—. Dir. Lab. Inmunología y Biología Molecular, 2006—11. Mem.: Asociación Colombiana de Parasitología y Medicina Tropical. Avocation: dance. Office: Carrera 32 #29-31 Oficina 419 Bucaramanga Santander AA678 Colombia Office Fax: 57-7-6322416. E-mail: claraisa27@yahoo.com.

GONZALEZ, EMILIO BUSTAMANTE, rheumatologist, educator; b. Asuncion, Paraguay, Jan. 9, 1949; came to U.S., 1974; s. Emilio Gonzalez-Jovellanos and Clara (Bustamante) Gonzalez; m. Elizabeth Ferreira, Jan. 4, 1973; 1 child, Daniel BS Scis. and Humanities, C.A.L. Coll., Asuncion, 1972; MD summa cum laude, Nat. U., Asuncion, 1972. Diplomate Am. Bd. Internal Medicine, Am. Bd. Rheumatology, Am. Bd. Allergy and Immunology. Intern U. Hosp., Asuncion, 1973—74; resident Danbury Hosp., Conn., 1975—78; tchg. fellow allergy and clin. immunology U. Pitts. Sch. Medicine and VA Med. Ctr., 1978—79; mem. staff allergy and clin. immunology Nat. Jewish Hosp. and U. Colo. Affiliated Hosps., Denver, 1979—80; mem. staff clin. immunology and rheumatology U. Tex. Med. Br., Galveston, 1980—81, clin. instr. dept. medicine, 1981—82, asst. prof. medicine, 1982—89, assoc. prof. medicine, 1989—, dir. rheumatology, 2004—, prof. medicine, 2004—; chief rheumatology svc. Grady Meml. Hosp. and Emory U. Sch. Medicine, Atlanta, 1989—; attending physician rheumatology sect. med. svc. VA Med. Svc., Emory U., Decatur, Ga., 1989—; attending physician divsn. rheumatology

Emory U. Hosp., Atlanta, 1989—; cons., part-time mem. divsn. rheumatology Emory Clinic and Emory U., Atlanta, 1989—; dir. rheumatology Atlanta Med. Ctr., 1998—2004. Bd. dirs. Arthritis Found., Ga., sci. com.; presenter in field Contbr. articles to profl. jours.; reviewer in field:. Fellow ACP, Am. Coll. Rheumatology; mem. AMA, Am. Acad. Allergy and Immunology, Ga. Rheumatism Soc. (program chmn. 1993-94), Ga. Soc. Rheumatology (pres. 1995-96), Sigma Xi Office: Univ Tex Med Branch Dir Rheumatology 301 University Blvd Galveston TX 77555-1165 Office Phone: 409-772-2863. Office Fax: 409-772-7355. Business E-Mail: ebgonzal@utmb.edu.

GONZALEZ, FRANK J., medical researcher; b. Tampa, Fla., Nov. 30, 1953; BA, U. South Fla., 1975, MA, 1977; PhD, U. Wis., 1981; DSc (hon.), Mahidol U., 2001. Grad. rsch. assoc. dept. microbiology U. South Fla., Tampa, 1977; postdoctoral fellow McArdle Lab. for Cancer Rsch., Madison, Wis., 1981—82; staff fellow lab. devel. pharmacology Nat. Inst. Child Health and Human Devel., NIH, Bethesda, Md., 1982—84; sr. staff fellow Lab. Molecular Carcinogenesis Nat. Cancer Inst., NIH, Bethesda, 1984—88, acting chief Nucleic Acids Sect., 1986—88, chief Nucleic Acids Sect., 1986—96, supervisory rsch. chemist, 1988—90, acad. full prof., 1990—96, chief Lab. Metabolism, head Nucleic Acids Sect, 1996—. Cons. in field. Recipient Promotion of Sci. short-term fellowship, Japanese Soc. for Promotion of Sci., 1998, George Scott award, Toxicology Forum, 1995, Vis. Prof. Travel award, Japanese Ministry of Sci. and Edn., 1995, Hon. lectureship, Nat. Sci. Coun, China, 1993, John J. Abel award in pharmacology, Am. Soc. for Pharmacology and Exptl. Therapeutics, 1992, Rawls-Palmer Progress in Medicine award, Am. Soc. for Clin. Pharmacology, 1991; named hon. vis. prof., Mahidol U., 1997. Mem.: Sr. Biomed. Rsch. Svc. Office: Ctr Cancer Rsch Lab Metabolism Bldg 37 Rm 3106 37 Convent Dr Bethesda MD 20892 Office Phone: 301-496-9067. Office Fax: 301-496-8419. E-mail: fjgonz@helix.nih.gov. *

GONZALEZ, GISELA, immunologist, researcher; Scientist Cuban Ctr. Molecular Immunology. Achievements include development of CinmaVax EGF vaccine for lung cancer. Office: Calle 15 esq 216 Siboney Playa Havana Cuba 10400

GONZALEZ, HECTOR HUGO, nursing educator; b. Rome, Tex., Mar. 9, 1937; s. Amadeo Lorenzo and Carlotta (Trevino) G. BSN, Incarnate Word Coll., 1963; MSN, Cath. U. Am., 1966; PhD in Edn., U. Tex., 1974. VR-RN, Tex. Staff nurse Santa Rosa Med. Ctr., San Antonio, 1962-65; asst. dir. nursing divsn. Incarnate Word Coll., San Antonio, 1968-72; prof., chmn. dept. nursing San Antonio Coll., 1972-92, dir. Ctr. for Assoc. Degree Edn. Rsch. and Svc., 1987-92, prof. and chmn. emeritus, 1993—. Cons. NIMH, 1973, FDA, 1989-93, mem. anesthesiology and respiratory devices panel, mem. dispute resolution panel, 2000—01; numerous cdnl. instns. and hosps. in U.S., Mex., P.R., Kuwait; mem. Nat. Adv. Coun. on Alcohol Abuse and Alcoholism, 1976-80; vis. prof. Facultad Enfermería, U. Autónoma Nuevo Leon, 1980-1990; mem. nat. adv. coun. nurses edn. and practice, 1992-96; mem. panel on nursing practice U.S. Pharmacopeia, 1985-2000. Contbr. articles to profl. jours.; peer reviewer Nursing Outlook, 1983, Advancing Clinical Care. Mem. legis. affairs adv. com. State Senator Glen Kothman, San Antonio, 1983; bd. dirs. Family Svcs. Assn. San Antonio; mem. multidisciplinary academic external com. U. Autonoma de Nuevo Leon, Mex., 1986-88. Capt. nurse corps U.S. Army, 1966-68. Recipient cert. of appreciation Citizens of Bexar County, San Antonio, 1970, Nat. Student Nurses Assn., 1977. Mem. ANA (mem. adv. bd. minority fellowship program 1976-80, Trail Blazer award Minority Fellowship Program 2004), Nat. Assn. Hispanic Nurses (pres. 1982-84, bd. dirs. 1995-97, CEO San Antonio chpt. 1998-2008, project dir. breast cancer tng. grant Am. Cancer Soc. and Nat. Assn. Hispanic Nurses 1992-96, historian 2000—08), Nat. League for Nursing (bd. dirs. 1973-81). Democrat. Roman Catholic. Home: 114 Magnolia Dr San Antonio TX 78212-3115 Office Phone: 210-733-7460. Personal E-mail: hhgzz@sbcglobal.net.

GONZALEZ, JORGE JOSE, medical educator; b. Valdivia, Chile, Aug. 13, 1945; came to U.S., 1973; s. Manuel and Emma (Clasing) G.; m. Barbara Hayworth, May 22, 1971; children: Carla Andrea, Maria Cristina. MD, U. Chile, 1971. Resident in internal medicine New Hanover Meml. Hosp., Wilmington, N.C., 1973-76; fellow in endocrinology Med. U. S.C., Charleston, 1976-78; from asst. prof. to assoc. prof. medicine U. N.C. Sch. Medicine, Chapel Hill, 1978-92, prof. medicine, 1992—2007. Program dir. Internal Medicine Tng. Program, Wilmington, 1991-2001. Recipient N.C. Pub. Health Assn. Adult Health Promotion Sect. Spl. commendation, 1989. Fellow Am. Coll. Clin. Endocrinology; mem. Am. Diabetes Assn., Endocrine Soc., Am. Assn. Clin. Endocrinology. Episcopalian. Home: 4921 Nicholas Creek Cir Wilmington NC 28409-3295 Office: Ptnrs Endocrinology & Diabetes 1612 Doctors Cir Wilmington NC 28401-7406 Office Phone: 910-762-9701. Business E-Mail: jgonzalez@partnersed.com.

GONZALEZ, JUAN MIGUEL, medical educator; b. San Juan, Jan. 16, 1975; MD, U. PR, 2001; MTR, U. Pa., 2009. Asst. prof. Wayne State U. Sch. Medicine, 2009—. Recipient Excellence Tchg. Faculty award, Wayne State U. Fellow: Fellow Am. Coll. Ob-Gyn. Home: 22 Woodward Heights Blvd Upper Flat Pleasant Ridge MI 48069 Business E-Mail: jgonzale@med.wayne.edu.

GONZALEZ, RAQUEL MARIA, pharmacist; b. Veguitas, Oriente, Cuba, June 1, 1952; d. Ernesto Esteban and Evora Cristina (Ramirez) G. BS in Biology, Ga. Coll., 1974; BS in Pharmacy, Mercer U., 1977. Registered pharmacist, Ga., Fla., Tenn.; registered pharmacist cons., Fla. Staff pharmacist Cobb Gen. Hosp., Austell, Ga., 1978, VA Hosp., Nashville, 1978-79, Decatur, Ga., 1979-81, Lewisburg Cmty. Hosp., Tenn., 1981-89; pharmacist Pharmacy Staffing Svcs. Inc., Brentwood, Tenn., 1989—; chief pharmacist Super D Drug Store # 50, Fayetteville, Tenn., 1989-93; chief of pharmacy Fred's Pharmacy, Lewisburg, Tenn., 1993—. Relief pharmacist Farmer's Market Pharmacy (Kroger), Nashville, 1989—. Mem. Tenn. Pharmacist Assn., Ducks Unltd., Atlanta Ski Club. Republican. Roman Catholic. Avocations: piano, white water rafting, skiing, snorkeling, gardening. Home: RR 1 Box 35 Belfast TN 37019-9801 Office: Fred's Pharmacy 1800 Mooresville Hwy Lewisburg TN 37091-2010 Office Phone: 931-270-6775. Business E-Mail: p2226@fredsinc.com.

GONZÁLEZ, RICARDO, surgeon, educator; b. Buenos Aires, June 26, 1943; s. Salvador María and Clyde Alcira (Prevettoni) González; m. Barbara Magda Ludwikowski; children: Diego Andres, Carlos Ricardo, Alexander Serif Ludwikowski. BA, Coll. Nat. San Isidro, 1959; MD, U. Buenos Aires, 1965. Diplomate Am. Bd. Urology, cert. spl. competence in pediat. urology Am. Bd. Urology. Resident in surgery Hosp. Mil. Ctr., Buenos Aires, 1966—68; intern in surgery U. Minn., Mpls., 1969—70, resident, med. fellow in urologic surgery, 1970—74, from instr. to prof. urology, 1974—85, prof. urology, 1985—94, prof. pediat., 1993—94; chief, pediat. urology Children's Hosp. of Mich., Detroit, 1994; prof. urology Wayne State U., Detroit, 1995—99; prof. urology and pediat., chief pediat. urology divsn. U. Miami /Jackson Meml. Hosp., Fla., 1999—2002; dir. pediat. urology fellowship Thomas Jefferson U., Wilmington, Del., 2002—08, cons., 2008—, prof. urology Phila., 2002—; internat. cons. Italian Hosp., Buenos Aires, 2007—; sr. cons. pediat. urology Children's Hosp. U. Zurich, Switzerland, 2008—; cons. pediat. urologist Hannoversche Kinderheilanstralt, Hannover, Germany, 2010—. Pres. Pediat. Urology P.C., Detroit, 1995-00; vis. prof. Harvard U., Cambridge, Mass., 1994, John Hopkins U., Balt., 1995, U. Washington, Seattle, 1995, U. Calif., San Francisco, 1996, Cornell U., NY, 1998, U. Montreal, 2000, McGill U., 2000, U. Vienna, Austria, 2003, Chinese U. Hong Kong, 2003, SUNY Upstate Med. Coll., Syracuse, 2003, U. Zurich, Switzerland, 2005, 06, U. Belgrade, 2005, U. SD Sanford Sch. Medicine, 2007; vis. prof., acting chief pediatric urology Kinderspital U. Zurich, Switzerland, 2006, 07, mem., U. Gabrielle D'Amunzio, Pescara, Italy, U. Alexandria, Egypt, 2010. Contbr. over 360 articles to profl. jours., over 50 chpts. to books; editor 3 books. Am. Acad. Pediat. fellow, 1981, Nat. Kidney Found. rsch. fellow 1974-76; co-prin. investigator USPHS cancer grant 1976-78; recipient medal, European Soc. Paediatric Urology, 2003, Soc. Iberoamericana Urologia Pediática, 2000, prize for tchg. in pediatric urology, CIPESUR, 2007. Fellow Am. Acad. Pediat. (exec. sect. on urology com. 1995-98); mem. Am. Urol. Assn., Mex. Coll. Urology (hon.), Venezuelan Soc. Spina Bifida, Argentine Confedn. Urology, Societé Internat. d'Urologie, Ibero-Am. Soc. Pediat. Urology (pres. 1995-98, Medal of Merit 2000), Soc. Pediat. Urol. Surgeons (by invitation), European Soc. Paediat. Urology (hon.), Swiss Assn. Pediatric Surgeons. Avocations: opera, music, language, reading, writing. Home: Papenstieg 13 Hannover D-30171 Germany Personal E-mail: ricardo_gonzalez33154@yahoo.com.

GONZALEZ, RICHARD, psychology professor; BA in Psychology, UCLA, 1985; PhD in Psychology, Stanford U., 1990. Asst. prof. Dept. Psychology U. Washington, 1990—96, assoc. prof. Dept. Psychology, 1996—97, adj. assoc. prof. mgmt. and org. Sch. Bus., 1996—97, dir. Ctr. for Judgment and Decision Making, 1993—97; vis. assoc. prof. Dept. Psychology Princeton U., 1996—97; vis. assoc. prof. (summers) U. Chgo. Grad. Sch. Bus., 1998, 99, assoc. prof. Dept Psychology U. Mich., 1997—2001, adj. assoc. prof. Dept. Statistics, 1997—2001, prof. mktg. Bus. Sch., 2001—, prof. Dept. Statistics, 2001—, prof. Dept. Psychology, 2001—, chmn. Dept. Psychology, 2002—04; faculty assoc. Rsch. Ctr. for Group Dynamics Inst. for Social Rsch., U. Mich., 1997—2004, rsch. prof. Rsch. Ctr. for Group Dynamics, 2004—. Assoc. editor Theory and Decision, 2002—04, editl. bd. Psychological Rev., 1997—, Jour. Experimental Psychology: Learning, Memory and Cognition, 2000—, Psychological Methods, 2002—, Psychological Sci., 2003—, Jour. of Personality and Social Psychology, 2000—05, Personal Relationships, 1997—2001. Mem.: Inst. Math. Statistics, Am. Statistical Assn., Soc. Psychological Study of Social Issues, Soc. Personality and Social Psychology, Soc. Math. Pscyhology, Soc. for Judgment and Decision Making, Am. Psychological Soc., APA, Psychonomic Soc., Soc. Experimental Social Psychologists. Office: Dept Psychology Univ Michigan 525 E University Ann Arbor MI 48109 Office Phone: 734-647-6785. Office Fax: 734-764-3520. E-mail. gonzo@umich.edu.

GONZÁLEZ, RODRIGO VALENZUELA, physician, surgeon, medical auditor; b. Talca, Province of Maule, Chile, May 12, 1947; s. Pedro Valenzuela Messina and Marta González Orellana; m. Ana María Gacitúa Medina, Aug. 6, 1974; children: Victoria Valenzuela Gacitúa, Loreto Valenzuela Gacitúa. MD, Chile U., 1973; postgrad. in Gastroenterology, Complutente U., 1984—85. Adminstrn. diplomate Chile U., 1994. Chief medicine svc. Calama Hosp., Province El Loa, Chile, 1974—78, chief emergency svc., 1977—79, chief surgery svc., 1987—2005. Fellow: Chilean Soc. Surgeons; mem.: Lions Internat. Club (dist. gov. 2001—02). Achievements include development of a prepared tissue as surgical mesh. Avocations: travel, painting. Home: La Cascada 1551 Villa Ascotan Provincia El Loa Calama Cas 301 Chile Office: Calama Clinic Granaderos 1640 Provincia El Loa Calama Cas 301 Chile Office Fax: 55-342052. Personal E-mail: docroro12@hotmail.com.

GONZALEZ, RUBEN RENE, biochemist, researcher, educator; s. Rafael Angel Gonzalez-Carabia and Maria del Rosario Perez-Rivera; m. Margarita Perla Ramos-Garcia, Dec. 2, 1996; children: Ruben Gonzalez-Ramos, Rene Gonzalez-Ramos, Frank Angel Gonzalez-Ramos, Roni-Shanon Gonzalez-Ramos. Biochemist, U. Havana, 1974, PhD, 1985. Scientist Nat. Inst. Endocrinology, Havana, Cuba, 1987—96; vis. scientist Boston Biomed. Rsch. Inst., Watertown, Mass., 2000—02, instr., 2002—; assoc. scientist Vincent Ctr. for Reproductive Biology Mass. Gen. Hosp., Boston, 2003—; rsch. asst. prof. Morehouse Sch. Medicine, Atlanta, 2006—, assoc. prof., 2009. Rschr. fellow in enzymology-microbiology Moscow Rsch. Inst. Food Sci., 1978—79; rsch. fellow enzymology-microbiology INSA, Toulouse, 1983—84; rsch. fellow immunoassay-reproductive hormones Karolinska Inst., Stockholm, 1989, U. Oulu, Finland, 1989—90; fellow in vitro fertilization technologies IVI-Madrid, 1999; rsch. fellow embryo implantation Inst. of Mother and Child Rsch. U. Chile, Santiago, 1996—2000; rsch. fellow embryo implantation U. Geneva, 1998—99; rsch. fellow embryo implantation IVI-Valencia U. Valencia, Spain, 1998—99; adj. scientist Boston Biomed. Rsch. Inst., 2006; affiliate scientist CRSCR, MSM, Atlanta, 2007—; spkr. in field. Contbr. articles to profl. jours. Sci. adviser, rev. com. WHO-Rockefeller Found. Initiative on Embryo Implantation Rsch., 2000—04; sci. reviewer CONRAD Twinning Program, 2003. Recipient Disting. Cancer Scientist award, Georgia Cancer Coalition, 2008—; grantee, Susan G. Komen Found., 2005—07, Cancer Rsch. and Prevention Found., 2005—07, NIF, NCI, 2008—; CONRAD Grant, Leptin Peptide Antagonists, 2002—08, grant, UAB Breast Cancer Spore, 2008—. Mem.: Ga. Acad. Sci., Am. Assn. for Cancer Rsch., Am. Soc. Biochemistry and Molecular Biology, Spanish Soc. Fertility (assoc. Serono Sci. prize XIII Nat. Congress 2000), Am. Soc. Reproductive Medicine (assoc.). Achievements include development of novel inhibitors of leptin function; discovery of expression of leptin and leptin receptor by human and rabbit endometrium; patents in field; research in leptin role in embryo implantation; blockade of leptin signaling for cancer prevention and treatment. Office: Morehouse Sch Medicine Dept Microbiology Immunology and Biochem 720 Westview Dr SW Atlanta GA 30310 Office Fax: 404-752-1179. Personal E-mail: rrglez@yahoo.com. Business E-Mail: rgonzalez@msm.edu.

GONZALEZ, STEVAN ALFREDO, physician; b. Ithaca, NY, Sept. 14, 1973; MD, Dartmouth Med. Sch., 2000; MS, Columbia U., 2007. Attending physician Baylor All Saints Med. Ctr., 2008—. Advanced Hepatology fellowship, Am. Assn. Study Liver Diseases. Mem.: Internat. Liver Transplantation Soc., Am. Soc. Transplantation, Am. Gastroent. Assn., Am. Assn. Study Liver Diseases. Office: 1250 8th Ave Ste 515 Fort Worth TX 76104 Business E-Mail: stevan.gonzalez@baylorhealth.edu.

GONZALEZ, WILLIAM G., healthcare advisor; s. William G. and Blanche Irene; m. Shirley Ann Mos, Aug. 15, 1964; children: Dana Lynn, Liane Renee. BA, Rutgers U., 1964; MBA, Cornell U., 1966; cert., Sloan Inst. Hosp. Adminstrn., 1966; MPA, NYU, 1980. Bus. adminstr. U. Calif.-San Francisco Med. Ctr., 1966-68, asst. dir., various positions, 1968-74; dep. dir. Capital Dist. Psychiat. Ctr., Albany, NY, 1974-79; instr. Albany Med. Coll., 1974-79; adj. asst. prof. SUNY-Albany, 1978-79; dir. U. Calif.-Irvine Med. Ctr., Orange, 1979-85; sr. lectr. Grad. Sch. Mgmt. and Calif. Coll. Medicine, U. Calif., Irvine, 1980-85; bd. dirs. Hosp. Coun. So. Calif., 1983-85; pres., chief exec. officer Butterworth Health Corp. and Butterworth Hosp., Grand Rapids, Mich., 1985-99; pres., CEO Spectrum Health, Grand Rapids, 1999-2000; healthcare advisor Wm. Gonzalez & Assocs., Chgo., 2000—. Adj. prof. health svcs. adminstrn. Mich. State U. Coll. Human Medicine, 1985—; mem. gov.'s Task Force on Access to Health Care, 1987-89; mem. nursing task force Joint Commn. on Accreditation Health Care Orgns., 1988-90; trustee Mich. Hosp. Assn., 1990-96; chmn. M in Mgmt. adv. coun. Aquinas Coll., Grand Rapids, 1992-95; bd. dirs. Grand Rapids Area Med. Edn. Ctr., chmn., 1995-97; mem. accreditation coun. grad. med. edn., 1994-98, Am. Hosp. Assn., coordinating Com. on Med. Edn.; regent ACHE Area B., Mich., 1994-98. Bd. dirs. Grand Rapids Pub. Edn. Fund, 1993-99; bd. dirs. Old Kent Fin. Corp., 1994-2000; active Health Professions Coun., San Francisco, 1971-74; active Planned Parenthood-World Population, Alameda Calif. and San Francisco, 1972-74; mem. coun. of dels. sect. on met. hosps. Gov.'s Coun., 1989-92; mem. regional policy bd. AHA, 1990-93. Served with M.C. U.S. Army, 1961-64. William Stout scholar, 1964; Alfred P. Sloan scholar, 1964-65; N.Y. State Regents scholar, 1964-65; Rotary Internat. exchange fellow in hosp. adminstrn. Australia, summer 1982 Fellow: Commn. on Accreditation of Healthcare Mgmt. Edn. (staff cons. 2004—08, site visitor 2006—). Office: Wm Gonzalez & Assocs 500 N Michigan Ave Ste 300 Chicago IL 60611 Office Phone: 312-396-4088.

GONZALEZ-ANGULO, ANA MARIA, medical educator; b. Popayan, Colombia, Feb. 9, 1971; m. Manuel E. Caicedo-Mosquera. MD, U.del Cauca, Popayan, 1995. Lic. med. oncology Am. Bd. Internal Medicine. Asst. prof. M.D. Anderson Cancer Ctr., Houston, 2004—. Office: Box 1354 1515 Holcombe Blvd Houston TX 77030 Office Phone: 713-563-0767

GONZÁLEZ ISASI, ANA, psychologist; b. Vitoria-Gasteiz, July 17, 1977; PhD in Psychology, U. del País Vasco, 2000. Clín. psychologist Hosp. Santiago Apóstol de Vitoria Gasteiz, 2001—04, Hosp. U. Insular de Gran Canaria, 2004—. Office: Avenida Marítima Las Palmas de Gran Canaria 35016 Spain E-mail: anagonis@hotmail.com.

GONZALEZ-LIMA, ERIKA MUSIOL, mental health counselor, psychotherapist; b. Caracas, Venezuela, June 9, 1956; MEd, U. Tex., Austin, 1981; PhD, Tex. A&M U., 1989. Health edn. coord. Student Health Ctr., Tex. A&M U., 1989—91; health and human svcs. sr. planner Austin, Travis County Health and Human Svcs. Dept., 1992—2002; grad. studies lectr., dept. psychology U. Tex., Austin, 2004—08, program coord. dept. psychology, 2002—, exec. edn. faculty, McCombs Sch. Bus. Found., 2008—. Nat. bd. cert. counselor, 1989—; lic. profl. counselor, Tex., 2009—. Recipient Cert. of Achievement and Teamwork award, Austin, Travis County Health and Human Svcs. Dept. Mem.: Am. Translators Assn., ACA, Internat. Network Children and Families. Avocation: swimming. Office: 5739 Merrywing Cir Counseling Office Austin TX 78730 Personal E-mail: erikalima@gmail.com.

GONZÁLEZ LOMBIDE, EDUARDO, public health service officer; b. Bilbao, Bizkaia, Spain, Sept. 21, 1953; s. Alfonso González-Garzia and Amelia Lonbide-Herrera; m. María del Mar Lertxundi-Etxebarria, Feb. 2, 1979; children: Ioritz González-Lertxundi, Naroa González-Lertxundi. MD, Med. Sch. U. Basque Country, Bilbao, 1978; M in Bus. Adminstrn., IESE, 2005. Cert. hosp. mgmt. expert U. Deusto, 1984. Zumarraga hosp. chief exec. Osakidetza, 1984—88, family physian Azkoitia, Gipuzkoa, Spain, 1980—84, 1988—95; cons. edn. min. Basque Govt., Gasteiz, Araba, Spain, 1991—92; cons. gen. dir. Local Govt. Gipuzkoa, Donostia-San Sebastián, Spain, 1995—2000; chief exec. Osakidetza - Ekialde, Donostia - San Sebastián, Gipuzkoa, 2000—. Bd. sec. Bank Gipuzkoa, Donostia-San Sebastián, 2000—02; bd. mem. Europistas Hwy. Mgmt., Madrid, 2000—02; evaluation com. mem. EUSKALIT - Basque Found. Quality Mgmt., Zamudio, Bizkaia, 2008—; mem. forum INNOBASQUE - Basque Found. Innovation, Zamudio, 2008—. Contbr. articles to profl. jours. Mem. Aranzadi Nature Scis. Soc., Donostia-San Sebastián, 1980—2010. Mem.: Spanish Soc. Healthcare Quality, Spanish Soc. Primary Healthcare Dist. Dir. Home: Auzmendi bidea 38 Azkoitia Gipuzkoa E20720 Spain Office: Osakidetza - Ekialde Nafarroako Hiribidea 14 20013 Donostia-San Sebastián Spain Business E-Mail: correo.gerenciaekialde@osakidetza.net.

GONZALEZ-LOPEZ, LAURA, rheumatologist, researcher; b. Guadalajara, Jalisco, Mex., June 26, 1963; d. Jesus Ruben Gonzalez-Ulloa and Esperanza Lopez-Cortes; m. Jorge Ivan Gamez-Nava; children: Jorge Ivan Gamez-Gonzalez, Laura Esthela Gamez-Gonzalez. MD, U. Guadalajara, Jalisco, 1988, MS, 1998; DSc, U. Colima, Mex., 2002. Speciality in rheumatology U. Nacional Autonoma Mex., 1992, cert. Rheumatologist Mexican Coll. Rheumatology, 2008. Consulting rheumatologist Mexican Inst. Social Security, Guadalajara, 1992—, assoc. rschr. clin. and epidemiology focusing in rheumatic disorders, 1997—, adj. prof. rheumatology in the family medicine residency program, 2004—; postdoc. fellow U. Alberta, Canada, 1996—97; rschr. Nat. Coun. Sci. and Tech., Guadalajara, 1998—; prof. pub. health scis. postgrad. program U. Guadalajara, 2004—. Contbr. articles to profl. jours. (Nat. Rsch. award, Nat. Soc. Rheumatology-Novartis, 2001, 2003). Recipient award, Presidency of

Republic, 1992, Fundacion IMSS-AFORE XXI Nat. award, 2007; grant, Nat. Coun. Sci. and Tech., 1998, 2003, Mexican Inst. Social Security, 1999, 2004—07. Mem.: Jalisco Coll. of Rheumatology (assoc.), Mexican Coll. of Rheumatology (assoc.). Office: Justo Sierra 2076 Int 10 Jalisco Guadalajara 44680 Mexico Business E-Mail: lguragl@mail.edg.mx. E-mail: dralauragonzalez@prodigy.net.mx.

GONZALEZ-MARQUEZ, HUMBERTO, biologist, educator; b. Mexico, Nov. 8, 1859; Degree, U. Autonoma Met., 1981, U. Henri Pincaré, 1997. Prof. U. Autónoma Met., 1982—. Rsch. grant, Nat. Sys. Rschrs. (Conacyt). Master: Rsch. Acad. Reproductive Biology; mem.: Mexican Soc. Tenetics. Avocations: music, guitar. Office: San Rafael Atlixco 186 Col Vicntina México 09340 Mexico Office Fax: 5255 58044727. Business E-Mail: hgm@xanum.uam.mx.

GONZALEZ-MARTIN, JULIAN, microbiologist, consultant; b. St. Feliu de Codines, Barcelona, Dec. 18, 1957; Degree in Medicine, U. Autonomous Barcelona, 1982; PhD, U. Barcelona, 1996. Med. microbiology resident Microbiology Dept., Hosp. Clinic Barcelona, 1985—88, specialist, 1989—95, sr. specialist, 1996—2002, cons., 2003—09, sr. cons., 2010—. Assoc. prof. med. microbiology Faculty Medicine, U. Barcelona, 1990. Recipient Rsch. Upjohn award; grants, Health Investigations Fund, Health and Sci. Ministries, Internat. Health Cooperation, La Caixa Found. Mem.: Tb Clin. Trials Consortium, Spanish Respiratory and Thoracic Surgery Soc., Spanish Clin. Microbiology and Infectious Diseases Soc. Avocations: literature, painting, walking. Office: Villarroel 170 Barcelona 08036 Spain Office Fax: 34932279372. Business E-Mail: juliangonzalez@ub.edu.

GONZÁLEZ-MORENO, SANTIAGO, surgical oncologist; b. Segovia, Spain, May 31, 1968; s. Marcelino González-Galindo and María Teresa Moreno-Martín; m. María Alonso-Zarraga, Apr. 18, 1998; children: Alba González-Alonso, Julen González-Alonso, Nerea González-Alonso. MD, U. Autonoma Madrid Med. Sch., 1986—92; Diploma in Study Design & Stats. Health Scis., U. Autonoma Barcelona, 1997; PhD, U. Navarra Med. Sch., Pamplona, Spain, 2003. Diplomate Spanish Govt., European Union, 1992, cert. bd surgical oncologist European Union, 2004. Gen. surgery resident Hosp. U. Octubre, Madrid, Madrid, 1993—98; surg. oncology fellow Wash. Cancer Inst., Washington, 1999—2001; vis. asst. prof. U. Tex., MD Anderson Cancer Ctr., Houston, 2005; Surg. oncology coord., Ctr. Oncologico MD Anderson I. España, Madrid, 2001—03, attending surg. oncologist, 2001—, chmn. dept. surg. oncology, 2010—. Instr., surgery U. San Pablo-CEU, Madrid, 2006—08; bd. mem. Spanish Soc. Surg. Oncology, Madrid, 2004—, v.p., 2009—; editl. cons. Clin. & Translational Oncology, Madrid, 2005—; exec. com. mem. European Soc. Surg. Oncology, Brussels, 2008—; sr. editor Surg. Oncology, Clin. & Translational Oncology, 2010—. Contbr. scientific papers. With Spanish Navi, 1993, Madrid, Spain. Decorated Naval Merit award Spanish Navy; grant, Spanish Assn. Surgeons, 1998, 1999. Mem.: Internat. Gastric Cancer Assn., Internat. Coll. Surgeons, Internat. Soc. Surgery, Spanish Assn. Surgeons, Spanish Soc. Surg. Oncology, European Soc. Surg. Oncology, Soc. Surg. Oncology, Am. Soc. Clin. Oncology. Roman Cath. Avocations: travel, languages, reading, photography. Office: Ctr Oncológico MD Anderson I España Calle Arturo Soria 270 Madrid Spain Office Phone: 34917878600 ext. 1827. Office Fax: 34 91 768 0681. Personal E-mail: sgmaz@telefonica.net. Business E-Mail: sgonzalez@mdanderson.es.

GONZALEZ-PEREZ, OSCAR, medical educator, researcher; b. Colima, Mex., Apr. 1, 1971; 2 children. PhD, U. Colima, 2002. Asst. prof. U. Guadalajara, Jalisco, Mexico, 2003—05, assoc. prof., 2005—07, mem. PhD program admission com., 2006—; prof. U. Colima, 2007—, head, psychology academic bd., 2007—. Head Lab. Neurosci., Colima, 2007—. Contbr. scientific papers. Recipient medal, Diario de Mex. Mexican Coun. Sci. and Tech., 1994, Outstanding Achievement, Am. Coll. Rheumatology, 1999, Best Rsch. award, Found. Pedro Sarquis Merrewe, 2002; named Best Med. Student, U. Colima, 1994, Best Grad. Student, 1998; Postdoc. Stipend fellowship, U. Calif. Inst. Mex. and US, 2003, Rsch. grant, Found. Ramón Álvarez Buylla de Aldana, 2007—08, Mexican Coun. Sci. and Tech., 2006—08. Mem.: Soc. Cirugía Exptl., Soc. Ciencias Fisiológicas, Soc. Neurosci. Achievements include patents pending for design of an acetate mold for electron microscopy inclusion; discovery of a novel mechanism to guidance the new neurons migration in the forebrain. Avocations: travel, chess. Office: Univ Colima Ave Universidad 333 Colima 28040 Mexico Office Phone: 52 312 316 1091. Office Fax: 52 312 316 1091. Personal E-mail: osglez@gmail.com. Business E-Mail: osglez@ucol.mx.

GONZALEZ-SCARANO, FRANCISCO ANTONIO, neurologist, virologist; b. Ponce, PR, Mar. 23, 1950; s. Francisco and Genoveva (Scarano) Gonzalez-Hernandez; m. Barbara Jean Turner, June 23, 1979; children: Genevieve Carre, Stephanie Katharine, Lisa Frances. BA, Yale U., 1971; MD, Northwestern U., Chgo., 1975; MA (hon.), U. Pa., Phila., 1988. Diplomate Am. Bd. Neurology. Intern Hosp. U. Pa., 1975-76, resident in neurology, 1976-79; fellow U. Pa., Phila., 1979-82, NIMR, London, 1981-82; asst. prof. depts. neurology and microbiology U. Pa., Phila., 1982-88, assoc. prof., 1988-94, prof., 1994—2010, prof. emeritus, 2010—; dean, v.p. med. affairs, John P. Howe Disting. chair U. Tex. Health Sci. Ctr., San Antonio, 2010—. Vice-chair rsch. neurology dept. U. Pa, 1998-99, chair 1999—2010; co-dir. Pa. Ctr. for HIV and AIDS, 1998-2007, Pa. Neurosci. Ctr., 2006—2010; chmn. bd. sci. counselors Nat. Inst. Neurol. Diseases and Stroke, Bethesda, Md., 1993-97, Nat. Adv. Neurol. Diseases and Stroke Coun., 2004—08. Assoc. editor Viral Pathogenesis, 1997; editl. bd. Jour. Neurovirology, 1996—, Virus Rsch., 1997—, AIDS, 1995-2002, GLIA, 1999—, Jour. Virology, 2000—, Virology, 2004—. Trustee Swarthmore Presbyn. Ch., 1997-2000, session 2004-07. Harry Weaver scholar Multiple Sclerosis Soc., NYC, 1982-87. Fellow: Phila. Coll. Physicians; mem.: Inst. of Medicine, Am. Soc. Clin. Investigation, Am. Acad. Neurology (mem. sci. issues com. 1985—89, profl. and pub. issues com. 1987—93), Am. Neurol. Assn. (exec. coun. 2001—03, chair sci. prog. com. 2005—07, v.p. 2008—), Scroll & Key, John Morgan Soc., Penn Club, Alpha Omega Alpha. Presbyterian. Avocation: photography. Office: University Tex Health Sci Ctr 7703 Floyd Curl Dr San Antonio TX 78228-3900 Office Phone: 210-567-4422. Office Fax: 210-567-3435. Business E-Mail: scarano@uthscsa.edu. *

GONZÁLEZ STÄGER, MARÍA ANGÉLICA, nutritionist, educator; b. San Antonio, Chile, Oct. 11, 1952; BS in Nutrition, U. Chile, 1978, MS in Nutrition, 1996. Assoc. prof. U. del Bío-Bío, 1976—. Dir., MECESUP project Ministry of Edn., Chile, 2007—. Recipient Global Nutrition award, Swedish Internat. Devel. Cooperation Agy., 2004. Mem.: Confederación Latinoamericana Nutricionistas y Dietistas, Coll. Nutricionistas U. Chile AG, Soc. Chilena Nutrición. Avocations: farming, cooking, reading. Office: Avenida Andrés Bello Chillán Biobio Chile Office Fax: 56 42 253142. Business E-Mail: magonzal@ubiobio.cl.

GOO, YONGSOOK, physiologist, educator; b. Seoul, Republic Of Korea, Feb. 19, 1964; d. Geonwhoi Goo and Jinsoon Oh. MD, Seoul Nat. U., Rep. Korea, 1988, PhD, 1993. Asst. prof. Chungbuk Nat. U., Cheongju, Chungcheongbuk-do, Republic of Korea, 1994—96, assoc. prof., 1999—2004, prof., 2004—; vis. asst. prof. Tulane U. Med. Sch., New Orleans, 1996—98. Office Phone: 82-43-261-2870.

GOOD, LARRY IRWIN, gastroenterologist, educator; b. NYC, Feb. 8, 1948; s. Samuel and Lillie (Sternlight) G.; m. Judy Chafetz, Aug. 16, 1969; children: Adam Eric, Lauren Elyse, Bryan Scott, Allison Jill. BA, Colgate U., 1969; MD, Med. U. of SC, 1973. Diplomate Am. Bd. Internal Medicine, Am. Bd. Gastroenterology. Intern in medicine Tchg. Hosp. Med. U. of SC, 1973-74, resident in medicine Tchg. Hosp., 1974-75, chief resident in medicine Tchg. Hosp., 1975-76; fellow in gastroenterology U. Pa., 1976-78; with Hempstead (NY) Gen. Hosp., 1978—, Nassau County Med. Ctr., East Meadow, NY, 1978—, South Nassau Cmtys. Hosp., Oceanside, NY, 1978—, chief divsn. gastroenterology dept. medicine, 1989. Asst. prof. Sch. of Medicine, SUNY, Stony Brook, 1978; mem. health adv. bd. Hofstra Health Dome Uniondale, NY, 1983; with Lydia E. Hall Hosp., Freeport, NY, 1978-86, Mercy Hosp., Rockville Centre, NY, 1978-80. Contbr. articles to Am. Jour. Gastroenterology, The Papilla Vateri and its Diseases, Med. Times, New Eng. Jour. Medicine., Gastroenterology, Alpha Omega Alpha. Trustee, dir. Little Village Sch. & House, Garden City, NY, 1985—. Recipient Rsch. Svc. award NIH, 1977. Fellow Am. Coll. Gastroenterology; mem. AMA, ACP, L.I. Gastroenterologic Assn., Am. Gastroenterologic Assn. Jewish. Home: 444 Merrick Rd Lynbrook NY 11563 Office Phone: 516-766-0300. Personal E-mail: goodlb@optonline.net.

GOOD, LAURANCE FREDERIC, retired hospital administrator; b. Wheeling, W.Va., Sept. 26, 1932; s. Sidney Samuel and Jeannette (Berg) G.; m. Barbara S. Mayer, Oct. 18, 1959 (dec.); children: Philip (dec.), Jay, Paul, Jenny, Heidi. BA, Brown U., 1954; postgrad., U. Va. Law Sch., 1955. CLU, ChFC, cert. employee benefits specialist, CEBS, health ins. assoc.; registered health underwriter, LUTCF. V.p., gen. mdse. mgr. L.S. Good & Co., Wheeling, 1961-80, exec. v.p., 1969-80, vice chmn., sec. bd., 1961-80, Good's of Wheeling, W.Va., Steubenville, Ohio, St. Clairsville, Ohio, Gables, Altoona, Pa., Knapps, Lansing, Miss., Jackson, Miss., Fowler's, Binghamton, NY, Kann's, Wash., DC, Arlington, Va., Purcell's, Lexington, Ky., D.M. Christian Co., Owasso, Mich., Smith-Bridgeman, Flint, Mich., Grand Blanc, Mich., Robinson's Battle Creek, Mich.; pres. Personal History Sys.; life underwriter Equitable Life Assurance Soc. Am., 1983-89; health and welfare cons. Mockenhaupt, Mockenhaupt, Cowden & Parks, 1989; employee benefit specialist, life underwriter Lincoln Fin. Svcs., Inc., Pitts., 1990; exec. dir. Wheeling Works, Inc., Wheeling, W.Va., 1993-95; dir. Office of Gift Planning Med. Park Found., Wheeling, W.Va., 1995—2006; dir. devel. Wheeling Hosp. Mem. Million Dollar Roundtable, 1985-86; pres. Personal History Systems. Producer: Wheeling Rediscovered; Author: My Lifetime Book. Bd. dirs. Wheeling Symphony Soc., 1964-67, 68-73; with Ohio Valley Indsl. and Bus. Devel. Corp., Wheeling, 1971; chmn. Brown U. Alumni Program, 1954-88, W.Va.; Christmas seals chmn. Tb Assn. Ohio Valley, 1973; co-chmn. United Jewish Appeal, 1971-73; v.p., chmn. fin. com. Temple Shalom, 1986-89; co-founder Good Zoo in memory of eldest son, Philip; co-founder, pres. Good Zoo Friends, 1974-78; chmn. establishment com. Wheeling Devel. Conf.; bd. found. W. Liberty State Coll., 1971; creator Kraft-Good Archives; bd. dirs. Wheeling Hosp., 1972-87, hon. bd. dirs., 1988-96; bd. visitors Bethany Coll., 1972-77; trustee Oglebay Inst., 1972-90; mem. Estate Planning Coun. of Ohio Valley and Pitts.; co-chair Greater Wheeling/Bel-o-Mar Empowerment Zone/Enterprise Community Initiative, 1994; campaign dir. Toward the Next Century, Wheeling Hosp., 1998, dir. capital funds campaign, 2004. With USN, 1955-57. Charter recipient Disting. West Virginian award, 1976; named Master Gardener, W.Va. U., 2007. Mem. NAACP (charter life mem.), Nat. Retail Mchts. Assn. (dir. merchandising div. 1966-71, del. conf. 1969), Ohio Valley Assn. Life Underwriters (pres. 1987), W.Va. Assn. Life Underwriters (regional dir. 1988). Personal E-mail: good-for-you@comcast.com. *

GOOD, MICHAEL IAN, psychiatrist, educator; b. New Ulm, Minn., May 23, 1944; s. Rudolph I. and Raleigh (Aaronson) G.; m. Bambi Zimmerman. BA summa cum laude, U. Minn., 1966; MD, Harvard U., 1970; grad., Psychoanlytic Inst. New Eng. East, 1990. Diplomate Am. Bd. Psychiatry and Neurology. Resident in psychiatry Mass. Mental Health Ctr., Boston, 1971-74, fellow in child psychiatry, 1974-76; resident in psychiatry Peter Bent Brigham Hosp., Boston, 1973-74; dir. child psychiatry West-Ros-Park Mental Health Ctr., Boston, 1976-91; mem. sr. psychiat. staff Medfield (Mass.) State Hosp., 1991-92, Westborough (Mass.) State Hosp., 1992—. Clin. instr. psychiatry Harvard U. Med. Sch., Boston, 1976-81, asst. clin. prof., 1981-97, assoc. clin. prof., 1998—; candidate in child psychoanalysis Boston Psychoanalytic Inst., Psychoanalytic Inst. New Eng., 1991—; mem. faculty Psychoanalytic Inst. New Eng., East, 1994—. Contbr. articles to profl. jours. Fellow Am. Psychiat. Assn. (named Disting. Fellow); mem. Am. Acad. Child Psychiatry, Am. Psychoanalytic Assn., Mass. Psychiat. Soc., New England Coun. Child and Adolescent Psychiatry. Home and Office: 74 Craftsland Rd Chestnut Hill MA 02467-2632

GOOD, MICHAEL LOWELL, anesthesiologist, educator, dean; m. Danette M. Good; 5 children. BS in Computer and Comm. Sci., U. Mich., Ann Arbor, 1980, MD, 1984. Diplomate Am. Bd. Anesthesiology, cert. Nat. Bd. Med. Examiners. Chief resident dept. anesthesiology U. Fla. Coll. Medicine, Gainesville, 1986—87, rsch. fellow dept. anestesiology, 1987—88, asst. prof. dept. anestesiology, 1988—93, prof. anesthesiology, 1999—, sr. assoc. dean for VA affiliations, 2004—05, sr. assoc. dean for clin. affairs, 2005—08, interim dean, 2008—09, dean, 2009—; chief anesthesiology svc. Malcom Randall Vet. Affairs Med. Ctr., Gainesville, 1994—96, chief of staff, 1996—99; pres. U. Fla. Health Services Inst., Gainesville, 2007—08; chief of staff Shands HealthCare at the U. Fla. and Alachua Gen. Hosp., 2007—08. Inventor human patient simulator. Mem.: AMA, Fla. Med. Assn., Alachua County Med. Soc., Am. Soc. Echocardiography, Am. Soc. Anesthesiologists. Roman Catholic. Office: U Fla Coll Medicine PO Box 100215 Gainesville FL 32610-0215 Office Phone: 352-273-7500. E-mail: good@anest.ufl.edu. *

GOOD, ROBERT PAUL, orthopedist, educator; MD, Thomas Jefferson Univ., 1973. Lic. Pa., 1974, Calif., 1976, diplomate Am. Bd. Orthopaedic Surgery, 1980. Intern gen. surgery Thomas Jefferson Univ. Hosp., 1974, resident orthop. surgery, 1979, clin. prof. orthop. surgery; orthop. specialist Bryn Mawr Hosp., 1978; hosp. affiliations include Bryn Mawr Rehab. Hosp., 1980, Paoli Hosp., 1997. Recipient Osler award for tchg., Thomas Jefferson Univ.; named one of the Top Doctors, Phila. Mag., 2010—11. Fellow: ACS; mem.: Am. Acad. Orthop. Surgeons, Am. Assn. Hip and Knee Surgeons, Arthroscopy Assn. N.Am., Eastern Orthop. Assn., Phila. Orthop. Soc. (past pres.). Office: Bryn Mawr Hospital 27 S Bryn Mawr Ave Bryn Mawr PA 19010 Office Phone: 610-527-2727. Office Fax: 610-527-1588.

GOOD, WILLIAM VANCE, medical educator; b. Covington, Va., Sept. 28, 1951; MD, Cin. U., 1977. Clin. prof. U. Calif., San Francisco, 2005—. Fellow: Am. Assn. Pediatric Ophthalmology & Strabismus. Avocations: sports, reading. Office: 2340 Clay St San Francisco CA 94115 Office Fax: 415-458-2481. Personal E-mail: wvgood@gmail.com.

GOODE, ERICA TUCKER, internist; b. Berkeley, Calif., Mar. 25, 1940; d. Howard Edwin and Mary Louise (Tucker) Sweeting; m. Bruce Tucker (div. 1971); m. Barry Paul Goode, Sept. 1, 1974; children: Adam Nathaniel, Aaron Benjamin. BS summa cum laude, U. Calif., Berkeley, 1962, MPH, 1967; MD, U. Calif., San Francisco, 1977. Diplomate Am. Bd. Internal Medicine. Chief dietitian Washington Hosp. Ctr., Washington, 1968; pub. health nutritionist Dept. Human Resources, Washington, 1969—73; intern Children's Hosp. (now Calif. Pacific Med. Ctr.), San Francisco, 1977—78, resident, 1978—80, chief med. resident internal medicine, 1979—80; pvt. practice internal medicine San Francisco, 1980—. Expert witness med.-legal issues, Calif., 1990—; lectr., tchr. med. house staff Calif. Pacific Med. Ctr. Hosp., 1982—; assoc. prof. medicine U. Calif., San Francisco, 1984—; apptd. mem. Calif. Commn. on Aging, 2003—. Contbr. articles to profl. publs. Co-chair Physicians for Clinton, No. Calif., 1992, 96 Mem. AMA, ACP, Calif. Med. Assn., Calif. Soc. Internal Medicine, San Francisco Med. Soc. (mem. editl. bd.), U. Calif. Alumni Assn. (del.), Alpha Omega Alpha (named Best Doctor's list 1996-). Office: CPMC Inst for Health & Healing Clinic 2300 California St # 204 San Francisco CA 94115-2754 Office Phone: 415-876-5230. Business E-Mail: goodee@sutterhealth.org. *

GOODENBERGER, DANIEL MARVIN, medical educator; b. McCook, Nebr., Apr. 24, 1948; s. Marvin Eugene and Mary Ellen (Marshall) Goodenberger; children: James Michael, Katherine Elizabeth. BS, U. Nebr., Lincoln, 1970; MD, Duke U., Durham, NC, 1974. Diplomate Am. Bd. Internal Medicine, Am. Bd. Emergency Medicine (examiner 1983-95), Am. Bd. Pulmonary Disease, Am. Bd. Critical Care Medicine. Intern Peter Bent Brigham Hosp., Boston, 1974-75, resident in internal medicine, 1975-76; clin. assoc. Nat. Cancer Inst., Bethesda, Md., 1976-78; fellow pulmonary and critical care medicine Boston U. Med. Ctr., 1985-88; assoc. dir. emergency dept. Arlington Hosp., Va., 1979-82; edn. dir. emergency dept. Georgetown U. Hosp., Washington, 1982-85; dir. emergency svcs. U. Hosp., Boston, 1986-87; dir. pulmonary and critical care fellowship Washington U. Med. Schs., St. Louis, 1989-93; dir. pulmonary cons. svcs. Barnes Hosp., St. Louis, 1990-93, dir. internal medicine residency program, 1992—2006; assoc. prof. medicine Washington U., St. Louis, 1995-99; dir. divsn. med. edn. Washington U. Sch. Medicine, 1998—2006, prof. medicine, 1999—2006; prof., chair dept. medicine U. Nev. Sch. Medicine, Las Vegas, 2006—07; chief med. svc. Dallas VAMC, 2008—; prof., vice-chair, dept. medicine U. Tex., Southwestern Sch. Medicine, 2008—. Chief Wood-Moore Firm, Barnes-Jewish Hosp., 1996-2001. Editor Careers, 1996-98. Lt. comdr. USPHS, 1973-78. Winthrop Breon and Am. Coll. Chest Physicians scholar, 1987. Master ACP; fellow Am. Coll. Chest Physicians; mem. AMA, Am. Thoracic Soc., Am. Clin. and Climatological Assn., St. Louis Met. Med. Soc. (councilor 1997-2000), St. Louis Club, Harbor Point Yacht Club, Phi Beta Kappa, Alpha Omega Alpha. Methodist. Avocations: theater, music, travel, sailing. Home: 6371 Vickery Blvd Dallas TX 75214 Office: Dallas VAMC 4500 S Lancaster Rd Dallas TX 75216

GOODENDAY, LUCY SHERMAN, cardiologist, educator; b. NYC, Oct. 2, 1937; d. Leo Daniel and Winnie Victoria (Bornstein) Sherman; m. Kenneth Benjamin Goodenday, Aug. 31, 1958. AB, Bryn Mawr Coll., 1959; MD, N.Y. Med. Coll., 1963. Diplomate cardiovasc. disease Am. Bd. Internal Medicine; cert. nuclear cardiology. Clin. instr. U. Calif., San Francisco, 1969-71, asst. clin. prof., 1971-75; asst. prof. medicine U. Mich., Ann Arbor, 1975-78; assoc. prof. med. Med. Coll. Ohio, Toledo, 1979—2002; prof. medicine U. Toledo Coll. Medicine, 2003—. Editor: Hypertension in the Community, 1971; author: (movie, booklet) Current Approach to the Hypertensive Patient, 1970, (tape) Pro and Con Views on Routine Exercise Testing, 1977, Nuclear Cardiology Interactive Learning System, 1996—; editor-in-chief Studies in Nuclear Cardiology, 2001—; contbr. articles to profl. jours. Trustee N.W. Ohio AHA, 1983—96, mem. rsch. rev. bd., 1988—96; trustee Ohio Valley affil. AHA, mem. exec. com., 1996—99; mem. GE Healthcare, 2006—09. Fellow NIH, 1965-68, AAUW, 1968-69, Med. Coll. Ohio Tchg. Scholars Fellow, 2000; grantee VA, 1973-78, Am. Heart Assn., 1977-84, Warner Lambert, 1976, Nycomed Amersham, 2000-01. Mem. Am. Fedn. for Clin. Rsch., Am. Soc. Nuclear Medicine, Am. Soc. Nuclear Cardiology (founding mem.), Am. Coll. Cardiology. Mem. Soc. Of Friends. Avocation: horse breeding and training. Office: Univ Toledo Med Ctr 1192 Hospital Bldg 3000 Arlington Ave Toledo OH 43614 Business E-Mail: lucy.goodenday@utoledo.edu. *

GOODFELLOW, ROBIN IRENE, surgeon; b. Xenia, Ohio, Apr. 14, 1945; d. Willis Douglas and Irene Linna (Kirkland) G. BA summa cum laude, Western Res. U., Cleve., 1967; MD cum laude, Harvard U., 1971. Diplomate Am. Bd. Surgery. Intern, resident Peter Bent Brigham Hosp., Boston, 1971-76; staff surgeon Boston U., 1976-80, asst. prof. surgery, 1977-80; pvt. practice medicine specializing in surgery Jonesboro, La., 1980-81; practice medicine specializing in surgery Albion, Mich., 1984-87, Coldwater, Mich., 1987—97; ringside physician USA Boxing, 2003—. Bd. Overseers Case Western Res. U., 1977-82. AAUW fellow, 1970. Fellow Am. Coll. Ringside Medicine (treas.), ACS; mem. AMA, Internat. Med. Commn. (mem. Olympic style boxing, 2008-, sec. 2009-), Phi Beta Kappa. Republican. Methodist. Personal E-mail: robinigoodfellow@hotmail.com.

GOODFRIEND, THEODORE L., physician; b. Phila., Sept. 30, 1931; BA, Swarthmore Coll., 1953; MD, U. Pa., 1957. Prof. emeritus, medicine and pharmacology U. Wis. Sch. Medicine, 1965—2011; assoc. chief staff rsch. Dept. Vets. Affairs, 1975—. Mem.: Coun. High Blood Pressure Rsch., Am. Heart Assn. (Lifetime Achievement award, Irvine Page, Alva Bradley award). Avocations: bicycling, reading, music. Office: Research Service VA Hosp 2500 Overlook Ter Madison WI 53705 Business E-Mail: theodore.goodfriend@va.gov.

GOODHUE, PETER AMES, retired obstetrician, gynecologist, educator; b. Ft. Fairfield, Maine, Feb. 26, 1931; s. Lawrence and Zylpha (Ames) G.; m. Edith Ann Helfenstein, June 21, 1958; children: Lisa Grace, Scott Ames. BA, Amherst Coll., 1954; MD, U. Vt., 1958. Diplomate Am. Bd. Ob-Gyn. Intern Bellevue Hosp., NYC, 1958-59; resident Yale-New Haven Med. Ctr., 1959-62; pvt. practice medicine specializing in ob-gyn. Stamford, Conn., 1964—2010. Assoc. clin. prof. ob-gyn. N.Y. Med. Coll., 1984—98; asst. clin. prof. ob-gyn. Columbia Presbyn. Hosp., 1999—2004; mem. Conn. State Maternal Mortality Com., 1971—2007, chmn., 1981—83. Contbr. articles to profl. jours. Served to capt. USAF, 1962-64. Recipient Carbee prize U. Vt., 1958. Fellow ACOG (chmn. Conn. sect. 1976, pres. Conn. sect. 1973-76), ACS, Am. Fertility Soc., Am. Soc. for Colposcopy and Cervical Pathology, Am. Assn. Gynecologic Laproscopists; mem. Conn. Med. Soc., Conn. Soc. Am. Bd. Obstetricians and Gynecologists (pres. 1973-76), Fairfield County Med. Soc., Fairfield County Gynecol. and Obstet. Soc., Stamford Med. Soc. (pres. 1989-90). Republican. Episcopalian. Home Phone: 203-655-3029.

GOODHUE, WILLIAM WALTER, JR., pathologist, military officer, educator; b. St. Louis, Feb. 5, 1945; s. William W. and Rose Marie (Vahousek) Goodhue. BS cum laude, Georgetown U., DC, 1966; MD, Cornell U. Med. Sch., NYC, 1970. Diplomate Am. Bd. Pathology. Anat. pathology intern N.Y. Hosp.-Cornell Med Ctr., NYC, 1970-71, resident anat. pathology, 1971-74; chief resident pediatric pathology Columbia-Presbyn. Med. Ctr., NYC, 1974-75; resident clin. pathology Tripler Army Med. Ctr., Honolulu, 1976—78, chief pathology grad. med. edn., dir. electron microscopy, 1994—97, asst. chief dept. pathology and area lab. svcs., 1997—2001; first dep. med. examiner, ex officio mayoral cabinet mem. City and County of Honolulu, 2001—09, acting chief med. examiner, 2009—. Chief dept. pathology U.S. Army Hosp., Ft. Campbell, Ky., 1978—80; chief dept. pathology, med. dir. Sch. Med. Tech., dir. pathology residency tng. Gorgas Army Hosp., Panama; C.Z. and assoc. prof. med. tech. Panama Canal Coll., 1980—82; resident officer U.S. Army Command and Gen. Staff Coll., Ft. Leavenworth, Kans., 1982—83; divsn. surgeon 2d Inf. Divsn., 1983—84; dep. comdr. clin. svcs., chief dept. primary care and cmty. medicine, staff pathologist, acting comdr. Bayne-Jones Army Hosp., Ft. Polk, La., 1984—85; chief dept. pathology and area lab. svcs., dir. pathology residency tng. Dwight David Eisenhower Army Med. Ctr., Ft. Gordon, Ga., 1985—94; clin. assoc. prof. pathology Med. Coll. Ga., Augusta, 1986—94, Sch. Medicine U. Hawaii, Honolulu, 1997—; cons. in pathology Eisenhower Health Svc. Region to Comdg. Gen.; cons. ARC, 1978—80; rep. All. Army Med. Dept. Coll. Am. Pathologists Ho. of Dels., Am. Soc. Clin. Pathologist Adv. Coun., 1990—2001; mem. profl. adv. bd. Med. Lab. Observer, 1993—95; Army councillor-at-large Armed Forces Med. Lab. Scientists, 1993—2001; v.p. Land Bd. R.W. Meyer, Ltd. Assoc. editor: Hawaii Med. Jour., 2003—04; contbr. articles to profl. jours. Col. M.C. US Army, 1975—2001. Decorated Order Mil. Med. Merit, Hon. Order of Ky. Col.; recipient Surgeon Gen.'s "A" designator med. splty. excellence, 1997; fellow Rsch., USPHS, 1971—74. Fellow: Coll. Am. Pathologists, Am. Soc. Investigative Pathology, Nat. Assn. Med. Examiners, Am. Soc. Clin. Pathologists (lab. accreditation insp. & accreditation program 1988—), Am. Acad. Forensic Scis.; mem.: AMA (Physicians Recognition award 1976, 1978, 1980, 1982, 1986, 1989, 1992, 1995, 1998, 2001, 2004, 2007, 2010), U.S.-Can. Acad. Pathology, Clin. Lab. Mgrs. Assn. (bd. dir. 1989—92), Alliance Française, Assn. U.S. Army, Soc. Armed Forces Med. Lab. Scientists, NY Acad. Sci., Hawaii Soc. Pathologists, Soc. Ultrastructural Pathology, Am. Assn. Blood Banks, Assn. Mil. Surgeons U.S., Med. Assn. Isthmian Canal Zone (v.p. 1980—81), Soc. Pediat. Pathology, The Plaza Club Hawaii, Makani Kai Yacht Club, Outrigger Canoe Club, Cornell Club NY. Independent. Roman Catholic. Home: 45-995 Wailele Rd # 52 Kaneohe HI 96744-3041 Office: Dept Med Examiner 835 Iwilei Rd Honolulu HI 96817 Office Phone: 808-768-3090. Personal E-mail: WWGJRMD@aol.com. Business E-Mail: wgoodhue@honolulu.gov.

GOODIN, JULIA C., forensic specialist, state official; d. Vitus Jack and Geneva Goodin. BS, Western Ky. U., 1979; MD, U. Ky., 1983. Diplomate Am. Bd. Clin. and Anatomic Pathology, Am. Bd. Forensic Pathology. Intern Vanderbilt U. Med. Ctr., Nashville, 1983, resident in anatomic and clin. pathology, 1984-87; fellow in forensic pathology Med. Examiner's Office, Balt., 1987-88; asst. med. examiner Office of Chief Med. Examiner, Balt., 1988-90; dep. chief med. examiner State of Tenn., 1990-94; asst. med. examiner Nashville, 1990-93; chief med. examiner, 1993-94; asst. med. investigator State of N.Mex., Albuquerque, 1994-96; asst. prof. U. N.Mex., Albuquerque, 1994-96; clin. assoc. prof. U. of South Ala. Sch. Medicine, 1996-99; state med. examiner Ala. Dept. Forensic Scis., Mobile, 1996-99; chief state med. examiner State of Iowa, Des Moines, 1999—. Clin. prof. U. Md. Med. Sch., Balt., 1988-90, Vanderbilt U. Med. Ctr., 1990-94. Capt. USNR, 1985—. Mem. Am. Acad. Forensic Sci., Assn. Mil. Surgeons of U.S., AMA. Avocations: long-distance running, weightlifting, photography, studying French. Office: 2250 S Ankeny Blvd Ankeny IA 50023-9023 Home: 5241 Woodland Ave Des Moines IA 50312-1943 Office Phone: 515-725-1400.

GOODING, CHARLES ARTHUR, retired radiologist, physician, educator; b. Cleve., Feb. 28, 1936; s. Joseph J. and Florence G. (Pitt) G.; m. Gretchen Wagner, June 19, 1961; children: Gunnar, Justin, Britta. BA, Western Res. U., 1957; MD, Ohio State U., 1961. Intern Ohio State U. Hosp., 1961-62; resident in radiology Peter Bent Brigham Hosp., Children's Hosp. Med. Center, both Boston, 1963-65; rsch. fellow radiology Harvard Med. Sch., Boston, 1962, tchg. fellow, 1965-66; Harvard Med. Sch. fellow Hosp. for Sick Children, London, Karolinska Hosp., Stockholm, 1966; faculty U. Calif. Med. Center, San Francisco, 1969—2009, prof. radiology and pediatrics, 1976—2009, exec. vice-chmn. dept. radiology, 1974—2001, prof. emeritus, 2009. Pres. Radiology Rsch. and Edn. Found., 1973-96, Radiology Outreach Found., 1988-2002, pres. emeritus 2002—; hon. mem. faculty Francesco Maroquin U. Sch. Medicine, Guatemala City. Contbr. chpts. to books.; Editor: Pediatric Radiology, 1973—96; editor: Diagnostic Radiology, 1972-92; contbr. articles to profl. jours. Capt. M.C. USAR, 1967-68. Recipient Outstanding Alumni award Brigham Women's Hosp. Harvard Med. Sch., 1994, Disting. Alumnus award Ohio State U., 1986, Case Western Res. U., 1999, Beclere medal Internat. Soc. Radiology, 1998; named to Disting. Alumni Hall of Fame Cleve. Heights H.S., 1999, Top Pediat. Radiologist San Francisco mag., 2001. Fellow Am. Coll. Radiology, Royal Coll. Radiologists London (hon.), Armenian Radiol. Soc. (hon.); mem. Am. Roentgen Ray Soc., Assn. Univ. Radiologists, European Soc. Pediat. Radiologists (hon.), Pacific Coast Pediat. Radiologists Assn. (past pres.), Radiol. Soc. N.Am., Polish Radiology Soc. (hon.), Hungarian Radiology Soc. (hon.), San Francisco Med. Soc., Soc. Pediat. Radiology (v.p. 1994, pres. 1997 pres. SPR rsch. and edn. found. 1993-96, chmn., bd. dirs. 1998, Gold medal, 2009), Rocky Mountain Mountain Radiol. Soc. (hon.), Australian Soc. for Pediatric Imaging (hon.), Chinese Radiol. Soc. (hon.), Swiss Radiol. Soc. (hon.), Malaysian Radiol. Soc. (hon.), Vietnamese Radiol. Soc. (hon.), Thailand Radiology Soc. (hon.), French Soc. Radiology (hon.), Indian Radiol. and Imaging Soc. (hon.), Radiol. Soc. Pakistan (hon.), Indonesian Radiol. Soc. (hon.), Mongolian Nat. Radiol. Assn. (hon.), Nepal Radiol. Soc. (hon.), Armenian Med. Diagnostic Assn. (hon.), Brazilian Coll. Radiology (hon.), Cuban Radiol. Soc. (hon.), Indonesian Pediatric Radiol. Soc. (hon.), Asian and Oceanean Radiol. Soc. (gold medal 2004, Project Hope Hall of Fame, 2007), African Radiology Soc. (hon.). E-mail: charles.gooding@radiology.ucsf.edu.

GOODING, CHARLES THOMAS, psychologist, educator, retired academic administrator; b. Tampa, Fla., Nov. 18, 1931; s. Charles T. and Gladys (Bingman) G.; m. Shirley Ann Puckett, June 7, 1953; children: Steven Thomas, Carol Ann, David Lee, Mark Charles. BA, U. Fla., 1954, M.Ed., 1962, Ed.D., 1964; postgrad., U. Tampa, 1956-58. Tchr. Meml. Sch., Tampa, 1956-58, asst. prin., then prin. St. Mary's Sch., Tampa, 1958-62; grad. fellow U. Fla., Gainesville, 1962-63, instr., 1963-64; assoc. prof., then prof. SUNY, Oswego, 1964-79, prof. psychology, 1980-98, assoc. dean grad. studies, 1982-89, dean grad. studies and rsch., 1989-95, provost, v.p. for acad. affairs, 1995-98, emeritus, 1998—. Vis. prof. U. Liverpool, Eng., 1979-80; mem. SUNY Chancellor's Task Force on Tchr. Edn., 1984. Author: Learning Theories in Educational Practice, 1971; contbg. author: Florida Studies in the Helping Professions, 1969, Questioning and Discussion: A Multidisciplinary Study, 1988, Research Matters to the Science Teacher, 1992; contbr. articles to profl. jours. Trustee U. of South, 2002-05; bd. dirs. Oswego Coll. Found., 1996-, Bishop Gray Inns Found., 2008-. Served to 1st lt. USAR, 1954-56. SUNY Rsch. Found. grantee, 1966, 69-70, NY State Dept. Edn. grantee, 1971-72, 88-94, NSF grantee, 1980-81, 85-88, 90-95. Mem. APA, Ea. Ednl. Rsch. Assn. (v.p. 1979-81, treas., dir. 1983-85, pres.-elect 1987-88, pres. 1989-91, editl. bd. 1991-2000), Am. Ednl. Rsch. Assn. (chair ednl. enterprises SIG, 1994-96). Home: 603 Wild Pine Way Venice FL 34292-4618 E-mail: tgooding@comcast.net.

GOODING, DIANE CAROL, psychology educator, researcher; b. NYC, July 27, 1963; d. Conrad Lynwood and Anne Danforth Gooding. AB, Harvard U., 1985; PhD, U. Minn., 1996. Sr. rsch. asst. Murray Rsch. Ctr., Cambridge, Mass., 1985—87; asst. prof. U. Wis., Madison, 1996—2002, assoc. prof., 2002—07, prof., 2007—. Bd. dirs. Nat. Alliance for Mentally Ill, 1999-2005 Recipient Young Investigator award Internat. Congress Schizophrenia Rsch., 1999, Van Hise Outreach Disting. Tchg. award U. Wis., Madison, 2008, Outstanding Women Color award, 2010; dissertation fellow Ford Found., Nat. Rsch. Coun., 1992. Mem. N.Y. Acad. Sci., Sigma Xi. Office: U Wis-Madison 1202 W Johnson St Madison WI 53706 Home Phone: 608-238-3132, Office Phone: 608-262-3918. E-mail: dgooding@wisc.edu.

GOODING, GRETCHEN ANN WAGNER, physician, educator; b. Columbus, Ohio, July 2, 1935; d. Edward Frederick and Margaret (List) Wagner; m. Charles A. Gooding, June 19, 1961; children: Gunnar Blaise, Justin Mathias, Britta Meghan. BA magna cum laude, Ohio Dominican U., 1957; MD cum laude, Ohio State U., 1961. Diplomate Am. Bd. Diagnostic Radiology. Intern Univ. Hosps., Columbus, 1961-62; rsch. fellow Boston City Hosp., 1962-63, Boston U., 1963-65; with dept. radiology U. Calif., San Francisco, 1975—, assoc. prof. in radiology, 1981-85, prof., vice chmn., 1986—2003, prof. emeritus, 2009; asst. chief radiology VA Med. Ctr., San Francisco, 1978-87, chief radiology, 1987—2003, chief ultrasonography, 1975—2009. Chair com. acad. pers. U. Calif., San Francisco, 1993-94, bd. dirs. commn. accreditation vascular labs., 1993-96; with NIH Study Sect., Diagnostic Radiology, 1993-96, NIH Grant Reviewer, 2005-09; reviewer NIH, 2005-08, 10. Co-editor Radiologic Clinics of N.Am., 1993—; mem. editl. bd. San Francisco Medicine, 1986-2009, Applied Radiology, 1987-89, Current Opinion in Radiology, 1992-93, The Radiologist, 1993—, Emergency Radiology, 1993-2003, Jour. Clin. Ultrasound, 1997—; guest editor Emergency Radiology, 1999; contbr. articles to profl. jours. Mem. NIH Study Section, 1993—96, NIH Initial Review Group, Radiology, 1996, NIH Biomed. Imaging Grant Review Panels, 2005—10. Recipient Recognition award Inter Societal Commn. for Accreditation of Vascular Labs., 1997, Disting. Alumna award, Ohio State U. Coll. Medicine and Pub. Health, 2001, Alice Ettinger Disting. Achievement award, 2003; named Reviewer Extraordinaire, Jour. Ultrasound in Medicine, 2006, award, 2011. Fellow Am. Coll. Radiology (mem. commn. on ultrasound 1984-2000, chair stds. com. commn. on ultrasound 2004—, chmn. com. practice guidelines and tech. standards 2004—), Am. Inst. Ultrasound in Medicine (bd. govs. 1981-84, chair conv. program 1986-88, Presdl. Recognition award 1984), Am. Soc. Emergency Radiology, Soc. Radiologists U.S.; mem. AMA, San Francisco Med. Soc. (chmn. membership com. 1992-94, bd. dirs. 1996—), RSNA (course com. 1984-88, tech. exhibit com. 1992-96, mem. site med. advisor 2005-06), Bay Area Ultrasound Soc. (pres. 1979-80), Soc. Radiologists Ultrasound (chair membership com. 1991-93, chair corp. com. 1996-97), ARRS, AUR, CRS, Calif. Med. Assn., Am. Assn. Women Radiologists (pres. 1984-85, trustee 1991-94, Alice Ettinger Disting. Achievement award 2003), VA Chiefs of Radiology Assn. (pres.-elect, pres. 1994-95), San Francisco Radiol. Soc. (pres. 1990-91), Hungarian Radiol. Soc. (hon.), Pakistan Radiol. Soc. (hon.), Cuba Radiol. Soc. (hon.). Home Phone: 415-388-0536. Personal E-mail: gretchengoodingmd@gmail.com.

GOODKIN, ROBERT, neurosurgeon, educator; Diploma, Coll. William and Mary, 1958, NYU, 1960; MD, Chgo. Med. Sch., 1964. Diplomate Nat. Bd. Med. Examiners, 1965, Am. Bd. Neurol. Surgeons, 1973. Intern Bellevue Hosp. Ctr. NYU, NYC, 1964—65, resident in neurology Bellevue Hosp. Ctr., 1965—66, resident in neurol. surgery Bellevue Hosp. Ctr., 1966—71; attending staff Barrow Neurol. Inst., Phoenix, 1971—76; adj. assoc. prof. divsn. neurol. surgery U. Fla., Gainesville, 1976—78; assoc. prof. and chief divsn. neurol. surgery Jacksonville (Fla.) Hosps. Ednl. Program, U. Fla., 1976—78; chief dept. neurol. surgery U. Hosp. Jacksonville, 1976—78; pvt. practice neurosurgery Hollywood, Fla., 1978—81; clin. assoc. prof. dept. neurol. surgery U. Miami, Fla., 1978—82; clin. prof. dept. neurol. surgery U. So. Calif., LA, 1981—2000; dir. dept. neurol. surgery City of Hope Nat. Med. Ctr., Duarte, Calif., 1981—86; assoc. prof. neurol. surgery U. Wash. Med. Sch., Seattle, 1987—2003, prof. neurol. surgery, radiation oncology, 2003—06, prof. emeritus neurol. surgery, radiation oncology, 2007—; chief neurosurgery Madigan Army Med. Ctr., Tacoma, 1987—89; chief neurosurgery sect. VA Puget Sound Health Care Sys., Seattle, 1989—2003. Faculty U. Wash. Med. Sch., Seattle, 1987—; mem. neurosurg. cons. com. surg. svc. VA Ctrl. Office-Hdqrs., Washington, 2000—05, chmn., 2000—03; co-dir. gamma knife radiosurgery ctr. Harborview Med. Ctr., 2004—06; cons. med., legal affairs Office Vet. Affairs Western NY Healthcare Sys., 2006—; assoc. editor-in-chief Surg. Neurology Internat., 2010—. Mem. editl. bd.: Surg. Neurology, 2004—07, assoc. editor:, 2007—09. Mem.: Soc. for Neuro-Oncology, Internat. Spinal Cord Soc., Movement Disorder Soc., N.Am. Skull Base Soc., Am. Assn. Stereotactic and Functional Neurosurgery, N.Y. Acad. Scis., Congress Neurol. Surgeons, Neurosurg. Soc. Am. (pres. 1997—98), Acad. Spinal Card Injury Profls., Inc., World Soc. Stereotactic and Functional Neurosurgery, Am. Assn. Neurol. Surgeons. Office: UWMC-Harborview Medical Center Box 359766 325 9th Ave Seattle WA 98104 Office Phone: 206-744-9300.

GOODMAN, ALVIN IRWIN, internist, nephrologist, educator; b. NYC, July 12, 1929; s. Morris and Fanny (Rifkin) G.; m. Suzanna Elizabeth Gebhard; children: Nadine, Derek, Danielle, Leslie, Reva. BA, NYU, 1949; MD, U. Geneva, 1955. Diplomate Am. Bd. Internal Medicine, Am. Bd. Nephrology. Intern Jewish Hosp. Bklyn., 1956, resident in medicine, 1957—58; fellow in medicine Yale U. Sch. Medicine, New Haven, 1960—62, resident in medicine, 1962—63; dir. nephrology and renal ctr. Westchester County Med. Ctr., Valhalla, 1963—2000; prof. medicine, dir. nephrology N.Y. Med. Coll., Valhalla, 1975—2000, prof. med., 1963—2005, emeritus prof. med., 2005—. Dir. endstage renal disease program Bur. Quality Assurance, USPHS, Rockville, Md., 1974-75. Contbr. numerous articles to medl jours. Capt. M.C., U.S. Army, 1958-60. Recipient President's award Nat. Kidney Found., 1977, Cardinal Cook award N.Y. Med. Coll., 1986, Disting. Svc. award N.Y. Med. Coll., 2002. Fellow ACP; mem. Am. Soc. Nephrology, Internat. Soc. Nephrology, Am. Soc. Transplant Physicians, N.Y. Soc. Nephrology (pres. 1980-81), Beta Lambda Sigma. Avocation: travel. Personal E-mail: dralvingoodman@aol.com.

GOODMAN, COREY SCOTT, neuroscientist, biotechnologist, educator; b. Chgo., June 29, 1951; s. Arnold Harold (dec.) and Florence (Friedman) G.; m. Marcia M. Barinaga, Dec. 8, 1984. BS in Biology, Stanford U., Calif., 1972; PhD in Neurobiology, U. Calif., Berkeley, 1977. Postdoctoral fellow U. Calif., San Diego, 1979; asst. prof. dept. biol. scis. Stanford U., 1979-82, assoc. prof., 1982-87; prof. neurobiology and genetics U. Calif., Berkeley, 1987—2005, co-founder Helen Wills Neurosci. Inst., 1997, Evan Rauch prof. neuroscience, 1999—2001; dir. Helen Wills Neurosci. Inst., 1999—2000; co-founder Exelixis, Inc., 1995, Renovis Inc., 2000, Ven Bio LLC, PhyloTech, 2009; pres., CEO Renovis Inc., 2001—07; adj. prof. anatomy & biochemistry U. Calif., San Francisco, 2005—; pres. biotherapeutics & bioinnovation ctr. Pzifer, NYC, 2007—09; chair bd. dirs. Limerick BioPharma, iPierian, PhyloTech, Oligasis, Ossianix and NuMedii; mem. bd. dirs. NeuroTherapeutics Pharma, Mirnd Therapeutics. Investigator Howard Hughes Med. Inst., 1988—2001; chair bd. life sci. NRC, 2001—06; mem. bd. Biotech. Industry Orgn., 2005—09, Bay Bio, 2005—, Bay Area Sci. and Innovation Constorium, 2006—; mem. Calif. Coun. Sci. & Tech., 2007—; mem. bd. Pacific Inst., 2009—; mem. SAB Spinal Muscular Atrophy Found., 2005—, QB3 VCSF Industry Adv. Bd., 2007—, Stanford BioX Bioscis. Adv. Coun., 2008—, SAB, Stanley Ctr. Psychiat. Rsch., MIT, Harvard, 2009—. Contbr. more than 200 articles to profl. jours. Pres. McKnight Found. Endowment Fund Neurosci., 2000—05, v.p., 2005—. Recipient Charles Judson Herrick award, 1982, Alan T. Waterman award Nat. Sci. Bd., 1983, Javits Neurosci. Investigator award NIH, 1985, 92, NIH Merit award, 1985, Found. IPSEN Neuronal Plasticity prize, 1996, J. Allyn Taylor Internat. prize in medicine, 1996, Gairdner Found. Internat. award, 1997, Ameritec Found. Basic Rsch. Toward Cure Paralysis prize, 1997, Wakeman award for rsch. in neuroscis., 1998, March-Of-Dimes prize in Devel. Biology, 2001, Rsch. medal Reeve-Irvine, 2007. Fellow Am. Acad. Arts and Scis.; mem. NAS, Am. Philos. Soc. Office: venBio 1700 Owens St 5th Fl San Francisco CA 94158 Business E-Mail: corey.goodman@ne.com.

GOODMAN, CYNTHIA DIANE, physical medicine, rehab physician; b. Odessa, Tex., Oct. 11, 1954; d. Edwin Lloyd and Dorothy Jean Coventon; m. Sanford Jay Goodman, Oct. 26, 2003. BS, Dallas Bapt. U., 1977; MD, U. Tex., San Antonio, 1983; MS, SUNY, Buffalo, 1998. Cert. Am. Bd. Phys. Medicine and Rehab., 1990. Staff physician various NYC hosps., 1983—88; physiatry Work Well, Pitts., 1988—89; cons. Dept. Human Svcs., Oklahoma City, 1990—95; fellow preventive medicine SUNY, Buffalo, 1995—98; fellow pub. health HCFA, Dallas, 1998—2000; pub. health physician Pa. Health Dept., Harrisburg, Pa., 2000—10, Osteo Relief Inst. Dallas, 2011. Fellow: Am. Coll. Preventive Medicine, Am.-Coll. Soc. Preventive Medicine; mem.: Am. Assn. Physical Med. & Rehab, Med. Assoc., Am. Assn. Pub. Health Physicians, Dallas County Med. Soc., Am. Med. Assn. Republican. Jewish. Home: 12123 Heritage Park Rd #167 Oklahoma City OK 73120 Personal E-mail: cynthia.goodman3@gmail.com.

GOODMAN, DANIEL F., ophthalmologist; BS with highest distinction, Univ. Mich., Ann Arbor, Mich.; MD with highest distinction, Univ. Mich. Med. Sch. Resident, ophthalmology divsn. Univ. Calif., San Francisco, co-dir. Corneal Surgical Svc., 1988—90, assoc. clinical. prof. ophthalmology, Calif. Pacific Med. Ctr.; fell. Johns Hopkins Univ. Hosp.; pvt. practice ophthalmologist San Francisco, 1990—. Team ophthalmologist San Francisco Giants. Mem.: Am. Coll. Surgeons, AMA, Calif. Med. Assn., San Francisco Med. Soc., Am. Bd. Ophthalmology, Am. Acad. Ophthalmology, Internat. Soc. Refractive Surgeons, Am. Society of Cataract and Refractive Surgeons, Calif. Max Fine Cornea Society. Avocation: speed-skating.

GOODMAN, JESSE, physician, director, public health facility administrator, research scientist; BS, Harvard U.; MD, Albert Einstein Coll. of Medicine; MPH, U. Minn. Prof. medicine, dir. US Govt. Interagency Task Force Antimicrobial Resistance, 1998—2000; sr. advisor to commr. FDA, 1998—99, dep. dir. medicine Ctr. Biologics, Evaluation, and Rsch., 1999—2000, dir. Ctr. Biologics, Evaluation, and Rsch., 2003—, prof. medicine, 1997—2001; dir. divsn. infectious diseases U. Minn. Med. Sch., 1998—2001. Adj. prof. medicine U. Minn., Howard U.; attending physician NIH Clin. Ctr. and Walter Reed Army Med. Ctr. Mem.: Inst. Medicine of Nat. Acad. Sci., Am. Soc. for Clin. Investigation. Office: Ctr Biologics Evaluation and Rsch FDA 1401 Rockville Pike Ste 200N Rockville MD 20852-1448 Business E-Mail: jesse.goodman@fda.hhs.gov.

GOODMAN, LARRY J., health facility administrator; b. Detroit, 1950; Degree with distinction, U. Mich., MD, 1976. Diplomate Am. Bd. Internal Medicine, Am. Bd. Infectious Disease. Intern Rush Presbyn.-St. Luke's Med. Ctr., Chgo., 1976—77; resident in internal medicine Rush U. Med. Ctr., Chgo., 1977—79, chief resident, 1979, fellow in infectious disease, 1979—81, mem. faculty and staff, 1981—87, former prof., assoc. dean med. student programs, former dir. divsn. specialized tng. programs, dir. interinstnl. affairs, sr. v.p. for med. affairs, 1998—2002; Henry R. Russe dean, prof. Rush Med. Coll., Chgo., 2000—02; pres., CEO Rush U. Med. Ctr., 2002—; med. dir. Cook County Hosp., Chgo., 1996—98. Pres. Rush U., Chgo.; prin. officer Rush Bd. Trustees; CEO, chmn. bd. dirs. Rush Sys. for Health; mem. site survey team Liaison Com. on Med. Edn. Contbr. articles to profl. jours. Office: Rush U Med Ctr 1650 W Harrison St Chicago IL 60612 *

GOODMAN, MICHAEL, surgeon; b. NYC, July 2, 1979; BS, Duke U., 2001; MD, U. Cin., 2005. Resident, dept. surgery U. Cin., 2005—. Office: 231 Albert Sabin Way ML 0558 Cincinnati OH 45267 Business E-Mail: goodmamd@uc.edu.

GOODMAN, ROBERT L., internist, epidemiologist, educator; BS, Rutgers U.; MD, UMDNJ, Newark. Resident Albert Einstein Coll. Montefiore Med. Ctr., 1988—92, asst. prof., 2006—; clinical faculty Columbia-Presbyterian, dir. PCIM residency program. Office: 111 E 210th St Rm NW849 Bronx NY 10467 Office Phone: 718-920-5775. E-mail: rgoodman@montefiore.org.

GOODMAN, ROBERT MERWIN, microbiologist, botanist, educator; b. Ithaca, NY, Dec. 30, 1945; s. Robert Browning and Janet Edith (Pond) G.; 1 child, Nathan Mansfield. Student, Johns Hopkins U., 1963-65; B.Sc., Cornell U., 1967, PhD, 1973. Vis. rsch. fellow John Innes Inst., Norwich, Eng., 1973-74; asst. prof. U. Ill., Urbana, 1974-78, assoc. prof., 1978-81, prof., 1981-83; exec. v.p. R&D Calgene, Inc., Davis, Calif., 1982-90; vis. prof. U. Wis., Madison, 1990—91, prof., 1991—2005, prof., chair undergrad. program molecular biology, 1993—2005; prof., exec. dean agr. and natural resources Rutgers U., 2005—, exec. dean Sch. Environ. and Biol. Scis., 2005—; exec. dir. NJ Agrl. Experiment Sta., 2005—. Sr. scholar-in-residence NRC, 1990-91; mem. Bd. on Agr., NRC, 1986-91, chair com. on exam. plant sci. rsch. programs U.S., 1990-92, Commn. on Life Sci.; bd. dirs. Cornell Rsch. Found., Inc.; mem. NSF Task Force: Biology, Behavioral and Social Scis. Looking to 21st Century, 1990-91; cons. W.K. Kellogg Found., 1990-94; chmn. oversight com. collaborative crop rsch. program McKnight Found. Editor: Expanding the Use of Soybeans, 1976; assoc. editor Virology, 1976-94; mem. editl. bd. Plant Molecular Biology-Molecular Breeding, 1994-2004, Environ. Microbiology, 1997—. Pres. Channing-Murray Found., Urbana, Ill., 1976-78; bd. dirs. Sacramento Sci. Ctr., 1989-90. NSF-NATO postdoctoral fellow, 1973. Mem. AAAS, Am. Chem. Soc., Internat. Soc. Plant Molecular Biology, Internat. Soc. Molecular Plant Microbe Interactions, Am. Soc. Microbiology, Soc. Gen. Microbiology. Office: Rutgers Univ Cook Campus 88 Lipman Dr STe 104 New Brunswick NJ 08901

GOODMAN, ROBERT RICHARD, neurosurgeon, educator; Studied, Johns Hopkins U., 1982. Diplomate Am. Bd. Neurol. Surgery. Intern Columbia Presbyn. Med. Ctr., resident, 1984—89; fellow Meml. Sloan-Kettering Cancer Ctr.; with Neurosurgical Assocs. PC, Valley Hosp., Hackensack Univ. Med. Ctr., Columbia Univ., assoc. prof. neurol. surgery. Office: Columbia University Ste 426 710 W 168th St New York NY 10032 Office Phone: 212-305-3774. Office Fax: 212-305-3629.

GOODMAN, STEVEN MICHAEL, conservation biologist; b. Detroit, Aug. 3, 1957; BS, U. Mich., 1984; PhD, U. Hamburg, 2000; HDR, U. Paris-Sud XI, 2005. Mac Arthur field biologist Field Mus. Natural History, Chgo., 1989—. Prof. U. Antananarivo, Madagascar, 1994—; coord. ecology tng. program WWF Madagascar, 1994—. Author: The Birds of Egypt, 1989; editor: Natural Change and Human Impact in Madagasar, 1997; co-editor, lead author The Natural History of Madagascar, 2004. Grantee John and Catherine MacArthur Found., 1995-98, Nat. Geographic Soc.; named MacArthur fellow, John D. and Catherine T. MacArthur Found., 2005. Office: Field Mus of Natural History Roosevelt Rd/Lake Shore Dr Chicago IL 60605

GOODMAN, STEVEN N., medical educator; AB in Applied Math. and Biochemistry, Harvard Coll., 1976; MD, NYU Sch. Medicine, 1981; MHS in Biostatistics, John Hopkins Sch Hygiene and Pub Health, 1986; PhD in Epidemiology, John Hopkins Sch Hygiene and Pub. Health, 1989; grad. work in math. biology, Courant Inst., 1978—79. Cert. Pediat., lic. Mo., Md. Biomathematician, lab for applied studies NIH, 1977, 1979; rsch. assoc. NAS, Com. Risk and Decision Making, Washington, 1980—81; resident, pediat. St. Louis Children's Hosp., Washington U., 1981—84; instr., dept. oncology, divsn. biostatistics (joint appt. in epidemiology) John Hopkins Sch. Medicine, 1988—90, dir., neuroblastoma screening project, 1988—90, group statistician, lung cancer study group, 1988—90, asst. prof., dept. oncology, divsn. biostatistics (joint appt. in epidemiology and biostatistics), 1990—96, assoc. prof., dept. oncology, divsn. biostatistics (joint appt. in epidemiology and biostatistics), 1996—. On faculty of John Hopkins Ctr. for Clin. Trials, 1991—, John Hopkins Grad. Tng. Program in Clin. Investigation, 1994—, John Hopkins Inst. for the History and Philosophy Sci., 1995—, John Hopkins Bioethics Inst., 1998—; assoc. dir. Baltimore Cochrane Ctr., 1994—98; co-dir. John Hopkins Evidence-Based Practice Ctr., 1997—; pediat. staff mem. Sinai Hosp., 1984—91, Union Meml. Hosp., 1984—89; pediat. preceptor John Hopkins Hosp., Harriet Lane Clinic, 1984—85; children and youth clinic physician, part-time John Hopkins Hosp., 1985—86; served on a wide variety of nat. panels, including Inst. Medicine's Com. on Veterans and Agent Orange, Com. on Immunization Safety, Medicare Coverage Adv. Commn., Surgeon General's committees to write the 2001 and 2002 reports on Smoking and Health.; chairs a nat. panel on the health outcomes of children born using assisted reproductive technologies sponsored by the Am. Acad. Pediat. & Am. Soc. Reproductive Medicine; represents the Am. Acad. Pediat. on the Med. Adv. Panel of the Nat. Blue Cross/Blue Shield Tech. Evaluation program; cons. in field. Reviewer for several profl. jours., assoc. editor (statistics) Annals of Internal Medicine, 1987—, assoc. editor Journal of General Internal Medicine, 1999—2001, editor-in-chief Clinical Trials: Journal of the Society for Clinical Trials, 2003—; contbr. several articles to profl. jours. Recipient Nat. Rsch. Svc. award, 1984—88; Harvard Nat. Scholar, 1972. Mem.: Soc. Epidemiological Rsch., Am. Statistical Assn., Inst. Math. Statistics, Soc. for Clin. Trials (bd. dirs. 2001—, chair, student scholarship com. 1999—2003), St. Louis Physicians for Social Responsibility (pres. 1982—84), Delta Omega. Office: Dept Oncology Divsn Biostatistics John Hopkins Sch Medicine 550 No Broadway Ste 1103 Baltimore MD 21205 Address: Rm E-6146 Dept Epidemiology John Hopkins Sch Pu 615 N Wolfe St Baltimore MD 21205 Office Phone: 410-955-4596. Office Fax: 410-955-0859. Business E-Mail: sgoodman@jhmi.edu.

GOODMAN, WAYNE K., psychiatrist, researcher; BS in Elec. Engring., Columbia U.; MD, Boston U. Intern, resident & fellow Yale U. Med. Sch.; founder & chief Yale U. Clinical Neuroscience Rsch. Unit Obsessive Compulsive Disorders Clinic; chmn. U. Fla. Dept. Psychiatry; dir. NIMH Div. Adult Translational Rsch. & Treatment Devel.; chmn. psychiatry Mt. Sinai Sch. Med. Co-founder Obsessive Compulsive Found.; acting chmn. FDA Psychopharmacologic Drug Adv. com.; mem. Fla. Gov. Coun. on Suicide Prevention. Recipient Mysell Lecture award, Harvard U. Fellow: Am. Psychiatric Assn.; mem.: Am. Coll. Neuropsychopharmacology. Achievements include development of Y-BOCS rating standard for OCD. Office: 6001 Executive Blvd Rm 7123 MSC 9632 Bethesda MD 20892 Office Phone: 301-435-8031. E-mail: goodmanw@mail.nih.gov.

GOODNICK, PAUL JOEL, psychiatrist; b. Phila., Sept. 29, 1950; BA magna cum laude, U. Pa.; MD with honors, SUNY Downstate Med. Ctr., Bklyn. Diplomate Am. Bd. Psychiatry and Neurology. Resident Washington U., St. Louis, Columbia U., NYC; fellow Mt. Sinai Hosp., NYC; asst. prof. psychiatry Wayne State U., Detroit, 1980-81, U. Chgo., 1981-84, Columbia U., NYC, 1984-87, U. Miami, Fla., 1987-89, clin. assoc. prof. psychiatry, 1989-90, assoc. prof., 1990-93, prof., 1993—2002, clin. prof. of psychiatry, dir. mood disorders program, dept. psychiatry, 1989—2003; dir. clin. svc. Carrier Clinic, Belle Mead, NJ, 2003—; clin. prof. psychiatry U. Medicine and Dentistry, NJ, 2004—. Dir. outpatient svcs. and affective disorders program Fair Oaks Hosp., Boca/Delray, Fla., 1987-90; cons. APA, 1991. Assoc. editor jour. Lithium, 1989-94; editor: Chronic Fatigue and Related Immune Deficiency Syndromes, 1993, Predictors of Response in Mood Disorders, 1996, Mania, 1998; editor Expert Opinion on Pharmacotherapy, 1999—, Annals of Clinical Psychiatry, 2000-05, Expert Opinion on Drug Safety, 2001—, Therapy, 2005-. Mem. nat. adv. bd. Jerusalem Health Ctr. Recipient Clin. Excellence award N.Y. Alliance for Mentally Ill, 1987, SUNY Downstate award, 2001. Fellow Am. Psychopathol. Assn., Am. Psychiat. Assn., Internat. Soc. Affective Disorders; mem. AAAS, Soc. Biol. Psychiatry, N.Y. Acad. Sci., Am. Acad. Clin. Psychiatry, KP. Office: Carrier Clinic 252 Rte 601 POB 147 Belle Mead NJ 08502 Office Phone: 908-281-1484. Personal E-mail: pgoodnick@aol.com.

GOODRICH, EDWARD (NED) OLIN, surgeon, educator; b. New Haven, May 7, 1925; s. Edward Olin and Laura May (MacKay) G.; m. Gladys Patricia Murphy, July 1, 1950 (div. May, 1974); children: Edward, Timothy, Jonathan; m. Alfreda Leona Verratti, May 20, 1974 (dec. May, 1990); children: Alfred James, Claudia Goodrich Bender. Student, Yale U., 1943-44; MD, N.Y. Med. Coll., 1949. Diplomate Am. Bd. Surgery. Surg. intern Albany (N.Y.) Hosp., 1950, asst. resident in surgery, 1952—53; asst. resident in surgery and surg. rsch. Albany VA Hosp., 1953—56; resident in surgery Albany VA Hosp, 1956—57; attending surgeon St. Vincent Hosp., Santa Fe, 1959—81; asst. resident pathology Med. Coll. Ohio, Toledo, 1983—84; resident in phys. medicine and rehab. Hosp. U. Penn, Phila., 1984; pvt. gen. practice, Ardmore, Pa., 1984-85. Guest rschr. Health Rsch. Lab., Los Alamos, N.Mex., 1962-81; instr. in phys. medicine and rehab. U. Pa., 1987—88; staff Cmty. Vols. in Medicine, West Chester, Pa., 2004—. Author: Your Stomach is a Liar, 2006. Founding trustee Santa Fe Prep. Sch., 1961—70. Col. M.C. USAR, 1949—83, ret. USAR, 1951. Decorated Silver Star. Fellow: ACS (mem. oper. rm. environ. com.); mem.: Surg. Infection Soc., Internat. Surg. Soc., Southwestern Surg. Congress, Am. Soc. Metabolic Bariatric Surgery (sr.), Masons. Achievements include research in clean air, skin cell growth, liver transplantation, obesity, pollution effects on liver, diabetes. Home: 28 Simpson Rd Ardmore PA 19003-2211 *

GOODRICH, ISAAC, neurosurgeon, educator; b. Milledgeville, Ga., Sept. 19, 1939; s. Ellis and Frieda (Bergman) G.; m. Dianne L. Brittain, Aug. 28, 1965; children: Mindy Anne, Scott David, Jennifer Gale. AA, Ga. Mil. Coll., 1959; BS, U. Ga., 1961; MD, Med. Coll. Ga., 1964. Cert. Am. Bd. Neurol. Surgery. Intern Columbia-Presbyn. Med. Ctr., NYC, 1964-65; resident in neurosurgery Yale-New Haven Med. Ctr., 1967-71; practice medicine specializing in neurosurgery New Haven, 1971—. Instr. neurosurgery, Yale U. Med. Sch., 1970-71, asst. clin. prof., 1978-86; assoc. clin. prof., 1986—; attending neurosurgeon Yale-New Haven Hosp., 1973—, Hosp. St. Raphael, 1971—. Contbr. articles to profl. jours. Capt. U.S. Army, 1965-67. Decorated Bronze Star, Air Medal; recipient Disting. Alumni award Ga. Mil. Coll., 1980. Fellow: ACS, Royal Soc. Medicine, Internat. Coll. Surgeons; mem.: AAAS, AMA (Physicians Recognition awards for Continuing Med. Edn.), Vets. Fgn. Wars, Cyber Knife Soc., New Haven County Med. Assn. (pres. 1998—99), Conn. State Med. Soc. (v.p. 2000—01, pres.-elect 2001—02, pres. 2002—03), Conn. State Neurosurg. Soc. (pres. 2001—03), Am. Assn. Neurol. Surgeons, New Eng. Neurosurg. Soc. (pres. 1997—99), Congress Neurol. Surgeons, Veterans of Fgn. Wars, New Haven City Med. Assn. (pres. 1989—90), 28th Inf. Assn., Soc. 1st Inf. Divsn., Am. Legion. Jewish. Home: 84 Links Way Oxford CT 06478 Office: 330 Orchard St Ste 316 New Haven CT 06511-4430 Office Phone: 203-781-3400.

GOODRICH, JAMES TAIT, neuroscientist, neurosurgeon; b. Portland, Oreg., Apr. 16, 1946; s. Richard and Gail (Josselyn) Goodrich; m. Judy Loudin, Dec. 27, 1970. Student, Golden West Coll., 1971—72; AA, Orange Coast Coll., 1972; BS cum laude, U. Calif., Irvine, 1974; PhD, Columbia U., 1970, MPhil, 1979; MD, Coll. Mt. St. Vincent, 2005; DSc honoris causa, Burdenro Neuro. Inst., Moscow, 2008. Diplomate Am. Bd. Neurol. Surgery, Am. Bd. Pediatric Neurosurgery. Intern Columbia-Presbyn. Med. Ctr., NYC, 1980—81; resident in neurol. surgery N.Y. Neurol. Inst., NYC, 1981—86; assoc. Montefiore Med. Ctr., Bronx, NY, 1986—; mem. staff Jacobi Med. Ctr., 1986—; assoc. Weiler Hosp. Albert Einstein Coll. Medicine, NYC, 1986—, prof. nuerosurgery, 1998—. Prof. neurosurgery U. Palermo, Sicily, Italy, 1992—. Editor: Jour. Child Nervous Sys., Neurosurgery; contbr. scientific papers to profl. jours. Recipient Roche Labs. award in Nuersci., 1978, Mead-Johnson award, 1978, Bronze medal, Alumni Assn. Coll. Physicians and Surgeons, 1980, Sandoz award for Outstanding Rsch., 1980, NYC Mayor's award sci. and tech., 2004, Maj. Gen. John L. Russell Leadership award, US Marine Corps U. Found., 2006, Guide to Am.'s Top Surgeons, Consumers Coun. Am., 2008, 2009, Best Med. Drs. in NY, NY Mag., 2008; named Disting. Alumnus, U. Calif., Irvine, 2007, Commencemend Spkr. Giaouating Class, Bronx Leadership Acad. II, 2005, Dep. Comdt.'s Guest of Honor, Evening Parade USMC Barracks, Washington, 2007; named one of Best Med. Drs. in NY, NY Mag., 2006, 2007—09; named to Guide to Am.'s Top Surgeons, Consumers Coun. Am., 2002, Best Drs. in Am., 2003, Best Drs. in America, 2009; Willamette Industries scholar, NIH grantee. Fellow: Royal Soc. Medicine (London); mem.: AMA, AAAS, Dionysius Coun. Presbyn. Hosp. N.Y.C., Les Amis du Vin, Am. Osler Soc., Soc. Ancient Medicine, Columbia Presbyn. Med. Soc., Soc. Bibliography Natural History (London), ISIS History Sci. Soc., Med. History Soc. N.J., Congress Neurol. Surgeons, Am. Assn. Neurol. Surgery (chmn. sect. history neurol. surgery), N.Y. Acad. Scis., Brit. Brain Rsch. Assn., Am. Assn. History Medicine (Sir William Osler medal 1977—78), N.Y. Acad. Medicine (Melicow award 1980), Internat. Soc. Pediat. Neurosurgeons, European Brain Rsch. Assn., Am. Soc. Pediat. Neurosurgeons, Am. Epilepsy Soc., Am. Assn. Neurol. Surgeons, U. Calif. Alumni Assn., Friends Columbia U. Librs., Worshipful Soc. Apothecaries (London), South Coast Wine Explorers Club (past chmn.), Sigma Xi, Alpha Gamma Sigma. Achievements include research in neuronal regeneration, brain reconstruction and craniofacial reconstruction. Home: 125 Tweed Blvd Nyack NY 10960-4913 Office: Albert Einstein Coll Medicine Montefiore Med Ctr Div Pediat Neurosurg 111 E 210th St Bronx NY 10467-2401 Office Phone: 718-920-4197. Business E-Mail: goodrich@aecom.yu.edu.

GOODRIDGE, ALAN GARDNER, research biochemist, educator; b. Peabody, Mass., Apr. 2, 1937; s. Lester Elmer and Gertrude Edith (Gardner) G.; m. R. Ann Funderburk, Aug. 19, 1960; children— Alan Gardner Jr., Bryant C. BS in Biology, Tufts U., 1958; MS in Zoology, U. Mich., 1963, PhD in Zoology, 1964. Rsch. fellow dept. biol. chemistry Harvard Med. Sch., Boston, 1964—66; asst. prof. physiology U. Kans. Med. Ctr., Kansas City, 1966-68; assoc. prof. Banting and Best dept. med. rsch. U. Toronto, Ont., Can., 1968-76, prof. Banting and Best dept. med. rsch., 1976-77; prof. pharmacology and biochemistry Case Western Res. U., Cleve., 1977-87; prof., head dept. biochemistry U. Iowa, 1987-96; prof. biochemistry Ohio State U., 1996—2001, dean Coll. Biol. Scis., 1996-2001, exec. dean Colls. of Arts and Sci., 1999-2001; prof. biol. scis. and pharmacology U. Toledo, 2002—06, provost, 2003—06, exec. v.p. academic affairs and enrollment svcs., 2002—06, prof., biochemistry and cancer biology, 2006—; provost and acting pres. Alfaisal U., Saudi Arabia, 2007—09. Assoc. editor Jour. Biol. Chemistry, 1990-2002, Ann. Rev. of Nutrition, 1994-99, Jour. Lipid Rsch., 1995-99; contbr. numerous articles to profl. jours. Mem. bd. trustees Toledo Opera Assn. 2009-. Served with US Army, 1958—61. Grantee Med. Rsch. Coun. Can., 1968-77, NIH, 1966-68, 77-97, USDA 1986-90, 93-97; Josiah Macy Jr. faculty scholar, 1975-76. Mem. AAAS, Am. Soc. Biochemistry and Molecular Biology. Home: 10 Exmoor Ottawa Hills OH 43615-2156 Home Phone: 419-537-1635; Office Phone: 419-383-5291. Business E-Mail: alan.goodridge@utoledo.edu.

GOODWIN, ANDREW WIRT, II, radiologist; b. Oil City, Pa., Feb. 4, 1932; s. Frank Bert and Florence Bickford (Green) G.; m. Anita Faye Adkins, May 27, 1987; children: Andrew, Victoria, Mary Elizabeth, Mark H., Martha J., Lisa R. BA, Colgate U., 1953; MD, U. Mich., 1957. Diplomate Am. Bd. Radiology, Am. Bd. Nuclear Medicine. Intern Mary Hitchcock Meml. Hosp., Hanover, NH, 1957-58; resident in radiology Mayo Clinic, Rochester, Minn., 1958-61, resident, 1958-61; radiologist Associated Radiologists, Inc., Charleston, W.Va., 1961-86, Radiol. Physicians Assn., Fairmont, W.Va., 1988—2002; pvt. practice. Republican. Episc. Home Fax: 304-926-0851. Personal E-mail: agoodwinii@aol.com.

GOODWIN, BEATRICE, nursing educator, consultant; d. David and Myrtle Goodwin. BS in Nursing, Vanderbilt U., 1955; MA, NYU, 1960, PhD, 1970; PhD (hon.), Valparaiso U., 2003. RN NY, 1958. Prof. nursing CUNY, NYC, 1970—98; vis. prof. Catholic U. Chile, Santiago, 1972—73, U. Conception, Chile, 1984—88, U. Los Andes, Santiago, 1999—2000, U. Chile, Santiago, 2006—, U. Andres Bello, Santigo, Chile, 2006—; adj. prof. nursing NYU, NYC, 1998—. External reviewer U. Ottawa, Canada, 1978; cons. clin. nursing Surgeon Gen., US Air Force, DC, 1980—82; cons. curriculum in baccalaureate nursing World Health Orgn., DC, 1986—88; dir. Latin Am. projects NYU Coll. Nursing, NYC, 1998—; keynote spkr. Nat. Colloquium Nursing Rsch., Bogota, Colombia, 2001, Internat. Nursing Conf., Chile, 2002, Colombia, 04; curriculum cons. programs in nursing Colombian Assn. Faculties Nursing, Chile, 2006—; vis. prof. U. Andrés Bello, Santiago, Chile, 2006—, U. Chile, Santiago, 2006—. Founding editor: Jour. Nursing Scholarship, 1964—69. Mem. Career Devel. Bd., US Air Force Nurse Corps, DC, 1979—81, NYU Nurse Alumni Assn., NYC, 2002—. Decorated Meritorious Svc. Medal US Air Force. Mem.: Internat. Ctr. Nursing Rsch., Chilean Assn. Nursing Edn. (hon.), Chilean Assn. Edn. in Nursing (hon.), Sigma Theta Tau (life), Kappa Delta Pi (life). Home: 220 E 65th St Apt 21K New York NY 10065 Office Phone: 212-998-5321. Personal E-mail: beagoodwin@aol.com.

GOODWIN, JEAN MCCLUNG, psychiatrist; b. Pueblo, Colo., Mar. 28, 1946; d. Paul Stanley and Geraldine (Smart) McClung; m. James Simeon Goodwin, Aug. 8, 1970; children: Laura (dec.), Amanda Harding Goodwin, Robert Caleb, Paul Joshua, Elizabeth Cronin Goodwin. BA in Anthropology summa cum laude, Radcliffe Coll., 1967; MD, Harvard U., 1971; MPH, UCLA, 1972. Diplomate Am. Bd. Psychiatry and Neurology, Am. Bd. Forensic Psychiatry, cert. adult psychoanalysis Am. Psychoanalytic Assn. Resident in psychiatry Georgetown U. Hosp., Washington, 1972-74, U. N.Mex. Sch. Medicine, 1974-76, asst. dir., dir. psychiat. residents tng., 1979-85; prof.

Med. Coll. Wis., 1985-92, U. Tex. Med. Br., Galveston, 1992-98, prof. clin. psychiatry, 1998—; pvt. practice in gen. psychiatry, psychoanalysis. From instr. to assoc. prof. dept. psychiatry U. N.Mex. Sch. Medicine, 1976-85; cons. protective services Dept. Human Services, N.Mex., 1976-84; faculty Houston-Galveston Psychoanalytic Inst., 1999—; founding bd. dirs. Houston-Galveston Trauma Inst.; lectr. in field Author: Effects of High Altitude on Human Birth, 1969, Sexual Abuse: Incest Victims and Their Families, 1982, 2d edit., 1989, Rediscovering Childhood Trauma: Historical Casebook and Clinical Applications, 1993, Mischief and Mercy, 1993; co-author (with Reina Attias) Splintered Reflections: Images of the Body in Trauma, 1999; mem. editl. bd. Jour. Traumatic Stress, 1985-93, Dissociation, 1988-98, Psychotherapy Rev., 1998-2000, Trauma and Dissociation, 2000—; contbr. articles to profl. jours. Chmn. work group on child sexual abuse Surgeon Gen.'s Conf. on Violence and Pub. Health, Leesburg, Va., 1985; mem. adv. bd. Nat. Resource Ctr. on Child Sexual Abuse, 1989-96. Recipient Esther Haar award Am. Acad. Psychoanalysis, 1990, Cornelia Wilbur award Internat. Soc. for Study of Dissociation, 1994; Nat. Cen. Child Abuse and Neglect grantee, 1979-82, Nat. Inst. Aging grantee, 1980-85. Fellow Internat. Soc. Study Dissociation (exec. com. 1991-96), Am. Psychiat. Assn. (dist. br. treas., sec. N.Mex. br. 1980-82, exhibits and programs subcoms. 1985-91) Democrat. Roman Catholic. Office: 4925 Fort Crockett Blvd Apt 510 Galveston TX 77551-5949 Office Phone: 409-762-1101. Personal E-mail: jmgoodwin@aol.com.

GOODWIN, PAMELA J., oncologist, educator; Scientist Samuel Lunenfeld Rsch. Inst., chmn. breast rsch.; prof. med. U. Toronto Mt. Sinai Hosp.; dir. Marvelle Koffler Breast Ctr. Office: Marvelle Koffler Breast Centre Mount Sinai Hospital 600 University Ave 12th Fl Toronto ON Canada M5G 1X5 Office Phone: 416-586-8799.

GOODWIN, SCOTT CRAIG, interventional radiologist; b. Gardena, Calif., July 15, 1957; s. Alfred Boree Goodwin and Dorothy Tena Curtis; m. Suzie May El-Saden, Aug. 7, 1993; children: Alexander Boree, Adam El-Saden. BS magna cum laude with dept. honors, UCLA, 1979; MD, Harvard U., 1984. Intern in internal medicine St. Luke's Hosps./Wash. U., St. Louis, 1984-85; resident in diagnostic radiology UCLA Med. Ctr., 1985-88, fellowship in cardiovascular and interventional radiology, 1988-89, vis. asst. prof. radiology, 1989, from asst. prof. to assoc. prof., 1989—2001, prof. radiology, 2001—, chief vascular, interventional radiology, 1994-2001, vice chmn. radiology, 2003—07; chief angiography and interventional radiology Daniel Freeman Hosp., Inglewood, Calif., 1989-91; vice chmn. imaging svcs. Irvine (Calif.) Med. Ctr., 1991-92; chmn., prof. radiology Wayne State U., Detroit, 2001—02; chmn. radiology Greater L.A. VA Med. Ctr., 2002—07; vice chmn. radiology UCLA Med. Ctr., 2002—07; chmn. prof. radiology UCI Med. Ctr., Orange, Calif., 2007—. Lectr. in field. Author (with others): Uterine Fibroid Embolization, 2009; contbr. articles to profl. jours. Recipient numerous rsch. grants. Office: UCI Med Ctr 101 The City Drive S Rt 140 Orange CA 92868 Office Phone: 714-456-5033. Business E-Mail: sgoodwin@mednet.ucla.edu, sgoodwin@uci.edu.

GOODYEAR, LAURIE J., physiologist, educator; BS, Springfield Coll., 1981; MS in Exercise Physiology, U. South Calif., 1983; PhD in Cell Biology, U. Vt., 1989. Fellow U. Vt. Dept. Med., 1989—90, Harvard Med. Sch., 1990—92, instr., 1992—95, asst. prof., 1995—2001, assoc. prof., 2002—; fellow Joslin Diabetes Ctr., 1990—92, rsch. assoc. metabolism section, 1992—93, investigator, 1993—2002, metabolism section head, 2000—, sr. investigator, 2002—, transgenic core dir. Reviewer various NIH Study Sections; editorial bd. various med. Jours. Fellow: Am. Coll. Sports Med. (chmn. molecular & cellular regulatory mechanisms interest group 1997—2000); mem.: AAAS, Am. Physiological Soc., Am. Diabetes Assn (vice chmn. exercise coun. 2003—). Office: One Joslin Pl Boston MA 02215 Mailing: 17 Ledge Hill Rd Southborough MA 01772 Office Fax: 617-732-2650. E-mail: laurie.godoyear@joslin.harvard.edu.

GOOLEY, TED ALAN, statistician; b. Spokane, Wash., July 22, 1962; BS, Wash. State U., 1984; PhD, U. Ariz., 1990. Mem. Fred Hutchinson Cancer Rsch. Ctr., 1992—. Office: 1100 Fairview Ave N PO Box 19024 Seattle WA 98109-1024 Business E-Mail: tgooley@fhcrc.org.

GOOLKASIAN, PAULA A., psychologist, educator; b. Methuen, Mass., Aug. 9, 1948; d. Paul K. and Sadie T. (Touma) G.; m. Francis C. Martin, July 29, 1978; 1 child, Christopher. BA, Emmanuel Coll., 1970; MS, Iowa State U., 1972, PhD, 1974. Asst. prof. U. N.C., Charlotte, 1974-79, assoc. prof., 1979-85, prof. psychology, 1985—, pres. faculty, 1989—. Cons. in field. Exec. editor: Jour. Gen. Psychology. NDEA fellow, 1971-74; grantee NSF, NIH, numerous others. Fellow APA, Assn. Psychol. Scis.; mem. Cognitive Sci. Soc., Psychonomics Soc., Soc. Computers in Psychology (sec.-treas. 1989-91, pres. 1994), Sigma Xi, Phi Kappa Phi. Office: U NC Dept Psychology 9201 University City Blvd Charlotte NC 28223

GOOSBY, ERIC PAUL, ambassador, epidemiologist; b. Aug. 28, 1952; MD, U. San Francisco, 1978. AIDS activity divsn. attending physician San Francisco Gen. Hosp., 1986, assoc. med. dir. AIDS Clinic, 1987; dir. HIV Svcs. US Pub. Health Svc., Health Resources and Svcs. Adminstrn., Washington, 1991—94; dir. Office HIV/AIDS Policy US Dept. Health and Human Services, Washington, 1994—2000; interim. dir. Nat. AIDS Policy Office, The White House, Washington, 1997, acting dep. dir., 2000; CEO, chief medical officer Pangaea Global AIDS Found., San Francisco, 2001—09; amb. at-large, coord. US Govt. Activities to Combat HIV/AIDS Globally US Dept. State, Washington, 2009—. Prof. clin. medicine U. Calif., San Francisco. Office: US Dept State Office of US Global AIDS Coord 2201 C St NW Washington DC 20520 *

GOOSKENS, ROBERT HENRICUS JOHANNUS, pediatric neurologist; b. Eindhoven, Brabant, The Netherlands, Nov. 4, 1948; s. Theo M. and Anne Elisabeth (Gimbrère) G. MD, U. Utrecht, The Netherlands, 1975, PhD, 1988. Resident in neurology Univ. Hosp. Utrecht, 1975-81, resident in clin. neurophysiology, 1981-82; rsch. child neurologist Univ. Children's Hosp., Utrecht, 1982-84, cons. child neurologist, 1984—. Cons. child neurologist Psychiat. Child Clinic, Vught, The Netherlands, 1984-94, Rehab. Ctr. De Hoogstraat, Utrecht; med. mgr. Sylvia Toth Ctr., 1999—, mem. compaints authority U. Hosp. Utrecht. Contbr. articles to internat. med. jours. Recipient award Jour. Ultrasound Medicine and Biology, 1995, Best Clin. paper award World Fedn. for Ultrasound in Medicine and Biology, 1995; rsch. grantee Prevention Fund The Netherlands, 1987, 91, Catharyne Found., 1998, Johannes Found. Fund, 1998, Jan Ivo Found., 2001, De Phelps Found., 2003. Mem. Dutch Child Neurology Soc. (bd. dirs. 1990—), Dutch Spina Bifida Soc. (sec. 1990—), Internat. Child Neurology Assn., Internat. Soc. Rsch. into Hydrocephalus and Spina Bifida, Internat. Cerebral Palsy Soc., European Ultrasound Soc., Dutch Soc. of Tech. Svcs. Roman Catholic. Avocations: skiing, golf, hockey, sculpture, travel. Home: Prins Hendriklaan 35 3583 EC Utrecht Netherlands Office: U Childrens Hosp Child Neur Lundlaan 6 3584 EA Utrecht Netherlands Office Phone: 31 88 755 4000. Office Fax: 31 88 755 5350.

GOPAL, DEEPAK VENU, gastroenterologist; b. Birmingham, Eng., Aug. 14, 1968; s. Candade Srinivas and Sama Parthasarathy (Usha) Venugopal; m. Lalitha Venkateshwaran Iyer, Sept. 11, 2000. MD, Meml. U. Newfoundland, St. John's, Can., 1993. Diplomate Am. Bd. Internal Medicine, Am. Bd. Gastroenterology. Resident in internal medicine U. Toronto, Ontario, Canada, 1993—96; chief med. resident in internal medicine Sunnybrook Health Scis. Ctr.-U. Toronto, Ontario, Canada, 1996—97; fellow divsn. gastroenterology Oregon Health & Sci. U., Portland, Oreg., 1997—2000, asst. prof. medicine divsn. gastroenterology, 2001—. Contbr. articles to profl. jours. Recipient Rsch. award, U. Toronto, 1996, Resident Rsch. award, 1997; fellow Janssen Gi fellow, World Congress of Gastroenterology, Austria, 1998; scholar Bursary scholar, Canadian Internat. Devel. Agy., 1991, GI fellow/resident Reporter scholar, Wyeth-Ayerst: Digestive Diseases Week, Calif., 2000. Fellow: Royal Coll. Physicians & Surgeons Canada; mem.: AMA, ACP (Best Clinical Vignette 1997), Oregon Cancer Inst., Can. Soc. Internal Medicine, Am. Gastroenterology Assn., Am. Coll. Gastroenterology, Am. Soc. Gastrointestinal Endoscopy, Oreg. Med. Assn. Office: Oregon Health and Sci Univ PV-310, 3181 SW Sam Jackson Park Rd Portland OR 97201-3098 also: 2978 Bosshard Dr Fitchburg WI 53711-5855 Business E-Mail: gopalde@ohsu.edu.

GOPE, RAJALAKSHMI, geneticist, educator; b. Uthamapalayam, Tamil Nadu, India, Feb. 21, 1952; d. Irudayamary Savarimuthu and Savarimuthu Antony; m. Mohan Lal Gope, Dec. 17, 1982; 1 child, Abhisar. BSc, Bangalore U., 1972, MSc, 1976; PhD, Indian Inst. Sci., 1981. Cert. rsch. scientist Indian Inst. of Sci., 1981. Asst. prof. NIMH and Neuroscis., Bangalore, Karnataka, India, 1997—2001, assoc. prof., 2001—. Sr. rsch. assoc. Northwestern U., Chgo., Mich. State U., East Lansing; asst. prof. Creighton U., Omaha; postdoctoral fellow U. Tex. Health Sci. Ctr., San Antonio, 1981—83, Baylor Coll. Medicine, Houston, 1983—86, Creighton U., Omaha, 1987—88; reader M.S. U., Baroda, India; sr. rsch. fellow Indian Inst. Sci., Bangalore, Karnataka, 1976—78, jr. rsch. fellow, 1978—81. Contbr. articles to profl. and sci. jours. Recipient John C. Henefick Faculty Devel. award, Health Future Found., 1990; grantee, Nebr. Dept. Health, 1990, Life Scis. Rsch. Bd., Dept. Biotech., Govt. India, 2000—03, 2001—04; fellow, Indian Inst. Sci., 1978—81, 1976—78. Mem.: AAAS, Indian Soc. Cell Biology (life), Soc. Biol. Chemists India (life), Indian Sci. Congress Assn. (life), Indian Soc. Human Genetics (life). Achievements include research in For the first time demonstrated that the sodium butyrate treatment changes the methylation pattern of the RB1 gene in human colon tumor cell line HT29; For the first time published data showing that the growth factor PDGF AA might be limiting the EGF-mediated wound repair process; For the first time provided evidence that the sodium butyrate treatement alters the expression of RB1 and p53 genes and the expression and the phosphorylation of Rb protein; For the first time demonstrated that the level of total Rb protein and the level of phosphorylated form of the Rb protein are increased in human colon carcinomas; For the first time shown that the level of RB1 and p53 gene expressions can be used for the classification of human colon carcinomas; For the first time shown the increased expression of RB1 gene in human colon carcinomas compared to the normal colonic mucosa; For the first time shown the subgenome length packaged DNA in bacteriophage p22 using agarose gel electrophoresis; For the first time showed the rate of DNA entry into capsids in bacteriophage p22 in vitro DNA packaging; Showed the involvement extrachromosomal DNA in the formation of parasporal crystalline proteinaceous toxin in Bacillus thuringiensis var. thuringiensis. Home: NIMH and Neuroscis Qtrs No 36 Type IV Bl 2 Karnataka Bangalore 560 029 India Office: NIMH and Neuroscis Dept Human Genetics 2900 Hosur Rd Karnataka Bangalore 560 029 India Office Fax: 091 08 2656 4830. E-mail: rgope@nimhans.kar.nic.in.

GOPPELT, JOHN WALTER, physician, psychiatrist; b. Saginaw, Mich., Jan. 20, 1924; s. Paul Gustave and Marion LeRoy (Payne) G.; m. Martha Keller Rowland, Mar. 31, 1956; 1 child, Edmund H. S.B., MIT, Cambridge, Mass., 1949; MD, U. Pa., Phila., 1955. Diplomate Am. Bd. Psychiatry and Neurology. Intern Bryn Mawr Hosp., Pa., 1955—56; resident in psychiatry Inst. of Pa. Hosp., Phila., 1956-59; practice medicine, specializing in psychiatry Haverford, Pa., 1959—. Contbr. articles to profl. jours. Chmn. Drug and Alcohol Coun. Del. County, Media, Pa., 1979—83; committeeman Rep. Party, Haverford Twp., Pa., 1980. With US Army, 1943—46. Recipient Legion of Honor award Chapel of Four Chaplains. Mem. AMA, Am. Psychiat. Assn., NY Acad. Scis., Math. Assn. America, Sigma Xi. Avocation: mathematics. Address: 369 Exeter Rd Haverford PA 19041-1084 Office Phone: 610-649-2047.

GORALCZYK, JERZY WLODZIMIERZ, physician, researcher; b. Krakow, Poland, Feb. 10, 1934; s. Franciszek and Katarzyna Goralczyk; m. Marta Kozik, Sept. 1, 1979; children: Katarzyna, Zachariasz Jerzy, Anita. MD, Med. Acad., Krakow, 1957. Obstetrician asst. Dist. Hosp., Zagan, Poland, 1957—60; sr. surg. asst. Pulmonary Hosp., Zakopane, Poland, 1960—71, dept. head, 1984—2002; sr. profs. asst. Chest Surgery Clinic, Zakopane, Poland, 1972—77; sr. surg. asst. County Hosp., Tarnow, Poland, 1977—79; sr. profs. asst. Inst. of Oncology, Krakow, Poland, 1979—80, II Dept. of Thoracic Surgery, Zakopane, Poland, 1980—83, II Chest Surgery Clinic, Zakopane, Poland, 1980—83; ret., 2002. Dir. postgraduate edn. Ctr. of Postgraduate Medicine, Warszawa, Poland, 1981—2001; oncological surgeon County Gen., Nowy Sacz County, Poland, 1983—98. Recipient Gold Disting. Cross, The Cavaliers Cross of Restitution of Poland, 1976, 1989. Fellow: Polish Bd. of Thoracic Surgery; mem.: Polish Soc. of Oncological Surgery, Polish Oncological Assn., Soc. of Polish Surgeons. Home: Chramcowki 2 Zakopane 34-500 Poland Office: Pulmonary Hosp Ul. Gladkie 1 34-500 Zakopane Poland Office Fax: +48 1820 14632, +48 1820 14632. Personal E-mail: goral_zak@interia.pl.

GORARD, DAVID A., gastroenterologist; b. London, Dec. 23, 1960; s. William J. and Antonia Gorard; m. Philippa M. Cooper, June 7, 1986; children: Lucy, Camilla, Henry. MB, BChir, St. Mary's Hosp. Med. Sch., London, 1984; MD, U. London, 1994. Registrar Westminster & Queen Mary's Hosp., London, 1987-89; rsch. fellow St. Bartholomew's Hosp., London, 1990-94; sr. registrar Royal London Hosp., 1994-96; cons. physician Wycombe Hosp., Bucks, England, 1996—. Contbr. articles to profl. jours. Mem. Royal Coll. Physicians, British Soc. Gastroent. Office: Wycombe Hosp High Wycombe Bucks HP11 2TT England

GORBACHEV, ANTON, biomedical researcher; b. Russia, Dec. 7, 1970; MS, Moscow State U., 1991, PhD, 1995. Project scientist Cleve. Clinic, 1998—. Scientist Devel. grant, Am. Heart Assn. Mem.: Am. Assn. Immunologists. Office: 9500 Euclid Ave Cleveland OH 44195 Business E-Mail: gorbaca@ccf.org.

GORBIEN, MARTIN JOHN, medical educator, geriatrician; b. Chgo., Dec. 24, 1955; MD, Autonomous U., Guadalajara, Mexico, 1983. Cert. internal medicine 1996, geriatric medicine 1998, palliative care 2008. Intern to resident, geriatric medicine Mercy Hosp. and Med. Ctr., Chgo., 1984—87; fellowship, geriatric medicine UCLA, 1987—89; asst. prof. medicine U. Chgo. Pritzer Sch. Medicine, Chgo., 1994—98; assoc. prof., dir. Rush Med. Coll., St. Lukes Med. Ctr., Geriatric Dept., Chgo., 1998—. Office: Rush U Med Ctr 1725 W Harrison St Ste 955 Chicago IL 60612 Office Phone: 312-942-3362, 312-942-5321. Business E-Mail: mgorbien@rush.edu.

GORBUNOVA, VERA ANDREEVNA, oncologist; d. Audrey Gorbunov and Gelena Gorbunova; m. Anatoliy Podobed; children: Audrey Podobed, Svetlana Kobina;. Diploma, Second Moscow Med. Inst., 1970; D of Med. Scis., Cancer Rsch. Ctr. Russia, 1985. Cert. prof. 1995. Resident dept. chemotherapy N.N. Blokhin Russian Cancer Rsch. Ctr., Moscow, 1970—72, postgrad., 1973—75, rsch. asst., 1975—79, sr. rsch. asst., 1979—85, leading rsch. asst., 1985—89, chief dept. chemotherapy, 1989—. Recipient Hon. Worker of Sci., Russian Fedn., 2001; named Laureate, 2001. Achievements include research in chemotherapy of solid tumors. Office Phone: 007-495-324-9479. Personal E-mail: veragorbunova@mail.ru.

GORBY SCHMIDT, MARTHA LOUISE, pharmacologist, researcher; d. Charles and Louise Gorby. BS in Nursing, Villanova U., 1983. RN Pa., 1983; cert. paralegal. Clin. rsch. asst. Scirex, Blue Bell, Pa., 1996—97; mgr. data quality compliance Aventis Pharma/Rhone Poulenc Rorer, Bridgewater, NJ, 1998—2001; mgr. clin. data rev. Premier Rsch. Worldwide, Phila., 1997—98; assoc. dir. Yamanouchi Pharma Am., Paramus, NJ, 2001—04; global project data mgr. Merck Rsch. Labs., Blue Bell, 2004—07, sr. clin. rsch. specialist-clin. rsch. oncology, 2007—. Meddra blue ribbon panel Northrup Grumman, Alexandria, Va., 2003; spkr. in field. Editor: Pen and Ink Mag. (Svc. Award, 1979). Office vol. adminstr. Ch. Good Samaritan, Paoli, Pa., 1990—94, 12 step group facilitator, 1990—94, music dir. sch. com., advt. chmn., 1990—94. Mem.: NAFE, AACN, ANA, N.Y. Acad. Scis., Oncology Nurse Soc., Am. Chem. Soc., Am. Heart Assn., Assn. Clin. Rsch. Profls., Soc. Clin. Data Mgmt., Regulatory Affairs Profl. Soc., Drug Info. Assn. (spl. interest action com. 2003—), Am. Soc. Clin. Oncology (assoc.). Episcopalian. Achievements include research in oncology-early to late stage development. Avocations: music, travel, reading, comedy, hiking. Office: Merck Rsch Labs PO Box 1000 UC-72 North Wales PA 19454 Personal E-mail: mlgs2327@verizon.net. Business E-Mail: martha_schmidt@merck.com.

GORDIS, ENOCH, retired science administrator, internist; b. NYC, Feb. 21, 1931; s. Robert and Fannie (Jacobson) Gordis. BA, Columbia U., 1950, MD, 1954. Fellow Dazian Found., NYC, 1958—59; clin. fellow Mt. Sinai Hosp., NYC, 1959, chief resident dept. medicine, 1960; assoc. prof. dept. medicine Mt. Sinai Sch. Medicine, NYC, 1971—79, prof. medicine, 1979—; guest investigator Rockefeller U., NYC, 1961—62, rsch. assoc., 1962—63, assoc. prof., 1965—71, prof. clin. medicine, 1971—; dir., mem. treatment prevention study sect. Nat. Inst. on Alcohol Abuse and Alcoholism, Rockville, Md., 1986—2001. Extensive pub. appearances in U.S. and abroad on topics related to alcoholism and addiction. Co-author: Controversies in Clinical Care, 1981, Current Therapy in Gastroenterology and Liver Disease, 1986; manuscript reviewer: Annals Internal Medicine, Butterworth Inc., Clin. Textbook of Addictive Disorders, European Jour. Clin. Investigation, Jour. Clin. Investigation, Jour. Lipid Rsch., Jour. Studies in Alcohol, Med. Letter, others, assoc. editor: Alcoholism: Clin. and Exptl. Rsch., 1979—, mem. editl. bd.: U. Medicine and Dentistry of N.J., —, N.J. Med. Sch., —; contbr. articles, abstracts to profl. jours. Corr. Com. on Human Rights, 1988—89. Capt. M.C. US Army, 1955—57. Fellow: ACP; mem.: Rsch. Soc. on Alcoholism, Inst. of Medicine of NAS (corr. com. human rights 1988—89), Am. Physiol. Soc., Am. Soc. Addiction Medicine, Am. Gastroent. Assn., Am. Fedn. for Clin. Rsch., Am. Coll. Neuropsychopharmacology, Adv. Group on Fellowships in Alcohol and Drug Abuse, Phi Beta Kappa, Sigma Xi.

GORDIS, LEON, physician; b. NYC, July 19, 1934; s. Robert and Fannie (Jacobson) Gordis; m. Hadassah Cohen, June 14, 1955; children: Daniel, Elihu, Jonathan. BA, Columbia, 1954; BHL, Jewish Theol. Sem., 1954; MD, SUNY, 1958; MPH, Johns Hopkins U., 1966, DrPH, 1968. Intern, then resident in pediat. Jewish Hosp., Bklyn., 1958—61; fellow in pediat. Sch. Medicine Johns Hopkins U., 1962—66, instr. Sch. Medicine, 1966—68, assoc. prof. epidemiology, Sch. Hygiene and Pub. Health, 1971—73; asst. med. dir. ambulatory care Sinai Hosp., Balt., 1966—68, chief dept. community medicine, 1968—69; prof. epidemiology Johns Hopkins, 1973—, chmn. dept. epidemiology, 1975—93; prof. pediat., 1992—; assoc. dean admissions & Acad. affairs Johns Hopkins Sch. Medicine, 1993—99. Vis. prof. med. ecology Hebrew U., Jerusalem, 1969—71. With USPHS, 1961—65. Fellow: AAAS, Am. Acad. Pediat.; mem.: APHA, Assn. Tchrs. Preventive Medicine, Am. Heart Assn., Soc. Pediatric Rsch., Am. Pediatric Soc., Am. Epidemiol. Soc. (pres. 1983—84), Soc. Epidemiologic Rsch. (pres. 1979—80), Inst. Medicine NAS. Home: 105 Swanhill Ct Baltimore MD 21208-1608 Office: 615 N Wolfe St Baltimore MD 21205-2103 Business E-Mail: lgordis@jhsph.edu.

GORDON, BENJAMIN DICHTER, pediatrician, health facility administrator, educator; b. Bklyn., Mar. 4, 1927; s. Abraham S. and Selma F. (Dichter) G.; m. Ellen M. Nimaroff, June 10, 1951; children: Wendy, Marcy, Amanda. AB, Amherst Coll., 1947; MD, U. Md., 1951. Diplomate Am. Bd. of Pediatrics. Rotating intern Kings County

Hosp., Bklyn., 1951-52, asst. resident in pediatrics, 1953-54, Maimonides Hosp., Bklyn., 1952-53; research fellow Irvington House, Irvington-on-Hudson, NY, 1954-55; practice medicine specializing in pediatrics Stratford & Bridgeport, Conn., 1955-73; assoc. attendant, emergency dept. Bridgeport Hosp., 1973-78; asst. dir. emergency dept. Danbury (Conn.) Hosp., 1978-82; clin. dir. Union Carbide Corp., Danbury, 1982-87; med. dir Chesebrough-Ponds, Inc., Trumbull, Conn., 1987-90. Asst. prof. occupational medicine Yale U.; chmn. Rheumatic Fever com. Conn. State Heart Assn.; cons. to cosmetic industry and product-testing labs.; former attending occupl. med. clinic Milton (Mass.) Hosp.; attending occupl. med. clinic Jordan Hosp., Plymouth, Mass.; cons. Clin. Rsch. Ctr. Cape Cod. Author: Practical Guide for New Parents, 1970, (poetry) The Nohnlove, Common Sense Weight Control; contbr. articles to profl. jours. Past chmn., Bd. Health, Town of Yarmouth, Mass.; mem. Regional Emergency Planning Com. for Barnstable County. Served with USNR, 1945-46. Fellow: Am. Coll. Occupl. and Environ. Medicine, Am. Acad. Pediats.; mem.: Barnstable Dist. Med. Soc. (com. on violence), Mass. Med. Soc., Occupl. Med. Assn. Conn. (pres. 1987—88), Fairfield County Med. Soc. (past chmn. pub. health com.), Conn. State Med. Soc. (past chmn. comty. pub. health), Williams Club (N.Y.C.). Jewish. Avocations: music, dance, reading, history, golf. Home: 14 Hillsea Rd Yarmouth Port MA 02675-1111 Personal E-mail: b.gordonmd@comcast.net.

GORDON, CRAIG JEFFREY, oncologist, educator; b. Detroit, Feb. 10, 1953; s. Maury Allen and Shirley Phoebe (Jacoby) G.; m. Susan Ann Blase, Aug. 3, 1980; children: Sari, Scott, Brittany. BS, Oakland U., 1978; DO, U. Osteo. Med. and Health Scis, Des Moines, 1983. Diplomate Am. Bd. Internal Medicine, Am. Bd. Med. Oncology. Intern-chief Botsford Gen. Hosp., Farmington Hills, Mich., 1983-84, resident, 1984-87; fellow in hematology and oncology Wayne State Univ. (affiliated Hosp.'s Prog.), Detroit, 1987-90, fellow-chief, 1989-90; clin. asst. prof. dept. medicine Wayne State U., Detroit, 1990—; dir. divsn. hematology and oncology Botsford Hosp., Livonia, Mich., 1992—; med. dir. Angela Hospice, 1993—98; pres. Clin. Oncology Assocs., 1998—; dir. Botsford Hosp. Cancer Ctr., 2008—; prin. investigator Detroit Clin. Rsch. Ctr. Mem. extrarenal transplantation com. Mich. Dept. Pub. Health; physician advisor Gilda's Club Mich., 1993—2001; mem. Greater Detroit Area Health Care Coun. on Cancer Care. Contbr. articles to profl. jours. Named Intern of the Yr. Botsford Hosp. Staff, 1984, Resident of the Yr., 1985-87; named to Best Doctors in Metro Detroit Hour Mag., 2005, 2007-2010; clin. fellow Am. Cancer Soc., 1987-90. Fellow Am. Coll. Osteo. Internists; mem. Am. Osteo. Assn., Mich. Assn. Osteo. Physicians and Surgeons, Mich. Soc. Hematology and Oncology, Am. Soc. Clin. Oncologists, Oakland County Osteo. Assn. Avocations: sports, popular music, astronomy, electronics. Office: 27900 Grand River Ave Farmington MI 48336 Home Phone: 248-538-7922. Personal E-mail: gordondo@comcast.net.

GORDON, FRANK JEFFREY, medical educator; b. Washington, Dec. 5, 1948; married; 2 children. Attended, Case Western Reserve U., 1966-69; BS in Biology, N.Mex. State U., 1972, MA in Psychology, 1974; PhD in Biopsychology, U. Iowa, 1980. Interdisciplinary rsch. fellow U. Iowa, Iowa City, 1978-80, postdoctoral rsch. fellow Dept. Internal Medicine, 1980-81, rsch. scientist, 1981-82; asst. prof. dept. pharmacology Emory U. Sch. Medicine, Atlanta, 1982-88, assoc. prof., 1988—. Spkr. in field. Editl. bd. Am. Jour. Physiology, 1989-93. Mem. com. on risk factors Iowa Heart Assn., 1982. USPHS predoctoral fellow, 1978-80, post-doctoral fellow, 1980-82; rsch. starter grantee Pharm. Mfgs. Assn. Found., 1983-85. Fellow Coun. High Blood Pressure Rsch.; mem. Am. Physiol. Soc., Am. Soc. Pharmacology and Exptl. Therapeutics, Am. Heart Assn. (rsch. investigatorship Ga. affiliate 1987-88, AHA established investigator 1989-94), Soc. Neurosci., Sigma Xi. Achievements include research in brain and spinal cord regulation of peripheral cardiovascular systems in normal and pathological states. Office: Dept Pharmacology Rollins Rsch Ctr Rm 5011 Atlanta GA 30322-0001 Office Phone: 404-727-5893.

GORDON, HAROLD M., pediatrician, educator; MD, Tufts U. Sch. Medicine. Diplomate Am. Bd. Pediatrics, 1982. Intern St. Christopher's Hosp. for Children, resident; lectr, instr. family practice residency program Bryn Mawr Hosp., hosp. affiliations include, 1980, Lankenau Med. Ctr., 1995, Paoli Hosp., 1995; sch. physician Radnor and Upper Merion Townships; instr. critical care course for neonatal nurses. Mem.: Valley Forge Pediatric Soc., Am. Acad. Pediats., Diplomate of the Nat. Bd. Office: Bryn Mawr Hospital 130 South Bryn Mawr Ave Bryn Mawr PA 19010 Office Phone: 484-337-3000.

GORDON, JEFFREY IVAN, gastroenterologist, educator, molecular biologist, researcher; b. New Orleans, Oct. 4, 1947; BA in Biology, Oberlin Coll.; MD, U. Chicago-Pritzker Sch Medicine, 1973. Intern, medicine Barnes Hosp., St. Louis, 1973—74, jr. asst. resident, medicine, 1974—75, sr. asst. resident. medicine, 1978—79; rsch. assoc. biochemistry lab, gastrointestinal medicine Nat. Cancer Ins., NIH, Bethesda, Md., 1975—78; chief med. resident Wash. U. Medical Service, John Cochran VA Hospital, St. Louis, 1978—79; fellow in medicine, gastroenterology Wash. U. Sch. of Medicine, St. Louis, 1979—81, asst. prof. medicine and biol. chemistry, 1981—84, assoc. prof. medicine and biol. chemistry, 1985—87, prof. medicine and biol. chemistry, 1987—90, head molecular biology & pharmacology dept., 1991—, Robert J. Glaser Disting. U. Prof., 2002—, dir. Ctr. Genome Sciences, 2004—. Contbr. articles to profl. publications. Recipient Young Investigator award, Am. Federation Clinical Rsch., 1990, NIDDK Young Scientist award, 1990, Marion Merrell Dow Disting. prize in Gastrointestinal Physiology, 1994, Janssen Sustained Achievement award in Digestive Sciences, 2003, Sr. Scholar award in Global Infectious Diseases, Ellison Medical Found., 2003; named Wellcome Vis. Prof. in Basic Med. Sciences, 1998, Horace W. Davenport Disting. Lecturer, Am. Physiological Assn., 2003, Sir Arthur Hurst Lecturer, British Soc. Gastroenterology, 2004; John A. & George L. Hartford Found. Fellowship, 1981—84, Established Investigatorship, Am. Heart Assoc., 1985—90. Fellow: AAAS, Am. Acad. Arts and Scis., Am. Acad. Microbiology; mem.: NAS, Inst. Medicine, Am. Gastroenterology Assn. (Morton I. Grossman Disting. Lectr. 1999, Disting. Achievement award 1992, 1992), Assn. Am. Physicians. Achievements include internationally known for research on gastrointestinal development and how gut bacteria affect normal intestinal function and predisposition to health and to certain diseases. Office: Dept Molecular Biology & Pharmacology Wash U Campus Box 8510 4444 Forest Park Saint Louis MO 63108 Office Phone: 314-362-7243. Business E-Mail: igordon@molecool.wustl.edu.

GORDON, LARRY JEAN, sanitarian, environmental health consultant; b. Tipton, Okla., Oct. 16, 1926; s. Andrew J. and Deweylee (Stewart) G.; m. Nedra Callender, Aug. 26. 1950; children: Debra Gordon Dunlap, Kent, Gary. Student, U. Okla., 1943-44; BS, U. N.Mex., 1949, MS, 1951; DHL (hon.), U. N.Mex., Albuquerque, 2007; MPH, U. Mich., 1954. Diplomate laverde Am. Acad. Sanitarians, 2003, emeritus 2008. High sch. sci. tchr., N.Mex., 1949-50; various positions N.Mex. Dept. Health, 1950-55; commd. officer USPHS, 1957—, advanced through grades to Dir. Grade (Navy capt.), dir. Albuquerque Environ. Health Dept., 1955-68, 82-86; dir. Environ. Improvement Agy., Santa Fe, 1968-73; adminstr. for health and environ. programs N.Mex. HHS Dept., Santa Fe, 1976-78; dir. N.Mex. Sci. Lab. System, Albuquerque, 1973-76; dep. sec. N.Mex. Health and Environ. Dept., Santa Fe, 1978-82, sec., 1987-88; vis. prof. pub. adminstrn. U. N.Mex., Albuquerque, 1988—, adj. prof. polit. sci., 1997—, sr. fellow Inst. for Pub. Policy, 1997—. Chmn. N.Mex. Water Quality Commn., 1971-73, New Mex. Coal Surface Mining Commn., 1971-73 Asst. editor Jour. Environ. Health, 1975-78; cons. editor Environ. News Digest, 1970-82; editl. cons. Jour. Pub. Health Policy, 1980-96, Underwriters Labs., 1996; contbr. over 240 articles to profl. jours. With USN, 1944—46. Recipient Samuel J. Crumbine award for Outstanding Devel. of Comprehensive Program for Environ. Sanitation, 1959 and 65, Sanitarians Disting. Service award Internat. Assn. Milk, Food, and Environ. Sanitarians, 1962, Outstanding Contrbn. award N.Mex. Assn. Pub. Health Sanitarians, 1967, Boss of Yr. award Santa Fe chpt. Nat. Secs. Assn., 1970, Walter F. Snyder award For Achievement in Environ. Quality, 1978, Commendation for Leadership in Health Care N.Mex. Hosp. Assn., 1981, N.Mex. Outstanding Pub. Svc. award, 1988, Zimmerman award U. N.Mex. Alumni, 1993, L.A. County Breslow award L.A. County Dept. Health Svcs., 1994, Outstanding Leadership in Environ. Adminstrn. award Am. Soc. for Pub. Adminstrn., 1994. Hon. Doctor of Humane Letters award, U. New Mexico Bd. Regents, May 2007 Mem. APHA (exec. bd. 1975-82, pres. 1980-81, John J. Sippy Meml. award 1962, other coms., Sedgwick award 1987), Am. Acad. Sanitarians (founder, David Calvin Wagner Excellence award 1984), N.Mex. Pub. Health Assn. (past pres., Disting. Svc. award 1970, Spl. award, 1978, D.A. Larrazola award 1989), N.Mex. Environ. Health Assn., (past pres.), Am. Lung Assn. N.Mex. (bd. dirs. 1982-94, Clinton P. Anderson award for Oustanding Contbn. to Lung Health 1987), Nat. Accreditation Coun. Environ. Health Curricula, Nat. Audubon Soc. (pres. coun. 1982-86), U. Mich. Sch. Pub. Health Alumni Assn. (bd. govs. 1985-88, Outstanding Alumnus award 1995), Royal Soc. Promotion of Health, London (hon.), N.Mex. Soc. Pub. Adminstrn. (Disting. Pub. Adminstr. award 1996), Am. Acad. Sanitarians (diplomate emeritus), Delta Omega, Phi Kappa Phi, Phi Sigma. Independent. Avocations: fishing, travel, golf, genealogy. Home: 1674 Tierra Del Rio NW Albuquerque NM 87107-3259 Office Phone: 505-343-9845. Personal E-mail: larrygordon1016@gmail.com.

GORDON, LORI HEYMAN, psychotherapist, author, educator; b. S.I., NY, Jan. 31, 1929; d. Julius and Bertha (Hahn) Heyman; m. Morris Gordon, Sept. 5, 1982 (dec.); children: Beth, Jonathan, David, Seth. BS, Cornell U., 1950; MSW, Cath. U. Am., 1963; PhD, Summit U. La., 1993. Lic. clin. social worker, accredited supr., Va. Founder/dir. Family Rels. Inst., Falls Church, Va., 1969; condr. psychoednl. tng. seminars nat. and internat. PAIRS (Practical Application Intimate Relationship Skills), Falls Church. Instr. family therapy Am. U. Grad. Sch. Counseling Edn., Washington; field supr. Cath. U. Am. Sch. Social Work, Washington; presenter profls. cons. Am. Assn. Marriage and Family Therapy Conf., 1988-91, Va. Assn. Marriage and Family Therapy Conf., 1989, ABA Family Law divsn. ptnrs. program, 1994; founder Ctr. for Separation and Divorce Mediation, 1980; founder, dir. PAIRS Ltd., 1984, PAIRS Inst., 1990; founder, exec. dir. PAIRS Found., Inc., 1991, dir. tng., 1995 Author: Love Knots--How To Untangle Daily Frustrations, 1990, Passage to Intimacy, 1993, rev. edit., 2001, If You Really Loved Me, 1996, Pairs Participant Handbook, Pairs Curriculum Guide and Training Manual vol. I, II, revised, 1999, The Peers Experience, 1999, Breaking the Code of Jealousy: Seven Steps to Healing, 2004; co-author: Prepairs, A Guide for Catholic Couples, 1999, Preventive Approaches to Couples Therapy, 1999, Prepairs, A Guide for Jewish Couples, 2001, Prepairs: A Guide for Christian Couples, 2001, Christian Pairs, 2002, Dare to be: The Autobiography of Rabbi Morris Gordon, 2006; contbr. articles to profl. jours. and mags., chpts. to books. Mem. Internat. Human Lng. Resource Network, Avanta-The Va. Satir Tng. Orgn., Inst. Noetic Scis., Coalition Marriage, Family and Couples Edn. (bd. dirs.). Office: PAIRS Found Ltd 1675 Market St Ste 207 Weston FL 33326-3681 Home Phone: 954-384-2829; Office Phone: 954-385-1775. Personal E-mail: pairsline@aol.com.

GORDON, MARSHA L., dermatologist; b. Annapolis, Md., 1958; BA, Rutgers U., 1980; MD, U. Pa., 1984. Diplomate Am. Bd. Dermatology. Intern Cooper Med. Ctr., Camden, 1984—85; resident in dermatology Mt. Sinai Med. Ctr., NYC, 1985—88, chief cons., 1988—, vice chair dermatology, 1996—. Asst. prof. Mt. Sinai Sch. Medicine, NYC, 1988—97, assoc. clin. prof., 1997—. Office: Mount Sinai Med Ctr Box 1048 5 E 98th St New York NY 10029-6501 Office Phone: 212-241-9773. Office Fax: 212-987-1197. Business E-Mail: marsha.gordon@mssm.edu.

GORDON, MORRIS AARON, medical mycologist; b. Waterbury, Conn., Apr. 3, 1920; s. Samuel and Anna (Rubinstein) G.; m. Ruth Kathryn McKee, May 22, 1945 (div. 1970); children: Barbara Jean, David Spencer, Sarah Elizabeth. BS, City Coll. N.Y., NYC, 1940; MS, U. Chgo., 1942; PhD, Duke U., 1949. Diplomate Am. Bd. Microbiology; cert. lab. dir., N.Y. Lab. officer Regional Hosp., U.S. Army, Camp Blanding, Fla., 1945-46; mycologist Communicable Disease Ctr., Atlanta, 1949-54; lectr. Emory U., 1952—53; biol. warfare specialist Chem. Corps Training Command, Fort McClellan, Ala., 1954-55; assoc. prof. microbiology Med. Coll. S.C., Charleston, 1955-59; sr. to prin. rsch. scientist, dir. mycology labs. N.Y. State Dept. Health, Albany, 1959-87, dir. clin. microbiology & mycology labs., 1983-87, dir. emeritus clin. microbiology and mycology labs., 1987—96. Study sect. NIH, Washington, 1971-75; adv. com. Brown-Hazen Awards, N.Y.C., 1974-78; cons. VA Hosp., Albany, 1959-96; rsch. prof. Albany Med. Coll., 1975-90. Author: Laboratory Identification of Pathogenic Fungi, 1970; founder/editor Bull. Med. Mycol. Soc. Ams., 1976-94; contbr. over 150 articles to numerous profl. jours. Lt. comdr. USPHS, 1949-54. Recipient various rsch. grants NIH, teaching fellowship Duke U., 1947-49; Fulbright prof., Uruguay, 1978, Inter-Am. fellow La. State U., 1959. Mem. Med. Mycol. Soc. Ams. (pres. 1978-79, Benham award 1988), Internat. Soc. Human and Animal Mycology (v.p. 1982-85, Georg award 1991), Am. Soc. Microbiology (pres. mycology sect.), Phi Beta Kappa, Sigma Xi (pres. Albany chpt. 1972). Achievements include invention of latex test for cryptococcosis; initiation of diagnostic immunofluorescence for human fungal diseases; cultured pathogenic lipophilic yeasts; establishment of first presence in North America and first presence in humans of Dermatophilus infection. Address: 251 Springmoor Dr Raleigh NC 27615

GORDON, PHILIP HARRY, physician; b. Saskatoon, Can., Sept. 13, 1942; MD, U. Sask., Can., 1966. Diplomate Am. Bd. Surgery, Am. Bd. Colon and rectal surgery; FRCS (Can.), FRSM, FACS, FASCRS, FCSCRS. Intern Jewish Gen. Hosp., Montreal, Canada, 1966-70, resident, 1971-72, Montefiore Hosp., Pitts., 1970-71; vice-chmn., dept. surgery, dir. colon/rectal surgeons Sir Mortimer B. Davis Jewish Gen. Hosp., Montreal. Prof. surgery and oncology, dir. colon and rectal surgery McGill U., Montreal; lectr in field. Editl. bd. numerous jours.; author four textbooks; contbr. articles to profl. jours., chpts. to books. Mem.: ACS (adv. coun. for colon and rectal surgery 1990—95, vice chair 1992—95), Am. Bd. Colon and Rectal Surgery (pres. 1999—2000), Can. Soc. Colon and Rectal Surgeons (founding pres. 1982—86), Royal Coll. Physicians and Surgeons of Can. (chmn. splty. com. in colon and rectal surgery), Am. Soc. Colon and Rectal Surgeons (pres. 1994—95). Office: Jewish Gen Hosp 3755 Cote St Catherine Rd Montreal PQ Canada H3T 1E2 Office Phone: 514-342-1772. Business E-Mail: philip.gordon@mcgill.ca.

GORDON, RITA, research scientist; b. Donetsk, Ukraine, Oct. 5, 1947; DSc, Donetsk State U., 1970; PhD, Inst. Cell Biophysics Russian Acad. Sci., 2000. Leading scientist Inst. Cell Biophysics Russian Acad. Scis., 2002—. Recipient Commendation award, Russian Acad. Scis. Avocations: travel, cooking. Office: Institutskaya 3 Pushchino Moscow 142290 Russia Office Fax: 7-4967-33-05-09. Personal E-mail: ritagordon@yandex.ru.

GORDUS, ANDREW GEORGE, ecotoxicologist; b. Oshkosh, Wis., Oct. 5, 1956; s. George and Margaret Gordus; 3 children. BS, Humboldt State U., 1980, MS, 1985; PhD, U. Calif., Davis, 1992. Wildlife biologist trainee U.S. Fish & Wildlife Svc., 1978-80, wildlife biologist, 1980-81; grad. rsch. intern Smithsonian Inst., 1982; post-grad. rschr. U. Calif., Davis, 1988-90, staff rsch. assoc., 1990-93; ecotoxicologist, wildlife biologist H.T. Harvey & Assocs., Fresno, Calif., 1993—2000; sr. environ. scientist, water quality, food safety biologist Calif. Dept. Fish and Game, Fresno, Calif., 2000—. Hunter safety instr. Calif. Dept. Fish & Game, 1992-94. NSF grad. fellow, 1981-84, grad. opportunity fellow U. Calif.-Davis, 1984-86; Calif. State scholar, 1977-79, Ernest & Mildred Lanini scholar Humboldt State U., 1981-82. Mem. Wildlife Disease Assn., Dixon Sportsmen Assn. (bd. dirs. 1992-94), Soc. Environ. Toxicology and Chemistry, The Wildlife Soc. Achievements include notable findings lyme disease in Northeast California, Food Safety-Wildlife for E. coli 0157:H7 and Salmonella, mitigate selenium impacts to birds, algal toxins in fish, Wildlife lead poisoning, salt toxicosis in birds; designed shorebird and waterfowl wetlands, wetland and wildlife habitat restoration plans. Office: Calif Dept Fish and Game 1234 E Shaw Ave Fresno CA 93710 Office Phone: 559-243-4014. Business E-Mail: agordus@dfg.ca.gov.

GORE, STEVEN LOWELL, accountant; b. Paducah, Ky., June 22, 1953; BS in Acctg., Lipscomb U., Nashville, 1975. CPA Tenn. Analyst fiscal svcs. King Faisal Hosp., Riyadh, Saudi Arabia, 1976—77; facility acct. Am. Retirement Corp., Nashville, 1983; staff auditor Hosp. Corp. Am., Nashville, 1984—87; contr. Sumner Regional Med. Ctr., Gallatin, Tenn., 1987—2003; devel. officer Genetics Assocs., Inc., Nashville, 2003—05; freelance cons. Nashville, 2005—; examiner Dept. Commerce and Ins., Nashville, 2005—. Vol. Margaret Maddox YMCA-East, Nashville, 1997—2000; poll ofcl. Metro-Davidson County Election Commn., Nashville, 1999. Recipient Appreciation Letter for Svc. United Way of Sumner County, 1997-2000. Mem.: IEEE, AAAS, Am. Math. Soc., Math Assn. Am., NY Acad. Sci., Am. Pub. Health Assn., Am. Chem. Soc. Mem. Christian Ch. Avocations: fishing, reading, jogging. Office: Tenn Dept Commerce and Ins 500 James Robertson Pkwy Ste 750 Nashville TN 37243-1169 Home: 3704 B Belmont Blvd Nashville TN 37215-1615 Office Phone: 615-741-2677. Personal E-mail: stevengore@msn.com.

GORE, TUSHAR, marketing professional; s. Balkrishna and Anuradha Gore; m. Ramya Kumbale, June 10, 1996. BSChemE, Indian Inst. of Tech., Bombay, 1994; PhD in Chem. Engring., U. Minn., 2000. Assoc. cons. McKinsey and Co., Florham Park, NJ, 2000—02; assoc. dir. bus. analyst Novo Nordisk Pharm. Inc., Princeton, NJ, 2003—. Presenter in field. Contbr. articles to profl. publs. Project coord. Am. India Found., NYC, 2001. Grantee, U. Minn. Mem.: NY Acad. Scis. Avocations: scuba diving, model railroad, guitar, photography.

GOREN, ELIHU N., endocrinologist; MD, Yeshiva U., 1973. Hosp. affiliations include Chestnut Hill Hosp., Montgomery Hosp., Mercy Suburban Hosp., Montgomery Hosp. Med. Ctr., Chestnut Hill Hosp. Mem.: Hormone Found., Am. Assn. of Clin. Endocrinologists. Office: Montgomery Hospital 1301 Powell St Norristown PA 19401 Office Phone: 610-270-2000.

GOREN, RONALD C., infectious disease physician; MD, Temple U., 1973. Diplomate Am. Bd. Internal Medicine, Am. Bd. Internal Medicine-infectious disease. Resident George Washington Univ. Hosp.; fellow infectious disease Veterans' Adminstrn. Hosp., Wash. Recipient Dr. Stanley J. Skromak award, 2011. Office: Aria Health 9501 Roosevelt Blvd Ste 208 Philadelphia PA 19114 Office Phone: 215-464-9634. Office Fax: 215-969-2327.

GORENEK, BULENT, cardiologist, educator; b. Ankara, Turkey, Sept. 20, 1965; m. Emine Sevil Gorenek, Oct. 23, 1993. Staff cardiologist Dept. Cardiology Osmangazi U., Eskisehir, Turkey, 1991—, prof. Dept. Cardiology, 1991—. Home: PK115 Koprubasi Eskisehir 26311 Turkey Office: Osmangazi University School of Medicine Cardiology Department Meselik Eskisehir 26120 Turkey Office Fax: 902222395370. Personal E-mail: bulent@gorenek.com.

GOREVIC, PETER D., immunologist, rheumatologist, educator; MD, NYU Sch. Med., 1970. Diplomate Am. Bd. Allergy and Immunology, Am. Bd. Internal Medicine, cert. diagnostic lab. immunology. Resident internal medicine Univ. of Chgo. Hosps., Bellevue Hosp. Ctr., NYU Sch. Med., 1971—74, fellow rheumatology, 1974—76, fellow allergy and immunology, 1976—77; prof. medicine Mt. Sinai Sch. Med., chief divsn. of rheumatology. Co-editor: (publ.) Cyoglobulinemic and noncryoglobulinemic neuropathy in chronic hepatitis C virus (HCV) infection, 2000, Cryoglobulinemia, Cryofibrinogens and Pyroglobulinemia, 2006, Eprodisate for the Treatment of AA Amyloidosis. Named one of Best Doctors, NY Mag., 2009. Office: Mount Sinai Medical Center Department of Medicine Rheumatology 5 E 98th St 11 Fl New York NY 10029 Office Phone: 212-241-1671. Office Fax: 212-849-2574. E-mail: peter.gorevic@mountsiani.org.

GORGE, JOHN ANTHONY, health corporation executive; b. New Kensington, Pa., July 11, 1948; s. Moses and Veronica (Raymond) George; m. Leah Diane George, Oct. 30, 1971 (div. 1992); m. Carolyn D. Dozier, Sept. 22, 2000. BS, Duquesne U., Pitts., 1970; MBA, U. Pitts., 1973; MS in Taxation, Robert Morris Coll., Pitts. CFP. Asst. adminstr. mental health and mental retardation program Western Psychiat. Inst. and Clinic, Pitts., 1971-72; adminstrv. dir. Latrobe Area Hosp., Pa., 1973-76; asst. dir. Presbyn. U. Hosp., Pitts., 1976-80; owner, prin. George-Anstey Food Distbg. Corp., Pitts., 1978-81; mgmt. cons. Arthur Young & Co., Pitts., 1980-82; exec. dir. Ea. Allegheny County Health Corp., 1982-85; pres. Alpha Health Network, 1985-88; pres., bd. dirs. Intergroup Svc. Corp., 1988—. Bd. dir. Health Coalition Ptnrs.; pres., bd. mgrs. USAccess; lectr. in field. Contbr. articles to profl. jours. Mem.: Am. Assn. Prepared Provider Orgns. Roman Catholic. Home: 5121 Ellsworth Ave Pittsburgh PA 15232-1419 Office: 401 Shady Ave Suite B108 Pittsburgh PA 15206-4450 Personal E-mail: john_w_george@yahoo.com.

GORHAM, MILLICENT, medical association administrator; BA, Simmons Coll., Boston, 1976. Health legis. asst., Rep. Louis Stokes US House of Reps., Washington; coord. Congl. Black Caucus Health Brain Trust; exec. dir. Nat. Black Nurses Assn., 1995—. Mem. FDA Consumer Consortium, Fannie Mae Osteoporosis Bus. Coun.; mem. adv. bd. Capital Area Rural Health Roundtable. Editor: NBNA News; mem. editl. bd.: Nursing Spectrum mag. Recipient State Offices Rural Health award, 1995, Disting. Mem. award, Women in Govt. Rels., 1998. Office: Nat Black Nurses Assn 8630 Fenton St Ste 330 Silver Spring MD 20910-3803 Office Phone: 301-589-3200. Office Fax: 301-589-3223. *

GORIN, SUSAN, medical association administrator; Asst. exec. dir. Coun. for Exceptional Children, 1981—93; exec. dir. Nat. Assn. Sch. Psychologists, Bethesda, Md., 1993—. Adv. bd. Ctr. on Personnel Studies in Spl. Edn. Office: Nat Assn Sch Psychologists Ste 402 4340 East West Hwy Bethesda MD 20814 Office Phone: 301-347-1640. Business E-Mail: sgorin@naspweb.org. *

GORMAN, KAREN MACHMER, optometric physician; b. Poughkeepsie, NY, June 4, 1955; d. James Andrew and Joan (Benton) Machmer; m. D.L. McCartney III, Aug. 16, 1976 (div. June 1982); m. N. David Gorman, Oct. 16, 1985; 1 stepchild, Danette Y. Gorman. BS in Optometry, U. Houston, 1976, OD, 1978; therapeutic pharm. lic., U. Mo., St. Louis, 1993. Nat. Bd. Optometry; lic. optometrist, Colo., Mo., Tex. Pvt. practice, Dallas, 1978-83, 1984-85, Hurst, Tex., 1984-85, St. Joseph, Mo., 1986-2000; councilwoman, chmn. pub. safety com. City Coun., City of St. Joseph, 1997—2006, chmn. parks exec. com., 2005—06; pvt. practice Maryville, Mo., 1999—. Charter mem. optometric adv. panel Pearle, Inc., 1991-93; lectr. on eyecare to community groups; free-lance journalist St. Joseph News-Press, Benson (N.C.) Rev., jazzreview.com, Jazz Amb. mag.; with Fly In, Washington, 2001-2005. Contbr. poetry to lit. jours. including Nat. Libr. of Poetry, Typo mag., Edge mag., articles to profl. jours. including St. Joseph News Press and Benson (N.C.) Review; lead actress (play) None Come Back Innocent, Robidoux Resident Theatre, St. Joseph, 1990, Hay Fever, 1991, The Best Man, 1992, Wedded But No Wife, 1993, Mousetrap, 1993, Diary of Anne Frank, 1994, Death and the Maiden, 1995, Veronica's Room, 1996, Plaza Suite, 1997, Dial M for Murder, 2000, The Laramie Project, 2002, The Atonement, Grace Evangelical Church, 2005, On Golden Pond, 2006, Agnes of God, 2008, Heaven's Gates, Hell's Flames, 2004-11; narrator Sing for The Cure, St. Joseph Cmty. Chorus, 2008. Vol. Dallas Humane Soc., 1981, YWCA Women's Abuse Shelter; patron Robidoux Resident Theatre, St. Joseph, 1988-2010, St. Joseph Animal Shelter; patron Second Harvest Food Bank, 1998-2010; sponsor, coach, cheerleader and drill team Mo. Western State Coll., St. Joseph, 1985-86; legis. corr. Humane Soc. U.S., 1990-2010; mem. St. Joseph (Mo.) City Coun., 1997—2006, chmn. landfill and water pollution com., 1998-2005, parks and recreation com., 2005-06, pub. safety com., chmn., City Conwal Com. Puppy Mill Legis., 2011; bd. dirs. Robidoux Resident Theater, 2006—09, mus. oversight bd. City St. Joseph, 2008-11, chmn., 2009-, judge Regional HS Speech and Drama Concert, 2008. Recipient Optometric Recognition awards Pearle, Inc., 1986-90; U. Houston scholar, 1972-76 Mem.: DAR (Pony Express chpt.), Nat. Soc. Newspaper Columnists, U. Houston Alumni Assn., Grace Evangelical Ch., Evangelism & Prayer Coms., Tau Sigma. Avocations: reading, writing, poetry. Office: 1713 S Main Maryville MO 64468 Office Phone: 660-582-8911. E-mail: eyedrkim@aol.com.

GORMAN KOCH, COLLEEN, anesthesiologist, educator; BA in Hist., Marquette U.; MS in Clinical Rsch. Design & Statistical Analysis, U. Mich. Sch. Pub. Health; MD, U. Cin. Coll. Med. Cert. anesthesiology Nat. Bd. Echocardiography. Intern Cleveland Clinic Found.; resident Brigham & Women's Hosp. Harvard Med. Sch., clinical instr. of anesthesiology; cardiothoracic anesthesiologist Cleveland Clinic, clinical assoc. echocardiography. Med. sch. admissions com. Cleveland Clinic Lerner Coll. Med. Case Western U.; vice chmn. rsch. & edn. Cleveland Clinic Dept. Cardiothoracic Anesthesia; leadership coun. Anesthesia Inst.; assoc. editor Annals of Thoracic Surgery Cardiothoracic Anesthesiology. Contbr. chapters to books. Recipient Bruce Hubbard Stewart Fellowship award, Cleveland Clinic. Fellow: Am. Coll. Cardiology; mem.: Internat. Anesthesia Rsch. Soc. (bd. trustees), Nat. Soc. Cardiovascular Anesthesiologists (vice chmn. scientific program com.). Office: Cleveland Clinic 9500 Euclid Ave Mail Code J4-331 Cleveland OH 44195 Office Phone: 216-445-7418.

GORNEY, RODERIC, psychiatrist, educator; b. Grand Rapids, Mich., Aug. 13, 1924; s. Abraham Jacob Gorney and Edelaine (Roden) Harburg; m. Carol Ann Sobel, Apr. 13, 1986. BS, Stanford U., 1948, MD, 1949; PhD in Psychoanalysis, So. Calif. Psychoanalytic Inst., 1977. Diplomate Am. Bd. Psychiatry and Neurology. Pvt. practice psychiatry, San Francisco, 1952-62; asst. prof. UCLA, 1962-71, assoc. prof., 1971-73, prof. psychiatry, 1980—, dir. psychosocial adaptation and the future program, 1971—85; psychoanalytic mem. emeritus New Ctr. Psychoanalysis, 2005—. Faculty So. Calif. Psychoanalytic Inst. Author: The Human Agenda, 1972. Served with USAF, 1943-46. Fellow AAAS, Acad. Psychoanalysis, Am. Psychoanalytic Assn., Internat. Psychoanalytic Assn., Am. Psychiatric Assn. (essay prize 1971), Group for Advancement of Psychiatry, New Ctr. for Psychoanalysis. Avocation: music. Office: Semel Inst Neurosci and Human Behavior 760 Westwood Plz Los Angeles CA 90095-8353 Office Phone: 310-476-3099, 310-825-0463. Business E-Mail: preadapt@ucla.edu.

GOROG, FRANÇOISE, psychoanalyst; b. Lyon, France, July 26, 1946; d. Léonard Massaux and Anne Royer; m. Jean-Jacques Gorog, May 13, 1978; 1 child, Mathias. D, Faculté De Médecine, Lyon, 1963. Cert. psychiatrist. Chef de svc. Hopital Sainte-Anne, Paris, 1988—; doctor mental health and deafness Paris, 2003—. Dir. review: Corrélats, Paris, 2000. Author: (book) La psychose maniaco-dépressive, 1988, Coupable ou Non Coupable en Des Mélancolies, Editions du Champ Lacanien, 2001. Mem.: Team Psychoanalysis and Medicine, Internationale des Forums du Champ Lacanien. Home: 10 Avenue Des Gobelins 75005 Paris France Office: Centre Hospitalier Sainte-Anne 1 Rue Cabanis 75014 Paris France Office Phone: 0145658088. Office Fax: 0145658944. Business E-Mail: gorog@chsa.broca.inserm.fr.

GOROSPE, EMMANUEL CRUZ, physician, medical researcher; BS in Pub. Health cum laude, U. Philippines, Manila, 2000, MD, 2005; grad. cert. in Health Care Ethics, Rush U., Chgo., 2005; MPH, U. Nev., Las Vegas, 2007. Cert. Ednl. Commn. Fgn. Med. Grads., 2006, in basic & advanced cardiac life support Am. Heart Assn., 2009, lic. US, cert. Am. Bd. Internat. Medicine, 2010, lic. Minnesota Bd. Med. Practise, 2010 Rschr. U. Philippines, Nat. Inst. Health, Manila, 2000—01; med. intern U. Philippines, Philippines Gen. Hosp., Manila, 2004—05; rsch. fellow Harvard Med. Sch., Brigham & Women's Hosp., Boston, 2005; transplant and rsch. coord. Children's Nephrology Clinic, Las Vegas, 2006—07; postdoc. fellow Johns Hopkins U. Sch. Medicine, Balt., 2007—10; medicine housestaff Johns Hopkins Bayview Med. Ctr., Balt., 2007—10; instr. medicine Mayo Clinic Coll. Medicine, Rochester, Minn., 2010—; fellow gastroenterology and hepatology Mayo Grad. Sch. Medicine, 2010—. Cons. Nev. Ctr. Ethics and Health Policy, Reno, 2005, PalCare Found., Inc., Manila, 2004—07; co-investigator Johns Hopkins-Fraunhofer IIS EndoCAD Collaboration, 2008—. Author: Diagnosis Made Simple for Parents, 2006; reviewer in field:; contbr. articles to profl. jours., chapters to books. Cons. bioethics Nev. Multicultural Coalition End-of-Life Issues, Las Vegas, 2005—07; advisor Ednl. Commn. Fgn. Med. Grads. Internat. Med. Grads. Advisors Network, 2007—. Recipient Chancellor's List, 2006, Dean's award, U. Nev. Sch. Public Health, 2007, Patrick Murphy award, Johns Hopkins Medicine, 2010; Presdl. scholar, U. Philippines, 2000. Mem.: Am. Assn. Study Liver Diseases, Am. Gastroent. Assn., Am. Soc. Gastrointestinal Endoscopy, Am. Coll. Gastroenterology, U. Philippines Med. Alumni Soc. Am., Internat. Club Ascites, Sigma Xi Sci. Rsch. Soc., Nat. Scholars' Honor Soc., Phi Sigma Biol. Honor Soc., Phi Kappa Phi Honor Soc. Roman Catholic. Achievements include development of the first university-based palliative care volunteer program in the Philippines; the first bilingual Filipino-English advance directives document in Nevada. Avocations: martial arts, piano, travel. Business E-Mail: gorospe.emmanuel@mayo.edu.

GORROD, JOHN WILLIAM, biopharmacy research educator; b. London, Oct. 11, 1931; s. Ernest Lionel and Carrie Rebecca (Richardson) G.; m. Doreen Mary Collins, Apr. 3, 1954; children: Julia Caroline, Simon Jonathon William, Nicholas Ernest Freeman. Diploma, Chelsea Coll., London, 1961; PhD, London U., 1979, DSc, 1982. Tech. officer Chester Beatty Rsch. Inst., London, 1955-65; rsch. fellow biochemistry U. Bari, Italy, 1964; rsch. fellow Royal Commn. Exhibition of 1851, 1965-67; lectr. biopharmacy Chelsea Coll., London, 1968-80, reader biopharmacy, 1980-84; prof., head Dept. of Pharmacy King's Coll., London, 1984-90, head div. Health Scis. Faculty of Life Sci., 1988, 1989, rsch. prof., 1990-97, prof. emeritus, 1997, elected fellow, 1996—; prof. toxicology U. Essex, England, 1997—. Dir. Drug Control and Tchg. Ctr., Sports Coun., 1985-91; vis. prof. U. Bologna, U. Bari, U. Kebangsan, Malaysia, Chinese Acad. of Preventive Medicine, 1991; Can. MRC vis. prof. U. Man., U. Sask., 1988; adv. coun. tobacco sci. & health Inst. Sci. & Health, St. Louis; sci. adv. bd. Philip Morris Internat., 2006—. Author: Biological Oxidation of Nitrogen in Organic Molecules, 1972, Drug Metabolism in Man, 1978, Biological Oxidation Nitrogen, 1978, Drug Toxicity, 1979, Testing for Toxicity, 1981, Biological Oxidation of Nitrogen in Organic Molecules, Development of Drugs and Modern Medicines, 1986, (with others) Metabolism of Xenobiotics, 1988, Molecular Aspects of Human Disease, vols. 1 and 2, 1989, Biological Oxidation of Nitrogen in Drug Molecules, 1990, Molecular Basis of Neurological Disorders and Their Treatment, 1991, Nicotine and Related Alkaloids, 1993, Analytical Determination of Nicotine and Related Compounds and Their Metabolites, 1999; contbr. articles to profl. jours.; editl. bd. Xenobiotica, European Jour. Drug Metabolism and Pharmokinetics, Drug Metabolism Revs., Anti Cancer Rsch. Recipient Gold medal of Comenius, U. Bratislava, 1991. Fellow Pan-Hellenic Assn. Pharmacists (hon.), Turkish Pharm. Soc. (hon.), Royal Coll. Pathologists, Royal Soc. Chemistry, Inst. Biology; mem. Internat. Soc. Study Xenobotics (founder, mem. coun., pres. 2000, 2001), Sch. Pharmacy U. London (hon. fellow), Pharm. Soc. Gt. Britain (hon.), German Pharm. Soc. (corr.), Athenaeum Club. Avocations: travel, reading. Home: Rest Orchard School Ln Polstead Heath Suffolk CO6 5BG England Business E-Mail: jgorr@essex.ac.uk.

GORSEN, ROBERT MARC, neurosurgeon; b. Phila., Mar. 10, 1953; s. Herman Irving Gorsen and Marilyn Joyce Freedman; m. Sharon Virginia Grant, May 13, 1989; children: Devin Marily, Dillon Robert. BA, Haverford Coll., 1975; PhD, Thomas Jefferson U., 1980, MD, 1982. Internship Lenox Hill Hosp., NYC, 1982—83; neurosurgery resident Thomas Jefferson U. Hosp., Phila., 1983—88; pvt. practice Fairfax County, Va., 1988—. Named one of Top Drs., Washingtonian Mag., 1993, 1995, 1999, 2002, 2005, 2008, 2010, Top Spine Specialists, 2003. Achievements include patents for cervical traction collar; posture lumbar traction device; traction colllor and its method of use; protective and theropeutic body gear. Office: Robert M Gorsen MD PHD PC 3301 Woodburn Rd Annandale VA 22003 Office Phone: 703-573-4700. Personal E-mail: neusur@aol.com.

GORSKY, ALEX, pharmaceutical executive; b. 1960; BS, US Mil. Acad., West Point, 1982; MBA, U. Pa., 1996. Sales rep. Janssen Pharmaceutica Inc., 1988, pres.; group chmn. Europe, the Middle East & Africa Johnson & Johnson, 2003—04; COO, head gen. medicines Novartis Pharmaceuticals Corp., 2004—05, CEO, head Pharma North America, 2005—08; worldwide chmn. medical devices & diagnostics group (MD&D), mem. exec. com. Johnson & Johnson, 2009—11, vice chmn. exec. com., 2011—. Mem. Doylestown Hosp. Bd. Served to capt. US Army. Named Honorable Mentor, Healthcare Businesswomen's Assn., 2009. Mem.: Phila. Coll. Pharmacy, Nat. Alliance on Aging, Nat. Alliance for the Mentally Ill. Avocation: running. Office: Johnson & Johnson 1 Johnson & Johnson Plaza New Brunswick NJ 08933 *

GORSKY, MEIR, clinical oral pathologist; b. Katovitz, Poland, Mar. 7, 1946; arrived in Israel, 1950; s. Leon Goldberger and Irena (Glicksman) G.; m. Hana Geisler, July 9, 1947; children: Mody, Sharon, Idan. DMD, Hebrew U., 1972; cert. in oral medicine, U. Calif., San Francisco, 1982. Dir. oral medicine clinic Tel Aviv U., 1977—, coord. sect. oral pathology & medicine sch. dental medicine, 1982-87, full prof., 1995—. Vis. prof. U. Calif., San Francisco, 1985, 88, 89, 98, 99 Cancer Agy., B.C. Vancouver, Can., 1997, UI Chgo. 2002-08; dir. retraining program Ministry Health and Tel Aviv U., 1976-77; cons. in oral medicine Tel Hashomar Hosp., Ramat Gan, Israel, 1977—; dir. dept. evaluation for splty. in oral medicine Israel Dental Assn., 1995, chmn. oral medicine com., 1990-95; bd. dirs. Sch. Dental Med. Tel-Aviv U. Contbr. chpts. to books and articles to profl. jours. Mem. bd. examinations Ministry Health, Israel, 1985—; mem. pub. rels. com. sch. dental medicine Tel Aviv U., 1985-88, mem. curriculum com. to upgrade profl. knowledge in dentistry, 1990, mem. coun. faculty medicine, 1996—. Capt. Israeli Med. Forces, 1972-95. Grantee Alpha Omega, 1981. Fellow Am. Acad. Oral Medicine, Am. Acad. Oral Pathology, Internat. Assn. Dental Rsch. Avocations: photography, music. Office: Tel Aviv U Sch Dental Medic Sect Oral Pathology Tel Aviv 69978 Israel

GORSUCH, RICHARD LEE, psychologist, educator, minister; b. Wayne, Mich., May 14, 1937; s. Culver C. and Velma L. Gorsuch; m. Sylvia S. Coalson, Aug. 18, 1961; children: Eric, Kay. BA, Tex. Christian U., 1959; MA, U. Ill., 1962, PhD, 1965; MDiv, Vanderbilt U., 1968. Lic. psychologist, Calif; ordained min., Disciples of Christ, 1968. Asst. prof. of psychology Vanderbilt U., 1966-68, dir. statis. consultation, 1966-68; asst. prof., then assoc. prof. psychology George Peabody Coll. for Tchrs., 1968-73; assoc. prof. Inst. Behavioral Rsch. Tex. Christian U., 1973-75; assoc. prof., then prof. psychology U. Tex., Arlington, 1975-79; prof. psychology Fuller Theol. Sem., Pasadena, Calif., 1979—2006, sr. prof., 2006—; CEO Uni Mult Inc. Author: Factor Analysis, 2d edit., 1983, Integrating Psychology and Spirituality?, 2002; co-author: Psychology of Religion, 1996, 3d edit., 2003; editor Jour. For. Sci. Study of Religion; cons. editor Ednl. and Psychol. Measurement, Multivariate Behavioral Rsch.; contbr. article to Ann. Rev. Psychology, 1988. Fellow APA (coun. of reps. 1984-85, 89-90, pres. divsn. 36, 1990-91, William James award 1986), Soc. Sci. Study Religion; mem. Religious Rsch. Assn., Soc. of Multivariate Exptl. Psychology. Achievements include development of UniMult statistics package. Office: Fuller Theol Sem Grad Sch Psychology 180 N Oakland Ave Pasadena CA 91001 Office Phone: 626-584-5527. Business E-Mail: rgorsuch@fuller.edu. *

GORTATOWSKI, MELVIN JEROME, retired chemist; b. Chgo., Oct. 30, 1925; s. Walter Harry and Anna Martha (Santowski) Gortatowski. BS, U. Ill., 1950, PhD, 1956; MS, Wash. State U., 1952. Research instr. biochemistry U. Utah, Salt Lake City, 1955-58, research assoc. psychiatry, 1958-59, research instr. biochemistry, chemist VA Hosp., 1959-65; assoc. investigator, asst. rsch. prof. pediatrics, biochemistry U. So. Calif. Children's Hosp., Los Angeles, 1965-71; dir. bur. clin. chemistry Utah State Health Lab., Salt Lake City, 1971-87, safety officer, 1980-87. Contbr. articles to profl. jours. With US Army, 1944—46. Eastman Kodak fellow, U. Ill., 1954. Mem.: Mineral Collectors Utah, Am. Chem. Soc., Utah Numismatic Soc. (bd. dirs. 1976—77), Phi Lambda Upsilon, Sigma Xi. Roman Catholic. Avocations: photography, stamp collecting/philately, music, mineral collecting, swimming. Home: 4015 Foubert Ave Salt Lake City UT 84124-3410

GOS, TOMASZ, forensic pathologist, educator; b. Gdansk, Pomerania, Poland, Sept. 22, 1958; MD, Med. U. Gdansk, 1983, habilitation, 2009. Asst. prof. Med. U. Gdansk, 1991—. Postdoc. rschr. U. Magdeburg, Germany, 2004—05. Recipient award, Polish Ministry Health, 2010. Mem.: Polish Soc. Forensic Medicine and Criminology, Polish Neurosci. Soc. Avocation: history. Office: Debowa 23 Gdansk Pomerania 80-204 Poland Business E-Mail: gost@gumed.edu.pl.

GOSEKI-SONE, MASAE, nutrition educator, researcher; b. Tokyo, May 6, 1956; d. Yoshimichi and Chieko Sone; m. Atsushi Goseki, 1983. B of Home Econs., Japan Women's U., 1979, M of Home Econs., 1981; PhD in Dentistry, Tokyo Med. and Dental U., 1989. Registered dietitian with qualification Ministry of Health and Welfare, 1984, radiation protection supr. qualification first class Sci. and Tech. Agy., 1997. Ednl. asst. Tokyo Med. and Dental U., Tokyo, 1981—97; lectr. Japan Women's Univeristy, Tokyo, 1998—2001; assoc. prof. Japan Women's U., 2002—08, prof., 2009—. Trustee Japan Soc. of Metabolism and Clin. Nutrition, Tokyo. Grantee Sci. Rsch. grantee, Ministry Edn., Culture, Sports, Sci. and Tech., 1990—93, 1998—99, 2008—. Mem.: Am. Soc. for Bone and Mineral Rsch. Achievements include discovery of registration of the novel gene (Cbfa1, rat partially); patents for the prediction method of bone mineral density and the gene polymorphism analysis (tissue non-specific alkaline phosphatase). Avocation: reading. Office: Japan Women's Univ 2-8-1 Mejirodai Bunkyo-ku Tokyo 112-8681 Japan Business E-Mail: goseki@fc.jwu.ac.jp.

GOSLINGS, J. CAREL, emergency physician, surgeon; b. Leiden, Zuid-Holland, Netherlands, Sept. 13, 1968; s. Bernard and Antoinette (Mees) G.; m. Karin van Gilst; children: Wessel Oege, Milou Lucia Noor. M in Medicine, U. Amsterdam, 1991, MD, 1993. Intern dept. traumatology Acad. Med. Ctr., Amsterdam, 1989—91, surg. resident, 1998—2000, attending surgeon trauma unit dept. surgery, 2001—, chief trauma unit dept. surgery, 2004—; intern Burn Ctr. Zuiderziekenhuis, Rotterdam, Netherlands, 1991; surg. resident St. Lucas Hosp., Amsterdam, 1995—98. Helicopter emergency med. svc. physician Lifeliner 1 Traumacenter NW Netherlands, Amsterdam, 2003—. Mem. editl. bd. Netherlands Jour. Surgery, 1998—; contbr. articles to profl. jours.; patentee in field. 1st med. lt. The Netherlands Army, 1995. Lt. med. officer US Army, 1994—95, Nunspeet, Netherlands and Vitez, Bosnia-Hercegovina. Mem. Netherlands Soc. Traumatology, Netherlands Soc. Surgery. Achievements include research in Trauma Surgery, Distal Radius Fractures. Avocations: running, bicycling, ice skating. Office: Acad Med Ctr 9 Meibergdreef Amsterdam 1105 AZ Netherlands Office Fax: *31-20-6914858. Personal E-mail: goslings@knmg.nl. E-mail: j.c.goslings@amc.uva.nl.

GOSS, JEROME ELDON, craftsman, retired cardiologist; b. Dodge City, Kans., Nov. 30, 1935; s. Horton Maurice and Mary Alice (Mountain) G.; m. Lorraine Ann Sanchez, Apr. 20, 1986. BA, U. Kans., 1957; MD, Northwestern U., 1961. Diplomate Am. Bd. Internal Medicine, Am. Bd. Cardiology, fine bookbinding Glasgow Met. Coll., 2004-05; Higher Nat. cert. Intern Met. Gen. Hosp., Cleve., 1961-62; resident in internal medicine Northwestern U. Med. Ctr., Chgo., 1962-64; fellow in cardiology U. Colo., Denver, 1964-66; asst. prof. medicine U. N.Mex., Albuquerque, 1968-70; pvt. practice N.Mex. Heart Clinic, Albuquerque, 1970—99, Presbyn. Med. Group, Albuquerque, 2000—02; with Presbyn. Heart Group, Albuquerque, 2003—05; propr. fine bookbinding and repair, 2005—. Bd. alumni counsellors Northwestern U. Med. Sch., 1977-89, nat. alumni bd., 1991-97; chief dept. medicine Presbyn. Hosp., Albuquerque, 1978-80, exec. com., 1980-82, dir. cardiac diagnostic svcs., 1970-96. Contbr. articles to profl. jours. Bd. dir. Presbyn. Heart Inst., Ballet West N.Mex., N.Mex. Symphony Orch., N.Mex. Cancer Ctr. Found., 2008-10; pres. Albuquerque Mus. Found., 1983-96, Corrales Hist. Soc. (pres. 2002-05, 2008-09). Lt. comdr. USN, 1966-68. Nat. Heart Inst. research fellow, 1965-66; named one of Outstanding Young Men Am., Jaycees, 1970; recipient Alumni Service award Northwestern U. Med. Sch., 1986, Disting. Achievement award Albuquerque Mus. Found., 1997, Sr. Svc. award Presbyn. Healthcare Sys., 1999; named Disting. Physician, Presbyn. Healthcare Sys., 2010. Fellow ACP, ACC, Coun. Clin. Cardiology of Am. Heart Assn., Soc. Cardiac Angiography, Am. Soc. of Geriatric Cardiology; mem. Albuquerque-Bernalillo County Med. Soc. (sec. 1972, treas. 1975, v.p. 1980), Guild Book Workers, Alpha Omega Alpha. Republican. Methodist. Office Phone: 505-792-1516. Personal E-mail: jegoss@comcast.net.

GOSSAIN, SUNITA RANI, dermatologist, researcher, medical educator; d. Duni Chand and Uma Devi Gossain; m. Arvind Mohan. MBBS, Guy's & St Thomas' Med. Sch., London, 1992—97. MRCP Royal Coll. of Physicians, UK, 2000, MRCGP Royal Coll. of Gen. Practitioners, 2002, DFFP Royal Coll. of Ob-gyn., 2002. Physician - internship Guy's & St Thomas' Hosp., London, 1997—98; physician - internal medicine St George's Hosp., London, 1998—2000; fellowship Fitznells Manor Surgery, Epsom, Surrey, 2000—01; prin. Family Medicine, England, 2002—04; clin. fellow dermatology St. Mary's Hosp., Portsmouth, England, 2006; dermatology registrar Churchill Hosp., Oxford, 2007—; specialist registrar in dermatology London KSS Deanery, 2007—. Sub-internship Johns Hopkins Sch. of Medicine, Balt., 1996; fellow - clin. rsch. Fla. Skin Cancer Ctr., Tallahassee, 1999; presenter in field. Editor: (jour.) Guy's Hosp. Gazette; contbr. articles to profl. jours. Editor & rep. Student Med. Edn. Com., London, 1994—96; com. mem. Academic Bd.: United Med. & Dental Schools, London, 1996—97. Recipient Distinction, in contention for Frazer Rose Medal: Ranked in Top Twelve in Dr. in UK, Royal Coll. of Gen. Practitioners, 2002, Ranked First in Audit /Rsch.: Osteoporosis, Primary Care Trust, 2002. Mem.: Royal Coll. Gen. Practitioners, Royal Coll. Physicians, British. Assn. Dermatology (assoc.). Achievements include research in real time analysis of skin cancer, lentigo maligna; diabetes mellitus & sialic acid. Personal E-mail: sunitagossain@hotmail.com. Business E-Mail: sunitagossain@doctors.org.uk.

GOSSELIN, BENOIT JEAN, otolaryngologist, facial plastic surgeon, head and neck reconstructive surgeon; b. Quebec City, Can., Oct. 24, 1962; BSc, U. Ottawa, 1983, MD, 1988. Diplomate Am. Bd. Otolaryngology, Bd. of Facial Plastic & Reconstructive Surgery. Resident in otolaryngology U. Ottawa, Canada, 1989-93; fellow head and neck surgery U. Toronto, Canada, 1993-94; fellow in microvascular and facial plastic surgery Mercy Hosp. Pitts., 1994-95; asst. prof. surgery Dartmouth Coll., Hanover, NH, 1995—; staff otolaryngology sect. Dartmouth-Hitchcock Med. Ctr., Lebanon, NH, 1995—; staff otolaryngologist, head and neck surgeon VA Med. Ctr., White River Junction, Vt., 2002—; dir. comprehensive head and neck cancer program Norris Cotton Cancer Ctr., Lebanon, 2003—. Fellow ACS, Royal Coll. Surgeons (Can.), Am. Soc. Head and Neck Surgery; mem. AMA, Am. Acad. Otolaryngology, Head and Neck Surgery, Am. Acad. Facial Plastics and Reconstructive Surgery, Am. Rhinologic Soc., Am. Soc. Univ. Otolaryngologists, Can. Soc. Otolaryngology, Head and Neck Surgery, Can. Med. Assn. Office: Dartmouth-Hitchcock Med Ctr Sect Otolaryngology One Medical Ctr Dr Lebanon NH 03755 Office Phone: 603-650-8112. *

GOSTIN, LAWRENCE O., lawyer, educator; b. Oct. 19, 1949; s. Joseph and Sylvia (Berkman) G.; m. Jean Catherine Allison, July 30, 1977; children: Bryn Gareth, Kieran Gavin. BA summa cum laude, SUNY, Brockport, 1971; LLD (hon.), SUNY; JD, Duke U., 1974. Bar: N.Y. 1981, Coun. Europe. Legal dir. Nat. Assn. Mental Health, London, 1975-82; vis. fellow U. Oxford Ctr. for Criminol. Rsch., 1982-83; gen. sec. Nat. Coun. Civil Liberties, London, 1983-85; sr. fellow in health law Harvard U. Sch. Pub. Health, 1985—. Vis. prof. social policy McMaster U., Hamilton, Ont., Can., 1978-79; exec. dir. Am. Soc. Law, Medicine, and Ethics, Boston, 1987-94; adj. assoc. prof. Sch. Pub. Health, Harvard U., 1988—, adj. prof., 1990—, lectr. Law Sch., 1990—; vis. prof. Georgetown U. Law Ctr., 1993-94, assoc. prof., 1994-95, prof., 1996—, John Carroll rsch. prof., 2004-05, assoc. dean for rsch. and acad. programs, 2005-; Linda and Timothy O'Neill prof. Global Health Law, 2008-, prof. Johns Hopkins Sch. Hygiene and Pub. Health, 1994—; co-dir. Georgetown/Johns Hopkins Program on Law and Pub. Health; dir. CDC Collaborating Ctr. on Law and the Pub.'s Health; legis. coun. U.S. Senate Labor and Human Resources Com., Washington, 1987, 88; bd. dirs., nat. exec. com. Am. Civil Liberties Union, 1987—; assoc. dir. Harvard U. WHO Internat. Collaborating Ctr. on Health Legis., 1989— Western European editor Internat. Jour. Law and Psychiatry, London, 1978-81; editor in chief: Law Medicine & Health Care; exec. editor: Am. Jour. Law and Medicine; sect. editor Jour. AMA; editor: Secure Provision, 1985, AIDS and the Health Care System, 1990, Surrogate Motherhood: Politics and Privacy, 1990, Implementing the Americans with Disabilities Act, 1993; co-editor: Law, Science and Medicine, 2d edit., 1996; author: Human Rights and Public Health in the AIDS Pandemic, 1997, The Rights of Persons with HIV Disease, 1996, Mental Health Services: Law and Practice, 1986, Institutions Observed, 1986, Mental Health: Tribunal Procedure, 1984, 2d edit., 1992, A Human Condition, 1975, 2d vol., 1977, Civil Liberties in Conflict, 1988, Public Health Law: Power, Duty, Restraint, 2000, 2nd edit., 2008, The AIDS Pandemic: Complacency, Injustice and Unfulfilled Expectations, 2004; editor Public Health law and Ethics: A Reader, 2002, 2nd edit. 2009, The Human Rights of Persons with Intellectual Disabilities: Different But Equal, 2003, Public Health Ethics, 2007, Biosecurity in the Global Age, 2008, Principles of Mental Health Law and Policy, 2010. Legal affairs com. Internat. League Socs. for Mentally Handicapped, Brussels, 1980—, prin. mental health law, 2010; trustee Cobden Trust, London, 1983-85; chmn. Advocacy Alliance, London, 1981-84; sec. All Party Parliamentary Civil Liberties Group, London, 1984-85; bd. dirs. ACLU, 1986—, exec. com., 1988—; mem. com. experts drafting conventions on human experientation UN, Siracusa, Italy, 1980-82. Recipient Rosemary Deldridge Meml. award Nat. Consumer Coun. U.K., 1983; fellow Kennedy Inst. Ethics, 1994—, Fulbright fellow U. Oxford, 1974-75. Avocations: climbing, vegetable growing. Home: 10413 Masters Ter Potomac MD 20854-3862 Office: Georgetown U Law Ctr 600 New Jersey Ave NW Washington DC 20001-2075 Business E-Mail: gostin@law.georgetown.edu.

GOSTON, JANAINA LAVALLI, nutritionist; b. Belo Horizonte, Minas Gerais, Aug. 28, 1977; Degree in Nutrition, Newton Paiva U., 2003; MSc in Food Sci., Fed. U. Minas Gerais, Belo Horizonte, 2008, DPH, 2008—; postgrad. in Exercise Physiology, UVA-RJ. Nutritionist specialist, sports ASBRAN, 2004—. Home: R Turvo N03 Apt 03 Lagoinha Belo Horizonte Minas Gerais 31210-110 Brazil Personal E-mail: jananutricao@yahoo.com.br.

GOSWAMI, GAURAV K., radiologist; b. Kota, India, Sept. 3, 1964; MD, Grant Med. Ctr., 1987. Pres., CEO Precise Intervention, 2010—. Recipient Resident Rsch. award, Radiologic Soc. N.Am. Mem.: Soc. Interventional Radiology. Achievements include development of newer devices to improve the lives of my patients. Avocations: travel, movies, writing. Office: 2284 N State College Blvd Fullerton CA 92831 Office Fax: 714-990-4376. Business E-Mail: drgmit@gmail.org.

GOSWAMI, NILESH J., cardiologist; b. London, Oct. 15, 1969; BS, Purdue U., 1991; MD, Southern Ill. U., 1995. Dir., CCU and chest pain ctr. Prairie Cardiovasc. Cons., Ltd., 2003—, exec. com. mem., 2011. Named one of Best Drs. America. Fellow: Soc. Cardiovasc. Angiography and Interventions, Am. Coll. Cardiology; mem.: Soc. Vascular Medicine. Avocations: scuba diving, cooking. Office: Prairie Heart Inst 619 E Mason Springfield IL 62794 Office Fax: 217-525-2535. Business E-Mail: ngoswami@prairieheart.com.

GOTFRYD, ALBERTO, orthopedist; b. Santos, Brazil, July 26, 1978; M, Santa Casa São Paulo Med. Sch., 2008, PhD. Preceptor, orthops. & spine dept. Santa Casa Santos Hosp., 2007—. Mem.: Brazilian Spien Soc. Office: Ave Ana Costa 259/51 Santos Sao Paulo 11060-907 Brazil Personal E-mail: albertocoluna@yaho.com.br.

GOTLIEB, JAQUELIN SMITH, pediatrician; b. Washington, Oct. 20, 1946; d. Turner Taliaferro and Lois Barbara (Fisk) Smith; m. Edward Marvin Gotlieb, June 25, 1970; children: Sarah Ruth, Aaron Franklin, David Jacob. BS in Zoology, Duke U., 1968; MD, Med. Coll. Va., 1972. Diplomate Am. Bd. Pediat. Rotating intern Med. Coll. Va. Hosps.-Va. Commonwealth U., Richmond, 1972—73, resident in pediat., 1973—74; pvt. practice Richmond, 1974—75, Stone Mountain, Ga., 1976—86, 1987—; resident in pediat. U. Colo., Denver, 1975—76; med. dir., cons. CIGNA Healthplan Ga., Atlanta, 1986—87. Sch. physician Richmond City Schs., 1974-75. Bd. dirs. Ga. Health Found., Atlanta, 1985-95, vice chmn., 1995-99, chmn., 1999-2005. Recipient Tee Rae Dismukes award, 2003. Fellow Am. Acad. Pediat. (Ga. chpt. bd. dirs. 1996-99, coord. state chpt. Pediat. Rsch. in Office Settings, 1996—, mem. steering com. Pediat. Rsch. in Office Settings, 2005—); mem. Med. Assn. Ga., Ga. Perinatal Assn. (bd. dirs. 1994-2002, pres. 1999-2000), DeKalb Med. Soc. (chmn. com. 1976). Office: Pediatric Center of Stone Mountain LLC 5405 Memorial Dr Ste D Stone Mountain GA 30083-3236 Home Phone: 770-564-2339; Office Phone: 404-296-3800. *

GOTO, HIROSHI, ophthalmologist, educator; b. Tokyo, Nov. 15, 1959; MD, Tokyo Med. U., 1978. Prof., chmn. Tokyo Med. U. Hosp., 2008—, v.p., 2009—. Recipient award, Japanese Ocular Histopath. Study. Mem.: Am. Acad. Ophthalmology, Japanese Ophthal. Soc. Avocation: running. Office: 6-7-1 Nishi-shinjuku Shinjuku-ku Tokyo 160-0023 Japan Office Fax: 81-3-3342-8430. Business E-Mail: goto1115@tokyo-med.ac.jp.

GOTO, MASAMI, medical researcher; MD, Kawasaki Med. Sch., Okayama, Japan, 1979, PhD. Prof. Kawasaki U. Med. Welfare, 2007—. Fellow: Am. Heart Assn. Achievements include patents for nitric oxide catheter. Home Phone: 81 0 086-273-4574; Office Phone: 81 0 086-462-1111. Office Fax: 81086-462-1193. Personal E-mail: mkiringoto@gmail.com. Business E-Mail: goto@me.kawasaki-m.ac.jp.

GOTO, NOBORU, neuroanatomist, neuropathologist, neurologist; b. Tokyo, Jan. 4, 1940; s. Iwao and Momoko Goto; m. Naoe Sekine, Aug. 23, 1964; 1 child, Jun. BS, Nihon U. Sch. Medicine, Tokyo, 1966, MD, 1967, PhD, 1971. Intern U. Hosp., 1966—67, asst. dept anatomy, 1967—71, sr. lectr., 1972; post grad. fellow Nat. Hosp., Queen Sq., London, 1973—75; abroad fellow Nihon U. Sch. Medicine, 1973—75, assoc. prof. anatomy, 1977—91; prof. and chmn. Showa U. Sch. Medicine, Tokyo, 1991—2005. Hon. pres. Koriyama Profl. Tng. Coll. Health Scis., 2005—. Achievements include discovery of pathogenesis of presbyacusis, aging of nerve fibers. Home: 28-10 Soshigaya 6 Setagaya-ku Tokyo 157-0072 Japan Office: Koriyama Profl Tng Coll 9-3 Zukei 2 Koriyama Fukushima 963-8834 Japan Office Fax: 81-24-936-7778. Personal E-mail: goto@sea.plala.or.jp. Business E-Mail: n-goto@k-tohto.ac.jp.

GOTTA, ALEXANDER WALTER, anesthesiologist, educator; b. Bklyn., Apr. 10, 1935; s. A. Walter and Helen C. (Bruskewic) G.; m. Colleen A. Sullivan, July 17, 1965; 1 child, Nancy C. BS summa cum laude, St. John's U., 1956; MD, NYU, 1960. Diplomate Am. Bd. Anesthesiology, Am. Bd. Med. Examiners. Intern U. Chgo., 1960-61; resident in surgery Boston City Hosp., 1961-62; resident in anesthesiology N.Y. Hosp.-Cornell U., NYC, 1962-64; instr. anesthesiology Cornell U., 1965-66; adj. prof. St. John's U., 1977—79; dir. anesthesia St. Mary's Hosp., Bklyn., 1968-78; from asst. prof. to prof. SUNY, Bklyn., 1968—97; prof. emeritus, 1997—; mem. dean's adv. bd. St. John's Coll., 2003—07. Dir. anesthesia L.I. Coll. Hosp., Bklyn., 1983-90, Kings County Hosp. Ctr., 1990-97; spkr. in field. Editor: Anesthesiology Clinics Trauma, 1996; contbr. articles to profl. jours. Capt. U.S. Army, 1966-68, Vietnam. Fellow N.Y. Acad. Medicine (chmn. anesthesia sect. 1990, recognition for svc. to urban medicine 1997), Am. Coll. Anesthesiologists, Am. Soc. Anesthesiologists (ho. dels. 1986-97, chmn. refresher course com. 1995); mem. N.Y. Soc. Anesthesiologists (bd. dirs. 1983-97, chmn. sci. program com. 1991-93, chmn. PGA 1994-96, v.p. 1994, pres.-elect 1995, pres. 1996, Disting. Svc. award, 2010), N.Y. Soc. Critical Care Medicine (pres. 1985), Assn. Univ. Anesthesiologists, Acad. Anesthesia. Republican. Roman Catholic. Home: 29 Ascot Ridge Rd Great Neck NY 11021-2912 Office: Kings County Hosp Ctr 451 Clarkson Ave Brooklyn NY 11203-2097 E-mail: alexwg@optonline.net.

GOTTENGER, EMANUEL EZEQUIEL, physician; s. Andre and Amalia Gottenger; m. Patricia Margarita Babilonia, Mar. 2, 1996; children: Leonardo Issac, Deborah. BS, Coll. Moral y Luces Herzl Bialik, Caracas, Venezuela, 1980—85; MD, U. Ctrl. de Venezuela, Caracas, 1986—93. Cert. Fla., 2001, diplomate Am. Bd. Urology, 2003. Physician Ministry of Health and Social Assistance, Caracas, Venezuela, 1993—94; rsch. scholar Baylor Coll. Medicine, Houston, 1994—95; surg. intern Beth Israel Med. Ctr., NYC, 1995—96, surg. resident, 1997—98, urology resident, 1998—2001; urologic oncology, laparoscopy fellowship Dept. Veterans Affairs Med. Ctr., West Palm Beach, Fla., 2001—02, attending urologist, physician-in-charge laparoscopic urology, 2002—05, Advanced Urology of South Fla., LLC, 2005—. Contbr. articles to profl. jours., chapters to books. Recipient Scholars in Urology Award, Pfizer Corp., 1999, 2000. Fellow: ACS; mem.: Fla. Urol. Soc., Am. Urol. Assn. South Eastern Sect. Avocations: computers, travel, bicycling. Office: 5350 W Atlantic Ave Ste 102 Delray Beach FL 33484 Office Phone: 561-496-4444. Office Fax: 561-496-2001. Business E-Mail: urologist4u@comcast.net.

GOTTESMAN, IRVING I., psychologist, educator; b. Cleve., Dec. 29, 1930; s. Bernard and Virginia (Weitzner) G.; m. Carol Applen, Dec. 23, 1970; children: Adam M., David B. BS, Ill. Inst. Tech., 1953; PhD, U. Minn., 1960. Diplomate in clin. psychology and psychol. assessment; lic. psychologist, Va. Intern clin. psychology VA Hosp., Mpls., 1959—60; lectr. depts. social rels. and psychology Harvard U., 1960—63; USPHS fellow in psychiat. genetics Inst. Psychiatry, London, 1963—64; assoc. prof. psychiat. & genetics, dept. psychiatry U. N.C., 1964—66; prof. dept. psychology, psychiatry and genetics U. Minn., 1966—80; prof. dept. psychiatry and genetics Washington U., St. Louis, 1980—85; Commonwealth prof. psychology U. Va., Charlottesville, 1985—94, Sherrell J. Aston prof. psychology, prof. clin. pediats., 1994—2001, Sherrell J. Aston prof. emeritus, 2001—; sr. fellow psychology, Drs. Irving and Dorothy Bernstein prof. adult psychiatry U. Minn., 2001—. Cons. NIMH, Washington, 1975-79, 92-96, NIMH Nat. Plan for Schizophrenia, 1988-89; mem. Pres.'s Commn. on Huntington Disease, 1977; tng. cons. VA, Washington, 1968-85, 2001—10, MPLS, 2010-; fellow Ctr. for Advanced Studies in the Behavioral Scis., Stanford, Calif., 1987-88; Inst. of Medicine Com. cons. Vietnam War Experience Study, 1987-88, Med. Follow-Up Agy., 2000—10; NRC cons. Workshop on Schizophrenia, 1995-96; cons. human rights Equal Opportunities Commn., Hong Kong, 1999-2003, 05-06; mem. Inst. Medicine Follow-up Agy., 2000—10; chair twins com. Inst. Medicine, 2000-07, mem. com. on genomics and the public's health in the 21st century, 2004-05, Bd. Health Select Populations, 2005-10; cons. Inst. Psychology, Chinese Acad. Scis., 2011-. Author: Schizophrenia and Genetics, 1972 (Hofheimer prize), Schizophrenia The Epigenetic Puzzle, 1982, Schizophrenia Genesis: The Origins of Madness, 1991 (transl. into Japanese and German, William James Book award, Phi Beta Kappa U. Va. Book award 1992), Schizophrenia and Genetic Risks, 1992, 3d edit., 1999, Schizophrenia and Manic Depressive Disorder: Biological Roots of Mental Illness Revealed by Study of Identical Twins, 1994, transl. into Japanese, 1998, Seminars in Psychiatric Genetics, 1994, Psychiatric Genetics and Genomics, 2002, revised, 2004; editor: Man, Mind and Heredity, 1971, Vital Statistics, Demography and Schizophrenia, 1989. Served with USNR, 1949-53, 56-61; USN, 1953-56. Guggenheim fellow U. Copenhagen, 1972; recipient R. Thornton Wilson prize Ea. Psychiat. Rsch. Assn., 1965, Stanley Dean award Am. Coll. Psychiatrists, 1988, Eric Strömgren medal Danish Psychiat. Soc., 1991, Kurt Schneider prize, Bonn, 1992, Alexander Gralnick prize Am. Assn. Suicidology, 1992, Jonathan Logan award Nat. Alliance for Mentally Ill, 1995; David C. Wilson lectr. U. Va. Sch. Medicine, 1967, Lifetime Achievement award Internat. Soc. for Psychiat. Genetics, 1997; Parker lectr. Ohio State U. Sch. Medicine, 1983, 93, Gralnick award Res. severe Mental Illness, NARSAD, Lieber prize, others. Fellow APA (Disting. Scientist award divsn. 12, sect. 3 1994, Disting. Sci. Contbns. award 2001), AAAS, Am. Psychopathol. Assn., Royal Coll. Psychiatrists (hon. fellow), Am. Psychol. Soc. (human capital initiative task force for psychopathology rsch. agenda 1993-96); mem. Minn. Human Genetics League (v.p. 1969-71), Soc. Study Social Biology (v.p. 1976-80), Behavior Genetics Assn. (pres. 1976-77, J. LeJeune lectr. 2007, T. Dobzhansky award 1990), Am. Soc. Human Genetics (editl. bd. 1967-72), Soc. Rsch. in Psychopathology (pres. 1993, Joseph Zubin award 2001), Japanese Soc. Biol. Psychiatry (spl. lecture award 2001), Inst. of Psychiatry (14th Eliot Slater Lectr., 2002), Am. Psychol. Found. (Life Achievement Gold medal, 2007), Soc. Biol. Psychiatry. Business E-Mail: gotte003@umn.edu.

GOTTESMAN, LESTER, colon and rectal surgeon, educator; MD, U. Pitts., Pa., 1978. Diplomate Am. Bd. Surgery, 1984, Am. Bd. Colon and Rectal Surgery, 1993. Resident surgery St. Luke's Roosevelt Hosp. Ctr., NYC, 1978—83; fellow surgery Mem. Sloan Kettering Cancer Ctr., NYC, 1984—85; fellow colon & rectal surgery Ferguson Clinic, Grand Rapids, Mich., 1986—87; assoc. prof. surgery Columbia Univ. Coll. Physicians and Surgeons. Named Top Doctor, Castle Connolly NYC, 2009; named one of Bst Doctors, NY Mag., 2010. Office: St. Luke's Roosevelt Hospital Center 425 W 59th St Suite 9A New York NY 10019 Office Phone: 212-523-8417. Office Fax: 212-523-8186.

GOTTESMAN, MICHAEL MARC, biomedical researcher; b. Jersey City, Oct. 7, 1946; s. Jacob Joseph and Frieda (Shapiro) Gottesman; m. Susan Kemelhor, Feb. 5, 1966; children: Daniel Eric, Rebecca Fran. AB, Harvard Coll., 1966; MD, Harvard Med. Sch., 1970. Diplomate Am. Bd. Internal Medicine. Med. intern, resident Peter Bent Brigham Hosp., Boston, 1970-71, 74-75; rsch. assoc. NIH, Bethesda, Md., 1971-74, sr. investigator, Nat. Cancer Inst., 1976-80, chief molecular genetics sect., Lab. Molecular Biology, 1980-90, chief Lab. Cell Biology, 1990—, acting dir. Nat. Ctr. Human Genome Rsch., 1992—93, acting sci. dir., 1993, dep. dir. intramural rsch., 1993—, head multidrug resistance sect. Asst. prof. dept. anatomy Harvard Med. Sch., 1975—76; asst. surgeon gen. USPHS. Recipient

Milken Family Found. award for cancer rsch., 1988, C.E. Alken prize, 1991, Samuel G. Taylor III award for excellence in cancer rsch., 1991, Jefferson Cancer Inst. prize, 1991, Rosenthal Found. award, 1992, Am. Soc. Pharmacology & Exptl. Therapeutics (ASPET) award, 1997. Fellow: AAAS. Office: Nat Cancer Inst Lab Cell Biology 37 Convent Dr Bldg 1A09 Bethesda MD 20892-4255 Office Phone: 301-496-1530. Office Fax: 301-402-0450. Business E-Mail: mgottesman@od.nih.gov. *

GOTTESMAN, SUSAN, federal agency administrator; BA magna cum laude, Radcliffe Coll., Cambridge, Mass., 1967; PhD, Harvard U., 1972. Postdoc. fellow Lab. Molecular Biology, Nat. Cancer Inst., NIH, Bethesda, Md., 1971—74, rsch. chemist, sr. investigator, 1976—85, acting chief biochemical genetics sect., 1985—86, chief biochemical genetics sect., 1987—; rsch. assoc. dept. biology MIT, 1974—76. Mem. adv. com. NIH Office Rsch. Svcs., 1986—89; mem. EPA Biotechnology Sci. Adv. Com., 1987—89, chair subcom. pre-manufacture notification, 1995; mem. bd. sci. advisors Jane Coffin Childs Meml. Fund Med. Rsch., 1988—96; mem. rsch. scholars adv. program panel com. Howard Hughes Med. Inst., 1989—92, mem. rsch. tng. fellowships med. students review com., 1995—97; mem. scholars adv. panel Fogarty Internat. Ctr., 1990—94, chair scholars adv. panel, 1992—94. Mem. editl. bd. Jour. Bacteriology, 1987—89, assoc. editor, 1989—99, mem. editl. bd. Genes & Develop., 1992—; contbr. articles to profl. jours. Nat. Merit Scholar, 1963, NSF postdoctoral fellow, 1969, Jane Coffin Childs Meml. fund for med. postdoctoral fellow, 1971. Mem.: AAAS (coun. mem. 1992—95), NAS (coun. mem. 2006—09), Am. Soc. Biochemistry & Molecular Biology (coun. mem. 1992—95), Am. Soc. Microbiology (chmn. divsn. genetics and molecular biology 1985—86, chair ethical practices com. 1991—97), Genetics Soc. America, Am. Acad. Microbiology. Office: Lab Molecular Biology Nat Cancer Inst NIH Bldg 37 Rm 5132 37 Convent Dr MSC 4255 Bethesda MD 20892-4255 Office Phone: 301-496-3524. Office Fax: 301-496-3875. Business E-Mail: susang@helix.nih.gov.

GOTTFRIED, EUGENE LESLIE, physician, educator; b. Passaic, NJ, Feb. 26, 1929; s. David Robert and Rose (Chill) G.; m. Phyllis Doris Swain, Aug. 16, 1957. AB, Columbia U., 1950, MD, 1954. Cert. Nat. Bd. Med. Examiners, Am. Bd. Internal Medicine. Intern Presbyn. Hosp., NYC, 1954-55, asst. resident in medicine, 1957-58; resident Bronx (N.Y.) Mcpl. Hosp. Ctr., 1958-59, fellow in medicine, 1959-60; asst. instr. medicine Albert Einstein Coll. Medicine Yeshiva U., NYC, 1959-60, instr., 1960-61, assoc., 1961-65, asst. prof., 1965-69; assoc. prof. medicine Cornell U. Med. Coll., NYC, 1969-81, assoc. prof. pathology, 1975-81; clin. prof. dept. lab. medicine U. Calif., San Francisco, 1981-93, prof., 1993-99, vice chmn. dept. lab. medicine, 1981-98, prof. emeritus, 1999—. Hosp. appointments include asst. vis. physician Bronx Mcpl. Hosp. Ctr. 1960-66, assoc. attending physician, 1966-69; assoc. attending physician N.Y. Hosp., N.Y.C., 1969-81, assoc. attending pathologist, 1975-81, dir. lab. clin. hematology, 1969-81; chief lab. medicine San Francisco Gen. Hosp. Med. Ctr., 1981-98, dir. clin. labs., 1981-98. Assoc. editor Jour. Lipid Research, 1971-72, 75-77; mem. editorial bd. Jour. Lipid Research, 1972-77. Dir. Rescue One Found., 1998—, Moraga-Orinda Fire Protection Dist., 2002—, Lt. comdr. M.C. USNR, 1955—57, with Ready Res. USNR, 1957—64. Recipient Career Scientist award Health Research Council City of N.Y., 1964-72; Named Volunteer of Yr. Orinda, 2007. Fellow ACP, Am. Soc. Hematology, Internat. Soc. Hematology, Acad. Clin. Lab. Physicians and Scientists, Nat. Com. Clin. Lab. Stds. (chair area com. on hematology 1995-00), Orinda Pub. Safety Adv. Commn., Rotary (pres. Orinda club 2004-05), Phi Beta Kappa, Alpha Omega Alpha. Business E-Mail: eugene.gottfried@ucsf.edu.

GOTTLANDER, ROBERT JAN LARS, dental company executive; b. Bohuslan, Sweden, Sept. 5, 1956; came to U.S., 1986; s. Jan H. K. and Ragnhild S.E. (Rutgerson) G.; m. Eva L.M. Svenson, July 4, 1987; children: Daniel J.R., Magdalena A.E., Linnea E.R. Student, Kongahalla Coll., Sweden, 1975; candidate of odontology, U. Gothenburg, Sweden, 1976, DDS, 1980. Dentist Swedish Health Care, Trollhattan, Sweden, 1980-82; asst. prof. dept. orthodontics Community Dentistry, Trollhattan, 1982-84; mgr. tng. and edn. Nobelpharma AB, Gothenburg, 1984-85, product mgr., 1985; v.p., mgr. edn. and product Nobelpharma USA Inc., Waltham, Mass., 1986-87, v.p. profl. affairs, 1987-88, v.p., gen. mgr. Chgo., 1988—2002; v.p. global mktg. Nobel Biocare AB, Gothenburg, Sweden, 2002; exec. v.p. global mktg. Nobel Rnocare AB, 2005. Pres. V-Dal Union of Dentists, Trollhattan, Sweden, 1982-84; chmn. V-Dal Dental Soc., Sweden, 1983-84, sec. 1981-82; v.p. global mktg. Nobel Biocare AB, Sweden, 2001, exec. v.p., 2005. Lt. Swedish Royal Navy, 1976-79. Mem. AMA, Swedish Dental Soc., Swedish Orthodontic Soc.; affiliate mem. ADA, Acad. of Osseointegration. Lutheran. Avocations: sailing, skiing, tennis, reading. Home Phone: 41446801538; Office Phone: 41432114237. Business E-Mail: robert@gottlander.com.

GOTTLIEB, ALICE B., dermatologist, rheumatologist; PhD in Immunology, Rockefeller U., 1979; MD, Cornell U., 1980. Diplomate Am. Bd. Dermatology, bd. cert. rheumatology and internal medicine. Fellow in rheumatology Cornell U. Hosp. for Spl. Surgery, NYC, 1982—84; resident in internal medicine N.Y. Hosp., NYC, 1980—82, resident in dermatology, 1990—93; chair dermatology, dermatologist-in-chief Tufts Med. Ctr., Boston, 2006—; Hanvey B Ansell prof. dermatology Tufts U. Sch. Med. Office: Tufts Med Ctr 800 Washington St Box 114 Boston MA 02111 Office Phone: 617-636-0156.

GOTTLIEB, BETH SUSAN GLASS, pediatric rheumatologist; MS, Yeshiva U.; MD, Tel Aviv U., 1992. Diplomate Am. Bd. Pediatrics, Am. Bd. Pediatrics-pediatric rheumatology. Intern Schneider Children's Hosp., 1993, resident, 1995, fellow, 1998; hosp. affiliations include LI Jewish Med. Ctr., North Shore Univ. Hosp., Steven and Alexandra Cohen Children's Med. Ctr. of NY. Named one of Best Doctors, NY Mag. Office: Steven and Alexandra Cohen Children's Medical Center of New York 269-01 76th Ave New Hyde Park NY 11040 Office Phone: 718-470-3530. Office Fax: 718-831-0182.

GOTTLIEB, GARY LLOYD, healthcare system administrator, psychiatrist; b. May 6, 1955; m. Derri Shtasel; 2 children. BS cum laude, Rensselaer Poly. Inst., Troy, NY, 1975; MD, Albany Med. Coll., NY, 1979; MBA Health Care Adminstrn., with distinction, Wharton Sch., U. Pa., 1985. Diplomate American Bd. Psychiatry and Neurology, cert. in psychiatry and geriatric psychiatry. Intern NYU Med. Ctr., NYC, 1979-80, resident in psychiatry, 1980-82, chief resident in psychiatry, 1982-83; Robert Wood Johnson Found. clin. scholar U. Pa., Phila., 1983-85; instr. to assoc. prof. dept. psychiatry U. Pa. Sch. Medicine, 1985-94, clin. prof. psychiatry, 1994—98; dir., CEO Friends Hosp., Phila., 1994—2002; prof. psychiatry Harvard Med. Sch., Boston, 1998—; pres. Brigham & Women's Hosp., Boston, 2002—09; pres., CEO Partners Healthcare Sys. Inc., Boston, 2010—. Assoc. dean managed care U. Pa. Med. Ctr., 1992—94, interim chair dept. psychiatry, 1993—94; Ascher-Globus vis. prof. Cornell U. Sch. Medicine, 1993. Mem. editl. bd. Internat. Jour. Geriatric Psychiatry, asst. editor American Jour. Geriatric Psychiatry; contbr. articles to profl. jours. Recipient Earl Bond award for teaching excellence, U. Pa., 1999, Christian R. and Mary F. Lindback Found. award for disting. tchg., 1991. Mem.: Soc. Health & Human Values, Gerontol. Soc. America, Assn. Acad. Psychiatry, American Assn. Geriatric Psychiatry (bd. dirs. 1987—90, pres. 1993—95), Alzheimer's Assn., American Assn. Gen. Hosp. Psychiatrists, American Geriatrics Soc., American Psychiat. Assn., Inst. Medicine, Beta Gamma Sigma. Office: Partners Healthcare System 800 Boylston St Boston MA 02199-8185 *

GOTTLIEB, MARISE SUSS, physician, epidemiologist; b. NYC, July 16, 1938; d. Lester J. and Fannie (Freeman) Suss; m. A. Arthur Gottlieb, June 8, 1958 (dec.); children: Mindy Cheryl Davidson, Joanne Meredith. AB, Barnard Coll., 1958; MD, NYU, 1962; MPH, Harvard U., 1966. Diplomate Am. Bd. Preventive Medicine. Intern medicine Mass. Meml. Hosp., 1962—63; resident preventative medicine dept. epidemiology Harvard U. Sch. Pub. Health, 1965—68; instr. dept. medicine Harvard Med. Sch., Boston, 1969—70; fellow, asst. Medicine Peter Bent Brigham Hosp.; dir. chronic disease control N.J. Dept. Health, Trenton, 1970—75; asst. prof. dept. cmty. medicine Rutgers Med. Sch., Piscataway, NJ, 1972—75; assoc. prof. dept. medicine Tulane U. Sch. Medicine, New Orleans, 1975—91; assoc. prof. dept. epidemiology Sch. Pub. Health, 1975—80; chief chronic disease control La. Dept. Health and Human Resources, Tulane U., New Orleans, 1975—85; dir. clin. and regulatory affairs, v.p. med. affairs Imreg Inc., New Orleans, 1985—98; sec. treas. Pres. Endeavor Corp., 1998—; mem. bd. alumni coun. Harvard U. Sch. Pub. Health, 2005—; mem. epidemiology and disease control study sect. NIH, Bethesda, 1982—85; NIH traineeship, 1965—66; spl research fellow Nat. Inst. Arthritis, Metabolism and Digestive Diseases, 1966—68. Contbr. articles to profl. jours. Fellow: Am. Coll. Epidemiology, Am. Coll. Preventive Medicine; mem.: Am. Pub. Health Assn., Am. Fedn. Med. Rsch., Soc. Epidemiol. Rsch., Am. Diabetes Assn. Home: 215 Chestnut Hill Rd Chestnut Hill MA 02467-1313 Business E-Mail: marsgott@massmed.org.

GOTTLIEB, MICHAEL NORMAN, internist, educator, health facility administrator; b. Bklyn., July 26, 1943; s. Louis and Grace Gottlieb; m. Anne A. Appelman, Dec. 25, 1965; children: Brian, Elizabeth. BA, SUNY, Binghamton, 1964; MD, SUNY, Bklyn., 1968. Diplomate Am. Bd. Internal Medicine. Intern Univ. Hosp. U. Calif., San Diego, 1968-69, resident Univ. Hosp., 1969-71, clin. fellow in nephrology, 1971-72, 1971-72; rsch. fellow in medicine Harvard Med. Sch., Boston, 1972-73; spl. fellow Peter Bent Brigham Hosp. NIH, Boston, 1972-73; instr. in medicine Peter Bent Brigham Hosp., Harvard Med. Sch., Boston, 1974-77; asst. clin. prof. medicine Harvard Med. Sch., Boston, 1976—; ptnr. Commonwealth Nephrology Assn., Boston, 1977—; assoc. chair dept. medicine Metrowest Med. Ctr., Framingham, Mass., 1992-95, chief med. officer, 1995—; dir. West Suburban Artifical Kidney Ctr., 1980—2010. Assoc. in medicine Peter Bent Brigham Hosp., Boston, 1975—82; med. dir. West Suburban Artificial Kidney Ctr., Framingham, Mass., 1980—, The Kidney Ctr., Boston, 2001—04, MetroWest Artificial Kidney Ctr., Waltham, Mass., 1990—2006, active staff, 1992—; assoc. physician Brigham and Women's Hosp., Boston, 1982—; courtesy staff Norwood (Mass.) Hosp., 1994—; bd. dirs. End Stage Renal Disease Network #1. Contbr. to med. textbooks, numerous articles to profl. jours. Mem. AMA, ACP, Am. Soc. Nephrology, Am. Soc. Artificial Internal Organs, Mass. Med. Soc., Am. Soc. Enteral and Parenteral Nutrition, Am. Coll. Physician Execs., Internat. Soc. Artificial Organs. Avocations: boating, sailing. Office: Metrowest Med Ctr 67 Union St Natick MA 01760-6056 Office Phone: 508-650-7155. E-mail: michael.gottlieb@mwmc.com.

GOTTO, ANTONIO MARION, JR., dean, internist, medical educator; b. Nashville, Oct. 10, 1935; s. Antonio M. and Reather (Gray) Gotto; m. Anita Louise Safford, July 21, 1959; children: Jennifer, Gillian, Teresa. BA magna cum laude, Vanderbilt U., 1957, MD, 1965; DPhil, Oxford U., Eng., 1961; LLD (hon.), Abilene Christian U., 1979; MD (hon.), U. Bologna, 1982. Diplomate Am. Bd. Internal Medicine. Intern Mass. Gen. Hosp., Boston, 1965—66, resident, 1966—67; practice medicine specializing in internal medicine, 1967—; head molecular disease br. Nat. Heart and Lung Inst. NIH, Bethesda, Md., 1969—71; dir. and prin. investigator Lipid Rsch. Clinic, Houston, 1971—77; prof. medicine, chief dir., arteriosclerosis and lipoprotein rsch. Baylor Coll. Medicine, Houston, 1971—96; dir., prin. investigator specialized ctr. rsch. in arteriosclerosis Nat. Heart, Lung and Blood Inst., 1971—96, dir., prin. investigator Spl. Ctr. Rsch. Arteriosclerosis, 1971—96; J.S. Abercrombie prof. Baylor Coll. Medicine, 1976—96, Disting. Svc. prof., 1985—96; sci. dir. Meth. Hosp. and Baylor Nat. Rsch. and Demonstration Ctr., 1974—83, 1987—90; Bob and Vivian Smith prof. and chmn. dept. medicine Baylor Coll. Medicine, 1977—96; chief internal medicine svcs. The Meth. Hosp., 1977—96; provost med. affairs Cornell U., 1997—, dean Weill Med. Coll., 1997—. Hon. guest lectr. various med. socs., schs. and hosps., 1972—; mem. nat. diabetes adv. bd. HEW (now HHS), 1977—84; mem. steering com. Italian-Am. com. on cardiovascular disease NIH, 1978—; mem. adv. coun. Nat. Heart, Lung and Blood Inst., 1987—91; hon. prof. U. Buenos Aires, 1985. Author (with Michael E. DeBakey): The Living Heart, 1977; author: The Living Heart Diet, 1984, The New Living Heart Diet, 1996, The New Living Heart, 1997; editor: Current Atherosclerosis Reports, 1998—, Current Practice of Medicine, 1999—; co-editor: Atherosclerosis Rev. Series, 1976—92, Jour. Cardiovasc. Risk, 1994—; mem. editl. bd.: Jour. Biol. Chemistry, 1976—81, Advanced in Lipid Rsch., 1973—78, Am. Heart Jour., 1981—, Arteriosclerosis, 1981—89, Circulation Rsch., 1974—79, Cardiovascular Rsch. Ctr. Bull., 1972—; contbr. articles on biochem. and cardiovascular rsch. to profl. publs. Mem. sci. adv. bd. Fondation Cardiologique Princesse Liliane, Brussels, 1976—, Lorenzini Found., Milan, Fritz Thyssen Found., Cologne, Germany; mem. Mission of Houston Econ. Devel. Coun., 1985; walkathon chmn. Juvenile Diabetes Found., 1986. With USPHS, 1967—69. Decorated knight Order of Merit, Italy, Order of the Lion Finland; recipient Albert Weinstein award, 1965, Laurea ad Honorem, U. Bologna, Seale Harris award, So. Med. Assn., 1995; named hon. cons., Adm. Bristol Hosp., Istanbul, Turkey, Houston Internat. Exec. Yr., 1987; named one of New York's Influentials, New York Mag., 2006; grantee, John A. Hartford Found., 1971—75. Fellow: Am. Coll. Cardiology; mem.: Am. Longevity Assn., Am. Assn. Rhodes Scholars, Am. Bd. Internal Medicine, Am. Heart Assn. (pres. 1983—84, past pres. 1984—86, Paul Ledbetter award for disting. svc., Paul Dudley White award for outstanding contbns., Gold Heart award 1989), Am. Diabetes Assn., Am. Soc. Biol. Chemists, Am. Assn. Physicians, Internat. Soc. Atherosclerosis (pres. 1985—, Achievement award 1982), So. Soc. Clin. Investigation, Am. Soc. Clin. Investigation (v.p. 1980—81), Inst. Medicine of NAS, River Oaks Country Club, Alpha Omega Alpha. Presbyterian. Office: Weill Med Cornell U 1300 York Ave Rm F 105 New York NY 10021-4805 Office Phone: 212-746-6005. Business E-Mail: dean@med.cornell.edu. *

GOTTS, EDWARD EARL, psychologist, researcher; s. Earl and Norma Noma Gotts; m. Shirley Jean Lund, Sept. 10, 1955; children: Gregory, Gary, Kimberly. BA, Whitworth Coll., Spokane, 1960, MA, 1962; PhD, U. Tex., Austin, 1966. Lic. psychologist Ind., diplomate Am. Bd. Assessment Psychology, Am. Bd. Profl. Psychology. Asst. prof. edn. psychology U. Tex., Austin, 1966—67; rsch. coord., asst. prof. inst. child study Ind. U., Bloomington, 1967—69, prof., psychol. dir. Devel. Tng. Ctr., 1972—74; dir. divsn. childhood & parenting Appalachian Edn. Lab., Charleston, W.Va., 1974—83; chief psychology, clin. prof. Marshall Med. Sch., Huntington, W.Va., 1983—86; chief psychologist, internship dir. Madison State Hosp., Ind., 1986—2003; adj. faculty Mass. Sch. Profl. Psychology, Boston, 2004—. Mem. Child Mental Health Adv. Bd., Indpls., 1968—76, chair, 1973—74; mem. Gov.'s Mental Health Adv. Bd., Indpls., 1974—76, Mental Health & MR Planning Commn., Indpls., 1974—76. Author: The Clinical Application of MMPI Special Scales, 1995, The Clinical Interpretation of the MMPI-2, 2005; gen. editor: The Home Visitor's Kit, 1977. Bd. dirs. First Steps Program, Madison, 1994—97; lay leader, lay spkr. N. United Meth. Ch., Madison, 1999—. Capt. USAF, 1953—57. Fellow, U. Colo. Med. Ctr., 1971—72; USPHS fellow, U. Tex., 1965—67. Fellow: APA, AERA; mem.: Soc. Personality Assessment, Ind. Psychol. Assn. (editor 1996—97), Rotary (bd. dirs. Madison chpt. 1989—90). Avocations: travel, gardening, hiking. Office: PO Box 856 Madison IN 47250

GOTTSCHALL, CARLOS SANTOS, veterinarian, educator; b. Porto Alegre, Rio Grande do Sul, Brazil, Sept. 14, 1967; s. Carlos Antonio Mascia and Elisabete Maria Santos Gottschall; m. Catarina Andreatta Gottschall, July 20, 1996; 1 child, Carolina Andreatta. Diploma in vet. medicine, U. Fed. do Rio Grande do Sul, Porto Alegre, 1991, MS, 1994. Adv. in animal prodn. Autonomous, Porto Alegre, Rio Grande do Sul, Brazil, 1993—; prof. U. Luterana, Canoas, Rio Grande do Sul, 1994—; instr. in animal prodn. Senar / Rs, Porto Alegre, 1996—98. Plan and projects in animal prodn. Fundação U. Empresa Technologica e Ciências, Porto Alegre, 1995—98. Author: Desmame de terneiros de corte. Como? Quando? Porquê?, 2002, Gestao e Manejo para a bovinocultura lerteira, 2002, Produção de Novilhos Precoces: Nutrição Manejo e Custos de produção, 2005, 2d edit.; editor: Veterinaria em Foco; contbr. articles to profl. jours. Home: Rua Des Augusto L Lima 129 / 402 Rio Grande do Sul Porto Alegre 90 470-120 Brazil Office: Univ Luterana do Brasil Av Farroupilha Rio Grande do Sul Canoas 92 450-900 Brazil Personal E-mail: carlosgott@cpovo.net.

GOU, DAO DI, medical educator; b. Qing-Dao, China, Mar. 8, 1971; PhD, Peking U., 2010. Lectr. Peking U., 1997. Office: 38 Xue-Yuan Rd Hai-Dian Dist Beijing 100191 China Business E-Mail: b.gou@bjmu.edu.cn.

GOUDESEUNE, SCOTT, medical association administrator; Dir. learning, devel., US sales Coors Brewing Co., Golden, Colo.; v.p. US sales Reebok CCS Fitness, Aurora, Colo., 1997—2000; v.p. sales, new bus. Am. Coun. on Exercise, San Diego, 2000—03, v.p. ops., 2003—05, COO, 2005—06, pres., CEO, 2006—. Mem.: Nat. Coalition Promoting Phys. Activity (bd. dirs.). Office: Am Coun on Exercise 4851 Paramound San Diego CA 92123 Office Phone: 858-279-8227. Office Fax: 858-279-8064. *

GOUGH, JANET, writer, consultant; b. NYC; BA in English, Montclair St U., 1982; MA in English, Seton Hall U., 1986. Cons. systems, documentation and tng. for biotech., device and pharm. cos.; dir. tech. comm. Cerus Corp., Concord, Calif., 2000—02; prof. English Seton Hall U., South Orange, NJ, Rutgers U., New Brunswick, NJ; course dir. tech. writing, process writing, ESL and electronic record keeping for profl. tng. orgns. Author: Write It Down: Guidance for Preparing Effective and Compliant Documentation, 2000, 2d edit., 2004, Hosting a Compliance Inspection; co-author: Electronic Record Keeping: Achieving and Maintaining Compliance with 21 CFR Part II and 45 CFR Parts 160,162, 164, The Internal Quality Audit, The External Quality Audit, The Clinical Trial Manual; contbr. articles to profl. jours. Mem.: Tchrs. of English to Spkrs. of Other Langs., Am. Med. Writers Assn., Regulatory Affairs Profl. Soc. Office Phone: 973-252-3731. E-mail: janetgough@optonline.net.

GOULART, DARIO GRECHI, ophthalmologist; b. São Paulo, Brazil, July 8, 1971; MD, Faculdade da Santa Casa de Sao Paulo, 1994; PhD, U. Sao Paulo, 2008. Cert. retina and vitreous specialist. Assoc. MD Retina and Vitreous Sector, Hosp. da Santa Casa de São Paulo, 2001—07; chmn. retina and vitreous sector Hosp. Metropolitano de São Paulo, 2002—08, chmn. dept. ophthalmology, 2005—08, chmn. ophthalmological urgencies, 2005—08; chmn. Centro Paulista da Visão, 2007—. Vol. cataract surgeon MD Corumbá Campaigns (MT), 1998—2000. Retina & Vitreous fellowship, Santa Casa de Sao Paulo Ophthalmology Dept., 1998—2000. Mem.: Conselho Brasileiro de Oftalmologia, Sociedade Brasileira de Retina e Vítreo, Am. Acad. Ophthalmology. Roman Catholic. Office: Ctr Paulista da Visão R Mário Borin 559 Vl Va Jundiaí São Paulo 13209030 Brazil Home: Ave Prof Mucio Lobo Costa 82 C4 Jundiai SP 13208-710 Brazil Office Phone: 551145212166. Office Fax: 551145212492. Personal E-mail: dggoulart@gmail.com. Business E-Mail: cpvisao@gmail.com.

GOULD, BRUCE ELLIOTT, physician, academic administrator, educator; b. Queens, NY, 1954; BA, Cornell U.; MD, SUNY, Syracuse, 1979. Intern U. Mass. Med. Ctr., Worcester, resident in medicine, fellow in medicine; prof. gen. internal medicine U. Conn. Sch. Medicine, assoc. dean primary care; med. dir. St. Francis Hosp./U. Conn. Primary Care Ctr. Burgdorf /Fleet Health Ctr., Hartford, Hartford Dept. Health and Human Svcs. Dir. Conn. area health edn. ctr. program U. Conn. Sch. Medicine, 1997—, founder, participant Migrant Farm Workers program, 1998—; chair nat. adv. coun. migrant health U.S. Dept. HHS, 2004—. Mem.: AMA Found. (Pride in Profession award 2004). Office: Burgdorf Health Ctr 131 Coventry St Hartford CT 06112 Address: U Conn Health Ctr 263 Farmington Ave Farmington CT 06030-2926 Office Phone: 860-679-4322. Fax: 860-679-1101. E-mail: gould@adp.uchc.edu. *

GOULD, LANCE K., medical scientist, professor; s. Kenneth Newton and Elizabeth May (Barrett) G.; m. Helene Freiin von Eckardstein, Sept. 28, 1970; 1 son, Stefan Anton. MD, Case Wes. Res., Cleve., 1964. Martin Bucksbaum disting. U. chair cardiovasc. medicine U. Tex. Med. Sch. Houston, 1979—, exec. dir. Weatherhead Heart Ctr.; exec. dir. Weatherhead P.E.T. Ctr. Preventing & Reversing Atherosclerosis. Mem. editorial bd. Circulation, 1988-92, Circulation Res., 1982-87, 2004—, Jour. Am. Coll. Cardiology, 1982-88, 2004—, Am. Jour. Cardiology, 1978-86; assoc. editor Circulation, 1993-2003; contbr. articles to profl. jours Lt comdr. US Army, 1967—69, Atlanta, GA and Hawaii-Pacific Trust Territories. Recipient George von Hevesy prize, 1978, ACC Young Investigators award, 1983 Fellow Am. Coll. Cardiology (trustee 1984-89), Am. Heart Assn. (chmn. coun. on circulation, Brown Meml. lectr. 1990); mem. Am. Soc. Clin. Investigation, Soc. Nuclear Medicine, N.Am. Soc. Cardiac Radiology, Am. Physiologic Soc., Assn. Am. Physicians, Assn. Univ. Cardiologists, NIH diagnostic radiol. study sect., Houston Cardiol. Soc. (pres. 1983) Democrat. First to report the concept of coronary flow reserve for defining stenosis severity, quantification of stenosis fluid dynamics in vivo, pharmacologic stress perfusion imaging, experimental and clinical positron emission tomography (PET) of coronary artery stenosis, improved PET perfusion defects in patients with CAD after both short and long term lipid lowering, the basic principles of and mathematical structure of the coronary artery tree, the longitudinal base to apex perfusion abnormality of diffuse coronary atherosclerosis before localized stenosis, the resting perfusion heterogeneity of endothelial dysfunction due to early CAD and an 80% reduction in coronary events in CAD after intense combined pharmacologic and lifestyle treatment compared to usual care & leader in cardiac Positron Tomography. Office: Univ Texas Med School 6431 Fannin Rm 4256MSB Houston TX 77030 Office Fax: 713-500-6615. Business E-Mail: k.lance.gould@uth.tmc.edu.

GOULD, LISA, surgeon; b. Elmhurst, Ill., Oct. 2, 1959; BA, Knox Coll., 1977; MD, PhD, U. Ill., 1990. Asst. prof. Med. Coll. Wis., 1999—2001; assoc. prof. U. Tex. Med. Br., 2001—07, U. South Fla., 2007—; staff physician James A Haley Vets. Hosp., 2007—. Oral examiner Am. Bd. Plastic Surgeons, 2010—. Spinal Cord Injury Hypothesis Devel. grant, Dept. Def., grant, NIA/Hartford Found., VA. Fellow: ACS; mem.: Am. Assn. Hand Surgeons, Am. Soc. Surgery Hand, Am. Soc. Plastic Surgeons, Wound Healing Soc. (bd. dirs. 2004—07, sec. 2010—). Avocation: sailing. Office: 13000 Bruce B Downs Blvd Tampa FL 33612 Business E-Mail: lisa.gould@va.gov.

GOULD, MADELYN S., psychiatric epidemiologist, professor; BS, Bklyn. Coll., 1972; MA, Princeton U., NJ, 1974; MPH, Columbia U. Sch. Pub. Health, NYC, 1976; PhD, Columbia U., 1980. Fellowship in psychiat. epidemiology Columbia U., 1976—79; prof. clin. epidemiology in psychiatry Columbia U. Coll. Physicians & Surgeons; dep. dir. rsch. training program in child psychiatry NY State Psychiat. Inst. Mem. Pres.'s Commn. Mental Health, 1978, Sec.'s Task Force Youth Suicide, US Dept. Health & Human Svcs., 1989; founding mem. NY State Suicide Prevention Coun. Mem. editl. bd. Jour. Am. Acad. Child & Adolescent Psychiatry, contbg. author Surgeon Gen.'s Nat. Suicide Prevention Strategy, 1999; contbr. articles to profl. jours. Recipient Edwin A. Schneidman award, Am. Assn. Suicidology, 1991, Established Rschr. award, Am. Found. Suicide Prevention, 2001, Rsch. award, 2006, NY State Office Mental Health, 2002, W.T. Grant Found. Faculty Scholar award. Achievements include research in the epidemiology of youth suicide, as well as the evaluation of suicide prevention interventions. Office: NY State Psychiat Inst 1051 Riverside Dr Unit 72 New York NY 10032 Office Phone: 212-543-5329. Office Fax: 212-543-5966. E-mail: GOULDM@childpsych.Columbia.edu, msg5@columbia.edu. *

GOURAS, PETER, ophthalmology educator; b. NYC, Apr. 15, 1930; s. Demetrius and Julia (Crowley) G.; m. Ute Keppler, Aug. 29, 1959; children: Eckhart, Gunnar, Roswitha. AB, Johns Hopkins U., 1951, MD, 1955; PhD Honoris Causa, U. Athens, Greece. Intern Johns Hopkins Hosp., Balt., 1955-56; rsch. scientist NIH, Bethesda, Md., 1956-58, staff scientist, 1960-68, chief neurophysiology sect. ophthal. br., 1968-70; fellow Cambridge (Eng.) U., 1958-59; chief neurophysiology sect. Nat. Eye Inst., Bethesda, 1971-78; assoc. prof. dept. ophthalmology Columbia U., NYC, 1978-81, prof. dept. ophthalmology, 1981—. Humboldt prof., Freiburg, Fed. Republic Germany, 1974-75; prof. ophthamology U. P.R., San Juan, 1979; dir. retinitis pigmentosa ctr. Columbia Presbyn. Med. Ctr., N.Y.C., 1979—; mem. sci. adv. bd. N.Y. Eye Bank, N.Y.C, editl. bd. mem., Graches Rsch. Clin. Expert Opthal., 2003-. Author: Neurocircuitry of the Retina, 1985, The Perception of Colour, 1991; co-author: (with S. Federman) The Retina and Vitreous, 1993; mem. editorial bd. Clin. Vision Scis. Chmn. vonSallmann Prize com., N.Y.C., 1980—. Served to med. dir. USPHS, 1956-78. Recipient Professorship award Research to Prevent Blindness, 1978-83, Sr. Sci. Investigator award, 1990, Alcon Rsch. Inst. award, 1990. Home: 5225 Sycamore Ave Bronx NY 10471-2835 Office: Columbia U Dept of Ophthalmology 630 W 168th St Dept Of New York NY 10032-3795 *

GOURGUECHON, PRUDENCE LEIB, psychoanalyst; BA, Yale U., 1973; MD, U. Mich., 1979; grad., Inst. Psychoanalysis, Chgo., 1995. Cert. Psychiatry, 1985, Psychoanalysis, 1997. Resident in psychiatry Northwestern U. Med. Sch., 1979—83, chief resident, 1983; private practice Ill., 1983—; faculty dept. psychiatry and behavioral sciences Northwestern U. Med. Sch.; faculty Inst. Psychoanalysis, Chgo., Wis. Provisional Psychoanalytic Inst., 2005—, training and supervising analyst, 2005—. Mem.: Am. Psychoanalytic Assn. (editor The American Psychoanalyst 2000—04, sec. 2004—08, chair task force on psychoanalysis and undergraduate edn. 2004—, pres. 2008—10), Am. Coll. Psychoanalysts. Mailing: 540 Frontage Rd Ste 2120 Northfield IL 60093 Office Phone: 847-441-1395. *

GOURI, RAGHU MANGALA, pathologist, educator; b. Bangalore, Karnataka, India, Sept. 22, 1964; MBBS, DCP, Kempegowda Inst. Med. Scis., MD, 1987; diploma, JJM Med. Coll., Kuvempu U., Davanagere, 1992, MD in Pathology, 1993. Prof. MS Ramaiah Med. Coll., 1994—. Project guide STS ICMR. Mem.: Indian Assn. Pathologists and Microbiologists (Karnataka) (sec., treas. 1998—2000). Avocations: yoga, exercise. Home: Hanumaiah layout Sanjaynagar Bangalore Karnataka 560094 India Personal E-mail: mangalagouri22@yahoo.com.

GOURLAY, DAVID, pediatrician, educator; b. San Francisco, Calif, Oct. 24, 1971; BA, U. Calif., Santa Barbara, 1993; MD, Med. Coll. Wis., Milw., 1997. Asst. prof. surgery Children's Corp. Ctr. Med. Coll. Wis., 2006—. Prin. investigator Children's Rsch. Inst., 2006; med. dir. trauma Children's Hosp. Wis., 2008. Maj. USAR, 1998. Decorated Iraq Campaign medal with Bronze Campaign Star USAR, Armed Forces Res. medal with M Device; recipient Brave Hearts Award, ARC; named one of Top 40 Under 40, Milwaukee's Bus. Jour. Fellow: ACS; mem.: Am. Pediatric Surg. Assn., Shock Soc., Am. Acad. Pediat., Assn. Academic Surgeons, Alpha Omega Alpha. Office: Med Coll Wis Children's Corp Ctr Ste C410 999 N 92nd St Milwaukee WI 53226 Office Fax: 414-266-6579. Business E-Mail: dgourlay@chw.org.

GOURLEY, DICK R., dean, pharmacy educator; b. Franklin, Ky., Dec. 26, 1944; m. Greta Ann Kimbrough, Dec. 7, 1968; 1 child, Kristin Marie. BS, U. Tenn. Coll. Pharmacy, 1969, PharmD, 1970. Lic. pharmacist Tenn. Asst. prof. clin. pharmacy Mercer U. Sch. Pharmacy, Atlanta, 1970-72, prof., dean., 1984-89; asst. prof. U. Nebr., Nebr. Med. Ctr., Coll. Pharmacy, Omaha, 1972-73, assoc. prof., 1973-81, prof., 1981-84, chmn. dept. pharmacy practice, 1972—84; prof., dean. Coll. Pharmacy U. Tenn. Health Sci. Ctr., Memphis, 1989—. Cons. Grady Meml. Hosp., Atlanta, 1971—72, Ga. Narcotic Treatment Prog., 1971—72, Shannondale Nursing Home, Knoxville, Tenn., 1971—72, Tri-County Meml. Hosp., Lexington, Nebr., 1975—76, Luth. Med. Ctr., Omaha, 1975—84, Nebr. State Dept. Pub. Instns., 1976—84; bd. dirs. Greater Omaha Pharmacists Assn., 1974—77; vis. prof. U. Sydney, 1978; vis. tutor Ctrl. Inst. Tech., Upper Hutt, New Zealand, 1978; mem. Bd. Pharm Specialists, 1993—, chair, 1995—97. Co-author: Practicing Pharmacist Handbook: Guidlines for the Establishment of High Blood Pressure Control Services by the Practicing Pharmacist, 1977, Handbook for Institutional Pharmacy Practice, 1979, Handbook of Non-Prescription Drugs, 1979, Pharmaceutics and Pharmacy Practice, 1981, Applied Therapeutics for Clinical Pharmacists, 1982, Pharmacy Technicians' Manual, 1988, numerous others; editor: numerous textbooks, ednl. material; contbr. articles to profl. jours., chapters to books. Judge Greater Nebr. Sci. & Engring. Fair, 1973—79; chmn. UNMC Coll. Pharmacy United Way Campaign, 1979—81. Mem.: Fedn. Internat. Pharm., Internat. Found. Pharmacy Edn., Tenn. Pharmacists Assn., Am. Pharm. Assn., Am. Assn. Colleges of Pharmacy, Am. Coun. Pharm. Edn., Am. Soc. Hosp. Pharmacists (bd. dirs. 1981—84), Assn. Pub. Health Observatories, APHA (bd. trustees 2008—10), Rho Chi, Phi Delta Chi. Office: U Tenn Coll Pharmacy 847 Monroe Ave Memphis TN 38103-4901 Office Phone: 901-448-6036. Business E-Mail: dgourley@uthsc.edu. E-mail: dgourley@bellsouth.net.

GOUS, PETRUS NJ, ophthalmologist, consultant; b. Pretoria, South Africa, Feb. 15, 1963; s. Andre and Mimi Gous; m. Jutta Therese Carpenter-Kling, Dec. 6, 1986; children: James Nicholas, Michael Alexander, Christopher Matthew. MB, BChir cum laude, U. Pretoria, 1986, MD cum laude, 1994. Glaucoma cons. dept. ophthalmology U. Pretoria, 1995—; pvt. practice ophthalmologist Pretoria Eye Inst., 1995—. Chmn. rsch. com. Pretoria Eye Inst., 1996—, chmn., 2003—04; founding mem., past pres., exec. mem. South African Glaucoma Soc, 1996—2006; founding mem. Exco South African Soc. Ocuoplastic Surgery, 2007—. Recipient Pro Patria medal, South African Nat. Def. Force Med. Svcs., 1989. Fellow: Coll. Ophthalmology South Africa; mem.: South African Vitreoretinal Soc., South African Glaucoma Soc. (founder), South African Cataract and Refractive Soc., Ophthal. Soc. South Africa, Internat. Cataract and Refractive Surgery, Assn. for Rsch. in Vision and Ophthalmology, Am. Acad. Ophthalmology, South African Med. Assn., Ophthalmology Alumni Soc. of U. Pretoria. Achievements include patents for Eyeborn Bioceramic orbital implant; orbital implant injection delivery device; ophthalmic eyedrop dispenser; first to publish sutureless phacotrabeculectomy in combined cataract and glaucoma; sutureless extended scleral tunnel Ahmed valve implants; sutureless scleral tunnel express implants. Office: Pretoria Eye Inst Po Box 56184 Arcadia 7 Pretoria South Africa Office Fax: +27-12-343 8038; Home Fax: +27-12-460 6570. E-mail: pgous@global.co.za.

GOUTAGNY, STEPHANE, neurosurgeon; b. Saint Symphorien sur Coise, Mar. 9, 1975; MD, U. Paris 7, 2005, PhD. Neurosurgeon Assistance Publique Hôpitaux de Paris, 2007—. Office: 100 Blvd du Genral Leclerc Clichy Ile de France 92110 France E-mail: stephane.goutagny@bjn.aphp.fr.

GOUTARO, KATSUNO, medical educator; b. Japan, Sept. 6, 1970; MD, Okayama U. Med. Sch., PhD, 1998. Asst. prof. Juntendo U. Urayasu Hosp., 2006—. Mem.: Soc. Am. Gastrointestinal and Endoscopic Surgeons. Avocation: snowboarding. Office: 2-1-1 Tomioka Urayasu Chiba 2790021 Japan E-mail: gkatsuno4596@sd5.so-net.ne.jp.

GOUTZANIS, LAMPROS, oral and maxillofacial surgeon professor; b. Boeotia, May 17, 1963; DDS, U. Thessaloniki, MD, 1986; MSc, U. Athens, PhD, 1996. Lectr. U. Athens, 2008—; oral and maxillofacial surgeon Evangelismos Hosp., 2009—. Named Eminent Scientist of Yr., IRPC, 2010. Mem.: Internat. Assn. Oral and Maxillofacial, European Assn. Oral and Maxillofacial Surgeons. Avocations: fishing, photography, music. Home: Zaloggou 33 Korydallos Athens Attica 18120 Greece Personal E-mail: lgoutzan@dent.uoa.gr.

GOUVERIS, HARALAMPOS, otolaryngologist; s. Theodoros Gouveris and Hionia Gouveri; m. Maria Zissiopoulos, Oct. 9, 2004. MD, U. Patra, Greece, 1996. Physician U. Mainz Clinics, Germany, 1998—. Clin. instr. Head and Neck Surgery Found., Inc. Contbr. articles to profl. jours. Mem.: German Soc. Otolaryngologyt. Achievements include research in otology and neurotology. Avocations: travel, singing, dance. Home: Augustinerstr 31 Mainz 55116 Germany Office Fax: +49-6131-176637. E-mail: gouveris@hno.klinik.uni-mainz.de.

GOVENDER, DHIRENDRA, pathologist; b. South Africa, Aug. 11, 1961; MBChB, U. Natal, 1985; PhD, U. KwaZulu-Natal, 2009. Assoc. prof. U. Natal, 2000—03; prof. pathologist divsn. anat. pathology U. Cape Town, 2003—. Web editor Jour. Clin. Pathology, 2003—; pres. South African divsn. Internat. Acad. Pathology, 2008—10. Harry Crossley Sr. Clin. Rsch. fellowship, U. Cape Town, grant, Oppenheimer Meml. Trust, Rsch. grant, Nat. Health Lab. Svc. Rsch. Trust. Master: Royal Coll. Pathologists (internat. advisor 2006—); fellow: Colls. Medicine South Africa (hon. registrar 2009—11). Office: University Cape Town Divsn Anatomical Pathology Observatory Cape Town Western Cape 7925 South Africa Office Fax: 27214047611. Business E-Mail: dhiren.govender@uct.ac.za.

GOVIER, FRED EVERETT, surgeon; b. Broken Bow, Nebr., Dec. 27, 1954; MD, U. Nebr., 1979. Urologist Va. Mason Med. Ctr., 1987—, chief surgeon, 2007—. Fellow: ACS. Avocations: surfing, golf. Office: Va Mason Medical Ctr 1100 Ninth Ave Seattle WA 98111 Office Phone: 206-223-6178. E-mail: fred.govier@vmmc.org.

GOVINDARAJAN, RAGHAV, neurologist; b. India, Mar. 23, 1983; MD, Bangalore Med. Coll., 2007. Clin. resident Cleve. Clinic Fla., 2009—. Bd. mem. Fla. Soc. Neurology, 2010. Recipient Cert. of Appreciation, Lions Internat., Best abstract winner, AMA-WPC, 2011, Jr. mem. recognition award, AWA-WPC, 2011, Best Doc. Award, Arnold P. Gold Found.; named Resident of the Yr., Cleve. Clinic Fla., 2010—11; travel grant, Am. Neurol. Assn., 2010, Fla. Soc. Neurology, 2010. Mem.: AMA, Am. Assn. Neuromuscular and Electrodiagnostic Medicine (Jr. mem. Recognition award 2011), Am. Acad. Neurology. Avocations: golf, reading. Office: 2950 Cleve Clinic Blvd Weston FL 33331 Personal E-mail: raghav316g@gmail.com.

GOVINDJEE, biophysics, biochemistry, and biology professor; b. Allahabad, India, Oct. 24, 1933; arrived in US, 1956, naturalized, 1972; s. Vishveshwar Prasad and Savitri Devi Asthana; m. Rajni Varma, Oct. 24, 1957; children: Anita Govindjee, Sanjay Govindjee. BSc, U. Allahabad, 1952, MSc, 1954; PhD, U. Ill., 1960. Lectr. botany U. Allahabad, 1954-56; grad. fellow U. Ill., Urbana, 1956-58, rsch. asst., 1958-60, USPHS postdoctoral trainee biophysics, 1960-61, mem. faculty, 1961—, assoc. prof. botany and biophysics, 1965-69, prof. biophysics and plant biology, 1969-99, disting. lectr. Sch. Life Scis., 1978, emeritus prof. biophysics, plant biology and biochemistry, 1999—. Author (with E. Rabinowitch): Photosynthesis, 1969; editor: Bioenergetics of Photosynthesis, 1975, Photosynthesis: Energy Conversion by Plants and Bacteria; Carbon Assimilation and Plant Productivity, 2 vols., 1982 (Russian transl. 1987); co-editor: The Oxygen Evolving System of Photosynthesis, 1983, Light Emission by Plants and Bacteria, 1986, Excitation Energy and Electron Transfer in Photosynthesis, 1989, Molecular Biology of Photosynthesis, 1989, Photosynthesis: From Photoreactions to Productivity, 1993, Concepts in Photobiology: Photosynthesis and Photomorphogenesis, 1999, Chlorophyll a Fluorescence: A Signature of Photosynthesis, 2004, reprinted, 2010, Discoveries in Photosynthesis, 2005, Photosynthesis in Silico, 2009, Abiotic Stress Adaptation in Plants, 2010; editor Hist. Corner: Photosynthesis Rsch., 1989—99; guest editor spl. issue Biophys. Jour., 1972, Photochemistry and Photobiology, 1978, Photosynthesis Research, 1993, 96, 2002-04, 09; editor-in-chief Photosynthesis Rsch., 1985-88; founding series editor: Advances in Photosynthesis and Respiration, vol. 1, 1994, vol. 2, 1995, vols. 3, 4 and 5, 1996, vols. 6 and 7, 1998, vol. 8, 1999, vol. 9, 2000, vols. 10 and 11, 2001, vol. 12, 2002, vol. 13, vol. 14, 2003, vols. 15, 16, 17, 19, 2004, vols. 18, 20, 22, 2005, vols. 23-25, 2007, vols. 26-28, 2008, vols. 29 & 30, 2009, vols. 31 & 32, 2010, vols. 33 & 34, 2011; contbr. articles to profl. jours., also Sci. Am. Founder, Govindjee and Rajni Govindjee Award for excellence in Biol. Rsch. U. Ill., Urbana-Champaign. Recipient Lifetime Achievement award, Rebeiz Found., 2007, Comm. award, Internat. Soc. Photosynthesis Rsch., Lifetime Achievement award, Liberal Arts & Scis., U. Ill., Urbana Champaign, 2008; named to Past and Present Eminent Indian Botanists, 2010; Fulbright Scholar, 1956—61, 1996—97. Fellow AAAS, NAS (India); mem. Am. Soc. Plant Biologists, Biophys. Soc. Am., Am. Soc. Photobiology (coun. 1976, pres. 1981), Internat. Photosynthesis Soc. (exec. com., publ. com. 1995-01, hon. pres. 13th Internat. Photosynthesis Congress 2004), Sigma Xi (emeritus). Achievements include discovery of several new fluorescing forms of chlorophyll a; the presence of chlorophyll a in what is now called Photosystem II; the two-light effects on chlorophyll a fluorescence; Emerson Enhancement in NADP reduction; the time (in picoseconds) taken by the reaction center of Photosystem II to undergo primary charge separation; the theory for the molecular mechanism of thermoluminescence in plants; an understanding of chlorophyll a fluorescence changes with time; the unique role of bicarbonate ions in the electron and proton transfer on the electron acceptor side of Photosystem II. Avocation: photography. Office: University Ill Dept Plant Biology 265 Morrill Hall 505 S Goodwin Ave Urbana IL 61801-3707 Home Phone: 217-337-0627; Office Phone: 217-333-1794. Business E-Mail: gov@illinois.edu.

GOWANS, SIR JAMES LEARMONTH, retired science administrator, immunologist; b. Sheffield, Eng., May 7, 1924; s. John Gowans and Selma Ljung; m. Moyra Leatham, July 28, 1956; children: William, Jenny, Lucy. MB, BS, U. London, 1947; MA, DPhil, Oxford U., 1953; ScD (hon.), Yale U., New Haven, 1966; DSc (hon.), U. Chgo., 1971, U. Birmingham, Eng., 1978, U. Rochester, NY, 1987; MD (hon.), U. Edinburgh, Scotland, 1979, U. Sheffield, Eng.; DM (hon.), U. Southampton, Eng., 1987; LLD (hon.), U. Glasgow, Scotland, 1988. Rsch. prof. sch. pathology Oxford U., 1962-77, dir. med. rsch. coun., cellular immunology unit, 1963-77; sec., CEO UK Med. Rsch. Coun., 1977-87; cons. global prog. on AIDS WHO, Geneva, 1987-88; rsch. programs adv. com. Nat. Multiple Sclerosis Soc., NYC, 1988-90; sec.-gen. Human Frontier Scis. Program, Strasbourg, France, 1989-93. Mem. gov. coun. Internat. Agy. Rsch. on Cancer, Lyon, France, 1980—87; chmn. European Med. Rsch. Coun., 1985—87; DIR. Charing Cross Sunley Rsch. Ctr., London, 1989—91; dir. European Iniative Communicators of Sci., Munich, 1995—99. Contbr. articles to profl. jours. Recipient Gairdner Found. Internat. award, 1968, Paul Ehrlich prize, 1974, Feldberg award, 1979, Wolf Found. prize in medicine, Israel, 1980, Medawar prize, 1990. Fellow: Royal Soc. (Royal medal 1976); mem.: NAS (fgn. assoc.), Am. Soc. Leukoryte Biology (hon.), Am. Assn. Immunologists (hon.). Avocations: music, gardening, old books. E-mail: jamesgowans@btinternet.com. *

GOY, ANDRE, medical oncologist, educator; Attended, Grenoble U. Med. Ctr., France. Intern Grenoble Univ. Med. Ctr., resident; fellow Albert Michallon Univ. Med. Ctr., Meml. Sloan-Kettering Cancer Ctr., NY; asst. prof. M. D. Anderson cancer ctr. Tex. Univ., Houston; assoc. prof. biosciences grad. sch. Univ. of Medicine and Dentistry of NJ, Piscataway; chief lymphoma divsn. John Theurer cancer ctr. Hackensack Univ. Med. Ctr., NJ, 2010—, dir. tissue repository John Theurer cancer ctr., 2010—, dir. clin. and translational cancer rsch. John Theurer cancer ctr., 2010—, dep. dir. John Theurer cancer ctr., 2010—. Reviewer for jour. clin. oncology Clin. Cancer Rsch. Reviewer Am. Jour. of Hematology. Mem.: Am. Soc. of Clin. Oncology, Am. Soc. of Hematology. Achievements include development of small-molecule therapy in mantle cell lymphoma and the proteomics of cancer; research in predictive biomarkers in lymphoma. Office: Hackensack University Medical Center John Theurer Cancer Center 30 Prospect Ave Hackensack NJ 07601 Office Phone: 201-996-2000.

GOYAL, MANISH, physiologist; b. Gwalior, Madhya Pradesh, India, Jan. 1, 1980; MBBS, G. R. Med. Coll., Gwalior, 2003; MD, King Geoge's Med. U., Lucknow, Uttar Pradesh, 2008. Physiologist All India Inst. Med. Scis., 2008—, sr. demonstrator, physiology, 2008—11. Recipient Prashasti-patra award, Dept. Family Welfare, Delhi Govt., Honour award, G. R. Med. Coll., Gwalior. Mem.: Assn. Med. Practitioners India, Indian Soc. Chronobiology, Assn. Physiologists and Pharmacologists India (H. H. Loescheke Nat. award 2007). Avocation: writing. Office: Dept Physiology AIIMS Ansari New Delhi 110029 India Personal E-mail: drmanishgoyal@rediffmail.com.

GOYER, ROBERT ANDREW, pathology educator; b. Hartford, Conn., June 2, 1927; s. Andrew R. and Cecelia P. (Castonquay) G.; m. Mary Ellen Wilke, Feb. 4, 1955; children: Barbara, John, Peter, Ellen. BS, Holy Cross Coll., 1950; MD, St. Louis U., 1955. Diplomate: Am. Bd. Pathology. Intern St. Francis Hosp., Hartford, 1955-56; resident in pathology St. Louis U. Hosps., 1956-60; practice medicine specializing in pathology St. Louis, 1956-65; instr. pathology St. Louis U., 1960-62, asst. prof., 1962-65, Sch. Medicine, U. NC, Chapel Hill, 1965-68, assoc. prof., 1968-71, prof. pathology, 1971-74, adj. prof. pathology, 1979-87; clin. pathologist Cardinal Glennon Meml. Hosp. for Children, St. Louis, 1961-62, dir. labs., 1962-64; staff pathologist NC Meml. Hosp., Chapel Hill, 1965-74; chief pathology U. Hosp., London, Ont., Canada, 1974-79; prof. pathology Health Scis. Centre, U. Western Ont., Canada, 1974-79, 87-92, prof. emeritus, 1992—; dept. dir. Nat. Inst. Environ. Health Scis., Research Triangle Park, NC, 1979-87; pvt. cons. health effects, toxic metals Chapel Hill, 1992—. Nat. assoc. Nat. Acads.; mem. com. WHO/IPCS, NAS, NRC. Contbr. articles to profl. jours.; mem. editl. bd. Yearbook Pathology, 1979-88, AMA Archives of Pathology, 1973-82. Served with USN, 1945-47. Recipient Merit award, Soc. Toxicology, 2004; Nat. Found. fellow, 1959—60. Mem. Coll. Am. Pathology, Am. Assn. Pathologists, Internat. Acad. Pathology, Soc. Exptl. Biology and Medicine, Soc. Toxicology (Merit award 2004). Roman Catholic. Achievements include research in experimental pathology and metal toxicology. Office: 6405 Huntingridge Rd Chapel Hill NC 27517 Office Phone: 919-419-1804. Personal E-mail: robert_goyer@msn.com.

GOZAL, DAVID, pediatrician, educator; b. Morocco, June 14, 1955; MD, Hadassah Med. Sch., 1979. Prof. pediat. Tulane U., 1994—99, prof., rsch. vice-chair U. Louisville, 1999—2000; Herbert Abelson endowed prof., chmn. pediat. U. Chgo., 2009—. Chief physician Comer Children's Hosp., 2009. Recipient Disting. Faculty award, U. Louisville, Chevalier de l'Ordre du Merite, Presidency of Cameroon. Mem.: Am. Acad. Sleep Medicine, Soc. Pediat. Rsch., Assn. Am. Physicians, Am. Pediat. Soc., Am. Thoracic Soc. (Amberson lectr.). Office: University Chgo 5721 S Maryland Ave MC 8000 Ste K-160 Chicago IL 60637 Office Fax: 773-702-4523. Business E-Mail: dgozal@uchicago.edu.

GOZON, RICHARD C., pharmaceutical executive, retired paper distribution executive; b. Pitts., Oct. 9, 1938, s. Frank J. and Helen (Franklin) G.; m. Fran A. Burmeister, June 21, 1940; children: Cheryl, Michael, Diana. BS in Bus., Valparaiso U., 1960; advanced mgmt. program, Harvard U., 1978. With sales dept. Champion Internat., Hamilton, Ohio, 1959-61; dir. sales Nationwide Papers, Chgo., 1961-72; pres. Rourke Eno Paper Co., Hartford, Conn., 1972-78; exec. v.p. Unisource Corp., Phila., 1978-79, pres., 1979-85; v.p. Alco Standard Corp., Phila., 1982, dir., 1983, exec. v.p., COO, 1987, pres., COO, 1988—93; pres. Alco Paper & Office Products, Phila., 1983, Paper Corp. of Am., Phila., 1985-87; exec. v.p., CEO Alco Standard Corp., Valley Forge, Pa., 1988; exec. v.p. Weyerhaeuser Co., 1994—2002; bd. dir. AmerisourceBergen Corp., 2001—, chmn., 2006—. Trustee Richard Roberts Real estate Growth Trus I, Avon, Conn.; dir. UGI Corp., UGI Utilities, Inc., Triumph Group, Inc. and Amerigas Partners LP. Dir., World Affaris Coun. of Phila. Mem. Sales & Mktg. Execs. Club. Clubs: Merion Golf (Ardmore, Pa.); Pine Valley golf (Clementon, N.J.); Harvard Bus. Sch. Republican. Lutheran. Avocations: golf, tennis, skiing. Mailing: AmerisourceBergen Corp Bd Directors PO Box 959 Valley Forge PA 19482 *

GOZUM, MARVIN ENRIQUEZ, internist; b. Phila., Jan. 01; s. Filemon Terzon and Teresita Van G. BS in Biology, Ateneo de Manila, The Philippines, 1980; MD, Fatima Coll. of Medicine, The Philippines, 1984. Intern The Bklyn.-Caledonian Hosp. div. Downstate Med. Ctr., N.Y., 1984-85, resident in internal medicine N.Y., 1985-87; attending physician Thomas Jefferson U. Hosp., Phila., 1987—; clin. instr. Jefferson Med. Coll., Phila., 1987-89, rsch. assoc. Ctr. for Rsch., 1989—, clin. asst. prof. medicine, 1989—, chief med. informatics div. internal medicine, 1989—; med. cons. Wills Eye Hosp., Phila., 1987—, chief med. cons., 1990—. Adv. bd. computers in medicine com. Thomas Jefferson U. Hosp., 1987—; adv. bd. computer com. Wills Eye Hosp., 1987; adv. bd. curriculum devel. com. Thomas Jefferson U., Phila., 1988; adv. bd. Continuing Med. Edn. Com. Internal Medicine, 1991—. Developer: (computer programs) Diagnosticon Computer Assisted Diagnosis, 1982, Fluid/Electrolyte Calculator, 1984, Preoperative Evaluation, 1987; co-developer: (computer program) VACAD Image Processor, 1987. Named to Osteoporosis Project, Health Sci. Inst., 1990. Mem. AAAS, Am. Med. Informatics Assn., Soc. Gen. Internal Medicine. Achievements include development of computer assisted preoperative evaluation, automated report generation for preoperative evaluations, automated medical diagnosis, pocket intensive care calculator. Office: Jefferson Med Coll 1025 Walnut St Philadelphia PA 19107-5001

GRABER, MARK L., internist; m. Deborah Graber; children: Lauren, Emily. BS, Yale U., 1971; MD, Stanford U., 1975. Diplomate Am. Bd. Internal Medicine, 1978. Prof. emeritus SUNY, Stony Brook, NY; sr. scientist RTI Internat. Home: 1 Breezy Hollow Saint James NY 11780 Business E-Mail: mgraber@rti.org. *

GRABOW, THEODORE SCOTT, physician; b. Madison, Wis., Oct. 8, 1966; BA, Carleton Coll., 1989; MD, SUNY Buffalo Sch. Medicine, 1994. Dir., pain medicine fellowship program Johns Hopkins U. Sch. Medicine, 2000—03, dir., pain treatment ctr., 2001—03, asst. prof., 2000—03, adj. asst. prof., 2003—11; assoc. staff St. Joseph Med. Ctr., 2003—11; clin. staff Greater Balt. Med. Ctr., 2007—11; v.p. Pain Medicine Specialists, 2003—. Bd. cert. pain medicine ABA Subspecialty Bd. Pain Mgmt., 2000—; bd. cert. anesthesiology Am. Bd. Anesthesiology, 1999. Recipient Braun award, Am. Soc. Regional Anesthesia, 1st prize Overall, Midwest Anesthesia Resident's Conf., Recognition Svc. award, St. Joseph Med. Ctr., St. Clare Med. Outreach. Mem.: Internat. Assn. Study Pain, Am. Soc. Anesthesiologists. Avocations: soccer, reading. Office: 8322 Bellona Ave Ste 330 Towson MD 21204 Office Fax: 410-825-8974. Business E-Mail: tgrabow@jhmi.edu.

GRACHEK, MARIANNA KERN, healthcare administrator; b. Amsterdam, The Netherlands, Oct. 6, 1949; d. Johannus J. and Paulina G. (DeHaas) Kern; m. Kenneth A. Grachek, June 12, 1971; children: Ellen, Brett. Grad., St. Vincent Med. Ctr., Toledo, 1971; BSN, U. Toledo, 1978; MSN, Med. Coll. of Ohio, 1987. Lic. nursing home adminstr.; cert. gerontol. nurse; cert. DON Nat. Assn. Dirs. of Nursing Adminstrn; cert. nursing home adminstr. and assisted living adminstr., ACHCA. Clinician gerontol. nursing, staff devel. educator St. Vincent Med. Ctr., Toledo, 1982-87; dir. nursing svcs. Lake Park Nursing Care Ctr., Sylvania, Ohio, 1987-90; nursing home adminstr. St. Luke's Transitional Care Ctr., Maumee, Ohio, 1990—96; aasoc. administr. St. Francis, Ohio, 1996—97; long term care surveyor Joint Commn. Accreditation Health Care Orgns., Oakbrook, Ill., 1993—97, exec. dir. long term care accreditation program, 1997—2006; pres., CEO Am. Coll. Health Care Adminstr., 2006—. Recipient Sigma Theta Tau (Zeta Theta Chpt.) Rsch. award, 1987 Alzheimer's Assn. (pres. N.W. Ohio chpt. 1991-93), ACHCA (bd. dirs. 1999-2003), NADONA (member of the Yr. 2008). Office Phone: 202-536-5120. Personal E-mail: mgrachek@grachek.com. Business E-Mail: mgrachek@achca.org. *

GRACHEV, STANISLAV ALEXANDROVICH, chemist, researcher; b. Komsomolsk, Russia, Mar. 7, 1935; s. Alexandr Matveevich and Efrosinia Ivanovna Grachev; m. Liudmila Mikhailovna Romanova, June 10, 1960; 1 child, Helena Stanislavovna Gratcheva. Cand. of Chem. Sci., Leningrad State U., Russia, 1962; D of Chem. Sci., Technol. Inst. Lensoveta, Leningrad, 1982. Jr. sci. worker Petersburg Nuc. Physics Inst., Gatchina, Russia, 1962—65, sr. sci. worker, 1965—67, head lab. chem. synthesis, 1967—, prof., 1982—2003. Contbr. articles to profl. jours. Rsch. grantee, Acad. Sci. USSR, 1983—95, Russian Acad. Sci., 1983—95. Achievements include discovery of synthesis organic compounds of polonium, non-toxic radioprotectors with prolonged effect. Office: Petersburg Nuclear Physics Inst RAS Orlova Roscha Leningrad district Gatchina 188350 Russia Home: AP 164 ul. Podryadchikova 11 188306 Gatchina Lyeningradskaya obl. Russia Office Fax: (7-813-71)313-47. Personal E-mail: grachev@gtu.ru. Business E-Mail: grachev@omrb.pnpi.spb.ru.

GRACIA, CLARISA R., gynecologist, educator, oncologist, reproductive endocrinologist; BA in English, Amherst Coll., Mass., 1993; MD, SUNY, Buffalo, 1997; MSCE in Epidemiology and Biostatistics, U. Pa., Phila., 2004. Diplomate Am. Bd. Ob-Gyn. Intern Hosp. of the Univ. Pa., resident, fellow, asst. prof. ob-gyn. Co-author: Ovarian Cryopreservation, 2002, Presumed diagnosis of ectopic pregnancy, 2002, Molecular basis of pubertal abnormalities, 2003, Usefulness of pipelle endometrial biopsy in the diagnosis of women at risk for ectopic pregnancy, 2003, Hormones and menopausal status as predictors of depression in women in the transition to menopause, 2004, various others. Named one of Top Docs, Phila. Mag., 2011. Mem.: Endocrine Soc., Soc. Reproductive Endocrinology and Infertility, Am. Soc. Reproductive Medicine, Am. Coll. Obstetricians and Gynecologists. Office: Hospital of the University of Pennsylvania Penn Fertility Care 3701 Market St Ste 800 Philadelphia PA 19104 Office Phone: 215-662-2963. Office Fax: 215-349-5512. Business E-Mail: cgracia@obgyn.upenn.edu.

GRADOS, MARCO ANTONIO, psychiatrist, researcher, s. Oscar and Mayela Grados; m. Judy Johnson, May 21, 1996; children: Marco Sebastian, Ana Mayela. MD, Cayetano Heredia, Lima, 1990; MPH, Johns Hopkins U., Balt., 2001. Assoc. prof. Johns Hopkins U., 2010—. Grantee Rsch. Career Devel. award, NIMH, 2002—07. Mem.: Am. Acad. Child & Adolescent Psychiatry (pres., Md. chpt. 2003—05). Home: 2309 Siena Way Woodstock MD 21163 Office: Johns Hopkins Univ SOM 600 N Wolfe St CMSC 346 Baltimore MD 21287 Office Phone: 443-287-2291.

GRADWELL, DAVID PETER, physician, physiologist, medical educator; b. Salisbury, Wiltshire, England, July 5, 1953; s. James and Evelyn Rosemary Gradwell; m. Jane Elisabeth Risdall, Apr. 20, 2002; children: Robert Matthew, Christopher Andrew. BSc in Physiology with honors, U. Dundee, Scotland, 1976, B Surgery B Medicine, 1981; PhD in Physiology, United Med. and Dental Schs. Guy's and St. Thomas, London, 1993. Accredited cons. UK, 1993, diplomate in aviation medicine Royal Coll. Physicians, 1988. Commd. RAF, 1984, advanced through grades to group capt., 2003; cons. adviser in aviation medicine RAF Ctr. Aviation Medicine, Henlow, England, 1998—2009, officer commdg. aviation medicine wing, 1998—. Hon. prof. aviation medicine King's Coll. London, London; whittingham prof. aviation medicine Roy Coll. Physicians, London. Editor: (textbook) Ernsting's Aviation Medicine; author: Aviation Medicine, 2006, Human Factors for Pilots, 1996. Gov. Adam's Grammar Sch., Newport, England, 2006—; trustee Stewart Meml. Trust, London, 2000—. Recipient Louis H. Bauer Founders award, Aerospace Med. Assn., 2005, Eric Liljencrantz award, 2006, Richard Fox-Linton Meml. prize, RAF, 1996; named Stewart Meml. lectr., Stewart Trust, 1999. Fellow: RCP, FOM; mem.: Royal Coll. Surgeons Eng. (Lady Cade medal 2000). Mem. Church Of England. Achievements include research in physiological protection at high altitude. Avocations: off-shore sailing, aviation history, surfing. Office: RAF Ctr Aviation Medicine SG16 6DN Henlow SG16 6DN England

GRADY, DENISE, reporter; b. NYC, Apr. 23, 1952; 2 children. BS in Biology, SUNY, Stony Brook, 1973; MA in English, U. NH, 1978. Asst. editor New England Journal of Medicine, 1979—80, Physics Today, 1974—75; freelance writer for Science, Discover, Time, Scientific American, Vogue, Reader's Digest, American Health, Parenting, and Self, 1988—98; staff writer for medicine Time Mag.; assoc. editor The Sciences Mag., 1984—85; contributing writer Discover Mag., 1983—84, staff writer, 1980—83, 1985—87; freelance writer science dept. The New York Times, 1996, contract writer, 1997, science news reporter, 1998—, health editor. Instructor in writing U. NH, 1978. Author: Deadly Invaders: Virus Outbreaks Around the World, from Marburg Fever to Avian Flu. Recipient Nat. Soc. of Profl. Engrs., 2nd Pl. 16th Ann. Journalism award, 1981, William Harvey award, 3rd Pl., American Med. Writers Assn., the Nat. High Blood Pressure Edn. Program and Squibb Corp., 1982, Nat. Council for Geographic Edn. bet geographic article in a nongeographic publication, 1983, Commendation from the Newspaper Guild for Choice and Excellence of Crusading Journalistic Contribution in the areas of science and medicine, 1986, Golden Block award, Nat. Stuttering Project, 1990, Nat. Media award, American College of Allergy, Asthma and Immunology, 1993, Nat. Headliner award, 1994, Media award, American Soc. of Anesthesiologists, 1998, Victor Cohn prize for Excellence in Med. Sci. Reporting, 2009. Avocations: reading, hiking, mountain biking, swimming, gardening. Office: The New York Times 620 8th Ave New York NY 10018 Business E-Mail: grady@nytimes.com.

GRADY, KIMBERLY ANN, medical technologist; b. St. Paul, Mar. 16, 1962; d. Paul William and Carol Ann Prokop; m. Michael Edward Grady Jr., Sept. 15, 1984; children: Amanda Carol, Joseph Michael. Med. Lab. Tech., Med. Inst. Minn., Mpls., 1980—82; BS bus. mgmt. with hon., U. Phoenix, 1999—2003; MBA, Benedictine U., Lisle, Ill. Cert. clinical lab. scientist Nat. Certifying Agy. for Clin. Lab. Pers., clin. lab. asst. Nat. Certifying Agy. for Lab. Pers., registered med. technologist Internat. Soc. for Lab. Tech. Pvt. practice, Wood Dale, Ill., 1996—; sr. med. technologist, safety officer Smith Kline Beecham Clin. Laboratories, Atlanta, 1988—96; med. technologist Memphis Clin. Lab., 1986—88; med. lab. technician Boyce & Bynum Pathology Lab., Columbia, Mo., 1984—86; supr. anat. pathology client svcs. Quest Diagnostics, 2005—. Contbr. articles to profl. jours. Active Girl Scouts, Atlanta, 1995—96, Lady KC, Algonquin, Ill., 1996—2003; historian Theresians Internat., 1991—98; coord. Magnificat, Atlanta, 1994—96; leader Cursillo, Atlanta, 1994—96. Recipient Citizenship Medal, LEGIONARIES, 1976, Safety Award, Smith Kline Beecham, 1994. Mem.: Am. Soc. For Clin. Pathology (assoc.), Am. Soc. For Clin. Lab. Sci. (assoc.), Clin. Lab. Mgmt. Assn. (assoc.), The Nat. Assn. For Female Executives (assoc.). Republican. Roman Catholic. Avocations: golf, swimming, sewing, reading. Home: 9941 Thornton Way Huntley IL 60142-2383 Personal E-mail: snoopykg1@aol.com.

GRADY, M. SEAN, neurosurgeon; BA in Biology, U. Calif. San Diego, 1977; MD, Georgetown Medical Sch., 1981. Intern dept. surgery U. Va. Sch. Medicine, 1981—82, resident neurological surgery, 1982—87; faculty mem., investigator U. Wash., 1987—99; chmn. dept. neurosurgery U. Pa. Health System, 1999—; Charles Harrison Frazier Prof. Neurosurgery U. Pa. Editorial bd. Journal of Neurosurgery. Named one of Phila. Top Doctors, Philadelphia Mag., 2002, 2004—. Mem.: American Bd. Neurological Surgery (chmn. 2008—09), Neurological Soc. America, Congress Neurological Surgery, American Assn. Neurological Surgery, American Coll Surgeons, American Academy Neurological Surgery, Soc. Neurological Surgeons. Office: Hosp U Penn 3 Silverstein 3400 Spruce St Philadelphia PA 19104 *

GRADY, PATRICIA A., federal agency administrator; BSN, Georgetown U., Washington, 1967; MSN, U. Md., 1968, PhD in Physiology, 1977; grad. mgmt. prog., Harvard U. John F. Kennedy Sch. Govt., Cambridge, Mass., 1994. Cert. in nursing St. Francis Hosp. Sch. Nursing, 1964. Instr. Washington Hosp. Ctr. Sch. Nursing, 1966-67; instr. to asst. rsch. prof. U. Md. Sch. Nursing, Bethesda, 1968-88; rsch. assoc. U. Md., Bethesda, 1976-77; health sci. adminstr. Nat. Inst. Neurol. Disorders & Stroke (NINDS), NIH, Bethesda, 1988-92, asst. dir. NINDS, 1992-93, dep. dir., 1993—95, acting dir., 1993-94, dir. Nat. Inst. Nursing Rsch. (NINR), 1995—. Co-chair NIH Pub. Trust Initiative, 2004—. Recipient Rozella M. Schlottfeld Disting. Lecture award, Case Western Reserve U., 1994; fellow NIH, 1973—76. Fellow: Am. Heart Assn. (Excellence in Nursing award 1995); mem.: ANA, AAAS, Inst. Medicine, Neurotrauma Soc., Soc. Neuroci., Am. Neurol. Assn., Am. Acad. Neurology, Am. Soc. Profl. & Exec. Women, Am. Lung Assn., Am. Acad. Nursing, Sigma Theta Tau. Office: NINR 31 Center Dr Rm 5B05 Bethesda MD 20892-2178 Office Phone: 301-496-8230. Office Fax: 301-594-3405. Business E-Mail: patricia.grady@nih.gov. *

GRAFFAGNINO, CARMELO, neuroscientist, emergency physician; MD, U. Western Ont., Can., 1985. Cert. Neurology, Vascular Neurology. Resident in internal medicine U. Western Ont., 1968—88, resident in neurology, 1988—91, stroke clin. fellow, 1991; stroke molecular genetics fellow Duke U. Med. Ctr., Durham, NC, 1992—94, dir. neurosciences critical care unit. Fellow: Royal Coll. Physicians Can. Office: Duke U Med Ctr 2946 Durham NC 27710 Office Phone: 919-684-5650. Office Fax: 919-684-6514.

GRAFMAN, IRENE, cosmetic dentist; DDS, NYU, 1998; studied, Dawson Ctr., Pankey Inst. Established Smile Health Spa, 1998. Named one of Top Cosmetic Doctors and Dentists, Castle Connolys, Americas Top Dentists, 2003—04; named to Who's Who in America. Mem.: ADA, Peninsula Hosp. Dental Soc., Am. Acad. of Cosmetic Dentistry, NY County Dental Soc. Office: Smile Health Spa Ste 1 F 120 East 36th St New York NY 10016 Office Phone: 212-532-5377. Office Fax: 212-532-5371. Business E-Mail: drgrafman@smilehealthspa.com.

GRAFT, DAVID F., allergist, consultant; b. Pitts., Dec. 11, 1953; BA, Johns Hopkins U., 1975, MD, 1978. Cons. Pk. Nicollet Clinic, 1987—. Pres. Joint Coun. Allergy Asthma and Immunology, 2000—02. Contbr. scientific papers. Recipient Rsch. award, Inst. Rsch. and Edn. HealthSys. Minn., 1997, Educator award, Pk. Nicollet Inst., 2007. Fellow: Am. Coll. Allergy Asthma and Immunology, Am. Acad. Allergy Asthma and Immunology. Office: 3800 Park Nicollet Blvd Minneapolis MN 55436 Business E-Mail: graftd@parknicollet.com.

GRAHAM, ANNA REGINA, pathologist, educator; b. Phila., Nov. 1, 1947; d. Eugene Nelson and Anna Beatrice (McGovern) Chadwick; m. Larry L. Graham, June 29, 1973; 1 child, Jason. BS in Chemistry, Ariz. State U., 1969, BS in Zoology, 1970; MD, U. Ariz., 1974. Diplomate Am. Bd. Pathology. With Coll. Medicine U. Ariz., Tucson, 1974—, asst. prof. pathology, 1978-84, assoc. prof. pathology, 1984-90, prof. pathology, 1990—2008, prof. emeritus, 2008—, scholar-in-residence Ariz. intermedicine program, 2009—. Fellow Am. Soc. Clin. Pathologists (bd. dirs. Chgo. chpt. 1993-2003, sec. 1995-99, v.p. 1999-2000, pres.-elect 2000-01, pres. 2001-02), Internat. Acad. Pathology, Am. Telemedicine Assn., Coll. Am. Pathologists; mem. Ariz. Soc. Pathologists (pres. Phoenix chpt. 1989-91), Ariz. Med. Assn. (treas. Phoenix chpt. 1995-97). Republican. Baptist. Avocations:

motorcycles, piano, choir. Office: Ariz Health Scis Ctr Dept Pathology 1501 N Campbell Ave Tucson AZ 85724-5105 Office Phone: 520-626-7345. Business E-Mail: agraham1@email.arizona.edu.

GRAHAM, COLIN ALEXANDER, emergency physician; b. Irvine, Ayrshire, Scotland, Aug. 18, 1971; s. Alexander and Mary Graham; m. Jacqueline Amberton, Oct. 1, 1999; children: Clive, David. MBChB, U. Glasgow, 1994, MPH, 2002, MD, 2007. Specialist registrar in emergency medicine So. Gen. Hosp., Glasgow, 1999—2004; clin. rsch. fellow in emergency medicine Scottish Coun. for Postgrad. Med. and Dental Edn. Chief Scientist Office, Glasgow, 2001—03; assoc. prof., accident and emergency medicine academic unit Trauma Ctr. Chinese U. Hong Kong, Prince of Wales Hosp., Shatin, Hong Kong, 2004—07, prof., 2007—. Editor-in-chief European Jour. Emergency Medicine, 2009—. Contbr. articles to profl. jours. Recipient BASICS Gold Medal award, Royal Coll. of Surgeons of Edinburgh, 1997. Fellow: RCP (Edinburgh), Am. Coll. Chest Physicians, Hong Kong Acad. Medicine, Hong Kong Coll. Emergency Medicine, Royal Coll. Physicians and Surgeons Glasgow, Royal Coll. Surgeons Edinburgh, Coll. Emergency Medicine London; mem.: European Soc. Emergency Medicine (coun. mem. 2009—). Office: Accident and Emergency Medicine Academic Unit Chinese U Hong Kong Trauma Ctr Prince of Wales Hosp Shatin New Territories Hong Kong SAR Office Phone: 852 2632 1033. Business E-Mail: cagraham@cuhk.edu.hk.

GRAHAM, DAVID G., preventive medicine physician, psychiatrist; b. Nov. 17, 1949; s. Thomas and Catherine G.; m. Katherine A. Graham; children: Brigitte, John. BA magna cum laude, Walsh U., 1971; MD, Ctrl. U., 1980; MPH, Columbia U., 1985. Diplomate Am. Bd. Preventive Medicine, Am. Bd. Clin. Psychiatry. Intern, then resident in psychiatry SUNY, Stony Brook, 1980-84, resident in preventive medicine, 1984-86, assoc. prof. preventive medicine, 1985—; attending physician VA Med. Ctr., Northport, NY, 1985—; dir. pub. health Suffolk County Dept. Health Svcs., NY, 1986—, chief dep. health commr. NY, 2005—. Author: Medieval Minds, 1985, Profiles in Protest, 1987, Statistics, 1987, Mental Status Manual, 1989. Fellow Am. Coll. Preventive Medicine; mem. APHA, Am. Psychiatric Assn., Am. Assn. Pub. Health Physicians, Alumni Assn. Columbia U. Avocations: gardening, antiques, tennis, reading, outdoor recreation.

GRAHAM, DAVID RICHARD, orthopedic surgeon; b. Detroit, May 15, 1940; s. Lewis J. and Elberta Y. Graham; m. Dorothy T. Young, June 11, 1966; children: Rebecca, Jeffrey. BA cum laude, Harvard U., 1962; MD, U. Rochester, 1966. Diplomate Am. Bd. Orthop. Surgery. Intern Highland Hosp., Rochester, NY, 1966—67, resident in surgery, 1967—68; resident in orthopaedic surgery Henry Ford Hosp., Detroit, 1970—72; orthopaedic surgeon Elmira (N.Y.) Orthopaedic Assocs., P.C., 1972—2001, pres., 1992—2001; orthop. cons. US Dept. Vet.'s Affairs, 2009—. Pres. Arnot Ogden Med. Staff, Elmira, 1990; clin. assoc. Sch. Medicine & Dentistry U. Rochester, 1992—. Lt. comdr. U.S. Navy, 1968-70. Fellow Am. Coll. Surgeons, Am. Acad. Orthop. Surgeons; mem. AMA, Med. Soc. State N.Y., Ea. Orthop. Assn., Am. Coll. Sports Medicine, Chemung County Med. Soc. (pres. 1993-94), Elmira Torch Club (pres. 1990). Republican. Presbyterian. Home and Office: 690 W Clinton St Elmira NY 14905-2226

GRAHAM, DAVID TREDWAY, medical educator, physician; b. Mason City, Iowa, June 20, 1917; s. Evarts Ambrose and Helen (Tredway) G.; m. Frances Jeanette Keesler, June 14, 1941; children: Norma VanSurdam, Andrew Tredway, Mary Brewster. BA, Princeton U., 1938; MA, Yale U., 1941; MD, Washington U., St. Louis, 1943. Intern Barnes Hosp., St. Louis, 1944, asst. resident medicine, 1944-45, 47-48; research fellow medicine Cornell U. Med. Coll., 1948-51; asst. prof. medicine Washington U. Med. Sch., 1951-57, asst. prof. psychiatry, 1956-57; assoc. prof. medicine U. Wis. Med. Sch., 1957-63, prof. medicine, 1963-85, prof. emeritus, 1986—, assoc. chmn. dept., 1969-71, chmn., 1971-80, asst. dean and/or chmn. med. sch. admissions, 1964-69; adj. prof. psychology U. Del., 1986-93. Vis. prof. psychiatry U. Va. Sch. Medicine, 1960; Ripley lectr. U. Wash., 1976 Editor: Clin. Research Procs. 1954-59. Alt. del. Democratic Nat. Conv., 1968. Served to capt., M.C. AUS, 1945-47. Recipient Emeritus Faculty award U. Wis. Med. Alumni Assn., 1992. Fellow ACP; mem. Am. Fedn. Clin. Research, Am. Psychosomatic Soc. (council 1952-55, 64-67, pres. 1978-79), Soc. Psychophysiol. Research (bd. dirs. 1964-67, pres. 1969-70), Central Soc. Clin. Research (emeritus) Office: University of Delaware Dept Psychology Newark DE 19716 *

GRAHAM, GEORGE ANDREW, JR., psychologist, consultant; b. Bakersfield, Calif., Dec. 7, 1930; s. George Andrew Graham and Mary Pearl Sandidge; m. Patricia Anne Phillips, June 19, 1953; children: G. Andrew III, Ronald Glen, Holly Anne Meikle. BA, U. Redlands, 1952; BD, Andover Newtown Theol. Sch., 1956; MA, Boston U., 1956; M in Sacred Theology, Union Theol. Sch., NYC, 1957; postgrad., U. Chgo., 1957-60, 69-70; PhD, Marquette U., 1974. Lic. psychologist, Wis. Min. young adults Old S. Ch., Boston, 1952-55; min. youth 1st Bapt. Ch., Mt. Vernon, NY, 1955—57, min., chaplain Iowa City, 1960-63; lab sch. psychologist U. Chgo., 1957-60; chaplain U. Redlands, Calif., 1963-70; assoc. McGinley & Co., Milw., 1970-73; asst. v.p. personnel divsn. 1st Wis. (became Firstar, then US Bank), Milw., 1973-75, dir. employment and devel., 1975-77, v.p., 1977-81, 1st v.p., 1981-85, dir. employment, counseling, devel. and tng., 1985-88; 1st v.p. Firstar Corp., 1988-92; pres. Graham Consulting, Waukesha, Wis., 1992—. Adj. prof. U. Wis., Milw., 1978-88. Pres. Wis. chpt. Leukemia Soc. Am., Wis. Epilepsy Assn., Lad Lake; bd. dirs. Wis. Sch. Profl. Psychology, Wis. Conservatory Music, Wis. Coun. Econ. Edn.; personnel com. ARC; chmn. pers. com. United Way, Milw.; exec. com. Potawatomi Area coun. Boy Scouts Am. Recipient Silver Beaver award Boy Scouts Am., 1988. Mem. Am. Psychol. Assn., Soc. Indls. and Orgnl. Psychologists. Republican. Home and Office: N8W30095 Woodcrest Dr Waukesha WI 53188 Office Phone: 262-968-5814. E-mail: g1207@msn.com.

GRAHAM, GINGER L., consulting firm executive, former pharmaceutical executive; b. Springdale, Ark., Nov. 18, 1955; m. John Graham; 3 stepchildren. BS in Agrl. Economics, U. Ark., 1979; MBA, Harvard U., 1986. With Elanco Eli Lilly & Co., 1979—92, pres., CEO Advanced Cardiovascular Systems, 1993—2000; group chmn., Office of Pres. Guidant Corp., 2000—03; pres., CEO Amylin Pharmaceuticals Inc., San Diego, 2003—06, CEO, 2006—07; pres., CEO Two Trees Consulting, Ventura, Calif., 2008—. Sr. lectr. bus. adminstrn. Harvard Bus. Sch.; bd. dirs. Amylin Pharmaceuticals Inc., 1995—2010, Genomic Health Inc., 2008—, Walgreen Co., 2010—, Pharmaceutical Rsch. & Manufacturers of America, Calif. Coun. on Sci. and Tech.; mem. advisory bd. Kellogg Ctr. for Exec. Women; bd. dean's adv. Harvard Bus. Sch., health industry alumni bd.; health sciences adv. bd. U. Calif. San Diego; spkr. in field. Recipient Emerging Co. Exec. of Yr. award, Pharmaceutical Achievement Awards, 2005, Woman of Valor award, American Diabetes Assn., 2006; named 100 of the Most Inspiring People, Pharma VOICE, 2006; named one of The 40 Most Influential People in the Industry, World Pharmaceuticals Mag., 2007. Office: Two Trees Consulting 1746 South Victoria Ave Ventura CA 93003

GRAHAM, GLORIA FLIPPIN, dermatologist; b. Durham, NC, Mar. 3, 1935; d. James Meigs and Ida Mae (Boyd) F.; m. Douglas Graham (div.); 1 child, Wayne Meigs Graham; m. James Herbert Graham, July 29, 1989. BS, Wake Forest U., Winston-Salem, NC, 1957; MD, Bowman-Gray Sch. Medicine, 1961. Diplomate Am. Bd. Dermatology. Intern Sch. Medicine Vanderbilt U., Nashville, 1961—62; resident dermatology U. Va. Med. Ctr., Charlottesville, 1962—65; pvt. practice Columbia, SC, 1965—66; physician, owner Wilson Dermatology Clinic, NC, 1966—94; physician, dermatologist Grahams' Dermatology Svcs., Morehead City, 1992—2005; attending physician Crystal Coast Dermatology Svcs., P.A., Morehead City, 2000—01; physician, dermatologist Down East Med. Assocs., Morehead City, 2005—; dermatopathologist Wake Forest U. Sch. Medicine, 2009. Cons. Carteret Gen. Hosp., Morehead City, 1986-2000; clin. attending prof. Bowman Gray Sch. Medicine, Winston-Salem, NC, 1991-2000; adj. clin. prof. U. NC Sch. Medicine, Chapel Hill, 1995-2001; assoc. prof. dermatology Wake Forest U. Med. Sch., 2001-20, bd. visitors, 2003—; lectr. cryosurgery World Congress Dermatology, Argentina, 2007, World Congress CryoSurgery, China, 2007. Co-exhibitor: Two Hereditary Osseocutaneous Syndromes, Acad. Dermatology, 1965 (Silver award), So. Med. Assn. Exhibit Hereditary Acrokeratotic Poikiloderma, 1970 (3d Pl. award). Recipient Gold award, Internat. Soc. Dermatology, 2007; named Woman of Yr., Women's Residence Coun. Wake Forest U., 1982, Practitioner of Yr., Dermatology Found., 1998. Mem.: Dermatopathology Libr. Website, Wake Forest U. Sch. Medicine, Internat. Soc. Cryosurgery (v.p. 2001—05, honorary mem. 2005), Women's Dermatologic Soc. (pres. 1997—98, Rose Hirschler award 2001), Am. Dermatologic Assn. (elect), Am. Acad. Dermatology (bd. dirs. 1991—96, audit com. 1996—2000, ethics com. 1996—2001, nominating com. 2002—, chair nominating com. 2003, honorary mem. 2005, Fox award 2003), N.Am. Clin. Dermatologic Soc. (bd. dirs. 1995—2001), World Congress Dermatology (co-chmn. cryosurgical symposium 1997, 2001), Wake Forest U. Sch. Medicine Alumni Assn. (bd. dirs. 2003—, Disting. Achievement award 2007). Avocations: travel, fishing. Home: 106 Cypress Dr Pine Knoll Shores NC 28513-6706 Personal E-mail: ggfgraham@aol.com.

GRAHAM, GREGORY DANE, psychiatrist, psychoanalyst, educator; b. Oakland, Calif., Aug. 9, 1947; BA in Philosophy, U. Calif., Santa Cruz, 1969; MD, U. Erlangen Nuremberg, Germany, 1978. Diplomate Am. Bd. Psychiatry and Neurology. Resident in internal medicine U. Tex. Health Sci. Ctr., Houston, 1979—80, resident in psychiatry, 1980—83; asst. prof. psychiatry Baylor Coll. Medicine, Houston, 1983—85, clin. asst. prof. psychiatry, 1985—94, clin. assoc. prof. psychiatry, 1994—2004, clin. prof. psychiatry, 2005—. Tng. and supervising analyst Houston Galveston Psychoanalytic Inst., 1998. Fellow: Am. Psychiatric Assn.; mem.: Am. Psychoanalytic Assn. (cert. in psychoanalysis). Office: 4550 Post Oak Pl # 300 Houston TX 77027 Office Phone: 713-622-5430.

GRAHAM, JAMES CHRISTOPHER, research scientist, statistician, psychologist, consultant; s. J. Keith and Barbara Ann Graham; m. L. Jill Graham, Mar. 21, 1998; 1 child, Eben. BA magna cum laude, Wichita State U., 1980; MA, U. Tex., 1994, PhD, 1997. Rsch. specialist Tex. Dept. Protective and Regulatory Services, Austin, 1997—2000; statistician, rsch. mgr. State of Wash. Dept. of Social and Health Svcs., Office Children's Adminstrn. Rsch., Seattle, 2000—05; rsch. scientist, statistician U. Wash. Sch. Social Work, Child Welfare Rsch. Group, Seattle, 2005—10; statistician, program evaluator U. Wash. Sch. Medicine, Fetal Alcohol and Drug Unit, 2008—; IT mgr. data & reporting analyst State of Wash. Dept. Social and Health Svcs., Children's Adminstrn., 2010—. Contbr. articles to profl. jours.;, author reports in field. Dir. Friends Along the Rd., Fort Myers, Fla., 2002—. Fellow, U. Tex., Austin, 1982—84; Leader scholar, Wichita State U., 1976—80, Postdoctoral fellow, NIH, 2001—03. Mem.: Soc. Prevention Rsch., Wash. State Pub. Health Assn., Puget Sound Mycol. Soc., Sigma Xi. Office: Children's Adminstrn Tech Svcs PO Box 45605 Olympia WA 98504-5605 Business E-Mail: jcgraham@u.washington.edu.

GRAHAM, JEWEL FREEMAN, social worker, lawyer, educator; b. Springfield, Ohio, May 3, 1925; d. Robert Lee and Lula Belle Freeman; m. Paul N. Graham, Aug. 8, 1953; children: Robert, Nathan. BA, Fisk U., 1946; student, Howard U., 1946-47; MS in Social Svc. Adminstrn., Case Western Res. U., 1953; JD, U. Dayton, 1979; LHD (hon.), Meadville-Lombard Theol. Sch., 1991. Bar: Ohio; cert. social worker. Assoc. dir. teenage program dept. YWCA, Grand Rapids, Mich., 1947-50, coord. met. teenage program Detroit, 1953-56; dir. program for interracial edn. Antioch Coll., Yellow Springs, Ohio, 1964-69, from asst. prof. to prof., 1969-92, prof. emeritus, 1992—. Mem. Ohio Commn. on Dispute Resolution and Conflict Mgmt., 1990-92. Mem. exec. com. World YWCA, Geneva, 1975-83, 87-95, pres., 1983; bd. dirs. YWCA of the U.S.A., 1970-89, pres., 1979-85; bd. dirs. Antioch U., 1994-96. Named to Greene County Women's Hall of Fame, 1982, Ohio Women's Hall of Fame, 1988; named 1 of 10 Outstanding Women of Miami Valley, 1987; recipient Ambassador award YWCA of the U.S.A., 1993. Mem. ABA, Nat. Assn. of Social Workers (charter), Nat. Coun. of Negro Women (life), Alpha Kappa Alpha. Democrat. Unitarian Universalist. Avocations: bicycling, swimming, walking, needlecrafts. E-mail: jewelg@aol.com.

GRAHAM, JOHN H., IV, association executive; BA, Franklin and Marshall Coll., 1971. Mem. Valley Forge coun. Boy Scouts Am., 1971—79; exec. dir. Am. Diabetes Assn., Phila., 1979—83, dir. devel. divsn. NYC, 1983—85, asst. exec. v.p. Alexandria, Va., 1985—88, dep. exec. v.p., 1988—90, CEO, 1990—2003; pres., CEO Am. Soc. Assn. Executives, Washington, 2003—. Mem.: Combined Health Appeal, Independent Sector, Greater Washington Soc. Assn. Execs., Nat. Health Coun., Am. Soc. Assn. Execs. Office: Am Society of Assn Executives 1575 I St NW Washington DC 20005

GRAHAM, JOHN WALLACE, pathologist; MD, McGill U., Montreal, Que., Can., 1960. Diplomate Am. Bd. Pathology. Intern L.A. County-U. So. Calif. Med. Ctr., 1960-61; resident in pathology U. Oreg. Health Sci. Ctr., Portland, 1961-63, V.A. Med. Ctr. West Los Angeles, 1963-65; fellow in forensic pathology Office Med. Examiner, Balt., 1965-66, dep. med. examiner LA, 1966-67, chief div. forensic medicine, 1968, 1983-84, asst. med. examiner Dallas, 1975-78, dep. chief med. examiner Calgary, Alt., Can., 1984-86; dir. Calif. Toxicology Service Inc., LA, 1969-75; chief med. examiner State of Utah, Salt Lake City, 1978-83. Asst. clin. prof. pathology, U. So. Calif., 1970-75, U. Tex. Southwestern Med. Sch., 1975-78; assoc. clin. prof. U. Utah, 1979-84, U. Calgary, 1986-88. Fellow Am. Acad. Forensic Scis., Coll. Am. Pathologists. Home: 1571 Tomahawk Dr Salt Lake City UT 84103-4228

GRAHAM, OLIVE JANE, retired medical/surgical nurse; b. Waterford, Wis., Mar. 23, 1932; d. Theodore Joseph Auterman and Edna Wilhelmina Sophia Boldt-Auterman; m. Charles E. Briggs (div.); children: Charles E. Briggs Jr., Joette A. O'Neill, Michael W. Briggs; m. Albert Frank Graham, Sept. 1, 1986. Diploma, St. John's Sch. Nursing, 1952. Cert. oper. room nurse, in oper. room tech., Johns Hopkins Hosp., 1953. Staff nurse Gibson Cmty. Hosp., Gibson City, Ill., 1952—53, Wesley Mem. Hosp., Chgo., 1953—54, Mercy Hosp., Champaign, 1954—55, Ho. Good Samaritan Hosp., Watertown, 1955; oper. rm./emergency rm. supr. Gibson Comty., Gibson City, 1956—58; staff nurse Cole Hosp., Champaign, 1958—59; office nurse Dr. Paul Sunderland, Gibson City, 1960—61; staff nurse Jefferson County Hosp., Ft. Atkinson, Wis., 1962—63, Charleston Meml. Hosp., Ill., 1964—68; tchr. Lamaze Dr. Pearman, Dr. Ferneau, Columbia, Mo., 1968—69; staff nurse Boone Hosp. Ctr., 1969—72, Harry S. Truman Meml. VA, 1972—92; ret. Co-dir.: (video) Pre-Operative Visit, 1982. Asst. leader Green Meadows Coun. Girl Scouts Am., Gibson City, 1958—59, neighborhood chmn., 1959—60; mem. Federated Jr. Womans Club, 1955—61, v.p. 17th dist., 1961—62; vol. blood drives ARC, 1993—2000; mem. bd. Rainbow Ho., Temporary Home for Children in Crisis, Columbia, 1996—2005, pres., 1998—99; mem. Lois Mikeut Century Cir. Internat. ORder King's Daus. and Sons., Inc., 1997—; mem. bd. King's Daus. Home, Mexico, 2001—03; docent Boone County Hist. Mus., 1995—; mem. U. Mo. Ext. Wives, 1993—2011; vol. Mo. State Show-ME Games, 1995—2011; candidate Columbia City Coun., 1977; mem. choir, prayer chain, care givers Trinity Luth. Ch., Columbia, 1968—; mem. United Meth. Women, 1993—2001. Mem.: Nat. Assn. Fed. Retirees, U. Mo. Alumni Assn., U. Mo. Quarterback Club, Beta Kappa (master), Beta Sigma Phi (charter pres. Xi Epsilon Theta, coun. pres., Girl of Yr. 1984). Lutheran. Avocations: walking, reading, bridge.

GRAHAM, PHILIP LAMAR, epidemiologist, physician; b. Seattle, June 18, 1969; s. Philip L. Graham and Burnley D. Dame; m. Dara K. Sicherman, Sept. 20, 2003; children: Arla Marisol, Rosa Clementine. BA, Trinity Coll., Hartford, Conn., 1992; MD, George Wash. U., DC, 1998; MSc, Columbia U. Sch. Pub. Health, NYC, 2003. Cert. N.Y., 1999. Pediatric resident Columbia U. Med. Ctr., NYC, 1998—2001, pediatric infectious disease fellow, 2001—03, asst. prof., pediat., 2003—; attending physician, asst. hosp. epidemiologist Children's Hosp. N.Y., NYC, 2003—. Epidemiologist pediat. hosp. NY Presbyn. Weill Cornell Med. Ctr., adj. asst. prof. pediats., 2002—; quality & patient safety officer children's health NY Presbyn. Hosp., 2009—. Office: Columbia Univ Med Ctr 622 W 168 St New York NY 10032

GRAJETZKI, HANS, retired anesthesiologist; b. Berlin, Germany, May 29, 1938; s. Egon and Charlotte Grajetzki; children: Daniela, Ina. MD, Humboldt U., Berlin, 1968. Anaesthesiologist Berlin, 1973, cert. Diving and Hyperbaric Medicine Physician German Hyperbaric and Diving Medicine Soc., 1998. Resident Templin Cmty. Hosp., Germany, 1968—73; staff physician, hyperbaric med. ctr. Krankenhaus im Friedrichshain, Berlin, 1973—2000; dir. berlin ctr. for diving and hyperbaric medicine Vivantes Klinikum im Friedrichshain, Berlin, 2000—03. Fellow: Assn. of German Sport Divers (Diving Medicine Physician award 2003). Home: Frankfurter Allee 32 Berlin 10247 Germany Office: Vivantes Klinikum im Friedrichshain Matthiasstrasse 7 Berlin 10249 Germany Office Fax: +49 30 42108760. Personal E-mail: hgrajetzki@t-online.de. E-mail: druckkammer@khf.de.

GRALOW, JULIE RUTH, physician; b. Sanford, Fla., Feb. 10, 1959; d. Richard Thomas and Ruth Haas Gralow; m. Hugh Willison Allen. BS, Stanford U., 1981; MD, U. So. Calif., 1988; residency, Brighman Women's, Harvard, 1991. Cert. internal medicine 1991, med. oncology 1995. Rsch. asst. Becton Dickinson Monoclonal Ctr., Mountain View, Calif., 1981—83, Stanford U. Sch. Medicine, 1983—84; rsch. fellow U. So. Calif. Sch. Medicine, 1985; acting instr. U. Wash., Fred Hutchinson Cancer Rsch. Ctr., Seattle, 1994—97, asst. prof., 1998—2002, assoc. prof. med. oncology, 2002—. Dir. breast cancer inst. U. Wash. and Fred Hutchinson Cancer Rsch. Inst., Seattle, 2003—; assoc. program head breast cancer Fred Hutchinson Cancer Rsch. Ctr., 2001—. Author: (jour. article) Jour. Immunology, 1984, New Eng. Jour. Medicine, 1984; co-author: Breast Fitness: An Optimal Exercise and Health Plan for Reducing Your Risk of Breast Cancer; contbr. several articles to profl. jours.; helped launch (traveling exhibit of art by women with breast cancer) Living Well With Cancer Series and Innervisions. Cons. program for appropriate tech. in health USAID Ukraine Breast Cancer Assistance Project, 1997—2000; co-chair breast cancer com. Southwest Oncology Group, 2000—; del. U. Wash. Ctr. for Women and Democracy, 2003; med. dir., team physician Team Survivor Northwest (exercise and fitness program for women cancer survivors). Recipient Career Devel. award, Am. Soc. Clin. Oncology, 1995—98, Clin. Career Devel. award, Am. Cancer Soc., 1995—98, Irving I. Lasky award, 1988, Janet M. Glasgow Achievement award, Am. Med. Women's Assn., 1988; U.S.C. Rsch. Fellowship, 1984—85, 1985—86. Mem.: Wash. State Med. Oncology Soc., Am. Soc. Breast Disease, Susan G. Komen Found. Breast Cancer Rsch., Nat. Alliance Breast Cancer Orgn., Puget Sound Oncology Group, Am. Assn. Cancer Rsch., Am. Soc. Clin. Oncology (Pub. Issues Com. 1999—, co-chair, Pub. Issues Com. 2000—02, liaison, Health Svcs. Rsch. Com. 2000—, chair, Patient Communication Com.), AMA. Office: (SCCA) Seattle Cancer Care Alliance 825 Eastlake Ave E PO Box 19023 Seattle WA 98109-1023 Office Phone: 206-288-7722.

GRAMMATIKOS, ALEXANDROS, physician, researcher; b. Thessaloniki, Greece, Jan. 2, 1978; MD, Med. Sch., AUTH, Greece, 2001, PhD, 2009; MSc in Integrated Immunology, U. Oxford, 2005. Countryside physician Kato Idrousa Rural Surgery, 2001—03; physician Greek Armed Forces, 2003—04; specialist tng. in internal medicine Gennimatas Gen. Hosp., 2006—10; rsch. fellow BIDMC, Harvard Med. Sch., 2010—. Hon. specialist registrar ST3 position Clin. Immunology Dept. John Radcliffe Hosp., Oxford, 2009. Fellowship, FEBS, 2005, BIDMC, Harvard Med. Sch. Mem.: UK Med. Coun., Greek Med. Coun., ESID, CIS, EAACI. Avocations: chess, computers, bicycling. Home: 78 Saint Paul St Brookline MA 02446 Personal E-mail: alex.grammatikos@gmail.com.

GRAMPUROHIT, NIRMALA DATTATRAYA, pharmacognosist, educator; d. Rajaram J. and Malati R. Desai; m. Dattatraya Appanbhat Grampurohit, May 28, 1978; children: Namrata, Shweta. BS in Pharm., U. Mumbai; MS in Pharm., 1976; PhD, Shrimati Nathibai Damodar Thackersy Women's U., 1992. Lectr. in pharm. Bombay Coll. Pharm., Mumbai, India, 1972—81; lectr. in pharm. C.U. Sham Coll. Pharm. Shrimati Nathibai Damodar Thackersy U., Mumbai, 1981—92, reader in pharm. C.U. Sham Coll. Pharm., 1992—; prin., prof. pharmacognosy Dr. Bhanuben Nanavati Coll. Pharmacy, Vile Parle, Mumbai, 2006—. Mem. academic coun. SNDT Women's U., 2000—05; mem. panel inspectors Pharmacy Coun. India; external examiner various instns. Contbr. articles to profl. jours. Recipient Best Tchr. award, Maharashtra State Govt., 2003, Prof. M.L. Khorana award, Indian Jour. Pharm. Scis., 2004; grantee, U. Grants Commn., 1998—2000, 2001—03, 2001, All India Coun. Tech. Edn., 2000—03, 2002—04. Mem.: Indian Pharm. Assn. (Best Rsch. Paper award 2000), Indian Soc. Pharm. (mem. exec. com. Indian Jour. Nat. Products 2000—), Indian Drug Manufacturer's Assn. (mem. sci. com. 1999—, mem. sci. com. Indian Herbal Pharmacopoeia, Best Rsch. Paper award 1999), Assn. Pharm. Tchrs. India (life), Indian Soc. Tech. Edn. (life), Assn. Pharm. (life). Avocations: painting, drawing, knitting. Home: F 208 Hrushikesh Swami Samarth Nagar Andheri Mumbai 400053 India Office: SVKM Coll Pharmacy V M Road 400 056 Mumbai India Office Phone: 022-26132905, 91-022-55747086, 26134557/58. Personal E-mail: drnirmalag@yahoo.com.

GRAN, JAN TORE, medical educator; b. Oslo, Apr. 29, 1949; MD, U. Oslo, PhD, 1977. Prof., dept. rheumatology Oslo U. Hosp., Rikshospitalet, 2001—. Office: Rikshospitalet Sognsvannsveien Oslo 1027 Norway Business E-Mail: jan.tore.gran@ous-hf.no.

GRANADOS, VANDERLEY, surgeon, educator; b. São Paulo, Brazil, June 26, 1950; s. Jose Antonio and Irene Ferrarezi Granados; m. Amelia Hortensia Otto, Feb. 12, 1978; children: Cindy Lis, Leroy Otto. Attended, Ensino Adventist Inst., São Paulo, 1966—68; MD, Fed. U. Pará, Belem, 1974. Missionary med. dir. Manaus Adv. Clinic, 1978—83; missionary surgeon Silvestre Adventist Hosp., Rio de Janeiro, 1987—, vice-dir. medicine, 2000—; also bd. dirs. Treas. Brazilian Soc. Laparoscopic Surgery, 1994—97; relief missionary physician Malamulo Adventist Hosp., Malawi, 1987, Mwami Adv. Hosp., Zambia, 1987. Fellow: ACS; mem.: Rio De Janiero Soc. Bariatric Surgery (sec. 2004—05), Internat. Soc. Bariatric Surgery, Brazilian Coll. Surgeons. Adventist. Avocations: jogging, classical music. Office: Silvestre Adventist Hosp Lad dos Guararapes 263 22241-220 Rio de Janeiro Brazil Home: Rua Cosme Velho 415 - Apt 603 22241-090 Rio de Janeiro RJ Brazil Office Phone: 011-55-21 3526-0212. Personal E-mail: vanderley_granados@yahoo.com.br. Business E-Mail: vdiretoria@hasilvestre.org.br.

GRANBERG, SETH, obstetrician, researcher, gynecologist; b. Oulu, Finland, Nov. 22, 1945; s. Seth Ferdinand Granberg and Maj Gretchen Wallin. MD, U. of Aarhus, Denmark, 1977; PhD, U. Gothenburg, Sweden, 1989. Assoc. prof. U. Gothenburg, 1991, head ultrasound unit dept. ob/gyn., 1987—90; physician varous hosps., 1983; obstetrician/gynecologist Sahlgren Hosp., Gothenburg, 1983—2000; head, reproductive medicine and ultrasound Karolinska Hosp., Stockholm, 2001—, prof. ultrasound, 2002—; prof. Karolinska U., Stockholm, 2002. Grantee medical rsch., 1991. Achievements include research in gynecological ultrasound, oncology, infertility, cervical physiology. Avocations: skiing, golf, fishing, travel. Home: Karolinskav 11 Solna 17164 Sweden Office: Karolinska Hospital Dept Ultrasound and Reprod Medicine Stockholm 17176 Sweden Business E-Mail: seth.granberg@telia.com.

GRANDI, EDWARD, medical association administrator; BA in Liberal Arts, St. John's Coll., 1977. Broker, v.p. Assurance, Inc., 1977—93, pres., CEO, 1993—96; sr. acct. exec. Hilb, Rogal, Hobbs Ins., 1996—2000; devel. dir. Safe Have Outreach Ministry, 2000—04, Interfaith Conf. Met. Washington, 2002—03; exec. dir. Am. Sleep Apnea Assn., Washington, 2004—. Office: American Sleep Apnea Assn 6856 Eastern Ave NW Ste 203 Washington DC 20012-2119 Office Phone: 202-293-3650. Office Fax: 202-293-3656. *

GRAÑENA, ALBERT, hematologist, educator; b. Barcelona, Sept. 26, 1947; s. Pedro and Antonia (Batista) Grañena; m. Asuncion Aracil (div. Nov. 1988); children: Albert, Marc, Ariadna; m. Olga Millon Grañena, 2008. MD, U. Barcelona, 1969, PhD summa cum laude, 1979, Specialist Internal Medicine, 1981, Specialist Hematology, 1981. Asst. physician Hosp. Clinic, Barcelona, 1970—72, specialist in hematology, 1972—79, sr. cons. in Hematology, head Marrow Transplant Program, 1979—93; prof. medicine U. Barcelona, 1993—; head hematology svc. Inst. Catala Oncologia, Barcelona, 1993—, Hosp. Bellvitge, Barcelona, 2004—. Assoc. prof. Escuela Farreras Valenti, Barcelona, 1974—; prof. U. Barcelona, 1985—; cons. Inst. I/ Dexeus, Barcelona, 1998—; lectr. to nat. and internat. med. congresses. Contbr. articles to internat. jours., to nat. jours. Bd, dirs. Fundacio Josep Carreras. Recipient IX DuPont prize, Oviedo, Spain, 1999; named Main investigator Joint Com. Spanish EEUU for sci. coop.; Presidential grant, Fundacio Josep Carreras, Barcelona, 1995—2001. Mem.: European Bone Marrow Tranplantation Soc., Internat. Soc. Hematology, Am. Soc. Hematology. E-mail: 5755agb@comb.cat.

GRANET, KENNETH M., internist; b. Manhasset, NY, Mar. 22, 1957; s. Irving and Arlene Granet; m. Wendy Granet. BA summa cum laude, Hofstra U., Hempstead, NY, 1979; MD, SUNY-Downstate Med. Ctr., Bklyn., 1984. Diplomate Am. Bd. Internal Medicine. Intern/resident in medicine North Shore Univ. Hosp., Manhasset, 1984-87, Meml. Sloan Kittering Cancer Ctr., NYC, 1984-87; pvt. practice LI, N.Y., 1987-93, Eatontown, N.J., 1993—; asst. program dir. dept. medicine Monmouth Med. Ctr., Long Branch, N.J., 1993—; clin. asst. prof. medicine Hahnemann U. Sch. Medicine, Phila., 1993—; section chief dept medicine Monmouth Med. Ctr., Long Branch, NJ. Med. dir. Cerebral Palsy, Monmouth, 1993—; lectr. in field; chmn. ethics com. Monmouth Med. Ctr. Contbr. articles to profl. jours. Organizer/founder 5 mile Spring Health Run, North Shore Univ. Hosp., 1987-92. Recipient Dean's Spl. award Hahnemann U. Sch. Medicine, 1995, Best Doctors award Consumer Reports; named Attending of the Yr., Dept. Medicine, Monmouth Med. Ctr., 1993-94, Best MD, NJ Monthly, 1995. Fellow ACP (preceptor/mentor program); mem. N.J. Med. Soc., Monmouth County Med. Soc. (exec. com. 1994—), Phi Beta Kappa. Office: 166 Morris Ave Long Branch NJ 07740 Office Phone: 712-229-2020.

GRANGAARD, DANIEL ROBERT, psychologist; b. Fond du Lac, Wis., Jan. 7, 1950; s. Lawrence Robert and Dorothy Ruth (Giove) G.; m. Becky Anne Byas, June 16, 1979; children: Dawn Michelle, Scott Robert. BA, Baylor U., 1972, MS, 1974, EdD, 1976. Lic. psychologist; lic. specialist in sch. psychology. Teaching fellow Baylor U., Waco, Tex., 1974-76; assoc. sch. psychologist Edn. Svc. Ctr. Region XII, 1976-77; sch. psychologist Austin Ind. Sch. Dist., 1977-85; dir. testing, internship tng. Minirth-Meier Tunnell & Wilson Clinic, 1989-94; pvt. practice, 1985—89, 1994—2000. Psychologist Genesis unit Shoal Creek Hosp., Austin, 1987—92, 1994—95; cons. psychologist Charter Hosp., Austin, 1984—94, United Cerebral Palsy Assn., 1992—98, Genesis Behavioral Health Clinic, Austin, 1994—95, Austin Child Guidance Ctr., 1995—96; adj. prof. psychology Austin C.C., 1995—, coll. assoc. student svcs., 2001—; adj. prof. psychology St. Edwards U., 1997—2001. Author: psychology textbook supplements; contbr. chpts. to books, articles to profl. jours.; webpage designer Austin C.C., 1999—2007. Westcreek rep. Austin Neighborhood Coun., 1980; coach YMCA Little League Baseball, 1995-99; dir. counseling First Evangel. Free Ch., Austin, 1994-95, elder, 1993-96. Recipient Excellence award, Nat. Inst. Staff and Orgnl. Devel. Austin CC, 2007. Mem. APA, Soc. Tchg. Psychology, Tex. CC Tchrs. Assn., Phi Delta Kappa. Republican. Mem. Evangelical Free Ch. Avocations: golf, basketball, exercise. Office: Austin CC Rio Grande Campus 1212 Rio Grande St Austin TX 78701-1710 Office Phone: 512-223-3131. Business E-Mail: dgran@austincc.edu.

GRANGE, LAURENT, rheumatologist, director; b. Annecy, France, Nov. 1, 1967; MD, Med. Sch. Grenoble, 2000; PhD, U. Joseph Fourrier, 2006. Unit dir. Ambulatory Platform Rheumatology Dept. Med. Sch. Hosp. of Grenable, France, 2004—. Pres. Assoc. Francaise Lutte Anti Rhumatismale, 2010. Mem.: Soc. Francaise Rhumatologie. Office: Clinique Universitaire Rhumatologie Grenoble Hosp Rheumatology Dept Echirolles Rhone Alpes 38434 France Office Fax: 33476765602. Business E-Mail: lgrange@chu-grenoble.fr.

GRANGER, CARL V., physician, educator; b. Bklyn., Nov. 26, 1928; s. Carl Victor and Marie Henson Granger; m. Helen Bolden (div. 1983); m. Joanne Champion (dec. 1994); m. Eloise Morrow, Sept. 1, 1995; children: Glenn, Marilyn. BA, Dartmouth Coll., 1948; MD, NYU, 1952. Bd. cert. in phys. medicine and rehab. Intern Nassau County Med. Ctr., Hempstead, N.Y., 1952-53; resident in phys. medicine and rehab. Walter Reed Army Med. Ctr., Washington, 1955-58; asst. prof. Yale U., New Haven, 1961-68; prof., chmn. Tufts U., Boston, 1968-76; prof. Brown U., Providence, 1977-83, U. Buffalo, 1983—, prof., chmn. rehab. medicine, 1998-2001. Contbr. articles to profl. jours. Maj. U.S. Army, 1954-61. Office: Uniform Data Sys Med Rehab Ste 300 270 Northpointe Pkwy Amherst NY 14228 Business E-Mail: CGranger@udsmr.org. *

GRANICK, MARK S., plastic surgeon, medical educator; b. New York, NY, July 7, 1951; m. Carol Singer, Feb. 17, 1994. BA cum laude, Cornell U., 1973; MD, Harvard Med. Sch., 1977. Cert. Am. Bd. of Plastic Surgery, 1984, Am. Bd. Otolaryngology - Head and Neck Surgery. Intern surgery Harvard Surgical Svc., New England Deaconess Hosp., 1977—78, resident otolaryngology, 1978—79; resident plastic surgery Mass. Eye and Ear Infirmary, Boston, 1979—82; resident U. Pitts., 1982—84; chief plastic surgery Med. Coll. Pa.; prof. surgery Hahnemann U., 1990—2000; chief plastic surgery, plastic surgery residency program dir., prof. surgery U. Medicine and Dentistry of NJ (UMDNJ)-NJ Med. Sch., 2001—. Contbr. articles to med. jours. Fellow: ACS; mem.: Northeastern Soc. Plastic Surgeons (bd. mem.), Am. Assn. Plastic Surgeons, Am. Soc. Plastic Surgeons. Office: UMDNJ 140 Bergen St Ste E1620 Newark NJ 07103 Office Fax: 973-972-8268. Personal E-mail: mgranickmd@umdnj.edu.

GRANIERI, ENRICO GAVINO, neurologist, educator; b. Sassari, Sardinia, Mar. 5, 1946; MD, Sassary U., 1971. Cert. specialization in neurology Parma U., 1976. Resident dept. neurology Sch. Neurology U. Parma, 1972—76; asst. prof. dept. neurology faculty medicine Sassari U., 1972—79; assoc. prof. Dept. Neurology Faculty Medicine, Ferrara U., 1979—89, prof., 1999—, dir., 2001—11; dir. Multiple Sclerosis Ctr. Ferrara U., 2004—11, dir. master of epilepsy, 2006—11, dir. master clin. neurophysiology, 2006—09; dir. Clin. Neurophysiology Ctr. Ferrara U. Hosp., 1990—2000. Grant, Associazione Italiana Sclerosi Multipla, Fondazione Italiana Sclerosi Multipla, Ferrara U. Mem.: Italian League Against Epilepsy, Italian Soc. Neurology. Achievements include research in clinical, epidemiological and experimental demyelinating disease with an emphasis on multiple sclerosis-the commonest potentially disabling disease of young adults. Avocation: music. Office: Corso della Giovecca 203 Ferrara 44100 Italy Office Fax: 39532205525. Business E-Mail: enrico.granieri@unife.it.

GRANNIS, FREDERIC WINSLOW, JR., thoracic surgeon; b. San Antonio, Oct. 6, 1943; s. Frederic Winslow and Mary Grannis; m. Patricia Harris, Feb. 11, 1967; children: Jennifer, Frederic Francis, Luke, Jessica. BS in Biology, Boston Coll., 1965; MD, N.Y. Med. Coll., 1969; degree in Gen. Surgery, Mayo Grad. Sch. Medicine, Rochester, Minn., 1974; degree in Thoracic Surgery, Mayo Grad. Sch. of Medicine, Rochester, Minn., 1978. Diplomate Am. Bd. Thoracic Surgery, Am. Bd. Surgery. Intern Mayo Grad. Sch. Medicine, Rochester, 1970; ptnr. Hayes, Silver and Grannis Med. Corp, Arcadia, Calif., 1978—96; with dept. thoracic surgery City of Hope Nat. Med. Ctr., Duarte, Calif., 1996—; sci. adv. com. mem. Tobacco Related Disease Rsch. Project, 2008—; caring ambassadors Long Cancer Med. Writers Cir., 2009; clin. prof. Thoracic Surgery, Hope, 2010, pres. elect, med. staff, 2009. Voluntary asst. clin. prof. dept. surgery U. Calif., San Diego, 1998—; mem. guideline panel on non-small-cell lung cancer Nat. Comprehensive Cancer Network, Rockledge, 1998—; mem. steering com. Internat. Early Lung Cancer Action Project (I-ELCAP), NYC, 2001—, mem. thoracic surg. com., 2001—. Author: (book) Medical, Surgical and Radiation Oncology, edits. 1-6, 1996, Minimal Access Thoracic Surgery, 1998, Surgical Oncology, 2000, (web page) The Lung Cancer and Cigarette Smoking Web Page, 1996, The Young People's Cyber-Library, 1998, Cyber-Gallery: Images of Disease Caused by Tobacco Products, 2001; contbr. articles to profl. jours. Mem. Pasadena Tobacco Prevention Coalition, 1997—2000; mem. cancer control com. San Gabriel Valley unit Am. Cancer Soc., Pasadena, Calif., 1997—2002. Asst. chief surgery USPHS, 1974—76. Fellow: ACS, Am. Coll. Chest Physicians (sci. adv. com., Calif. Tobacco Related Disease Rsch. Project 2006—10, health and sci. policy com.); mem.: Am. Coll. Chest Physicians, GLOBALink - The Internat. Tobacco-Control Network, Internat. Union Against Cancer, Trudeau Soc. Am. Lung Assn. L.A. County (David Salkin award 2000), Calif. Med. Assn., Soc. of Surg. Oncologists, Internat. Assn. for Study of Lung Cancer, Am. Thoracic Soc., Calif. Thoracic Assn., We. Thoracic Surg. Soc., L.A. Surg. Soc., Soc. Thoracic Surgeons, Gen. Thoracic Surg. Club. Democrat. Avocations: informatics, history, travel. Office: City of Hope Nat Med Ctr 1500 E Duarte Rd Duarte CA 91010 Office Phone: 626-359-8111. Business E-Mail: fgrannis@coh.org.

GRANOTT, NIRA, psychologist, researcher; b. Petah-Tikva, Israel; came to U.S., 1987; d. Jacob and Celia Granott; children: Guy A. Farber, Bali Farber MA, Tel Aviv U., 1983; EdM, Harvard U., 1988; PhD, MIT, 1993. Dir. multi-media project Edn. TV, Tel-Aviv, 1974—80; sr. analyst, software developer Control data Corp., Tel-Aviv, 1983—86; asst. prof. psychology U. Tex. Dallas, Richardson, 1993—95, dir. microdevel. lab., 1993—2002, asst. prof. psychology, 1997—2002; co-founder, pres. OORIM, LLC, 2000—. Vis. prof. psychology and lectr. edn. Harvard Grad. Sch. Edn., Cambridge, Mass., 1996-97; grant cons. Harvard U., 1995-96. Editor: (spl. issue) New Ideas in Psychology, 2005—06. Rsch. grantee NSF, 1999, Tex. Higher Edn. Bd., 2000, Timberlawn Rsch. Found., 1999; vis. scholar Tufts U., 2002-04, 05-06. Mem. Am. Psychol. Soc., Soc. for Rsch. on Child Devel Avocations: painting, photography, dance, yoga. Personal E-mail: ngranott@aol.com.

GRANSTEIN, RICHARD DAVID, dermatologist; b. Detroit, July 24, 1952; s. Harry and Estella Leah Granstein; m. Ilene Siegal, Nov. 24, 1985; children: Justin, Alicia. SB, MIT, 1974; MD, UCLA, 1978. Diplomate Nat. Bd. Med. Examiners, Am. Bd. Dermatology. Intern Harbor-UCLA Med. Ctr., Torrance, 1978-79; resident in dermatology Mass. Gen. Hosp., Boston, 1979-81, rsch. fellow, 1982-84, NCI-Frederick (Md.) Cancer Rsch. Facility, 1981-82; asst. prof. dermatology Harvard Med. Sch., Boston, 1984-90, assoc. prof. dermatology, 1990-96; dermatologist-in-chief N.Y. Presbyn. Hosp., NYC, 1995—; chmn., prof. dermatology Weill Med. Coll., Cornell U., NYC, 1995—. Cons. Connetics Corp., Palo Alto, Calif., 1995—98, Zeneca, Wilmington, Del., 1999—2000, Med. Pharm. Corp., Scotsdale, Ariz.; sci. adv. bd. AGI Dermatics, Freeport, NY, 1998—2008; sci. adv. Sigaun Bioscis., Princeton, NJ, 2008—. Editor: Mechanisms of Immune Regulation, 1994. Fellow Am. Acad. Dermatology, N.Y. Acad. Medicine, N.Y. Dermatol. Soc.; mem. Soc. Investigative Dermatology (bd. dirs. 1995-2000), Am. Soc. Clin. Investigation, Alpha Omega Alpha. Avocations: skiing, tennis. Office: Weill Med Coll Cornell U 1300 York Ave Rm F 342 New York NY 10021-4805 Home Phone: 914-725-5103; Office Phone: 646 962-7546. Business E-Mail: rdgranst@med.cornell.edu.

GRANT, ALFRED DAVID, orthopaedic surgeon, educator; b. NYC, June 12, 1933; s. Charles Meyer and Lillie (Eigen) G.; m. Ellen M. Michels, Apr. 16, 1961; children: Susan, Michele, Laura. BA, Emory U., 1952; MD, Chgo. Medical, 1957. Cert. Nat. Bd. Medical Examiners. Intern 4th surg. divsn. Bellevue Hosp, NYC, 1957-58; resident gen. surgery Montefiore Hosp, Bronx, N.Y., 1958-59; resident orthopaedic surgery Hosp. for Joint Diseases/Orthopaedic Inst., NYC, 1959-62; instr., prosecutor gross anatomy Chgo. Medical Sch., 1954-57; assoc. orthopaedic surgery Tulane Medical Sch., 1962-64, pvt. practice orthopaedic surgery, 1964—; with Hosp. Joint Diseases/Orthopaedic Inst., NYC, 1964—, emeritus chief neuromuscular sect. dept. orthopaedics, 1973—, emeritus med. dir. first chance child devel sch., 1974—, med. dir. Muscular Dystrophy clinic, 1974—, emeritus dir. ctr. neuromuscular and devel. disorders, 1979—97, assoc. dir. orthopaedic surgery, 1982—98; clin. asst. prof. orthopaedic surgery Albert Einstein Coll., 1970-79; asst. prof. orthopaedic surgery Mt. Sinai Sch. of Medicine, 1981—87; clin. prof. orthopedic surgery NYU Sch. Medicine, 1987-95; clin. prof., 1995—. Vis. surgeon Boston Children's Hosp., 1989, Shriner's Hosp., Springfield, Mass., 1989; asst. attending Montefiore Hosp., 1964—66, Morrisania Hosp., Bronx, NY, 1964—66, Albert Einstein Coll. Hosp., 1969—73; chief orthopaedic surgery United Hosp., Port Chester, NY, 1964—81, cons., 1981—; orthopaedic cons. St. Vincent's Hosp. Westchester Divsn., 1966—81, Rye Psychiat. Hosp., 1968—83, Staten Island (N.Y.) Devel. Ctr., 1976—89, Osborne Meml. Home, Rye, 1973—89; attending orthopaedist Rose Kennedy Ctr. Human Devel. and Retardation, Bronx, 1970—73; attending orthopaedics and birth defects clinic Albert Einstein Coll. Hosp., 1969—93; dept. surgery, orthopaedics sect. Beth Israel Hosp., NY, 1979—98. Edit. bd. Bulletin Hosp. Joint Diseases/Orthopaedic Inst.; lectr., presenter numerous courses, papers, symposia in field, U.S., Eur.; contbr. articles, chpts. profl. jours. Bd. trustees United Cerebral Palsy of Westchester, 1982—. HEW grant, 1974-77. Fellow N.Y. Acad. Medicine; mem. AMA, Am. Bd. Orthopaedic Surgery (examiner 1984—), N.Y. Med. Soc., Am. Soc. Surgery Foot and Ankle, Am. Ortho. Assn., Am. Acad. Orthopaedic Surgery (rehab. com. 1984-87), Am. Coll. Surgeons (trauma com. Westchester chpt. 1973-76), Am. Acad. Cerebral Palsy and Devel. Medicine (credential's com. 1987-89, sci. program com., 1986-88, rsch. and awards com., 1995-97), Pediatric Orthopaedic Club of N.Y. (pres. 1988-89, sec. 1986-87, pres.-elect 1987-88), N.Y. County Med. Soc., N.Y. State Soc. Orthopaedic Surgeons, Pediatric Orthopaedic Soc. No. Am., No. Am. Assn. Study and Application of Methods of Ilizarov, Israel Ortho. Assn. (hon.). Office: Hosp Joint Diseases Orthopaedic Inst 301 E 17th St New York NY 10003-3804 Personal E-mail: adgrant01@aol.com.

GRANT, HUGH, agricultural products executive; b. Mar. 1958; BS in Molecular Biology and Agrl. Zoology with honors, Glasgow U., Scotland; MS, Edinburgh U., Scotland; MBA, Internat. Mgmt. Ctr., Buckingham, Eng. Co-pres. agrl. sector Pharmacia Corp., 1998; v.p., COO Monsanto Co., 2000, exec. v.p., COO, 2000—03, chmn., pres., CEO, 2003—. Mem. exec. com. Microedit Summit Campaign; mem. internat. adv. bd. Scottish Enterprise. Bd. govs. United Way St. Louis; bd. trustee Donald Danforth Plant Sci. Ctr.; mem. Civic Progress. Mem.: Biotechnology Industry Orgn., Internat. Policy Coun. on Agr., Food and Trade, CropLife Internat. (mem. of the President's adv. group). Address: Monsanto Co 800 N Lindbergh Blvd Saint Louis MO 63167

GRANT, PETER RAYMOND, biologist, researcher, educator; b. London, Oct. 26, 1936; arrived in US, 1978; m. Barbara Rosemary Matchett, Jan. 4, 1962; children: Nicola, K. Thalia. BA with honors, Cambridge U., Eng., 1960; PhD in Evolutionary Biology, U. B.C., Vancouver, Can., 1964; PhD (hon.), U. Uppsala, 1986; DSc (hon.), McGill U., 2000, U. San Francisco, Quito, 2005, U. Zürich, 2007. Postdoctoral rsch. fellow Yale U., 1964—65; asst. prof. McGill U., Canada, 1965—68, assoc. prof., 1965—68, prof., 1973—77, U. Mich., Ann Arbor, 1977—85, chmn., dept. ecology and evolutionary biol., 1981—83; prof. Princeton U., NJ, 1985—2008, assoc. chmn., biology dept. NJ, 1987—88, dir., program in ecology, evolution and behavior NJ, 1988—90, Class of 1877 Prof. of Zoology NJ, 1989—2008, Class of 1877 Prof. of Zoology Emeritus NJ, 2008—, chmn., dept. ecology and evolutionary biology NJ, 1990—91. Vis. prof. Universities of Uppsala and Lund, Sweden, 1981, U. Uppsala, Sweden, 1985. Author: Ecology and Evolution of Darwin's Finches, 1986, 99; co-author: Evolutionary Dynamics of a Natural Population: The Large Cactus Finch of the Galapagos, 1989 (Wildlife Publication award, Wildlife Soc., 1991), How and Why Species Multiply: The Radiation of Darwin's Finches, 2008; editor: Evolution on Islands, 1998; co-editor: Molecules, Molds and Metazoa, 1992; assoc. editor Ecology, 1968-70, Evolutionary Theory, 1973-, Biological Journal of the Linnean Society, 1984-, Philosophical Transactions of the Royal Society of London, 1990-93; contbr. articles to profl. jours. Recipient Alexander von Humboldt Found. Sr. Scientist Rsch. prize, 1996; co-recipient Leidy medal, Acad. Natural Sciences Phila., 1994, Loye & Alden Miller award, Cooper Ornithological Soc., 2003, Balzan prize in Population Biology, 2005, Outstanding Scientist award, Am. Inst. Biol. Sciences, 2005, Darwin-Wallace medal, Linnean Soc., 2008, Kyoto prize for Basic Sci., Inamori Found., 2009. Fellow AAAS, Royal Soc. London (Darwin medal, 2002), Royal Soc. Can., Am. Ornithologists' Union (Brewster medal, 1983), Linnean Soc. London; mem. Am. Philos. Soc., NAS (fgn. assoc.), Royal Soc. Sciences (fgn.), Am. Acad. Arts & Sciences, Am. Soc. Naturalists (hon., pres. 1999, past pres. 2000, E.O. Wilson Naturalist award, 1998), Soc. for the Study of Evolution, Ecological Soc. America, Soc. Behavioral Ecology, Charles Dawin Found. (Gen. Assembly, Millenial medal for Conversation in Galapagos, 2000), Nuttall Ornithological Soc. (hon.) Office: Princeton U Dept Ecology & Evolutionary Biology 105 Eno Hall Princeton NJ 08544-1003 Office Phone: 609-258-5156. Business E-Mail: prgrant@princeton.edu.

GRANT, RONALD ALFRED, psychiatrist, pastoral counselor, psychoanalyst; b. Providence, May 28, 1938; s. Alfred Edward and Althea G.; children: Andrew Edward, Kathryn Caroline. AB, Tufts U., 1959; MDiv, Andover Newton Theol. Sem., 1963, STM, 1964, D in Ministry, 1972; MD, Boston U., 1969. Cert. psychoanalysis, med. psychotherapy, group therapy. Intern Mary Imogene Bassett Hosp. (affiliate Columbia U. Med. Ctr.), Cooperstown, NY, 1969—70, resident, 1970—71, N.Y. State Psychiat. Inst. and Columbia Med. Ctr., NYC, 1971—73; pvt. practice pastoral counselor, 1972—; pvt. practice psychiatry, Westport, Greenwich, Conn., 1973—; pvt. practice psychoanalysis, 1981—. Mem. faculty, tng. and supervisory analyst C.G. Jung Inst. N.Y., 1981—, med. dir., 1983—87; bd. dirs., sec., 2007—08; psychiat. cons. Montessori Sch., Wilton, Conn., 1987—97; staff psychiatrist, supr. Temenos Inst., Westport, Conn., 1987—, med. dir., 1998—2000; mem. adj. faculty Andover Newton Theol. Sem., 1991—98. Mem. editorial bd. Human Devel. Jour., 1986-94. Named one of Outstanding Young Men in Am., 1970. Mem. AMA, Am. Psychiat. Assn., Am. Inst. Homeopathy, NY Assn. Analytical Psychology, Internat. Assn. Analytical Psychology, Inclusion Teaming (former mem. bd. dirs., cons.). Avocations: stamp collecting/philately, sports, reading, skiing, golf. Office: 45 E Putnam Ave Greenwich CT 06830-5438 also: 1465 Post Rd E Westport CT 06880

GRANT, WALTER MATTHEWS, retired lawyer; b. Winchester, Ky., Mar. 30, 1945; s. Raymond Russell and Mary Mitchell (Rees) G.; m. Ann Carol Straus, Aug. 5, 1967; children: Walter Matthews II, Jean Ann, Raymond Russell II. ABJ, U. Ky., Lexington, 1967; JD, Vanderbilt U., 1971. Bar: Ga. 1971, Tenn. 1992. Assoc. Alston & Bird, Atlanta, 1971-76, ptnr., 1976-83; v.p., gen. counsel, sec. Contel Corp., Atlanta, 1983-91; sr. v.p., gen. counsel Smith & Nephew Inc., Memphis, 1991-93; sr. v.p., gen. counsel, sec. The Actava Group Inc., Atlanta, 1993-96, Bruno's Supermarkets, Inc., Birmingham, Ala., 1996—2002; bd. chmn. Florence McDonnell Ctr., Atlanta, 2007—10; mem. bd. trustees Alliance Christian Media Atlanta, 2008—. Editor in chief Vanderbilt Law Rev., 1970-71, Ga. State Bar Jour., 1979-82. Baptist.

GRASSI, ALDRIGO, retired psychiatrist; b. Bergamo, Italy, May 22, 1947; s. Camillo Grassi and Lidia Parossi; m. Renata Roella, Aug. 25, 1972 (div. 2000); 1 child, Matteo. MD, U. Pavia, Italy, 1971, D in Psychiatry, 1975; degree in Pub. Health and Preventive Medicine, U. Bologna, Italy, 1980. Dept. head Emilia-Romagna Region, Bologna, 1978—84, Local Health Unit 30, Cento, Italy, 1985—90; gen. mgr. Local Health Unit 4, Parma, Italy, 1991—92; dir. Mental Health Ctr., Bologna, 1993—95, 2000—04; dept. head Mental Health Dept., Bologna, 1997—99, ret., 2004. Author: Guida agli interventi sulle tossicodipendenze, 1982, La programmazione sanitaria, 1985, Giovani e Disagio psichico, 1989, All'ombra dell'mltimo Sole, 2007, La Quinta Stagione, 2008, La terza b: una banda di assassini, 2011. Com. mem. Inst. Ortopedico-Rizzoli, Bologna, 1983—85. Mem.: SIEP (cons. 1990—).

GRATSIANSKY, NIKOLAI, cardiologist; b. Irkutsk, Russia, Aug. 9, 1942; MD, 2nd Moscow Med. Inst., 1965, PhD, 1970. Instr., lectr. internal medicine 2nd Moscow Med. Inst., Clinic Internal Medicine 1, 1970—77; sr. rschr. dept. urgent cardiology Inst. Clin. Cardiology, USSR Cardiology Rsch. Ctr., Moscow, 1977—82, leading rschr. dept. cardiovasc. surgery, 1987—89; head clin. dept., dept. Ischemic heart disease Inst. Preventive Cardiology, USSR Cardiology Rsch. Ctr., Moscow, 1982—86; chief lab. clin. cardiology and ctr. atherosclerosis Inst. Physico-Chem. Medicine FMBA, 1989—. Fellow: European Soc. Cardiology; mem.: Soc. Cardiology Russian Fedn. Home: Leninsky prospekt 123 korp1 kv84 Moscow 117513 Russia Home Fax: 74954387440. Personal E-mail: n.gra@athero.ru.

GRATTON, GABRIELE, neuroscientist, psychology professor; MD, U. Rome; PhD, U. Ill. Assoc. prof. psychology dept. U. Ill. Urbana-Champaign, faculty, Beckman Inst. Contbr. articles profl. jours. Fellow: Assn. Psychol. Sci.; mem.: Soc. Psychophysiol. Rsch. (pres. 2009—10). Office: Univ Ill 519 Psychology Bldg 603 E Daniel St Champaign IL 61820 Business E-Mail: grattong@illinois.edu. *

GRAVALLESE, ELLEN M., rheumatologist, educator; b. Boston, Sept. 3, 1955; BA, Harvard Coll., 1977; MD, Columbia Coll. Physicians and Surgeons, 1981. Assoc. prof. medicine Harvard Med. Sch., 1981—2006; chief, divsn. rheumatology, prof. medicine U. Mass. Med. Sch., 2006—. Bd. dirs. Am. Coll. Rheumatology, 2003—06. Recipient Marion Ropes award, Arthritis Found.; grant, NIH. Mem.: ASBMR, ACR. Avocation: travel. Office: Lazare Research Bldg Ste 223 364 Worcester MA 01605 Office Fax: 508-856-8878. Business E-Mail: ellen.gravallese@umassmed.edu.

GRAVER, MARY KATHRYN, medical/surgical nurse; b. Rehrersburg, Pa., Nov. 8, 1934; d. Levi B. and Emma A. (Sensenig) Gibbel; m. C. W. Graver, June 27, 1959; children: Elizabeth Ann, Craig Warren, Timothy John, Kathryn Renate. RN, Coatesville Hosp., Pa., 1956; BA, Eastern Coll., St. Davids, Pa., 1994. Staff nurse pediatrics unit Phila. Gen. Hosp., 1956; staff nurse med./surg. unit Coatesville Hosp., 1957; staff nurse maternal and med./surg. units Ephrata (Pa.) Hosp., 1958-59; staff/clinic nurse Bryn Mawr (Pa.) Hosp., 1976-93, vol., 2001—.

GRAVES, JENNIFER A. MARSHALL, genomics and genetics researcher; b. Adelaide, Australia, Nov. 24, 1941; d. Theo John and Ann (Nicholls) Marshall; m. John Wagner Graves, July 16, 1966; children: Alison, Erica. BS, Adelaide U., 1962, MS, 1967; PhD, U. Calif., Berkeley, 1971. Lectr. La Trobe U., Melbourne, Australia, 1971-77, sr. lectr., 1978-85, reader, 1986-91, prof., 1991-2001; sr. prof. rsch. sch. of biol. scis. Australian Nat. U., Canberra, 2001—, dir. ARC Ctr. Kangaroo Genomics. Professorial fellow U. Melbourne, 2001—. Editor: Mammals From Pouches and Eggs, 1990, Sex Chromosomes and Sex Determining Genes, 1993, Mammalian Genomics, 2004; contbr. over 360 articles to profl. jours. Fulbright scholar Internat. Edn. Found., 1965-71; recipient Sir Ronald A. Fisher award U. Adelaide, 1963, Ian Potter grants Ian Potter Found., Melbourne, 1988, 92, Ormonde Lectureship, U. Queensland, Brisbane, 1990, L'oréal-UNESCO Women in Science award, 2006, Offer in The Order of Australia, 2010, Mackfarlane Burnet medal, 2006, numerous govt. and pvt. grants. Fellow Australian Acad. Scis.; mem. Genetics Soc. Australia (v.p. 1993-94, pres. 1994—96), Cell Biology Soc. Victoria (pres. 1981-83), Australian and New Zealand Soc. for Cell Biology (pres. 1984-85), Am. Soc. Human Genetics, Royal Soc. Victoria, others. Avocations: songwriter, singer. Office Phone: 61261252492. Office Fax: 61 3 8344 7909.

GRAVES, KATHRYN LOUISE, dermatologist; b. Kansas City, Kans., Mar. 9, 1949; d. Jack Clair and Ruth Marjory (Prentice) Schroll; m. Jeffery Jackson Graves, Mar. 31, 1973; children: Jeffery Justin, Jonathon Tyler, Kathryn Camille. BA, U. Kans., 1971; MD, U. Kans., Kansas City, 1974. Diplomate Am. Bd. Dermatology. Intern St. Lukes Hosp., Kansas City, 1975-76, resident in internal medicine, 1976; resident dermatology Sch. Medicine U. Kans., Kansas City, 1976-79; dermatologist Hutchinson (Kans.) Clinic P.A., 1979—; mem. med. staff Hutchinson Hosp., 1979—. Fellow Am. Acad. Dermatology; mem. AMA, Kans. Dermatology Soc., Kans. Med. Assn., Hutchinson C. of C., Gamma Phi Beta (standards chair 1973—). Republican. Methodist. Avocations: reading, walking, tennis, needlepoint. Home: 130 Hyde Park Dr Hutchinson KS 67502-2840 Office: Hutchinson Clinic 2101 N Waldron St Hutchinson KS 67502-1197 Office Phone: 620-669-2570.

GRAVES, SCOTT STOLL, research scientist, educator; b. Oxnard, Calif., Sept. 11, 1952; BS, U. Calif., Davis, 1974; PhD, U. Ga., 1984. Sr. scientist II NeoRx Corp., 1987—2002; staff scientist, rsch. assoc. prof. Fred Hutchinson Cancer Rsch. Ctr., U. Wash., 2003—. Affiliate asst. prof. U. Wash., 1994—95; sci. advisor KLIP Pharma, 2010—. Recipient Dale A Porter award, Animal Disease Workers Southern States; Rsch. grant, NCI, NIH. Avocations: skiing, fly fishing, carpentry. Office: Fred Hutchinson Cancer Rsch Ctr Seattle WA 98109 Personal E-mail: scttgraves@gmail.com.

GRAVINO, FRANK NICHOLAS, cardiologist; BS, Boston U., MD, 1974. Diplomate Am. Bd. Internal Medicine, Am. Bd. Internal Medicine-cardiovasc. disease, Am. Bd. Internal Medicine-nuclear cardiology. Intern internal medicine Boston City Hosp., 1975, resident internal medicine, 1978; fellow cardiology Ronald Reagan Univ. Calif. LA Med. Ctr., 1980; hosp. affiliations include Holy Cross Hosp., Wash. Adventist Hosp., Md. Heart P.C. Named one of Top Doctors, Washingtonian Mag., 2011. Office: Maryland Heart PC Ste 200 6410 Rockledge Dr Bethesda MD 20817 Office Phone: 301-897-5301.

GRAVITZ, HERBERT L., clinical psychologist, writer; b. Washington, Aug. 18, 1942; s. Phillip Benjamin and Sophie (Korin) G.; m. Leslie Ann Gravitz; children: Brian Eric, Aaron David, Jason Michael. BS, U. Md., 1964; MA, U. Tenn., Knoxville, 1966, PhD, 1969. Diplomate Am. Bd. Forensic Examiners, in psychotherapy Am. Acad. Experts in Traumatic Stress; lic. clin. psychologist; bd. cert. in illness trauma. Asst. dir. Counseling Ctr., U. Calif., Santa Barbara, 1972—79, counseling program dir., 1979-80, coord. tng., 1980-81; cons. psychologist Psychiat. Emergency Team, Santa Barbara, 1980-81, Sanctuary House, Inc., Santa Barbara, 1980-82; core faculty Suzanne Somers Inst., Palm Springs, Calif., 1989—93; pvt. practice Santa Barbara, 1979—. Asst. prof. psychology U. Windsor, Ont., Can., 1969-72. Author: Obsessive Compulsive Disorder: New Help for the Family, 1998, 2nd edit., 2005, Facing Adversity: Words that Heal, 2005, Mental Illness and the Family: Unlocking the Doors to Triumph, 2005; co-author: Recovery: A Guide for Adult Children of Alcoholics, 1985, Genesis: Recovery from Childhood Traumas, 1988; author: The Bright Side of Illness. Fellow Am. Acad. Experts in Traumatic Stress; mem. Calif. State Psychol. Assn. Avocations: music, writing, meditation, stamps. Office: Ste 217 2020 Alameda Padre Serra Santa Barbara CA 93103-1756 Office Phone: 805-963-9309. Business E-Mail: gravitz@earthlink.net.

GRAVLEE, GLENN P(AGE), anesthesiologist, educator, director; b. Birmingham, Ala., Aug. 15, 1950; BS in Medicine, Northwestern U., 1972, MD, 1974. Diplomate Am. Bd. Anesthesiology, Nat. Bd. Echocardiography. Intern Hartford Hosp., Conn., 1974—75; resident anesthesiology Mass. Gen. Hosp., Harvard Med. Sch., Boston, 1975—77, chief resident, cardiac anesthesia fellow, 1977—78, instr., 1978—79; from asst. prof. to prof. Wake Forest U., 1978—94; prof. Allegheny U. Health Scis., Pitts., 1994—99, chair, 1994—99; prof. dept. anesthesiology Coll. Med. and Pub. Health, Ohio State U., Columbus, 1999—, chmn. dept. anesthesiology Coll. Med. and Pub. Health, 1999—2002, vice chmn., 2002—06; prof. Health Scis. Ctr. U. Colo., 2006—, dir. edn. Dept. Anesthesiology Health Scis. Ctr., 2006—. Editor: Cardiopulmonary Bypass: Principles and Practice, 1994, 2000; co-editor: A Practical Approach to Cardiac Anesthesia, 2003, Year Book of Anesthesia, 2004; contbr. articles to profl. jours. Mem.: Am. Soc. Anesthesiologists, Internat. Anesthesiology Rsch. Soc., Soc. Cardiovasc. Anesthesiologists (pres. 2003—05), Am. Bd. Anesthesiologists (dir. 1999—). Office: Univ Colo Health Scis Ctr Dept Anesthesiology 4200 E 9th Ave B113 Denver CO 80262 Business E-Mail: glenn.gravlee@uchsc.edu.

GRAY, BRADFORD HITCH, health service researcher; b. Greenwich, Conn., Dec. 31, 1942; s. John Bradford and Joyce (Hitch) G.; m. Anne Morgan, Aug. 6, 1966 (div. 1980); children: Carrie Elizabeth, Joshua Bradford; m. Helen Darling, Jan. 15, 1983. BS, Okla. State U., 1964; PhD, Yale U., 1973. Asst. prof. U. N.C., Chapel Hill, 1971-74; staff sociologist Nat. Commn. for the Protection of Human Subjects of Rsch., Washington, 1975-77; study dir. Inst. of Medicine NAS, Washington, 1977-88; prof. pub. health Yale Sch. Medicine, New Haven, 1989-96; exec. dir. Program on Non-Profit Orgns. Yale U., New Haven, 1989-96, dir. Inst. for Social and Policy Studies, 1992-96; dir. divsn. health and sci. policy N.Y. Acad. Medicine, NYC, 1996—2004; prin. rsch. assoc. Urban Inst., Washington, 2004—. Author: Human Subjects in Medical Experimentation, 1975, The Profit Motive and Patient Care, 1991; editor: New Health Care for Profit, 1983, For-Profit Enterprise in Health Care, 1986. Grantee Lilly Endowment, Indpls., 1990, Ford Found., N.Y., 1989, Rockefeller Bros. Fund, N.Y., 1989, Robert Wood Johnson Found., 1989, 93, 96, Commonwealth Fund, 1997. Mem.: Inst. of Medicine, Grolier Club, Yale Club of N.Y. Office: Urban Inst 2100 M St NW Washington DC 20037 Home: 1648 32nd St NW Washington DC 20007

GRAY, DARREN J., epidemiologist; b. Brisbane, Australia, Aug. 21, 1978; BSc, U. Queensland, 1999, PhD, 2008. Rsch. fellow Griffith U. & Queensland Inst. Med. Rsch., 2009—. Adj. assoc. prof. Hunan Inst. Parasitic Diseases, China, 2010. Named Publ. of Yr., Griffith U., 2010; Rsch. fellowship, grants, Nat. Health and Med. Rsch. Coun., Australia. Mem.: Am. Soc. Tropical Medicine and Hygiene, Queensland Tropical Health Alliance, Australian Soc. Parasitology (JD Smyth Travel award). Office: 300 Herston Rd Brisbane Queensland 4006 Australia Business E-Mail: darren.gray@qimr.edu.au.

GRAY, DONALD MELVIN, molecular and cell biology educator; b. Milton, Pa., Apr. 4, 1938; s. Harry Seal and Edith Sophia (Larrison) G.; m. Carla Christine Winlund, Sept. 10, 1970. BA, Susquehanna U., 1960; MS, Yale U., 1963, PhD, 1967. Postdoctoral fellow U. Calif., Berkeley, 1967—70; asst. prof. molecular and cell biology U. Tex. at Dallas, Richardson, 1970—76, assoc. prof., 1976—83, prof., 1983—, program head, 1989—95, 2004—07. Contbr. articles to profl. jours. Fogarty Sr. Internat. fellow European Molecular Biology Lab., Heidelberg, Fed. Republic of Germany, 1977-78; NIH grantee U. Tex. at Dallas, 1972-93, NSF grantee, 1994-98, Welch Found. grantee, 1972—2010. Fellow AAAS; mem. Am. Chem. Soc., Biophys. Soc. Office: Univ Tex at Dallas Molecular and Cell Biology 800 W Campbell Rd Richardson TX 75080

GRAY, EDMUND WESLEY, physician; b. Colville, Wash., Nov. 9, 1928; s. Wesley Harold and Helen (Corridan) G.; m. Jane Bloomfield, June 20, 1953; children: Timothy Paul, Sarah Jane, Terrence Wesley. Student, Gonzaga U., Spokane, Wash., 1946—49; MD, U. Wash., Seattle, 1953. Diplomate Am. Bd. Family Practice. Intern Indpls. Gen. Hosp., 1953-54; pvt. practice Colville, 1956—. Health officer N.E. Tri-County Health Dept., Colville, 1973—; med. dir. N.W. Alloys, ALCOA, Addy, Wash., 1975—; cons., mem. Wash. State Physicians Ins. Assn., Seattle. Mem. joint select com. on basic health Wash. Ho. of Reps., Olympia, 1986-87; mem. Wash. Bd. Health, 1986-88, 2001-06; mem. Wash. Basic Health Commn., 1988-. Capt. M.C., USAF, 1954-56. Recipient Disting. Alumni award Gonzaga U., 1988, U. Wash. Sch. Medicine, 1992, Colville HS, 1997, Achievement in Pub. Health award Wash. Pub. Health Ofcls., 1988, Warren Featherstone Reid award State of Wash., 1995, Recognition of Merit in Medicine Washington State Senate, 2007. Mem. AMA (del. 1980-87, Nathan Davis award, 2006), Am. Acad. Family Practice, Wash. Acad. Family Practice, Wash. Pub. Health Assn., Wash. Med. Assn. (past sec., v.p., pres. 1985-86), Stevens County Med. Assn. (You Made a Difference award 1987), Spokane County Med. Assn. (hon. life), Colville C. of C. (pres. 1966), Elks (exalted ruler Colville 1964, dist. dep. 1968), Providence Health Car Bd. Democrat. Roman Catholic. Avocations: golf, water and snow skiing, crafts. Home: 860 E 1st Ave Colville WA 99114-3218 Office: NE Wash Med Group 1200 E Columbia Ave Colville WA 99114-3354 Business E-Mail: ewgray@ultraplix.com. *

GRAY, HARRY BARKUS, chemistry professor; b. Woodburn, Ky., Nov. 14, 1935; s. Barkus and Ruby (Hopper) Gray; m. Shirley Barnes, June 2, 1957; children: Victoria Lynn, Andrew Thomas, Noah Harry Barkus. BS, Western Ky. U., 1957; PhD, Northwestern U., 1960, DSc (hon.), 1984, U. Chgo., 1987, U. Rochester, 1987, U. Paul Sabatier, 1991, U. Göteborg, 1991, U. Firenze, 1993, Columbia U., 1994, Bowling Green State U., 1994, Ill. Wesleyan, 1995, Oberlin Coll., 1996, U. Ariz., 1997, Carleton U., 2001, U. SC, 2003, U. Copenhagen, 2003, U. Edinburgh, 2006. Postdoctoral fellow U. Copenhagen, 1960—61; faculty Columbia U., 1961—66, prof., 1965—66; prof. chemistry Calif. Inst. Tech., Pasadena, 1966—, now Arnold O. Beckman prof. chemistry and founding dir. Beckman Inst. Vis. prof. Rockefeller U., Harvard U., U. Iowa, Pa. State U., Yeshiva U., U. Copenhagen, U. Witwatersrand, Johannesburg, South Africa, U. Canterbury, Christchurch, New Zealand, U. Hong Kong; George Eastman prof. Oxford (Eng.) U., 1997—98; cons. govt., industry; Kistiakowsky lectr. Harvard U., 1999. Author: Electrons and Chemical Bonding, 1965, Molecular Orbital Theory, 1965, Ligand Substitution Processes, 1966, Basic Principles of Chemistry, 1967, Chemical Dynamics, 1968, Chemical Principles, 1970, Models in Chemical Science, 1971, Chemical Bonds, 1973, Chemical Structure and Bonding, 1980, Molecular Electronic Structures, 1980, Braving the Elements, 1995. Recipient Franklin Meml. award, Stanford U., 1967, Fresenius award, Phi Lambda Upsilon, 1970, Shoemaker award, U. Louisville, 1970, award for excellence in tchg., Mfg. Chemists Assn., 1972, Centenary medal, Royal Soc. Chemistry, 1985, Nat. medal of Sci., 1986, Alfred Bader Bioinorganic Chemistry award, 1990, Gold medal, Am. Inst. Chemists, 1990, Linderstrom-Lang prize, 1992, Priestly award, Dickinson Coll., 1991, Chandler medal, Columbia U., 1999, Harvey prize, Technion Israel Inst. Tech., 2000, Benjamin Franklin medal in Chemistry, Franklin Inst., 2004, Wolf prize in chemistry, Wolf Found., Israel, 2004; named Calif. Scientist of Yr., 1988, Achievement Rewards for Coll. Scis. Man of Sci., 1990;

Guggenheim fellow, 1972—73, Phi Beta Kappa scholar, 1973—74. Fellow: AAAS; mem.: NAS (Nichols medal 2003, award in chem. scis. 2003), Acad. Nat. Linceia, Royal Danish Acad. Scis. and Letters, Am. Philos. Soc., Royal Soc. (London), Royal Swedish Acad., Am. Chem. Soc. (award pure chemistry 1970, Harrison Howe award 1972, award inorganic chemistry 1978, Remsen Meml. award 1979, Tolman medal 1979, award for disting. svc. in advancement of inorganic chemistry 1984, Pauling medal 1986, Priestley medal 1991, Willard Gibbs medal 1992, Wolf prize for chemistry 2004, Benjamin Franklin medal in chemistry 2004, City of Florence prize in molecular scis. 2006, Pupin medal 2008, Schulich prize 2008, Antonimi award 2008), Phi Lambda Upsilon, Alpha Chi Sigma. Office: Calif Inst Tech 408 Beckman MC 127-72 1200 E California Blvd Pasadena CA 91125-0001

GRAY, HERMAN B., hospital administrator; m. Shirley Mann; children: Monifa, Dara. MD, U. Mich., Ann Arbor; MBA, U. Tenn. Chief pediatric resident Children's Hosp. of Mich., v.p. grad. med. edn., dir. Pediatric Residency Prog., chief staff, COO, clin. assoc. prof. pediatrics, pres., 2005—. Med. cons. Mich. Dept. Cmty. Health, Children's Specialized Health Svcs.; v.p., med. dir. clin. affairs Blue Care Network. Fellow: Am. Acad. Pediatrics; mem.: AMA, Wayne County Med. Soc., Mich. State Med. Soc. Office: Children's Hosp MIch 3901 Beaubien Detroit MI 48201

GRAY, KRIS DIANE, nursing consultant, forensic specialist; ASN, Fresno C.C., 1993; BA in Biology, Calif. State U., 1985. Diplomate Am. Bd. Medicolegal Death Investigators (registered), lic. paramedic Calif., cert. emergency nurse Bd. Cert. Emergency Nursing, flight nurse Bd. Cert. Emergency Nursing; RN Calif. Cardiac rsch. assoc. U. Calif. San Francisco, Fresno, 1984—85; paramedic Fort Bend County Emergency Svcs., Rosenberg, Tex., 1987—90, Am. Med. Svcs., Fresno, 1990—94; RN Sierra View Dist. Hosp., Porterville, Calif., 1994—2004; instr. Porterville C.C., 1994—95; RN Holland Am.-West Tours Inc., Seattle, 1996—2000; owner Gray Forensics and Consulting, Visalia, Calif., 2003—; co-owner Mobile Blood Draws, Visalia, Calif., 2007—. Peer counselor Ctrl. Valley Emergency Svcs. Support Team, Fresno, 1990—95; forensic autopsy asst. Tulare County Sheriff's Office, Visalia, 1998—; safety officer Disaster Mortuary Ops./Recovery Team, Washington, 2002—; founding mem. Dept. Homeland Security U.S. Govt.; presenter in field; founding mem. Soc. Medicolegal Death Investigators. Rschr. (book) Visalia's Fabulous Fox, 2000, unit prodn. mgr. (feature film) Legend of Jake Kincaid, 2001, interviewer (oral history project) Tulare County and WWII, 2004; editor: Commendation From Sher H. Bill Wittmen Tulare County Sheriffs Office. Crisis counselor Help in Emotional Trouble, Fresno, 1983—85; bd. dirs. Citizens Adv. Bd., Visalia, 1987. Mem.: Western Pacific Forensic Response Inst. (bd. mem. 2007—), Am. Bd. Forensic Nurses, Air and Surface Transport Nurses Assn., Am. Bd. Forensic Examiners (cert. med. investigator), Am. Assn. Legal Nurse Consultants, Calif. State Coroners Assn. (assoc.). Avocations: golf, snorkeling, guitar. Office: Gray Forensics and Consulting 2115 S Ashton Ct Visalia CA 93277 Office Phone: 559-734-3980, 559-901-6546. Personal E-mail: kgraybar@sbcglobal.net E-mail: kg@foxforensics.net.

GRAY, MARTIN PETER, pediatrician, consultant; b. Ormskirk, Lancashire, Sept. 12, 1967; MBChB, Glasgow U., 1993. Cons. pediat. intensivist St Georges Healthcare NHS Trust, 2006—. Mem.: RCP (London). Office: St Georges Hosp Blackshaw Rd Tooting London SW170QT England Office Fax: 442087250089. Business E-Mail: martingray2@nhs.net.

GRAY, MARY JANE, retired obstetrician, gynecologist; b. Columbus, Ohio, June 13, 1924; BA, Swarthmore Coll., 1945; MD, Wash. U., 1949; DMS, Columbia U., 1954. Diplomate Am. Bd. Ob-Gyn. Intern Barnes Hosp., St. Louis, 1949-50; resident in ob-gyn. Presbyn. Hosp., NYC, 1950-56; fellow Columbia U., 1953—54, instr., 1956-60; asst. prof. ob-gyn. Coll. Medicine U. Vermont, 1960-63, assoc. prof., 1963-69, prof., 1969-76; adj. prof. U. N.C., 1976-85, prof., asst. dean Coll. Medicine, 1985-90, prof. emeritus ob-gyn., 1990—; ret., 1996. Mem. AMA, Am. Coll. Ob-Gyn., Soc. Gynecol. Investigation.

GRAY, PAULETTE STYLES, federal agency administrator, biologist; b. Chattanooga, Feb. 21, 1944; d. Paul Styles and Louise (Hill) Dennis; m. Walter Leonard, May 10, 1964; children: Walter Leonard Jr., Daniel Allen. BS in biology, Tuskegee Inst., 1966; MS in mycology, Atlanta U., 1976, PhD in cellular and devel. biology, 1978. Asst. prof., dir. electron microscopy lab. Atlanta U., 1978-79; research assoc. U. Kaiserslautern, Germany, 1979-81; instr. U. Maryland, Kaiserslautern, 1980-82; supr. clin. microbiology sect. Landstuhl Army Regional Med. Ctr., Germany, 1981-82; exec. sec. Divsn. Extramural Activities, Nat. Cancer Inst., NIH, Bethesda, Md., 1983-84, spl. review officer, 1984, chief rev. logistics br., 1988, assoc. dir. extramural applications, dep. dir., 1997—2005, acting dir., 2003—05, dir., 2005—. Tchr. Sun. Sch. Alfred St. Bapt. Ch., Alexandria, Va., 1982-89, supt., 1988-89; judge sci. and engring. fair Fairfax County pub. schs., 1984-89; speaker Med. Coll. Ga., Augusta, 1985. Recipient Lederle Labs. award, 1977, H.E. Finley Meml. award Atlanta U., 1978, Outstanding Performance award Nat. Cancer Inst., 1983; Josiah Macy Jr. fellow, 1979, Hon. Fulbright Hays fellow, 1979-81, Spl. Act. of Achievement award, 1992, 93, EEO Spl. Recognition award, 1991, NIH Dir.'s award, 1990, Cert. Recognition and Spl. Achievement award, HHS, 1988-93. Mem. Am. Soc. Zoology, Nat. Inst. Sci., Atlanta U. Ctr. Honor Soc. (biology), Am. Assn. Cancer Rsch., Inc., Am. Assn. Cell Biology, Internat. Platform Assn., Women in Cancer Rsch., Assn. Women in Govt., Nat. Assn. Exec. Women. Avocations: cooking, reading, jogging, writing. Office: Nat Cancer Inst Divsn Extramural Activities 6116 Executive Blvd Rockville MD 20852 Office Phone: 301-496-5147. E-mail: pg36f@nih.gov. *

GRAY, ROBERT C., insurance company executive; Positions with Highmark Blue Cross Blue Shield, Pitts., 1987—, exec. v.p, Fin. & Subs. Svc., treas., CFO, 1998—2006, exec. v.p.; pres., CEO Highmark's Vision Holding Co., 2006—. Recipient CFO Excellence Award, CFO Magazine, 2001. Office: Highmark 120 5th Ave Ste 2015 Pittsburgh PA 15222-3001

GRAY, RONALD H., medical educator; b. Sydney, NSW, Australia, Aug. 28, 1941; s. Max and Eva Gray; m. Maria J. Wawer, May 5, 1992; children: Owen J., Aviva R. MB, BS, MSc, DTM&H, Sydney U. Med. resident Sydney Hosp., 1966—68, Papua New Guinea, Health Dept., Liagam, 1969—70; lectr. London Sch. Hygiene and Tropical Medicine, 1971—79; scientist WHO, Geneva, 1977—79; prof. pop., family and reproductive health, epidemiology, and internat. health Johns Hopkins Bloomberg Sch. Pub. Health, Balt., 1980—, William G. Robertson Jr. prof. pop. and family planning, 2002—. Contbr. scientific papers. Grantee, NIH, Gates Found., Doris Duke Charitable Found., WHO, CDC. Achievements include research in reproductive and perinatal health with a focus on HIV prevention. Office: Johns Hopkins U Rm E4132 615 N Wolfe St Baltimore MD 21205 Office Phone: 410-955-7818. Office Fax: 410-614-7386. E-mail: rgray@jhsph.edu.

GRAY, SHEILA HAFTER, psychiatrist, researcher; b. NYC, Oct. 19, 1930; MD, Harvard U., 1958. cert. Washington Psychoanalytic Inst., 1969. Intern St. Elizabeths Hosp., Washington, 1958-59; resident McLean Hosp., Belmont, Mass., 1959-61; clin. and rsch. fellow Mass. Gen. Hosp., Boston, 1961-62; staff psychiatrist Chestnut Lodge, Inc., Rockville, Md., 1962-64; practice medicine, specializing in psychiatry and psychoanalysis Washington, 1964—; clin. asst. prof. psychiatry U. Md. Sch. Medicine, Balt., 1968-75, clin. assoc. prof., 1975-83, clin. prof., 1983-96; instr. Washington Psychoanalytic Inst., 1971-75, tchg. analyst, 1975-96, Balt.-Washington Inst. for Psychoanalysis, 1996—; clin. prof. psychiatry Uniformed Svcs. U. Health Scis., 1997-99, adj. prof. psychiatry, 1999—. Staff U. Md. Hosp., Balt., 1970-96; physician mem. Commn. on Mental Health, Superior Ct. of D.C., 1972-98; bd. govs. Nat. Capital Reciprocal Ins. Co., 1981-98; treas. NCRIC Physicians Orgn., 1994-97; cons. Walter Reed Army Med. Ctr., Washington, 1983—. Active Mayor's Adv. Com. on Mental Health Svcs. Reorgn., Washington, 1984; adv. panel Mayor's Environ. Design Awards Program, 1988-89; exec. com. D.C. Fedn. Civic Assns., 1984—, asst. rec. sec., 1985, rec. sec., 1986-88, 2d v.p., 1989-90, pres., 1991-92, del.-at-large, 1993—; v.p. programs Women's Equity Action League Met. D.C., 1986; commr. D.C. Adv. Neighborhood Commn., 1986-88; mem. Met. Washington Coun. of Govt.'s Partnership for Regional Excellence, 1992; trustee Accreditation Coun. for Psychoanalytic Edn., Inc., 2002—, sec., 2004-08, pres., 2008-. Fellow: Am. Psychiat. Assn. (chair com. quality assurance and improvement, Coun. on Econ. Affairs, 1996—97, disting. life fellow); mem.: Washington Psychoanalytic Soc. (chmn. bd. dirs. psychoanalytic clinic and councillor ex officio 1987—90), Med. Soc. D.C. (exec. bd. 1982, ho. dels 1992—97), Washington Psychiatric Soc. (councillor 1981—83), Am. Acad. Psychoanalysis (trustee 1996—99, pres.-elect 1999—2000, pres. 2000—01, editl. bd. jour. 2002—), Am. Psychoanalytic Assn. (parliamentarian 2006—, diplomate Bd. Profl. Stds.), Palisades Citizens Assn. (bd. dirs. 1980—, treas. 1983—84, pres. 1984—86). Office: PO Box 40612 Palisades Sta Washington DC 20016 Office Phone: 202-338-1955.

GRAZI, RICHARD VICTOR, reproductive endocrinologist, educator; MD, SUNY, Buffalo, 1981. Diplomate Am. Bd. Ob-Gyn, cert. reproductive endocrinology. Resident NYU Med. Ctr., 1982—85; fellow Univ. of Medicine and Dentistry of NJ, 1985—87, Am. Coll. of Ob-Gyn.; assoc. clin. prof. ob-gyn. Mt. Sinai Sch. Med.; dir. reproductive endocrinology and infertility Maimonides Med. Ctr. Office: Maimonides Medical Center 1355 84th St Brooklyn NY 11228 Office Phone: 718-283-8600. Office Fax: 718-283-6580.

GRAZIANI, LEONARD JOSEPH, pediatric neurologist, researcher; b. Phila., Nov. 17, 1929; m. Amelia Honeyford, June 29, 1956; children: Paul, Amy, Virginia, David. BA, LaSalle Coll., Phila., 1951; MD, Jefferson Med. Coll., Phila., 1955. Diplomate Am. Bd. Pediat., Am. Bd. Psychiatry and Neurology. Intern Valley Forge (Pa.) Army Hosp., 1956; resident Brooke Army Hosp., San Antonio, 1959; chief pediatric svc. Ireland Army Hosp., Ft. Knox, Ky., 1960 61; neurology fellow Bronx Mcpl. Hosp. Ctr., 1961-64; interdisciplinary fellow Albert Einstein Coll. Medicine, Bronx, 1964-66, asst. prof. pediat. and neurology, 1964-68; career scientist Health Rsch. Coun., NYC, 1967-68; attending pediatrician, neurologist Thomas Jefferson U. Hosp., Phila., 1968—2004; chief div. pediatric neurology dept. pediat. Jefferson Med. Coll., Thomas Jefferson U., Phila., 1974-99, vice chair dept. pediat., 1988-96, prof. pediat., neurology, 1968—98, emeritus prof., 1998—. Cons. neurologist Woods Svcs., Langhorne, Pa., 1968—; staff E.I. duPont Inst., Wilmington, 1984-2004. Contbr. articles to profl. jours. Capt. U.S. Army, 1955-61. Fellow Am. Acad. Neurology, Am. Acad. Pediat.; mem. Am. Pediatric Soc., Soc. Pediatric Rsch., Child Neurology Soc., Alpha Omega Alpha, Sigma Xi.

GRAZIANO, KATHLEEN, pediatrician; b. Phoenix, Feb. 24, 1969; MD, Columbia Coll. Physicians and Surgeons, 1996. Physician Pediat. Surgeons Phoenix, 2006—. Fellow: ACS, Am. Acad. Pediat.; mem.: Coller Surg. Soc., Am. Pediat. Surgery Assn. Office: 1920 E Cambridge Ste 201 Phoenix AZ 85006 Office Fax: 602-254-2185. Business E-Mail: kathy.graziano@cox.net.

GRBAC-IVANKOVIC, SVJETLANA, nuclear medicine physician; b. Rijeka, Croatia, July 28, 1960; d. Ranko and Larisa Grbac; 1 child, Andrej Ivankovic. MD, Croatia, 1983; PhD in Nuc. Medicine, Sch. Medicine, U. Rijeka, 2006. Specialist in nuc. medicine 1990. Rsch. fellow UCONN Health Ctr., Farmington, 1992—94; head functional unit dept. nucelar medicine Clin. Hosp. Ctr. Rijeka, 2005—; assoc. prof. U. Rijeka, Sch. Medicine, 2007—, head, clin. dept. nuc. medicine, 2011—. Musician piano player. Office: Clinical Hosp Ctr Rijeka Kresimirova 42 51-000 Rijeka Croatia Office Fax: 385-51-658-365. Personal E-mail: svjetlana.grbac@medri.hr.

GRDISA, MIRA, biochemist, researcher; b. Jastrebarsko, Croatia, Dec. 21, 1948, d. Mirko and Katarina (Boricevic) Diksic; m. Stjepan Grdisa, May 10, 1975; children: Mario, Martina. BS in Organic Chemistry, Faculty Tech., Croatia, 1972; MS in Molecular Biology, U. Zagreb, Croatia, 1975; PhD in Chemistry, Rudjer Buskovic Inst., Croatia, 1988. Cert. engr. Asst. Ruder Bošković Inst., Zagreb, 1972-75, rsch. asst., 1975-88, higher rsch. asst., 1988-94, rsch. assoc., 1994-98, sr. rsch. assoc., 1998—2005, assoc. prof., 2003—10, sr. scientist, 2005—, prof., 2010—. Postdoctoral fellow McGill U., Montreal, Can., 1990-92, vis. scientist, 1995; vis. scientist Montreal Neurol. Inst., 1994; sabbatical Hosp. Hotel Dieu, Paris, 1999-2000. Inventor in field; contbr. articles to profl. jours. Mem. Croatian Biochemists Soc., Croatian Soc. Human Genetic, Soc. Subcell Pathologists. Roman Catholic. Avocations: music, embroidery, sewing. Office: Rudjer Boskovic Inst Bijenicka Cesta 54 10000 Zagreb Croatia Home Phone: 385 1 299 4676; Office Phone: 385 1 4560964. E-mail: grdisa@irb.hr.

GREASER, MARION LEWIS, science educator; b. Vinton, Iowa, Feb. 10, 1942; s. Lewis Levi and Elisabeth (Sage) G.; m. Marilyn Sue Pfister, June 12, 1965; children— Suzanne, Scott BS, Iowa State U., 1964; MS, U. Wis., 1967, PhD, 1969. Postdoctoral fellow Boston Biomed. Research Inst., 1968-71; asst. prof. sci. U. Wis., Madison, 1971-73, assoc. prof., 1973-77, prof., 1977—, Cambell-Bascom prof., 2004—. Contbr. articles to profl. jours. Recipient Outstanding Researcher award Am. Heart Assn.-Wis., 1985 Mem. AAAS, Am. Soc. Biochem. Molecular Biology, Biophys. Soc., Am. Meat Sci. Assn. (Disting. Rsch. award 1981), Am. Soc. Animal Sci. (Meat Rsch. award 2000). Home: 2374 Branch St Middleton WI 53562-2809 Office: U Wis Muscle Biology Lab 1805 Linden Dr W Madison WI 53706-1110 Business E-Mail: mgreaser@ansci.wisc.edu.

GREAVES, ROGER F., health and medical products executive; b. 1937; BA, Calif. State U., Long Beach, 1962. With Allstate Ins. Co., Chgo. and Pasadena, Calif., 1962-68; various positions, then v.p. human resources Blue Cross So. Calif., 1968-82; pres., CEO Health Net, Inc., Woodland Hills, Calif., 1982—91, chmn. bd., 1989—, co-pres., co-CEO, 1991—95. Mem. Calif. Wellness Found. (bd. dirs.). Office: Health Net Life Insurance Co 21281 Burbank Blvd Woodland Hills CA 91367-6607 *

GRECO, RICHARD JUDE, plastic and reconstructive surgeon; b. Hazleton, Pa., Jan. 8, 1960; s. Victor Frank and Mary Jean Greco; m. Robin Emma Robinson, Jan. 30, 1981; children: Richard, Blake, Apryl, Dean. BS in Biology summa cum laude, Ursinus Coll., Collegeville, Pa., 1979; MD magna cum laude, Thomas Jefferson Med. Coll., Phila., Pa., 1983. Diplomate Am. Bd. Plastic Surgery, Am. Bd. Gen. Surgery; cert. Hand Surgery. Resident in gen. surgery Thomas Jefferson U. Hosp., Phila., 1983-88; fellow, hand surgery Hand Ctr., Phila., 1986—87; fellow, plastic surgery U. Pitts., 1988—90; asst. prof. surgery U. Pitts. Sch. Medicine, 1990—93; fellow, aesthetic surgery Manhattan Eye and Ear Hosp., NYC, 1990; dir. Telfair Breast Ctr. Candler Hosp., Savannah, Ga., 1993-97; CEO, pvt. practice Ga. Inst. for Plastic Surgery, Savannah, 1998—. Adv. bd. Consumer Guide to Plastic Surgery; hosp. appointment Meml. U. Hosp., Candler/St. Joseph Healthcare Sys.; presenter in field. Editor: Emergency Plastic Surgery, 1993; contbr. articles to profl. jours.; author med. textbooks; featured in Allure, Wall St. Jour., London Times, Oprah mag., Cosmopolitan and others. Polit. adv. People for Pub. Edn., Savannah, 1997. Burroughs Welcome-AMA fellow, 1991. Fellow ACS; mem. AMA, Am. Soc. Plastic Surgery (past chmn. Pub. Edn. Com., mem. new device and tech. com., mem. online com.mem. adv. com. pub. edn. campaign), Am. Soc. Aesthetic Surgery (vice-chmn. pub. edn. com.), Lipoplasty Soc., Am. Soc. for Surgery Hand, Ga. Med. Soc., Jefferson Hand Club, Alpha Omega Alpha. Republican. Roman Catholic. Holds two patents relating to surg. practices. Office: Ga Inst Plastic Surgery 5361 Reynolds St Savannah GA 31405-6014 Office Phone: 800 260-7135. E-mail: plastxdoc@aol.com, greco@mycosmeticsurgeon.md.

GREDIG, DANIEL, social work professor; b. Erstfeld, Uri, Switzerland, June 22, 1964; s. Arnold Gredig and Martha [illegible] Wäckerlin. PhD, U. Zurich, Switzerland, 1999. Lic. U. Fribourg, Switzerland, 1991; diploma Kanton Fribourg, 1992. Social worker Johannesstift Spandau, Berlin, 1989—91; asst., dept. social work U. Fribourg, 1991—93; asst. Inst. Edn., U. Zurich, 1993—2000; head inst. integration and participation Sch. Social Work, U. Applied Scis. Northwestern Switzerland, Olten, 2000—10, head master studies, 2010—. Pres. Swiss Aids Fedn., Zurich, 1997—2007. Found. Dessaules, Biel-Bienne, Switzerland, 1997—, co-founder, mem. exec. bd. Verein Förderung des Sozialen Arbeit als Akademische Disziplin, Soc. Social Work, Bern, Switzerland; mem. adv. bd. Series Grundlagen Soziale Arbeit, Edit. Schneider Hohengehren, Baltmannsweiler, Germany. Mem.: Internat. AIDS Soc., German Soc. Ednl. Sci., Swiss Soc. Social Work. Office: UAS Northwestern Switzerland Riggenbachstrasse 16 Olten CH 4600 Switzerland Office Phone: 41 62 311 96 76. Business E-Mail: daniel.gredig@fhnw.ch.

GREEN, ANDREW, orthopaedic surgeon, educator; b. NYC, June 5, 1961; s. Alvin and Miriam Blau Green; m. Amy Louise Feldman, June 12, 1988; children: Elliot Loeb, Liza Rachel, Lucy Feldman. BA, Princeton U., NJ, 1983; MD, Columbia U. Coll. Physicians and Surgeons, NYC, 1987. Diplomate orthopaedic surgery Am. Bd. Orthopaedic Surgery, 1995. Asst. prof. orthopaedic surgery Warren Alpert Med. Sch., Brown U., Providence, 1993—2003, assoc. prof. orthopaedic surgery, 2003—, chief divsn. shoulder and elbow surgery. Bd. governors RISD Mus., Providence, 2007—08, fine arts com., 2005—08. Mem.: New Eng. Shoulder and Elbow Soc., Orthopaedic Trauma Assn., Academic Orthopaedic Assn., Am. Acad. Orthopaedic Surgeons, Am. Shoulder and Elbow Surgeons. Office: Univ Orthopedics Inc 2 Dudley St Ste 200 Providence RI 02905 Business E-Mail: agshoulder@aol.com.

GREEN, BARBARA STRAWN, psychotherapist; b. Cleve., May 31, 1938; d. Charles Everard and Dorothy Haring (Strawn) G. BA, Pa. State U., 1960; MS, Columbia U., 1962; postgrad. in psychotherapy and psychoanalysis, Postgrad. Ctr. for Mental Health, NYC, 1975. Ordained Dharma tchr., 2003; cert. social worker, NY; cert. Rutgers Summer Sch. Alcoholism Studies, 1982; ordained Buddhist priest, 2007. Social worker VA, NYC, 1962-66; sr. psychiat. social worker in child psychiat. Downstate Med. Ctr., Bklyn., 1966-71; staff therapist Inst. for Contemporary Psychotherapy, NYC, 1971-73; pvt. practice psychotherapy NYC, 1973—2006; social worker Lower East Side Svc. Ctr., NYC, 1975-77; intake coord. alcoholism program Postgrad. Ctr. for Mental Health, NYC, 1981-82; program coord. Bowery Residents Com., NYC, 1984—; interpreter Van Cortlandt Manor, Croton-on-Hudson, 2003—. Sec. alcoholism com. NYC chpt. NASW, 1987 89. Author: Jogging the Mind, 1995. Sec. Middle-Way Mediation Ctr., Danbury, Conn.; leader Buddhist meditation group Fed. Correctional Inst., Danbury, 2000—; participant NYC Marathon, 1991, 1992. Avocations: pottery, travel. Home: 1301 Nutmeg Dr Carmel NY 10512

GREEN, BARTH, neurosurgeon; b. Shoemaker, Calif., 1945; m. Kathy Green; children: Jeremy, Jared, Jenna. BA, Ind. U., 1966; MD, Ind. U. Sch. Medicine, 1969. Diplomate Am. Bd. Neurological Surgeons. Intern, general surgery Henry Ford Hosp., Detroit, 1969—70; resident, neurosurgery Northwestern U. Sch. Med., Chgo., 1970—75; joined U. Miami Med. Ctr., 1975; prof., chmn., dept. neurological surgery U. Miami Sch. Medicine, prof. orthopedics and rehabilitation; chief neurosurgery Jackson Meml. Hosp., VA Med. Ctr., Miami. Vis. prof. at several Am. and internat. universities and med. schools. Mem. editl. bd. Spine Universe. Pres., bd. dir. Ctr. for Haitians Studies and Health Services; co-founder, chmn. bd. Shake-a-Leg, Miami, 1995—; founder Miami Project to Cure Paralysis, 1985—, pres.; co-founder Project Medishare, Haiti. Lt. Col. US Army Med. Reserve. Recipient Spirit Excellence award, Miami Herald, Spl. medal, Soviet Acad. Sciences, Health Care Hero award, New Miami Mag., St. Marten De Porres Social Justice award, Southern Dominican Order of Preachers, Joseph R. Narot award for Cmty. Svc., Temple Israel, Karolinska Inst. Large Silver medal, Stockholm; named to Spinal Cord Injury Hall of Fame, Nat. Spinal Cord Injury Assn., 2006. Fellow: Am. Coll. Surgeons. Office: U Miami Dept Neurological Surgery 1095 NW 14th Terr Miami FL 33136 Office Phone: 305-243-3254.

GREEN, BERT FRANKLIN, JR., retired psychology professor; b. Honesdale, Pa., Nov. 5, 1927; s. Bert Franklin and Emily May (Brown) Green; m. Hasseltine Beck Robinson, Apr. 29, 1961 (div. 1974); children: Malcolm, Edward. AB, Yale, 1949; MA, Princeton, 1950, PhD, 1951. Mem. psychology group Lincoln Lab., MIT, 1951-62, leader, 1958-62; cons. RAND Corp., 1961; prof. psychology Carnegie Inst. Tech., Pitts., 1962-69, head psychology dept., 1962-67; prof. Johns Hopkins, Balt., 1969—93, prof. emeritus, 1993—. Author: Digital Computers in Research, 1963. Mem.: APA, Am. Edn. Rsch. Assn. (Lindquist award for Excellence Rsch. Measurement 2001), Psychometric Soc., Am. Statis. Assn. Home: 311 Eastway Ct Baltimore MD 21212-4710 Personal E-mail: bfgreen@verizon.net. Business E-Mail: bfgreen@jhu.edu.

GREEN, CHARLES BRUCE, career military officer, surgeon; b. Topeka, Kans., June 1, 1955; BS in Chemistry, U. Wis., Parkside, 1974; MD, Med. Coll. Wis., 1978; MPH, Harvard U., 1988. Captain USAF, 1978, advanced through grades to lt. gen., 2009; family practice resident Eglin Regional Hosp., Eglin AFB, Fla., 1978—81, resident family practice, 1981; flight surgeon US Air Force Hosp., Mather AFB, Calif., 1981—84; officer in charge Family Practice Clinic, Wheeler AFB, Hawaii, 1984—85; chief of clinic svcs. Hickam AFB, Hawaii, 1985—87; resident aerospace medicine USAF Sch. Aerospace Medicine, Brooks AFB, Tex., 1988—89; chief aerospace medicine, comdr. 657th Tactical Hosp., Clark AFB, Philippines, 1989—91; comdr. 65th Med. Group, Lajes Field, Portugal, 1991—93, 366th Med. Group, Mountain Home AFB, Idaho, 1993—95, 96th Medical Group, Eglin AFB, Fla., 1995—97; command surgeon North Am. Aerospace Defense Command (NORAD), US Space Command and Air Force Space Command, Peterson AFB, Colo., 1999—2001, US Transp. Command (USTRANSCOM) and Hdqs. Air Mobility Command, Scott AFB, Ill., 2001—03; comdr. 59th Med. Wing, Wilford Hall Med. Ctr., Lackland AFB, Tex., 2003—05; asst. surgeon gen. for health care ops. USAF, Bolling AFB, DC, 2005—06, dep. surgeon gen., 2006—09, surgeon gen., 2009—. Decorated Defense Superior Svc. Medal with oak leaf cluster, Legion of Merit, Defense Meritorious Svc. Medal, Airman's Medal, Meritorious Svc. Medal with four oak leaf clusters, Joint Svc. Commendation Medal, Air Force Commendation Medal with two oak leaf clusters, Air Force Achievement Medal, Nat. Def. Svc. Medal with bronze star, Armed Forces Expeditionary Medal, Humanitarian Svc. Medal with bronze star, Philippine Bronze Cross. Fellow: Am. Acad. Family Physicians, Aerospace Med. Assn.; mem.: AMA, Assn. Mil. Surgeons of US, Air Force Assn., Soc. USAF Flight Surgeons (former pres.), Aerospace Med. Assn., Uniformed Svcs. Acad. Family Physicians, Am. Coll. Physician Execs. Office: USAF Office of Surgeon Gen Bolling AFB DC 20032 *

GREEN, DANA I., retail executive, lawyer; b. 1949; BA, Ind. U., 1971, JD, 1974; LLM in Taxation, DePaul U., 1990. Bar: Ill. 1974. Atty. through dept. dir., employee rels. Walgreen Co., 1974—98, div. v.p., employee rels., 1998—2000, corp. v.p., human resources, 2000—04, sr. v.p., 2004—05, sr. v.p., gen. counsel, corp. sec., 2005—10, exec. v.p., gen. counsel, 2010—. Office: Walgreen Co 200 Wilmot Rd Deerfield IL 60015 Office Phone: 847-914-2500. Office Fax: 847-914-2804. E-mail: dana.green@walgreens.com. *

GREEN, DANIEL MICHAEL, pediatric oncologist; b. Seattle, May 30, 1946; s. Daniel Marie and Margaret Ann (Johnson) Green; m. Lydia Ann Betz, Jan. 7, 1984; children: Amy Lynn, Sarah Ann, Daniel Joseph. BS, MIT, 1969; MD cum laude, St. Louis U., 1973. Diplomate Am. Bd. Pediatrics, in pediatric hematology-oncology Am. Bd. Pediatrics. Intern in pediat. Boston City Hosp., 1973-74, resident in pediat. hematology-oncology, 1974-75; fellow in pediatric oncology Sidney Farber Cancer Inst., Boston, 1975-78; fellow in hematology/oncology Children's Hosp. Med. Ctr., Boston, 1975-78; rsch. fellow in pediat. Med. Sch. Harvard U., Boston, 1975-78; cancer rsch. pediatrician II Roswell Park Meml. Inst., Buffalo, 1978-90; attending physician Roswell Pk. Cancer Inst., Buffalo, 1990—2008; spl. cons. in hematology-oncology Children's Hosp. Buffalo, 1978-85, from asst. attending to assoc. attending physician, 1985-89, attending physician, 1989—2008; rsch. asst. prof. Sch. of Medicine and Biomed. Scis. SUNY, Buffalo, 1978-82, from asst. prof. to assoc. prof., 1982-90, prof., 1990—2008. Author: Diagnosis and Management of Malignant Solid Tissues in Infants and Children, 1985, Long Term Complications of Treatment for Cancer During Childhood and Adolescence, 1989; mem. editl. bd. Pediatric Blood and Cancer, ad hoc reviewer Am. Jour. Pediatric Hematology/Oncology, Jour. Clin. Oncology, Cancer, Pediat., Med. and Pediatric Oncology; contbr. articles to profl. jours. Recipient, Buffalo Bills Found., 1988—90, Nat. Cancer Inst., 1991—; grantee, ACS Instnl., 1980—81, Dorothea Haus Ross, 1984—85, AROCC, 1985—90. Mem.: St. Jude Children's Rsch. Hosp. (mem. dept. epidemiology & cancer control 2008—), Soc. Pediat. Rsch., N.Y. Acad. Scis., Am. Soc. Hematology, Am. Pediat. Soc., Am. Soc. Pediat. Hematology-Oncology, Am. Acad. Pediat. (exec. com. 1992—94, oncology-hematology sect.), Internat. Soc. Pediat. Oncology (sci. com. 1989—95, sec. gen. 1999—2005), Am. Fedn. Clin. Rsch., Am. Assn. Cancer Rsch., Am. Soc. Clin. Oncology. Office: Dept Epidemiology and Cancer Control St Jude Children's Rsch Hosp 262 Danny Thomas Pl Mail Stop 735 Memphis TN 38105-2794 Office Phone: 901-595-5915. Office Fax: 901-595-5845. Business E-Mail: daniel.green@stjude.org.

GREEN, DANIEL WILLIAM, pediatrician; b. Calif., Sept. 26, 1963; BS, Trinity Coll., 1985; MD, U. Tex. Med. Br., 1998. Attending pediat. orthop. surgeon Hosp. Spl. Surgery, 1998—. Office: 535 E 70th St New York NY 10021 Office Fax: 212-774-2776. Personal E-mail: taylor682002@yahoo.com.

GREEN, DAVID, hematologist; b. Phila., 1934; AB, U. Pa., 1956; MD, Jefferson Med. Coll., 1960; PhD, Northwestern U., 1974. Cert. Am. Bd. Internal Medicine, 1967, in Hematology 1972. Intern Cook County Hosp., Chgo., 1960—61; resident, internal medicine Jefferson Hosp., Phila., 1961—63, fellow, hematology, 1963—64; prof. Northwestern U., 1975—. Office Phone: 312-695-4442.

GREEN, ERIC DOUGLAS, federal agency administrator, cell biologist, genetics and pathology researcher; b. St. Louis, 1959; married; 2 children. BS, U. Wis., Madison, 1981; MD, Washington U., St. Louis, 1987, PhD in Cell Biology, 1987. Resident lab. medicine Washington U. Sch. Medicine, St. Louis, 1987—92, fellow dept. genetics, 1988—92, asst. prof. pathology, genetics and internal medicine, co-investigator Human Genome Ctr., 1992—94, adj. instr. dept. genetics, 1994—99; head phys. mapping sect. Nat. Human Genome Rsch. Inst. (NHGRI), NIH, 1994—2010, dir. DNA sequencing core, 1995—97, NIH sr. investigator, 1996—2010, chief Genome Tech. Br., 1996—2009, founding dir. Intramural Sequencing Ctr., 1997—2009, sci. dir. NHGRI, 2002—09, acting sci. dir. NHGRI, 2009—10, dir. NHGRI, 2009—. Contbr. articles to profl. jours. Mem.: Am. Assn. Physicians, Am. Soc. Clin. Investigation. Office: National Human Genome Research Institute Rm 2408 49 Convent Dr Msc 4431 Bldg 49 Bethesda MD 20892-0001 Office Phone: 301-496-0844. Office Fax: 301-402-0837. E-mail: eric.green@nih.gov. *

GREEN, GEORGE EDWARD, retired surgeon; b. NYC, Jan. 18, 1932; s. Robert and Hannah Augusta (Berkowitz) G.; m. Sheila Ellen Greenwald, Feb. 18, 1960; children: Samuel, Benjamin. Student, Yale Coll., 1952, MD, 1956. Diplomate Am. Bd. Thoracic Cardiovascular Surgery, Am. Bd. Surgery. Asst. attending surgeon NYU Hosp., NYC, 1968—70; attending surgeon St. Lukes Roosevelt Hosp., 1970—94, Columbia Presbyn. Hosp., NYC, 1992—94; attending surgeon, chief cardiothoracic surgery L.I. Jewish Hosp., NYC, 1982—83; prof. clin. surgery Columbia U., NYC, 1992—94; ret., 1994. Author: Originator of Internal Thoracic Artery-LAD Anastomosis; author, editor: Surgical Revascularization of the Heart, 1991; contbr. articles to profl. jours. Lt. comdr. USN, 1962-63. Rsch. grantee Nat. Heart and Lung Inst. NIH, 1966-68. Mem. Am. Assn. Thoracic Surgery, Soc. Thoracic Surgeons, Soc. Vascular Surgery, Internat. Cardiovascular Soc. Democrat. Jewish. Home: 175 Riverside Dr New York NY 10024 Personal E-mail: georgegreen@hotmail.com.

GREEN, HAROLD DANIEL, dentist; b. Scranton, Pa., Feb. 4, 1934; s. Harold Charles and Viola Mildred (Brown) G.; m. Cornelia Ann Ellis, Aug. 1, 1959; children: Scott Alan, Mary Ann. BA, Beloit Coll., Wis., 1956; DDS, Northwestern U., 1960. Gen. practice dentistry, Beloit, Wis., 1964—. Dir. Beloit Savs. Bank, chmn. trust com., 1989—; mem loan com. Blackhawk State Bank, mem. fin. com., 1993. Contbr. articles to profl. jours. Active Wis. div. Am. Cancer Soc., 1964-75; 1st pres., co-organizer Citizen's Council Against Crime, Beloit; past officer, chmn. membership Beloit YMCA; pres. Beloit Brewers, chmn. bd., 1982-2002, class A midwest league affiliate of Milw. Brewers baseball team, 1986-87; chmn. Student Achievers Program, Wis., No. Ill.; mem. adv. bd. Salvation Army; chmn. Beloiters for Coun.-Mgr., 1989; stateline chmn. Student Achiever Program, 1988, 93; bd. dirs. Greater Beloit Found., 1989—; chmating com. Greater Beloit Community Trust, Inc., 1991,93; chmn. adminstrv. bd., chmn. Council of Ministries, First United Methodist Ch., Beloit, pastor parish rels., 1995—; chmn. ann. dinner, bd. dirs., nominating com., fundraising, pub. speakers Beloit Crime Stoppers, 1993—, chmn., 1995-96; chmn. facilities study com. Sch. Dist. Beloit, 1991—; chmn. Eagle Scout bd. rev. Sinnisippi coun. Boy Scouts Am., 1995-96; vice chair spkrs. bur. Beloit Sports Hall of Fame, 1998-99, chmn., 1999. Recipient award for creativity in dentistry Johnson & Johnson Co., 1970; 3 citations for Cmty. Svc. United Givers Fund, 1970-75; Disting. Svc. citation Greater Beloit Assn. Commerce; named to Rock County Hall of Honor, 2000 Fellow Acad. Gen. Dentistry, Internat. Coll. Dentists. (Wis. editor), Am. Acad. Dental Practice Adminstrn. (past chmn. profl. liaison; mem. ADA (chmn. council on dental practice 1982-84), Wis. Dental Assn. (pres. 1979-80, trustee 1968-74), Wis. Dental Assn. Found., Rock County Dental Soc. (pres. 1976), Wis. Council of Professions (bd. dirs. 1974-80, pres. 1973-75), Chgo. Dental Soc., Greater Milw. Dental Assn., Fedn. Dentaire Internationale, Pierre Fauchard Acad., Am. Acad. History of Dentistry, Lions (beloit programs, 1993—, past pres.), Delta Sigma Delta. Avocations: bicycling, golf, basketball, running, fishing. Home: 2207 Collingswood Dr Beloit WI 53511-2332 Office: 419 Pleasant St Beloit WI 53511-6249 *

GREEN, HOWARD A., dermatologist; Grad., George Wash. U.; MD, Boston U., 1985. Diplomate Am. Bd. Internal Medicine, 1988, Am. Bd. Dermatology, 2004. Resident internal medicine Thomas Jefferson Univ. Hosp., Phila., 1986—88; fellow mohs surgery Boston Univ. Med. Ctr., Boston, 1992—93; resident dermatology Harvard Med. Sch. Boston Mass. Gen. Hosp., Boston, Beth Israel Hosp., Children's Hosp., Lahey Clinic, New Eng. Deaconess Hosp., Brigham and Women's Hosp., Harvard Cmty. Health Plan., 1988—92; staff Dermatology Assocs., P.A. of the Palm Beaches; hosp. affiliation include St. Mary's Med. Ctr. Author publs. dozens of sci. papers on mutagenesis, skin cancer, lasers and wound healing, and has several med. patents. Named one of America's Top Doctors, Castle Connolly Med., LTD. Office: Dermatology Associates PA of the Palm Beaches 120 A Butler St West Palm Beach FL 33407 Office Phone: 561-659-1510.

GREEN, JEFFREY, cardiologist; Attended, NY Med. Coll., 1998. Diplomate Am. Bd. Internal Medicine, Am. Bd. Cardiology-cardiovascular disease. Resident in internal medicine Montefiore Med. Ctr., Bronx, NY, 1999—2001, fellow in cardiovascular disease, 2002—04; cardiologist Stamford Hosp. Office: Stamford Hospital The Heart Physicians P C 80 Mill River St Stamford CT 06902 Office Phone: 203-348-7410. Office Fax: 203-961-8488.

GREEN, LARRY ALTON, physician, educator; b. Ardmore, Okla., Mar. 27, 1948; s. Thomas Alton and Mary Lou (Gauntt) Green; m. Margaret Joyce Ball, Mar. 27, 1971; children: Nathaniel, Katherine. BA, U. Okla., 1969; MD, Baylor Coll. Medicine, Houston, 1973. Diplomate Am. Bd. Family Practice. Intern then resident U. Rochester, Highland Hosp., NY, 1973—76; asst. prof. U. Colo., Denver, 1972—82, assoc. prof., 1982—85, prof., 1985—, chmn. dept., 1985—99, Woodward-Chisholm chair, 1989—99, dir. AAFP Ctr. for Policy Studies in Family Practice and Primary Care, 1998—. Vis. prof. various univrs., U.S., New Zealand, U.K., Republic of South Africa, 1982—; dir. residency Mercy Med. Ctr., Denver, 1980—85; founding pres. Ambulatory Sentinel Practice Network, Denver. Contbr. articles to profl. jours. Elder Presbyn. Ch., Denver. With USPHS, 1976—77. Grantee, USPHS, 1978—, Kellogg Found., 1982—87. Mem.: American Bd. Family Medicine (bd. dirs. 2005—10, chair elect 2008—09, chair 2009—10), IOM, Tchrs. Family Medicine, Am. Acad. Family Physicians, N.Am. Primary Care Rsch. Group (bd. dirs. 1989—93, pres. 1997—), Assn. Depts. Family Medicine (pres. 1987—89). Avocation: fly fishing. Office: PO Box 6508 Aurora CO 80045-0508

GREEN, LAWRENCE WINTER, public health educator; b. Bell, Calif., Sept. 16, 1940; s. Clifton Lawrence and Ora Elizabeth (Winter) G.; children: Beth Allison Green Levin, Jennifer Laurie Garcia-Green; m. Judith Marilyn Ottoson, May 1, 1982. BS, U. Calif., Berkeley, 1962, MPH, 1966, DrPH, 1968; DSc (hon.), U. Waterloo, Can., 2005. Project assoc. Ford Found., Dacca, Bangladesh, 1963-65; lectr. U. Calif. Sch. Pub. Health, 1968-70; asst. prof., assoc. prof., prof. Johns Hopkins U. Sch. Pub. Health, Balt., 1970-81, asst. dean, head div. health edn., 1972-79; dir. U.S. Office Health Info. and Health Promotion, Washington, 1979-81; vis. lectr. Harvard U. Ctr. for Health Policy, Boston, 1981-82; prof., dir. Ctr. for Health Promotion Rsch. U. Tex., Houston, 1982-88; v.p. Henry J. Kaiser Family Found., Menlo Park, Calif., 1988-91; prof., dir. Inst. Health Promotion Rsch. U. B.C., Vancouver, Canada, 1991—99. Vis. prof. U. Limburg Sch. Health Sci., Maastricht, The Netherlands, 1987-91; cons. WHO, Geneva, 1974, 82-83, NIH, Bethesda, Md., 1975-88, UN Fund for Population Activities, Beijing, 1984, UNICEF, Beijing, 1991; vis. rsch. social scientist Inst. for Health Policy Studies, U. Calif. Sch. Medicine, San Francisco 1991. Author: Dacca Family Planning Experiment (Beryl Roberts award 1973), Health Education Planning, 1980, Measurement and Evaluation, 1986, Community and Population Health, 1973, 8th edit., 1999, Health Promotion Planning, 1991, Drug Abuse Prevention, 1993, Participatory Research, 1994, Health Program Planning, 2005, elected mem. Inst. Medicine, Nat. Acad. Sci. 2009. Recipient Disting. Svc. citation U.S. Asst. Sec. Health, 1981, commendation Nat. Ctr. for Health Edn., 1986, Jacques Perisot medal Internat. Union Health Edn.; scholar Assn. for Advancement Health Edn., 1986, AAHPERD, 1988-89, Alumnus of Yr. award U. Calif., Berkeley, 1994. Fellow APHA (governing coun. 1974-76, Disting. Career award 1978, Excellence award 1994), Acad. Behavioral Medicine Rsch., Soc. for Pub. Health Edn. (disting., pres. 1984-85), Am. Sch. Health Assn. (hon.), Soc. for Behavioral Medicine (bd. dirs. 1985-88), Am. Acad. Phys. Edn. (assoc.), Pacific Inst. Rsch. Evaluation (bd. dirs. 2008-), Eta Sigma Gamma, Delta Omega. Avocations: sports, chess, ukelele. Office: Univ of Calif at San Francisco 185 Berry St Ste 6600 Box 0981 San Francisco CA 94143 Home: 66 Santa Paula Ave San Francisco CA 94127 Personal E-mail: lwgreen@comcast.net. Business E-Mail: lgreen@cc.ucsf.edu.

GREEN, LINDA GAIL, retired international healthcare and management consultant, nursing educator; b. Kalamazoo, Nov. 29, 1951; d. Jesse Floyd and Mattie Dean (Fulcher) G. BS in Nursing, Fla. State U., Tallahassee, 1974; postgrad., Nova U., Ft. Lauderdale, Fla. Staff nurse med./surg. unit St. Mary's Hosp., West Palm Beach, Fla., 1974, staff nurse coronary care, 1974-75, relief charge nurse ICU, 1975-76, asst. nursing care coord. post anesthesia recovery rm., 1976-78, insvc. instr., 1978-81, asst. dir. staff devel. and edn., 1981-83; dir. insvc. H.H. Raulerson Hosp., Okeechobee, Fla., 1983-84; adminstr. Med. Personnel Pool, Palm Beach, Fla., 1984-90; regional exec. healthcare divsn. Interim Svcs., Inc. (formerly Pers. Pool of Am., an H&R Block Co.), Ft. Lauderdale, 1990-93; pres. L.G.I. Consulting/Cmty. Health Educator, West Palm Beach, 1993—2000. Dir. ednl. svcs., nurse educator, dir. ednl. svc. Intracoastal Health Svcs., Inc., Good Samaritan Med. Ctr., St. Mary's Med. Ctr., West Palm Beach, Fla., 1998—2000; bd. dirs. at large Earthworkers Unltd., Inc., 2005—; spkr. in field. Author: Sexual Harassment in Home Healthcare, 1993. Past bd. dirs. Vinceremos Therapeutic Riding Ctr., Inc. for Physically and Mentally Challenged, 1990-95; chair Helen K. Persson Endowment Scholarship, 1999-2000; mem. Palm Beach County Workshop Devel. Bus. Partnership Coun., 1999. Mem. ANA, AHA (heart walk industry leader 1994, 95), Palm Beach County Health Educators (past sec.), Palm Beach County Patient Educators (pres. 1989, Leadership and Spirit awards 1989), Royal Palm Beach Bus. Assn., Palms West C. of C. (v.p. 1987-88, Dedicated and Outstanding Svc. award 1989, Cert. of Appreciation 1986, 87), Zonta Internat. (pres. 1994-95, past v.p. Palms West chpt., del. to internat. conf., Hong Kong, 1992).

GREEN, LOUIS HARRY, retired surgeon; b. Houston, Jan. 21, 1923; MD, U. Tex. Med. Br., 1947. Diplomate Am. Bd. Surgery. Intern D.C. Gen. Hosp., Washington, 1947—48; resident surgery Meml. Hosp., Houston, 1948—49, Houston VA Hosp., 1951—54, Baylor Affiliated Hosps., Houston; emeritus clin. assoc. prof. Baylor Coll. Medicine, Houston; emeritus staff Meth., St. Luke's Episcopal, Tex. Children's, Hermann Hosps. Commencement keynote spkr., natural scis. and math. U. Houston, 2005, 05, commencement spkr., selector MSM, 07, scholar, 07. Named Disting. Alumnus U. Houston, 1989, Great Texan Chron's and Colitis Found. Am., 1975. Fellow: ACS; mem.: AMA, Houston Surg. Soc. (pres. 1991—92). Personal E-mail: barbara.louis@gmail.com.

GREEN, MAURICE, molecular biologist, educator, virologist; b. NYC, May 5, 1926; s. David and Bessie (Lipschitz) G.; m. Marilyn Glick, Aug. 20, 1950; children: Michael Richard, Wendy Allison Green Lee, Eric Douglas. BS in Chemistry, U. Mich., 1949; MS in Biochemistry and Chemistry, U. Wis.-Madison, 1952, PhD in Biochemistry and Chemistry, 1954. Instr. biochemistry U. Pa. Med. Sch., Phila., 1955-56; asst. prof. St. Louis U. Health Scis. Ctr., 1956-60, assoc. prof., 1960-63, prof. microbiology, 1963-77; prof., chmn. Inst. for Molecular Virology, 1964—. Office: E A Doisy Rsch Ctr Inst Molecular Virology 1100 S Grand 6th Fl Rm 633 Saint Louis MO 63104-1015 Business E-Mail: green@slu.edu.

GREEN, MAURICE RICHARD, neuropsychiatrist; b. Chgo., Oct. 28, 1922; divorced; children: Melissa, Suzanne, Constance. BS, Northwestern U., 1942; BM, Northwestern U. Med. Sch., 1945, MD, 1946; cert. in Psychoanalytic Tng., William Alanson White Inst., NYC, 1954. Diplomate Am. Bd. Psychiatry and Neurology. Intern Passavant Hosp., Chgo., 1945-46; resident in psychiatry Bronx (N.Y.) VA Hosp., 1948-51; cons. psychiatrist Brookwood Hall, East Islip, L.I., N.Y., 1955-58; staff psychiatrist Psychiatric Clinic Ct. Spl. Sessions, 1956-60; cons. psychiatrist Bleuler Psychotherapy Ctr., Queens, N.Y., 1956-68; rsch. psychiatrist, mem. psychiat. epidemiology sect. William Alanson White Inst., NYC, 1968-72; attending geriat. psychiatrist Albert Einstein Med. Sch., 1974-76; attending child and adolescent psychiatry Harlem Hosp. of Columbia Presbyn. Med. Ctr., NYC, 1974-75; med. dir. geriat. and family psychiatry Lincoln Hosp., 1974-76; chief psychiatrist Family Ct. Svcs. divsn. South Beach Psychiat. Ctr., SI, N.Y., 1976-80; sr. attending psychiatrist Columbia-Presbyn. at St. Luke's-Roosevelt Hosp., NYC, 1978—; cons. psychiatrist Liaison-Consultation Svc. NYU Med. Ctr., NYC, 1985-86; psychiatrist spl. evaluation and treatment unit Rockland Psychiat. Ctr., 1985-87. Mem. faculty William Alanson White Inst., N.Y.C., 1957—09; cons. Goddard Coll., 1961-68; assoc. attending psychiatrist Bellevue Hosp., 1962-85; clin. prof. psychiatry NYU Med. Sch., 1964—2003; mem. med. bd. Roosevelt Hosp., 1965-76; prin. investigator Diamox-Thiamine Research Unit Nathan S. Kline Research Inst., 1987; project dir. Brain Chemistry of Schizophrenia at Nathan Kline Inst., 1988-93; med. dir. Neurologic Sys., Inc., 1987; presidium Inst. for Brain Function Rsch., Inc., 1987; mem. Treatment Innovations Task Force-Soc. for Traumatic Stress Studies, 1987. Author: Interpersonal Psychoanalysis: Selected Papers of Clara Thompson, 1971, Psicoanalisi interpersonale, 1972, L'Esperiencze Prelogica, 1972, Violence and the Family, 1980; (with Edward S. Tauber) Prelogical Experience, 1959; assoc. editor Contemporary Psychoanalysis jour., 1968-80; contbr. articles to profl. jours. Project dir. Nathan Kline Rsch. Inst., 1988—. Fellow: N.Y. Acad. Medicine, Am. Acad. Child and Adolescent Psychiatry (com. on hospitalization of children, nat. legis. network 1982—86), Am. Psychiat. Assn. (com. on aging N.Y. Dist. br.), Am. Orthopsychiat. Assn. (publs. com. Anniversary Vol. 1968—71); mem.: Am. Acad. Psychoanalysis, Am. Assn. Geriat. Psychiatry, Internat. Soc. Psychoneuroendocrinology, Am. Assn. Psychosocial Rehab., Soc. Biol. Psychiatry, Nat. Assn. Patients Rights and Advocacy, Physicians for Social Responsibility, N.Y. Soc. Clin. Psychiatry, N.Y. Coun. Child Psychiatry. Home and Office: 275 Central Park W Apt 15 D New York NY 10024-3058 Office Phone: 212-595-9774. Personal E-mail: mauriegreen@msn.com.

GREEN, MICHAEL D., pediatric infectious disease physician; MD, U. Ill., 1983; MPH, U. Pitts., 1989. Diplomate Am. Bd. Pediatrics, Am. Bd. Pediatrics-pediatric infectious diseases. Resident Children's Hosp. of Pitts. of UPMC, 1986, fellow, 1989; hosp. affiliation include/s Magee-Womens Hosp. of UPMC, Children's Hosp. of Pitts. of UPMC. Recipient Clinical Infectious Diseases award. Fellow: Infectious Disease Soc. of America; mem.: Am. Soc. of Microbiology, Pediatric Infectious Disease Soc., Soc. for Pediatric Rsch., Am. Soc. of Transplantation, Internat. Pediatric Transplantation Assn., Am. Pediatric Soc. Office: Childrens Hospital of Pittsburgh of UPMC 1 Childrens Hospital Drive 4401 Penn Ave Pittsburgh PA 15224 Office Phone: 412-692-7438. Office Fax: 412-692-5071. E-mail: greemd@chp.edu.

GREEN, MORRIS, retired pediatrician, educator; b. Indpls., May 27, 1922; s. Coleman and Rebecca (Oletnick) Green; m. Janice Barber Gorton, Mar. 11, 1955; children: David Schuster, Alan Coleman, Carolyn Ann, Susan Elaine, Marcia Ruth, Sylvia Rebecca. AB, Ind. U., 1942, MD, 1944. Intern Ind. U. Med. Ctr., 1945; resident pediat. U. Ill. Rsch. and Ednl. Hosps., 1947—49; instr. pediat. U. Ill. Coll. Medicine, 1949—52; asst. prof. Yale Sch. Medicine, 1952—57; faculty Ind. U. Sch. Medicine, Indpls., 1957—2006, Perry W. Lesh prof. pediat., 1963—2006; chmn. dept. pediat., physician-in-chief James Whitcomb Riley Hosp. for Children, Indpls., 1967—88. Commr. health State of Ind., 1990—91. Author: Pediatric Diagnosis, 6th edit., 1998, co editor: Ambulatory Pediatrics, 1968, 5th edit., 1999, Bright Futures, 2d edit., 2000; mem. editl. bd.: Pediat. Rev., Contemporary Pediat., Current Problems Pediat., Jour. Devel. Behavioral Pediat., Jour. Ambulatory Pediat. Assn., Social Work in Health Care, nat. adviser: Children Today. Served to capt. M.C. US Army, 1945—47. Recipient George Armstrong award in ambulatory pediat., 1971, C. Anderson Aldrich award in child devel., 1982, Irving S. Cutter award, Phi Rho Sigma, 1984, Ross award for pediat. edn., 1985, Simon Wile award, Am. Acad. Child and Adolescent Psychiatry, 1990, Joseph W. St. Geme award, Fedn. Pediat. Orgns., 1992, Disting. Career award, Ambulatory Pediat. Assn., 1996, Lifetime award for disting. svc. in years of health advancement, Ind. Pub. Health Found., 2003. Mem.: AMA (Abraham Jacobi award 1990), Soc. Rsch. Child Devel., Inst. Medicine, Am. Orthopsychiat. Assn., Am. Acad. Pediat. (Abraham Jacobi award 1990), Am. Fedn. Clin. Rsch., Soc. Pediatric Rsch., Am. Pediatric Soc., Alpha Omega Alpha, Sigma Xi, Phi Beta Kappa. Home Phone: 301-869-2978. Personal E-mail: maunderw@iupui.edu.

GREEN, PHILIP P., mathematician, educator, computer scientist; BA in Math., Harvard U.; PhD in Math., U. Calif., Berkeley. With Princeton U.; asst. prof. math. Columbia U.; vis. mem. Inst. Advanced Study; postdoctoral work, pathology dept. U. NC, Chapel Hill; with Collaborative Rsch. Inc., Waltham, Mass.; with genetics dept. Washington U., St. Louis; with U. Washington, Seattle, 1994—, prof. genome sciences, adj. prof. computer science and engring.; investigator Howard Hughes Med. Inst., 2000—. Contbr. articles to profl. jours. Recipient Gairdner Found. Internat. award, 2002. Mem.: NAS. Office: U Washington Dept Genome Sciences Box 357730 1705 NE Pacific St K-343B Health Science Seattle WA 98195-7730 Office Phone: 206-685-4341. Office Fax: 206-685-9720. Business E-Mail: phg@u.washington.edu. *

GREEN, ROBERT CASTLEMAN, neurologist; b. Richmond, Va., Oct. 21, 1954; s. Robert C. and Meredith (Wilkinson) G.; m. Sally E. McNagny, July 6, 1985; children: Nathanial, Courtney, Lachlan. BA in Biology and English, Amherst Coll., Mass., 1976; MD, U. Va. Med. Sch., 1980; MPH, Emory U., Atlanta, 2000. Diplomate Am. Bd. Psychiatry & Neurology. Intern in medicine RI Hosp., Providence, 1980—81; pub. health training Johns Hopkins Sch. Pub. Health, Balt., 1981—82; resident/chief resident neurology Harvard Med. Sch./Beth Israel Hosp., Boston, 1982—85, fellow divsn. neurosci. and behavioral neurology, 1985—86; fellow pediatric and adult epilepsy Children's Hosp., Boston, 1986—87; asst. prof. neurology Emory U. Sch. Medicine, 1988—94, assoc. prof. neurology, asst. prof. psychiatry and behavioral scis., Ctr. Genetics, 1994—96; vis. prof. Ga. State U. Coll. Health & Human Scis., 1996—99; assoc. prof. neurology Boston U. Sch. Medicine, 1999—2003, prof. neurology and medicine, 2003—, prof. epidemiology, Sch. Pub. Health, 2003—, dir. Alzheimer's disease clin. rsch. program, 2004—. Dir. neurobehavioral program Emory U. Sch. Medicine, 1988-96. Author: (book) Diagnosis and Management of Alzheimer's Disease and Other Dementias, 2001; mem. editl. bd. Jour. Neuroscis., 1995—, Medscape Neurology, 2001—; contbr. articles to profl. jours. Grantee Nat. Inst. Aging, 1991—. Mem. Am. Acad. Neurology, Am. Neuropsych. Assn., Behavioral Neurology Soc. Avocations: running, scuba, choral singing. Office: Boston U Med Sch Genetics Program/Alzheimer's Disease Ctr 715 Albany St L 320 Boston MA 02118 Office Phone: 617-638-5362. *

GREEN, TRACEY D., public health service officer; BA in Psychology and Biology, U. Nev., MD. Diplomate American Bd. Family Practice. Resident family practice Altoona Hosp. - Hershey Med. Ctr., Pa.; assoc. prof. sch. medicine U. Nev.; med. dir. frontier and rural health program Nev. Dept. Health & Human Services, Carson City, med. dir. women;s health connection, med. supr. of nursing sexually transmitted disease program, state health officer, 2009—. Office: Nevada Department Health & Human Services 4150 Technology Way Carson City NV 89706-2009 Office Phone: 775-684-4200. Office Fax: 775-684-4211. *

GREEN, WILLIAM R., medical educator, researcher, former dean; BS, U. Mich., 1983; PhD, Case Western Reserve U. Rschr. Johns Hopkins U., Fred Hutchinson Cancer Rsch. Ctr., U. Wash., Seattle; scientist Dartmouth Med. Sch., 1983—, chair dept. microbiology and immunology, 2002—08, 2010—, dean, 2008—10, dir. Dartmouth Cmty. Med. Sch., 2010—. Prin. investigator NIH Ctrs. of Biomedical Rsch. Excellence. Mem.: Assn. Med. Sch. Microbiology and Immunology Chairs, Am. Assn. Immunologists. Office: Dartmouth Med Sch Borwell Rsch Bldg HB 7556 1 Medical Dr Lebanon NH 03756 E-mail: william.r.green@dartmouth.edu. *

GREENBAUM, LARRY MARC, rheumatologist; b. NYC, Feb. 26, 1958; s. Arthur and Roslyn Greenbaum. MD, SUNY, Bklyn., 1984. Diplomate in internal medicine and rheumatology Am. Bd. Internal Medicine. Intern, resident in internal medicine Winthrop U. Hosp., Mineola, NY, 1984-87; fellow rheumatology U. Cin., Cin., 1987-89; physician Med. Specialists, Inc., Zanesville, Ohio, 1989-93; physician, rheumatologist Ind. Internal Medicine Cons., Greenwood, 1993—. Columnist Rheumatology News. Avocations: gardening, reading, music. Office: Ind Internal Medicine Consultants 701 E County Line Rd Ste 101 Greenwood IN 46143 Office Phone: 317-885-2860. Office Fax: 317-885-2869.

GREENBAUM, LENNARD D., radiologist; MD, Temple Univ., 1970. Intern Washington Hosp. Ctr., 1971; resident, diagnostic radiology Univ. Mich. Univ. Hosp., 1974; sr. ptnr. Med. Ctr. Radiology Group, Orlando, Fla.; and. co-dir. Hughes Ctr. for Fetal Diagnositcs, Arnold Palmer Hosp. for Children and Women, 1992—; and chief, sect. diagnostic ultrasound, dept. radiology Orlando Regional Healthcare. Fellow: Am. Inst. Ultrasound Medicine (pres. 2005—07), Soc. Radioogists in Ultrasound, Am. Coll. Radiology; mem.: Internat. Soc. Ultrasound in Obstetrics and Gynecology, Radiological Soc. N. Am., Am. Roentgen Ray Soc., AMA. Office: Medical Ctr Radiology Group 20 W Kaley St Orlando FL 32806

GREENBAUM, STEVEN S., dermatologist; Grad., Tulane U., New Orleans, 1983. Diplomate Am. Bd. Dermatology. Resident Abington Meml. Hosp., 1984, Henry Ford Hosp., 1987; fellow Univ. of Calif., San Francisco, 1988; dermatologist Skin & Laser Surgery Ctr. of Pa. Office: Skin & Laser Surgery Center of PA Ste 1101 1528 Walnut St Philadelphia PA 19102 Office Phone: 215-735-4994. Office Fax: 215-735-8376.

GREENBERG, ALEX MICHAEL, oral and maxillofacial surgeon; BS in Biology, Lafayette Coll., Easton, Pa., 1979; D in Dental Surgery, Columbia U. Sch. of Dental and Oral Surgery, 1983. Cert. Am. Bd. Oral and Maxillofacial Surgery, Northeast Regional Bd. Dental Examiners, lic. NY. Resident, gen. dentistry Beth Israel Med. Ctr., 1983—84, asst., oral and maxillofacial surgery, dept. dentistry, 1987—; resident, oral and maxillofacial surgery Mt. Sinai Sch. Medicine, NY, 1986—87, chief resident, oral and maxillofacial surgery NY, 1986—87, clin. instructor, oral and maxillofacial surgery, dept. dentistry NY; fellow, maxillofacial surgery U. Basel, Switzerland, 1988; asst. clin. prof., oral and maxillofacial surgery Columbia U. Sch. Dental and Oral Surgery. Asst., dept. dentistry Cabrini Med. Ctr., 1988—91; asst. attending, divsn. oral and maxillofacial surgery Presbyn. Hosp. Dental Svc., Columbia Presbyn. Med. Ctr., NY, 1988—; asst., dept. dental/oral surgery City Hosp. Ctr. Elmhurst, 1988—97; asst., divsn. oral and maxillofacial surgery, dept. dentistry Mt. Sinai Hosp., 1988—; lectr. in field. Author numerous publs., including several peer-reviewed articles; contbr. chapters to books; editor: Craniomaxillofacial Fractures: Principles of Internal Fixation Using The AO/ASIF Technique, 1993; author: Craniomaxillofacial Reconstructive and Corrective Bone Surgery: Principles of Internal Fixation Using the AO/ASIF Technique, 2002. Fellow: NY Acad. Dentistry; mem.: Am. Assn. Oral and Maxillofacial Surgeons, NY State Soc. Oral and Maxillofacial Surgeons, Dental Soc. NY State, Am. Dental Assn., NY County Dental Soc. Achievements include patents in field. Office: 18 E 48th St Ste 1702 New York NY 10017 Office Fax: 212-319-9778. Business E-Mail: info@dralexgreenberg.com.

GREENBERG, BARRY H., cardiologist, medical educator; b. Bklyn., June 24, 1944; s. Reuben and Blanche (Ross) G.; m. Jennifer Keithly, Feb. 18, 1984; children: Lauren, Miranda. BA, Bklyn. Coll., 1966; MD, SUNY, Syracuse, 1970. cert. internal medicine and cardiovascular diseases Am. Bd. Internal Medicine. Resident medicine Yale-New Haven Hosp., Conn.; postdoctoral fellow cardiology U. Calif., San Francisco; staff assoc. heart, lung and blood, lipid metabolism br. Nat. Insts. Health, 1971; dir. coronary care unit Oreg. Health Scis. U., Portland, 1977-95; prof. medicine, dir. advanced heart failure treatment program U. Calif., San Diego, 1995—. Assoc. Jour. of Am. Coll. Cardiology; charter mem. U. Calif., San Diego/Salk Inst. Molecular Medicine. Editor: Valvular Heart Disease, 1987, Congestive Heart Failure, 2001. Named to Best Doctors in Am., 1995—. Mem.: HFSA (pres.), ACC, AHA. Office: U Calif San Diego 200 W Arbor Dr San Diego CA 92103-8411 Office Phone: 619-543-7751. E-mail: bgreenberg@ucsd.edu.

GREENBERG, BENJAMIN D., psychiatrist, educator; b. NYC, Aug. 16, 1956; BA, Amherst Coll., 1979; MD, U. Miami, 1987. Postdoc. fellow U. Calif., San Diego, 1980—84; fellow, interdisciplinary programs health Harvard Sch. Pub. Health, 1984—85; chief, adult obsessive-compulsive disorder rsch. unit NIMH, 1992—99; assoc. prof. psychiatry Brown U. & Butler Hosp., 2000—. Clin. faculty, dept. psychiatry Johns Hopkins U., 1992—. Recipient Rsch. Mentor award, Brown U. Dept. Psychiatry, Young Investigator award, Am. Neuropsychiatric Assn. Mem.: AMA, Am. Psychiat. Assn., Soc. Biol. Psychiatry. Office: 345 Blackstone Blvd Providence RI 02906 Office Fax: 401-455-6442. Business E-Mail: bgreenberg@butler.org.

GREENBERG, CAROLYN PHYLLIS, retired anesthesiologist; b. San Francisco, July 7, 1941; AB, Stanford U., 1962; MD, U. Calif., San Francisco, 1966. Diplomate Am. Bd. Anesthesiology. Rotating intern L.A. County Hosp., 1966-67; resident in anesthesiology Presbyn. Hosp., NYC, 1967-69, vis. fellow in anesthesiology, 1969-70, asst. attending anesthesiologist, 1971-90, assoc. attending anesthesiologist, 1990-99, med. dir. ambulatory surgery, 1986-96, attending anesthesiologist, 1999; asst. attending anesthesiologist NY Hosp., 1970-71; attending anesthesiologist NY Presbyn. Hosp., 1999—2006; ret., 2006. Instr. anesthesiology Cornell Med. Sch., 1970—71; assoc. anesthesiology Columbia U., NYC, 1971—74, asst. prof. clin. anesthesiology, 1974—90, assoc. prof. clin. anesthesiology, 1990—99, prof. clin. anesthesiology, 1999, prof. emerita anesthesiology, 1999—; clin. prof. anesthesiology Cornell Med. Sch., 1999—2006. Contbr. book chpts., articles to profl. jours. Mem. Am. Soc. Anesthesiologists, NY State Soc. Anesthesiologists (Media award 1992), Med. Soc. NY, Soc. Ambulatory Anesthesia (treas. 1994-98, 2nd v.p. 1998-99, 1st v.p. 1999, Ambulatory Anesthesia Rsch. Found. award 1992), Malignant Hyperthermia Assn. of US (hotline cons. 1983-99, partnership award 1996). Jewish. Avocations: swimming, reading, piano, travel. Personal E-mail: cgfcalvin@yahoo.com.

GREENBERG, DAVID, pediatrician, educator; b. Haifa, Israel, Apr. 9, 1960; MD, Ben Gurion U., 1992. Assoc. prof. cons. pediat. infectious diseases Soroka U. Med. Ctr., Ben-Gurion U. Negev, 1999—. Home: Tamar 39 Omer 84965 Israel Home Fax: 086232334. Personal E-mail: dudi@bgu.ac.il.

GREENBERG, E. PETER, microbiologist; BA in Biology, Western Wash. U., 1970; MS in Microbiology, U. Iowa, 1972; PhD in Microbiology, U. Mass., 1977. With Cornell U., U. Iowa, 1988—2004, Sheppard prof. molecular pathogenesis; chair dept. microbiology U. Wash. Sch. Med., 2005—07, prof. microbiology, 2007—. Sci. advisor Genelux, San Diego, 2007—; chief sci. officer Quorum Scis., 1998—2001. Editor: Jour. Bacteriology; assoc. editor Annual Reviews Microbiology. Mem.: Am. Acad. Microbiology, AAAS, NAS. Office: U Wash Sch Medicine Dept Microbiology 1705 NE Pacific St Box 357242 Rm K-359A Seattle WA 98195-7242 Office Phone: 206-616-2881. Business E-Mail: epgreen@u.washington.edu.

GREENBERG, HARLY E., pulmonologist, educator; Attended, NYU Sch. Medicine, 1982. Diplomate Am. Bd. Internal Medicine, Am. Bd. Internal Medicine-pulmonary disease. Intern North Shore Univ. Hosp., Manhasset, NY, resident in internal medicine, 1982—85, with; fellow in pulmonary disease NYU Bellevue Hosp. Ctr., 1985—87; assoc. prof. medicine Albert Einstein Coll. Medicine; pulmonologist LI Jewish Med. Ctr. Office: Long Island Jewish Medical Center 410 Lakeville Rd Ste 107 New Hyde Park NY 11042 Office Phone: 516-465-3899. Office Fax: 516-616-4124.

GREENBERG, IRA ARTHUR, psychologist; b. Bklyn., June 26, 1924; s. Philip and Minnie (S.) G.; m. Martha Estella Cantrell, 1949 (div. 1950); m. Judith Linda Burgard Rials, 1952 (div. 1954); m. Monita Ruth Niborod, 1961 (div. 1965). Grad. Scouts and Raiders Sch., US Naval Amphibious Tng. Base, 1944; BA in Journalism, U. Okla., 1949; MA in English, U. So. Calif., 1962; MS in Counseling, Calif. State U., LA, 1963; PhD in Psychology, Claremont Grad. Sch., 1967; Grad., Marine Corps Inst.'s Command and Staff Coll., 1992. Editor Ft. Riley Guidon, Kans., 1950—51; copy editor, reporter Columbus Enquirer, Ga., 1951—55; reporter Louisville Courier-Jour., 1955—56, LA Times, 1956—62. Counselor Claremont Coll. Psychol. Clinic and Counseling Ctr., 1964-65; lectr. psychology Chapman Coll., Orange, Calif., 1965-66; psychologist Camarillo State Hosp., 1967-69, supervising psychologist, 1969-73, clin. psychologist, 1973-93; asst. prof. edn. San Fernando Valley State Coll., Northridge, Calif., 1967-69, lectr. psychodrama, social welfare U. Calif. Extension Divsn., Santa Barbara, 1968-69; vis. prof. edn. U. Nev., Reno, 1977-92; vol. psychologist Free Clinic, LA, 1968-70; staff dir. Calif. Inst. Psychodrama, 1969-71; tng. cons. Topanga Ctr. for Human Devel., 1970-75; faculty Calif. Sch. Profl. Psychology, 1970-80; founder, exec. dir. Behavioral Studies Inst., mgmt. cons., LA, 1970—; founder, exec. dir. Psychodrama Ctr. for LA, Inc., 1971—, Group Hypnosis Ctr., LA, 1976—; prodr., host TV talk show Crime and Pub. Safety, Time Warner Cable, 1983-2008; cons. in field. Author: Psychodrama and Audience Attitude Change, 1968; editor (author): Psychodrama: Theory and Therapy, 1974, Group Hypnotherapy and Hypnodrama, 1977, The Hebrew National Orphan Home: Memories of Orphanage Life, 2001. Vol. humane officer State of Calif., 1979-89; res. officer LA Police Dept., 1980-86; bd. dirs. Humane Educators Coun., 1982-86; active Nat. Coun. Employer Support of Guard and Res., 1998-2008. With AUS 78th inf. divsn., 1943, army specialized tng. program, 1944, 11th engr. combat battalion XXI corps 7th Army, ETO, 1944-46; USAR, 1950-51, sgt. 1st class; capt. Calif. State Mil. Res., 1986-93, maj., 1993-2000; lt. col. US Svc. Command, 2000-02; col. Emergency Disaster Assistance Corps, 2002—; col. Am. Vol. Res., 2006—. Fellow Am. Soc. Clin. Hypnosis, Am. Soc. Group Psychotherapy and Psychodrama; mem. APA, Calif. Psychol. Assn., LA County Psychol. Assn., So. Calif. Soc. Clin. Hypnosis (pres. 1977-78), Group Psychotherapy Assn. So. Calif. (pres. 1987-88), So. Calif. Psychotherapy Affiliation (dir. 1976-85), Am. Soc. Psychical Rsch., Assn. Rsch. and Enlightenment, Peace Officers Assn., LA County; Acad. TV Arts and Scis., Nat. Acad. Cable Programming, UDT/SEAL Assn., Navy Amphibious Scouts and Raiders Assn., 11th Engr. Combat Battalion Assn., 78th Infantry Divsn. Assn., VFW, Am. Legion, Jewish War Vets. (sr. vice comdr. JWV Post 617, Culver City, Calif., 2011), State Def. Forces Assn. Am., Mensa, Am. Zionist Fedn., NRA, Calif. Rifle and Pistol Assn., SW Pistol League, Animal Protection Inst. Am., LA SPCA, Hebrew Nat. Orphan Home Alumni Assn., Sigma Delta Chi, Sierra Club, Greater LA Press Club, B'nai B'rith Club, Beverly Hills Gun Club Office Phone: 310-472-2662.

GREENBERG, JUDITH HOROVITZ, geneticist; b. Phila., Apr. 2, 1947; d. Monty B. and Evelyn (Cohen) Horovitz; m. Warren Greenberg, June 8, 1969; 1 child, Elyssa H. BS in Biology, U. Pitts., 1967; MA in Biology, Boston U., 1970; PhD in Biology, Bryn Mawr Coll., 1972. Rsch. assoc. ARC, Bethesda, Md., 1971—74; postdoctoral fellow NIH, Bethesda, 1974—75, sr. staff fellow, 1975—81, health scientist adminstr., 1981—88; dir. divsn. genetics and devel. biology NIH, Nat. Inst. Gen. Med. Scis., Bethesda, 1988—; acting dir. Nat. Inst. Gen. Med. Scis. NIH, Bethesda, 2002—03, 2011—. Recipient

Pub. Health Svc. Spl. Recognition award, 1991, Presdl. Meritorious Exec. award, 1999, NIH Dirs. award, 2004, 2006-08. Mem. AAAS, Sigma Xi. Office: NIGMS NIH Bldg 45 Natcher Bldg 2AS25J 45 Center Dr Bethesda MD 20892-6200 E-mail: judith.greenberg@nih.gov. *

GREENBERG, MARK A., cardiologist, educator; MD, U. Ill. Coll. Medicine, 1973. Diplomate Am. Bd. Internal Medicine, Am. Bd. Cardiology-cardiovascular disease, Am. Bd. Cardiology-interventional cardiology. Clin. prof. medicine Albert Einstein Coll. Medicine; resident in internal medicine Montefiore Med. Ctr., Bronx, NY, 1973—76, fellow in cardiovascular disease, 1976—78, cardiologist Henry and Lucy Moses divsn. Office: Montefiore Med. Ctr. MMC Greene Medical Arts Pavilion 3400 Bainbridge Ave Bronx NY 10467 Office Phone: 718-920-4212. Office Fax: 718-920-7447.

GREENBERG, MICHAEL RICHARD, urban studies and community health educator; b. NYC, Aug. 22, 1943; s. Sidney Saul and Mildred (Saletra) Greenberg; m. Gwendolyn Barker, Jan. 19, 1978; children: Seana Pappas, Heather Wilkerson, Joshua Suggs, Alexandra Farsiou. BA, CUNY, 1965; MA, Columbia U., 1966, PhD, 1969. Asst. prof. Columbia U., NYC, 1969-71; assoc. prof. Rutgers U., New Brunswick, NJ, 1971-73, prof., 1973-78, disting. prof., 1978-82, prof. urban studies and cmty. health, 1982—, assoc. dean faculty, 2000—. Co-dir. pub. health N.J. Grad. Progam in Pub. Health, New Brunswick, 1983—. Author: Urbanization and Cancer Mortality, 1983, Public Health and the Environment, 1988, Environmental Risk and the Press, 1989 (award 1988), Environmental Reporter's Handbook (award 1989), Environmentally Devastated Neighborhoods, 1996, Restoring America's Neighborhoods, 1999; Editor in Chief. Risk Analysis: An Internat. Jour. Recipient Spl. Merit award, EPA, 1977, Dennis Sullivan award, Pub. Health Assn., 2001. Mem. APHA, Assn. of Am. Geographers (Disting. Scholars award 1997 Disting. Achievement award 2003), Soc. for Risk Analysis. Avocation: walking. Office: Rutgers U Dept Urban Studies Civic Sq Bldg 33 Livingston Ave Ste 100 New Brunswick NJ 08901-1900 E-mail: mrg@rci.rutgers.edu.

GREENBERG, RAYMOND SETH, academic and health facility administrator, educator; b. Chapel Hill, NC, Aug. 10, 1955; s. Bernard George and Ruth Esther (Marck) G.; m. Leah Daniella Dacus, Oct. 23, 1988. BA in Chemistry, U. N.C., 1976, PhD in Epidemiology, 1983; MD, Duke U., 1979; MPH, Harvard U., 1980; DMS (hon.), The Citadel, 2001; DS (hon.), Simpson Coll., 2002. Asst. prof. sch. medicine Emory U., Atlanta, 1983-86, assoc. prof., 1986-90, dep. dir. Winship Cancer Ctr., 1985-90, chair epidemiology/ biostat., 1988-90, prof., dean sch. pub. health, 1990-95; v.p. for acad. affairs, provost Med. U. SC, Charleston, 1995-99, pres., 2000—. Chair preventive medicine Nat. Bd. Med. Examiners, Phila., 1991-93; chair epidemiology study sect. NIH, Bethesda, Md., 1992-94; bd. sci. counselors Nat. Inst. for Dental and Craniofacial Rsch., Bethesda, 1994-99, mem. blue ribbon panel on rsch. tng. and career devel., 1999; chair adv. coun. Prudential Ctr. for Health Care Rsch., Atlanta, 1994-96; chair Harvard Adv. Com. on Electromagnetic Fields and Human Health, Boston, 1994-98; adv. com. on rsch. and med. grants, Am. Cancer Soc., Atlanta, 1994-96; breast and cervical cancer early detection and control adv. com., Ctrs. for Disease Control and Prevention, Atlanta, 1996-2000; adv. com. on agrl. health risks, Harvard Ctr. for Risk Analysis, Boston, 1996-99; clin. adv. bd. Deloitte and Touche Healthcare Consulting Group, 1997-99; chair sci. adv. panel 3M Corp., 1998-2002; chair bd. trustees S.C. Gov.'s Sch. Sci. and Math., 2004-08; bd. sci. counselors Nat. Ctr. Health Stat., 2004-08; mem. adv. bd. McKesson Corp., 2005—, Soc. Fellows and Scholars, Nat. Ctr. Minority Health; mem. S.C. Commn. on Healthcare Access, 2004-05. Author: Medical Epidemiology, 1993, 4th edit., 2005, Epidemiologia Medica, 1995, 3d edit., 2004; contbr. articles to profl. jours. Bd. dirs. Ga. divsn. Am. Cancer Soc., 1987-93, Carolina Art Assn., 1996-98, Trident United Way, 1999-2002, Trident Urban League, 2006—; mem. Gov.'s Task Force on Higher Edn., 2006., chair bd. mem. Sea Grant, 2008-, bd. SC Rsch. Authority, 2000-Recipient SC Order of Palmetto, 2005; named hon. alumnus, Med. U. S.C. Coll. Medicine Alumni Assn., 2006. Fellow Am. Coll. Epidemiology (pres. 1990-91); mem. APHA, Am. Epidemiology Soc. Democrat. Jewish. Office: Med U SC Colcock Hall 179 Ashley Ave Charleston SC 29425 Office Phone: 843-792-9005. Business E-Mail: greenber@musc.edu.

GREENBERG, RICHARD E., urologist; MD, Cornell U., 1976. Diplomate Am. Bd. Urology. Resident gen. surgery dept. NY-Prsbyn. Hosp., resident urology, Meml. Sloan-Kettering Cancer Ctr., NY; joined Fox Chase Cancer Ctr., 1983, urologist, chief urologic oncology dept. Fellow: ACS; mem.: Phila. Urol. Soc., Am. Urol. Assn., Soc. of Urologic Oncology. Office: Fox Chase Cancer Center 333 Cottman Ave Philadelphia PA 19111-2497 Office Phone: 888-369-2427.

GREENBERG, ROSALIE, child psychiatrist; b. Bklyn., Dec. 21, 1950; d. Sam and Molly Greenberg. BA, NYU, 1972; student, Upstate Med. Ctr., Syracuse, 1972—73; MD, Columbia U., 1976. Intern Overlook Hosp., Summit, NJ, 1976—77; resident gen. psychiatry Columbia Presbyn. Med. Ctr., NY, NY State Psychiatric Inst., 1977—80, fellow in child and adolescent psychiatry, 1979—81, dep. dir. pediat. psychiatry outpatient clinic, 1981—82; dir. child and adolescent outpatient svcs. Fair Oaks Hosp., Summit, NJ, 1982—. Instr. Columbia U., 1981—. Mem.: AMA, Am. Acad. Child and Adolescent Psychiatry, Am. Psychiat. Assn. Office: Fair Oaks Hosp 19 Prospect St Summit NJ 07901-2531

GREENBERG, SHELDON BURT, plastic and reconstructive surgeon; b. Bklyn., July 8, 1948; s. Morris and Lillian (Liss) G.; m. Andrea R. Levy, Feb. 10, 1991; children: Matthew, Joshua. BS, Muhlenberg Coll., 1970; MD, Chgo. Med. Sch., 1974. Diplomate Am. Bd. Otolaryngology, Plastic Surgery. Resident in surgery Lenox Hill Hosp., NYC, 1974-75; resident in otolaryngology Met. Hosp., Manhattan Eye and Ear Hosp., NYC, 1978; resident in plastic surgery Akron (Ohio) City Hosp., 1978-80, fellow in hand surgery, 1980; pvt. practice Norwalk, Conn., 1981—; chief, plastic surgery Norwalk Hosp., 1996—. Fellow Am. Coll. Surgeons, Am. Soc. Plastic Surgeons; mem. Conn. Med. Soc., Fairfield County Med. Soc., Fairfield Men's Club. Republican. Jewish. Avocations: tennis, american history, gardening. Office: 761 Main Ave Suite 101 Norwalk CT 06851 Office Phone: 203-845-2244. Business E-Mail: sgreenbergmd@sbcglobal.net.

GREENBERG, SHELDON STUART, psychiatrist; b. Chgo., Mar. 19, 1944; Children: Geoffrey, Adam, Orly. Degree, U. Ill., Chgo., 1964; MD, Loyola U., 1968. Diplomate Am. Bd. Psychiatry and Neurology, Am. Bd. Addiction Medicine; cert. addiction medicine, 1993, 2003. Intern Cook County Hosp., Chgo., 1968-69; resident in psychiatry Northwestern U., Chgo., 1969-72; pvt. practice Chgo., 1973—; medical staff Lewis Weiss Hosp., 1985—. Asst. prof. dept. psychiatry Chgo. Med. Sch., 1974-76; clin. asst. prof. Abraham Lincoln Sch. Medicine U. Ill., 1977-80; cons. psychiatrist Orchard Ctr. for Mental Health and Turning Point, 1972-74; staff psychiatry Nat. Tng. Labs., Bethel, Maine, 1974-75; staff psychiatrist Ravenswood Hosp. Med. Ctr., Chgo., 1977-93, dir. psychiat. unit, 1977-80; cons. psychiatrist various ins. cos., 1979-; nat med. dir. Lifeline Drug Dependency Program Louis Weiss Meml. Hosp., Chgo., 1984—2002; attending psychiatrist Charter-Barclay Hosp., Chgo., 2000-01; med. dir. Compsych Health Resource Corp., Anixter Found. Maj. U.S. Army, 1972-74. Mem. Am. Psychiat. Soc., Ill. Psychiat. Soc., Am. Acad. Addiction Psychiatry. Office: Ste 200 2835 W Sheffield Chicago IL 60657 Office Phone: 773-561-3365. Personal E-mail: ssgmdsc@gmail.com.

GREENBERG, STEPHEN BARUCH, dean, medical educator; b. May 24, 1944; BA, Johns Hopkins U., 1966; MD, U. Md., 1970. Herman Brown tchg. prof. Baylor Coll. Medicine, Houston, 1990—, vice chmn. dept. medicine, 1990-1999, sr. v.p., dean of med. edn., 2006—; chief medicine svc. Ben Taub Gen. Hosp., Houston, 1990, assoc. chief staff, 1990, assoc. chmn. Dept. Medicine, 2000, chair, 2004—06. Office: Baylor Coll Medicine One Baylor Plaza Houston TX 77030 E-mail: stepheng@bcm.edu. *

GREENBERG, STEPHEN TODD, plastic surgeon; b. Manhasset, NY, Sept. 22, 1962; BS, George Washington U., DC, MD, 1988. Diplomate Nat. Bd. Med. Examiners. Resident in surgery NY Hosp.-Cornell U. Med. Ctr., NYC, 1989—93; resident in plastic surgery Hosp. of U. Pa., Phila., 1993—95, fellow, 1996; dir. NY Premier Plastic Surgery, NYC and Woodbury, NY. Asst. clin. prof. surgery. Fellow: Am. Coll. Surgeons; mem.: AMA, Nassau County Med. Soc., NY Med. Soc., Am. Cleft Palate-Craniofacial Assn., Am. Soc. Plastic and Reconstructive Surgeons. Office: NY Premier Plastic Surgery 195 Froelich Farm Blvd Woodbury NY 11797 Home Phone: 516-364-1400; Office Phone: 516-364-4200. E-mail: docstg@aol.com.

GREENBERG, STEVEN M., physician; b. NYC, June 26, 1956; s. Nathan and Jean Greenberg; m. Elizabeth Anne Attanasio, June 6, 1999; children: Aaron, Adam, Lauren. BS, SUNY, 1977; MD, Albany Med. Coll., 1983. Lic. N.Y., 1984, diplomate Nat. Bd. Med. Examiners, 1983, Am. Bd. Internal Medicine, 1986, Am. Bd. Internal Medicine Subspecialty in Cardiovasc. Disease, 1989, cert. NASPE, 1994, IBHRE, 2006. Intern, resident internal medicine Bronx Med. Hosp. and Hosp. of Albert Einstein Coll. of Medicine, 1983—86; dir. clin. evaluation unit Weiler Hosp. of Albert Einstein Coll. of Medicine, Bronx, 1986, asst. attending physician, 1986; rsch. fellow cardiology Albert Einstein Coll. of Medicine, Bronx, 1986—87; asst. attending physician Queens Hosp. Ctr., 1986—89, Bronx Mcpl. Hosp. Ctr., 1986—90; fellow cardiology Mt. Sinai Hosp., NYC, 1987—90, attending physician NY, 1989—90, St. Francis Hosp., Roslyn, NY, 1990—, co-dir., pacemaker ctr., 1990—, coord., pacemaker ctr. Roslyn, NY, 1991, dir. CCU, 1994—. Cons. in field. Co-author articles in numerous profl. jours. Trustee Village of Old Westbury, NY. Fellow: Heart Rhythm Soc., Am. Coll. Physicians, Am. Coll. Cardiology. Avocations: kayaking, coin collecting/numismatics. Office: St Francis Hosp PO Box 9000 Roslyn NY 11576-9000

GREENBERG, WILLIAM MICHAEL, psychiatrist; b. Bklyn., Oct. 19, 1946; s. Benjamin Greenberg and Marilyn (Berger) Hamberg; m. Wendy Faith Megerman, June 14, 1992. BA, Queens Coll., 1968; postgrad., U. Medicine & Dentistry N.J., 1974—76; MD, Albert Einstein Coll. Medicine, 1978. Diplomate Am. Bd. Psychiatry Neurology, Am. Bd. Geriatric Psychiatry, 2006, Am. Bd. Forensic Psychiatry, 2009, Am. Bd. Addiction Psychiatry, 2008, cert. clin. psychopharmacology 2003. Computer programmer We. Electric Co., NYC, 1970—73; rsch. asst. Bklyn. Jewish Hosp., 1973—74; resident psychiatry Bronx Mcpl. Hosp. Ctr., NY, 1978—83, pres. house staff, 1981—82; acting med. dir. Met. Ctr. Mental Health, NYC, 1983; staff psychiatrist Bronx Psychiat. Ctr., 1983—84; dir. psychiatry clinic North Ctrl. Bronx Hosp., 1984—88; psychiatrist, cons. Montefiore Mental Health Svcs. Rikers Island, East Elmhurst, NY, 1985—86; pvt. practice Bronx, NY, 1985—88, NJ, 1997—; mem. spkr.'s bur. Bergen Pines County Hosp. (now Bergen Regional Med. Ctr.), Paramus, NJ, 1988—2000; chief psychiatrist, attending staff mem. Bergen Regional Med. Ctr., Paramus, 1988—96, dir. psychiat. rsch., 1993—2000, interim med. dir. psychiatry, 1996—98, dir. psychiatry residency tng. program, 1997—2000, chmn. instrnl. rev. bd., 1996—2000; dir. outpatient rsch. ctr. Nat. Kline Inst., Orangeburg, NJ, 2001—07; assoc. dir. clin. devel. Forest Rsch. Inst., 2007—09, dir. clin. devel., 2009—. Asst. clin. prof. Albert Einstein Coll. Med., Bronx, NY, 1988—90; vis. asst. prof. Med. Coll. Pa., 1990—94, adj. asst. prof., 1994—2000; adj. assoc. prof. Drexel U. Coll. Medicine, 2000—04; adj. assoc. prof. environ. medicine NYU Sch. Medicine, 2001—02; prin. investigator clin. drug trials; clin. assoc. prof. psychiatry NYU Sch. Medicine, 2002—08; prof. psychiatry St. George U. Sch. Medicine, 2009—. Editor: N.J. Psychiatrist, 2001—; asst. editor: Cmty. Psychiatrist, 1985—89, mem. editl. bd.: Einstein Quar. Jour. Biology and Medicine, 1987—2000; contbr. articles to profl. jours. Union rep. Cmty. Interns Residents, NYC, 1979—81; spkr.'s bur. Physicians Social Responsibility, NYC, 1982—84. Recipient Psychiatrist Recognition award, NJ Alliance Mentally Ill, 1996; scholar Rock Sleyster Mem., AMA, 1977. Mem.: AAAS, NJ Psychiat. Assn. (pres. 2004—05), Assn. Advancement Philosophy Psychiatry, Am. Psychiat. Assn. (assembly mem. 2007—, Bruno Lima Disaster Psychiatry award 2007). Avocations: meditation, photography, philosophy, computers. Office: Forest Rsch Inst Jersey City NJ 07311

GREENBERGER, ELLEN, psychologist, educator; b. NYC, Nov. 19, 1935; d. Edward Michael and Vera (Brisk) Silver; m. Michael Burton, Aug. 26, 1979; children by previous marriage: Kari Edwards, David Silver. BA, Vassar Coll., 1956; MA, Harvard U., 1959, PhD, 1961. Instr. Wellesley (Mass.) Coll., 1961—67; sr. rsch. scientist Johns Hopkins U., Balt., 1967-76; prof. psychology and social behavior U. Calif., Irvine, 1976—, prof. emeritus & rsch. prof., 2007—. Author: (with others) When Teenagers Work, 1986; contbr. articles to profl. jours. USPHS fellow, 1956-59; Margaret Floy Washburn fellow, 1956-58; Ford Found. grantee, 1979-81; Spencer Found. grantee, 1979-81, 87, 88-91. Fellow Am. Psychol. Assn., Am. Psychol. Soc.; mem. Soc. Rsch. in Child Devel., Soc. Rsch. on Adolescent Devel. Office: University Calif 4546 Social & Behavioral Sci Gateway Irvine CA 92697-7085 Office Phone: 949-824-6328. Business E-Mail: egreenbe@uci.edu. *

GREENBERGER, JOEL S., radiation oncologist educator; MD, Harvard Coll., Boston. Resident Joint Ctr. for Radiation Therapy; prof., chair radiation oncology dept. Univ. of Pitts. Sch. of Medicine; co-dir. Lung and Esophageal Cancer Program Univ. of Pitts. Cancer Inst. Recipient Sara Stone Burns award, Am. Cancer Soc. Mass. Divsn. Office: University of Pittsburgh Physicians Shadyside Radiation Oncology 5230 Centre Ave Pittsburgh PA 15232 Office Phone: 412-623-6720.

GREENBERGER, MARTIN, biotechnologist, information scientist, educator; b. Elizabeth, NJ, Nov. 30, 1931; s. David and Sidelle (Jonas) G.; m. Ellen Danica Silver, Feb. 2, 1959 (div. June 1974); children: Kari Edwards, David Silver; m. Liz Attardo, Dec. 11, 1982; children: Beth Jonit, Jonah Ben, Jilly Sal. Grad. with hons., USAF Officer Candidate Sch., 1953; AB with honors, Harvard U., 1955, AM, 1956, PhD in Applied Math. and Economics, 1958. Teaching fellow, resident adviser, staff mem. Computation Lab., Harvard U., Cambridge, 1954-58; mgr. applied sci. Cambridge IBM, 1956-58; asst. prof. mgmt. Mass. Inst. Tech., Cambridge, 1958-61, assoc. prof., 1961-67; prof., chmn. computer sci., dir. info. processing Johns Hopkins U., Balt., 1967-72; prof. math. scis., sr. research assoc. Center for Met. Planning and Research, 1972-75, prof. math. scis., 1978-82; IBM chair in tech. and info. systems UCLA Anderson Grad. Sch. Mgmt., 1982—; dir. UCLA Ctr. Digital Media, 1995-2000; pres. Council for Tech. and the Individual, 1985—; sr. fellow Milken Inst., 1999—; faculty mem. & advisor Singularity U., NASA AMES, 2009—. Mgr. systems program Electric Power Research Inst., Palo Alto, Calif., 1976-77; Isaac Taylor vis. prof. Technion-Israel Inst. Tech., Haifa, 1978-79; vis. prof. Internat. Energy Program, Grad. Sch. Bus., Stanford U., 1980, MIT Media Lab., 1988-89, Harvard U., 2001; computer sci. and engring. bd. NAS, 1970-72; chmn. COSATI rev. group NSF, 1971-72; evaluation com. Internat. Inst. for Applied Systems Analysis, Laxenburg, Austria, 1980; adv. panels, Office Tech. Assessment, GAO, U.S. Congress; adv. com. Getty Info. Inst.; cons. IBM, AT&T, CBS, Rand Corp., Morgan Guaranty, Arthur D. Little, TRW, Munger Tolles, Bolt, Beranek & Newman, Brookings Inst., Resources for Future, Electric Power Rsch. Inst., Atlantic Richfield, Rockwell Internat., Security Pacific Corp., John F. Kennedy Sch. of Govt. Harvard U., Bell Atlantic Corp., Sony Corp., Applied Minds, Mitchell Silberberg and Knupp, Am. Online, Kirkland and Ellis, Vertex Pharmaceuticals, Nat. Cancer Inst. Author: (with Orcutt, Korbel and Rivlin) Microanalysis of Socioeconomic Systems: A Simulation Study, 1961; (with Jones, Morris and Ness) On-Line Computation and Simulation: The OPS-3 System, 1965; (with Crenson and Crissey) Models in the Policy Process: Public Decision Making in the Computer Era, 1976; (with Brewer, Hogan and Russell) Caught Unawares: The Energy Decade in Retrospect, 1983; editor: Management and The Computer of the Future, 1962, republished as Computers and the World of the Future, 1964; Computers, Communications, and the Public Interest, 1971; (with Aronofsky, McKenney and Massy) Networks for Research and Education, 1973; Electronic Publishing Plus: Media for a Technological Future, 1985, Technologies for the 21st Century, Vol. 1, On Multimedia, 1990, Vol. 3, Multimedia in Review, 1992, Vol. 5, Content and Communication, 1994, Vol. 7, Scaling Up, 1996. Mem. overseers' vis. com. Harvard U., 1975-81; founder and mem. working groups Energy Modeling Forum, Stanford U., 1978-81; mem. adv. com. Nat. Center Analysis of Energy Systems Brookhaven Nat. Lab., 1976-80, chmn., 1977; mem. rev. com. Energy and Environment div. Lawrence Berkeley Lab., 1983, applied sci. div., 1986-88; chmn. forum on electronic pub. Washington program Annenberg, 1983-84; co-founder ICC Forum, 1985; chmn. CTI Roundtable Digital Media, 1990-99; chmn. CTI Roundtable Healthy Aging, 2006; trustee Educom, Princeton, N.J., 1969-73, chmn. council, 1969-70. With USAF, 1952-54, USAFR, 1954-60. Named a Disting. Grad. Officer Candidate Sch., USAF, 1953; NSF fellow, 1955-56; Guggenheim fellow U. Calif., Berkeley, 1965-66. Fellow: AAAS (v.p., chmn. sect. T 1973—75); mem.: Sigma Xi, Phi Beta Kappa. Office: UCLA Anderson Grad Sch Mgmt 110 Westwood Plz Los Angeles CA 90095-1481

GREENBERGER, PAUL ALLEN, allergist, immunologist, educator; b. Pitts., May 28, 1947; s. Lawrence Fred and Jean (Half) Greenberger; m. Rosalie Simon, Dec. 29, 1974; children: Rachel, Daniel. BS, Purdue U., West Lafayette, Ind., 1969; MD, Ind. U. Sch. Medicine, 1973. Diplomate Am. Bd. Internal Medicine, Am. Bd. Allergy & Immunology, cert. in diagnostic lab. immunology. Intern medicine Clarian Meth. Hosp., Indpls., 1973—74; resident internal medicine Barnes Jewish Hosp./Washington U., St. Louis, 1974—76; allergy/immunology fellow McGaw Med. Ctr., Chgo., 1976-78; asst. prof. medicine Northwestern U. Feinberg Sch. Medicine, Chgo., 1979-83, assoc. prof., 1983-88, prof., 1988—. Contbr. articles to profl. jours. Named one of Top Doctors in Chgo. Metro Area, Castle Connolly Med. Ltd., 2000—03, America's Top Doctors, 2002—07. Fellow: ACP, Soc. Clin. Rsch., Am. Coll. Allergy Asthma & Immunology, Am. Acad. Allergy, Asthma & Immunology (pres. 2009—10), Am. Coll. Chest Physicians, Am. Thoracic Soc. Office: Feinberg Sch Medicine 240 E Huron McGaw Rm M 316 Chicago IL 60611 Office Phone: 312-695-4000. Business E-Mail: p-greenberger@northwestern.edu. *

GREENBLATT, DAVID J., pharmacologist; b. Boston, Apr. 8, 1945; s. Milton and Gertrude A. (Rogers) G.; m. Lisa L. von Moltke, Nov. 29, 1991. BA, Amherst Coll., 1966; MD, Harvard Med. Sch., 1970. Diplomate Am. Bd. Clin. Pharmacology. Intern in medicine Montefiore Hosp., Bronx, NY, 1970-71; resident in medicine Harvard Med. Svc. Boston City Hosp., 1971-72; fellow clin. pharmacology Mass. Gen. Hosp., Boston, 1972-74, mem. staff clin. pharmacology unit, 1974-76, chief clin. pharmacology unit, 1976-79; dir. clin. pharmacology program Tufts Med. Ctr., Boston, 1979—; prof. pharmacology/exptl. therapeutics, psychiatry, medicine, anesthesia Sch. Medicine, Tufts U., Boston, 1979—; chmn. dept. pharmacology and exptl. therapeutics Sch. Medicine, Tufts U., Boston, 1994—2010, Louis Lasagna prof. pharmacology and exptl. therapeutics, 1997—. Author, co-author 11 books; contbr. over 800 articles to profl. jours. Recipient T. George Bidder award UCLA, 1988. Fellow Am. Coll. Clin. Pharmacology (bd. regents 1987-91, McKeen-Cattell award 1985, Disting. Svc. award 2001, pres.-elect 1994-96, pres. 1996-98, Dist. Investigator award 2002); mem. Am. Soc. Clin. Pharmacology and Therapeutics (bd. dirs. 1983-85, Rawls-Palmer award 1980), Am.

Soc. Clin. Investigation, Am. Coll. Neuropsychopharmacology, Am. Assn. Pharm. Scientists (Clin. Scis. Rsch. Achievement award 2005) Avocation: baseball. Office: Tufts U Sch Medicine 136 Harrison Ave Boston MA 02111-1817 Office Phone: 617-636-6997. Business E-Mail: dj.greenblatt@tufts.edu.

GREENBLATT, HELLEN CHAYA, immunologist, microbiologist; b. Frankfurt au Main, Germany; d. Gedaljie and Sara (Glass) Greenblatt. BA, CCNY, 1968; MS, U. Okla., 1971; PhD, SUNY Downstate Med. Ctr., Bklyn., 1977. Microbiologist Walter Reed Army Inst., Washington, 1978-80; sr. rsch. immunoparasitologist Merck Sharp & Dohme, Rahway, NJ, 1980-81; assoc. Albert Einstein Coll. Medicine, Bronx, NY, 1981-84; dir. rsch. and devel. Clin. Scis. Inc., Whippany, NJ, 1984-86, dir. new bus. and sci. devel., 1986-88; sr. devel. virology E.I. DuPont, Wilmington, Del., 1988-90; mng. dir. M-CAP Techs. Internat./DCV, Wilmington, 1990-93; tech. rep. BTR Separations, Wilmington, 1993-94; v.p. R & D, DCV Biol. Scis., Wilmington, 1994-97; v.p. devel. Life Scis. divsn. DCV BioNutrition, Wilmington, 1997-2000; v.p. Legacy USA, Melbourne, Fla., 1999—2002; exec. v.p. Legacy for Life, 2002—04, chief sci. officer, 2004—11; dir. Anti Aging Anti Inflammator Strategies. Numerous internat. and domestic tech. presentations, 2011. Contbr. chpt. to book, numerous articles to peer-review profl. jours. Recipient Outstanding Young Woman award Competitive Resident Rsch. Coun., Washington, 1978, Amanda Cox Spirit of Life award; grantee NRC, 1978-80; fellow NRC. Mem.: Internat. Soc. Exercise & Immunology, Inflammation Rsch. Assn., NY Acad. Scis. Achievements include patents for gastroprotective, anti-inflammatory and anti-diarrheal properties of immune egg; among the foremost authorities on polyvalent hyperimmune egg for human and pet applications. Office Phone: 800-746-0300, 302-265-3870. Business E-Mail: hgreenblatt@legacyforlife.net, hcgreenblatt@hotmail.com, dehellen@dehellengreenblatt.info.

GREENBLATT, MICHAEL NOEL, hospital administrator, primary care internist; b. Bklyn., Oct. 29, 1937; s. Lazarus and Pearl (Hichenka) G.; married; children: Sheldon Howard, Kenneth Bruce. BS in Pharmacy, Columbia U., 1959; MD magna cum laude, SUNY, Bklyn., 1963. Diplomate Am. Bd. Internal Medicine. Straight med. intern Mt. Sinai Hosp., NYC, 1963-64, resident in internal medicine, 1964-65; chief USPHS Outpatient Clinic, Chgo., 1965-67; asst. resident in medicine Case Western Res. U./Univ. Hosps. of Cleve., 1967-68, resident in gastroenterology, 1968-69, tchg. fellow dept. medicine, 1968-69; asst. prof. clin. medicine SUNY Coll. Medicine, Stony Brook, 1972—2005. Asst. attending Nassau County Med. Ctr., 1970-77, assoc. attending, 1977 2005; mem. staff Mid-Island Hosp., Bethpage, N.Y., 1970-99, New Island Hosp., Bethpage, 1999-2006, Winthrop Hosp., 1993-2006, North Shore U. Hosp., Plainview, Nassau County Med. Ctr., East Meadow, 1970—2005; med. dir. Mid-Island and N.I. Hosp., 1988-2005; physician adviser case mgmt. Lenox Hill Hosp., N.Y.C., 2005—. Lt. comdr. USPHS, 1965-67. Fellow ACP, Am. Coll. Gastroenterology; mem. AMA, N.Y. State Med. Soc., Nassau County Med. Soc., Am. Coll. Physician Execs. Jewish. Avocations: bicycling, walking, hiking, kayaking. Office: Lenox Hill Hosp 100 E 77th St New York NY 10075 Home Phone: 516-798-4121; Office Phone: 212-434-2972. Personal E-mail: mngreenblatt@aol.com. Business E-Mail: mgreenblatt@lenoxhill.net.

GREENE, BOB, exercise physiologist, weight loss and nutrition expert; b. Cherry Hill, NJ, Dec. 8, 1958; m. Urania Greene, 2005; 1 child, Kylee. BA in Phys. Edn., U. Del.; MA in Exercise Physiology, U. Ariz. Cert. personal trainer. Founder, creator The Best Life Diet & Fitness Plan, Bestlife Foods, Bestlife Supplements & Vitamins. Author: Get With the Program!: Getting Real About Your Weight, Health, and Emotional Well-Being, 2003, Get With the Program! Guide to Good Eating; Great Food for Good Health, 2003, The Get With The Program! Guide to Fast Food and Family Restaurants, 2003, Keep the Connection: Choices for a Better and Healthier Life, 2004, Bob Greene's Total Body Makeover: An Accelerated Program of Exercise and Nutrition for Maximum Results in Minimum Time, 2004, The Best Life Diet, 2006 (#1 Diet Book, Consumer Reports, NY Times bestseller), The Best Life Diet Cookbook: More than 175 Delicious, Convenient, Family-Friendly Recipes, 2008, The Life You Want: Get Motivated, Lose Weight, and Be Happy, 2010, The Best Life Guide to Managing Diabetes and Pre-Diabetes, 2010, 20 Years Younger: Look Younger, Feel Younger, Be Younger!, 2011; co-author (with Oprah Winfrey): A Journal of Daily Renewal: The Companion to Make the Connection, 1996, Make the Connection: Ten Steps to a Better Body and a Better Life, 1999; regular contbr. O: The Oprah Mag. Mem.: American Coun. Exercise, American Coll. Sports Medicine. Mailing: c/o Simon & Schuster Inc 1230 Ave of Americas New York NY 10020 *

GREENE, CHARLES SIDNEY, dentist, educator; b. Aug. 21, 1937; BS, U. Chgo., 1958; DDS, U. Ill., Chgo., 1963. Clin. prof. U. Ill. Coll. Dentistry, 1995—. Office: UIC Coll Dentistry Dept Orthodontics 801 South Paulina Chicago IL 60612 Business E-Mail: cgreene@uic.edu.

GREENE, DAVID, surgeon, researcher; b. NYC, Nov. 15, 1966; s. Martin and Carole Greene; m. Denise Altman; children: Rachael children: Jonathan. BA magna cum laude, Harvard U., 1989; MD, Yale U., 1993. Diplomate Am. Bd. Med. Examiners, Am. Bd. Otolaryngology, Am. Bd. Facial Plastic Surgery. Rsch. fellow NIH, Bethesda, Md., 1990—90; resident otolaryngology head and neck surgery U. Calif., San Francisco, 1993—98, chief resident head and neck surgery, 1997—98; fellow facial plastic surgery Stanford U., Calif., 1998—99; clin. instr. facial plastic surgery Stanford U. Med. Ctr., 1998—99; staff surgeon Palo Alto Vets. Health Sys., 1998—99; staff otolaryngologist, head and neck surgeon Physicians Regional Med. Ctr. (formerly Cleveland Clinic), Naples, Fla., 1999—, chmn., 2001—. Contbr. articles to profl. jours. Recipient Spl. Thanks and Recognition award, VA, 1999, Physician Recognition award, AMA, 2001, Am. Top Doctors, Consumer Rsch. Coun. America; named Am. Top Physician, Consumer Rsch. Coun. America; named one of Best Physicians Am., Castle-Connolly's Top Drs.; John Harvard scholar, Harvard U., 1986, Harvard Coll. scholar, 1986, Harvard Detur scholar, 1985. Fellow: Am. Rhinologic Soc., Am. Acad. Otolaryngology (Achievement award 2001); mem.: ACS, Am. Acad. Facial Plastic Surgery (Best Clin. Rsch. Paper award 1999), Phi Beta Kappa. Office: 1000 Goodlette Rd N Ste 200 Naples FL 34102 Office Phone: 239-434-6200. Office Fax: 239-434-5741. *

GREENE, DONALD RICHARD, dermatologist, educator; b. Buffalo, Aug. 20, 1947; s. Norman Sanborn and Helen Jean (Secord) Powers; m. JoAnne D'Amico, Mar. 5, 1982; children: Patrick Ryan, Claire Elizabeth. BA, SUNY, Buffalo, 1970, MD, 1974. Diplomate Am. Bd. Dermatology. Intern Buffalo Gen. Hosp., 1974-75; resident Hosp. of U. Pa., Phila., 1975-76, Yale-New Haven Hosp., 1976-79, chief resident, 1978-79; clin. instr. Yale U. Sch. Medicine, New Haven, 1979-82, clin. asst. prof., 1982—. Attending physician Yale-New Haven Hosp., Hosp. St. Raphael, 1979—; med. bd. Branford (Conn.) Health Care Ctr., 1983—. Named one of America's Top Drs., Consumer Rsch. Coun. America, 2008—11, Top Dermatologists, Conn. Mag., 2008—11; grantee, Am. Cancer Soc., 1972. Fellow Am. Acad. Dermatology (Leadership Cir. for Volunteerism); mem. AMA, Conn. State Med. Soc. (pres. dermatology sect. 1984-85), New Haven County Med. Assn., New Haven City Med. Assn., New Eng. Dermatologic Soc., Dermatology Found. (Leaders Soc.), NY Acad. Sci., Assn. Attendings at Yale U. Sch. Medicine, Mensa, Yale Club New Haven, Penn Club NY, Mory's Assn. Episcopalian. Office Phone: 203-481-3419.

GREENE, JERRY GEORGE, retired physician; b. Regina, Sask., Can., May 13, 1937; came to U.S., 1962, naturalized, 1981; s. David Robert and Fae (Woodman) G.; m. Waltra Laguniak, Feb. 27, 1960; children: Deidre, Cheryl, Michael. MD, U. Man., 1960; MS in Med., U. Wis., Madison, 1990. Diplomate: Am. Bd. Internal Medicine. Rotating intern St. Boniface Hosp., Winnipeg, Man., Canada, 1960-61, jr. asst. resident medicine, 1961-62; teaching fellow U. Man., 1961-62; fellow in medicine Mayo Clinic, 1962-66, asst. in pulmonary diseases, 1966; chief pulmonary lab. St. Joseph's Hosp., St. Paul, 1966-69; asst. prof. medicine U. Minn. St. Paul, 1968-71; practice medicine specializing in internal medicine, 1966-68, Med. Assos. Saranac Lake, NY, 1972-78; asso. cardiac catheterization lab. St. Mary's Hosp., Mpls., 1967, dir. inhalation therapy program, 1967, chief pulmonary disease St. Paul Ramsey Hosp., 1968-71; med. dir. Will Rogers Hosp., Saranac Lake, NY, 1971-72; chief dept. medicine Saramac Lake Gen. Hosp., 1977-78; chief pulmonary disease sect. VA Hosp., Fargo, ND, 1978-90; clin. assoc. prof. Mt. Sinai Sch. Medicine, 1991—2000. Asst. prof. medicine in internal medicine U. Minn., 1968-71; prof. medicine U. ND Sch. Medicine; chief pulmonary svc. VA Hosp., Fargo, 1978-91; chief of staff VAMC, Castle Point, NY, 1991-96; past med. dir. VA Upstate NY Healthcare, NY, 1996-99; cons. ND Lung Assn., P3RO, Blue Cross/Blue Shield ND; adv. com. med. edn. NIH 1980—, pulmonary acad. award com. on pulmonary testing 1979-84; comdr. 105th USAF Clinic, Stewart Field, Newburgh, NY. Assoc. editor RT mag.; contbr. articles to profl. jours. Bd. dirs. ND Lung Assn., 1979. Served with RCAF, 1960-62; to lt. col. M.C., USAF, Air N.G., 1982, comdr. Air Nat. Guard, 2000-04, ret. col. USAF, 2004. Recipient Recognition award Mayo Clin. Fellow's Assn., 1966, Pulmonary Acad. award NIH, 1978 Fellow A.C.P., Am. Coll. Chest Physicians (com. on respirator pathophysiology); mem. VA Pulmonary Physicians, Mayo Clinic Alumni Assn.

GREENE, JOHN NORMAN, epidemiologist, educator; b. Hialeah, Fla., May 2, 1960; MD, U. South Fla. Coll. Medicine, 1986. Prof. medicine, sect. chief, divsn. infectious diseases, tropical medicine Moffitt Cancer Ctr., 1991—. Dir., employee health H. Lee Moffitt Cancer Ctr. & Rsch. Inst., Tampa, Fla., 1991—; dir., epidemiology U. South Fla. Coll. Medicine, 1997—. Named one of Best Doctors America, 2007—08; nominee Alumni award, USF Coll. Medicine, 2011. Fellow: ACP; mem.: Nat. Comprehensive Cancer Network, Soc. Healthcare Epidemiology America, Infectious Disease Soc. America. Avocations: fishing, boating. Office: Moffitt Cancer Ctr 12902 Magnolia Dr Tampa FL 33612 Office Fax: 813-745-8468. Business E-Mail: john.greene@moffitt.org.

GREENE, LOREN WISSNER, endocrinologist; Attended, NYU, 1971—75. Diplomate Am. Bd. of Internal Medicine, 1978, Am. Bd. of Internal Medicine-endocrinology, Am. Bd. of Internal Medicine-diabetes & metabolism. Resident Bellevue Hosp., 1975—78, fellow, 1978—80; clin. assoc. prof. dept. of medicine NYU Langone Med. Ctr. Office: NYU Langone Medical Center and School of Medicine 550 1st Ave New York NY 10016 Office Phone: 212-263-7300.

GREENE, LYNNE JEANNETTE, wellness consultant, artist; b. Albany, NY, Aug. 27, 1938; d. Zebulon Stevens and Helen Matilde (Maier) Robbins; m. Stanley E. Greene, Jan. 31, 1962 (dec. June 27, 1987); 1 child, Stuart Nathaniel; m. Michael Alan Karlan, Sept. 29, 1991. Student, Goucher Coll., 1956-57; BA with honors, Parsons Sch. Design, 1960. Asst. designer Haymaker Sportswear (David Crystal), NYC, 1959-61; designer Craig Craely Sportswear and Dresses, NYC, 1961-63, Flair Lingerie, NYC, 1964-66; designer, owner Kaleidoscope Lingerie, NYC, 1966-67; head designer Contessa/Monique/Fisher Lingerie, NYC, 1967-71; creative dir. Eye of the Peacock Sportswear, N.J., 1968-72; head designer, owner Lynne Greene Designs Retail, Montclair, N.J., 1972-74; designer, pres. Little Greene Apples Inc., Montville, NJ, 1971—2005; designer, dir. mktg. Lady Lynne Lingerie, Guy Laroche Lingerie, NYC and Paris, 1973-93, Paris, 1973—93, Val Mode by Lynne Greene, NYC, 1993-97; v.p. design and merchandising The Intapp Group/Go Figure, NYC, 1997-99; pres. Vital Advantage LLC, 1999—, owner, 1999—. Lingerie critic Pratt Inst., 1984-2001. Patentee in field; illustrator books, pamphlets in fashion and packaging fields; comml. artist and illustrator Home & Office Design. Active participant Montville Soccer Assn, 1972-88, fund drives for Am. Heart Assn., Cancer Inc., March of Dimes, Spl. Olympics, creator of Share Ed. by the Book, 2000. Recipient Lace Designer of the Yr., French Lace Coun., 1975, 1980, Humanitarian award, Polar Bear Project, Nikken Inc., 2003, honors in field; named Designer of Yr., French Lace Coun., 1975—80. Mem.: Powerful You! Women's Exec. Network, The Fashion Group, 200 Club N.J., Kiwanis (pres. 2004—05, Kiwanian of Yr. 2002—03). Republican. Avocations: sketching, portraiture, cooking, sewing, painting. Personal E-mail: maklynne@optonline.net.

GREENE, MARK W., plastic surgeon; Med. degree, U. Tex. Health Sci. Ctr., San Antonio; dental degree, U. Tenn. Ctr., Memphis. Diplomate Am. Bd. Plastic Surgery, Am. Bd. Oral and Maxillofacial Surgery. Intern in anesthesia Univ. Tex. Health Sci. Ctr., San Antonio, resident in oral and maxillofacial surgery; resident in surgery Methodist Med. Ctr., Ohio; resident in plastic and reconstructive surgery Northeast Ohio Univ. Coll. Medicine, Akron. Named to, New Beauty Mag., 2010. Mem.: Bexar County Med. Soc., Tex. Soc. Plastic Surgeons, Am. Soc. Aesthetic Plastic Surgery, Am. Soc. Plastic Surgeons. Office: Mark W Greene M D Remington Oaks Office Bldg Ste 110 525 Oak Centre Dr San Antonio TX 78258 Office Phone: 210-653-4993. Office Fax: 210-599-4626.

GREENE, MICHAEL FURMAN, obstetrician; m. Greene. BA, Rutgers U., 1970; MD, SUNY, 1976. Maternal Fetal Medicine Mass., 1982. Intern, ob-gyn. Boston Hosp. Women, 1976—77, resident, maternal fetal medicine, 1977—80; fellow Brigham-Womens Hosp., Boston, 1980—82, staff, ob-gyn., 1982—94; chief obstetrics, dept. ob-gyn. Mass. Gen. Hosp., Boston, dir. maternal fetal medicine, 1994—; prof. obstetrics, gynecology and reproductive biology Harvard Med. Sch.; staff mem. Vincent ob-gyn. svc., Mass. Office: Mass Gen Hosp Vincent ob-gyn 55 Fruit St YAW 4 Boston MA 02114

GREENE, MONICA LYNN BANKS, psychologist; b. Washington, Sept. 24, 1969; d. John Thomas and Priscilla (Sneed) Banks. BS in Microbiology, Howard U., Washington, 1986; MBA/MGA, U. Md., College Park, 2000, PhD, 2005. Cert. therapeutic recreation specialist, activity cons. Therapeutic recreation specialist Dept. Human Svcs., Washington, 1986-91; dir. activities, vols., transp. Independence Ct. Hyattsville, Md., 1991-93; dir. therapeutic activity svcs. Asbury Meth. Village, Gaithersburg, Md., 1993—; dir. therapeutic activities and vol. svcs. Presdl. Woods Health Care Ctr., Adelphi, Md.; owner, pres. Excell Eldercare Mgmt., Inc.; asst. adminstr. St. Thomas More Nursing & Rehab. Ctr., Hyattsville, Md.; exec. dir. Morningside HOuse of St. Charles, Waldorf, Ind., 2003—; pvt. practice psychology Largo, Md., 2005—; clin. psychologist, therapist Laurel Regional Hosp.; owner It's All About Us! LLC, Excell ElderCare Mgmt., Inc. Mem.: Alpha Kappa Alpha. Democrat. Baptist. Avocations: swimming, jet skiing, horseback riding, snorkeling. Home: 1210 Blue Wing Ter Upper Marlboro MD 20774 E-mail: monicagreen01@comcast.net.

GREENE, WALTER BLAIR, pediatric orthopedist; b. Fayetteville, NC, July 21, 1946; BS, Davidson Coll.; MD, Univ. NC Med. Sch., 1972. Cert. Am. Bd. Orthopaedic Surgery. Intern in orthopaedic surgery Parkland Meml. Hosp., Dallas, 1972—73; resident in pediatric orthopaedics Univ. NC Sch. Med., Chapel Hill, 1973—77; fellow in pediatric orthopaedic surgery Newington Children's Hosp., Conn., 1977—78; assoc. prof. pediatrics & orthopaedic surgery Univ. NC Sch. Med., Chapel Hill, 1983—89, prof. pediatrics & orthopaedic surgery, 1989—95; J. Vernon Luck prof. orthopaedic surgery Univ. Mo. Sch. Med., Columbia, 1996—2003, chmn. Dept. Orthopaedic Surgery, 1996—2002; pediatric orthopaedic surgeon OrthoCarolina, Charlotte, NC, 2003—06, Cape Fear Orthopaedic Clinic, Fayetteville, NC, 2007—. Editor: Netter's Orthopaedics, author: Essentials of Musculoskeletal Care; co-author: Clinical Measurement of Joint Motion; contbr. articles to profl. jours.; mem. editl. bd. Jour. of Pediatric Orthopaedics. Mem.: Am. Acad. Orthopaedic Surgeons, Pediatric Orthopaedic Soc., Am. Med. Soc. Office: Cape Fear Orthopaedic Clinic Ste 801 4140 Ferncreek Dr Fayetteville NC 28314 also: Ste 108 6000 Ramsey St Fayetteville NC 28311 Office Phone: 910-484-2171, 919-484-3222.

GREENE, WARNER CRAIG, medical educator, administrator; b. Mexico, Mo., June 13, 1949; BA, Stanford U.; MD, PhD, Washington U. Sch. Medicine, St. Louis, 1977. Lic. physician Md., N.C., Calif., diplomate Am. Bd. Allergy and Immunology, Am. Bd. Internal Medicine. Intern, medicine Mass. Gen. Hosp., Boston, 1977—78, resident, allergy and immunology, 1978—79; investigator metabolism br. Nat. Cancer Inst., NIH, Bethesda, Md., 1979—83, sr. investigator metabolism br., 1983—86; investigator Howard Hughes Med. Inst., Chevy Chase, Md., 1987—92; prof. medicine Duke U. Sch. Medicine, Durham, NC, 1987—92; prof. medicine, microbiology and immunology U. Calif., San Francisco, 1992—, dir. & sr. investigator Gladstone Inst. for Virology and Immunology, 1992—, co dir., Gladstone Ctr. for AIDS Rsch., 1994—, Nick and Sue Hellmann Dist. Prof. Translational Medicine, 2006—. Cons. Merck Pharms., Whitehouse Station, NJ, Eli Lilly Inc., Indpls., Abbott Pharms., Abbott Park, Ill., Hoffman LaRoche, Nutley, NJ, Sagres Pharm., Alliance Pharms., Inc., San Diego, Pfizer, Inc., NYC; mem. Nat. Inst. Allergy and Infectious Diseases, AIDS Rsch. Rev. Com., 1988—90; co-chair Keystone AIDS Symposium, 1995; mem. postdoctoral fellowship rev. com. Pfizer, 1995—; mem. adv. bd. exec. com. Inst. Human Virology, 1999—; Syntex lectr. Laurentian Hormone Conf., 1987; Kroc vis. prof. rheumatology UCLA, 1989; Plenary lectr. Sandoz Symposium on Human Retroviruses, 1990; keynote address Calif. Acad. Scis., 1994; pres. Academic Alliance Found. Assoc. editor: Jour. of Acquired Immune Deficiency Syndromes, mem. editl. bd.: Cytokine, Growth Factors, 1987, Blood, others, 1987, assoc. editor: Jour. of Immunology, 1984—88; contbr. several articles to profl. jours. Recipient rsch. grants in field, Washington Acad. of Scis. Award in Biol. Scis., 1984; named one of 100 Most Cited Scientists, Inst. for Sci. Info., 1981—88. Fellow: AAAS, Am. Rheumatism Assn. (Young Investigator award 1988); mem.: ACP, Inst. Medicine, Assn. Am. Physicians, Calif. Acad. Medicine, Am. Soc. for Clin. Investigation (v.p. 1993—94), Am. Assn. Immunologists, Am. Fedn. for Clin. Rsch. (Outstanding Investigator award 1987), Alpha Omega Alpha, Sigma Xi. Achievements include research in basic scientific studies aimed at further understanding how HIV grows and interacts with its cellular host; biology of NF-kB, an inducible eukaryotic transcription factor that is capable of activating HIV replication. Office: Gladstone Inst Virology and Immunology 1650 Owens St San Francisco CA 94158-2261 Office Phone: 415-734-4805. Office Fax: 415-355-0153. E-mail: wgreene@gladstone.ucsf.edu.

GREENE, WAYNE KENNETH, science educator, researcher; b. Perth, Australia, Nov. 29, 1965; s. Kenneth and Elizabeth Greene; m. Izabella Pawlowski, May 6, 1989; children: Elysia, Brendan. PhD, U. Western Australia, Perth, 1987—91. Sr. lectr. Murdoch U., Perth, 1998—. C.J. Martin fellowship, Nat. Health and Med. Rsch. Coun., 1994—99. Achievements include research in human canine lymphoma leukemia. Office: Murdoch Univ South St 6150 Perth Australia Office Fax: 08 9310 4144. Business E-Mail: w.greene@murdoch.edu.au.

GREENFIELD, GEORGE B., radiologist; b. NYC, May 4, 1928; s. Jacob and Rose (Wolf) G.; m. Barbara Anne O'Driscoll, Mar. 3, 1956; children: Edward James, Sheelagh Anne. BA, NYU, 1949; MD, State U. Utrecht, Netherlands, 1956. Diplomate: Am. Bd. Radiology, Am. Bd. Nuclear Medicine. Intern Bridgeport (Conn.) Hosp., 1956-57; resident radiology Presbyn.-St. Lukes Hosp., Chgo., 1957-60; practice medicine, specializing in radiology Chgo., 1960—; radiologist Cook County Hosp., 1961-66, asst. dir. diagnostic radiology, 1966-69; assoc. prof. radiology U. Ill., 1966-69; prof., chmn. dept. radiology Chgo. Med. Sch., 1969-74, Mt. Sinai Hosp. Med. Center, 1969-89; prof. diagnostic radiology Rush Med. Coll., 1975-87; pres. med. staff Mt. Sinai Hosp. Med. Center, 1983-85; prof. radiology Cook County

Grad. Sch. Medicine., Chgo. Med. Sch., 1987-89, vice chmn. dept. radiology, 1988-89; prof. radiology U. South Fla., Tampa, 1989—2003, prof. emeritus, 2004—. Attending radiologist H. Lee Moffitt Cancer Ctr. & Rsch. Inst., Tampa, 1989—2006. Author: Radiology of Bone Diseases, 5th edit., 1990; sr. author: A Manual of Radiographic Positioning, 1973, Computers in Radiology, 1985, Imaging of Bone Tumors, 1995 Imaging of Arthritis, 2001; contbr. articles to profl. jours. Trustee Mt. Sinai Hosp., 1986-89. Served with U.S. Army, 1951. Fellow Am. Coll. Radiology; mem. AMA, Chgo. Med. Soc., Chgo. Roentgen Soc., Am. Roentgen Ray Soc., Radiol. Soc. N.Am., Inst. Medicine Chgo., Internat. Skeletal Soc., Soc. Skeletal Radiology, Sigma Xi.

GREENFIELD, JOSEPH CHOLMONDELEY, JR., physician, educator; b. Atlanta, July 20, 1931; s. Joseph Cholmondeley and Agnes (Game) Greenfield; m. Mary Ruth Fordham, Aug. 13, 1955; children: Mary Agnes, Ruth Ann, Susan Lee. AB in History, Emory U., 1954, MD, 1956. Intern, resident in medicine Duke Med. Ctr., Durham, NC, 1956—59, mem. staff, 1962—2001, asst. prof. medicine, 1962—65, assoc. prof. medicine, 1965—70, prof. medicine, 1970—, dir. heart sta., 1972—2001, James B. Duke disting. prof., 1981—, chief cardiovasc. divsn., 1981—89, chmn. dept. medicine, 1983—95; staff., dir. heart sta. VA Med. Ctr., Durham, 1962—; clin. assoc. NIH, USPHS, 1959—62, mem. cardiovasc. and pulmonary study sect., 1974—78, chmn., 1975—78. Author: A Quail Hunter's Odyssey, 2004, 2009, Duke Cardiology Fellows Training Program, Origin to the Present, 2004, Bawna Babu, 2005, Duke Chief Medical Residents, 2005; contbr. 200 articles to profl. jours. Fellow: ACP, Am. Coll. Cardiology (disting. sci. award 1985); mem.: NRA (life), Inst. Medicine, Assn. Am. Physicians, Am. Physiol. Soc., Am. Soc. Clin. Investigation, SCV, Safari Club Internat., Kappa Alpha, Alpha Omega Alpha, Phi Beta Kappa. Methodist. Home: 1212 Virginia Ave Durham NC 27705-3264 Office: Duke U Med Ctr PO Box 3246 Durham NC 27715-3246 Office Phone: 919-286-6951. Business E-Mail: green045@mc.duke.edu.

GREENFIELD, LAZAR JOHN, surgeon, educator; b. Houston, Dec. 14, 1934; s. Robert G. and Betty B. (Greenfield) Heath; m. Sharon Dee Bishkin, Aug. 29, 1956; children: John, Julie, Jeff. Student, Rice U., 1951-54; MD, Baylor U., 1958. Diplomate Am. Bd. Surgery, Am. Bd. Thoracic Surgery, cert. gen. vascular surgery, 1991. Intern Johns Hopkins Hosp., Balt., 1958-59, resident, 1961-66; chief surgery VA Hosp., Oklahoma City, 1966-74; prof. dept. surgery U. Okla. Med. Center, 1971-74; Stuart McGuire prof., chmn. dept. surgery Med. Coll. Va., Richmond, 1974-87; F.A. Coller prof., chmn. dept of surgery U. Mich., 1987—2002; CEO U. Mich. Health System, 2002—03; interim exec. v.p. med. affairs U. Mich. Med. Sch., 2002—03; sabbatical FDA, 2003—04. Mem. surgery A study sect. NIH; dir. Am. Bd. Surgery, 1976-82, pres. elect. Am. Coll. Surgeons, 2010-. Author: Surgery in the Aged, 1975; editor-in-chief Surgery, Scientific Principles and Practice, 1993, 96, 3rd edit., 2001, Surgery News, 2004-; editor Complications in Surgery and Trauma, 1983, 2nd edit., 1990; contbr. to profl. publs. With USPHS, 1959—61. Recipient Disting. Alumni award Rice U., 1999, Jacobson Innovation award, 2010; Thomas R. Franklin scholar, 1952, John and Mary Markle scholar in med. sci., 1968-73. Mem. Inst. Medicine NAS, Am. Surg. Assn., Am. Assn. Thoracic Surgery, Assn. Acad. Surgery, Soc. U. Surgeons, Am. Coll. Surgeons, Johns Hopkins Soc. Scholars, Phi Delta Epsilon. Home: 7011 E Calle Arandas Tucson AZ 85750 Home Phone: 734-668-7571; Office Phone: 734-936-6398.

GREENFIELD, LINDA SUE, nursing educator; b. Dover, Del., Aug. 5, 1950; d. Norman Raymond and Eleanor Henrietta (Harmon) Connell; m. Douglas Herman Greenfield, Dec. 27, 1976; children: Leah, Paige. BSN, Cath. U., 1972; MSN cum laude, Boston U., 1977; postgrad., Coll. New Rochelle, 1986-88; PhD, Adelphi U., 1998. RN NY. Staff nurse emergency rm. and ICU Washington Hosp. Ctr., 1974-75; operating rm. nurse Mass. Eye & Ear, Boston, 1975; ICU nurse Peter Bent Brigham Hosp., Boston, 1975-76; surg. nurse practitioner Kingsbrook Jewish Hosp., Bklyn., 1976-79; nurse anesthetist student Metropolitan Hosp., 1979—81; cert. registered nurse anesthetist Brookdale Hosp., Bklyn., 1981-92, Winthrop U. Hosp., Mineola, N.Y., 1992-94; adj. prof. Adelphi U., Garden City, N.Y., 1995-99; adj. prof. nursing NY Inst. Tech., Old Westbury, 1998-99; clin. supr. Midtown Ctr. Complementary Care, NYC, 1999-2000; clin specialist St. Francis Hosp., Roslyn, N.Y., 2000-01; assoc. prof. nursing Adelphi U., 2001—07; assoc. prof. U. Vt., 2008—11, Columbia U., NY, 2011—. Contbr. articles to profl. jours. Bd. officer Manhasset Newcomers, N.Y., 1988-90; bd. dirs. Friends of Manhasset Libr., N.Y., 1990-94; mem. Make a Wish Found., N.Y., 1990—. Lt. U.S. Army, 1970-74. Recipient Disting. Faculty Excellence award, Adelphi U., 2005; nominee Teaching Excellence award, 2007, US Prof. of Yr. award, Carnegie Found. the Advancement Tchg., 2007. Mem.: ANA, Nat. Assn. U. Women, Nat. Assn. for Holistic Nurses, Nat. Assn. Homeopathy, Noetic Soc., Sch. Cmty. Assn., Am. Assn. Nurse Anesthetists, Sigma Theta Tau. Avocations: skiing, sailing, dance. Home: 2500 Johnson Ave Apt 17K Riverdale NY 10463 Personal E-mail: sue.greenfield@gmail.com.

GREENFIELD, RUSSELL HOWARD, physician, educator; b. Abington, Pa., Apr. 3, 1958; MD, Chgo. Med. Sch., 1984. Resident & fellow, emergency medicine Harbor-UCLA Med. Ctr., 1984—87, fellow, emergency medicine, 1987—88; fellow, integrative medicine U. Ariz. Coll. Medicine, vis. asst. prof.; emergency medicine resident program Carolinas Med. Ctr.; dir. emergency dept. Presbyterian Hosp. Matthews; asst. clinical prof. U. NC Chapel Hill Sch. Medicine; founding dir. Carolinas Integrative Health. Co-author: Healthy Child, Whole Child, 2001. Recipient Golden Apple award, Carolinas Med. Ctr. Mem.: Alpha Omega Alpha. Office: PO Box 245153 Tucson AZ 85724-5153 Office Phone: 520-626-6417. Office Fax: 520-626-3518.

GREENFIELD, SHELLY FAITH, psychiatrist, educator; MD, Harvard Coll., Cambridge, Mass., 1986; MPH, U. NC, 1992. Diplomate Am. Bd. Psychiatry and Neurology-psychiatry, Am. Bd. Psychiatry and Neurology-addiction psychiatry, lic. Mass., 1987. Intern psychiatry McLean Hosp., Belmont, Mass., 1987, resident psychiatry, 1990, assoc. clin. dir. alcohol and drug abuse treatment program, chief academic officer, dir. clin. and health svcs. rsch. and edn. in the alcohol and drug abuse program divsn. on alcohol and drug abuse, dir. outpatient substance abuse treatment program and consultation svcs.; fellow NC Meml. Hosp.; dir. med. sch. Harvard Coll., Cambridge, Mass., prof. psychiatry med. sch. Mem.: Am. Coll. of Psychiatrists, Am. Acad. of Addiction Psychiatry, Am. Psychiat. Assn. (mem. coun. on addiction psychiatry). Office: McLean Hospital 115 Mill St Belmont MA 02478 Office Phone: 617-855-2241. Office Fax: 617-855-2699. E-mail: sgreenfield@mclean.harvard.edu.

GREENGARD, PAUL, neuroscientist, educator; b. NYC, Dec. 11, 1925; married; 3 children. AB in Math. & Physics, Hamilton Coll., Clinton, NY, 1948; PhD in Biophysics, Johns Hopkins U., Balt., 1953. NSF fellow in neurochemistry Inst. Psychiatry, U. London, 1953—54; Nat. Found. Infantile Paralysis fellow Molteno Inst., Cambridge U., England, 1954—55; Paraplegia Found. fellow Nat. Inst. Med. Rsch., England, 1955—56; fellow Nat. Inst. Neurological Diseases & Blindness, NIH, Bethesda, Md., 1956—58, vis. scientist Nat. Heart Inst., 1958—59; dir. dept. biochemistry Geigy Rsch. Labs., Ardsley, NY, 1959—67; prof. pharmacology & psychiatry Yale U. Sch. Medicine, New Haven, 1968—83; Vincent Astor prof., head. Lab. Molecular & Cellular Neurosci. Rockefeller U., NYC, 1983—, dir. Fisher Ctr. for Alzheimer's Disease Rsch., 1995—. Vis. assoc. prof., prof. pharmacology Albert Einstein Coll. Medicine, NYC, 1961—70; vis. prof. Vanderbilt U., Nashville, 1967—68; Andrew D. White prof.-at-large Cornell U., Ithaca, NY, 1981—81; mem. bd. sci. governors Scripps Rsch. Inst., La Jolla, Calif. Co-founder Pearl Meister Greengard Prize ann. award for women scientists; bd. dirs. Michael Stern Parkinson's Rsch. Found. Recipient Dickson Prize & Medal in Medicine, U. Pitts., 1977, Ciba-Geigy Drew award, 1979, Award in Biology & Medical Sciences, NY Acad. Sciences, 1980, 3M Life Scis. award, Fedn. Am. Societies Exptl. Biology, 1987, Bristol-Myers award for Disting. Achievement in Neuroscience Rsch., 1989, Goodman & Gilman award in receptor pharmacology, 1992, Karl Spencer Lashley prize, American Philos. Soc., 1993, Biochem. Soc. Thudichum medal, 1996, Award for Pioneering Achievements in Health, Charles A. Dana Found., 1997, Mayor's award for Excellence in Sci. & Tech., NYC, 1998, Award for Medical Rsch., Met. Life Found., 1998, Sr. Scholar award, Ellison Med. Found., 1999, Nobel Prize in Physiology/Medicine, The Nobel Found., 2000. Mem.: NAS, Nat. Alliance Rsch. Schizophrenia & Depression (Lieber prize 1996), Soc. Neurosci. (Gerard prize 1994), AAAS, American Neurol. Assn. (hon.). Office: Rockefeller U Lab Molecular & Cellular Neuroscience 1230 York Ave New York NY 10021-6399 Business E-Mail: Paul.Greengard@rockefeller.edu. *

GREENGART, ALVIN, cardiologist; Attended, Mt. Sinai Scg. Medicine, 1974. Diplomate Am. Bd. Internal Medicine, Am. Bd. Cardiology-cardiovascular disease. Resident in internal medicine Brookdale Med. Ctr., Bklyn., 1975—77, fellow in cardiovascular disease, 1977—79; dir. non-invasive cardiology Maimonides Med. Ctr. Author: (jours.) A new electrocardiographic criteria for the indentification of the culprit vessel in inferior wall myocardial infarction, The relationship between anterior ST depression and coronary collateral in patients with inferior myocardial infarction. Fellow: Am. Coll. Cardiology; mem.: Am. Soc. Echocardiography, NY Heart Assn., Am. Heart Assn. Office: Maimonides Medical Center 4802 10th Ave Brooklyn NY 11219 Office Phone: 718-283-6473. Office Fax: 718-871-4780.

GREENLEAF, JOHN EDWARD, human research consultant; b. Joliet, Ill., Sept. 18, 1932; s. John Simon and Julia Clara (Flint) G.; m. Carol Lou Johnson, Aug. 28, 1960. MA, N.Mex. Highlands U., 1956; BA in Phys. Edn., U. Ill., 1955, MS, 1962, PhD in Physiology, 1963. Tchg. asst. N.Mex. Highlands U., Las Vegas, 1955-56; engring. draftsman Allis-Chalmers Mfg. Co., Springfield, Ill., 1956-57; tchg. asst. in phys. edn. U. Ill., Urbana, 1957-58, rsch. asst. in phys. edn., 1958-59, tchg. asst. in human anatomy and physiology, 1959-62; summer fellow NSF, 1962; pre-doctoral fellow NIH, 1962-63; rsch. physiologist Life Scis. Directorate, NASA, Ames Rsch. Ctr., Moffett Field, Calif., 1963—66; rsch. physiologist Space Scis. directorate NASA/Ames Rsch. Ctr., Moffett Field, Calif., 1967—2002; postdoctoral fellowship Karolinska Inst., Stockholm, 1966-67. Adj. prof. biology dept. San Francisco State U., 1988-2002; adj. prof. dept. exercise sci. U. Calif., Davis, 1996-01; adj. prof. dept. human performance San Jose State U., 2002—; Japan Soc. for Promotion of Sci. vis. prof. Kyoto Prefectural U. Medicine, 1997; mem. internat. adv. bd. Medicina Sportiva. Author: Springfield High School Hall of Fame, Biographies of Awardees, 1968-2008, 2010; mem. editorial bd. Jour. Applied Physiology, 1989-99, Med. Sci. Sports Exercise, 2000-02; contbr. articles to profl. jours. Pub. dir. N.Mex. Highlands U. Found., 1999—2006, life mem. Bronze Cir.Coll. Liberal Arts & Scis., U. Ill., Urbana Campaign. Served with U.S. Army, 1952-53. Recipient Disting. Alumni award N.Mex. Highlands U., 1990, Disting. Alumni award dept. molecular and integrative physiology U. Ill., 1998, Am. Coll. Sports Medicine Citation award, 1999, Water and Medicine prize Internat. Cannes and Nestle Water Inst., 2003; exch. fellow NAS, 1973-74, 77, 89, NIH, 1980; named to Springfield HS Hall of Fame, Ill., 2005. Fellow AIAA (assoc.), Am. Coll. Sports Medicine (trustee 1984-87), Aerospace Med. Assn. (Harold Ellingson award 1981-82, Eric Liljencrantz award 1990), NASA Ames Assn. (assoc.); mem. Am. Physiol. Soc. (mem. com. on coms. 1984-87, long range planning com. 1987-90, internat. physiol. com. 1997-00, environ. and exercise physiology sect. Honor award, 2004, Living History Project award), Polish Soc. Sports Medicine (hon.), Nat. Rifle Assoc.(endowment mem.), Shooting Sports Rsch. Coun. (internat. shooters devel. fund 1984), Sigma Xi. Achievements include patents in field. Home: 12391 Farr Ranch Ct Saratoga CA 95070-6527 Office Phone: 408-867-5680.

GREENLEE, KATHY JO, federal agency administrator; b. 1960; BA in Bus. Adminstrn. and Bus. Law, U. Kans. Gen. counsel Dept. Ins., State of Kans., Topeka, 1999—2002, asst. sec. for aging, 2002—04, long-term care ombudsman, 2004—06, sec. for aging, 2006—09; asst. sec. for aging US Dept. Health & Human Services, Washington, 2009—. Adminstr. Cmty. Living Assistance Supports & Services (CLASS), 2011—; bd. dirs. Nat. Assn. State Units on Aging, Kans. Health Policy Authority, KansasWorks; former chief of staff, chief ops. to Gov. Kathleen Sebelius, Topeka. Office: USHHS 200 Independence Ave SW Washington DC 20201 Office Phone: 202-401-4634. E-mail: Kathy.Greenlee@aoa.hhs.gov. *

GREENOUGH, WILLIAM BATES, III, medical educator; b. Providence, Jan. 3, 1932; s. William Bates Jr. and Dorothy Garrison (Rand) G.; m. Jane Cheney Woodruff, Aug. 14, 1954 (dec. 1964); children: William Beckley, Kate, Thomas Clark, Elisabeth Bates; m. Quaneta Ahmed, 1965; 1 child, Zarin Farah Naz. BA magna cum laude, Amherst Coll., 1953; MD cum laude, Harvard U., 1957. Intern, asst. resident Columbia U. Coll. Physicians and Surgeons, NYC, 1957-59; sr. rsch. fellow Mary Imogene Bassett Hosp., Cooperstown, NY, 1959-61; sr. resident Peter Bent Brigham Hosp., Boston, 1961-62; staff assoc. Nat. Heart Inst. Cholera Rsch. Lab., Dhaka, Bangladesh, 1962-65; chief infectious diseases div. Johns Hopkins U. Sch. Medicine, Balt., 1970-76, dir. Robert Wood Johnson Clin. Scholars Program, 1974-77, prof. medicine, 1983—, prof. internat. health sch. pub. health, 1985—; dir. Internat. Ctr. for Diarrhoeal Disease Rsch., Dhaka, Bangladesh, 1979-85; mem. geriatric medicine div. Johns Hopkins U., 1985—. Mem. bacteriology and mycology study sect. NIH, 1972-76, chmn., 1974-76; ad hoc study group on enteric disease Walter Reed Army Inst. Rsch., 1975-77; pres. Bangladesh Info. Ctr., Washington, 1971-84; adv. coun. Bangladesh Found., Chgo., 1972; active Md. Gov.'s Commn. on Phys. Fitness and Marathon Commn., 1971-77; pres., chmn. bd., trustee Internat. Child Health Found., Columbia, Md., 1985-95, pres., 1998—2000; chmn. Internat. Ctr. for Diarrheal Disease Rsch., Bangladesh Endowment Fund, 1997—; cons. Cera Products Inc., 1993—, chmn. sci. adv. bd., 2002—; cons. in field, spkr. in field. Editor Infection and Immunity, 1975-78, Topics in Infectious Disease, 1976—, Jour. Diarrhoeal Disease Rsch., 1983-85, Jour. Health & Population Rsch., 93-2000; internat. adv. Kuwait Med. Jour., Jour. Health Population and Nutrition, 2000-; contbr. articles to profl. jours., chpts. to books Sr. surgeon USPHS, 1962-67. Recipient Internat. prize in medicine, King Faisal Found., 1984, Hajj, 1989, Maurice Pate prize UNICEF, 1984, recognized for svc. to children, 1983; Howard Florey Meml. lectr. Haji, 1989, U. Adelaide, 2001, Paul G. Rogers Soc. Ambassador Global Health Rsch., 2006; Outstanding svc. Award, Bangladesh American Found. Inc., 2007. Fellow: ACP, AAAS, Infectious Diseases Soc. Am. (mem. internat. affairs com. 2000—03); mem.: Bangladesh Med. Soc., Am. Soc. Microbiology, Bangladesh Assn. for Advancement Scis., Am. Geriatric Soc., Am. Soc. for Clin. Investigation, Assn. Am. Physicians. Muslim. Achievements include patents in field. Home: 1300 Hollins Ln Baltimore MD 21209-2237 Office: Johns Hopkins Geriatrics Ctr 5505 Hopkins Bayview Cir Baltimore MD 21224-6822 Office Phone: 410-550-0782, 410-550-0785. Personal E-mail: wgreenou@hotmail.com. Business E-Mail: wgreeno2@jhmi.edu.

GREENOUGH, WILLIAM TALLANT, psychobiologist, educator; b. Seattle, Oct. 11, 1944; s. Harrison and Maryon C. (Whitten) G.; 1 dau., Jennifer Anne. BA, U. Oreg., 1964; MA, UCLA, 1966, PhD, 1969. Instr. U. Ill., Urbana-Champaign, 1968-69, asst. prof., 1969-73, assoc. prof., 1973-77, chair neural and behavioral biology program, 1977-87, prof. psychology, psychiatry, cell and devel. biology, 1978—, dir. neurosci. program, 1999—2001, dir. Ctr. Advanced Study, 2000—09; assoc. dir. Beckman Inst. for Advanced Sci. and Tech., 1987-91; prof. U. Ill. Ctr. Advanced Study, 1997—, Swanlund prof. psychology, psychiatry, cell and devel. biology, bioengineering, 1998—. Vis. prof. psychobiology U. Calif., Irvine, 1972; vis. prof. psychology U. Wash., 1975-76; program chmn. Winter Conf. on Brain Rsch., 1984-85, conf. chair, 1994-95; panel mem. integrative neural sys. NSF, 1987-91; dir. NSF Ctr. of Neurobiology of Learning and Memory, 1989-94; v.p., exec. com. Forum on Rsch. Mgmt., Fed. Behavioral, Psychol. and Cognitive Sci., 1991-93; mem. sci. adv. bd. Am. Psychol. Assn. Sci. Directorate; mem. NSF Biol. Sci. Directorate Adv. Com. Editor: (with R.N. Walsh) Environments as Therapy for Brain Dysfunction, 1976, (with J.M. Juraska) Developmental Neuropsychobiology, 1987; co-editor jour. Neurobiol. Learning and Memory, 1984-2004; contbr. numerous articles to profl. jour. Recipient William Rosen award for rsch. Nat. Fragile X Found., 1998, Mathew J. Wayner- NNOXE Pharms. award, 2006, FRAXA Res. Fdn. Dedication award, 2008; Cattell Found. fellow, 1975-76; USPHS and NSF grantee, 1969—; U. Ill. sr. scholar, 1985-88. Fellow AAAS (chair sect. I, Psychology 2001-02), Soc. for Rsch. into Child Devel. (disting. Sci. Contbn. award 2003, APA (Disting. Sci. Contbn. award 1999), Am. Psychol. Soc. (William James Fellow award 1998), Soc. Exptl. Psychology, Am. Acad. Arts & Sciences; mem. NAS, Soc. Neurosci. (councilor 1990-94, treas. 2003-05), Soc. Devel. Neurosci., Soc. Devel. Psychobiology (bd. dirs. 1977-80), Sigma Xi. Achievements include rsch. interests in morphological plasticity of cerebellum, experience and learning-based synapse formation, molecular mechanisms of mental retardation, and plasticity of glial cells. Office: U Ill Beckman Inst 405 N Mathews Ave Urbana IL 61801-2325 Office Phone: 217-333-4472. E-mail: wgreenou@illinois.edu.

GREENSPAN, DEBORAH, dental educator; BDS, U. London, 1960, BDS, 1964; LDS, Royal Coll. Surgeons, Eng., 1964; ScD (hon.), Georgetown U., 1990; DSc, U. London, 1991; DDS, U. Sheffield, Eng., 2008; DSc, Kings Coll., London, 2007. Registered dental practioner, U.K.; diplomate Am. Bd. Oral Medicine. Vis. lectr. oral medicine U. Calif., San Francisco, 1976-83, asst. clin. prof., 1983-85, assoc. clin. prof., 1985-89, clin. prof., 1989-96, prof. clin. oral medicine, 1996—, interim chair dept. orofacial scis. Sch. Dentistry, 2004—05, interim chair dept. orofacial scis., 2004—07, chair orofacial scis., 2007—. Lectr. in oral biology, U. Calif., San Francisco, 1972, clin. dir. Oral AIDS Ctr., 1987—, active Sch. Dentistry coms. including admissions com., 1985—, chair task force on infection control, 1987—; cons. Joint FDI/WHO Working Group on AIDS, 1989—, EEC, 1990, WHO, 1990, 91, Dept. Health State Calif., 1991, others; ad hoc reviews Epidemiology and Disease Control Sect. Div. Rsch. Grants NIH, 1987—, Rsch. Am. Global Ambassador; mem. programs adv. com. Nat. Inst. Dental Rsch., 1989—, mem. spl. ad hoc tech. rev. panel, 1991, mem. panel Fed. Drug Adminstrn., 1991-94; other svc. to govtl. agys.; participant numerous sci. and profl. workshops, meetings, and continuing edn. courses, numerous radio, TV, and press interviews concerning AIDS and infection control in dentistry. Author: (with J.S. Greenspan, Pindborg, and Schiødt), AIDS and the Dental Team, 1986 (transl. German, French, Italian, Spanish, Japanese), AIDS and the Mouth, 1990, (with others) San Francisco General Hospital AIDS Knowledge Base, 1986, Dermatologic Clinics, 5th edit., 1987, Infectious Disease Clinics of North America, 2nd. edit., 1988, Oral Manifestations of AIDS, 1988, Contemporary Periodontics, 1989, Opportunistic Infections in AIDS Patients, 1990, AIDS Clinical Review, 1990, Oral Manifestations of Systemic Disease, 1990, others; mem. editl. bd. rev. Jour. Am. Coll. Dentists, 1991; mem. editl. bd. Oral Diseases, 1999; ad hoc referee Jour. Oral Pathology, 1983—, Cancer, 1985—, Jour. Acad. Gen. Dentistry, 1986—, European Jour. Cancer & Clin. Oncology, 1986, Archives of Dermatology, 1988—, Jour. AMA, 1988—, AIDS, 1991; contbr. numerous articles to profl. jours. Mem. dental subcom. of profl. edn. com. Calif. div. Am. Cancer Soc., 1982-90, profl. health care providers task force, 1991. Nat. Cancer Inst. fellow, 1978-79, Am. Coll. Dentists fellow, 1988; recipient Woman of Distinction award, London, 1986, Commendation cert. Asst. Sec. for Health, 1989; named Seymour J. Kreshover lectr. Nat. Inst. Dental Rsch., 1989, Hon. Lectr. United Med. and Dental Schs. of Guys and St. Thomas

Hosps., U. London, 1991. Fellow AAAS, Royal Soc. Medicine, Royal Coll. Surgeons; mem. ADA (vis. lectr. speaker's bur. 1988—, cons. coun. on dental therapeutics 1988—, mem. coun. sci. affairs 1999—), Am. Assn. Dental Rsch. (session chair 1986-87, constitution com. 1988-91, chair 1990-91, pres. San Francisco sect. 1990—, treas. 1992—), Am. Acad. Oral Pathology, Am. Soc. Microbiology, Am. Assn. Women Dentists, Am. Acad. Oral Medicine, Am. Assn. Dental Schs., Internat. Assn. Dental Rsch. (pres. exptl. pathology group 1989-90, v.p. 2004-05, other coms. and offices), Internat. Assn. Oral Pathologists, Internat. Assn. for Dental Rsch. (v.p. 2005—), Internat. Dental Assn. for Dental Rsch. (pres., 2007-08), Calif. Dental Assn., San Francisco Dental Soc., Internat. AIDS Soc., Inst. of Medicine. Achievements include rsch. on oral candidiasis in HIV infection, on HIV-associated salivary gland disease, on oral hairy leukoplakia, and on the prevalence of HIV-associated gingivitis and periodontitis in HIV-infected patients. Office: U Calif Sch Dentistry Dept Orofacial Scis S 612 513 Parnassus Ave Box 0422 San Francisco CA 94143-0422

GREENSPAN, FRANCIS S., retired physician; b. Perth Amboy, NJ, Mar. 16, 1920; s. Philip and Francis (Davidson) G.; m. Bonnie Jean Fisher, Oct. 25, 1945; children: Richard L., Robert H., Susan L. BA, Cornell U., 1940, MD, 1943. Diplomate Am. Bd. Internal Medicine. Mem. endocrinology staff U. Calif.-San Francisco; chief endocrinology Stanford (Calif.) Hosp., 1949-59; chief thyroid clinic U. Calif. Med. Ctr., San Francisco, 1959—2011, now clin. prof. medicine and radiology; practice medicine specializing in endocrinology San Francisco; chief of staff U. Calif. Hosps. and Clinics, San Francisco, 1976-78. Editor: Textbook of Endocrinology; contbr. articles to med. jours. Served with USNR, 1944-45. Mem. San Francisco Med. Soc., Calif. Med. Assn., AMA, Endocrine Soc., Am. Thyroid Assn., Western Soc. Clin. Rsch., Western Assn. Physicians, Calif. Acad. Medicine. Home: 2431 Mariner Square Dr #306 Alameda CA 94501 Home Phone: 415-751-7570; Office Phone: 415-353-2350. E-mail: frankg@medicine.ucsf.edu.

GREENSPAN, LOUISE CATHERINE, pediatrician; b. London, Apr. 19, 1969; 2 children. BA, Univ. Calif., Berkeley; MD, Cornell Univ., 1995. Cert. Am. Bd. Pediatrics, 1998, in pediatric endocrinology Am. Bd. Pediatrics, 2001. Resident in pediatrics Univ. Calif., San Francisco, 1995—98, fellow in pediatric endocrinology, 1998—2001; pediatric endocrinologist Permanente Med. Group, San Francisco, 1998—; asst. clin. prof. Univ. Calif., San Francisco, 2001. Mem.: Am. Acad. Pediatrics, Am. Diabetes Assn., Endocrine Soc., Lawson Wilkens Pediatric Endocrinology Soc. Office: Permanente Med Group 8th Fl N 2200 O'Farrell St San Francisco CA 94115 Office Phone: 415-833-4625.

GREENSPAN, VALEDA CLAREEN, nursing educator, consultant; b. Ellsworth, Kans., Sept. 10, 1940; d. Theodore Frederick and Clara Lydia (Weinhardt) Steinle; m. Edward Phil Fabricius, June 10, 1962 (div. 1973); children: Craig Philip, Sheri Kay; m. Barney Greenspan, June 7, 1999. BS, Ft. Hays State U., 1962; M Nursing, Ind. U., 1966; cert. in gerontology, North Tex. State U., 1980, PhD, 1982. Instr. Bartholomew County Hosp., Columbus, Ind., 1971-72; asst. prof. Ft. Hays State U., Hays, Kans., 1973-74, Tex. Woman's U., Denton, 1974-80, Minot (N.D.) State U., 1980-82, dean, 1982—99; mem. clin. faculty George Mason U., Fairfax, Va., 2003; curriculum cons. Boise (Idaho) State U., 2004— Cons., expert witness Zuger & Bucklin, Bismarck, N.D., 1982-83; mem. N.D. adv. bd. No. States Power Co., 1989-92; treas. health bd. 1st Dist., 1994-97. Matthews fellow North Tex. State U., 1979; grantee Bush Found., 1983-84; recipient Excellence in Writing award Am. Jour Nursing, 1987. Mem. ANA (del. 1986-87), Nat. League Nurses (bd. rev. 1992-95, baccalaureate higher degree programs site visitor 1983-1998), Nat. Gerontol Assn., N.D. Nurses Assn. (treas. dist. 2 1982-84, nominating com. 1984-85, 93-94, v.p. 1989-92, Phi Delta Kappa, Sigma Theta Tau. Avocations: reading, sewing, cooking, crafts, hiking. Home: 2250 E Mozart Ct Meridian ID 83646-1124 Office Phone: 208-426-5398. Business E-Mail: valgreenspan@boisestate.edu.

GREENSTEIN, BRUCE D., public health service officer, state official; b. 1968; m. Cindy Greenstein; children: Kennedy, Kyla. MS in Healthcare Policy & Pub. Adminstrn., Fla. State U. Assoc. regional adminstr., dir. waivers & demonstrations US Dept. Health & Human Services (HHS); mng. dir. worldwide health Microsoft Corp.; v.p. CSNI; analyst GAO; sec. La. Dept. Health & Hospitals, Baton Rouge, 2010—. Office: Louisiana Department of Health and Hospitals 682 N 4th St Baton Rouge LA 70802 Office Phone: 225-342-9500. Office Fax: 225-342-5568. *

GREENSTEIN, JEFFREY IAN, neurologist; b. Durban, South Africa, July 27, 1947; s. Joseph and Miriam (Shamos) G. MD, U. Cape Town, S. Africa, 1971. Diplomate Am. Bd. Neurology and Psychiatry. Asst. to assoc. prof. neurology Temple U. Sch. Med., Phila., 1983-89, prof., 1989—2002, chmn. neurology, 1989—2000; pres. Multiple Sclerosis Inst., 2002—. Chmn. dept. neurology Grad. Hosp., 2002—06; clin. prof. of neurology Drexel U. Sch. Medicine. Pres. Multiple Sclerosis Rsch. Inst., 2004—. Mem. AAAS, Am. Acad. Neurology, N.Y. Acad. Sci., Nat. Multiple Sclerosis Soc. (chmn. profl. adv. com. Phila. 1992-95, bd. of trustees, Del. Valley Chpt. 1996-2004). Office: 1341 N Delware Ave #212 Philadelphia PA 19125 Office Phone: 215-985-2245, 267-597-3830.

GREENSTEIN, STUART MARK, surgical educator; b. Bklyn., Feb. 16, 1955; s. Saul and Anne (Stillman) G.; m. Gayle Suzette Shulman (div. Jan. 1987); 1 child, Samuel; m. Sylvia Redner, July 2, 1989; children: Brian Liedman, Leah Chaya Ruth, Talia Miriam Rachel. BS, CUNY, 1976; MD, Harvard U., 1979. Diplomate Am. Bd. Surgeryy. Intern, instr. surgery NYU Med. Ctr., NYC, 1979-80; resident in surgery, clin. instr. U. Med. and Dentistry N.J., Newark, 1980-84; instr. vascular surgery Hosp. of U. Pa., Phila., 1984-85; clin. asst. instr. SUNY Downstate Med. Ctr., Bklyn., 1985-86; asst. prof. surgery Hahnemann U., Phila., 1986-88, Albert Einstein Coll. Medicine, Yeshiva U., Bronx, N.Y., 1988-93, assoc. prof. surgery, 1993—2002, prof. surgery, 2002—. Mem. staff Montefiore Med. Ctr., Bronx, 1988—. Contbr. articles to med. jours. Salk scholar CUNY, 1975. Fellow ACS (1st prize N.J. chpt. 1982, 2d prize 1983); mem. AAAS, Am. Soc. Transplant Surgeons, Transplantation Soc., N.Y. Acad. Scis. Democrat. Achievements include construction of a competent phonatory neoepiglottis using cervical skin flaps. Office: Montefiore Headache Center 1575 Blondell Ave Ste 225 Bronx NY 10461-2662 Office Phone: 718-920-8146. *

GREENSTREET, YVONNE, pharmaceutical executive; b. UK; MD in medicine, U. Leeds, UK; MBA, INSEAD, Fontainbleau, France. Med. student St. Thomas, St. Mary's Univ. Coll. and St. Bartholomew Hospitals, London; obstetrics and gynecology practitioner UK Nat. Health Svc.; joined GlaxoSmithKline, 1992, v.p., med. dir. UK pharm. bus., v.p., head European clin. devel. and med. affairs, chief med. officer Europe, sr. v.p., head of Musculoskeletal, Inflammation Gastrointestinal & Urogenital Medicine Devel. Ctr., sr. v.p., chief strategy., rsch. & devel., 2008—11; sr. v.p., head medicines devel. for specialty care bus. unit Pfizer, Inc., 2011—. Former mem. adv. com. topic selection NICE, UK; former mem. global product mgmt. bd. and rsch. & devel. exec. com. GlaxoSmithKline; bd. dirs. Molecular Insights Pharmaceuticals, Cambridge, Mass., 2008—. Former mem. Assn. of Brit. Pharm. Industry Med. Com., Prescription Medicines Code of Practice Authority Appeal Bd., UK. Office: Pfizer Inc 500 Arcola Rd Collegeville PA 19426-3982 *

GREENWALD, ALFRED EMANUEL, retired cosmetic surgeon; b. New Brunswick, NJ, Feb. 25, 1920; s. Louis and Ethel (Weiss) G.; m. Leatrice Joy Fleishman, June 15, 1947 (div. June 1995); children: Melvin Alan, Bryna Jane Pomp. Student, George Washington U., 1938-40; BA, NYU, 1942, MS in Chemistry, 1943; MD, N.Y. Med. Coll., 1947, postgrad. in Surgery, 1951. Diplomate Am. Bd. Surgery, Am. Bd. Cosmetic Surgery, Nat. Bd. Med. Examiners. Rotating intern Newark Beth Israel Hosp., NJ, 1947-48; surg. intern Flower and Fifth Avenue Hosps., NYC, 1948-49; resident, surgery Hackensack (N.J.) Hosp., 1949—50, Dept. Grad. Surgery, NY Med. Coll., 1950—51; resident in surgery Martland Med. Ctr.-Univ. Hosp., Newark, 1951-54; gen. practice medicine Hackensack, 1950-51; pvt. practice surgery, Paramus, N.J., 1954; pvt. gen. surgery practice New Brunswick, 1957—74; cosmetic surgery, 1974—92; ret., 1992. Examining physician 1 N.Y. State Workers' Compensation Bd., Bklyn., 1994-95; emeritus staff mem. Middlesex Same Day Surg. Ctr., Robert Wood Johnson Univ. Hosp., St. Peter's Univ. Hosp., Meml. Med. Ctr. South Amboy, N.J., Surgicare Ctrl. Jersey. Author: The Aging Face, 1985; contbr. articles to med. jours. Capt. M.C., U.S. Army, 1955-57, with Hosp. Ft. Bennigs, Ga. Mem. AMA, Am. Assn. Cosmetic Surgeons, Am. Soc. Cosmetic Surgeons, Am. Acad. Cosmetic Surgery, Pan Am. Med. Assn., Internat. Coll. Surgeons, Internat. Soc. Cosmetic, Plastic and Reconstructive Surgery, Internat. Acad. Cosmetic Surgery, French Soc. Esthetic Surgery, Med. Soc. N.J., N.J. Soc. Cosmetic Surgery, Phila. Soc. Facial Plastic Surgeons, Middlesex County Med. Soc., Am. Physicians Fellowship for Israel Med. Assn., Med. Amateur Radio Coun. (founder 1965, treas. 1986-00, conf. chmn. 1984), Amateur Astronomers, Inc., Princeton Personal Computer Users Group, Astronomers, Inc. Jewish. Achievements include pioneer work on malar augmentation for high cheek bones and the lip lift cheilopexy for cheiloptosis. Home: Ten Llewellyn Pl New Brunswick NJ 08901-3027 Home Phone: 732-247-5578. Personal E-mail: alfredgr@aol.com.

GREENWALD, BLAINE, geriatrician, psychiatrist, educator; MD, NY Med. Coll., 1978. Diplomate Am. Bd. Psychiatry and Neurology, 1983, Am. Bd. Psychiatry and Neurology-geriatric psychiatry, 2000. Resident psychiatry Mt. Sinai Hosp., 1979—82, fellow geriatric psychiatry, Bronx VA Hosp., 1982—83; hosp. affiliation includes The Zucker Hillside Hosp.; assoc. prof. psychiatry Albert Einstein Coll. of Medicine. Office: North Shore University Hospital 300 Community Dr Manhasset NY 11030-3816 Office Phone: 516-562-0100.

GREENWALD, BRUCE MICHAEL, pediatrician; b. Bklyn., Feb. 5, 1955; BS, Univ. Mich., 1977; MD, NYU Sch. Med., 1982. Cert. Am. Bd. Pediatrics, 1987, pediatric critical care med. Am. Bd. Pediatrics, 1990. Resident in pediatrics NYU Med. Ctr. & Bellevue Hosp. Ctr., NYC, 1982—85, chief resident in pediatrics, 1985—86; fellow in pediatric critical care med. NY Hosp. Cornell Med. Ctr., NYC, 1986—88; chief divsn. pediatric critical care med. NY Presbyterian Hosp. Weill Cornell Med. Ctr., NYC, 1999—; prof., exec. vice chmn. Dept. Pediatrics Weill Cornell Med. Coll., NYC; attending pediatrician Meml. Hosp. Sloan Kettering Cancer Ctr. Mem.: Soc. Critical Care Med. (mem. exec. com. pediatrics sect.), NY Soc. Pediatric Critical Care (pres. 1993—95). Office: NY Presbyterian Hosp Weill Cornell Med Ctr 525 E 68th St New York NY 10065 Office Phone: 212-746-3056. Office Fax: 212-746-8332.

GREENWALD, PETER, federal agency administrator, cancer prevention physician, epidemiologist, researcher; b. Newburgh, NY, Nov. 7, 1936; s. Louis and Pearl (Reingold) Greenwald; m. Harriet Reif, Sept. 6, 1968; children: Rebecca, Laura, Daniel. BA, Colgate U., 1957; MD, SUNY Coll. Medicine, 1961; MPH, Harvard U., 1967, DrPH, 1974. Intern LA County Hosp., 1961-62; resident in internal medicine Boston City Hosp., 1964-66; asst. in medicine Peter Bent Brigham Hosp., 1967-68; mem. epidemiology and disease control study sect. NIH, 1974-78; mem. NY State Gov.'s Breast Task Force, 1976-78; dir. NY State Dept. Health, Albany, 1968-76; dir. epidemiology N.Y. State Dept. Health, Albany, 1976-81; prof. medicine Albany Med. Coll., 1976-81; attending physician Albany Med. Ctr. Hosp., 1968-81; adj. prof. biomed. engring. Rensselaer Poly. Inst., Troy, NY, 1976-81; assoc. scientist Sloan-Kettering Inst. for Cancer Research, NYC, 1977-81; dir. divsn. cancer prevention Nat. Cancer Inst., NIH, Bethesda, Md., 1981—97, 1998—. Mem. VA Merit Rev. Bd. Med. Oncology, Washington, 1972-74 Editor-in-chief Jour. Nat. Cancer Inst., NIH, 1981-87; contbr. articles to profl. jours. Rear adm. USPHS, 1962-64, 81—. Recipient Disting. Svc. award NY State Dept. Health, 1975; Redway medal and award for med. writing NY State Jour. Medicine, 1977, NY State Gov.'s Citationfor pub. health achievement, 1981, PHS commendation 1983, 88, Disting. Svc. medal, 1993, Disting. Svc. award, Am. Cancer Soc., 1997, Outstanding Rsch. award Am. Inst. Cancer Rsch., 1997, Pub. Svc. award Cancer Treatment and Rsch. Found., 1997; named to SUNY Honor Roll of Disting. Grads., 1997. Fellow ACP, APHA (epidemiology sect. chmn. 1981), Am. Coll. Preventive Medicine, Am. Soc. Nutritional Scis.; mem. Am. Assn. Cancer Rsch. (DeWitt Goodman lectr. 1998), Am. Soc. Clin. Oncology, Am. Coll. Epidemiology (bd. dirs. 1981-82), Am. Soc. Preventive Oncology (Disting. Achievement award 1998), Internat. Epidemiology Soc., Nat. Acad. Scis. (food and nutrition bd. 1982-88), Am. Cancer Soc. (Cancer Prevention award 2002). Office: NIH/NCI Divsn Cancer Prevention EPN/2040 6130 Exec Blvd Bethesda MD 20892-7309 Home Phone: 301-652-8044; Office Phone: 301-496-6616. Business E-Mail: pg37g@nih.gov, greenwap@mail.nih.gov. *

GREENWALD, THERESA MCGOWAN, health services administrator, rehabilitation nurse; b. Scranton, Pa., Feb. 8, 1950; d. Robert Bell and Agnes (Butler) McGowan; m. David Jeffrey Greenwald, Oct. 26, 1996; 1 child, Jennifer Emilie Nicole Drescher. Diploma nursing, Hosp. U. Pa., 1970. RN, Ohio; cert. rehab. nurse, case mgr. Staff nurse, asst. head nurse Riddle Meml. Hosp., Media, Pa., 1971-80; rehab. nurse, mgr. Upjohn Rehab. Scvs., Phila. and Cin., 1980-85; cons., life care planner Occupl. Health Resources, Cin., 1985-87, Springfield, Va., 1987-88; dir. life care planning Rehab. Experts, Vienna, Va., 1988-89; program mgr., account exec. Comprehensive Rehab. Assocs., Cin., 1989-93; dir. managed care case mgmt. Sheakley Med. Mgmt. Sys., Cin., 1993-95; clin. program coord. Mayfield Clinic and Spine Inst., Cin., 1996—2005; sr. mgr. health svcs. Cin. Bell, 2005—08, health & productivity cons., 2008—09; dir. Nat. Bd. Certification Continuity of Care, 1998-99; mgr., disability mgmt., employee health Christ Hosp., 2009—10; wellness and absence mgmt. cons. McG Consulting, LLC, 2010—. Mem. cmty. adv. bd. Drake Ctr., Inc., 1998-2000. Mem. Nurse Case Mgrs. of S.W. Ohio (membership chair 1994-99), Case Mgmt. Resource Network (v.p., pres. elect, 2005). Office Phone: 513-910-9905. Personal E-mail: tmcg@nuvox.net.

GREENWAY, HUBERT T., dermatologist; MD, Med. Coll. Ga., 1974. Diplomate Am. Bd. Dermatology, 1982. Intern family medicine Med. Coll. of Ga. Hosp. and Clinics, 1975; resident dermatology Naval Med. Ctr., San Diego, 1979—82; fellow mohs surgery Univ. Wis. Med. Ctr., Madison, Wis., 1981; chmn. mohs and dermatologic surgery Scripps Clinic; hosp. affiliation include Scripps La Jolla Hosps. and Clinics. Office: Scripps Clinic Torrey Pines 10666 N Torrey Pines Rd MS 112A La Jolla CA 92037 Mailing: Scripps Clinic Rancho Bernardo 15004 Innovation Dr S97 San Diego CA 92128 Office Phone: 858-554-8646, 858-487-1800.

GREENWOOD, JANET KAE DALY, psychologist, academic administrator, marketing professional; b. Goldsboro, NC, Dec. 9, 1943; d. Fulton Benton and Kelminy Ethel Esther (Ball) Daly; 1 child, Gerald Thompson. AA, Peace Coll., 1963; BS in English and Psychology, East Carolina U., 1965, MEd in Counseling, 1967; postgrad., N.C. State U., 1967-69, U. London, 1969; PhD in Counseling and Higher Ednl. Adminstrn., Fla. State U., 1972. Tchr. English Kinston (N.C.) City Schs., 1965-66, Goldsboro City Schs., 1966-67; counselor and psychometrist primary and secondary schs. County of Wake, NC, 1967-69; coord. Am. Inst. for Fgn. Study, 1969; supr. student tours in Eng., France, Switzerland, Italy, and Capri, 1969; counselor Fla. State U., Tallahassee, 1969-72; asst. dir. counseling Rutgers U., New Brunswick, NJ, 1972-73, cons. to v.p. for student svcs., 1973-74, lectr. in counseling psychology, 1972-74; coord. and assoc. prof. counselor edn. U. Cin., 1974-77, adviser to grad. students, 1974-77, vice provost student affairs, 1977-81; pres. Longwood Coll., Farmville, Va., 1981-87, U. Bridgeport, Conn., 1987-92; cons., ptnr., dir. Heidrick & Struggles, Washington, 1992-2000; v.p. A.T. Kearney, Inc., 2000—04; owner, pres. Greenwood & Assocs., Inc., 2004—. Guidance cons. South Plainfield Pub. Schs., 1973-76; adviser Parents without Ptnrs., 1976; bd. dirs. Hydraulic Co.; mem. Gov.'s Partnership To Prevent Substance Abuse in the Workforce, mem. audit com. and cmty. and govt. rels. com. Contbr. articles to profl. jours. Mem. Gov.'s Ad Hoc Edn. Com. on Tchr. Edn. and Counselor Edn., State of Ohio, 1975; mem. state planning commn. Nat. Identification of Women Project; chair Twin Rivers Tenants Rights Assn., 1972-74; bd. dirs. Bridgeport Hosp., Bridgeport Bus. Coun.; mem. adv. com. Bridgeport Pub. Edn. Fund; bd. dirs. Conn. Ballet Theatre, chair South End steering com; mem. mgmt. adv. com. City of Bridgeport; mem. adv. com. United Way Tri-State; chair South End Partnership Com; mem. The Schiavone Steering Com./Downtown Bridgeport Project, YWCA Bd., Champion/United Way, United Way Community Human Svcs. Planning Coun., Bridgeport Symphony Bd., Bridgeport Opera Bd., Bridgeport Area Coll./Univ. Consortium, Conn. Conf. Ind. Colls., The Newcomen Soc. of U.S., The United Way Ea. Fairfield County; mem. adv. bd. Sacred Heart/St. Anthony Sch., Roosevelt Sch; mem. ct. com. Regional Plan Assn. Fairfield 2000; bd. dirs. Conn. Ballet Theatre; chair The Bridgeport Regional Bus. Coun. Brass Ring Task Force on Leadership; bd. govs. Fairfield County Study; mem. hon. bd. dirs. Conn. Earth Day 20, Inc.; chair L.I. Sound Western Regional Coun.; founding mem. L.I. Sound Assembly; mem. membership com., campus partnership subcom. Drugs Don't Work program, 1989-91. Recipient Spl. award Black Arts Festival, Meritorious Svc. award Am. Assn. State Colls. and Univs. Mem. AAUP, Am. Coll. Pers. Assn. (editor and chair media bd. 1975—), Am. Pers. and Guidance Assn., Cin. Pers. and Guidance Assn., Ohio Psychol. Assn., Cin. Psychol. Assn., Organizational Behavior Assn., Am. Sch. Counselors Assn., Ohio Sch. Counselors Assn., Assn. for Women Faculty, Ohio Counselor Edn. and Supervision Assn., Kappa Delta Pi.

GREENWOOD, JOHN EDWARD, surgeon, researcher; b. Oldham, Lancashire, Eng., June 15, 1963; s. Edward John and Barbara Ann Greenwood; m. Helen Mary Fanning, Aug. 2, 1986; children: Emma Catharine, Sam John. BSc in anatomy with honors, Victoria U., Manchester, Eng., 1986, MB, ChB, 1989, MD, 1996. Ho. officer Stepping Hill Hosp., Stockport, Cheshire, England, 1989—90; demonstrator in anatomy Victoria U., Manchester, 1990—91; sr. ho. officer in surgery South Manchester Surg. Rotation, 1991—94; surg. rsch. fellow U. Hosp. South Manchester, 1994—96; registrar in plastic surgery Manchester/Preston Plastic Surgery Rotation, Manchester & Preston, Lancashire, England, 1996—2001; dir. burns unit Royal Adelaide Hosp., South Australia, Australia, 2001—; assoc. prof. discipline surgery faculty health scis., Sch. Medicine U. Adelaide, 2009—; dir. Noroskin Pty Ltd., Adelaide, 2010, NovoWound Pty Ltd., Melbourne, 2010. Bd. dirs. Skin Pty. Ltd., Adelaide, 2005—; clin advisor PolyNovo Biomaterials Pty. Ltd., Melbourne. Contbr. articles to profl. jours., chapters to books. Founder Julian Burton Burns Trust, Adelaide, 2003; South Australian plan for mass burn casualties com. Dept. of Health, Adelaide, 2006. Recipient award, Order of Australia Assn., 2003, Inaugural Burke/Yannas Bioengineering award, 2011. Fellow: Royal Australasian Coll. Surgeons, Royal Coll. Surgeons Eng.; mem.: Am. Burn Assn., Lions Clubs Australia (hon., James D. Richardson honour award 2007). Achievements include design and development of burn and wound healing products employing the NovoSorb (novel biodegradeable polymer) platform. Avocations: guitar, music. Office: Burns Unit Royal Adelaide Hosp North Terr 5000 Adelaide SA Australia Office Fax: 0061 - 8 - 82225676. Business E-Mail: john.greenwood@health.sa.gov.au.

GREENWOOD, M.R.C., academic administrator, biologist, nutrition educator; b. Gainesville, Fla., Apr. 11, 1943; d. Stanley James and Mary Rita (Schmeltz) Cooke; m. (div. 1968); 1 child, James Robert. AB summa cum laude, Vassar Coll., 1968; PhD, Rockefeller U., 1973; LHD (hon.), Mt. St. Mary Coll., 1989. Rsch. assoc. Inst. of Human Nutrition, Columbia U., NYC, 1974-75, adj. asst. prof., 1975-76, asst. prof., 1976-78; assoc. prof. dept. biology Vassar Coll., Poughkeepsie, NY, 1978-81, prof. biology, 1981-86, dir. animal model, CORE Lab. of Obesity Rsch. Ctr., 1985-89, dir. undergrad. rsch. summer inst., 1986-88, dir. Howard Hughes biol. scis. network program, 1988, chmn. of biology dept., John Guy Vassar prof. natural scis., 1986-89; prof. nutrition and internal medicine, dean grad. studies U. Calif. Davis, 1989—96, prof. nutrition and internal medicine dept. nutrition, 2005—09, dir. Food Health Initiative, 2008—09; chancellor U. Calif. Santa Cruz, 1996—2004, prof. biology, 2005—; provost, sr. v.p. academic affairs U. Calif. Sys., 2004—05; pres. U. Hawaii Sys., 2009—. Mem. nutrition study sect. NIH, 1983-87; mem. NRC; assoc. dir. for sci. White House Office Sci. and Tech., 1993-95. Editor: Obesity, Vol. 4, 1983; contbr. over 250 articles and abstracts to profl. jours., 1974-89. Recipient Rsch. Career Devel. award NIH, 1978-83; Mellon scholar-in-residence St. Olaf Coll., Northfield, Minn., 1978; NY State Regents fellow, 1968. Mem. AAAS (pres. 1998-99), NRC (policy and global affairs divsn. chair 2004-), Inst. Medicine of Nat. Acad. Scis. (chair food and nutrition bd., diet and health subcom. 1986—), N.Am. Soc. Study of Obesity (pres. 1987-88), Am. Inst. Nutrition (BioServ 1982), Am. Physiol. Soc., The Harvey Soc., Am. Diabetes Assn., Am. Acad. Arts and Scis., Internat. Assn. Study of Obesity (treas. 1991—). Home: 5033 El Cemonte Ave Davis CA 95616 Office: U Hawaii Sys Bachman 204 2444 Dole St Honolulu HI 96822 Office Phone: 808-956-8207. Office Fax: 808-956-5286. E-mail: mrcgreenwood@hawaii.edu.

GREENWOOD, ROBERT SAMUEL, pediatric neurologist; b. Frederick, Okla., June 12, 1943; s. Gorman and Ruth (Dittmar) G.; m. Dana Sue Reno, Aug. 20, 1966; children: Holly, Brian. BS, U. Tex., 1965, MD, 1968. Cert. Am. Bd. Pediatrics, 1974, in child neurology Am. Bd. Neurology, 1979. Intern Children's Hosp., St. Louis, 1968—69, resident in pediatrics, 1969—70, resident in pediatric neurology, 1970—71, 1973—75; chief mil. pediatrician Andrew Rader Clinic, Washington, 1971-73; fellow pediatrics, asst. neurologist Washington U., St. Louis, 1975-77, rsch. instr., neurosurgery, 1977; asst. prof. neurology Univ. NC, Chapel Hill, 1977-83, assoc. prof. to prof. neurology, 1983—. Med. dir. Epilepsy and Anticonvulsant Drug Rsch. Lab., 1980-87. Author: Pediatric Neurology, 3rd. edit., 1983; contbr. articles to med. jours. Recipient Nat. Rsch. Svc. award Nat. Inst. Neurologic and Communicative Disorders and Stroke, 1975-77, co-investigator rsch. grantee, 1984-91; prin. investigator rsch. grantee NIDR, 1989—. Mem. AAAS, Am. Acad. Pediatrics (exec. com. computer and other techs. 1990—), N.C. Neurol. Soc. (v.p. 1990—), N.C. Epilepsy Assn. (profl. adv. bd. 1977—), N.Y. Acad. Scis., Child Neurology Soc., Soc. for Neurosciences. Office: Univ NC Dept Neurology Ste 751 101 Manning Dr Chapel Hill NC 27599 Office Phone: 919-966-8160. Office Fax: 919-966-2922.

GREER, DAVID STEVEN, dean, educator, physician; b. Bklyn., Oct. 12, 1925; s. Jacob and Mary (Zaslawsky) Greer; m. Marion Clarich, June 25, 1950; children: Jeffrey, Linda. BS, U. Notre Dame, 1948; MD, U. Chgo., 1953; MA (hon.), Brown U., 1975; LHD (hon.), Southeastern Mass. U., 1981. Diplomate Am. Bd. Internal Medicine. Intern Yale-New Haven Med. Center, 1953—54; resident in medicine U. Chgo. Clinics, 1954—57; instr. endocrinology and medicine U. Chgo., 1957; practice medicine specializing in internal medicine Fall River, Mass., 1957—74; chief staff dept. medicine Fall River Gen. Hosp., 1959—62; med. dir. Earle E. Hussey Hosp., Fall River, 1962—75; chief staff dept. medicine Truesdale Clinic and Truesdale Hosp., Fall River, 1971—74, pres. med. staff, 1968—70; sr. clin. instr. medicine Tufts U. Coll. Medicine, 1969—71, asst. clin. prof., 1971—78; clin. asso. prof. community health Brown U., 1973—75, dir. family practice residency program, 1975—78, prof. community health, 1975—93, prof. emeritus, 1993—, assoc. dean medicine, 1974—81, dean medicine, 1981—92, dean emeritus, 1992—, chmn. sect. community health, 1978—81. Mem. Gov.'s Task Force on Quality of Care, Medicaid Program, Commonwealth of Mass., 1969—70; del. White House Conf. Aging, 1971, 81; pres. Ind. Living Authority, State of R.I., 1975—81; mem. exec. com. Cancer Control Bd. R.I., 1975—80; mem. R.I. Gov.'s Task Force for Inst. of Mental Health, 1976—81; bd. dirs. Health Planning Coun., Inc., Providence, 1976—78; chmn. com. on aging Jewish Fedn. R.I., 1978—80; chmn. Gov.'s Commn. on Provision of Comprehensive Mental Health Svcs. in R.I., 1980—81; trustee Southeastern Mass. U., 1970—81, chmn., 1973—74, Providence Mayor's Sr. Citizens Task Force, 1975; bd. dirs. Assn. Home Health Agys. R.I., 1975—80; founding dir. Internat. Physicians for Prevention of Nuc. War, Inc., 1980—85; vis. prof. dept. medicine Georgetown U., 1992—93; scholar-in-residence Assn. Am. Med. Colls., 1992—93. Contbr. articles to profl. jours. Recipient Outstanding Svc. award, Mass. Easter Seal Soc., 1970, Outstanding Citizens award, Jewish War Vets. Aux., 1973, Disting. Svc. award, U. Chgo. Med. Alumni Assn., Cutting Found. medal, Andover Newton Theol. Sem., 1976, Lifetime Achievement award, Mass. Med. Soc.; named Prof. of the Yr., Brown U., 1992; fellow in health, Kellogg Found. Internat., 1986—89, vis. fellow, Green Coll. Oxford U., 1985. Master: ACP; mem.: R.I. Med. Soc., Internat. Soc. Rehab. Medicine, Am. Congree Rehab. Medicine, Gerontol. Soc., Inst. Medicine. Jewish. Office: Brown U Box G Providence RI 02912 Office Phone: 401-729-3644. Business E-Mail: David_Greer@brown.edu.

GREER, FRANK ROLAND, pediatrician, neonatologist; b. Gainesville, Fla., Gainesville, FL, Mar. 3, 1946; s. Charles Francis and Elizabeth French Greer; m. Catherine West, June 15, 1946; children: Natalie Greer Nicholson, Jonathan West. BS, Washington & Lee U., 1968; MD, U. Pa., 1972. Pediatrics Am. Bd. of Pediat., Chapel Hill, NC, 1977, Neonatal-Perinatal Medicine Am. Bd. of Pediat., NC, 1981. Resident in pediats. Cin. Children's Hosp., 1972—75, fellow in neonatal-perinatal medicine, 1978—80; prof. of pediat. U. of Wis., Madison, Wis., 1980—. Maj. Med Corps US Army, 1975—78. Office: Dept Pediats Univ Wisconsin 600 Highland Ave Madison WI 53792 also: Wisconsin Perinatal Ctr Meriter Hosp Madison WI 53711 Business E-Mail: frgreer@pediatrics.wisc.edu. E-mail: frgreer@wisc.edu. *

GREER, ROBERT BRUCE, III, orthopedist, educator; b. Butler, Pa., 1934; BA, Haverford Coll., 1956; MD, Harvard U., 1960. Diplomate Am. Bd. Orthopaedic Surgery (bd. dirs. 1985-94, pres. 1990-91). Intern Mich. Med. Ctr., 1960-61, resident in surgery, 1961-62; resident in orthopaedic surgery U. Pitts. Med. Ctr., 1964-67, asst. prof. orthopedic surgery, 1967-71; orthopaedist MS Hershey Med. Ctr., Pa.; prof., chief orthopaedic surgery Pa. State U., 1971-91; ret. Med. dir. Howmedica, Inc., 1997-99. Capt. USAR, 1962-64. Mem. ACS, Am. Acad. Orthopaedic Surgeons, Am. Orthopaedic Assn., Ea. Orthopaedic Assn., Alpha Omega Alpha.

GREER, WILLIAM R., internist; MD, U. Pa. Diplomate Am. Bd. Internal Medicine. Intern Univ. of Pa. Hosp., resident, fellow; attending physician; internal medicine rep. morbitity and mortality com. Paoli Meml. Hosp.; internal medicine rep. Sepsis Clinical Pathway team Main Line Health, internal medicine rep. Stroke Clinical Pathway Team. Named one of the Top Doctor, Phila. Mag., 2002, 2011. Mem.: ACP, Main Line Health (Bylaws Com.). Office: Main Line Health Ste 200 21 Industrial Blvd Paoli PA 19301 Office Phone: 610-651-0370. Office Fax: 610-651-7758.

GREGANTI, MAC ANDREW, physician, educator; b. Cleveland, Miss., Apr. 13, 1947; s. Mack Americo and Grace Margaret (Barbati) G.; m. Susan Taylor, Aug. 8, 1971; children: Paul Andrew, Mack Taylor, Mary Catherine. BS summa cum laude, Millsaps Coll., 1969; MD summa cum laude, U. Miss., 1972. Diplomate Am. Bd. Internal Medicine, Am. Bd. Geriat. medicine. Intern U. Rochester, NY, 1972-73, resident NY, 1973-75; instr. dept. medicine U. Miss. Sch. Medicine, Jackson, 1975-76, asst. prof., 1976-77, U. N.C. Sch. Medicine, Chapel Hill, 1977-83, assoc. prof., 1983-90, prof., 1990—, chief div. gen. medicine, 1986-91, assoc. chair for clin. affairs, 1991-99, acting chmn., 1999-2000, vice-chmn., 2000—. Dir. med./pediatric residency U. N.C. Dept. Medicine, Chapel Hill, 1980-86, dir. medicine residency, 1981-86. Contbr. articles on med. edn. and patient care to profl. jours. Fellow: ACP; mem.: Am. Geriatrics Soc., Alpha Omega Alpha. Roman Catholic. Avocations: tennis, golf, photography, computers. Office: Univ NC Chapel Hill Dept Medicine 125 Macnider Hall Cb 7005 Chapel Hill NC 27599-7005 Office Phone: 919-966-3063.

GREGG, ROBERT LEE, retired pharmacist; b. White River, SD, Mar. 2, 1932; s. C.W. and Margaret (Maguire) G.; m. Julie D. Tyler, June 7, 1956; children: Allen, Mark, Susan. BS, S.D. State U., 1958. Registered pharmacist, S.D. Owner, mgr., pharmacist Kennebec (S.D.) Drug, 1958—79, Gregg Drug, Chamberlain, SD, 1978—2003; ret., 2003. Adv. coun. Coll. Pharmacy, S.D. State U., Brookings, 1985-98; pres. S.D. Bd. Pharmacy, Pierre, 1992-93. Past sec. Indsl. Devel. Corp., Kennebec; pres. Lake Francis Case Devel. Corp., Chamberlain, 1984-85, Brule County unit Am. Cancer Soc., 1992-2004. With Med. Svc. Corps. US Army, 1953—55, Republic of Korea. Named S.D. Horseperson of Yr., S.D. Horse Coun., 1999. Mem. S.D. Pharm. Assn. (pres. 1985-86, Bowl of Hygeia award 1992, S.D. Pharmacist of Yr. 1996), Nat. Assn. Retail Druggists, Chamberlain C. of C., NRA (life), VFW (life, quartermaster Kennebec 1965-76, Outstanding Post Quartermaster award 1965), Am. Legion (life), Am. Quarter Horse Assn., S.D. Trail Riders (bd. dirs. 1986-97), KC (4th degree). Republican. Roman Catholic. Avocations: equestrian activities, trail riding, big game hunting. Personal E-mail: rjgregg@midstatesd.net.

GREGG, SHEA CHRISTOPHER, surgeon, educator; b. Nashua, NH, July 15, 1976; MD, Dartmouth, Brown Med. Program, 2002. Asst. prof., surgery Warren Alpert Sch. Medicine, Brown U., 2008—. Mem.: ACS. Office: Rhode Island Hosp 593 Eddy St APC 435 Providence RI 02903 Office Fax: 401-444-6681. Business E-Mail: sgregg@lifespan.org.

GREGGS, ELANORA, social worker; b. Barnwell County, SC, Nov. 10, 1933; d. Daniel and Georgia (Cobb) Young; children: John, Christopher, Paulette, Doris. BA, Coll. New Rochelle, 1985; MSW, Yeshiva U., 1987. Para-profl. Bd. Edn., Bklyn., 1965—67; salesperson Tira Exclusive, Laurelton, NY, 1982—85, Mary Kay Cosmetics, Stanley Home Products; human svcs. supr. Cath. Charities, Bklyn., 1986—87, social work supr. Jamaica, NY, 1987—95, Jamaica Support Sys., 1995. Tchr. Maranatha Bible Inst., 2001—; cons., spkr. in field. Author: Broken Pieces, 1998. Alumni Coll. New Rochelle, NY, 1985—, Yeshiva U., NYC, 1987—; pub. rels. Lake Arbor Found., Mitchellville, Md., 2000—; vol. in nursing homes, 1996—; active Christian Women of Faith, Mitchellville, Md., 2001—; acting min. Evangel Cathedral, 1995—. Avocations: reading, writing, walking, swimming, gardening.

GREGOR, PAVEL, cardiologist; b. Policka, Svitavy, Czech Republic, Jan. 12, 1952; s. Robert and Marie (Stylova) G.; m. Marie Lysakova, June 19, 1977; children: Martin, Pavlina. Dr., Charles U., 1976, DSc, 1992. Physician Hosp. Kralovske Vinohrady, Prague, Czech Republic, 1976-81, cardiologist, 1981—; asst. prof. 3rd Sch. of Medicine, Prague, 1981-91, assoc. prof., 1991-95, prof. medicine, 1995—, head dept. of cardiology, 1991—. Author: Echocardiography, 1983 (Prize Presidium Czech Med. Soc., Ann. award of pub. 1984), 2d edit., 1991 (Prize Czech Soc. Cardiology 1991), Hypertrophic Cardiomyopathy, 1992 (Prize Czech Lit. Found. 1992), Cardiology, 1994. Mem. academical senate 3rd Sch. of Medicine, 1990-95, 1998-2001. Fellow European Soc. of Cardiology; mem. Czech Soc. Cardiology. Roman Catholic. Avocations: motorcycling, classical music, books. Office: Cardio Ctr 3d Internal Clin Srobarova 50 10034 Prague 10 Czech Republic

GREGOREK, HANNA, medical analyst; b. Torun, Pomorze, Poland, Nov. 25, 1949; d. Arnold and Wacjawa Buss; m. Wojciech Jan Gregorek, Dec. 17, 1981; 1 child, Agata. Med. analyst, Med. Sch., Lódz, Poland, 1972; specialist of med. analysis II, Med. Sch., Warsaw, Poland, 1980; doctor, Med. Sch., 1986. Asst. Country Hosp., Torun, 1972-74, head hematology lab., 1976-81; sel-reliant asst. Postgrad. Med. Edn. Ctr., Bydgoszcz, Poland, 1974-76; asst. dept. immunology Children's Meml. Health Inst., Warsaw, 1981-86, asst. prof., 1986-95, head humoral immunology lab., 1996—2002, head immunology lab., 2003—. Scientific sec. Polish Com. of Immunology, Warsaw, 1996-98. Asst. editor: Central European Jour. Immunology, 1991-99; contbr. articles to profl. jours. Avocations: classical music, theater, painting, swimming. Home: Bukowskiego 1 03-982 Warsaw Poland Office: Childrens Meml Health Inst Al. Dzieci Polskich 20 04-730 Warsaw Poland Office Phone: 48-22-815-70-29. Fax: 48-22-815-7156. E-mail: h.gregorek@czd.pl.

GREGORY, DANIEL HAYES, gastroenterologist; b. Waterton, NY, Dec. 18, 1933; AB, Hamilton Coll., 1957; MD, U. Va., 1962. Intern Med. Coll. of Va., Richmond, 1962—63; resident in internal medicine U. Minn. VA Hosp., Mpls., 1963—66, fellow in gastroenterolgy, 1966—68; assoc. chmn. to dept. Med. Coll. Va., Richmond, 1972—79; chief of medicine VA Hosp., 1975—79; assoc. Allegheny Gastro Assocs., Pitts., 1979—90; assoc. prof. medicine Med. Coll. Pa., 1980—90; med. dir. E.J. Noble Noble Hosp., Alexandria Bay, NY, 1990; pres. med. staff Bassett Healthcare, 1992—94, chief digestive diseases, 1996—2001, sr. attending physician, 1991—; assoc. prof. medicine Columbia U., NYC, 2002—. Adv. faculty Merck, Sharp & Dohme, 1982—; program dir. GI fellowship Allegheny Gen. Hosp., Pitts., 1979-90; bd. dirs. River Hosp., Alex Bay, N.Y., 2002-05, bd. trustees emeritus, 2005-. Contbr. over 50 articles on hepatocellular metabolism and clin. gastroenterology to profl. jours. Mem. med. adv. Am. Liver Found., Pitts., 1985—; mem. Am.'s Registry Outstanding Profls., 2002-03. Mem. Am. Assn. Study Liver Disease, Am. Gastroenterology Assn., Am. Coll. Gastroenterology, Am. Men. Sci., Am. Soc. Gastrointestinal Endoscopy, Allegheny County Med. Soc. (pres. 1989—, chmn. bd. 1990).

GREGORY, STEPHANIE ANN, hematologist, educator; b. Vineland, NJ, June 23, 1940; d. Andonetta Gregory; m. Sheldon Chertow; children: Elizabeth Chertow, Jennifer Chertow, Daniel Chertow, Erica Chertow. BS cum laude, Boston Coll., 1961; MD cum laude, Med. Coll. Pa., 1965. Diplomate in internal medicine and hematology Am. Bd. Internal Medicine. Internal medicine intern Presbyn.-St. Luke's Hosp., Chgo., 1965-66, resident in internal medicine, 1966-68, fellow in hematology, 1969—72; chief resident in internal medicine Presbyn.-St. Lukes Hosp., Chgo., 1968-69; chief spl. morphology lab. sect. hematology Rush-Presbyn.-St. Luke's Med. Ctr., Chgo., 1972-76, dir. sect. hematology divsn. hematology/oncology, 1994—, Elodia Kehm prof. medicine, dir. hematology and stem cell transplantation, 1995—; from asst. prof. medicine to assoc. prof. medicine Rush Med. Coll., Chgo., 1972-86, prof. medicine, 1986—; adminstr., dir. Consultants in Hematology Rush U. Med. Ctr., Chgo., 1985—, sr. attending physician, 1982—, dir. sect. hematology, 2004—; chair Internat. Workshop Nuc. Oncology, Bayer Health Care-Bayer Schering Pharma, Budapest, Hungary, 2007, Madrid, 2008. Coord. continuing edn. sect. hematology Rush-Presbyn.-St. Luke's Med. Ctr., Chgo., 1970-76, dir. transfusion therapy svc. sect. hematology, 1972-76, asst. chmn. dept. medicine, 1972-77, clin. dir. Sheridan Rd. Pavilion, 1976-77, acting dir. sect. clin. hematology, 1980-81, assoc. dir. sect. hematology, 1993-94, asst. chair dept. medicine, 1993-94; co-dir. Lymphoma Ctr., Rush Univ Medical Ctr., Chgo., 1992—; mem. UN Security Coun. Commn. Experts, 1994; mem. med. adv. bd. Leukemia Rsch. Found., 1996—, Leukemia/Lymphoma Soc. Am., Lymphoma Rsch. Found.; chair B-cell Edn. Malignancies program, 2005-. Recipient award Am. Women's Med. Assn., 1965, William B. Peck Sci. award for rsch. in hematopoietic stem cell studies Sci. Assembly of Interstate Postgrad. Med. Assn., 1973, Outstanding Alumni award MCP-Hahneman Med. Sch., 1998, Excellence in Medicine award Rush U. Med. Ctr., 2006; grantee Schweppe Found. Rsch., 1969-72, NIH tng. grantee Nat. Heart, Lung and Blood Inst., 1974-79; Schweppe fellow, 1969-72. Fellow ACP (mem. Ill. coun. 1994—, mentor physician mems. for advancement to fellowship designation ann. meeting 1996, Ill. Laureate award 1996); mem. AMA, Internat. Soc. Hematology (Inter-Am. divsn.), Internat. Soc. Exptl. Hematology (charter), Leukemia Soc. Am. (bd. trustees Ill. chpt. 1987—, chmn. patient aid com. Ill. chpt. 1988-90, treas. Ill. chpt. 1992-93, chairperson patient fin. aid com. Ill. chpt. 1992—, v.p. Ill. chpt. 1991-94, mem. med. adv. bd. Ill. chpt. 1996—), Am. Soc. Clin. Oncology, Am. Soc. Hematology (co-editor, 2005-, co-editor self-assessment program, 2005-), Ea. Coop. Oncology Group, Inst. Medicine Chgo., Chgo. Soc. Internal Medicine (exec. com. 1992—, sec.-treas. 1992-93, v.p. 1993-94, pres. 1994-95), Aplastic Anemia Found. Am. (hon. bd. trustees 1988—), Mark H. Lepper M.D. Soc. Tchrs. (elected), Alpha Omega Alpha, Sigma Xi. Office: Rush Univ Medical Ctr 1725 W Harrison St Ste 834 Chicago IL 60612-3861 Office Phone: 312-942-5982. Business E-Mail: stephanie_gregory@rush.edu.

GREGSON, NIGEL CHRISTOPHER, pharmaceutical executive, consultant; b. Hythe, Hampshire, Eng., June 5, 1964; s. Christopher Allen Candy and Susan Mary Gascoigne Storer; m. Trudy Ellen Hauser, Nov. 12, 1988; children: Jordan James, Theo Jacob, Lauren Elise. BA in Bus. Adminstrn. with honors, Loughborough U., Eng., 1986; cert. in Health Econ., U. Aberdeen, 2001. CPA Ill. Sr. auditor KPMG Peat Marwick, London, 1986—89, supervising sr. auditor Phila., 1990—90; operational cons. SmithKline Beecham, Phila., 1990—96, assoc. dir. planning and fin., global mktg., 1996—97, dir. global pricing and econ. analysis, 1998—2000; group dir. global pricing and reimbursement strategy GlaxoSmithKline, Phila., 2001—03; co-founder, prin. PriceSpective LLC, Blue Bell, Pa., 2003—. Author: Pricing Medicines: Theory and Practice, Challenges and Opportunities. Mem.: Internat. Soc. for Pharmacoeconomics and Outcomes Rsch. (assoc.), Inst. Chartered Accountants in Eng. and Wales (assoc.). Home: 1228 Turnbury Ln North Wales PA 19454 Office: PriceSpective LLC 620 Sentry Pkwy Ste 100 Blue Bell PA 19422 Office Fax: 610-862-6007. Personal E-mail: ngregson@comcast.com. Business E-Mail: ngregson@pricespective.com.

GREIDER, CAROLYN WIDNEY, molecular biologist, educator; b. San Diego, Apr. 15, 1961; BA in Biology, U. Calif., Santa Barbara, 1983; PhD in Molecular Biology, U. Calif., Berkeley, 1987. Fellow Cold Spring Harbor Lab., NY, 1988-90, asst. investigator NY, 1990-92, assoc. staff investigator NY, 1992-94, investigator NY, 1994-97; assoc. prof. dept. molecular biology and genetics Johns Hopkins U. Sch. Medicine, Balt., 1997—99, prof., 1999—2003, prof. oncology, 2001—, interim dir. dept. molecular biology and genetics, 2002—03, Daniel Nathans prof. & dir. dept. molecular biology and genetics, 2003—. Vis. lectr. SUNY, Stony Brook, 1991—97; mem. sci. adv. bd. Geron Corp., 1992—96; mem. Nat. Bioethics Adv. Commn., 1996—2001; organizer Gordon Rsch. Conf. Nucleic Acids, Providence, 1998; cons. Amgen, Inc., 1998—2002. Mem. editl. bd. Cancer Cell, 2001—, Molecular Cancer Rsch., 2003—; contbr. numerous articles and revs. to profl. jours., chapters to books. Recipient Sr. Scholar award, Ellison Med. Found., 1998, Gairdner Found. Internat. award, 1998, Passano Found. award, 1999, Lewis S. Rosenstiel award, Brandeis U., 1999, Lila Gruber Cancer Rsch. award, 2006, Wiley prize in biomed scis., 2006, Albert Lasker award for Basic Med. Rsch., 2006, Louisa Gross Horwitz prize, Columbia U., 2007, Nobel prize in physiology/medicine, 2009; Regents scholar, U. Calif., 1981, Pew Biomed. Scis. scholar, 1990—94. Fellow: AAAS, American Acad. Microbiology, American Acad. Arts & Scis.; mem.: NAS (Richard Lounsbery award 2003), Inst. Medicine, American Soc. Biochemistry & Molecular Biology (Schering-Plough Sci. Achievement award 1997), American Soc. Microbiology, American Assn. Cancer Rsch. (Gertrude Elion Cancer Rsch. award 1994, Cornelius Rhoads award 1996), American Soc. Cell Biology (coun. mem. 1998—2001, Glenn Found. award 1995), Phi Beta Kappa. Achievements include along with Elizabeth Blackburn, discovery of telomerase, a key enzyme in cancer and anemia research. Office: Johns Hopkins U Sch Med Dept Molecular Biology & Genetics 601 PCTB 725 N Wolfe St Baltimore MD 21205 Office Phone: 410-614-6506. Office Fax: 410-614-2987. Business E-Mail: cgreider@jhmi.edu.

GREINER, JACK VOLKER, ophthalmologist, physician, surgeon, educator, research scientist, investor; b. Fountain Hill, Pa., Aug. 25, 1949; s. Harry Sandt and Vera Lilian G.; m. Cynthia Ann Mis, May 17, 1980; children: Ashley Lauren, Logan Nicholas Jack, Jordan Dean Jack. AA, Valley Forge Mil. Coll., 1969; BA, U. Vt., 1971; MS in Anatomy, Purdue U., 1974; PhD, U. Toledo, 1975; OD, New Eng. Coll. Optometry, 1978; DO, Midwestern U., 1982. Diplomate Am. Bd. Physician Specialties. Rsch. fellow ophthalmology Howe Lab. Ophthalmology Harvard Med. Sch. and Mass. Eye and Ear Infirmary, Boston, 1974—76; rsch. fellow ophthalmology Harvard Med. Sch., Boston, 1975—78, instr. ophthalmology, 1988—90, clin. instr., 1991—; rsch. fellow cornea and external diseases of eye Schepens Eye Rsch. Inst., Retina Found., 1976—78, clin. assoc. scientist, 1991—; rsch. assoc. ophthalmology U. Ill. Eye and Ear Infirmary, Chgo., 1979—81, rsch. asst. prof. ophthalmology, 1981—83; med. intern Cook County Hosp., Chgo., 1982—83; resident ophthalmology Georgetown U. Med. Ctr., 1983—86; clin. prof. surgery U. New Eng. Coll. Osteo. Medicine, 2010—; asst. clin. prof. dept. ophthalmology Tufts U. Sch. Medicine, Boston, 2000—. Adj. asst. scientist Eye Rsch. Inst., Retina Found., Boston, 1978; adj. asst. prof. ophthalmic pathology Midwestern U., 1978-82, asst. prof. dept. pathology, 1982-83, assoc. prof., 1983-87; co-dir. Eye Rsch. Lab., Chgo. Osteo. Hosp., 1980-87; clin. fellow ophthalmology Harvard Med. Sch./Mass. Eye and Ear Infirmary, 1986-88; med. staff Winchester Hosp., Lawrence Meml. Hosp., Medford, Melrose-Wakefield Hosp., Spaulding Rehab. Hosp., Boston; founder, staff Laser Eye Ctr. Boston, 1996—; founder, bd. dirs. Ocular Rsch. Boston, Inc.; founder & dir. Boston Ocular Surface Ctr., Boston, Windchester; prin. investigator or sub investigator over 100 clin. rsch. FDA drug approval trials, 1980— Mem. editl. bd. Internat. Jour. Biomed. Sci., 2005—; contbr. chpts. to books, over 150 articles to profl. jours.; patentee in ophthalmology and dermatology. Capt. C.E. USAR, 1971-78. Fight For Sight grantee, 1980-82, Nat. Soc. to Prevent Blindness grantee, 1981-82, NIH Nat. Eye Inst. grantee, 1982-85, 92-97. Fellow Am. Acad. Osteo. Surgeons (pres. 1995-96), Am. Acad. Optometry, Am. Acad. Ophthalmology (Achievement award 2001), Am. Acad. Specialists in Surgery (pres. 2002-04, sec. 2001-02, Physician of Yr. 2003); mem. AMA (Physicians Recognition award 1985-87, 89-91, 94-97, 99), Internat. Soc. Refractive Surgeons, Am. Soc. Cataract and Refractive Surgery, Mass. Soc. Eye Physicians and Surgeons, Am. Assn. Physician Specialists, Nat. Acads. Practice (editl. bd. Jour. Nat. Acad. Practice Forum 1993-96, named Disting. Practitioner), Am. Assn. Physician Specialists (bd. dirs. 2002-06), Nat. Soc. Prevent Blindness (bd. dirs. Prevent Blindness Mass., 1994-2004), Contact Lens Assn. Ophthalmologists, Assn. Rsch. in Vision and Ophthalmology, Tear Film and Ocular Surface Soc., Mass. Med. Soc., Sigma Xi, Phi Kappa Phi, Sigma Sigma Phi, Am. Bd. Physician Specialists(bd. cert.) Office: Harvard Med Sch Schepens Eye Research Inst 20 Staniford St Boston MA 02114-2508 Home Phone: 781-721-0390, Office Phone: 617-248-3875. Business E-Mail: jackvgreiner@schepens.harvard.edu.

GREINER, KENNETH DONALD, JR., retired management consultant, health facility administrator; b. Cushing, Okla., Aug. 19, 1938; s. Kenneth Donald Greiner and Billie Alene (Williams) Greiner; m. Leitner Louise Jarrell, Sept. 2, 1961; children: Katherine Louise Pierce, Kenneth Donald III, Jennifer Lee Burrell, Cheryl Sue Gumerson. BS in Econs., Okla. State U., 1960; MBA, Harvard U., 1962; BS in Health Care Adminstrn., Okla. Bapt. U., 1977. Adminstrv. asst. Doric Corp., Oklahoma City, 1962-64; asst. to treas. Skelly Oil Co., Tulsa, 1964-66; loan officer AID, Lahore, Karachi, Pakistan, 1966-69; ptnr. Resource Analysis and Mgmt. Group, Oklahoma City, 1969-74; v.p., dir. Texas Internat. Co., Oklahoma City, 1974-76; chmn. Grace Living Ctrs. (formerly Amity Care Corp.), Oklahoma City, 1976—2002; pres. Grouper Mgmt. Co., (Formerly Nursing Home Properties), 2002—; ptnr. Ams. Mgmt. Svcs. LLC, 2003—06. Asst. bankruptcy trustee Four Seasons Nursing Ctrs. Am., 1972—73; bd. dirs. Cmty. bnk Warr Acres, 1972—82, Will Rogers Bank, 1983—94; br. adv. dir. Oklahoma City Nations Bank, 1994—97; bankruptcy trustee Gulf South Corp., 1974, Cleanerator Corp., 1974, Preferred Commodity Options Corp., 1974—75; bd. dirs. Secret Harbour Beach Resort, 2004—07. Treas., bd. dirs. Neighborhood Svcs. Orgn., Oklahoma City Met. Area, 1978—83; chmn. bd. New World Sch., Oklahoma City, 1973—74; mem. Putnam City Sch. Bd., 1988—93, pres., 1992—93; dir. Cowboy Golf, Inc., 1992—2003; trustee Hillcrest Hosp., Oklahoma City, 1989—93; dir. Emergency Med. Svcs. Authority, Oklahoma City, Tulsa, 1998—2001; mem. bd. govs. Okla. State U. Found., 1994—, trustee, 1998—2009, vice chmn., 2004—05, chmn. bd., 2005—07, Papal Found. Investment Com., 2007—, Opportunity Internat. Bd. Govs., 2008—, Cath. Social Ministries, Archdiocese of Oklahoma City, 1977—86. Mem.: Nat. Assn. Bds. Examiners Nursing Home Adminstrs. (pres. 1994—96), Okla. State Bd. Nursing Homes (bd. dirs. 1988—92), Nursing Home Assn. Okla. (exec. bd. 1988—2003, v.p. 1990—92), Okla. State U. CBA Assocs. (pres. 1993—94), Equestrian Order Holy Seplechre, Ski Island Lake Inc. (pres. 1984—87), Quail Creek Golf and Country Club (v.p., dir. 1998—2001), Bus. Boosters Club (pres. 1985), Harvard Bus. Sch. Alumni Club (pres. Oklahoma City 1970—71), Phi Delta Theta Alumni (pres. Oklahoma City 1969—71). Republican. Roman Catholic. Office: 4350 Will Rogers Pkwy Ste 350 Oklahoma City OK 73108

GREISCH, JOHN J., medical products executive; BBA, Miami U., Ohio; M in Mgmt., Northwestern U. CPA. With Price Waterhouse; various positions, including pres., Materials Handling Group, CFO The Interlake Corp., Lisle, Ill., treas., pres., Largest Bus., pres., European Ops.; pres., CEO Fleetpride Corp., Deerfield, Ill.; v.p. Tisco, Inc.; prin. acctg. officer Baxter International, Inc., v.p., fin. and strategy, BioScience Bus., v.p., fin., Renal Bus., 2002—03, pres., Bioscience Divsn., 2003—04; corp. v.p. Baxter Healthcare Corp-.(subs. Baxter Internat. Inc.), 2004; sr. v.p. Baxter International, Inc., 2004, CFO, 2004—06, pres., internat. ops., corp. v.p., 2006—09; corp. v.p. Baxter World Trade Corp. (subs. Baxter Internat. Inc.), 2007; pres., CEO, mem. bd. dirs. Hill-Rom Holdings, Inc. (formerly Hillenbrand Industries, Inc.), 2010—. Bd. dirs. TomoTherapy, Inc., 2008—10. Bd. trustees John G. Shedd Aquarium, Chgo.; bd. dirs. Children's Meml. Hosp. Found., Chgo. Office: Hill-Rom Holdings Inc 1069 State Route 46 E Batesville IN 47006 Office Phone: 812-934-7777. Office Fax: 812-934-8189. Business E-Mail: John.Greisch@hill-rom.com. *

GREISMAN, STEWART GEORGE, rheumatologist, educator; Studied, Yale U., New Haven, 1981. Diplomate Am. Bd. of Internal Medicine, 1984, Am. Bd. of Internal Medicine-rheumatology, 1986. Resident internal medicine Yale New Haven Hosp., 1982—84; fellow rheumatology Hosp. for Spl. Surgery, 1984—86, with, Lenox Hill Hosp.; asst. prof. of medicine coll. of physicians and surgeons Columbia Univ.; assoc. attending prof. dept. of medicine St. Luke's Roosevelt Hosp. Ctr. Named one of Top Doctors NY Metro Area, Castle Connolly's, 2009. Office: St. Luke's Roosevelt Hospital Center 457 W 57th St New York NY 10019 Office Phone: 212-265-1471. Office Fax: 212-265-9724.

GREKOS, ZANNOS G., cardiologist; b. Jersey City, Apr. 27, 1965; BS in Chemistry and Biology, Fla. Atlantic U., Boca Raton, 1986; MD, U. South Fla. Coll. Medicne, 1990. Diplomate Am. Bd. Internal Medicine, cert. in cardiovasc. diseases. Intern, resident internal medicine Tampa Gen. Hosp./U. South Fla. H. Lee Moffitt Cancer & Rsch. Inst., 1990—94, fellow cardiovasc. diseases, 1993—96; assoc. clin. prof. cardiology Nova Southeastern U., Ft. Lauderdale, Fla.; dir. Regenocyte Therapeutic Stem Cell Clin. Ctr., Naples, Fla. Mem. sci. adv. bd. US Repair Stem Cell Inst. Fellow: Am. Acad. Pediat., Am. Acad. Cardiology; mem.: Internat. Soc. Stem Cell Rsch. Achievements include development of many protocols used for adult stem cell therapy throughout the world; using adult stem cell therapy to treat congestive heart failure, cardiomyopathy, peripheral artery disease, coronary artery disease, kidney disease, ischemic heart disease, pulmonary disease and early senile dementia. Office: Regenocyte Therapeutic 9500 Bonita Beach Rd Ste 210 Bonita Springs FL 34135 Office Phone: 239-333-1239. Office Fax: 239-333-2891. *

GRELLET, JEAN, medical educator; b. Melle, France, Oct. 9, 1955; s. Jacques and Simone Grellet; m. Muriel Mounier, July 17, 1985; children: Jerome, Virginie. PharmD, U. Bordeaux II, France, 1982; M in rsch., U. Bordeaux II, 1984, PhD, 1987. Resident U. Hosp., Bordeaux, France, 1982—87, hosp. pharmacist, 1992—; tchr. U. Bordeaux II, 1989—, head pharm. dept., 2008—. Mem.: European Soc. of Clin. Pharm. (assoc.). Achievements include research in cardiology; impact of left ventricular hypertrophy on myocardial perfusion and performance; infectiology: intracellular activity of antiinfective agents in an in vitro model of infected monocyte/macrophage cell; pharmacokinetics: intracellular penetration of drugs and transplacental transfer. Avocations: travel, caving, skiing, mountain climbing. Office: U Hosp Place a Raba Leon 33000 Bordeaux France Office Fax: (33)0556795674. Business E-Mail: jean.grellet@chu-bordeaux.fr.

GRELSAMER, RONALD P., orthopedist, surgeon, educator; BS in Bioengring., Brown U., 1971—75, BA in French Lit., 1971—75; MD, Columbia U., 1975—79. Diplomate Am. Bd. of Orthopaedic Surgeons, 1987, Am. Bd. of Orthopaedic Surgeons, 1996. Resident orthopaedic surgery Columbia Presbyn. Med. Ctr., 1981—84, fellow hip and knee surgery, 1984—85; assoc. prof. orthopaedic surgery Mt. Sinai Sch. of Medicine; with Maimonides Med. Ctr., Hosp. for Joint Diseases, Mt. Sinai Med. Ctr. Author: What your knee doctor won't tell you, 1996, The Patella - A Team Approach, 1998; co-author: (publs.) The medial-lateral position of the patella in routine MR imaging, 1998, The Anatomy and Biomechanics of the Patella, 1998, and numerous other publications. Recipient Career Devel. award, Orthopaedic Rsch. and Edn. Found. Mem.: French Acad. of Orthopaedic Surgeons, European Sports Medicine Soc., Orthopaedic Rsch. Soc., State Orthopaedic Soc., State Med. Soc. Office: Mount Sinai Medical Center Box 1188 5 E 98th St New York NY 10029 Office Phone: 212-241-2914. Office Fax: 212-534-6202.

GREMIAO, MARIA PALMIRA DAFLON, pharmacologist, educator; b. Rio de Janeiro, Dec. 4, 1957; Degree in Pharmacy, Faculty Pharm. Sci., 1982; PhD, Chemistry Inst., 1995. Prof. U. Estadual Paulista, 1986—. Office: Rodovia Araraquara - Jaú km 1 Araraquara Sao Paulo 14801-902 Brazil Office Fax: 1633016975. Business E-Mail: pgremiao@fcfar.unesp.br.

GREMSE, DAVID ALBERT, pediatrician, educator; b. Montgomery, Ala., Oct. 14, 1956; s. Albert Rudolph and Jean (Faust) Gremse; m. Diane Blackwell, June 13, 1981; children: Jennifer, Albert, Christopher. BChE summa cum laude, Ga. Inst. Tech., 1979; MD, U. South Ala., 1983. Lic. Ala., Nev., diplomate Am. Bd. Pediat. and Pediat. Gastroenterology, Nat. Bd. Med. Examiners. Prof., chair pediats. U. Nev. Sch. Medicine, 2004—; dir. pediats. U. South Ala. Gastroenterology and Nutrition Divsn., 1990—2003. Asst. prof., assoc. prof. Pediat. U. South Ala., Mobile, 1990—99, asst. prof. Pharmacology, 1997—99, prof. pediat., 1999—2003, assoc. prof. Pharmacology, 1999—2003. Mem. editl. bd.: Paediatric Drugs, 2001—, reviewer: profl. jours., —; contbr. chpts. in books, articles to profl. jours. Recipient Eagle Scout award, Boy Scouts Am., 1970; grantee, Cystic Fibrosis Found., 1994—95, 1996—97, TAP Holdings, Inc., 1998—99, 1998, 2002, Cell Pathways, Inc., 1999—2000, AstraZeneca, Inc., 1999—2000, Glaxo Wellcome, 1999—2000, 2000—01, 2001—03, Omnicare Clin. Rsch., Inc., 2001, 2002, Wyeth Ayerst, 2002, GlaxoSmithKline, 2002—04; fellow, Child Hops. Med. Ctr., Cin., 1987—90. Fellow: Am. Coll. Gastroenterology (Pediat. Gastroenterology com. 2001, credentials com. 2001—); mem.: AMA (Physician's Recognition award 1997—2000), Soc. Pediat. Rsch. (reviewer Gastroenterology Abstract 2003), So. Soc. Pediat. Rsch. (moderator Gastroenterology session ann. meeting 1994, moderator Clin. Pharmacology ann. meeting 1997), Crohn's and Colitis Found. Am., Med. Soc. Mobile (Bd. Censors 1995—97), Mobile Pediat. Soc. (pres. 1994—95), Am. Bd. Pediat. (assoc.; sub. bd. pediat. gastroent. 2007—), So. Med. Assn., Med. Assn. State of Ala., N.Am. Soc. Pediat. Gastroenterology and Nutrition (sec., treas. 2008—), Am. Gastroent. Assn., Am. Acad. Pediat. (chmn. Acad. Issues com. Ala. chpt. 1997—, Com. mem. Gastroenterology and Nutrition Edn. sect. 2001—, Nutrition com. 2001—, exec. bd. dist. VII rep. Ala. chpt. 2001—, v.p. Nev. chp. 2006—), Alpha Omega Alpha, Tau Beta Pi, Phi Kappa Phi, Phi Eta Sigma. Home: 4885 Staranger Ln Las Vegas NV 89147 Office: U Nev Med Sch 2040 W Charleston Blvd Ste 402 Las Vegas NV 89102 Office Phone: 702-671-2231.

GRENDELL, JAMES HENRY, medical educator; b. Cleve., Dec. 7, 1949; married; 3 children. BS in Biology magna cum laude, John Carroll U., 1971; MD cum laude, Ohio State U., 1975. Diplomate Nat. Bd. Med. Examiners, Am. Bd. Internal Medicine with subspecialty in gastroenterology; lic. physician, N.Y. Intern in medicine Beth Israel Hosp., Boston, 1975-76, resident in medicine, 1976-78; fellow in gastroenterology U. Calif., San Francisco, 1978-81, asst. prof. medicine and physiology, 1981-88, assoc. prof., 1989-94; chief gastroenterology sect. San Francisco VA Med. Ctr., 1990-94; prof. medicine Cornell U., NYC, 1994—99; chief divsn. digestive diseases New York Hosp.-Cornell U. Med. Ctr., NYC, 1994-98; chief divsn. gastroenterology, hepatology and nutrition Winthrop U. Hosp., Mineola, NY, 1999—; prof. medicine SUNY, Stony Brook, 2003—. Mem. gastroenterology subsplty. bd. Am. Bd. Internal Medicine, 1995-99; lectr. in field. Editor: Current Diagnosis and Treatment in Gastroenterology, 1996, 2003; assoc. editor Internat. Jour. Pancreatology, 1989—, Pancreas, 1993—; cons. editor Gastroenterology, 1982; ad hoc referee Sci. Jour. of Clin. Investigation, Annals of Internal Medicine, Gastroenterology, Am. Jour. Physiology, Digestive Diseases and Scis., Neuroendocrinology, Western Jour. Medicine, Fedn. Proc., Can. Jour. Physiology and Pharmacology, Endocrinology, Am. Jour. Gastroenterology, Jour. Lab. and Clin. Medicine; contbr. numerous articles and abstracts to profl. jours., chpts. to books. Mem.: ACP (gastroenterology subcom. med. knowledge self-assessment program IX 1989—91), Internat. Assn. of Pancreatology, Western Assn. Physicians, Western Soc. for Clin. Investigation, Am. Pancreatic Assn. (governing coun. 1989—95, pres. 1993—94), Gastroenterology Rsch. Group, Am. Gastroenterol. Assn. (com. on tng. and edn. 1990—94, chmn. tng. subcom. 1991—94, Fall postgrad. course assoc. dir. 1992, co-chair pancreatic disorders sect. 1993—95, chair 1995—97, coun. 1997—2000, governing bd. 1997—2000, course dir. 1998, pub. affairs and advocacy com. 2003—), Am. Fedn. Clin. Rsch., Landacre Soc., Alpha Omega Alpha. Office Phone: 516-663-4624. Business E-Mail: jgrendel@winthrop.org.

GRENEVICKI, LANCE FRANCIS, surgeon; b. Plainfield, NJ, May 21, 1967; s. Lawrence Francis and Joann Frances (Bengivenga) Grenevicki; m. Amy Lavonne Bridgers, Apr. 13, 1996; children: Anna Lavonne, Lance Francis Jr. BS, Va. Poly. Inst. and State U., 1989; DDS cum laude, Med. Coll. Va., 1993; MD, U. Mo., Kansas City, 1997. Diplomate Am. Bd. Oral and Maxillofacial Surgery. Intern Truman Med. Ctr., Kansas City, Mo., resident, 1993-99; attending med. staff, chmn. med. records com. Holmes Regional Med. Ctr., Melbourne, Fla., past chief surgery, chair surg. quality improvement com., mem. med. staff, chmn. med. records com.; courtesy clin. asst. prof. surgery U. Fla., 2001—06; active med. staff mem. Wuesthoff Hosp., Melbourne, Fla.; adj. clin. prof. U. Ctrl. Fla., Sch. Medicine. Mem. adv. coun. Fla. Cancer Control and Rsch., med. quality com., 2006—10, bd. quality com., 2006—; bd. dirs. Isaac Walton League of Am., Christiansburg, Va., 1988—89. Recipient Victim's Advocate award, State Atty.'s Office, 2002; named Surg. Resident of Yr., Isaac Walton League Am., 1997. Fellow: ACS, Am. Acad. Cosmetic Surgery, Am. Coll. Oral and Maxillofacial Surgeons, Am. Assn. Oral and Maxillofacial Surgeons (del. Fla.); mem.: ADA, AMA (Brevard County del.), Fla. Soc. Dental Anesthesiology (pres. 2006), Brevard County Med. Soc. (pres. 2011—), Brevard County Dental Soc. (adv. com. cancer control and rsch. 2005—, pres. 2009, chair), So. Med. Assn., Ctrl. Dist. Dental Soc., Fla. Dental Assn., Fla. Med. Assn. (Brevard county del., chair rules credentials com. 2008), Fla. Soc. Oral and Maxillofacial Surgeons (trustee 2001—06, pres. 2008, Young Eagle award 2001), Southeastern Soc. Oral and Maxillofacial Surgeons, Psi Omega, Alpha Omega Alpha, Pi Kappa Alpha. Roman Catholic. Avocations: trap and skeet shooting, hunting, fishing. Office: Inst Facial Surgery 1093 S Wickham Rd Melbourne FL 32904-1652 Home: 2306 N Riverside Dr Indialantic FL 32903-3619 Office Phone: 321-674-3900.

GRENIER, PHILIPPE ANDRÉ, radiologist, educator; b. Paris, Dec. 24, 1949; s. Albert Grenier and Marie-Jeanne Grenier-Gimello; m. Dominique Brigitte Heritier, Mar. 18, 1994; m. Brigitte Dezoteux, 1972 (div. 1993); children: Antoine Alexandre, Clément Albert, Adrien Constant, Camille. Baccalaureat, Lycée Bayonne, France, 1966; degree in Medicine, U. Paris, 1977. Rsch. fellow Med. Sch. Xavier Bichat, Paris, 1978—82, assoc. prof., radiology, 1982—88; prof., radiology Med. Sch. Bobigny U. Paris XIII, France, 1988—89, Med. Sch. U. Pierre Marie Curie, Paris, 1989—, v.p., 1998—2001, chmn., dept. radiology, 1989—, Hosp. Pitié-Salpetriere, Paris, 1989—, chmn. and vice chmn., exec. com., 2007—. Author: (book) Imagerie Thoracique de l'Adulte (Herman Fishgold prize, 1996), Imaging of the Airways; contbr. scientific papers (Giovanni DiChiro award, 1999). No rank no br. Recipient Lucien Mallet medal, Fondation de France, 1996. Master: Radiol. Soc. N.Am. (vice-chair of internat. adv. bd. 2007—, Cum Laude 1996), European Assn. Radiology (coms. edn. and subspecialties 1997—2006, Gold medal 2007), Soc. Française Radiology (gen. sec. 2006—07), European Soc. Thoracic Imaging (pres. 2007—08), Fleischner Soc. (pres. 2002—03), European Congress Radiology (pres. 2002—03, Magna Cum Laude 2002, Cum Laude 2004, Gold medal 2007); fellow: Royal Coll. Radiology, Internat. Soc. Strategic Studies Radiology; mem.: U. Buenos Aires, Soc. Canadienne Française Radiologie, Swedish Soc. Med. Radiology, Japan Radiol. Soc., Italian Soc. Radiology, Austrian Soc. Radiology, Soc. Argentina Radiologia. Achievements include research in postprocessing techniques and image analysis for airway and lung disease. Office: Hosp Pitie-Salpetriere Radiologie 47/83 Bd de l'Hosp Paris 75013 France Office Fax: 33 1 42 17 82 24. Business E-Mail: philippe.grenier@psl.aphp.fr.

GRESHAM, GLEN EDWARD, physician; BA, Harvard Coll., 1953; MD, Columbia U., 1958. Intern, then resident in internal medicine Univ. Hosps., Cleve., 1958-60, 62-64; asst. prof preventive medicine Ohio State U., Columbus, 1964-69; asst. prof. medicine Yale U., New Haven, 1969-70; assoc. prof. rehab. medicine, medicine and cmty. medicine Tufts U., Boston, 1970-78; prof., chmn. dept. rehab. medicine SUNY, Buffalo, 1978-98, prof. emeritus, 1998—, Gresham vis. prof., 1989, med. dir. Erie County Med. Ctr., 1990-92. With USPHS, 1960—62. Recipient Disting. Svc. award Mass. Council Orgns. Handicapped, 1972, Walter P. Cooke award SUNY Buffalo, 2007; Nat. Found. fellow rehab., 1962-64. Fellow ACP, Am. Coll. Rheumatology (emeritus); mem. Am. Acad. Phys. Medicine and Rehab. (hon.), Columbia U. Club NYC, Harvard Club Boston. Achievements include research in epidemiology chronic disease, functional assessment, stroke disability. Home Phone: 239-472-4031; Office Phone: 716-898-3218. Personal E-mail: greshdoc@aol.com.

GRESHAM, JAMES STEVE, hospital administrator; b. Greenville, SC, Oct. 13, 1951; s. James William and Ruby Etta (Ayers) G.; m. Sharon Dee Barfield, Nov. 15, 1975 (dec. 1989); children: Ashley Lynn, David Bruce; m. Kathleen Perry Jennings, Sept. 8, 1990; 1 child, James Steven Jennings. BS, Clemson U., 1973; MBA, Pacific Western U., 1984. Cert. profl. Acad. Healthcare Mgmt. Mgmt. assoc. Citizens & So. Nat. Bank, Greenville, 1973-75; dir. spl. svcs. USAF, Nellis AFB, Nev., 1975-77; med. squadron cmdr. USAF Hosp., Columbus AFB, Miss., 1977-80; cmdr. 70th Aeromed. Evacuation Squadron, Niagara Falls, N.Y., 1980-82; dir. ops. 72d Aeromed. Evacuation Squadron, McGuire AFB, N.J., 1982-85; dir. health svcs. Headquarters 14th Air Force, Marietta, Ga., 1985-90; adminstr. cancer ctr. Greenville Hosp. Sys., 1990—. Author: Disaster Casualty Management, 1979. Mem. Res. Officers Assn., Am. Acad. Med. Adminstrs., Assn. Cancer Execs., Am. Coll. Oncology Adminstrs., So. Air Force Res. Med. Svc. Corps Officers, Assn. Mil. Surgeons U.S. Methodist. Office: Cancer Ctr Greenville Hosp Sys 701 Grove Rd Greenville SC 29605-5601 *

GRESS, RONALD E., oncologist, medical researcher; MD, Baylor Coll. Medicine, Tex., 1975. Diplomate Am. Bd. Internal Medicine, Am. Bd. Med. Oncology. Resident in internal medicine Johns Hopkins Hosp., Balt., 1975—78, fellow in oncology, 1978—79, asst. chief svc., 1982—83; clin. assoc. immunology Ctr. Cancer Rsch., Nat. Cancer Inst., NIH, Bethesda, Md., 1979—82, sr. investigator exptl. immunology br., 1983—2004, chief exptl. transplantation and immunology br., 2000—, chief med. oncology clin. rsch. unit, 2001—, dep. dir. Mem.: Am. Soc. Clin. Investigation. Office: Nat Cancer Inst Bkdg 10 CRC, Rm 3-3332 10 Center Dr Bethesda MD 20892-1203 Office Phone: 301-496-1791. Office Fax: 301-480-4354. Business E-Mail: gressr@mail.nih.gov. *

GRESSNER, OLAV AXEL, physician; b. Aachen, Germany, July 14, 1978; Grad. in Med. Studies, Heidelberg U., Germany, Edinburg U., Scotland, Mt. Sinai Sch. Medicine, NY; MD, Heidelberg U., Germany, 2005. Bd. cert. med. specialist lab. medicine 2011. With U. Hosp. Bonn, Dept. Internal Medicine I, 2005—07, U. Hosp. Aachen, Dept. Clin. Chemistry & Pathobiochemistry- Ctrl. Lab., 2007—10, Wisplinghoff Med. Lab., Cologne, 2010—. Recipient Ismar-Boas award, German Soc. Digestive & Metabolic Diseases, 2006, Ivar-Trautschold award, German Soc. Clin. Chemistry & Lab. Medicine, 2008, Numerous Poster Prizes, Am. Gastroent. Assn. and many more, 2000—, Young Investigator award, Asian Pacific Assn. Study Liver, 2009; Danone Internat. Travel grant, 2010. Mem.: Am. Assn. Clin. Chemistry, German Soc. Clin. Chemistry & Lab. Medicine, Am. Assn. Study Liver Diseases. Achievements include research in role of TGF-beta and connective tissue growth factor in fibrogenic diseases and the discovery of their inhibition by methylxanthines. Personal E-mail: olavgressner@yahoo.com.

GREY, MARGARET, dean, nursing educator; b. Easton, Pa., Sept. 25, 1949; m. Michael Lauterbach. BS, U. Pitts.; MSN in Pediatric Nursing, Yale U.; DPH, Columbia U. Nursing educator U. Pa., Columbia U., Yale U. Sch. Nursing, 1993—, assoc. dean scholarly affairs, dir., Ctr. Self and Family Mgmt., Annie Goodrich prof., dean, 2005—. Chairperson Nursing Sci. Review Com. Nat. Inst. Nursing Rsch., 1995—97. Contbr. articles to profl. jours. Rudin Clin. Nursing Rsch. scholar, Disting. Fellow, NAPNAP, 1990, Robert Wood Johnson Exec. Nurse Fellowship, 1999-2001; Sch. Nursing Teaching award, UPenn., 1990, Virginia Herderson award for Outstanding Contributions to Nursing Rsch., 1997, Applied Nursing Rsch. award, Coun. Nurse Researchers, ANA, 1998, Disting. Alumni award, U. Pitts. Sch. Nursing, 1999, Achievement in Rsch. award, Natl. Org. Nurse Practitioner Faculties, 2000, Excellence in Nursing Rsch. award, Assn. Faculties of PNP Programs, 2000. Fellow Soc. Behavioral Medicine, Am. Acad. Nursing; mem. ANA (mem. coun. nurse researchers, primary care providers), NAPNAP (membership com.), APHA, Am. Diabetes Assn., Am. Sociol. Assn., Nat. Assn. Pediatric Nurse Assocs. and Practitioners (pres. 1992-93), Inst. Medicine; Sigma Theta Tau. Office: Yale U Sch Nursing 100 Church St S, Rm 206 PO Box 9740 New Haven CT 06536 Office Phone: 203-785-2393. Office Fax: 203-785-3554. Business E-Mail: margaret.grey@yale.edu.

GREY, ROBERT DEAN, biology professor, former academic administrator; b. Liberal, Kans., Sept. 5, 1939; s. McHenry Wesley and Kathryn (Brown) G.; m. Alice Kathleen Archer, June 11, 1961; children: Erin Kathleen, Joel Michael. BA, Phillips U., 1961; PhD, Washington U., 1966. Asst. prof. Washington U., St. Louis, 1966-67; from asst. prof. to full prof. zoology U. Calif., Davis, 1967—, chmn. dept., 1979-83, dean biol. scis., 1985—93, interim provost, 1993-95, provost, exec. vice chancellor, 1995—2001, sr. advisor to chancellor, 2001—02, provost, exec. vice chancellor emeritus, 2002—, exec. asst. to chancellor health affairs Riverside, 2005—07, acting chancellor, 2007—08; interim provost U. Cal Sys., 2008—09. Author: (with others) A Laboratory Text for Developmental Biology, 1980; contbr. articles to profl. jours. Recipient Disting. Tchg. awrd Acad. Senate U. Calif., Davis, 1977, Magnar Ronning award for tchg. Associated Students U. Calif., Davis, 1978, Disting. Alumnus award Phillips U., 1991. Avocations: music, hiking, gardening. Business E-Mail: rdgrey@ucdavis.edu.

GREYSON, CLIFFORD RUSSELL, internist; b. NYC, 1958; AB, Harvard Coll., 1980; MSEE, Stanford U., 1985, MD, 1987. Cert. internal medicine and cardiovascular diseases, critical care medicine. Resident in internal medicine Stanford U. Hosp., 1987-90, fellow in critical care, 1990-91; fellow in cardiovasc. disease U. Calif., San Francisco, 1991-95, faculty cardiology divsn., 1995-99, U. Colo. Health Scis. Ctr., Denver, 1999—. Co-dir. med. intensive care unit San Francisco VA Med. Ctr., 1998-99. Elected to city coun. Town of Woodside, Calif., 1995. Recipient Clinician Scientist award Am. Heart Assn., 1995-96, Clin. Investigator Devel. award NIH, 1996-01, R01 rsch. award NIH, 2003. Fellow Am. Coll. Cardiology, ACP; mem. Western Soc. Clin. Investigation. Office: Denver VA Med Ctr Cardiology 111B 1055 Clermont St Denver CO 80220-3808

GRIBETZ, MICHAEL ELLIOT, urologist, educator; BS summa cum laude, City Coll. of NY, 1971; MD, Albert Einstein Coll. of Medicine, 1973. Diplomate Am. Bd. Urology. Resident surgery Montefiore Med. Ctr., Bronx, NY, 1973—75; resident urology Mt. Sinai Hosp., NY, 1975—78; attending urologist Mount Sinai Med. Ctr. Asst. clin. prof. urology Mount Sinai Sch. of Medicine. Recipient, Phi Beta Kappa, NY's Best Doctors, NY mag., How to Find the Best Doctors, Castle-Conoly, Guide to Top Doctors. Mem.: AMA, Soc. for the Study of Impotence, Soc. of Clin. Urologists, Soc. of Pediatric Urology, NY State and County Med. Socs., Am. Urological Assn. Office: Mount Sinai Medical Center One Gustave L Levy Pl New York NY 10029 Office Phone: 212-241-6500.

GRICHNIK, JAMES MICHAEL, dermatologist; b. Memphis, May 10, 1961; BA summa cum laude, Washington U., 1982; PhD, Baylor Coll. Medicine, Houston, 1988; MD, Harvard Med. Sch., Boston, 1990. Intern Beth Israel Hosp., Boston, 1990—91; resident Duke U. Med. Ctr., Durham, NC, 1991—94, asst. prof. divsn. dermatology dept. medicine, 1994—2000, assoc. prof. divsn. dermatology dept. medicine, 2000—08; prof. dept. dermatology U. Miami, 2008—. Contbr. articles to profl. jours. NIH-MSTP predoctoral fellow, 1982-86, Dept. Cell Biology predoctoral fellow, 1986-87, Postdoc. fellow, 1987-88. Mem.: Pan Am. Soc. Pigment Cell Rsch., Am. Assn. Cancer Rsch., Am. Acad. Dermatology, Soc. Investigative Dermatology. Office: Univ Miami Rm 912 BRB 1501 NW 10th Ave Miami FL 33136

GRIDLEY, MARK CHARLES, psychologist; b. Detroit, Jan. 5, 1947; s. Frederick William and Helen Lucille (Jones) Gridley. BS, Mich. State U., 1969; MS, Case Western Res. U., 1970, PhD, 1977. Psychometrist, research asst. Case Western Res. U. Hosp., 1971-73; saxophonist/flutist free-lance Cleve., 1969—; cons., psychologist Cleve. Bd. Edn., 1977-81; vis. asst. prof. John Carroll U., University Heights, Ohio, 1981-84; prof. psychology Heidelberg Coll., Tiffin, Ohio, 1987—2008; adj. prof. Cleve. State U., 2008—; tchg. fellow Case Western Res. U., 2009—. Author: Jazz Styles: History and Analysis, 1978, 1985, 1988, 1991, 1994, 1997, 2000, 2003, 2005, 2008, 2011, Concise Guide to Jazz, 1992, 2003, 2006, 2009; contbr. articles to profl. jours. Recipient Best Flutist award, Notre Dame Collegiate Jazz Festival, 1968, Disting. Achievement award, Ednl. Press Assn. Am., 1987. Mem.: Soc. Am. Music, Col. Music Soc.

GRIEPP, RANDALL BERTRAM, cardiothoracic surgery educator; b. Marshall, Minn., Mar. 11, 1940; s. Frank Rudolph and Muriel Camella (Hawes) G.; m. Eva Botstein, Aug. 23, 1968; 1 child, Matthew Michael. BS, Calif. Inst. Tech., 1962; MD, Stanford U., 1967. Diplomate Am. Bd. Surgery, Am. Bd. Thoracic Surgery. Intern in internal medicine Bellevue Hosp., NYC, 1967-68; resident in gen., thoracic and cardiovascular surgery Stanford U. Hosp., Stanford, Calif., 1968-73; asst. prof. surgery Stanford (Calif.) U., Stanford, 1973-76; prof. surgery SUNY, Bklyn., 1976-85, chief cardiothoracic surgery, 1976-85, acting chmn. dept. surgery, 1977-79; prof. surgery, chief cardiothoracic surgery Mt. Sinai Sch. Medicine, NYC, 1985—2001, chmn. cardiothoracic surgery, 1991—2001, prof. chmn. emeritus, 2002—; chief cardiac surgery Beth Israel Med. Ctr., NYC, 1989-90. Mem. rev. bd. for clin. evaluation of temp. left ventricular assist devices and preclin. testing of permanent left ventricular assist devices, Nat. Heart & Lung & Blood Inst., Bethesda, Md., 1980—85; reviewer surgery and bioengring. study sect NIH, 1985-89, 91—95, chmn., 1993-95. Mem. editorial bd. Jour. Cardiac Surgery, 1989—2005. Mellon Found. fellow, 1973-76. Fellow ACS; mem. Soc. Clin. Surgery, Soc. Thoracic Surgeons, Am. Surg. Assn., Soc. Univ. Surgeons, Thoracic Surgery Dirs. Assn. (exec. com. 1985—), Am. Assn. Thoracic Surgery (chmn. membership com. 1988-90), N.Y. Soc. Thoracic Surgery (pres. 1989-90), Harvey Soc. Avocation: sailing. Office: Mt Sinai Med Ctr 1190 Fifth Ave New York NY 10029-6500 Office Phone: 212-659-9495.

GRIES, FRIEDRICH ARNOLD, internist, endocrinologist; b. Essen, Germany, Nov. 4, 1929; s. Carl Friedrich and Adele (Pflitsch) G.; m. Helga Stumpp, Oct. 4, 1957; children: Sylvia, Jutta, Carola, Gundula. MD, U. Marburg, 1956. Specialist in internal medicine, endocrinology, and diabetes. Rsch. fellow U. Munich, 1958—61; resident U. Düsseldorf, Germany, 1961—64, lectr., 1967, prof. medicine, 1971, chmn. medicine, 1973; head German Diabetes Rsch. Inst., 1973—96; head dept. endocrinology U. Düsseldorf, 1994—96. Rsch. fellow Harvard Med. Sch., Boston, 1964—65; spkr. German Rsch. Coun., 1973—88; dir. Inst. Nutrition Counseling, 1983—99. Coauthor: Adipositas, 1976, Diabetes, 1993, 3d edit., 2004, Textbook of Diabetic Neuropathy, 2003; editor 10 books; contbr. articles to profl. jours., chpts. to books Recipient medal U. Helsinki, 1990, Celal Öker medal Turkish Diabetes Assn., 1997, Order of Merit 1st Class Fed. Rep. of Germany, 2002, Neurodiab Life Time Achievement award, 2008. Mem. Internat. Assn. Study of Obesity (v.p. 1992-98), German Nutrition Assn. (hon., v.p. 1980-86), German Diabetes Assn. (hon., pres. 1977-78, Paul Langerhans plaque 1988), German Obesity Assn. (hon; pres. 1993-96), Am. Diabetes Assn., German Soc. Internal Medicine, Diabetic Neuropathy Study Group EASD (hon. chmn. 1994-97), European Assn. Study of Diabetes (vice chmn. diabetes and nutrition study group 1984-86), Lions Internat. Düsseldorf-Hösel (pres. 1984-85). Avocations: sailing, hiking. Office: U Düsseldorf Auf'm Hennekamp 65 40225 Düsseldorf Germany Home Phone: 49 2131 39576. Home Fax: 0 2131 153561. Personal E-mail: hfagries@t-online.de.

GRIEVE, WILLIAM ROY, psychologist, educator, educational administrator, researcher; b. NYC, Mar. 15, 1917; s. Walter Stuart and Grace G.; m. Harriet Bush, Mar. 30, 1978; children: Leslie Lynne Grieve Bainbridge, Davelyn Anne Grieve Sandhowe. Student, SUNY, Oswego, 1934—35; BS, NYU, 1937, MA, 1938; EdD, Rutgers U., 1954. Tchr. secondary edn., NYC, 1938—48; rsch. fellow Ohio State U., Columbus, 1942; ind. arts editor High Point Mag. N.Y.C. Bd. Edn., 1984—85, textbook and instrnl. materials com., 1954—65, curriculum specialist Bur. Curriculum Rsch., 1948—50, supr., adminstr. secondary edn., 1950—65; prof. NYU, NYC, 1965—72, ombudsman Sch. Edn., 1969—71, rsch. predictive testing specialist in vocat./tech. edn.; prof. grad. program NYU/U. PR, NYC, 1966—79; ESSA, ESAA, and ESEA evaluation studies in reading, math., ESL and indsl. edn. NY, NJ, Conn., Mass., Md., 1970—83; assoc. dir. evaluation studies divsn. Psychol. Corp., 1972—75; dir. Ednl. Planning and Rsch. Inc., Boston, 1975—83, pres. Glencove, NY, 1983—, Stuart, Fla., 1983—. Asst. examiner ind. edn., supervision, guidance lics., NYC Bd. Edn., 1950-72; chmn. ind. edn. standing com. Bd. Supts., NYC, 1960-65; adj. prof. psychology L.I. U., Bklyn., 1965-70; adj. prof. edn. NY Inst. Tech., Westbury, 1981-86, SUNY, Westbury, 1986-89; cons. NY C.C. orthotics and prosthetics, 1966, NC State U., 1968, Pub. Edn. Assn./Nat. Alliance Businessmen, NY, 1968-72, Citibank, PR, 1970, Met. Mus. Art (The Art of Black Africa), NYC, 1970, Sta. UFT-TV, NY, 1970; Young and Raubicam, NY, 1974; cons. Cautaulds Internat., Mobile, Ala., 1975, Rheem Mfg., Chgo., 1975, Bankers Trust, NYC, 1975, Republic Steel, Akron and Canton, Ohio, 1977, Rheem Mfg, Chgo, 1979, S.W. Regional Lab., Calif., 1980, N.Y. State Dept. Edn., 1985—, job and task analysis, equal opportunity test devel., alt. edn. programs, coop. edn., work study, career edn., tng. and devel., 1990—; prof., U. PR, Rio Piedras, 1966-67, rsch. predictive testing specialist, 1970-83; cons., industry and commerce in pers. analysis, job and tittle description, hiring and promotion, 1999-2010. Contbr. articles to profl. jours. Bd. mgrs. Prospect Park YMCA, Bklyn., 1960-65; adviser desegregation measures Boston Pub. Schs., 1976-81. With U.S. Army, 1944-45. Mem.: Am. Psychol. and Guidance Assn., Am. Assn. Tchr. Educators, Am. Vocat. Assn., Am. Vocat. Ednl. Rsch. Assn. (charter), N.Y. Schoolmasters Club, Kappa Delta Pi, Kappa Phi Kappa, Epsilon Pi Tau, Phi Delta Kappa. Home: 5684 SE Riverboat Dr Stuart FL 34997 Office Phone: 772-220-6010. Personal E-mail: haribil@aol.com.

GRIFFEN, DANIEL LEONARD, III, cardiologist; MD, U. Iowa, 1982. Diplomate Am. Bd. Internal Medicine, Am. Bd. Internal Medicine-cardiovasc. diseases, Am. Bd. Internal Medicine-advanced echocardiography. Resident Nat. Naval Med. Ctr., fellow; tng. echocardiography lab. Duke Univ.; chmn. cardiology Laurel Regional Hosp. Named one of Top Doctors, Washingtonian Mag., 2011. Fellow: Am. Coll. of Cardiology. Office: Laurel Regional Hospital 7300 Van Dusen Rd Laurel MD 20707 Office Phone: 301-725-4300. Office Fax: 410-792-2270.

GRIFFENHAGEN, GEORGE BERNARD, trade association executive; b. Portland, Oreg., June 9, 1924; s. Richard Bernard and Clara (Schoenian) G.; m. Joan Helen Houston, June 21, 1946 (dec. June 23, 2009); children: Gary Bernard, Gordon Wesley, Barbara Clare. BS in Pharmacy, U. So. Calif., 1949, MS, 1950; student, Fresno State Coll., 1946, U. London, 1948. Dir. research Nion Corp., Hollywood, Calif., 1950-52; curator div. med. scis. Smithsonian Instn., Washington, 1952-59; sec. sect. history of pharmacy Am. Pharm. Assn., Washington, 1952-59, pres. local chpt., 1958-59, assoc. exec. dir., 1959-89, hon. pres., 1990-91; trustee Am. Pharm. Assn. Found., Washington, 1989-94; editor Jour. Am. Pharm. Assn., Washington, 1960-76; sec.-gen. 4th Pan Am. Congress Pharmacy and Biochemistry, Washington, 1957; sec. organizing com. 31st Internat. Congress Pharm. Scis., Washington, 1971; sec.-gen. Internat. Congress History of Pharmacy, Washington, 1983, Japan-U.S. Congress of Pharm. Scis., Honolulu, 1987; v.p. Pan Am. Pharm. and Biochem. Fedn., 1963-82, 85-91, Pharmacy World Congress, Washington, 1991. U.S. del. Internat. Pharm. Fedn. Gen. Assemblies, London, 1955, Brussels, 1958, Copenhagen, 1960, Vienna, 1962, Amsterdam, 1964, Hamburg, 1968, Geneva, 1970, Lisbon, 1972, Rome, 1974, Warsaw, 1976, Cannes, 1978; U.S. del. FIP Coun., Bucharest, 1969, Dublin, 1975, Montreal, 1985, Helsinki, 1986, Amsterdam, 1987, Sydney, 1988, Munich, 1989, Istanbul, 1990, Lyon, 1992, Tokyo, 1993, Lisbon, 1994, Jerusalem, 1996, Vancouver, 1997, The Hague, 1998, Barcelona, 1999, Vienna, 2000; congress coord., The Hague, 1977; U.S. del. Pan Am. Fedn. Pharmacy Congress, Mexico City, 1963, Buenos Aires, 1966, Caracas, 1969, Panama, 1972, Guatemala City, 1985, Santo Domingo, 1988, Buenos Aires, 1994, San Jose, Costa Rica, 1997, Rio de Janeiro, 2000; U.S. del. Internat. Congress History of Pharmacy, Budapest, Hungary, 1981, Fedn. Asian Pharm. Assns. Congress, Seoul, Korea, 1982; mem. Nat. Action Com. on Drug Edn., Office of Edn., 1970-71, Va. Gov.'s Coun. on Narcotic and Drug Abuse Control, 1970-72. Editor: Scalpel and Tongs, 1972-73; Contbr. articles to profl. jours. Mem. Fairfax County Rep. Com., Va., 1962-97; adminstrv. asst. to chmn. Va. State Rep. Com., 1969-71; life mem. Rep. Nat. Com., 1979—; founding pres. Nat. Coord. Coun. on Drug Edn., 1968-69. Served with C.E. AUS, World War II, ETO. Recipient Pfizer Merit award U.S. CD Coun., 1964, U. So. Calif. Alumnus award, 1969; Hugo H. Schaefer award Am. Pharm. Assn., 1984; Disting. Svc. award Pharmacy Guild of Australia, 1988, Internat. Pharmacy Jour. Editor's prize, 1989, 95, Remington Honor medal Am. Pharm. Assn., 1991; named to Nat. Philatelic Writers Hall of Fame, 1990. Mem. Am. Inst. History of Pharmacy (pres. 1960-61, Edward Kremers award 1969, sec. 1991-2005, hon. pres. 2008-), Friends of Hist. Pharmacy (pres. 1957-58), Pharm. Wholesalers Assn. (Distinguished Service award 1971), Am. Topical Assn. (1st v.p. 1972-75, pres. 1976-79, pres. med. subjects unit 1969-72, Distinguished Topical Philatelist award 1970, Myrtle Watt Med. Philately Topicalist award 1980, editor Topical Time 1992—2009), Am. Philatelic Congress (Jere Hess Barr award 1969), Am. Philatelic Soc. (sec.-treas. Writers Unit 1982—; U.S. commr. to Internat. Exhbn. Thematic Philately, Basel, Switzerland 1983, Luff award 2003), Am. Revenue Assn. (named to Sterling Meml. Roll of Disting. Fiscalists 1979), Council Philatelic Orgns. (treas. 1983-91), Internat. Pharm. Fedn. (hon.), Philatelic Lit. Assn., Academie Internationale d'Histoire de la Pharmacie (treas. 1971-81, 1989-97), Pharm. Soc. Gt. Britain (hon.), Sigma Xi, Rho Chi, Phi Kappa Psi. Office: Am Pharm Assn 2215 Constitution Ave NW Washington DC 20037-2907 Home: 12226 Cathedral Dr Woodbridge VA 22192-2232 Business E-Mail: dcsmith3477@gmail.com.

GRIFFETH, LANDIS KING, nuclear medicine physician; b. Greenville, SC, Aug. 3, 1956; s. Jesse Ellis and Mary Alice (King) G.; m. Terri Blount, Aug. 6, 1978. BA in Chemistry and Zoology summa cum laude, Duke U., 1977, PhD in Pharmacology, 1983, MD, 1984. Diplomate Am. Bd. Nuc. Medicine. Postdoctoral rsch. fellow Duke U. Sch. Pharmacology, Durham, NC, 1983-84; resident in diagnostic radiology Mallinckrodt Inst. of Radiology, Washington U., St. Louis, 1984-86, resident in nuclear medicine, 1986-87, chief resident in nuc. medicine, 1987-88, asst. prof. radiology, 1988-93; dir. nuc. medicine Baylor U. Med. Ctr., Dallas, 1993—; med. dir. North Tex. Clin. P.E.T. Inst., Dallas, 1998—. Dir. nuc. medicine and P.E.T., Am. Radiology Assn., Dallas, 1993—, nat. med. dir., P.E.T., U.S. Oncology, 2000—. Assoc. editor Radiology Jour., 1993-2000; cons. to editor Radiology, 2000-02; contbr. numerous articles to profl. jours; reviewer med. jours; edit. bd. Molecular Imagingand Biology, 2004-. Mem. Univ. Park United Meth. Ch.; bd. dirs. Cavalier Health Found.; mem. devel. coun. Tex. A&M Coll. Vet. Medicine. Mem. Am. Coll. Radiology, Am. Coll. Nuc. Physicians, Soc. Nuc. Medicine, Acad. Molecular Imaging (nat. patient adv. com.), Inst. for Clin. P.E.T., Radiol. Soc. N.Am., Am. Soc. for Law Enforcement Tng., Tex. Med. Assn., Tex. Radiol. Soc., Dallas County Med. Soc., Phi Lambda Upsilon, Alpha Omega Alpha. United Methodist. Avocations: target shooting, reading, dogs, travel. Office: Baylor U Med Ctr 3500 Gaston Ave Dallas TX 75246-2096 Office Phone: 214-826-8822. Business E-Mail: lk.griffeth@baylorhealth.edu.

GRIFFIN, BRIAN PIUS, cardiologist; b. County Galway, Ireland, Dec. 31, 1956; MD with honors, Nat. U. Ireland, Galway, 1979, MD higher degree, 2004. Cert. internal medicine and cardiovasc. diseases Am. Bd. Internal Medicine. Intern U. Coll. Hosp., Galway, Ireland,

1979—80, resident, 1980—81, St. Vincent's Hosp.-Dublin, 1981—82, Guys & St. Thomas Hosp., London, 1981—82; fellow Mater Misericordiade Hosp., Dublin, Irish Heart Found., Dublin, Cedars-Sinai Med. Ctr., LA, Harvard Med. Sch.; resident Boston Med. Ctr., 1987—89; fellow Mass. Gen. Hosp., Boston, 1989—91; asst. prof. medicine Dartmouth Med. Sch., Hanover, NH; assoc. dir. echocardiography lab Dartmouth Hitchcock Clinic and Hosp.; dir. cardiovasc. tng. program Cleve. Clinic, 1994—, staff cardiologist dept. cardiology, cardiovasc. imaging, 1994—, vice chmn. dept. cardiovasc. medicine, 2003—. Reviewer Circulation, Jour. Am. Coll. Cardiology; co-dir. Intensive Review Course Cardiology Cleve. Clinic Found. Recipient Stokes medal, Irish Cardiac Soc., 2002; named Tchr. of Yr., Cleve. Clinic Found., 1997. Fellow: Am. Coll. Cardiology; mem.: Am. Coll. Cardiology (mem. workforce and tng. com.), Royal Coll. Physicians Ireland, Am. Heart Assn. (mem. coun. on clinical cardiology, mem. laennec com.). Office: Cleveland Clinic Dept Cardiology 9500 Euclid Ave Cleveland OH 44195 Office Phone: 216-444-6812. Office Fax: 216-445-5499.

GRIFFIN, DIANE EDMUND, research physician, virologist, educator; b. Iowa City, Ia., May 12, 1940; d. Rudolph William and Doris Irene (Swanson) Edmund; m. John Wesley Griffin, June 13, 1965; children: Christopher Todd, Erik Edmund. BA, Augustana Coll., Rock Island, Ill., 1962; MD, Stanford U., Calif., 1968, PhD, 1970. Diplomate Am. Bd. Internal Medicine, cert. in pediatric infectious diseases. Intern, resident medicine and infectious disease Stanford U. Hosp., 1968-70; fellow Johns Hopkins U., Balt., 1970-73, asst. prof. Sch. Medicine, 1973-79, assoc. prof., 1979-86, prof., 1986—94, W. Harry Feinstone prof. and chair dept. molecular microbiology and immunology, Bloomberg Sch. Pub. Health, 1994—, also Disting. Svc. prof., Alfred & Jill Sommer chair dept. molecular microbiology and immunology, dir. Malaria Rsch. Inst. (JHMRI), 2001—07. Investigator Howard Hughes Med. Inst., 1973—79; mem. virology study sect. NIH, 1982—86, mem. microbiology and infectious diseases rsch. adv. com., 1989—92, chair, 1992—94; mem. adv. com. Nat. Multiple Sclerosis Soc., 1986—92. Editor: Jour. Virology; mem. editl. bd. Virology, Virus Rsch., Jour. Neurovirology; contbr. articles to profl. jours., chapters to books. Recipient Javits Neurosci. Investigator award, Nat. Inst. Neurological Disorders & Stroke; named to Md. Women's Hall of Fame, 2009. Fellow: AAAS, Infectious Diseases Soc. America; mem.: NAS (coun. mem. 2010—), Am. Acad. Microbiology, Inst. Medicine, Am. Soc. Virology (coun. mem. 1987—89), Am. Soc. Clin. Investigation. Democrat. Lutheran. Avocation: gardening. Office: Bloomberg Sch Pub Health Bldg Ste E 5132 615 N Wolfe St Baltimore MD 21205-2103 Office Phone: 410-955-3459. Office Fax: 410-955-0105. E-mail: dgriffin@jhsph.edu.

GRIFFITH, B(EZALEEL) HEROLD, retired plastic surgeon, educator; b. NYC, Aug. 24, 1925; s. Bezaleel Davies and Henrietta (Herold) G.; m. Jeanne B. Lethbridge, 1948; children: Susan, Tristan. BA, Johns Hopkins U., [illegible], MD, Yale U., [illegible]. Cert. Am. Bd. Plastic Surgery, 1959, diplomate Nat. Bd. Med. Examiners. Asst. in anatomy Yale U., New Haven, 1947—48, asst. in surgery, 1948—49; intern Grace New Haven Cmty. Hosp.-Yale U., 1948-49; resident in surgery VA Hosp., Newington, Conn., 1949-50; asst. resident in surgery 2d (Cornell) Surg. Divsn., Bellevue Hosp., NYC, 1952-53; instr. surgery Cornell U., 1956; resident in plastic surgery VA Hosp., Bronx, 1953-55; resident (sr. registrar) in plastic surgery U. Glasgow, Scotland, 1955; chief resident in plastic surgery N.Y. Hosp. Cornell Med. Ctr., NYC, 1956; rsch. fellow in plastic surgery Cornell U. Med. Coll., 1956-57; pvt. practice specializing in plastic surgery Chgo., 1957-96; attending plastic surgeon Northwestern Meml., Children's Meml., VA Lakeside hosps., Rehab. Inst. Chgo.; instr. surgery Northwestern U., 1957-59, assoc. in surgery, 1959-62, asst. prof. surgery, 1962-67, assoc. prof., 1967-71, prof., 1971-96, prof. emeritus, 1996, chief divsn. plastic surgery, 1970-91; chief plastic surgery Shriners Hosp. for Crippled Children, Chgo., 1994-96; ret., 1996. Chmn. Am. Bd. Plastic Surgery, 1981—82. Mem. editl. bd.: Plastic and Reconstructive Surgery, 1972—78; contbr. articles to profl. jours. Lt. M.C. USNR, 1950—52. Fellow ACS, Am. Assn. Plastic Surgeons, Chgo. Surg. Soc., Royal Soc. Medicine; mem. AAAS, AMA, Am. Bd. Plastic Surgery (dir. 1976-82), Am. Burn Assn., Am. Soc. Plastic and Reconstructive Surgeons (sec. 1972-74), Brit. Assn. Plastic Surgeons (hon.), Plastic Surgery Rsch. Coun. (chmn. 1969), Am. Cleft Palate Assn., N.Y. Acad. Scis., Ill., Chgo. Med. Socs., Midwestern Assn. Plastic Surgeons, Soc. Head and Neck Surgeons, Soc. Med. History of Chgo., Chgo. Hist. Socs., Civil War Round Table, Evanston Hist. Soc. (trustee 1974-78), Masons, Yale Club (Chgo.), Nathan Smith Club, Sigma Xi (pres. Northwestern U. 1986-87, 94-95), Plastic Surgery Ednl. Found. (v.p. 1969). Achievements include research in transplantation, skin tumors, cleft palate, paraplegia.

GRIFFITH, LAWRENCE STACEY CAMERON, cardiologist, educator; b. Wash., Sept. 16, 1937; s. Ernest Stacey and Margaret Dyckman (Davenport) G.; m. Anne Gorman Young, June 20, 1959; children: Lawrence, John, Melinda, Gordon. BA, Haverford Coll., Pa., 1959; MD with honors, U. Rochester, NY, 1963. Diplomate Am. Bd. Internal Medicine, Am. Bd. Cardiovascular Disease. Intern in medicine and surgery Strong Meml. Hosp., Rochester, NY, 1963—64, asst. resident in surgery, 1964—65, asst. and assoc. resident in medicine, 1967—69; rsch. fellow in cardiology Johns Hopkins U., Balt., 1969—71, asst. prof. medicine Sch. Medicine, 1971—76, asst. prof. radiology, 1974—80, assoc. prof. medicine, 1976—88, prof. medicine, 1988—; med. dir. Johns Hopkins Medicine Internat., 1999—. Cons. VA Coop. Study Surgery for Coronary Artery Disease, Program on Surg. Control of Hyperlipidemias, U. Minn. Contbr. articles to profl. jours. Bd. dirs. Julia Dyckman Andrus Meml., Inc., Yonkers, NY, 1971—, chmn., 1976-2007; bd. dirs. John E. Andrus Meml. Home for Aged, Hastings-on-Hudson, NY, 1974-97; bd. dirs. Surdna Found., NYC, 1976—, v.p., 1988-94; chmn. adv. bd. Balt. Pastoral Counseling Svc., 1971-80. With USPHS, 1965-67. Fellow ACP, Coun. Clin. Cardiology of Am. Heart Assn., Am. Coll. Cardiology; mem. Alpha Omega Alpha. Democrat. Methodist. Home: 802 W Saint Georges Rd Baltimore MD 21210-1409 Office: Johns Hopkins Hosp Halsted 500 600 N Wolfe St Baltimore MD 21287-0005 Office Phone: 410-955-6173.

GRIFFITHS, BARBARA LORRAINE, psychologist, marriage and family therapist, writer; b. Glendale, Calif., July 15, 1927; d. David William and Mabel Augusta (Gaarder) G.; m. Dale Elmo Rumbaugh, Mar. 28, 1948 (div. 1957); 1 child, David Wynn; m. Knute Flint, Nov. 13, 1964. AA in Journalism, Valley C.C., 1958; BA in Psychology, U. Calif. Riverside, 1972; MS in Rehab. Counseling, Calif. State U., 1976; PhD in Clin. Psychology, Calif. Grad. Inst., 1984. Cert. Diplomate Am. Psychotherapy Assn., 1998, cert. addicition specialist, Marriage and Family Therapist 1979. Alcoholism counselor Kaiser Permanente, LA, 1976-82; pvt. practice Hollywood, L.A., 1979-89, Glendale, Burbank, Calif., 1989-97, LA, 1997—2005. Mem. State of Calif. Med. Diversion Evaluation Com., 1998—2003; screener 6th and 7th Prism awards Entertainment Industry Coun. Film, 2001—02; sci. expert reviewer 6th annual Prism Awards Entertainment Industry Coun., 2002—03; reviewer 6th and 7th Ann. PRISM awards Entertainment Industry Coun. Film, 2002; clinical psychologist Calif. Youth Authority, 2002—03. Editor (child abuse newsletter): Directions, 1976—86; writer, prodr.: (short film) Silver Bullet Kid, 2003; contbr. short stories, feature articles, columns to various mags., newspapers and profl. mags.; editor: Sunrise Sunset Memories, 2010. Mem. Glendale Rotary, 1990-95, Verdugo BPW, 1988-91; Nat. Ski Patrolwoman #122, 1952-56. Recipient Editor's Choice award for poetry, 1997. Mem. APA (assoc.), Los Angeles County Psychol. Assn., Douglas County Nev. Sr. Adv. Coun. Avocations: script writing, tennis, skiing, swimming and water sports, reading. Home and Office: 1344 E Wales Ct Gardnerville NV 89410 Personal E-mail: bgriffiths1287@charter.net.

GRIFO, JAMES (JAMIE) A., obstetrician, gynecologist; b. Paterson, NJ, Dec. 16, 1955; m. Anne Borsch; 1 child, Christopher. PhD in Biochemistry, Case Western Res. U., Cleve., 1982; MD, Case Western Res. U. Sch. Mdicine, 1984. Diplomate Am. Bd. Obstetrics & Gynecology, cert. in reproductive endocrinology/infertility. Intern ob-gyn. Weill Cornell Med. Coll., NYC, 1984-85, reproductive endocrinology resident, 1985-88, asst. prof., 1990—95; fellow in reproductive endocrinology Yale Med. Sch., New Haven, 1988-90; prof. ob-gyn., dir. divsn. reproductive endocrinology NYU Sch. Medicine, 1995—, co-founder, program dir. NYU Fertility Ctr., 1995—. Contbr. med. articles to profl. jours. Recipient President's award, RESOLVE Nat. Infertility Assn., 1996; named one of Best Doctors in NY, NY Mag., 1997—, 401 Best Doctors for Women in America, Good Housekeeping mag. Mem.: Soc. Assisted Reproductive Tech. (past pres.), Am. Soc. Reproductive Medicine, Phi Beta Kappa. Office: NYU Fertility Ctr 660 First Ave at 38th St New York NY 10016 Office Phone: 212-263-7978. Office Fax: 212-263-7978. Business E-Mail: James.Grifo@nyumc.org. *

GRIGIENE, RUTA, radiologist, researcher; d. Konstantinas Valuckas and Auksuole Valuckiene; m. Andrius Grigas, Oct. 9, 1994; children: Indre Grigaite, Algis Grigas. MD, Vilnius U., Lithuania, 1997, PhD, 2006. Radiologist, rschr. Oncology Inst. Vilnius U., 2000—06, head, radiology dept., 2006—, mem. bd., 2007—. Mem.: Lithuanian Radiology Assn. Achievements include research in cervical cancer, cancer imaging, angiogenesis imaging, prognostic, predicting factors in cancer. Avocations: travel, reading, skiing. Office: Vilnius Univ Oncology Inst Santariskiu G. 1 8406 Vilnius Lithuania Office Fax: 370 5 2786790. Business E-Mail: ruta.grigiene@vuoi.lt.

GRIGOLO, BRUNELLA, research scientist; b. Rovereto, Trento, Italy, Jan. 6, 1956; Grad., 1975; degree in Biol. Sci., U. Bologna, 1980. Physiopathology and cartilage regeneration Rizzoli Orthop. Inst., 1991—, responsible lab. preclinical studies, 2010—. Mem.: Italian Soc. Knee Surgery, Arthroscopy, Sport, Cartilage and Orhopaedic Technologies, Osteoarthritis Rsch. Soc., Internat. Cartilage Repair Soc. Avocations: skiing, diving. Office: Via di Barbiano 1/10 Bologna 40136 Italy Office Fax: 00390516366807. Business E-Mail: brunella.grigolo@ior.it.

GRIGOROPOULOS, VLASSIS G., ophthalmologist, consultant; b. Athens, Greece, May 25, 1964; s. George Grigoropoulos and Maria Grigoropoulou; m. Anabel I. Quijada, Apr. 19, 1999; children: Maria Nefeli Grigoropoulou, Emilio. Degree, Med. U. Athens, Greece, 1989, PhD, 2008. Diplomate Greek Ophthal. Soc., 1998. Sr. house officer Charing Cross Hosp., London, 1992—93, Conquest Hosp., Hastings, East Sussex, 1994—95, U. Athens, Gen. Hosp., 1995—98, vitreoretinal fellowship, 1998—99, Gloucester & Cheltenham Gen. Hosp., 1999—2000, St Thomas' Hosp., London, 2001—01, sr. mem. tchg. program, 2000—01; vitreoretinal fellowship Moorfields Eye Hosp., London, 2001—02; cons. opthalmologist Kent County Ophthalmic & Aural Hosp., Maidstone, 2001—01, Henry Dunant Hosp., Athens, 2003—. Sr. mem. tchg. program Med. Sch., U. Athens, 1998—99, Cheltenham Gen. Hosp., 1999—2000, Ophthalmology Dept., U. Patra, Greece, 2004—, Greek Ophthal. Soc., Athens, Greece, 2004—. Contbr. scientific papers. Csultant ophthalmologist Red Cross, Athens, 2003—09. Recipient award, Scottish Exec. & Diabetes. Mem.: European Vitreoretinal Soc., Am. Soc. Retina Specialists, Am. Acad. Ophthalmology, Greek Vitreoretinal Soc., Greek Ophthal. Soc. Achievements include research in diabetic retinopathy detection and effect of JPEG image. Avocations: sailing, photography, music, computers. Office: Vlassis Grigoropoulos Seuitelou 1 115 28 Athens Greece Office Phone: 30 210 7791879.

GRIGORY, FASTOVTSOV, psychiatrist; b. Volgograd, July 14, 1962; MD, Volgograd, 1975. Physician Serbsky Nat. Rsch. Ctr. Social and Forensic Psychiatry, 2003—. Office: Kropotkinskiy 23 Moscow 119991 Russia Business E-Mail: fgrigo@yandex.ru.

GRILLNER, STEN ERIK, neurophysiology educator, researcher; b. Stockholm, June 14, 1941; s. Vilhelm and Karin Maria Grillner; m. Lena I.K. Hegnelius, Aug. 3, 1963; children: Pernilla, Katja. MB, U. Goteborg, Sweden, 1962, MD-Phd, Docent, U. Goteborg, Sweden, 1969. Instr. physiology med. faculty U. Göteborg, 1963-69, rsch. assoc., docent med. faculty, 1969-75; vis. scientist Acad. Sci., Moscow, 1971; prof. physiology Karolinska Inst., Stockholm, 1975-86, prof., chmn. Nobel Inst. Neurophysiology, 1986—, prof., chmn. dept. neurophysiology and behavior, 1993—. Adj. mem. Nobel Com. Physiology and Medicine, 1987—, dep. chmn., 1992—94, chmn., 1995—97, dep. chmn., 2004, chmn. Nobel assembly, 2005—; Forbes lectr. Woodshole, 1993; mem. adv. bd. RIKEN Inst., Tokyo, 1998—; hon. prof. Beijing Med. U., 2000. Recipient Greater Nordic prize of E. Fernström U., Lund, Sweden, 1990, Disting. Achievement award in neuroscience, Bristol Myers Squibb, 1993, Reeve-Irvine medal, NY, 2002, Neuronal Plasticity award, Found. IPSEN, Paris, 2003, Ralph Gerard prize, Soc. for Neuroscience, 2005; co-recipient Kavli prize for neuroscience, Norwegian Acad. Sci. and Letters in partnership with the Kavli Found. and the Norwegian Ministry of Edn. and Rsch., 2008. Mem.: NAS (fgn. assoc.), Royal Spanish Acad. Medicine, Inst. Medicine, Nat. Acad., Am. Acad. Arts and Scis. (hon. fgn.), Norwegian Acad. Sci., Royal Swedish Acad. Scis., Acad. of Sci. in Europe. Home: Norrtullsgat 3 S-11329 Stockholm Sweden Office: Department of Neuroscience Nobel Institute for Neurophysiology Retzius Vag 8 171 77 Stockholm Sweden Office Phone: 46-8-52486900. Office Fax: 46-8-349544. Personal E-mail: Sten.Grillner@ki.se.

GRILLONE, GREGORY ANGELO, otolaryngologist, educator; b. NYC, Feb. 17, 1953; s. Gregory and Rose Marie Grillone; m. Diane Marie Raymond, May 29, 1988; children: Gregory James, Deanna Rose. BA, NYU, 1975; MD, Mt. Sinai U., NYC, 1983. Diplomate Am. Bd. Otolaryngology. Intern otolaryngology/gen. surgery Tufts-New Eng. Med. Ctr., Boston, 1983—84; resident otolaryngology, head and neck surgery Boston U. Med. Ctr., 1984—88; staff Boston VA Hosp., 1988, Boston Children's Hosp., 1988, Boston City Hosp., 1988—96; residency prog. dir., vice chmn. dept. otolaryngology Boston U. Med. Ctr., 1996—; assoc. prof. dept. otolaryngology Boston U. Sch. Medicine, 2004—, dir. Ctr. Voice & Swallowing, 2006—. Sr. clin. instr. Tufts. U. Sch. Medicine. Contbr. articles to profl. jours. Fellow: ACS; mem.: AMA, Am. Acad. Otolaryngology (Honor award 2000), Soc. Univ. Otolaryngologists, Am. Head & Neck Soc., Voice Found., Mass. Soc. Otolaryngology (bd. dirs. 1992), New Eng. Otolaryn. Soc. (sec., treas. 1994—99, v.p. 1999—2000, pres. 2000—01). Office: Dept Otolaryngology Boston Univ Med Ctr 820 Harrison Ave 4th Fl Boston MA 02118 Office Fax: 617-638-7965; Home Fax: 617-638-7965. Personal E-mail: gregory.grillone@bmc.org. Business E-Mail: drgrillone@hoarseness.org.

GRIM, CHARLES W., former federal agency administrator; b. Okla., 1958; DDS, U. Okla. Coll. Dentistry, 1983; MA in Health Services Adminstrn., U. Mich., 1992. Clin. assignment Claremore Svc. unit Indian Health Svc., US Dept. Health & Human Services, Okmulgee, Okla., asst. area dental officer Oklahoma City, area dental officer, 1989—92, dir. divsn. oral health Albuquerque, 1992, acting svc. unit dir., dir. divsn. clin. services and behavioral health, acting exec. officer, assoc. dir. office of health programs Phoenix, 1998—99, acting dir. Oklahoma City, 1999—2000, area dir., 2000—02, interim dir. Rockville, Md., 2002—03, dir., 2003—07. Rear adm. Commd. Corps USPHS. Mem.: ADA, Soc. Am. Indian Dentists, Am. Assn. Pub. Health Dentistry, Am. Bd. Dental Pub. Health, Commd. Officers Assn. E-mail: charles-grim@cherokee.org.

GRIMBY, GUNNAR LARS, physician, researcher; b. Stockholm, Apr. 6, 1933; s. Paul and Mary (Holm) Grimby; div.; children: Lars, Hans, Anna; m. Agneta Elisabet Holström, Mar. 31, 1985. MD, Göteborg (Sweden) U., 1960, PhD in Med. Sci., 1962; specialization in clin. physiology, specialization in rehab. medicine. Med. diplomate. Resident Sahlgrenska U. Hosp., Göteborg, 1960-65, cons., 1966-72; assoc. prof. Göteborg U., 1973-83, prof., 1983-99. Chmn. expert com. on rehab. Swedish Bd. Health and Social Welfare, 1994-98. Editor-in-chief Jour. Rehab. Medicine, 1999—; contbr. over 420 articles to profl. publs.; contbr. chpts. to books. Bd. dirs. Coll. Phys. Edn., Stockholm, 1995-97. Sr. rsch. fellow Harvard Sch. Pub. Health, 1965-66. Fellow Royal Coll. Physicians; mem. Swedish Soc. Rehab. and Phys. Medicine (vice chmn. 1990-93, chmn. 1994-95), Japanese Assn. Rehab. Medicine (corr.), German Soc. Phys. Medicine and Rehab. Avocations: skiing, outdoor activities, boating. Office: Sahlgrenska U Hosp Rehab Medicine 413 45 Goteborg Sweden E-mail: gunnar.grimby@rehab.gu.se.

GRIMBY-EKMAN, ANNA ELISABETH, statistician; b. Sweden, Dec. 28, 1967, PhLic in Stats., Gothenburg U., 1997, PhD, 2010. Statistician dept. occupl. & environ. medicine Sahlgrenska U. Hosp., 1999—. Cons. Jour. Rehab. Medicine, 2009. Mem.: Soc. Epidemiol. Rsch., Swedish Soc. Statisticians Promotion, Swedish Epidemiologic Soc. Avocation: running. Office: Box 414 Gothenburg SE 405 30 Sweden Business E-Mail: anna.ekman@amm.gu.se

GRIMES, JERRY SPEIGHT, orthopedist; b. France, Sept. 17, 1964; MD, U. Tex. Med. Branch, 1999. Asst. prof. dept. orthopedics Tex. Tech Health Scis. Ctr., 2005—09; physician Ctr. Orthop. Surgery, 2009—. Mem.: Am. Orthop. Foot and Ankle Soc., Am. Acad. Orthop. Surgeons. Office: 4642 N Loop 289 Ste 101 Lubbock TX 79416 Office Fax: 806-792-8588. Business E-Mail: speight@grimesmd.com.

GRIMES, PEARL E., dermatologist, educator; MD, Wash. U., St. Louis, 1974. Diplomate Am. Bd. Dermatology, 1979. Resident dermatology Howard Univ., Washington, 1976—79; established The Vitiligo and Pigmentation Inst. of Southern Calif., 1990; clin. prof. dermatology David Geffen Sch. of Medicine UCLA; hosp. affiliation include Ronald Reagan UCLA Med. Ctr. Author over 100 publs. and abstracts; asst. editor, mem. editl. bd. (jour.) Jour. of the Am. Acad. of Dermatology, mem. editl. bd. Jour. of Clin. Dermatology; contbg. editor: (jour.) Cosmetic Dermatology. Established Coalition for At-Risk Youth, 2005. Named one of The Best Doctors of America. Mem.: Women's Dermatologic Soc., Internat. Pigment Cell Soc., Dermatology Found., Soc. of Investigative Dermatology, Am. Dermatological Assn., Am. Soc. of Dermatologic Surgery, Am. Acad. of Dermatology. Office: The Vitiligo and Pigmentation Institute of Southern CA Ste 650 5670 Wilshire Blvd Los Angeles CA 90036 Office Phone: 323-467-4389.

GRIMHOLT, UNNI, geneticist; b. Oslo, Oct. 20, 1960; s. Svein Jørgen and Marit Ingeborg (Iversen) G.; m. Eirik Ruben. MS, U. Oslo, 1988; PhD, Norwegian Coll. Vet. Medicine, 1994. Rsch. fellow Agrl. U. of Norway, 1988-90, Norwegian Coll. of Vet. Medicine, 1991-94, rschr., 1994—. Contbr. articles to profl. jours. Mem. Norwegian Biochem. Soc. Phone: 22 96 47 87. Office: CEES Univ Oslo Dept Biology PO Box 1066 Blindern OSLO 0316 Norway also: Univ Oslo CEES-Dept Biology Postboks 1066 Blindern 316 Oslo Norway Business E-Mail: unni.gri@ulrik.uio.no.

GRIMLEY, JEFFREY MICHAEL, dentist; b. Alton, Ill., Feb. 3, 1957; s. John Richard and Joyce Imogene (Mallin) G.; m. Julie Ellen Gardner, Aug. 2, 1980; children: Joel Michael, Christopher Mark, Benjamin Jeffrey. BS, U. Iowa, 1979, DDS, 1983; cert., Miami Valley Hosp., Dayton, Ohio, 1984. Gen. practice dentistry, Naperville, Ill., 1984—. Mem. ADA, Acad. Gen. Dentistry, Ill. Dental Soc., Chgo. Dental Soc. Methodist. Avocations: sports, photography. Office: Ste 112 1980 Three Farms Ave Naperville IL 60540-5365 Home Phone: 630-416-9583; Office Phone: 630-369-6980. Personal E-mail: grimleydds1@aol.com.

GRINBERG, RAUL, internist; b. Buenos Aires, Aug. 15, 1922; came to U.S., 1958; s. David Grinberg and Ana Tabachicoff; m. Raquel Funes, Feb. 12, 1945 (div. 1962); children: George Anibal, Ricardo Adrian, Diego Xavier. Bachelor's degree, Mariano Moreno, Buenos

Aires, 1939; MD, Buenos Aires Med. Sch., 1946. Rsch. assoc. Columbia U., NYC, 1958-62; sr. internist Roswell Pk. Meml. Inst., Buffalo, 1963-64; clin. instr. SUNY, Binghamton, N.Y., 1970-74; pvt. practice Binghamton, 1970—. Vis. prof. Cornell U., Ithaca, N.Y., 1964-66; mem. adv. bd. oncology N.Y. State Med. Soc., Lake Success, 1970-96. Author: (books) Computers and Obesity, 1989, Sexual Education for Doctors, 1998, The Secret Life of a Doctor, 2003; artist (one man shows) include SUNY Art Gallery, Binghamton, 2000, Jewish Cmty. Ctr., 2002, Gallery Unitarian Universalist Ch., Binghamton, NY, 2007. Mem. Roberson Art Mus., Binghamton, 1964-99, H. Johnson Art Mus., Ithaca, 1980-99, Philharmonic Orch., Binghamton, 1964-99; Met. Mus., N.Y.C., 1997-99. Recipient Bronze award Am. Cancer Soc., 1997. Fellow ACP; mem. Endocrine Soc., Am. Assn. for Cancer Rsch. (emeritus mem. 2011, 2011), Am. Coll. Forensic Examiners, Inc., Meml. Sloan-Kettring Milenium Cir., Antiques Soc. (Broome County), Am. Indian Relief Coun. Avocations: painting, writing, collecting antiques. Home and Office: Apt 3A Bldg 4 201 Evergreen St Vestal NY 13850

GRINBLATT, DAVID LEE, internist, hematologist, oncologist; b. Columbus, Ohio, July 14, 1959; Grad., MIT, 1981; MD, Case Western Res. U., 1986. Resident in internal medicine Rush-Presbyn.-St. Lukes, Chgo., 1986-89; fellow hematology and oncology Northwestern U., Chgo., 1989-92; attending physician Weiss Meml. Hosp., Chgo., 1992—, U. Chgo. Hosps., 1992—; exec. officer Cancer & Leukemia Group B, Chgo., 1995—; asst. prof. U. Chgo., 1992-99, assoc. prof., 1999—. Mem. ACP, ACS, Am. Soc. Clin. Oncology, Am. Soc. Hematology. Office: U Chicago-Weiss Meml Hosp 4646 N Marine Dr Chicago IL 60640-5759

GRINDE, TURID VOGT, psychologist, researcher; b. Trondheim, Norway, Nov. 23, 1923; d. Fredrik and Signe (Fjalstad) Vogt; m. Hans Grinde, Jan. 4, 1946; children: Geir, Bjørn, Gunner. Candidate of psychology, U. Oslo, 1948; MPH, U. Calif., Berkeley, 1976. Rsch. asst., lectr. U. Oslo, 1949-51; clinician, rschr. Ctr. Inst. Cerebral Palsy, Oslo, 1960-66; sch. psychologist Baerum, Norway, 1967-69; cons. Ministry Health and Social Affairs, Oslo, 1969-79, head of child welfare, 1979-83; project mgr. Nordic Coun. of Ministers, 1983-89; sr. rschr. Ministry of Children and Family Affairs, Oslo, 1989—, Norwegian Social Rsch., Oslo, 1989—2000, Comparative Norwegian Child Welfare Rsch., 2000—04. Organizer, participant Nordic and internat. confs. Author: Children and Child Welfare in the Nordic Countries, 1989, The Knowledge Base of Child Welfare, 1993, Child Welfare Complaints and Legal Rights, 1996; editor: Nordic Child Welfare: The Threshold for Measures and the Proceedings in Compulsory Decisions, 2004; contbr. articles to profl. jours.; author: Nordic Child Welfare Services: Variations in Norms, Attitude and Practice, 2008. Main author proposal law for psychologists, Norwegian Parliament, 1972. Mem. APA (affiliate), Norwegian Psychol. Assn. (chmn. 1963-65, 68-69), Norwegian Rschrs., Internat. Soc. Prevention Child Abuse and Neglect, Assn. Child Psychology and Psychiatry. Avocations: family and grandchildren, travel. Office: Norwegian Social Rsch Munthes gt 29 0260 Oslo Norway Home: Claude Monet's allé 21 Sandvika 1338 Norway Office Phone: (0047) 416 92 248. E-mail: turid.v.grinde@nova.no, tvg@live.no.

GRINES, CINDY LEE, health facility administrator, cardiologist; b. Kalamazoo, Mich., May 17, 1955; children: Jessica, Derek. BS cum laude, Ohio State U., 1977, MD cum laude, 1980. Intern, resident Ohio State U. Hosps., Columbus, 1980-84; fellow cardiology U. Mich. Hosp., Ann Arbor, 1984—87, instr. internal medicine divsn. cardiology, 1986-87; assoc. investigator rsch. dept. VA Med. Ctr., Ann Arbor, 1986-89, Lexington, Ky., 1986-89; asst. prof. medicine divsn. cardiology U. Ky., Lexington, 1987-90; dir. cardiac catheterization lab. William Beaumont Hosp., Royal Oak, Mich., 1990—, dir. interventional cardiology fellowship program. Com. mem. Nat. Heart, Lung, Blood Inst., FDA; researcher in field. Contbr. articles to profl. jours. Named to Best Doctors in America. Fellow Am. Coll. Cardiology (mem. planning bd.); mem. Am. Heart Assn. (coun. clin. cardiology, mem. planning bd.), Am. Coll. Angiology, Am. Coll. Physicians, Detroit Heart Club, Alpha Omega Alpha. Avocations: skiing, hiking, water sports. Office: William Beaumont Hosp Divsn Cardiology 3601 W 13 Mile Rd Royal Oak MI 48073-6712 Office Phone: 248-898-4163. Office Fax: 248-898-5596.

GRINNELL, ALAN DALE, neuroscientist, educator; b. Mpls., Nov. 11, 1936; s. John Erle and Swanhild Constance (Friswold) Grinnell; m. Verity Rich, Sept. 30, 1962 (div. 1975); m. Feelie Lee Grinnell, Dec. 23, 1996. BA, Harvard U., Cambridge, Mass., 1958, PhD, 1962. Jr. fellow Harvard U., 1959-62; rsch. assoc. biophysics dept. Univ. Coll. London, 1962-64; asst. rsch. zoologist UCLA, 1964-65, from asst. prof. to prof. dept. biology, 1965-78, prof. physiology, 1972—; dir. Jerry Lewis Neuromuscular Research Ctr. UCLA Sch. Medicine, 1978—2003; head Ahmanson Lab. Cellular Neurobiology UCLA Brain Research Inst, 1977—; dir. tng. grant in cellular neurobiology UCLA, 1968—2006, rsch. assoc. Fowler Mus. Cultural History, 1990—, chmn. dept. physiol. sci., 1997—2001. Author: Calcium and Ion Channel Modulation, 1988, Physiology of Excitable Cells, 1983, Regulation of Muscle Contraction, 1981, Introduction to Nervous Systems, 1977, others; contbr. editorial revs. to profl. jours., pub. houses, fed. granting agys. Guggenheim fellow, 1986; recipient Sr. Scientist award Alexander von Humboldt Stiftung, 1975, 79, Jacob Javits award NIH, 1986. Mem. AAAS (mem.-at-large neurosci. steering group 1998-2002), Muscular Dystrophy Assn. (mem. med. adv. com. LA chpt. 1980-92), Soc. for Neurosci. (councilor 1982-86), Am. Physiol. Soc. (mem. neurophysiol. steering com. 1981-84), Soc. Fellow, Phi Beta Kappa, Sigma Xi, others. Avocations: music, anthropology, archaeology, travel. Home: 510 E Rustic Rd Santa Monica CA 90402-1116 Office: UCLA Sch Medicine Dept Physiology Los Angeles CA 90095-0001 Office Phone: 310-825-4468. Business E-Mail: agrinnell@mednet.ucla.edu.

GRINNEY, JAY, health facility company executive; b. Racine, Wis., Mar. 20, 1951; s. Leo Richard and June Louise (Christensen) G.; children: Naomi Hope, Rachel June, Matthew Jay; m. Ellen Heath, May 4, 1988. BA in Psychology, St. Olaf Coll., 1973; MHA, Washington U., Saint Louis, Mo., 1981, MBA, 1981. Adminstrv. resident The Meth. Hosp. System, Houston, 1982-83, asst. v.p., 1982-84, sr. v.p., 1985; CEO, Rosewood Med. Ctr. HCA Healthcare Co., Houston, 1990—92, COO, Houston region, 1992—93, pres., Houston region, 1993—96, pres., Eastern group Nashville, 1996—2004; pres., CEO HealthSouth Corp., Birmingham, 1999—, bd. dirs., 2004—. Treas., bd. dirs. The People's Community Clinic, St. Louis, 1979-81; adj. instr. Washington U., Houston, 1988—. Mem. allocations com. Houston United Way, 1988. Mem. Am. Coll. Healthcare Execs. (mem. regent's adv. coun. 1986—), Am. Hosp. Assn., Tex. Hosp. Assn., Greater Houston Hosp. Coun. (fin. com. 1985). Avocations: weightlifting, running, skiing, horseback riding. Office: HealthSouth Corp One HealthSouth Pkwy Birmingham AL 35243 Office Phone: 205-967-7116. Office Fax: 205-969-3543. Business E-Mail: jay.grinney@healthsouth.com. *

GRISEZ, JAMES LOUIS, physician, plastic surgeon; b. Modesto, Calif., Feb. 25, 1935; s. John Francis and Josephine Marie (Tournahu) G.; m. Diane Madeline Skidmore, Mar. 7, 1989; children: James, Stephen, Suzanne, Kathleen. MD, St. Louis Sch. Medicine, 1960. Diplomate Am. Bd. Plastic and Reconstructive Surgery. Intern D.C. Gen. Hosp., Washington, 1960-61; resident med. ctr. Georgetown U., Washington, 1961-64; resident plastic and reconstructive surgery ctr. St. Francis Meml. Hosp., San Francisco, 1964-66; military surgeon Brook Army Med Ctr., San Antonio, 1966, Second Gen. Hosp., Landstuhl, Germany, 1966-69; pvt. practice Napa, Calif., 1969-82, Salinas, Calif., 1982-90, Kailua-Kona, Hawaii, 1990-93, South Valley Plastic Surgery, Gilroy, Calif., 1993—2002; provl. staff French Hosp. San Luis Obispo, 2002—03; active staff Arroyo Grande Cmty. Hosp., 2003—. Active staff mem. St. Louise Regional Hosp.; chief of staff South Valley Hosp., Hazel Hawkins; chief staff St. Helena Hosp., 1977-78, exec. com. 1973-80; radio talk show host All About Plastic Surgery, sta. KRNY, 1986-88. Contbr. articles to med. jours. Mem. Am. Cancer Soc. (pres. 1988-90), Am. Soc. Plastic Surgeons, Calif. Soc. Plastic and Reconstructive Surgeons, Hawaii Plastic Surgery Soc. Home: 1595 Chesapeake Pl Arroyo Grande CA 93420 Office: Plastic Reconstructive & Hand Surgery 200 B Station Way Arroyo Grande CA 93420 *

GRISWOLD, NANCY J., federal judge; b. 1960; BA, La. State U., 1980; JD, Baylor U. Law Sch., 1983. Pvt. law practice, Dallas, Shreveport, La.; chief judge La. Workers Compensation Ct., 1990—93; adminstrv. law judge Office Hearings & Appeals Social Security Adminstrn. (SSA), Shreveport, La., 1995—2002, chief adminstrv. law judge, 2002—04, regional chief adminstrv. law judge Boston, 2004—06, dep. chief adminstrv. law judge Office Disability Adjudication & Review Washington, 2006—10; chief adminstrv. law judge Office Medicare Hearings & Appeals US Dept. Health & Human Services, Washington, 2010—. Mem.: Colo. Bar Assn., La. Bar Assn., Tex. Bar Assn. Office: Office Medicare Hearings & Appeals US Dept Health & Human Services (HHS) 1700 N Moore St Ste 1800 Arlington VA 22209 Office Phone: 703-235-0635. Office Fax: 703-235-0700. E-mail: nancy.griswold@hhs.gov. *

GRITZ, ELLEN R., behavioral scientist, educator; PhD, U. Calif., San Diego, 1971. Prof., dir. cancer control divsn. UCLA Johsson Comprehensive Cancer Ctr., 1986—93; prof., chair behavioral sci. U. Tex. M.D. Anderson Cancer Ctr., Houston, 1993—, Olla S. Stribling disting. chair cancer rsch. Bd. pop. health and pub. health practice Inst. Medicine, 1995—2005, nat. cancer policy bd., 1997—99; bd. dirs. Am. Legacy Found., 2002—. Recipient Elkins Faculty Achievement award in Cancer Prevention, U. Tex. M.D. Anderson Cancer Ctr., 2002. Fellow: APA, Soc. Behavioral Medicine; mem.: Inst. Medicine, Soc. for Rsch. on Nicotine and Tobacco (pres. 2006—07), Am. Soc. Preventive Oncology (pres. 1993—95, Joseph W. Cullen Meml. award, Disting. Achievement award 2001). Office: Dept Behavioral Sci UT MD Anderson Cancer Ctr Unit 1330 PO Box 301439 Houston TX 77230-1439

GRIVER, JEANETTE A., psychologist, consultant; b. NYC, July 2, 1932; d. Lawrence Maurice Rosenthal and Selma Demby-Rosenthal; m. David M Griver, Mar. 15, 1951 (div. Apr. 1991). BA Psychology, UCLA, 1961; MA Psychology Human Factor, U. So. Calif., 1964. V.p. Jan Engring. Electronic Components, Santa Monica, 1955—62; pres. Jan Engring. Human Factors Divsn., Santa Monica, 1962—89; CEO Compsych Sys., Inc., LA, 1962—. Cons. to several orgns., 1962—. Author: Applied Problem Analysis Plus, 1988, Oh No! Not Another Problem, 2000, Curio a Shetland Sheepdog Meets the Crow, 2004, Curio a Shetland Sheepdog and Friends, 2005, Curio a Shetland Sheepdog and Her Pals, 2007, Curio a Shetland Sheepdog Meets the Cat, 2009; contbr. articles to jours. Mem. Pacific Palisades C. of C., 1990—2003. Mem.: Internat. Assn. Nanotech., Human Factors Soc. (sec. 2003), Lions Club Pacific Palisades (pres. 1990). Avocations: travel, tennis. Office: Compsych Systems Inc PO Box 1568 Pacific Palisades CA 90272 Office Phone: 310-454-6426, 310-454-2646. Business E-Mail: res04wq4@gte.net.

GRJIBOVSKI, ANDREJ M., biomedical researcher, consultant; b. Severodvinsk, Russia, Nov. 27, 1975; s. Mechislav V. Grjibovski and Tatjana E. Grjibovskaja; m. Natalia M. Andronova, Aug. 13, 2002. MD, No. State Med. U., Arkhangelsk, Russia, 2000; MPhil, U. Oslo, Norway, 2003; PhD, Karolinska Inst., Stockholm, Sweden, 2005. Rschr. Karolinska Inst., 2005; sr. advisor Nat. Inst. Pub. Health, Oslo, 2006—. Lectr. Internat. Sch. Pub. Health, Arkhangelsk, Russia, 2007—08, dir., 2008—; prof. U. Tromso, Norway, 2009—. Achievements include research in sociodemographic determinants of pregnancy outcomes and infant growth in transitional Russia.

GROAH, LINDA KAY, nursing administrator, educator; b. Cedar Rapids, Iowa, Oct. 5, 1942; d. Joseph David and Irma Josephine (Zitek) Rozek; m. Patrick Andrew Groah, Mar. 20, 1975; 1 child, Kimberly stepchildren: Nadine, Maureen, Marcus. Diploma, St. Luke's Sch. Nursing, Cedar Rapids, 1963; student, San Francisco City Coll., 1976-77; BA, St. Mary's Coll., Moraga, Calif., 1978; BSN, Calif. State U., 1986; MSN, U. Calif., 1989. Staff nurse to head nurse U. Iowa, 1963-67; clin. supr., dir. oper. and recovery rm. Michael Reese Hosp., Chgo., 1967-73; dir. oper. rms. Med. Ctr. Ctrl. Ga., Macon, 1973-74; dir. oper. and recovery rms. U. Calif. Hosps. and Clinics, San Francisco, 1974-90, asst. dir. hosps. and clinics, 1982-86; v.p. patient care svcs., COO Kaiser Found. Hosp., San Francisco, 1990—2004, COO, nurse exec., 2004—07; exec. dir. AORN, Denver, 2007—. Asst. clin. prof. U. Calif. Sch. Nursing, San Francisco, 1975—; cons. to oper. rm. suprs. and divsn. ednl. resources and programs Assn. Am. Med. Colls., 1976—; condr. seminars. Author: Perioperative Nursing Practice, 1983, 3d edit., 1996; contbr. articles to profl. jours., chapters to books; author, prodr. audio-visual presentations; author: computer software. Recipient Calif. Excellence in Nursing Leadership award, Nursing Spectrum, 2005, award for Nursing Leadership, Calif. Nurse Week, 2005; named Most Influential Women in Bus., San Francisco Bus. Times, 2006. Fellow: Am. Acad. Nursing; mem.: ANA (vice chmn. oper. rm. conf. group 1974—76), Nat. League Nurses, Assn. Oper. Rm. Nurses (mem. com. nominations 1979—84, treas. 1985—87, 1993—95, bd. dirs. 1991—93, pres.-elect 1995—96, pres. 1996—97, pres. found. 1992—95, trustee found. 1995—97, Excellence award in Preoperative Nursing 1989), San Francisco C. of C. Home: 5 Mateo Dr Belvedere Tiburon CA 94920-1071 Office: 3020 Bridgeway Ste 399 Sausalito CA 94965-2839 Home Phone: 415-786-4533; Office Phone: 800-755-2676. Personal E-mail: lindag1005@aol.com. Business E-Mail: lgroah@aorn.org.

GROB, GEORGE FREDERICK, independent program evaluator; M in Math., Georgetown U., 1969. Comptr. Office of Asst. Sec. Def.; ops. rsch. analyst Office of Asst. Sec. Navy for Fin. Mgmt.; dir. planning and policy coordination Office of Asst. Sec. Planning and Evaluation, USHHS, 1976-88; chair evaluation and inspection round table PCIE, Washington, 1994—2002; dep. insp. gen. for evaluation and inspections USHHS, Washington, 1988—2002, asst. insp. gen. for evaluation and inspections, 2004—05, dep. insp. gen. mgmt. and policy, 2002—05; exec. dir. Citizens Health Care Working Group, 2005—06; pres. Ctr. for Pub. Program Evaluation, 2006—. Mem. Am. Evaluation Assn. Home and Office: 38386 Millstone Dr Purcellville VA 20132-3739 Office Phone: 540-454-2888. E-mail: georgefgrob@cs.com.

GROB, GERALD N., historian, educator; b. NYC, Apr. 25, 1931; s. Sidney and Sylvia G. Grob; m. Lila Kronick, Dec. 25, 1954; children: Bradford S., Evan D., Seth A. BS, CCNY, 1951; MA, Columbia U., 1952; PhD, Northwestern U., 1958; D.Litt. (hon.), Clark U., 2002. From instr. history to prof. Clark U., Worcester, Mass., 1957—69; Henry E. Sigerist prof. of the history of medicine Rutgers U., New Brunswick, NJ, 1969—, chmn. dept., 1969—71, 1973—74, 1981—84. Mem. fellowship adv. com. NEH, 1975—76; chmn. study sect. history of medicine NIH, 1975—77, 1987—89, 1993—98. Author: Ed Jarvis and the Medical World of 19th Century America, 1978, Workers and Utopia, 1961, The State and the Mentally Ill, 1966, Mental Institutions in America, 1973, Mental Ilness and American Society, 1875-1940, 1983, The Inner World of American Psychiatry, 1890-1940, 1985, From Asylum to Community, 1991, The Mad Among Us, 1994, The Deadly Truth: A History of Disease in America, 2002, The Dilemma of Federal Mental Health Policy, 2006, Diagnosis Therapy & Evidence, 2009; contbr. articles to profl. jours. Elected to inst. medicine NAS. With US Army, 1955—57. Grantee, NIH, 1960—65, 1967—81, 1984—92; fellow, NEH, 1972—73, 1989—90, Am. Coun. Learned Socs., 1976—77, Guggenheim fellow, 1980—81, Davis Ctr., Princeton U., 1985—86. Mem.: Orgn. Am. Historians, Am. Antiquarian Soc., Am. Assn. History of Medicine (coun. mem. 1978—81, v.p. 1994—96, pres. 1996—98, William H. Welch medal 1986, Lifetime Achievement award 2006). Jewish. Home: 821 Starview Way Bridgewater NJ 08807-1824 Office: Rutgers U Inst Health Care Policy 30 College Ave New Brunswick NJ 08901-1293 Office Phone: 732-932-8377. Business E-Mail: ggrob@rci.rutgers.edu.

GROBLER, SIAS RENIER, oral biology and dental materials researcher; b. Bloemfontein, South Africa, Mar. 30, 1948; s. Anna Fourie Grobler, Dec. 11, 1971; children: Liza, Renier. BSc, UOFS, South Africa, 1969, BSc (hon.), 1970, MSc, 1971, DSc, 1976; PhD, Univ Stellenbosch, Stellenbosch, 1983. Sr. lectr. U. W.C., Bellville, 1973-81, U. Stellenbosch, 1981-91, asst. dir., 1991—, emeritus prof., 2004—; dir. prof. Oral & Dental Rsch. Inst. Mem. IADR, DASA, SAIADR. Office: Oral and Dental Rsch Inst Faculty Dentistry University Western Cape Tygerberg South Africa Home: 35 Granula Pl Sunset Beach Cape Town South Africa Business E-Mail: srgrobler@uwc.ac.za.

GROBMAN, ARNOLD BRAMS, retired biology educator, academic administrator; b. Newark, Apr. 28, 1918; s. Samuel H. and Sophia (Brams) G.; m. Hulda Gross, Feb. 20, 1944; children: Marc Ross, Beth. BS, U. Mich., 1939; MS, U. Rochester, 1941, PhD, 1943. Instr. zoology U. Rochester, 1943—44, rsch. assoc. Manhattan project, 1944—46; from asst. prof. to assoc. prof. biology U. Fla., 1946—59; rsch. participant Oak Ridge Inst. Nuc. Studies, 1950, rsch. specialist, med. center study, 1951—52; dir. Fla. State Mus., 1952—59; dir. biol. scis. curriculum study U. Colo., 1959—65, dean Coll. Arts and Scis.; prof. zoology Rutgers U., New Brunswick, NJ, 1965—72, dean, 1966—72; vice chancellor for acad. affairs, prof. biol. scis. U. Ill., Chgo., 1973—74, spl. asst. to pres., 1974—75; chancellor U. Mo.-St. Louis, 1975—85, chancellor emeritus, 1985—, prof. biology, 1975—, rsch. prof., 1986—; adj. curator Fla. Mus. Natural History, 1982—. Vis. lectr. Utah State U., Ind. U./Purdue U., U. So. Ill., Nat. Taiwan Normal U., U. Campinas, Brazil, U. New Delhi, India, U. No. Sumatra, Indonesia, U. Sind, Pakistan, Chulalongkorn U., Bangkok, Thailand, U. Singapore, Sophia U., Japan, Internat. Christian U., Japan, Chiang Mia U., Thailand; cons. to govt., industry, founds. and ednl. instns., 1954—; Mem. divsn. biology and agr. NRC-NAS, 1954-58, com. adult edn., 1956-58; sec. U.S. nat. com. Internat. Union Biol. Scis., 1966-69; chmn. Ednl. Opportunity Ctr. Met. St. Louis, 1976-78; mem. adv. team sci. soc., Thailand, 1971; fgn. observer Treaty Plebiscite, Gov. Panama, 1977-78; mem. Commn. on Adult Learner Author: (with others) Island Life: A Study of the Land Vertebrates of Eastern Lake Michigan, 1948, Our Atomic Heritage, 1951, Genetics Effects of Chronic X-irradiation Exposure in Mice, 1960, BSCS Biology Implementation in the Schools, 1964, The Changing Classroom, 1969, Urban State Universities, 1988; editor: Social Implications of Biological Education, 1970; also articles to profl. jours., encys. and newspapers. Bd. dirs. St. Louis United Way, Laumeier Sculpture Park, Narcotics Svc. Coun., Regional Commerce and Growth Assn., St. Louis Higher Edn. Ctr., St. Louis Pub. Libr.; v.p. St. Louis Conf. Edn., 1980-82; adv. bd. Indian River County Pub. Libr., 1997-2003 Recipient Fred H. Stoye prize Am. Soc. Ichthyologists and Herpetologists, 1941, Cressy Morrison prize N.Y. Acad. Scis., 1943; Macalaster award Nat. Assn. Biology Tchrs., 1966, award of merit Urban League, 1984, Commanders Cross, Order of Merit, Germany, 1985 Mem. Acad. Zoology India (exec. com. 1967-69), Am. Assn. Higher Edn., AAAS (coun. 1961-65), Am. Assn. Museums (mus. tng. com. 1960-63), Am. Assn. State Colls. and Univs. (urban affairs com. 1977-85), Am. Ednl. Rsch. Assn., Am. Inst. Biol. Scis. (exec. com. 1958-61, Disting. Svc. award 1984), Am. Soc. Ichthyologists and Herpetologists (bd. govs. 1952—, pres. 1964), Am. Soc. Naturalists, Am. Soc. Zoologists, Assn. Am. Med. Colls., Assn. Southeastern Biologists, ASCD, Assn. Tropical Biology, Asian Assn. Biol. Edn., Biol. Scis. Curriculum Study (chmn. steering com. 1965-69), Biol. Soc. China, Biol. Soc. Washington, Coun. Fgn. Rels., NEA, Edn. Programs Improvement Corp. (trustee 1970-74), Colo.-Wyo. Acad. Sci., AAUP, Explorers Club, Fla. Acad. Sci., Fla. Found. Future Scientists (chmn. 1957-59), Herpetologists League, Mo. Coun.

Pub. Higher Edn. (exec. com. 1977-82, v.p. 1978, pres. 1979), Mo. Bot. Garden, Nat. Coun. Accreditation Tchr. Edn. (chmn. 1970-71), Genetics Soc., Herpetologists League, Philippine Assn. Sci. Tchrs., Nat. Assn. Biology Tchrs. (pres. 1966, editl. bd. 1974-77, dir. 1978-80), Nat. Assn. Rsch. Sci. Tchg., Nat. Assn. State Univs. and Land Grant Colls. (exec. com. 1979-80, coun. acad. affairs 1974-76, chmn. divsn. urban affairs 1978-79), NSTA, Nature Conservancy, Newcomen Soc., N.J. Acad. Scis., Orgn. Tropical Studies, Sci. Soc. Thailand, Soc. Study Amphibians and Reptiles, Soc. Study Evolution, Soc. Systematic Zoology, Soc. Vertebrate Paleontology, Southeastern Museums Conf. (pres. 1955-57), Phi Beta Kappa, Sigma Xi, Phi Kappa Phi, Phi Sigma, Alpha Sigma Lambda, Alpha Epsilon Delta. Home: Oak Hammock 5000 SW 25th Blvd Apt 1115 Gainesville FL 32608

GROBOSCH, T., toxicologist; Degree in Chem. Engring., U. Applied Scis., Berlin, 1990; PhD in Chemistry, U. Potsdam, Germany, 1998. Clk. George Moll, Berlin, 1993—94; freelancer GUQ, Berlin, 1994—95; dispensing technician Heinz Haupt, Berlin, 1996—98, 1998; postdoctoral rschr. dept. chemistry U. Surrey, England, 1998; sci. asst. Pencef, Berlin, 1999—2000, Inst. Clin. Toxicology and Poision Control Ctr., Berlin, 1998—2000, supr., 2000—. Contbr. articles to profl. jours. Achievements include patents in field. Office: Berliner Betrieb Zent Gesundheitlic Inst Toxicology Clin Toxicology Oranienburger Str 285 Berlin 13437 Germany

GRODMAN, MARC D., medical laboratory and research executive; BA, U. Pa., 1973; MD, Columbia U. Coll. Physicians & Surgeons, NYC, 1977. Asst. prof. clin. medicine Columbia U. Coll. Physicians & Surgeons; asst. attending physician NY Presbyn. Hosp.; founder, pres., CEO, chmn. Bio-Reference Labs., Inc., Elmwood Park, NJ, 1981—. Primary care clin. fellow Mass. Gen. Hosp., 1980—83; med. cons. metal trades dept. AFL-CIO, 1982—84; bd. dirs. Bio-Reference Labs. Inc., 1981—, American Clin. Lab. Assn., 2005—. Office: Bio-Reference Labs Inc 481 Edward H Ross Dr Elmwood Park NJ 07407-3118 Office Phone: 201-791-2600, 201-791-1941. Business E-Mail: mgrodman@bioreference.com. *

GRODNITSKAYA, ELENA, endocrinologist, researcher; b. Ulan Ude, Republic of Buryatia, Apr. 17, 1978; MD, Voronezh State Med. Acad., 2001; PhD, Rsch. Ctr. Endocrinology, Russian Acad. Med. Scis., 2006. Reproductive endocrinologist Ctr. Family Planning and Reprodn., Moscow City Health Protection Dept., 2006—. Mem.: Internat. Soc. Gynecol. Endocrinology. Office: Sevastopolskiy Prospect 24 A Moscow 117209 Russia Business E-Mail: elena1778@mail.ru.

GRODY, WAYNE WILLIAM, physician, educator; b. Syracuse, NY, Feb. 25, 1952; s. Robert Jerome and Florence Beatrice (Kashdan) G.; m. Gaylen Ducker, July [illegible]. BA, Johns Hopkins U., 1974, MD, Baylor Coll. Medicine, 1977, PhD, 1981. Diplomate Am. Bd. Pathology, Am. Bd. Med. Genetics; lic. physician, Calif. Intern, resident UCLA Sch. Medicine, 1982-85, postdoctoral fellow, 1985-86, asst. prof., 1987-93, dir. DNA Diagnostic Lab., 1987—, assoc. prof., 1993-97, prof. depts. pathology and lab. medicine, pediat., human genetics, 1997—. Panelist Calif. Children's Svcs., 1987—, U.S. FDA, Washington, 1989—; DNA tech. com. Pacific Southwest Regional Genetics Network, Berkeley, Calif.; mem. task force genetic testing, NIH, 1987—; med., tech. cons., writer Warner Bros., NBC, Tri-Star, CBS, Twentieth Century Fox, Universal, others, 1987—; chair, molecular genetics com. Coll. Am. Pathologists, Assn. Molecular Pathology; chmn. genomic medicine adv. com. VA and others. Contbg. editor, film critic: MD Mag., 1981-91; assoc. editor Diagnostic Molecular Pathology, 1993—; contbr. articles to profl. jours., chpts. to books. Recipient best paper award L.A. Soc. Pathology, 1984, Joseph Kleiner Meml. award Am. Soc. Med. Technologists, 1990; Basil O'Connor scholar March of Dimes Birth Defects Found., 1989, Nakamura Lecturship Scripps Clinic, 1996, Moss Lectureship LSU, 1998, Stop Cancer Fdn. Rsch. award, 1998, Hill Lectureship Baylor Coll. Medicine, 2003, Lifetime Achievement award, Coll. Am. Pathology, 2010, Leader award Am. Soc. Clin. Pathology, 2010-; named One of Am.'s Top Doctors, 2001—. Mem. AAAS, AMA, Am. Soc. Clin. Pathology (Leadership award 2010), Am. Soc. Human Genetics, Am. Coll. Med. Genetic(chair, bd. dirs. 2001-2006, pres. 2011-) Soc. Inherited Metabolic Disorders, Soc. Pediat. Rsch. Democrat. Jewish. Achievements include application of molecular biology to clinical diagnosis and genetic screening, molecular genetics research and AIDS and cancer research. Office: UCLA Sch Medicine Divsns Med Genetics and Molecular Pathology Los Angeles CA 90095-1732 Home Phone: 310-573-0268; Office Phone: 310-825-5648. Business E-Mail: wgrody@mednet.ucla.edu.

GROEN, HARRY J.M., chest physician; b. Utrecht, The Netherlands, Feb. 3, 1953; s. Jan Groen and Netty Van Hooren; m. Hermke Kuipers, June 18, 1980; children: Wendy, Lise, Pauline, Hannah. MD, Utrecht U., The Netherlands, 1980; PhD, U. Groningen, The Netherlands, 1995. Physician Min. Fgn. Affairs, Hague, Netherlands, 1980-82, med. supt., 1982-84; chest physician Univ. Hosp., Groningen, 1984—. Home: Doorrid 11 9751 Haren Netherlands Office: Univ Hosp Hanzeplein 1 9700 Groningen Netherlands Office Phone: 31503616161. Business E-Mail: hjmgroen@int.umcg.nl.

GROENEMEYER, DIETRICH H.W., radiologist, medical educator; b. Clausthal-Zellerfeld, Germany, Nov. 12, 1952; s. Wilhelm Karl-Dietrich and Hella Carin (von Hunnius) G.; m. Christa Enste, Oct. 28, 1977. MD, U. Kiel, Germany, 1981; PhD, U. Witten-Herdecke, Muelheim an der Ruhr, Germany, 1990. Asst. prof. biomed. tech. Biomed. Tech. U., Kiel, 1978-82; asst. prof. radiology U. Kiel, 1982-84, U. Witten-Herdecke, 1984-88, asst. med. dir. thoracic clinic, 1987-88, dir. Inst. of Diagnostic and Interventional Radiology, 1988-90, chmn. Inst. Diagnostic and Interventional Radiology, 1990-96, asst. prof., 1988-90, assoc. prof., 1990-96, chmn. med. computer sci., 1990-96, prof. radiology, 1996—, chmn. dept. radiology and microtherapy, 1997—. Dir. Muelheim Krankenhaus Inst., Germany, 1988-96, Gionemayos-Inst., 1997-, Rsch. Devel. Ctr. Microtherapy, Germany, 1990—, R & D Ctr. Minimally Invasive Therapy, Berlin, 1995-97; vis. prof. Harvard U. Med. Sch., Boston, 1996; adj. prof. Georgetown U. Med. Ctr., 2001. Author: Interventionelle Computer Tomographie, 1989, Interventional Computed Tomography, 1990; mem. editl. bd. Minimally Invasive Therapy, 1991—, Open Field MRI, 1999, Med. in Deutschland, 2001, Mein Rückenbuch, 2004, Gesundheitswirtschaft. Die Zukunft für Deutschland, 2004, Mensch bleiben, 2005, Kapital Gesundheit. Für eine menschliche Medizin, 2005, Der kleine Medicus, 2005, Lebe mit Herz und Seele. Sieben Haltungen zur Lebenskunst, 2006. Named Hon. Citizen of Ruhr-District of North-Rhine Westfalia, 2000. Recipient World Future award, 2003. Avocations: reading, writing, sports, travel. Office: U Witten-Herdecke Inst Microtherapy Universitätsstr 142 44799 Bochum Germany also: U Witten-Herdecke Alfred Herrhausenstrasse 50 58448 Witten Germany

GROGAN, PAUL BERNARD, journalist, advocate; b. Brisbane, Australia, Apr. 14, 1963; s. Bernard Michael and Lesly June Grogan; m. Chrys Psaromatis, June 10, 2000; children: Michael, Emmanuel. Journalism Australian Journalists Assn., 1997. Media and policy adviser Australian Govt., Sydney, Canberra, Nsw, Act, Australia, 1997—2003; advocacy mgr. The Cancer Coun. Australia, Sydney, Nsw, Australia, 2004—. Consulting Freelance, Sydney, 1999—2004. Mem.: Australian Journalists Assn. Home: Clovelly Rd NSW Sydney 2026 Australia Office Fax: 61 2 9036 3101. Business E-Mail: paul.grogan@cancer.org.au.

GROHEUX, DAVID, nuclear medicine physician; b. Rennes, Ile et Vilaine, France, Apr. 20, 1974; s. Jean-Yves Groheux and Danielle Le Quilliec. D in Nuc. Medicine, U. Medicine, Rennes; MS in Med. Imaging, U. Paris, Paris XII; diploma in Imaging Oncology, U. Medicine, Paris XI. Cert. European Sch. Nuc. Medicine, Vienne. Physician and clin. rschr. Hopital St. Louis, Paris, Ile de France; physician and sci. dir. Petscan Ctr., La Rochelle, Charente Maritime. Mem.: Assn. Medicine Practitioners Nuc. (Ile de), Union Nuc. Medicine, French Soc. Nuclear Medicine and Molecular Imaging, European Assn. Nuc. Medicine, Coun. Med. Soc. Charente Maritime, Soc. Nuc. Medicine, Tennis Club La Rochelle. Achievements include research in nuclear medicine and positron emission tomography computed tomography and the role of 18F-FDG PET/CT in patients with breast cancer. Office: Hosp Saint Louis 1 Ave Claude Vellefaux Paris Ile de France 75475 France Home Phone: (33) 0630603009; Office Phone: (33) 0142499411. Office Fax: (33) 0142499405. Personal E-mail: dgroheux@yahoo.fr.

GROLLI, FRANK THOMAS, retired pharmacist; b. Bklyn., July 25, 1933; s. Frank and Theresa D. G.; m. Maria T. Cerbone, Mar. 30, 1974. BS in Pharmacy, Bklyn. Coll. Pharmacy, 1956. Registered pharmacist Ferro's Pharmacy, Bklyn., 1959-61; mgr., owner Associated Drugs, NYC, 1961-66; mgr., pharmacist Frank's Pharmacy, Staten Island, 1966-76; asst. mgr., pharmacist Savon SuperX, Staten Island, 1976-84, asst. mgr., pharmacy supr., 1984-88, pharmacy coord., 1988-94; n.e. region pharmacy coord. H.S.I., Rutherford, NJ, 1994; pharmacy supr. Revco D.S., Carteret, NJ, 1994-95, ret., 1995. Col. Med. Svc. Corps, 1961-86. Decorated Nat. Def. Svc. medal. Army Reserve Comp. Achievement medal, Meritorous Svc. medal. Mem. APHA, Pharm. Soc. NY, N.Y.C. Pharm. Soc., Italian Pharm. Soc., Res. Officers Assn., Assn. Mil. Surgeons. Avocations: gardening, stamp collecting/philately, fishing, home repairs.

GROLLMAN, JULIUS HARRY, JR., cardiovascular and interventional radiologist; b. LA, Nov. 26, 1934; s. Julius Harry and Alice Carolyn (Greenlee) G.; m. Alexa Jule Silverman, May 20, 1959; children: Carolyn, David, Elizabeth. BA, Occidental Coll., 1956; MD, UCLA, 1960. Diplomate Am. Bd. Radiology. Intern L.A. VA Hosp., 1960-61; resident in radiology UCLA Med. Ctr., 1961-64; chief cardiovascular radiology Walter Reed Gen. Hosp., 1965-67; chief cardiovascular radiology Ctr. Health Svcs. UCLA, 1967-78; chief cardiovascular and interventional radiology Little Company of Mary Hosp., Torrance, Calif., 1978—2005, retired, 2005; clin. prof. radiol. sci. UCLA, 1978—2010. Contbr. over 150 articles to profl. jours., 9 chpts. to med. books. Fellow Soc. Cardiac Angiography and Interventions (trustee 1992-95), Am. Coll. Radiology, Coun. Cardiovascular Radiology, Am. Heart Assn., Soc. Cardiovascular and Interventional Radiology; mem. AMA, Am. Roentgen Ray Soc., Radiol. Soc. N.Am., Western Angiographic and Interventional Soc. (pres. 1976-77), N.Am. Soc. for Cardiac Imaging (pres. 1991-92). Republican. Presbyterian. Home: 211 S Guadalupe Ave Unit 3 Redondo Beach CA 90277

GROLLMAN, SIGMUND SIDNEY, physiology educator; b. Stevensville, Md., Feb. 12, 1923; s. Ellis Phillip and Rachel Naomi (Krystal) G. BS, U. Md., 1947, MS, 1949, PhD, 1952. Cert. biochem. physiology. Tchg. asst. dept. zoology U. Md., College Park, 1947-49, instr., 1949-51, asst. prof., 1952-55, assoc. prof., 1955-58, prof., 1958-84, chair div. physiology, 1966-73, dir. grad. studies, 1973-83, prof. emeritus, 1984; pres. Sigmund Grollman Ltd., Balt., 1970—. Author: (textbook) The Human Body--Its Structure and Function, 1964, 4th rev. edit., 1984, (manual) Anatomy and Physiology, 1960-84, Experimental Mammilian Physiology, 1971-83; contbr. articles to profl. jours. Sgt. US Army, 1940-43, ETO. Fellow Am. Coll. Sports Medicine; mem. Soc. Exptl. Biology and Medicine, NY Acad. Sci., Sigma Xi. Home: 4001 N Charles St Baltimore MD 21218-1749 Office Phone: 410-235-5598.

GROMACKI, SUSAN JEAN, optometrist; b. Greenfield, Mass., Oct. 03; d. George Peter and Jean Klocko Gromacki; m. Scott David Lathrop, June 2, 2001; 1 child, Stephanie Elizabeth; 1 child, Sarah Jean Lathrop. BS, U. Notre Dame, 1989; OD, Ohio State U., 1993, MS in Physiol. Optics, 1993. Lic. optometrist. Resident in hosp.-based optometry U. S. Dept. of Veterans Affairs Med. Ctr., Chillicothe, Ohio, 1993—94; asst. prof. optometry New Eng. Coll. Optometry, Boston, 1994—98; faculty dept. ophthalmology and visual scis. U. Mich., Ann Arbor, 1998—2001; optometrist Hudson Valley Eye Surgeons, Fishkill, NY, 2002—03, Kaiser Permanente, Fairfax, Va., 2004—05, Huron Ophthalmology, 2006—. Speakers' bur. Vistakon (Johnson & Johnson), Jacksonville, Fla., 1995—2003, Sunsoft Contact Lens Co., Albuquerque, 1996—99; adv. bd. Cooper Vision, Rochester, NY, 1996—; examiner Nat. Bd. of Examiners in Optometry, 1998—; speakers' alliance. Alcon, 2004—; speakers' bur. CIBA Vision, 2006—, Bausch & Lomb, 2007—; cons. in field. Contbr. articles to profl. jours. V.p. Mil. Coun. of Cath. Women, West Point, NY, 2002—03; mem. parish coun. Most Holy Trinity Parish, West Point, NY, 2002—03; provider Vision USA, Various, 1994—. Recipient Contact Lens Achievement award, CIBA Vision, 1993, Harold F. Kohn award, Am. Optometric Found., 1993, Allergan Optometry award, Allergan, 1993, Wesley-Jessen award for Excellence, Wesley-Jessen, 1993, Alcon NOVA award, Alcon, 1993, America's Top Optometrists, Consumers' Rsch. Coun. of Am., 2002, 2003, 2004, 2005; Ednl. grant, Vistakon/ Johnson & Johnson, 1992, Optometry Class of 1953 Endowed scholarship, Ohio State U., 1992, U. of Notre Dame scholar, U. of Notre Dame, 1985—89, Bausch & Lomb Contact with the Future Ednl. Travel grant, Bausch & Lomb, 1992. Fellow: Am. Acad. Optometry (nat. comm. com. 2001—); mem.: Va. Optometric Assn., Ohio Optometric Assn., Mass. Soc. Optometrists, Mich. Optometric Assn., NY State Optometric Assn., Am. Optometric Assn., Assn. Contact Lens Educators, Ohio State U. Alumni Assn., U. Notre Dame Alumni Assn. (Boston bd. dirs. 1996—98), Epsilon Psi Epsilon. Roman Catholic. Avocations: physical fitness, golf, tennis, cooking, travel.

GROMOV, IRINA, psychiatrist, educator; b. Russia, Mar. 30, 1961; MD, Kishinev Sch. Medicine, 1984; PhD, Moscow Inst. Hematology and Blood Transfusion, 1994. Fellow addiction psychiatry HMS, Mass. Gen. Hosp., Dept. Psychiatry, 2002—03, clin. instr., physician on staff, 2003—04; med. dir. Urschel Recovery Sci. Inst., 2004—; pvt. practice, 2010—. Clin. asst. prof. psychiatry U. Tex. Southwestern Med. Sch., 2008—. Recipient Best Drs. in America, 2010, Excellence award, HMS, MGH, Dept. Psychiatry. Mem.: NTSPP, ASAM, Am. Psychiat. Assn. Avocations: travel, opera, yoga. Office: 5425 W Spring Creek Pky Ste 210 Plano TX 75024 Office Fax: 972-473-9600. Business E-Mail: gromov@recovery-science.com.

GRØNBECH, JON ERIK, surgeon; b. Mo i Rana, Norway, May 22, 1949; MD, U. Bergen, 1975, PhD, 1988. Chmn., dept. gastrointestinal surgery St Olav U. Hosp., 2001—. Prof. Norwegian U. Sci. & Tech., 1995. Office: Olav Kyrres gt 17 Trondheim N-7038 Norway E-mail: jon.e.gronbech@ntnu.no.

GRÖNBLAD, MATS ÅKE, physician, educator; b. Karhula, Finland, Dec. 31, 1951; s. Kaj Hjalmar Grönblad and Ulla Anita Qvist; m. Mariko Teramura, Nov. 18, 2006; 1 child, Mikael. MD, PhD, U. Helsinki, Finland, 1983. Cert. pain mgmt. specialist Finnish Doctors Assn., 1999, prof. competence in rehab. medicine U. Gothenburg, Sweden, 2000, in rehab. medicine U. Uppsala, Sweden, 2000. Sr. lectr. U. Helsinki, 1989—97, assoc. prof., 1993—. Sr. clin. cons. U. Ctrl. Hosp., Helsinki, 1993—. Nat. coord. Bone and Joint Decade, 2000—10, Bone and Joint Decade Amb., 2010—. Mem.: Am. Acad. Pain Medicine, Internat. Soc. Study Lumbar Spine, NY Acad. Scis. Office: Univ Ctrl Hosp Sairaalakatu 1 POB 900 Helsinki 00029 HUS Finland

GROOPMAN, JEROME, medical educator; b. Jan. 11, 1952; MD, Columbia Coll. Physicians and Surgeons. Diplomate Am. Bd. Internal Medicine with subspecialties in hematology and med. oncology. Resident in internal medicine Mass. Gen. Hosp., Boston; clin. fellow in medicine Harvard Med. Sch., Boston; fellow divsn. of hematology/oncology U. Calif.; rsch. fellow Boston Children's Hosp.-Sidney Farber Cancer Ctr.; prof. medicine Harvard Med. Sch., Dina and Raphael Recanati chair; chief exptl. medicine, dir. AIDS oncology program, dir. Mapplethorpe Lab. Beth Israel Deaconess Med. Ctr. Contbr. articles; staff writer: New Yorker, 1998—; author: The Measure of Our Days, 1997, Second Opinions, 2000, The Anatomy of Hope, 2003, How Doctors Think, 2007. Recipient Victor Cohn prize, Excellence in Med. Reporting, Coun. for Advancement of Sci. Writing, 2006. Fellow: Am. Acad. Arts and Sciences; mem.: Inst. of Medicine of NAS. Office: Beth Israel Deaconess Med Ctr Rm 351 4 Blackfan Cir Boston MA 02115 Office Phone: 617-667-0070. Office Fax: 617-975-5244. E mail: jgroopma@bidmc.harvard.edu.

GROSE, CHARLES FREDERICK, pediatrician, epidemiologist; b. Faribault, Minn., Apr. 15, 1942; s. Frederick G. and Marie A. (Swelland) G. BA, Beloit Coll., 1963; MD, U. Chgo., 1967. Bd. cert. in pediatric infectious disease. Resident Albert Einstein Coll. Medicine, Bronx, NY, 1967-68, fellow, 1970—75, U. Calif., San Francisco, 1975-76; asst. prof. Health Sci. Ctr. U. Tex., San Antonio, 1976-84; prof. pediatrics U. Iowa Hosp., Iowa City, 1985—. Cons. NIH, Bethesda, Md., 1988—. Editor Pediat. Infectious Disease Jour., 2003—; mem. editl. bd. Virology Jour.; contbr. articles to profl. and sci. jours. Capt. U.S. Army Med. Corps., Vietnam, 1968-70. Grantee NIH, 1978—. Fellow Infectious Disease Soc. Am., Pediatric Infectious Disease Soc., Am. Acad. Pediatrics, Am. Soc. Virology. Achievements include research on diagnosis and treatment of chickenpox and shingles, and on the etiologic agent which is varicella virus. Office: U Iowa Hosp Pediatrics 200 Hawkins Dr Iowa City IA 52242-1009 Business E-Mail: charles-grose@uiowa.edu.

GROSFELD, JAY LAZAR, surgeon, educator; b. NYC, May 30, 1935; m. Margie Faulkner; children: Lisa, Denise, Janice, Jeffrey, Mark. AB cum laude, NYU, 1957, MD, 1961. Diplomate Am. Bd. Surgery (spl. qualification Pediatric Surgery). Gen. surgery intern Bellevue and Univ Hosps. NYU, NYC, 1961—62; resident in gen. surgery Bellevue and Univ. Hosps. NYU, NYC, 1962—66; resident in pediatric surgery Ohio State U. Coll. Medicine, Children's Hosp., 1968—70; instr. surgery Ohio State U. Coll. Medicine, 1968—70; clin. instr. surgery NYU Sch. Medicine, NYC, 1965—66, asst. prof. surgery and pediatrics, 1970—72; prof., dir. pediatric surgery Ind. U. Sch. Medicine, Indpls., 1972—2005, chmn. dept. surgery, 1985—2003, Lafayette F. Page prof., 1981—2005, Lafayette F. Page prof. emeritus, 2005—; surgeon-in-chief James Whitcomb Riley Hosp. Children, 1972—2005; Lafayette Page prof. surgery, chmn. emeritus Ind. U. Sch. Medicine, Indpls., 2005—. Editor-in-chief Jour. Pediat. Surgery, 1994—. Author: Common Problems in Pediatric Surgery, 1991, Central Surgical Association: The First 50 Years, 1991, Progress in Pediatric Trauma, 1992, Essentials of Pediatric Surgery, 1995, Pediatric Surgery, 6th edit., 2006, The Surgery of Childhood Tumors, 1999, Principles of Pediatric Surgery, 2003, The Surgery of Childhood Tumors 2nd Edit., 2008; contbr. over 600 papers, reports, book chpts., articles for med. jours. Capt. MC US Army, 1966—68. Decorated Commendation medal; recipient numerous fellowships, grants, teaching awards; named Sagamore of the Wabash, 2002. Fellow: ACS (bd. govs. 1985—91), Am. Acad. Pediat. (exec. com. surg. sect. 1989—95, chmn. surg. sect. 1994—95, sec. surg. sect., William E. Ladd medal 2002—), European Pediatric Surgeons (hon.), Royal Coll. Sugeons (Ireland) (hon.), Royal Coll. Physicians and Surgeons Glasgow (hon.), Royal Coll. Surgeons of Eng. (hon.); mem.: AMA, Ajm. Surg. Assn. Found., World Fedn. Perdiatric Surgical Assns. Found., Southern Surg. Assn., Halsted Soc. (v.p. 1995—96, pres. 1996—97), Accreditation Coun. Grad. Med. Edn. (surg. residency rev. com. 1996—2001, vice chair 2000—01), Am. Bd. Med. Specialities, World Fedn. Assns. Pediat. Surgeons (pres. 1998—2001, v.p.), Am. Bd. Surgery (bd. dirs. 1989—97, vice chair 1995, chmn. 1996—97, chmn.-elect), Am. Pediatric Surg. Assn. Found. (chmn. bd. dirs., bd. trustees), Internat. Soc. Surgery (sec., treas. Internat. Soc. Surgery Found. 2001—), Western Surg. Assn. (pres. 1997—98), Soc. Surg. Oncology, Brit. Assn. Pediat. Surgeons (exec. coun. 1990—93, Denis Browne Gold medal 1998), Ctrl. Surg. Assn. (sec. 1987—, pres.-elect 1988, pres. 1990), Soc. Surgery Alimentary Tract, Am.

Trauma Soc., Ind. State Med. Assn., British Assn. Pediat. Surgeons (hon.), Marion County Med. Soc., Soc. Univ. Surgeons, Am. Surg. Assn. (first v.p. 2005—, pres. 2006—), Am. Pediat. Surg. Assn. (pres. 1994—95, 2005, bd. govs., pres.-elect), N.Y. Cancer Soc., Assn. Acad. Surgery, Pediat. Surgery Biology Club, Alpha Omega Alpha, Phi Beta Kappa. Office: J W Riley Childrens Hosp 702 Barnhill Dr Rm 2500 Indianapolis IN 46202-5128 Business E-Mail: jgrosfel@iupui.edu.

GROSH, WILLIAM W., internist; b. NYC, Aug. 22, 1949; MD, Columbia U. Physicians and Surgeons, 1974. Diplomate Am. Bd. Internal Medicine. Intern Vanderbilt U. Med. Ctr., 1974-75, resident, 1975-77; fellow in oncology Vanderbilt U., Nashville, 1980-83, instr., 1983-84, asst. prof. medicine, 1984-88, Univ. Va., 1988-93, assoc. prof. internal medicine, 1993—. Mem. AMA. Office: Univ Va Dept Medicine Divsn Hematology/Oncology PO Box 800716 Charlottesville VA 22908-0466 Office Phone: 434-924-1904. Office Fax: 434-243-6086. Business E-Mail: wwg9u@virginia.edu.

GROSS, ANDRES, psychiatrist, educator; b. Viljandi, Estonia, Aug. 26, 1963; s. Villem and Mai Gross; m. Mairi Luht, Jan. 8, 1999; children: Karoline, Villem, Werner; m. Katrin Gross (div.); 1 child, Oskar. MD, U. Tartu, Estonia, 1987; specialist in gen. adult psychiatry, 1996. Cert. psychiatrist U. Helsinki, Finland, 1996. Med. nurse, ward pulmonology Tartu U. Clinic, Estonia, 1983—84; paramedic Tartu, 1985—87; intern Tartu U. Psychiatric Clinic, 1987—89; psychiatry trainee U. Hosp. Tartu, 1987—89, psychiatrist, 1989—92, Tammiharju Hosp., Finland, 1992—96; sr. lectr. U. Helsinki, 2000—02; cons. psychiatrist Linden House Care Prins. Ltd., Market Weighton, England, 2004—05, Nottinghamshire Healthcare Nat. Health Svc. Trust, England, 2005—06; sr. lectr. U. Helsinki, 2007—. Lectr. and presenter in field. Contbr. articles to profl. jours. Achievements include Fluent in English, Estonian, Finnish, Russian and Swedish. Avocation: skiing. Office: Helsinki Univ Ctrl Hosp Valskarinkhtu 12A 00260 Helsinki Finland

GROSS, C.W., otolaryngologist, educator; b. Covington, Va., Nov. 9, 1930; s. Charles Calvin and Frances (Field) Gross; m. Catherine Elizabeth McCombs, Dec. 8, 1979; children: Charles, William, Alice, Nicholas, Catherine. BS, U. Ky., 1953; MD, U. Va., 1961. Diplomate Am. Bd. Otolaryngology. Intern U. Va.; resident Mass. Eye and Ear Infirmary, Boston; instr. Midway Jr. Coll., 1956—57; tchg. fellow Harvard Sch. Medicine, Boston, 1965—66, asst. in otolaryngology, 1966—67; asst. prof. U. Cin. Sch. Medicine, 1967—68; prof. U. Tenn. Sch. Medicine, 1968—70, chmn. dept. otolaryngology, 1970—77; prof. otolaryngology-head and neck surgery and pediat. U. Va. Sch. Medicine, 1989—; pvt. practice Memphis, 1977—89. Mem. editl. bd. Am. Jour. Rhinology and ENT Jour. Active short-term Christian med. missions Haiti, Belize, Bolivia, El Salvador, India, Nigeria, Charlottesville; founding mem. bd. dirs. Albemarle 1st Bank; past chmn. bd. Covenant Sch., Charlottesville. Served USN, 1953—56, lt. j.g. beachmaster USNR, 1956—61. Mem.: Internat. Rhinological Soc. (Lifetime Achievement award 2000), Am. Rhinologic Soc. (pres. 2000, Better Hearing Inst. Disting. Svc. award 1982), Triologic Soc. (pres. 2000), Am. Acad. Otolaryngology-Head and Neck Surgery (pres. 1984, Disting. Svc. award 1998), U. Va. Med. Alumni Assn. (bd. dirs., treas., trustee, sec. Med. Sch. Found., chmn. med. adv. program). Avocations: Bible study, tennis, gardening, U.Va. basketball and football. Home: Box 318 Ivy VA 22945 Office: University Va Health Sys PO Box 800713 Charlottesville VA 22908-0713 Office Phone: 434-924-5934. Business E-Mail: cwg9u@virginia.edu. *

GROSS, EITAN MOSHE, surgeon, educator; b. Tel Aviv, Apr. 30, 1954; s. Chaim and Aliza Gross; m. Shalvit Landau, Feb. 5, 1978; children: Matan Akiva, Naama, Yair. MD, Hadassah Hebrew U., Israel, 1986. Cert. in Gen. Surgery Israel, 1992, in Pediatric Surgery Israel, 1997, diplomate Gen. Surgeon Israel, Pediatric Surgeon Israel. Intern Hadassah U. Hosp., Jerusalem, 1985—86, resident in gen. surgery, 1986—92, fellow, pediatric surgery, 1992—97; resident in gen. surgery Mount-Sinai Med. Ctr., NYC, 1988—89; fellow, gen. and oncological pediatric surgery U. Tenn., Le Bonheur Children's Med. Ctr., St. Jude Children's Rsch. Hosp., 1994—96; attending in pediatric surgery Hadassah Med. Ctr., Jerusalem, 1997; sr. lectr. pediatric surgery Hadassah Hebrew U., Jerusalem, 2000—, head pediat. surg. oncology unit, 2007—. Mem. Nat. Coun. for Pediat., Israel, 1998. Lt. col. Navy, 1972, Israel. SOUDAVAR Meml. scholarship, Meml. Sloan-Kettering Cancer Ctr., 2005. Mem.: Internat. Soc. Pediatric Surg. Oncology (assoc.), Israel Surg. Assn. (assoc.), Israel Med. Assn. (assoc.), Pediatric Surgery Soc. (assoc.). Jewish. Avocations: swimming, hiking, diving. Office: Hadassah Hebrew U Med Ctr Ein Kerem 91999 Jerusalem Israel Office Fax: 972-2-6446483. Business E-Mail: eitangr@hadassah.org.il.

GROSS, GARY NEIL, allergist, physician; b. Fort Lewis, Wash., July 25, 1944; s. Norman Harold and Dorothy Naomi (Bercie) G.; m. Elaina Wee, Mar. 23, 1974; children: Risa, Lara. BA, U. Tex., 1967; MD, Southwestern Med. Sch., Dallas, 1969; MBA, Southern Methodist U., Dallas, 1987. Diplomate Am. Bd. Internal Medicine, Am. Bd. Allergy and Clin. Immunology. Intern U. Utah Med. Ctr. Hosp., Salt Lake City, 1969-70, resident, 1970-71; fellow Nat. Jewish Hosp., Denver, 1971-74; founding physician Dallas Allergy and Asthma Ctr., Tex., 1979—; med. dir. Pharm. Rsch. and Cons., Dallas, 1992—; clin. prof. internal medicine Southwestern Med. Sch., Dallas, 1994—. Contbr. articles to profl. jours. Bd. dirs. Am. Jewish Com., Dallas, 1990-94, Am. Lung Assn., 1978-88, Temple Emanuel Brotherhood, 1978-80. Fellow Am. Coll. Physicians, Am. Acad. Allergy Asthma and Immunology (chmn. seminars com., 1987-88, chmn. pub. edn. com., 1989-90, Outstanding Vol. Clin. Faculty award 2004, Disting. Svc. award 2003); mem. Fedn. Regional State Local Allergy Socs. (gov. reg. 5, 1992-, chmn. 1993-94), Joint Coun. Allergy Clin. Immunology (sec. bd. dirs. 1992-96, exec. v.p. 1998-). Jewish. Avocations: bicycling, skiing, photography. Office: 5499 Glen Lakes Dr Ste 100 Dallas TX 75231-4383 Office Phone: 214-691-1330. Personal E-mail: gary.gross@daac-prc.com.

GROSS, HARVEY R., physician, educator; Studied, Boston U., 1970. Diplomate Am. Bd. Family Practice, cert. geriatric medicine. Resident SUNY, Buffalo, Stony Brook; resident family medicine Southside Hosp., 1972—74; with Holy Name Hosp., Bergen Regional Med. Ctr.; asst. clin. prof. medicine Mt. Sinai Shc. Med.; chief dept. of family practice Englewood Hosp. and Med. Ctr. Named Best Doctor, NJ Monthly Mag., NY Mag. and Castle Connelly. Office: Englewood Hospital and Medical Center Ste 102 370 Grand Ave Englewood NJ 07631 Office Phone: 201-567-3370. Office Fax: 201-816-1265.

GROSS, IAN, academic pediatrician, neonatologist; b. Pretoria, Oct. 15, 1943; came to U.S., 1971; s. Kenneth and Gladys Bakst (Cooper) G.; m. Melanie Belman, Dec. 3, 1967; children: David Anthony, Adam Charles. BS, U. Witwatersrand, Johannesburg, Republic of South Africa, 1963, MBBCh, 1967. Diplomate Am. Bd. Pediat., Am. Bd. Neonatal-Perinatal Medicine. Rotating intern Johannesburg Gen. Hosp., 1968; pediatric resident U. Witwatersrand Hosps., Johannesburg, 1970-71, Children's Hosp. Harvard Med. Sch., Boston, 1971-72; postdoctoral fellow in pediat. Harvard Med. Sch., Boston, 1972-73; postdoctoral fellow in pediatrics Yale U., New Haven, 1973-74; asst. prof. Yale U. Sch. Medicine, New Haven, 1974-78, assoc. prof., 1978-85, prof., 1985—. Dir. newborn spl. care unit Yale-New Haven Hosp., 1982—; mem. study sect. NIH, Bethesda, Md., 1981-85; mem. adv. bd. Hood Found., Boston, 1988-94. Editor Pediat. Rsch., 1992-98, Seminars in Perinatology, 1997—; contbr. chpts. to books, numerous articles to profl. jours. Named Most Disting. Med. Grad. U. Witwatersrand, Johannesburg, 1967, Mentor of Yr., Ea. Soc. Pediatric Rsch., 2005; James Hudson Brown fellow, Yale U., 1973; rsch. grantee NIH and Am. Heart Assn. Fellow Am. Acad. Pediat.; mem. Soc. Pediatric Rsch., Am. Physiol. Soc. Avocations: bicycling, photography. Office: Yale Sch Medicine 333 Cedar St New Haven CT 06520-8064 E-mail: ian.gross@yale.edu.

GROSS, JOERG PAUL, psychiatrist; b. Oberhausen, Germany, Jan. 29, 1967; s. Paul and Wilfriede Gross; m. Daniela Wolfert, Sept. 18, 1992; children: Johanna, Christoph, Stefan. Psychiatrist Würzburg Germany, 2001. Pvt. practice Practice for Psychiatry, Würzburg, Germany, 2001—03. Chmn. Office: Practice For Psychiatry Münzstraße 10 Germany Würzburg 97070 Germany Home: Platenstva Be 6 Wurzburg Germany Office Phone: 0931/4679990. Office Fax: 0931/4679992. E-mail: praxis.blocherundgross@t-online.de.

GROSS, PAUL ALLAN, health products executive; b. Va., Oct. 1, 1937; s. Albert and Cynthia (Saxe) G.; m. Gail Byrd, Nov. 19, 1966; children: Lorri, Garry, Randy. Degree, U. Richmond, 1959; BA, U. Ga., 1961; MHA, Va. Commonwealth U., 1964; cert. in hosp. adminstrn., U. Miami, Jackson Meml. Hosp. Adminstrv. resident in hosp. adminstrn. Tampa Gen. Hosp., Fla., 1964; adminstrv. asst. Dallas County Hosp. Dist., 1964-66, asst. adminstr., 1966-69, sr. asst. adminstr., 1969-70, assoc. adminstr., 1971-72; clin. assoc. prof. hosp. med. care U. Tex. Southwestern Med. Sch., 1964-72, Sch. Allied Health Scis., Dallas, 1964-72; exec. dir. Humana Inc. Suburban Hosp., Louisville, 1972-76; v.p. Fla. region Humana Inc., Miami, 1976-81; sr. v.p. Pacific Region Humana Inc., Newport Beach, Calif., 1981-84, exec. v.p., pres. hosp. div., 1984-92; ret. Humana Inc., 1992; prof., health adminstr. Va. Commonwealth U./Med. Coll. Va., 1992-95, prof. emeritus, 1996—. Nat. cons. emeritus Surgeon Gen. USAF, 1987—; vice chmn. bd. trustees MedEcon, Inc., Louisville, 1993-96, also bd. dirs.; bd. dirs. St. Anthony Pub. Co., Washington, 1993-96; advisor KBL Healthcare Inc., Comprehensive Med. Mgmt., Inc., N.Y.C. 1993-96. Contbr. articles to profl. jours. Mem., chmn. U.S. Selective Svc. System Local Bd. 154, Newport Beach, 1983, Bd. 13, Louisville, 1982-2002; bd. assocs. U. Richmond, Va., 1990-96; bd. dirs. St. Francis High Sch., Louisville, 1989-92; bd. dirs. Louisville Zool. Found., 1989-96, chmn. investment com., 1992; mem. adv. bd. Sch. Nursing, 1992-96, Spalding U., 1997; chmn. devel. bd. Jefferson County C.C., Kentuckiana Edn. and Work Force Com.; bd. dirs U.S. Selective Svc. Bd., 1981-2002, emeritus 2002—; preceptor Fellowship Program-Edn. with Industry, USAF, 1986-92; bd. dirs. Spaulding U., 1996-97, Lake/Sumter County United Way, 2005-07, LifeStream Behavioral Ctr., 2004-; bd. mem., treas. chair fin. com. Comprehensive Med. Mgmt. Inc, 1993-96; bd. dirs. Med. Coll. Va. Found., chmn. audit and applications com., 1993-2000; pres. bd. dirs. Pelican Cove Two Condo Assn.; bd. dirs. Hospice of Lake and Sumter County, Fla, 2005-; CRA adv. bd., mem, chmn. City of Tauares Fla., 2005-08. With USNR, 1955—63. Recipient Humana Club award, Ctrl. Region, Louisville, 1974—76, Presdl. medallion, Va. Commonwealth U., 1995; named Outstanding Adminstr., Ctrl Region Humana, 1975, 1976. Fellow Am. Coll. Health Care Execs. (ethics com., chmn. inv. droped sect. 1993—); mem. Tex. Hosp. Assn., Hosp. Coun. So. Calif. (chmn. multi-instnl. corp. liaison com. 1983—), United Hosp. Assn. Calif., Fedn. Am. Healthcare Sys. & Am. Hosp. Assn. (hon. life). Home: PO Box 311 Terra Ceia FL 34250-0311 E-mail: pagross144@comcast.net.

GROSS, PETER ALAN, epidemiologist, researcher; b. Newark, Nov. 18, 1938; s. Meyer P. and Nathalie (Bass) Denburg) G.; m. Regina Teri Gittlin, May 30, 1964; children: Deborah Karen, Michael Philip, Daniel Brian. BA cum laude, Amherst Coll., 1960; MD, Yale U., 1964. Diplomate Am. Bd. Internal Medicine. Intern Yale-New Haven Hosp., 1964-65, jr. resident, 1965-66; sr. resident Peter Bent Brigham Hosp., Boston, 1968-69; research and edn. assoc. Va Hosp., West Haven, Conn., 1971-73, acting chief infectious disease sect., 1972-73; chief infectious disease sect. VA Hosp., West Haven, Conn., 1973-74, Hackensack U. Med. Ctr., NJ, 1974—, chmn. dept. medicine, 1980—2007, chmn. med. bd., 1986, exec. v.p., chief med. officer, 2006—, exec. v.p., 2010—; prof. medicine NJ Med. Sch., Newark, 1981—, vice chmn. dept. medicine, 1994—2006, preventive medicine and cmty. health, 2007—, prof. preventive medicine and cmty. health, 2007—. Asst. prof. medicine Yale U. Sch. Medicine, New Haven, 1971—74; asst. clin. prof. Columbia U. Coll. Physicians and Surgeons, NYC, 1974—77, assoc. clin. prof. medicine, 1977—81; ad hoc reviewer rsch. grants NIH, Nat. Inst. Allergy and Infectious Diseases; investigator Ctr. for Biologic Evaluation and Rsch. FDA, 1974—95; chmn. drug safety and risk mgmt. adv. com. Ctr. for Drug Evaluation and Rsch. FDA, 2002—06; mem. clin. indicators task force Joint Commn. on Accreditation of Healthcare Orgns., 1987—89, chmn. pneumonia clin. adv. panel, 1999—2001; chmn. Sentinel Event Adv. Group, 2004—06, mem., 2006—; project dir. Phase I-111 Robert Wood Johnson Found. and Inst. for Healthcare Improvement; mem. expert panels on cmty.-acquired pneumonia, HCQIP and surg. dir. prevention HCQIP Ctrs. for Medicare and Medicaid Svc., 1998—; co-chmn. N.J. Quality Improvement Adv. Com.; mem. Mahimal quality forum Steering Com. Healthcare Associated Infections, 2006—. Author: Gram Strain Recognition, 1975, 2d edit., 1980, Managing Your Health, 1991; past assoc. editor: Clinical Performance and Quality Health Care; mem. editorial bd. Jour. Clin. Microbiology, 1980—, Infection Control, 1980-90; mem. editl. bd. Managed Care, 1998—; past editl. bd. Joint Commn. Jour. Quality Improvement. Served to lt. comdr. USPHS, CDC, 1966-68. NIH fellow Yale U., 1969-71. Fellow Infectious Diseases Soc. Am. (clin. affairs com., past chair practice guidelines com., councillor 2000-02); mem. ACP (task force on adult immunization), Am. Acad. Microbiology, Am. Soc. Virology, Am. Soc. Microbiology, Soc. Healthcare Epidemiologists Am. (councillor 1986-88, v.p. 1992, pres.-elect 1993, pres. 1994, past pres. 1995), Assn. Profs. Medicine, Prof. Preventive Medicine & Cmty. Health. Office: Hackensack U Med Ctr Dept Med Adminstrv Affairs Hackensack NJ 07601

GROSS, STANLEY MERHL, chiropractor; b. Breese, Ill., June 27, 1953; s. Walter Frank and Priscilla Dean (Myers) G.; m. Katherine Ferlisi, June 27, 1993; children: Timothy, Carisa, Geno, Zachary. BS in Biomed., Washington U., St. Louis, 1982; PhD, Harvard U., 1983; BS in Biology, Logan Coll., Chesterfield, Mo., 1986, D Chiropractic, 1988. Diplomate Advanced Chiropractic Technique; cert. acupuncture Community Chiropractic Ctr. Pvt. practice, chief staff Community Chiropractic Ctr., O'Fallon, Mo., 1988—; instr., lectr. Logan Coll. Chiropractic, Chesterfield, Mo., 1988—. Author: Bio-Synergistic Integration, 1984, The Physician Within, 1997. Dir. Ankylosing Spondytitis Assn., St. Louis, 1988—; alderman ward II, St. Paul, Mo., 1993—. Recipient Star Scholarship Logan Alumni Assn., Chesterfield, 1987. Mem. Acad. Advancement Sci., Am. Chiropractic Assn., Toastmasters Internat. (Most Able award 1992). Avocations: gardening, swimming, fishing. Office: 305A O Fallon Plz O Fallon MO 63366 Home: 70 Timber Oaks Trl O Fallon MO 63368-8178

GROSS, STEPHEN MARK, pharmacist, dean; b. Bklyn., July 31, 1938; s. Arthur S. and Hazel F. (Marks) Gross; m. Susan S. Farber, Nov. 5, 1961; 1 child, Julie S. BS, Columbia U., 1960, MA, 1969, EdD, 1975; DSc (hon.), LI U., 2008. Registered pharmacist N.Y., 1961. Pharmacist/mgr. C.O. Bigelow Chemists Inc., NYC, 1960-65, Bigelow-Americana Chemists Inc., NYC, 1963-65; asst. to dean Coll. Pharm. Scis. Columbia U., NYC, 1965—68, asst. dean, 1968—71, assoc. dean, 1971—72, acting dean, 1972—74, dean, 1974—76; dean grad. studies Arnold & Marie Schwartz Coll. Pharmacy and Health Scis. LI U., 1976—79; dean Sch. Bus. and Pub. Adminstrn., Bklyn. Ctr. LI U., 1983—84; dean grad. studies and rsch. Conolly Coll. LI U., 1979—83, dean Faculties Pharmacy and Health Professions, 1984—88, dean Schwartz Coll. Pharmacy, 1985—2008, dean Sch. of Health Professions, 1990—2007, dean emeritus, sr. advisor to the pres., 2009—. Mem. health care quality improvement steering com. Island Profl. Rev. Orgn., 1995—2000; mem. NY State Bd. Pharmacy, 1991—2001, chmn., 1997—98, extended mem., 2001—. Mem. editl. bd. U.S. Pharmacist, 1978—80, Am. Druggist, 1989—92; contbr. articles to profl. publs. Recipient numerous grants instnl. improvement. Mem.: Am. Soc. Health-Sys. Pharmacists, Nat. Cmty. Pharmacists Assn., Pharm. Soc. State N.Y., Am. Assn. Colls. Pharmacy (chmn. sect. continuing edn. 1979—80), Am. Pharm. Assn., Soc. Am. Magicians (v.p. N.Y. Assembly 1981—83, pres. 1983—84). Home: 43 Knott Dr Glen Cove NY 11542-4116 Office: LI U 1 University Plz Brooklyn NY 11201-5301 Office Phone: 718-488-1004, 718-488-1227. Business E-Mail: stephen.gross@liu.edu.

GROSSBERG, GEORGE THOMAS, psychiatrist, educator; b. Hungary, Aug. 20, 1948; came to the U.S., 1957; s. Henry and Barbara (Rothman) G.; m. Darla Jean Brown, June 13, 1976; children: Jonathan, Anna-Leah, Aviva, Aliza Rebecca, Jeremy. BA, Yeshiva U., 1971; MD, St. Louis U., 1975. Diplomate Am. Bd. Psychiatry and Neurology in Psychiatry and Geriatric Psychiatry. Chief resident in psychiatry St. Louis U., 1978-79, instr., 1979-81, asst. prof., 1982-86, assoc. prof., 1986-90, prof., 1990-98, Samuel W. Fordyce prof. and chmn. dept. psychiatry, 1995-98, Samuel w. Fordyce prof., dir. divsn. geriat. psychiatry, 1998—. Cons. on aging U.S. VA Hosps. Assn., Washington, 1990—. Contbr. articles to profl. jours. Adv. bd. St. Louis Alzheimers Assn., 1983-, St. Louis Sr. Olympics, 1998-; bd. dir. St. Louis Jewish Cmty. Ctr., 2000-08. Recipient Pub. Svc. award, St. Louis Alzheimers Assn., 1989, Donovan-Shear award, St. Louis Mental Health Assn., 1999, Fleischman-Hilliard award, Jewish Ctr. for Aged, 2000, Physician of Year award, Mo. Adult Daycare Assn., 2001. Mem. Am. Assn. Geriat. Psychiatry (pres. 1989-90), Am. Psychiat. Assn. (cons. on aging 1990—, Falk fellow 1977-79), Am. Geriat. Soc., Gerontol. Soc. Am., Internat. Psychogeriat. Assn. (treas. 1997—, pres. 2003-05). Avocations: antique collectibles, art, skiing. Office: Saint Louis U Sch Medicine 1438 S Grand Saint Louis MO 63104-1016 Office Phone: 314-977-4850, 314-977-4829. Business E-Mail: grossbgt@slu.edu.

GROSSER, BERNARD IRVING, psychiatrist, educator; b. Boston, Apr. 19, 1929; s. John and Katherine (Russman) G.; children: Steven, Mark, Minda; m. Karen Grosser. BA, U. Mass., Amherst, 1950; MS, U. Mich., Ann Arbor, 1953; MD, Case Western Res. U., Cleve., 1959. Diplomate Am. Bd. Psychiatry and Neurology. Intern U. Utah, 1959-60, resident in psychiatry, 1960-65; asst. prof. psychiatry U. Utah Sch. Medicine, Salt Lake City, 1967-71, assoc. prof., 1971-75, prof., 1975—, chmn. dept., 1978—2007. Mem. pre-clin. and clin. psychopharm. rev. com. NIMH, Washington, 1974-79, 80-84, mem. Intramural NIMH sci. adv. bd., 1984-88; mem. merit rev. bd. VA, Washington, 1988-91; sr. sci. advisor Alcohol, Drug Abuse and Mental Health Adminstrn., Washington, 1987-88; ad hoc mem. Mental Health Clin. Rsch. Ctr. rev. com. NIMH, 1997, ad hoc mem. mental health clin. contracts rev. com., 1998, NIMH ad hoc mem. spl. emphasis panel, 2000-06; rev. panel R13, 2005, R03, 2006, Extramural LRP, 2008-10. Contbr. chpts. to books, articles to profl. jours. Capt. USAF, 1965-67. Grantee NIMH, 1959-84, FDA, 1985-88; recipient Exemplary psychiatrist award Nat. Alliance for Mentally Ill, 1997. Fellow Am. Psychiat. Assn. (disting. life); mem. Internat. Soc. Psychoneuroendocrinology (treas. 1974-88), Utah Psychiat. Assn. (pres. 1995-96), Psychiat. Rsch. Soc. (pres. 1986-87), Soc. Neurosci., NY Acad. Scis., Collegium Internat. Neuro-psychopharmacologicum, Am. Assn. Psychiatry Dept. Chairmen (coun. 1997-2005, sec.-treas. 2005-06). Republican. Jewish. Home: 511 Perrys Hollow Rd Salt Lake City UT 84103-4245 Office: U Utah Sch Medicine Dept Psychiatry 50 N Medical Dr Salt Lake City UT 84132-0001 Office Phone: 801-581-7953. Business E-Mail: bernard.grosser@hsc.utah.edu.

GROSSETT, DEBORAH LOU, psychologist, consultant; b. Alma, Mich., Feb. 16, 1957; d. Charles M. and Margaret A. (Roethlisberger) Grossett, Charles M. and Margaret A. (Roethlisberger) Grossett. BS, Alma Coll., Mich., 1979; MA, Western Mich. U., Kalamazoo, 1981, PhD, 1984. Lic. psychologist, Tex.; cert. in diagnostic evaluation, Tex.; bd. cert. behavior analyst, Tex. Grad. rsch. and tchg. asst. Western Mich. U., 1979-84; asst. group home supr., cmty. outreach Residential Opportunities, Kalamazoo, 1982-84; psychologist Richmond State Supported Living Ctr., Tex., 1984-87, cons., 2010—; psychologist Shapiro Devel. Ctr., Kankakee, Ill., 1987-88; clin. coord. Monroe Devel. Ctr., Rochester, NY, 1988; chief psychologist Denton State Sch., Tex., 1989-90; dir. psychol./behavioral svcs. Ctr. for the

Retarded, Houston, 1990—2002, 2008—; psychologist Mental Health and Mental Retardation Authority of Harris County, Houston, 2002—08, Behavior Treatment and Tng. Ctr., 2005—06; pvt. practice, 2004—. Behavioral cons. Ctr. for Developmentally Disabled Adults, Kalamazoo, 1984, Goodman-Wade Enterprises, Houston, 1987; instr. psychology Houston C.C., 1985-86, U. Houston-Clear Lake, 1987, 92, 95—. Contbr. chpt. to book, articles to profl. jours. Western Mich. U. fellow, 1984. Mem. Am. Psychol. Assn., Am. Assn. on Intellectual and Devel. Disabilities, Assn. for Behavior Analysis (chair Outreach Bd. 1989-91), Tex. Assn. for Behavior Analysis (bd. dirs. 1989-91, program chair 1996, pres. 1997). Democrat. Presbyterian. Avocations: golf, camping, gardening. Home: 9750 Ravensworth Dr Houston TX 77031-3130 Office: The Center 3550 W Dallas Houston TX 77019 Office Phone: 713-525-8467. Business E-Mail: dgrossett@thecenterhouston.org.

GROSSI, ROBERT J., vascular surgeon; Grad., U. Medicine and Dentistry of NJ-Sch., Newark, 1981. Diplomate Am. Bd. Surgery, 1987, recertified 1995, 2006, Am. Bd. Surgery-vascular surgery, 1989, recertified 1996, 2006. Residency tng. gen. surgery St. Vincent's Hosp., NYC, 1982—86; fellowship Temple Univ. Hosp., Phila., 1986—87; vice chair surgery dept. Beth Israel Med. Ctr. Office: Beth Israel Medical Center 1st Ave16th St New York NY 10003 Office Phone: 212-420-2000.

GROSSINI, ELENA, medical researcher; b. Novara, July 28, 1970; Degree in Medicine, U. Turin, 1995; PhD, U. East Piedmont, 2000. Rschr. U. East Piedmont, 2001—. Recipient Start Cup, Torino Piemonte, 2010. Mem.: APS. Achievements include research in neural and hormonal control of the cardiovascular system and protection against ischemia-reperfusion injuries. Avocations: swimming, reading. Office: via Solaroli Novara 28100 Italy Business E-Mail: grossini@med.unipmn.it.

GROSSMAN, ANDREW, pediatrician, educator; b. Phila., Oct. 23, 1975; BA, Duke U., 1998; MD, UMDNJ, 2002. Attending physician, clin. asst. prof. pediat. Children's Hosp. Phila., 2008—. Mem.: AGA, NASPGHAN, CCFA. Office: Children's Hosp Phila 34t Philadelphia PA 19104 Office Fax: 215-590-3606. Business E-Mail: grossmanan@email.chop.edu.

GROSSMAN, ELMER ROY, pediatrician; b. LA, Jan. 30, 1929; s. Harry and Reta (Frankel) G.; m. Rosalind Nagin, June 24, 1951 (div. 1976); children: Deena, Marianna; m. Pamela Canfield Antoncich, July 29, 1976; stepchildren: Camilla Sutter, Michael A. Antoncich. AB, U. Calif.-Berkeley, 1949; MD, U. Calif. Sch. Medicine, San Francisco, 1953. Intern Orange County Gen. Hosp., Orange, Calif., 1953-54; resident U. Calif. Hosps., San Francisco, 1957-59; practice medicine specializing in pediatrics Berkeley Pediatric Med. Group, Calif., 1959-92. Assoc. clin. prof. health and med. scis, U. Calif., Berkeley, 1978-80; clin. prof. pediat. emeritus U. Calif. Sch. Medicine, San Francisco; chmn. dept. pediat. Alta Bates Hosp., Berkeley, 1972-74, chmn. infant care ethics com., 1984-90. Author: Everyday Pediatrics, 1993, Everyday Pediatrics for Parents, 1996; columnist The Everyday Pediatrician; contbr. articles to nat. mags. Mem. Berkeley Schs. Master Plan Com., 1966—68, Berkeley Schs. Child Care Com., 1968—70, Berkeley Cmty. Environ. Adv. Commn., 2000—02, Berkeley Cmty. Health Commn., 2002; pres. Temple Beth El, Berkeley, 1970—72. Served to capt USAF, 1954—56. Fellow Am. Acad. Pediatrics; mem. Alameda-Contra Costa Med. Assn., Physicians for Social Responsibility, Physicians for a Nat. Health Program. Democrat. Jewish. Avocations: wine making, gardening. Home and Office: 899 Euclid Ave Berkeley CA 94708-1305 Office Phone: 510-526-9614. Personal E-mail: elmer@grossmanfamily.com.

GROSSMAN, HERBERT BARTON, urologist, researcher; b. Tampa, Fla., June 25, 1945; s. Benjamin and Pauline (Mattis) G.; m. Amy C. Becker, Aug. 24, 1969; children: Beth, Sara, Rebecca. BA, La Salle Coll., Phila., 1966; MD, Temple U., 1970. Diplomate Am. Bd. Urology. Surg. intern U. Mich. Med. Ctr., Ann Arbor, 1970-71; surg. resident St. Joseph Mercy Hosp., Ann Arbor, 1973-74; urology resident U. Mich. Med. Ctr., Ann Arbor, 1974-77; instr. U. Mich. Med. Sch., Ann Arbor, 1977-78; rsch. and clin. fellow Meml. Sloan-Kettering Cancer Ctr., NYC, 1978-80; asst. prof. U. Mich. Med. Sch., Ann Arbor, 1980-85, assoc. prof., 1985-90, prof., 1990-94; dir., urologic oncology U. Mich. Cancer Ctr., Ann Arbor, 1986-94; prof. U. Tex. M.D. Anderson Cancer Ctr., Houston, 1994—2010; dep. chair Dept. Urology U. Tex. MD Anderson Cancer Ctr., 1998—2008, clin. prof., 2011—. Cons. Taubman Med. Libr., 1985—94, The Med. Letter, 1991, Jour. Vascular Surgery, 1991; reviewer VA Merit Rev. Bd. for Surgery, 1986, NIH Pathology B Ad Hoc (SI) Study Sect., 1988, NIDDK Ad Hoc Rev. Groups 12 and 13, 1992, Med. Rsch. Coun., UK, 1999, Dutch Cancer Soc., 1999, 2001, NCI Spl. Emphasis Panel, 1999, 2000, 2003—04, 2010—11; spl. reviewer NIH Exptl. Therapeutics Study Sect., 1986, reviewer spl. study sect., 95, reviewer cancer ctr. support grant, 96; reviewer NCI Rev. Group/subcom. 4, 1997; external reviewer Alta. Cancer Bd., 1998; mem. surg. quality control and edn. com SW Oncology Group, 1980—90, GU com., 1980—, organ site chmn. for local bladder cancer, 1991—2000; surg. oncology adv. com. dept. surgery U. Mich. Med. Ctr., Ann Arbor, 1981—82, dept. surgery computer sys. adv. com., 1983—88, cancer ctr. clin. rsch. com., 1987—94, laser safety com., 1987—94, med. sch. admissions com., 1988—94, patient care com., 1989—90, hosps. quality mgmt. com., 1990—94, rsch. coord. sect. urology, 1991, fin. adv. com., adv. promotion com. for primary rsch. staff dept. surgery, 1993—94; med. practice subcom. U. Tex. M.D. Anderson Cancer Ctr., Houston, 1994—2010, grad. med. edn. com., 1994—2004, surveillance com., 1994—95, dir. clin. rsch., 1994—2004, dep. chmn. dept. urology, 1998—2008, clin. study sect. rev. grants program, 2002—10, vice chmn., 2002—03, chmn., 2003—04; prostate cancer adv. com. Mich. Dept. Pub. Health, 1993—94; clin. rsch. com. mem., 1994—2000, chmn., 1997—2000, dir. bladder cancer multidisciplinary rsch. program, 1999—2004; mem. sci. adv. bd. Anthra Pharms., Inc., 1994—2004, Fujirebio Diagnostics Inc., 2003—07; cons. NCI early detection rsch. network, 2002, PhotoCure, 2003—, Viventia Biotech., 2006—, Ferring Pharms., 2007—, Oncomethylome, 2009—; ad hoc reviewer NCI subcom. E, 2003—04, US Army Med. Rsch. and Materiel Command, 1999; mem. NCI program for assessment of clin. cancer tests strategy group, 2003—, co-chair, 2006—; mem. NCI PACCT strategy group, 2004—; molecular biology rev. panel FAMRI, 2001—06, chair therapeutic intervention; chmn. Tengion Data Safety Monitoring Bd., 2010—. Mem. editl. bd. Oncology Reports, 1998—, Jour. Urology, 1999—2007, sect. editor Urologic Oncology, 2000—, Molecular Oncology, 2007—; contbr. articles to profl. jours., chapters to books. Capt. USAF, 1971—73. Recipient 2d prize Ferdinand C. Valentine Urology Essay Contest, 1980, also numerous rsch. grants; named to W.A. "Tex" and Deborah Moncrief, Jr. Disting. Chair in Urology, 1994, Vis. Professorship award in urology, Pfizer/AUA, 2004; Ferdinand C. Valentine fellow N.Y. Acad. Medicine, 1979-80, clin. fellow Am. Cancer Soc., 1979-80. Office: U T MD Anderson Cancer Ctr 1515 Holcombe Blvd # 1373 Houston TX 77030-4009 Office Phone: 713-792-3250.

GROSSMAN, JOHN A. I., orthopedist; b. Norfolk, Va., Dec. 3, 1951; Diploma, Norfolk Acad., 1969; AB in Middle East Studies, Dartmouth Coll., 1973; MD, U. Va, Sch. Medicine, 1978. Diplomate Am. Bd. Plastic Surgery, 1989, lic. State NY, 1990; cert. added qualifications in hand surgery 1990. Resident surgery George Wash. U. Med. Ctr., 1978—79; surgeon Miami Children's Hosp., Fla., 1996—, Baptist Hosp., Miami, 1996—, Doctors Hosp., Fla., 1996—, NYU Hosp. Joint Diseases, NY, 2005; resident surgery Cleveland Clinic Found., 1979—81; sr. resident Mass. Gen. Hosp., 1981—82; resident instr. plastic reconstrn Shriner's Burn Inst. Eastern Va. Sch. Medicine, 1983—85; hand fellow French Hand Inst., 1982—83; asst. prof. plastic surgery Brown U., 1986—90, NYU Sch. Medicine, 1990—96, assoc. prof. clin. surgery, 1996—97, clin. asst. prof. orthopedic surgery, 2006—10, clin. assoc. prof. orthopedic surgery, 2010. Editl. mem. Annals Hand Surgery, 1983—90, Jour. Brachial Plexus & Peripheral Nerve Injury; co-dir. Brachial Plexus Program, NYU Med. Ctr., 1992—96, Pediatric Upper Extremity Program, NYU Med. Ctr., 1992—96; assoc. dir. Hand Surgery Fellowship, NYU Med. Ctr., 1992—96; med. dir. Hand Rehabilitation Unit, NYU Med. Ctr., 1992—96; dir. Peripheral Nerve Unit, Doctor's Hosp., 1997—99, Brachial Plexus Program, Miami Children's Hosp., 1997—; invited lectr. in fields. Contbr. chapters to books. Recipient Friends Dartmouth Libr. award, 1972, Lower award, Cleve. Clinic Found., 1980, Poster prize, Internat. Fedn. Socs. Surgery Hand, 2001, NYU Hosp. Joint Diseases Eleanor Kauffman award, 2009; fellow, Dartmouth Coll., 1972—73, Allergan grant, 2005, Falk grant, 2002—04, Medical Trust grant, 2002—04. Mem.: ACS, NY Acad. Medicine Iberoamerican Acad. Pediatric Neurology (program com. mem. 2000), Groupe d Etude de la Main Plastic Surgery Rsch. Coun. NY Soc. Surgery Hand, Am. Soc. Surgery Hand Residents & Fellows Com., Am. Soc. Peripheral Nerve Program Com., Am. Assn. Plastic Surgery, Am. Assn. Hand Surgery (program com. mem. 1992—94, time & Pl. com. mem. 1995—96), Am. Assn. Clin. Anatomists. Achievements include research in peripheral nerve and brachial plexus surgery, upper extremity reconstruction. Home: PO Box 43 0942 Miami FL 33243

GROSSMAN, JOYCE RENEE, pediatrician, internist; b. Bklyn., Nov. 15, 1951; d. Norman and Sydell (Rashbaum) Katz; m. Arthur Robert Grossman (div.); 1 child, Justin BS, Bklyn. Coll., 1973; MS, Cornell Med. Coll., Ithaca, NY, 1980; MD, Downstate Med. Coll., 1986. Adj. prof. Downstate Med. Ctr., Bklyn., 1994—; attending physician N.Y. Hosp. Network, Bklyn., 1996—97, Beth Israel Med. Ctr., Bklyn., 1997; assoc. med. dir. Cigna of N.Y., NYC, 1998—. Author: (with others) Pediatric Aspects of Tuberculosis & Clinical Handbook, 1995 Fellow: Am. Acad. Physicians, Am. Acad. Pediat. Achievements include patents for gene therapy, antibiotics and chemotherapeutic agents.

GROSSMAN, MELANIE, dermatologist; AB in Biology, Princeton U., NJ, 1984; MD, NYU, 1988. Diplomate Am. Bd. Dermatology. Intern Yale U. Med. Ctr., New Haven, 1988—89; resident in dermatology Presbyn. Hosp./Columbia U., NYC, 1989—92; fellow in laser dermatology and photodynamic therapy Mass. Gen. Hosp. and Wellman Labs., Boston, 1993—95, asst. attending dermatologist NY Hospital, NYC, 1998, Cornell Univ., 1998; pvt. practice dermatology NYC, 1992—. Asst. attending dermatology Presbyn. Hosp., NYC, 1992—, Cornell U., NYC, 1998—, NY Hosp., NYC, 1998—, St. Luke's Roosevelt Hosp. Ctr., NYC, 1995—; attending physician dept. plastic surgery NY Eye and Ear Infirmary, NYC, 1996—; assoc. clin. in dermatology Columbia U., NYC, 1992—; dir. clin. and laser rsch. studies Laser and Skin Surgery Ctr. of NY, NYC, 1995; clin. affiliate dermatology NY Hosp., NYC, 1996—97; clin. instr. dermatology Cornell U. Med. Ctr., NYC, 1996—97; clin. fellow dermatology Mass. Gen. Hosp.-Harvard Med. Sch., Boston, 1993—95. Contbr. articles to profl. jours. Fellow: Am. Soc. for Dermatologic Surgery, Am. Soc. for Laser Medicine and Surgery (socioecon. affairs com. 1997—2000, nominating com. 2000); mem.: Women's Dermatologic Soc., Women's Med. Soc. NY, Dermatologic Soc. Greater NY (comm. com., exec. com.), Med. Soc. State of NY, Am. Acad. Dermatology (chair photobiology task force 1998—99, melanoma task force, comm. com. 1998—2000, comm. study group for 21st century, sports ad hoc com., chair socioecon. affairs com. 1999—2000). Office: 161 Madison Ave Ste 4 NW New York NY 10016 Office Phone: 212-725-8600. Office Fax: 212-725-8620.

GROSSMAN, MICHAEL, economics professor; b. Bklyn., July 12, 1942; s. Mortimer and Doris (Orent) G.; m. Ilene Joy Gordon, Sept. 11, 1966; children: Sandra Diane, Barri Lynn. BA, Trinity Coll., Hartford, Conn., 1964; PhD, Columbia U., 1970. Asst. prof. Ctr. Health Adminstrn. Studies, Grad. Sch. Bus., U. Chgo., 1969-71; rsch. assoc., co-program dir. health econs. rsch. Nat. Bur. Econ. Rsch., NYC, 1972—; prof. econs. CUNY Grad. Sch., 1974, disting. prof. econs, 1988. Mem. population sci. study sect. Nat. Inst. Child Health and Human Devel., Washington, 2003—; mem. bd. sci. counselors Nat. Ctr. for Health Stats., Hyattsville, Md., 2004—; cons. in field. Author: (Book) The Demand for Health: A Theoretical and Empirical Investigation, 1972 (Nomination for Kulp Award of the American Risk and Insurance Association, 1976); editor: The Economic Analysis of Substance Abuse: An Integration of Econometric and Behavioral Economic Research, 1999, Economic Analysis of Substance Use and Abuse: The Experience of Developed Countries and Lessons for Developing Countries, 2001, Substance Use: Individual Behaviour, Social Interactions, Markets and Politics, 2005; co-editor: Review of Economics of the Household, 2005—; assoc. editor Jour. Health Econs., Amsterdam, Netherlands, 1982—; contbr. articles to profl. jours. Mem. Social Scis., Nursing, Epidemiology and Methods Study sect. Ctr. for Sci. Rev., NIH, Washington, 2000—01. Recipient Victor R. Fuchs award, Am. Soc. Health Economists, 2008; Ford Found. fellow, Columbia U. Mem.: APHA, Health Econs. Rsch. Orgn., Population Assn. Am., Internat. Health Econs. Assn., Am. Econ. Assn., Pi Gamma Mu, Phi Beta Kappa. Independent. Jewish. Avocations: tennis, skiing, boating. Home: 115 E 9th St Apt 14C New York NY 10003 Office: Nat Bur Econ Rsch 365 5th Ave 5th Flr New York NY 10016-4309 Office Phone: 212-817-7959. Business E-Mail: mgrossman@gc.cuny.edu.

GROSSMAN, ROBERT GEORGE, neurosurgeon, department chairman; b. NYC, Jan. 24, 1933; s. Ferenc and Vivian (Isenberg) Grossman; m. Ellin Friedman, June 26, 1955; children: Amy, Kate, Ruth. BA, Swarthmore Coll., 1953; MD, Columbia U., 1957. Diplomate Am. Bd. Neurosurgery. Intern Strong Meml. Hosp., Rochester, NY, 1957-58; resident Presbyn. Hosp., Columbia U., NYC, 1960-63; acad. practice medicine, specializing in neurol. surgery Houston, 1973—; from instr. to assoc. prof. neurol. surgery U. Tex. S.W. Med. Sch., 1963-68; from assoc. prof. to prof. neurol. surgery Albert Einstein Coll. Medicine, 1969-73; prof., chmn. div. neurol. surgery U. Tex. Med. Br., Galveston, 1973-80; prof., chmn. dept. neurol. surgery Baylor Coll. Medicine, 1980—2005; assoc. dean clin. affairs Baylor Coll. Medicine, 2002—05; dir. Neurol. Inst., chmn. dept. neurosurgery Meth. Hosp., Houston, 2005—. Chmn. neurology B study sect. USPHS, NIH, 1972—74; mem. bd. sci. counsellors Nat. Inst. Neurol. Diseases and Strok, NIH, 1993—96. Author (with W. D. Willis): Medical Neurobiology, 3d edit., 1981; chmn. editl. bd.: Jour. Neurosurgery, 1987. With US Army, 1958—60. Mem.: ACS, Soc. Neurol. Surgeons (pres. 1995), Am. Acad. Neurol. Surgery (v.p.), Am. Bd. Neurol. Surgery (chmn. bd. dirs. 1989—90), Soc. Univ. Surgeons, Am. Assn. Neurol. Surgeons. Home: 2002 Sunset Blvd Houston TX 77005-1651 Office: Tex Med Ctr Scurlock Tower 6560 Fannin St Ste 944 Houston TX 77030-2706 Office Phone: 713-441-3800. Business E-Mail: rgrossman@tmhs.org.

GROSSMAN, ROBERT IVIN, dean, neuroradiologist, scientist, educator; b. NYC, Sept. 28, 1947; BS, Tulane U., 1969; MD, U. Pa., 1973. Cert. Radiology, Neuroradiology. Intern Beth Israel Hosp., Boston, 1973-74; resident in neurosurgery U. Pa. Med. Sch., Phila., 1974-76, resident in radiology, 1976-79; fellow in neuroradiology Mass. Gen. Hosp., Boston, 1979-81; asst. prof. radiology U. Pa. Med. Sch., Phila., 1981-84, assoc. prof., 1984-87, prof. radiology, neurosurgery and neurology, 1987; chief neuroradiology U. Pa. Med. Ctr., 1987, chmn. Diagnostics Radiology Study Sect., 1997—2000; Louis Marx prof. radiology, chmn. Dept. Radiology, prof. neurosurgery, neurology, physiology and neuroscience NYU Sch. Medicine, 2001—, Saul J. Farber dean, 2007—; CEO NYU Langone Med. Ctr., 2007—. Mem. Diagnostic Radiology Study Sect. NIH, 1995—2000, chmn., 1997—2000, mem. Nat. Adv. Coun. Biomedical Imaging and Bioengineering, 2003—07. Author: Neuroradiology: The Requisites, 1994, Magnetic Resonance Techniques in Clinical Trials in Multiple Sclerosis, 1999; assoc. editor Magnetic Resonance Medicine, 1991—; contbr. articles to med. jours. Recipient Javits Neuroscience Investigator Award, NIH, 1999, Outstanding Contributions in Rsch. Award, Am. Soc. Neuroradiology Edn. and Rsch. Found., 2004. Fellow: Internat. Soc. Magnetic Resonance in Medicine, Am. Coll. Radiology; mem.: Am. Soc. Neuroradiology (pres.-elect 2005—06, former v.p.), Alpha Omega Alpha. Office: Rusk Inst Rm 229 560 First Ave New York NY 10016 Office Phone: 212-263-3269. Office Fax: 212-263-8137. E-mail: Robert.Grossman@nyumc.org. *

GROSSMAN, STANLEY LAWRENCE, surgeon; b. Bklyn., Aug. 14, 1929; MD, SUNY, Bklyn., 1954; MPH, N.Y. Med. Coll., 1986. Diplomate Am. Bd. Surgery. Intern Maimonides Hosp., Bklyn., 1954-55, resident in surgery, 1955-59; with St. Lukes Hosp., Newburgh, N.Y., Cornwall Hosp., N.Y. Fellow ACS, N.Y. Acad. Medicine; mem. AMA, Med. Soc. State N.Y. Office: 460 Gidney Ave Newburgh NY 12550-3117 *

GROSSMAN, ZVI, medical researcher; b. Haifa, Israel, Mar. 24, 1941; PhD, Reali, 1958, Tel Aviv U., 1972. Prof. Tel Aviv U., 1986; adj. rschr. NIH, 1998. Home: 10006 Hurst St Bethesda MD 20814 Personal E-mail: grossmanz@niaid.nih.gov.

GROUDINE, MARK TERRY, oncologist; married. BS in Zoology, U. Wis., 1970; MD, U. Pa., 1975, PhD, 1976. Lic. physician Wash., 1990. Vis. scientist dept. molecular biology Swiss Inst. Exptl. Cancer Rsch., Lausanne, Switzerland, 1972—73; vis. fellow dept. biochem. scis. Princeton U., Princeton, NJ, 1975—76; intern and resident in radiation oncology U. Wash. Sch. Medicine, Seattle, 1976—80, asst. prof. radiation oncology, adj. asst. prof. dept. pathology, 1979—83, assoc. prof. radiation oncology, adj. assoc. prof. pathology, 1983—86, full prof. radiation oncology, adj. full prof. pathology, 1986—; asst. mem. basic scis. divsn. Fred Hutchinson Cancer Rsch. Ctr., 1979—83, assoc. mem. basic scis. divsn., 1983—86, program head molecular medicine program, 1986—95, full mem. basic scis. divsn., 1995—, dep. dir., 1998—2010, interim pres., dir., 2010—. Mem. bd. sci. counselors divsn. cancer treatment Nat. Cancer Inst., 1986—91. Recipient, Allison Eberlein Fund award, 1989; fellow Clin. fellow, Am. Cancer Soc., 1979—80, Leukemia Soc. fellow, 1977—79, Med. Scientist Tng. Program fellow, NIH, 1970—72. Fellow: Am. Acad. Arts & Sciences, AAAS; mem.: Nat. Acad. Sci. and Inst. Medicine (life). Office: Fred Hutchinson Cancer Rsch Ctr 1100 Fairview Ave N A2M-015 PO Box 19024 Seattle WA 98109-1024 Office Phone: 206-667-4497. Office Fax: 206-667-6525. E-mail: markg@fhcrc.org.

GROVE, JEFFREY SCOTT, family practice physician; b. Paxton, Ill., Sept. 21, 1964; s. Ronald Edwin and Delores Ann (Martensen) G.; m. Karen Beth Hanlon, June 17, 1989; children: Garrett Jeffrey, Victoria May. BS in Biology, Fla. So. Coll., 1986; DO, Southeastern Coll. Osteo Med., North Miami Beach, Fla., 1990. Diplomate Am. Bd. Quality Assurance and Utilization Rev. Physicians; bd. cert. family practice and in geriatrics. Intern Suncoast Hosp., Largo, Fla., 1990-91, resident in family practice, 1991-93; pvt. practice SunCoast Family Med. Assocs., Largo, 1993—. Med. dir. Barrington Properties, Largo, 1994-97, Oak Manor Nursing Ctr., Largo, 1993-2000, Drew Village Nursing Ctr., Clearwater, Fla., 1996-99, Highland Pines Nursing Ctr., 1999-2000; rep.-at-large exec. com. Suncoast Hosp., 1995-2000, chief adminstrv. resident, 1992-93, family practice tchg. staff, geriatrics program dir., 1993-96, faculty devel. com., 1994—2006, legal compliance comm., 1998—2006; mem. quality assurance/utilization rev. com., 1993—2006, med. dir. of quality assurance/utilization rev. dept., 1995—06; bd. dirs. Suncoast Cmty. Care PHO, Largo, 1994-98, med. dir., 1998; clin. asst. prof. family medicine Nova Southeastern U. Coll. Osteo. Medicine, North Miami Beach, 1994-2000, clin. assoc. prof., 2000—; clin. instr. Kirksville Coll. Osteo. Medicine, 1993—; trustee SunCoast Hosp. Found., 1996-2002, SunCoast Hosp., 1998—06; regional med. dir. Tampa Bay for Elder Health. Vice-chmn. bd. trustees SCH Found., 1997-98, chmn., 1998-99; trustee St. Paul's Sch., 2003—09, chmn. devel. com., 2005—07; bd. trustees health professions divsn. Nova Southeastern U., 2009-. Named to Outstanding Young Men of Am.; recipient Disting. Trustee award SCH Found., 2000. Mem.: Am. Coll. Osteopathic Family Practitioners (nat. bd. govs. 2004—, v.p. 2011—, Fellows award 2002), Pinellas County

Osteo. Med. Soc. (bd. govs. 1995—, treas. 1996—99, pres. 2000—03, Physician of Yr. 2002—03, Distinguished Svc. award 2007), Fla. Soc. Am. Coll. Osteo. Family Physicians (chmn. membership com. Fla. chpt. 1997—99, trustee 1997—2010, treas. 1999—2000, v.p. 2000—01, pres. 2001—02, Physician of Yr. 2003—04, Distinguished Svc. award 2009), Fla. Osteo. Med. Assn. (trustee 2001—, exec. com. 2005—, 1st v.p. 2009—10, pres. 2011—), Am. Osteo. Assn. (mem. coun. continuing med. edn. 2006—09, vice-chmn. coun. on continuing med. edn. 2006—, chmn. coun. continuing med. edn. 2009—, mem. Bur. of State Govt. Affairs), Nova Southeastern U. Coll. Osteo. Medicine Alumni Assn. (v.p. 2000—01, pres. 2002—03, Disting. Alumni award 2001, Disting. Alumni Achievement award 2003), Scouting Res., Nat. Eagle Scout Assn. (life). Republican. Methodist. Avocations: golf, stamp collecting/philately, travel, skiing. Office: SunCoast Family Med Assocs 12020 Seminole Blvd Largo FL 33778 also: 120 Medical Blvd Ste 103 Spring Hill FL 34609 Office Phone: 727-588-9572.

GROVER, ASHOK KUMAR, ophthalmologist; b. Agra, Uttar Pradesh, India, Oct. 30, 1955; s. Ishar Dass and Santosh Grover; m. Poonam Grover; children: Apoorv, Tushar. MBBS, Maulana Azad Med. Coll., New Delhi, 1976; MD Ophthalmology, All India Inst. Med. Sci., 1980. Sr. resident All India Inst. Med. Sci., New Delhi, 1981—83; mem. Nat. Acad. Med. Sci., 1982; asst. prof. Maulana Azad Med. Coll., New Delhi, 1984—88, assoc. prof., 1988—92; sr. cons. dept. ophthalmology Sir Ganga Ram Hosp., New Delhi, 1992—, chmn. dept. ophthalmology. Councilor Asia Pacific Acad. Ophthal., Afro Asian Acad. Ophthal. Recipient Padma Shri award, Pres. India. Fellow: Internat. Coun. of Ophthalmology, Internat. Med. Sci. Acad., Royal Coll. Physicians and Surgeons Glasgow; mem.: Asia Pacific Soc. of Oculoplastic and Reconstructive Surgery (past v.p.), Afro Asian Acad. of Ophthalmology (bd. mem.), Asia Pacific Acad. of Ophthalmology (councillor at larger), All India Ophthal. Soc. (pres.), Delhi Ophthalmic Soc. (past pres.), Ocular Trauma Soc. India (hon. gen. sec.), Indian Intraocular Implant and Refractive Surgery Soc., Oculoplastic Assn. India (past pres.), Fedn. Ophthalmic Rsch. and Edn. Ctrs. (past pres.). Home: 11/1 E Patel Nagar New Delhi 110008 India Office: Vision Eye Centre 12/27 W 110 008 New Delhi India Office Phone: 911125882129, 25887228. Personal E-mail: akgrover55@yahoo.com.

GROVER, CHANDER, physician, educator; b. Delhi, Apr. 25, 1976; MD, DNB, Maulana Azad Med. Coll., MNAMS, 2002. Lectr. U. Coll. Med. Scis., 2009—. Office: University Coll Med Scis Delhi 110095 India Business E-Mail: chandergroverkubba@rediffmail.com.

GROVER, NEETA DHAR, physician, pharmacologist, educator; b. Srinagar, Kashmir, India, Feb. 27, 1971; MBBS, Grant Med. Coll., Mumbai, 1996, MD, 2001. Tutor Grant Med. Coll., 1998—2001, lectr., 2001; asst. prof. DY Patil Med. Coll., Kolhapur, India, 2003—07, Bharati Vidyapeeth U. Med. Coll. and Hosp., Sangli, India, 2007—08, assoc. prof., 2008—, 2008—10. Recipient Servier Young Investigator award, Inst. Rschs. Internat., Servier, France. Mem.: Indian Pharmacol. Soc. Avocations: knitting, reading. Home: 43-B Rama Udyan Phase 3 Pandarpur Rd Miraj Maharashtra 416410 India Personal E-mail: neetadhargrover@hotmail.com.

GROVER, SANJAY, plastic surgeon; b. Calif. married; 3 children. BS, UCLA, 1990; MD, U. Calif., San Diego, 1994. Cert. Med. Bd. Calif., 1995, diplomate Am. Bd. Plastic Surgery, 2002. Surg. intern Stanford U. Med. Ctr., 1994—95, plastic surgery resident, 1997—99, chief resident, 1998—99; surg. resident Stanford Health Svcs., 1995—97; fellow in aesthetic surgery PACES Plastic Surgery, Atlanta, 1999; pvt. practice Newport Beach, Calif., LA. Affiliated Hoag Meml. Hosp. Presbyn., Irvine Multi Specialty Surgery Care Surgery Ctr., Newport Beach Surgery Ctr., Laguna Hills Surgery Ctr. Featured on (TV series) Good Day LA: Style File with Jillian Barbieri, 2002. Fellow: Am. Coll. Surgeons; mem.: Calif. Soc. Plastic Surgeons, Rhinoplasty Soc., Orange County Soc. Plastic Surgeons (past pres.), Am. Soc. for Laser Medicine & Surgery, Am. Soc. for Aesthetic Plastic Surgery, Am. Soc. Plastic Surgeons. Office: Ctr for Aesthetic Plastic Surgery Ste 507 360 San Miguel Dr Newport Beach CA 92660 Office Phone: 949-759-9551. E-mail: inquiry@doctorgrover.com.

GRSKOVIC, BRANKA, geneticist; b. Zagreb, Croatia, Aug. 8, 1973; BSc, U. Zagreb, 1997, MSc, 2002, PhD, 2005. Rsch. scientist asst. Sch. Medicine, U. Zagreb, 1997—2008; DNA expert Forensic Sci. Ctr. Ivan Vucetic, Gen. Police Directorate, Ministry of Interior, 1998—. Asst. prof. U. Ctr. Forensic Scis., U. Split, Croatia, 2011. Recipient Rector's award, U. Zagreb; CEEPUS scholarship, Ministry of Sci. and Tech., Zagreb. Mem.: Croatian Soc. Human Genetics, European Soc. Human Genetics. Avocations: dance, travel, reading. Office: Ilica 335 Zagreb 10000 Croatia Office Phone: 38514887-334. Office Fax: 38513788051. Business E-Mail: bgrskovic@mup.hr.

GRU, ALEJANDRO ARIEL, pathologist; b. Buenos Aires, May 22, 1979; MD, U. Buenos Aires, 2004. Fellow in anatomic pathology, physician Barnes-Jewish Hosp., 2006—11. Named one of Best Resident, Fellow, Am. Soc. Dermatopathology. Mem.: US and Can. Acad. Pathology (Stowell-Orbinson Cert. of Merit), Am. Soc. Clin. Pathology, Coll. Am. Pathologists. Home: 1068 E Linden Ave Saint Louis MO 63117 Business E-Mail: agru@path.wustl.edu.

GRUBB, ROBERT L., JR., neurosurgeon; b. Charlotte, NC, May 9, 1940; MD, U. N.C., 1965. Intern Barnes Hosp., St. Louis, 1965-66, resident in gen. surgery, 1966-67, resident in neurosurgery, 1969-73; fellow NIH, Bethesda, Md., 1968-69; mem. staff Barnes-Jewish Hosp., St. Louis, St. Louis Children's Hosp.; prof. neurosurgery Washington U., St. Louis. Fellow ACS; mem. Am. Acad. Neurol. Surgery, AANS, CNS, SNS. Office: Washington U Sch Medicine 660 S Euclid Ave Box 8057 Saint Louis MO 63110-1093 Home Phone: 314-965-1330; Office Phone: 314-362-3567. Business E-Mail: grubbr@nsurg.wustl.edu.

GRUBER, IRMHILD, embryologist, director; b. Ramsau Hainfeld, Nov. 22, 1968; MSc, U. Vienna, 1996, DSc, 2002. Biomed. asst. AKH Vienna, 1992—95; scientist CCRI St. Anna Hosp., 1995—96; IVF lab. dir. Landesklinikum St. Pölten, 1997—. Recipient Wissenschaftspreis Ärztekammer NÖ 2002, Ärztekammer NÖ. Mem.: Embryologenforum Austria (chmn. 2004—06, co-chmn. 2006), ESHRE. Avocations: gardening, music, literature. Office: Prost-Fuehrer-Strasse 4 Sankt Pölten Lower Austria A-3100 Austria Office Fax: 43 2742 300 12429. Business E-Mail: irmhild.gruber@stpoelten.lknoe.at.

GRUBER, JONATHAN H., economist; b. Sept. 30, 1965; m. Andrea Gruber, 1991; children: Sam, Jack, Ava. BS MIT, 1987; PhD, Harvard U., 1992. Asst. prof. economics MIT, Cambridge, Mass., 1992—95, Castle Krob assoc. prof. economics, 1995—97, prof. economics, 1997—, assoc. head economics dept., 2006—08. Undergraduate program coord. MIT Economics Dept., 1994—; faculty rsch. fellow Nat. Bur. Econ. Rsch., 1992—98, dir. Program on Children, 1996—2009, rsch. assoc., 1998—, dir. Program on Health Care, 2009—; academic adv. com. Ctr. Am. Progress, 2004—. Author: Pub. Finance & Pub. Policy, 2005, 2d edit., 2007; assoc. editor Jour. Pub. Economics, 1997—2001, co-editor, 2001—, Jour. Health Economics, 1998—2001, assoc. editor, 2001—, mem. adv. bd. Social Sci. Rsch. Network (SSRN) Abstracts in Health Economics, 1998—, SSRN Jour. Unemployment Ins., 2004—, mem. editl. bd. Berkeley Electronic Jours. in Econ. Analysis & Policy, 2001—; contbr. articles to profl. jours. Dep. asst. sec. econ. policy US Treasury Dept., 1997—98; mem. Congl. Budget Office long term modeling adv. group, 2000—, Bd. of Commonwealth Health Ins. Connector Authority, 2006—. Recipient Kenneth Arrow award, Am. Pub. Health Assn., 1995, FIRST award, Nat. Inst. Aging, 2003; named 19th Most Powerful Person in US Health Care, Modern Healthcare Mag., 2006; Rsch. fellow, Sloan Found., 1995, Presdl. Faculty fellow, NSF, 1995, Margaret MacVicar faculty fellow, MIT, 2007. Fellow: Am. Acad. Arts and Sciences; mem.: Nat. Acad. Social Ins., Inst. Medicine, Phi Beta Kappa. Office: MIT Dept Economics E52-355 50 Memorial Dr Cambridge MA 02142-1347 Office Phone: 617-253-8892. Office Fax: 617-253-1330. E-mail: gruberj@mit.edu.

GRUBER, RONALD P., plastic surgeon, researcher; b. London, Apr. 13, 1941; came to U.S., 1946; s. Paul and Edith (Lieblein) G.; m. Gloria Lynn Rubel, June 4, 1967; children: Alicia, Brandon, April, Amanda. BA in Speech, U. Calif., Berkeley, 1962; MD, U. Calif. Sch. Medicine, San Francisco, 1966. Diplomate Am. Bd. Plastic Reconstructive Surgery. Intern Maimonides Med. Ctr., NYC, 1966-67; resident, gen. surgery Montefiore Med. Ctr., NYC, 1967-68; resident, surgery U. Calif., San Francisco, 1970-71, Stanford U. Med. Ctr., 1971-73, Bank of Am. Giannini fellow, dept. plastic surgery Calif., 1972—73, chief resident, plastic surgery, 1973-74, clin. instr., surgery Calif., 1974—96; NIH fellow Stanford U., 1971—72, clin. asst. prof. Calif., 1996—; chief, clin. and exptl. br., biphysics lab. Edgewood Arsenal Biophysics Lab., Md., 1968-70; clin. asst. prof. U. Calif., San Francisco, 2002—. Asst., neuropharmacological rsch., Langley Porter Inst., San Francisco, 1965-66, Moses Inst. Rsch., NYC, 1967-68; assoc. staff Alta Bates Hosp., Berkeley, 1974-, mem. med. edn. com. 1974-75, Children's Hosp., Oakland, Calif., 1974-92; active staff Summit Hosp., Oakland, Calif., 1974-, Oakland Hosp., Calif. 1974-; mem. med. edn. com., 1974-76, ambulatory surgery com., 1978-84, exec. com. 1983-85, peer review com., 1988; mem. med. edn. com. Merritt Hosp., 1976-84; adj. clin. faculty, Stanford U. Med. Ctr., 1996-; vis./traveling professorships U. So. Calif., 1994, U. Calif. San Diego, 1994, U. Tex. Houston, 1996, Brown U., 1998, 2001, U. Miami, 1998, Loma Linda U., 2001, U. Va., 2001, U. Cinn., 2001, John Hopkins U., 2001, Georgetown U., 2001, Wash. U., 2002, NY Soc. Plastic Surgery, 2002, St. Barnabas Med. Ctr., 2002; presenter in fields of plastic surgery rsch. and physics rsch. Editl. cons. Annals of Plastic Surgery, 1986-, Plastic & Reconstrucive Surgery, 1992-; Aesthetic Surgery Jour. 1996-; reg. editor Aesthetic Plastic Surgery Jour., 2000-; co-author: Rhinoplasty: State of the Art, 1993; contbr. numerous articles to scientific jours., including Plastic & Reconstructive Surgery, Annals of Plastic Surgery, Clin. Plastic Surgery, others; co-author numerous videos; contbr. numerous chpts. to books. Major, U.S. Army, Edgewood Arsenal, Md., 1968-70. Maj. Oakland Army Base-Reserve Duty, 1970—72. Recipient Am. Cancer Soc. award, 1978, Hon. Thomas Jefferson Prof. Plastic Surgery, U. Va., 2001; named to Best Doctors in America, 1996, Best Plastic and Reconstructive Surgeons, 1999; named one of Top Doctors in the Bay Area, San Francisco Mag., 1999. Mem. AAAS, AMA, ACS, Royal Soc. Medicine, Psychonomic Soc., Am. Physicians Fellowship Inc., Internat. Coll. Surgeons (regent, Northern Calif. 1984, local host chmn. 1988, v.p., 1988), Am. Soc. Plastic and Reconstructive Surgeons(scientific program com. 1981, 1982, 1994-95, 1998 exhibits com. 1994, 1995, scientific exhibit/poster com. 1996, technical exhibits com. 1998, N.Y. Acad. Scis., Internat. Soc. Study of Time, Am. Soc. Aesthetic Plastic Surgery (traveling prof. 2001-03, scientific com., 1983, 1988, strategic planning com., 1986, chmn. audiovisual com., 1987-88, scholarship com., 1984-87, local arrangements com., 1988, ethics com. (western US) rep. 1990-93, scientific program com. 1994-95, 1998, 1999, technical exhibits com., 1998, edn. com., 1999, regional editor jour., Walter Scott Brown award, best video or film, 1983), Am. Soc. Maxillofacial Surgeons (traveling prof.), Am. Assn. Plastic Surgeons (by invitation), Am. Physics Soc., Calif. Med. Assn., Alameda Contra Costa County Med. Assn.(mediation com. 1976-, ethics com. 1990-96), Calif. Soc. Plastic Surgeons (Insurance mediation com., 1983, scientific com. 1982, chmn. scientific com., 1986, 1987, 1988, mktg. com. 1986, awards com. 1996, best overall paper award, Rhinoplasty Soc. (founding mem. 1995, sec. 1996, v.p., 1997, pres.-elect 1998, pres. 1999-2000, immediate past pres.), Lipolysis Soc. N.Am., Northwestern Soc. Plastic & Reconstructive Surgery (hon. mem. by invitation), Plastic Surgery Edn. Found. (curriculum com., 1988, rsch. grant com, 1988, instructional course com. 1987, 1988, silicone rsch. com., 1992), Am. Cancer Soc. (bd. dirs. ad hoc 1981-84, Surgery Ctr. Oakland, Calif. bd. dirs. 1985-91). Achievements include development of the periareolar subpectoral augmentation mammaplasty; innovations include Gruber Open Rhinoplasty Retractor, 1996, Gruber Rhinoplasty Set, Nasal Tip Graft Sizes, 2001, Mucoperichondrial elevator/knife combination, 2002, Columella Retractor, 2002, Cartilage Carving Block, 2002; pioneer of the open rhinoplasty. Office: East Bay Aesthetic Plastic Surgery Ctr 3318 Elm St Oakland CA 94609 Office Phone: 510-654-9222. Office Fax: 510-654-2349. Business E-Mail: rgrubermd@pacbell.net.

GRUBER, SABINE ELISABETH, plastic surgeon; b. Salzburg, Austria, July 24, 1969; d. Fritz Leopold and Cecilia Elisabeth Gruber. Grad., U. Vienna, Austria, 1994. Intern Hosp.-Barmherzige Brüder, Salzburg, 1994—96, resident, 1996—2001, cons., 2001—09, attending in plastic surg. unit, 2002—; organizer Congress Plastic Surgery, Salzburg, 2001—02; vis. prof. U. So. Calif., U. Calif., Irvine. Contbr. articles to profl. jours. Grantee, Mayo Clinic, Rochester, Minn., 1999, Munich, 2001. Mem.: Soc. Plastic, Aesthetic and Reconstructive Surgery (Austria) (award 2007), Soc. Plastic Surgery (tng. program supr. 1999—2009). Avocations: classical music, opera, paintings, skiing, golf. Office: Ernest-Thunstraße 12 5020 Salzburg Austria

GRUDEN POKUPEC, JOSIPA SANJA, physician; b. Zagreb, Croatia, Dec. 11, 1973; d. Vladimir Georgio and Zdenka Ivanka Gruden; m. Josipa Sanja Gruden Pokupec, July 18, 1998; children: Maximilian Pokupec, Iva Pokupec. Degree, High Med. Sch., Zagreb, 1997. Docent stomatology Clinic Stomatology, Coll. Zagreb, Croatia, 2008—; asst. stomatology Acad. Stomatology, Coll. Split, Croatia, 2009. Contbr. articles to profl. jours. Home: Dedici 76 Zagreb 10000 Croatia Office: Policlinic Stomatology Ulica Ivana Perkovca 3 10-000 Zagreb Croatia Business E-Mail: jspokupec@net.hr.

GRUDZINSKI, IRENEUSZ PIOTR, pharmacist, toxicologist, researcher; b. Kozienice, Poland, May 19, 1961; s. Kazimierz Wladyslaw Grudzinski and Leokadia Grudzinska; m. Janina Maria Kucharska, Oct. 18, 1986; children: Monika, Klaudia. MPharm, Med. Acad., Lodz, Poland, 1986; DSc, Mil. Inst. Hygiene and Epidemiology, Warsaw, 1989. Rsch. assoc., postdoctoral fellow Simon Fraser U., Burnaby, B.C., Canada, 1994, 1996—98; scientist (rsch. asst.) Mil. Inst. Hygiene and Epidemiology, Warsaw, 1987—93, 1998—; sr. specialist Warsaw Pharm. Works Polfa S.A., 2002—. Contbr. articles to profl. jours. Mem.: Polish Soc. Toxicology. Roman Catholic. Achievements include research in biochemical mechanisms of gastrointestinal toxicity of inorganic nitrates and nitrites; biochemical mechanisms of gastrointestinal toxicity of N-nitrosodiethylamine; biochemical mechanisms of nitrite-induced energy disturbances in cells; effects of sodium nitrite on programmed cell death in murine small intestinal mucosa; effects on N-nitrosodiethylamine on crypt cell survival in the small intestinal mucosa of gamma irradiated animals; role of nitric oxide in N-nitrosodiethylamine-induced radioresistance in murine liver and small intestinal mucosa; role of nitric oxide from L-arginine in N-nitrosodiethylamine-induced hepatocarcinogenesis; anti-oxidant effects of diallyl sulfide from garlic, coenzyme Q10, and polyamines in sodium nitrite and/or N-nitrosodiethylamine-poisoned animals. Avocation: classical music. Home: # 5/26 Horbaczewskiego E 03-984 Warsaw Poland Business E-Mail: ipgbiotechplus@pro.onet.pl.

GRUEN, ALISON BRETT, dermatologist; b. NYC, Jan. 15, 1974; d. John Fredrick and Judith Smith Gruen; m. Adam Laurence Evans, July 29, 2005. BA in History magna cum laude, Princeton U., 1996; MD, Yale U., 2000. Diplomate Am. Bd. Dermatology, 2004. Resident in dermatology Health Sci. Ctr., Bklyn., 2001—04, chief resident, 2003—04; pvt. practice New York, NY. Recipient Outstanding Physician award, King's County Hosp. Ctr., 2003, Fifteenth Ann. Conrad Stritzler Meml. Resident Competition First Pl. award, Dermatologic Soc. Greater NY, 2004. Mem.: Women's Dermatologic Soc., Am. Acad. Dermatology, Alpha Omega Alpha. Avocations: skiing, fly fishing, cooking. Office: 1020 Park Ave New York NY 10028 also: 35 E 35th St New York NY 10016

GRUEN, GERALD ELMER, psychologist, educator; b. Granite City, Ill., July 19, 1937; s. Elmer George and Velma Pearl G.; m. Karol Jane Selvidge, Mar. 20, 1960; children— Tami Jane, Christy Lynn. BA, So. Ill. U., 1959; MA, U. Ill., 1963, PhD, 1964. Postdoctoral fellow Heinz Werner Inst. Devel. Psychology, Clark U. and Worcester (Mass.) State Hosp., 1964-66; asst. prof. dept. psychol. scis. Purdue U., West Lafayette, Ind., 1966-69, assoc. prof., 1969-74, prof., 1974—2005, head dept. psychol. scis., 1987-97, prof. emeritus, 2005—. Author: (with T. Wachs) Early Experience and Human Development; contbr. chpt. to The Structuring of Experience, 1977; contbr. articles to profl. jours. Deacon Calvary Baptist Ch., West Lafayette. Recipient USPHS rsch. awards, 1968-71, Nat. Rsch. Svc. award NIMH, 1976-80, Research award Nat. Insts. Child Health and Human Devel., 1981—; recipient Ind. Psychol. Assn. Gordon Barrows award for disting. career contbns., 2000. Fellow APA, Am. Psychol. Soc. (charter mem.); mem. Midwestern Psychol. Assn., Soc. for Rsch. in Child Devel., Sigma Xi. Home: 3738 Westlake Ct West Lafayette IN 47906 Office: Purdue U Psychology Dept West Lafayette IN 47907 Office Phone: 765-463-5560. Personal E-mail: jjgruen@comcast.net. Business E-Mail: gruen@psych.purdue.edu. *

GRUENSTEIN, STEVEN, hematologist, educator, oncologist; MD, U. Genoa, Italy, 1984. Diplomate Am. Bd. Internal Medicine, Am. Bd. Internal Medicine-med. oncology. Resident internal medicine Met. Hosp. Ctr., NYC, 1984—87; fellow hematology and oncology Beth Israel Med. Ctr., NYC, 1987—90; assoc. clin. prof. medicine, hematology and med. oncology Mt. Sinai Sch. Medicine; attending physician Mt. Sinai Hosp., Lenox Hill Hosp. Recipient Patient's Choice Award, Compassionate Doctor's Award; named an Outstanding Clin. Hematologist/Oncologist, NY Met.; named one of Best Doctors, NY Mag., Best Doctors in US and NY, Castle Connelly. Mem.: Am. Soc. of Breast Diseases, Am. Soc. of Hematology, Am. Soc. of Clin. Oncology. Office: Mount Sinai Medical Center One Gustave L Levy Place New York NY 10029 Office Phone: 212-241-6500.

GRUFT, JAMES HARRIS, physiatrist, educator; s. Miriam and Mortimer Gruft; m. Ewa Gruft; children: Monet, Leandra. BA in Psychology, SUNY Suffern, 1976; MD, George Wash. U. Sch. of Medicine, 1986. Cert. Am. Acad. of Phys. Medicine & Rehab., 1992, diplomate Am. Bd. Pain Medicine. Med. dir. pain mgmt. program Marianjoy Rehab. Hosp. and Clinics, Oakbrook Terrace, Ill., 1990—2004; pres., med. dir. Complete Pain & Rehab. Mgmt., LLC, Hinsdale, Ill., 2003—08, From Pain to Wellness LLC, Oakbrook Terrace, Ill., 2008—. Asst. prof. Rush Med. Coll., Chgo., 1990—. Author: (book) Understanding Pain and Healing (Schmerz verstehen und heilen), From Pain to Wellness, 2008. Named Best Drs., 2002—. Fellow: Am. Acad. Phys. Medicine & Rehab.; mem.: Am. Soc. Composers, Authors and Pubs, Am. Acad. Pain Medicine, Internat. Assn. for Study of Pain, Dramatist Guild. Avocations: back-packing, music. Office: 1 Trans Am Plz Dr Ste 100 Oakbrook Terrace IL 60181-4286 Office Phone: 630-627-7500. Office Fax: 630-627-7502. Business E-Mail: information@frompaintowellness.com.

GRUMBACH, MELVIN MALCOLM, pediatrician, educator; b. NYC, Dec. 21, 1925; s. Emanuel and Adele (Weil) G.; m. Madeleine F. Butt, Dec. 1, 1951; children: Ethan Malcolm, Kevin Lawrence, Anthony Havemeyer. Student, Columbia U., 1945, MD, 1948; DM honoris causa (hon.), U. Geneva, 1991; D honoris causa (hon.), U. René Descartes Paris V, 2000, U. Athens, 2008. Diplomate Am. Bd. Pediatrics, Am. Bd. Pediatric Endocrinology (com. mem. 1975-79). Resident in pediatrics Babies Hosp., Presbyn. Hosp., Columbia U. Med. Ctr., NYC, 1949-51; trainee Oak Ridge Inst. Nuc. Studies, 1952; postdoctoral fellow, asst. pediatrics Johns Hopkins Sch. Medicine, 1953-55; mem. faculty Columbia U. Coll. Physicians and Surgeons,

NYC, 1955-65, from instr. to assoc. prof. pediatrics, 1961-65; from asst. to assoc. attending pediatrician Babies Hosp. and Vanderbilt Clin., Columbia-Presbyn. Med. Ctr., 1955-65, founding head postdoctoral tng. program, Pediat. Endocrinology & Pediat. Endocrine Divsn., 1955—65; dir. pediatric svc. U. Calif. Hosps., 1966-86; prof. pediatrics, chmn. dept. U. Calif. Sch. Medicine, San Francisco, 1966-86, first Edward B. Shaw prof. pediatrics, 1983-94, acting dir. Lab. Molecular Endocrinology, 1987-89, Edward B. Shaw disting. prof. emeritus pediatrics (active), 1994—. Vis. prof. Vanderbilt U., 1961, Emory U., 1962, U. Western Ont., 1962, U. NC, 1963, 82, U. Rochester, 1972, UCLA, 1981, U. Tex., Dallas, 1983, Peking Union Med. Coll. and Hosp., 1986, U. Hong Kong, 1986; cons. Letterman Gen. Hosp., 1966-94, Children's Hosp., San Francisco, U.S. Naval Hosp., Oakland, Calif., 1966-94, HEW, NIH, 1961-, Nat. Bd. Med. Examiners, 1964-68; human embryology and devel. study sect. NIH, 1962-66, endocrinology study sect., 1967-71; bd. sci. counselors Nat. Inst. Child Health and Human Devel., 1971-75; gen. clin. rsch. ctrs. com., divsn. rsch. resources NIH, 1976-80, com. for rev. Clin. Ctr., 1984-85, IOM com. study AIDS rsch. program NIH, 1989-91, nat. adv. coun. Nat. Inst. Child Health and Human Devel., 1991-96; sci. adv. com., clin. rsch. adv. com. Nat. Found.-March of Dimes, 1969-94, chmn. clin. rsch. adv. com., 1974-82, Basil O'Connor starter scholar rsch. award comm., 1995-99, grant screening com., 2000-; awards com. Lita Annenberg Hazen Award for Excellence in Clin. Rsch., 1981-86; sci. adv. bd. Scripps Clinic and Rsch. Found., 1977-78, Princesse Marie Christine Found., Brussels, 1981-91, U. Mich. Ctr. for Human Growth and Devel., 1982-89, U. Colo. Health Scis. Barbara Davis Ctr., 1986-93, Rsch. Inst. Hosp. for Sick Children, Toronto, 1984-88, Children's Hosp. LA, 1987-92; sci. and med. adv. bd. Whittier Inst. Diabetes and Endocrinology, 1987-92; adv. bd. Nat. Pituitary Agy., 1965-69; sci. adv. com. Nat. Inst. Environ. Health Scis., 2007-; mem. NIH Evaluation of Endocrinology and Metabolic Diseases, 1977-79; Dean's bd. vis. Mt. Sinai Sch. Medicine, NYC, 1986-87; sci. adv. coun. Cin. Children's Hosp. Rsch. Found., 1997-98; pres. bd. trustees Internat. Pediat. Rsch. Found., Inc., 1984-89; sci. coun. Aid Pour la Recherche Medicale a l'enfance, Paris, 1981-89; com. future pub. health Inst. Medicine, 1986-87; del. to Chinese Acad. Med. Scis., 1986; assoc. editor Internat. Jour. Pediatric Endocrinology, 2008-; lectr. in field; chmn. various confs. Assoc. editor, mem. editl. bd. Jour. Clin. Endocrinology Metabolism, 1957-70, 2006-09; adv. editor Jour. Pediat., 1966-73, mem. editl. bd., 1973-79; assoc. editor Pediat. Rsch., 1970-84, Barnett Pediatrics, 14th-15th edits., Rudolph Pediatrics, 16th-23rd edits., Current Topics in Experimental Endocrinology, 1968-72, Internat. Jour. Pediat. Endocrinology, 2008-; mem. internat. editl. bd. pediat. and pediatric surgery: Excerpta Medica, 1974-2000; mem. editl. bd. Biology of Reproduction, 1968-70, Endocrinologic Clinica Metabolism, 1981—, Pediat. in Rev., 1982-84, Jour. Endocrinol. Investigation, 1982-90, Endocrine Revs., 1984-88, Jour. Pediat. Endocrinology Metabolism, 1984—, Trends in Endocrinology, 1989-2010, Monographs on Endocrinology, Springer-Verlag, 1975-90, Clinical Pediat. Endocrinology, 1992—, Jour. Endocrine Genetics, 1999—, Internat. Jour. Pediat. Endocrinology, 2009-; contbr. articles to profl. jours. Capt. USAF, 1951—53. Postdoctoral fellow Nat. Found. Infantile Paralysis, 1953-55; recipient Joseph M. Smith prize Columbia U., 1962; Career Scientist award Health Research Coun. City N.Y., 1961-66; Silver medal Bicentennial Columbia Coll. Physicians and Surgeons, 1967, Gold medal, 1988; Clin. Endocrinology Trust medal (U.K.), 1983, Centennial Medallist award Babies Hosp., Columbia-Presbyn. Med. Ctr., 1987, Coll. de France medal, 1979, Winthrop award, Am. Fertility Soc., 1981, Sci Patron, Liggins Inst. Faculty Med. Health Sci., U. Auckland, New Zealand, 2001—, UCSF medal, U. Calif., San Francisco, 2010. Fellow: AAAS, NY Acad. Scis. (liason nat. rsch. coun. mem. 2011—), Am. Acad. Pediats. (Bordon award 1971, Lifetime Achievement award 1996), Am. Acad. Arts and Scis.; mem.: Nat. Acad. Scis. (mem. nominating com. 2007, 2010, liaison, Nat. Rsch. Coun. 2011—), Am. Pediat. Soc. (pres.-elect 1988—89, pres. 1989—90, John Howland award 1997), Calif. Acad. Medicine, Western Assn. Physicians, Internat. Neuroendocrinology Soc., Internat. Endocrine Soc. (del. to ctrl. com. 1976—92, exec. com. 1984—92, hon. pres. 2000—04), Endocrine Soc. (coun. 1968—71, pres. elect 1980—81, coun. 1980—83, pres. 1981—82, Robert H. Williams Disting. Leadership award 1980, Fred Conrad Koch award 1992), Teratology Soc., Soc. Pediat. Rsch., Western Soc. Pediat. Rsch. (pres. 1978—79), Lawson Wilkins Pediat. Endocrine Soc. (pres. 1975—76, Inaugural Judson Van Wyk prize 2006), Harvey Soc., Am. Soc. Human Genetics, Assn. Am. Physicians, Am. Soc. Clin. Investigation, Assn. Med. Sch. Pediat. Dept. Chmn. (exec. coun. 1967—72, pres. 1973—75, task force on Pediat. Scientist Tng. Program 1984—91, chmn. selection com. 1986—91), Inst. Medicine US Nat. Acad. Scis. (mem. pub. health com. 1985—87, mem. AIDS rsch. com. 1989—91, chmn. adolescent devel. and biology of puberty 1998—99, mem. com. on understanding the biology of sex and gender differences 2000—01), Soc. Française de Pediatrie (corr.), European Soc. Pediat. Endocrinology (corr.), Italian Soc. Pediat. Endocrinology & Diabetology (hon.), Israel Endocrine Soc. (hon.), Pacific Coast Fertility Soc. (hon.), Japanese Soc. Pediat. Endocrinology (hon.), Can. Soc. Endocrinology and Metabolism (hon.), Argentine Soc. Endocrinology and Metabolism (hon.), Johns Hopkins U. Soc. Scholars, U. Club NYC, Alpha Omega Alpha, Sigma Xi. Office: Univ Calif Sch Medicine Dept Pediatrics S672 San Francisco CA 94143-0434 Office Phone: 415-476-2244. Business E-Mail: grumbach@peds.ucsf.edu.

GRUNBERG, ROBERT LEON WILLY, nephrologist, educator; b. Bucharest, Romania, July 23, 1940; arrived in U.S., 1972, naturalized, 1977; s. William A. and Isabelle L. (Rosen) Grunberg; m. Donna M. Fishman, Oct. 19, 1975; children: Wendie I., Andrea B. MD, U. Orleans-Tours, France, 1969. Diplomate Am. Bd. Internal Medicine, Am. Bd. Nephrology, cert. hypertension specialist in clin. hypertension. Intern, then resident in cardiology Vichy Hosp., France, 1968-72; resident in internal medicine Albert Einstein Med. Ctr., Phila., 1972-74; fellow in nephrology-hypertension Hahnemann Univ. Hosp., Phila., 1974-76, sr. clin. instr. then asst. clin. prof. div. nephrology, 1976; pvt. practice Allentown, Pa., 1976—. Attending physician St. Luke's Hosp., Bethlehem, Pa., Lehigh Valley Ctr. (name now Lehigh Valley Hosp.), Allentown; attending charge divsn. nephrology Easton Hosp., Pa., dir. Renal Dialysis Ctr., 1989; courtesy staff Hahnemann U. Hosp.; chief dialysis Warren Hosp., Phillipsburg, NJ, 1999. Fellow: ACP; mem.: AMA (Physician's Recognition award 1975, 1979, 1982, 1985, 1988—98, 2001), NY Acad. Scis., Nat. Kidney Found., Internat. Soc. Peritoneal Dialysis, Assn. Advancement Med. Instrumentation, Internat. Soc. Nephrology, Internat. Soc. Artificial Organs, Am. Soc. Parenteral and Enteral Nutrition, Internat. Soc. Hypertension, Am. Soc. Artificial Internal Organs, Am. Soc. Nephrology, Pa. Med. Soc. Office: 50 S 18th St Easton PA 18042-3912 also: 401 N 17th St Allentown PA 18104-5034 Office Phone: 610-258-3608.

GRUNBERGER, IVAN, urologist, educator; MD, NYU Sch. of Medicine, 1980. Diplomate Am. Bd. Urology. Resident surgery North Shore Univ. Hosp., Manhasset, NY, 1981—82; resident urology NYU Med. Ctr., NY, 1982—86; urologist Bklyn. Heights Urology. Assoc. clin. prof. State Univ. Of NY Downstate. Office: Brooklyn Urology PC One Prospect Pk W Ste C Brooklyn NY 11215 Office Phone: 718-230-7788.

GRUNDER, FRED IRWIN, retired industrial hygienist, consultant; b. Detroit, Aug. 17, 1940; s. Fritz and Mary Kathrine (Irwin) G.; m. Barbara Ann Ward, May 7, 1966; children: John Frederick, Robert William. BS in Engr. Physics, U. Mich., 1963, MS in Physics, 1967. Diplomte Am. Bd. Indsl. Hygiene; cert. indsl. hygienist. Rsch. assoc. U. Mich., Ann Arbor, 1960-69; chemist G.D. Clayton & Assocs., Southfield, Mich., 1969-72; lab. dir. Bethlehem Steel Corp., Pa., 1972-85; dir. indsl. hygiene Am. Med. Labs., Fairfax, Va., 1985-92; mgr. lab. accreditation programs Am. Indsl. Hygiene Assn., Fairfax, 1992—2002; indsl. hygiene cons. Fishersville, Va., 2002—; v.p. SAW Habitat for Humanity. Sect. editor: Methods for Biological Monitoring, 1988. Scoutmaster Boy Scouts Am., Bethlehem, 1972-84; pres. U. Mich. Club, Lehigh Valley, 1980-84; mem. toxic planning and oversight panel Chesapeake Rsch. Consortium, Solomons Island, Md., 1990-91, lab. assessor AIHA Lab. Accreditation Avg. LLC, 1992, 2004—; bd. dirs. Nat. Coop. Lab. Accreditation, 1997-98, pres., 1998-2000, past pres., 2000-01, evaluation coord., 2004-07. Fellow Am. Indsl. Hygiene Assn.; mem Am. Chem. Soc., Am. Acad. Indsl. Hygiene. Democrat. Methodist. Avocations: reading, stamp and coin collecting, gardening. Personal E-mail: fgrunder@ntelos.net.

GRUNDFAST, KENNETH MARTIN, otolaryngologist; b. Bklyn., Mar. 12, 1944; s. Theodore Harvey and Anne Gertrude (Goldberg) G.; m. Ruthanne Blatt Grundfast, May 26, 1974; children: Rena Brett, Dara Beth. BA, Johns Hopkins U., 1965; MD, SUNY, Syracuse, 1969. Cert. Am. Bd. Otolaryngology, 1977. Clin. instr. dept. of community medicine Georgetown U. Sch. of Medicine, Washington, 1972-74, prof. depts. otolaryngology and pediat., 1996-99, interim chmn. dept. otolryngology; resident otolaryngology Boston U. Hosp., 1974-77; fellow in pediatric otolaryngology Childrens Hosp. of Pitts., 1977-78, staff otolaryngologist, 1978-79, asst. prof. of otolaryngology, 1978-79; prof. dept. otolaryngology, 1980-96; chmn. dept. otolaryngology Children's Nat. Med. Ctr., Washington, 1980-94, vice-chmn., 1994-96, prof., chmn. dept otolaryngology Sch. Medicine Boston U., 1999—; chmn. ethics com. Boston Med. Ctr., 2004—. Lectr. in field. Author: (with others) Ear Infections in Your Child, 1987, Pediatric Otology/Neurotology, 1997; contbr. articles to profl. jours. Lt. comdr. USPHS, 1971-73. Recipient Sylvan Stool Achievement award Sentac, 2000. Fellow ACS, Am. Acad. Pediat.; mem. AMA (Humanitarian award 1973), Soc. Ear, Nose and Throat Advancement in Children (bd. dirs. 1985, v.p. 1988, pres. 1989), Am. Bronchoesophagologic Soc., Soc. U. Otolaryngologists, Am. Neurotology Soc., Trilogical Soc. (hon. mention clin. rsch. thesis), Am. Soc. Pediatric Otolaryngology (pres. 1993-94), Am. Acad. Otolaryngology (v.p. 1994-96, sec.-treas. 2004-, Presdl. Citation award 1996), Nat. Med. Honor Soc., Assn. Acad. Depts. Otolaryngology (pres.-elect). Avocations: swimming, bicycling. Office: Dept Otolaryngology One Boston Med Ctr Pl Boston MA 02118-2393 Office Phone: 617-638-7934. E-mail: kenneth.grundfast@bmc.org.

GRUNDON, RACHAEL, veterinarian; b. Bedford, Eng., Apr. 4, 1969; BSc, U. London, Charing Cross and Westminster Med. Sch., 1991; VetMB, U. Cambridge, 1995. Cert. in vet. radiology RCVS, 2000, in vet. ophthtal. RCVS, 2007. Resident vet. ophthalmology Animal Eye Care, Melbourne, Victoria, Australia, 2008—. Mem.: Royal Coll. Vet. Surgeons, Australian Coll. Vet. Scientists. Office: 181 Darling Rd East Malvern Melbourne Victoria 3145 Australia Business E-Mail: vetrg@aol.com.

GRUNEBAUM, MICHAEL F., psychiatrist, educator; b. Boston, Sept. 17, 1960; MD, Harvard Med. Sch., 1991. Asst. prof. clin. psychiatry Columbia U., 2000. Office: NY State Psychiatric Inst New York NY 10032 Business E-Mail: mfg14@columbia.edu.

GRUNFELD, LAWRENCE, reproductive endocrinologist, educator; MD, Mt. Sinai Sch. of Medicine, 1979. Diplomate Am. Bd. Ob-Gyn, cert. reproductive endocrinology. Intern Mt. Sinai Hosp.; resident Albert Einstein Colle. Hosp., fellow, Yale-New Haven Hosp.; with Lenox Hill Hosp.; assoc. clin. prof. ob-gyn. Mt. Sinai Sch. Med.; dir. of fellowship tng. Mt. Sinai Med. Ctr., NYC, 1986—. Co-dir. Reproductive Medicine Assocs. of NY. Recipient Harold Schulman award for Excellence in Rsch., Am. Fertility Assn. Family Bldg. award, 2001; named one of Best Doctors, NY Mag., 2003—07. Office: Mount Sinai Medical Center 635 Madison Ave 10th Fl New York NY 10022 Office Phone: 212-756-5777. Office Fax: 212-756-5770.

GRUNNET, MARGARET LOUISE, retired pathologist, educator; b. Mpls., Feb. 20, 1936; d. Leslie Nels and Grace Harriet (Thomson) Grunnet; m. Irving Noel Einhorn, Mar. 10, 1972; stepchildren: Jeffrey Allan, Franne Ruth, Eric Carl, Stanley Glenn. BA summa cum laude, U. Minn., Mpls., 1958; MD, U. Minn., 1962; MS, Ohio State U., 1969. Resident in psychiatry U. Pa. Sch. Medicine, Phila., 1963-64; resident anatomic pathology Presbyn.-U. Pa. Med. Ctr., Phila., 1965-66; fellow neuropathology Phila. Gen. Hosp., 1967, Ohio State U. Hosp., Columbus, 1968-69; instr. Ohio State U., 1969; asst. prof. U. Utah Sch. Medicine, Salt Lake City, 1970-76, assoc. prof., 1976-80; assoc. prof. pathology U. Conn. Sch. Medicine, Farmington, 1980-90, prof., 1990—2006, prof. emeritus, 2006. Contbr. articles to profl. jours. Mem. Am. Med. Women's Assn., Internat. Soc. Neuropathology, Conn. Soc. Pathologists, World Muscle Soc., Am. Assn. Neuropathologists, Phi Beta Kappa, Alpha Omega Alpha. Mem. Ch. of Christ. Avocations: reading, music, travel. Office: U Conn Health Ctr Dept Pathology Farmington CT 06032 Home: 275 Steele Rd B415 West Hartford CT 06117-2805 Business E-Mail: grunnet@nso1.ucnc.edu.

GRUNOW, JOHN EDWARD, pediatrician, educator; b. St. Louis, Oct. 27, 1949; BS, Valparaiso U., 1971; MD, U. Tex., 1975. Chief, pediatric gastroenterology, hepatology and nutrition Okla. U. Med. Ctr., 1992—, prof., 1995—. Office: 1200 N Phillips Ave Ste 14401 Oklahoma City OK 73104 Business E-Mail: john-grunow@ouhsc.edu.

GRUPP, STEPHAN, medical researcher, director; b. Cin., July 25, 1959; MD, PhD, Cin. U., 1987. Dir. of translational rsch. Children's Hosp. of Phila., 1996—. Home: 107 Llandaff Rd Havertown PA 19083 Business E-Mail: grupp@email.chop.edu.

GRUSS, PETER, molecular biologist; b. Alsfeld, Germany, June 28, 1949; s. Heinrich and Ursula (Nowotka) Gruss; children: Daniel, Julia. Diploma, U. Darmstadt, Germany, 1973; PhD in Biology, magna cum laude, Heidelberg U., Germany, 1977. Postdoc. fellow Inst. Virus Rsch., Heidelberg, 1977-78, Lab. Molecular Virology, NIH, Bethesda, Md., 1978-80, expert cons., 1980-81, vis. scientist, 1981-82; assoc prof. microbiology Heidelberg U., 1982-86, dir. Ctr. Molecular Biology, 1983-86; dir. Max Planck Inst. Biophysical Chemistry, Goettingen, Germany, 1986—; hon. prof. Goettingen U., 1990—; pres. Max Planck Soc. Advancement of Sci., Munich, 2002—. Mem. EMBO Fund Com., 1988—92, DFG Senate Com. Animal Exptl. Rsch., 1992—96; mem. sci. adv. bd. Boehringer Ingelheim Found., 1990—94, Randall Inst., London, 1995—98, Rsch. Inst. Molecular Pharmacology, Berlin, 1997—2000, Welcome/CRC Inst., Cambridge, 2000, King's Coll./Guy's Hosp., London; trustee German Cancer Rsch. Ctr., Heidelberg, Germany, 1994—98; pres. EMBL Coun., 2000—02. Assoc. editor Cell, 1990—99; mng. editor Mechanisms of Devel., 1990—2001; editl. adv. bd. mem. Trends in Genetics, 1992—96, bd. reviewing editors Science, 1995—2000; contbr. articles to profl. jours. Recipient Robert Koch Career Devel. award, 1983, Feldberg prize, 1992, Gottfried Wilhelm Leibniz prize, German Rsch. Found., 1994, Louis Jeantet Prize for medicine, 1995, Pres.'s prize for tech. & innovation, Germany, 1999, Berthold medal, U. Göttingen, 2002. Mem.: German Acad. Natural Scientists, Bavarian Acad. Scis., Am. Acad. Arts & Scis. (fgn. hon.), Acad. Scis. (Goettingen), Acad. Europaea, NY Acad. Sci., Am. Soc. Differentiation, European Molecular Biology Orgn., Internat. Soc. Devel. Biology (pres. 1994). Office: Max Planck Inst Biophysical Chemistry Am Faßberg 11 D 37077 Göttingen Germany also: Max Planck Soc Hofgartenstr 8 80539 München Germany Office Phone: 49 551 201 1211. Office Fax: 49 551 201 1222. E-mail: peter.gruss@gv.mpg.de. *

GRUSZCZAK, ANNA, neurologist; b. Lublin, Poland, Feb. 19, 1978; MD, Med. U. Lublin, PhD, 2004. Asst. Clin. Hosp. Lublin, 2006—. Mem.: Polish Neurol. Soc. Home: Jana Sawy 10/7 Lublin Lubeskie 20-632 Poland Personal E-mail: agruszczak@op.pl.

GRÜTZMEIER, SVEN SAHLGREN, health clinic administrator, physician; b. Norresundby, Denmark, Sept. 20, 1950; arrived in Sweden, 1977; s. Anton Grützmeier and Ingegärd Sahlgren. MD, Aarhus U., Denmark, 1977; specialist internal medicine/hematology, Linköping (Sweden) U., 1986, specialist clin. chemistry, 1989, specialist in infectious diseases, 2001; postgrad., Karolinska Inst., Stockholm. Lic. physician. Resident Main Hosp., Norrköping, Sweden, 1977—81, Univ. Hosp., Linköping, 1981—89; dir. Gay Men's Health Clinic, Linköping, 1985—91; specialist Gay Men's Health Clinic-South Hosp., Stockholm, 1990—; asst. dir. Gay Men's Health Clinic, Stockholm, 1992—; Cons. Stockholm County Orgn. Against AIDS, 1990—, Mus. Natural History, 1994—, Maria Regina Hospice, 1994—, med. dir., 1994—99; cons. Konsultant Med. Clinic, Norrkoping Hosp., 2001—05; arranger Yearly Gay Health Confs. for Physicians, 1988—; cons., mem. Swedish Med. Assn. Group of Physicians, 2004—; donator, co-founder chair in sexual health Univ. Minn., 2004, tchr. program human sexuality, 08; mem. group to reform edn. sys. for med. students Karolinska Inst., 2006—; sr. cons., dept. hematology Gövle Hosp., 2010—. Contbr. articles to med. jours. Arranger confs. for physicians and dentists on health issues for gay men and lesbians, 1988—; med. support cons. Worldpride, Stockholmpridefestivals, 1998—; mem. group reforming edn. sys. med. students Karoinska Inst., 2006—. Recipient Gold Medal award Royal Soc. Pro Patria, 1998; rsch. fellowship Karolinski Inst., 2000—. Fellow European Soc. Med. Oncology, Swedish Hematol. Soc., N.Y. Acad. Scis.; mem. AAAS, Swedish Gay Physicians (pres. 1988—), Royal Soc. Pro Patria (Gold Medal award 1998). Avocations: opera, ballet, cooking, history, trains. Office: Gay Men's Health Clinic Dept Dermatology South Hosp S-118 83 Stockholm Sweden Home Phone: +46 8849616; Office Phone: +46 8 6162465. Business E-Mail: sven.grutzmeier@mtc.ki.se.

GRYLLI, VASILEIA, psychologist; b. Athens, Greece, June 21, 1976; Degree in Psychology, U. Athens, 1999; PhD in Psychology, U. Vienna, 2006. Rsch. scientist U. Clinic Neuropsychiatry Childhood & Adolescence, Vienna, 2001—05; clin., health psychologist Childrens' Protection Ctr. 'Michalineio', 2007—. Clin. rsch. scientist U. Athens, Sch. Medicine, Psychiat. Clinic, Eating Disorders Outpatient Clinic, 2009—10. Mem.: Assn. Greek Psychologists. Avocations: swimming, bicycling, dance, meditation. Home: Papadiamanti 7 Marousi Athens 15126 Greece Personal E-mail: vasileia_grylli@hotmail.com.

GRYSON, JOSEPH ANTHONY, orthodontist; b. Rahway, NJ, Feb. 11, 1932; s. Elmer Joseph Anthony and Joyce Asher (Toms) G.; m. Patricia Ann Huddleston, Nov. 22, 1961; children— Karen Ann, David Joseph. BSChemE, Cornell U., 1954; D.D.S., U. Calif., San Francisco, 1964. Diplomate: Am. Bd. Orthodontics. Engr. div. refinery tech. service Standard Oil of Calif., Richmond, 1954, 58-60; individual practice dentistry specializing in orthodontics San Rafael, Calif., 1964-96; clin. instr. orthodontics U. Calif., San Francisco, 1965-87, assoc. clin. prof. orthodontics, 1987-99, clin. prof. orthodontics, 1999—. Referee Am. Jour. Orthodontics and Dentofacial Orthopedics. Contbr. articles to profl. jours. Treas., pres., dir. Homeowners Assn., San Rafael, 1970-74. Served as carrier pilot USN, 1954-58. Mem. ADA, Pacific Coast Soc. Orthodontists (dir. 1980-85, pres. 1985-86, award of merit 1992), Am. Assn. Orthodontists (ho. of dels. 1982-87, 94-95, spkr. ho. of dels. 1988-91, James E. Brophy Disting. Svc. award 1996), Calif. Dental Assn. (Disting. Svc. award 1994), E.H. Angle Soc. (sec. No. Calif. component 1992-96) Home: 1060 Lea Dr San Rafael CA 94903-3726 Personal E-mail: jagryson@comcast.net.

GRZESKIEWICZ, JOSEPH LEONARD, plastic surgeon; Attended, US Naval Acad., 1979—80; BS in Math. cum laude, James Madison U., 1983; MD, U. Va., 1987. Diplomate Am. Bd. Medical Examiners, 1988, Am. Bd. Plastic Surgery, 2000, lic. Calif., 1989. Designated naval flight surgeon (number4217) US Naval Aerospace Med. Inst., Pensacola, Fla., 1989; basic course microvascular surgery US Naval Hosp., San Diego, 1992, intern surgery, 1988; cons. surgeon plastic and reconstructive surgery US Naval Med. Ctr., San Diego, 1999—2004; resident plastic surgery Univ. of Mo. Hosps. and Clinics, Columbia, Mo., 1995—96; fellow plastic and orthopaedic surgery (hand) Univ. of Va. Health Sciences Ctr., Charlottesville, Va., 1998—99; flight surgeon med. dept. Marine Aircraft Group 39, Camp Pendleton, Calif., 1989—92, dep. head, 1990—91, med. student clin. preceptor, tng. officer CME dept.; squadron flight surgeon Marine Helicopter Light Attact Squadron 169, Camp Pendleton, Calif., 1989—91; founder and med. dir. Luminesse Med. Spa, 2006—07; plastic surgery divsn. Scripps Meml. Hosp., La Jolla, Calif., 1999—; plastic surgeon cosmetic surgery divsn. LA Jolla Cosmetic Surgery Ctr., Calif., 2005—. Contbr. various pub. Lt. active duty USNR, 1987, commd. as ensign USNR, 1983, lt. comdr. USNR, 1991, Hon. Discharge USNR, 1992. Fellow: ACS; mem.: San Diego County Med. Soc., San Diego Plastic Surgery Soc., Calif. Med. Assn., Am. Soc. of Plastic Surgeons, Boy Scouts of America (eagle scout 1976). Office: La Jolla Cosmetic Surgery Center 9850 Genesee Ave Ste 480 La Jolla CA 92037 Office Phone: 858-215-4622.

GU, JIINSONG, research scientist; b. Jinan, Shandong, China, Jan. 23, 1970; PhD, Shandong U., 2002. Assoc. prof. U. Jinan, 1996—. Mem.: Chinese Soc. Microbiology. Avocations: swimming, tennis, movies. Office: Sch Med & Life Sci Jinan Shandong 250022 China Office Fax: 86-531-8973-6818. E-mail: jingsong_gu@yahoo.com.

GU, YANHONG, pediatrician, researcher; d. ChangYou and Feng-Zhen Gu; m. YeMing Li, May 5, 1989; 1 child, Lixin Li. BM, SE U., Nanjing, China, 1988; MS in Health Sci., U. Tokyo, 1999, PhD in Health Sci., 2002. Diplomate Beijing Gen. Rlwy. Hosp., 1988. Pediatrician Beijing Gen. Rlwy. Hosp., Haidian-qu, Beijing, 1988—90; rsch. fellow Boshi-Aiiku-Kai, Minato-ku, Tokyo, 2001—02; postdoctoral fellow Japan Soc. Promotion Sci., Tokyo, 2002—04. Rsch. fellow Nat. Rsch. Inst. for Child Health and Devel., Setagaya-ku, Tokyo, Japan, 2005—. Recipient Rsch. award, U. Tokyo, 2001, Young Investigator's award, Asian Soc. Pediatric Rsch., 2005, Encouraging prize, Japanese Soc. Inherited Metabolic Diseases, 2007, Rsch. Nomiyama award, Japanese Soc. for Biomedical Rsch. on Trace Elements, 2008; scholar, Asian Devel. Bank-Japan Scholarship Program, 1997—99; Postdoctoral fellowship, Japan Soc. Promotion of Sci., 2002—04, Travel grant, Internat. Congress In born Errors Metabolism, San Diego, 2009. Mem.: Japanese Soc. Child Health (councilor 2007—09). Achievements include discovery of the incidence of Menkes disease in Asia; an alu insertion in the gene of Menkes disease; eighty percent of mothers of Japanese patients with Menkes disease were carriers; research in no association between genetype and phenotype in classical Menkes disease; no association between genotype and phenotype in Aisian homozygous for R778L patients with Wilson disease; the onset of Wilson disease in Chinese children is not related to ApoE epsilon 3/3. Office: Dept Health Policy NCCHD 2-10-1 Okura Setagaya-ku Tokyo 157-8535 Japan Personal E-mail: tecchanworld3@live.jp. Business E-Mail: gyh@nch.go.jp.

GUADAGNI, ANNA MARIA, children's diseases physician, researcher; b. Monterchi, Arezzo, Italy, Nov. 18, 1940; d. Michele and Rosa (Mari) G.; m. Sandro Ceccagnoli, Sept. 9, 1962; children: Cristiana, Marco, Riccardo. Pharm. Chemist, U. Perugia, Italy, 1964; MD, U. Rome, 1976. Specialist in children's diseases, newborn's diseases., anaesthetics and resuscitation. Intern, resident Policlinico Umberto 1 U. La Sapienza, Rome, 1976-77, physician, 1976-83; dep. dir. NICU Bambino Gesu Hosp., Rome, 1983—2006, tchr. Sch. for Nursing, 1986—2006; with Villa Stuart Clinic. Co-author: Neonatology, 1982, Newborn in the NICU, 1997. Recipient award De Tony, Com. Nat. Rsch., Rome, 1980. Avocations: cine club, tennis, golf, music. Office: Villa Stuart Clinic 00135 Rome Via Trionfale Rome 5952 Italy Home: Via Trionfale 6316 135 Rome RM Italy Home Phone: 390635455117; Office Phone: 390635528200. Personal E-mail: guadagnia@yahoo.it.

GUAN, DA-WEI, pathologist, educator; b. Qiqihae, Heilongjiang, Jan. 27, 1963; MD, China Med. U., 1988, PhD, 1994. Dep. dean China Med. U. Sch. Forensic Medicine, 2001—10, prof., 2001, dean, 2011—. Recipient 5th Nat. award, Fok Ying Tong Edn. Found., Hong Kong. Mem.: Chinese Assn. Forensic Medicine. Office: 92 Beier Rd Heping Dist Shenyang Liaoning 110001 China Office Fax: 86-24-23267698. Business E-Mail: dwguan@mail.cmu.edu.cn.

GUAN, YANGTAI, neurologist, educator; b. Jiangxi Province, China, Aug. 15, 1964; MD, PhD, Fudan U., Shanghai, 1997. Attendant physician Shanghai Changhai Hosp., 1994—2001, assoc. prof., assoc. sr. physician, 2001—07, prof., sr. physician, 2007—. Dir. Shanghai Inst. Prevention and Treatment Cerebravascular Diseases, 2009—11, legar rep., 2010—11. Decorated awards Gen. Logistics Dept. People's Liberation Army; recipient, Shanghai Sci. and Tech. Com. Master: Shanghai Gerontology Soc. (CVD br.); fellow: Shanghai Integrative Chinese and Western Medicine Acad. (Neurology br.), Shanghai Med. Assn. (Neurology br.); mem.: Chinese Immunology Assn. (Neuro-Immunology br.), Chinese Med. Assn. (Neurology br.). Avocation: badminton. Office: Changhai Rd 168 Shanghai 200433 China Office Fax: 086-021-81873516. E-mail: yangtaiguan@hotmail.com.

GUANÀ, RICCARDO, pediatrician; b. Turin, June 9, 1976; Degree in Medicine, U. Turin, 2001, degree in Pediat. Surgery, 2006. Cons. Santa Chiara Hosp., Trento, 2008—09, Regina Margherita Children's Hosp., Turin, 2009—. Mem.: Italian Soc. Pediat. Surgery. Avocations: swimming, skiing. Office: Piazza Polonia 94 Turin 10126 Italy E-mail: riccardoguan@gmail.com.

GUANGBIN, SUN, physician; b. Tonghua, Jilin, Apr. 20, 1965; D, 2nd Med. U., 2004. Physician Shanghai Pudong New Area Gongli Hosp., 1990—. Home: lingshan Rd 866-12-901 Shanghai 200135 China Personal E-mail: sgb223@hotmail.com.

GUANGYAO, SU, science educator; b. Wenzhou City, Zhejiang Province, Sept. 2, 1981; MS, Zhejiang Gongshang U., 2007, D candidate. Lectr. Zhejiang Gongshang U., 2007—. Recipient 1st prize, People's Govt. of Zhejiang Province. Office: 18 Xuezheng St Hangzhou Zhejiang Province 310018 China E-mail: suguangyao@yahoo.com.cn.

GUANGYING, ZHU, oncologist, educator; b. Jiangsu, China, Oct. 26, 1963; MD, Peking Union Med. Coll., CAMS, Beijing, PhD, 2000. Attending physician, dept. radiation oncology Xuzhou Med. Coll. Cancer Inst., China, 1990—96, assoc. prof., dir. dept. radiation oncology, 1996—2001; dep. dir. radiation oncology, chief physician, prof., PhD supr. Beijing Cancer Hosp., 2001—11, dir. radiation oncology, chief physician, prof., PhD supr., 2011—; vis. prof., dept. radiation oncology MD Anderson Cancer Ctr., 2004—05. Fellow Chinese Jour. Neuro-Oncology, Chinese Jour. Cancer Palliative Medicine, Chinese Jour. Cancer; vis. prof., dept. radiation oncology MD Anderson Cancer Ctr., 2004—05. Recipient Outstanding Young and Mid. Oncologist award, Oncology Br., Chinese Med. Soc., 1997, 2003, Higher Edn. Tchg. Achievement award, Peking U. Med. Sci. Ctr., 2009; named Outstanding Tchr., Edn. Com. Jiangsu Province, 1996, Peking U. Med. Sci. Ctr., 2002. Fellow: Chinese Soc. Clin. Oncology, Chinese Med. Assn. Avocations: reading, singing, sports. Office: 52 Fucheng Rd Haidian Dist Beijing 100142 China Office Fax: 86 10 88196120. Personal E-mail: zgypu@yahoo.com.cn.

GUARENTE, LEONARD P., medical geneticist, educator; b. Chelsea, Mass., June 6, 1952; s. Leonard and Norma Guarente; m. Barbara Weiffenbach, Sept. 6, 1981 (div. 1985); 1 child, Jeffrey. BS in Biology, MIT, Cambridge, 1974; PhD in Molecular Genetics, Harvard U., 1978. Jane Coffin Childs postdoc. fellow Harvard U., 1978—81; asst. prof. biology MIT, 1981—85, assoc. prof., 1985—91, prof., 1991—2000, Novartis prof. biology, 2000—, dir. Glenn Lab. for Sci of Aging, 1982—. Founder, dir. Elixir Pharm., Cambridge, 2000—; co-chair sci. adv. bd. Sirtris Pharm., Inc., Cambridge, 2007—. Author: (autobiography) Ageless Quest: One Scientist's Search for Genes That Prolong Youth, 2003; assoc. editor Nucleic Acids Rsch., 1983—88, Molecular & Cellular Biology, 1986—88, 1989—91, mem. editl. bd. Genes & Devel., Trends in Genetics, Jour. of Anti-Aging Medicine, Sci. Mag. SAGE KE, Devel. Cell; contbr. articles to profl. jours.; spkr. in field. Recipient Presdl. Young Investigator award, NSF, 1984—89, Thomas D. and Virginia W. Cabot Career Devel. Professorship, 1989—92, Earle P. Charlton Lectureship, 1998; named Investigator of 2001, Acad. Am. Soc. Healthy Aging, Ida Beam Disting. Lectr., 2001; scholar, Ellison Med. Found., 1999—2002. Fellow: Am. Acad. Arts & Scis., Am. Acad. Microbiology. Achievements include research in the underlying causes of aging at the cellular level; discovery of a gene that regulates aging; patents in field. Office: MIT Bldg 68-280 77 Massachusetts Ave Cambridge MA 02139 Office Phone: 617-253-6965. Fax: 617-253-8699. E-mail: leng@mit.edu. *

GUARESCHI, ADRIANA, psychiatrist; b. Parma, Italy, Sept. 9, 1924; m. Carlo Lorenzo Cazzullo; children: Anna, Alessandra. MD, U. Milan, 1949, Prof. Child Neuropsychiatry, 1975. Assoc. prof. U. Milan, Italy, 1963—75, prof., 1975—99; dir. Inst. Child Neuropsychiatry/U. Milan, 1973—2000; dir. Sch. Specialization in Child Neuropsychiatry U. Milan, 1979—. Founder, dir. Jour. Devel. neuropsychiatry, 1981-97; v.p. Legrenzi Found., Milan, 1997—; emeritus prof. child neuropsychiatry U. Milan, 2001 Editor: (books) La Depressione Infantile, 1992, Processi Mentali In Eta Evolutiva, 1995, neuropsicofarmacologia Clinica In Eta Pediatrica, 1996, Neurologia E Psichiatria Dello Sviluppo, 1998. Recipient award Golden Lions for Rsch. and Prophylaxis of Neuropsychic Deficits, 1972; decorated Croix-Rouge Bulgare, 1975. Mem. WHO (com. for internat. classification of psychiat. disorders in childhood 1980), Italian Child Neuropsychiatrists (del. 1995—, pres. Italian collegium 1992-98). Office: Inst Child/Adoles Neurol Psyc Scis/Via GF Besta 1 20161 Milan Italy Home Phone: 39-072-76005793; Office Phone: 39-02-64445177. E-mail: arsmilano@tiscalinet.it, guareschi.cazzullo@tin.it.

GUARINI, LUDOVICO, pediatrician, educator, hematologist, oncologist; Studied, Universita Di Napoli, Italy, 1974. Diplomate Am. Bd. of Pediatrics, cert. pediatric hematology-oncology. Resident Beth Israel med. ctr. Columbia Presbyn. Med. Ctr., 1978—81, fellow Beth Israel med. ctr., 1981—84; dir. pediatric hematology-oncology Maimonides Med. Ctr., acting chmn. pediat. With exec. com. pediatric faculty practice bd. and edn. com. dept. pediat. Maimonides Med. Ctr., tchr. pediatric residency program and med. student program dept. of pediat. Office: Maimonides Medical Center 6300 8th Ave Brooklyn NY 11220 Office Phone: 718-765-2671. Office Fax: 718-765-2679.

GUARINO, ANTHONY MICHAEL, pharmacologist, educator, consultant, counselor; b. Framingham, Mass., Dec. 11, 1934; s. Alfred V. and Nellie L. (Beatrice) G.; m. Aida Iris Gerena, Nov. 9, 1957; children: Theresa, Elizabeth, Barbara, Cathy, Tom, Gregory, Paula, Phil, Richard, Paul. BS in Chemistry, Boston Coll., 1956; MS in Chemistry, U. R.I., 1963, PhD in Pharmacology and Toxicology, 1966; MA in Counseling, Liberty U., Lynchburg, Va., 1993. Lic. profl. counselor. Lt. comdr. USPHS, 1966, advanced through grades to capt., 1979; staff fellow pharmacology-toxicology rsch. assoc. program Nat. Heart Inst., NIH, Bethesda, Md., 1966-68; rsch. pharmacologist NCI Nat. Cancer Inst., NIH, Bethesda, Md., 1968-73, chief lab. toxicology, 1973-80; regulatory pharmacologist Ctr. for Drugs and Biologics-FDA, Md., 1980-84; lab. dir. fishery rsch. br. FDA, Dauphin Island, Ala., 1984-93; marriage and family counselor Cath. Social Svcs., Mobile, Ala., 1993—2006, The Carpenter's House, Mobile, 2007—. Adj. prof. U. South Ala. Coll. Medicine, Mobile, 1996-; vice chmn. com. on animals as monitors in environ. hazards NAS. Contbg. author: Handbook of Experimental Pharmacology—Concepts in Biochemical Pharmacology, 1971, Handbook of Experimental Pharmacology, Antineoplastic and Immunosuppressive Agents, 1974, Methods in Cancer Research, 1979, Pesticides and Xenobiotics Metabolism in Aquatic Organisms, 1979, Pesticides and Xenobiotics Metabolism in Aquatic Organisms, 1979, Cisplatin—Current Status and New Developments, 1980, Modern Pharmacology, 1982; contbr. 106 articles to profl. jours. Mem. Am. Soc. Pharmacology and Exptl. Therapeutics, Soc. Toxicology, Am. Chem. Soc., Am. Assn. Christian Counselors. Roman Catholic. Home: 968 Westbury Dr Mobile AL 36609-3332 Office: Carpenter's House PC 601 Bel Air Blvd Ste 409 Mobile AL 36606 Office Phone: 251-476-9994. Business E-Mail: amguarino@earthlink.net.

GUBER, MYLES STUERT, surgeon; b. Denver, July 3, 1956; s. Frank Friday Guber and Celia Elsie Kramish; m. Deborah Ann Bishop, Aug. 25, 1996; children: Michael Albert, Samuel David, Halle Anderson. BS, Northwestern U., 1978, MD, 1980. Diplomate Am. Bd. Surgery, Am. Bd. Thoracic Surgery. Staff cardiac surgeon Porter Meml. Hosp., Denver, 1987—. Fellow: Am. Coll. Surgeons; mem.: Western Thoracic Surg. Assn., County Thoracic Surgeons. Jewish. Avocations: skiing, golf, climbing, basketball. Home: 355 Ash St Denver CO 80222 Office: Colo Cardiovascular Surg Assocs Ste 550 950 E Harvard Ave Denver CO 80210 Office Phone: 303-778-6527. Office Fax: 303-733-1288. Personal E-mail: mgube@aol.com. *

GUBLER, DUANE J., virologist, educator, researcher; b. Santa Clara, Utah, June 4, 1939; s. June and Thelma (Whipple) G.; m. Bobbie J. Carroll, Mar. 1, 1958; children: Justin Chase, Stuart Jefferson. BS, Utah State U., 1963; MS, U. Hawaii, 1965; ScD, Johns Hopkins U., 1969; AS, So. Utah State U., 1962, DSc (hon.), 1988. Asst. prof. pathobiology Sch. Hygiene Johns Hopkins U., Balt. and Calcutta, 1969-71; assoc. prof. tropical medicine Sch. Medicine U. Hawaii, Honolulu, 1971-75; head virology dept. Naval Med. Rsch. Unit Number 2, Jakarta, Indonesia, 1975-78; assoc. prof. entomology and microbiology U. Ill., Urbana, 1978-79; rsch. microbiologist divsn. vector-borne viral diseases Ctrs. for Disease Control and Prevention, Fort Collins, Colo., 1980-81, dir. San Juan (P.R.) Labs., 1981-89, dir. divsn. vector-borne infectious diseases Ft. Collins, Colo., 1989—2003; dir. Asia Pacific Inst. Tropical Medicine and Infectious Diseases, U. Hawaii, Honolulu, 2004—; prof., chair, dept. tropical medicine, med. microbiology, and pharm. U. Hawaii Sch. Medicine, 2004—; dir. Duke U. Nat. U. Singapore Grad. Med. Sch., 2007—. Cons. NRC, 1972, South Pacific Commn., 1972-76, WHO, Geneva, New Delhi and Manila, 1974—, AID, Washington, 1977—, Pan Am. Health Orgn., 1981—, Internat. Devel. Rsch. Ctr., Ottawa, Can., 1977—, Rockefeller Found., NYC, 1987—, US Dept. Defense, 1992-, Nat. Inst. of Allergy and Infectious Diseases, 2002-, numerous nat. ministries of health, 1972—; Bailey K. Ashford meml. lectr. U. P.R. Sch. Medicine, 1999; chmn. bd. coun. Pediat. Dengue Vaccine Initiative, 2002-; mem. sci. adv. bd. Novartis Inst. Tropical Diseases, 2003—, Hawaii BioTech., Inc., 2006-, Environ. Health Inst., Singapore, 2006-08; sci. advisor Inviragen Inc., 2006-, mem. Strategic and Tech. Adv. Group on Neglected Tropical Diseases, WHO, 2007-. Contbr. numerous articles to profl. jours. Lt. USN, 1975—77. Recipient Commendation medal, 1984, Outstanding Svc. medal, 1988, Honorary Dr. of Sci., Southern Utah State U., 1988, Meritorious Svc. medal, 1991, Outstanding Unit citation, 1995, 98, 2000, Outstanding Alumni award for sci. and rsch. Johns Hopkins U. Sch. Pub. Health, 1997, Chuck Alexander Operational award La. Mosquito Control Assn., 1998, Disting. Svc. award Dept. HHS, 1996, 2000, 01, 03, Charles Shepard award in Sci., Ctr. for Disease Control, 2001; selected as one of 90 Illustrious Alumni in celebration of U. Hawaii's 90th year, 1997, Woodward Lectr. award USN Preventive Medicine Unit, 2000. Fellow Infectious Disease Soc. Am., Am. Assn. for Advancement of Sci., Am. Soc. Tropical Medicine (Charles Franklin Craig lectr. 1988, pres.-elect 1998, pres. 2000), Am. Mosquito Control Assn., Entomol. Soc. Am. (highlights in med. entomology lecture 1979, 95), Soc. Vector Ecologists, Rotary (Rotarian of Yr. San Juan chpt. 1986, Meritorious Svc. award Rotary Found., Evanston, Ill. 1990, Svc. Above Self award Fort Collins Club 1999, Internat. Svc. Above Self award 2000); mem. AAAS. Office: U Hawaii Sch Medicine Kaka'ako Campus BSB 320 651 Ilalo St Honolulu HI 96813 Office Phone: 808-692-1606. Business E-Mail: dgubler@hawaii.edu.

GUCKERT, NORA JANE GASKILL, medical/surgical nurse, hospice nurse, holistic consultant; b. Pitts., June 17, 1945; d. James E. and Nora L. (McAllister) Gaskill; m. Ray H. Guckert, Aug. 1, 1964 (div. May 2001); children: Brian K. Sr., Bruce M., Brenda L. Jansen. LPN, C.C. Allegheny County, Pitts., 1976, AS in Nursing, 1982; BS, Clayton Coll. Holistic Med., 1998, MS, 1999, PhD, 2001. Staff nurse St. Margaret's Meml. Hosp., Pitts., 1976-86; vis. nurse Personal Touch Home Care, Pitts., 1986-87, Norfolk, Va., 1995-98; pvt. practice, 1988—; staff nurse Kimberly Quality Home Care/Portsmouth Naval Hosp., Va., 1988-90; liason Sentara Home Health, 1992; cons. Holistic Health of Tidewater, Inc., Va., 1995-99; dir. nursing Med. Staff Svcs., Inc., Va. Beach, 1997-98; hospice dir. Personal Touch Home Care, 1997—99; home health nurse Tender Loving Care/Staff Builders Inc., 2000—02; dir. nursing edn. Virginia Beach, Newport News and Richmond campsuses Med. Careers Inst., 2000—03; home health nurse Comfort Care Home Health, 2003—; cons. Holistic Health of Virginia Beach Cons. Svc., 1997—; correctional med. svc. supr., chronic care nurse Virginia Beach Correctional Ctr., 2003—; weekend supr. Virginia Beach Health Care and Rehab. Ctr., 2007—. Dir. 1st holistic conf. by profls., Virginia Beach, 1997; cons. Holistic Health of Va. Beach Cons. Svc., 1997—. Author materials on nutritional needs. Vol. Chesapeake Indigent Care Clinic. Home: 3280 Winterberry Ln Virginia Beach VA 23453-5910 Personal E-mail: nonniejphd@cox.net.

GUDAVALLI, MADHU, neonatal-perinatal doctor, educator; Diplomate Am. Bd. Pediatrics, Am. Bd. Pediatrics-neonatal-perinatal medicine. Resident in pediat. NY Infirm, 1974—76, Booth Meml. Hosp., NY, 1976—77; fellow in neonatal- perinatal medicine Bellevue Hosp., NY, 1977—79; chief of neonatology NY Meth. Hosp., 1992; clin. assoc. prof. of pediat. Weill Cornell Med. Coll. Mem.: Dept. of Pediat. (adv. com.), Bklyn. Pediatric Soc., NY Meth. Hosp. Physician's Alumni Assoc., NY Perinatal Soc. (pres.). Office: New York Methodist Hospital 506 Sixth St Brooklyn NY 11215 Office Phone: 718-780-3000.

GUDAYOL FERRE, ESTEVE, research scientist, educator; b. Barcelona, Aug. 13, 1971; Degree in Psychology, U. Autonoma de Barcelona, 1995; PhD in Med. Rsch., Inst. Polit. Nat., 2011. Prof., rschr. U. Michoacana de San Nicolas de Hidalgo, 2000—. Mem.: Asociacion Mexicana de Neuropsicologia. Avocation: reading. Home: Bosque de Oyameles 845 1 A col bosqiie Morelia Michoacan 58200 Mexico Personal E-mail: egudayol14@yahoo.com.mx.

GUDJONSSON, BIRGIR, physician; b. Akureyri, Iceland, Nov. 8, 1938; s. Gudjon and Kristjana (Jakobsdottir) Vigfusson; m. Heidur Anna Vigfusdottir, Oct. 21, 1961; children: Asdis, Gunnar, Sigrun. MD, U. Iceland, 1965. Diplomate internal medicine and gastroenterology. Intern Stamford Hosp., Conn., 1966—67, resident in internal medicine, 1967—68; asst. prof. Yale U. Med. Sch., 1972—73, 1977—78, 1982; physician internal medicine and gastroenterology Reykjavik, Iceland, 1974—; asst. prof. Cons. in field. Author (with H.M. Spiro): Controversies in Internal Medicine, 1980; contbr. articles to profl. jours. Judge various athletic and gymnastic events; active Icelandic Athletic Fedn., 1981—. Master: ACP; fellow: Am. Gastroenterol. Assn., Royal Soc. Medicine, Royal Coll. Physicians London; mem.: AAAS, Internat. Hepato Pancreato Biliary Assn., Reykjavik Athletic Club. Lutheran. Achievements include research in pancreatic cancer. Home: Alftamyri 51 108 Reykjavik Iceland Office: Med Clinic Alfheimum 74 Reykjavik 104 Iceland Office Phone: 0113545356800.

GUEDES, ALEX, surgeon, educator; b. Salvador, Brazil, Sept. 4, 1970; PhD, Faculdade de Ciências Médicas da Santa Casa de São Paulo, 2007. Physician Escola Bahiana de Medicina e Saúde Pública, 1993; preceptor, dept. surgery Medicine Faculty Bahia Fed. U. Bahia, 2002—09, substitute prof., dept. exptl. surgery and splty. surgery, 2009—10, adj. prof., dept. exptl. surgery and splty. surgery, 2011—. Oncologic orthops. cons. Santa Casa da Misericórdia da Bahia, 2000—11. Recipient Comendador award, Câmara Mcpl. de Salvador.

Mem.: Soc. Brasileira de Ortopedia, Soc. Latino Americana de Tumores Músculo-Esqueléticos, Associação Brasileira de Oncologia Ortopédica, Soc. Brasileira de Cirurgia do Joelho, Soc. Brasileira de Artroscopia. Avocations: chess, music, travel. Home: Avenida Juracy Magalhães Júnior N° 2426 Salvador Bahia 41940-060 Brazil Home Fax: 55-71-32037270. Personal E-mail: alexguedes2003@yahoo.com.br.

GUENTSCH, ARNDT, dentist, researcher; b. Saalfeld, Thuringia, Germany, Apr. 23, 1976; s. Helmut and Maritta Guentsch; m. Daniela Wagner, July 31, 2004; 1 child, Ansgar Marlon. Grad., Friedrich-Schiller-U., 2001. Dentist, rschr. Sch. Dental Sciences, Jena, Germany, 2001—. Recipient Meridol prize, 2006. Achievements include research in pathogenesis of periodontitis. Home: Boecklinstrasse 8 Thuringia Erfurt 99096 Germany Office: Sch Dental Sciences An der alten Post 4 Thuringia Jena 07743 Germany Office Fax: 493641934411. Personal E-mail: zahnarzt-guentsch@t-online.de. Business E-Mail: arndt.guentsch@med.uni-jena.de.

GUERET, GILDAS, physician; b. Neuilly, May 14, 1965; B, Quimper U., 1984; MD, U. Hosp., 1999; PhD, Brest U., 2005. Mem.: European Soc. Intensive Care Medicine, French Anesthesiology Soc. Office: 5 Ave Foch Brest 29609 France E-mail: gildas.gueret@chu-brest.fr.

GUERETTE, NATHAN L., medical educator, director; b. NYC, Sept. 4, 1968; MD, SUNY Stony Brook, 1997. Dir., urogynecology Pa. Hosp. UPENN, Phila., 2005—08; assoc. fellowship dir., urogynecology Drexel U., Phila., 2008—09; dir. Female Pelvic Medicine Inst. VA and Med. Coll. Va., Richmond, 2009—, assoc. prof., 2009—. Fellowship, urogynecology and reconstructive surgery Cleve. Clinic, 2005. Contbr. chapters to books & articles to profl. jours. Recipient Outstanding Fellowship Rsch. award, Am. Urogynecologic Soc., 2006. Fellow: IUGA (com. mem. 2007—10), ICS, AUGS. Achievements include development of pelvic reconstruction procedures. Avocations: skiing, golf. Office: Female Pelvic Medicine Inst VA 1467 Johnston Willis Dr Richmond VA 23235 Office Fax: 804-323-5070.

GUERIN, NEWTON, foundation administrator; m. Jane Guerin. Degree in psychology, U. Ala., Birmingham. Field rep. Birmingham chpt. American Cancer Soc., nat. rep., dep. exec. v.p. Ala. divsn.; various positions of increasing responsibility including chief of staff Nat. Multiple Sclerosis Soc.; exec. v.p., COO American Liver Found., 2007—, interim pres., CEO, 2011—. Office: American Liver Found 39 Broadway Ste 2700 New York NY 10006 Office Phone: 212-668-1000. Office Fax: 212-483-8179. *

GUERRA, ALDO BENJAMIN, plastic and cosmetic surgeon; b. Managua, Nicaragua, Dec. 10, 1969; arrived in U.S., 1981; s. Aldo Antonio and Nelly Beatriz Guerra. BS in Biology, U. Calif., San Diego, 1992, MD, 1996. Diplomate Am. Bd. of Plastic Surgery. Chief cosmetic surgeon (face and boby) Aesthetic Surg. Assocs., Metairie, La., 2004—; chief cosmetic surgeon (face and body) McCollough Inst. Appearance and Health, Gulf Shores, Ala., 2004—; dir., chief cosmetic surgery Ab Guerra Plastic Surgery Clinic and Skin Care Ctr., Phoenix. Asst. prof. La. State U., New Orleans, 2002—04. Author: Cosmetic Surgery: A Consumer's Guide to Aesthetic Plastic Surgery, 2004; contbr. articles to profl. jours. Hipanic role model, cmty. outreach Hispanic Med. Assn. of La., Metairie, 2003—05. Named one of Top 100 Hispanic, New Orleans Metro Area, Vocero News Mag., 2004. Mem.: Hispanic Med. Assn. of La. (assoc.). Achievements include first to use new reconstructive techniques in children. Avocations: traveling, sailing. Home: 40402 N Copper Basin Trl Anthem AZ 85086-1836 Office Fax: 602-249-1282. Personal E-mail: aldissimo1@hotmail.com. E-mail: drguerra@gmail.com.

GUERRA, FERNANDO A., pediatrician, health facility administrator; b. San Antonio, 1939; m. Beverly Guerra; 6 children. BA, Univ. Tex.; MD, Univ. Tex. Med. Br., Galveston, 1964; MPH, Harvard Univ, Diplomate Am. Bd. Pediatrics. Intern San Francisco Gen. Hosp., 1964—65; resident U. Tex. Hosps., Galveston, 1967—69, U. Tex. Bexar County Tchg. Hosps., San Antonio, 1969—71; staff pediatrician Santa Rosa Children's Hosp., San Antonio, 1970—; fellow in pub. health Harvard U., Boston, 1982—83; founder, med. dir. Barrio Family Health Clinic, San Antonio; dir. health MetroHealth, San Antonio, 1987—. Clin. prof. pediatrics Univ. Tex. Health Sci. Ctr., San Antonio; bd. trustees Urban Inst., Inst. Medicine Bd. on Children and Families, CDC Adv. Com. on Immunization Practices; founding scholar Pub. Health Leadership Inst.; adj. prof. Univ. Tex. Sch. Pub. Health, USAF Sch. Aerospace Med., Brooks AFB. Contbr. numerous articles to profl. jours. Fellow: Am. Acad. Pediats. (spokesman for Internat. Yr. of the Child 1979); mem.: APHA, Tex. Med. Assn., Inst. of Medicine of NAS. Office: MetroHealth 332 W Commerce San Antonio TX 78205-2489 Office Phone: 210-207-8731.

GUERRERO, REUBEN CASTRO, oncologist, internist; b. Manila, Philippines, Aug. 22, 1935; came to U.S., 1962, naturalized, 1978; s. Jacobo Tolentino and Francisca Claravall (Castro) G.; m. Celina V. Sison, June 18, 1962; children: Chiarina, Leonora, Anthony Paul. AA, U. Philippines, Manila, 1952; MD, U. Philippines, 1957. Intern Philippine Gen. Hosp., Manila, 1956-57; mem. faculty Coll. Medicine, U. Philippines, 1957-62; resident Ch. Home and Hosp., Balt., 1962-64, chief resident, 1965-66; asst. prof. medicine, chief chemotherapy divsn. Philippines and Cancer Inst., 1968-73; med. oncologist, chmn. cancer com., chmn. dept. hematology Straub Clinic & Hosp., Honolulu, 1973—. Clin. assoc. prof. John A. Burns Sch. Medicine, U. Hawaii; chmn. research Philippine Cancer Soc., 1969-73; pres. Hawaii-Pacific div. Am. Cancer Soc., 1989-90; CME coord. Aloha Med. Misson. Contbr. articles to profl. jours. With Philippine Army, Res.,1957 58. Postdoctoral fellow medicine Johns Hopkins Hosp., Balt., 1964-65, postdoctoral fellow med. oncology, 1966-68. Fellow ACP; mem. Am. Soc. Internat. Medicine, Am. Soc. Clin. Oncology, Philippine Soc. Med. Oncology, Honolulu County Med. Soc., Hawaii Med. Assn. (cancer commn.), Philippine Med. Assn. Hawaii (pres. 1998-99), AMA, Am. Geriatric Soc., Aerospace Med. Assn., Honolulu Marathon Assn., Honolulu Club. Republican. Roman Catholic. Home: 2159 Okoa St Honolulu HI 96821-2647 Office: Straub Clinic and Hosp 888 S King St Honolulu HI 96813-3083 Office Phone: 808-522-3808. Personal E-mail: reubenguerrero@aol.com. Business E-Mail: rguerrero@straub.net.

GUERRERO, RODRIGO V., epidemiologist; MD, Harvard U., MS, 1966, PhD, 1968. Dean divsn. health Univ. of the Valley, dir.; sec. mcpl. health and dir. Univ. Hosp. of the Valley, Cali, Colombia; dir. Carvajal Found., Cali, Colombia, 1984—92; mayor City of Cali, Colombia, 1992—94; bd. pres. VallenPaz, 2002—. Regional advisor in health and violence Pan-Am. Orgn. of Health, Washington, 1995—98; founder, dir. Med. the Colombia mag. Mem.: Inst. of Medicine of NAS. Office: Fundacion Carvajal Carrera 25 #2-01 Cali Colombia Home: Calle 7 Oeste # 3-140 Apt 601 Edificio El Alfil Cali Colombia Home Phone: 011 572 893 4985; Office Phone: 011 572 882 1933. E-mail: guerrerr@yahoo.com.

GUERTIN, SHAWN M., health facility administrator; V.p. fin. Coventry Health Care, Inc., Bethesda, Md., 1998—2003; sr. v.p. Coventry Health Care, 2003—04, exec. v.p., CFO, treas., 2005—09, cons., 2010—. Fellow: Soc. Actuaries; mem.: Am. Acad. Actuaries. Office: Coventry Health Care Inc 6705 Rockledge Dr Ste 900 Bethesda MD 20817 *

GUERTIN, TIMOTHY E., medical products executive; b. 1949; BS in Elec. Engring. & Computer Scis., U. Calif., Berkeley, 1971. With Singer Bus. Machines; Joined Varian Medical Systems, Inc., Palo Alto, Calif., 1976; gen. mgr. customer support Varian Med. Systems, Inc., 1982—89, gen. mgr., pres. Oncology Systems, 1990—2005, corp. v.p., 1992—99, exec. v.p., 1999—2005, pres., COO, 2005—06; pres., CEO Varian Medical Systems, Inc., 2006—. Chmn. bd. dirs., mem. Silicon Valley/No. Calif. Coun. Am. Electronics Assn.; bd. dirs. Diagnostic Imaging sect., chmn. Therapy Systems divsn. Nat. Elec. Mfrs. Assn.; mem. corp. coun. Am. Soc. Therapeutic Radiology and Oncology, Can. Assn. Radiation Oncologists; bd. dirs. Varian Med. Systems, Inc., 2005—. Served in USAR. Recipient AeA/Stanford Alumni of the Yr. award, 2008. Office: Varian Med Systems 3100 Hansen Way Palo Alto CA 94304 Office Phone: 650-493-4000. Office Fax: 650-842-5196. *

GUERY, SEBASTIEN JEAN-BAPTISTE, medical researcher; b. Laxou, Meurthe et Moselle, France, July 26, 1976; s. Robert Guery and Betty Turchet. MSc in Medicinal Chemistry, Louis Pasteur U., Strasbourg, France, 2000, PhD in Organic Chemistry, 2003; student, IMD, Lausanne, Switzerland, 2009. Postdoc. rschr. Novartis Inst Biomedical Rsch., Basel, Switzerland, 2004—05; sr. scientist GlaxoSmithKline, Verona, VR, Italy, 2005—08, rschr. medicinal chemistry. Contbr. articles to profl. med. jours. Recipient Exceptional Sci. award, GlaxoSmithKline, 2007, Best Poster award, 2007; MENRT grant, Ministere l'Education Nationale, la Rsch. la Tech., 2000. Mem.: Am. Chem. Soc. Achievements include patents for pyrimidines derivatives for the treatment of GABA B mediated nervous system disorders; 3 patents published and 1 patent in field; patents filed for new chemical entities for the treatment of psychiatric disease (still confidential). Home: 6 route d'Allarmont Celles sur Plaine Vosges 88110 France Office: IMD Internat Chemin Bellerive 32 Lausanne CH 1001 Switzerland Office Phone: 00 41079477 9923. Personal E-mail: guery_sebastien@yahoo.fr. Business E-Mail: sebastien.guery@mba2009.imd.ch.

GUETTLER, JOSEPH HENRY, medical association administrator, researcher; b. Royal Oak, Mich., July 20, 1970; BS, Valparaiso U., 1992; MD, Northwestern U., 1996. Dir., sports medicine edn., rsch. Beaumont Hosp., 2003—. Pres. Mich. Orthop. Soc., 2010—11; head team physician and assoc. clin. prof. Oakland U., 2010—11; edn. com. Am. Orthopedic Soc. Sports Medicine, 2011—. Recipient Herodicus Rsch. award, AOSSM. Fellow: Am. Orthop. Assn., Am. Acad. Orthop. Surgeons; mem.: Arthroscopy Assn. N.Am. Avocations: sports, fishing. Home: 2979 River Valley Dr Troy MI 48098 Personal E-mail: jguettlermd@wideopenwest.com.

GUEVARA HURTADO, HELLEN ASTRID, pharmacologist; b. Bogota, Aug. 31, 1982; Degree in Pharm. Chemistry, Nat. U. Colombia, Bogota, 2009. Cert. Colombian Red Cross, 2009. Tchr. program aux. pharm. svcs. Ednl. Instn. Campo Alto, 2009—09; R&D leader pharm. chemistry Pronabell Labs. Ltd, 2010—. With XII Colombian Congress of Pharmacology and Therapeutics, 2009; conf. asst. Gattefosse and Global Trends in The Natural Cosmetics Market, 2011. Avocations: soccer, volleyball, reading. Home: Calle 47b sur #23b - 70 Apt 148 Bogota 11001000 Colombia Office Phone: 8260288.

GUGGENHEIM, FREDERICK GIBSON, psychiatrist, educator; b. Chgo., July 8, 1935; s. Melvin Elias and Marjorie Stone (Gibson) G.; m. Bethany Reed (div. Apr. 1976); m. Olivia Rogers, Nov. 23, 1984; children: Jennifer, Hannah, Russell Alderson, Rhoades Alderson. BA, Yale U., 1957; MD, Columbia U., 1961. Resident in medicine Bellevue Hosp., NYC, 1961-63, Columbia Presbyn. Med. Ctr., NYC, 1963-64; clin. assoc. NIMH, Bethesda, Md., 1964-66; resident in psychiatry Strong Meml. Hosp., Rochester, NY, 1966-69; asst. prof. Harvard Med. Sch., Boston, 1970-79; from asst. in psychiatry to assoc. psychiatrist Mass. Gen. Hosp., Boston, 1969-79; assoc. prof. Southwestern Med. Sch. in Tex., Dallas, 1979-85; Marie Wilson Howells prof. and chair dept. psychiatry U. Ark. for Med. Scis., Little Rock, 1985-2000, prof., 2001—02, prof. and chair emeritus, 2004—; chief psychiat. cons. svc. Univ. Hosp., Little Rock, 2001—02; staff psychiatrist East Bay Mental Health Ctr., Providence, 2002—05; psychiatrist Butler Hosp., 2005—; clin. prof. psychiatry Warren Alpert Sch. Medicine, Brown U., Providence, 2006—. Mem. nat. adv. com. clin. scholars program Robert Wood Johnson Found., Princeton, N.J., 1988-94; mem. com. on career devel. awards VA, Washington, 1990-95; mem. nat. adv. coun. Substance Abuse and Mental Health Svcs. Adminstrn., 1993-96; chief of staff U. Hosp., 1992-94, sec. med. bd., 1998-2000. Recipient Allison travel fellowship, Yale U., 1956, 1957, Saybrook Fellows prize, 1957, Nancy CA Roeske cert. of recognition for excellence in med. student edn., 2002, Irma Bland MD award for excellence in tchg. residents, 2005, Lifetime Achievement award, Assn. Acad. Psych., 2005. Fellow (Disting. life) Am. Psychiat. Assn., Am. Coll. Psychiatrists, Acad. Psychosomatic Medicine (Disting. fellow), Assn. Acad. Psychiatry (Disting. life, pres. 1992-93, Life Achievement award 2005); mem. So. Assn. Rsch. in Psychiatry (pres. 1991-92), Am. Assn. Chairmen of Depts. Psychiatry (pres. 1995-96), Ark. Psychiat. Soc. (pres. 1988-89), Cosmos Club of Wash., Alpha Omega Alpha (faculty). Home: 690 Angell St Providence RI 02906-5552 Office: Butler Hosp Partial Hospitalization Program 345 Blackstone Blvd Providence RI 02906 Office Phone: 401-455-6408.

GUGGENHEIMER, JAMES, dentist, educator; b. Belgrade, Yugoslavia, Mar. 4, 1936; came to U.S., 1938; s. Siegfried and Eta (Rubowitz) G.; m. Constance Fitzgerald, Mar. 27, 1969; children: Paul, Peter, Gregor. BS, CCNY, 1958; DDS, Columbia U., 1962. Diplomate Am. Bd. Oral Medicine. Intern VA Hosp., Albany, N.Y., 1962-63; resident oral surgery Strong Meml. Hosp., Rochester, N.Y., 1963-64; fellow oral medicine Phila. (Pa.) Gen. Hosp., 1964-66; asst. prof. Univ. Pitts. (Pa.) Sch. Dental Medicine, 1966-70, assoc. prof., 1970-76, prof., 1976—. Cons. staff Presbyn. Univ. Hosp., Pitts., 1968—, Montefiore Univ. Hosp., Pitts., 1968—; mem. Pitts. Cancer Inst., 1986—. Mem. tobacco control com. Am. Cancer Soc., Pitts., 1986; bd. dirs. Am. Chronic Pain Assn., Pitts., 1989. Mem. APHA, Am. Assn. Dental Rsch., Am. Acad. Oral Medicine, Omicron Kappa Upsilon. Office: Univ Pitts Sch Dental Med 3501 Terrace St Pittsburgh PA 15261-0001 Home: 210 Kensington Ct Pittsburgh PA 15238 Office Phone: 412-648-8627. E-mail: guggen@pitt.edu. *

GUICE, KAREN SUE, federal agency administrator; b. El Paso, Tex., Nov. 26, 1951; MD, U. N.Mex. Sch. Medicine, 1977; MA of Pub. Policy, Duke U., Durham, NC. Gen. surgery tng. U. Wash., Seattle; mem. surg. faculty U. Tex. Med. Br., Galveston, U. Mich., Med. Coll. Wis.; prof. surgery Duke U.; exec. dir. Fed. Recovery Coordination Program, US Dept. Veterans Affairs, 2008—11; prin. dep. asst. sec. for health affairs / prin. dep. dir. TRICARE Mgmt. Activity Mil. Health Sys., US Dept. Def., 2011—. Staff mem. US Senate Labor Com., 1998—99; dep. dir. President's Commn. Care for America's Returning Wounded Warriors, 2007. Contbr. articles to profl. jours., chapters to books. Recipient W.W. Coon Surg. Residents award for Tchg. Excellence, U. Mich., 1988, Outstanding Alumna award, Coll. Arts & Sciences, N.Mex. State U., 1993, Outstanding Achievement award, US Dept. Def., 2007, Commendation, US Dept. Veterans Affairs, 2009; grantee NIH, Emergency Med. Services for Children Program; Robert Wood Johnson Health Policy fellow, 1997—98. Fellow: ACS (dir. fellowship svcs. 1999—2001); mem.: Assn. Women Surgeons (Disting. Mem. award 1999), Assn. Academic Surgery (pres. 1993). Office: Military Health System US Dept Defense 1400 Defense Pentagon Washington DC 20301 *

GUICHET, JEAN-MARC GEORGES OLIVIER, orthopedic surgeon; b. Marseille, France, May 11, 1961; s. Pierre Edmond Henry Guichet and Janine Marie Maximilienne Bancal; m. Sophie Maréchel, June 17, 1995; children: Adrien, Alexandre, Cécile. MD, u. diploma anatomy surg. techniques, U. Burgundy, Dijon, France, 1988; M in Human Biology, U. Aix-Marseilles II, France, 1986, diploma of further studies, 1988, PhD, 1991; diploma of surgery, U. Burgundy, 1993; u. diploma of microsurgery, U. Lorraine, France, 1995; PhD, NYU, 1999. Cert. Nat. Med. Bd.; nat. competitive exam. of hosp. practitioner Health Ministry, Paris. Intern in gen. surgery Faculty of Medicine, Marseille, 1980-85, extern hosp., 1980-85, instr. in anatomy, 1986-88; resident in orthopedic surgery Univ. Hosp. Ctr., Dijon, 1986-88, 91-93, internat. rsch. fellow Hosp. for Joint Diseases Orthopedic Inst., NYC, 1988-91; resident in orthopedic surgery U. Burgundy, 1985-88, 91 92; fellow in pediat. orthopedic surgery U. Lorraine, Nancy, 1992-98; sr. lectr., hon. cons. pediatric limb reconstrn. svc. Children's Hosp., Sheffield, England, 1998—2000, cons. orthop. surgery Nancy, France, 2000—04, CHP Beauregard Marseille, 2004—. Engr., cons. Medinov Co., Roanne, France, 1989-91; cons. Landos Co., Chaumont, France, 1991-97, Depuy Co., Lyon, France, 1997-98. Contbr. numerous chpts., articles and papers to profl. jours. and books; patentee in field. Vol. Nat. Mil. Active Svc., Ministry of Coop., N.Y., 1988-90; mem. choir and orch. Bach of Fürstenfeldbruck, Munich, 1977—. Grantee Hoover Found., 1989, engr. grantee Rsch. Ministry, 1990, inventor grantee Anvar-Rsch. Ministry, 1998. Mem. French Assn. Orthopedic Surgeons, French Assn. Pediat. Orthopedic Surgeons, French Soc. Orthopedics and Trauma, French Soc. Biomechanics, N.Y. Acad. Scis. Roman Catholic. Avocations: classical music, photography. Office Phone: 33.491.777547. Business E-Mail: jeanmarcguichet@sfr.fr. E-mail: j.guichet@wanadoo.fr.

GUIDA, ROBERT ANTHONY, otolaryngologist, plastic surgeon; b. New Kensington, Pa., May 19, 1957; BA in Biology, U. Steubenville, 1975—79; MD, Hahnemann U., 1979—83. Intern internal medicine Lankenau Hosp., Phila., 1983 84; resident in gen. surgery Grad. Hosp. U. Pa., Phila., 1984—85; resident NY Eye & Ear Infirmary, NYC, 1985—89; fellow facial plastic and reconstructive surgery Oregon Health Sci. U., Portland, 1989—90; assoc. prof. otolaryngology Cornell Med. Coll., 1990—99; dir. divsn. facial plastic and reconstructive surgery Cornell Med. Ctr., NY, 1992—99; asst. attending surgeon Dept. Otorhinolaryngology Manhattan Eye, Ear and Throat Hosp.; attending surgeon Lenox Hill Hosp.; pvt. practice NYC, 1999—. Named one of Top Doctors in NY, NY Mag., 2004, 2005. Fellow: Am. Coll. Surgeons, Am. Acad. Facial Plastic and Reconstructive Surgery; mem.: Phila. County Med. Soc., Pa. Med. Soc., Med. Strollers Soc., NY County Med. Soc., Med. Soc. State NY, NY Facial Plastic Surgery Soc. (mem., bylaws com.), Am. Soc. Hair Restoration Surgery, Am. Soc. Laser Medicine and Surgery, Am. Cleft-Palate-Craniofacial Assn., Am. Soc. Dermatologic Surgery, Am. Acad. Otorhinolaryngology-Head and Neck Surgery, AMA. Office: 880 Fifth Ave New York NY 10021 Office Phone: 212-871-0900. Office Fax: 212-871-0909. Business E-Mail: info@drguida.com.

GUIDRY, JIMMY, public health service officer; BS, Southwestern Univ., 1974; MD, La. State Univ., 1978. Cert. Am. Bd. Pediatrics. Residency Earl K. Long Med. Ctr., 1978—81; private practice, 1981—84; dir. adolescent svc. Earl K. Long Hosp., 1985—90; med. dir. Acadian region La. Dept. Health & Hospitals, 1990—91, asst. sec. office public health, 1996—2000, med. dir. & state health officer, 2000—. Recipient LPHA award, 1997. Fellow: Am. Acad. Pediatrics. Mailing: Dept Health & Hospitals PO Box 629 Baton Rouge LA 70821-0629

GUILE, JEAN-MARC J. M., psychiatrist, neuroscientist; b. Nantes, France, Feb. 18, 1956; s. Yvette A. Hauray; m. Pierryle M. Guile, Oct. 25, 1986; children: Christophe Guile-Servin, Clemence Guile-Servin, Andreane Guile-Servin, Marine Guile-Servin, Domitille Guile-Servin. MD, U. Paris XI, 1989; MSc in Anthropology, Sch. High Studies Social Scis., Paris, 1989. Ces France, 1989, Cspq Can., 1992, lic. hosp. psychiatrist France, 1998. Asst. psychiatrist-in-chief CHU, Brazzaville, Republic of the Congo, 1984—85; staff psychiatrist CHR, Baie-Comeau, Canada, 1986—90, psychiatrist-in-chief, 1990—91; chief svc. Douglas Hosp., Montreal, Canada, 1992—96, dir. child psychiatry divsn., 1997—2001; med. dir. CCCA-CMPP, Crepy-en-Valois, France, 2001—. Asst. prof. psychiatry McGill U., Montreal, 1986—; clin. assoc. prof. psychiatry U. Montreal, Montreal, 2001—; assoc. rschr. Fernand Seguin Ctr. Rsch., Montreal, 2005—; rschr. lab. psychology and cognitive neurosci. Nat. Ctr. Sci. Rsch., U. Paris V, 2006—; assoc. rschr. McGill Rsch. Ctr., Montreal, 1986—2001. Editor: Mag. Neuropsychiatry of Child and Adolecent, 2006—; bd. editors Mag. Neuropsychiatry Childhood and Adolescence, 2006—; editor-in-chief: Perspectives Psychiatriques, 2007—. Bd. dirs. Can. Assn. Sovereign Order Malta, Ottawa, Canada, 1997—; hospitaller Malteser Internat., Rome, 1999—2005. Decorated Merit Cross medal Sovereign Mil. Order Malta, Knight; recipient Grant arms award, Can. Heraldic Auth., 1997. Mem.: French Adolescent Soc. Child Psychiatry (corr.), Can. Acad. Child and Adolescent Psychiatry (assoc.), Paris Med. Soc. Psychology (assoc.), Am. Acad. Child and Adolescent Psychiatry (assoc.). Personal E-mail: jmguile@total.net.

GUILL, MARGARET FRANK, pediatrician, educator, medical researcher; b. Atlanta, Jan. 18, 1948; d. Vernon Rhinehart and Margaret N. (Tichenor) Frank; m. Marshall Anderson Guill III, July 6, 1974; children: Daniel Marshall, Laura Elizabeth. BA, Agnes Scott Coll., 1969; MD, Med. Coll. Ga., 1972. Diplomate Am. Bd. Pediatrics, Am. Bd. Pediatrics subbd. pulmonology, Am. Bd. Allergy and Immunology, Nat. Bd. Med. Examiners. Resident in pediatrics Kaiser Found. Hosp., San Francisco, 1976-78, fellow in allergy, 1978-79; staff physician Waipahu (Hawaii) Clinic, 1973-76; intern in internal medicine Med. Coll. Ga., Augusta, 1973, resident in pediatrics, 1974, fellow in allergy and immunology, 1979-80, from asst. prof. to prof. pediatrics, 1981—2009, also chief sect. pediatric pulmonology and dir. Asthma Ctr., dir. Cystic Fibrosis Ctr., 1990—2009, vice chair dept. pediat., 2000—09, Dorothy A. Hahn chair pediats., 2001—09, pediat. prof. emeritus, 2010—; prof. pediat. Dartmonth Med. Sch., 2010—; co-dir. pediat. cystic fibrosis prog. Dartmouth Hitchcock Med. Ctr., 2010—, interim chief allergy & pediat. pulmonology, 2010—. Pres. Physician Practice Group, 2001—04; pres. staff Childrens Med. Ctr. Hosp., 2000—01; spkr. in field. Host Healthwatch weekly program WJBF-TV, 1982-83; contbr. articles to profl. jours. Active Reid Meml. Presbyn. Ch.; vol. tchr. Episcopal Day Sch., 1982-85; career day participant Acad. Richmond County, 1982, 83; med. advisor Augusta Area Allergy and Asthma Support Group, 1984-86; adv. bd. East Cen. br. Am. Lung Assn. Ga., 1985—, program of work com., 1987—, bd. dirs., 1987—, program coordinating com., 1990-91, exec. bd., 1989-91; med. staff Camp Breathe Easy, 1985—2008, med. dir., 1996-98. Recipient Mosby Book award, 1973; grantee rsch. grantee, BRSG, 1981—86, Del Labs., 1982, Merrell-Dow, 1983—84, Elan Pharms., 1986, Am. Lung Assn. Ga., 1986—87, Hollister-Stier, 1986, Fisons Corp., 1989, 1991—93, 1995, Med. Coll. Ga., 1989, Am. Heart Assn., 1991, Genentech, 1991—2005, Miles, 1992, Clintrials, 1990—95, PathoGenesis, 1995—2004, SmithKline Beecham, 1996, Kaleida Health, 2002, Chiron, 2002, Corus Pharma, 2005—06, Chiron, 2005—06; Rsch. grantee, CFF Therapeutics, 2005—09. Fellow Am. Acad. Pediat., Am. Coll. Chest Physicians, Am. Acad. Allergy, Asthma and Immunology, Am. Coll. Allergy, Asthma and Immunology; mem. Am. Thoracic Soc., Alpha Omega Alpha. Office: Dartmouth Hitchcock Med Ctr 1 Med Ctr Dr Lebanon NH 03756 Home: 2 Woodrow Rd Hanover NH 03755 Office Phone: 603-653-9884. Business E-Mail: margaret.f.guill@hitchcock.org.

GUILLAMA-ALVAREZ, NOEL JESUS, merchant banker, healthcare executive; b. Havana, Cuba, Nov. 30, 1959; arrived in US, 1966, naturalized, 1981; s. Jesus Mario Guillama and Rosa Maria Alvarez Guillama; 1 child, Jahziel Mikhail Guillama. Student, Fla. Internat. U., Miami, Palm Beach C.C., Lake Worth, Fla., 1978—80; BS in Constrn. Mgmt., Allstate Coll., Tampa, Fla., 1983; postgrad., MIT, Cambridge, Mass., 1997—99, Palm beach Atlantic U. Mathematical Orgn., Wellington, Fla., 2003—07. Cert. bldg. contractor, Fla.; lic. real estate broker, mortgage broker, gen. ins. agt. Dir. programing Teleprompter Corp., West Palm Beach, Fla., 1976-79; pres., CEO JMG Holdings Inc, Palm Beach, Fla., 1980-90; chmn., CEO Tektonica, Inc., Tequesta, Fla., 1984—; chmn. Medtronics, Inc., Wellington, 1984—; v.p. ops. Quality Care Networks, Boca Raton, Fla., 1990-95; v.p. devel. Medpartners, Inc., Birmingham, Ala., 1995; pres., CEO Met. Health Networks (Amex:MDF), West Palm Beach, 1995-2000; chmn. The Quantum Group (Amex: QGP), Wellington, Fla., 2000—, TargitInteractive, Portsmouth, NH, 2000—02; dir. Da Vinci Ventures Group, Inc., 2003. Vice-chair Palm Beach County Adv. Bd., West Palm Beach, 1990—92; co-founder, vice-chair Lake Worth Cmty. Devel. Corp., 1990—92; co-founder Project Lake Worth, 1989—92. Writer weekly column Palm Beach Latino Newspaper, 1991-92. Mem. Palm Beach County Edn. Commn., 2007; trustee Palms West Hosp., Loxahatchee, Fla., 2005—; dir., treas. and chmn. fin. and investment com. Fla. Internat. U., 2004—, mem. biomed. engring. adv. bd., 2005—, chmn. bus., tech. and edn. advancement bd., 2002—, Western Cmtys., Palm Beach County, 2003—07; mem. Wellington Fla. Edn. Com., 2005—07; committeeman Rep. Exec. Com., Palm Beach County, Fla., 2005—06; bd. dirs. Palm Beach CC Found., Lake Worth, Fla., 2005—, Cultural Trust Palm Beaches, 2006—07. Recipient award Leukemia Soc. Am., 1979, Chin de Plata award Todo Mag., Miami, Fla., 1978. Mem.: Health Info. Mgmt. Soc., Med. Group Mgmt. Assn., Am. Fin. Assn., Am. Coll. Healthcare Execs. (assoc.), Rotary. Republican. Avocations: scuba diving, tennis, golf, fishing. Office Phone: 561-798-9800.

GUILLEMIN, ROGER CHARLES LOUIS, physiologist, academic administrator; b. Dijon, France, Jan. 11, 1924; arrived in U.S., 1953, naturalized, 1963; BA, U. Dijon, 1941, BSc, 1942; MD, Faculty of Medicine, Lyons, France, 1949; PhD, U. Montreal, 1953; PhD (hon.), U. Rochester, 1976, U. Chgo., 1977, Baylor Coll. Medicine, 1978, U. Ulm, Germany, 1978, U. Dijon, France, 1978, Free U. Brussels, 1979, U. Montreal, 1979, U. Man., Can, 1984, U. Turin, Italy, 1985, Kyung Hee U., Korea, 1986, U. Paris, Paris, 1986, U. Barcelona, Spain, 1988, U. Madrid, 1988, McGill U., Montreal, Can., 1988, U. Claude Bernard, Lyon, France, 1989, Laval U., Quebec, Can., 1990, PhD (hon.), 1996, Sherbrooke U., Quebec, 1997, U. Franche-Comté, France, 1999. Intern, resident Univ. Hosps., Dijon, 1946—47; rsch. asst., assoc. dir., asst. prof. Inst. Exptl. Medicine & Surgery, U. Montreal, 1949—53; asst. prof. physiology Baylor Coll. Medicine, Houston, 1953-57, assoc. prof., 1957—63, prof., dir. labs. neuroendocrinology, 1963-70; resident fellow, rsch. prof., chmn. labs. neuroendocrinology Salk Inst., La Jolla, Calif., 1970-89, dean, 1972—73, 1976—77, disting. prof., 1989—, interim pres., 2007—09. Cons. physiology VA Hosp., Houston, 1954—60, 1967—70; lectr. exptl. endocrinology dept. biology Rice U., Houston, 1958—60; cons. biochemistry MD Anderson Hosp. & Tumor Inst., Houston, 1967—70; bd. dirs. ICN Pharms., 1987—89, 1994—2001, SPI Pharm., 1989—95, Prizm Pharm., 1992—98, Viratek, 1992—95, Jonas Salk Fedn., 1995—2005; disting. scientist Whittier Diabetes Inst., San Diego, 1989—97, sci. & med. dir., 1993—94; adj. prof. medicine U. Calif., San Diego, 1994—97. Decorated chevalier Legion d'Honneur France, officer de la Légion d'Honneur; recipient Gold medal, 1st Internat. Congress Pharmacology, Stockholm, 1961, Saintour award for exptl. endocrinology, Coll. de France, Paris, 1961, Disting. Scientist award, Nat. Diabetes Rsch. Coalition, 1966, La Madonnina award for medicine, Carlo Erba Found., 1974, Gairdner Found. Internat. award, 1974, Lasker award for basic med. rsch., 1975, Dickson prize in medicine, 1976, Nobel prize in medicine, 1977, Nat. Medal Sci., 1977, Barren Gold medal, 1979, Dale medal, Soc. Endocrinology, 1980, Ellen Browning Scripps Soc. medal, Scripps Meml. Hosp. Found., 1988; scholar, John & Mary R. Markle Found., NY, 1952—56. Fellow: AAAS; mem.: NAS, Tex. Med. Ctr. Rsch. Soc. (pres. elect 1959, pres. 1960, hon. 1970), Am. Inst. Biol. Sci., Western Soc. Clin. Rsch., Internat. Soc. Neurosci. (charter), Acad. Sci., French Acad. Scis., Am. Acad. Arts & Scis., Soc. Neuroscis., Internat. Soc. Rsch. Biology Reprodn., Internat. Brain Rsch. Orgn., Soc. Exptl. Biology & Medicine, Endocrine Soc. (coun. 1969—73, nominating com. 1974—75, pres. 1986), Assn. Am. Physicians, Am. Physiol. Soc., Soc. Francaise d'Endocrinologie (hon.; pres. 1982—83), Soc. Biology Paris (hon.), Internat. Soc. for Immunology of Reproduction (hon.), Howard Florey Inst. Exptl. Physiology and Medicine (hon.), Can. Soc. Endocrinology and Metabolism (hon.), Swedish Soc. Med. Sci. (hon.), Am. Peptide Soc. (hon.), Club of Rome. Office: The Salk Inst 10010 N Torrey Pines Rd La Jolla CA 92037-1099 Address: The Salk Inst PO Box 85800 San Diego CA 92186-5800 Business E-Mail: guillemin@salk.edu.

GUILLET, JACQUES ANDRE, physician, medical researcher; b. Cauterets, France, Apr. 16, 1948; s. Auguste Victor and Gloria (Otal) G.; m. Catherine Michele Casse, Jan. 17, 1979; children: Audrey Valerie, Cecile Pauline. MD, Faculty Medicine, Bordeaux, France, 1978. Resident physician Bordeaux San. Region, Agen, France, 1973-78; resident pediatrics Faculty Medicine, Bordeaux, 1979, resident biophysics, biology, 1984; resident nuclear medicine Nat. Inst. Nuclear Scis. and Techs., Paris, 1980, lectr., 1988—; resident biophysics nuclear Bordeaux II U., 1982-86; medicine lectureship Pellegrin Hosp., Bordeaux, 1982-86; biologist, head depts. biophysics, nuclear medicine St Esprit Hosp, Agen, France, 1985—, head depts. biology, med. imaging, pharms., 2005—; lectr. Conservatoire Nat. Arts et Metiers, Agen, 1984—, Nat. Edn. Ctr. for Radiol. Risks, 1994—; head rsch. ctr. Radioactivity Rsch./Supervision Ctr., Agen, 1994-99. Bd. dirs. Hosp. Centre, Agen, 1991-94 biology, med. imaging and pharmacy mgr., 2005—; hon. mem., med. advisor French Assn. Thyroid Patients, 2000—. Author: Nuclear Medicine and Biology: 5 books in French, 1984-93, Prostatic Specific Antigen, 1987-88, Atlas of Bone Scintigraphy, 1993, Thyroid autoantibodies, 1997; contbr. more than 300 articles to profl. jours. Recipient awards Amersham-Buchler, Europe, 1983, French Soc. Nuclear Energy, Sfen, Paris, 1992. Mem. European Assn. Nuclear Medicine, French Soc. Biophysics, French Soc. Radio Protection, Pediatric Nuclear Medicine, French Pediat. Soc., Concerted Activity in Nuclear Medicine, French Assn. Thyroid Patients (hon., med. adv., 2000—). Office: Hosp St Esprit Rt de Villeneuve 47923 Agen France

GUILLORY, SAMUEL L., ophthalmologist, educator, pediatrician; BSEE, Northrop Inst. of Tech., 1967; MD, Mt. Sinai Med. Sch., 1975. Diplomate Am. Bd. Ophthalmology. Resident pediat. Mt. Sinai Hosp., 1975—76, resident ophthalmology, 1976—79; fellow Cornell Med. Ctr., 1979—81; assoc. clin. prof. ophthalmology Mt. Sinai. Med. Sch., assoc. clin. prof. pediat. Recipient pediat. award, Bella Schick Soc. Mem.: Pediatric Soc. of NY, Am. Acad. of Ophthalmology. Office: The Mount Sinai Medical Center One Gustave L Levy Place New York NY 10029-6574 Office Fax: 212-241-6500.

GUILLOTREAU, JULIEN, urologist; b. Lorient, Apr. 12, 1978; MD, Faculté Médecine Toulouse, 2008. Cert. urologist Faculté Médecine Toulouse, 2009. Resident gen. surgery CHU Toulouse, Dept. Urology, 2003—08, clin. fellow, 2008—10; rsch. asst. CNRS UMR 5089, IPBS, 2008—09; rsch. fellow urology Cleve. Clinic Found., 2010—. Regional rep. French Soc. Resident in Urology, 2006—08, pres., 2008—10; residents rep. U. Toulouse Paul Sabatier III, Sch. Medicine, 2007—09, vice chmn., 2009—10. Recipient Resident award, French Urol. Assn. Nat. Meeting, Lasserre's prize, Paul Sabatier U., Sch. Medicine Toulouse III. Mem.: French Assn. Urologists. Avocations: rugby, travel. Office: Glickmann Inst 9500 Euclid Ave Cleveland OH 44195 E-mail: julienguillotreau@gmail.com.

GUILOFF, ROBERTO JAIME, neurologist; b. Santiago, Chile, Mar. 4, 1943; arrived in U.K., 1972; s. Angel Guiloff-Luder and Blanca Eva Davis; m. Feb. 3, 1968 (div. 1997); children: Claudio Ivan, Carolina Adela; m. Heather Angus-Leppan, Apr. 6, 1999; children: Vivien Veronica, Angelica Elizabeth, David Vincent. BSc in Biology, U. of Chile, Santiago, 1960, MD, 1967, L Philosophy, 1967. Trainee, asst. prof. neurology U. Chile, 1967-72; registrar in neurology Nat. Hosps. for Neurology and Neurosurgery, London, 1974-76; sr. registrar Nat. Hosp., Queen Sq. and King's Coll. Hosp., London, 1976-80; cons. neurologist Westminster and St. Stephen's Hosps., London, 1981-93, Hammersmith Hosps. Trust, Chelsea & Westminster Hosp., London, 1993—2008, Charing Cross Hosp. Imperial Coll. Healthcare NHS Trust, 2008—; dir. neuromuscular unit Charing Cross Hosp., London, 1993—2008, dir. motor neuron disease care and rsch. ctr., 1994—2008; prof. clin. neurology Faculty Medicine, U. Chile, 2008—. Hon. sr. lectr. medicine Charing Cross and Westminster Sch., London, 1987; hon. cons. neurologist Royal Brompton Hosp., London, 1993—2005. Mem. editl. bd. Jour. Neurology, Neurosurgery and Psychiatry, 1989-94, ALS and other Motor Neuron Diseases, 1999-2008; editor: CPD Neurology, 1998-2002, Clinical Trials in Neurology Springer-Verlag, 2001; author: Sense Perception in Idealism and the Neurological Theory, 1968; contbr. articles to profl. jours., chpts. to books. Recipient Col. Med. prize Chilean Coll. Physicians and Surgeons, 1967, Queen Sq. prize in neurology Inst. Neurology, 1977; Queen Elizabeth II scholar Brit. Coun., 1972-73. Fellow Royal Coll. Physicians, Royal Soc. Medicine (sect. of clin. neuroscis., internat. sec. 1993-99, sec. 1991-92, pres. 2000-01); mem. World Fedn. Neurology (sec. treas. com. motor neuron diseases 1998—), Brit. Soc. for Clin. Neurophysiology (mem. coun. 1994—2000, sec. 1998-2000), Assn. Brit. Neurologists, Brit. Peripheral Nerve Soc. (mem. coun. 2007-10), West London Medico-Chirurgical Soc., (pres. 2003-04). Avocations: opera, classical music, tennis. Office: Charing Cross Hosp Fulham Palace Road W6 8RF London England Office Phone: 44-020-8846-1196. Business E-Mail: r.guiloff@imperial.ac.uk.

GUIMARÃES, ANA BEATRIZ PEDRIALI, psychologist, educator; b. Londrina, Paraná, Brazil, June 19, 1978; Degree in Psychology, PUC-PR, 2001; PhD in Scis., USP, 2009. Prof. PUC-PR U. & Unibrasil. Author: (book) A Past That Lives: Family History of Alcoholic Women, 2010. Recipient Young Rschr. award, NIDA, 2009; fellowship, U. Ala., NIH. Achievements include research in Pparanaense network of tobacco women control. Avocation: ballet. Home: Deputado Mario Barros 752 Ap 81 Curitiba Paraná 80530-280 Brazil Office Phone: (41) 3016-5077. Personal E-mail: pedrialiguimaraes@yahoo.com.br.

GUIMARÃES, FERNANDO SILVA, physical therapist, educator; b. Niterói, Rio de Janeiro, Apr. 14, 1969; Degree in Phys. Therapy, Escola Superior Ensino Helena Antipoff, 1992; PhD, Fed. U. Rio de Janeiro, 2003. Grad. diploma in physiotherapy Brazilian Assn. Rsch. Assoc. prof. Fed. U. Rio de Janeiro, 1996—. Fellow: Brazilian Assn. Cardiopulmonary Phys. Therapy and Physiotherapy in Intensive Care; mem.: European Respiratory Soc. Avocations: saxophone, volleyball. Office: Coordenação do Curso de Fisioterapia Rua Luiz Fagundes Rio de Janeiro 21941-913 Brazil Office Fax: 55 21 25622223. Business E-Mail: fguimaraes_pg@yahoo.com.br.

GUIMARÃES, JOSÉ GUILHERME ANTUNES, dentist, educator; b. Niteroi, Rio de Janeiro, Aug. 3, 1963; MSc in Dental Materials, U. São Paulo, 2000, PhD in Restorative Dentistry, 2004. Adj. prof. U. Fed. Fluminense, 1991—. Pvt. practice, 1985—. Mem.: Brazilian Laser in Dentistry Assn., Brazilian Oral Rsch. Soc. Office: R Mario Santos Braga 30/3° andar Centro Niteroi Rio de Janeiro 24020-140 Brazil Business E-Mail: jgag@vm.uff.br.

GUIMARAES, PATRICIA NEVES, psychology professor; b. Montes Claros, Minas Gerais, Brazil, May 27, 1966; B in Social Work, Pontificia Universidade Catolica, Minas Gerais, 1987; PhD in Psychiatry, Fed. U. Sao Paulo, 2010. Asst. prof. State U. Montes Claros, 2001—. Coord. ctr. conciliation parties, families jurisdiction tribunal Ct. Justice, Minas Gerais, 1994. Scholarship, McGill U., Can., CAPES- Brazil Govt. Found. Avocation: piano. Home: Av Vicente Guimaraes 130 Apt 501 Montes Claros Minas Gerais 39403410 Brazil Personal E-mail: pnguimaraes@yahoo.com.br.

GUINAN, MARY ELIZABETH, dean, physician, researcher; b. NYC, Sept. 23, 1939; d. Michael and Mary (Lyne) Guinan; m. Peter M. Schantz, July 19, 1979; children: Aimee, Erica, Brendan. BA, Hunter Coll., 1961; PhD, U. Tex., Galveston, 1969; MD, Johns Hopkins U., 1972. Cert. American Bd. Internal Medicine, American Bd. Preventive Medicine and Pub. Health. Rsch. scientist Ctrs. for Disease Control, Atlanta, 1978-86, asst. dir. for sci., 1986-90, AIDS rschr., 1990—98, chief urban health rsch ctrs., 1995—98; state pub. health officer Nev. Dept. Health and Human Services, Carson City, 1998—2002, Nev. Dept. Health & Human Services, 2008—09; exec. dir. Nev. Pub. Health Found; dean U. Nev. Las Vegas Sch. Pub. Health, 2004—09, U. Nev. Las Vegas Sch. Cmty. Health Sciences, 2009—. Mem. pub. health commn. Nev. State Med. Assn., 1999—. Writer women's health column Jour. American Med. Women's Assn., 1988-94. Mem. American Med. Women's Assn. (pres. 2011-), Infectious Disease Soc. America. Avocations: jogging, skiing, birding. Office: UNLV Sch Pub Health 4505 Maryland Pky Box 453063 Las Vegas NV 89154-3063 Office Phone: 702-895-5090. *

GUINN, JANET MARTIN, psychologist, consultant; b. Rapid City, SD, Aug. 16, 1942; d. Verne Oliver and Carolyn Yetta (Clark) Martin; m. David Lee Guinn, Oct. 27, 1962 (div. June 1988); children: Cynthia Gail, Kevin Scott, Garrett Lee. BS in Psychology, U. Alaska, 1980, MS in Counseling Psychology, 1983; PhD in Clin. Psychology, Calif. Sch. Profl. Psychology, 1988. Lic. psychologist, Alaska, Nev. Pvt. practice, Anchorage, 1988-93, Carson City and Reno, Nev., 1993—; clinician Behavior Medicine Cons., 1983-84; pvt. practice clinician, 1983-84; supr. Southcentral Counseling Ctr., Anchorage, 1984-85; cons. City/Borough of Juneau, Alaska, 1988; psychologist youth treatment program Alaska Psychiat. Inst., Anchorage, 1989-90; psychologist Nev. Mental Health Inst., Sparks, 1994-97. Cons. in field; cons. Alaska Small Bus. Coalition, Anchorage, 1990-92; reviewer Blors Corp. Contbr. articles to profl. jours. Active in politics. Mem. APA, Am. Coll. Forensic Examiners, Nev. Psychol. Assn., Internat. Neuropsychol. Soc., Rotary, Psi Chi. Republican. Avocations: skiing, gourmet cooking, dance.

GUINOUARD, DONALD EDGAR, psychologist; b. Bozeman, Mont., Mar. 31, 1929; s. Edgar Arthur and Venabell (Ford) G.; m. Irene M. Egeler, Mar. 30, 1951; children: Grant M., Philip A., Donna I. BS, Mont. State U., Bozeman, 1954; MS, Mont. State U., 1955; EdD, Wash. State U., Pullman, 1960; postdoctoral, Stanford U., 1965; grad., Indsl. Coll. of the Armed Forces, 1964, Air War Coll., 1976. Lic. psychologist, Ariz., counselor, Wash., Mont.; cert. secondary tchr. and sch. adminstr., Wash., Mont.; diplomate Am. Psychotherapy Assn., Am. Bd. Forensic Counselors, Am. Bd. Psychol. Specialities. Advanced through grades to col. USAFR, 1946-84, ret., 1984; dir. counseling Consol. Sch. Dist., Pullman, Wash., 1955-60; assoc. prof. Mont. State U., Bozeman, 1960-66; field selection officer Peace Corps, U.S., S.Am., 1962-68; prof. counseling, counseling psychologist Ariz. State U., Tempe, 1966-90; prof. emeritus, 1990; co-owner Forensic Cons. Assocs., Tempe, 1970—; pvt. practice, 1990—. Admissions liaison officer USAF Acad., Colo. Springs, 1967-84; assessment officer Fundamental Edn. Ctr. for the Devel. of the Latin American Community, Patzcuaro, Mex., 1963-64; expert witness on vocat. and psychol. disability for fed. and state cts. Contbr. articles to profl. jours. Mem. Ariz. Psychol. Assn., Am. Assn. Counseling & Devel., Reserve Officers Assn., Am. Psychotherapy Assn., Am. Coll. Forensic Examiners. Democrat. Methodist. Avocations: photography, woodworking, camping, fishing, silversmithing. Home and Office: 112 E Cairo Dr Tempe AZ 85282-3606 E-mail: donaldg516@aol.com.

GUINSBURG, PHILIP FRIED, alcohol and substance abuse counselor; b. NYC, Sept. 13, 1946; s. Theodore and Elena (Fried) G.; m. Debrah Josias Guinsburg, June 15, 1968; children: Mark, Michael. BA, Columbia Coll., 1968; MA, U. ND, Grand Forks, 1970, PhD, 1973. Diplomate Am. Bd. Med. Psychotherapy; lic. alcohol and drug abuse counselor. Clin. dir. Nashville Drug Treatment Ctr., Dede Wallace Ctr., 1973-78; pvt. practice Nashville, 1974—. Asst. clin. prof. psychiatry Vanderbilt U., Nashville, 1987-93; cons. Crisis Intervention Ctr., 1974-99; pres. Dreammakers, Inc., Nashville, 1989-91; cons. Campus For Human Devel. Co-author: Making Love Safe, 2003. Baseball coach Brentwood Civitan Little League, Tenn., 1982-92. Recipient Voices in Recovery award, Tenn. Assn. Drug and Alcohol Svcs., 2006; named to Hall of Fame, Howlett Woodmere Alumni Assn., 2006. Mem. ACA, Am. Group Psychotherapy Assn., Am. Acad. Psychoterhapists (pres. 2005-06), Assn. for Spiritual, Ethical and Religious Values in Counseling, Nat. Assn. Addiction

Counselors (Profl. of Yr. award, 2004), Tenn. Assn. Alcohol and Drug Abuse Counselors (pres., Tenn. Profl. of Yr. 2002, Lifetime Achievement award 2003), Voices in Recovery. Jewish. Avocations: gardening, sports, gourmet foods. Home: 8121 Maryland Ln Brentwood TN 37027-7341 Office: 2313 21st Ave S Nashville TN 37212-4908 Home Phone: 615-972-1046; Office Phone: 615-386-3333. Personal E-mail: pfg1946@aol.com.

GUION, ROBERT MORGAN, psychologist, educator; b. Indpls., Sept. 14, 1924; s. Leroy Herbert and Carolyn (Morgan) Guion; m. Mary Emily Firestone, June 8, 1947; children: David Michael, Diana Lynn, Keith Douglas, Pamela Sue, Judith Elaine. BA, State U. Iowa, 1948; MS, Purdue U., 1950, PhD, 1952. Vocat. counselor Purdue U., 1948-51, research fellow, 1951-52; mem. faculty Bowling Green (Ohio) State U., 1952—, prof. psychology, 1964—, univ. prof., 1983-85, univ. prof. emeritus, 1985—, chmn. dept., 1966-71. Vis. prof. U. Calif., Berkeley, 1963—64, U. N.Mex., 1965; tech. adviser Dept. Pers. Svcs., State of Hawaii, 1970; vis. rsch. psychologist Ednl. Testing Svc., 1971—72; cons. in field. Author: (book) Personnel Testing, 1965, Assessment, Measurement and Prediction for Personnel Decisions, 1998, 2nd edit., 2011; editor: Jour. Applied Psychology, 1983—88; co-author (with Scott Highhouse): Essentials of Personnel Assessment and Selection, 2006. With AUS, 1943—46. Recipient Stephen E. Bemis award, Internat. Pers. Mgmt. Assn., 2000. Mem.: APA (pres. divsn. 14 1972—73, pres. divsn. 5 1982—83, James McKeen Cattell award divsn. 14 1965, 1981, Disting. Sci. Contbn. award divsn. 14 1987, Disting. Svc. award divsn. 14 1993, Lifetime Contbn. award divsn. 5 1997), Assn. Psychol. Scis. (James McKeen Cattell award 2000). Methodist. Home: 632 Haskins Rd Bowling Green OH 43402-1615 Personal E-mail: rmguion@wcnet.org.

GUIORA, ALEXANDER ZEEV, psychologist; b. Nyiregyhaza, Hungary, June 13, 1925; came to U.S., 1963, naturalized, 1968; s. Solomon and Theresa (Gottlieb) G.; m. Susie N. Neuser, Jan. 20, 1955. Docteur d'Universite, Sorbonne U., Paris, 1951. Prof. psychiatry, psychology and linguistics U. Mich., Ann Arbor, 1964-85; prof. psychology, dir. grad. program in clin. psychology U. Haifa, Israel, 1985-87, dean of research authority, 1987-91, prof. emeritus, 1994-97; pres. Coll. of Yizrael, Israel. Vis. prof. U. Negev, Israel, 1971; vis. prof., chmn. dept. med. psychology Technion Israel Inst. Tech., 1976-77; vis. prof. Hebrew U., Jerusalem, 1983— Editor: (with Marrvin Brandwin) Perspectives in Clinical Psychology, 1968, Epistemology for the Language Sciences, 1983; gen. editor: Lang. Learning: Jour. of Rsch. in Lang. Studies; contbr. articles to profl. jours. Mem. Am. Psychol. Assn., Israeli Psychol. Assn., Azazels Club Jewish. Office: U Haifa Haifa 31999 Israel Home: 1222, 7 Hapalmach St Po Box 30900 Zikhron Yaaqov Israel Office Phone: 972-4 829-665. Business E-Mail: aguiora@umich.edu, aguiora@research.haifa.ac.il.

GUIQIU, CAO, physician; b. Kolar, Dec. 16, 1972; B, Xinjiang Med. U., 1996, PhD, 2011. Assoc. chief physician 5th Affiliated Hosp. Xinjiang Med. U., 1996—. Office: Henan West Rd Urumqi Xinjiang 830011 China Office Fax: 0991-7922957.

GUIS, SANDRINE, rheumatologist, educator; d. Max and Aline Guis. MD, U. Méditerranée, Marseille, France, PhD, 2008. Cert. rheumatologist Marseille, 1997. Assoc. prof. U. Méditerranée, 2003—07, medicine prof., 2008—. Treas. AFPER, Marseille, 2006. Office: Hôsp Conception 147 boulevard Baille Marseille 13385 France E-mail: sandrine.guis@ap-hm.fr.

GUJRATHI, SHEILA, medical products executive; BS Biomedical Engring., Northwestern U., MD. Cert. Internal medicine internship and residency Brigham and Women's Hosp., Harvard Med. Sch.; tng. Univ. of Calif., San Francisco; tng. in allergy and immunology fellowship program Stanford Univ.; mgmt. cons. McKinsey and Co.; with Genentech; v.p. global clin. devel. group in immunology Bristol-Myers Squibb (BMS); chief. med. officer Receptos, Inc. Office: Receptos Inc. Ste 205 10835 Rd to the Cure San Diego CA 92121 Office Phone: 858-652-5700. Office Fax: 858-587-2659.

GUL, MUSTAFA, dean; b. Kahramanmaras, Turkey, Apr. 14, 1968; D, Istanbul U. Cerrahpasa Med. Faculty, 1992. Assoc. prof. Kahramanmaras Sutcuimam U. Med. Faculty, 2007, vice dean, 2010—. Office: Yoruk Selim MahGazi Mustafa Kuscu Cad Kahramanmaras Merkez 46050 Turkey Office Fax: 90-344-2212371. Personal E-mail: mustafagultr@yahoo.com.

GULATI, MARTHA, health facility administrator, cardiologist; b. Lions Head, Ont., Can., May 14, 1969; BSc in Gen. Sci., McMaster U., Hamilton, Can., 1990; MD, U. Toronto, 1995; MS in Health Studies Clin. Profls., U. Chgo., 2002. Lic. Med. Coun. Can., 1997, internal medicine resident 1998, diplomate in cardiology, Am. Bd. Internal Medicine, 2005, Nat. Bd. Med. Examiners, 2004, lic. physician Ill., Ohio. Clin. assoc., medicine, dept. medicine, divsn. cardiology U. Chgo., 2001—02; asst. prof., dept. medicine, divsn. cardiology Rush U. Med. Ctr., Chgo., 2002—04, asst. prof., preventative medicine, 2002—05, asst. dir., Cardiology Consult Svc., 2003—04, rsch. dir., Heart Ctr. Women, 2003—04; asst. prof., preventive medicine Northwestern U., Chgo., 2005—10, assoc. med. dir., 2005—10, Lawrence E. and Nancy S. Glick family disting. physician, 2008—10, assoc. prof., medicine, 2010; assoc. prof., dept. internal medicine, divsn. cardiology Ohio State U., Columbus, 2010—, Sarah Ross Soter chair, women's cardiovasc. health, 2010—, sect. dir., 2010—, assoc. prof., Coll. Pub. Health, divsn. epidemiology, 2011—. Contbr. chapters to books, articles to numerous profl. jours. Vol. Girls On The Run, 2003—10, adv. bd. mem., 2009—10, med. dir. Chgo. Area Runners Assn., 2007—08. Recipient Dr. Delbert S. Hoare award, U. Toronto, 1995, AstraZeneca Young Cardiovasc. Investigator award, 2002—04, Young Investigator award, Am. Soc. Nuc. Cardiology, 2004, Inspiring Women award, Women's Nat. Basketball Assn., 2007; named one of Chgo.'s Top 40 under 40 in Bus., Crain's Chgo. Bus., 2005; fellowship, U. Chgo., 2001, Rsch. grant, Northwestern U. Inst. Women's Health. Fellow: Am. Coll. Cardiology (mem., women cardiology coun. 2009—, chair 2008—10, vice chair 2008—10, First Annual Heart Women's Health Credo award 2011); mem.: Inst. Women's Health Rsch. (Pioneer award 2009—10), Am. Med. Women's Assn. (Gender Equity award 2010), Am. Coll. Sports Medicine, Am. Heart Assn. (mem. go red women com., Chgo. 2002—10, mem. go red women com., Columbus 2010—, bd. dirs., mem., sister to sister Ill. chpt. 2008—10), Tennis Club, Sigma Xi, U. Chgo. chpt., Alpha Phi (Ursa Major award 2010). Avocation: running. Office: Ohio State University 473 W 12th St Ste 200 Columbus OH 43210 Office Phone: 614-688-5559. Office Fax: 614-293-5614. Business E-Mail: martha.qulati@osumc.edu.

GULBAHAR, OKAN, physician; b. Izmir, Turkey, Jan. 1, 1970; s. Nukhet and Osman Gulbahar; m. Selmin Cinar, May 20, 1969; 1 child, Canbora. MD, Ege U. Faculty of Medicine, 1993; specialist in Internal Medicine, Ege U. Faculty of Medicine Dept. of Internal Medicine, 1999; subspecialist in Immunology, Ege U., Dept. of Internal Medicine Divsn. of Immunology, 2003; subspecialist in Allergy, Ege U., Dept. Internal Medicine Divsn. Allergy, 2004. Diplomate Ege U. Faculty of Medicine, 1993. Student advisor in erasmus project Ege U., Izmir, Turkey, 2002—. Contbr. articles to profl. jour. Grantee Travel Grant, European Acad. of Allergology and Clin. Immunology (EAACI), 2002, World Allergy Orgn.-IAACI (WAO), 2003. Mem.: Turkish Nat. Soc. Allergy and Clin. Immunology, Am. Coll. Allergy, Asthma & Immunology (ACAAI), EAACI (Travel Grant 2002). Office: Ege Univ Dep Internal Medicine Bornova 35100 Izmir Izmir Turkey Office Fax: +902323438140. E-mail: ogulbahar@yahoo.com, gulbahar@med.ege.edu.tr.

GULBRANDSEN, PATRICIA HUGHES, physician; b. May 9, 1940; d. Patrick Boland and Anne Hughes; m. Jon Alf Gulbrandsen, Mar. 6, 1972 (dec. Oct. 1984). BA, Cornell U., 1962; MD, U. Pa., 1967; MPH, Johns Hopkins U., 1980. Cert. Am. Bd. Disability Analysts; diplomate Am. Bd. Phys. Medicine and Rehab., Am. Bd. Occupl. Medicine. Rotating intern Chgo. Wesley Meml. Hosp., 1967-68; resident in neurology Pa. Hosp., Phila., 1968-69, Georgetown U. Hosp., Washington, 1972-74; fellow in gynecologic endocrinology Chelsea Hosp. for Women, London, 1969-71; resident in phys. medicine and rehab. Good Samaritan Hosp., Phoenix, 1974-76; commd. maj. U.S. Army, 1979, advanced through grades to lt. col., 1982; with Walter Reed Army Med. Ctr., Washington, 1979-81; occup. medicine officer U.S. Army/Army Environ. Hygiene Agy., Aberdeen Proving Ground, Md., 1981-83; resigned U.S. Army, 1983; med. dir. USN/Naval Surface Warfare Ctr., White Oak, Md., 1984-89, NASA Hdqs., Washington, 1990-93; acting chief med. officer Hdqs. FBI, Washington, 1995; med. officer Orgn. Am. States, Washington, 1999—2001; occupl. health phys., cons. Def. Intelligence Agy., Bolling AFB, Washington, 2001—03; NIOSH occupl. medicine physician Dept. Energy Worker Advocacy Program, 2004; pvt. practice Gulbrandsen Energy Medicine, LLC, 2006—. Occupl. medicine Profl. Occupl. Health Svcs., 1997-98; staff physiatrist, head consultation svc. New Eng. Med. Ctr. Hosps., Boston, 1977-78; instr. neurology and phys. medicine and rehab. Tufts U. Sch. Medicine, Boston, 1977-78; med. cons. Fairfax County (Va.) Health Dept., 1990, Hummer and Assocs., Cleve., 1990-93, Allied Med. Cons., Inc., Washington, 1994-95, AspenMed Svcs., Inc., 1995-96, 01-03, The Westwood Group, 2004, Gulbrandsen Energy Medicine, LLC, 2006—, Occu Save, Inc., Lanham, Md., 1996, staff privileges Drs. Cmty. Hosp., 1996-98, Hummer Whole Health Mgmt., 1998-99. Office Phone: 757-426-6074. Personal E-mail: mddocg@yahoo.com

GULCHER, JEFFREY ROBERT, genomics company executive; b. Jan. 25, 1960; PhD, U. Chgo., 1986, MD, 1990. Cert. Neurology, 1998. Staff mem., dept. neurology Beth Israel Hospital, Boston, 1993—98, Harvard U. Med. Sch., 1993—98; resident, neurology, Longwood program, neurology dept. Harvard Medical School, 1996; co-founder deCODE Genetics, Reykjavik, Iceland, 1996, v.p., rsch. & devel., 1996—2003, chief sci. officer, 2003, v.p., product devel. Office: deCODE Genetics Sturlugata 8 IS-101 Reykjavik Iceland Office Phone: 0113545701900. Office Fax: 0113545701903. Business E-Mail: jgulcher@decode.com.

GULEC, SEZA, surgeon, educator; b. Ankara, Turkey, Aug. 20, 1961; MD, Ankara U. Sch. Medicine, 1984. Prof. surgery, nuc. medicine, chief surg. oncology Fla. Internat. U. Herbert Wertheim Coll. Medicine, 2007—. Fellow: ACS; mem.: Soc. Nuc. Medicine, Soc. Surg. Oncology. Office: 11200 SW 8th St HLS II 693 Miami FL 33199 E-mail: sezagulec@gmail.com.

GULER, NURHAN, dentist, educator; b. Konya, Mar. 1, 1970; DDS, PhD, Selcuk U., 2000. Assoc. prof. faculty dentistry Yeditepe U., 2000—. Recipient Best Presentation award, Hong Kong, Seattle. Fellow: Internat. Oral And Maxillofacial Surgeons. Avocation: swimming. Office: Bagdat Cad 238 Goztepe Istanbul 34728 Turkey Office Fax: 90 216 3626211. Business E-Mail: nguler@dr.com.

GULERIA, SANJAY, agricultural studies educator, researcher; b. Joginder Nagar, Himachal Pradesh, India, June 10, 1971; PhD, GSSS, Joginder Nagar, 1992. Asst. scientist HPAU, Palamur, Himachal Pradesh, 2000—07; assoc. prof. SK U. Agrl. Scis. and Tech., Jammu, India, 2007—. Recipient award, HPAU Palampur. Mem.: Indian Soc. Agrl. Biochemists. Avocations: reading, music. Office: Divsn Biochem and Plant Physiol Main Campus Chatha Jammu Jammu and Kashmir 180009 India Personal E-mail: guleria71@rediffmail.com.

GULESERIAN, KRISTINE JANE, surgeon, thoracic surgeon, educator; AB in Classics-Greek, Harvard Coll., 1990; MD, Boston U. Sch. Medicine, 1994. Cert. Am. Bd. Thoracic Surgery, Am. Bd. Surgery. Resident, gen. surgery Brown U. Sch. Medicine, 1994—99; resident, thoracic surgery Washington U. Sch. Medicine, 2001—03; fellow, cardiovascular tissue engring. Children's Hosp. Boston, 1999—2001, fellow, pediat. cardiovascular surgery, 2003—04; asst. prof., cardiothoracic surgery Southwestern Med. Sch. Contbr. several articles to profl. jours. Recipient Outstanding Chief Resident award, Brown U. Dept. Surgery, 1999, Kaplan Cardiovascular Rsch. award, Children's Hosp. Boston, 2000, Corgentech Clin. Rsch. Scholarship, Soc. Thoracic Sugery, 2004, Hudson Found. Clin. Rsch. award, Children's Med. Ctr. Dallas, 2006. Mem.: Am. Heart Assn., Soc. Heart Valve Disease, So. Thoracic Surgical Association, Internat. Soc. Heart & Lung Transplantation, Soc. Thoracic Surgeons. Achievements include led team of doctors responsible for the heart and liver transplant of 3 year old girl at Children's Medical Center at Dallas in 2005, 7 year old in 2009. Address: U Tex Southwestern Med Ctr Dallas 5323 Harry Hines Blvd Dallas TX 75390-8835 Office: Childrens Med Ctr Dallas 1935 Medical District Dr Dallas TX 75235 Office Phone: 214-456-5000. Office Fax: 214-456-5015.

GULHANE, SUSHMA RAJESH, pathologist, educator; b. Bhandara, Nov. 10, 1976; MBBS, IGMMC&H, Nagpur, 2000; MD in Pathology, GMC, Nagpur, DNB in Pathology, 2005. Asst. prof. MGIMS, Sevagram, 2005—09; specialist pathologist cum asst. prof. ESI-PGIMSR, Andheri, 2010—. External faculty NIIMS, Hyderabad, 2009—; reviewer numerous jours. Contbr. to profl. publs. Mem.: All India ESIC Specialist Assn., VAPM, IAPM. Avocations: gardening, reading, writing. Home: ESIC Model Hosp Qutr 12 Type IV Mumbai Maharashtra 400093 India Personal E-mail: drsushmagulhane76@gmail.com.

GULICK, PETER GREGORY, medical educator; b. Youngstown, Ohio, July 12, 1950; s. Peter and Sophie (Kudera); m. Charlotte Ann Chubick, July 21, 1973; children: Gregory, Jeff, Laurie, Scott. BS in Biology and Chemistry, Mt. Union Coll., Alliance, Ohio, 1972; DO, Chgo. Osteo. Coll., 1976. Diplomate Am. Bd. Osteo. Examiners. Intern Detroit Osto. Hosp., 1976-77; internal medicine resident Cleve. Clinic Found., 1977-80; infectios disease fellow Cleve. Clinic Found, 1981-83, med. oncology fellow, 1983-84, Roswell Park Meml. Inst., Buffalo, 1980-81; clin. assoc. primary care Cleve. Clinic Found, 1983-84; asst. prof. medicine Mich. State U., East Lansing, 1984-90, assoc. prof. medicine, 1990—, dir. HIV/AIDS.Hepatitis C Clinic, 2000—; dir. MSU Sparraw Hosp., 2008—; med. dir. Ingham County, Health DEpt HIV/Heapatitis Clinic, 2007. Rsch. instr. medicine, SUNY, Buffalo, 1980-81; instr. biology Cleve. State U., 1982-83; dir. med. edn. Lansing (Mich.) Gen. Hosp., 1987-92, assoc. dir. med. edn., 1992—. Author: Clinics of North America, 1983. Mem. Mich. State AIDS Task Force, Lansing, 1986, Mich. State Breast Cancer Task Force, 1986, Lansing area AIDS Network, 1988. Mem. AMA, Am. Osteo. Assn., Mich. Assn. Osteo. Physicians, Am. Microbiology Assn., Am. Fedn. Clin. Rsch., Am. Coll. Physicians, Infectious Disease Soc. Am., Am. Microbiology Assn., Am. Acad. HIV Medicine. Democrat. Roman Catholic. Avocations: weightlifting, swimming, walking, fishing. Home: 1839 Pine Knoll Dr Okemos MI 48864-3802 Office: Mich State U Coll Medicine Dept Internal Medicine B318 W Fee Hall East Lansing MI 48824-1315 Office Phone: 517-353-3211. Business E-Mail: gulick@msu.edu.

GULICK, WALTER LAWRENCE, psychologist, educator, retired academic administrator; b. Summit, NJ, July 4, 1927; s. Walter Lawrence and Carol (Dewey) G.; m. Winifred Bourn Frazee, Oct. 18, 1952; children: Hans, Tod, Kristina. AB, Hamilton Coll., Clinton, NY, 1952; MA, U. Del., 1955; PhD, Princeton U., 1957; MA (hon.), Dartmouth Coll., 1968; LHD (hon.), St. Lawrence U., 1989. Mem. faculty U. Del., 1957-65, prof. psychology, 1963-65, chmn. dept., 1964-65; prof. psychology Dartmouth Coll., Hanover, NH, 1965-74, chmn. dept., 1970-73, 74-75, Disting. Class of 1925 prof., 1973-75; dean of coll. Hamilton Coll., 1975-79, prof. psychology, 1975-81, William R. Kenan prof., 1979-81; pres. St. Lawrence U., 1981-87, Gulick Assocs., 1987—. Vis. prof. U. Vt., 1977; resident scholar U. Del., 1988-02; cons. Presbyn. Hosp., Phila., 1961-63; editl. cons. Oxford U. Press, 1963—, McGraw-Hill Pub. Co., 1966-67, Harper & Row, 1971-73, Cambridge U. Press, 1979—. Author: Hearing: Physiology and Psychophysics, 1971, Human Stereopsis: Psychophysical Analysis, 1976, Hearing: Physiological Acoustics, Neural Coding and Psychoacoustics, 1989, Dark Harbor: A Chesapeake Bay Mystery, 2009; contbr.: Ency. of Human Behavior, 1994; contbr. articles to profl. jours. Mem. Hanover Sch. Bd., 1972-75, Dresden Bd. Sch. Dirs., 1972-75; mem. grad. coun. Princeton U., 1972-75; mem. adv. coun. Nat. Inst. for Humanities, 1975-; mem. tchg. evaluation project HEW. Served with U.S. Merchant Marine, 1945-46 AUS, 1946-48. Recipient Nat. Svc. award 1955, 81, Dale prize Hamilton Coll., 1952, Alumnni Achievement medal, 1995; Theta Delta Chi fellow U. Del., 1953-55, Psychology scholar Princeton U., 1955-57. Mem. N.Y. Acad. Scis., Ea. Psychol. Assn., Psychonomic Soc., Phi Beta Kappa, Omicron Delta Kappa, Sigma Xi (pres. Dartmouth chpt. 1967-68, Gold Medal Lifetime Achievement award 1995), Psi Chi (pres. U. Del. chpt. 1954-55). Achievements include research in vision and hearing. Home: 347 Greenbriar Ln West Grove PA 19390 Personal E-mail: w.gulick@verizon.net.

GULKO, EDWARD, healthcare executive, consultant; b. Paterson, NJ, Nov. 22, 1950; s. Benjamin and Anita (Yankelevsky) G.; m. Judith Ilene Lee, May 29, 1977. BS in Indsl. Engring., N.J. Inst. Tech., 1972; MBA, Temple U., 1974. Cert. healthcare exec., med. practice exec.; lic. nursing home adminstr. Health program analyst Morrisania Hosp., Bronx, NY, 1974—75; assoc. dir. Mission Health Ctr., San Francisco, 1976; supervising sys. analyst Health and Hosp. Corp., NYC, 1977—78; dep. exec. dir. Greenpoint Hosp., Bklyn., 1978—82; assoc. exec. dir. Woodhull Med. Ctr., Bklyn., 1982—84; adminstr. Montclair Med. Group, NJ, 1984—87; asst. adminstr. Summit Med. Group, NJ, 1987—91; adminstr. Wooster Clinic, Inc., Ohio, 1991—96; COO Grove Hill Med. Ctr., New Britain, Conn., 1996—99; exec. dir. Old Bridge-Sayreville Med. Group, NJ, 1999—2002; adminstr. Digestive Healthcare Ctr. and Ctrl. Jersey Ambulatory Surgery Ctr., Hillsborough, NJ, 2002—03; exec. dir. Englewood Orthop. Assocs., NJ, 2003—. Trustee Society Hill Townhouse Assn., 1986-90, v.p., 1987-88, pres., 1988-89; bd. dirs. Residential Support Svcs., 1993-96, v.p. 1993-96. Lt. cmdr. Med. Svcs. Corps, USNR, 1982—2004 Fellow: Am. Coll. Healthcare Execs., Am. Coll. Med. Practice Execs.; mem.: NJ Med. Group Mgmt. Assn. (exec. bd. 2000—07, treas. 2003—04, v.p. 2004—05, pres. 2006—07), Am. Acad. Med. Adminstrs. (N.J. state dir. 2000—), Naval Res. Assn. (dist. v.p. 1987—91), Med. Group Mgmt. Assn. (nat. comm. com. 1993—95, jour. editl. bd. 2000—03, sec.-treas. orthop. practice assembly 2007—08, pres. 2008—09), Assn. Mil. Surgeons US (exec. com. N.J. chpt. 1985—87, pres. 1988—89). Democrat. Home: 230 Seton Hall Dr Freehold NJ 07728-8878 Office: 401 S Van Brunt St Englewood NJ Office Phone: 201-569-2770.

GULLO, STEPHEN PERNICE, psychologist, corporate executive; b. NYC; s. Anthony V. and Rose (Pernice) G. PhD Columbia U. Pres., chmn. bd. Inst. Health and Weight Scis., NYC, 1980—; co-dir. Family Bereavement Project Columbia U. Med. Sch., NYC. Asst. clin. prof. Columbia-Presbyn. Med. Ctr., 1980-96; chair Nat. Obesity and Weight Control Edn. Inst., Am. Inst. for Life-Threatening Illness, Columbia U., 1996-98; chair profl. adv. bd. Am. Inst. for Life Threatening Illness, Columbia-Presbyn. Med. Ctr., 1996-2000; mem. com. grants and profl. edn. NYC region Am. Cancer Soc., 1980-99; mem. sci. adv. com. Inst. Cancer Rsch.; co-chmn. Internat. Conf. Child and Health, Columbia-Presbyn. Med. Ctr., NYC, 1979; co-chair Nat. Obesity Symposium, Am. Inst. for Life Threatening Illness, Columbia U. Med. Ctr., 1994; expert witness City Coun. NY. Author: (with J. Schowalter et al) When People Die, 1978, The Child and Death, 1983, Education in Thanatology, 1984, Loveshock: How to Survive a Broken Heart and Love Again, 1988, Thin Tastes Better, 1995, (with T. Van Italie, A. Simopoulos and W. Futterweit) Obesity, 1995; cons. editor Jour. Thanatology, 1974-80, Archives Found. Thanatology, 1974—; chmn. editl. bd. Thanatology Abstract Series,

1974-76; cons. editor Advances in Thanatology, 1980-97; assoc. editor Loss, Grief & Care, 1990, Illness, Crises and Loss; contbg. editor: SELF, 1994-2002; contbr. articles and chpts. to med. textbooks. Vice chair ann. dinner Boys' Town of Jerusalem, 1981, assoc. chmn. ann. dinner Girls' Town Jerusalem, 1984; co-chmn. fundraising com. Found. Thanatology, 1982—; life hon. mem. Foss Found. Recipient gran croce al merito Accademia Italiana per lo Sviluppo Economico e Souale, Rome, 1985, Schoenberg award Am. Inst. for Life Threatening Illness, 1990; Knight Order St. John of Jerusalem, 1986; Patterson Found. fellow, 1972-73; NIH Rsch. grantee, 1973-75. Mem. NY Acad. Scis., Found. Thanatology (exec. bd., profl. adv. bd.), Columbia U. Coll. Physicians and Surgeons, Rolls Royce Owners Found. Office Phone: 212-734-7200.

GULMI, FREDERICK ANTHONY, hospital administrator; b. Bklyn., June 13, 1955; MD, U. Ctrl. Del Caribe, 1981. Chmn., residency program dir. Brookdale U. Hosp. and Med. Ctr., 1989—. Editl. rev. bd. mem. Jour. Urology, 2000—. Mem.: Am. Urologic Assn. (NY sect.) (Bklyn. rep. to bd. dirs. 2004—08, sec. 2008—11, sect. secs. membership coun. 2008—11, pres. elect. 2011—), Urologic Diagnostic and Therapeutic Intervention Com., Nat. Urology Ultrasound Faculty. Avocation: golf. Office: One Brookdale Plz Brooklyn NY 11212 Business E-Mail: fgulmi@brookdale.edu.

GULOTTA, STEPHEN J., cardiologist; b. Bklyn., Mar. 5, 1933; s. Vito and Dora Gulotta; m. Lee Scaringella Gulotta, June 27, 1954; 1 child, Stephen Gulotta Jr.; children: Ronald, Eric. BS in Chemistry, Bklyn. Coll., 1954; MD, SUNY, Bklyn., 1958. Diplomate Am. Bd. Internal Medicine with subspeciality in cardiovascular diseases. Med. intern Montefiore Hosp., Bronx, NY, 1958—59, resident in medicine, 1959—61; fellow in cardiology N.Y. Hosp. Cornell Med. Ctr., NYC, 1961—62; chief cardiology North Shore Univ. Hosp., Manhasset, NY, 1967—79; dir. catheterization labs. St. Francis Hosp., Roslyn, NY, 1979—2000. Mem. editl. bd. Circulation, Jour. Am. Coll. Cardiology, 1962—, Am. Jour. Cardiology, —; contbr. over 50 articles to profl. jours. Pres. Nassau Heart Assn., 1978—80, Am. Heart Assn., N.Y. Affiliate, 1981—83; bd. dirs. Commn. on Human Rights, Mt. Vernon, NY, 1964—70. Recipient Disting. Svc. award, Am. Heart Assn., 2000. Fellow: Am. heart Assn. Coun. of Clin. Cardiology, Am. Coll. Chest Physicians, Soc. Coronary Angiography and Interventions, Am. Coll. Cardiology, Am. Coll. Physicians. Avocations: skiing, collecting 20th Century American painters. Office Phone: 516-365-5599.

GÜLPINAR, MEHMET ALI, medical educator; b. Gaziantep, Turkey, Jan. 12, 1970; Postgrad in Physiology, Marmara U., Sch. Medicine, 2001; PhD, Yildiz Tech. U., Inst. Social Sci., 2007. Rsch. asst. dept. physiolgy Marmara U. Sch. Medicine, 1998—2001, vice dean, 2010; instr. Marmara U. Sch. Medicine, Dept. Med. Edn., 2001—10, assoc. prof., 2010—, head dept., 2010. Mem.: Assn. Med. Edn. Europe. Office: Marmara University Sch Medicine Istanbul 34668 Turkey E-mail: mali.gulpinar@gmail.com.

GULYA, AINA JULIANNA, otologist, neurotologist, skull base surgeon; b. Syracuse, NY, Feb. 3, 1953; d. Aladar and Sylvia E. Gulya; m. William R. Wilson, May 21, 1983. AB cum laude, Yale Coll., 1974; MD with distinction in rsch., U. Rochester, 1978. Diplomate Am. Bd. Otolaryngology. Intern, jr. resident in gen. surgery Beth Israel Hosp., Boston, 1978-80; resident in otolaryngology Mass. Eye and Ear Infirmary, Boston, 1980-83; fellow in otology/neurotology Bapt. Hosp. Ear Found., Nashville, 1983-84; asst. prof. surgery George Washington U., Washington, 1984-87, assoc. prof. surgery, 1987-90, clin. prof. surgery, otolaryngology, head and neck surgery, 1998—2005; assoc. prof. otolaryngology and head and neck surgery Georgetown U., Washington, 1990-94, prof., 1994-96; chief clin. trials br. Nat. Inst. on Deafness and other Comm. Disorders, Bethesda, Md., 1996-2000, chief clin. trials epidemiology biostats. sect., 2000—; ret., 2005; clin. trials project officer NIH. Assoc. examiner Am. Bd. Otolaryngology, 1993-97, bd. dirs., 1997-2002, oral exam. leader for otology, 2000-02, chair neurotology sub-specialty cert. com., 2000-02, cons. Nat. Inst. on Deafness and Other Comm. Disorders. Co-author: Anatomy of the Temporal Bone With Surgical Implications, 1986, 95, author, 2007; contbr. articles, to profl. jours., 2007; assoc. editor Am. Jour. Otology, 1989-99; co-editor Surgery of the Ear, 5th edit., 2002, 6th edit., 2009, sr. editor, 2010. Bd. dirs. Deafness Rsch. Found., 1994—2001. Recipient Libr. award, Rochester Acad. Medicine, 1975, presdl. citation, Am. Otol., Rhinol. and Laryngol. Soc., 1999. Mem.: Am. Acad. Otolaryngology, Head and Neck Surgery (bd. dirs. 1995—97, Honor award 1991, Disting. Svc. award 2001), Am. Neurotology Soc. (coord. for continuing med. edn. 1990—95), Am. Otological Soc. (coun. 1993—, editor-libr. 1995—2000, trustee rsch. fund 1993—2001, pres.-elect 1999—2000, pres. 2000—01). Avocation: water-skiing. Home: 111 Pleasant Grove Rd Locust Grove VA 22508

GUMMARAJU, SRINIVAS CHAKRAVARTHY, oncologist, hematologist; b. Hyderabad, India, July 2, 1967; came to U.S., 1993; s. H.P. Sundar Gummaraju and Subhadra Devi Vemaraju; m. Aruna, Jan. 23, 1997; children: Hala Chakravarthy. MB, BS, Osmania Med. Coll., India, 1989. Diplomate Am. Bd. Internal Medicine, Am. Bd. Hematology and Medical Oncology. Intern Osmania Gen. Hosp., India, 1990-91; physician Chakravarthy Clinics, India, 1991-93; resident Cook County Hosp., Chgo., 1993-96; fellow U. Calif., Davis, 1996—99; sr. cons. Apollo Hosps., India, 2000—03; asst. prof. U. Calif., Davis, 2003—. Chmn. Med. Care Rev. bd. Cook County Hosp., Chgo., 1994-96; organizer State Med. Exhbn. Osmania Med. Coll., 1988; chmn. cancer com. Fremont Rideout Health Group, 2004-05; cancer liaison physician ACS, 2003-05. Illustrator: Children's Book of Knowledge, 1986; contbr. poems to mags. Sec. Children's Universe, India, 1986-88; adult educator Govt. Aksharajyoti Movement, India, 1992; representative House Staff Assn. Cook County Hosp., Chgo., 1994-96. Recipient Spl. commendation Govt. India, 1990; in 99th percentile for Quality of Care By a Physician USA Wide Press-Ganey Survey, 2006. Mem. ACP, AMA (Physician Recognition award 1999), Am. Soc. Clin. Oncologists, Indian Med. Assn. (life). Avocations: rare book collecting, travel, languages, golf. Home: 3-4-491/1 Barkatpura Hyderabad 500027 India Personal E-mail: gummaraju02@sify.com.

GUMUDAVELLI, SRIDHAR, pharmacist, researcher; b. Warangal, Andhrapradesh, India, Feb. 26, 1967; arrived in U.S., 2002; s. Krishnamurthy and Annapoorna Gumudavelli; m. Padmasree Gunda, Feb. 11, 1996; children: Srinija children: Sricharan. M in Pharmacy, Kakatiya U., Warangal, 1992. Post Graduate In Packaging Technology Mumbai, India, 1999, Diploma In Export Management Bangalore, India, 1997. Prodn. mgr. Trident Pharmaceuticals Ltd., Hyderabad, India, 1992—95; dep. mgr. R&D Biological, Ltd., Hyderabad, 1995—99; mgr. R&D Cadilla Pharmaceuticals, Ahmedabad, Gujurat, India, 1999—2002; sr. mgr., head R&D Intas Pharmaceuticals Ltd., Ahmedabad, 2002—03; sr. mgr., head novel drug delivery systems Alembic Ltd., Vadodara, Gujurat, India, 2003—03; dir. tech. Capricorn Pharma Inc., Frederick, Md., 2003—05, Pharmaceutics Internat. Inc., Balt., 2005—. Prodn. cons. Adjuvant Pharmaceuticals, Hyderabad, 1994—. Author: (scientific journal) Sneezing Facts & Myths (Best Author award, 1986). Cmty. helper Warangal Youth, 1984—92. Mem.: Am. Assn. Pharm. Scientist. Achievements include patents for The Process For Manufacturing Of Clear Liquid Pharmaceutical Composition Of Azithromycin; patents pending for Site Specific Bioadherent Controlled Release Self Microemulsion Drug Delivery Composition; Pharmaceutical Zinc Acetate Dihydrate Rapid Mouth Disintegrating Mucoadherent Dosage Form Coposition And Process; Microosmosealed Controlled Drug Delivery Formulation & Process; A Process Of Preparaing Liquisolid Molecular Adsorption Compact Solid Dosage Forms Containing Loratidine; A process of preparing extended release osmo microsealed venelafaxine HCl; A Process Of Preparing Capsule Dosage Form Of Azithromycin Monohydrate; A process of preparing lozenges of bupropion HCl; A Process Of Preparing Sildenafil Citrate Trandermal Gel; A Process Preparing Of Azithromycin Microparticules By Evaporation Precipitation Method; A Process Preparing Of Antihistaminic Mucoadhesive Liquid; A Process Preparing Of Bupropion Chewing Gum. Office: Pharmaceutics Internat Inc Hunt Valley MD 21031 Home: 5 Spring Glen Ct Cockeysville MD 21030-2440 Personal E-mail: sricharan21@hotmail.com.

GUMUS, ILKNUR INEGOL, medical educator; b. Turkey, Apr. 2, 1973; MD, Istanbul U. Med. Sch., 1997. Asst. prof. Fatih U. Med. Sch., 2005—. Office: Ciftlik Cd 57 Ankara Emek 06510 Turkey Office Fax: 90 3122213672. Personal E-mail: ilknurinegol@yahoo.com.

GUNABUSHANAM, GOWTHAMAN, radiologist; s. Gunabushanam Narasimhan and Malarkodi Gunabushanam. MB, Jawaharlal Inst. Postgrad. Med. Edn. and Rsch., Pondicherry, India, 1996—2002; MD, All India Inst. Med. Sciences, New Delhi, 2005. Registered Tamil Nadu Med. Coun., India, 2002, diplomate Ednl. Commn. Fgn. Med. Graduates, US, 2006. Sr. resident BBR Hospitals, Hyderabad, India, 2005—07; fellow radiology Yale U. Sch. Medicine, New Heaven, 2007—09, prof., 2009—. Contbr. papers to profl. jours. and pubs. Grantee, Radiol. Soc. N.Am., Oak Brook, Ill., 2006. Fellow: Royal Coll. Radiologists. Achievements include patents for remote health management system; public health surveillance system. Office: Diagnostic Radiology Yale Univ 333 Cedar St PO Box 208042 New Haven CT 06520-8042

GUNASEKAR, PALUR G., toxicologist, director; b. Vellore, Tamil Nadu, India, Jan. 26, 1956; s. Palur G. Govindachari and Palur G. Ranganayaki; m. Bhagyalakshmi G. Palur; children: Palur G. Himaja, Palur G. Viswas. PhD, Madras U., India, 1987. Asst. prof. Tex. Southern U., Houston, 2004—07; tech. dir. NHRC Det-EHEL, WPAFB, Dayton, Ohio, 2007—. Scientist Operational Toxicology, WPAFB, Dayton, Ohio, 2001—03. Rsch. grant, Am. Parkinson Found. Assn., 2003, NIH, 2004, Office Naval Rsch., 2010, Traumatic Brain Injury & Prevention. Mem.: Soc. Reproductive Biology & Comparative Endocrinology, Soc. Neurosci., Soc. Toxicology. Home: 6638 Averell Dr Dayton OH 45424 Office: NHRC Det-EHEL 2729 R St Area B Bldg 837 WPAFB Dayton OH 45434 Office Fax: 937-904-9412. Business E-Mail: palur.gunasekar@wpafb.af.mil.

GUNBIN, KONSTANTIN, geneticist; b. Omutninsk, Kirov, Russia, June 9, 1980; MS, Udmurt State U., Izhevsk, Russia, 2002; PhD, Inst. Cytology and Genetics SB RAS, Novosibirsk, 2007. Staff rsch. scientist Inst. Cytology and Genetics SB RAS, Novosibirsk, 2005—. Office: Lavrentyev Ave Novosibirsk 630090 Russia Personal E-mail: genkvg@gmail.com.

GUNDAVARAM, PAWAN, oncologist; b. India, Aug. 21, 1979; BSc, Jawaharlal Nehru Med. Coll., MD, 2003. Med. resident Rush U., 2008; physician Resurrection Med. Ctr., Chgo., 2008—09, St James Med. Ctr., Ill., 2008—09, Dept. Hematology-Oncology, Montefiore Med. Ctr., Bronx, NY, 2009—. Non-exec. ind. dir. Kaveri Seed Co. Ltd., 2006—11. Mem.: Indian Med. Coun., AMA, ACP, Am. Soc. Hematology, Am. Soc. Clin. Oncology. Avocations: opera, motorcycling. Home: 175 E 96th St Apt 19C New York NY 10128 Home Fax: 773-527-2772. Business E-Mail: pgundava@montefiore.org.

GUNDERSON, CLARK ALAN, orthopedic surgeon; b. Watertown, SD, Aug. 27, 1948; s. Harvey Alfred and Eugenie (Tulson) G.; m. Robbie Gunderson; children: Ashley, Camille Student, U. Minn., 1966-69; BS, U. S.D., 1971; MD, Baylor Coll. of Medicine, 1973. Diplomate Am. Bd. of Orthopaedic Surgery, 1979. Intern in gen. surgery Charity Hosp., New Orleans, 1973-74, resident in orthopedic surgery, 1974-78; chief of surgery Lake Charles (La.) Meml. Hosp., 1980-83, 90-91, sec., treas. med. staff, 1983-87, pres. med. staff, 1992-93, also trustee, 90-94, chief of surgery, 1998-99; clin. assoc. prof. La. State U. Sch. of Medicine, New Orleans, 1987-90. Bd. dirs. Arthritic Found. La., 1987. Mem. AMA, ACS, Am. Acad. Orthopaedic Surgeons (bd. councilors 2002, com. on state com. 2002), La. Orthopaedic Assn. (pres. 1995-96), Calcasieu Parish Med. Soc., La. State Med. Soc., N.Am. Spine Assn., Mid Am. Orthopaedic Assn., La. Orthopaedic ASsn. (exec. com. 1993—), Lake Charles Country Club (pres. 1987-89), Clin. Orthopedic Rsch. Soc., Sigma Chi. Avocation: golf. Office: 2615 Enterprise Blvd Lake Charles LA 70601-7675 *

GUNEYI, UMIT AHMET, physician, consultant; b. Kirikkale, Turkey, Dec. 22, 1957; arrived in U.S., 1958; s. Selim S. and Muazzez A. Guneyi. BS in Molecular Biology, U. Hawaii, 1981; MD, U. Tech. Santiago, Santo Domingo, Dominican Republic, 1985; MS in Health Svcs. Adminstrn., U. St. Francis, 2003. Cert. terrorism tng. Reno Citizens Police Acad., 2005, Fed. Emergency Mgmt. Agy. cert. Nat. Incident Mgmt. Sys. Dept. Homeland Security, 2006. Surgeon Washoe Med. Ctr., Reno, 1990—91; dep. coroner Washoe County Coroners Office, Reno, 1991; chief instr. med. terminology Truckee Meadows C.C., Reno, 1994—2000; ind. rschr. dept. biomed. engring. U. Nev., Reno, 2000—06; lectr. Associated Counter-Threat Edn. Specialists, Reno, 2003—, cons. bio-terrorism, 2003—; exec. med. dir. Wellness Ctr. at Progreso Latino, Inc., Central Falls, RI, 2006—; mem. bd. dirs. STEP-1 Inc., 2008—; mem. bd. dirs., dir. USAN Western Region, 2009—; pres. CEO First Health Care Strategies Group, 2009—; pres. chmn. bd. NVTAA, 2008—. Adv. Helping Angels Home Healthcare Svcs., Sparks, Nev., 2002—03; founder, CEO Gulee Enterprises, Reno-Sparks, 1994—98; exec. v.p. med. svcs. Homeland Security Def. Coalition, Rochester, NY; mem. hwy. watch Dept. of Homeland Security, 2006—; mem. nutrition adv. com. U. RI, 2006—; mem. adv. com. RI Dept. Health, 2006—; mem. RI Homeland Security Cmty. Coun. Work Group, 2006—. Author numerous TV Show. Active Dept. Homeland Security Hwy. Watch, 2006; mem. Nev. Washoe County Citizen Homeland Security Coun., 2003—, Nev. Washoe County Cmty. Emergency Response Team, 2004—, Truckee Meadows Police Acad. Citizens; lobbyist, co-dir. com. establish state P.A. program Carson City, Nev., 2002—; del. convs. Rep. Party, Nev., 1996, 2000, rep. presdl. task force, poitl. cons. Washington, 1996—, rep. nat. senatorial com., 1996—. Scholar, Pacific Health Rsch. Inst., 1978. Fellow: Am. Coll. Internat. Physicians; mem.: Am. Fedn. Tchrs., Assn. For Intelligence Officers, Reno Citizens Inst., Am. Acad. Family Physicians, Am. Coll. Emergency Physicians, Planetary Soc. Republican. Achievements include research in designing artificial pancreas; design of proto-type for artificial pancreas. Avocations: astronomy, parapsychology, coin collecting/numismatics, stamp collecting/philately, antiques. Home: 3025 Socrates Dr Reno NV 89512 Office Phone: 401-728-5920 ext. 320, 775-813-6442, 775-772-9705. Personal E-mail: uguneyi@sbcglobal.net. Business E-Mail: bguneyi@progresolatino.org.

GUNGOR UGURLUCAN, FUNDA, obstetrician, gynecologist, educator; b. Edirne, Turkey, Oct. 14, 1977; MD, Istanbul U., 2001. Ob-gyn. resident Istanbul U., 2006, specialist, med. faculty, dept. ob-gyn., 2008—. Office: Istanbul Tip Fakultesi Kadin Dogum Mill Istanbul Fatih 34810 Turkey

GUNN, ALBERT EDWARD, JR., internist, health facility administrator, lawyer, educator; b. Port Washington, NY, Oct. 31, 1933; s. Albert Edward and Esther Frances (Williams) G.; m. Joan Marie Jacoby, May 18, 1968; children: Albert Edward III, Emily Williams Gunn, Andrew Robert, Clare Margaret Gunn Berchelmann, Catherine Ann, Philip David. BS, Fordham Coll., 1955, LLB, 1958; MB BCh BAO, Nat. U. Ireland, Galway, 1967. Bar: NY 1958, US Ct. Mil. Appeals 1959, DC 1972, US Supreme Ct. 1972, US Ct. Appeals (DC cir.) 1972; diplomate Am. Bd Internal Medicine, lic. physician Pa., NY, Va., Tex., Eng., Wales. Owner, agt. Albert E. Gunn Ins. Agy., Port Washington, 1953-65; 2nd lt. USAF, 1955, active to 1st lt., 1958—61, SAC served in res., 1961—75, capt., 1962; intern Montefiore Hosp., NYC, 1967-68; resident in medicine Roosevelt Hosp., NYC, 1968-70; USPHS trainee in neurology U. Rochester, NY, 1970-72; asst. dir. govtl. rels. AMA, Washington, 1972-74; med. dir. Geriat. Svcs. Suffolk County, Hauppauge, NY, 1974-75, Rehab. Ctr., U. Tex./M.D. Anderson Cancer Ctr., 1975-88, chief rehab. sect., 1988-93, chief geriat. sect., 1993-2000, dep. chmn. dept. internal med. spltys., 1998-2000; prof. mgmt. and policy scis. U. Tex. Houston Sch. Pub. Health, 2001—. Asst. prof. medicine U. Tex. Med. Sch., Houston, 1976-80, assoc. prof., 1980-2000, prof., 2000-08, assoc. dean for admissions, 1979-2006, spl. adv. to the President, 2006-08; med. dir. Region IV, Tex. Med. Found., 1986-93; del.-at-large White House conf. on Handicapped Individuals, 1977; pres. Mus. Med. Sci., 1990; cons. CDC, Legal Svcs. Corp., Nat. Libr. Medicine. Co-author: Rehabilitation of the Cancer Patient, 1976, AIDS in Africa, 1988; editor, contbg. author: Cancer Rehabilitation, 1984; mem. editl. bd. Cancer Bull., 1977-90, Gerontology and Geriatrics Edn., 1984-2003, Linacre Quar.; contbr. articles to profl. jours Pres. Cath. Evidence Guild, Fordham, NY, 1953-54; mem. nat. adv. health coun. HEW, 1974-75; mem. adv. com. Nat. Inst. Law Enforcement and Criminal Justice, Law Enforcement Assistance Adminstrn., U.S. Dept. Justice, 1974-76; mem. bd. regents Nat. Libr. Medicine, NIH, 1983-87, chmn., 1986-87, chmn. lit. selection tech. adv. com., 1988-91; bd. dirs. Right to Life Advs., 1977-78, Tex. Med. Ctr. Libr., 1990. Mem. Tex. Med. Assn. (hon. mem. 2010-, trustee ins. trust, chmn. bd. trustees 1997-2000), Harris County Med. Soc. (hon. mem. 2010-, exec. bd. 1986-90, v.p. 1998), Royal Coll. Physicians London (licentiate), Royal Coll. Surgeons Eng., Houston Acad. Medicine (bd. dirs. 1986-90, pres. 1990), Houston Bar Assn. (50 Yr. Svc. award 2008), DC Bar, Cath. Med. Assn. (regional bd. dirs. 1992—, Thomas Linacre award 1997), NRA (life), Res. Officers Assn. (life), Am. Legion (life), KC, Army and Navy Club, Cosmos Club, Petroleum Club Houston, Fellowship Cath. Scholars. Home and Office: 3514 Glen Haven Blvd Houston TX 77025-1306

GUNN, JOAN MARIE, health facility administrator; b. Binghamton, NY, Jan. 29, 1943; d. Andrew and Ruth Antoinette (Butler) Jacoby; m. Albert E. Gunn Jr., May 18, 1968; children: Albert E. III, Emily Williams Gunn, Andrew R., Clare M. Berchelmann, Catherine A.B., Philip D. Diploma, Binghamton State Hosp., 1966; BS summa cum laude, Tex. Women's U., 1983; MSN, U. Tex., Houston, 1989. RN, NY, Tex., Va. Staff nurse Columbia/Presbyn. Med. Ctr., NYC, 1966-67; head nurse, ICU Montefiore Hosp. and Med. Ctr., NYC, 1967-68; staff nurse Nat. Orthopedic and Rehab. Hosp., Arlington, Va., 1972-73, Woman's Hosp. of Tex., Houston, 1976-80; staff nurse geriatrics St. Anthony's Ctr., Houston, 1985-86; charge nurse gero psychiatry Bellaire Gen. Hosp., Houston, 1986; from head nurse gero psychiat. unit to dir. patient svcs. Harris County Psychiat. Ctr. U. Tex., Houston, 1986—2001, dir. patient svs. Harris County Psychiat. Ctr., 2001—07. Mem. NRA, Nat. Soc. Colonial Dames of the XVII Century, Daus. of Union Vets. of Civil War. Roman Catholic. Avocation: reading history. Home: 3514 Glen Haven Blvd Houston TX 77025-1306

GUNNARSSON MÉRIAUX, BENITA EVY CAROLA, school nurse practitioner, educator; b. Katrineholm, Södermanlands län, Sweden, Dec. 2, 1965; d. Evert Bror Pettersson and Yvonne Evy Viola Håkansson, Bo Ingvar Håkansson (Stepfather); m. Anton Håkan Mériaux; 1 child, Lina Evy Sofie Mériaux Gunnarsson. MSc in MSN and Health scis., Sch. Health Scis., U. Coll. Borås, 2001. RN Swedish Nat. Bd. Health and Welfare., 1998. Coordinating sch. nurse Sch. Health Svcs., Vingåker, Södermanlands Län, Sweden, 1998—2000, sch. nurse Mölndal and Göteborg, Västra Götalandsregionen, Sweden, 2000—04. Contbr. articles to profl. jours. Achievements include development of treatments of children in the health promotion and prevention work against obesity in school health services; intervention research in dementia care, development of non-pharmacological treatment method; research in children with obesity.

GUNTER, JACK PERSHING, plastic surgeon, otolaryngologist; b. Ft. Smith, Ark., Oct. 7, 1937; s. Jack and Charlene Gunter; m. Deborah Dawson, Mar. 21, 1992; children: Ashley, Page, Courtney. BA, Westminster Coll., Fulton, Mo., 1959; MD, U. Okla., Oklahoma

City, 1963; postgrad. in Facial Plastic and Reconstructive Surgery, Mercy Hosp., Pitts., 1968-69. Diplomate Am. Bd. Otolaryngology, Am. Bd. Plastic Surgery. Intern U. Ark. Med. Ctr., 1963-64, resident in gen. surgery, 1964-65; resident in otolaryngology Tulane U. Eye, Ear, Nose & Throat Hosp., New Orleans, 1965-68; NIH fellow in facial, plastic and reconstructive surgery Mercy Hosp., Pitts., 1968-69; assoc. prof. otolaryngology U. Tex. Health Sci. Ctr., Dallas, 1969-76, chmn. divsn. otolaryngology, 1971-74, clin. assoc. prof. otolaryngology, 1976-91; resident in plastic surgery U. Mich. Hosp., Ann Arbor, 1978-80; clin. prof. otolaryngology U. Tex. Health Sci. Ctr., Dallas, 1991—; clin. asst. prof. plastic surgery U. Tex. Southwestern Med. Sch., Dallas, 1980-86, clin. assoc. prof., 1986-91, clin. prof., 1991—; pvt. practice Dallas, 1981—. Guest lectr. in field; founder, chmn. Dallas Rhinoplasty Symposium. Co-editor, pub. Dallas Rhinoplasty: Surgery by the Masters, 2nd edit. Recipient Westminster Coll. Alumni Achievement award, 1990; named to Best Doctors in America, 1993—. Fellow ACS; mem. Am. Soc. Plastic and Reconstructive Surgery (Aesthetic award for video tape of Primary Rhinoplasty via the Open Approach, 1993), Am. Soc. Plastic Surgeons (President's award, 2004), Am. Assn. Plastic Surgeons, Am. Soc. for Aesthetic Plastic Surgery (Tiffany award for best paper, 1989), Am. Acad. Facial Plastic and Reconstructive Surgery, Am. Acad. Facial Plastic and Reconstructive Surgery, Am. Acad. Otolaryngology, AMA, Dallas County Med. Soc., Tex. Med. Assn., Tex. Soc. Plastic Surgeons, Rhinoplasty Soc., Inc. (founding mem. 1996). Avocation: golf. Office: 8144 Walnut Hill Ln Ste 170 Dallas TX 75231 Office Phone: 214-369-8123. Office Fax: 214-369-2984. Business E-Mail: drgunter@gunter-center.com, info@gunter-center.com.

GUNTHEROTH, WARREN GADEN, pediatrician, cardiologist, educator; b. Hominy, Okla., July 27, 1927; s. Harry William and Callie (Cornett) G.; m. Ethel Haglund, July 3, 1954(dec. 2007); children: Kurt, Karl, Sten; m. Sally Comish, Nov. 28, 2009. Attended, Harvard Coll., 1945—51; MD, Harvard U., 1952. Diplomate: Am. Bd. Pediatrics, Am. Bd. Pediatric Cardiology, Nat. Bd. Med. Examiners. Intern Peter Bent Brigham Hosp., Boston, 1952-53; fellow in cardiology Children's Hosp., Boston, 1953-55, resident in pediatrics, 1955-56; rsch. fellow physiology and biophysics U. Wash. Med. Sch., Seattle, 1957-58, mem. faculty, 1958—, prof. pediatrics, 1969—, head divsn. pediatric cardiology, 1964-91. Author: Pediatric Electrocardiography, 1965, How to Read Pediatric ECGs, 1981, 4th edit., 2006, Crib Death (Sudden Infant Death Syndrome), 1982, 3d edit., 1995, Climbing With Sasha, a Washington Husky, 1995, Paradise Found and Lost, 2009, My Life Loves and Battles, 2010; also more than 330 articles; mem. editl. bd. Am. Heart Jour., 1977-80, Circulation, 1980-83, Am. Jour. Noninvasive Cardiology, 1985-94, Jour. Am. Coll. Cardiology, 1988-94, Am. Jour. Cardiology, 1977 ; sect. editor Practice of Pediatrics, 1979-87, Pediatric Cardiology, 2004-07. Served with USPHS, 1950-51. Spl. research fellow NIH, 1967. Mem. Soc. Pediatric Rsch., Biomed. Engring. Soc. (charter), Am. Heart Assn. (chmn. N.W. regional med. rsch. adv. com. 1978-80), Cardiovascular System Dynamics Soc. (charter), Am. Coll. Cardiology. Democrat. Home: 13201 42nd Ave NE Seattle WA 98125-4626 Office: U Wash Med Sch Dept Pediatrics PO Box 356320 Seattle WA 98195-6320 Office Phone: 206-543-3186. Business E-Mail: wgg@uw.edu.

GUNVEN, PETER MAGNI, surgical oncologist; b. Karlsborg, Sweden, Sept. 9, 1944; s. Magni and Greta (Karlsson) G.; m. Siri Leithoff, May 25, 1973; children: Louise, Asa, Jakob. MD, DSc, Karolinska Inst., Stockholm, 1974. Docent in tumor biology Karolinska Inst., Stockholm, 1975, surgeon, 1975-80, Sabbatsberg City Hosp., 1980-89; docent in surgery Karolinska Inst., Stockholm, 1987; acad. tchr. surgery Karolinska U. Hosp., Stockholm, 1989-96, sr. surgeon, 1996—2000, oncologist, 2000—; vis. prof. liver and stomach cancer surgery Nat. Cancer Ctr. Hosp. and Nat. Matsudo Hosp., Tokyo, 1985-91. Chmn. Stockholm Regional Group Gastric Cancer, 1995—2007, Nat. Group Cancer Unknown Primary, 2007—; mem. Bd. Health Tech. Assessment, Stockholm County Coun. Contbr. over 80 articles to profl. jours. and chpts. to textbooks. Lt. Med. Corps, 1991. Recipient Silver medal Swedish Army Vol. Officers' Tng., 1991, Gold medal Assn. Cavalry and Commando Officers of the Swedish Army, 1993. Mem. Swedish Cancer Soc. (sec. sci. bd. 1974-87), Acad. Lancisiana (Rome, hon.). Office: Karolinska U Hosp Radiumhemmet Dept of Oncology SE-17176 Stockholm Sweden E-mail: peter.gunven@karolinska.se.

GUO, FENG-BIAO, biology professor; b. HeNan, China, Oct. 5, 1979; PhD, TianJin U., 2006. Assoc. prof. U. Electronic Sci. and Tech. China, 2008—. Reviewer Jour. Theoretical Biology Bio-Sys. JBSD, 2009. Grant, NSFC. Mem.: AAAS, Internat. Soc. Computational Biology. Office: 4 Sect 2 North Jianshe Rd ChengDu SiChuan 610054 China

GUO, HOW-RAN, physician, educator; MD, Taipei Med. Coll., 1981—88; MPH, Harvard U., Boston, 1988—89, MS, 1989—90, DSc, 1989—94. Lic. doctor Dept. Health, Taiwan, ROC, 1989, cert. diagnosis and treatment of occupl. diseases 1997, spl. bd. occupl. medicine 2002. Epidemic Intelligence Svc. officer Nat. Inst. Occupl. Safety & Health Ctrs. Disease Control & Prevention, Cin., 1992—94; asst. prof. U. Cin., 1995—96; assoc. prof. Nat. Cheng Kung U., Tainan, Taiwan, 1996—2002, prof. occupl. and environ. medicine, 2003—. Recipient Best Spkr. award, Taipei Med. Coll., 1988, Spl. Act or Svc. award, Dept. Health and Human Svcs., 1994, Rschr. award, Nat. Sci. Coun., Taiwan, 1996—98; grantee Travel Grant award, The 15th Internat. Sci. Meeting Internat. Epidemiol. Assn., 1999. Mem.: Internat. Assn. Radiopathology, Asian Assn. Occupl. Health (sec. gen. 2000—02, first v.p. 2003—05), Taiwan Pub. Health Assn., Taiwan Epidemiology Assn. (coun. mem. 2002—), Taiwan Environ. & Occupl. Medicine Assn. (sec. gen. 2000—04, exec. coun. mem. 2004—08, pres. 2008—), Internat. Soc. Environ. Epidemiology (East Asia chpt. chair 2005—), Am. Coll. Occupl. & Environ. Medicine, Taiwan Occupl. Health Assn. (life), Soc. Environ. Geochemistry & Health (life). Office: Nat Cheng Kung Univ 138 Sheng-Li Rd Tainan 70428 Taiwan

GUO, WEI, orthopedist, educator; b. Qingdao, Shandong, China, Feb. 6, 1958; MD, Qingdao Med. Coll., 1984; MS, Zhongshan Med. U., Guangdong, China, 1989; PhD, Beijing Med. U., 1993. Resident Qingdao Med. Coll., 1984—90; asst. attending People's Hosp., Beijing, 1990—95, assoc. attending, 1995—2000, attending, 2000—, chief orthop. oncology, 2001—. Fellow Meml. Sloan-Kettering Cancer Ctr., NYC, 1996—98; prof. People's Hosp., 2001—. Contbr. articles to profl. jours. Mem.: Asia Pacific Orthop. Soc., Chinese Orthop. Soc., Internat. Soc. Limb Salvage. Achievements include research in mechanism of methotrexate resistance in osteosarcoma; development of new adjurant chemotherapy in osteosarcoma and Ewingsarcoma into China; new techniques for reconstruction of pelvic ring after resection of pelvis and sacrum tumors. Office: Dept Orthop Surgery 100044 Beijing China Business E-Mail: bonetumor@sohn.com.

GUO-QING, ZHENG, neurologist, educator; b. China, Apr. 5, 1975; PhD, Guangzhou U. Chinese Medicine, MD, 2004, Tianjin Med. U., China, PhD, 2010. Resident physician, dept. neurology Guangdong Provincial Hosp. TCM, China, 2001—03; sr. rsch. coord. Sch. Chinese Medicine Li Ka Shing Faculty Medicine U. Hong Kong, 2009—10; assoc. prof. Ctr. Neurology 2nd Affiliated Hosp. Wenzhou Med. Coll., Wenzhou, China, 2004—. Res. leader, subject Integrated Medicine Key Dept. Cerebrovascular Disease Zhejiang Provincial Adminstrn. TCM, 2005—; young and mid. aged academic leader Wenzhou Med. Coll., 2008—; mng. editl. bd. mem. Frontiers in Biosci., 2009—. Recipient 3rd award, Med. Sci. and Tech. Zhejiang Province, 2010, 3rd Sci. and Tech. award, Traditional Chinese Medicine Zhejiang Province, 2010. Mem.: China Elder Health Care Assn., Brain Health Care (profl. academic com.), China Assn. Chinese Medicine (profl. com. encephalopathy, profl. com. thrombosis, 3rd Sci. and Tech. award 2008), Dr. Soc. Integrative Medicine Chinese MD Assn. (profl. com. neurology), Chinese Assn. Integrative Medicine (profl. com. neurology). Office: 109 Xueyuan W Rd Wenzhou Zhejiang 325027 China Office Fax: 86-577-88832693. E-mail: gq_zheng@sohu.com.

GUOYONG, HU, physician; b. Hubei Province, China, Sept. 29, 1977; MD, PhD, Shanghai Jiaotong U., 2010. Resident Yangzhou No.1 People's Hosp., 2003—07; attending physician Shanghai Tenth People's Hosp., Tongji U. Sch. Medicine, 2010—. Office: 301 Yanchang Rd Shanghai 200072 China E-mail: huguoyongyz@yahoo.com.cn.

GUPTA, ABHAY, plastic and reconstructive surgeon, medical educator; b. Glasgow, Scotland, Dec. 10, 1970; arrived in U.S., 1999; s. Daya Krishna and Chander Kanta Gupta. MD, U. We. Ont., Can., 1994. Diplomate Am. Bd. Plastic and Reconstructive Surgery, Royal Coll. Physicians and Surgeons Can. Resident surgeon dept. plastic and reconstructive surgery U. We. Ont., London, Canada, 1994—98, chief resident dept. plastic and reconstructive surgery, 1998—99; jr. faculty assoc. U. Tex. M.D. Anderson Cancer Ctr., Houston, 1999—2000; assoc. staff dept. plastic surgery Cleve. Clinic Fla., Ft. Lauderdale, 2000—01; asst. prof. dept. surgery, chief reconstructive microsurgery U. Tex. Health Sci. Ctr., San Antonio, 2001—04; voluntary clin. asst. prof., dept. surgery U. Calif., San Diego Med. Sch., 2004—; active staff, dept. plastic surgery Sharp Meml. Hosp., San Diego, 2004—, Sharp Mary Birch Hosp., San Diego, 2004—, TriCity Med. Ctr., Oceanside, Calif., 2004—, Pomerado Hosp., Poway, Calif., 2004—, Scripps Meml. Hosp., La Jolla, Calif., 2004—, Encinitas, 2004—, Inland Valley Regional Med. Ctr., Wildomar, Calif., 2007—, Rancho Springs Med. Ctr., 2007—, U. Health Sys., San Antonio, 2001—04, Christus Santa Rosa NW Hosp., San Antonio, 2001—04, Christus Santa Rosa Childrens Hosp., San Antonio, 2001—04, Audie L. Murphy Meml. Va. Hosp., San Antonio, 2001—04, Meth. Hosp., San Antonio, 2001—04, Bapt. Health Sys., San Antonio, 2002—04. Chief resident dept. plastic and reconstructive surgery U. We. Ont., London, 1998—99; chief adminstrv. fellow dept. plastic and reconstructive surgery U. Tex. M.D. Anderson Cancer Ctr., Houston, 1999—2000; asst. dir. postgrad. resident edn. div. plastic surgery U. Tex. Health Sci. Ctr., San Antonio, 2001—04; med. dir. Gupta Plastic Surgery, San Diego, 2008—. Author: (books) The Unfavorable Results in Plastic Surgery. Avoidance and Treatment, 3rd edit., 2001; contbr. articles to profl. jours. Active Hindu Soc. San Antonio, 2001. Recipient Can. Scholarship award, Govt. Can., 1988—90. Fellow: ACS, Royal Coll. Physicians and Surgeons Can.; mem.: AMA, Calif. Soc. Plastic Surgeons, Am. Soc. Reconstructive Microsurgery, Can. Med. Assn., Internat. Soc. Plastic Surgeons, Tex. Med. Assn., Tex. Soc. Plastic Surgeons, Can. Soc. Plastic Surgeons, Am. Soc. Plastic Surgeons. Avocations: golf, tennis, running, scuba diving. Office Phone: 858-621-6000. Office Fax: 858-621-6340.

GUPTA, AMIT, plastic surgeon; MBBS with honours, Maulana Azad Med. Coll., India, 1994—99, CM in Gen. Surgery, 2003. Fellowship with Dr. Ruth Graf, Curitiba, Brazil; fellowship with Dr. Ana Zulmira Centro Medico Athena, Brazil; with Dr. Milton Daniel Curitiba, Brazil; with Dr. Julio Fernandis; with Dr. Manuel Athayade; with Dr. Sirlei Costa Porto Alegre, Brazil; with Dr. Carlos Uebel Uebel Clinic, Porto Alegre, Brazil, 1986; with Dr. Patrick Tonnard Belgium; cons. plastic & cosmetic surgeon Divince Cosmetic Surgery, New Delhi. Recipient Best All Around Med. Grad., Lt. Governor's Trophy, 1999, Best Contbr. to Corp. Life of Coll., Dr. KB Sharma. Achievements include first Plastic Surgeon in Delhi, Gurgaon, Noida offering VASER, short scar Face lift, Breast Lift, Tummy tuck etc. Office: Divine Cosmetic Surgery L-7 GF South Ext Part II New Delhi 110049 India Personal E-mail: guptamit76@gmail.com. *

GUPTA, ANOOP KUMAR, cardiologist; b. Gandhidham, Kutch, India, June 21, 1967; s. Arvind K. and Rekha Gupta; m. Sharmishtha Sengupta, Dec. 2, 2000. MBBS, JLN Med. Coll., Ajmer, Rajasthan, India, 1991; MD, U. Rajasthan, 1995; DM in Cardiology, U. Mumbai, 1999. Resident in internal medicine SMS Med. Coll., Jaipur, Rajasthan, India, 1992—95; fellow in cardiology KEM Hosp., Mumbai, 1996—99, asst. prof. cardiology, 1999—2000; fellow in electrophysiology Mich. State U., East Lansing, 2000—01; cons. electrophysiologist Krishna Heart Inst., Ahmedabad, Gujarat, India, 2002—03; cons. cardiologist and electrophysiologist Apollo Hosp., Ahmedabad, Gujarat, India, 2003—. Dir. electrophysiology Apollo Hosp., Ahmedabad, Gujarat, India, 2003—, Krishna Heart Inst., Ahmedabad, Gujarat, India, 2002—03. Assoc. editor: Indian Pacing Electrophysiology Jour., 2002, mem. editl. bd.: Indian Heart Jour., 2003—; contbr. articles. Recipient Gold medal, JLN Med. Coll. Ajmer, 1991, Internat. Excellence in Cardiology award, UNO, 2003. Fellow: Am. Coll. Cardiology (life); mem.: Indian Med. Assn. (life). Office: Apollo Hosp 1A Bhat GIDC Estate Gandhinagar 382428 India Personal E-mail: anoopgupta@msn.com.

GUPTA, ARUN KUMAR, ophthalmologist, consultant; s. Madan Sarup and Indra Wati Gupta; m. Divya Bansal Gupta, Mar. 8, 1985; children: Ankur, Monica. MBBS, All India Inst. Med. Sci., 1978, MD, 1981. Resident to sr. resident All India Inst. Med. Sci., New Delhi, 1979—85; cons. Bukenial Gen. Hosp., Saudi Arabia, 1986—89; with Regional Hosp., Waterford, Ireland, 1991—92, registrar, 1992—94; sr. registrar Aberdeen Royal Infirmary, Scotland, 1994—95; cons. Ashford Hosp., West Middlesex U. Hosp., 1995—. Contbr. articles to profl. jours. Mem.: Am. Acad. Soc. Cataracts and Refractive Surgery, Am. Acad. Ophtholmology, Royal Coll. Ophtholmologists, Royal Coll. Surgeons. Avocations: photography, swimming. Home: 86 the Ave Middlesex Sunbury-on-Thames TW16 5EX England Office: Ashford Hosp London Rd Middlesex Isleworth TW15 3AA England Fax: 01784-884640. Personal E-mail: a.gupta44@gmail.com.

GUPTA, ASHOK K., biology professor; b. Jammu, Sept. 18, 1953; BSc in Med. Tech., PGI, Chandigarh, 1973; PhD in Microbiology, Nat. Inst. Virology, Pune U., 1987. Prof., 1981—; rsch. officer, sr. rsch. officer, microbiologist & asst. dir. Nat. Inst. of Virology, Pune, 1981—2003; microbiologist Ibn-Sena Hosp., SIRT, LIBYA,Fgn. Assignment Govt. India Permission, 1992—97; assoc. prof. microbiology Rural Med. Coll., PIMS, Loni, 2004—06, prof. microbiology, 2006. Prof., mem. bd. studies, core com. mem. rntcp, i/c bw manage't & inf'n control, resource person on je, panel examiners, reviewers RMC, NICD, ICMR, UGC & IJMR, Virus Rsch. Vaccine, 1990. Recipient Young Scientist award, Indian Soc. Parasitology. Mem.: Soc. Scientists Exptl. Animals, IIS, NIV Res. Found., BSI, IAMM, IVS, Indian Soc. Parasitology. Avocations: reading, travel. Office: Microbiology Dept Rural Med Coll PIMS, Loni Maharashtra 413736 India Office Fax: 91-2422-273413. Business E-Mail: drashok.gpt@gmail.com.

GUPTA, MADAN LAL, cardiologist; b. New Delhi, Dec. 25, 1938; came to U.S., 1969; MD, Rajasthan U., Jaipur, India, 1961. Diplomate Am. Bd. Internal Medicine, Am. Bd. Cardiovasc. Disease. Resident internal medicine Flushing Hosp., NYC, 1969-70, Brooklyn VA Hosp., NYC, 1971-72; resident cardiology Grasslands Hosp., Valhalla, N.Y., 1970-71; fellow cardiology Maimonides Med. Ctr., NYC, 1972-73; staff St. Marys Hosp., Galesburg, Ill., 1973—, Galesburg Clinic, 1973—. Fellow ACP, Am. Coll. Cardiology. Office: Galesburg Clinic 3315 N Seminary St Galesburg IL 61401-1224 Office Phone: 309-344-1000. *

GUPTA, MANISH, oncologist, educator; b. Dagshai, Solan, June 5, 1973; MBBS, IGMC Shimla, 1997, MD in Radiation Oncology, 2006. Asst. prof., dept. radiation oncology RCC Shimla, 2003. Mem.: IAPC, AROI (fellowship). Avocations: reading, travel. Office: Dept Radiotherapy IGMC Shimla RCC Shimla Himachal Pradesh 171001 India E-mail: mg9122@rediffmail.com.

GUPTA, MONESHA, pediatrician, educator; arrived in U.S., 1993; d. Surendranath Kedarnath and Vijayalaxmi Gupta; m. Sanjay Malhotra, June 29, 2001. MBBS, Grant Med. Coll., Bombay, 1989. Diplomate in pediatrics and in pediatric cardiology Am. Bd. Pediatrics. Clin. instr. Mich. State U., Flint, 1993—96; pediatric cardiologist NY Presbyn. Hosp., NYC, 1996—99, U. Tex., Houston, 2002—. Cons. pediatric cardiologist U. Minn., Mpls., 2000—02, U. Tex., 2002—; adj. faculty Rockefeller U., NYC, 2001—02. Contbr. articles to profl. jours. Treas. Sci. of Spirituality, Naperville, Ill., 1989. Med. officer Signals Rgt. Indian Army, 1989—90. Fellow: Am. Coll. Cardiology, Am. Acad. Pediat. Avocations: painting, travel, volleyball. Office: Univ Tex Med Sch Houston Divsn Pediat Cardiology 6410 Fannin St UTPB Ste 425 Houston TX 77030 Home Phone: 713-436-9683; Office Phone: 713-500-5743. Business E-Mail: monesha.gupta@uth.tmc.edu.

GUPTA, NALINA, physical therapist, educator; b. Jammu, Jammu and Kashmir, India, Apr. 6, 1979; d. Shakti and Kamla Gupta; m. Sameer Singh. BS in Physiotherapy, Manipal U., 2003, MS in Physiotherapy, Neuroscis., 2006. Lectr. Sardar Bhagwan Singh Postgrad. Inst. Biomed. Sci. and Rsch., Dehradun, India, 2006—09; sr. lectr. Coll. Applied Edn. and Health Sci., Meerut, India, 2009—10, head, dept. physiotherapy, 2010—. Contbr. articles to profl. jours. & publs. GSE team mem. Rotary Internat., RI Dist., Italy, 2008. Recipient Shobha Alva Meml. Gold medal, Karnataka, 2003. Mem.: Internat. Spinal Cord Soc., SCIPT, Indian Fedn. Neuro-Rehab., Indian Assn. Physiotherapist, Spinal Cord Soc. (Indian chpt.). Avocations: music, cooking, travel. Office: Coll Applied Education and Health Sci Gangotri Roorkee Rd Meerut Uttar Pradesh 250001 India Personal E-mail: nals235@yahoo.co.in.

GUPTA, NEERU, ophthalmologist, educator; b. Oct. 14, 1962; MD, U. Manitoba, Winnipeg, 1986; PhD in Experimental Pathology, U. BC, Vancouver, Can. Diplomate Am. Bd. Ophthalmology. Ophthalmology resident U. Toronto, fellow ophthalmic pathology; glaucoma fellowship U. Calif., San Diego; prof. ophthalmology & vision scis. and lab. medicine & pathobiology U. Toronto. Dir. glaucoma & nerve protection unit St. Michael's Hosp., Toronto. Editor vision sci. sect. Can. Jour. Ophthalmology, mem. editl. bd. Internat. Glaucoma Rev., Jour. Eye & Brain; contbr. articles to profl. jours. Sci. adv. bd. mem. Glaucoma Found. Fellow: Royal Coll. Surgeons Can.; mem.: Can. Glaucoma Soc. (sec.-treas.), Glaucoma Rsch. Soc. Can. (bd. dirs.), Assn. Internat. Glaucoma Patient Organizations (mem. adv. com.), Am. Acad. Ophthalmology, Asia-Pacific Acad. Ophthalmology, Am. Glaucoma Soc., Assn. Rsch. Vision & Ophthalmology. Office: St Michaels Hosp 30 Bond St Ste 8 072 CCW Toronto Ontario M5B 1W8 Canada Office Phone: 416-864-5444. Office Fax: 416-864-5208. Business E-Mail: guptan@smh.toronto.on.ca. *

GUPTA, P. K., biomedical researcher; b. Moga, Punjab, India, Feb. 14, 1943; s. Roop Lal and Vidhya Wati Aggarwal; m. Rakesh Bansal, Nov. 18, 1967; children: Vikas, Pankaj. B in Vet. Sci. and Animal Husbandry, Punjab Agrl. U., Hisar, India, 1965, MSc in Medicine, 1967, PhD in Pharmacology and Toxicology, 1971. Cert. computer application Upkar Computer Sci. Ctr., 2005. Asst. rsch. officer Postgrad. Inst. Med. Edn. and Rsch., Chandigarh, 1967—68; lectr., officer in-charge animal house dept. biophysics Punjab U., Chandigarh, India, 1970—73; project dir., scientist-in-charge pharmacology and toxicology sponsored chems. Indsl. Toxicology Rsch. Ctr., Coun. Sci. Indsl. Rsch., New Delhi, 1973—80; chmn., prof. divsn. pharmacology and toxicology Indian Vet. Rsch. Inst., Indian Coun. Agrl. Rsch., New Delhi, 1980—2003; dir. Toxicology Consulting Svcs. Inc., Bareilly, India, 2003—. Vis. prof./scientist dept. drug toxicology U. Tenn. Ctr. Health Scis., Memphis, 1977—78, W.Va. U., Morgantown, 1977—78; expert cons. WHO, Geneva, 1981, 1991—92, adviser, 2003—06; expert cons. Internat. Atomic Energy Agy., Vienna, 1985, UN FAO, Rome, 1992; cons. Ministry Agr., New Delhi, 2003—. Author: Basis of Organ and Reproduction Toxicity, 1985, Adverse Effects of Xenobiotics, 1985, Immuno and Clinical Toxicology, 1985, Veterinary Toxicology, 1986, Know Your Society, 1986,

Advances in Toxicology and Environmental Health, 1988, Pesticides in the Indian Environment, 1988, Directory Society Toxicology, 2005; contbr. chapters to books, articles to profl. jours.; founding editor: Tox Letter, 1983—94, assoc. editor:, Jour. Environ. Biology, 1985—91, mem. editl. bd.: Clin. Toxicology, Indian Jour. Pharmacology, Indian Jour. Environ. Toxicology and Health; book review editor Marcel Dekker. Recipient Gold medal, Indian Vet. Jour., 1991—92, Best Tchr. award, Indian Coun. Agrl. Rsch., 1990—91, Astra Zeneca award, 2004. Fellow: Nat. Acad. Vet. Scis. (founder), Soc. Toxicology (gen. sec. 1980—83, pres. 1983—85, 1986—87, founder, editor-in-chief Indian Jour. Toxicology 1994—2003, founder, editor-in-chief Toxicology Internat. 2003—, Gold medal 1987, 1991, 1997, Lifetime Achievement award 2003, 2007—08), Acad. Environ. Biology (v.p. 1986—89), Acad. Scis. Animal Welfare (life; founding pres. 2002—, founder), Am. Coll. Vet. Toxicologists; mem.: Acad. Scis. Environ. Biol., Soc. Pesticides, Indian Pharmacol. Soc., Indian Assn. Vet. Scientists, Soc. Vet. Physiologists, Biochemists and Pharmacologists India, Soc. Biol. Chemists India, Internat. Union Toxicology (councillor 1980—83, founding dir. 1980—83, hon. auditor 1983, councillor 1983—86, 1986, mem. nominating com. 2004—07, Travel award 2004). Office: Toxicology Consulting Svcs C-44 Rajendra Nagar Bareilly 243 122 India Office Phone: 91 581 2300628.

GUPTA, PARMESHWAR RAM, cardiologist, educator; b. Mau, Uttar Pradesh, India, June 20, 1946; MBBS, MD, Inst. Med. Scis., Banaras Hindu U., 1968. Head dept. cardiology Banaras Hindu U., India, 1998—2011, prof. cardiology, 2002—. Recipient Shikshha Ratan award, Internat. Friendship Soc., New Delhi; named one of Best Citizen, India Pub. House, New Delhi, 2010. Fellow: Indian Acad. Echocardiography, Indian Coll. Cardiology, Indian Soc. Cardiology; mem.: Cardiological Soc. India. Avocation: reading. Home: B 31/83 -29-30 Rashni Nagar Lanka Varanasi Uttar Pradesh 221005 India Personal E-mail: sumitraprg2000@yahoo.com.

GUPTA, PURSHOTTAM DAS, endocrinologist, consultant; b. Jaipur, Rajasthan, India, Aug. 10, 1939; s. Kalyan Baksh and Jamuna Devi Gupta; m. C. K. Gupta, July 4, 1961 (dec. Dec. 1998); children: Kalpana, Sanjay, Alpana. BS, Maharaja's Coll., Jaipur, 1961; MS, U. Rajasthan, Jaipur, 1963; PhD, Panjab U., Chandigarh, India, 1968. Rsch. assoc. Med. Sch. U. Pa., Phila., 1970—72; asst. prof. All India Inst. Med. Sci., New Delhi, 1972—79; asst. dir. Ctr. Cellular and Molecular Biology, Hyderabad, 1979—89, dep. dir., 1989—95, dir., 1995—99, Iladevi Cataract and IOL Rsch. Ctr., Ahmedabad, 1999—2006; founder Atmiya Inst Gerontology Rsch., Gujarat, India, 2006—, dir., 2006—. Vis. prof. Tottori U., Yonago, Japan, 1987—. Author numerous books, editor; contbr. articles to profl. jours.; organizer and author: Science for the Society, 1993. Recipient Guest Lecture award, Alberta Heritage Found., 1994, Best Invention award, Gov. of Andhra Pradesh, 2005; fellow, Max Plank Inst. Exptl. Endocrinology, 1994. Fellow: Nat. Acad. Scis., Royal Microscopic Soc. Eng., N.Y. Acad. Sci. India; mem.: Soc. Endocrinology. Achievements include invention of protein estimation at nano level. Home: 833 Churukon ka Rasta Jaipur Rajasthan 302003 India Office: Atmiya Inst Gerontol Rsch Rajkot Gujarat India Home Phone: 91 141 2328041; Office Phone: 91-281-2562681. Personal E-mail: pdg2000@hotmail.com.

GUPTA, RAJENDRA PRASAD, physician; b. Marhura, India, May 19, 1948; naturalized, 1981; s. Ramji Das and Somvati Devi Gupta; m. Vinod K. Gupta, Dec. 14, 1974; children: Vanita, Vikram, Vishal. BSc, Agra U., Mathura, 1964; B Medicine B Surgery, Rajisthan U., Udiapur, India, 1969, MD, 1973; MBA, U. South Fla., 1999. Diplomate Am. Bd. Internal Medicine, Am. Bd. Gastroenterology, Am. Bd. Utilization and Quality Review Physicians. Rotating intern R.N.T. Med. Coll., Udaipur, Ind., 1969-70, resident in internal medicine, 1970-71, casualty med. officer in internal medicine, 1972; med. officer Seema Nursing Home, Udaipur, 1972, cons. physician, 1972-73; resident tng. in internal medicine Nat. Health Svc. Hosps., 1973-75; resident in internal medicine category "C" St. Francis Med. Ctr., Trenton, NJ, 1975-77; fellow in gastroenterology U. Medicine and Dentistry of N.J., Newark, 1977-79; pvt. practice in gastroenterology and internal medicine Trenton, 1979—; practice medicine Hopewell Valley Med. Group PA, Trenton, NJ. Tchr. Ravindra Nath Tagore Med. Coll.; clin. instr. U. Medicine and Dentistry of NJ, 1977-79, Robert Wood Johnson Med. Sch., Piscataway, NJ, 1992-95; clin. sr. instr. Hahneman Med. Coll., Phila., 1981-92; asst. prof. Robert Wood Johnson Med. Sch., Piscataway, 1995—; affiliated Capital Health Sys., Trenton, Robert Wood Johnson at Hamilton Hosp., NJ; chmn. audit com. Mercer Med. Ctr., Trenton, 1982-83, chmn. utilization rev., 1983-88, mem. constitution and bylaws, 1984-88, med. records com., 1983-85, exec. com., 1985-88, chmn. risk mgmt. com., 1987—, chief gastroenterology sect., 1993-95, chmn. com. sect. chiefs, 1995-97, chmn. physician/hosp. orgn. com., 1993-94, steering com., 1994-95, computer com., 1993, co-chmn. joint conf. com., 1995—, strategic planning com., 1995-96, chmn. dept. medicine, 1995-97, search com., med. dir., 1995, pres. med. staff, 1995-96, fin. com., 1995-97; assoc. med. dir. Ctrl. NJ Mercer, Middlesex Preferred Orgn., Prucare, 1985-86; pres. Healthpath Mercer County, Aetna Health Plan Ind. Practice Assocs., Mt. Laurel, NJ, 1992-94; chmn. med. adv. bd. Morris Hall Home for Aged, Lawrenceville, NJ, 1987-90; treas. Physician's Healthcare Plan NJ, Lawrenceville, 1993-95, sec., 1995-96, v.p., 1996-97, fin. com., 1993-97; cons. gastroenterology Bd. Med. Examiners, Trenton, 1990—. Active Am. Cancer Soc. Mercer County chpt., 1990-92; bd. trustees Chapin Sch., Princeton, NJ, 1993-94; mem. Healthcare Adv. Group for Christie Whitman, 1993; chmn. Capital Health Sys. Found., Trenton, NJ, 2003—, Med. Soc. NJ (pres. 2008-). Fellow ACP, Internat. Coll. Physicians, Am. Coll. Gastroenterology, Coll. Utilization Rev. Physicians; mem. AMA (category I award cert. 1979—, Physician Outreach award Presentation 1997, 99), Am. Soc. Gastrointestinal Endoscopy, Acad. Medicine NJ, Med. Soc. NJ (trustee 1996—, legis. com. 1992-94, 2d v.p. 2005-06, internat. med. grad. com. 1992-93, pres. coun. 1992-93, vice-chmn. internat medicine grad. com. 1993-94, chmn. reference com. B ho. of dels. 1993, chmn. house of dels. 1994, vice-chmn. coun. on legis. 1994-95, del. organized med. staff sect. 1995—, exec. com. coun. on legis. 1996—, cons. coun. legis. 1996—, pres. 2008-), NJ Gastrointestinal Soc., Mercer County Med. Soc. (v.p. 1990-91, chmn. numerous coms., pres. 1992-93), Capital Health Found. Republican. Hindu. Avocations: tennis, swimming, skiing. Office: Hopewell Valley Med Group PA 1871 Pennington Rd Trenton NJ 08618-1208

GUPTA, RAMJI, dermatologist; b. Faizabad, Sept. 26, 1951; Diploma in Dermatology & Venerology, S N Med. Coll., 1977; MD, AIIMS, 1980. Registrar AIIMS, 1980—83; sr. cons. dermatologist Indraprastha Apollo Hosp., 2008. Recipient Best Photography award, DMA & IADVL, Prem Kumari award; GSK Oration grant, IADVL. Mem.: Indian Assn. Dermatologists Venereologists and Leprogists, Pemphigus and Pulse Therapy Found. Avocations: swimming, writing. Home: 47 C Pocket B Sidharth Ext New Delhi Delhi 110014 India Personal E-mail: drramjigupta@yahoo.co.in.

GUPTA, SANJAY, neurosurgeon, medical correspondent, journalist; b. Novi, Mich., Oct. 23, 1969; s. Subhash and Damyanti Gupta; m. Rebecca Olson, May 15, 2004; children: Sage Ayla, Sky, Neal. BS in Biomedical Scis., U. Mich., Ann Arbor; MD, U. Mich. Med. Ctr., 1993. Diplomate American Bd. Neurol. Surgery, cert. med. investigator. Neurosurgical fellowship Semmes-Murphy Clinic, Memphis, U. Mich. Med. Ctr.; White House fellow, spl. advisor to First Lady, 1997—98; asst. prof. dept. neurol. surgery Emory U. Sch. Medicine, Atlanta, 2001—; health & med. news reporter Cable News Network (CNN), Atlanta, 2001—, chief med. corr. Founder, dir. CNN's Fit Nation Initiative, 2006—; assoc. chief neurosurgery svc. Grady Meml. Hosp., Atlanta; neurosurgeon Emory U. Hosp. Author: Chasing Life: New Discoveries in the Search for Immortality to Help You Age Less Today, 2007 (NY Times bestseller), Cheating Death: The Doctors and Medical Miracles that Are Saving Lives Against All Odds, 2009 (NY Times bestseller); host (TV series) House Call with Dr. Sanjay Gupta, CNN, 2005—, Fit Nation, 2008—, (podcast) Paging Dr. Gupta, CNN.com, guest host CBS News Sunday Morning, 2007, Larry King Live, 2009, spl. corr. CBS News, columnist TIME mag., reg. contbr. health & med. news reports Anderson Cooper 360°, American Morning, 60 Minutes. Bd. dirs. Lance Armstrong LiveStrong Found. Recipient Humanitarian award, Nat. Press Photographers Assn., 2003, News & Documentary Emmy award, 2006, Health Comm. Achievement award, AMA Med. Comm. Conf., 2009, Mickey Leland Humanitarian award, Nat. Assn. Multi-Ethnicity in Comm., 2009; named Journalist of Yr., Atlanta Press Club, 2004; named a Pop Culture Icon, USA Today, 2003; named one of Sexiest Men Alive, People Mag., 2003, Ten Most Influential Celebrities, Forbes mag., 2011. Mem.: Coun. Fgn. Rels., Congress Neurol. Surgeons, American Assn. Neurol. Surgeons. Achievements include in 2004, covering the tsunami disaster in Sri Lanka that took more than 155,000 lives in Southeast Asia, contributing to the 2005 Alfred I. DuPont-Columbia award for CNN; in 2006, contributing to CNN's Peabody award-winning coverage of Hurricane Katrina, revealing that official reports that Charity Hospital in New Orleans had been evacuated were incorrect; consideration for the position of Surgeon General of the US by President Barack Obama in 2009. Office: Grady Memorial Hospital 80 Jesse Hill Dr SE Atlanta GA 30303 also: Cable News Network PO Box 105366 One CNN Ctr Atlanta GA 30348 Office Phone: 404-778-1398. *

GUPTA, SHAILENDRA, information technology executive; B in Mech. Engring., Birla Inst. Tech. and Sci.; MBA, Indian Inst. Mgmt. Held various mgmt. roles, mfg. plant Godrej & Boyce Mfg. Co. Ltd., India; mng. dir. Tech. Pacific Group, India, 1995—2001, CEO, 2001; joined as COO, Ingram Micro Asia-Pacific Ingram Micro, Inc., 2004, sr. v.p., Ingram Micro Asia-Pacific, 2007—08, exec. v.p., pres., Ingram Micro Asia-Pacific, 2007—; CEO Tech Pacific Australia Pty Ltd., 2001—, Tech Pacific Ltd., 2001—. Office: Ingram Micro Inc 1600 E St Andrew Pl Santa Ana CA 92705 Office Phone: 714-566-1000. Office Fax: 714-568-0138. Business E-Mail: shailendra.gupta@ingrammicro.com.

GUPTA, SUNETRA, science professor, writer; b. Kolkata, West Bengal, India, Mar. 15, 1965; d. Dhruba and Minati Gupta; m. Adrian Vivian Sinton Hill, Sept. 3, 1994; children: Isolde Urmila Natasha Hill, Olivia Nisha Maud Hill. AB, Princeton U., NJ, 1987; PhD, Imperial Coll., London, 1992. Prof. U. Oxford, Oxfordshire, England, 1999—. Author: (novel) A Sin of Colour (Southern Arts prize, 2000), Moonlight into Marzipan, The Glassblower's Breath, Memories of Rain, So Good in black, 2011. Recipient Sci. medal, Zool. Soc. London, 2007, Rosalind Franklin award, Royal Soc., 2009, Wolfson Merit award, 2010. Office: Univ Oxford South Parks Road OX1 3PS Oxford England

GUPTA, VIKAS, physician, director; b. Pathankot, Punjab, India, Aug. 6, 1976; s. Rajinder Pal and Adarsh Gupta. MBBS, Govt. Med. Coll., Amritsar, Punjab, 2000. Cert. DNB. Med. officer Mahajan Clinic, Amritsar, 2001—06; grad. asst. Sch. Pub. Health, Houston, 2007—08. Scholarship, State Govt., 1995. Mem.: APHA, AMSA, SEIS, U. Tex. Sch. Pub. Health Student Assn. (adminstrv. dir. pub. rels. 2008—), Nat. Scholars Honor Soc. (life). Hindu. Office: Univ Tex Sch Pub Health 1200 Herman Pressler Houston TX 77054 Home: 7900 Cambridge St Apt #4-2G Houston TX 77054 Personal E-mail: vikasguptadr@gmail.com.

GUPTAN, RAJ, physician, researcher; s. Rajkumar and Sumalika. MD, Maulana Azad Med. Coll., India, 1990. Dir. Venous Rsch. Found., Schaumburg, Ill., 2003—. Dir. rsch. Vein Clinics Am., Schaumburg, Ill., 2001—03; founder, dir. Venous Rsch. Found. Contbr. articles to more than 80 rsch. publs., chapters to books. Fellow: Royal Soc. Medicine (London); mem.: Am. Coll. Phlebology, Indian Soc. Gastroenterology (life). Achievements include development of original clinical research, medical device invention, and hypertext medical publishing. Home: 5500 Carriageway Dr Ste 214 Rolling Meadows IL 60008 Office: Venous Rsch Found PO Box 59444 Schaumburg IL 60008 Personal E-mail: rguptan@hotmail.com. E-mail: rguptan@venousresearchfoundation.com.

GURA, KATHLEEN MARIE, pediatric pharmacist, educator; b. Worcester, Mass., Aug. 17, 1960; d. Philip J. and Catherine Joyce Kozak; m. Scott Gura, May 5, 1984; children: Alessandra Jeanne, Samantha Anne. BS, Mass. Coll. Pharmacy and Allied Health Scis., 1982; PharmD, Mass. Coll. Pharmacy and Health Scis., 1999. Registered pharmacist Mass. Bd. Pharmacy, 1982, D.C. Bd. Pharmacy, 1983, bd. cert. nutrition support pharmacist Bd. Pharm. Specialties, 1993. Clin. staff pharmacist Children's Hosp. Nat. Med. Ctr., Washington, 1982—84; clin. pharmacy specialist GI/nutrition Children's Hosp. Boston, 1984—; course dir., dept continuing edn. Harvard Med. Sch., 2007—. Adj. assoc. prof. Mass. Coll. Pharmacy, Boston, 1999—; adj. asst. prof. Northeastern U., Boston, 2002—; preceptor for experiential edn. U. N.C. Coll. Pharmacy, Chapel Hill, 2003—, Wash. State U., 2004—, adj. faculty, preceptor for experiential edn. Sch. Pharmacy, U. Wash., Seattle, 2004—; preceptor U. Conn., 2006—. Author: (textbook) Manual of Pediatric Nutrition, 2000, 2005, Pediatric Nutrition in Your Pocket, 2002, Geriatric Nutrition, The Health Professional's Handbook, 3d edit., 2004, Nutrition in Pediatrics, 4th edit., 2007, Clinical Management of Intestinal Failure, 2011. Leader Girls Scouts Am., Norfolk, Mass., 1999. Recipient Innovatice Pharmacy Practice award, 2007, Boston Globe award, 2007, Stanley Serlick award, 2008, Drug Therapy Rsch. award, ASHP, 2009, Svc. award, MSHP, 2010. Fellow: Pediat. Pharmacy Advocacy Group (bd. dirs. 2000—04, v.p., finance 2004—05), Am. Soc. Health System Pharmacists (ho. dels. 1996—2003, chair coun. profl. affairs 2000—01); mem.: European Soc. for Clin. Nutrition and Metabolism, Am. Coll. Clin. Pharmacy, Am. Soc. for Parenteral and Enteral Nutrition, Mass. Soc. of Health Sys. Pharmacists (pres. 2000—01, bd. dirs. 2005—10, Practitioner Excellence award 1994), Rho Chi, Rho Pi Phi (sec. 1980—81, US pharm. conv. ad hoc adv. panel 2007, bd. pharm. specialties 2011—). Avocations: travel, photography. Home: 5 Barnstable Rd Norfolk MA 02056 Office: Children's Hospital Boston 300 Longwood Ave Boston MA 02115 Business E-Mail: kathleen.gura@childrens.harvard.edu.

GURDON, SIR JOHN BERTRAND, cell biologist; b. Dippenhall, Hampshire, Eng., Oct. 2, 1933; s. William Nathaniel and Elsie Marjorie (Byass) G.; m. Jean Elizabeth Curtis, June 25, 1965; Elizabeth Aurea, William John. BS in Zoology, Oxford U., 1956, DPhil in Embryology, 1960; DSc (hon.), U. Chgo., 1978; D (hon.), U. Rene Descartes, Paris, 1982; DSc (hon.), Oxford U., 1988, U. Hull, 1998, U. Glasgow, 2000; DSc, U. Glasgow, Cambridge, Uk, 2007; Fellow Magdalene Coll. (hon.), Cambridge, 2003, Fellow (hon.) Churchill Coll., 2007; Fellow Christ Church Coll. (hon.), Oxford. Beit Meml. fellow dept. zoology Oxford U., 1958—61, rsch. fellow England, 1961-71; Gosney rsch. fellow Calif. Inst. Tech., 1961—62; rsch. fellow Christ Church, 1963—64; mem. staff Med. Rsch. Coun., Lab. Molecular Biology, Cambridge, England, 1972—83, head cell biology divsn., 1979—83; John Humphrey Plummer prof. cell biology U. Cambridge, 1983—2001; master Magdalene Coll., Cambridge, 1995—2002; Fullerian prof. physiology and comparative anatomy Royal Instn., 1985—; Charles M. and Martha Hitchcock professorship U. Calif., Berkeley, 2005—06. Lectr. dept. zoology Oxford U., 1965-72; vis. rsch. fellow Carnegie Instn., Balt., 1965; fellow Churchill Coll., Cambridge, 1974-94, Eton Coll., Windsor, Eng., 1978-; chmn. Wellcome Trust and Cancer Rsch. Campaign Inst. Cancer and Devel. Biology, Cambridge, 1988-2001, Co. Biologists; gov. The Wellcome Trust, London, 1995-2000; group leader Wellcome CR UK Inst., Cambridge, 2001-. Author: Control of Gene Expression in Animal Development, 1974; contbr. papers to sci. jours. Hon. fellowhip Christ Church, Oxford, 1985; recipient Albert Brachet prize Belgian Royal Acad., 1968, sci. medal Zoological Soc., 1968, Feldberg Found. award, 1975, Paul Ehrlich prize, Germany, 1977, Nessim Habif prize U. Geneva, 1979, Ciba medal, prize Biochemical Soc., 1980, Comfort Crookshank triennial award for cancer rsch. Middlesex Hosp. Med. Sch., 1983, Prix Charles Leopold Mayer prize, Acad. Scis., France, 1984, William Bate Hardy triennial prize Cambridge Philos. Soc., 1984, Ross Harrison prize Internat. Soc. Devel. Biology, 1985, Emperor Hirohito Internat. Biology prize, Japan, 1987, Wolf prize in medicine, 1989, Jan Waldenstrom medal Swedish Oncology Soc., 1991, Disting. Svc. award, Miami, 1992, Jean Brachet Meml. prize Internat. Soc. Differentiation, 2000, Conklin medal Am. Soc. Devel. Biology, 2001, Pioneer in Stem Cell award Frontiers in Human Embryonic Stem Cell Organizing Com., 2004; co-recipient Albert Lasker Basic Med. Rsch. award, Lasker Found., 2009. Fellow Royal Soc. London (Croonian lectr., John Jaffe prize 1976, Royal medal 1985, Copley medal 2003, Rosenstiel prize, 2009); mem. Inst. of Medicine, Am. Acad. Arts and Scis. (hon. fgn. mem.), Academie des Sciences, Institut de France (fgn. assoc.), Academia Europaea, Lombardy Acad. Sci. (fgn. mem.), Belgian Royal Acad. Sci., Letters and Fine Arts (fgn. assoc.), Am. Philos. Soc. (fgn. mem.), UGoldsmiths Club London (liveryman 1986). Mem. Ch. Eng. Office: U Cambridge Dept Zoology Downing St Cambridge CB2 3EJ England also: Gurdon Inst Univ Cambridge Tennis Court Rd Cambridge England Office Phone: 44-1223-334-090. E-mail: jbg1000@cam.ac.uk. *

GURE, TANYA RUFF, medical educator; b. Cin., Jan. 5, 1971; BS, Yale Coll., 1993; MD, Ohio State U. Coll. Medicine & Pub. Health, 2000. Asst. prof. U. Mich. Sch. Medicine, 2008—. Recipient Clin. Transl. & Sci. award, NIH. Mem.: ACP, Soc. Gen. Internal Medicine, Am. Geriat. Soc. Office: 300 N Ingalls Bldg Rm 925 Ann Arbor MI 48109-2007 Office Fax: 734-936-2116. Business E-Mail: tanruff@umich.edu.

GUREWITSCH, EDITH DIAMENT, gynecologist, educator; b. Bklyn., Apr. 16, 1965; BA, Columbia U., 1987, MD, 1991. Assoc. prof. gynecology, obstetrics & biomed. engring. Johns Hopkins U. Sch. Medicine, 1997—. Rsch. grant, Ctr. Disease Control. Fellow: Am. Bd. Obstetricians & Gynecologists; mem.: AMA, Am. Coll. Obstetricians & Gynecologists, Royal Coll. Medicine, Soc. Maternal Fetal Medicine. Avocation: bicycling. Office: Johns Hopkins Hosp Phipps 217 600 Baltimore MD 21208 Office Fax: 410-614-8305. Business E-Mail: egurewi@jhmi.edu.

GURJAR, MOHAN, physician, educator; b. Jaipur, Oct. 30, 1975; MD, GIC, 1998. Asst. prof. SGPGIMS, 2008—. Office: SGPGIMS Rae Bareli Rd Lucknow Uttar Pradesh 226014 India Business E-Mail: mohan@sgpgi.ac.in.

GURLAND, MARK A., orthopedist, surgeon; Attended, NYU, 1979. Diplomate Am. Bd. of Orthopedic Surgery, Am. Bd. of Orthopedic Surgery-hand surgery. Resident surgery Hosp. Univ. Pa., 1979—80; resident orthopaedic surgery Hosp For Joint Disease, 1980—84; fellow hand surgery Thomas Jefferson Univ. Hosp., 1984; with Englewood Hosp. & Med. Ctr., Hackensack Univ. Med. Ctr. Office: Hackensack University Medical Center 30 Prospect Ave Hackensack NJ 07601 Office Phone: 201-996-2000.

GURMAN, ANDREW WILLIAM, orthopedic surgeon; b. NY, May 20, 1952; m. Nancy Gurman; 2 children. Grad., Syracuse U., NY; MD, SUNY Upstate Med. U., Syracuse, 1980. Diplomate American Bd. Orthop. Surgery. Surg. intern Montefiore Hosp., Bronx, NY, 1980—81, orthop. resident, 1981—85; fellow hand surgery Hosp. Joint Diseases Orthop. Inst., NYC, 1985—86; solo practice Altoona, Pa. Mem.: ACS, AMA (vice-spkr. 2007—11, bd. dirs. AMA Found. 2008—, spkr. House of Delegates 2011—, spkr. 2011—), American

Soc. Surgery of Hand, American Acad. Orthop. Surgeons, Blair County Med. Soc. (past pres.), Pa. Med. Soc. (spkr. House of Delegates 2002—07). Office: Andrew W Gurman MD 1701 12th Ave Ste C 2 Altoona PA 16601 *

GURSKAYA, OLESYA, physiologist; b. St. Petersburg, Russia, Sept. 10, 1974; MS in Medicine, I.I. Mechnikov (formerly St. Petersburg State Med. Acad.), 1997; PhD in Medicine, Pathophysiology, St. Petersburg Med. Acad. Postgrad. Edn., 2003. Intern in therapy I.I. Mechnikov, 1997—98; physician in clin. residency program, dept. clin. physiology and functional diagnostics St. Petersburg Med. Acad. Postgrad. Edn., 1998—2000, asst., dept. clin. physiology and functional diagnostics, 2003—09, physician in functional diagnostics; head, dept. functional diagnostics Russian Acad. Scis., Inst. Human Brain, 2009—. Physician in functional diagnostics Inst. Human Brain, 2009—11. Avocations: travel, fishing, walking. Office: 9 Akademika Pavlova St Saint Petersburg 197376 Russia Office Fax: 78122343247. Business E-Mail: gurskaya_olesya@mail.ru.

GURUBHAGAVATULA, MOHAN JAGAN, rheumatologist, physician; MD, U. Health Sciences Coll. of Osteo. Medicine, 1998. Diplomate Am. Bd. Internal Medicine-internal medicine, rheumatology, lic. to practice Pa., 2003. Hosp. affiliation includes Chestnut Hill Hosp, Pa.; fellow rheumatology Hahnemann Univ. Hosp., Phila.; resident internal medicine Med. Coll. Pa., Phila. Office: Chestnut Hill Hospital 8835 Germantown Ave Philadelphia PA 19118 Office Phone: 215-248-8200.

GURUNATHAN, BASKAR, engineering educator; b. Kumbakonam, May 24, 1977; BTech, Bharathidasan U., 1999; MTech, Annamalai U., 2006. Lectr. Dr. Navalar Neducnchezhiyan Coll. Engring., 1999—2004; assoc. prof. St. Joseph's Coll. Engring., Chennai, Tamil Nadu, India, 2006—. Mem. bd. examiners Annamalai U., 2008, Pondichery U., 2009, Anna U. Tech, Coimbatore, 2009. Recipient Best paper award, Inst. Chem. Tech., Mumbai. Fellow: Soc. Applied Biotech. (India); mem.: European Fedn. Biotech., Indian Soc. Tech. Edn., Indian Inst. Chem. Engrs., Biotech. Rsch. Soc. India. Avocations: badminton, reading. Office: St. Joseph's Coll Engring Dept Biotechnology Chennai Tamil Nadu 600119 India Personal E-mail: basg2004@gmail.com.

GURUNATHAN, RAMESH, surgeon, consultant; b. Klang, Selangor, Malaysia, July 3, 1966; s. Gurunathan Kailasam and Prabhawathy Kannan; m. Vanitha Renganathan, Mar. 23, 1997; children: Kanesha Ramesh, Delishaa Ramesh. MBBS, Mangalore U., India, 1992; MS in Surgery, Nat. U. Malaysia, 2000. Cons. upper gastrointestinal surgeon Tuanku Jaafar Hosp., Seremban, Malaysia, 2005—, founder, stomach cancer support group; chmn. Malaysian Upper Gastrointestinal Club, Seremban, 2007—. Nat. chmn. Upper Gastrointestinal Surg. Tng., Kuala Lumpur, Malaysia, 2005—. Contbr. articles to profl. jour. Fellow: RCS (Ireland); mem.: Acad. Medicine, Malaysia. Achievements include development of largest series of laparoscopic surgery for reflux disease in Malaysia. Office: Tuanku Jaafar Hosp Dept Surgery Jalan Rasah Seremban N Sembilan 70300 Malaysia Home: Jalan Sikamat 238A 70400 Seremban Malaysia Personal E-mail: rameshgtn77@yahoo.com.

GURUSWAMY, VELUPANDIAN, anesthesiologist; b. Trichy Tamil Nadu, India, June 17, 1968; s. Guruswamy Shunmugavelu and Pounambal Guruswamy; m. Uma Maheshwari Deivasigamani, May 18, 1997. MBBS, U. Madras, 1991, DA, 1996. Sr. registrar anaesthetics Nat. U. Hosp., 2002—03; specialist registrar anaesthetics Mersey Rotation, Liverpool, England, 2003—. Fellowship paediatric anaesthesia Royal Liverpool (England) Childrens Hosp., 2004—05. Contbr. articles to profl. jours. Recipient award, Chengalpattu Med. Coll., India, 1987. Fellow: RCSI; mem.: Assn. Anaesthetists Great Britain. Achievements include research in ultrasound in paediatric regional anaesthesia.

GUSI, NARCIS, science educator; b. Barcelona, Dec. 7, 1963; s. Elena Gusi; life ptnr. Yolanda Garcia; 1 child, Queralt. Postgrad. in Applied Stats., U. Politechnic Catalonia, Barcelona, 1992; MS in Sport Psychology, U. Autonoma Barcelona, 1993; PhD in Exercise Physiology, U. Barcelona, 1994; MS in Health Econ. & Pharmaeconomics, U. Pompeu Fabra, Barcelona, 2007. Tchr. secondary sch. Govt. Catalonia, Barcelona, 1988—94; prof. U. Extremadura, Caceres, Spain, 1994—, head rsch. group, 1994—. Dir. health svc. Regional Govt. Extremadura, Caceres, 2006—. Contbr. articles to profl. sci. jours. Grant, European Union, Spanish Gov, Regional Gover, 1988—. Mem.: EuroQol, Health Enhancing Phys. Activity WHO. Achievements include design of exercise looks after You (exercise service linked to primary care for elderly and child with obesity, diabetes, depression, fibromyalgia, etc.). Avocations: running (marathon, cross), basketball, dance, golf. Office: Univ Extremadura Faculty Sport Scis 10071 Caceres Spain Business E-Mail: ngusi@unex.es.

GUSTAFSSON, JAN-ÅKE, molecular endocrinologist, medical nutritionist; b. Stockholm, Aug. 4, 1943; s. Oscar Åke and Anna Ingegerd (Skog) G.; m. Ulla Nilsson, May 23, 1967 (div. 1987); 1 child, Jan Carl-Otto Åke. MB, Karolinska Inst., Stockholm, 1964, PhD, 1968, MD, 1971. Assoc. prof. in chemistry Karolinska Inst., Stockholm, 1971-78, prof., chmn. dept. med. nutrition, 1978—, dir. ctr. biotechnology, 1985—, mem. Nobel Assembly. Chief sci. councillor Karobio Inc., Stockholm, 1987—; adj. prof. dept. cell biology Baylor Coll. Medicine, Houston, 1987—; lectr. in field. Mem. editl. bd. Molecular Endocrinology, Breast Cancer Rsch. and Treatment, Molecular Pharmacology, Cancer Rsch., Cell Metabolism and The Prostate. Recipient Svedberg prize in chemistry, 1982, Fernstrom prize, 1983, Anders Jahre prize, 1992, Gregory Pincus medal, 1994, Soderberg prize, 1998, Koch award, 2002, Bristol-Myers award in nutrition, 2004, Descartes Rsch. prize, 2005. Mem. Japanese Biochem. Soc. (hon.), Am. Soc. for Biochemistry and Molecular Biology, Swedish Acad. Scis., Swedish Acad. Engring. Scis., AAAS (hon.), US Nat. Acad. Sci. (hon.). Achievements include patents for osteoporosis treatment with estrogen receptor beta antagonist; molecular cloning, cDNA sequences, and therapeutic uses of mammalian estrogen receptor beta; OR-1 orphan receptors belonging to the nuclear receptor family. Office: Karolinska U Hosp NOVUM Dept Biosciences and Nutrition Karolinska Inst S-14186 Stockholm Sweden also: 3013 Sci and Engineering Ctr Bldg 545 Room 3026 Houston TX 77204-5056 Home Phone: +46-8-333644; Office Phone: +46-8-58583746. Business E-Mail: jan-ake.gustafsson@ki.se.

GUSTIN, MARK DOUGLAS, retired healthcare executive; b. Bklyn. BS in Acctg., N.Y. Inst. Tech., 1969, MBA in Bus. Mgmt., 1973; M Profl. Studies, L.I. U., 1975; residency diploma in hosp. adminstrn., Kings County Hosp. Ctr., 1979; health care fin. mgmt. cert., Molloy Coll., 1993, elder care studies cert., 1994. Cert. Behavioral Healthcare Exec. 1983. Acct. Fass, Tuchler & Muster, NYC, 1969-74; asst. adminstr. Manhattan Kidney Ctr. Nat. Nephrology Found., Inc., NYC, 1974-76; adminstr. Carter Cmty. Health Ctr., Jamaica, NY, 1976-77; resident in hosp. adminstrn. Kings County Hosp. Ctr., N.Y.C. Health and Hosps. Corp., Bklyn., 1978-79, evening dir. (asst. dir.), 1979-80, assoc. dir., 1980-92; sr. assoc. dir. Kings County Hosp. Ctr., NYC Health and Hosps. Corp., Bklyn., 1992—2008. Panel mem. surrogate decision making program N.Y. State Commn. on Quality of Care for the Mentally Disabled, 1993—; mem. Nat. Coun. Cmty. Behavioral Healthcare, 1999-2001, bd. dirs. 1999-2001; mem. bd. visitors LI Devel.Disabilities Svcs. Office, 2007-. Vol. Disaster Psychiatry Outreach, PC, 2004—. Fellow Am. Acad. Med. Adminstrs., Am. Coll. Healthcare Execs., Assn. Behavioral Healthcare Mgmt. (pres. N.Y. chpt. 1999-, adv. coun. chair 2000-01, adv. coun. mem. 2003-, Harold Piepenbrink award 2003), Am. Coll. Managed Care Adminstrs.; mem. Mental Health News (adv. coun. mem. 2002-), Mental Health Assn. in N.Y. State (bd. chair 2004-06, Caroline Cash award, 2004), Praxis Housing Initiatives (bd. dirs. 2009-). Home: 32 Jasmine Ln Valley Stream NY 11581-2412

GUSZCZYN, TOMASZ, physician, medical biochemist, researcher; b. Bialystok, Poland, Apr. 3, 1974; s. Piotr and Eugenia Guszczyn; m. Emilia Bankowska-Guszczyn, Dec. 14, 1978; 1 child, Julia. DDSD, Med. Acad. Bialystok, 1998, MD, 2004, PhD, 2005. Dentist, Bialystok, 1998—2002; asst. Dept. Med. Biochemistry, Bialystok, 2002—05, asst. Dept. Children's Orthop. and Traumatology Med. U. Bialystok, 2005—. Office: Dept Children's Orthop & Traumatology Ul. Jerzego Waszyngtona 17 15-269 Bialystok Poland Business E-Mail: tombial@mp.pl.

GUTENTAG, PATRICIA RICHMAND, social worker, family counselor, occupational therapist; b. Newark, Apr. 10, 1954; d. Joseph and Joan (Miller) Leflein; m. Herbert Norman Gutentag; children: Steven, Jesse. BS in Occupational Therapy, Tufts U., 1976; MSW, Boston Coll., 1979. Lic. family and marriage counselor, lic. clin. social worker, N.J.; diplomate Am. Bd. Examiners in Clin. Social Work; registered occupational therapist, N.J. Social worker Jewish Family Svc., Salem, Mass., 1979-82; pvt. practice family and marriage counselor Westfield and Red Bank, N.J., 1982—. Cons. high stress, Westfield and Red Bank, 1982—. Fellow N.J. Soc. for Clin. Social Work; mem. NASW, Am. Occupational Therapists Assn., Registered Occupational Therapists Assn., Soc. for Advancement Family Therapy in N.J., Am. Anorexia-Bulimia Assn., Am. Assn. Marriage and Family Therapy. Avocation: reading. Office: 200 Maple Ave Red Bank NJ 07701-1732

GUTH, CARYL JOY, retired anesthesiologist; b. Peoria, Ill., 1935; m. John Falstad, 1988 (dec. 2001). AA, Mars Hill Coll., 1955, BS, Wake Forest U., 1957, MD, 1962. Diplomate Am. Bd. Anesthesiology. Intern U. Kans. Med. Ctr., Kansas City, 1962-63; resident in anesthesiology U. Pa. Hosp., Phila., 1963-65; instr. dept. anesthesiology Wake Forest U. Bapt. Hosp., Winston-Salem, NC, 1965; fellow in anesthesiology Queen Victoria Hosp., Sussex, Eng., 1966; instr. U. Nijmegan, Netherlands, 1966; bd. dirs. Mills Hosp., San Mateo, Calif., 1994—96, Mills-Peninsula Health Sys., Burlingame, 1994—2002; former chmn. dept anesthesiology Mills-Peninsula Hosps., San Mateo, Calif., ret. Mem. bd. sci. and policy advisors Am. Coun. Sci. and Health, 1995—; ind. Nikken wellness cons., 1996-; holistic and integrative medicine physician San Mateo, 1998-2003, Advance, NC, 2003-. Bd. visitors Wake Forest U. Bapt. Med. Ctr., Winston-Salem, NC, 2004—. Recipient Crisp-Casey award for best female athlete, Wake Forest U., 1957. Mem. AMA, Am. Soc. Anesthesiology (del. 1976-2000, chair com. on comms. 1987-90, chair com. profl. diversity 1995-97, ann. meeting program organizer 1983-84, 87-88, 94, 97), Calif. Med. Assn. (chair com. splty. socs. 1983-84), Calif. Soc. Anesthesiology (past pres., editor bull. 1976-79, asst. treas. 1979-81, pres.-elect 1981-82, pres. 1982-83, Disting. Svc. award 2006), San Mateo County Med. Assn. (bd. dir. 1984-86, chair med. staff affairs com. 1985-86), Coy C. Carpenter Philanthropic Soc., Wake Forest U. Soc., Pres.'s Club Wake Forest U. (endowed WFU womens golf scholarship 2007—), Wake Forest U. Deacon Club (bd. dirs. 2008-, named Deacon Club Mem. of Yr. award 2010), Wake Forest U. Med. Alumni Assn. (bd. dir. 1999—, sec. 2003-04, pres.-elect 2004-05, pres. 2005-06, dean's leadership coun. 2006—; Disting. SVc. award 2010). Achievements include established and endowed chair in complementary and integrative medicine Wake Forest U. Bapt. Med. Ctr., 2002. Home: 105 Willowbrook Pl Advance NC 27006-9480 Office Phone: 336-998-6112. Personal E-mail: cguth@triad.rr.com. Business E-Mail: drguth@yahoo.com.

GUTH, SHERMAN LEON (S. LEE), psychologist, educator; b. NYC; s. Arthur and Caroline (Laub) G.; children from previous marriage: Melissa, Victoria; m. Ling Zhao; 1 child, Lillian. BS, Purdue U., 1959; MA, U. Ill., 1961, PhD, 1963. Lectr. dept. psychology Ind. U., Bloomington, 1962-63, instr., 1963-64, asst. prof., 1964-67, assoc. prof., 1967-70, prof., 1970—; dir. research and grad. devel. Sch. Optometry, 1980-88, chmn. dept. visual scis., 1982-85. Vis. assoc. prof. psychology Mich. State U., 1968-69; NIH spl. research fellow in psychology U. Calif., Berkeley, 1971-72; NSF program dir. for sensory physiology and perception, 1977-78 NIH research grantee, 1964—70, NSF research grantee, 1963—86. Fellow Optical Soc. Am. Achievements include being the creator of the ATD model for visual adaption and color perception. Office: Ind U Dept Psychology Bloomington IN 47405 Business E-Mail: guth@indiana.edu.

GUTHEINZ, JOSEPH RICHARD, JR., criminal justice educator, consultant, lawyer, board member; b. Camp Lejune, NC, Aug. 13, 1955; s. Joseph R., Sr. and Rita C. (O'Leary) Gutheinz; m. Lori Ann Bentley, Jan. 16, 1976; children: Joseph IV, Christopher, Michael, Jim, Bill, Dave. AS, AA, Monterey Peninsula Coll., Calif., 1975; BA, Calif. State U., Sacramento, 1978, MA, 1979; postgrad., U. Calif., Davis, 1979-80; grad. U.S. Army Mil. Intelligence Officer Basic Course, U.S. Army Tactical Intelligence Sch., 1980; grad., U.S. Army Flight Sch., 1984; MS in Sys. Mgmt., U. So. Calif., 1985; JD, S. Tex. Coll. Law, 1996; grad. Criminal Investigators Basic Course (hon.), Fed. Law Enforcement Tng. Ctrs., 1988; grad. (disting.), Fed. Law Enforcement Tng. Ctrs. Office Inspector Gen., 1989. Bar: Tex. Supreme Ct. 1997, U.S. Dist. Ct. (so. dist.) Tex. 1997, U.S. Armed Forces Ct. Appeals 1998, U.S. Ct. Appeals (5th, 10th, 11th and fed. cirs.) 1998, U.S. Tax Ct. 1998, U.S. Supreme Ct. 2001; lic. FAA comml. pilot, cert. fraud examiner, tchr. aeronautics, mil. sci., bus. and indsl. mgmt., pub. svcs. and adminstrn., sociology and police sci. Calif., in network and networking for agents and sys. 1999. Officer U.S. Army, Kitzigen, Fed. Rep. Germany, 1980-82, capt., mil. intelligence officer Stuttgart, Fed. Rep. Germany, 1982-84, capt., aviator Ft. Polk, La., 1984-86; spl. agt. civil aviation security FAA, Oklahoma City, 1986-87; spl. agt. U.S. Dept. Transp., Denver, 1987-90; sr. spl. agt., acting sr. resident agent in charge Office Insp. Gen. NASA, Houston, 1990-2000; partner Gutheinz Law Firm LLP, Houston, 1997—; mentor, instr. organized crime U. Phoenix, 2002—; instr. criminal justice Alvin C.C., 2004—, mem. paralegal bd. of advisors, 2006—; expert witness Gary Mckinnon case Eng. High Ct., 2009; cons. Colorado Sch. Mines Mus. Criminal justice instr.; guest spkr. in field; police sci. instr. Ctrl. Tex. Coll., Nelligan, 1983; case agt. in charge of investigating space shuttle temperature transducers which grounded Shuttle Fleet, 91; nine agy. task force leader Omniplan Investigation, 1992—97; lead NASA OIG criminal investigation MIR Space Station Fire and Crash, 1997; lead investigator Jerry Whittredge, The Astronaut Impersonator, 1998; under cover agent Operation Lunar Eclipse, 1998; investigative cons. U.S. Attorney's Office, Little Rock, 2002; aptd. mem. adv. com. on offenders with med. and mental impairments Tex. Dept. Criminal Justice, 2004—08; affiliated atty. Thomas More Law Ctr., 2005—; mem. Tex. State Bar Assn. Aviation Law Sect., 2008—, Mock Trial Charles Rabys Capital Murder Trial Friendswood Mcpl. Ct., 2010; instr., supr. Moon Rock Project, Colo. and West Va. Goodwill Moon Rocks, 2010; cons. Colo. Sch. Mines Mus., 2010. Author: Moon Rock Con, 2003, Is it Legal to Privately Own Space ShuttleTiles, 2002, Stealing the Dream, 2002, In Search of the Goodwill Moon Rocks, 2004, There Will Be a Day After Tomorrow, 2004, Building 265, 2005, Marketing an Asteroid Threat, 2005, The Great Astronaut Impersonator, 2005, Cover-up in Space, 2005, Cumbre Vieja: A Terrorist Time Bomb, 2005, Making Safety a Priority: NASA's Path to Mars, 2005, NASA's Plutonium Gamble, 2006, NASA's Fallen Star: The Investigation of Omniplan Corporation, 2006, NASA is for Lovers, Psychos and Homicidal Maniacs, 2007, Grand Jury System's a Bad Joke on Justice, 2008, A Home Away From Home: Settling the Moon, 2008, A Call for Compassion in the Gary McKinnon Case, 2008; mil. editor: The Conservative Voice, 2005—08; actor: (TV films) Moon for Sale, 2007; contbr. columns in newspapers; co-author (with Joseph Patriot Gutheinz IV): Hubble Telescope Mankinds Spyglass On the Universe, 2008; co-author: Sinkhole deMayo Mystery of a Famas Tex. Sinkhole, 2009, Tarmac Delays Are Unlawful Restraint Of Passengers, 2009; co-author: (with Joseph Philip Gutheinzv) Confusing Science with Science Fiction: The Remarketing of an Asteroid Threat, 2010; co-author: (with Emma Gutheinz) Where Dinosaurs Were, Dreams Remain, 2010. Pres. Calif. State U. United Students for Life, 1976—79; chairperson Calif. Rally for Life, 1980; atty./activist against San Jacinto C.C. spl. election to annex parts of Clear Lake Texas, 2003; proponent Calif. Pro-Life Initiative, 1977; rally organizer Morton Downey Dem. Presdl. Campaign rallies, 1979; del. Tex. senatorial resolutions com. Rep. Party, 2000, 2004, del. conv. Tex., 2004; bd. dirs. Sea Isle Property Owners, 2001—02, Instrumental Placing Canadian Goodwill Moon Rock Canada Sci. & Tech. Mus., Ottawa, 2009; briefed Pres. Yeltsin's econ. advisors, 1995. Decorated Meritorious Svc. medal US Army, Commendation medal; recipient Cert. Spl. Achievement, US Dept. Transp., 1989, Letter of Commendation, FBI Dir. Louis Freeh, 1995, Tex. Spl. Commendation, US Atty. Office So. Dist., 1996, Exceptional Svc. medal, NASA, 2000, Pres.'s Coun. Integrity and Efficiency Career Achievement award, 2000, cert. of appreciation, US Atty. (so. dist.) Tex., 2003, cert. of commendation, U. Phoenix, 2003, writing honorarium, 2004, 2005, 2006, 2007, 2008, 2009, 2010, Excellence in Tchg. cert., Phi Theta Kappa, 2005, Merit scholar, S. Tex. Coll. Law; named Hon. Lt. Gov., Okla., 1987, World's Foremost Authority on Stolen Moon Rocks, Irish Mail Newspaper, 2007, Hon. Deputy Sheriff, Harris County, Texas, 2008. Mem.: Am. Bar Assn., Tex. Pro Bono Coll., Harris County Lawyers assn., Nat. Rep. Lawyers Assn. (mem. spkrs. panel on Calif. recall election), Tex. Criminal Def. Lawyers Assn., Tex. State Bar Assn., Cert. Fraud Examiners. Republican. Roman Catholic. Avocations: reading, teaching, public speaking, political activism, helping the poor. Office: 205 Woodcombe Houston TX 77062 Office Phone: 281-488-1280. Personal E-mail: jgutheinz@sbcglobal.net.

GUTHRIE, DIANA FERN, nursing educator; b. NYC, May 7, 1934; d. Floyd George and A. May (Moler) Worthington; m. Richard Alan Guthrie, Aug. 18, 1957; children: Laura, Joyce, Tammy. AA, Graceland Coll., 1953; RN, Independence Sanitarium, Mo., 1956; BS in Nursing, U. Mo., 1957, MS in Pub. Health, 1969; EdS, Wichita State U., Kans., 1982; PhD, Walden U., 1985. Cert. diabetes educator, bd. cert. advanced diabetes mgmt.; RN Mo., Kans., cert. holistic nursing, RN advanced practitioner; lic. profl. counselor Kans., cert. stress mgmt. edn., clin. hypnosis, healing touch, lic. marriage and family therapist. Instr. red cross U.S. Naval Sta., Sangley Point, Philippines, 1961-63; acting head nurse newborn nursery U. Mo., Columbia, 1963-64, birth defect nurse dept. pediat., 1964-65, nursing dir. clin. research ctr., 1965-67, research asst., 1967-73; diabetes nurse specialist Sch. Medicine U. Kans., Wichita, 1973—, asst. then assoc. prof. Sch. Medicine, 1974-85, prof. dept. pediat. and psychiatry Sch. Medicine, 1985-99, prof. emeritus, 2000; prof. dept. nursing Kans. U. Med. Ctr., Wichita, 1985-99, ret., 1999. Nurse cons. diabetes Mo. Regional Med. Program, Columbia, 1970-73; nat. advisor Human Diabetes Ctr. for Excellence, Lexington, Ky., 1982-90, Phoenix, 1983-92, Charlottesville, Ky., 1990-95; adj. prof. Sch. Nursing Wichita State U., 1985—. Author: Nursing Management of Diabetes, 1977, 5th edit., 2002, 6th edit., 2008, The Diabetes Source Book, 1990, 5th edit., 2003, Alternative and Complementary Diabetes Case, 2000, Diabets Hidden Secrets, 2006; contbr. articles to profl. jours. Health adv. bd. Mid-Am. All Indian Ctr., Wichita, 1978-80, bd. dirs. Wichita Urban Indian Health Clinic, 1980-82; bd. trustees Graceland U., Lamoni, Iowa, 1996-2001, bd. trustees emeritus, 2002—. Recipient Disting. Hon. Nursing Alumnus award, Wichita State U. Sch. Nursing/Nursing Alumni Soc., 2007; named Kans. Counselor of Yr., Kans. Counseling Assn., 2006. Fellow: Am. Nurse Assn., Am. Assn. Diabets Edn., Am. Assn. Diabetes Educators (Kans. area Disting. Svc. award 1999, Living Legend award), Am. Acad. Nursing; mem.: APHA, ANA, Am. Assn. Med. Psychotherapists (profl. adv. bd. 1985—), Am. Diabetes Assn. (Kans. area prof. edn. and youth com. 1988—, affiliate bd. dirs. 1979—83, pres. Kans. affiliate 1980—81, 1990—91, Outstanding Educator award 1979, Regional Outstanding Svc. award 1984, South Ctrl. Kans. Counselor of Yr. 2006, Kans. Counselor of Yr. 2006), Sigma Theta Tau (Exemplary Recognition award Epsilon Gamma chpt. 1996). Democrat. Mem. Cmty. Of Christ Ch. Avocations: harp, piano, painting, crafts, reading. Office: 200 S Hillside Wichita KS 67211-2127 Business E-Mail: dguthrie@kumc.edu.

GUTIERREZ, FERNANDO R., medical educator; b. Manzanillo, Cuba, Aug. 8, 1947; MD, Valladolid, Spain, 1947. Prof. radiology Wash. U. Sch. Medicine, 1979—. Named Lectr. of Yr., Radiol. Soc. Finland, 2008; named one of Best Drs. in America, 2005—11. Mem.: Radiol. Soc. N.Am. Office: 510 S Kingshighway Blvd Saint Louis MO 63110 Business E-Mail: gutierrezf@mir.wustl.edu.

GUTIERREZ, RAMIRO LUIS, internist; b. Santurce, PR, Apr. 4, 1972; BS, Cornell U., 1994; MD, Uniformed Svcs. U., 1998. Internist, infectious diseases, undersea medicine US Navy, 2009—. Asst. prof., medicine Uniformed Svcs. U., 2006. Fellow: ACP; mem.: Infectious Diseases Soc. America, Alpha Omega Alpha Honor Med. Soc. Office: 8901 Wisconsin Ave Bethesda MD 20889 Business E-Mail: ramiro.gutierrez@med.navy.mil.

GUTIERREZ-AGUIRRE, CESAR HOMERO, hematologist, educator; b. Monterrey, Feb. 22, 1968; MD, U. Autónoma Nuevo León, 1993. Hematologist U. Autónoma Nuevo León, 2000, cert. in internal medicine Hosp. U. Prof. Hosp. U., 2003—. Mem.: Internat. Soc. Hematology. Office: Madero y Gonzalitos Monterrey Nuevo León 64460 Mexico E-mail: hematohu@yahoo.com.

GUTIN, PHILIP H., neurosurgeon; MD, U. Pa., Phila., 1971. Diplomate Am. Bd. Neurol. Surgery. Resident Univ. Calif., San Francisco, 1972—79; fellow Nat. Cancer Inst., 1973—76; co-exec. dir. Brain Tumor Ctr.; chmn. neuro-oncology Meml. Sloan-Kettering Cancer Ctr., chmn. dept. of neurosurgery. Office: Memorial Sloan-Kettering Cancer Center 1275 York Ave New York NY 10065 Office Phone: 212-639-8556.

GUTTMACHER, ALAN EDWARD, federal agency administrator, physician, educator; b. Balt., Nov. 24, 1949; s. Manfred Shanfarber Guttmacher and Carola (Blitzman) Eisenberg; m. Diane Highum, 1978 (div. 1988); m. Brigid Mary Coles, Sept. 22, 1990. AB, Harvard Coll., 1972; MD, Harvard Med. Sch., 1981. Intern Children's Hosp. Boston, 1981-82, pediat. resident, 1982-85; fellow med. genetics Children's Hosp. Boston/Harvard Med. Sch., 1985-87; dir. Vt. Regional Genetics Ctr., assoc. prof. pediat. medicine U. Vt. Coll. Medicine, Burlington, 1987-90; sr. clin. adv. to dir. Nat. Human Genome Rsch. Inst. (NHGRI), NIH, Bethesda, Md., 1999—2002, dep. dir., 2002—08, acting dir., 2008—10, Nat. Inst. Child Health and Human Devel. (NICHD), Bethesda, Md., 2010, dir., 2010—. Co-founder Genetic Resources On the Web (GROW), 1999; pres. bd. dirs. The Guttmacher Inst., NYC, 1998—; overseer US Surgeon Gen.'s Family Hist. Initiative, Nat. Coalition Health Profl. Edn. in Genetics. Co-editor (with Francis S. Collins): (series in New Eng. Jour. Medicine) Genomic Medicine, 2003; contbr. articles to profl. jours., chapters to books. Mem. exec. com. Vt. chpt. March of Dimes, 1987—91; vol. pediatrician Vt. Spl. Olympics, 1990—93; pres. bd. dirs. Planned Parenthood No. New Eng., Williston, Vt., 1992—94; mem. global rsch./med. adv. bd. HHT Found. Internat., Monkton, Md., 1993—; bd. dirs. Planned Parenthood Fedn. of America, NYC, 1995—. Recipient Nat. Rsch. Svc. award, USPHS, 1985. Fellow: Am. Coll. Med. Genetics, Am. Acad. Pediat.; mem.: Inst. Medicine, Am. Soc. Human Genetics, Am. Pub. Health Assn., Alpha Omega Alpha. Office: NICHD Bldg 31, Rm 2A32, MSC 2425 31 Center Dr Bethesda MD 20892-2425 Office Phone: 301-402-0911. Office Fax: 301-402-2218. Business E-Mail: guttmach@mail.nih.gov. *

GUTTMAN, HELENE NATHAN, biomedical consultant, transpersonal counselor; b. NYC, July 21, 1930; d. Arthur and Mollie (Bergovoy) Nathan. BA, Bklyn. Coll., 1951; AM, Harvard U., 1956; MA, Columbia U., 1958; PhD, Rutgers U., 1960. Registered and cert. profl. past-life regression therapist; bd. cert. nutrition specialist; bd. cert. and registered hypnotherapist; registered and cert. transpersonal counselor; cert. and registered neurolinguistic therapist. Rsch. technician Pub. Health Rsch. Inst., NYC, 1951-52; control bacteriologist Burroughs-Wellcome, Inc., Tuckahoe, NY, 1952-53; vol. rschr. Haskins Labs., NYC, 1952-53, rsch. asst., 1953-56, rsch. assoc., 1956-60, staff microbiologist, 1960-64; lectr. dept. biology Queens Coll., NYC, 1956-57; rsch. collaborator Brookhaven Nat. Labs., Upton, L.I., NY, 1958; guest investigator Botanisches Institut der Technisches Hochschule, Darmstadt, Germany, 1960; rsch. assoc. dept. biol. scis. Goucher Coll., Towson, Md., 1960-62; vis. asst. rsch. prof. dept. medicine Med. Coll. Va., Richmond, 1960-62; asst. prof., then assoc. prof. dept. biology NYU, 1962-67; from assoc. prof. to prof. dept. biol. scis. U. Ill.-Chgo., 1967-75, prof., 1969-75; prof. dept. microbiology U. Ill. Med. Sch., 1969-75; assoc. dir. for rsch. Urban Systems Lab. U. Ill., 1975; expert Office of Dir. Nat. Heart, Lung and Blood Inst., NIH, Bethesda, Md., 1975-77, coord. rsch. resources Office Program Planning and Evaluation, 1977-79; dep. dir. Sci. Adv. Bd., Office of Adminstr., EPA, 1979-80; program coord., post-harvest tech., food safety and human nutrition, sci. and edn. adminstrn. USDA, 1980-83, assoc. dir. Beltsville (Md.) Human Nutrition Rsch. Ctr., Agrl. Rsch. Svc., 1983-89; pres. HNG Assocs., 1983—; nat. animal care coord. Nat. Program Staff Agr. Rsch. Svc./USDA, Beltsville, 1989-95. Bd. advisors The Monroe Inst., 1993—. Sr. author: Experiments in Cellular Biodynamics, 1972; co-editor (procs.) First Joint USA-USSR Joint Symposium on Blood Transfusion, Moscow, 1976, DHEW Publ. No. (NIH) 78-1246, 1978; editl. bd. Jour. Protozoology, 1972-75, Jour. Am. Med. Women's Assn., 1978-81, Methods in Cell Sci., 1994-2004; sr. editor: Science and Animals: Addressing Contemporary Issues, 1989; editor: Guidelines for Well-being of Rodents in Research, 1990, Rodents and Rabbits: Current Research Issues, 1994; (with others) Rodents and Rabbits: Addressing Current Issues, 1994; contbr. articles to profl. jours. Edn. com. Ill. Commn. on Status Women, 1974-75; cons. EPA, sci. adv. bd., 1974-79; bd. dirs. Du Page County Comprehensive Health Care Agy., 1974-75. Andelot fellow Harvard U., 1956, Rutgers U. scholar, 1960; recipient Thomas Jefferson Murray prize Theobald Smith Soc., 1959; Spl. award for work in Germany Deutscher Forschungs Gemeinschaft, 1960; Fellow Dazian Found., 1956; rsch. grantee. Fellow: AAAS, N.Y. Acad. Scis., Am. Acad. Microbiology, Am. Inst. Chemists (past chmn. com.); mem.: Monroe Inst. (bd. sci. advisors 1992—), Univ. and Coll. Women Ill. (past v.p.), Fed. Orgn. Profl. Women (past chmn. task force, past pres.), Assn. Women in Sci. (past chmn. com.), Soc. Protozoology (past mem. exec. com., past com. chmn.), Am. Soc. Clin. Nutrition, Am. Soc. Cell Biology (past com. chmn.), Am. Soc. Microbiologists, Neuroscis. Soc., Am. Soc. Biol. Chemistry and Molecular Biology, Tissue Culture Assn. (com. chmn. Nat. Capital Area br. 1988—90), Soc. Sci. Exploration, Soc. for In Vitro Biology (chmn. constn. and bylaws com. 1994—2002, Disting. Svc. award 1995, 1999), Assn. for Transpersonal Psychology (profl. mem.), Soc. Am. Bacteriologists (pres.'s fellow), Internat. Assn. Regression Therapies (life profl.), Am. Running and Fitness Assn. (mem. bd. advisors 1993—95, bd. dirs., mem. editl. bd.), Sigma Xi, Sigma Delta Epsilon (past coord. regional ctrs.). Home and Office: 5607 Mclean Dr Bethesda MD 20814-1021 Office Phone: 301-656-8980. Business E-Mail: hguttman@soundbalance.net.

GUTTMANN-BAUMAN, INES, pediatrician, educator; b. Zagreb, Croatia, Mar. 15, 1965; MD, U. Zagreb Med. Sch., 1988. Cert. in internat. devel. Sch. Advanced Internat. Studies, Johns Hopkins U. Asst. prof. pediat. Children's Hosp. Akron, NEOUCOM, 1998—2000, Children' s Nat. Med. Ctr., George Washington University, 2000—04; clin. assoc., divsn. pediatric endocrinology Johns Hopkins U., 2004—. Mem.: AMA, Lawson Wilkins Pediatric Endocrine Soc. Office: 200 N Wolfe St Baltimore MD 21287 Office Fax: 410-955-9773. Business E-Mail: igbauman@pol.net.

GÜVEN, KASIM CEMAL, marine biologist; b. Nov. 20, 1925; s. Osman and Gülsum Güven; m. OK Nermin, Aug. 30, 1954; children: Haldun, Kemal. PhD, Istanbul U., Turkey. Prof. faculty pharmacy U. Istanbul, Turkey, 1965—, dean, 1965—69; prof. Inst. Marine Sci., Istanbul, 1991—2011. Editor: Acta Pharmaceutica Sciencia, 1955—, Jour. Black Sea/Mediterranean Environ., 2005—11. Home: Basak Sok 37/8 34140 Bakirkoy Istanbul Istanbul Turkey Home Phone: 90 212 573 0388. Personal E-mail: kcguven@yahoo.com. Business E-Mail: kcguven@istanbul.edu.tr.

GUYER, CHARLES GRAYSON, II, psychologist; b. High Point, NC, May 22, 1949; s. Charles Grayson Sr. and Mildred Louise (Wrokman) G.; m. E.R. Ward, June 24, 1986; children: Charles Grayson III, Jarvis Griffith. BA, Appalachian State U., 1972, MA, 1974; EdD, Coll. William & Mary, 1978. Bd. cert. in counseling psychology and family psychology Am. Bd. Profl. Psychology; cert. in forensic medicine Am. Coll. Froensic Examiners Bd., in med. psycotherapy Am. Bd. Med. Psychotherapists, clin. hypnosis cons. Am.Soc. Clin. Hypnosis, in forensic psychology The Am. Bd. Psychol. Specialtie, Profl. Psychology-Assn. State and Provincial Psychology Bds., Interjurisdictional Practice Assns. State Provincial Psychology Bds. Postdoc. No. Wyo. Mental Health, Buffalo, 1978-80; pvt. practice High Point, N.C., 1980-83, Greensboro, NC, 1988—98; chief sch. psychologist Perquimans County Schs., Hertford, NC, 1998—2002; pvt. practice Jacksonville, NC, 2002—08; clin. dir. Substance Abuse Rehabilitation program Dept. Mental Health Naval Hosp. Camp Lejeune, NC, 2008—. Pres. Am. Bd. Family Psychology, 1992-94, bd. dirs., 1991-96, 2000-03, sec. family bd., 2000-03, Am. Bd. Counseling Psychology, 1991-93; exec. bd. mem. The Am. Bd. Forensic Psychol. Specialties (1986-1990); mem. Am. Psychol. Assn. Taske Force Veteran's Administration Psychologist (1990-1991), NC Licensing Act Task Force (1994-1995), NC Governor's Bd. Chronically Mentally Ill (1980); examiner American Bd Family Psychology American Board Profl. Psychology, 1990-, American Bd. Counseling Psychology, 1986-; offio bd dirs. Am. Psychol. Assn.-Divn. Family Psychology, 1995-1996. Contbr. chapters to books, articles to profl. jours. Bd. dirs. mem. Pine Valley United Meth. Ch. Lt. USN, 1983—88. Recipient Nay Achievement medal, Am. Bd. Profl. Psychology, 1992, Disting. Svc. award, 1995, Achievement award, 1996, Irving I. Sector award, Am. Soc. Clin. Hypnosis, 1997. Fellow APA, Am. Soc. Clin. Hypnosis (chmn. ethics com. 1993-97), Acad. Family Psychology (pres. 1995-96, re-elected sec. 2009-11), Acad. Family Psychology (found. sec. 1991-94, pres. 1995-96), Am. Acad. Counseling Psychology (bd. dirs. 1991-93, founding pres. 1993-95), Soc. Clin. Exptl. Hypnosis; mem. Am. Group Psychotherapy Assn., Va. Acad. Clin. Psychologists, Va. Psychol. Assn., NC Soc. Clin. Hypnosis, NC Psychol. Assn., Guilford County Psychol. Assn. (treas. 1997-98). Methodist. Achievements include inovator in psychotherapy approach utilizing a combined hypnotherapy and cognitive psychotherapy approach implementing age regression in the treatment of sex offenders and violent offenders. Avocations: running, reading, basketball. Home: 103 Tryon Ct Jacksonville NC 28546 Office: Pvt Practice 1 Mathew Ct Jacksonville NC 28546 also: Substance Abuse Rehab Program Naval Hosp Camp Lejeune 100 Brewster Ln Mental Health Dept Camp Lejeune NC 28547 Office Phone: 910-450-6531, 910-353-4991, 910-353-6410. Personal E-mail: drguyerii@yahoo.com. Business E-Mail: charles.guyer@med.navy.mil.

GUYNN, ROBERT WILLIAM, psychiatrist, educator; b. Streator, Ill., Oct. 27, 1942; s. William Digby and Helen Louise (Dancey) G. BA, Mich. State U., 1963; MD, Johns Hopkins U., 1967. Diplomate Am. Bd. Psychiatry and Neurology. Clin. fellow Nat. Inst. of Mental Health, Washington, 1970-73; asst. prof. Dept. of Psychiatry and Behaviorial Scis. U. Tex., Houston, 1973-76, assoc. prof., 1976-83, vice-chmn., prof. psychiatry, 1983—2010, interim chmn., 1987-89, chmn., 1989—2007, prof. emeritus, 2010—. Dir. U. Tex. Mental Scis. Inst., 1987—2007; exec. dir. Harris County Psychiat. Ctr., 1988—2007; sr. oral examiner Am. Bd. Psychiatry and Neurology, 1994—2003, mem. written exam com., 1998—2007, chair, 2008—; dir. Acad. Psychiatry, 2008—, editl. bd., 2006—08. Contbr. articles to profl. jours. and book chpts.; mem. editl. bd. Internat. Rev. Psychiatry, 1988-93, editor-in-chief, 1989-93. Bd. dirs. Vols. of Am., Houston, 1982—88; with Passages, 1991—94; mem. adv. bd. The Gathering Place, The Club House, 2004—07. Surgeon USPHS, 1970—73. Recipient Psychiat. Excellence award, Tex. Soc. Psychiat. Physicians, 2000. Fellow Am. Psychiat. Assn. (disting.), Am. Coll. Psychiatrists; mem. Am. Soc. Biol. Chemistry, Tex. Rsch. Soc. on Alcoholism (pres. 1985-87), Tex. Soc. of Am. Assn. Psychiat. Adminstrs. (treas. 1990-91, pres. 1992-93), Biochem. Soc., Rsch. Soc. on Alcoholism, Houston Psychiat. Soc. (v.p. 1989-90, pres. 1991-92), Harris County Med. Soc. (bd. ethics 1989-92), Tex. Dept. Mental Health and Mental Retardation (med. adv. com. 1997—2003), Mental Health and Mental Retardation Auth. (adv. bd. 1992—). Avocations: printmaking, painting. Office: U Tex Health Sci Ctr PO Box 20708 Houston TX 77225-0708 Office Phone: 713-500-2554. Business E-Mail: robert.w.guynn@uth.tmc.edu.

GUYTON, ROBERT A., cardiothoracic surgeon, medical educator; BS in Physics with great distinction, U. Miss., 1967; MD magna cum laude, Harvard Med. Sch., 1971. Bd. cert. Am. Bd. Surgery, Am. Bd. Thoracic Surgery, lic. Ga. Asst. resident, surgery Mass. Gen. Hosp., Boston, 1971—73, 1975—77, sr. resident, surgery, 1977—78, clin. fellow, surgery, 1977—78, chief resident, cardiothoracic surgery, 1979; clin. assoc. surgery Branch Nat. Heart & Lung Inst., Bethesda, Md., 1973—75; chief resident, cardiothoracic surgery Children's Hosp. Med. Ctr., Boston, 1978—79; asst. prof. surgery Emory U. Sch. Medicine., Atlanta, 1980—84, assoc. prof. surgery, 1984—90, Disting. Charles Ross Hatcher, Jr. prof. surgery, 1990—, dir., cardiothoracic residency training program, 1990—, chief, Divsn. Cardiothoracic Surgery, Dept. Surgery, 1990—; dir., Cardiothoracic Rsch. Lab. Carlyle Fraser Heart Ctr., Crawford Long Hosp., Atlanta, 1980—85, chief, cardiac surgery, 1987—95; co-dir. Emory-Georgia Tech. Biomedical Tech. Rsch. Ctr., Atlanta, 1986—92; chief, cardiothoracic surgery Emory U. Hosp., Atlanta, 2006—. Mem., transfusion com. Crawford Long Hosp., 1980—91, mem., infection control com., 1980—91, chmn., surgical intensive care unit com., 1980—91, critical pathway com. for cardiac surgery, 1993—95; co-dir. Emory-Ga. Tech. Biomedical Tech. Rsch. Ctr., Atlanta, 1986—90; chmn., new program develop., long range planning com. Emory U. Sch. Medicine, 1986—88, mem., univ. priorities com., 1988—91, mem. faculty com. on appointments and promotions, Office of the Dean, 1995—98; bd. dirs. exec. com. Emory Clinic, 1990—98, 1991—93; critical pathway task force for cardiac surgery Emory U. Hosp., 1994—; mem. Emory U. Sys. Healthcare Internet Com., 1995—97; chmn. Am. Coll. Cardiology/Am. Heart Assn. com. on guidelines for coronary artery bypass, 1997—2006; mem. Emory Healthcare Info. Tech. Com., 1999—2001, Emory Healthcare Managed Care Contract Com., 1999—; mem. valve adv. bd. Medtronic, Inc., 1999—; bd. dirs. Thoracic Surgery Found. for Rsch. and Edn., 2006—; invited lectr. in field. Co-editor: Cardiopulmonary Bypass Principles and Techniques of Extracorporeal Circulation; mem. editl. bd. Clin. Cardiology, 1989—, guest editor The Annals of Thoracic Surgery, 1988—98, Seminars in Thoracic and Cardiovascular Surgery, 1995, manuscript reviewer Jour. Am. Coll. Cardiology, Circulation, Am. Jour. Thoracic and Cardiovascular Surgery; contbr. articles to med. jours. Lt. comdr. US Pub. Health Svc., 1973—75. Recipient Award for Outstanding Rsch., Harvard Med. Sch., Mass. Med. Soc., 1971. Fellow: ACS; mem.: So. Surgical Assn., Am. Soc. for Artificial Internal Organs, Soc. for Thoracic Surgery End., Andrew G. Morrow Soc., Am. Heart Assn., AMA, Ga. Med. Assn., Atlanta Med. Assn., Thoracic Surgery Found. for Rsch. and Edn. (bd. dirs.), Thoracic Surgery Dirs. Assn., So. Thoracic Surgical Assn., Soc. Thoracic Surgeons (mem. program com. 1988—91, com. on edn. and resources 1989—91, chmn., com. on scientific program for 1990 interim meeting 1990, chmn., program com. 1990—91, treas.-elect 1996—97, internet liaison com. 1997—2000, treas. 1997—2002, mem. exec. com. 1997—2004, first-v.p. 2002—03, mem. Coun. on Health Policy & Relationships, chair, workforce on comm. 2005—, chair Workforce on Comm.), Am. Surgical Assn., Am. Coll. Cardiology, Am. Assn. Thoracic Surgeons (Evarts A. Graham Meml. Traveling Fellowship Com. 1990—94, mem. governing coun. 1992—95, Evarts A. Graham Meml. Traveling Fellowship Com. 1993—94, co-chmn., com. on continuing med. edn. 1995—96), Alpha Omega Alpha, Omicron Delta Kappa, Phi Kappa Phi. Achievements include patents pending in field. Office: The Emory Clinic Inc Bldg A Rm 2223 1365 Clifton Rd NE Atlanta GA 30322 Office Phone: 404-778-3836. Office Fax: 404-778-5039.

GUYURON, BAHMAN, plastic surgeon, educator; b. Tabriz, Iran, Mar. 24, 1946; MD, U. Tehran Med. Sch., 1971. Cert. Am. Bd. Surgery, Am. Bd. Plastic Surgery. Intern, craniofacial surgery Flushing Hosp., NY, 1973—74; resident, gen. surgery Boston U., 1974—78; resident, plastic surgery Cleve. Clinic Found., Ohio, 1978—80, dir., sect. craniofacial surgery Ohio, 1981—83; fellow, craniofacial surgery Toronto U. Hosp. for Sick Children, 1980—81; staff mem. Cleve. Clinic Hillcrest Hosp.; chief, divsn. plastic surgery Mt. Sinai Med. Ctr., 1986—93; med. dir. Zeeba Surgery Ctr., Lyndhurst, Ohio, 1997—; clin. prof., surgery Case Western Reserve U., Ohio; chief Divsn. Plastic Surgery Univ. Hosps. Case Med. Ctr., Ohio, 2005—; Kiehn-Deprez prof. and chmn., dept. surgery Case Med. Sch. and U. Hospitals Case Med. Ctr., Ohio; pres. Bahman Guyuron MD, Inc., 1982—. Bd. dirs. Noteworthy Med. Sys., Inc.; independent dir., mem. stock option com. Morgan's Food Inc., Cleve., 2003—; presenter in field. Contbr. several articles to peer-reviewed jours., chapters to books; pub. two textbooks, sr. editor Aesthetic Surgery Jour. Mem.: Aesthetic Surgery Edn. and Rsch. Found. (pres.-elect), Am. Assn. Plastic Surgeons (trustee), Plastic Surgery Endowment Fund (trustee), Plastic Surgery Edn. Found. (trustee), Am. Soc. Plastic Surgery (trustee), Northeast Ohio Soc. for Plastic and Reconstructive Surgeons (pres.), Ohio Soc. for Plastic and Reconstructive Surgeons, Rhinoplasty Soc., Am. Soc. Maxillofacial Surgeons (past pres.), Am. Bd. Plastic Surgery (dir.). Achievements include being one of the leaders in the investigation and surgical treatment of migraine headaches; invention of multiple medical and non-medical devices. Office: 29017 Cedar Rd Lyndhurst OH 44124 Office Phone: 440-461-7999. Office Fax: 440-461-4713. E-mail: bguyuron@aol.com.

GUZICK, DAVID S., academic administrator, hospital administrator; b. 1952; MD, NYU, 1979, PhD. Resident in ob-gyn. John Hopkins Hosp., 1979—83; fellow in reproductive endocrinology U. Tex. Southwestern Med. Sch., 1983—85; dir. divsn. reproductive endocrinology Magee Women's Hosp., U. Pitts.; assoc. prof. U. Pitts., 1986—94, prof., 1994—95; chief svc. ob-gyn. Strong Meml. Hosp., Rochester, NY; Henry A. Thiede prof. and chair ob-gyn. U. Rochester Sch. Medicine and Dentistry, 1995—2002, dean and prof. ob-gyn., 2002—09; sr. v.p. health affairs U. Fla., 2009—; pres. UF & Shands Health Sys., 2009—; bd. chmn. UF Shands and Shands Jacksonville, 2009—. Named one of America's Best 400 Doctors for Women, Good Housekeeping mag. Mem.: Inst. Medicine, Soc. Assisted Reproductive Tech., Soc. Reproductive Endocrinologists, Am. Soc. Reproductive Medicine, The Endocrine Soc., Am. Bd. Obstetrics and Gynecology, Coun. Chairs of Obstetrics and Gynecology, Soc. Gynecologic Investigation, Am. Gynecologic and Obstetric Soc., Soc. Scholars. Office: UF & Shands The University Fla Academic Health Sys 1600 SW Archer Rd Gainesville FL 32608 *

GUZY, PETER MICHAEL, cardiologist, educator; b. Monongahela, Pa., Oct. 30, 1940; BS in Chemistry, U. Notre Dame, 1962; PhD in Biochemistry, U. Ky., 1970; MD, Med. Coll. of Ohio, 1973. Resident McMaster U., Hamilton, Ont., Can., 1973-75, U. Toronto, Ont., Can., 1975-76; fellow in cardiology UCLA Sch. Medicine, 1976-79; asst. prof. medicine UCLA div. Cardiology, 1979-83, assoc. prof. medicine, 1984-90, clin. prof. medicine, 1990—. Dir. UCLA Pacemaker Clinic, 1980-95. Bd. dirs. Am. Heart Assn., 1984-87.

Named Tchr. of Yr., UCLA Dept. Medicine, 1981—82. Fellow Am. Coll. Cardiology, Royal Coll. Physicians, Surgeons of Can. Office: 100 UCLA Med Plz Ste 535 Los Angeles CA 90095 Office Phone: 310-209-7450.

GUZZARDI, GIUSEPPE, radiologist; b. Sanremo, Aug. 18, 1970; MD, U. Pavia, 1996. Vascular surgeon, radiologist U. Torino, 2002. Med. asst. Inst. Interventional Radiology A. Avogadro U., 1997—. Avocation: golf. Office: Corso Mazzini 18 Novara 28066 Italy Business E-Mail: guz@libero.it.

GWAK, YOUNG SEOB, biomedical researcher; b. Busan, Republic of Korea, Mar. 3, 1967; arrived in US, 2002; s. Byung Ok Gwak and Dae Kum Chung; m. Jong Eun Kwon, Aug. 19, 1972. BS, U. Incheon, 1994, MS, 1996; PhD, Yonsei U., Seoul, 2002. Lic. biomed. rschr. U. Tex. Med. Br. Rsch. assoc. Yonsei U. Sch. of Medicine, Seoul, 1996—99; postdoctoral fellowship U. of Tex. Med. Br., Galveston, 2002—, sr. rsch. scientist, 2007—. Contbr. articles to profl. jours. Mem.: Gulf Coast Pain Consortium, Soc.for Neurosci., Sigma Xi. Office: Univ Tex Med Br MRB 4 301 University Blvd Galveston TX 77555-1043 Business E-Mail: ysgwak@utmb.edu.

GWELY, NOURELDIN, thoracic surgeon, educator; b. Mansoura, Egypt, Oct. 16, 1965; MD, Mansoura, 1999. Resident, 1991—95; asst. lectr., 1995—2000; lectr., 2000—05; asst. prof, 2005—10; prof., cardiothoracic surgery Faculty Medicine, Mansoura U., 2010—. Cons. Health Ministry, 2000—. Mem.: Egyptian Soc. Cardiothoracic Surgery. Office: Bank Misr St Mansoura 1254 Egypt E-mail: dr.noureldin_noaman@yahoo.com.

GWIZDALA, ADRIAN, cardiologist; b. Poland, Jan. 21, 1977; D, U. Med. Scis., 2002. Physician Poznan U. Med. Scis., 2010—. Mem.: Polish Cardiac Soc., European Soc. Cardiology. Office: Dluga 1/2 Poznan Wielkopolska 610848 Poland E-mail: adrian.gwizdala@gmail.com.

GYAMFI, CYNTHIA, gynecologist, obstetrician, maternal-fetal medicine specialist; b. Dusseldorf, Germany, Oct. 28, 1972; arrived in U.S., 1977; d. Anthony Ransford and Mary Gyamfi. BS, U. Miami, 1994, MD, 1998. Diplomate Am. Bd. Ob-gyn., bd. cert. ob-gyn. 2006. Intern ob-gyn. U. Miami, Jackson Meml. Hosp., 1998—99, resident ob-gyn., 1999—2002; attending ob-gyn. Elmhurst Hosp. Ctr., NY, 2002—05; asst. clin. prof. maternal-fetal medicine Columbia U., 2005—. Fellow maternal fetal medicine Mt. Sinai Med. Ctr., NYC, 2002—05. Contbr. articles to profl. jours. Mem.: Nat. Med. Assn., Am. Inst. Ultrasound Medicine, Am. Coll. Ob-Gyn. (jr. fellow, sec.-treas. Dist. II 2003—04, jr. fellow, vice chmn. dist. II 2004—05, jr. fellow, chmn. dist. II 2005—06), Soc. Maternal Fetal Medicine (assoc.; pres.). Office: Columbia U Divsn Maternal-Fetal Medicine Dept Ob-Gyn 622 W 168th St PH-16 New York NY 10032 Home: 301 W 110TH ST APT 5R New York NY 10026-4061 Personal E-mail: drcynthiagyamfi@yahoo.com.

GYENES, GÁBOR, physician, educator; b. Budapest, Dec. 14, 1959; s. George and Marianne (Ferenczi) G.; m. Erika Müllner, July 13, 1991; children: Balázs, Dóra. MD, Semmelweis U. Med. Sch., Budapest, Hungary, 1984; postgrad., Karolinska Inst., Stockholm, 1994-97. Asst. prof. 3rd Dept Med. Semmelweis Med. U., 1984-98; clin. fellow adult cardiology U. Toronto, Ont., Can., 1998-2001; asst. prof. divsn. cardiology U. Alta., Edmonton, Canada, 2001—07, assoc. prof., 2007—. Author: Pharmindex Kompendium, 1995, Hypertension: Data and Facts, 1997, Handbook of Coronary Angiography and Angioplasty, 2001; editor: Cardiology, 2000; co-author, editor: 25 Landmark Trials in Cardiology, 2006, 2nd edit., 2008. Recipient Eminent Young Scientist award Internat. Rsch. Promotion Coun., 2000. Mem. Hungarian Soc. of Cardiology, Hungarian Soc. Internal Medicine, Can. Cardiovascular Soc. Avocations: rock and classical music, tennis, soccer. Office: U Alta Walter Mackenzie Health Ctr 2C2 Edmonton AB Canada T6G 2B7 Office Phone: 780-407-7929. Personal E-mail: gyenesgabor@hotmail.com. Business E-Mail: gabor.gyenes@capitalhealth.ca.

GYSBERS, NORMAN CHARLES, counselor, educator; b. Waupun, Wis., Sept. 29, 1932; s. George S. and Mabel (Landaal) Gysbers; m. Mary Lou Ziegler, June 23, 1954 (dec. July 1997); children: David(dec.), Debra, Daniel; m. Barbara K. Townsend, May 12, 2001 (dec. June 2009); m. Elinor Arendt Gysbers, Apr. 2, 2011. AB, Hope Coll., 1954; MA, U. Mich., 1959, PhD, 1963. Tchr. Elem. and Jr. H.S., Muskegon Heights, Mich., 1954-56; lectr. edn. U. Mich., 1962-63; prof. counseling psychology U. Mo., Columbia, 1963—, now curators' prof. Cons. U.S. Office Edn.; mem. nat. adv. coms. ERIC Clearinghouses in Career Edn. and Counseling and Pers. Svcs.; rsch. and devel. com. for CEEB, Am. Insts. for Rsch. Project on Career Decision Making, Comprehensive Career Edn. Model, TV Career Awareness Project KCET-TV, L.A.; dir. 10 nat. rsch. projects and state projects in career devel.-guidance; Francqui prof. Universite Libre de Bruxelles. Editor: Vocat. Guidance Quar. 1962-70; (with L. Sunny Hansen) spl. issue Personnel and Guidance Jour., May 1975, Jour. Career Devel., 1979-2006, (with E. Moore and W. Miller) Developing Careers in the Elementary School, 1973, (with E. Moore and H. Drier) Career Guidance: Practices and Perspectives, 1973; author: (with E. Moore) Improving Guidance Programs, 1981, Designing Careers, 1984, (with E. Moore) Career Counseling, 1987, (with P. Henderson) Developing and Managing Your School Guidance Program, 1988, 4th edit., 2006, (with C. McDaniels) Counseling for Career Development, 1992, (with P. Henderson) Guidance Programs that Work, 1997, (with M. Heppner and J. Johnston) Career Counseling, 1998, 3rd edit. 2009(translated into Italian, Japanese, Korean and Chinese), (with P. Henderson) Leading and Managing Your School Guidance Program Staff, 1998, (with P. Henderson) Implementing Comprehensive School Guidance Programs, 2002;(with Richard Lapan) Strengths-Based Career Development for Comprehensive School Gudiance and Counselling Programs 2009, Remembering the Past, Shaping the Future: A History of School Counseling, 2010; contbr. articles to profl. jours. and chpts. to textbooks. Elder Presbyn. Ch. Served with arty. U.S. Army, 1956-58. Recipient Am. Spirit award, USAF, 1987, Pillar of Excellence Ten Yr. award, Coll. Edn. U. Mo., 2003, Excellence in Tchg. award, Gov., 2004, Disting. Faculty Alumn award, 2008, Disting. Friend of Coll. award, 2011; William T. Kemper Excellence in Tchg. fellow, U. Mo., 2002. Mem.: ACA (pres. 1977—78, disting. profl. svc. award 1983), Internat. Assn. Ednl. and Vocat. Guidance, Mo. Guidance Assn. (outstanding svc. award 1978), Am. Vocat. Assn. (v.p. 1979—82, merit award guidance divsn. 1978), Am. Sch. Counselor Assn. (post-secondary sch. counselor of yr. 2001, Mary Geheke Lifetime Achievement award 2004), Assn. for Counselor Edn. and Supervision, Nat. Career Devel. Assn. (pres. 1972—73, nat. merit award 1981, Eminent Career award 1989, Disting. Faculty Alumn award 2008). Office: U Mo 201 G Student Success Ctr Columbia MO 65211-6060 Home: 4008 Fall Ridge Dr Columbia MO 65203 Office Phone: 573-882-6386. E-mail: gysbersn@missouri.edu. *

HA, CHUL-WON, medical educator; MD, PhD, Seoul Nat. U. Prof. Samsung Med Ctr., Sungkyunkwan U. Sch. Medicine, Seoul, 2004, prof., in-house staff, 2009—. Editl. bd. mem. Jour. Korean Orthopedic Assn., Seoul, 2007—. Author: (surgical video) AAOS Orthopedic Surgery Videotape Libr.; editl. bd. mem. (jour.) Korean Orthop. Rsch. Soc., Seoul, 2005—. Recipient Seoul Meml. award, SICOT, 2006, Excellent Paper award, 2007, Best Paper award, 2008. Mem.: Korean Orthop. Assn. (info. rsch. com. mem., editl. bd. mem. 2007—), Korean Knee Soc., Korean Arthroscopy Soc. (sci. bd. mem. 2006—). Achievements include invention of cartistem, a mesenchymal stem cell & hydrogel complex for the treatment of articular cartilage defects. Office: Samsung Med Ctr Dept Orthop Surg KangNam Gu IRWon Dong 50 Seoul 135-710 Republic of Korea Office Fax: 82 2 3410 0061. Business E-Mail: hacw@skku.edu.

HA, EUN HYE, psychologist, educator; m. Ki Hong Park; children: Se Won Park, Se Hyun Park. D in Philosophy, Yonsei U., Seoul, Korea, 2000. Lic. psychologist Dept. Nat. Health and Welfare, 1997. Assoc. prof. Dept. Child Welfare Sookmyung Women's U., 2004—. Mem.: Korean Psychol. Assn. Achievements include research in problems of topiramate compared to cabamazepine as monotherapy for Children with Benign Rolendic Epilepsy; effects of Cognitive-Behavioral Group Therapy for Depressive Mothers of Children with Behavior Problems. Office: Sookmyung Women's Univ 53-12 Chungpa-Dong 2-Ga Yongsan-Gu Seoul 140-742 Republic of Korea Office Fax: 82-2-710-9209. Business E-Mail: graceha@sookmyung.ac.kr.

HA, KWON-SOO, medical educator; b. Republic of Korea, Aug. 15, 1961; PhD, U. Tex., Austin, 1991. Rschr. Howard Hughes Med. Inst., Vanderbilt U. Sch. Medicine, 1992—93; prin. investigator Korea Basic Sci. Inst., 1994—2002; prof. Kangwon Nat. U. Sch. Medicine, 2002—. Recipient Premier award, Ministry of Sci. & Tech., Pres. award, Kangwon Nat. U., Best Tech. award, Korea Basic Sci. Inst. Mem.: Korean Biochip Soc., Korean Soc. Molecular & Cellular Biology, Human Proteome Orgn., Am. Soc. Cell Biology. Avocations: bicycling, running. Office: Kangwondaehak-Gil 1 Chuncheon Kangwon 200-701 Republic of Korea Office Fax: 82-33-250-8807. Business E-Mail. ksha@kangwon.ac.kr.

HA, SEUNG YEON, pathologist, educator; d. Man Jong Ha and Hyo Kon Park; m. Jin Kyu Choi; children: Jeong Eun Choi, Young Il Choi. MS, Chungnam U., Republic of Korea, 2000; DS, Korea U., Seoul, 1989, MD, PhD, 2003. Lic. Ministry for Health, Welfare and Family Affairs, 1989, cert. pathologist Ministry for Health, Welfare and Family Affairs, 1991, Clin. chief dept. pathology Gil Hosp., Incheon, 1994—99; instr. Gachon U., Incheon, 1999—2001, asst. prof., 2001—05, assoc. prof., 2005—, dir., dept. pathology. Vis. scholar Stanford U. Hosp., Calif.; rsch. fellow U. Calif., San Diego, 2003—04. Contbr. med. poster to exibitions (Best Poster, Japan-Korean Joint Meeting Diagnostic Cytopathology, 2007). Mem.: Korean Soc. Cytology, Korean Soc. Pathologist. Business E-Mail: syha@gilhospital.com.

HA, SUNG-JAE, research scientist, director; b. Republic of Korea, May 4, 1975; PhD, Kwangwoon U., 2006. Sr. engr. Samsung Thales, 2006—10; dir. R&D Ctr. Planning ICT Co. Ltd, 2011—. Avocation: golf. Home: Dream&Green Apt 102-309 Jung-Gye Dong Seoul 139-229 Republic of Korea Personal E-mail: sungjea@hanmail.net.

HA, TAE KYUNG, physician, surgeon; b. Seoul, Republic of Korea, Aug. 21, 1973; s. Jung Woo Ha and Jung Soon Lee; m. Youn Kyoung Seo, Dec. 20, 1998; children: Hyeri, Yuna, Dagyeom. PhD, Hanyang U. Coll. Medicine, Seongdong-ku, Haengdang-dong, 2007. Diplomate Ministry Health, Welfare and Family Affairs, 1998. Clin. asst. prof. Hanyang U. Med. Ctr., Seoul, Republic of Korea, 2008—09, asst. prof., 2010—. Contbr. articles to profl. jours. Capt. Mil. Army, 2003—06. Recipient Best Poster award, Korean Gastric Cancer Assn., 2007; Clin. Rsch. grant, Korean Soc. Clin. Oncology. Mem.: Korean Gastric Cancer Assn., Korean Soc. Clin. Oncology, Korean Surg. Soc., Korean Cancer Assn., Korean Soc. Endoscopic & Laparoscopic Surgeons. Home: Jungrang-gu Jungwha 1 dong 281-26 Seoul 131-875 Republic of Korea Office: Hanyang University Coll Medicine 17 Haengdang-dong Seongdong-ku Seoul 133-781 Republic of Korea Office Phone: 82-2-2290-8443-5. Office Fax: 82-2-2281-0224. Personal E-mail: 981220black@hanmail.net. Business E-Mail: missurgeon@hanyang.ac.kr.

HA, TAE-SUN, pediatrician, educator; b. Seoul, Republic of Korea, Feb. 6, 1962; s. Rak-Pyung Ha and Soon-Ran Kwon; m. Sun-Min Kim, Aug. 25, 1989; children: Jeong-Yoon, Dong-Soo. B in Med. Sci., Seoul Nat. U., 1987, M in Med. Sci., 1992, MD, 1995. Resident Seoul Nat. U. Hosp., Republic of Korea, 1988—91; instr., asst. prof., assoc. prof. Chungbuk Nat. U., Cheongju, Republic of Korea, 1992—2003, prof., 2003—. Mem. adv. bd. Korean Rsch. Found., Seoul, 2004—; mem. editl. bd. Korean Jour. Pediat., 2007—. Mem. editl. bd. Jour. Korea Soc. Pediat. Nephrology, 2003—07, editor-in-chief Chungbuk Med. Jour., 2003—07; contbr. articles to profl. jours. Rsch. grant, Health Technology Planning and Evaluation Bd., 1998—2000, Korean Soc. Nephrology, 2002, Korea Sci. and Engring. Found., 2002—05, 2007—, Korean Pediat. Soc., 2006, Nat. Rsch. Found. Korea, 2010—. Mem.: European Renal Assn., Internat. Pediat. Nephrology Assn., Am. Soc. Nephrology (corr.). Avocations: tennis, travel, movies. Office: Chungbuk Nat U Coll Medicine Dept Pediat 62 Gaeshin-Dong Cheongju 361-763 Republic of Korea Office Phone: 82 43 269 6374. Business E-Mail: tsha@chungbuk.ac.kr.

HA, YOON, biology professor; b. Seoul, Republic Of Korea, Aug. 19, 1968; s. Chong Hyun Ha and Mi Ja Park; m. Hee Jeong Kim, Apr. 6, 2004; 1 child, Su Rim. MD, Yonsei U., Korea, 1994, PhD, 2002. Cert. neurosurgeon Korean Neurosurgical Soc., 1999. Asst. prof., dept. neurosurgery Inha U., Incheon, Republic of Korea, 2004—08, Yonsei U., Seoul, 2008—. Artwork abstract painting and photograph. Capt. Airforce, 1999—2002, ChungJu. Recipient Student Rsch. award, Yonsei U., 1993, Severance award, 1994, Dir. award, Seoul Dist. Hosp., 2002, Young Neurosurgeon award, Korean Neurosurgical Soc., 2002, Synthes award, Congress Neurol. Surgeons, San Francisco, 2004, L'Oréal Best Poster award, Tissue Engring. Soc. Internat., Lausanne, Switzerland, 2004, Woo Jeong Hyun Meml. award, Korean Neurosurgical Soc., Seoul, 2004, 3rd Pl., Basic Sci. Rsch. award, Cervical Spine Rsch. Soc., Boston, 2004, Best Poster award, 2004, Best Rsch. award, Korean Tissue Engring. Soc. & Regenerative Medicine, Seoul, 2006, Korean Spinal Neurosurgery Soc., Seoul, 2006; grantee Tissue Engring. and Cell Therapeutics Devel., Ministry Commerce, Industry and Energy, Korea, 2005, Frontier project, Ministry Sci. and Tech. Korea, 2008; New Faculty grant, Korea Rsch. Found., 2003, Tissue engring. grant, Ministry Health and Welfare, Korea, 2005, Basic Rsch. grant, Ministry Sci. and Tech. Korea, 2006. Mem.: Asia Pacific Cervical Spine Soc., Asia Pacific Symposium Neural Regeneration, Cervical Spine Rsch. Soc., Korean Soc. Spinal Neurosurgery, Korea Inst. Sci. and Tech., Soc. Neurosci., Aerospace Med. Assn. Korea, Korean Cervical Spine Rsch. Soc., Congress Neurol. Surgeons. Achievements include research in cytokine therapy which improves neurologic functions in spinal cord injured patients; patents for role of autologous bone marrow cell transplantation; discovery of hypoxia inducible gene expression system; patents pending for tissue engineering technique. Avocations: painting, photography, music, travel. Home: Dangsandong 1 ga Yeondeungpogu Seoul 150-041 Republic of Korea Office: Yonsei Univ Dept Neurosurgery Shinchondong Seodaemungu Seoul 120-749 Republic of Korea Business E-Mail: hayoon@yuhs.ac.

HAAB, FRANCOIS, urologist, educator; b. Paris, Apr. 8, 1964; s. Michel and Marie Haab; m. Virginie Bardou-Jacquet, Mar. 10, 1990; children: Emilie, Dimitri. Cert. MD, prof.urology Paris Med. Sch., U. Pierre et Marie Curie Paris VI, 1995. Prof. urology Tenon Hosp., Paris, 2001—07, prof. urology, chmn. urology dept., 2008—. Adviser polit. party leader MODEM, Paris, 2001—. Recipient Award, French Acad. Surgery, 1995. Roman Cath. Avocations: running, tennis, golf. Home: 5 Rue Du Bel Air Paris 75012 France Office: Urology dept Tenon Hosp 4 Rue De La Chine Paris 75020 France Home Fax: 33156017306. Business E-Mail: francois.haab@tnn.aphp.fr.

HAAGA, JOHN R., radiologist; b. July 6, 1945; MD, Ohio State Univ. Coll. Med., 1970. Cert. Am. Bd. Radiology. Residency in diagnostic radiology Cleve. Clinic. Found.; chmn. Radiology Dept. & med. dir. Univ. Hospitals of Cleveland; Castele Prof. of radiology Case Western Reserve Univ. Office: UH Case Med Ctr 11100 Euclid Ave Cleveland OH 44106 Office Phone: 216-844-3858. Office Fax: 216-844-5922.

HAAGE, PATRICK, radiologist; b. Kiel, Germany, Oct. 4, 1967; s. Horst and Un Aie Ulrike Haage. MD, U. Düsseldorf, Germany, 1994; MBA, U. Aix-Marseille, France, 2003. Resident in radiology Med. U., Essen, Germany, 1995-97, U. Tech., Aachen, Germany, 1997-2000, fellow, 2000—02, assoc. prof., 2002—; chmn. dept. diagnostic and interventional radiology U. Witten/Herdecke, Wuppertal, Germany, 2006—. With German Army, 1987-88. Achievements include first demonstration of gadolinium-enhanced ventilation assessment in magnetic resonance imaging in large animals and in humans. Office: U Hosp Witten/Herdecke Heusnerstrasse 40 42283 Wuppertal Germany Home: Schanzenstraße 115 40549 Düsseldorf Germany Office Phone: 49 202 896 2565. Business E-Mail: patrick.haage@helios-kliniken.de.

HAAS, ERIC M., colon and rectal surgeon; b. Freeport, NY, Dec. 7, 1969; BA in Biology, U. Tex., Austin, 1993; MD, U. Tex., 1997. Pres. Colorectal Surg. Assoc., Ltd. LLP, 2003—. Program dir., minimally invasive colon & rectal surgery U. Tex. Med. Sch., Houston, 2008. Named one of Top Drs., Castle Connolly Med. Ltd., 2009, 2010, Best Physicians, Health and Fitness Sports Mag., 2008, 2009, Houston's Top Drs., H Tex. Mag., 2007, 2008, 2009, America's Top Surgeons, Consumer's Rsch. Coun. Am., 2010, 2011. Fellow: ACS, ASCRS; mem.: SAGES, MIRA, CRSA. Office: 7900 Fannin Ste 2700 Houston TX 77054 Office Fax: 713-790-0616. Business E-Mail: ehaasmd@houstoncolon.com.

HAAS, INGRID ELIZABETH, physician; b. Portland, Oreg., June 5, 1953; d. Fred F. and Anastasia Haas; children: Kristen, Lauren. BS, Oreg. State U., 1975; MD, U. Oreg., 1978. Diplomate Am. Bd. Ob.-Gyn. Physician CIGNA Healthplan, Phoenix, 1982-84, chief of staff, 1984-85; pvt. practice Scottsdale, Ariz., 1985—2011; v.p. spirit abd ward, 2011—. Chmn. ob.-gyn. dept. Scottsdale Meml. Hosp. North, 1987-88, chief of surgery, 1988-89, chmn. laser com., 1990—92; adv. bd. Scottsdale Meml. Office Community Health Edn., 1990—92, chmn. perinatal subcom. 1992; ball chmn. Desert Found., 2010; proctor Mentor Corp. for Advanced Pelvic Surgery; spkr. in field; cons. in field. Trustee emeritus SMH Found.; physician mem. Ariz. Med. Bd. 2002-05, med. cons. 2005—; mem. aux. bd. Desert Found; chmn. DFA Ball, 2010, Honor Ball, 2003. Named Scottsdale 101 Best Dr. of Yr., Americas Top Obstetricians & Gynecologists; named one of Best Drs. in Am., 2004, 2005—06, 2009—, 2010—11, Ind. Best Drs., 2005—06, Best Drs., Phoenix Mag., 2005—10. Mem. Am. Coll. Ob-Gyn., Am. Assn. Gynecologic Laparoscopists, Ariz. Med. Assn. Independent. Lutheran. Avocation: skiing. Office Phone: 480-483-9011.

HAAS, JERE DOUGLAS, nutritional sciences educator, researcher; b. Lancaster, Pa., Sept. 15, 1945; s. Jacob Charles and Dorothy Louise (Graeter) H.; m. Sharon Faye Pitt, June 22, 1968; children: Jeremy Michael, Jonathan Andrew. AB, Franklin and Marshall Coll., 1967; MA, Pa. State U., 1970, PhD, 1973. Trainee in human biology USPHS, Peru, 1971-73; asst. prof. anthropology U. Mass., Amherst, 1973-75; asst. prof. nutrition Cornell U., Ithaca, N.Y., 1975-80, assoc. prof., 1980-87, prof., 1987—; Nancy Schlegel Meinig prof. maternal and child nutrition; dir. human biology program, dir. divsn. nutritional scis. Cornell U., Ithaca, NY, 1998—2003. Hon. rsch. fellow anatomy dept. U. Aberdeen, Scotland, 1982, vis. prof. Food Rsch. Inst., Stanford (Calif.) U., 1988-89; mem. com. on nutrition during pregnancy and lactation Inst. Medicine, NAS, 1988-90; advisor panel on nutrition WHO, 1991—; chair subcom. on maternal anthropometry, 1991-94; tech. adv. group on food and nutrition Pan Am. Health Orgn., 1996—2009; dir. divsn. nutrition and health Nat. inst. Pub. Health, Cuernavaca, Mex., 1998. Mem. editl. bd. Human Biology, 1984-88, Annals Human Biology, 1985—, Am. Jour. Human Biology, 1990-2002; contbr. more than 200 articles to profl. jours., chpts. to books. Rsch. grantee NSF, Bolivia, Peru, 1975-96, NIH, N.Y., Kans., Guatemala, 1978-94, 1998-2003, 2006—, USDA, 1996-2010, Micronutrient Initiative, Philippines, 2001-05, India 2009-, IFPRI CIAT Mex. India, 2008-. Fellow AAAS, Human Biology Assn. (exec. com. 1981-85); mem. Am. Assn. Phys. Anthropologists (v.p. 1992-94, pres. 1995-97), Am. Soc. Nutrition, Publs. Mgmt. Com., Soc. Internat.

Nutrition Rsch. (exec. coun. 2000-04), Assn. Nutrition Depts. and Programs (treas. 1998-2003, chair 2003). Office: Cornell U 220 Savage Hall Ithaca NY 14853-6301 Business E-Mail: jdh12@cornell.edu.

HAAS, MARK, pathologist; b. NYC, Jan. 30, 1955; s. Alvin and Ruth (Heller) H. BA, Duke U., 1977, PhD, MD, 1982. Diplomate Am. Bd. Pathology. Assoc. rschr. dept. physiology Duke U., Durham, NC, 1983; resident dept. pathology Yale-New Haven Hosp., 1983-85; postdoctoral fellow dept. physiology Sch. Medicine Yale U., New Haven, 1985-86; asst. prof. pathology Yale U., New Haven, 1986-89, U. Chgo., 1989-93, assoc. prof., 1993—99, dir. renal pathology, 1994—99; assoc. prof., dir. electron microscopy lab. Johns Hopkins U., Balt., 1999—2009, dir. renal pathology, 2004—09, prof., 2004—; staff pathologist Cedars Sinai Med. Ctr., LA, 2009—10; prof. Cedars Sinai Acad. Series, 2010—. Sect. editor Clin. Nephrology, 2010—. Reviewer: Am. Jour. Physiology, 1984—, mem. editl. bd., 1993-99; reviewer: Jour. Membrane Biology, 1985—, Jour. Biol. Chemistry, 1987—, Jour. Clin. Investigation, 1990—, Sci., 1991—, Jour. Am. Soc. Nephrology, 1995—, Am. Jour. Pathology, 1998-, Am. Jour. Transplantation, 2006-; mem. editl. bd. Am. Jour. Kidney Diseases, 1999-2001, Kidney Internat., 2002-; sect. editor Clin. Nephrology, 2010-; contbr. articles to profl. jours, chpts. to med. books. Recipient Established Investigator award, Am. Heart Assn., 1992-97; rsch. grantee NIH, Am. Heart Assn., Cystic Fibrosis Found.; fellow John A. Hartford Found., 1986-89. Mem. Am. Soc. for Investigative Pathology, U.S. and Canadian Acad. Pathology, Am. Soc. Nephrology, Renal Pathology Soc. (concillor 2003-06, v.p. 2007, pres. 2008), Alpha Omega Alpha (v.p., organizer symposium 1981-82). Office: 8700 Beverly Blvd Rm 8742 Los Angeles CA 90048 E-mail: mark.haas@cshs.org.

HAASE, ASHLEY THOMSON, microbiology professor, researcher; b. Chgo., Dec. 8, 1939; s. Milton Conrad and Mary Elizabeth Minter (Thomson) H.; m. Ann DeLong, 1962; children: Elizabeth, Stephanie, Harris. BA, Lawrence Coll., 1961; MD, Columbia U., 1965. Intern Johns Hopkins Hosp., Balt., 1965—67; clin. assoc. Nat. Inst. Allergy and Infectious Disease, Bethesda, Md., 1967—70; vis. scientist Nat. Inst. Med. Rsch., London, 1970—71; chief infectious disease sect. VA Med. Ctr., San Francisco, 1971—84, med. investigator, 1978—83; prof. microbiology U. Minn., Mpls., 1984—99, head dept., 1984—, Regents' prof., 1999—. Mem. fellowship screening com. Am. Cancer Soc., San Francisco, 1978-81; mem. UNESCO Internat. Cell Rsch. Orgn., India, 1978; mem. nat. adv. coun. Nat. Inst. Allergy and Infectious Diseases, 1986-91, mem. task force on microbiology and infectious diseases, 1991, Method to Extend Rsch. in Time investigator, 1989—, chair AIDS rsch. adv. com., 1993-96, chmn. vaccine subcom.; Javits neurosci. investigator Nat. Inst. Neurol. and Communicative Disorders and Stroke, 1988-95; chmn. panel on AIDS, 1988-95, U.S.-Japan Coop. Med. Sci. Program, 1988-95, chair US Delegation, 2005-; mem. OAR AIDS Rsch. Evaluation Working Group, 1995-96; mem. adv. com. for career awards in biomed. scis. Burroughs-Wellcome Fund, 1995-2000; trustee Lawrence U., 1997-2000; adv. coun. NIH Office AIDS Rsch., 2002—05, Inst. Medicine, 2003—. Editor: Microbial Pathogenesis, 1988-94; contbr. articles on AIDS pathogenesis and other topics in neurovirology to profl. jours. Recipient Lucia R. Briggs Disting. Achievement award Lawrence Coll., 1990. Mem. AAAS (coun. del. sect.on med. scis. 2006—), Am. Soc. Microbiology, Assn. Am. Physicians, Am. Soc. Clin. Investigation, Am. Soc. Virology, Assn. Med. Schs. Microbiology Chmn., Infectious Diseases Soc. Am., Nat. Multiple Sclerosis Soc. (adv. com. 1978-84), Am. Assn. Immunologists, Phi Beta Kappa, Alpha Omega Alpha Democrat. Home: 14 Buffalo Rd Saint Paul MN 55127-2136 Office: U Minn Dept Microbiology 420 Delaware St SE Minneapolis MN 55455-0374 Business E-Mail: haase001@umn.edu.

HAASE, JUERGEN, cardiologist, professor of medicine; b. Wuerzburg, Germany, Apr. 15, 1954; s. Werner and Jutta Haase; m. Renate Haase, July 15, 1985; children: Jeannine, Wolfgang. MD, Tech. U., Munich, 1981; PhD, Erasmus U., Rotterdam, 1993. Lic. Germany, 1980, cert. in medicine Germany, 1986, in cardiology Germany, 1988, lic. Netherlands, 1991. Resident in medicine Kempfenhausen Hosp., Munich, 1980—84; resident in cardiology Bogenhausen Hosp., Munich, 1984—91; rsch. fellow in cardiology Erasmus Med. Ctr., Rotterdam, 1991—93; sr. cardiologist Red Cross Hosp., Frankfurt, 1993—94, cons. in cardiology, 1995—; sr. cardiologist Heart Ctr., Frankfurt, 1994—96, cons. in cardiology, 1997—2000. Dir. annual course Global Cardiovascular Interventions, 1997—2006; lectr. Johann-Wolfgang-Goethe-U., Frankfurt, 2001—; assoc. editor Jour. Interventional Cardiology, 2005—10; prof. Goethe U., Frankfurt, 2007—. Editor: (text book) Cardiovascular Interventions in Clinical Practice. Fellow: Am. Coll. Cardiology, European Soc. Cardiology. Achievements include research in experimental and clinical validation of quantitative coronary angiography systems; investigation of new interventional devices. Office: Kardiocentrum Frankfurt Pfingstweidstr 11 Frankfurt Germany 60316 Office Phone: 49-69-94434-153. Business E-Mail: j.haase@kardiocentrum.de.

HABAL, NIZAR, oncologist, surgeon, educator; b. NY, Nov. 1, 1965; s. Saleh and Munawar Habal; m. Razan Istwany, Jan. 8, 1998; children: Yasmine, Kamal. BA, Cornell U., Coll. Arts Sciences, Ithaca, NY, 1983—87; MS, Columbia U., Sch. Human Nutrition, NY, 1987—88; MD, NY Med. Coll., Valhalla, 1989—93. Cert. Am. Bd. Surgery, 1999. Attending surgeon Pitt County Meml. Hosp., Greenville, NC, 2000—; adj. prof. dept. clin. nutrition NY Inst. Tech., Westbury, 1988; coord. AIDS edn. program dept. health NY Med. Coll., Westchester County, Valhalla; resident surgeon The NY Hosp., Cornell Med. Ctr., New York, 1993—98; sr. clin. fellow John Wayne Cancer Inst., Santa Monica, Calif., 1998—2000. Cons. Physicians East Breast Cancer Ctr., Greenville, NC, 2002—. Author: (rsch.) Annals Of Surgical Oncology, Seminars In Oncology, Anticancer Research, Journal Of Surgical Oncology. Recipient, Alpha Omega Alpha Honor Med. Soc., 1991; fellow Fellow, Am. Bd. of Surgery, 2003; scholar, NY Med. Coll. Bd. Of Trustees, 1990-1993. Fellow: ACS; mem.: Am. Bd. Surgery, Am. Soc. Gen. Surgeons, NC Med. Soc. (county del. 2002—02), Am. Soc. Breast Surgeons, Soc. Surg. Oncology. R-Liberal. Muslim. Office: Carolina Breast and Oncologic Surgery 2223 Hemby Ln Greenville NC 27834 Business E-Mail: nh.cbos@earthlink.net.

HABBOUSHE, MUDHAFER PETROS, orthopedist, educator; b. Nineveh, Mosul, Iraq, Apr. 9, 1935; s. Petros Behnam Habboushe and Nejma Yousif Simble; m. Hayfa Faraj Al-Shiekh; children: Rowaida, Raya, Rana. MBBCh, Baghdad U., 1961; MS in Orthop., Liverpool U., 1973. Lic. in med. surgery and midwifery Soc. Apothecaries London, 1968. Gen. Iraqi Armed Forces Med. Svcs., 1961—2003, gen., Iran-Iraq War, 1981—88; sr. house officer surgery Rasid Mil. Hosp., Iraq, 1961—65, cons. orthops., 1974—80; head accident and orthops. dept. Rashid Mil. Hosp., 1981—93; registrar orthops. Lord Mayor Treloar's Hosp., England, 1965—69; cons., comdr. orthops. Habaniya Air Force Hosp., Iraq, 1969—74; lectr. orthops. Coll. Medicine, Iraq, 1993—2003; with Advaclinic Amman Jordon, 2011—. Traumatologist, team drs. Bin Sina Predl. Hosp., 1976—2003; cons., orthop. and trauma Ministry of Def., Iraq, 1990—2003, Arab Med. Ctrs., Amman, Jordan, 2003—08, Jordan Orthop. and Spinal Ctr., Amman; pvt. practice Advaclinic Amman Jordon. Contbr. articles to numerous profl. jours. Named Plaque Iraqi Orthop. Bd., 1993, Plaque Iraqi Med. Svcs., 1968. Fellow: RCS (Eng.), ACS; mem.: Brit. Med. Assn., Jordanian Med. Assn., Iraqi Orthop. Bd., Iraqi Med. Assn. Home: 3142 Albany Dr Sterling Heights MI 48310 Office: P.O. Box 101 11831 Amman Jordan Personal E-mail: umran_ibrahim@yahoo.com.

HABENICHT, JOANNE ELIZABETH, radiation therapist educator; d. Thomas J. Habenicht and Gertrude Gaynor Habenicht. BS, St. Joseph's Coll., Patchogue, NY, 1988; MPA, LI U., Greenvale, NY, 1995. Cert. in radiology, radiation therapy, mammography Am. Registry of Radiologic Technologists, Minn., 1972. Radiographer, radiation therapist Syosset Hosp., NY, 1972—79; radiation therapist LI Jewish Med. Ctr., New Hyde Pk., NY, 1979—90; radiation therapy tech. program dir. NY Meth. Hosp., Bklyn., 1990—97, Manhattan Coll., Riverdale, NY, 1997—. Chairperson radiation therapy com. Assn. Educators Radiologic Sci. State NY, 1996—2006; moderator Radiol. Sci. Soc. Manhattan Coll., Co-Curricular Club, Riverdale, NY, 1997—; tech. advisor NYSDOH Radiol. Bur. Environ. Radiation, Troy, NY, 2005—08. Mem.pres. Cathedral Gardens Coop., Hempstead, NY, 2002—05. Recipient Pi Alpha Alpha award, LI U., 1993, Lambda Nu award, Manhattan Coll., 2008. Mem.: NY State Soc. Radiologic Scis., AERT of SNY, NSSRT, AIERS, NESRT, ASRT, ASTRO. Avocations: reading, dog breeding. Office: Manhattan Coll 4513 Manhattan Coll Pwy Mem 428 Bronx NY 10471 Business E-Mail: joanne.habenicht@manhattan.edu.

HABER, PIERRE-CLAUDE, psychologist; b. Landau, Germany, June 8, 1931; arrived in US, 1943, naturalized, 1949; s. Kurt S. and Hedwig (Kuhn) Haber. BA, Bklyn. Coll., 1952; MA, Duke U., 1953; PhD, U. Paris, 1956. Counselor, dir. adult edn. Ctrl. Sch. Dist. 2, Yorktown Heights, NY, 1956—59; psychologist Manpower Devel. Program, Bklyn., 1959—65; asst. prof. Queens Coll., 1965—70; exec. sec., exec. dir. Psychology Soc., NYC, 1970—; cons. forensic psychologist NY, 1978—; assoc. prof. Jersey City State Coll., 1967—80. Organizer biennial overseas study and visitation trips. Author: The Social and Political Attitudes of Andre Gide, 2000; contbr. articles to profl. jours. & Compton's Ency. Bd. advisors Nat. Reference Inst. Mem.: APA, NY Assn. Pub. Sch. Adult Educators, Am. Psychology Soc., NY State Pers. and Guidance Assns. (v.p. 1957—59), Pi Delta Phi. Republican. Jewish.

HABER, RALPH NORMAN, psychology consultant, researcher, educator; b. Lansing, Mich., May 15, 1932; s. William and Fannie (Gallas) Haber; m. Ruth Lea Boss, 1961 (div. 1974); children: Sabrina Beth, Rebecca Ann; m. Lyn R. Roland, 1974. BA, U. Mich., 1953; MA, Wesleyan U., Middletown, Conn., 1954; PhD, Stanford U., 1957; Postdoctoral fellow, Med. Research Council, Applied Psychology Unit, Cambridge, Eng., 1970-71. Rsch. assoc. Inst. for Comm. Rsch., Stanford, 1957-58; instr. psychology San Francisco State Coll., Calif., 1957-58; asst. prof. psychology Yale, 1958-64; assoc. prof. psychology U. Rochester, NY, 1964-67, prof. psychology NY, 1967-70, prof. psychology and visual sci. NY, 1970-79, chmn. dept. psychology NY, 1967-70, mem. faculty senate NY, 1968-70, sec., mem. steering com. NY, 1969-70; prof. psychology U. Ill., Chgo., 1979-91, rsch. prof., 1991-94, rsch. prof. emeritus, 1994—; ptnr. Human Factors Cons., Swall Meadows, Calif., 1988—; rsch. assoc. psychology U. Calif., Santa Cruz, 1990. Chmn., divisional maj. III Yale, 1959—64; vis. asst. prof. New Sch. Social Rsch., 1963; rsch. cons. VA, 1967—71; adv. editor exptl. psychology Holt, Rinehart & Winston Book Pubs., 1969—77; vis. scientist Med. Rsch. Coun. Applied Psychology Unit, Cambridge, England, 1970—71; ptnr. Human Factors Cons., Highland Park, Ill., 1979—94; vis. prof. Air Force Human Resources Lab., Williams AFB, Ariz., 1981—83; adj. prof. U. Calif., Riverside, 1997—99. Author (with Hershenson): The Psychology of Visual Perception, 1973, 2d edit., 1980; author: (with Fried) An Introduction to Psychology, 1975; author: (with others) Discovering Psychology, 1977; co-author (with Lyn Haber): Challenges to Fingerprints, 2009; editor: Current Research on Motivation, 1966, Contemporary Theory and Research on Visual Perception, 1968, Information Processing Approaches to Visual Perception, 1969; contbr. articles to profl. jours. Commr. Wheeler Crest Fire Prevention Dist., Swall Meadows, Calif., 1995—2000; founder, 1st pres., bd. dirs. Eastern Sierra Conservancy, 2000—02; bd. dirs. Andrea Lawrence Inst. Mountains and Rivers, 2005—09; mem. Mono County Grand Jury, 2010—11; committeeman 18th ward Birghton Dem. Com., NY, 1967—70; founding mem., trustee Admission Prep. Program, Rochester, 1968—70. Recipient Outstanding Achievement award, U. Mich., 1977; grantee, NSF, NIH, Nat. Inst. Edn., Air Force Office Sci. Rsch., Dept. Army; Behavioral Sci. fellow, Ford Found., 1953—54. Fellow: AAAS, APA, Am. Psychol. Soc.; mem.: Internat. Assn. Identification, Human Factors and Ergonomics Soc., Optical Soc. Am., Brit. Psychol. Assn., Psychonomics Soc., Am. Contract Bridge League (dir. Bishop unit 517 1996—), Sigma Xi, Pi Lambda Pi. Home Phone: 760-387-2458; Office Phone: 760-387-2458. Business E-Mail: ralph@humanfactorsconsultants.com.

HABERAL, MEHMET, surgeon; b. Rize, Turkey, Oct. 29, 1944; Medical Diploma, Ankara U. Med. Sch., Turkey, 1967; DSc (hon.), U. Karachi, Pakistan, 2006; DS (hon.), Azerbaijan Med. U., 2006. Gen. surgeon Hacettepe U., 1971; fellow Shriner's Burn Inst., Galveston, Tex., 1973, Colo. Univ. Med. Sch., 1974—75; founder burn and transplantation unit Hacettepe U., Ankara, Turkey, 1975, assoc. prof. of gen. surgery, 1976—; mem. editl. bd. Burn Care and Rehab. Mem. editl. bd. Internat. Med. Jour. and Jour. of Investigative Surgery, Clin. Transplantation, Transplantation Procs.; mem. adv. bd. Saudi Jour. Kidney Diseases and Transplantation; founder Turkish Organ Tranaplantation and Burn Found. Hosp., 1985, Baskent U., Haberal Ednl. Found., 1993; mem. editl. bd. Burn Care andRehabilitation; vis. prof. The Mass. Gen. Hosp., Boston, 2006, The Johns Hopkins U., 2006. Editor-in-chief: jours. Dialysis, Transplantation and Burn, Jour. of Exptl. and Clin. Transplantation; guest editor Transplantation Procs., 1996, 1998, 2000, 2002, 2004, 2005, 2006, Urology Jour., 2004, mem. editl. bd Jour. Burn Care and Rehab., Urology Jour., 2004. Recipient Everett Idris Evans Meml. award, Am. Burn Assn., 1985, Millenium medal, Transplantation Soc., Rome, 2000; fellow, FACS, 1987. Fellow: Internat. Coll. Surgeons (hon.), Am. Surg. Assn. (hon.); mem.: Internat. Soc Burn Injuries (pres. 2006—08), Mediterranean Burns Club (founding mem. 1984), Turkish Organ Transplantation and Burn Found. (founder), Mid. East Burn and Fire Disaster Soc. (founder 1998, pres. 2006—), Turkish Burn and Fire Disaster Soc., N.Y. Acad. Sci., Turkish Transplantion Soc (founder, pres. 1990), Middle East Soc. for Organ Transplantation (founder, pres. 1987). Achievements include first to perform an organ transplantation in Turkey; performed the first living-related kidney transplantation in Turkey in 1975 and the first successful cadaver-liver transplantation in Turkey and the region in 1988; performed the first cadaver kidney transplantation in Turkey with an organ provided by Eurotransplant; first domestic cadaver kidney trasplantation in Turkey; first pediatric segmenteal living-related liver transplantation in Turkey, region and Europe; first adult segmental living-related liver transplantation in the world; first combined liver-kidney transplantation from a living related donor in the world; research in cadaver-kidney with cold ischemia time up to 111 hours. Office: Baskent Univ 1 6490 Ankara Turkey Office Phone: 90 312 2127393. E-mail: rektorluk@baskent-ank.edu.tr.

HABERMANN-HORSTMEIER, LOTTE H., medical educator, director; b. Horbach, Hesse, Germany, 1959; d. Robert Rudolf and Magdalena Cäcilia Habermann; m. Gerrit Horstmeier, 1984; children: Katja Magdalena Horstmeier, Lukas Maximilian Horstmeier. PhD in Neurophysiology, Philipps-U., Marburg, Germany, 1986. Cert. in orthopedagogy U. Hagen, 1986, in psychobiology Deutsches Inst. Fernstudien U. Tuebingen, 1987, in anthropology 1993, diplomate in acupuncture NPA, 2004, Landesaerztekammer Baden-Wuerttemberg, Stuttgart, Germany, 2008, in phytotherapy BTB Remscheid, 2005, in nutrtional medicine Deutsche Acad. Ernaehrungsmedizin, Freiburg, Germany, 2008. Med. writer Dr. Carl GmbH, Stuttgart, 1986—; lectr. Several Colls. Further Edn., Marburg, 1986—, Saarbrücken, Germany, Rottweil, Germany; dep. dir. STZ Unternehmen & Fuehrungskraefte, Villingen-Schwenningen, Germany, 2005—; lectr. physiology, anatomy, functional food nutrition Furtwangen U., Germany, 2008—. Mem. adv. coun. Landesstiftung Baden-Wuerttemberg, 2008—. Mem.: Bundesverband deutscher Ernaehrungsmediziner. Office: STZ Unternehmen & Fuehrungskraefte Klosterring 5 Villingen-Schwenningen 78050 Germany Business E-Mail: stz952@stw.de.

HABICHT, JEAN PIERRE, public health educator; b. Geneva, Dec. 15, 1934; s. Max H. and Elizabeth (Peterson) Herzog; m. Pat Hinxman, Jan. 3, 1959 (div. Oct. 1990); children: Heidi, Christopher, Oliver; m. Gretel H. Pelto, June 13, 1997. MD, U. Zurich, Switzerland, 1964; MPH, Harvard U., 1968; PhD, MIT, 1969. Cert. in clin. nutrition Am. Bd. Nutrition. Biochem. rsch. asst. Merck, Sharpe, and Dohme, Rahway, NJ, 1958; pediat. intern Children's Hosp. Med. Ctr., Boston, 1965—66; med. officer WHO, Guatemala, 1969—74; prof. maternal and child health U. San Carlos, Guatemala, 1972—74; spl. asst. Nat. Ctr. Health Stats., Washington, 1974—77; James Jamison prof. Cornell U., Ithaca, NY, 1977—2005, emeritus grad. prof. nutritional epidemiology, 2005—. Cons. pub. health issues nat. and internat. govt., profl. agy., 1975—; mem. expert com. nutrition WHO, Geneva, 1975—, mem. com. epidemiology and disease prevention, 1986—89, chmn. expert com. phys. status, 1991—93; chmn. expert com. optimal duration exclusive breast feeding, 2001; mem. tech. adv. com. Child and Adolescent Health and Devel., 2001—05; mem. epidemiology and disease control study sect. NIH, Washington, 1980—83; mem. joint nutrition monitoring and evaluation com. HHS-USDA, 1982—86; mem. adv. group coordinating subcom. nutrition UN, 1983—89, chmn., 1986—87; mem. food and nutrition bd. NAS, Washington, 1981—84, mem. com. internat. nutrition, 1975—79, mem. com. uses dietary reference intakes Inst. Medicine, 1997—2000. Contbr. articles to profl. jours., chapters to books. Fellow: Soc. Internat. Nutrition Rsch. (pres. 2002—04, Kellogg prize 1994), Am. Soc. Nutrition (Atwater Meml. lectr. 1998, Conrad A. Elvehjem award 1999, McCollum Internat. lectureship 2006—07), Am. Coll. Epidemiology; mem.: APHA, Internat. Soc.. Environ. Epidemiology, Internat. Soc. Rsch. Human Milk and Lactation (exec. com. 1995—96), Internat. Epidemiol. Assn., Soc. Epidemiologic Rsch., Am. Soc. Clin. Nutrition, Delta Omega, Gamma Sigma Delta, Sigma Xi. Office: 129 Eastlake Rd Ithaca NY 14850 E-mail: gp32@cornell.edu.

HACHIYA, AKIRA, research scientist; b. Nagasaki, Japan, Apr. 21, 1972; s. Makoto and Kimiyo Hachiya; m. Kaoru Nakajima, July 1, 1975; children: Akane, Shiori Gloria. PhD in Med. Sci., Tokyo Med. U., 2007. Cert. in Biol. Sci. Lab. Kao Corp., Tokyo. Rschr. Kao Corp. Biol. Sci. Lab., Haga-gun, Tochigi, Japan, 1997—2003, rsch. mgr. Cin., 2004—. Contbr. articles to profl. sci. jours. Mem.: Japanese Soc. Pigment Cell Rsch. (nagoya, Japan 1997—2008). Achievements include patents for human skin substitutes, photo aged skin model, pigmentation spot model; methods for gene transfer to mammals. Avocations: fishing, tennis, travel. Office Phone: 81-258-68-7490. Business E-Mail: hachiya.akira@kao.co.jp.

HACHTEN, RICHARD ARTHUR, II, healthcare system executive; b. LA, Mar. 24, 1945; s. Richard A. and Dorothy Margaret (Shipley) H.; m. Jeanine Hachten, Dec. 12, 1970; children: Kristianne, Karin. BS in Econs., U. Calif., Santa Barbara, 1967; MBA, UCLA, 1969. Mgmt. intern TRW Systems Group, Redondo Beach, Calif., 1969-72; adminstrv. asst. Meth. Hosp., Arcadia, Calif., 1972-73, asst. adminstr., 1973-74, assoc. adminstr., 1974-76, v.p. adminstrn., 1976-80; exec. v.p., adminstr., 1980-81; pres., adminstr., 1981-84; CEO Tri-City Hosp. Dist., Oceanside, 1984-91; pres. Bergan Mercy Health Sys., Omaha, 1991-95, Algent Health, Omaha, 1996—. Instr. health care mgmt. Pasadena (Calif.) City Coll. Bd. dirs., pres. Hospice of Pasadena, Inc.; bd. dirs. ARC, Arcadia, Mercy Housing Midwest, Omaha, Metropolitan Cmty. Coll. Found.; bd. governing mems. Omaha Symphony. Fellow Am. Coll. Healthcare Execs.; mem. Hosp. Coun. San Diego and Imperial Counties (chmn., bd. dirs.), Nebr. Hosp. Assn. (chmn. bd. dirs., chmn. dist. 1), Calif. Assn. Hosps. and Health Sys. (bd. dirs.), Am. Hosp. Assn. (policy bd. mem.), Rotary, Beta Gamma Sigma. Republican. Methodist. Office: Alegent Health 12809 W Dodge Rd Omaha NE 68154 Home: 1895 NW Perspective Dr Bend OR 97701-8305 Home Phone: 402-393-6988; Office Phone: 402-343-4420. Business E-Mail: richard.hachten@alegent.org.

HACKBARTH, GLENN M., human services administrator; BA, Pa. State U.; MA, JD, Duke U. Atty. advisor to asst. sec. for planning and evaluation HHS, 1981—84; dep. adminstr. Health Care Financing Adminstrn., HHS, 1986—88; sr. v.p. Harvard Cmty. Health Plan, 1988—97; founder, CEO Harvard Vanguard Med. Assocs., Boston, 1997—98; chmn. Medicare Payment Adv. Commn., Washington, 2001—. Cons. The Bard Group, 2000—01. Office: Medicare Payment Advisory Commn 601 New Jersey Ave NW Ste 9000 Washington DC 20001 *

HACKEL, EMANUEL, science educator; b. Bklyn., June 17, 1925; s. Henry N. and Esther (Herbstman) H.; m. Elisabeth Mackie, June 24, 1950 (dec. Apr. 1978); children: Lisa M., Meredith Anne, Janet M.; m. Rachel A. Fisher, Oct. 18, 1981; stepchildren: Daniel E., Tabitha A., and Jessica K. Harrison. Student, N.Y. U., 1941—42; BS, U. Mich., 1948, MS, 1949; PhD, Mich. State U., 1953. Fisheries biologist Mich. Dept. Conservation, 1949; mem. faculty Mich. State U., East Lansing, 1949—, prof. natural sci., 1962-74, chmn. dept. natural sci., 1963-74, prof. medicine, 1974-95, prof. emeritus, 1995—, prof. zoology, 1974-95, prof. emeritus, 1995—. Asst. dean coll. 1958-63; rsch. fellow Galton Lab., U. Coll., London, 1970-71, 77-78; vis. investigator blood group rsch. unit Lister Inst., London, 1956-57; cons. Mpls. War Meml. Blood Bank, 1983-95. Author: Guide to Laboratory Studies in Biological Science, 1951, Studies in Natural Science, 1953, Natural Science, 1955, Vols. 1, 2, 3, 1952-63. Editor: The Search for Explanation-Studies in Natural Science, Vols. 1, 2, 3, 1967-68, Laboratory Manual for Natural Science, Vol. 1, 2, 3, 1967-68, Human Genetics, 1974, Theoretical Aspects of HLA, 1982, Bone Marrow Transplantation, 1983, HLA Techniques for Blood Bankers, 1984, Human Genetics 1984: A Look at the Last Ten Years and the Next Ten, Transfusion Management of Some Common Heritable Blood Disorders, 1992, Advances in Transplantation, 1993, HLA Typing Section, Clinical Laboratory Medicine, 1994, Human Genetics '94: A Revolution in Full Swing, 1994; contbr. articles on genetics, human blood group immunology and chem. nature of blood group antigens, human biochem. genetics, tissue typing, human histocompatibility antigens to sci. jours. Served to lt. (j.g.) USNR, 1943-47; now lt. comdr. USNR Ret. Recipient Cooley Meml. award Am. Assn. Blood Banks, 1969, Elliott Meml. award Am. Assn. Blood Banks, 1987, alumni disting. faculty award Coll. Natural Sci. Mich. State U., 1995. Mem. Assn. Gen. and Liberal Studies (sec.-treas. 1962-65), AAUP, AAAS, Genetics Soc. Am., Am. Soc. Human Genetics, Am. Assn. Blood Banks (dir. 1983-84, chmn. sci. sect. 1983-84), Mich. Assn. Blood Banks (v.p. 1970, pres. 1975-77), Am. Inst. Biol. Sci., Biometric Soc., Transplantation Soc. Mich. (dir. 1975-84), Am. Assn. for Clin. Histocompatability Testing, N.Y. Acad. Scis., Sigma Xi, Phi Kappa Phi. Home: 244 Oakland Dr East Lansing MI 48823-4747

HACKER, KAREN, internist, adolescent medicine, educator; MD, Northwestern U., Evanston, 1982. Diplomate Am. Bd. Internal Medicine, 1985, Am. Bd. Internal Medicine-adolescent medicine, 2004. Resident internal medicine Boston City Hosp., 1983—85; fellow adolescent medicine LA Children's Hosp., 1985—87; asst. prof. medicine Harvard Med. Sch.; physician Cambridge Health Alliance Physician Orgn. (CHAPO); exec. dir. Inst. for Cmty. Health. Fellow: LA Childrens Hosp. Office: Institue for Community Health 163 Gore Ave Cambridge MA 02141 Office Phone: 617-499-6681.

HACKER, WILLIAM D., state agency administrator, public health service officer; b. Manchester, Ky. BS, Univ. Ky., 1968, MD, 1972. Cert. Am. Bd. Pediatrics, Certifying Commn. Med. Mgmt. Residency in pediatrics Univ. Ky., 1972—75; private practice Corbin, Ky., 1975—93; chief medical officer Appalachian Regional Healthcare, Lexington, Ky., 1993—99; medical dir. Ky. Health Select, Lexington, 1999—2000; physician cons. Ky. Dept. Public Health, Frankfort, 2001—02, mgr. public health preparedness, 2002—03, dir div. laboratory svc., 2003—04, commr., 2004—. Fellow: Am. Acad. Pediatrics. Office: Ky Dept Pub Health 275 E Main St Frankfort KY 40621

HACKNEY, JACK DEAN, physician; b. Marion, Ill., Oct. 11, 1924; s. William F. and Betty (Monical) H.; m. Dorothy Anne Stublefield, Sept. 8, 1946; children: Richard W., Robert J. Student, So. Ill. Univ., 1941-43, Yale U., 1943; MD, St. Louis U. Sch. Medicine, 1948. Diplomate Am. Bd. Internal Medicine, Acad. Toxicol. Scis. Resident in internal medicine VA Hosp., St. Louis, 1949-51, White Meml. Hosp., LA, 1953-54; rsch. assoc. Loma Linda U., LA, 1954-57, asst. to assoc. prof., 1957-69; prof. medicine U. So. Calif., LA, 1969-94, prof. emeritus, 1994—; dir. pulmonary lab. Rancho Los Amigos Med. Ctr., Downey, Calif., 1969-92, chief environ. health, 1970-94, emeritus, 1994—. Mem. EPA Sci. Adv. Bd., Washington, 1984-86; cons., 1986-92. Editor/author: Inhalation Toxicology of Air Pollution, 1993; contbg. author: Bronchial Asthma: Mechanics and Therapeutics, 1985, 93; contbr. articles to profl. jours. Mem. air quality adv. com. Dept. Health Svcs., State of Calif., 1974-94, med. adv. panel South Coast Air Quality Mgmt. Dist., 1985-92. 1st lt. AMC, 1951-53, Korea. Recipient Calif. medal Am. Lung Assn. Calif., 1992. Fellow Am. Coll. Chest Physicians, Am. Coll. Toxicology; mem. Am. Physiol. Soc., Am. Thoracic Soc., Alpha Omega Alpha, Sigma Xi. Achievements include development of indirect method for measuring respiratory ventilation; extraction of gases from blood for Gas Chromatographic analysis; control of exposure facilities and methods to study human inhalation toxicology and use of these facilities to demonstrate ozone toxicity, adaptation to ozone, and determine exposure responses to many inhaled gas and particle pollutants. Home: 5181 Duenas Laguna Hills CA 92637-1878 Office: Environmental Health Svc RLAMC 7601 Imperial Hwy # 51 Downey CA 90242-3456

HADDAD, GHADA, endocrinologist; MD, St. Joseph's U. Diplomate Am. Bd. Internal Medicine, Am. Bd. Internal Medicine-endocrinology, diabetes and metabolism. Intern Cooper Univ. Hosp.; fellow Hosp. of the Univ of Pa.; head divsn. of endocrinology, diabetes and metabolism Cooper Univ. Hosp., assoc. prof. of medicine; physician Cooper Univ. Office: Cooper University Hospital 1210 Brace Rd Suite 107 Cherry Hill NJ 08034 Office Phone: 856-795-3597. Office Fax: 856-795-7590.

HADDAD, HESKEL MARSHALL, ophthalmologist, educator; b. Baghdad, Iraq, Sept. 26, 1930; came to US, 1953, naturalized, 1962; s. Moshe M. and Masuda (Cohen) H.; m. Doris I. Fatzer, July 4, 1963; children: Ava Masuda Geffen, Andreas Moshe, Michael Albert. MBCHB, Royal Coll. Medicine, Baghdad, 1950; MD, Hebrew U., Jerusalem, 1953. Diplomate Am. Bd. Pediatrics, Am. Bd. Ophthalmology; ordained rabbi, 1997. Intern Donolo Hosp., Jaffo-Tel Aviv, Israel, 1950-51; rotating intern Hadassah U. Hosp., Jerusalem, 1951-53; pediatric resident Children's Med. Center, Boston, 1953-56; fellow in pediatric endocrinology Johns Hopkins Hosp., Balt., 1956-58; fellow in clin. endocrine br. Nat. Inst. Arthritis and Metabolic Diseases, NIH, Bethesda, Md., 1958-59, pediatrician sect. clin. endocrinology, 1959-60; asst. prof. pediatrics sch. medicine Howard U., Washington, 1959-60; resident, asst. dept. ophthalmology sch. medicine Washington U., St. Louis, 1960-64; leave of absence, 1962-63; fellow pediatric ophthalmology Inst. Visual Sci., San Francisco, 1962; research fellow Hôpital des Quinze-Vingts, Laboratoire de Physiologie de Vision, Ecole des Hautes Etudes, Paris, 1962-63; ophthalmologist Hôpital Beni Messous, Algiers, Algeria, 1964; asst. attending ophthalmic surgeon, also asst. prof. ophthalmology Mt. Sinai Hosp. and Sch. Medicine, NYC, 1964-67; dir. dept. ophthalmology Beth Israel Med. Center, NYC; also assoc. prof. ophthalmology Mt. Sinai Sch. Medicine, 1967-71; clin. prof. ophthalmology NY Med. Coll., 1971—. Author: Endocrine Exophthalmos, 1973, Metabolic Eye Diseases, 1974, Metabolic-Peditric Eye Diseases, 1979, Metabolic Ophthalmology: Diagnostic Techniques Vols. I and II, 1985, Jews of Arab and Islamic Countries: History, Problems and Solutions, 1984, (autobiography) Flight from Babylon, 1986, Born in Baghdad, 2005; editor-in-chief: Metabolic Ophthalmology, 1976-79, Metabolic and Ophthalmology, 1976-79, Metabolic and Pediatric Ophthalmology, 1979-82, Metabolic, Pediatric and Systemic Ophthalmology, 1982—; contbr. articles to profl. jours.; holder 7 US patents. Pres. Am. Com. for Rescue and Resettlement of Iraqui Jews, World Orgn. Jews from Arab Countries, Parents' Assn. of Sch. of Performing Arts, 1980-83. Fellow ACS, Am. Inst. Chemists; mem. Am. Endocrine Soc., Am. Fedn. Clin. Research, Assn. Research Ophthalmology and Vision, AMA, NY County Med. Soc., AAAS, Am. Acad. Ophthalmology, NY Acad. Medicine, NY Acad. Scis., NY Soc. Clin. Ophthalmology, Soc. Eye Surgeons, Société Française d' Ophthalmologie, German Ophthal. Soc., Internat. Soc. Metabolic Eye Disease (founder, sec.-treas. 1973—), World Soc. on Systemic Ophthalmology (founder, sec.-treas. 1982, chmn.), NY County Med. Soc. (chmn. com. fgn. med. grads. 1985-90, del. NY State Med. Soc. 1985-86, chmn. rev. commn. 2005—). Achievements include patents in field. Office: 1125 Park Ave New York NY 10128-1243 Office Phone: 212-427-1246. Personal E-mail: optoedcorp@aol.com.

HADDAD, JOSEPH, JR., pediatric otolaryngologist; b. Torrington, Conn., Oct. 30, 1956; MD, NYU, 1983. Diplomate Am. Bd. Otolaryngology. Resident in surgery Presbyn. Hosp., NYC, 1983-85, resident in otolaryngology, 1985-88; fellow in pediatric otolaryngology Children's Hosp., Pitts., 1988-90; dir. pediatric otolaryngology Columbia Coll. P&S, 1990—, assoc. prof. to Lawrence Savetsky prof., vice chmn. clin. otolaryngology, 1996—; dir. pediatric otolaryngology Morgan Stanley Children's Hosp., Columbia-Presbyn. Med. Ctr., NYC. Named a Best Doctor, NY Mag.; named one of America's Top Doctors, Castle Connolly. Mem. AMA, Am. Acad. Otolaryngology-Head and Neck Surgery, Am. Coll. Surgeons, Am. Acad. Facial Plastic and Reconstructive Surgery, Am. Soc. Pediatric Otolaryngology. Office: Morgan Stanley Children's Hosp BHN 5th Fl 3959 Broadway New York NY 10032 Office Phone: 212-305-[illegible] Office Fax: 212-305-6142.

HADDAD, STEVEN L., orthopaedic surgeon; BS in Biology with honors, U. Mich, Ann Arbor, 1985; MD, John Hopkins U., Balt., 1989. Diplomate Am. Bd. Orthop. Surgery, lic. Ill. Intern, gen. surgery Georgetown U., 1989—91, resident, orthop. surgery, 1991—95; fellow, foot and ankle surgery Union Meml. Hosp., Balt., 1995—96; instructor, clin. orthop. surgery Northwestern U. Med. Sch., Chgo., 1996—2000, asst. prof., clin. orthop. surgery, dept. orthop. surgery, 2000—05, assoc. prof., clin. orthop. surgery, dept. orthop. surgery, 2005—. Active attending, chief, sect. foot and ankle surgery Evanston Northwestern Healthcare, Ill., 1996—; active attending Rush North Shore Med. Ctr., 2003—; mem. design team, champion surgeon Agility Ankle, DePuy Corp. (Johnson & Johnson Co.); physician Trinity Irish Dance Co., 1996—, bd. dirs., 2000—; physician Giordano Dance Co., 1997—; invited lectr., presenter in field. Assoc. editor Lawyers' Medical Cyclopedia:Third Edition, 1993, guest editor Arthrodesis of the Foot and Ankle, Foot and Ankle Clinics, 2002, asst. sect. editor (foot and ankle) Orthopaedic Quarterly, 2001—, assoc. editor Foot and Ankle International, 2003—, asst. editor for clin. tips & surgical techniques, 2005—; editor: Workers' Compensation Manual, American Orthopaedic Foot and Ankel Society, 2004; reviewer Clinical Orthopaedic and Related Research, 2005—; contbr. chapters to books. Lector Our Lady of Perpetual Health, 2003—. Mem.: N.Am. Foot and Ankle Assn., Assn. Bone and Joint Surgeons, Orthop. Foot Club, AMA, Am. Acad. Orthop. Surgeons (mem. foot and ankle sub-committee 1999—2006, mem. leadership fellows program 2004—05, mem. profl. liability com. 2005—, mem. foot and ankle program subcommittee 2007—, mem. continuing med. edn. courses com. 2007—, chmn. ann. meeting subsection on foot and ankle, cons. reviewer for journal 2005—, editor, The Athlete's Ankle 2008, sect. editor, Your Orthopaedic Connection 2007—), Am. Orthop. Assn., Am. Orthop. Foot and Ankle Soc. (mem.-at-large young physician's sect. 1997—98, chmn.-elect young physician's sect. 1999—2000, chmn. young physician's sect. 2000—01, mem. nominating com. 2001, bd. dirs. (mem.-at-large) 2001—03, chmn. occupational health com. 2001—03, chmn. individual donors, standing com. on outreach and edn. fund 2001—03, membership services com. 2003—05, program chair 2004—05, mem. edn. com. 2006—, chmn., edn. com. 2007—), Sigma Xi, Phi Beta Kappa. Office: Illinois Bone & Joint Inst Ltd Glenview Medical Arts Bldg 2401 Ravine Way Glenview IL 60025-7645 also: 2350 Ravine Way Glenview IL 60025 also: 1144 Wilmette Ave Wilmette IL 60091 Office Fax: 847-998-5680, 847-998-6365.

HADDEN, JOHN WINTHROP, immunopharmacology educator; b. Berkeley, Calif., Oct. 23, 1939; s. David Rodney Hadden; m. Elba Mas, July 31, 1964; children: John W. II, Paul J. BA, Yale U., 1961; MD, Columbia U., 1965. Asst. prof. pathology U. Minn., Mpls., 1972-73; assoc. prof. Cornell Grad. Sch., NYC, 1973-82; assoc. mem., dir. lab. immunopharmacology Sloan-Kettering Meml. Cancer Inst., NYC, 1973-82; prof. medicine, dir. div. immunopharmacology U. South Fla., Tampa, 1982-99; founder, chief sci. officer IRX Therapeutics, NYC, 1999—. Cons. in field.; vis. prof. U. South Fla. Med. Coll., Nat. Cancer Inst., Mex. Assoc. editor Internat. Jour. Immunopharmacology, 1978-86, editor, 1986-99; editor 12 textbooks; contbr. chpts. to books, more than 300 articles to profl. jours. Mem. Am. Assn. Immunologists, Am. Soc. Pharm. & Exptl. Therapy, Internat. Soc. Immunopharmacology (v.p. 1982-85, pres. 1985-88, publ. officer 1988-99, treas. 1999-2002), Tampa Yale Club (v.p. 1986-91) Achievements include patents for 10 methods of imparting immunomodulating activity. Home: 428 Harbor Rd Cold Spring Harbor NY 11724-2108 Office: Immuno-Rx Inc 140 W 57th St Ste 9C New York NY 10019-3326 Office Phone: 212-582-1199. E-mail: jwhadden@optonline.net.

HADDOCK, CHRISTOPHER KEITH, research scientist, former psychology professor; b. Columbia, Tenn., May 3, 1962; s. Jerry Lynn and Sara (Lentz) H.; m. Risa Jean Stein; 1 child, Justin Christopher. BA, David Lipscomb U., Nashville, 1984; MAR, Harding U., Memphis, 1987; MS, U. Memphis, 1991, PhD, 1993. Lic. clin. psychologist, Tenn. Clin. asst. prof. U. Tex. Health Sci. Ctr., San Antonio, 1995-97; prof. of psychology and medicine U. Mo., Kansas City, 1997—; co-dir. behavioral cardiology MidAm. Heart Inst.; CEO Health Rsch. Group. Behavior sci. cons. Henry M. Jackson Found., Washington, 1994-96. Contbr. articles to profl. jours. Capt. USAF, 1992-97. NIH Co-prin. investigator, 1994, 99; Van Vleet fellow U. Memphis, 1989-91. Mem.: APA, Am. Heart Assn., Soc. Internat. Nutrition Rsch., Am. Statistical Assn., Am. Soc. Nutritional Scis., Am. Soc. Clin. Nutrition, Soc. for Rsch. on Nicotine and Tobacco, Soc. of Air Force Clin. Psychologists, Soc. Behavioral Medicine. Libertarian. Avocations: running, weightlifting. Home: 2336 SW Feather Ridge Rd Lees Summit MO 64082-4085

HADDY, FRANCIS JOHN, internist, educator; b. Walters, Minn., Sept. 6, 1922; s. Thomas J. and Frances (Shaheen) H.; m. Theresa Eileen Brey, Sept. 21, 1946; children: Richard, Carol, Alice. Student, Luther Coll., Decorah, Iowa, 1940-42; BS, U. Minn., 1943, M.B., 1946, MD, 1947, MS in Physiology, 1949, PhD in Physiology (Am. Heart Assn. fellow), 1953. Diplomate Am. Bd. Internal Medicine. Intern Mpls. Gen. Hosp., 1946—47; fellow internal medicine Mayo Found., 1949—51; asst. prof. physiology and medicine Northwestern U. Med. Sch., 1953—61; clin. investigator VA Rsch. Hosp., Chgo., 1957—59; prof. physiology, chmn. dept., assoc. prof. medicine U. Okla. Med. Center, 1961—66; prof. physiology, chmn. dept. Mich. State U., East Lansing, 1966—76; prof. physiology Uniformed Svcs. U., Bethesda, Md., 1976—99, chmn. dept. physiology, 1976—87; mem. Mayo grad. faculty dept. physiology and biomed. engring. Mayo Clinic Coll. Medicine, Rochester, Minn., 2003—. Mem. cardiovasc. study sect. NIH, 1963-69; tng. com. Nat. Heart and Lung Inst., NIH, 1970-73; mem. atherosclerosis and hypertension adv. com. Nat. Heart, Lung and Blood Inst., NIH, 1983-86; rsch. com. Am. Heart Assn., 1974-80; mem. life scis. adv. com. NASA, 1986-92, chmn., 1988-92, mem. aerospace med. adv. com. 1988-93, mem. NASA-NIH adv. com., 1993-95; sr. scientist NASA/Johnson Space Ctr. SC med. scis. divsn., Houston, 1989-90; cons., peer rev. adminstr. for cardiopulmonary, integrative physiology, and clin. areas NASA, 1995—. Mem. editl. bd. Am. Jour. Physiology, 1963-69, 80-86, Jour. Applied Physiology, 1963-69, Procs. Soc. Exptl. Biology and Medicine, 1969-72, Circulation Rsch., 1975-81, Microvascular Rsch., 1978-81, Hypertension, 1978-81, Jour. Am. Coll. Nutrition, 1993-99, author: Flight Surgeon & Intern, 2005, Chronology of Recent Health Care Legislation, 2010, co-author: (with Theresa B. Haddy) Minnesota Physicians in the 1862 Sioux Uprising, 2011 Recipient Med. Sci. Achievement award Am. Heart Assn., 1987, Scientist Emeritus awrd Soc. Exptl. Biology and Medicine, 1996-97, Disting. Alumnus award Mayo Found., 2003, Disting. Svc. award Luther Coll., 2004. Fellow Am. Coll. Nutrition (coord. hypertension and cardiovasc. diseases 1992-98, bd. dirs. 1993-97, publs. com. 1994-99, ann. award 1986); mem. Am. Physiol. Soc. (steering com. circulation group 1972-75, chmnm. com. on coms. 1974-77, coun. 1976-79, pres. 1981, fin. com. 1983-89, chmn. fin. com. 1985-89, select com. on animal care 1988-91, chmn. long range planning com. 1990-93, hon. com. 1993-95, chmn. 1995, Carl J. Wiggers award 1966), Am. Soc. Clin. Investigation, Fedn. Am. Socs. Exptl. Biology (bd. dirs. 1980-83, treas. 1990-92, rep. to Am. Assn. Accreditation Lab. Animal Care trustees 1993-96, exec. com. 1995-96, Bay G. Daggs award, 2009), Internat. Union Physiol. Scis. (US nat. com. 1976-79, 81-84), Nat. Hypertension Assn. (trustee 1979—, v.p. 2003—), NAS (basic biomed. scis. panel, com. on nat. needs for biomed. and behavioral rsch. pers. Inst. Medicine 1983-86), Assn. Chairmen Depts. Physiology (chmn. animal welfare com. 1986-87), Aerospace Med. Assn. (publ. com. 1994-95), Am. Soc. for Gravitational and Space Biology (awards com. 1994-99), Montgomery County Art Assn. (pres. 1997-98), Mayo Found. (Disting. Alumnus award, 2003). Achievements include left heart catherization, small vein and artery catherization, mechanisms of pulmonary edema, fluid flux across the capillary membrane, local regulation of blood flow, ionic action on blood vessels, and low renin hypertension. Home: 211 2nd St NW Apt 1607 Rochester MN 55901-2896 Business E-Mail: tbhaddy@aol.com.

HADDY, THERESA BREY, pediatrician, hematologist, oncologist, educator; b. Wabasso, Minn., Feb. 27, 1924; d. Francis William and Elizabeth Katherine (Daub) Brey; m. Francis John Haddy, Sept. 21, 1946; children: Richard Ian, Carol Haddy Froelich, Alice Haddy Hellen. BS, U. Minn., 1944, MB, 1946, MD, 1948. Diplomate in pediatrics and in pediatric hematology/oncology Am. Bd. Pediatrics. Intern Mpls. Gen. Hosp., 1947—48; resident in pediat. U. Minn., Mpls., 1950—52; fellow in hematology U. Okla., 1962—64; practice medicine, specializing in gen. pediatr. Des Plaines, Ill., 1954—61; asst. prof., dir. pediat. hematology oncology U. Okla., Oklahoma City, 1961—66; chief child health Mich. Dept. Pub. Health, Lansing, 1966—69; assoc. prof., dir. pediat. hematology oncology Mich. State U., East Lansing, 1969—76; expert in blood diseases NIH, Bethesda, Md., 1977—79; assoc. prof., dir. pediat. hematology oncology Howard U., Washington, 1979—87, prof., 1987—89, prof. emeritus, 1989—. Guest rschr. pediat. oncology br. NIH, NCI, Bethesda, 1989-2001; mem. acad. adv. staff Children's Nat. Med. Ctr., Washington, 2000—. Author: (books) Country Doctor and City Doctor: Father and Daughter, 2006; co-author: (with Francis J. Haddy) Minnesota Physicians in the 1862 Sioux Uprising, 2011; contbr. over 100 articles to profl. jours. Mem. Am. Soc. Hematology, Am. Soc. Pediat. Hematology/Oncology (publs. com. 2002-04), Nat. Hypertension Assn. (adv. bd. 2002—), Am. Soc. Clin. Oncology, NIH Alumni Assn. Episcopalian. Personal E-mail: tbhaddy@aol.com.

HADEF, HYSHAM, physician; b. Mohammedia, Oct. 8, 1972; MD, U. Strasbourg, PhD, 2002. Physician SAMU, 1998. Master: CHU (Strasbourg). Office: 70 Engelbreit St Strasbourg Alsace 67091 France

HADJIYANNAKIS, EVAGELOS YIANNIS, surgeon; b. Kastelorizo, Rodos-Dodecanese, Greece, Dec. 25, 1938; s. Yiannis Vasilios Hadjiyannakis and Anastasia Evangelos Stamatiou; m. Katerina Koniavitou, Dec. 26, 1967 (div. 1994); children: Yiannis, Vasia; m. Bouli Estratiadou-Koster; children: Hercules, Demetrios. MD, Athens

U., Greece, 1961, PhD, 1964, postgrad., 1973. House officer 1st surg. univ. clinic Laiko Hosp., Athens, 1962-64, univ. asst. 1st surg. univ. clinic, 1964-66, 1st asst. univ. clinic, 1966-68, lectr. 1st surg. dept., 1969-75, asst. prof. univ., 1973—; sr. hosp. registrar Cambridge, England, 1969-71. Cons. 2d dept. transplant unit Tzanio Gen. Hosp., Pireus, Greece, 1975—86, 1st surg. dept. transplant unit Evagelismos Hosp., Athens, 1986—2002, Athens Med. Ctr., 2003—; assoc. prof. Athens U., 1983—2000, prof., 2000. Author: (book) Surgical Emergencies Complications of Liver Transplantation, 1982, Kidney and Liver Transplantation, 1995, Internal Medicine: Kidney, Pancreas, Liver, Cardiac and Lung Transplantation, Prevention and Early Diagnosis of Decay Diseases, 2002, 2d edit., 2003; contbr. articles to profl. jours. Pres. Kastelorizian World Assn., Pireus, 1983—90, World Transplant Athletics, Athens, 1982—; chmn. European Forum Immunosuppression, Athens, 1989, European Congress Transplant Soc., Rodos, 1993, World Transplant Olympics, Athens, 1982; pres. Internat. Hippokratous Found. Kos, 2000. Recipient Gold medal, Patriarch Athenagoras Constantinople, 1963, Panhellenic Transplant Assn., 2001, Gold cross, Patriarch Venediktos, Jerusalem, 1978, Gold medal, 1980, Laudation, European Internat. Hepatobilliary Assn. Congress Athens, 1995. Fellow: Am. Coll. Vascular Surgery; mem.: N.Y. Acad. Scis., Hellenic Surg. Soc. (pres. 2002), Transplantation Soc., Internat. Coll. Surgery, Hellenic Tranplantation Soc. (founding pres.), Yachting Club (Vouliagmenis), Nat. Yachting Club (Pireus), Rotary. Avocation: sculpting. Office: Athens Med Ctr Distomou 5-7 15125 Athens Greece

HADLEY, H. ROGER, urologist, educator, dean; MD. Cert. Am. Bd. Urology, Am. Bd. Surgery. Resident in urology UCLA, fellowship in neurourology, urodynamics and female urology; faculty mem. Loma Linda U. Sch. Med., 1983—, chief of urology, 1990—2002, dean, 2002—; exec. v.p. med. affairs Loma Linda U. Adventist health Sciences Ctr. Contbr. articles to profl. jours., chapters to books. Achievements include research in female urinary incontinence. Office: Office of Dean Med Sch Loma Linda Univ Med Ctr 11234 Anderson St Loma Linda CA 92354 *

HADLEY, JEFFERY, cosmetic dentist; m. Jennifer Hadley; 3 children. Studied in Biology and Internat. Rels., Brigham Young U.; grad., U. So. Calif., 1993; student, Acad. of Gen. Dentistry. With US Navy; gen. practice resident Gt. Lakes Naval Hosp.; sr. dental officer 1st marine divsn. Camp Le Lejeune; navy dentist Guantanamo Bay; comdr. US Navy Dental Corps. Mem. Cardinal & Gold. With Ch. of Jesus Christ of Latter— Day Saints. Avocations: camping, reading, snowboarding. Office: Jeffery W. Hadley DDS Ste A-140 3910 Pecos McLeod Las Vegas NV 89121 Office Phone: 702-454-7695.

HADLEY, MARK N., medical educator; b. San Francisco, Feb. 14, 1956; BA in Economics, Stanford U., 1978; MD, Albany Med. Coll., 1982. Charles A. & Patsy W. Collat prof. neurol. surgery U. Ala., Birmingham, 1991—. Office: UAB Divsn Neurosurgery 510 20th Birmingham AL 35294-3410 Office Fax: 205-975-6081. Business E-Mail: mhadley@uabmc.edu.

HADLEY, WILLIAM MELVIN, retired dean; b. San Antonio, June 4, 1942; s. Arthur Roosevelt and Audrey Merle (Barrett) H.; m. Dorothy J. Hadley, Jan. 21, 1967 (div. July 1989); children: Heather Marie, William Arthur; m. Jane F. Walsh, Oct. 13, 1990. BS in Pharmacy, Purdue U., West Lafayette, Ind., 1967, MS in Pharmacology, 1971, PhD in Toxicology, 1972. Teaching and grad. asst. Purdue U., West Lafayette, 1967-72; asst. prof. U. N.Mex., Albuquerque, 1972-76, assoc. prof., 1976-82, prof., 1982—2002, asst. dean Coll. Pharmacy, 1984-86, acting dean Coll. Pharmacy, 1985, dean Coll. Pharmacy, 1986—2002; prof. and dean emeritus Coll. Pharmacy, 2002—. Vis. scientist Lovelace Inhalation Toxicology Inst., Albuquerque, 1981, adj. scientist, 1991-2002, sr. scientist, 2002—; adv. bd. Waste Edn. Rsch. Consortium, Las Cruces, N.Mex., 1989-2003; dirs. adv. com. Nat. Ctr. for Eviron. Health, CDC, 2002-04, mem. NIH Proposal Rev. Panels, Bethesda, Md., 1983-84; mem. Gov.'s PCB Expert Adv. Panel, Santa Fe, 1985-86; sci. adv. bd. Carlsbad Environ. Monitoring Ctr., 1992-97; sci. adv. com. S.W. Regional Spaceport, Las Cruces, 1992-94; bd. dirs. Ctr. Excellence Hazardous Materials Mgmt., Carlsbad, N.Mex., 2005—; cons. in field. Steering com. United Fund, U.N.Mex., 1987, key person, 1988—97. NIH grantee, 1974-80, 83-87; Bowl of Hygeia, N.Mex. Pharm. Assn., 1998. Mem. AAAS, Am. Pharm. Assn., Am. Assn. Colls. of Pharmacy, Soc. Toxicology (pres. Rocky Mt. chpt. 1990-91). Republican. Achievements include research in biotransformation of xenobiotics with emphasis on nasal tissue; effects of heavy metals on biotransformation with emphasis on cadmium; toxic effects of xenobiotics on the immune system. Office Phone: 623-465-1813. Personal E-mail: wmhadley@aol.com.

HAEFNER, DON PAUL, retired psychology educator; b. Albany, NY, Mar. 7, 1928; s. Carl William and Mary Theresa (Diamond) H.; m. Allegra Ouida Turner, June 11, 1951 (dec. Oct. 1981); children: Carol, Ann, Thomas; m. Cynthia Jean Stewart, May 29, 1982. AB in psychology, Clark U., 1951; PhD, U. Rochester, 1956. Chief soc. psychologist Vets. Adminstrn. Ctr., Bath, NY, 1956—57; rsch. soc. psychologist VA Hosp., Brockton, Mass., 1957—60, U.S. Pub. Health Svc., Washington, 1960—62; rsch. assoc., lectr. to prof. U. Mich. Sch. Pub. Health, Ann Arbor, 1962—93, asst. dean, 1968—84, prof. emeritus, 1993—. Vis. instr. U. Rochester, N.Y., 1956-57; lectr. psychology Boston U., 1958-60; reviewer profl. jours., 1975-94; cons. to health orgns., 1975-85. Contbr. articles to profl. jours. Fellow APHA, Soc. Pub. Health Edn.; mem. APA, Sigma Xi, Delta Omega. Unitarian Universalist. Avocations: travel, photography, choral singing. Home: 2250 Pine Grove Ct Ann Arbor MI 48103-2338

HAEMISCH, YORK, physicist; b. Dresden, Saxony, Germany, June 18, 1962; s. Peter and Ute Haemisch; life ptnr. Fong-Yih Kao; 1 child, Robert. MS, Tech. U., Dresden, 1989; PhD, Ludwig-Maximilians-Univ., Wuerzburg, 1994; MS in Engring., U. Pa., 2002. Product specialist pet ctrl. europe GE Med. Sys., Frankfurt, Germany, 1993—96; sales mgr. Germany ADAC Lab., Maarssen, Netherlands, 1997—98, product mgr. Europe, 1998—99, product mgr. global Milpitas, Calif., 1999—2001; dir. pet sci. Philips Med. Sys., Milpitas, 2001—02, product mgr. in-vivo-imaging Best, Netherlands, 2002—. Active mem. Neues Forum, Dresden, Germany, 1989. Home: Uglitscher Strasse 3 Hessen Idstein D-65510 Germany Office: Philips Medizinsysteme Hewlett-Packard Strasse 2 Boeblingen D-71034 Germany Office Fax: +49 6126 58 37 57. Business E-Mail: york.haemisch@philips.com.

HAFEY, JOSEPH MICHAEL, retired health association executive; b. Annapolis, Md., June 25, 1943; s. Edward Earl Joseph and Verna (Hedlund) H.; m. Mary Kay Miller, Dec. 30, 1978; children: Erin Catherine, Ryan Michael. BA, Whittier Coll., 1965; MPA, UCLA, 1967. Sr. asst. health officer HHS, Washington, 1967-69; dir. govt. relations Alliance for Regional Community Health, St. Louis, 1969-71; exec. dir. Contra Costa Comprehensive Health Assn., Richmond, Calif., 1971-74, Bay Area Comprehensive Health Planning Coun., San Francisco, 1974-76, Western Ctr. for Health Planning, San Francisco, 1976-86, Western Consortium for Pub. Health, Berkeley, 1980-95; pres., CEO Pub. Health Inst. (formerly Calif. Pub. Health Found.), 1985—2009. Chmn. Contra Costa Pub. Health Adv. Body, Martinez, Calif., 1987-93; founder Calif. Coalition for Future of Pub. Health, Sacramento, 1988—; co-founder Calif. Healthy Cities Program, Berkeley, 1987—. Chmn. United Way Com. for the Uninsured, San Francisco, 1985-93; bd. dirs. Eugene O'Neill Found., 1980-89. With USPHS, 1967-69. Recipient fellowship WHO, Geneva, 1987. Mem. Am. Pub. Health Assn. (governing coun. 1984-87), Am. Health Planning Assn. bd. dirs., chmn. annual meeting 1982). Avocations: jogging, tennis, skiing, collecting political campaign buttons. Home: 1749 Toyon Rd Lafayette CA 94549-2111 Office: Pub Health Inst 555 12th St Oakland CA Office Phone: 510-285-5531. Business E-Mail: joehafey@phi.org.

HAFEZ, MAHMOUD A., orthopedist, educator; MB BCh, MSc, Cairo U. Med. Sch., Egypt, 1985. Cert. diploma SICOT, 2005. Prof., orthop. head orthopaedic dept. Cairo U., Egypt, 2006—; part-time cons. arthroplasty surgeon Al Helal Hosp., Egypt, NHS Hosps., England; examiner SICOT Diploma Soc. Internat. de Chirurgie Orthopedique et de Tramatologie; mem. AO Found. Peer Review Panel, Switzerland; mem. bd. govs., ex- v.p. Am. Fracture Assn., Ill.; pres. Middle East Soc. Computer Assisted Orthopaedic Surgery, Egypt. Regional v.p. and uk del. Am. Fracture Assn., Chgo., 2001—03. Author (poet): (poetry, medical bioengineering writing) Insall-Scott, JBJS Br, F (Japanese-SICOT, BOA, Pfizer, AFA, ES-PRC). Recipient Hap Paul award, Internat. Soc. Tech. Arthroplasty, 2010, Cert. Recognition Tchg., Arab Med. Union, Egypt, 2010, Exemplary Surgeon award, Ministry of Health, Egypt, 2009, Cert. Recognition, Med. Sch., Oct. 6 U., Egypt, 2008, Japanese SICOT award, 2005, Travel award, Brit. Orthopaedic Assn., 2004, Pfizer Acad. award, Eng., 2004; Rsch. grant, EPSRC, 2001. Fellow: RCS; mem.: BMA, AFA, Int Soc. CAOS, ORS, SICOT, EOA, COA, BOA. Muslim. Achievements include patents pending for Computer assisted templating in knee surgery; research in Orthopedic Surgery; design of Computer assisted orthopaedic surgery tools. Office Fax: 2 02 2391 8993.

HAFFEY, THOMAS ANTHONY, cardiologist, consultant; b. Hazleton, Pa., June 13, 1951; s. James John and Mary Agnes Haffey; m. Marilyn Ann Michelcavage, Apr. 23, 1977; children: Marie Victoria, Thomas Patrick. DO, Phila. Coll. Osteo. Medicine, 1977; BS, Kings Coll. Cert. DO Am. Osteo. Assn./IL, 1977, in cardiovasc. disease 1989, in internal medicine 1989, in clin. lipidology 2005. Clin. prof. internal medicine Western U., Ponoma, Calif., 1996—; intern Pontiac Osteopathic Hosp., 1977—78, resident, 1978—80; fellowship Cardiology William Beaumont Hosp., Royal Oak. Fellow: Am. Heart Assn., Nat. Lipid Assn., Am. Coll. Cardiology (colo. chpt., gov. 2010), Am. Coll. Osteo. Internists (pres. sect. cardiology 1999—2001); mem.: SW Lipid Assn. (bd. mem.). Conservative. Roman Catholic. Achievements include research in Investigator LIFE Study. Avocation: photography. Office: Western Cardiology Ste 140 9141 Grant St Thornton CO 80229 Home: 10933 Meade Way Westminster CO 80031-2129 Personal E-mail: thaffey@yahoo.com.

HAFFNER, ALDEN NORMAN, academic administrator; b. Bklyn., Oct. 3, 1928; s. Irving and Irene (Gutfleisch) H. AB, Bklyn. Coll., 1948; OD, Pa. Coll. Optometry, 1952; MPA, NY U., 1960, PhD, 1964; DOS (hon.), Mass. Coll. Optometry, 1960; ScD (hon.), Pa. Coll. Optometry, 1973. Exec. dir. Optometric Ctr. NY, NYC, 1957—; acting chief adminstrv. officer State Coll. Optometry, SUNY, NYC, 1970-71, dean, 1971-76, pres., 1976-78; assoc. chancellor for health scis. SUNY, Albany, 1978-82, vice chancellor for research, grad. studies and profl. programs, 1982-87, pres. coll. optometry, 1987—. Pub. svc. prof. health poligy Rockefeller Coll., SUNY-Albany, 1986; chmn. NY State Com. on Health Personnel and Productivity, 1990—; cons. in field. Contbr. articles in field to profl. jours. Mem. adv. com. Commn. for Blind and Visually Handicapped, State Dept. Social Services, 1966-70; mem. bd. nat. study commn. on optometry Nat. Commn. on Accrediting, 1968-70; mem. health manpower planning com. Comprehensive Health Planning Agy., NYC, 1969-73; project dir. Fed. Program of Identification, Counseling, Guidance and Recruitment of Minority Students in Profession of Optometry, 1968-74; mem. Mayor's Com. for Study of Aging, NYC, 1958; chmn. bd. trustees Manhattan Health Plan, Inc., 1976-81. Served to 1st lt. USMC Army, 1953-55. Recipient Albert Fitch Meml. award, 1962; Prof. Frederick A. Woll Meml. award, 1961; Disting. Achievement award Alumni Assn., NY U. Grad. Sch. Pub. Health Adminstrn., 1974 Fellow Am. Pub. Health Assn., AAAS, Am. Sch. Health Assn., Am., N.Y. Acad. Optometry; mem. NY Acad. Scis., Group Health Assn. Am., Am. Pub. Welfare Assn., Am. Soc. Pub. Adminstrn., Nat. Rehab. Assn., Illuminating Engring. Soc., Am. Optometric Assn., NY State Optometric Assn., Gerontol. Soc., Am. Assn. Univ. Adminstrs., Pub. Health Assn. City of NY (dir. 1967—), Nat. Assn. Land Grant Colls. and State Univs. (com. health affairs 1981), Cmty. Family Planning Coun., Am. Coun. on Edn., Assn. Cad. Health Ctrs., Hermann Biggs Soc., Beta Sigma Kappa (Gold Medal award 1974), Home: 201 E 36th St New York NY 10016-3668 Office: SUNY Coll Optometry 33 W 42nd St New York NY 10036-8003

HAFFNER, WILLIAM H.J., obstetrician, gynecologist; b. Jersey City, Mar. 31, 1939; s. William S. and Jean W. (Krueger) H.; m. Marlene E. Brings, Aug. 17, 1963; children: Stephanie E., Andrea J. AB, Wesleyan U., 1961; MD with distinction, George Washington U., 1965. Diplomate Am. Bd. Ob-Gyn., Nat. Bd. Med. Examiners. Surg. intern George Washington U. Hosp., Washington, 1965-66; resident ob-gyn. Sloan-Columbia-Presbyn. Hosps., NYC, 1966-71; head ob-gyn. Gallup Indian Med. Ctr., N.Mex., 1971-81; staff Nat. Naval Med. Ctr., Bethesda, Md., 1981—; attending staff ob-gyn. Uniformed Svcs.-U. Health Scis., Bethesda, 1981—, residency program dir. ob-gyn., 1985-94, prof., 1992—, chmn., 1992—2003, acting assoc. dean faculty devel., 2006—08. Chief med. officer Office of Surgeon Gen. USPHS, 1990—94. Editor: Obstetric Neonatal and Gynecologic Care, 1993—2007, Mil. Medicine, 2006—. Fellow AMA, Am. Coll. Ob-Gyn. (Disting. Svc. award 2002), Am. Soc. Reproductive Medicine; mem. Assn. Profs. Gynecology and Obstetrics (coun. mem. 2000—08, sec.-treas. 2003—06, pres. elect 2005-06, pres. 2006—07), Alpha Omega Alpha. Office: Uniformed Svcs-U Health Sci Dept Ob-Gyn Bethesda MD 20814-4799 Office Phone: 301-295-3886. Personal E-mail: whaffner@usuhs.mil.

HAFKENSCHIEL, JOSEPH HENRY, JR., retired cardiologist; b. Youngstown, Ohio, Apr. 2, 1916; s. Joseph Henry and Anna Marie (Conroy) H.; m. Lucinda Buchanan Thomas, July 18, 1942 (dec. 1983); children: Joseph Henry III, Benjamin A. Thomas, Mark Conroy, John Proctor; m. Carol MacDonald Smith Rush, Jan. 25, 1985 (div. April 4, 2007). AB, Swarthmore Coll., 1937; MD, Johns Hopkins U., 1941. Diplomate Am. Bd. Internal Medicine. Intern U. Pa. Hosp., Phila., 1941-42; instr. pharmacology U. Pa. Sch. Medicine, 1946-47; resident U. Pa. Hosp., 1948-49, fellow in cardiology, 1949; instr. medicine U. Pa. Sch. Medicine, 1949-51; cardiovasc. disease physician, pvt. practice, 1949-65; assoc. medicine U. Pa. Sch. Medicine, 1951-66; med. dir. West Coast Office Sandoz Pharm., San Francisco, 1965-67; clin. instr. medicine Stanford U., 1966-69, staff physician Cowell Student Health Svcs., 1967-69; cardiovasc. disease physician, pvt. practice Palo Alto, 1969-78; asst. to assoc. prof. Stanford U., 1969-84, emeritus clin. assoc. prof. medicine, 1984—; ret. Staff physician Extended Care Svc. VA Med. Ctr., Palo Alto, 1978-84. Contbr. articles to profl. jours., to profl. publs. Pres. Peninsula Meml. and Funeral Soc., Palo Alto, 1984. Maj. M.C., USAAF, 1942-46. Fellow ACP, Coll. Physicians Phila., Am. Heart Assn., Am. Physiol. Soc.; mem. Air Force Assn., Am. Irish Hist. Soc., San Francisco Golf Club, Ballybunion Golf (Ireland) Club, Am. Legion (post comdr. 1960-62), Sigma Xi. Republican. Roman Catholic. Avocations: golf, gardening, travel. Home: Apt 16 501 Portola Rd Portola Valley CA 94028-8226 Home Phone: 650-529-8156.

HAFT, GAIL KLEIN, pediatrician; b. NYC, Mar. 5, 1938; d. Herbert and Pearl (Mittleman) Klein; m. Jacob I. Haft, Mar. 27, 1964; children: Bethanne, Ian. AB in Chemistry, Vassar Coll., 1959; MD, U. Rochester, 1963. Diplomate Nat. Bd. Med. Examiners, Am. Bd. Pediatrics. Intern Albert Einstein Coll. Medicine, NYC, 1963-64, resident, 1964-65, Mt. Sinai Hosp., NYC, 1967-68; pediatrician Dept. Health, Staten Island, NY, 1965-67, Head Start, Englewood, NY, 1969-71, Dept. Health, Hackensack, NJ, 1970-71; utilization rev. physician Hosp. Corp., NYC, 1973-76; pediatrician Westchester County Health Dept., NY, 1974-76; sch. physician Bd. Edn., Yonkers, NY, 1974-76; bus. mgr. Heartronics, Newark, 1980-94; chief med. officer Bergen County Spl. Svcs., Paramus, NJ, 1984—; physician Tenafly (N.J.) Sch. Bd. Edn., 1990-94. Mem. Tenafly Bd. Edn., 1983-89, pres., 1986-88.

HAGA, TATSUYA, neuroscientist, researcher; b. Tokyo, Feb. 14, 1941; s. Ko and Yasu (Tadokoro) Haga; m. Kazuko Tsutsumi, Apr. 4, 1969. BS, U. Tokyo, PhD, 1970. Instr. U. Tokyo, 1969-74, prof., 1988-2001, prof. emeritus, 2001—; assoc. prof. Hamamatsu (Japan) U., 1974-88; prof. Gakushuin U., Tokyo, 2001—11. Co-author: Receptor Biochemistry, 1990; editor: G Protein-Coupled Receptors, 1999, G Protein-Coupled Receptors, Structure, Function, and Ligand Screening, 2005. E-mail: tatsuya.haga@jcom.home.nc.jp.

HAGAN, JOHN CHARLES, III, ophthalmologist; b. Mexico, Mo., Oct. 7, 1943; s. John Charles Hagan II and Cleta L. (Book) Neely; m. Rebecca Jane Chapman, July 15, 1967; children: Carol Ann, Catherine Elizabeth. BA, U. Mo., 1965; MD, Loyola U., Chgo., 1969. Diplomate Am. Bd. Ophthalmology. Intern Med. Coll. Wis., Milw., 1969-70; resident in ophthalmology Emory U., Atlanta, 1972-75; practice medicine, Kansas City, Mo., 1975—. Cons. Am. Running and Phys. Fitness Assn., Washington, 1973—. Editor: Mo. Medicine: The Jour. of the Mo. State Med. Assn.; contbr. over 130 articles to profl. jours Capt. M.C., USAF, 1970-72. Fellow ACS; mem. AMA, Am. Soc. Cataract and Refractive Surgery, Mo. Soc. Eye Physicians and Surgeons (pres. 1998), Kansas City Soc. Ophthalmology, Greater Kans. City Met. Med. Assn. (pres., 2010) Office: Discover Vision Ctrs 9401 N Oak Trafficway Kansas City MO 64155 Office Phone: 816-478-1230.

HAGEBOUTROS, ALEXANDRE, oncologist, educator; MD, St. Joseph U., Lebanon. Diplomate Am. Bd. Internal Medicine, Am. Bd. Internal Medicine-med. oncology, Am. Bd. Internal Medicine-hematology, lic. NJ. Intern Cooper Univ. Hosp., resident, assoc. head, divsn. hematology/oncology, assoc. prof. medicine, physician; fellow Temple Univ. Hosp. Office: Cooper Unviersity Hospital Ste M 900 Centennial Blvd Voorhees NJ 08043 Office Phone: 856-673-4575. Office Fax: 856-325-6777.

HAGEMANN, ROBERT A., clinical laboratory services executive; BS in Acctg., Rider U., Lawrenceville, NJ; MBA in Fin., Seton Hall U., South Orange, NJ. Formerly with Crompton & Knowles, Inc., Ernst & Young LLP, Prime Hospitality, Inc.; various sr. fin. positions Quest Diagnostics, Inc. (formerly Corning Life Sciences, Inc.), 1992—96, v.p., corp. contr., 1996—98, CFO, 1998—, sr. v.p., 2003—. Bd. dirs. Zimmer Holdings, Inc., 2008—. Office: Quest Diagnostics Inc 3 Giralda Farms Madison NJ 07940 Office Phone: 973-520-2700. Personal E-mail: rhagemann@questdiagnostics.com. *

HAGEN, MICHAEL DALE, family physician educator; b. St. Louis, Nov. 11, 1949; s. Hubert Dale and Gwendel (Carden) Hagen; m. Barbara Carroll Keifer, Aug. 21, 1971; children: Laura Carrol, Sandra Ann. BS in Biology, Denison U., 1971; MD cum laude, U. Mo., Columbia, 1975. Cert. family practice bd. Pvt. practice Family Medicine Assocs., Aurora, Mo., 1978—81; asst. prof. dept. family practice U. Ky., Lexington, 1981—87, assoc. prof. dept. family practice, 1987—92, prof. dept. family practice, 1993—, interim chmn. dept. family practice, 1992—93, assoc. chmn. dept. family practice, 1993—97, project dir., computer-based assessment, 1996—; assoc. dir. assessment methods Am. Bd. Family Practice, 2003—05; v.p. assessment methods devel. Am. Bd. Family Medicine, 2005—07, sr. v.p., 2008—. Fellow clin. decision making New Eng. Med. Ctr., Boston, 1987—89; at-large dir. Am. Bd. Family Practice, Lexington, 1991—96, pres., 1995—96; residency rev. com. family practice Accreditation Coun. for Grad. Med. Edn., Chgo., 1994—97. Author: Saunders Review Family Practice, 1992, 1997, 2002; contbr. articles to profl. jours. Mem.: AMA, Omicron Delta Kappa, Soc. for Med. Decision Making, Am. Acad. Family Physicians (clin. policies task force 1994—95), Phi Kappa Phi, Alpha Omega Alpha. Presbyterian. Avocations: amateur radio, gardening. Home: 2012 Blairmore Rd

Lexington KY 40502-2435 Office: Am Bd Family Medicine 1648 McGrathiana Pky 5th Fl Lexington KY 40511 Office Phone: 888-995-5700. Business E-Mail: hagen@theabfm.org. E-mail: hagenmd@prodigy.net.

HAGEN, MONIKA ELISABETH, surgeon, researcher; b. Giessen, Germany, Feb. 18, 1976; d. Peter Karl Anton and Heidrun Hagen. Dr. med., Philipps U., Marburg, Germany, 1998, Med. U. Luebeck, Germany, 2002; MBA, U. Wales, Cardiff, Fernuniversitaet, Hagen, Germany, 2002. Bd. cert. rescue medicine Landesaerztekammer Hessen, Germany, 2003, bd. cert. in surgery 2008, cert. Ednl. Commn. Fgn. Med. Grads., 2006. Surg. resident Regionalspital Surselva, Ilanz, Switzerland, 2002—04, Kantonsspital Muensterlingen, Switzerland, 2004—06; rsch. fellow U. Hosp., Geneva, 2006—07, rsch. faculty, 2007—08; vis. sr. fellow U. Calif., San Diego, 2008—. Sci. spkr. Assn. North-West German Urologists, Berlin, 2000, German Assn. Urology, Hamburg, 2000, German Assn. Endoscopy and Imaging Procedures, Munich, 2001, Global Awareness Soc. Internat., Accra, Ghana, 2001, Washington, 03, Chgo., 06, Soc. Laparoendoscopic Surgeons, Boston, 2006, Arbeitsgemeinschaften Minimal Invasive Chirurgie, Interlaken, Switzerland, 2007, SAGES, Las Vegas, Switzerland, 2007, Digestive Disease Week, Washington, 2007, European Assn. Endoscopic Surgery, Athens, Greece, 2007, Minimal Invasive Robotic Assn., Rome, 2007, Quebec, 09, SAGES, Phila., 2008, Digestive Disease Week, San Diego, 2008, EAES, Stockholm, 2008, Moscar, San Francisco, 2008; instr. robotic surgery U. Hosp., Geneva, 2006; invited spkr. LASRCC, Geneva, 2008, Spanish Soc. Laparoscopic Surgery, Valencia, 2008, ASIMC, Geneva, Swiss Surg. Soc., Basel, Switzerland, 2008, Inselspital, Bern, Switzerland, 2008, Medeserv, Hamburg, Germany, 2008, D-NOTES, Hamburg, 2008; cons. EPFL, Lausanne, Switzerland, 2008. Author: (book) Operationsberichte für Einsteiger, Chirurgie; contbr. articles to numerous profls. jours. Recipient Best Poster Presentation award, Arbeitsgemeinschaft Minimal Invasive Chirurgie, 2007, Outstanding Poster Presentation award, EAES, 2007; grantee, 2007—08, NOSCAR, 2008. Mem.: European Assns. Endoscopic Surgery, Minimal Invasive Robotic Assn. (NYC) (sci. spkr. 2007), Soc. Surgery Alimentary Tract. Achievements include research in Multiple findings of research in the field of robotic surgery; Multiple findings of research in the field of Natural Orifice Translumenal Endoscopic Surgery. Office Phone: 714-655-6557. Personal E-mail: monikahagen@aol.com.

HAGER, GEORGE V., JR., health services executive; BA in Economics, Dickinson Coll., 1978; MBA, Rutgers U. CPA. Ptnr., health care practice KPMG, LLP, Phila., 1989—92; v.p. Genesis Health Ventures, Inc., Kennett Square, Pa., 1992-94, CFO, 1992—2003, sr. v.p., 1994-99, exec. v.p., CFO, 1999—2003; exec. v.p. Genesis HealthCare Corp., v.p., 1992—94, CFO, 1992—2003, sr. v.p., 1994, chmn, CEO, 2003—. Bd. dirs. Adolor Corp., REACH Med. Holdings, Inc. Bd. trustees U. of the Sciences; bd. dirs., mem., strategic planning com. Nat. Investment Ctr.; bd. dirs. Del. Valley Chapter of the Alzheimer's Assn. Recipient Cain Bros. award Cain Bros. & Modern Healthcare Mag., 1996. Mem. AICPA, PICPA. Office: Genesis HealthCare Corp 101 E State St Kennett Square PA 19348 Office Phone: 610-444-6350. Office Fax: 610-925-4000. Business E-Mail: george.hager@genesishcc.com. *

HAGER, GORDON LEE, molecular biologist, researcher; b. Girard, Kans., Dec. 5, 1942; BS cum laude in Chemistry and Math., U. Kans., 1964; postgrad., U. Wash., 1964-68, Inst. de Biologie Moleculaire, Geneva, 1968-69; PhD in Genetics, U. Wash., 1970. Postdoctoral fellow Inst. de Biologie de Moleculaire U. Geneva, 1970-71; postdoctoral fellow Dept. Biochemistry and Biophysics U. Calif., San Francisco, 1971-73, Gianinni Found. fellow Dept. Biochemistry and Biophysics, 1973-75, assoc. rsch. biochemist, 1976; expert cons. Lab. of Tumor Virus Genetics Nat. Cancer Inst., NIH, 1977-79, chief viral immunogenetics sect., 1980-83, chief Hormone Action and Oncogenesis Sect., 1983—, chief Lab. Receptor Biology and Gene Expression, Ctr. Cancer Rsch. Adj. prof. Grad. Program in Genetics, George Washington U., 1983—; preceptor Pharmacology Rsch. Assoc. Program, Nat. Inst. Gen. Med. Scis., 1986—. Assoc. editor Virology, 1983-85, Molecular Carcinogenesis, 1987-92, Cancer Rsch., 1989-91, Receptor, 1991-97, Molecular Endocrinology, 1992-93; mem. editorial bd. Jour. of Molecular and Cell Biochemistry, 1983-89, Jour. of Biol. Chemistry, 1993-94. Recipient Pub. Health Svc. Spl. Recognition award for Disting. and Unique Accomplishments in Basic Cancer Rsch., Dept. Health and Human Svcs., 1982, NATO Internat. Coop. fellowship, 1987; named R.Q. Brewster Outstanding Chemistry fellow U. Kans., 1961, Summerfield scholar U. Kans., 1962, Pfizer fellow Inst. de Recherches Cliniques de Montreal, 1984, fellow AAAS, 1993. Mem. AAAS, Am. Soc. Biol. Chemists, Am. Soc. for Microbiology, Internat. Assn. for Breast Cancer Rsch., The Endocrine Soc. Office: Ctr Cancer Rsch Lab Receptor Biology and Gene Expression 41 Library Dr Rm B-602 Bethesda MD 20892 Office Phone: 301-496-9867. Office Fax: 301-496-4951. E-mail: hagerg@dce41.nci.nih.gov. *

HAGER, LOWELL PAUL, biochemistry educator; b. Girard, Kans., Aug. 30, 1926; s. Paul William and Christine (Selle) H.; m. Frances Erea, Jan. 22, 1949; children: Paul, Steven, JoAnn. AB, Valparaiso U., 1947; MA, U. Kans., 1950; PhD, U. Ill., 1953. Postdoctoral fellow Mass. Gen. Hosp., Boston, 1953-55; asst. prof. biochemistry Harvard U., Cambridge, Mass., 1955-60; mem. faculty U. Ill., Urbana, 1960—, prof. biochemistry, 1965—, head biochem. div., 1967-89, dir. Biotech. Ctr., 1987—. Chmn. physiol. chemistry study sect. NIH, 1965—; vis. scientist Imperial Cancer Rsch. Fund, 1964; cons. NSF, 1976. Editor life scis. Archives Biochemistry and Biophysics, 1966—; assoc. editor Biochemistry, 1973—; mem. editorial bd. Jour. Biol. Chemistry, 1874—. With USAAF, 1945. Guggenheim fellow U. Oxford, Eng., 1959-60, Max Planck Inst. Zellchemie, 1959-60. Mem. NAS (elected), Am. Chem. Soc., Am. Soc. Biol. Chemists, Am. Soc. Microbiology (chmn. physiology divsn. 1967). Achievements include rsch. in enzyme mechanisms, intermediary metabolism, tumor virus. Home: 5 Fields East Champaign IL 61822 Office Phone: 217-333-9686. Business E-Mail: l-hager@uiuc.edu.

HAGGERTY, ROBERT JOHNS, pediatrician, educator; b. Saranac Lake, NY, Oct. 20, 1925; s. Gordon Abbott and Nina (Johns) H.; m. Muriel Ethel Protzmann, Oct. 29, 1949; children: Robert, Janet, Richard, John. AB, Cornell U., 1946, MD, 1949; AM (hon.), Harvard U., 1975; DSc (hon.), Ind. U., 1990. Diplomate Am. Bd. Pediat. Intern Strong Meml. Hosp., Rochester, NY, 1949-51; from resident to chief resident pediat. Children's Hosp. Med. Ctr., Boston, 1953-55; med. dir. family health care program, asst. prof. pediat. Harvard Med. Sch., 1953-64; prof. pediat., chmn. dept. U. Rochester Sch. Medicine, 1964-75; Roger I. Lee prof. health svcs., chmn. dept. health svcs. Harvard Sch. Pub. Health, 1975-78; prof. pediat. Harvard Med. Sch., Boston, 1975-78, clin. prof., 1978-80; pres. William T. Grant Found., NYC, 1980-92; clin. prof. pediat. Cornell U. Med. Sch., NYC, 1980-92; prof. pediat. emeritus U. Rochester Sch. Medicine, 1992—; exec. dir. Internat. Pediatric Assoc., 1993-98. Dir. gen. pediat. acad. devel. program Robert Wood Johnson Found., 1978-88; mem. health svcs. rsch. sect. USPHS, 1964-70, 82-84, chmn., 1968-70, 82-84; mem. N.Y. State Health Planning Adv. Coun., Carnegie Coun. on Children, 1972-77; chmn. panel health scis. rsch., com. on nat. needs for biomed. and behavioral rsch. per. NRC, 1975-78; mem. bd. U.S. Com. on UNICEF, 1981-87; mem. Gov.'s Coun. on Grad. Med. Edn., N.Y. State, 1989-93. Editor: (with M. Green) Ambulatory Pediatrics, 1968, 5th edit., 1999, (with J. Lucey) Pediatrics, 1973-80, Pediatrics in Rev., 1978-2004, Bull. N.Y. Acad. Medicine, 1992-99; assoc. editor New Eng. Jour. Medicine, 1959-64; contbr. articles to med. jours. Mem. vis. com. Grad. Sch. Edn., Harvard U., 1982-88; bd. dirs. Grantmakers in Health, 1985-89; bd. overseers, social scis. dept., Tufts U., 1990-94; bd. visitors U. Okla. Sch. Pub. Health, 1991-94. Capt. USAF, 1951-53. Recipient Martha M. Eliot award Am. Pub. Health Assn., 1976, Disting. Alumni award Cornell U. Med. Coll., 1987, 6 awards various pediatric socs., 1989, Primary Care Achievement award PEW Found. Health Professions Commn., 1994; Markle scholar in acad. medicine, Markle Found., N.Y.C., 1962-67; fellow Ctr. for Advanced Study Behavioral Scis., Stanford, Calif., 1974-75, Children award Soc. Rsch. Child Devel., 2009, Disting. Career award Academic Pediat. Assn., 2009. Mem.: Soc. Rsch. Child Devel. (Disting. Contbn. award 2009, Lifetime Achievement award 2009), Academic Pediat. Assn. (Lifetime Achievement award 2009, Disting. Career award 2009), Alliance for Health Care for All (trustee 1991—94), Am. Health Fedn. (trustee 1989—92), NY Acad. Medicine (trustee, sec. 1989—92), Inst. Medicine (coun. 1974—77, chmn. com. on prevention of mental illness 1992—93, chmn. steering com. nat. study quality assurance programs 1975—76, Gustave Lienhard award 1989), Soc. Pediat. Rsch. (v.p. 1970—71, Disting. award 2009), Internat. Epidemiol. Assn., Assn. Am. Med. Colls., Ambulatory Pediat. Assn. (chmn. 1963—64, George Armstrong award 1969), Am. Pediat. Soc. (Joseph St. Geme award 1989, John Howland award 1998, E.H. Christopherson award for internat. child health 2001, Alfred I. Du Pont award 2004), Am. Acad. Pediat. (v.p., pres. 1983—85, Grulee award 1981, Dale Richmond award 1981, Aldrich award 1986, Job Smith award 1987, Abraham Jacobi award 1996, E.H. Christopherson award for internat. child health 2001, Lifetime Edn. award 2002), Am. Assn. Poison Control Ctrs. (pres. 1962—64), Assn. Med. Sch. Pediat. Dept. Chairmen (pres. 1969—70), Royal Coll. Pediats. and Child Health (hon.), Harvard Club N.Y.C., Alpha Omega Alpha, Phi Beta Kappa. Personal E-mail: robert_haggerty@urmc.rochester.edu.

HAGGIE, JOHN, surgeon, educator; b. Manchester, Eng. MB ChB, Victoria U. Mancester Sch. Medicine, Eng., MD, 1977; grad. studies in gen. surgery, PhD, 1987. Cert. Royal Coll. Surgeons Eng. Physician Univ. Hosp., South Manchester, England; tutor Victoria U. Manchester Sch. Medicine; mem. South Manchester Surg. Tng. Scheme; registrar Hope Hosp. Salford, England, Chester Hosp., England, Mersey Region, England; consulting surgeon Grenfell Region Health Services, St. Anthony, Nfld., Canada, 1993—97; pvt. practice in gastrointestinal, vascular & thoracic surgery, urology and orthopaedics Great North Peninsula and Labrador, Canada, 1993—97; attending surgeon in gen. and vascular surgery James Paton Meml. Hosp., Gander, Nfld., 1997—2008, chief dept. surgery, 1999—, chief of staff, 2008—. Mem.: Can. Med. Assn. (mem. coun. on health policy and economics 2005—09, bd. dirs. 2006—09, pres. 2011—, former mem. com. on edn. and profl. devel., former chmn. ad hoc working group on pharm. issues), Nfld. and Labrador Med. Assn. (bd. dirs., com. mem. 1996—, chmn. comm. com. 1998—99, pres. 2002—03, mem. profl. services com. 2003—05). Office: James Paton Meml Hosp Dept Surgery 125 Trans Canada Hwy Gander NF Canada A1V 1P7 *

HAGIWARA, KEIJI, pediatrician; b. Tenri, Nara, Japan, Jan. 15, 1948; s. Shiro and Fumie Hagiwara; m. Sachie Nishijima, Feb. 10, 1978; children: Fumito, Tasuku, Ryo MD, Yamaguchi U., Ube, Japan, 1975; PhD, Yamaguchi U., 1985. Med. lic., Japan. Intern Yamaguchi U. Hosp., Ube, 1975, 1975; pediatrician Yamaguchi Ctrl. Hosp., Hofu, Japan, 1976—79; sr. ho. staff Yamaguchi U. Sch. Medicine, Ube, 1978—87, lectr. dept. pediat., 1987—97; pediatrician Kami-Ube Pediat. Clinic, Ube, 1997—. Guest rschr. Cath. U. Louvain, Brussels, 1985-87; health cons. The Japanese Sch. Brussels, 1985-87, Ministry Fgn. Affairs, 1987; vice dir. dept. pediat. Yamaguchi U. Sch. Medicine, 1988-97; cons. Kotoshiba Elem. Sch., Ube, 1997— Recipient Konishi award, 1989; sci. grantee Ministry Edn. Japan, Tokyo, 1989, Ministry Edn. and Culture Japan, Tokyo, 1997 Mem.: Japan Med. Assn., Japan Pediat. Soc., Am. Soc. for Microbiology. Office: Kami-Ube Pediat Clinic Tokiwadai 1-20-2 Ube 755-0097 Japan Office Phone: 81-836-29-1155. Office Fax: 81-836-29-1156. Business E-Mail: keiji-hagiwara@umin.ac.jp.

HAGIWARA, SHIN-ICHI, health facility administrator; b. Mashikomachi, Tochigi, Japan, Feb. 12, 1958; s. Toshio and Mitsu Hagiwara; m. Takako Kyoden; children: Shiori, Akiyo. BS, Ibaraki U., Mito Japan, 1981; MB, Toyama Med. and Pharmaceutical Coll., Toyama Japan, 1990; MD, Jichi Med. Sch., Tochigi Japan, 2000. Diplomate. Asst. Jichi Med. Sch., Minamikawachimachi, Tochigi, Japan, 1995—2000; gen. mgr. Honda Engring. Health Care Ctr., Hagamachi, Tochigi, Japan, 2000—. Mem.: Am. Thoracic Soc. Avocations: skiing, golf. Home: 4-12-10 Shimotsukeshi Tochigi 329-0433 Japan Office: Honda Engring Health Care Ctr 6-1 Hagadai Hagamachi Tochigi 321-3395 Japan Home Phone: 81-285-44-6890; Office Phone: 81-28-677-5527. Office Fax: 81-28-677-6955. Business E-Mail: Shinichi_Hagiwara@hondaeg.co.jp.

HAGOOD, JAMES SMALL, pediatrician, educator; b. Barranquilla, Colombia, Aug. 26; BA, U. NC, Chapel Hill, 1983, MD, 1987. Resident, pediat. Vanderbilt U. Med. Ctr., 1987—90, chief resident, pediat., 1990—91; rsch. fellowship, pediatric pulmonology U. Ala., Birmingham, 1991—94; asst. prof., pulmonary divsn. dept. pediat. UAB Sch. Medicine, Birmingham, Ala., 1994—2001, asst. dir., Pediatric Pulmonary Ctr., 2001—05, dir., Pulmonary Ctr., 2005—09, assoc. prof., pulmonary divsn. dept. pediat., 2001—06, prof., pulmonary divsn. dept. pediat., 2006—09; founding co-dir., translational rsch. Normal and Disordered Devel. Program UAB, 2008—09; divsn. chief, prof., dept. pediat. divsn. respiratory medicine U. Calif. San Diego, 2009—. Recipient Robert C. Boerth award, Vanderbilt U., 1988, Housestaff Clin. Tchg. award, 1990, Ralph E. Tiller Disting. Faculty award, UAB Dept. Pediat., 2006, Rud Polhill Sr. Investigator award, Children's Ctr. Rsch. and Innovation, 2006, 2009, Dean's award, U. Ala., Birmingham, 2008; named one of America's Top Pediatricians, Consumer's Rsch. Coun. America's Guide to America's Top Pediatricians, 2002; named to Best Drs. in America, 2005—; Clin. Investigation grant, Nat. Heart, Lung and Blood Inst., 1994—99, grant, Am. Lung Assn., 2002—05. Mem.: Am. Soc. Matrix Biology, Am. Thoracic Soc., Phi Beta Kappa, Phi Eta Sigma. Office: Rady Children's Hosp San Diego 3020 Children's Way MC 5070 San Diego CA 92123 also: University Calif San Diego 9500 Gilman Dr MC 0731 La Jolla CA 92093-0731 Office Fax: 858-966-5846. Business E-Mail: jhagood@ucsd.edu.

HAGSTROM, JACK WALTER CARL KLING, retired pathology educator; b. Rockford, Ill., Dec. 2, 1933; s. Walter Carl Paul Hagstrom and Loretta Christine (Kling) Pearson; life ptnr. Thomas J. Fleming. AB, Amherst Coll., 1955; MD, Cornell U., 1959. Instr. dept. pathology Cornell U. Med. Coll., NYC, 1962-65, asst. prof., 1965-68; assoc. prof. Case We. Res. U., Cleve., 1968-70, Columbia U., NYC, 1970-75, prof. pathology, 1975-91, prof. emeritus, 1991—. Attending pathologist Univ. Hosp., Cleve., 1968—70, Presbyn. Hosp., NYC, 1981—91; dir. dept. pathology Harlem Hosp., NYC, 1981—91; hon. curator modern poetry Amherst Coll. Libr., Amherst, Mass., 1981—. Author: Thom Gunn: A Bibliography, 1979, Dana Gioia: A Descriptive Bibliography with Critical Essays, 2002, James Merrill: A Descriptive Bibliography, 2009; contbr. articles to profl. jours. Mem. corporator Holden Arboretum, Mentor, Ohio; chmn. Friends of Amherst Coll. Libr., 1973—90. Fellow: Am. Coll. Cardiology; mem.: Pvt. Librs. Assn., Acad. Am. Poets, Printing History Soc., Bibliograph. Soc. London, Bibliograph. Soc. U. Va., Bibliograph. Soc. Am., Kiambu Club, Northport Yacht Club, Durban Club, Jockey Club, Club Odd Vols., Grolier Club, Pratts Club, Travellers' Club, Garrick Club. Episcopalian. Home: PO Box 105 Seven Ponds Towd Rd Water Mill NY 11976

HAHM, DAE-HYUN, engineering educator; b. Wonju, Kangwon-do, Republic of Korea, July 25, 1966; s. Jaekyu Hahm and Bongsoon Ha; m. Helen Yoo; 1 child, Kevin. PhD, Korea Advanced Inst. Sci. & Tech., Taejeon, 1994. Postdoc. Korea Rsch. Inst. Biosci. & Biotech., Taejeon, 1994—95, sr. rschr., 1997—99; postdoc. Stanford U., Sch. Medicine, Palo Alto, Calif., 1995—97; instr. Kyung Hee U., Younginsi, Republic of Korea, 1999—2005, asst. prof., 2006—. Chief tech. officer Avixgen Co., Seoul, Republic of Korea, 2000—08, cons. KIBO, Seoul. Contbr. articles to numerous sci. jours. CTO Avixgen (Bioventure Co.), Seoul, 2000—08. Grantee Acupuncture & Meridian Sci. Rsch. Ctr., Ministry of Edn., Sci. & Tech., 2005; HIV grant, Korea Sci. Found., 2000, Rsch. grant, Ministry of Edn., Sci. & Tech., 2002. Mem.: Korean Soc. Microbiology & Biotech. (Honor of Poster Presentation 2002), Soc. Neurosci. Achievements include discovery of legionella pneumoniaee MreB like protein and MreA like protein genes, complere cds. Avocations: snowboarding, skiing, swimming. Home: Sanghyun-dong Youngin Kyunggi-do 448-519 Republic of Korea Office: Kyung Hee Univ Hoegi-dong 1 Seoul 130-701 Republic of Korea Office Fax: 82-2-966-2175. Personal E-mail: dhahm@paran.com. Business E-Mail: dhhahm@khu.ac.kr.

HAHM, JONG RYEAL, medical educator; b. Jinju, Gyeongsangnam, Republic of Korea, June 26, 1964; s. Lee Hahm; m. Yoon Ju Kim, Apr. 18, 1993; children: Seung Hee, Yeon Soo. PhD, Gyeongsang Nat. U., Jinju, 1999. Med. fellow Samsung Med. Ctr., Sungkyounkwan U. Medicine, Seoul, 1998—2000; asst. prof. dept. medicine Gyeongsang Nat'l U. Coll. Medicine, Jinju, 2000—. Office: Gyeongsang Nat Univ Hosp Chilam-Dong # 90 660-280 Jinju Gyeongsangnam-do Republic of Korea Office Fax: 82-55-758-9122. Business E-Mail: jrhahm@medimail.co.kr.

HAHM, THOMAS X., plastic surgeon; Grad., MD, Emory U., Atlanta; tng. in Gen. Surgery and Plastic Surgery, U. Louisville; surg. tng. in Craniofacial and Cosmetic Surgery, Johns Hopkins U., Balt. Staff plastic surgeon Roper/St. Francis Hosp. System, Trident Health System, East Cooper Hospital; plastic surgeon Carolina Aesthetic Plastic Surgery Inst. Mem.: Am. Soc. of Aesthetic Plastic Surgery (candidate mem.), Am. Soc. of Plastic Surgery (candidate mem.), AMA, SC Med. Assn., Alpha Omega Alpha. Office: Carolina Aesthetic Plastic Surgery Institute 900 Bowman Rd Ste 101 Mount Pleasant SC 29464 also: Carolina Aesthetic Plastic Surgery Institute 9213-C University Rd Charleston SC 29406 Office Phone: 843-884-1400.

HAHN, BEATRICE H., virologist, biomedical researcher; Grad., U. Regensburg, Germany; MD, U. Munich Med. Sch., 1981. Postdoc. fell Nat. Cancer Inst., Bethesda, Md., 1982—85; prof. medicine and microbiology U. Ala., Birmingham, 1985—2010, sr. scientist, Comprehensive Cancer Ctr., assoc. dir. devel. resources, Ctr. AIDS Rsch.; clin. assoc. Penn Ctr. AIDS Rsch., U. Pa. Sch. Medicine, 2011—. Mem. editl. bd. Jour. Virology; contbr. articles to profl. jours. Named one of the Top 50 Women in Sci., Discover Mag., 2002. Mem.: Inst. Medicine. Achievements include research in the origins and evolution of human and simian immunodeficiency viruses, and in studying HIV/SIV gene function and disease mechanisms from an evolutionary perspective; development of the first molecular clone of HIV-1; discovery of the origins of HIV-1 and HIV-2 in non-human primate species in Africa, determining the pathogenic impact of SIV infection on wild chimpanzee populations. Office: Univ Pennsylvania School Medicine 3600 Market St Philadelphia PA 19104 also: Penn Center AIDS Research 522 Johnson Pavilion 3610 Hamilton Walk Philadelphia PA 19104 *

HAHN, DAVID MICHAEL, orthopedic surgeon; b. Bristol, England, Apr. 22, 1960; s. John and June Hahn; m. Jane Ann Canning, Feb. 22, 1990; children: Jamie, Ben, Sophie. MbChB, Birmingham U., England, 1984. Resident othopedic surgeon Queens Med. Ctr., Nottingham, England, 1990—95, cons. orthopedic surgeon, 1996—; orthopedic trauma fellow Carolinas Med. Ctr., Charlotte, NC, 1995—96. Clin. dir. trauma Queens Med. Ctr., 2004—. Contbr. chpt. to book. Fellow: Royal Coll. Surgeons Eng. (assoc.). Office: Nottingham U Hosp NHS Trust Queens Medical Centre Derby Road NG7 2UH Nottingham NG7 2UH England Business E-Mail: david.hahn@nuh.nhs.uk.

HAHN, MARC B., dean, physician, educator; b. Providence, 1958; m. Robin Hahn; 2 children. BS in Biology, Syracuse U.; DO, Des Moines U., 1984. Intern Walter Reed Army Med. Ctr., Washington, 1984-85, resident in anesthesiology, 1985-87; fellow in pain mgmt. Nat. Inst. Health, Bethesda, Md., 1987-88; prof. dept. anesthesiology & dir. pain medicine fellowship program Pa. State U. Coll. Medicine, Hershey, 1995—2001, chief pain medicine and palliative care divsn., Milton S. Hershey Med. Ctr.; Robert Wood Johnson Health Policy fellow Inst. Medicine Nat. Acad. Sciences, Washington, 1998—99; prof. surgery and pathology/anatomy, sr. v.p. health affairs U. North Tex. Health Sci. Ctr., Ft. Worth, 2001—08, dean Texas Coll. Osteopathic Med., 2001—08; scholar-in-residence Am. Med. Colls. (AAMC), Washington, 2009, Am. Assn. Colls. of Osteo. Medicine (AACOM), Chevy Chase, Md., 2009; sr. v.p. health affairs, dean U. New Eng. Coll. Osteopathic Medicine, Biddeford, Maine, 2009—. Lectr. in fields of anesthesiology, pain medicine, med. edn. and health policy; oral examiner and question writer Am. Bd. Anesthesiology, 1993—. Reviewer Anesthesia and Analgesia Jour., Jour. of Gastroenterology, Am. Jour. Physical Medicine and Rehabilitaion; author: (textbook) Regional Anesthesia: An Atlas of Anatomy and Technique. Served to maj. US Army. Mem.: Pa. Soc. Anesthesiologists (bd. dirs.), Internat. Assn. Study of Pain, Am. Acad. Pain Medicine (pres. 2002—03, bd. dirs., chmn. membership com., chmn. clin. practice com.), Am. Soc. Anesthesiologists (peri-operative pain guidelines com., govt. affairs com., economics com.), Am. Pain Soc., Am. Osteo. Assn., AMA. Office: University New Eng Coll Osteopathic Medicine Office of Dean 11 Hills Beach Rd Biddeford ME 04005 *

HAHN, SANG JUNE, physiology professor; b. Seoul, Republic of Korea, June 30, 1958; s. Gap Su and Chun Ja (Jo) Hahn; m. Ihn Kyung Joo; 1 child, Ji One. MD, Cath. U. Med. Coll, Seoul, 1983; PhD, Cath. U. Grad. Sch., Seoul, 1992. Cert. in physician Ministry Health & Social Affairs, 1983. Chmn. Dept. Physiology, Cath. U. Med. Coll, 2003—. Contbr. articles to profl. jours. Internat. Fogarty fellowship, Fogarty Internat. Ctr., USA, 1994. Office: Physiol Catholic Univ Med Coll 505 Banpo-dong Socho-gu Seoul 137-701 Republic of Korea Office Fax: 82-2-532-9575. Business E-Mail: sjhahn@catholic.ac.kr.

HAHN, SANG KI, geneticist; b. Chungyang, Choongnam, Korea, Aug. 12, 1933; came to U.S., 1978; s. Noh Soo and Dong Jin (Chung) H.; m. Jung Ja Kim, Aug. 27, 1956; children: Young-Soon, Sok-Chul, Joong-Hee, Jung-Yun. BS, Seoul U., Republic of, 1957, MS, 1959; postgrad., U. Minn., 1960-61; PhD, Mich. State U., 1967. Chartered biologist Inst. Biology, London. Lectr. Seoul Nat. U., 1961-65, asst. prof., 1965-71; assoc. plant breeder/genetist Internat. Inst. Tropical Agr., Ibadan, Nigeria, 1971-72, asst. dir., plant breeder, genetist, 1972-83, dir., plant breeder, genetist, 1983-91, dir. emeritus, 1991—, acting head biotech. rsch. unit, 1992-93. Mem. Field Crop Varietal Nomination Com. of South Korea, 1969-71; mem. Project Evaluation Team, U.S. AID, Zaire, 1983, Ea. and So. Africa, 1988; sci. adviser Internat. Found. for Sci., Sweden, 1984—; adj. prof. plant breeding dept. plant breeding and biometry Cornell U. 1989-94; external examiner PhD thesis U. Queensland, Australia, 1990; hon. scientist Rural Devel. Adminstrn., South Korea, 1992—; external examiner for MPhil thesis U. West Indies, 1990; sec. Internat. Sweet Potato Testing Group. Author: Africa: A Continent of Mystery, 1990; editor: Integrated Pest Management, 1990; editl. adv. bd. Jour. Root Crops, Indian Soc. Root Crops, 1977—, Jour. Agr., Ecosys. and Environ., The Netherlands, 1985—; editl. bd. Sci. Tech. Rev., 1979-92, Jour. Food and Agr., 1986-93; author discovery of polyploid cassava, theoretical and applied genetics, 1990; developer improved varieties of cassava, 1982 (Guinness award for sci. achievement 1982); contbr. articles to profl. jours. Recipient Korea Presdl. award of merit, 1982, Traditional Chieftaincy Title Seriki Agbe (King of Farmers), Oba of Ikire, Nigeria, 1983, Sang-Huh award Sang-Huh Cultural Found., Republic of Korea, 1992, Hon. Internat. Alumni award Mich. State U., 1993. Fellow Inst. Biology (London), Am. Soc. Agronomy, Nigeria Inst. Biology (exec. com. coun. 1990—); mem. Crop Sci. Soc. Am., Am. Soc. Hort. Sci., Internat. Soc. Horticulture Sci. (exec. mem. 1979—, exec. com. and coun. 1991—), Internat. Soc. Tropical Root Crops (pres. 1991—, found. mem. 1979—, Disting. Svc. award 1983), Internat. Soc. Tropical Crop Rsch. and Devel. (v.p. 1990—), Africa Plant Biotech. Network (sec. gen. 1990-93). Avocations: poetry, jogging, gardening, meditation. Home: 1352 Homestead Creek Dr Broadview Hts OH 44147-2581 *

HAHN, SEUNG S., oncologist, educator; b. Pusan, Republic of Korea, Aug. 15, 1952; MD, Seoul nat. U., 1976. Prof. SUNY Upstate Med. U., 2003—. Recipient Best Tchr. award, Assn. Residents Radiation Oncology. Mem.: Syracuse U. Oratorio Soc., ACR, ASTRO. Avocations: singing, golf, guitar. Office: 4526 Lamplighter Ln Manlius NY 13104

HAHN, STEPHEN M., radiation oncologist educator; BA in Biology, Rice U., 1980; MD, Temple U., 1984. Diplomate Am. Bd. Internal Medicine, Am. Bd. Radiology-radiation oncology, Am. Bd. Radiology-hematology/oncology. Intern, resident internal medicine San Francisco hosp. Univ. of Calif., 1984—87, chief resident internal medicine San Francisco hosp., 1987—88; med. oncology fellowship medicine br. Nat. Cancer Inst., Bethesda, Md., 1988—91, resident radiation oncology, 1991—94; chmn. dept. radiation oncology Univ. of Pa., Henry K. Pancoast prof., dir. photodynamic therapy program, co-program leader radiation biology. Co-author numerous publs. Named one of Top Docs, Phila. Mag., 2002, 2007, 2010—11, Best Doctors in America, 2003—10, America's Top Doctors, 2007—08, 2010. Office: Perelman Center for Advanced Medicine Concourse Level 3400 Civic Center Blvd Philadelphia PA 19104 Office Phone: 800-789-7366.

HAHN, TAE W., ophthalmologist, director; b. Seoul, Republic of Korea, Oct. 22, 1957; s. Chong M. Hahn and Chun H. Park; m. Kyongok Rosa Ryu, Jan. 21, 1982; children: Aidan Dongheon, Kayle Dongyun. MD, Cath. U. Med. Coll., Seoul, 1982; PhD, Med. Grad. Sch. Cath. U., 1993. Prof. Cath. U. Med. Coll., 1989—2000; rsch. fellow Wilmer Eye Inst. John Hopkins U., Seoul, 1993—95; dir. Apgujong St. Mary's Eye Ctr., Seoul, 2000—. Exec. dir. Korean External Eye Disease Soc., Seoul, 2000—, Korean Soc. Cataract and Refractive Surgery, Seoul, 2000—. Co-author: (textbook) Surgical techniques in anterior and posterior lamellar keratoplasty. Vol. ophthalmologist Joseph Hosp., Seoul, 1989—93. Recipient Topcon Academic award, Topcon Co., 1994. Mem.: Korean Ophthalmologists Assn. (pres. 2007—09). Roman Catholic. Avocations: golf, photography, travel. Home: 61-2 Hansol Villa 108 Bundang-dong Seongnam 463-831 Republic of Korea Office: Apgujong St Mary's Eye Ctr 621-3 Sinsa-dong Kangnam-gu Seoul 135-894 Republic of Korea Office Phone: 82-2-3445-3457. Office Fax: 82-2-533-1750; Home Fax: 82-31-701-9846. Personal E-mail: twhahn@hotmail.com.

HAI, HU, physician, director; b. Xianju County, Zhejiang, China, Dec. 24, 1960; MD, PhD, Med. Coll. Shanghai Jiaotong U., 1992. Dir. dept. minimally invasive surgery Tongji U. Affiliated Shanghai East Hosp., 2004. Recipient China Outstanding Leadership award, Evaluation Com. Endos Award in Medicaol Sci. & Tech., China Outstanding Yong Dr. award. Avocations: reading, chess, swimming. Office: 150 Jimo Rd Pudong New Dist Shanghai 200120 China Office Fax: 58798999.

HAI, TAO, ophthalmologist, educator; b. Yunnan, China, Nov. 10, 1968; MD, Peking U., PhD, 2008. Assoc. prof., assoc. chief physician Armed Police Gen. Hosp. China, 2003—. Office: Dept Ophthalmology 69 Yongding Haidian Beijing 100039 China Office Fax: 86-010-68211329.

HAIGHT, DAVID HULEN, ophthalmologist; b. Highland Park, Ill., Mar. 30, 1954; s. Thomas Hulen and Virginia Ellen (Olsson) H. AB in Biochemistry magna cum laude, Brown U., 1976; MD, Johns Hopkins U., 1980. Diplomate Am. Bd. Ophthalmology. Resident ophthalmology Manhattan Eye, Ear and Throat Hosp., NYC, 1981-84, fellow in cornea dept., 1984-85, resident instr., ophthalmology, 1985-87, residency coord., 1989-91, chief Contact Lens Clinic I, 1986—2007, chief coord. investigator, 1991—, with laser rsch. study, 1991—. Quality assurance com. Manhattan Eye, Ear and Throat Hosp., N.Y.C., 1987-2007, chmn. ophthalmology credentials com. 1993-2007; surgeon dir. Manhattan Eye, Ear and Throat Hosp., 1997-2007, dir. refractive surgery, 1997—; mem. adv. bd. N.Y. Eye Bank for Sight Restoration, N.Y.C., 1992—; sec. med. adv. bd. N.Y. Eye Bank for Sight Restoration, 1995-97; skills transfer adv. com. Am. Acad. Ophthalmology, San Francisco, 1992-96; lectr. ophthalmology Columbia U., NYC, 1997—; clin. asst. prof. ophthalmology N.Y. Weill-Cornell Med. Coll., NYC, clin. prof. ophthalmology NYU Sch. Medicine. Contbg. author: Corneal Surgery, 1986, 4th edit., 2008, Color Atlas of Ophthalmology, 1999. Fellow Am. Acad. Ophthalmology (honor award 1993, Sr. Achievement award 2007); mem. Med. Soc. of State of N.Y., N.Y. State Ophthalmologic Soc., Internat. Soc. Refractive Surgery, Am. Soc. Cataract and Refractive Surgery, Phi Beta Kappa, Sigma Xi (assoc.). Avocations: photography, golf, travel, aviation, birding. Office: 155 E 72nd St New York NY 10021-4371 Office Phone: 212-772-9474. E-mail: dhaight@laserlasik.com.

HAIKERWAL, MUKESH CHANDRA, physician; b. Lucknow, India, Dec. 28, 1960; m. Karyn Haikerwal; 3 children. MBChB, U. Leicester, 1986. Chair, drs. mental health program Beyondblue: Nat. Depression Initiative, 2009; head clin. leadership & engagement Nat. E-Health Transition Authority, 2009; pres. Australian Med. Assn., 2005—07; chair World Med. Assn. Coun., 2011—. Prof. sch. medicine Flinders U., 2009. Named to Officer in the Order of Australia, Gov. Gen. Australia. Fellow: Royal Australian Coll. Gen. Practitioners, Australian Med. Assn. Avocations: films, cooking, bicycling. Office: Unit 2 / 174 Millers Rd Altona N Melbourne Victoria 3025 Australia Office Fax: 61393153199. Business E-Mail: mckehaik@bigpond.net.au.

HAILPARN, DIANA FINNEGAN, psychotherapist, writer; b. Newark, Jan. 25, 1949; d. Thomas Patrick Finnegan and Aurora Floyd Durden; m. Michael Hailparn, May 10, 1973. BA, William Paterson U., 1971; MA, Fairleigh Dickinson U., 1973; MS, Columbia U., 1975. LCSW, diplomate Clin. Social Work Assn. Psychotherapist Bonniel Brae Residential Treatment Ctr., 1973—75, Clifton Mental Health Clinic, NJ, 1975—79, Diana Assoc., Mahwah, NJ, 1975—. Author: Fear No More: A Psychotherapist's Guide to Overcoming Anxiety and Panic, 2000; contbr. articles to profl. med. jours. Named one of Am.'s Best Therapists, Psychology Today. Mem.: NASW (licentiate), Dictionary Internat. Biography, NJ Assoc. Social Workers, Columbia U. Sch. Social Work Alumni Assn. Avocations: travel, art, writing. Office: Diana Assoc 19 N Bayard Ln Mahwah NJ 07430-2236 Office Phone: 201-661-8815. Personal E-mail: leaurore@yahoo.com.

HAIMOV-KOCHMAN, RONIT, gynecologist, reproductive endocrinologist; b. Tel Aviv, Oct. 22, 1965; d. Rafael and Denise Haimov; m. Tuvia Kochman, Sept. 15, 1986; children: Yoav Kochman, Naama Kochman, Amit Kochman. MD, Hadassah Hebrew U. Sch. Medicine, Jerusalem, Israel, 1989. Resident Hadassah Hebrew U. Med. Ctr., Jerusalem, 1995—2000, sr. physician. divsn. reproductive endocrinology and infertility, dept. obs.-gyn., 2004—. Contbr. articles to profl. jours. Adminstr. tchg. program dept. ob.-gyn. Hebrew U. Sch. Medicine, 2004. Capt. Israeli Def. Forces, 1991—94. Grantee, Hadassah Med. Orgn., 2004—05; fellow, U. Calif., Dept. Cell and Tissue Biology, San Francisco, 2003—04; scholar, Hebrew U. Sch. Medicine, 1986—89. Mem.: Jerusalem Obstetrics and Gynecology Soc. (rsch. coord. 2005), Israel Menopause Soc., Israeli Soc. Fertility and Reproduction, Soc. of Gynecologic Investigation. Achievements include research in characterization of heparanase in human placenta and in the corpus luteum. Office: Hadassah Hebrew U Med Ctr 24035, Mt Scopus Pob 91999 Jerusalem Israel Office Fax: 972-2-581-4210. E-mail: kochman@hadassah.org.il.

HAINES, ANDREW PAUL, medical educator, researcher; b. London, Feb. 26, 1947; s. Charles George and Lilian Emily (Buck) Haines; m. June Marie Power, Feb. 12, 1982 (div. 1989); m. Anita Berlin, Mar. 14, 1998; children: Alex, Adam. MB, BS with honors in Surgery, Pathology, Pharmacology, Therapeutics, Kings Coll., London, 1969; MD, U. London, 1985. House physician, surgeon King's Coll. Hosp., London, 1969—70; sr. house officer U. West Indies, Kingston, Jamaica, 1970-71, Nat. Hosp. for Nervous Diseases, London, 1972; med. officer Britain-Nepal Med. Trust, Biratnagar, Nepal, 1973; mem. sci. staff Med. Rsch. Coun., Harrow, Eng., 1974-86; sr. lectr. St. Mary's Hosp. Med. Sch., London, 1984-87; prof. primary care Univ. Coll. London, 1987—2000; dir. R & D N.E. Thames Regional Health Authority, London, 1993—94, Nat. Health Svc. Exec., London, 1994—96; dean London Sch. Hygiene and Tropical Medicine, London, 2001—05, dir., 2005—. Chmn. steering group on trial of screening of elderly Med. Rsch. Coun., London, 1993—2000, mem., 1996—, chmn. health scis. rsch. and pub. health bd., 1996—98; mem. group on health effects of climate change WHO, Geneva, 1993—96; mem. ctrl. R & D com. UK Nat. Health Svc., 1995—2000; mem. UN Intergovtl. Panel on Climate Change, 1996—2000; mem. WHO adv. com. on Health Rsch., 2004—; chair health and social care policy com. Univ. UK Health and Social Care, 2007—. Co-editor: Critical Condition-Human Health and the Environment, 1993, Climate Change and Human Health, 1996, Evidence-Based Practice in Primary Care, 1998, Getting Research Findings into Practice, 1998; contbr. over 200 articles to sci. and profl. jours.; chpts. to books Mem. internat. coun. Internat. Physicians for Prevention of Nuc. War, Boston, 1982-85; mem. internat. coun. Pugwash Orgn. of Sci. and World Affairs, London, 1987-92; v.p. Medact, London, 1992—; mem. scientific strategy com. Assn. of Med. Rsch. Charities, 1998-2004. Co-recipient Nobel Peace prize, 1985; Rsch. grantee Wellcome Trust, 1990-92, Med. Rsch. Coun., 1986, 92, 99-2000, Nat. Health Svc. Rsch. and Devel. Programme, 1995-96, 98-99, named Knight of Brit. Empire Queen's New Year's Honors List, 2005. Fellow: Acad. Med. Scis., Faculty Pub. Health, Royal Coll. Gen. Practitioners, Royal Coll. Physicians; mem.: Inst. Medicine (fgn. assoc.). Avocations: foreign travel, environmental issues. Office: London Sch Hyg Trop Medicine Keppel St London WC1E 7HT England Office Phone: 0044 2079272278. Business E-Mail: andy.haines@ishtm.ac.uk.

HAINES, CINDY D., physician, consultant; BS in Biology & Psychology, St. Louis U., MD. Diplomate family medicine Am. Bd. Family Practice. Resident St. Louis Family Medicine; asst. clinical prof. dept. cmty. & family medicine St. Louis U. Sch. Medicine; pres. Haines Med. Comm.; chief med. officer HealthDay News; mng. editor HealthDay-Physician's Briefing. Recipient Geriatric Scholar's award, St. Louis U. Mem.: Healthcare Businesswoman's Assn. (dir. pub. rels. 2007—08), St. Louis Acad. Family Physicans (v.p. bd.), Am. Acad. Family Physicans, Internat. Mensa Soc. Office: SLUCare Family Medicine 1034 S Brentwood Blvd Ste 1120 Saint Louis MO 63117 also: Saint Louis University Donco Bldg 2nd Fl 1402 South Grand Blvd Saint Louis MO 63104 Office Phone: 314-977-4600, 314-977-8480. Office Fax: 314-977-5268. E-mail: drcindy@hainesmedicom.com.

HAINES, IAN EDWIN, oncologist; b. Melbourne, Victoria, Australia, Nov. 23, 1954; s. Eric Edwin and Dorothy Haines; m. Wendy Lee Harmer; children: Joanna Emily, Scott Lindsay Edwin, Cameron James, Michael Harmer. MBBS, U. Melbourne, Australia, 1978. Clin., rsch. fellow med. oncology Meml. Sloan-Kettering Cancer Ctr., NYC, 1985—87; founder and head, Melbourne oncology group Cabrini Med. Ctr., Malvern, Victoria, 1987—; assoc. prof. Monash U., Melbourne, 1991—; vis. med. oncologist Alfred Hosp., Melbourne, Victoria, Australia, 1987—; mem. ethics subcom. Med. Oncology Group Australia, 2007—; with Cabrini Hosp., Melbourne; mem. Acute Inpatient Palliative Care Svc. Cabrini Hosp., Melbourne; steering com. mem. Cabrini Hosp. Vis. Domiciliary Care Nursing Svc., 1999. Subcommittee mem. Cancer Coun. Victoria, Melbourne, 1988—; reviewer Med. Jour. Australia & Internal Med. Jour. RACP. Contbr. medical review and research manuscripts, articles to profl. jours. With Leadership Victoria, Melbourne, 2007—08. Fellow: Royal Australasian Coll. Physicians, Australian Assn. Palliative Medicine; mem.: Med. Oncology Group of Australia (mem. ethics sub-com. 2007—), Am. Soc. Clin. Oncology. Achievements include established and published details of first undergraduate teaching courses in palliative care at Melb University in 1987, and Monash University in 1991 with Drs John Buchanan, Nathan Chernt & Carrie Le. Avocations: golf, tennis, bicycling, reading, walking. Office: Cabrini Med Ctr Suite 45 183 Wattletree Rd Malvern Victoria 3144 Australia Office Phone: 61-3-9509-3744. Office Fax: 61-3-9509-5644. Business E-Mail: melbonc@bigpond.net.au.

HAINES, KATHLEEN ANN, pediatrician, educator; b. NYC, July 28, 1949; d. George Raymond and Gertrude Ann (Driscoll) H.; m. Emil Claus Gotschlich, May 24, 1975; 1 child, Emily Claire. BA in Biology, Hunter Coll.-CUNY, 1971; MD, Albert Einstein Coll. Medicine, 1975. Diplomate Am. Bd. Pediatrics, Am. Bd. Allergy and Immunology. Intern, resident NY Hosp./Cornell U., NYC, 1975-77, fellow in allergy/immunology, 1977-80; from instr. in pediatrics to assoc. prof. Sch. Medicine NYU, NYC, 1980—91, assoc. prof. clin. pediatrics and medicine Sch. Medicine, 1991—2005, adj. assoc. prof. Sch. Medicine, 2005—; dir. pediat. rheumatology Hosp. Joint Diseases/NYU Med. Ctr., 1994—2002; dir. clin. immunology lab. Hosp. Joint Diseases, 1995—2002; sect. chief pediat. immunology Hackensack U. Med. Ctr., NJ, 2002—; assoc. prof. pediat. U. Medicine and Dentistry NJ/NJ Med. Sch., 2005—. Mem. rsch. coun. NY Heart Assn., 1988-90; program com. Am. Coll. Rheumatology, 2000-03, vis. prof., 2001. Contbr. articles to profl. jours., chpts. to books in field. Med. and Scientific Com. N.Y.C. chpt. Arthritis Found., 1993-99. Grantee, N.Y. Arthritis Found., 1990, 1996, NIH, 1993—98. Fellow Am. Acad. Allergy and Immunology, Am. Acad. Pediatrics (mem. exec. com. rheumatology sect., 2003—); mem. Am. Fedn. Med. Rsch., Allergy, Asthma and Immunology Soc. of Greater N.Y. (sec. 1995-97, pres.-elect 1997-98, pres. 1998-99), Harvey Soc., Soc. Pediatric Rsch., Clin. Immunology Soc. Office: Hackensack U Med Ctr 30 Prospect Ave Hackensack NJ 07601 Home Phone: 212-722-6380; Office Phone: 201-996-5306. Business E-Mail: khaines@humed.com. *

HAINES, RICHARD FOSTER, retired psychologist; b. Seattle, May 19, 1937; s. Donald Hutchinson and Claudia May (Bennett) H.; m. Carol Taylor, June 17, 1961; children: Cynthia Lynn, Laura Anne. Student, U. Wash., 1955-57; BA, Pacific Luth. Coll., Tacoma, 1960; MA, Mich. State U., 1962, PhD, 1964. Predoctoral rsch. fellow NIH, 1964; Nat. Acad. Sci. postdoctoral resident rsch. assoc. Ames Rsch. Ctr./NASA, Moffett Field, Calif., 1964-67, rsch. scientist, 1967-86, chief of space human factors office, 1987-88, rsch. scientist Rsch. Inst. Advanced Computer Sci., 1988-90; assoc. prof. dept. psychology San Jose State U., 1988-89; computer scientist RECOM Techs., Inc., Moffett Field, Calif., 1993-2000, Raytheon Corp., 2000—01; ret., 2001. Rsch. cons. to NASA Foothill Coll.; cons. Stanford U. Sch. medicine, 1966-67, TRW-Systems Group, 1969-70; mem. adv. com. on vision NRC; founding mem. advanced tech. applications com. Calif. Coun. AIA and NASA, 1975-80; mem. adv. bd. Space Scis. Ctr.-Foothill Coll., 1976-78; bd. advisors Fund for UFO Rsch., Washington; chmn. bd. Novosibirsk Christian Pub.-Calif., 1993-2007; chief scientist Nat. Aviation Reporting Ctr. on Anomalous Phenomena, 2001—. Author: UFO Phenomena and the Behavioral Scientist, 1979, Observing UFOs, 1980, Melbourne Episode: Case Study of a Missing Pilot, 1987, Advanced Aerial Devices Reported During the Korean War, 1990, Night Flying, 1992, Project Delta, 1994, Close Encounters of the Fifth Kind, 1999, Aviation Safety in America - A Previously Neglected Factor, 2000, Sudden Loss: Earthquake Realities, 2009, Spherical UAP and Aviation Safety: A Critical Review (Edn.), 2010; mem. editl. and sci. bd. Jour. UFO Studies, Internat.

UFO Reporter, Cuadernos de Ufologica; contbr. articles to profl. jours. Mem. Palo Alto (Calif.) Mayor's Com. on Youth Activities, 1967; chmn. adv. coun. Christian Cmty. Progress Corp., Menlo Park, Calif.; v.p., dir. Ctr. Counseling for Drug Abuse, Menlo Park; bd. dirs., chmn. sci. adv. team Threshold Found.; founding co-dir. Joint Am.-Soviet Aerial Anomaly Fedn., 1991—97. Named Alumnus of Yr., Pacific Luth. U., 1972 Fellow Aerospace Med. Assn. (assoc.); mem. Optical Soc. Am., Sigma Xi. Achievements include patents for device of advanced detection of glaucoma, optical projector of vision performance data for design engineers, visual simulator optical alignment device, grooming aid for use by astronauts in space.

HAINES, STEPHEN JOHN, neurosurgeon; b. Burlington, Vt., Sept. 4, 1949; s. Gerald Leon and Frances Mary (Whitcomb) H.; m. Jennifer Lea Plombon; children: Christopher, Jeremy. AB, Dartmouth Coll., 1971; MD, U. Vt., 1975. Diplomate Am. Bd. Neurol. Surgery; diplomate Nat. Bd. Med. Examiners. Intern U. Minn., Mpls., 1975—76; resident neurol. surgery U. Pitts., 1976—81; from asst. prof. to prof. U. Minn., Mpls., 1982—93, prof. neurosurgery, otolaryngology and pediatr., 1993—97, head divsn. pediat. neurosurgery, 1985—97, chmn. and head dept. neurosurgery, 2003—; prof. neurosurg., Lyle A. French chair, head dept. neurosurg. U. Minn. Med. Sch., 2003—; prof. neurol. surgery, otolaryngology and pediats., chmn. dept. neurol. surgery Med. U. S.C., 1997—2003. Adv. panel FDA Neurologic Devices, 2002—05, chair, 2005; mem. Com. Postmarket Surveillance Pediat Med. Devices, Inst. Medicine, 2004—05. Contbr. articles to profl. jours. Recipient Disting. Academic Achievement award, 2010. Fellow ACS; mem. AMA, Am. Assn. Neurol. Surgeons (Van Wagenen fellow 1981), Congress Neurol. Surgeons (pres. 1996), Soc. Clin. Trials, Neurosurg. Soc. Am., Am. Acad. Neurol. Surgery, Soc. Neurol. Surgeons, Am. Soc. Pediat. Neurosurgery (hon. mem. 2008-). Office: Dept Neurosurgery MMC 96 420 Delaware St SE Minneapolis MN 55455 Office Phone: 612-626-5767. Business E-Mail: shaines@umn.edu, headneurosurg@umn.edu.

HAIRSTON, ILANA, psychiatrist, educator; b. Jamaica, July 11, 1966; PhD, Stanford U., 2004. Rsch. asst. prof. U. Mich., 2009—. Mem.: Rsch. Soc. Alcoholism, Assn. Psychol. Sci., Soc. Neurosci., Sleep Rsch. Soc. Office: University Mich Psychiatry 4250 Ann Arbor MI 48105 Business E-Mail: ilanahai@med.umich.edu.

HAIT, GERSHON, pediatric cardiologist; b. May 10, 1927; came to U.S., 1952, naturalized, 1965; s. Nahum and Leah H.; m. Doris J. Coburn, Mar. 20, 1957; children: Jonathan, Yael. MD, U. Lausanne, Switzerland, 1952. Intern Michael Reese Hosp., Chgo., 1952-53; resident Cook County Hosp., Chgo., 1961-62, fellow in pediatric cardiology, 1954-56, 59-60; instr. pediatrics, NIH fellow in pediatric cardiology Albert Einstein Coll. Medicine, Bronx, NY, 1962-64, dir. pediatric cardiology, 1966-85, prof. pediatrics, 1979—2005, prof. emeritus, 2005—. Mem. staff Bronx Mcpl. Hosp. Center, Montefiore; cardiac cons. to depts. of health of Bronx, SI, and Rockland counties. Contbr. articles to profl. jours. Served to lt. M.C. Israeli Army, 1956-59. Grantee NIH; Grantee Am. Heart Assn.; Grantee others. Mem. Am. Physiology Soc., Soc. for Pediatric Research, Am. Acad. Pediatrics, Am. Fedn. Clin. Research, Am. Heart Assn., Am. Coll. Cardiology, Sleep Rsch. Soc., Am. Acad. Sleep Medicine. Jewish. Home: 14 Withington Rd Scarsdale NY 10583 3306 Office: Childrens Hosp Montefiore 3415 Bainbridge Ave Bronx NY 10467 Personal E-mail: gershonhait@aol.com.

HAIZINGER, BETTINA MARIA, pediatric cardiac anesthesiologist, emergency physician; b. Weyregg, Austria, Oct. 25, 1958, d. Friedrich and Eva Haizinger. MD, U. Innsbruck, Austria, 1984. Diplomate gen. practitioner Austrian Med. Chamber, Vienna, 1989, in emergency medicine Austrian Med. Chamber, 1989, in anesthesiology Austrian Med. Chamber, Vienna, 1997, in anaesthesiology intensive care European Acad. Anesthesiology, Zurich, Switzerland, 1997, competence in perioperative TEE Nat. Bd. Echocardiography, Inc., Dallas, 2004. Resident, dept. neurology U. Clinic Innsbruck, 1984—85; resident Gen. Hosp. Vöcklabruck, Austria, 1985—89; gen. practitioner Rehab. Ctr. Cardiac and Vascular Diseases, Bad Schallerbach, Austria, 1989—91; resident, dept. anesthesiology intensive care medicine Gen. Hosp. Linz, Austria, 1991—97, helicopter emergency physician, 1997—, staff mem., dept. anesthesiology intensive care medicine, 1997—. Guest physician, cardiac intensive care unit Children's Hosp. Boston, 1999; guest physician U. Calif., San Francisco, 1999, Gt. Ormond St. Hosp. Children, London, 2005. Contbr. articles to profl. jours. Mem.: European Soc. Anesthesiology, Am. Soc. Anesthesiology. Avocations: swimming, mountain climbing, reading, mountain biking. Office: General Hosp Linz Krankenhausstraße 9 Upper Austria Linz 4021 Austria Home: Beim Amthof 1/8 Seewalchen 4863 Austria Office Fax: 43 0 732 7806 2154. Personal E-mail: bettina.haizinger@cablevision.et. Business E-Mail: bettina.haizinger@akh.linz.at.

HAIZLIP, JULIE A., pediatrician, educator; b. NC, Aug. 5, 1969; BS in Pharmacy with Honors, U. NC, 1992, MD, 1996. Assoc. prof., pediat. U. Va., 2003—. Fellow: Am. Acad. Pediat.; mem.: Am. Acad. Comm. Healthcare, Soc. Critical Care Medicine. Office: University Va Dept Pediatrics PO Box 300386 Charlottesville VA 22908-0386 Office Fax: 434-982-3843. E-mail: julie_haizlip@yahoo.com.

HAJDU, MICHAEL A., cardiologist; b. Washington, Mar. 4, 1955; s. Stephen Hajdu and Margaret Patricia Hadju. BA, Knox Coll., 1978; PhD, U. Nebr., 1988; MD, U. Iowa, 1997. Resident Fletcher Allen Health Care, U. Vt., Burlington, 1997—2000, cardiology fellow, 2000—02; cardiologist Cardiology Cons., Kans. City. Named a Kans. City Super Doctor, Kans. City mag., 2007. Avocations: fishing, bicycling.

HAJNALKA, SZABO, pediatrician, b. Hadad, Romania, July 26, 1965; Degree in Med., Semmelweis U. Budapest, 1990; PhD, U. Szeged, 2010. Head dept. neonatological, pediat. U. Szeged, 2005—11. Mem.: European Respiratory Soc. Office: University Szeged Dept Pediatrics Korányi fasor 14-15 Szeged 6720 Hungary Business E-Mail: szabohaj@pedia.szote.u-szeged.hu.

HAKALEHTO, EINO ELIAS, microbiologist, researcher; b. Lahti, Finland, Feb. 23, 1961; s. Jukka Joseppi and Riitta Kyllikki (Salmi) H.; m. Hanna Kaarina Nokelainen Hakalehto, Nov. 11, 1986; children: Lauri Sakari Miikael, Jukka-Pekka Daniel. MS, U. Helsinki, Finland, 1983; diploma in biotech., U. Canterbury, Eng., 1985; PhD, U Kuopio, Finland, 2000. Rsch. trainee State Rsch. Ctr., Espoo, Finland, 1981-83; asst. tchr. U. Helsinki, Finland, 1984; project rschr. Valio Dairies Coop., Helsinki, Finland, 1986; course leader in biotechnology U. Kuopio, Finland, 1987-88; vis. scientist Hebrew U., Jerusalem, 1989-90; project dir. U. Kuopio, Finland, 1992—, adj. prof. biotech. microbe analytics, 2008—. Mng. dir. Finnoflag Oy, Finland, 1993—, R & D dir. Samplion Oy Finland, 2009-; scientific adv., Finnoflag Oy, Finland, 1997—, Kerox Oy, Finland, 1997-99, Maitomaa Coop., Finland, 1997—, Modelon Oy, Finland, 1999-2005, Biometz Finland Oy, 2009, Biopollo Sys. Oy, 2009-. Inventor in field; contbr. articles to profl. jours. Mem. bd. Student Union U., Helsinki, Finland, 1983-84; 1st chmn. environ. sect., 1983-84; sec. toxicology and microbiology sect. Scientific Com. of Nat. Def., Finland, 1994-97, active, 1998-2003. Grantee Acad. Finland, 1989-90, Scientific Com. on Nat. Def., Finland, 1992-96, Finnish Nat. Fund, 1992-95, Regional Coun. of Savo, Finland, 1997—. Achievements include invention of portablemicrobe enrichment unit equipment. Avocations: nature, literature. Office: FinnoFlag Oy PL 262 FIN70101 Kuopio Finland

HAKALO, JERZY, orthopedist; b. Szczecin, June 9, 1958; MD, Med. U., Bialystok, 1983; PhD, Med. U., Wroclaw, 2004. Head, orthop. dept. County Hosp. Ltd. Slubice, 2011—. Cons., dept. neurosurgery Provincial Hosp., Zielona Gora, 2000—04, cons., dept. orthop., RSA, Polokwane, 2004—05. Mem.: Polish Spine Surgery Soc. Avocations: computers, photography. Home: Konarski 16 Swiebodzin Lubuskie 66-200 Poland Personal E-mail: hakalo@poczta.onet.pl.

HAKEEM, A. HUSSAIN, physician, consultant; b. India, Feb. 2, 1974; MBBS, Govt. Med. Coll., Srinagar, Kashmir, India, 2000, MS, 2005. Cons. Prince Aly Khan Hosp., Mumbai, 2006—10, Fortis Cancer Ctr., Mumbai, 2011—. Recipient SBS Man Gold medal, NWZ AOI, India; Fellowship, Narotum Sakseria Found. Mem.: Assn. Surgeons India, Assn. Med. Cons. Mumbai, Found. Head and Neck Oncology. Avocations: sports, reading. Office: Fortis Cancer Ctr Mulund Goregaon Link Rd Mumbai Maharashtra 400 078 India Office Fax: 91-22-6799 4242. E-mail: drahhakim@gmail.com.

HAKEL, MILTON DANIEL, JR., psychologist, educator, writer, consultant; b. Hutchinson, Minn., Aug. 1, 1941; s. Milton Daniel and Emily Ann (Kovar) H.; m. Lee Ellen Pervier, Sept. 1, 1962; children: Lane, Jennifer BA, U. Minn., 1963, PhD, 1966. Diplomate in Indsl. and Orgnl. Psychology Am. Bd. Profl. Psychology. Prof. psychology Ohio State U., Columbus, 1968-85, U. Houston, 1985-91, chmn. dept., 1987-91; pres. Orgnl. Rsch. and Devel., 1977—2006; ptnr. Applied Rsch. Group, 1984-87; Ohio Bd. Regents eminent scholar, prof. Bowling Green State U., 1991—2009, prof. emeritus, 2009—. Trustee Am. Bd. Profl. Psychology, 1987-90; mem. US nat. com. Internat. Union Psychol. Sci., 1997-01, mem. com. on assessment and tchr. quality NRC, 1999-00, mem. bd. testing and assessment, 1999-05, evaluate advanced tchr. cert. Co-author (sr.): Making It Happen: Doing Research with Implementation in Mind, 1982; author: Beyond Multiple Choice: Evaluating Alternatives to Traditional Testing, 1998; editor Current Directions in Psychol. Sci., 1998-99, Personnel Psychology, 1973-84, pub. 1984-2004; co-editor: Applying the Science of Learning to University Teaching and Beyond, 2002; editor (sr.): Assessing Accomplished tch.: Advanced Level cert. program, 2008; contbr. 40 articles to profl. jours. Chair Human Capital Initiative Coordinating Com., 1991-99, co-chair Applying Sci. Learning to U. Edu. conf. steering com. Recipient James McKeen Cattell award, 1965; Fulbright-Hays Sr. scholar, 1978, NSF grantee, 1966-73, Disting. Svc. Contbrs. award, 1995. Fellow Assn. for. Psychol. Sci. (founding bd. dirs., co chair Lifelong Learning at Work and at Home 2006—), Soc. Indsl. and Orgnl. Psychology (pres. 1984), Am. Assn. Adv. Sci., Internat. Assn. Applied Psychology (bd. dirs. 2004-10), Summit Conf., Alliance Orgnl. Psychology (pres. 2010-); mem. Ohio Bd. Regents Com. Higher Learning Accountability and Productivity (chair 2006-09). Presbyterian. Home: 1435 Cedar Ln Bowling Green OH 43402-1476 Office: Bowling Green State U Dept Psychology Bowling Green OH 43403-0001 Office Phone: 419-372-8144. Business E-Mail: mhakel@bgsu.edu.

HAKIM, ALAN JAMES, rheumatologist, acute medicine physician, consultant; b. London, Mar. 4, 1968; s. Lalit K Hakim and Anne M Sadler. BA, Cambridge U., 1989, MA, MA, Cambridge U., 1992. Sr. house physician Addenbrookes Hosp., Cambridge, England, 1992—94; specialist, rheumatology & medicine U. Coll. London Hosps., 1994—2000; arthritis rsch. campaign clin. fellow St. Thomas' Hosp., 2000—03; cons. rheumatologist, physician Whipps Cross U. Hosp., 2001—, dir. rheumatology rsch., 2007—, assoc. clin. dir. emergency medicine, 2008—; hon. cons. rheumatologist U. Coll. London Hosps., 2003—. Chmn. Rheumatology Trainees Com., 1999—2001; med. advisor Hypermobility Assn., 2003—, Ehler's Danlos Soc., 2005—. Author: (medical textbook) Oxford Handbook of Rheumatology (Brit. Med. Assn. Book Award, 2003). Named Advanced Med. Leader, Brit. Assn. Med. Mgrs., 2007. Fellow: Royal Coll. Physicians, Royal Soc. Medicine (coun. mem. divsn. rheumatology and rehab. 2000—); mem.: Whipps Cross Med. Assn. (chmn. 2006—). Achievements include research in genetics of soft tissue rheumatic disorders; epidemiology and clinical research in the field of heritable disorders of connective tissue. Office: Whipps Cross Hosp Dept Rheumatology Whipps Cross Hospital Whipps Cross Road E11 1NR London England Office Fax: 020 8535 6504. Personal E-mail: alanhakim@aol.com. E-mail: alan.hakim@whippsx.nhs.uk.

HAKIM, NADEY SUBHY, surgeon; b. Beirut, Apr. 9, 1958; arrived in Eng., 1975; s. Subhy Elias Hakim and Katy Namur; m. Nicole Antoine Abounader, Feb. 14, 1992; children: Alexandra, David, Andrea. MD, Paris Descartes U., 1984; PhD, London U., 1991; D, Charles U., Prague, Czech Republic, 1999; D (hon.), U. Lima, Peru, 2005. Surg. fellow Mayo Clinic, Rochester, Minn., 1987-90; surg. registrar Guy's Hosp. London, 1990-93, 94-97; transplant fellowship U. Minn. Hosp., 1993-95; cons. surgeon, surg. dir. West London transplant unit Imperial Coll. Healthcare NHS Trust, London, 1995—. Hon. cons. surgeon Royal Free Hosp., London, 1995, Hammersmith Hosp., London, 1999; pediat. transplant surgeon Gt. Ormond St. Hosp., London, 1996; vis. prof. U. Hong Kong, 1996, U. Taipei, Taiwan, 1996, U. Rome, 1998, U. Prague, 1998, U. Tbilisi, Ga., 1999; hon. prof. surgery U. São Paulo, Brazil, 1999, Baskent U., Ankara, Turkey, Lyon U., France; tutor London Sch. Surgery, 2009. Author: Enteric Physiology of the Transplantated Intestine, 1974, Introduction to Organ Transplantation, Current Immunosuppression: An Update, 1997, History of Organ and Cell Transplantation, 1999, Access Surgery, 2000, Pancreas Transplantation, 2000, Transplantation Surgery, 2000, Composite Tissue Allograft, 2006, Haemostasis, 2007; editor: Euronews, 1997—; mem. editl. bd. Transplantation Procs., 1997—, Graft Transplant Jour., 1998—, Georgian Jour. Surgery, 1999—, Internat. Surgery, 1998—99, editor-in-chief, 2000—. Recipient J. Wesley Alexander prize for outstanding rsch. in field of transplantation, 2007, Bailiff Order of St. John Jerusalem, 2010, Grand Cross St. John, 2010. Fellow: ACS, Royal Soc. Medicine, Russian Surg. Soc., Am. Soc. Transplant Surgeons, Am. Soc. Transplant Physicians, Internat. Med. Scis. Acad. (hon.), Czech Purkine Surg. Soc. (hon.), Internat. Coll. Surgeons (hon.; v.p. 2001—02, pres.-elect 2003—04, pres. 2004—06, Max Thorek prof. surgery 2008—), Georgian Transplantation Soc. (hon.), Royal Soc. Medicine (pres. transplant sect. 2001—02, mem. coun. 2010—), Royal Coll. Surgeons London, Royal Coll. Surgeons Ireland; mem.: Assn. Fellows of Mayo Grad. Sch. Medicine, Brit. Transplant Soc., Brit. Med. Assn., Internat. Pancreas & Islet Transplant Assn., French Clin. Soc., Internat. Soc. Surgery UK, Acad. Surg. Rsch., Assn. European Young Med. Scientists (founding mem.). Achievements include representing Britain in the international team which has performed the worlds first arm transplant. Avocations: music, sculpture, horseback riding. Office: Imperial Coll Healthcare NHS Trust The Bays South Wharf Rd St Marys Hosp London W2 1NY England E-mail: nadey@globalnet.co.uk.

HAKIM, OSSAMA MAHMOUD, ophthalmologist, consultant; b. Alexandria, Egypt, Jan. 6, 1962; s. Mahmoud Hakim Mohamed and Latifa Mostafa Hasan; m. Amal Ahmed Mekawey, June 29, 1990; children: Mohamed Ossama Mahmoud, Reem Ossama Mahmoud. MD, Zagazig Faculty Medicine, Egypt, 1985; MD in Ophthalmology, Ain Shams U., 1992; highest degree in ophthalmology, Egyptian Univs., 2006. Intern Zagazig U. Hosp., 1986—87; resident ophthalmologist Kobry Al Kobba Mil. Hosp., 1987—89, Ain Shams U. Hosp., 1990—92; sr. registrar ophthalmologist Magrabi Eye Hosp., Jeddah, 1996—99; fellow Irvine U., Calif., 1999; cons. pediatric ophthalmology and oculoplasty Magrabi Eye Ctr., Madina Munwara, Saudi Arabia, 1999—. Dir. Magrabi Eye Ctr., 2002—. Contbr. articles to profl. jours. Fellow: Royal Coll. Surgeons (assoc.); mem.: Pan Am. Assn. Ophthalmology (assoc.), European Strabismological Assn. (assoc.), Internat. Soc. Genetic Eye Diseases (assoc.), Am. Acad. Ophthalmology (assoc.), Internat. Strabismological Assn. (assoc.), Am. Acad. Pediatric Ophthalmology & Strabismus (assoc.). Home: 4 Belbisis St Elmontaza Zagazig Egypt Office Fax: 96648423346. Personal E-mail: oshakim@hotmail.com. E-mail: osshakim@gmail.com.

HAKIMI, RAINER, physician, consultant; b. Karim and Ursula Hakimi; m. Regina Hakimi; 1 child, David. MD, U. Tubingen, 1988. Specialist in occupl. medicine, emergency medicine, sports medicine, med. quality mgmt., naturopathy, psychotherapie, family medicine. Head med. svcs. Hallesche Krankenrersicherung, Germany, 1993—. Cons. Mayo Clinic, Selbsthilfe, 2001—03. Contbr. articles to profl. jours. Protestant. Avocations: travel, windsurfing, writing. Office: Hallesche Krankenversicherung Reinsburg Str 10 70178 Stuttgart Germany Business E-Mail: rainerhakimi@aol.com.

HAKOLA, HANNU PANU AUKUSTI, psychiatry educator; b. Lapua, Finland, Feb. 22, 1932; s. Aukusti Jalmari and Toini Kyllikki (Tikkanen) H.; m. Maija-Leena Salo, Apr. 19, 1954; children: Jouni, Marja, Jorma, Jaakko. MD, U. Turku, Finland, 1956, MA, 1960, PhD, 1972. Diploma in health adminstrn. Nat. Bd. Health, Finland, 1979. Asst. physician Neuropsychiat. Clinic, Turku, 1956-60; chief psychiatrist Harjamäki Hosp., Siilinjärvi, Finland, 1960-69, Niuvanniemi Hosp., Kuopio, Finland, 1969-83; prof. forensic psychiatry U. Kuopio, Finland, 1983-95. Med. dir. Harjamäki Hosp., Siilinjärvi, 1960-69. Author: On Environmental Conditions of Criminal Psychopaths, 1959, Clinical Aspect of a New Hereditary Disease, 1972, Polycystic Lipomembranous Osteodysplasia with Sclerosing Leukoencephalopathy, 1990, Duraljan Vocabulary, 1997, 1000 Duraljan Etyma, 2000, (with H. Assadian) Sumerian and Proto-Duraljan, 2003, Duraljan Hypothesis: Towards the Mother Tongue of Man, 2006, Lexical Affinities between Tamil and Finnish, 2009; editor: Symposium on Forensic Psychiatry, 1988; inventor Carbamazepine in Schizophrenia, 1982, Duraljan Superfamily, 1989, 1000 Duraljan Etyma, 2000; editl. bd. Med. Jour. Duodecim, 1975-81; contbr. over 300 articles to profl. jours. and chpts. in books. Bd. dirs. Kuopio U. Ctrl. Hosp., 1985—89, 1993—2002. Decorated knight Finnish Order of White Rose; comdr. Finnish Order of Lion; Paulo Found. grantee, Helsinki, Finland, 1971, Aaltonen Found. grantee, Tampere, Finland, 1973; recipient Prize, Acta Psychiat. Scandinavia, 1972. Mem. Finnish Med. Assn. (hon. 2002-, del. com. 1964-97, exec. bd. 1980-84), Med. Assn. North-Savo (hon.), Rotary (pres. Puijo club 1974, Paul Harris fellow 1982, Blue Stone fellow 1995, hon. 2003). Avocations: music, hunting. Home: Satamakatu 3 D 49 FIN-70100 Kuopio Finland Office: Niuvanniemi Hosp FIN 70240 Kuopio Finland

HÁLA, MARTIN, anesthesiologist; b. Brno, May 9, 1971; MD, Masaryk U., 1995. Anaesthesiologist Ctr. Cardiovasc. Surgery & Transplantation, 2001—. Mem.: Czech Med. Chamber. Home: Chopinova 11 Brno Jm 623 00 Czech Republic Home Phone: 777 657 649. Personal E-mail: haalis@seznam.cz.

HALAMA, NIELS, physician, researcher; b. Göttingen, Germany, Aug. 6, 1977; s. Klaus and Erika Halama; m. Silke Grauling-Halama. Gen. qualification for univ. entrance, Goethe Gymnasium, Bensheim, 1997; MD, U. Heidelberg, Germany, 2005. Vis. med. student Tex. Heart Inst., Houston, 2002; final yr. trainee Med. U. of Ohio, Toledo, 2005; resident internal medicine Nat. Ctr. for Tumor Diseases, Heidelberg, Germany, 2006—; postdoc. rsch. fellow German Cancer Rsch. Ctr., 2007—. Editor: Medicle, 2004—, author poetry. Group leader YMCA, Bickenbach, Germany, 1995—2001. Scholar, Studienstiftung des deutschen Volkes, 1980. Fellow: Helmholtz Alliance Immunotherapy Cancer. Achievements include research in Characterization of a novel genetic syndrom with abdominal benign tumors; Characterization of candidate genes for diabetic nephropathy; development of Bioinformatical software for the analysis of gene-structure; cancer immunology research analyzing cancer-host interedition in cancer patients with chemotherapy treatment. Avocations: canoeing, piano, guitar. Home: Im Schecken 33 Hessen Seeheim-Jugenheim 64342 Germany Personal E-mail: nhalama@gmx.net.

HALATEK, TADEUSZ, medical researcher; b. Lodz, Poland, Aug. 28, 1947; Degree in Pharmacy, Med. U. Lodz, 1972; PhD, Nofer Inst. Occupl. Medicine, 1974. Rsch. scientist Nofer Inst. Occupl. Medicine, 1974—. Office: Swietej Teresy 8 Lodz 91-348 Poland Business E-Mail: halatek@imp.lodz.pl.

HALATSCH, MARC-ERIC, academic neurosurgeon; b. Hannover, Germany, Oct. 25, 1967; s. Johannes and Vera Halatsch; m. Ursula Schmidt, June 27, 1996; children: Jakob-Leonhard, Johannes-Hendrik. MD, Georg August U. Med. Sch., Göttingen, Germany, 1993, PhD in Exptl. Neurooncology, 2004. Bd. cert. neurosurgeon Georg August U. Med. Sch., Göttingen, 2003. Rsch. fellow Mt. Sinai Sch. Medicine, NYC, 1993, post-doctoral rsch. fellow, 1996-98; attending neurosurgeon Ruprecht Karls U. Med. Sch., Heidelberg, Germany, 2005—09; vice chmn., prof. dept. neurosurgery U. Ulm Med. Sch., Ulm, Germany, 2009—. Chair, co-chair sci. sessions internat. oncology meetings; assoc. internet editor neuro-oncology World Fedn. Neurosurg. Socs. Sci. Adv. Bd., Internat. Inst. Anticancer Rsch. Contbr. articles and invited rev. to profl. jours. Recipient Genomic Pioneers award, Human Genome Orgn., 2008; Merit scholar, German Nat. Scholarship Found., 1987—93. Mem.: German Spine Soc., German Cancer Soc., European Assn. Neurosurgical Socs. (German rep. 2004—08, Young Neurosurgeons' Com.), German Soc. Neurosurgery, Händel Music Soc., Am. Assn. Cancer Rsch. Achievements include development of a gene therapeutic approach to specifically target an activated oncogene in a subset of malignant brain tumors by retrovirus-mediated transfer of a hairpin ribozyme; research in characterization of oncogenes and tumor suppressor genes in human cancer; patent for adjuvant medical treatment of a subset of malignant brain tumors. Avocations: literature, history, theater, photography. Office: Ulm Med Sch University Steinhövelstrasse 9 Ulm D-89075 Germany Home Phone: 49 731 1431685.

HALBREICH, URIEL MORAV, psychiatrist, educator; b. Jerusalem, Nov. 23, 1943; arrived in US, 1978, naturalized, 1982; s. Mordechai and Zipora (Tennenbaum) H.; m. Judith Thadine, 1987; children: Jasmine, Bethany. MD, Hebrew U., 1969. Diplomate Tel Aviv U. Psychiatry and Psychotherapy. Intern gen. medicine Hadassah U. Hosp., Jerusalem, 1968; comdr., vice-chief med. officer Israeli Navy, 1970—72, chief psychiatrist, 1977—78; resident, 2d then 1st asst. Hadassah Hosp. Hebrew U., Jerusalem, 1972—78; temp. chief physician Hadassah U. Hosp., Jerusalem, 1978; asst. prof., rsch. psychiatrist Columbia U., NYC, 1978—80; assoc. prof., dir. divsn. biol. psychiatry Albert Einstein Coll. Medicine, NYC, 1982—85; prof. psychiatry, dir. biobehavioral rsch. SUNY, Buffalo, 1985—, prof. ob-gyn., 1988—; pres., CEO IN-CLINE Rsch. Edn. & Devel., 2006—; chair PEMRN, 2008—. Vis. prof. Harvard U., 1996-98, exec. cons. dept. psychiatry, 1998-2001; chmn. 1st Internat. Congress on Hormones, Brain and Neuropsychopharmacology, 1993, chmn. sect. on interdisciplinary collaboration World Psychiat. Assn., 1997—, others; chmn. 2d Congress on Hormones, Brain and Neuropsychopharmacology, 2000; chmn. bd. dirs. Internat. Inst. Edn. in Mental Health and Psychopharmacology, 1997-2006; cons. in field. Editor: Transient Psychosis, 1983, Resistance to Treatment with Antidepressant Drugs, 1986, Hormones and Depression, 1987, Multiple Sclerosis: A Neuropsychiatric Disorder, 1992, Psychopharmacology of Women, 1996, Psychiatric Issues in Women, 1996, Training in Psychiatry and Psychopharmacology, 1998, Psychopharmacology of Mood Anxiety and Cognition, 2000, Psychiatry and the Law in Eastern Europe, 2000, Womens Mental Health, 2002; contbr. over 350 articles to profl. jours., chpts. to books. Combat physician Golani Brigade IDF, 1968—69, vice chief med. officer Israel Navy, 1970—72, chief psychiartist Israeli Navi, 1976—78. Recipient Ben Gurion award Gen. Fedn. Labor, 1976, Yair Gon award Hebrew U. Hadassah Med. Sch., 1978, Nat. Rsch. Svc. award NIH, 1978, Svc. award Internat. Soc. Psychoneuroendocrinology, 2003; grantee NIMH, 1982—. Fellow: Am. Coll. Psychiatrists, Am. Psychiat. Assn. (disting.), Coll. Internat. Neuropsychopharmacology (co-chmn. edn. com. 1994—96), Am. Psychopathology Assn., Am. Coll. Neuropsychopharmacology (chmn. rules and constitution com. 1996); mem.: World Psychiatric Assn. (founding chair sect. interdisciplinary collaboration 1999—), Hormones, Brain and Neuropsychopharmacology (pres.), Endocine Soc., Assn. Med. Psychiatry (chmn. edn. com. 1992—96, councilor 1992—96), Soc. Biol. Psychiatry (chmn. program com. 1992—93), Am. Coll. Psychiatrists, Internat. Assn. Women's Mental Health (pres. 2001—04), Internat. Soc. Psychol. Neurol. Endocrinology (chmn. 21st congress 1990, pres. 1999—2002). Jewish. Office Phone: 716-316-4440. Personal E-mail: uhalbreich@gmail.com.

HALDER, AJANTA, geneticist, educator; b. Agartala, Tripura, Aug. 22, 1964; PhD, Netaji Subhas Vidyaniketan, 1987, Calcutta U., 2004, MSc. Assoc. prof. Ramakrishna Mission Seva Pratishthan, 1996—. Home: 33/1 Sarat Ghosh Garden Rd Dhakuria Kolkata West Bengal 700031 India Personal E-mail: ajantahaldar@yahoo.com.

HALDER, ANDREAS MATTHIAS, orthopedist, director; b. Berlin, Aug. 22, 1965; s. Günter Eugen and Annelies Halder; m. Konstanze Schiefer, Sept. 30, 1995; children: Marie Luise, Sophie Charlotte, Caroline. PhD, Westfälische Wilhelms U., Münster, 1992, MD, 1994. Specialist in orthop. Landesärztekammer Brandenburg, 1997, specialist in traumatology 2006, cert. prof. U. Magdeburg, 2004. Resident Free U., Berlin, 1991—93; cons. Orthop. Clinic, Birkenwerder, Germany, 1994—2000; rsch. fellow Mayo Clinic, Rochester, Minn., 1998—99; med. dir. Klinik Endoprothetik, Sommerfeld, Germany, 2001—. Vorsitzender Lenkungsausschuß Qualitätssicherung, Brandenburg, 2004—05, Leitlinieukoumission DG00C, 2009—, Branderburger Orthopadische Gesellschsft, 2009—. Mem.: Sana Kliniken Med. Bd. (Munich), Mayo Alumni Assn. Achievements include patents for total knee replacement and total hip replacement. Office: Klinik Endoprothetik Waldhausstr. 1 16766 Sommerfeld Germany Office Fax: 49-33055-52203. Personal E-mail: orthopaede@yahoo.de.

HALDERMAN, BRENT L., psychologist; b. Norton, Kans., July 6, 1957; BA, Ft. Hays State U., 1982; PhD, U. Mo., Kans., 1990. Clin. mgr. New Directions Behavioral Health, 1999—. Pvt. practice, 1993—2011. Recipient Best Practices award, URAC. Mem.: APA, Kans. Psychol. Assn. Office: 7011 W 121st Ste 105 Overland Park KS 66209 Office Fax: 913-345-1464. Business E-Mail: bhalderman@ndbh.com.

HALDERMAN, JAMES ROBERT, anesthesiologist, consultant; b. Little Rock, Nov. 30, 1966; s. Robert Marvin and Mary Sue Halderman; m. Karen Lynn Barnett; children: Brandy Lynn Griffin-Bagno, Rachel Hannah. BS, U. Ark., Little Rock, 1991, MD, 1995. Diplomate Am. Soc. Anesthesiologists, 2008. Cons., anesthesiology and pain medicine Tracy Anesthesia and Pain Medicine Group, Calif., 2000—, med. dir. & exec., 2003—04; cons., membership devel. Coop. Am. Physicians Mut. Protection Trust, LA, 2007—. Bd. dirs. San Joaquin Med. Soc., Stockton, Calif., 2005—, past pres., 2010—; house del. Calif. Med. Assn., Sacramento, 2006—. Mem.: CMA, AMA. Home: James Robert Halderman MD Inc 325 Covey Ln Tracy CA 95376-4670

HALE, DANIEL G., lawyer, insurance company executive; b. 1946; B in English, Kenyon Coll., Ohio; JD cum laude, Capital U., Ohio. Past ptnr., chmn. Drinker Biddle and Reath, Phila.; past sr. v.p., gen. counsel Holy Cross Health Sys.; gen. counsel Trinity Health, Novi, Mich., 1996—2007; exec. v.p. Trinity Inst. for Health and Cmty. Benefits, Novi, Mich., 2009—. Adj. prof. law Capital Univ. Law Sch., Columbus, Ohio; chair health reform initiatives com. Catholic Health Assn.; bd. trustees Ohio Cancer Found.; frequent spkr., lectr. and author on various aspects of health care law. Spkr., lectr. and author various aspects of health care law. Mem.: ABA, Nat. Health Lawyers Assn. Office: Trinity Health 27870 Cabot Dr Novi MI 48377 Office Phone: 248-489-6000. *

HALE, DAVID FREDRICK, biotechnology executive; b. Gadsden, Ala., Jan. 8, 1949; s. Millard and Mildred Earline (McElroy) Hale; m. Linda Carol Sadorski, Mar. 14, 1975; children: Shane Michael, Tara Renee, Erin Nicole, David Garrett. BA, Jacksonville State U. Dir. mktg. Ortho Pharm. Corp. divsn. Johnson & Johnson, Raritan, NJ, 1978—80; v.p. mktg. BBL Microbiology Sys. divsn. Becton Dickinson & Co., Cockeysville, Md., 1980—81, v.p., gen. mgr. BBL Microbiology Sys. divsn., 1981—82; sr. v.p. mktg. and bus. devel. Hybritech, Inc., San Diego, 1982, pres., 1983—86, CEO, 1986—87; pres., CEO, dir. Gensia Sicor, Inc., San Diego, 1987—97; pres., CEO Women First HealthCare, Inc., 1998—2000; pres., CEO, dir. Cancer-Vax Corp., Carlsbad, Calif., 2000—06; chmn. Hale BioPharms Ventures LLC, 2006—. Chmn. bd. Santarus, Inc., Somaxon Pharms., SkinMedica, Metabasis Therapeutics; bd. dirs. Verus Pharms., BIO, Children's Hosp., San Diego Econ. Devel. Corp., BIOCOM San Diego, Connatus Pharm., Neurelis Inc.; co-founder, chmn. Connect. Mem.: Chief Exec.'s Orgn., World Pres.'s Orgn. Republican. Episcopalian. Home: PO Box 8925 17079 Circa del Sur Rancho Santa Fe CA 92067 Office: 1042 B W El Camino Rd Ste480 Encinitas CA 92024 Office Phone: 858-756-2480.

HALE, RALPH WEBSTER, obstetrician, gynecologist; b. Princeton, W.Va., Nov. 30, 1935; s. Ralph and Mabel (Burton) Hale; m. Jane Esther Towner, Sept. 2, 1956; 3 children. BS, U. Ill., Urbana-Champaign, 1957; MD, U. Ill., Chgo., 1960. Diplomate American Bd. Obstetrics and Gynecology. Intern Akron Gen. Hosp., Ohio, 1960-61; gen. med. officer Naval Air Sta. Barbers Point, Oahu, Hawaii; resident Kapiolani Med. Ctr., Honolulu, 1965-68; clin. instr. dept. ob-gyn John A. Burns Sch. Medicine, U. Hawaii, Honolulu, 1968-70, instr., 1970-71, asst. prof., 1971-72, assoc. dean student affairs, 1972-73, assoc. prof., 1973-76, assoc. dean clin. affairs, 1973-77, prof., chmn. dept. ob-gyn, 1976—93; exec. v.p. American Coll. Obstetricians & Gynecologists, Washington, 1993—; vice chair bd. dirs. US Anti-Doping Agy., Colorado Springs, Colo., 2000—03, chair, 2003—10. Chief ob-gyn svc. Kapiolani-Children's Med. Ctr., 1974—85; chmn. Honolulu Ob-Gyn Soc., 1976—79; pres. Pacific Coast Fertility Soc., 1980—81. Mem. editl. bd. Obstetrics & Gynecology; contbr. articles to profl. jours. Mem. exec. bd. US Olympic Com., 1984—2000, v.p., 1992—96; mem. US/USSR Anti-Doping Commn., 1989—92; mem. US del. staff Olympic Games, 1992, 1994, 1996, 1998, US Chef de Mission Atlanta, 1996. Served with USN. Recipient Disting. Svc. award, AMA, 2010. Mem.: American Coll. Sports Medicine, Assn. Professors Gynecology & Obstetrics (v.p. 1978—79, pres.-elect 1989—90, pres. 1990—91), American Fertility Soc., American Assn. Gynecol. Laparoscopists. Mailing: c/o American College of Obstetricians and Gynecologists PO Box 96920 Washington DC 20090

HALE, VICTORIA G., chemist, pharmaceutical executive; m. Ahvie Herskowitz. BS in Pharmacy, Univ. Md., 1983; PhD in Pharma. Chemistry, Univ. Calif., San Francisco, 1990. Sr. reviewer U.S. FDA, 1990—94; scientist Genentech Inc., 1994—97; co-founder, chief scientific officer Axiom Biomedical Inc., 1999—2000; founder, chmn., CEO Inst. for OneWorld Health, San Francisco, 2000—. Adj. assoc. prof. biopharmaceutical sciences Univ. Calif., San Francisco, 2002—; mem. indsl. adv. bd. Calif. Quantitative BioMedical Rsch. Group; adv. WHO; expert reviewer NIH. Recipient Exec. of the Yr., Esquire mag., 2005, Innovation award for social & econ. innovation, The Economist mag., 2005, Skoll award for social entrepreneurship, Skoll Found., 2005; named one of Most Outstanding Social Entrepreneurs, Schwab Found. for Soc. Entrepreneurship, Switzerland, 2004, Scientific Am. 50, 2004; fellow, Ashoka Innovators for the Pub., 2006; MacArthur Fellow, John D. and Catherine T. MacArthur Found., 2006. Mem.: Inst. Medicine, World Tech. Network (World Tech. award for Social Entrepreneurship 2006). Office: Inst for OneWorld Health Ste 500 50 California St San Francisco CA 94111 Office Phone: 415-421-4700. Office Fax: 415-421-4747.

HALE, WILLIAM WALLACE, III, psychologist, researcher; b. Ridgewood, NJ, Jan. 9, 1966; arrived in The Netherlands, 1985; s. William Wallace Hale Jr and Joan Beverly (McLean) Wallace; m. Cornelia Dorothea Van Roon, June 13, 1987; children: Ian James William, Peter John Christiaan, Mark Paul Luke. MA, U. Utrecht, The Netherlands, 1993; PhD, U. Groningen, The Netherlands, 1997. Rschr. Acad. Hosp. Groningen, 1993-99; asst. prof. psychology U. Maastricht, 1999-2001, U. Utrecht, 2001—. Contbr. articles to profl jours. Mem.: Dutch Inst. Psychology. Office: U Utrecht Rsch Ctr Heidelberglaan 1 3584 CS Utrecht Netherlands Business E-Mail: b.hale@uu.nl.

HALEY, DAVID ALAN, healthcare executive; b. St. Louis, Aug. 29, 1943; s. John David and Helen Ermyl (Richardson) H.; children: Trisha Lynn, Jason Alan, Eric Nathan. BA, So. Ill. U., Edwardsville, 1966; MPH magna cum laude, UCLA, 1971. Adminstrv. asst. Kaiser Found. Hosp., Panorama City, Calif., 1971; assoc. adminstr. Our Lady of Lourdes Hosp., Pasco, Wash., 1971-74, Garfield Hosp., Monterey Park, Calif., 1974-75; assoc. exec. dir. Gen. Hosp., Ft. Walton Beach, Fla., 1976-79; v.p. ops. Our Lady of the Lake Regional Med. Ctr., Baton Rouge, 1979-88; pres. Phoenix Connection, Baton Rouge, 1988-89; CEO Gibson Gen. Hosp., Princeton, Ind., 1989-93; pres., CEO Four States Physicians Assn., Joplin, Mo., 1993-94; exec. dir. MedQuest Health Resources, Inc., 1995-96; pres., CEO The Haley Group, Frankfort, Ill., 1996—2004; CEO St. Anthony's Hospice, Henderson, Ky., 2004—06; v.p., COO Ctr, for Hospice and Palliative Care, South Bend, Ind., 2006—. Mem. Four Rivers Comprehensive Health Planning Agy., Richland, Wash., 1972-74; treas. S.E. Wash. State Hosp. Coun., Pasco, 1973, v.p. 1974; corp. mem. Mid La. Health Systems Agy., Baton Rouge, 1979-82; gubernatorial appointee La. Statewide Health Coord. Coun., Baton Rouge, 1984; gubernatorial appointee, Healthcare Facility Adminstrn. Bd., Indpls., 1991-93; sec.-treas. S.W. Ind. Hosp. Coun., Evansville, 1992-93. Served with USNR, 1967-69. USPHS fellow, 1969-71. Fellow Am. Coll. Healthcare Execs.; mem. Healthcare Fin. Mgmt. Assn., La. Hosp. Assn. (council on planning, 1984-87), Ind. Hosp. Assn. (mem. coun. pub. rels. 1992-93), Vis. Nurse Assn. Southwestern Ind. (bd. dirs. 1992-93), La. Assn. Bus. and Industry (health care council 1987); Kiwanis, Rotary. Republican. Home and Office: The Haley Group 3628 Raleigh Ct Mishawaka IN 46545

HALIBURN, JOAN MARIE, psychiatrist, consultant; b. Podanur, India, June 10, 1939; Degree, Holy Cross Coll., India, 1956; MBBS, Madras Med. Coll., India, 1962. Physician, child health svcs. Western Health Region, Sydney, 1972—75; vis. physician Adolescent Svcs., Western Health Region, Sydney, 1975—82; vis. psychiatrist Westmead Hosp., Australia, 1990—2011; dir. tng. Australia & New Zealand Assn. Psychotherapy, 1992—2009; cons. psychiatrist Pvt. Practice & Western Health Region, 1987—; sr. clin. lectr. U. Sydney, 1997—2011. Sec. Australian Soc. Adolescent Psychiatry, 1987—90; editl. bd. mem. Youth Clearinghouse, Tasmania, 1989—91; faculty supr. Australia & New Zealand Assn. Psychotherapy, 1990—2011, pres., 1998—2011; keynote spkr. 25th Jubilee Congress. Recipient Svc. award, Lions Club, Mt. Druitt, Sydney. Fellow: Royal Australian & New Zealand Coll. Psychiatry; mem.: SERFAC, Faculty Child & Adolescent Psychiatry, Internat. Soc. Study Personality Disorders, Am. Psychiat. Assn. Avocations: music, travel. Office: 2 Marlborough St Drummoyne NSW 2047 Australia Office Fax: 61-02-97191230. Business E-Mail: jhalibur@bigpond.net.au.

HALIL, SUSAN TERRELL, dental hygienist; b. Bessemer, Ala., June 23, 1949; d. Jack Ingram Terrell and Betty May Hardiment; m. Donald William Halil, Sr., Sept. 29, 1972; children: Donald William, Douglas Winston, Melissa Marie. AS, Pensacola Jr. Coll., 1969. Registered dental hygienist Fla. Bd. Dentistry. Dental hygienist Dr. Maxwell de la Rua, Pensacola, Fla., 1969—70, Dr. Reuben Groom, Jacksonville, Fla., 1970—72, Dr. A.J. Bauknecht, Jacksonville, 1972—86; new patient orientation/dental hygienist Dr. Bruce Kanehl, Jacksonville, 1986—87; periodontal dental hygienist Dr. Lamar Pearson, Jacksonville, 1987—89; ins. assoc. Capital Ins. Agy., Jacksonville, 1989—91; dental hygienist Dr. Eric Townsend, Ponte Vedra, Fla., 1991—2001, new patient coord., dental hygienist, 2003—, orofacial myologist, 2010—; new patient coord., dental hygienist Dr. Joseph Barton, Jacksonville, 2001—02. Presenter in field, cmty. svc. Newsletter editor:. Pres. San Jose Cath. Women's Guild, Jacksonville, 1983—84, San Jose Cath. Parish Coun., Jacksonville, 2001—03, coun. pres., 2000—03, pres. coun., 2002; catechist, 2004—07; lector, 1983—. Mem.: N.E. Fla. Dental Hygiene Assn. (first v.p. 1972—73, pres. 1973—74, newsletter editor 1973—74, mem. at large 1979—80, newsletter editor 1980—81, mem. at large 2007—08, 2011—, corr. sec. 2011—, Svc. award 1970—71, 1979—80, Achievement award 1995, Svc. award 2007—08), Fla. Dental Hygiene Assn. (N.E. Fla. rep. coun. on govtl. affairs 1991—97, N.E. Fla. del. 1992—97, v.p. 1994—95, pres. elect 1995—96, pres. 1996—97, immediate past pres. 1997—98, mem. nominating com. 1997—2007, co-chair membership com. 2007—08, Disting. Svc. award 2002, Component Outstanding Mem. award 2002, 2004, Yvette Blum Lifetime Mentor award), Am. Dental Hygienists' Assn. (alt. del. 1970—71, nat. del. 1971—73, 1994—97, chairperson nat. del. 1996—97, liaison Inst. for Oral Health 1998—99). Republican. Avocations: gardening, walking, bicycling, dance, yoga. Home: 7104 St Augustine Rd Jacksonville FL 32217 Office Phone: 904-285-7711. Personal E-mail: shalil@bellsouth.net.

HALL, ALAN, molecular biology educator; b. Barnsley, U.K., May 19, 1952; s. Roland and Edith (Wright) H.; m. Eileen Henderson, Jan. 4, 1975; children: Graham Andrew, Alison. BA in Chemistry, Oxford U., 1974; PhD in Chemistry, Harvard U., 1977. Postdoctoral scientist U. Edinburgh, Scotland, 1977-79, U. Zürich, Switzerland, 1979-81; group leader scientist Inst. of Cancer Rsch., London, 1981-93; prof. molecular biology U. Coll. London, 1993—2001, prof., dir. cell biology unit, Med. Rsch. Coun. Lab. for Molecular Cell Biology, 2001—05; chmn., cell biology progra, Meml. Sloan-Kettering Cancer Ctr., NY, 2005—. Contbr. numerous articles to profl. jours. Recipient Feldberg Found. prize Med. Rsch. Coun., 1993, Gairdner Internat. Found. award, 2006. Mem. European Molecular Biology Orgn., Academia Europaea. Office: Meml Sloan Kettering Cancer Ctr 1275 York Ave New York NY 10021 *

HALL, BARRY G., evolutionary biologist; b. New York, July 17, 1942; m. Susan M. (Werlein), May 2, 1964; children: Steven, Scott, Rebecca Hathaway. BS in Genetics, U. Wis, Madison, 1968; PhD in Genetics, U. Wash., Seattle, 1971. Asst. prof. Meml. U. Nfld. and Med. Sch., St. John's, Canada, 1974—77; asst. to assoc. to prof. U. Conn., Storrs, 1977—89; prof. U. Rochester, NY, 1989—2003, prof. emeritus, 2003—; dir. Bellingham Rsch. Inst., Wash., 2004—; adj. prof. Ctr. Genomic Sci., Allegheny-Singer Rsch. Inst., Pitts., 2009—. Author: Phylogenetic Trees made easy: A how-to manual for molecular biologists, 2001, 4th edit., 2011; editor-in-chief: Molecular Biology and Evolution, 1993—98; contbr. articles to sci. jours. Grantee, NIH, 1978—86, 1986—92, 1992—96, 2000—04, NSF, 1989—93, Am. Cancer Soc., 1996—98; NIH Rsch. and Career Devel. awardee, 1980, Fulbright Sr. scholar, 1984. Achievements include patents for the determination of identity between two organisms by subjecting a restriction endonuclease digest of genomic DNA to electrophoresis and hybridization; Barlow-Hall method of experimentally predicting evolution of antibiotic resistance genes (method of determining evolutionary potential of mutant resistance genes/use thereof to screen drug efficacy); method of identifying putative antibiotic resistance genes; one of the founders of the field of experimental evolution. Home: 218 Chuckanut Point Rd Bellingham WA 98229 Personal E-mail: barryhall@zeninternet.com. Business E-Mail: drbh@mail.rochester.edu.

HALL, BRIAN KEITH, biology professor, writer; b. Port Kembla, NSW, Australia, Oct. 28, 1941; s. Harry J. and Doris (Garrad) Hall; m. June Denise Priestley, May 21, 1966; children: Derek Andrew, Imogen Elizabeth. BSc, U. New Eng., Australia, 1963, BSc with honors, 1965; PhD, U. New Eng., 1968, DSc, 1978. Teaching fellow U. New Eng., Armidale, 1965-68; asst. prof. biology Dalhousie U., Halifax, N.S., Canada, 1968-72, assoc. prof., 1972-75, prof., 1975—, chmn. dept. biology, 1978-85, Killam rsch. prof., 1990-95, faculty sci., Killam prof. biology, 1996-2001, George S. Campbell prof. of biology, 2001—, univ. rsch. prof., 2002—07; Killam rsch. fellow, 2003; univ. rsch. prof. emeritus, 2007—. Vis. prof. U. Guelph, 1975, U. Queensland, Australia, 1981, Southampton U., England, 1982; mem. adv. com. on life scis. Natural Scis. and Engring. Rsch. Coun. Can., 1985; Turner-Newall lectr. U. Manchester, England, 1985; Frontiers in Biology lectr. Tex. A&M U., 1992; Von Hofsten lectr. Uppsala U., Sweden, 1993; Plenary lectr. Internat. Congress Vert. Morphol., 1994; Fry lectr. Can. Soc. Zoologists, 1994; Sarnat lectr. UCLA, 1994; Miller vis. res. prof. U. Calif., Berkeley, 1997; Landsdowne vis. prof. U. Victoria, 1998; Glaser Disting. vis. prof. Fla. Internat. U., 2000; Rayne mem. vis. prof. U. Western Australia, 1993, 2006. Author: (book) Developmental and Cellular Skeletal Biology, 1978; author: (with N. MacLean) Cell Commitment and Differentiation, 1987; author: The Neural Crest, 1988, Evolutionary Developmental Biology, 1992, Evolutionary Developmental Biology, 2d edit., 1998, The Neural Crest in Development and Evolution, 1999, 2nd edit., 2008; editor: Cartilage, 3 vols., 1983; author: Bones and Cartilage, 2005;; author: (with B. Hallgrimsson) Strickberger's Evolution, 5th edit., 2011; author: Exolutioun: Principles and Processes, 2010; editor: Bone, A Treatise, 9 vols., 1990—94; editor: (with S. Newman) (book) Cartilage: Molecular Aspects, 1991; editor: (with J Hanken) The Vertebrate Skull, 3 vols., 1993, Homology: The Hierarchical Basis of Comparative Biology, 1994; editor: (with M. H. Wake) The Origin and Evolution of Larval Forms, 1999; editor: (with W. Olson) Keywords and Concepts in Evolutionary Development Biology, 2003; editor: (with W. R. Pearson and G. Muller) Environment, Development and Evolution, 2003; editor: (with B. Hallgrimsson) Variation, 2005; editor: Fins and Limbs: Development, Evolution and Transformation, 2006; editor: (with B. Hallgrimsson) Epigenetics, 2011. Recipient Young Scientist of Yr. medal, Atlantic Provinces Interuniv. Com. in Scis., 1974, Fry medal, Can. Soc. Zoologists, 1994, Craniofacial Biology Rsch. award, 1996, Alexander Kowalvsky medal, 2001, award of excellence in rsch., Govt. of Can., 2002, Killam prize, Govt. Can., 2003—05; fellow, Nuffield Found., 1982, Warwick James, London U., 1989, Ctr. Human Biology, U. Western Australia, 1993—; Killam Rsch. fellow, Govt. Can., 2005—, Hall of Fame, 2009. Fellow: Royal Soc. Can.; mem.: Am. Acad. Arts and Sci. (hon. fgn.). Home: 15/6770 Jubilee Rd Halifax NS Canada B3H 2H8 Office Phone: 902-494-3522. Business E-Mail: bkh@dal.ca.

HALL, ELLA TAYLOR, clinical school psychologist; b. Macon, Miss., Nov. 30, 1948; d. Essex and Mamie (Roland) Taylor; children: Banyikaai Monique (dec.), Motiqua Shante. BA, Fisk U., 1971, MA, 1973; PhD, George Peabody Coll., 1978. Mental health specialist behavioral sci. divsn. Meharry Med. Coll., Nashville, 1976-77; assoc. psychologist Bronx (N.Y.) Psychiat. tr., 1979; clin. psychologist Wiltwyck Residential Treatment Ctr., Ossining, N.Y., 1979-81; clin. cons. Abbott House, Irvington, N.Y., 1982-85; sch. psychologist Abbott Union Free Sch. Dist., 1985—. Cons. psychologist Youth Theater Interactions, Inc., N.Y.; rschr in the field. Author: (poetry) Double Twister, Somebody, Clinging Tears, 1994, Maple Tree at Dawn, 1995, Down My Three Rows, 1995, Mama Sis, 1995, These Times, 1995, Ordinary, 1996, Young Wilted Flower, 2000, Secret Garden, 2000, Blood Silence, 2000; (art) In My Mind, 1994, Picking Cotton, 1995, contbr. poems to anthology. Lay reader, acolyte Episcopal Ch.; mem. Com. on Spl. Edn., sponsor, Kids Program Africa. NIMH tng. grantee, Kendall grantee; Crusade fellow. Mem. Schomburg Ctr. for Rsch., N.Y. State Psychol. Assn., N.Y. Bot. Soc., Wildlife Conservation Soc., Delta Sigma Theta, Abbott Sch. Tchrs. Assn. (pres. elect, 2008), Seamen's Ch. Inst. (vol. knitter). Avocation: photography.

HALL, ERIC J., physicist, educator; b. Great Britian, July 5, 1933; married, July 27, 1957; 1 child. BSc with honors in Physics, U. Coll., London, 1953; DPhil in Radiobiology, Oriel Coll., Oxford U., Oxford, 1962, MA honoris causa, 1966, DSc honoris causa, 1977. Asst. physicist Churchill Hosp., Oxford, 1955—56, sr. physicist, 1957—62, prin. physicist, 1963—68; asst. physicist Cardiff Radiotherapy Ctr., 1956—57; prof. radiology Columbia U., NYC, 1968—86; radiation biologist, radiation oncology svc. Presbyn. Hosp., NYC, 1983—; dir. Ctr. for Radiological Rsch., NY, 1984—, prof., radiation oncology and radiology NY, 1986—, Higgins Prof., radiation biophysics NY, 1993—. Fulbright Exchange Scholar, vis. asst. prof. radiological physics U. Colo., 1962—63; mem. radiation adv. com. NASA, 1971—75; mem. therapeutic radiology test com. Am. Bd. Radiology, 1974—; mem., Com. 40 Nat. Coun. on Radiation Protection & Measurement, 1979—88, mem. coun., 1982—, mem. fin. com., 1984—88, mem., Com. 1, 1988—, mem., Com. 1-3, 1990—93, mem. bd., 1993—99, mem., Com. SC 1-6, 1995—99; mem. radiation study sect. NCI, 1974—78, mem. cancer ctr. support review com., 1985—89, sect. chmn., plan for radiation rsch., 1987; mem. study sect. on prevention, diagnostic and treatment Am. Cancer Soc., 1986—90; chmn., radiotherapy search com. Columbia-Presbyn. Med. Ctr., 1983—85; Gilbert H. Fletcher Disting. Prof. M.D. Anderson Cancer Ctr., Houston, 1995; Raymond S. Bush Vis. Professorship Ont. Cancer Inst. Princess Margaret Hosp., Canada, 1995; John S. Laughlin Vis. Professorship Meml. Sloan-Kettering Cancer Ctr., NY, 2000; mem. prog. com. Internat. Conf. on Protectors and Anticarginogens; mem. institutional safety com. Coll. Physicians & Surgeons, Columbia U., mem. faculty coun.; mem. environ. health & safety com. Columbia-Presbyn. Med. Ctr., Presbyn. Hosp.; chmn., joint radiation safety com. Presbyn. Hosp., 1985—, chmn., radioactive drug. rsch. com., 1985—; invited lectr. in field. Contbr. articles to profl. jours.; co-author: Californium-252 in Teaching and Research International Atomic Energy Agency, 1974, Principles and Practice of Brachytherapy; using afterloading systems, 2001; co-author: (with D.J. Brenner) Making Radiation Therapy Decision, 1996; author: Radiation and Life (1st ed. 1978, 2nd ed. 1984, French ed. 1979, arabic ed. 1980, Russia ed. 1989), Radiobiology for the Radiologist (1st ed. 1973, 2nd ed. 1978, 3rd ed. 1988, Japanese ed. 1979, 4th ed. 1994, 5th ed. 2000). Recipient Marie Curie Gold medal, Health Physics Soc., Great Lakes Chpt., 1983, Janeway medal, Am. Radium Soc., 1992, Gold medal, Juan Del Regato Found., 1997, John B. Little award, Harvard Sch. Pub. Health, Boston, 2000, Henry S. Kaplan Disting. Scientist award, 12th Internat. Congress Radiation Rsch., Australia, 2003. Fellow: Am. Soc. for Therapeutic Radiology and Oncology (mem. long range planning com. 1986—, sec. 1993—95, mem. prog. com. 1995, mem. constitution & bylaws com. 1995, Gold medal 1993), Soc. Radiological Protection (hon.), Royal Coll. Radiologists (hon.), Am. Coll. Radiology (hon.; mem. radiation adv. group 1997—98); mem.: NAS (BEIR V com. 1986—89, BRER Com. 1987—90, 1993—98, BEIR VI Com. 1993—98, Boron Neutron Capture Therapy Com. 1990), Internat. Assn. of Radiation Rsch. (councillor 1983—87, chmn., nominating com. 1987, pres.-elect 1995—99, pres. 1999—2003), Am. Radium Soc. Inc. (mem. exec. com. 1990—92, mem. prog. com. 1992, 1995—96, sec. 1996—97, chair, prog. com. 1997—99, pres. 1999—2000), Radiation Rsch. Soc. (mem. prog. com. 1975, councillor 1977—80, mem. fin. com. 1981, pres.-elect 1983, mem. prog. com. 1983—84, pres. 1984—85, 1984—85, mem. honors and awards com. 1986—90, mem. prog. com. 1988—90, 1992, Failla award 1991), Soc. for Pediatric Radiology (hon.), Radiological Soc. N.Am. (chairman, subcom. on radiation therapy & radiobiology of the prog. com 1985—87, second v.p. 1989, award of honor, annual oration in radiation oncology 1990, Gold medal 1992, Outstanding Researcher award 1996), European Soc. for Therapeutic Radiology & Oncology, Assn. for Radiation Rsch. (Weiss medal 1990), British Inst. Radiology (Roentgen award 1976, Barclay medal 1983). Office: Ctr for Radiological Rsch VC 11-230 630 W 168th St New York NY 10032 Office Phone: 212-305-5660. Office Fax: 212-305-3229. Business E-Mail: ejh1@columbia.edu.

HALL, JAMES BRYAN, gynecologist, oncologist; b. Dayton, Ohio, Nov. 24, 1946; s. Mitchell Z. and Moyne L. H.; m. Edith Miller, Mar. 22, 1975; children: James B. Jr., William B. AB, Taylor U., 1969; MD, Med. U. S.C., 1974. Diplomate Am. Bd. Ob-Gyn., Oncology. Rotating intern Miami Valley Hosp., Dayton, 1974-75; resident in ob-gyn. Wright State U.-Miami Valley Hosp., 1975-78, chief resident in ob-gyn., 1977-78; fellow in gynecologic oncology, asst. in gynecology Mass. Gen. Hosp., Boston, 1978-80; pvt. practice Charlotte, N.C., 1988-95. Instr. ob-gyn. Harvard U., Boston, 1978-80; dir. gynecologic oncology, dept. ob-gyn. Carolinas Med. Ctr., 1980—, dir. gynecology, Blumenthal Cancer Ctr., coord. med. student clerkship, 1982-87, acting dir. dept. ob-gyn., 1987-88, assoc. prof., 1986-88; asst. prof. U. N.C., Chapel Hill, 1980-86, assoc. prof., 1986-88, clin. prof., 1995—; spkr. at profl. confs. Contbr. numerous articles to med. jours. Named Best Doctor in America, 2011. Fellow ACS, Am. Coll. Ob-Gyn.; mem. Am. Soc. Clin. Oncology, Soc.Gynecologic Oncology, Charlotte Gynecol. and Obstetrical Soc. (sec.-treas. 1984-86, v.p. 1986-87, pres. 1987-88, treas. 1998-2000), Am. Cancer Soc. (bd. dirs. Mecklenburg County chpt., chmn. profl. edn. com., exec. com.), AMA, N.C. Med. Soc., James H. Nelson Jr. Oncology Soc. (pres.), Mecklenburg County Med. Soc. (bd. dirs., 2007-, treas., 2011-). Republican. Evang. nondenominational. Avocations: tennis, gourmet cooking. Office: Blumenthal Cancer Ctr Leviene Cancer Inst Carolina Med Ctr 1000 Blythe Blvd Charlotte NC 28203-5812 Office Phone: 704-355-2884.

HALL, KATHY, health facility administrator; b. Covington, Ky., Feb. 15, 1953; d. Joseph B. and Mary Louise (Weindel) Dusing; m. Harold G. Hall, Oct. 6, 1973; children: Becky, Amy, Sarah. AA, Eastern Ky. U., 1973, BS in Nursing, 1978; MS in Nursing, Bellarmine U., 1999. Med.-surg. staff nurse Good Samaritan Hosp., Lexington, Ky., 1973; infection control nurse Pattie A. Clay Hosp., Richmond, Ky., 1975-93, orientation instr., 1978-82, quality assurance dir., 1982-93; nurse epidemiologist U. Ky. Chandler Med. Ctr., Lexington, 1993—99; edn. dir. Shriners Hosp. for Children, Lexington, 1999—2002; dir. continuing edn. and devel. Coll. Health Sci. Ea. Ky. U. Mem.: NNSDO, KNA, ANA, Ctrl. KY Staff Devel. Group, Sigma Theta Tau. Office: CHS Continuing Edn and Devel 202 Perkins Bldg Ea Ky U 521 Lancaster Ave Richmond KY 40475-3102 Office Phone: 859-622-2143. Business E-Mail: Kathy.Hall@eku.edu.

HALL, LISABETH S., ophthalmologist, pediatrician; MD, State U. NY, 1992. Diplomate Am. Bd. of Ophthalmology, 2009. Intern Mt. Sinai Hosp., 1992—93; resident Manhattan EE&T Hosp., 1993—96; fellow Univ. Calif., 1996—97; instr. dept. of ophthalmology NYU Langone Med. Ctr. Office: NYU Langone Medical Center and School of Medicine 550 1st Ave New York NY 10016 Office Phone: 212-263-7300.

HALL, PAMELA ELIZABETH, psychologist; b. Jacksonville, Fla., Sept. 10, 1957; d. Gary Curtiss and Ollie (Banko) H. BA, Rutgers U., 1979; MS in Edn., Pace U., NYC, 1981, D in Psychology, 1984. Lic. psychologist, NY, NJ, Calif., Conn. Psychology extern St. Vincent's Med. Ctr., NYC, 1981—82; intern in clin. psychology Elizabeth Gen. Med. Ctr., NJ, 1982—83, staff psychologist, 1983—85, J.F.K. Med. Ctr., Edison, NJ, 1985-87; pvt. practice Summit and Perth Amboy, NJ, 1985—; sr. supervising psychologist Muhlenberg Med. Ctr., Summit, 1987—90; prof. psychology Nyack Coll., Nyack, NY, 2001—. Rsch. affiliate, internat. lectr. NIMH field trials on assessment of dissociative disorders Yale Sch. Medicine, Yale U., New Haven, 1990—2002; adj. prof. psychology Pace U., NYC, 1979-99; exec. bd. dir. Nat. Coun. on Alcoholism and Drug Dependence of Middlesex County, 2000-02. Mem. Mayor's Com. on Substance Abuse, Perth Amboy, 1987-89. Henry Rutgers scholar, 1979; named to Hall of Fame Perth Amboy HS, 2005. Mem. Am. Soc. Clin. Hypnosis, Internat. Soc. for Study of Trauma and Dissociation (founder, pres. NJ chpt. 1988—, dir. component socs.), Pace U. Alumni Assn., Rutgers U. Alumni Assn., Psi Chi. Avocations: crew, swimming, weightlifting, art. Office: 12 Kent Place Blvd Summit NJ 07901-1907 Office Phone: 908-277-2383. E-mail: dr.pamelahall@hotmail.com.

HALL, ROBERT JOSEPH, internist, educator; b. Buffalo, June 4, 1926; s. Joseph M. and Florence C. (Kirst) H.; m. Dorothy Nowak, Aug. 28, 1948; children: Thomas R., Kathleen A. Hall Noble, Mary J. Hall Stuart, Michael F., Steven E. Student, Canisius Coll., Buffalo, 1943-45; MD, U. Buffalo, 1948. Diplomate Am. Bd. Internal Medicine, Sub Bd. Cardiovascular Disease (mem. cardiovascular disease sect. 1969-75). Intern Mercy Hosp., Buffalo, 1948-49; commd. 1st lt. M.C. U.S. Army, 1948, advanced through grades to col., 1966; resident in internal medicine Walter Reed Gen. Hosp., Washington, 1949-52, resident in cardiovascular diseases, 1956-57; asst. cardiovascular research Walter Reed Army Inst. Research, 1957-58; service in Korea and Japan, 1952-55; chief cardiology service Brooke Gen. Hosp., Ft. Sam Houston, Tex., 1961-66, Walter Reed Gen. Hosp., 1966-69; ret., 1969; clin. assoc. prof. medicine Georgetown U. Med. Sch., 1967-69; clin. prof. medicine Baylor U. Coll. Medicine, Houston, 1969—, prof. emeritus, 2004—; clin. prof. medicine U. Tex. Med. Sch., Houston, 1977—; med. dir. Tex. Heart Inst., Houston, 1969-93, chmn. exec. com. profl. staff, 1969-93; dir. div. cardiology St. Luke's Episcopal Hosp., Houston, 1969-95, assoc. chief med. service, 1970-83; dir. edn., cardiology Tex. Heart Inst. Tex. Heart Inst. and St. Luke's Episcopal Hosp., 1992—2002, dir. emeritus, 2002—. Cons. Tex. Children's, VA, Brooke Gen. hosps., M.D. Anderson Hosp. and Tumor Inst.; mem. cardiovascular study sect. NIH, 1958-61; mem. phys. evaluation team Gemini project NASA, 1958-61; mem. nat. adv. heart counseil Dept. Def., 1966-69; adv. council Mended Hearts, 1970-78 Contbr. numerous articles med. jours. Mem. President's Adv. Panel Heart Disease. Decorated Legion of Merit; recipient Disting. Alumnus award Canisius Coll., 1995. Fellow A.C.P., Am. Coll. Cardiology (gov. 1968-71-74, chmn. bd. govs. and trustee 1973-74); mem. Am. Heart Assn. (fellow council clin. cardiology; pres. Houston chpt. 1974-75, advisor corp. cabinet 1980-86), Assn. Mil. Surgeons U.S., Assn. Advancement Med. Instrumentation, Pan Am. Med. Assn. (chmn. sect. cardiovascular diseases 1978-81), Assn. Univ. Cardiologists, Tex. Med. Assn., Tex. Cardiology Club, Harris County Med. Soc., Houston Cardiology Soc. (chmn. 1976-77), Houston Soc. Internal Medicine, Alpha Omega Alpha, 1948—. Home: 5504 Sturbridge Dr Houston TX 77056-1623 Office: 6624 Fannin St Ste 2480 Houston TX 77030-2309 Business E-Mail: rjhall@wt.net.

HALL, ROBERT STEVENS, retired dentist; b. Hartford, Conn., Apr. 19, 1938; s. Llewellyn and Caroline (Doane) Hall; m. Marcia Smith, June 29, 1963; children: Gretchen Ashley, Robert Stevens Jr., Sabra Lee. AB, Middlebury Coll., 1960; DDS, U. Pa., 1964. Pvt. practice dentist, Hartford, 1966—73, Farmington, Conn., 1973—2008; ret. Instr. U. Conn. Sch. Dental Medicine, 1973—85, 2000—, mem., admissions com., 2008—; gov. Soc. Descendants Founders Hartford, 2005—. Capt. US Army, 1964—66. Recipient Order of St. John, Priory US, 2007. Master: Acad. Gen. Dentistry; fellow: Am. Coll. Dentists; mem.: Hartford Dental Soc. (dentist peer rev./patient rels. 1980—, chmn. ethics com. 1998—). Avocations: travel, sports, photography. Home: 53 Sunset Farm Rd West Hartford CT 06107-1332

HALL, SEAN MICHAEL, health facility administrator; s. Michael J. and Vittoria C. Hall. Grad. cert., U. NSW, Sydney, 2004; Cert., Harvard U., Mass., 2006, MIT, 2006. Cert. Australian Inst. Co. Dirs. NSW, 2004. Sales dir. FIT-BioCeuticals Ltd., Sydney, 1999—2004, chief ops. officer, 2004—, CEO, 2006—. Dir. FIT-BioCeuticals Ltd., 1999—, exec., decision maker. Fundraising, cross promotions Canteen Childrens Charity, Sydney, 2003. Recipient Recognition in the field of Functional Medicine, Inst. Functional Medicine, 1998. Mem.: AICD. Liberal. Roman Catholic. Avocations: sailing, kendo, scuba diving. Office: FIT BioCeuticals Pty Ltd 16/37-41 O'Riordan St NSW Alexandria 2015 Australia Personal E-mail: sean.hall@fit.net.au.

HALL, SIMON JOHN, urologist, department chairman; b. Oxford, Eng., May 24, 1961; BA, Columbia Coll., 1983; MD, Coll. Physicians & Surgeons, Columbia U., 1988. Chmn., dept. urology Mt. Sinai Sch. Medicine, 2004—. Fellow: NY Acad. Medicine. Office: 5 E 98th St New York NY 10029 Office Fax: 212-876-3246. Business E-Mail: simon.hall@mssm.edu.

HALL, WESLEY W., plastic surgeon, educator; MD, U. Nev. Diplomate Am. Bd. Plastic Surgery. Gen. surgery tng. Univ. Colo.; radiology tng. Johns Hopkins Hosp., plastic surgery tng. Pa. State Univ., 1999; pvt. practice Hall and Wrye Plastic Surgeons, Nev. Author: various publs. Recipient Regents' Outstanding Student, Bd. of Regents, various others. Fellow: ACS; mem.: Am. Soc. of Plastic Surgeons, Alpha Omega Alpha. Office: Hall and Wrye Plastic Surgeons 635 Sierra Rose Dr Ste A Reno NV 89511 Office Phone: 775-284-8296. Office Fax: 775-332-6583.

HALL, WILLIAM STERLING, psychology educator; b. Lonoke County, Ark., July 6, 1934; s. Joseph William and Mattie (Brock) H. AB, Roosevelt U., 1957; PhD, U. Chgo., 1968. Instr., asst. prof. ednl. psychology NYU, NYC, 1966-68; assoc. rsch. psychologist Ednl. Testing Svc., Princeton, N.J., 1968-70; asst. prof. psychology Princeton U., 1970-73; assoc. prof. Vassar Coll., Poughkeepsie, N.Y., 1973-74, Rockefeller U., NYC, 1974-78; prof. psychology and ednl. psychology U. Ill., Urbana-Chamaign, 1978-81, co-dir. Ctr. for Study Reading, 1978-81; prof. psychology U. Md., College Park, 1981—2007, chmn. dept., 1993—2006; co-dir. Inst. Comparative Human Devel. Mem. study sect. NIMH, 1977-81; mem. grad. evaluation panel NRC; Henry B. Luce vis. prof. psychology Williams Coll., 1985; chair Coun. of Grad. Depts. Psychology, 2000. Bd. dirs. Lazurus awards com. NRMA, N.Y.C., 1975-82, Nat. Coll. Adv. Svc., N.Y.C., 1982—2002. Recipient AERA award, 1982; grantee Carnegie Corp., 1975, 77, Ford Found., 1975. Fellow APA, N.Y. Acad. Scis., Am. Psychol. Soc.; mem. AAAS (sci. fellows selection com.), Soc. for Rsch. in Child Devel., Cosmos Club, Sigma Xi, Alpha Phi Alpha. Office: Univ Md Dept Psychology College Park MD 20742-0001

HALL, ZACH WINTER, former scientist and research administrator; b. Atlanta, Sept. 15, 1937; s. Dixon Winter and Marjorie Elizabeth (Owens) H.; m. Anne Browning, June 1958 (div. Aug. 1960); m. Marion Nestle, Dec. 1973 (div. June 1985); m. Julie Ann Giacobassi, Nov. 9, 1987. BA, Yale U., 1958; PhD, Harvard U., 1966. Asst. prof., then assoc. prof. Harvard Med. Sch., Boston, 1968-76; prof. U. Calif., San Francisco, 1976-94; dir. Nat. Inst. Neurol. Disorders and Stroke, Bethesda, Md., 1994-97; assoc. dean for rsch. U. Calif., San Francisco, 1997-98, vice chancellor rsch., 1998-2000, exec. vice chancellor, 2000—01; pres., CEO EnVivo Pharms., Inc., 2001—02; sr. assoc. dean for rsch. Keck Sch. Medicine, U. So. Calif., 2002—05; pres. Calif. Inst. Regenerative Medicine, 2005—07. Med. Adv. Bd., Chevy Chase, Md., 1995-99, Howard Hughes Med. Inst.; Alexander Forbes lectr. Grass Found., 1994; David Nachmanson lectr. Weizmann Inst., Rehovath, Israel, 1996; adv. coun. RIKEN Inst., Tokyo, 2001-. Author, editor: Molecular Neurobiology, 1992; editor jour. Neuron, 1988-94. Recipient Purkynje medal for sci. achievement, Czech Acad. Sci., 2003. Fellow AAAS; mem. Am. Acad. Arts and Scis., Inst. Medicine. Home: PO Box 519 575 N Fall Creek Rd Wilson WY 83014-0519 Home Phone: 307-739-3026. Personal E-mail: zwhall@gmail.com.

HALLANI, MERVAT, writer, researcher; b. Beirut, Nov. 9, 1970; 3 children. BS in Advanced Sci. with honors, U. NSW, Kensington, 1997; PhD, U. Sydney, 2002. Rsch. scientist Westmead Hosp., Wentworthville, NSW, Australia, 2005—07; med. writer Datapharm Australia, Drummoyne, NSW, 2007—. Contbr. articles to profl. jours. Postgrad. scholarship, Australian Govt., 1998—2000, grant, Westmead Millennium Inst., 2000, Travel grant, Thoracic Soc. Australia & New Zealand, 2001, 2002. Mem.: Assn. Regulatory & Clin. Scientists (Australia), Australasian Med. Writers Assn., Thoracic Soc. Australia & New Zealand. Achievements include discovery of calcium activated chloride channel in rat olfactory neurons; research in route of breathing and perception in healthy and mild asthmatic subjects. Avocations: writing, reading, architecture, walking, cooking. Home: 91 Davenport Dr Wallacia NSW 2745 Australia Office: Datapharm Australia 56-56A Thompson St Drummoyne NSW 2047 Australia Office Fax: 61 9719 2811. Personal E-mail: mervat@swiftdsl.com.au. Business E-Mail: mervathallani@datapharm.com.au.

HALLAUER, ARNEL ROY, geneticist; b. Netawaka, Kans., May 4, 1932; s. Roy Virgil and Mabel Fern (Bohnenkemper) H.; m. Janet Yvonne Goodmanson, Aug. 29, 1964; children: Elizabeth, Paul BS, Kans. State U., 1954; MS, Iowa State U., 1958, PhD, 1960. Rsch. agronomist USDA, Ames, Iowa, 1958-60, geneticist Raleigh, NC, 1961-62, rsch. geneticist Ames, 1963-89; prof. Iowa State U., 1990—2002, C.F. Curtiss Disting. prof. agr. emeritus, 2003—. Author: (with J.B. Miranda) Quantitative Genetics in Maize Breeding, 1981, 2d edit., 1988, 3d edit., 2010; editor: Specialty Corns, 1994, 1st edit., 2000. 2d lt. US Army, 1954-56. Recipient Applied Rsch. and Ext. award 1981, Henry A. Wallace award for disting.svc. to agr., 1992, Disting. Alumni Achievement citation, 1996, Iowa State U., Genetics and Plant Breeding award Nat. Coun. Plant Breeding, 1984, Gov.'s Sci. medal State of Iowa, 1990, Burlington No. Career Rsch. Achievement award Iowa State Found., 1991, Centennial medal Phi Kappa Phi, 1997, Verdent Plant Genetics award Verdent Ptnrs., Chgo., 2001, Hall of fame, Horton HS, KS, 2006; named to USDA/Agrl. Rsch. Sci. Hall of Fame, 1992; named one of 150 Visionaries Iowa State U., 2007; honored Inter-Am. Inst. Coop. Agr. significant contbns. to agr., Washington, 2003, Arnel R. Hallauer Internat. Symposium plant breeding, Mexico City, 2003; USDA grantee, 1982, 85, 87, 90. Fellow Am. Soc. Agronomy (Agronomic Achievement award for crops 1989, Agronomic Rsch. award 1992), Crop Sci. Soc. (Dekalb Pfizer Crop Sci. award 1981, Pres.'s award 2002), Iowa Acad. Sci. (disting. fellow 1985); mem. NAS, 1988, Nat. Agri-Mktg. Assn. (nat. award for excellence in rsch. 1993), Kans. State U. Alumni Assn. (alumni fellow 1997), Iowa State Alumni Assn. (faculty citation 1987, Disting. Achievement Citation 1995), Gamma Sigma Delta (Disting. Svc. to Agr. award 1990, Rsch. Award of Merit 1999). Republican. Lutheran. Home: 516 Luther Dr Ames IA 50010-4735 Office: Iowa State U 1505 Dept Agronomy Ames IA 50010 Office Phone: 515-294-8520, 515-294-7823. Business E-Mail: hallauer@iastate.edu.

HALLBERG, INGALILL RAHM, medical/surgical nurse; b. Kristianstad, Sweden, Nov. 20, 1944; RN, Kristanstad U., Sweden, 1969, RNT, 1974; PhD, Umea U., Sweden, 1990. Cert. RN 1969. Various to rsch. asst. Care Rsch. and Devel. Unit, Kristianstad, Sweden, 1985—87, sr. lectr., 1986—97; prof. in caring sci. Lund U., Sweden, 1997—, head dept. nursing, 2000—01; dep. dean at the medicine faculty Lund. U., Sweden, 2000—05, asst. vice chancellor; dir. Vardal Inst., 2002—; asst. vice chancellor Lund U. Author: (novels) Narrative Gerontology, 2001, Delirium, 2001; contbr. articles to profl. jours. Fellow: European Nurse Acad. (pres.). Home Phone: 46 46 389730; Office Phone: 46 46 222 1932. E-mail: ingalill.rahm_hallberg@rektor.lu.se.

HALLÉN, ANUND ANDREAS, geriatrician; b. Stockholm, July 16, 1932; s. Arne and Ada (Nordin) H.; m. Liliane Strindberg, June 23, 1967; children: Clara, Frida, Andreas, Carolina. MD, Karolinska Inst., Stockholm, 1960; PhD in Med. Chemistry, U. Uppsala, Sweden, 1974. Specialist competence in clin. chemistry, 1972, in geriat., 1981. docent in med. chemistry, 1974. Asst. med. chemistry Karolinska Inst., 1955-60; rsch. fellow Harvard U., Mass. Gen. Hosp., Boston, 1961-63; physician, clin. chemist St. Göran Hosp., Stockholm, 1964-69; rsch. fellow med. chemistry U. Uppsala, 1969-75; med. staff various geriatric hosps., Uppsala, 1975-85, geriatric clinics, Sollentuna, Sweden, 1985-99. Mem. AAAS, Swedish Med. Assn. Achievements include contributions in the connective tissue field, and studies on the aging of human intervertebral disc; development of theory that aging depends on a progressive accumulation of cross-linked insoluble protein, that hampers cellular functions, forming a gel which excludes macromolecules and organelles from part of the water volume. Home: Måsvägen 12A SE-18357 Täby Sweden Office: Dept Med Biochem Box 582 SE-75123 Uppsala Sweden Personal E-mail: anund.hallen@swipnet.se.

HALLETT, MARK, neurologist, educator, researcher; b. Phila., Oct. 22, 1943; s. Joseph Woodrow and Estelle (Barg) H.; m. Judith E. Peller, June 26, 1966; children: Nicholas L., Victoria C. BA magna cum laude, Harvard U., 1965, MD cum laude, 1969. Diplomate Am. Bd. Psychiatry and Neurology. Resident in neurology Mass. Gen. Hosp., Boston, 1972-75; Moseley fellow Harvard U., London, 1975-76, lectr., assoc. prof. neurology Boston, 1976-84; head clin. neurophy. lab. Brigham and Women's Hosp., Boston, 1976-84; clin. dir. Nat. Inst. Neurol. Disorders and Stroke NIH, Bethesda, Md., 1984-2000, chief human motor control sect. NINDS, 1984—. Author: (with others) Entrapment Neuropathies, 1990, 3d edit., 1998; editor: (with M.F. Brin and J. Jankovic) Scientific and Therapeutic Aspects of Botulinum Toxin, 2002, (with S. Chokroverty) Magnetic Stimulation in Clinical Neurophysiology, 2d edit., 2005, (with others) Psychogenic Movement Disorders. Neurology and Neuropsychiatry, 2006; editor-in-chief Clin. Neurophysiology, 2000-07, World Neurology, 2008-; assoc. editor Brain, 2006-; contbr. numerous articles to profl. jours. Bd. dirs. Easter Seals Rsch. Found., Chgo., 1985-87; mem. med. adv. bd. Nat. Parkinson Found., Miami, 1985—2009, Dystonia Med. Rsch. Found., Chgo., 1989-93, 2000-03, Benign Essential Blepharospasm Rsch. Found., Beaumont, 1990—, Myoclonus Rsch. Found., Fort Lee, N.J., 1989-2003. Recipient Physician Rschr. of Yr. award, Physicians Profl. Adv. Com. to Surgeon Gen. of Pub. Health Svc., 1999, Adrian lecture, Internat. Fedn. Clin. Neurophysiology, 1999, Geoffrey Parr Meml. lecture, British Soc. Clin. Neurophysiology, 2004. Mem. Am. Assn. Electrodiagnostic Medicine (pres. 1991-92, Disting. Rschr. Award 2002), Am. Acad. Neurology (v.p. 2001-05, Movement Disorders Rsch. award 2005), Am. Neurol. Assn., Am. Clin. Neurophysiology Soc. (Pierre Gloor award 2004), Soc. for Neurosci., Movement Disorder Soc. (pres. 1999-2000, C. David Marsden lectr. 2006), Deusche Gesellschaft Für Neurologie (Wilhelm-Erb-Gedenkmünze, 2007), Internat. Fed. Clin. Neurophysiology (hon. fellow 2010, Great Wall Friendship award 2011), Phi Beta Kappa, Alpha Omega Alpha. Democrat. Jewish. Home: 5147 Westbard Ave Bethesda MD 20816-1413 Office: NINDS NIH Msc 1428 Bldg 10 Rm 7D37 10 Center Dr Bethesda MD 20892-1428 Office Phone: 301-496-9526. Business E-Mail: hallettm@ninds.nih.gov.

HALLFORD, H. GENE, medical educator; b. Okla., Dec. 25, 1957; MA, U. Ctrl. Okla., 1997; PhD, U. Okla., 2011. Clin. instr. U. Okla. Health Scis. Ctr., 1989—. Mem.: APA, Am. Anthrop. Assn. Office: OU Children 1200 N Phillips Ave Ste 12100 Oklahoma City OK 73104 Office Fax: 405-271-8697. Business E-Mail: gene@hallford.com.

HALLIDAY, WILLIAM ROSS, retired physician, speleologist, writer; b. Atlanta, May 9, 1926; s. William Ross and Jane (Wakefield) H.; m. Eleanore Hartvedt, July 2, 1951 (dec. 1983); children: Marcia Lynn, Patricia Anne, William Ross III; m. Louise Baird Kinnard, May 7, 1988. BA, Swarthmore Coll., 1946; MD, George Washington U., 1948. Diplomate Am. Bd. Vocat. Experts. Intern Huntington Meml. Hosp., Pasadena, Calif., 1948-49; resident King County Hosp., Seattle, Denver Children's Hosp., L.D.S. Hosp., Salt Lake City, 1950-57; pvt. practice Seattle, 1957-65; with Wash. State Dept. Labor and Industries, Olympia, 1965-76, med. dir., 1970—96, Wash. State Div. Vocat. Rehab., 1976-82; staff physican N.W. Occupational Health Ctr., Seattle, 1983-84; med. dir. N.W. Vocat. Rehab. Group, Seattle, 1984, Comprehensive Med. Rehab. Ctr., Brentwood, Tenn., 1984-87. Dep. coroner King County, Wash., 1964—66. Author: Adventure Is Underground, 1959, Depths of the Earth, 1966, 2d edit., 1976, American Caves and Caving, 1974, 82, Floyd Collins of Sand Cave, 1998; co-author: (with Robert Nymeyer) Carlsbad Cavern: The Early Years, 1991; editor Jour. Spelean History, 1968-73, Hawaiian Volcanoes, 2005; contbr. articles to profl. jours. Cons. Egyptian Environ. Affairs Agency; v.p. North Cascades Conservation Coun., 1962—63; pres. Internat. Speleological Found., 1981—87, Internat. Union Speleol. Com. on Volcanic Caves, 1992—98, hon. pres., 1998—; asst. dir. Internat. Glaciospeleological Survey, 1972—76; mem. Gov.'s North Cascades Study Com., 1967—76; chmn. Hawaii Speleol. Survey, 1989—97; dir. We. Speleol. Survey, 1957—83, dir. rsch., 1983—96. Served to lt. USNR, 1949—50, served to lt. comdr USNR, 1955—57. Recipient medal Geol. Soc. China; named Alumnus of Yr., George Sch., 1992. Fellow Am. Coll. Chest Physicians, Nat. Speleological Soc. (hon., bd. govs. 1950-2001), Explorers Club; mem. Nat. Trust (Scotland), Geol. Soc. Am., Mars Soc., Ukrainian Speleological Soc. (hon.), Seattle Tennis Club, Internat. Union Conservation Nature World Com. on Protected Areas.

HALLMANN, ARMIN, biochemist, biologist; b. Niederhatzkofen, Bavaria, Germany, Aug. 31, 1965; s. Georg and Marianne (Zieglmeier) H. Diploma in Biology, U. Regensburg, Germany, 1991, PhD, 1995. Tutor in biochem. scis. U. Regensburg, 1991—94, mem. rsch. staff, rsch. scientist, 1995—2002, asst. prof., 1995—2002, educator biochem. scis., 1995—2002, head biochemistry/molecular biology lab, 1996—2002; prof., head dept. cellular devel. biology of plants U. Bielefeld, Germany, 2003—. Contbr. articles to profl. jours. Recipient scholarshp Nissen Found., Germany, 1992-94, Richard-Winter Found., Germany, 1992-95, OBAG prize, Germany, 1996, Junkmann Found., Germany, 2000. Mem. Verband Deutscher Biologen, Gesellschaft Biochemie Molekularbiologie, Am. Soc. for Biochemistry and Molecular Biology, Deutscher Hochschulverband. Home: Walterstr 16 D 33824 Werther Germany Office: U Bielefeld Dept Cellular Devel Biology of Plants Universitatsstr 25 D 33615 Bielefeld Germany E-mail: armin.hallmann@gmx.de, armin.hallmann@uni-bielefeld.de.

HALLORAN, PHILIP FRANCIS, nephrologist, immunologist; b. Hamilton, Ohio, June 14, 1944; MD, Univ. Toronto, 1968; PhD, Univ. London, Eng., 1978. Asst. prof. Univ. Toronto, 1975—80, assoc. prof., 1980—86, prof., 1986—87; dir., renal transplantation Toronto Gen. and Mount Sinai Hosp., 1975—87; staff phys. Tri-Hosp. Nephrology Svc., 1975—87; med. dir., HOPE program Univ. Alberta Hosp., 1987—99, dir., tissue typing lab., 1987—99, med. dir., transplantation programs, 1987—99; dir., divsn. nephrology, immunology Univ. Alberta, 1987—2003, prof., med. microbiology, immunology, 1987—, prof., dept. medicine, 1987—, Muttart chair, clin. molecular immunology & autoimmunity, 1993—; dir. Alberta Transplant Inst., 2002—. Vis. prof., immunology Hammersmith Hosp., Imperial Coll. Sch. Medicine, London, 2002. Recipient Medical award, Kidney Found. Can., 1991, Commemorative Medal, 1993, Medal of Excellence in Rsch., 2000, Disting. Scientist award, Can. Soc. Clin. Investigation, 2006; named Officer of the Order of Can., 2005; named one of Top 100 Physicians of Century in Alberta, 2005. Fellow: Acads. Arts, Humanities and Scis. Can., Royal Soc. Can., Royal Coll. Phys.and Surgeons of Can. (Medal in Medicine 1985); mem.: AAAS, Internat. Soc. Nephrology, Fedn. Am. Soc. Experimental Biology, Can. Inst. Academic Medicine, Can. Transplantation Soc. (pres. 1988—89, Lifetime Achievement award 2005), Can. Soc. Nephrology, Can. Soc. Immunology, Can. Med. Assn., Brit. Transplantation Soc., Brit. Soc. Immunology, Am. Soc. Transplant Surgeons, Am. Soc. Transplantation (Roche Ernest Hodge Disting. Achievement award 2007), Am. Soc. Clin. Investigation, Am. Assn. Immunologists, Alta. Med. Assn. Office: Nephrology & Transplantation Immunology Univ Alberta 250 Heritage Medical Research Centre Edmonton AB T6G 2S2 Canada Business E-Mail: phil.halloran@ualberta.ca.

HALLSTRÖM, INGER KRISTENSSON, pediatrics nurse, educator; b. Hässleholm, Skane, Sweden, Nov. 17, 1955; d. Karl Holger and Ebba Maj Kristensson; m. Per Hallström, June 2, 1979; children: Anton, Olof, Elinor. PhD, Lund U., 1998. RN 1977. RN dept. neurosurgery U. Hosp., Lund, Skane, Sweden, 1978—84, registered sick children's nurse dept. pediatric surgery, 1984—98; clin. lectr. dept. nursing Lund U. Hosp., Lund, Sweden, 1998—, assoc. prof. dept. pediat., 2002—; prof. pediat. nursing Med. Faculty Lund U., 2008. Head nurse Dept. Pediatric Surgery U. Hosp., Lund, 1992—98. Author: Parental Participation in Paediatric Surgical Care, 1998 (Quality Assurance, U. Hosp., 1995), Children's Health Care, 2003. Office: Lund Univ Dept Health Sci Box 157 221 00 Lund 221 00 Sweden Home Phone: 46 46 12 86 44.

HALPERIN, EDWARD CHARLES, dean, physician; b. Somerville, NJ, Nov. 15, 1953; s. Irving M. and Ruth (Jacobs) H.; m. Sharon F. Rosenblatt, Sept. 6, 1981; children: Rebecca, Jennifer, Alison. BS, U. Pa., 1975; MD, Yale U., 1979. Diplomate Am. Bd. Radiology. Intern Stanford U. Hosp., Calif., 1979—80; resident Mass. Gen. Hosp., Boston, 1980—83; asst. prof. Duke U., Durham, NC, 1983—85, assoc. prof., 1985—93, prof., 1993—, chmn. dept., 1996—2003, vice dean Sch. Medicine, 2002—06; dean Sch. Medicine, Ford Found. prof. med. edn. and prof. radiation, oncology, pediat. and history U. Louisville, 2006—. Author: Pediatric Radiation Oncology, 1989, Russian edit., 1999, Principles and Practice of Radiation Oncology; contbr. articles to profl. jours. Recipient Career Devel. award Am. Cancer Soc., 1986; fellow Am. Coun. on Edn., 1992. Fellow Am. Coll. Radiology. Office: Office of the Dean Sch Medicine U Louisville 323 E Chestnut St Abell Adminstn Ctr Louisville KY 40202 Office Phone: 502-852-5184. *

HALPERIN, JEROME ARTHUR, retired pharmaceutical executive; b. Paterson, NJ, Feb. 21, 1937; s. Harry Nathan and Frieda (Niestat) Halperin; m. Barbara Anne Hott, Sept. 1, 1963; children: Alicia Jennifer Odom, Rachel Elizabeth Halperin Montgomery. BS, Rutgers U., 1958; MPH, Johns Hopkins U., 1962; MS, MIT, 1974; DSc (hon.), Mercer U., 1993, Mass. Coll. Pharmacy, 1995, Phila. Coll. Pharmacy and Sci., 1996; DHL (hon.), Western U. Health Scis., 2000. Commd. officer USPHS, 1958, advanced through grades to rear admiral, 1983; staff pharmacist USPHS Hosps., Dept. HEW, Albuquerque and NYC, 1958-61; radiol. health specialist Calif. Health Dept., Berkeley, 1962-65; agreement states coord. Bur. Radiol. Health, Rockville, Md., 1965-66; dir. indsl. radiation and air hygiene Kans. Dept. Health, Topeka, 1966-68; regional rep. Bur. Radiol. Health, Chgo., 1968-71; dir. Northeastern Radiol. Health Lab., FDA, HEW, Winchester, Mass., 1971-73; dep. assoc. dir. new drug evaluation Bur. Drugs, FDA, HEW, Rockville, 1974-77, dep. dir., 1977-82; acting dir. Office of Drugs Nat. Ctr. Drugs and Biologics FDA, Rockville, 1982-83; v.p. tech. CIBA Consumer Pharms., Edison, NJ, 1983-89; exec. dir. U.S. Pharmacopeial Conv., Inc., Rockville, 1989-95, exec. v.p., CEO, 1995-2000; pres., CEO Food & Drug Law Inst., Washington, 2000—06; ret., 2006. Chmn. Conf. Pharmacy 21st Century Va., 1984; cons. WHO, 1979—; trustee Davis and Elkins Coll., 2003—. Contbr. articles to profl. jours. Mem. Bd. Health, Hoffman Estates, Ill., 1971; bd. dirs. Perspective Woods Citizen Assn., Olney, Md., 1977—80. Recipient Outstanding Svc. award, Federally Employed Women's Assn., 1983, Disting. Career award, Drug Info. Assn., 2001, Career Achievement award, Profl. Fraternities Assn., 2001, Disting. Alumni award, FDA, 2002; named Alumnus of Yr., Rutgers U. Coll. of Pharmacy, 1981, Disting. Person of Yr., Pharmaceutical Planning Svc., Inc., 1998. Fellow: APHA, AAAS, Am. Pharm. Assn. (Remington Honor medal 2001), Am. Assn. Pharm. Scientists; mem.: Food & Drug Adminstrn. Alumni Assn. (bd. dir.), Internat. Pharm. Fedn. (expert mem. bd. pharm. scis.). Jewish. Personal E-mail: jeromehalperin@comcast.net.

HALPERN, ABRAHAM LEON, psychiatrist; b. Warsaw, Feb. 2, 1925; came to U.S., 1957, naturalized, 1962; s. Rubin M. and Helen (Perelman) H.; m. Marilyn Lois Benjamin; children: Howard, Lon, Marnen, Heather Halpern Schneid, Mark, Emily Halpern Lewis, John. MD, U. Toronto, Ont., Can., 1952. Diplomate Am. Bd. Psychiatry and Neurology with cert. in forensic psychiatry, Am. Bd. Forensic Psychiatry; cert. mental hosp. adminstr.; cert. correctional health profl. Intern Toronto Western Hosp., 1952-53; resident Warren (Pa.) State Hosp., 1957-60, Ea. Pa. Psychiat. Inst., Phila., 1959; assoc. research scientist Mental Health Research Unit, Syracuse, NY, 1961-62; commr. mental health Onondaga County, 1962-67; practice medicine specializing in psychiatry Mamaroneck, NY, 1967—; dir. psychiatry United Hosp. Med. Ctr., Port Chester, 1967-91; attending psychiatrist Beth Israel Hosp., NYC, 1968-73, Westchester County Med. Ctr., 1971—; cons. forensic psychiatry High Point Hosp., Port Chester, 1969-93; cons. St. Vincent's Hosp., Harrison, NY, 1973-93; clin. assoc. prof. psychiatry N.Y. Med. Coll., Valhalla, NY, 1973-80, clin. prof. psychiatry, 1980-94, prof. emeritus of psychiatry, 1994—; cons. Rye (N.Y.) Hosp. Ctr., 1994—; attending psychiatrist Kirby Forensic Psychiat. Ctr., Ward's Island, NY, 1994-95; attending psychiatrist dept. alcohol/substance abuse treatment Yonkers (N.Y.) Gen. Hosp., 1995-96; clin. dir. mental health svcs. Dept. Correctional Program, Westchester County, NY, 1996; staff psychiatrist Bedford Hills Correctional Facility, NY, 2003—05. Clin. asst. prof. SUNY, Syracuse, 1964-67; asst. clin. prof. Mt. Sinai Sch. Medicine, 1970-74; clin. prof. forensic psychiatry, NY Sch. Psychiatry, 1979-82; med. adv. com. Vis. Nurse Assn., Syracuse, 1962-67; mem. NY State Mental Hygiene Med. Rev. Bd., 1982-86; bd. govs. High Point Hosp., 1989-92. Assoc. editor Bull. Am. Acad. Psychiatry and the Law, 1982-88, Jour. Am. Acad. Psychiatry and the Law, 2002-05; mem. editorial bd. Psychiat. Jour. of U. Ottawa, 1979-91; mem. exec. editorial com. Psychiat. Quar., 1982-90, assoc. editor, 1990—. Chmn. Syracuse chpt. Com. to Abolish Capital Punishment, 1962-65; mem. profl. adv. com. N.Y. State Assn. for Mental Health, 1964-67; mem. N.Y. State Law Revision Adv. Com. on the Insanity Def., 1979-80; mem. Westchester County Community Mental Health Bd., 1976-78, chmn., 1977-78; mem. Westchester County Hosp. Bd., 1992-99; bd. visitors Harlem Valley Psychiat. Center, 1978-82; mem. N.Y. State Correction Med. Rev. Bd., 1980-87, N.Y. State Mental Hygiene Med. Rev. Bd., 1982-85; bd. dirs. Westchester Council on Alcoholism, 1980-85. Served to surgeon lt. comdr. Royal Can. Navy, 1942-45, 53-57. Recipient Citizenship award, NY State Bar Assn., 1966, Liberty Bell award, Onondaga County Bar Assn., 1966, Falun Dafa Appreciation award, 2000. Fellow ACP (William C. Menninger Meml. award for Disting. Contbns. to the Sci. of Mental Health, 2004), Royal Coll. Psychiatrists (hon.), Am. Acad. Forensic Scis., Am. Coll. Psychiatrists, Am. Psychiat. Assn. (com. psychiatry and law 1973-75, com. on abuse and misuse psychiatry and psychiatrists 1993-2003, com. on jud. action, 2006—09, Human Rights award 2000, Warren Williams Assembly award, 2009), Am. Assn. Psychoanalytic Physicians (dir. 1978-84, Sigmund Freud award 2002) Can. Acad. Psychiatry and Law (Bruno Cormier award 2006) Am. Pub. Health Assn., Academia, Medicinae and Psychiatriae Found. (charter); mem. AMA, N.Y. State Med. Soc. (com. on mental health, com. bioethical issues, com. on child abuse and domestic violence, Pres.'s Citizenship award, 2003), Internat. Assn. Forensic Psychotherapy, Soc. Correctional Physicians, Pan Am. Med. Assn. (mem. council sect. on psychiatry 1983-85), Westchester County Med. Soc., Westchester Psychiat. Soc. (pres. 1973-74), Soc. Med. Jurisprudence (trustee 1980-85), Internat. Acad. Law and Mental Health (pres. 1983-87), Am. Acad. Psychoanalysis (sci. assoc. 1987), Am. Acad. Psychiatry and Law (councilor 1978-81, pres. elect 1981-82, pres. 1982-83, Golden Apple award 1987), Accreditation Coun. on Fellowships in Forensic Psychiatry (pres. 1990-93), Internat. Coun. on Prison Med. Svcs. (v.p. 1991-2003). Home and Office: 720 The Pky Mamaroneck NY 10543-4227 Office Phone: 914-698-2136. Personal E-mail: ahalpernmd@verizon.net.

HALPERN, ALLAN, dermatologist, educator; MD, Albert Einstein Coll. of Medicine, 1977—81; BA in Biology, U. Pa., 1973—77, MS in Epidemiology, 1988—91. Resident internal medicine dept. Montefiore Hosp. and Med. Ctr., NY, 1981—84, chief resident internal medicine dept. NY, 1984—85; asst. instr. Pa. Univ., 1985—87, asst. prof. dermatology dept., 1990—97; resident dermatology dept. Univ. of Pa. Hosp., Phila., 1985—87, dir. gen. dermatology clinic, 1988—92, dir. pigmented lesion group, 1990—97, acting dir. gen. dermatology clinic., 1994—95; assoc. attending physician and chief dermatology svc. medicine dept. Meml. Hosp. Cancer Ctr. of Allied Diseases, NYC, 1997—2004, attending physician, 1997—; assoc. mem. Meml. Sloan-Kettering Cancer Ctr., NYC, 1997—2003, mem., 2003—; assoc. prof. dermatology dept. Cornell Univ., NYC, 1997—2004, prof. dermatology dept., 2004—. Lectr. dermatology dept. Pa. Univ., 1987—89. Co-author: (publs.) Confocal mosaicing microscopy in skin excisions: a demonstration of rapid surgical pathology, 2009. Mem.: Manhattan Met. Dermatology Soc. (v.p.

1999—2000), Internat. Soc. Digital Imaging of the Skin (pres. 2002—), Am. Cancer Soc. (vice-chmn. 1997—), Soc. for Investigative Dermatology. Office: Meml. Sloan-Kettering Cancer Ctr 1275 York Ave New York NY 10065 Office Phone: 212-639-2000.

HALPERN, JOSEPH ALAN, physician; b. Bklyn., Feb. 28, 1952; s. Lester A. and Adele Janet (Tax) H.; m. Cynthia Gould, Sept. 1, 1979; 1 child, Elyza. AB, Bard Coll., Annandale on Hudson, NY, 1974; MD, N.Y. Med. Coll., Valhalla, 1978. Diplomate ABEM, ABIM. Resident family practice SUNY, Buffalo, 1978-79; resident in medicine Norwalk (Conn.) Hosp., 1979-81, chief resident medicine, 1981-82; emergency physician Kent and Queen Anne Hosp., Chestertown, Md., 1982-83, North Arundel Hosp., Glen Burnie, Md., 1983-85; attending emergency physician Johns Hopkins Hosp., Balt., 1986-87; emergency physician Anne Arundel Med. Ctr., Annapolis, Md., 1987—, assoc. chief emergency medicine, 1994—99; referral physician Divers Alert Network. Attending physician Bayview Med. Ctr., Balt., 1992-94. Fellow Am. Coll. Emergency Physicians; mem. ACP, Med. Chi. Md. Avocations: sailing, bicycling, scuba diving. Office: Anne Arundel Med Ctr 2001 Medical Pkwy Annapolis MD 21401 Office Phone: 443-481-1293. E-mail: jhalp228@aol.com.

HALSEY, JEAN MICHELE, nursing educator; b. St. Louis, Oct. 16, 1949; d. Martha Idabelle Halsey and George Orlander Johnson; 1 child, Rene' Erle Jordan. Diploma, St. Louis Mcpl. Sch. of Nursing, 1972. RN Mo., 1972, Wyo., Calif., 1979, Fla., Okla., 1982, Wash., 2004. Staff nurse St. Louis City Hosp., 1972—75, St. Louis U. Hosp., 1975—78; travel nurse Comprehensive Nursing Svcs., St. Louis, 1979; staff nurse Cedar Sinai Med. Ctr., LA, 1979—82; critical care instr. Los Altos Hosp., Long Beach, Calif., 1981—82; staff nurse City of Faith, Tulsa, Okla., 1982—83, St. Mary's Hosp., West Palm Beach, Fla., 1983—85, PRN Nursing Agy., Clearwater, Fla., 1985—. Vol. nurse educator Am. Heart Assn., West Palm Beach, Fla., 1982—85. Prayer ptnr. City of Faith, Tulsa, Okla., 1982—83. Republican. Achievements include research in the effects of intravenous inderal on the outcome of post myocardial infarction patient; the effects of streptokinase, urokinase and tissue plasminogen activator on myocardial infarction patients; the effects of intravenous nitroglycerine, intravenous amiodarone, intravenous dopamine, intravenous dobutrex, and intravenous nitropresside on the outcomes of cardiogenic shock patients; the use of angioplasty on post myocardial infarction patients; the use of various types of Swan Ganz catheters in the treatment of myocardial infarction patients. Avocations: domestic and European travel, gardening, reading, gourmet cooking. Office: PRN Nursing Agy Ste 102 13575 58th St N Clearwater FL 33760 Personal E-mail: jhals3@aol.com.

HALSTEAD, LUCINDA ANN, otolaryngologist, educator; b. Pasadena, Calif., Oct. 2, 1952; MD, George Wash. U., 1981. Assoc. prof., dept. otolaryngology, head, neck surgery Med. U. SC., 1986—. Laryngologist Spoleto Festival, 1988. Mem.: Am. Acad. Otolaryngology Head & Neck Surgery. Avocations: singing, ice skating, sewing. Office: 135 Rutledge Ave PO Box 250550 Charleston SC 29425 Office Fax: 843-792-0546. Business E-Mail: halstead@musc.edu.

HALTMAYER, MEINHARD, medical educator; b. Linz, Austria, July 7, 1952; s. Hans and Maria Haltmayer; m. Maria Huber, Dec. 25, 1952; 1 child, Eva. MD, U. Innsbruck, Austria, 1978. Lab. dir. Konventhospital Barmherzige Brueder, Linz, Austria, 1992—2005, Core Lab., Linz, 2006—. Chmn. Ctrl. Lab. Hosp. Barmherzige Brueder, Linz, 1992—2005, cons. transfusion medicine, 1994; assoc. prof. medicine lab. Paracelsus Private Medicine U., Salzburg, Austria, 2005—. Fellow: OEGLMKC, mem.: Internat. Athorosclerosis Soc., Am. Heart Assn., Am. Assn. Clin. Chemistry, Internat. Fedn. Clin. Chemistry. Office: BS Coorp Lab Seilerstaette 4 Linz A-4020 Austria Office Fax: +43-732-7677-3799. Business E-Mail: meinhard.haltmayer@bs-labor.at.

HALVER, JOHN EMIL, nutritional biochemist; b. Woodinville, Wash., Apr. 21, 1922; s. John Emil and Helen Henrietta (Hansen) Halver; m. Jane Loren, July 21, 1944; children: John Emil, Nancylee Halver Hadley, Janet Ann Halver Fix, Peter Loren, Deborah Kay Halver Hanson. BS, Wash. State U., 1944, MS in Organic Chemistry, 1948; PhD in Med. Biochemistry, U. Wash., 1953. Plant chemist Assoc. Frozen Foods, Kent, Wash., 1946-47; asst. chemist Purdue U., 1948—49; instr. U. Wash., Seattle, 1949—50, affiliate prof., 1960—75; prof. U. Wash. Sch. Fisheries, 1978—92; prof. emeritus U. Wash., 1992—. Condr. research on vitamin and amino acid requirements for fish; identified aflatoxin B1 as specific carcinogen for rainbow trout hematoma; identified vitamin C2 for fish; dir. Western Fish Nutrition Lab. U.S. Fish and Wildlife Service, Dept. Interior, Cook, Wash., 1950—75, sr. scientist, nutrition, Seattle, 1975—78; cons. FAO, UNDP, Internat. Union Nutrition Scientists, Nat. Fish Research Inst., Hungary, World Bank, Euroconsult, UNDP, IDRC; affiliate prof. prof. U. Oreg. Med. Sch., 1965—69; vis. prof. Marine Sci. Inst. U. Tex., Port Aransas; pres. Fisheries Devel. Technology, Inc., 1980—90, Halver Corp., 1978—. Lay leader Meth. Ch., 1965—70. Capt. US Army, World War II, col. USAR. Decorated Purple Heart, Bronze Star with oak leaf cluster, Meritorious Service Conduct medal. Fellow: Am. Inst. Nutrition, Am. Inst. Fishery Research Biologists; mem.: NAS, Hungarian Acad. Sci., World Aquaculture Soc., Am. Fishery Soc., Am. Chem. Soc., Am. Sci. Affiliation, Soc. Exptl. Biol. Medicine, Rotary, Alpha Chi Sigma, Pi Mu Epsilon, Phi Lambda Upsilon. Achievements include founder JE Halver Fellowship at University of Washington; founder JE Halver Lecture at Washington State University. Home: 16502 41st Ave NE Seattle WA 98155-5610 Office: U Wash Box 355100 Sch Fisheries and Aquatic Scis Seattle WA 98195-5100 Office Phone: 206-543-9619. Business E-Mail: halver@u.washington.edu.

HALVERSON, PAUL KENNETH, state agency administrator, public health service officer; b. Downey, Calif., Mar. 21, 1959; s. Kenneth Gunnar and Doris M. (Laury) H.; m. Andrea Edwina Stenken, June 14, 1980; children: Melissa Nathalie, Kara Elizabeth. AA, Glendale Coll., 1980; BS, Ariz. State U., 1982, M of Health Svcs. Adminstrn., 1984; D Health Policy and Adminstrn., U. N.C., 1994. Various clin. positions John C. Lincoln Hosp., Phoenix, 1975-79; adminstr. Lincoln Inst. Surgery & Truama, Phoenix, 1979-84; adminstrv. resident Health Cen. System, Mpls., 1984; v.p. Mercy Med. Ctr., Coon Rapids, Minn., 1984-86; pres., chief exec. officer Cen. Mich. Community Hosp., Mt. Pleasant, Mich., 1986-92; asst. prof. dept. health policy and adminstrn. U. N.C., Chapel Hill, 1993—97, sr. fellow Ctr. for Pub. Health Practice, 1994—97, exec. liaison Office of Dean Sch. Pub. Health, 1995—97; pres., CEO Health Faculty Cons., Inc., Chapel Hill, 1993—97; dir. div. public health systems & mem. sr. sci. staff Ctr. for Disease Control, Atlanta, 1997—2004; prof. & chmn. health policy & mgmt. dept. Boozman Coll. Public Health, Univ. Ark., 2004—05; dir. div. health Arkansas Dept. of Health and Human Svc., Little Rock, 2005—. Sr. hosp. mgmt. specialist Rsch. Triangle Inst., Research Triangle Park, N.C., 1995-97; adj. prof. Ctrl. Mich. U., Mt. Pleasant, 1986-92; pres., CEO Meridian Home Care, Inc., Mt. Pleasant, 1988-92. Chmn. bd dirs. Ctrl. Mich. Health Policy Coun., 1987-92; bd. dirs. United Way of Isabella County, Mt. Pleasant, 1987-92, Am. Heart Assn., Mt. Pleasant, 1988-92. Mem. Am. Hosp. Assn., Am. Mgmt. Assn., Med. Group Mgmt. Assn., Am. Coll. Healthcare Execs. (mem. regent's adv. coun. 1989—), Pres.'s Assn., Mich. Hosp. Assn. Republican. Avocations: photography, microcomputers, travel. Office: Health Div 4815 W Markham St Little Rock AR 72205-3867 Home Phone: 501-954-9990; Office Phone: 501-661-2400. Business E-Mail: phalverson@healthyarkansas.com.

HALVERSTADT, DONALD BRUCE, urologist, educator; b. Cleveland, July 6, 1934; s. Lauren Oscar and Lillian Frances (Jones) H.; m. Margaret Ann (Marcy), Aug. 4, 1956; children: Donna, Jeffrey, and Amy. BA magna cum laude (hon.), Princeton U., 1956; MD cum laude (hon.), Harvard U., 1960. diplomate Am. Bd. Urology. Intern, then resident in surgery Mass. Gen. Hosp., Boston, 1960—62, resident in urology, 1964—67; pvt. practice medicine specializing in urology Okla City, 1967; chief pediatric urology svc. Okla. Children's Meml. Hosp., Okla. City, 1967; clin. prof. urology and pediat. U. Okla. Med. Sch., 1970; chief staff Okla. Children's Meml. Hosp., Okla. City, 1974—79; interim provost U. Okla. for Health Sci., Okla. City, 1979—80; CEO State of Okla. Tchg. Hosp., 1980—83; spl. asst. to pres. for Hosp. affairs Okla. U., 1980—84; vice chair dept. urology U. Okla. Med. Sch., 1982; bd. dir. State of Okla. Tchg. Hosp.; CEO State Regents for Higher Edn., 1988—93. Mem. U. Okla. Bd. Regents, 1993-2000, (chmn. 1999); founder, vice chmn., dir. Lincoln Nat. Bank, Oklahoma City, 1984-2003; bd. dir. BancFirst of Okla., 2004-, Compensation Comm., 2010, vice chair bd. gov. Okla. Med. Ctr. Hosp. Sys., 1998—; bd. dir. Triad Hosp., Inc., chair compliance com., 2000—2007, nominating com. dir. Legacy Hosp. Partners Inc., Chair, Compliances com., 2008-. Contbr. articles to med. journals. Vice chair bd. gov. Univ. Health Ptnrs.; pres., chmn. bd. Okla. Ind. Phys. Svc. Corp., 1986-96; trustee Columbia Presbyn. Hosp., 1990-96, chmn., 1995-96; bd. dir. Nat. Assn. Basketball Coaches FDTN, athletic dir. adv. coun. U. Okla., 2003. Fellow ACS; mem. AMA (Physicians Recognition Award 1969, 72, 79, 82, 85, 91, 94, 96, 99, 2002), Am. Urol. Assn., Am. Acad. Pediat., Soc. Pediat. Urology, Am. Soc. Nephrology, Soc. Univ. Urologists, So. Med. Assn., Okla. Med. Assn., Okla. County Med. Soc., Okla. State Regents for Higher Edn., Am. Coll. Physician Exec., Assn. Governing Bd. Coll. and Univ. (bd. dir., sec. 1996-97, treas. 1997-98). Presbyterian. Home: 2932 Lamp Post Ln Oklahoma City OK 73120-6105 Office: 715 Aberdeen Rd Edmond OK 73025-2719 Business E-Mail: donald-halverstadt@ouhsc.edu.

HALVORSON, GEORGE CHARLES, healthcare insurance company executive; b. Fargo, ND, Jan. 28, 1947; s. George Charles and Barbara Theone (Johnson) H.; m. Mary Elizabeth Probst, June 27, 1986; children: Jonathan Dale, Seth Gregory, George Charles IV, Michael Thomas. BA, Concordia Coll., Moorhead, Minn., 1968. Cert. health cons., 1981. Successively mgr. market rsch., mgr. corp. planning, dir. planning and budget, v.p. planning and budget, sr. v.p. Blue Cross & Blue Shield, St. Paul, 1968-76; exec. dir. HMO Minn., St. Paul, 1976-83; pres. Sr. Health Plan, St. Paul, 1983-86, Health Accord, Inc., Mpls., 1983-86, Group Health, Inc., Mpls., 1986—2002; pres., CEO HealthPartners, Mpls.; chmn., CEO Kaiser Permanente, 2002—. With Value & Sci.-Driven Health Care Inst. of Medicine Roundtable; with Adv. Com. on Health Reform American Hosp. Assn.; with Performance Health System Commonwealth Fund Commn.; bd. mem. America's Ins. Plans, Alliance of Cmty. Health Plans; chair Health Plans Internat. Fedn.; co-chair Quality Improvement in Health Care Inst. for Healthcare Improvement Ann. Forum; ops. dir. HMO/Jamaica, Kingston, 1985-86; cons. AIG/American Internat. Health, Washington, 1987-88; chair World Economic Forum's Health Govs. Meeting, Davos, 2009; lectr. in field; adv. to govts. of Uganda, Great Britain, Jamaica and Russia. Author: Health Care Will Not Reform Itself: A User's Guide to Refocusing and Reforming American Health Care, Health Care Reform Now!, Health Care Co-ops in Uganda, Epidemic of Care, How to Cut Your Company's Health Care Costs, 1987; contbr. articles to profl. journals. Chmn. Boy Scout Food Drive, St. Paul, 1988; fund raiser United Way, Mpls., 1987-88. Recipient CEO IT Achievement award Modern Healthcare/Health Info. and Mgmt. Sys. Soc., Internship award Wall St. Jour. Newspaper Fund, 1968, Louis Sullivan award Workgroup for Electronic Data Interchange, 2009. Mem. Nat. Coop. Bus. Assn. (bd. dirs.), Minn. Bus. Partnership (bd. dirs.), Group Health Assn. American, Minn. Coun. HMO's (bd. dirs.), Decathlon Club (Bloomington, Minn.), Mpls. Club. Avocations: writing, hunting, chess. Address: Kaiser Permanente Oakland 1 Kaiser Plaza Oakland CA 94612 Office Phone: 510-271-5910. Business E-Mail: George.C.Halvorson@kp.org. *

HAM, OK KYUNG, professor; b. Incheon, Republic of Korea, Jan. 19, 1966; d. Kyung Keun Ham and Soon Wha Lim; m. Jin Bae Kim, Oct. 8, 1988; 1 child, Byung Soo Kim. BS, Coll. Nursing, Yonsei U., Seoul, Republic of Korea, 1988; MPH, Grad. Sch. Pub. Health, Yonsei U., Seoul, Republic of Korea, 1997; PhD in Health Studies, Tex. Woman's U., Denton, 2002. Cert. health edn. specialist Nat. Commn. Health Edn. Credentialing, 2005; RN Korea Ministry Health & Welfare, 1988. Rsch. asst. Nursing Policy Rsch. Inst., Yonsei U., 2000—03; asst. prof. Kyungpook Nat. U., Daegu, Republic of Korea, 2003—06, INHA U., Dept. Nursing, Incheon, 2006—09, assoc. prof., 2009—. Contbr. articles to profl. jours. Mem.: Korea Nurses Assn., Soc. Pub. Health Educators. Home: Samho Garden Mansion E-501 Banpo Dong Seocho Gu Seoul 137-933 Republic of Korea Office: INHA Univ Dept Nursing #253 Yonghyun Dong Nam Gu Incheon 402-751 Republic of Korea Office Phone: 82-32-860-8211. Office Fax: 82-32-874-5880. Business E-Mail: okkyung@inha.ac.kr.

HAM, O(SCAR) EMERSON, JR., neurologist; b. Atlanta, Feb. 22, 1940; s. O. Emerson and Ruth Roan (McCurry) H.; m. Mary Little Schofield, Sept. 12, 1964; children: O. Emerson III, Stephen B. BA, Emory U., 1960, MD, 1964. Diplomate Am. Bd. of Psychiatry and Neurology; lic. M.D. Minn., Fla., Ga. Intern. in medicine U. Fla. Tchg. Hosp., Gainesville, 1964-65; fellow in neurology Mayo Clinic, Rochester, Minn., 1965-68; staff neurologist Wilford Hall USAF Hosp., San Antonio, Tex., 1968-70; pvt. practice neurology Neurol. Assn., Savannah, Ga., 1970-77; group practice neurology Neurol. Inst., Savannah, 1977—. Clin. instr. neurology U. Tex. Sch. Medicine, San Antonio, 1968-70; assoc. clin. prof. Med. Coll. Ga., Augusta, 1978-95. Contbr. articles to profl. jours. Grad. Leadership Savannah; bd. trustees, vice chmn. Ga. Infirmary, Savannah. Capt. USAF, 1968-70. Mem. AMA, Am. Acad. Neurology, Am. EEG Soc., Ga. Med. Soc. (past pres.), So. Med. Assn., Med. Assn. Ga., Ga. Neurol. Soc. (past pres.), Savannah Rotary, Alpha Omega Alpha. Episcopalian. Avocations: boating, hunting, hiking, skiing. Office: Neurol Inst Savannah 4 E Jackson Blvd Savannah GA 31405-5810

HAMADEH, RANDAH RIBHI, dean; b. Jerusalem, May 22, 1954; BSc, Am. U. Beirut, 1975; DPhil, U. Oxford, 1988. Prof., chair dept. family and cmty. medicine Arabian Gulf U., 2005—10, asst. dean grad. studies and rsch., 2010—. Temp. advisor WHO/EMRO, 1999—; advisor to asst. undersecretary tng. and planning Ministry of Health, Bahrain, 2005—. Rsch. Tng. fellowship, Internat. Agy. Rsch. on Cancer, Rsch. grant, Arabian Gulf U. Mem.: Bahrain Cancer Soc., Anti-Smoking Soc. (Bahrain), GLOBALink, Soc. Social Medicine, Internat. Epidemiologic Assn. Avocations: reading, embroidery, writing. Office: Arabian Gulf University PO Box 22979 Manama 000 Bahrain Office Fax: 97317230730. Business E-Mail: randah@agu.edu.bh.

HAMANAKA, SATOKO, psychiatrist; d. Toshiaki and Sachiko Hamanaka; m. Masamoto Yokoyama. MD, PhD, Kitasato U. Sch. Medicine, Japan, 2006. Cert. Bd. Am. Acad. Anti Aging Medicine, 2007, basic proficiency in chelation therapy Am. Coll. Advancement in Medicine, 2007, anti aging medicine specialist World Soc. Anti-Aging Medicine, 2008, Japanese Bd. Anti-Aging Regenerative Medicine, 2006. Resident Kitasato U. Hosp., Sagamihara-shi, Japan, 2000—02; staff Kameda Med. Ctr., Kamogawa, Japan, 2002—03; lectr. Internat. U. Health and Welfare Atami Hosp., Atami-shi, Japan, 2006—07; vice dir. AAC Clinic Ginza, Tokyo, 2007—. Cons. Anti-Aging Network, Ginza, 2007—. Office: AAC Clinic Ginza Ginza AS Bldg 5F 3-5-8 Ginza Chuo-ku Tokyo 104-0061 Japan Office Phone: 81-3-5250-7333. Business E-Mail: hamanaka@aac-clinic.com.

HAMASHITA, TOMOHIRO, research scientist; b. Osaka, Japan, Aug. 21, 1976; PhD, Osaka Prefecture U., 2011. Rsch. scientist Taisho Pharm. Co., Ltd., 2002—. Office: 1-403 Yoshino-sho Kita-ku Saitama 331-9530 Japan Business E-Mail: tomohiro.hamashita@po.rd.taisho.co.jp.

HAMBARTSOUMIAN, EDOUARD, obstetrician, researcher, embryologist; b. Erevan, Armenia, Sept. 29, 1955; arrived in U.S., 1995; s. Martin Andreas Hambartsoumian and Raya Magaki Stepanian; children: Lily, Vahakn. MD (hon.), Erevan U., Armenia, 1981; cert. in fetal medicine, U. Paris, 1994. Chief ob-gyn. dept Aragats Dist. Hosp., Tsakhkahovit, Armenia, 1981—85; chief ob-gyn. dept. Erebouni Hosp., Erevan, Armenia, 1985—88, Maternity #3, Erevan, Armenia, 1988—93; scientist Hosp. Antoine Belcere, Paris, 1993—95; sr. scientist Boston U./Fertility Ctr. New England, 1995—. Embryologist Fertility Ctr. New England, Boston, 2000—01. Contbr. articles to profl. jours. Organist local ch. Named Honorary Inventor of USSR, Governement of USSR, 1978; grantee Travel grant, NIH, 1997. Mem.: Soc. Study Reprodn. (assoc.). Avocation: music. Office: Fertility Ctr New England 20 Pond Meadow Dr Reading MA 01867 Home: 66 Maywood St Roxbury MA 02119-2125 Personal E-mail: hambartsoumian@hotmail.com

HAMBRICK, ERNESTINE, retired colon and rectal surgeon; b. Griffin, Ga., Mar. 31, 1941; d. Jack Daniel Hambrick and Nanni (Harper) Hambrick Rubens. BS, U. Md., 1963; MD, U. Ill., 1967. Diplomate Am. Bd. Colon and Rectal Surgery, Am. Bd. Surgery. Intern in surgery Cook County Hosp., Chgo., 1967-68, resident in gen. surgery, 1968-72, fellow colon and rectal surgery, 1972-73, attending surgeon, 1973-74, part-time attending surgeon, 1974-80; pvt. practice colon and rectal surgery Chgo., 1974-97; pres. med. staff Michael Reese Hosp., Chgo., 1990-92, chief surgery, 1993-95; founder, chmn. STOP Colon/Rectal Cancer Found., 1997—2009; hospice physician, 2009—. Mem. Nat. Colorectal Cancer Round Table, 1997—2007, mem. steering com., 2000—06. Contbr. articles to profl. jours. Trustee Rsch. and Edn. Found. Michael Reese Med. Staff, Chgo., 1994—98, treas., 1994—98. Fellow: ACS, Am. Coll. Gastroenterology, Am. Soc. Colon and Rectal Surgeons (v.p. 1992—93, trustee Rsch. Found. 1992—98). Avocations: travel, photography, scuba diving, flying, writing. Office: 1340 S Damen Ave Chicago IL 60608 Home Phone: 312-944-4636; Office Phone: 312-997-7200. Personal E-mail: ehcrsone@aol.com.

HAMBRICK, GEORGE WALTER, JR., dermatologist, educator; b. Charlottesville, Va., Dec. 4, 1922; s. George W. and Sallie Anna (McCallum) H BS, Concord Coll., 1944; MD, U. Va., 1946. Intern Hosp. U. Iowa, 1946—47; asst. resident dermatology U. Va. Hosp., 1947—48; resident Columbia-Presbyn. Hosp., NYC, 1950—51; fellow dermatology Duke U., Durham, NC, 1951—52, assoc. dermatology, 1953; instr. Columbia U., NYC, 1953—55, assoc., 1955—57, asst. prof., 1957—62; assoc. prof. U. Pa., 1962—66, Johns Hopkins U., Balt., 1966—69, prof., 1969—76; dir. dermatology Johns Hopkins Med. Inst. Johns Hopkins U., 1967—76; prof. U. Cin., 1976-81, dir. dermatology, 1976-81; prof. Cornell U. Coll. Medicine, NYC, 1981—96; chief dermatology N.Y. Hosp., 1981—96, prof emeritus, 1996—; sr. lectr. Columbia U., 2001—. Capt. AUS USMC, 1948—50. Fellow ACP; mem. AMA (del. 1981-90), Soc. Investigative Dermatology (pres. 1971-72, hon. mem.), Dermatology Found. (trustee, pres. 1974), Assn. Profs. Dermatology, Am. Dermatol. Assn. (hon.), Am. Acad. Dermatology (hon. dir. 1978), Am. Skin Assn. (pres. 1988-93, 2000-), Johns Hopkins Med. Sch. (disting. med. alumni), Alpha Omega Alpha. Office: Am Skin Assn 346 Park Ave S New York NY 10010 Home Phone: 434-978-2172; Office Phone: 212-889-4858.

HAMBURG, DAVID A., psychiatrist, foundation administrator; b. Evansville, Ind., 1925; MD, Ind. U., 1947, D.Sc. (hon.), 1976, Rush U., 1977, Mt. Sinai Sch. Medicine, 1980, U. Rochester, 1981, U. Ill., Chgo., 1984, Albert Einstein Sch. Medicine, 1985, U. Pitts., U. So. Calif., Hahnemann U., 1986; LHD (hon.), Ramapo Coll., 1991, Duke U., 1993, So. Indiana U., 2000. Diplomate Am. Bd. Psychiatry and Neurology. Intern Michael Reese Hosp., Chgo., 1947-48, resident in psychiatry, 1949-50, Yale U.-New Haven Hosp., 1948-49; staff psychiatrist Brooke Army Hosp., San Antonio, 1950-52; practice medicine specializing in psychiatry, 1950-75; research psychiatrist Walter Reed Army Inst. Research, Washington, 1952-53; assoc. dir.

Psychosomatic and Psychiat. Inst., Michael Reese Hosp., Chgo., 1954-56; fellow Center for Advanced Study in Behavioral Scis., Palo Alto, Calif., 1957-58, 67-68; chief Adult Psychiat. Br. NIMH, Bethesda, Md., 1958-61; prof., chmn. dept. psychiatry Stanford U. Med. Sch., 1961-72, Reed-Hodgson prof. human biology, 1972-76; Sherman Fairchild Disting. scholar Calif. Inst. Tech., Pasadena, 1974-75; pres. Inst. Medicine Nat. Acad. Scis., Washington, 1975-80; dir. div. health policy research and edn., John D. MacArthur prof. health policy and mgmt. Harvard U., Cambridge, Mass., 1980-82; pres. Carnegie Corp., NYC, 1983-97, pres. emeritus, 1997—; dist. scholar Weill Cornell Med. Coll., 2004—; sr. scholar Woodrow Wilson Ctr. Internat. Scholars, 2010—. Adv. com. med. rsch. WHO, 1975-86; mem. exec. panel adv. com. Chief of Naval Ops, 1984-92; chmn. sci. adv. bd. NIMH, 1986-87; sec. Energy Adv. Bd., 1990-94; mem. Ctr. for Naval Analysis, 1990-93. Author: No More Killing Fields: Preventing Deadly Conflict, 2002, Learning to Live Together: Preventing Hatred and Violence in Child and Adolescent Development, 2003. Bd. dirs. Rockefeller U., 1979—, Mt. Sinai Med. Ctr., N.Y.C., 1984—; trustee Stanford U., 1988-94, Internat. Devel. Rsch. Ctr., Ottawa, Ont., Can., 1990-94, Am. Mus. Natural History, N.Y.C., 1990—; co-chmn. Carnegie Commn. on Preventing Deadly Conflict, 1994-99; mem. Pres.'s Com. of Advisors on Sci. and Tech., 1994-2001; dep. chmn. Fed. Res. Bank N.Y., Def. Policy Bd., U.S. Dept. Def., 1994-95; chmn. to sec. gen. prevention genocide United Nations Adv. Com., 2006-. Recipient numerous awards including: Pres.'s medal Michael Reese Med. Ctr., 1974, Peace award Cranbrook Found., 2003; A.C.P. award, 1977; MIT Bicentennial medal, 1976, Presdl. Medal of Freedom, 1996; Disting. Presdl. fellow for internat. activities Nat. Acads., 2002.; co-recipient Sarnat prize in Mental Health, Inst. Medicine, 2007. Mem. Am. Psychiat. Assn. (Vestermark award 1977, Disting. Svc. award 1991, Pres.'s medal Bank St. Coll. 1994, Charter medallion Radcliffe Coll. 1994), Nat. Acad. Scis. (com. on internat. security and arms control 1981-86, Pub. Welfare medal 1998, Fgn. Policy Assocs. medal 2004), AAAS (pres. 1984-85, chmn. bd. 1985-86), Assn. Rsch. Nervous and Mental Disease (pres. 1967-68), Am. Philos. Soc., Am. Acad. Arts and Scis., Phi Beta Kappa, Alpha Omega Alpha. Office: Weill Cornell Med Coll Dept Psych 525 E 68th St Box 171 New York NY 10065 Business E-Mail: dah2013@med.cornell.edu.

HAMBURG, MARGARET ANN (PEGGY HAMBURG), federal agency administrator, former public health administrator; b. Chgo., July 12, 1955; d. David Alan and Beatrix Ann (McCleary) Hamburg; m. Peter Fitzhugh Brown, May 23, 1992; children: Rachel Ann Hamburg Brown, Evan David Addison Brown. BA magna cum laude, Radcliffe Coll., Harvard U., Cambridge, Mass., 1978; MD, Harvard U., 1983. Diplomate American Bd. Internal Medicine, Nat. Bd. Med. Examiners. Intern, resident internal medicine NY Hosp., Cornell Med. Coll., NYC, 1983-86; spl. asst. to the dir., Office Disease Prevention & Health Promotion, US Dept. Health & Human Services, Washington, 1986-88, asst. sec. planning & evaluation, 1997—2001; spl. asst. to dir. Nat. Inst. Allergy & Infectious Diseases, NIH, Bethesda, Md., 1988-89, asst. dir., 1989-90; dep. commr. family health services NYC Dept. Health, NYC, 1990-91, commr. health, 1991-97; v.p. biological programs Nuclear Threat Initiative (NTI), Washington, 2001—05, sr. scientist, 2005—09; commr. FDA, Silver Spring, Md., 2009—. Guest investigator Rockefeller U., NYC, 1985—86; clin. instr. dept. medicine Georgetown U. Sch. Medicine, Washington, 1986—90; mem. steering com. women & aids NIH, 1991; asst. prof. clin. pub. health Columbia U. Sch. Pub. Health, NYC, 1991—97; adj. asst. prof. medicine Cornell U. Med. Coll., NYC, 1991—97; bd. govs. Greater NY Hosp. Assn., 1991—97; mem. sci. adv. bd. Nat. Pub. Radio, 1992—97; adv. bd. mem. Medunsa Trust, Inc., Med. U. So. Africa, 1993—97; bd. mem. sci. counselors Nat. Ctr. Infectious Diseases, US Centers Disease Control (CDC), 1994—97; bd. dirs. NYC Health Systems Agy., Med. & Health Rsch. Assn., Health Hosps. Corp., Nat. Coun. Women's Health, Primary Care Devel. Corp. Mem. editl. bd. Jour. NY Acad. Sci., 1992—97, The Bull. (NY Acad. Medicine), 1992—97, Current Reviews in Pub. Health, 1993—97; contbr. articles to profl. jours. Vol. attending physician Washington Free Clinic, 1988—90; trustee Rockefeller Found. Recipient Spl. Recognition award, USPHS, 1990, Women's Club NY cert. of honor, 1993, Robert F. Wagner Pub. Svc. award, NYU, 1993; named one of The 100 Most Powerful Women in DC, Washingtonian mag., 2009. Fellow: ACP, AAAS; mem.: NAS, APHA, Women in Health Mgmt., Soc. Social Biology, Pub. Health Assn. NYC, NY Acad. Medicine, Coun. Fgn. Rels., Am. Med. Women's Assn. Office: FDA 10903 New Hampshire Ave Silver Spring MD 20903-0002 E-mail: Margaret.Hamburg@fda.hhs.gov. *

HAMBURGER, ROBERT N., pediatrician, educator, consultant; b. NYC, Jan. 26, 1923; s. Samuel B. and Harriet (Newfield) H.; m. Sonia Gross, Nov. 9, 1943; children: Hilary (dec.), Debre (dec.), Lisa. BA, U. NC, 1947; MD, Yale U., 1951. Diplomate Am. Bd. Pediatrics, Am. Bd. Allergy and Immunology. Instr., asst. clin. prof. sch. medicine Yale U., New Haven, 1951-60; assoc. prof. biology U. Calif. San Diego, La Jolla, 1960-64, assoc. prof. pediatrics, 1964-67, prof., 1967-90, prof. emeritus, 1990—, asst. dean sch. medicine, 1964-70, lab. dir., 1970-98, head fellows tng. program allergy and immunology divsn., 1970-90; pres., CEO RNA and Co., Inc., 2002—; emeritus chmn., bd. dirs. BioVigilant Sys. Inc., 2009—. Cons. various cos., Calif., Sweden, Switzerland, 1986—. Author 1 book; contbr. articles to profl. jours. Vol. physician, educator Children of the Californias, Calif. and Baja California, Mex., 1993-2009, Baker Sch. Free Clinic, 1999-2009. 1st lt. Air Corps, U.S. Army, 1943-45, PTO. Decorated Air medal with oak leaf clusters, Purple Heart; grantee NIH and USPHS, 1960-64, 64-84; Fulbright fellow, 1980, Disting. fellow Am. Coll. Allergy, Asthma, Immunology, 1986. Mem. U. Calif. San Diego Emeriti Assn. (pres. 1992-94). Achievements include patentee for allergy peptides, allergen detector, Pathogen Detector System and Methods. Avocations: flying, skiing, writing. Office: U Calif San Diego Revelle Coll Sch Medicine La Jolla CA 92093-0950 Office Phone: 858-534-7555. Business E-Mail: rhamburg@ucsd.edu.

HAMDI, HAMID S., neurologist, neurorehabilitation specialist, consultant, researcher; b. Karachi, Sind, Pakistan, May 5, 1959; s. Mohammad Abul Aas, Habiba Bano Aas; m. Imrana Y. Hamdi, Mar. 26, 1959; children: Mia, Samiha. MBBS, Dow Med. Coll., Karachi, Pakistan, 1978—84. Med. officer Civil Hosp. and Dow Med. Coll., Karachi, Sind, Pakistan, 1986—88, Saudi Ministry Health, Riyadh, Saudi Arabia, 1988—93; resident Lincoln Med. Ctr., Bronx, NY, 1993—94; resident in Neurology Nassau County Med. Ctr., East Meadow, NY, 1994—97; fellow in neurorehabilitation Hosp. Joint Diseases, NYC, 1997—99; clin. asst. prof. neurology Ind. U., 2003—. Cheif resident in Neurology Nassau County Med. Ctr., East Meadow, NY, 1996—97; investigator Antegren trial Hosp. for Joint Diseases, NYC, 1997—99, site prin. investigator-KEEPER trial, 2000—01; investigator-Betaserone trial Heartland Neurology Associates, 2000—01; faculty mem. NYU Sch Medicine, NYC, 1999—99; vis. lectr. Purdue U., West Lafayette, 2000—01; clin. asst. prof. Ind. U. Sch. Medicine, Ind.; spkr. in field. Author: (Reveiw article) Neurocysticercosis- a reveiw., 1997; editor: (Periodical) NCMC Proceedings, 1996. Speaker National MS Soceity Indiana Chapter, West Lafayette, IN, 2000—00, Renssalaer, IN, 2001—01, Stroke Support Group, Lafayette, IN, 2001—01. Mem.: AMA, Am. Acad. Neurology, Am. Soc. Neurorehab. Office: Heartland Neurology Assocs 1345 Unity Pl #365 Lafayette IN 47905 Home: 340 Augusta Way Fort Wayne IN 46825-2171 Office Phone: 765-446-5300.

HAMDY, AMAL MOHAMED, cardiologist, educator; b. Cairo, Aug. 23, 1955; d. Mohamed Hamdy Mahmoud. MD in Cardiology, Ain-Shams U., Cairo, 1996. Physician Ain-Shams U. Specialized Hosp., Cairo, 1981—84, cardiologist, 1984—98; prof. cardiology Faculty Medicine, Al-Azhar U., Cairo, 2007—. Contbr. articles to profl. sci. jours. Recipient, Egyptian Med. Syndicate, 1986; named Establishment Specialized Hosp., Ain-Shams U., 1984. Mem.: European Soc. Cardiology. Achievements include research in echocardiography and tissue doppler imaging. Office: Al-Zahraa Univ Hosp Al-Zahraa Hosp St Abasseya Cairo 17516 Egypt Personal E-mail: amhamdy55@hotmail.com.

HAMDY, RONALD CHARLES, geriatrician; b. Alexandria, Egypt, July 31, 1946; came to U.S., 1985; s. Charles and Mary Hamdy; m. Eleanor Gertrude Hamdy, Aug. 19, 1977; children: Conrad, Gerard, Ronan. MB, ChB with honours, U. Alexandria, 1968, DM, 1971. Rotating intern U. Alexandria, 1968-69; resident in internal medicine Al-Gomhouriya Gen. Hosp., Alexandria, 1969-70; resident registrar internal medicine U. Alexandria Main Tchg. Hosp., 1970-72; sr. ho. officer geriatric and internal medicine Farnborough (Eng.) Hosp., Kent, 1972-73; registrar in geriatric medicine Bromley (Eng.) Group of Hosps., Kent, 1974; sr. registrar in geriatric medicine King's Coll. Group Hosps., London, 1975-77; consulting physician St. John's Hosp. Richmond (Eng.), Twickenham & Roehampton Health Authority, 1977-85, chmn. dept. clin. gerontology, ethics rsch. com., 1981-85; prof. internal medicine, Cecile Cox Quillen prof. geriatric medicine, head divsn. gerontology East Tenn. State U., Mountain Home, 1985—, Cecile Cox Quillen prof. geriatric medicine, head divsn. gerontology, 1990—, dir. osteoporosis ctr., 1997—; chief geriat. VA Med. Ctr., Mountain Home, 1985-88, assoc. chief of staff geriatric and extended care, 1988—2004. Hon. sr. lectr. geriatric medicine St. George's Hosp. Med. Sch., U. London, 1981-85; planning team for elderly Wandsworth Health Care, 1982-85; med. dist. initiated peer rev. orgn. VA Hosps., Dist. 8, 1986-89; vis. prof. Health Care for Elderly, U. London, 1991-93; Burroughs Wellcome vis. prof. geriatric medicine Royal Soc. Medicine, 1994-95; co-chmn. pharmacy and therapeutics com. VA Med. Ctr., Johnson City, Tenn., chmn. adverse drug reaction com.; chmn. program com. Coll. Medicine Continuing Med. Edn., East Tenn. State U.; mem. Gov.'s task force on Alzheimer's Disease, Tenn., task force on edn., prevention and detection of osteoporosis; mem. advisor to pub. guardian 1st Tenn. Devel. Dist.; adv. bd. Colonial Hill Health Care Ctr., Johnson City, Golden J-55, Johnson City Med. Ctr. Hosp., Inc.; sr. health adv. com. 1st Tenn. Regional Health Office; adj. clin. prof. divsn. clin. nutrition and psychiatry East Tenn. State U., editor in chief, Jours. Clin. Densitometry, 2010-. Author: Diuretic Therapy in the Older Patient, 1978, Paget's Disease in Bone, Assessment and Management, 1981, Geriatric Medicine: A Problem Oriented Approach, 1984; editor: (with J. Turnbull, M. Lancaster, L. Norman) Alzheimer's Disease: A Handbook for Caregivers, 1990, 3d edit., 1998; mem. editl. adv. bd. Revs. Clin. Gerontology, South Med. Jour., Geriatria; reviewer for med. jours.; contbr. chpts. to books, articles to profl. jours. Fellow ACP (com. geriat. 1987-90, chmn. com. geriat. MKSAP IX 1991-94), Royal Coll. Physicians, Royal Soc. Medicine; mem. Internat. Soc. Clin. Densitometry, Am. Geriat. Soc. (membership com., reviewer jour., ann. meeting planning com. 1993), Gerontol. Soc. Am., Royal Coll. Surgeons, So. Med. Assn. (vice-chmn. coun. 1995-96, chmn. coun. 1996-97, v.p. 1997-98, pres.-elect 1998-99, pres. 1999-2000, editor geriatric medicine sect. Dial-Access program, from assoc. councilor to councilor state Tenn., chmn. adv. com. sci. activities, reviewer jour., assoc. editor So. Med. Jour. 1995-2000, editor 2000-2010, editor in chief, Jour. Clin. Deusitometry), So. Assn. Geriatric Medicine (pres. 1990-92), So. Assn. for Primary Care (editor clin. revs.), Tenn. Med. Assn. (reviewer jour.), Tenn. Geriat. Soc. (founding), Brit. Med. Assn., Brit. Geriat. Soc., Bone and Mineral Soc., Alzheimer's Assn. (pres. bd. dirs. N.E. Tenn. chpt. 1990-91). Office: Ea Tenn State U Coll Medicine PO Box 70429 Johnson City TN 37614-1704 Office Phone: 423-439-8830. Business E-Mail: hamdy@etsu.edu.

HAMED, M. RAOUF, pharmacologist, toxicologist, educator, writer; b. Cairo, June 20, 1948; s. Hamed Ismail and Souad Mousa; m. Salwa Abdalla Metwally, July 22, 1975; children: Mourad, Omneia. BA in Pharmacy and Pharm. Sci., Alexandria U., Egypt, 1970; PhD in Pharmacology, Inst. Drug Rsch. and Control, Warsaw, Poland, 1977; diploma in Ops. Rsch., Cairo U., 2000. Rsch. asst. Drug Rsch. and Control Ctr., Giza, Egypt, 1970—74; lectr. faculty pharmacy Al Fatah U., Tripoli, Libya, 1978—83; prof. pharmacology and toxcology Nat. Orgn. Drug Control and Rsch., Giza, 1984—; prof. pharmacology, dean of rsch. and postgrad. studies Asmara Coll. Health Scis., 2009—. Asst. sec. gen. Pugwash - Egyptian Br., Cairo, 1987—94; sec. gen. bd. dirs. Nat. Orgn. Drug Control and Rsch., Cairo, 1988—94, founder, gen. dir. Drug Bioavailability Ctr., 1990—94. Author: Management of Knowledge: A Futural Perspective (Best Book in Futural studies in Egypt, 1998). Cons. Forum Intercultures dialogue, Coptic Evang. Orgn. Social Svcs, Cairo, 1997—2008; mem. Egyptian Coun. Fgn. Affairs, Cairo, 2005—, head com., 2007—09; mem. of directors Al Rouad (The Initiators), Cairo, 2002—08; mem. sci. culture com. Supreme Coun. Culture, Cairo, 2001—08, head of com., 2007—09; mem. divsn. peaceful use and strategic studies Coun. Space Rsch., Egyptian Acad. Sci. and Tech., Cairo, 2001—07; cons. Ahwal Misreya Mag., Al Ahram Orgn., Cairo, 2000—08, Sotour mag., Cairo, 1999—2007. Scholar, Ministry Health Poland, Inst. Drug Rsch. and Control), 1974. Mem.: Top Mgmt. Soc., Pharmacists Syndicate. Achievements include research in line on pharmacology of capasaicin and its interaction with drug safety and efficacy; development of new research units nationaly and regionaly; research in influence of protein malnutrition on safety and efficacy of drugs. Avocation: music. Office: Nat Orgn Drug Control and Research 6 Abo Hazem St Pyramides Avenue Giza Egypt Home: 453, King Faysal St 12111 Giza Giza Egypt Office Fax: 00235855582. Business E-Mail: mraoufh@yahoo.com.

HAMEED, AFSHAN BATOOL, cardiologist, educator; b. Pakistan, Mar. 13, 1968; MD, King Edward Med. U., 1989. Asst. prof., maternal fetal medicine & cardiology U. Calif., Irvine, 2005—, dir. perinatal svcs., 2010—. Office: 101 City Dr Bld 56 Ste 800 Orange CA 92868 Business E-Mail: ahameed@uci.edu.

HAMID, SAIMA, healthcare educator; b. Rawalpindi, Aug. 13, 1967; MPH, Health Svcs. Acad., Islamabad, 2001; PhD, Karolinska Inst., Stockholm, Sweden, 2010. Rsch. asst. Health Svcs. Acad., Ministry of Health, 1998—2000, instr., 2000—07, asst. prof., 2007—, tchr., rschr. Mem.: Population Assn. Pakistan. Avocation: reading. Home: House 106 96 I-8/4 Islamabad 44000 Pakistan Home Fax: 92519255592. Personal E-mail: saima_hamid@yahoo.com.

HAMIDI, REYHANEH, dermatologist; b. Tehran, Iran, Feb. 28, 1980; BA, UCLA, 2003; MD, U. SC, 2008. Resident, dermatology Harbor-UCLA Med. Ctr., 2009—. Recipient Dean's Recognition award, Keck Sch. Medicine, U. SC. Mem.: Women's Dermatologic Soc., Am. Soc. Dermatologic Surgery, Am. Acad. Dermatology, Alpha Omega Alpha Honor Soc. Home: 1500 Highland Ave Manhattan Beach CA 90266 Personal E-mail: reyhamidi@yahoo.com.

HAMILTON, CARLOS ROBERT, JR., endocrinologist, academic administrator, consultant; b. Houston, June 12, 1939; s. Carlos Robert and Berta (Denman) H.; m. Carolyn Burton, Aug. 12, 1961; children: Carlos R. III, Patricia Frances. BA, U. Tex., 1961; MS, MD with honors, Baylor Coll. Medicine, 1966. Diplomate Am. Bd. Internal Medicine, Am. Bd. Endocrinology and Metabolic Diseases. Intern in internal medicine Johns Hopkins Hosp., Balt., 1966-67, asst. resident in internal medicine, 1967-69, chief resident in medicine, 1970-71; clin. and rsch. fellow Harvard Med. Sch./Mass. Gen. Hosp., Boston, 1969-70; asst. prof. medicine Johns Hopkins U. and Hosp., Balt., 1971-72; staff endocrinologist Wilford Hall USAF Med. Ctr., San Antonio, 1972-74; clin. prof. medicine Baylor Coll. Medicine, Houston, 1974—; clin. prof. medicine Med. Sch. U. Tex., Houston, 1999-2000, prof. internal medicine, 2000—, spl. asst. to pres., 2000—. Cons. endocrinology and internal medicine Med. Clinic of Houston, L.L.P., 1974—2000; med. advisor employee benefit com. Southwestern Bell Tel. Co., 1975—93; attending physician in endocrinology Ben Taub Gen. Hosp./Baylor Coll. Medicine, 1980—; attending physician, mem. active staff The Meth. Hosp./Meml.-Hermann Hosp., Houston, 1974—; mem. active staff St. Luke's Episcopal Hosp., 2000—, Meml. Hermann Hosp., 2000—; practicing physicians adv. coun. U.S. Dept. HHS, 2003—07; mem. health, sci. and rsch. com. World Anti-Doping Agy., Montreal, 2003—07. Contbr. articles to profl. jours. Dist. and coun. chair, area pres., regional bd. dirs., v.p. Boy Scouts Am., Houston, Atlanta, Irving, Tex., 1980—; bd. regents Tex. Woman's U., 1999-2001; chair, bd.dirs. Mus. Health and Med. Sci., Houston, 2006-08. Recipient Dist. award of merit, Silver Beaver award, Silver Antelope award, Disting. Eagle Scout award, Silver Buffalo award Boy Scouts Am., 1982-99. Fellow ACP (bd. dirs. Tex. chpt., Mead-Johnson Residency scholar 1970, bd. dirs. Tex. Acad. Internal Medicine and ACP-ASIM health and pub. policy com., Tex. Laureate award 2003, Named Advocate of Yr., 2006), Am. Coll. Endocrinology (trustee 1999-2000, sec.-treas. 2001-02, chancellor 2005-06, pres. 2007-08); mem. SAR (bd. dirs. Paul Carrington chpt. 1992—, pres. 1993), Am. Soc. Internal Medicine (bd. dirs. polit. action com. 1995-98, Key Congl. Contact of Yr. 1996), Am. Assn. Clin. Endocrinologists (bd. dirs. 1995—, chair legis. and regulatory com. 1998-2000, sec. exec. com. 2000-01, treas. 2001-02, v.p. 2002-2003, pres.-elect 2003-04, pres. 2004-05, Disting. Svc. award, 2010), Tex. Med. Assn. (exec. com. polit. action com. 1989-01, chair 1995, 96), Harris County Med. Soc. (bd. dirs. 1992-99, pres.-elect 1998, pres. 1999), Kiwanis (bd. dirs. Houston chpt. 1986-95, pres. 1995), Alpha Omega Alpha, Sigma Xi; Master ACE. Office: U Tex Health Sci Ctr 7000 Fannin Rm 1535 Houston TX 77030 Office Phone: 713-500-3825. Business E-Mail: carlos.r.hamilton@uth.tmc.edu.

HAMILTON, JAMES PETER ADAM, medical educator; b. New Haven, Apr. 26, 1971; MD, U. Md., 2000. Asst. prof. Johns Hopkins U. Sch. Medicine, 2007—. Recipient Mentored Clinician Scientist award, NIH, NIDDK. Mem.: AGA, AASLD. Office: 720 Rutland Ave Ross Bldg Rm 918 Baltimore MD 21205 Office Fax: 410-955-9677. Business E-Mail: jpahamilton@jhmi.edu.

HAMILTON, KIRK LEE, medical educator, researcher; BS, MA, U. Tex.- Arlington, 1978; PhD, Utah State U., Logan, 1982. Rsch. instr. med. br. U. Tex., Galveston, 1982—86; rsch. instr. Sch. Medicine U. Ala., Birmingham, 1986—89; vis. asst. prof. Colby Coll., Waterville, 1989—89; rsch. asst. prof. Fla. Inst. Tech., Melbourne, 1989—90; asst. prof. Xavier U. La., New Orleans, 1990—94; sr. lectr. Sch. Med. Scis. U. Otago, Dunedin, 1994—. Editl. bd. mem. Am. Jour. Physiology - Renal Physiology, 2007—; rschr. HS and JC Anderson Trust, New Zealand, 2006—; vis. scholar U. Pitts. Sch. Medicine, 2002, 08. Contbr. 100 articles to profl. jours. Recipient Nat. Svc. Rsch. award, US Pub. Health Svc. (NIH), 1985—87, Rsch. Devel. award, Cystic Fibrosis Found., 1988—90; Rsch. grant, Am. Heart Assn. Tex. Affiliate, 1985—88, NIH, 1992—95, Dean's Strategic Rsch. Fund - U. Otago, 1995, 2001—06, U. Otago, 2004—05. Mem.: Internat. Physiology Com. Am. Physiol. Soc. (alt. mem. 2008—), Med. Sciences New Zealand (sci. programme co-organizer 2005—08, co-chair 2007), Gen. Soc. Physiologists, Biophys. Soc., Physiol. Soc. New Zealand (coun. mem. 2003), Am. Physiol. Soc. (mem.comm. 2005—07). Office: Univ Otago Sch - Physiology 270 Gt King St Dunedin New Zealand Office Fax: 6434797323. Business E-Mail: kirk.hamilton@otago.ac.nz.

HAMILTON, LEONARD DERWENT, physician, molecular biologist; b. Manchester, Eng., May 7, 1921; came to U.S., 1949, naturalized, 1964; s. Jacob and Sara (Sandelson) H.; m. Ann Twynam Blake, July 20, 1945; children: Jane Derwent, Stephen David, Robin Michael. BA, Balliol Coll., Oxford U., Eng., 1943, BM, 1945, MA, 1946, DM, 1951; MA, Trinity Coll., Cambridge U., Eng., 1948, PhD, 1952. Diplomate Am. Bd. Pathology. USPHS rsch. fellow U. Utah, 1949-50; staff Sloan-Kettering Inst., NYC, 1950-79, head isotope studies sect., 1957-64, assoc. scientist, 1965-79; staff Meml. Hosp., NYC, 1950-65; faculty Sloan-Kettering div. Grad. Sch. Med. Scis. Cornell U., 1956-64; sr. scientist, head divsn. microbiology Med.

Research Ctr. Brookhaven Nat. Lab., Upton, NY, 1964-76; head biomed. and environ. assessment divsn. Office. Environ. Policy Analysis, 1973-94. Attending physician Hosp. Med. Rsch. Ctr., 1964-85; dir. WHO Collaborating Ctr. for Assessment of Health and Environ. Effects of Energy Systems, 1983-97, WHO focal point on health and environ. effects of energy systems, 1983-2005, mem. WHO expert adv. panel on environ. hazards, 1983-98; prof. medicine Health Sci. Ctr., SUNY, Stony Brook, 1968—; adj. prof. biometry and epidemiology Med. U. S.C., Charleston, 1996—; cons. HEW, Ctr. Disease Control, Nat. Inst. Occupational Safety and Health, epidemiology study of Portsmouth Naval Shipyard, 1978-88; vis. fellow St. Catherine's Coll., Oxford U., 1972-73; internat. panel experts on fossil fuel UN Environment Programme, 1978, panel on nuclear energy, 1978-79, panel on renewable sources and comparative assessment of different sources, 1980; com. mem. Nat. Acad. Sci.-NRC, Washington, 1975-80; mem. NYC Mayor's Tech. Adv. Com. on Radiation, 1963-77, NYC Commr. of Health Tech. Adv. Com. on Radiation, 1978—; energy panel WHO Commn. on Health and Environment, 1990-91; mem. Internat. Expert Group 3, Comparative Environ. and Health Effects of Different Energy Systems for Electricity Generation, 1990-91; sr. expert Symposium on Electricity and the Environ., Helsinki, Finland, 1991. Editor: Gerrard Winstanley, Selections from His Works, 1944; Physical Factors and Modification of Radiation Injury, 1964; The Health and Environmental Effects of Electricity Generation-a Preliminary Report, 1974. Recipient Fed. Lab. Consortium award, 1990; Am. Cancer Soc. scholar, 1953-58; Commonwealth Fund grantee, 1955-62. Mem. AMA, Am. Assn. Cancer Rsch., Am. Soc. Clin. Investigation, Am. Soc. for Investigative Pathology, Soc. for Risk Analysis, Harvey Soc., Cosmos Club (Washington). Office: Brookhaven Nat Lab Upton NY 11973 Office Phone: 631-344-2004. Personal E-mail: leonardhmltn@aol.com. Business E-Mail: lhamilton@bnl.gov.

HAMILTON, STANLEY RALPH, pathologist; b. Ft. Wayne, Ind., Dec. 2, 1948; s. Ralph Albert and Anita (Lunsford) Hamilton; m. Cheryl Lynn Fitzpatrick, Oct. 30, 1971; children: Brian, Kimberly, Mark. AB in Zoology, Ind. U., 1970, MD, 1973. Diplomate in anat. and clin. pathology Am. Bd. Pathology. Intern, resident in pathology and lab. medicine Johns Hopkins U. Sch. Medicine and Hosp., Balt., 1973—79; from asst. prof. to prof. pathology & oncology Johns Hopkins U. Sch. Medicine, Balt., 1979—98; prof., head pathology and lab. medicine U. Tex. M. D. Anderson Cancer Ctr., Houston, 1998—. Editor: Br. Jour. Cancer, Jour. Pathology, Archives Pathol. Lab. Medicine. Recipient Lifetime Achievement award, Collaborative Group of Americas on Inherited Colorectal Cancer. Mem.: Am. Soc. Clin. Oncology, Arthur Purdy Stout Soc. Surg. Pathologists, Am. Assn. Cancer Rsch., Gastrointestinal Pathology Soc., U.S. and Can. Acad. Pathology, Am. Gastroent. Assn., Am. Soc. Investigative Pathology, Alpha Omega Alpha, Phi Beta Kappa. Office Phone: 713-792-2040. Business E-Mail: shamilto@mdanderson.org.

HAMILTON, STEVEN M., plastic surgeon; b. Houston, Aug. 25, 1954; MD, Baylor U., 1983. Cert. Plastic Surgery, 1992. Resident U. Tex. Health Sci. Ctr.; pvt. practice Houston; staff mem. St. Luke's Episcopal Hosp. Avocation: fishing. Office: 6624 Fannin St Ste 1650 Houston TX 77030 also: 22999 Highway 59, N, Ste 250 Kingwood TX 77339 Office Phone: 713 797 1007, 713 348-3344. Office Fax: 713 797 0633.

HAMILTON, THOMAS ALAN, medical association administrator; b. Phila., Feb. 2, 1950; BA, U. Colo., 1971; PhD, U. Oreg., 1976. Dept. chair Cleve. Clinic, 1987—. Prof. Case Western U. Sch. Medicine, 1998—2011; editor-in-chief Jour. Interferon and Cytokine Rsch., 2002—. Fellow: AAAS; mem.: Am. Assn. Immunology, Internat. Soc. Interferon and Cytokine Rsch., Soc. Leukocyte Biology. Office: Cleve Clinic 9500 Euclid Ave Cleveland OH 44195 Office Fax: 216-444-9329. Business E-Mail: hamiltt@ccf.org.

HAMLAT, ABDERRAHMANE, neurosurgeon; b. Tizi-Ouzou, Algeria, June 4, 1952; s. Larbi Hamlat and Tassadit Ben-Meziani. MD, Algiers U., 1973—79. Neurosurgeon Algiers U., 1981. Resident in neurosurgery Hopital Ait IDIR, Algiers, 1979—83, neurosurgeon, 1980—88, Hosp.Pontchaillou, Rennes, 1988—, Praticien Hospitalier, Rennes, 2006—. Cons. Ait Idir, 1998—. Contbr. scientific papers. Mem.: Societe De Neurooncology Bretonne, Algerian Soc. Neurosurgery, French Soc. Neurosurgery (assoc. Grand Diplome de neurosurgery 1993). Office: Hosp Pontchaillou Svc de neuroch Rue Henri le Guilloux 35000 Rennes France Office Fax: +33(0)299284180. Personal E-mail: hamlat.abd@wanadoo.fr. Business E-Mail: abderrahmane.hamlat@chu-rennes.fr.

HAMLIN, ROBERT HENRY, public health service officer, educator, management consultant; b. Cambridge, Mass., Apr. 2, 1923; s. Howard E. and Margaret E. (Henry) H.; m. Beate Kraschewski, Dec. 16, 1960; 1 son, Andrew Werner. AB summa cum laude, Ohio State U., 1944; BSM., Northwestern Med. Sch., 1945, B.M., 1946, MD with honors, 1947; M.P.H. magna cum laude, Harvard, 1952, JD, 1953. Diplomate: Am. Bd. Preventive Medicine. Intern Johns Hopkins Hosp., Balt., 1946-47; cons. Mass. commn. reporting, preparing and promulgating legislation on pub. and mental health and pub. welfare, 1950-53; 1st asst. to commnr. pub. health Mass., 1952-53; asst. prof. legal medicine Harvard Law Sch., 1952-57; lectr. pub. health law and adminstrn. Harvard Sch. Pub. Health, 1952-57, asso. prof. pub. health adminstrn., 1959-62, Roger Irving Lee prof. pub. health, 1962-65, chmn. dept. pub. health practice, 1963-65; v.p. Booz, Allen and Hamilton (mgmt. cons.), 1965-67; ind. mgmt. cons., 1968; chmn. bd. MACRO Systems, Inc. (mgmt. cons.), Washington, 1969-80; clin. prof. dept. comprehensive medicine Coll. Medicine, U. South Fla., 1980-83; acting dir., prof. pub. health program Coll. Pub. Health, U. South Fla., 1983; pres. United Health Techs., Inc. (mgmt. cons.), 1981—. Adj. prof. health adminstrn. Columbia U. Sch. Public Health and Adminstrv. Medicine, 1972-80; cons. Rockefeller Found., 1959-61; staff dir. spcl. commn. Harvard health services, 1953-54; mem. U.S. Commn. for UNESCO, 1958-60; dir. pub. health, Brookline, Mass., 1953-57; cons. Hoover Commn. II, 1954-55; asst. to sec. health, edn. and welfare, 1957-59; vis. lectr. pub. health adminstrn. and law Harvard, 1957-59 Contbr. articles profl. publs. U.S. del. 10th session gen. conf. UNESCO, Paris, 1958, pub. health adminstrn. cons. to pvt. orgns., state and local govts. Served as apprentice seaman USN, 1943-46; lt. (j.g.) M.C. USNR, 1947-49. Fellow Am. Pub. Health Assn.; mem. Mass. Med. Soc., Phi Beta Kappa, Phi Eta Sigma, Alpha Epsilon Delta, Alpha Omega Alpha, Delta Omega. Home Fax: 330-952-1615. Business E-Mail: rbhamlin@zoominternet.net.

HAMMADIEH, NAHED M., obstetrician, gynecologist; s. Mouhammed A. Hammadieh and Asma E. Ebrahem; m. Dareen A. Ganema, Aug. 31, 2004; children: Tarek N., Rama N. MD, Damascus U., Syria, 1989, U. Birmingham, 2005; student, Inst. Learning and Tchg. Higher Edn., 2004. Clin. rsch. fellow Birmingham (England) Women's Hosp., 1999—2001; sr. registrar Dept. Ob-gyn. Cardiff (Wales) U., 2002—. Faculty bd. endoscopic surgery team Dept. Ob-gyn. Cardiff (Wales) U., 2002—. Mem.: Brit. Arab Med. Assn. (mem. exec. com. 2003—05), Royal Coll. Ob-gyn. Achievements include research in the affect of transvaginal hydrosalpix aspiration on the IVF outcome. Office: Cardiff Univesity Department of Obstetrics & Gynaecology Heath Park Cardiff CF14 4XN England Home: 6 Lismore Drive B17 0TP Birmingham England Office Fax: 0044(0)292074722. Personal E-mail: nahed@doctors.org.uk. Business E-Mail: nhammadieh@cf.ac.uk.

HAMMAMI, MOUHANAD, pediatrician; b. Jan. 1967; Past pres. Mich. chpt. Nat. Arab Am. Med. Assn., exec. dir., 2008—. Recipient Leadership award (Internat. Grad. Physician), AMA Found., 2006. Office: Nat Arab Am Med Assn Ste 208 801 S Adams Rd Birmingham MI 48009 Home Phone: 734-524-0331; Office Phone: 248-646-3661. Business E-Mail: mhammami@naama.com.

HAMMAR, BJÖRN F.C., ophthalmologist; b. Sverige, June 3, 1963; MD, PhD, Karolinska Inst., 1993, Linköping U., 2008. Sr. cons. Skåne U. Hosp., 2003—. Mem.: EUNOS. Office: Skåne University Hosp Dept Ophthalmology Lund SE-22185 Sweden E-mail: hammar.lyngby@gmail.com.

HAMMAR, SHERREL LEYTON, retired medical educator; b. Caldwell, Idaho, May 21, 1931; m. Shirley; children: Kathryn M., David Jefferson. BA, Coll. Idaho, 1953; MD, U. Wash., 1957. Intern Mpls. Gen. Hosp., 1957-58; resident U. Wash., Seattle, 1958-60; instr. dept. pediat. U. Wash. Sch. Medicine, Seattle, 1962-64, asst. prof. dept. pediat., 1964-69, assoc. prof. dept. pediat., 1969-71, U. Hawaii, Honolulu, 1971-73; prof. U. Hawaii Sch. Medicine, Honolulu, 1973—2001; interim dean John A. Burns Sch. Medicine U. Hawaii, Honolulu, 1996-99, emeritus prof., 2001—06. Chief adolscent clinic U. Wash., 1964-65, acting dir. clin. tng. unit devel. & mental health ctr., 1964, asst., 1965-71, acting dir. clin. tng. unit child devel. and mental retardation ctr., 1970-71; dir. ambulatory pediatric svcs., chief adolescent medicine Kauikeolani Children's Hosp., Honolulu, 1971-72, dir. med. svcs. and tng., 1972-73, chief pediat., 1973—, dir. pediatric med. edn., 1979—; chmn. dept. pediat. U. Hawaii, 1973-97, residency program dir., 1973-97; cons. in field. Contbr. articles to profl. jours. Fellow U. Wash., 1960-62. Fellow APHA, Am. Acad. Pediat. (com. youth 1967-73, 75-81, sect. adolescent health, exec. coun. 1978-80, com. early childhood, adoption and dependent care 1990-92, task force on AIDS 1990-92); mem. AMA (med. sch. sect.), Western Soc. Pediatric Rsch., Hawaii Med. Assn. (pres. 2003-04), Ambulatory Pediatric Assn., Seattle Pediatric Soc., Honolulu County Med. Soc. (pres. 2005), Alpha Omega Alpha. Home Phone: 808-955-4735. Personal E-mail: lerram@aol.com.

HAMMEN, CONSTANCE L., psychology professor; PhD, U. Wis. Prof. clin. psychology UCLA, chmn. Dept. Clin. Psychology, 1993—2006, disting prof. psychology and psychiatry and biobehavioral sciences. Contbr. articles to profl. jours. Office: Dept Clin Psychology UCLA 1285 Franz Hall Box 951563 Los Angeles CA 90095-1563 Office Phone: 310-825-6085. Office Fax: 310-206 5895. E-mail: hammen@psych.ucla.edu.

HAMMER, GREGORY BENSON, anesthesiologist, pediatrician, educator; b. Chgo., June 1, 1955; s. Robert A. Hammer and Kate (Schamberg) Shapiro; m. Christina Pahl, Apr. 11, 1982; children: Maxfield Pahl, Alexa Lee. BS, U. Wis., 1977; MD, U. Ill., Chgo., 1982. Diplomate Am. Bd. Anesthesiology, Am. Bd. Pediatrics, Am. Bd. Critical Care Medicine. Intern Children's Hosp., Oakland, Calif., 1982-83, resident in pediatrics, 1983-85; resident in anesthesiology U. Pa. Hosp., Phila., 1985-87; fellow in critical care medicine, pediatric anesthesiology Children's Hosp., Phila., 1987-88; dir. pediatric anesthesiology, dir. pediatric ICU Calif. pacific Med. Ctr., San Francisco, 1988-95; assoc. dir. pediatric ICU Lucile Packard Children's Hosp.-Stanford (Calif.) U. Med. Ctr., 1995—. Prof. anesthesiology, Stanford U., LA, 2003-. Editor: Pediatric Neurosurgical Intensive Care, 1997. Mem. Am. Soc. Anesthesiologists, Am. Acad. Pediatrics, Soc. Critical Care Medicine, Soc. Pediatric Anesthesiologists. Office: Stanford U Med Ctr Pediatric Critical Care/Anesthesiology Dept Anesthesiology Stanford CA 94305-5640 Office Phone: 650-723-7835. Business E-Mail: ham@stanford.edu.

HAMMER, JOHN HENRY, II, retired hospital administrator; b. Bartlesville, Okla., Dec. 27, 1943; s. John Henry and Lucy (Macias) H.; children: John Henry, Erica, Megan. BBA, St. Joseph's Coll., 1966; student, U. Md., Europe, 1968-69; MBA, U. Ill., 1984. Project mgr. Econ. & Manpower Corp., NYC, 1971-73; asst. dir. human resources St. Catherine Hosp., East Chicago, Ind., 1974-80; pres. Employees Credit Union, East Chicago, Ind., 1974-80; dir. pers. Lakeview Med. Ctr., Danville, Ill., 1980-84, v.p., 1984-88, United Samaritans Med. Ctr., Danville, Ill., 1988-95; ret., 2007; asst. dir. ops. & maintenance U. Ill., 1997—2007. Bd. dirs. East Cen. Ill. Health Systems Agy., East Cen. Ill. Health Planning Orgn., Vermilion Area Cmty. Health Ctr. Chmn. De La Garza Career Ctr. Program Com., 1974-80, bd. dirs. Jr. Achievement of Danville, 1990-95, vice chmn., 1991, chmn. 1993-95; mem. adv. bd. McKinley Health Ctr., 2002-07; mem. edn. commn. St. Mary's Sch., Westville, Ill., 2009-10. Capt. USAF, 1967-71, to lt. col. USAFR, 1974-93. Mem. Ind. Soc. Hosp. Personnel Adminstrn. (chmn. 1976-77, dir. 1977-79, pres. 1979-80), Am. Coll. Healthcare Execs., Rotary (bd. dirs. 1990-92, pres. 1991). Roman Catholic. Avocations: photography, writing. Home: 218 W Ellsworth St Westville IL 61883-1232 Personal E-mail: hammer.martel@yahoo.com.

HAMMER, TERENCE MICHAEL, physician; b. Chgo., May 7, 1946; s. Albert S. and Minnetta Elizabeth (Nichols) H.; 1 child, Kathryn Gyo Hammer. BS, U. Ill., 1968; MD, Stanford U., 1973. Diplomate Am. Bd. Family Practice. Intern L.A. County-U. So. Calif. Med. Ctr., 1973—74; med. dir. Long Beach Health Dept. Drug Program, Calif., 1974—75; resident family medicine Contra Costa Med. Svcs., Martinez, Calif., 1975—77; pvt. practice family medicine Redondo Beach Med. Group, Calif., 1977—81, Family Practice Assocs., Torrance, Calif., 1981—96, Med. Inst. Little Co. of Mary Hosp., Torrance, 1996—2008, Family Med. Ctr. Torrance, Calif., 2009—; clin. asst. prof. family practice Sch. Medicine, U. Southern Calif., 2010—. Lectr. in field. Bd. trustees Peninsula Edn. Found., Palos Verdes, Calif., 1991-99; bd. examiners Malcolm Baldridge Nat. Quality Awards, 1999, 2001. Recipient Patient Choice's award, 2010; named Calif. Rep. of Yr., 2001; named one of America's Top Family Drs., Consumers Rsch. Coun. Am., 2002. Mem. Am. Coll. Physician Execs., Premier Health Med. Group (pres. 1991—), South Bay Ind. Physicians Med. Group (pres. emeritus). Lutheran. Avocations: fishing, art, swimming, writing. Office: Family Med Ctr Torrance 2900 Lomita Blvd Torrance CA 90505 Office Phone: 310-326-8600. Personal E-mail: hefish1@aol.com.

HAMMER, WADE BURKE, retired oral and maxillofacial surgeon, educator; b. Lakeland, Fla., Apr. 21, 1932; s. Orval Seown and Lilly Pearl (Wade) H.; m. Betty Dean Webb, June 22, 1956 (dec.); children: Robert Burke Hammer, Joanna Wade Hammer Dykes. AA, U. Fla., 1956; D.D.S., Emory U., 1960. Diplomate Am. Bd. Oral and Maxillofacial Surgery; Merchant Marine Master. Pvt. practice dentistry, Orange Park, Fla., 1960-61; resident in oral and maxillofacial surgery U. Pa. Grad. Sch. Medicine, Phila., 1961-62, Grady Meml. Hosp., Atlanta and Emory U., 1962-65; practice dentistry specializing in oral and maxillofacial surgery Atlanta, 1965-68; mem. staff Med. Coll. of Ga. Hosp., Augusta; asst. prof. oral and maxillofacial surgery Med. Coll. Ga., Augusta, 1968-71, assoc. prof., 1971-75, prof., 1975-93, prof. emeritus oral and maxillofacial surgery, 1993. Staff VA Hosp. Complex, Augusta, 1969-99; cons. Ft. Gordon Army Med. Ctr., 1970-93, Univ. Hosp., Augusta, 1968-93. Contbr. articles to profl. jours. Chmn. exec. com. Gen. Faculty Orgn. Med. Coll. Ga., 1988; mem. USCG Auxiliary. With USN, 1950-54, col. USAR, 1976-92, ret. Decorated Legion of Merit, Meritorious Svc. medal, Army Commendation medals (5), Bailiff and Grand Prior of Grand Priory of US, Hospitaler Order St. John of Jerusalem, Knight Sovereign Mil. Order of the Temple of Jerusalem. Fellow Am. Assn. Oral and Maxillofacial Surgeons (life), Am. Coll. Dentists, Am. Soc. Dental Anesthesiology; mem. ADA (life), Internat. Assn. Dental Rsch., Ga. Dental Assn., Ea. Dist. Dental Assn., Am. Assn. Dental Schs., Augusta Dental Soc., Ga. Soc. Oral and Maxillofacial Surgeons, Southeastern Soc. Oral and Maxillofacial Surgeons (pres. 1984-85), Res. Officers Assn. (Nat. Dental Surgeon 1990-92, Dept. of Ga. Pres. 1998-99, nat. councilman, 2003-06), Interallied Confedn. of Res. Officers (US. del. 1992-2002), Assn. Mil. Surgeons (life), USCG Aux., Exptl. Aircraft Assn.(pvt. pilot, mcht. marine master), Am. Legion, VFW, U.S. Army Order Mil. Med. Merit, U.S. Sailing Assn., Boat-U.S., Mil. Officers Assn. Am., Sigma Xi, Omicron Kappa Upsilon (pres. Supreme chpt. 1980-81). Methodist. Personal E-mail: wbhammer@aol.com.

HAMMERGREN, JOHN H., health products executive; BBA, U. Minn.; MBA, Xavier U. With Baxter Healthcare Corp./Am. Hosp. Corp. and Lyphomed Inc., 1981-91; pres. med./surgical divsn. Kendall Healthcare Products Co., Mansfield, Mass., 1991-96; corp. exec. v.p., pres., CEO supply mgmt. bus. McKesson HBOC, Inc., 1996-99; group pres, McKesson Health Systems, 1997—99; chief exec. officer supply chain mgmt. McKesson Corp. (formerly McKesson HBOC, Inc.), 1997—99; dir. McKesson Corp., 1999—; co-pres, co- CEO McKesson Corp. (formerly McKesson HBOC, Inc.), 1999—2001; pres., CEO McKesson Corp., 2001—, chmn. bd., 2002—. Dir. Nadro, S.A. de C.V., Mexico, Verispan LLC; bd. trustee Healthcare Leadership Coun. Recipient Cap Gemini Ernst & Young Leadership award for Global Integration, 2004, Warren Bennis award for Leadership, 2004. Office: McKesson Corp One Post St San Francisco CA 94104 *

HAMMERMAN, MARC RANDALL, nephrologist, educator; b. St. Louis, Sept. 29, 1947; s. Elmer and Lillian Hammerman; m. Nancy Tutt, Aug. 9, 1974; children: Seth, Megan. AB, Washington U., St. Louis, 1969, MD, 1972. Intern Barnes Hosp., St. Louis, 1972-73, resident, 1973-74, Mass. Gen. Hosp., Boston, 1976-77; instr. Washington U., St. Louis, 1977-78, asst. prof., 1979-84, assoc. prof., 1984-89, prof., 1989—, dir. renal div. Sch. Medicine, 1991—. Mem. study sect. NIH, 1990-95, investigator Am. Heart Assn., 1984; dir. Wash. U. O'Brien Ctr., 2007—. Contbr. over 200 sci. articles, revs. to profl. publs., chpts. to books. Lt. comdr. USPHS, 1974-76. NIH grantee, 1980—. Mem. Am. Fedn. for Clin. Rsch., Am. Soc. Clin. Investigation, Assn. Am. Physicians. Achievements include research in xenotransplantation of animal organs to treat kidney failure and diabetes in humans; the use of embryonic animal cells to prevent the rejection of transplanted organs by the human immune system; first to cure diabetic rats through the transplantion of embryonic pig pancreatic cells. Avocations: writing short stories, jewelry-making. Office: Washington U Sch Medicine Renal Div Box 8126 660 S Euclid Ave Saint Louis MO 63110-1010 Business E-Mail: mhammerm@domwustl.edu.

HAMMILL, STEPHEN CHARLES, cardiologist, medical educator; b. Denver, Feb. 26, 1948; s. Kenneth Milton and Virginia Bell Hammill; m. Karen Falbe; children: Noel Thomas, Eric Falbe, Stephen Gregory, Daniel Kenneth. MD, U. Colo., 1974. Diplomate Bd. Medicine Colo., 1974. Dir., heart rhythm svc. Mayo Clinic, Rochester, Minn., 1988—2006, prof. medicine, 1981—. Pres. Heart Rhythm Soc., Washington. Named Henry Plummer Disting. Physician, Mayo Clinic, 2008. Fellow: Heart Rhythm Soc. (Disting. Svc. award 2008), Am. Coll. Cardiology. Office: Mayo Clinic 200 First St SW Rochester MN 55906

HAMMMOND, KATE, biochemist, educator; b. Eng., Nov. 30, 1944; BSc with honors, London, 1966; PhD, Witwatersrand, 1977. Postdoc. rschr. St. Mary's Hosp. Med. Sch., London, 1978—80; rsch. officer South African Inst. Med. Rsch., 1981—82; lectr., sr. lectr., assoc. prof. U. Witwatersrand, 1982—99, prof., 2005—, United Arab Emirates U., 2000—05. Newsletter editor South African Assn. Clin. Biochemists, 1989—93, sec., 1993—98; project reviewer, evaluator Nat. Rsch. Found. South Africa, 1993. Rsch. grant, Nat. Cancer Assn. South Africa, South African Med. Rsch. Coun., Nat. Rsch. Found. South Africa, H. E. Griffin Cancer Trust, Terry Fox Cancer Rsch. Fund. Mem.: Assn. Clin. Biochemists (London), South African Assn. Clin. Biochemists, South African Biochem. Soc., Internat. Soc. Differentiation, Biochem. Soc. (London). Avocations: travel, photography, reading. Home: 31 Gleneagles Rd Greenside Johannesburg Gauteng 2193 South Africa Business E-Mail: kate.hammond@wits.ac.za.

HAMMON, JOHN WILLIAM, JR., medical educator, thoracic surgeon; b. Springfield, Mo., Mar. 9, 1942; m. Mary Lisa Hammon; children: Ian, Dudley, Daniel. BA, Drury Coll., 1964; MD, Tulane U., 1968. Diplomate Am. Bd. Surgery, 1978, Am. Bd. Thoracic Surgery, 2008. Intern Duke U. Med. Ctr., Durham, NC, 1968—69, resident,

1969—70, resident, gen./thoracic surgery, 1972—77, tchg. scholar cardiac surgery, 1977—78; asst. prof. surgery Vanderbilt U., Nashville, 1978—83, assoc. prof. surgery, 1983—89, prof. dept. cardiac and thoracic surgery, 1989—91; chief cardiac and thoracic surgery VA Hosp., Nashville, 1987—91; Howard Holt Bradshaw prof., chmn. Bowman Gray Sch. Medicine, Winston-Salem, NC, 1991—95; prof. surgery Sch. Medicine Wake Forest U., Winston-Salem, NC, 1995—2009; prof. surgery emeritus Walce Forest U. Sch. Med. Winstonsalem, NC, 2009—. Prin. investigator NIH Grants, 1979—2008; fed. drug. admstr. Cardiac Devices Panel, 2009—. Mem. editl. bd. Jour. Surg. Rsch., 1986—91, Cardiac Chronicle, 1986—91, Annals of Thoracic Surgery, 1991—2002, Jour. Cardiac Surgery, 1993—, Jour. Thoracic and Cardiovascular Surgery, 2006—. Lt. comdr US Naval Hosp., 1970—77. Recipient Disting. Alumni award, Drury Coll., 1989, 2001; scholar, NIH, 1974. Mem.: ACS (gov. 2002, membership com. 2002—04), Soc. Thoracic Surgeons (standard and ethics com. 2008—), N.C. Surg. Assn. (pres. 2006—07), Winston-Salem Surg. Assn. (pres. 1999—2000), So. Thoracic Surg. Assn. (v.p. 1999—2000, pres. 2007—08, pres.'s award for best sci. paper 1985), Am. Assn. Thoracic Surgery (residents com. 1999—2003, membership com. 2002—05, sci. and govt. affairs com. 2007—, sci. affairs and govt. relation com. 2007—), Omicron Delta Kappa. Avocations: golf, fishing. Office: Dept Cardiothoracic Surgery Medical Ctr Blvd Winston Salem NC 27157-1096 Office Phone: 336-716-6002. Office Fax: 336-716-3348. Business E-Mail: jhammon@wfubmc.edu. *

HAMMOND, CHARLES BESSELLIEU, obstetrician, gynecologist, educator; b. Ft. Leavenworth, Kans., July 24, 1936; s. Claude G. and Alice (Sims) H.; m. Peggy A. Hammond, June 21, 1958; children: Sharon L., Charles B. BS, The Citadel, 1958; MD, Duke U., 1961. Diplomate Am. Bd. Ob-Gyn. Intern in surgery Duke U., 1961-62, resident in ob-gyn, 1962-63, 66-69, fellow in reproductive endocrinology, 1963-64, asst. prof. dept. ob-gyn, 1969-73, asso. prof., 1973-78, prof., 1978-81, E.C. Hamblen prof. emeritus, 1981—, chmn., 1980—2002. Contbr. in field. Served with USPHS, 1964-66. Fellow Royal Coll. Ob-gyn. (ad eundeum), Soc. Ob-gyn. Can. (hon.); mem. AMA, Am. Fertility Soc. (pres. 1985), ACOG (chmn. dist. IV 1997-2000, pres. 2002), Am. Assn. Ob-Gyn. Found. (pres. 1996-2002), Assn. Profs. Obstetrics and Gynecology, Am. Gynecol. and Obstet. Soc. (pres. 1993-94), Soc. Gynecol. Investigation, Am. Gynecol. Soc., Am. Assn. Obstet. and Gynecology, N.C. Med. Soc., N.C. Soc. Obstetricians and Gynecologists (pres. 1985), Am. Gynecol. Club (pres. 1994), Inst. of Medicine. Presbyterian. Home: 2827 McDowell Rd Durham NC 27705-5604 Office: Duke U Med Ctr PO Box 3853 Durham NC 27710 Business E-Mail: hammo005@mc.duke.edu.

HAMMOND, DENNIS CLYDE, plastic surgeon, educator; b. Saginaw, Mich., May 2, 1959; BS with honors in Biology, U. Mich., Ann Arbor, 1981; MD with Distinction, U. Mich. Med. Sch., Ann Arbor, 1985. Cert. Am. Bd. Plastic Surgery, lic. Mich., 1986, Tenn., 1990, Wis., 1991, diplomate Nat. Bds., 1986. Intern and resident, gen. surgery Blodgett Meml. Med. Ctr., St. Mary's Health Svcs., Grand Rapids, Mich., 1985—88; resident, plastic and reconstructive surgery Grand Rapids Area Med. Edn. Ctr., Grand Rapids, Mich., 1988—90; fellow, aesthetic and reconstructive breast surgery and cosmetic surgery Inst. for Aesthetic and Reconstructive Surgery, Baptist Hosp., Nashville, 1990—91; fellow, hand and microvascular surgery Med. Coll. Wis., Milw., 1991—92; pvt. practice Ctr. Breast Body Contouring, Grand Rapids, Mich.; asst. clin. prof., dept. surgery Mich. State U., East Lansing. Invited visiting professorships; presenter in field. Contbr. several articles to profl. jours., chapters to books. Recipient Best Paper award, Pharmacological Manipulation of Rat Flaps: Fact or Friction, Ann. Plastic Surgery Senior Residents Conf., NY, 1990, First prize President's award, Am. Roentgen Ray Soc., 1991, Clifford C. Snyder award, Computerized Morphologic Analysis of Tissue Expander Shape Using a Biomechanical Model, best paper, Ann. Mtg. Plastic Surgery Rsch. Coun., Charlottesville, Va., 1991, Doran Scholar award for rsch. project and publication, Endoscopic Tattooing of the Colon: Clinical Experience, 1992; named one of America's Top Plastic Surgeons, MORE Mag., Country's Top Breast Surgeons, America's Top Doctors. Mem.: Am. Assn. Plastic Surgeons, Am. Cancer Soc. (bd. dirs.), Mich. Acad. Plastic Surgeons (First prize clin. award 1994, First prize basic sci. award 1988), Mich. State Med. Soc., Kent County Med. Soc., Midwest Assn. Plastic Surgeons (First prize clin. award 1988, First prize clin. award for Latissimus Dorsi Musculocutaneous Flaps and Tissue Expanders/Implants Immediate Breast Reconstruction 1995), Am. Soc. for Aesthetic Plastic Surgery, Am. Soc. Plastic and Reconstructive Surgeons, ACS, Gilda's Club of Grand Rapids (mem. adv. bd.). Achievements include invention of revolutionary SPAIR technique. Office: Ctr Breast Body Contouring 4070 Lake Dr SE Ste 202 Grand Rapids MI 49546 Office Phone: 616-464-4420. Office Fax: 616-464-4354. E-mail: office@dennischammond.com.

HAMMOND, DOUGLAS ALAN, physician; b. Florence, Ala., Jan. 18, 1965; s. Harold Jerry and Peggy Ann (Newbern) Hammond; m. Kathy Dale Belue, Aug. 6, 1988; children: William, John, Christian. BS, U. Ala., 1986; MD, U. Ala. Sch. Medicine, 1991. Cert. Am. Bd. Surgery, 1997, Nat. Bd. Med. Examiners. Surgery resident Meth. Hosps., Memphis, 1991—94, U. Tenn., 1994—96; ptnr. Jackson Surg. Assocs., Montgomery, Ala., 1996—2001, Memphis Surg. Specialists, 2001—. Cons. Wyeth Pharms., 2003. Fellow: Southeastern Surg. Congress, Am. Coll. Surgeons; mem.: AMA. Presbyn. Avocations: reading, travel. Office: Memphis Surg Specialists 1325 Eastmoreland Ste 410 Memphis TN 38104 Office Phone: 901-725-1921.

HAMMOND, GRAEME LORD, surgeon, educator; b. NYC, Jan. 30, 1933; married; 2 children. BS, Denison U., Granville, Ohio, 1958; MD, McGill U., Montreal, Can., 1962. Diplomate Am. Bd. Surgery, Am. Bd. Thoracic Surgery; lic. surgeon, N.Y., Mass., Conn. Intern in surgery Royal Victoria Hosp., Montreal, 1962-63; resident in surgery Mass. Gen. Hosp., Boston, 1963-65, 66-68, clin. rsch. fellow in surgery, 1965-66; from asst. prof. to assoc. prof. surgery Yale U. Sch. Medicine, New Haven, 1969—79, prof. surgery, 1979—2006, sr. rsch. scientist, 2006—08, prof. surgery emeritus, 2008; attending surgeon Yale-New Haven Hosp., 1969—2008, prin. investigator lung transplant program, 1988—2008. Vis. rsch. scientist dept. biochemistry Hormone Rsch. Lab., U. Calif., San Francisco, 1981-82; mem. examining bd. Nat. Bd. Med. Examiners, 1987-90. Mem. editorial bd. Thoracic and Cardiovascular Surgery, 4th edit., 1982, 5th edit., 1990, 6th edit., 1996. With U.S. Army, 1953-55. Fellow USPHS, 1965-66. Mem. Am. Surg. Assn., Soc. Univ. Surgeons, Am. Assn. Thoracic Surgery, Am. Coll. Surgeons, Am. Heart Assn. (fellow coun. cardiovascular surgery, established investigator 1972-76), Am. Soc. for Biochemistry and Molecular Biology, New England Surg. Soc., Internat. Soc. Cardiovascular Surgery, Internat. Soc. Heart Rsch., Assn. Acad. Surgery, Soc. Thoracic Surgeons, Internat. Soc. for Heart and Lung Transplantation, The Transplantation Soc., The European Assn. for Cardio-Thoracic Surgery, Soc. Vascular Surgery. Office Phone: 203-285-2702. Business E-Mail: graeme.hammond@yale.edu.

HAMMOND, HAROLD LOGAN, oral and maxillofacial pathologist, retired educator; b. Hillsboro, Ill., Mar. 18, 1934; s. Harold Thomas and Lillian (Carlson) Hammond; m. Sharon Bunton Hammond, Aug. 1, 1954 (dec. 1974); 1 child, Connie; m. Pat J. Palmer, June 3, 1986. Student, Millikin U., 1953—57, Roosevelt U., Chgo., 1957—58; DDS, Loyola U., Chgo., 1962; MS, U. Chgo., 1967. Diplomate Am. Bd. Oral & Maxillofacial Pathology. Intern. U. Chgo. Hosps., Chgo., 1962—63, resident, 1963—66, chief resident oral pathology, 1966—67; asst. prof. oral pathology U. Iowa, Iowa City, 1967—72, assoc. prof., 1972—80, assoc. prof., dir. surg. oral pathology, 1980—83, prof., dir., 1983—2004, prof. emeritus oral pathology, radiology and medicine, 2004; dir. emeritus, Surg. Oral Pathology Lab., 2004—. Cons. pathologist Hosp. Gen. de Managua, Nicaragua, 1970—90, VA Hosp., Iowa City, 1977—2004; cons. editor Revista de la Assn., Nicaragua, 1970—71; revista de la Federacion Odontologica de Centroamerica, Panama. Contbr. articles to profl. jours. Scholar, Mosby Pub. Co., 1962. Fellow: AAAS; mem.: AAUP, Am. Assn. Dental Rsch., Am. Dental Assn., North America Soc. Head & Neck Pathologists, Internat. Assn. Dental Rsch., Internat. Assn. Oral Pathologists, NY Acad. Scis., Am. Men & Women of Sci., Am. Acad. Oral & Maxillofacial Pathology. Avocations: antiques, collecting gambling paraphernalia, collecting toys. Home: 1732 Brown Deer Rd Coralville IA 52241-1157 Office: U Iowa Dental Sci Bldg Iowa City IA 52242-1001

HAMMOND, JANET, pharmaceutical executive; m. Peter Potgieter. ScM in Clin. Investigation, Johns Hopkins U.; PhD, MD, Capetown U., South Africa. Head clin. drug discovery virology GlaxoSmith-Kline; med. leader early clin. rsch. team HIV Early Devel. and Virology Life Cycle Mgmt.; group dir. Bristol-Myers Squibb; sr. v.p. global med. affairs Valeant Pharmaceuticals Internat., chief med. officer; attending physician West LA Veterans Andminstrn. Hosp.; v.p. translational medicine-virology in pharmaceutical rsch. and early devel. Hoffmann-La Roche Inc., Nutley, NJ, 2011—. Adj. faculty mem. UCLA. Reviewer Lancet, European Jour. of Med. Microbiology, various publs. Recipient numerous awards. Mem.: Southern African Critical Care Soc., Infectious Diseases Soc. of America, Internat. Soc. of Infectious Diseases, Coll. of Medicine of South Africa, Global Safety Bd. (chair). Achievements include launch preparations for 3 new drugs; contbn. in new drug applications and mktg. authorization application. Office: Hoffmann-La Roche Incorporated 340 Kingsland St Nutley NJ 07110 Office Phone: 973-235-5000.

HAMMOND, RAYMOND WILLIAM, retired pharmacotherapy specialist; b. Port Arthur, Tex., May 16, 1944; s. Woodrow Wilson and Anna Mary (Brockman) H.; m. Sandra Louise Borel, Feb. 1, 1964; children: Cynthia Lynn, Jeffrey Carl. BS in Pharmacy, U. Houston, 1973; PharmD, U. Tenn. Ctr. Health Scis., 1981. Lic. pharmacist, Tex.; cert. pharmacotherapy specialist. Staff pharmacist USPHS Hosp., SI, NY, 1974-75; dep. chief pharmacist Med. Ctr. Fed. Prisoners, Springfield, Mo., 1975-77, USPHS Outpatient Clinic, Savannah, Ga., 1977-78, chief pharmacist, 1978-79, USPHS Outpatient Clinic, Port Arthur, Tex., 1981; pharmacist USPHS Indian Hosp., Whiteriver, Ariz., 1981-83; asst. chief inpatient clin. pharmacy services W.W. Hastings Indian Hosp., Tahlequah, Okla., 1983-91; chief customer svc. and quality assurance br. divsn. Supply Mgmt. Indian Health Svc., Albuquerque, 1991-94; asst. prof. pharmacy, experiential programs coord. Coll. Pharmacy, U. N.Mex., dir. drug utilization rev. program, 1994-97; clin. pharmacy corrd. Sierra Med. Ctr., El Paso, Tex., 1997-98; clin. assoc. prof. pharmacy coop. pharmacy program U. Tex., Austin and El Paso, 1998-99; assoc. dean practice programs Coll. Pharmacy U. Houston, 1999—2010; ret., 2010. Clin. resource speaker SW Okla. State U. Sch. Pharmacy, 1984-91; adj. asst. prof. Northeastern State U. Coll. of Optometry, Tahlequah, Okla., 1986-90; adj. assoc. prof., 1991; mem. Pharmacotherapy Splty. Coun., 1994-2000; mem. adv. bd. Cherokee County Elder Care. Contbr. chpt. to books and articles to profl. jours. Mem. instl. rev. bd. NE State U., Tahlequah, 1985-91; bd. dir. Cherokee County Hospice Assn., 1986-87. Capt. USPHS, 1974-94. Fellow Am. Coll. of Clin. Pharmacists; mem. Am. Soc. Health Systems Pharmacists, Tex. Soc. Health-Sys. Pharmacists, N.Mex. Soc. Hosp. Pharmacists (pres. 1997), Commd. Officers Assn. USPHS, Mensa, Rho Chi., Am. Pharmacists Assn., Military Officers Assn. America Roman Catholic. Avocations: photography, backpacking, fishing, beer and winemaking, golf, woodworking, guitar. Home: 3015 Marble Falls Dr Pearland TX 77584-7067

HAMOLSKY, MILTON WILLIAM, retired physician; b. Lynn, Mass., May 25, 1921; s. Israel and Sophie (Cremer) H.; m. Sandra Oelbaum, Feb. 18, 1979; children: Deborah Lynne, John Stephen, David James, Joy, Robin. AB, Harvard U., 1943, MD, 1946; Ad Eundum, Brown U., 1964. Diplomate Am. Bd. Internal Medicine. Intern Beth Israel Hosp., Boston, 1946-47, resident, 1947-48, 50-51, asst. physician, dir. endocrine clinic, 1957-63; instr. Harvard U. Med. Sch., 1951-55, asst. prof. medicine, 1955-63; prof. med. sci. Brown U., 1963-87, prof. emeritus, 1987—2008; physician-in-chief R.I. Hosp., Providence, 1963-87, W&I Hosp., Providence, 1981-87, U.S. Vets. Adminstrn. Hosp., 1981-87. Vis. asst. prof. biochemistry Brandeis U., 1958-59; vis. Commonwealth fellow Coll. de France, 1960-62; chief adminstrv. officer R.I. Bd. Med. Licensure and Discipline, 1987-2001; mem. Providence Pub. Sch. Bd., 2003-06, v.p., 2004-06; bd. govs. Lifespan Hosps., 2003-08; mem. Bd. Home and Hospice Care RI, 2007-08; exec. com. Diet Counseling Svc. Obstet. Health Care Com.; pres. Zlinkoff Found. Med. Edn. and Rsch., 1989-95; pres. Dolen Found., 1989-95; chmn. adv. com. Comty. Health Ctrs., 1990-08; bd. trustees R.I. Hosp., 1986-97, hon. trustee, 2004-08; cons. Roger Univ. Bradley Hosps.; acting dir. R.I. Dept. Health, 1995. Author: Thyroid Testing, 1968; contbr. numerous articles on endocrinology to profl. publs. Trustee Planned Parenthood, Providence, R.I. Child Guidance Clinic, Camp Jori, Providence, R.I. Hosp., 1986-97; mem. Bd. Pub. Schs. Edn. Com., 2003-, v.p., bd. 2004-. Served as capt. M.C., U.S. Army, 1948-50. Recipient Henry A. Christian award Harvard U. Med. Sch., 1946, Mallinckrodt award as founder nuclear medicine, 1977, W.W. Keen disting. svc. award Brown U., Am. Heart Assn. Hon. John Chafee award Cmty. Svc., 2002; named to R.I. Heritage Hall of Fame, 1996; Milton Hamolsky Ann. Outstanding Physician of Yr. award named for him, 2001-; tchg. fellow Tufts U., 1950-51, Harvard Univ., 1950-51, rsch. fellow 1951-52, Damon Runyon rsch. fellow 1951-52. Mem. A.C.P. (master gov. R.I. chpt., Milton W. Hamolsky lifetime svc. award 1999), AMA, Am. Thyroid Assn., Endocrine Soc., Am. Physiol. Soc., Soc. Clin. Investigation, Am. Fedn. Clin. Research, R.I. Diabetes Soc. (pres.), R.I. Heart Assn. (pres.) Home: 150 Arlington Ave Providence RI 02906-2330

HAMORI, CHRISTINE, plastic surgeon, educator; MD, Tulane U. Diplomate Am. Bd. Plastic Surgery, state lic. Mass. Intern gen. surgery Boston Univ., resident gen. surgery; asst. prof., surgery Boston Med. Ctr., 1996—2002; fellow plastic surgery Univ. Pa., clin. instr., 2004—06; pvt. practice Christine Hamori Cosmetic Surgery + Skin Spa; hosp. affiliations include South Shore Hosp., Jordan Hosp., Nantucket Cottage Hosp. Appeared in (TV shows) WCVBTV, Channel 5 News, The Montel Williams Show, The Doctors. Fellow: Am. Coll. of Surgeons; mem.: Am. Soc. for Aesthetic Plastic Surgery, Am. Soc. of Plastic Surgeons. Office: Christine Hamori Cosmetic Surgery + Skin Spa Ste 28 95 Tremont St Duxbury MA 02332 Office Phone: 781-934-2200. Office Fax: 781-934-7301.

HAMOS, JULIE E., state official, former state legislator; b. Hungary, 1949; m. Alan Greiman. BA, Washington U., 1972; JD, George Washington U., 1975. Staff atty. Subcommittee on Oversight US House Ways & Means Com., 1975—77; founder Legislature Support Ctre. Low-income Families & Minorities, 1977—79; legis. dir., polit. action dir. America Fedn. State, County, & Municipal Employees, Chgo., 1979—81; legis. liaison, policy adv. Cook County State's Atty., 1981—84, dir. Child Support Enforcement Divsn., 1984—88; dep. campaign mgr. Richard M. Daley for Mayor, 1988—89; founder Julie E. Hamos & Associates, 1988—; mem. Dist. 18 Ill. House of Reps., 1999—2010; chmn. Workforce Devel. Task Force, 1999—2010; mem. Appropriations Human Services Com., 1999—2010; dir. Ill. Dept. Health Care & Family Services, Chgo., 2010—. Recipient Nat. award, American Pub. Transp. Assn., 2008; named Woman of Yr., Jewish News, 2008; named a Woman to Watch, Crain's Chgo. Bus., 2011; named one of 25 Women to Watch, 2007; fellow Harvard U. John F. Kennedy Sch. Govt. for Sr. Executives in State & Local Govt., 2004. Democrat. Office: Ill Dept Healthcare & Family Services 210 South Grand Ave East Springfield IL 62763 *

HAMPEL, KLAUS ERICH, retired gastroenterologist; b. Leipzig, Germany, Mar. 18, 1932; s. Erich and Maria (Baldus) H.; 1 son, Dierk Johannes. MD, SUNY, Stony Brook, 1960; Habilitation, Free U., Berlin, 1967. Med. asst. Med. Clinic, Free U., Berlin, 1960-67; lectr., sr. registrar Free U. Med. Sch., 1967-69, prof., head gastroent. unit, 1969-97, head diet sch., 1977-97; dean U. Klinikum Charlottenburg, 1976-78; ret., 1997; with dept. medicine, divsn. nephrology intensive med. care U. Berlin, 2001. Author papers on cytogenetics, hematology, gastroenterology, ethical problems in medicine. Mem. Am. Gastroenterol. Assn. (sr.).

HAMPTON, JAMES WILBURN, hematologist, oncologist; b. Durant, Okla., Sept. 15, 1931; s. Hollis Eugene and Ouida (Mackey) Hampton; m. Carol McDonald, Feb. 22, 1958; children: Jaime, Clay, Diana, Neal. BA, U. Oklahoma, 1952, MD, 1956. Int. U. Okla. Hosps., 1956-57, res.; instr. to prof. U. Okla., Oklahoma City, 1959-77; clin. prof. med., 1977—. Mem. admissions bd., 1965—; bd. dirs., 1995—2006; head hematology/oncology, 1972—77; head hematology, mem. Okla. Med. Rsch. Found., Oklahoma City, 1972—77; dir. cancer prog. and med. oncology Bapt. Med. Ctr., 1977—85; med. dir. Cancer Ctr. S.W., 1985—94, Troy and dollie Smith Cancer Ctr., 1994—; mem. Internat. Com. Thrombosis and Hemostasis; cons. NIH, Biomed. and Nat. Cancer Inst., Karolinska Inst., Stockhom; vis. scientist Career Devel. Award, 1966—67; vis. prof. U. NC, Chapel Hill, 1966; founder Stewart Wolf Soc., 1967, pres., 1990—92; founder Robert Montgomery Bird Soc., 1973, pres., 1996—98. Contbr. articles to profl. jours. Chmn. Network Cancer Prevention and Control Rsch. Am. Indians/Alaska Natives Nat. Cancer Inst.; mem. Interncultural Cancer Coun., 1996—, chair-elect, 2000—01, chair, 2001—02; initiator Hospice Oklahoma County, 1990—; bd. dirs. Am. Cancer Soc., mem. at large, nat. bd. dirs., 1990—96; mem. com. task force Cancer Socio-Economically Disadvantaged, 1990—2002; chmn. Okla. divsn. svc. and rehab. com., collaborating ptnr. Pres. Bush Dialogue on Cancer, 1999—; chmn. Okla. Pain Initiative, 1996; mem. adv. com. Office Minority Health NIH, 1996—99; co-chmn. Save St. Paul's Episcopal Cathedral Com., 1983; chmn. bishop's Okla. com. Indian work, mem. province VII Indian com., alt. del. Diocesan Conv. Okla., 1991—95, 2000—05; mem. coun. combating racism Epis. Ch. Am., 1995—97, del. to elect bishop to Okla., 2007, del. to Diocesan Conv., 2007. Recipient Humanitarian award, ACS, 1999, honor by Lakota Tribe at Mayo Clinic, 1999, Leap of Faith award, Intercultural Cancer Coun., 2006; named Physician of the Yr., U. Okla. Alumni Assocs., 1998; Career Devel. grantee, NIH, 1966—76. Fellow: ACP; mem.: AMA (mem. minority affairs consortium, mem. steering com. 1997—2000), Intercultural Cancer Coun. (chairperson 2003), Am. Psychosomatic Soc., So. Soc. Clin. Investigation, Am. Soc. Clin. Oncology, Am. Soc. Hematology, Assn. Am. Pathologists, Am. Phyhsiol. Soc., Assn. Am. Indian Physicians (pres. 1978—79, 1988—89, Indian Physician of the Yr. award 1987), Internat. Soc. Thrombosis and Hemostasis, Oklahoma County Med. Soc. (editor bull. 1981—, bd. dirs. 1982—85, 1989—91), Ctrl. Soc. Clin. Rsch. (assoc. editor Jour. Lab. and Clin. Med. 1975—76), Am. Fedn. Clin. Rsch. (pres. midwest sect. 1970—71), English Speaking Union, Blue Cord Club, Oklahoma City Golf and Country Club, Chaine des Rotisseurs. Home: 1414 N Hudson Ave Oklahoma City OK 73103-3721 Office: Mercy Cancer Ctr 4205 McCenly Blvd Ste 375 Oklahoma City OK 73120 Office Phone: 405-749-0415. Business E-Mail: james.hampton@mercy.net.

HAMRA, SAMEER T., plastic surgeon, educator; b. Ponca City, Okla., July 16, 1937; MD, U. Okla., 1963. Diplomate Am. Bd. Surgery, 1970, Am. Bd. Plastic Surgery, 1977. Intern gen. surgery U. Okla., 1963—64, resident plastic surgery, 1964—68, NYU Med. Ctr., NYC, 1970—73; fellowship surgery U. Lausanne, Switzerland, 1965—66; staff mem. Mary Shiels Hosp., Dallas; assoc. clin. prof. plastic surgery U. Tex. Southwestern Med. Ctr., Dallas. Mem.: Am. Soc. Plastic Surgeons, Am. Assn. Plastic Surgeons, Am. Soc. Aesthetic Plastic Surgery. Office: 9301 North Central Expressway #551 Dallas TX 75231-9080 Home: 9301 N Central Expy Ste 551 Dallas TX 75231-0819 Office Phone: 866-773-9181. Office Fax: 214-754-9080. E-mail: drhamra@drhamra.com.

HAMREN, NANCY VAN BRASCH, office manager; b. LA, Feb. 2, 1947; d. Milton Carl and Winifred (Taylor) Van Brasch; m. Jerome Arthur Hamren, Feb. 14, 1981; children: Emily Allison, Meredith Ann. Student, Pasadena City Coll., 1964-65, San Francisco State Coll., 1966-67, U. Oreg., 1975-79. Bookkeeper/office mgr. Springfield Creamery, Eugene, Oreg., 1969—, mem.; past pres., bd. dirs. Oreg. Dairy Industries. Originator Nancy's Yogurt, Nancy's Cultured Dairy Products. Active Oreg. Shakespearean Festival, Ashland, 1986, Planned Parenthood, Sta. KLCC Radio; mem. Willamette Valley Sustainable Food Alliance; pres. Oreg. Dairy Industries; bd. dir., v.p. Internat. Probiotics Assn. Mem.: Slow Food Movement, Oreg. Country Fair, Provender Alliance, Conservation Internat., Oreg. Pub. Broadcasting, Wilderness Soc., N.Am. Truffling Soc. Democrat. Avocations: gourmet cooking, gardening, walking, wine tasting, reading.

HAMRICK, HARVEY J., pediatrician; b. Rutherfordton, NC, July 8, 1940; MD, U. NC Sch. Medicine, 1967. Intern, pediat. NC Meml. Hosp., Chapel Hill, 1967—68, resident, pediat., 1968—70, chief resident, pediat., 1970—71, fellow, pediat., 1972; hosp. appointment U NC Hosps., Chapel Hill, dir., pediat. residency tng. program; prof., pediat. U NC Sch. Medicine. Contbr. articles to profl. jours. Office: U NC Pediat Edn Office 30137 NC Womens Hosp 101 Manning Dr CB# 7593 UNC Sch Medicine Chapel Hill NC 27599-7593 Fax: 919-966-8419.

HAMSAYEH, NILOUFER G., dentist; 1 child. BA in Psychol., UC, San Diego, BSDS; DDS, UC, San Francisco. Private practice dentist, San Francisco. Mem. bd. dir. San Francisco Food Bank. Office: 500 Sutter St Ste 615 San Francisco CA 94102 *

HAMVAS, AARON, medical educator; b. Yankton, SD, Aug. 19, 1956; BS, Rensselaer Poly. Inst., 1977; MD, Wash. U. Sch. Medicine, 1981. Prof., pediat. Wash. U. Sch. Medicine, 1990—. Mem.: Am. Thoracic Soc., Am. Pediatric Soc. Avocations: bicycling, tennis. Office: Divsn Newborn Medicine Box 8116 Saint Louis MO 63110 Office Fax: 314-454-4633. Business E-Mail: hamvas@kids.wustl.edu.

HAMZA, AHMED MOHAMED, pediatrician, researcher; b. Cairo, Aug. 17, 1971; s. Mohamed Hamza Sayed El-Ahl and Sawsan Ahmed Ragha; m. Hala Mostafa El-Tamimi, Feb. 25, 2007; 1 child, Mohamed. MBBCh, Ain-Shans U., 1996; MSc, Zagazig U., 2002; MHSC, Inst. Health Mgmt., 2003. House officer Ain-Shams U. Hosp., Cairo, 1996—97; registrar Mil. Med. Acad., Cairo, 1997—98, Zagazig U. Hosp., Egypt, 1998—99; sr. registrar Tabarak Hosps. Group, Cairo, 2000—01, chief med. officer, 2001—04, adv. bd., 2002—, v.p., 2004—. Asst. rschr. Nat. Rsch. Ctr., 2006—. Contbr. articles to profl. jours. Bd.mem. Eqyptian Soc. Prevention and Treatment of Disease, 2001—, treas., 2003—; bd. mem. Egyptian Judo Aikido & Sumo Fedn., [illegible], 2004—, treas., 2007—. Mem.: SPIE, Inst. Healthcare Mgmt., Am. Telemedicine Assn., Egyptian Soc. Preventive Medicine (treas.), Egyptian Soc. Neonatology, MEETUS Alumni Network. Moslem. Achievements include research in application of a laser for diagnosis and treatment of neonatal jaundice; invention of mobile LED photography for treatment of neonatal jaundice. Avocation: Judo (nat. champion 1990-96). Office: Tabarak Childrens Hosp 3, Hussain Zohdi St Golfland Hiliopolis 11361 Cairo Egypt Office Fax: 00202-26903274. Personal E-mail: ahmed_hamza_1999@yahoo.com.

HAN, ANTHONY, anesthesiologist; b. Seoul, Republic of Korea, Apr. 3, 1960; s. Jung Keun Han and Sun Bok Woo; m. Susan Han; children: A.J., Ricky, James. BS, Seoul Nat. U., 1981, MD, 1985; MS in Anesthesiology, Cath. U., Seoul, 1998, PhD in Physiology, 2001. Cert. Am. Bd. Anesthesiology (subspecialty in pain mgmt.), Am. Bd. Family Practice, Am. Acad. Pain Medicine, Korean Bd. Family Practice, Korean Bd. Pain Medicine, Korean Bd. Anesthesiology. Intern in family medicine East Tenn. State U. Coll. Medicine, Kingsport, 1988—89; resident in family medicine U. Tenn. Coll. Medicine, Memphis, 1989—91; resident in anesthesiology U. Miss. Med. Ctr., Jackson, 1991—93; fellow in anesthesiology and pain medicine, instr. U. Md. Med. Ctr., Balt., 1994; pvt. practice N.W. Med. Ctr., Balt., 1995; staff anesthesiologist, dir. pain mgmt. ctr. Samsung Med. Ctr., SungKyunKwan U., Seoul, 1995—2001, instr. anesthesiology and pain medicine, 1997—99, asst. prof. anesthesiology and pain medicine, 1999—2001; assoc. prof. Hangang Sacred Heart Hosp., Hallym U. Coll. Medicine, Seoul, 2001—, staff anesthesiologist, 2001—. Mem. rsch. proposal rev. bd. Korea Rsch. Found., 2002, 05; mem. clin. pharmacology unit proposal rev. bd. Korean Health Tech. Planning and Evaluation Bd., 2004; spkr. in field. Contbr. articles to profl. jours.; co-author: Pain Management Preview, 1998, Textbook of Intravenous Anesthesia, 1998, Pain Medicine, 2000, Basics of Anesthesia, 2000, IV-PCA Guide, 2001, On the Study and Practice of Intravenous Anesthesia, 2002. Vol. med. svc. Rafael Cath. Migratory Fgn. Workers Clinic, 2005—. Recipient Physician's Recognition award, AMA, 2003, Silver medal, Mighty Hallym Photography Contest, Seoul, 2004, Bronze medal, 2005, 2d pl. art exhbn., Am. Soc. Anesthesiologists, 2005; grantee, Organon, Inc., 2002, Il Song Rsch. Inst., 2004, 2005, Korean Rsch. Found., 2005, Korean Health Industry Devel. Inst., 2005. Fellow: Am. Acad. Family Physicians; mem.: AMA, Korean Pain Soc. (bd. exams. com. 1998—2001, publs. com. 1998—2001, jour. publs. com. 1999—2001), Korean Soc. Anesthesiologists (med. ins. com. 2000—02, sec. med. terminology rev. com. 2003, task force team for practice guidelines 2003—04, Abbott Young Investigators award 2004), European Soc. Anesthesiologists, Am. Acad. Regional Anesthesia and Pain Medicine, Internat. Assn. for Study of Pain, Am. Acad. Pain Medicine, Am. Acad. Anesthesiologists, Soc. Tchrs. Family Medicine. Avocations: landscape photography, trekking, swimming. Home: 207-803 Hyundai 2d apt Gae Po-Ding Gang Nam-Ku 135-240 Seoul Republic of Korea E-mail: athan@unitel.co.kr.

HAN, BYUNG IN, neurologist; b. Gyungsan, Gyeongsangbuk-do, Republic of Korea, Feb. 27, 1965; s. Jong Gun Han and Jung Hee Kim; m. Hye Young Chung, Mar. 1, 1999; 1 child, Yoon Sik. MD, Kyungpook Nat. U., Daegu, 1990. Cert. med. dr. Ministry Health and Welfare, Korea, 1990. Chmn. Daegu Hapkido Assn., 2007—. Cons. Fieldwork Internat. Healthcare, Seoul, Republic of Korea, 2007—. Exhibitions include Painting; contbr. articles to profl. jours. First lt. Med. Divsn., 1991—94, Jeollabuk-do, Muju-gun. Mem.: Asian Neurosonology Rsch. Group, Am. Tinnitus Assn., Korean Fedn. Environ. Movement, Korean Neurol. Assn. Achievements include invention of a vessel model of the circle of Willis; research in trans cranial doppler, vertigo, pressure ulcer. Office: Do Neurology Clinic 11th Fl Namsandong 925-2 Banwol Med Tower Daegu 700-440 Republic of Korea

HAN, CHANG WHAN, orthopedist, educator; b. Kunsan, Republic of Korea), Oct. 13, 1964; s. Lee Do Han and Jung Dan Park; m. Ji Sook Lee, July 1, 1989; children: Jung Hyun, Soo Hyun. MD, Cath. U. Korea, Seoul, 2006—06, PhD, 2006. The chmn. of the arthritic ctr. Daejeon St. Mary's Hosp., Daejeon, 2002—. Contbr. articles to profl. jour. Grantee, Korean Seoul city Tissue Engring., 2005—.

HAN, CHUNHUI, physicist; b. China, Apr. 12, 1976; PhD, U. Mich., 2003. Med. physicist, Hope, 2004. Mem.: Am. Assn. Physicists Medicine. Office: 1500 Duarte Rd Duarte CA 91010 Personal E-mail: hanchunhui@gmail.com.

HAN, DENNIS, ophthalmologist, educator; b. Ishpeming, Mich., May 22, 1957; AB, U. Mich., 1978, MD, 1981. Prof. ophthalmology Med. Coll. Wis., 1988—, retina sect. head, 1999—. Fellow: Am. Acad. Ophthalmology (Sr. Achievement award); mem.: Macula Soc., Retina Soc., Am. Soc. Retina Specialists (hon.), Am. Ophthal. Soc. Office: 925 N 87th St Milwaukee WI 53226 Business E-Mail: dhan@mcw.edu.

HAN, DONG-HOO, dental educator; b. Seoul, Republic Of Korea, Dec. 20, 1953; m. Hyun-Hee Seo, Nov. 26, 1983; children: Seok-Bum, Jae-Bum. DDS, Yonsei U., Seoul, 1978, MSD, 1981, PhD, 1987. Intern & resident, dept. prosthodontics Yonsei Dental Hosp., Seoul, 1978—81; prof., dept. prosthodontics Coll. Dentistry Yonsei U., 1984—; adjuctive asst. prof. Coll. Dentistry U. Iowa, Iowa City, 1989—90; vis. faculty Ctr. Prosthodontics & Implant Dentistry Loma Linda U., Calif., 1996; vis. prof., dept. implantology Coll. Dentistry Jilin U., Changchun, China, 2004, hon. prof., 2004—. Dir., acad. affair Korean Acad. Prosthodontics, Seoul, 1997—99, sec., 2003—05, v.p., 2007—, Korean Acad. Stomatognatic Function, Seoul, 2002—04, Korean Acad. Oral Maxillofacial Implantology, Seoul, 2002—06; dental cons. pres. Cheongwadae, Seoul, 1998—2003; pres. Yonsei Inst. Dental Implantology, Seoul, 2002—06; chmn. ITI Sect. Korea, Seoul, 2006—. Capt. Korean Army, 1981—84. Recipient Pres.'s award, Republic of Korea, 2003. Fellow: Internat. Team Implantology. Office: Dept Prosthodontics Coll Dentistry Yonsei University 250 Seongsanno Seodaemun-gu Seoul 120-752 Republic of Korea Office Phone: 82-2-2228-3163. Office Fax: 82-2-312-3598. Business E-Mail: donghoohan@yuhs.ac.

HAN, DOUG HYUN, medical educator; b. Seoul, Republic Of Korea, Aug. 26, 1970; s. Won Sun Han and Sook Kyung Choi; m. Seong Hyun Kim; children: Seong A., Seong Min. MD, Chung Ang U., Seoul, 1997, PhD, 2004. Clin. fellow Seoul Nat. U. Hosp., 2005—06; rsch. fellow Brain Imaging Ctr., Harvard Med. Sch., Belmont, Mass., 2006—08, asst. prof. Chung Ang U. Med. Sch., Republic of Korea, 2008—. Cons. Hyun Dai Unicorns profl. baseball team, Suwon, 2004—05. Contbr. articles to numerous profl. jours. Fellow: NIDA (dir. 2006, Invest fellowship 2006). Office: Chung Ang Univ Hosp Han Gang Ro 2 Ga Seoul 140-757 Republic of Korea Office Fax: 82-2-792-8307. Personal E mail: hduk@yahoo.com.

HAN, EUN-TAEK, parasitologist, educator; b. Incheon, Republic of Korea, Mar. 20, 1968; PhD, Seoul Nat. U., 2003. Prof. Kangwon Nat. U. Sch. Medicine, 2003—. Recipient award, Assn. Basic Med. Scientists, 2008. Mem.: Korean Soc. Parasitologists, Am. Soc. Tropical Medicine and Hygiene. Office: 192-1 Hyoja 2-dong Dept Parasitology Chuncheon Gangwon 200-701 Republic of Korea Office Fax: 82-33-255-8809. Business E-Mail: ethan@kangwon.ac.kr.

HAN, IN HO, neurosurgeon, educator; b. Busan, Republic of Korea, Dec. 4, 1973; MS, Pusan Nat. U., 2001. Intern, resident Dept. Neurosurgery, Pusan Nat. U. Hosp., 1998—2003, asst. prof. Sch. Medicine, 2009—; chief Armed Forces Busan Hosp. Dept. Neurosurgery, 2004—06, dir. Busan St. Marys Med. Ctr., 2006—07, clin. and rsch. fellow Youngdong Severance Spine Hosp., Yonsei U., Coll. Medicine, 2007—08. Editl. bd. mem. Korean Jour. Spine, 2010—. Mem.: Korean Spinal Neurosurgery Soc., Korean Neurosurg. Soc. (Academic award). Avocations: baseball, reading. Office: Pusan Nat University Hosp 305 Gudeok-Ro Seo-gu Busan 602-739 Republic of Korea Office Fax: 82-51-244-0282. Business E-Mail: farlateral@hanmail.net.

HAN, JAEHONG, biology professor; b. Yechon, Republic of Korea, Apr. 10, 1970; PhD, U. Mich., 2001. Assoc. prof. Chung-Ang U., 2008—. Mem.: Korean Soc. Applied Biol. Chemistry. Office: Naeri 72-1 Ansung Gyeonggi 456-756 Republic of Korea Business E-Mail: jaehongh@cau.ac.kr.

HAN, JIN SUK, medical educator, researcher; b. Seoul, Republic of Korea, Aug. 11, 1953; s. Chang Kyo Han and Jong Hyun Kim; m. Mi Kyung Choo, Nov. 21, 1956; children: Hee Kyung, Soo Jung, Han-Joo Song, Yong-hun Lee, Hyun Soo. MD, Seoul Nat. U., 1978, PhD, 1988. Diplomate Korean Bd. Medicine, Korean Bd. Internal Medicine, Korean Bd. Nephrology. Chmn. dept. internal medicine Masan Province Hosp., Kyungsangnam-do, 1983—86; vis. fellow renal mechanisms sect. Lab. Kidney Electrolyte Metabolism, NHLBI, Bethesda, Md., 1990—92; intern Seoul Nat. U. Hosp., 1978—79, resident dept. internal medicine, 1979—83, dir. dialysis unit, 1996—2004, chief divsn. nephrology, 2001—04; lectr. dept. internal medicine Seoul Nat. U. Coll. Medicine, 1986—88, asst. prof. dept. internal medicine, 1988—94, assoc. prof. dept internal medicine, 1994—99, prof. dept. internal medicine, 1999—. Coun. mem. Coun. Drug Evaluation Com., Ministry Health and Welfare, Seoul, 1994—98. Contbr. articles to profl. jours., chapters to books (2 times, 2006). Capt. Korean Army, 1983—86. Recipient 1st Abbott Excellent Rsch. award, Korean Soc. Nuc. Medicine, 1986, Excellent Rsch. award, Korean Fedn. Scis. and Tech. Socs., 1997, 2003. Mem.: Internat. Soc. Nephrology (corr.), Am. Physiol. Soc. (corr.), Am. Soc. Nephrology (corr.), Korean Soc. Nephrology (life; editor-in-chief jour. 1994—96, sec. gen. 1996—98, dir. sci. program com. 2000—02, dir. collaboratory study com. 2004—06, pres. elect. 2011—, Abstract of Excellence award 2001, 2002). Achievements include research in Pathogenic mechanisms of transporters defect in RTA, DI and Gitelman's syndrome. Office: Intern Med Seoul Nat Univ Coll Medicine 28 Yongon-dong Chongno-gu Seoul 110-744 Republic of Korea Office Fax: 82-2-741-4876. Personal E-mail: jshan@snu.ac.kr.

HAN, JONG KYU, radiologist; b. Seoul, Republic of Korea, Sept. 23, 1966; MD, Soonchunhyang U., 1996, MMS, PhD, 2010. Radiologist Soonchunhyang U. Cheonan Hosp., 2003—; instr. Soonchunhyang U. Med. Coll., 2004—07, asst. prof., 2007. Mem.: Korean Soc. Musculoskeletal Radiology, Korean Soc. Radiology. Avocations: mountain climbing, swimming. Office: 8 Soonchunhyang 2 Gil Cheonan ChoonchungNam 330-721 Republic of Korea Business E-Mail: mdhjk@schmc.ac.kr.

HAN, KIHWAN, plastic surgeon; b. Daegu, Republic of Korea, Apr. 7, 1954; m. Shinhyang Kim, Sept. 29, 1978; children: Soeun, Hyoeun. MD, Kyungpook Nat. U., 1978, MSc in Medicine, 1981, PhD, 1989. Cert. plastic surgeon Korean Bd. Plastic & Reconst. Surgery, 1983. Intern Dongsan Med. Ctr., Daegu, Republic of Korea, 1978—79, resident in plastic surgery, 1979—83; prof. Keimyung U. Coll. Medicine, Daegu, 1986—94; chief dept. plastic & reconstructive surgery Dongsan Med. Ctr., 1994—. Vis. prof. Harvard Med. Sch., Boston, 1990—91, Chang Gung Meml. Hosp., Taiwan, 2007; CEO Gyeongju Dongsan Hosp., 2009—11, Daegu Dongsan Hosp., 2011—. Author: Plastic and Reconstructive Surgery, 1994, Aesthetic Plastic Surgery, 1998, Plastic Surgery for Student, 1999, Plastic Surgery (Sabiston Textbook of Surgery), 2003, (Korean edit.) Daniels Rhinoplasty, 2005, New Plastic Surgery for Student, 2009, Cleft Lip and Palate, 2005, (Korean edit.) Nahai's Aesthetic Surgery, 2007, (book) Clinical Photography, 2008, Cosmetic and Reconstructive Oculoplastic Surgery, 2009, Current Trends in Asian Rhinoplasty: Operation Guide, 2011. Capt. Daegu Military Med. Ctr., 1983—86. Mem.: Asian Pacific Cranio-Facial Assn., Am. Cleft Palate-Craniofacial Assn., Am. Soc. Plastic & Reconstructive Surgeons. Home: 156-1 Nungsung-dong Daegu 701 530 Republic of Korea Office: Dongsan Med Ctr Dept Plastic & Reconstructive Surgery Dongsan-Dong 194 700-712 Daegu Daegu Republic of Korea Office Phone: 82(53)250-7633, 82 10 9507 7633. Business E-Mail: khh@dsmc.or.kr, kihwanhan54@gmail.com.

HAN, KI-HWAN, anatomist, educator; b. Seoul, Republic of Korea, May 6, 1970; s. Won-Sik Han and In-Soon Kwon Han; m. Ja-Hee Kim; children: Ji-Yong, Jia. BA, Cath. U., Seoul, 1992; MD, Cath. U. Sch. Medicine, Seoul, 1996, PhD, 2005. Diplomate Korean Med. Assn., 1996. Intern Kangnam St. Mary's Hosp., Seoul, 1996—97; tchg. asst. Cath. U. Sch. Medicine, 1997—2004; asst. to assoc. prof. Ewha Woman's U. Sch. Medicine, Seoul, 2004—. Pub. health svc., Busan, Republic of Korea, 2000—03. Mem.: Korean Soc. Nephrology (corr.), Korean Assn. Anatomists (corr.), Am. Physiological Soc. (corr.), Internat. Soc. Nephrology (corr.), Am. Soc. Nephrology (corr.). Office: Ewha Woman's Univ Sch Medicine 911-1 Mok-6-dong Yangcheon-ku Seoul 158-710 Republic of Korea Office Fax: 82-2-2650-5711. Business E-Mail: khhan@ewha.ac.kr.

HAN, LIANG, surgeon, educator; b. Tianjin, Dec. 9, 1961; MS in Medicine, Tianjin Med. U., 1995. Prof. Tianjin Med. U. Cancer Hosp. 2000—, dir. gastrointestinal surg. dept., 2004. Recipient award, Tianjin State Govt. Master: Chinese Gastric Cancer Assn. (dep. chmn.); mem.: Chinese Anti-Cancer Assn. Avocation: sports. Office: Huanhu Xi Lu Tiyuanbei He Xi Dist Tianjin 300060 China Office Fax: 0086-22-23359983. Business E-Mail: tjlianghan1961@126.com.

HAN, SANGYEUL, research scientist; b. Republic of Korea, Oct. 31, 1969; PhD, Seoul Nat. U., 2001. Rsch. fellow Mass. Gen. Hosp., 2002—08, asst., 2008—10; instr. Harvard Med. Sch., 2008—10; prin. rsch. scientist Samsung Advanced Inst. Technologies, Samsung Electronics Inc., 2010—. Grant, Nat. Inst. Health. Mem.: Soc. Neurosci., Am. Soc. Cell Biology. Avocations: travel, soccer, jogging. Home: 66 Sylvester Ave Winchester MA 01890 Business E-Mail: syhan69@partners.org.

HAN, SEHJIN, plastic surgeon; b. Daegu, Republic of Korea, Oct. 22, 1974; MD, U. Chgo., 2000. Facial plastic surgeon, otolaryngologist Kaiser Permanente, 2006—08, Wash. Twp. Med. Group, 2008—10; facial plastic surgeon Otolaryngology Assocs., 2010—. Co-founder Human Practice Inc., 2010. Recipient Ill. Jr. Poet Laureate award, Gwendolyn Brooks; AAO-HNSF Ortho-McNeil grant. Mem.: Am. Acad. Otolaryngology and Head and Neck Surgery, Am. Acad. Facial Plastic and Reconstructive Surgery. Avocations: painting, photography. Office: 233 East Erie St Ste 804 Chicago IL 60611 Office Fax: 312-944-6420. Personal E-mail: sehjin@hotmail.com.

HAN, SEUNG HWAN, cardiologist, educator; b. Busan, Republic of Korea, Oct. 18, 1966; MD, Korea U., PhD, 1992. Prof., chief cardiology Gil Hosp., Gachon U. Medicine and Sci., 2009—. Editl. mem. Korean Jour. Internal Medicine, 2008—10; bd. mem., academic com. Korean Vascular Biology Working Group, 2008—11; bd. mem., sci. com. ENCORESEOUL, 2008—11; bd. mem., edn. com. Korean Atherosclerosis and Lipid Soc., 2008—11; bd. mem., rsch. com. Korean Soc. Cardiology, 2009—11. Recipient Young Investigator award, Ascian Soc. Lipidology. Mem.: Korean Soc. Interventional Cardiology, Korean Soc. Cardiology, Korean Soc. Internal Medicine. Office: 1198 Guwol-dong Namdong-gu Incheon 405-760 Republic of Korea Personal E-mail: shhan@gilhospital.com.

HAN, SEUNG-KYU, medical educator; b. Seoul, Republic of Korea, Sept. 2, 1962; s. Joong-Hee Han and Seung-Yeol Lee Han; m. Hee-Youn Hwang, Feb. 22, 1990. BA, Korea U., 1987, MSc, 1990, PhD, 1994. Diplomate Korean Bd. Plastic Surgery. Intern Korea U. Med. Ctr., Seoul, 1987—88, resident in plastic surgery, 1988—92, clin. instr., 1992—95; lectr., asst. prof. Korea U. Coll. Medicine, Seoul, 1995—2002, assoc. prof., 2002— ; vis. scholar, rsch. scientist Stanford U., 1997—99; fellow Plastic Surgery Ctr. of the Pacific, Honolulu, 1999. Dir. plastic rsch. lab. Korea U. Med. Ctr., Seoul, 1999—; chmn. sci. com. Korean Rsch. Group for Wound Care, Seoul, 2003—; editl. com. Korean Med. Assn., Seoul, 2001—03; sci. com. Korean Soc. Plastic Surgeons, Seoul, 2000—02; editl. com. Korean Soc. Reconstructive Hand Surgery, Seoul, 2000—02. Editor: Advances in Wound Care, 2002; contbr. articles to profl. jours. Rsch. grant, Korea U., 1996, 2000, Ministry of Health and Welfare, 2003. Fellow: European Acad. Cosmetic Surgery; mem.: World Biomaterials Congress, Internat. Soc. Aesthetic Plastic Surgery, Am. Soc. Plastic Surgeons (corr.), Internat. Soc. Plastic and Reconstructive Surgery. Avocations: travel, golf. Office: Korea Univ Guro Hosp 97 Guro-Dong Guro-Ku Seoul 152-703 Republic of Korea Office Fax: + 82 2 868 6698. Business E-Mail: pshan@kumc.or.kr.

HAN, SHUHONG, research scientist; b. China, Feb. 24, 1972; PhD, Peking U., 2001. Scienstist U. Fla., 2008—. Mem.: Clin. Immunology. Avocations: reading, sports. Office: University Fla 1600 SW Archer Rd Gainesville FL 32610 Business E-Mail: hansh72@ufl.edu.

HAN, SOO HONG, surgeon, educator; b. Jeju, Republic of Korea, Sept. 12, 1964; MD, Kyung-Hee U., Seoul, Republic of Korea, 1989, PhD, 2004. Assoc. prof. Dept. Orthop. Surgery, CHA Bundang Med. Ctr., CHA U., 2004—. Editor chief Jour. Korean Soc. Microsurgery, 2010. Mem.: Korean Soc. Microsurgery (Excellent Article award), World Soc. Reconstructive Microsurgery, Korean Soc. Surgery Hand, Korean Orthop. Assn. Office: 351 Yatap-dong Bundang-gu Seongnam Gyeonggi 463-712 Republic of Korea

HAN, SUNG-SIK, surgeon; b. Seoul, Apr. 6, 1970; MD, Seoul Nat. U., 1996, PhD, 2008. Staff surgeon Nat. Cancer Ctr., Republic of Korea, 2006—. Mem.: Korean Surg. Soc. Office: 111 Jungbalsan-ro madu-1 dong Goyang Gyeonggi 410-769 Republic of Korea Business E-Mail: sshan@ncc.re.kr.

HAN, WONSHIK, medical educator; b. Seoul, Republic of Korea, Jan. 15, 1970; MD, Seoul Nat. U., 1994, PhD, 2005. Asst. prof. Seoul Nat. U. Coll. Medicine, Republic of Korea, 2004—; intern, gen. surgery residency Seoul Nat. U. Hosp., 1994—99; clin. prof. Seoul Nat. U. Medicine, 2004—05, asst. prof., dept. surgery, 2006—09, assoc. prof., dept. surgery, 2010—; joint faculty mem. Seoul Nat. U. Cancer Rsch. Inst., 2009—. Fellowship, Seoul Nat. U. Hosp., 2002—04. Office: Seoul Nat Univ Coll Medicine 28 Yongon-dong Chongno-gu Seoul 110-744 Republic of Korea Home: Walkerhill Apt 23-1101 Seoul Republic of Korea Office Fax: 82 2 766 3975. Business E-Mail: hanw@snu.ac.kr.

HAN, YONG MOON, pharmacology educator, dean, consultant; s. Chang Sung and Yoon Sook (Park) Han; m. Soo Kyung Kim, June 10, 1958; children: Britta Jean, Eric Young. BS, Chung-Ang U., Seoul, 1979; MS, Calif. State U., Sacramento, 1987; PhD, U. Nev., Reno, 1991. Lic. pharmacist. Postdoctoral rschr. Mont. State U., Bozeman, 1992—94, asst. prof., 1995—2000; assoc. prof. Dongduk Women's U. Coll. Pharmacy, Seoul, 2001—06, prof., dean, 2007—. Cons. LygoCyte Pharm. Co., Bozeman, 1998—2000, FDA, Seoul, 2001—. Editor: Archives of Pharmacal Rsch. Named Scientist of Yr., Fedn. Korean Microbiol. Socs., 2004; Predoctoral scholar, NIH, 1987. Mem.: Pharm. Soc. Korea (assoc.), Am. Soc. Microbiology (assoc.). Achievements include patents for development of fungal vaccines. Business E-Mail: ymhan@dongduk.ac.kr.

HAN, YOUNG-HOON, research scientist; b. Jeju, Republic of Korea, Jan. 5, 1967; PhD, Seoul Nat. U., 1997. Prin. investigator Korea Inst. Radiol. & Med. Scis., 2006—. Office: Nowon-gil 75 Nowon-gu Seoul 139-706 Republic of Korea Business E-Mail: yhhan@kirams.re.kr.

HANABUSA, HIDEJI, epidemiologist; b. Hiroshima, Japan, Mar. 23, 1955; MD, Keio U., 1980, PhD, 1992. Chair Ogikubo Hosp., 2008—. Adj. prof. Keio U., 2009—11. Recipient Outstanding Rev. award, Jour. Clin. Infectious Disease. Mem.: ISTH. Avocation: swimming. Office: 3-1-24 Imagawa Suginami Tokyo 167-8515 Japan Office Fax: 81-3-3399-1107. Business E-Mail: hanabusa@muh.biglobe.ne.jp.

HANAFUSA, NORIO, physician, educator; b. Okayama, Japan, June 24, 1969; MD, U. Tokyo, PhD, 2002. Assoc. prof. U. Tokyo Hosp., Bunkyo-ku, 2006—08, lectr., 2008—. Fellow: Japanese Soc. Dialysis Therapy, Japanese Soc. Internal Medicine. Office: Dept Hemodialysis & Apheresis Univ Tokyo Hosp 7-3-1 Hongo Bunkyo-ku Tokyo 113-8655 Japan Office Fax: 81-3-3818-3762. Business E-Mail: hanafusa-tky@umin.ac.jp.

HANAHAN, DOUGLAS, biochemist, educator; b. 1951; s. Donald J. and Lillian Marie H. BS in Physics, MIT, 1976, MA, 1976; MA in Biophysics, Harvard Univ., 1983, PhD, 1983. Sr. staff scientist Cold Spring Harbor Lab., 1983—88; assoc. prof. biochemistry and biophysics and Hormone Rsch. Inst. U. Calif., San Francisco, 1988—93, prof. biochemistry and biophysics and Hormone Rsch. Inst., 1993—, exec. com. Helen Diller Family Comprehensive Cancer Ctr., 2006—, mem. Diabetes Ctr.; rsch. prof. Am. Cancer Soc., 2001—; prof. life sciences Swiss Fed. Institutes of Tech., 2009—; dir. Swiss Inst. Experimental Cancer Rsch., 2009—. Fellow: Am. Acad. Arts and Scis.; mem.: Inst. Medicine. Office: Dept Biochemistry UCSF PO Box 0534 San Francisco CA 94143-0534 Office Phone: 415-476-9209, 415-476-4661.

HANAKAWA, TAKASHI, physician, researcher; b. Tokushima, Japan, Aug. 17, 1965; MD, Kyoto U., 1991, PhD, 1999. Resident Kyoto U. Hosp., 1991—92; physician Tenri Hosp., Nara, Japan, 1992—96; clin. fellow NINDS Nat. Inst. Health, Md., 2000—02; asst. prof. Kyoto U. Grad. Sch. Medicine, 2002—05; sect. chief Inst. Neurosci. Nat. Ctr. Neurology and Psychiatry, 2005—, dir. dept. molecular imaging Integrated Brain Imaging Ctr., 2011—. Rschr. Japan Sci. and Tech. Agy., 2008—. Recipient Young Investigator award, Japan Neurosci. Soc.; NINDS Intramural fellowship, Nat. Inst. Health. Fellow: Am. Acad. Neurology; mem.: Soc. Neurosci. Office: 4-1-1 Ogawahigashi Kodaira Tokyo 187-8502 Japan Business E-Mail: hanakawa@ncnp.go.jp.

HANAMEY, ROSEMARY T., nursing educator; b. Detroit, May 16, 1937; d. Albert Edward and Catherine Margaret (Shaheen) Hanamey. BSN, Mercy Coll., Detroit, 1959; MS, Boston Coll., 1963; postgrad., U. Mich., 1982; PhD student, U. Mich., Sch. Edn. RN Mich., 1959. Staff nurse Mt. Carmel Mercy Hosp., Detroit, 1959—60, Mass. Gen. Hosp., Boston, 1960—63; instr. nursing Mercy Coll., Detroit, 1963—65, asst. prof., 1967—69; asst. exec. sec. Mich. Nurses Assn., Lansing, 1965—67; exec. sec. Mich. Conf. AAUP, Detroit, 1969—70; instr. nursing Madonna Coll., Livonia, Mich., 1972—76; asst. prof. nursing Ea. Mich. U., Ypsilanti, 1976—80; vol. parish nurse St. Joseph Cath. Ch., Dexter, Mich., 1997—. Mem. careers com. Mich. League Nursing, Detroit, 1977—97; cons. Detroit Practical Nurse Ctr., 1980—85; mem. parish nurse partnership St. Joseph Mercy Health Sys., Ann Arbor, Mich., 1997—. Author: (videotape) Intravenous Therapy: Monitoring and Problem Solving, 1977 (2nd place, 1978), Intravenous Therapy: Basic Concepts, 1977 (3rd place, 1978). Trustee Brenden Walsh; precinct del. Dem. Party, Detroit, 1966—69. Grantee, USPHS, 1961—62; scholar, Marygrove Coll., Detroit, 1955—56. Mem.: Dexter Kiwanis Club. Avocations: swimming, walking. Home: 8074 Huron St Unit 1 Dexter MI 48130-1053 Home Phone: 734-426-8483.

HANANO, RALPH, biologist, consultant; b. Hannover, Germany, Feb. 23, 1963; s. Ismail and Monika Hanano; 1 child, Melanie. BSc in Biology, U. Wuerzburg, Germany, 1987, MSc in Biology, 1992; PhD, U. Ulm, Germany, 1999. Cert. Human Biologist U. Ulm, Germany, 1997. Sci. asst. U. Ulm, Germany, 1997—99; mgr. sci. cooperations Paul Hartmann AG, Heidenheim, Germany, 1999—2001, group leader corp. R&D, 2001—05; dir. Ralno - Biomedical Consulting & Svcs., Ichenhausen, Germany, 2005—. Competence team Paul Hartmann AG, Heidenheim, Germany, 2000—04. Author 23 sci. publs. Scholar Talents for Biomolecular Medicine, U. of Ulm, 1993 - 1995. Mem.: German Assn. Wound Healing, Assn. German Biologist. Achievements include patents for Biologically Active Wound Dressing. Avocations: nature, sports, travel, science. Office: Ralno - Biomedical Consulting & Services Bei der Sandhuehl 18 Bavaria Ichenhausen 89335 Germany Office Fax: 49-(0)8223-962408. Business E-Mail: ralno-consult@email.de.

HANAWALT, PHILIP COURTLAND, biology professor, researcher; b. Akron, Ohio, Aug. 25, 1931; s. Joseph Donald and Lenore (Smith) H.; m. Joanna Thomas, Nov. 2, 1957 (div. Oct. 1977); children: David, Steven; m. Graciela Spivak, Sept. 10, 1978; children: Alex, Lisa. Student, Deep Springs Coll., 1949-50; BA, Oberlin Coll., 1954, ScD (hon.), 1997; MS, Yale U., 1955, PhD, 1959; PhD (hon.), U. Seville, Spain; doctorate honoris causa, U. Bio Bio, Concepcion, Chile, 2006; PhD (hon.), U. Seville, Spain, 2008. Postdoctoral fellow U. Copenhagen, Denmark, 1958-60, Calif. Inst. Tech., Pasadena, 1960-61; rsch. biophysicist, lectr. Stanford U., Calif., 1961-65, assoc. prof., 1965-70, prof., 1970—, Howard H. and Jessie T. Watkins univ. prof., 1997—2002, chmn. dept. biol. scis., 1982-89, Dr. Morris Herzstein prof. biology, 2009—; faculty dept. dermatology Stanford Med. Sch., 1979—. Mem. Stanford Comprehensive Cancer Ctr.; mem. physiol. chemistry study sect. NIH, Bethesda, Md., 1966—70, mem. chem. pathology study sect., 1981—84; mem. sci. adv. com. Am. Cancer Soc., NYC, 1972—76, Coun. for Extramural Grants, 1998—2001; chmn. 2d ad hoc senate com. on professoriate Stanford U., 1988—90; mem. NSF fellowship rev. panel, 1985; mem. carcinogen identification com. Calif. EPA, 1995—98; mem. toxicology adv. com. Burroughs-Welcome Fund, 1995—2001, chmn., 1997—2000; mem. sci. adv. bd. Fogarty Internat. Ctr., NIH, 1995—99; chmn. Gordon Conf. on Mutagenesis, 1996, Gordon Conf. on Mammalian DNA Repair, 1999; mem. bd. on radiation effects rschr. NAS Commn. on Life Scis., 1996—98, 2005—; mem. internat. adv. bd. Chulabhorn Rsch. Inst., Bangkok; trustee Oberlin Coll., 1998—2007; lectr. Curie Inst., Paris, 2003; keynote lectr. for conf. on DNA repair & mutagenesis Am. Soc. Microbiology, 2004; pres., chair organizing com. 9th Internat. Conf. on Environ. Mutagens, San Francisco, 2005; vis. scholar Grad. Sch. Frontier Bioscis., Osaka U., Japan, 2007; edit. bd. mem. Genes & Environ. DNA Repair Mechanism Ageing & Devel.; sr. editor Cancer Rsch., 2003—; edit. bd. mem. Proceedings Nat. Acad. Scis. Author: Molecular Photobiology, 1969; author, editor: DNA Repair: Techniques, 1981, 83, 88, Molecular Basis of Life, 1968, Chemical Basis of Life, 1973, Molecules to Living Cells, 1980; mng. editor DNA Repair Jour., 1982-93; sr. editor Jour. Cancer Rsch., 2003—; assoc. editor Jour. DNA Repair, Molecular Carcinogenesis, Environ. Health Perspectives, Mechanism of Aging and Development; bd. rev. editors Sci.; mem. editl. bd. Procs. of NAS, 2003—; contbr. more than 400 articles to profl. jours. Recipient Outstanding Investigator award Nat. Cancer Inst., 1987-2001, Excellence in Tchg. award No. Calif. Phi Beta Kappa, 1991, Environ. Mutagen Soc. Ann. Rsch. award, 1992, Peter and Helen Bing award for Disting. Tchg., 1992, Am. Soc. for Photobiology Rsch. award, 1996, Internat. Mutation Rsch. award, 1997, Ellison Found. Sr. scholar award, 2001-04, John B. Little award in radiation scis. Harvard Sch. Pub. Health, 2002; Hans Falk lectr. Nat. Inst. Environ. Health Scis., 1990, Severo Ochoa Meml. Hons. lectr. NYU, 1996, IBM-Princess Takamatsu lectr. Japan, 1999, Sonnebonn lectr. Ind. U., 2002; Fogarty sr. rsch. fellow, 1993. Fellow: AAAS, Am. Acad. Arts and Sciences, Am. Acad. Microbiology; mem.: NAS, European Molecular Biology Orgn. (fgn. assoc.), Radiation Rsch. Soc., Environ. Mutagen Soc. (pres. 1993—94, Student Mentoring award 2001), Am. Soc. Biochemistry and Molecular Biology, German DNA Repair Network (hon.), Biophys. Soc. (exec. bd. 1969—71), Genetics Soc., Am. Soc. for Photobiology, Am. Assn. Cancer Rsch. (bd. dirs. 1994—97). Achievements include co-discovery of DNA excision-repair and transcription-coupled DNA repair; research on the role of DNA changes in human genetic disease and aging. Office: Stanford U Dept Biol Herrin Biology Labs 371 Serra Mall Stanford CA 94305-5020 Office Phone: 650-723-2424. Business E-Mail: hanawalt@stanford.edu.

HANAZAKI, MOTOHIKO, anesthesiologist, researcher; s. Tomoo and Motoko Hanazaki; MD, Okayama U., 1992, PhD, 2000. Lic. Japan, 1992. Resident Okayam U. Hosp., 1992—94; anesthesiologist Kochi Pref. Ctrl. Hosp., Japan, 1994—97; rsch. fellow Mayo Clinic, Rochester, Minn., 1997—99; asst. prof. Okayama U. Med. Sch., 2005—; sr. asst. prof. Hoshi U., 2009—. Contbr. rsch. articles to profl. jours. Mem.: Japan Soc. Pain Clinicians, Soc. Cardiovasc. Anesthesiologists, Internat. Anesthesia Rsch. Soc., Japanese Soc. Cardiovasc. Anesthesiologists, Japanese Soc. Intravenous Anesthesia, Japanese Pharmacological Soc., Am. Soc. Anesthesiologists, Japanese Soc. Intensive Care Medicine, Japanese Assn. Acute Medicine, Japan Soc. Smooth Muscle Rsch., Japanese Soc. Anesthesiologists. Achievements include research in airway smooth muscle. Office: Dept Anesthesiology Kawasaki Med Sch 2 1 80 Nakasange Kitaku Okayama 700 8505 Japan Office Fax: 81862356984. E-mail: motohiko@hanazaki.com.

HANBALI, FADI, neurosurgeon, educator; b. Beirut, July 12, 1967; s. Samir Hanbali and Dunia Ghossayni; m. Rana N Kronfol. BS, Am. U. Beirut, Lebanon, 1988; MD, Am. U., Beirut, 1992. Resident neurol. surgery Beirut Med. Ctr. Am. U., 1992—98; fellow complex spine surgery Cleve. Clinic Found., 1998—99; fellow neurosurgery and oncology MD Anderson Cancer Ctr., Houston, 1999—2001; asst. prof. neurosurgery and orthop. surgery U. Tex. Med. Br., Galveston, 2001—06; asst. prof. neurosurgery Tex. Tech. U. HS, El Paso, 2006—08, assoc. prof. neurosurgery, 2008—. Contbr. articles to profl. jours., chapters to books. Mem.: AMA, Am. Coll. Surgeons, World Assn. of Lebanese Neurosurgeons, Singleton Surg. Soc., Congress of Neurol. Surgeons. Office: Tex Tech U HSC 4800 Alberta Ave El Paso TX 79905 Business E-Mail: fadi.hanbali@ttuhsc.edu.

HANCOCK, BARRY WILLIAM, retired medical educator; b. London, Jan. 25, 1946; s. George Llewellyn and Sarah (Collins) H.; m. Christine Diana Helen Spray, July 5, 1969; children: Carole Ruth, David Christopher. MBChB, U. Sheffield, 1969, DCH, MD, 1977. Med. registrar therapeutics Nat. Health Svc. Royal Infirmary Hosp., Sheffield, 1973-74; lectr. medicine, sr. registrar med. oncology Nat. Health Svc. Royal Hallamshire Hosp., Sheffield, 1974-78; sr. lectr. in medicine, hon. cons. physician and oncologist Nat. Health Svc. Royal Hallamshire and Weston Park Hosps., Sheffield, 1978-86, reader in medicine, hon. cons. physician and oncologist, 1986-88; prof. clin. oncology U. Sheffield, 1988—2009, emeritus prof. clin. oncology, 2009, dir. oncology, 1997-2000. Dir. Supraregional Gestational Trophoblastic Tumour Screening and Treatment Svc. Sheffield, 1991-2009; divsnl. surgeon St. John Ambulance Brigade, North Derbyshire, 1982-86; trial coord. Brit. Nat. Lymphoma Investigation, London, 1983-2008; lead cancer clinician North Trent Cancer Network, 2001-2005; dir. cancer rsch. U. Sheffield/Yorkshire Cancer Rsch., 1993-2009. Co-author: Lecture Notes on Clinical Oncology, 2nd edit., 1986; editor: Assessment of Tumour Response, 1982, Cancer Care in the Community, 1996, Cancer Care in the Hospital, 1996; co-editor: Lymphoreticular Disease, 2nd edit., 1985, Immunological Aspects of Cancer, 1985, Gestational Trophoblastic Disease, 1997, 2nd edit., 2003, 3rd edit., 2009, Malignant Lymphoma, 2000. Recipient R.S. Morton Cup Univ. Med. Soc., 1974, New Years' hon. award Lord Mayor Sheffield, 1999, Sheffield Cmty. Hero award, 2002, U. Sheffield Centenary Achievement medal, 2005, Gold medal Internat Soc. Study Trophoblast, 2009, Pfizer Excellence Oncology Lifetime Achievement award, 2008, Named officer Brit. Empire OBE, 2009, Sheffield City Legend award, 2010 Fellow Royal Coll. Physicians (London and Edinburgh), Royal Coll. Radiologists; mem. Assn. Cancer Physicians, Assn. Profs. Oncology (chmn. 1995-2001), Nat. Cancer Rsch. Inst. Renal Clin. Studies Group (chmn. 2001-08), Brit. Oncol. Assn., U.K. Coord. Com. on Cancer Rsch. Renal Group (chmn. 1999-2001), Brit. Assn. Cancer Rsch., European Soc. Med. Oncology, Am. Soc. Clin. Oncology, Med. Soc. (hon. pres. 1988), Med. Rsch. Coun. (chmn. renal cancer planning group, 1996-98), Internat. Soc. Study Trophoblast (pres. 2007-09). Methodist. Avocations: railways, photography, stamp collecting/philately, tennis. Home: Treetops 253 Dobcroft Rd Sheffield S11 9LG England Office: Weston Park Hosp YCR Clin Oncology Whitham Road S10 2SJ Sheffield England Home Phone: (114) 2651433; Office Phone: (114) 2265007. Business E-Mail: b.w.hancock@sheffield.ac.uk.

HAND, PETER JAMES, neurobiologist, educator; b. Oak Park, Ill., Jan. 5, 1937; s. James Harold and Edna Mae (Watson) H.; m. Mary Minnis, Sept. 16, 1958; children: Katherine Patricia, Carol Jane, Margaret Anne, Robin Lynn, Stephen Douglas, Peter James; m. Carol Louise Corson, Oct. 23, 1976; m. Christine L. Arnold, Sept. 19, 1986. VMD, U. Pa., 1961, PhD, 1964. Mem. faculty U. Pa., Phila., 1964—, prof. anatomy, 1979-99, head dept. anatomy, 1980-87, 91-97, emeritus prof., 1999—. Mem. NIH rev. com. Regional Primate Ctrs., 1985-89; mem. nominating com. Lifu Acad. award in Chinese Medicine; adj. faculty Indian River C.C., 2003-; COO Hand Wine Cons., Inc. Contbr. articles to profl. jours. Pres. coun. USO, Cape May, NJ, 1972—73, nat. del.; wine columnist Hometown News, 2005; mem. ch. coun. Jupiter First Ch., 2002—05; trustee Mid-Atlantic Ctr. for Arts, Cape May, NJ, 1973—74; bd. dirs. Cape May Taxpayers Assn., 1972—74, University City Hist. Soc., Phila., 1978—80; v.p. bd. dirs. Arbors Village Assn., 2002—03, chmn. environ. com., 2003—04. NIH grantee, 1970-82, 86-92, 95—2003, Riverview Grounds Com., 2008-. Mem. Am. Assn. Anatomists, Am. Assn. Vet. Anatomists, Soc. Neurosci. (pres. Phila. chpt. 1984-85), Internat. Brain Rsch. Orgn., World Assn. Vet. Anatomists, Internat. Assn. for Study of Pain, Am. Coll. Acupuncture (pres. 1997-98), Internat. Coll. Acupuncture and Electro-Therapeutics, Sigma Xi, Alpha Psi (trustee 1965-87). Democrat. Home Phone: 610-717-1630. Personal E-mail: handpain@comcast.net.

HAND, ROGER, physician, educator; b. Bklyn., Sept. 25, 1938; s. Morton and Angela (Belvedere) H.; m. Susan Hand; children: Christopher, Jessica. BS, NYU, 1959, MD, 1962. Intern, then resident in internal medicine NYU Med. Ctr., 1962-68; postdoctoral fellow, asst. prof. Rockefeller U., NYC, 1968-73; clin. asst. prof. medicine Cornell U. Med. Coll., NYC, 1970-73; asst. prof., then assoc. prof. medicine McGill U., Montreal, Que., Canada, 1973-80; prof. medicine, dir. McGill Cancer Ctr., 1980-84; sr. physician Royal Victoria Hosp., Montreal, 1980-84; chmn. internal medicine Ill. Masonic Ctr., Chgo., 1984-88; prof. medicine U. Ill., Chgo., 1984—, chief sect. gen. internal medicine, 1988-95, prof. health policy and adminstrn. Sch. Pub. Health, 1995—2002. Prin. clin. coord. Ill. Found. Quality Health Care, Chgo., 1996-00; physician advisor OLR Med. Ctr., Chgo., 2000-01, ret., 2001-. Contbr. articles to profl. jours. Brig. gen. USAR, 1963-71, 85-03, ret.; diaster relief-search-and-rescue pilot auxs. USCG, USAF; vol. disaster relief programs ARC, FEMA. Decorated Air medal, Meritorious Svc. medal, Army Commendation medal, Legion of Merit; med. rsch. grantee. Fellow ACP, Royal Coll. Physicians and Surgeons, Am. Coll. Med. Quality; mem. Am. Soc. Clin. Investigation, Am. Soc. Biol. Chemists, Am. Assn. Cancer Research, Am. Soc. Clin. Oncology, Infectious Disease Soc., Can. Soc. Clin. Investigation, Cen. Soc. Clin. Rsch., Am. Cancer Soc.(bd. dirs. Ill. div.), Am. Health Quality Assn. Office Phone: 847-926-8229. E-mail: buckgeneral@ameritech.net.

HANDA, AMIT, neurosurgeon; b. New Delhi, Nov. 29, 1969; DNB in Surgery, St. Stephen's Hosp., Delhi, 2001, DNB in Neurosurgery. Maj., surgeon Army M.C., Indian Army, 1999—2004; jr. specialist St. Stephen's Hosp., 2006—. Mem.: United Svcs. Instn. India, Nat. Acad. Med. Scis. Avocations: mountain climbing, scuba diving. Home: 289 Aravali Apts Alaknanda New Delhi Delhi 110019 India Personal E-mail: dramithanda@yahoo.com.

HANDAL, JOHN A., orthopaedic surgeon; Attended, Med. Coll. Pa., 1979. Diplomate Am. Bd. Orthopaedic Surgery. Intern gen. surgery State Univ., NY, 1980; fellow sports medicine Hershey Med. Ctr., 1984; fellow emergency medicine Emergency Medicine Ctr. Inst., 1985; resident orthop. surgery Albert Einstein Med. Ctr., 1984, physician. Named one of the Top Doctors, Phila. Mag., 2011. Office: Albert Einstein Medical Center Willowcrest Bldg 4th Fl 5501 Old York Philadelphia PA 19141 Office Phone: 215-456-7900. Office Fax: 215-456-3428.

HANDEL, DAVID JONATHAN, health facility administrator; b. NYC, Jan. 2, 1946; s. Milton M. and Ruth (Stamer) H.; m. Julia Elizabeth Noll, June 26, 1971; chldren: Daniel, Jennifer. BS, Cornell

U., 1966; MBA, U. Chgo., 1968. Assoc. planning coordinator for health scis. Northwestern U., Chgo., 1970-73, adminstr. Northwestern U. Med. Clinics and Med. Assocs., 1973-76; dir. planning and implementation Mid-Ohio Health Planning Fedn., Columbus, Ohio, 1976-79; assoc. hosp. adminstr. Vanderbilt U. Hosps., Nashville, 1979-82, assoc. dir. ops., 1982-85; dir. Ind. U. Hosps., Indpls., 1985-96; exec. v.p., COO Clarian Health Ptnrs., Inc., Indpls., 1997—2004. V.p. United Hosp. Svcs., Indpls., 1986-88, pres., 1989-90, Bedford Reg. Med. Ctr., 1997-2004, La Porte Regional Health Sys., Inc., 1998-2004; chmn. Rehab. Hosp. Ind., 2002-07; with Goshen Health Sys., 2000-2004; bd. dirs. Ruth Lilly Health Edn. Ctr., Indpls; sr. v.p. bus. devel. and strategy Sisters of St. Francis Health Svc., Inc., 2007-; dir. MHA program Ind. U., 2004-07, exec. in residence, 2007-09, assoc. dir. Ctr. Dir. Health Policy, 2009-. Contbr. articles to profl. jours. Sr. asst. health svcs. officer USPHS, 1968-70. Fellow Am. Coll. Health Care Execs.; mem. Ind. Hosp. Assn. (bd. dirs. 1994-97). Office: Ind U BS4085 801 W Michigan St Indianapolis IN 46202 Business E-Mail: dhandel@iupui.edu.

HANDEL, NEAL, plastic surgeon, researcher, educator; b. LA, Sept. 2, 1947; s. Max and Ruth H. BA, Columbia U., 1969; MD, Yale U., 1973. Diplomate Am. Bd. Plastic Surgery, 1981. Resident surgery UCLA Sch. Medicine, 1973—75; resident, 1975—76, Tulane U., New Orleans, 1976—78, U. Colo., Denver, 1978—96; plastic and reconstructive surgeon The Breast Ctr., Van Nuys, Calif., 1982—99, assoc. med. dir., 1982—99; assoc. clin. prof. Divsn. Plastic Surgery David Geffen Sch. Med., UCLA. Mem. adv. bd. Ctr. for Devel. Biology Calif. State U., Northridge, 1985—. Featured on Body Work series, Plastic Surgery Beverly Hills, The Learning Channel, 2005, contbr. articles to profl. jours. Rsch. grantee Am. Soc. Aesthetic Plastic Surgery, 1991. Fellow ACS; diplomat, Am. Bd. Plastic Surgery; mem. Calif. Am. Soc. Plastic Surgeons, Am. Soc. Aesthetic Plastic Surgery, Am. Assn. Plastic Surgeons. Office: Neal Handel MD 13400 Riverside Dr Ste 101 Sherman Oaks CA 91423-2513 Office Phone: 818-788-3113. Office Fax: 805-862-9101.

HANDELSMAN, JOHN ELLIS, pediatric orthopedist, surgeon; b. Johannesburg, Dec. 14, 1930; arrived in U.S., 1977; s. Maurice Handelsman and Rose Betty Braude; m. Barbara Jan Ebenstein, June 24, 1979; children: Sarah Rose, Leanne Beth, Risa Carlyn. MBBChir, Witmatersrand U., 1953; CM in Orthopedics, Liverpool U., Eng., 1963; MD, SUNY, 1977; MA (hon.), Brown U., 1982. Diplomate Am. Bd. Orthop. Surgery, 1978. Intern Gen. Hosp. and Baragwanath Hosp., Johannesburg, 1954—56; resident gen. surgery War Meml. Hosp., High Wycombe, 1957—58, Whipps Cross and St. James Hosps., London, 1957—58; resident orthopedic Nuffield Orthopedic Ctr. and Radcliffe Infirmary, Oxford, England, 1959—61, Royal Victoria Hosp., Montreal, Canada, 1961—62, St. Bartholomew's Hosp., Rochester, England, 1962; fellow Liverpool (Eng.) U. and Walton Hosp., 1963, orthop. surgeon Baragwanath Hosp., Johannesburg, 1964—65, sr. prin. orthop. surgeon Johannesburg Gen. Hosp., 1966—67; chief pediat. orthopedics U. Hosp., Stony Brook, NY, 1977—81; dir. pediat. orthopedics Nassau County Med. Ctr., East Meadow, NY, 1977—81, R.I. Hosp., Providence, 1981—86; chief pediat. orthopedics Schneider Children's Hosp., New Hyde Park, NY, 1986—2002, attending orthopedics and pediatrics, 2002—. Contbr. articles to profl. jours. Fellow: Royal Coll. Surgeons (Eng.); mem.: Pediatric Orthop. Soc. N.Am. (emeritus), Am. Orthop. Assn. (sr.; mem. com. 1985—), Am. Acad. Orthop. Surgeons (mem. com. 1978—). Achievements include research in a neuromuscular cause for club foot; the use of the small A.O. external fixator in osteotomies of the femur, tibia and humerus. Avocations: swimming, bicycling, music, reading, woodworking. Office: Pediat Orthop Surgery 2500 Marcus Ave Ste 103 Lake Success NY 11042 Office Phone: 516-488-5885. Office Fax: 516-352-0819. Personal E-mail: jhandelsman@verizon.net.

HANDRA-LUCA, ADRIANA-ALINA, pathologist, educator; b. Cluj-Napoca, Romania, Apr. 4, 1970; d. Viorel and Anuta Handra-Luca. BS, U. Medicine and Pharmacy, Cluj-Napoca, 1994; MD, U. Medicine, Cluj-Napoca, 1994; PhD, U. Paris 6, 2004. Asst. prof. Pub. Assistance Hosp. U. Paris 5, Clichy, France, 2000—01, Pub. Assistance Hosp. U. Paris 6, 2001—03, Pub. Assistance Hosp. U. Paris 13/Nord, Bobigny Bondy, France, 2003—05, assoc. prof., 2005—. Contbr. articles to profl. jours. Achievements include research in tumor type description. Home: 19 rue George Sand Paris 75016 France Office: Dept Pathology APHP Hospital Avicenne 125 route de stalingrad 93000 Bobigny France Office Phone: 0033 148955606. Business E-Mail: adriana.handra-luca@jvr.aphp.fr.

HANDZEL, ZEEV THEODOR, immunologist, allergist; MD, Hebrew U., 1964. Rsch. fellow NIH, Bethesda, Md., 1971—73; sr. physician dept. pediat., dep. chmn. Kaplan Hosp., Rehovot, Israel, 1974—82, head clin. immunology and allergy unit, 1982—2002; dir. Pediat. Rsch. Inst., Rehovot, 1990—2002. Dir. clin. trials with Thymic Humoral Factor, 1977-87; sr. lectr. pediat. Hebrew U. and Hadassah Med. Sch., Jerusalem, 1979, assoc. prof., 1983; vis. scientist Pasteur Inst. London Sch. Tropical Medicine, London, Paris, 1986-87, U. Wis. Clin. Ctr., 1994-95; sr. cons. Biopharma; chief med. officer Modus Biol. Membranes, 2004—; med. dir. Modus Biol. Membranes Ltd., 2004. Editor: Allergy, 1996; contbr. articles to profl. jours. Grantee Agis Industries, 1991, Heiser Found. for Leprosy, 1992, Israeli League against Tb, 1994-96, Israel Ministry Health, 1999-2000; recipient AIDS Rsch. Internat. award World Acad. Population and Health Scis., 1987, Internat. Rsch. Project on Susceptibility to Tb. Mem. Internat. AIDS Soc., European Soc. of Immunodeficiency (rep., pres.-elect); fellow Am. Acad. Allergy and Clin. Immunology, Israel Soc. Allergy and Clin. Immunology, N.Y. Acad. Scis. Office: Pediatric Rsch Inst Kaplan Hosp 76100 Rehovot Israel Office Phone: 972-8-9441571. Business E-Mail: zthandzel@clalit.org.il.

HANI, ANTOINE GEORGE, psychiatrist, psychoanalyst; b. Beirut, May 1, 1925; came to U.S., 1953; s. George Antoine Hani and Marie Haddad; m. Virginia Helen Ahlstrom; children: George, Valerie; m. Théa Jeitani Hani, Oct. 6, 1984; 1 child, Stéphanie. MD, St. Joseph U., Beirut, 1953. Bd. cert. Adult Psychoanalysis and Child and Adolescent Psychoanalysis. Pvt. practice, Chevy Chase, Md., 1958—; supervising and tng. analyst Washington Psychanalytic Inst., 1981—, dir., 1996-99. Tchg. analyst Washington Psychanalytic Inst., 1969, supervising and tng. analyst, 1981—, dir., 1996—99; clin. prof. psychiatry and behavorial scis. George Washington U., 2002—; tchg. and supervising psychoanalyst IPA Eastern European Psychoanalytic Inst., 2002—. Contbr. articles to profl. jours. Cross fertilizing rels. Fedn. European Psychoanalysts, Fedn. Latin Am. Psychoanalysts. Recipient cert. of honor, Washington Psychoanalytic Soc., Inst. and Found., 2002. Fellow: Am. Coll. Psychoanalysts (honor 1999), APA (disting. life, honor 1973); mem.: Washington Psychoanalytic Soc. (pres. 1987—89, honor and recognition for disting. career in psychoanalysis), Am. Psychoanalytic Assn. (fellow bd. on profl. stds. 1993—99), Internat. Psychoanalytic Assn. (mem. new groups com. 1995—, chmn. com. to develop psychoanalysis in Mid. East 1995—2007), Cosmos Club. Roman Catholic. Home: 8501 Thornden Ter Bethesda MD 20817 Office: 5480 Wisconsin Ave # 1619 Chevy Chase MD 20815 Home Phone: 301-365-3957; Office Phone: 301-656-4765. E-mail: antoinehani@aol.com.

HANIFIN, JON M., dermatologist, educator; MD, U. Wis., Madison, WI, 1965. Diplomate Am. Bd. Dermatology, 1970. Resident dermatology Univ. of Calif. Med. Ctr., San Francisco, 1966—69, fellow clin. & lab. immunology; prof. dermatology Oreg. Health & Sci. Univ., hosp. affiliation include. Office: OR Health & Science University Deprtment of Dermatology 3303 SW Bond Ave MC CH16D Portland OR 97239 Office Phone: 503-418-3376.

HANIHARA, TUNEHIKO, anthropologist, educator; b. Sapporo, Aug. 21, 1958; MD, Yamagata U., 1985; PhD, U. Tokyo, 1991. Prof. Kitasato U. Sch. Medicine, 2009—. Mem.: Anthrop. Soc. Nippon, Am. Assn. Phys. Anthropologists. Office: 1-15-1 Kitasato Minami-ku Sagamihara Kanagawa 252-0374 Japan Office Fax: 81-042-778-9022. Business E-Mail: hanihara@med.kitasato-u.ac.jp.

HAN-JUNG, CHAE, pharmacist, educator; b. Seoul, Seoul, Republic of Korea, Nov. 5, 1965; m. Kim Hyung-Ryong, Aug. 8, 1993. PhD, ChonBuk Med. Univercity, Jeon-Ju, Republic of Korea, 2001. Pharmacist South Korea Pharmacy Soc., 1989. Post-doc fellow The Burnham Inst., 2001—02; prof. ChobBuk U., Jeon-Ju, Jellabukdo, Republic of Korea, 2000—01, ChobBuk Nat. U. Med. Sch., Jeon-Ju, 2002—. Contbr. articles to profl. jours. Achievements include research in contributing to the knowledge of apoptosis in cardiomyocycle. Home: Seo-Sin Dong Dae-Chang @102/1006 JeollaBukDo Jeon-Ju 560-181 Republic of Korea Office: ChonBuk Nat l Univ Medical school Keum-am Dong 560-181 Jeonju Chonbuk Republic of Korea Office Fax: 63-275-2855; Home Fax: 63-275-2855. Personal E-mail: hjchae@chonbuk.ac.kr.

HANKIN, ELAINE KRIEGER, psychologist, researcher; b. Scranton, Pa., Oct. 17, 1938; d. Maurice and Beatrice (Blumberg) Krieger; m. Abbe Hankin, Dec. 22, 1957; children: Susan Hankin-Birke, Elyse Rae Burton. BA, Temple U., 1979, MEd, 1980; PhD, Bryn Mawr Coll., 1984. Therapist Comac Youth Service Bur., Willow Grove, Pa., 1975-76; therapist, supr. interns Aldersgate Youth Service Bur., Willow Grove, 1975-84; staff psychologist, coord. diagnostic testing Buck's County Guidance Ctr., Doylestown, Pa., 1981-84; psychologist, clin. dir. Abington (Pa.) Psychol. Assocs., 1984-99; v.p., adminstr. dir. Corp. Devel. Systems, Abington, 1984-86; supervisor psychology interns Friends Hosp., Abington, 1996—99; pvt. practice psychology, 1985—. Mem. Willow Grove, Pa., 1986-98, Eugenia Hosp., Ft. Washington, 1986-99, Progression Inst., Ft. Washington, 1986-90, Westmeade Ctr., 1990-95, Friends Hosp., 1996-99. Mem. adv. bd. for Women and Minority Bus. President's scholar Temple U., 1979, Alumnae scholar Bryn Mawr Coll., 1982. Fellow Pa. Psychol. Assn., Phila. Soc. Clin. Psychologists (mem. membership com.); mem. AAUW, Am. Psychol. Assn., Nat. Coun. on Family Rels., Fla. Psychol. Assn., Phi Beta Kappa, Psi Chi. Office: 8713 Ferrara Ct Naples FL 34114 Office Phone: 215-887-1113, 239-331-2107.

HANKINS, CHRISTOPHER LOVELL, plastic surgeon; b. Dallas, Sept. 13, 1955; s. Hayden Lovell Hankins and Helen Louis Holmes; m. Xiaoqing Tang, Sept. 7, 2002; m. Mary Grace Piniones, Oct. 4, 1986 (div. July 10, 1992). BS cum laude, U. Tex., Dallas, 1978; MD, U. Tex. Med. Br., Galveston, Tex., 1982. Aesthetic surgery fellow Stamford Hosp., London, 2000—01; clin. fellow plastic surgery St. George's Hosp., London, 2001—02; ceo Plastic Surgery Enterprises Ltd., Leeds, England, 2002—05; plastic surgery fellow Baylor Coll. Medicine, Houston, 2005—06; assoc. Houston Hand House, 2006—; attending plastic surgeon Cornerstone Hosp., Houston, 2008, Foun. Surgical Hosp., 2008. Bd. edit. Open Reconstruction and Cosmetic Surgery Jour., 2008—, Open Jour. Local and Regional Anesthesia and Analgesia, 2008—, open Jour. Infection and Drug Resistance, 2008—. Vol. plastic surgeon Agris and Zindles Children's Found., Bolivia Med. Mission, 2008, House Charity, Pakisthan Med. Mission, 2008. Recipient Rsch. Found. award, Baylor U. Med. Ctr., 1984; named Cert. Outstanding Achievement Aerospace Rsch., NASA, Dallas, 1974. Avocations: drawing, painting, music, singing. Office: Houston Hand House 6560 Pannin St Ste 1730 Houston TX 77030 Home Phone: 832-633-2044.

HANLEY, FRANK LOUIS, surgeon, educator; b. Providence, May 19, 1952; BA, Brown U.; MD, Tufts U. Sch. Medicine, 1978. Diplomate Am. Bd. Surgery, Am. Bd. Thoracic Surgery. Resident, surgery U. Calif., San Francisco, 1978—81, resident, cardiothoracic surgery, 1986—88, fellow, 1981—84, prof., chief divsn. cardiothoracic surgery, 1993—2001; assoc. prof. Harvard Med. Sch., Boston Children's Hosp., 1989—92; prof., cardiothoracic surgery, dir. heart ctr. Stanford U. Med. Ctr., Calif., 2001—; svc. chief, pediat. cardiothoracic surgery Lucile Packard Children's Hosp., Stanford, Calif., dir., Children's Heart Ctr., Lawrence Crowley, MD, Endowed Prof. in Child Health, 2004—, exec. dir., Pediat. Heart Ctr. Invited guest lectr. Editor: (books) Cardiac Surgery in the Neonate and Infant, Cardiac Surgery, Pediatric Cardiac Intensive Care, Infant-Annals of Thoracic Surgery; contbr. several articles to profl. publs. Recipient Excellence in Tchg. Award, Dept. of Surgery, U. of California-San Francisco, 1992-1994, Outstanding Surg. Chief Resident Award, U. of California-San Francisco, 1986, Outstanding Resident Tchg. Award, 1986, Alpha Omega Alpha Med. Soc., 1986, Outstanding Graduating Studen in Surgery (Martin J Loeb Award), Tufts Sch. of Medicine, 1978. Mem. Am. Assn. for Thoracic Surgery (adv. editl. bd.), Am. Heart Assn., Congenital Heart Surgeons' Soc. Data Ctr., Soc. Thoracic Surgeons, Thoracic Surgery Dirs. Assn., Howard C. Naffziger Surgical Soc., Western Thoracic Surgical Assn., Alpha Omega Alpha. Office: Stanford U Sch Medicine Falk Cardiovasc Rsch Bldg 300 Pasteur Dr Falk CVRB MC 5407 Stanford CA 94305 Address: U Calif 505 Parnassus Ave S-549 San Francisco CA 94143 Office Phone: 650-724-2925, 650-723-0190. Office Fax: 415-476-9678, 650-725-0707. Business E-Mail: frank.hanley@stanford.edu, fhanley@stanford.edu.

HANLEY, HENRY GORMAN, cardiologist; b. Providence, Feb. 11, 1941; s. James Lawrence and Mary Rose (Gorman) Hanley; m. Linda Ellis, June 20, 1970 (div. Jan. 1989); children: Tara, April; m. Kathy Davis, Nov. 18, 1989; children: Eric, Alan. AB, Harvard U., 1962; MD, Yale U., 1966. Diplomate Am. Bd. Internal Medicine, Am. Bd. Cardiovascular Diseases, Am. Bd. Interventional Cardiology. Asst. prof. Baylor Coll. Medicine, Houston, 1971-76, asst. prof. dept. cell biophysics, 1974-76; assoc. prof. medicine U. Ky. Coll. Medicine, Lexington, 1976-80; prof., chief sect. cardiology La. State U. Med. Ctr., Shreveport, 1980—2002; cardiologist Freedman Meml. Cardiology LLC, Alexandria, La., 2002—. Contbr. articles to profl. jours. Fellow: Am. Coll. Cardiology (mem. exec. coun. La. chpt. 1997—98, gov. La. chpt. 2000—03); mem.: Am. Heart Assn. (pres. La. chpt. 1988—90). Roman Catholic. Avocations: golf, travel. Office: Freedman Meml Cardiology LLC Doctors Bldg Ste 112 3311 Prescott Rd Alexandria LA 71301 Home: 6400 Genevieve Alexandria LA 71303 Home Phone: 318-442-1739; Office Phone: 318-767-0960. E-mail: hghanley@aol.com.

HANLEY, THOMAS PATRICK, obstetrician, gynecologist; b. St. Louis, Apr. 16, 1951; s. Thomas P. and Virginia Barbara (Lydon) H.; m. Patricia Ann McHargue, Dec. 27, 1975; children: Colleen, Thomas III, Timothy, Matthew. BA, St. Louis U., 1973, MD, 1977. Diplomate Am. Bd. Ob-gyn. Intern St. Louis U., 1977-78, resident, 1978-81; practice medicine speciailizing in ob-gyn St. Louis, 1981—; med. dir. Informatics SSMPO, St. Louis, 2007—; pres. med. staff St. Mary's Health Ctr., 1993; mem. staff Mo. Bapt. Hosp., St. Clare Hosp., Fenton, Mo.; clin. prof. St. Louis U. Med. Sch., 1983—. Mem. AMA (Physicians Recognition award 1981—), Am. Coll. Ob-Gyn. (Physicians Excellence award 1986—), Mo. State Med. Soc., St. Louis Gynecol. Soc. (pres. 1989-90), St. Louis Met. Med. Soc. Independent. Roman Catholic. Avocation: golf. Office: 3555 Sunset Office Dr 107 Saint Louis MO 63127 Office Phone: 314-238-9000.

HANN, LUCY E., radiologist, educator; b. 1946; MD, Harvard Med. Sch., 1973. Cert. diagnostic radiology 1977. Resident U. Pa. Hosp., Mass. Gen. Hosp.; radiologist, dir. ultrasound Meml. Sloan-Kettering Cancer Ctr., NYC; prof. radiology Weill Med. Coll., Cornell U. Office: Meml Sloan-Kettering Cancer Ctr 1275 York Ave Rm C278 New York NY 10021

HANNA, ADEL SHAFIK, dermatologist, venereologist, consultant; b. El-Menia, Egypt, Jan. 19, 1947; s. Shafik Hanna and Evon Kamel (Hendy) Demian; m. Faten Kamel Badawy, Jan. 25, 1981; children: Sherif, Sally. MD, U. Alexandria, Egypt, 1970, diploma Skin and Venereology Disease, 1978; MS in Pub. Health, High Inst. Pub. Health, 1992. Med. diplomate in dermatology and Sexually Transmitted Disease and AIDS. House officer Ministry of Health Hosps., Alexandria, 1971-72, registrar, 1973-78, specialist skin and venereology disease, 1978-83; gen. practitioner Rural Health Ctrs., Tanta, Egypt, 1972-73, head skin and venereology disease dept. El-Moassat Hosp., Alexandria, 1984-85; clin. adminstr. Alexandria Skin and Venereology Disease Clinic, Alexandria, 1986-88. Cons. health ins., Alexandria, 1989-96; cons., dir. Ministry of Health, Alexandria, 1997—. Mem. Egyptian AIDS Prevention Soc. Avocations: music, travel, reading. Home: El Moaskar El Romany Dobat Mostafa Kamel Bldg 11 Alexandria Egypt Office: 12 Bobastes St Celeopatra Hamamat Alexandria Egypt Office Phone: 002-03-5424153. E-mail: adel_shafik47@yahoo.com.

HANNA, MICHAEL GEORGE, JR., immunologist, pharmaceutical executive; b. Cleve., July 7, 1936; s. Michael George and Camella (Karem) Hanna; m. Barbara Ann Pearson, Sept. 6, 1958; children: Michael George, Christina, Suzanne Kathleen. BS in Biology, Baldwin-Wallace Coll., 1958; MS in Biology, Notre Dame U., 1960; PhD, U. Tenn., 1964; DSc (hon.), Baldwin-Wallace Coll., 2000. Rsch. biologist biology div. Oak Ridge Nat. Lab., 1964-68, dir. immunology carcinogenesis group, 1968-75; dir. cancer biology program, head host tumor interaction sect. cancer biology program Nat. Cancer Inst. Frederick (Md.) Cancer Rsch. Facility, 1975-79, dir., Cancer Rsch. Ctr., 1979—83; dir. Litton Inst. Applied Biotech., Rockville, Md., 1983—85; sr. v.p., Akzo Nobel Organon Teknika Biotech. Rsch. Inst., Rockville, Md., 1985-94; pres., CEO PerImmune, Inc., Rockville, Md., 1994-98; founder, chmn., pres., chief sci. officer Intracel, Frederick, 1998—2002, chmn. emeritus, chief sci. officer, 2002—07; founder, chmn., CEO Vaccinogen Inc., 2007—10, founder, chmn., 2011—. Cons. NASA Lunar Receiver Lab., 1968—70; chmn. tech. adv. com. biotech. U.S. Dept. Commerce, 1985—90; mem. working group biotech. U.S. Dept. Def., 1985—90; mem. bd. overseers Ctr. Advanced Rsch. Biotech., 1984—88; commencement spkr. Baldwin-Wallace Coll., 2000. Gen. editor: Contemporary Topics in Immunobiology, 1971—85, Vaccine Rsch., 1991—96, mem. editl. bd.: Immunopharmacology, 1978—2003, Cancer Rsch., 1978—92, Jour. Biol. Response Modifiers, 1982—2002, Cancer Metastasis, 1984—; contbr. articles to profl. jours., 250 publs. Chmn. local emergency planning com. homeland security Frederick County, 2002—04; trustee Baldwin-Wallace Coll., 1998—. Recipient Charles Thornton award, Litton Industries, 1984, Ohio Found. Ind. Colls. Career Excellence award, 2005. Mem.: Internat. Soc. Immunopharmacology (coun. 1991—), Am. Assn. Immunologists, Am. Assn. Cancer Rsch., Soc. Exptl. Pathology. Achievements include 14 patents in cancer biology and immunotherapy; development and registration for TICE-BCG treatment of bladder cancer; development of technology platform for Oncovax autologous tumor cell vaccine for treatment of stage II colon cancer. Office: Vaccinogen Inc 5300 Westview Dr Ste 406 Frederick MD 21703 Office Phone: 301-668-8400. Business E-Mail: mghannajr@vaccinogeninc.com.

HANNER, JEAN P., retired California state civil servant; b. Toronto, Ont., Can., July 19, 1940; arrived in US, 1953; d. Joseph William and Dorothy Candy; m. Frank M. Beverley (dec.); m. Charles L. Hanner (dec.); 1 child, Anthony David. AS in Nursing, Chaffey Coll., Alta Loma, 1978; BA in Pub. Admin., Calif. Poly., Pomona, 1982. RN Calif., Fla. Dir. psychiat. nursing edn. Lanterman Devel. Ctr., Pomona, Calif., 1964—2003; owner Pat Hanner Art Gallery, Ont., Calif., 1964—. Bd. dirs. psychiat. nursing edn. Pacific Fed. Credit Union, Pomona; bd. dirs. Here We Grow Child Care Ctr., Pomona. Author: (book) Ontario City Sewer System, 1980, A Miracle in the Making, 1993, (book) Continuous Quality Improvement, New Am. Gov., 2009. Doner Parkinsons Resource Ctr., Palm Springs, Calif., Life Outreach Internat., Joyce Myers Ministry, Father Flannigan's Boys Town, Feed The Children, Am. Red Cross, Am. Cancer Soc., Faith Cmty. Home Ch. Named Employee of the Month, Lanterman

Devel. Ctr., 2003, Employee of the Yr., 2003. Mem.: ARC. Avocations: art, gardening, aerobics, swimming. Home and Office: Pat Hanner Art Gallery 911 W Rosewood Ct Ontario CA 91762 Personal E-mail: phanner1@excite.com.

HÄNNINEN, KARI ERKKI, psychiatrist, researcher; b. Helsinki, Finland, Dec. 13, 1963; s. Eino Olavi and Ritva Marita Hänninen; life ptnr. Mari Helena Valkamo; 1 child, Joel Karinpoika. MD, U. Helsinki, 1989. Cert. psychiatrist U. Helsinki, 1997, competence of adminstrn. U. Helsinki, 2003. Dept. psychiatrist Rauha Hosp., Joutseno, Finland, 1990—95; asst. psychiatrist Helsinki U. Ctrl. Hosp., 1995—97; asst. chief psychiatrist South Karelia Ctrl. Hosp., Lappeenranta, 1997—2000, chief psychiatrist, 2000—. Dir. adult psychiatry South Karelia Ctrl. Hosp., 2002—. Grantee, U. Helsinki, 1999, South Karelia Ctrl. Hosp., 2001, U. Tampere, 2003. Mem.: South Karelia Med. Soc. (assoc. Rsch. award 2003), Vyborg Tb Assn. (assoc. Rsch. award 2003), Vyborg Student Assn. (assoc. Rsch. award 2003). Achievements include research in Studies on molecular genetics of schizophrenia. Avocations: sports, Porsche's. Office: South Karelia Ctrl Hosp Valto Käkelän katu 14C/6 Lappeenranta 53130 Finland E-mail: kari.hanninen@ekshp.fi.

HANO, TAKUZO, medical educator; b. Wakayama, Japan, Feb. 7, 1952; s. Senjiro and Sadako Nishimura; m. Taemi Hano, May 3, 1983; children: Shimpei, Chihiro. MD, Wakayama U. Sch. Medicine, Japan, 1977, PhD, 1981. Diplomate med., cardiological, nephrological, gerontol. Rsch. assoc. Wakayama Med. U., 1981—82, adj. asst. prof., 1982—91, asst. prof., 1991—95, assoc. prof. dept. medicine divsn. cardiology, 1995—2006, prof. Ctr. for Ednl. R&D, 2006—. Rsch. assoc. U. So. Calif., L.A., 1986-87. Author: Biosignaling in Cardiac and Vascular System, 1987, Contribution to Nephrology, 1990, Genetic Hypertension, 1992. Recipient Seishu award Wakayama Med. Soc., 1982. Internat. fellow Am. Heart Assn.; mem. Internat. Soc. Hypertension, Internat. Soc. Nephrology, Am. Soc. Hypertension, Japanese Soc. Hypertension (coun. mem. 1992—), Japanese Soc. Nephrology (coun. mem. 1991—), Japanese Coll. Angiology (coun. mem. 1991—), Japan Geriatric Soc. (coun. mem. 1992—). Office: Wakayama Med Univl 811-1 Kimiidera Wakayama 641-8510 Japan

HANRAHAN, LAWRENCE MARTIN, healthcare consultant; b. Cin., Mar. 9, 1961; adopted s. Robert Donald and Mary Francis (Doran) Hanrahan, s. Barry Wright and Kathryn Regina Kinkaid; m. Madeleine Carol Routon. AB in Chemistry, Miami U., 1983; MD, U. Cin. Coll. Medicine, 1988; MBA, U. Tex. Grad. Sch. Bus., 1992. Founder, owner Landscaping group, Cin., 1975—85; chief ultrasound tech., instr., rsch. assoc. Good Samaritan Hosp. Peripheral Vascular Lab., Cin., 1983—84; instr., technologist Clin. Vascular Lab. Christ Hosp., Cin., 1986; tech. cons., instr. Biosound, Inc., Indpls., 1983—89; surg. rsch. fellow divsn. surgery Boston U. Sch. Medicine; instr. peripheral vascular technologist Seton Med. Ctr., Austin, 1991; summer assoc. health care ops. Deloitte & Touche, Houston, 1991, cons. health care ops., 1991—92, sr. cons., 1992—94, mgr. health care ops., 1994—; sr. assoc. healthcare provider cons. William M. Mercer, Inc., Houston, 1995—97; co-founder Hanrahan Williams LLC, Houston, 1997—2000; dir. Genesis Healthcare Internat., Inc., Houston, 2000—01; co-founder, chmn. Interna Quality Healthcare, Profl. Connection, L.P., Houston, 2001—04; sr. mgr. Capgemini US LLC, 2004—05, Accenture, 2005—, global head health facility devel., 2005—10; prin. PWC, 2010—. Founder, chmn., pres. MLH Industries, Inc. (formerly CORE Med. Techs., Inc.), Houston, 1992—; sr. mgr., treas. Miami Med. Edn. and Devel., Miami U., 1975-79; com. mem. Disting. Lecture Series, U. Tex. Sch. Bus., Austin, 1990-91; founding pres. Tex. Bus. Hall of Fame Found. Scholarship Alumni Assn., 1992-93; bd. dirs., exec. com., 1992-93; mem. adv. bd. Healthcorp MBA, Owen Sch., Vanderbilt U., 2005-06; lectr. healthcare adminstrn. program U. Houston, 2002—. Contbr. articles to profl. jours. Finalist ACS resident competition, 1990, San Diego State U. Entrepreneurship competition; winner New Eng. Surg. Soc. resident competition, 1990; Tex. Bus. Hall of Fame Found. scholar, 1991, Abell-Hanger Endowed presdl. scholar, 1991, Accenture HLS Innovation award, 2006. Mem. AMA, Soc. for Vascular Tech., Mass. Med. Soc., Harris County Med. Soc., Med. Student Surg. Soc., Tex. Med. Assn. (chair com. on physician access 1999-2006, alt. del. 2003-06, del. 2006-, cons. coun. on med. edn. 2006—), Harris County Med. Soc., Greater Houston Partnership, Engring. Health Issue Com., Beta Theta Pi. Achievements include patents in field. Avocation: jazz music. Office: 1201 Louisiana Ste 2900 Houston TX 77002 Office Phone: 713-837-1311, 281-610-6258, 713-356-4206. Business E-Mail: lawrence.m.hanrahan@us.pwc.com.

HANRATTY, CARIN GALE, pediatric nurse practitioner; b. Dec. 31, 1953; d. Burton and Lillian Aleskowitz; children: Tyler James, Alison Erin. BSN, Russell Sage Coll., 1975; postgrad., U. Calif., San Diego, 1980, St. Joseph's Cool., 2002—. Cert. CPR instr.; cert. NALS; cert. specialist ANA. PNP day surgery unit Children's Med. Ctr., Dallas, 1981-85; clin. mgr. pediatrics Trinity Med. Ctr., Carrollton, Tex., 1985-86; pediatric drug coord. perinatal intervention team for substance abusing women and babies Parkland Meml. Hosp., Dallas, 1990-97; sch. nurse practitioner Dallas Ind. Sch. Dist., 1997-98; pediat. nurse Sub Sch. NP@Carroll ISD, Southlake, Tex., 1998—2002, Agape Clinics of Tex., 2003—04, Healthcare Med. Assocs., 2004—06, Home Health Care, 2006—08, Dr. Levy Pediat. Med. Edge Health Care, Hurstitx, Tex., 2008—. Guest talk show Morning Coffee, Sta. KPLX-FM, various TV programs. Rep. United Way, 1988-97, blood donor chair Parkland Hosp., 1990-97, chair March of Dimes, 1992-97; bd. dirs., med. cons. KIDNET Found. Mem. ARC (profl., life), Nat. Assn. PNPs (v.p. Dallas chpt. 1982-83), Tex. Nurses Assn. Avocations: sewing, swimming. Home: 2021 Huntington Dr Arlington TX 76010-7631 Personal E-mail: caring1231@yahoo.com, carinhanratty@sbcglobal.net.

HANSBARGER, L. CLARK, dean; b. Welch, W.Va. m. Christine Hansbarger. Grad., Duke U. Sch. Economics and Bus. Adminstrn., Durham, NC, Med. Coll. of Va. Sch. Medicine. Dir. W.Va. Dept. Health, 1981—85; divsn. dir. gen. pediat. U. N.Mex., med. dir. of pediat. ambulatory services, dean grad. med. edn.; assoc. v.p. health sciences, dean sch. medicine, dir. med. edn. W.Va. U., Charleston, 2002—. Office: WVa University Sch Medicine Robert C Byrd Health Sciences Ctr 3110 MacCorkie Ave SE Charleston WV 25304-3110 Office Phone: 304-347-1206. Office Fax: 304-347-1298. Business E-Mail: chansbarger@hsc.wvu.edu. *

HANSEL, WILLIAM, biology professor; b. Vale Summit, Md., Sept. 16, 1918; s. John W. and Helen M. (Sperlein) H.; m. Milbrey Downey, Aug. 16, 1942; children: Barbara, Kay. MS, Cornell U., 1947, PhD, 1949. Asst. prof. Cornell U., Ithaca, N.Y., 1949-52, assoc. prof., 1952-61, prof., 1961-90, Liberty Hyde Bailey prof., 1983-90, chmn. physiology dept., 1978-83; Gordon D. Cain prof. La. State U., Baton Rouge, 1990—. Scientific adv. Merck, Sharp and Dohme, Rahway, 1980-85, Smith, Kline, Beecham, Westchester, Pa., 1986-91. Author: Genetic Engineering of Animals, 1990, Nutrition and Reproduction, 1998; contbr. over 300 articles to profl. jours. Maj. U.S. Army, 1941-46, ETO. Recipient 13 nat. or internat. rsch. and svc. awards including first Pharmacia and Upjohn Internat. award for life time rsch. in ruminant reproduction, 1998. Fellow AAAS; mem. Soc. Study Reprodn. (pres. 1976), Am. Physiol. Soc., Endocrine Soc., Soc. Exptl. Biology and Medicine (treas. 1975), Gamma Sigma Delta, Sigma Xi, Phi Kappa Phi. Achievements include isolation and identification of cusative agent of bovine x-disease; development of successful technique for estrous cycle regulation in cattle; pioneered development of assays for hormones in blood of animals; discovery of control mechanisms for corpus luteum function in cattle; demonstrated the relationships between nutrition and reproduction in cattle; development of successful targeted treatment for human prostate, breast, ovarian and testes cell tumors and metastases grown in test mice. Office: Pennington Biomed Rsch Ctr 6400 Perkins Rd # B1047 Baton Rouge LA 70808-4124 Home Phone: 225-767-1372; Office Phone: 225-763-3198. Business E-Mail: hanselw@pbrc.edu.

HANSELL, JOHN ROYER, retired pathologist; b. Phila., June 30, 1931; s. Henry Lewis and Elizabeth (Campbell) H. AB, U. Pa., Phila., 1953; MD, Jefferson Med. Coll., 1957. Diplomate Am. Bd. Pathology, Am. Bd. Nuclear Medicine (chmn. 1988-89). Intern Germantown Hosp., Phila., 1957-58, resident, pathologist, 1956-61, Bryn Mawr Hosp., Pa., 1961-62; pathology fellow New Eng. Deaconess Hosp., Boston, 1962-63; resident Mayo Clinic, Rochester, Minn., 1966-67; chief nuclear medicine VA Med Ctr., Phila., 1967-93. Contbr. chpts. to books and articles to profl. jours. Comdr. USPHS, 1963-66. Fellow Soc. Nuclear Medicine, Coll. Am. Pathologists. Republican. Avocations: antiques, gardening.

HANSELL, PHYLLIS SHANLEY, nursing educator, administrator, researcher, consultant; b. NYC, Jan. 3, 1947; s. Peter James and Jewell Mae (Altis) S.; m. Robert Lewis Hansell, June 16, 1984; children: Benjamin, Christopher. BS, Fairleigh Dickinson U., 1972; MEd, Columbia U., 1975, EdD, 1981. RN. Staff nurse Mountainside Hosp., Montclair, NJ, 1967-69; head nurse NY Med. Coll., NYC, 1970-72, clin. instr., 1972-75; instr. Seton Hall U., South Orange, NJ, 1975-77, asst. prof., 1977-79, prof. nursing, 1986-94, 96—, dir. nursing rsch., 1986-94, dept. chair, 1996-99, acting dean, 1999-2000, dean Coll. Nursing, 2000—, dean, prof. Coll. Nursing, 2000; dir. nursing rsch. Meml. Sloan-Kettering, NYC, 1984-86. Chair NJ Assn. of Baccalaureate and Higher Degree Programs in Nursing; commr. Nat. Commn. for VA Nursing, 2002—04; mem. adv. coun. Future of Nursing in NJ, 2002—04. Contbr. articles to profl. jours., chpt. to book. Bd. dirs. Jr. League, Montclair, 1992-94, chair grants and corp. devel., chair Newark Teen Arts Festival, Montclair and Newark, 1994-95. Recipient Gov.'s merit award Gov. NJ, 1994. Fellow: Am. Acad. Nursing; mem.: ANA (chair rsch., Gov.'s award 1994), NJ State Nurses Assn. (mem. coun., Rsch. award 1994), Am. Acad. Practice (Disting. Practitioner 2000), Sigma Theta Tau (v.p. Gamma Nu chpt. 1994—96, Rsch. award 1983). Avocations: opera, ballet, skiing, tennis, golf. Office: Seton Hall U 400 S Orange Ave South Orange NJ 07079-2697

HANSELL, RICHARD STANLEY, obstetrician, gynecologist, educator; b. Indpls., Nov. 18, 1950; s. Robert Mathey and Jewell (Martin) H.; m. Cathy C., Oct. 7, 1995; children: Elizabeth, Victoria. BA, DePauw U., 1972; MD, Ind. U., 1976. Cert. Am. Bd. Obstetrics and Gynecology. Practice medicine specializing in ob-gyn. Cedarwood Med. Ctr., St. Joseph, Mich., 1980-86; asst. prof. ob-gyn. Ind. U., Indpls., 1986-93, assoc. prof., 1993—2002, prof., 2002—. Instr. Western Mich. U., Kalamazoo, 1980-86; med. bd. Planned Parenthood, Benton Harbor, Mich., 1980-86; med. dir. Planned Parenthood of Ctrl. Ind., 1991-95; examiner Am. Bd. Ob-gyn., 1994—. Mem. Am. Coll. Ob-gyn., Assn. of Profs. of Gynecology and Obstetrics, Ind. State Med. Soc., Ctrl. Assn. Ob-gyn., Indpls. Med. Soc. Presbyterian. Avocations: golf, fishing. Office: Ind U Med Sch Dept Ob-Gyn 1001 W 10th St Indianapolis IN 46202-2859 Home Phone: 317-823-4235; Office Phone: 317-630-6280. Business E-Mail: rhansell@iupui.edu.

HANSEN, ANDREAS, educational psychologist, researcher; b. Harstad, Troms, Norway, Feb. 14, 1947; s. Hans Andreas and Klara Jonette Hansen; m. Kirsti Bjørg Koppen; children: Andrea Hansine Koppen, Olai Karl-Vegar Koppen, Iver Lars-Håvard Koppen, Oystein Westermann, Ingeborg Westermann. D in Polit. Edn., U. Tromsø. Ednl.-psychol. counsellor Ednl.-Psychol Svcs., Harstad, Troms, 1983—96, Nat. Support Sys. Spl. Edn. N-Norway, Harstad, 1996—. Tchr. Compulsory Sch., Different Cities, Norway, 1971—83. Contbr. articles to profl. jours. Mem.: Internat. Assn. Cognitive Edn. and Psychology. Office: Ednl-Psychol Svcs / PPD Pb 253 9483 Harstad Norway Home Phone: 47 77072027; Office Phone: 47 77028968. Office Fax: 47 77028961. Personal E-mail: andhanse@online.no. Business E-Mail: andreas.hansen@statped.no.

HANSEN, DOMINIQUE, medical researcher; b. Bilzen, Belgium, Apr. 28, 1980; D in Rehab. Scis., Vrije U. Brussel, 2009. Rschr. cardiovasc. medicine, rehab. Jessa Hosp., Hasselt, Belgium, 2004—; docent Hasselt U., 2009. Recipient Student award, ACSM Internat., 2008, Vice Belgian Judo champion, 1996. Mem.: European Soc. Cardiology, Belgian Soc. Cardiology. Home: Beekstraat 7 Sint Truiden 5800 Belgium Personal E-mail: hansen_dominique@yahoo.com. Business E-Mail: dominique.hansen@jessazh.be.

HANSEN, JAMES EDWARD, medical educator, researcher; b. Green Bay, Wis., Sept. 4, 1926; s. James Christian and Helen Dorothy (Terp) H.; m. Beverly May Kapke, June 5, 1948; children: Barbara Parry, Patricia Begley, Linda DeGroot, James H. Student, St. Norbert's Coll., 1942-43, U. Wis., 1943-44, Marquette U., 1944-45; MD, Johns Hopkins U., 1945-49. Diplomate Am. Bd. Internal Medicine. Intern, then resident Letterman Army Med. Ctr., San Francisco, 1949-53; commd. 1st lt. U.S. Army, 1949, advanced through grades to col. Kans., Colo., London, Japan, France, and Jordan, 1975, physician Kans., Colo., London, 1950-62; chief physiology div. U.S. Army Med. Rsch. and Nutrition Lab., Denver, 1962-65; sci. dir. U.S. Army Rsch. Inst. Environ. Medicine, Natick, Mass., 1965-71; chief clin. investigation svcs. Tripler Army Med. Ctr., Honolulu, 1971-75; assoc. prof. dept. medicine UCLA, Torrance, 1976-78, prof. dept. medicine, 1978-86, emeritus prof. dept. medicine, 1986—. Instr., asst. prof. U. Colo., 1961-65; liaison mem. applied physiology study sect. NIH, 1965-71; cons. environ. medicine U.S. Army Surgeon Gen., Washington, 1965-73; lectr. environ. medicine Johns Hopkins U., Balt., 1966-71; clin. prof. physiology U. Hawaii, 1972-75; cons., MET Test. Author: Pulmonary Functionn Testing and Interpretation, 2011, Pulmonary Function Testing and Interferetation, 2011; co-author: Principles of Exercise Testing and Interpretation, 1986, 4th rev. edit., 2005; contbr. numerous articles to profl. jours. Chmn. congregation St. Matthew's Luth. Ch., Aurora, Colo., 1962-64, Gloria Dei Luth. Ch., Pearl City, Hawaii, 1972-74; sch. supt. Luth. Ch., Natick, 1967-69; elder, mission com. chmn. St. Peter's By the Sea Presbyn. Ch., Rancho Palos Verdes, Calif., 1992-95, mem. bd. dirs., SHAWL San Pedro, 1996-; mem. bd. dirs. Vol. Am., LA, 2005-. Pulmonary fellow Fitzsimons Army Med. Ctr., 1960, UCLA Ctr. Health Scis., 1975-76; recipient Sustaining Membership award Assn. Mil. Surgeons, 1970, Calif. medal Am. Lung Assn., 1996; named Layperson of Yr., South Coast Interfaith Coun., 2004, Disting. Scientist Honor Lectr. Am. Coll. Chest Physicians, 2008. Fellow ACP, Am. Coll. Chest Physicians; mem. Am. Physiol. Soc., Am. Thoracic Soc. (sci. adv. bd. 1983-00), Calif. Thoracic Soc. (pulmonary chmn. 1980-83, physiology com), Internat. Soc. Exercise Intolerance Rsch. and Edn. (founding mem. 2005-, advisor bd. dirs. 2005-08). Avocations: piano, tennis. Home: 1692 Morse Dr San Pedro CA 90732-4336 Office: Harbor-UCLA Med Ctr PO Box 405 1000 W Carson St Torrance CA 90502-2004 Office Phone: 310-222-3803. Personal E-mail: jimandbev@cox.net.

HANSEN, JENNIE CHIN, medical association administrator; b. NY, 1948; BS in Nursing, Boston Coll., 1970, D (hon.), 2008; MSN, U. Calif., San Francisco, 1971. RN. Exec. dir., CEO On Lok Sr. Health Services, San Francisco, 1980—2004; sr. fellow U. Calif. San Francisco Ctr. Health Professions; pres. Am. Assn. Retired Persons (AARP), 2008—10; CEO Am. Geriatrics Soc., 2010—. Prof. nursing, part-time faculty San Francisco State U., 2005—; bd. dirs. SCAN Found., 2009—; commn. mem. Robert Wood Johnson Found./Inst. Medicine Inititative on Future of Nursing, 2009—; bd. officer Nat. Acad. Social Ins.; fed. commr. Medicare Payment Adv. Commn. (MedPAC); nat. adv. com. mem. Robert Wood Johnson Exec. Nurses Program. Recipient Maxwell Pollack award for Productive Living, Gerontological Soc. America, 2002, Adminstr.'s Achievement award, Ctr. Medicare & Medicaid Services, 2005; named Women's Healthcare Exec. Woman of Yr., No. Calif., 2000. Fellow: Am. Acad. Nursing; mem.: Am. Soc. Aging (past pres.). Office: Am Geriatrics Soc Empire State Bldg 350 Fifth Ave Ste 801 New York NY 10118 Office Phone: 202-308-1414. Office Fax: 212-832-8646. *

HANSEN, JO-IDA CHARLOTTE, psychology professor, researcher; d. Gordon Henry and Charlotte Lorraine (Helgeson) Hansen; m. John Paul Campbell. BA, U. Minn., 1969, MA, 1971, PhD, 1974. Asst. prof. psychology U. Minn., Mpls., 1974-78, assoc. prof., 1978-84, prof., 1984—, dir. Ctr. for Interest Measurement Rsch., 1974—, dir. counseling psychology program, 1987—, dir. Vocat. Assessment Clinic, 1997—, prof. human resources and indsl. rels., 1997—, assoc. dean for rsch. and grad. studies Coll. Liberal Arts, 2005—. Author: User's Guide for the SII, 1984, 2d edit., 1992, Manual for the SII, 1985 2d edit. 1994; editor: Measurement and Evaluation in Counseling and Development, 1993-2000; editor Jour. Counseling Psychology, 1999-2005; contbr. over 160 articles to profl. jours., chpts. to books. Recipient early career award U. Minn., 1982, E.K. Strong, Jr. gold medal, 1984, Leona Tyler award, Am. Counseling Assn. Extended Rsch. award. Fellow APA (coun. reps. 1990-93, 97-99, pres. divsn. counseling psychology 1993-94, chmn. joint com. testing practices 1989-93, com. to revise APA/Am. Ednl. Rsch. Assn. Nat. Coun. Ednl. Measurement Evaluating Psychologing Testing Stds. 1993-99, 2009-, exam. com. Assn. State Provincial Psychology Bds. 1996-99, bd. sci. affairs, 2003-05, chair coun. of editors 2003-04; Leona Tyler award for rsch. and profl. svc. 1996, Psychology Lifetime Achievement award, 2009, Minn. Psychol. Assn. Grad. Student Mentor award 2011), ACA (extended rsch. award 1990, disting. rsch. award 1996), ARA, ACS; mem. Assn. for Measurement and Evaluation (pres. 1988-89, Exemplary Practice award 1987, 90). Avocations: golf, theater, music, water and downhill skiing, spectator sports. Office: U Minn Dept Psychology Ctr Interest Measurement 75 E River Rd Minneapolis MN 55455-0280 Office Phone: 612-625-3873, 612-625-2081. Business E-Mail: hanse004@umn.edu.

HANSEN, KARINA HELENE AIMEE, economist, director; b. Glostrup, Denmark, Sept. 10, 1973; d. Claus Unn Hansen and Josee Helene Aimee Hansen Caron. BSc, Copenhagen U., 1996, MSc, 1998; MPH, U. Paris 1 Pantheon-Sorbonne, 1999; PhD, U. Paris XI, 2005. Rsch. mgr. H. Lundbeck, Paris, 2000—02, pharmacoecon. mgr., 2002—05, sect. head, 2006—07, dir., 2007—. Reviewer PEDS, England, 2006—. Contbr. articles to profl. jours., chapters to books. Avocations: sailing, running. Office: H Lundbeck 37 Ave Pierre 1er de Serbie Paris 75008 France Business E-Mail: khan@lundbeck.com.

HANSEN, LISE LOTTE, geneticist, educator; b. Aarhus, Denmark, July 6, 1956; MSc, Aarhus U., 1986, Phd, 1994. Assoc. prof. Aarhus U., 1996—. Bd. mem. inst. human genetics Aarhus U., 2001—04, asst. head dept., inst. human genetics, 2003—04, dep. head danish centre molecular gerontology, 2005—07, bd. mem. inst. human genetic, 2009—. Recipient Rsch. award, Kbm. Rasmussen & Wife, Karen Krieger Found., Holger & Inez Petersens Meml. award, Ms. Astrid Taysens award. Mem.: Danish Soc. Clin. Genetics, Danish Soc. Cancer Rsch., Am. Assn. Cancer Rsch. Office: University Aarhus Wilhelm Meyers Allé 4 Aarhus 8000 C Denmark Office Fax: 45 8612 3173. E-mail: lotte@humgen.au.dk.

HANSEN, MARY MINCER, healthcare consultant, former state agency administrator; b. Norfolk, Va., Mar. 8, 1948; d. Dale Francis and Mildred Irene (Thomas) Mincer; m. Roger V. Hansen; 1 child, Raymond. BSN, Creighton U., 1970; MSN, Tex. Woman's U., 1981; PhD, Iowa State U., 1993. RN, Iowa. Staff nurse Mercy Hosp., Des Moines, 1970-72; instr. Mercy Sch. Nursing, Des Moines, 1972-86; asst. prof. divsn. nursing Grand View Coll., Des Moines, 1981-84; asst. prof. to assoc. prof. dept. nursing Drake U., Des Moines, 1986—2003; dir. Iowa Dept. Public Health, Des Moines, 2003—07; pres. Hansen Health Consultation, 2007—. Bd. dirs. Drake Ctr. Health Issues; rsch. fellow Iowa Dept. Public Health 2000-2003; part-time faculty mem. Des Moines U. Dept. Global Health. Contbr.: Nurse Manager Problem Solver, 1994. Presdl. appointee Pres.'s Adv. Com. on Arts; mem. Senator Tom Harkin's Health Adv. Group, 1990—,

Nat. Health Policy Coun., 1993—; past dir. Drake Ctr. Health Issues; past pres. Iowa Public Health Found.; co-chmn. Iowans United for Healthy Future. Mem. Assn. State & Territorial Health Officials (pres. elect 2005), Iowa League for Nursing (pres. 1991-93), Iowa Nurses Assn. (dist. pres. 1995-97, Theresa Christy award), Sigma Theta Tau, Phi Delta Kappa Internat., Phi Kappa Phi. Office: Hansen Health Consultation 5210 Tamara Pt Panora IA 50216-8611 Business E-Mail: mchansen@netins.net.

HANSEN, RONALD C., dermatologist, educator; MD, U. Iowa, 1968. Diplomate Am. Bd. Pediatrics, 1974, Am. Bd. Dermatology, 1980. Fellow dermatology Univ. Med. Ctr., Tuscon, Ariz., 1978—80; resident pediat. Childrens Hosp., LA, 1969—70, Stanford Univ. Med. Ctr., Stanford, Calif., 1970—72; prof. dermatology Univ. Ariz. Coll. Medicine; hosp. affiliation include Phoenix Children's Hosp. Office: Phoenix Childrens Hospital Department Dermatology 1919 E Thomas Rd Main West Bldg Fl 2 Phoenix AZ 85006 Office Phone: 602-546-0895.

HANSEN, THOMAS NANASTAD, hospital administrator, pediatrician; b. Neenah, Wis., Oct. 11, 1947; m. Cheryl Bailey, June 9, 1979; children: Elaine Christ, William Thomas. BS in Physics summa cum laude, Tex. Christian U., 1970; MD, Baylor Coll. Medicine, 1973. Diplomate Am. Bd. Pediatrics. Intern in pediatrics Baylor Coll. Medicine, Houston, 1973-74, resident in pediatrics, 1974-76, postdoctoral fellow in neonatal perinatal medicine, 1976-78; postdoctoral fellow in pediatric pulmonary disease U. Calif., San Francisco, 1978-81; asst. prof. pediatrics Baylor Coll. Medicine, 1978-84, assoc. prof. pediatrics, 1984-89; prof. pediatrics and cell biology Tex. Children's Hosp. Found., Houston, 1989-95; head sect. on neonatology Baylor Coll. of Medicine, 1987-95, vice-chmn. rsch. dept. pediatrics, 1994-95, dir. child health rsch. ctr., 1994-95, co-dir. ctr. for tng. in molecular medicine, 1994-95; chmn. pediat., CEO Children's Hosp., Columbus, Ohio, 1995—2005; pres., CEO Children's Hosp. and Regional Med. Ctr., Seattle, 2005—. Mem. exam com. Am. Bd. Pediatrics, 1982—, sub-bd. neonatal-perinatal medicine, 1992—, chmn. credentials com., 1993—, chmn.-elect sub-bd. neonatal perinatal medicine, 1994. Contbr. numerous articles to profl. jours. Trustee Tex. Women's Hosp., 1988-91. Mem. Western Soc. for Pediatric Rsch., So. Soc. for Pediaatric Rsch., Soc. for Pediatric Rsch. (sec.-treas. 1986-91, chmn. student rsch. com. 1990—, trustee internat. chpt. 1992—), Am. Physiol. Soc., Am. Pediatric Soc., Am. Fedn. for Clin. Rsch., Am. Thoracic Soc., Am. Acad. of Pediatrics, N.Y. Acad. of Scis., Am. Soc. for Cell Biology, Assn. of Med. Sch. Pediatric Dept. Chmn., Sigma Xi. Office: Children's Hosp and Regional Med Ctr PO Box 5371 Seattle WA 98105-0371

HANSEN-FLASCHEN, JOHN HYMAN, medical educator, researcher; b. Hamilton, Ohio, June 25, 1950; s. Steward Samuel and Joyce (Davies) Flaschen; m. Susan Laurella Hansen, Aug. 22, 1951; children: Lynn, Lauren. AB, Brown U., 1972, MD, NYU, 1976. Diplomate in internal medicine, pulmonary medicine, critical care medicine Am. Bd. Internal Medicine. Resident in medicine U. Pa., Phila., 1976-79, chief resident in medicine, 1980-81, pulmonary fellow, 1979-80, 81-82, attending physician, 1982—, asst. prof. medicine, 1982-87, assoc. prof., 1988-98, prof., 1999—, dir. edn. and tng. programs in pulmonary and critical care, 1983-90, dir. pulmonary and critical care divsn., 1990-98, chief pulmonary, allergy and critical care divsn., 1998—, dir. Penn Lung Ctr., 1996— Mem. editl. bd. Clin. Pulmonary Medicine, Respiratory Medicine, UpToDate; editor Pulmonary and Critical Care MKSAP 13, ACP; contbr. articles to profl. jours. Steering com. Nat. Emphysema Treatment Trial, 1997—2003. Recipient Spl. Investigator award Am. Heart Assn., 1982-84, Lindback Tchg. award U. Pa., 1999, others; Measey Found. fellow, 1982-83. Fellow ACP, Am. Coll. Chest Physicians, Coll. Physicians Phila.; mem. Am. Thoracic Soc. (chmn. postgrad. edn. com. 1995—, clin. problems long range planning com. 1997-99, Clinician Educator award 2004), Soc. for Critical Care Medicine, Soc. for Bioethics Consultation, Laennec Soc. Phila. (pres. 1990-91), Drinker Soc. for Critical Care in Phila. (founder, 1st pres. 1988-90), Sigma Xi, Alpha Omega Alpha. Democrat. Home: 365 Penn Rd Wynnewood PA 19096-1401 Office: Hosp U Pa 873 Mahoney Bldg 3400 Spruce St Philadelphia PA 19104-4206 Office Phone: 215-662-6003.

HANSHAW, JAMES BARRY, pediatrician, educator, artist; b. Scarsdale, NY, Dec. 23, 1928; s. George Lee and Kathryn Frances (Reilly) H.; m. Marian Christine Kernan, Aug. 14, 1954; children: Thomas, Lee, Elizabeth, John, Margaret. AB, Syracuse U., NY, 1950; MD, SUNY, Syracuse, 1953, DSc (hon.), 1991. Intern Cin. Gen. Hosp., 1953-54; resident pediatrics U. Rochester Med. Center, 1956-58; Nat. Found. postdoctoral fellow virology Harvard U. Sch. Pub. Health, 1958-60; academic medicine, specializing in pediatrics Rochester, NY, 1960-75; instr. to prof. pediatrics and microbiology U. Rochester Sch. Medicine, 1960-75; prof., chmn. dept. pediatrics U. Mass., Worcester, 1975-85, interim vice chancellor, acad. dean, 1985-86; interim chancellor, 1987; provost, dean U. Mass., 1986-89, dean and provost emeritus, 1989—2010, prof. pediat., 1975—2010, emeritus prof. pediat., 2010—, interim chmn. dept. pediatrics, 1997-98; chmn. dept. pediatrics Meml. Health Care, 1993-98. Lectr. pediatrics Harvard U. Med. Sch., 1975-2002; vis. prof. Inst. Child Health, London U. and Hosp. for Sick Children, London, 1971-72; coll. health physician WPI, 1990—2010. Author: (with J.A. Dudgeon) Viral Infections Fetus and Newborn, 1978, 2d edit. (with Dudgeon and W.C. Marshall), 1985, The Art of J. Barry Hanshaw: Forty Favorite Works with Reflections From the Artist, 2009. Served with USAF, 1953-56. Recipient Career Rsch. Devel. award NIH, 1962-72, Disting. Alumnus award Upstate Med. U., 2003, Career Achievement award Worcester Dist. Med. Soc., 2004, Disting. Resident Alumnus award U. Rochester Med. Ctr., 2006; Buswell fellow U. Rochester, 1960-62; NIH grantee, 1962-75. Mem. AMA, Am. Pediatric Soc., Soc. Pediatric Research, Am. Acad. Pediatrics, Infectious Diseases Soc. Am., New Eng. Pediatric Soc., Sigma Xi, Alpha Omega Alpha. Home: 18 Baypath Dr Boylston MA 01505-1427 Home Phone: 508-869-6038.

HANSON, ARTHUR STUART, physician, consultant; b. Mpls., Mar. 10, 1937; s. Arthur Emanuel and Frances Elenor (Larson) H.; m. Gail Joan Taylor, June 16, 1963; children: Marta Eileen, Peter Arthur. BA, Dartmouth Coll., 1959; MD, U. Minn., 1963. Diplomate Am. Bd. Internal Medicine, Am. Bd. Pulmonary Disease. Intern Hennipen County Med. Ctr., 1963-64; resident in internal medicine U. Minn., 1964-65, 68-70, fellow pulmonary disease, 1970-71; cons. in pulmonary and critical care medicine Park Nicollet Clinic, Mpls., 1971—2011, med. dir., 1975-82, v.p. legis. and cmty. affairs, 1982-86; dir. med. edn. Park Nicollet Med. Found., Mpls., 1982-86; pres., CEO Park Nicollet Inst., Mpls., 1986—2002. Bd. dirs. Minn. Health Data Inst., 1993-03. Pres., bd. chair Minn. Smoke Free Coalition, 1985-88, 96-98, 2005-07; vice chair Minn. Partnership for Action Against Tobacco, 1998-2003; chmn. bd. Smoke Free Generation Minn., 1984-90. Recipient Cmty. Leadership award, Am. Lung Assn. Hennepin County, 1987, Harvey H. Rogers Meml. award, Minn. Pub. Health Assn., 1988, award for excellence in health promotion, Minn. Health Commr., 1989, Physician of Excellence award, Park Nicollet Health Svcs., 2000, Lynn Smith 25-Yr. award, Am. Cancer Soc., 2001, Harold S. Diehl Lifetime Achievement award, U. Minn. Med. Found., 2007, Physician of Excellence award, Park Nicollet Methodist Hosp, 2000. Fellow ACP, AMA (del., chmn.), Am. Coll. Chest Physicians; mem. Minn. Med. Assn. (pres. 1992-93, Stop the Violence award 1994, Disting. Svc. award 1998), Minn. Healthcare Coalition on Violence, Hennepin Med. Soc. (pres. 1990-91, Charles Bolles Bolles-Rogers award 1998, Shotwell award 2007). Unitarian Universalist. Avocations: birding, gardening, physical fitness, reading, travel. Office: Park Nicollet Clinic Ste 300 6490 Excelsior Blvd Minneapolis MN 55426 Home Phone: 612-676-1591; Office Phone: 952-993-3242. Business E-Mail: hansoa@parknicollet.com.

HANSON, DANIEL R., psychiatrist, educator; b. Fargo, ND, Jan. 26, 1947; s. Ralph and Lila H.; children: Erik, Matthew, Kendra. BA, U. Minn., 1969, PhD, 1974, MD, 1983. Diplomate Am. Bd. Med. Examiners Psychiatry. Assoc. prof. psychiatry & psychology U. Minn., Mpls., 1987—; chmn. dept. psychiatry Regions Hosp., St. Paul, 1991—2002; staff psychiatrist VA Med. Ctr., Mpls., 2002—. Chairperson dept. psychiatry St. Paul Ramsey Med. Ctr., 1991—, bd. dirs., 1993—. Author: Schizophrenia: The Epigenetic Puzzle, 1982. Grantee, Stanley Med. Found., 2003—06. Fellow: Am. Psychopathological Assn., Assn. Psychol. Sci., Am. Psychiat. Assn. (disting. fellow). Office: Dept Psychiatry F 282/2A W 2450 Riverside Ave Minneapolis MN 55454 Office Fax: 612-273-9779. Business E-Mail: drhanson@umn.edu.

HANSON, DENNIS MICHAEL, retired health facility administrator; b. Cleve., Aug. 20, 1943; s. John Joseph and Victoria (Tucholski) H. BBA, Cleve. State U., 1971; MPH, U. Pitts., 1974. Asst. adminstr. Huron Rd. Hosp., Cleve., 1974—76; adminstr. asst. Mt. Sinai Med. Ctr., Cleve., 1976—80; dir. radiology U. Louisville, 1980—84, assoc. prof., 1982—86; sr. cons. Honeywell, Mpls., 1986—87; mgr. radiology U. N.C., Chapel Hill, 1987—90; mgr. diagnostic imaging Kaiser Hosp., Honolulu, 1990—97; cons. Dowdy Mgmt. and Consulting, Cocoa Beach, Fla., 1999—2000; radiol. technician Norton Healthcare, Louisville, 2000—04; ret., 2005. Councilman City of Meadowbrook Farm, Ky., 1982-86. With USAF, 1961-65. Named Ky. Colonel, 1984. Fellow Am. Coll. Healthcare Execs.; mem. Am. Hosp. Radiology Adminstrs. Home: Unit 103 3901 Yardley Ct Louisville KY 40299-7355

HANSON, LAURA C., geriatrician, educator; MD, Harvard U., 1986. Diplomate Am. Bd. Internal Medicine, 1989, Am. Bd. Internal Medicine-geriatric medicine, 2002, Am. Bd. Internal Medicine-hospice & palliative medicine, 2009. Resident internal medicine Brigham & Women's Hosp., 1986—88, Univ. NC Hosp., 1988—89, fellow geriatric medicine, 1989—91; assoc. prof. geriatric medicine Univ. NC Sch. of Medicine, co-dir. palliative care program. Office: University of North Carolina Hospitals 101 Manning Dr Chapel Hill NC 27514-4220 Office Phone: 919-966-4131. E-mail: lhanson@med.unc.edu.

HANSON, VICTOR ARTHUR, gerontologist, retired surgeon; b. Syracuse, NY, May 5, 1933; s. Victor Arthur Sr. and Dorothy (Burns) H.; m. Mary Diane Nadijcka, Sept. 13, 1985. AB, Princeton U., 1955; MD, U. Pa., 1959. Diplomate Am. Bd. Surgery. Intern then resident, instr. surgery U. Pa. Hosp., Phila., 1964-69, chief resident, 1968-69; instr. surgery SUNY, Syracuse, N.Y., 1969-71, asst. prof. surgery, 1971-78, clin. asst. prof. surgery, 1978-80; asst. prof. surgery Thomas Jefferson U., Phila., 1980-88; pvt. practice Syracuse, 1969-80; dir. rsch. VA Med. Ctr., Wilmington, Del., 1983-87; pvt. practice Wilmington, Del., 1987-90; staff surgeon HMO, Atlanta, 1990-96; pvt. practice in geriatrics Atlanta, 1996—; ret. surgeon. Contbr. articles to profl. jours. Lt., naval flight surgeon, USN, 1961-64, Vietnam. Grantee Am. Heart Assn., 1975, FDA, 1988, Merit Rev. X Z Vets. Adminstn. Hosp. System. Fellow ACS; mem. AMA, Med. Assn. Ga., Med. Assn. Atlanta, Soc. Surgery of the Alimentary Tract, So. Med. Assn. Avocations: tennis, model railroading. Home: 3875 W Nancy Creek Ct NE Atlanta GA 30319-4803 Office Phone: 404-255-6894. Personal E-mail: vahanson@bellsouth.net.

HANSRAJ, KENNETH KARAMCHAND, surgeon, research scientist; b. Georgetown, Guyana, Oct. 28, 1961; arrived in U.S., 1974; s. Augustus and Anjanie Hansraj; m. Marcia Dee Griffin, Aug. 1, 1998; 1 child, Jonathan. BS, Fairleigh Dickinson U., 1982; grad., Columbia U. Sch. General Studies; MD, Hahnemann U., 1987. Cert. Am. Bd. Minimally Invasive Spinal Medicine and Surgery, 1999, Am. Bd. Orthopedic Surgeons, 2001, Nat. Bd. Med. Examiners, 1989, lic. N.Y., 1996, Calif., 1991. Fellow in biomechanics Hosp. for Special Surgery, NYC, 1987—88; gen. surgery tng. Mt. Sinai Hosp., NYC, 1988—90; resident orthopaedic surgery King/Drew Med. Ctr., LA, 1990—95; fellow in minimally invasive spinal surgery Calif. Ctr. for Minimally Invasive Spine Surgery, Thousand Oaks, Calif., 1995; fellow in scoliosis and spinal surgery Hosp. for Special Surgery, NYC, 1995—96; spinal surgeon, dir. NY Spine Surgery & Rehab. Medicine PLLC, Poughkeepsie, NY, 1997—. Attending orthopaedic surgeon St. Francis Hosp., Poughkeepsie, NY, 1997—, St. Vincent's Hosp., Staten Island, NY, 1997—, Bailey Seton Hosp., Staten Island, NY, 1997—; jr. attending orthop. surgeon Hosp. for Special Surgery, NYC, 1995—96, New York Hosp., NYC, 1995—96, Meml.-Sloan Kettering Med. Ctr., NYC, 1995—96; presenter in field. Editor: Surgical Techniques International; contbr. articles to profl. and med. jours. Fellow: Am. Acad. Orthopaedic Surgeons. Office: NY Spine Surgery & Rehabilitation Medicine PLLC Ste 202 243 North Rd Poughkeepsie NY 12601 Home Phone: 845-471-1551; Office Phone: 845-471-9200. Office Fax: 845-471-1551. Personal E-mail: specialspine@aol.com.

HAO, CHUNHAI, pathologist, researcher; arrived in Can., 1986, naturalized; s. Chang Cheng Hao and Shu Jun Song; 1 child, Jason Z. MD, Jilin Med. Coll., China, 1982; MSc, Norman Bethune U. Med. Scis., Chang Chun, China, 1985; PhD, U. Sask., Can., 1991. Lic. Med. Coun. Can., med. lic. Ga. Resident neuropathology U. We. Ontario, Canada, 1992—97; asst. prof. neuropathologist U. Alta. and Hosps., Edmonton, Canada, 1997—2002, assoc. prof. neuropathologist, 2002—04, Emory U. and Hosp., Atlanta, 2004—. Clin. investigator Alberta Heritage Found. Med. Rsch., 2000—04. Named Disting. scholar, Ga. Cancer Coalition, 2005—. Fellow: Royal Coll. Physicians & Surgeons Can. (licentiate; specialist cert. in neuropathology); mem.: Soc. Neuro-Oncology, Am. Soc. Investigative Pathology, Am. Soc. Biochemistry and Molecular Biology, Am./Can. Assn. Neuropathologists, Am. Assn. Cancer Rsch. Achievements include understanding of pathobiology of human cancers. Office: Emory Univ Winship Cancer Inst 1365-C Clifton Rd NE Atlanta GA 30322 Office Fax: 404-778-5550. Business E-Mail: chao@emory.edu.

HAO, SHOUGANG, science educator; b. Beijing, Apr. 2, 1942; M, Peking U., 1981. Prof. Peking U., 1992—2006. Mem.: Palaeontological Soc. China. Office: Sch Earth & Space Scis Peki Beijing 100871 China Business E-Mail: sghao@pku.edu.cn.

HAO, XI-SHAN, hospital administrator; b. 1946; Grad., Tianjin Med. U. Prof. oncology Tianjin Med. Univ., pres., 1994—; academician Chinese Acad. of Engring., 2003—. Recipient State Progress of Sci. and Tech. in Med. Sci. award, 2nd prize, Med. Sci. and Tech. award, 1st prize. Office: Tianjin Medical University Hospital Ti-Yuan-Bei Huan-Hu-Xi Road He-Xi District Tianjin 30060 China Office Phone: 862223340123. *

HAPNER, BYRON, gynecologist; b. Knoxville, Tenn., Sept. 19, 1963; DO, NY Coll. Osteo. Medicine NY Inst. Tech., 1990. Clin. asst. prof., ob-gyn. U. Pa. Health Sys., 1994—2010; co-owner Premier Women's Health South Jersey, 2010—. Fellow: Am. Coll. Ob-Gyn. Office: 155 Bridgeton Pike Ste C Premier Women Mullica Hill NJ 08062 Office Phone: 856-223-8930. E-mail: bhapner@pwhsj.com.

HAPP, ERIK M., medical educator; MD, Hahnemann U. Diplomate Am. Bd. Opthalmology. Intern Nat. Naval Med. Ctr.; resident Univ. Pitts. Med. Ctr.; instr. surgery Drexel Univ.; fellow Allegheny Gen. Hosp., practice, physician. Named one of Top Doctors, Pitts. mag., 2011. Office: Allegheny General Hospital 320 E N Ave Pittsburgh PA 15212 Office Phone: 412-359-3131. Office Fax: 412-359-4108.

HAQUE, IKRAM, medical educator; b. Karachi, Pakistan, Mar. 25, 1970; MBBS, Dow Med. Coll., U. Karachi, 1994. Assoc. prof. & divsn. chief U. Tex. health, 2009—. Fellow: Am. Acad. Pediat. Office: 6431 Fannin St MSB 3228 Houston TX 77030 Office Fax: 713-500-0588. Business E-Mail: ikram.haque@uth.tmc.edu.

HAQUE, KAMRUL, research scientist; b. Narsingdi, Bangladesh, Feb. 3, 1968; BSc in Biochemistry with honors, 1991, PhD in Food and Nutritional Scis., 2005. Rsch. scientist U. Coll. Cork, Ireland, 2006—10. Recipient Dean's Hon. award, Dhaka U., Bangladesh. Avocations: reading, sports, movies. Home: Genazzano Bendemeer Pk Magazine Rd Cork Ireland Personal E-mail: kamrul67@yahoo.com.

HAQUE, MALIKA HAKIM, pediatrician; b. Madras, India; arrived in US, 1967; d. Syed Abdul and Rahimunisa (Hussain) Hakim; m. C. Azeez Haque, Feb. 5, 1967; children: Kifizeba Haque Akbar, Masarath Haque Khan, Asim Zayd Haque. MBBS, Madras Med. Coll., 1967. Diplomate Am. Bd. Pediatrics. Rotating intern Miriam Hosp. Brown U., Providence, 1967-68; resident in pediatrics N.J. Coll. Medicine Childrens Hosp., 1968-70; fellow in devel. disabilities Ohio State U., 1970-71; acting chief pediat. Nisonger Ctr., 1973-74; staff pediatrician Children and Youth Project Children's Hosp., Columbus, Ohio; clin. asst. prof. pediatrics Ohio State U., 1974-80, clin. assoc. prof. pediatrics, 1981-99, clin. assoc. prof. dept. internat. health Coll. Medicine, 1993-99, clin. prof. pediatrics and internat. health Coll. Medicine, 1999—, med. dir. Noor cmty. clinic, Rardin family practice ctr. Columbus, Ohio, 2010—. Pediatrician Children's Hosp. Physician Health Ctrs. Children's Hosp., Columbus, 1982—; dir. Pediat. Academic Assn., 1992-2002; cons. Ctrl. Ohio Head Start Program, 1974-79; med. cons. Bur. Rehab. and Devel. Disabilities for State of Ohio, 1990—. Contbr. articles to profl. jours. and newspapers. Charter founder Ronald Reagan Rep. Ctr.; trustee Asian Am. Health Alliance Network, Columbus, 1994-01; bd. trustee Islamic Found. Ctrl. Ohio, 2006-09; bd. regents Islamic Medical Assn. North Am., 2007—. Recipient Physician Recognition award, AMA, 1971—86, 1988—99, 2002—05, Gold medals in surgery, radiology, pediat. and ob-gyn., Presdl. medal of Merit, Pres. Ronald Reagan, 1982, Nat. Leadership award, Nat. Rep. Congl. Com., 2001, Physician of the Yr. award, 2003, Outstanding Svc. award, CAIR Ohio, 2005, Islamic Medical Assn. North Am., 2005; named one of Americas Top Pediatrician, Consumer's Rsch. Coun. America, 2008—. Fellow Am. Acad. Pediatrics; mem. Islamic Med. Assn., Noor Islamic Cultural Ctr. (Ohio) (Outstanding Svc. and Contbn. award 2008), Am. Assn. Physicians Indian Origin, Pediat. Acad. Assn. (dir. 1992-02), Ambulatory Pediat. Assn., Ctrl. Ohio Pediatric Soc., Culturally Diverse Patient Care, Joint Commn. Hosps. Accreditation Healthcare Orgns. (expert adv. panelist 2008-). Achievements include research on enuresis and tumors caused by human papilloma viruses. Office: 700 Childrens Dr Columbus OH 43205-2664 Home: 5095 Noor Park Cir Dublin OH 43016

HARA, KOJI, medical educator; b. Fukuoka, Japan, Aug. 11, 1969; MD, U. Occupl. and Environ. Health, PhD, 2000. Asst. prof., dept. anesthesiology U. Occupl. and Environ. Health Sch. Medicine, 2000—. Office: 1-1 Iseigaoka Yahatanishiku Kitakyushu Fukuoka 807-8555 Japan Business E-Mail: kojihara@med.uoeh-u.ac.jp.

HARADA, SHOJI, medical researcher; BS, MA, U. Tokyo, Bunkyo-ku, PhD, 1972. Rsch. assoc. Kyorin U., Sch. Medicine, Mitaka, Shinkawa, Japan, 1972—76; prof. U. Tsukuba, Cmty. Medicine, Ibaraki, Japan, 1976—2002; dir. sci. bd. SRL, Inc., Tokyo, 2002—. Fellow, Alexander-Humbolt Found., Germany, 1976—79. Achievements include discovery of ALDH2 polymorphism.

HARADA, TASUKU, medical educator; b. Japan, Feb. 20, 1958; MD, Tottori U., PhD, 1983. Ob-gyn. prof., faculty medicine Tottori U., 2008—. Avocations: reading, golf. Office: Nishi cho 36-1 Yonago Tottori 683-8504 Japan Business E-Mail: tasuku@med.tottori-u.ac.jp.

HARADA, TSUTOMU, pharmaceutical executive; b. Saitama, Japan, Jan. 20, 1967; MSc in Engring., Osaka Prefecture U., 1992; PhD in Pharmacology, Mukogawa Women's U., 2010. Sr. rschr. Formulation Rsch. Lab. Kawashima Rsch., Eisai Co., Ltd., 1992—2008; sr. mgr., planning and ops. dept., Discovery & Devel. Rsch. Hdqs. Japan Eisai Co., Ltd., 2008—09, sr. mgr., customer joy dept., Eisai Japan Planning & Operation Sect., 2009—. Vis. lectr. Syowa U., 2011.

Recipient HHC award, Eisai Co., Ltd., 2007. Avocations: music, travel. Office: Koishikawa 5-5-5 Bunkyo Tokyo 112-8088 Japan Office Fax: 81-3-3811-8837. Business E-Mail: t-harada@hhc.eisai.co.jp.

HARANATH, PALEPU SITA RAMA KRISHNA, pharmacologist, educator; b. Gajapathinagaram, Andhra Pradesh, India, Nov. 9, 1927; s. Gumpaswami and Perindevi P.; m. Kasturi Namboori, Feb. 10, 1950 (dec. Jan. 1953); m. Savithri Mocherla, Feb. 2, 1955; children: Jagannath, Manikyam. MBBS, Andhra Med. Coll., Visakhapatnam, 1949, MD in Pharmacology and Therapeutics, 1952, DSc in Pharmacology, 1960; Doc. (hon.), NTR Med. U., 2009. Prof. pharmacology Kurnool (India) Med. Coll., 1957-79; prof. Osmania Med. Coll., Hyderabad, India, 1974-75, Arab Med. U., Benghazi, Libya, 1984-86; prof. emeritus Nat. Inst. of Nutrition, Hyderabad, India, 1987-88; prof. Annamalai U., Annamalainagar, India, 1988-92; prof. pharamacology Arab Med. U., Benghazi, Libya, 1992-94. Dir. med. edn. Andhra Pradesh State, Hyderabad, 1981-83, additional dir. med. edn., 1979-81; prin. Kurnool Med. Coll., 1975-79, vice prin., 1966-74; mem. Med. Coun. of India, 1978-84. Contbr. articles to profl. jours. Fellow WHO, 1958-59, 68-69; recipient Dr. Achanta Lakshmipathi award Nat. Acad. Med. Scis., India, 1992, Dr. B.C. Roy award for eminent med. tchr. Med. Coun. India, 1979, Dr. B.N. Ghosh Oration award Indian Pharmacol. Soc., 1980, Dr. Yellapragada Subbarao Oration award Indian Med. Assn., 1980, Dr. Gurraju Meml. Oration award, 1980. Fellow Nat. Acad. of Med. Scis., Internat. Med. Scis. Acad.; mem. British Pharmacol. Soc., Ind. Coun. of Med. Rsch. Home: Flat 22 Alka 15th Rd Mumbai 400 054 India

HARARY, KEITH, research scientist, writer, science journalist; b. NYC, Feb. 9, 1953; s. Victor and Lillian (Mazur) H.; m. Darlene Moore, Oct. 22, 1985. BA in Psychology, Duke U., 1975; PhD, Union Inst., 1986. Crisis counselor Durham Mental Health Ctr., NC, 1972-76; rsch. assoc. Psychical Rsch. Found., Durham, 1972-76; rsch. assoc. dept. psychiatry Maimonides Med. Ctr., Bklyn., 1976-79; dir. counseling Human Freedom Ctr., Berkeley, Calif., 1979; rsch. cons. SRI Internat., Menlo Park, Calif., 1980-82; design cons. Atari Corp., Sunnyvale, Calif., 1983-85; pres. rsch., exec. dir. Inst. for Advanced Psychology, 1986—; freelance sci. journalist, 1988—; editor-at-large Omni Mag., 1996-98; sr. v.p., rsch. dir. Capital Access, 1996—2001; exec. v.p. Owl Pals, 2003—; editl. dir. NETSPLORER, 2004—. Invited lectr. Duke U., 1995; lectr. in field; adj. prof. Antioch U., San Francisco, 1985-86; guest lectr. Lyceum Sch. for Gifted Children, 1985-89; vis. rschr. USSR Acad. Scis., 1983; rsch. cons. Am. Soc. for Psychical Rsch., 1971-72, sci. applications Internat. Corp., 1991-93; psychol. cons., nat. media spokesperson for Budget Rent A Car Corp., 1997-99; psychol. cons., media spokesperson Sears Corp., 1997; psychol. cons. Microsoft Corp., 1998-99. Author: Owl Pals children's book series, 2007—; Co-author: The Mind Race, 1984, 85, 30-Day Altered States of Consciousness Series, 1989-91, rev. edit., 1999; co-author: Who Do You Think You Are? Explore Your Many-Sided Self With the Berkeley Personality Profile, 1994, rev. edit., 2005, CD-ROM edit., 1996; monthly columnist Omni Mind Brain Lab in Omni Mag., 1995-98; contbr. over 100 articles to profl. jours. and other publs. Mem. APA, Assn. for Media Psychology, Am. Soc. for Psychical Rsch. (bd. dirs. 1994—). Achievements include development of reflective approach to personality profiling; development of advanced human perception research, including original training methodologies in altered states induction, and extended perception; development of original scientific terminology in specialized theoretical areas in advanced perceptual research, including extended perception, extended human abilities, mental noise, paranormal hysteria, stress apparitions, others; development of original clinical approaches to crisis intervention. Home and Office: PO Box 4601 Portland OR 97208

HARASZTHY, VIOLET IBOLYA, dentist, researcher; b. Palic, Serbia-Montenegro, May 29, 1960; d. Vilmos and Rozsa Farkas; m. Gary Geza Haraszthy, Jan. 23, 1987. DDS, Szegedi Orvostudomanji Egjetem, Szeged, Hungary, 1984; MS, SUNY, Buffalo, 1993, DDS, 2001, PhD, 1999. Cert. Prosthodontist SUNY, Buffalo, 1998, Periodontist SUNY, Buffalo, 1994; RN Nursing Sch. Subotica, Yugoslavia, 1979. Dentist Mezohegyes (Hungary) Hosp.; clin. asst. prof. SUNY, Buffalo, 1993—99, asst. prof., 1999—. Lab. dir. SUNY, Buffalo, 2001—. Contbr. articles to profl. jours. Grantee Colgate, 2002—03; Rsch. grantee, Am. Acad. of Dentistry, 2001. Republican. Achievements include identifying the role of iron in actinobacillus actinomycetemcomitans; identifying bacteria associated with periodontal disease and their geographical distribution; research in the connections between heart disease and periodontal disease; the distribution of highly toxic actinobacillus actinomycetemcomitans. Office: SUNY 3435 Main St Buffalo NY 14214 E-mail: vh1@acsu.buffalo.edu.

HARBISON, SEAN, surgeon, educator; BA in Biology, LaSalle Coll., Phila., Pa., 1982; MD, Temple U., 1986. Diplomate Am. Bd. Surgery. Intern in gen surgery Grad. Hosp., Phila., Pa., 1987; fellow Meml. Sloan-Kettering Cancer Ctr., NYC, 1992; prof. surgery Temple Univ. Sch. of Medicine; hosp. affiliations include: Temple Univ. Hosp., Roxborough Meml. Hosp., Jeanes Hosp. Named Best Doctors, 2009—10, 2011—12, Top Docs, Phila. Mag., 2010, 2011. Office: Temple University Hospital 3401 N Broad St Philadelphia PA 19140 Office Phone: 215-707-2000. E-mail: harbison@temple.edu.

HARDAN, ANTONIO, medical educator; b. Lebanon, Mar. 1964; MD, St. Joseph U., 1988; degree in Child Psychiatry, U. Pitts., 1995. Assoc. prof. Stanford U., 2006—. Office: 401 Quarry Rd Stanford CA 94305 Business E-Mail: hardanay@stanford.edu.

HARDAWAY, ERNEST, II, oral and maxillofacial surgeon, public health service officer; BS, Howard U., 1957, DDS, 1966, cert. in oral and maxillofacial surgery, 1972; MPH, Johns Hopkins U., 1973. Intern, then chief resident oral and maxillofacial surgery Howard U. Med. Ctr., Washington, 1969-72; asst. prof., mem. attending staff Howard U. Coll. Medicine and Med. Ctr., Washington, 1974—; with Bur. Quality Assurance, HHS, Washington, 1974-77; various adminstrv. positions Bur. Med. Services and Health Services Adminstrn., USPHS, 1977-80; dep. commr., then commr. pub. health City of Washington, 1982-84; acting v.p. fin. and adminstrv. affairs Mile Sq. Health Ctr., Inc., 1984; asst. to regional health adminstr. Fed. Employee Occupl. Health Program, 1985, dir., 1986—89, Chgo. and Kansas City, 1989—90; mem. CFO coun. com. on entrepreneurial govt. Office Mgmt. and Budget, Washington, 1991—2001; chmn. com. on acad. affairs Coll. Bus. U. Ill., 2001—. Profl. staff Com. on Ways and Means, U.S. Ho. of Reps., 1972; spl. asst. to dir. Office Policy Planning and Evaluation, HEW, 1973; presenter in field. Contbr. articles to profl. jours. Mem. D.C. Emergency Med. Care Adv. Com., D.C. Long-Term Planning Group, 1983, D.C. Health Coordinating Council, D.C. Commn. on Homelessness, 1984; mem. adv. bd. Rosemont Health Ctr., 1984; sec. D.C. Commn. on Licensure to Practice Healing Art, 1983; bd. dirs. United Black Fund, 1984, Potomac Valley Myastenia Gravis Found., 1984; mem. com. human rsch. Instnl. Rev. Bd., Chgo., 1994-2001; chmn. com. acad. affairs U. Ill., 2002. Global Community Health fellow HEW, 1971, Louise C. Ball fellow, 1969; recipient Meritorious Service award USPHS, 1982, J.B. Johnson Nursing Ctr. award, 1983, Outstanding Service placque D.C. Village Choir, 1984, Disting. Service cert. Concerned Citizens for Alcohol Abuse, 1984, Whitman-Walker award for AIDS effort, 1984, Exceptional Accomplishment award Regional Health Adminstr., 1987. Fellow Am. Assn. Oral and Maxillofacial Surgeons (ho. of dels. 1977-80), Internat. Coll. Dentistry, Royal Soc. Health, Acad. Dentistry Internat., Am. Coll. Dentistry; mem. ADA (cons. council hosp. dental care 1976-77), D.C. Soc. Oral and Maxillofacial Surgeons (sec.-treas. 1979-81), Nat. Dental Assn. (Dentist of Yr. 1983, 1st ann. Disting. Service award 1984), Omicron Kappa Upsilon, Chi Delta Mu, Sigma Pi Phi. Home: 88 W Schiller St Apt 1204 Chicago IL 60610-2037 Personal E-mail: drehardaway@aol.com.

HARDAWAY, ROBERT MORRIS, III, retired surgeon; b. Camp John Hay, The Philippines, Jan. 9, 1916; s. Robert Morris and Olive (Gray) Hardaway; m. Lee H. Harkey, June 12, 1939; children: Robert Morris IV, Elizabeth J., Thomas G. II, Christopher L. AB, U. Denver, 1936; postgrad., U. Colo. Med. Sch., 1935-37; MD, Washington U., St. Louis, 1939. Diplomate Am. Bd. Surgery. Commd. 1st lt., M.C. U.S. Army, 1939, advanced through grades to brig. gen., 1970; ward officer, surg. svc. Fitzsimons Gen. Hosp., Denver, 1940-41, resident surgery, 1949-50; ward officer, surg. svc. N. Sector Gen. Hosp., Hawaii, 1941-43; tchr. Med. Field Service Sch., Carlysle Barracks, Pa., 1943-45; surg. trainee Nichols Gen. Hosp., Louisville, 1945-46; resident surgery Madigan Gen. Hosp., Tacoma, 1946-47; chief surg. service 34th Gen. Hosp., Republic of Korea, 1947-49, Sta. Hosp., Ft. Belvoir, Va., 1950-54; chief surg. svc. 97th Gen. Hosp., Frankfurt, Germany, 1954-58, comdg. officer, 1967-70; chief surg. service Martin Army Hosp., Ft. Benning, Ga., 1958-60; dir. divsn. surgery Walter Reed Army Inst. Rsch., Washington, 1960-67; comdg. gen. William Beaumont Army Med. Ctr., El Paso, 1970-75; prof. surgery Tex. Tech U. Sch. Medicine, El Paso, 1976—2002; staff R.E. Thomason Gen. Hosp., El Paso, 1975—2002; ret., 2002. Author: Syndromes of Disseminated Intravascular Coagulation, 1966, Clinical Management of Shock, Surgical and Medical, 1968, Capillary Perfusion in Health and Disease, 1981, Shock-the Reversible Stage of Dying, 1988, Treatment of Wounded in Vietnam, 1988, Blood Problems in Critical Care, 1989; contbr. articles to profl. jours. Decorated Legion of Merit with oak leaf cluster, DSM; recipient 2d prize for exhbn., AMA, 1964, Silver award exhibit, Am. Soc. Clin. Pathologists-Coll. Am. Pathologists, 1964, cert. of Outstanding Achievement, U.S. Army Sci. Conf., 1964. Fellow: ACS, Microcirculation Assn., Am. Assn. Surgery Trauma, Am. Coll. Angiology; mem.: AMA, Assn. Mil. Surgeons U.S., Alpha Omega Alpha. Episcopalian. Achievements include research in intravascular coagulation and hemorrhagic shock.

HARDELAND, RUDIGER HERMANN HORST, retired biology educator; b. Lodz, Poland, June 23, 1943; arrived in Germany, 1944; s. Hermann August Franz and Gertrud (Rohrer) H.; m. Gisa Volling, Mar. 27, 1968; children: Ingrid, Ulrike. D in Natural Scis., Georg-August U., Gottingen, Fed. Republic Germany, 1968. Rsch. scholar Georg-August U., Gottingen, 1969-70, asst., 1971-73, lectr., 1973-75, assoc. prof., 1975-78, prof. biology, 1978—2008. Dean faculty biology U. Gottingen, 1983-85, chmn. deans faculties math. and natural scis., 1983-85; v.p. Georg-August U., Gottingen, 1989-91. Co-author: Allgemeine Biologie, 1975; editor-in-chief Jour. Interdisciplinary Cycle Rsch., 1978-86; cons. editor Biol. Rhythm Rsch., Jour. Pineal Rsch.; contbr. articles to sci. jours. Mem.: Soc. Reproductive Biology and Comparative Endocrinology, Indian Pineal Study Group, Soc. Francophone de Chronobiol., European Pineal and Biol. Rhythms Soc., Deutsche Zoologische Gesellschaft, Leibniz-Sozietaet. Avocations: painting, jazz, music. Home: Hambergstr 7B 37124 Rosdorf Germany Office: U Gottingen Inst Zoology and Anthropology Berliner Str 28 37073 Göttingen Germany Office Phone: 49 551 395414. Personal E-mail: rhardel@gwdg.de.

HARDEN, ANITA JOYCE, nurse; b. Jackson, Tenn., May 17, 1947; d. Percy Lawrence and Marjorie (Robinson) H.; 1 child, Brian Robinson Weir. BSN, Ind. U., 1968, MBA, 1989; MSN, Ind. U.-Purdue U., Indpls., 1973. Staff nurse Indpls. Hosps., 1968-71; instr. Ind. U. Sch. Nursing, 1973-75; dir. continuing care Gallahue Mental Health Ctr., Indpls., 1975-80; mgr. psychiatry Cmty. Hosp., Indpls., 1980-87, product line mgr. for psychiat. and mental health svcs., 1986—; dir. psychiat. svcs. Cmty. Hosp. North, 1987-89, v.p., 1990-94; exec. dir. mental health svcs. Cmty. Hosps. of Ind., Inc., 1989-90; exec. dir. mental health St. Vincent-Cmty. Health Network, 1994-96; exec. dir. behavioral care svcs. Cmty. Hosps. Indpls., 1996-2001, v.p. behavioral health, 2001—03; pres. Cmty. Hosp. East, 2003—05; interim CEO Cmty. Health Network Found., 2009—10; pres. CEO Interim Exec. LLC, 2011—. Clin. asst. prof. Ind. U., 1977-82, clin. assoc. prof., 1982—; clin. assoc., trainer Suicide Prevention Svc., Indpls., 1974-77; chmn. adv. bd. deinstitutionalization project Cen. State Hosp., Indpls., 1978-79; bd. dirs. Safe Sitter, Behavioral Sys. LLC, InteCare; adj. assoc. prof. Ind. U. Sch. Nursing, 1998—. Contbr. articles to profl. jours. Active Ind. County Cmty. Mental Health Ctr., 1979-80; bd. dirs. Marion County Mental Health Assn., Citizens Energy Group, Choices Inc., Indpls. Zoo, Alternatives in Madison County, Jackson-Peoples Living Ctr.; bd. trustees Christian Theol. Sem., 2005—. Recipient Outstanding Achievement in Professions award Ctr. Leadership Devel., 1981, Clin. Excellence award Ind. U. Sch. Nursing, 1989. Mem. Ind. U. Alumni Assn., Christian Women's Fellowship, 500 Festival Assocs., Greater Indpls. Orgn. Nurse Execs. (v.p.), Coalition 100 Black Women (bd. dirs.), Neal-Marshall Aumni Club, Alpha Kappa Alpha, Sigma Theta Tau, Chi Eta Phi. Home: 7607 Newport Bay Dr Indianapolis IN 46240-3370 Office Phone: 317-355-5526. Business E-Mail: aharden@ecommunity.com. *

HARDEN, JANET KULA, nursing educator; b. Bay City, Mich., Nov. 21, 1950; MSN, Madonna U., MSA, 1998; PhD, U. Mich., 2004. Dir., nursing, CEO Kern Hosp., 1989—94; asst. prof. Wayne State U., 1994—. Cons. Best, Heyns, Klaeren & Schroeder PC Attys. Law, 2004—11; bd. dirs. Blue Care Network Mich., 2005—11. Recipient New Investigator's Rsch. award, U. Mich. Mem.: Oncology Nursing Soc. (Rsch. grant), Sigma Theta Internat. Lambda Chpt. Avocations: reading, gardening, walking. Office: 5557 Cass Ave Rm 372 Detroit MI 48202 Business E-Mail: jharden@wayne.edu.

HARDIMAN, GARY T., medical educator; b. Ireland, May 9, 1967; BSc with honors, Nat. U. Ireland, 1989, PhD, 1993. Assoc. prof. dept. medicine UCSD, 2009—. Office: Dept Medicine 9500 Gilman Dr MC 0724 La Jolla CA 92093-0724 Office Fax: 858-822-6430. E-mail: gthardiman@gmail.com.

HARDIN, BRYAN DAVID, occupational safety and health specialist; b. Clinton, Okla., July 4, 1944; s. Everett Tirey and Alma Jewell (Carmichael) H.; children: Bryan David Jr., Erin Elizabeth; m. Mary Victoria Broun, Sept. 30, 1996. BS in Math., Okla. U., 1966, BS in Zoology, 1970, MS in Zoology, 1972; PhD in Environ. Health Sci., U. Cin., 1983. Commd. officer USPHS, 1972, advanced through grades to asst. surgeon gen., 1999; criteria document mgr. Nat. Inst. for Occupl. Safety and Health, Rockville, Md., 1972-75, grad. trainee Cin., 1975-77, rsch. biologist (toxicologist), 1977-86, sr. reviewer divsn. standards devel. and tech. transfer, 1986-87, br. chief, 1987-90, acting AIDS coord. Atlanta, 1988, dep. dir divsn. stds. devel. and tech. transfer Cin., 1990-92, asst. dir. Washington, 1992—93; spl. asst. to asst. Sec. of Labor for Occpl. Safety & Health, Washington, 1993—94; sr. scientist Office of Dir. Nat. Inst. Occupl. Safety and Health, Washington, 1994-95, acting dep. dir. Atlanta, 1996, lead sr. scientist Office of Dir. Washington, 1996-98, dep. dir. Atlanta, 1998-2000, Bryan Hardin Consulting, Hilton Head, SC, 2000—03; sr. cons. GlobalTox, Inc., Redmond, Wash., 2001—04; prin. Veritox, Inc., Redmond, 2004—. Mem. reproductive and devel. toxicology work group Nat. Toxicology Program, 1980—86; mem. Toxic Substances Control Act Interagy. Testing Com., 1987—89, vice chmn., 1988, chmn., 89; mem. working groups on evaluation of carcinogenic risk of chemicals to humans Internat. Agy. for Rsch. on Cancer, 1985, 92; mem. task group for environ. health criteria documents Internat. Program on Chem. Safety, WHO, 1989; mem. working group drafting Prins. and Methods for the Assessment of Risk from Exposure to Chemicals, 1990; chmn. expert consultation Harmonization of Chem. Hazard Comm., 1991; mem. steering com. Internat. Hazard Datasheets on Occupations, ILO, Internat. Occupl. Safety and Health Info. Ctr., 1995—98; mem. endocrine disruptor screening and testing adv. com. USEPA, 1996—98; adv. bd. for the risk edn. project Am. Chem. Soc., 1997—2000; adj. assoc. prof. environ. and occupl. health Rollins Sch. Pub. Health Emory U., Atlanta, 2000—01; mem. AIHA Emergency Response Planning Com., 2001—, sec., 2009—11, vice chair, 2011—. Contbr. articles and abstracts to profl. jour. 1st lt. US Army, 1966—68, capt. USAR, 1968—72. Recipient Surgeon Gen.'s Exemplary Svc. medal, 1993, 1997, Career Scientist of Yr. award, USPHS, 1999, DSM, 2001, Disting. Svc. award, Internat. Safety Equipment Assn., 2001; named Sci. Fed. Employee of Yr., Greater Cin. Fed. Exec. Bd. and Fed. Bus. Assn., 1983. Fellow: Acad. Toxicol. Scis.; mem.: Am. Coll. of Toxicology, Am. Coll. Occupl. and Environ. Medicine, Soc. Toxicology (elected councilor Occupl. & Pub. Health Specialty section 2004—06), Am. Indsl. Hygiene Assn., Teratology Soc. (pub. affairs com. 1985—88, constn. and bylaws com. 1993—96), Sigma Xi. Avocation: vocal music. Home: 337 Greenwood Dr Hilton Head Island SC 29928 Office: 33 Office Park Rd Ste 4A PMB 344 Hilton Head Island SC 29928 Office Fax: 843-363-9465. Business E-Mail: bhardin@veritox.com.

HARDIN, SALLY BROSZ, dean, nursing educator; BSN, U. Ill., Chgo., 1966, MSN, 1968; PhD, U. Ill., Urbana, 1976. Assoc. prof. U. Ill., Chgo., 1976—86; prof. to disting. prof. U. SC, Columbia, 1986—94; prof., dir. PhD nursing program U. Mass., Amherst, 1994—98, U. Mo., St. Louis, 1998—2003; prof., dean U. San Diego Sch. Nursing and Health Sci., 2003—. Contbr. articles to profl. jours. Fellow: Am. Acad. Nursing. Office: U San Diego Sch Nursing 5998 Alcalá Park San Diego CA 92110-2492 Office Phone: 619-260-4550. E-mail: shardin@sandiego.edu.

HARDING, CLIFFORD VINCENT, III, medical educator; b. Arlington, Va., Jan. 31, 1957; s. Clifford Vincent Harding, Jr. and Drusilla Ruth (Van Hoesen) Harding; m. Mina Kay Chung, May 7, 1983; children: Clifford Vincent IV, Andrew Richard. BA magna cum laude, Harvard U., 1979; MD, PhD, Washington U., 1985. Diplomate Nat. Bd. Med. Examiners. Resident in pathology Washington U., St. Louis, 1985—89, chief resident in pathology, 1989—90, instr. pathology, 1989—90, asst. prof. pathology, 1990—93, Case Western Res. U., Cleve., 1993—96, assoc. prof. pathology, 1996—99, prof. pathology, 1999—, chair pathology, 2008—, dir. med. scientist tng. program Cleve., 2001—; med. staff physician U. Hosps. Cleve., Cleve., 1993—2003, 2008—; adj. staff Cleve. Clinic Found., 2004—. Reviewer NIH study sects. NIH, Bethesda, Md., 1996—, chmn. AITC study sect., 1999—2001. Mem. editl. bd.: Advances in Anatomic Pathology, 1994—2000, Traffic, 1998—2001, Cellular Microbiology, 1998—. Recipient Jr. Faculty Rsch. Award, Am. Cancer Soc., 1991; grantee, NIH, 1994—; scholar, Pfizer, Inc, 1991. Mem.: AAAS, Am. Soc. Microbiology, Am. Soc. for Investigative Pathology (Am. Assn. Pathologists Exptl. Pathology-in-Tng. award 1989), Am. Soc. for Cell Biology, Am. Assn. Immunologists, Phi Beta Kappa. Achievements include research in immunology; cell biology. Office: Case Western Reserve Univ Pathology Wolstein 6522 2103 Cornell Rd Cleveland OH 44106-7288 Business E-Mail: cvh3@cwru.edu.

HARDING, FRANCES M., federal agency administrator; b. 1957; m. Robert M. Harding; children: Rachael, Madeline. Various positions of increasing responsibility including assoc. commr. divsn. prevention & recovery NY State Office of Alcoholism & Substance Abuse Services, 1982—2008; dir. Ctr. Substance Abuse Prevention (CSAP) Substance Abuse & Mental Health Services Adminstrn. (SAMHSA), Washington, 2008—, dir. Ctr. Mental Health Services (CMHS), 2010—11. Mem. adv. coun. Network Addressing Collegiate Alcohol & Other Drug Issues, US Dept. Edn., 2008; NY State rep., bd. dirs. Nat. Assn. State Alcohol & Drug Abuse Directors. Contbr. articles to profl. jours. Recipient Sci. to Practice award, Internat. Soc. Prevention Rsch., 2004. Office: Substance Abuse & Mental Health Services Administration 1 Choke Cherry Rd Rockville MD 20857 Office Phone: 240-276-2420. *

HARDMAN, ROLAND, pharmacognosy educator; b. Bolton, Eng., Nov. 22, 1923; s. Albert and Florence Ina (Coppard) H.; m. Margaret Madeline Sharp, Aug. 7, 1948; children: Paul David, Barbara Anne. B in Pharmacy, U. Coll. Nottingham, 1945; BSc in Chemistry, Sir John

Cass Tech. Inst., London, 1948; PhD in Non-Clin. Med. Pharmacy, U. Nottingham, 1958. Rsch. pharmacist Allen & Hanbury Co. Ltd., Ware, 1945-49; lectr. in pharmacog. dept. pharmacy U. Nottingham, 1949-68; head pharmacy dept. Obafemi Awolowo U., Ife, Nigeria, 1961-63; reader and head pharmacognosy U. Bath, England, 1968-84; cons. pharmacog. Agros Assoc., Muir of Ord, 1968—. Vis. external examiner univs. of London, Cardiff, Nottingham, Sunderland, Belfast, Dublin, Cairo, Nairobi, Ife and Kano, 1966-86; cons. Joint Com. for Methods of Evaluating Plant Drugs of the Pharm. Soc. and the Soc. of Analytical Chemistry, London, 1969-72; vis. cons. to plant based pharm. industry Indian Commn. to EU, Brussels, 1985; UK rep. Com. Utilization Medicinal and Aromatic Plants in the EU, 1988-95, exec. dir. Barbara E Norwitz CRC Press Taylor & Francis Group. Contbr. articles to profl. jour.; creator and series editor: Medicinal and Aromatic Plants - Industrial Profiles, 1994—, Traditional Herbal Medicines for Modern Times, 1998—. Rsch. grantee EU, U. Ife, 1961-63, Nat. Rsch. Devel. Corp. UK, 1964-72, Brooke Bond Liebig Co. Ltd., 1971-74, Min. of Agr. with Nat. Seed Devel. Corp. with Weed Rsch. Orgn. UK, 1973-84. Fellow Royal Pharm. Soc. G.B.; mem. Internat. Pharm. Fedn. (sect. sec.-treas., pres. 1980-95, creator programs and lectr., rep. programs for world congresses on medicinal and aromatic plants for human welfare, 1992, 97), Phytochem. Soc. Europe, Am. Botanical Soc. Achievements include patents in field. Avocations: gardening, music, physical fitness, history. Home: Green Hedges 215 Norwich Rd Wroxham Norwich NR12 8RZ England Mailing: Barbara E Norwitz CRC Press Taylor and Francis Group 6000 Broken Sound Pkwy NW Ste 300 Boca Raton FL 33487 Office Phone: 44-1603-781 119. Fax: 561-998-2559. Business E-Mail: r.hardman@bath.ac.uk.

HARDWICK, DAVID FRANCIS, pathologist; b. Vancouver, BC, Can., Jan. 24, 1934; s. Walter H. W. and Iris L. (Hyndman) H.; m. Margaret M. Lang, Aug. 22, 1956; children: Margaret F., Heather I., David J. MD, U. B.C., 1957, LLD (hon.), 2001. Intern Montreal (Que., Can.) Gen. Hosp., 1957-58; resident Vancouver Gen. Hosp., 1958-59, Children's Hosp., Los Angeles, 1959-62; research assoc. U. So. Calif., 1961-62; clin. instr. U. B.C., Vancouver, 1963-65, asst. prof. pathology, 1965-69, assoc. prof., 1969-74; prof. U. BC, 1974—99; head dept. pathology U. B.C., 1976-90, assoc. dean rsch. and planning, 1990-96; dir. labs. Children's Hosp., Vancouver, 1969-92, Vancouver Gen. Hosp., 1976-90; chmn. M.A.C., Children's Hosp., 1970-87; interinstitutional planning U. B.C. Medicine, 1996-98, spl. advisor on planning, 1999—. Adj. prof. Chinese U. Hong Kong; mem. U. B.C. Senate, 1966-71. Author: Acid Base Balance and Blood Gas Studies, 1968, Intermediary Metabolism of Liver, 1971, Directing the Clinical Laboratory, 1990, Laboratory Supervision and Management, 2d edit., 2002; contbr. numerous articles to profl. publs. Bd. dirs. Children and Family Rsch. Inst., BC, 1998—2008, Women's Hosp. Found., 1997-2000, BC Transplant Found., 1993-2006. Recipient Queen's Centennial medal Govt. Can., 1978, U. B.C. Faculty Citation award, 1987, Wallace Wilson Leadership award, 1990, William Boyd Lectureship award Canadian Assn. Path, 1994, Sydney Israels Founders award B.C. Rsch. Inst. Children and Family, 1997, Univ. medal for Outstanding Svc., U. B.C., 1997; Sydney Farber lectr., Soc. Ped. Path., 1998, Excellence award Coll. Physicians & Surgeons, 2008, Disting. Pathologist award Assn. Pathology Chairs, 2010, Disting. Svc. award NA Chairs Pathology, 2010, award W & M Webber Faculty Medicine UBC, 2010, Med. Undergrad. Soc. UBC, 2010, other awards. and honorsch Fellow Royal Coll. Physicians (Can. assoc. pathology chair, Excellence award 2010), UBC Faculty Medicine (Lifetime Achievement award 2010), MUS MAA (Bronze award 2010), Coll. Am. Pathologists, mem. Internat. Acad. Pathology (pres. 1996, v.p. N.Am. 1998—2006, sec. 2006-, Gold medal 2002, sec. 2006-), Can. Med. Assn., BC Assn. Lab. Medicine, BC Med. Assn., NY Acad. Sci., Soc. Pediat. Pathology, Internat. Acad. Pathology (sec. 2006-, Disting. Svc. award 1994, Gold Medal award 2004), US and Can. Acad. Pathology (Pres.'s award 2004), U BC Alumni (Lifetime Achievement award 2007), BC Transplant Found. (chmn. bd. 2000—06), Med. Student and Alumni Ctr. Soc. (chair 2001-05), Alpha Omega Alpha. Office: U BC Dept Pathology 2211 Wesbrook Mall Vancouver BC Canada V6T 1W5 Home: Deans Office Medicine University BC 217-3194 Health Scis Mall Vancouver BC Canada V6T 123 Business E-Mail: david.f.hardwick@ubc.ca.

HARDY, BRITTA, biomedical researcher; b. Russia, Apr. 23, 1946; d. Issack and Rosa Kogut; m. Amos Andrash Hardy, Apr. 16, 1967; children: Einat Hardy-Alrod, Irit Singer. PhD in Life Scis., Weizmann Inst. Sci., Rehovot, Israel, 1975. Fellow hematology Stanford U. Med. Ctr., Calif., 1976—79; head rsch. lab. Felsenstein Rsch. Ctr., Tel-Aviv U. Sch. Medicine, Petach-Tikva, Israel, 1980—. Fellow pediat. nephrology Stanford U. Med. Ctr., 1985; chief scientist, cons. CureTech Biotechnology Ltd., Yavne, Israel, 2001—03. Contbr. articles to profl. jours. Recipient Chaim Weizmann award for post-doctoral studies, Weizmann Inst. Sci., 1975—78, Outstanding Achievement award, Internat. Jour. Oncology, 2001; grantee, Ministry Sci. and Devel., 1983—87, Chief Scientist Ministry Health, 1989—91, 1995—97, Israel Cancer Assn., 1992—94, Ministry Energy and Found. Rsch., 1992—94. Mem.: Internat. Soc. Heart Rsch., Am. Assn. Cancer Rsch. (corr.), Am. Soc. Hematology (corr.), Israeli Soc. Hematology (assoc.), Israeli Soc. Immunology (assoc.). Achievements include invention of antibody for cancer immunotherapy; patents for novel compounds for tumor immunology; patents pending for novel peptides for therapeutic angiogenesis; research in applied medicine using novel compounds for the alleviation of ischemia. Avocation: music. Office: Felsenstain Med Rsch Ctr Rabin Medical Center Beillinson Campus Petah Tiqwa 49100 Israel Office Fax: 972-3-9216979. Personal E-mail: bhardy@post.tau.ac.il.

HARDY, LARRY W., pharmacologist, director; b. Anderson, SC, Jan. 25, 1954; SB, MIT, 1976; PhD, U. Calif., Berkeley, 1983. Rsch. dir., pharmacology Sunovion Pharms., 2004—. Mem.: Soc. Neurosci., Am. Chem. Soc. Avocation: singing. Home: 122 River Rd Sturbridge MA 01566 Personal E-mail: lhardy@charter.net.

HARDY, R. DOUG, epidemiologist, educator; m. Michelle Hardy; 3 children. Assoc. prof. U. Tex. Southwestern Med. Ctr.; dir. U. Tex. Southwestern South Africa Clinical Fellowship Program. Office: University of Texas Southwestern Medical Center 5323 Harry Hines Blvd Dallas TX 75390-9113 Office Phone: 214-648-9914. Office Fax: 214-648-2741.

HARDY, RICHARD ALLEN, JR., psychologist, educator; b. Danville, Va., Feb. 11, 1944; s. R. Allen and Jeanne Arthur Hardy; 1 child from previous marriage, Monica. BA, Fla. State U., Tallahassee, 1966; MS, Auburn U., Ala., 1968, PhD, 1971, postdoctoral student, 1979—81. Rsch. assoc. HumRRO, Columbus, Ga., 1971—73; unit psychologist Partlow State Sch. and Hosp., Tuscaloosa, Ala., 1973—79; psychologist dept. corrections Marion Correctional Inst., Ocala, Fla., 1986—94, Tomoka Correctional Inst., Daytona Beach, Fla., 1994; exec. dir. Success Unlimited, 1992—; tchr. Duvl County Sch. Bd., Jacksonville, Fla., 1995—. Internat. sports cons.; regional rep. Assn. for Internat. Cultural Exch. Programs, 1991—98. Author: (book, tng. manual) Innovative Olympic Training, 1996. VIP 25th Olympiad, Barcelona; co-capt. Team USA World Fitness Festival, Moscow, 1991—92; capt. Team USA, 1992; amb. Mel Whitfield, Washington, 1995; goodwill amb. First African Games, Zimbabwe, 1995; capt. Team USA, 1992; mem. Team USA vs. Team USSR Adult Fitness Competition, Moscow, 1990, Team USA vs. Team Spain Family Fitness Tour, Madrid; performer World's Fair, Seville, Spain, 1992. Capt. USAR, 1967—68. Mem.: Runners For Christ, World Fitness Fedn. (founder), Sigma Xi. Republican. Avocations: running, track and field. Office Phone: 904-743-3322.

HARDY, RICHARD EARL, rehabilitation counseling educator; b. Victoria, Va., Oct. 11, 1938; s. Clifford E. and Louise (Hamilton) H.; 1 son, Jason Elliott. BS, Va. Poly. Inst. and State U., 1960, MS, 1962, EdD, 1966. Rehab. counselor State of Va., Richmond, 1961-63; rehab. advisor HHS, Washington, 1964-66; chief psychologist S.C. Dept. Rehab., Columbia, 1966-68; prof. chmn. dept. rehab. counseling Med. Coll. Va., Richmond, 1968-96, prof. and chair emeritus, 1996—. Former bd. mem. S.C. State Bd. Psychology, former ABPP candidate examiner; internat. cons. to numerous countries including Turkey, Iraq, Peru, Uruguay, South Africa, Brazil, Thailand Author, editor: International Rehabilitation: Approaches and Programs, Hemingway: A Psychological Portrait, 1988, Gestalt Psychotherapy, 1991, Hispaniola Episode: A Mental Health Allegory, 1992, (with J.G. Cull) The Brass Chalice: Drug Prevention Stories and Information for Children and Youth, 1994, Counseling in the Rehabilitation Process, 1999, Woodpeckers Don't Get Headaches: The Psychology of Stress, Relationships, and Addiction, 2001, numerous others. Recipient Nat. award Nat. Rehab. Assn., 1976; recipient Nat. award Am. Assn. Workers for Blind, 1976, Outstanding Grad. award Med. Coll. Va./Va. Commonwealth U., Dept. Rehab. Counseling, 1997, Richard E. Hardy endowed scholarship Med. Coll. Va., 1998, Outstanding Scholar award U. Md. Sch. Edn., 2006. Fellow Am. Psychol. Soc., Assn. Allied & Preventive Psychology; mem. Am. Assn. Vol. Action Scholars, Phi Kappa Phi. Office: Va Commonwealth U 6962 Forest Hill Ave Richmond VA 23225

HARE, HENRY PHILLIP, JR., psychiatrist; b. Paris, Tex., Apr. 4, 1925; s. Henry P. and Bertha (McIntosh) H.; children: Elizabeth Anne, John Keble. Student, Rice U., Houston, 1941-43; BA, U. Tex., Galveston, 1945, MD, 1947; Sr. Status Student, Keble Coll. Diplomate Am. Bd. Psychiatry and Neurology. Rotating intern U.S. Marine Hosp., Balt., 1947-48; fellow in psychiatry Menninger Sch., Topeka, 1951; staff to chief psychiatry USPHS Hosp., Ft. Worth, 1951-54; dir. psychotherapy Beverly Hills Clinic, Dallas, 1954-60; lectr. psychiatry Mansfield Coll., U. Oxford, Eng., 1960-61; assoc. to dir. Tulsa Psychiat. Found., 1961-63; pvt. practice Nix Med. Ctr., San Antonio, 1963—; clin. prof. psychiatry U. Tex. Health Sci. Ctr., San Antonio, 1965—; med. dir., chief profl. staff San Antonio State Hosp., 1989-93, forensic psychiatrist, 1993-97; mem. rev. bd. on manifest dangerousness TDMHMR, 1993—2003. Psychiat. examiner to Episcopal Bishop W. Tex., San Antonio, 1963—; psychiat. rep. to med. bd. Humana Met. Hosp., San Antonio, 1989-90; sr. status student Keble Coll. Contbr. articles to profl. jours. Mem. Bexar County Bd. Trustees for Mental Health and Mental Retardation, San Antonio, 1969-74; mem. distbns. com. San Antonio Area Found., 1975-78. Capt. USPHS, 1947—. Named Layman of Yr., Episcopal Diocese Dallas, 1959; named to Most Venerable Order of the Hosp. of St. John Jerusalem, 2001. Fellow Am. Psychiat. Assn. (disting. life), So. Psychiat. Assn., Royal Soc. Health; mem. Bexar County Psychiat. Soc. (pres. 1967-68), Alcuin Club. Democrat. Avocations: sailing, stamp collecting, ecclesiology and ecumenics. Home: 10314 Severn Rd San Antonio TX 78217-3945 Office: 1122 Nix Med Ctr San Antonio TX 78205 Office Phone: 512-222-1409.

HARE, JOSHUA MICHAEL, cardiologist, educator; b. South Africa, Apr. 4, 1962; s. Philip and Isadora Hare; m. Lee Susan Cohen, Oct. 17, 1999. BA in Biochemistry with honors, U. Pa., Phila., 1984; MD, Johns Hopkins U., Balt., 1988. Cert. FLEX, diplomate Am. Bd. Internal Medicine, 1991, Am. Bd. Cardiovasc. Disease, 1995. Intern in medicine Johns Hopkins Hosp., 1989; fellow in internal medicine Johns Hopkins U., Boston, 1991; resident in medicine Johns Hopkins Hosp., Boston, 1991; fellow in cardiovasc. disease Brigham and Women's Hosp., Boston, 1994; rsch. fellow in medicine Harvard U., 1994; asst. prof. medicine Johns Hopkins U. Sch. Medicine, Balt., assoc. dir. cardiac transplant program, prof. medicine and biomedical engring.; Louis Lemberg prof. medicine Miller Sch. Medicine, U. Miami, 2006—, chief divsn. cardiology, 2006—, dir. interdisciplinary stem cell inst., 2006—. Recipient Young Investigator award, Am. Coll. Cardiology, Clin. Investigator Devel. award, Nat. Heart Lung and Blood Inst., SmithKline Beecham Jr. Faculty award. Fellow: Am. Heart Assn.; mem.: Am. Soc. Clin. Investigation, Assn. U. Cardiologists. Achievements include being one of the main pioneers in cardiovasc. stem cell therapy. Office: Clin Rsch Bldg Miller Sch Medicine U Miami 1120 NW 14th St11th Fl Miami FL 33136 Office Phone: 305-243-1998. Office Fax: 305-243-1894.

HARE, JULIA, educational psychologist, author, consultant; b. Tulsa, Okla. m. Nathan Hare. BA in Music, Langston U., Okla., 1960; MA in Music Edn., Roosevelt U., Chgo., 1962; PhD in Edn., Calif. Coast U., Santa Ana, 1987. Elem. sch. tchr., Chgo.; dir. ednl. progs. Oakland Mus., Calif.; pub. rels. dir. local fed. housing prog. San Francisco; co-founder, nat. exec. dir. The Black Think Tank, San Francisco, 1979—. Numerous TV appearances including CNN & Co., C-SPAN, Tony Brown's Jour., Inside Edition; spkr. Congl. Black Caucus. Co-author (with husband): The Endangered Black Family, 1984, Bringing the Black Boy to Manhood: The Passage, 1985, Crisis in Black Sexual Politics, 1989, The Miseducation of the Black Child, 1991, How to Find and Keep a BMW (Black Man Working), 1995, The Sexual and Political Anorexia of the Black Woman, 2008; contbr. articles to newspapers and mags.; spkr. in field. Recipient Abe Lincoln award for outstanding broadcasting, Carter G. Woodson Edn. award, Harambee award, Assn. Black Social Workers', Lifetime Achievement award, Internat. Black Writers & Artists Union, Presdl. citation, Nat. Assn. Equal Opportunity in Higher Edn.; named Educator of Yr., Washington DC Jr. C. of C., Scholar of Yr., Assn. African Historians; named one of 10 Most Influential African Americans in San Francisco Bay Area; named to Power 150, Ebony mag., 2008.

HAREZI, ILONKA JO, medical technology research executive; b. Princeton, Ind., Jan. 17, 1949; d. Joseph and Helen Marie Fullop; m. John O. Schofield, Dec. 14, 1971 (div. Dec. 1982); 1 child, Franceska; m. Courtland Reeves, Nov. 26, 1986; children: Bryan, Katharine. PhD, Chgo. Sch. Design, 1969. Mktg. ptnr. Fullop and Assocs., 1983-85; founder, sec., treas. Kinetic Energy Ltd., 1985-90; freelance set designer Ilonka Creative Environments, 1974-84; founder, v.p. Harezi Internat., 1980-84; founder, sec., treas. Elf Cocoon Corp., 1984-86; founder, pres., chmn. Elf Cocoon Internat. Ltd., 1985-92; founder, pres. Elfworks, Inc., 1991-94, Elfworks, Nev., 1994-96; pres., dir. Allied Fund for Capital Appreciation, Inc., 1994—98; v.p. Phillip Stein Teslar, 2001—; pres. Nanogy, Inc., 2003—. Interviewed by radio, TV, and newspapers on design and extremely low frequency electromagnetic tech.; presenter tech. sems. on ELF, the Quantum and scalar phenomena. Author: The Resonance in Residence, (DVD) A Soul, Breathing and Steppin' into the Rain, 2007; contbr. articles to profl. jours. Mem. UN Bus. Orgn., New York, NY, 2001—03. Fellow N.Y. Acad. of Sci.; mem. NAFE, ACLU, AAAS, Am. Inst. Interior Designers, Women's Internat. League for Peace and Freedom, Nat. Assn. Against Health Fraud, Nat. Narcotics Officers Assns. Coalition, N.Y. Acad. Sci., UN-USA Bus. Coun., Knights of Malta (dame), Knights of Africa (dame), U.S. Acad. Polit. Sci., Am. Craft Coun. Achievements include patents pending for transdermal pump and teslar chip. Office: 169 E Flagler 17th Fl Miami FL 33101 Office Phone: 305-933-6768. Personal E-mail: ilonkaharezi@aol.com.

HARFORD, ROBERT R., dermatologist; s. Victor and Cossil Harford; m. Ruby Harford; 1 child, Mercedes. BS, Ala. A&M U., 1980; MD, SUNY, Bklyn., 1988. Diplomate Am. Bd. Dermatology, Am. Bd. Pathology and Dermatology. Commd. officer USN, 1981—2005, advanced through grades to comdr.; head med. dept. Naval Med. Clinic, Antarctica, 1989—90; health sci. rsch. med. officer, clin. investigator Naval Med. Rsch. Inst., Bethesda, Md., 1991—93; resident in dermatology Nat. Naval Med. Ctr., Bethesda, Md., 1993—96, head dermatopathology, 2000—02; head dermatology Naval Hosp. Guam, Agana, 1996—99, dir. med. svcs., 1998—99; head dermatopathology, dir. dermatology mohs micrographic surgery lab. Naval Med. Ctr., San Diego, 2002—05. Asst. prof. dermatology Uniformed Services U. of the Health Sciences, Bethesda, 2001—; asst. clin. prof. medicine U. Calif., San Diego, 2003—. Cons. for first ann. women health fare Soroptomist Internat. Guam, Agana, 1998; med. advisor Este Magi Le Atua Care, San Jose, Calif., 2005; physician vol. Cheyenne River Reservation, Eagle Butte, SD, 1992. Decorated Meritorious Svc. medal, Navy Commendation medal (5), Achievment medal USN. Fellow: Am. Acad. Dermatology; mem.: Assn. Mil. Surgeons of the US (life). Achievements include research in relationship between changes in serum thyrotropin and lipoprotein cholesterol with prolonged antarctic residence; effects of cold weather on memory, thyroid function, and oxygen consumption. Avocation: travel.

HARIG, FRANK P., cardiac surgeon, consultant; b. Dortmund, Germany, Aug. 2, 1964; s. Horst D. Heinrich and M. Harig; m. Kerstin Maria Staudinger, Mar. 23, 1995. MD, J.W.Goethe U., Frankfurt Main, Germany, 1992; PhD in Cardiac Surgery, FA U. Erlangen, 2011. Lic. surgeon Bavarian Bd. Surgery, Germany, 2002. Resident cardiothoracic surgery St.Johannes Hosp., Dortmund, Germany, 1993—95; cons. cardiac surgery U. Hosp., Erlangen, Germany, 1995—, gen. leader remia legendo, 2011. Cons. in field. Co-editor: Guideline for Using Extracorporeal Circulation. Achievements include research in cytokines and clinical outcome after cardiac surgery. Office: Univ Hosp Erlangen FAU Maximiliansplatz 91054 Bavaria Erlangen Germany Office Fax: +49(0)9131.853.3982. Personal E-mail: frank.harig@web.de. Business E Mail: frank.harig@uk-erlangen.de.

HARI KUMAR, K. V.S., endocrinologist; b. Konidena, Andhra Pradesh, Sept. 29, 1972; MD, AFMC, Pune, India, 2002; DNB in Endocrinology, Medwin Hosps., 2011. Classified med. specialist, endocrinologist Ministry of Def., Indian Army, 2009—. Asst. prof. AFMC, 2002—03. Recipient Smt Harimalini Joshi Meml. Gold medal, U. Pune, Lt. Gen. Inder Singh Meml. Gold medal, AFMC, Col. SN Prabhakaran Gold medal. Mem.: RSSDI, ISPAE, ESI, APPES, ISBMR, API, AACE (Internat. Tng. fellow), Endocrine Soc. India (Dr AR Seth Meml. Gold medal). Avocations: swimming, travel. Office: Command Hosp Dept Endocrinology Lucknow Uttar Pradesh 226002 India E-mail: hariendo@rediffmail.com.

HARIRI, AMIR, surgeon; b. Clamart, Apr. 6, 1981; MD, Paris Descartes U., 2010. Physician Ctr. Chirurgie Orthopedique et de la Main, 2010—. Prof. Surgery Sch. Paris, 2007—11. Mem.: GEM-French Soc. Hand Surgery, SOFCOT-French Soc. Orthop. Surgery. Avocations: tennis, guitar. Office: 10 Ave Achille Baumann Illkhirch Graffenstaden Alsace 67400 France E-mail: amirhariri@aol.com.

HARIRI, ROBERT JOSEPH, neurosurgeon, researcher; m. Maggie Meade; 3 children. Grad., Columbia Coll., Columbia U. Sch. Engring. and Applied Sciences; PhD, MD, Cornell U. Founder Anthrogenesis Corp. (acquired by Celgene Corp.), 1997—2002; surgical tng. NY Hosp.-Cornell Med. Ctr.; CEO Celgene Cellular Therapeutics Divsn., Celgene Corp., pres.; founder LifebankUSA, a Celgene Co., Cedar Knolls, NJ, 1998, chmn., chief scientific officer, pres. Bd. dir. Semorex, Inc., Vemics, Plasmasol Corp.; advisor to many pharma. and med. device enterprises. Exec. prodr. (with wife): Off the Black, 2006; guest appearance MSNBC, Connected Coast to Coast, ABC, World News Tonight. Achievements include being a recognized leader in the development of new human cellular and tissue therapeutics; development of proprietary technological solutions to enhance the processes involved in the collection, testing and storage of umbilical cord blood cells; patents pending for in all areas of cell processing and surgical devices and techniques. Avocation: avid pilot, Rocket Racing League. Office: LifebankUSA 45 Horsehill Rd Cedar Knolls NJ 07927

HARISDANGKUL, VALEE, physician; b. Bangkok, June 20, 1941; came to U.S., 1976; s. Sin Fong Wong and Samandsri Harisdangkul. MD, Siriraj Hosp., Bangkok, 1966; PhD, Columbia U., 1971. Diplomate Am. Bd. Internal Medicine and Rheumatology. Fellow in rheumatology Hosp. for Spl. Surgery, NYC, 1971-73; asst. prof. Mahidol U., Bangkok, 1973-75, assoc. prof., 1975-76; fellow in rheumatology Michael Reese Med. Ctr., Chgo., 1976-77; resident in internal medicine U. Miss. Med. Ctr., Jackson, 1977-79, asst. prof.,

1979-85, assoc. prof., 1985-94, prof., 1994—2006, prof. emeritus, 2006—, dir. rheumatology lab., 1982-90, chief. div. rheumatology, 1983-92, dir. fellowship tng. program divsn. rheumatology, 1993—2006. Contbr. articles to profl. jours. Rockefeller Found. scholar, 1967-71; recipient Gold medal Siriraj Med. Sch., 1966, nominated Best Doctor in U.S.A., 2002, 03, 04 Fellow ACP, Am. Coll. Rheumatology; mem. Thai Med. Assn., Thai Rheumatology Assn. Office: Univ of Miss Med Ctr 2500 N State St Jackson MS 39216-4500 Office Phone: 601-984-5540. Business E-Mail: vharisdangkul@medicine.umsmed.edu.

HARITON, JO ROSENBERG, psychotherapist, educator; b. Albany, NY, June 12, 1948; d. Irving H. and Madeline P. Rosenberg; m. Frank J. Hariton; 2 children. BA, Goucher Coll., Towson, Md., 1970; MS, Columbia U., 1973; PhD, NYU, 1992; postgrad., Postgrad. Ctr. Mental Health, NYC, 1979. Cert. psychoanalyst. With maternal and child health dept. Bronx (N.Y.) Mcpl. Hosp. Ctr., 1973-76, coord. emergency svcs. children's dept. child psychiatry, 1976-79; field work instr. NYU Sch. Social Work, 1977-79; sr. psychiat social worker divsn. child and adol. psychiatry Westchester divsn. N.Y. Hosp.-Cornell Med. Ctr., White Plains, N.Y., 1979-82, social work coord., 1982-98; mem. faculty Cornell U. Med. Sch., 1982—; prof. assoc. NYPH; pvt. practice psychotherapy. Dir. Social Skills Tng. Program Contbr. articles on group therapy to profl. jours. Fellow N.Y. State Soc. Clin. Social Work Psychotherapists; mem. NASW, Acad. Cert. Social Workers, Am. Group Psychotherapy Assn. Home: 1065 Dobbs Ferry Rd White Plains NY 10607-2212 Office: NY Presby Hosp Westchester Divsn 21 Bloomingdale Rd White Plains NY 10605-1596 Office Phone: 914-997-5957. Business E-Mail: jhariton@med.cornell.edu.

HARITOS-FATOUROS, MIKA MARIA, psychologist, psychotherapist; BA in Psychology, U. Coll., London, 1954; MA in Ednl. Psychology, London U., 1963. Assoc. prof. Aristotle U., Thessaloniki, Greece, 1975, prof., 1978, emeritus prof., 1999, rschr., 1999—2008. Vis. prof. psychology Panteion U., Athens, 1999—. Author: Violence Workers: Police Torturers and Murderers Reconstruct Brazilian Atrocities, 2003 (award New Eng. Coun. Latin Am. Studies, 2003, award Am. Soc. Criminology's Divsn. Internat. Criminology, 2003), Psychological Origins of Institutional Torture. Pres. com. for licence in psychology and psychotherapy Greek Ministry of Health, Athens, 1993—2001. Mem.: Greek Assn. Behavioral Rsch. & Therapy (pres.), European Assn. Counselling (v.p. 2007—). Achievements include research in street children, counselors without frontiers. Office: Aristotle Univ Thessaloniki Univ Campus Salonika Greece Office Phone: 2310-997313, 30210 7224625. Office Fax: 30 2310 842774; Home Fax: 30 210 7224625.

HARK, WILLIAM HENRY, retired federal agency administrator, aerospace physician; b. Charleston, W.Va., Nov. 1, 1932; s. Zundel and Esther Sylvia (Henry) H.; m. Claudette Berkley Watson, Apr. 14, 1961; 1 child, William Tucker. AB, W.Va. U., 1954, BS, 1955; MD, Med. Coll. Va., 1957; MPH, Harvard U., 1963. Diplomate Am. Bd. Preventive Medicine. Intern Walter Reed Gen. Hosp., Washington, 1957-58; resident in aerospace medicine U.S. Army, 1962-65, advanced through grades to col., physician, aviation med. cons., 1957-76, ret., 1976; mgr. med. specialties divsn. FAA, Washington, 1980-92, dep. fed. air surgeon, 1992-99. Adv. group for aerospace R&D, NATO, Brussels, 1969-71; mem. joint com. on aviation pathology Dept. of Def., Washington, 1969-71. Decorated Legion of Merit, Air medal, Bronze Star, Vietnam Campaign medal U.S. Army, 1968. Fellow Am. Coll. Preventive Medicine, Aerospace Med. Assn.; mem. Assn. Mil. Surgeons U.S. Avocations: photography, computers. Home: 4317 Southwood Dr Alexandria VA 22309-2822

HARKIN, TOM (THOMAS RICHARD HARKIN), United States Senator from Iowa; b. Cumming, Iowa, Nov. 19, 1939; s. Patrick and Frances H.; m. Ruth Raduenz, 1968; children: Amy, Jenny. BS in Govt. & Economics, Iowa State U., 1962; JD, Cath. U. Am., 1972. Bar: Iowa 1972. Staff mem. US House Select Com. on US Involvement in Southeast Asia, 1970; atty. Polk County Legal Aid Soc., 1973—74; mem. US Congress from 5th Iowa Dist., 1975—85; US Senator from Iowa, 1985—; chmn. US Senate Agrl., Nutrition, & Forestry Com., 2001, 2001—03, 2007—09, US Senate Health, Edn., Labor, & Pensions Com., 2009—. Co-author: (with C.E. Thomas) Five Minutes to Midnight: Why the Nuclear Threat is Growing Faster than Ever, 1990. Dem. candidate for Presidency of U.S., 1992. Served with USN, 1962—67, served with USNR, 1968—74. Named Outstanding Young Alumnus Iowa State U. Alumni Assn., 1974; recipient Excellence in Public Svc. award Am. Acad. Pediatrics, 1991, Disting. Public Svc. award Med. Libr. Assn., 1995, William Steiger Meml. award American Conf. Govtl. Indsl. Hygienists, 1996, President's award Nat. Corn Grower's Assn., 2001, Richard and Barbara Hensen Leadership award and Disting. Lectureship U. Iowa Coll. Public Health, 2001, Friend of Seniors award Nat. Com. to Preserve Social Security & Medicare, 2002, Morris K. Udall award Pub. Svc. Parkinson's Action Network, 2002, Chronicles of Courage award VSA Arts, 2002, Spl. Recognition award AHA, 2003, Capitol Dome award American Cancer Soc., 2003, Disting. Cmty. Health Champion Nat. Assn. Cmty. Health Centers, 2005, Fred Rogers Integrity award Campaign for Commercial-Free Childhood, 2005, Nathan Davis award for Outstanding Govt. Svc., AMA, 2008. Mem.: Am. Legion. Democrat. Roman Catholic. Office: US Senate 731 Hart Senate Bldg Washington DC 20510-0001 also: Federal Bldg Ste 733 210 Walnut St Des Moines IA 50309-2106 Office Phone: 202-224-3254, 515-284-4574. Office Fax: 202-224-9369, 515-284-4937. E-mail: tom_harkin@harkin.senate.gov. *

HARKNESS, JOAN ANN V., retired health educator; b. Trenton, NJ, Sept. 14, 1937; d. William H. and Letitia C. (Fenton) Van Noy; m. David S. Harkness, June 3, 1961; children: A. Elizabeth, Lynne A., David W., Jonathan H., William F. Diploma, Mercer Hosp. Sch. Nursing, 1958; AA with highest honors, Trenton Jr. Coll., 1961; BA in History summa cum laude, Trenton State Coll., 1978; MEd in Counseling and Personnel Svcs., Trenton State Coll.(now the Coll. NJ), 1983. RN, NJ; cert. sch. nurse, NJ; cert. in alcoholism counseling Trenton State Coll., 1990. Gen. staff nurse Mercer Med. Ctr., Trenton, NJ, 1958—59, Princeton Med. Ctr., NJ, 1960; substitute sch. nurse Pennington Prep. Sch., NJ, 1961; substitute instr. Pennington Presbyn. Nursery Sch., 1974-75; substitute sch. nurse Hopewell Valley Regional Sch. Dist., Pennington, 1974-83; substance abuse counselor, intern Met. Clinic of Counseling, Trenton, 1988-89; health educator Blue Cross Blue Shield Health Ctrs., BCBS NJ(now Horizon BCBS NJ), Trenton and Quakerbridge, 1985—96. Recipient Dean of Faculty award for high scholarship, Trenton Jr. Coll., 1961. Mem. Am. Counseling Assn., Am. Assn. for Adult Devel. and Aging, NJ Profl. Counselors Assn., NJ Assn. for Adult Devel. and Aging, Capital Health Sys. Mercer Nurses Alumnae Assn., Student Nurse Com. Capital Health Sys. Aux. Mercer (assoc.), Chi Sigma Iota Counseling Acad. and Profl. Honor Soc. Internat. Alpha Epsilon Chpt., The Coll. of NJ., Sigma Tau Sigma (hon. mem.), Nat. Hon. Soc. Students Social Scis. Home: 422 Burd St Pennington NJ 08534-2701

HARLAN, LINDA CAROL, epidemiologist; b. Glasgow, Mont., Feb. 24, 1950; d. Norman Joseph Mavencamp and Bernice Audrene Klingler; m. William Robert Harlan, Aug. 23, 1980; 1 child, Nicole Porter. BSN, Mont. State U., 1972; MPH, U. Mich., 1981, PhD, 1985. RN Calif., 1972. Project coord. U. Calif., Davis, 1973—80; sr. rsch. analyst Westat, Inc., Rockville, Md., 1981—82; rsch./tchg. asst. U. Mich., Ann Arbor, 1983—84, post-doctoral fellow, 1985—87; biostatistician, epidemiologist Henry Ford Hosp., Detroit, 1984—85; cancer epidemiologist Nat. Cancer Inst., Bethesda, Md., 1987—; nat. coordinating coun. Cancer Surveillance, 2009—. Mem. editl. bd.: Jour. Clin. Oncology, 2003—06; contbr. articles to profl. jours. Mem.: ACS (mem. commn. on cancer 2005—10). Office: Nat Cancer Inst Ste 4005 6130 Executive Blvd Bethesda MD 20892-7344 Business E-Mail: lh50w@nih.gov.

HARLAN, WILLIAM ROBERT, JR., internist, educator, researcher; b. Richmond, Va., Nov. 1, 1930; s. William Robert and Helen J. (Weaver) H.; m. Linda Carol Mavencamp, Aug. 23, 1980; children: Elizabeth, William, Christopher, Nicole. BA, U. Va., 1951; MD magna cum laude, Med. Coll. Va., 1955. Diplomate Am. Bd. Internal Medicine, Am. Bd. Family Practice. Intern U. Wis., Madison, 1955-56; resident in medicine Duke U. Hosp., Durham, NC, 1958-62; dir. Clin. Rsch. Ctr., Med. Coll. Va., 1963-70; asso. dean U. Ala. Med. Sch., 1970-72; prof. medicine and community health scis. Duke U., 1972-74; prof. medicine and postgrad. medicine U. Mich., Ann Arbor, 1974-88, asst. dean Med. Sch.; dir. div. epidemology and clin. applications Nat. Heart, Lung and Blood Inst., 1988-91; assoc. dir. for disease prevention NIH, Bethesda, 1991—2002; expert NIMH, 2001—06, sr. advisor, 2001—05; cons. Nat. Libr. Medicine, 2006—09. Cons. World Bank; mem. sci. adv. bd. U.S. Air Force; mem. Armed Forces Epidemiology Bd., NIH study sects. and adv. councils. Contbr. articles to med. jours. Lt. USMC, 1956—58, US Naval Sch. Aerospace Medicine. Fellow ACP, Am. Coll. Preventive Medicine, Am. Acad. Family Practice, Am. Heart Assn.; mem. N.Y. Acad. Sci., Sigma Xi, Alpha Omega Alpha (Markle Scholar in Acad. Medicine). Democrat. Episcopalian. Avocations: tennis, golf, skiing. Home: 3503 Windsor Pl Chevy Chase MD 20815-4001 also: 155 N Sea Pines Dr Hilton Head Island SC 29928-5804 Personal E-mail: wharlan@starpower.net.

HARLE, THOMAS STANLEY, radiologist; b. Detroit, Aug. 17, 1932; s. Edward John and Daisy Odell (Bacon) H.; m. Barbara Janette Chrestman, Oct. 15, 1960; children: Blair Thomas, Timothy John. Student, Mich. State U., 1950-53; BS, Northwestern U., 1954; MD, Northwestern U., Chgo., 1957. Diplomate Am. Bd. Radiology (trustee 1987-99). Intern Passavant Meml. Hosp., Chgo., 1957-58; radiology resident Brooke Army Med. Ctr., San Antonio, 1958-61, asst. chief radiology, 1964-65; radiologist Ft. Detrick, Frederick, Md., 1961-62, Kelsey Seybold Clinic, Houston, 1965-66; chief of radiology Irwin Army Hosp., Ft. Riley, Kans., 1962-64; asst. prof., then assoc. prof. Baylor Coll. Medicine, Houston, 1966-69; assoc. prof. Duke U. Med. Ctr., Durham, NC, 1969-71; prof. U. Tex. Med. Sch., Houston, 1975-78, 80-82, chmn. dept. radiology, 1975-78; prof. Mich. State U., East Lansing, 1978-80, U. Tex. M.D. Anderson Cancer Ctr., Houston, 1982-1997, asst. v.p. acad. affairs, 1982-90, assoc. v.p. acad. affairs, 1990-94; prof. dept. radiology Wake Forest U., Winston Salem, NC, 1997—, Isadore Meschan disting. prof. radiology, 2001—. Contbr. articles to profl. jours., chpts. to books. Maj. U.S. Army, 1958-65. Fellow Am. Coll. Radiology; mem. Assn. Univ. Radiologists (pres. 1983-84), Radiol. Soc. N.Am. (pres. 1993), European Assn. Radiologists (hon.), Faculty of Radiologists, Royal Coll. Surgeons in Ireland (hon.), Brit. Inst. Radiology (hon.). Republican. Baptist. Avocation: architecture. Office: Wake Forest U Medical Center Blvd Winston Salem NC 27157-0001 Office Phone: 336-716-4316. Business E-Mail: tharle@wfuhmc.edu.

HARLEMAN, JOHANNES HENDRIKUS, experimental pathologist; b. Rotterdam, The Netherlands, Sept. 9, 1953; s. Johannes H. Harleman and Elisabeth J. Steenbergen; m. Helene Maria Bijloo, Feb. 27, 1976; children: Eden J.F., Marie C.E. DVM cum laude, State U. Utrecht, The Netherlands, 1977; PhD, U. Ill., 1982. Bd. cert. in Vet. Pathology, Toxicologic Pathology, and Toxicology, The Netherlands. Rsch. assoc. U. Ill., Urbana-Champaign, 1978-82; pathologist Ciba Geigy AG, Basel, Switzerland, 1982-83; sr. pathologist Smith Kline & French, Welwyn, England, 1983-86; head pathology ASTA Medica AG, Halle, Germany, 1986-99; head toxicology-pathology Novartis Pharma AG, Basel, 1999—2001; head preclinical safety Eu Novartis Pharma AG, 2001—04, global head pathology, 2005—06; head pathology Merck KGaA, Darmstadt, Germany, 2006—07, global head toxicology, 2007—09; sr. dir. pathology, global discipline leader ASTRA Zenera Safety Assessment Macclesfield Oheshine, England, 2009—. Co-author (Internat. Agy. Rsch. on Cancer, WHO) International Classification of Rodent Tumors-Haematopoietic System, 1993, International Classification of Rodent Tumors-Male Genital System, 1997, International Classification of Rodent Tumors-Female Genital System, 1997; hon. lectr. dept. pathology Vet. Sch., Hannover, Germany, 2000-03; hon. prof. toxicologic pathology Tieraerztliche Hochschule, Hannover, 2004. Mem. editl. bd. Toxicological Pathology, 1997-2003. Bd. mem. Christian Reformed Ch., Champaign, 1980-81, Christliche Gemeinschaft Bielefeld, 1992-99. Mem. German Soc. Toxicologic Pathology (v.p. 1992-2002), European Soc. Toxicological Pathology (pres. 2002-04), Royal Netherlands Vet. Assn., Internat. Fedn. Societies of Toxicologic Pathology (pres.-elect 2004-07, pres. 2007-09, past pres. 2009-), Phi Kappa Phi. Avocations: cooking, hiking, reading. Office: Safety Assessment Uk Rereside Alderely Pk Macclesfield Cheshire SK 104 TG England Home: 21 Manchester Rd Macclesfield Cheshire 2EH England Office Phone: 0049-6151-723664.

HARLEY, DAVID H., facial plastic surgeon; Grad. cum laude, Dartmouth Coll.; MD, Vanderbilt U. Diplomate Am. Bd. Otolaryngology, Am. Bd. of Facial Plastic and Reconstructive Surgery. Residency Vanderbilt Univ. Med. Ctr.; residency plastic and reconstractive surgery Methodist Hosp., Houston; plastic surgery residency St. Joseph Med. Ctr.; trained cancer reconstructive surgery MD Anderson Med. Ctr.; tng. plastic surgery, head and neck surgery ACGME; staff physician Charles George VA Med. Ctr., Asheville, 2008—. Recipient Hospital award of Excellence, Dean's award of Distinction. Mem.: Alpha Omega Alpha (Vanderbilt chpt.). Office: Biltmore Plastic Surgery 1249 Hendersonville Rd Asheville NC 28803 Mailing: Biltmore Plastic Surgery 902 N Church St Greenville SC 29601 Office Phone: 828-274-1009, 864-232-2332. Office Fax: 828-274-4418, 828-274-4418.

HARMAN, ANDREW N., research scientist; b. Epsom, Eng., Aug. 7, 1974; BSc with 1st class honors, U. Coll. London, 1997; PhD, U. Cambridge, 2002. Postdoc. fellow Westmead Millennium Inst., 2002—. Recipient prize, Westmead Millennium Inst. Avocation: winemaking. Office: Westmead Millennium Inst PO Box 41 Westmead NSW 2145 Australia Business E-Mail: andrew.harman@sydney.edu.au.

HARMATA, MICHAEL, chemistry professor, researcher; b. Chgo., Sept. 22, 1959; AB, U. Ill., Chgo., 1980; PhD, U. Ill., Champaign-Urbana, 1985. Norman Rabjohn disting. prof. chemistry U. Mo., Columbia, 1986—. Adj. prof. Inst. Nano and Molecular Medicine, 2010; Liebig hon. prof. U. Giessen, 2010. Recipient Prose award, Assn. Am. Pubs., Inc.; Big 12 Faculty fellowship, U. Tex., Austin, Rsch. fellowship, Alexander von Humboldt Found. Fellow: Japan Soc. Promotion Sci.; mem.: Internat. Soc. Heterocyclic Chemistry, Am. Chem. Soc., Sigma Xi, Phi Kappa Phi, Phi Beta Kappa. Avocations: reading, model building, stamp collecting/philately. Office: 601 S College Ave Columbia MO 65211 Office Fax: 573-882-2754. Business E-Mail: harmatam@missouri.edu.

HARMEL, MEREL HILBER, anesthesiologist, educator; b. Cleve., May 19, 1917; s. Louis and Hermine (Greenbaum) H.; m. Armide Chilcoat, July 2, 1944 (dec. 1988); children: Nancy Armide, Ruth Courtney, Priscilla Gover, Mary Louise; m. Ernestine Friedl Levy, Dec. 27, 1990. BA, Johns Hopkins U., 1938, MD, 1943; PhD in Sci. (hon.), Downstate Med. Ctr., SUNY, 2010; DSc (hon.), SUNY, Downstate, 2010. Diplomate Am. Bd. Anesthesiology. Fellow in anesthesiology NRC; anesthesiologist-in-chief Albany Med. Ctr., 1948-52, Kings County Med. Ctr., Bklyn., 1952-68, pres. med. bd., 1958-62, chmn. exec. com., 1964-65; cons. L.I. Jewish, St. Albans Naval, Maimonides, St. John's Episcopal, VA hosps., N.C. Eye and Ear Hosp., Durham; assoc. prof. anesthesiology (surgery) Albany Med. Coll., 1948-52; prof., chmn. dept. anesthesiology SUNY Downstate Med. Ctr., 1952-68, Pritzker Sch. Medicine, U. Chgo., 1968-71; prof. anesthesiology Duke Med. Ctr., Durham, NC, 1971—, chmn. dept. anesthesiology ctr., 1971-83, prof. anesthesiology, 1983-87, Merel H. Harmel prof. anesthesiology, 2002, prof. emeritus, 1987—; prof. anesthesiology Duke U. Med. Ctr., Durham, 2002—; lectr. Duke U., 2010; Roderick Calverly lectr., 2009. Vis. prof. dept. anesthesiology Sch. Medicine, Johns Hopkins U., 1985—. Contbr. articles to profl. jours. Named Disting. Med. Alumnae Johns Hopkins Sch. Medicine, 2003; Commonwealth fellow Oxford U., 1961-62, hon. mem. Sr. Common Rm., Pembroke Coll., 1961; named Merel Harmel vis. lectureship in his honor Duke U. Med. Ctr., 1983, Merel H. Harmel chair dept. anesthesiology in his honor, 2003, Tribute honor, SUNY Downstate Med. Ctr., 2008. Fellow Am. Coll. Anesthesiology (bd. govs.), Royal Coll. Anaesthesia Faculty; mem. AMA, Am. Soc. Anesthesiologists (Living History Series), Assn. Univ. Anesthetists, Duke U. Med. Ctr. Founders Soc., Johns Hopkins U. Soc. Scholars, Japan Soc. Anesthesiologists (hon.), Assn. Anesthesiologists Français (hon.), Oxford Soc. Carolinas (hon. sec. 1990—, W.G. Anlyan Lifetime Achievement award 1999). Business E-Mail: harme001@mc.duke.edu.

HARMELINK, HERMAN, III, minister, writer, religious studies educator; b. Sheldon, Pa., Dec. 26, 1933; s. Herman, II and Thyrza (Eringa) Harmelink; m. Barbara Mary Conibear, Aug. 11, 1959; children: Herman Alan IV, Lindsay Alexandra. BA cum laude, Central Coll., 1954; MA, Columbia U., 1955; postgrad., U. London, 1955; MDiv, New Brunswick Theol. Sem., 1958; World Coun. Chs. scholar, U. Heidelberg, 1959; STM magna cum laude, Union Theol. Sem., NYC, 1964, MPhil, 1978. Ordained to ministry Ref. Ch. Am., 1959. Min. Cmty. Ch., Glen Rock, NJ, 1959-64, Woodcliff Cmty. Ch., Woodcliff-on-Hudson, NJ, 1964-71, Reformed Ch., Poughkeepsie, NY, 1971—; ecumenical officer Internat. Coun. Cmty. Chs., 2000—. Adj. faculty philosophy SUNY, Marist Coll.; chaplain Holland-Am. Line; chmn. interch. rels. Ref. Ch. Am., 1964—71; pres. Synod of NJ, 1969; vice chmn. faith order commn. Nat. Coun. Chs., 1976—79, mem. commn. regional and local ecumenism, 1981—84, del. Gen. Assembly, 1999—, mem. faith and order commn., mem. exec. bd., 2000—, mem. interfaith commn., 2010—; chmn. ecumenical rels. commn. Internat. Coun. Cmty. Chs., 1994—; del. 18th and 19th Plenary Consultation Ch. Union, St. Louis, 1999—2008, 20th Plenary Consultation Ch. Union, Ft. Lauderdale, 2011; mem. steering com. reconciliation ministries task force Chs. Uniting in Christ, 2002—; pres. Dutchess Interfaith Coun., 1977—78, devel. retirement cmty. com., 1989—, bd. dirs.; del. gen. coun. World Alliance Ref. Chs., Frankfurt, 1964, Nairobi, 70, Grand Rapids, 2010; adv. Gen. Assembly World Coun. Chs., Uppsala, Sweden, 1968; US del. 50th Anniversary Faith and Order Commn., Lausanne, Switzerland, 1977; del. gen. assembly World coun. Chs., Porto Allegre, Brazil, 2006. Author: Ecumenism and the Reformed Church, 1968, The Reformed Church in New Jersey, 1969, Another Look at Frelinghuysen and His Awakening, 1969; contbg. author: Concord Makes Strength, 2002, Piety and Patriotism, 1976, Vision from the Hill, 1984, The Livingston Legacy, 1987. Nat. bd. dirs. Literacy Vols. Am.; participant US-South African Leader Exch. Program, 1971; bd. dirs. Dutchess County Arts Coun., 1976—80, Bardavon 1869 Opera House, 1978—79; mem. allocation and planning divsn. United Way. Dutchess County; mem. Dutchess County Execs. Com. Med. Ethics; sec. bd. dirs. Rehab. Programs, Inc., 1977—79; bd. dirs. Anderson Ednl. Found., Collingwood Repertory Theatre, 1978—80, Mid-Hudson Meml. Soc., 1981—84; pres. Poughkeepsie Generating Cmty., 1974—; bd. dirs. Literacy Vol. Dutchess County, pres., 1987—89; bd. dirs. Literacy Vols. Am., NY, chmn. pers. comm., mem. program com., pres.-elect, 1992—93, pres., 1993—96, Ranfurly Libr. Svc. NY Inc.; adv. bd. Wartburg Luth. Svcs., 1993—; chmn. Anderson Sch. Wine Showcase; chmn. fin. com. Town of Poughkeepsie Dem. Com., Dutchess County Dem. Com.; ecumenical adv. del. Presbyn. Ch. Gen. Assembly, Long Beach, Calif., 2000, Episc. Gen. Conv., Mpls., 2003, Columbus, 2006, Anaheim, 2009, United Meth. Gen. Conf., 2004; trustee Peter A. Lindsay Trust Imperial Coll. U. London; trustee St. Francis Hosp., mem. exec. com. bd.; bd. dirs. Poughkeepsie Rural Cemetery, chmn. fin. com. Lt. USNR, 1957—61. Decorated knight Order of the Temple of Jerusalem; Fulbright Travel grantee, Germany, 1958—59. Mem.: Most Traveled People, Mercersburg Soc., Co. of Pastors, Presbyn. Hist. Soc., Am. Soc. Ch. History, N.Am. Acad. Ecumenists, Nat. Ecumenical Officers Assn. (sec. 2007—), Dutchess County Hist. Soc. (life; bd. dirs. 1974—78), Ctr. Lifetime Study, Poughkeepsie C. of C., Fulbright Assn. (life), Mil. Order Fng. Wars US (life), Dutchess Interfaith Coun., English Speaking Union, Fjord Club, The Club, Circumnavigators Club (NYC), Poughkeepsie Social Reading Club (past pres.), Dutchess county Clergy Club, Travelers Century Club (life), Witherspoon Soc., Royal Overseas League (London), Chevalier du Tastevin (France), Lumanites (sec.-treas.), Poughkeepsie Rotary (pres. 1977—79, sec. 1979—, sec. Dist. 721 1980—81, gov. 1982—83, chmn. World Cmty. Svc., Internat. Coun. Legis. 1983, internat. pres.'s rep. to dist. confs. 1984, 1988, sect. leader internat. conv. 1990, Paul Harris fellow), Friends St. George's and Descs. Knights of Garter (life), St. George's Soc. NY (life). Office: 70 Hooker Ave Poughkeepsie NY 12601

HARMON, GLYNN, medical educator; b. Hollister, Calif., Nov. 4, 1933; BA, MA, U. Calif. at Berkeley, 1963; MSIS, PhD, Case Western Res. U., 1970. Aviator, Russian interpreter, cuban blockade USN, 1955—64; prof. biomed., nursing and pub. health informatics U. Tex. at Austin, 1970—. Bd. govs. Grad. Sch. Integrative Medicine, 2004—. Decorated Pacific Svc. and Cuban Blockade Medals US Navy. Mem.: Tailhook Assn., Med. Libr. Assn. Home: 6910 Hart Ln # 107 Austin TX 78731 Business E-Mail: gharmon@ischool.utexas.edu.

HARMON, ROBERT GERALD, public health executive; b. Barnsdall, Okla., Mar. 20, 1944; s. Thomas Frederick and Eleandor Virginia (Colley) H.; children: Rex, Susan. BA in Zoology, Washington U., 1966, MD, 1970; MPH, Johns Hopkins U., 1977. Diplomate Am. Bd. Preventive Medicine. Intern, then resident U. Colo. Med. Ctr., Denver, 1970-73; asst. prof. health svcs. and internal medicine U. Wash., Seattle, 1977-80; chmn. dept. community medicine Maricopa Med. Ctr., Phoenix, 1980-85; dep. dir. Maricopa County Divsn. Pub. Health, Phoenix, 1980-82, dir., 1983-85; dir. Dept. Health State of Mo., Jefferson City, 1986-90; clin. prof. U. Mo. Sch. Medicine, Columbia, 1986-90; adminstr. Health Resources Svcs. Adminstrn. USPHS/HHS, Rockville, Md., 1990-93; sr. v.p. MetraHealth Ctr. for Corp. Health Inc., Oakton, Va., 1994-95; v.p., nat. med. dir. Optum divsn. United-Health Group, McLean, Va., 1996—2004; dir., chief med. officer Ctr. for Health Care Policy and Evaluation Ingenix/United Health Group, Eden Prairie, Minn., 2004—05; dir. Duval County Health Dept., Jacksonville, 2006—. Clin. prof. Sch. Medicine, U. Fla., 2007-. & Col. Health, U North Fla, Jacksonville, 2009-. Contbr. over 50 articles to profl. jours. Bd. dirs. Partnership for Prevention, DC, 1996-2005, Nat. Bd. Pub. Health Examiners, DC, 2005-2010; with commd. corps USPHS, 1974-75, 90-93. Decorated Meritorious Svc. medal USPHS. Fellow Am. Coll. Preventive Medicine (pres. 2003-05); mem. Nat. Assn. County Health Ofcls. (pres. 1983-85), Assn. State and Territorial Health Ofcls. (exec. com. 1987-90), Ariz. County Health Ofcls. Assn. (founder, pres. 1984-85), Omicron Delta Kappa, Delta Omega. Avocation: sports. Office: 900 University Blvd N Jacksonville FL 32211 Office Phone: 904-253-1010. E-mail: robert_harmon@doh.state.fl.us.

HARMS, NANCY ANN, nursing educator; d. Orval M. and Ruth Marie (Nelson) H.; m. Gerhart J. Wehrbein. Diploma, Bryan Meml. Hosp., 1971; BS in Natural Sci., Nebr. Wesleyan U., 1971; BSN, U. Nebr., 1975, MSN, 1977, PhD, 1988. RN, Nebr. Staff nurse, asst. supr., ins. coord. Brewster Hosp., Holdrege, Nebr., 1971-72; instr. Immanuel Sch. Nursing, Omaha, 1972-73; coord. nursing care plan devel. Hosp. Info. Sys. U. Nebr. Med. Ctr., Omaha, 1975; asst. chair dept. Coll. St. Mary, Omaha, 1975-80; curriculum coord. Midland Luth. Coll., Fremont, Nebr., 1980-88, chair nursing divsn., 1988—2007, prof. Mem. ANA (mem. Ho. of Dels.), Nebr. Nurses' Assn. (Nurse Excellence award, Excellence in Writing award jour., adv. Nebr. Student Nurses Assn., mem. various coms.), Nat. League Nursing, Sigma Theta Tau (theta omega, gamma pi chpts.). Business E-Mail: gjwanh@cox.net.

HARMSEN, LOTTE, physician; b. Copenhagen, Jan. 28, 1977; MD, U. Copenhagen, 2005, PhD, 2010. Jr. physician dept. respiratory medicine, gastroent. & vascular surgery, & gen. practice Region Zealand Hosps., 2005—07; rschr. Respiratory & Allergy Rsch. Unit Copenhagen U. Hosp., Bispebjerg, 2007—10, jr. physician dept. ob-gyn. Hvidovre, 2011—. Grant, Copenhagen U. Hosp., HS Rsch. Found., Christian X Found., Danish Lung Assn. Mem.: Danish Med. Soc., Danish Med. Assn. Home: Skyttedal 2 Nærum 2850 Denmark Business E-Mail: l.harmsen@dadlnet.dk.

HARNICK, JOEL, cardiologist; b. Oceanside, NY, Apr. 9, 1969; MD, Ea. Va. Med. Sch., 2001. Pediatric cardiologist Good Samaritan Hosp. Med. Ctr., 2008—. Fellow: Am. Acad. Pediat., Am. Coll. Cardiology. Office: 655 Deer Pk Ave Babylon NY 11702 Office Phone: 631-321-2130. Office Fax: 631-321-2156. Business E-Mail: joel.harnick@chsli.org.

HARNOD, TOMOR, neurosurgeon, educator; b. Taipei, Taiwan, Dec. 5, 1963; married, Feb. 2, 1994. Cert. Taiwan Neurosurgical Soc., 1996. Neurosurgeon Vet. Gen. Hosp., Taipei, 1990—96; clin. observer Barrow Neurol. Inst., Phoenix, 1996; attending neurosurgeon Cardinal Tien Hosp., Taipei, 1996—99; attending neurosurgeon, epilepsy ctr. dept. ns Tzu Chi Gen. Hosp., Hualien, Taiwan, 1999—, dir. neurosurgery ward, 2005—; clin. asst. prof. Dept. Medicine, Tzu Chi U., Hualien, 2002—. Office: Tzu Chi Gen Hosp Dept NS 707 Sec 3 Chung-Yang Rd Hualien 970 Taiwan Office Fax: 886-3-8577161. Business E-Mail: nsha@tzuchi.com.tw.

HARNOIS, VERONICA D'URSO, psychologist, educator; d. John Joseph and Vera Shannon D'Urso; children: Kent, Kathleen Duquette, Sheila Foley, Carol Recor, Jeanne, John. BA, Merrimack Coll., North Andover, Mass., 1957; MEd, Am. Internat. Coll., Springfield, Mass., 1971, cert. advanced grad. studies, 1991, D of Edn., 2003. Cert. sch. psychologist Mass., lic. ednl. psychologist Mass. Substitute tchr., tchr. Springfield Pub. Schs., 1958—69; co-dir., cons., tchr. Miss Barker's Sch., 1969—75; ednl. dir., tchr. Osborn Day Sch., Agawam, 1975—83; vocat. counselor, examiner Urban League, Springfield, 1984—85; clin. specialist, sch. psychologist Kolburne Sch., New Marlborough, 1986—94; dir. sch. program Brightside, Inc., Springfield, 1994—96; cons., psychol. examiner May Inst., West Springfield, 1997—98; sch. psychologist Springfield Pub. Schs., 1998—. Instr. psychology, spl. edn. and reading Am. Internat. Coll., 1991—. Author: The Harnois Program, 1994. Recipient Medallion award for leaders of distinction, Acad. Notre Dame, Tyngsboro, Mass., 2008. Mem.: Pioneer Valley Reading Coun. (bd. dirs. 1988—2007), Nat. Assn. Sch. Psychologists, Western Mass. Counseling Assn., Delta Kappa Gamma. Roman Catholic. Avocation: reading. Home: 38 Nassau Dr Springfield MA 01129 Office: Springfield Pub Schs 195 State St Springfield MA 01103 also: 1550 Main St Springfield MA 01103 Personal E-mail: harnoisv@verizon.net.

HARNSBERGER, JEFFREY R., colon and rectal surgeon, educator; MD, U. Toledo, Ohio, 1987. Diplomate Am. Bd. Surgery, 1993, Am. Bd. Surgery, 2001, Am. Bd. Colon and Rectal Surgery, 1994, Am. Bd. Colon and Rectal Surgery, 2005. Intern Dartmouth-Hitchcock Med. Ctr., Lebanon, NH, resident in gen. surgery, 1987—92; fellow in colon and rectal surgery St. Louis Univ. Med. Ctr., Mo., 1992—93; asst. prof. surgery med. sch. Dartmouth Coll.; hosp. affiliations include Elliot Hosp., Dartmouth-Hitchcock Med. Ctr., Manchester, NH. Office: Dartmouth-Hitchcock Medical Center 100 Hitchcock Way Manchester NH 03104 Office Phone: 603-695-2840. Office Fax: 603-695-2985.

HAROLD, JOHN GORDON, cardiologist, internist; s. John and Anne (Callaghan) H.; m. Ellen Teresa Cox, Dec. 28, 1977. BS, CCNY, 1977; MD, SUNY, Stony Brook, 1979. Diplomate Nat. Bd. Med. Examiners, Am. Bd. Internal Medicine, Am. Bd. Cardiovascular Disease, Am. Bd. Critical Care Medicine, Am. Bd. Geriatric Medicine. Intern medicine Mt. Sinai Hosp., NYC, 1979-80, resident medicine, 1980-82; cardiology fellow div. cardiology, dept. medicine Cedars-Sinai Med. Ctr., LA, 1982-85, assoc. cardiologist, 1985—90, chief staff, 2004—05; asst. clin. prof. medicine Sch. Medicine UCLA, 1987-93, assoc. clin. prof. sch. medicine, 1993-99, clin. prof. medicine, 1999—. Attending physician Cedars-Sinai Heart Inst.; vice-chair pharmacy and therapeutics com. Cedars-Sinai Med. Ctr., 1990—2001, mem. med. exec. com., 1996—2010, 1999—, clin. chief cardiology, 1998—99, clin. chief medicine, 1999—2001, vice chief of staff, 2002—03, chief Staff, 2004—05; vis. faculty Beijing Med. U., 1st Tchg. Hosp. of Beijing Med. U., 1989. Editor: Two-Dimensional Echocardiography and Cardiac Doppler, 1990; book reviewer; contbr. articles to profl. jours. Active Nat. Eagle Scout Assn.; mem. Rep. Nat. Com., Washington, 1982—; bd. dirs. Beverly Hills Affiliate Am. Heart Assn., 1995—99; bd. dirs. Cedars-Sinai Med. Ctr., Save A Heart Found., LA, UCLA Sch. Medicine Clin. Faculty Assn., 1998—. Recipient Nat. Rsch. Svc. award NIH, 1984-85; named Alumnus of Yr. Cedars-Sinai, 2005, Alumni award, Sch. Med. Stony Brook, 2007. Master: ACP, Am. Coll. Cardiology (v.p. 2011—); fellow: AHA, AHA LA Divsn. (LA affiliate bd. dirs. 2005—, pres. 2008—10, coun. on clin. cardiology 2009—, Passion Heart award 2007), Am. Coll. Chest Physicians, Am. Coll. Cardiology (Southern Calif.) (comm. chair Calif. chpt. 2001—05, gov. 2006—, chair. bd. govs. 2009—10, sec. 2009—, mem. exec. com. bd. trustees 2009—, pres. Calif. Chpt.); mem.: Nat. Geog. Soc., AMA (Physicians Recognition award 1998, 2001), ACC (sec. 2009—10), Am. Bd. Internal Medicine (bd. dirs. 2006, mem. exec. com. 2010—), L.A. County Med. Assn. Republican. Roman Catholic. Avocation: flying. Office: Cedars Sinai Med Office Towers Ste 750 Los Angeles CA 90048-6101 Office Phone: 310-659-2030. Office Fax: (310) 659-1369.

HAROON, MUHAMMAD, rheumatologist; b. Faisalabad, Pakistan; MBBS, King Edward Med. Coll., Lahore, Pakistan; MMedSc. Fellow, specialist registrar rheumatology South Infirmary, Victoria U. Hosp., Cork, Ireland, 2005—07, Waterford Regional Hosp., Ireland, 2007—. Enthusiastic young rschr.; clinician in rheumatology field. Contbr. scientific papers. Mem.: RCP (Ireland), Irish Soc. Rheumatology. Achievements include research in wide range of adverse events with newer biologic agents, have also investigated the role of vitamin D in rheumatology patients. Home: 15 Bracken Dr Waterford Ireland Office: Waterford Regional Hosp Ardkeen Waterford Ireland Personal E-mail: mharoon301@hotmail.com.

HARPER, GLENN R., cardiac electrophysiologist; Grad., Med. Coll. of Pa. Diplomate Am. Bd. Internal Medicine, 1988, Am. Bd. Internal Medicine-cardiovasc. disease, 1993, Am. Bd. Internal Medicine-clin.cardiac electrophysiology, 1994. Intern Med. Coll. of Pa., resident; fellow Hahnemann Univ.; with Bryn Mawr Hosp., 1991, Lankenau Med. Ctr., 1995; campus chief electrophysiology Paoli Hosp. Office: Bryn Hospital MOB N Ste 105 830 Old Lancaster Rd Bryn Mawr PA 19010 Office Phone: 866-225-5654.

HARPER, LYNN D., biologist; children: Travis, Christopher, MacKenzie. BA, MS in Cell and Molecular Biology, U. Bridgeport. Tech. writer, asst. mgr. Bionetics Corp., Washington, 1982—83; tech. dir. space sys. divsn. Gen. Electric Mgmt. and Tech. Svcs. Co., Washington, 1983—86; program mgr. advanced missions and spl. projects space life scis. divsn. NASA, 1986—89, dep. project mgr. Search Extraterrestrial Intelligence; chief advanced life support divsn. NASA Ames Rsch. Ctr., 1990—93, acting chief advanced life support divsn., 1993—94, sr. sys. engr. space scis. divsn., 1994—96, lead, integrative studies astrobiology, 1996—2000, lead astrobiology advanced concepts and technologies, 2000—05; lead integrative studies astrobiology space rsch., 2005—08. Contbr. scientific papers. Recipient Exceptional Leadership medal, NASA, 6 other achievement awards. Achievements include co-founding the science of Astrobiology, Space Portal, and RosettaSpace; significant contributions to in space experiments on Space Shuttle, Mir, Space Station, Stardust, Mars missions; contributor to human exploration of the solar system studies. Office: NASA Ames Rsch Ctr MS 555-3 Bldg 555 Rm 3 Moffett Field CA 94035 *

HARPER, SHIRLEY FAY, nutritionist, educator, consultant, lecturer; b. Auburn, Ky., Apr. 23, 1943; d. Charles Henry and Annabelle (Gregory) Belcher; m. Robert Vance Harper, May 19, 1973 (dec. Mar. 2000); children: Glenda, Debra, Teresa, Suzanna, Cynthia. BS, Western Ky. U., 1966, MS, 1982. Cert. nutritionist and lic. dietitian, Ky. Dir. dietetics Logan County Hosp., Russellville, Ky., 1965-80; cons. Western State Hosp., Hopkinsville, Ky., 1983-84, instnl. dietetic adminstr., 1984-88; dietitian Rivendell Children's Psychiat. Hosp., Bowling Green, Ky., 1988-90; instr. nutrition Western Ky. U., Bowling Green, 1990-92. Cons. Auburn (Ky.) Nursing Ctr., 1976-95, Belle Meade Home, Greenville, Ky., 1980—, Brookfield Manor, Hopkinsville, 1983—2010, Sparks Nursing Ctr., Ctrl. City, Ky., 1983—, Muhlenberg Cmty. Hosp., Greenville, 1989-2000, Russellville Health Care Manor, 1978-83, 92-2011, Westlake Regional Hosp., Columbia, Ky., 1993-, Franklin-Simpson Meml. Hosp., Franklin, Ky., 1993-2003, Lakeview Health Care Ctr., Morgantown, Ky., 2001-03, Morgantown Care and Rehab. Ctr., 2003-04, Trigg County Personal Care Home, Cadiz, 2002-, Gainsville Manor, Hopkinsville, 2002-; nutrition instr. Madisonville (Ky.) C.C., 1995-98, Covington's Convalescent Ctr., Hopkinsville, 2007-. Mem. regional bd. dirs. ARC of Ky., Frankfort, 1990-96; vice chair ARC of Logan County, 1992-93, chmn., 1993-96, 97—; bd. dirs. Logan County ARC United Way, 1993—; co-chair adv. coun. devel. disabilities Lifeskills, 1992-93, adv. coun. Lifeskills Residential Living Group Home, 1993-2000, human rights adv. coun., 1994-2000; chair Let's Build our Future Campaign; nutrition del. Citizen Am. Program to USSR, 1990; adv. chair for vocat. edn., Russellville; mem. adv. coun. for home econs. and family living, We. Ky. U., 1990-93; bd. dirs. ARC of Logan County for United Way, 1993—; del. 24th Internat. Congress on Arts and Comm., Oxford (Eng.) U., 1997. Recipient Outstanding Svc. award Am. Dietetic Assn. Found., 1993, Outstanding Svc. award Barren River Mental Health-Mental Retardation Bd., 1987, Svc. Appreciation award Logan-Russellville Assn. for Retarded Citizens, 1987, Internat. Woman of Yr. award for contbn. to Nutrition and Humanity, Internat. Biog. Assn., 1993-94, World Lifetime Achievement award Am. Biog. Inst., 1995; inaugurated Lifetime Dep. Gov., Am. Biog. Rsch. Bd., 1995, Pres.'s award ARC of Logan County, 1996, award of excellence Oxford, Eng. Internat. Congress on Arts and Comm., Internat. Sash of Acad., Am. Biog. Inst., 1997. Mem. Am. Dietetic Assn., Nat. Nutrition Network, Ky. Dietetic Assn. (pres. Western dist. 1976-77, Outstanding Dietitian award 1984), Bowling Green-Warren County Nutrition Coun., Nat. Ctr. for Nutrition and Dietetics (charter), Ky. Nutrition Coun., Logan County Home Economist Club (sec. 1994-95, 1999-2000, v.p. 1995-96, 2000-01, pres. 1996-97, 2001—), Internat. Biog. Assn., Internat. Platform Assn., Diabetes Care and Edn., Cons. Dietitians in Health Care Cmtys., Phi Upsilon Omicron (pres. Beta Delta alumni chpt. 1994-96, Outstanding Alumni award 1997). Avocations: music, poetry, reading, drawing. Home and Office: 443 Hopkinsville Rd Russellville KY 42276-1286

HARPER, WILLIAM R., medical association administrator; b. Fairfield, Calif., May 13, 1969; MD, Northwestern U., 1995. Asst. prof. to assoc. prof. U. Chgo. Pritzker Sch. Medicine, 1998—2010; clin. assoc. medicine U. Chgo., 2011—. Co-founder, co-pres., & chief med. officer Engaged Health Solutions, LLC, 2009. Recipient David E. Rogers award, Soc. Gen. Internal Medicine. Mem.: Phi Beta Kappa, Alpha Omega Alpha (chpt.). Office: 5841 S Md Ave MC 9038 Chicago IL 60637 Business E-Mail: wrharper@uchicago.edu.

HARPREET, BARINGA SINGH, anti-aging and regenerative medicine, aesthetic medicine, family medicine, sexual medicine consultant, clinical pharmacologist; s. Baringa Singh Labh and Baringa Kaur Barjinder; m. Baringa Kaur Paramdeep, Sept. 24, 1993; children: Baringa Singh Yash Karan, Baringa Singh Roop Karan. MBBS, Miss Edith Brown Christian Med. Coll. & Hosp., Ludhiana,Punjab. India, 1988; MD, Dayanand Med. Coll. & Hosp., Ludhiana, 1991; DFM, Royal Coll. Gen. Practitioners, 2008; MD in Internal Medicine, Tever Acad. Med. Edn. & Rsch., Russia, 2007. Diplomate Am. Bd. Anti-aging & Regenerative Medicine, 2009, Am. Acad. Aestethic Medicine, 2009. Lectr. pharmacology Dayanand Med. Coll. & Hosp., Ludhiana, 1991—92; dir. Sgtb Homeo Med. Coll. & Hosp., Patiala, Punjab, 1996—99; prof. head dept. Bjs Dental Coll. Hosp. & Rsch. Inst., Ludhiana, 1999—; chair person, chief cons., dir. Skin Kraft & Vital Life Derma Cosmetology & Wellness Ctr., Ludhiana, 2009—. Contbr. scientific papers. Recipient Gold medal, Cmty. Welfare, 1995, Vashisht award, 1996, Param Chikitsak award, 1997; fellow Dermatology fellow, Ctrl. Rsch. Inst. Med. Scis., 2008. Fellow: Royal Coll. Gen. Practitioners; mem.: Lodhi Club, Sutluj Club. Hindu Sikh. Achievements include development of cocktails for mesotherapy. Avocations: travel, gardening, music, stamp collecting/philately. Office: Skin Kraft Derma Cosmetology Ctr 23-A Sarabha-Nagar Ludhiana Punjab 141001 India Home: 23-A 141 001 Ludhiana India Office Phone: 91-161-4648888. Personal E-mail: doctorharpreet8@yahoo.com Business E-Mail: dryash456@yahoo.com.

HARRIBANCE, SEAN LALSINGH, parapsychologist; b. Fyzabad, Trinidad and Tobago, Nov. 11, 1939; arrived in U.S., 1969; s. Harribance Singh and Sampatia Batchasingh; m. Christine Ann Comyn, Feb. 28, 1971; children: Linnea Christine, Sean Lalsingh Jr. Cashier Trinidad Bus Svc., San Fernando, 1959—69; part-time rschr. Parapsychology Lab., Dr. Hamlyn Dukhan, Trinidad, 1966—69; parapsychol. rsch. subject Found. for Rsch. on Nature of Man, Durham, NC, 1969—73; part-time rsch. subject Psychical Rsch. Found., Durham, NC, 1969—73, 1980; pres. Sean Harribance Inst. for Parapsychology, Inc., 1980—. Part-time parapsychology rsch. subject Laurentian U., Sudbury, Ont., Can., 1996, 97, 2000, 09; hon. dir. Sean Harribance Inst. for Parapsychology Rsch., Inc., Tex., Sean Harribance Inst. Parapsychology Found., Trinidad; affiliated with engring. dept. Duke U., 1975; symposium contbr., Am. Psychol. Assn., 2008. Co-author: This Man Knows You, 1976; contbr. articles to profl. jours. including jours. Neuroquantology, jours. Consciousness Exploration & Rsch., Internat. Jour. Psychophysiology, Internat. Jour. Neuroscience, Perceptual and Motor Skills, Jour. Parapsychology, Jour. Am. Soc. for Psychical Rsch., Jour. Neuropsychiatry and Clin. Neuroscience, Procs. Parapsychol. Assn., Rsch. in Parapsychology, symposium APA 116th Ann. Convention, 2008, Jour. Consciousness Exploration & Rsch., Neuroquantology Jour. Named Hon. Citizen, recipient Key to City, City of Baton Rouge, 1975, hon. lt. col. aide-de-camp, Ala. State Militia, 1975. Home: PO Box 908 Sugar Land TX 77487-0908 Office Phone: 281-980-3860. Personal E-mail: harribance@yahoo.com.

HARRIGAN, JOHN THOMAS, JR., physician, obstetrician, gynecologist; b. Perth Amboy, NJ, Apr. 20, 1929; s. John T. and Mary E. (Czapp) H.; m. Marlene Lulka, Apr. 14, 1961 (div.); children: John, Alisa, Edmund; m. Karen Tiejen, Aug. 23, 1992 (dec. 2003), Barbara Kolarsick, 2008. Student, U. Va., 1946-49; MD, George Washington U., 1953. Diplomate Am. Bd. Ob-Gyn. Intern Doctors Hosp., Washington, 1953-54; resident in ob-gyn Luth. Hosp., Balt., 1954-55, Providence Hosp., Washington, 1957-58, Free Hosp. for Women, Boston, 1958-59; practice medicine specializing in ob-gyn, sub specialist in maternal-fetal medicine Jersey City, 1960-65, Colonia, NJ, 1962-70, Madison Twp., NJ, 1965-70; asst. attending in ob-gyn Margaret Hague Hosp., Jersey City, 1960-65; attending physician in ob-gyn Rahway Hosp., N.J., 1962-70, South Amboy Hosp., N.J., 1965-73, sec. to med. staff, 1970; attending in ob-gyn Martland Hosp. Unit, Newark, 1970-74; dir. dept. ob-gyn Monmouth Med. Ctr., Long Branch, NJ, 1974-76, dir. regional perinatal edn. program, 1975-78; dir. Monmouth Perinatal Ctr., Long Branch, 1975-78; sr. attending in ob-gyn St. Peter's Med. Ctr., 1978—; assoc. prof. ob-gyn Hahnemann

Med. Coll., Phila., 1975-78; prof. dir. div. maternal-fetal medicine Rutgers Med. Sch., Piscataway, NJ, 1978—, prof. ob-gyn., dir. div. maternal-fetal medicine, 1978-86, U. Medicine and Dentistry N.J., Robert Wood Med. Sch., 1986—. Cons. in maternal-fetal medicine to physicians, Eastern N.J.; mem. maternal and infant care services com. N.J. Dept. Health, 1975—; dir. statewide premature delivery prevention project; med.-legal expert cons.; tech. adv. panel Healthstart program, N.J. Health Dept. Contbr. articles to med. jours.; reviewer med. jours. Mem. task force on biomed. causes and pub. rels. Gov.'s Coun. on Prevention Mental Retardation, N.J., task force on genetics and fetal defects, 1984—; mem. pub. affairs com. MOD Birth Defects Found.; pres. Perinatal Assn. N.J., 1991-93; mem. N.J. Commn. of Health and Parental and Child Health adv. Com., 1993—, vice chair, 1995—. Capt. M.C. U.S. Army, 1955-57. Fellow ACOG (vice chmn. N.J. sect. 1979-82, chmn. N.J. sect. 1982—, nat. adv. coun. 1982—, legis. rep., treas. dist. III 1986); mem. AMA, Med. Soc. N.J. (maternal infant care com. 1988—), Am. Inst. Ultrasound in Medicine (legis. com. 1994), Am. Fertility Soc., N.J. Perinatal Assn. (v.p. 1980-90, pres. 1990), N.J. Perinatal Tech. adv. Com. Baker channing Soc., N.J. Ob-gyn. Soc. (coun.), N.J. Maternal Fetal Medicine Soc. (pres. 1994-95). Democrat. Roman Catholic. Home: 301 Sussex Ave Spring Lake NJ 07762-1231 Office: Jersey Shore Med Ctr Perinatal Inst 301 Sussex Ave Spring Lake NJ 07762-1231 Personal E-mail: j.harrigan@verizon.net.

HARRIGAN, ROSANNE CAROL, medical educator; b. Miami, Fla., Feb. 24, 1945; d. John H. and Rose (Hnatow) Harrigan; children: Dennis, Michael, John. BS, St. Xavier Coll., 1965; MSN, Ind. Univ., 1974, EdD in Nursing and Edn., 1979. Staff nurse, recovery rm. Mercy Hosp., Chgo., 1965, evening charge nurse, 1965—66; head nurse Chgo. State Hosp., 1966—67; nurse practitioner Health and Hosp. Corp. Marion County, Indpls., 1975—80; assoc. prof. Ind. U. Sch. Nursing, Indpls., 1978—82; nurse practitioner devel. follow up program Riley Hosp. for Children, Indpls., 1980—85; prof. Ind. U. Sch. Nursing, Indpls., 1982—85; chief nursing sect. Riley Hosp. Child Devel. Ctr., Indpls., 1982—85; chmn., prof. maternal child health Loyola U., Niehoff Sch. Nursing, Chgo., 1985—92; dean sch. nursing U. Hawaii, Honolulu, 1992—2002; nurse practitioner Waimanalo Health Ctr., Hawaii, 1998—2002; Frances A. Matsuda chair women's health John A. Burns Sch. Medicine U. Hawaii Manoa, Honolulu, 2000—05, chair faculty devel., 2002—, chair dept. Complementary and Alternative Medicine, 2002—, prof. pediat., 2003—. Lectr. Ind. U. Sch. Nursing, 1974-75, chmn. dept. pediat., family and women's health, 1980-85; adj. prof. of pediat. Ind. U. Sch. Med., 1982-85; editl. bd. Jour. Maternal Child Health Nursing, 1984-86, Jour. Perinatal Neo-natal, 1985—, Jour. Perinatology, 1989—, Loyola U. Press, 1988-92; adv. bd. Symposia Medicus, 1982-84, Proctor and Gamble Rsch. Adv. Com. Blue Ribbon Panel; sci. rev. panel NIH, 1985; mem. NIH nat. adv. coun. nursing rsch., 2000-; cons. in field. Contbr. articles to profl. journals. Bd. dir. March of Dimes Ctrl. Ind. Chpt., 1974-76, med. adv., 1979-85; med. and rsch. adv. March of Dimes Nat. Found., 1985—, chmn. Task Force on Rsch. Named Nat. Nurse of Yr. March of Dimes, 1983; faculty rsch. grantee Ind. U., 1978, Pediatric Pulmonary Nursing Tng. grant Am. Lung Assn., 1982-85, Attitudes, Interests, and Competence of Ob-Gyn. Nurses Rsch. grant Nurses Assn. Am. Coll. Ob-Gyn., 1986, Attitudes, Interests, and Priorities of Neo-natal Nurses Rsch. grant Nat. Assn. Neonatal Nurses, 1987, Biomedical Rsch. Support grant, 1988; Doctoral fellow Am. Lung Assn. Ind. Tng. Program, 1981-86. Mem. AAAS, ANA (Maternal Child Nurse of Yr. 1983), Assn. Women's Health, Obstetrical and Neonatal Nursing (chmn. com. on rsch. 1983-86), Am. Nurses Found., Nat. Assn. Neo-natal Nurses, Nat. Perinatal Assn. (bd. dir. 1978-85, rsch. com. 1986), Midwest Nursing Rsch. Soc. (theory devel. sect.), Ill. Nurses Assn. (commn. rsch. chmn. 1990-91), Ind. Nurses Assn., Hawaii Nurses Assn., Ind. Perinatal Assn. (pres. 1981-83), N.Y. Acad. Sci., Ind U. Alumni Assn. (Disting. Alumni 1985), Sigma Xi, Pi Lambda Theta, Sigma Theta Tau (chpt. pres. 1988-90). Home Phone: 808-728-2904. Business E-Mail: harrigan@hawaii.edu.

HARRINGTON, ELIZABETH B., vascular surgeon educator; MD, NY Med. Coll.; grad. magna cum laude, Barnard Coll. Diplomate Am. Bd. Surgery-gen. vascular, Am. Bd. Surgery. Residency surgery Mount Sinai Hosp., fellowship vascular surgery; assoc. clin. prof. Mt. Sinai Sch. of Medicine. Co-author numerous publs. Recipient Author H. Aufses Sr Prize in Surgery, 1980. Mem.: NY Vascular Soc. (pres. 1998—2000), Alpha Omega Alpha (hon.). Office: Mount Sinai Medical Center Ste 1D 1225 Pk Ave New York NY 10128 Office Phone: 212-876-7400. Office Fax: 212-831-8090.

HARRINGTON, JOHN TOLAN, internist, nephrologist, educator, retired dean; b. Fall River, Mass., Dec. 30, 1936; s. John J. and Elizabeth C. (Tolan) Harrington; m. Gertrude Rose Hargraves, Aug. 27, 1960; children: Gertrude, Kathleen, Daniel, Ann, John, Mark, Timothy. BA magna cum laude, Coll. of the Holy Cross, 1958; MD cum laude, Yale U., 1962. Diplomate Am. Bd. Internal Medicine. Intern, resident in internal medicine N.C. Meml. Hosp., Chapel Hill, 1962-65; clin. and rsch. fellow in nephrology Tufts Med. Ctr. (formerly New Eng. Med. Ctr.), Boston, 1965-68, nephrologist, dir. hemodialysis unit, 1971-81, chief gen. medicine divsn., 1981-86, sr. nephrologist, 2003—; chmn. dept. medicine Newton (Mass.)-Wellesley Hosp., 1986-94; dean academic affairs Tufts U. Sch. Medicine, Boston, 1994-95, asst. prof. medicine, 1971-75, assoc. prof. medicine, 1975-79, prof. medicine, 1979—, dean ad interim, 1995-96, dean, 1996—2002, dean emeritus, 2003—, dir., internat. affairs, 2008—. Author: Acid-Base, 1982; editor: Nephrology Forum Kidney Internat., 1979—2005, World Kidney Forum, Am. Kidney Diseases, 2007—; contbr. articles to profl. jours. Pres. Hummocks Cmty. Orgn., Portsmouth, RI, 1978—80, Nat. Kidney Found., Mass., 1988. Master: ACP (gov. Mass. chpt. 1989—93); fellow: Royal Irish Coll. Physicians (hon.); mem.: Am. Soc. Nephrology, Internat. Soc. Nephrology, Holy Name Soc. Democrat. Roman Catholic. Avocations: sailing, swimming, Irish poetry and drama, baseball. Office Phone: 617-636-0355. Personal E-mail: gertrudeharrington123@comcast.net. Business E-Mail: john.harrington@tufts.edu.

HARRINGTON, KATHLEEN FLEEGE, medical educator; b. Frankfurt, Germany, Sept. 26, 1950; BA, St. Mary's Coll., Notre Dame, Ind., 1972; PhD, U. Ala. Birmingham, MPH, 2006. Project dir. U. Ala. Birmingham, 1998—2006, asst. prof., 2007—. Ednl. rsch. cons. UAB Lung Health Ctr., 2006—11; adv. com. mem. Children's Hosp. Pediatric Pulmonary Ctr., 2007—11; cons. evaluator Heal Inc., 2008—11; bd. mem. UAB Palliative Care Cmty. Adv. Bd., 2009—11. R21 Devel. grant, NIH Nat. Inst. Nursing Rsch., grant, HRSA Maternal and Child Health Bur. Mem.: Am. Thoracic Soc., Kappa Delta Pi. Avocations: tennis, kayaking. Office: 618 20th St South OHB 143 Birmingham AL 35294-7447 Office Fax: 205-975-6118. Business E-Mail: kharring@uab.edu.

HARRINGTON, ROBERT A., cardiologist; MD, Tufts U. Sch. Med., 1986. Resident. U. Mass. Med. Ctr., 1986—90; resident Duke U. Med. Ctr., 1990—93; dir. Duke Clinical Rsch. Inst. Assoc. editor Am. Heart Jour.; editorial bd. mem. Jour. Am. Coll. Cardiology. Co-editor: Am. Coll. of Chest Physicians Consensus Panel on Antithrombotic & Thrombolytic Drugs 8th Ed., Antiplatelet Therapy in Clinical Practice. Fellow: Soc. Cardiovascular Angiography, Am. Heart Assn., Am. Coll. Cardiology. Office: 2400 Pratt St Rm 7028 Durham NC 27705 Office Phone: 919-668-8749. Office Fax: 919-668-7072.

HARRIS, C. MARTIN, information technology executive; BA, MD, MBA, U. Pa. Fellowship Hosp. of U. Pa., Phila., internship, residency; chief info. officer University of Pennsylvania Health Systems, 1991—96; staff mem., Dept. Gen. Internal Medicine Cleveland Clinic Foundation, chief info. officer, 1996—, chmn., info.-tech. divsn., 1996—2010. Former bd. dirs. CareScience, Inc., Phila.; past chmn. found. bd. E-Health Initiative; adv. to dir. Nat. Inst. Health; bd. dirs. Inst. for Healthcare Improvement, Boston; exec. dir. E-Cleveland Clinic, 2000; bd. dirs. Invacare Corp., 2003—; commr. (appt. by pres.) Commn. on Systemic Interoperability, 2005—. Adv. bd., Better Health 2010 Com. Assn. Am. Med. Coll.; judge for case studies in medicine The Computerworld Smithsonian Honors Program. Mem.: Am. Med. Informatics Assn., Healthcare Info. and Mgmt. Systems Soc. (chmn., nat. health info. infrastructure task force). Achievements include raising awarenss of impact of information technology in practice of medicine. Office: Cleveland Clinic Foundation 9500 Euclid Ave Cleveland OH 44195 Office Phone: 216-445-2200.

HARRIS, CURTIS CRAIG, medical researcher; BA in Zoology, U. Kans., 1965, MD, 1969. Intern Dept. Medicine UCLA Hosp., 1969—70; resident and trainee in clin. oncology VA Hosp., Washington, 1973—76; rsch. assoc. Lung Cancer Inst. Divsn. Cancer Cause and Prevention, Nat. Cancer Inst., NIH, Bethesda, Md., 1970—72, head Ultrastructure Unit, Pathogenesis Sect., Lung Cancer Br., 1972—75, head Human Tissue Studies Sect., Lab. Exptl. Pathology, 1975—81, assoc. chief Lab. Exptl. Pathology, 1979—81; chief Lab. Human Carcinogenesis Ctr. Cancer Rsch., Nat. Cancer Inst., NIH, Bethesda, Md., 1981—, head Molecular Genetics and Carcinogenesis Sect., 1981—. Clin. prof. medicine and oncology Georgetown U. Sch. Medicine. Recipient Alton Ochsner Award Relating Smoking and Health, Alton Ochsner Med. Found. and Am. Coll. Chest Physicians, 1993, Walter Hubert Award and Lectr., Brit. Assn. Cancer Rsch., 1995, DSM, USPHS, 1999. Fellow: AAAS; mem.: Internat. Assn. for Study of Lung Cancer, Am. Soc. Differentiation, Am. Assn. Cancer Rsch., Am. Soc. Clin. Investigation, Internat. Soc. Gastroent. Carcinogenesis (Charles Heidelberger Award 1999). Office: Lab Human Carcinogenesis NCI Bethesda Bldg 37 Rm 3068A 37 Convent Dr Bethesda MD 20892 Office Phone: 301-496-2048. Office Fax: 301-496-0497. E-mail: curtis_harris@nih.gov. *

HARRIS, DAVID THOMAS, immunology educator; b. Jonesboro, Ark, May 9, 1956; s. Marm Melton and Lucille Luretha (Buck) Harris; m. Francoise Jacqueline Besencon, June 24, 1989; children: Alexandre M., Stefanie L., Leticia M. BS in Biology, Math. and Psychology, Wake Forest U., 1978, MS, 1980, PhD in Microbiology and Immunology, 1982. Fellow Ludwig Inst. Cancer Rsch., Lausanne, Switzerland, 1982-85; rsch. asst. prof. U. NC, Chapel Hill, 1985-89; assoc. prof. U. Ariz., Tucson, 1989—2004, prof., 1996—. Cons. Teltech, Inc. Mpls., 1990—, Advanced Biosci. Resources, 1994-95; bd. sci. advisors Cryo-Cell Internat., 1992-95; bd. dir. Ageria, Inc., Tuscon; dir. Cord Blood Stem Cell Bank, 1992—; mem. Ariz. Cancer Ctr., Steele Meml. Children's Rsch. Ctr., Ariz. Arthritis Ctr. Program, sci. adv. bd. Cord Blood Registry, Inc., chief sci. div. Cord Blood Registry, Inc.; founder ImmuneRegen BioScis., Inc., 2002, Advanced Genetic Tools (Quregen, Inc.), 2004. Co-author chpts. to sci. books, articles to profls. jour.; reviewer sci. jour.; co-holder 9 scientific patents. Grantee numerous grants, 1988—. Mem. AAAS, Am. Assn. Immunologists, Reticuleondothelial Soc., Internat. Soc. Hematotherapy and Graft Engring., Internat. Soc. Devel. and Comparative Immunology, Scandanavian Soc. Immunology, Sigma Xi, Democrat. Church Of Christ. Avocations: tennis, hiking, jogging, skiing, travel. Office: Univ Ariz Dept Immunology POBox 245221 Tucson AZ 85724 Office Phone: 520-626-5127. Business E-Mail: davidh@U.Arizona.edu.

HARRIS, ELAINE K., medical consultant; b. NYC, Mar. 17, 1924; d. Julius and Bertha (Wecker) Kirschbuam; m. Herbert Harris, Aug. 1, 1948; children: Gail, Linda, Geoffrey. AB Bus. Economics cum laude, Hunter Coll.; AM Bus. Edn., Columbia U. Lic. tchr. bus. NY. Founder, pres. Sjogren's Syndrome Found., 1983-91, exec. dir., 1991-94. Cons. in field; v.p. exec. bd. Nat. Alliance for Oral Health; developer Sjogren's Syndrome Ednl. Symposia for lay and profls., nat. and internat. support group network. Editor: Moisture Seekers Newsletter, 1984-94, Sjogren's Syndrome Handbook: An Authoritative Guide for Patients, 1989; editor: The New Sjogren's Syndrome Handbook, 1998; contbg. author: Sjogren's Syndrome: Clinical and Immunologic Aspects, 1987, Self-Help, Concepts and Applications, 1992; contbr. articles to profl. jours. Founded Nassau-Suffolk Chpt. Hunter Coll. Alumni Assn., 1949; past treas. Youth Employment Svc., Great Neck (N.Y.) Pub. Schs., former chair Broader Horizons Com., PTA, Great Neck Pub. Sch., others; active Jewish communal field. Recipient Women's Living Legacy, Women's Internat. Ctr., 1994, Third Internat. Conf. on Sjogren's Syndrome, Greece, 1991; elected to Hunter Coll. Hall of Fame, 1989. Avocations: gardening, baking, photography. Personal E-mail: elaine.hh@verizon.net.

HARRIS, GARDINER, journalist; Grad., Yale U., New Haven. Appalachian reporter, Eastern Ky. bur. chief Louisville Courier-Jour., 1995—98; pharm. industry reporter Wall St. Jour., NYC, 1999—2003; bus. reporter The New York Times, 2003—04, sci. reporter, 2004—. Author: (novels) Hazard, 2010. Recipient Worth Bingham Prize for investigative journalism, Nieman Found. Journalism, 1999, George Polk award for environ. reporting, 1999. Office: NY Times 620 Eighth Ave New York NY 10018 E-mail: gardiner@nytimes.com. *

HARRIS, GERALD DAVID, surgeon; b. Olney, Ill., July 3, 1947; s. Gerald Craver and Juanita Harris; m. Mary Josephine Burke, Sept. 6, 1970. MD, U. Ill., Chgo., 1973; MBA, Northwestern U., Evanston, Ill., 1995. Resident Northwestern U., Chgo., 1973—79; asst. Northwestern Meml. Hosp., Chgo., 1978—79; asst. clin. prof. Northwestern U., Chgo., 1980—98, assoc. clin. prof., 1999—. Asst. clin. prof. dept. surgery Northwestern U., Chgo., 1980—98, assoc. clin. prof. dept. surgery, 1998—. Contbr. chpts. to books and articles to profl. jours. Fellowship, U. Calif., San Francisco, 1979. Mem.: Soc. for Reconstructive Microsurgery, Am. Soc. for Surgery of the Hand. Avocations: weightlifting, aerobics, team sports. Home: 800 N Michigan Apt 3801 Chicago IL 60611 Office Phone: 312-337-6960. Office Fax: 312-337-3961. Business E-Mail: gharris@chicagohandsurgery.com.

HARRIS, HENRY WILLIAM, physician; b. Catawba, NC, Jan. 6, 1919; s. Henry William and Katie (Coulter) H.; m. Margaret Ann Roberts, Nov. 29, 1950; children: Henry William, John R., James P. BA, U.N.C., 1940; MD cum laude, Harvard U., 1943. Diplomate: in pulmonary disease Am. Bd. Internal Medicine. Intern Harvard Med. Service, Boston City Hosp., 1944-45, asst. resident medicine, 1945-46; resident fellow Thorndike Meml. Lab., 1944, 46; resident chest service Bellevue Hosp., NYC, 1947; staff physician Gundersen Clinic, LaCrosse, Wis., 1948-53; asst. prof. medicine U. Utah Coll. Medicine, 1955-59, asso. prof., 1959-60; chief pulmonary disease service VA Hosp., Salt Lake City, 1955-60; prof. chmn. dept. medicine Woman's Med. Coll. of Pa., 1960-67; chmn. dept. medicine Catholic Med. Center Bklyn. and Queens, 1967-70; asso. prof. clin. medicine N.Y.U. Sch. Medicine, 1969-70, prof., 1970—. Adj. staff chest svc. Bellevue Hosp., N.Y.C.; hon. staff Tisch Hosp., N.Y.C.; sr. coms. Bur. Tb, Dept. of Health, N.Y.C., 1989-2004. Mem. editorial bd.: Annals of Internal Medicine, 1976-80; Contbr. articles to profl. publs. Bd. dirs. Am. Lung Assn., 1961-79, v.p., 1972-73; bd. dirs. N.Y. Lung Assn., 1974-95, v.p., 1983—, pres. 1987-90; bd. dirs. Am. Bur. Med. Advancement in China, 1978-2005, v.p., 1983-87, pres. 1987-92, chmn. H. Wm. Harris vis. prof. com., 1986-96. Served to capt., M.C. AUS, 1953-55. Fellow ACP; mem. Am. Thoracic Soc. (pres. 1962-63). Home: 4 Birchwood Ct Apt 3L Mineola NY 11501-4513 Home Phone: 516-742-5136.

HARRIS, J(ACOB) GEORGE, health products executive; b. Kings Mountain, NC, Sept. 5, 1938; s. James A. and Carolyn (Hord) H.; m. Sondra Gilbert, Mar. 29, 1959; children: Cynthia, Susan, David. BA in Math., Duke U., 1960. With Am. Hosp. Supply Corp., 1960-84, region mgr. South San Francisco, 1964-67, pres. Port Credit, Ont., Canada, 1967-70, v.p. ops. Evanston, Ill., 1970-71, pres. dietary products div. McGaw Park, Ill., 1971-74, corp. v.p. Evanston, 1974-78, exec. v.p., 1978-84; chmn., chief exec. officer Health Group Inc., Nashville, 1984-85; founder, pres., CEO Pinnacle Care Corp. (merged Mariner Health Group), 1985-94; pres., COO Mariner Health Group, 1994; ret., 1994; formerly bd. dirs. Mariner Health Group. Bd. dirs. Union Spl. Corp., Chgo., Monoclonal Antibodies, Inc., Mountain View, Calif., Electro Neucleonics Inc., Health Group, Electro-Biology Inc., Dialogic Comm. Corp. Bd. dirs. Highland Park (Ill.) Hosp., 1981-84; trustee McCormick Sem., Chgo. Mem. Scientific Apparatus Mfrs. Assn. (bd. dirs.), Richland Country Club. Home: 1204 Beddington Park Nashville TN 37215-5810 Office Phone: 615-370-9191. Personal E-mail: bocaj1938@aol.com.

HARRIS, JAN CAPLAN, health facility administrator; b. Ithaca, NY, Jan. 15, 1944; d. Frank and Shirley Ellen (Rickard) Caplan; m. Sonny G. Harris, Mar. 23, 1990; children: Josh, Greg, Ginger, Morgan, John BSN, Cornell U., 1966; MA in Liberal Studies, Dartmouth Coll., 1974; MS in Healthcare Adminstrn., U. Colo., 1989; DHA candidate, U. Ctrl. Mich., 2008. Coord. fed. programs, dir. instrn., dir. tech. ctr. Northwest Arctic Sch. Dist., Kotzebue, Alaska, 1976-82; dir. planning and devel., interim pres., ops. exec. Maniilaq Assn., Kotzebue, 1985-93; adminstr., v.p. health svcs. Maniilaq Health Ctr., Kotzebue, 1993-97; sr. health care quality improvement coord. PRO-West, Anchorage, 1998—2001, mgr. Medicare ops., 1998—2001; sr. health sys. specialist Alaska Ctr. for Rural Health/Inst. for Circumpolar Health Studies U. Alaska, Anchorage, 2001—03, dir. health workforce devel., 2003—05, assoc. dean Coll. Health and Social Welfare, 2005—08, vice provost, health programs, 2008—. Cons. Walrus Works, Anchorage, 1982-85, Harris Consulting, 1986—. Bd. dirs. Anchorage Neighborhood Health Ctr., 1999—2005, chair, 2000—02. Recipient Svc. award PHS/Indian Health Svc. Fellow: Am. Coll. Healthcare Execs. (Regents sr. level exec. award 2006, Svc. award 2009); mem.: APHA, Alaska Pub. Health Assn. (Meritorious Svc. award 2009), Alaska Healthcare Execs. Network (pres. 2001—03). Home: 6900 Oakwood Dr Anchorage AK 99507 Office Phone: 907-786-4595.

HARRIS, JEFFREY PAUL, otolaryngologist; b. Quincy, Mass., July 10, 1949; BA, Case Western U., 1971; MD, U. Pa., 1974, PhD in Immunopathology, 1976. Cert. Am. Bd. Atolaryngology, 1979, Am. Bd. Neurotology, 2004, diplomate Nat. Bd. Med. Examiners, Am. Bd. Otolaryngology. Intern, surgical house officer U. Pa. Hosp., Phila., 1975—76; resident in otolaryngology Mass. Eye and Ear Infirmary/Harvard Med. Sch., Boston, 1976—79; clin. fellow in otolaryngology Harvard Med. Sch., 1978—79; fellow in neurotology and skull base surgery Hosp. of U. Zurich, Switzerland, 1983; asst. prof. surgery & otolaryngology U. Calif. Sch. Medicine, San Diego, 1979—85, assoc. prof. surgery & otolaryngology, 1985—89, chief otolaryngology & head-neck surgery, 1986—, prof. surgery and chief otolaryngology, 1989—, dir. neurotology fellowship program, divsn. otolaryngology-head & neck surgery, 2004—, dir. otolaryngology residency program, dir. neurotology residency program, divsn. otolaryngology-head & neck surgery. Attending U. Calif. Med. Ctr., San Diego, 1979—, chief of staff, 1991—93; attending VA Med. Ctr., 1979—, Children's Hosp. & Med. Ctr., San Diego, 1990—98, Thornton Hosp., 1993—, chief of staff, 1993—94; active Green Hosp. of Scripps Clinic, La Jolla, Calif., 1997—, Alvarado Hosp. Med. Ctr., San Diego, 1998—2001; courtesy Scripps Meml. Hosp., La Jolla, 1991—2000, Kaiser Permanente, Calif., 1991—99; invited presenter in field. Editl. bd. mem. for several journals; contbr. articles to several peer-reviewed journals.; scientific and manuscript reviewer; co-editor: Immunobiology of the Head & Neck, 1984, Immunobiology in Otology, Rhinoogy & Laryngology, 1992, Head and Neck Manifestations of Systemic Disease, 2007; editor: Meniere's Disease, 1999; contbr. chapters to books. Recipient Sam Sanders award for Clinical Rsch., Am. Acad. Otolaryngic Allergy, 1985; named to Best Doctors in the US, Towne & Country Mag., Best Doctors in America, Am. Health Mag., America's Top Doctors, Castle Connolly, 2003—. Fellow: ACS, Trilogical Soc.; mem.: ACP (former pres.), Assn. Academic Departments of Otolaryngology-Head & Neck Surgery, Soc. Univ. Otolaryngologists-Head & Neck Surgeons, Am. Neurotology Soc., Pacific Coast Oto-Ophthalmological Soc., Pan-American Assn. of Oto-Rhino-Laryngology-Head & Neck Surgery, San Diego

County Med. Soc., Calif. Med. Assn., San Diego Acad. Otolaryngology-Head & Neck Surgery, Am. Acad. Otolaryngology-Head & Neck Surgery (Honor award, Disting. Svc. award), Assn. for Rsch. in Otolaryngology (pres. 1991—92), Am. Otological Soc. (pres. 2003—04), Alpha Omega Alpha, Phi Beta Kappa. Achievements include patents in field. Office: University of California-San Diego 200 W Arbor Dr Dept 8895 San Diego CA 92103-8895 Office Phone: 619-543-7896. Office Fax: 619-543-5521.

HARRIS, JEFFREY SAUL, physician, consultant, health facility administrator; b. Pitts., Mar. 13, 1949; s. Aaron Wexler and Janet Mary (Wexler) Harris; m. Mary V. Anderson, Jan. 2, 1981; children: Sarah Ariel, Noah Aaron, Susannah Leia. BS in Molecular Biophysics/Biochemistry, Yale U., New Haven, Conn., 1971; MD, U. N.Mex., Albuquerque, 1975; MPH, U. Mich., Ann Arbor, 1982; MBA, Vanderbilt U., Nashville, 1988. Diplomate Am. Bd. Preventive Medicine in Occupl. Medicine and Gen. Preventive Medicine, Am. Bd. Emergency Medicine. Gen. med. officer USPHS, Juneau, Alaska, 1976-78; clin. dir. S.E. Alaska Native Health Corp, Juneau, 1978-79; asst. to commr. Tenn. Dept. Health and Environ., Nashville, 1980—83; dir. health care mgmt. Northern Telecom Inc., Nashville, 1983—88; pres. HDM, Inc., Nashville, 1988—90; med. dir. Aetna Health Plans of Tenn., Nashville, 1990-91; nat. practice leader, health strategy Alexander & Alexander Cons. Group, San Francisco, 1991-94; chief prevention, health and disability officer Indsl. Indemnity, San Francisco, 1994-97; pres. J. Harris Assocs., Inc., Mill Valley, Calif., 1979—; CEO Med-Fx, LLC, 1999—2004; sr. physician Permanente Med. Group, San Rafael, Calif., 2000—. Pres., chmn. Collaborative for Excellence in Occupl. Medicine, Mill Valley, Calif., 2005—. Author: Strategic Health Management, 1994; author, editor: Managed Care in Occupational Medicine, 1998, Quick Reference to Practice Guidelines in Occupational Medicine, 1999, author, co-editor: Occupational Medicine Practice Guidelines: Evaluation and Management of Common Health Problems and Functional Recovery in Workers, 1997, 2004, 2008, Integrated Health Management, 1998, Managing Employee Health Care Costs, 1992, Manual of Occupational Health and Safety, 1992, 1996, 2004—, Health Promotion in the Work Place, 1994, 2001, 2003, mem. editl. bd.: Am. Jour. Health Promotion, 1985—, editl. reviewer: JAMA, BMJ, Am. Jour. Pub. Health, Occupl. Medicine, JOEM, Cochrane Collaborative, ACP, Am. Pain Soc.; contbr. articles to profl. jours., chapters to books. Fellow Am. Coll. Occupl. Environ. Medicine (dir. 1982-2009, chmn. practice guidelines com. 1992-98, Presdl. award 1996, Felton Authorship award 1998, Achievement award 2004), Western Occpl. Environ. Med. Assn. (Authorship award 1997, Rutherford B. Johnstone award 2006). Avocations: skiing, running, music, painting, writing. Home: 386 Richardson Way Mill Valley CA 94941-4053 Personal E-mail: jharrismvl@aol.com.

HARRIS, JUDITH ANN WHITE, occupational health nurse, educator; b. Springfield, Ohio, Mar. 6, 1939; d. Willie and Tennessee Belle (Poole) Martin; m. Allen G. Harris, Mar. 21, 1986; 1 child by previous marriage, Denise Marian Womble. Student, U. South Fla., 1978-85, BS/MS in Psychology, 2000. RN, Fla.; cert. tchr., Fla. Nurse Dr. Robert Tapogna, Springfield, Ohio, 1960-62, Springfield City Hosp., 1962-65, Dr. Robert Beam, Springfield, 1965 75; ednl. coord., instr. med. assisting Sarasota Vocat. Ctr., Fla., 1977-82, instr. med assisting program, chmn. dept., 1982-84, 89-91, instr. health svc. oocupations, placement coord. health occu, 1985-88; dept. chmn. Allied Health, 1989-95; v.p. Jara Villas Commous Assn., 2008—; pres. Jora III Villas, 2008—. Bd. dirs Fla Bd Inc.; pres. J.W. Harris Pub. Co.; cruise ship lectr. for Princess, Royal Caribbean and Celebrity Cruise Lines; v.p., sec. Al Harris Pest Control, Inc. 1996 ; dir. adv. & mktg., 2000-. Author: J.W. Harris Medical Assisting Review Manual, 1995, Templin, 2002; contbr. articles to profl. jours. Vol. Children's Breath Clinic, Sarasota, 1977-79, Kidney Found., Sarasota, 1982, ARC, Sarasota, 1976-88, dir. Spl. Care Unit, 1984-88; v.p. Sons of Norway, 1993-95; choir soloist Beneva Christian Ch., 1989—, deaconess, 1993-96, elder 1997—, chmn. Health Care Svcs. Dept., 1996—, vice chmn. bd. dirs., 2001-02, chmn. bd., 2002—; asst. state dir. Fla. Good Sons, 1993-94; bd. dirs. Fla. Bd. Camping Assn., Inc., sec., 1999--, newsletter editor, 1996—; chmn. FVA Leadership Forum, 1992—; parish nurse and chmn. health svcs. dept. Beneva Christian Ch., 1995—; pres. FVA Post Pres.'s Club, 1999—; 1st v.p. Sarasota Bay Republican Women's Club Federated, 1998-2001; mem. Sarasota Tiger Bay Club, 1999—, Sarasota Homebuilders Assn., 1999—; sec. Acorn Glass Bowling League, 2000—. Named Outstanding Vocat. Tchr. Sarasota County Sch. Bd., 1985, Woman of Impact for Edn., Sarasota County Commn. on the Status of Women, 1995. Mem. Am. Vocat. Assn. (Outstanding Vocat. Tchr. region II 1985, Vocat. Tchr. Yr. 1987), Health Occupations Educators (vice chmn. policy com. 1985-86), Nat. Assn. Health Occupations Tchrs. (v.p. region II 1984-86, pres. elect 1988, pres. 1989-91), Fla. Vocat. Assn. (bd. dirs. 1983-85, pres. 1987-88, Pres. award 1984, Outstanding Vocat. Educator region 23 award 1982, Sarasota Mayors award 1984, Gov.'s Proclamation for Outstanding Tchg. 1987, chmn. leadership forum 1993—), Health Occupations Educators Assn. Fla. (pres. 1983-84, chmn. legis. com. 1985-93, Outstanding Tchr. 1983), Sarasota County Vocat. and Adult Edn. Assn. (pres. 1978-80, editor newsletter 1978-83), Am. Assn. Med. Assts., Good Sams Inc. Fla. (asst. state dir. dist. 12 1993-95), Fraternal Order of Eagles Aux. (dist. 3 auditor 1995-96, eagle nurse 1995-97, chair health care dept. 1995—, condr. 1996—), Sarasota Bay Republican Women's Club (life; v.p. 1998—), Women's Coun. Realtors (ways and means chair 2002-, corr. sec. 2003, rec. sec. 2004), Sarasota Assn. Realtors, Ladies of Oriental Shrine N.Am., Sunrise Rotary Club (Paul Harris fellow, 2002-, Rotary Internat. Sustaining Mem. 2002-), Tara Country Club (soc. com. mem., co-chair commn. com. 2011-) Tiger Bay Club, Delta Kappa Gamma, Phi Kappa Phi. Avocations: swimming, camping, knitting, sewing, biking. Home: 6417 Liberty Ave Bradenton FL 34203

HARRIS, LOUIS SELIG, pharmacologist, researcher; b. Boston, Mar. 27, 1927; s. Max Selig and Pearl (Oppochinski) Harris; m. Ruth Irma Schaufus, Aug. 22, 1952; 1 child, Charles Allan. BA, Harvard U., 1954, MA, 1956, PhD, 1958. Sect. head, sr. rsch. biologist Sterling-Winthrop Rsch. Inst., Rensselaer, NY, 1958-66; lectr. in pharmacology Albany (N.Y.) Med. Coll., 1959-66; from assoc. prof. to prof. U. N.C., Chapel Hill, 1966-73; Harvey Haag prof. Med. Coll. Va./Va. Commonwealth U., Richmond, 1972—, chmn. pharmacology, toxicology dept., 1972-92, assoc. v.p. health scis., 1996—2003; acting assoc. dir. Nat. Inst. on Drug Abuse, Rockville, Md., 1987-88. Hon. prof. U. P.R. Sch. Medicine, 1972—, Beijing Med. U., 1990—; mem. com. problems drug dependence NAS/NRC, 1973—77; bd. dirs. Com. Problems Drug Dependence, Inc., 1977—93, chmn., 1990—92, bd. dirs., 1998—2002, pres., 2001—03; Sterling Drug vis. prof., 1983; rschr. in field. Editor: NIDA Monographs, Proceedings, Committee on Problems of Drug Dependence, 1979—2002; contbr. chapters to books. Chmn. bd. dirs. Found. Pharmacology, Harris Family Found.; bd. dirs. Human Resources Inc., VCU Intellectual Property Found., 2002, Med. Coll. Va. Found., 1999—2010, bd. dirs. emeritus, 2010—. Recipient Hartung Meml. award, U. N.C., 1981, Univ. Excellence award, Med. Coll. Va./Va. Commonwealth U., 1984, Outstanding Faculty award, 1984, Nathan B. Eddy award, Com. Problems Drug Dependence, 1985, Abe Wikler award, Nat. Inst. Drug Abuse, 1991, Gov.'s award Drug Abuse Rsch., 1992, Presdl. medallion, Va. Commonwealth U., 1993, Wayne medal, 2010, Life Achievement award in Sci. and Industry, Commonwealth of Va., 1997, Disting. Svc. award, 1999. Fellow: Collegium Internationale Neuro-Psychopharmacologicum, Coll. Problems Drug Dependence, Am. Coll. Neuropsychopharmacology; mem.: AAAS, Va. Acad. Sci., Internat. Soc. Study Pain, Internat. Soc. Biochemistry Pharmacology, Soc. Neuroscience, Internat. Narcotic Enforcement Officers Assn., Elisha Mitchell Sci. Soc., Mex. Pharmacology Soc. (hon.), Assn. Harvard Chemists, Am. Soc. Clin. Pharmacology and Therapeutics (emeritus mem.), Am. Pharm. Assn., Am. Pain Soc. (charter 1977), Am. Assn. Med. Sch. Pharmacology, Am. Chem. Soc., Am. Soc. Pharmacology and Exptl. Therapeutics, Cosmos Club Washington, Harvard Club Boston. Home: 7830 Rockfalls Dr Richmond VA 23225-1049 Office: Va Commonwealth U PO Box 980027 Richmond VA 23298-0027 Office Phone: 804-828-2075. Business E-Mail: harris@hsc.vcu.edu.

HARRIS, MATTHEW NATHAN, surgeon, educator; b. NYC, Dec. 20, 1931; s. Saul and Deborah (Moskowitz) H.; m. Frances Wicentowski, June 27, 1954; children: Amy Rachel, Julie Rebecca, Daniel Charles. BA, NYU, 1952; MD, Chgo. Med. Sch., 1956. Diplomate Am. Bd. Surgery, Nat. Bd. Med. Examiners; lic. physician, N.Y. Intern Bellevue Hosp. Ctr., NYC, 1956-57, resident in gen. surgery, 1957-58, 60-63; sr. clin. trainee in cancer USPHS, NYC, 1963-64; instr. anatomy NYU, NYC, 1966-68, dir. elective surg. anatomy, 1973-74; prof. surgery, dir. surg. oncology NYU Sch. Medicine, NYC, 1979—2001. Vis. surgeon Bellevue Hosp. Ctr.; attending surgeon Tisch Hosp.; cons. and lectr. in field.; cons. surgeon Manhattan V.A. Hosp. Contbr. articles to Jour. ACS, Breast Disease, Cancer, Annals Surgery, Radiology, N.Y. State Jour. Medicine, Cancer Rsch., Surgery, Jour. Lab. Investigations, others. Mem. bd. trustees Rosalind Franklin U. Medicine and Sci. Capt. USAR, 1958—60, Korea. Chgo. Med. Sch. scholar, 1955. Fellow ACS (cancer liaison fellow, N.Y. state chmn.); mem. AMA, Am. Soc. Clin. Oncology, Am. Assn. Clin. Anatomists, Am. Radium Soc., N.Y. Cancer Soc., N.Y. Surg. Soc. (pres. 1991-92), N.Y. Med. Soc., N.Y. Met. Breast Cancer Group, Soc. Surg. Oncology, N.Y. Cancer Programs Assn., Inc., Pan-Am. Med. Soc., Soc. Cons. Armed Forces, 38th Parallel Med. Soc. (Korea), Pan Pacific Surg. Assn., Internat. Pigment Cell Soc., Assn. Cancer Edn., Assn. Academic Surgery, So. Alumni Bellevue Hosp., Chgo. Med. Sch. Alumni Assn. (mem. bd.), Alpha Omega Alpha, Sigma Xi, Beta Lambda Sigma. Achievements include research in cytologic evaluation breast diseases by stereoactic aspiration, malignant melanoma vaccine, primary surgical management malignant melanoma. Office: NYU Clin Cancer Ctr 160 E 34th St New York NY 10016 Office Phone: 212-731-5413. Business E-Mail: matthew.harris@nyumc.org.

HARRIS, MAURICE DANIEL, internist; b. NYC, Feb. 3, 1950; MD, SUNY, 1977. Diplomate Am. Bd. Internal Medicine. Intern Emory Heart & Vascular U. Affiliated Hosps., Atlanta, 1977—78, resident in internal medicine, 1978-80, fellow in cardiology, 1980-82, staff DeKalb Med. Ctr., Decatur, Ga., Rockdale Hosp., Decatur, Piedmont Hosp., Decatur. Mem. Am. Coll. Cardiology. Office: 2675 N Decatur Rd Ste 200 Decatur GA 30033-6132 Office Phone: 404-296-1256

HARRIS, MICHAEL BERTRAM, pediatrician, educator; b. NYC, Dec. 20, 1943; s. Harry Hayim and Rose Harris; m. Freida Guttman, Jan. 4, 1969; children: Miera Beth, Aimee Gail, Jonathan Seth, Aaron Kenneth. BA, Yeshiva U., 1965; MD, Albert Einstein Coll. Medicine, 1969. Diplomate Nat. Bd. Med. Examiners. Intern, resident Childrens Hosp., Phila., 1969—71, fellow in pediatric hematology, 1971—74; asst. attending in pediatrics Beth Israel Med. Ctr., NYC, 1974—76; instr. pediatrics U. Pa. Sch. Medicine, 1972—74; chief pediatric hematology-oncology Children's Hosp., Pitts., 1976—77, Mt. Sinai Hosp., NYC, 1977—87; asst. attending pediatrics, asst. prof. pediatrics Mt. Sinai Sch. Medicine, 1977—83, assoc. prof., assoc. attending pediatrics, 1983—87; asst. prof. pediatrics U. Pitts. Sch. Medicine, 1976—77; assoc. prof. pediatrics NJ Med. Sch., 1987—96, prof., 1996—. Dir. Tomorrows Childrens Inst.; attending pediatrician Hackensack U., NJ; chief Pediatric Hematology-Oncology, Joseph M. Sanzari Childrens Hosp., Hackensack U. Med. Ctr., NJ. Contbr. articles to med. jours. Mem.: AAAS, Harvey Soc., Soc. Study Blood, New York Pediatric Soc., Children's Oncology Group, Am. Soc. Hematology, Am. Acad. Pediatrics, NY Acad. Sci., Am. Soc. Clin. Oncology. Office: Hackensack Pediatrics 177 Summit Ave Hackensack NJ 07601-1311 also: Hackensack University Med Ctr. Tomorrow Childrens Inst 30 Prospect Ave Hackensack NJ 07601 Office Phone: 201-996-5437. Business E-Mail: mbharris@humed.com. *

HARRIS, MICHAEL GENE, optometrist, lawyer, educator; b. San Francisco, Sept. 20, 1942; s. Morry and Gertrude Alice (Epstein) H.; m. Dawn Block; children: Matthew Benjamin, Daniel Evan, Ashley Beth, Lindsay Meredith. BS, U. Calif., 1964, M in Optometry, 1965, D in Optometry, 1966, MS, 1968; JD, John F. Kennedy U., 1985. Bar: Calif., U.S. Dist. Ct. (no. dist.) Calif. Assoc. practice optometry, Oakland, Calif., 1965-66, San Francisco, 1966-68; instr., coord. contact lens clinic Ohio State U., 1968-69; asst. clin. prof. optometry U. Calif., Berkeley, 1969-73, dir. contact lens extended care clinic, 1969-83, chief contact lens clinic, 1983—, assoc. clin. prof., 1973-76, from asst. chief to assoc. chief contact lens svc., 1970—, from lectr. to sr. lectr., 1978—, vice chmn. faculty Sch. Optometry, 1983-85, 95—, prof. clin. optometry, 1984-86, clin. prof., 1986—, dir. residency program, 1993-95, asst. dean, 1994-95, assoc. dean, 1995—2005, acting dean, 2000, dir. policy and planning, 2003—07, prof. emeritus, 2007—, assoc. dean emeritus, 2007—. Peter's Meml. lectr. U. Calif. Sch. Optometry, 2000; vis. prof. City U., London, 1984; vis. rsch. fellow U. NSW, Sydney, 1989; sr. vis. rsch. scholar U. Melbourne, Victoria, Australia, 1989, Victoria, 92; mem. ophthalmic devices panel med. device adv. com. FDA, 1990—, interim chmn., 1994; lectr., cons. in field; mem. regulation rev. com. Calif. Bd. Optometry; cons. hypnosis Calif. Optometric Assn., Am. Optometric Assn.; cons. Nat. Bd. Examiners in Optometry, Soflens divsn. Bausch & Lomb, 1973—2007, Barnes-Hind Hydrocurve Soft Lenses, Inc., 1974—87, Pilkinton-Barnes Hind, 1987—94, Contact Lens Co., 1977—2001, Palo Alto, Va., 1980, Primarius Corp., Cooper Vision Optics, 1979—2007, Alcon, 1980—2007, CIBA, 1976—2007, Vistakon, 1980—2000; co-founder Morton D. Sarver Rsch. Lab., 1986. Editor current comments sect. Am. Jour. Optometry, 1974-77; editor Eye Contact, 1984-86; assoc. editor The Video Jour. Clin. Optometry, 1988-92; cons. editor Contact Lens Spectrum, 1988—; author: Contact Lenses: Treatment Options for Ocular Disease, Contact Lenses for Pre & Post-Surgery; editor: Problems in Optometry, Special Contact Lens Procedures; Contact Lenses in Ocular Disease, 1990; mem. editl. bd. Contact Lens and Anterior Eye Jour.; contbr. chpts. to books, articles to profl. jours. Planning commnr. Town of Moraga, Calif., 1986, vice-chmn. Calif., 1987—88, chmn., 1988—90; mem. Town Coun., Moraga, 1992—96; mem. adv. planning commn. Medi-Cal., 1993—95, chmn., 1994—96, with managed care commn., 1995—, chmn. managed care commn., 1996—98; life mem. Bay Area Coun. for Rescue & Recovery, 1976; grantor Michael G. Harris Family Endowment Fund U. Calif., Dr. Michael G. Harris Tchg. award U. Calif.; commr. Sunday Football League Contra Costa County, 1974—78; planner, fin. advisor College Pk. HS Track Project; mem. Pleasant Hill C. of C., Friends of Rodgers Ranch, Friends of Libr.; mem. adv. bd. Mt. Diablo Regional YMCA, 2003—04, co-chair, 2008—; vice-mayor Town Coun., Moraga, 1994—95; city county rels. com. Contra Costa County, Calif.; planning commr. City of Pleasant Hill, Calif., 1999—2002, coun. mem. Calif., 2002—; vice chair Redevel. Agy., Pleasant Hill, 2002—, chair, 2007—08, vice mayor, 2003—04, mayor, 2004—05, 2008—09; founding mem. Young Adults divsn. Jewish Welfare Fedn., 1965—69, chmn., 1967—68; charter mem. Jewish Cmty. Ctr. Contra Costa County; founding mem. Jewish Cmty. Mus. San Francisco, 1984; pararabinnic Temple Isaiah, Lafayette, Calif., 1987, bd. dirs., 1990, Jewish Cmty. Rels. Coun. Greater East Bay, 1979—83, Campolindo Homeowners Assn., 1981—85, League of Calif. Cities East Bay Divsn., 2002—; bd. dirs. East Bay divsn. League of Calif. Cities, pres., 2007—08. Recipient Eminent Svc. award, Am. Acad. Opometry, 2003; named Alumnus of Yr., U. Calif. Sch. Optometry, 1999, John F. Kenndey Univ. Sch. of Law, 2005; U. Calif. fellow, 1971, Calif. Optometric Assn. scholar, 1965, George Schneider meml. scholar, 1964. Fellow: Prentice Soc. (pres.-elect 1994—96, pres. 1996—98), Assn. Schs. and Colls. Optometry (coun. on acad. affairs), British Contact Lens Assn., Am. Acad. Optometry (mem. contact lens com. 1974—80, vice-chmn. contact lens sect. 1980—82, chmn. sect. 1982—84, immediate past chmn. 1984—86, chmn.jud. com. 1989—2001, chmn. bylaws com. 1989—2003, ethics taskforce 1999—, mem., bd. dirs. 2010—, diplomate cornea and contact lens sect., chmn. contact lens papers, Eminent Svc. award 2003); mem.: Nat. Acads. of Practice (Distin. Scholar 2004—), Contra Costa Bar Assn., Calif. Acad. Sci., Calif. State Bd. Optometry (regulation rev. com.), Internat. Soc. Contact Lens Rsch., Mex. Soc. Contactology (hon.), Nat. Coun. on Contact Lens Compliance, Am. Optometric Found., Internat. Assn. Contact Lens Educators, Assn. Optometric Contact Lens Educators, Calif. Optometric Assn., Am. Optometric Assn. (proctor 1969—79, cons. on hypnosis, cons. editor Jour., mem. com. on opthalmic stds., subcom. on testing and certification, position papers com.), Internat. Assn. Contact Lens Educators, Robert Gordon Sproul Assn. U. Calif., Benjamin Ide Wheeler Soc. U. Calif., JFK U. Sch. Law Alumni Assn., U. Calif. Optometry Alumni Assn. (life), Pleasant Hill C. of C. Democrat. Business E-Mail: mharris@berkeley.edu.

HARRIS, MILDRED CLOPTON, clergy member, educator; b. Chgo., May 27, 1936; d. Jordan and Willa Mildred Clopton; m. Herbert Curlee Harris, Feb. 4, 1928. BA, DePaul U., 1957; MA, Columbia U., 1963, Governors State U., 1975; MPS, Loyola U., Chgo., 1985; D in Min., Bible Inst. Sem., Plymouth, Fla., 1985. Ordained to ministry Ind. Assemblies of God. Tchr. Gary (Ind.) Pub. Schs., 1957-93; founder, pres. God First Ministries, Chgo., 1978—. Organizer Chgo. March for Jesus, 1995-97. Author: Traits of an Intercessor, 1991, Educating Your Child God's Way, 1991, The Productive Prayer Guide, 1991; exec. prodr. (cassette) tribe of Judah En Danse, 1995-96 (ASCAP award); host (TV show) Born Again, (radio show) WCFJ 1470 AM; commr. Chgo. Housing Authority Radio Show, Great Lakes Gospel Radio. Bd. dirs. Midwestern U., Chgo., 1989-97, Goodman Theater, Chgo., 1994—, Make a Wish Found., Chgo., 1994-97, Windows of Opportunity, Chgo., 1997—; mem. exec. adv. com. Chgo. Housing Authority, 1995-99, commr., 1999—; overseer Gary (Ind.) Educators for Art, 1990—; adv. bd. mem. to Lisa Madigan Atty. Gen. Ill.; adv. bd. mem. to Daniel Hynes Comptr., Ill. Recipient CHANCE award Chgo. Housing Authority, 1998, Seniors-Gladys Reed award, 1998; Mary Herrick scholar Du Sable H.S. Alumni, 1998, Jefferso TV award, NBC, 2005. Mem. ASCAP, Nat. Soc. Fundraising Execs., Religious Conf. Mgmt. Assn., Nat. Coun. Negro Women (life), Afro Am. Coun. for Ill. State Teras, Union League Club Chgo., Chgo. Ill. Links Inc. Avocations: travel, interior decorating. Home: 7246 S Luella Ave Chicago IL 60649-2514

HARRIS, MITCHEL BRION, orthopedist, surgeon; b. Chgo., Dec. 19, 1958; MD, U. Ill., 1984. Cert. Orthop. Surgery, 1992. Intern surgery U. Ill. Hosps., Chgo., 1984—85; resident orthop. surgery Dartmouth Hitchcock Med. Ctr., Hanover, NH, 1989, Sunnybrook & Womens Coll. Health Scis. Ctr., 1990; attending U. Hosp., La. State U., New Orleans, 1990, Charity Hosp., New Orleans, 1990; chief orthop. trauma Brigham and Women's Hosp., Boston. Asst. prof. La. State U., 1990—95, assoc. prof., 1995, HAMARD, 2005; spkr. in field. Contbr. articles to med. jours. Named a Top Doctor, Boston Mag., 2006, 2007. Office: Brigham and Women's Hosp Dept Orthopedic Surgery 75 Francis St Boston MA 02115 Office Phone: 617-732-5385. Office Fax: 617-264-5226. Business E-Mail: mbharris@partners.org.

HARRIS, PATRICE A., III, physician, public health service officer; b. Bluefield, W.Va. B in Psychology, W.Va. U., M in Counseling, MD. Resident in psychiatry Emory U., Ga., fellow in child psychiatry; sr. policy fellow Emory U. Sch. Law; pvt. practice physician Ga.; med. dir. Fulton County Dept. Behavioral Health and Devel. Disabilities, Ga.; dir. health services Fulton County Govt., Ga. Founding pres. Ga. Psychiatry PAC. Mem.: AMA (mem. governing coun. on legis. 2003—, chair governing coun. on legis. 2010—11, bd. trustees 2011—, mem. governing coun. Women Physicians Congress), American Psychiatric Assn. (bd. mem., del. to the AMA), Med. Assn. Ga.

(mem. coun. on legis., mem. com. on constn. and by-laws), Ga. Psychiatric Physicians Assn. (bd. mem., pres.), Alpha Kappa Alpha. Office: Fulton County Health and Human Services 141 Pryor St Atlanta GA 30303 *

HARRIS, PHILIP EDWARD, endocrinologist; b. Plymouth, Devon, Eng., May 7, 1954; s. Roy Edward and Mary Eleanor Harris; m. Munire Kologlu, May 30, 1987; children: Levent Edward, Murat Simon, Metin Alexander. BSc in Physiology, U. Wales, Cardiff, 1976, PhD, 1986; MB, BChir, Welsh Nat. Sch. Medicine, Cardiff, 1979. Tng. fellow Med. Rsch. Coun., Cardiff, 1982—85; med. registrar St. Bartholomews Hosp., London, 1985—87; 1st asst. U. Newcastle, Newcastle-upon-Tyne, 1988—94; MRC traveling fellow Harvard U., Boston, 1990—91; sr. lectr. King's Coll. Hosp., London, 1994—2001; med. dir. Pharmacia Corp., Peapack, NJ, 2001—03; hon. cons. physician U. Hosp. Lewisham, London, 2002—; early clin. lead Pfizer Corp., NYC, 2003—; clin. devel. sr. dir. Pfizer Ltd., Sandwich, England, 2003—07; v.p. med. scis., endocrinology Ipsen Biopharm. Ltd., Slough, Berkshire, 2007—. Editor: (book) Endocrinology in Clinical Practice, 2003, CME Bull., 1998. Fellow: Royal Coll. Physicians; mem.: Growth Hormone Rsch. Soc., European Neuroendocrine Assn., Endocrine Soc. Anglican. Achievements include research in G protein and G protein coupled receptor mutations in endocrine neoplasia. Avocations: running, tennis, scuba diving. Office: Ipsen Biopharm Ltd 190 Bath Road SL1 3XE Slough England Office Phone: 44(0)1753627700. Office Fax: 441753627701. Business E-Mail: philip.harris@ipsen.com.

HARRIS, PHILIP ROBERT, management and space psychologist; b. Bklyn., Jan. 22, 1926; s. Gordon Roger and Esther Elizabeth (Delahanty) H.; m. Dorothy Lipp, July 3, 1965 (dec. 1997); m. Janet Belport, Feb. 14, 2001. BBA, St. John's U., 1949; MS in Psychology, Fordham U., 1952, PhD, 1956; spl. student, NYU, 1948-49, Syracuse U., 1961. Lic. psychologist U. of State of N.Y., 1959, N.Y. Dir. guidance St. Francis Prep. Sch., NYC, 1952-56; dir. student personnel, v.p. St. Francis Coll., NYC, 1956-63; exec. dir. Assn. Human Emergency-Thomas Murray Tng. Program, 1964-66; vis. prof. Pa. State U., 1965-66; vis. prof., cons. Temple U.; sr. assoc. Leadership Resources Inc., 1966-69; v.p. Copley Internat. Corp., La Jolla, Calif., 1970-71; pres. Mgmt. and Orgn. Devel. Inc. (now Harris Internat. Ltd.), La Jolla, 1971—; edn. dir. Air/Space Am., 1988; sr. scientist Netrologic, Inc., La Jolla, Calif., 1990-93; prof. Calif. Internat. Bus. U., 2005—. Rsch. assoc. Calif. Space Inst., U. Calif., San Diego, 1984-90; adj. prof. Pepperdine U., U. No. Colo., Calif. Sch. Internat. Mgmt., 2005-07; acad. adv. Command Coll., Commn. on Peace Officers Stds. and Tng. State of Calif., Dept. Justice, 1986-94; past cons. Westinghouse, N.V. Philips, I.B.M., Computer Sci. Corp. Control Data, govt. agys.; chmn. bd. dirs. United Socs. in Space, Inc., 1993-97; adj. prof. Calif. Internat. Bus. U., 2005. Author, 52 vols. including: Effective Management of Change, 1976, Improving Management Communication Skills, 1978, Managing Cultural Differences, 1979, 8th edit., 2011, New Worlds, New Ways, New Management, 1983, Managing Cultural Synergy, 1982, Management in Transition, 1985, Living and Working in Space, 1992, 2d edit., 1996, High Performance Leadership, 2d edit., 1994, New Work Culture, 1998, Launch Out, 2003, Human Pioneers, 2011, (autobiography) You Only Have One Life To Live, 2011; co-author: Transcultural Leadership, 1993, Developing Global Organizations, 1993, 2d edit., 2001, Multicultural Management 2008, 5th edit., 2011, Multicultural Law Enforcement, 1995, 4th edit., 2007, Space Enterprise Living and Working Offworld in The 21st Century, 2009, Toward Human Emergence, 2009, Managing the Knowledge Culture, 2005; editor: Innovations in Global Consultation, 1980, Global Strategies in Human Resource Development, 1983; author (series) New Work Culture, 3 vols., 1994-98; co-editor Manging Cultural Differences Series, 1993-2009, Butterworth-Heinemann/Elsevier Sci., 1979-2007, Developing High Performance Leaders; mem. editl. bd. European Bus. Rev., 1996-2006; founding editor emeritus Space Governance Jour., 1993-98; contbr. 260 articles to profl. jours. V.p. Bklyn. Downtown Renewal Effort, 1957-59. Recipient Literati Club award for excellence, 2005; named to Gulf Pub. Author Hall of Fame, 1999; Fulbright prof. to India U.S. State Dept., 1962; NASA faculty fellow, 1984. Fellow AIAA (assoc.); mem. ASTD (Torch award 1975), Aviation Space Writers Assn. (journalism awards 1986, 88, 89, 93), World Bar Assn. (Space Humanitarian award 1992, 2011), Nat. Space Soc., United Socs. in Space (dir. emeritus), Soc. for Human Performance in Extreme Environments, Fulbright Assn., YMCA. Independent. Home and Office: 2702 Costebelle Dr La Jolla CA 92037-3524 Personal E-mail: philharris@aol.com.

HARRIS, PHILLIP JOHN, cardiologist; b. Sydney, May 18, 1945; MBBS, U. Oxford, 1973, PhD, 1970. Fellow Duke U., 1977—79; head, dept. cardiology Royal Prince Alfred Hosp., 1985—2006, head, divsn. medicine, 1996—2000; clin. dir., cardiovasc. svc. Sydney Local Health Dist., 2008—. Chair, governing coun. South Western Sydney Local Health Dist., 2010; clin. prof. Ctrl. Clin. Sch., U. Sydney, 1992; pres. Cardiac Soc. Australia and New Zealand, 1996—98, Nat. Heart Found. Australia, 1996—2003, dep. nat. pres., 1997—2003. Recipient Sir John Loewenthall award, Nat. Heart Found. of Australia. Fellow: Am. Heart Assn., Am. Coll. Cardiology, Cardiac Soc. Australia and New Zealand, Royal Australian Coll. Physicians. Avocation: golf. Office: Dept Cardiology RPA Hosp Missen Camperdown NSW 2050 Australia Business E-Mail: phil.harris@email.cs.nsw.gov.au.

HARRIS, RACHEL LOUISE, therapeutic radiographer, researcher; b. Liskeard, Cornwall, Eng., Jan. 22, 1965; d. Clark and Rosamund Lilian (Doidge) Badham; m. Trevor Wayne Harris, May 30, 1987. Diploma in therapeutic radiography, Portsmouth Sch. Radiography, 1988; MSc in Social Rsch., Plymouth U., Eng., 1993. Radiographer Cornwall Health Authority, Truro, Eng., 1988-89; sr. II Plymouth Health Authority, 1990-94, supt. rsch. radiographer in oncology, 1995—2004; freelance cons. and presenter, 2005—; profl. officer (rsch.) Soc. and Coll. of Radiographers, 2006—. Conf. presenter in field Contbr. articles to profl. jours. Mem. Coll. Radiographers, European Soc. Therapeutic Radiology and Oncology (com.). Anglican. Avocations: walking dogs, reading. Office Phone: 020 77407225. Business E-Mail: rachelh@sor.org.

HARRIS, RAYMOND CLEMENT, nephrologist, educator; b. Nashville, Tenn., Mar. 26, 1952; s. Raymond Clement and Elizabeth Lay Harris; m. Paula Jean Messenheimer, Sept. 26, 1982; children: Matthew Clement, William Alexander. BS, Yale U., 1974; MD, Emory U., 1978. Intern U. Calif., San Francisco, 1978—79, med. resident, 1979—81; renal fellow Brigham & Women's Hosp., Boston, 1982—86; asst. prof. Vanderbilt U. Hosp., Nashville, 1986—91, assoc. prof., 1991—98, prof., 1998—, dir. divsn. nephrology & hyptertension; dir. Vanderbilt O'Brien Ctr. for Study of Kidney Disease, Nashville. Office: Vanderbilt U Med Ctr Medicine Dept D-3100 Med Ctr N Nashville TN 37232-0001 Home Phone: 615-385-4575; Office Phone: 615-322-2150.

HARRIS, ROGER CLARK, psychiatrist, consultant; b. Washington, Aug. 27, 1938; s. Lester Wilbur and Margaret Elizabeth (Gilligan) H.; m. Ann Marie Dorman, Sept. 22, 1962; children: Laura Colleen, Gregory Scott Henry. BS, U. Md., 1961, postgrad., 1961—62, MD, 1968. Diplomate Am. Bd. Med. Examiners, Am. Bd. Psychiatry and Neurology. Intern Washington Hosp. Ctr., 1968—69; resident in psychiatry U. Md. Med. Sch., 1969—72; staff psychiatrist Portsmouth Psychiat. Ctr., Va., 1972—73, Larry H. Dizmang and Assoc., Annapolis, Md., 1973—74; pvt. practice Annapolis, 1974—75; prin. Roger C. Harris Group Practice of Psychiatry and Assocs., Annapolis, 1975—; pres. Chesapeake Comprehensive Counseling Ctrs., Inc., Washington and Balt., 1988—96. Co-founder Psychiatry Consultation Svc. of Baltimore City Police Dept., 1970-72; chief psychiatry svc. Anne Arundel Gen. Hosp., Annapolis, 1978-81; asst. clin. prof. psychiatry U. Md. Sch. Medicine, 1973—; acting dir. of outpatient clinic U. Md. Emergency Psychiat. Svcs., 1971-72, chief resident, 1971-72; primary founder psychiatry dept. Anne Arundel Gen. Hosp. Mem. Disability Rev. Bd. for Anne Arundel County, 1985-87, Orgn. of Physicians for Social Responsiblity, 1985—. Recipient Cert. Appreciation Arundel Lodge, Inc., Annapolis, 1988, Mitchell Scholarship, Alpha Tau Omega Social Fraternity, College Park, Md., 1960. Mem. Chesapeake Bay Psychiat. Soc., Am. Psychiat. Assn., Md. Psychiat. Soc., Anne Arundel County Med. Soc., Am. Group Psychotherapy Assn., Orthopsychiat. Assn., Epping Forest Boat Club, Young Foresters Orgn., Alpha Tau Omega (sec. 1958-60). Democrat. Presbyterian. Avocations: boating, swimming, body surfing, bodyboard surfing, classical music. Home: 212 Eareckson Ln Stevensville MD 21666-3040 Office: 1511 Ritchie Hwy Ste 201 Arnold MD 21012-2410 Home Phone: 410-643-1262; Office Phone: 410-757-1511.

HARRIS, STEVEN M., urologist; b. Port Chester, NY, Aug. 19, 1952; s. Jules Franklin and Belle Diane Harris; m. Chantal Harris, Aug. 26, 2001; children: Hillel, Adena, Rafi, Rebecca. BA in Physics, SUNY, Buffalo, 1973; MD, Albert Einstein Coll. Medicine, Bronx, 1976. Resident urology Mt. Sinai Sch. Medicine, NYC, 1981; chief urology Long Beach Med. Ctr., NY, 1996—, attending urologist, South Nassau Cmtys. Hosp., Mercy Hosp. Pres. med. staff LBMC, NY, 2005—06, pres. med. bd., 2007—08; profl. tennis registry, 1996—. Physician liaison Future Physician Club, Long Beach HS, 1984—. Mem.: Profl. Tennis Registry (instr. 1996—2006). Avocations: tennis, golf. Office: 711 Lincoln Blvd Long Beach NY 11561 Office Phone: 516-431-9800.

HARRIS, WILLIAM HAMILTON, orthopedic surgeon; b. Gt. Falls, Mont., Nov. 18, 1927; s. John H. and LaRue (Hamilton) H.; m. Johanna Alderfer, June 8, 1952; children: William Hamilton Jr., Kristin, Jonathan, David. AB, Haverford Coll., Pa., 1947, DSc, 2000; MD, U. Pa., 1951. Intern U. Pa. Hosp., 1951-52; resident in orthop. surgery Children's Med. Ctr., Boston, 1955, Mass. Gen. Hosp., Boston, 1957, Royal Nat. Orthopedic Hosp., London, 1959-60; mem. faculty Harvard U. Med. Sch., 1960—, clin. prof. orthop. surgery, 1975—, Alan Gerry clin. prof. orthop. surgery, 1997—; orthop. surgeon, founder Harris Lab. Mass. Gen. Hosp., 1960—2004, emeritus dir., 2004—, chief adult reconstructive unit, 1974—2002, chief emeritus adult reconstructive unit, 2002—. Sr. lectr. MIT, Cambridge, 1969—. Contbr. more than 520 articles to various publs., chpts. to books. Capt. M.C., USAF, 1952-54. Fellow, Nat. Found., 1959-60, Sprague Found., 1960-61, Med. Found. Boston, 1961-64, Clementine Cope fellow Haverford Coll., 1947, traveling fellow Am. Orthop. Assn., 1965; recipient Kappa Delta award for Orthop. Rsch., 1970, 76, M.E. Mueller Lifetime Achievement award in orthopaedic surgery, Lifetime Achievement award, The Hips Soc., 2008. Mem. AMA, Internat. Hip Soc. (past pres., a founder), Hip Soc. (a founder, 1st pres. 1969), Am. Acad. Orthopedic Surgeons, Interurban Orthopedic Club, Mass. Med. Soc., Phi Beta Kappa, Alpha Omega Alpha. Home: 665 Concord Ave Belmont MA 02478-2027 Office: Mass Gen Hosp 32 Fruit St Boston MA 02114-2620

HARRISL, LAUREN JULIUS, psychology professor; b. Chgo., July 9, 1940; BS, U. Ill., 1961; PhD, U. Minn., 1965. Prof. psychology Mich. State U., 1965—. Mem., editl. bd. Jour. Brain and Cognition, Jour. Devel. Neuropsychology, Jour. Laterality Asymmtries Body, Brain, & Cognition. Recipient Disting. Faculty award, Mich. State U. Fellow: AAAS, APA. Home: Michigan State University Dept Psychology East Lansing MI 48824 Business E-Mail: harrisl@msu.edu.

HARRISON, CHRISTOPHER JOSEPH, pediatrician, educator; b. Dayton, Ky., Aug. 21, 1947; BS, U. Ky., 1967, MD, 1971. Assoc. prof., pediat. Cin. Children's Hosp. Med. Ctr., 1983—91; prof., pediat. Creighton U. Sch. Medicine, 1991—2000, U. Louisville, 2000—05, Children's Mercy Hosp., U. Mo., Kans. City, 2005—, dir., infectious diseases rsch. lab. Recipient VTEU Pediat. Sub award, DMID, NIH; grant, NIAID, NIH. Fellow: Soc. Pediat. Rsch., Am. Acad. Pediat.; mem.: Infectious Diseases Soc. America, Pediat. Infectious Diseases Soc. (Breese award), Am. Soc. Microbiology. Avocations: bass, fishing, running, jogging. Office: 2104 Gillham Rd Kansas City MO 64108 Business E-Mail: cjharrison@cmh.edu.

HARRISON, DAVID GLENN, medical educator, cardiologist; BS, Okla. State U., Stillwater, 1970; MD, U. Okla., Okla. City, 1974. Cert. internal medicine Nat. Bd. Examiners, 1976, cardiovasc. diseases 1979. Intern Duke Hosp., Durham, NC, 1974—75, resident, 1975—77; fellow Duke U., 1977—79; clinical instr. U. NC, Charlotte, 1979—80; clinical cardiologist Nalle Clinic, Charlotte, 1979—80, U. Iowa, Iowa City, 1980—90, fellow, 1980—82, assoc. in cardiovasc. Coll. Medicine, 1980—82, asst. prof. medicine, 1982—87, dir. sect. cardiology, 1984—89, assoc. prof. medicine, 1987—90; prof. medicine Emory U. Sch. Medicine, Atlanta, 1990—, interim dir., 1999—2000, dir. cardiology, 2000—; dir. sect. cardiology Atlanta VA Hosp., 1991—94, 1998—2000. Mem. Iowa affiliate study sect. Am. Heart Assn., 1982—85, mem. Great Plains regional review com. study sect., 1983—88, mem. com. regional and nat. rsch., 1987—88, chmn. Great Plains regional review study sect., 1987—88, mem. nat. review com. study sect., 1987—90, chmn. credentials com., 1992—94, mem. vascular biology study sect., 1991—94, mem. nat. study sect. vascular biology, 1992—95, chmn. marcus selection com., 1993—95, mem. exec. com. coun. on circulation, 1993—95, chmn. sci. conf. planning com., 1993—95, vice chmn. exec. com. coun. on circulation, 1995—98, chmn. exec. com. coun. on circulation, 1998—99, mem. program com. coun. basic cardiovasc. sciences, 1999—2000, mem. rsch. planning and evaluation com., 2000—01, fellow coun. basic cardiovasc. sciences, 2001—, mem. rsch. com., 2002—04; mem. med. student adv. com. U. Iowa, 1983—84, mem. house staff adv. com., 1983—90, mem. U. aminal care com., 1983—90, mem. house staff evaluation com., 1986—90, mem. promotions com., 1988—90; chmn. merit review study sect. VA, 1990—94; mem. NIH experimental cardiovasc. sciences study sect., 1992—97, 1993—95; mem. sci. adv. com. Atherogenics, Inc., 1995—; mem. rsch. planning Emory U. Health Svcs. Ctr., 1997; mem. rsch. strategic planning, dept. medicine Emory U., 2000; mem. sci. adv. bd. VasoPharm, Inc., 2000—; mem. adv. bd. Novartis Angiotensin/ARB, 2000—; mem. heart ctr. steering com. Emory Heart Ctr., 2002—; mem. governing bd. Carlyle Frazier Heart Ctr. Crawford Long Hosp., 2003—; mem. Proteomics, Chemical and Structural Biology Strategic Planning com., 2003—. Mem. editl. bd. Circulation, 1990—94, Journal of Cardiovascular Pharmacology, 1991—, Trends in Cardiovascular Medicine, 1992—93, Endothelium, 1992—96, Journal of Vascular Medicine and Biology, 1993—98, Circulation Research, 1995—, Journal of Clinical Investigation, 1997—, Arteriosclerosis, Thrombosis and Vascular Biology, 1999—, Hypertension, 2000—. Recipient Individual Nat. Rsch. Svc. award, NIH, 1980, Clinical Investigator award, 1981, Clinician Scientist award, Am. Heart Assn., 1981, Established Investigator award, 1987, Novartis award for Hypertension Rsch., 2004, Disting. Achievement award, 2003, J. Willis Hurst Internal Medicine Residency Program Mentorship award, Emory U., 2004. Mem.: Oxygen Soc., Am. Assn. U. Cardiologists, Soc. Vascular Medicine and Biology, Am. Soc. Clinical Investigation, Am. Physiol. Soc. (fellow cardiovasc. sect. 1988—), Ctrl. Soc. Clinical Rsch., Am. Fedn. Clinical Rsch. Midwest Sect., Assn. Am. Physicians. Office: Woodruff Meml Bldg Rm 319 Emory U 1639 Pierce Dr Atlanta GA 30322 Office Phone: 404-727-8386. Office Fax: 404-727-3585. Business E-Mail: dhar02@emory.edu.

HARRISON, DEAN M., hospital administrator; BS, Ind. U., Bloomington; MBA, St. Francis Coll. Pres., COO Univ. of Chgo. Health System, 1998; spl. advisor Merrick Ventures, LLC.; sr. v.p. corp. ops. Northwestern Meml., 1998; pres., CEO Northwestern Meml. Hosp., 2002—, Northwestern Meml. HealthCare, 2006—; bd. dirs. Univ. HealthSystem Consortium, United Way Met. Chgo., Ill. Hosp. Assn., Assn. of Am. Med. Colleges' Coun. of Tchg. Hosps. and Health Sys. Recipient Nat. Healthcare award, B'nai B'rith Internat., 2008, U.S. Dept. of Commerce Minority Bus. Devel. Agy., Chgo. Minority Enterprise Devel. Coun., 2010 CEO Leadership Cir. of Excellence award. Mem.: Bus. Leadership Group for Workforce Chgo. 2.0., The Inst. of Medicine of Chgo., World President's Orgn., The Comml. Club of Chgo., The Econ. Club of Chgo. Office: Northwestern Memorial Hospital 251 E Huron Chicago IL 60611 Office Phone: 312-926-3112.

HARRISON, LYNN HENRY, JR., cardiovascular surgeon, educator; b. Oklahoma City, Jan. 8, 1944; s. Lynn Henry and Vera Alice (Pritchett) H.; m. Lura Ann Wright, June 21, 1969; children: Parker, Tyler. BA, Yale U., 1966; MD, U. Okla., 1970. Diplomate Am. Bd. Surgery, Am. Bd. Thoracic Surgery. Clin. assoc. surgery Nat. Heart and Lung Inst., Bethesda, Md., 1972-74; resident surgery Duke University, Durham, NC, 1970-72, 74-78, teaching scholar surgery, 1978-79; asst. prof. surgery U. Okla. Sch. Medicine, Oklahoma City, 1979-84; clin. asst. prof. La. State U. Sch. Medicine, New Orleans, 1986-89, clin. assoc. prof., 1989, assoc. prof. surgery, chief sect. cardiovascular surgery, 1993-98, prof. surgery, 1998—, Craighead chair surgery, 2002; ptnr. The O'Neill Surg. Group, New Orleans, 1984-91; pres. Crescent Surg. Assocs., Marrero, La., 1991-93; prof., chief cardiac surgery U. Mass., Worcester, 2006—09; clin. dir. cardiac surgery Baptist Health Cardiac & Thoracic Surgical Group, Miami, 2009—. Pres. Southern Soc. Clin. Surgeons, Washington, 2005—06. Contbr. articles to numerous profl. publs. Bd. dirs. Ballet Okla., Oklahoma City, 1983-85. With, 1972—74, Bethesda, Md. Recipient Alan J. Stanley prize, U. Okla. Sch. Medicine, 1967. Fellow ACS (counselor La. chpt. 1988—, pres. 1995, gov. 1998-2004); mem. Assn. Acad. Surgery, Soc. Thoracic Surgeons, Am. Assn. Thoracic Surgery, So. Surg. Assn., Surg. Assn. of La. (pres. 1996), Andrew G. Morrow Soc., David C. Sabiston Jr. Surg. Soc., Timberlane Country Club (bd. dirs.). Avocations: golf, hunting. Office: Baptist Health 8900 N Kendall Dr Miami FL 33176 Office Phone: 786-596-5991. *

HARRISON, NEDRA JOYCE, surgeon; b. Buffalo, Apr. 16, 1951; d. Herman Lloyde and Gertrude (Newsom) H. BS, Rosary Hill Coll., 1973; MD, SUNY, Buffalo, 1977. Diplomate Am. Bd. Surgery. Resident in surgery Millard Fillmore Hosps., Buffalo, 1977-82, mem. active attending staff in gen. surgery, 1983—2000; practice medicine specializing in gen. surgery Buffalo, 1982—2000; courtesy staff Scottsdale (Ariz.) Healthcare, 2000—. Cons. staff Bry-Lyn Hosp., 1986-89; provisional staff in gen. surgery St. Joseph Intercommunity Hosp., 1986-87, active staff, 1995-2000; courtesy staff Scottsdale (Ariz.) Healthcare, Shea, Ariz., 2001—, Osborn, Ariz., 2001— Chmn. United Thank Offering, Episcopal Ch., Buffalo, 1982; bd. dirs. Niagara Luth. Home, 1987-2000; mem. alumni bd. dirs. SUNY at Buffalo Sch. Medicine, 1986-92. Recipient Best Rsch. Paper in Gen. Surgery award Millard Fillmore Hosps., 1978, 81. Fellow ACS; mem. AMA, Am. Med. Women's Assn., Maricopa County Med. Soc., Christian Med. Soc., Am. Soc. Breast Surgeons, Delta Epsilon Sigma. Episcopalian. Office: 10210 N 92nd St Scottsdale AZ 85258 Office Phone: 480-551-2528.

HARRISON, RICK E., pediatrician; b. Seattle, Wash., Nov. 12, 1953; BA cum laude, Univ. Wash., 1976, MD, 1980. Cert. Am. Bd. Pediatrics, 1986, in pediatric critical care Am. Bd. Pediatrics, 1987. Intern in pediatrics Phoenix Hospitals, 1981—83, resident in pediatrics, 1982—83; co-chief resident Maricopa Med. Ctr., Phoenix, 1982—83; fellowship in pediatric critical care Children's Hosp. of LA, 1983—85; prof. clin. pediatrics David Geffen Sch. Med., UCLA, 1985—, vice chair clin. affairs dept. pediat.; med. dir., pediatric critical care Mattel Children's Hosp., UCLA; chief of med. staff UCLA Med. Ctr., 2002—04. Three time recipient, Robert Neerhout Tchg. award. Mem.: Soc. Critical Care Med., Phi Beta Kappa. Office: Mattel Children's Hosp Div Pediatric Critical Care MDCC 12-494 10833 LeConte Ave Los Angeles CA 90095 Office Phone: 310-825-6752.

HARROP, JAMES S., neurosurgeon, director; MD, Thomas Jefferson U., Phila. Diplomate Am. Bd. Neurol. Surgery. Lectr.; intern in gen. surgery Thomas Jefferson Univ. Hosp., Phila., resident in neurosurgery; resident in pediatric neurosurgery Children's Hosp. Pa.; fellow in neurosurgical and orthopaedic spine Cleve. Clinic; asst. prof. neurosurgery Jefferson med. coll. Thomas Jefferson Univ. Hosp., dir. adult reconstructive spine divsn. Mem.: AMA, SpineUniverse (editl. bd. mem.), Pa. Neurol. Soc., Congress of Neurol. Surgeons, Am. Assn. of Neurol. Surgeons. Office: Thomas Jefferson University Hospital 2nd Fl 909 Walnut St Philadelphia PA 19107 Office Phone: 215-955-7000. Office Fax: 215-503-9170.

HART, CECIL WILLIAM JOSEPH, otolaryngologist, surgeon; b. Bath, Somerset, Eng., May 27, 1931; came to U.S., 1957. s. William Theodore Hart and Paulina Olive (Adams) Gilmer; m. Brigid Frances Molloy, June 15, 1957 (dec. Nov. 1984); children: Geoffrey Arthur, Paula Mary, John Adams; m. Doris Crystel Katharina Alm, Mar. 14, 1987; children: Kristen-Linnea Alm, Erik Alm, Britt-Marie Alm. BA, Trinity Coll., Dublin, Ireland, 1952, MB, BCH, BAO, 1955, MA, 1958. Diplomate Am. Bd. Otolaryngology. Intern Dr. Steevens Hosp., Dublin, Ireland, 1956, Little Co. Mary Hosp., Evergreen Park, Ill., 1957, mem. staff, 1958-59; resident in otolaryngology U. Chgo. Hosp. and clinic, 1959-62; instr. U. Chgo. Med. Sch., 1962-64, asst. prof., 1964-65; practice medicine specializing in otolaryngology Chgo., 1958—; mem. staff Northwestern Meml. Hosp., 1972-97, Rehab. Inst. Chgo., 1965-97, Children's Meml. Hosp., 1972-97, Little Co. of Mary Hosp., 1977-94, LaGrange (Ill.) Comty. Meml. Hosp., 1977-94, Loyola U. Med. Ctr., 1997—. Tchg. assoc. Cleft Palate Inst., 1968, dir. otolaryngology, 1969-92; asst. prof. dept. otolaryngology-head and neck surgery Northwestern U. Med. Sch., 1965-75, assoc. prof., 1975-92, prof., 1992-97, prof. emeritus, 1997—; lectr. dept. otorhinolaryngology Loyola U., 1972, prof. otolaryngology, head and neck surgery, 1997-2001; med. adv. bd. So. Hearing and Speech Found., Nat. Inst. of Deafness and Other Communicative Disorders, 1989-95. Producer videos, movie; contbr. numerous articles to profl. jours. and mags.; also guest appearances various radio and TV talk shows. NIH fellow U. Chgo., 1962-63; NIH grantee, 1985-88. Fellow Am. Neurotology Soc. (pres. 1974-75, chmn. editorial review & publ. com. 1978-79, constn. and bylaws com. 1979-97), Am. Acad. Otolaryngology-Head and Neck Surgery (chmn. subcom. on Equilibrium 1980-86, computer com. 1987-90), ACS, Inst. Medicine Chgo., Soc. for Ear, Nose and Throat Advances in Children; mem. AMA, Brit. Med. Assn., Ill. State Med. Soc., Chgo. Med. Soc., Am. Cleft Palate Assn., Am. Council Otolaryngology, Am. Otological Soc., Chgo. Laryngological and Otological Soc. (v.p. 1975-76), Northwestern Clin. Faculty Med. Assn. (vice chmn. 1976-78, pres. 1979-81), Barany Soc., Royal Soc. Medicine, Irish Otolaryngological Soc., So. Hearing and Speech Found (med. adv. bd.), Chgo. Hearing and Balance Assn. (pres.), Sigma Xi. Roman Catholic. Avocations: travel, baroque music, symphony, opera, tennis. E-mail: cwjhart@aol.com.

HART, JOSEPH PATRICK, academic vascular surgeon; s. Thomas J.X. and Patricia A.M. Hart. BA in Biology, Grinnell Coll., 1991; MD, Northwestern U., 1995. Diplomate in vascular surgery Am. Bd. Surgery. Intern Med. Coll. Wis., Milw., 1995—96, resident in surgery, 1995—2003, chief resident in surgery, 2002—03, vascular surgery fellow, 2003—05; rsch. fellow cardiothoracic surgery Columbia U., NYC, 1997—2000; clin. and rsch. fellow carotid and peripheral intervention AZ St. Blasius, Belgium, 2005—06; specialist registrar in vascular surgery Limerick Regional Hosp., Ireland, 2001; asst. prof. surgery, divsn. vascular surgery U. Rochester Sch. Medicine and Dentistry, 2006—08; asst. prof. surgery, divsn. vascular surgery and interventional radiology, chief endovascular surgery Med. U. SC, Charleston, 2008—. Attending surgeon Med. U., SC, Ralph A. Johnson Vets. Affairs Med. Ctr. Contbr. articles to profl. jours. Recipient William Gore award, Soc. Vascular Tech., 1993, Marco Polo scholarship, Soc. Vascular Surgery, 2005. Fellow: ACS; mem.: Southern Assn. Vascular Surgery, Am. Heart Assn., Regis Alumni Assn., Nat. Eagle Scout Assn., Soc. Vascular Ultrasound, Assn. Academic Surgery, Tissue Engring. Regenerative Medicine Internat. Soc., Internat. Soc. Vascular Surgery, Peripheral Vascular Surgery Soc., Soc. Vascular Surgery, European Soc. Vascular Surgery (corr.). Achievements include research on ventricular function during cardiac surgery and vascular/endovascular surgery. Office: Med Univ SC Dept Surgery Divsn Vascular Surgery 25 Courtenay Dr Ste 7018 MSC 295 Charleston SC 29425 Home: 498 Albemarle Rd #402 Charleston SC 29407 Office Phone: 843-876-4855. Personal E-mail: josephphart@aol.com. Business E-Mail: hartjp@musc.edu.

HART, RONALD WILSON, radiobiologist, educator, toxicologist, business adviser; b. Syracuse, NY, Mar. 23, 1942; s. Wilson and Annabell Hart. BS, Syracuse U., 1967; MS, U. Ill., 1970, PhD, 1971; postgrad. (Nat. Cancer Inst. trainee), Oak Ridge Nat. Lab., 1973. USPHS trainee, 1970-71; asst. prof. dept. radiology Ohio State U., Columbus, 1971-75, dir. radiation biology rsch. divsn., 1971-82, assoc. prof. depts. biology, biophysics, preventive medicine, 1976-78, assoc. prof. pharmacology, medicinal chemistry dept. preventive medicine, 1977-78, dir. chem., biomed. environ. rsch. group dept. preventive medicine, 1977-82, prof. depts. radiology, preventive medicine, pharmacology, medicinal chemistry, vet. pathobiology, 1978-82; dir. Nat. Ctr. for Toxicological Rsch., Jefferson, Ark., 1980-92, Disting. scientist in residence, 1992-2000; rsch. prof. Strang Cancer Prevention Rsch. Ctr. Rockefeller U., 2000—04, dir., hart mgmt., 2008—; venture ptnr. Sail Venture Capital, 2008—. Disting. prof. U. Poona, India, 1978—2004, Cairo U., 1989—; disting. prof. carcinogenesis Guang Zhou Med. Coll., China, 1988—; adj. prof. U. Ark. Med. Sci., 1980—, U. Tenn. Health Scis., 1983—; adj. prof. pharmacology Coll. Pharmacy U. Ark., 1997—; cons. Oak Ridge Nat. Lab., 1971—75, Brookhaven Nat. Lab., 1975—78, Argonne Nat. Lab., 1975—78, EPA, 1976, 78, Am. Indsl. Health Coun., 1978, PPG Industries, 1978, Informatics, 1978—80, FDA, 1980; mem. NAS/NRC Bd. Toxicology and Environ. Health Hazards, 1976—82; mem. insteragy. staff group Office Sci. and Tech. Policy Exec. Office of Pres., 1982—85, chmn., 1983—85; chmn. bd. dirs. Ark. Sci. and Tech. Authority, 1983—84, mem., 1985—88; bd. dirs. Miltos Pharms., 2006—08, Water Chef, Inc., 2007—08, SpectRX, 2006—, Immunovative, Inc., 2007—08, SNTech., 2007—, WNKO Battery, 2007—, Geo Vidio, LLC, 2007—, ZUMA, 2008—09; St. R. adv. bd. Miss. State U., 1987—96; adv. bd. Petrotech, 1991—92, VoiceNet, 1998—99, Waterchef, Inc., 2001—03, Micromed Labs., 2002—06, Biomed, 2002—08, Applied DNA Sci., Inc., 2003—05, Fla. A&M U. Rsch. Ctr., 1985—2004, Omega Foods, 2004—05, Met. Area Networks, 2004, Ship OK, LLC, 2004—06, Biophora, Inc., 2005, Neogenix Ind., 2006—, Ice Energy, 2007—, Flex Energy, 2009—, Therapy's Solutions, 2009—, Motor Excellence, 2009—; bd. visitors Memphis State U., 1984—90; chair task force risk assessment/risk mgmt. HHS, 1985, chmn. com. coordinate environ., health and related programs, 1985—88; chmn. sci. panel Agt. Orange working group, 1986—88; mem. USAF toxicology rev. panel, 1987; chmn. intergovtl. Task Force Tech. Transer, 1987—88, DHHS Task Force Tech. Transfer, 1987—88; mem. Inter Govt. Commn. Competitiveness, 1987—94; apptd. del. US-USSR Emerging Leaders Summit; chmn. Sci. and Tech. Commn., 1988; disting. adj. prof. Moscow State U., 1989—, Guanzou Med. U., China, 1988—, U. Udina, Italy, 1999—2002; chmn. Ark. Sch. Math. and Sci. Found., 1997—2003; adv. bd. Regeneris, 2009—; bd. dirs. Motor Excellence LLC, 2010—, G Thum Inc., 2011—. Editor-in-chief: Toxicology Indsl. Health, 2000—; contbr. chapters to books, articles to profl. jours. Recipient Hopkins award for grad. rsch., 1971, Japanese Med. Assn. award, 1978, Karl-August-Forester award, West Germany, 1980, award of merit, FDA, 1982, 1985, 1986, Sr. Exec. Svc. award, 1982, 1984, 1985, Commr.'s Spl. citation, 1987, Superior Svc. award, USPHS, 1983, Gov.'s award Outstanding Svc., State of Ark., 1985, Letter of Commendation, Pres. of US, 1985, Pres. Rank award Outstanding Accomplishment, Guangzhou Med. Coll., 1988, Bose medal, Bose Inst., 1994, Ednl. medal, U. Ark., 2005; named Outstanding Alumnus, Syracuse U., 1976. Fellow: AAAS, Am. Assn. Clin. Chemistry, Risk Analysis Soc., Gerontol. Soc., Am. Coll. Toxicology (past pres.); mem.: Sr. Execs. Assn., Photochem. and Photobiol. Soc., Biophys. Soc., Radiation Rsch. Soc., Sigma Xi. Office: 4821 Crestwood Little Rock AR 72207 Personal E-mail: rhart99@comcast.net.

HARTER, DONALD HARRY, neurologist, medical educator; b. Breslau, Germany, May 16, 1933; came to U.S., 1940; naturalized, 1945; s. Harry Morton and Leonor Evelyne (Goldmann) H.; m. Lee Grossman, Dec. 18, 1960 (div. 1976); children: Kathryne, Jennifer, Amy, David; m. Rikki Horne, May 18, 1985 (div. 1986); m. Marjorie Brandt Dahlin, Oct. 12, 1990. AB, U. Pa., 1953; MD, Columbia U., 1957. Diplomate Am. Bd. Psychiatry and Neurology. Intern in medicine Yale-New Haven Med. Center, 1957-58; asst. resident, then resident neurology N.Y. Neurol. Inst., 1958-61; guest investigator Rockefeller U., 1963-66; mem. faculty Columbia Coll. Physicians and Surgeons, 1960-75, prof. neurology and microbiology, 1973-75; vis. fellow Clare Hall, Cambridge, England, 1973—74; attending neurologist N.Y. Neurol. Inst., Presbyn. Hosp., 1973-75; Charles L. Mix prof. Northwestern U., 1975-85, Benjamin and Virginia T. Boshes prof. neurology, 1985-87, chmn. dept. neurology, 1975-87, Northwestern Meml. Hosp., Chgo., 1975-87; dir. rsch. scholars program Howard Hughes Med. Inst./NIH, Bethesda, 1989-2000; with dept. neurology George Washington U. Med. Ctr., Washington, 1987—. Vis. sci. officer Howard Hughes Med. Inst., 1986—87, sr. sci. officer, 1987—2000; clin. prof. neurology George Washington U. Sch. Medicine and Health Scis., 1987—2001, prof. emeritus clin. neurology, 2001—03; prof. emeritus neurology in residence George Washington U., 2004—; vis. rsch. fellow Dept. Pathology U. Cambridge, England, 1973—74, 2000—01; vis. life mem. Clare Hall, 2000—01, mem. adv. com. on fellowships Nat. Multiple Sclerosis Soc., 1976—79, chmn., 1977—79, rsch. programs adv. com., 1989—94, mem. Nat. Commn. on Venereal Disease, HEW, 1970—72; mem. med. adv. bd. Am. Parkinson Disease Assn., 1976—90, Myasthenia Gravis Found., 1980—87; mem. sci. adv. coun. Nat. Amyotrophic Lateral Sclerosis Found., 1978—85; mem. bd. sci. counselors Nat. Inst. Dental Rsch. NIH, 1990—95; sr. sci. advisor Amyotrophic Lateral Sclerosis Assn., 1992—2000. Mem. editorial bd. Neurology, 1976-82, Anns. of Neurology, 1983-89; mem. adv. bd. Archives of Virology, 1975-81. Recipient Joseph Mather Smith prize Columbia U., 1970, Lucy G. Moses award, 1970, 72, Donald W. Mulder award The ALS Assn., 1998; Am. Cancer Soc. scholar, 1973-74; USPHS spl. fellow, 1963-66, Guggenheim fellow, 1973. Fellow: AAAS, Am. Acad. Neurology, Infectious Diseases Soc. Am.; mem.: Am. Soc. Virology, Am. Soc. Microbiology, Deutsche Gesellschaft fur Neurologie (corr.), Am. Neurol. Assn., Am. Soc. Clin. Investigation, Univ. Club Washington, Yale Club N.Y.C., Cosmos Club, Phi Beta Kappa. Office: George Washington U Med Ctr Ste 7-404 2150 Pennsylvania Ave NW Washington DC 20037-3201 Business E-Mail: dharter@mfa.gwu.edu.

HARTIG, GREGORY K., otolaryngologist, educator; b. Detroit, Aug. 31, 1962; m. Kimberly Judith Howe. MD, U. Mich., Ann Arbor, 1988. Diplomate Am. Bd. Otolaryngology, 1993. Prof. surgery U. Wis., Madison, 1994—2009. Office: University Wis Hosp 600 Highland Ave Madison WI 53792

HARTIGAN-GO, KENNETH YU, toxicologist, consultant; b. Manila, Philippines, Oct. 4, 1960; s. Modesto Yao and Lily Yu Hartigan-Go; m. Catherine Chungunco, Sept. 27, 1998; 1 child, Kaylee. MD, U. Philippines, 1985, U. Newcastle-Upon-Tyne, 1998. Lic. Profl. Regulation Commn., 1986. Asst. prof. Pharmacology and Toxicology dept. U. Philippines, Manila, 1990—95; exec. dir. Zuellig Found., Makati City, Philippines, 2001—; cons. Health Tech. Assessment Com. Philippine Health Ins. Corp., Pasig, 1999—; assoc. prof. Pharmacology and Toxicology dept. U. Philippines, Manila, 1995—2001; cons. toxicologist Nat. Poisons Control and Info. Svcs. Philippine Gen. Hosp., Manila, 1990—2005; dep. dir. Bur. Food and Drugs Dept. Health, Muntinlupa, Philippines, 1999—2001, mgr. Philippine Nat. Drug Policy Program Manila, 1999—2001; vice chmn. Dangerous Drugs Bd., Manila, 2001—01; project leader Adverse Drug Reactions Monitoring Programs Dept. Health, Manila, 1994—97; hon. clin. rsch. fellow Wolfson Unit Clin. Pharmacology U. Newcastle-upon-Tyne, England, 1992—94; prof. pharmacology and toxicology dept. U. Philippines, Manila, 2001—05. Bd. mem. Philippine Coalition Against Tb, Quezon City, Philippines, 2001—, Corp. Network for Disaster Response, Makati City, 2002—; mem. adv. com. Safety of Medicinal Products WHO, Geneva, 2003—. V.p. ops. League of Corp. Founds., Makati City, 2002. Fellow: Philippine Soc. Occupl. & Clin. Toxicology (pres. 2001), Philippine Soc. Exptl. and Clin. Pharmacology (v.p. 2006—), Philippine Coll. of Physicians (life Diplomate 1992); mem.: Asia Pacific Assn. Med. Toxicology (vice-president 2001), Philippine Med. Assn. (life), Drug Info. Assn. (Outstanding Svc. Award 2001), Pi Gamma Mu, Phi Kappa Phi. Office Fax: +63-2-8922871. Business E-Mail: hartigan@zuelligfoundation.org.

HARTING, MATTHEW TIHEN, surgeon; b. Austin, Tex., Sept. 23, 1976; BA, U. Tex., Austin, 1999; MD, U. Tex., Houston, 2003. Adminstrv. chief resident, dept. surgery U. Mich., 2010—. Bd. dirs. Tex. 4000, 2005—. Recipient Arnold Coran Tchg. award, U. Mich., 2009, 2011, Golden Beeper award, Mich. Alumni Soc., Nat. Trauma Rsch. Svc. award, NIH, UT Med. Sch., Houston, Adult Stem Cell Tng. Grant award, NIH, U. Minn. Mem.: ACS (resident mem.), Internat. Soc. Stem Cell Rsch. Office: 1500 E Med Ctr Dr Ann Arbor MI 48109 Business E-Mail: mharting@umich.edu.

HARTL, FRANZ-ULRICH, biochemist, educator; b. Essen, Germany, Mar. 10, 1957; arrived in US, 1991; s. Franz and Ruth (Walter) Hartl; m. Manajit Hayer, Aug. 7, 1987. MD summa cum laude, U. Heidelberg, Germany, 1982; MD, U. Heidelberg Inst. Biochemistry, 1985; D of Med. Habilitation, U. Munich Inst. Physiological Chemistry, 1990. Postdoc. fellow U. Munich Inst. Physiological Chemistry, 1985—86, group leader, 1987-89, academic coun., 1990-91; postdoc. fellow, fellow German Rsch. Coun., UCLA, 1989—90; assoc. mem. prog. cellular biochemistry & biophysics, Sloan-Kettering Inst., NYC, 1991—92, tenure mem. prog. cellular biochemistry & biophysics, 1993—97; assoc. prof. cell biology and genetics Cornell U. Grad. Sch. Med. Scis., NYC, 1991—92, prof., 1993—97; William E. Snee chair cellular biochemistry Meml. Sloan-Kettering Cancer Ctr., NYC, 1995—97; sci. dir. Max-Planck Inst. Biochemistry, Martinsried, Germany, 1997—, mng. dir. Germany, 2002—. Assoc. investigator Howard Hughes Med. Inst., Chevy Chase, Md., 1994—97. Contbr. numerous articles to profl. jours. Recipient Vinci award, LVMH Sci. for Art Competition, 1996, Lipmann award, Am. Soc. Biochemistry & Molecular Biology, 1997, Acad. prize, Acad. Sci. Berlin-Brandenburg, 1999, Wilhelm Vaillant Rsch. prize, 2000, Gottfried Wilhelm Leibniz prize, German Rsch. Coun., 2002, Feldberg prize, 2003, Ernst Jung prize for medicine, 2005, Koerber European Sci. award, 2006, van Gysel prize, 2009, Dr H.P. Heineken prize, Royal Netherlands Acad. Arts & Scis., 2010, Albert Lasker Basic Med. Rsch. award, Lasker Found., 2011; co-recipient (with Arthur L. Horwich) Gairdner Found. Internat. award, Canada, 2004, (with Arthur L. Horwich) Wiley prize in biomedical sci., 2007, (with Arthur L. Horwich) Lewis S. Rosenstiel award for disting. work in basic med. sci., 2008, (with Arthur L. Horwich) Louisa Gross Horwitz prize, Columbia U., 2008; named Twenty-Seventh Ann. Cynthia Ann Chan Meml. Lectr., U. Calif., Berkeley, 2010. Fellow: AAAS; mem.: Max Planck Soc. (chmn. biomedical sect. 2005—), Bavarian Acad. Scis., German Acad. Scis., Acad. Sci. North Rhine-Westphalia (fgn. mem.), German Soc. Biochemistry & Molecular Biology (pres. 2003—05, Otto Warburg medal), Am. Chem. Soc., Protein Soc. (Stein & Moore award 2006), Am. Acad. Arts & Scis. (fgn. mem.), Japanese Biochem. Soc. (hon.), Harvey Soc. Achievements include research in the complete pathway by which molecular chaperones fold proteins in the living cell. Office: Max Planck Institute of Biochemistry Am Klopferspitz 18 82152 Martinsried Germany Office Phone: 49 89 8578 2233, 49 89 8578 2244. Office Fax: 49 89 8578 2211. Business E-Mail: uhartl@biochem.mpg.de. *

HARTLEY, CELIA LOVE, author, consultant, retired nursing educator, administrator; b. Colfax, Wash., Oct. 25, 1935; d. Thomas Warren and Ella Marie (Kerkman) Love; m. Lawrence Dosser (div.); children: Laurie Denise Draper, Byron Garth Dosser; m. Gordon E. Hartley, Dec. 17, 1977 (dec.). Diploma, Deaconess Hosp. Sch. Nursing, Spokane, Wash., 1956; BSN, U. Wash., Seattle, 1965, MSN, 1968. RN, Wash., Calif. Staff nurse Deaconess Hosp., Spokane, 1956-62; charge nurse Northgate Gen. Hosp., Seattle, 1963-65; hosp. supr. Stevens Meml. Hosp., Edmonds, Wash., 1965-66; prof. nursing Shoreline C.C., Seattle, 1967-73, dir. nursing edn., asst. div. chmn. health occupations, 1973-92; chair health sci. divsn. Coll. of the Desert, Palm Desert, Calif., 1992-99, prof. emerita, 1999—; nursing curriculum cons. Pres. Coun. on Nursing Edn. in Wash. State, 1992; adv. com. Antioch West and Seattle U., 1979-81, Nursing Edn. Com. Higher Edn. Coordinating Bd., 1990, Western Wash. U. Nursing, 1984, Seattle Pacific U. Nursing, 1992; other coms. various orgns., 1979—; presenter in field. Author: (with Janice Ellis) Nursing in Today's World; Trends, Issues, and Management, 1980, Managing and Coordinating Patient Care, 1991, 5th edit., 2009; mem. editl. bd. Assoc. Degree Nurse, 1987-91, Jour. Nursing Edn., 1991—2010; contbr. articles to profl. jours.; chpts. to books. Recipient Dedicated Svc. award, Western Regional Assn. of Constituent Leagues for Nursing, 1987; named to Hall of Fame, Coll. of Desert Alumni Assn., 1999. Fellow Acad. Nurse Edn.; mem. Nat. League of Nursing (bd. dirs. 1981-84, appeal panel Coun. AD Programs 1988-91, 95-98, chmn.-vice chmn. various coms.), Wash. Constituent League (v.p. 1986-87, chmn. nominating com. 1984-85, chmn. membership com. 1985-86), Sigma Theta Tau, Safe Harbor Free Clinic (bd. dirs. 2009-), Wash. Free Clinic Assn. (bd. trustee 2009-). Home: 3234 Mabana Rd Camano Island WA 98282 Office Phone: 360-387-0822. Personal E-mail: cegohart@wavecable.com.

HARTMAN, CHARLES HENRY, highway safety, transportation and not-for-profit executive, educator; b. Red Lion, Pa., Feb. 1, 1933; s. Earl Eugene and Jeannette (Kline) Hartman; m. Patricia A. Cooper, Aug. 3, 1956 (div. May 1974); children: Elizabeth Jean, Amy Joan; m. Catherine M. Wheeler, June 7, 1975 (div. Apr. 1994); children: Eric Michael, Jennifer Leigh, David Wheeler, Scott Andrew; m. Andrea S. Anderson, July 8, 2000. BS, Millersville State Tchrs. Coll., 1954; MA, Mich. State U., 1958, EdD, 1962. Cert. assn. exec. Tchr. Hollidaysburg Pub. Schs., Pa., 1956—57; assoc. prof. Ill. State U., Normal, 1959—62; vis. lectr. edn. U. Wis., Madison, 1962—63, Milw., 1963—64; dir. edn. Automotive Safety Found./Hwy. Users Fedn., Washington, 1964—70; dep. adminstr. Nat. Hwy. Traffic Safety Adminstrn., U.S. Dept. Transp., Washington, 1970—73; pres. Motorcycle Safety Found., Irvine, Calif., 1973—84, Touchstone Mgmt. Svcs., Delta, Pa., 1984—88; exec. v.p. AAHPERD, Reston, Va., 1988—90; exec. dir. Am. Coll. Health Assn., Balt., 1990—98; pres. Nonprofit Orgn. Mgmt. and Consultation, 1998—2002; dir. transp. and support svcs. Red Lion Area Sch Dist., Pa., 2003—04; office mgr. Andrea S. Anderson Law Offices, P.C., 2004—. Cons. Nat. Assn. Women Hwy. Safety Leaders, Md. State Dept. Edn., 1969—70; dir. Nat. Safety Coun., Chgo., 1976—79; vice chmn. traffic conf., 1976—78; presdl. appointee Nat. Hwy. Safety Adv. Com., Washington, 1977—80; gov.'s appointee Pa. Task Force Alcohol and Hwy. Safety, 1981—82; vice chmn. Alliance Traffic Safety, 1981—83, chmn., 1983—85; mem. policy com. Hwy. Users Fedn.; lectr. bus. adminstrn. Capital Campus Pa. State U., Middletown, 1987—88; bd. dirs. Lincoln Intermediate Unit # 12, 1987—89, 1991—93; sr. cons. York Nonprofit Mgmt. Devel. Ctr., 1998—2000; spkr. in field. Sch. dir. Red Lion (Pa.) Area Schs., 1986—2003, pres. sch. bd., 1988, 1996—2003, v.p., 1989—95; mem. York 2000 Commn.; trustee Nat. Motorcycle Fund; pres. Howard County C. of C., Columbia, Md., 1985—87. With US Army, 1954—56. Recipient Traffic Safety Educator of the Yr. award, Wis. Traffic Edn. Assn., 1972, Sec.'s award, U.S. Dept. Transp., 1973; named to Hall of Fame, Red Lion Area Sch. Dist., 1993. Fellow: Am. Acad. Safety Edn.; mem.: NRA, Am.

Legion, Pa. Sch. Bds. Assn., Assn. Advancement Automotive Medicine, Am. Driver and Traffic Safety Edn. Assn., Pres. Assn./Am. Mgmt. Assn., Soc. Automotive Engrs., Am. Soc. Assn. Execs. (vice-chmn. evaluation com. 1984—85, chmn. 1985—86), Phi Sigma Pi, Phi Delta Kappa. Republican. Home: 122 E McKinley Rd Delta PA 17314 Office: 901 Delta Rd Red Lion PA 17356-9179 Business E-Mail: charley@asa-law.com.

HARTMAN, DEANNA MEARS, retired family counselor, addiction counselor; b. Norfolk, Va., Aug. 11, 1937; d. James Gordon Jr. and Sarah Talmadge (Johnson) Mears; m. David Luther Brinkley Jr. (div.); children: Kim Brinkley Hebebrand, David III, Jeffrey Lawrence Brinkley; m. Shirish Ramachandra Pandya, June 7, 1978 (dec.). AA, U. Akron, 1980; BA, Va. Wesleyan, 1983; MA, Antioch U., 1994. Cert. cognitive behavioral therapist; nat. cert. counselor. Dir. edn. svcs. Va. Coun. on Alcoholism, Drugs, Norfolk, 1985-87, exec. dir., 1990-93; outpatient program specialist Maryview Psychiat. Hosp., Portsmouth, Va., 1988-89; clin. therapist City of Portsmouth, 1988-89; educator, therapist City of Va. Beach, 1984-86, 93-95; mental health counselor Glasgow High Wellness Ctr., Newark, Del., 1995; family counselor, addiction specialist Williamsburg Pl., Farley Ctr., Williamsburg, Va., 1997—. Founder Survivors of Suicide, Virginia Beach, 1982-86, vol. educator AARP Bear, Del., 1995. Contbr. articles to profl. jours., various presentations. Bd. dirs. Hospice of Virginia Beach, 1983-85, Safe Place, 1988-90, Civitan Internat., 1990-92, comty. adv. coun. for curriculum Coll. of Edn., Old Dominion U., Norfolk, 1991-92. Named Rookie of Yr., Civitan Internat., 1991; recipient Disting. Svc. award Va. Alcohol and Drug Abuse Counselors, 1992. Avocations: reading, writing, walking, birdwatching. Home: 19208 Cedar Crest Ct North Fort Myers FL 33903-6602

HARTMAN, GARY EDWIN, pediatric surgeon; b. Wis. Rapids, Wis., Feb. 10, 1948; m. Susan Hartman; 1 child, Emi. BA in Psychology, U. Wis., 1970; MBA in Info. Tech., George Washington U. Sch. Bus. & Pub. Mgmt., 2000; MD, U. Wis. Med. Sch., 1974. Cert. Am. Bd. Surgery, added qualifications in surgical critical care, Am. Bd. Surgery, spl. competence in pediatric surgery, Am. Bd. Surgery, Nat. Bd. Med. Examiners, lic. Calif. Rotating internship, U. Calif. San. Francisco affiliate program Highland Gen. Hosp., Oakland, Calif., 1974—75, gen. surgery resident, U. Calif. San Francisco affiliate program, 1975—79; pediatric surgery and critical care resident Stanford U. Med. Ctr., Calif., 1979—81, asst. prof. surgery and pediatrics, divsn. pediatric surgery, 1983—91, assoc. prof. surgery and pediatrics, divsn. pediatric surgery, 1991—93; pediatric surgery resident Okla. Children's Meml. Hosp., U. Okla. Health Sci. Ctr., Okla. City, 1981—83; chmn. pediatric surgery Children's Nat. Med. Ctr., Washington, 1993; assoc. prof. surgery and pediatrics George Wash. Sch. Med., DC, 1993—97, prof. surgery and pediatrics, 1997—2004; clin. prof. surgery Stanford U. Sch. Medicine, Calif., 2004—. Assoc. dir., pediat. intensive care unit Lucile Salter Packard Children's Hosp. at Stanford, 1991—93, pres.-elect, med. staff, 1992—93, v.p., med. staff, 2006—; assoc. dir., pediatric critical care Children's Nat. Med. Ctr., DC, 1993—2004, chmn., dept. pediat. surgery, 1995—2004, mem. perioperative leadership group, 1995—2004, pres.-elect, med. staff, 2002—04; chief, divsn. pediat. surgery Georgetown U. Med. Ctr., 1999—2004; dir., regional pediat. surg. svcs. Stanford U., 2004—, Lucile Packard Children's Hosp., 2004—; examiner Am. Bd. Surgery, 1994—. Contbr. articles to profl. jours., chapters to books. Named one of Best Doctors in Am., Best Doctors Inc., 2005—07, Guide to America's Top Surgeons, Consumer's Rsch. Coun. America, 2007; Ruth Rader Meml. Fellowship for Med. Rsch., Okla. U. Health Scis. Ctr., 1982, Andrew W. Mellon Found. Fellow, Stanford U. Sch. Medicine, 1988—90. Mem.: Santa Clara County Med. Soc., Montgomery County Pediat. Soc., Northern Va. Pediat. Soc., Calif. Med. Assn., Surg. Infection Soc., Soc. Critical Care Medicine, Pacific Assn. Pediat. Surgeons (mem. program com. 1993—94), Assn. for Academic Surgery, Am. Pediat. Surg. Assn. (mem. critical care com. 1994—98, mem. publications com. 1998—2000, mem. nominating com. 2004—), ACS, Am. Acad. Pediatrics (Surg. Sect. and Critical Care Sects.), Acad. Surg. Rsch., Assn. Pediat. Surgery Tng. Dirs. (sec., treas. 1999—2004, pres. 2004—06), Assn. Pediat. Surgery Program Directors (pres. 2003—06). Achievements include leading team of surgeons to successfully separate conjoined twins in 2004 & 2007; has done five surgeries in total to separate conjoined twins. Office: Stanford University Sch Medicine Dept Pediat Surgery 780 Welch Rd Ste 206 Stanford CA 94305 Office Phone: 650-723-6439. Office Fax: 650-725-5577. Business E-Mail: ghartman@lpch.org.

HARTMAN, NANCY LEE, physician; b. Philipsburg, Pa., July 29, 1951; Grad., Barbizon Sch. Modeling, 1970; AA Med. Tech., Harcum Jr. Coll., 1971; BA Biology and Med. Tech., Lycoming Coll., 1974; MS Med. Biology, L.I. U., 1977; MD, Am. U. Caribbean, Plymouth, Montserrat, W.I., 1981. Cert. med. technologist Am. Soc. Clin. Pathologist. Med. technologist Lock Haven Hosp., Pa., 1971—72, Williamsport Hosp., Pa., 1972—73, Renovo Hosp., Pa., 1974; med. technologist microbiology Jersey Shore Hosp., Pa., 1974; microbiologist N.Y. Hosp. and Cornell Med. Ctr., NYC, 1974—75, Drekter and Heisler Labs., NYC, 1975, North Shore Labs., Inc., Syosset, NY, 1976—78; lab. technician North Shore Hosp., Manhasset, NY, 1981—82, Nat. Health Labs., Inc., Bethpage, NY, 1982; resident internal medicine program Interfaith Med. Ctr., Bklyn., 1983—84; med. cons. Shapiro & Baines, Mineola, NY, 1985—88; resident pathology program Lenox Hill Hosp., NYC, 1986—87; resident clin. pathology Beth Israel Med. Ctr., NYC, 1988—89; resident internal medicine Lenox Hill Hosp., 1990; med. specialist, pres. Advt. Ltd., Glenwood Landing, NY, 1990—92. Med. cons. Leader Mfg., Inc., Quebec, Can., 1988-89, Meiselman, Boland, Reilly and Pittoni, Mineola, 1988-92, Law Office Sybil Shainwald, N.Y.C., 1989-91, Reichenbaum and Silberstein, Great Neck, N.Y., 1990-92, Audio Visual Med. Mktg., Inc., N.Y.C., 1990-92, Law Office Peter D. Kolbrener, Westbury, N.Y., 1990-92, Siben & Siben, Bayshore, N.Y., 1990-92, 93-94, Whiteman & Gorray, Uniondale, N.Y., 1990-92, Law Office Jed Neil Kirsch, Mineola, 1990-92, Gandin, Schotsky & Rappaport, Melville, N.Y., 1990-92, Doniger, Garland & Engstrand, N.Y.C., 1991-92, Law Office Steven Miller, Mineola, 1991-92, Law Office Harry Organek, Westbury, 1991-92, Law Office Michael Flomenhaft, N.Y.C., 1991-92, Damashek, Godosky & Gentile, N.Y.C., 1991-92, Easton & Clark, Levittown, N.Y., 1991-92, Tomas, Simonhoff, O'Brien, and Adourian, Haddonfield, N.J., 1993-94, Med. Surveillance, Inc., Westchester, Pa., 1993-94; rsch. fellow Rockefeller U., N.Y.C., 1996; med. cons. specializing in med. malpractice & personal injury & product liability cases, 1996-. Author: The Pocket Handbook of Infectious Agents and Their Treatments, 1987; contbr. articles to profl. jours. Allied Health Professions Traineeship grant, 1975—77. Mem. AMA, Am. Med. Women's Assn., Am. Soc. Clin. Pathologists (registered med. technologist), Internat. Platform Assn., Am. Soc. Microbiology. Avocations: jogging, scuba diving, flying, tennis, golf. Home: PO Box 374 Roslyn NY 11576-0374

HARTMAN-ABRAMSON, ILENE, medical educator; b. Detroit, Nov. 8, 1950; d. Stuart Lester and Freda Vivian (Nash) Hartman; m. Victor Nikolai Abramson, Oct. 24, 1941. BA, U. Mich., Ann Arbor, 1972; MEd, Wayne State U., Detroit, 1980; PhD in Higher Edn., Wayne State U., 1990. Cert. continuing secondary tchr., Mich. Program developer and instr. William Beaumont Hosp., Royal Oak, Mich., 1972—74; vocat. counselor for emigres Jewish Vocat. Svc. and Cmty. Workshop, Detroit, 1974—81; program developer and cons. Detroit Psychiat. Inst., 1982; instr. for foreign students Oakland C.C., Farmington Hills, Mich., 1983-99. Mem. adv. bd. Mich. Dept. Edn., Detroit, 1981; lectr. Internat. Conf. Tchrs. English to Speakers of Other Langs., 1981; chair profl. stds. and measures com. Mich. Devel. Edn. Consortium, editor newsletter, 1997; mem. rehab. adv. coun. State of Mich.; guest lectr. med. edn./residency tng. initiatives Detroit Med. Ctr. Hutzel Hosp., Providence Hosp., Beaumont Hosp., Detroit Med. Ctr., Harper Hosp.; adj. faculty Wayne State U., 2000; adj. prof. internat. comms. Lawrence Tech. U., 2000—; grant reviewer HRSA Bur. Primary Health Care, 2008—; presenter in field; with S.E. Mich. Coun. Bouts Exec. Comm.; mem. bd. respiratory care Rules Com., 2009—; mem. dept. cmty. health Mich. Bd. Pharmacy, 2009—11, State Mich. Bd. Respiratory, 2009—; guest spkr., facilitator Ctr. Behavioral & Decision Scis. Medicine, 2010—11; co-investigator Soc. Tchrs. Family Medicine, 2011—. Mem. editl. bd. Mensa Rsch. Jour.; contbr. articles to prof. jours. Mem. Am. Acad. on Communication Healthcare, Am. Mensa (rsch. rev. com.). Jewish. Avocations: self-defense for women, Karate. Personal E-mail: ihabramson@aol.com.

HARTMANN, LYNN C., physician, educator; b. Chgo. Student, U. Ill., 1976-79; MD with distinction, Northwestern U., 1983. Bd. cert. Nat. Bd. Med. Examiners. Internal medicine intern and resident U. Iowa Hosps. and Clinics, 1983-86; med. oncology fellow Mayo Clinic, 1986-88; clin. investigator Biol. Response Modifiers Program Nat. Cancer Inst., Frederick, Md., 1988-89; asst. prof. Mayo Med. Sch., 1989-93, assoc. prof., 1993—, dir. women's cancer program, cons. dept. oncology, 1992—; assoc. dir. edn. Mayo Cancer Ctr., 1995—. Contbr. chpts. to books and articles to profl. jours. Recipient Career Devel. award Am. Cancer Soc., 1991-94; Am. Cancer Soc. clin. fellow, 1987-88; grantee Dept. Def. Breast Cancer Initiative, 1994-98, Oliver and Jennie Donaldson Charitable Trust, 1995-98, Nat. Cancer Inst., Kamen Found. Fellow Am. Cancer Soc.; mem. AMA, ACP, AAAS, Am. Assn. for Cancer Rsch., Am. Assn. for Cancer Edn., Am. Soc. Clin. Oncology (edn. com.), Am. Soc. Preventive Oncology, Am. Med. Womens Assn., Soc. Gynecologic Oncology, Women in Cancer Rsch., Alpha Omega Alpha, Rho Chi. Avocations: bird watching, literature. Office: Mayo Clinic 200 1st St SW Rochester MN 55905-0002

HARTMANN, MICHAEL, pharmacist, health economist; b. Paderborn, Germany, Sept. 21, 1960; s. Anneliese and Franz Hartmann; m. Dorothee Hartmann, Nov. 23, 1990. MBA, MPH, PhD, PharmD. Lic. pharmacist Germany, 1985. Dir. Hosp. Pharmacy, U. Jena, Germany, 1995—. Office: Univ Hosp Jena Erlanger Allee 101 7747 Jena Germany E-mail: apotheke@med.uni-jena.de.

HARTMANN, ROBERT SANKEY, health facility administrator, not-for-profit fundraiser; b. June 9, 1948; s. Robert Trowbridge and Roberta (Sankey) H.; m. Ruth Eva Satterthwaite, Dec. 2, 1978; children: Daniel Satterthwaite, David Trowbridge. BA in Speech/Drama cum laude, Occidental Coll., 1969, MA in Speech/Drama, 1971; student, Guildhall Sch. Music & Drama, 1970; mgmt. devel. course, Harvard Bus. Sch., 1974. Spl. asst. to chmn. Nat. Endowment for Arts, Washington, 1973—78; lobbyist for Daniel J. Edelman Washington, 1978; creative dir., lobbyist Hill and Knowlton, Washington, 1978—81; sr. v.p. Ruder Finn & Rotman, Washington, 1981—84; dir. pub. rels. World Wildlife Fund, Washington, 1984—86; sr. v.p. and dir. pub. rels. Abramson Assocs., Inc., 1986—90; v.p. pub. affairs, mktg. and devel. Nat. Rehab. Hosp., Washington, 1990—. Chmn. bd. dirs. Met. Meth. Nursery Sch., 1989—94. Named Outstanding Young Man Am., 1983. Mem. Pub. Rels. Soc. Am. (Thoth award 1984), Internat. Assn. Bus. Communicators (Gold Quill award 1984), Westmoreland Citizens Assn. (pres. 1992-93), Nat. Press Club, Capitol Hill Club. Home: 5023 Worthington Dr Bethesda MD 20816-2748 Office: Nat Rehab Hosp 102 Irving St NW Washington DC 20010-2949 Office Phone: 202-877-1776. Business E-Mail: robert.s.hartmann@medstar.net.

HARTRICK, CRAIG T., physician, educator; b. Pontiac, Mich., May 24, 1954; BS in Chem. Engring., Mich. State U., 1976; MD, Wayne State U., 1980. Diplomate Am. Bd. Anesthesiology. Dir., anesthesiology rsch. Beaumont Hosps., 1999; discipline dir. pharmacology Oakland U. William Beaumont Sch. Medicine, 2010—, prof., biomed. scis., prof., anesthesiology, 2010; clin. prof., health scis. pharmacology Oakland U. Editor-in-chief Pain Practice, 2005; bd. examiner World Inst. Pain, 2004. Fellow: Added Qualifications Pain, Am. Bd. Anesthesiology, Interventional Pain Practice; mem.: Sec. World Inst. Pain Found. Avocations: fly fishing, guitar. Office: Oakland University Willam Beaumont Hosp SOM Rochester MI 48309 Business E-Mail: chartrick@beaumont.edu.

HARTSFIELD, JAMES KENNEDY, JR., orthodontist, geneticist; b. Decatur, Ala., Feb. 12, 1955; s. James Kennedy and Shirley Joann (Bridwell) H.; m. Karen Lee Whitaker, May 8, 1977; 1 child, Kennedy Whitaker. BS in Biology cum laude, U. SC, Columbia, 1977; DMD in Dental Medicine, Med. U. SC, Charleston, 1981; MS in Med. Genetics, Ind. U., Indpls., 1983; MMSc in Oral Biology, Harvard U., Boston, 1987; PhD in Med. Scis., U. South Fla., Tampa, 1993. Diplomate Am. Bd. Med. Genetics., Am. Bd. Orthodontics. Intern Hillsborough Dental Rsch. Clinic, Tampa, Fla., 1981-82; clin. fellow Ind. U., Indpls., 1982-83; rsch. fellow Harvard U., Boston, 1983-86, Mass. Gen. Hosp., Boston, 1984-86; clin. fellow U. South Fla., Tampa, 1986-87, asst. prof., 1987-93; assoc. prof. Sch. Dentistry and Sch. Medicine, Ind. U., Indpls., 1993—99, prof. Sch. Dentistry and Sch. Medicine, 1999—2008, adj. prof. Sch. Dentistry and Sch. Medicine, 2008—; prof., E. Preston Hicks Endowed Chair in Orthodontics and Oral Rsch., Coll. Dentistry U. Ky., 2008—, prof., Coll. Medicine, 2010—. Adj. prof. U. Ill. at Chgo. Coll. Dentistry; dir. Teratogen Info. Svc., U. South Fla., 1987-93; dir. oral facial genetics divsn. Sch. Dentistry Ind. U., 1993-, acting chmn. oral facial devel., 1998-99, chmn., 1999-2002, interim chmn. orthodontics and oral facial genetics, 2007—; pres. Meridian Orthodontics, PC, 2003-08; dir. orthodontic program rsch. & hereditary genomics lab. U. Ky. Coll. Dentistry, 2008—, dir. grad. orthodontic program residency, 2011; editl. rev. bd. mem. Am. Jour. Orthodontics and Dentofacial Orthops., 2008-, Angle Orthodontist, 2011-. Mem. editl. bd. Jour. Dental Rsch., 2007-09; rev. bd. mem. Internat. Jour. Oral Maxillofacial Implants; contbr. articles to profl. jours. Med. adv. coun. Osteogenesis Imperfecta Found., 2007—. Recipient Physician-Scientist award NIH, 1989, 1st Ind. Rsch. Support and Transition award, 1996, B.F. Dewell Meml. Biomed. Rsch. award Am. Assn. Orthodontists Found., 2001, Disting. Faculty award Ind. U. Sch. Dentistry Alumni Assn., 2003; named Outstanding Faculty of Yr., Ind. Dental Assn., 2004. Fellow Am. Coll. Med. Genetics (founding), Am. Coll. Dentists, Coll. of Diplomates of Am. Bd. Orthodontics; mem. ADA, Am. Soc. Human Genetics, Am. Assn. for Dental Rsch., Edward H. Angle Soc. Orthodontists (Midwest Component), Internat. Assn. Dental Rsch. (v.p. craniofacial biology group 2003-04, pres. 2005-06), Internat. Coll. Dentists, Soc. Craniofacial Genetics (pres. 1989-90), Am. Dental Edn. Assn., Am. Cleft Palate Assn., Am. Assn. Orthodontists, Harvard Soc. for Advancement of Orthodontics (v.p. 2006-07, pres. 2007-09), Confs. on Orthodontic Advances in Sci. and Tech. (bd. dirs. 2006—). Presbyterian. Avocations: music, boating. Office: U Ky Coll Dentistry Rm D-406 800 Rose St Lexington KY 40536-0297 Office Phone: 859-323-5371. Office Fax: 859-257-8878. Personal E-mail: drHartsfield@post.harvard.edu. Business E-Mail: James.Hartsfield@uky.edu.

HARTUNG, OLIVIER, thoracic surgeon; b. Marseille, France, July 14, 1966; MD, U. la Méditérranée, 1997. Vascular surgeon Assistance Pub.-Hosp. Marseille, 1999—. Office: Chirurgie Vasculaire Hôpital Universitaire Nord chemin des bourrelly Marseille 13015 France Office Fax: (33)491968370. Business E-Mail: olivier.hartung@ap-hm.fr.

HARTUNG, ROLF, environmental toxicology educator, researcher, consultant; b. Bremen, Germany, Mar. 1, 1935; came to U.S., 1952, naturalized, 1958. BS in Wildlife Mgmt., U. Mich., 1960, M in Wildlife Mgmt., 1962, PhD in Wildlife Mgmt., 1964. Diplomate Am. Bd. Toxicology. Instr. in wildlife mgmt. U. Mich., Ann Arbor, 1963, lectr. in indsl. health, 1964, asst. prof. indsl. health, 1965—69, assoc. prof. environ. and indsl. health, 1969—73, prof. environ. toxicology, 1973—97, prof. emeritus, 1997—, chmn. toxicology program, 1974—80. Com. or sub-com. mem. Nat. Acad. Scis., 1971-72, 79-97, Mich. Dept. Natural Resources, 1977-97; mem. Mich. Environ. Rev. Bd., 1982-86; mem. hazardous materials com. U.S. Congress Office Tech. Assessment, 1980-83; chmn. com. on environ. effects, transport and fate of sci. adv. bd. EPA, 1982-87, mem. exec. com. of sci. adv. bd., 1982-87. Editor, contbg. author: Environmental Mercury Contamination, 1972; assoc. editor Jour. Toxicology and Indsl. Health, 1984-87, Ency. of Toxicology, 1998; contbr. chpts. to books and articles to profl. jours. Recipient H. M. Wight award U. Mich., 1963; NSF fellow, 1960-64. Mem. Am. Indsl. Hygiene Assn., Mich. Indsl. Hygiene Assn., Soc. Environ. Toxicology and Chemistry, Soc. Toxicology, Wildlife Disease Assn., Wildlife Soc., Sigma Xi, Phi Sigma, Phi Kappa Phi. Home: University Mich 3125 Fernwood Ave Ann Arbor MI 48108-1955 Office Phone: 734-395-1113. Business E-Mail: rhartung@umich.edu.

HARTWELL, LELAND HARRISON (LEE HARTWELL), geneticist, educator; b. LA, Oct. 30, 1939; s. Majorie (Taylor) Hartwell; m. Theresa Naujack. BS, Calif. Inst. Tech., Pasadena, 1961; PhD in Biology, MIT, 1964. Postdoc. fellow Salk Inst. Biol. Studies, La Jolla, Calif., 1964-65; asst. prof. U. Calif., Irvine, 1965-67, assoc. prof., 1967-68, U. Washington Sch. Medicine, Seattle, 1968-73, prof. genome scis., 1973—2010, Am. Cancer Soc. rsch. prof. genetics, 1990—2010, adj. prof. medicine, 2003—10; faculty Fred Hutchison Cancer Rsch. Ctr., Seattle, 1996—97, pres., dir., 1997—2010; faculty, Virginia G. Piper chair personalized medicine Ariz. State U., Tempe, 2010—, co-dir., chief scientist Biodesign Inst. Ctr. Sustainable Health, 2010—. Chmn. sci. adv. bd. Canary Found. Mem. editl. bd. Jour. Cell Biology, 1988—91, Molecular Biology of the Cell, 1991—93, Molecular & Cellular Biology; contbr. articles to profl. jours. Recipient Eli Lilly award in microbiology and immunology, 1973, NIH Merit award, 1990, Alfred P. Sloan award, GM Cancer Rsch. Found., 1991, Hoffman LaRoche Mattia award, 1991, Gairdner Found. Internat. award, 1992, Simon Shubitz award, U. Chgo., 1992, Rosenstiel award, Brandeis U., 1993, Katherine Berkan Judd award, Meml. Sloan Kettering Cancer Ctr., 1994, Warren Triennial prize, Mass. Gen. Hosp., 1995, Carnegie Mellon Dickson award, 1996, Louisa Gross Horwitz prize, Columbia U., 1995, Albert Lasker award for basic med. rsch., 1998, Komen Brinker award for sci. distinction, Susan G. Komen Breast Cancer Found., 1998, Disting. Alumni award, Calif. Inst. Tech., 1999, Am. Cancer Soc. medal of honor, 1999, Léopold Giffuel prize, Assn. Rsch. Cancer, France, 2000, Nobel prize in physiology/medicine, 2001, Massry prize, Meira & Shaul G. Massry Found., Wash. State Medal of Merit, 2003; fellow John Simon Guggenheim Meml. Found., 1983—84; scholar Am. Cancer Soc.; 1996 Laureate, Passano Found., Inc. Mem.: NAS, Am. Assn. Cancer Rsch., Am. Acad. Microbiology, Genetics Soc. America (pres. 1990), Am. Soc. Cell Biology (Keith Porter award 1995), Am. Soc. Microbiology, Am. Acad. Arts & Scis. Achievements include patents in field. Office: Ariz State U Biodesign Inst PO Box 875001 1001 S McAllister Ave Tempe AZ 85287 Office Phone: 480-727-0779. E-mail: Lee.Hartwell@asu.edu. *

HARTZBAND, PAMELA IRENE, endocrinologist, internist; b. Elizabeth, NJ, June 6, 1952; m. Jerome Groopman. MD, Harvard Med. Sch., 1978. Diplomate Am. Bd. Internal Medicine, cert. in endocrinology & metabolism. Intern internal medicine Mass. Gen. Hosp., Boston, 1978—79, resident internal medicine, 1979—80; endocrinology metabolism resident UCLA Med. Ctr., 1980—81, fellow in endocrinology, diabetes & metabolism, 1981—83; attending physician Beth Israel Deaconess Med. Ctr., Boston, 1984—; asst. prof. medicine Harvard Med. Sch. Contbr. articles to profl. jours. Fellow: ACP; mem.: Am. Assn. Clin. Endocrinologists, Hormone Found. Office: Beth Israel Deaconess Med Ctr 330 Brookline Ave Boston MA 02215 Office Phone: 617-667-8878.

HARTZELL, CHARLES R., science foundation director, cell biologist, biochemist; b. Butler, Pa., Aug. 12, 1941; s. Charles R. and Ada Grace (Giles) H.; m. Marguerite K. Getty; children: Scott David, Amy Lynette. BS, Geneva Coll., 1963; PhD, Indiana U., 1967; MDiv, Union Theol. Sem., 2002. Post-doctoral fellow Ind. U., Bloomington,

1967; rsch. fellow Commonwealth Sci, and Industry Rsch. Orgn., Melbourne, Australia, 1967-68; rsch. fellow, asst. rsch. prof. U. Wis., Madison, 1968-71; asst. prof. Pa. State U., University Park, 1971-75, assoc. prof., 1975-78; sr. rsch. scientist Alfred I. DuPont Inst., Wilmington, Del., 1978-80, dir. rsch., 1981-97, Nemours Children's Clinics, Fla., 1987—2001; rsch. mgr. The Nemours Found., Jacksonville, 1987—2001; prof. pediat. Jefferson Med. Coll., Phila., 1989—; dir. Cross Heart Ministries, Inc., Wilmington, 2002—. Contbr. articles to profl. jours. NIH fellow, 1968-70; established investigator Am. Heart Assn., 1970-75. Presbyterian. Avocations: ballroom dancing, music, exercise, cabinet making. Office: Cross-Heart Ministries Inc 34 Colefax Ct Wilmington DE 19804-2950 Office Phone: 302-593-4832. Personal E-mail: chartzell1@verizon.net. Business E-Mail: chartzell@juno.com.

HARTZELL, IRENE JANOFSKY, psychologist, mediator; d. Leonard S. and Annelies Janofsky; 1 child, Mark. BA, U. Calif., Berkeley, 1963, MA, 1965; PhD, U. Oreg., 1970. Cert. in advanced paralegal Edmonds CC Wash., 2010. Psychologist Lake Washington Sch. Dist., Kirkland, Wash., 1971-72; staff psychologist VA Med. Ctr., Seattle, 1970-71, Long Beach, Calif., 1973-74; dir. parent edn. Children's Hosp., Orange, Calif., 1975—78; clin. psychologist Kaiser Permanente, Woodland Hills, Calif., 1979—94; clin. instr. pediats. Coll. Medicine U. Calif., Irvine, 1975—78; ret., 1994; small claims ct. mediator Riverside County, Calif., Pierce County, Wash., 2008—. Author: The Study Skills Advantage; contbr. articles to profl. jours. Intern Oreg. Legis., 1974—75. U.S. Vocat. Rehab. Adminstrn. fellow, U. Oreg., 1966—67, 1969. Personal E-mail: irene.hartzell@gmail.com.

HARUTA, TETSURO, physician, educator; b. Kagoshima, Japan, Nov. 22, 1956; s. Masayoshi Haruta and Fumiko Nagatomo; m. Kayo Murai; 1 child, Saaya. MD, Shiga U. Med. Sci., 1984, PhD, 1992. Asst. prof. Toyama Med. and Pharm. U., Japan, 1997—2001, lectr. dept. medicine, 2001—. Achievements include research in mechanism of insulin resistance.

HARVEY, BIRT, retired pediatrician, educator; b. Teheran, Iran, Nov. 24, 1928; five children. BA, Johns Hopkins U., 1948; MD, N.Y.U., 1952. Pvt. practice, 1958-88; prof. pediat. emeritus Stanford U., Palo Alto, Calif., 1995—. Past sr. fellow Inst. Health, Policy Studies, U. Calif., San Francisco. Mem. Inst. Med. Nat. Acad. Scis. (emeritus), Am. Acad. Pediatrics (past pres.), Am. Pediat. Soc. (emeritus).

HARVEY, BRIAN HERBERT, pharmacologist, researcher; s. Michael Frederick and Wamey Harvey; m. Marinda Magda Du Toit, Apr. 4, 1987; children: Amy, Jesse Brian Michael. BPharm, Rhodes U., 1982; BSc with hons., Potchefstroom U., 1986; MSc, Stellenbosch U., 1988, PhD, 1992. Registered pharmacist South African Pharmacy Coun., 1981. Clin. pharmacist Tygerberg Hosp., Cape Town, South Africa, 1986—89; sr. rschr. South African Med. Rsch. Coun., Cape Town, 1989—93; products advisor Eli Lilly, Johannesburg, 1994—97; assoc. prof. North-West U., Potchefstroom, South Africa, 1998—2001, prof., 2002—. Contbr. articles to profl. jours. Lt. med. svcs. South African Def. Force, 1981—85. Decorated Pro Patria South African Def. Force, Svc. medal; grantee, Nat. Rsch. Found., 2003—05, 2006—, South African Med. Rsch. Coun., 2004—. Fellow: Collegium Internat. Neuropsychopharmacologicum (Best Poster award 2000), mem.: Internat. Soc. Lithium Rsch., South African Acad. Pharm. Scis. (Best Publication award 2001, 2002, 2004), South African Pharmacology Soc. (Best Publication award 2005), Internat. Brain Rsch. Org. Achievements include advancing current knowledge of the neurobiology of depression, post traumatic stress disorder and other anxiety disorders; development of animal models of anxiety and stress-related disorders. Office: North-West U Hofman St 2520 Potchefstroom 2520 South Africa Office Fax: +27 18 299 2225. Business E-Mail: brian.harvey@nwu.ac.za.

HARVEY, JOHN ADRIANCE, psychologist, pharmacologist, researcher, educator; b. NYC, Oct. 14, 1930; s. John Adriance Harvey and Paula Ann (Truhar) Oestreich; m. Rhoda S. Sadigur, Dec. 20, 1958; children: David Alexander(Dec.), Andrew Martin, Michael Allen. AB, U. Chgo., 1955, PhD, 1959. Research assoc. U. Chgo., 1959-61, asst. prof., 1961-67, assoc. prof., 1967-68; prof. psychology and pharmacology U. Iowa, Iowa City, 1968-88; prof. pharmacology and physiology, chief div. behavioral neurobiology Drexel U. Coll. Medicine, Phila., 1988—, chair dept. pharmacology and physiology, 2006—08, prof. emeritus, 2010—. Guest worker Maudsley Hosp., London, 1966-67; chmn. biopsychology rsch. rev. com. NIH, 1983-85; chmn. behavioral neurobiology rsch. rev. com. NIMH, 1986-90, mem. adv. panel; mem. extramural sci. adv. bd. Nat. Inst. on Drug Abuse, 1990—. Author: Behavioral Analysis of Drug Action, 1971, (with Barry Kosofsky) Cocaine: Effects on the Developing Brain; editor Jour. Pharmacology and Exptl. Therapeutics, 1990-98; contbr. numerous articles to profl. jours. Recipient Rsch. Devel. award, NIMH, 1963—68, Rsch. Scientist award, 1969—74. Fellow APA (pres. divsn. 28 1984-85), Am. Coll. Neuropsychopharmacology; mem. Am. Soc. for Pharmacology and Exptl. Therapeutics (editl. adv. bd.), Soc. for Neurosci. (fin. com.), Soc. for Neurochemistry, European Soc. for Neurochemistry, Pavlovian Soc., Soc. for Biol. Psychiatry, Behavioral Pharmacol. Soc. (pres. 1996-98). Office: Drexel U Coll Medicine Dept Pharmacology/Physiol 245 N 15th St Mail Stop 488 Philadelphia PA 19102 Home: 2401 Pennsylvania Ave 11B24 Philadelphia PA 19130 Office Phone: 215-880-0663. Business E-Mail: john.harvey@drexelmed.edu.

HARVEY, JOHN COLLINS, internist, educator; b. Youngstown, Ohio, Sept. 11, 1923; s. J. Paul and Mary J. (Collins) H.; m. Adele Dillon, Nov. 26, 1949 (dec. Feb. 23, 2010); children: Elizabeth V.R. (Mrs. Charles Yon), John Collins Jr., William Charles II, Amy L.R. (Mrs. L. F. Reese), Margaret J.B. (Mrs. Gregory Granitto). Grad., Phillips Exeter Acad., 1941; BS, Yale U., 1944; MD, Johns Hopkins U., 1947; DSc (hon.), Barry U., 1952; MLA, Johns Hopkins U., 1968; MAS, Johns Hopkins, 1974; MA, St. Mary's U., 1975, PhD in Theology, 1988. Diplomate Am. Bd. Internal Medicine, 1952. Successively house officer, asst. resident, resident Osler Med. Service, Johns Hopkins Hosp., 1947-53, physician, 1953-73; successively instr., asst. prof., asso. prof., prof. medicine Johns Hopkins, 1953-73; prof. medicine Georgetown U., Washington, 1973-89, prof. medicine emeritus, 1989—; sr. rsch. scholar Kennedy Inst. of Ethics, Georgetown U., Washington, 1989—, Ctr. for Clin. Bioethics, Georgetown Med. Ctr., 1993—. Vis. prof. medicine U. Ibadan, Nigeria, 1964; hon. assoc. prof. medicine Guy's Hosp., London, 1973 Co-editor: Catholic Perspectives on Medical Morals, Catholic Studies in Bioethics; Contbr. articles to profl. publs. Mem. various local, state and nat. govt. med. adv. coms.; trustee emeritus Washington Home for Incurables; mem. emeritus med. adv. com. Sacred Congregation for Causes of Saints, Holy See, Vatican City. Col. (ret.) M.C., USAR. A. Blaine Brower Traveling fellow ACP to Guy's Hosp. London, 1956; sr. scholar Kennedy Inst. Ethics, Georgetown U., 1973-89. Fellow ACP (master); mem. AAAS, AMA, Am. Clin. and Climatol. Assn., Biophys. Soc., Johns Hopkins Soc. Scholars, Tudor and Stuart Club (Balt.), Cosmos Club, Knights of St. Gregory, Knights of Malta, Phi Beta Kappa, Sigma Xi, Alpha Omega Alpha. Republican. Roman Catholic. Home: 8300 Burdette Rd Foxhill Apt 469 Bethesda MD 20817 Office Phone: 202-687-1160. Office Fax: 202-687-8955. Personal E-mail: jcviola@aol.com. Business E-Mail: harveyjc@georgetown.edu.

HARVEY, JOHN FRANCIS, geneticist, director; b. Birkenhead, Wirral, Eng., Mar. 19, 1949; s. Reginald and Kathleen Harvey; m. Hilary June Gibbs, May 1, 1976; children: Clare Alexandra, Faye Victoria Halls, Richard Anthony. BSc in Applied Biology with honors, Liverpool Poly. U., 1979; PhD in Bacterial Steroid Degredation, Liverpool Poly. U./CAMR, 1983. Supr. Glaxo Ops. Eng., Liverpool, 1975—79; rsch. scientist Ctr. for Applied Microbiology and Porton Down, Salisbury, Wilts, England, 1983—84; rschr. dept. molecular genetic Wessex Regional Cytogenetics Lab., Salisbury, 1984—89; dir. molecular genetics, co-dir. ngrl Wessex Regional Genetics Lab., Salisbury Dist. Hosp., 1990—. Co-inaugurator CMGS, 1998; nat. assessor for molecular genetics Royal Coll. Pathology, London, 1993—; insp. molecular diagnostic labs. Clin. Pathology Accreditation, 1999—2005; co-dir. nat. genetics ref. lab. Wessex Regional Genetics Lab. SDH, 2002—; internat. spkr. in field; chmn. Tng. Accreditation Bd. UK Clin. Scientists, 1988—92; inaugurator SCOBEC, 2003. Contbr. articles to profl. jours. Fellow: Royal Coll. Pathology; mem.: Brit. Soc. Human Genetics. Avocations: travel, squash, singing. Office: Wessex Regional Genetics Lab SDH Odstock Salisbury SP2 8BJ England Home: 136 Winterslow Road SP4 0JX Salisbury England Home Fax: 01722 338095. Business E-Mail: john.f.harvey@salisbury.nhs.uk.

HARVEY, LEWIS O., JR., psychology professor, department chairman; BA, Williams Coll., Williamstown, Mass., 1964; MS, Pa. State U., 1966, PhD, 1968. Post-doctoral fellow, rsch assoc. Mass. Inst. Tech., Cambridge; sci. co-worker Inst. Perception, Soesterberg, Netherlands; faculty mem. Mass. Coll. Optometry, U. Colo., Boulder, 1974—, prof. psychology, chmn., dept. psychology, faculty fellow, inst. cognitive sci., affiliated faculty, ctr. neuroscience. Guest prof. Ludwig-Maximilian U. Inst. Med. Psychology, Munich, Albert-Ludwigs U., Freiburg im Breisgau, Germany, U. Nijmegen Inst. Cognition and info., Netherlands. Office: Dept Psychology and Neuroscience Univ Colo 345 UCB Boulder CO 80309-0345 Office Phone: 303-492-4420. Office Fax: 303-492-2967. Business E-Mail: lharvet@psych.colorado.edu.

HARVEY, PETER WILLIAM, healthcare educator; b. Adelaide, South Australia, Apr. 4, 1953; BEd, UNISA, 1978; PhD, UWA, 2001. Assoc. prof. Flinders U., 2007—. Mgr. Statewide Gambling Therapy Svc., 2007. Mem.: Flinders U. Ctr. Gambling Rsch. Office: Flinders Dr Bedford Park South Australia 5042 Australia Office Fax: 61 8 84842101.

HARVEY, RALPH CLAYTON, anesthesiologist; b. Knoxville, Tenn., July 12, 1952; DVM, U. Tenn., 1981, MS, U. NC, Chapel Hill, 1981. Anesthesiologist U. Tenn. Coll. Vet. Medicine, 1985—, faculty senate, 2001—04. Mem.: Tenn. Vet. Med. Assn. (Outstanding Faculty Mem. award), AVMA, Am. Coll. Vet. Anesthesiologists (exec. sec. 1991—94, mem. exec. bd. 1998—2002). Avocations: running, scuba diving, kayaking. Office: University Tenn Coll Veterinary Medicine C247 Veterinary Med Ctr Knoxville TN 37996 Office Fax: 865-974-5554. E-mail: harvey_ralph@yahoo.com.

HARVEY, WILLIAM M., psychologist, director; BA, Tougaloo Coll., Miss., 1954; PhD, Wash. U., St. Louis, 1966. Chief, clin. psychology unit St. Louis State Hosp., 1964—69; founder and exec. dir. Narcotics Svc. Coun., St. Louis, 1969—95; project dir. Multicultural Resource Ctr. - Nat. Inst. Drug Abuse, LA, 1975—79; adj. prof. sociology Wash. U., 1977—86; exec. editor, assoc. pub. Miss. Enterprise Newspaper, Jackson, 1977—88; sr. rsch. scientist Mo. Inst. Mental Health, U. Mo., St. Louis, 1994—2004; dir. Tanzanian Royalty Exploration Co., Sharon, Conn., 2003—. Mem. Nat. Adv. Coun., Nat. Inst. Drug Abuse, Washington, 1976—80, Presdl. Commn. Mental Health, Washington, 1977—78; pres. Nat. Coordinating Coun. Drug Edn., Washington, 1977—79; cons. Office Juvenile Justice and Delinquency Prevention, Dept Justice, Washington, 1986—90, Ctr. Substance Abuse Prevention, Dept Health and Human Svc., Rockville, Md., Nat. Inst. Alcoholism and Alcohol Abuse, Rockville, 1988—94, Am. Inst. Rsch., Washington, 1989—95. Sci. adv. bd. mem. D.A.R.E. Aemrica, Washington, 1992—2000. Mem.: APA. Office: Tanzania Royalty Exploration 99 Amenia Union Rd Sharon CT 06069 Office Fax: 860-364-0673; Home Fax: 860-364-2014. Business E-Mail: wh108@usa.net.

HARWOOD, VIRGINIA ANN, retired nursing educator; b. Lawrenceville, Ohio, Nov. 5, 1925; d. Warren Leslie and Ruth Ann (Wilson) H.; m. Kenneth Dale Juillerat, Dec. 21, 1946 (div. 1972); children: Rozanne Augsburger, Vicki Anderson, Carol Mann, Karen Albaugh. RN, City Hosp. Sch. Nursing, Springfield, Ohio, 1946; BSN, Ind. U., 1968; MS in Edn., Purdue U., 1973, PhD, 1982. Cert. psychiat./mental health nurse, ANA. Staff nurse various hosps., 1946-60; pub. health nursing supr. Whitley County Health Dept., Columbia City, Ind., 1960-65; nursing supr., coordinator staff devel. Ft. Wayne (Ind.) State Hosp., 1965-69; faculty sch. nursing Parkview Hosp., Ft. Wayne, 1969-74; faculty dept. nursing Ball State U., Muncie, Ind., 1974-77; dir. nursing program Thomas More Coll., Ft. Mitchell, Ky., 1977-79; faculty sch. nursing Purdue U., West Lafayette, Ind., 1979-80; dean sch. nursing Ashland (Ohio) Coll., 1980-83; retired, 1983-86; charge nurse admission psychiat. unit VA Med. Ctr., Marion, Ind., 1986-93, ret., 1994—. Active Rep. Nat. Com., 1978—, U.S. Senatorial Club, 1984—; ch. coun. Grace Luth. Ch., Gas City, Ind., 1993-96; bd. dirs. Luth. Ctr., Ball State U., Muncie, Ind., 1994-96; bd. mgrs. Covington Creek Condominium Assn., 1997-2001; vol. Foellinger-Freeman Bot. Conservatory, 1993—. With Cadet Nurse Corps, 1944—46. Mem. Am. Nurses Found., Ohio State Nurses Assn. (pres. Mohican dist. 1981-83), Mensa, Intertel, Sigma Theta Tau, U.S. Amateur Ballroom Dancing Assn. (bd. dirs. Ft. Wayne chpt. 1998-2001, v.p. 2000, pres. 2001. Avocations: travel, reading, dance, orchid culture. Home: 2815 W Old Trail Rd Columbia City IN 46725 Personal E-mail: kalbaugh@maplenet.net.

HAR ZION, GILAD, orthodontist, educator; b. Safed, Israel, Dec. 27, 1968; s. Hedva Har Zion and Moti Semo (Stepfather); m. Ziva Lurie; children: Ronili, Yael, Roi. BSc in Medicine, Hebrew U., Jerusalem, 1990, DMD, 1992; MSc, Hebrew U. Sch. Dental Medicine Hadassah, Jerusalem, 2000. Cert. specialist in orthodontics Israel Dental Assn., 2001. Tchr. orthdontics Hebrew U., Faculty Dental Medicine, 2000—. Maj. MC Israeli Army, 1992—. Mem.: Am. Assn. Orthodontists, World Fedn. Orthodontists, European Orthodontic Soc., Israeli Orthodontic Soc. Home: Carmel Mevaseret Zion 90805 Israel Office: Alfasi 19 Jerusalem 92302 Israel Office Phone: 972-77-5561065. Office Fax: 972-2-5663222. Business E-Mail: gilad9@012.net.il.

HASAN, AHMED ABUL KASHEM, cardiologist, physician scientist; b. Faridpur, Bangladesh, Jan. 7, 1955; s. Adeluddin Ahmed and Hamida Begum Hasan; m. Tahmina Ferdaus Hasan, Mar. 2, 1984; children: Jishan Adel, Joshua Adel. HSC, Dhaka Coll., Bangladesh, 1973; MD Diploma with Honors, Moscow 2nd Med. Inst., 1980; PhD in Internal Medicine, Cardiology, Acad. Med. Scis., Moscow, 1986. splst.-cardiologist, Moscow, 1986; gen. practitioner internal medicine, Moscow, 1980; cardiologist, gen. med. practitioner Bangladesh Med. Coun., 1981. House physician Hosp. Inst. Internal Medicine Acad. Med. Scis., Moscow, 1980-82, staff cardiologist, fellow Hosp. Inst. Clin. Cardiology, 1982-86; cardiology cons. Dhaka, Bangladesh, 1986-87; postdoct., rsch. assoc. dept. biochemistry and thrombosis rsch. Temple U., Phila., 1987-91; rsch. asst., prof. dept. med. biochemistry Temple U. Sch. Medicine, Phila., 1991; rsch. investigator dept. internal medicine U. Mich. Med. Ctr., Ann Arbor, 1991-96, asst. rsch. scientist, asst. prof. dept. internal medicine, 1996—2002; founder, v.p., dir. rsch. Thromgen, Inc., Ann Arbor, 1995—2002; med. officer Nat. Heart, Lung and Blood Inst., NIH, Bethesda, Md., 2002—, program adminstr., 2002—06, program dir., med. advisor divsn. cardiovasc. diseases, 2006—; acting depy. br. chief Atherothrombosis & Coronary Artery Disease Br., 2007—. Spkr. in field. Contbr. numerous articles to sci. and med. jours., chpts. to books including Jour. Biol. Chemistry, Procs. NAS, Blood, Thrombosis & Haemostasis, Am. Jour. Physiology, Biochemistry, Circulation; reviewer Am. Inst. Biol. Scis., Am. Nat. Acad. Scis., Am. Jour. Physiology, Jour. Am. Med. Assn. Recipient Outstanding Svc. Merit award, NIH, 2005, Merit award, 2006, Dir. Honor award, 2006, Excellence in Rsch. & Adminstrn. Merit award, 2011. Fellow Am. Coll. Cardiology; mem. AHA (coun. on clin. cardiology 1986, coun. on Arteriosclerosis Thrombosis and Vascular Biology 1990), AAAS. Achievements include five us patents in fields cardiovascular medicine. Office: NHLBI/NIH 6701 Rockledge Dr RKL II Bethesda MD 20892 Home: 18318 Buccaneer Ter Leesburg VA 20176-8474 Office Phone: 301-435-0064. Personal E-mail: josh0323@verizon.net. Business E-Mail: hasana@nhlbi.nih.gov.

HASAN, AISHA NASREEN, medical educator; b. New Delhi, Oct. 1, 1970; MBBS, Topiwala Nat. Med. Coll., 1996. Asst. prof. Meml. Sloan-Kettering Cancer Ctr., 2010—. Adj. asst. prof. Weill Cornell Med. Coll., 2010. Nominee Young Investigator award, Am. Soc. Hematology; Pediat. Hematology-Oncology fellowship, Weill Cornell Med. Coll., MSKCC, 2007. Mem.: Am. Soc. Bone Marrow Transplantation. Achievements include research in study of T-cell biology to develop techniques for broader application of targeted adoptive immunotherapies for treatment of cancer and lethal viral infections. Avocation: running. Office: Memorial Sloan-Kettering Cancer Ctr New York NY 10065 Office Fax: 212-717-3239. Business E-Mail: hasana@mskcc.org.

HASAN, MURAD, epidemiologist; b. Dhaka, Bangladesh, Dec. 9, 1963; came to U.S., 1993; s. Zia and Reba Hasan; m. Runa R. Hasan, July 21, 1993; 1 child, Lamisa. MB BS, Dhaka Med. Coll., 1991; MS in Epidemiology, U. Tex. Sch. Pub. Health, Houston, 1997, postgrad., 1998—. Resident Dhaka Med. Coll. Hosp., 1991-92; med. officer Miami and Sundarban Garments, Dhaka, 1992-93; data mgr. Sch. Pub. Health U. Tex., Houston, 1993-94, rsch. asst., 1994-97, data and clin. tng. mgr., 1997—. Cons. WHO, Dhaka, 1999; mem. internat. adv. com. Nat. Inst. for Rsch. in Sex Edn., Counseling, and Therapy, Mumbai, India, 1997—. Recipient Excellence award Cardiff Software, 1998. Mem. Am. Assn. Pub. Health. Avocations: the internet, computer graphics, database management, homepage building, visual basic.

HASAN, SAIYID AKBAR, ophthalmologist, consultant; b. Lucknow, India, July 18, 1970; BA, U. Ky., 1991, MD, 1995. Asst. prof. ophthalmology Mayo Clinic, 2002—11, cons., 2002—. Mem.: Fla. Soc. Ophthalmology (named Outstanding Young Ophthalmologist), Am. Acad. Ophthalmology (Achievement award), Am. Soc. Cataract and Refractive Surgeons. Avocations: tennis, basketball, reading. Home: 504 Honey Locust Ln Ponte Vedra Beach FL 32082 Personal E-mail: jaxcornea@yahoo.com.

HASAN, SANAH, medical educator, researcher; b. Palestine, Nov. 5, 1967; BSc in Pharmacy, Kans. U., 1994, PharmD, 2002; PhD in Pharmacy, Monash U., 2011. Lic. in pharmacy Kans. State Bd. Pharmacy, 1994. Staff pharmacist Hays Med. Ctr., Kans., 1994—98, pharmacy clin. coord., 1998—2000; clin. pharmacy lectr. Dubai Pharmacy Coll., United Arab Emirates, 2003; clin. pharmacy lectr., instr. Gateway Inst., Dubai, United Arab Emirates, 2004—05; rschr., clin. pharmacy, lectr. Sharjah U. Coll. Pharmacy, 2005—. Cons. Sharjah U. Med. Coll. Sharjah Tchg. Hosp., 2005—10; pharmacy practice rsch. collaborator United Arab U. Al-Ain, United Arab Emirates, 2009—11, Am. U. Sharjah, United Arab Emirates, 2010—11. Recipient Quest Recognition award, Hays Med. Ctr. Patient Care Team, 1998; grant, Sharjah U. Coll. Grad. Studies and Rsch., 2006—09. Mem.: Women and Mental Health Rsch. Group Coll. Health Scis. (Sarjah), Pharm. and Clin. Scis. Rsch. Group Coll. Pharmacy (Sharjah), Am. U. Sharjah Women's Assn., Am. Pharmacists Assn., Rho Chi Honor Soc. Avocations: exercise, swimming, walking, aerobics, reading. Office: Sharjah University Coll Pharmacy Sharjah 266666 United Arab Emirates Office Fax: 97165585812. Business E-Mail: shasan@sharjah.ac.ae.

HASAN, SYED HAMIDDUDDIN, medical researcher, consultant; b. Hyderabad, India, Nov. 2, 1935; arrived in U.S., 1995; s. Syed Samiullah and Zohra Khatoon; m. Amina H. Rasul, Oct. 15, 1960; children: Roomana, Afzia, Humaira, Syed Fareed. BSc Chemistry,

Botany and Zoology, Osmania U., Hyderabad, 1956; PhD Pharmacology, Bristol U., Eng., 1968. Lectr. Bristol U., 1966—68, U. Ibadan, Nigeria, 1968—69; sr. rsch. assoc. Schering AG, Berlin, 1969—95. Vis. scientist Worcester Found., Mass., 1969—70, Cornell U., NYC, 1973, Ohio State U., Columbus, 1974, U. Man., Winnipeg, Canada, 1976; cons. UN devel. programme U. Karachi, Pakistan, 1983; cons. Ohio State U., Columbus, 1984—95. Contbr. articles to profl. jours. Mem.: Pharmacol. Soc. Pakistan, Am. Chem. Soc., Am. Endocrine Soc., Brit. Endocrine Soc., German Endocrine Soc. Achievements include patents pending for antiprogestinins; research in pharmacological studies and effects of progesterone-antagonists, clinical and pharmacological properites of cyproterone acetate. Avocations: gardening, photography, reading, travel, cooking. Home: 1671 Orchard Ln Northfield IL 60093

HASAN, SYED MISBAHUL, medical educator; b. Nagpur, Maharashtra, Feb. 22, 1969; PhD in Pharm. Chemistry, Faculty Pharmacy, Jamia Hamdard, New Delhi, 1999. Asst. prof., coord. dept. pharm. chemistry Coll. Pharmacy, Jouf U., 1999—. Tchr., rschr. Jamia Hamdard U., 1999. Jr. Rsch. fellow, All India Coun. Tech. Edn., New Delhi, U. Grants Commn., New Delhi. Avocations: reading, sports. Home: PO Box 2994 Sakaka Al-Jouf 42421 Saudi Arabia Personal E-mail: misbahhasan@yahoo.com.

HASAN, WALEED ALI, urologist, consultant; s. Ali Hasan; m. Susan Hasan, July 1, 1999; 1 child, Lydia Iman. Diploma in Laparoscopic Surgery, European Inst. Telesurgery, Strassbourg, France, 2002. Cert. urologist Bd. Urology, Saudi Arabia, 2001. Cons. urologist SMC, Manama, Bahrain, 2003—, NHS Hosp., London, 2005. Contbr. articles to internat. med. jours. Mem. Bahrain Cancer Soc., Manama, 2008. Fellow: RCS (Edinburgh) (lectr. surgery 2008), European Bd. Urology (Netherlands). Achievements include research in hydrojet assissted surgery. Office: Salmaniya Med Complex Po Box 12 Manama Bahrain Office Fax: 973 17828269. Personal E-mail: mrwaleedali@hotmail.com.

HASE, MAMORU, medical educator; b. Hokkaido, Japan, Feb. 11, 1965; MD, Sapporo Med. U. Sch. Medicine, 1990, PhD, 2005. Asst. prof., dept. traumatology and critical care medicine Sch. Medicine, Sapporo Med. U., 2006—. Fellow: Japanese Coll. Cardiology. Avocation: hockey. Office: South 1 West 16 Chuo-ku Sapporo Hokkaido 060-8543 Japan Office Fax: 81-11-611-4963. Business E-Mail: hase@sapmed.ac.jp.

HASEGAWA, KAZUHIRO, physician; b. Utsunomiya, Tochigi, Japan, Sept. 5, 1962; s. Kusuo and Itsuko Hasegawa; m. Emi Saito, Feb. 11, 1989; 1 child, Rei. MD, Niigata U. Sch. Medicine, 1987, PhD, 1992—96, Ind. U., 1996. Cert. Ministry of Health and Welfare, Japan, 1987. Resident in orthopedic surgery Niigata U. Sch. Medicine and Affil. Hosps., 1987—92; rsch. fellow dept. anatomy and biomechs. rsch. ctr. Ind. U., 1992—94; clin. fellow in orthopaedic surgery Niigata U. Sch Medicine, 1994—97; lectr., dir. dept. orthopaedic surgery Niigata U. Sch. Medicine, Niigata City, Japan, 2002—. Dir., spine surgery sect. Niigata U. Hosp., Niigata City, Japan, 1999—2005. Coord., scoliosis exam. for children Niigata Edn. Office, Niigata City, Japan, 1999—2003. Scholar, Niigata Med. Assn., 1998. Mem.: N.Am. Spine Soc. (corr.). Office: Niigata Spine Surgery Ctr Kameda Daiichi Hosp 2-5-22 Nishimachi Niigata City Niigata 950-0165 Japan Office Fax: +81-25-382-7311. Personal E-mail: kazu3795jp@yahoo.co.jp.

HASEGAWA, NAKABA, physician, director; b. Kariya, Japan, Aug. 18, 1962; s. Kou and Kimiko Hasegawa; m. Kaori Hasegawa, May 3, 1991; children: Aya, Nozomi, Megumi. MD, Nagoya U., 1989, PhD, 1999. Resident Kariya (Japan) Gen. Hosp., 1989—94; clin. fellow Nagoya (Japan) U., 1994—97; asst. dir. Tosei Gen. Hosp., Seto, Japan, 1997—. Office: Tosei General Hosp 160 Nishioiwake Aichi Seto 489-8642 Japan Office Fax: 81-561-82-9139. Business E-Mail: public@tosei.or.jp.

HASEGAWA, NOBORU, medical educator, medical researcher; b. Nagoya, Japan, Feb. 14, 1956; s. Hitoshi and Kinue Hasegawa; m. Keiko Hara, Feb. 24, 1985; children: Masaki, Chiaki. BA, Tokyo Coll. of Pharmacy, 1980; MS, Nagoya City U., 1982; PhD, Fujita Health U., Aichi, 1990. Cert. pharmaceutist Japan, 1980. Asst. Fujita Health U., Toyoake, Japan, 1982—89; asst. prof. Nagoya Bunri Coll., Japan, 1990—, assoc. prof., 1993—2001, prof., 2002, Nagoya Bunri U., Inazawa, Japan, 2003—04, Gifu Women's U., Japan, 2005—. Councilor Japan Soc. Home Econs., Tokyo, 2002—03. Grantee Elizabeth Arnold Fuji Found., 2003. Mem.: Japanese Biochem. Soc., Japanese Pharmacological Soc., Physiol. Soc. Japan, Pharm. Soc. Japan. Office: Gifu Womens Univ 80 Taromaru Gifu 501 2592 Japan Office Phone: 81-58-229-2211. Business E-Mail: hsgwn@ishikawa-nu.ac.jp.

HASELTINE, FLORENCE PAT, federal agency administrator, gynecologist, obstetrician; b. Phila., Aug. 17, 1942; d. William R. and Jean Adele Haseltine; m. Frederick Cahn, Mar. 12, 1964 (div. 1969); m. Alan Chodos, Apr. 18, 1970; children: Anna, Elizabeth. BA in Biophysics, U. Calif., Berkeley, 1964; PhD in Biophysics, MIT, 1969; MD, Albert Einstein Coll. Medicine, NYC, 1972. Diplomate Am. Bd. Ob-Gyn., Am. Bd. Reproductive Endocrinology. Intern U. Pa.; resident Brigham & Women's Hosp., Boston; asst. prof. dept. ob-gyn. & pediat. Yale U., New Haven, 1976—82, assoc. prof., 1982—85; dir. Ctr. Population Rsch., Nat. Inst. Child Health & Human Devel. NIH, Bethesda, Md., 1985—. Founder Haseltine System, Inc., Alexandria, Va., 1995; founding sr. editor Jour. Women's Health. Co-author: Woman Doctor, 1976, Magnetic Resonance of the Reproductive System, 1987; contbr. articles to profl. jours. Bd. dirs. Older Women's League, 1998—, Am. Women in Sci., 1998—. Fellow: AAAS; mem.: Soc. Cell Biology, Soc. Women's Health Rsch. (founder 1990, bd. dirs.), Soc. Gynecol. Investigation, Inst. Medicine. Office: NICHD Ctr Population Rsch 6100 Exec Blvd Rm 8B07D MSC 7510 Bethesda MD 20892-7510 Office Phone: 301-496-1101. Office Fax: 301-496-0962. Business E-Mail: florence.haseltine@nih.gov. *

HASH, MICHAEL M., federal agency administrator; BA in Polit. Sci., Washington & Lee U., Lexington, Va. Staff mem. American Hosp. Assn., 1973—80, dep. dir. Washington office, 1980—85; prin. Health Policy Alternatives, Inc., Washington, 1985—98, 2001—08; dep. adminstr. Health Care Financing Adminstrn., 1998—2000; sr. advisor Office Health Reform, US Dept. Health & Human Services, 2009—11, dir. Office Health Reform, 2011—. Sr. staff assoc. US House Subcom. Health & Environment, 1990—95. Vol. bd. dirs. Providence Hosp., Washington, chmn. bd., 2008—09. Served as capt. US Army. Mem.: Nat. Acad. Social Ins. Democrat. Mailing: US Dept Health & Human Services (HHS) 200 Independence Ave SW Washington DC 20201 *

HASHIKURA, YASUHIKO, medical association administrator; b. Azumino, Japan, Sept. 6, 1957; MD, Tokyo Med. Coll., 1983; PhD, Shinshu U., 1995. Asst. prof. Shinshu U. Sch. Medicine, 2003—04; prof., divsn. organ transplantation Shinshu U. Hosp., 2004—05, dir., Transplantation Ctr., 2005—08; dep. dir. Nagano Prefectural Hosp. Orgn. Hdqs. Ctr. Med. Edn., 2010—. Mem.: Internat. Liver Transplantation Soc. (Rising Star award), Transplantation Soc. Avocation: mountain climbing. Office: Suzaka 1332 Suzaka Nagano 382-0091 Japan Office Fax: 81-26-246-5559. Personal E-mail: ykmyh@live.jp.

HASHIM, SABET W., cardiothoracic surgeon, educator; MD, St. Joseph's U., 1975. Diplomate Am. Bd. Thoracic Surgery. Intern St Luke's Hosp. Ctr., 1976, resident in gen. surgery, 1979; instr. sch. medicine Columbia Univ., NY, 1979; resident in cardiothoracic surgery Yale-New Haven Hosp., Conn., 1981; assoc. prof. cardiac surgery sect. Yale Med. Group, dir. cardiac valve surgery, clin. chief cadiac surgery sect.; cardiothoracic surgeon Yale-New Haven Hosp. Named one of Top Doctors, NY Mag., 2010. Fellow: ACS; mem.: Soc. of Thoracic Surgeons. Office: Yale-New Haven Hospital 800 Howard Ave New Haven CT 06519 Office Phone: 203-785-6214. Office Fax: 203-785-7288.

HASHIM, YUMI ZUHANIS HAS-YUN, medical researcher, educator; b. Kangar, Perlis, Malaysia, July 15, 1977; d. Hashim Mohamad and Ampuan Hamzah; m. Mohamad Zainuddin Hussien, Nov. 16, 2000; children: Muhammad Hakim Has-Yun Zainuddin, Nur Fatihah Has-Yun Mohamad Zainuddin, Sufian Has-Yun Mohamad Zainuddin. Degree in Biomed. Scis., U. Kebangsaan, Kuala Lumpur, Malaysia, 1999; MS in Bioprocess Engring., U. Tech., Skudai, Johor, Malaysia, 2002; PhD in Nutrition and Cancer, U. Ulster, Coleraine, Northern Ireland, 2007. Rsch. officer Chem. Engring. Pilot Plant, Skudai, Malaysia, 1999—2000; lectr. Internat. Islamic U. Malaysia, Kuala Lumpur, 2000—; postdoc. rsch. fellow U. Coll. Dublin, 2007—. Adminstr. Biomed Network, Kuala Lumpur, 2008. Scholar Skim Latihan Acad. Bumiputra, Ministry High Edn., Malaysia, 2004—07. Mem.: Biochem. Soc., Soc. Chem. Industry, Inst. Biomedical Scis. Achievements include research in olive oil phenolics having anti-invasive effects on colon cells in vitro. Avocations: reading, travel. Business E-Mail: yumi.hashim@ucd.ie.

HASHIMOTO, ISAO, medical researcher; b. Tokyo, Mar. 29, 1940; MD, Hokkaido U., 1966; PhD, U. Tokyo. Dir., dept. psychophysiology Tokyo Inst. Psychiatry, 1992—2000; vis. prof. Nat. Inst. Physiol. Scis., 1997—2000, Kanazawa Inst. Tech., 2005, sr. scientist, 2000—05; sci. and tech. coord. Hokuriku Innovation Cluster Health Sci., 2008—. Grant, Japan Med. Assn. Fellow: Japan Biomagnetism and Bioelectromagnetics Soc., Japanese Soc. Clin. Neurophysiology; mem.: Soc. Neurosci. Avocations: golf, reading. Office: Ishikawaken Kioikaikan 4-8 Kojimachi Chiyoda-ku Tokyo 102-0083 Japan Office Fax: 81-3-5212-2212. Business E-Mail: ihashi@ael.kanazawa-it.ac.jp.

HASHIMOTO, KEN, dermatologist, educator; b. Niigata City, Japan, June 19, 1931; came to U.S., 1956; m. Noriko Sakai, Oct. 3, 1961; children: Naomi, Martha, Eugene, Amy. MD, Niigata U., 1955. Cert. Am. Bd. Dermatology, 1968, Dermatopathology, 1972. Asst. prof. dermatology Tufts U. Sch. Medicine, Boston, 1965-68; assoc. prof. medicine, anatomy U. Tenn., Memphis, 1968-70, prof. medicine, assoc. prof. anatomy, 1970-77, dir., dermatopathology, prof., 1975-77; prof., dir. dermatology, prof. anatomy Wright State U., Dayton, Ohio, 1977-80; chief, dermatology sect., dir. elec. microscopy lab. VA Med. Ctr., Dayton, 1977-80; dermatologist in chief Detroit Med. Ctr., 1987—; prof., chmn. dermatology Wayne State U., Detroit, 1980-99, prof. emeritus, 1999—. Mem. dermatol. drugs adv. com. FDA. Fulbright scholar, 1956-59; participant med. investigatorship career devel. program VA, 1969-77. Mem. Am. Soc. Dermatopathology (pres. 1986-87), Nat. Bd. Med. Examiners, Japanese Soc. Investigative Dermatology (hon.), Memphis Dermatological Soc. (pres. 1973-74), Soc. Investigative Dermatology (v.p. 1980-81, chmn. program com. 1985-86), Soc. Francaise de Dermatologie et de Syphilographie (corr. 1989), Japanese Assn. Dermatology (hon.). Office: Wayne State U Sch Medicine Dept Dermatology 540 E Canfield St Detroit MI 48201-1928

HASHIMOTO, NOBOU, hospital administrator; Grad., Kyoto U., 1973, grad., 1980, MD. Pres. Nat. Cardiovasc. Ctr., Japan. Co-author: (publs.) Quantitative cerebral bloodflow measurements using stable Xenon/CT: Clinical Applications, 1995, Advances in Interventional Neuroradiology and Intravascular Neurosurgery, 1996. Office: National Cardiovascular Center Office of the President 571 Fujishiro-dai Suita Osaka 565 8565 Japan Office Phone: 81668335012. *

HASHIMOTO, PAULO HITONARI, anatomist, educator, physician; b. Amagasaki, Hyogo, Japan, Mar. 23, 1930; s. Sohei and Otei (Asakura) H.; m. Maria Elizabeth Yoshiko Inoue, May 5, 1960; children: Yoneichi, Kazuko, Hideko, Muneaki, Narutoshi. MD, Osaka U., Japan, 1953, DMSc, 1960. Intern Osaka U., 1953—54, instr. Med. Sch., 1957-60, asst. prof., 1960-65, assoc. prof., 1965-74, prof. anatomy, 1974-93, hon. prof., 1993—; prof. Koshien U., Japan, 1993-98. Postdoc. fellow Harvard Med. Sch., Boston, 1963-65. Contbr. articles to profl. jours. Mem. Am. Assn. Anatomists (emeritus), Japanese Assn. Anatomists (hon.), Japanese Soc. Electron Microscopy, Japanese Soc. Microcirculation (coun.). Roman Catholic. Avocation: vocal music.

HASHIUCHI, TOMOHISA, medical researcher; b. Japan, Aug. 26, 1970; PhD, Fukuoka, 1996; MD, Nara Med. U., PhD, 2011. Rschr. Nara Med. U., 1996—2011. Office: 5-2-6 Hyakurakuen Nara 631-0024 Japan Office Phone: 81-742-43-3333. Office Fax: 81-742-46-8607. Personal E-mail: thashiuchi@aol.com.

HASHIZUME, RINTARO, medical researcher; b. Tokyo, Mar. 8, 1965; MD, St. Marianna U., 1990, PhD, 1996. Instr. St. Marianna U. Sch. Medicine, 1990—2004; postodoc. rschr. U. Tex., MD Anderson Cancer Ctr., 1997—99; asst. rschr. U. Calif., San Francisco, 2009—. Recipient 2010 Rsch. award, Childhood Brain Tumor Found., 2010—, Rsch. Encouragement award, Japanese Breast Cancer Soc., Young Investigator award. Mem.: Japanese Cancer Assn., Japanese Surg. Soc., Soc. Neuro-oncology, Am. Assn. Neurol. Surgeons, Am. Assn. Cancer Rsch. Office: 1450 3rd St HD 200 Hellen Diller San Francisco CA 94158 Business E-Mail: rintaro.hashizume@ucsf.edu.

HASHMI, ZUBAIR ALI, surgeon; b. Hyderabad, India, Sept. 4, 1978; BS, U. Ill., 1998; MD, Ross U., 2003. Surgeon cardiothoracic surgery Allegheny Gen. Hosp., 2009—11; surgeon cardiothoracic surgery transplant Duke U. Med. Ctr., 2011—. Mem.: Internat. Soc. Heart Lung Transplantation, Am. Assn. Thoracic Surgery, Cardiothoracic Surgery Network, Am. Coll. Chest Physicians, Soc. Thoracic Surgeons, Golden Key Nat. Honor Soc., Phi Kappa Phi, Phi Eta Sigma. Avocations: travel, pool, flying. Office: Duke University Med Ctr #3392 Durham NC 27710 E-mail: z_hashmi@yahoo.com.

HASKETT, ROGER F., psychiatrist, educator; b. Penzance, Eng., Nov. 24, 1944; MD, U. Melbourne, 1968. Asst. prof. psychiatry U. Tex. Med. Br., Galveston, 1979—81; asst. to assoc. prof. psychiatry U. Mich. Med. Sch., 1981—92; prof. psychiatry U. Pitts. Sch. Medicine, 1992—. Recipient President's award, Pa. Psychiat. Soc.; named Exemplary Psychiatrist, NAMI. Fellow: Am. Psychiat. Assn.; mem.: Am. Coll. Psychiatrists, Internat. Soc. Electroconvulsive Therapy and Neurostimulation, Soc. Biol. Psychiatry. Avocations: sailing, travel, gardening. Office: 3811 Ohara St Western Psychiatric I Pittsburgh PA 15213-2593 Office Fax: 412-246-5520. Business E-Mail: haskettrf@upmc.edu.

HASSAN, FRED, health products executive; b. Pakistan, Nov. 12, 1945; arrived in US, 1970; s. Syed Fida and Zeenat (Hussain) Hassan; m. Noreen Shah, Mar. 15, 1969. BS in Chem. Engring. with honors, Imperial Coll. of Sci. and Tech., 1967; MBA, Harvard U., 1972. Chem. engr., sales mgr. Dawood Corp., Lahore, Pakistan, 1967-70; sales rep. Richardson-Vicks, NYC, 1970; project mgr., corp. planning Sandoz Pharms. Corp., East Hanover, NJ, 1972-74; mgr. planning Dorsey Labs. div. Sandoz Pharms. Corp., Lincoln, Nebr., 1974-76, dir. mktg., 1975-80; CEO Sandoz Pakistan, Karachi, Pakistan, 1980-83; gen. mgr. Sandoz Pharms. Corp., East Hanover, NJ, 1984—86, COO, 1986—87, CEO, 1987-89; pres. Wyeth Ayerst Labs., St. David's, Pa., 1989-93; sr. v.p. global pharm. Am. Home Products, Madison, NJ, 1993—95, exec. v.p., 1995-97; CEO Pharmacia Corp., Peapack, NJ, 1997—2003, chmn., 2001—03; chmn., CEO Schering-Plough Corp., Kenilworth, NJ, 2003—09; chmn. Bausch & Lomb, 2010—. Bd. dirs. Avon Products, Inc., 1999—, Schering-Plough Corp., 2003—09, Time Warner, Inc., 2009—; chmn. Health Care Inst. of NJ. Named CEO of Yr. in global pharmaceutical industry, Financial Times, 1999. Mem.: Pharm. Rsch. & Mfrs. Am. (former chmn.), Alliance for Aging Rsch. (former bd. dir.). Office: Bausch & Lomb One Bausch & Lomb Pl Rochester NY 14604-2701 Office Phone: 585-338-6000. Office Fax: 585-338-6007. *

HASSAN, IBRAHIM MOHAMMED, nuclear medicine physician; b. Basrah, Iraq, July 1, 1947; arrived in New Zealand, 1995; s. Ibrahim Mohammed and Zahra Hassan; m. Faiza Abdulsahib Ali; children: Farah, Halah, Nour. B Medicine B Surgery, Mosul U., Iraq, 1970; PhD (hon.), U. Birmingham, Eng., 1982. Asst. prof. faculty medicine U. Kuwait, 1985—90, assoc. prof., 1990, U. Libya, Tripoli, 1991—95, U. Malaysia, Kuala Lumpur, 1995—96; cons. Auckland (New Zealand) Hosp., 1997—. Coord. Kuwaiti Bd. Nuc. Medicine, 1988—90; presenter more than 50 abstracts at internat. confs. Contbr. numerous articles to profl. jours. With Iraqi armed forces, 1971—72. Fellow: Australian and New Zealand Soc. Nuc. Medicine, Am. Soc. Nuc. Medicine; mem.: European Nuc. Medicine Soc. Muslim. Avocations: swimming, football, volleyball. Office: Auckland Hosp Park Rd Auckland New Zealand Home: 17 Ardee Close 2016 Auckland New Zealand Office Phone: 64 (9) 307 4949 X4210 or 24535. Fax: 64-9 274 3530. E-mail: ibrahimh47@yahoo.com.

HASSAN, KHAMIS AHMED, dental educator; b. Alexandria, Egypt, Jan. 4, 1952; s. Ahmed Mohamed Hassan and Fatehia Abbas Hamza; m. Salwa Ebaid Khier, Feb. 9, 1978; children: Islam Khamis, Marwa Khamis. BDS, Alexandria Univ., 1975, MS in Conservative Dentistry, 1979, PhD in Conservative Dentistry, 1982; postdoctoral tng. cert. in operative dentistry and dental materials, Marquette U., 1985. Clin. instr. conservative dentistry faculty dentistry Mansoura (Egypt) U., 1976—79, asst. lectr. conservative dentistry, 1979—82, asst. prof. conservative dentistry, 1982—84, assoc. prof., chmn. conservative dentistry dept., 1988—92, prof., chmn. conservative dentistry, 1997—2001, chmn. conservative dentistry dept., vice dean for postgraduate studies, 1999—2001; postdoctoral fellow dental materials dept. Marquette U. Sch. Dentistry, Milw., 1985—86, sr. postdoctoral rsch. assoc. dental materials dept., 1986—88; assoc. prof. conservative dentistry King Saud U., Coll. Dentistry, Riyadh, Saudi Arabia, 1992—94, prof. conservative dentistry, 1994—97, prof., head operative dentistry divsn., restorative dental sciences dept., 2001—. Dir. first ann. table clinics program Mansoura U., 1999—2001. Editor-in-chief: Laureate Restorative Dentistry Newsletter. Mil. dental specialist, 1976—77, Mil. Gen. Hosp., Alexandria, Egypt. Grantee Dental Rsch. Project, Shofu Dental Co., US Br., 1987; Peace fellow, U.S./Egypt, 1984—85. Fellow: Acad. Dentistry Internat.; mem.: Am. Acad. Cosmetic Dentistry, Am. Acad. Operative Dentistry, Saudi Restorative Dental Club (assoc.), Egyptian Dental Assn. (assoc.), Saudi Dental Soc. (assoc.), Internat. Assn. for Dental Rsch., Alexandria Sporting Club (life). Muslim. Achievements include research in comparison of two composite finishing and polishing systems. Avocations: swimming, soccer, camping, fishing. Office: King Saud Univ Coll Dentistry PO Box 60169 Riyadh 11545 Saudi Arabia

HASSAN, ZURIDAH, healthcare educator; b. Teluk Intan, Perak, Malaysia, May 23, 1956; BSc, U. Sains Malaysia, Penang, 1982; PhD, U. Putra Malaysia, Serdang, Selangor, 2004. Sr. microbiologist Ministry Health Malaysia, 1982—; assoc. prof. U. Tech. MARA, 2006, coord. postgrad. studies faculty health scis., 2007—. Recipient Diamond prize, U. Tech. MARA; Internat. fellowship, Ministry Sci. and Innovation Malaysia, Rsch. grant, Ministry Higher Edn. Malaysia. Avocations: gardening, reading, cooking. Office: Puncak Alam Puncak Alam Selangor 42300 Malaysia Office Fax: 603-32584599. Business E-Mail: drzuridah@salam.uitm.edu.my.

HASSELMEYER, EILEEN GRACE, medical researcher; b. Bklyn., May 23, 1924; d. Edwin Allen and Margaret Grace (Cody) H. RN, Bellevue Sch. Nursing, 1946; BS, NYU, 1954, MA, 1956, PhD, 1963. Mem. staff Pediatric Metabolic and Nutritional Rsch. Svc., NYU Children's Med. Svc., Bellevue Hosp., NYC, 1946-56, study coord., 1951-56; rsch. nursing supr. Met. Hosp., NYC, 1951; lectr. pediatric nutrition rsch. U. Tex. Sch. Nursing, 1952-53; nursing dir.

nutritional rsch. studies Children's Hosp. of John Seely Hosp. (U. Tex. Med. Br.), Galveston, 1952-53; lectr. and nursing rsch. assoc. nutritional svc. pediat. dept. Hosp. Infantile, Mexico City, 1953; nursing dir. rsch. unit Willowbrook State Sch., SI, 1953-54; commd. USPHS, 1956, advanced through grades to asst. surgeon gen.-rear adm., 1981; ret. 1989; nurse cons. Divsn. Nursing Resources, Bur. Med. Svcs., USPHS, Washington, 1956-59; prin. investigator Handling and Premature Infant Behavior project, NYU, NYC, 1961-63; sr. nurse cons. Div. Nursing, Bur. State Svcs., USPHS, Washington, 1963; spl. asst. for prematurity Office of Dir., Nat. Inst. Child Health and Human Devel., Bethesda, Md., 1963-66, acting dir. perinatal biology and infant mortality program, extramural programs, 1967-68, dir., 1969-74, asst. to dir. for perinatology, 1974-80; chief pregnancy and infancy br. Ctr. for Rsch. for Mothers and Children, 1974-79, acting chief clin. nutrition and early devel. br., 1979-80; assoc. dir. for sci. rev. Office of Dir., 1979-89; spl. asst. to dir. N.C. for Nursing Rsch., 1986-89; exec. dir. Uniform Svcs. U. Health Sci., Fed. Coll. Nursing Feasability Study Task Force, 1989-92. Annie W. Goodrich vis. prof. Yale U. Sch. Nursing, New Haven, 1968-69; asst. surgeon gen. USPHS, Dept. Health and Human Svcs., 1981-89, chmn. interagy. panel on sudden infant death syndrome, 1974-82, others. Contbr. articles to profl. jours. Recipient NICHD Recognition of Outstanding Performance, 1973, plaque for 25 yrs. dedicated svc., 1987, Chief Nurse Officer's medal USPHS, 1989; USUHS Commendable Svc. medal, 1990; USPHS Surgeon Gen.'s Cert. of Appreciation, 1990; HEW-USPHS Commendation medal, 1975; recipient Perinatal Research Soc. award, 1979; NYU Sch. Edn., Health, Nursing and Arts Professions Creative Leadership award, 1980; Achievement award Nat. Sudden Infant Death Syndrome Found., 1987, Eileen G. Hasselmeyer Disting. Sci. Achievement award Sudden Infant Death Syndrome Alliance, 1990; Outstanding Performance award NCNR, 1987, Meritorious Svc. medal HHS-USPHS, 1989; cert. appreciation NIH-NCNR, 1989; Nat. League for Nursing Commonwealth fellow, 1959-62; NIH fellow, 1962-63; Am. Nurses Found. grantee, 1962-63; State of Conn. Maternal and Infant Program grantee, 1969; Sigma Theta Tau research grantee, 1969-71; Yale U. Sch. Nursing developmental grantee, 1969; disting. alumnae award Bellevue Alumnae Assn., 1997. Mem. Pub. Health Svc. Commd. Officers Assn., Bellevue Alumnae Assn.

HASSELMO, ANN HAYES DIE, executive recruiter, psychologist, academic administrator, consultant, educator; b. Baytown, Tex., Aug. 15, 1944; d. Robert L. and Dorothy Ann (Cooke) Hayes; 1 child, Meredith Anne. BS with highest honors, Lamar U., 1966; MEd, U. Houston, 1969; PhD, Tex. A&M U., 1977. Lic. psychologist. Asst. prof. dept. psychology Lamar U., Beaumont, Tex., 1977—82, assoc. prof., dir. Psychol. Clinic, 1982—86, prof., dir. Psychol. Clinic, 1986—88, Regents prof. psychology, 1986, dir. grad. programs in psychology, 1981—86, pres. faculty senate, 1985—86; pvt. practice clin. psychology Beaumont, 1979—87; prof. Tulane U., New Orleans, 1988—92, dean Newcomb Coll., 1988—92, assoc. provost, 1991—92; pres., prof. psychology Hendrix Coll., Conway, Ark., 1992—2001, pres. emerita, 2001—; v.p., ptnr. higher edn. practice A.T. Kearney, Inc., Alexandria, Va., 2001—02; mng. dir. Acad. Search Consultation Svc., Washington, 2002—06; pres. Am. Acad. Leadership Inst., 2006—. Adminstr. adolescent residential unit Mental Health/Mental Retardation S.E. Tex., 1979-80, mem. cmty. adv. com., 1981-87; cons. in field; coordinating bd. Tex. Coll. and Univ. Sys. Internship, 1986, chair, bd. dirs. Ednl. and Instl. Ins. Adminstrs., 2000-02; bd. dirs. Nat. Merit Scholarship Corp., Acxiom Corp., Found. for Ind. Higher Edn., Air U., USAF. Contbr. articles to profl. jours. Mem. cmty. adv. com. Beaumont State Ctr. Human Devel., 1981-88; chair So. Collegiate Athletic Conf., 1996-97; participant Nat. Identification Program for Women, Am. Coun. on Edn., 1985, mem. govt. rels. commn., 1993-96, chmn., 1994-96, chmn. coun. of fellows, 1995-96, bd. dirs., 1997-2000; bd. dirs. Beaumont Civic Opera, Lamar U. Wesley Found., Tulane U. Wesley Found.; bd. govs. Isidore Newman Sch., 1991-92; trustee Robert Morris Coll., 1990-98, chmn. edn. com., 1990-94, chmn. pers. com., 1994-98, mem. exec. com., 1990-98; mem. univ. senate United Meth. Ch., 1993-01, chair commn. on instnl. rev., 1997-01; 1st v.p. Nat. Assn. Schs. & Colls. United Meth. Ch., 1996, pres. 1997-98; bd. dirs. Ouachita coun. Girl Scouts U.S., 1996-2000; mem. bd. visitors Air U., USAF, 1999—; mem. Internat. Women's Forum, 1995—, Ark. Women's Leadership Forum, 1999-02, pres. 2000-01; mem. Ark. Commn. to Streamline State Govt., 1996-98; mem. pres. commn. NCAA, 1997-01, chmn. div. III, 1999-2001, mem. exec. com. 1999-2001; chair Assoc. Coll. of the South, 1997-99; bd. dirs. Ark. Repertory Theatre, 2000-01, United Way of Faulkner County, 2000-01. Am. Coun. Edn. fellow Coll. William and Mary, 1986-87; recipient Regents Merit award, 1979, Coll. Health and Behavioral Sci. Merit award, 1982, Lamar U.; named one of Top 100 Women in Ark., Ark. Bus., 1995-99. Mem. APA, Southwestern Psychol. Assn., Family Svcs. Assn. (bd. dirs. 1988-89), Tex. Psychol. Assn. (dir. divsn. acad. psychologists 1986), S.E. Tex. Psychol. Assn. (treas. 1978-80, pres. 1983), Mental Health Assn. Jefferson County, Nat. Register Health Svc. Providers in Psychology, Nat. Assn. Ind. Colls. and Univs. (bd. dirs., vice chmn. 1995, chair 1996). Address: 1825 K St NW Ste 705 Washington DC 20006

HAST, MALCOLM HOWARD, biomedical scientist, educator; b. NYC, May 28, 1931; s. Irving William and Rose Lillian (Berlin) H.; m. Adele Krongelb, Feb. 1, 1953; children: David Jay, Howard Arthur. BA, Bklyn. Coll., 1953; postgrad., U. So. Calif., LA, 1955—57; MA, Ohio State U., Columbus, 1958; PhD (NIH fellow), Ohio State U., 1961; CBiol, FSB, Gt. Britain, 1991. Instr. U. Iowa, 1961-63; NIH spl. fellow U. Iowa Coll. Medicine, 1963-65, asst. prof., 1965-69; assoc. prof. otolaryngology-head and neck surgery Northwestern U. Feinberg Sch. Medicine, Chgo., 1969—74, prof., 1974—; dir. research otolaryngology Northwestern U. Med. Sch., Chgo., 1969-93, prof. cell and molecular biology (anatomy), 1977—2001; prof. basic and behavioral scis. Northwestern U. Dental Sch., 1989-2001; assoc. med. staff Northwestern Meml. Hosp., 1969-90, health profl., 1990-93; rsch. assoc. zoology Field Mus. Natural History, 1995—; assoc. editor Clinical Anatomy, 1995—. Mem. faculty appeals panel Northwesten U., 1974-83, chmn., 1999-2001, med. sch. appt. promotion and tenure com., 1986-91, gen. faculty benefits com., 2004—; mem. exec. com. of med. admissions com. Feinberg Sch. Medicine, 1991-2003, chmn., 1998-2003; mem. task force on new materials Am. Bd. Otolaryngology, 1969-72; dir. Ill. Soc. Med. Rsch., 1973-77; guest scientist Max Planck Inst. für Psychiatrie, 1976, Zoologisches Forchungsinstitut und Mus. A. Koenig, 1988; mem. Internat. Anat. Nomenclature Com., 1983-91; mem. screening & admissions com. Med. Scientist Tng. Program, 2002-; Brodel meml. lectr. Assn. Med. Illustrators, 1995; mem. Chgo. Clin. Ethics Programs; vis. prof. Royal Coll. Surgeons Eng., 1980-86, U. Edinburgh, 1987. Editor Annotated Translation of Vesalius' Fabrica, 1995-, elec. edit., 2003; contbr. articles to profl. jours., chpts. to books. Mem. adv. bd. Ctr. Deafness, 1977-80; bd. dirs. Cliff Dwellers Arts Found., 1979-82; trustee Wilmette Libr. Bd., 1982-83, Wilmette Bd. Health, 1999-2007; med. adv. bd. Lincoln Pk. Zool. Gardens, 1983-2008. Served with US Army, 1953-55. NATO sr. fellow in sci. Oxford U., Eng., 1978; NIH rsch. grantee, 1964-84, 95—2004, NSF rsch. grantee, 1975-77, NEH grantee, 1995-2002; recipient Gould Internat. award, 1971, Disting. Alumnus award of Honor, Bklyn. Coll., 1977, Alumnus of Yr. award, 1984; Arnott demonstrator Royal Coll. Surgeons Eng., 1985. Fellow AAAS, Linnean Soc. London, Soc. Biology, Am. Speech-Hearing Assn., Royal Soc. Medicine; mem. AMA, AAUP (chpt. pres. 1977-82), Am. Physiol. Soc. (animal care and experimentation com. 1976-82), Am. Assn. Clin. Anatomists, Chgo. Laryngol. and Otol. Soc. (coun. 1988-89), Am. Soc. Mammalogists, Anat. Soc. Gt. Britain and Ireland, Am. Assn. History Medicine, Soc. Med. History Chgo., Amnesty Internat. (coord. Chgo. Health profls. group 1986-87), Am. Assn. Anatomists, Nat. Eagle Scout Assn., Sigma Xi (chpt. pres. 1971-72), Sigma Alpha Eta. Achievements include research on neuromuscular physiology, embryology and comparative anatomy of the larynx, history of medicine. Office: 303 E Chicago Ave Chicago IL 60611-3008 Office Phone: 312-503-1595. Business E-Mail: m-hast@northwestern.edu.

HASTINGS, JOHN WOODLAND, biologist, educator; b. Salisbury, Md., Mar. 24, 1927; s. Vaughan Archelaus and Kathrine (Stevens) H.; m. Hanna Machlup, June 6, 1953; children: Jennifer, David, Laura, Karen. BA, Swarthmore Coll., 1947; MA, Princeton U., 1950, PhD, 1951; MA, Harvard U., 1966. AEC postdoctoral fellow Johns Hopkins, 1951-53; instr. to asst. prof. biol. scis. Northwestern U., 1953-57; from asst. prof. to prof. biochemistry U. Ill. at Urbana, 1957-66; prof. biology Harvard, 1966-87, Paul C. Mangelsdorf prof. natural scis., 1987—; master Pforzheimer House, 1976-96. Summer rsch. participant Oak Ridge Nat. Lab., 1958; vis. lectr. biochemistry Sheffield (Eng.) U., 1961-62; instr. physiology Marine Biol. Lab., Woods Hole, Mass., 1961-66, dir., 1962-66, dir. marine ecology, 1989-91, mem. corp., 1961, trustee, 1966-74, exec. com., 1968-74; guest prof. Rockefeller U., 1965-66, Inst. Biol. Phys. Chemistry Paris, 1972-73, U. Konstanz, Ger., 1979-80, Nat. Biology Inst., Okazaki, Japan, 1986, U. Munich, 1993; Disting. vis. scientist Calif. Inst. Tech., 2000, Jet Propulsion Lab., 2000-04; mem. panel molecular biology NSF, 1963-66, mem. adv. com. biology and medicine, 1968-71; com. postdoctoral fellowships chemistry Nat. Acad. Scis., 1965-67, com. photobiology, 1965-71, com. on phototherapy, 1971-73, com. on low frequency radiation, 1975-77; mem. Commn. Undergrad. Edn. in Biol. Scis., 1965-66; space biology com. NASA, 1966-71; biochemistry tng. com. Nat. Inst. Gen. Med. Scis., 1968-72; mem. internat. adv. bd. Marine Biol. Lab., Eilat, Israel, 1968—; faculty assoc. Calif. Inst. Tech., 2000. Contbr. profl. jours. With USN, 1944—45. Guggenheim fellow, 1965-66, NIH fellow, 1972-73, Yamada Found. fellow, Osaka, Japan, 1986, Humboldt fellow, 1993, recipient Alexander von Humboldt prize, 1979, Lifetime Achievement award, Am. Soc. Photobiology, 2003, Peter C. Farrell Sleep Medicine prize, Harvard Med. Sch., 2006. Fellow AAAS, Am. Soc. Biol. Chemists, Biophys. Soc., Soc. Am. Microbiologists, Am. Soc. Photobiology (pres. 1999-2001), Soc. Gen. Physiology (pres. 1963-65), Soc. Chemi- and Bio-luminescence (founding pres. 1994-98), Pierian Sodality(pres. 1999—2001), Johns Hopkins Soc. Scholars, mem. Nat. Acad. Scis., Am. Acad. Arts and Scis., Phi Beta Kappa (hon.) (Alpha Info chpt.). Home: 14 Concord Ave Apt #809 Cambridge MA 02138-2356 Office: 16 Divinity Ave Cambridge MA 02138-2020 Office Phone: 617-495-3714. Business E-Mail: hastings@fas.harvard.edu.

HATA, JUN-ICHI, research and development company executive, medical educator; b. Kyoto, Sept. 9, 1940; s. Makoto and Ito Hata; m. Misako Ishida, Aug. 15, 1943; children: Shigeki, Mayumi Ono. MD, Keio U., 1968, PhD, 1969. Assoc. prof. Sch. Medicine Tokai U., Kanagawa, 1975—84; dir. Nat. Children's Med. Rsch. Ctr., Tokyo, 1984—90; prof. Sch. Medicine Keio U., Tokyo, 1990—2001, Coll. Human Sci. Tokiwa U., 2008—; gen. dir. Nat. Ctr. Child Health and Devel. Rsch. Inst., Tokyo, 2001—05, pres., 2005—07, emeritus pres., 2007—. Emeritus. prof. sch. medicine Keio U., 2007—. Mem.: Internat. Acad. Pathology (corr.). Avocations: tennis, music. Home: 2 13 10 Nishigotanda Shinagawa Tokyo 141 0031 Japan Office: Nat Ctr Child Health and Dev 2 10 1 Okura Setagaya Tokyo 157 8535 Japan Office Phone: 81-29-232-2517. Office Fax: 81-3-3416-0336; Home Fax: 81-3-3491-5649. Personal E-mail: jhata99@gmail.com. Business E-Mail: jhata@nch.go.jp.

HATA, TSUYOSHI, oral surgeon, educator; b. Okayama-city, Japan, Apr. 28, 1957; s. Isamu and Yoshiko Hata; m. Yohko Fujiwara; children: Megumi, Saori. DDS, Niigata U., Japan, 1981; PhD, Kawasaki Med. Sch., Japan, 1995. Asst. prof. Kawasaki Med. Sch., 1989—. Composer: (haiku) Ginka saijiki (Ginka no kai). Office: Dept Oral Surgery Matsushima 577 Kurashiki-city Okayama 7010192 Japan Office Fax: 81 86 462 1199. Business E-Mail: dentahata@med.kawasaki-m.ac.jp.

HATA, YUTAKA, medical educator; b. Kawasaki, Feb. 15, 1957; MD, U. Tokyo, 1982, PhD, 1991. Prof. Tokyo Med. & Dental U., 1999—. Office: 1-5-45 Yushima Bunkyo-ku Tokyo 1138519 Japan Business E-Mail: infommch@tmd.ac.jp.

HATANAKA, YOSHIHIKO, pharmaceutical executive; b. Apr. 20, 1957; B in Economics, Hitotsubashi U., Japan, 1980. Joined Fujisawa Pharm. Co., Ltd., Japan, 1980, v.p. corp. planning, 2003—05, Astellas Pharma Inc., 2005—06, corp. exec., 2005—08, pres., CEO Astellas US LLC and Astellas Pharma US, Inc., 2008—09, sr. corp. exec., 2008—11, CFO, chief strategy officer, 2009—11, rep. dir., pres., CEO, 2011—. Office: Astellas Pharma Inc 2-3-11 Nihonbashi Chou-ku Tokyo 103-8411 Japan *

HATANO, SADASHI, molecular biology educator; b. Kobe, Japan, Apr. 12, 1929; s. Yoriaki and Kimiko Hatano; m. Kimie Hatano, May 27, 1958; children: Kazuko, Fumiko. BS, Osaka U., Japan, 1954, MS, 1956, DSc, 1959. Rsch. assoc. Osaka U., 1959-60, Nagoya (Japan) U., 1961-71, assoc. prof., 1971-75, prof., 1975-93, prof. emeritus, 1993—. Editor: Cell Motility, 1979, 86, Molecular Biology of Physarum, 1986. Avocations: travel, photography, music.

HATCH, DANIEL, medical association administrator; b. Ill., Sept. 13, 1952; DPM, ICPM, 1978. Pres. Foot and Ankle Ctr., 1980—. Past pres. Am. Coll. Foot and Ankle Surgeons, 2007—08. Fellow: ACFAS. Office: 1931 65th Ave Ste A Greeley CO 80634 Business E-Mail: dhatch@footandanklecolorado.com.

HATCH, DAVID A., urologist; m. Susan Paxman; children: Aaron, Chandler, Colin. BA, Brigham Young U., 1976; MD, U. Utah, 1980. Cert. Urology, 1988. Intern Oreg. Health Sciences U., Portland, 1980—81, resident in urologic surgery, 1981—86; fellow in pediatric urology Children's Meml. Hosp., Chgo., 1986—87; prof., chief pediatric urology Loyola U. Stritch Sch. Medicine. Fellow: ACS, Am. Acad. Pediat. (Urology sect.); mem.: Am. Urological Assn. (North Ctrl. sect.), Am. Soc. Transplant Surgeons, Soc. Pediatric Urology, Soc. Fetal Urology, Soc. U. Urologists, Urologic Soc. Transplantation and Vascular Surgery (pres. 1995—96), Am. Assn. Pediatric Urologists, Chgo. Urologic Soc. Office: Dept Urology Loyola U Med Ctr 2160 S First Ave Maywood IL 60153 Office Phone: 708-216-6266.

HATCH, FREDERICK TASKER, research scientist; b. Boston, Aug. 27, 1924; s. Frederick Southard and Beatrice (Tasker) H.; m. Virginia Weeks, Mar. 3, 1946; children: Daniel F., Daphne A., Deborah J., Douglas E. BA, Dartmouth Coll., 1944; MD, Harvard U., 1948; PhD, MIT, 1960. Diplomate Nat. Bd. Med. Examiners. Intern Roosevelt Hosp., NYC, 1948-49; rsch. fellow Columbia U., NYC, 1949-52; established investigator Am. Heart Assn./Mass. Gen. Hosp., Boston, 1960-65; sr. scientist, sect. leader Lawrence Livermore Nat. Lab., Calif., 1965-80, asst. assoc. dir. Calif., 1980-87, cons. Calif., 1987—2006. Mem. lipid metabolism adv. com. Nat. Heart, Lung and Blood Inst., Bethesda, Md., 1968-73. Assoc. editor Lipids Jour., 1964-73; author chpts. in books; contbr. numerous articles to profl. jours. Sec. Land Conservation Task Force, Meredith, N.H., 1989-90, chmn. Transp. Adv. Com., 1994—2008, mem. Project Advisory Com. NH DOT, 2008-. Capt., Army Nutrition Lab., Denver, USAR, 1952-55. Fellow Am. Inst. Chemists; mem. Am. Chem. Soc., Am. Soc. Biochemistry and Molecular Biology, Environ. Mutagen Soc.; fellow Arteriosclerosis, Thrombosis and Vascular Biology, Coun. of Am. Heart Assn. (exec. com. 1971-73). Lipid and lipoprotein metabolism; coronary heart disease risk factors; satellite DNA structure; mutagens and carcinogens in cooked foods; genetic toxicology of heterocyclic and aromatic amines. Home and Office: 27 Pease Rd Meredith NH 03253-5506 Personal E-mail: fhatch@metrocast.net.

HATCH, SANDRA SUE, physician, educator; MD, UTHSC, Houston, 1987. Prof. UTMB, Galveston, Tex., 1997—, endowed chair, 2007—. Office: Univ Texas Medical Br 301 University Blvd Galveston TX 77555

HATCHER, CHARLES ROSS, JR., surgeon, health facility administrator; b. Bainbridge, Ga., June 28, 1930; s. Charles Ross and Vivian Elizabeth (Miller) Hatcher; m. Phyllis Gregory Slappey, July 9, 1988; children from previous marriage: Marian Barnett Thorpe, Charles Hatcher III. BS magna cum laude, U. Ga., 1950; MD cum laude, Med. Coll. Ga., 1954. Intern Johns Hopkins Hosp., Balt., 1954-55; resident surgery Peter Bent Brigham Hosp., Boston, 1955-56, Johns Hopkins Hosp., 1958-62; prof. surgery, chief cardiothoracic surgery Emory U. Sch. Medicine, Atlanta, 1971-90, dir., CEO Emory Clinic, Atlanta, 1976-84; v.p. health affairs, dir. Woodruff Health Scis. Ctr., Emory U., 1984-96, dir. emeritus; chmn., CEO Emory HealthCare, 1995-96. Bd. dirs. Life of the South Corp., Japan Am. Soc. Contbr. Capt. US Army, 1956—58. Mem.: ACS, So. Thoracic Surg. Assn. (pres. 1984), So. Surg. Assn., Am. Cancer Soc., Soc. Thoracic Surgeons (pres. 1986—87), Am. Assn. Thoracic Surgery, Am. Surg. Assn., Am. Coll. Chest Physicians (bd. regents 1977—81, bd. govs. 1974—77), Am. Coll. Cardiology (bd. govs. 1976—80), Johns Hopkins Soc. Scholars, Gov.'s Club Tallahassee, Fla., Bainbridge Country Club, Piedmont Driving Club, Rotary Club (bd. dirs. Atlanta chpt. 1976—80), Capital City Club, Alpha Omega Alpha, Sigma Xi, Phi Beta Kappa. Methodist. Home: 1105 Lullwater Rd NE Atlanta GA 30307-1245 Office: Emory U Woodruff Health Scis Ctr 1440 Clifton Rd NE Ste 318 B Atlanta GA 30322-1013 also: 1440 Clifton Rd NE Ste 318B Atlanta GA 30322 Office Phone: 404-778-5860. Business E-Mail: charles.hatcher@emoryhealthcare.org.

HATEM, GHALEB FAYEZ, ophthalmologist, hospital administrator; b. Al-Sowieda, Syria, Dec. 24, 1947; s. Fayez S. and Hadieh Y. Hatem; m. Layla Jarmakani, Nov. 13, 1987; children: Sami, Dina, Ziena, Sara. PCB, Damascus U., Syria, 1966, MD, 1972. Diplomate Am. Bd. Ophthalmology. Vice chmn. dept. EENT Oakwood Hosp., Dearborn, Mich., 1991-95, chmn., 1997—2004. Mem. adv. com. Arab Chaldean Coun., Detroit, 1994—. Recipient Disting. Svc. award, Am. Druze Soc., 1986; named to Top Docs List, Detroit Hour mag., 2007. Fellow: Am. Soc. Retina Specialists, Arab Am. Med. Assn. (nat. pres. 2002—, Disting. Svc. award 1994, Top Docs List, Hour Mag. 2007), Am. Acad. Neurology, Am. Acad. Ophthalmology. Office: 4655 S Telegraph Rd Dearborn Heights MI 48125-1936 Office Phone: 313-295-2888.

HATFULL, GRAHAM F., microbiologist, educator; BSc in Biol. Sci., Westfield Coll., U. London; PhD in Molecular Biology, Edinburgh U., Scotland, 1981; postdoctoral studies, Yale U., Cambridge U., UK. Prof. to Eberly Family Prof. U. Pitts., 1988—, chmn. Dept. Biological Sci. Mem. editl. bd. Jour. of Bacteriology, jour. Molecular Microbiology, jour. Molecular Microbiology & Biotechnology. Grantee professorship, Howard Hughes Med. Inst., 2002—. Office: 376 Crawford Hall Univ Pitts 4249 5th Ave Pittsburgh PA 15260 Office Phone: 412-624-6975, 412-624-6976. Office Fax: 412-624-4870. E-mail: gfh+@pitt.edu.

HATOUM, HIND TELLAWI, medical educator; b. Damascus, Syria, Feb. 10, 1947; BS in Pharmacy, Pharm. Scis., Damascus U., 1970; PhD, U. Miss., 1980. Prof. pharmacy adminstrn. and pharmacy practice U. Ill. Chgo., 1981—93, adj. prof., 1994—; sr. dir. GD Searle, 1994—97; pres. Hind T. Hatoum & Co., 1997—. Mem.: Internat. Soc. Pharmacoeconomics, Phi Kappa Phi. Avocation: reading. Office: 1758 N Wilmot Ave Chicago IL 60647 E-mail: htliatoum@sbcglobal.net.

HATSOPOULOS, NICHOLAS G., biomedical researcher, educator; BA in Physics, Williams Coll., 1980; ScM in Psychology, Brown U., 1991, PhD in Cognitive Sci., 1992. Fellow Calif. Inst. Tech. Computational Neuroscience Program, Brown U. Dept. Neuroscience, asst. prof. rsch.; asst. prof. U. Chgo. Dept. Organismal Biology & Anatomy; co-founder Cyberkinetics Neurotechnology Sys. Chmn. Computational Neuroscience & Neurobiology com.; prin. investigator U. Chgo. Hatsopoulos Lab. Office: 1027 E 57th St Rm 202 Chicago

IL 60637 Office Phone: 773-702-5594, 773-702-5024. Office Fax: 773-702-0037. E-mail: nicho@uchicago.edu.

HATTA, MOCHAMMAD, biomedical researcher, educator; b. Makassar, South Sulawesi, Indonesia, Apr. 16, 1957; s. Rahmat Naziruddin and Madaniah Jakob; m. Ratnawati Saardi; children: Muhammad Reza Primaguna, Ressy Dwiyanti, Andini Febrianty, Rizki Amelia Noviyanthi, Ade Rifka Junita. MD, Hasanuddin U., Makassar, Indonesia, 1983; PhD, Toyama Med. and Pharm. U., Japan, 1992; degree, Indonesian Clin. Microbiology Collogium, 2001. Head clin. microbiology installation of Tchg. Hosp. Hasanuddin U., 1994—98, chmn. dept. microbiology Faculty Medicine, 1998—; head dept. clin. microbiology Hasanuddin Tchg. Hosp., Makassar, South Sulawesi, 1998—. Head blood transfusion, Makassar, South Sulawesi, Indonesia, 1983—87; med. coord. Foster Parents Plan Internat., Makassar, 1983—87; disting. expert blood transfusion NATO, Brussels, 1992; project leader leprosy rsch. programme NSL, Amsterdam, 1992—; project leader Japan Indonesia Leprosy Rsch., Tokyo, 1993—; rsch. project leader INCO-DC European Commn., Brussels, 1998—; Indonesia project leader KNAW, Amsterdam, 2002—; rsch. project leader Royal Netherlands Acad. Art and Sci., Amsterdam, 1995—; vis. prof. Kobe U., Japan, 2005, 08, vis. rschr. sr., 07. Contbr. exhibition Japanese Culture (Entrustmen award Toyama Gov., 1992), articles (Rsch. Publ. Program URGE award, 1996, West Pacific Allergy award, 1997, Sci. and Tech. Agy. award, 1995). Recipient Molecular genetic, Latrobe U., Merlbourne, Australia, 1994; vis. scholar, Kobe U., Japan, 2005—07; Vis. rsch. scholar, Royal Tropical Inst., Netherlands, 1993, Vis. fellowship, Imperial Coll., London, UK, 1997, Rsch. collaborative on recombinant BCG vaccine grantee, Nagasaki U., 1998. Fellow: Internat. Soc. Blood Transfusion (hon. Young rsch. fellow 1995); mem.: Internat. Epidemiology Assn. (Travelling rsch. award 1996), Internat. Soc. Devel. and Coop. Immunology. Achievements include development of molecular epidemiology tools for infectious diseases; design of clinical trials of typhoid vaccine; research in molecular biology and immunology approach for diagnostic tools of infectious diseases; Development of recombinant BCG vaccine; chemoprophylaxis of leprosy; genetic analysis of human infectious diseases; patents for Simple dipstick assay for diagnostic of typhoid fever. Home: BTN Antara B6/6 Km9 South Sulawesi Makassar 90224 Indonesia Mailing: Hasanuddin Univ Faculty Medicine Dept Med Microbiology JlPerintis Kemerdekaan Km 10 Makassar South Sulawesi Indonesia Home Phone: 62-411-5204009. Office Fax: +62-411-586971. Personal E-mail: hattaram@indosat.net.id.

HATTERY, ROBERT RALPH, radiologist, educator; b. Phoenix, Dec. 15, 1939; s. Robert Ralph and Goldie M. H.; m. D. Diane Sittler, June 18, 1961; children: Angela, Michael. BA, Ind. U., Bloomington, 1961; MD, Ind. U., Indpls., 1964; cert. in diagnostic radiology, U. Minn. Mayo Grad. Sch. Medicine, Rochester, 1971. Diplomate Am. Bd. Radiology. Intern Parkland Meml. Hosp.-Southwestern Med. Sch., Dallas, 1964-65; fellow Mayo Clinic, Rochester, Minn., 1967-70, cons., 1970-81, chmn. dept. diagnostic radiology, 1981-86; instr. radiology Mayo Med. Sch., 1973-75, asst. prof. radiology, 1975-78, assoc. prof. radiology, 1978-82, prof. radiology, 1982—. Chair Mayo Group Practice Bd., 1991-93; chmn. bd. govs Mayo Clinic, Rochester, 1994-98; trustee Mayo Found., 1992-2002; trustee Am. Bd. Radiology. Author numerous jour. articles and abstracts, book chpts. Capt. USAF, 1965-67, Willford Hall Hosp., San Antonio. Fellow Am. Coll. Radiology; mem. Radiol. Soc. N.Am. (bd. dirs. 1999—), Am. Roentgen Ray Soc., Soc. Computed Body Tomography (pres. 1982-83), Soc. Genitourinary Radiography (pres. 1986-88), Am. Bd. Radiology (exec. dir. 2002-08, sr. advisor 2008-). Office: American Bd Radiology 5441 E Williams Blvd Tucson AZ 85711 Business E-Mail: rhattery@theabr.org.

HATTORI, HIDENORI, neurologist, researcher; s. Yasunori and Fumiko Hattori. MD, Keio U., Tokyo, 1999; PhD, Keio U., 2003. Clin. fellow Keio U. Sch. Medicine, 2003—05; rsch. fellow Harvard U., Boston, 2005—08; instr. Keio U., 2008—09; chief physician Saitama City Hosp., 2009—. Grantee, Japanese Govt., 2003. Mem.: Japanese Soc. Neurology (cert. specialist). Office: Saitama City Hosp 2460 Mimuno Midoritu Saitama 336-8522 Japan Office Phone: 81-48-873-4111. Personal E-mail: hidehatt@1999.jukuin.keio.ac.jp.

HATTORI, TOSHIO, medical educator; b. Shizuoka City, Japan, July 1, 1949; MD, Kyoto U., 1974, PhD, 1981. Prof. Grad. Sch. Medicine Tohoku U., 1998—. Cons. prof. Harbin Med. U., 2004; coord. Rsch. Network AIDS TB SubSahara Pince, 2011. Recipient Heilongjiang Provincial Sci. award. Mem.: Am. Soc. Immunology, Am. Soc. Microbilogy. Avocation: swimming. Home: 1-3-5-701 Kamisugi Aoba-ku Sendai Miyagi 980-0011 Japan Home Fax: 81-22-713-0294. Personal E-mail: ps84b9@bma.biglobe.ne.jp.

HAUBEN, MANFRED, physician; b. NYC, Apr. 9, 1959; s. Richard and Zora (Soumerai) Hauben. BA in Chemistry, NYU, 1980; MD, NY Med. Coll., 1984, MPH, 1990, DTMH, 1989. Diplomate Nat. Bd. Med. Examiners, Am. Bd. Preventive Medicine, Am. Bd. Clin. Pharmacology. Resident dept. pathology Columbia Presbyn. Med. Ctr., NYC, 1985-86; resident in cmty. and preventive medicine Our Lady Med. Ctr., NYC, 1987-89, fellow clin. preventive medicine and chief resident, 1989-90; assoc. med. dir. Sterling-Winthrop, Inc., NYC, 1990-94; assoc. med. dir. safety evaluation and epidemiology Pfizer, Inc., 1994-00, med. dir., team leader safety evaluation and epidemiology, 2000-01, med. dir. med. safety evaluation, 2001—03, med. dir. risk mgmt. strategy, 2003—08; sr. dir. Risk Mgmt. Strategy, 2008—, Worldwide Safety Strategy, 2010—. Adj. clin. asst. prof. family and cmty. medicine NY Med. Coll., 1993—; clin. asst. prof. dept. medicine NYU Sch. Medicine, 2000—, adj. clin. prof. pharmacology, 2000—; assoc. prof., editl. bd. Sch. Info. Sys., Computing and Math., Brunel U. Peer reviewer, mem. editl. bd., referee, contbr. articles to profl. jours. Mem.: AMA (Physician Recognition award), Math. Assn. America, Internat. Soc. Pharmacovigilance, Am. Statis. Assn., Am. Soc. Clin. Pharmacology and Therapeutics, Drug Info. Assn., Am. Coll. Clin. Pharmacology, Internat. Soc. Pharmacoepidemiology, Am. Phys. Soc., Alpha Omega Alpha.

HAUCH, KENNETH W., otolaryngologist, educator; married; 2 children. Grad., US Military Acad., NY, 1968, George Wash. U., 1975. Diplomate Am. Bd. Otolaryngology. Cheif otolaryngology svc. Fort Hood, Tex., 1982; intern Walter Reed Army Med. Ctr., Wash., 1976, resident, 1980, asst. chief otolaryngology-head and neck surgery svc., specialty cons. to the White House, col.; chief otolaryngology Holy Cross Hosp., Silver Spring, Md., Washington Adventist Hosp., Takoma Park, Md.; clin. appointment divsn. of otolaryonglogy/head and neck oncology Nat. Inst. on Deafness and Other Communication Disorders; assoc. clin. prof. Sch. of Medicine George Wash. Univ. Adj. assoc. prof. clin. surgery Uniformed Svcs. Univ. of Health Sciences. Named one of the Top Doctors, Washingtonian Mag., 2011. Fellow: ACS, Am. Acad. of Otolaryngology — Head and Neck Surgery; mem.: Am. Acad. of Facial Plastic and Reconstructive Surgery. Office: Hauck, Bianchi & Driscoll PA Number 203 2415 Musgrove Rd Silver Spring MD 20904 Office Phone: 301-989-2300. Office Fax: 301-236-5357.

HAUCK, WILLIAM EDWARD, retired education educator; b. Pa., July 5, 1932; s. Lewis William and Margaret Alice (Freas) H. BS in Math. and Physics, U. Pitts., 1954, MEd in Edn. Psychology, 1962; PhD in Counseling & Edn. Psychology, U. Wis., Madison, 1969. Cert. tchr. in English, math., phys. scis., social studies; cert. sch. psychology, counseling, Pa.; lic. psychologist, Pa. Dir., overseas adult edn. Armed Svcs., Kassel, Fed. Republic Germany, 1954-57; tchr., math. and English Churchill Area Schs., Pitts., 1957-61; rsch. assoc. Bucknell U., Lewisburg, Pa., 1961-63; rsch. assoc., teaching asst. U. Wis., Madison, 1963-67; assoc. coord., Project SESAME-Title III Bucknell U., Lewisburg, Pa., 1967-69, from prof. edn. to prof. emeritus, 1969—95, prof. emeritus, 1995, chair dept. edn., 1989—95; psychologist Five-County Psychol. Svcs., Lewisburg, Pa., 1985—. Author: Fractions, 1966, Decimals and Percents, 1966, Review of Trigonometry, 1968; co-author: (manual) Brief Algebra Review Manual, 1967, Algebra Review Manual, 1967; reviewer Harper Collins Publishers, 1990—; contbr. numerous rsch. articles to refereed jours. With U.S. Army, 1954-56. Recipient Lindback award, Bucknell U. Mem. Am. Ednl. Rsch. Assn. (div. rsch. and instrn., div. counseling), APA (div. sch. psychology, div. counseling), Nat. Assn. Sch. Psychologists. Avocations: travel, skiing, reading. Home: 117 Oakwood Dr Winfield PA 17889 Office: 115 Farley Cir Ste 304 Lewisburg PA 17837 Office Phone: 570-523-6224, 570-522-6237. Personal E-mail: wehauck@dejazzd.com.

HAUG, CHARLOTTE J., editor, educator; Editor-in-chief Jour. Norwegian Med. Assn.; adj. assoc. Stanford Ctr. for Health Policy-Primary Care & Outcomes Rsch. Office: Postboks 1152 Sentrum 107 Oslo Norway N-0107 Office Phone: 47-2310-9045. Office Fax: 47-2310-9040. E-mail: charlotte.haug@legeforeningen.no.

HAUGAN, GERTRUDE M., clinical psychologist; b. New Richland, Minn. d. Henry Albert and Ella Pauline (Gardson) H. BA, George Washington U., 1952, MA, 1956; PhD, U. Md., 1970. Lic. psychologist, D.C., Md. Research psychologist New Eng. Med. Ctr., Boston, 1959-62; intern clin. psychology Hall Psychiat. Inst., Columbia, SC, 1968-69; fellow in pediatrics Sch. Medicine Johns Hopkins U., Balt., 1970-71; clin. psychologist adloescent program Devel. Services Ctr., Washington, 1971-72, chief children's unit, 1972-85; chief Devel Services Ctr., Washington, 1986-94. Cons. in psychology Ea. Shore State Hosp., Cambridge, Md., 1969-71, in child psychology Ctr. for Spl. Edn., Annapolis, Md., 1972-76; instr. in child psychology Montgomery Coll., Rockville, Md., 1977-78. Contbr. articles to profl. jours. Mem. APA, D.C. Psychol. Assn., Am. Assn. on Mental Retardation, Phi Beta Kappa. Home: 4720 S Chelsea Ln Bethesda MD 20814-3720 Personal E-mail: trudyhaugan@aol.com.

HAUGEN, DAVID LEE, surgeon; b. Portland, Oreg., Dec. 14, 1935; MD, U. Oreg./Health Scis. U., 1962. Diplomate Am. Bd. Surgery. Intern Santa Clara County Hosp., San Jose, Calif., 1962-63; resident U. Oreg. Hosp. - Clinics, 1965-70, Karolinska Hosp., Stockholm, 1968-69; staff Sutter Roseville Comm. Hosp., Calif., 1970—; sr. staff Mercy San Juan Hosp., Carmichael, Calif., 1970—; courtesy staff Sutter Hosp., 1970—2010. Mem. Am. Coll. Surgeons, Calif. Med. Assn. Office: 15366 De La Cruz Dr Rancho Murieta CA 95683 Office Phone: 916-965-6570. *

HAUMSCHILD, MARK JAMES, pharmacist; b. West Bend, Wis., Apr. 6, 1951; s. James Harlow and Helen Marie (Bohn) H.; m. Mary Jo Snider, Oct. 15, 1976; 1 child, Ryan James. BA in Chemistry, Fla. Atlantic U., 1973; BS in Pharmacy, U. Fla., 1976; MS in Mgmt., U. South Fla., 1982; PharmD, Mercer U., 1984. Cert. nuc. pharmacist; cert. nutritional support pharmacist; cert. geriatric pharmacist. Continuing edn. instr. St. Petersburg (Fla.) Jr. Coll., 1977-81; staff pharmacist Morton F. Plant Hosp., Clearwater, Fla., 1976-78, nuclear pharmacy coordinator, 1978-83, clin. pharmacist, 1984-86, resident, 1984-85; ctr. mgr. Foster Infusioncare, St. Petersburg, 1986-88; gen. mgr. Healthinfusion Inc., St. Petersburg, 1988-95; pres. Pharm D. Cons., Largo, Fla., 1984—; regional dir. ops.-Fla. UPC Health Network, Clearwater, Fla., 1995-98; scientific mgr. Aventis, Inc., Largo, 1998—2004; dir. Sanofi-Aventis, Inc., 2005—. Adj. instr. Coll. Pharmacy, U. Fla., Gainesville, 1980-86, 2003-. Fellow Am. Soc. Cons. Pharmacists; mem. Am. Soc. Hosp. Pharmacists, S.W. Soc. Hosp. Pharmacists, Am. Pharm. Assn. (cert. in nuclear pharmacy), Soc. Nuclear Pharmacy, Am. Coll. Hosp. Adminstrs., S.W. Fla. Soc. Hosp. Pharmacists (cert. nuclear pharmacist), Beta Gamma Sigma, Phi Kappa Phi. Republican. Avocations: golf, walking, reading, snowboarding, surfing. Home and Office: Sanfi-Aventis Inc 12494 104th Ter Seminole FL 33778-3407

HAUPT, RICHARD M., pharmaceutical executive; Grad., U. Md., 1979. Exec. dir. med. affairs Merck Div. Vaccines. Office: 126 E Lincoln Ave Rahway NJ 07065

HAUPTMAN, PAUL J., cardiologist, educator; MD, Cornell U., 1987. Diplomate Am. Bd. Internal Medicine-cardiovasc. disease, 2003. Resident internal medicine Brigham & Women's Hosp., Boston, 1992—93, fellow internal medicine, 1988—90; fellow cardiovasc. disease Mt. Sinai Hosp., NYC, 1990—92; fellow Harvard Med. Sch.; prof. medicine St. Louis Univ., asst. dean clin. and trans. rsch. Office: Saint Louis University School of Medicine 3635 Vista Ave Saint Louis MO 63110-0250

HAUPTMANN, RANDAL MARK, biotechnologist; b. Hot Springs, SD, July 6, 1956; s. Ivan Joy and Phyllis Maxine (Pierce) H.; m. Beverly Kay Suko, May 22, 1975; 1 child, Erich William. BS, SD State U., 1979; MS, U. Ill., 1982, PhD, 1984. Postdoctoral rschr. Monsanto Corp. Rsch., St. Louis, 1984-86; vis. rsch. scientist U. Fla., Gainesville, 1986-88; asst. prof. No. Ill. U., DeKalb, 1988-90, dir. plant molecular biology ctr., 1989-90; sr. rsch. scientist Amoco Life Sci. Techs., Naperville, Ill., 1990-94; dir. advanced tech. Seminis Vegetable Seeds, Woodland, Calif., 1994-98; gen. mgr. Ball Helix, West Chicago, Ill., 1998—2003; pres. Varro Inc., Chgo.; head raw product rsch. Fresh Express, Salinas, Calif. Author: (with others) Methods in Molecular Biology, 1990; contbr. articles to profl. jours. Mem. Internat. Assn. Plant Tissue Culture, Internat. Soc. Plant Molecular Biology, Am. Soc. Plant Physiologists, Tissue Culture Assn. (Virginia Evans award 1982), Sigma Xi, Gamma Sigma Delta. Democrat. Home Phone: 831-384-7388; Office Phone: 630-464-5791. Business E-Mail: randal.hauptmann@mac.com.

HAUQUITZ, ALAN CRAIG, medical educator; s. Fred and Elva Jennings Hauquitz; m. Gillian Denise Bowman, July 27, 1975; children: Astra Katherine Ciobo, Nova Elizabeth Dunworth. AS, SUNY, Morrisville, 1978; BA, SUNY, Plattsburgh, 1980; M in Health Sci., Johns Hopkins U., Balt., 1983, DSc, 1989. Health planner Md. Health Resources Planning Commn., Balt., 1982—88; rsch. assoc. Johns Hopkins U. Sch. Hygiene and Pub. Health, Balt., 1989; asst. prof., health care mgmt. Bond U. Sch. Bus., Gold Coast, Queensland, Australia, assoc. dir., health care studies, 1990—91; mgr. Queensland Health, Brisbane, Australia, 1992—96; sr. lectr. James Cook U. Sch. Pub. Health and Tropical Medicine, Townsville, Queensland, 1997—. Hosp. & provincial advisor PNG Health Svcs. Support Program Pty. Ltd., Brisbane, 2002—04; rsch. adviser PNG Nat. HIV/AIDS Support Project, Port Moresby, National Capital, Papua New Guinea, 2005, team leader, rev. of provincial hiv programs, 06; short term adviser, neglected tropical diseases WHO Pacific Regional Office, Manila, 2007, 09. Dir., internat. svc. Rotary Internat., Madang, Papua New Guinea, 2003—04. Recipient Am. Inst. Chemists award, SUNY, Plattsburgh, 1980, Nat. Rsch. Svc. award, NIH, 1983—88, Tchg. Excellence award, Bond U. Sch. Bus., 1990, Recognition award, Australian Coll. Educators, 2008. Mem.: Australian Health Economics Soc., Australasian Soc. HIV Medicine Inc., Rotary Internat. Club, Phi Theta Kappa. Avocations: reading, bicycling, travel. Office: James Cook University Anton Breinl Ctr 4811 Townsville QLD Australia Business E-Mail: alan.hauquitz@jcu.edu.au.

HAUSER, GEORGE, biochemist, educator; b. Vienna, Dec. 13, 1922; came to U.S., 1939. s. Hans Joseph and Juliane Therese (Gleissner) H.; m. Louise Jean Russo, July 2, 1955. BS, Ohio State U., 1949; PhD, Harvard U., 1955. Mem. faculty Harvard Med. Sch., Boston, 1952-55, from rsch. assoc. to prof., 1955-93, prof emeritus, 1993—; from asst. biochemist to biochemist McLean Hosp., Belmont, Mass., 1957-93, sr. biochemist, 1993—; rsch. affiliate Mass. Inst. Tech., 2000—08. Mem. editl. bd. Neurochem. Rsch; adv. and editl. bd. Jour. Neurochemistry, 1977-86, dep. chief editor, 1986-92; interim dir. Ralph Lowell Labs., McLean Hosp., Belmont, 1983-93; reviewer many sci. jours.; cons. NIH, NSF, MIT. Co-editor: Inositol & Phosphoinositides: metabolism & metabolic regulation. Mem., treas. Dem. Ward Com., Newton, Mass., 1976—. With U.S. Army, 1943-48. Recipient Austrian Cross Honor Sci. and Art, 2000; grantee Nat. Insts. Health, 1965-92, Nat. Sci. Found., 1980-82, Chevalier French Legion of Honor, 2009; fellow Japan Soc. for the Promotion of Sci., 1988. Mem. Biochem. Soc., Am. Soc. Biochemistry and Molecular Biology, Internat. Soc. Neurochemistry, Am. Soc. Neurochemistry (coun. 1983-87), Soc. Neurosci. Democrat. Jewish. Home: 47 Windermere Rd Auburndale MA 02466-2521 Office: McLean Hosp 115 Mill St Belmont MA 02478-9106 Office Phone: 617-855-2408. Business E-Mail: george_hauser@hms.harvard.edu.

HAUSER, ROBERT G., cardiologist, medical products executive; BS, U. Cin.; MD with honors, U. Cin. Coll. Med., 1968. Dir. Pacemaker Surveillance Clinic, 1987—2003; pres. & CEO Cardiac Pacemakers Inc, 1988—92; sr. cons. cardiologist Mpls. Heart Inst., 1992—; pres. cardiovascular svcs. div. Abbott Northwestern Hosp., 1995—96, 2003—04; dir. SonoSite, 2004—. Fellow: Heart Rhythm Soc. (founder & former pres.), Am. Coll. Cardiology. Office: 21919 30th Dr S E Bothell WA 98021-3904 Office Phone: 425-951-1200.

HÄUSER, WINFRIED, psychosomatic medicine; Cons. Klinikum Saarbrücken, Germany, 2000—. Grant, German Ministry Edn. and Rsch., 1999—2005, German Celiac Soc., 2004—05, German League Against Rheumatism. Master: German Interdisciplinary Assn. Pain Therapy. Office: Klinikum Saarbrücken Winterberg 1 Saarbrücken D-66119 Germany

HAUSMAN, KEITH LYNN, health facility administrator, physical therapist; b. Cleve., Nov. 20, 1949; s. Harold Herbert and Betty (Reed) H.; 1 child, Sierra Dawn. BS, Loma Linda U., 1972, MA in Pub. Health, 1975. Lic. real estate broker; cert. instrument multiengine flight instr., air transport pilot. Acting adminstr. Thomas Rehab. Hosp., Asheville, NC, 1976-77; pres. Marion County Hosp., Jefferson, Tex., 1977-81, Jellico (Tenn.) Cmty. Hosp., 1981-91; health care cons., 1991—; pres. Premier Rehab., Inc., 1994—, Premier Vending, Inc., 2000—09, Premier Vending Wholesale, Inc., 2002—07, Med. Sales & Supplies of Tenn., Inc., 2006—09. Bd. dirs. Pvt. Indsl. Coun. SDA4, Tenn., 1989-2000, Ardmore Adventist Hosp., 1977-81, Meml. Hosp., Manchester, Ky., 1981-91, Takoma Adventist Hosp., Greenville, Tenn., 1981-91. Fellow Am. Coll. Health Care Execs.; mem. Tenn. Hosp. Assn. (sec., Mid-East dist 1990, bd. dirs. 1991, pres., Mid-East dist. 1991), Campbell County C. of C. (bd. dirs. 1989-92). Republican. Seventh-Day Adventist. Home: PO Box 541 Jellico TN 37762-0541 Personal E-mail: hausmank@bellsouth.net.

HAUSMAN, STEVEN JACK, health science association administrator; b. Phila., May 20, 1945; s. Leo and Bella Hausman. BA, U. Pa., 1967, MS, 1968, PhD, 1972. Postdoctoral fellow Inst. for Cancer Rsch., Phila., 1972-75; staff fellow Nat. Inst. on Aging, Balt., 1975-77; spl. asst. to assoc. dir. Nat. Inst. Arthritis, Metabolism and Digestive Diseases, Bethesda, Md., 1977-78, dir. ctrs. program, 1978-86; dep. dir. extramural program Nat. Inst. Arthritis and Musculoskeletal and Skin Diseases, Bethesda, 1986-90, dep. dir., 1990—2007, dir. extramural program, 1997—2002; pres. Hausman-Tech Consulting, 2007—. Mem. AAAS, Am. Assn. Immunologists, Soc. In Vitro Biology, Am. Chem. Soc., Am. Soc. for Cell Biology. Office: NIAMS-NIH 31 Center Dr Msc2350 Bldg 31 Bethesda MD 20892-0001 Office Phone: 301-402-1691.

HAUSNER, LAURENCE, health science association administrator; BS in Mktg., Univ. RI, MBA in Mktg. Mgmt. Various positions including v.p. mktg., v.p. plans & ops., then chief of staff Nat.l Multiple Sclerosis Soc., 1986—2000; v.p. strategic partnerships HopeLink, Menlo Pk., Calif., 2000—03; various positions including gen. mgr. orgnl. devel., chief strategic devel. officer, then COO Leukemia & Lymphoma Soc., NY, 2003—07; CEO Am. Diabetes Assn., Alexandria, Va., 2007—. Office: Am Diabetes Assn 1701 N Beauregard St Alexandria VA 22311 *

HAVA, MILOS, retired pharmacologist, medical educator; b. Prague, Czech Republic, Oct. 15, 1927; arrived in U.S., 1968, naturalized, 1983; s. Emanuel and Eta Hava; m. Maria M. Hava, Sept. 5, 1951. MD, Charles U., Prague, 1952, PhD in Pharmacology, 1955. Cert. Ednl. Coun. for Fgn. Med. Grads., 1974. Asst. prof. pharmacology Charles U., 1952—55; sr. rsch. worker Czech Acad. Sci., 1955—58; dir. dept. pharmacology Rsch. Inst. Natural Products, Prague, 1958—68; assoc. prof. pharmacology U. Kans., Kansas City, 1968—73; prof. pharmacology U. Ill., Peoria, 1973—75; asst. med. dir. Marion Labs., Kansas City, 1975—79; dir. clin. rsch. Carter-Wallace, Cranbury, NJ, 1979—82, Wyeth, Phila., 1982—94; ret. Adj. prof. diagnostic imaging Temple U. Med. Sch., Phila., 1983—. Co-author: The Vinca Alkaloids, 1973; contbr. articles to profl. jours. Mem.: Am. Soc. Pharmacology and Exptl. Therapy. Avocations: reading, music, tennis, swimming, tai chi. Home: 126 South St Philadelphia PA 19147 Personal E-mail: havam@verizon.net.

HAVEL, RICHARD JOSEPH, physician, educator; b. Seattle, Feb. 20, 1925; s. Joseph and Anna (Fritz) Havel; m. Virginia Johnson, June 25, 1947; children: Christopher, Timothy, Peter, Julianne. BA, Reed Coll., 1946; MS, MD, U. Oreg., 1949. Intern Cornell U. Med. Coll., NYC, 1949—50, resident in medicine, 1950—53; clin. assoc. Nat. Heart Inst., NIH, 1953—54, rsch. assoc., 1954—56; faculty Sch. Medicine, U. Calif., San Francisco, 1956—, prof. medicine, 1964—; assoc. dir. Cardiovasc. Rsch. Inst., 1961—73, dir., 1973—92. Chief metabolism sect., dept. medicine Sch. Medicine, U. Calif., San Francisco, 1967—97; dir. Arteriosclerosis Specialized Ctr. Rsch., 1971—96; mem. bd. sci. counselors Nat. Heart, Lung and Blood Inst., 1976—80; chmn. food and nutrition bd. NRC, 1987—90; pres. Lipid Rsch., Inc., 1999—. Editor: Jour. Lipid Rsch., 1972—75; assoc. editor: Am. Jour. Clin. Nutrition, 1997—2007, mem. editl. bd.: Jour. Biol. Chemistry, 1981—85, Jour. Arteriosclerosis Thrombosis Vascular Biology, 1980—; contbr. chapters to books, articles to profl. jours. Established investigator Am. Heart Assn., 1956—61, chmn. coun. on arteriosclerosis, 1977—79. With USPHS, 1951—53. Recipient Disting. Achievement award, Am. Heart Assn., 1993, Bristol-Myers award for nutrition rsch., 1989, Gold medal, Charles U. Med. Faculty, Prague, Czech Republic, 1996, Commemorative Gold medal, Charles U., Prague, Czech Republic, 2007. Fellow: AAAS (Theobald Smith award 1960), Am. Inst. Nutrition; mem.: NAS, Western Soc. Clin. Investigation (Mayo Soley award 1997), Am. Soc. for Clin. Investigation, Assn. Am. Physicians, Am. Soc. Clin. Nutrition (McCollum award 1993), Am. Acad. Arts and Scis., Inst. Medicine of NAS, Alpha Omega Alpha, Phi Beta Kappa. Office: U Calif San Francisco Cardiovascular Rsch In San Francisco CA 94143-0130 Home Phone: 415-461-8583. Business E-Mail: richard.havel@ucsf.edu.

HAVHANNISYAN, VAHAN, physicist; b. Yerevan, Armenia, Dec. 19, 1983; PhD, 2009. Sci. rschr. A. I. Alikhanyan Nat. Sci. Lab., 2009—. Office: Alikhanian Brothers 2 Yerevan 0036 Armenia Business E-Mail: vahmer@rambler.ru.

HAVIGHURST, CLARK CANFIELD, law educator; b. Evanston, Ill., May 25, 1933; s. Harold Canfield and Marion Clay (Perryman) H.; m. Karen Waldron, Aug. 28, 1965; children: Craig Perryman, Marjorie Clark. BA, Princeton U., 1955, JD, Northwestern U., 1958. Bar: Ill. 1958, N.Y. 1961. Assoc. Debevoise Plimpton Lyons & Gates, NYC, 1958, 61-64; assoc. prof. law Duke U., Durham, NC, 1964-68, prof., 1968-86, William Neal Reynolds prof., 1986—2002, emeritus, 2005—; interim dean Duke U. Sch. Law, 1999. Dir. Program on Legal Issues in Health Care Duke U., 1969-88; adj. scholar Am Enterprise Inst. Pub. Policy Rsch., 1976-2005; resident cons. FTC, Washington, 1978, Epstein, Becker & Green, Washington, 1989-90; scholar in residence Inst. Medicine of NAS, Washington, 1972-73, RAND Corp., Santa Monica, 1999. Author: Deferred Compensation for Key Employees, 1964, Regulating Health Facilities Construction, 1974, Deregulating the Health Care Industry, 1982, Health Care Law and Policy, 1988, 2d edit., 1998, Health Care Choices: Private Contracts as Instruments of Health Reform, 1995; editor Law and Contemporary Problems jour., 1965-70. With U.S. Army, 1958-60. Mem. Inst. Medicine of Nat. Acad. Sci., Order of Coif Home: 1109 Fearrington Post Pittsboro NC 27312 Office: Duke U Sch Law PO Box 90360 Durham NC 27708-0360 Office Phone: 919-613-7061. Business E-Mail: hav@law.duke.edu.

HAWGOOD, SAM, dean, pediatrician, medical educator; married. MD with honors, U. Queensland. Pediat. intern Royal Children's Hosp., Brisbane, Australia; neonatal fellow Queen Victoria Hosp., Melbourne, U. Calif. San Francisco; faculty mem. U. Calif. San Francisco Sch. Medicine, 1984—, head divsn. neonatology, 1994—2006, chair dept. pediat., 2004—09, interim dean, 2007—09, dean, 2009—, vice chancellor med. affairs, 2009—; physician in chief U. Calif. San Francisco Children's Hosp., 2003—09; pres. U. Calif. San Francisco Med. Group. Sr. staff mem. U. Calif. San Francisco Cardiovascular Rsch. Inst. Office: Univeristy Calif Sch Medicine S-224 Campus Box 0410 513 Parnassus Ave San Francisco CA 94143-0410 Office Phone: 415-476-2342. Office Fax: 415-476-0689. E-mail: sam.hawgood@ucsf.edu. *

HAWK, ERNEST T., federal agency administrator; BS, MD, Wayne State U., Detroit; MPH, Johns Hopkins U., 1994. From intern to resident to sr. accoc. medicine Emory U. Sch. Medicine, Atlanta, 1985—91; fellow in med. oncology U. Calif., San Francisco, 1991—93; cancer prevention fellow Nat. Cancer Inst., NIH, 1993, various positions in Chemoprevention Br., chief Gastrointestinal and Other Cancers Rsch. Group, Divsn. Cancer Prevention, 1999—2004, dir. Office of Centers, Training and Resources, 2004—. Office: UT MD Anderson Cancer Ctr 1515 Holcombe Blvd Unit 1371 Houston TX 77030 Business E-Mail: ehawk@mdanderson.org.

HAWKE, ROBERT FRANCIS, dentist; b. Pasadena, Calif., Oct. 26, 1946; s. George Herbert and Mildred Estelle (Wood) H.; m. Emily Sue Wilkins, Aug. 17, 1973; 1 child, Kristen. BA, U. Ariz., 1969; DDS, Baylor U., Dallas, 1973. Assoc. B.J. Barber, Tucson, 1976-78; ptnr. Barber-Hawke, P.C., Tucson, 1978-87; pvt. practice Tucson, 1987—. Bd. dirs., pres. Delta Dental Ariz., Phoenix, 1985-91. Mem. Tucson Bus. Alliance, 1981—, pres., 1983, 94, Cmty. Auto Immune Deficiency Syndrome Adv. Coun., Tucson, 1987-90, Auto Immune Deficiency Syndrome Edn. Project, Tucson, 1988-90. Maj. U.S. Army. Fellow Am. Coll. Dentists, Internat. Coll. Dentists; mem. ADA (alt. del. 1988-92, del. 1994-2000, 14th dist. chmn. polit. action com. 1995-98), Ariz. State Dental Assn. (trustee 1988, v.p. 1991, pres.-elect 1992-93, pres. 1993-94, past pres. 1994-95, mem. legal liaison com. 1993-94, chmn. coun. on constitution and bylaws 1996-97, chmn. coun. on budget planning 1992-93, chmn. coun. on ins. 1998-2003, Svc. award 2002), So. Ariz. Dental Soc. (bd. dirs. 1983-89, pres. 1987-88), Pierre Fauchard Acad., Acad. Laser Dentistry, Acad. Gen. Dentistry, Tucson Advanced Cosmetic & Restorative Study Club, World Clin. Laser Inst., Give Kids a Smile Day (So. Ariz. chmn. 2003-04), Care Doctor Cerec Club Tucson, Rotary (Paul Harris fellow), Beta Beta Beta. Republican. Evangelical. Avocations: golf, jogging, tennis, racquetball, reading. Home: 6745 E Tivani Dr Tucson AZ 85715-3348 Office: 1575 N Swan Rd Ste 200 Tucson AZ 85712-4068 Office Phone: 520-323-3842. Personal E-mail: hawkerobertf@qwestoffice.net.

HAWKER, RICHARD ELKINGTON, pediatric cardiologist, consultant; b. Bathurst, New South Wales, Australia, Sept. 24, 1941; s. Bernard Hugh Elkington and Mary Isbel Hawker; m. Robyn Gwendoline Kay, Oct. 1, 1966; children: Danielle Kirsten, Kieran Richard, Lucas Kendall, Katrina Sheridan. B Medicine B Surgery with honors, U. Sydney, Australia, 1965. Cardiology registrar Royal Prince Alfred Hosp., Sydney, 1968—70; fellow pediatric cardiology Royal Alexandra Hosp. Children, Sydney, 1971; fellow cardiology Hosp. for Sick Children, Toronto, Ont., Canada, 1971—72; pediatric cardiology fellow Johns Hopkins U. Hosp., Balt., 1972—73; hon. assoc. physician Royal Prince Alfred Hosp., Sydney, NSW, 1976—; staff cardiologist Children's Hosp. at Westmead, 1974—; vis. med. officer John Hunter Children's Hosp., Newcastle, Australia, 1982—; mem. staff Sydney Children's Hosp., 2006—. Contbr. articles to med. jours. Mem. Operation Open Heart program for developing countries. Recipient Cert. Appreciation, Australian Govt., 2002. Fellow: Cardiac Soc. Australia and New Zealand, Royal Australasian Coll. Physicians (mem. pediat. written exam. com.). Office: Children's Hosp at Westmead Locked Bag 4001 NSW Westmead 2145 Australia Home: 16 Denison St Parramatta NSW 2150 Australia Office Phone: 61 2 9845 2345. Office Fax: 61 2 9845 2163. E-mail: rich@chw.edu.au.

HAWKINS, BARBARA REED, retired mental health nurse; b. Burgettstown, Pa., July 20, 1945; d. John Francis Reed and Iona Elinor Spring; m. Hal Kenneth Hawkins, Sept. 6, 1969; children: David, Heidi, Brian, Russell. BS in Nursing, Duke U., 1968; MSN, U. N.C., 1973; postgrad., Houston Montessori Ctr., 1992—95. RN N.C., 1968. Staff nurse pediatrics Duke U. Med. Ctr., 1968—69; psychiatric nurse, group co-therapist Durham County Mental Health Ctr., 1971—72; counselor Durham Crisis and Suicide Ctr., 1972—73; lectr. psychiat. nursing U. N.C., Sch. Nursing, Chapel Hill, 1972; lectr. U. N.C., 1972—73, instr., 1973—77; therapist Psychiat. Assocs. Chapel Hill, 1975—79; head nurse, nursing supr., acting unit dir. Ga. Mental Health Inst., 1979—80; coord. career devel. Emory U. Hosp., 1980—81; tchr. Sugar Creek Children's Montessori Sch., Sugarland, Tex., 1992—95. Cons. in field. Contbg. author Patterson Family Favorites, 1998. Vol. Tex. Wildlife and Rehab. Ctr., 1983—2004; vol. cons. in counseling crisis intervention, 2000—. Recipient Internat. Peace prize, United Cultural Conv., 2010; named Women of Yr., Am. Biog. Inst. Bd. Internat. Rsch., 2011. Avocations: shell collecting, gourmet cooking, gardening, interior decorating, crafts. Home: 5440 N Braeswood Blvd Apt 937 Houston TX 77096

HAWKINS, DAVID RAMON, psychiatrist, writer, researcher, spiritual teacher; b. Milw., June 3, 1927; s. Ramon Nelson and Alice-Mary (McCutcheon) H.; m. Susan Humphrey; children: Sarah Humphrey. BS, Marquette U., 1950; MD, Med. Coll. Wis., Milw., 1953; PhD, Columbia Pacific U., 1995. Med. dir. North Nassau Mental Health Ctr., Manhasset, NY, 1956-80; dir. rsch. Brunswick Hosp., LI, NY, 1968-79; pres. Acad. Orthomolecular Psychiatry, NYC, 1970-80; dir. Inst. Spiritual Rsch., Sedona, Ariz., 1979-88, The Rsch. Inst., Sedona, 1988—. Chmn. Inst. Advanced Theoretical Rsch., 1993—; guest on TV shows including McNeal-Lehrer, Barbara Walters, Today; chief of staff Mingus Mountain RTC, 1995; lectr. in field; cons. in field. Author (with Linus Pauling): Orthomolecular Psychiatry, 1973; author: Power vs. Force, 1995, The Eye of the I, 2001, I, 2002, Truth vs. Falsehood, 2005, Transcending the Levels of Consciusness, 2006, Devotional Non-Duality, 2006. With USN, 1945—46. Recipient Mosby Book award, 1953; named knight, Sovereign Order St. John of Jerusalem, Tae Ryoung Sun Kak Tosun, Mount Bo Jing and Radasanti Meditation Ctr., 2006; nominee Templeton prize, 2006. Mem. AMA, APA, Ariz. Med. Soc., Ariz. Psychiat. Soc., Alpha Omega Alpha. Avocation: architecture. Office: Rsch Inst PO Box 3516 W Sedona Ave Sedona AZ 86340 Business E-Mail: info@veritospub.com.

HAWKINS, GREGORY, insurance company executive; BA in Acctg., U. Mich., Flint. CPA. Held various operational mgmt. positions Univ. Mich. Health System, Blue Cross Blue Shield Mich.; sr. v.p., CFO M-CARE, Ann Arbor; CFO Priority Health, 2007—. Office: Priority Health 1231 E Beltline NE Grand Rapids MI 49525 *

HAWKINS, HAL KENNETH, pathologist; b. Bartlesville, Okla., Aug. 11, 1945; s. Guy Rodgers and Sarabeth (Barbour) H.; m. Barbara Patterson Reed, Sept. 6, 1969 (div. Apr. 1992); children: David, Heidi, Brian, Russell. PhD, Duke U., 1971, MD, 1972. Asst. prof. Duke U. Med. Sch., Durham, N.C., 1973-79, Emory U. Sch. Medicine, Atlanta, 1979-83, Baylor Coll. Medicine, Houston, 1983-93; assoc. prof. U. Tex. Med. Br., Galveston, 1993—2002, prof., 2002—. Pathologist Shriners Burns Hosp., Galveston, 1996-. Mem. U.S. Canadian Acad. of Pathology. Office: 300 University Blvd Rt 0747 Galveston TX 77550 Office Phone: 409-770-6635. Business E-Mail: hhawkins@utmb.edu.

HAWKINS, JOELLEN MARGARET BECK, nursing educator; b. Harvey, ND, Dec. 15, 1941; d. Charles Joel and Gertrude Adelaide (Waits) Beck; m. Charles Albert Watson, June 27, 1964 (div. 1978); children: John Charles, Andrew Bruce; m. David Gene Hawkins, Oct. 4, 1978. Student, Oberlin Coll., 1959—61; diploma, Chgo. Wesley Meml. Hosp. Sch. of Nursing, 1964; BSN, Northwestern U., Chgo., 1964; MS, Boston Coll., 1969, PhD, 1977. Cert. women's health nurse practitioner. Staff nurse Sheboygan Meml. Hosp., 1964-65; instr., staff Boston Lying in Hosp., 1965-66, 68-69; staff nurse Brookline Vis. Nurse Assn., 1968, Guy's Hosp., London, 1968; campus nurse Roger Williams Coll., Bristol, RI, 1969-70; instr. Salve Regina Coll., Newport, RI, 1970-74; faculty Roger Williams Coll., Bristol, RI, 1974-75; prof. U. Conn., Storrs, 1978-83; asst., assoc. prof. William F. Connell Sch. Nursing Boston Coll., Chestnut Hill, Mass., 1975-78, prof., 1983—2008, emeritus prof., 2008—; writer in residence, dept. nursing Simmons Coll. Sch. Nursing & Health Studies, 2008—. Women's health nurse practitioner Crittenton Hastings House, 1984-2000, U. Conn. Student Health Women's Clinic, 1978-83, Sidney Borum Health Ctr., 2000—09, Pine St. Inn Women's Clinic, 2000-06, chief nursing cons., Taber's Cyclopedic Med. Dictionary 2010-. Author: Maternal-Newborn Nursing: Pretest Self-Assessment and Review, 1978, Clinical Experience in Collegiate Nursing Education: Selection of Clinical Agencies, 1981, Health Care of Women: Gynecological Assessment, 1982, Women and the Menopause, 1983, Linking Nursing Education and Practice: Collaborative Experiences in Maternal Child Health, 1987, Dictionary of American Nursing Biography, 1988, Nursing and the American Health Care Delivery System, 4th edit., 1993, Nurse-Social Worker Collaboration in Managed Care: A Model of Community Case Management, 1998, The Advanced Practice Nurse: Current Issues, 5th edit., 2000, Guidelines for Nurse Practitioners in Gynecologic Settings, 10th edit., 2011—(Book of Yr. award Am. Jour. Nursing, 2004); editor: Linking Nursing Education and Practice, 1987 (Book of Yr. award Am. Jour. Nursing, 1988), Clin. Excellence for Nurse Practitioners: Internat. Jour. of NPACE, 1996—2005, Diversity in Health Care Research: Strategies for Multisite, Multidisciplinary, and Multicultural Projects, 2003; nursing chief cons.: Taber's Medical Dictionary, 2005—07, 2010—; contbr. over 100 articles to profl. jours., chapters to books;, co-author 36 books. Recipient Disting. Alumni award North H.S., North St. Paul, Minn., 1989, Miriam Manisoff award Planned Parenthood Fedn. Am., 1997, Disting. Alumna award Chgo. Wesley Meml. Hosp. Sch. Nursing, 1999; named Nurse Practitioner of Yr. Am. Acad. of Nurse Practitioners, 1995. Fellow Am. Acad. Nursing, Am. Acad. Nurse Practitioners, Nat. Acads. Practice (Nicholas A. Cummings award 2006); mem. ANA, Mass. RNs Assn. (Disting. Nurse Rschr. award 1984, Lucy Lincoln Drown Nursing History award 1994), Sigma Theta Tau (Elizabeth Russell Belford Founder's award 1993). Democrat. Unitarian Universalist. Home: 151 Stanton Ave Auburndale MA 02466-3005 Office Phone: 617-552-4252. Personal E-mail: joellenhawkins@mac.com. Business E-Mail: hawkinsj@bc.edu.

HAWKINS, KATHERINE ANN, hematologist, educator, lawyer; b. Teaneck, NJ, Oct. 25, 1947; d. Howard Robert and Helen Ann (Foley) Hawkins; m. Paul Jonathan Chrzanowski, June 29, 1974; children: Eric, Brian. AB, Manhattanville Coll., Purchase, NY, 1969; MD, Columbia U., 1973; JD, Fordham U., Sch. of Law, 2002. Intern Presbyn. Hosp., NYC, 1973, Roosevelt Hosp., NYC, 1974-75, resident, 1975-77; fellow NYU, 1977-79; attending hematologist Sickle Cell Ctr. St. Luke's Hosp., NYC, 1985-87; assoc. attending physician St. Luke's - Roosevelt Hosp. Ctr., NYC, 1989—, sr. attending physician, 2007—; asst. clin. prof. medicine Columbia U., NYC, 1987-94, assoc. clin. prof., 1994—96; assoc. dir. dept. medicine, dir. med. edn. St. Luke's Hosp., NYC, 1991-96; assoc. residency program dir. Beth Israel Med. Ctr., NYC, 1996—; assoc. prof. clin. medicine Albert Einstein Coll. Medicine Yeshiva U., NYC, 1996—. Mem. attending staff Beth Israel Hosp., N.Y.C., St. Luke's-Roosevelt Hosp. Ctr., N.Y.C.; exec. sec. Bd. Profl. Med. Conduct. Contbr. articles to profl. jours. Fellow ACP, Am. Coll. Legal Medicine; mem. ABA, Am. Soc. Hematology, Am. Soc. Clin. Oncology, NY State Dept. Health-(exec. sec. bd. profl. med. conduct 2009-). Roman Catholic. Office: NYS Dept of Health 90 Church St 4th Fl New York NY 10007 Office Phone: 212-417-4445.

HAWKINS, RICHARD ALBERT, medical educator, administrator; b. Greenwich, Conn., Mar. 27, 1940; s. Albert Rice and Florence Marie Elizabeth (Hansen) H.; m. Enriqueta Elias, May 9, 1964; children: Richard Alfred, Paul Andrés. BSc magna cum laude, San Diego State U., 1963; PhD, Harvard U., 1969; LHD (hon.), U. Phoenix, 1994. Rsch. fellow Metabolic Rsch. Lab. Radcliffe Infirmary, Oxford (Eng.) U., 1969-71; staff fellow in neurochemistry St. Elizabeth Hosp., Washington, 1971-72, NIMH/NIAAA sr. staff fellow in neurochemistry, 1972-74; chief phys. sci. br. FDA, Rockville, Md., 1974-76; assoc. prof. neurosurgery and physiology NYU Med. Ctr., NYC, 1976-77; prof. anesthesia and physiology Pa. State U., Hershey (Pa.) Med. Ctr., 1977-88; prof., chmn. physiology and biophysics The Rosalind Franklin U. Medicine and Sci., North Chicago, Ill., 1988-93, prof., 1988—; exec. v.p. acad. affairs, chief academic officer Herman M. Finch U. Health Scis./Chgo. Med. Sch., North Chicago, Ill., 1993-98, provost, 1998, pres., CEO, 1999—2003, pres. emeritus, 2003. Hon. prof. U. Valencia, Spain, 1989—. Contbr. numerous articles to profl. jours. Recipient Meritorious Rsch. award Morris Parker Found., 1992. Fellow Am. Heart Assn.; mem. Am. Physiol. Soc., Am. Soc. Neurochemistry, Biochem. Soc., Soc. for Neurosci., Alpha Omega Alpha. Home: 950 N Michigan Ave Chicago IL 60611 Office: Rosalind Franklin U Med and Sci 3333 Green Bay Rd North Chicago IL 60064-3037 Business E-Mail: rah@post.harvard.edu.

HAWKINS, ROLAND BENTON, oncologist; b. St. Louis, Feb. 10, 1940; BS in Physics, Wash. U., St. Louis, 1962, PhD, MD, 1967. Physician, radiation oncologist Ochsner Med. Sys., 1989—. Mem.: Am. Soc. Therapeutic Radiology And Oncology. Office: Ochsner Cancer Inst 1514 Jefferson New Orleans LA 70121 Office Fax: 504-842-2037. Business E-Mail: rhawkins@ochsner.org.

HAWKINS, STACY SUSAN, research scientist, consultant; b. Stamford, Conn., Aug. 1, 1967; d. Charles Everett and Norma Jean (Crook) H. BSEE, MIT, Cambridge, Mass., 1989; PhD in Biomed. Engring., Rutgers U., Piscataway, NJ, 1994. Rsch. asst. Rutgers U., Piscataway, 1992-94, postdoctoral fellow, 1994-95, vis. asst. prof., 1995-96. Cons. Colgate Palmolive, Piscataway, N.J., 1994-95; cons. dept. oral biology U. Medicine and Dentistry of N.J., Newark, 1995-96; rsch. scientist Unilever Rsch., Edgewater, N.J., 1996—. Contbr. chpt. to book, articles to profl. jours. Pianist Christ Cmty. Baptist Ch., 1992—, music dir. 1994—. Recipient Thomas J. Watson Meml. scholarship I.B.M. Corp., 1985-89, Music Piano scholarship MIT, 1986-87. Mem. IEEE, Engrng. in Medicine and Biology Soc., Soc. Christian Design Profls. (assoc.). Avocations: running, volleyball, basketball, piano, choir. Home: 350 Shore Rd Stratford CT 06615-7000

HAWS, ELIZABETH ANNE, psychologist, director; b. Willingboro, NJ, Mar. 30, 1970; d. William Joseph and Mary Ruth (Datko) Haws. BA in Edn. of the Handicapped, Kean U., 1992; MA in Sch. Psychology, Rowan U., 1998, supr. curriculum and instrn., 2000, EdS, 2001. Spl. edn. tchr. Willingboro Bd. Edn., 1992—98, peer mediation supr., 1994—95, peer mediation coord., 1996—98, sch. psychologist, 1998—2000, Mt. Laurel Bd. Edn., NJ, 2005—08; supr. Union County ESC, Westfield, NJ, 2000—03; dir. spl. svcs. Eastampton Bd. Edn., NJ, 2003—05; cons. sch. psychologist, 2005—08; CEO Koala Ednl. Consulting, 2007—, sch. psychologist, 2008—; chemistry tchr. Lawrence BOE, 2008—10. Mem. crisis response team Burlington County Sch.; mem. Burlington County Red Cross Disaster Relief Team. Mem.: NASP, N.J. Prin. and Supr. Assn., N.J. Assn. Sch. Psychologists, Coun. Exceptional Children (chpt. 461 programming com. 1988—89, pres. 1989—91, treas. 1991—92), Profl. Assn. Dive Instructors, Cara Irish Soc., Alpha Epsilon Lambda, Sigma Beta Chi. Republican. Roman Catholic. Avocations: writing, bicycling, walking, travel, golf, scuba diving. Home: 202 E Union St Burlington NJ 08016-1717 Personal E-mail: lizhaws@aol.com.

HAWVER, DENNIS A., psychologist, consultant; s. Carl F. and Frances J. H.; children: Timothy, Laura, Derek; m. Judith M. Anderson, Jan. 28, 1977. BA, U. Akron, 1964, MA, 1965; PhD, Temple U., Phila., 1964-70. Dir. rsch. Temple U., Phila., 1964-70, instr. Grad. Sch., 1968-70, internal cons., 1964-70; mng. ptnr. Cardall Assocs., Princeton, N.J., 1970-72; nat. program dir. The RHR Inst., NYC, 1972-80; pres. The Hawver Group, NYC and Princeton, 1980—. Pres. The Hawver Group, N.Y.C. and Princeton, 1980-; pres. Princeton chpt. Inst. Mgmt. Cons. Author: How to Improve Your Negotiating Skills, 1983; contbr. to bus. and profl. jours.; developer rsch. and tng. programs; internat. cons. in exec. identification and devel. and bus. negotiations. Chmn. Leadership Devel. Com. of Princeton C. of C. Mem. APA, Soc. Indsl. and Organizational Psychology, Internat. Assn. Applied Psychology, Inst. Mgmt. Cons. (CMC), Soc. Assessment Sys. Practitioners, Internat. Pers. Mgmt. Assn. Assessment Coun. Office: Hawver Group 19 Melville Rd Princeton Junction NJ 08550-2807 E-mail: hawvergrp@aol.com.

HAWWA, AHMED F., pharmacist, educator; b. Ajman, United Arab Emirates, Sept. 13, 1980; s. Fayeq M. Hawwa and Shamsa A. Abu Nasrah. BSc in Pharmacy with honors, U. Jordan, Amman, 2003; PhD in Clin. Pharmacy, Queen's U. Belfast, Northern Ireland, 2007. Cert. in pharmacy Jordanian Pharm. Assn., 2003. Formulator, R & D dept. Hikma Pharm. Ltd., Amman, Jordan, 2003—03; tchg. asst. Sch. Pharmacy, U. Jordan, Amman, 2003—04; postdoc. rsch. fellow Sch. Pharmacy, Queen's U. Belfast, 2007—09; lectr. clin. pharmacy Sch. Pharmacy, Queen's U. Belfast, 2009—. Contbr. articles to profl. jours. (Brit. Coun. Travel grant, 2007, award, 2007). Recipient Abdul-Rahim Jardaneh award, U. Jordan, 2003, award, Hikma Pharm. Ltd., 2003. Mem.: Jordanian Pharm. Assn., Children's Medicine Rsch. Group, Rsch. Forum Child, Child Health & Welfare Recognised Rsch. Group. Achievements include research in influence of genetic polymorphisms on tacrolimus nephrotoxicity and dosage requirements in children with liver transplants. Avocations: running, tennis, surfing internet. Office: Queen's Univeristy Belfast Sch Pharmacy 97 Lisburn Rd Belfast BT9 7BL Northern Ireland Business E-Mail: a.hawwa@qub.ac.uk.

HAYAKAWA, TORU, neurosurgeon; b. Osaka, Japan, Sept. 24, 1934; s. Tetsuo and Shizu Hayakawa; m. Naoko Oda, May 30, 1969; children: Takashi, Makoto. MD, Osaka U., 1959, PhD, 1964. Intern Osaka (Japan) U. Med. Sch., 1959-60, resident, 1960-64; surgeon Sakai City Hosp., 1964-65, resident, 1965-67; asst. Osaka U. Med. Sch., 1967-77; assoc. dept. neurology U. Minn., Mpls., 1973-75; sr. neurosurgeon Ctr. for Adult Diseases, Osaka, 1977-80; asst. prof. Osaka U. Med. Sch., 1981-89, assoc. prof., 1989-90, prof. and chmn. dept. neurosurgery, 1990—98; dir. Kansai Rosai Hosp., 1998—2005. Mem. Japanese Neurosurg. Soc. (mem. neurosurg. bd.). Home: 1-2-10-704 Mikage Yamate Higachinada Kobe 658 Japan Office: Kansai Rosai Hosp 3-1-69 Inabaso Amagasaki 660-8511 Japan Home Phone: +81-78-843-4323; Office Phone: 81-6-6416-1221.

HAYASE, TOSHIYUKI, engineering educator, researcher; b. Nagoya, Japan, Jan. 30, 1956; Deng, Nagoya U., 1980. Prof. Tohoku U., 2000—. Dir. Inst. Fluid Sci., 2008—. Fellow: Japan Soc. Mech. Engrs. Avocations: walking, bicycling. Office: 2-1-1 Katahira Sendai Miyagi 980-8577 Japan Business E-Mail: hayase@ifs.tohoku.ac.jp.

HAYASHI, PAUL HIDEYO, medical association administrator, educator; b. Denver, Oct. 11, 1960; BA, U. Calif., LA, 1983; MD, U. Calif., San Diego, 1987. Transplant hepatologist U. NC, 2006—. Mem.: Am. Assn. Study Liver Diseases. Home: 8011 Burnett-Womack Bldg Chapel Hill NC 27516 Business E-Mail: paul_hayashi@med.unc.edu.

HAYASHI, SHOGO, anatomist, educator; b. Japan, Feb. 13, 1976; MD, Aichi Med. U., 2002; PhD, Tokyo Med. U., 2007. Asst. prof., 1st dept. anatomy Tokyo Med. U., 2002—07; lectr. Med. Edn. Ctr., Sch. Medicine, Aichi Med. U., 2007—. Mem.: Japanese Assn. Anatomist, Japan Soc. Med. Edn. Office: Yazako-Karimata 21 Nagaku Aichi 480-1195 Japan Business E-Mail: shogo@aichi-med-u.ac.jp.

HAYASHI, YOSHIHIKO, dental educator, researcher; b. Moji, Fukuoka, Japan, Jan. 11, 1952; s. Morio and Sachiko (Kunizawa) H.; m. Ryoko Kinoshita, Oct. 14, 1979; children: Mitsuhiko, Yoko. DDS, Tokyo Med. and Dental U., 1976; PhD, Kyushu U., Fukuoka, 1982. Instr. Showa U., Tokyo, 1976-77, Kyushu U., 1981-86, asst. prof., 1986-92, assoc. prof., 1992-95; prof. Nagasaki U., 1995—, counselor, 2002—04; chief Nagasaki U. Dental Hosp., 1995—2005; dir. dental sect. Nagasaki U. Hosp., 2005—07; dean Nagasaki U. Sch. Dentistry, 2007—. Lectr. Japan Internat. Cooperation Agy., Fukuoka, 1994—2004; organizer Scanning Microscopy 1996 meeting, Bethesda, Md., 1997 meeting, Chgo.; moderator Internat. Congress on Biol. Med. Engring., Singapore, 2002; pres. 121st Ann. Mtg. Japanese Soc. Conservative Dentistry, Nagasaki, 2004. Contbr. articles to profl. jours. Italian Govt. scholar, 1983-84; fellow Japanese Min. of Edn., 1991, 95, 97, 2002. Mem. Japanese Assn. for Conservative Dentistry (dir. 1996—), Japanese Assn. Endodontics (bd. dirs. 2000—, pres., 32nd Ann. Meeting, Nagasaki 2011); Japanese Soc. Chitin and Chitosan. Office: Nagasaki U Grad Sch Biomed Scis Sakamoto 1-7-1 Nagasaki 852-8588 Japan Business E-Mail: hayashi@nagasaki-u.ac.jp.

HAYASHIDA, NOBUAKI, biologist, educator; b. Ohtawara, Tochigi, Japan, Aug. 21, 1961; PhD in Biology, Nagoya U., Japan, 1989. Rschr. plant molecular biology RIKEN (Inst. Phys. and Chem Rsch.), Tsukuba, Ibaraki, Japan, 1989—96; assoc. prof. biotech. Divsn. Gene Rsch., Shinshu U., Ueda, Nagano, Japan, 1996—2009; prof. applied biology Faculty Textile, Sci. & Tech., Shinshu U., Ueda, 2009—. Councilor Japanese Soc. Plant Physiology, Kyoto, 2004—07. Achievements include discovery of sequences of plant genes, plant protein kinases; Pcb2, a gene for Chlorophyll synthesis; novel interpretation of thylakoid structure in photosynthesis. Office: Divsn Gene Rsch Shinshu Univ 3-15-1 Tokida Ueda Nagano 386-8567 Japan Office Fax: 81-268-21-5660.

HAYATA, EIJIRO, gynecologist; b. Kyoto, Dec. 25, 1978; Degree, Nat. Def. Med. Coll., 2003. Physician dept. ob-gyn. Japan Self Def. Forces Ctrl. Hosp., 2010—. Mem.: Japan Soc. Perinatal Neonatal Medicine, Japan Soc. Obstetrics and Gynecology. Office: Ikejiri 1-2-24 Setagaya Tokyo 154-8532 Japan Office Phone: 3-3411-0151. Personal E-mail: e_hayata@hotmail.com.

HAYDEN, MICHAEL R., medical geneticist, educator; Grad. in medicine, U. Cape Town, South Africa, 1975, PhD, 1979; ScD (hon.), U. Alta., Can., 2009. Cert. in internal medicine and clin. genetics. Post-doc. fellow, tng. in internal medicine Harvard Med. Sch., Mass.; Killam prof. med. genetics, Can. rsch. chair in human genetics & molecular medicine U. BC, Vancouver, Canada; chmn. Ctr. Molecular Medicine & Therapeutics, Vancouver; founder NeuroVir, Xenon Genetics, Aspreva Pharmaceutics, Inc. Co-leader Can. Pharmacogenomics Network Drug Safety. Contbr. articles to profl. jours. Mem. selection panel Gairdner Med. Rev.; bd. mem. American Soc. Human Genetics, American Soc. Clin. Investigation. Decorated Order of BC, Order of Can.; recipient Lifetime Achievement award, Huntington Soc., Can., 2001, Leadership and Rsch. Excellence award, Nat. Centres Excellence, 2004, Prix Galien, 2007, Jacob Biely prize, U. BC, 2010, Gairdner Wightman award, Gairdner Found., Can., 2011. Mem.: Royal Soc. Can., Can. Acad. Arts and Sciences. Office: University BC Ctr Molecular Medicine and Therapeutics 950 W 28th St Rm 3025 Vancouver BC Canada V5Z 4H4 Office Phone: 604-875-3535. Office Fax: 604-875-3819. Business E-Mail: mrh@cmmt.ubc.ca. *

HAYES, ALICE BOURKE, academic administrator, biologist, researcher; b. Chgo., Dec. 31, 1937; d. William Joseph and Mary Alice (Cawley) Bourke; m. John J. Hayes, Sept. 2, 1961 (dec. July 1981). BS, Mundelein Coll., Chgo., 1959; MS, U. Ill., 1960; PhD, Northwestern U., Evanston, Ill., 1972; DSc (hon.), Loyola U., Chgo., 1994; HHD (hon.), Fontbonne Coll., St. Louis, 1994; LHD (hon.), Mount St. Mary Coll., 1998; DSc (hon.), St. Louis U., 2002; EdD (hon.), Providence Coll., 2004; DLH (hon.), U. San Francisco, 2006; DHL, Aquinas Inst. Theology, 2008, Lewis U., 2008, HHD (hon.). Rschr. Mcpl. Tb San., Chgo., 1960-62; faculty Loyola U., Chgo., 1962-87, chmn. dept., 1968-77, dean natural scis. divsn., 1977-80, assoc. acad. v.p., 1980-87, v.p. acad. affairs, 1987-89; provost, exec. v.p. St. Louis U., 1989-95; pres. U. San Diego, 1995—2003, pres. emerita, 2003—. Mem. space biology program NASA, 1980—86; mem. adv. panel NSF, 1977—81, Parmly Hearing Inst., 1986—89; del. Bot. Del. to South Africa, 1984, to People's Republic of China, 1988, to USSR, 1990; reviewer Coll. Bd. and Mellon Found. Nat. Hispanic Scholar Awards, 1985—86; bd. dirs. Jack-in-the-Box, 1999—2008, ConAgra, 2000—07, Pulitzer Inc., 1994—2004; mem. Ill. Bd. Higher Edn., 2004—11. Co-author books; contbr. articles to profl. publs. Campaign mem. Mental Health Assn. Ill., Chgo., 1973-89; trustee Chgo.-No. Ill. divsn. Nat. Multiple Sclerosis Soc., 1981-89, bd. dirs., 1980-88, com. chmn., sec. to bd. dirs., vice chmn. bd. dirs.; trustee Regina Dominican Acad., 1984-89, Civitas Dei Found., 1987-92, Rockhurst Coll., Loyola U., Chgo., San Diego Found.; trustee St. Ignatius Coll. Prep. Sch., bd. dirs., 1984-89, sec., vice chmn.; bd. dirs. Urban League Met. St. Louis, St. Louis Sci. Ctr., 1991-95, Cath. Charities St. Louis, 1992-95, St. Louis County Hist. Soc., 1992-95, Cath. Charities San Diego, 1996—2003, San Diego Hist. Soc., 1996—2003; bd. dirs., trustee Old Globe Theater, 1996—2003, Chirst The King Coll. Prep, 2008- Named to Tchrs.' Hall of Fame Blue Key Soc.; fellow in botany U. Ill., 1959-60; fellow in botany NSF, 1969-71; grantee Am. Orchid Soc., 1967; grantee HEW, 1969, 76; grantee NSF, 1975; grantee NASA, 1980-85, Coffey award, Chgo., 2007, Hesburgh award, Cath Coll. & U., 2008, Reischauer Internat. Edn. award., Japan Soc. San Diego & Tijuana, 2010 Mem. AAAS, AAUP (corp. rep. 1980-85), Am. Assn. for Higher Edn., Am. Assn. Univ. Adminstrs. (mem. program com. nat. meeting 1988), Am. Soc. Gravitational and Space Biology, Assn. Midwest Coll. Biology Tchrs., Am. Soc. Plant Physiology, Bot. Soc. Am., Am. Inst. Biol. Scis. Acad., Chgo. Network, Soc. Ill. Microbiologists (edn. com. 1969-70, Pasteur award com. 1975, pub. rels. com. 1974, chair speakers' bur. 1974-79), Chgo. Assn. Tech. Socs. (acad. liaison 1982-85, awards com. 1984-89), Am. Coun. on Edn. (corp. rep. higher edn. panel), Ctr. Rsch. Librs. (nominating com. 1986), N.C. Assn. Colls. and Schs. (cons., evaluator Commn. on Higher Edn. 1984-95, commr.-at-large 1988-94), Mo. Women's Forum Club, North Ctrl. Assn. Schs. and Colls., Western Assn. Schs. and Colls., N.W. Assn. Schs. and Colls., Sigma Xi, Delta Sigma Rho, Sigma Delta Epsilon, Phi Beta Kappa, Alpha Sigma Nu. Roman Catholic. Home: 6801 N Loron Chicago IL 60646 Personal E-mail: alicehayes@sbcglobal.net.

HAYES, ERNEST M., podiatrist; b. New Orleans, Jan. 21, 1946; s. Ernest M. and Emma Hayes; m. Bonnie Ruth Beigle, Oct. 16, 1970. BA, Calif. State U., Sacramento, 1969; BS, Calif. Coll. Podiat. Medicine, San Francisco, 1971, DPM, 1973. Diplomate Am. Coun. Podiatric Physicians and Surgeons., 2008; Bd. cert. Am. Bd. Lower Extremity Surgeons. Resident in surg. podiatry Beach Cmty. Hosp., Buena Pk., Calif., 1973-74, dir. residency program, 1974-75; pvt. practice Anaheim, Calif., 1974-80, Yreka, Calif., 1980-95, Machias, Lubec and Calais, Maine, 1995—. Courtesy staff Down East Cmty. Hosp., 1997—2004; sr. clin. instr. So. Calif. Podiatric Med. Ctr., LA, 1975—78; vice chmn. podiatry dept. Good Samaritan Hosp., Anaheim, Calif., 1978—79; mem. med. staff Mercey Med. Ctr., Mt. Shasta, Calif.; CEO, Siskiyou Foot Group, Yreka, 1980—95, Nature's Pace, 1995, Underground Food and Seed, LLC, 1995; pres. Down East Podiatry, Machias, Maine, 1995—. Registrar POSM Horse Registry, 2000; bd. dir. Little Bogus Ranches Home Owners Assn., 1981—83, pres., 1983—84. Fellow: Am. Coll. Lower Extremity Surgeons, Am. Coll. Lower Extremity Surgeons, Nat. Coll. Foot Surgeons; mem.: Am. POSM Horse Assn. (trustee 1995), Am. Assn. Podiatric Physicians and Surgeons, 1989. Baptist. Home: PO Box 538 Lubec ME 04652-0538

HAYES, LESLIE ALLYSON, pediatrician, adolescent medicine; MD, Mt. Sinai Sch. of Medicine, 1986. Cert. addiction medicine 2005, adolescent medicine. Intern Children's Hosp. Nat. Med. Ctr., resident pediat. Washington, 1986—89; fellow adolescent medicine Univ. of Medicine and Dentistry of NJ Med. Ctr., Newark, 1989—91; physician The Bklyn. Hosp. Ctr. Office: The Brooklyn Hospital Center Children's Health Center 121 Dekalb Ave Brooklyn NY 11201 Office Phone: 718-250-6594. Office Fax: 718-250-6894.

HAYES, MARK, lawyer, former legislative staff member; b. Shelbina, Mo., 1966; m. Katherine Hayes. BS in Pharmacy, U. Mo., Kansas City, 1988; JD, American U. Washington Coll. Law, 2006. Staff asst. to Senator Kit Bond US Senate, 1989—99; sr. adv. to Senator Kit Bond US Senate Small Bus. Com., Washington, 1994—95; health policy advisor to Senator Jim Jeffords US Senate Health, Edn., Labor & Pensions Com., Washington, 2001; health policy advisor, Senator Charles Grassley US Senate, 2003—04; v.p. St Louis 2004, 1996—2000; sr. health policy advisor & legis. aide, Senator Olympia Snowe US Senate, 2001—02; health policy adv. to Senator Charles Grassley US Senator, Washington, 2002—04; health policy dir. to Senator Charles Grassley US Senate, 2004—06, health policy dir., chief health counsel to Senator Charles Grassley, 2006—10; asst. dir. fed. govt. affairs Hoffman-LaRoche, Inc., 1995—96; shareholder Greenberg Traurig LLP, Washington, 2010—. Asst. adj. prof. George Washington U. Mem.: ABA, Republican Nat. Lawyers Assn., Fed. Bar Assn., American Health Lawyers Assn. Republican. Office: Greenberg Traurig LLP 2101 L St NW Ste 1000 Washington DC 20037 Office Phone: 202-331-3164. Office Fax: 202-261-4759. E-mail: hayesml@gtlaw.com. *

HAYES, MAXINE DELORES, public health service officer, physician, pediatrician; b. Nov. 29, 1946; children: Leon Williams, Kevin Williams. AB in Biology, Spelman Coll., 1969; MD, SUNY Buffalo, 1973; MPH, Harvard U., 1977; DSc (hon.), Spelman Coll., 2000. Intern pediat. Vanderbilt Hosp., Nashville, 1973-75; resident Children's Hosp., Boston, 1975-76; dir. Divsn. Parent-Child Health Svcs., Olympia, Wash., 1988-90, asst. sec., 1990-93, Cmty. and Family Health, Olympia, 1993-2000, acting health officer, 1998-2000; state health officer Wash. State Dept. Health, 2000—. Pres. Assn. Maternal and Child Health Programs, Washington, 1995-97; nat. program dir. Robert Wood Johnson Child Health Initiative, 1994-97; chair, Comprehensive Health Edn. Found. Bd. Dir., Seattle Recipient Outstanding Contbns. in Field of Pub. Health award Wash. State Pub. Health Assn., 1994, Guardian of Women's Health award Aradia Women's Health Ctr., 1996, Stockton Kimball award for medicine SUNY, Buffalo, 2000, Dr. Nathan Davis award AMA, 2002, Richard P. Nelson Lecture Series award Iowa Pub. Health Assn., 2002, Lifetime Achievement award Wash. Health Found., 2003. Fellow Am. Acad. Pediatrics; mem. APHA (Helen Rodriguez-Trias Social Justice award 2007), Inst. Medicine. Avocations: opera, art, science. Office: Wash State Dept Health PO Box 47890 Olympia WA 98504-7890 Office Phone: 360-236-4018. Business E-Mail: maxine.hayes@doh.wa.gov.

HAYES, MELANIE, dental hygienist, educator; b. Australia, Nov. 15, 1980; B in Oral Health, U. Newcastle, 2007, B in Health Sci. with honor, 2008. Dental hygienist Maitland Dental Care, 2007—10, Hunter Periodontics and Implants, 2009—11; lectr. U. Newcastle, 2009—. Recipient Faculty medal, Faculty Health, U. Newcastle, Golden Scaler award, Hu Friedy. Mem.: Internat. Assn. Dental Rsch., Am. Dental Edn. Assn., Dental Hygienists Assn. Australia. Avocation: reading. Office: 10 Chittaway Rd Ourimbah NSW 2258 Australia Office Phone: 61 2 4349 4514. Business E-Mail: melanie.hayes@newcastle.edu.au.

HAYES, MONICA PRASAD, medical educator; b. Northampton, Mass., Sept. 25, 1971; BS, Cornell U., 1993; MD, SUNY Upstate Med. U., 1997. Asst. prof., divsn. gynecologic oncology Mt. Sinai Sch. Medicine, 2006—. Recipient Robert E Nesbitt award, SUNY Upstate Med. U., Best Resident Tchg. award, Berlex Lab., Disting. Housestaff award, NY Presbyn. Hosp., Weill Cornell Med. Coll. Fellow: Am. Coll. Ob-Gyn.; mem.: ACS, Alpha Omega Alpha. Avocations: tennis, travel. Office: 1190 Fifth Ave Box 1173 New York NY 10029 Office Fax: 212-241-7462. Business E-Mail: monica.prasad@mssm.edu.

HAYES, WILBUR FRANK, retired biology professor; b. Rhinelander, Wis., Nov. 10, 1936; s. Wilbur Mead and Evelyn (Stritesky) H.; m. Dawn Olivia Waldorf, July 21, 1979 (div. Feb. 1991); stepchildren: Lynn, Robert, Dana, Richard, Gary, Kevin. BA, Colby Coll., Waterville, Maine, 1959; MS, Lehigh U., Bethlehem, Pa., 1961, PhD, 1965. Postdoctoral fellow Yale U., New Haven, 1965-67; asst. prof. biology Wilkes Coll., Wilkes-Barre, Pa., 1967-71, assoc. prof., 1971-99, assoc. prof. emeritus, 2000—. Vis. prof. Northeastern U., Boston, 1987-88. Contbr. articles to profl. jours. Chmn. bd. dirs. N.E. Pa. chpt. Am. Heart Assn., Wilkes-Barre, 1986-87. Mem. Soc. for Integrative and Comparative Biology, Pa. Acad. Sci., Microscopy Soc. Am., Sigma Xi (pres. Wilkes Coll. chpt. 1976-77, sec.-treas. 1984-87, 88-91). Republican. Congregationalist. Avocations: photography, travel, skiing. Home: 47 Stanley St Wilkes Barre PA 18702-2308 Office: Wilkes U Dept Biology Wilkes Barre PA 18766

HAYES GLADSON, LAURA JOANNA, psychologist; b. Winnebeau, NC, Mar. 26, 1943; d. Victor Wilson and Pansy Lorraine (Springsteen) Hayes; m. Jerry Allen Gladson, June 20, 1965 (div. Mar. 1992, remarried Dec. 27, 1997); children: Joanna Kaye, Paula Rae. BA, So. Coll., 1965; MEd, U. Tenn., Chattanooga, 1977; EdD, Vanderbilt U., 1985. Lic. psychologist, Ga. Psychol. intern Lakeshore Mental Health Inst., Knoxville, Tenn., 1985-86; counselor, psychologist Tara Heights Enterprises, Atlanta, 1986—; psychologist, owner Assoc. Psychol. Svcs., Inc., Ringgold, Ga., 1990—. Bd. dirs. Theraplay, Inc., Ringgold; founder Abused Children in Therapy, Inc., 1997. Mem. APA, Christian Assn. for Psychol. Studies, Ga. Psychol. Assn. Democrat. Home: 327 Homestead Cir Kennesaw GA 30144-1335 Office: Assoc Psychol Svcs Box 700 479 Cotter St Ringgold GA 30736-5149 Office Phone: 706-937-5180. Personal E-mail: lauragladson@yahoo.com.

HAYFLICK, LEONARD, cell biologist, biogerontologist, microbiologist, educator, writer; b. Phila., May 20, 1928; s. Nathan Albert and Edna H.; m. Ruth Louise Heckler, Oct. 3, 1954; children: Joel, Deborah, Susan, Rachel, Anne. BA in Microbiology and Chemistry, U. Pa., 1951, MS in Med. Microbiology, 1953, PhD in Med. Microbiology and Chemistry, 1956. McLaughlin rsch. fellow in infection and immunity, dept. microbiology U. Tex. Med. Br., Galveston, Tex., 1956-58; assoc. mem. Wistar Inst. Anatomy and Biology, Phila., 1958-68; asst. prof. rsch. medicine U. Pa., Phila., 1966-68; prof. med. microbiology Stanford U. Sch. Medicine, Calif., 1968-76, senator-at-large, Basic Med. Scis., 1970-73, chmn. gen. rsch. support grant com., 1972-74; sr. rsch. cell biologist Children's Hosp., Oakland, Calif., 1976-81; prof. zoology, prof. microbiology and immunology U. Fla., Gainesville, 1981-87, dir. Ctr. for Gerontol. Studies, Coll. Liberal Arts and Scis., 1981-87; prof. anatomy U. Calif. Sch. Medicine, San Francisco, 1988—. Mem. subcom. on mycoplasmataceae Internat. Com. Bacteriol. Nomenclature, 1965-78; mem. steering com. cell and devel. biology film program MIT, 1970-73; chmn. Calif. State Com. Health White Ho. Conf. Aging, 1971-72, Calif. state rep., 1972; Nat. Cancer Planning Com. Nat. Cancer Inst., NIH, 1972; chmn., adult devel. and aging rsch. and tng. com. Nat. Inst. Child Health and Human Devel., NIH, 1972-73; non-resident fellow Inst. Higher Studies, Santa Barbara, Calif., 1973—; mem. Argonne Nat. Lab. rev. com. biol. and med. rsch. div. Argonne Nat. Lab., 1973-76; mem. rsch. adv. com. Tchrs. Ins. and Annuity Assn. Am.-Coll. Retirement Equities Funds, NYC, 1974-80; founding mem. Nat. Adv. Coun. on Aging, Nat. Inst. on Aging, NIH, Bethesda, Md., 1975; cons. Office of Dir. Nat. Cancer Inst., Bethesda, 1963-74; vis. scientist Ctr. for Aging Weizmann Inst. Sci., Rehovoth, Israel, 1980, 86; mem. adv. bd. Internat. Exchange Ctr. Gerontology, Fla. Univ. System, Tampa, 1982-86; mem. jury for Sandoz prize in gerontology and geriatrics, 1985-89; bd. dirs. Ctr. for Climacteric Studies, Inc., Gainesville, 1985-88; expert cons. various coms. US Congress, vis. prof. Oita Med. U., Japan, 1991-95, U. Parma, Italy, 1991, Kurume U. Med. Sch., Japan; lectr. in field. Author: How and Why We Age, 1996; editor: Biology of the Mycoplasmas, 1969, Handbook of the Biology of Aging, 1977; sr. editor Biol. Scis. Microfiche Collection Info. on Gerontology and Geriatric Medicine Univ. Microfilms Internat., Ann Arbor, Mich., 1984-98; editor-in-chief Exptl. Gerontology, 1984-98; asst. editor In Vitro jour. Tissue Culture Assn., 1969-75; editor biol. scis. sect. Jour. Gerontology, 1975-80; assoc. editor Cancer Rsch., 1972-80; mem. editorial bd. Jour. Bacteriology, 1964-72, Jour. Virology, 1967-70, Infection and Immunity jour., 1968-78, Exec. Health Report, 1970—, Mechanisms of Aging and Devel., 1972—, Gerontology and Geriatrics Edn., 1980—, A Revista Portuguesa de Medicina Geriatrica, 1987—; mem. adv. com. Bergey's Manual of Determinative Bacteriology, 1965-78; bd. dirs., mem. editorial bd. Bollettino Dell Instituto Sieroterapico Milanese, Archivo de Microbiologia ed Immunologia, Milan, Italy, 1968—; contbr. numerous articles in field to profl. jours. Staff sgt. US Army, 1946-48. Recipient Samuel Roberts Noble Found. Rsch. Recognition award, 1984; co-recipient Sandoz prize Internat. Assn. Gerontology, 1991, Biomed. Scis. & Aging award U. So. Calif., 1974, Rsch. Recognition award Samuel Roberts Noble Found., 1984; Karl-Forster lectr. Acad. Sci. and Lit., Mainz, Germany, 1983, Hoffman-LaRoche lectr. Waksman Inst. Microbiology Rutgers U., 1984, Wadworth Meml. Fund lectr. Rush-Presbyn.-St. Luke's Med. Ctr., Chgo., 1984, hon. lectr. Rosenfield Program Pub. Affairs Grinnell Coll., 1989, invited speaker Sandoz lectrs. in Gerontology, Basle, Switzerland, 1986, 92, numerous other lectureships U.S.A., Can. and Europe, 1970—, Career Devel. award Nat. Cancer Inst., NIH, 1962-70, Lifetime Achievement award Soc. In Vitro Biology, 1996, Van Wezel prize Euro. Soc. Animal Cell Technology, 1999, Lord Cohen of Birkinhead medal Brit. Soc. Rsch. on Aging, 1999, Life Extension prize, Regenerative Medicine Secretariat, 2001. Fellow AAAS, Gerontol Soc. Am. (program and awards com. 1972-77, chmn., exec. com. biol. scis. sect. 1972-74, com. on internat. rels. 1980-82, pub. policy com. 1980-82, pres. 1982-83, ann. Robert W. Kleemeier award 1972, Brookdale award 1980); mem. Am. Soc. for Microbiology, Tissue Culture Assn. (hon., trustee 1966-68, program com. 1970, mem. coun. 1972-74, v.p. 1974-76, pres. Calif. chpt. 1971-73), Soc. for Exptl. Biology and Medicine (councillor 1984-88), Assn. for Advancement of Aging Rsch. (adv. coun. 1970-71), Am. Aging Assn., Am. Cancer Soc. (virology and cell biology study sect. 1974-76), Internat. Assn. Microbiol. Standardization (sec. cell culture com. 1963-73, chmn. 1985—, mem. coun. 1987-89), Internat. Orgn. for Mycoplasmology (Presdl. award 1984), Am. Gerontol. Soc. (v.p., coun. 1972-74, 81-83, program com. 1977-79, bdu. dirs. 1981-83), Am. Fedn. Aging Rsch. (bd. dirs., exec. com., rsch. adv. com. 1981—, chmn. study sect. 1987—, v.p. 1988—, Leadership award 1983), Fedn. Am. Socs. for Exptl. Biology, Aging Prevention Rsch. Found. (sci. adv. bd. dirs.), Am. Assn. for Cancer Rsch., Am. Soc. Pathologists, Calif. Found. for Biomed. Rsch., Am. Longevity Assn. (sci. adv. bd. dirs. 1981—), Western Gerontology Assn. (coun. 1972-74, bd. dirs. 81-83), Internat. Assn. Gerontology (mem. Am. exec. com. 1972-75, treas., exec. com. 1985-89, co-recipient Sandoz award gerontology 1991), Found. on Gerontology (sci. adv. bd. 1985—), Soc. Medicine and Natural Sci., Ukrainian Acad. Med. Scis. (fgn., Academician 1991, 2005), French Biol. Soc. (fgn.), Euro. Soc. Animal Cell Tech. (Van Wezel prize), Brit. Soc. Rsch. on Aging (Lord Cohen of Burkinhead medal), France Soc. Biology. Achievements include first prototype of inverted microscope for tissue culture use acquisitioned by Smithsonian National Museum of American History in 2006, discoverer of the mortality of cultured normal cells known as the Hayblick Limit, developer of the human cell strain WI-38 used for production of most of the worlds human virus vaccines, discourses cause of walking pneumonia to be a mycoplasma the smallest free living microorganism. Office: U Calif 36991 Greencroft Close PO Box 89 The Sea Ranch CA 95497-0089 Personal E-mail: lenh38@aol.com.

HAYMAN, MARTIN ARTHUR, psychiatrist, educator; b. NYC, Dec. 5, 1929; s. Louis and Cecelia (Klatzkin) H.; m. Traude E. Sighartner, June 9, 1957; children: Douglas, Kenneth. BA cum laude, NYU, 1951, MD, 1955. Diplomate Am. Bd. Psychiatry and Neurology, Nat. Bd. Med. Examiners. Intern Meadowbrook Hosp., East Meadow, NY, 1955-56; pvt. practice Nassau County, 1959-73; sr. physician VA Med. Ctr., Northport, 1973; resident in psychiatry SUNY Med. Ctr., Stony Brook, 1974-77, asst. prof. clin. psychiatry, 1977—. Dir. psychiatry South Brookhaven Health Ctr., Patchogue, NY, 1977—91; attending physician Brookhaven Meml. Hosp. Med. Ctr., 1977—91. Reviewer jour.; contbr. articles to profl. jours. Mem. ad hoc com. Helping Older People Emotionally, Suffolk County, 1981-82. Capt. M.C., USAF, 1956-58. Fellow Acad. Psychosomatic Medicine; mem. AMA (Physician's Recognition awards 1970—), Am. Psychiat. Assn., Med. Soc. N.Y., Suffolk County Med. Soc., Phi Beta Kappa, Beta Lambda Sigma (vice chancellor 1951). Home and Office: 20 Redwood Dr PO Box 626 Great River NY 11739-0626 Office Phone: 631-277-9850. Personal E-mail: mhayman@pol.net, mthayman@optonline.net.

HAYMOND, MOREY WILLIAM, pediatrician, endocrinologist; b. Greeley, Colo., Apr. 29, 1943; MD, Wash. U., St. Louis, 1969. Intern, pediat. endocrinology St. Louis Children's Hosp., Wash. U., 1969—70, resident, 1970—71; fellow, medicine St. Louis Children's Hosp., 1971—73; cons. Mayo Clinic, Rochester, 1978—90; prof. pediat. Mayo Med. Sch., Rochester, Minn., 1984—90, 1990—96, U. Fla., Jacksonville, 1990—96; dir. Nemours Children's Clinic, 1990—96; section chief pediatric endocrinology & metabolism Baylor Coll. Medicine, prof. & vice chmn. rsch. dept. pediatrics, 1996, program dir. Child Health Rsch. Ctr. & Clinical Scientist Training Program; dir. Diabetes Care Ctr. Tex. Children's Hosp. Scientific adv. com. Patton Med. Devices; editorial bd. Diabetes, Nutrition & Metabolism, Endocrine Practice, Diabetes Care, Jour. Clinical Endocrinology & Metabolism; assoc. editor Mayo Clinic Proceedings. Office: Baylor College of Medicine Children's Nutrition Research Center 1100 Bates St Houston TX 77030 also: Patton Medical Devices 3108 N Lamar Blvd Austin TX 78705 E-mail: mhaymond@bcm.tmc.edu.

HAYNES, MOSES ALFRED, physician; b. Guyana, Nov. 17, 1921; came to U.S., 1947, naturalized, 1955; s. Milton Alphonso and Charlotte Mildred (Alleyne) Haynes; m. Hazel Louise Edgecombe, July 1, 1951; 1 child, Theresa Sue Aldrich. BS, Columbia U., 1951; MD, SUNY, 1954; MPH, Harvard U., 1963. Intern St. John's Episcopal Hosp., Bklyn., 1954-55; physician USPHS Indian Hosp., Cheyenne Agy., SD, 1955-59; asst. prof. community medicine U. Vt., 1959-64; assoc. prof. Sch. Pub. Health, Johns Hopkins, 1966-69; prof. preventive and social medicine and pub. health UCLA, 1969-77; assoc. dean Drew Postgrad. Med. Sch., Los Angeles, 1969-77, chmn. dept. cmty. medicine, 1969-74, acting dean, 1975-76, dean, pres., 1979-86; dir. Drew/Meharry/Morehouse Consortium Cancer Ctr., 1986-90. Pres. SECON Inc., 1977-79; vis. prof. Med. Coll., Trivandrum, Kerala, India, 1964-66; mem. cancer support rev. com. Nat. Cancer Inst. Chmn. health task force Urban Coalition, 1968—69; mem. Pres.'s Com. Health Edn., 1972; exec. dir. Nat. Med. Assn. Found., 1968—69; mem. bd. sci. counselors, divsn. cancer prevention and control Nat. Cancer Inst., 1989—93, chmn., 1991—93; mem. adv. com. Nat. Ctr. Health Stats., 1974—76; bd. dirs. Ptnrs. for Prevention, 1991—92; chmn. bd. dirs. Charles Drew U. Medicine and Sci., 2001—03; mem. adv. bd. Fogarty Internat. Ctr., 1992—93; mem. U.S. Preventive Svcs. Task Force, 1985—86. With USPHS, 1955—59. Fellow Am. Coll. Preventive Medicine, (pres. 1983-85); fellow AAAS; mem. Inst. Medicine of Nat. Acad. Sci. (internat. health bd., com. human rights 1986-89), Inst. Medicine (council 1983-86), Johns Hopkins Soc. Scholars, Alpha Omega Alpha. Home: 4161 Harbortown Ln Corona CA 92883 E-mail: malfredh@sbcglobal.net.

HAYNES, WILLIAM FORBY, JR., retired internist, cardiologist, educator; b. Newark, June 6, 1926; s. William Forby and Grace (Brien) H.; m. Constance Simpson, July 2, 1960; children: William, Suzanne, David; m. Aline Linehan James, Aug. 25, 1984. BS, U.S. Mcht. Marine Acad., 1946; AB, Princeton U., 1950; MD, Columbia U., 1954; MA in Theology, La Salle U., 2001. Diplomate Am. Bd. Internal Medicine (subcert. in cardiovasc. diseases), Nat. Bd. Med. Examiners. Intern St. Luke's Med. Ctr., NYC, 1954—55, 1957—59, fellow cardiology, 1959—60; ship's med. officer U.S. Navy, 1955—57; fellow in cardiology N.Y. Heart Assn., NYC, 1959-60; pvt. practice specializing in internal medicine/cardiology Princeton, N.J., 1960-97; ret., 1997. Asst. clin. prof. medicine Robert Wood Johnson Med. Sch., 1972—; sr. attending internal medicine Princeton Med. Ctr., 1960-89, ret., hon. staff, 1997—; lectr. on spirituality and med. practice, 1982—; mem. adv. coun. Ctr. for Study of Religion, Princeton U., 2000—09, pres. class of 1950, 2010-; adj. prof. theology, LaSalle U, guest lectr. Princeton Theological Seminary, med. resident NY Heart fellowship, 1959-60, sr. attending intern med., 1960-1997, pres. class 1950 Princeton U. Author: (books 4) A Physician's Witness to the Power of Shared Prayer, 1990, (book) Minding the Whole Person: Cultivating a Healthy Lifestyle from Youth Through the Senior Years, 1994, "Sea Time" Life on Board Supply & Troop Ships During World War II & Its Aftermath, 2007, Daily Word, 2010, Love Letters to God; contbr. articles to profl. jours.; co author: (with Geffery B. Kelly) "Is There a God in Health Care?" Toward a New Spirituality of Medicine., 2006. Vestry Trinity Episcopal Ch., Princeton, NJ; lt. Navy Med. Corps., med. officer USN, 1955-57, cadet Pacific Theater, 1944-45 Recipient Archbishop Theodore McCarrick award Disting. Svc., 1997, 250th Anniversary award, Princeton Swimming and Diving Team, 2000, LaSalle Grad. Religion Achievement award, 2001, Golden Merit award, Med. Soc. N.J., 2004; named Outstanding Profl. Achievement award, US Merchant Marine Acad. Found., 2006. Fellow: ACP, Am. Coll. Chest Physicians, Am. Coll. Cardiology, Theta Alpha Kappa; mem.: U.S. Masters Swimming Assn. (top ten), Princeton U. Friends of Swimming (pres. 1975—87), Princeton Officers Soc. (chaplain), Princeton U. Alumni Coun. Athletics, Third Order of St. Francis, Mercer County Heart Assn. (trustee 1964—76, v.p. 1970, Cardiologist of Yr. 1995), Old Guard at Princeton (pres. 2004—06), Nassau Club, Univ. Cottage Club Princeton. Episcopalian. Co-inventor GI String for detecting intestinal bleeding, 1960. Home and Office: 6 Skyfield Dr Princeton NJ 08540-7403 Personal E-mail: williamfhaynes@gmail.com.

HAYNIE, THOMAS POWELL, III, physician; b. Hearne, Tex., Aug. 9, 1932; s. Thomas Powell Jr and Sue Cummings Haynie; m. Bette Flossel, Mar. 10, 1956 (dec. Apr. 2002); children: David Powell, Amy Cummings, Sue Cummings, Garner Powell; m. Charlotte Peters, Dec. 18, 2004. Student, U. South, Sewanee, Tenn., 1949-51, U. Tex., Austin, 1951-52; MD, Baylor U., 1956. Diplomate Am Bd Internal Med, Am Bd Med Oncology, Am Bd Nuclear Med. Intern, then resident in internal medicine U. Mich. Med. Center, Ann Arbor, 1956-60, instr., 1960-62; asst. prof. medicine, dir. nuclear med. service U. Tex. Med. Br., Galveston, 1962-65; assoc. prof. medicine U. Tex.-M.D. Anderson Cancer Ctr., Houston, 1965-75; prof. U. Tex.-M.D. Anderson Hosp. and Tumor Inst., Houston, 1975-95, James E. Anderson prof. nuclear medicine, 1988-95, prof. emeritus of nuclear medicine, 1995—, chief sect. nuclear medicine, 1967-84, chmn. dept. nuclear medicine, 1984-93, head dept. internal medicine, 1977-84. Adj prof radiology Baylor Col Med, Houston, 1996—; pres Am Col Nuclear Med, 1993—94; consult in field. Contbr. articles in field, chapters to books; editor: Jour Nuclear Med, 1985—89. Mem.: AMA, ACP, AAAS, Am. Coll. Radiology, Tex. Assn. Physicians Nuclear Medicine, Tex. Med. Assn., Soc. Nuclear Medicine, Assn. Univ. Radiologists, Am. Thyroid Assn., Radiol. Soc. N.Am., Am. Coll. Nuclear Medicine, Am. Coll. Nuclear Physicians, Order St. Lazarus of Jerusalem, Sigma Xi, Phi Gamma Delta. Episcopalian. Office: U Tex-MD Anderson Cancer Ctr 1515 Holcombe Blvd Houston TX 77030-4009 Home: 771 Lakewood Ct Lewisville TX 75077-8686 Personal E-mail: thaynie@swbell.net. Business E-Mail: thaynie@mdanderson.org.

HAYNSWORTH, ROBERT FRANCIS, JR., anesthesiologist; b. El Paso, Tex., Aug. 11, 1954; MD, U. Tex., Houston, 1981. Cert. in anesthesiology, specialty in pain mgmt. Flex intern Tex. Tech. U. Health Sci. Ctr., Lubbock, 1981-82, resident in anesthesiology, 1982-84, chief resident in anesthesiology, 1983-84; fellow in pain mgmt. U. Tex. S.W. Med. Sch., Dallas, 1984—85; attending anesthesiologist Baylor U., Tex., 1992—2002, attending physician Tex., 1992—2002; clin. dir. Baylor Pain Mgmt. Ctr., 1992—. Office: 530 Clara Barton Blvd Ste 215 Garland TX 75042-5740

HAYWOOD, ANNE MOWBRAY, pediatrician, virologist, educator; b. Balt., Feb. 5, 1935; d. Richard Mansfield and Margaret (Mowbray) H. BA in Chemistry, Bryn Mawr Coll., 1955; MD, Harvard U., 1959. Cert. Am. Bd. Pediat. Intern U. Calif. Med. Ctr., San Francisco, 1959-60; fellow biochemistry dept. Columbia U., NYC, 1961-62; fellow divsn. biology Calif. Inst. Tech., Pasadena, 1960-61, 62-64; asst. prof. microbiology, microbiology dept. Northwestern U. Med. Sch., Chgo., 1964-66, Yale U. Med. Sch., New Haven, 1966-73; resident in pediat. U. Wash., Seattle, 1974-75, pediat. infectious disease fellow, 1975-76, Vanderbilt U., Nashville, 1976-77; assoc. prof. Dept. Pediat. and Microbiology, Immunology U. Rochester, NYC, 1977—. Vis. asst. prof. Rockefeller U., N.Y.C., 1971-72; vis. scientist biophysics unit Agrl. Rsch. Coun., Cambridge, Eng., 1972-74, Inst. for Immunology and Virology, U. Zürich, Switzerland, 1987; vis. assoc. prof. dept. zoology U. Calif., Davis, 1986; vis. assoc. prof. McArdle Lab. for Cancer Rsch., U. Wis., 1999-2000; adj. scientist Nat. Inst. Child Health and Human Devel., NIH, 2004-05. Co-author: Practice of Pediatrics, 1977, Infections in Children, 1982, Liposome Letters, 1983, Practice of Pediatrics, 1987, Molecular Mechanisms of Membrane Fusion, 1988, Membrane Fusion, 1991, Encyclopedia of Human Biology, 1991, 2d edit., 1997, Cell and Model Membrane Interactions, 1991, Infections of the Central Nervous System, 2004. Fogarty Internat. Ctr. Sr. fellow NIH, 1987, European Molecular Biology Orgn. fellow, 1973-74, NIH Spl. fellow, 1971-73, Am. Cancer Soc. Postdoctoral fellow, 1960-62; Harvard Med. Sch. scholar, 1955-59, Harriet Judd Sartain scholar, 1955-59, N.Y. Alumnae scholar Bryn Mawr Coll., 1951-55. Democrat. Office: U Rochester Med Ctr Dept Pediatrics PO Box 777 Rochester NY 14642-8777 Office Phone: 585-275-7945. Business E-Mail: anne_haywood@urmc.rochester.edu.

HAYWOOD, B(ETTY) J(EAN), anesthesiologist; b. Boston, June 1, 1942; d. Oliver Garfield and Helen Elizabeth (Salisbury) H.; m. Lynn Brandt Moon, Aug. 29, 1969 (div. Aug. 1986); children: Kaylin, Kristan, Kelly, Kasy R BSc, Tufts U., 1964; MD, U. Colo., 1968; MBA, Oklahoma City U., 1993; Grad., Air War Coll., 1997. USAF 1st female intern Wilford Hall AFB, San Antonio, 1968-69; resident in pediatrics U. Ariz., Tucson, 1971-72, resident in anesthesiology, 1972-74; dir. anesthesia dept. Pima County Hosp., Tucson, 1975-76; staff anesthesiologist South Community Hosp., Oklahoma City, 1977—, Moore (Okla.) Mcpl. Hosp., 1981-94, chief of anesthesia, 1990-94; staff anesthesiologist St. Anthony Hosp., Oklahoma City, 1982—; instr. dept. anesthesia U. Okla. Health Sci. Ctr., Oklahoma City, 1999—; col. USAF, active duty for Op. Enduring Freedom Wilford Hall Med. Ctr., Lackland AFB, Tex., 2001—02; 1st Ferak intern USAF. Chief of ethics com. S.W. Med. Ctr., 1996. Bd. dirs. N.Am. South Devon Assn., Lynnville, Iowa, 1978—86; mem. med. com. Planned Parenthood Okla., 1992—94; col. USAFR, 1968—2007. Mem. ASA, World South Devon Assn. (U.S. rep. 1985, 88), Tufts U. Alumni Assn. (rep.), Chi Omega (treas. 1963-64) Republican. Presbyterian. Avocations: skiing, sailing. Home: 705 NW 144th St Edmond OK 73013-1878 Personal E-mail: Beej1942@sbcglobal.net.

HAYWOOD, H(ERBERT) CARL(TON), psychologist, educator; b. Taylor County, Ga., July 2, 1931; s. Howard Chapman and Rosebud (Smith) H.; m. Nancy Patricia Roberts, Oct. 5, 1951 (div. Mar. 1971), children: Carlton, Terence, Elizabeth, Kristin; m. Dona June Wooldridge Tapp, Sept. 6, 1993 (div. Mar. 2000). AB, San Diego State Coll., 1956, MA, 1957; PhD, U. Ill., 1961. Lic. clin. psychologist Tenn. Mem. faculty George Peabody Coll. (merged with Vanderbilt U. 1979), Nashville, 1962—94, Alexander Heard disting. svc. prof., 1993-94, prof. psychology, 1969-93, prof. spl. edn., 1975-79, prof. emeritus, 1994—, dir. mental retardation rsch. tng. program, 1968-70; dir. Inst. Mental Retardation and Intellectual Devel., 1970-73, Office Rsch. Adminstrn., 1974-76, John F. Kennedy Ctr. Rsch. Edn. and Human Devel., 1971-83; prof. neurology Vanderbilt U. Sch. Medicine, 1971-93; prof. psychology and edn., dean grad. sch. edn. & psychology Touro Coll., NYC, 1993-2000. Vis. prof. U. Toronto, 1965-66; sr. fellow Vanderbilt Inst. Pub. Policy Studies, 1983-88; chmn. Nat Mental Retardation Research Center Dirs., 1979-82; adv. bd. Ill. Inst. Developmental Disabilities, Chgo., 1970-78, Eunice Kennedy Shriver Center Mental Retardation, Waltham, Mass., 1973-80, Tenn. Dept. Mental Health, 1964-92; mem. nat. child health and human devel. council NIH, 1983-88; cons. President's Com. on Mental Retardation, 1968-73; mem. sci. rev. com., health research facilities br., div. edn. and research facilities NIH, 1967-71 Author (with Brooks and Burns): Bright Start: Cognitive Curriculum for Young Children, 1992; editor: Brain Damage in School Age Children, 1968; author (with Lidz): Dynamic Assessment in Practice, 2007; editor: Social Cultural Aspects of Mental Retardation, 1970; editor: (with Begab and Garber) Prevention of Retarded Development in Psychosocially Disadvantaged Children; editor: (with J.R. Newbrough) Living Environments for Developmentally Retarded Persons, 1981; editor: (with D. Tzuriel) Interactive Assessment, 1992; editor: (with S. Friedman) Developmental Follow-Up: Domains, Concepts, and Methods, 1994; editor: Am. Jour. Mental Deficiency, 1969—79, Jour. Cognitive Edn. and Psychology, 1999—2006; mem. editl. bd.: Jour. Abnormal Child Psychology, 1973—89, Contemporary Psychology, 1982—85, Acta Paedologica, 1983—87, Jour. Mental Deficiency Rsch., 1984—2001, Internat. Rev. Rsch. in Mental Retardation, 1982—97; contbr. articles on child devel., motivation, cognitive edn., psycho assessment and mental retardation to profl. jours. Trustee Am. U. Rome, 2000—04. With USN, 1950-54. Recipient Myrtle Wreath Citation of Honor, So. Region Hadassah, 1979. Fellow Am. Assn. Mental Retardation (v.p. psychology 1975-77, 1st v.p. 1978-79, pres. 1980-81, Leadership award, 1985, Rsch. award, 1989), APA (pres. Div. 33 1978-79, mem. Coun. of Reps. 1980-82, Edgar A. Doll award, 1988), Assn. for Psychol. Sci.; mem. Internat. Assn. Cognitive Edn. (pres. 1988-92, Disting. Svc. award, 1995), Soc. Rsch. in Child Devel., Inst. Medicine. Democrat. Episcopalian. Avocations: piano, organ, choral conducting. Business E-Mail: carl.haywood@vanderbilt.edu.

HAYWOOD, L. JULIAN, cardiologist, educator; b. Reidsville, NC, Apr. 13, 1927; s. Thomas Woodly and Louise Viola (Hayley) H.; m. Virginia Elizabeth Paige, Dec. 3, 1953; 1 child, Julian Anthony. BS, Hampton Inst., 1948; MD, Howard U., DC, 1952. Intern St. Mary's Hosp., Rochester, NY, 1952-53; resident L.A. County Hosp., 1956-58; fellow cardiology White Meml. Hosp., 1959-61; traveling fellow U. Oxford, England, 1963; instr. medicine Loma Linda (Calif.) U., 1960-61, asst. prof., 1961-73, assoc. clin. prof., 1973-82, clin. prof., 1982—; asst. prof. medicine U. So. Calif., 1963-67, assoc. prof., 1967-76, prof., 1976—2010; dir. EKG dept. L.A. County/U. So. Calif.

Med. Ctr., prof. emeritus, 1998—2010. Past dir. coronary care unit, physicians tng. program Regional Med. Programs L.A. County/U. So. Calif. Med. Ctr, 1970-75; cons. Los Angeles County Coroner, Indsl. Accident Bd. Calif., Health Care Tech. Divsn., USPHS, Nat. Heart and Lung Inst.; past mem. cardiology adv. com. divsn. heart and vascular diseases; bd. dirs., pres. Sickle Cell Diseases Found.; mem. Armed Forces Epidemiol. Bd., 1996-2006; active U. So. Calif. Salerni Collegium, 1997-98; bd. dirs. Charles Drew U. Medicine and Scis., 1999—. Contbr. articles profl. jours.; Mem. editorial bds.: Jour. Nat. Med. Assn. Past pres., hon. mem., bd. dirs. Am. Heart Assn. Greater L.A., 1989—. With M.C. USNR, 1954-56. Recipient award of merit L.A. County Heart Assn., 1968, 69, 73, 75, 78, 79, 95, Recognition award, Horvard U. Med. Alumni Assn., 1977, Appreciation award, 1990, Recognition award, 2002, Disting. Alumnus award Howard U. Sch. Medicine, 1982, Disting. Svc. award, 1996, Disting. Health Educator award, 2003, Louis B. Russel award Am. Heart Assn., 1988, Merit award, 1991, Heart of Gold award Am. Heart Assn./Greater L.A. Affiliate, 1989, Dedicated Svc. award, 1991, 93, Award of Achievement in Rsch., 1994, 20th Anniversary Founder's award Assn. Black Cardiologists, 1994, Cert. of Appreciation, Armed Forces Epidemiology Bd., 2001, Eagle Cert. of Excellence award Nat. Med. Fellowships, N.Y.C., 2004, Disting. Svc. award, 2004, Professorship award, 2010, Cert. of Appreciation, Office of Def., 2006, Disting. Svc. award Black History Month, LA County/U. So. Calif. Med. Ctr., 2007; J.B. Johnson Meml. lectr., 1975, 88; honoree Internal Medicine sect. Nat. Med. Assn., 1988; named Alumnus of Yr.-at-Large, Hampton U., 1993; nat. med. fellow Gala West 2004, 2004, Lifetime Achievement award Sickle Cell Diseases Found., 2007; 50 Yrs. Svc. award Loma Linda U, 2009. Master ACP; fellow AAAS (Disting. Svc. award 2007), L.A. Acad. Medicine, Am. Coll. Cardiology (Disting. Svc. award 2001, Cert. of Merit 2003, Cert. of Appreciation 2003), Am. Heart Assn. (coun. on clin. cardiology, coun. on atherosclerosis, exec. com. coun. on epidemiology, long range planning com., dir., past sec., v.p. Greater L.A. affiliate, pres.); mem. AMA, AAUP, Am. Fedn. Clin. Rsch., Western Soc. Clin. Investigation, Assn. Advancement Med. Instrumentation, Nat. Med. Assn. (Charles Drew Med. Soc.), N.Y. Acad. Scis., Hampton Inst. Alumni Assn. (past pres. L.A. chpt.), Med. Faculty Assn. U. So. Calif. Sch. Medicine (past pres.), Assn. Physicians L.A. County Hosp. (pres. 1991-2006), Western Assn. Physicians, Fedn. Am. Scientists, Assn. Black Cardiologists (Walter Booker Innovation award 1990), Assn. Acad. Minority Physicians (councilor, pres.-elect 1992-93, pres. 1993-94), Alpha Omega Alpha, Am. Coll. Physicians (Laureate award So. Calif. Region I 1997). Office: LACt USC Med Ctr 2020 Zonal Ave Intern Resident Room 332 Los Angeles CA 90033-1029 Office Phone: 323-226-7116. Business E-Mail: jhaywood@hsc.usc.edu.

HAYWOOD, THEODORE JOSEPH, physician, educator; b. Monroe, NC, Feb. 13, 1929; s. Jesse Beman and Mary (McDonald) H.; m. Nancy Hume Ferguson, Dec. 21, 1959; children: Elizabeth Linscott, Keene McDonald, Mark Shepard. BS, The Citadel, 1948; MD, Vanderbilt U., 1952. Diplomate: Am. Bd. Pediatrics, Am. Bd. Allergy and Immunology. Pvt. practice allergy, Houston, 1958—; mem. staff Tex. Children's Hosp., 1958—, mem. active staff Pediatrics, 1963—; mem. faculty Baylor U. Coll. Medicine, 1958—, clin. assoc. prof. pediatrics and allergy, 1977—. Assoc. mem. U. Tex. McDonald Obs., 2000—, bd. visitors dept. astronomy, 2007—. Served with M.C. AUS, 1955-57. Fellow Am. Coll. Allergists, Am. Acad. Allergy and Immunology, Am. Acad. Pediatrics; mem. Sigma Xi. Clubs: River Oaks Country (Houston). Republican. Episcopalian. Home: 2923 Ferndale Pl Houston TX 77098-1117 Office: McGovern Allergy & Asthma Clinic 4710 Bellaire Blvd Ste 200 Bellaire TX 77401-4505 Home Phone: 713-522-5600; Office Phone: 713-661-1444. Business E-Mail: mac@mcgovernallergy.com.

HAYWORTH, SCOTT DAVID, physician; b. NYC, Apr. 4, 1956; s. Henry Charles and Anne (Sinnreich) H.; m. Nan Alison Sutter, June 21, 1981; children: William, John. AB, Princeton U., 1978; MD, Cornell U., 1984. Diplomate Am. Bd. Ob/Gyn., Nat. Bd. Med. Examiners. Intern Mt. Sinai Hosp., NYC, 1984-85, resident physician, 1985-87, chief resident, 1987-88; physician Mt. Kisco (N.Y.) Med. Group, 1988—, v.p., 1995-96, pres., 1996—, acting med. dir., 1996-98, CEO, 1998—. Co-chmn. laser com. No. Westchester Hosp., 1991-95, mem. pharmacy and therapeutics com., 1990-04, mem. med. cabinet, 2002-04; found. bd., 2005-; mem. nat. physician adv. bd. Aetna, 2004-; clin. asst. prof. Mt. Sinai Sch. Medicine, NYC, 2005—, nat. exec. bd. Am. Coll. Ob-Gyn., 2008- Consulting editor Contemporary Ob-Gyn., 2006—; contbr. chpt. to book and articles to profl. jours. Bd. dirs. No. Westchester Hosp. Found., 2005—, Cmty. Mut. Savs. Bank, 2010; sr. advisor Arsenal Capital Ptnrs., 2009—. Recipient award of merit Vis. Nurse Assn. Hudson Valley, 2005; NIH fellow, 1981, David Bar fellow, 1981. Fellow Am. Coll. Ob-Gyn. (chmn. Hudson Valley sect. 2000-01, sec. Dist. II-NY 2002, treas. Dist. II-NY 2002-04, vice chair Dist. II-NY 2004-, vice chair 2004-2008, chair 2008-, Dist. Svc. award 2002, Am. Coll. OB-Gyn. Nat., 2007, vice chmn. Finance Com., Nat. Compensation Com., 2007); mem. Westchester Obstet. and Gynecol. Soc. (sec.-treas. 1995-96, co-pres. 1996-97, pres. 1997-99), Internat. Soc. Gynecol. Endoscopy, Gynecol. Laser Soc., Am. Med. Group Assn. (bd. dir. 2005—, chmn. membership com. 2005—, found. bd. dirs. 2006-, exec. com. bd. dir. 2008-, sec. 2009, chair 2011). Office: Mt Kisco Med Group 90 S Bedford Rd Mount Kisco NY 10549-3412 Office Phone: 914-241-1050.

HAZARIKA, SUKANYA, lawyer; b. Guwahati, Assam, Aug. 24, 1984; LLB, Delhi U., 2008; LLM attending, Harvard Law Sch., 2011—. Mgr. academic programmes Pub. Health Found. India, 2006—08, legal officer, 2008—. Adj. prof. Indian Inst. Pub. Health, Delhi, 2010—. Avocations: dance, reading, singing. Home: D 1/10 Hauz Khas Market New Delhi 110016 India Personal E-mail: sukanya.hazarika@ymail.com.

HAZBOUN, VIVECA, psychiatrist; b. Ramallah, Jordan, Nov. 2, 1949; arrived in U.S., 1966; d. Albert Anthony and Helen Hazboun. BS in Chemistry, Immaculate Heart Coll., LA, 1970; MD, U. So. Calif., 1976. Diplomate in adult psychiatry Am. Bd. Psychiatry and Neurology, 1982, in child psychiatry Am. Bd. Psychiatry and Neurology, 1984. Tchg. asst. Grad. Sch. U. So. Calif., LA, 1970—72; intern in internal medicine Huntington Meml. Hosp., Pasadena, Calif., 1976—77; resident in adult psychiatry LA County-U. So. Calif. Med. Ctr., 1977—79, fellow in child and adolescent psychiatry, 1979—81, chief child resident, 1980—81, asst. prof. clin. psychiatry, 1981—85, clin. instr., 1980—81; practice adult, child and adolescent psychiatry LA, 1980—; supr. mental health UN Relief and Work Agy., 1990—95; founder and dir. adult and child psychiatry and neurology Guidance and Tng. Ctr., 1994—2008. Ward chief children's inpatient Los Angeles County-U. So. Calif. Med. Ctr. Psychiat. Hosp., 1981—85; cons. staff Edgemont Psychiat. Hosp., LA, 1982—85; cons. Medecins sans Frontieres, Jerusalem, Medecins du Monde, Jerusalem; project dir. World Vision. Contbr. articles to med. jours. Recipient Papal award, Rome, 1968, recognition awards Child Guidance Clinic, 1980, Women in Data Processing, 1983; fellow Child Guidance Clinic, 1980. Mem. WHO (steering com., thematic group, 2003—), Am. Acad. Child Psychiatry, So. Calif. Psychiat. Soc., So. Calif. Soc. Child Psychiatry, Internat. Assn. Child and Adult Psychiatry (sci. com.), Ea. Mediterranean Child and Adult Psychiatry Assn. (ethics com.), Am. Arab Univ. Grads. Office: PO Box 14016 Jerusalem Israel Office Phone: 310-543-0105. Business E-Mail: gtc@p_ol.com.

HAZEL, WILLIAM A., JR., orthopedist; m. Cindy Hazel; children: W. Andrew Jr., Susanne D. BS in Civil Engring., Princeton U., 1978; MD, Duke U., 1983. Orthopedic resident Mayo Clinic, 1988; orthopedic surgeon Commonwealth Orthopaedics and Rehabilitation, Vienna, Va.; asst. orthopedic surgeon Washington Redskins, 1988—95, DC United, 1995—2005. Mem.: AMA (alt. delegate Va. Delegation 1993—96, vice chmn. Va. Delegation 1996—98, chair Va. Delegation 1999—2003, bd. trustees 2004—10), Va. Orthopedic Surgery Soc., Va. Med. PAC, Med. Soc. Va. (past speaker and pres.), Fairfax County Med. Soc., Am. Med. Soc., Am. Coll. Surgeons, Am. Assn. Orthopedic Surgeons, Fairfax C. of C., Duke U. Davidson Club, Mayo Clinic Alumni Assn. Office: Commonwealth Orthopaedics & Rehabilitation Ste 220 13350 Franklin Farm Rd Herndon VA 20171 Office Phone: 703-471-5300. Office Fax: 703-471-4391. *

HAZENFIELD, HUGH NORMAN, surgeon; b. Indpls., May 6, 1942; s. Harold Henry and Pearle Esther (Attig) H.; m. Barbara Lynn Shellabarger; Aug. 15, 1964; children: Anthony Michael, Andrew Bradley. BA, U. Chgo., 1964, MD, 1968. Diplomate Am. Bd. Otolaryngology. Chmn. divsn. otolaryngology Cook County Hosp., 1975—79, assoc. med. dir., 1978—79; chmn. divsn. otolaryngology Head and Neck Surgery Michael Reese Hosp., Chgo., 1979—89, assoc. v.p. profl. affairs, 1987—89; chmn. dept. surgery Wahiawa Gen. Hosp., 1989—92, Kapiolani Med. Ctr. for Women and Children, 1989—2005, St. Francis Med. Ctr. West, 1990—2006, Kapiolani Med. Ctr. at Pali Momi, 1993—, vice chief-of-staff, 2004—06, chief of staff, 2006—08, chief med. officer, 2009—. Attending surgeon Children's Meml. Hosp., Chgo., 1976-89; cons. Larabida Hosp., Chgo., 1984-89. Contbr. articles to med. jours. Bd. dirs. St. Mary's Sch., Evanston, Ill., 1981-84, Lincoln Opera, Chgo., Wahiawa Hosp., 1989-2009, Wahiawa Hosp. Assn., 1991-2009, chmn., 1995-97; bd. dirs. Hawaii Opera Theatre, 1997—, v.p., 2001-09. Served with USN, 1969-71. Fellow Am. Acad. Otolaryngology, ACS, Chgo. Laryngological and Otological Soc., Hawaii Soc. Otolaryngology—Head and Neck Surgery. Avocations: computer science, sailing, classical music, motorcycling. Office: 98-1079 Moanalua Rd Exec Office Aiea HI 96701-4714 Office Phone: 808-485-4544. Personal E-mail: hawaiibiker@gmail.com.

HAZZARD, WILLIAM RUSSELL, geriatrician, educator; b. Ann Arbor, Mich., Sept. 5, 1936; s. Albert Sidney and Florence Bernice (Woolsey) Hazzard; m. Ellen Bennett Friedman, June 10, 1961; children: Susan Lovejoy Roque, Russell Holden, Rebecca Cornell Oliver, Daniel Bennett. AB, Cornell U., 1958, MD, 1962. Diplomate Am. Bd. Internal Medicine, Am. Bd. Geriatrics. Resident in internal medicine U. Wash. Sch. Med. and Affiliated Hosps., Seattle, 1966—67, fellow in endocrinology and metabolism, 1965—66, 1967—69; from instr. to prof. medicine U. Wash., Seattle, 1969—82, dir. Northwest Lipid Rsch. Clinic, 1972—78; investigator Howard Hughes Med. Inst., U. Wash., Seattle, 1972—80; chief divsn. gerontology and geriatric medicine, 1978—82; prof. medicine, assoc. dir. dept. medicine Johns Hopkins Med. Instns., Balt., 1982—86, dir. ctr. on aging, 1983—86; prof., chmn. dept. internal med. Bowman Gray Sch. Medicine of Wake Forest U., Winston-Salem, NC, 1986—98; dir. J. Paul Sticht Ctr. on Aging of Wake Forest U., Winston-Salem, NC, 1987—97; sr. adv. J. Paul Ctr. On Aging of Wake Forest U., 1998—; prof. medicine U. Wash., Seattle, 1999—; dir. geriatrics and extended care VA Puget Sound Health Care Sys., 1999—. Vis. lectr., hon. sr. registrar Oxford (Eng.) U., 1977—78, St. Thomas Sch. Medicine, London, 1977—78; dir. sect. gerontology and geriatric medicine VA Puget Sound Health Care Sys., Seattle, Tacoma, Wash., 1999—. Editor: Principles of Geriatric Medicine and Gerontology, 1984, 1989, 1993, 1999, 2003, 6th edit., 2009; contbr. over 200 articles to jours. in field. Lt. USNR, 1963—65. Fellow: ACP; mem.: Nat. Inst. on Aging (mem. nat. adv. coun. 1995—99, aging rev. com. 1990—94, Geriatric Medicine Acad. award 1980), Am. Clin. and Climatol. Assn., Assn. Am. Physicians, Am. Soc. Clin. Investigation (mem. emeritus), Am. Fedn. Biomed. Rsch. (mem. emeritus), Am. Heart Assn. (coun.on arteriosclerosis), Gerontol. Soc. Am. (chmn. clin. med. sect. 1984), Am. Geriatrics Soc. (bd. dirs. 1988—94, pres. 1993), Inst. Medicine of NAS. Avocations: gardening, conservation and nature study, music, athletics. Home: 3515 E Conover Ct Seattle WA 98122-6426 Office: VA Puget Sound Health Care Sys Geriatric Extended Care 1660 S Columbian Way Seattle WA 98108-1532 E-mail: william.hazzard@med.va.gov.

H'DOUBLER, FRANCIS TODD, JR., surgeon; b. Springfield, Mo., June 18, 1925; s. Francis Todd and Alice Louise (Bemis) H'D; m. Joan Louise Huber, Dec. 20, 1951 (dec. Dec. 1983); children: Julie H'Doubler Thomas and Sarah H'Doubler Muegge (twins), Kurt, Scott; m. Marie Ruth Duckworth, Jan. 18, 1986 Student, Washington U., St. Louis, 1943, Miami U., Oxford, Ohio, 1943-44; BS, U. Wis., 1946, MD, 1948. Intern Milw. Hosp., 1948-49; resident in surgery U.S. Naval Hosp., Oakland, Calif., 1950-51; practice medicine specializing in alternative medicine Springfield, Mo., 1952—; mem. courtesy staff St. John's Hosp., Springfield, L.E. Cox Hosp., Springfield. Bd. dirs. Union Planters Bank. Active Singing Doctors; chmn. fundraising drive YMCA, 1960-61, Sch. Bond and Tax Levy Com., 1958, Greene County Rep. Com., 1974-75; past bd. trustees Shriners Hosps., past chmn. spinal cord injury com., past chmn. rsch. com., past chmn. long range planning com., emeritus mem. rsch. com.; mem. Commn. to Reapportion Mo. Senate, 1971, Rep. State Fin. Com., 1972-75, steering com. Wilson's Creekl Battlefield Nat. Park, 1951-61, pres.'s adv. coun. Sch. Ozarks, Point Lookout, Mo., 1975-89; trustee Cottey Coll., Nevada, Mo., past bd. chmn.; bd. trustees Forest Inst. With USNR, 1943-46, 49-51. Decorated Bronze Star with V, Purple Heart with oak leaf cluster; recipient Disting. Service award Mo. Jaycees, 1959; Humanitarian award S.W. Mo. Drug Travelers Assn., 1971; named Young Man of Yr., City of Springfield, 1959 Fellow Am. Coll. Nuclear Medicine (founder's group); mem. AMA, Greene County Med. Assn., Mo. Med. Soc., Southwestern Surg. Congress, Mo. Surg. Assn., Soc. Nuclear Medicine, Am. Thyroid Assn., Springfield Jr. C. of C. (past pres.), Springfield C. of C., DAV, VFW, SAR, Am. Legion, Green Gang (co-founder), Sigma Nu (Outstanding Alumnus nat. award 1980), Nu Sigma Nu. Clubs: Hickory Hills Country. Lodges: Mason (33 deg.), Shriners (imperial potentate 1980-81), Red Cross of Constantine, Order DeMolay Legion Honor (hon.), Royal Order Scotland. Presbyterian.

HE, DALIN, surgeon, educator; b. China, Mar. 17, 1960; MD, Xi'an Jiaotong U., 2001. Dir., prof. First Hosp. Xi'an Jiaotong U., 1991. Office: Yanta West Rd 277 Xi'an Shaanxi 710061 China E-mail: dalinhexjtu@yahoo.com.cn.

HE, GUANGXUE, epidemiologist, educator; b. China, Feb. 28, 1963; BS in Pub. Health, Baotou Med. Coll., 1985; MSc in Med. Sci., Peking Union Med. Coll., 1991. Asst., dept. epidemiology Inner Mongolia Med. Coll., 1985—88; assoc. prof., dir., dept. tb control & prevention Beijing Rsch. Inst. Tb Control, 1991—2001; prof., dir., dept. internat. coop. & rsch. Nat. Ctr. Tb Control & Prevention, Chinese Ctr. Disease Control & Prevention, 2002—. Sec. & mem. Chinese TB Operational Rsch. Com., 2003; standing mem. exec. coun. Beijing Anti-Tuberculosis Assn., 2003; sec. & mem. Consultative Com. TB Experts Chinese Ministry Health, 2004; vice-dir. Chinese TB Ethical com., 2006; assoc. editor-in-chief Jour. Chinese Anti-Tuberculosis Assn., 2007—11. Recipient award, Beijing Peoples Govt., Chinese Antituberculosis Assn. Mem.: Internat. Union Against TB & Lung Disease. Avocations: ping pong/table tennis, football, video games. Office: No 155 Changbai Rd Changping Dist Beijing 102206 China Office Fax: 86 1058900556. Business E-Mail: heguangxue@chinatb.org.

HE, RUI, mechanical engineer; b. Chongqing, China, Oct. 30, 1975; PhD in Mech. Engring., U. Mich., Ann Arbor, 2007. Sr. mech. R & D engr. Boston Sci., 2007—. Contbr. to profl. publs. Avocation: soccer. Home: 4215 Comstock Ln N Minneapolis MN 55446 Business E-Mail: ruihe@umich.edu.

HE, XIAOQIONG, healthcare educator; b. Hunan, China, Nov. 15, 1964; MD, Tongji Med. U., MPH, 1989. Assoc. prof. Inst. Nutrition and Food Sci. Kunming Med. U., China, 1989—2006; vis. scientist Ctr. Cancer Prevention and Control Flinders U., Australia, 2006—07; rsch. assoc., rsch. scientist Mich. State U., 2008; prof. Sch. Pub. Health Kunming Med. U., 2009—. Bd. dir. Yunnan Nutrition Soc., 1994—2004, China Nutrition Soc., 1998—2002. Grant, China Natural Sci. Fund Com., Yunnan Sci. and Tech. Dept., Yunnan Edn. Dept. Mem.: China Nutrition Soc. Office: 191 Western Renmin Rd Kunming Yunnan 650031 China

HE, YONG, medical researcher; b. Shandong, China, Sept. 22, 1975; PhD, Chinese Acad. Scis., 2005. Investigator Beijing Normal U., 2008—. Recipient 'Scopus Young Scientist' award, Elsevier, Beijing Natural Sci. award; fellowship, Montreal Neurol. Inst., McGill U. Mem.: Soc. Neuroscience, Orgn. Human Brain Mapping. Avocations: basketball, movies, music. Office: 19 Xinjiekouwai St Beijing 100875 China Business E-Mail: yong.he@bnu.edu.cn.

HE, YU-GUANG, physician, educator; b. China, July 16, 1956; MD, MS, Tongji Med. U., China, 1982. Assoc. prof. U. Tex. Southwestern Med. Sch. at Dallas, 2001—. Program dir. Vitreal Retinal Svc., 2004—. Fellow: Am. Acad. Opthalmology. Office: 5323 Harry Hines Blvd Dallas TX 75390-9057 Office Fax: 214-648-2382. Business E-Mail: yuguang.he@utsouthwestern.edu.

HEAD, JONATHAN FREDERICK, cell biologist; b. Syracuse, NY, Nov. 23, 1949; s. Arthur Everard and Lillian Myrtle (Hendra) H.; m. Priscilla Catherine Tambone, July 28, 1984; 1 child, Catherine Elizabeth. BS in Zoology, Syracuse U., 1971; MA in Biology, Bklyn. Coll., 1977; PhD in Biology, Fordham U., 1985. Rsch. asst. Naylor Dana Inst. Disease Prevention/Am. Health Found., Valhalla, NY, 1974-78, Cornell U. Med. Coll., NYC, 1978, Mt. Sinai Sch. Medicine, NYC, 1978-84, rsch. assoc., 1984-86, rsch. asst. prof., 1986-87; dir. tumor cell biology Ctr. Clin. Scis./Internat. Clin. Labs., Nashville, 1986-89; pres. Mastology Rsch. Inst., Baton Rouge, 1989—, Oncbiomune, LLC, Baton Rouge, 2005—. High Complexity Clin. Lab. dir. Am. Bd. Bioanalysis, 1988—; med. lab. dir. Clin. Chemistry, State of Tenn., 1988—; clin. lab. scientist/specialist, State of La., 1995—; adj. assoc. prof. Tulane U. Sch. Medicine, New Orleans, 1989—, La. State U. Vet. Sch., Baton Rouge, 2005-; adj. prof. Delta State U., Cleve., Miss., 1992—; dir. R&D Med. Thermal Diagnostics, Baton Rouge, 1995-2001, Innovative Dug Techs., Edmond, Okla., 1999-2005; rschr. and lectr. in field of cancer. Contbr. articles, abstracts and chpts. to sci. publs. Mem. State of La. Adoption Cmty. Adv. Bd., 1992-95. Mem. AAAS, Am. Assn. Cancer Rsch., Am. Soc. Clin. Oncology, Am. Acad. Thermology, Soc. Immunotherapy of Cancer, Am. Soc. Breast Disease, European Soc. Med. Oncology, NY Acad. Scis. Methodist. Home: 6144 Hagerstown Dr Baton Rouge LA 70817-3917 Office: Mastology Rsch Inst 17050 Med Ctr Dr 4th Fl Baton Rouge LA 70816 Home Phone: 225-753-4939; Office Phone: 225-755-3070. Business E-Mail: jhead@eehbreastca.com.

HEAGARTY, MARGARET CAROLINE, retired pediatrician; b. Charleston, W.Va., Sept. 8, 1934; d. John Patrick and Margaret Caroline (Walsh) H. BA, Seton Hill Coll., 1957; BS, W.Va. Sch. Medicine, 1959; MD, U. Pa., 1961; DSc honoris causa, Iona Coll., 1989. Diplomate: Am. Bd. Pediatrics. Intern Phila. Gen. Hosp., 1961—62; resident in pediatrics St. Christopher's Hosp. for Children, Phila., 1962—64; dir. pediatric ambulatory care services N.Y. Hosp.-Cornell Med. Ctr., NYC, 1969—78; dir. pediatrics Harlem Hosp. Ctr. Columbia U., NYC, 1978—2000, prof. pediatrics coll. physicians & surgeons, 1987—2000, prof. emerita coll. physicians and surgeons, 2000—. Cons. Dept. HEW Promotion of Child Health, Washington; mem. Com. Community Oriented Primary Care Inst. Medicine, Washington; mem. Robert Wood Johnson Found. Program for Prepaid Managed Health Care, 1984; mem. governing council Inst. Medicine, Nat. Acad. Scis., 1986 Author: Changing the Medical Car System-Report of an Experiment, 1974, Medical Sociology: A Systems Approach, 1975, Child Health: Basics for Primary Care, 1980. Grantee Commonwealth Found., 1981, Robert Wood Johnson Found., 1983, Ctr. for Disease Control, 1985, Health Rsch. and Svc. Adminstrn., 1988, Nat. Inst. Allergy/Infectious Disease, 1988. Fellow Inst. Medicine (steering group for nat. forum on future of children and their families 1987—); mem. Ambulatory Pediatric Assn. (pres. 1976-77), Soc. Pediatric Research, Am. Pediatric Soc., Am. Acad. Pediatrics (com. on hosp. care 1988—), Assn. Pediatric Program Dirs., Nat. Bd. Med. Examiners. Home: 2520 Kingsland Ave Bronx NY 10469-6108

HEALEY, JOHN HENRY, orthopaedic surgeon, researcher; b. Lowell, Mass., Aug. 25, 1952; s. Robert Cummings and Ruth Elizabeth (Burckel) H.; m. Paula Olsiewski, Oct. 9, 1977; children: Georgia, Vivian. BS in Biology, Yale U., 1974; MD, U. Vt., 1978. Intern New Eng. Med. Ctr. Hosp., Tufts U.; resident in orthopedic surgery Hosp. for Spl. Surgery, 1979-83; fellowship in surg. oncology Meml. Sloan Kettering Cancer Ctr., 1983-84; attending surgeon Meml. Sloan Kettering Cancer Ctr., Hosp. Spl. Surgery, NYC, 1984—, chief orthopaedic surgery, 1991—; prof. surgery Cornell U. Med. Coll., NYC, 1984—, Alpha Omega Alpha, 1978; vice chair edn. dept. surgery, 2009—; prof. orthop. surgery Weill Med. Coll. Cornell U., 1999—. Rsch. exec. bd. mem. Hosp. Spl. Surgery, NYC, 1994-96. Editor: Diagnosis and Management of Pathologic Fractures, 1993, dep. editor Clin. Orthop. Rel. Res., 2008-, pres. Assn. Bone Joint Suurgeons, 2010-, bd. dirs. Mem. spl. gifts com. Yale U., New Haven, 1994. NIH grantee; recipient Career Devel. award Am. Cancer Soc., 1986, Disting. Academic Achievement award, U. Vt., 2003. Mem. Internat. Soc. Limb Salvage (pres. 1995-96, bd. dirs. 1983-2005), Orthopaedic Rsch. Soc. (bd. dirs. 1994-96), Orthopaedic Rsch. Edn. Found. (Zimmer award Orthopaedic Rsch. 1984, grant rev. com. 1995-98), America Acad. Orthop. Surgeons Rsch. Devel. Com., Korean Orthop. Soc. (hon. 2001), Peking U. Hon. Prof., Italian Soc. Orthop. & Traumatology. Avocation: baseball. Office: Meml Sloan Kettering Cancer Ctr 1275 York Ave New York NY 10065-6094 Office Phone: 212-639-7610. Business E-Mail: healeyj@mskcc.org. *

HEALY, PATRICIA COLLEEN, social worker; b. Denver, Aug. 24, 1935; d. Cecil John and Gracia Maude (Walker) Schulte; m. John Patrick Healy III, Aug. 3, 1957 (div. Jan. 1972); 1 child, Sean Patrick. BA, Sacred Heart Coll., Wichita, 1957; MSW, U. Kans., 1983; postgrad., Wichita State U., 1974, 75, 89, Emporia U., Kans., 1990, U. Kans., 1998. Lic. specialist clin. social worker, Kans.; cert. in spinal cord injury medicine. Proofreader Wichita Pub. Co., 1953; clk. typist Nat. Sales, Inc., Wichita, 1954-58, Dept. of Army, Ft. Leavenworth, Kans., 1958-60, Air Force, McConnell AFB, Kans., 1962-63; clk., typist VA Regional Office, Wichita, 1963-66; self-employed typist Wichita, 1966-70, ward clk., typist VA Regional Office and VA Med. Ctr., Wichita, 1970-73; vets. benefits counselor VARO, Wichita, 1973-83; social worker VA Med. Ctr., Wichita, 1983-2000; ret.; pvt. practice Wichita, 2000—. Author filmstrip, columns, book revs., feature stories and poetry. Former mem. Ctrl. Plains AAA Coun. on Aging; mem. Clin. Social Work Assn., 2003—; vol. Sr. Svcs.; bd. dirs. Ind. Living Ctr. South Ctrl. Kans., 1990—96, Sedgwick County Dept. Aging Cmty. Svc. Adv. Bd.; cmty. svcs. adv. bd. mems. Older Adult Alliance, Visioneering Wichita, Ctrl. Plains Area Agy. Aging, 2008. Roman Catholic. Avocations: writing, reading, photography, music, knitting and sewing.

HEAN, TAY KHOON, surgeon; MBBS, Singapore, 1988. Surg. fellowship Royal Coll. Surgeons, Glasgow, Singapore, 1995, Edinburgh, 1995; travelling fellowship scholarship understudy prof. Alfred Cushieri in ninewells hosp. for advance laparoscopic surgery Royal Coll. Surgeons Glasgow, Dundee, Scotland; fellowship Internat. Coll. Surgeons, 1995; advanced surg. tng. in gen. surgery Acad. Medicine Singapore (AMS), 1998; subspecialty tng. under 2 world renowned surgeons; health manpower devel. programme (HMDP) with prof. Bernard Launois at Pontchaillou hosp. Univ. de Rennes, Brittany, France; vis. dr. nat. cancer ctr. Singapore Gen. Hosp. (SGH); dir. Tay Khoon Hean Surgery Pte. Ltd., Singapore, Coun. mem. North West Cmty. Devel. Coun. (CDC). Recipient Sportsman of the Yr. Meritorious award, Singapore Nat. Olympic Coun., Sportsboy of the Yr., 1981, 1983; named one of the Top 40 in the World for 50m Freestyle, 1985. Mem.: Singapore Swimming Assn., WHO, Acad. of Tropical Surgery. Achievements include represented Singapore at various internat. meets including the Olympic Games, Commonwealth Games, Asian Games, SEA Games from 1979 to 1987. Office: Tay Khoon Hean Surgery Pte Limited Gleneagles Medical Centre 6 Napier Rd Number 08-02 258499 Singapore Office Phone: 6564711221. Office Fax: 6564711621. *

HEATH, JOHN ANDREW, oncologist, researcher; b. Washington, Sept. 10, 1962; s. William Carick Heath and Ann Mary Brenan; m. Annabel Mary Hawkins, Nov. 28, 1992. BVSc with honors, U. Melbourne, Australia, 1984, PhD, 1990, MBBS, 1993; MSc in Clin. Epedemiology, Harvard U., Boston, 2002. Cert. in Clin. Effectiveness Harvard U., 2000. Vet. surgeon U. Melbourne, Australia, 1985; intern St. Vincent's Hosp., 1994; basic tng. pediat. Royal Children's Hosp., 1995—97; advanced tng. hematology-oncology Children's Cancer Ctr., 1998; Robert Steele clin. rsch. fellow Meml. Sloan-Kettering Cancer Ctr. N.Y. Presbyn. Hosp., NYC, 1999—2001; neuro-oncologist Dana Farber Cancer Inst. Children's Hosp., Boston, 2001—02; sr. rsch officer Murdoch Children's Rsch. Inst., Melbourne, 2002; dir. clin. rsch. Children's Cancer Ctr., 2002—. Mem. med. and sci. adv. com. Leukemia Found. Victoria, Melbourne, Australia, 2002—, Telstra on Trac at PeterMac; mem. palliative care bd. Cancer Coun. Victoria, 2002—, mem. neuro-oncology com.; examiner Australia Med. Coun., 2002—; cons. Merck Pharms., NJ, 2003; spkr. at nat. and internat. confs.; peer reviewer Leukemia Found. NSW, Leukemia Found. Victoria, Nat. Health and Med. Rsch. Coun. grants, Jour. Pediat. and Child Health, 2002—, Internat. Soc. Pediat. Neuro-oncology Sci. Mtg., 2004—, Am. Jour. Pathology, Jour. Pathology, Jour. Clin. Neurosci. Mem. animal experimentation ethics com. Royal Children's Hosp., 2002—04; philanthropic advisor Harvard Club of Australia, 2005. Recipient Palliative Care award, Nat. Health and Med. Rsch. Coun., 2005; named Grad. of Yr., CIBA-GEIGY, 1993; grantee, Cancer Coun., 2004, Murdoch Children's Rsch. Inst., 2004; fellow, DHS, 2004, Nat. Health and Med. Rsch. Coun., 2005; scholar, Fedn. European Cancer Socs. - Am. Assn. Cancer Rsch. - ASCO, 1999, Am. Assn. Cancer Rsch., 2001. Fellow: Royal Australasian Coll. Physicians (Cottrell fellow 2005); mem.: Am. Soc. Hematology, Am. Soc. Pediat. Hematology and Oncology, Am. Assn. Cancer Rsch., Am. Soc. Clin. Oncology (Merit award 2001), Children's Oncology Group (prin. investigator 2003—, Young Investigator award 2004), Australia and New Zealand Children's Haematology and Oncology Group (dir. 2002—, dir. Tumor Not the Target com. 2004—). Avocations: travel, horse racing, golf, tennis. Home: Floradale 319 Springs Rd Terip Terip 3719 Australia Office: Childrens Cancer Ctr Royal Childrens Hosp Flemington Rd Parkville 3052 Melbourne Australia Office Phone: 613 9345 4864. Office Fax: 613 9345 6524. E-mail: john.heath@rch.org.au.

HEATHER, BREAM-ROUWENHORST, pharmacist; b. Clinton, Iowa, Apr. 10, 1982; PharmD, U. Iowa Coll. Pharmacy, 2005. Asst. prof. U. Iowa Coll. Pharmacy, 2007—; clin. pharmacy specialist Vets. Affairs Med. Ctr., 2007—. Mem.: Iowa Pharmacy Assn., Am. Pharmacists Assn., Am. Soc. Health-Sys. Pharmacists, Soc. Critical Care Medicine, Am. Coll. Clin. Pharmacy, Rho Chi. Office: Veterans Affairs Med Ctr 601 Hwy 6 W Iowa City IA 52241 Business E-Mail: heather-bream@uiowa.edu.

HEATON, CHARLES LLOYD, dermatologist, educator; b. Bryan, Tex., May 8, 1935; BS, Tex. A&M U., 1957; MD, Baylor U., 1961; MA (hon.), U. Pa., 1973. Diplomate Am. Bd. Dermatology. Intern Jefferson Davis Hosp., Houston, 1961-62; resident Baylor U., 1962-65; sr. attending physician Phila. Gen. Hosp., 1965-69, chief of svc., 1970-77; mem. dept. dermatology U. Pa. Sch. Medicine, 1966-78; assoc. prof. dermatology U. Pa., 1973-78, U. Cin., 1978-85, prof., 1985—2007, prof. emeritus, 2007—, interim dir. dept. dermatology, 1998; staff UC Health U. Hosp., 1978—. Author: Audiovisual Course in Venereal Disease, 1972, (with D.M. Pillsbury) Manual of Dermatology, 1980; contbr. 35 articles to profl. jours., 12 chpts. to books. Served to lt. comdr. USPHS, 1965-67. Recipient Disting. Svc. award, Ohio Dermatol. Assn., 2010, Career Achievement award, UC Health U. Hosp.; named Ohio Dermatologist of Yr., 2000. Fellow ACP, AAD, Coll. Physicians Phila.; mem. AMA, Soc. Investigative Dermatology, Am. Venereal Disease Assn., Am. Dermatol. Assn., Cin. Dermatol. Soc., Alpha Omega Alpha. Home: 5534 E Galbraith Rd Apt 25 Cincinnati OH 45236-2840 Office: University Cin Coll Medicine Dept Dermatology 231 Albert Sabin Way Cincinnati OH 45229-2827 Business E-Mail: charles.heaton@uc.edu.

HEBDEN, JOAN NARER, medical association administrator; b. Balt., Dec. 22, 1953; BS, U. Md. Sch. Nursing, 1975, MS, 1985. Nurse clinician, team leader, oncology ICU acute care U. Md., Med. Ctr., 1978—81, clin. nurse, open heart recovery rm, 1981—83, nurse epidemiologist, 1983—92, infection control mgr., 1992—99, dir., infection prevention and hosp. epidemiology, 1999—. Govs. task force HIV exposure correctional facilities, Md., 1997; consultative faculty, infection control Am. Healthcare Inst., 1997—2007; clin. faculty U. Md. Sch. Nursing, 2000—; infection prevention cons. U. Splty. Hosp., 2006—; editl. bd. Am. Jour. Infection Control, 2007—. Recipient Best Rsch. award, U. Md. Grad. Sch., 1985; grant, Ctrs. Disease Control, 1995—96. Mem.: Soc. Healthcare Epidemiologists Am., Assn. Profls. Infection Control, Sigma Theta Tau. Avocations: travel, reading. Home: 1302 W Lake Ave Baltimore MD 21210 Home Fax: 410-328-0089.

HEBER, DAVID, clinical nutritionist, medical educator; b. Celle, Germany, Apr. 26, 1948; naturalized, 1956; s. Max and Fela (Hendel) Heber; m. Anita Weinberg, Aug. 15, 1970; children: Marc Alan, Adrianna Michelle. BS in Chemistry, magna cum laude, UCLA, 1969, PhD in Physiology, 1978; MD, Harvard Med. Sch., Boston, 1973. Diplomate American Bd. Internal Medicine, cert. in endocrinology & metabolism, cert. specialist clin. nutrition American Bd. Nutrition. Med. intern Beth Israel Hosp., Boston, 1973-74; resident internal medicine Harbor-UCLA Med. Ctr., Torrance, Calif., 1974-76, fellow endocrinology & metabolism, 1976—78; asst. prof. medicine UCLA Sch. Medicine/Harbor UCLA Med. Ctr., 1978—83; assoc. prof. medicine UCLA Sch. Medicine, 1983—91, chief divsn. clin. nutrition, 1983—, prof. medicine, 1991—, dir. Ctr. Human Nutrition, 1996—. Nutritional cons. Calif. State Bd. Medicine, 1982—; vis. prof. nutrition Nat. Dairy Coun., 1985—91; dir. American Bd. Nutrition, 1994—2000; mem. Calif. Cancer Adv. Coun., 1998—2000. Author: Natural Remedies for a Healthy Heart, 1998, The Resolution Diet, 1999, What Color Is Your Diet?, 2001, The LA Shape Diet, 2004; mem. editl. bd. Obesity Rsch., 1995—, American Jour. Clin. Nutrition, 1997—2003, Alternative Medicine Alert, 2002—; contbr. articles to profl. jours.; med. expert KABC Radio/ABC Radio Network, 1984—86, KCBS TV LA, 1986—87, Discovery Health Channel Nat. Body Challenge, 2001—, TV appearances include CBS, NBC, MSNBC, CNN. Mem. patient care com. American Inst. Cancer Rsch., 1996—; chair nutrition adv. com. Calif. Avocado Commn., 1996—. Recipient Rsch. Career Devel. award, NIH, 1982—87, CaPCure Investigator award, Assn. Cure Prostate Cancer, 1994, Creativity award, Prostate Cancer Found., 2010. Fellow: ACP, American Coll. Nutrition; mem.: American Soc. Nutrition (Roland S. Weinsier award in Med./Dental Sch. Nutrition Edn. 2009), American Soc. Clin. Nutrition, American Soc. Enteral & Parental Nutrition, Sigma Xi, Alpha Omega Alpha, Phi Beta Kappa (dir.). Achievements include research in obesity treatment and nutrition for cancer prevention and treatment. Office: UCLA Ctr Human Nutrition David Geffen Sch Medicine 900 Veteran Ave Rm 12 217 Los Angeles CA 90095 Office Phone: 310-206-1987. Office Fax: 310-206-5264. *

HEBER, GEOFFREY, cosmetics executive; b. Sydney, Oct. 28, 1953; s. Kenneth Royce Heber and Madeleine Patricia Davidge; m. Deborah Isabelle Davis, Apr. 12, 1982; children: Katrina Claire, Thomas Geoffrey, Oliver James. MBBS with honors, U. NSW, Sydney, 1979; MBA, U. Sydney, 1989. Registered Med. Bd. NSW, 1980. Ptnr. Heber Davis Skin Clinic, Sydney, New South Wales, 1988—; exec. dir. Doctors Formula Pty. Ltd., Sydney, 1991—2001; exec. chmn. Ultraceuticals Pty. Ltd., Sydney, 2001—; fellow, faculty medicine Australasian Coll. Cosmetic Surgery, 2002. Mem.: Australian Med. Assn. Achievements include patents for Cross-Linked polysaccharide compositions; patents pending for Cross-Linked polysaccharide gels and method for dermal regeneration. Office: Heber Davis 37 Bay St Broadway New South Wales 2007 Australia

HEBLING, EDUARDO, medical educator; b. Piracicaba, Brazil, Feb. 14, 1968; Degree in Dentistry, Piracicaba Dental Sch., 1986. Assoc. prof. U. of Campinas, 2002—. Mem.: IADR. Avocations: tennis, running, golf. Office: Caixa Postal 52 Piracicaba Sao Paulo 13414018 Brazil Office Fax: 55-21-19-21065218. Business E-Mail: hebling@fop.unicamp.br.

HECHT, ANDREW C., orthopedist, surgeon, educator; MD, Harvard U., 1994. Diplomate Am. Bd. of Orthopaedic Surgery. Intern gen. surgery New England Deaconess Hosp.; resident orthopaedic surgery Mass. Gen. Hosp., 1995—99, Harvard Combined Orthopaedic Program; fellow spinal surgery Emory Univ. Spine Ctr., 2000—01; asst. prof. orthopaedics Mt. Sinai Sch. of Medicine, asst. prof. neurosurgery; spine surgical cons. NY Jets, NY Islanders, NY Dragons; spine surgical cons. numerous collegiate teams Hofstra Univ. and Molloy Coll.; dir. Nat. Football League spine care program for retired players Mt. Sinai Med. Ctr., co-dir. spine surgery; founder and med. co-dir. Newton-Wellesley Spine Ctr.; dir. spine surgery fellowship Mass. Gen. Hosp. Named Top Physician, Consumer Rsch. Coun. of America; named one of Top Doctors, NY Mag., Top Doctors for NY Metro Area, Castle and Connolly, Top Doctors in America, Super Doctors, NY Times, Best Doctors in America. Mem.: North Am. Spine Soc. Office: Mount Sinai Medical Center Department of Orthopaedic Surgery 9th Fl 5 E 98th St New York NY 10029 Office Phone: 212-241-8892. Office Fax: 212-423-0827. E-mail: andrew.hecht@mssm.edu.

HECHT, DAVID A., facial plastic surgeon; BS, Coll. William and Mary, 1989; MD, NYU, 1993. Diplomate Am. Bd. Otolaryngology, cert. Nat. Bd. Medical Examiners, facial plastic and reconstructive surgery, lic. Ariz. (lic. number 28516), 2000. Intern and resident gen. surgery dept. Georgetown Univ. Med. Ctr., Washington, 1993—95, resident otolaryngology - head and neck surgery dept., 1995—99; fellow and clin. instr. facial plastic and reconstructive surgery divsn. Univ. of Ill. at Chgo., 1999—2000. Co-author: (publs.) Effects of the novel a v integrin antagonist SM256 and cis-platinum on growth of murine squamous cell carcinoma PAM LY8, 2000, Skeletal modifications in rhinoplasty, 2000, Atypical presentations of cat scratch disease in the head and neck, 2001, Management of the middle ear hemangiomas, 2001, Preoperative rhinoplasty: evaluation and analysis, 2002; contbr. and numerous others. Recipient People's Choice Doctor, 101 North Mag., 2006; named one of the Best Doctors in America, 2007—08, Top Doctors, Phoenix Mag., 2007. Mem.: Ariz. Soc. of Otolaryngology-Head and Neck Surgery (pres. 2005—07), Am. Acad. of Otolaryngology-Head and Neck Surgery, Am. Acad. of Facial Plastic and Reconstructive Surgery, Phi Betta Kappa Nat. Honor Soc. Office: Ste 250 20201 N Scottsdale Healthcare Dr Scottsdale AZ 85255 Office Phone: 480-374-2935. Office Fax: 480-374-2940.

HECHT, MICHAEL H., chemistry professor; b. NYC, Jan. 2, 1956; BA, Cornell U., 1977; PhD, MIT, 1984. Prof. chemistry Princeton U., 1990—. Office: Princeton University Dept Chemistry Princeton NJ 08544 Business E-Mail: hecht@princeton.edu.

HECK, ALBERT FRANK, retired neurologist; b. Balt., Oct. 9, 1932; s. Albert Franklin and Dorothy Mary Heck; divorced; children: Albert William, Karl Andrew, Robert Conrad, Paul Christopher. AB, Johns Hopkins U., 1954; MD, U. Md., 1958. Diplomate: Am. Bd. Psychiatry and Neurology. Intern Mercy Hosp., 1958-59; NIH fellow in neurology U. Md., Balt., 1959-62, faculty, instr. to prof., 1964-77; prof., chmn. dept. neurology U. Tenn. Center for Health Scis., Memphis, 1977-82, dir. neurosci. program, 1978-82; prof. neurology W. Va. U., 1982-2000; ret., 2000. Vis. prof. Medezinische Hochschule Hannover, W. Ger., 1973-74 Contbr. writings to profl. publs. Served with M.C. U.S. Army, 1962-64. Recipient jr. investigator award NIH, 1965, U.S. sr. scientist award, 1973; Humboldt Found. prize Fed. Republic Germany, 1973-74 Fellow Am. Acad. Neurology, ACP, Stroke Council Am. Heart Assn.; mem. Am. Neurol. Assn., Alpha Omega Alpha. Achievements include research in field.

HECKADON, ROBERT GORDON, plastic surgeon; b. Brantford, Ont., Can., Jan. 30, 1933; s. Frederick Gordon and Laura (Penrose) Heckadon; m. Camilla Joyce Russell, July 11, 1959; children: David, Louise, Peter, William, Barbara. BA, U. Western Ont., 1954; MD, 1960; postgrad., U. Toronto, 1960—66, U. Vienna, 1966. Intern Toronto Gen. Hosp., 1960—61, asst. resident, 1962—63, Toronto Western Hosp., 1961, Toronto Wellesley Hosp., 1962; resident in plastic surgery St. Michael's Hosp., Toronto, 1963, Toronto Western Hosp., 1964, Toronto Gen. Hosp., 1964, Toronto Hosp. for Sick Children, 1965; asst. resident orthop. Toronto East Gen. Hosp, 1965—66; practice medicine specializing in plastic surgery, Windsor, Ont. Mem. surg. staff Hotel Dieu Grace, Windsor, Windsor Regional Hosp.; med. dir. Workplace Safety & Ins., Windsor. Served with RCAF, 1951—56. Fellow: ACS; mem.: Can. Soc. Plastic Surgeons, Royal Coll. Physicians and Surgeons, Windsor Acad. Surgery, Essex County Med. Assn., Ont. Med. Assn., Canadian Med. Assn.

HECKLER, FREDERICK ROGER, plastic surgeon; b. NYC, Mar. 7, 1942; s. Frances George; children: Jeremy, Michael, Adrienne, Lauren. Student, Tufts U., 1959-62, MD, 1966. Diplomate Nat. Bd. Med. Examiners, Am. Bd. Surgery, Am. Bd. Plastic Surgery with qualification in surgery of the hand. Intern in surgery U. Chgo. Med. Ctr., 1966-67; resident in gen. surgery Tufts New Eng. Med. Ctr., Boston, 1967-69; fellow in surgery Malmo (Sweden) Gen. Hosp., 1969-70; resident in plastic surgery Wilford Hall USAF Med. Ctr., San Antonio, 1973-75; fellow in hand surgery Denver Gen. Hosp., 1976-77; chief surgery USAF Hosp., Taiwan, 1976-77; asst. prof. surgery U. Miss. Med. Ctr., Jackson, 1977-79, chief divsn. plastic surgery, 1979-82; dir. divsn. plastic surgery Allegheny Gen. Hosp., Pitts., 1982—; clin. assoc. prof. plastic surgery U. Pitts. Sch. Medicine, 1982—. Active med. staff Miss. Cripple Children's Treatment and Tng. Ctr., Miss., 1981-82; dir. cleft palate clinic Allegheny Gen. Hosp., Pitts., 1982-88; attending physician St. Margaret Meml. Hosp., Pitts., 1984-89, Montefiore Hosp., Pitts., 1986-89, Divine Providence Hosp., Pitts., 1991—, North Hills Passavant Hosp., Pitts., 1993; cons. med. staff Harmarville Rehab. Ctr., Inc., Pitts., 1985; cons. in plastic surgery VA Hosp., Pitts., 1993—, Miss. Meth. Rehab. Ctr., Jackson, 1977-82, VA Hosp., Jackson, 1977-82; dir. burn unit U. Miss. Med. Ctr., Jackson, 1979-82, co-dir. hand surgery svc., 1979-82; mem. med. staff Miss. Crippled Children's Treatment and Tng. Ctr., Jackson, 1981-82; presenter in field. Contbr. numerous articles to profl. publs., chpts. to books; assoc. editor Jour. Plastic and Reconstructive Surgery. Lt. col. USAF, 1972-76. Mem. AMA, ACS, Am. Soc. Plastic and Reconstructive Surgeons, Am. Assn. Plastic Surgeons, Assn. Mil. Plastic Surgeons, Soc. Air Force Clin. Surgeons, Am. Burn Assn., Internat. Soc. for Burn Injuries, Am. Cleft Palate Assn., Plastic Surgery Rsch. Coun., Am. Soc. for Surgery of Hand, Am. Assn. Hand Surgery, Royal Soc. Medicine, Assn. Acad. Chmn. of Plastic Surgery, Lipolysis Soc. N.Am., Allegheny County Med. Soc., Pa. Med. Soc., Ohio Valley Plastic Surg. Soc., Pitts. Surg. Soc. Office: Allegheny Gen Hosp 320 E North Ave Pittsburgh PA 15212-4756 Office Phone: 412-359-4352.

HECTOR, ARANIBAR, cardiologist; b. Santiago, Chile, June 14, 1966; MD, Pontificia U. Catolica De Chile, 1991, degree in pediatrics, 1997. Chief cardiopulmonary resuscitation tng. unit Clinica Alemana De Santiago, 2008—. Editl. bd. mem. Thorax Mag., 2010—. Fellow:

Am. Acad. Chest Physicians; mem.: Am. Heart Assn., European Respiratory Soc. Avocation: mountain climbing. Home: Colina La Gloria 2446 Las Condes Santiago Met 7600726 Chile Personal E-mail: haranibarm@gmail.com.

HEDGES, JERRIS R., dean, medical educator, researcher; m. Susan Hedges. AA in Gen. Sci., Centralia Coll., Wash., 1969; B in Astronautics and Aeronautics, U. Wash., Seattle, M in Chemistry, MD; M in Med. Mgmt., U. So. Calif. Marshall Sch. Bus., LA. Residency Med. Coll. Pa.; faculty mem. U. Cin. Sch. Medicine; from assoc. prof. to prof. Oreg. Health & Scis. U., Portland, chmn. dept. emergency medicine, 1997—2005, vice-dean Sch. Medicine, 2005—08; dean John T. Burns Sch. Medicine U. Hawai'i at Manoa, Honolulu, 2008—. Editor: (med. jour.) Acad. Emergency Medicine, 1993—97; co-editor: (med. textbook) Clinical Procedures in Emergency Medicine; contbr. articles to profl. jours. Recipient Disting. Alumnus award, Centralia Coll., 2010. Mem.: Nat. Acad. Scis. Inst. of Medicine, Assn. Academic Chairs Emergency Medicine (former pres.), Soc. Acad. Emergency Medicine (former pres.). Achievements include research in the evaluation of Trauma System impact and effectiveness. Office: University Hawaii John A Burns Sch Medicine 651 Ilalo St Med Edn Bldg Office of Dean 2d Fl Honolulu HI 96813 Office Phone: 808-692-0881. Office Fax: 808-692-1247. Business E-Mail: jerris@hawaii.edu. *

HEDGES, MARK STEPHEN, clinical psychologist; b. Chgo., Feb. 15, 1950; s. Norman T. and Doris Mae (Walters) H.; m. Janice Finnie, Aug. 16, 1975; children: Anna, Miriam. BS, Purdue U., 1972; MA, U. S.D., 1974, PhD, 1977. Psychology intern Western Mo. Mental Health Ctr., Kansas City, 1975-76; psychologist, dir. psychol. svcs. Northeastern Mental Health Ctr., Aberdeen, SD, 1977—2003; psychologist Luth. Social Svcs., Aberdeen, SD, 2003—; sch. psychologist Aberdeen Pub. Schs., 2003—. Mem. Justice Children Com. Mem. APA, S.D. Assn. Sch. Psychologists, Phi Beta Kappa, Psi Chi, Phi Kappa Phi. Methodist. Office: Aberdeen Pub Sch 1224 S 3rd St Aberdeen SD 57401 Office Phone: 605-725-7148. Business E-Mail: mark.hedges@k12.sd.us.

HEDLEY-WHYTE, JOHN, anesthesiologist, educator; b. Newcastle-upon-Tyne, Eng., Nov. 25, 1933; arrived in U.S., 1960, naturalized, 1965; s. Angus and Nancy (Nettleton) H.-W.; m. Elizabeth Tessa Waller, Sept. 19, 1959. Student, Harrow Sch., 1947-52; BA (Rothschild scholar Clare Coll.), Cambridge U., 1955, MB, 1958, MA, 1959, MD, 1972; AM (hon.), Harvard U., 1967. House surgeon St. Bartholomew's Hosp., London, 1958-59; resident in anesthesia Mass. Gen. Hosp., 1960-62, hon. anesthetist, 1977—; clin. asst. anesthesia Harvard U., 1961-63, instr., 1963-65, clin. assoc., 1965-67, assoc. prof., 1967-69, prof., 1969-76, 1st David S. Sheridan prof. anaesthesia and respiratory therapy, 1976—; prof. dept. health policy and mgmt. Harvard U. Sch. Pub. Health, 1988-2000, mem. leadership coun., 2003—06; chmn. faculty seminar in health and medicine Harvard U., 1975—76, 2003—; anesthetist-in-chief Beth Israel Hosp., Boston, 1967-88, chmn. com. on rsch., 1976-82. Cons. in field; mem. tech. adv. bd. on med. devices tech. Am. Nat. Stds. Inst., 1973-83; U.S. del. Internat. Electrotech. Commn., 1989-91, 92—; leader U.S. del. Internat. Orgn. Standardization, Geneva, 1973-89, 2010-, chmn. com. TC 121, SC 3 on anaesthetic and respiratory equipment, 1978—, ISO sec. gen. citation, 2007. Author: Respiratory Care, 1965, Applied Physiology of Respiratory Care, 1976, Continuous Anesthesia Vapor Monitoring, 1990, Operating room and Intensive Care Alarms and Information Transfer, 1992, editl. bd. mem., Ulster Med. Jour., 2011-; contbr. articles to profl. jours. Recipient Hichens prize St. Bartholomew's Hosp., London, 1957, tech. com. award Am. Assn. Adv. Med. Instrumentation, 2008. Fellow ACP (life), German Soc. Anaesthesia and Intensive Care Medicine (hon., life), ASTM (hon., chmn. com. F29 1983-89, 2010-, Merit award 1994, user vice chmn. 2000-05, membership sec. 2006—2010), Royal Coll. Anaesthetists (hon., life); mem. Am. Physiol. Soc., Abernethian Soc. (past pres.), Am. Soc. Anesthesiologists (chmn. com. mech. equipment 1977-82, chmn. com. on equipment and standards 1982-84), Mass. Soc. Anesthesiologists (pres. 1973-74), Am. Soc. Pharmacology and Exptl. Therapeutics, Roxbury Soc. Med. Improvement (libr. 1970-88, sec.-treas. 1988—), Mass. Med. Soc. (coun. 1975-78), Fairhaven Preservation Assn. (pres. 1990—), Boodle's Club, Carlton Club (hon., life), The Country Club (exempt, life), Somerset Club, Harvard Club of Boston, Harvard Travellers' Club, Vicarage Club. Democrat. Episcopalian. Achievements include discovery that human blood has a constant relative solubility for oxygen. Office: VA Med Ctr 1400 VFW Pkwy Boston MA 02132-4927

HEDLOVÁ, DANA, epidemiologist; b. Prague, May 31, 1961; MD, Charles U., Prague, Czech Republic, 1986; degree in Epidemiology, Inst. Postgrad. Med. Edn., Czech Republic, 1995. Physician, epidemiol. unit health care facilities State Hygiene Svc., Prague, 1986—96; hosp. epidemiologist, head hosp. hygiene dept. Ctrl. Mil. Hosp. Prague, 1996—. Mem. bd. nat. register HAI Ministry Health, Czech Republic, 2005—, mem. working group patient safety, Czech Republic, 2010—; nat. contact point surg. site infection ECDC, Czech Republic, 2009—; mem. ctrl. coordination group nat. antibiotic program Nat. Inst. Pub. Health, Czech Republic, 2010—. Mem.: Czech Med. Assn. JE Purkyne (mem. subcom. antibiotic policy 2009—), Soc. Med. Microbiology. Avocations: photography, gardening, travel. Office: U Vojenské nemocnice 1200 Prague 16902 Czech Republic Business E-Mail: dana.hedlova@uvn.cz.

HEDRICK, WYATT SMITH, pharmacist; b. Roswell, N.Mex., Sept. 28, 1951; s. Wyatt Smith and Roberta Walker (Stuart) H. BS in Pharmacy, U. N.Mex., 1974; MS in Hosp. Pharmacy, U. Houston, 1978. Registered pharmacist, N.Mex., Tex. Pharmacy intern St. Mary's Hosp., Roswell, N.Mex., 1973, Ea. N.Mex. Med. Ctr., 1973-74, U-SAVE Drug, 1974-75; pharmacy resident U. Tex. Med. Br. Hosps., Galveston, 1977-78; staff pharmacist Meml. Gen. Hosp., Las Cruces, N.Mex., 1978, Las Palmas Med Ctr., El Paso, Tex., 1978—. Mem. Am. Soc. Health-Sys. Pharmacists, Tex. Soc. Health-Sys. Pharmacists, El Paso Area Soc. Health-Sys. Pharmacists. Avocations: reading, travel, physical fitness. Home: 1028 Quinault Dr El Paso TX 79912-1223 Personal E-mail: whedr34182@aol.com.

HEE-JIN, HWANG, physician, educator; b. Seoul, Republic of Korea, Jan. 3, 1974; MD, Yonsei U. Coll. Medicine, 2000; MS, Yonsei U. Grad. sch., 2009. Asst. prof. dept. family medicine Kwandong U. Coll. Medicine, 2010—. Mem.: Korean Assn. Family Medicine. Office: Hwajung-dong Dukyang-gu 697-24 Goyang Gyonggi 412-270 Republic of Korea Office Fax: 82-31-969-0500. Business E-Mail: yonseimd@hanmail.net.

HEER, MARTINA, nutritionist, researcher; d. Marliese Heer; m. Gerd Wilhelm Meister, Jan. 28, 2008. PhD, RFW U. Bonn, Germany. Head space physiology divsn. German Aerospace Ctr., Cologne, Germany, 2003—09; adj. assoc. prof. RFW U. Bonn, 2004—; dir. Nat. Health Profil Inst. Metabolic Rsch., 2009—. Cons. european space agy. European Space Agy. and European Astronaut Ctr., Cologne, 1998—. Recipient Sci. award, German Aerospace Ctr., 2000, Otto Lilienthal award, Soc. Friends and Supporters DLR, 2007. Mem.: ESPEN, German Sect. ISMNI, Am. Soc. Nutrition, Am. Soc. Bone and Mineral Rsch., Internat. Acad. Astronautics. Office: Profil Inst Metabolic Rsch Hellesburg Str 9 Neuss 417460 Germany Office Phone: 4921314018253. Personal E-mail: drmheer@aol.com. Business E-Mail: martina.heer@profil-research.de.

HEERENS, ROBERT EDWARD, physician; b. Evanston, Ill., July 2, 1915; s. Joseph and Karen (Larsen) H.; m. Martha Virginia Lysne, Aug. 21, 1943; children: Kisti Lyn, Martha Jill, Nancy Ann, Robin Jan, Sara Bryce. AB, Kalamazoo Coll., 1938; postgrad., U. Ala. Med. Sch., 1939-41; MD, Northwestern U., 1944. Diplomate Am. Bd. Family Practice. Intern U.S. Naval Hosp., Great Lakes, Ill., 1943-44, resident, 1946-47; gen. practice medicine Rockford, Ill., 1947—; pres. med. staff Swedish-Am. Hosp.; mem. staffs St. Anthony, Rockford hosps.; clin. assoc. prof. family medicine Rockford Sch. Medicine, also dir. ind. studies, mem. exec. com.; mem. admissions com. U. Ill. Coll. Medicine, 1970—, promotions com., 1973-75, mem. Senate Med. Ctr., 1975-77, also mem. acad. council, mem. adv. com. on family practice. Bd. dirs. Rockford Community Chest, 1954-60, Vis. Nurse Assn.; pres. Winnebago Tb Assn., 1960-61, Winnebago County Bd. Health, 1961-69; mem. Rockford Community Devel. Com.; mem. Community Action Com., 1969-71; pres. Northwestern Area Agy. on Aging, 1991-93. Served with M.C., USN, 1942-47. Recipient Disting. Svc. award Pub. Health Winnebago County Health Dept., 1997, Unique Achievement award Gov. of Ill., 1992, Betty Henry award for Cmty. Svc., 2000; Sr. of Yr. award Lifescape Cmty. Svcs., 2000, Super Sr. of Yr., 2006; Svc. Above Self award Rotary, Rockford, 2007. Mem. AMA, Am. Acad. Family Physicians (Ill. del. to congress of dels. 1959-71, mem. pub. relations com. 1967-74, chmn. pub. relations com. 1971-74, bd. dirs. 1970-73, exec. com. 1972-73, v.p. 1974), Ill. Acad. Gen. Practice (pres. 1958), Ill. Acad. Family Physicians (Pres.'s award 2000), Ill. Med. Soc. (chmn. pub. relations com. 1961-62, Pub. Svc. award 1994), Winnebago County Med. Soc. (v.p. 1965, pres. 1966), Rockford C. of C. (pres. 1962, chmn. edn. com.), Phi Beta Phi Home: 5664 Spring Brook Rd Rockford IL 61114-5553

HEESACKER, MARTIN, psychologist, educator; b. Warwick, Va., Apr. 25, 1956; s. Bernard Andrew and Mary (NeCasek) H. BS with highest honors, U. So. Miss., 1977; MS in Psychology Counseling, U. Mo., 1981, PhD in Psychology Counseling, 1983. Lic. psychologist, Ohio, Fla. Counselor, intern U. Mo., Columbia, 1981-83; asst. prof. psychology So. Ill. U., Carbondale, 1983-86, Ohio State U., Columbus, 1986-89; assoc. prof. psychology U. Fla., Gainesville, 1989—95, prof. psychology, 1995—, chmn., dept. psychology, 2000—07. Cons. Covington Industries, Opp, Ala., 1983-84, North Fla. Evaluation and Treatment Ctr., Gainesville, 1996—, SOAR Am., Inc., Melbourne, Fla., 1990—; lectr. in field. Editorial bd. Jour. Counseling Psychology, 1987-95, Contemporary Psychology, 1995—; editor Profiles of Adjustment, 1994; contbr. articles to profl. jours., chpts. to books. Recipient Grad. Rsch. award Mo. Psychol. Assn., 1982, Davis Productivity award Fla. Tax Watch, 1994; Fulbright scholar USIA, 1987; Lilly fellow Eli Lilly Endowment, 1988. Fellow APA (counseling psychology divsn., co-chair Gt. Lakes regional conf. 1987-88, new profls. com. 1986-87, Early Career award 1989); mem. Midwestern Psychol. Assn., Soc. Advancement Social Psychology, Soc. Exptl. Social Psychology, Sigma Xi. Avocations: sailing, jogging, swimming. Office: Dept Psychology U Fla 027 Psychology Bldg PO Box 112250 Gainesville FL 32611-2250 Office Phone: 352-273-2136. Business E-Mail: heesack@ufl.edu.

HEE SOON, CHO, medical educator; b. Yeongcheon, Kyeongsangbuk-do, Republic of Korea, May 16, 1970; d. Cho Moo Hwan and Jang Wol Sun; m. Lee Kwang Hee, Jan. 28, 1995; children: Lee Yong Sun, Lee Jung Ah. MS in Medicine, Yeungnam U. Coll. Medicine, Daegu, 1998; DMS, Kyungpook Nat. U., Daegu, Republic of Korea, 2009. Cert. Korean Nat. Bd. Medicine, 1994, Korean Bd. Lab. Medicine, 1999. Resident Yeungnam U. Med. Ctr., Daegu, 1995—99, fellow, 2001—04; instr. Yeungnam U. Coll. Medicine, Daegu, 2004—07, asst. prof., 2007—11, assoc. prof., 2011—. Contbr. articles to profl. jours. Mem.: Korean Soc. Lab. Medicine, Korean Soc. Hematology (sec. hereditary hemolytic anemia working party 2006—). Roman Catholic. Office: Yeungnam University College of Medicine 317-1 Deamyung-Dong Namgu 705-035 Daegu Daegu Republic of Korea Office Fax: 82-53-620-3297. Business E-Mail: chscp@med.yu.ac.kr.

HEESTAND SKINNER, DIANE ELISSA, medical educator; b. Boston, Oct. 9, 1945; d. Glenn Wilson and Elizabeth (Martin) Heestand. BA, Allegheny Coll., 1967; MA, U. Wyo., 1968; edn. specialist, Ind. U., 1971, EdD, 1979; MPH, U. Ark. Med. Sci., 2007. Asst. prof. communication Clarion (Pa.) State Coll., 1971; asst. prof. learning resources Indiana U. of Pa., 1971-72; asst. prof. communication U. Nebr. Med. Ctr., Omaha, 1972-74; assoc. prof. learning resources Tidewater Community Coll., Virginia Beach, Va., 1975-78; ednl. cons. U. Ala. Sch. Medicine, Birmingham, 1978-81; dir. learning resources, assoc. prof. med. edn. Mercer U. Sch. Medicine, Macon, Ga., 1981-88; asst. dean ednl. devel. and resources Ohio U. Coll. Osteopathic Medicine, 1989-90; assoc. prof. clin. med. edn., dir. biomed. communications U. So. Calif. Sch. Medicine, LA, 1990-95, acting chair dept. med. edn., 1992-95; prof., dir. office ednl. devel. U. Ark. for Med. Scis., Little Rock, 1995—2007; prof., assoc. dean. Coll. Health Related Prof., U. Ark. for Med. Scis., 2008—. Cons. Lincoln (Pa.) U., summer, 1975; vis. fellow Project Hope/China, Millwood, Va., summer, 1986. Author (teleplay) Yes, 1968 (award World Law Fund 1968); producer, dir. (slide tape) Finding a Way, 1980 (1st Pl. award HESCA 1981, Susan Eastman award 1981). Rsch. sect. chair So. Group on Ednl. Affairs, 1998—2000. Grantee, Porter Found., 1984, Ark. Dept. Higher Edn., 1996—97, UAMS Spl. Devel., 1997—99; Family and Preventive Medicine fellow, Health Resources and Svcs. Adminstrn., 2003—. Mem. Health Scis. Comm. Assn. (bd. dirs. 1982-86, pres.-elect 1987-88, pres. 1988-89, Spl. Svc. award 1990), Assn. Ednl. Comm. and Tech. (pres. media design and prodn. div. 1985-86), Assn. Biomed. Comm. Dirs. (bd. dirs. 1993-95), Soc. of Dirs. of Rsch. in Med. Edn. (steering com. 2000—, chair-elect 2002, chair 2003), Generalists in Med. Edn. (steering com. 1998-2001, chmn. 1999-2000). Democrat. Presbyterian. Avocations: tennis, gardening, golf. Office Phone: 501-686-5720. Business E-Mail: heestanddianee@uams.edu.

HEETUN, ZAID SHAH, physician; b. Curepipe, Plaine Williams, Mauritius, Sept. 16, 1982; s. Shaheyzahan and Yasmin Heetun. MB BCh, BAO BA, Trinity Coll. Dublin, 2006. Cert. dr. Irish Med. Coun., 2006. Sr. house officer U. Coll. Hosp. Galway, Ireland, 2007—08, St. James Hosp., Dublin, 2008—. Rsch. asst. Adelaide and Meath Hosp., Tallaght, Dublin, 2006—07. Contbr. articles to profl. jours. Recipient Clin. Honors, Trinity Coll. Dublin, 2006. Home: Apt 2 61 Cork St Dublin 053 Ireland Office: Saint James Hosp James St Dublin 953 Ireland Personal E-mail: heetunz@gmail.com.

HEFFERNAN, MICHAEL P., dermatologist; b. Portsmouth, NH, June 11, 1967; BS, U. Notre Dame, 1989; MD, U. Mich. Sch. Medicine, 1993. Asst. to assoc. prof. Wash. U. Sch. Medicine, 1999—2005; chmn., divsn. chief, dept. dermatology Wright State U., 2005—09; dermatologist Ctrl. Dermatology, 2009—. Bd. dirs. Wright State Physicians, 2005—09. Named Dermatology Tchr. of Yr., Wash. U. Fellow: Am. Acad. Dermatology; mem.: AMA, Med. Dermatology Soc. (bd. dirs. 2008, pres. 2005—06). Avocation: golf. Office: 1034 S Brentwood Blvd Ste 600 Saint Louis MO 63130 Office Fax: 314-721-6122. Business E-Mail: michael.heffernan@centralderm.com.

HEFFEZ, DAN, neurosurgeon; b. Cairo, Dec. 10, 1954; DCS, McGill U., 1975, MD, 1979. Asst. prof. Johns Hopkins U., 1986—90; dir., cerebrovasc. surgery CINN Med. Group, 1990—2003; assoc. prof. Rush U., 1998—2005; ptnr. Milw. Neurol. Inst., 2004—. Med. dir., Wis. Chiari Clinic Columbia St. Mary's Hosp., 2008; cons. KLS Martin, 2010, Aesculap, 2011. Recipient Clinician Scientist award, Johns Hopkins U.; named Upjohn Resident of Yr., Johns Hopkins Hosp.; Fogarty Rsch. fellowship, NIH. Fellow: RCS (Can.); mem.: Congress Neurol. Surgeons, Am. Assn. Neurol. Surgeons. Avocations: reading, skiing, bicycling. Office: 960 N 12th St Milwaukee WI 53233 Office Fax: 414-278-9005. Business E-Mail: dheffez@mni-wi.org.

HEFNER, DAVID STUART, health facility administrator, academic administrator; b. Boston, Tex., July 20, 1954; s. John Hardin and E. Patricia (Schwartz) H.; div. 1984; children: Tonia Marie, Brandi Lynn. BBA, U. Tex., 1976; M in Personnel Adminstrn., Brigham Young U., 1982. Founder, CEO Cons. Concepts, Inc., Salt Lake City, 1978, mng. ptnr., 1978—94; hosp. adminstr. Crook County Hosp., Sundance, Wyo., 1978-80, Tooele Valley Hosp., Utah, 1980-82; program mgr. BSL Tech., Salt Lake City, 1982-85; acting exec. dir., COO Penn State Milton S. Hershey Med. Ctr., Hershey, 2003, exec. dir., COO, 2003—06; sr. ptnr. CSC Global Health Solutions, 2006; pres. U. Chgo. Med. Ctr., 2006—09; sr. adv. Assn. American Med. Colleges (AAMC), Washington, 2009—; exec. v.p. clinical affairs Ga. Health Sciences U., Augusta, Ga., 2011—; CEO MCG Health Inc., Augusta, Ga.; CEO, chief strategy & transformation officer Physicians Practice Group, Augusta, Ga., 2011—. Mem.: Am. Arbitration Assn. (panel arbitrator). Office: Georgia Health Sciences University 1120 15th St Augusta GA 30912 *

HEGGERS, JOHN PAUL, retired surgery, immunology and microbiology educator; b. Bklyn., Feb. 8, 1933; s. John and May (Hass) H.; m. Rosemarie Niklas, July 30, 1977; children: Arn M., Ronald R., Laurel M., Gary R., Renee L., Annette M. BA in Bacteriology, Mont. State U. now U. Mont., 1958; MS in Microbiology, U. Md., 1965; PhD in Bacteriology and Pub. Health, Wash. State U., 1972. Diplomate Am. Bd. Bioanalysis; cert. wound specialist Am. Acad. Wound Mgmt.; cert. Advanced Burn Life Support provider. Med. technologist U.S. Naval Hosp., St. Albans, N.Y., 1951-53; bacteriologist Hahnemann Hosp., Worcester, Mass., 1958-59; commd. 2d lt. U.S. Army, 1959, advanced through grades to lt. col., 1975; mem. staff dept. bacteriology 1st U.S. Army Med. Lab., NYC, 1959-60; chief clin. lab., food svc. divsn. & diet kitchen U.S. Army Hosp., Verdun, France, 1960-63; chief virology and rickettsiology div. dept. microbiology 3d U.S. Army Med. Lab., Ft. McPherson, Ga., 1965-66; instr. bacteriology Basic Lab. Sch., Ft. McPherson, 1965-66; chief diagnostic bacteriology 9th Med. Lab., Saigon, Vietnam, 1966-67; chief microbiology div. dept. pathology Brooke Gen. Hosp., Ft. Sam Houston, Tex., 1967-69; chmn. dept. microbiology U.S. Army Sch. Med. Tech., Ft. Sam Houston, 1967-69; instr. bacteriology evening div. San Antonio Jr. Coll., 1969; lab. scis. officer Office Surgeon Gen., Washington, 1972-74; microbiologist spl. mycobacterial disease br. div. geog. pathology Armed Forces Inst. Pathology, Washington, 1973, spl. asst. to dir., 1973-74; chief clin. rsch. lab. clin. rsch. svc. Madigan Army Med. Ctr., Tacoma, 1974-76, asst. chief clin. investigation svc., 1976-77; instr. immunology, parasitology and mycology Clover Park Vocat. Tech. Inst., 1976-77; ret., 1977; assoc. prof. dept. surgery U. Chgo., 1977-80, prof., 1980-83; prof. surgery Wayne State U., Detroit, 1983-88; prof. surgery, microbiology and immunology U. Tex. Med. Br., 1988—2005; ret., 2005. Dir. clin. microbiology Shriners Burn Hosp., Galveston, Tex., 1988-2005. Author: Current Problems in Surgery, 1973, Quantitative Bacteriology, 1991; contbr. articles to profl. jours.; contbg. editor: Jour. Am. Med. Tech., 1972-2000. Pres. Aloe Rsch. Found., 1989-92, vice-chmn. 1992-95; Svc. award dedicator. Decorated Bronze Star; Legion of Merit; recipient cert. of appreciation A.C.S., 1969, cert. appreciation Armed Forces Inst. Pathology, 1974, Valley Forge Honor cert. Freedoms Found., 1974 Fisher award in med. tech., Fisher Scientific, Am. Med. Techs., 1968, 82, Gerard B. Lambert award, 1973, Ednl. Found. Rsch. award Am. Soc. Plastic and Reconstructive Surgery, 1978, Alumni Achievement award Wash. State U., 1993, Disting. Alumni award U. Mont., 1994, cert. appreciation for volunteering for operations Noble Eagle and Enduring Freedom, U.S. Army Reserve Command Personnel, 2002. Fellow NY Acad. Sci., Am. Acad. Microbiology, Royal Soc. Tropical Medicine and Hygiene, Am. Geriat. Soc.; VFW (life), mem. Nat. Registry Microbiologists (chmn. exec. coun. 1976-79), Am. Soc. Microbiology (chmn. com. tellers 1974-75), Wash. Soc. Am. Med. Technologists (pres. 1975-77), Wash. Soc. Med. Tech. (chmn. sect. microbiology sci. assembly, dir. 1975-77), Assn. Mil. Surgeons U.S. (life), Am. Soc. Clin. Pathologists (assoc.), Am. Med. Technologists (Disting. Svc. award 1975, Exceptional Merit award 1976, nat. dir. 1979-80, nat. sec. 1980-82, nat. v.p. 1982-84, Technologist of Yr. 1983), Am. Burn Assn. (chmn. rsch. com., 2d v.p. bd. trustees 2002, plaque of appreciation for dedicated svc., 2004, Pres.'s continuing edn. award 1981, At Large award 1986, Robert B. Lindberg award 1991, 92, 2004, Curtis P. Artz Disting. Svc. award 1996), Plastic Surgery Rsch. Coun., Surg. Infection Soc. (charter), Am. Assn. Bioanalysts (William N. Reich Outstanding Achievement award

2007), Ill. State Soc. Med. Technologists (v.p. 1979), Internat. Soc. Burn Injuries, Vietnam Vets. Assn. (life), Masons (32d degree, knight comdr. Ct. Honor), Shriners (ritualistic potentate), Sigma Xi

HEH, SHU-SHYA, nursing educator; d. Shang-Cheng Heh and Yu Lin; m. Chia-Yang Shiau, Mar. 24, 1984; children: Gwo-Harn Shiau, Gwo-Shiuan Shiau. MPhil, Oxford Brookes U., Eng., 1999; PhD, Nat. Taiwan U., 2011. RN Dept. Health, Taiwan, 1983. Lectr. Nat. Def. Med. Ctr., Tapei, Taiwan, 1987—91; asst. prof. Fu-jen Cath. U., Taipei County, 1995—. Contbr. scientific papers. Hon. citizen Vets. Affairs Commn., Taiwan, 1991—. Recipient Rsch. award, Nat. Sci. Coun., Taiwan, 1987. Mem.: Lambda Beta-at-Large, Sigma Theta Tau. Office: Nursing Dept Fu-Jen Catholic Univ 510 Chung-Cheng Rd Taipei County 242 Taiwan Office Phone: 886-2-29053427. Business E-Mail: 039752@mail.fju.edu.tw.

HEHN, MICHELE, pharmacist; b. France, Sept. 30, 1967; PharmD, Strasbourg, France, 1995. Pharmacist CH de St. Denis & RESAH-IDF, 2004—. Office: 2 Rue du Dr Delafontaine Saint-Denis Seine Saint-Denis 93205 France Business E-Mail: michele.hehn@ch-stdenis.fr.

HEICK, ALEX, physician, neurologist; b. Copenhagen, Jan. 25, 1949; s. Bent Heick and Ruth Preisler (Jensen) Hansen; m. Annelise Dal, Feb. 2, 1978; children: Lykke, Frederikke, Esben. M in Psychology, U. Copenhagen, 1978, MD, 1979. Cert. specialist of neurology. Intern dept. orthopedic surgery Kommune Hosp., Copenhagen, 1980-81; intern dept. medicine Bispebjerg Hosp., Copenhagen, 1981-82; intern dept. anaesthesiology Rønne Sygehus, Denmark, 1982-83; resident dept. neurosurgery Rigs Hosp., Copenhagen, 1983-85; resident dept. neurology Roskilde (Denmark) Hosp., 1986-93; with dept. neurology Glostrup U. Hosp., Denmark, 1994-99; cons. dept. neurology Holbaek Hosp., 1999-2001, Frederiksberg Hosp., 2001—08, Glostrup U. Hosp., 2008—. Chmn. polit. adv. group Minister of Health, Copenhagen, 1994-96; chmn. bd. Gladsaxe Gymnasium, Denmark, 1994-96, 98-2001; chmn. BL-TV, Copenhagen, 1998—. Author: (book) Sundhedens Pris (about Health Politics), 1995, Danmark 2020 (on the future of Denmark), 2004; contbr. articles to profl. jours. Ctr. Dem. Party candidate for European Parliament, Denmark, 1994; chmn. Dist. City Coun. of Bispebjerg, Denmark, 1998—. Decorated UN medals for mil. svc., Queen's Silver medal, 2005. Mem. Danish Neurol. Soc., Masons. Lutheran. Avocations: music, painting, basketball. Home: Tonemestervej 9 Copenhagen NV 2400 Denmark Office: Glostrup Univ Hosp Dept Neurology Copenhagen Denmark Personal E-mail: alexheick@dadlnet.dk.

HEIDLER, STEFAN, urologist; b. Bruck an der Mur, Aug. 28, 1977; MD, Med. U. Vienna, 2005. With, dept. urology Med. U. Graz, 2007—09, Donauspital, 2009—10; urologist Kaiser Franz Josef Spital, 2010—. Recipient Eiugen Rehfisch prize, Forum Urodynamikum, award, Österreichisch-Bayerischer Urologenkongreß. Office: Kundratstrasse 3 Vienna 1100 Austria Business E-Mail: stefanheidler@ymail.com.

HEIKEN, JAY PAUL, physician; b. NYC, Aug. 31, 1952; s. Martin and Sylvia (Fisher) H.; m. Barbara Ellen Rayburn, Dec. 11, 1976 (div. 1982); m. Francine J. Rosen, Apr. 29, 1990 (div. 2007); 1 child, Lauren M. BA, Williams Coll., 1974; MD, Columbia U., 1978. Intern Emory U. Hosp., Atlanta, 1978-79; resident in radiology Columbia-Presbyn. Med. Ctr., NYC, 1979-82; fellow abdominal radiology Mallinckrodt Inst. Radiology, St. Louis, 1982-83; asst. prof. Washington U. Sch. Medicine, St. Louis, 1983-87, assoc. prof., 1988-93, prof., 1993—. Dir. abdominal imaging Mallinckrodt Inst. Radiology, St. Louis, 1995-2009; mem. Washington U. Cancer Ctr, editor Pancreatic Cancer, 2009. Author, editor: Manual of Clinical Magnetic Resonance Imaging, 1986, 2d edit., 1991; editor: Computed Body Tomography with MRI Correlation, 1998, 4th edit., 2006; contbr. articles to profl. jours. Mem. Radiol. Soc. N.Am., Am. Roentgen Ray Soc., Am. Coll. Radiology, Greater St. Louis Soc. Radiologists, Soc. Computed Body Tomography and Magnetic Resonance (pres. 2003-04), Soc. Gastrointestinal Radiologists (pres. 2010-11, bd. dirs.), Assn. Univ. Radiologists, Internat. Cancer Imaging Soc.(pres. 2007-08, trustee) Avocations: skiing, tennis, softball, wine tasting. Home: 157 Gay Ave Saint Louis MO 63105-3665 Office: Mallinckrodt Inst 510 S Kingshighway Blvd Saint Louis MO 63108-1356 Office Phone: 314-362-1053. Business E-Mail: heikenj@mir.wustl.edu.

HEILAND, MAX, maxillofacial surgeon; b. Bad Soden, Germany, June 24, 1971; s. Gertraude and Frank Heiland; m. Sabrina Schulz, Jan. 30, 1998; children: Ida children: Anna, Paul. MD, U. Hamburg, Germany, 1999, DMD, 2001, PhD, 2004. Resident oral and maxillofacial surgery U. Hosp. Hamburg-Eppendorf, Germany, 1998—2004, sr. resident, 2005—09, prof. oral and maxillofacial surgery, 2006—07; head, dept. oral and maxillofacial surgery Gen. Hosp. Bremerhaven, 2007—10, U. Med. Ctr., Hamburg, Eppendorf, 2010—. Contbr. articles to profl. jours. Mem.: Internat. Assn. Dentomaxillofacial Radiology, Deutsche Gesellschaft für Computer und Roboterassistierte Chirurgie, Deutsche Gesellschaft für Schädelbasischirurgie, Deutsche Gesellschaft für Plastische und Wiederherstellungschirurgie, Deutsche Gesellschaft für Zahn, Mund und Kieferheilkunde, Deutsche Gesellschaft für Mund, Kiefer und Gesichtschirurgie. Office: Univ Hosp Hamburg-Eppendorf Martinistr 52 Hamburg 20246 Germany Home: Julius-Vosseler-Strasse 75P Hamburg 22527 Germany Office Phone: 49-40-74105-3259. Office Fax: 49-40-74105-5467. Personal E-mail: max.heiland@t-online.de. Business E-Mail: m.heiland@uke.de.

HEILEMAN, JOHN PHILLIP, retired endocrinologist; b. Phoenix, Feb. 2, 1930; s. Leonidas McHaffie and Rose Madelaine (Murphy) H.; m. Ann Frances O'Hara, Nov. 4, 1961; children: Jeanne Marie, James Andrew, Denise Ann, Matthew John. BS, Ariz. State U., 1951; MD, Loyola U., Chgo., 1955; postgrad., USN Sch. Aviation Medicine, Pensacola, Fla., 1956. Diplomate Am. Bd. Internal Medicine, subspecialty in endocrinology. Intern U.S. Naval Hosp., Gt. Lakes, Ill., 1955-56; resident in internal medicine Cook County Hosp., Chgo., 1958-60, Vet. Rsch. Hosp., Chgo., 1960-61; fellow in endocrinology, 1961-62; practice medicine specializing in internal medicine and endocrinology Phoenix, 1962—97; pres. Endocrinology Assocs. P.A., Phoenix, 1971-97. Pres. Ariz. chpt. Am. Diabetes Assn., 1975-77; bd. dirs., Ariz. Kidney Found., 2002-11. Lt. comdr., flight surgeon USNR, 1955-58. Fellow ACP, Am. Coll. Clin. Endocrinologists; mem. Ariz. Med. Assn. (sec. 1967-69), Maricopa County Med. Soc., Ariz. Soc. Internal Medicine, Ariz. Kidney Found. (bd. mem.), Ariz. Country Club. Republican. Roman Catholic. Avocations: tennis, skiing.

HEILICSER, BERNARD JAY, emergency physician; b. Bklyn., Jan. 19, 1947; s. Murray and Esther (Dubrow) H.; m. Marcia Cherry, June 2, 1976; children: Micah, Seth, Jacob. BA, SUNY, Binghamton, 1968; MS, Hahnemann Med. Coll., Phila., 1971; DO, Coll. Osteo. Medicine/Surgery, Des Moines, 1976. Diplomate Am. Bd. Emergency Medicine. Instr. anatomy and physiology U. Pa. and Hahnemann Med. Coll., Phila., 1971-73; staff physician Va. Inst. Tech., Blacksburg, 1977-78; asst. prof. emergency medicine Chgo. Coll. Osteo. Medicine, 1979; emergency physician St. Margaret Hosp., Hammond, Ind., 1979-83, Michael Reese Med. Ctr., Chgo., 1989-91, Ingalls Hosp., Harvey, Ill., 1983—; project med. dir. South Cook County Emergency Med. Svc., Harvey, 1984—. Faculty Chgo. Osteo. Med. Ctr., 1987-99; faculty trauma nurse specialist St. James Hosp., Chicago Heights, Ill., 1980—; preceptor nurse practitioners Purdue U., Hammond, 1981-90; fellow MacLean Ctr. Clin. Med. Ethics, U. Chgo., 1993-94; chmn. ethics com., hosp. med. ethicist Ingalls Hosp., Harvey, Ill., 1994—; cons. Nat. Bd. Osteo. Med. Examiners, Harvey, 1994-95, ethics com. Am. Coll. Osteo. Emergency Physicians, 1997—; chmn. disaster com. Ill. Region 7 Emergency Med. Svcs./Trauma, 1997—; chair Ill. Region VII EMS Adv. Coun., 2001-04; adj. faculty Coll. Health Professions, Govs. State U., 1999—01; exec. coun. Ill. Med. Emergency Response Team, 1999—, dep. med. dir., dep. comdr, 2008-; med. advisor Combined Agy. Response Team, 1999—. Vol. fireman Flossmoor (Ill.) Fire Dept., 1985—, Matteson (Ill.) Fire Dept., 1980-90; lead physician, mgr. med. team Ill. Task Force One Urban Search and Rescue, 2004—. Recipient Spl. Recognition award, Met. Chgo. Healthcare Coun., 1992, Emergency Nursing award, Ill. Nurses Assn., 2001, Behind the Scenes award, Emergency Nurses Assn., 2009. Fellow Am. Coll. Emergency Physicians, Am. Coll. Osteo. Emergency Physicians (Robert Aranosian award 2008); mem. Am. Osteo. Assn., Nat. Assn. Emergency Med. Svcs. Physicians, Nat. Assn. Emergency Med. Technicians, Sigma Sigma Phi. Jewish. Avocations: running, basketball. Office: Ingalls Hosp One Ingalls Dr Harvey IL 60426 Office Phone: 708-915-6900. E-mail: bernardh47@yahoo.com.

HEILMAN, MARLIN STEPHEN, medical products executive; b. Tarentum, Pa., Dec. 25, 1933; s. Glenn Harold and Hilda Barnes; m. Drusilla Caswell, Aug. 18, 1956; children: Philip, Glenda, Carl Barnes, Stephen James, Karen. BA, U. Pa., 1955, MD, 1959. Pvt. practice, Pitts., 1963—65; cons. Westinghouse R & D, Pitts., 1965—67; pres. Medrad, Inc., Pitts., 1968—80, Intec Systems, Inc., Pitts., 1980—84; chmn., CEO Medrad/Intec, Inc., Pitts., 1984—86; chmn. bd. dirs., CEO Vascor, Inc., Pitts., 1986—, Lifecor, Inc., Pitts., 1986—. Founder Medrad, Intec, Medrad/Intec, Vascor & Lifecor, chmn. Alle-Kiski Med. Ctr. Contbr. articles to profl. jours. Capt. USAF, 1961—63. Recipient Michel Mirowski Excellence in Cardiology award, 1992; named Entrepreneur of Yr., Arthur Young/Venture Mag., 1987; named to Nat. Inventors Hall of Fame, 2002. Office: Vascor Inc 566 Alpha Dr Pittsburgh PA 15238-2912

HEIMBERG, MURRAY, pharmacologist, biochemist, physician; b. Bklyn., Jan. 5, 1925; s. Gustav and Fannie (Geller) H.; children by previous marriage: Richard G., Steven A.; m. Anna Frances Langlois Knox, July 12, 1964; stepchildren: Larry M. Knox, David S. Knox. BS, Cornell U., Ithaca, NY, 1948, MNS, 1949; PhD in Biochemistry (NIH fellow), Duke, 1952; MD, Vanderbilt U., 1959. NIH Postdoctoral fellow in biochemistry Med. Sch. Washington U., St. Louis, 1952-54; research asso. physiology Med. Sch. Vanderbilt U., 1954-59, asst. prof. to prof. pharmacology, and asst. prof. medicine, 1959-74; prof., chmn. dept. pharmacology, prof. medicine U. Mo., 1974-81; prof. and chmn. dept. pharmacology, prof. medicine, endocrinology and metabolism U. Tenn., Health Sci. Ctr., Memphis, 1981-96; Van Vleet prof. pharmacology U. Tenn., Memphis, 1986-96, Disting. prof. pharmacology and medicine, 1996-99, disting. prof. pharmacology and medicine emeritus, 2000—. Cons. NSF, NIH; cons., established investigator Am. Heart Assn.; attending physician U. Tenn. Hosps. and Memphis VA Hosp.; dir. emeritus lipid metabolism clinic U. Tenn. Med. Group. Contbr. articles to profl. jours. Served with inf. AUS, 1943—45, ETO. Decorated Purple Heart, Bronze Star; recipient Lederle Med. Faculty award; research grantee. Fellow AAAS, AHA, Am. Coll. Clin. Pharmacology, Am. Heart Assn.; mem. Am. Soc. Biol. Chemistry and Molecular Biology, Am. Soc. Pharmacology and Exptl. Therapeutics, Endocrine Soc., Am. Diabetes Assn., So. Soc. Clin. Investigation. Home: 105 Devon Way Memphis TN 38111-7711 Office Phone: 901-448-4748. Personal E-mail: mheimberg1@comcast.net. Business E-Mail: mheimberg@uthsc.edu.

HEIMKE, JOHN, dentist, educator; DMD, Case Western Res. U., Cleve., 1989; MPH, Emory U. Resident advanced edn. program in gen. dentistry, Ft. Benning, Ga.; resident dental implant prosthetic Misch Implant Inst.; clin. instr. coll. dentistry NYU; dentist The Facial Aesthetic Designers, Ohio. Named one of Cleve.'s Top Cosmetic Dentists, Cleve. Mag., 2008—10. Fellow: Pierre Fuchard Acad.; mem.: Acad. of Cosmetic Dentistry, Acad. of Gen. Dentistry, Greater Cleve. Dental Soc., Ohio Dental Assn., ADA. Office: The Facial Aesthetic Designers 2615 S Campbell St Sandusky OH 44870 also: The Facial Aesthetic Designers 21851 Center Ridge Rd Ste 302 Rocky River OH 44116 Office Phone: 888-219-8176, 888-219-8176.

HEIMLICH, HENRY J., physician, surgeon, educator; b. Wilmington, Del., Feb. 3, 1920; s. Philip and Mary (Epstein) Heimlich; m. Jane Murray, June 3, 1951; children: Philip, Janet, Elisabeth. BA, Cornell U., 1941, MD, 1943; DSc (hon.), Wilmington Coll., 1981, Adelphi U., 1982, Rider Coll., 1983, Alfred U., 1993. Diplomate Am. Bd. Surgery, Am. Bd. Thoracic Surgery. Intern Boston City Hosp., 1944; resident VA Hosp., Bronx, 1946—47, Mt. Sinai Hosp., NYC, 1947—48, Bellevue Hosp., NYC, 1948—49, Triboro Hosp., Jamaica, NY, 1949—50; attending surgeon divsn. surgery Montefiore Hosp., NYC, 1950—69; dir. surgery Jewish Hosp., Cin., 1969—77; prof. advanced clin. scis. Xavier U., Cin., 1977—89; assoc. clin. prof. surgery U. Cin. Coll. Medicine, 1969—78. Pres. Heimlich Inst.; mem. Pres.'s Commn. on Heart Disease, Cancer and Stroke, 1965; pres. Nat. Cancer Found., 1963—68, bd. dirs., 1960—70; founder Heimlich Inst. Found. Author: Postoperative Care in Thoracic Surgery, 1962; author: (with M.O. Cantor, C.H. Lupton) Surgery of the Stomach, Duodenum and Diaphragm, Questions and Answers, 1965; contbr. chapters to books, articles to profl. jours.; prodr.(film): Esophageal Replacement with a Reversed Gastric Tube (Medaglione Di Bronzo Minerva, 1961), Reversed Gastric Tube Esophagoplasty Using Stapling Technique, How to Save a Choking Victim: The Heimlich Maneuver, 1976, 1982, How to Save a Drowning Victim: The Heimlich Maneuver, 1981, Stress Relief: The Heimlich Method, 1983, (video): Dr. Heimlich's Home First Aid Video, 1989 (Vira award, 1989); editl. bd. films Reporte's Medicos, 1962. Cmty. Devel. Found., 1967—70; Save the Chidlren FEdn., 1967—68; United Cancer Coun., 1967—70. Served to lt. (s.g.) USNR, 1944—46. Recipient Lasker award for Pub. Svc., Lasker Found., 1984, China-Burma-India Vets. Assn. Americanism award, 1988, 1st Heimlich Humanitarian award, Spirit of Am. Festival, 1994, Heimlich Inst. established in perpetuity by Deaconness Assns., Inc. Fellow: ACS (chpt. pres. 1964), Am. Coll. Gastroenterology, Am. Coll. Chest Physicians; mem.: AMA (cons. to jour.), Ctrl. Surg. Assn., Collegium INternat. Chirurgiae Digestive, Pan Am. Med. Assn., Am. Gastroent. Assn., Soc. Surgery Alimentary Tract, N.Y. Soc. Thoracic Surgery, Cin. Soc. Thoracic Surgery, Soc. Thoracic Surgeons (founding mem.). Achievements include development of Heimlich Operation (reversed gastric tube esophagoplasty) for replacement of esophagus; invention of Heimlich chest drain valve, Heimlich Micro-Trach (HMT) for COPD, emphysema and cystic fibrosis; development of Heimlich Maneuver to save lives of victims of food choking and drowning and prevents and overcomes asthma attacks (listed in Random House, Oxford Am. and Webster dictionaries); Computers for Peace, a program to maintain peace throughout world and A Caring World. Personal E-mail: hjheimlich@fuse.net.

HEIN, KAREN KRAMER, pediatrician, epidemiologist; b. NYC, Feb. 2, 1944; d. Irving W. and Ruth (Eisenberg) Kramer: m. Ralph Dell, Aug. 28, 1983; children: Ethan, Molly. BA, U. Wis., 1966; B of Med. Sci., Dartmouth Med. Sch., 1968; MD, Columbia U., 1970. Intern Bronx Mcpl. Hosp., Bronx Mcpl. Hosp. Ctr., 1970, resident, 1971-73; dir. adolescent AIDS program Montefiore Med. Ctr., NYC, 1987-94; clin. prof. pediat. Albert Einstein Coll. Medicine, NYC, 2003—, prof. epidemiology and social medicine, 1993—2003, clin. prof. pediat., epidemiology and population health, 2003—08; exec. officer Inst. Medicine NRC, Washington, 1995—98; pres. William T. Grant Found., NYC, 1998—2003. Cons. NYC Dept. Health, 1980-85, NYC Bd. Edn., 1987-93; bd. dirs. Dartmouth Med. Sch., Hanover, NH, Consumers Union, 1998-, Childfund Internat., 2005-, Internat. Rescue Com., 2005-, Nat. Bd. Med. Examiners, 2002—09. Author: AIDS: Trading Fears for Facts Consumer Reports Books, 1989. Named Outstanding Physician, Dept. Health and Human Svcs., 1989, Adminstrs. Citation award, 1993. Fellow Am. Bd. Pediat.; mem. Am. Pediatric Soc., Soc. for Pediatric Rsch., Am. Acad. Pediat., Soc. for Adolescent Medicine (pres. 1992-93). Address: Box 607 Jacksonville VT 05342

HEINEMANN, ALLEN W., rehabilitation psychologist; PhD, U. Kans., Lawrence, 1977—82. Lic. clin. psychologist Ill., 1984. Prof. Feinberg Sch. Medicine, Northwestern U., Chgo., 1985—; dir. ctr. rehab. outcomes rsch. Rehab. Inst. Chgo., 1988—. Pres. Am. Congress Rehab. Medicine, Indpls., 2004—05. Recipient Essie Morgan Excellence award, Am. Assn. Spinal Cord Injury Psychologists & Social Workers, 2003. Fellow: Am. Congress Rehab. Medicine (Disting. Mem. award 2006); mem.: APA (pres. rehab. psychology divsn. 2004—05, Harold Yuker award for rsch. excellence 2004, Roger Barker Disting. Career award 2000). Office: Rehab Inst Chgo 345 E Superior St Chicago IL 60611 Office Phone: 312-238-2802. Business E-Mail: a-heinemann@northwestern.edu.

HEINEY, JAKE P., orthopedist; b. Toledo, Jan. 16, 1975; s. Ronald Keith and Kathy Heiney. BS, Ctrl. Mich. U., Mt. Pleasant, 1997; MS, Wayne State U., Detroit, 1998, MD, 2002. Resident physician Akron Gen. Med. Ctr., Ohio, 2002—07; trauma fellow Orthopaedic Trauma & Fracture Specialists, San Diego, 2007—08; orthopaedic surgery clin. instr. U. Calif., San Diego, 2007—08; orthopaedic surgeon ProMedica Health Sys., Toledo. Reviewer Jour. Orthopaedic Trauma, Tampa, Fla., 2009. Orthopaedic Ednl. grant, Biomet, Inc, 2006. Mem.: Arbeitsgemeinschaft Osteosynthesefragen faculty, Akron Gen. Ho. Staff Assn. (treas. 2003—04, v.p. 2004—05, pres. 2005—07), Calif. Orthopaedic Assn., Am. Acad. Orthopaedic Surgeons, Orthopaedic Trauma Assn., Alpha Omega Alpha Honor Med. Soc. (jr. inductee 2000—01, pres. 2001—02). Office: ProMedica Health Sys 2109 Hughes Dr Jobst Tower Ste 840 Toledo OH 43606 Office Fax: 419-480-6151. Business E-Mail: jake.heineymd@promedica.org, jakeheiney@ameritech.net.

HEINKE, MATTHIAS HERBERT, biomedical engineer, researcher; s. Herbert and Ruth Heinke; m. Kerstin Heinicke, Aug. 1, 1981; 1 child, Tobias. Diploma in Engring., Tech. U. Ilmenau, Germany, 1983, ED, 1989, PhD in Biomed. Engring., 1989; PD Dr.-Ing. med. habil.; Priv. Doz., U. Jena, 2009. Cert. in fachingenieur der medizin Akademie Arztliche Fortbildung Berlin, 1989. Rsch. asst. cardiac electrophysiology, biomed. engr., dept. internal medicine U. Jena, Germany, 1983—. Contbr. articles to profl. jours. Avocations: travel, music, tennis, volleyball. Office: Internal Medicine I Univ Jena Erlanger Allee 101 7747 Jena Germany Office Phone: 0049-3641-9324532. Personal E-mail: matthias.heinke@web.de. Business E-Mail: matthias.heinke@med.uni-jena.de.

HEINLEIN, CATHERINE R., medical educator; b. Calif., May 3, 1956; M, U. So. Calif., 1995; PhD, U. La Verne, 2007. Clin. dietitian, diabetes prof. Huntington Hosp. Pasadena, 1987—2005; asst. prof. Azusa Pacific U., 2001—. Cons. Webb Sch., 2008. Decorated Commendation medal US Army, Achievement medal. Mem.: Am. Assn. Diabetes Educators, Am. Diabetes Assn., Am. Dietetic Assn., Sigma Theta Tau Internat. Avocations: hiking, cooking, drawing. Office: 701 E Foothill Blvd Sch Nursing Azusa CA 91702 Business E-Mail: cheinlein@apu.edu.

HEINRICH, BERND, biologist, educator; b. Bad Polzin, Poland, Apr. 19, 1940; came to US, 1950, naturalized, 1951; s. Gerd Hermann and Hildegard Maria (Bury) H. BA in Zoology, U. Maine, 1964, MS in Zoology, 1966; PhD in Zoology, UCLA, 1970; PhD (hon.), U. Maine, 1999, Unity Coll., Maine, 1986, PhD (hon.), 2000; MA in Philosophy and Human Ecology, Coll. Atlantic, 2006. Teaching and research asst. UCLA, 1966-70; asst. prof. entomology U. Calif., Berkeley, 1971-75, assoc. prof., 1975-78, prof., 1978-80; prof. biology U. Vt., Burlington, 1981—2003, prof. emeritus, 2004—. Author: Bumblebee Economics, 1979, Insect Thermoregulation, 1981, In a Patch of Firewood, 1984, One Man's Owl, 1987, Ravens in Winter, 1989, The Hot-Blooded Insects, 1993, A Year in the Maine Woods, 1994, The Thermal Warriors, 1996, The Trees in My Forest, 1998, Mind of the Raven, 1999, Racing the Antelope, 2001, Why We Run, 2001, The Winter World, 2003, The Geese of a Beaver Bog, 2003, The Snoring Bird, 2007, The Summer World, 2009, Nesting Season, 2010; co-author: Biology, 1979; contbr. numerous articles to sci. jours. Recipient Burroughs, Winship and Rutstrums Author's awards, 1984,

95; Guggenheim fellow, 1976-77, von Humboldt fellow, 1988-89. Mem. Am. Ornithological Union, NAS, Sigma Xi; Fellow Am. Acad. Arts & Sciences. Office: U Vermont Dept Biology Marsh Life Science Bui Burlington VT 05405-0001

HEINRICHS, HARVEY L., plastic surgeon, educator; b. Saskatoon, Sask., Can., 1942; BS, Walla Walla Coll.; MD, Loma Linda U., 1968. Cert. Am. Bd. Plastic Surgery, 1976. Intern gen. surgery Loma Linda Hosp., Calif., 1968—69, resident plastic surgery Calif., 1969—72; resident U. Calif., Irvine, 1972—74, former chief resident plastic surgery; staff mem. Hoag Meml. Hosp. Presbyn., Newport Beach, Calif., Newport Beach Surgery Ctr., James Irvine Surgical Ctr., Hoag Lido Surgical Ctr., Hoag Newport Surgicare. Asst. clin. prof. plastic & reconstructive surgery Loma Linda U., U. Calif., Irvine. Contbr. articles to med. jours. Fellow: ACS; mem.: AMA, Calif. Med. Assn., Calif. Soc. Plastic Surgeons, Am. Soc. for Aesthetic Plastic Surgery, Am. Soc. Plastic Surgeons, Alpha Omega Alpha Med. Honor Soc. Office: 1441 Avocado Ave Ste 601 Newport Beach CA 92660 Office Fax: 714-644-8763.

HEIR, STIG, orthopedist; b. Oslo, Apr. 19, 1961; MD, U. Bergen, Norway, 1987, PhD. Head, dept. knee and shoulder surgery Martina Hansens Hosp., 1997—. Office: Martina Hansens Hosp PB 23 Baerum N-1306 Norway Business E-Mail: stighei@online.no.

HEIRD, WILLIAM CARROLL, pediatrician, educator; b. Decatur, Tenn., Jan. 27, 1936; s. C.T. and Mary Edna (Ward) H.; m. Jane Ray, Aug. 21, 1960. BS, Maryville Coll., Tenn., 1958; MS, Vanderbilt U., Nashville, 1963, MD, 1964. Intern Vanderbilt U. Med. Ctr., Nashville, 1964-65; resident Babies Hosp. Columbia-Presbyn. Med. Ctr., NYC, 1965-67; asst. prof. pediatrics Coll. Physicians and Surgeons Columbia U., NYC, 1971-77, assoc. prof. pediatrics Coll. Physicians and Surgeons, 1977-89; prof. pediatrics Baylor Coll. Medicine, Houston, 1990—; pediatrician Children's Nutrition Rsch. Ctr., Houston. Co-editor: Protein and Energy Needs During Infancy, 1987; editor: Nutritional Needs of the 6-to-12 Month Old, 1991; contbr. numerous articles to profl. publs., chpts. to books. Capt. USAF, 1967-69. Mem. Am. Pediatric Soc., Soc. for Pediatric Rsch., Am. Soc. Nutrition, Am. Acad. Pediatrics. Office: Children's Nutrition Rsch Ctr 1100 Bates St Houston TX 77030-2600 Office Phone: 713-798-7177. Business E-Mail: wheird@bcm.edu.

HEITGER, MARCUS HANS WALTER, neuroscientist; b. Mannheim, Germany, Dec. 30, 1968; arrived in New Zealand, 1998; MS in Biology, U. Heidelberg, Germany, 1998; PhD, U. Otago, Dunedin, New Zealand, 2005. Rsch. scientist Christchurch (New Zealand) Neurotechnology Rsch. Programme, 2000—09, Van der Veer Inst. for Parkinson's and Brain Rsch., U. Otago, Christchurch, 2004—05; postdoc. fellow Van der Veer Inst. Parkinson's and Brain Rsch., U. Otago, Christchurch, 2005—09; postdoc. fellow, dept. biomed. kinesiology Katholieke U., Leuven, Belgium, 2009—. Contbr. chapters to books, articles to profl. jours. PhD scholar, U. Otago, 1999—2002, Neurotechnology Rsch. Doctoral scholar, Christchurch Neurotechnology Rsch. Programme, 2000—04, AMI McKessar fellow, Canterbury Med. Rsch. Found., New Zealand, 2000, 2003, Post-Doctoral fellow, U. Otago, New Zealand, 2005—09. Office: Motor Control Lab Rsch Ctr Movement Control & Neuroplasticity Tervuurse Vest 101 bus 01500 3001 Leuven Belgium Office Phone: 003216329098. Business E-Mail: marcus.heitger@faber.kuleuven.be, marcus.heitger@gmail.com.

HEITMAN, ELIZABETH, healthcare educator, anesthesiologist; PhD in Religious Studies, Rice U., 1988. Dir. Responsible Conduct of Rsch. Vanderbilt U. Med. Ctr., assoc. prof. Ctr. for Clinical & Rsch. Ethics, assoc. prof. medicine & anesthesiology. Co-author: The Ethical Dimensions of the Biological & Health Sciences. Mem.: Assn. Schs. Pub. Health. Office: University of Mississippi Center for Psychiatric Neuroscience 2500 N State St Jackson MS 39216-4505 Office Phone: 601-815-4727. Office Fax: 601-984-5885. E-mail: elizabeth.heitman@vanderbilt.edu.

HEITZENRATER, JAMES F., hospital administrator; BA, Marshall U., W. Va.; MA in healthcare adminstrn., Ctrl. Mich. U. Asst. adminstr. Colin Anderson Ctr., W.Va.; adminstr. Marcum & Wallace Meml. Hosp., Irvine, Ky., Methodist Sugar Land Hosp.; pres. St. Mary's Medical Ctr. Campbell County, 2010—. Mem. Program Planning Com. DePelchin Children's Ctr.; bd. mem. Fort Bend Econ. Devel. Coun., Fort Bend C. of C. Fellow: Am. Coll. Healthcare Exec. (diplomat). Office: St Marys Med Ctr Campbell County 923 E Ctrl Ave La Follette TN 37766 *

HEJAL, RANA B., critical care specialist; MD, Am. Univ. of Beirut, 1988. Diplomate Am. Bd. Internal Medicine, 2004, Am. Bd. Internal Medicine- pulmonary disease, 2004, Am. Bd. Internal Medicine-critical care medicine, 2005. Resident in internal medicine Metro-health Med. Ctr., Cleve., 1989—91; resident in pulmonary diseases Univ. Hosps. of Cleve., 1991—94, rsch. fellow in pulmonary disease, 1994—95; med. dir. Univ. Hosps. Case Med. Ctr. Office: UNiversity Hospitals Case Medical Center 11100 Euclid Ave Cleveland OH 44106 Office Phone: 216-844-3201.

HELDGAARD, POUL ERIK, physician, researcher; b. Svendborg, Denmark, Sept. 16, 1945; s. Ernst Storm and Ingeborg Kirstine Lindegaard; life ptnr. Elin Kallestrup; children: Thomas, Julie Kirstine, Anne Kathrine Bach. MD, U. Copenhagen, 1973, PhD, 2006. Lic. specialist in gen. practice Danish Med. Bd., 1994. Family physician Ørum Health Ctr., Tjele, Denmark, 1979—; rsch. fellow rsch. unit, dept. gen. practice U. Copenhagen, 1997—. Mem. Health Rsch. Com. Viborg County, Denmark, 2002—. 2d lt. M.C. Danish Army, 1976—77. Grantee, Found. Devel. Quality in Gen. Practice Viborg County, 1997—2000, Health Ins. Found., Gen. Practitioners' Found. Devel. and Edn., Danish Heart Found. and Danish Diabetes Assn., 1997—2005; scholar, Danish Found. Rsch. Found. Gen. Practice, 2000—05. Office: Ørum Health Ctr Vestergade 25 Ørum Tjele DK-8830 Denmark Office Fax: +45 86 65 25 44; Home Fax: +45 86 65 25 44. Personal E-mail: poul.erik@heldgaard.net. E-mail: peh@oerumlaegerne.dk.

HELDIN, CARL-HENRIK, cancer research scientist; b. Växjö, Sweden, Aug. 9, 1952; s. C. Lennart and G. Kristina (Fredriksson) H.; m. Paraskevi Papanikolaou, July 10, 1982; children: C. Johan, P. Angelos. Student, Uppsala U., Sweden, 1971-75, BSc, 1981, PhD in Med. and Physiol. Chemistry, 1980. Jr. scientist Uppsala U., 1980-83, sr. scientist, 1984-85, prof. molecular cell biology, med. faculty, 1992—; dir. Ludwig Inst. Cancer Rsch., Uppsala, 1986—. Mem. sci. adv. com. Inst. of Danish Cancer Soc., 1996—, European Molecular Biology Lab., Heidelberg, 1998—2004, European Inst. for Oncology, Milan, 1998—, Max Planck Inst. for Biochemistry, Martinsried, 1998—, Bio City, Turku, 2003—, Uppsala BIO-X, 2004—, Inst. Molecular Biology, Copenhagen, 2004—, Biotech. Ctr., Oslo, 2005—. Asst. editor Growth Factors, 1988, Molecular Biology of the Cell, 1989—, Cancer Rsch., 1993—; contbr. articles to profl. jours. Recipient Swedberg prize Swedish Biochem. Soc., 1984, Anders Jahre's prize U. Oslo, 1986, Prix Antoine Lacassagne, French Nat. Orgn. Against Cancer, 1989, K. Fernstrom's prize Med. Faculty Uppsala U., 1989, K. Fernstrom's Large Nordic prize, Med. Faculty Lund U., 1993, Meyenburg prize German Cancer Ctr., 1999, Pezcoller-AACR Cancer Rsch. award, 2002 Rudbeck award, 2003. Mem. European Molecular Biology Orgn. (medal 1992), Royal Swedish Acad. Sci., Academia Europea, European Rsch. Coun. (mem. scientific coun.). Home: Rättarvägen 12 S-75645 Uppsala Sweden Office: Ludwig Inst for Cancer Rsch Uppsala U Box 595 Biomed Ctr S-75124 Uppsala Sweden Office Phone: 46 18 160401. E-mail: C-H.Heldin@licr.uu.se.

HELDMAN, BETTY LOU FAULKNER, retired health facility administrator; b. Washington, NC, June 3, 1937; d. Basil Frank Faulkner and Willie Mae Rose; m. Arthur Charles Heldman Jr., Aug. 23, 1959; children: Ruth Victoria, Andrew Basil. BS in Biology, Davis and Elkins Coll., Elkins, W.Va., 1959; MS in Med. Biology, C.W. Post Coll., 1978. Cert. eye bank technician Eye Bank Assn. Am. Lab. asst. Portsmouth (Va.) Gen. Hosp., 1954—58; lab. technician Johnson & Johnson Rsch., New Brunswick, NJ, 1959—62; med. assoc. Brookhaven Nat. Lab., Upton, NY, 1973—86; adminstrv. dir. Lions Eye Bank for L.I., Great Neck, NY, 1986—97; ret. Presenter in field; pres., v.p. exec. bd. Brookhaven Women in Sci., 1979—86; chairperson United Fund Brookhaven Nat. Lab., 1983—84; elected mem. lectr. com. Brookhaven Lab., 1978—84; exec. bd. Sunsel GAP, Cosby, Tenn., 2007—; founder and coord. Stitch & Chatter (Charity Sewing), 1999—. Author, pub.: Faulkner, Cannon, Rose, Brickell-Families of Eastern North Carolina, 2003; contbr. rsch. papers to profl. jours. Vol. King Genealogy Libr.; pres. bd. Sunset Gap Mission program. Recipient Outstanding Svc. in Sci. award, Town of Islip, 1985, Plaque of Appreciation, Lions and Lioness Clubs, 1991, Disting. Recognition award, Knights of the Blind, 2004. Mem.: Assn. for Women in Sci. Home: 2146 Seaton Springs Rd Sevierville TN 37862 Personal E-mail: blink406@wildblue.net.

HELENIUS, ILKKA, surgeon; b. Finland, Sept. 7, 1973; MD, U. Helsinki, PhD, 1998. Asst. prof. U. Helsinki, 2005; vice chmn., dept. surgery Turku Children's Hosp., 2009—. Recipient Hibbs award, Scoliosis Rsch. Soc., 2005. Avocations: jogging, boating. Office: Turku Children's Hosp Kiinamyllynka Turku Varsinais-Suomi 20900 Finland Business E-Mail: ilkka.helenius@helsinki.fi.

HELFAND, ARTHUR ERWIN, podiatrist; b. Phila., Jan. 12, 1935; s. Nathan H. and Esther Helfand; m. Myra Werner, May 23, 1976; children: Jennifer Bess, Lewis Aaron. DPM, Temple U., 1957. Diplomate AM. Bd. Podiatric Pub. Health, Am. Bd. Podiatric Orthop. & Primary Podiatric Medicine (bd. dirs. 1992-95), Am. Bd. Podiatric Orthop. Pvt. practice, Phila., 1957—2002; active staff James C. Giuffre Med. Ctr., Phila., 1958-89, coord. dept. podiatry, 1959-68, co-chief, 1968-78, chief, 1978-89, dir. podiatric edn., 1968-89; dir. clin. rsch. Pa. Coll. Podiatric Medicine, Phila., 1963-64, prof. podiatry, coord. clinics, 1964-70, prof. podiatry, chmn. dept. community health and aging, 1970—2002, prof. podiatric medicine, podiatric orthopedics, 1998—2002; prof. Sch. Podiatric Medicine Temple U., Phila., 1998—2002, prof. emeritus, 2002—. Mem. staff Thomas Jefferson U. Hosp., Phila., 1973—2002, hon. staff, Temple U. and Temple U. Children's Hosp., 2002—; cons. podiatry dept. surgery Phila. VA Hosp., 1973—82; adj. prof. depts. orthopedic surgery and medicine Jefferson Med. Coll., Phila., 1976—2002, adj. prof. orthopedic surgery, podiatry, vis. assoc. prof. cmty. health and preventive medicine, 1977—79; adj. prof. medicine Temple U., 2003—; cons. staff Willis Eye Hosp., 1980—2002; affiliate staff Joslin Ctr. Diabetes, Boston, 1993—96, Joslin Ctr. Diabetes at Wills and Jefferson, 1993—96; hon. staff Temple U. Hosp.; cons. staff Temple U. Children's Hosp.; cons. Dept. Vets. Affairs, Podiatric Svc., Washington; cons. in field. Mem. editl. bd. Rehab. Today, 1990—93; contbr. chapters to books, articles to profl. jours.; editor: 10 textbooks. Bd. dirs. Pa. Diabetes Acad., 1988—2002, treas., 1991—93, 1995—97, chmn., 1993—95; bd. dirs. Phila. Corp. Aging, 2005—, bd. chair, 2007—, chmn., 2007—. Recipient Lifetime Achievement award, Podiatry Mgmt., 1991. Fellow: ACP, Royal Soc. Health, Am. Pub. Health Assn. (emeritus, mem. task force aging), Pa. Pub. Health Assn., Am. Geriatrics Soc. (emeritus); mem.: AMA, Am. Assn. Colls. Podiatric Medicine, Internat. Acad. Preventive Medicine, Gerontol. Soc., Delware Valley Geriatrics Soc. (bd. dirs. 1989—2004, pres. 1999—2000), Am. Assn. Hosp. Podiatrists, Am. Soc. Podiatric Dermatology, Phila. County Podiatry Soc., Pa. Podiatry Assn., Am. Podiat. Med. Assn. (pres. 1982—83), Am. Soc. Podiatric Medicine (pres. 1994—95), Am. Coll. Foot Orthopedists, Temple U. Alumni Assn. Business E-Mail: arthur.helfand@temple.edu.

HELFENBEIN, ERIC D., electrical engineer, researcher; s. Abraham and Muriel Helfenbein; m. Cheryl Anton; children: L., A. BS in Math. and Computer Sci., UCLA, 1977; MS in Elec. Engring. and Computer Sci., MIT, 1980. Programmer/analyst Tech. Svc. Corp., Santa Monica, Calif., 1974—77; rsch. asst. UCLA Brain/Computer Interface Lab., 1976—77, MIT Lab. for Info. and Decision Systems, Cambridge, Mass., 1978—80; cons. Cardio-Dynamics Labs., Santa Monica, Calif., 1978; clin. engr. Mass. Gen. Hosp., Boston, 1979—80; engr. / project leader Hewlett-Packard Patient Monitoring Divsn., Waltham, Mass., 1980—93; rsch. engr. Hewlett-Packard Rsch. Labs, Palo Alto, Calif., 1993—2000; engr. / rsch. scientist Agilent Technologies Rsch. Labs, Palo Alto, Calif., 2000—01; engr. /scientist Philips Med. Systems - Advanced Algorithm Rsch. Ctr. - Cardiology, Milpitas, Calif., 2001—. Contbr. articles to profl. jours., conf. procs. Scholar, UCLA scholar, 1977. Mem.: IEEE, Drug Info. Assn., Internat. Soc. of Computerized Electrocardiology. Achievements include patents for Intramyocardial Wenckebach activity detection in high-resolution ECGs; determination of respiratory effort from muscle tremor in ECG signals; time-diversity filter for removal of electromagnetic interference from ECGs; real-time physiologic artifact removal from respiratory waveforms. Home: Philips Med Systems 3860 N 1st St San Jose CA 95134-1702 E-mail: eric.helfenbein@philips.com.

HELIKER, DIANE, nursing researcher; b. NY, Nov. 24, 1944; BSN, Tex. Women's U., 1981; PhD in Nursing, Loyola U., Chgo., 1995. Prof. U. Tex., Galveston, 1995—2010; dir., edn. and tng. China Sr. Care, Inc., 2010. Grant, NIH-NINR. Mem.: ANA, Gerontol. Soc. America, Sigma Theta Tau Internat. (Alpha Delta chpt., Nursing Rsch. award). Avocations: travel, reading, yoga. Home: 275 E Railrd Ave Unit 303 Bartlett IL 60103 E-mail: dheliker@utmb.edu.

HELINSKI, DONALD RAYMOND, biologist, educator; b. Balt., July 7, 1933; s. George L. and Marie M. (Naparstek) H.; m. Patricia G. Doherty, Mar. 4, 1962; children: Matthew T., Maureen G. BS, U. Md., 1954; PhD in Biochemistry, Western Res. U., 1960; postdoctoral fellow, Stanford U., 1960-62. Asst. prof. Princeton (N.J.) U., 1962-65; mem. faculty U. Calif., San Diego, 1965—, prof. biology, 1970—, chmn. dept., 1979-81, dir. Ctr. for Molecular Genetics, 1984-95, assoc. dean Natural Scis., 1994-97, prof. emeritus, 2006—. Mem. com. guidelines for recombinant DNA research NIH, 1975-78 Author papers in field. Mem. Am. Soc. Biol. Chemists, Am. Soc. Microbiology, AAAS, Am. Acad. of Arts and Scis., Am. Acad. Microbiology, Nat. Acad. Scis., European Molecular Biology Orgn. (assoc.). Office: Bonner Hall 9500 Gilman Dr La Jolla CA 92093-0322

HELLBERG, DAN GUNNAR, obstetrician, gynecologist; b. Uppsala, Sweden, Oct. 11, 1953; s. Gunnar Birger and Kerstin Mariana (Persson) H.; children: Marten, Maja; m. Natalija Casovskiha, Mar. 3, 2001. MD, Uppsala U., 1978, PhD, 1987. From jr. physician to ob-gyn. trainee Falun (Sweden) Hosp., 1978—87, cons. dept. ob/gyn., 1987-92, scientist, 1992—2002, assoc. prof., 1998, supr. Centre for Clin. Rsch., 2002—; assoc. prof. dept. women's and children's health Uppsala U., Sweden, 1998, prof. dept. women's and children's health, 2008; prof. ob-gyn. Stromstad Acad., Sweden, 2011. Cons. Los Alamos (N.Mex.) Nat. Lab./NIH, 1993—, WHO Collaborating Ctr. for STDs and Their Complications, Uppsala, 1993—; supr. Ctr. for Clin. Rsch., Falun, 2002—; collaborator Am. Health Found., N.Y.C., 1984—; founder Riga Youth Health Centre, Latvia, 1997, prof. dept. Womens and Childrens Health, Uppsala U. Sweden. Co-author: Genital Papillomavirus Infectious and their Sequelae, 1987, Bacterial Vaginosis, 1994, Clinical Bacteriology, 1995; author: On Some Possible Etiological Factors of Cervix and Penis Cancer, 1987; co-author, editl. com.; Sexually Transmitted Diseases, 1994; Editor: Histological and Serological Tumor Markers and Their Clinical Usefulness in Cancer. Uppsala Ctr. for STD Rsch. fellow, 1993—. Fellow Scandinavian Soc. for Travel Medicine, Swedish Soc. Medicine, Internat. Fedn. Obstetricians and Gynecologists; mem. Internat. Fedn. of Cervical Pathology, N.Y. Acad. Sci., Latvian Family Planning Assn., Dalarna Beer Acad. Achievements include research in focus on smoking and womens health. Avocations: golf, cultural events. Office: Ctr Clinical Rsch Nissers vag 3 79182 Falun Sweden Office Phone: 0046(0) 70 0915316. E-mail: dan.hellberg@ltdalarna.se.

HELLBOM, EINAR ERIK OSKAR, medical products executive; b. Ovansjo, Sweden, Jan. 21, 1929; BA, U. Stockholm, 1981. Product mgr. Merck, Schering Corp. Janssen, Lundbeck, 1956—96. Avocation: gardening. Home: Saningsvagen 86 Jarfalla SE.17552 Sweden

HELLE, KAREN BLAAUW, physiology educator; b. Bergen, Norway, Jan. 24, 1934; d. Trygve and Ingeborg Zimmer Blaauw; m. Knut Helle, 1957 (div. 1985); children: Trygve, Brit. Degree in bioChemistry, U. Bergen, 1961, PhD in Physiology, 1971. Asst. prof. biochemistry U. Bergen, 1963—69, asst. prof. physiology, 1969—73, assoc. prof. physiology, 1974—82, prof. gen. physiology, 1984—2004. Mem. med. sect. Norwegian Rsch. Coun., Oslo, 1987—90; v.p. Norwegian Coun. for Fisheries, Trondheim, Norway, 1988—91. Author, editor: The Nansen Symposium on New Concepts in Neuroscience, 1987, Chromogranins, 2000; author, editor ChromograninA and its Derived Peptides, 2004; contbr. 130 papers to peer-reviewed jours. Chairperson Heart Found., U. Bergen, Bergen, 1998—; bd. dirs. local br. Kredittkassen-Fisheries, Bergen, 1980—93. Mem.: Scandinavian Physiol. Soc. (mem. editl. bd. 1992—2000), Physiol. Soc. London, Norwegian Acad. for Sci. and Letters (elected 1994), Soc. for Prevention of Crib Death, Soc. for Advancement of Sci. Office: U Bergen Dept Biomed Jonas Lies ver 91 Bergen 5009 Norway Office Phone: 47 55586416. Business E-Mail: karen.helle@biomed.uib.no.

HELLER, AXEL RÜDIGER, anesthesiologist, researcher; b. Giessen, Hessen, Germany, Sept. 25, 1969; s. Gerhard and Adelheid Heller; m. Susanne Christine Novotny, Oct. 2, 1992; children: Sebastian Johannes, Tobias Florian, Michael Jonas. MD, U. Giessen, Germany, 1994, Dr. Medicine, 1998; postgrad., U. Heidelberg, Germany, 1994—98; Dr. Medicine habilitation, PhD, U. Dresden, Germany, 2002; postgrad., Dresden Internat. U., 2006—. Diploma European Acad. Anesthesiology, 2002, cert. emergency physician, chief emergency and disaster physician, in intensive care medicine, in operating rm. mgmt. Intern U. Hosp., Mannheim, Germany, 1994—95, resident, 1995—98, U. Dresden, 1998—2001, fellow anesthesiology, 2001—, head exptl. rsch. lab. dept. anesthesiology and intensive care medicine, 1999—2005, vice chair anesthesiology, 2006—, assoc. prof. anesthesiology, 2002—, full prof. anesthesiology, 2007. Author: Immunomodulation in Systemic Inflammation and Acute Lung Injury, 2002; editor: several books. Mem.: Internat. Anesthesia Rsch. Soc., European Soc. Anesthesiology (Tchg. Recognition award 2005), Assn. German Anesthesiologists, German Soc. Anesthesiology and Critical Care Medicine (Thieme Tchg. award 2005). Roman Catholic. Achievements include patent on device for stress measurement; patent on gas recycling. Avocations: long distance running, mountain climbing, skiing. Office: U Hosp Dresden-Dept Anesthesiology Fetscherstrasse 74 01307 Dresden Germany E-mail: heller-a@rcs.urz.tu-dresden.de.

HELLER, LOIS JANE, physiologist, educator, researcher; b. Detroit, Jan. 4, 1942; d. John and Lona Elizabeth (Stockmeyer) Skagerberg; m. Robert Eugene Heller, May 21, 1966; children: John Robert, Suzanne Elizabeth. BA, Albion Coll., 1964; MS, U. Mich., 1966; PhD, U. Ill., Chgo., 1970. Instr. med ctr. U. Ill., Chgo., 1969-70, asst. prof., 1970-71, U. Minn., Duluth, 1972-77, assoc. prof., 1977-89, prof., 1989—. Author: Cardiovascular Physiology, 7th edit., 2010; contbr. numerous articles to profl. jours. Mem. Am. Physiol. Soc., Am. Heart Assn., Soc. Exptl. Biology and Medicine, Internat. Soc. Heart Rsch., Sigma Xi. Avocation: birding. Home: 9129 Congdon Blvd Duluth MN 55804-0005 Office: Univ Minn Sch of Medicine Duluth MN 55812

HELLER, MARY BERNITA, psychotherapist; b. Roland, Iowa, Feb. 11, 1934; d. Casper and Blanche (Hanson) Stenberg; m. John R. Heller, June 7, 1958; children: Kristen, Jonathan, Kathryn. BA, St. Olaf Coll., 1956; MSW, Fordham U., 1970. Lic. Social Worker NY, Bd. Cert. Diplomate in Social Work. Psychiat. social worker Beloit Children's Home, Ames, Iowa, 1957—58; caseworker Luth. Cmty. Svcs., NYC, 1958—59, Soc. Seamen's Children, SI, NY, 1971—75; psychiatric social worker S.I. Mental Health, 1971—75; psychotherapist Mid-Hudson Cons. Ctr., Wappinger Falls, NY, 1976—84; pvt. practice Poughkeepsie, NY, 1977—; psychotherapist Windsor Counseling Group, New Windsor, NY, 1989—2003. Supr. Luth. Cmty. Svcs., NYC, 1987-96. Bd. dirs. Children's Home of Poughkeepsie, 1983-88; bd. dirs. Seafarers and Internat. House, N.Y.C., 1990-96, v.p., 2002-2005, pres., 2005-08; mem. candidacy com. Met. N.Y. Synod, N.Y.C., 1986-94, v.p., 1992-2002, pres. 2005-08, chair Strategic Planning Com., 2008-09; mem. coun. Hudson Valley Philharm., Poughkeepsie, 1983-88; mem. Mission Devel. Bd., Metro NY Sqnod, 2004-09. Fellow Am. Orthopsychiat. Assn.; mem. NASW, Acad. Cert. Social Workers. Democrat. Lutheran. Avocation: skiing. Home: 24 Thornwood Dr Poughkeepsie NY 12603-4633 Office: 55 Wilbur Blvd Poughkeepsie NY 12603-3424 Home Phone: 845-473-5451; Office Phone: 845-452-3714. Personal E-mail: maryheller211@hotmail.com.

HELLERSTEIN, DAVID JOEL, psychiatrist, researcher, writer; b. Cleve., Dec. 30, 1953; s. Herman Kopel and Mary Leah (Feil) H.; m. Lisa Perry, Oct. 16, 1983; children: Sarah Nicole, Benjamin, Jason Samuel. AB, Harvard U., Cambridge, Mass., 1976; MD, Stanford U., Calif., 1980. Intern, then resident psychiatry NY Hosp. Cornell Med. Ctr., 1980-84; fellow pub. psychiatry Columbia Presbyn. Med. Ctr.-N.Y. State Psychiat. Inst., NYC, 1984-85; attending psychiatrist Beth Israel Med. Ctr., NYC, 1985-2000; instr. psychiatry Mt. Sinai Med. Ctr., NYC, 1985-88, asst. prof. psychiatry, 1988-93; physician in charge psychiat. outpatient svcs. Beth Israel Med. Ctr., NYC, 1989-96, chief outpatient psychiatry divsn., 1996-2000; asst. prof. psychiatry Albert Einstein Coll. Medicine, NYC, 1993-96, dir. mood disorders rsch. unit, 1994-2000, assoc. prof. psychiatry, 1996-2000; assoc. prof. clin. psychiatry Columbia U. Coll. Physicians and Surgeons, NYC, 2000—10; prof. clin. psychiatry Columbia U. Coll. Physicians & Surgeons, NYC, 2011—; rsch. psychiatrist Columbia U. Psychiatry Depression Evaluation Svc., 2007—. Clin. dir. NY State Psychiatric Inst., 2000—05; dir. mood disorders rsch. unit St. Luke's Roosevelt Hosp. Ctr., 2001—07; med. dir. clin. trials program Columbia Psychiatry, 2005—2007, dir. med. comm., 2007—. Author: (novels) Loving Touches, 1987, Stone Babies, 2000, (essay collection) Battles of Life and Death, 1986, (non-fiction) A Family of Doctors, 1994, Heal Your Brain, 2011; contbr. articles to profl. jours.; contbg. editor N.Am. Rev., 1981—, Sci. Digest, 1986-87, 7 Days mag., 1988-90, M.D. Mag., 1990-95. MacDowell Colony fellow, 1984, 86, 88, 2009. Fellow APA (disting.); mem. PEN, Am. Psychiat. Assn. (editor NY County Dist. newsletter, 1989-2001; chmn. publs. com. N.Y. County chpt. 1989-2001, pres.-elect 1997-98, pres. 1998-99), Author's Guild. Democrat. Jewish. E-mail: djh102@columbia.edu.

HELLERSTEIN, LEWIS JAN, hematologist, oncologist, consultant; b. Denver, Sept. 27, 1938; s. Louis A. and Lenoara Brilliant Hellerstein; m. Peggy Henry Hellerstein, Feb. 4, 1962; children: Raymond Trent, Julia K. Connel, Kimberly Helen Segelke, Jason Lee. Student, Ohio State U., 1956—57; BA, U. Colo., 1960, MD, 1964. Diplomate Am. Bd. Internal Medicine, 1972, Am. Bd. Hematology, 1972. Extern Gen. Rose Meml. Hosp., Denver, 1962—64; intern DC Gen. Hosp. George Washington U., 1964—65, from jr. asst. resident to asst. resident in medicine, instr. phys. diagnosis, 1965—66, fellow in medicine, 1966; fellow in hematology and oncology Beth Israel Hosp., Boston, 1968—69; fellow in coagulation Beth Israel Hosp., Children's Med. Ctr., Boston, 1969—70, sr. fellow in coagulation, instr., 1970—71; assoc. in medicine Harvard Med. Sch., Boston, 1969—70, instr., 1970—71, Albany Med. Coll., NY, 1969—70; clin. instr. Baylor Coll. Medicine, Houston, 1971—80; clin. asst. prof. U. Tex. Med. Sch., Houston, 1974—76, clin. assoc. prof., 1976—. Contbr. articles to profl. jours. Med. officer USAF, 1966—68. Achievements include research in LDH isoenzyme fractionation in clinical medicine; use of Kr 95 in diagnosis of right to left shunts and pulmonary function; effects of hormones in tissue culture of cancerous and non-cancerous origin; guanethidine in spasticity; patents for intracorporal vacular prosthetic blood irradiator. Office: 11506 Habersham Ln Houston TX 77024-6518

HELLMAN, SAMUEL, radiologist, educator; b. NYC, July 23, 1934; s. Henry Sidney and Anna (Egar) Hellman; m. Marcia Sherman, June 30, 1957; children: Jeffrey, Richard, Deborah Susan. BS magna cum laude, Allegheny Coll., 1955, DSc (hon.), 1984; MD cum laude, SUNY, Syracuse, 1959, DSc (hon.), 1993; MS (hon.), Harvard U., 1968. Med. intern Beth Israel Hosp., Boston, 1959—60; asst. resident radiology Yale Sch. Medicine and Grace-New Haven Hosp., 1960—62, postdoctoral fellow radiotherapy and cancer research, 1962—64; postdoctoral fellow Inst. Cancer Research and Royal Marsden Hosp., London, 1965—66; asst. prof. radiology Yale Sch. Medicine, 1966—68; assoc. prof. radiology Harvard Med. Sch., 1968—70; dir. Joint Center for Radiation Therapy, 1968—83, assoc. prof., chmn. dept. radiation therapy, 1971, prof., chmn. dept., 1971—83, also Alvan T. and Viola D. Fuller-Am. Cancer Soc. prof.; physician-in-chief Meml. Sloan Kettering Cancer Ctr., 1983—88, Benno Schmidt chair in clin. oncology, 1983—88; dean div. biol. sci. and Pritzker Sch. Medicine, v.p. for Med. Ctr. U. Chgo., 1988—93, Pritzker prof., 1988—93, Pritzker disting. svc. prof., 1993—2006, Pritzker disting. svc. prof. emeritus, 2006—. Chmn. bd. sci. counselors divsn. cancer treatment Nat. Cancer Inst., 1980—84; bd. govs. Argonne Nat. Lab., 1990—93; trustee Brookings Inst., 1992—; bd. dirs. Varian Med. Systems Inc., Insightec; mem. sci. adv. bd. Ludwig Inst. for Cancer Rsch. Contbr. numerous articles to med. jours. Trustee Allegheny Coll., 1979—98, chmn. bd. trustees, 1987—93. Recipient Rosenthal award for cancer rsch., 1980, medal, City of Paris, 1986, award for Outstanding Contbns. to Cancer Care, Assn. Cmty. Cancer Ctrs., 1993. Fellow: AAAS; mem.: N.Y. Acad. Scis., Soc. Chmn. Acad. Radiology Depts., Inst. Medicine NAS, Assn. Am. Physicians, Am. Cancer Soc., Am. Soc. Hematology, Am. Assn. Cancer Rsch., Am. Soc. Clin. Oncology (pres. 1986, David A. Karnovsky lectr. 1994), Assn. Univ. Radiologists, Am. Coll. Radiology (gold medal 2003), Am. Soc. Therapeutic Radiologists (pres. 1983, Gold medal 1991), Am. Radium Soc., Alpha Omega Alpha, Sigma Xi, Phi Beta Kappa. Home: 1122 N Dearborn St Apt 25H Chicago IL 60610 Office: U Chgo Divsn Biol Scis 5841 S Maryland Ave Chicago IL 60637-1463 Office Phone: 773-702-4346. Business E-Mail: s-hellman@uchicago.edu.

HELLSTRÖM, INGEGERD, medical researcher; b. Stockholm; permanent resident, US, 1966, US citizen, 1996; m. Karl Erik Hellström; children: Katarina Elisabet, Per Erik. MD of Medicine, Karolinska Inst. Med. Sch., Stockholm, 1964, PhD of Medicine (Tumor Biology), 1966. Rsch. assoc. (docent), dept. Tumor Biology Karolinska Inst. Med. Sch., Stockholm, 1959-66, asst. prof. dept. tumor biology, 1966; asst. prof. microbiology U. Wash., Seattle, 1966—, rsch. assoc. prof. microbiology, 1969-72, prof. microbiology/immunology, 1972—85, adj. prof. pathology, 1972—85, affiliate prof. pathology, 1985—2005, prof. emeritus, 2006—; mem. and program head, divsn. tumor immunology Fred Hutchinson Cancer Rsch. Ctr., Seattle, 1975—83; sr. scientist Oncogen, Seattle, 1983—85, lab. dir., 1985—86; v.p. Oncogen/Bristol-Myers Squibb, Seattle, 1986-90; v.p. immunological diseases Bristol-Myers Squibb Pharm. Rsch. Inst., Seattle, 1990—97; pron. investigator Pacific Northwest Rsch. Inst., Seattle, 1997—2004. Patents in the field: 17 US patents and 1 UK Patent; mem. editl. adv. bd., Jour. of Nat. Cancer Inst.; assoc. editor, Cancer Research, 1980-87, 1988-93, 1995-; mem. editl. bd., Anticancer Research; mem. gen. assembly, GM Cancer Rsch. Found.; mem. external adv. com, Specialized Ctr. for Cancer Rsch., U. Ill. at Chgo., Coll. Medicine, 1991-; contbr. to 450 sci. publs. Recipient Lucy Wortham James award, Ewing Soc., 1971, Matrix Table award, 1972, Pap award Outstanding Contbn. Cancer Rsch., Papanicolaou Cancer Rsch. Inst., 1973, Am. Cancer Soc. Nat. award 1974, RNO (Knight of Northern Star, First Class Swedish Order of Merit), 1976, Humboldt award to Sr. US Sci., Humbolt Stiftung Bonn, W. Germany, 1980. Mem. AMA, Am. Assn. Immunologists, Am. Fedn. Clin. Rsch., Am. Assn. Cancer Rsch., Soc. Biol. Therapy. Office: Harborview Med Ctr Box 359939 325 Ninth Ave Seattle WA 98104-2499 Office Phone: 206-897-5908. Business E-Mail: ihellstr@u.washington.edu.

HELLSTRÖM, KARL ERIK, science educator, researcher; b. Stockholm; permanent resident, US, 1966, US Citizen, 1996; m. Ingegerd Hellström; children: Katarina Elisabet, Per Erik. Candidate of medicine, Karolinska Inst. Med. Sch., Stockholm, 1955, MD, PhD, Karolinska Inst. Med. Sch., Stockholm, 1964. Rsch. fellow, dept. histology Karolinska Inst. Med. Sch., Stockholm, 1953—57, rsch. assoc., dept. histology, 1957, docent in tumor biology, 1958—62, asst. prof., dept. tumor biology, 1962—66; investigator in cell biology funded by Swedish Medical Rsch. Coun, 1964—66; assoc. prof. pathology U. Wash. Sch. Medicine, Seattle, 1966—69, prof. pathology, 1969—83, adj. prof. microbiology and immunology, 1984—2005, affiliate prof. pathology, 1984—2005, prof. emeritus, 2006—; prin. investigator Pacific Northwest Rsch. Inst., Seattle, 1997—2004, mem. and head, program of tumor immunology Fred Hutchinson Cancer Rsch Ctr., Seattle, 1975—83; sr. scientist Oncogen, Seattle, 1983—85, lab. dir., 1985—86; v.p. Oncogen/Bristol-Myers, 1986—90; v.p. oncology drug discovery Bristol-Myers Squibb Pharm. Rsch. Inst., 1990—95, v.p. immunotherapeutics drug discovery, 1995—97. Bd. dirs. Seattle Genetics, Inc.; sci. adv. coun. Cancer Rsch. Inst. Inc. Editl. bd.: Cancer Immunology and Immunology; contbr. to 460 sci. publs. Assessor Anti-Cancer Coun., Victoria, BC, Canada; Can. reviewer Netherlands Cancer Found. Recipient Lucy Wortham James award, Ewing Soc., 1971, Parke Davis award in Exptl. Pathology, 1972, Pap award for Outstanding Contbn. in Cancer Rsch., Papanicolaou Cancer Rsch. Inst., Miami, Fla., 1973, Nat. award for Cancer Rsch., Am. Cancer Soc., 1974, RNO (Knight of the Northern Star, 1st Class, Swedish Order of Merit), 1976, Humboldt award to Sr. US Sci., Humboldt Stiftung, Bonn, Germany, 1980. Mem.: Clin. immunology Soc., Am. Assn. for Clin. Rsch., AAAS, Am. Assn. of Immunologists, Am. Assn. Exptl. Pathology, Am. Assn. for Cancer Rsch., NY Acad. Sciences, Sigma XI, The Sci. Rsch. Soc., Alpha Omega Alpha, U. Wash. Chap. Achievements include patents in field. Office: Harborview Med Ctr Box 359939 325 Ninth Ave Seattle WA 98104-2499 Office Phone: 206-897-5907. Business E-Mail: hellsk@u.washington.edu.

HELLSTRÖM, MIKAEL, radiologist, educator, researcher; b. Stockholm, Dec. 2, 1950; MD, U. Lund, 1975; PhD, U. Gothenburg, 1986. Prof., cons. radiologist Sahlgrenska Acad., Gothenburg U., 2001—. Sci. adv. com. Swedish Coun. Health Tech. Assessment (SBU, Statens Beredning Medicinsk Utvärdering), 2008—. Mem.: Swedish Soc. Radiology, European Soc. Gastrointestinal and Abdominal Radiology, European Soc. Urogenital Radiology, European Soc. Radiology. Avocations: squash, tennis. Office: Dept Radiology Sahlgrenska University Hospital Gothenburg 413 45 Sweden Business E-Mail: mikael.hellstrom@xray.gu.se.

HELLWAGNER, KLAUS GERHARD, anesthesiologist, emergency physician; b. Wien, Austria, Apr. 10, 1966; MD, Med. U. Vienna, Wien, 1993; LLM, Med. U. Vienna, 2009. Staff anesthesiologist Med. U. Vienna, Wien, Austria, 1993—2005, Wiener Gebietskrankenkasse, 2005—09. Chief emergency physician ASBÖ, Wien, 2004—09; emergency physician Vienna EMS, 2009—. Med. officer Austrian Mil., 2001—. Achievements include research in Medical Law; Dreams during anesthesia; Resuscitation. Office: Ma 70 Wienen Bcufsruettung Radetzkystrusse 1 Wien 1030 Austria Business E-Mail: klaus.hellwagner@mafwien.gu.ut.

HELMAN, LEE J., medical researcher; married; 2 children. BA with distinction, George Wash. U., Washington, 1976; MD magna cum laude, U. Md., 1980. Cert. in internal medicine 1983, in med. oncology 1985, lic. Md. Intern in internal medicine Barnes Hosp., Washington U., St. Louis, 1980—81, jr. resident in internal medicine, 1981—82, sr. asst. resident, 1982—83; chief resident Washington U. Med. Svc., St. Louis VA Med. Svc., 1982; med. staff fellow pediatric br. and medicine br. Nat. Cancer Inst., NIH, Bethesda, Md., 1983—84, med. staff, biotech. & sr. staff fellow and med. officer molecular genetics sect., pediatric br., 1984—92, head molecular oncology sect., pediatric oncology br. Ctr. Cancer Rsch., 1993—, acting dep. chief pediatric br., 1995—96, acting chief pediatric oncology br., 1996—97, chief pediatric oncology br., 1997—2007, dep. dir. Ctr. Cancer Rsch., 2001—, acting chief med. oncology Ctr. Cancer Rsch., 2005—07, acting sci. dir. clin. rsch. Ctr. Cancer Rsch., 2005—07, sci. dir. clin. rsch. Ctr. Cancer Rsch., 2007—, acting clin. dir. Ctr. Cancer Rsch., 2008—09; assoc. prof. pediat. Uniformed Services of Health Sciences, F. Edward Hébert Sch. Medicine, Bethesda, 1994—98; part-time prof. pediat. and oncology Johns Hopkins U., Balt., 1999—. Contbr. articles to profl. jours. Mem.: American Assn. Cancer Rsch., American Soc. Clin. Oncology, Connective Tissue Oncology Soc. Office: Nat Cancer Inst Bldg 31, Rm 3A11 31 Center Dr MSC 2440 Bethesda MD 20892-2440 Office Phone: 301-496-4257. Office Fax: 301-480-4318. E-mail: helmanl@nih.gov. *

HELMECKE, GERD, physician, consultant, astrophysicist; b. Duisburg, Germany, Apr. 5, 1949; s. Fritz and Hannelore Helmecke; m. Brigitte Kern, Sept. 8, 1973; 1 child, Sabrina. Vet. degree, Friedrich-Wilhelms U., Germany, 1976. Asst. physician Marien Hosp., Euskirchen, Germany, 1978; head physician Maria-Htilf Hosp., Rheinbach, Germany, 1979—83; pvt. practice Hennef, Germany, 1983—. Cons. in field. Author: Basic Cosmos Model, 2003. With German mil., 1970. Achievements include invention of safety bathpad; research in spl. treatment dialysis and pregnancy. Avocation: sports. Home: Erfurtstr 33 St Augustin 53757 Germany Office: Koenigstr 4 Hennef 53773 Germany Office Phone: 02242-82424. Personal E-mail: dokhelmecke@t-online.de.

HELMS GUBA, LISA MARIE, nursing administrator; b. Sioux City, Iowa, Nov. 24, 1962; d. Dean Edward and Betty Lou Victoria (Guenther) H. BA in Nursing, Carroll Coll., Helena, Mont., 1986; postgrad., Calif. State U., Sacramento, 1990-92; MSN, Incarnate Word Coll., 1996. Cert. pediatric nurse. Enlisted U.S. Army, 1981, advanced through grades to lt. col., 2004, nurse San Francisco, 1986-90, Calif. Nat. Guard, San Francisco, 1990-92, Rio Linda (Calif.) Union Sch. Dist., 1990-92; enlisted USAF, 1992—2008; mem. A.F. Nurse Corps Wilford Hall Med Ctr., Lackland AFB, Tex., 1992-96; asst. nurse mgr. and critical care aeromed. transp. team nurse dir. Malcolm Grow Hosp., Andrews AFB, Md., 1996-2000; dir. Nurse Triage Ctr., 2001—03; nursing exec. Internal Medicine and Women's Health, Dover AFB, 2003—03, case mgr., 2004—06; nurse mgr. multi svcs. unit Malcolm Grow Med. Ctr., Andrews AFB, Md., 2006—08; comdr. Air Staging Facility, Andrews AFB, Md., 2007—08. Deployed to Guantanamo Bay, Cuba, July to Oct. 1994 for Operation Sea Signal, Operation Safe Haven; provider med. care to Haitian/Cuban migrants, 2009-, perinatal nurse, fetal & infant mortality review coord. Anne Anndel County Health Dept., Annapolis, Md., 2009-. Decorated Army Commendation medal; recipient Merit medal, USAF, Air Force Commendation medal. Mem. AAN. Office Phone: 410-222-7223. Personal E-mail: lisaguba@sprintmail.com. Business E-Mail: hdhelmoo@aacounty.org.

HELMY, MOHAMED MOHAMED, dermatologist, consultant; b. El-Mansoura, Egypt, Nov. 26, 1948; s. Mohamed Helmy Abdel-Aziz and Amina Fahmy El-Said; m. Magda Moustafa Ibrahim, Nov. 28, 1974; children: Rania Mohamed, Raouf Mohamed. MB, BChir, Al-azhar U., Cairo, 1972, M in Dermatology & Venereology, 1982, PhD in Dermatology & Venereology, 1989. Ho. officer El-Hussein U. Hosp., Cairo, 1973—74, resident in dermatology and venereology, 1978—82; resident in internal medicine Gamal Abdel-Naser Hosp., Alexandria, Egypt, 1974—74; resident in dermatology Kuwait Hosp., Dubai, United Arab Emirates, 1974—78, dermatovenereologist, 1982—95; cons. dermatoligist, head depts. derma, stds. and andrology Electricity Hosp., Cairo, 1996—. Gen. sec. in divsn. dermatology & venereology Emirates Med. Assn., Dubai, 1993—95; adv. bd. drugs Electricity Hosp., Cairo, 1997—. Contbr. articles to profl. jours. Chmn. sci. com. Egyptian Club, Dubai, United Arab Emirates, 1992—95. Recipient Cert. of Appreciation, Fourth Asian Dermatol. Congress, 1996, Kuwait Hosp., Dubai, 1997, Ministry of Health, United Arab Emirates, 1997. Fellow: Am. Acad. Dermatology; mem.: Asian Dermatol. Assn., Internat. Soc. Dermatology. Avocations: football, tennis, swimming, classical music, reading. Home: 19 Abdel-hamid Badawy St Heliopolis Cairo 11351 Egypt Office: Private Clinic 58 El-Hegaz St Heliopolis Cairo 11351 Egypt Office Fax: (+202) 6373509. Personal E-mail: mhelmy_aziz@yahoo.com.

HELMY, SANAA MOUHAMED HUSSEIN, geneticist, educator; b. Cairo, May 1, 1953; BSc, Cairo U., 1980, PhD in Genetics, 2001. Asst. prof., dr. cytogenetics Nat. Rsch. Ctr., Cairo, 2009—. Mem.: Nat. Human Genetics Soc., Arabic Med. Rsch. Soc., Egyptian Soc. Genetics Children, Brit. Soc. Human Genetics, Internat. Soc. Prenatal Diagnosis. Avocation: travel. Office: ElBouhousse St Cairo Gizza 12311 Egypt Office Fax: 00 202 33388481.

HELTIANU, CONSTANTINA, chemist; b. Pitesti, Romania, Sept. 27, 1941; Degree in Chemistry, Bucharest U., Romania, 1965; PhD in Chemistry, Gh. Asachi Tech. U., Iasi, Romania, 1985. Asst. prof. Faculty Natural Scis., Pitesti, 1965—66; sci. investigator Inst. Endocrinology C. I. Parhon, Bucharest, Romania, 1966—78; sci. rschr. Inst. Cellular Biology and Pathology, Nicolae Simionescu, Bucharest, 1978—92, sr. sci. rschr., 1992—, sci. bd. mem., 1993—. Fulbright rschr. Yale U., New Haven, 1981—82; vis. rschr. U. Coll. London, 1993—98, Ctr. Transgene Tech. and Gene Therapy, Leuven, Belgium, 1997—97, Dept. Genetic, Cochin Port Royal Sch. Medicine, Rene Descartes U., Paris, 1999—2004. Recipient Gheorghe Marinescu award, Romanian Acad., Bucharest, Emil Racovita award, award, Assn. Overcoming Lysosomal Diseases, Paris, Romanian Soc. Diabetes Nutrition and Metabolic Diseases, Bucharest. Mem.: Romanian Soc. Cell Biology, Romanian Acad. Med. Scis. Avocations: reading, travel, sports. Office: 8 BPHasdeu Bucharest 050568 Romania Business E-Mail: ina.heltianu@icbp.ro.

HELZER, JAMES DENNIS, retired health facility administrator; b. Fresno, Calif., Apr. 27, 1938; s. Alexander and Katherine (Scheidt) H.; children: Amy, Rebecca. BS, Fresno State Coll., 1960; M.Hosp. Adminstrn., U. Iowa, 1965. Adminstrv. asst. Twilight Haven, Fresno, Calif., 1960-61, adminstr. resident, 1964-65; asst. adminstr. U. Calif. Hosps. and Clinics, San Francisco, 1965-68, Fresno Community Hosp., 1968-71, exec. adminstr., 1971-82, pres., chief exec. officer, 1982-91, Community Hosps. Cen. Calif., 1982-91, cons., 1991-95; adminstr. Veterans Home of Calif., Yountville, Calif., 1995-99; ret., 1999. Served with U.S. Army, 1961-63. Fellow Am. Coll. Hosp. Adminstrs.; mem. Am., Calif. hosp. assns. Clubs: Rotary. Presbyterian. Home: 1164 Secret Lake Loop Lincoln CA 95648-8404

HEMILÄ, HARRI OLAVI, biochemist, epidemiologist, researcher; b. Valkeakoski, Finland, June 16, 1958; s. Simo Olavi and Anja Heleena (Innala) H.; life ptnr. Teija Tuulikki Koivula; children: Joonas, Mikko, Antti. MSc, U. Helsinki, Finland, 1983, PhD, 1993, MD, 1999. Rsch. assoc. U. Helsinki, 1986-90, 95—, docent in biochemistry, 1996—, lectr. in pub. health, 2002—. Contbr. articles to profl. jours. Achievements include research on the role of Vitamin C and Vitamin E and beta-carotene on infections diseases and on the role of Vitamin E on mortality. E-mail: harri.hemila@helsinki.fi.

HEMINGWAY HALL, PATRICIA A., health insurance company executive; b. 1952; d. Ernest Hemingway. BSN, Mich. State U., East Lansing, 1975; MA in Pub. Health, Health Planning & Adminstrn., U. Mich., 1979. Intensive care unit nurse; with A. Foster Higgins, Aetna/Ptnrs. Health Plans, Voluntary Hosps. America, Blue Cross Blue Shield Fla.; head utilization mgmt. and network mgmt. divsn. Blue Cross Blue Shield Tex., 1993—94, COO NE Tex. geographic bus. unit, 1994—98, sr. v.p. geographic bus. units and health care mgmt., 1998—2001, pres., 2001—06; sr. cons. Gorman Health Group LLC; dir. fin., subscriber svcs., enterprise process mgmt., info. tech., actuarial and treasury divsns. Health Care Svc. Corp., exec. v.p. internal ops., 2006—07, pres. Tex. divsn., COO, 2007—08, pres., 2007—, CEO, 2008—. Bd. dirs. NRG Texas, LLC, 2003—, Manpower Group, 2011—, Prime Therapeutics, LLC, MEDecision, Blue Cross Blue Shield Assn., Blue Cross Blue Shield Fin. Corp., America's Health Ins. Plans, Nat. Inst. for Health Care Mgmt., Salvation Army Adv. Bd., Health Care Leadership Coun. Named one of Top 25 Woman to Watch, Crain's Chgo. Bus., 2008, 2010—, Top 25 Women in Healthcare, Modern Healthcare mag., 2009, The 100 Most Powerful People in Healthcare, Modern Healthcare, 2009—10. Office: Health Care Service Corporation Blue Cross Blue Shield of Illinois 300 E Randolph St Chicago IL 60601-5099 Office Phone: 312-653-6000. Office Fax: 312-938-4209. *

HEMMING, VAL G., retired dean, educator; b. Rexburg, Idaho, July 9, 1937; m. Alice Bell Hemming; children: Heidi, Julie, Jill, Patrick. BA in Entomology, U. Utah, 1962; MD, U. Utah Coll. Medicine, 1966. Diplomate Am. Bd. Pediatrics, Nat. Bd. Med. Examiners. Commd. 2d lt. USAF, 1965, advanced through grades to col.; pediatric intern U. Utah Affiliated Hosps., 1966—67; resident physician in pediatrics Wilford Hall USAF Med. Ctr., Lackland AFB, Tex., 1968—70; staff pediatrician USAF Hosp., Wiesbaden, Germany, 1970—74; chmn., dir. pediatric residency tng. David Grant USAF Med. ctr., Travis AFB, Calif., 1976—80; assoc. prof. dept. pediatrics Uniformed Svcs. U. Health Scis., Bethesda, Md., 1980—84, prof. dept. pediatrics, 1984—87, prof., chmn. dept. pediatrics, 1987—95, from interim dean to dean F. Edward Hebert Sch. Medicine, 1995—2002, prof. emeritus in pediats., 2002—; splty. cons. in pediatrics to Air Force Surgeon Gen., 1983—90; ret., 1990. Cons. in pediatrics to the asst. sec. for health affairs Dept. of Def., 1988-91; adv. coun. Nat. Inst. of Child Health and Human Devel. Contbr. numerous articles to profl. jours. Mem. Am. Acad. Pediatrics, Am. Pediatric Soc., Infectious Disease Soc. of Am., Western Soc. for Pediatric Rsch., Pediatric Infectious Disease Soc., Lancefield Soc., Internat. AIDS Soc., Am. Soc. for Microbiology. Office: Uniformed Svcs U Health Scis 4301 Jones Bridge Rd Bethesda MD 20814-4712 Home Phone: 301-942-5566; Office Phone: 301-295-3742. Business E-Mail: vhemming@usuhs.mil.

HEMMINGSEN, BARBARA BRUFF, retired microbiologist; b. Whittier, Calif., Mar. 25, 1941; d. Stephen Cartland and Susanna Jane Bruff; m. Edvard Alfred Hemmingsen, Aug. 5, 1967; 1 child, Grete. BA, U. Calif., Berkeley, 1962, MA, 1964; PhD, U. Calif., San Diego, 1971. Lectr. San Diego State U., 1973-77, asst. prof., 1977-81, assoc. prof., 1981-88, prof., 1988—2004; ret., 2004. Vis. asst. prof. Aarhas U., Denmark, 1971—72; cons. AMBIS, Inc., San Diego, 1984—85, Woodward-Clyde Cons., 1985, 1987—91, Novatron, Inc., 2000—06. Author (with others): (book) Microbial Ecology, 1972; contbr. articles to profl. jours. Mem. Planned Parenthood, San Diego. Mem.: AAAS, Civil War Round Table, San Deigo, San Diego Assn. Rational Inquiry (sec. 1998—2001, treas. 2002—), Am. Women Sci., Am. Soc. Microbiology, Daus. of Union Vets. of Civil War (patriotic instr. Nancy Lincoln Tent 2007—09), Brit. Isles Geneal. Rsch. Assn. (sec. 2006—09), Phi Beta Kappa (corr. sec. Nu chpt. Calif. 1994—2002, historian 2003—, past pres.), Sigma Xi. Democrat.

HEMPFLING, LINDA LEE, retired nurse; b. Indpls., July 28, 1947; d. Paul Roy and Myrtle Pearl (Ward) H. Diploma, Meth. Hosp. Ind. Sch. Nursing, 1968; postgrad., St. Joseph's Coll., Jaliet Jr. Coll. Cert. in profl. healthcare mgmt. 2009; med. audit specialist, 2000. Charge nurse Meth. Hosp., Indpls., 1968; staff nurse operating rm. Silver Cross Hosp., Joliet, Ill., 1969, charge nurse oper. rm. Huntington Hosp., 1969-73; night supr. oper. rm., post anesthesia care unit Hermann Hosp., Houston, 1973-76, unit mgr., purchasing coord. oper. rms., 1976-83; RN med. auditor, quality improvement, tng. coord. Nat. Healthcare Rev., Inc., Houston, 1984—98; RN med. auditor RelayHealth, 1999—2011. Future Nurses Am. scholar, 1965, Nat. Merit scholar, 1965. Mem.: Am. Assn. Med. Audit Specialists, Tex. Med. Auditors Assn., Assn. PeriOperative Registered Nurses. Home Phone: 713-729-7303. *

HEMSLEY, STEPHEN J., healthcare company executive; b. 1952; BS, Fordham U., 1974. Gen. mgr. tech. activities and knowledge initiatives Arthur Andersen and Co., mng. ptnr. strategy and planning; CFO Arthur Anderson Worldwide Arthur Anderson and Co.; sr. exec. v.p. UnitedHealth Group, Inc., Detroit, 1997—98, COO, 1998—2006, pres., 1999—, bd. dirs., 2000—, CEO, 2006—. Bd. dirs. Provell, Inc., 1997—2001; bd. trustee Univ. of St. Thomas, Minn., Minn. Pub. Radio. Trustee Minn. Pub. Radio, 2002—. Office: UnitedHealth Group Inc PO Box 1459 Minneapolis MN 55440-1459 also: UnitedHealth Group Inc 9900 Bren Rd E Minnetonka MN 55343 Office Phone: 800-328-5979. *

HENCHEY, CHRIS, insurance company executive; MBA, Southern NH U. Co-founder, chief operations officer Choicelinx Corp., bd. dirs., 1999—2005; v.p. MVP Health Care, NH, exec, v.p., COO, 2008—. Office: MVP Health Care 625 State St PO Box 2207 Schenectady NY 12301-2207

HEND, MAGDY F. A., reproductive and infertility endocrinologist, consultant, health facility administrator; b. Cairo, June 19, 1955; arrived in Eng., 1972; s. Fawzy Ahmed Hend and Hania Hafez Hasan; m. Dina Kayali-Hend, Apr. 27, 1992; children: Lena, Clara, Omar. MB BChir, Ain Shams U., Cairo, 1979. Registrar ob-gyn. Chase Farm Hosp., London, 1983—88; med. officer Manor House Hosp., London, 1989—90; pvt. cons. Tally Ho Med. Ctr., London, 1990—93; cons. med. dir. London Regency Hosp., 1993—97, Brit. Hormone Ctr., London, 1997—2000; med. dir. Cairo Heliopolis Hosp., Cairo, 1998—; cons. med. dir. Brit. Fertility and Virility Ctrs., London, 2000—; cons. Gynecol. Cosmetic Surgery. Cons., med. dir. Regency Clinic, London. Author: (book) The Royal College of General Practice Reference Book, 1993, National Association of Fund Holding Practices, 1995, The Medical Book, 1995. Recipient cert., Al-Azhr U., 1998. Fellow: Lottery Club; mem.: Am. Soc. for Reproductive Medicine, European Soc. Human Reproduction, Brit. Andrology Soc., Brit. Fertility Soc., Royal Coll. Gynecologists U.K., Royal Coll. Physicians and Surgeons Glasgow (licentiate), Royal Coll. Surgeons Edinburgh (licentiate), Royal Coll. Physicians Edinburgh (licentiate). Achievements include first to testosterone replacement therapy; fallopian tube catheterization as an alternative treatment for test tube baby in cases of blocked tubes; research in sexual difficulties, hormone replacement, infertility in both sexes, and polycystic ovaries. Avocations: photography, listening to classical music and opera, computers. Office Phone: 44 207 490 0505. Office Fax: (0044) 207 490 4490. Personal E-mail: magdyhend@yahoo.co.uk.

HENDEE, WILLIAM RICHARD, medical physics educator, academic administrator, radiologist; b. Owosso, Mich., Jan. 1, 1938; s. C.L. and Alvina M. H.; m. Jeannie Wesley, June 16, 1960; children: Mikal, Shonn, Eric, Gareth and Gregory (twins), Lara and Karel (twins). BS, Millsaps Coll., Jackson, Miss., 1959; PhD, U. Tex., 1962; DSc (hon.), Millsaps Coll., Jackson, Miss., 1988. Diplomate Am. Bd. Radiology, Am. Bd. Health Physics. AEC fellow Nat. Reactor Testing Sta., Idaho Falls, Idaho, 1960; asst. prof., then assoc. prof. physics Millsaps Coll., 1962-65, chmn. dept., 1964-65; instr. Miss. State U. (extension), 1963; asst. prof., then assoc. prof. radiology (med. physics) U. Colo. Med. Center, 1965-73, prof., 1974-85, chmn. dept., 1978-85; mem. staff VA Hosp., Denver, 1970-85, Mercy Hosp., 1971-85, Denver Gen. Hosp., 1971-85, Beth Israel Hosp., 1974-85; v.p. sci. and tech. AMA, Chgo., 1985-1991; prof. radiology, biophysics, radiation oncology, bioethics Med. Coll. Wis., Milw., 1991—2006, clin. prof. radiology and biophysics, 1985-91, sr. assoc. dean, v.p., 1991—2005, dean grad. sch., 1995—2006, pres. rsch. found., 2005—06, disting. prof. radiation oncology, biophysics, cmty. and public health, 2006—. Prof. bioengring. Marquette U., 1993—; vis. lectr. Oak Ridge Assoc. Univs., 1964; adj. prof. radiology Northwestern U. Sch. Medicine, 1986-91; adj. prof. elec. engring. U. Wis.-Milw., 2003-, adj. prof. radiology U. Colo., 2009-, clin. prof. radiology, U. N.M, 2007-; adj. prof. Mayo Clinic, Rochester, 2011-. Editor Med. Phys., 2005—; contbr. 375 articles to profl. jours., author/editor 24 books. Served with USMC, 1957-62. Recipient Disting. Alumnus award Millsaps Coll., 1967, Disting. Svc. award Nat. Wildlife Fedn., 1990, Wright Langham Meml. award U. Ky., 1991, Gold medal Am. Roentgen Ray Soc., 2005, Med. Coll. Sic. Disting. Svc. award, 2005; Gilbert X-ray fellow, 1960-62, summer fellow NSF, AEC; campus assoc. Danforth Found., gold medal Am. Roentgen Ray Soc., 2005; Disting. Svc. award, Med. Coll. Wis., 2005, Gold medal Radiol. Soc. N.Am., 2007. Fellow Am. Coll. Radiology (Gold medal 2010), Am. Inst. Med. and Biol. Engring. (pres. 1998-99); mem. AAAS, Health Physics Soc. (chmn. coms., Elda E. Anderson award 1972), Am. Assn. Physicists in Medicine (pres. 1976-77, Robert S. Landauer Meml. award 1977, William D. Coolidge award 1989), Nat. Wildlife Fedn. (Disting. Svc. award 1990), Soc. Biomed. Engring., (sr. mem.), Soc. Nuclear Medicine (pres. 1980-81, Benedict Cassen Meml. award 1984), Am. Acad. Home Care Physicians (Disting. Svc. award 1991), Am. Bd. Radiology (trustee 1995-05, pres. 2002-04, found. dir. 2007-, chair 2009-11), Omicron Delta Kappa, Theta Nu Sigma. Office: PO Box 7319 Rochester MN 55903-7319 Home: 725 11th St NW Rochester MN 55901 Business E-Mail: whendee@mcw.edu.

HENDERSON, BERTRAM DONALD, medical geneticist, educator; b. Bloemfontein, South Africa, June 2, 1958; MBChB, UFS, 1982, MMED, 1993. Prin. specialist, sr. lectr. FPA, UFA, 2000—09, head clin. unit, med. genetics, 2009—. Councillor Coll. Medicine South Africa, 2009—. Mem.: Lysosomal Storage Disease Med. (South Africa) (adv. bd.), Med. and Sci. Adv. Bd. South African Cystic Fibrosis Assn. Office: PO Box 339 G11 Bloemfontein Free State 9300 South Africa Office Fax: 27862705512. Business E-Mail: gnmgbdh@ufs.ac.za.

HENDERSON, BRIAN EDMOND, preventive medicine physician, educator, former dean; b. San Francisco, June 27, 1937; s. Edward O'Brien and Antoinette (Amstutz) H.; m. Judith Anne McDermott, Sept. 3, 1960; children: Sean, Maire, Sarah, Brian John, Michael. BA, U. Calif.-Berkeley, 1958; MD, U. Chgo., 1962. Resident Mass. Gen. Hosp., Boston, 1962-64; chief arbovirology Ctr. Disease Control, Atlanta, 1969-70; assoc. prof. pathology U. So. Calif., LA, 1970-74, prof. pathology, 1974-78, prof. preventive medicine, dept. chmn., 1978-88, dir. Kenneth Norris Jr. Comprehensive Cancer Ctr., 1983—93, rschr., 1994—96, prof. dept. preventative medicine, Kenneth T. Norris Chair in Cancer Prevention, 1996—, dir. Zilkha Neurogenetic Inst., 2002—; dean Keck Sch. Medicine, U. So. Calif., LA, 2004—07, disting prof. preventive medicine, Kenneth T. Norris, Jr. chair in cancer prevention, 2007—; pres. Salk Inst. Biol. Studies, La Jolla, Calif., 1993—94. Established LA Cancer Surveillance Program, U. So. Calif., 1972, Hawaii-LA Multiethnic Cohort, 1993; cons. WHO, South Pacific Commn., U.S.-Japan-Hawaii Cancer Program; mem. Charles S. Mott selection com. Gen. Motors Cancer Research Found., 1982-88; bd. councillors Nat. Cancer Inst., 1979-82; mem. sci. council Internat. Agy. for Rsch. on Cancer, 1982-86 Contbr. articles to profl. jours., chpts. to books; mem. editorial bd. Jour. Clin. Oncology; assoc. editor: Cancer Research. Served to lt. col. USPHS, 1964-69 Nat. Acad. Sci. disting. scholar to China, 1982; recipient Richard & Hinda Rosenthal Found. award, Am. Assn. Cancer Research, 1987, Rsch. Excellence in Cancer Epidemiology and Prevention Award, Am. Acad. Cancer Rsch., U. Chgo. Disting. Svc. Award, Presdl. Medallion., U. So. Calif., 1999. Fellow Los Angeles Acad. Medicine; mem. AAAS, NAS, Inst. Medicine, Infectious Disease Soc. Am., Am. Epidemiol. Soc., Alpha Omega Alpha. Democrat. Roman Catholic. Office: Keck School Medicine Comprehensive Cancer Ctr 1441 Eastlake Ave # 44 Los Angeles CA 90089-0112 Office Phone: 323-442-4325. Office Fax: 323-442-7891, 323-865-0127. E-mail: brian.henderson@keck.usc.edu.

HENDERSON, CHRISTOPHER, pathologist, educator, neuroscientist; PhD, U. Cambridge, England, 1979. Dir. rsch. CNRS, Montpellier, France; vis. scientist Genentech Inc., San Francisco; co-founder Trophos S.A., Marseille, France; co-dir. Columbia U. Motor Neuron Ctr.; prof. pathology & cell biology in neurology Columbia U. Assoc. editor Neuron; joint editor-in-chief European Jour. Neuroscience. Named Disting. Prof., NY State Office Sci., Technol., & Acad. Rsch. Office: Center for Motor Neuron Biology and Disease Hammer Health Sciences Bldg 6th Fl Rm 616/602 New York NY 10032 Office Phone: 212-342-4086. E-mail: ch2331@columbia.edu.

HENDERSON, DONALD AINSLIE, public health service officer; b. Lakewood, Ohio, Sept. 7, 1928; s. David Alexander and Grace Eleanor (McMillan) Henderson; m. Nana Irene Bragg, Sept. 1, 1951; children: Leigh Ainslie, David Alexander, Douglas Bruce. BA, Oberlin Coll., Ohio, 1950; MD, U. Rochester, 1954; MPH, Johns Hopkins U., 1960; LDS (hon.), U. Rochester, 1977, Oberlin Coll., Ohio, 1978, U. Ill., 1979, U. Md., 1980, Yale U., 1986, Albany Med. Coll., 1989, Lafayette Coll., 1991, U. Mo., 1992, Clarkson U., 2006; LLD (hon.), Marietta Coll., Ohio, 1978; MD (hon.), U. Geneva, 1977; LHD (hon.), SUNY, 1981, Johns Hopkins U., 1994, Towson State U., 1994; LLD (hon.), U. Minn., 2003, U. S.C., 2004, U. Medicine and Dentistry N.J., 2004; DS (hon.), Clarkson U., 2006. Diplomate Am. Bd. Preventive Medicine. Intern, then resident Mary Imogene Bassett Hosp., Cooperstown, NY, 1954-55, 57-59; chief epidemic intelligence service Center Disease Control, USPHS, Atlanta, 1955-57, chief surveillance sect., 1960-66; chief med. officer smallpox eradication WHO, Geneva, 1966-77; dean Johns Hopkins U. Sch. Hygiene and Pub. Health, 1977-90; assoc. dir. Office Sci. and Tech. Policy, Exec. Office Pres. of U.S., Washington, 1991-93; dep. asst. sec., sr. sci. advisor HHS, Washington, 1993—95; prof. Johns Hopkins U. Sch. Pub. Health, Balt., 1977—; dir. Hopkins Ctr. Civilian Biodefense Strategies, 1998—2001; dir., prin. advisor Office of Pub. Health Emergency Preparedness Dept. Health and Human Svcs., 2001—03; disting. scholar Ctr. for Biosecurity U. Pitts. Med. Ctr., 2003—; prof. medicine and pub. health U. Pitts. Sch. Medicine, 2003—. Vis. prof. Mayo Clinic, 2006. Contbr. articles to profl. jours. Decorated knight Grand Cross Order of Direkgunabhorn; recipient Ernest Jung Found. prize, 1976, Govt. India-Indian Soc. Malaria and Other Communicable Diseases award, 1975, Rosenhaus Internat. award for excellence, 1975, George MacDonald medal, London Sch. Hygiene and Tropical Medicine, Royal Soc. Tropical Medicine and Hygiene, 1976, Health medal, Govt. Afghanistan, 1976, Spl. Albert Lasker Pub. Health Svc. award, WHO, 1976, Health for All medal, 1990, Joseph C. Wilson award in internat. affairs, 1978, James D. Bruce Meml. award, 1978, Outstanding Alumnus award, Delta Omega, 1980, Disting. Alumnus award, Johns Hopkins U., 1982, Dean's medal, 2002, Internat. Merit award, Gairdner Found., 1983, Albert Schweitzer Internat. prize for medicine, 1985, Nat. Medal Sci., 1986, Richard T. Hewitt award, Royal Soc. Medicine, 1986, Edward Jenner medal, 1996, Charles Dana Found. award for pioneering achievement in health, 1986, Japan prize in preventative medicine, 1988, Health medal 1st Grade, People's Republic China, 1988, Medal of Abnegation Uruguay, 1988, Honor award, Pan Am. Health Orgn., 1990, Abraham Lilienfeld award, Am. Coll, Epidemology, 1991, Award of Excellence, Ronald McDonald Children's Charities, 1992, Surgeon Gen.'s medallion, USPHS, 1992, City of Medicine award, 1993, Waltor Reed medal, Am. Soc. Tropical Medicine and Hygiene, 1993, Merit award, Nat. Coun. Internat. Health, 1993, Gold medal, Albert B. Sabin Found., 1994, Oswaldo Cruz Gold medal of merit, Govt. of Brazil, 1995, Soc. citation, Infectious Diseases Soc. Am., 1996, L. Frank Calderone prize, Columbia U. Sch. Public Health, 1999, Takeru Higuchi Meml. award, U. Kans., 1999, Presdl. Medal Freedom, 2002, Joseph Smadel Medal, Infectious Diseases Soc. Am., 2002, Arthur Kornberg Rsch. award, U. Rochester, 2002, Disting. Alumnus award, 2003, Silver medal, Govt. Italy Ministero Della Salute, 2004, Hutchinson Medal for Disting. Pub. Svc., U. Rochester, 2005, Ailanthus award, State U. NY, Coll. Med., 2008; named Burroughs Wellcome Vis. Prof., Royal Soc. Medicine, 1996, Internat. Hero of Pub. Health, U. Calif., Berkley, 2007; fellow Paul Harris fellow, Rotary Internat., 1993. Fellow: Nat. Acad. Arts and Scis., Nat. Acad. Medcine Mex. (hon.), N.Y. Acad. Medicine (hon. John Stearns award 1995, Annapolis Ctr. Sci. award 2000, Silvia and Herbert Berger award 2001), London Sch. Tropical Medicine and Hygiene (hon.), Am. Acad. Pediat. (hon.), Royal Coll. Physicians (hon.); mem.: APHA, Indian Soc. Malaria and Other Communicable Diseases, Royal Soc. Tropical Medicine and Hygiene, Royal Coll. Physicians Edinburgh (Eng.), Internat. Epidemiol. Assn., Inst. Medicine NAS (Pub. Welfare medal 1978). Home: 3802 Greenway Baltimore MD 21218-1825 Office: U Pitts Med Ctr Ctr for Biosecurity The Pier IV Bldg Ste 210 Baltimore MD 21202 Office Phone: 443-573-3323. E-mail: dahzero@aol.com.

HENDERSON, HAROLD, medical educator; b. Clarksdale, Miss., Apr. 6, 1956; BS, Tulane U., 1979; MD, LSU Sch. Medicine, 1984. Prof. medicine U. Miss. Med. Ctr., 1991—. Recipient Clinician, Educator Yr., HIV Medicine Assn., 2005; named one of Best Doctors in America. Fellow: ACP; mem.: HIV Medicine Assn., Infectious Diseases Soc. America. Office: University Mississippi Med Ctr Jackson MS 39216 Office Fax: 601-815-4014. Business E-Mail: hhenderson@umc.edu.

HENDERSON, ISAAC CRAIG, oncologist, researcher; b. Paullina, Iowa, Aug. 10, 1941; s. Isaac C. and Ora E. (Tjossem) H.; m. Mary Turner Henderson, June 11, 1966; children: Isaac Craig, Amy Hudson. AB, Grinnell Coll., Iowa, 1963, DSc, 1994; MD, Columbia U., 1970. Cert. internal medicine, 1977, med. oncology, 1979. Intern Presbyn. Hosp., NYC, 1970-71; resident, 1971-72; rsch. assoc. NIH, 1972-74; instr. medicine Harvard U. Med. Sch., Boston, 1975-76; asst. prof., 1976-84; assoc. prof., 1984-92; founder, dir. Breast Evaln. Ctr., Dana Farber Cancer Inst., 1980—92; prof. medicine U. Calif., San Francisco, 1992-95; dep. dir. Cancer Ctr., San Francisco; chmn., CEO Sequus Pharm., Inc., Menlo Park, Calif., 1995—99; sr. med. advisor and mem. bd. of dir. Alza Corp., Mountain View, Calif., 1999—2002; CEO Access Oncology, NY, 2001—04; pres. Keryx Biopharmaceuticals, Inc., NYC, 2004—08. Chair FDA Oncologic Drugs Adv. Com., 1989-92; adj. prof., U. Calif., San Francisco, 1995-. Contbr. articles to profl. jours. Mem. med. adv. panel Nat. Blue Cross-Blue Shield Assn., 1991-, mem. medicare adv. panel 1997-; bd. trustees Grinnell Coll., 2000-; bd. dirs. San Francisco Opera, 2001-. Served with USPHS, 1972-74. Fulbright Rsch. scholar, 1964-65; Merck, Sharp & Dohme Internat. fellow, 1966; named one of Best Drs. in America, 1992-. Fellow ACP; mem. Am. Soc. Clin. Oncology, Am. Assn. Cancer Rsch., Soc. Friends. Achievements include research on clin. protocols evaluating new treatment of breast cancer. Office: 1373 Bay St San Francisco CA 94123-2201 Office Phone: 415-674-5148. E-mail: ichenderson@hotmail.com.

HENDERSON, J. NEIL, medical anthropologist; b. Sulphur, Okla. m. Carson Henderson; children: Matt, Kara, Gabriela. BA in Sociology and Anthropology, U. Ctrl. Fla., 1973; MS in Psychol. Anthropolgy, Fla. State U., 1975; PhD in Medical Anthropology, U. Fla.,

1979. Prof. U. Okla. Health Scis. Ctr., Oklahoma City. Faculty advisor Native Am. Pub. Health Student Assn., 2001—; external adv. bd. ctr. health equality, ctr. excellence in partnership for cmty. outreach U. Ariz., Tucson, 2006; cons. ethnogeriatrics nat. com. US Bur. Health Professions; grant reviewer NIH; project coord. U. South Fla. Geriatric Edn. Ctr.; dir. Am. indian Dibetes Prevention Ctr. Contbr. articles to profl. jours., chapters to books; co-author: The Culture of Long-Term Care: Nursing Home Ethnography, 1995, Social and Behavioral Foundations of Public Health, 2001. Pres. Assn. Anthropology and Gerontology, 1996; oversight com. diversity Nat. Alzheimer's Assn., 2004—; com. mem. Kellogg/ASPH disparities task force Am. Schs. Pub. Health, 2005—; com. mem. prevention rsch. workgroup Ctrs. Disease Control Nat. Pub. Health Action Plan to Promote and Protect Brain Health, 2006—. Recipient Outstanding Employee award, U. South Fla. Suncoast Gerontology Ctr., Achievement award in Native Am. health, U. Okla. Coll. Pub. Health, 2006, Leadership in Prevention award Native. Am. Health, Loma Linda U. Sch. Pub. Health, 2006; Okla. Ctr. Am. Indian Diabetes Health Disparities grant, NIH, 2007—. Mem.: Choctaw Nat. Okla. Achievements include research in health and disease in Native American/Alaska Native populations, Hispanics and African Americans; the cultural construction of health and disease; intercultural health communication; impact of organizational culture on health care dynamics; institutional and informal long term care strategies in rural and urban communities; development of a needs assessment project on cardiovascular health and service needs for large Native American tribes; developed and conducted cultural competence workshops for Native American tribes; developed and operated multicultural support groups for caregivers to victims of dementing diseases such as Alzheimer's. Office: 801 NE 13th St # 253 Oklahoma City OK 73104-5005 Office Phone: 405-271-7500, 405-397-9336. Business E-Mail: neil-henderson@ouhsc.edu, twohawkinstitute@cox.net.

HENDERSON, JOHN MICHAEL, surgeon; b. Edinburgh, Feb. 4, 1945; MBChB, St. Andrews U., 1969. Dept. chair Cleve. Clinic, 1992—2004, chief quality officer, 2005—. Grant, NIH. Fellow: RCS (Edinburgh). Office: 9500 Euclid Ave E32 Cleveland OH 44195 Office Fax: 216-444-8510. Business E-Mail: henderm@ccf.org.

HENDERSON, MAUREEN MCGRATH, medical educator; b. Tynemouth, Eng., May 11, 1926; arrived in U.S., 1960; d. Leo E. and Helen McGrath Henderson. MB BS in Medicine and Surgery, U. Durham, Eng., 1949, DPH, 1956. Prof. preventive medicine U. Md. Med. Sch., 1968—75, chmn. dept. social and preventive medicine, 1971—75; assoc. epidemiology Johns Hopkins U. Sch. Hygiene and Pub. Health, 1960—75; prof. epidemiology and medicine U. Wash. Med. Sch., 1975—96, prof. emeritus epidemiology and medicine, 1996—, asst. v.p. and assoc. v.p. health scis., 1975—81, head cancer prevention rsch. program Fred Hutchinson Cancer Rsch. Ctr., 1983—94; mem. Nat. Inst. Environ. Health Scis. Adv. Coun., 1994—97. Chmn. epidemiology and disease control study sect. NIH, 1969—82; chmn. clin. trial rev. com. Nat. Heart Lung and Blood Inst., 1975—79; mem. Nat. Cancer Adv. Bd., 1979—84; mem. bd. Robert Wood Johnson Health Policy Fellowship, 1989—93; bd. radiation effects rsch. NRC, 1991—97. Assoc. editor Hour. Cancer Rsch., 1984—88, mem. editl. bd. Jour. Nat. Cancer Inst., 1988—, mem. editl. adv. bd. Cancer Detection and Prevention, 1992—. Decorated Order of Brit. Empire; recipient John Snow award, Am. Pub. Health Assn., 1990; scholar Luke Armstrong, 1956—57, John and Mary Markle, Acad. Medicine, 1963—68. Mem.: NAS, Inst. Medicine, Nat. Rsch. Coun. (report rev. com. 1996—2002, mem. com. rsch. priorities for airborne particulate matters 1998—2000), Am. Epidemiol. Soc. (pres. 1990—91), Internat. Coun. Cancer Rsch. (sci. adv. bd. 1989—92), Soc. Epidemiol. Rsch. (chmn. 1969—70), Assn. Tchrs. Preventive Medicine (pres. 1972—73), Am. Coll. Epidemiology. Home: Mirabella #1220 116 Fairview Ave N Seattle WA 98109 Home Phone: 206-254-1872. E-mail: mhenders@w-link.net, mhenders@broadstripe.net.

HENDERSON, MELFORD J., infectious disease epidemiologist, genetic epidemiologist, molecular biologist, chemist; b. Birmingham, Ala., Dec. 28, 1950; BS, Bishop Coll., Dallas, 1972; MA, Johns Hopkins U., 1976; student, NYU Dental Sch., 1977—79; MPH, Yale U., 1984. Ordained min. Rsch. assoc. Bishop Coll., 1972-73; rsch. assoc. Sch. of Pharmacy U. Md., Balt., 1976-77; microbiologist Torigian Labs., Queens, NY, 1979-81; pub. health analyst internat. program cardiovasc. diseases NIH, Bethesda, Md., 1984, epidemiologist, analyst, Task Force on Black and Minority Health, 1985—; disting. scholar, lectr., pub. health ofcl. Health Promotion & Disease Prevention, Cost & Financing, Cost-Effectiveness Rsch.; epidemiologist, program ofcl. & extramural project officer Agy. Healthcare Quality and Rsch., Rockville, Md., 1990—. Epidemiologist DC Govt., DC Health Dept., 1985-88; sr. rsch. assoc. Prospect Assocs., 1989; with Mayor's Health Policy Coun., Washington, 1986; fed. govt. ofcl. to asst., restructuring DC Health Care Sys. Author 10 scholarly sci. publs.; contbr. articles to profl. sci. jours., chapters to books. Founder Apostles Ch. Jesus Christ Internat., A Worldwide Prophetic-Apostolic Ministry, bishop, apostle, prophet, evangelist, tchr., pastor. Recipient numerous awards in chemistry and pub. health; NIH fellow, 1973-76, USPHS fellow, 1982-84, rsch. fellow Assn. Black Cardiologists, 1984-85. Mem. APHA, Md. Pub. Health Assn., Blacks in Govt., Soc. for Epidemiol. Rsch., Assn. Black Cardiologists, John Hopkin's U. Alumni Assn., John Hopkin's U., SOc. Black Alumni, Yale U. Alumni Assn., Beta Kappa Chi. Business E-Mail: mhenders@ahrq.gov.

HENDERSON, RALPH HALE, physician; b. NYC, Mar. 5, 1937; s. Ralph Ernest and Clifford West (Sellers) H.; m. Ilze Sarma, May 21, 1966. AB, Harvard U., 1959, MD, 1963, MPH, 1970, M.Pub. Policy, 1972. Intern, then resident in internal medicine Boston City Hosp., 1963-65; joined USPHS, 1965, capt., 1973-81, asst. surgeon gen., 1981-90, svc. in U.S. and West Africa, 1965-69. Asst. chief venereal disease br., state and cmty. svcs. divsn. Ctrs. Disease Control, Atlanta, 1972-73; dir. venereal disease control divsn. Bur. State Svcs., 1973-76; program mgr. expanded program on immunization WHO, Geneva, 1977-78, dir. expanded program immunization, 1979-89, asst. dir. gen., 1990-98, spl. advisor to dir. gen., 1998-99; Lilly lectr. Royal Coll. Physicians, 1989; lectr. disting. lecture series Baylor Coll. Medicine, 1995. Contbr. to med. publs. Trustee Dermatology Found., 1975-77. Recipient Commendation medal USPHS, 1969, Meritorious Svc. medal, 1984, Disting. Svc. medal, 1990, Donald MacKay Meml. medal Royal Soc. Tropical Medicine and Hygiene, 1990, Internat. Child Survival award U.S. Com. UNICEF and the Task Force for Child Survival and Devel., 1992, Ann. Pub. Health Forum award London Sch. of Hygiene and Tropical Medicine, 1994. Mem. Am. Coll. Preventive Medicine. Home: 1098 Mcconnell Dr Decatur GA 30033-3402

HENDERSON, TARA O., physician, educator; b. NYC, Apr. 22, 1973; d. Joseph P. and Virginia C. Olive; m. M. Todd Henderson, Aug. 29, 1998; children: Charlotte N., Andrew G. AB, Princeton U., NJ, 1995; MD, U. Chgo. Pritzker Sch. Medicine, 1999; MPH, Harvard Sch. Pub. Health, Boston, 2005. Instr. pediatric hematology oncology Harvard Med. Sch. Dana-Farber Cancer Inst. Children's Hosp., 2005, U. Chgo. Pritzker Sch. Medicine, 2005—. Dir. U. Chgo. Childhood Cancer Survivors Ctr., 2005—. Mem.: Children's Oncology Group (steering com. Hodgkin's com., vice chair high risk Hodgkin's study), Am. Soc. Clin. Oncology. Achievements include research in Study of Second Cancers in Childhood Cancer Survivors. Office: University Of Chicago Pathology 5550 S Shore DR Apt 1006 Chicago IL 60637-5057 Office Fax: 773-207-9881. E-mail: thenderson@uchicago.edu. *

HENDERSON, VICTOR WARREN, behavioral and geriatric neurologist, epidemiologist, researcher, educator; s. Philip and Jean (Edsel) H.; m. Barbara Curtiss; children: Gregory, Geoffrey, Stephanie, Nicole. BS, U. Ga., 1972; MD, Johns Hopkins U., 1976; MS, U. Wash., 1996. Diplomate Am. Bd. Psychiatry and Neurology, 1981, United Coun. Neurologic Subspecialties, 2006. Intern Duke U., Durham, NC, 1976—77; resident Washington U., St. Louis, 1977—80; fellow Boston U., 1980—81; asst. prof. neurology U. So. Calif., LA, 1981—86, assoc. prof. neurology, gerontology and psychology, 1986—93, prof. neurology, gerontology and psychology, 1993—2001, chief divsn. cognitive neurosci. & neurogerontology, 1989—2001, Kenneth and Bette Volk prof. neurology, 1999—2001; prof. geriat., neurology, pharmacology and epidemiology U. Ark. Med. Scis., Little Rock, 2001—04, vice chair dept. geriat., 2001—04; prof. health rsch. and policy and neurology and neurological scis. Stanford U., 2004—, dir. grad. program in epidemiology, 2004—, chief dvsn. epidemiology, 2010—. Dir. NIH Alzheimer's Disease Rsch. Ctr. Clin. Core, 1985—2001, Rural Aging and Memory Study, 2001—04; dir. neurobehavior Clinic/Bowles Ctr. for Alzheimer's and Related Diseases, 1988—2001; chair neurology dept. Los Angeles County/U. So. Calif. Med. Ctr., 1992—97; vis. scientist MIT, 1988—89; vis. prof. U. Melbourne, 2002; co-dir. State of Calif. Alzheimer's Disease Rsch. Ctr. U. So. Calif., 1999—2001, NIH Alzheimer's Disease Ctr., 2001—03; Kearney vis. prof. Mental Health Rsch. Inst. Victoria, Australia, 2002; prof. fellow dept. psychiatry U. Melbourne, 2003—08; assoc. chief of staff geriat. and extended care Ctrl. Ark. Vets. Healthcare Sys., 2003—04; lectr. and spkr. in field. Author: (with others) Principles of Neurologic Diagnosis, 1985, Hormone Therapy and the Brain, 2000, Hormones, Cognition and Dementia, 2009; mem. editl. bd. profl. jours.; contbr. articles to profl. jours. Recipient Simons Lecture, Alzheimer's Assn. (Boston chpt.), 1995, Solvay Lecture, British Menopause Soc., 1997, Rsch. award, Alzheimer's Assn. (LA chpt.), 1998, Faculty Recognition award, Phi Kappa Phi, 2001, Vis. Rsch. Scholars award, U. Melbourne Collaborative Research Program, 2002; grantee, Alzheimer's Assn., Calif. Dept. Health Svcs., Adminstrn. on Aging, NIH, French Found., 1984—. Fellow: Am. Acad. Neurology (chair, geriatric neurology sect. 2000—11, Lawrence McHenry award 2007); mem.: Soc. Epidemiologic Rsch., N.Am. Menopause Soc. (trustee 2002—09, treas. 2005—06, pres. 2007—08), French Found. Alzheimer Rsch., Nat. Aphasia Assn., Internat. Menopause Soc. (treas., Coun. Affiliated Menopause Socs. 2008—11, bd. mem. 2011—), Soc. for Behavioral and Cognitive Neurology, Gerontol. Soc. Am., Am. Neurol. Assn. Office: Stanford U Sch Medicine 259 Campus Dr HRP Redwood Bldg Stanford CA 94305-5405

HENDERSON, WILLIAM REED, JR., allergist, immunologist, educator; MD, U. Calif., 1973. Diplomate Am. Bd. Internal Medicine, 1976, Am. Bd. Allergy and Immunology, 1979, lic. Wash., 1978. Resident internal medicine Stanford Med. Ctr., 1974—75, Nat. Inst. Health, 1975—76, fellow allergy & immunology, 1976—78; prof. medicine Univ. of Wash.; hosp. affiliations includes Univ. of Wash. Med. Ctr. Co-author: (publs.) Eosinophil cysteinyl leukotriene synthesis mediated by exogenous secreted phospholipase A2 group X, 2010, An update on the role of leukotrienes in asthma, 2010, Relationship between levels of secreted phospholipase A2 groups IIA and X in the airways and asthma severity, 2011, and other numerous publications. Named one of Top Doctors, Seattle Mag., 2010, Seattle Met. Mag., 2011. Office: University of Washington Medical Center Box 356151 1959 NE Pacific St Seattle WA 98195-6151 Office Phone: 206-598-3300.

HENDLER, NELSON HOWARD, physician, health facility administrator, director; b. NYC, Aug. 15, 1944; s. Albert and Winifred (Siff) H.; m. Lee Meyerhoff, Oct. 20, 1974 (div. Nov. 2005); children: Lee Samuel, Alexander, Lindsay, Josepha. BA, Princeton U., 1966; MD, U. Md., 1972, MS, 1974. Diplomate Am. Bd. Psychiatry and Neurology. Resident in psychiatry Johns Hopkins Hosp., Balt., 1975; asst. prof. neurosurgery sch. medicine Johns Hopkins U., 1975—2006; owner, clin. dir. Mensana Clinic, Stevenson, Md., 1978—2006; assoc. prof. physiology sch. dental surgery U. Md., 1986—2006; CEO, Mensana Clinic Diagnostics, 2006. Pres. Reflex Sympathetic Dystrophy Syndrome of Am., 1995-97. Author: Diagnosis and Non-Surgical Management of Chronic Pain, 1981; (with others) Coping with Chronic Pain, 1979; editor Diagnosis and Treatment of Chronic Pain, 1982; contbr. articles to profl. jours., chpts. to books; co-patentee direct current motor protector. Bd. dirs. Md. Mental Health Assn., Balt., 1976-78, Balt. Zool. Soc., 1978-85; bd. dirs. Am. Orgn. Rehab. through Tng., 1983—, pres. Balt. chpt.; bd. dirs. Am. Technion Soc., 1980-92, pres. Balt. chpt. Recipient Janet Travell award Am. Acad. Pain Mgmt.; Falk fellow Am. Psychiat. Assn., 1975. Fellow Acad. Psychosomatic Medicine, Am. Psychiatric Assn.; mem. Am. Inst. Stress (v.p. 1978-89), Internat. Soc. Study of Pain, Am. Acad. Pain Mgmt. (bd. dirs. 2002—, pres. 2006), Am. Pain Found. (bd. dirs. 1997-01), Israeli Pain Soc. (hon.), Princeton U. Alumni Assn. Md. (bd. dirs., pres.), Princeton Club NYC, Safari Internat. Club, Loch Raven Skeet and Trap Club. Republican. Jewish. Avocations: bird hunting, skeet and trap shooting, fishing, record big game hunter. Office: Mensana Clinic 1718 Greenspring Valley Rd Stevenson MD 21153-0642 Office Phone: 410-653-2403. Personal E-mail: docnelse@aol.com.

HENDREN, ROBERT LEE, psychiatrist, educator; b. Boise, June 30, 1949; s. Robert Lee and Merlyn (Churchill); m. Mary Noele de Vibraye Hendren, May 18, 1984. Student, U. Idaho, 1967—69; BA, U. Utah, 1971; DO, Kirksville Coll., 1975. Diplomate Am. Bd. Psychiatry and Neurology. Resident in psychiatry Mayo Grad. Sch. Medicine, Rochester, Minn., 1976—79; fellow in child psychiatry Yale Child Study Ctr., New Haven, 1979—81. Asst. prof. psychiatry George Washington U., 1981—85, assoc. prof. psychiatry, 1985, U. N. Mex., 1986—91, prof. psychiatry, 1991—96; prof., dir. child and adolescent psychiatry Robert Wood Johnson Sch. Medicine, 1996—2001; prof. chief, child and adolescent psychiatry U. Calif. Davis; exec. dir. M.I.N.D. Inst., Sacramento, 2001—09; vice-chair & prof. U. Calif. San Fransisco, 2009—. Contbr. chapters to books. Mem.: Soc. Profl. Child and Adolescent Psychiatry (pres. 2002—04), Assn. Academic Psychiatry, Am. Acad. Child Psychiatry (pres. 2007—09), Am. Psychiat. Assn. Avocations: skiing, sailing, tennis. Home Phone: 415-924-9397; Office Phone: 415-476-7198. E-mail: robert.hendren@ucsf.edu.

HENDRICKS, DOUGLAS L., plastic surgeon; BA in Microbiology with high honors, cum laude, U. Md., 1978; MD, U. Louisville, 1982. Diplomate Am. Bd. Surgery, 1988, Am. Bd. Surgery, 1998, Am. Bd. Plastic Surgery, 1992, cert. added qualification in surgery of the hand 1993, qualified med. evaluator 1993, radiology supr. 1997, lic. Ky., 1983, Pa., 1987, Calif., 1990. Intern gen. surgery Univ. of Louisville Hosp., Ky., 1982—83, resident gen. surgery Ky., 1983—86, chief resident gen. surgery Ky., 1986—87; resident plastic surgery Univ. of Pitts., 1988—90, rsch. fellow plastic surgery, 1987—88; co-dir. microsurgery tchg. lab. Loma Linda Univ. Med. Ctr., Calif., 1990—2000, co-dir. complex wound ctr., 1990—2000; sect. chief plastic and reconstructive surgery Jerry L. Pettis Veterans Adminstrn. Hosp., Calif., 1990—2000, dir. difficult wound team, 1990—2000; asst. prof. plastic and reconstructive surgery divsn. Loma Linda Univ./Sch. of Medicine, Calif., 1990—94, dir. residency program, 1996—98, ret. assoc. clin. prof. plastic and reconstructive surgery divsn., 1994—; pvt. practice Pacifica Cosmetic Surgery Ctr., Newport Beach, Calif.; hosp. affiliation include Hoag Meml. Presbyn. Hosp., Newport Beach, Calif., 2000—. Contbr. numerous peer reviewed jours. Mem.: ACS, AMA, Am. Assn. Surgery of the Hand, Loma Linda Univ. Med. Ctr. (wound care com., office practice com.), Am. Soc. of Reconstructive Microsurgery, Calif. Soc. of Plastic Surgeons, Am. Soc. of Plastic Reconstructive Surgeons, Plastic Surgery Rsch. Coun., Am. Soc. for Peripheral Nerve, Wound Healing Soc., San Bernardino County Med. Soc., Calif. Med. Assn., Hiram C. Polk Surg. Soc., Westmoreland County Med. Soc., Pa. Med. Soc. Office: Pacifica Cosmetic Surgery Center 280 Newport Center Dr Ste120 Newport Beach CA 92660 Office Fax: 800-372-2156.

HENDRICKS, GILBERT L., III, neuroendocrine immune physiologist, researcher; b. Richmond, Va., 1959; s. Gilbert L. Jr. and Ina Mae Hendricks. BS in Biology, Pa. State U., 1981, BS in Microbiology, 1984, MS in Physiology, 1989, PhD in Physiology, 1994. Surg. technician Lewistown (Pa.) Hosp., 1982-85; grad. rsch. asst. Pa. State U., University Park, 1987-94, postdoctoral rsch. scientist Biotech. Inst., University Park, 1995-96; instr., rsch. assoc. Pa. State U., University Park, 1998—. Advisor to MS candidates Pa. State U., 1993-94, instr. U.S.-AID Egypt project, 1994, advisor to PhD candidates, 2000—. Contbr. articles to profl. jours. Mem. SAR, Sons of Confederate Vets., Gamma Sigma Delta. Methodist. Achievements include development of assay to measure hormone production by leukocytes; determined corticotropin releasing factor (CRF) stimulates adrenocorticotropic hormone by chicken leukocytes, identified macrophage as primary leukocyte responsible for immune adrenocorticotropic hormone production, cloned chicken adiponectin.

HENDRICKS-MUNOZ, KAREN D., neonatal-perinatal doctor, educator; MPH, MD, Yale U. Obstetric intern Yale New Haven Hosp., pediatric intern, pediatric. resident, 1979—81; fellow neonatology Strong Meml. Hosp., 1981—84; post doctorate tng. in neonatal-perinatal medicine Univ. of Rochester Sch. of Medicine, NY; asst. prof of pediat. Strong Meml. Hosp., Rochester, NY, 1984, clin. dir. Neonatal ICU, 1986; asst. prof. of pediat. Univ. of Miami, 1988; chief divs. of neonatology NYU Med. Ctr., 1996; assoc. prof. pediat. NYU. Named Best Pediatrician, Neonatal-Perinatal Medicine, 2001, NY's Best Doctor, 2001. Mem.: Neonatology Divsn. Translational Lab., ACGME Neonatal- Perinatal Fellowship Tng. Program (founder). Office: New York University Langone Medical Center 560 First Ave H 533 New York NY 10016 Office Phone: 212-263-7477. Office Fax: 212-263-0134.

HENDRICKSON, CLIFFORD DANIEL, sports medicine physician; b. Bryn Mawr, Pa., Feb. 5, 1963; BS, Pa. State U., 1985; MD, Pa. State U., Hershey, 1989. Adj. clin. prof. U. Mich., 1998, dir. med. svcs., head, athletics team physician, 1998—. Staff physician U. Health Svcs., 1998. Mem.: Am. Med. Soc. Sports Medicine (Best Conf. award, NCAA-AMSSM Conf.). Avocations: golf, sports. Home: 7095 Wapiti Way Saline MI 48176 Business E-Mail: cdhendrx@umich.edu.

HENDRICKSON, GREGG, cosmetic dentist; Grad., Arthur A. Dugoni Sch. of Dentistry, Misch Internat. Implant Inst.; attended, Las Vegas Inst. for Advanced Dentals Studies. Resident, Las Vegas, Nev., 1965—. Fellow: Internat. Congress of Oral Implantologists; mem.: ADA, Am. Acad. of Dental Sleep Medicine, Dental Org. of Conscious Sedation, Las Vegas Inst. Dentist, Am. Acad. of Cosmetic Dentistry, Nevada Dental Assn., Southern Nev. Dental Soc. Office: Gregg C. Hendrickson DDS Ste 100A 2790 W Horizon Ridge Pky Henderson NV 89052 Office Phone: 702-735-3284.

HENDRICKSON, ROBERT FREDERICK, pharmaceutical company executive; b. Cambridge, Mass., Jan. 5, 1933; s. Charles H. and Ruth E. Hendrickson; m. Virginia H. Emery, Apr. 27, 1963; children: Karen, Susan, Douglas. AB in Econs. magna cum laude, Harvard U., 1954, MBA, 1958. Engaged in prodn. planning, internat. div. Internat. Latex Corp., Dover, Del., 1958-61; mgr. prodn. planning and control Merck Sharp & Dohme, West Point, Pa., 1961-66, dir. long-range planning, 1966-68, exec. sec. new products com., 1968-69, dir. prodn. planning and control, 1969-71, dir. ops., 1971-72, v.p. ops., 1972-80; sr. v.p. Merck & Co., Inc., Rahway, N.J., 1981-85, sr. v.p. mfg. and tech., 1985-90, ret., 1990; mfg. cons., 1990—. Bd. dir. Cytogen, Inc., Unigene, Inc.; trustee Carrier Found., 1992—. Bd. dir. Lenape Valley Mental Health Found., 1972-80, pres., 1976-77; trustee N.J. State Safety Coun., 1980-90, New Eng. Hist. Geneal. Soc., 1999—, Ctr. Theol. Inquiry, 2005—, N.Y. Geneal. and Biog. Soc., 2005—. With AUS, 1954-56. Mem. North Pa. C. of C. (bd. dirs. 1974-77), Pharm. Mfg. Assn. (chmn. prodn. and engring. sect. 1980-81), NOW Legal,

Def. and Edn. Fund (bd. dirs. 1987-93), N.J. State C. of C. (bd. dirs. 1985-90), N.J. Coun. for the Humanities (trustee 1992-96). Presbyterian. Home: 50 Constitution Hl W Princeton NJ 08540-6774

HENDRICKSON, WAYNE A(RTHUR), biochemist, educator; b. Spring Valley, Wis., Apr. 25, 1941; s. Olaf and Margaret (Oare) H.; children: Helen Margaret, Inga Marie. BA, U. Wis., River Falls, 1963; PhD in Biophysics, Johns Hopkins U., 1968; PhD (hon.), Uppsala U., 1995. Rsch. assoc. Johns Hopkins U., Balt., 1968-69; postdoctoral rsch. assoc. Naval Rsch. Lab., 1969-71, rsch. biophysicist, 1971-84; prof. biochemistry and molecular biophysics Columbia U. Coll. Physicians and Surgeons, NYC, 1984—; investigator Howard Hughes Med. Inst., 1986—. Sci. adv. bd. mem. Progenics Pharms., 1987—; sci. adv. bd. mem., Kinetix Pharms., 1997—; sci. policy com. Stanford Linear Accelerator Ctr., 1992-94; program evaluation bd. Advanced Photon Source, 1988—; biomed. adv. com. for Pitts. Supercomputing Ctr., 1987-92; DOE Synchrotron Rev. Com., 1987-88; proposal rev. panel Cornell High Energy Synchrotron Source, 1987—; mem. NSF Molecular Adv. Panel, 1980-83, NIH Biophys. Chemistry Study Sct., 1986-89; mem. sci. adv. bd. Burnham Inst., 1995—; mem. nat. adv. Gdn. Med. Scis. Coun., 1997—; mem. sci. adv. vom. European Synchrotam Radiation Facility, 1997—, Rutgers Ctr. Advanced Biotech. & Medicine, 1998—; investigator, Howard Hughes Med. Inst. Mem. editl. bd. Jour. Biomolecular Structure and Dynamics, 1986-91; assoc. editor Jour. Molecular Biology, 1987-93; editor Current Opinion in Structural Biology, 1989—, Macromolecular Structures, 1990—, Structure, 1993—; contbr. numerous articles to profl. jours. Recipient Biol. Scis. award Washington Acad. Scis., 1976, Meritorious Civilian Svc. award U.S. Navy, 1978, Arthur S. Flemming award Outstanding Young Fed. Employees, 1979, Aminoff prize Royal Swedish Acad. Scis., 1997, Anfinsen award Protein Soc., 1997, Arthur H. Compton award, Advanced Photon Source, 2001, Gairdner Found. Internat. award, 2003. Fellow AAAS, Am. Acad. Arts and Scis; mem. NAS (Alexander Hollaender award 1998), Am. Crystallographic Assn. (chmn. biol. macromolecules group 1980, A.L. Patterson award 1981, Fankuchen award com. 1982), Am. Soc. Biochemistry and Molecular Biology (mem. pubs. com. 1997—, Fritz Lipmann award 1991), Biophys. Soc. (coun. mem. 1987-90, mem. publs. com. 1989—), Internat. Union Crystallography (commn. on biol. macromolecules 1981-87, commn. on crystallographic computing 1984-87, commn. on synchrotron radiation, 1990-93). Achievements include rsch. in macromolecular structure and function, in principles of protein structure, dynamics and assembly, in properties of specific proteins, in diffraction methods, in crystallographic computing, and in synchrotron radiation. Office: Columbia U Dept Biochem & Molecular Biophys 650 W 168th St Black Bldg 203 New York NY 10032-3795 Office Phone: 212-305-3456. Office Fax: 212-305-7379. Business E-Mail: wayne@convex.hhmi.columbia.edu. *

HENDRIX, SHERMAN SAMUEL, biology professor, researcher; b. Bridgeport, Conn., June 1, 1939; m. Carol Ann Seibel, June 10, 1961; children: Marc, Robin. BA in Biology, Gettysburg Coll., 1961; MS in Zoology, Fla. State U., 1964; PhD in Zoology, U. Md., 1972. Instr. biology Gettysburg (Pa.) Coll., 1964-70, asst. prof., 1970-77, assoc. prof., 1977-90, prof., 1990—2010, emeritus prof., 2010, chmn. dept., 1985—90, 1997—2001, coll. marshal, 2000—10. Contbr. articles to profl. jours. Bd. dirs. United Way Adams County, Gettysburg, 1983-86; trustee Brayton H. Ransom Meml. Trust Fund, 2004—. Interam. fellow in tropical medicine NIH, 1973. Mem. Am. Soc. Parasitologists (mentor com. 2003-06, chair 2004-06, memorian com. mem. 2009-, chair 2011), Helminthological Soc. Washington (pres. 1984, v.p. 2002-04, corr. sec.-treas. 2005—, editl. bd. 1985-2002, editor jours. 1993-98, Anniversary award 1998), Pa. Acad. Sci. (treas. 1986-90, pres. 1990-92, mem. editl. bd. 2006—, Lifetime Achievement award 1998), Am. Malacological Soc. Lutheran. Achievements include research on aquatic animal parasites. Office: Gettysburg Coll Dept Biology Gettysburg PA 17325

HENDRY, JEAN SHARON, psychopharmacologist; d. Clarence Richard and Frances Lee (Manger) Shaver; 1 child, Robert Andrew. BA, Hunter Coll., NY, 1976; MA in Psychology, Princeton U., NJ, 1978, PhD in Psychology, 1980. Rsch. asst. Hunter Coll., NYC, 1974-75; asst. instr. Princeton U., Princeton, NJ, 1976—79; postdoctoral fellow in pharm. Med. Coll. Va., Richmond, 1979—82; psychology instr. U. Richmond, 1985-86, Pa. State U., Media, Pa., 1987—88; exec. dir. Mira Found USA Inc., 2007—09; cons. Jean Hendry and Assocs., 2009—. Guest reviewer various psychological and pharmacological jours. Contbr. numerous articles to profl. jours. Active Arts Coun. of Moore County, World Wildlife Assn., Weymouth Ctr. Arts & Humanities. Mem.: Princeton U. Alumni Coun. (alumni coun. mem. 2009—, exec. com. mem. 2009—, vice chair grad. alumni rels. com.), Assn. Psychol. Sci., Assn. Princeton Grad. Alumni (elected to bd. 2006, 2009, serving another term mem. 2009—), Nature Conservancy, Nat. Audubon Soc., Nat. Wildlife Fedn., Carolina Triangle Club of Princeton (co-chair 2007—), Sigma Xi, Phi Beta Kappa. Avocations: tennis, exercise, reading. Business E-Mail: jhendry@alumni.princeton.edu.

HENEIN, RAFICK GARAS, former pharmaceutical company executive, pharmacist; b. Cairo, Apr. 18, 1940; s. Garas and Daisy (Badir) H.; m. Nelly Bishara, July 27, 1963; children: Tarik, Natalie. BS in Pharmacy, Cairo U., 1960, diploma in Indsl. Pharmacy, 1961; MS in Pharm. Scis., Budapest U., 1970; PhD in Pharm. Tech., Acad. Scis., Hungary, 1971; diploma in Mgmt., McGill U., Montreal, 1977, MBA, 1982. Chief pharmacist Egyptian Air Force, 1961-62; head extraction dept., liquids and ointments dept., packaging dept., Chem. Industries Devel., Cairo, 1962-65; dir. pharm. research and devel. Chinoin Labs., Budapest, Hungary, 1970-71; adminstrv. asst. to plant mgr. Ayerst Labs., Inc., Montreal, Que., 1971, prodn. control mgr., 1972-73, asst. dir. prodn., 1973-76, dir. prodn., 1977-79, dir. prodn. ops., 1980, v.p. materials mgmt., 1980-82, v.p. plant, distbn. ops., 1983-86, sr. v.p. plant, distbn. ops., 1987-88; exec. v.p. NovoPharm Ltd., Scarborough, Ont., Can., 1988—; former pres., CEO Zenith Goldline; pres., CEO IVAX Pharmaceuticals, 2001—06. Bd. dirs. Ayerst Organics, Ltd. div. of API Lab. Products, Ltd., GeoPharma Inc., 2007-; lectr. U. Montreal Dept. Pharmacy, 1980—, John Abbott Coll., St. Anne de Bellevue, Que., 1982—. Mem. Order Pharmacists of Que., Pharm. Mfrs. Assn. (vice chmn. 1980-81, chmn. plant ops. sect. 1981-82, past chmn. 1982-83). Mem. Coptic Ch. Avocation: tennis. Office Phone: 954 629 0909. Personal E-mail: rhenein@aol.com.

HENG, K S, surgeon; B Med. Sci., MD, Nat. U., Malaysia; M in Medicine, Nat. U., Singapore. Fellowship Royal Coll. Surgeons, Edinburgh; with plastic surgery depts. Numerous Med. Instns.; lead investigator Singapore Gen. Hosp. and Exptl. Lab.; founder NICANOR Clinic, pvt. practice, cosmetic surgeon. Lectr. surgery dept. Nat. Univ., Malaysia; article contbr. Cosmetic-Related Publs.; mem. cosmetic related researches. Office: NICANOR Clinic Merchant Square A-1-3A Jalan Tropicana Selatan 1 PJU 3 Selangor Malaysia Office Phone: 60378830989. *

HENG, MADALENE C., dermatologist; b. Singapore, 1942; MD, Med. Sch., Singapore, 1967. Chief divsn. dermatology UCLA San Fernando Valley Program, 1978—2003; clin. prof. medicine, dermatology UCLA Sch. Medicine, 1978—2003; dermatologist Ctr. Family Health, Cmty. Meml. Hosp., 2006—. Recipient Tchg. awards, UCLA San Fernando Valley Program. Fellow: Am. Acad. Dermatology, Australasian Coll. Dermatology, Royal Australasian Coll. Physicians. Avocations: badminton, ping pong/table tennis, tennis. Office: 2361 E Vineyard Ave Oxnard CA 93036 Office Fax: 805-981-3767. E-mail: madaleneheng@aol.com.

HENG, WAN, physician; b. Sichuan, July 7, 1983; MD, West China Hosp. Med. Sci., 2005. Dr.-in-charge West China Fourth Hosp. Sichuan U., 2007—. Office: 18 Sect 3 Renmin Nanlu Chengdu Sichuan 10041 China

HENG, WEE JIN, surgeon; MBBS, MMed; FAMS, Singapore; FRCSEd, UK; FACS, USA. Cornea & refractive surgery fellowship tng. Wills Eye Hosp., Philadelphia; joined Tan Tock Seng Hosp., 1996, head cornea svc., 2004, head refractive surgery, 2007, sr. cons. cornea ans refractive surgery, dep. dir. Spkr. med. conf. on cornea, refractive surgery and cataract surgery Various Countries; with specialist tng. Com. for Opthalmology; with contact lens practitioner bd. Coll. of Opthalmologist; with Soc. of Opthalmology, Singapore; examiner local and overseas opthalmology examinations; instr. lasik and opthalmic microsurgery courses. Co-author: (book) Colour Atlas and Synopsis of Cornea and External Eye Diseases, 2003. Recipient Cornea and Refractive Surgery Educator award, Asia Pacific Assn., Spring Singapore Excellence Svc. award; grantee Human Manpower Devel. Plan Overseas Fellowship, Ministry of Health. Office: Tan Tock Seng Hospital LASIK Centre Level 1 Clinic 1A 11 Jalan Tan Tock Seng Hospital Singapore 308433 Singapore Office Phone: 6563572255. *

HENINGER, GEORGE ROBERT, psychology professor, researcher; b. LA, Nov. 15, 1934; s. Owen P. and Rachel (Cannon) H.; m. Julie Hawkes, June 27, 1957; children: Steven, Catharine, Karen, Brian. BS, U. Utah, 1957, MD, 1960. Diplomate Am. Bd. Psychiatry and Neurology. Intern Boston City Hosp., 1960-61; resident in psychiatry Mass. Mental Health Ctr., 1961-63, chief resident, 1963-64; clin. assoc., clin. neuropharmacology rsch. ctr. St. Elizabeth's Hosp. NIMH, Washington, 1964-65, program specialist, office of dir. Bethesda, Md., 1965-66; asst. prof. psychiatry, assoc. chief rsch. ward Yale U., New Haven, 1966-71, assoc. prof., 1971-76, chief rsch. ward, 1971-78, prof. clin. psychiatry, 1976-78, prof. psychiatry, dir. Abraham Ribicoff Rsch. Facilities, 1978-93, assoc. chmn. rsch. dept. psychiatry, 1988-93, dir. lab. clin. and molecular neurobiology, 1993—. Cons. NIMH, 1975-86, 88-94, NIH, 1987, McGill U., 1989, VA, 1990-94, Nat. Rsch. Coun. Can., 1991-93, Nat. Inst. Aging, 1992-93, Wellcome Trust, 1992-94, Pfizer Inc., Merck, Sharp & Dohme, Inc., The Upjohn Co., Hoffman La Roche, Inc., Burroughs Wellcome Co., Bristol-Meyers Co., Squibb Corp., Kali DuPhar, Inc.; bd. sci. advisors, Neurogen Corp. REviewer manuscripts Archives Gen. Psychiatry, Am. Jour. Psychiatry, Psychiatry Rsch., Biol. Psychiatry, Jour. Affective Disorders, Jour. Clin. Psychopharmacology, Life Scis., Neurochemistry Internat., Psychiatry, Schizophrenia Bull., Psychoneuroendocrinology, Jour. AMA. Sr. asst. surgeon USPHS, 1964-66. Recipient Rsch. Sci. Devel. award Type II, NIMH, 1971, 1st prize Anna Monika Found., 1995; grantee NIMH, 1971, 74, 77, 82, 85, 89, 91. Fellow Am. Coll. Neuropsychopharmacology, Am. Psychiat. Assn.; mem. AAAS, Am. Psychopath. Assn., Soc. Neurosci., Soc. Biol. Psychiatry, Psychiat. Rsch. Soc., N.Y. Acad. Scis., Conn. Psychiat. Soc., Sigma Xi, Phi Kappa Phi, Alpha Omega Alpha. Avocation: running. Office: Yale U 34 Park St New Haven CT 06511

HENKIN, ROBERT ELLIOTT, nuclear medicine physician; b. Pitts., June 7, 1942; s. Hyman and Nettie (Jaffee) H.; m. Denise Dulberg, June 26, 1966 (dec. 1985); children: Gregory, Joshua, Steven; m. Renae Marley, Nov. 27, 1988 (dec. Nov. 2006). Student, Cornell U., 1960-62; BA, NYU, 1965, MD, 1969. Diplomate Am. Bd. Nuclear Medicine, Nat. Bd. Med. Examiners. Internship gen. surgery Bellevue Med. Ctr., NYU, NYC, 1969—70; resident in diagnostic radiology Northwestern U., Chgo., 1970—72, resident in nuc. medicine, 1972—74, asst. prof. radiology, 1974—76; from asst. prof. to assoc. prof. radiology Loyola U., Maywood, Ill., 1976—80, dir. nuc. medicine, 1976—98, prof. radiology, 1980—2005, acting chair dept. radiology, 2000—02, dir. nuc. medicine, 2002—05, vice chair dept. radiology, 2002—05, prof. emeritus radiology, 2006—. Fellow Am. Coll. Radiology, Am. Coll. Nuc. Physicians (pres. 1990); mem. AMA, Am. Coll. Physician Execs., Soc. Nuc. Medicine (bd. dirs., trustee 1983-89, 2000-04, v.p. 1995-96, ho. dels. 1998-2004). Home and Office: UNM Ltd 1952 W Cuyler Ave Ste 404 Chicago IL 60613-2404 Personal E-mail: unm@mindspring.com.

HENKIN, ROBERT IRWIN, neuroscientist, internist, nuclear medicine physician, medical products executive; b. LA, Oct. 5, 1930; s. William and Ida Mildred (Scher) H.; m. Marsha Lynn Jacobs, May 15, 1964 (div. Jan. 1982); children: Amanda Joan, Michael Jonathan, David Gorman, Joshua Adam, Elizabeth Madeline, Hannah Deborah; m. Jane M. Pettit, 2007; stepchildren: William Christopher Pettit, Sara Jane Pettit, Andrew Scott Pettit. AB cum laude, U. So. Calif., 1951; MA, UCLA, 1953, PhD, 1956, MD, 1959. Intern in medicine U. Calif. Hosp., LA, 1959-60; resident in medicine Jackson Meml. Hosp., U. Miami (Fla.), 1960-61; commd. officer USPHS, 1961, advanced through grades to sr. surgeon, resigned, 1975; rsch. assoc. Nat. Inst. Mental Health, NIH, Bethesda, Md., 1961-63, sr. investigator, 1963-69; chief sect. on neuroendocrinology Nat. Heart and Lung Inst., NIH, Bethesda, 1969-75; dir. Ctr. Molecular Nutrition and Sensory Disorders Georgetown U. Med. Ctr., Washington, 1975-85, assoc. prof. pediat. and neurology, 1975-82, prof., 1982—, dir. Taste and Smell Clinic, 1985—. Pres., CEO Sialon Corp., Washington, 1987—; cons. Campbell Soup Co., 1969-74, USDA/NIH, 1975—, Hooker Chem. Co., Buffalo, 1976-77, Washington Cont. for Zinc, 1985—, Florasynth, NYC, 1986-91, Squibb Pharm. Co., NYC, 1986-87, Blue Cross/Blue Shield, 2003—, Quigley Pharma, 2004-06, Becton-Dickson, 2006—; guest worker NIH, Bethesda, Md., 2005-. Author: Zinc, 1975; editor Biol. Element Rsch., Nutrition; contbr. articles to profl. jours.; patentee saliva, taste diagnostics, wound healing protein, drugs to treat taste/smell disorders. Recipient Vicennial medal Georgetown U., 1984; Atwater Kent fellow UCLA, 1957; grantee Dept. Def., USDA, NIH, 1969—. Fellow Am. Coll. Nutrition; mem. Biophys. Soc. (charter), Am. Physiol. Soc., Am. Soc. Nutrition, Am. Fedn. Med. Rsch., Am. Soc. Clin. Investigation, Composers Guild Am., Cosmos Club, Phi Beta Kappa, Sigma Xi (nat. lectr. 1984-87, Giovanni di Chiro Sci. award 1998). Avocations: tennis, running, skiing. Home: 6601 Broxburn Dr Bethesda MD 20817-4709 Office: Ctr Mol Nutrn/Sensory Disorders Taste and Smell Clin 5125 MacArthur Blvd NW Ste 20 Washington DC 20016-3300 Home Phone: 301-229-0388; Office Phone: 202-364-4180. Office Fax: 202-364-9727. Business E-Mail: doc@tasteandsmell.com.

HENLEY, DOUGLAS E., medical association administrator; b. Hope Mills, NC, Jan. 1, 1951; m. Mary Henley. MD, U. NC Sch. Medicine, Chapel Hill, 1977. Diplomate Am. Bd. Family Medicine. Resident NC Meml. Hosp., Chapel Hill, NC, 1977—80; pvt. practice Hope Mills, NC, 1980—2000; assoc. clin. instr. U. NC Sch. Medicine; exec. v.p., CEO Am. Acad. Family Physicians, 2000—. Mem. NC Cervical Cancer Task Force; mem. tech. adv. panel Office Tech. Assessment, US Congress. Mem. editl. bd. Family Practice News, Jour. Family Practice, mem. current procedural terminology editl. panel AMA. Fellow: American Acad. Family Physicians (bd. dirs. 1991—97, chmn. 1993—94, 1996—97, pres. 1995—96). Office: AAFP 2021 Massachusetts Ave NW Washington DC 20036 Business E-Mail: dhenley@aafp.org. *

HENLEY, RICHARD JAMES, healthcare executive; b. Wroclaw, Poland, May 31, 1956; came to US, 1959; s. Henry and Lidia Horczak. BA and MA summa cum laude, CCNY, 1978. Asst. v.p. fin. Mt. Sinai Med. Ctr., NYC, 1978-80, dir. fin. planning, 1980-81, assoc. dir. fin., 1982-84, dir. fin. profl. svcs., 1984-85; v.p. fin., treas. Vassar Bros. Med. Ctr., Poughkeepsie, NY, 1985-92, sr. v.p. for adminstrn., treas., 1992-97, exec. v.p., treas., 1997—2005; exec. v.p., COO, CFO Health Quest, Poughkeepsie, 1999—2005; pres. and CEO Pocono Health Sys., East Stroudsburg, Pa., 2005—08, Pocono Med. Ctr., Pa., 2005—08, Healthcare Strategic Solutions, LLC, 2008—. Treas. VBH Corp., Poughkeepsie, 1986-99, Found. Vassar Bros. Med. Ctr., 1986-2003, VBH Ins. Co., Ltd., 1988-2005, pres., 1991—2005, Riverside Diversified Svc., Inc., 1986-92, pres., 1992—2005, Riverside Mgmt. Svc., Inc., 1986-92, pres., 1992—2005, Alamo Amulance Svc., 1986-92, pres., 1992-2005; pres. Hudson Valley Home Care, Inc.; pres. HealthServe, LLC; bus. adv. coun. SUNY, New Paltz, 1999—2005; bd. dir. Dutchess County Econ. Devel. Corp., chmn., 2003-05. Contbr. articles to profl. jours. Treas. Bardavon 1869 Opera House, Poughkeepsie, 1986-91, Family Svcs. Dutchess County, Poughkeepsie, 1987-88, Samuel F. B. Morse Hist. Site, 1998-99; pres. Hudson Terr. Owners' Corp., Poughkeepsie, 1987-88. Fellow Healthcare Fin. Mgmt. Assn. (nat. life mem. 2000, nat. dir. 1994-96, nat. sec. 1996-97, nat. treas. 1997-98, nat. chmn. elect 1998-99, nat. chmn. 1999-2000, cost effectiveness award 1979-80, William G. Follmer Merit award 1986, Robert H. Reeves Merit award 1989, Fredric T. Muncie Mert award 1991, Medal of Honor award 1994, Stephen A. Ryan Meml. award 2003), Am. Heart Assn. (bd. dirs.), Am. Coll. Health Exec. (regent Hudson Valley Adirondack 2002-06, bd. govs. 2006-09, Disting. Svc. award, 2008), Pocono Mountains C. of C. (dir. 2006-08). Office Phone: 203-220-9382. Personal E-mail: richardhenley@optonline.net. Business E-Mail: rjh@healthcarestrategicsolutions.com.

HENN, FRITZ ALBERT, psychiatrist; b. Alden, Pa., Mar. 26, 1941; s. Fredrich and Luise (Kimm) H.; m. Suella Weiland, Aug. 1, 1964; children: Sarah, Stephen. BA, Wesleyan U., Middleton, Conn., 1963; PhD, Johns Hospkins U., 1967; MD, U. Va., 1971. Dir. rsch. tng. U. Iowa Hosps. and Clinics, Iowa City, 1975; asst. prof. U. Iowa, Coll. of Medicine, Iowa City, 1974-78, assoc. prof., 1978-81, prof. dept. psychiat., 1981; prof., chmn. SUNY, Stony Brook, 1982-94; dir. L.I. Rsch. Inst., Stony Brook, 1982-83, Inst. of Mental Health Rsch., Stony Brook, 1983—; prof. psychiatry U. Heidelberg, Germany, 1994; dir. Ctrl. Inst. for Mental Health, Germany, 1994; assoc. dir. life scis. Brookhaven Nat. Lab, Upton, NY, 2006—. Pres. Winter Conf. on Brain Rsch., 1990-92. Mem. editorial bd. Jour. Neurochemistry, 1980-90, Archives Gen. Psychiatry, 1983—. Cons. Project Dawn Justice Dept., 1973-74. Fellow Life Ins. Medicine Rsch. Fund, 1968-71, Falk fellow Am. Psychiat. Assn., 1972-74. Fellow Am. Coll. Neuropsychopharmacology, Am. Coll. Psychiatrists; mem. AMA, Soc. for Neurol. Sci., Psychiat. Rsch. Soc. (pres. 1992), Am. Soc. Neurochemistry, Sigma Xi, Alpha Omega Alpha. Office: Brookhaven Nat Lab Bldg 490 Bell Avw Upton NY 11973-5000 Office Phone: 49 621 1703739. Office Fax: 49 621 1703760. Business E-Mail: henn@zi-mannheim.de, fhenn@nnl.gov.

HENNA, PEARL, dermatologist; b. Mar. 10, 1981; BS, U. Ga., 2003; degree in Medicine, Med. Coll. Ga., 2007. Dermatologist Med. Coll. Ga., 2009. Home: 1040 Alexander Dr Apt 2333 Augusta GA 30909 Personal E-mail: hennapearls@yahoo.com.

HENNEBERG, ALEXANDRA EHRENGARD, neuropsychiatrist, neuroimmunologist; b. Braunschweig, Germany, Oct. 28, 1956; d. Baron Horst-Henning Hans and Baroness Margarete Hildegard (Küpper) Kirchbach; m. Hans-Joachim Heinrich Henneberg, Oct. 27, 1988; children: Felix Karl Viktor, Julius Horst Friedrich, Sophia Ingeborg Amalie. 2d med. exam, U. Tübingen, Germany, 1977; 3d med. exam., U. Bonn, Germany, 1982; habilitation in neurology, U. Ulm, Germany, 1993. Guest worker Med. Rsch. Ctr., London, 1979-80; asst. physician dept. psychiatry Hosp. of Psychiatry, Cologne, Germany, 1987-88; asst. physician dept. neurology U. Ulm, Germany, 1982-87, 89-92, asst. med. dir. dept. neurology, 1992-95; med. dir. Hosp. for Parkinson's Disease, Bad Nauheim, Germany, 1995—2002; cons. Hosp. for Neurology, Bad Homburg Tannenwaldallee, Germany, 2002—03, Dr. Baumstark Hosp., Bad Homburg, 2003—04, Klinik Rodenstein, Bensheim, 2005, Rot-Kreuz-Maingau Hosp., Frankfurt, Germany, 2005—; prof. U. Giessen, Germany, 1999—. Mem. Neurology Rsch. Lab., Ulm, 1982—87; head Neuroimmunology Rsch. Group, Ulm, 1989—95, Epileptology, 1998, Phys. Therapy, 1999; del. German Soc. Med. Dirs., 2000—, Dist. and Nat. Med. Soc., 2000—; mem. awards com. Studienstiftung des Deutschen Volkes, Fritz-Strauch Award, 2004—06; mem. study group videotape-assisted therapy on Parkinson's disease; initiator study group magnetic pulse stimulation in Parkinson; mem. study group ear acupuncture in

Parkinson's disease. Author: Immunological Alterations in Psychiatric Diseases, 1997, Parkinson-zu neuem Gleichgewicht finden, 1997, (with J. Komm and K. Prokein) Parkinson na und?, 1998, (with L. Johner) Parkinson-Lexikon fur Patienten.; contbr. articles to med. jours. Hon. justice Hessen Fin. County Ct., 2002—; cons. Red Cross Hosp., Frankfurt, 2005—. Recipient award, Winter Workshop on Schizophrenia, London, 1992; grantee, Hertiestiftung, Frankfurt, Germany, 1987, Stanley Found., Arlington, Va., 1993; scholar, Studienstiftung Deutschen Volkes, Bonn, 1974—82. Mem.: German Soc. Electrotherapy (sci. com.), N.Y. Acad. Scis., German Soc. Neurogenetics, German Soc. Neuropathology, German Soc. Neurochemistry, German Soc. Psychiatry, German Soc. Immunology, German Soc. Neurology (Poster prize 1999), Internat. Soc. Neuroimmunomodulation, Internat. Soc. Pathophysiology. Avocations: playing violin, dance, riding, reading. Office: Scheffelstr 31 D-60318 Frankfurt Germany Office Phone: 0049-69-59795430. Business E-Mail: henneberg-neuropsych@t-online.de.

HENNEMAN, STEPHEN CHARLES, psychotherapist; b. Chgo., June 17, 1949; s. Charles Philip Jr. and Marion Louise (Eichberger) Henneman; m. Patricia Anne York, Feb. 14, 1975 (div. Sept. 1980); 1 child, Charles Philip III; m. Marion Jean McDermand, Oct. 4, 1980; stepchildren: Ervin F. Jr. Schrock, Lisa Ann Schrock, Thomas M. Schrock. BA in Journalism, Colo. State U., 1971; MA in Counseling, U. N.D., 1987. Cert. profl. counselor, Am. Counseling Assn. Commd. 2d lt. USAF, 1971, advanced through grades to maj., 1984; missile launch officer 570th Strategic Missile Squadron, Davis Monthan AFB, Ariz., 1972-76; info. officer 321st Strategic Missile Wing, Grand Forks AFB, ND, 1976-79; missile combat crew flight comdr. 446th Strategic Missile Squadron, Grand Forks AFB, 1980-82; missile combat crew comdr. evaluator 321st Strategic Missile Wing, Grand Forks AFB, 1982, wing nuclear surety officer, 1982-83, chief weapon safety branch, 1983-85; asst. ops. officer 320th Strategic Missile Squadron, F E Warren AFB, Wyo., 1985-86; dep. wing inspector 90th Strategic Missile Wing, F E Warren AFB, 1986-88; ops. officer 319th Strategic Missile Squadron, F E Warren AFB, 1988-89; dep. chief war res. materiel div. Hdqrs. U.S. Air Forces in Europe, Ramstein Air Base, Fed. Republic Germany, 1989-92; vol. and outreach coord. Safe House/Sexual Assault Svcs., Inc., Cheyenne, Wyo., 1992-93; quality control investigator Dept. Employment State of Wyoming, Cheyenne, 1993-95; counselor Wyo. State Penitentiary, Rawlins, 1995-96, counseling team leader, 1996-97; residential counselor Aurora (Colo.) Cmty. Mental Health Ctr., 1997-99, mental health clinician, 1999-2001, profl. counselor, 2001—. Advocate, counselor Safehouse/Sexual Assault Svcs., Inc., Cheyenne, 1985-89; sec., bd. dirs. Carbon County Citizens Organized to See Violence Ended, 1996-97. Mem. ACA, Am. Mental Health Counselors Assn., Colo. Counselors Assn., Nat. Cert. Counselors. Avocations: photography, popular music recordings collecting, reading. Office Phone: 303-617-2756. Business E-Mail: schenneman@comcast.net.

HENNER, JULIE, surgeon; b. Paris, Nov. 17, 1971; MD, Claude Bernard Lyon 1 U., 2006, DESC, 2009. Chief clinique Hôpital femme mère enfant, Lyon U. Hosp., 2006—08, Grenoble U. Hosp., 2008—09; praticien hospitalier Albertville Hosp., 2009—. Avocation: mountain climbing. Office: 253 Rue Pierre De Coubertin Albertville Savoie 73200 France Business E-Mail: a.pinaroli.j.henner@wanadoo.fr.

HENNESSEY, WILLIAM JOSEPH, physician; b. Troy, NY, Mar. 8, 1947; BS, Rensselaer Poly. Inst., 1969, MD, Albany Med. Coll., 1973. Resident in ob-gyn Albany (N.Y.) Med. Ctr. Hosp., 1973—76; pvt. practice specializing in gynecology Green Island, NY, 1976—. Office Phone: 518-272-9140. E-mail: whennessey@aol.com.

HENNIGAR, WILLIAM GRANT, JR., dentist; b. Buffalo, Dec. 25, 1947, s. William Grant and Donnette (Glaeser) H.; m. Jennie Carcaud, Mar. 22, 1975 (div.), children: William Grant III, Charlotte Carcaud, Travis Welshofer(dec.), Brittany Lines. AB, Colgate U., 1970; DMD, U. Pa., 1973; cert., U. Rochester, 1975; JD, Cleve. State U., 1992. Bar: Mass., NY 1993; cert. provider Invisalign 2005. With Harvard U. Health Inc., Cambridge, Mass., 1974; ptnr. Am. Family Dental Group, P.C., Cheektowaga, NY, 1982-97; pres. Grand Island, Cheektowaga, NY, 1988—. Bd. dirs. West River Homeowners Assn., Grand Island, 1985-88, Alumni Bd. Nichols Sch., Buffalo, 1988-89; com. mem. Nichols Sch. Athletic Hall of Fame, 2010, Spl. Advancement Com., Eastman Inst. Oral Health U. Rochester. Long range planning com., Town of Grand Island, NY, 1998. Lic. capt. USCG, 1989—. Named to Athletic Hall of Fame, Nichols Sch., 2005. Fellow Acad. Gen. Dentistry, ADA; mem. ABA, NY State Bar Assn., Internat. Assn. Orthodontics, Am. Acad. Dental Group Practice, US Dental Inst. (cert. 1985), Erie County Bar Assn., Erie County Dental Soc., NY State Dental Soc., Am. Dental Assn., Buffalo Launch Club (Grand Island), Phi Kappa Psi, Psi Omega, U.S. Power Squadron. Libertarian. Episcopalian. Avocations: volleyball, boating, softball, geneology, running. Home: PO Box 691 Grand Island NY 14072-0691 Office: Am Family Dental Group 2025 Whitehaven Rd Grand Island NY 14072-2024

HENNINGSEN, NELS CHRISTIAN, medical researcher; b. Aarhus, Denmark, Aug. 14, 1943; arrived in Sweden, 1970; s. Nicolai Christian and Gerda Henningsen; m. Birgitta Anne Hemming, Sept. 5, 1970; children: Eva, Jesper, Karin. MD, U. Copenhagen, 1970; PhD, U. Lund, Sweden, 1980. Resident dept. medicine U. Malmö, Sweden, 1971—76, chief resident, 1976—90, head dept., 1990—95; specialist Gustav Adolf Group, Malmö, 1995—2002, group leader, 2002—05; specialist Ellenbogen, Malmö, 2005—, chmn. bd., 2007—. Contbr. articles to numerous profl. publs. Capt. Danish Army, 1970—72. Mem.: Am. Soc. Hypertension, Internat. Soc. Preventive Medicine, Internat. Soc. Hypertension, Rotary (pres. 1999). Avocations: skiing, gardening, reading. Office: Laegegruppen Ellenbogen Baltzarsgatan 23 211 36 Malmö Sweden Office Phone: 0046-40-208000.

HENNOSY, MARK W., systems analyst; b. Columbus, Ohio, Mar. 30, 1965; Degree in Bus., Columbus State CC, 1986. Bus. sys. analyst Ohio Dept. Mental Health, 1987—. Avocation: volleyball. Office: 30 E Broad St Columbus OH 43215 Business E-Mail: mark.hennosy@mh.ohio.gov.

HENNY, CHARLES JOSEPH, biologist, researcher; b. Salem, Oreg., Mar. 20, 1943; s. Joseph and Mildred Henny; m. Susan Carol Jenkins, June 17, 1967; children: Cheryl Anne Evan, Sharon Marie Kolb. BS in Fisheries and Wildlife, Oreg. State U., Corvallis, 1965, MS in Wildlife Mgmt., 1967, PhD in Wildlife Ecology, 1970. Rsch. biologist US Fish and Wildlife Svc., Laurel, Md., 1970—74, Denver, 1974—76, Corvallis, 1976—93, US Geol. Survey, Corvallis, 1993—2011. Courtesy prof. Oreg. State U., 1977—2010; assoc. editor Journal Raptor Rsch., 1991—2002; editl. bd. mem. Bulletin Environ. Contamination Toxicology, 2003—11. Contbr. scientific papers. Ind. sci. rev. panel Pacific NW Electric Power and Conservation Planning Coun., Portland, Oreg., 2005—11. Fellow: Am. Ornithologists Union; mem.: Waterbird Soc., Northwestern Field Naturalists, Northwestern Scientific Assn., Wilson Ornithological Soc., British Ornithologists Union, Wildlife Soc., Raptor Rsch. Found. (Hamerstrom award for Lifetime Achievement 2006). Avocations: travel, birdwatching, book collecting. Office: US Geological Survey 3200 SW Jefferson Way Corvallis OR 97331 Home: 1907 NW Cascade Heights Dr Albany OR 97321 Office Fax: 541-757-4845. Business E-Mail: hennyc@usgs.gov.

HENNY, CHRISTIAAN PIETER, emergency physician, researcher; b. Den Haag, Netherlands, Apr. 18, 1946; s. Maria Adelia Montessori and Jan Jacob Henny; m. Cornelia Anna Zwart, June 12, 1960; children: Maurits Sebatiaan children: Isa Andrea, Cristiaan Alexander. MD, U. of Amsterdam, The Netherlands, 1975—83, PhD, 1983—87; degree Anesthesiology, U. of Amsterdam, The Netherelands, 1986—90; degree Intensive Care Medicine, U. of Amsterdam, The Netherlands, 1990—92, degree Emergency Medicine, 1994—96. Medical The Netherlands, 1983, Anesthesiology The Netherlands, 1990, Intensive Care Medicine The Netherlands, 1992, Emergency Medicine The Netherlands, 1996. Sr. staf anesthesiology Academic Med. Ctr., Amsterdam, Netherlands, 1992—; sr. lectr. U. of Amsterdam, Amsterdam, Netherlands, 1998—; chmn. dept. high care Academic Med. Ctr., Amsterdam, Netherlands, 1994—2004, sr. rschr., 1997—, bd. blood transfusion com., 1998—; chmn. nat. com. guidelines blood transfusion Nat. Inst. for Quality Assesment, Utrecht, Netherlands, 2000—; bd. com. medications Academic Med. Ctr., Amsterdam, Netherlands, 1997—, bd. com. emergency medicine and traumatology, 1994—; chaiman com. investmens and materials Academical Med. Ctr., Amsterdam, Netherlands; reviewer sevral internat. med. journals Academic Med. Ctr., Amsterdam, Netherlands, 2000—. Author: Hereditary ATIII deficiency and heparin(Thromb Res), (book) Plasminogen and antiplasmin: relevant parameters for monitoring fibrinolytic therapy?, Disseminated intravascular coagulation, Bloodloss, transfusion and fluid management in the postoperative period, (scientific paper) Use of a new heparinoid as anticoagulant during acute hemodialysis of patients with bleeding complications(Lancet), Acquired ATIII deficiency in the course of toxic shock syndrome(Neth J Med), A review of the importance of acute multidisciplinary treatment following spontaneous rupture of the livercapsule during pregnancy(Surg Gynaecol Obstet), contbr. over 60 sci. papers in field. Fellow: European soc. of Intensive Care Medicine, Royal soc. for the advancement of Sci. Rsch.; mem.: Dutch soc. of Traumatology, Dutch soc. on the treatment of Pain, Soc. For Advancement of Blood Mgmt., Dutch soc. of Thrombosis and Haemostasis, World assn. of Cardiothoracic and Vascular Anesthesia (licentiate), Internat. soc. of Oxygen Transport to Tissue, Dutch soc. of Intensive Care Medicine, Network for the Advancement of Transfusion Alternatives, Dutch soc. of Anesthesiology, Alph Tau Omega (life). Office: Acad Med Ctr Meibergdreef 9 1105 AZ Amsterdam Netherlands Office Fax: 31 20 6979441. Business E-Mail: c.p.henny@amc.uva.nl.

HENRICHS, RONALD A., medical association administrator; BS in Business, Univ. Wis. Cert. Certified Assn. Exec. (CAE). Staff liaison State Med. Soc. Wis., dir., divsn. comm., mng. editor, Wis. Med. Jour.; dir., young physician svcs. AMA; exec. dir. Am. Acad. Physical Medicine and Rehabilitation, 1989—2004, Am. Acad. Dermatology, Schaumburg, Ill., 2004—. Mem.: Am. Assn. Med. Soc. Execs. (past sec., past mem. exec. com.), Assn. Forum of Chicagoland, Am. Soc. Assn. Execs. Office: AAD PO Box 4014 Schaumburg IL 60168-4014 Office Phone: 847-330-0230. Business E-Mail: rhenrichs@aad.org *

HENRIKSEN, EVA HANSINE, retired anesthesiology educator; b. Petaluma, Calif., Jan. 1, 1929; d. Peder Henrik Boas and Karen (Nielsen) Henriksen; m. Daniel Edward MacLean, Aug. 25, 1957 (dec. Dec. 1981), m. Roger S. Johnson, July 25, 2009; children: Elizabeth Brown, Mary Laverty. AA, U. Calif., Berkeley, 1948, BA, 1950; MD, Yale U., 1954. Diplomate Am. Bd. Anesthesiology. Intern, resident Los Angeles County Hosp., LA, 1954-57; from instr. to asst. prof. anesthesia Loma Linda U. (formerly Coll. Med. Evangelists), LA, 1957-68; from instr. to assoc. prof. surgery anesthesiology Sch. Medicine U. So. Calif., LA, 1957-94, assoc. prof. anesthesiology emeritus, 1994—2009. Anesthesia cons. L.A. Coroner's Office, 1992—2009. Governing coun. Angelica Luth. Ch., 1992—2000, 2002—07. Democrat. Avocation: patchwork quilt making. Home: 14643 Tumble Weed Ln Royal Oaks CA 95076-9259

HENRIKSEN, JENS HENRIK, physician, educator, medical researcher; b. Copenhagen, Aug. 23, 1945; s. Jens Einar and Christa Marie Louise (Sahl) H.; m. Karin Højer-Pedersen Dahi. Degree in Medicine, U. Copenhagen, 1972, D in Med. Sci., 1982. Bd. cert. clin. physiology and nuclear medicine. Registrar Kommunehospitalet/Bispebjerg Hosp., Denmark, 1973—76; registrar/sr. registrar clin. physiology Hvidovre Hosp., 1976—80, registrar/sr. registrar internal medicine, 1980—82, chief physician dept. clin. physiology, 1984; sr. registrar/cons. Bispebjerg Hosp./Rigshospitalet, Denmark, 1982—84; prof. clin. physiology U. Copenhagen, 1994—. Pres. Soc. Theoretical and Applied Therapy, Copenhagen, 1989-90, Danish Soc. Clin. Physiology and Nuc. Medicine, Copenhagen, 1991-93. Author: Pathogenesis of Ascites in Cirrhosis, 1982, Ernest Henry Starling (1866-1927), Physician and Physiologist-A Short Biography, 2000, E.H. Starling, His Contemporaries and the Nobel Prize-100 Years with Hormones, 2003, Basal Indicator Kinetics, 2007, Professor Biography I, 2011; author, editor: Degradation of Bioactive Substances, 1991, Basel Indicator Kinetics in Whole-body, Organs and Tissues, 2007, Clin. Physiology Nuc. Medicine - 40 Yr. Review, 2008; prof. biography I, 2011; assoc. editor Liver, 1986-91; editor Scandinavian Jour. Clin. and Lab. Investigation, 1988—; rev. editor Clin. Physiology, 1991-97; contbr. articles to profl. jours. Recipient Kommunitetet, U. Copenhagen, 1968—72, Tode award, Danish Soc. Medicine, 1995, Klein award, Copenhagen Soc. Medicine, 1997, Juhl Meml. award, Rsch. Found., 2002—03, Niels A. Lassen prize, 2003, Knighthood award, Order of Dannebrog, 2009; Rsch. grantee, John and Birthe Meyer Found., 1990, 1992, 1994, 1997, H:S grantee, 2001. Fellow Internat. Coll. Angiology; mem. Internat. Assn. Study Liver, European Assn. Study Liver, Internat. Union Physiol. Scis. (bd. coun. clin. physiology 1993—2005), N.Y. Acad. Scis., Italian Liver Found. (sci. and cons. com.). Home: Fasanhaven 16 DK-2820 Gentofte Denmark Office: Hvidovre Hosp U Copenhagen Dept Clin Physiology 239 DK-2650 Hvidovre Denmark Home Phone: +4539681816; Office Phone: +4536322203.

HENRIKSON, DONALD MERLE, forensic pathologist; b. Walla Walla, Wash., May 2, 1947; s. James Christan and Carol Jean (DuBois) H.; m. Eileen Ruth Mikita, Oct. 12, 1980. BA, Harvard U., 1969; MD, U. Calif., Davis, 1981. Diplomate Am. Bd. Pathology. Assoc. pathologist Lab. Medicine Cons., Inc., Auburn, Calif., 1986-87, FPMG, Inc., 1987-88; owner, pathologist FFPMG, 1989-94; assoc. pathologist NCFP, Inc., Sacramento, 1994—2002; pathologist Placer County Coroner's Office, Auburn, 2002—. Mem. med. staff Sierra Valley Dist. Hosp., Loyalton, Calif., 1992-95, Oroville Hosp. and Med. Ctr., 1986-95, Sierra Nev. Meml. Hosp., Grass Valley, Calif., 1986-94, Sutter Auburn Faith Hosp., 1986—; asst. clin. prof. U. Calif. Sch. of Medicine, Davis, 1994-2002. Mem. Placer County Child Death Rev. Team, Auburn, 1990—; mem., former chair Sacramento County Child Death Rev. Team, Sacramento, 1994-2001; mem. Nevada County Child Death Rev. Team, Nevada City, 1996—. Sgt. U.S. Army, 1969-71. Fellow Coll. of Am. Pathologists; mem. AMA, AAAS, Am. Acad. Forensic Scis., Am. Soc. for Clin. Pathology. Avocations: hiking, golf, piano. Office: Placer County Coroner Auburn Justice Ctr 2929 Richardson Dr Auburn CA 95603 Office Phone: 530-889-7807.

HENRION, ROSEMARY PROVENZA, psychotherapist, educator; b. Greenville, Miss., Oct. 2, 1929; d. Vincent and Camille (Portera) Provenza; m. Albert Joseph Henrion, Sept. 8, 1956 (dec.); 1 child, Albert Joseph Jr. BSN, U. Tex., Galveston, 1963; MSN in Psychiat./Mental Health Nursing, Vanderbilt U., 1972; MEd in Secondary Edn., U. So. Miss., 1974. RN Tex.; cert. logotherapist, profl. psychotherapist. Psychotherapist St. Mary's Hosp., Galveston, Tex., 1951—52, office and pvt. duty surg. nurse, 1952—53; supr. ob-gyn. nursing Greenville Gen. Hosp., 1954—56, head nurse, ob-gyn. and med.-surg. nursing, 1953—54; instr. nursing Providence Hosp. Sch. Nursing, Waco, Tex., 1957—59; dir. inservice edn., asst. dir. nursing svc. Meml. Hosp., Gulfport, Miss., 1966—67, dir. nursing svc., 1967—68; psychiat. clin. nurse specialist Biloxi VA Med. Ctr., Miss., 1972—89, in-house cons., 1975—92, assoc. chief nursing svc., 1989—92; clin. nurse specialist VA Outpatient Ctr., Pensacola, Fla., 1992—98; adj. clin. prof., psychiat.-mental health nursing La. State U., New Orleans, 1975—76; adj. clin. prof. grad. nursing program U. So. Miss., Hattiesburg, 1983—92, liaison prof., logotherapy course Vienna, 1985; faculty V.F. Inst. Logotherapy, Berkeley and San Jose, Calif., 1983—92, Abilene, Tex., 1993—; clin. instr. grad. nursing program U. So. Ala., 1998—99. Mem. Internat. Acad. Behavioral Medicine, COunseling & Psychotherapy Inc., 1990—; internat. bd. dirs. V. F. Inst. of Logotherapy, 1992—; instr. advanced clin. logotherapy course World Congress Logotherapy, Dallas, 1993—; first guest lectr. internat. program on logotherapy U. South Africa, Pretoria, 2005; co-founder Inst. Meaningful Living, 2003—; educator, cons. St. Joseph Homes, Mobile, Ala., 2004—07, St. Mary's Homes, Mobile, 2007—, quality assurance specialist. Co-author: The Power of Meaningful Intimacy: Key to Successful Relationships, 2003, 2004; contbg. author: International Forum for Logotherapy, 1983—2006, Favorite Counseling and Therapy Techniques, 1997, Favorite Counseling and Therapy-Homework Assignments, 2000, Existential Psychotherapy of Meaning, 2009, Meaningful Living Continued Despite Lymphedema Diagnosis, 2010. Mem. Pope John Paul II Cultural Ctr. Mem.: AAUW, Nat. Mus. Women Arts, Women's Mus.: Inst. for the Future (charter mem. 2000—11), Am. Assn. Med. Psychotherapists and Psychodiagnosticians, U. Southern Miss. Alumni Assn., Nat. Women's History Mus. (charter mem. 2000—), Women's Mus. (Smithsonian affiliate mem. 2009—), Miss. Bd. Nursing (pres. 1977—79), The Wilson Assocs., Vanderbilt Alumni Assn., Sigma Theta Tau Internat. (Iota chpt. 1972—). Home and Office: 19 Wenmar Ave Pass Christian MS 39571-3144 Office Phone: 228-860-4570. Personal E-mail: rhenrion@cableone.net.

HENRÍQUEZ-HERNÁNDEZ, LUIS ALBERTO, research scientist; b. Las Palmas de Gran Canaria, Spain, Apr. 4, 1978; PhD, U. de Las Palmas de Gran Canaria, 2001. Rsch. scientist, vet. U. de Las Palmas de Gran Canaria, 2008—. Office: C/ Dr Pasteur S/N 6th Fl Las Palmas de Gran Canaria Las Palmas 36016 Spain Business E-Mail: lhenriquez@dcc.ulpgc.es.

HENRY, G. WILLIAM, pediatrician; b. 1951; MD, Ind. Univ., 1977. Cert. Am. Bd. Pediatrics, 1982, in pediatric cardiology Am. Bd. Pediatrics, 1985. Intern in pediatrics Ind. Univ., Indpls., 1977—78, resident in pediatrics, 1978—79; fellowship in pediatric cardiology Univ. NC, Chapel Hill, 1979—82, prod. of pediatrics, chief of pediatric cardiology div., dir. Children's Heart Ctr. Office: UNC Sch Med 5160Q Bioinformatics Bldg 130 Mason Farm Rd Chapel Hill NC 27599-7220 Office Phone: 919-966-4601. Office Fax: 919-966-6894.

HENRY, J. MYRLE, retired pharmacist; b. Jacksonville, Fla., Aug. 30, 1938; s. Joseph Mason and Ovieda Ida (Dossey) H.; m. Tommie Claire Williams, Aug. 28, 1959; children: Cheri Kim, Kathy Lynn. BSP, U. Fla., 1961. Registered pharmacist Fla. Pharmacist Barwick Drugs, Plant City, Fla., 1961, Magnolia Pharmacy, Plant City, 1962-66, pharmacist, co-owner, 1966-80; co-owner H&R Drug Ctr., Plant City, 1973-85, owner, 1985-93, Herring Drug, Plant City, 1977-86; pharmacist, owner Magnolia Pharmacy, 1980-2000; pharmacist Kash n Karry Pharmacy, Plant City, 2000—08. Past mem. Hillsborough County Citizens Adv. Com.; past pres. The Fla. Opry, East Hillsboro Hist. Soc.; Plant City Down Town Bus. and Merchants Assn.; past mem. Am. Pharm. Assn.; founder, past pres. Bapt. Towers Plant City, Inc.; deacon 1st Bapt. Ch.; past pres. Christian Living Ctr., Inc.; trustee So. Fla. Bapt. Hosp., Evangelical U. and Sem.; past bd. dirs. Hillsborough County unit Am. Cancer Soc., past chmn. Plant City br.; founder, past chmn. Strawberry Classic Car Show. Recipient Wyeth Bowl of Hygeia Cmty. Svc. award for Fla., 2007; named Plant City's Citizen Yr., group of 10 clubs Kiwanis, Civitan, Rotary, C. of C., Pilot, Optimist, Lions, Womans, Jr. Womans and Rotary Daybreak, 2001. Mem.: East Hillsborough C. of C. (past bd. dirs., past treas.), Fla. State Pharm. Assn., Hillsborough County Pharmacy Assn. (past pres.), Plant City Lions Club (past pres.), Kappa Psi. Avocation: gardening. Home: 3716 Keene Rd Plant City FL 33565-5408

HENRY, MICHEL CAMILLE, cardiologist; b. Fresse sur Moselle, France, Sept. 8, 1939; s. Albert and Germaine Henry; m. Annick Paulette Lebacle, June 26, 1964; children: Isabelle Marcelle, Brigitte Gilberte Blanchet. MD, Faculté de Médecine, Nancy, France, 1969, degree, 1973. Interventional cardiologist Cabinet de Cardiologie, Nancy, 1973—; chief patron Vascular Inst., Apollo Clinic, Hyderabad, India, 2001. Contbr. articles to profl. jours. Capt. Armée de terre, 1966—2005, France. Fellow: Indian Soc. Cardiology, Russian Cardiovasc. Soc. (life), Am. Soc. Angiology (life), Am. Heart Assn. (life). Roman Catholic. Achievements include development of protection devices and stents. Home: 4 allée des Roches Nancy 54000 France Office: Cabinet de Cardiologie 80 rue Raymond Poincaré Nancy 54000 France Home Phone: 33 3 83 96 1837; Office Phone: 33 3 83 41 1739. Office Fax: 33 3 83 28 75 26; Home Fax: 33 3 83 98 25 78. Personal E-mail: m.henryilrmdt@wanadoo.fr.

HENRY, MITCHELL L., surgeon, educator; b. Lincoln, Nebr., Nov. 7, 1954; m. Margie L. Henry; children: Erin, Lucas. BS, U Nebr., Lincoln, 1976, MD, 1979. Prof. surgery Ohio State U., Columbus, chief divsn. transplantation, 2005—. Office: Ohio State Univ 395 W 12th One Doan Office Tower #130 Columbus OH 43210 Business E-Mail: henry.6@osu.edu.

HENRY, STEPHEN LEWIS, retired lieutenant governor, orthopedic surgeon, educator; b. Owensboro, Ky., Oct. 8, 1953; s. Virgil Lewis and Wanda (Harper) Henry; m. Heather Reneé French, Oct. 27, 2000. BS, We. Ky. U., 1976; MD, U. Louisville, 1981. Diplomate Am. Bd. Orthopaedic Surgery. Intern gen. surgery U. Louisville Med. Ctr., 1981-82, resident, 1982-86, instr. orthopedic surgery, 1986—; lt. gov. Commonwealth of Ky., 1995—2003. Clin. investigator Richards Med. Co., Memphis, 1986—; athletic physician football teams U. Louisville, 1987—, Seneca High Sch., 1987—, Ky. State Football Championships, 1986—; commr. "A" dist. Jefferson County, 1992-95. Editor: Sports Medicine; contbr. abstracts and articles to profl. jours., chpts. to books. Treas. Louisville Tyler Park Neighborhood Assn., 1983-88, pres., 1988-89 Recipient best paper award So. Med. Assn., 1985, best clin. rsch. award U. Cin., 1986, outstanding resident rsch. award U. Louisville, 1988, Edwin G. Bovill rsch. award Orthopaedic Trauma Assn., 1989, Bell award for outstanding vol., Louisville, 1989, Presdl. recognition Nat. Vol. Week, The White House, 1989; named Outstanding Young Leader in Ky., 1988, One of 10 Outstanding Young Ams., U.S. Jaycees, 1989, Bell award, 1989, Jefferson award, 1989, Owensboro award for excellence, 1990, Lawrence-Grever award, 1990; grantee Richards Med. Co., 1986, Dept. Navy, 1989. Mem. Jefferson County Med. Soc., So. Orthopedic Assn., Ky. Med. Assn., Founder and Pres. Future Fund Land Trust and Endowment, Founder and Pres. Ky. Prostate Cancer Coalition, Fouder and Exec. Dir. Rosemary Clooney House and Mus. Democrat. Home: PO Box 4729 Louisville KY 40204-0729 Office Phone: 502-376-1967.

HENSCHKE, CLAUDIA INGRID, physician, radiologist; d. Ulrich Konrad and Gisela Franziska H. BA in French, So. Meth. U., 1962, MS in Math. Stats., 1966; PhD in Stats., U. Ga., 1969; MD, Howard U., 1977; Radiologist, Harvard U., 1981. Diplomate Am. Bd. Radiology. Internship, residency dept. radiology Harvard Med. Sch./Brigham and Women's Hosp., 1977-81, clin. fellow in radiology, 1977-81; rsch. fellow in radiology Brigham and Women's Hosp., 1979—80, Harvard Med. Sch., Boston; rsch. fellow in epidemiology Harvard Sch. of Pub. Health, 1981-82; assoc. radiologist Brigham and Women's Hosp., 1982-83, co-dir. Thoracic Divsn., 1983; asst. attending radiology to assoc. radiologist The N.Y. Hosp. - Cornell Med. Ctr., 1983-87, 87-92, sect. chief, chest imaging to chief of divsn., 1988-92, 92-95, attending radiologist, 1992, chief, Divsn. of Health Care Policy and Tech. Assessment, 1995—, chief, Divsn. of Chest Imaging, 1995—2000. Various acad. positions to prof. radiology, Cornell U. Med. Coll., 1992—; cons. Rockefeller U., 1986—96, Med. Program Devel. and Med. Computer Systems Planning, 1986—; lectr. in field; mem. numerous coms. in field; vis. prof. numerous unvis., including Columbia U., 1999, Roy Castle Internat. Ctr. for Lung Cancer Rsch., Liverpool, Eng., 1999, Washington U., 1999, Clinica U., Pamplona, Spain, 1999, U. Rochester, N.Y., 1999, radiologist, Mt. Sinica Sch. Medicine, 2009-, others. Mem. editl. bd. Complications in Surgery, 1995—, Investigative Radiology, 1990-94, Clin. Imaging, 1988—, Acad. Radiology, 1994—, others; reviewer Am. Jour. Cardiology, 1982—, Chest, 1992—, Radiology, 1993—, Jour. of Computed Assisted Tomography, 1995—, Am. Jour. of Radiology, 1995—, others; contbr. numerous books, including: Women's Complete Handbook, 1994, Introduction to Statistics and Computer Programming, 1975, Instructions for General Purpose Program Package, 1971, First and Second Biomedical Computing Symposium 1965 and 1966, 1967; contbr. numerous articles to profl. jours. and publs. Named Ky. Col. by Gov. of Ky., 1963; grantee in field. Mem. Am. Statis. Soc., Am. Assn. Women Radiologists (Marie Curie award/2d place 1994), Radiol. Soc. N.Am., Am. Coll. Radiology, Soc. Thoracic Radiology, Sigma Xi, Phi Kappa Phi. Office Phone: 212-580-3189. Business E-Mail: chenschke@earlydxvx.org.

HENSGEN, HERBERT THOMAS, retired medical technologist; b. Cin., May 28, 1947; s. Herbert and Carolyn Elizabeth (Stites) H. BS, U. Cin., 1973, MS, 1978; AAS, Cin. State Tech. and C.C., 1981. Reg. med. technologist. Grad. tchg. asst. U. Cin., 1976-77; lectr. Xavier U. (formerly Edgecliff Coll.), Cin., 1977-78; tech. Our Lady of Mercy Hosp. (now Mercy Hosp. Anderson), Cin., 1979-81, med. lab. tech., 1981—84, med. technologist, 1984—86; rsch. asst. Cin. Children's Hosp. Med. Ctr., 1986—2010. Instr. Cin. State Tech. and C.C., 1984-85. Contbr. article to Gen. and Comparative Endocrinology; co-author abstracts for Soc. for Pediat. Rsch., Endocrine Soc. Deacon Madisonville Bapt. Ch., 1977. Mem. Am. Soc. Clin. Pathology, Triple Nine Soc., Am. Mensa Ltd. Achievements include production of data suggesting lack of insulin-like growth factor-1 (IGF-I) may mediate growth retardation in the neonatal rat; discovery of evidence that IGF-I may be one of several growth factors regulating differentiation of the fetal brain; demonstration that the antigonadal effect of prolactin in the lizard Anolis carolinensis is directed toward the smaller ovarian follicles; research on effects of IGF-I and its binding proteins on fetal and neonatal development. Home: 7420 Drake Rd Cincinnati OH 45243-1422

HENSHER, ROBERT WILLIAM, oral and maxillofacial surgeon, consultant; b. London, Aug. 26, 1948; s. Walter Hensher and Elsie Alice Wright; m. Judith Caroline Candy, Oct. 17, 1987; 1 child, Charles. B in Dental Surgery, U. Liverpool, Eng., 1972; MB, ChB with honors, U. Liverpool, 1978. Dental ho. officer Liverpool Hosps., 1972, ho. officer, 1978; registrar Westminster & Roehampton Hosps., 1980—81; resident oral and maxillofacial surgery Charity Hosp. New Orleans/La. State U., 1981, ZMK Klinik Münster/ Gt. Ormond St. Hosp. UCH London, 1982—86; cons. oral and maxillofacial surgery NHS Cheltenham & Gloucester, England, 1986—2000; pvt. practice London, 2000—. Cons. NHS, 1986—2000, hon. cons., 2000—. Contbr. articles to profl. jours. Fellow: Brit. Assn. Oral and Maxillofacial Surgeons, Royal Coll. Surgeons England & Edinburgh); mem.: Am. Soc. TMJ Surgeons. Anglican. Avocations: fox hunting, motorcycling, bass, ballet. Office: 11 Harcourt House 19A Cavendish Square W1G 0PN London England Office Phone: 442074990891. Office Fax: 442074990889. E-mail: roberthensher@aol.com.

HENSLE, TERRY W., pediatric urologist; b. NYC; BS, Univ. Pa., 1964; MD, Cornell Univ., 1968. Cert. Am. Bd. Urology, 1978. Intern Boston City Hosp., 1968—69, resident in urology, 1969—73; resident in pediatric urology Mass. Gen. Hosp., Boston, 1973—76; fellow in pediatric urology Great Ormand St. Hosp., London, 1977, Mass. Gen. Hosp., Boston, 1976—77; prof. urology Columbia Univ. Coll. P&S, NYC, 1978—, vice-chmn. Urology Dept.; urologist Columbia Univ. Med. Ctr., Columbia-Presbyterian Hosp., NYC. Vis. prof. more than 40 universities; past pres. NY Acad. Med., Urology sect., Soc. for Pediatric Urology. Contbr. articles to profl. jours., chapters to books. Gen. surgeon USAF, 1970—72. Recipient Lifetime Achievement award, Nat. Kidney Found., 1996. Mem.: Am. Coll. Surgeons, Am. Urological Assn., Am. Acad. Pediatrics, Soc. Pediatric Urological Surgeons, Am. Assn. Genitourinary Surgeons, NY State Urological Soc., NY Med. & Surgical Soc., NY Clinical Soc., Societe Internationale d'Urologie, Soc. Univ. Urologists, Am. Assn. Clinical Urologists, Am. Assn. for Parenteral & Enteral Nutrition (past pres.), Northeast Med. Assn. Office: Columbia Univ Med Ctr 2-219N 3959 Broadway New York NY 10032 Office Phone: 212-305-8510. Office Fax: 212-305-4421.

HENSLEY, ELIZABETH CATHERINE, nutritionist, educator; b. Mpls., Feb. 27, 1921; d. Erich Christian and Lulu Mabel (Elliott) Selke; m. Eugene B. Hensley, June 10, 1954 (dec. 1992). BS in Edn., U. N.D., 1942; MS, Cornell U., 1944, postgrad., 1950-51. Instr. food and nutrition U. Del., 1944-47; asst. prof. Okla. A&M U., 1947-50; mem. faculty U. Mo., Columbia, 1951—, prof. food and nutrition, 1954-84, prof. emeritus, 1984—, chmn. dept. home econs., 1954-55, head dept. food and nutrition, 1955-65, co-chmn. dept. human nutrition, 1973-76. Author: Basic Concepts of World Nutrition, 1981. Mem. Am. Home Econs. Assn., Nutrition Today Soc., Mo. Home Econs. Assn., Boone County Hist. Soc., PEO, Pi Lambda Theta, Omicron Nu, Phi Upsilon Omicron, Gamma Sigma Delta, Kappa Alpha Theta Mem. Christian Ch. (Disciples Of Christ). Home: 802 Greenwood Ct Columbia MO 65203-2841

HENSLEY, MARY LYNNE FLOYD, academic medical center administrator; b. Covington, Ky., June 6, 1952; d. Robert Forsythe and Maysie McDowell (Williams) Floyd; m. Carl Evans Hensley II, Apr. 15, 1972; children: Carl Evans III, John Thomas, James Michael. Student, Am. U., DC, 1970-71; AS, U. State of N.Y., Albany, 1983; BBA with high distinction, U. Iowa, 1985; cert., U. Iowa Advanced Mgmt. Inst., 1990; cert. exec. program in healthcare mgmt., Ohio State U., 1993; M Accountancy, U. Iowa, 1998. Cert. instl. leadership devel. program U. Iowa Hosps. & Clinics, 2001. Acctg. technician R&D VA Med. Ctr., Iowa City, 1982-86; adminstr. dept. neurology U. Iowa, Iowa City, 1986-98, interim assoc. dir. faculty practice plan Coll. Medicine, 1994—95, asst. to head dept. radiology, 1998-99, asst. to head dept. neurology and Inst. Neurol. Diseases, 1999—2006; adminstrv. ctr. dir. depts. psychiatry, neurology, neurosurgery and otolaryngology Clin. Neurosci. Ctr. Med. Sch. U. Minn., Mpls., 2006—, with dept. otolaryngology, 2009. Adj. lectr. dept. health mgmt. and policy Coll. Pub. Health U. Iowa, 1999—2008, 2011-, grad. program in hosp. and health adminstrn., 1994-99, tchg. asst. dept. acctg., 1997-98; mem. EEG adv. com. Kirkwood Community Coll., Cedar Rapids, Iowa, 1986-98; internship preceptor, project preceptor, mentor grad. program in hosp. and health adminstrn. U. Iowa, 1992—2006; coop. edn. preceptor Coll. Bus. Adminstrn., U. Iowa, 1989, 93-98, with, HFMAs exchange, 2006-07, HFMA & People To People Delegation Russia, 2008. Mem. PTA, Iowa City, 1982—98; pack com. chmn. Boy Scouts Am., 1987—88, pack treas., 1988—89, den leader, 1986—89, troop merit badge instr., 1989—98; past mem. Iowa Med. Group Mgmt. Assn. Am. U. scholar, 1970-71, E. Lester Williams scholar, U. Iowa, 1984-85, Ponder Fund scholar U. Iowa, 1985, Am. Coll. Med. Practice Execs. scholar, 1997; recipient Fedn. of Schs. of Accy. award U. Iowa, 1997, Healthcare Fin. Mgmt. High Scorer award, 1998. Fellow: Accrediting Commn. Edn. Health Svcs. Adminstrn., Healthcare Fin. Mgmt. Assn. (bd. examiners 1999—2002, leader splty. group on fin. mgmt. of physician pratices 2001—02, cert., mem. best article judging com. 2011—, Follmer Bronze award 2001, Silver Reeves award 2005, Muncie Gold award 2011, mem. US exchange 2006—07, people to people del. russia 2008), Am. Coll. Healthcare Execs. (diplomate 1996, bd. cert.), Am. Coll. Med. Practice Execs. (cert.); mem.: ANA (pres. Acad. Neurology Adminstrs., with Assn. Univ. Profs. Neurology 2000—01), Med. Group Mgmt. Assn. (pres.-elect Neurosci. Adminstrn. Assembly 2001—02, pres. 2002—03, past pres. 2003—05), Inst. Mgmt. Accts. (past mem.), Phi Eta Sigma, Beta Gamma Sigma, Alpha Sigma Lambda, Beta Alpha Psi, Omicron Delta Kappa, Mortar Bd. Independent. Methodist. Avocations: hiking, history, art, music, travel, gardening. Office: U Minn Med Sch Campus Delivery Code 2721 Ste 900 A Rm 910 2829 Univ Ave SE Minneapolis MN 55414 Office Phone: 612-625-8681. Office Fax: 612-626-4700. Business E-Mail: hensley@umn.edu.

HENSON, ANNA MIRIAM, retired otolaryngologist, retired medical educator; b. Springfield, Mo., Nov. 7, 1935; d. Bert Emerson and Esther Miriam (Crank) Morgan; m. O'Dell Williams Henson, Aug. 1, 1964; children: Phillip, William. BA, Park Coll., Parkville, Mo., 1957; MA, Smith Coll., 1959; PhD, Yale U., 1967. Instr. Smith Coll., Northampton, Mass., 1960-61; rsch. assoc. Yale U., New Haven, 1967-74; instr. U. N.C., Chapel Hill, 1975-78, rsch. asst. prof., 1978-83, rsch. assoc. prof., 1983-86, prof. Sch. Medicine dept. otolaryngology, 1986—2001; ret., 2001. Mem. study sect. on hearing rsch. NIH, Bethesda, Md., 1990-93. Contbr. articles to profl. jours. Fulbright scholar, Australia, 1959-60; NIH grantee, 1975—2003. Mem. Assn. for Rsch. in Otolaryngology, Sigma Xi. E-mail: mmhenson@med.unc.edu.

HENSON, MICHELLE, medical association administrator; b. Erie, Pa.,, PA, May 9, 1967; BA in Acctg., Alaska Pacific U., 2002. Adminstr. Anchorage Cmty. Internists, 2000—02, Culpeper Med. Assocs., 2003—06, Va. Orthopaedic Ctr. PC, 2006—. Mem.: Am. Acad. Orthop. Execs., Med. Group Mgmt. Assn. Office: 663 Sunset Ln Culpeper VA 22701 Business E-Mail: michellehenson@ymail.com.

HENSON, O'DELL WILLIAMS, JR., retired anatomy educator; b. Kansas City, Mo., Jan. 11, 1934; s. O'Dell Williams and Natalie (Smith) H.; m. Miriam Morgan, Aug. 1, 1964; 1 child, Phillip William. BA, U. Kans., 1957, MA, 1960; PhD, Yale U., 1964. From instr. to assoc. prof. dept anatomy Yale U., New Haven, 1964-74; prof. dept cell biology and anatomy U. N.C., Chapel Hill, NC, 1974—2004, ret., 2004. Chmn. Commn. Anatomy, N.C., 1982-2003. Recipient Phi Sigma award 1960, Alexander Von Humbolt award 1982, Cen. Carolina Bank Excellence in Tchg. award 1982, NIH-Nat. Inst. Deafness and Other Communicative Disorders Claude Pepper award, 1989. Fellow AAAS. Home: 317 Reade Rd Chapel Hill NC 27516-1509 E-mail: owh@med.unc.edu.

HENSSGE, CLAUS, retired forensic specialist; b. Dresden, Germany, June 3, 1936; MD, Humboldt U., Berlin, 1962. Cons. Inst. Forensic Medicine, Berlin, 1975—83, Munster, Germany, 1984—86, prof. Cologne, Germany, 1986—93, dir. Essen, Germany, 1993—2003. Adv. bd. mem. Internat. Jour. Legal Medicine, Berlin, 1990—2007, Forensic Sci. Internat., Amsterdam, 1990—. Contbr. articles to profl. publs. Avocations: bicycling, chess. Home: Franzensbader Strasse 24 Berlin D 14193 Germany Personal E-mail: c.henssge@t-online.de.

HENTSCHEL, DIRK M., nephrologist; b. Berlin, May 18, 1970; MD, Freie U., Berlin, 1998. Dir., interventional nephrology Birgham & Women's Hosp., 2008. Mem.: Am. Soc. Diagnostic & Interventional Nephrology, Am. Soc. Nephrology. Office: Brigham & Women's Hosp 75 Francis Boston MA 02115 Business E-Mail: dhentschel@partners.org.

HEO, MOON YOUNG, education educator; b. Seoul, Republic of Korea, June 18, 1954; s. Nam Kyung Heo and Ok Ju Ha; m. Young Sook Min, Mar. 15, 1953; children: Sung Woo, Isu. BS, Chungang U., Seoul, 1976, MS, 1982, PhD, 1985. Pharmacist Korea Ministry of Health and Social Affairss, 1976. Asst. prof. Kangwon Nat. U., Chunchon, Republic of Korea, 1985—89, assoc. prof., 1989—93, dir., 1993—95, dean, 1997—99, prof., 1993—. Vis. prof. Univ of Tex. Med. Br., Galveston, 1989—2000; dir. Nat. Com. of Cosmetics, Seoul, 2000—02; councilor Kangwon Nat. U., Chunchon, Republic of Korea, 2001—02. Mem. editl. bd. Jour. Environ. Mutagen & Carcinogen, 1999—; author: (poetry) Hedgehoggy Love. Mem. Chun Environ. Movement Assn., Chunchon, 1996—2003; v.p. Chunchon Lit. Assn., 2002—; councilor Kangwon Lit. Assn., 2003—. Recipient Excellent Rsch. award, Korea Environ. Mutagen Soc., 1998; grantee Grant, Korea Ministry of Health and Welfare, 1997—2000, Korea Rsch. Found., 1997—98, Korea Ministry of Health and Welfare, 1998—2000, Korea Ministry of Sci. & Tech., 2001—; fellow Vis. Prof. Abroad, Kangwon Nat. U., 1989—90, 1999—2000. Achievements include patents for Anti-inflammatory carboxycyclic acetal pregnane derivatives; Whitening agent containing chestnut innershell; Flavonoids as cancer chemopreventive agent; Mungbean extract which cotains vitexin and isovitexin, ane its production method; Biological active mixture of vegetables and its antioxidative and free radical scavenging effect; Biological active mixture of Cassiae seed and its antioxidative and free radical scavenging effect; Cosmetic mixture which contains mungbean extract; Face washing mixture which contains mungbean flavonoid and protein; Safflower extract as blood circulator; Safflower extract as analgegics. Home: Greentown 102-405 Toegyedong Kangwon Chunchon 200-752 Republic of Korea Office: Coll Pharmacy Kangwon Natl Univ Hyojadong 200-701 Chunchon Gangwon-do Republic of Korea Office Fax: 033-253-9647; Home Fax: 033-253-9647. Personal E-mail: myheo@kangwon.ac.kr.

HEPPNER, DONALD GRAY, JR., biomedical executive, immunology research physician, army officer; b. Lynchburg, Va., Jan. 17, 1956; s. Donald Gray Sr. and Nathalie (Ward) H.; m. Mary Virginia Leach, June 12, 1983; children: Charlotte Nathalie, Virginia Dearing, William Lynch. BA in Biochemistry/German Lit., U. Va., 1978, MD, 1983. Diplomate Am. Bd. Internal Medicine, 1986, Am. Bd. Infectious Diseases, 1990, 2003, Gen. Staff Coll, Ft. Leavenworth, Tex., 1993. Commd. capt. U.S. Army, 1987, advanced through grades to col., 2002; intern in internal medicine U. Minn. Hosps. and Clinics, Mpls., 1983-84, resident in internal medicine, 1984-86; rsch. assoc. Dight Lab., U. Minn., Mpls., 1987; with emergency medicine dept. Abbot North Western Hosp., Mpls., 1986-88; fellow infectious diseases U. Md., Balt., 1988-90; infectious disease officer Dept. Immunology, Walter Reed Army Inst. of Rsch., Washington, 1990-93; asst. chief dept. immunology Armed Forces Rsch. Inst. Med. Scis., Bangkok, 1993-94, chief dept. immunology and medicine, 1994-97; overseas malaria vaccine trial coord. dept. immunology Walter Reed Army Inst. Rsch., Forest Glen, Md., 1997-99, chief dept. immunology, 2001—06; dir. U.S. Army Malaria Vaccine Program, 2001—07, acting dir. divsn. communicable diseases and immunology, 2006, dir. divsn. of malaria vaccine devel., 2006—08; dep. comdr. Walter Reed Army Inst. Rsch., 2008—11; v.p. clin. devel. Crucell Biologics, Johnson & Johnson Co., Rockville, Md., 2011—. Attending physician Walter Reed Army Med. Ctr., Washington, 1991-93, 2003-06; advisor NRC, 1995-97. Contbr. more than 97 articles to profl. jours. Mem. Com. on Fgn. Rels., Charlottesville, Va., 1983—. Decorated Order Mil. Med. Merit; recipient Legion of Merit, Kiwanis Internat. World Svc. medal, 2009; named Alumnus of Yr., Va. Episcopal Sch., 2011; finalist Berry prize, Fed. Medicine, 2008. Fellow: ACP, Royal Asiatic Soc., Royal Geog. Soc.; mem.: VFW (life), Coun. Fgn. Rels.(Wash.), Sons Revolution Va. Soc., Order of St. John (officer 2010—, bd. gov. 2010—, hospitaller 2009—), Armed Forces Infectious Disease Soc. (life), Sons Am. Revolution Va. Soc., Soc. Colonial Wars State of Va., Aztec Club 1847, Am. Soc. Tropical Medicine and Hygiene, Soc. War 1812, U. Va. Alumni Assn. (life), Philos. Soc. Washington, Am. Legion, Mil. Order Fgn. Wars. Achievements include development and testing of malaria vaccines for military and public health benefit. Office: Crucell Biologics Ste 305 6110 Executive Blvd Rockville MD 20852-3903 Office Phone: 301-945-0940. Business E-Mail: gray.heppner@crucell.com.

HEPPNER, GLORIA HILL, research administrator, educator; b. Gt. Falls, Mont., May 30, 1940; d. Eugene Merrill and Georgia M. (Swanson) Hill; m. Frank Henry Heppner, June 6, 1964 (div. 1975); 1 child, Michael Berkeley. BA, U. Calif., Berkeley, 1962, MA, 1964, PhD, 1967. Damon Runyon postdoctoral fellow U. Wash., Seattle, 1967—68; asst. and assoc. prof. Brown U., Providence, 1969-79, Herbert Fanger meml. lectr., 1988; chmn. dept. immunology, dir. labs., sr. v.p. Mich. Cancer Found., Detroit, 1979-91; dir. breast cancer program Karmanos Cancer Inst., 1991—2003, dep. dir., 1994—2003; assoc. chair for rsch. dept. internal medicine Wayne State U. Sch.

Medicine, Detroit, 1991—2001, asst. dean cancer program, 2002—03, spl. asst. to dean, Karmanos Cancer Inst., 2003, assoc. v.p. rsch., 2003—, interim v.p. rsch., 2006—07. Mem. external adv. com. basic sci. program M.D. Anderson Hosp. and Tumor Clinic, Houston, 1984-94; mem. external adv. com. Case Western Res. U. Cancer Ctr., Cleve., 1988—, Roswell Park Meml. Inst., Buffalo, 1991-98; Sarah Stewart meml. lectr. Georgetown U., Washington, 1988; bd. sci. counselors Nat. Inst. Dental Rsch., 1993-97. Editor: Macrophages and Cancer, 1988; mem. editl. bd. Cancer Rsch., 1989-93, Jour. Nat. Cancer Inst., 1988, Sci., 1988-92; contbr. over 200 articles to sci. jours. Bd. dirs. Lyric Chamber Ensemble, 1996-99, Detroit Symphony Orch., 2005-. Recipient Mich. Sci. Trail-Blazer award State of Mich., 1987; fellow Damon Runyon-Walter Winchell Found., 1967-69. Mem. AAAS, Am. Assn. for Cancer Rsch. (bd. dirs. 1983-86, chmn. long-range planning com. 1989-91), Am. Assn. Immunologists, Metastasis Rsch. Soc. (bd. dirs. 1985-89), Women in Cancer Rsch. (nat. pres.), Internat. Differentiation Soc. (v.p. 1990-92, pres. 1992-94), LWV (bd. dirs. Grosse Pointe, Mich. 1989-95). Democrat. Avocations: music, theater. Office: 5057 Woodward Detroit MI 48201 Home Phone: 313-886-9038; Office Phone: 313-577-8848. E-mail: heppnerg@wayne.edu.

HEPTINSTALL, ROBERT HODGSON, physician; b. Keswick, Eng., July 22, 1920; s. James A. and Mabel (Sanders) H.; m. Ann Enraght Porter, Jan. 25, 1950; children: Gillian, Jonathan, James, Caroline. MB, BS, London U., 1944, MD, 1948. Intern, house surgeon Charing Cross Hosp., London, 1944; jr. lectr. pathology St. Mary's Hosp., London, 1947-50, sr. lectr. pathology, 1950-60; vis. prof. pathology Washington U., St. Louis, 1960-62; assoc. prof. pathology Johns Hopkins Med. Sch., Balt., 1962-67, prof. pathology, 1967—69, 1988—92, Baxley prof. pathology, dir. dept. Balt., 1969-88; pathologist in chief Johns Hopkins Hosp., 1969-88, disting. svc. prof. pathology, 1992—2008, emeritus prof., 2008—. Pathology study sect. NIH, 1963-67, pathology tng. com., 1967-71; sci. adv. bd. Nat. Kidney Found., 1969-73. Author: Pathology of the Kidney, 1966, 6th edit., 2007; editor Lab. Invest, 1976-81. With M.C., Royal Army, 1944-47. Recipient gold medal Danish Surg. Soc., 1984, David M. Hume Meml. award Nat. Kidney Found., 1986. Mem.: Renal Pathology Soc. (pres. 1980—83), Internat. Soc. Nephrology (v.p. 1981—84, Jean Hamburger award 1999), Am. Soc. Nephrology (pres. 1972—73, John P. Peters award 1993), Internat. Acad. Pathology (Maude Abbott lectr. 1983, Disting. Pathologist award 2002), Danish Soc. Nephrology (hon.), Alpha Omega Alpha.

HER, SONG, biotechnologist, director; b. Seoul, Republic of Korea, Feb. 14, 1961; BS in Food Engring., Yonsei U., 1985, MS in Biotech., 1991, PhD in Biotech., 1996; postdoc. in Psychiatry, Stanford Med. Sch., 1996—99, Harvard Med. Sch. Mclean Hosp., 1999—2000. Dir. bio imaging ctr. Korea Basic Sci. Inst., 2006—, rschr. Nat. Agenda Program, 2001—; rsch. fellow Dept. Cellular & Structural Biology, UTHSCSA, Tex., 1991—93; rsch. assoc. Dept. Psychiatry & Behavioral Sci., Stanford U. Sch. Medicine, 2000—05; prin. investigator Bioimaging, Korea Basic Sci. Inst., Republic of Korea, 2006—; adj. prof. Dept. Biomed., Hallym U., Republic of Korea, 2008—; mem. Mental Heathe Food R & D Project, Korea Food Rsch. Inst., 2001—, Brain longevity Project, Korea Inst. Oriental Medicine, 2001—; rschr. Ministry Health & Welfare, Republic of Korea, 2004—05, Basic Rsch. Promotion Fund Korea Govt., 2006—09; mem. Rsch. Fund, 2001—, INNO Biz Small & Medium Bus. Administrn., 2007—09. Peer reviewer Jour. Life Sci. Archives Pharmacal Rsch., Exptl. Neurobiology, Clin. Endocrinology, Jour. Microbiology & Biotech. Contbr. articles to profl. publs. Recipient award, Stanford U., 1998, Membership Soc. Neurosci., 1997; Postdoc. fellowship, Korean Rsch. Found., 1997. Achievements include research in molecular mechanisms associated with in vivo dynamic GR signaling in animal models using molecular imaging technologies; unites molecular biology and in vivo imaging; visualization of the cellular function and the follow-up of the molecular process in living organisms without perturbing; development of molecular imaging technology with significant technological advances that permit imaging at the nano, cellular or whole organism levels; enable the use of novel drugs to visualize events or genetic engineering of novel reporter genes both in vitro and in vivo. Office: Korea Basic Sci Inst 192-1 Hyoja 2 Dong Chuncheon Gangwon Do 200 701 Republic of Korea

HERB, EDMUND MICHAEL, optometrist, educator; b. Zanesville, Ohio, Oct. 9, 1942; s. Edmund G. and Barbara R. (Michael) H.; divorced; children: Sara, Andrew; m. Jeri Herb. OD, Ohio State U., 1966. Pvt. practice optometry, Buena Vista, Colo., 1966—; past prof. Timberline campus Colo. Mountain Coll.; past clin. instr. Ohio State U. Sch. Optometry. Mem. Am. Optometric Assn., Colo. Optometric Assn. Home: 16395 Mt Princeton Rd Buena Vista CO 81211-9505 Office: 115 N Tabor St Buena Vista CO 81211 Office Phone: 719-395-6356.

HERBACZYNSKA-CEDRO, KRYSTYNA MARIA, physiologist; b. Warsaw, Jan. 28, 1939; d. Wojciech and Maria Herbaczynski; m. Adrzej Cedro (div. 1982); children: Krzysztof, Wojciech; m. Leszek Ceremuzynski, 1985. Cert. physician, Med. Sch. Warsaw, 1963; MD, Polish Acad. Scis., Warsaw, 1968, PhD, 1975. Hosp. physician, Warsaw, 1963-68; rsch. asst. Med. Rsch. Ctr.-Polish Acad. Scis., Warsaw, 1964-72, asst. prof., 1975-80, 1983-88, prof., 1988—. Vis. scientist Wellcome Rsch. Labs., Beckenham, England, 1982; lectr. Postgrad. Med. Sch., Warsaw, 1990—; mem. coun. European Soc. Clin. Investigation, 1974—76, v.p., 1976—77. Contbr. articles to profl. jours. including Nature, Cardiovascular Rsch., Am. Jour. Cardiology, others. Organizer Solidarity Union, Warsaw, 1980. Wellcome Trust rsch. fellow Royal Coll. Surgeons, London, 1972-74, Med. Rsch. Inst., Midhurst, Eng., 1981-82. Mem. Internat. Soc. Heart Rsch. Achievements include research in hormonal and metabolic response to acute myocardial infarction, in therapeutic implication of experimental studies. Office: Polish Acad Sci Med Rsch Ctr Ul. Prof. Adolfa Pawinskiego 5 02-106 Warsaw Poland E-mail: ceremuzynska@cmdik.pan.pl.

HERBERMAN, RONALD BRUCE, medical association administrator, immunologist; b. Bklyn., Feb. 26, 1940; married, 1963; children: Steve, Holly. BA, NYU, 1960, MD, 1964; MD (hon.), U. Rome, 1986. Intern, asst. resident medicine Mass. Gen. Hosp., 1964-66; clin. assoc. immunologist USPHS, 1966-68; sr. investigator immunology br. Nat. Cancer Inst. NIH, Bethesda, Md., 1968-71, head cellular and tumor immunolology sect. Lab. Cell Biology, 1971-74, chief Lab. Immunodiag., 1975-81, chief biol. therapeutic br., 1981-85; prof. medicine and pathology Sch. Medicine U. Pitts., 1985—; founder U. Pitts. Cancer Inst., 1985; assoc. vice chancellor Cancer Rsch. U. Pitts. Sch. Medicine, Hillman prof. oncology, prof. medicine; chief med. officer oncology Intrexon Corp., 2009—. Acting assoc. dir. biol. response program Nat. Cancer Inst., NIH, 1981-85, dir. immunodiag. contract program, 1972-76; mem. FDA rev. panel diagnostic tests, 1979-83; mem. AIDS clin. drug devel. com. Nat. Inst. Allergy and Infectious Disease, 1986—. Sect. editor: Jour. Immunology, 1974-77; assoc. editor Cancer Rsch., 1975-80, Clin. Immunoology and Immunopathology, 1978-85, Jour. Immunol. Methods and Clin. Immunol. Therapy, 1980-90, Jour. Clin. Immunology, 1981—, Jour. Nat. Cancer Inst., 1972-80. Recipient Lifetime Sci. Award, Inst. for Advanced Studies in Immunology and Aging. Fellow Am. Acad. Microbiology, Clin. Immunol. Soc., Soc. Biol. Therapy (pres. 1996-98), Am. Soc. Clin. Oncology; mem. Soc. Leukocyte Biology (pres. 1984), Am. Soc. Clin. Investigation, Am. Assn. Immunologists, Am. Assn. Cancer Rsch., Internat. Soc. Interferon Rsch. Achievements include research in cancer immunology and immunotherapy; immunodiagnstic tests for cancer; natural killer cells characterization and in vivo role in resistance to cancer and AIDS. Office: Intrexon Corp 1872 Pratt Dr Blacksburg VA 24060 Home Phone: 412-963-0846; Office Phone: 540-961-0725. Business E-Mail: herbermanrb@upmc.edu. *

HERBERT, MICHAEL E. (MICKEY), retired insurance company executive, health care consulting executive; m. Jackie Curkan Herbert; children: Eleni, Christopher, Stephanie, Mickey, Charlie. BA, Swarthmore Coll., Pa., 1967; MBA, Harvard U., 1969; LHD (hon.), U. Bridgeport. With one of the leading healthcare reform and healthcare mgmt. orgns., 1971; fellow tng. program HMO Wharton Sch. Univ. of Pa., 1976; sr. fellow exec. program in managed care Univ. of Mo.; founder, CEO Physicians Health Svc. Inc. (sold to HealthNet, Inc.), 1976—98; v.p., corp. sec. InterStudy, 1971—76; past chair America's Health Insurance Plan (formerly American Assn. of Health Plans), dir., mem. exec. strategy task force; past chmn. Bridgeport Regional Bus. Coun., mem. exec. com.; past chair American Managed Care and Rev. Assn.; charter chmn. Acad. for Healthcare Mgmt.; bd. dirs. UroCor Inc., Patient Care, Milw., 2002—, chair, 2011—; pres., CEO ConnectiCare, 2005—10; co-chair. Conn. Health Insurance Policy Coun., 2006. Past adj. prof. U. Conn.; past pres. Barnum Mus. and P.T. Barnum Found., dir.; former pres., CEO, majority owner Bridgeport Bluefish Baseball Club; officer Atlantic League; gen. ptnr. Phila. Barrage, BridgeSports; mem. com. of trustees Hopkins Sch.; bd. dirs. Labyrinth Healthcare Group. Past chmn. Bridgeport Area Found., Conn., United Way Ea. Fairfield County, bd. dirs., dir. emeritus; past pres. bd. associates U. Bridgeport; past bd. mem. Bayer Inst.; chmn. Greater Bridgeport Area Found.; dir. Sch. Ethical Edn.; mem. honorary bd. dir. Spl. Olympics Conn.; with local boards of YMCA and Jr. Achievement; mem. Entrepreneurial Hall of Fame, Charlotte, NC. Recipient won many athletic awards, West Point Soc. award, Wash. DC, Good Scout award, Fairfield County Boy Scouts of America, Entrepreneur of the Year award, Southern New Eng. Excellence in Tourism Image award, Coastal Fairfield County Conv. & Visitor Bur., 2001, Excellence in Partnership award, BridgeSports, 2001, Trustee's Merit award, Housatonic Cmty. Coll., 2002; named Boy of the Year, Prince Georges County, Bridgeport's City Champion, State of Conn.; named one of Fastpitch Hall of Fame, Conn. Amateur Softball Assn. Mem.: Assn. of Conn. HMOs (charter pres.). Office: Patient Care 633 W Wisconsin Ave Ste 1310 Milwaukee WI 53203 Office Phone: 414-271-1790. *

HERBST, ARTHUR LEE, obstetrician, gynecologist; b. NYC, Sept. 14, 1931; s. Jerome Richard and Blanche (Vatz) H.; m. Lee Ginsburg, Aug. 10, 1958. AB magna cum laude, Harvard Coll., 1953, MD cum laude, 1959; DSc (hon.), N.E. Ohio U., 2001. Diplomate Am. Bd. Ob-gyn. (bd. dirs. 1985-93, dir. div. gynecol. oncology 1989-91). Intern Mass. Gen. Hosp., Boston, 1959—60, resident, 1960—62; resident in ob-gyn. Boston Hosp. for Women, 1962—65; instr., assoc. prof. ob-gyn. Mass. Gen. Hosp. and Harvard U. Med. Sch., Boston, 1965—76; Joseph B. DeLee prof. ob-gyn. U. Chgo., 1976—84, Joseph B. DeLee Disting. Service prof., 1984—2005, disting. prof. emeritus, 2005—; chmn. dept. ob-gyn. Chgo. Lying In Hosp., 1976—2001; chmn. exec. com. U. Chgo. Hosps. and Clinics, 1980. Chmn. dean's adv. bd. U. Ariz. Coll. Sci., 2006—. Contbr. articles to profl. jours. Fellow Royal Coll. Obstetricians and Gynecologists (hon.), Inst. Med., Nat. Acad. Scis.; mem. AMA, ACS, ACOG, Am. Gynecol. and Obstet. Soc. (pres. 1997-98), Am. Assn. Profs. Ob-Gyn., Ctrl. Assn. Obstetricians and Gynecologists, Chgo. Gynecologic Soc., Soc. Pelvic Surgeons, Endocrine Soc., Infertility Soc., Soc. Gynecologic Oncologists, Inst. Advanced Multicultural & Minority Medicine (bd. mem. 2008-). Office: U Chgo Med Ctr 5841 S Maryland Ave MC2050 Chicago IL 60637-1463 Home: 4451 N Camino Sumo Tucson AZ 85718

HERBST, JEFFREY HOWARD, psychologist; b. Balt., May 27, 1965; s. Nathan and Rita H. Herbst; m. Elise Rachel Bennett, June 18, 1989; children: Nathaniel Robert, Sarah Mina. BA, U. Md. Baltimore County, 1987, PhD, 1996. Rsch. asst. U. Md. Baltimore County, Catonsville, Md., 1986-87, grad. tchg. asst., 1987-91; psychologist Nat. Inst. on Aging, Balt., 1987—. Guest rschr. Union Meml. Hosp., Balt., 1996; adj. asst. prof. psychology Loyola Coll., Columbia, 1998—. Reviewer: Pacing and Clin. Electrophysiology; contbr. articles to profl. jours. Com. mem. Temple Oheb Shalom, Balt., 1997. Mem. APA, Phi Kappa Phi. Avocations: model trains, stamp collecting/philately, genealogy, computers. Office: Nat Inst on Aging 5600 Nathan Shock Dr Baltimore MD 21224-6825 Home: 11025 Kimball Crest Dr Alpharetta GA 30022-6494 Fax: (410) 558-8307. E-mail: jh202f@nih.gov.

HERDEG, HOWARD BRIAN, retired physician; b. Buffalo, Oct. 14, 1929; s. Howard Bryan and Martha Jean (Williams) H.; m. Beryl Ann Fredricks, July 21, 1955; children: Howard Brian III, Erin Ann Kociela. Student, Paul Smith's Coll., 1947-48, U. Buffalo, 1948-50, Canisius Coll., 1949; DO, Phila. Coll. Osteo. Medicine, 1954; MD, U. Calif., Irvine, 1962. Diplomate Am. Acad. Pain Mgmt. Intern Burbank (Calif.) Hosp., 1954-55; practice medicine specializing in gen. medicine, surgery and pain mgmt., Woodland Hills, Calif., 1956—; ret., 2004. Chief med. staff West Park Hosp., Canoga Park, Calif., 1971-72, trustee, 1971-73; chief family practice dept. West Hills Hosp. and Med. Center (formerly Humana Hosp. West Hills, 1982-85, 88-89), exec. com., 1984-85, 88-89. Mem. Hidden Hills (Calif.) Pub. Safety Commn., 1978-82; bd. dirs. Hidden Hills Cmty. Assn., 1971-73, pres. 1972; bd. dirs. Hidden Hills Homeowners Assn., 1973-75, pres. 1976-77; bd. dirs. Woodland Hills Freedom Season, 1961-67, pres. 1962; mem. Hidden Hills City coun., 1984-2001, mayor pro tem, 1987-90, mayor, 1990-92. Recipient Disting. Svc. award Woodland Hills Jr. C. of C., 1966. Mem. Woodland Hills C. of C. (dir. 1959-68, pres. 1967), Calabasas C. of C., Tustin Hist. Soc., Tustin Santa Ana Rotary Club, Rotary (pres. elect 2005-06, pres. 2006—, dir. 2007-), Theta Chi, Gamma Pi. Republican. Home: 13368 Savanna Tustin CA 92782-9143 Personal E-mail: docherdeg@cox.net.

HERDMAN, ROGER C., physician, policy analyst; b. Newton, Mass., Sept. 22, 1933; s. Gordon Walker Herdman and Florence Elizabeth Watson; m. Ellen Tifft, May 13, 1957; children: Jennifer, Lisa, Prudence, Betsey. BS, Yale U., 1955; MD, Yale U. Sch. Medicine, 1958. Intern U. Minn., resident in pediat. Mpls., 1958-61, fellow in pediat., 1962-65, asst. prof., 1965-69; prof. pediat. Albany Med. Coll., NY, 1969-79; dep. health commr. N.Y. State Dept. Health, Albany, 1969-77, dir. pub. health, 1977-79; v.p. profl. affairs Meml. Sloan-Kettering Cancer Ctr., NYC, 1979-83; asst. dir. Congl. Office Tech. Assessment, Washington, 1983—92, acting dir. to dir., 1993-96; sr. scholar Inst. Medicine-Nat. Academies, Washington, 1996-2000, dir. Nat. Cancer Policy Bd., 2000—, dir., Health Care Services Bd., 2005—; dir. NRC Nat. Cancer Policy Bd., 2000—05. Bd. dirs. InHealth, 2006—. Author: Organ Transplantation, 1997, Safety of Silicone Breast Implants, 1999; contbr. numerous articles to med. jours. Lt. USNR, 1959-61. Office: Inst Medicine 500 5th St NW Keck 758a Washington DC 20001 Office Phone: 202-334-1302.

HERESCO-LEVY, URIEL AUREL, psychiatrist, researcher; b. Bucharest, Romania, June 15, 1954; arrived in Israel, 1972; s. Tsalik Haim and Mariana A. (Moscovitch) Heresco-L.; m. Tal Fuchs, July 12, 1989; children: Lior, Yuval. BA, Hebrew U., Jerusalem, 1977; MD, Tel Aviv U., 1986. Israel sci. coun. accreditation in psychiatry; U.S.A. ednl. commn. for fgn. med. graduates accreditation. Resident psychiatry Ezrath-Nashim-Herzog Meml. Hosp., Jerusalem, 1986-90, sr. psychiatrist, 1990-93, dir. women psychiatry divsn., 1993—, dir., psychiatry dept., 2004—; fellow biol. psychiatry and psychopharmacology rsch. Albert Einstein Coll. Medicine, NYC, 1991-93. Vis. scientist, lectr. Brown U., Providence, 1990; cons. psychiatry, res. officer Israel Def. Forces, 199-98—; sci. mem. Latner Inst. Rsch. in Psychiatry, Jerusalem, 1993-; mem. admission com. Hadassah Med. Sch., Hebrew U., Jerusalem; assoc. prof., 2006-. Contbr. articles to profl. jours. Sci. grantee Eli Lilly & Co., Indpls., 1996, Scottish Rite Schizophrenia Rsch. Program, Lexington, Mass., 1996, Stanley Found. US, 2005, Israel Acad. Scis., 2009; recipient Young Scientist award Nat. Alliance for Rsch. on Schizophrenia & Major Depression, Chgo., 1997, 99, Independent Investigator award NAt. Alliance Rsch. Schizophrenia & Major Depression, NY, 2006. Fellow Israel Soc. Biol. Psychiatry, Collegium Internat. Neuro-Psychopharmacologycum; mem. European Coll. Neuropsychopharmacology. Achievements include invention of patent for use of glutemmergic amino acids in movement Aisorsers, 2010. Avocations: literature, music. Office: Ezrath Nashim Herzog Meml Hosp Ghivat Shaul POB 3900 91035 Jerusalem Israel Office Phone: 972 2 5310900. Business E-Mail: heresco@md.huji.ac.il.

HERGENROEDER, ALBERT C., pediatrician, educator, BS, U. Pitts., 1976, MD, 1980. Diplomate Am. Bd. Pediatrics, 1993, Am. Bd. Pediatrics-sports medicine, 2004, Am. Bd. Pediatrics-adolescent medicine, 2009. Resident pediat. Duke Univ. Med. Ctr., Durham, 1981—83; fellow adolescent medicine Univ. Washington, Seattle, 1984—85, head of sports medicine sects. Baylor Coll. Med., head of adolescent medicine, prof. pediat.; chief young women's clinic Tex. Children's Hosp., chief sports medicine clinic, chief adolescent medicine svc. Fellow: Soc. for Adolescent Medicine, Am. Acad. of Pediat., Am. Coll. of Sports Medicine; mem.: Soc. for Pediatric Rsch., Am. Bd. of Pediat. Office: Texas Children's Hospital Clinical Care Center 11th Fl 6701 Fannin St CC 1710.00 Houston TX 77030 Office Phone: 832-822-4887.

HERKNER, BERNADETTE KAY, occupational health nurse; b. East Liverpool, Ohio, Apr. 29, 1947; d. Charles R. and Anna G. (Parr) Geon. Diploma in nursing, East Liverpool City Hosp., 1973; BS in Applied Sci., Youngstown U., Ohio, 1976. RN, Ohio, Mich., Fla; cert. in audiometrics, siprometry, ICD-9-CM; cert. case mgr.; cert. occupl. health nurse specialist. Charge nurse emergency rm. East Liverpool City Hosp., 1976-78; sr. occupl. health nurse specialist Dow Chem. N.Am., Midland, Mich., 1978-2000. Active Vol. Action Ctr. Midland County. Recipient Best Bedside Nurse, Centennial award for svc. to humanity, 1973, Ctrl. Mich. Outstanding Occupl. Health Nurse of Yr. award, 1993; named Miss Hope Columbiana County unit Am. Cancer Soc., 1977. Mem. Am. Assn. Occupl. Health Nurses (cert.), Mich. Assn. Occupl. Health Nurses (bd. dirs.), Emergency Nurses Assn., Mich. Nurses Assn., Ctrl. Mich. Assn. Occupl. Health Nurses (bd. dirs., corr. sec. 1986-90, rec. sec. 1990-91, pres. 1991-95, legis. chmn. 1995-96), East Ctrl. Mich. Emergency Nurses, Ohio Emergency Nurses Assn. (membership sec.), Case Mgmt. Soc. Am.

HERLIHY, JAMES P., critical care specialist, educator; MD, Georgetown U., 1984. Diplomate Am. Bd. Internal Medicine, 1987, Am. Bd. Internal Medicine- pulmonary disease, 2004, Am. Bd. Internal Medicine- critical care medicine, 2005. Resident in internal medicine Letterman AMC, San Francisco, 1985—87; fellow in cardiovascular disease Mass. Gen. Hosp., Boston, 1991—95; assoc. clin. prof. Baylor Coll. of Medicine; hosp. affiliation includes St. Luke's Episcopal Hospital. Office: Saint Luke's Episcopal Hospital 6624 Fannin Ste 1700 Houston TX 77030 Office Phone: 713-526-5511. Office Fax: 713-790-9408. E-mail: phka@aol.com.

HERLIHY-CHEVALIER, BARBARA DOYLE, retired mental health nurse; b. Cambridge, Mass., June 28, 1935; d. William A. and Aloyse V. (Mahoney) Doyle; m. Timothy J. Herlihy, Aug. 20, 1955 (dec. Oct. 1983); children: Michael, Ann-Marie, Sharon, Ellen, Stephen, Kathleen, James; m. Robert J. Chevalier, May 28, 1994 (dec. Oct. 1995); 1 stepchild, Ron. RN, Mass. Gen. Hosp., 1956; BS in Human Svcs., N.H. Coll./So. N.H. U., 1983; MS in Nursing, Anna Maria Coll., 1987. Nat. cert. instr. and coord. remotivation therapy. Pvt. duty nurse N.E. Bapt. Hosp., MGH, Boston, 1956, St. John's Hosp., Lowell, Mass., 1966—70; charge nurse Tewksbury Hosp. Mass. Dept. Pub. Health, Mass., 1970—76; coord. remotivation therapy Danvers State Hosp., Mass., 1976—79; registered cmty. mental health nurse Mass. Dept. Mental Health, Lawrence, 1979—91; ret., 1991. Mental health nurse Lowell Adult Day Treatment, Mass., 1991—94; bd. dirs. New Eng. Gerontol. Assn., 2009. Fellow Nat. Remotivation Therapy Orgn. (nat. instr., coord., Dorothy Hoskins

Smith honorarium 2001); mem. Internat. Adv. Coun. Remotivation Therapy, Nat. Remotivation Therapy Orgn., Inc., Bay State Remotivation Coun. Home Phone: 603-883-3702. Personal E-mail: barbhc@comcast.net.

HERLIN, GUNNAR, radiologist; b. Stockholm, Feb. 8, 1951; s. Gunnar Herlin and Gudrun Ekman; m. Gudrun Ekman, Sept. 23, 1995; children: David Ekman, Alice Ekman. Degree, Karolinska Inst., Stockholm, 1977. Lic. Karolinska Inst., 1979, specialist clin. chemistry Karolinska Inst., 1985, specialist radiology Karolinska Inst., 1992. Specialist Dr. Radiology Dept. Karolinska U. Hosp. Huddinge, Stockholm, 1992—98; sr. radiologist Karolinska U. Hosp., 1998—. Contbr. scientific papers. Office: Karolinska University Hosp Huddinge Glömstavägen Stockholm 141 86 Sweden

HERLING, IRVING MARC, internal medicine educator, cardiologist; b. NYC, Jan. 7, 1949; MD, U. Pa., 1974; degree in Biology magma cum laude, City Coll. NY. Diplomate Am. Bd. Internal Medicine, Am. Bd. Cardiovasc. Disease. Intern Hosp. of U. Pa., Phila., 1974-75, resident in internal medicine, 1975-77, fellow in cardiology, 1977; mem. faculty U. Pa. Sch. Medicine, 1977—, assoc. prof. medicine. Fellow ACP, Am. Coll. Cardiology; mem. Am. Heart Assn. (fellow coun. clin. cardiology). Office: U Pa Med Ctr Penn Tower #800 3400 Spruce St Ste 907 Philadelphia PA 19104-4206 also: 250 King of Prussia Rd Radnor PA 19087 Office Phone: 215-662-7700, 610-902-2273.

HERLONG, H. FRANKLIN, retired physician; b. Augusta, Ga., Apr. 16, 1948; BA, Duke U., 1970; MD, Med. U. SC, 1974. Assoc. prof. medicine Johns Hopkins Sch. Medicine, 1974—, assoc. dean student affairs, 1992—2007. Chmn. student affairs sect. Thirteen Sch. Consortium Med. Schs., 2005—07. Mem.: ACP, Am. Assn. Study Liver Disease. Avocation: gardening. Office: 4940 Eastern Ave Baltimore MD 21224 Office Fax: 410-550-7861. Business E-Mail: hherl@jhmi.edu.

HERMAN, DAVID CHRISTOPHER, ophthalmologist; b. Mpls., Oct. 25, 1957; s. Wallace Martin and Katherine Ann Herman; m. Karen Herman; children: Nicole Marie, Daniel Christopher. BS, U. Ill., Urbana, 1979; MD, Mayo Med. Sch., Rochester, Minn., 1983; MS in Med. Mgmt., U. Texas, Dallas, 2000. Cert. Am. Bd. Ophthalmology, 1988. Sr. staff fellow NIH, Bethesda, Md., 1987—88; cons. in ophthalmology Mayo Clinic, Rochester, 1988—2011; dir. Mayo Clinic Employee & Cmty. Health, 2007—11, Mayo Clin. Affiliated Network, 2010—11; pres., COO U. Health Sys. Eastern Carolina, Greenville, NC, 2011—. Bd. mem. Minn. Bd. Med. Practice, Mpls., 1990—99; bd. trustees Minn. Med. Assn., Mpls., 1994—96; med. dir. Mayo Clinic Rochester, 2003—07, exec. bd., 2007—10; bd. dirs. Immanuel-St. Joseph's Health Sys., Mankato, 2005—11, Inst. Clin. Sys. Improvement, Bloomington, Minn., 2006—11, St. Mary's Hosp., Rochester, 2007—10, Rochester Meth. Hosp., 2007—11, Mayo Health Sys., 2009—11. Mem. Ronald McDonald House, Rochester, 2004—, Ronald McDonald House Charities, 2011—. Fellow: Am. Acad. Ophthalmology. Avocation: aviation. Office: University Health Systems Eastern Carolina 2100 Stantonsburg Rd PO Box 6028 Greenville NC 27835-6028 Home: 3007 Westview Dr Greenville NC 27834

HERMAN, DAVID JAY, orthodontist; b. Rome, NY, Oct. 4, 1954; s. Maurice Joseph and Bettina S. (Stiener) H.; m. Mary Beth Appleberry, Apr. 11, 1976; children: Jeremiah D., Kellin A. BA in Biology, San Jose State U., 1976; DDS, Emory U., 1981; MS in Orthodontics, U. N.C., 1992, MPH, 1992. Comdr. USPHS, 1981-97; advanced gen. practice resident Gallup (N. Mex.) Indian Med. Ctr., 1983-84; Navajo area dental br. chief Window Rock, Ariz., 1986-89; mem. grad. residency com. U. NC, Chapel Hill, 1990—92; Navajo area orthodontic specialist Shiprock, N.Mex., 1992-97; clin. dir. Nizhoni Smiles Inc., 1992—98; pvt. practice Farmington, N.Mex., 1998—; pres. Four Corners Orthodontics, Inc., 1998—. Mem. health adv. bd. Navajo Reservation Headstart, 1986—89; health promotion/disease prevention cons. USPHS/Indian Health Svc. Navajo Area, Window Rock, 1986—89; cons. Ariz. IHS Periodontal Health Task Force, 1986—90. Asst. wrestling coach Winslow (Ariz.) H.S., 1984-86, Gallup High Sch., 1987-89, Chapel Hill H.S., 1991-92, Farmington H.S., 1992—, Aztec H.S., 1998-2000; mem. H.S. Youth Wrestling Program, 1992-2000. Recipient Healthy Mothers/Healthy Babies Disease Prevention award, 1988, USPHS Achievement medal, 1985, Headstart Achievement award, 1989, Ariz. Pub. Health Assn. Hon. award, 1989; Nat. Health Svc. Corp. scholar Emory U., 1977-81. Mem. ADA, Am. Assn. Orthodontists, Rocky Mountain Soc. Orthodontists, N.Mex. Dental Soc. Orthodontists (pres. 1998-99), Northwestern Dental N.Mex. Soc. (pres. 1995-96, 2009-10, v.p. 2008-09), Navajo Area Dental Soc. (pres. 1985), Am. Assn. Mil. Orthodontists (sec.reas. 1992, v.p. 1993-94, pres. 1995-97). Avocations: wrestling, weightlifting, jogging, scuba diving, backpacking.

HERMAN, JOAN ELIZABETH, retired health insurance company executive; b. NYC, June 2, 1953; d. Roland Barry and Grace Gales (Goldstein) Herman; m. Richard M. Rasiej, July 16, 1977. AB, Barnard Coll., 1975; MS, Yale U., New Haven, 1977. Actuarial student Met. Life Ins. Co., NYC, 1978-82; asst. actuary Phoenix Mut. Life Ins. Co., Hartford, Conn., 1982-83, assoc. actuary, dir. underwriting rsch., 1983-84, 2nd v.p., 1984-85, v.p., 1985-89, sr. v.p., 1989-98; pres. splty. bus. WellPoint Health Networks, Woodland Hills, Calif., 1998, grp. pres., 1999—2001, pres. splty., sr. and state sponsored progs. divsn., 2002—04; pres., CEO, splty. sr. and state sponsored bus. divsn. WellPoint, Inc., Indpls., 2004—08; pres. Herman & Associates LLC, 2008—. Bd. dirs. PM Holdings, Inc., Phoenix Grp. Holdings, Inc., Phoenix Am. Life Ins. Co., Emprendimiento Compartido, S.A., MRV Communications Inc., 2009—, chmn. bd. dirs., 2009—; v.p. BC Life & Health Co., Profl. Claims Svcs. Inc., Proserv., MEDIX. Contbr. articles to profl. jours. Bd. dirs. Health Ins. Assn. Am., 2002—03; capt. fundraising team Greater Hartford Arts Coun., Hartford, 1986; bd. dirs. Children's Fund Conn., 1992—98, My Sister's Pl. Shelter, Hartford, 1989—94, Western Mass. Regional Nat. Conf. Conn., 1995—98, Greater Hartford Arts Coun., 1997—98, Hartford Ballet, 1989—95, corporator, 1995—98; bd. dirs. Leadership Greater Hartford, 1989—94, chmn. bd. dirs., 1993—94; bd. dirs. So. Calif. Leadership Network, 2003—, South Ctrl. Scholars Found., 2007—; mem. bd. founders Am. Leadership Forum Hartford, 1991—98; corporator Hartford Sem., 1994—98; bd. dirs. Ctr. Dance Arts, 2009—, Am. Red Cross Greater LA, 2010—, Hadassah, Glastonbury, Conn., Temple Beth Hillel, South Windsor, Conn., 1983—84. Fellow: Soc. Actuaries (chair health sect. coun. 1994—95); mem.: Bayer Med. Care (strategic adv. bd. mem.), Vital Data Tech. (strategic adv. bd. mem.), Ctr. Dance Arts (bd. dirs. 2008—), Am. Leadership Forum, Am. Acad. Actuaries (bd. dirs. 1994—97). Jewish. Avocations: reading, swimming, bicycling, jogging, aerobic dancing, hiking. Office Phone: 818-388-5181. Personal E-mail: hermaj1@verizon.net.

HERMAN, MARTIN JOSEPH, orthopaedic surgeon, educator; MD, Columbia U., NY, 1990. Diplomate Am. Bd. Orthopaedic Surgery, lic. NJ, 1992, Pa., 1996. Resident orthop. surgery Robert Wood Johnson Univ. Hosp., 1995; fellow pediatric orthopaedics Campbell clinic Univ. Tenn., 1996; assoc. prof. orthop. surgery and pediat. Drexel Univ.; hosp. affiliation include St. Luke's Hosp.; attending orthop. surgeon St. Christopher's Hosp. for Children. Named one of the Top Doctors, Phila Mag., 2010—11. Office: Saint Christopher's Hospital for Children 3601 A St Philadelphia PA 19134 Office Phone: 215-427-5000. Office Fax: 215-427-5555.

HERMAN, MARY MARGARET, neuropathologist; b. Plymouth, Wis., July 26, 1935; d. Elmer Fredolein and Esther Lydia (Bross) H.; m. Lucien Jules Rubinstein, Jan. 31, 1969. BS in Med. Sci., U. Wis., 1957, MD, 1960. Diplomate Nat. Bd. Med. Examiners, Am. Bd. Anatomic Pathology, Am. Bd. Neuropathology. Intern Mary Hitchcock Meml. Hosp., Hanover, NH, 1960-61; resident in neurology U. Wis. Hosps., 1961-62; intern in pathology Yale U., New Haven, 1962-63, asst. resident in pathology, 1963-64, fellow in neuropathology, 1964-65, rsch. assoc. pathology, 1967-68; fellow in neuropathology Stanford U., Palo Alto, Calif., 1965-66, fellow, acting instr. neuropathology, 1966-67, asst. prof. pathology, 1967-74, assoc. prof., 1974-81; prof., co-dir. divsn. neuropathology U. Va. Sch. Medicine, Charlottesville, 1981-91, prof. clin. pathology, 1991-92; spl. expert neuropathology in clin. brain disorders br. NIMH, Washington, 1991-96, sr. staff scientist, 1996—; neuropathologist NIMH Brain Collection, 1992—, Stanley Fund Brain Collection, 1992—2002. Vis. asst. prof. Albert Einstein Coll. Medicine, Bronx, NY, 1971—72; mem. program project rev. com. Nat. Inst. Neurol. and Communicative Diseases NIH, 1973—77; cons. lab. svc. VA Hosp., Salem, Va., Ctrl. Va. Tng. Ctr., Lynchburg, 1982—92, ad hoc mem. pathology A study sect., 1986—91; cons. neuropathologist DC Med. Examiner's Office, Washington, 1992—, Med. Examiner's Office, No. Va. Dist., Fairfax, 2000—, DC Gen. Hosp., 1992—2002, Howard U. Hosp., 2009—; mentor scientist NIH Intramural Rsch. Tng. award, Fogarty Fellows, Howard Hughes Med. Inst./MCPS/NIH student and tchr. internships program, Stanley Found. scholar's program, Mont. County Pub. Schs. HS Sci. Internship Program. Mem. editl. bd.: Jour. Neuropathology and Exptl. Neurology, 1989—93, 2001—08; contbr. over 200 articles to profl. jours. Recipient Rsch. Career Devel. award, NIH, 1967—72, Staff Recognition award, 2000—06, Faculty Devel. award, Merck Found., 1969. Mem.: AAAS, AMA, Am. Assn. Anatomists, Soc. Biol. Psychiatry, Am. Assn. Neuropathologists (Weil award 1974), Am. Soc. for Investigative Pathology, Soc. for Devel. Biology, Internat. Soc. Neuropathology, Am. Soc. Cell Biology (rsch. fellowship program, mentor scientist summer tchr. 1994), Internat. Acad. Pathology, Soc. In Vitro Biology, Soc. Neurosci. Achievements include research in neuropathology of major mental disorders, neurodegeneration and aluminum neurotoxicity, and embryonal tumors of the CNS. Avocations: tennis, gardening, music. Home: 10008 Stedwick Rd Apt 304 Montgomery Village MD 20886-3718 Office: NIMH NIH 49 Convent Dr Rm BIB80 MSC 4425 Bethesda MD 20892-4425 Office Phone: 301-480-0042. Office Fax: 301-480-0023. Business E-Mail: mh230t@nih.gov.

HERMAN, ROBERTA, insurance company executive; MD, Master's equivalent degree in epidemiology and biostatistics, McGill U., Montreal, Can. Resident internal medicine Royal Victoria Hosp., Montreal, Canada; fellow cmty. medicine McGill U.; practicing internist Harvard Cmty. Health Plan; chief internal medicine Cambridge Ctr.; sr. v.p. health services, chief med. officer Harvard Pilgrim Health Care, 2008—09, interim COO, 2009—10, COO, 2010—. Former chair Chief Med. Officers Leadership Coun. of the Assn. of Health Ins. Plans; former pres. Alliance for Health Care Improvement; guest lectr. Harvard Sch. of Pub. Health. Bd. mem. Planned Parenthood League of Mass. Mem.: American Heart Assn. Greater Boston (bd. chmn.). Office: Harvard Pilgrim Health Care Inc 93 Worcester St Wellesley Hills MA 02481 *

HERMANEK, PAUL, pathologist, educator; b. Vienna, Mar. 8, 1924; s. Karl and Ilse (Steiner) H.; m. Christine Zimmermann, Mar. 5, 1954; children: Peter, Eva. MD, U. Vienna, 1950, U. Münster, 1994. Assoc. prof. U. Vienna, 1966-69; head dept. surg. pathology U. Erlangen, Germany, 1969-72, prof. surg. pathology, 1972-90; emeritus, 1990—. Author: Surgical Oncology, 1986; editor: TNM Classification of Malignant Tumours, 1987, 92, TNM Supplement, 1993, Prognostic Factors in Cancer, 1995, Manual Tumor Documentation, 1995, 2001, Recipient award German Cancer Soc., 1988, European Soc. Surg. Oncology, 1994. Mem. German Soc. Endoscopy (pres. 1983-84), Austrian Soc. Pathology (hon.), German Soc. Surgery (hon.). Roman Catholic. Office: U Erlangen Dept Surgery Krankenhausstr 12 91054 Erlangen Germany Home Phone: 0049-9131-13636; Office Phone: 0049-9131-8533269, 0049-9131-8533279. Office Fax: 0049-9131-8536887. Business E-Mail: susanne.merkel@uk-erlangen.de.

HERMAN-GIDDENS, MARCIA EDWINA, physician associate; b. Washington, Sept. 17, 1941; d. Edwin Parker and Lucy Marshall (Price) Herman; m. G. Scott Herman-Giddens, Sept. 17, 1960; children: Gregory, Marcus, Melantha, Huong; m. Douglas G. Berg, Nov. 8, 1997. B.Health Sci., Duke U., Durham, NC, 1978; MPH, U. N.C., Chapel Hill, 1985, DrPH, 1994. Cert. physician asst. Lab. tech. U. Ala. Med. Ctr., Birmingham, 1962-64; rsch. asst. genetics U. NC, Chapel Hill, 1968-69, dir. injury rsch., 1994-95, adj. prof., sch. pub. health, 1995—; exec. dir. NC Women's Polit. Caucus, Chapel Hill, 1972-73; sr. physician assoc. Duke U. Med. Ctr., Durham, NC, 1979-81, asst. clin. prof. pediat., 1983—94, asst. clin. prof. cmty., family medicine, 1984—89; child maltreatment cons. Pittsboro, NC, 1998—2005; sr. fellow NC Child Advocacy Inst., Raleigh, 2000—05; child and family health cons. Pittsboro, 2005—. Med. dir. Duke U. Med. Ctr. Child Protection Team, 1986—89, N.C. State Child Fatality Prevention Team, Office Chief Med. Examiners, 1995—98; med. cons. Program on Childhood Trauma and Maltreatment, Chapel Hill, 1993—2004; prin. investigator numerous studies on child maltreatment and puberty; mem. Numerous Sci. Orgn., NC Vector Borne Disease Task Force, 2007—. Author: Assignment of Sexual Maturity Stages, 1992, Assessment of Sexual Maturity Stages in Boys, 2005, Assessment of Sexual Maturity Stages in Girls and Boys; contbr. articles to profl. jours., chapters to books; editl. asst.: Medicine and Pediatrics in One Book, 1998, reviewer: numerous med. jours. Chair med. com. NC Child Fatality Task Force, Raleigh, 1991—93, mem., 1991—95; mem. bd. adjustment Town Chapel Hill, 1980—85; chair Chapel Hill Coop. Presch., 1969—71; pres. Tick-borne Infections Coun. NC, 2005—; bd. dirs. Planned Parenthood, Orange County, 1989—95, Durham County, 1989—95. Recipient Svc. award for outstanding svc. to the health of North Carolinians, U. N.C. Sch. Pub. Health, 1994, Outstanding Indirect Svc. award APHA, 1997; named Alumna of the Yr., Duke U. Physician Asst. Program, 1983, Hall of Fame, 2002. Mem. Ambulatory Pediatric Assn., Sigma Xi. Achievements include research on child fatality in North Carolina that assisted with the formation of legislatively appointed task force and child fatality prevention sys., research on child sexual abuse and child abuse homicides, research on onset of puberty in children in U.S. Office: 1450 Russell Chapel Rd Pittsboro NC 27312 Office Phone: 919-542-5573. Personal E-mail: medherman@gmail.com. Business E-Mail: mherman-giddens@unc.edu.

HERMANN, ROBERT CHARLES, JR., neurologist, educator; b. Temple, Tex., Aug. 1, 1944; s. Robert Charles and Jewel Irene Hermann; m. Mary Frances Goggans; children: Robert Charles III, Randall Scott. MD, U. Tex., Galveston, 1965—69. Cert. neurologist Am. Bd. Neurology/Psychiatry, 1979, in electromyography Am. Assn. Electrodiagnostic Medicine, 1988, clinical neurophysiologist Am. Bd. Neurology/Psychiatry, 1996. Med. internship U. Tex. Med. Br., 1969—70, assoc. prof., 2002—03; neurology resident Mayo Clinic, Rochester, Minn., 1970—75, cons. neurology, asst. prof, 1975—88, 1990—2002, cons. neurology Scottsdale, Ariz., 1988—90, emeritus prof. Rochester, 2002—06; clin. prof. neurology/medicine U. Tex. Health Sci. Ctr., San Antonio, 2003—. Dir. electromyography lab. U. Tex. Med. Br., 2002—03; emg lab. dir. UTHSCSA, San Antonio, 2003—. Contbr. articles to profl. jours., chapters to books. Maj. USAF, 1971—73, Lackland AFB. Recipient Woltman award for outstanding resident in neurology, Mayo Clinic, 1975, Tchr. of Yr. award, Mayo Med. Fellows Assn., 1982, 1984, 1991, 1997, Outstanding Tchr. award in basic scis., Mayo Med. Sch., 1985, Tchg. Hall of Fame, Mayo Med. Fellows Assn., 1997, Spl. Recognition award for tchg. in clin. neurophysiology, Mayo Clinic, 2002, Hall of Fame, Taylor HS, 2003, Taylor Legends award, 2006; named Super Doctor, Tex., 2010. Fellow: Am. Acad. Neurology; mem.: Am. Assn. Neuromuscular and Electrodiagnostic Medicine. Office: Univ Tex Health Sci Ctr SA 4647 Medical Dr San Antonio TX 78229 Business E-Mail: hermannr@uthscsa.edu.

HERMANN, ROBERT EWALD, retired surgeon; b. Highland, Ill., Jan. 28, 1929; s. Ewald E. and Erna (Pabst) H.; m. Barbara Bower, Aug. 23, 1952 (dec. Aug. 1980); m. Polly Dreher, Mar. 8, 1986; childrn: Robert Jr., Barry, Monty. AB cum laude, Harvard U., 1950; MD, Washington U., St. Louis, 1954. Diplomate Am. Bd. Surgery. Intern, resident Univ. Hosps., Cleve., 1954-61; chmn. gen. surgery Cleve. Clinic, 1969—94, emeritus cons. dept. gen. surgery, 1994—96; clin. prof. surgery Case Western Res. Sch. Medicine, Cleve., 1970—96. Dir. Am. Bd. Surgery, Phila., 1975-81; mem. Residency Rev. Com., Chgo., 1975-81. Author: Surgery of Gallbladder, Bile Ducts, Pancreas, 1979, Surgical Practice of Cleveland Clinic, 1985; contbr. over 180 articles to med. jours., 53 chpts. to books. Trustee Cleve. Clinic Found., 1976-77. Capt. M.C. U.S. Army, 1956-57. Recipient Roswell Park Gold medal Buffalo Surg. Soc., 1993. Mem. ACS (gov. 1981-87, v.p. 1996-97, Disting. Svc. award 1994), Am. Surg. Soc., German Surg. Soc. (hon.), Internat. Surg. Soc., Internat. Coll. Surgeons (hon.), Soc. Surg. Oncology, Soc. Surgery Alimenatary Tract (pres. 1988-89), Assn. Program Dirs. Surgery (pres. 1979-81), Ea. Surg. Soc. (pres. 1985-86), Pan-Pacific Surg. Assn. (v.p. 1991-93), Joint Commn. on Accreditation of Healthcare Orgns. (bd. commrs. 1997-2002). Republican. Avocations: tennis, golf, sailing, music. Home: 1 Bratenahl Pl Apt 1403 Bratenahl OH 44108-1156 Office: Cleve Clinic A-80 9500 Euclid Ave Cleveland OH 44195-0001 Personal E-mail: rhermannmd@aol.com.

HERMINGHAUSEN, ELFRIEDE GERDA, physician; Abitur, U., Celle, Germany; PhD in Medicine, Munich. Lic. medicine practitioner Munich, pilot PPLA, Munich, cert. internal medicine Munich, aviation medicine Munich, travel medicine. Tng. as specialist Internal Medicine in Various Hosps.; pvt. practice, 1981—. Mem.: AIOPA, Am. Aerospace Med. Assn., German Aerospace Med. Assn., German Assn. Internal Medicine.

HERNANDEZ, JOSE YOLANDO BALAGTAS, surgeon; b. Manila, Philippines, Dec. 30, 1938; came to U.S., 1964; s. Pablo Manio and Leoncia (Balagtas) Hernandez; m. Minerva Cuadrante, Dec. 17, 1966; children: Jay, Myra, Maureen. MD, U. St. Thomas, Manila, Philippines, 1962. Diplomate Am. Bd. Surgery, Am. Bd. Colon-Rectal Surgery, Internat. Bd. Proctology. Fellow: Soc. Philippine Surgeons in Am., Southeastern Surgical Congress, Internat. Acad. Proctology, InterAm. Coll. Physicians and Surgeons, Internat. Coll. Surgeons, Am. Soc. Colon Rectal Surgeons, Am. Soc. Abdominal Surgeons; mem.: AMA, Coll. Internat. Chirurgiae Digestiva, Endoscopic Surgeons, Am. Gastroent. Roman Catholic. Avocations: ballroom dancing, golf, music. Home and Office: 3053 Carlow Cir Tallahassee FL 32309-3302

HERNANDEZ, MARIBEL, cardiac electrophysiologist; Grad., Stanford U. Diplomate Am. Bd. Internal Medicine, 1989, Am. Bd. Internal Medicine-cardiovasc. disease, 1991, Am. Bd. Internal Medicine-clin. cardiac electrphysiology, 1994. Intern Santa Clara Valley Med. Ctr.; resident New England Deaconess Hosp., Harvard Med. Sch.; fellow Med. Coll. of Pa., Lankenau Hosp.; with Bryn Mawr Hosp., 1999, Lankenau Med. Ctr., 1999; clin. asst. prof medicine Thomas Jefferson Univ. Hosp. Author: (article) Heart Disease in Women. Mem.: ACP, Am. Coll. of Cardiology, N. Am. Soc. of Pacing & Electrophysiology. Office: Lankenau Medical Center MOB E Ste 556 100 Lancaster Ave Wynnewood PA 19096 Office Phone: 610-649-6980. Office Fax: 610-649-6990.

HERNANDEZ, MINERVA CUADRANTE, physician, consultant; d. Arsenio Francisco Cuadrante and Mercedes Rontas Relunia; m. Jose Yolando Balagtas Hernandez, Dec. 17, 1966; children: Jay, Myra, Maureen. MD, U. St. Tomas, Manila, 1962. Intern St. Clare's Hosp., Schenectady, NY, 1964—65; jr. resident Springfield Hosp., Mass., 1965—66; pediatric resident Trumbull Meml. Hosp., Warren, Ohio, 1966—69; resident, gen. pathology Allentown Hosp., Pa., 1969—70; staff physician Fla. State Hosp., Chattahoochee, 1974—78, Southwestern State Hosp., Thomasville, Ga., 1980—85; physician advisor Profl. Found. for Health Care, Tampa, Fla., 1985—89; staff physician Tricare Clinic, Atlantic Beach, Fla., 1993—97; med. dir. Spectrum Health Care Partnership, Cecil Field, Fla., 1995—96; physician Fla. State U., Thagard Student Clinic, Tallahassee, 1997—2004. Mem. Springtime Tallahassee, 1983. Fellow: Am. Bd. Disability (analyst), Am. Coll. Utilization Rev. Physicians; mem.: Panhandle Med. Soc., Assn. Am. Philippine Physicians, Am. Acad. Family Physicians. Avocations: ballroom dancing, creative writing, reading. Home: 3053 Carlow Cir Tallahassee FL 32309 Office: Fla State Univ Thagard Student Health Ctr Tallahassee FL 32309

HERNANDEZ ALTEMIR, FRANCISCO, surgeon; b. Burjasot, Spain, Apr. 8, 1937; s. Jose Hernandez and Maria Altemir; m. Maria Luz Montero, Mar. 18, 1965; children: Susana, Sara, Sofia, Elena, Rebeca. Licenciado en medicina y cirugia, Madrid, 1961; Licenciado medico estomatologo, Facultad de Estomatologia, Madrid, 1963; MD, Facultad de Medicina, Zaragoza, Spain, 1978. Peds. cons. Facultad Medicina, Madrid, 1971—, tramatology and orthopaedics cons., 1971—, plastic surgery cons., 1970—; head dept. oral and maxillofacial surgery Hosp. Miguel Servet, Zaragoza, 1975—. Head dept. maxillofacial surgery Red Cross Hosp., Zaragoza, 1976—; extraordinary collaborator prof. U. Zaragoza. Patentee in field; contbr. articles to profl. jours. such as Jour. Maxillofacial Surgery, 1986, Jour. Cranio-Maxillofacial Surgery, 1998, 2000; contbr articles to jours. Mem. ECMFS, SECOM, Royal Medicine Acad. Achievements include invention of immediately voluntary lenthening device for tennis rackets and other perfections that modify the racket aesthetic and dynamics; patents for endotracheal tube; nasotracheal tube for exploration and intubation; perfectioned surgical drainage; device for auscultation of the air flow to facilitate endotracheal intubation; design of security device for a better control of impacted third molars during exodontias; development of submental route visted using the laryngael mask airway; submental intubation with bronchial fibroscopy; modifications of nasotracheal intubation with a new orotracheal tube; technique to facilitate the extraction of the permanent dental structures in pollicular phase; endotracheal tube modified to make easy nasotracheal intubation; subzygomaticomalar endotracheal intubation in selected cases; design of new method of installing ectopic digestive catheter in different medical and veterinary specialities; endotracheal ectopic intubations; ectopic digestive probes; interocclussal oral wedge of curved jugal surface with space; device to isolate from the surgical field the possible orotracheal commissural tube with or without lingual malleable retractor; patents for proposal of endoscopic surgery to the skull base with submental access a new way; proposal for the application on the new terms accesibility and inaccesibility in the classic and renowned TNM Staging and in what we refer to as G(n): TNM. Avocations: basketball, tennis, fishing. Office: Planta O B Calle Fray Luis Amigo no 8 50006 Zaragoza Aragon Spain Office Phone: 976-270719. Personal E-mail: drhernandezaltemir@yahoo.es. Business E-Mail: drbernandejaltemir@yahoo.es.

HERNANDEZ-ANDRADE, EDGAR ARMANDO, physician, researcher; b. Mexico City, May 29, 1961; s. Armando Hernandez Guzman and Aurora Andrade Martinez; life ptnr. Donatella Luisa Gerulewicz Vannini; children: Citlali Hernandez, Maria Fernanda Hernandez, Ana Lucia Hernandez, Natalia Aurora Hernandez. MD, Nat. Inst. Tech., Mex., 1984; M in Med. Sci., Autonomous U. Mex., Mexico City, 1997; PhD, U. Lund, Sweden, 2001. Cert. obstetrics and gynecology Mex., perinatal medicine Mex. Specialist in obstetrics and gynecology Women Hosp., Mexico City, 1991—95; fetal medicine specialist Nat. Inst. Perinatal Medicine, Mexico City, 1992—, assoc. prof. perinatal medicine, sr. rschr., 1997—, coord. fetal therapy program, 2003—; postdoctoral rschr. Kings Coll. Hosp., London, 2001—03; fetal medicine rsch. coord. Vall D Hebron U. Hosp., Barcelona, 2003—. Rsch. advisor Nat. Coun. Sci., Santiago, Chile, 2003—; coord. fetal medicine found. Fetal Medicine Found., Mexico City, 2003—; guest rschr. dept. obstetrics and gynecology Lund U. Hosp., 2003—; dir. early fetal devel. rsch. program Nat. Inst. Perinatal Medicine, Mexico City, 2004—. Recipient 1st prize in clin. rsch., Nat. Congress Obstetrics and Gynecology, Mex., 1995, Young Rsch. award, Internat. Fedn. Obstetrics and Gynecology, 1997, Juan de la Cierva Rsch. award, 2005; named Best Resident in Obstetrics and Gynecology, Nat. Coun. Health, Mex., 1991, Best Resident in Perinatal Medicine, Nat. Inst. Perinatal Medicine, Mex., 1992; named one of the Best Nat. Young Specialist, Pres. of Mex., 1992; fellow, Fetal Medicine Found., 2001—03; scholar, Nat. Coun. Sci. and Tech., 1997-2001; ATL-Phillips Rsch. grantee, 1998, Cerebra Orgn. grantee, 2004, Thrasher Rsch. grantee, 2005. Achievements include development of ultrasound method to quantify fetal organs blood perfusion; Ultrasound method to track the fetal blood; research in Doppler method to select anemic fetuses; fetal brain blood perfusion; fetal brain development; fetal amino acids; fetal organ blood perfusion; fetal cardiac abnormalities; middle cerebral artery peak systolic velocity in the management of the anemic fetus; fetal brain blood perfusion. Avocations: music, athletics, travel, movies.

HERNÁNDEZ GARRIDO, MARITA, medical educator, researcher; b. Dortmund, Germany, Feb. 2, 1970; PhD in Medicine, 2000. Prof., rschr. U. Valladolid, Spain, 2010—. Avocation: photography. Office: IBGM Sanz y Forés 3 Valladolid 47003 Spain Office Fax: 34983184800. Business E-Mail: maritahg@ibgm.uva.es.

HERNÁNDEZ-ZAMORA, EDGAR, medical researcher; b. Mexico City, Apr. 26, 1969; PhD, Escuela Nacional de Ciencia Bilogicas, Inst. Politécnico Nacional, 2008. Prof. U. Autónoma Metropolitana Xochimilco, 1993—96; técnico lab. clínico Hosp. Infantil Méx. Federico Gómez, 1996—97; master specializing in biochemistry Escuela Nacional de Ciencias Biológicas, Dept. Bioquímica. Inst. Politécnico Nacional, 1997—99; rsch. fellow Ctr. Médico Nacional siglo XXI, 1998—2000; rschr. med. scis. Inst. Nacional de Rehab., 2000—. Prof. Escuela Preparatoria Oficial No. 30, 1992—93, Ctr. Cultural U. Justo Sierra, 1999—2001, U. Tecnológica Méx., 2004—05, Escuela Superior Rehab., 2005—11. Recipient Tchg. Merit, Centro Cultural U. Justo Sierra. Fellow: Soc. Mexicana Genética; mem.: Sistema Institucional de Investigadores Secretaría de Salud, Sistema Nacional Investigadores, Agrupación Mexicana para el estudio de la Hematología, Soc. Mexicana de Bioquímica. Avocations: movies, running. Home: Sur 167 1716 Mexico Cty 08020 Mexico Personal E-mail: edgarhz1969@gmail.com.

HERNDON, CHRISTOPHER N., physician; BS in Biochemistry and Cell Biology, U. Calif., San Diego, 1999; MD Cum Laude, Yale U. Sch. Medicine, 2004. Diplomate Am. Bd. Og-gyn., 2009, lic. Med. Bd. Calif., 2008. Clin. fellowship reproductive endocrinology & infertility U. Calif. San Francisco, 2008—; integrated res. program ob-gyn. & reproductive medicine Brigham & Women's Hosp. Mass. Gen. Hosp., 2004—08. Rep. Com. Global Medicine, Mass. Med. Soc., 2005—06; co-dir. founder Med. Student Clin. Skills & Simulation Tng. Ob-Gyn., 2008—; instr. Med. Student Clin. Anatomy Tchg. Sessions, 2009—; CPX instr. U. Calif., 2009—, rep. Med. Student Edn. Coun, 2010—, preceptor PISCES Longitudinal Integrated Curriculum, 2010—; dir. ethnomedine Northeast Amazon Program Amazon Cons. Team, 2000—06; co-founder, exec. editor Yale Jour. Health Policy, Law & Ethics, 1999—2001. Contbr. articles to profl. publs., chapters to books. Recipient award, Conservation, Food & Health Found., 2001—03, Devel. Marketplace Competition winner, World Bank, 2003—04, award, Fred Found., 2004, Outstanding Leadership award, Dept. Ob-gyn. & Reproductive Scis. U. Calif., San Francisco, 2011; fellow, William H. Scout Meml., 1998, UC San Diego Rsch. Adv. Group, 1999; Travel fellow, Downs Internat. Health, 2000, Rsch. fellow, Yale U. Student Rsch., 2000—02, Pfeiffer Rsch. fellow, 2003—04, Kanbar Ctr. Simulation Ednl. grant, U. Calif., 2010. Achievements include research in low cost and complexity in vitro fertilization, national & global disparities in access to infertility care; gene expression analysis of endometrium in women with adenomyosis; effectiveness of a focused OB/GYN clinical skills workshop for medical students; disease concepts and treatment by tribal healers of an Amazonian forest culture. Home: 22 Terra Vista Ave Apt B4 San Francisco CA 94115

HERNDON, JAMES HENRY, orthopedic surgeon, educator; b. LA, Oct. 31, 1938; s. James Greene and Kathleen Theresa (Murphy) H.; m. Geraldine Grace Armiger, Feb. 26, 1971; chidlren: Jennifer, Jonathan. BS, Loyola U., LA, 1961; MD, UCLA, 1965; MA, Brown U., 1979; MBA, Boston U., 1990; MA (hon.), Harvard U., 1999; DHL (hon.), Loyola-Marymount U., 2004. Diplomate Am. Bd. Orthopaedic Surgery (bd. dirs., pres. 1991-92). Intern Hosp. of U. Pa., Phila., 1965-66, resident in surgery, 1966-67; resident in orthopaedics Mass. Gen. Hosp., Boston, 1970, chief resident in orthopaedics, 1967-70; asst. clin. prof. orthopaedic surgery Mich. State U., Grand Rapids, 1974-77, assoc. clin. prof., 1977-78; prof., chmn. dept. orthopaedics Brown U., Providence, 1979-88; surgeon-in-chief dept. orthopaedic surgery R.I. Hosp., Providence, 1979-88; chief dept. orthopeadics and rehab. Presbyn. U. Hosp., Pitts., 1988-98; Silver prof., chmn. dept. orthopaedic surgery U. Pitts., Pitts., chief orthopaedics, 1988-98, assoc. sr. vice chancellor health svcs., 1995; v.p. med. svcs. Pitts. Edn. Ctr., 1995-98; chmn. ptnrs. dept. orthopaedic surgery Mass. Gen. Hosp., 1998—2004, Brigham and Women's Hosp., 1998—2004. Examiner Am. Bd. Orthopaedic Surgery, Chgo., 1977—2004, pres., 1990-91; William H. and Johanna A. Harris prof. orthop. surgery Harvard Med. Sch., 2004-. Reviewer Jour. Bone and Joint Surgery, 1975—, bd. trustees, 2005-, treas., 2007—, JBJS trustees-tres., 2006-09, chmn., 2008; contbr. articles to profl. jours., chpts. to books; author books in field. Trustee Meeting St. Sch., Providence, 1984-88, Harmarville Rehab. Hosp., Pitts., 1989-95; mem. bd. govs. Arthritis Found., Providence, 1984-88, Pitts., 1989—98, Boston, 1998-2004; bd. dirs. Make A Wish Found., chmn., 1998-99; bd. trustee, chmn. JBJS, 2008-. Recipient Edith and Carl Lasky Meml. award UCLA Med. Sch., 1965, Bronze award Am. Congress Rehab. Medicine, 1972, Clin. Rsch. award N.Y. Med. Soc., 1974. Fellow ACS, Am. Acad. Orthopaedic Surgeons (treas. 1994-97, pres. 2003—04), Royal Coll. Surgeons, Eng.; mem. Am. Orthopaedic Assn. (pres. 1999-00), Orthop. Rsch. Soc., Residence Rev. Com. Orthopaedic Surgery (past chmn.), Am. Soc. Surgery of Hand, Internat. Soc. Orthopaedic and Traumatology (chmn. US sect., 1996-2006), Internat. Soc. for Quality in Health Care, Brasilian Soc. Orthopaedics and Traumatology, Hellenic Assn. Orthopaedic and Traumatology, Romanian Soc. Surgery of the Hand, Assn Bone and Joint Surgeons. Office: Massachusetts Gen Hosp White 542 55 Fruit St Boston MA 02114-2696

HERNEZ-BROOME, GINA, sports psychologist; B in Psychology, U. Colo., Colorado Springs; M in Indsl. & Orgnl. Psychology, PhD in Indsl. & Orgnl. Psychology, Colo. State U. Faculty U. Rockies, LLC, 2009—. Program mgr., design and delivery faculty team, mem., rsch. faculty team Ctr. for Creative Leadership, Colorado Springs, Colo. Office: University of the Rockies LLC 555 E Pikes Peak Ave Colorado Springs CO 80903-3612 Office Phone: 719-442-0505. Business E-Mail: hernez-broomeg@rocky.edu. *

HERNIGOU, PHILIPPE, orthopedist, educator; b. France, Jan. 11, 1950; Prof. orthop. surgery U. Paris, 1988—. Chief orthop. dept. Hosp. Henri Mondor. Office: Hosp Henri Mondor 51 Ave Du Marec Paris 75015 France Office Fax: 33 1 49812608. Business E-Mail: philippe.hernigou@wanadoo.fr.

HEROS, ROBERTO COSME C., neurosurgeon; b. Havana, Cuba, Sept. 27, 1942; m. Deborah O.; children: Elsa, Rob, Carlos. MD, U. Tenn., Memphis, 1968. Diplomate Am. Bd. Neurol. Surgery. Intern in surgery Mass. Gen. Hosp., Boston, 1968-69; asst. resident gen. surgery, 1969-70; resident in neurosurgery, 1972-77; asst. in neurosurgery, 1976-77; attending neurosurgeon Presbyn. U. Hosp., Pitts., 1977-79; assoc. chief neurosurgery, 1979-80; asst. prof. neurosurgery U. Pitts., 1977-80, dir. neurosurgery residents ednl. program, 1979-80; asst. prof. surgery Harvard Med. Sch., Boston, 1980-83; assoc. prof. surgery, 1983-89; prof. surgery, 1989-90; Lyle A. French prof., chmn. dept. neurosurgery U. Minn., 1990-95; prof., chair dept. neurol. surgery U. Miami, 1995—. Dir. U. Miami Internat. Health Ctr. Chmn. editl. bd. Neurosurgery, 1988; contbr. articles to profl. jours. Chmn. Brain Attack Nat. Coalition, neurovasc. com. World Fedn. Neurosurg. Soc. Maj. USAF, 1970—72. Recipient Medal of Surgery U. Tenn., 1968, Dean's medal, 1968. Fellow: ACS; mem.: World Congress Neurol. Surgeons (v.p. 1986—87, pres. 2005—09), Neurosurg. Soc. Am., Am. Acad. Neurol. Surgeons (pres. 2001), Am. Assn. Neurol. Surgeons (pres. 2002), Alpha Omega. Office: U Miami Med Sch 1095 NW 14th Terr Miami FL 33136-1407 Office Phone: 305-243-4572. E-mail: rheros@med.miami.edu.

HEROUX, ALAIN, cardiologist, educator; MD, Universite Laval, Can., 1981. Diplomate Am. Bd. Internal Medicine, Am. Bd. Internal Medicine-cardiovasc. disease. Resident internal medicine Laval Univ. Med. Ctr., Quebec, Canada, 1982—85; resident cardiovasc. disiease Royal Victory Hosp., Quebec, Canada, 1986—87; asst. prof. medicine Rush Med. Coll.; prof. medicine cardiology Loyola Medicine, med. dir. heart failure and heart transplantation. Office: Loyola University Medical Center Bldg 111 - Rm 1110 2160 S 1st Ave Maywood IL 60153 Office Phone: 708-327-2738.

HERRELL, STANLEY DUKE, surgeon, educator; b. Arlington, Va., Sept. 12, 1964; BA in Chemistry with Summa cum laude, U. Richmond, 1986; MD, U. Va. Sch. Medicine, 1990. Asst. prof. Med. U. SC, 1997—2000, U. Kans. Med. Ctr., 2000—01; assoc. prof., dept. urologic surgery Vanderbilt U. Med. Ctr., 2001—, med. dir., med. ctr. east oper. suites, 2005—, bd. mem., 2009—. Dir. & fellowship dir. Vanderbilt Endourology-Minimally-Invasive Urologic Surgery & Robotics, 2001—; chmn., robotics com. Vanderbilt U. Sch. Medicine, 2003—; mem., practice guidelines & practice guidelines oversight coms. Am. Urol. Assn., 2007—. Recipient Tchg. award, U. Va., Dept. Urology. Mem.: ACS, Am. Urol. Assn., Soc. Laparoendoscopic Surgeons, Endourological Soc., Am. Urol. Assn., Phi Beta Kappa, Alpha Omega Alpha. Avocations: computers, cooking. Office: A-1302 MCN VUMC Dept Urologi Nashville TN 37232-2765 Office Fax: 615-322-8990. Business E-Mail: duke.herrell@vanderbilt.edu.

HERRERA, GUILLERMO ANTONIO, pathologist, educator, researcher; b. Havana, Cuba, Mar. 16, 1952; came to U.S., 1967; s. Guillermo S. and Olga (Del Castillo) H.; m. Elba A. Turbat, Dec. 23, 1972; 1 child, Marlene F. Student, U. Miami, 1970; MD cum laude, U. P.R., 1975. Diplomate Am. Bd. Pathology, Am. Bd. Anat. and Clin. Pathology; cytopathology added qualification bd.; lic. physician Fla., N.Mex., Ala., Miss., La., Mo. Intern categorical pathology Brooke Army Med. Ctr., Ft. Sam Houston, Tex., 1975-76, resident pathology, anatomic and clin., 1975-79, chief resident, 1978-79; asst. prof. dept. pathology Sch. Medicine and Dentistry U. Ala., Birmingham, 1982-87, scientist II Nephrology Rsch. and Tchr. Ctr. Sch. Medicine, 1982-88, dir. nephropathology Schs. Medicine and Dentistry, 1987-88, assoc. prof. dept. pathology, 1987-88, prof. pathology, head surg. pathology, 1991-95, sr. scientist Comprehensive Cancer Ctr., 1991-95, acting med. dir. Sch. Cytotech., 1991-93, faculty mem. Grad. Sch., 1991-95; assoc. prof., head surg. pathology U. Miss. Med. Ctr., 1989-91; head surg. pathology, attending pathologist VA Hosp., Birmingham, 1991-95; sr. scientist, co-dir. EM Core Facility Comprehensive Cancer Ctr. Ala., 1991-95; prof. pathology, medicine, cell biology La. State U., Shreveport, 1996—2006, chmn. dept. pathology, 1996—2006; prof. St. Louis (Mo.) U., 2006—, chmn. dept. pathology, 2006—. Assoc. pathologist Palm Beach Pathology, Good Samaritan Hosp., West Palm Beach, Fla., 1988-89; faculty Grad. Sch. U. Miss., 1989-91; cons. pathologist VA Hosp., Jackson, 1990-91; attending pathologist, head surg. pathology VA Hosp., Birmingham, 1991-95; acting med. dir. Sch. Cytotech., U. Ala., Birmingham, 1991-93, acting head cytopathology, 1991-93, faculty mem. Grad Sch., 1991-95; sr. scientist Comprehensive Cancer Ctr. Ala., co-dir. EM Core facility, 1991-95; cons. Overton Brooks VA Hosp., Shreveport, La. Mem. editl. bd.: Ultrastructural Pathology and Pathology Case Revs., 1995—, Human Pathology and Applied Immunohistochemistry and Molecular Morphology, 2001—, manuscript reviewer: Applied Pathology, Diagnostic Cytopathology, Am. Jour. Medicine, Am. Jour. Kidney Diseases, Archives of Pathology and Laboratory Medicine, 2005, Ultrastructural Pathology, Stain Tech. and Histochemistry, Am. Jour. Clin. Pathology, Pathobiology, Human Pathology, Cancer, Kidney Internat., Pathology Rsch., Practice and Annals of Saudi Medicine, Am. Jour. Pathology, mem.: NIH rev. panel, assoc. editor: Ultrastructural Pathology Jour., 2004—; contbr. articles to profl. jours., chpts. to books. Maj. M.C., U.S. Army, 1974-82, col. USAR, 1988-96, ret. Grantee U. P.R., 1972-75, Brooke Army Med. Ctr., Ft. Sam Houston, 1978-79, U. Ala., Birmingham, 1983-86, 87-88, Universita Degli Studi di Milano, 1984, VA, 1986—, Nat. Cancer Inst., 1991—, NIH, 1992—, Ala. Kidney Found., 1992-93, Leukemia Soc. Am., 1997-99. Mem.: N.Y. Acad. Scis., Birmingham Soc. Pathologists (v.p. 1987—88), Tex. Electron Microscopy Soc., Internat. Acad. Pathology, Arthur Purdy Stout Soc. Surg. Pathologists, Am. Soc. Nephrology, Rsch. Soc., Soc. Advancement Sci., Renal Pathology Soc. (chmn. tng. com. 1996—98, sec.-treas. 1999—2005), Soc. Ultrastructural Pathology (sec.-treas. 1988—91, treas. 1991—99), Electron Microscopy Soc. Am., Armed Forces Soc. Lab. Scientists, Am. Soc. Clin. Pathology, Alpha Omega Alpha. Roman Catholic. Home: 3583 Conroy Rd Apt 1117 Orlando FL 32839 Office Phone: 314-577-8475. Business E-Mail: gherrer1@slu.edu.

HERRERA-LLERANDI, RODOLFO EDUARDO, surgeon, educator; b. Guatemala City, Guatemala, Aug. 6, 1915; s. Carlos and Chusita (Llerandi) H.; m. Odette Lefebre, June, 1954 (div. 1961); m. Evelina Gonzalez, 2003. BA, Paris U., 1932, BA, BPh, 1934; BS, MIT, 1938; MD, Harvard U., 1942; D (hon.), Francisco Marroquin U., Guatemala, 1995. Diplomate Am. Bd. Surgery. Resident and fellow in surgery Mass. Gen. Hosp., Boston, 1942-47; instr. in surgery Harvard Med. Sch., Boston, 1945-47; chief of surgery Hosp. San Vincente, Guatemala City, Guatemala, 1948-58; hon. prof. surgery U. De San Carlos, Guatemala City, 1955-67, Hosp. Mil., Guatemala City, 1955-67; dean and prof. surgery U Francisco Marroquin Sch. of Medicine, Guatemala City, 1978—; surgeon in chief U. Hosp. Esperanza, 1963—. Pres. Nat. Congress Medicine, 1956-57, Nat. Anti-TB Assn., Guatemala, 1960-62, Fund. Chusita Llerandi de Herrera, Guatemala, 1972—. Contbr. articles to profl. jours, sci. mags. Cons. Nat. Anti-TB Assn., Guatemala, Child Welfare Assn., Guatemala. Capt. Guatemalan Army. Decorated comdr. Legion of Honor France, chevalier Order St. Fortunat, Order Rodolfo Robles, Order Elisa Molina de Stahl Guatemala; recipient Orden del Quetzal, Gold medal, Mass. Gen. Hosp., 1961, U. San Carlos, 1967, Disting. Citizen diploma, Municipality de Guate, Guatemala, 1980, Banco Indsl., S.A., 1989, Rotary Club Guatemala, 1989. Mem. Internat. Soc. Surgery (nat. del. 1977-91), Am. Assn. Thoracic Surgeons (hon.), Coll. of Physicians and Surgeons of Guatemala. Avocations: helicopter pilot, collector mayan relics, Russian icons. Office: F Marroquin U Med Sch Med 6a Ave 7-55 Zona 10 01010 Guatemala City Guatemala Office Phone: 2415-9000 ext. 1513. Business E-Mail: llerandi@ufm.edu.gt.

HERRERO, CLEMENTE, social sciences educator; b. Spain, June 29, 1942; PhD in Philosophy and History, U. Valencia, 1973. Prof. social scis. U. Autonoma Madrid, 1997—.

HERRERO DE LUCAS, ANGEL, medical educator, consultant; b. Madrid, June 30, 1969; s. Angel Herrero Munoz and Maria del Milagro de Lucas Valdor; m. Cristina Baraja Bargueño, Dec. 27, 2003; children: Covadonga Herrero Baraja, Silvia Herrero Baraja. BS in Medicine and Surgery, U. Complutense Madrid, 1994, PhD cum laude, 2004; BS in Pharmacy, U. C.E.U. San Pablo Madrid, 2000. Cert. superior tech. expert in contingency of industrial and health risks

Escuela Internat. Alta Dirección Hosp., 2005, in doping control CSD (Superior Bd. Sports, Spain), 2006, orthop. specialist U. Alcalá de Henares, Madrid, 2002, clin. trial monitor Ofcl. Coll. Pharmacists, Madrid, 2001, gen. practitioner Ministry of Edn. Spain, 1994. House officer, gen. medicine Royal Albert Edward Infirmary, Wigan, Lancanshire, England, 1995; house officer, orthop. surgery Gen. Hosp., Birmingham, England, 1995; house officer, gen. surgery Walsall Manor Hosp., England, 1995—96; demonstrator, anatomy Charing Cross Hosp., London, 1996; sr. ho. officer Oldchurch Hosp., Oldchurch, London, England, 1996—97; physician Nat. Championships of Kiokushinkai, Madrid, 1997; cons. physician Fedn. Football, Madrid, 1998—99; physician, chmn. med. svcs. CD Leganes, SAD, Madrid, 1999—2005, FEH (Spanish Weightlifting Fedn.), Madrid, 2004—06; clin. trials monitor Roche Pharma, SA, Madrid, 2001—02, clin. rsch. assoc.; cons. pharmacist Pharmacy Sierra Picos de Europa, Madrid, 2001—; sr. lectr. anatomy Faculty Medicine. U. Complutense Madrid, 2002—; dir. pharmacy Metro Madrid, SA (Underground Svc.), 2002—04; cons. physician Ctr. Geriat. Valdeluz, Madrid, 2004; physician Feminine Master Series Tennis, Madrid, 2005—, Club Atlético de Madrid, SAD, 2005—08, COE (Spanish Olympic Com.), Almeria, Andalucia, Spain, 2005, European Weightlifting Fedn., Madrid, 2005—06, Mediterranean Weightlifting Fedn., Madrid, 2005—06, Masculine Master Series Tennis, Madrid, 2005—; sr. lectr. ofcl. mastery pharm. Faculty of Pharmacy. U. San Pablo CEU, Madrid, 2005—; sr. lectr. ofcl. master, sports orthop. and traumatology U. Catolica San Antonio, Murcia, Spain, 2006—, sr. lectr. dr.'s degree prevention and rehab. injury in sportsman, 2006—; sr. lectr. anatomy Faculty of Odontology. U. San Pablo CEU, Madrid, 2006—; sr. lectr. course joints and health in sport performance: prevention and therapeutics Nat. Bd. Phys. Edn. Cataluna, Spain, 2007—; sr. lectr. prostheses and orthotics Faculty of Medicine. U. San Pablo CEU, 2008—, prof. med. and surg. pathology III, 2008—, chmn. co-dir. Summer Sch., 2008—. Chmn. med. svcs. XVII Spanish Championships of Kiokushinkai, Madrid, 1997; treas. XXX Congress Iberian Soc. of Biomechanics and Biomaterials, Madrid, 2007; sec. III Internat. Interuniversitary Congress on Health and Sports Scis., Madrid, 2007, mem. sci. com., 07; lectr. Internat. Soc. Advancement of Kinanthropometry, Madrid, 2007; cons. dr. Masculine, Feminine and Sr. Master Series Tennis of Rome, 2007. Author: (book) Kinanthropometry: Corporal Composition and Somatotype of Football Players Developing their Physical Activity in Teams of the Autonomous Community of Madrid; contbr. scientific papers (numerous prizes, III Internat. Interuniversitary Congress on Health and Sport Scis., 2007). Mem. Medicus Mundi, Madrid, 1994—2008, Pharm. Mundi, Madrid, 2000—08. Fellow: RCP (Madrid), Ofcl. Coll. Pharmacists, Madrid; mem.: Spanish Assn. Pharm. Industry Drs., AEMEF (Spanish Assn. Drs. Football Team). Achievements include research in valuation of the nutritional status in human populations and their clinical, epidemiological and health promotion applications; numerous patents and pending applications for patents; patents for herceptin as treatment for breast cancer. Office: Univ Complutense Madrid Avenida Ramon y Cajal Madrid 28040 Spain Home: Calle Leopoldo Alas Clarin 6 10 A 28035 Madrid Spain Office Fax: (34) 913 943 4 97; Home Fax: (34) 916 104 934. Business E-Mail: aherrero@med.ucm.es. E-mail: aherrero@ceu.es.

HERRICK, SYLVIA ANNE, health facility administrator; b. Minot, ND, Oct. 5, 1945; d. Sylvester P. and Ethelina (Harren) Theis; m. Michael M. Herrick, Nov. 8, 1969; children: Leo J., Mark A. BSN, U. N.D., 1967; MS in Pub. Health Nursing, U. Colo., Denver, 1970; sch. nurse credential, San Jose State U., 1991; postgrad., Golden Gate U. RN Calif., cert. pub. health nursing, health svc., prof. in healthcare quality. Pub. health nurse Dept. Pub. Health City of Mpls.; instr. nursing San Francisco State U., 1975-88; cons. exec. search Med-Power Resources, Alameda, 1988; coord. health svcs. Alameda Unified Sch. Dist., 1988-91; team mgr. home care nursing and program devel. coord. Vis. Nurse Assn. and Hospice of No. Calif., 1991-99; mgr. disease mgmt. and health awareness East Bay Med. Network, Emeryville, Calif., 1999-2000, interim dir. med. mgmt., 2000; dir. utilization and quality mgmt. Children First Medical Group, Oakland, Calif., 2001—. Spkr. in field; edn. com. mem. Mem.: Calif. Assn. Healthcare Quality, Nat. Assn. Healthcare Quality, Calif. Sch. Nurses Orgn. (bd. dirs., chair edn. Bay Coast sect.), Delta Kappa Gamma. Home: 1711 Encinal Ave Alameda CA 94501-4020 Office Phone: 510-428-3473. Office Fax: 510-450-5868. Business E-Mail: sherrick@mail.cho.org.

HERRINE, STEVEN K., gastroenterologist, educator; BA in Math. and History with highest honors, Oberlin Coll., 1982; MD, Jefferson Med. Coll., 1990. Diplomate Am. Bd. Internal Medicine, 1993, Am. Bd. Internal Medicine-gastroenterology, 1995, Am. Bd. Internal Medicine-transplant hepatology, 2006, lic. Commonwealth of Pa., 1992. Intern Hosp. Univ. Pa., resident; asst. dean. acad. affairs dept. Jefferson Med. Coll., 1995; fellow Thomas Jefferson Univ. Hosp., prof. medicine dept., assoc. med. dir. liver transplantation. Co-author: Use of Over-the-counter Analgesics In Patients With Chronic Liver Disease, 2008, Future Trends in Hepatology: Challenges and Opportunities, 2008, Pegylated Interferon 2a and 2b In Combination With Ribavirin For the Treatment of Chronic Hepatitis C In HIV Infected Patients, 2008, Safety of Peginterferon In The Treatment of Chronic Hepatitis C, 2008, Serologic Markers Do Not Predict Histologic Severity or Response To Treatment In Patients With Autoimmune Hepatitis, 2009, various publs. Named one of the Top Doctors, Phila. Mag., 2010. Fellow: Am. Gastroent. Assn. (2006). Office: Thomas Jefferson University 1020 Walnut St Philadelphia PA 19107 Office Phone: 215-955-6000.

HERRING, SUSAN WELLER, dental educator, anatomist; b. Pitts., Mar. 25, 1947; d. Sol W. and Miriam (Damick) Weller; m. Norman S. Wolf, May 27, 1995. BS in Zoology, U. Chgo., 1967, PhD in Anatomy, 1971. NIH postdoctoral fellow U. Ill., Chgo., 1971-72, from asst. prof. to prof. oral anatomy and anatomy, 1972-90; prof. orthodontics U. Wash., Seattle, 1990—. Vis. assoc. prof. biol. sci. U. Mich., Ann Arbor, 1981; cons. NIH study sect., Washington, D.C., 1987-89; sci. gov. Chgo. Acad. Sci., 1982-90; mem. pub. bd. Growth Pub. Inc., Bar Harbor, Maine, 1982—. Mem. editl. bd. Cells, Tissues, Organs, 1989-2004, Jour. Dental Rsch., 1995-98, 2003—05, Jour. Morphology, 1997—, Integrative Biology 2000—05;, Archives of Oral Biology, 2003-; contbr. articles to profl. jours. Predoctoral fellow NSF, 1967-71; rsch. grantee NIH, 1975-78, 81—, NSF, 1990-92, 94-95. Fellow AAAS; mem. Internat. Assn. Dental Rsch. (dir. craniofacial biology group 1994-95, v.p. 1995-96, pres.-elect 1996-97, pres. 1997-98, Craniofacial Biology Rsch. award 1999), Soc. Integrated Comp. Biol.(chmn. vertebrate zoology 1983-84, exec. com. 1986-88), Am. Soc. Biomechanics, Am. Assn. Anatomists (chmn. Basmajian com. 1988-90), Soc. Vertebrate Paleontology, Internat. Soc. Vertebrate morphology (convenor 4th congress 1994, pres. 1994-97), Sigma Xi. Avocation: violin. Office: U Wash Box 357446 Seattle WA 98195-7446 Business E-Mail: herring@uw.edu. E-mail: herring@u.washington.edu.

HERRLING, PAUL, pharmaceutical executive, researcher, educator; PhD, U. Zurich, Switzerland, 1975. Rschr. Sandoz Pharma, Basel, Bern, Switzerland, 1975—85, dir. Sandoz Rsch. Inst. Berne and dir. preclin. CNS rsch. dept., 1985—92, dir. preclin. rsch. Basel, 1992—94, dir. corp. rsch., 1994—96; head global rsch., mem. pharma exec. com. Novartis Pharma, Basel, 1996—2002, head corp. rsch., 2002—; chmn. of bd. Novartis Inst. Tropical Disease, Singapore; dir. Novartis Institutes Developing World Med. Rsch., 2010—. Post doctorate fellow UCLA Neuropsychiatric Inst.; prof. drug discovery sci. U. Basel; full adj. prof. Harold Dorris Neurobiol. Inst., Scripps Rsch. Inst., La Jolla, Calif.; dir. Friedrich Miescher Inst., Basel, Novartis Rsch. Found. Genomics Inst., La Jolla; mem. working group on rsch. and devel. WHO. Bd. trustees Novartis Found., London, Fondation Maison de la Chimie, Paris, Scripps Rsch. Inst., La Jolla; bd. dirs. Chiron, Emeryville, Calif., Swiss Fed. Institutes Tech., Zurich, TBAllince, NYC, Drug for Neglected Diseases Initiative, Geneva; mem. strategic adv. bd. Agilent, Palo Alto, Calif. Office: Novartis Internat AG 4002 Basel Switzerland *

HERRMANN, PAUL C., physician, chemist; b. Radford, Va., Oct. 7, 1968; s. E. Clifford and Marilyn H.; m. Sarah E. Herrmann, July 7, 1996. BS in Chemistry, Andrews U., 1991; PhD in Chemistry, Stanford U., 1996; MD, Loma Linda U., 2000. Printer's apprentice Quick Print, Loma Linda, Calif., 1983-87; waste water lab. analyst Andrews U., Berrien Springs, Mich., 1987-89, boiler rm. water analyst, 1987-89; rschr. indsl. coop. LECO Corp., St. Joseph, Mich., 1989; sci. and engring. rsch. participant Oak Ridge (Tenn.) Nat. Lab., 1990; tchg. and rsch. asst. Stanford (Calif.) U., 1991-96, rsch. assoc., 1997; clin. fellow NIH, Bethesda, Md., 2000—06; assoc. prof. Loma Linda U. Contbr. articles to profl. jours.; lectr. in field. Mem. AMA, NY Acad. Scis., Phi Kappa Phi, Phi Lambda Epsilon, Pi Mu Epsilon, Sigma Xi. Avocations: archery, history, literature, hiking. Home: 25190 Birch St Loma Linda CA 92354 Business E-Mail: pherrmann@llu.edu. *

HERROD, HENRY GRADY, III, pediatrics professor, allergist, immunologist; b. Oakland, Calif., Apr. 30, 1945; MD, U. Ala., 1972. Cert. allergy and immunology; cert. pediats. Intern U. Wash., Seattle, 1972-73, resident in pediats., 1973-74; resident rsch. assoc. in allergy and immunology NIH, Bethesda, Md., 1974-76; fellow in allergy and immunology Duke U., Durham, 1976-78; physician Le Bonheur Childrens Med. Ctr., Memphis; prof. U. Tenn., Memphis, dean, 1998—2005; fellow Urban Child Inst., Memphis, 2005—. Mem. AAAI, AAI, AAP, APS. Office: Urban Child Inst 600 Jefferson # 221 Memphis TN 38105 Home Phone: 901-685-6016; Office Phone: 901-576-1355. Business E-Mail: hherrod@utmem.edu.

HERSCHMAN, HARVEY ROY, medical educator, researcher; b. Cleve., June 22, 1940; s. Nathan B. and Ida R. Herschman; m. Betty Jean Cox. PhD, U. Calif. San Diego, 1967. Postdoc. fellow Brandeis U., Waltham, Mass., 1967—69; asst. prof. to disting. prof. David Geffen Sch. Medicine, UCLA, 1969—; dir. basic rsch. Jonsson Comprehensive Cancer Ctr. Achievements include discovery of COX-2 enzyme; research in identification of biomarker for malignant melanoma. Office: David Geffen Sch Medicine UCLA 341 Boyer Hall 611 Charles E Young Dr Los Angeles CA 90025 Office Fax: 310-825-1447. Business E-Mail: hherschman@mednet.ucla.edu. *

HERSH, PETER, ophthalmologist, educator; MD John's Hopkins U., 1982. Diplomate Am. Bd. of Ophthalmology. Resident mass. eye & ear infirmary Harvard Med. Sch., fellow mass. eye & ear infirmary; fellow Am. Acad. of Ophthalmology, Am. Coll. of Surgeons, Cornea Soc.; dir. The Cornea and Laser Eye Inst.; prof. ophthalmology UMDNJ-NJ Med. Sch., dir. cornea and refractive surgery. Vis. rsch. collaborator dept. of mech. and aerospace engring. Priceton Univ. Recipient Honor award, Am. Acad. of Ophthalmology, Pioneer in Refractive Surgery award, Summit Tech. Inc., Sr. Honor and Achievement award, Am. Acad. of Ophthalmology; named Tchr. of the Year, Mass. Eye & Ear Infirmary, Harvard Med. Sch.; named one of Best Doctors in NJ, NJ Monthly, NJ Life, Best Doctors in NY, NY Mag.; named to Best Doctors in America; fellow, Am. Ophthal. Soc. Mem.: NJ Acad. of Ophthalmology, Am. Ophthal. Soc., Am. Soc. for Cataract and Refractive Surgery, Internat. Soc. of Refractive Surgery. Office: The University Hospital 150 bergen St C 431 Newark NJ 07103 Office Phone: 973-972-4300.

HERSH, STEPHEN PETER, psychiatrist, psycho-oncologist, chronic pain expert, educator, mitochondrial disorders clinical research facilitator; b. NYC, Aug. 11, 1940; s. Joseph Harrison and Lillian (Berk) H.; m. Jean Ann Lehrke, Apr. 10, 1969; children: Damon, Katharine, Justin, Tessa. BA, Amherst Coll., 1962; MD, NYU, 1967. Diplomate Am. Bd. Psychiatry and Neurology. Pediatric intern NYU-Bellevue Med. Ctr., NYC, 1967-68, fellow in child psychiatry, 1970-72; resident in psychiatry U. Pa., Phila., 1968-70; chief Ctr. for Studies in Child and Family Mental Health, NIMH, Rockville, Md., 1972-73, spl. asst. to dir., 1973-74, asst. dir., 1975-79; dir. div. children and youth St. Elizabeths Hosp., Washington, 1981; co-founder, co-dir., chmn. bd. Med. Illness Counseling Ctr., Chevy Chase, Md., 1982-94, exec. med. dir., 1995—, pres., 2002—; behavioral health and medicine cons. Marriott Internat., 1996—99. Clin. prof. psychiatry and pediat. George Washington U. Med. Ctr., Washington, 1989—; cons. pediat. br. Nat. Cancer Inst., Bethesda, Md., 1972-99; nat. adv. coun. Nat. Anthrop. Film Ctr., Smithsonian Instn., Washington, 1979-81; chmn. sci. adv. bd. St. Jude Children's Rsch. Hosp., Memphis, 1980-82; attending physician Children's Hosp. Nat. Med. Ctr., 1984-97; dir., prin. investigator HIV Neuropsychology R&D project Nat. Cancer Inst., 1988—; med. staff clin. ctr., NIH, 1992-99; dir. rsch. grant J.W. and Alice S. Marriott Found., 2002—; cons. Edison Pharma, 2007—, strategic adv., 2008-, Mayo Clinic Individualized Medicine Leadership Group, 2008-; med. advisor Alice S. and J. W. Marriott Found., 2011-. Author: The Executive Parent, 1979, The Physician and the Mental Health of the Child, 1981, Beyond Miracles, 2000; contbg. editor Journeys, 1994-96; contbr. articles to profl. jours., chpts. to books. Svcs. com. Am. Cancer Soc., Washington, 1974-79; mem. com. on traffic Somerset (Md.) Town Coun., 1975-78; bd. dirs. Barker Found., Washington, 1984-87; mem. med. bd. Lupus Found. Greater Washington, 1988-92, My Image After Breast Cancer, 1995-2000; bd. med. advisors Multimedia Med. Sys., 1997; vol. emergency response physician Md. Dept. Health and Mental Hygiene, 2003; profl. adv. bd. Wellness Cmty., Washington, 2005—, bd. govs. Med. Alumni Coun., NYU Sch. Medicine, 2004-11. Recipient spl. award Nat. Consortium for Child Mental Health Svcs., 1979, Alumni Leadership award NYU Sch. Medicine, 2005; nominee one of Top Drs., Greater Wash., 2008. Fellow, Am. Psychiat. Assn. (disting. life, Significant Achievement award 1993); mem. APA, Internat. Assn. Study Pain. Democrat. Achievements include facilitating expansion of research in mitochondrial disorder; development of pain curriculum at NYU School of Medicine; achievement award for creating an out-patient facility for specialized services for persons with medical illnesses and disabilities and innovation in improving health care quality management. Home: 421 Kent Square Rd Gaithersburg MD 20878-5711 Office: Med Illness Counseling Ctr 2 Wisconsin Cir Ste 650 Chevy Chase MD 20815-7003 Office Phone: 301-654-3638 ext. 203. Personal E-mail: sphersh@covad.net.

HERSHBERGER, RAY E., cardiologist, educator; b. Lincoln, Nebr., Sept. 22, 1953; BA, Goshen Coll., 1975; MD, U. Nebr., 1978. Cert. Internal Medicine, 1981, Cardiovascular Disease, 1989. Resident internal medicine Washington Hosp. Ctr., DC, 1978—79, U. Kans. Sch. Medicine, Wichita, 1979—81; fellowship cardiology U. Utah Hosp., Salt Lake City, 1985—90; fellowship cardiac transplant Utah Cardiac Transplant Program, Salt Lake City; dir. cardiac transplantation, prof. medicine in cardiology Oreg. Health & Sci. U., Portland; prof. medicine, assoc. chief cardiology, dir. Advanced Heart Failure Therapies Program, dir. Translational Cardiovascular Genetic Medicine Miller Sch. Medicine, U. Miami, 2007—. Founder, prin. investigator Familial Dilated Cardiomyopathy Rsch. Project. Office: U Miami PO Box 019132 Miami FL 33101 Office Phone: 305-243-7067. Office Fax: 305-243-7069. E-mail: rhershberger@med.miami.edu.

HERSHEY, GERALD LEE, psychologist, educator; b. Detroit, Mich., Mar. 7, 1931; s Von Waltz and Clementine H.; m. Shirley Gauld, Oct. 2, 1954; children: Bruce, Dale, James. Student, UCLA, 1949-54; BA with honors, Mich. State U., 1957, MA, 1958, PhD, 1961. Asst. instr., research assoc. Mich. State U., East Lansing, 1958-61; mem. faculty dept. psychology Fullerton Coll., Calif., 1961—, prof., 1965—, chmn. dept., 1980—; vis. prof. Chapman Coll., Calif., 1962-69. Co-author: Human Development (2d edit.), 1978, Living Psychology (3d edit.), 1981. Served to 1st lt. AUS, 1954-56. Mem. NEA, APA, Assn. Humanistic Psychology, Lions. Office: Fullerton Coll 321 E Chapman Ave Fullerton CA 92832-2011 Office Phone: 714-992-7011. E-mail: jhersey@fullcoll.edu.

HERSHEY, NATHAN, lawyer, educator; b. NYC, Apr. 28, 1930; s. Harry and Hannah (Horwitz) Hershey; m. Carol Fine, July 13, 1958; children: Suzanne, Madeleine. AB, NYU, 1950; LLB, Harvard U., 1953. Bar: D.C. 1953, Pa. 1977. Individual practice law, NYC, 1955—56; rsch. assoc. in health law U. Pitts., 1956—58, asst. prof., 1958—63, assoc. prof., 1963—68, prof., 1968—; mem. Pa. Bd. Med. Edn., 1974—80; of counsel Markel, Schafer, and Goldman P.C., Pitts., 1977—2005, Post & Schell, Phila., 1984—94. Cons. Pa. State Com. on Pub. Health and Welfare, 1973—80; v.p. U. Pitts. Senate, 1995—98, pres., 1998—2001. Author (with others): Hospital Law Manual, 1959; author: (with Robert D. Miller) Human Experimentation and the Law, 1976; author: Hospital-Physician Relations, 1982; editor: Hosp. Law Newsletter; contbr. articles to profl. jours. Bd. dirs. Women's Health Svcs., 1976—91, bd. v.p., 1982—91; bd. dirs. Hill House Assn., Pitts., 1964—71. With US Army, 1953—55. Mem.: Am. Pub. Health Assn., Soc. Hosp. Attys. Western Pa. (dir. 1974—85, past pres.), Am. Soc. Hosp. Attys. (past pres.), Inst. Medicine of NAS. Democrat. Jewish. Office: 2200 Lawyers Bldg Pittsburgh PA 15219 Home: 6315 Forbes Ave Apt 1101 Pittsburgh PA 15217-1749 Home Phone: 412-421-0151.

HERSHKO, AVRAM, biochemist, educator; b. Karcag, Hungary, Dec. 31, 1937; arrived in Israel, 1950; s. Moshe and Shoshana Margit (Manci) Hershko; m. Judith Leibowitz, 1963; children: Daniel, Yair, Oded. MD, Hebrew U. Hadassah Med. Sch., Jerusalem, 1965, PhD, 1969. Postdoc. fellow U. Calif., San Francisco, 1969—72; assoc. prof. Technion-Israel Inst. Tech., Haifa, 1972—80, prof., 1980—, disting. prof. biochemistry, Rappaport Faculty Medicine, 1998—. Vis. rschr. Fox Chase Cancer Ctr., Phila., 1978—81. Contbr. articles to numerous sci. and profl. jours. With Israel Def. Forces, 1965—67. Recipient Weizman prize for scis., Israel, 1987, Israel prize in biochemistry, 1994, Wachter prize, U. Innsbruck, Austria, 1999, Gairdner Found. Internat. award, 1999, Alfred P. Sloan, Jr. prize, GM Cancer Rsch. Found., 2000, Albert Lasker award for basic med. rsch., 2000, Wolf Found. prize in medicine, Israel, 2001, Louisa Gross Horwitz prize, Columbia U., 2001, Nobel prize in chemistry, 2004. Mem.: NAS (fgn. assoc.), Am. Acad. Arts & Scis. (fgn. hon.), European Molecular Biology Orgn. Achievements include discovery of the significance of the body's mechanism for destroying proteins which plays a key role in immunity, inflammation and cancer; ubiquitin-mediated protein degradation. Office: Technion Israel Inst Tech Rappaport Inst 9697, 1 Efron St Po Box 31999 Haifa Israel Office Phone: 9724 8295344. Business E-Mail: hershko@tx.technion.ac.il. *

HERSHON, JAMES J., critical care specialist; MD, U. Vt., 1976. Diplomate Am. Bd. Internal Medicine, 1979, Am. Bd. Internal Medicine- pulmonary disease, 1982, Am. Bd. Internal Medicine-critical care medicine, 2002. Resident in internal medicine Highland Hosp., Oakland, Calif., 1976—79; fellow in pulmonary critical care medicine Calif. Pacific Med. Ctr., San Francisco, 1976—79, hosp. affiliation includes. Office: California Pacific Medical Center 2351 Clay St Ste 501 San Francisco CA 94115 Office Phone: 415-923-3421.

HERSHOW, RONALD C., epidemiologist, educator; BA in Biology, Hofstra U.; MD, Cornell U. Cert. infectious diseases. Hosp. epidemiologist U. Ill. Chgo., 1987—99, assoc. prof. epidemiology, clinical assoc. prof. med. Office: UIC School of Public Health 1603 W Taylor St Rm 987 Chicago IL 60612 Office Phone: 312-996-4759. Office Fax: 312-996-0064. E-mail: rchersho@uic.edu.

HERTZ, KENNETH THEODORE, healthcare executive; b. Jackson Heights, NY, Aug. 19, 1951; s. Irwin R. and Dorothy S. H.; m. Debra Pitre, July 12, 1997. BA in Spl. Studies, SUNY, Fredonia, 1974; cert. med. and dental practice mgmt., Loyola U., 1992. Cert. med. practice exec.; fellow Am. Coll. Med. Practice Execs., 2010. Gen. mgr. Cape Cod Symphony, West Barnstable, Mass., 1974-75; mng. dir. Tulsa Philharm., 1975-78; pres., gen. mgr. Atlanta Ballet, 1979-89; instr. continuing edn. Oglethorpe U.; dir. Atlanta Great Artists

Series, 1989-90, Atlanta Arts Devel. Svcs., 1989-90; exec. dir. New Orleans Symphony, 1990-91; adminstr. M.D. Care, Inc., New Orleans, 1991-95; dir. acquisitions and network devel. Tenet Healthcare, New Orleans, 1995-96, area mgr. practice ops., 1996-97; adminstr. MacArthur Surg. Clinic, Alexandria, La., 1977—2002, KTH Cons. LLC, 2003—05; sr. cons. MGMA Health Care Cons. Group, 2005—08, prin., 2008—; med. assoc. MGMA Med. Group. Mem. dance panel City of Atlanta, 1983-89, Ga. Coun. for Arts, 1984-88, NEA, 1985-87; dir. Dance/USA, 1985-89; mem. adv. bd. cert. program in med./dental practice mgmt. Loyola U., 1993—; mem. Pres.'s Adv. Coun., De La Salle H.S., 1993-2000. Chmn. Atlanta C. of C. Cultural Programming Task Force, 1987—89, Atlanta C. of C. "Arts Alive", art celebration, 1986, Ga. Profl. Arts Caucus, 1983—85; bd. dirs. Big Bros./Big Sisters, 1988—89, Arts Festival Atlanta, BVA, 1986—90, Bus. Vols. for Arts, New Orleans Ballet Assn., 1996—98, Rapides Symphony Orch., 1998—2000, Ballet Alexandria, 2000—, Am. Jewish Com., Atlanta, 1967. Mem. Midtown Bus. Assn. (dir. 1984-89), Ga. Citizens for Arts, Am. Symphony Orch. League, La. Med. Group Mgmt. Assn. (bd. dirs. 2001—, sec. 2003—, v.p., 2004-05), Ctrl. La. Med. Group Mgmt. Assn. (v.p. 2001-02, pres. 2002—), Alpha Phi Omega Office Phone: 348-729-3460. E-mail: khertz@mgma.com.

HERTZBERG, HENRY, retired radiologist; b. Bklyn., Oct. 21, 1933; s. Louis and Bessie (Eisman) H.; m. Dori Balter, June 10, 1962; children: Richard, Lisa. BS, CCNY, 1955; MD, SUNY, Bklyn., 1959. Diplomate Am. Bd. Radiology. Intern Kings County Med. Ctr., Bklyn., 1959-60; resident Roosevelt Hosp., NYC, 1960-63; dir. radiology Fort Gordon (Ga.) Army Hosp., 1963-65; pvt. practice Green Brook, N.J.; assoc. dir. dept. radiology Somerset Med. Ctr., Somerville, N.J., 1975-85; dir. dept. radiology Muhlenberg Med. Ctr., Plainfield, NJ, 1985-92, attending radiologist, 1992—2002. Clin. asst. prof. radiology Rutgers U. Med. Ctr., 1985—. Capt. M.C., U.S. Army, 1963-65. Mem. AMA. Avocation: travel. Home: 182 Deer Run Watchung NJ 07069-6222 Office: Assoc Radiologists PA 239 Us Highway 22 Green Brook NJ 08812-1916

HERTZIG, MARGARET E., psychiatrist; b. NYC, Feb. 9, 1935; d. Morris and Grace Koenig Hertzig; m. Herbert George Birch, Dec. 11, 1961 (dec. Feb. 5, 1973); children: Sarah Ellen Birch, Martin Lawrence Birch. AB, Vassar Coll., 1956; MD, NYU, 1960. Diplomate psychiatry Am. Bd. Psychiatry and Neurology, 1968, child psychiatry Am. Bd. Psychiatry and Neurology, 1975. Rotating intern Jewish Hosp. Bklyn., 1960—61, pediat. resident, 1961—62; psychiatric resident Bellevue Psychiat. Hosp., 1962—64; rsch. fellow NYU Sch. Medicine, 1964—66; assoc. prof. psychiatry Cornell U. Med. Coll., NYC, 1977—95; assoc. attending psychiatrist N.Y. Hosp.-Cornell Med. Ctr., NYC, 1977—95; dir. child and adolescent outpatient dept. Payne Whitney Clinic-N.Y. Presbyn. Hosp., NYC, 1977—2002; prof. psychiatry Weill Med. Coll. Cornell U., NYC, 1995—, interim vice-chair child and adolescent psychiatry, 2002—09; attending psychiatrist N.Y. Presbyn. Hosp., Weill Cornell Med. Ctr., NYC, 1995—. Cons. Spl. Citizens Inc., NYC, 1980—. Fellow, NYU Sch. Medicine, 1964—66. Fellow: Am. Acad. Child and Adolescent Psychiatry. Office: Weill Med Coll Cornell Univ 525 East 68th St New York NY 10021 Office Phone: 212-746-5712. Business E-Mail: mehertzi@med.cornell.edu.

HERVÁS, FRANCISCO IGNACIO, microbiologist, educator; b. Madrid, Aug. 9, 1951; s. Carlos and María Luisa Hervás; m. María Francisca Dotor, Dec. 6, 1989; m. María Concepción Martín, July 19, 1978 (dec. Oct. 23, 1986). MD, U. Granada, Spain, 1976; specialist in clin. pathology, U. Complutense, Madrid, 1981, specialist in clin. microbiology, 1982, MD, 1976; PhD (hon.), Ministry Defence, 2005. Officer Spanish Army Med. Corp Sch., Madrid, 1977—78; med. corp units officer Ministry of Def., Madrid, 1978—79; microbiology specialist Hosp. Militar 41, Barcelona, 1983—87; microbiology sect. chief Hosp. Ctrl. de la Defensa, Madrid, 1987—97, microbiology dept. dir., 1997—. Assoc. prof. clin. microbiology U. Complutense, Madrid, 1992—2004; dir. tchg. unit Ministry of Health, Spain, 1995; dir. Geclobor Cons., Madrid, 1998—; with U. Complutense Madrid; collaborator Circulo Ahumada, 1999—. Author: Procedimientos de Inteligencia Artificial en el Estudio de las Enfermedades Infecciosas, 1999 (Excellence in Health Care prize, 2005), Modelos de Gestión para Médicos de Familia, 2005, Hospital Empresa y Sanidad Asistencial Calidad y Rentabilidad, 2007, Midiendo la Infección, 2008, Ensalada de cosas, 2009, Michino, 2010; mem. editl. bd.: Revista de Medicina Militar, 2003; contbr. articles. Lt. Col. Med. Corp, 1977—2011, Madrid. Mem.: Soc. Espanola de Quimioterapia (assoc.), European Soc. for Clin. Microbioloy and Infectious Diseases (assoc.), Soc. Española de Enfermedades Infecciosas y Microbiología Clínica (assoc.), VIP Club (assoc.). Roman Catholic. Achievements include research in cluster analysis sys. for bacterial growth simulations. Avocations: opera, mathematics, writing, gardening, walking. Office: Hosp Central de la Defensa Glorieta Del Ejército S/N Madrid 28047 Spain Office Fax: 34 914222172. Business E-Mail: fhermal@oc.mde.es.

HERVE, JEAN-CLAUDE, biologist, researcher; b. Saint Gilles du Mené, France, July 25, 1947; s. Ernest Hervé and Marie-Joseph Moro; m. Michelle Marchand, Dec. 19, 1981; children: Erwann, Morgane, Gwénaëlle. DSc, U. Poitiers, France, 1984. Rsch. visitor U. Paris VI, 1978—79; rsch. worker CNRS-U. Poitiers, 1979—88, rschr., 1990—; rsch. visitor U. Oxford, England, 1988—90. Exec. editor Bentham Sci. Pubs., Hilversum, Netherlands, 2002; guest editor Elsevier, Amsterdam, 2003—04. Recipient Sci. rsch. award, Fondation de France, 1975. Mem.: Physiol. Soc., Am. Physiol. Soc. Avocation: travel. Home: 218 route de Nouaille 86550 Mignaloux Beauvoir France Office: UMR 6187 CNRS-Univ Poitiers 40 avenue du R Pineau 86022 Poitiers France Office Fax: (33) 549 45 37 51; Home Fax: (33) 549 46 21 16. Business E-Mail: jean.claude.herve@univ-poitiers.fr.

HERZ, NATHAN (BEN), occupational therapy professor; BS in Occupational Therapy, Eastern Ky. U., 1990; MBA, Averett U., Danville, Va., 1999; D of Occupational Therapy, Creighton U., Omaha, 2004. Chair rehabilitation svcs. Jefferson Coll. Health Scis., Roanoke, Va., 2000—04; asst. prof., program dir. dept. occupational therapy Med. Coll. Ga., 2004—. Bd. dirs. Columbia Parkinson's Support Group, SC. Recipient Disting. Svc. award, Med. Coll. Ga., 2008. Mem.: Ga. Occupational Therapy Assn., Am. Occupational Therapy Assn. Achievements include research in Parkinson's disease and the use of interaction video gaming systems, such as Wii and Wii Fit game systems, and how it relates to rehabilitation. Office: Med Coll Ga Dept Occupational Therapy 1120 15th St Augusta GA 30912 E-mail: nherz@mcg.edu. *

HERZBERG, MARGARET ANN, adult nurse practitioner, orthopaedic nurse; b. Bellmore, NY, Dec. 11, 1957; d. Ann Dorothy (Meehan) Herzberg. BS cum laude, Adelphi U., 1980, MS in Nursing Adminstrn., 1996; post-masters adult nurse practitioner, 1999. RN, N.Y. Nurse, office mgr. East Side Sports Medicine Ctr., NYC, 1980-81; staff nurse Nassau County Med. Ctr., East Meadow, 1981—85; pvt. practice orthopedic nurse researcher North Bellmore, 1988—; dir. program devel. PRO-FORM Sports Medicine, P.C., St. James, 1988—93; owner Creative Concepts Cons. Svcs., North Bellmore, 1993—; pvt. practice med./legal cons. North Bellmore, 1993—; coord. nursing Resource Ctr. Skills Lab and Computer Ctr. Adelphi U. Sch. Nursing, Garden City, 1993—98; nurse practitioner pvt. practice, Enrico Mango MD, PC, Smithtown, 1996—; dir. med. svcs. The Helen Keller Nat. Ctr., Sands Point, 2004—. Mem. vol. med. staff Victory Games, U.S. Orgn. of Disabled Athletes, Uniondale, N.Y., 1990—96, Atlanta Paralympic Games. Mem. Nat. Assn. Orthopaedic Nurses (v.p. L.I. Orthopaedic Nurses 1994-98), Nat. Assn. Strength and Fitness Profls. (nat. sec. 1990-91), Sigma Theta Tau (chpt. exec. bd., newsletter editor 1982-87, 88-89). Republican. Roman Catholic. Avocations: writing, water sports, art, physical fitness. Office: The Helen Keller Nat Ctr 141 Mid Neck Rd Sands Point NY 11050 Office Phone: 516-944-8900 ext. 236. E-mail: pegherz@optonline.net.

HERZBERGER, EUGENE E., retired neurosurgeon; b. Sotchi, USSR, June 7, 1920; came to U.S., 1957, naturalized, 1964; s. Eugene S. and Mary P. H.; married; children— Henry, Monica MD, U. King Ferdinand I, Cluj, Rumania, 1947. Diplomate Am. Bd. Neurol. Surgery. Intern Univ. Hosp., Cluj, Rumania, 1946-47, resident in surgery, 1947-48; resident in neurosurgery Beilinson Hosp., Tel Aviv, 1949-53; chief neurosurgeon Tel Hashomer Govt. Hosp., Tel Aviv, 1953-57; research asst. Yale U., 1958-59; instr. neurosurgery Med. Coll. Ga., 1959-60; attending neurosurgeon St. Clare Hosp., Monroe, Wis., 1960-76, Mercy Hosp. and Finley Hosp., Dubuque, Iowa, 1976-94; ret., 1994. Contbr. articles to med. jours. Mem. Am. Assn. Neurol. Surgeons, Iowa Midwest Neurosurg. Soc., Congress Neurol. Surgeons, Am. Acad. Neurology, Iowa State Med. Soc.

HERZLINGER, REGINA, economist, educator, writer; m. George Herzlinger. BS, MIT; Doctorate, Harvard Bus. Sch. Economist, Washington; v.p. Various Cons. Firms, Cambridge; asst. sec. Gov. Commonwealth Mass.; prof. Harvard Business School, Boston, 1971—. Pub. bd. dirs. 13 cos. Author: (books) Market-Driven Health Care, 2000, Consumer-Driven Health Care, 2004, Who Killed health Care?, 2007, 4 other books. Avocations: art, gardening, aerobics. Office: Harvard Bus Sch Soldier's Field Boston MA 02163 Business E-Mail: rherzlinger@hbs.edu. *

HERZOG, BERNARD MAURICE JEAN, radiology educator; b. Nancy, Meurthe et Moselle, France, Dec. 28, 1935; s. Eugène and Elisabeth (Dufour) H.; m. Anne-Marie Vlasak (div. 1974); children: Xavier, Bertrand, Hedwige; m. Christine Renaud, 1984; 1 child, Irvin. Licencié-ès sciences, Facultè des sciences, Nancy, 1961; Doctorat en Médecine, Facultè de Médecine, Nancy, 1961; nat. degree in electroradiology, Paris, 1963. Biophysics research chief Facultè de Médecine, Nancy, 1961-63, asst. electroradiologist Grenoble, France, 1964-66, prof. electroradiology Nantes, France, 1966-2000; head radiology depts. Nantes Hosp. System, 1966-92. Consistent research in med. pathology and immunology, Nancy, 1959-64, musicotherapy and psychoanalysis, Nantes, 1975-2000. Author: Death, Love, and Dreams, 1987, The Cancerous Imaginary, 1987, Gold of Ashes, 1991, The Birdcatcher and the Amazon, 1992, AIDS and Cancer by the Light of Psychoanalysis, 1993, New Tracks to Cure Cancer, 2000, Transgenic = The Beginning of Catastrophic Disorder, 2000, Life Despite Death, 2001, The 7 Banes: Ecological Peril, 2003, Torments of the Soul, Illnesses of the Body: A New Psychosomatic Medicine, 2005, Western Medicine's Downfall Pleading for a more Humanistic Apporach, 2008. Avocations: art, music, literature, philosophy.

HERZOG, DAVID BRANDEIS, psychiatrist; b. Newark, Oct. 18, 1946; s. Harry William H.; m. Jennifer Mary Rathbun; children: Jonathan Rathbun, Matthew Alden. BA, Rutgers U., 1966; MD with highest honors, U. Mex., 1973. Intern in pediatrics U. Wis. hosp., Madison, 1973-74, resident in pediatrics, 1974-75; sr. resident in pediatrics Boston City Hosp., 1975-76; resident in child psychiatry Children's Hosp. Med. Ctr. & Judge Baker Guidance Ctr., Boston, 1976-78; chief resident psychosomatic unit Children's Hosp. Med. Ctr., 1977-78; resident in adult psychiatry Mass. Gen. Hosp., Boston, 1978-80, dir. psychosomatic outpatient clinic, 1980-81, chief consultation and liaison svc., 1980—2000, dir. eating disorders unit, 1981—. Pres. and founder Harvard Eating Disorders Ctr., 1994-, pres. Eating Disorders Coalition for Rsch. Policy and Action; prof. psychiatry, Harvard U., Boston, 1998—. Author 185 refereed articles, revs., chpts. and two books. Grantee, NIMH, 1987, 93. Fellow Am. Acad. Pediatrics, Am. Acad. Child and Adolescent Psychiatry, mem. AMA (Joseph B. Goldberger award 1994), Am. Psychiat. Assn. (Blanche F. Ittleson award 1992), New Eng. Coun. Child and Adolescent Psychiatry (bd. dirs. 1983-87).

HERZOG, DENNIS NEIL, psychologist, supervisor; b. Cleve., Dec. 29, 1956; s. Charles Martin and Lois Shirley Herzog; m. Lisa Anne Steinberg, May 27, 1990; children: Joshua Robert, Daniel Isaac. BA in Psychology, Long Beach State U., Calif., 1981, MS in Counseling, 1985. Sch. psychologist credential Calif. Commn. Tchr. Credentialing, 1985, lic. ednl. psychologist Calif. Bd. Behavioral Scis., 2001. Sch. psychologist supr. Irvine Unified Sch. Dist., Calif., 1985—; pvt. practice Tustin, 2001—; psychologist Cmty. Day Sch., Huntington Beach Union HS Dist., 2008—. Invited participant Oxford Round Table, England, 2005; founding mem. Orange County Psychologist Suprs., Irvine, Calif., 2006—. Vol. coach youth sports; bd. mem. U. Synagogue, Irvine, 2004—06, Disability Awareness Found., Mission Viejo, Calif., 2000—05, The Hope Inst., Costa Mesa, 2001—04. Named Big Brother of Yr., Big Bothers of Orange County, 1981, Outstanding Supporter of Prevention, Irvine Prevention Coalition, 2003, Man of Yr., Tustin Meadows Cmty. Assn., 2004. Mem.: Orange County Assn. Sch. Psychologists, Calif. Assn. Sch. Psychologist, Nat. Assn. Sch. Psychologists. Avocations: weightlifting, martial arts, football. Office: Irvine Unified Sch Dist 5050 Barranca Pkwy Irvine CA 92604 Personal E-mail: dandlherzog@sbcglobal.net. Business E-Mail: dherzog@iusd.org.

HESS, DARLA BAKERSMITH, cardiologist, educator; b. Valparaiso, Fla., June 4, 1953; d. James Barry and Irma Marie (Baker) Bakersmith; m. Leonard Wayne Hess, July 20, 1988; 1 child, Ever Marie. BS, Birmingham So. Coll., 1975; MD, Tulane U., New Orleans, 1979. Diplomate Am. Bd. Internal Medicine, Am. Bd. Cardiovascular Disease. Commd. ensign USNR, 1979, advanced through grades to lt. comdr., 1988; resident in internal medicine Portsmouth Naval Hosp., Va., 1979-82, cardiologist, head non-invasive cardiology Va., 1986-88; fellow in cardiology San Diego Naval Hosp., 1982-84; cardiologist, head med. officer in charge ICU Camp Lejeune Naval Hosp., N.C., 1984-85; dir. noninvasive sect. cardiology, dir. fetal echocardiography U. Mo., Columbia, 1991—99; asst. prof. medicine U. Miss. Med. Ctr., Jackson, 1988-91, asst. prof. ob/gyn., 1990-91; co-dir. fetal echocardiogaphy U. Mo., Columbia, 1991—99, co-dir. Adult Congenital Heart Disease Clinic, 1991—99, assoc. prof. medicine, assoc. prof. ob/gyn., 1998—2001; cardiologist Lehigh Valley Heart Specialists, Pa., 2006—07. Clin. assoc. prof. Pa. State U., 2006—07; cardiologist, 2008—; assoc. prof. Va. Tech. Carilon Sch. Medicine, 2009. Author: (with others) Obstetrics and Gynecology Clinics, 1992, Clinical Problems in Obstetrics & Gynecology, 1993, General Medical Disorders During, 1991; co-editor: Fetal Echocardiography, 1999; contbr. articles to So. Med. Jour., Ob/Gyn. Clinics N.Am., Soc. Perinatal Obs., Jour. Reproductive Medicine, others. Fellow Am. Coll. Cardiology, Fellow Am. Heart Assn. (fellow stroke coun.), Fellow Am. Soc. Echocardiography; mem. Am. Assn. Nuclear Cardiology, Phi Beta Kappa, Alpha Omega Alpha. Republican. Anglican. Home: PO Box 192 Franklin PA 16323-0192 Home Phone: 540-774-1496. Personal E-mail: darlabhess@msn.com.

HESS, EVELYN VICTORINE, medical educator; b. Dublin, Nov. 8, 1925; arrived in U.S., 1960, naturalized, 1965; d. Ernest Joseph and Mary (Hawkins) H.; m. Michael Howett, Apr. 27, 1954. MB, B.Ch, BAO, U. Coll., Dublin, 1949; MD, Univ. Coll., Dublin, 1980. Intern West Middlesex Hosp., London, Eng., 1950; resident Clare Hall Hosp., London, 1951-53, Royal Free Hosp. and Med. Sch., London, 1954-57; rsch. fellow in epidemiology of Tb Royal Free Med. Sch., London, 1955; fellow U. Tex. Southwestern Med. Sch., Dallas, 1958—59, asst. prof. internal medicine, 1960-64; assoc. prof. dept. medicine U. Cin. Coll. Medicine, 1964-69, McDonald prof. medicine, 1969—, dir. div. immunology, 1964-95. Sr. investigator Arthritis and Rheumatism Found., 1963-68; attending physician Univ. Hosp., VA Hosp.; cons. Children's Hosp., Cin., 1967—, Jewish Hosp., Cin., 1968—; mem. various coms., mem. nat. adv. coun. NIH; mem. various coms. FDA, Cin. Bd. Health. Contbr. articles to profl. jours., chapters to books. Active Nat. Pks. Assn., Smithsonian Instn., others. Recipient award Arthritis Found., 1973, 78, 83, Am. Lupus Soc., 1979, Am. Acad. Family Practice, 1980, State of Ohio, 1982, Spirit of Am. Women, 1989, Daniel Drake medal U. Cin., 2001, Gold medal Lupus Found., 2004, Lifetime Hess Rsch. award Lupus Found., 2005; fellow Royal Free Med. Sch., Scandinavia, 1956; Empire Rheumatism Coun. travelling fellow, 1958-59. Master ACP (gov. Ohio chpt. 1999-2003, Master Tchr. award 1995); fellow AAAS, Am. Acad. Allergy, Royal Soc. Medicine, ACR (master, Disting. Rheumatologist award 1996); mem. Heberden Soc., Am. Coll. Rheumatology, Pan-Am. League Assns. for Rheumatology (Gold medal 2003), Ctrl. Soc. Clin. Rsch., Am. Fedn. Clin. Rsch., Am. Assn. Immunologists, Am. Soc. Nephrology, Am. Med. Womens Assn. (Local Hero award 2004), Am. Soc. Clin. Pharmacology and Therapeutics, N.Y. Acad. Scis., Soc. Exptl. Biology and Medicine, Rheumatological Soc. Colombia (hon.), Rheumatological Soc. Peru (hon.), Rheumatological Soc. Italy (hon.), Clin. Immunol. Soc. Japan (hon.), Cuban Soc. Rheumatology (hon.), Alpha Omega Alpha. Achievements include research in immunology, rheumatic diseases. Home: 2916 Grandin Rd Cincinnati OH 45208-3418 Office: U Cin Med Ctr ML 563 ML 563 MSB Cincinnati OH 45267-0001 Office Phone: 513-558-4701. Business E-Mail: hessev@email.uc.edu.

HESSE, VOLKER, pediatrician; b. Röbel, Müritz, Germany, Aug. 18, 1942; s. Werner Walter and Marianne (Groß) H.; m. Gertraud Daniel, May 25, 1974; children: Lydia-Kathrin, Juliana. Med. degree summa cum laude, Friederich Schiller U., Jena, Germany, 1968, MD, 1969, Dr.sc.med., 1979. Head dept. pediatric endocrinology Univ. Children's Hosp., Jena, 1979-89; med. dir. Children's Hosp. Berlin-Lichtenberg, Germany, 1989-91; vice med. dir., chmn. dept. pediatrics Hosp. Berlin-Lichtenberg, 1991—96, head dept. social pediatrics, 1992—; head German ctr. growth and development in childhood and adolescence, 1993. Prof. pediatrics Friedrich Schiller U., 1988; hon. prof. Humboldt U., Berlin, 1989; chmn. German unification leading pediatricians, 2000-06; bd. mem. German longitudinal language development study. Editor: (textbook) Endocrinology in Childhood and Adolescence, 1982; author: Iodine and Rickets Proplylaxis 1976-1989; Goethe and Children, 2001; Pioneers of Modern Medicine (with C. Fleck, G. Wagner) 2004. 1990 (Finkelstein prize, Schlossman prize 1981); contbr. articles to profl. jours. Silbert scholar UCLA, 1984. Mem. European Soc. Pediatric Endocrinology (pres. 1990-91), Lawson Wilkins Pediatric Endocrine Soc., European Soc. for Pediatric Rsch., N.Y. Acad. Scis., North German Pediatric Soc. (hon., pres. 1996-97), Scientific Soc. Berlin, Academy of Pediatrics, Adolescence Med. (coun. mem., 2000-06), Acad. Sci. Erfurt (founder, 2007), Soc. Nature & Health Berlin (founder, 2006), Unifications Luriting Drs. Germany, Berlin Goethe Soc. (coun. mem.). Avocations: medical history, history of endocrinology, german classic literature, publications on the poets Goethe and Schiller. Office: Hosp Berlin Dept Pediatrics Gotlindestrasse 2-20 D-10365 Berlin Germany

HESSELMAR, BILL, pediatrician, educator; b. Gothenburg, Sweden, Jan. 1, 1955; MD, U. Gothenburg, Sweden, 1987. Cert. in paediat. 1994. Cons. paediatric pulmonology & allergology Queen Silvia Children's Hosp., Gothenburg, Sweden, 1994—. Assoc. prof. Sahlgrenska Acad., U. Gothenburg, Sweden, 2011. Mem.: Swedish Paediatric Soc., European Respiratory Soc. Office: Queen Silvia Childrens Hosp Gothenburg 41685 Sweden Office Fax: 46(0)313434760. Business E-Mail: bill.hesselmar@vgregion.se.

HESTER, THOMAS RODERICK, JR., plastic surgeon, educator; b. Cairo, Ga., Mar. 24, 1942; Grad., Emory U., Atlanta, 1963, MD, 1967. Cert. Am. Bd. Surgery, 1973, Am. Bd. Plastic Surgery, 1980. Intern surgery Grady Meml. Hosp., Atlanta, 1967—68; resident plastic reconstructive surgery Emory Affiliated Hosps., 1968—72; chief surgery Colquitt County Meml. Hosp., Moultrie, Ga., 1972—76; chief resident plastic surgery Emory U., 1976—78; assoc. prof. plastic and reconstructive surgery Emory U. Sch. Medicine, 1980—93, program dir. divsn. plastic surgery, 2001; asst. prof. plastic and reconstructive surgery Emory U., 2001—, chief divsn. plastic surgery, 2001—, William G. Hamm chair plastic surgery, 2005—; founder Paces Plastic Surgery, 1993—. Contbr. articles to med. jours., chapters to books. Maj. USAR, 1973—76. Recipient Best Jour. Article, Aesthetic Soc. Ednl. Rsch. Found., 1997. Fellow: Am. Coll. Surgeons; mem.: AMA, Southeastern Surg. Soc., So. Med. Assn., Med. Assn. Atlanta, Jurkiewicz Soc., James C. Thoroughman Surg. Soc., Ga. Med. Assn., Ga. Soc. Plastic Surgeons, Southeastern Soc. Plastic and Reconstructive Surgeons, Am. Assn. Plastic Surgeons, Am. Soc. Aesthetic Plastic Surgery (Simon Fredericks award 1992), Internat. Soc. Aesthetic Plastic Surgeons, Am. Soc. Plastic Surgeons, Alpha Omega Alpha Honor Med. Soc. Office: Paces Plastic Surgery 3200 Downwood Cir Ste 640A Atlanta GA 30327 also: Emory Divsn of Plastic and Reconstructive Surgery Emory Crawford Long Hosp 550 Peachtree St, SE, 8th Fl, Ste 4300 Atlanta GA 30308 Office Phone: 404-351-0051, 678-420-7045. Office Fax: 404-351-0632.

HESTON, JERRY D., child and adolescent psychiatrist, educator; MD, U. South Fla., Tampa, 1981. Diplomate Am. Bd. Psychiatry and Neurology, 1988, Am. Bd. Psychiatry and Neurology- child and adolescent psychiatry, 1989, Am. Bd. Pediatrics, 2004. Intern LeBonheur Children's Hosp., 1982, resident pediat. Memphis, 1982—84; resident psychiatry Univ. Tenn. Affiliated Hosp., Memphis, 1984—86, fellow child & adolescent psychiatry, 1986—88; clin. prof. psychiatry Univ.Tenn. Coll. Medicine. Office: The University of Tennessee Health Science Center 920 Madison Ave Memphis TN 38163 Office Phone: 901-448-3420. Business E-Mail: jheston@uthsc.edu.

HETSKO, CYRIL MICHAEL, internist; b. Montclair, NJ, May 25, 1942; s. Cyril Francis and Josephine (Stein) Hetsko; m. Theresa Hottenroth, Jan. 2, 1988; 1 child, Michael Dimitri. BA, Amherst Coll., 1964; MD, U. Rochester, 1968. Diplomate Nat. Bd. Med. Examiners, Am. Bd. Internal Medicine. Intern U. Wis. Hosps., Madison, 1968—69, resident internal medicine, 1969—72; clin. assoc. prof. medicine U. Wis., 1975—95, prof., 1995—; dean Care HMO, Inc., 1983—84; chmn. Dept. Medicine St. Mary's Hosp. Med. Ctr., Madison, 1985—87; dir. Physicians Ins. Co. Wis., Madison, 1990—93; tru. Trustee Internal Medicine Ctr. To Advance Rsch. and Edn., Washington, 1991—; mem. White House Health Profls. Outreach Group, 1993—94; dir. Nat. Commn. Office Lab. Accreditation, 1994—; pres. North Ctrl. Med. Conf., 1995—96; cons. Health Ministry, Ekaterinburg, Russia, 1996; mem. US Clin. Lab. Improvement Adv. Coun., 2002—05. Mem.: Wis. Soc. Internal Medicine, AMA (alt. del. 1983—93, del. 1994—2003, bd. trustees 2003—11), Am. Coll. Physicians (regent, treas. 1998—2004), Nat. Found. for Infectious Disease, New Eng. Soc. in City NY, NY Acad. Scis., Dane County Med. Soc., State Med. Soc. Wis, Assn. Mil. Surgeons US, Am. Soc. Microbiology, Am. Soc. Internal Medicine. Office: Dean Med Ctr 1313 Fish Hatchery Rd Madison WI 53715-1911 *

HETTINGER, MICHAEL EUGENE, corneal surgeon; b. Memphis, Sept. 20, 1946; s. Elmer Eugene and Jeanette M. Hettinger; m. Terry Carmack Hettinger, Oct. 9, 1976; children: Christian Andrew, Michael Eugene Jr., Rachel Elise. BA in Biology, Rhodes Coll., Memphis, 1968; MS in Pathology, U. Tenn., Memphis, 1971. Toxicologist City of Memphis Hosps., 1970—75, acting dir. toxicology lab., 1971—72, med. technologist clin. chemistry lab., 1972—75; MD U. Tenn. Ctr. for Health Sci., Memphis, 1972—75; intern Regional Med. Ctr. Memphis, 1975—76; resident in ophthalmology U. Ala., Birmingham, 1976—79; fellow anterior segment surgery Mass. Eye and Ear Infirmary, Boston, 1979—81; dir. corneal and external disease svc. Kans. U. Med. Ctr., 1981—84; med. dir. Kans. Eye Bank, 1981—89; ptnr. Kansas City Eye Clinic, Overland Park, Kans., 1983—; co-med. dir. Midwest Transplant Network Eye Bank, 1994—2006. Clin. fellow ophthalmology Harvard Med. Sch., Boston, 1979—81; asst. prof. ophthalmology Kansas City U. Med. Ctr., 1981—84, clin. asst. prof. ophthalmology, 1984—96; vis. grand rounds prof. dept. ophthalmology U. Tenn., 1983; vis. lectr. dept. microbiology U. Health Svcs., 1983; lectr. in field; fellow staff Mass. Eye and Ear Infirmary, Boston, 1979—81; mem. provisional staff New Eng. Bapt. Hosp., Boston, 1980—81; mem. med. staff VA Hosp., Kansas City, Mo., 1981—84; mem. staff dept. ophthalmology Kans. U. Med. Ctr., 1981—2000; mem. staff Shawnee Mission Med. Ctr., Kans., 1983—, Children's Mercy Hosp., Kansas City, Mo., 1985—93, Miami County Hosp., Paola, Kans., 1990—. Contbr. articles to profl. jours. Bd. dirs. Midwest Transplant Network, Kansas City. Recipient Spl. Achievement award, U. Tenn. Ctr. Health Scis., 1975, Fellowship award, Bausch and Lomb, 1979—80; named Best Drs. America, 2000—08, Am. Top Ophthalmologist award, 2008; grantee, USPHS, 1969—71, Nat. Soc. to Prevent Blindness, 1980—81; scholar, Omicron Delta Kappa, 1966—68. Fellow: ACS; mem.: Midwest Transplant Network (chmn. adv. bd. 2007—), Internat. Soc. Refractive Surgery, Cornea Soc., Am. Soc. Cataract and Refractive Surgery, Kansas City Soc. Ophthalmology and Otolaryngology, Kans. Med. Soc., Midwest Corneal Assn., Med. Soc. Johnson and Wyandotte Counties (treas. 2003, sec. 2004, pres-elect 2005, pres. 2006), Midwest Transplant Network (bd. dir. 2000—), Am. Acad. Ophthalmology (mem. coun. 2002—08), Eye Bank Assn. Am. (chmn. grievance com. 1981, mem. accreditation com. 1982—87, Paton Soc. 1982—, med. adv. bd. 1983—, fin. com. 1985—, bd. dirs. 1987—90, treas. 1990—98, bd. dirs. 1991—, exec. com. 1991—, legis. and regulatory affairs com. 1998—2002, chmn.-elect. bd. dirs. 2000—02, chmn. bd. dirs. 2002—04, R. Townley Paton award 2006), Kansas City Ind. Physicians Assn. (treas. 2004—06, bd. dirs.). Methodist. Avocations: golf, reading. Office: Kansas City Eye Clinic 7504 Antioch Overland Park KS 66204 Office Phone: 913-341-3100. Business E-Mail: mgalloway@kceyeclinic.com.

HEUER, MICHAEL ALEXANDER, dean, endodontist educator; b. Grand Rapids, Mich., Apr. 27, 1932; s. Harold Maynard and Gwendolyn Ruth (Kremer) H.; m. Barbara Margaret Naines, Nov. 23, 1955; children— Kristan M., Karin E., Katrina A. DDS, Northwestern U., 1956; MS, U. Mich., 1959. Diplomate Am. Bd. Endodontics, 1967. Pvt. practice, Chgo., 1959-86; asst. prof. Northwestern U., 1960-66; assoc. prof. Loyola U., Chgo., 1968-73; prof., chmn. dept. endodontics Northwestern U., 1974-83, assoc. dean acad affairs, 1983-88, sr. assoc. dean, 1988-93, dean, 1993-98, prof. emeritus, 1999—. Dir. Am. Bd. Endodontics, 1971-77, sec.-treas., 1973-76, pres., 1976-77, ednl. cons., 1977-92; chmn. subcom. Am. Nat. Standards Inst.; mem. com. on advanced edn. Commn. on Accreditation of Dental Edn., 1974-77, endodontic cons., 1986-91, curriculum cons., 1986-92. Contbr. articles in field to profl. jours. Served with USNR, 1956-58. Recipient Northwestern U. Alumni Merit award, 2001. Fellow Am. Coll. Dentistry (life, sec.-treas. Ill. sect. 1986-92, vice chair 1992-94, chair 1994-96), Internat. Coll. Dentistry, Am. Assn. Endodontists (life; exec. coun. 1967-71, sec. 1979-84, v.p. 1984-85, pres.-elect 1985-86, pres. 1986-87); mem. AAAS, ADA (life; coun. dental materials and devices 1972-78, chmn. 1977-78, sci. and edn. cons. 1980-97), Internat. Assn. Dental Rsch., Am. Assn. Dental Schs., Chgo. Odontographic Soc. (pres. 1982-84), Edgar D. Coolidge Endodontic Soc. (life, charter sec. 1961, pres. 1964, trustee), Phi Eta Sigma, Omicron Kappa Upsilon, Chi Psi, Delta Sigma Delta. Home: 1552 Treeline Ct Naperville IL 60565-2015 Personal E-mail: mikeaheuer@sbcglobal.net.

HEWES, ROBERT CHARLES, radiologist; b. Balt., Feb. 14, 1953; s. Gordon Cecil and Gladys Dorothy (Barringham) H.; m. Judith Renee Lacy, Mar. 23, 1975; children: Christy, Amy, Jeremy. Student, Columbia Union Coll., 1973, Kettering Coll. of Med. Arts, 1971; BS, Loma Linda U., 1976, MD. Diplomate Am. Bd. Med. Examiners, Am. Bd. Radiology, Am. Bd. Vascular and Interventional Radiology. Resident in radiology Loma Linda U., Calif., 1978-81, asst. prof. radiology, 1983-84, pres. house staff assn., 1980; fellow in orthopedic radiology Hosp. for Spl. Surgery Cornell U. Med. Ctr., NYC, 1981-82; fellow in interventional radiology Johns Hopkins U. Hosp., Balt., 1982-83; assoc. prof. Wright State U.; mem. staff Kettering (Ohio) Med. Ctr., 1984—2002, vice chmn. dept. radiology, 1985-87, chmn., 1988-95; pres. Patient First Imaging Network, 1994-95, med. dir., 1996-98; radiologist, mem. med. staff Hilton Head Hosp., 1999—2009, med. dir. dept. radiology, 2007—09; pres. radiology Hilton Head LLC, 2007—09; med. dir. dept. imaging radiology cons. Fla. Hosp. Meml. Med. Ctr. & Health Care Ptnrs., 2009—. Pres. Kettering Radiologists, Inc., 1987-95, 97-99, Alumni Assn. Spring Valley Acad., 1987-89, Housestaff Assn. Loma Linda Univ., 1980-81; bd. dirs. Spring Valley Acad., chmn. fin. mgmt. com., 1998-99; vol. radiology edn. program Micronesia, 1998-2004, 2008, Marshall Islands, 2009-11; med. dir. Carolina Conf. Seventh Day Adventist, 2006—09. Contbr. articles on radiology to profl. jours. Bd. dirs. Seventh Day Adventist Ch., Kettering, Ohio, Hilton Head Island, SC. Recipient Philip Wilson award Hosp. Spl. Surgery, 1982, Cert. of merit Am. Roentgen Ray Soc., 1983, Disting. Alumnus award Kettering Coll. Med. Arts, 1990; named Physician of Yr., Hilton Head Regional Med. Ctr., 2006. Mem.: Volusia County Med. Soc., Miami Valley Radiol. Soc. (pres. 1994), Soc. of Interventional Radiology, Radiol. Soc. N.Am., AMA, Alpha Omega Alpha (award). Republican. Adventist. Avocations: golf, travel, watersports. Office: PO Box 732037 Ormond Beach FL 32173 Office Phone: 386-231-3015. Personal E-mail: bobhewes@gmail.com. Business E-Mail: robert.hewes@fhmmc.org.

HEWITSON, WILLIAM CRAIG, physician, career officer; b. Park City, Utah, July 4, 1961; s. William Glenn and Darlene Marie Hewitson; m. Lisa Lynn Williams; children: William Brent, Staci Anne, Andrew Craig. BA with honors, U. Utah, 1986; MD, USUHS, 1991; MPH, Johns Hopkins U., 1995; BS, U. NY, 1995; MHA, Baylor U., 2006. Diplomate Am. Bd. Preventive Medicine. Officer U.S. Army, advanced through grades to col., 1986; transitional intern Fitzsimons Army Med. Ctr., Aurora, Colo., 1991—92; 2d brigade surgeon 7th Inf. Divsn., Ft. Ord, Calif., 1992—93, divsn. surgeon Ft. Lewis, Wash., 1993—94; resident in general preventive medicine Walter Reed Army Inst. Rsch., Washington, 1994—96; chief injuries and occupation illnesses U.S. Army Ctr. for Health Promotion and Preventive Medicine, Aberdeen Proving Grounds, Md., 1996—98; chief preventive medicine divsn. Gen. Leonard Wood Army Cmty. Hosp., Ft. Leonard Wood, Mo., 1998—2000; healthcare adminstrv. fellow Baylor U., Ft. Sam Houston, Tex., 2000—02; chief epidemiology and disease surveillance Brooke Army Med. Ctr., Ft. Sam Houston, Tex., 2002—03; chief cmty. health practices br. Army Med. Dept. Ctr. and Sch., Ft. Sam Houston, Tex., 2003—06; cons. to surgeon gen. for nuclear, biol. and chem. surety medicine U.S. Army Med. Command, Ft. Sam Houston, Tex., 2006—; chief, preventive medicine & force health protection TF 1st Med Bde, Baghdad, Iraq, 2009. Dir. The Preventive Health Care Mgmt. Group, Salt Lake City, 1996-97; cons. Med. Adv. Sys., Owings, Md., 1995-98. Contbr. articles to profl. jours. Advancement chmn. Big Piney dist., Boy Scouts Am., Waynesville, Mo., 1999, Four Rivers dist. health and safety com., 1998, Pack com. chmn., Ft. George G. Meade, 1995-97, health and safety com. Eagle dist., 2001-02; missionary, Argentina, 1980-82; mem. St. Thomas Episcopal Ch., San Antonio, Tex. Fellow Am. Coll. Preventive Medicine; mem. AMA (Physician Recognition award 1997, 2000, 03, 06), Assn. Mil. Surgeons U.S., Am. Coll. Healthcare Exec., Am. Coll. Occ & Env Med., Masons. Avocations: running, exercise, flying, golf, tennis. Office: 2050 Worth Rd Ste 25 Fort Sam Houston TX 78234 Office Phone: 210-221-7952, 210-221-7952. Business E-Mail: nbcdoc@satx.rr.com.

HEWITT, JACQUELINE N., astronomy educator; AB in Econs., Bryn Mawr Coll., 1980; PhD in Physics, MIT, 1986. Prof. physics MIT, 1989—; dir. MIT Kavli Inst. for Astrophysics and Space Rsch., 2002—. Recipient Annie Jump Cannon award in Astronomy, 1989; David and Lucille Packard fellow, 1990; Henry G. Booker prize award, 1993; Maria Goeppart-Mayer award Am. Phys. Soc., 1995; Alfred P. Sloan rsch. fellow, 1990. Fellow: Am. Phys. Soc. Office: MIT Kavli Inst Astrophysics & Space Rsch Rm 37-241 Cambridge MA 02139 Business E-Mail: jhewitt@mit.edu.

HEWSTON, RUTH, researcher, educator; b. Preston, England, June 8, 1976; d. Andrew and Linda Law; m. Andrew Hewston, Dec. 29, 2001; children: Laura, Emily. BA with hons. in Performing Arts, De Montfort U., 1997; MA in Psychol. for Musicians, U. Sheffield, 2000; PhD, U. Wolverhampton, 2005. Rsch. asst., music psychologist U. Leicester, England, 1999; rsch. asst. U. Wolverhampton, England, 2001—03, lectr., 2002—04; lectr. dance sci. Laban, Creekside, London, 2001—05, Royal Acad. Dance, London, 2004; sr. rsch. fellow Nat. Acad. Gifted & Talented Youth, Coventry, 2004—07, U. Warwick, 2007—; assoc. lectr. The Open U., 2007—. Lectr. in field; presenter in field. Contbr. articles to profl. jours. Mem.: Internat. Soc. Music Edn., Am. Ednl. Rsch. Assn., Performing Arts Medicine Assn., Brit. Psychol. Soc., Internat. Assn. Dance Medicine and Sci., European Soc. Cognitive Scis. Music, Soc. Edn., Music and Psychology Rsch., Nat. Childbirth Trust (vol. rsch. networker 2005—). Avocations: clarinet, saxophone. Office: Ctr Ednl Devel Appraisal and Rsch Univ Warwick Coventry CV4 7AL England Business E-Mail: r.hewston@warwick.ac.uk.

HEXIG, BAYAR, engineering educator; b. Inner Mongolia, China, Apr. 1, 1972; B, Normal U. Inner Mongolia, 1994; PhD, Tokyo Inst. Tech., 2005. Postdoc. fellow Nat. Inst. Health Scis., Japan, 2005—07; asst. prof. Tokyo Inst. Tech., 2007—. Mem.: Soc. Polymer Sci. (Japan), Japan Soc. Drug Delivery Sys., Japanese Soc. Biomaterials, Japanese Soc. Regenerative Medicine. Avocations: basketball, skateboarding. Home: Ogawa1-13-4 Coop Town 18-304 Machida Tokyo 194-0003 Japan Home Fax: 81-42-796-5077. Personal E-mail: hexig.b.aa@m.titech.ac.jp.

HEY, WAYNE ALBERT, urologic surgeon, medical association executive; b. Upper Darby, Pa., Jan. 20, 1950; s. Warren Albert and Doris Elanore Hey; m. Margaret Ann Davies, Mar. 17, 1972 (div. July 1993); children: Wayne, Lauren; m. Paula Jean Hey, May 26, 1994; children: Sarah, Zach, Joshua, Bethany. BA with honors, Temple U., 1971; DO, Phila. Coll. Osteo. Medicine, 1975. Cert. Am. Coll. Osteo. Surgeons. Intern Detroit Osteo. Hosp. Corp., 1975-76, resident urology, 1976-80; asst. prof. surgery Tex. Coll. Osteo. Medicine, Ft. Worth, 1980—, founder, dir. urology residency, 1986-94. Pres. DFW Urology Consultants, Ft. Worth, 1982—, Imaging Resources, Inc., Ft. Worth, 1984—; mng. gen. ptnr. Dallas Ft. Worth Imaging Partnership, 1984—. Deacon Bloomfield Hills (Mich.) Bapt. Ch., 1978-80; elder Pantego Bible Ch., Arlington, Tex., 1988-90. Recipient Meade Johnson award Meade Johnson Pharms., 1977. Fellow Am. Coll. Osteo. Surgeons; mem. Am. Urol. Assn., Tex. Osteo. Med. Assn. Republican. Avocations: jogging, singing, raising six children. Office: Dfw Urology 1101 University Dr Fort Worth TX 76107-3012 E-mail: wahfacos@airmail.net.

HEYDE, MARTHA BENNETT, psychologist; b. New Bern, NC, Jan. 31, 1920; d. George Spotswood and Katherine (McIntosh) Bennett; m. Ernest R. Heyde, Aug. 17, 1946. AB, Columbia U., 1941, MA, 1949, PhD, 1959. Instr. psychol. founds and svcs. Tchrs. Coll., Columbia U., NYC, 1957-59, rsch. assoc., 1960-70, cons., 1970-73. Contbg. author: (rsch. monograph) The Vocational Maturity of Ningh Grade Boys, 1960, Floundering and Trial After High Sch., 1967; co-author: Vocational Maturity During the High School Years, 1979. Mem. Barnard Coll. alumnae coun. Columbia U., 1956-61, 69—, pres. class, 1956-61, trustee, 1974-79, hon. vice chmn. Barnard Coll. Centennial, 1987-89. Lt. (j.g.) USCG, During WWII. Mem. APA, Sigma Xi, Kappa Delta Pi, Pi Lambda Theta. Home: 530 E 23rd St Apt 8E New York NY 10010-5030

HEYMAN, JOSEPH MARTIN, gynecologist; b. Bklyn., May 21, 1942; s. Ezekiel and Elaine Olga (Adelman) H.; m. Laurel Ann Taylor, June 10, 1967; children: Eve Renata, Todd Sanford. BS, CCNY, 1963; MD, SUNY, Bklyn., 1967. Diplomate, Am. Bd. Ob.-Gyn. Intern USPHS Marine Hosp., Staten Island, NY, 1967-68; chief outpatient dept., venereal disease control officer USPHS Northern Navajo Indian Hosp., Shiprock, N.Mex., 1968-70; resident in ob.-gyn. Sinai Hosp., Balt., 1970-73; staff ob.-gyn. Women's Health Care, West Newbury, Mass., 1973—2001, former pres.; pres. med. staff Anna Jaques Hosp., Newburyport, Mass., 1990-92; ob.-gyn. private practice; chair, nat. physician adv. bd. Optum Insight (formerly Ingenix), 2010—. Bd. dirs. Tufts Associated HMO, Waltham, Mass., 1986-96; exec. com. bd. trustees Anna Jaques Hosp., 1995-99; pres. Healthy Women and Babies, L.L.C.; mem. Health and Human Svcs. Practicing Physics Adv. Coun., 1999-2003; dir. Lower Merrimac Valley Physician Hosp. Orgn., 2001—; mem. steering com. Connecting for Health, 2003—; mem. bd. commrs. Joint Commn., 2003—11; dir. Joint Commn. Resources, 2006—11, treas. 2008—10. Contbr. articles to profl. publs. Pres., West Newbury PTA, 1978; mem. adv. com. Physician Edn. Ctr. Found., 1996—. Fellow: ACOG; mem.: AMA (chair Coun. on Med. Svc. 2000—01, bd. trustees 2002—11, chair-elect bd. trustees 2007—08, chair bd. trustees 2008—09), World Med. Assn. Coun., Whittier Ind. Practice Assn. (pres. 1985—95, exec. bd. 1985—), Mass. Med. Soc. (exec. bd. 1983—2004, spkr. house of dels. 1992—94, v.p. 1994—95, pres.-elect 1995—96, pres. 1996—97). Democrat. Avocations: computers, reading, music, politics. Office: 24 Morrill Pl Amesbury MA 01913 Office Phone: 978-388-1259. *

HEYMAN, JULES, psychologist, educator; PhD, NYU; MS, CCNY & YU. Cert. Biofeedback Certification Inst. America, 1992; lic. psycotherapist NYS, jr. HS. sci. tchr. Bd. Ed. NYC, cert. psychotherapist Group Rels. Ongoing Workshop, 1973, sch. psychologist NY State Ed. Dept., Eriksonion Hypnosis, Mass., in Hypnosis Harry Aarons, NJ, in counseling Inst. Disaster Mental Health, Red Cross, 2010. NOS & vets. counselor NY State Divsn. Pers.; pvt. practice-psychotherapy NYC; residential counselor Jewish Bd. Guardians, NYC; staff psychologist, adj. faculty Queens Coll., Flushing, NY; faculty Group Rels. Ongoing Workshop, NYC; adj. prof. Mercy Coll., Dobbs Ferry, NY, 1979—; prof. Touro Coll., NYC, 1989—. Pres. & founder Ctr. Self Improvement, NYC; assoc. adjunct prof CUNY. Contbr. scientific papers, to profl. publs. Mem.: EPA, APA, Am. Ednl. Rschrs. Assn., Internat. Psychol. Hist. Soc., Eastern Psychol. Assn. Achievements include being remarkably successful with underperforming students. Avocations: piano, painting. Home: 115-12 227th St Cambria Heights NY 11411 Office: 205 E 17 St New York NY 10003 Personal E-mail: julesheyman@yahoo.com.

HEYMAN, MELVIN BERNARD, pediatric gastroenterologist; b. San Francisco, Mar. 24, 1950; s. Vernon Otto and Eve Elsie Heyman; m. Jody Ellen Switky, May 8, 1988. BA in Econs., U. Calif., Berkeley, 1972; MD, UCLA, 1976, MPH in Nutrition, 1981. Diplomate in pediatrics and pediatric gastroenterology Am. Bd. Pediatrics. Intern, resident L.A. County-U. So. Calif. Med. Ctr., 1976-79; fellow UCLA, 1979-81; asst. prof. U. Calif., San Francisco, 1981-88, assoc. prof., 1988-94, prof., 1994—, chief pediatric gastroenterology, hepatology and nutrition, 1990—, dir. tng. program i pediatric gastroenterology and nutrition, 1997—, Anita Ow Wing endowed chair, 2006—. Mem. cons. staff San Francisco Gen. Hosp., Scenic Gen. Hosp., Modesto, Calif.; assoc. dir. Pediatric IBD Consortium 2000—. Contbr. articles to profl. jours. Chmn. sci. adv. com. San Francisco chpt. Crohn's and Colitis Found. Am., 1987-94, bd. dirs., 1986-03; mem. City and County San Francisco Task Force on Nutrition and Phys. Activity for Children, 2003-04; bd. dirs. Nat. PTA, 2005-07; chmn. bd. Inflammatory Bowel Diseas Summer Camp Found., 2005-. Recipient Investigator award, NIH-NIDDK, 2002—; rsch. grantee, Children's Liver Found., 1984—85, John Tung grantee, Am. Cancer Soc.,

1985—89, NIH-NIDDK grantee, 1998—, UC Mexus project grantee. Mem.: Am. Bd. Pediatric Gastroenterology (chair sub-bd. 2000—01), Am. Gastroenterol. Assn., Am. Inst. Nutrition, Am. Acad. Pediat. (com. on nutrition 1999—2006, exec. com. sect. on pediat. gastroenterology and nutrition 1999—, chair 2005—), N.Am. Soc. Pediat. Gastro Nutrition (chair patient care com. 1997—2000). Avocations: skiing, swimming, hiking, tennis, biking. Office: U Calif Dept Pediat PO Box 0136 San Francisco CA 94143-0136 Office Phone: 415-476-5892. Business E-Mail: mheyman@peds.ucsf.edu.

HEYMANN, STEVE, oncologist; b. Strasbourg, France, July 28, 1978; Diploma, Paris U., 2005; MD, Louis Pasteur U., 2007. Chief resident Ctr. Paul Strauss, 2007—09; praticien fellow, des ctrs. de lutte contre le cancer Inst. de Cancerologie Gustave Roussy Cancer Ctr., 2009—11, médecin spécialiste, des ctrs. de lutte contre le cancer, 2011—. Mem.: European Soc. Therapeutic Radiation Oncology, French Soc. Young Radiation Oncologist, Franch Soc. Gynecol. Cancers. Avocation: tennis. Office: 114 Rue Edouard Vaillant Villejuif Val De Marne 98400 France Personal E-mail: steveheymann@free.fr.

HEYMANN, WARREN R., dermatologist, educator; Attended, Albert Einstein Coll. of Medicine, Bronx, NY. Diplomate Am. Bd. Dermatology, Am. Bd. Dermatology-dermatopathology, Am. Bd. Dermatology-pediatric dermatology. Intern Bellevue - NYU Med. Ctr., NYC; resident Albert Einstein Coll. of Medicine, Bronx, NY; fellow dermatopathology Univ. of Pa., Phila.; clin. prof. dermatology Univ. Pa., Phila.; prof. medicine and pediatrics UMDNJ-Robert Wood Johnson Med. Sch., head divsn. of dermatology Cooper Hosp. Mem.: Soc. Pediatric of Dermatology, Am. Acad. of Dermatology, Pa. Acad. of Dermatology (former pres.), Phila. Dermatologic Soc. (former pres.). Office: Heymann Manders Green Halpern Ste 306 100 Brick Rd Marlton NJ 08053 Mailing: Heymann Manders Green Halpern Ste 215 Three Cooper Plz Camden NJ 08103 Office Phone: 856-596-0111, 856-342-2439. Office Fax: 856-596-7194, 856-968-7832.

HEYNEMAN, DONALD, parasitology and tropical medicine educator; b. San Francisco, Feb. 18, 1925; s. Paul and Amy Josephine (KLauber) H.; m. Louise Davidson Ross, June 18, 1971; children: Amy J., Lucy A., Andrew P., Jennifer K., Claudia G. AB magna cum laude, Harvard U., 1950; MA, Rice U., 1952, PhD, 1954. Instr. zoology UCLA, 1954-56, asst. prof., 1956-60; head dept. parasitology U.S. Navy Med. Research unit, Cairo, also co-dir. Malakal, Sudan, 1960-62; assoc. research parasitologist Hooper Found. U. Calif., San Francisco, 1962-64, assoc. prof., 1966-68, prof., 1968-91, prof. emeritus, 1991—, asst. dir. Hooper found., 1970-74, acting chmn. dept. internat. health, 1976-78, assoc. dean Sch. Pub. Health Berkeley and San Francisco, 1987-91, assoc. dean emeritus, 1991—, chmn. joint med. program, 1987-91, chmn. emeritus, 1991—. Research coordinator U. Calif. Internat. Ctr. Med. Research and Tng., Kuala Lumpur, Malaysia, 1964-66; cons. physiol. processes sect. NSF, 1966-91; environ. biology div. NIH, 1968-91; mem. tropical medicine and parasitology study sect. NIAID-NIH, 1973-76; mem. adv. sci. bd. Gorgas Meml. Inst., 1967-90; cons. WHO, 1967, mem. sci. tech. rev. com. on Leishmaniases, 1984; cons. UN Devel. Program, 1978-91, US-AID, others; panel reviewer Internat. Nomenclature of Diseases, 1984—; Am. cons. and U.S. prin. investigator U. Linkage Project, Egypt-U.S., 1984—; mem. Calif. Health Adv. Com., 1983—. Author: (with R. Boolootian) An Illustrated Laboratory Text in Zoology, 1962, An Illustrated Laboratory Text in Zoology, A Brief Version, 1977, International Dictionary Medicine and Biology, (with R. Goldsmith) Textbook of Tropical Medicine and Parasitology, 1989;co-author, contbg. editor Phytolacca dodecandra: Endod, 1984, Endod II, 1987; contbr. articles to jours., chpts. to books.; editorial cons. Am. Jour. Tropical Medicine and Hygiene, Jour. Parasitology, Jour. Exptl. Parasitology, Sci., 1968—, other jours. Served with AUS, 1943-46. NIH grantee, 1966-85. Mem. Am. Soc. Parasitologists (council 1970-74, pres. 1982-83), Am. Micros. Soc. (exec. com. 1971-75), Am. Soc. Tropical Medicine and Hygiene (councilor 1981-84), So. Calif. Parasitol. Soc. (pres. 1957-58), No. Calif. Parasitologists (sec.- treas. 1969-72, pres. 1977-78), Phi Beta Kappa. Home: 1400 Lake St San Francisco CA 94118-1036 Personal E-mail: dheyneman@me.com.

HEYWANG-KOEBRUNNER, SYLVIA H., radiologist, educator; b. Karlsruhe, Germany, July 31, 1956; d. Walter and Ditha (Bierwag) H.; m. Gerhard Köbrunner, Mar. 11, 1989; children: Sandra, Petra. MD, Ludwig-Maximilians U., Munich, Germany, 1981, Dr. med. habil, 1992. Bd. cert. physician, 1982, radiologist, 1990. Resident radiology Ludwig-Maximilians U., Munich, 1983-90, mem. staff, 1990-92, asst. prof., 1991-92, U. Leipzig, Germany, 1993; asst. prof., vice dir. diagnostic radiology U. Halle, Germany, 1994-96; assoc. prof., vice dir. diagnostic radiology Martin Luther U., Halle, Germany, 1996—2003; assoc. prof., head dept. breast imaging and intervention Tech. U., Munich, 2003—07; head Nat. Reference Ctr. Mammography, 2007—. Author: Contrast-enhanced MRI of the breast, 1990, 2d edit., 1996, Breast Imaging, 1996, 2d edit. in English, 2001, in German 2003, Handbook Diagnostic Radiology - Breast, 2004; mem. editl. bd. European Radiology, Diagnostic Imaging, Roentgenpraxis; reviewer Radiology, Jour. Computer Assisted Tomography, JMRI, European Jour. Radiology, Jour. Magnetic Resonance Imaging, Investig Radiology, European Radiology, Acta Radiologica, Roe Fo.; contbr. articles to profl. jours. Scholar breast imaging German Cancer Assn., 1982; recipient MR prize Internat. MR-Symposium, 1991, Holthusen Ring, German Roentgen Soc., 1992, European Yvette Mayent-Curie prize, 1999. Mem. German Radiol. Soc. (mem. breast imaging com., Holthusenring award 1992), German Senology Soc. (bd. mem. 1995—), Radiol. Soc. N.Am., European Assn. Radiology, European Soc. Magnetic Resonance Medicine, European Congress Radiology (head breast com. 2000—), N.Y. Acad. Sci. Achievements include inauguration of contrast enhanced breast MRI; introduction vacuum-assisted breast biopsy in Europe; patents for breast biopsy coil; substance for interstitial marker solution; minimal invasive breast biopsy using fluorescence marker; first MR-guided vacuum breast biopsy; fixation device for MRI of the breast; development of web-based data base and reporting system for documentation and reporting of breast screening (with KV Bayern); research in image-based clinical studies. Avocations: music, science. Office: Nat Reference Ctr Mammography Munich Einsteinstr 3 81675 Munich Germany Business E-Mail: heywangkoe@referenzzentrum-muenchen.de.

HICKMAN, CLEVELAND PENDLETON, JR., biology professor; b. Greencastle, Ind., Oct. 29, 1928; m. Ethel Rae Rickenbacher, Aug. 19, 1950; children: Andrew Richard (dec.), Diane Elaine. AB, DePauw U., 1950; MS, U. N.H., 1953; PhD in Zoology (B.C. Elec. scholar), U. B.C., 1958. Fishery researcher U. Wash., Seattle, 1954-55; asst. prof. U. Alta., 1958-63, asso. prof., 1963-67; assoc. prof. biology Washington and Lee U., Lexington, Va., 1967-70, prof., 1970-93, prof. emeritus, 1993—. Author: (with L.S. Roberts and A. Larson) Animal Diversity, 1995, 3rd edit., 2003, (with L.S. Roberts) Biology of Animals, 7th edit., 1998, (with L.S. Roberts, S.I. Keen, A. Larson, H. I'Anson and D. Eisenhour) Integrated Principles of Zoology, 14th edit., 2008, A Field Guide to Sea Stars and Other Echinoderms of Galápagos, 1998, A Field Guide to Marine Molluscs of Galápagos, 1999, A Field Guide to Crustaceans of Galapagos, 2000, A Field Guide to Corals and Other Radiates of Galapagos, 2008, (with William S. Hoar) A Laboratory Companion for General and Comparative Physiology, 3d edit., 1983; contbr. numerous articles to profl. jours. Nat. Rsch. Coun. Can. grantee, 1959-67; sr. rsch. fellow, 1965-66; NIH grantee, 1962-65; NSF grantee, 1970-74 Office: Washington and Lee U Dept Biology Lexington VA 24450 Personal E-mail: hickman.c@rockbridge.net. Business E-Mail: hickmanc@wlu.edu.

HICKMAN, ELIZABETH PODESTA, retired counselor; b. Livingston, Ill., Sept. 30, 1922; d. Louis and Della (Martin) Podesta; m. Franklin Jay Hickman, Mar. 17, 1944 (dec.); children: Virginia Hickman Hellstern, Franklin. BEd summa cum laude, Ea. Ill. State U.; MA, George Washington U., 1966, EdD, 1979; postgrad., U. Chgo., 1945, U. Va., 1964-66; postgrad. (fellow), Northeastern U., 1967-68; exxon, Found.Raskob Found. grantee. Lic. counselor, Va. Tchr. pub. schs., Ill., Ohio, Va., Naples, Italy, 1944-64; dir. coll. transfer guidance Mayrmount Coll. Va., Arlington, 1964-67, dir. Counseling Ctr., 1974-81, assoc. dean counseling and residence life, 1981-84; cmty. counselor Divsn. Mass. Employment Security, Newton, 1968-69; tchr. English conversation, Fuchu, Japan, 1969-73; placement dir., career counselor Coll. of Gt. Falls, Mont., 1973-74. Lectr. Far East divsn. U. Md., Fuchu, 1971-73; spl. advisor Internat. Ranger Camps, Denmark and Switzerland, 1974-81; spl. cons. Internat. Quaker Sch., Werkhoven, The Netherlands, 1959-63; mem. steering com. Pres.'s Com. on Employment of Handicapped, 1974-95. Vol., ARC, 1967-68, Family Svcs., 1954-75, White House Agy. Liaison, 1986—, Kennedy Ctr. Adminstrn., Washington, 1984—, Arlington Free Clinic, 2000-02. With WAVES, 1943-44. Recipient Disting. Alumnus award Ea. Ill. U., 1984, Pres.'s Vol. Svc. award Washington DC, 2007-, White House vol. award, 2008. Mem. Brent Soc., Rose Soc., Potomac (Ill) Soc., Italian Am. Soc., Marymount U. Angels Soc., Women's Com. Nat. Symphony Orch., Washington Opera Guild, Square Sigma Sigma, Pi Lambda Theta, Am. League. Roman Catholic. *

HICKNER, JOHN M., physician, department chairman; b. St. Cloud, Minn., Mar. 23, 1950; MD, Ind. U., 1975; M in Clin. Rsch. and Biostatistics, U. Mich., 1995. Chair, family medicine Cleve. Clinic, 2009—. Office: 9500 Euclid Ave G-10 Cleveland OH 44195 Personal E-mail: johnhickner@yahoo.com.

HICKNER, ROBERT, physiologist, educator; b. Ann Arbor, Jan. 31, 1962; BS in Biology, Ind. U., 1985; PhD in Physiology, Karolinsa Inst., 1995. Prof., exercise and sport sci., and physiology East Carolina U., 1997—, dir., PhD program, bioenergetics and exercise sci., 2008—. Recipient Rsch. award, East Carolina U. Fellow: Am. Coll. Sports Medicine; mem.: Am. Diabetes Assn. Office: 363 Ward Sports Medicine Blvd Greenville NC 27858 Office Fax: 252-737-4689. Business E-Mail: hicknerr@ecu.edu.

HICKOK, NOREEN J., medical educator; b. Pontiac, Mich., Oct. 12, 1953; SB, MIT, 1975; PhD, Brandeis U., 1981. Assoc. prof. Thomas Jefferson U., 1996—. Mem.: AAAS, Orthop. Rsch. Soc. Avocations: piano, ballet, sewing, knitting. Office: 1015 Walnut St Ste 501 Philadelphia PA 19107 Business E-Mail: noreen.hickok@jefferson.edu.

HICKS, ALLEN MORLEY, retired hospital administrator; b. Toronto, Iowa, May 11, 1928; s. Perle and Grace (Mowry) H.; m. Sue Hicks; children by previous ma rriage: David, Dennis, Wendy, Patricia. Student, Long Beach City Coll., 1949-50; BS, U. Iowa, 1952, MS, 1954. Adminstrv. resident St. Lukes Hosp., Davenport, Iowa, 1953-54; adminstr. Schmitt Meml. Hosp., Beardstown, Ill., 1954-57, Pekin (Ill.) Meml. Hosp., 1957-63, Ill. Masonic Hosp. and Med. Center, Chgo., 1963-72; pres. Community Hosp., Indpls., 1972-84, Meth. Health Care Systems, Memphis, 1984-85, VHA Enterprises, 1985-90; adminstr. Midwest Med. Ctr., Indpls., 1991-93. Sr. advisor St. Vincent's Hosp. and Health Care Corp.; chmn. bd. Vol. Hosps. Am., 1980-84, Multi-Mut. Ins. Cos. of Bermuda and Cayman Islands; bd. dirs. Am. Coll. Testing, Ind. Blue Cross, Am. Health Capital, Indpls. Conv. Ctr.; preceptor masters degree program in health and hosp. adminstrn. U. Iowa; chmn. com. extended care Coun. on Assn. Svc., 1963; pres. Chgo. Hosp. Coun., 1970-71. Campaign chmn., bd. dirs., chmn. indsl. divsn. United Fund, Pekin, Ill., 1959-64; pres. Tazwell County United Cerebral Palsy, 1960-61; chmn. Cancer Crusade, Pekin, 1960-61; svc. chmn. Tazewell County, 1958-60; chmn. bd. Tomahawk dist. Creve Coeur coun. Boy Scouts Am., 1963-64, bd. dirs. Crossroads council; bd. dirs. Cancer Soc., Hosp. Research and Devel. Inst., Inc.; pres. Meth. Health Sys. Memphis, 1984-85. H. With USNR, 1945- 49, 51-52. Recipient Outstanding Young Man of Year award State Ill., 1960; Distinguished Service award Pekin Jr. C. of C., 1960; Boss of Year award Marquette chpt. Nat. Secs. Assn., 1962 Fellow Am. Coll. Health Adminstrn.; mem. Am. Hosp. Assn. (del. 1971—, chmn. com. community relations), Ill. Hosp.Assn. (trustee, chmn. com. personnel relations), Am. Coll. Hosp. Adminstrs., Am. Assn. Maternal and Infant Health, Ill. Welfare Assn., Ill. C. of C., Am. Legion, Am. Vets., 500 Assn., Beta Gamma Sigma. Presbyterian (elder, trustee). Clubs: Mason, Elks, Kiwanis (bd. dirs. Internat. Found. 1981-85, pres. local chpt. 1983). Home Phone: 651-275-3635; Office Phone: 972-742-9872. Personal E-mail: allenm202@yahoo.com.

HICKS, JOCELYN MURIEL, laboratory medicine specialist; b. Leamington Spa, Warwickshire, Eng., Aug. 17, 1937; arrived in U.S., 1965; d. Harold Archie and Muriel Ellen (Cumberland) Bingley; m. John Geoffrey Hicks, Aug. 15, 1959 (div. Nov. 1965); m. Melvin Blecher, May 1, 1973. BS, U. London, 1959, MSc, 1962; PhD, Georgetown U., 1971, DSc (hon.), 2010. Fellow Georgetown U. Med. Ctr., Washington, 1969-71; dir. clin. chemistry Children's Hosp. Nat. Med. Ctr., Washington, 1971-75, chmn. dept. lab. medicine, 1975-90, chief of lab. medicine and pathology, 1990—2001, dir. clin. support svcs., 1995-99; asst. prof. George Washington U. Med. Ctr., Washington, 1972-74, assoc. prof., 1975-81, prof., 1981—2002, prof. emeritus, 2002—; mem. profl. staff The Hosp. for Sick Children, Washington, 1984—2001; exec. dir. Ctr. Complex Diseases, 1999-2001; exec. dir. emeritus Children's Nat. Med. Ctr., 2002—; COO genetics divsn. Genetics and IVF, Fairfax, Va., 2002—04; pres. JMBH Assocs., Washington, 2004—. Pres. Children's Faculty assocs. Children's Hosp., Washington, 1989—90, chmn. bd. dirs., 1990—93, chmn. exec. com., 1994—95; clin. affiliate Cath. U. Am., Washington, 1982—94; cons. Johnson and Johnson Clin. Diagnostics, Bayer Diagnostics, i-Stat Corp. Author: Selected Analyses of Clinical Chemistry, 1984, Textbook of Clinical Chemistry, 1984, Directory of Rare Analyses, 1986, 1987, 1990, 1992, 1994, 1997, 1998, 2000, 2005, The Neonate, 1974, Pediatric Reference Ranges, 1995, 1997; co-author: Biochemical Basis of Pediatric Disease, 1992, Biochemical Basis of Pediatric Disease, 2d edit., 1995; co-editor: Point-of-Care Testing, 1999, 2004; contbr. articles to profl. jours. Recipient Kone award, Assn. Clin. Biochemists, 1987, Roche award, Assn. Clin. Biochemists(UK), 2008. Fellow: Acad. Clin. Lab. Physicians and Scientists, Royal Coll. Pathologists U.K., Spanish Soc. Clin. and Molecular Pathology (hon.), Portuguese Soc. Clin. Pathologists (hon.), Am. Assn. Clin. Chemistry (hon.; bd. dirs. 1978—81, pres. 1981—82, chmn. publs. commn. 1982—87, Joseph H. Roe award 1976, Bernard Gerulat Meml. award 1983, Fisher award 1984, Van Slyke award 1988, Miriam Reiner award 1991, Outstanding Contbns. to Clin. Chemistry 1993, Outstanding Spkr. award 2002, Roger Boeckx Meml. lectr. 2002), Assn. Clin. Biochemistry (hon.), Israeli Soc. Clin. Biochemistry (hon.), Egyptian Soc. Lab. Medicine (hon.); mem.: Italian Soc. Clin. Biochemistry & Clin. Molecular Biology, Paraguayan Biochemistry Assn. (hon.), Croatian Soc. Med. Biochemistry (hon.), Egyptian Soc. Clin. Chemistry (hon.), Guatemala Assn. Chem. Biologists (hon.), South African Assn. Clin. Biochemistry (hon.), Internat. Fedn. Clin. Chemistry and Lab. Medicine (treas. 2003—05, 2003—05, pres. 2006—08, past pres. & bd. mem. 2009—, Concustell award, Spain 2006). Home and Office: JMBH Assocs 4329 Van Ness St NW Washington DC 20016-5625 Home Phone: 202-363-0373.

HICKS, JUDITH EILEEN, nursing administrator; b. Chgo., Jan. 1, 1947; d. John Patrick and Mary Ann (Clifford) Rohan; m. Laurence Joseph Hicks, Nov. 22, 1969; children: Colleen Driscoll, Patrick Kevin. BSN, St. Xavier U., Chgo., 1969; MSN, U. Ill., Chgo., 1971. Staff nurse Mercy Hosp., Chgo., 1969-70, nursing supr., 1970-73; cons. continuing edn. Ill. Nurses Assn., Chgo., 1974-75; dir. ob-gyn. nursing Prentice Women's Hosp. Northwestern Meml. Hosp., Chgo., 1975-81; v.p. nursing Children's Meml. Hosp., Chgo., 1981-86; pres. Children's Meml. Home Health, Inc., 1986—2001, Children's Meml. Nursing Svcs., 1986—2001; CEO Beechwood Health Solutions, LLC, 2009—. Pres. Allied & Children's Home Health and Nursing Svcs., 1988, CM Healthcare Resources, Inc., 1988—2001, The Pediat. Pl., Inc., 1994—2001, Focused Health Solutions, Inc., 2000—07, founder to CEO; dir. Near North Health Corp., Chgo., 1982—85; pres. Pediat. Excellence Program Svc.; bd. dirs. Infant Welfare Soc. Chgo., Nat. Breast Cancer Assn., Children's Meml. Med. Ctr., 1985—2007; mem. Sch. Pub. Health, Nutrition Rountable Harvard Sch. Pub. Health; mem., ledership coun. Harvard Sch. Pub. Health.; mem., dean adv. com. U. Illinois Sch. Nursing; bd. dirs. La Casa Norte. Mem. bd. trustees St. Xavier U., Chgo., 2005—. Recipient Jonas Salk Leadership award March of Dimes, 1998, Ernst and Young Outstanding Ill. Nurse Leader award, 1999, Entrepreneur of Yr. award Ernst and Young Midwest Region, 2006, Nursing Alumni of Yr. award, St. Xavier U., 2007; finalist Entrepreneur of Yr. award Ernst and Young, 2004. Mem. Am. Soc. Nursing Adminstrs., Women's Health Exec. Network (1984-85), Ill. Hosp. Assn. (chmn. coun. on nursing 1982-83), Inst. Medicine, Econ. Club of Chgo. Home: 2206 Beechwood Ave Wilmette IL 60091-1508 Office: Beechwood Health Solution LLC Wilmette IL 60091 Office Phone: 773-747-8356 Personal E-mail: judithhicks@mac.com. Business E-Mail: jhicks@beechwoodhealth.com.

HICKS, PATRICIA M., pediatrician, allergist, immunologist; Attended, Wilson Coll., Pa. State U., 1973. Diplomate Am. Bd. Allergy And Immunology, Am. Bd. Pediatrics. Resident pediat. Columbia-Presbyn. Med. Ctr., 1974—76, fellow allergy & immunology, 1979—81; with Valley Hosp. Office: Valley Hospital Ste 5 119 First St Ho Ho Kus NJ 07423 Office Phone: 201-444-5277.

HICKSON, GERALD BENNETT, pediatrician; b. Tifton, Ga., Apr. 22, 1952; BS, U. Ga.; MD, Tulane U. Sch. Medicine, 1978. Cert. Am. Bd. Pediat. Resident, pediat. Vanderbilt U. Med. Ctr., Nashville, 1978—81; fellow, gen. academic pediat. Vanderbilt U. Med. Ctr./Metro Nashville Gen. Hosp., Tenn., 1981—83; chief, pediat. Vanderbilt Clinic, Nashville, 1990—2003; health policy fellow Vanderbilt Inst. Pub. Policy Studies, Nashville, 1991; instr., pediat. Vanderbilt U. Sch. Medicine, Nashville, 1982—83, assoc. prof., 1997, prof., pediat., 1998, assoc. prof., pediat., 1990—98, prof., psychiatry, 2001, assoc. dean, clin. affairs, 2003—, prof., pediat., 2003—, dir., Ctr. for Patient and Profl. Advocacy; asst. prof. Vanderbilt Sch. Nursing, Nashville, 1990—92, assoc. prof., family and health sys. nursing, 1994—; dir., clin. risk and loss prevention Vanderbilt U. Med. Ctr. Vis. prof., pediat. U. Carabobo, Valencia, Venezuela, 1985; rsch. investigator Peabody Coll., Vanderbilt U., Tenn., 1988; bd. gov. Nat. Patient Safety Found.; chairperson, quality care com. Nat. Assn. Children's Hosp. and Related Inst. Mem.: Am. Acad. Pediat. (mem. com. on quality improvement). Office: Ctr for Patient & Profl Advocacy Vanderbilt U Med Ctr 405 Oxford House Nashville TN 37232-4200 Office Phone: 615-343-4500. Office Fax: 615-343-8580. Business E-Mail: gerald.hickson@vanderbilt.edu.

HIDA, RICHARD YUDI, ophthalmologist, educator; b. Botucatu, São Paulo, Brazil, Nov. 10, 1972; MD, U. Santo Amaro, 1996. Asst. prof. Santa Casa de Sao Paulo, 2003—, eye bank dir., 2009—. Mem.: Conselho Brasileiro de Oftalmologi, Am. Acad. Ophthalmology. Home: Rua Afonso de Freitas 488 Apt 61 Sao Paulo 04006-052 Brazil Personal E-mail: ryhida@mandic.com.br.

HIDAI, CHIAKI, medical educator, researcher; b. Tokyo, Sept. 22, 1961; s. Toshio and Aiko Hidai; m. Hiroko Yoshizawa, Apr. 27, 1990. MD, Hokkaido U. Sch. Meidicine, Japan, 1986, PhD. Instr. Nihon U. Sch. Medicine, Itabashi, Tokyo, 2000—. Home: 6-13-26 Ohizumi-gakuen-cho Nerima-ku Tokyo 178-0061 Japan Office: Nihon Univ Sch Medicine 30-1 Ohyaguchi-kami-cho Itabashi-ku Tokyo 173-8610 Japan Office Fax: 03-3972-8292. Business E-Mail: hidai@med.nihon-u.ac.jp.

HIDAJAT, RUDY RIDWAN, ophthalmology researcher; s. Agus and Kurniawati Hidajat; m. Rini Damayanthi Gunawan, Apr. 16, 1983; children: Ryan Marshall Holland, Jefferson Ray Tan Hidayat. BSc with honors, Massey U., Palmerston North, New Zealand,

1977—79; D of Medicine, Trisakti U., Jakarta, Indonesia, 1963—71; PhD, U. Canterbury, Christchurch, New Zealand, 1980—83. Cert. in Sci. Christchurch Tech. Inst., 1976. Lab. tech. Christchurch Drainage Bd., New Zealand, 1973—77; scientist Christchurch Hosp., New Zealand, 1983—. Rschr. Christchurch Hosp., New Zealand, 1983—; head, electrodiagnostic clinic Ophthalmology Dept., Christchurch Hosp., New Zealand, 1983—, coord. physics support for the nat. ocular melanoma svc., 1996—. Contbr. articles to profl. jours. Recipient Canterbury Dist. Health Bd. Quality and Innovation Supreme award, 2003, New Zealand Health Innovation awards, 2004, Asian Innovation award, 2004; Doctoral scholar, Lincoln Coll., 1980 - 1983, Travel grantee, Canterbury Med. Rsch. Found., 2002. Mem.: Australasian Coll. Phys. Scientists and Engrs. in Medicine, Internat. Soc. for Clin. Electrophysiology of Vision. Achievements include development of the automation of Farnsworth-Munsell 100 hue colour vision test in New Zealand. Office: Christchurch Hosp Riccarton Avenue Christchurch New Zealand

HIDAKA, HIROSHI, physician, educator; b. Sakai, Japan, Nov. 12, 1967; MD, Tohoku U., 1993, PhD, 1999. Jr. assoc. prof. Tohoku U. Hosp., 2009—. Mem. editl. bd. Japan Audiological Soc., 2009. Mem.: ARO, Japan Otolaryn. Soc. Office: 1-1 Seiryo-machi Aoba-ku Sendai Miyagi 980-8574 Japan Office Fax: 81-22-717-7306. Business E-Mail: zay00015@nifty.com.

HIDAKA, NORIAKI, orthopedist; b. Osaka, Aug. 30, 1958; MD, Osaka City U. Med. Sch., 1984. Chief dept. orthop. surgery Yodogawa Christian Hosp., 2008. Clin. prof. Osaka City U., Grad. Sch. Medicine, 2011. Master: Japanese Soc. Fracture Repair, Japanese Soc. Surgery Hand; mem.: Japanese Soc. Reconstructive Microsurgery, Japanese Orthop. Assn. Avocations: skiing, soccer. Office: 2-9-26 Higashi Yodogawa-ku Awaji Osaka 533-0032 Japan Business E-Mail: a108119@ych.or.jp.

HIDALGO, DAVID ARTHUR, plastic surgeon; b. Hartford, Conn., July 30, 1952; m. Mary Ann Tighe. BS in Biology, BA in Fine Arts magna cum laude, Georgetown U.; MD cum laude, Georgetown U. Sch. Medicine, 1978. Cert. Nat. Bd. Med. Examiners, 1980, Am. Bd. Surgery, 1984, Am. Bd. Plastic Surgery, 1987, lic. NY, 1980. Intern, surgery NYU Med. Ctr., NYC, 1978—79, resident, gen. surgery, 1979—83, resident, plastic surgery, 1983—85, fellow, microsurgery, 1985—86; affiliated with Meml. Sloan-Kettering Cancer Ctr., NYC, 1986—2000, asst. mem., 1987—92, assoc. mem., 1992—2000, chief, divsn. plastic and reconstructive surgery, 1992—2000; asst. attending surgeon Manhattan Eye, Ear & Throat Hosp., 1986—92, assoc. attending surgeon, 1992—; clin. asst. surgeon Meml. Hosp. for Cancer and Allied Diseases, 1986—88, asst. attending surgeon, 1986—92, assoc. attending surgeon, 1992—2000; asst. prof. surgery Cornell U. Med. Coll., 1986—93, assoc. prof. surgery, 1993—2001; affiliated with NY-Presbyn. Hosp., 1986—, Southampton Hosp., 2000—, cons., dept. surgery, 2000—; clin. prof., surgery Weill-Cornell U. Med. Coll., 2001—; pvt. practice aesthetic plastic surgery NYC, 2000—. Mem. breast search com. Meml. Hosp., 1993, mem. surgical quality assurance com., 96, mem. surgical exec. com., 1992—2000; lectr., presenter in field; spkr. on panels; vis. prof. U. Louisville, Ky., 1985, Johns Hopkins U., Balt., 1989, U. Pa., 1996, Yale U. Sch. Medicine, 2000, U. Chgo., 2000, Oreg. Health and Scis. U., 2002, U. Kansas, Mo., 2002, Northwestern U., 2002, U. Va., Charlorresville, 2002, Albany Med. Coll., NY, 2002, Brown U., RI, 2002, U. Manitoba, 2002, U. BC, 2002, U. Miami, Fla., 2002, Cedars-Sinai Med. Ctr. (Bernard G. Sarnat MD Lectureship), LA, 2003; nat. vis. prof. Plastic Surgery Ednl. Found., 2002, NYU, 2003; cons. Office of Profl. Conduct, NY State, 2004—. Contbr. Plastic and Reconstructive Surgery, Annals of Plastic Surgery;, author numerous chpt. in textbooks and other reference publ. in plastic surgery; co-author (with WW Shaw): Microsurgery in Trauma, 1987; publr. (videos on plastic surgery technique), guest appearances CBS News, ABC News & Fox News, quoted in numerous publs. Allure, Elle, Harper's Bazaar, Marie Claire, NY Times, Town & Country, Vogue, GQ, Tatler, Self and W, editl. cons. Plastic and Reconstructive Surgery, 1989—, mem. editl. bd., 2004—, editl. cons. Aesthetic Surgery Jour., 2001—, Annals of Plastic Surgery, 1995—2001, Head and Neck Surgery, 1991—95, Jour. Reconstructive Microsurgery, 1991—97, Annals of Surgical Oncology, 1993—96. Dir. med. com. Joan's Legacy Found., 2002—. Recipient First Prize, Plastic Surgery Ednl. Found. Nat. Sr. Resident's Conf., 1985, Best Surgical Technique Video awards, Health and Sci. Network, 1990, Clin. Rsch. award, Plastic Surgery Ednl. Found., 2001; named Best Cosmetic Doctors, NY Mag., 2003, The Producer, Elle mag., 2004; named one of Best Doctors in Am., Northeast Region, 1996—97, Top in plastic surgery specialty, America's Top Doctors, Best Doctors in NY, NY Mag., 1991, 1996, 1998, 2000, 2001, 2002; named to The List in plastic surgery, NY Times mag., 2005. Fellow: ACS; mem.: Am. Soc. Plastic and Reconstructive Surgeons (mem. CPT adv. com. 1995, mem. domestic symposia com. 1996, 1997), Soc. Surgical Oncology, Soc. Head and Neck Surgeons, Assn. for Academic Surgery, Am. Soc. for Reconstructive Microsurgery, AMA, NY Regional Soc. Plastic and Reconstructive Surgery, NY County Med. Soc., NY State Med. Soc., Am. Soc. Maxillofacial Surgeons (mem. scientific program com. 1992, mem. practice parameters com. 1992, Best Paper of Yr. award to appear in Plastic and Reconstructive Surgery 1989, Best Surgical Technique Video awards 1992, Best Paper of Yr. award to appear in Jour. Plastic and Reconstructive Surgery 2003), Am. Assn. Plastic Surgeons (mem. James Barrett-Brown award com. 1997, 1998, mem. scientific program com. 2000), Am. Soc. Aesthetic Plastic Surgery (mem. question writing subcom. for ABPS recertification examination 2000, mem. scientific program com. 2005—, mem. breast surgery immediate response com. 2005—), Am. Soc. Plastic Surgeons (James Barrett Brown award for Best Sci. Paper of Yr. 1992), Alpha Omega Alpha Med. Honor Soc. Avocations: art, painting. Office: 655 Park Ave New York NY 10021-5937 Office Phone: 212-517-9777. Office Fax: 212-517-2527. E-mail: info@drdavidhidalgo.com.

HIDEKI, ISHIHARA, medical researcher; b. Japan, Sept. 1, 1959; PhD, Hokkaido U., 1982. Exec. rschr. Sysmex Corp., 2007—. Supervising rsch. cancer diagnostic Ctrl. Rsch. Labs., 2000—. Office: 4-4-4 Takatsukadai Nishi-ku Kobe Hyogo 651-2271 Japan Business E-Mail: ishihara.hideki@sysmex.co.jp.

HIDEO, NAKAJIMA, oncologist, educator; b. Gunma, Japan, Nov. 18, 1963; MD, Tokyo Med. and Dental U., 1988. Assoc. prof. Kanazawa Med. U., 2005—. Lab. chief Nat. Inst. Longevity Sci., 2000—04. Avocation: swimming. Office: Daigaku1-1 Uchinada Ishikawa 920-0293 Japan Office Fax: 81-76-218-8283. Business E-Mail: hideonak@kanzawa-med.ac.jp.

HIDEYUKI, AKAZA, urologist, educator; b. Tokyo, 1946; MD, U. Tokyo, 1973. Guest asst. prof. U. Tenn., Memphis, 1982; lectr. urology U. Tokyo, 1986-90; asst. prof. urology U. Tsukuba, Japan, 1990-97, prof. urology, 1997—. Mem. Am. Urol. Assn., Soc. Internat. Urology, Japanese Urol. Assn. Office: Rsch Ctr Advanced Sci & Tech University Tokyo Rsch Campus 4 Rm 664-1 4-6-1 Komaba Meguro-ku Tokyo 153-8904 Japan Office Phone: 81 35452 5314. Fax: 81-298533223; Office Fax: 81 3 5452 5343. Business E-Mail: akazah@isbm.org, akazah@med.rcast.u-tokyo.ac.jp.

HIDEYUKI, OSHIGE, physician; b. Kyoto, Aug. 26, 1972; PhD, Postgrad. Sch., MD, 2007. Asst. Kansai Med. U. Hirakata Hosp., 2008—. Mem.: Japan Close-up Magician Assn., Japan Soc. Surgery Cerebral Stroke, Acad. Japan Osteopathy Assn., Japan Soc. Ctrl. Nervous Sys. Computed Imaging, Japan Neurosurg. Soc. Avocations: computers, magic. Office: Shinmachi 2-3-1 Hirakata Osaka 573-1191 Japan Office Fax: 072-804-2885. Business E-Mail: osge45645692@mx5.canvas.ne.jp.

HIDEYUKI, SAITO, medical educator; b. Tokyo, Mar. 31, 1964; MD, Keio U. Sch. Medicine, PhD, 1989. Asst. prof., dept. otorhinolaryngology Keio U. Sch. Medicine, 2007—. Avocations: music, winemaking. Office: 35 Shinanomachi Shinjuku-ku Tokyo 160-8582 Japan Office Fax: 81-3-3353-1261. Personal E-mail: hsaitorl@gmail.com.

HIDRON, ALICIA, internist, medical educator; b. Feb. 15, 1975; MD, CES Inst. Healt Scis., Columbia, 1999. Diplomate Am. Bd. Internal Medicine. Resident internal medicine Emory U. Sch. Medicine, Atlanta, 2002—05, chief resident, 2005—06, fellow divsn. infectious disease, 2006, asst. prof. medicine, 2007—. Contbr. articles to profl. jours. Mem.: ACP, Alpha Omega Alpha Honor Med. Soc. Office: Emory U Sch Medicine 201 Dowman Dr Atlanta GA 30322 also: 69 Jesse Hill Jr Dr SE Atlanta GA 30303 Office Phone: 404-616-7027. Business E-Mail: ahidron@emory.edu. *

HIEHLE, JOHN FREDERICK, JR., diagnostic radiologist; Grad., Harvard Med. Sch., 1987. Diplomate Am. Bd. of Radiology-diagnostic radiology, Am. Bd. of Radiology-interventional and vascular radiology, Am. Bd. of Radiology-neuroradiology. Intern Univ. of Hawaii, 1988; resident diagnostic radiology Hosp. of the Univ. of Pa., 1992, fellow neuroradiology, 1993. Office: Crozer Chester Medical Center Radiology Department 1 Medical Center Blvd Chester PA 19013 Office Phone: 610-579-3500. Office Fax: 610-579-3501.

HIELSCHER, ANDREAS HELMUT, biomedical engineer; b. Bremen, Germany, Feb. 15, 1964; arrived in U.S., 1991; s. Helmut Reinhardt and Inge Hielscher; m. Maria Anagnostopoulou, May 15, 1995; 1 child, Amélie Lukia Inge. BS in Physics, U. Hannover, Germany, 1989; MS in Applied Physics, U. Hannover, 1991; PhD, Rice U., Tex., 1995. Postdoctoral fellow Los Alamos Nat. Lab., N.Mex., 1995—98; asst. prof. SUNY - Downstate Med. Ctr., Bklyn., 1998—2001; adj. prof. Poly. U., 1999—2001; assoc. prof. of biomedical engring. and radiology Columbia U., NYC, 2001—. Contbr. articles to sci. and profl. jours. Recipient Shechao Charles Feng Meml. prize, SPIE Internat. Soc. of Optical Engring., 1997, Young Investigator award, Whitaker Found., 1999; grantee Optical Tomography Diagnosis Joint Diseases, Nat. Inst. Arthritis and Musculoskeletal and Skin Diseases, 1999—, Optical Tomographic Imaging Brain Injuries and Diseases, NYC Coun. Spkrs. Fund Biomed. Rsch., 1999—2003, Model Based Iterative Reconstruction Techniques Optical Tomography, Whitaker Found., 1999—2003, MRI Compatible Diffuse Optical Tomography Sys. for Small Animal Oximetry, Nat. Inst. for Biomedical Imaging and Bioengineering, 2003—, Small Animal Tomography Sys. Green Fluorescent Protein Imaging, Nat. Cancer Inst., 2007—; Dirs. Postdoctoral fellow, Los Alamos Nat. Lab., 1995, Dept. Biomed. Engring. and Laser Medicine fellow, Free U. of Berlin, 2003—08. Mem.: IEEE, SPIE Internat. Soc. of Optical Engring., Optical Soc. of Am. (chair of biomedical optical spectroscopy group 2001—03). Achievements include patents for Characterization of highly scattering media by measurement of diffusely backscattered polarized light, US Patent No. 6, 011, 626; patents pending for Iterative reconstruction scheme for optical tomography based on the equation of radiative transfer; A digital signal processor-based detection system for optical tomography. Office: Columbia Univ 500 W 120th St MC8904 New York NY 10027

HIER, DANIEL BARNET, neurologist; b. Chgo., Mar. 23, 1947; BA, Harvard U., 1969, MD, 1973. Medical intern Bronx Mcpl. Hosp., NYC, 1973-74; neurology resident Mass. Gen. Hosp., Boston, 1974-77, neurology fellow, 1977-79; neurologist Michael Reese Hosp., Chgo., 1979-89, chmn. neurology, 1987-89; head neurology U. Ill., Chgo., 1989—2003, assoc. prof. neurology, 1989-91, prof., 1991—; physician exec. Cerner Corp., 2010. Fellow Am. Acad. Neurology Home: 230 W 2nd St Apt 3106 Kansas City MO 64105-2176 Office Phone: 312-622-2776. E-mail: dbhier@gmail.com.

HIESHETTER, JANET, foundation administrator; BA in Health Sciences, Kalamazoo Coll., Mich. Dir. cmty. resource devel. TRIOLOGY, Inc.; sr. dir., interim exec. dir. Nat. Osteoporosis Found.; exec. dir. Dystonia Med. Rsch. Found., Chgo., 2004—. Office: Dystonia Med Rsch Found One E Wacker Dr Ste 2430 Chicago IL 60601-1905 Office Phone: 312-755-0198. Office Fax: 312-803-0138. Business E-Mail: jhieshetter@dystonia-foundation.org. *

HIGASHI, KOTARO, radiologist, department chairman; b. Ishikawa, Japan, Feb. 8, 1955; MD, Kanazawa Med. U., 1979. Prof., dept. radiology Kanazawa Med. U., 1991—98, vis. prof., 1998; chmn., dept. pet ctr. Asanogawa Gen. Hosp., 1998—. Mem.: Japanese Soc. Radiology, Japanese Soc. Nuc. Medicine. Avocation: tennis. Home: 1-16-1 Housai Kanazawa Ishikawa 920-0862 Japan Personal E-mail: h550208@kanazawa-med.ac.jp.

HIGASHI, TAKAHIRO, physician, educator; b. Japan, Nov. 17, 1972; MD, U. Tokyo, 1997; PhD, UCLA, 2005. Assoc. prof. U. Tokyo Grad. Sch. Medicine, 2009. Office: 7-3-1 Hongo Bunkyo Tokyo 113-0033 Japan Business E-Mail: thigashi@ncc.go.jp.

HIGBY, LAWRENCE M., medical products executive; BS, U. Calif. Exec. v.p. mktg., chmn. Orange County edit. LA Times, Times Mirror Co., 1986—94; group v.p., pres. & COO 76 Products Co. Unocal Corp., 1994—97; pres., COO Apria Healthcare Group, Lake Forest, Calif., 1997—2002, pres., CEO, 2002—08, advisor, vice chmn., 2008—. Office: Apria Health 26220 Enterprise Ct Lake Forest CA 92630-8405 Office Phone: 949-639-2000. Office Fax: 949-587-9363.

HIGGINBOTHAM, EDITH ARLEANE, radiologist, researcher; b. New Orleans, Sept. 14, 1946; d. Luther Aldrich and Ruby (Clark) H.; m. Terry Lawrence Andrews (div. 1979); m. Donald Temple Ford (div. 1989). BS, Howard U., 1967, MS, 1970, MD, 1974. Diplomate Am. Bd. Radiology, Am. Bd. Nuclear Medicine. Intern St. Vincent's Hosp., NYC, 1974-75, resident in diagnostic radiology, 1975-78, resident in nuclear radiology, 1978-79; asst. prof. radiology, chief nuclear medicine Howard U., Howard U. Hosp., Washington, 1979-82; assoc. prof. clin. radiology, dir. nuclear medicine U. Medicine and Dentistry N.J., Newark, 1982-90; locum tenems radiologist Sterling Med., Cin., 1991-94, Med. Nat., San Antonio, 1990-91; diagnostic radiologist Diagnostic Health Imaging Systems, Lanham, Md., 1994-95; locum tenens radiologist, 1995-97; radiologist, dir. radiology N.E. Wash. Med. Group, Colville, Wash., 1997—99; radiologist Mount Carmel Hosp., Colville, 1997-99, Barstow (Calif.) Cmty. Hosp., 1999, Queen of Peace Hosp., Mitchell, SD, 1999—2002, New Ulm Med Ctr., Minn., 2002—03, dir. radiology, 2003; radiologist Naeve Hosp., Albert Lea (Minn.) Med. Ctr., Mayo Health Sys., 2003—. Cons. Biotech. Rsch. Inst., Rockville, Md., 1989-94; profl. assoc. Ctr. for Molecular Medicine and Immunology, Newark, 1984-90; asst. prof. radiology George Washington U., Washington, 1990; counselor Am. Coll. Radiology, SD, 2001; presenter in field. Contbr. articles to profl. jours. Named Outstanding Working Woman, Glamour mag., 1981, Hon. Dep. Atty. Gen., State of La., 1982. Mem.: SD Med. Assn. (continuing med. edn. com. 2001), Freeborn County Med. Soc. (pres. 2005), Minn. Med. Assn. (continuing med. edn. com. 2005), Soc. Nuclear Medicine, Radiol. Soc. N.Am., Am. Coll. Radiology, Phi Delta Epsilon, Sigma Xi. Roman Catholic. Avocations: aerobics, reading, music, travel. E-mail: ehigginbothammd@charter.net.

HIGGINBOTHAM, EVE JULIET, academic administrator, dean, ophthalmologist; b. New Orleans, Nov. 4, 1953; d. Luther Aldrich and Ruby Edith (Clark) H.; m. Frank Christopher Williams, June 7, 1986. BSChE, MS in Engring., MIT, 1975; MD, Harvard U., 1979. Intern Pacific Med. Ctr., San Francisco, 1979-80; resident La. State U. Eye Ctr., 1980-83; fellow Mass. Eye and Ear Infirmary, Boston, 1983-85; asst. prof. U. Ill., Chgo., 1985-90; assoc. prof. U. Mich., Ann Arbor, 1990-94; prof., chair dept. ophthalmology and visual sciences U. Md., Balt., 1994—2005; dean Morehouse Sch. Medicine, Atlanta, 2005—09, sr. v.p. acad. affairs, 2005—09; sr. v.p., exec. dean health sciences Howard U., Washington, 2010—. Co-editor: Management of Difficult Glaucoma, 1994, Clinician's Guide to Comprehensive Ophtholomology, 1998; contbr. articles to profl. jours; mem. editl. bd. Jour. of Glaucoma, 1990-93, Archives of Ophthalmology, 1994—; sect. editor: Glaucoma in Principles and Practice of Ophthalmology. Bd. dirs. Prevent Blindness Am., Schaumburg, Ill., 1990-97, chair publs. com., 1990-95, chair scientific adv. com., 1995—. Fellow Am. Acad. Ophthalmology (trustee 1992-95); mem. Women in Ophthalmology (bd. dirs. 1990-99), Assn. Univ. Profs. Ophthalmology, Assn. in Rsch. in Vision and Ophthalmology, Inst. Medicine, Md. Soc. Eye Physicians and Surgeons (v.p. 1997-99, pres. 2000—), Balt. City Med. Soc. (treas. 1999-00, v.p. 2000—). Avocations: golf, piano. Office: Howard University 2400 Sixth St NW Washington DC 20059 Office Phone: 202-865-7470. Business E-Mail: eve.higginbotham@howard.edu. *

HIGGINS, GINA O'CONNELL, psychologist, writer; b. Bklyn. d. Paul Bernard Patrick Joseph and Virginia Payne (Conrad) O'Connell; m. James T. Higgins, Aug. 5, 1972 (div. June 1997); children: Caitlin, Taryn; m. R.D. Norton, June 13, 1998; children: Maya, Elias. BA magna cum laude, Tufts U., 1972, MEd, 1974; EdD, Harvard U., 1985. Lic. psychologist, Mass. Diagnostician, med. edn. and evaluation clinic North Shore Children's Hosp., 1982-87; psychotherapist, intake diagnostician, case cons. Mental Health Ctr., North Shore Children's Hosp., 1982-86; fellow Clin. Devel. Inst., Belmont, Mass., 1990—2002; staff psychologist Mass. Gen. Hosp., Boston, 1993—2001; pvt. practice psychotherapy and psychodiagnosis, Salem, Mass., 1993—2002. Lectr. Middlesex C.C., Bedford, Mass., 1974-75, Eliot Pearson dept. child study Tufts U., 1974-75; lectr. Lesley Grad. Sch., Cambridge, Mass., 1974-76, asst. prof., 1976-81; clin. assoc. Harvard Med. Sch./Mass. Gen. Hosp., Boston, 1994-2002. Author: Resilient Adults: Overcoming a Cruel Past, 1994. Recipient scholarship and fellowships. Mem APA, Mass. Psychol. Assn. Office: One Salem Green Ste 555 Salem MA 01970 Office Phone: 978-741-3459.

HIGGINS, GLORIA C., pediatrician; b. Grand Haven, Mich., Oct. 13, 1948; MD, Albert Einstein Coll. Med., 1983. Cert. Am. Bd. Pediatrics, 1987, in pediatric rheumatology Am. Bd. Pediatrics, 1992. Intern in pediatrics Children's Nat. Med. Ctr., Washington, 1983—84, resident in rheumatology, 1984—86; fellowship Univ. Tenn. Health Sciences Ctr., 1987—90; asst. prof. pediatrics Univ. Tenn.; pediatrician Nationwide Children's Hosp., Columbus, Ohio, 2000—; assoc. prof. clinical pediatrics Ohio State Univ. Coll. Med. Mem. exec. com. pediatric sect. Am. Coll. Rheumatology; mem. Ctrl. Ohio Chapter exec. bd. Arthritis Found.; mem. sci. rev. com. Childhood Arthritis & Rheumatology Rsch. Alliance; assoc. mem. Am. Bd. Pediatrics. Contbr. articles to profl. jours. Named one of America's Best Doctors, Castle Connolly, 2007. Office: Nationwide Childrens Hospice 255 E Main St Columbus OH 43215-5222 Office Phone: 614-722-5525. Office Fax: 614-722-3194.

HIGGINS, SHARON M., otolaryngologist; Undergraduate, Creighton U.; MD, U. Nebr., 1975. Intern, gen. surgery U. Okla. Health Sciences Ctr., otolaryngology head and neck surgery residency; asst. med. dir., bus. affairs Kaiser Permanente, otolaryngologist, head, neck surgeon, NW Permanente, 1979, chief, otolaryngology, 1987—99, v.p., ops. med. dir., specialty care, 1999—2005, pres., NW Permanente, PC, exec. med. dir., NW, 2007—. Bd. dirs. Tucker Maxon Oral Sch., Found. Med. Excellence. Named cert. head & neck surgery, Am. Bd Otolaryngology, 1979. Office: Kaiser Permanente Ste 100 500 NE Multnomah St Portland OR 97232 Office Phone: 503-813-2800. Office Fax: 503-813-4235. Business E-Mail: S.higgins@KP.org. *

HIGGINS, TERRENCE, plastic surgeon, educator; b. Las Vegas; MD, U. Tex. Diplomate Am. Bd. Plastic Surgery. Gen surgery tng. Mich. State Univ., plastic surgery tng., faculty mem.; with Cleveland Clinic, Ohio; pvt. practice Dr Anson and Dr Higgins Plastic Surgery Assocs., Nev. Recipient Most Outstanding Med. Student, Most Outstanding Resident Faculty Tchr. Mem.: Alpha Omega Alpha. Office: Dr Anson & Dr Higgins Plastic Surgery Associates 8530 W Sunset Ste 130 Las Vegas NV 89113 Office Phone: 702-822-2100. Office Fax: 702-822-2105.

HIGGS, JAY BRENT, rheumatologist; b. Bay City, Mich., Dec. 6, 1953; MD, U. Iowa, Coll. Medicine, 1980. Cert. ACP. Program dir., rheumatology fellow San Antonio Uniformed Svc. Health Edn. Consortium, 2006—. Assoc. prof. medicine Uniformed Svcs. U. Health Scis., 2002—11. Fellow: ACP, Am. Coll. Rheumatology. Avocation: violin. Home: 215 Rosemary Ave San Antonio TX 78209 Business E-Mail: jay.higgs@amedd.army.mil.

HIGH, KATHERINE ANN, physician, researcher; b. High Point, NC, July 27, 1951; d. Lacy Thacker and Joan (Davis) H.; m. George H. Steele Jr., May 26, 1984; children: Katherine T., Sarah C., John R. AB, Harvard Coll., 1972; MD, U. N.C., 1978; MA, U. Pa., 1993. Diplomate Am. Bd. Internal Medicine, hematology sect. Instr. hematology Sch. Medicine Yale U., New Haven, 1984-85; asst. prof. medicine & pathology U. N.C., Chapel Hill, 1985-91, assoc. prof., 1991-92; assoc. prof. pediatrics, pathology Sch. Medicine U. Pa., Phila., 1992-99, William H. Bennett assoc. prof. pediatrics, 1996-99, William H. Bennett prof. pediatrics, 1999—; investigator Howard Hughes Med. Inst., 2003—. Mem. hematology I study NIH, Bethesda, Md., 1994-98. Editl. bd. Am. Jour. Hematology, Detroit, 1988-98; contbr. articles to profl. jours. Adult edn. com. Ch. Redeemer, Bryn Mawr, Pa., 1995-97; schs. com. Harvard Club Phila., 1993—; mem. med. & sci. adv. bd. Nat. Hemophila Fedn., N.Y.C., 1997—; mem. exe. com. Am. Heart Assn., Dallas, 1995-97. Presdl. scholar, 1968, Nat. Merit scholar, 1968-72; recipient Individual Nat. Rsch. Svc. award NIH, 1982-84, clin. investigator award NHLBI, 1987-92, Excellence Acad. Medicine award Jefferson Pilot, 1988-92. Mem. AAAS, Inst. Medicine, Am. Soc. Clin. Investigation, Assn. Am. Physicians, Am. Soc. Hematology (molecular genetics edn. panel 1984-86, co-ordinating reviewer coagulation abstracts 1993, molecular biology clin. applications edn. panel 1994, nominee councillor 1995, co-ordinating reviewer disorders coagulation abstracts 1996, reviewer for coagulation abstracts 1997, mem. sci. subcom. on hemostasis 1997—, reviewer for gene therapy abstracts 1998, gene therapy edn. panel 1999), Am. Soc. Gene Therapy, Am. Heart Assn. (thrombosis rsch. study com. 1993-96, southeastern Pa. chpt. grant rev. panel 1994-97, exec. com. coun. thrombosis 1995-97), Coun. on Arteriosclerosis, Thrombosis, and Vascular Biology (membership/credentials com. 1998—). Office: Children's Hosp Phila 34th St & Civic Ctr Blvd Philadelphia PA 19104

HIGHMAN, BARBARA, dermatologist; b. Washington; d. Benjamin and Helen (Wienshienk) H. Student, Northwestern U., 1960—63; MD, U. Mich., 1967. Diplomate Am. Bd. Dermatology. Intern Baylor U. Affiliated Hops., Houston, 1967—68; dermatology residency Henry Ford Hosp., Detroit, 1968—71; fellow in dermatology Johns Hopkins U., Balt., 1971—72; pvt. practice Laurel, Md., 1972—2007. Staff North Charles Hosp., Balt., 1972-77, Laurel Regional Hosp.; cons. in dermatology U.S. Army, Ft. Myer, Va., 1972-77. Fellow: Am. Acad. Dermatology (continuing med. edn. award given every 3 years 1978—2010); mem.: Laurel Med. Soc., Med. and Chirugical Soc. State of Md. Office: 7520 Slade Ave Pikesville MD 21208 Office Phone: 301-498-4682. *

HIGLEY, BRUCE WADSWORTH, retired orthodontist; b. Iowa City, Dec. 1, 1928; s. Lester Bodine and Harriet (Wadsworth) H.; m. Marta Beatriz Velasco, Sept. 23, 1966. D.D.S., State U. Iowa, 1952, MS, 1953; student, Grinnell Coll., 1946-48, orthodontic certificate, 1953. Diplomate Am. Acad. Pain Mgmt. Research, instr. Iowa Dental U., 1952-53; practice dentistry, specializing in orthodontics South Miami, Fla., 1955—; Owner, chmn. bd. M.B.H. Enterprises, Inc., Miami, Fla., 1960—. Vice chmn. dist. coun. Boy Scouts Am., 1959-62; Mem. Personnel Bd., South Miami, 1959. 1st lt. Dental Corps AUS, 1953-55 Fellow Internat. Coll. Cranio-Mandibnlar ORthopaedics, World Fedn. Orthodontists; mem. Am. Assn. Orthodontics, Fla. Orthodontic Soc., So., Miami socs. orthodontists, Fla., Am. socs. dentistry for children, Fla., Fla. East Coast, Miami dental socs., Am., S. Dade dental assns., Fedn. Dentaire Internat., English Royal Acad., C. of C. (past dir., sec., treas.), Psi Omega, Omicron Kappa Upsilon. Presbyn. (deacon). Clubs: Rotarian (pres. 1961-62), Elk, Coral Reef Yacht, Coral Gables Country, Royal Palm Tennis; Bankers, Executive (Miami); Army-Navy. Home: 2000 Brickell Ave Miami FL 33129-1721 Office: 7210 S Red Rd Miami FL 33143-5321 Personal E-mail: drhigley@higleyorthodonticspecialist.com, brucehigley@att.net. *

HIGUCHI, RYUZO, pediatrics educator; b. Wakayama, Japan, Sept. 28, 1948; s. Kiyoshi and Toyoko (Inoue) H.; m. Kimi Imotani; children: Yuichi, Hisako, Ryoko. MD, Wakayama Med. Coll., 1974, PhD, 1992. Medical diplomate. Head pediatrician Hidaka Gen. Hosp., Gobo Wakayama, 1981-82; instr. Wakayama Med. Coll., 1983-85, head instr., 1986-88, assoc. prof., 1989—. Pres. Kinokuni Co-op Union, Wakayama, 1983—99. Contbr. articles to profl. jours. Chairperson Kinokuni Med. Coop. Union, Wakayama, 1985-98. Home: 89-4 Fuchu Wakayama 649-6338 Japan Office: Wakayama Med Coll/Pediat 811-1 Kimiidera Wakayama 641-0012 Japan E-mail: rhiguchi@wakayama-med.ac.jp.

HIGUCHI, TERUHIKO, hospital administrator; MD, PhD. Pres. Nat. Ctr. of Neurology and Psychiatry, Tokyo. Dir. Japanese Soc. for Mood Disorders; v.p. Japanese Soc. of Clin. Neuropsychopharmacology. Mem.: WHO. Achievements include research in Mood disorders; Psychopharmacology; Biological psychiatry. Office: National Center of Neurology and Psychiatry 4-1-1 Ogawa-Higashi Tokyo 1878502 Japan *

HILDEBRAND, JOHN GRANT, neuroscientist, educator; b. Boston, Mar. 26, 1942; s. John G. and Helen S. Hildebrand; m. Gail Deerin Burd, July 24, 1982. AB, Harvard U., 1964; PhD, Rockefeller U., 1969; Laurea Honoris Causa, U. Cagliari, Italy, 2000. Instr. neurobiology Harvard U. Med. Sch., Boston, 1970-72, asst. prof., 1972-77, assoc. prof., 1977-80, vis. prof., 1980-81; prof. biol. scis. Columbia U., NYC, 1980-85; prof. neurobiol., chemistry & biochemistry, entomology, molecular & cellular biology U. Ariz., Tucson, 1985—, Regents prof., 1989—, dir., Ariz. Rsch. Lab., divsn. neurobiology, 1985—2009, head dept. neurosci., 2009—. Assoc. behavioral biology Harvard U. Mus. Comparative Zoology, Cambridge, Mass., 1980-97; trustee Marine Biol. Lab., Woods Hole, Mass., 1981-89, mem. exec. com., 1981-88; Jan de Wilde lectr. U. Wageningen, The Netherlands, 1992; King Solomon lectr. Hebrew U., Jerusalem, 1995; K.D. Roeder lectr. Tufts U., 1995; Felix Santschi lectr. U. Zurich, Switzerland, 1995; Grandpierre Meml. lectr. Columbia U., 2002; Padykula lectr. Wellesley Coll., 2003; Cajal lectr. Cajal Inst., Madrid, 2004; Kravitz lectr. Marine Biol. Lab. Woods Hole, Mass., 2007, Martinez-Townsel lectr., 2009 Co-editor: Chemistry of Synaptic Transmission, 1974, Receptors for Neurotransmitters, Hormones, and Pheromones in Insects, 1980, Molecular Insect Science, 1990, Science and the Educated American: A Core Component of Liberal Education, 2010; devel. neurosci. sect. editor Jour. Neurosci., 1983-88; co-editor Jour. Comparative Physiology A, 1990—; mem. editorial bd. various other jours. Trustee Rockefeller U., N.Y.C., 1970-73. Recipient Javits Neurosci. award Nat. Inst. Neurol. and Communicative Disorders and Stroke, NIH, 1986-94, Merit award Nat. Inst. Allergy and Infections Diseases, NIH, 1986-97, R.H. Wright award Simon Fraser U., B.C., Can., 1990, Max Planck Rsch. award Max Planck Gesellschaft and Alexander von Humboldt-Stiftung of Germany, 1990, Founder's Meml. award Entomol. Soc. Am., 1997, award Humboldt Found., 1997, Manheimer Lectureship award Monell Chem. Senses Ctr., 2005, Henry and Phyllis Koffler prize, 2006, Outstanding Svc. to Biol. Scis. award Am. Inst. Biol. Scis., 2006, Lifetime Achievement award APA Diversity Program Neurosci., 2006; fellow Helen Hay Whitney Found., 1969-72, Einstein Professorship, Chinese Academy Sci., 2008, vis. scholar Phi Beta Kappa; grant A.P. Sloan Found., 1973-77. Fellow: AAAS, Entomol. Soc. America, Royal Entomol. Soc. UK; mem.: Nat. Acad. Scis., Am. Acad. Arts and Scis., Norwegian Acad. Sci. and Letters, Deutsche Akademie der Naturforscher Leopoldina, Internat. Soc. Chem. Ecology (pres. 1998—99), Soc. Integrative and Comparative Biology, Internat. Soc. Neuroethology (pres. 1995—98, Silver medal 2006), Soc. Neurosci. (treas. 1993—94), Assn. Chemoreception Sci. (pres. 2002—03, IFF Innovative Rsch. award 1997), Am. Soc. Biochemistry and Molecular Biology. Avocations: music, lower brass instruments. Home: 629 N Olsen Ave Tucson AZ 85719-5136 Office: U Ariz Dept Neurosci Coll Sci PO Box 210077 Tucson AZ 85721-0077

HILDRETH, EUGENE A., physician, educator; b. St. Paul, Mar. 11, 1924; s. Eugene A. V. and Lila K. (Clator) Hildreth; m. Dorothy Anne Myers, Mar. 23, 1946; children: Jeffrey Reed, William Myers, Anne Sarver, Katherine Clator. BS, Washington Jefferson Coll., 1943; MD, U. Va., 1947. Diplomate Am. Bd. Internal medicine, Am. Bd. Allergy and Immunology. Intern Johns Hopkins, 1947—48; resident in medicine Hosp. U. Pa., 1948—49, USPHS Postdoctoral Research fellow in cardio-vascular disease, 1949—51, chief resident in medicine, 1953—54, fellow in allergy and immunology, 1954—58, faculty, 1954—69, faculty, 1971—; instr. medicine U. Pa., Phila., 1953—54, asso. medicine, 1954—55, asst. prof. medicine, 1955—60, assoc. prof., 1960—69, assoc. dean U. Pa. (Sch. Medicine), 1964—69, prof. clin. medicine, 1971—90, prof. emeritus, 1990—, acting chmn. dept. research medicine, 1960—64. Chmn. dept. medicine Reading (Pa.) Hosp. and Med. Ctr.; cons. project site visitis USPHS, 1965—70; cons. VA Hosp. Phila., 1955—; nat. adv. com. Medic Alert Found Internat., 1964—83; cons. Citizens' Com. to Study Grad. Med. Edn., 1966, Am. Bd. Med. Spltys. rep. of subsplty. Bd. Allergy and Immunology of Am. Bd. Internal Medicine, 1969—72; mem. Am. Bd. Internal Medicine, 1969—72, 1975—82, cons., com. mem., 1972—75, chmn. certifying exam. com., 1978—81, mem. core exam. com., 1986—87, mem. exec. com., 1978—82, chmn., 1981—82; founding com. Am. Bd. Allergy and Immunology, 1970, mem., 1970—72, 1st co-chmn.; mem. rep. Am. Bd. Med. Spltys., 1976—83, chmn. nominating com., 1979—80; mem. med. adv. bd. Lupus Found. Del. Valley, 1979—; chmn. Federated Coun. Internal Medicine; appeals bd. liaison Coun. of Grad. Med. Edn., 1980—. Co-author: Low Fat Diet, 1953; mem. editl. bd.: Annals Internal Medicine, 1960—68, Postgrad. Medicine, 1969—75, Jour. Berks County Med. Soc., 1969—73, Internal Medicine Digest, 1971—75; contbr. chapters to books, articles to profl. jours. With USNR, 1943—45, with USNR, 1951—53. Grantee, USPHS; scholar John and Mary R. Markle scholar in acad. medicine, 1958—63. Master: ACP (mem. bd. regents 1985—92, chmn. bd. regents 1989—91, pres. 1991—92, immediate past pres. 1992—, mem. ethics com. 1986—90, chmn. com. to delineate privileges of med. procedures, mem. nominating 1997—); fellow: Am. Clin. and Climatologic Assn., Acad. Medicine of Singapore (hon.); mem.: ACGME (mem. residency rev. com. internal medicine), AAAS, Working Group on Disability of U.S. Presidents, Royal Soc. Medicine, Federated Coun. Internal Medicine, Am. Acad. Allergy, Inst. Medicine of NAS (mem. nominating com. 1982—84, mem. coun. 1986—90, chmn. nominating com. for coun. memberships 1989—90, mem. fin. com. 1988—90), N.Y. Acad. Scis., Fedn. AM. Socs. for Exptl. Biology, Peripatetic Soc., Phila. Art Mus. Home: 2000 Cambridge Ave Apt 129 Wyomissing PA 19610

HILDRETH, JAMES E.K., pharmacology and molecular science educator, dean; b. Camden, Ark. m. Phyllis D. King; children: Sophia, James. BS, Harvard U., 1979; PhD, Oxford U., Eng., 1982; MD, Johns Hopkins U., 1997. Asst. prof. pharmacology and molecular scis. Johns Hopkins U. Sch. Medicine, Balt., 1987, prof. pharmacology and molecular scis., 2002—05, assoc. dean grad. student affairs, adj. prof. pharmacology and molecular scis., 2005—; dir. Ctr. for AIDS Health Disparities Rsch. Meharry Med. Coll., Nashville, 2005—, prof. internal medicine, 2005—. Contbr. articles to profl. jours. Mem.: Inst. Medicine. Achievements include research on recognition and signaling in the immune system. Office: George Hubbard Hosp 5th FL 1005 Dr DB Todd Blvd Nashville TN 37208 Office Phone: 615-327-5754. Fax: 410-614-3386; Office Fax: 615-327-6929. E-mail: jhildret@som.adm.jhu.edu, jhildreth@mmc.edu.

HILGER, HANS HERMANN, cardiologist; b. Remscheid, Germany, Mar. 16, 1928; s. Robert and Elisabeth (Schaefer) H.; m. Dorothee Graf, Aug. 1, 1956 (dec. 1981; children: Karin, Renate; m. Renate Kullmann Bracht, Aug. 23, 1984; children: Sigrid, Detlef. MD, U. Bonn, Germany, 1955. Intern Univ. Hosp., Heidelberg, Germany, 1955-56; fellow Inst. Physiology U. Göttingen, Germany, 1956-58; resident in internal medicine Univ. Hosp., Bonn, 1958-64, from sr. registrar to prof., 1964-71, chairperson internal medicine Cologne, 1971-93; dean med. faculty U. Cologne, Germany, 1978-79. Author: Internal Medicine in Praxis and Clinic, 1973-91; author, editor: The Medical Profession in the Course of Time, 1990; editor: Signal Averaging Technique in Clinical Cardiology, 1981, Holter Monitoring Technique, 1985, Invasive Cardiovascular Therapy, 1987, Electrocardiography and Cardiac-Drug Therapy, 1989; contbr. articles to profl. jours. Chmn. bd. dirs. Hufeland Prize Found., Cologne, 1988-2003. Mem.: German Soc. Internal Medicine, German Austrian Soc. Internal Intensive Care Medicine, German Soc. Cardiology, North Rhine Westf Soc. Internal Medicine (hon.), Rotary Internat. Home: Rheingoldstr 19 50354 Huerth Cologne Germany Office: U Cologne Med Faculty Joseph Stelzmann Str 9 50924 Cologne Germany

HILKER, ROBERT REUBEN JOHN, medical educator, researcher, administrator, consultant; b. Le Mars, Iowa, Sept. 17, 1916; s. Roy Christian and Theresa Johanna (Ries) Hilker; m. Mary Esther Hynan. BA with honors, Morningside Coll., Sioux City, Iowa, 1938; student in Bus., Northwestern U., Ill., 1938—39; student, U. Colo., Boulder, 1945; BM with distinction, Northwestern U., Chgo., 1950, MD with distinction, 1951; DSc (hon.), Morningside Coll., Sioux City, Iowa, 2004. Diplomate Am. Bd. Internal Medicine, 1958, in occupl. medicine Am. Bd. Preventive Medicine, 1975. Intern St. Lukes Hosp., Chgo., 1950—51; resident internal medicine Chgo. Wesley Meml. Hosp., Chgo., 1951—53, fellow cardiology, 1953—55, asst. dir. Heart Sta., 1955—56; pvt. practice Chgo., 1956—82; from instr. to assoc. prof. emeritus Northwestern U., Chgo., 1957—74, prof. emeritus, 1974—; corp. med. dir. Ill. Bell Telephone Co., Chgo., 1962—82; cons. Chgo., 1982—. Mem. editl. adv. bd. Employee Health and Fitness, 1981. Editor: Jour. Occupl. Medicine; mem. editl. bd.: Alcoholism-Clin. and Rsch. Studies; contbr. over 40 articles to profl. jours. Lt. USNR, 1942—46. Recipient Alumni award, Morningside Coll., 1977, Krudsen award, 1994; named to Order of Morningside, Morningside Coll., 1980. Fellow: ACP, Inst. Medicine Chgo., Am. Occupl. Med. Assn. (pres., Meritorious Svc. award 1979), Am. Heart Assn., Am. Coll. Cardiology, Am. Acad. Occupl. Medicine, Am. Coll. Preventive Medicine; mem.: AMA, Internat. Coll. Cardiology, Chgo. Soc. Internal Medicine, Assn. Am. Med. Colls., Am. Soc. Internal Medicine, Am. Pub. Health Assn., Am. Med. Soc. Alchoholism, Am. Fedn. Clin. Rsch., Med. Dirs. Club Chgo. (pres.), Alpha Omega Alpha, Zeta Sigma. Independent. Avocation: photography. Home: 1355 St Catherines Cir Vero Beach FL 32967 Home Phone: 772-563-0107. Personal E-mail: rhilker@webtv.net.

HILL, CARLOTTA H., physician; b. Chgo., Apr. 8, 1958; d. Clarence Kenneth and Vlasta (Cizek) Hayes; m. Chester James Hill III, June 10, 1967 (div. 1974); m. Carlos A. Rotman, July 31, 1980; children: Robin Mercedes. BA magna cum laude, Knox Coll., 1969; MD with honors, U. Ill., 1973. Diplomate Nat. Bd. Med. Examiners, Am. Bd. Dermatology. Intern Mayo Sch. Medicine, Rochester, Minn., 1973-74; resident U. Ill., Chgo., 1975-78, asst. prof. clin. dermatology Coll. Medicine, 1978-93, assoc. prof. clin. dermatology Coll. Medicine, 1993—. Mem. U. Ill. Senate, Chgo., 1986-91, 99-2002; councilor Chgo. Med. Soc., 1990-96, 1999-2006. Contbr. articles to profl. jours. Bd. dirs. Summerfest St. James Cathedral, Chgo., 1986-91, YWCA, Lake Forest, Ill., 1995-, pres., 1998-2000; master gardner Chgo. Bot. Garden, Glencoe, Ill., 1994-98; bd. dirs. Lake Bluff Open Lands Assn., 1997-2006, Friends of Ryerson Woods, 2005—10, Lake Forest/Lake Bluff Hist. Soc., 2006-09; mem. Lake Bluff Libr. Bd., 2001-05. Recipient Janet Glascow award Am. Women's Med. Assn., 1973, named America's Top Physicians, 2003-06, America's Top Dermatologists, 2007-08, 09-10. Fellow Am. Acad. Dermatology, Mem. Herb Soc. Am. (ways and means No. Ill. unit 1992-94, treas. N. Ill. unit 1996-00, vice chair 2000-02, chair 2002-04, ctrl. dist. steering com. 2004-06, nat. herb garden com. 2006—), Chgo. Dermatol. Soc., Ill. Dermatologic Soc., Phi Beta Kappa, Alpha Omega Alpha, Royal Coll. Medicine Avocations: travel, cooking, gardening, reading. Office: Dept Dermatology 808 S Wood St Chicago IL 60612-7300 Office Phone: 312-996-6966. Business E-Mail: chhill@uic.edu.

HILL, CLARA EDITH, psychologist, educator; b. Shivers, Miss., Sept. 13, 1948; d. Fletcher Von and Anna (Teich) H.; m. James Gormally, May 25, 1974; children: Kevin, Katherine. BA, So. Ill. U., 1970, MA, 1972, PhD, 1974. Lic. psychologist, Md. Asst. prof. dept. psychology U. Md., College Park, 1974-78, assoc. prof. dept. psychology, 1978-85, prof. dept. psychology, 85—. Author: Therapist Techniques and Client Outcomes, 1989, Working with Dreams in Psychotherapy, 1996; author: (with Karen O' Brien) Helping Skills: Facilitating Exploration, Insight and Action 1st. edit., 1999; author: Helping Skills: The Empirical Foundation, 2001, Dream Work in Therapy: Facilitating Exploration, Insight and Action, 2004; co-author (with L.G. Castonguay): Insight in Psychotherapy, 2007; co-author: Helping Skills: Facilitating Exploration, Insight, and Action, 3rd edit., 2009; editor: Jour. Counseling Psychology, 1994—99, Psychotherapy Rsch., 2004—09. Recipient Outstanding Lifetime Achievement award, Soc. for Counseling Psychology, 2005; grantee, NIMH, 1983—92. Fellow APA (Leona Tyler divsn. 17 award 2002, Disting. Psychologist divsn. 29 award 2003); mem. Soc. Psychotherapy Rsch. (pres. N.Am. chpt. 1990, pres. internat. orgn. 1994-95, Disting. Rsch. Career award 2007), Internat. Assn. Study of Dreams, Soc. Exploration of Psychotherapy Integration. Avocations: reading, walking. Office: U Maryland Dept Psychology College Park MD 20742-0001 Business E-Mail: Hill@psyc.umd.edu.

HILL, DAVID JOHN, research scientist; b. Suva, Fiji, Aug. 12, 1942; MA, U. Melbourne, 1975, PhD, 1985. Dir., Ctr. for Behavioural Rsch. in Cancer Cancer Coun. Victoria, 1986—2002, CEO, 2002—11. Fellow U. Melbourne, 1998; adj. prof. Monash U., 1999; pres. Union for Internat. Cancer Control, 2008—10. Named Officer, Order of Australia. Fellow: Australian Psychol. Soc. (Ian Mathew Campbell prize); mem.: APHA. Office: Cancer Council Victoria 1 Rathdowne St Victoria Carlton 3053 Australia Office Phone: +61 9635 5656. E-mail: david.hill@cancervic.org.au.

HILL, GEORGE JAMES, physician, educator; b. Cedar Rapids, Iowa, Oct. 7, 1932; s. Gerald Leslie and Essie Mae (Thompson) H.; m. Helene (Zimmermann), July 16, 1960; children: James Warren, David Hedgcock, Sarah, and Helena Rundall. BA, Yale U., 1953; MD, Harvard U., 1957; MA, Rutgers U., 1999; DLitt, Drew U., 2005. Intern NY Hosp., 1957-58; fellow and resident in surgery Peter Bent Brigham Hosp. and Harvard Med. Sch., 1958-61, 63-66; clin. assoc. NIH, Bethesda, Md., 1961-63; instr. surgery U. Colo., 1966-67, asst. prof., 1967-72, asso. prof., 1972-73; prof. Washington Univ., 1973-76; prof., chmn. Marshall Univ., 1976-81; prof., dir. surg. oncology U. of Medicine and Dentistry of NJ, NJ Med. Sch., Newark, 1981-96; adj. prof. surgery Uniformed Svcs. U. of Health Scis., Bethesda, Md., 1989—; Am. Cancer Soc. prof. clin. oncology U. Medicine and Dentistry NJ, NJ Med. Sch., Newark, 1989-92; pres. faculty NJ Med. Sch., Newark, 1991-92; interim pres. Sterling Coll., Craftsbury

Common, Vt., 1996; prof. emeritus U. of Medicine and Dentistry of NJ, NJ Med. Sch., Newark, 1997—; rsch. coord. St. Barnabas Med. Ctr., Livingston, NJ, 1997-99. Adj. prof. history Kean U., Union, NJ, 2000-2001; hon. mem. med. sch. staff St. Barnabas Med. Ctr., 1999—; chmn. clin. cancer edn. com. Nat. Cancer Inst., 1978-80; vis. fellow in molecular biology, Princeton U., 1988; clin. prof. surgery Sch. Medicine Mt. Sinai U., 1999—. Author: Leprosy in Five Young Men, 1970, paperback edit., 1979; Outpatient Surgery, 1973, 3rd edit., 1988; Clinical Oncology, 1977, Edison's Environment, 2007, rev. edit., 2010; Intimate Relationships Church and State US and Liberia (VDM-Verlag, 2008), (heritage book) John Saxe, Loyalist (1732-1808) and His Descendants for Five Generations, 2010; contbg. 150 articles to med. journals. Active Nat. coun. Boy Scouts Am., 1968—2005, chmn. health career exploring com. Nat. coun., 1987—92; nat. dir. at large Am. Cancer Soc., 1989—96, mem. nat. exec. com., 1990—91, hon. life mem., 1996—, pres. W.Va. divsn., 1980—81; mem. NJ State Commn. on Cancer Rsch., 1983—84; pres. Tri State Area coun. Boy Scouts Am., Huntington, W.Va., 1980—82, v.p. Essex coun., 1983—89, exec. bd. mem. Northern NJ coun., 1998—; trustee Frost Valley YMCA, 1986—, NJ State Opera, v.p., 2006—08; pres. NJ divsn. Am. Cancer Soc., 1987—89; pres. Hill Family Trust, 1989—; trustee Sterling Coll., Craftsbury Common, Vt., 1990—2002, sec., 1993—96, interim pres., 1996; vestry Ch. of the Holy Innocents, 1994—96, 2002—05, warden, 2005—07. Capt. M.C. USNR, active duty USN, 1990—91, ret., 1992. Recipient Damon Runyon fellowship, 1957—58, Lederle Med. Faculty award, 1970, Civic Actions medal, Republic South Vietnam, 1972, Silver Beaver award, Boy Scouts Am., 1981, Nat. William Spurgeon III award, 1994, Silver Antelope award, 1998, Vigil honor, 2005, Disting. Eagle award, 2005, Am. Cancer Soc. Nat. Divisional award, St. George medal, 1992, Gorgas medal, Assn. Mil. Surgeons U.S., 1991, Outstanding Svc. medal, Uniformed Svcs. U. Health Scis., 1992, Meritorious Svc. medal, USN, 1993, N.J. Disting. Svc. medal, 2001; named Jerseyan of Week, Newark-Star Ledger, 1987, 1993. Fellow: Royal Soc. Medicine, Explorers Club; mem.: SAR (pres. N.J. Soc. 2001—02, nat. trustee 2002—03, trustee NJ state soc. 2004—, v.p. gen. 2005—06, Patriot medal 2003), AAUP (pres. chpt. 1988—89), ACS (com. on cancer 1987—93), Nat. Order Blue and Gray (v.p. gen. 2011—), Order of Indian Wars of the US, Nat. Soc. Sons & Daughters Pilgrims (gov. NJ Br. 2009—11, elder gen. 2011—), Jamestowne Soc., order of merovingian dynasty (surgeon gen. 2007—), Soc. Sons of Revolution (pres. NJ state soc. 2010—), NJ Med. Club (pres. 1999—2001), Med. Soc. NJ (chmn. com. cancer control 1985—94, sec. 1995—96), Essex County Med. Soc. (pres. 1995—96, historian 2009—, Delta award 2010), Oncology Nursing Soc. (hon.), Med. History Soc. NJ (v.p. 2000—02), Am. Assn. Cancer Rsch., Am. Assn. Cancer Edn. (pres. 1985—86, Edwards medal 1994), Ctrl. Surg. Assn., Soc. Surg. Oncology (exec. coun. 1985—88), Soc. Univ. Surgeons, Acad. Medicine NJ (pres. 1992—93), St. Andrew's Soc. (NY), Colonial Soc. Pa., Huguenot Soc. Am., Order Crown Charlemagne, St. Nicholas Soc. NY, Descs. of Founders of NJ (gov. gen. 2010—), Naval Res. Assn. (v.p. 3rd dist. 2004—06), Soc. of the Cin., Soc. Mayflower Descs. (gov. NJ state soc. 2007—08, dep. gov. gen. 2008—), Order Founders and Patriots of Am. (gov. NJ state soc. 2005—07, historian gen. 2008—), Soc. Colonial Wars (gov. NJ state soc. 2006—08, dep. gov. gen. 2009—), Soc. War of 1812 (pres., NJ State Soc. 2010—), Welcome Soc. Pa., Army and Navy Club, Harvard Club (NYC and Boston), Ancient and Hon. Arty. Co. Mass., Alpha Omega Alpha, Sigma Xi (chpt. pres. 1986—87). Republican. Episcopalian. Address: 3 Silver Spring Rd West Orange NJ 07052-4317

HILL, HELENE ZIMMERMANN, biologist, consultant; b. Phila., Apr. 10, 1929; d. Albert Walter and Barbara (Shoemaker) Zimmermann; m. George J. Hill, July 16, 1960; children: James Warren, David Hedgcock, Sarah, Helena Rundall. AB, Smith Coll., 1950; PhD, Brandeis U., 1964. Instr. Brandeis U., Waltham, Mass., 1963-64; postdoctoral fellow Med. Sch. Harvard U., Boston, 1964-66; postdoctoral fellow in biophysics Med. Sch. U. Colo., Denver, 1966-67, asst. prof. biophysics and genetics Med. Sch., 1967-72; assoc. prof. radiology Med. Sch. Washington U., St. Louis, 1973-76; from assoc. to prof. biochemistry Med. Sch. Marshall U., Huntington, W.Va., 1976-81; prof. radiology U. Medicine & Dentistry N.J., Newark, 1981—. Author: (chpt.) Cancer Biology & Biosynthesis, 1990; contbr. articles to Jour. Environ. and Molecular Mutagenesis, Jour. Pigment Cell Rsch. Recipient Lifetime Achievement award Baldwin Sch., 1991, Smith Coll. medal, 1997; grantee N.J. Commn. for Cancer Rsch., Ruth Eslrin Meml. for Cancer Rsch., 1986, Am. Cancer Soc., 1980-83, NIH, Nat. Cancer Inst., 1992-96. Mem. Am. Soc. for Photobiology, Radiation Rsch. Soc., European Soc. for Pigment Cell Rsch., Environ. Mutagen Soc. Achievements include research in radiobiology of melanoma as it relates to radiation resistance, photobiology of melanoma as it relates to pigmentation. Home: 3 Silver Spring Rd West Orange NJ 07052-4317 Office: U Medicine & Dentistry NJ 185 S Orange Ave Newark NJ 07103-2757 Office Phone: 973-972-3421.

HILL, JIM TOM, retired toxicology consulting firm executive; b. Cushing, Okla., Apr. 27, 1939; s. Wilburn C. and Susie (Ruckman) H.; m. Linda J. Archer, Aug. 30, 1963; children: Sheri, David, Susan. BS in Chemistry, Abilene Christian U., 1961; MS in Biochemistry, U. Tenn., 1964, PhD, 1968. Sr. rsch. scientist E.R. Squibb & Sons, New Brunswick, NJ, 1968-69, Lakeside Labs., Milw., 1969-75; sr. rsch. specialist Monsanto, St. Louis, 1975-78; dir. chemistry Covance, Vienna, Va., 1978-80; mgr. toxicology Phelps Dodge, Washington, 1980-81; dir. sci. affairs Chem. Specialties Mfrs. Assn., Washington, 1981-86, dir. product ingredient rev. program, 1987-97; v.p. Specialty Product Group SRS Internat., Washington, 1997—2003. Contbr. articles to profl. jours. Mem. Sigma Xi. Home: PO Box 1928 Stafford VA 22555-1928

HILL, KENT RICHMOND, foundation administrator, former federal agency administrator; b. Nampa, Idaho, May 24, 1949; s. Double E. and Helen Louise (Robertson) H.; m. Janice Elaine Hurn, June 12, 1972; children: Jennifer Lynn, Jonathan Kent. BA in History, N.W. Nazarene Coll., 1971; diploma for basic Russian lang., Def. Lang. inst., 1972; postgrad., Georgetown U., 1973-74; MA in Russian and East European Studies, U. Wash., 1976, PhD in History, 1980. Tchg. asst. in history N.W. Nazarene Coll., Nampa, Idaho, 1969-71; Russian translator US Army, 1972-74; tchg. asst. in history of Christianity U. Wash., Seattle, 1980, asst. prof. history, 1980-85; assoc. prof. history Seattle Pacific U., 1985-86; pres. Inst. on Religion and Democracy, Washington, 1986-92, Ea. Nazarene Coll., Quincy, Mass., 1992—2001; asst. administr. bur. for Europe and Eurasia US Agy. Internat. Devel (USAID), Washington, 2001—05, asst. adminstr. for global health, 2005—09, acting adminstr., 2009; v.p. for character devel. The John Templeton Found., Conshohocken, Pa., 2009—. Interviews, speaker, presenter in field. Author: The Puzzle of the Soviet Church: An Inside Look at Christianity and Glasnost, 1989, Turbulent Times for the Soviet Church, 1991, The Soviet Union on the Brink, 1991; contbr. articles to profl. publs. Bd. dirs. Peter Deyneka Russian Ministries, 1991-2001, Keston Coll., 1985-2001; mem. nat. exec. bd. World Without War Coun., Berkeley, Calif., 1986-2001; bd. advisors Inst. on Religion and Democracy, 1984-86, bd. dirs., 1993-2001; mem. ch. bd. 1st Ch. of Nazarene, Seattle, 1980-85; bd. trustees Russian-Am. Christian U., Moscow, 1998-2000; bd. dirs. Quincy Hist. Soc., 1997-2000. Named Alumnus of Yr., N.W. Nazarene Coll., 1988, to Presdl. Leadership list John Templeton Found., 1999; presented with Key to City, Mayor of City of Nampa, 1983; named Prof. of Yr. Seattle Pacific U., 1986; grantee Seattle Pacific U., 1981-82, 82-83, 84, 85, U. Wash., 1979-80; Nat. Def. Fgn. Lang. fellowship, 1976-77, Earhart fellow Internat. Rsch. and Exchs. fellow, 1978; recipient Pushkin award for Outstanding Scholarship, Def. Lang. Inst., 1972.

HILL, MARJORIE JEAN, health association administrator, psychologist; b. Bklyn., Aug. 8, 1956; d. Walter James and Laura Beulah (Cherry) H. AA, The Coll. of Staten Island, 1975; BA, Adelphi U., 1977, MA, 1979, PhD, 1981. Asst. dir. child psychiatry Kings County Hosp., Bklyn., 1981-88; internship coord., psychiatric edn. Lincoln Med. and Mental Health Ctr., Bronx, NY, 1988-90; dir. NYC Mayor's Office for the Lesbian & Gay Community, 1990-93; asst. v.p. NYC Health and Hosps. Corp., 1993; interim exec. dir. Gay Men's Health Crisis, NYC, 2006, CEO, 2006—. Asst. prof. psychiatry NY Med. Coll., Valhalla, 1988-90; adj. faculty Coll. New Rochelle, 1988-91; adj. clin. assoc. Pace U., NYC, 1989—; adj. clin. prof. Yeshiva U., Bronx, NY, 1989—. Bd. dirs. NY Civil Liberties Union, NYC, 1990, AIDS Films, NYC, 1991-93, Columbia County Youth Project, 1989—; mem. Black Leadership Commn. on AIDS, NYC, 1991—; mem. NYC Fair Housing Task Force, 1990; bd. dirs., nat. chair Unity Fellowship Ch. of Christ, Inc., 1993—; mem. WNET-Channel 13 Community Adv. Bd., 1990—. Recipient Community Organizer award WBAI NYC Learning Alliance, 1988, Community Svc. award Nat. Lesbian and Gay Health Found., 1988, Hall of Fame award Staten Island Community Coll., 1989, Community Svc. award Nat. Lesbian Conf., 1991, Bayard Rustin award Nat. Black Lesbian and Gay Leadership Forum, 1991, Woman of Power award NOW, 1993, Polit. Svc. award Stonewall Dem. Com., 1992, Community Svc. award Empire Pride Agenda, 1992. Mem. APA, Coalition of 100 Black Women NYC, Assn. Women in Psychology (steering com. 1987), Assn. Black Psychologists (pres. 1988, treas. 1990, bd. dirs., Nelson Mandela Psychologist of Yr. 1991), Nat. Black Gay and Lesbian Leadership Forum (bd. govs.). Avocations: grassroots organizing, bike riding, aerobics. Office: Gay Men's Health Crisis The Tisch Bldg 119 West 24th St New York NY 10011 Office Phone: 212-367-1000. Business E-Mail: marjorieh@gmhc.org. *

HILL, MARTHA N., dean, community health nurse; b. Boston, July 14, 1943; d. Paul Lawrence Norton and Margaret M. Hagerty; m. Gary S. Hill, June 18, 1966; children: Paul, Justin. Diploma, Johns Hopkins Hosp., Balt., 1964; BSN, The Johns Hopkins U., 1966, PhD, 1987; MSN, U. Pa., 1977; D (hon.), SUNY Downstate Sch. Nursing, 2001; D Honoris Causa (hon.), Göteborg U., 2004; DSc (hon.), U. Medicine and Dentistry, NJ, 2005. RN Md., 1964, Pa., 1974. Instr. Johns Hopkins Hosp. Sch. Nursing, Balt., 1966—73, clin. coord., adult nurse practitioner program, 1973—74; adult nurse practitioner and staff asst. Hosp. of U. Pa., Phila., 1974—76, nursing coord ambulatory care, 1975—76, nurse specialist in hypertension, rsch. assoc., 1977—80, dir., hypertension outreach program, 1978—80; asst. prof., divsn. nursing Johns Hopkins Univ. Sch. Continuing Studies, Balt., 1980—85, coord., divsn. nursing, 1983—85; asst. prof. Johns Hopkins Univ. Sch. Nursing, 1985—89, assoc. prof., 1989—97, acting dir. to dir., Ctr. Nursing Rsch., 1992—2002, dir. postdoctoral programs, 1992—98, interim dir. doctoral program, 1995—96, prof., 1997—, interim dean, 2001—02, dean, 2002—. Contbr. articles to profl. jours. Recipient Malcolm Alderfer Schweiker award, 1985, Ruth B. Freeman award, 1987, Disting. Alumni award Johns Hopkins U., 1997, Ptnr. in Pub. Health award Ctr. Disease Control and Agency Toxic Substances and Disease Registry, 1998, Pub. Svc. award Nat. Kidney Found. Md., 1999, Disting. Rsch. award Internat. Soc. on Hypertension in Blacks, 1999; named one of Top 10 Women's Health Heroes Readers Digest, 1999, 50 Pioneers of the Past, Present and Future Johns Hopkins Mag., 2000, Md. Top 100 Women Daily Record, 2006. Fellow Am. Acad. Nursing, Soc. Behavioral Medicine, Soc. Geriatric Cardiology, European Soc. Cardiology; mem. ANA (rep. to NIH high blood press coord. com.), Am. Heart Assn. (vice chmn. coun. cardiovasc. nursing 1989-91, pres. 1997-98; Nat. Svc. award 1993, 1996, Spl. award 1994, Award of Merit 1994, Chmn. Recognition award 1995, Martha N. Hill New Investigator award 1997, Sci. Coun. Disting. Achievement award 1997, Katherine A. Lembright award 2003), Inst. Medicine (coun. mem.), Internat. Soc. Hypertension, Am. Assn. Critical care Nurses (hon.), Delta Omega, Sigma Theta Tau (Nell J. Watts Lifetime Achievement in Nursing award 2003). Office: Johns Hopkins Univ Sch Nursing 525 N Wolfe St Rm 501 Baltimore MD 21205-2110 Office Phone: 410-955-7544. Office Fax: 410-955-4890. E-mail: mnhill@son.jhmi.edu.

HILL, NICHOLAS S., physician, researcher; b. Troy, NY, Dec. 27, 1949; s. Nicholas Snowden Hill, IV and Barbara Charlotte (Seim) Hill; m. Sophia P. Paraskos, Aug. 16, 1975; children: Kyra A., Alyssa N. AB, Harvard U., Cambridge, Mass., 1967—71; MD, Dartmouth Med. U., Hanover, NH, 1971—75. Diplomate in internal medicine, pulmonary and critical care Am. Bd. Internal Medicine. Resident in internal medicine Tufts-New Eng. Med. Ctr., Boston, 1975—77; sr. med. resident Boston VA Hosp., 1978; fellow in cardiovasc. medicine U. Mass. Med. Ctr., Worcester, 1979; fellow in pulmonary medicine Boston U., 1979—82; staff physician divsn. pulmonary critical care and sleep medicine RI Hosp., Providence, 1987—2002; chief divsn. pulmonary, critical care and sleep medicine Tufts-New Eng. Med. Ctr., Boston, 2002—. Author: (books) Pulmonary Hypertension Therapy, 2006; editor: Long-term Mechanical Ventilation, 2001, Ventilator Strategies in Critical Care, 2001, Noninvasive Ventilation, Principles and Practice; mem. editl. bd.: Am. Jour. Respiratory Critical Care Medicine, 1994—97, 2000—07, assoc. editor: Chest, 2005—. Recipient Henry Chadwick medal, Mass. Thoracic Soc., 2006, Disting. Scholar in Critical Care Medicine, Am. Coll. Chest Physicians, 2002; Parker B. Francis Fellow award, PFB Found., 1983. Fellow: Am. Coll. Chest Physicians (chair home care network 2002—04); mem.: Am. Physiology Soc., Mass. Thoracic Surgery (councilor Boston chpt. 1983—87), Am. Thoracic Soc. (mem. planning com. 2002—06, pres. 2011—). Achievements include research in evaluating clinical applcations of noninvasive ventilation; clinical applications of pulmonary hypertension therapies. Avocation: triathlons. Office: Tufts Med Ctr 800 Washington St # 257 Boston MA 02111 Office Fax: 617-636-5953. *

HILL, RONALD CHARLES, surgeon, educator; b. Parkersburg, W.Va., Sept. 4, 1948; s. Lloyd E. and Margaret (Pepper) H.; m. Lenora Jane Rexrode, June 12, 1971; children: Jeffrey, Mandy. BA with honors, W.Va. U., 1970, MD, 1974. Diplomate Am. Bd. Surgery, Am. Bd. Thoracic Surgery. Surg. intern Duke U. Med. Ctr., Durham, NC, 1974—75; resident in surgery Duke U., Durham, NC, 1974—85, rsch. assoc., 1976—79, tchg. scholar, 1984—85; asst. prof. surgery W.Va. U., Morgantown, 1985—90, assoc. prof., 1990—96, prof. surgery, 1996—2007, clin. prof. surgery Sch. Osteopathic Medicine, 1999—2007; chief cardiothoracic surgery VA Med. Ctr., Asheville, NC, 2009—; cons. prof., surgery Duke U. Sch. Medicine, 2007—. Cons. VA Med. Ctr., Clarksburg, W.Va., 1985—2007; dir. surg. rsch. dept. surgery W.Va. U., 1986—88, student coord. dept. surgery, 1986—97; mem. adh hoc com. merit rev. bd. for cardiovasc. studies VA, Washington, 1988—90; mem. Surg. Edn. and Self-Assessment Programs; chmn. instnl. rev. bd. Protection Human Subjects, 1994—2004, program dir. dept. surgery, 1998—2003, dir., thoracic surgery program, 2005—07; staff surgeon & chief CT surgery Veterans Adminstrn. Medical Ctr., Asheville, NC, 2007—. Contbr., co-contbr. numerous book chpts. and articles to profl. publs. Mem.-at-large adminstrv. bd. Drummond Chapel United Meth. Ch., Morgantown, 1987—89, 1993—95, fin. com., 1994—96, lay del. to ann. conf., 1995—97, chmn. coun. on evangelism, 1999—2001. Recipient Lange Med. Book award, 1971, 1973, 1974, Roche Med. award, 1972, Merck Med. Book award, 1974, Sowers award, Founders Soc. Duke U., 1992, Disting. Svc. award, W.Va. U., 2005; named Outstanding Attending Surgeon, 1998—99, Guide to America's Top Surgeons, 2008—, Top Surgeons, 2009—10; named one of Best Doctor Am., 2001—08. Fellow ACS (coun. W.Va. chpt. 1999-2001, sec.-treas. 2001-2002, 2d v.p. 2002-2003, 1st v.p. 2003-2004, pres. 2004-05, chmn. com. on applicants dist. 1 W.Va.), Southeastern Surg. Congress, Assn. Acad. Surgery, Sabiston Soc., Am. Coll. Cardiology, Am. Coll. Chest Physicians, So. Thoracic Surg. Assn. (program chmn. 1995-96, coun. 1999-2000), Soc. Thoracic Surgeons; mem. Am. Heart Assn. (v.p., pres. elect, pres. W. Va. affiliate 1994-96), Soc. Univ. Surgeons, Am. Assn. Thoracic Surgery, Internat. Surg. Soc., Assn. Programs Dirs. in Surgery, Assn. Surg. Edn., So. Surg. Assn., W.Va. Med. Assn., Monongalia County Med. Assn. (v.p. 1985-2007),Mended Hearts, Lakeview Country Club, Pines Country Club, Phi Beta Kappa, Alpha Omega Alpha (hon.), Alpha Epsilon Delta (hon.), Profl. Assn. Diving Instrs. Soc. (cert. master scuba diver). Republican. Avocations: fishing, photography, scuba diving, shell collecting. Office: VA Med Ctr Asheville NC 28805 Office Phone: 828-298-7911 ext. 5117. Business E-Mail: Ronald.Hill@va.gov.

HILL, STEPHEN A., pharmaceutical executive; Degree, Oxford U., Gordon Cornell Theol. Seminary. Med. adviser Roche products F. Hoffman-La Roche Ltd., U.K., med. dir. Roche products U.K., head internat. drug regulatory affairs Roche hdqs. Basel, Switzerland, mem. various exec. bds., head global drug devel.; pres., CEO ArQule, Inc., Woburn, Mass., 1999—2008; pres. Solvay Pharmaceuticals, Inc. - US, 2008—10. Non-exec. chmn. Novelos Therapeutics, Inc., 2008—. Office: Novelos Therapeutics Inc 3301 Agriculture Dr Madison WI 53716 *

HILL, VIRGINIA ANN, medical researcher; b. St. Cloud, Minn., Jan. 22, 1945; BS, St. Cloud State U., 1967. Sr. scientist Psychemedics Corp., 1990—. Office: 5832 Uplander Way Culver City CA 90230 Office Fax: 310-216-6662. Business E-Mail: virginiah@psychemedics.com.

HILLARD, CECILIA JANE, medical educator, director; b. Portsmouth, Va., Dec. 22, 1954; PhD, Med. Coll. Wis., 1983. Prof., pharmacology, dir., neurosci. rsch. ctr. Med. Coll. Wis., 1985—. Exec. dir. Internat. Cannabinoid Rsch. Soc., 2010. Office: Neurosci Rsch Ctr 8701 Water Tank Plank Rd Milwaukee WI 53226 Business E-Mail: chillard@mcw.edu.

HILLE, BERTIL, physiology educator; b. New Haven, Oct. 10, 1940; s. C. Einar and Kirsti (Ore) H.; m. Merrill Burr, Nov. 21, 1964; children: Erik D., J. Trygve. BS, Yale U., 1962; PhD, Rockefeller U., 1967, PhD hon causa, 2008. H.H. Whitney fellow Cambridge U., 1967-68; asst. prof. U. Wash., Seattle, 1968-71, assoc. prof., 1971-74, prof. physiology, 1974—. Vis. prof. U. Saarland, Hamburg, Germany, 1975-76. Author: Ion Channels of Excitable Membranes, 3d edit., 2001; mem. edit. bd.: Jour. Gen. Physiology, 1971—, Am. Jour. Physiology, 1984—87, Jour. Neurosci., 1984—87, Neuron, 1987—, Curr. Opinion Neurobiol., 1990—99, Procs. of NAS, 1996—99, Channels, 2006—; contbr. articles to profl. jours. Recipient Alexander von Humboldt Sr. Scientist award, 1975, Bristol-Myers Squibb award, 1990, (with Dr. Clay Armstrong) Louisa Gross Horowitz prize for biology or biochemistry Columbia U., 1996, (with Drs. Clay Armstrong and Roderick MacKinnon) Albert Lasker award for Basic Med. Rsch., Lasker Found., 1999, Gairdner Found. Internat. award, 2001. Mem. NAS, Biophys. Soc. (K.S. Cole award 1975), Am. Acad. Arts and Sci., Inst. of Medicine, Biophys. Soc., Soc. Neurosci. Home: 10630 Lakeside Ave NE Seattle WA 98125-6934 Office: U Wash Physiology & Biophysics Dept 1959 NE Pacific St HSB Rm G424 Box 357290 Seattle WA 98195-7290 E-mail: hille@u.washington.edu. *

HILLE, HANS-HEINO, gynecologist, consultant; s. Hans and Hedwig Hille; m. Susanne Roppel, June 15, 1990; m. Susanne Schneidermann (div.); children: Rubin, Sarah Schneidermann, Jurek, Lea Schneidermann. MD, U. Hamburg, 2003. Intern Hosp., Hamburg, 1975—81; cons. Hamburg, 1981—. Examiner, Germany, 2001—. Contbr. articles to profl. jours. Mem.: Deutsche Gesellschaft für Psychosomatik in Gynäkologie und Geburtshilfe (assoc.), Deutsche Gesellschaft Ultraschall in der Meditin (assoc.), Internat. Soc. Ultrasound Ob-gyn. (assoc.). Achievements include research in ultrasound in obstetrics and gynecology. Avocations: sailing, jazz, mountain climbing. Office: Lappenbergsallee 50 Hamburg D-20257 Germany Office Fax: 004940494336. Personal E-mail: heino.hille@t-online.de. E-mail: schulze-stadler-hille@gmx.de.

HILLEL, ZAHARIA, anesthesiologist; BS in Physics, City Coll. (CUNY), 1971; PhD in Biophysics, Albert Einstein Coll. Med., 1977; MD, U. Miami, 1981. Diplomate Am. Bd. Anesthesiology, Nat. Bd. of

Echocardiography. Resident in anesthesia Mount Sinai Med. Ctr., NYC, 1982-84, fellowship in cardiothoracic anesthesia, 1984-85; prof. clin. anesthesiology Coll. of Physicians and Surgeons, Columbia U. Office: St Luke's Roosevelt Hosp Ctr St Luke's Hosp Dept Anesth 1111 Amsterdam Ave New York NY 10025-1716 Office Phone: 212-523-2500. Fax: 212-523-3930. E-mail: zh2@columbia.edu.

HILLELSON, RUTH LEANNA, plastic surgeon; b. Providence, USA; m. Terr L. Whipple. Attended, Johns Hopkins U., 1971—75, U. Vt., 1975—77, Harvard U., 1977—79. Diplomate Am. Bd. Plastic Surgery, 1987. Intern Univ. Va., 1979—80, resident gen. surgery, 1980—81, fellow plastic, maxillofacial, and craniofacial surgery, 1981—82; resident gen. surgery Johns Hopkins Univ., 1982; resident plastic and maxillofacial surgery Univ. of Kans. Med. Ctr., 1983—85; project dir. NSF; hospital appointments include Johnston-Willis Hosp., Saint Mary's Hosp., Southside Regional Hosp.; co-founder Am. Self Ctr. for Cosmetic, Plastic and Orthopedic Surgery, dir. aesthetics and plastic surgery. Author: (publs.) Plastic and Reconstructive Surgery, Microangiographic Study of Hematoma-associated Flap, Necrosis and Salvage with Isoxsuprine. Recipient Best Meeting Presentation, Internat. Soc. of Plastic and Reconstructive Surgery-Brazil, 2006, Nat. Pinnacle award, Non-Invasive Radiofrequency, 2006—07. Mem.: Southeastern Soc. of Plastic and Reconstructive Surgery, Richmond Acad. of Medicine, Med. Soc. of Va., Am. Soc. of Plastic Surgeons, Am. Soc. of Laser Medicine and Surgery, Am. Soc. for Aesthetic Plastic Surgery, ACS, German Club. Achievements include research in Induced osteogenesis; Microangiographic study of hematoma-associated flap necrosis; Fascial tensile strength; Microangiographic study on pharmacologic skin flap delay; Radiofrequency on dorsal hand. Avocations: horseback riding, water-skiing, guitar, piano. Office: American Self PLC 9900 Independence Pk Dr Richmond VA 23233 Office Phone: 804-290-0060. E-mail: hillelson@americanself.com.

HILLIARD, CAROL, nurse, educator, consultant, researcher; d. Elias and Eula Mae (Holt) Hilliard. AAS, Bronx CC, 1971; BSN, Hunter-Bellevue Sch. Nursing, 1981, MSN, 1983. Staff nurse Fordham Hosp., NYC, 1971—73; per diem work in ER, ICU and post anesthesia care unit Columbia Presbyn. Hosp., 1973—90; per diem work in ER, ICU & PACU Lincoln Hosp., 1991—95, Bellevue Hosp., 1990, Lenox Hill Hosp., 1973—2003; from staff nurse to operating room instr. NY Med. Coll., NYC, 1974—78; from staff nurse to nurse edn. instr. ER, ICU, PACU Harlem Hosp., NYC, 1978—90; asst. prof. nursing Hostos CC, NYC, 1990—95; coord., nurse cons. The Exhale Nurse Cons., NYC, 1996—, The Exhale Nursing Review, 1998—. Tchr. state bd. review classes Megan Evers Coll., Bklyn., 1996—98. Instr. CPR & basic life support for health care profls. Am. Red Cross, 1980—. Mem.: NY Assn. Black Nurses, Critical Care Nurses Assn., NY State Nurses Assn., Emergency Dept. Nursing Assn., Am. Nursing Assn. Democrat. Baptist. Avocations: sewing, decorating, dance, jazz, computers. Home and Office: The Exhale Nurse Cons 1295 Grand Concourse Rm 3C Bronx NY 10452 Personal E-mail: budstallion@verizon.net.

HILLMAN, HAROLD HYRAN, retired physiologist; b. London, Aug. 16, 1930; s. David and Annie H.; m. Elizabeth Holland, Oct. 23, 1973; children: Alexander, Rachel, Benedict, Sophia. MB/BChir, MRCS, Middlesex Hosp., London, 1956; BS in Physiology, U. Coll., London, 1958; PhD in Biochemistry, Inst. Psychiatry, London, 1963. Rsch. asst., lectr. Inst. Psychiatry, London, 1958-62; rsch. fellow, docent Inst. Neurobiology, Goteborg, Sweden, 1962-64; lectr. Inst. Neurology, London, 1964-65; sr. lectr. Battersea Coll., London, 1965-68; reader in physiology U. Surrey, Guildford, Eng., 1968-95, dir. unity lab., 1970-95, founding editor, Resuscitation, 1972, editor-in-chief, 1972—85; med. adviser Inst. Biol. Psychiatry, Bangor, Wales, 1990-93. Sec. London Med. Postgrad., 1985-2000; vis. prof. Mahidol U., Thailand, 1995; physician Med. Found. for Care of Victims of Torture, 2003. Author: Certainty and Uncertainty in Biochemical Techniques, 1972, Living Cell, 1980, Cellular Structure Mammalian Brain, 1986, Atlas of Cellular Structure Human Nervous System, 1991, The Case for New Paradigms in Cell Biology and Neurobiology, 1991, Evidence Based Cell Biology and Some Implications for Clinical Research, 2008; contbr. 160 articles to profl. jours. Exec. mem. Brit. Amnesty, London, 1970-80; senator U. Surrey, Guildford, 1979-89; chmn. Surrey Assn. Univ. Tchrs., Guildford, 1978-89; chmn. Freedom to Care, 1997-2004; sec. Physicians for Human Rights, UK, 1997-2011; mem. Fgn. Office Com. Death Penalty, 2004-11. Recipient medal Free U. Brussls, 1975. Fellow Royal Soc. Medicine; mem. Physiol. Soc., Brit. Med. Assn. (chmn. Guildford divsn. 1995-99). Avocations: reading, writing. Home: 76 Epsom Rd 3 Merrow Dene GU1 2BX Guildford England Office Phone: 44-1483-568332. E-mail: harold.hillman@btinternet.com.

HILLMAN, JANICE K., adolescent medicine; MD, Cornell U., Ithaca, NY. Diplomate Am. Bd. Internal Medicine, 1987, Am. Bd. Family Medicine-adolescent medicine, 2004. Hosp. affiliations include Bryn Mawr Hosp., 1996—, Lankenau Med. Ctr., 1996—; intern Hosp. of the Univ. Pa., resident; fellow NY Hosp.-Cornell Med. Ctr.; clin asst. prof. medicine Hosp. of the Univ. Pa.; clin. care assoc. Univ. Pa. Health System. Named one of Top Docs, Phila. Mag., 2004—11. Office: Hospital ofthe University of Pennsylvania PennCare Ste 2J 250 King of Prussia Rd Radnor PA 19087 Office Phone: 610-902-2450.

HILLMAN, RICHARD EPHRAIM, pediatrician, educator; b. Pawtucket, RI, Oct. 6, 1940; s. Harold S. and Anne (Chernick) H.; m. Laura S. Smith, June 14, 1970; children: Helena, Stuart, Noah, Paul, Andrew, Anne. AB, Brown U., 1962; MD, Yale U., 1965. Diplomate: Am. Bd. Med. Examiners, Am. Bd. Pediatrics, Am. Bd. Human Genetics. Intern Grace-New Haven Hosp., 1965-66, resident, 1966-67; asst. prof. pediatrics Washington U., St. Louis, 1971-75, assoc. prof., 1975-78, prof. pediatrics, 1981-87, assoc. prof. genetics, 1977-81, prof. genetics, 1981-87; prof. biochemistry and child health U. Mo., Columbia, 1987—2000, prof. emeritus, dir. metabolic genetics rsch., 2000—. Chmn. mental retardation research com. Nat. Inst. Child Health and Human Devel., Bethesda, Md., 1983-87, assoc. chmn., 1995—. Lt. comdr. USN, 1969-71. Fellow Am. Acad. Pediatrics; mem. Soc. Pediatric Research (council), Am. Pediatric Soc., Am. Soc. Clin. Investigation, Soc. for Inherited Metabolic Disorders (pres.) Office: School of Medicine U Mo Columbia MO 65212

HIMBURG, SUSAN PHILLIPS, dietician, educator; b. Norfolk, Va., May 17, 1946; d. Claude Ralph Jr. and Sarah Ann (Gilbert) Phillips; m. James Donald Himburg, Feb. 9, 1968; 1 child, Karlene Susan. BS in Food and Nutrition, Fla. State U., 1968; M in Dietetics, Emory U., 1972; PhD in Edn., U. Miami, Fla., 1979. Dietetic intern Emory U., Atlanta, 1971; clin. dietitian Emory U. Hosp., Atlanta, 1972-73; from instr. to prof. Fla. Internat. U., Miami, 1973—, dir. coordinated program in dietetics, 1979-99, dir. health scis. recruitment and retention program, 1985—2007, chmn. dietetics and nutrition, 1992—97, SACS self-study dir., 1997—2000, SACS dir., 2006—. Grant reviewer disadvantaged assistance program HHS, Rockville, Md., 1989—; site visitor So. Assn. Colls. and Schs., Atlanta, 1987—. Author: (tng. manual) ADA Self-Study, 1988, 91, 95; contbr. articles to profl. jours. Recipient Univ. Svc. Medallion, Fla. Internat. U., 2000. Fellow Am. Dietetic Assn. (site visitor 1985-2006, chairperson commn. on accreditation 1992-93, medallion 1996); mem. Soc. Nutrition Edn., Fla. Dietetic Assn. (del. 1990-2000, Disting. Dietitian 1995), Miami Dietetic Assn. (mem. nominating com. 1989, Disting. Dietitian 1994), Phi Kappa Phi, Kappa Omicron Nu. Office: Fla Internat Univ Dietetics & Nutrition Miami FL 33199-0001 Home: P O Box 560847 Miami FL 33256-0847 E-mail: himburgs@fiu.edu.

HIMELSTEIN, RIMA H., pediatrician, gynecologist; MD, U. Pa., Phila., 1986. Diplomate Am. Bd. Pediatrics. Resident pediat. Mt. Sinai Hosp., fellow adolescent medicine; adolescent medicine physician Crozer Chester Med. Ctr. Office: Smedley Wellnes Center 1701 Upland St Ground Fl Wellness Center Chester PA 19013 Office Phone: 610-490-1755. Office Fax: 610-490-1883.

HIMLER, THOMAS CHARLES, psychologist; b. Cleve., June 30, 1942; s. Norbert and Grace Himler; m. Myra Stull (div.); 1 child, Tara. BS, Ohio State U., 1965; MA, John Carroll U., 1971; PhD, U. Akron, 1983. Nat. cert. sch. psychologist. Tchr. St. Barnabas Sch., Northfield, Ohio, 1965—68, Broadway Sch., Maple Heights, Ohio, 1968—69; sch. psychologist Lorain County, Elyria, Ohio, 1971—79, PSI Assocs., Cleve., 1980—82; asst. prof., adj. SD State U., Sioux Falls, 1985—87; sch. psychologist Sioux Falls Sch. Dist., 1982—; pvt. practice Sioux Falls, 1983—; forensic psychologist, 2009—. Mem. biomed. ethics com. Children's Care Hosp. and Sch., Sioux Falls, 1995—97; chmn. Sioux Falls Sch. Dist. Sch. Psychology Sect., 1995—97; chmn. psychology consulting staff Avera-McKennan Hosp., Sioux Falls, 1995—99, mem. med. exec. com, 1998—99. Mem.: APA, Internat. Assn. Sch. Psychologists, Nat. Assn. Sch. Psychologists, Mensa. Avocations: sailing, scuba diving, skiing, travel. Office: Sioux Falls Sch Dist 201 E 38th St Sioux Falls SD 57105 Office Phone: 605-332-3706.

HIMPENS, BERNARD JOSEPH EDMOND, physiologist, educator; b. Veurne, Belgium, Sept. 13, 1958; m. Lut Vantrappen, July 17, 1983; children: Pieter, Kristin, Inge, Joris. MD, U. Leuven, 1983, PhD, 1988. Postdoctoral fellow Pa, Muscle Inst. U. of Pa., Phila., 1986—88; postdoctoral mandate rsch. coun. U. Leuven, 1988—89, lectr. in physiology, 1989, asst. prof. physiology, 1990—91, assoc. prof., 1991—94, prof., 1994—97, prof. ordinarius, 1997—. Clin. asst. Dept. Internal Medicine (part-time) U. Leuven, Belgium, 1983—85, acad. sec. Faculty Medicine, 1996—2005, chmn. soc. acad. pers., 2003—05; aspirant Nat. Rsch. Coun. NFWO, Brussels, 1984—88, sr. asst. Nat. Rsch. Coun., 1989—91; dean faculty medicine K.U. Leuven, 2005. Chmn. Flemish Assn. of Profs., Leuven, 1999—2003. Recipient Internat. Raffeisen award, CERA, 1975, Golden Medal & Honour Medal City Veurne, Coll. Veurne Belgium, 1976, J.B. Van Helmont award Pathophysiology, Biophysics and Biochemistry, Royal Acad. Medicine Belgium, 1988—90, Dr. & Mw. G. Schamelhout-Koettlitz award for Sci. Med. Rsch., 1992, Sci. Merck Sharp & Dohme award, Nat. Rsch. Coun. Belgium, 1993, Medicine award, Alumni U. Found. Brussels, 1993; Grant Exch. U. Pa.- K.U. Leuven, 1985—86, Sci. Grant, NATO, 1986—87. Fellow Fogarty Ctr., NIH, 1987—88. Fellow: Belgian Soc. Physiology and Pharmacology (life); mem.: Royal Acad. Medicine (gen. sec. 2004), Am. Physiol. Soc. Home: Waversebaan 348 3001 Leuven Belgium Office: K U Leuven Campus Gasthuisberg 0&N2 Herestraat 49 bus 400 3000 Leuven Belgium Office Fax: 3216337487. E-mail: Bernard.Himpens@med.kuleuven.be.

HINCHEY, JUDITH, physician; b. Boston, May 31, 1962; MD, Tufts Med. Sch., 1990, MS. Dir. stroke svc. Caritas St. Elizabeth's Med. Ctr., 2000. Asst. prof. Tufts U., 2000. Home: 69 W Pine St Auburndale MA 02466 Home Fax: 617-789-5177. Business E-Mail: judith.hinchey@steward.org.

HIND, HARRY WILLIAM, pharmaceutical company executive; b. Berkeley, Calif., June 2, 1915; s. Harry Wyndham and B.J. (O'Connor) H.; m. Diana Vernon Miesse, Dec. 12, 1940; children: Leslie Vernon Hind Daniels, Gregory William. BS, U. Calif., Berkeley, 1939, LLD, 1968; DSc (hon.), U. Scis. Phila., 1982. Founder Barnes-Hind Pharms., Inc., Sunnyvale, Calif., 1939—. Pres. Hind Health Care, Inc. Contbr. articles to profl. jours.; designer ph meter and developer of ophthalmic solutions. Recipient Ebert award for pharm. rsch., 1948, Eye Rsch. Found. award, 1958, Helmholtz Ophthalmology award for rsch., 1968, Carbert award for sight conservation, 1973, Alumnus of Yr. award U. Calif. Sch. Pharmacy, 1965, Disting. Svc. award U. Calif. Proctor Found., 1985, Commendation by Resolution State of Calif., 1987, Pharmaceutical Achievements commendation State of Calif. Assembly, Hon. Recognition award Contact Lens Mfrs. Assn., 1990. Fellow AAAS; mem. Am. Pharm. Assn., Am. Optometric Assn. (Man of Yr. award Pharmacist's Planning Svc. 1987), Contact Lens Soc. Am. (Hall of Fame 1989), Am. Assn. Pharm. Scientists, Am. Chem. Soc., Calif. Pharm. Assn., NY Acad. Scis., Los Altos Country Club, Sigma Xi, Rho Chi, Phi Delta Chi.

HINDAR, JON, pharmaceutical executive; Rsch., develop. positions Alcatel, BP Chemicals; gen. mgr. chemical companies, 1982—92; mng. ptnr. Fondsfinana investment bank, Norway, 1997—2002; sr. v.p., life sci. divsn. Invitrogen Corp., Carlsbad, Calif., 2005; CEO NorSun AS. Office: NorSun SA Sommerrogaten 13-15 255 Olso Norway Office Phone: 760-603-7200. Office Fax: 760-602-6500.

HINDE, ROBERT AUBREY, biologist, psychologist, educator; b. Norwich, Eng., Oct. 26, 1923; s. Ernest Bertram and Isabella (Taylor) H.; m. Hester Cecily Coutts, Aug. 1968 (div. 1971); children: Francis Ronald John, Katharine Gwendolen Isabel, Jonathan Robert, Miranda Elizabeth; m. Joan Stevenson, May 5, 1971; children: Larissa Jane, Camilla Anne. BA with first class hons., Cambridge U., Eng., 1948, ScD, 1958; BSc, U. London, 1948; PhD, Oxford U., Eng., 1950; ScD (hon.), U. Libre, Brussels, 1974, Paris Nanterre, 1979, Stirling, 1991, Göteborg, 1991, Edinburgh, 1992, U. We. Ont., 1996, U. Oxford, 1998. Curator ornithol. field sta. dept. zoology Cambridge U., 1950-65; fellow St. John's Coll., Cambridge, 1951-54, 58-89; rsch. prof. Royal Soc., Cambridge, 1963-89; master St. John's Coll., Cambridge, 1989-94. Hon. dir. Med. Rsch. Coun. Unit on Devel. and Integration of Behaviour, 1970-89; Hitchcock prof. U. Calif., 1979; Green vis. scholar U. Tex., 1983; chairperson Brit. Pugwash Grp., 2003-. Author: Animal Behavior: A Synthesis of Ethology and Comparative Psychology, 1966, 1970, Biological Bases of Human Social Behaviour, 1974, Towards Understanding Relationships, 1979, Ethology, 1982, Individuals, Relationships and Culture, 1987, Relationships: A Dialectical Perspective, 1997, Why Gods Persist, 1999, Why Good is Good, 2002, Ending Wars, 2008; author: (with J. Rotblat) War No More, 2003; editor: Bending the Rules, 2007; contbr. numerous articles to profl. jours. Flight lt. RAF, 1940-45. Recipient Sci. medal Zool. Soc., 1961, Leonard Cammer award N.Y. Psychiat. Inst., Columbia U., 1980, award for psychiatry Albert Einstein Coll. Medicine, N.Y., 1987, Osman Hill medal Primate Soc. Gt. Britain, 1980, Huxley medal Royal Anthrop. Inst., 1990, Disting. Sci. Contbr. award Soc. Rsch. Child Devel., 1991, Disting. Career award Internat. Soc. Study Personal Rels., 1992, Frink medal Zool. Soc. of London, 1992, G. Stanley Hall medal APA, 1993, medal Assn. Study Animal Behaviour, 1997, Bowlby-Ainsworth award, 2003; named comdr. Brit. Empire, 1988, hon. fellow Balliol Coll., Oxford, 1986, Trinity Coll., Dublin, 1990. Fellow Royal Soc. (mem. coun. 1985-87, Croonian lectr. 1990, Royal medal 1996), Brit. Acd. (hon.), St. John's Coll. (mem. coun. 1965-67, master, 1989-94), Royal Coll. Psychiatry (hon.), Brit. Psychol. Soc. (hon.), Balliol Coll. Oxford (hon.), Am. Ornithologists Union (hon.); mem. U.S. Nat. Acad. Scis. (hon. fgn. assoc.), Am. Acad. Arts and Scis. (fgn., hon.), German Ornithol. Assn., Academia Europea. Office: St John's Coll Cambridge CB23 8AL England Home: Park Ln CB3 8AL Cambridge England Office Phone: 01223 339356. E-mail: rah15@cam.ac.uk.

HINDER, RONALD ALBERT, surgeon, researcher; b. Johannesburg, Jan. 14, 1942; came to U.S., 1987; s. Albert Julius and Anna (Ringgenberg) H.; m. Philla Johanna Möller, Nov. 21, 1968; children: Ingrid, Paul, Lisa. MB, BChir, Witwatersrand U., Johannesburg, 1965, PhD, 1976. House surgeon Coronation Hosp., Johannesburg, 1966; houseman Baragwanath Hosp., Johannesburg, 1966; sr. house surgeon in urology, orthop. and paediatric surgery Johannesburg Hosp., 1967, from surg. registrar to prin. surgeon, 1970-86; registrar in pathology South African Inst. for Med. Rsch., Johannesburg, 1968; surg. registrar Whipps Cross Hosp., London, 1969, Bethnal Green Hosp., London, 1969-70; assoc. prof. dept. surgery Creighton U., Omaha, 1987-91, prof. dept. surgery, 1991—2007, emeritus prof. dept. surgery, 2008—. Assoc. prof. dept. surgery Witwatersrand U., Johannesburg, 1984-87, bd. faculty medicine, 1977-86, senate animal ethics com., 1978-86, chmn. senate animal ethics com., 1982-83; dir. residency program in surgery Creighton U., Omaha, 1988—96, acting dir. surg. rsch., dir. esophageal and gastric function lab., 1990—96, attending staff VA med. Ctr., Omaha, cons. staff, Lincoln, Nebr.; courtesy staff Bergan Mercy Hosp., Omaha, Luth. Med. Ctr., Omaha, critical care com. St. Joseph Hosp., Omaha., 1988-93, med. policy bd., 1990-91, critical care com., med. policy bd., 1992-93; vis. prof., reviewer, lectr. and spkr. in field. Editor: Problems in General Surgery, 1992, Medical Intelligence Unit Gastroesophageal Reflux Disease, 1993; (with others) Current Problems in Surgery, 1992; co-author: Chest Surgery Clinics of North America, 1995, Seminars in Laparoscopic Surgery, 1995, Current Surgical Therapy Fifth Edition, 1995, Minimally Invasive Surgery of the Foregut, 1995, Operative Laparoscopy and Thoracoscopy, 1994, Practical Endoscopic Surgery for General Surgeons, 1994, Digestive Tract Surgery: A Text and Atlas, 1994, Principles of Laparoscopic Surgery, 1995, Hernia Fourth Edition, 1995, Color Atlas/Text of Advanced Laparoscopy for Surgeons, 1995, Laparoscopic and Thoracoscopic Surgery, 1995, Complications of Laparoscopic Surgery, 1995, Advances in Surgery, 1995, Surgery of the Esophagus, Stomach and Small Intestine, 1995, The Gastrointestinal Surgical Patient, 1994, Laparoscopic Abdominal Surgery, 1993, Perspectives in General and Laparoscopic Surgery, 1993, Problems in General Surgery, 1993, Surgery Annual, 1993, Surgery Clinics of North America, 1992, Current Surgical Therapy, 4th edit., 1991, Ambulatory Esophageal pH Monitoring: Practical Approach and Clinical Applications, 1991, Gastrointestinale Funktionsdiagnostik in der Chirurgie, 1991, Gastrointestinal Motility: Which Test?, 1989; mem. editl. bd. South African Jour. Surgery, 1983-87, Jour. Postgrad. Gen. Practice, 1986-87, Jour. Surg. Laparoscopy and Endoscopy, 1990—2006, The Mediterranean Jour. Surgery and Medicine, 1994—; contbr. articles to profl. jours. Travelling fellow U. Witwatersrand, 1975, 79, 85; Schweizerische Nationalfonds grantee Stadspital Triemli, Zurich, 1982; recipient numerous rsch. grants. Fellow ACS, Royal Coll. Surgeons, Am. Coll. Gastroenterology, Southwestern Surg. Congress; mem. AMA, Surg. Rsch. Soc. So. Africa (exec. com. 1982-87), South Africa Gastroenterology Soc. (hon. treas. 1978-85), Am. Gastroenterol. Assn., Soc. Internat. Surgery, Assn. Program Dirs. in Surgery, Am. Motility Soc., Soc. Am. Gastrointestinal Endoscopic Surgeons, Colegium Internat. Surgery Digestive, Soc. for Surgery of the Alimentary Tract (auditing com. 1992), Ctrl. Surg. Assn., Assn. for Acad. Surgery, Omaha Mid-West Clin. Soc. (vice-chmn. sect. on surgery 1988, chmn. surg. sect. 1989-90, sci. display awards com. 1991), Met. Omaha Med. Soc., North Ctrl. Cancer Treatment Group, Ea. coop. Oncology Group, Internat. Duodenal Club, Phi Beta Delta. Business E-Mail: hinder.ronald@yahoo.edu. *

HINDERLICH, HORST KLAUS, health facility administrator; b. Langewahl, Germany, Dec. 17, 1942; s. Herbert Heinz and Else Frieda (Liepe) H.; m. Hilde Johanne Scharf, June 14, 1969; 1 child, Hauke. BBA, U. Bremen, 1971; D (hon.), Univ. San Tomas, Bolivia, 1996; Senator (hon.), U. Applied Scis., Bremen, Germany, 2000. Bd. mem. HAG Gen. Foods, Bremen, Germany, 1969-86; cons. John Strk & Ptnr., Frankfurt, Germany, 1986-87; mng. dir. R&B Food Handels GmbH, Bremen, 1988-89, Rotes-Kreuz-Krankenhaus, Bremen, 1990—2004. Instr. Bus. Acad. Bremen, 1969-2003; chmn. supervisory bd. Ameos St. Salvator Hosp, 2004-07. Author: The Red Cross Hospital Writes History, 1999; contbr. articles to profl. jours. Chmn. C. of C. Bremen, 1970—2009; hon. judge Labor Ctr., Bremen, 1972—. Col. German Air Force, 1963—. Recipient Life Saving medal, City of Berlin, 1956, Hon. Cross in Gold, Ministry of Def., 1991, Gold Cross, KNBLO, 1996, Bolivian Navy Merit medal, 1996, Bolivian Air Force Merit medal, 1997, Peruvian Nat. Police Grand Officer Cross, 1999, German Merit Cross, 2001. Mem.: Hosp. Dirs.

Assn., German Mil. Res. Assn., Golf Club Worpswede. Lutheran. Avocations: golf, reading, travel, walking. Home and Office: Birkenheide 14 Osterholz-Scharmbeck 27711 Germany Business E-Mail: office-hinderlich@t-online.de.

HINDMARSH, KENNETH WAYNE, pharmacist, educator; b. Grandview, Man., Can., Aug. 13, 1941; s. Frederick Joseph and Mildred Olive (Clark) H.; m. Lois Irene Dies, July 9, 1966; children: Carla Anne, Ryan James. BSP, U. Sask, Saskatoon, Can., 1964, MSc, 1965; PhD, U. Alta., Edmonton, Can., 1970. Staff pharmacist U. Hosp., Saskatoon, Can., 1965-66; lectr. U. Sask., Saskatoon, Can., 1966-67; toxicologist Royal Can. Mounted Police, Regina, Can., 1970-71; mem. faculty U. Sask. Coll. Pharmacy, 1971—, prof., 1979—, asst. dean, 1987-92; dean faculty pharmacy U. Man., 1992-98, U. Toronto, Ont., 1998—2009; dean emeritus, 2009—; exec. dir. Can. Coun. Accreditation Pharmacy Programs, 2010—. Med. Rsch. Coun. vis. prof., Australia. Author: Nutritional Products, 1984, Drugs-What Your Kid Should Know, 1992, revised edit., 2000, Too Cool for Drugs, 1993; contbr. articles to profl. jours. Recipient Douglas M. Lucas award for excellence in forensic sci., 1999, Centennial Pharmacist award, 2007; Paul Harris fellow, 1970. Fellow Can. Soc. Forensic Sci. (pres. 1984); mem. Assn. Faculties Pharmacy of Can. (pres. 1977-78), Soc. Toxicology Can., Sask. Man. and Ont. Pharm. Assn., Can. Pharm. Assn., Can. Coun. Accreditation Pharmacy Programs (pres. 1993-95, 97-98). Baptist. Avocations: racquet sports, jogging, reading, music. Home: 801-62 Wellesley St W Toronto ON Canada M5S 2X3 Office: U Toronto Leslie Dan Faculty Pharmacy Toronto ON Canada M5S 3M2 Home Phone: 416-929-6146; Office Phone: 416-946-5055. Business E-Mail: wayne.hindmarsh@utoronto.ca.

HINES, COLLEEN M., clinical nurse specialist; d. David Walter Mullis and Jo Wilma Clary; m. Thomas E. Hines, Aug. 2, 1969. BS, Tex. Women's U., 1966, MS, 1979. RN Tex., cert. diabetes educator, childbirth educator, in thanotology. Staff nurse Parkland Hosp., Dallas, 1966—67, head nurse, 1967—75, nursing care supr., 1975—80, clin. nurse specialist, 1980—2003; program coord. Region 10 Edn. Svc. Ctr., Richardson, Tex., 2004—. Past mem. breastfeeding task force State of Tex. Dept. Health, Austin; mem. Nat. Head Start Assn.'s. Contbr. articles to profl. jours. Named Employee of Yr., Parkland Hosp., 1989. Mem.: Am. Assn. Diabetes Educators (past pres. local chpt., diabetes in pregnancy interest group), Tex. Nurses. Assn. (bd. dir. 2000—03, 2005—07, D-4 pres. 2009—, district pres. 2007—09, 2009—11), Am. Nurses Assn., Sigma Theta Tau (past pres. Tex. Women's U. chpt., Great 100 Nurse in Dallas 2008). Baptist. Avocations: reading, travel. Office Phone: 972-348-1614. Business E-Mail: colleen.hines@region10.org. E-mail: cmhteh@sbcglobal.net.

HINES, GEORGE LAWRENCE, surgeon; b. Bklyn., June 10, 1946; s. Frank and Ruth (Katzman) H.; m. Helene Anne Reitman, Aug. 23, 1969; children: Brian, Jennifer. BA, MD, Boston U., 1969. Diplomate Am. Bd. Gen. Surgery, Am. Bd. Thoracic Surgery, Am. Bd. Gen. Vascular Surgery. Intern Maimonides Med. Ctr., Bklyn., 1969-70; resident Sinai Hosp., Detroit, 1970-71; to chief resident L.I. Jewish Med. Ctr., NYC, 1971-74; cardiothoracic resident NYU Med. Ctr., NYC, 1974-76; attending physician Winthrop U. Hosp., Mineola, NY, 1976—, chief div. vascular surgery, 1995—; pvt. practice Mineola; prof. clin. surgery SUNY, Stony Brook. Maj. U.S. Army Res., 1970-79. Fellow ACS, (disting.)Soc. for Vascular Surgery; mem. Am. Assn. for Thoracic Surgery, Soc. Thoracic Surgeons. Democrat. Jewish. Avocations: jogging, piano. Office: Winthrop Cardiothoracic Vascular Surgery Group 120 Mineola Blvd Mineola NY 11501-4073 Office Phone: 516-663-4400.

HING, DAVID, plastic surgeon, educator; married; 2 children. MD, U. Mich. Diplomate Am. Bd. Plastic Surgery, cert. hand surgery. Resident in plastic surgery Univ. Chgo. Med. Ctr., Ill.; rsch. fellow in microcirculation Ralph K. Davies Med. Ctr., San Francisco, clin. fellow in microsurgery; academic plastic surgery tchg. staff Univ. Mich., Temple Univ., Phila., Univ. Calif., San Francisco; hosp. affiliations include St. Joseph Mercy Hosp., Forest Health Med. Ctr., Chelsea Cmty. Hosp.; plastic surgeon Ctr. for Plastic and Reconstructive Surgery, Mich. Mem.: Am. Soc. of Plastic Surgeons. Office: Center for Plastic and Reconstructive Surgery PO Box 994 5333 McAuley Dr Suites 5001 and 5008 Ann Arbor MI 48106 Office Phone: 734-712-2323. Office Fax: 734-712-2312.

HINGSON, RALPH W., medical educator; b. July 21, 1948; BA in Internat. Rels., Johns Hopkins U., 1969, ScD, 1974; MPH, U. Pitts., 1970. Prof. dept. social behavior sci. Boston U. Sch. Pub. Health, 1986—2007; dir. divsn. prevention and epidemiology Nat. Inst. on Alcohol Abuse and Alcoholism; past pres. Internat. Coun. Alcohol Drugs and Traffic Safety. Cons., Nat. Ctr. for Substance Abuse Prevention, Nat. Trans. Rsch. Bd., others; nat. bd. advs. MADD,; former v.p. Pub. Policy. Contbr. numerous articles to profl. jours. Recipient Hero award, MADD, 1995, Innovators Combating Substance Abuse award, Robert Wood Johnson Found., 2001, Widmark award, Internat. Coun. Alcohol Drugs and Traffic Safety, 2002, Ralph W. Hingson Rsch. in Practice Presdl. award, MADD, 2003, R. Brinkley Smith P3 Disting. Scientists award, Am. Soc. Addiction Medicine, 2008; named one of America's 10 Outstanding Young Men, U.S. Jaycees, 1984. Home: 4 Louisburg Sq Boston MA 02108-1203 Office: Nat Inst Alcohol Abuse and Alcoholism Rm 2077 5635 Fishers Ln Bethesda MD 20892-1706 Office Phone: 301-443-1274. Business E-Mail: rhingson@mail.nih.gov.

HINKLE, ALLEN JOSEPH, pediatrician, anesthesiologist, insurance company executive; b. Pittsburg, Calif., Nov. 30, 1950; s. Joseph Glenn and Marjorie Alice (Sweeney) H.; m. Aug. 3, 1974; 1 child: Melisse Paige. BS in Zoology magna cum laude with sr. honors, U. Mass., 1973; MD, Albert Einstein Coll. Medicine, 1976. Diplomate Am. Bd. Anesthesiology, Am. Bd. Pediatrics. Pediatrics intern Children's Hosp., Phila., 1976-77; pediatric resident Children's Hosp. Med. Ctr., Boston, 1977-79, staff anesthesiologist, 1981-82; anesthesiology resident Mass. Gen. Hosp., Boston, 1981-82; staff pediatric anesthesiologist Dartmouth-Hitchcock Med. Ctr., Hanover, N.H., 1982—; pediatric registrar St. Mary's Hosp. Med. Sch., London, 1978; dir. pediatric anesthesia Dartmouth Coll., 1982—, anesthesiology educator, 1983; chief med, officer Tufts Health Plan, Boston; chief med. dir. Blue Cross Blue Shield of Vermont; chief med. officer Anthem Blue Cross Blue Shield in NH; exec. v.p., chief med. officer MVP Health Care. Inventor anesthesia devices. Organizer pre-shc. edn., Lebanon, N.H., 1986-87. Recipient Merit award AMA, 1985. Mem. N.H./Vt. Soc. Anesthesiologists (v.p. 1986—), Am. Soc. Anesthesiology, Am. Acad. Pediatrics. Republican. Presbyterian. Avocations: tree farming, stained glass. Office: MVP Health Care 625 State St PO Box 2207 Schenectady NY 12301-2207 *

HINMAN, ALAN RICHARD, public health physician, epidemiologist; b. New Orleans, Mar. 23, 1937; s. E. Harold and Katharine Ellen (Fradenburgh) H.; m. Donna Virgene Graham, Dec. 21, 1959 (div. 1962); m. Lucy Winkler Householder, May 30, 1965; children: Johanna Mary, Katharine Emily. BA, Cornell U., 1957; MD, Western Res. U., 1961; MPH, Harvard U., 1969. Intern Cleve. Met. Hosp., 1961—62, resident in internal medicine, 1962—64, chief resident, 1964-65; with USPHS, 1965-70, 77-96; advanced through grades to asst. surgeon gen., 1988; epidemic intelligence svc. officer Ctr. for Disease Control, Calif. State Dept. Health, 1965-66; regional evaluation officer malaria eradication program Ctrs. for Disease Control, Atlanta, 1966-67, San Salvador, El Salvador, 1967-68, asst. chief viral diseases br. epidemiology program Atlanta, 1969-70; dir. Bur. Epidemiology, N.Y. State Dept. Health, Albany, 1970-71, asst. commr. epidemiology and preventive health svcs., 1971-75; asst. commr., dir. Bur. Preventive and Med. Svcs., Tenn. Dept. Pub. Health, Nashville, 1975-77; dir. divsn. immunization Ctr. for Prevention Svcs., Ctrs. for Disease Control, Atlanta, 1977-88; coord. nat. vaccine program Office of Asst. Sec. for Health, 1987-90; asst. surgeon gen. USPHS, 1988-96; dir. Nat. Ctr. for Prevention Svcs. Ctrs. for Disease Control, 1988-95; sr. advisor to dir. Ctrs. for Disease Control and Prevention, 1995-96; coord. CDC World Bank collaboration on immunizations Task Force Global HealthDecatur, Atlanta, 1996—2000; sr. pub. health scientist Task Force Child Survival and Devel., Atlanta, 1996—; prin. investigator All Kids Count, 2000—04; coord. PARTNERS TB ctrl. program, 2001—02; progarm dir. Uganda Immunization Tng. Program, 2008—. Adj. asst. prof. preventive and cmty. medicine Albany Med. Coll., Union U., 1970-75; adj. asst. prof. pub. health Rensselaer Poly Inst., 1971-75; assoc. clin. prof. dept. preventive medicine Vanderbilt U., 1975-77; clin. asst. prof. dept. cmty. medicine Divsn. Healthcare Svcs., U. Tenn., 1975-77; clin. asst. prof. dept. family and cmty. health Meharry Med. Coll., 1975-77; clin. assoc. prof. dept. preventive medicine-cmty. health Emory U. Sch. Medicine, Atlanta, 1978-90; vis. prof. Case Western Res. U. Sch. Medicine, 1984; adj. prof. Emory U. Sch. Pub. Health, 1990—; vis. lectr. Shanghai 1st Med. Coll., 1981; sr. pub. health scientist The Task Force for Child Survival and Devel., 1996—. Contbr. over 300 articles to profl. jours. Decorated D.S.M.; recipient Indian Health Svc. Dir. Spl. Excellence award, 1992. Fellow ACP, APHA (mem. gov. coun. 1975-77, mem. program devel. bd. 1984-86, mem. nominating com. 1984-86, chair 1985-86, chair-elect epidemiology sect. 1985-87, chair sect. 1987-89, past chair 1989-91, mem. exec. bd. 1991-95, spkr. governing coun. 1995-2007), Am. Acad. Pediat., Am. Coll. Epidemiology (mem. exec. bd. 1990-94, v.p. 1991-92, pres. 1992-93), Am. Coll. Preventive Medicine (regent 1974-75, 77-81, v.p. for pub. health 1975-76); mem. AMA, Am. Epidemiol. Soc., Am. Soc. Tropical Medicine and Hygiene, Am. Venereal Disease Assn. (bd. dirs. 1972-75, sec.-treas. 1975-77), Assn. Tchrs. Preventive Medicine, Infectious Diseases Soc. Am., Internat. Epidemiol. Assn., Physicians for Social Responsibility, Soc. Epidemiol. Rsch., Soc. Med. Decision Making. Home: 2194 Creek Park Rd Decatur GA 30033-2714 Office Phone: 404-687-5636. Business E-Mail: ahinman@taskforce.org.

HINNEBUSCH, ALAN GERARD, molecular geneticist; b. Pitts., June 26, 1954; s. Raymond Aloysius and Agnes Regina (McCrum) H.; m. Nancy Jane Andrews, Aug. 18, 1973; children: Amelia Jane, Alexander Joseph. BS in Biology, U. Dayton, 1975; PhD in Biochemistry/Molecular Biology, Harvard U., 1980. Postdoctoral fellow Cornell U., Ithaca, NY, 1980-82, MIT, Cambridge, 1982-83; sr. staff fellow Nat. Inst. Child Health & Human Devel., Bethesda, Md., 1983-87, sect. head lab. molecular genetics, 1987-95, chief, lab. eukaryotic gene regulation, 1995—2000, chief, lab. gene regulation and devel., 2000—, sect. head nutrient control of gene regulation, 2000—. Cons. BioTechnica Internat., Inc., Cambridge, 1981-85, Ribogene, Inc., Hayward, Calif., 1992—; Wellcome vis. prof. Med. Coll. Wis., 1995. Contbr. articles to profl. jours.; editor/asst. editor Genes Devel., Genetics, Molecular Cell Biology, Microbiology Rev., Molecular Microbiology, New Biologist. Named Md.'s Outstanding Young Scientist, Md. Sci. Ctr., 1994; recipient John E. Dlugos Jr. Award of Excellence in Biology, U. Dayton, 1975, Pub. Health Svc. Superior Svc. award NIH, 1991. Fellow Am. Acad. Microbiology; mem. Am. Soc. Microbiology, Genetics Soc. Am., Am. Acad. Arts & Sciences. Achievements include identification of the GCN4 transcriptional activator in the general animo acid control of S. cervisiae; elucidation of the mechanism of translational control of the GCN4 gene of S. cerevisiae; identification of the regulatory domain in translation initiation factor eIF2B. Office: NICHHD Lab Gene Regulation and Devel Bldg 18T Rm 106 Bethesda MD 20892 Office Phone: 301-496-4480. Business E-Mail: ahinnebusch@nih.gov.

HINSHAW, ADA SUE, nursing educator, former dean; b. Arkansas City, Kans., May 20, 1939; d. Oscar A. and Georgia Ruth (Tucker) Cox; children: Cynthia Lynn, Scott Allen Lewis. BS, U. Kans., 1961; MSN, Yale U., 1963; MA, U. Ariz., 1973, PhD, 1975; DSc (hon.), U. Md., 1988, Med. Coll. of Ohio, 1988, Marquette U., 1990, U. Nebr., 1992, Mount Sinai Med. Ctr., NY, 1993, U. Medicine and Dentistry N.J., 1995, Grand Valley State U., 1995, U. Toronto, Can., 1996, St. Louis U., 1996, Georgetown U., 1998. Instr. Sch. Nursing U. Kans., 1963-66; asst. prof. U. Calif., San Francisco, 1966-71; prof. U. Ariz., Tucson, 1975-87; dir. nursing rsch. U. Med. Ctr., Tucson, 1975-87; dir. Nat. Inst. Nursing Rsch. Pub. Health Svc., Dept. Health and Human Svcs., NIH, Washington, 1987—94; prof. U. Mich. Sch. Nursing, Ann Arbor, 1994—, dean, 1994—2006, dean emeritus, 2006—. Contbd. articles to profl. jours. Recipient Kay Schilter award U. Kans., 1961, Lucille Petry Leone award Nat. League for Nursing, 1971, Wolanin Geriatric Nursing Rsch. award U. Ariz., 1978, Alumni of the Yr award Sch. Nursing U. Kans., 1981, Disting. Alumni award Sch. Nursing Yale U., 1981, Alumni Achievement award U. Ariz., 1990, Disting. citation Kans. Alumni Assn., 1992, Health Leader of the Yr. award Pub. Health Svc., 1993, Centennial award Columbia Sch. Nursing, 1993, Presdl. Meritorious Exec. Rank award, 1994. Mem. ANA (Nurse Scientist of Yr. Award 1985, Salute to Nurses award 1994), Coun. Nurse Rschrs. (Nurse Scientist of Yr. Award 1985), Md. Nurses Assn., Western Soc. for Rsch. in Nursing, Am. Acad. Nursing, Inst. Medicine (mem. 1989-, coun. mem. 1999-04, mem. com. 1995-99, Walsh McDermott medal, 2005), Sigma Xi, Sigma Theta Tau (Beta Mu Chpt. award of Excellence in Nursing Edn., 1980, Elizabeth McWilliams Miller Excellence in Rsch. Award, 1987), Alpha Chi Omega. Avocations: hiking, camping, bicycling. Office: U Mich Sch Nursing 400 N Ingalls St Rm 4221 Ann Arbor MI 48109-2003 E-mail: ahinshaw@umich.edu.

HINSHAW, DANIEL BENJAMIN, surgeon, educator; b. LA, Jan. 25, 1957; BS, Loma Linda U., MD, 1978. Prof., surgery U. Mich. Med. Sch., 1987—. Cons., palliative medicine VA Med. Ctr. and U. Mich., 2001. Fellow: ACS. Office: Palliative Care Program 2215 Fuller Rd Ann Arbor MI 48105 Office Fax: 734-845-5681. Business E-Mail: hinshaw@umich.edu.

HINSHAW, STEPHEN P., psychology professor, department chairman; b. Columbus, Ohio, Dec. 1, 1952; s. Virgil Goodman Hinshaw, Jr. and Alene Pryor Hinshaw; m. Kelly M. Campbell, July 22, 2001; children: Evan R. Neukomm children: Jeffrey W., John W. Neukomm. AB in Psychology and Social Rels. summa cum laude, Harvard U., Cambridge, Mass., 1974; MA in Clin. Psychology, UCLA, 1979, PhD in Clin. Psychology, 1983. Licensure Bd. of Psychology, Calif., 1984. Program coord. Therapeutic Ctr., Mass. Mental Health Ctr., 1974—76; dir. Camp Freedom, Cambridge, Mass., 1975—77; clin. psychology intern, Neuropsychiatric Inst. UCLA, 1981—82, asst. prof. dept. psychology, 1986—90; psychologist child psychiatry divsn. U. Calif. Irvine Med. Ctr., 1982—83; postdoctoral fellow Langley Porter Inst. U. Calif., San Francisco, 1983—85; asst. clin. prof. dept. psychiatry U. Calif., San Francisco, 1984—86, clin. prof. dept. psychiatry, 2004—, vis. lectr. dept. psychiatry Berkeley, 1985—86, asst. prof. dept. psychology, 1990—91, assoc. prof. dept. psychology, 1991—95, prof. dept. psychology, 1995—, dir. clin. psychology tng., 1997—2001, chmn. dept. psychology, 2004—. Prin. investigator U. Calif., Berkeley, 1990—2003; pres. Profl. Group on Attention and Related Disorders, 1996—2000. Author: (book) The Years of Silence are Past: My Father's Life with Bipolar Disorder, Attention Deficits and Hyperactivity in Children; contbr. more than 130 articles to profl. jours. Recipient R.E. Harris award, U. Calif. San Francisco, 1985, Disting. Tchg. award, U. Calif., Berkeley, 2001, Disting. Profl. Contbn. award, The Help Group, 2004; named to Children and Adults with ADHD Hall of Fame, 2007; grantee, Nat. Inst. Mental Health. Fellow: AAAS, APA (pres., divsn. 53 2000—02), Assn. Psychol. Sci.; mem.: Internat. Soc. Rsch. in Child and Adolescent Psychopathology (pres. 1999—2001), Phi Beta Kappa. Achievements include contributor to multimodal treatment study of children with ADHD. Avocations: basketball, hiking. Office: Dept Psychology Univ Calif Tolman Hall #1650 Berkeley CA 94720-1650 Office Phone: 510-643-8586. Business E-Mail: hinshaw@berkeley.edu.

HINSON, JACK ALLSBROOK, research toxicologist, educator; b. Mullins, SC, Aug. 18, 1944; s. Layton Liston and Will (Allsbrook) H.; m. Joanne Edwards Kidd; children: Edward Thomas, Richard William. BS, Coll. of Charleston, 1966; MS, U. S.C., 1968; PhD, Vanderbilt U., 1972. Postdoctoral fellow Nat. Inst. of Health, Bethesda, Md., 1972-75, sr. staff fellow, 1975-80; rsch. toxicologist Nat. Ctr. Toxicological Rsch., Jefferson, Ark., 1980-90, chief biochem. mechanisms br., 1989-90; adj. prof. U. Ark. Med. Sci., Little Rock, 1980-90, prof., dir. div. toxicology. Dir. interdisciplinary toxicology program U. Ark. Med. Sci., 1990—; chmn. Ark. Toxicology Symposium, 1992-99; adj. assoc. prof. U. Tenn. Ctr. for Health Scis., Memphis, 1982-90; vis. fellow Middlesex Hops. Med. Sch., London, 1982; vis. prof. U. Leiden, The Netherlands, 1986. Editor Drug Metabolism Revs., 1997—, mem. editl. bd., 1995-97; mem. editl. bd. Toxicology and Applied Pharmacology, 1980-89, 96—, Jour. Toxicology and Environ. Health, 1991—; contbr. chpts. to books and articles to profl. jours. Mem. Soc. Toxicology (pres. South Ctrl. chpt. 1990-92), Am. Soc. Pharmacology and Exptl. Therapeutics, Internat. Soc. for Study of Xenobiotics. Episcopalian. Home: 8 Piedmont Ln Little Rock AR 72223-2232 Office: U Ark Med Sci Divsn Toxicology 4301 W Markham St # 638 Little Rock AR 72205-7101 Home Phone: 501-225-5671. Business E-Mail: HinsonJackA@uams.edu.

HINTERBERGER, MARGARETA, medical researcher; b. Vienna, Dec. 7, 1958; d. Stephan Maria and Margaretha Fischer; m. Wolfgang Alexander Hinterberger, Sept. 28, 1985; children: Alexander, Barbara, Stephan, Christoph, Lorenz. MD, Med. U., 1983. Trainee internal medicine Med. U. Vienna, 1983—91, sr. lectr. internal medicine, 1996; rschr., sci. writer L.Boltzmann Inst. Aging//Stem Cell Tx, Vienna, 1991—. Contbr. articles to profl. sci. publs. Mem.: Austrian Soc. Internal Medicine, Austrian Soc. Hematology and Oncology, Alumni Alma Mater Rudolphina, Austrian Alpine Club. Achievements include research in graft versus autoimmunity effect in allogeneic bone marrow transplantation; VITA-Study. Office: LBoltzmann Inst Aging/Stem Cell Tx Langobardenstraße 122 Vienna A-1220 Austria Business E-Mail: w.hinterberger@utanet.at.

HINTERBERGER-FISCHER, MARGARETA, oncologist, researcher; b. Vienna, Dec. 7, 1958; d. Stephan Maria and Margaretha Fischer; m. Wolfgang Alexander Hinterberger, Sept. 28, 1985; children: Alexander Wolfgang Hinterberger, Barbara Konstanze Hinterberger, Stephan Maria Hinterberger, Christoph Clemens Hinterberger, Lorenz Severin Hinterberger. MD, Med. U. Vienna, Austria, 1977—83, Specialist in Internal Medicine, 1983—91. Lic. sr. lectr. U. Vienna, 1996. Trainee U. Hosp., Vienna, 1983—91; rschr. Donauspital/ L.Boltzmann Inst. Stem Cell Transplantation, Vienna, 1992—, Donauspital/L. Boltzmann Inst. Aging Rsch. VITA-Study, Vienna, 2003—. Cons. rschr. Donauspital L.Boltzmann Inst. Aging Rsch., Vienna, 2003—. Contbr. scientific papers. Mem.: Austrian Soc. Hematology & Oncology, Soc. Internal Medicine, Alumni Alma Mater Rudolphina, Austrian Alpine Club. Roman Cath. Achievements include research in graft versus autoimmunity effect in allogeneic bone marrow tranplantation; folic acid and Alzheimer's disease VITA study. Avocations: mountaineering, mountain biking, skiing, photography, theater. Office: Boltzmann Inst Spiny Rsch Langobardenstrasse 122 Vienna A-1220 Austria Office Fax: 00431 28802 3280. Business E-Mail: w.hinterberger@utanet.at.

HINTERBUCHNER, CATHERINE N., physician, medical educator; b. Greece, Nov. 22, 1926; m. Ladislav P. Hinterbuchner, Dec. 10, 1955. MD cum laude, Nat. & Kapodistriakon U., Athens, Greece, 1951; DS (hon.), New Med. Coll., Valhalla, NY, 2002. Intern St. Luke's Hosp., 1953-54; resident in internal medicine French Hosp., 1954-55, Kingsbrook Jewish Med. Ctr., 1955-56, fellow in phys. medicine and rehab., 1956-57, N.Y. Med. Coll., 1956-57, N.Y. Med. Coll. and Met. Hosp. Ctr., 1959-60; acting cmn. dept. rehab. medicine N.Y. Med. Coll., Valhalla, 1970-71, prof., chmn. dept. rehab. medicine, 1971—2004, prof. emeritus rehab. medicine, 2005—; chief rehab. medicine, attending physician Met. Hosp. Ctr., NYC,

1964—2001; chief rehab. medicine Lincoln Med. and Mental Health Ctr., 2001—04. Fellow ACP, N.Y. Acad. Medicine, Am. Acad. Phys. Medicine and Rehab.; mem. AMA, N.Y. State Med. Soc., N.Y.C. Med. Soc., Am. Congress Rehab. Medicine, N.Y. Acad. Scis. *

HINTERBUCHNER, EUGEN K., neurologist, consultant; b. Bratislava, Slovak Republic, Feb. 10, 1949; s. Zoltan Hinterbuchner and Marta Hinterbuchnerova; life ptnr. Renata Lyerova; m. Eliska Cerna (div.); 1 child, Lukas P. MD, Charles U., Prague, 1976. Cert. neurologist Czech Physicians Chamber. Lectr., asst. prof. Inst. of Pathophysiology, Med. Sch., Brno, Czech Republic, 1979—81; house officer 1st Dept. of Internal Medicine, Med. Sch., Brno, 1981—84; consulting neurologist Neurosurg. Dept. Med. Sch., Brno, 1984—90; neurologist in chief Dist. Outpatient Dept., Brno, 1991—93; product specialist Schering Plough CEAG, Prague, Czech Republic, 1993—94; med. adviser Searle European Ltd., Prague, 1995—99; editor in chief postgrad. medicine Strategie / Mona / VNU, Prague, 1999—2001; med. dir. Slovakofarma, Prague, 2001—03; corp. med. info. mgr. Zentiva, Prague, 2003—. Med. cons. Grada Pub. Ho., Prague, 1999—2001; consulting neurologist Medicover, Prague, 2000—. Mem. ethical com. ARCOMed, Prague, 2002. Mem.: AAAS (assoc.), N.Y. Acad. of Scis. (assoc.). Home: Spesneho 1676 Roztoky 25263 Czech Republic Office: Zentiva Machova 18/838 Prague 12000 Czech Republic Personal E-mail: ehint@mybox.cz. E-mail: eugen.hinterbuchner@zentiva.cz.

HINZ, CARL FREDERICK, JR., immunologist, educator; b. Cleve., Apr. 9, 1927; s. Carl Frederick and Marie (Jones) H.; m. Joan Herndon, June 5, 1953; children— Elizabeth, Richard, Catherine, Gretchen. BS, Western Res. U., 1948, MD, 1951. Faculty dept. medicine Western Res. U. Sch. Medicine, Cleve., 1953-67, asst. prof., 1961-67, research asso. div. research in med. edn., 1964-67; prof., asso. dean U. Conn. Sch. Medicine, 1967-92, acting head dept. medicine, 1979-80, emeritus, 1992—. Mem. Conn. Med. Exam. Bd., 1976-80 Chmn. bd. dirs. blood svcs. Conn. region ARC, 1993-95, chair coun. of chairs North Atlantic area, 1995-98. Markle scholar, 1959-64; scholar-in-residence Inst. Medicine, Nat. Acad. Sci., 1987-88. Fellow ACP; mem. Am. Soc. Clin. Investigation, Am. Assn. Immunologists, Am. Soc. Hematology, Central Soc. Clin. Research, Am. Fedn. Clin. Research, Conn. Med. Soc., Hartford County Med. Assn. (dir. 1976-92, pres. 1986-87), Conn. Lung Assn. (pres. 1979-81)

HIOTIS, SPIROS P., surgeon, educator; MD, U. Md., 1992. Diplomate Am. Bd. Surgery. Resident in surgery Univ. South Fla. Med. Ctr., 1993—98; fellow in surgical oncology Meml. Sloan- Kettering Cancer Ctr., 1998—2000; asst. prof. surgery Mt. Sinai Sch. Med., asst. prof. oncological sciences; vice chmn. for surgical rsch. Mt. Sinai Med. Ctr. Author: Successful Limb Transplantation Across a Multi-Minor Barrier Facilitated by Preceding Engraftment of T-cell-Purged Donor and Recipient Bone Marrow, 1999, Captopril-Associated Cholestasis Complicating the Management of Pancreatic Cancer, 2000, Randomized Clinical Trials in Melanoma, 2002, Assessing the Predictive Value of Clinical Response to Combined Modality Therapy for Rectal Cancer; a Prospective Evaluation of 488 Patients, 2002, Magnetic Resonance Imaging of a Murine Model for Hepatocellular Carcinoma. Hepatology, 2003, Multiorgan Resection for Gastric Cancer: Intraoperative and Computed Tomography Assessment of Locally Advanced Disease is Inaccurate, 2004, Diagnostic Laparoscopy in the Evaluation of the Viral Hepatitis Patient with Potentially-Resectable Hepatocellular Carcinoma, 2005, Neoadjuvant chemotherapy, surgery, and adjuvant intraperitoneal chemotherapy in patients with locally advanced gastric or gastroesophageal junction carcinoma: a phase II study, 2005, Results following resection for stage IV gastric cancer; are better outcomes observed in selected patient subgroups?, 2007, Laparoscopic Staging for Liver, Biliary, Pancreas, and Gastric Cancer, 2007, various publs. Office: Mount Sinai Medical Center 5 E 98th St Fl 12 Box 1259 New York NY 10029 Office Phone: 212-241-2891. Office Fax: 212-241-1572.

HIRAGA, SEIGO, medical educator; b. Tokyo, Apr. 24, 1941; s. Masami and Sadako Hiraga; m. Michiko Itoh, Oct. 10, 1971; 2 children. MD, Tokyo Med. and Dental U., 1968, PhD, 1980. Jr. resident Tokyo Med. and Dental U., 1969-71, sr. instr., 1971-73, sr. instr., then asst. prof., 1977-80; dir. dept. urology Tokyo Rosai Hosp., 1973-77; asst. prof., then assoc. prof. Saitama (Japan) Med. Sch., 1980-85; assoc. prof. dept. transplantation Tokai U. Sch. Medicine, Isehara, Japan, 1985-97, dir. kidney ctr. assoc. prof. dept. surgery, divsn. transplantation surgery, 1997—; pres. Social Ins. Assns., Mishima (Japan) Hosp., 1997—. Vis. prof. Tokai U.; vis. asst. prof. Teikyo U., Kawasaki, Japan, 1985—; clin. fellow Karolinska U. Huddinge (Sweden) Hosp., 1986; postgrad. physician Meth. Med. Ctr., Baylor U. Med. Ctr., Dallas, 1989-90; pres. Internat. Transplant Coords. Meeting, Kyoto, Japan, 1994. Author: Clinical Transplants, 1986, Japan and North America Medical Exchange Foundation Review 1, 1991; contbr. articles to med. jours. Mem. Japanese Soc. for Renal Transplantation (chmn. 28th 1995), Transplantation Soc., Soc. Internationale D'urologie, Am. Soc. Transplant Physicians, Internat. Transplant Coords. Soc. (pres. 1994—), Soc. Organ Sharing (councillor). Zen Buddhist. Avocations: kendo, swimming, skiing, tennis, reading. Office: Social Ins Assns Mishima Hosp 20-9 Minamihoncho Mishima Shizuoka 411-0841 Japan

HIRAI, DENITSU, surgeon; b. Yokkaichi, Mie, Japan, July 27, 1943; came to U.S. 1969; s. Denyomu and Shizuo (Tanaka) H.; m. Fumiko Hada, June 14, 1969; 1 child, R. Lisa. MD, U. Tokyo, 1968; MBA, U. So. Calif., 2003. Diplomate Am. Bd. Surgery, Am. Bd. Quality Assurance and Utilization Rev. Physicians, Am. Bd. Surg. Critical Care; cert. nutrition support physician; cert. wound care specialist. Intern and residency Waterbury (Conn.) Hosp., 1969-74; fellow Mt. Sinai Hosp., 1974-75; asst. chief surgery VA Med. Ctr., Lincoln, Nebr., 1975-80, chief surgery, 1981-2000; asst. clin. prof. surgery Creighton U., Omaha, 1982-84, asst. prof. surgery, 1984-2000; clin. instr. U. Nebr., Omaha, 1986-88, clin. asst. prof. surgery, 1988-2000; assoc. prof. clin. surgery, mem. surgery staff Sch. Medicine U. So. Calif., LA, 2000—. Author: Brain Ticklers (Japanese), 1983. Fellow ACS, Am. Coll. Critical Care Medicine; mem. AAAS, AMA, ACS, Am. Soc. Parenteral and Enteral Nutrition, Soc. Am. Gastrointestinal Endoscopic Surgeons, Southwestern Surg. Congress, Soc. Critical Care Medicine, Assn. VA Surgeons. Avocations: photography, Karate. Office: LAOPC 351 E Temple St Los Angeles CA 90012 Personal E-mail: dhirai@usc.edu.

HIRAI, MAKIKO, physician; b. Kitakyushiyu, Fukuoka, Japan, Mar. 25, 1957; d. Yoshio and Fujiyo Sakamoto; m. Shinji Hirai, Feb. 8, 1986; 1 child, Takayuki. MD, Chiba U., Japan, 1983; DSc, Sch. of Medicine, Chiba, 1993. Diplomate Japanese Med. Bd., Japanese Bd. Ob-Gyn.; Ednl. Commn. for Fgn. Med. Grads. cert. Resident dept. ob-gyn. Chiba U., 1983, Kawasaki Steel Co.'s Hosp., Chiba, 1984-86; vis. fellow dept. diagnostic radiology Thomas Jefferson Univ. Hosp., Phila., 1993; chief in ob-gyn. Yokaichiba (Japan) City Hosp., 1993-95; internat. fellow dept. pediatric cardiology U. Miami (Fla.)-Jackson Meml. Med. Ctr., 1995; chief ob-gyn. Toyo Hosp., Chiba, Japan, 1996-97; with dept. gynecology Chiba Cancer Ctr., 1997—2004; with dept. ob-gyn Chiba U. Hosp., 2004—07; with dept. ob-gyn, dept. gynecology St. Luke's Internat. Hosp. Ctr. Preventive Medicine, Tokyo, 2008—10, Cancer Screening Ctr., Cancer Inst. Hospital of Japanese Found. Cancer Rsch., 2010—. Mem. Am. Roentgen Ray Soc.(sr.), Am. Inst. Ultrasound in Medicine, Japanese Cancer Assn., Japan Soc. Clin. Oncology, Japan Soc. Ob-Gyn., Japanese Soc. Med. Oncology, Japanese Soc. Gynecologic Oncology, Japanese Soc. Clin. Cytology. Home: 3-3-16 Kiminomori-Minami Oamishirasato Machi Sanbu gun Chiba 299-3241 Japan Office: 3-8-31 Ariake Koto ku Tokyo 135-8550 Japan Office Phone: 81-3-3570-0503. Business E-Mail: makiko-h@umin.ac.jp, makiko.hirai@jfcr.oc.jp.

HIRAI, YASUAKI, pharmacist, educator; b. Tokyo, Aug. 25, 1956; PhD, Showa U., 1984. Asst. prof. Showa U., 1984—91, assoc. prof., 1991—. Fellow: Japan Soc. Oriental Medicine, Japanese Cancer Assn., Pharm. Soc. Japan. Office: Kamiyoshida 4562 Fujiyoshida Yamanashi Prefecture 403-0005 Japan Office Fax: 81-555-30-0157. Business E-Mail: hirai@pharm.showa-u.ac.jp.

HIRAKAWA, KAZUTAKA, science educator; b. Ichikawa, Chiba, Japan, Jan. 14, 1973; s. Toshiko Hirakawa; m. Mami Hirakawa, Apr. 22, 2004; children: Nodoka, Momoka. BS, Toho U., Chiba, 1995; MS in Engring., U. Tokyo, 1997, PhD, 2000. Asst. prof. Mie U., Tsu, Japan, 2000—04; assoc. prof. Shizuoka U., Hamamatsu, Japan, 2004—. Contbr. articles to sci. jours. Grantee, Ministry Edn., Culture, Sports, Sci. and Tech. Japanese Govt., 2003—. Mem.: Japan Photodynamic Assn., Japanese Soc. Photomedicine and Photobiology, Japanese Photochemistry Assn., Chem. Soc. Japan. Achievements include research in fundamentals of photodynamic therapy. Office: Shizuoka Univ Naka-ku Johoku 3-5-1 Hamamatsu Shizuoka 432-8561 Japan Business E-Mail: tkhirak@ipc.shizuoka.ac.jp.

HIRAMATSU, NAOKI, medical educator; b. Kobe, Japan, Nov. 1960; s. Hiromitsu and Yoko Hiramatsu, Yonosuke (Stepfather) and Kiku Ueda (Stepmother); m. Yoko Ueda, Sept. 1998. M in Medicine, Osaka U., Japan, 1986, MD, 1994. Resident Osaka U. Hosp., 1986—87, med. staff gastroenterology, 1990—94, 1996—2003; resident Kansai Rosai Hosp., Hyogo, 1987—88; med. staff gastroenterology Osaka Koseinennkinn Hosp., 1988—90; rsch. fellow Tulane U. Med. Ctr., New Orleans, 1995—96; asst. prof. Osaka U. Grad. Sch. Medicine, 2003—, 2006—, assoc. prof., 2008 . Recipient Rsch. award, Japan Soc. Hepatology, 2007. Mem.: Am. Assn. Study Liver Diseases. Office: Osaka Univ Grad Sch Medicine Dept Gastroenterology & Hepatology 2-2 Yamadaoka Suita 565-0871 Japan Office Phone: 81-6-6879-3621. Office Fax: 81-6-6879-3629.

HIRANO, TETSUYA, general surgeon; b. Osaka, Japan, Nov. 11, 1951; s. Shunji and Masayo (Nakahara) H.; m. Kimiko Takeuchi, June 6, 1980; children: Haruka, Fuyuka, Ryutaro. MD, Kyoto U., 1979, PhD, 1992. Resident Kyoto U. Hosp., Japan, 1979, surg. fellow, 1991; resident Kurashiki (Japan) Ctrl. Hosp., 1979-82, surg. fellow, 1982-85; surg. staff Ohtsu Hosp., Osaka, Japan, 1985-88; rsch. fellow Harvard Med. Sch., Boston, 1989-90, Cambridge (Eng.) U., 1990-91; assoc. surgeon-in-chief Yoshioka Hosp., Kyoto, 1991-93, Kishiwada (Japan) Mcpl. Hosp., 1993—. Dir. surg. rsch. lab. Kishiwada Mcpl. Hosp., 1993—, Hirano Clin.; vis. asst. prof. Nagoyo City U. Sch. Medicine. Contbr. articles to profl. jours. Fellow ACS, Am. Coll. Gastroenterology, Am. Coll. Clin. Pharmacology, Internat. Coll. Angiology, Am. Coll. of Angiology, Internat. Coll. of Surgeons, Nat. Acad. Biochem., Molecular Medicine Soc.; mem. Japanese Gastrointestinal Surg. Soc. (bd. qualified), Am. Fedn. for Cin. Rsch., European Soc. for Clin. Investigation, European Soc. of Gastrointestinal Endoscopy, Japanese Surg. Soc. (bd. qualified), N.Y. Acad. of Sci., Soc. for Exptl. Medicine and Biology. Avocations: fishing, hiking, reading, listening to music. Office Phone: 0724-660359.

HIRANO, TOSHIO, medical educator; b. Osaka, Japan, Apr. 17, 1947; s. masami and Kaoru (Kubota) H.; m. Chiyoko Koyanagi, Dec. 8, 1974; 2 children. MD, Osaka U., Japan, 1972, PhD in Med. Sci., 1979. Vis. fellow, staff, gerontology rsch. ctr. Nat. Inst. Aging, NIH, Balt., 1973-76; med. staff, dept. internal medicine Osaka Prefectural Habikino Hosp., 1978—80; assoc. prof., dept. biochemistry, Inst. for Med. Immunology Kumamoto U. Med. Sch., 1980-84; assoc. prof., divsn. immunology, Inst. for Molecular and Cellular Biology Osaka U., 1984-89, prof., lab. develop. immunology, grad. sch. frontier biosciences, 2002—, prof., lab develop. immunology, WPI Immunology Frontier Rsch. Ctr., 2007—; prof., divsn. molecular oncology, Biomedical Rsch. Ctr. Osaka U. Med. Sch., 1989—2001; dir. Biomedical Rsch. Ctr., 1997—99; prof., dept. molecular oncology (now Lab. Develop. Immunology) Osaka U. Grad. Sch. Medicine, 2001—; group dir. RIKEN Rsch. Ctr. for Allergy and Immunology (RCAI), 2001—. Councilor mem. Osaka U., 2003—06, 2007—, dean, grad. sch. frontier biosciences, 2004—06, dean, grad. sch. medicine, 2008—. Author: Nature, 1986, Handbook of Experimental Pharmacology, 1990, The Cytokine Handbook, 1991, 2d edit., 1994; contbr. articles to profl. jours.; mem. editl. bd. Cytokine, London, 1989-, Internat. Immunopharmacology, 1995-; mem. assoc. editors Jour. Molecular Medicine, Berlin, 1994-. Recipient Erwin von Balz prize Boehringer, 1986, Rheumatism prize Japan Ciba-Geigy, 1990, prize for immunology Sandoz, Basel, Switzerland, 1992, Osaka Sci. prize, 1997, Mochida Meml. prize, 1998, ISI Citation Laureate award, 1981-98, 2000, Fujihara Found. Sci. prize, 2004, med. award, Japan Med. Assn., 2005, Emperor's Purple Ribbon medal, 2006; co-recipient Crafoord prize in polyarthritis, Royal Swedish Acad. Sciences, 2009, Japan prize, 2011. Mem. Japanese Soc. for Immunology (bd. mem. 1987-, mem. dir. bd. 1992-94, 1997-2000, 2003-2006, sr. coun. mem. 1992-94, 1997-2000, 2003-2006, pres. 2005-2006), Internat. Soc. Immunopharmacology (mem. coun. 1991—), Japanese Soc. for Cancer(bd. mem. 1995-), Japanese Soc. Molecular Biology, Japanese Biochemical Soc., Japanese Soc. Hematology, Am. Assn. Immunologists. Achievements include pioneering work with collegues to isolate interleukins, determine their properties and explore their role in the onset of inflammatory diseases. Office: Dept Molecular Oncology C7 Osaka U Grad Sch Medicine 2-2 Yamada-oka Suita Osaka 565-0871 Japan Office Phone: 81 6 6879 3880. Office Fax: 81 6 6879 3889. Business E-Mail: hirano@fbs.osaka-u.ac.jp. *

HIRAOKA, NOBUYA, hematologist; b. Japan, June 24, 1978; MD, Osaka Med. Coll., 2004. Clin. fellow Osaka Med. Coll., 2009—11. Mem.: Japanese Soc. Internal Medicine, Japanese Soc. Hematology. Avocation: fishing. Office: 2-7 Daigakumachi Takatsuki Osaka 569-0801 Japan

HIRASHIMA, DENISE E, ophthalmologist; b. Sao Paulo, Aug. 9, 1972; Degree in Medicine, Pontificia U. Catolica, Sao Paulo, 1996; degree in Ophthalmology, U. Mogi das Cruzes, 1999. Pvt. practice, 2003—. Mem.: ASCRS, Sociedade Brasileira de Catarata, Conselho Brasileiro de Oftalmologia. Avocations: golf, tennis. Office: R Sao Joao 410 Piracicaba São Paulo 13416 585 Brazil Personal E-mail: dehirashima@hotmail.com.

HIRATA, FUMIO, biology professor; b. Sasebo, Nagasaki, Japan, Mar. 17, 1947; B, Hokkaido U., 1969, DSc, 1974. Assoc. prof. Kyoto U., 1989—95; prof. Inst. Molecular Sci., 1995—. Dir. dept. theoretical and computational molecular sci. Inst. Molecular Sci., 2004—07, dir. rsch. ctr. computational sci., 2000—03, 2008—10. Recipient Sci. award, Chem. Soc. Japan; grant, Govt. Japan. Mem.: Phys. Soc. Japan, Chem. Soc. Japan. Avocations: tennis, skiing. Office: Inst Molecular Sci 38 Saig Okazaki Aichi 444-8585 Japan Office Fax: 81-564-53-4660.

HIRATA, KENJI, physician; b. Hokkaido, Oct. 9, 1977; MD, Hokkaido U., PhD, 2002. Clin. fellow Hokkaido U., 2006—. Office: Kita 15 Nishi 7 Kita-Ku Sapporo Hokkaido 060 8638 Japan Business E-Mail: khirata@med.hokudai.ac.jp.

HIRATSUKA, YOSHIMUNE, ophthalmologist; b. Shinjuku, Tokyo, Japan, Aug. 17, 1966; s. Sojin and Kyoko Hiratsuka; m. Ikuyo Mizutani, June 28, 1968; children: Mayuko, Sojun. MD, Yamagata U., Japan, 1991; MPH, Johns Hopkins U., 2000. From intern to med. staff Juntendo U. Sch. Medicine, Hongo, Bunkyo, Tokyo, Japan, 1991—93, med. staff dept. ophthalmology, 1993—. Mem. Japan Ophthalmol. Soc. Office: Juntendo Univ Dept Ophthal 3-1-3 Hongo Bunkyo Tokyo 113-8431 Japan Office Phone: 81-3-5802-1228. Business E-Mail: yoshi-h@tkf.att.ne.jp.

HIRATZKA, LOREN F., surgeon; MD, U. Iowa Coll. Medicine. Cert. Am. Bd. Surgery, 1978, Am. Bd. Thoracic Surgery, 2000. Internship LA County Harbor Gen. Hosp., residency in surgery; residency in thoracic and cardiovascular surgery rsch. U. Iowa Hospitals and Clinics, fellow in thoracic and cardiovascular surgery rsch.; surgeon Cardiac, Vascular and Thoracic Surgeons, Inc., Cin.; med. dir. cardiac surgery TriHealth, Inc., Cin., 1998—. Exec. com. mem., coun. on cardiothoracic and vascular surgery Am. Heart Assn./Am. Coll. Cardiology, mem. clin. practice guidelines task force. Contbr. articles to profl. jours. Fellow: ACS, Am. Coll. Cardiology, Am. Coll. Chest Physicians; mem.: AMA, Am. Heart Assn. (Chairman's award 2007, Samuel Kaplan Visionary award), Soc. Thoracic Surgeons, Am. Assn. Thoracic Surgery (pres., Southwestern Ohio affiliate), Soc. Univ. Surgeons, Assn. Academic Surgery, Internat. Soc. Cardiovascular Surgery, Cin. Acad. Medicine, Ohio Med. Soc. Office: Cardiac Vascular and Thoracic Surgeons Inc 4030 Smith Rd #300 Cincinnati OH 45209 Office Phone: 513-421-3494.

HIRAYAMA, AKI, nephrologist, educator; b. Tokyo, Feb. 26, 1967; s. Toshio and Takako Hirayama; m. Takako Koami; children: You, Kaoruko. MD, Tsukuba U., Japan, 1991, PhD, 1999. Vis. rsch. fellow, Inst. Urology and Nephrology Univ. Coll. London, 1996—97; asst. prof. nephrology, Inst. Clin. Medicine U. Tsukuba, 1999—2007; prof. medicine Ctr. Integrative Med., Tsukuba U. Tech., Kasuga, Japan, 2007—, dir., U. Healthcare Ctr. Contbr. articles to profl. jours. Recipient Young Scientist award, SFRR Japan, 2005. Mem.: Japanese Soc. Internal Medicine (Young Investigator award 2000), Soc. Free Radical Rsch. Internat. (Young Scientists award 2005), Soc. Electron Spin Sci. and Tech. (Young Investigator award 2005). Avocation: skiing. Office: Tsukuba U Tech Tsukuba 305-8521 Japan Office Phone: 81 29 858 9564. Business E-Mail: aki-hira@k.tsukuba-tech.ac.jp.

HIRNLE, PETER, radiation oncologist, gynecologist, researcher; b. Aug. 29, 1953; children: Christoph, Rita, Pauline. MD, Bonn U., Germany, 1983; PhD, Tübingen (Germany) U., 1991. Cert. med. sci. Project leader U. Bonn Konrad-Adenauer Grant, 1982-83; project leader Mildred Scheel Grant U. Tübingen, 1983-88, head lymphol. lab., prof., 1991—; dir. dept. radiation therapy and oncology Ctrl. Academic Hosp., Bielefeld, Germany. Author (with others): Lymph Stasis, 1991; chief editor: Our Opinion, 1981; co-editor: Lymphology; contbr. articles to profl. jours. German Rsch. Soc. grantee, Tübingen, 1985, Erwin Riesch grantee, 1988. Mem.: AAAS, others, N.Y. Acad. Scis., Internat. Soc. Lymphology, European Soc. Therapeutic Radiology and Oncology, Am. Assn. Cancer Rsch. Roman Catholic. Achievements include research in basic conditions for local treatment of lymph node metastases and lymphomas; use of liposomes as drug carriers for endolymphatic diagnosis and therapy. Office: Ctrl Academic Hosp Teutoburger Strasse 50 D-33604 Bielefeld Germany Business E-Mail: peter.hirnle@klinikumbielefeld.de.

HIROHASHI, SHINJI, radiologist, researcher; b. Higashi-osaka, Osaka, Japan, Aug. 2, 1957; s. Hisao and Nobuko Hirohashi; m. Rina Ohmichi, June 26, 1993; children: Shinta, Shinto. MD, Nara Med. U., Nara, 1985. Cert. radiologist Japan Radiol. Soc., 1995. Asst. prof. Nara Med. U., Kashihara, Japan, 1998—2003, assoc. prof., 2003—; chief radiologist Osaka Gyoumoikan Hosp., Japan. Home: 3-4-4 Momoyama-dai Osaka Suita 565-0854 Japan Office: Osaka Gyoumeikan Hosp 1-22-12 Kosodadenaka Kenohana Ku Osaka City Osaka 554-0022 Japan Office Fax: 81664626771; Home Fax: +81-6-6836-5305. Personal E-mail: hiroshima@gyoumeikan.or.jp. E-mail: shirohas@naramed-u.ac.jp.

HIROHITO, UMENO, medical educator; b. Fukuoka, Sept. 10, 1963; MD, Kurume-U., 1988. Assoc. prof. Kurume U. Sch. Medicine, 2004—. Mem.: Am. Broncho-Esophageal Assn. (Cho Family Endomed award 2007). Office: 67 Asahi-Machi Kurume Fukuoka 8300011 Japan Office Fax: 81-942-37-1200. Business E-Mail: umeno2@med.kurume-u.ac.jp.

HIROKI, TAKAHASHI, medical educator; b. Tokyo, June 18, 1959; MD, JIKEI U. Sch. Medicine, 1985; PhD, JIKEI Grad. Sch. Medicine, 1990. Assoc. prof. JIKEI U. Sch. Medicine, 1994—. Home: 3-26-8 Hatchobori Chuo-ku Tokyo 1040032 Japan Personal E-mail: hiroki@kk.iij4u.or.jp.

HIROKI, YOKOYAMA, physician, director; b. Shimonoseki, Sept. 15, 1959; MD, PhD, FJSIM, Kyusyu U., DMSc, 1985. Adminstrv. dir. Internal Medicine, Jiyugaoka Med. Clinic, 2000. Office: W6 S6-4-3 Obihiro Hokkaido 080-0016 Japan Office Fax: 81-155-20-5015. Business E-Mail: hiroki@m2.octv.ne.jp.

HIROKO, YANAGA, plastic surgeon, director; b. Japan, Jan. 25, 1954; MD, St. Marianna U., Sch. Medicine., 1983, PhD in Medicine, 1989. Resident Dept. Plastic & Reconstructive Surgery, St. Marianna U., 1983—85, lectr., 2001—11; asst., med. PhD St. Marianna U., 1985—92, asst. prof., lectr., 1992, Kurume U. Sch. Medicine, 1992—2001; dir. Yanaga Clinic and Tissue Culture Lab., 2001—. Dir. Hiroko Skin Sci. Lab., 2009—11; instr. divsn. plastic surgery, Osaka City Gen. Hosp., 2001—11. Grant-in-Aid, Ministry Edn. Mem.: Japan Soc. Plastic and Reconstructive Surgery, Internat. Cartilage Repair Soc., Internat. Soc. Burn Injuries, Internat. Soc. Aesthetic Plastic Surgery, Am. Soc. Plastic Surgeons. Achievements include development of new culture method for tissue-engineered chondrocytes. Avocation: diving. Office: 1-2-12 Tenjin Chuo-ku Fukuoka 810-0001 Japan Office Phone: 81-92-737-1177. Office Fax: 81-92-737-1178. Business E-Mail: yanaga@yanaga-cl.com.

HIROMATSU, SHINICHI, medical educator; b. Kumamoto-ken, Japan, Oct. 16, 1962; Sr. asst. prof. Kurume U. Sch. Medicine, 1987—. Office: 67 Asahi-machi Kurume-shi Fukuoka-ken 830-0011 Japan Office Fax: 81-942-35-8967. Business E-Mail: kaeru@med.kurume-u.ac.jp.

HIROMITSU, TANAKA, medical educator, researcher; b. Japan, May 26, 1963; Degree, Osaka City U., 1987; PhD, Kyoto Pharm. U., 1993. Assoc. prof. Nagasaki Internat. U., 2008—. Office: Osaka University Yamadaoka 3-1 Suita Osaka 565-0871 Japan Office Fax: 81-6-6879-4856. Business E-Mail: tanaka@biken.osaka-u.ac.jp.

HIRONAGA, MASAKI, dermatologist; b. Sakai, Osaka, Japan, Nov. 19, 1944; s. Shozabrow and Yukiko (Miyake) H.; m. Satsuki Nakai, Apr. 16, 1972; 1 child, Aki. MD, Wakayama Med. U., 1971, PhD, 1979. Med. diplomate; cert. ministry of Japan; bd. cert. dermatologist. Resident Wakayama Med. U., Wakayama, Japan, 1971—73, instr., 1973—78; asst. prof. Shiga U. Med. Sci., Otsu, Japan, 1978—82, vis. asst. prof., 1982—84; dermatologist Hironaga Dermatology Clinic, Moriyama, Japan, 1982. Co-author: Sexuality and Pathogenicity of Fungi, 1981; editor Japanese Jour. Med. Mycology, 1981-83. Mem. Internat. Soc. Human and Animal Mycology, Japanese Soc. Med. Mycology (councillor 1981-94), Japanese Dermatol. Assn. Avocation: collecting and researching antique japanese swords. Office Phone: 077 583 4153.

HIRONORI, KANEKO, surgeon, educator; b. Tokyo, Jan. 7, 1952; MD, Toho U., 1976, PhD, 1986. Prof. Toho U., Sch. Medicine Dept. Surgery, 2005—, chmn., 2008. Fellow: ACS. Avocations: golf, swimming. Office: 6-11-1 Omorinishi Otaku Tokyo 143-8541 Japan Office Fax: 81-3-3298-6578.

HIROSE, HITOSHI, medical educator; b. Narita City, Chiba, Japan, Dec. 8, 1965; s. Kohsen and Kin Hirose; m. Rika Akiyama. MD, Nagasaki U. Sch. Medicine, Japan, 1990; PhD, Juntendo U. Coll. Medicine, Tokyo, 2005. Cert. Japanese Bd. Surgery 2001, Japanese Thoracic Surgery Bd. 2002, Japanese Cardiovascular Surgery Bd., 2004. Surg. resident St. Luke's Roosevelt Hosp. Ctr., NYC, 1992—95, vascular surgery rsch. fellow, 1995—96; faculty mem. Nagasaki U. Hosp., 1997—98; staff surgeon Shin-Tokyo Hosp., Matsudo City, Japan, 1998—2000; chief cardiovasc. surgery Kobari Gen. Hosp., Noda City, Japan, 2000—02; clin. assoc. dept. cardiothoracic surgery Cleve. Clinic Found., 2002—04; faculty mem. dept. cardiothoracic surgery Drexel U. Coll. Medicine, 2004—08; assoc. prof., dept. cardiovasc. surgery Juntendo U., Tokyo, 2007—; assoc. prof. Thomas Jefferson U., 2008—. Contbr. articles to profl. jours.;, co-editor of sci. papers published in profl. jours. Fellow: Internat. Cardiothoracic Surgeons, Am. Coll. Anigology, Internat. Coll. Surgeons; mem.: Am. Coll. Cardiology, Am. Heart Assn., Internat. Soc. Artificial Organs, Internat. Cardiovascular Soc., Internat. Soc. Minimally Invasive Cardiac Surgry, Asian Soc. Cardiovasc. Surgery, European Assn. Cardiothoracic Surgery, Soc. Thoracic Surgeons, NY Acad. Sci. Office: Divsn Cardiothoraic Surgery Dept Surgery 1025 Walnut St Philadelphia PA 19107

HIROSE, MASAHIRO, medical association administrator, educator; b. Imabari, Japan, Mar. 12, 1955; MD, Ehime U. Sch. Medicine, 1985; PhD, Kyoto U. Sch. Pub. Health, 2005. Dir. Kyoto U. Hosp., Patient Safety Divsn., 2002—05; vis. scientist Harvard Sch. Pub. Health, 2005—06; lectr. special mission, dept. healthcare economics & mgmt. Kyoto U. Grad. Sch. Medicine, 2006—07; dir., edn. prof. Shimane U. Hosp., Ctr. Edn. Hosp. Medicine, 2008—. Adj. part-time prof. Kyoto U., Grad. Sch. Medicine, 2008; adj. prof., dept. med. informatics Kyoto U. Hosp., 2002—05. Abe fellowship, Social Sci. Rsch. Coun. Mem.: Internat. Soc. Pharmacoeconomics Outcomes & Rsch., Internat. Soc. Quality Health Care. Avocations: fishing, travel. Office: 89-1 Enya-Chou Izumo Shimane 693 8501 Japan Office Fax: 81 853 20 2405. E-mail: mhirose@med.shimane-u.ac.jp.

HIROSE, SUSUMU, geneticist, educator; b. Tokyo, July 22, 1943; PhD, U. Tokyo, 1971. Prof. Nat. Inst. Genetics, 1992—, vice dir. gen., 2004—07. Mem.: Am. Soc. Microbiology. Office: 1111 Yata Mishima Shizuoka-ken 411-8540 Japan Business E-Mail: shirose@lab.nig.ac.jp.

HIROSE, TERUO TERRY, surgeon educator, essayist, medical writer; b. Tokyo, Jan. 20, 1926; arrived in U.S., 1959; s. Yohei and Seiko (Ogushi) H.; m. Tomiko Kodama, June 1, 1976; 1 son, George Philamore. BS, Tokyo Coll., Japan, 1944; MD, Chiba U., Japan, 1948, PhD, 1958. Diplomate Am. Bd. Surgery, Am. Bd. Thoracic Surgery. Intern Chiba U. Hosp., Japan, 1948-49, resident in surgery, 1949-52; practice medicine specializing in surgery Chiba, Japan, 1952-53; resident in surgery Am. Hosp., Chgo., 1954; resident in thoracic surgery Hahnemann Med. Coll., Phila., 1955-56; chief of surgery Tsushimi Hosp., Hagi, Japan, 1958-59; tchg. fellow surgery NY Med. Coll., NYC, 1959-60; rsch. fellow advanced cardiovasc. surgery Hahnemann Hosp., Phila., 1959; asst. prof. surgery Chiba U., Japan, 1959; instr. NY Med. Coll., NYC, 1961-62, resident in thoracic surgery, 1961-62; sr. attending surgeon St. Barnabas Hosp., NYC, 1965-81; pvt. practice NYC, 1965-89, NJ, 1965-89; chief vascular surgery Union Hosp., Bronx, NY, 1966-67; attending surgeon Flower and Fifth Ave Hosp., NYC, 1973-80; clin. prof. surgery NY Med. Coll., NY, 1974-89; dir. cardiovasc. lab. St. Barnabas Hosp., NYC, 1975-84; attending surgeon Jewish Hosp. Med. Center, Bklyn., 1976-80, St. Vincent Hosp., NYC, 1976-88, Mamonides Hosp., Bklyn., 1976-78, Passaic Gen. Hosp., 1977-88, Westchester County Hosp., NY, 1977-78, Yonkers Profl. Hosp., NY, 1978-79, Westchester Sq. Hosp., 1978-84, Yonkers Gen. Hosp., Yonkers, NY, 1980-89, St. Joseph Hosp., Yonkers, NY, 1980-89; dir. KPMG Health Care, Japan, 1997—2001; chmn., prof. dept. head and health care admin. Shumei U., Tokyo, 1999—2006, prof. emeritus, 2006—, dean Premedical Tokyo, 2006—; health care, med. cons. Gerson Lehman Group, 2010—. Author: (in Japanese) A Chaos of American Medicine, 1987, Japanese Doctor, 1987, Where American Medicine Is Going, 1988, Major Surgery Without Blood Transfusion, 1990, Problems and Solutions of American Medicine, 1991, Warning for Modern Medical Science (New Medical Ethics), 1992, Comparative Studies of Medical System in the World, 1992, The Changing Face of Geriatrics, 1994, Monologue of Japanese American Physician, 1995, Environmental Medicine, 1998, Japan! Do Not Follow American Health Care System, 1998, Quality of Life in Modern Medicine, 1998, Medicine About Life and Death, 1998, 99, Why AIDS Can Not Be Conquered, 1999, Mechanism of Human Body, 2000, Comparison of Healthcare Systems Between U.S.A. and Japan, 2000, Medicine of Death, 2000, Lifestyle Related Medicine and Cutting Edge Technique, 2001, Alternative Medicine, 2001, Thanatology, 2000, Protect Japanese Health Care System By Health Care Reform, 2002, Basic and Practice of Health Care Administration, 2002, Better Understanding of Physician and Hospital, 2003, What Can We Learn from Medical Education System in USA, 2003, How Should We Take Care of Aged Population, 2004, Japanese Medicine in the 21st Century, 2005, How to Protect Japanese Health and Nursing Care Systems, 2007, Preventive Medicine for Life Related Disease, 2008, Desirable Type of Health and Nursing Care Systems Japan, 2009, Analysis of Medical Situations of The Entire World, 2010, How to Establish Long Lasting Health and Nursing Care Systems in Japan, 2011; editor Japanese Med. Planner Ltd.; contbr. more than 1500 articles to profl. jours. Recipient Hektoen Bronze medal, AMA, 1965, Gold medal, 1971. Fellow: NY Cardiol. Soc., NY Acad. Medicine, Internat. Coll. Surgeons, Am. Coll. Angiology, Am. Coll. Cardiology, Am. Coll. Chest Physicians; mem.: Am. Med. Assn., Assn. Ayurveda Integrated Medicine (chmn. pres. 2011—), Assn. Internat. Integrated Medicine (chmn., pres. 2010—), Am. Assn. Artificial Internal Organ, NY Soc. Cardiovasc. Surgery, Soc. Vascular Surgery, Japanese Assn. Health Care Adminstrs. (chmn., pres. 1999—), Am. Writers Assn., Am. Fedn. Clin. Rsch., Am. Geriatric Soc., Internat. Cardiovasc. Soc., Pan Pacific Surg. Assn., Soc. Thoracic Surgeon, Am. Assn. Thoracic Surgery, Japan PEN Club. Achievements include invention of single pass low prime oxygenator; pioneer coronary direct bypass surgery reconstruction of cardiac valves, open heart surgery without blood transfusion. Home Phone: 718-601-2191; Office Phone: 718-884-1071. Personal E-mail: coronarybypass@earthlink.net.

HIROSHI, GOTODA, engineering educator; b. Tokushima, Jan. 23, 1975; PhD, Keio U., 2003. Sch. sci. open & environ. sys. mem. Keio U., 2003—04; bldg., fire rsch. lab. Nat. Inst. Standards & Tech., 2004—05; mem. advanced energy techs. dept., environ. energy techs. divsn. Lawrence Berkeley Nat. Lab., 2005; fire suppression group mem. Nat. Rsch. Inst. Fire & Disaster, 2005—06; assoc. prof. dept. mech. engring. Ritsumeikan U., 2006—. Young Scientists grant, Ministry of Edn., Culture, Sports, Sci. & Tech. of Japan, fellow, Japan Soc. Promotion Sci., grant, Kumatani Sci. Tech. Found., Suzuki Found. Avocations: gymnastics, dance. Office: 1-1-1 Nojihigashi Kusatsu Shiga 525 8577 Japan Business E-Mail: gotoda@se.ritsumei.ac.jp.

HIROSHI, SHIMADA, retired surgeon; b. Chenogiu, Republic of Korea, Mar. 12, 1944; Degree, U. Sch. Medicine, Yokohama City U. Sch., 1963. Rsch. dir. med. divsn. Japan Labour Health and Welfare Orgn., 2009; dean Sch. Medicine Yokohama City U., 2005—08, prof. emeritus, 2010; dir. emeritus Harue Gen. Hosp., 2010—. Master: Internat. Soc. Digestive Surgery; fellow: Internat. Soc. Surgery, Am. Assn. Cancer Rsch., Soc. Surgery Alimentary Tract, Internat. Assn. Surgeons and Gestroenterologists. Avocations: sports, music, travel. Office: 5-62 Edomeshimoyashiki Harue-cho Sakai Fukui 919-0414 Japan Office Fax: 0776-51-6163. E-mail: hs440312@yahoo.co.jp.

HIROTA, EIZI, molecular scientist, educator, research scientist; b. Osaka, Japan, Aug. 5, 1930; s. Imaji and Kachi Hirota; m. Satoko Sahara, Dec. 12, 1959; children: Makiko, Yukiko Sakurai. BS in Chemistry, U. Tokyo, 1953, PhD, 1958. Rsch. assoc. U. Tokyo, 1958—62, lectr., 1962—64, assoc. prof., 1964—68; rsch. fellow Harvard U., Cambridge, Mass., 1960—62; prof. Kyushu U., Fukuoka, Japan, 1968—75; prof. emeritus Grad. U. Advanced Studies, Hayama, Kanagawa, Japan, 2001—; prof. Inst. Molecular Sci., Okazaki, Aichi, Japan, 1975—90, prof. emeritus, 1990—; v.p. Grad. U. Advanced Studies, Hayama, Kanagawa, Japan, 1990—95, pres., 1995—2001. Titular mem. Internat. Union Pure and Applied Chemistry, London, 1986—93; mem. Sci. Coun. Japan, Tokyo, 1997—2003; mem. adv. bd. Jour. Molecular Spectroscopy, Amsterdam, 1979—2009. Author: (book) High-Resolution Spectroscopy of Transient Molecules; contbr. book. Profl. mem. Sci. and Tech. Govtl. Bd., Tokyo, 1998—2001. Recipient Nishina award, Nishina Meml. Found., 1978, Acad. prize, Japan Acad., 1992, E.B.Wilson award in spectroscopy, Americal Chem. Soc., 2005, Spl. award, 153 Com. Plasma Material Sci., 2005. Mem.: Japan Soc. Applied Physics, Phys. Soc. Japan, Spectroscopical Soc. Japan (hon.; pres. 1999—2001), Chem. Soc. Japan (hon. award 1987, 1982). Avocations: mountain climbing, piano, travel, classical music, reading. Home: 2-22-16 Noge Setagaya Tokyo 158-0092 Japan Office: Grad Univ Advanced Studies Shonan Village Kanagawa Hayama 240-0193 Japan Office Phone: 81-468-58-1542. Office Fax: 81-46-858-1542. Personal E-mail: ehirota@triton.ocn.ne.jp.

HIROTA, MORIHISA, gastroenterologist, educator; b. Niigata, Japan, July 3, 1967; MD, PhD, Tohoku U. Grad. Sch. Medicine, 2000. Asst. prof. Divsn. Gastroenterology, Tohoku U. Hosp., 2007—. Mem.: Japanese Cancer Assn., Japanese Soc. Gastroenterology, Japan Pancreas Soc. Avocation: soccer. Office: 1-1 Seoryo-cho Aoba-ku Sendai Miyagi 980-8574 Japan Office Fax: 022-717-7177. Business E-Mail: morihirota@med.tohoku.ac.jp.

HIROTARO, IWASE, pathologist, educator; b. Kisarazu, Chiba, Japan, July 1, 1967; MD, U. Tokyo, PhD, 1993. Prof. Grad. Sch. Medicine, Chiba U., 2003—. Mem.: Japanese Soc. Legal Medicine. Office: Inohana 1-8-1 Chuo-ku Chiba 260-8670 Japan Business E-Mail: iwase@faculty.chiba-u.jp.

HIROYUKI, KATO, medical association administrator; b. Japan, Apr. 5, 1958; MD, Niigata U., 1984. V.p. Tokyo Women's Med. U. Med. Ctr. East, 2010—. Office: Tokyo Women's Med University MCE 2-1-1 Tokyo 116-8567 Japan Office Phone: 03-3810-1111. Office Fax: 03-38100933. Business E-Mail: hikatocl@dnh.twmu.ac.jp.

HIRSCH, HARVEY STUART, psychiatrist; b. NYC, Nov. 3, 1950; s. Leoanrd Samuel and Roberta Joan (Dreyer) H.; m. Linda Karen Green, Sept. 27, 1981; children: Daniel, Carly. BA, Columbia U., 1972; MD, Mt. Sinai Med. Sch., NYC, 1976. Diplomate Am. Bd. Psychiatry and Neurology, Nat. Bd. Med. Examiners, 1976. Intern Mt. Sinai Hosp., NYC, 1976, attending physician, 1979—; clin. instr. Mt. Sinai Med. Sch., NYC, 1979—; resident Mt. Sinai Hosp., NYC, 1977-79, chief resident, 1979—. Recipient Ams. Top Psychiatrists, Consumers Rsch. Coun. of Am., Wash., D.C., 2003. Mem. Am. Psychiat. Assn., Cum Laude Soc., Le Club (N.Y.C.), Phi Beta Kappa. Avocations: tennis champion, swimming champion. Office: 880 Fifth Ave New York NY 10021 Office Phone: 212-828-2213. Personal E-mail: hirschharvey@yahoo.com.

HIRSCH, JULES, physician, researcher; b. NYC, Apr. 6, 1927; Student, Rutgers U., 1943—45; MD, U. Tex., 1948; DSc (hon.), SUNY, 1988. Intern pathology and medicine Duke Hosp., NC, 1948—50; from asst. resident to resident coll. medicine SUNY, Syracuse, 1950—52; asst. prof., assoc. physician Rockefeller U., NYC, 1954—60, assoc. prof., physician, 1960—67, prof., sr. physician, 1967—98. Sherman Fairchild prof. Rockefeller U., 1988—98, emeritus, 1998—; sr. physician Rockefeller U. Hosp., 1967—, physician-in-chief, 1992—96, emeritus, 1996—. Recipient Robert H. Herman award, 1994, McCollum award, 1984. Fellow: ACP, Royal Coll. Physicians Edinburgh; mem.: Harvey Soc., Am. Fedn. Clin. Rsch., Assn. Am. Physicians, Am. Soc. Clin. Nutrition, Am. Soc. Clin. Investigation, Inst. of Medicine of NAS, AAAS, Assn. for Patient Oriented Rsch. (founding mem.). Achievements include research in obesity, human behavior, internal medicine, biochemistry and physiology of lipids, lipid metabolism and nutrition. Office: Rockefeller U 1230 York Ave New York NY 10065-6399 Business E-Mail: hirsch@mail.rockefeller.edu.

HIRSCH, LAWRENCE LEONARD, physician, retired educator; b. Chgo., Aug. 20, 1922; m. Donna Lee Sturm; children: Robert, Edward, Sharon. BS, U. Ill., 1943; MD, U. Ill., Chgo., 1950. Diplomate: Am. Bd. Family Medicine. Intern. Ill. Masonic Med. Ctr., Chgo., 1950-51; practice medicine specializing in family medicine Chgo., 1951-70; dir. ambulatory care Ill. Masonic Med. Ctr., Chgo., 1970-71, dir. family practice residency program, 1971-75; prof., chmn. dept. family medicine Chgo. Med. Sch., 1975-89, prof. emeritus, 1989—. Mem. med. licensing bd. State of Ill., 1982-94, chmn., 1988-94, hosp. licensing bd., 1994-2004; bd. dirs. Ill. Coun. for continuing Med. Edn., 1981-85, pres., 1986-87; cons. recombinant DNA Abbott Labs., 1980-87; lectr. in field; staff pres. Ill. Masonic Med. Ctr., 1970. Book rev. editor: Soc. of Tchrs. Family Medicine, 1979-89; book reviewer: Jour. AMA, 1969-; contbr. articles to profl. jours. Bd. dirs. Mid-Am. chpt. ARC, Chgo., 1978-88; nat. pres. Alpha Phi Omega, Kansas City, Mo., 1974-78; exec. com. Chgo. Found. Med. Care and PSRO, 1977-84, Ill. State Inter-Ins. Exchange, 1975-2006; bd. dirs. Crescent Counties Found. for Med. Care, 1985-91; commr. Northbrook (Ill.) Park Dist., 1987-91, pres., 1990—; mem. Village of Northbrook Planning Commn., 1987-89. With US Army, 1943—46. Recipient Silver Beaver award Boy Scouts Am., 1963; recipient Silver Antelope award Boy Scouts Am., 1967, Disting. Eagle award Boy Scouts Am., 1969, Brotherhood award Lakeview Interfaith Council, 1968, Physician Speaker award AMA, 1981; inducted into City of Chgo. Sr. Citizens Hall of Fame, 1991. Fellow AAAS, Am. Acad. Family Physicians (mem. congress of dels.); mem. Chgo. Med. Soc. (pres. 1979, Pub. Svc. award 1990), Ill. Acad. Family Physicians (pres. 1977), Assn. Depts. Family Medicine (exec. com.), Masons, Shriners, Kiwanis (dir. local club). Democrat. Unitarian Universalist.

HIRSCH, MARTIN, dentist; m. Noreen Hirsch; 2 children. BS, CUNY, 1968; DMD, U. Pa., 1972; splty. prosthodontics, U. Iowa, 1975; splty. maxillofacial prosthetics, U. Chgo., 1976. Cert. specialist in dental sleep medicine. Dental extern Coatsville Hosp., Pa., 1971—72; dental intern Mt. Sinai Hosp., NYC, 1972—73; resident VA Hosp., Iowa City, 1973—75, U. Chgo. Hosp. and Clinics, 1975—76; asst. prof. dept. otolaryngology Abraham Lincoln Sch. Medicine U. Ill. Med. Ctr., Chgo., 1976—77, dir. maxillofacial prosthetics clinic Craniofacial Anamolies Ctr., 1976—77; asst. prof. U. Ill. Coll. Dentistry, Chgo., 1977—93; staff dept. dentistry U. Ill. Hosp. Med. Ctr., Chgo., 1979—83; staff dept. surgery dental sect. Cuneo Hosp., Chgo., 1979—87; staff dept. surgery dental section Cabrini Hosp., Chgo., 1979—92; staff dept. dentistry Ill. Masonic Med. Ctr., Chgo., 1979—, mem. head and neck treatment ctr., 1981—; sr. staff dept. dental surgery Columbus Hosp., Chgo., 1979—98; pvt. practice gen., cosmetic and prosthetic dentistry Chgo., 1979—; attending Cath. Health Ptnrs., Chgo., 1998—2001, Resurrection Health Care St. Joseph's Hosp., 2001—. Adj. instr. U. Chgo. Hosps. and Clinics, 1975—76; spkr., presenter in field; pvt. practice sleep medicine Chgo. ENT. Spkr. Am. Cancer Soc., Chgo., 1981—87, chmn. profl. edn. com., 1981—85, mem. oral cancer com., 1982—86. Mem.: ADA, Colo. Prosthdontic Soc., Colo. Dental Soc., Chgo. Dental Soc., Ill. Dental Soc. Avocations: swimming, reading. Office: 2800 N Sheridan Rd Chicago IL 60657-6156 also: Advanced Ctr for Splty Care 3000 N Halsted St Ste 400 Chicago IL 60657 Office Phone: 773-248-6140. Personal E-mail: drmartinhirsch@gmail.com.

HIRSCH, MARTIN STANLEY, internist, epidemiologist, researcher; b. Cortland, NY, Apr. 16, 1939; s. Hans and Grete (Lipper) H.; m. Corinne Becker, Oct. 18, 1964; children: Tera Gretchen, Michael Edward. AB, Hamilton Coll., 1960; MD, Johns Hopkins U., 1964; MA, Harvard U., 1990. Diplomate Am. Bd. Internal Medicine, Am. Bd. Internal Medicine and Infectious Diseases. Intern in medicine U. Chgo. Clinics and Hosp., 1964-65, resident in medicine, 1965-66; fellow in virology Ctr. for Disease Control, Atlanta, 1966-68; fellow Nat. Inst. for Med. Rsch., London, 1968-69; fellow in infectious diseases Harvard U., Boston, 1969-71, asst. prof., 1971-76, assoc. prof., 1976-88, prof. medicine, 1988—; assoc. physician MGH,

Boston, 1981-87; physician Mass. Gen. Hosp., Boston, 1988—. Mem. sci. adv. bd. AM Found. for AIDS Rsch., 1987—; chmn. AIDS program adv. com. NIH, Bethesda, Md., 1989-92. Editor-in-chief: Jour. of Infectious Diseases, 2002—; contbr. more than 160 chpts. to books and 240 articles to profl. jours. Surgeon USPHS, 1966-68. Recipient Clin. Virology award, Pan-Am. Soc. Clin. Virology, 2000, Mentor award, Infectious Diseases Soc. Am., 2004, Maxwell Finland award, Nat. Found. Infectious Diseases, 2008, Lifetime Achievement award, Internat. Antiviral Soc. USA. Fellow Infectious Disease Soc. America, Am. Assn. Advancement Sci.; mem. Am. Soc. Clin. Investigation, Am. Soc. Virology, Assn. Am. Physicians, Phi Beta Kappa, Alpha Omega Alpha. Achievements include first isolation of HIV-1 from genital secretions, central nervous system and blood monocytes; pioneering treatment of human Herpes virus and HIV infections with agents used singly or in combination. Office: Mass Gen Hosp Infectious Disease Unit 65 Landsdowne St Cambridge MA 02139

HIRSCH, PHILIP FRANCIS, pharmacologist, educator; b. Stockton, Calif., June 24, 1925; s. Harold and Elsa (Frohman) H.; m. Eugenia Isaeff, Sept. 21, 1956; children— Steven, Lisa, Ken, Nancy. BS in Chemistry, U. Calif., Berkeley, 1950, PhD in Physiology, 1954. Lectr. physiology U. Calif., Berkeley, 1954-55; instr. pharmacology Sch. Dental Medicine, Harvard U., Boston, 1955-57, asso. in pharmacology, 1957-63, asst. prof. pharmacology, 1964; physiologist Lawrence Livermore Lab., 1964-66; asso. prof. pharmacology Sch. Medicine, U. N.C., Chapel Hill, 1966-70, prof., 1970-92; dir. dental research ctr. U. N.C., 1975-83, prof. dental ecology Sch. of Dentistry, 1988-92, prof. emeritus, 1992—. Mem. gen. medicine B study sect. NIH, 1974-78, clin. scis. study section, 1981-85. Contbr. articles to profl. jours. Bd. dirs. YMCA, Chapel Hill, 1981-83. Served with AUS, 1943-46. Mem. Endocrine Soc., Am. Soc. Pharmacology and Exptl. Therapeutics, Sigma Xi. Achievements include research in calcium metabolism parathyroid hormone and calcitonin. Home: 135 Carolina Meadows Villa Chapel Hill NC 27517-8512 Personal E-mail: pfhirsch@med.unc.edu.

HIRSCHHORN, KURT, pediatrics educator; b. Vienna, May 18, 1926; arrived in U.S., 1940, naturalized, 1945; s. Emanuel and Helen (Mayberger) Hirschhorn; m. Rochelle Reibman, Dec. 20, 1952; children: Melanie D., Lisa R., Joel N. Student, U. Pitts., 1944, BA, NYU, 1950, MD, 1954, MS, 1958. Intern Bellevue Hosp., NYC, 1954—55, resident, 1955—56; fellow NYU, 1956—57, U. Uppsala, Sweden, 1957—58; instr. NYU Sch. Medicine, 1956—58, asst. prof., 1958—63, assoc. prof., 1963—66; Arthur J. and Nellie Z. Cohen prof. genetics and pediat. Mt. Sinai Sch. Medicine, CUNY, 1966—76, Herbert H. Lehman prof., chmn. pediat., 1977—95, prof. pediat., human genetics and medicine, 1995—2007, emeritus prof., 2008—. Adj. prof. biology NYU, 1966—74; established investigator Am. Heart Assn., 1960—65; career scientist N.Y.C. Health Rsch. Coun., 1965—75. Author numerous sci. publs.; editor (with Harry Harris): Advances in Human Genetics, 1969—95; mem. editl. bd.: 16 sci. jours. Mem. coun. Village Cmty. Sch., 1968—73, chmn., 1972—73. With US Army, 1944—47. Recipient Rudolph Virchow medal, 1974, Alumni Achievement award, NYU Sch. Medicine, 1982, Jacobi medal, Mt. Sinai Med. Ctr., 1993, William Allan award, Am. Soc. Human Genetics, 1995, J. Lester Gabrilove award for significant contbns. to medicine, Mt. Sinai Sch. Medicine, 2001, The Col. Harland Sanders Genetics Lifetime Achievement award, The March of Dimes, 2006, Lifetime Achievement award, Mt. Sinai Sch. Medicine, 2009, Bergquist fellow, NYU, 1958. Fellow: AAAS, N.Y. Acad. Medicine, Am. Acad. Pediat.; mem.: Am. Cancer Soc. (coun. 1989—92), Am. Soc. Pediatric Chmn. (coun. 1983—86), Environ. Mutagen Soc. (coun. 1969—76), Genetics Soc. Am., Harvey Soc. (v.p. 1979—80, pres. 1980—81, coun. 1981—84), Am. Assn. Immunologists, Am. Soc. Human Genetics (pres. 1969, dir. 1964—65, 1968—71, Human Genetics Edn. Excellence award 2002), Am. Pediatric Soc. (John Howland award Disting. Svc. Pediats. 2006), Am. Assn. Physicians, Am. Soc. Clin. Investigation, Am. Coll. Med. Genetics, Inst. Medicine of NAS, Pediatric Travel Club, Alpha Omega Alpha, Sigma Xi, Phi Beta Kappa. Office: Mt Sinai Sch Medicine 1 Gustave L Levy Pl New York NY 10029-6500 Home: 20 Fifth Ave New York NY 10011 Office Phone: 212-241-4305. Business E-Mail: kurt.hirschhorn@mssm.edu.

HIRSCHHORN, ROCHELLE, genetics educator; b. Bklyn., Mar. 19, 1932; d. Hyman and Anna Reibman; m. Kurt Hirschhorn; children: Melanie D., Lisa R., Joel N. BA, Barnard Coll., 1953; MD, NYU, 1957. Cert. Am. Bd. Med. Genetics, 1987. Intern NYU-Bellevue Med. Divsn., NYC, 1958—59; rsch. fellow, tchg. asst. NYU Sch. Medicine, NYC, 1963—65, assoc. rsch. scientist, 1965—66, instr. medicine, 1966—69, asst. prof. medicine, 1969—74, assoc. prof. medicine, 1974—79, prof. medicine, 1975—, head divsn. med. genetics, 1984—98, prof. medicine & cell biology, 1996—2008, prof. emeritus medicine & cell biology, 2009—. Hon. fellow Galton Lab. Human Genetics & Biometry Univ. Coll., London, 1971—72; assoc. attending physician in medicine Beffevue Hosp., NYC, 1969—80, Univ. Hosp., NYU Sch. Medicine, 1974—81; attending physician Bellevue Hosp., 1980—2009, Univ. Hosp., 1981—; com. mem., study sect. NIH, 1973—97; vis. prof. Harvard U., 1995, U. Calif., San Francisco, 1995; mem. scientific search com. Barnard Coll., 2003—; internat. adv. bd. Peking U. Ctr. Med. Genetics, 2005—07. Trustee AIDS Med. Found./AMFAR; judge Westinghouse Nat. Sci. Talent Search; founding mem. Village Cmty. Sch.; senator NYU Senate, mem. pediatrics search com., 1987—89, human subjects instl. rev. bd., 1989—94, co-dir. second year med. genetics course, 1989—93, NYU appts. and promotions com., 1995—2002; adv. bd. mem. Genzyme Corp., Pompe, 2002—07. Recipient Alumni Berson award, NYU Sch. Medicine, Lifetime Achievement award, Jeffrey Modell Found., Master Scientist award, 2010; named Disting. Alumna, Barnard Coll., Hero of the Arthritis Found. Master: Am. Coll. Rheumatology; fellow: AAAS, Arthritis Found., Am. Coll. Med. Genetics (founding fellow); mem.: Inst. of Medicine of NAS, Am. Bd. Med. Genetics, Harvey Soc. (coun. 1989—92), Soc. for Inherited Metabolic Diseases, Peripatetic Soc., Interurban Clin. Club (pres. 1987—88), Am. Soc. Human Genetics, Am. Assn. Immunologists, Assn. Am. Physicians, Am. Soc. for Clin. Investigation, Alpha Omega Alpha (councillor Delta of N.Y. 1982—2002). Achievements include elucidation of pathophysiologic mechanisms, delineation of molecular and biochemical defects of genetic disorders including adenosine deaminase and glycogen storage disease type II; providing proof of principle of therapeutic options and cloning of the therapeutic molecule; identification of somatic mosaicism due to reversion to normal of inherited mutations and of increasing incidence and significance for gene therapy. Office: NYU Sch Medicine 550 1st Ave OBY C+D6 New York NY 10016 Mailing: 20 5th Ave Apt 14E New York NY 10011 Business E-Mail: hirscr01@med.nyu.edu.

HIRSCHLER, VALERIA, physician, researcher; b. Buenos Aires, Apr. 10, 1958; d. Esteban Hirschler and Adriana Bermann; children: Malena Cibils Madero, Carolina Cibils Madero, Javier Cibils Madero. MD, U. Buenos Aires, 1981. Cert. pediat. Residency Hosp. R. Gutierrez Soc. Physician Children's Hosp. R. Gutierrez, Buenos Aires, 1982—2000, Durand Hosp., Buenos Aires, 2000—. Rschr. Duran Hosp., Buenos Aires, 2000—. Mem.: Am. Diabetes Assn. Achievements include research in overweight and children. Home: Las Heras 1868 9 A Buenos Aires 1127 Argentina Office: Calle Maipu 5 M C1084ABA Buenos Aires Argentina Home Phone: 01148090363; Office Phone: 01148018387. Office Fax: 5411 48018287. Business E-Mail: vhirschler@intramed.net.

HIRSH, JACK, medical researcher; b. Melbourne, Australia, Jan. 5, 1935; Grad., U. Melborne Med. Sch.; DSc (hon.), McMaster U., 1999. Expanded knowledge of hematology at Washington U., St. Louis, London Postgraduate Med. Sch., U. Toronto; joined faculty of medicine McMaster U., Hamilton, Canada, 1973, prof. emeritus of medicine, chmn., dept. medicine; dir. Henderson Rsch. Ctr., Hamilton, Canada. V.p., med. Ontario Heart Found. Recipient Disting. Rsch. Professorship award, Heart and Stroke Found. Ontario, Trillium Clin. Scientist award, Ontario Ministry Health, Ham-Wasserman Lectureship, Am. Soc. Hematology, 1996, Editl. Excellence award, Am. Coll. Chest Physicians, 1996, Prix Galien award, 1999, Gairdner Found. Internat. award, 2000; named to Canadian Hall of Fame, 2000. Fellow. Royal Soc. Can.; mem.: Med. Rsch. Coun. Can. (coun. mem.), Internat. Soc. on Thrombosis and Haemostasis (chmn.), Order of Can. Office: Henderson Rsch Ctr McMaster U 711 Concession St Hamilton ON L8V 1C3 Canada Office Phone: 905-527-2299 42600. Office Fax: 905-575-2646. Business E-Mail: jhirsh@thrombosis.hhscr.org. *

HISAYUKI, UNEYAMA, pharmaceutical executive; b. Japan, Aug. 8, 1964; PhD, Tohoku U., 1995. Assoc. gen. mgr. Inst. Innovation, Ajinomoto Co., Inc., 2007—. Mem.: Japanese Pharmacological Soc., Soc. Neurosci., Japanese Pharm. Soc. Office: 1-1 Suzuki-Cho Kawasaki-Ku Kawasaki Kanagawa 210-8681 Japan Office Fax: 81-44-210-5893. Business E-Mail: hisayuki_uneyama@ajinomoto.com.

HISE, MARK ALLEN, dentist; b. Chgo., Jan. 17, 1950; s. Clyde and Rose T. (Partipilo) Hise. AA, Mt. San Antonio Coll., Walnut, Calif., 1972; BA with highest honors, U. Calif., Riverside, 1974; MS, U. Utah, 1978; DDS, UCLA, 1983. Instr. sci. NW Acad., Houston, 1978-79; chmn. curriculum med. coll. prep program UCLA, 1984—2009; instr. dentistry Coll. of Redwoods, Eureka, Calif.; pvt. practice Arcata, Calif., 1983—2001, Scotia, Calif., 2002—, Eureka, Calif., 2006—. Numerous radio and TV appearances; spkr. in field. Editor: Preparing for the MCAT, 1983—85; contbr. articles to profl. jours. Recipient awards for underwater photography, Best Dentist on North Coast, Times-Std. Newspaper, 2008—09; named, 2002, 2006, 2007; fellow, NIH, 1975—79; Henry Carter scholar, U. Calif., 1973, Regents scholar, 1973, Calif. State scholar, 1973—74. Mem.: ADA, AAAS, Calif. Dental Assn. Roman Catholic. Avocation: underwater photography. Office: 1600 Myrtle Ave Eureka CA 95501 Personal E-mail: mhise@aol.com.

HISHIKAWA, YOSHIO, health facility administrator; MD, Kobe U. Tchg. asst. Hyogo Coll. Medicine, Dept. Radiology, Japan, 1976—83, lectr., 1983—94, assoc. prof., 1994; counselor Hyogo Prefecture Gov., Health & Welfare, 1994; dir. Hyogo Ion Beam Med. Ctr., Tatsuuo-Shi, Japan, 2001—; prof. Kobe U. Grad. Sch. Medicine, Ion Beam Therapy, 2001. Vis. prof. Kobe U., Grad. Sch. of medicine, Hyogo, Japan, 2001. Recipient Estro-Nucletron Brachytycrapy award, 1990. Office: Hyogo Ion Beam Med Ctr 1-2-1 Kouto Shingu-Cho Hyogo Ibo-Gun 679-5165 Japan Office Fax: 81-791-58-2600. E-mail: y.hishikawa@hibmc.shingu.hyogo.jp.

HITCH, MELANIE AUDREY, orthopaedic nurse; b. Chgo., Sept. 19, 1947; d. Alden Edwards and Frances (Gillette) Snell; m. David C. Hitch, Sept. 2, 1972; children: Charles Joseph, Kathryn Elizabeth Frances. AA, Va. Intermont, Bristol, Va., 1967; BSN, U. Va., 1969; MS, U. Okla., 1982. Cert. in orthop. nursing 1988. Head nurse U. Va. Hosp., Charlottesville, 1969-73; clin. nurse specialist Sunnybrook Med. Ctr., Toronto, Ont., Can., 1973-75; staff nurse Bapt. Hosp., Memphis, 1975; head nurse Porter Meml. Hosp., Denver, 1976-78; physician's asst. Kaiser Permanent, Denver, 1978; clin. nurse specialist Okla. Children's Meml. Hosp., Oklahoma City, 1978-82; instr. Cazonovia (N.Y.) Coll., 1983; clin. nurse specialist Onondaga County Health Dept. Long Term Health Care, Syracuse, NY, 1983-89; supr. Pub. Health: Dayton & Montgomery County, Ohio, 1990—2010. Preceptor Syracuse U., 1986—89; adj. asst. prof. Sch. Nursing SUNY, Syracuse, 1988—89. Co-author: An Introduction to Orthopaedic Nursing: An Orientation Module, 1991; editor: (video) Total Hip Replacement-Patient Education (1st pl. Am. Jour. Nursing Patient Edn. Media award, 1994); reviewer: Orthopedic Nursing Jour., 2001—. Recipient Otto Au Franc award, Hip Soc., New Orleans, 1982; named Neonatal Intensive Home Care, Nat. Assn. Counties, 1987. Mem.: Dayton Area Orthop. Nurses (pres. 1992—93, 2004—05, 2010—), Orthop. Nurses Assn. (bd. dir. 1974—75, mem. nat. nominating com. 1975—77, v.p. 1977—78, sec. 1978—80), Nat. Assn. Orthop. Nurses (edn. approval com. 1984—, com. chair 1991, mem. nominating com. 1998—2001, chair 2000—01). Episcopalian. Avocations: skiing, gardening, sailing. Home: 4962 Walther Rd Kettering OH 45429-1944 E-mail: khitch@core.com.

HITCHENS, WILLIAM RANDOLPH (RANDY), healthcare executive; b. Logansport, Ind. s. William T. and Alberta J. Hitchens; m. Katherine J. Hitchens, Oct. 8, 1977; children: Cyrena, Chase, Carin. BS in Pharmacy, Purdue U., 1976; MBA, Ind. U., 1983. Pharmacist, mgr. Revco Drug, Ft. Wayne, Ind., 1981—83; assoc. product mgr. Boehringer Mannheim, Indpls., 1983, account mgr., 1984, product mgr., 1984—87, group mktg. mgr., 1987—90, sr. group product mgr., 1990—92, regional bus. mgr., 1992—94, nat. accounts managed care, 1994—97, dir. corp. partnership, 1997—98; corp. accts. dir. Roche, Indpls., 1998, nat. dir. corp. accounts, 1998—2004, dir. sales and mktg., 2004—05, area bus. dir., 2005—08, nat. sales dir., 2008—09, Dermal Life LLC, Tampa, 2009—, sr. v.p. bus. devel. Ofcl. U.S. Swimming, 1996-2004, bd. deacons, Second Presbyn. Ch. Indpls. Mem. Acad. Managed Care Pharmacists (legis. com. 1997-98, strategic mtkg. com. 1999). Presbyterian. Avocations: running, travel. Personal E-mail: wrhitchens@gmail.com.

HITOSUGI, MASAHITO, forensic pathologist, educator; b. Setagaya, Tokyo, July 3, 1969; s. Hitosugi Masaharu and Hitosugi Toshiko; m. Hamano Naoko Hitosugi; 1 child, Hitosugi Akari. MD, Grad. Sch. Medicine, Jikei U., Tokyo, 1994, PhD, DMS, 2000. Resident internal medicine Kawasaki Mcpl. Hosp., Kanagawa, Japan, 1994—96; physician Metropoltitan Police Dept. Tokyo, Tochigi Police, 1999—; rsch. asst. Jikei U. Sch. Medicine, Minato-ku, Tokyo, 2000—02; assoc. prof. Dokkyo Med. U. Sch. Medicine, Shimotsuga, Tochigi, Japan, 2002—; bd. mem. Internat. Traffic Medicine Assn., 2011—; assoc. prof. Tokyo City U., Japan, 2010. Councilor Japan Soc. Legal Medicine, Bunkyo-ku, 2004—; trustee Japan Assn. Med. English Edn., Shinjuku-ku, Tokyo, 2009—, Japan Coun. Traffic Sci., Chiyoda-ku, Tokyo, 2009—, Japan Soc. Biorheology, Bunkyo-ku, 2008—; lectr. Nagoya U., Japan, 2002—, Chiba U. Commerce, Ichikawa, Japan, 2008—; assoc. prof. Tokyo City U., Japan, 2010. Contbr. articles to profl. jours. Recipient Best Presentation award, Japan Soc. Automotive Engrs., 2008, Best Paper award, Japan Coun. Traffic Sci., 2010, Kenichi Uemura award, Japan Assn. Med. English Edn., 2010. Mem.: Internat. Traffic Medicine Assn. (bd. mem. 2011—). Achievements include patents for blood voscosity reducing agent; automatic foot-rest systems for drivers, new restraint system for vehicle passengers. Office: Dokkyo Med Univ Sch Med Kitakobayashi Mibu Shimotsuga-gun Tochigi 321-0293 Japan Office Phone: 81-282-87-2135. Office Fax: 81-282-86-7678. Business E-Mail: hitosugi@dokkyomed.ac.jp.

HITT, DAVID HAMILTON, SR., retired health facility administrator; b. Tuscaloosa, Ala., May 14, 1925; m. Frances Ford, Aug. 12, 1949 (dec.); children: David Hamilton, Kathryn Ann; m. Lola McKinney, Mar. 12, 1999 (dec.); m. Mary Chesser, July 10, 2004. BS, MS in Commerce and Bus. Adminstrn, U. Ala.; MHA, U. Minn., 1952. Hosp. adminstr. U. Ala. Hosp., 1947-50; various positions, including chief exec. officer Baylor U. Med. Center, 1952-79; sr. v.p. James A. Hamilton Assocs. (hosp. consultants), Dallas, 1979-84; pres., chief exec. officer Meth. Hosps. of Dallas, 1984-96, also bd. dirs., pres. emeritus; chmn. bd. dirs. Am. Rubber Tech. Inc., Jacksonville, Fla. Dir. emeritus Bapt. Med. Ctr., Jacksonville, Fla., Dallas Meth. Hosps. Found.; pres. Dallas Hosp. Coun., 1959; mem. adminstrv. bd. Coun. Tchg. Hosps. of Assn. Am. Med. Colls., 1972-79; assoc. clin. prof. Washington U., St. Louis, 1961-96; adj. assoc. prof. Trinity U., San Antonio, 1964-96. Contbr. numerous articles to profl. jours. Mem. exec. bd. council Boy Scouts Am.; v.p. Community Council Greater Dallas. Recipient Earl M. Collier award Distinguished Hosp. Adminstrn. Tex., 1973, Dean Conley award, Silver Beaver award Boy Scouts. Fellow Am. Coll. Healthcare Execs. (Gold medal award for excellence in healthcare mgmt. 1990, past regent, editl. bd. Frontiers Health Svcs. Mgmt. 1991-93); mem. Am. Hosp. Assn. (life, Citation for Meritorious Svc. 1987, Disting. Svc. award 1992, trustee, past chmn. coun. financing), Tex. Hosp. Assn. (trustee, treas., v.p., pres., chmn. ho. of dels. 1967), Am. Protestant Hosp. Assn. (past trustee), Alumni Assn. U. Minn. Program Hosp. Adminstrn. (past pres.), Marine Corps Assn., Exch. Club East Dallas (pres. 1957), Rotary (Dallas) (bd. dirs., dist. Ethics Bus. award 1993). Home: 14645 Preston Rd Apt 207 Dallas TX 75254 Personal E-mail: twintree75@yahoo.com.

HITT, RICARDO, physician; b. Cordoba, Argentina, Sept. 9, 1961; MD in Medicine, 1985, PhD in Medicine, 2001. Prof. Hosp. 12 de Octubre, 1990—. Adj. prof. U. Complutense de Madrid, 2004. Mem.: European Bd. Med. Oncology, European Bd. Internal Medicine, AACR, NYAS, ESMO, ASCO. Avocation: literature. Home: Velazquez 24 Las Matas Madrid 28290 Spain Personal E-mail: rhitt@telefonica.net.

HITZMAN, DONALD OLIVER, microbiologist; b. Milw., Dec. 2, 1926; s. Walter John and Irene (Smith) H.; m. Mary Elizabeth Neumann, Aug. 20, 1952; children: Murray W., Daniel C. AB, Carleton Coll., Northfield, Minn., 1948; MS, U. Ill., 1950, PhD, 1954. Resident microbiologist Texaco Co., Long Beach, Calif., 1951; sr. rsch. assoc. Phillips Petroleum Co., Bartlesville, Okla., 1954-85; v.p. rsch. Geo-Microbial Tech., Inc., Ochelata, Okla., 1985—. Contbr. articles to sci. publs. With USAAF, 1944-45. Fulbright scholar, Australia, 1951. Mem. Soc. Microbiology, Soc. Indsl. Microbiology, Am. Chem. Soc. Republican. Episcopalian. Achievements include over 60 patents; numerous fgn. patents. Office: Geo-Microbial Tech East Main St Ochelata OK 74051 Home Phone: 918-333-1717; Office Phone: 918-535-2281. E-mail: gmtgeochem@aol.com.

HIXSON, EDWARD GEORGE, general surgeon; b. Oneida, NY, Nov. 11, 1941; s. Edward George and Doris Elizabeth (Cummings) H.; m. Karen Agnes Rightmayer, June 13, 1981; children: Edward, Chris. BA, Middlebury Coll., Vt., 1963; MD, U. Vt., 1967. Diplomate Am. Bd. Surgeons; lic. N.Y. Intern Med. Ctr. Hosp. Vt., Burlington, N.Y., 1967-68, resident in gen. surgery; gen. surgeon Adirondack Med. Ctr., Saranac Lake, N.Y., 1973-90. Physician China-Everest Expedition, 1982, 84, Seven Summits Everest Expedition, 1983; surgeon 3d Bn. 172d Infantry (Mountain) Vt. Army Nat. Guard, Jericho, 1989—. Editor, author: (book) Winter Sportsmedicine, 1990; author: (with others) (books) Sports Neurology, 1987, Orthopedic Sportsmedicine, 1994. Maj. med. corps US Army, 1972—73, lt. col. MC N.C. US Army, ret., 2001. Fellow Am. Coll. Surgeons, Am. Coll. Sports Medicine; mem. AMA, Med. Soc. State of N.Y., Soc. Am. Gastrointestinal Endoscopic Surgeons, Soc. Laparandoscopic Surgeons, Ctrl. N.Y. Surgical Soc., Lake Placid Sportsmedicine Soc. (bd. dirs.). Republican. Episcopalian. Avocations: high altitude mountaineering, canoeing, skiing. Home: PO Box 278 Lake Clear NY 12945-0278 Office: Adirondack Surgical Group Ste 4 309 County Route 47 Saranac Lake NY 12983 Home Phone: 518-327-3643; Office Phone: 518-891-1610. E-mail: bphixsons@aol.com. *

HLATKY, MARK ANDREW, cardiologist, researcher; b. Windber, Pa., June 4, 1950; s. George Andrew and Rose Annette (Gonnella) H.; m. Donna Marie Alvarado, May 12, 1984; 1 child, Nicholas Michael. BS in Physics, MIT, 1972; MD, U. Pa. Sch. Medicine, 1976. Diplomate Am. Bd. Internal Medicine, Am. Bd. Cardiovasc. Disease; lic. physician, Calif. Intern, resident internal medicine U. Ariz., Tucson, 1976-79; Robert Wood Johnson clin. scholar U. Calif., San Francisco, 1979-81; fellow in cardiology Duke U. Med. Ctr., Durham, NC, 1981-83, assoc. medicine, cardiovascular divsn., 1983—86, asst. prof. medicine, cardiovascular divsn., 1986—89; assoc. prof. health rsch. and policy and of medicine (cardiovascular medicine) Stanford U. Sch. Medicine, Calif., 1989-96, prof. health rsch. and policy and of medicine (cardiovascular medicine) Calif., 1996—, chair, dept. health rsch. and policy Calif., 1996—2003. Dir., Health Services Rsch. Masters Degree Program 1989-; attending cardiovascular medicine svc., Stanford U. Med. Ctr., 1989-; co-dir., U. Calif. San Francisco-Stanford Evidence-based Practice Ctr., 1997-2002; co-dir., Donald W. Reynolds Cardiovascular Clin. Rsch. Ctr., 2000-01, dir., 2002-06; dir., Stanford-Kaiser Cardiovascular Outcomes Rsch. Ctr., 2008-. Contbr. articles to profl. jours.; editl. bds. Jour. Am. Coll. Cardiology, 1995—97, mem. editl. bds., 2002—, Am. Heart Jour., 1996—, Cardiac Electrophysiology Review, 1996—, Am. Jour. Medicine, 1997—, Jour. Invasive Cardiology, 1997—. Fellow Am. Coll. Cardiology; Am. Heart Assn. (fellow coun. on clin. cardiology), soc.Med. Decision-Making, Phi Beta Kappa. Achievements include research in outcomes after coronary surgery, coronary angioplasty, acute myocardial infarction, and cardiac arrhythmias. Home: 168 Rinconada Ave Palo Alto CA 94301-3725 Office: Stanford U Sch Medicine HRP Redwood Bldg Rm 150 Stanford CA 94305 Office Phone: 650-723-6426. E-mail: hlatky@stanford.edu.

HNATOW, DAVID A., emergency physician, educator; s. Anthony and Betty Hnatow; m. Brenda J. Hnatow, Mar. 28, 1987 (div.); children: Matthew, Sadie; m. Cynthia R. Hnatow, May 9, 1998; children: Anna, Andrew, Alexander. BS, Moravian Coll., 1981; MD, Georgetown U., 1985. Diplomate Am. Bd. Emergency Medicine. Staff Wilford Hall USAF Med. Ctr., Lackland AFB, Tex., 1991—93; asst. chmn. St. Luke's Luth. Hosp., San Antonio, 1993—94; asst. prof. U. Tex. Health Scis. Ctr., San Antonio, 1994—2003, assoc. prof., 2003—08, chief divsn. emergency medicine, 2001—08; med. dir. Univ. Hosp. Emergency Ctr., San Antonio, 2001—08; Greater San Antonio emergency physician, 2008—. Editor: (ednl. DVD) 91W Health Care Specialist, 2003; contbr. articles to profl. jours. Maj. USAF, 1985—93, Lackland AFB. Recipient Physican's Recognition award, AMA, 2002, 2005, 2008; Urgent Matters grantee, Robert Wood Johnson Found., 2003. Fellow: Am. Coll. Emergency Physicians, Am. Acad. Emergency Medicine. Avocations: scuba diving, skiing, boating, golf. Office: GSEP 8401 Datapoint Dr Ste 500 San Antonio TX 78229 Office Phone: 210-614-0180. Business E-Mail: dhnatow@satx.rr.com.

HO, BETTY JUENYÜ YÜLIN, retired musician, physiologist, educator; b. Nanking, China, Nov. 20, 1930; came to U.S., 1947; d. William Tien-Hu and Gwei-Hsin (Wang) Ho; m. Lajos Rudolf Elkan, Feb. 27, 1958 (div. Aug. 1967); children: Amanda, Anita, Julien (dec.), Raoul. Student, We. Coll., Oxford, Ohio, 1947—48; BS, Columbia U., 1952; postgrad., Lausanne U., Switzerland, 1955—56, piano studies with Maurice Perrin, Lausanne, 1956—58, CCNY, 1966—67, postgrad., 1972—74. Lab. technician Columbia U., NYC, 1953—54; ct. report typist Palais de Justice, Lausanne, 1956—57; pianist, accompanist Ecole de Ballet Mara Dousse, Lausanne, 1958—60; tchr. English Montcalme Inst., Lausanne, 1960—61; tchr. piano Le Manoir Inst., Lausanne, 1960—61, NYC, 1964—65. Rsch. dir. Juvenescent Rsch. Corp., N.Y.C., 1963— Author: The Living Function of Sleep, Life & Aging, 1967, The Origin of Variation of Races of Mankind & The Cause of Evolution, 1969, A Scientific Guide to Peaceful Living, 1972, A Chinese and Western Guide to Better Health and Longer Life, 1974, How to Stay Healthy A Lifetime Without Medicines, 1979, A Chinese & Western Daily Practical Health Guide, 1982, Immediate Hints to Health Problems, 1991, 101 Ways to Live 150 Years Young and Healthy, 1993, A Unique Guide for Health, Youth, and Longevity, 1993, A Unique Health Guide for Young People, 1994, How To Live a Long Life, 2004, Healing With Your Blood, 2008, Your Blood Keeps You Healthy, 2008, Immediate Suggestions to Good Health, 2008, Self-Help to Cheat Death, 2010, Treatise on The Living Body: A Synthetic Approach, 2011, How Your Body Truly Works, 2011. Named Citizen of Yr. Principality, Hutt River Province, Queensland, Australia, 1994, Royal Patronage Status for Life, 1995 Achievements include patents for infant feeding method. Home and Office: Juvenescent Research Corp 807 Riverside Dr Apt 1F New York NY 10032-7352 Office Phone: 212-543-2110. Personal E-mail: avan@earthlink.net.

HO, CHI-KUAN, immunologist, researcher; b. Macao, Macao, Dec. 31, 1944; s. Man-Kon and Man-Lee Ho; m. Mei-Yu Wu, Dec. 19, 1972. PhD, U. of Sask., Can., 1978. Rsch. assoc. Wash. U., St. Louis, Mo., 1978—80; assoc. investigator Veterans Gen. Hosp., Taipei, Taiwan, 1980—82, investigator, 1983—. Contbr. scientific papers (Disting. Paper Yr., Chinese Immunological Soc., 1991). Mem.: Internat. Soc. Cytokine and Interferon Rsch., Am. Assn. for Cancer Rsch. Achievements include patents for use of moscatilin as an anti-tumor drug. Office: Veterans Gen Hosp Taipei No 201 Sec 2 Shih-Pai Road Taiwan Taipei 11217 Taiwan Office Fax: 886-2-28757435. E-mail: cclin3@vghtpe.gov.tw.

HO, CHIU-MING, anesthesiologist, researcher; b. Hong Kong, Feb. 24, 1962; s. Keang-Wing Ho and Wong Chay Lee; m. Ling-Fang Wei, Feb. 21, 1992; children: Kuan-Yen, Kuan-Hsun. Diploma, Nat. Bd. Med. Examiners, Taiwan, 1991; MD, Nat. Def. Med. Ctr., Taiwan, 1991, PhD, 2001. Cert. Anesthesiologist Dept. Health, Exec. Yuan, Taiwan, 1995, in Pain Medicine Chinese Assn. Study Pain, Taiwan, 1996, in Intensive Care Medicine Taiwan Soc. Critical Care Medicine, Taiwan, 1999, in Cardiovascular Anesthesia Taiwan Soc. Cardiovasc. Anesthesia, Taiwan, 2002. Residency anesthesiology Taipei Veterans Gen. Hosp., Taiwan, 1991—96, attending anesthesiologist, 1996—; assoc. prof. Faculty Medicine, Nat. Yang-Ming U., Taipei, 2006—, asst. prof., 2002—06. Exec. editor Acta Anaesthesiologica Sinica, Taipei, 2001—02; reviewer Jour. Clin. Anesthesia, Falmouth, Mass., 2002—, Anesthesia and Analgesia, San Francisco, 2007—; editl. bd. Local & Regional Anesthesia, Chgo., 2008—. Contbr. articles to med. jours. Rsch. fellow, Nat. Sci. Coun., Taiwan, 1999, Rsch. grant, 2002—, Taipei Veterans Gen. Hosp., Taiwan, 1998—. Fellow: Internat. Coll. Surgeons, Taiwan; mem.: Taiwan Soc. Cardiovasc. Anesthesia, Taiwan Soc. Critical Care Medicine, Chinese Assn. Study Pain, Taiwan, Taiwan Soc. Anesthesiologists. Office: Taipei Veterans General Hosp 201 Sec 2 Shipai Rd Beitou Taipei 11217 Taiwan Office Fax: 886-2-28751597. Business E-Mail: cmho@vghtpe.gov.tw.

HO, CHRISTOPHER CHEE KONG, surgeon; b. Melaka, Malaysia, Jan. 24, 1975; MD, U. Kebangsaan Malaysia, 2000, MRCSEd, 2007, MS, 2008. Ho. officer Melaka Hosp., 2000—01; med. officer Hosp. Pakar Sultanah Fatimah, Muar, Malaysia, 2001—02, 2004—08, Hosp. Segamat, Malaysia, 2003; registrar Hosp. U. Kebangsaan Malaysia, Kuala Lumpur, 2004—08; surgeon Hosp. Pakar Sultanah Fatimah, Malaysia, 2008; urologist to lectr. U. Kebangsaan Malaysia Med. Ctr., 2008—. Contbr. articles to profl. jours. Mem.: Royal Coll. Surgeons Edinburgh, Malaysian Med. Assn. Office: Hospital Universiti Kebangsaan Malaysia Jalan Yaacob Latiff Bandar Tun Razak Cheras Kuala Lumpur 56000 Malaysia Office Fax: (603) 91737831. Personal E-mail: chrisckho2002@yahoo.com.

HO, DAVID (DA-I HO), research physician, virologist, scientific organization director; b. Taichung, Taiwan, Nov. 3, 1952; arrived in U.S., 1964; s. Paul and Sonia Ho; m. Susan Kuo Ho; children: Kathryn, Jonathan, Jaclyn. Student, MIT, 1970—71; BS summa cum laude, Calif. Inst. Tech., 1974; MD, Harvard, 1978; DSc (hon.), Bard Coll., 1997, Grad. Sch. CUNY, 1998, Swarthmore Coll., 1998, Tufts U., 1999, SUNY, Inst. Tech., 2000, Columbia U., 2000. Clin. tng. resident and chief resident internal medicine and infectious diseases Cedars-Sinai Med. Ctr., UCLA Sch. Medicine, 1978—82; clin. and rsch. fellow Infectious Disease Unit Mass. Gen. Hosp., 1982—85; rsch. fellow medicine Harvard Med. Sch., 1982—85; instructor in medicine Mass. Gen. Hosp. and Harvard Med. Sch., 1985—86; physician, rsch. scientist divsn. infectious diseases, dept. medicine Cedars-Sinai Med. Ctr., 1986—90; asst. prof. medicine in residence UCLA Sch. Medicine, 1986—89, assoc. prof. medicine in residence, 1989—90; prof. medicine and microbiology, co-dir. Ctr. for AIDS Rsch. NYU Sch. Medicine, 1990—96, dir., 1994—96; founding scientific dir., CEO Aaron Diamond AIDS Rsch. Ctr., NYC, 1990—, also bd. dir., 1998—; Irene Diamond prof., physician Rockefeller U., 1996—. Hon. prof. Peking Union Med. Coll., 1997, Chinese Acad. Med. Sciences, 1997, Wuhan U., 2002, Chinese Acad. Sciences, 2003, Fudan U., 2003; bd. dir. MIT Corp., 2003—. Contbr. articles to profl. jours. Bd. trustee Calif. Inst. Tech., 1997—; bd. overseers Harvard U., 1998—2004. Recipient Ernst Jung-Preis Fur Medizin (Germany), 1991, Mayor's award (N.Y.C.) for Excellence in Sci. and Tech., 1993, Squibb award, Infectious Disease Soc. Am., 1996, Bernard Field Meml. award, 1997, Scientific Honoree, NY Acad. Medicine, 1998, Golden Plate award, Am. Acad. Achievement, 1998, Hoechst Marion Roussel award, 1999, Presdl. Citizens medal, 2001, Friendship award, State Coun. People's Republic of China, 2003, Sydney Rubbo award, Australia Soc. Microbiology, 2003, Edward Ahrens award in Clin. Investigation, 2003, Lewis and Jack Rudin NY prize for Med. Rsch., 2003, Inspiration award, Asian Excellence award, 2006; named Man of Yr., TIME mag., 1996. Fellow: AAAS (Ernst Jung prize in medicine), Am. Acad. Microbiology, Am. Acad. Arts and Sciences; mem.: Chinese Acad. Engring. (fgn. mem. 2003—), Academia Sinica (Republic of China), NAS, IOM, NIH vaccine working group, Chinese Am. Leadership Orgn. (Chinese Am. leadership orgn., com. of 100 1990—), AmFAR (bd. dirs. sci. bd.). Office: Aaron Diamond AIDS Rsch Ctr 455 1st Ave 7th Fl New York NY 10016-9121 Address: Rockefeller U 1230 York Ave New York NY 10021 Office Phone: 212-448-5000. Office Fax: 212-725-1126. Business E-Mail: dho@rockefeller.edu.

HO, DONALD MING-TAK, pathologist, educator; b. Hong Kong, Mar. 21, 1952; s. Kam Kwong and Ruby Sook-Chun (Ngo) H.; m. Shufen Hung, Dec. 28, 1993; children: Tiffany, Dai-Cheng. MD, Nat. Def. Med. Ctr., Taipei, 1975; postgrad., U. London, 1979, Queen's U., Kingston, Can., 1979-85. Diplomate in anat. pathology and neuropathology Am. Bd. Pathology. Resident, chief resident Queen's U. and Kingston (Can.) Gen. Hosp., 1979-85; resident, chief resident, staff Vets. Gen. Hosp., Taipei, 1975-78, sect. chief surg. pathology, 1985-88, sect. chief neuropathology, 1989-93, sect. chief surg. pathology, 1993—2004; assoc. prof. Nat. Yang-Ming U. Sch. Medicine, 1992-2000, prof., 2000—, dir. Dept. Pathology and Lab. Medicine, 2004—. Contbr. articles to profl. jours. Grantee Taipei Vets. Gen. Hosp., Nat. Sci. Coun., 1992, 1994-, Nat. Sci. Coun. Fellow Royal Coll. Physicians Can. (specialist cert. in anat. pathology and neuropathology), Coll. Am. Pathologists; mem. Taiwan Soc. Pathology (specialist cert. in pathology, mem. splty. bd. exam. com., mem. quality assurance com. 1995-, pres. 2005-07), Internat. Assn. Pathology (pres. Taiwan divsn. 2005-07). Avocations: swimming, ping pong/table tennis, photography, bicycling. Office: Taipei Vets Gen Hosp Dept Pathology and Lab Medicine Taipei 11217 Taiwan Fax: (02) 2875 7056. E-mail: mtho@vghtpe.gov.tw.

HO, LAI YUN, medical educator; s. Yew Ping Ho and Chew Fun Leong; m. Shiew Shoo Ng, Oct. 15, 1977; children: Kok Tai, Kok On, Kok Ho. MBBS, U. Singapore, 1973, MD in Pediat., 1977; FAMS in Pediat., Acad. Medicine, Singapore, 1981. Lic. pediatrician and neonatologist Singapore Med. Coun., 1981. House officer Kandang Kerbau Hosp., Singapore, 1973, Singapore Gen. Hosp., 1973—74; med. officer Alexandra Hosp., Singapore, 1974, Kandang Kerbau Hosp., Singapore, 1974—75, Toa Payoh Gen. Hosp., Singapore, 1975; med. officer, paediatrics trainee Singapore Gen. Hosp., 1975—77; registrar in paediatrics Kandang Kerbau Hosp. and Tan Tock Seng Hosp., Singapore, 1977—80; fellow in neonatology Hosp. Sick Children, Toronto, Ont., Canada, 1981—82; sr. registrar Alexandra Hosp., Singapore, 1983—85; cons. pediatrician, dept. head Singapore Gen. Hosp., 1986—2004; clin. prof., assoc. dean Singapore Gen. Hosp., Nat. U. Singapore, 2004—. Founding head, dept. neonatology Singapore Gen. Hosp., 1986—2004, sr. cons., advisor, 2004—; mem. Specialists Accreditaton Bd., Singapore, 2005, Singapore Med. Coun., Singapore, 2005; co-chmn. Joint Com. Specialist Tng., Singapore, 2005—08. Mem.: editl. bds. to numerous jours. Advisor Club Rainbow, Singapore, 2000—08; bd. mem., chmn. Nat. Coun. Social Svc., Singapore, 2002—08; hon. cons., advisor IndoCare, Jakarta, Indonesia, 2004. Capt. 6th Field Hosp., 1975—98, Singapore Armed Forces. Recipient Svc. award, St. John's Ambulance Brigade, Singapore, 1991, Excellence for Singapore award, Singapore Govt., 2001, Pub. Svc. medal, 2006, Justice of Peace award, 2008, Gold Reviewer award, Acad. Medicine, Singapore, 2005, Outstanding Pediatrician Asia award, Assn. Socs. Southeast Asia Region; scholar Commonwealth Neonatology Tng. scholarship, Commonwealth Fund., Singapore, 1981—82. Fellow: Royal Coll. Physicians Thailand, Royal Coll. Paediatrics and Child Health, Royal Coll. Physicians London, Edinburgh, London, Singapore Acad. Medicine, Royal Australian Coll. Physicians (hon.), Royal Coll. Physicians Ireland (hon.), Am. Acad. Pediat. (hon.), Australian Coll. Paediatricians (hon.), Singapore Med. Assn. (life), Acad. Medicine Malaysia (hon.), Am. Coll. Physicians (hon.); mem.: Children's Charities Assn. (bd. dirs. 2000—04, chmn. 2001—02), Perinatal Soc. Singapore (life; pres. 1991—93, 1995—97, 1999—2001), Internat. Soc. Prevention Child Abuse and Neglect (Disting. Career award 2008, Disting. Career Award 2008), Med. Alumni Assn. (Med. Alumni award 2003), Singapore Children's Soc. (mem. exec. com. 1988—, vice-chmn. 2002—, Ruth Wong award 2003). Office: Singapore Gen Hosp Outram Rd Singapore 359647 Singapore Personal E-mail: holaiyun@pacific.net.sg. Business E-Mail: ho.lai.yun@sgh.com.sg.

HO, LOW-TONE, medical educator; s. Tzen and Jo-Hsiu (Yen) H.; m. Shu-Hsia Tu, Nov. 12, 1973; children: Pei-Ling, Pei-Shuan, Ming-Han. MD, Nat. Def. Med. Ctr., Taipei, 1971. Med. diplomate; lic. physician, Taiwan, U.S. Chmn. rsch. and edn. Taipei Vets. Gen. Hosp., Taipei, 1994—2009; prof. Nat. Yang-Ming U., Taipei, 1986, Nat. Def. Med. Ctr., Taipei, 1986—, Nat. Tsing-Hua U., Shin-Chu, Taiwan, 1999—. Prof. medicine Nat. Def. Med. Ctr., Taipei, 1986—, prof. nuclear medicine, 1991—; prof. medicine Nat. Yang-Ming U., Taipei, 1986—, prof. physiology, 1988—, dean Faculty Medicine, 1999-2004; prof. biomed. sci. Nat. Tsing-Hua U., Taipei, 1991—; prof. Grad. Inst. Clin. Medicine, NYMU, 1995—, prof. and dean, NYMU Sch. of Med., 1999-2004. Contbr. articles to profl. jours. Chmn. Med. Rsch. Ethics Found., Taipei, 2004. Col. Taiwan Nat. Def. Med. Ctr. Army, 1971—89, Taipei. Recipient Outstanding Rsch. Accomplishment award Nt. Sci. Coun., 1989-91; faculty fellow U. Mich., Ann Arbor, 1977-79; Nat. Health grantee, 1983-86. Mem. Diabetes Assn. China (exec. bd. 1988—), Endocrine Soc. China (exec. bd. 1988—), Soc. Lipid and Atherosclerosis China (exec. bd. 1994—). Achievements include research in First to show ET-1 causing insulin resistance. Avocations: chess, bridge, literature, computers, philosophy. Office: Taipei Vets Gen Hosp # 201 Shipai Rd Sec 2 Taipei 112 Taiwan Business E-Mail: ltho@vghtpe.gov.tw.

HO, MAC MENGFATT, biomedical researcher; s. Kum Weng Ho and Ping Chiow Chiu; m. Aipeng Lee, Feb. 1, 1990. BSc (hon.), Nat. U. Singapore, 1988; DPhil, U. Oxford, UK, 1995. Rsch. fellow Mass. Gen. Hosp., Harvard Med. Sch., Charlestown, Mass., 1998—2002; prin. investigator Nat. Cancer Centre, Singapore, 2002—. Reviewer:; contbr. articles to profl. jours. Grantee, Muscular Dystrophy Assn., 2005—, Nat. Med. Rsch. Coun., 2005—, Biomed. Rsch. Coun., 2006—; fellow, Wellcome Trust, 1995—98; scholar, Imperial Cancer Rsch. Fund, 1989—94. Achievements include patents for a blood-based assay for dysferlinopathies; dysferlin, a gene mutated in distal myopathy and limb girdle muscular dystrophy. Office: Nat Cancer Centre 11 Hospital Dr Singapore 169610 Singapore Office Phone: 6563275811. Office Fax: 6563720161. Business E-Mail: dmshmf@nccs.com.sg.

HO, REGINALD CHI SHING, medical educator; b. Hong Kong, Mar. 30, 1932; came to U.S., 1940; s. Chow and Elizabeth (Wong) Ho; m. Sharilyn Dang, Nov. 14, 1964; children: Mark, Reginald, Gianna Masca, Timothy. Student, St. Louis U., 1954, MD, 1959. Diplomate Nat. Bd. Med. Examiners, Am. Bd. Internal Medicine. Rotating intern U. Cin. Hosps., 1959-60, resident in internal medicine, 1960-62; fellow in hematology and oncology Barnes Hosp./Washington U., St. Louis, 1962-63; assoc. clin. prof., medicine JAB Sch. Medicine, 1977—2008; physician, dept. hematology and oncology Straub Clinic and Hosp., Honolulu, 1973—. Prin. investigator Hawaii Cmty. Clin. Oncology Program, Honolulu, 1983-86; adj. prof. clin. sci. Cancer Rsch. Ctr. Hawaii, 1989—, mem. various coms. Contbr. articles to med. jours. Bd. dirs. Cath. Svcs. for Families, 1987-91. Mem. AMA, ACP, Am. Cancer Soc. (divsn. del. 1982-93, del. dir. 1983-92, exec. com. 1989-94, chair med. and sci. exec. com. 1991-92, v.p. 1991-92, pres. 1992-93, immediate past pres. 1993-94, bd. dirs. Hawaii divsn. 1968—, pres. 1976-77, chmn. bd. dirs. 1977-78, hon. life mem. 1989—, bd. dirs.), Hawaii Med. Assn. (Hawaii cancer commn. 1980-85, chair cancer com. 1981-90), Alpha Omega Alpha. Roman Catholic. Avocation: tennis. Office: Straub Clinic Hosp 888 S King St Honolulu HI 96813-3083 Office Phone: 808-522-4000.

HO, TONY, surgeon; married; 3 children. MBBS. Fellowship Royal Coll. Surgeons, Glasgow, Scotland, Royal Coll. Surgeons Opthalmology, England, Acad. Medicine, Singapore; founder and dir. NIGHT-LASIK; specialist tng. Eye Inst., Glasgow, Scotland, Moorfields Eye Hosp., London, Bascom Eye Inst., Fla., with; sr. registrar Nat. Eye Centre, Singapore, 1991; surgeon Clearvision Eye Clinic & Lasik Centre, Singapore. Author: (spl. editl.) The Development of Refractive Surgery, pub. landmark sci. paper a method of iridotomy for angle closure glaucoma patients, numerous sci. papers on eye care, (books) The Complete Eye Care (Singapore Nat. Book Coun. Merit award, 1994), 18 Steps to Myopia Control, Childhood Myopia and Lasik Surgery. Recipient Pub. Svc. Commn. Merit Scholarship, Singapore, Scholar, Ministry of Health Manpower Devel. Plan for sub-specialty tng., 1990. Achievements include one of the early Singapore eye doctor to have a fully accredited USA eye fellowship certification who were the trail-blazers for many more doctors to follow; His "sequential Argon-Yag laser iridotomy" is now widely employed by doctors around the world as the de-facto standard method of iridotomies in dark brown irides. Office: Clearvision Eye Clinic & Lasik Centre 6 Nutmeg Rd Nutmeg Ct Singapore 228337 Singapore Office Phone: 6561002211. Office Fax: 6567336266. *

HO, VINCENT, gastroenterologist, educator; b. Sydney, Oct. 8, 1978; s. David and Sherry Ho. BSc in Medicine, U. NSW, Sydney, MBBS, 2002. Sch. prefect James Ruse Agrl. HS, Sydney, NSW, 1995—96, house capt., 1996; editor UNSW Med. Soc., Sydney, 1998; mem. edn. com. UNW Med. Faculty, Sydney, 2000; acad. bd. student rep. UNSW Acad. Bd., Sydney, 2000; pres. UNSW Med. Soc., 2000; intern Concord Hosp., Sydney, 2003; med. tutor U. Sydney Ctrl. Clin. Sch., Sydney, 2003; med. resident Tweed Heads Hosp., NSW, 2004; clin. assoc. lectr. U. Sydney No. Clin. Sch., 2004; med. registrar Wellington Hosp., New Zealand, 2005; advanced registrar gen. medicine Cairns Base Hosp., Queensland, Australia, 2006, gastroenterology registrar, 2007, Princess Alexandra Hosp., Brisbane, Queensland, 2008; clin. lectr. Sch. Medicine James Cook U., Cairns, 2006; clin. sr. lectr. James Cook U., Cairns, 2008—. Contbr. articles to profl. jours. Vol. Starlight found., Sydney, NSW, 2001—02. Recipient 1st prize, Australian Commn. & Media Law Assn., 2001, Presdl. Poster award, Am. Coll. of Gastroenterology, 2007; Travel grant, Gastroenterology Soc. Australia, 2007. Fellow: ACP, Am. Coll. Gastroenterology, Royal Australasian Coll. Physicians; mem.: Royal Australasian Coll. Med. Administrators, Gastroenterology Soc. Australia. Office: Townsville Hospital Level 1 Dept Gastroenterology Douglas Queensland 4814 Australia Home: 8 Abigail St Seven Hills 2147 Sydney NSW Australia Office Fax: (61) 7 4796 2381. Business E-Mail: vincent_ho@health.qld.gov.au.

HO, WAI MENG, anesthesiologist, researcher; b. Hong Kong, Feb. 25, 1952; s. Hei Ho and Shou Chun Wong; m. Mai Sha Wong, July 22, 1978; children: Zhi-Jun, Hung-Cheng. MD, Taipei Med. U., Taiwan,

1976. Resident in anesthesiology Taipei Vets. Gen. Hosp., 1979—82; chief resident, anesthesiology Taichung Vets. Gen. Hosp., Taiwan, 1982—83, acting staff, anesthesiology, 1983—84, attending staff, anesthesiology, 1984—2006, acting chair anesthesiology, 1996—98, chair anesthesiology, 1998—2004, Buddhist Tzuchi Taichung Gen. Hosp., 2006—. Assoc. prof. Chung Shan Med. U., Taichung, 1993—2006, TzuChi U., Hualien, 2007—. Contbr. articles to profl. jours. Recipient Quality Med. Specialist award and Med. prize, Nat. Med. Health and Biotech. Devel. Com., Taiwan, 2000. Fellow: Taiwan Soc. Cardiac Anesthesia, Taiwan Bd. Anesthesiology; mem.: Soc. Emergency and Critical Care Medicine Taiwan, Chinese Assn. Study of Pain, Soc. Anesthesiologists of Republic of China (standing coun. mem. 2000—02). Achievements include inventions in field. Avocations: reading, golf. Office: Buddhist Tzuchi Taichung Gen Hosp 66 Fongsing Rd Sec 1 Tanzih Township Taichung 427 Taiwan Personal E-mail: bmwho147@yahoo.com.tw. Business E-Mail: wmho@tzuchi.com.tw.

HOAG, JEFFREY B., physician, director; b. Evanston, Ill., Nov. 8, 1970; BS in Biology, U. Richmond, 1993; MD, Med. Coll. Va., 2001. Asst. prof. medicine Drexel U. Coll. Medicine, 2007; dir. critical care Cancer Treatment Ctrs. Am., 2010—. Dir. Drexel Adult Cystic Fibrosis Ctr., 2010—. Named one of Best Drs. in Am. List, Best Drs. Fellow: Am. Coll. Chest Physicians; mem.: Am. Thoracic Soc. Office: 1331 E Wyo Ave Ste 3170 Philadelphia PA 19124 Office Fax: 215-537-7710. Business E-Mail: jhoag@drexelmed.edu.

HOAGLAND, CHRISTINA GAIL, occupational therapist, industrial drafter; b. Long Beach, Calif., July 18, 1954; d. Joseph Richard and Dorothy Marian (Bell) H. BS in Occupl. Therapy, Loma Linda U., 1975; AS in Indsl. Drafting Tech., Mt. San Antonio Coll., 1985. Registered occupl. therapist; cert. brain injury specialist 2008. Occupl. therapist Yuka Mission Hosp., Zambia, Africa, 1976-77; staff occupl. therapist Hinsdale Sanitarium and Hosp., 1977—78, Glendale (Calif.) Adventist Med. Ctr., 1978-79; indsl. drafter Amerex Co., Riverside, Calif., 1985-88; re-entry occupl. therapist Rancho Los Amigos, Downey, Calif., 1989-90; staff occupl. therapist Corona (Calif.) Cmty. Hosp., 1990-92; occupl. therapist Linda R. Brown, Visalia, Calif., 1992; floating staff occupl. therapist Hilltop Rehab. Hosp., Grand Junction, Colo., 1992—95, St. Mary's Rehab. Ctr., Grand Junction, 1995—97; OTR, ind. living skills trainer supr. Interim Home Health Care, 1998—2008; floating staff occupl. therapist Grand Junction Cmty. Hosp., 2000—. Bd. mem. Brain Injury Trust Fund, 2006—10. Mem. Am. Occupl. Therapy Assn., Occupl. Therapy Assn. Colo. Nat. Mus. Women in Arts, Western Colo. Ctr. for the Arts. Democrat. Home: 578 N 26th St Grand Junction CO 81501-7961 Personal E-mail: cghtbi@yahoo.com.

HOANG THI BACH, BICH, hemobiologist; b. Thai Binh, Viet Nam, Aug. 8, 1945; arrived in France, 1963; d. Hoang Van Chau and Tran Thi Dong. MD, U. Strasbourg, 1971; specialization in hematology, U. Paris, 1980, specialization in transfusion, 1982. Intern, resident Strasbourg Hosp., 1968-71; asst. hemobiologist various hosps., Paris, 1972-81; hemobiologist Ministry of Health, Paris, 1981—. Cons. blood transfusion Ministry Edn. and Culture, Paris, 1993; advisor in medicine to dir. gen., Internat. Bibliog. Ctr., Cambridge, UK, 2003, dep. dir. gen., Europe divsn., 2004. Author: Physical Methods of Analysis, 1994; author lab. technique manuals Technics in Immunohematology, 1982, Technics of Preparation and Biological Constant Values of the Blood and its Derived Products, 1983, The Preparation and Preservation of Blood Product Components, 1995, Highest Degree Hospitals Practician, 2002. Mem. French Soc. Blood Transfusion, Am. Assn. Blood Bank, Internat. Soc. Blood Transfusion, N.Y. Acad. Scis. Home: Residence du Midi D 45 25 Rue Camille Blanc 94 400 Vitry-sur-Seine Ile France France Office: Assistance Publique Hosp Paris Univ Hosps Broussais-Georges Pompidou 20 rue Leblanc 75015 Paris France

HOASHI, TAKAYA, surgeon; b. Japan, Sept. 10, 1973; MD, Osaka U. Med. Sch., 1999, PhD, 2010. Surgeon Nat. Cardiovasc. Ctr., Japan, 2009—. Office: 5-7-1 Fujishirodai Suita Osaka 565-8565 Japan Office Phone: 81-6-6833-5012. Business E-Mail: thoashi@surg1.med.osaka-u.ac.jp.

HOBAIKA, ADRIANO BECHARA DE SOUZA, anesthesiologist; s. Bechara Nagib and Inaci Maria de Souza Hobaika; m. Lidiane Gomes Costa Hobaika, Nov. 26, 2002. MD in Medicine, U. Fed. Minas Gerais, Belo Horizonte, 2001; MSc in Medicine, Santa Casa de Misericórdia Belo Horizonte, 2008. CRMMG Conselho Regional Medicina Minas Gerais, 2001, título de especialista em anestesiologia Assn. Médica Brasileira, 2003, título superior em anestesiologia Soc. Brasileira Anestesiologia, 2007. Med. resident anesthesiology Hosp. Felício Rocho, Belo Horizonte, 2001—03; resident Anesthesiology Tchg. and Tng. Ctr. Santa Casa de Belo Horizonte, 2005—; staff anesthesiologist Hosp. Mater Dei, Belo Horizonte, 2008—. Contbr. articles to profl. jour. CNPq scholarship, Nat. Counsel Technol. and Sci. Devel., 1997—99. Mem.: Soc. Ambulatory Anesthesia, Soc. Brasileira Anestesiologia. Office: Hosp Mater Dei Rua Erê 23/401 Prado Belo Horizonte Minas Gerais 30410450 Brazil Business E-Mail: ahobaika@hotmail.com.

HOBAR, P. CRAIG, plastic surgeon, educator; b. Pitts., Oct. 21, 1954; MD, U. Miami, 1982. Cert. Am. Bd. Plastic Surgery. Resident gen. surgery Parkland Meml. Hosp., Dallas, 1982—87; resident plastic surgery U. Tex. Southwestern Health Sci. Ctr., Dallas, 1987—89; fellowship craniofacial surgery NYU Med. Ctr., NYC, 1989—90; pvt. practice Dallas, 1990—; founding ptnr. Dallas Plastic Surgery Inst.; head craniofacial surgery Children's Med. Ctr., Dallas; clin. assoc. prof. plastic surgery U. Tex. Southwestern Med. Ctr. Founder, med. dir. LEAP; affiliate plastic surgeon Dallas Stars. Named Dallas Cmty. Hero of 2000, Dallas Bus. Jour. Mem.: Christian Med. and Dental Soc., Am. Acad. Anti-Aging Medicine, Am. Assn. Plastic Surgeons, Am. Soc. Plastic and Reconstructive Surgeons, Am. Soc. Aesthetic Plastic Surgery (In Chul Song Award). Office: 411 N Washington Ave, Ste 6000 Dallas TX 75246 Office Phone: 214-832-8423. E-mail: chobar@earthlink.net.

HOBART, ANNA ZAMBON, psychologist; PhD in Psychology, U. Statale, Rome, 1973. Cert. in psycoanalitical tng. Tavistock Ctr. London, Rome, 1979, in psychol. tng. Inst. Neuropsichiatria Rome, 1984. Clin. psychologist Asssociazione Italiana Persone Down, Rome, 1979—97; several nat. & internat. conventions, spkr. on down syndrome, 1980—; promoter siblings group exec. com. mem. founder Fondazione, Italian Verso Il Futuro, 1985—; psychotherapist Pvt., Rome, 2000. Author: (book) La Persona Con Sindrome Down. Mem.: Guidelines Diagnosis Comm. ISS (v.p. 2009), Societa Psicoterapia Psicoanalitica Italiana. Home and Office: Vicolo del Cinque 38 153 Rome RM Italy

HOBBY, FREDERICK D., medical association administrator; m. Patricia King Hobby; children: Ashley, Brian, Ryan. B in History and Polit. Sci., Ky. State U., Frankfort; M in Sociology, Wash. U., St. Louis. Faculty mem. U. Louisville; exec., affirmative action dept. City of Louisville; adminstr. Humana, Inc.; clin. adminstr. Portsmouth Gen. Hosp., Va.; CEO Newport News Gen. Hosp.; various positions including adminstr. of clin. svcs., adminstr. guest, patient svcs., v.p. svc. excellence, chief diversity officer Greenville Hosp. Sys., Greenville, SC; pres., CEO Inst. Diversity in Health Mgmt., Chgo., 2005—. Faculty Snowmass Inst., 1997; gov. appointee SC State Health Planning Com.; bd. dir. Am. Hosp. Assn. Leadership Cir. on Eliminating Racial and Ethnic Disparities in Healthcare. Recipient Sr. Exec. Yr. award, Nat. Assn. Health Svcs. Execs., 1999. Office: Inst Diversity in Health Mgmt One N Franklin 30th Fl Chicago IL 60606 Office Phone: 312-422-2630. Office Fax: 312-895-2561. Business E-Mail: fhobby@aha.org. *

HOCH, ANNE Z., physiatrist, researcher, medical educator; b. Escanaba, Mich., Mar. 21, 1965; d. Byron K. and Betty A. Zeni; m. Stephen D. Hoch; 1 child, Hannah Anne. BS, Marquette U., Milw., 1987; DO, Mich. State U., East Lansing, 1992. Bd. cert. phys. medicine and rehab. Med. dir. sports rehab. dept. phys. medicine and rehab. Med. Coll. of Wis., Milw., 1997—2002, asst. prof. dept. phys. medicine and rehab. and orthop. surgery, 2002—, assoc. prof. dept. orthop. surgery, 2003—. Adj. prof. health edn. Wis. Luth. Coll., Milw., 1999—2001; adj. prof. dept. biomechanical engring. Marquette U., 2000—; rsch. comm. Strategic Health Initiative Am. Coll. Sports-Medicine, 2001—; dir. women's sports medicine program Froedtert Hosp. Med. Coll. Wis., Milw., 2002—, mem. women's faculty coun.-comm., 2001—03. Author: Medicine and Sci. in Sports and Exercise, 2003 (ERF Best Rsch. Paper award, 2003), 1998 (Sarah Baskin Rsch. Paper Writing award, 1997); contbr. articles to profl. jours. (Best Rsch. Paper by Physiatrist, JAMA, 1996). Contbr. Wis. Humane Soc., Milw., 2000—; vol. physician Mt. Mary Coll., 2000—; vol. team physician Divine Savior Holy Angels H.S., 2001—; pres. Wis. Women's Sports Found., 2001—. Recipient First prize poster, Passor-Midwest Regional Meeting, 1995; grantee phys. medicine and rehab., Med. Coll. of Wis., 2001, gen. clin. rsch. ctr., 2002—03, 2003—04. Fellow: Am. Acad. of Phys. Medicine and Rehab., Am. Coll. of Sports Medicine, Am. Coll. of Medicine; mem.: Acad. of Academic Physiatrists. Avocations: triathalon, kayaking, hiking, travel, reading. Office: Dept Orthop Surgery FEC 5th Fl 9200 W Wis Ave Milwaukee WI 53226 Office Phone: 414-805-7461.

HOCHBERG, MARK STEFAN, surgeon; b. Providence, Nov. 26, 1947; s. Robert and Gertrude (Meth) H.; m. Faith Shapiro, June 6, 1976; children: Alyssa T., Asher R. BA, Brown U., 1969; MD, Harvard U., 1973; MD (Honoris Causa), Chongqing Sch. Med. Sci., China, 1987. Diplomate Am. Bd. Thoracic Surgery, Am. Bd. Surgery. Chief resident cardiothoracic surgery Mass. Gen. Hosp., Boston, 1980; clin. fellow surgery Harvard Med. Sch., Boston, 1980; attending cardiac surgeon Newark Beth Israel Med. Ctr., 1981—93, dir. cardiac surgery, 1988—93; cons. cardiac surgeon Overlook Hosp., Summit, NJ, 1983—93; asst. prof. surgery U. Medicine and Dentistry N.J., Newark, 1981—87, assoc. prof. surgery, 1987—93; spl. asst. to pres., vis. prof. surgery George Washington U., Washington, 1993—94, dean univ. affairs, prof. surgery, 1994—95; sr. scholar Assn. Acad. Health Ctrs., 1995—96; pres. Healthcare Found. N.J., Roseland, 1996—2003; CEO Coll. Physicians Phila., 2003—05; adj. prof. surgery U. Pa. Med. Sch., 2003—05; prof. surgery NYU, 2005—; attending surgeon NYU Belleue Hosp., 2005—. Chmn. grant rev. com. N.J. affiliate Am. Heart Assn., New Brunswick, 1986-88, also bd. dirs.; mem. com. med. affairs Corp. of Brown U., Providence, 1987-2002 V.p. Temple B'nai Jeshurun, Short Hills, 1988-92; trustee Coun. N.J. Grantmakers, 1997-2002, pres. 2000-02 Fellow ACS, Am. Coun. Edn, Coll. Physicians of Phila., N.Y. Acad. Medicine; mem. Soc. Thoracic Surgery, Am. Assn. Thoracic Surgery, Alpha Omega Alpha. Office: NYU Sch Medicine Dept Surgery 550 First Ave NBV15 North 1 New York NY 10016

HOCHEDLINGER, KONRAD, biology professor, biomedical researcher; b. Austria; PhD, U. of Vienna, 2003. Rschr. Inst. Molecular Pathology, Whitehead Inst., 1999—2005; asst. prof. medicine Mass. Gen. Hosp. Ctr. Regenerative Medicine Laboratories, 2005—; asst. prof. Harvard Medical School; rschr., prin. faculty mem. Harvard Stem Cell Inst., 2005—. Mem. sci. adv. bd. iPierian, Inc., 2009—. Contbr. articles to profl. jours. Recipient Outstanding Young Investigator award, Internat. Soc. Stem Cell Rsch. (ISSCR); grantee Genzyme Postdoctoral Fellowship, Whitehead Inst., 2004. Office: Harvard Medical School 25 Shattuck St Boston MA 02115 also: HHMI Harvard Stem Cell Inst Mass Gen Hosp Richard B Simches Bldg 185 Cambridge St Boston MA 02114 Office Phone: 617-432-1000, 617-643-2075. Office Fax: 617-724-2662. Business E-Mail: khochedlinger@helix.mgh.harvard.edu. *

HOCHLERIN, DIANE, pediatrician, educator; b. NYC, Feb. 4, 1942; d. William J. and Bertha Hochlerin. BS, U. City of NY, 1962; MD, Med. Coll. Pa., 1966. Diplomate Am. Bd. Pediats. Intern Albert Einstein Hosp., Phila., 1966-67; resident Phila. Gen. Hosp., 1967-69; attending pediatrician St. Luke's Roosevelt Hosp., NYC, 1969—; now sr. attending physician St. Luke's Roosevelt Hosp, NYC; clin. assoc. prof. pediats. Columbia U., NYC, 1969—; asst. attending physician Cath. Med. Ctr., NYC, 1993-99. Faculty advisor Adelphi U., N.Y.C., 1994. Fellow Am. Acad. Pediats.; mem. N.Y. State Med. Soc., County Med. Soc. Home: 305 E 86th St New York NY 10028 Office: 66 W 94th St Ste 1A New York NY 10025 *

HOCHMAN, JUDITH SHERYL, cardiologist, researcher; b. NYC, Feb. 20, 1951; m. Richard Fuchs, June 28, 1981; children: Michael, Daniel, Benjamin. BA magna cum laude, Brandeis Univ., 1972; MA in Cellular and Develop. Biology, Harvard Univ., 1974; MD, Harvard Med. Sch., 1977. Resident, internal medicine Peter Bent Brigham Hosp.; chief med. resident Univ. Mass. Med. Ctr.; fellow, cardiovascular medicine John Hopkins Univ. Med. Ctr.; dir. cardiac care unit St. Lukes Roosevelt Hosp. Ctr., NYC, 1983—2003, dir. cardiac stepdown, 1992—2003, dir. cardiac rsch., 1997—2003, sr. attending in medicine, 1997—2003; assoc. prof. medicine Columbia Univ., NYC, 1996—2003; Harold Snyder Family Prof., Cardiology, dir., cardiovascular clin. rsch., clin. chief Leon H. Charney Divsn. Cardiology NYU Med. Ctr., NYU Sch. Medicine, NYC, 2003—. Com mem. NHLBT; adv. bd. Cardio Tech., Pine Brook, N.Y., 1997-, Bd. External Experts, 2007-; study chair, Occluded Artery and SHOCK Trials. Co-author: (chpt. in book) Textbook of Cardiovascular Medicine, 2006; editor: Cardiogenic Shock, AHA Clin. Senes, 2009; mem. editl. bds. Circulation, American Heart Journal, Critical Pathways in Cardiology, Acute Cardiac Care; contbr. articles to profl. jours. Fellow: Am. Coll. Cardiology, AHA/ACC Task Force Practice Guidelines; mem. Assn. U. Cardiologists, Assn. Am. Physicians, Phi Beta Kappa. Avocations: skiing, tennis, sailing. Office: NYU Sch Medicine 530 First Ave Skirball-9R New York NY 10016

HOCHSTER, HOWARD S., oncologist; b. Mpls., Dec. 30, 1953; MD, Yale U., 1980. Diplomate Am. Bd. Med. Oncology, Am. Bd. Hematology. Intern NYU-Bellevue Hosp., NYC, 1980—81, resident, 1981—83; fellow NYU Med. Ctr., 1983—85; Fulbright fellow Jules Bordet Inst., Brussels, 1985—86; oncologist NYU Med. Ctr., NYC, 1986—; mem. NYU Oncology Associates. Assoc. prof. medicine NYU Sch. Medicine, 1995—2002, prof., medicine, 2002—; dir., clin. trials NYU Cancer Inst., 2003—. Office: Clin Cancer Ctr 9th Fl 160 E 34th St New York NY 10016 Office Phone: 212-731-5100. E-mail: howard.hochster@nyumc.org.

HODES, RICHARD J., federal agency administrator, immunologist, researcher; b. NYC, Dec. 31, 1943; BA, Yale U., New Haven, 1965; MD, Harvard Med. Sch., Boston, 1971. Diplomate Am. Bd. Internal Medicine. Clin. tng. in internal medicine Mass. Gen. Hosp.; clin. investigator Nat. Cancer Inst. NIH, Bethesda, Md., dep. chief to acting chief immunology br., dir. Nat. Inst. Aging, 1993—, sr. investigator Exptl. Immunology Br. and head immune regulation sect., Ctr. Cancer Rsch. Program coord. US Japan Coop. Cancer Rsch. Program, 1982—; mem. sci. adv. bd. Cancer Research Inst., 1992—; mem. The Dana Alliance for Brain Initiatives, 1995—. Fellow: AAAS; mem.: NAS Inst. Medicine. Office: Nat Inst Aging Bldg 31C Claude D Pepper Bldg Rm 5C35 31 Center Dr MSC 2292 Bethesda MD 20892 Office Phone: 301-496-9265. Office Fax: 301-496-2525. E-mail: richard.hodes@nih.gov. *

HODESS, ARTHUR BART, cardiologist; b. NYC, Jan. 15, 1950; s. Samuel and Dora (Rosenkrantz) H.; m. Carol Yasuna, Aug. 31, 1969 (div. May 1985); children: Joshua David, Jeremy Scott; m. S. Christina Ellsworth, Dec. 23, 1987; children: Jonathan Ellsworth, Jason Dorian, Jordan Gottier. BA, Boston U., 1970; MD, Columbia U., 1974. Intern Hosp. of U. Pa., Phila., 1974-75, resident in medicine, 1975-77, fellow in cardiology, 1977-79; asst. instr. dept. medicine Hosp. U. of Pa., Phila., 1974-79, instr. physiology, dept. animal biology U. Pa., Sch. Veterinary Medicine, Phila., 1977-78; clin. assoc. dept. medicine U. Pa., Phila., 1979-81; attending cardiologist Brandywine Hosp., Coatesville, Pa., 1979—, dir. critical care, 1989—, chief of cardiology, 1990—, chmn. dept. medicine, 1991-95, bd. trustees, 2009—; pres. Brandywine Valley Cardiovascular Assocs., Thorndale, Pa., 1991—2010. Contbr. articles to profl. jours. V.p. Chestnut Hollow Homeowners Assn., West Chester, Pa., 1990-94, bd. dirs. 1995; bd. dirs. Beth Israel Congregation, Chester County, 1991-96. Fellow Clin. Coun. Cardiology Am. Heart Assn. Fellow: ACP, Am. Soc. Angiology, Am. Soc. Echocardiography, Am. Coll. Cardiology, Am. Coll. Chest Physicians; mem.: Brandywine Hosp. (bd. dirs. 2009), Soc. Cardiovasc. Computed Tomography, Soc. Critical Care Medicine, Cardiac Electrophysiology Soc. Office: Brandywine Valley Cardio 3025 Zinn Rd Thorndale PA 19372-1131 Office Phone: 610-384-2211. Business E-Mail: ahodess@bvcahearts.com.

HODGE, CHARLES JOSEPH, JR., neurosurgeon, educator; b. West Orange, NJ, Oct. 3, 1941; s. Charles Joseph and Marie Louise (Renton) H.; m. Caroline Von Hessert, Aug. 20, 1962 (div. 1981); children: Charles Joseph III, Frederich Sean, Jason Von Hessert; m. Linda Salvetti, Feb. 20, 1982. AB, Princeton U., 1963; MD, Columbia U., 1967. Intern Presbyn. Hosp., NYC, 1967-68; resident in surgery Yale-New Haven (Conn.) Hosp., 1968-69; resident in neurosurgery SUNY Upstate Med. Ctr., Syracuse, 1969-74; clin. fellow The London (Eng.) Hosp., 1974-75; asst. prof. dept. neurosurgery, Health Sci. Ctr. U. Syracuse, 1975-80, assoc. prof., 1980-84, prof., 1984—, chmn. dept., 1988—. Lt. Comdr. USN, 1963-75. Recipient Grass award for Rsch. Soc. Neurol. Surgery, 1987, rsch. grant Nat. Inst. Neurol. Communication Disorders, Bethesda, Md., 1986. Mem. Am. Assn. Neurol. Surgeons (sci. adv. bd. Rsch. Found. 1989—), N.Y. State Neurosurg. Soc. (bd. dirs. 1986-89), Am. Acad. Neurol. Surgery, Soc. for Neurosci., Soc. Univ. Neurosurgeons, Internat. Assn. for Study of Pain, University Club. Democrat. Episcopalian. Avocations: sailing, skiing, music. Office: SUNY Health Sci Ctr/Syracuse Dept of Neurosurgery 750 E Adams St Dept Of Syracuse NY 13210-2306 *

HODGE, JULIE A., dermatologist, educator; Grad., Stanford U.; MD, Tulane U., New Orleans. Diplomate Am. Bd. Dermatology. Intern internal medicine Ochsner Found. Hosp., New Orleans; resident dermatology Tulane Med. Ctr.; pvt. practice dermatologist Fullerton, Calif.; asst. clin. prof. Univ. Calif Irvine Med. Ctr. Bd. trustees Dermatology Found. Named Physician of Excellence, Orange County Med. Assn., 2009, Med. Expert, New Beauty Mag. Mem.: Women's Dermatologic Soc. (co-chair career devel.), Am. Soc. for Mohs Surgery, Am. Soc. for Laser Medicine and Surgery, Am. Soc. of Dermatologic Surgery, Am. Acad. of Dermatology. Office: Ste 300 1440 N Harbor Blvd Fullerton CA 92835 Office Phone: 714-526-7546. Office Fax: 714-526-7547.

HODGSON, ERNEST, toxicologist, educator; b. Durham, Eng., July 26, 1932; arrived in U.S., 1955; s. Ernest Victor and Emily (Moses) Hodgson; m. Mary Kathleen Devlin, Dec. 21, 1957 (dec.); children: Mary Elizabeth, Audrey Catherine, Patricia Emily Devlin, Ernest Victor Felix. BSc with honors, Kings Coll. U., Durham, Eng., 1955; PhD, Oreg. State U., 1959. Rsch. fellow Oreg. State U., Corvallis, 1955-59, U. Wis., Madison, 1959-61; asst. prof. N.C. State U., Raleigh, 1961-63, assoc. prof., 1963-65, prof. toxicology, 1965—, William Neal Reynolds prof., 1977—, chmn. toxicology dept., 1982-97, Disting. Alumni Rsch. prof., 1987-90; disting. prof. emeritus NC State U. Mem. adv. panel U.S. EPA, Washington, 1982—85; mem. toxicology study sect. NIH, Washington, 1985—89; mem. study sect. NIEHS, 1992—96, chmn., 1994—96; pres. Toxicology Comm., Raleigh, 1982—; vis. scientist U. Wash., Seattle, 1975; exec. dir. Found. Toxicology & Agromedicine. Author, editor: Introduction to Biochemical Toxicology, 1980, 4th edit., 2008, Modern Toxicology, 1987, 4th edit., 2010, Dictionary of Toxicology, Molecular and Biochemical Toxicology, 4th edit., 2008; editor: Revs. Biochemical Toxicology, 1979—, Revs. Environ. Toxicology, 1984—, Jour. Biochemical and Molecular Toxicology; mem. editl. bd. Chemico-Biol. Interactions; contbr. articles to profl. jours. Chmn. policy rev. com. Gov.'s Waste Mgmt. Bd., Raleigh, 1984. Grantee, NIH, 1962—, U.S. Army, 2000—. Mem.: AAAS, Internat. Soc. Study Xenobiotics (mem. coun. 1986—89, sec.-elect 1990—92, sec. 1992—94, pres.-elect 1996—97, pres. 1998—99, Disting. Svc. award 2004), Am. Chem. Soc. (Sterling Hendricks award USDA 1997, Burdick and Jackson Internat. award in pesticide chemistry), Am. Soc. Pharmacology (mem. drug metabolism com. 1981—84), Soc. Toxicology (pres. N.C. chpt. 1984—85, mem. edn. com. 1984—, pres. mechanisms sect. 1991—92, historian, archivist 2005—09, Edn. award 1984, Merit award 1994), Sigma Xi (chpt. pres. 1974). Democrat. Avocations: history, writing, travel. Office: NC State U Dept Toxicology PO Box 7633 Raleigh NC 27695-0001 Office Phone: 919-515-5295. Business E-Mail: ernest_hodgson@ncsu.edu.

HODGSON, JAN, geneticist, educator; b. Birmingham, Eng., June 6, 1958; BSc (hon.), Kingston U., 1997; PhD, U. Melbourne, 2006. Lectr. genetics counselling U. Melbourne, 2008—. V.p. Genetic Support Network Victoria, 2009; mem. com. mgmt. Down Syndrome Victoria, 2010. Mem.: Internat. Inst. Qualitative Methodology, Australasian Soc. Genetic Counsellors, Human Genetics Soc. Australasia. Office: Genetics Edn & Health Research Melbourne Victoria 3052 Australia Office Fax: 03 8341 6207. Business E-Mail: jan.hodgson@mcri.edu.au.

HODGSON, PAUL EDMUND, surgeon, department chairman; b. Milw., Dec. 14, 1921; s. Howard Edmund and Ethel Marie (Niemi) H.; m. Barbara Jean Osborne, Apr. 22, 1945; children: Ann, Paul. BS summa cum laude, Beloit Coll., 1943; MD cum laude, U. Mich., 1945. Diplomate: Am. Bd. Surgery. Intern U. Mich. Hosp., 1945-46, resident in surgery, 1948-52; mem. faculty dept. surgery U. Mich., 1952-62, assoc. prof., 1956-62; prof. surgery U. Nebr. Coll. Medicine, Omaha, 1962-88, prof. emeritus, 1988—, asst. dean for curriculum, 1966-72, chmn. dept. surgery, 1972-84. Trustee Beloit Coll., 1977-80 Served to capt. M.C. U.S. Army, 1946-48. Mem. A.C.S., Frederick A. Coller Surg. Soc., Soc. Univ. Surgeons, Central Surg. Assn., Soc. Surgery Alimentary Tract, Am. Assn. Surgery Trauma, Western Surg. Assn., Am. Surg. Assn. Presbyterian. Office: Dept Surgery Med Ctr 983280 Nebraska Medical Center Omaha NE 68198-3280

HODIS, JIRI, physician, educator; b. Prague, Sept. 26, 1971; MD, Charles U., Prague, 1997; M, Charles U., Hradec Kralove, 2005, PhD, 2011. Exec. head Hodis s.r.o., 2010—. Asst. dept. pharmacology Charles U. Prague, 2003. Office: V Plani 55/36 Lhotka Prague 14200 Czech Republic Office Phone: 420603179629. Office Fax: 420257922426. Business E-Mail: hodis@hodis.eu.

HODISH, ISRAEL, endocrinologist; b. Israel, Mar. 4, 1967; MD, Hebrew U., Jerusalem, 1996; PhD, Tel Aviv U., Israel, 2006. Asst. prof. U. Mich., 2009—. Co-founder Hygieia Inc., 2008. Office: 1000 Wall St Ann Arbor MI 48105 Business E-Mail: ihodish@umich.edu.

HODOBA, DANILO DANIEL, psychiatrist; b. Sr. Mitrovica, Vojvodina, Yugoslavia, Feb. 15, 1951; arrived in Croatia, 1970; s. Stjepan and Magdalena (Perković) H.; m. Nevenka Čakić, Feb. 28, 1976; 1 child, Ivan. MD, Zagreb U., Croatia, 1975, MSc, 1983, DSc, 1985. Physician in gen. practice, Croatia, 1975-78; psychiatrist Psychiat. Hosp. Vrapče, Zagreb, 1978-91, head dept. psychiat. rsch., 1991—, head psychophysiology dept., 1992—, pres. coun. experts, 1993-95, pres. bd. dirs., 1995-97. Pres. bd. dirs. Helios Ins. Co., Zagreb, 1992-94. Lectr. on sleep, epilepsy, aging; contbr. articles to profl. jours. Mem. Croatian Med. Assn., Internat. Psychogeriatric Assn., European Sleep Rsch. Soc., Croatian Sleep Rsch. Soc. (pres. 1994-2004), Croatian League Against Epilepsy (pres. 2004—), Acad. Med. Scis. Avocations: history of ancient civilizations, bicycling. Office: Psychiat Hosp Vrapče Bolnička 32 10090 Zagreb Croatia

HOEJGAARD, LISELOTTE, nuclear medicine physician, educator; b. Copenhagen, Mar. 19, 1957; d. Knud and Karen Hoejgaard; m. Jes Bruun Lauritzen, May 20, 1956; 1 child, Frederik. MD, DMSc, Copenhagen U., Denmark, 1982. Cert. specialist in clin.physiology and nuclear medicine Danish Nat. Bd. of Health, 1990. Chief physican Hvidovre Hosp., Copenhagen, 1995—98; chief physician Rigshospitalet, Copenhagen, 1998—2000, dir., prof., 2000—; editor in chief Jour. of the Danish Med. Assn., Copenhagen, 1996—2002; prof. in med. tech. Copenhagen U., Copenhagen, 2004—; sci. adv. bd. mem. Innovative Med. Initiative, Bruxellers, 2008—; adv. bd. mem. EU Commr. Sci., 2008—; mem. Conseil Adminstrn. Inst. Nat. La Sante Et La Rsch. Medicine, Paris, 2009—; with Knighthood, Denmark, 2006. Mem. nat. coun. for med. edn. Danish Nat. Bd. of Health, Copenhagen, 2000—; mem. polit. rsch. coun. Ministry of Rsch. and Edn., Copenhagen, 2003—; mem. European Strategic Forum for Rsch. Infrastructure, Bruxelles, Belgium, 2004—; chair European Med. Rsch. Coun., 2006—. Author (scientific author and editor) 150 publs. in med. jours. Recipient Prize of honour, Soc. Clin. Physiology and Nuclear Medicine, 2001, The Danish Medico prize, Orgn. of the Danish Med. Industry, 2004, Niels Lassen award, Min. ERNA Hamilton Arts and Sci., 2005. Mem.: Med. Soc. Copenhagen (pres. 1990—92, internat. com. med. jour. editors 1997—2002). Achievements include patents for A new method for gastric potential difference measurements. Office: Copenhagen Univ Rigshospitalet Blegdamsvej 9 2100 Copenhagen Denmark Office Phone: +45 3545 4215. Office Fax: +45 3545 4015. E-mail: lottepet@rh.dk.

HOENIG, JOHANNES FRANZ, plastic surgeon, educator; b. Dülmen, Germany, July 15, 1956; s. Johann Josef and Emy Bernadette (Gelshefarth) H. MD, U. Ulm, Germany, 1986, DMD, 1988; PhD, U. Goettingen, Germany, 1995. Diplomate German Bd. Plastic and Reconstructive Surgery. Resident U. Ulm, 1985-86, U. Würzburg, Germany, 1986-88; sr. resident U. Goettingen, 1989-93, instr. in plastic and reconstructive surgery, 1992, cons. in plastic and reconstructive surgery, 1993, clin. prof., chief plastic and reconstructive surgery, 1995; clin. prof. U Hosp. Med. Sch. Goettingen, 1999; prof., chief dept. craniofacial plastic surgery Paracelsus Clinic, Hannover, 2004. Lectr. craniofacial and plastic surgery U. Med. Sch. Goettingen, 1993-94; gen. mgr. Medline Pub., 1992. Author numerous books and more than 200 articles; editor, author: Plastic Surgery, 1994, Aesthetic Surgery, 2000; inventor multi-point contact osteosynthesis plate; patentee in field. Mem. Art Collection, Goettingen, 1991; founder Bernhard Rosevelt Gelschefarth Soc., Germany 1996. Mem. German Soc. Plastic and Reconstructive Surgery, Am. Soc. Plastic and Reconstructive Surgery, NY Acad. Sci., German Soc. Craniofacial Osteology (chmn. 1994-97), European Assn. Aesthetic Plastic Facial Surgeons (pres. 1997-2000). Avocations: painting, music, skydiving, horseback riding. Office: Univ Hosp Med Sch Robert Koch Str 40 37075 Göttingen Germany Office Phone: 49-511-450-3012.

HOENIG, MICHEL RAYMOND, cardiovascular physician, researcher; b. Homs, Syria, Oct. 24, 1980; s. Thomas Hoenig and Maha Aji. BS in Biomed. Sci.; MD, U. Queensland, Brisbane, Australia, 2004; PhD, U. Queensland, 2011. Lic. Mbbs Med. Bd. Queensland, 2005, cert. Med. Bd. Australia, 2010, lic. Med. Bd. Australia, 2010. Nat. Health and Med. Rsch. Coun. med. postgrad. scholar U. Queensland, 2006—11. Achievements include patents pending for novel therapies to induce angiogenesis to treat coronary disease, ischemic stroke and other vascular diseases; research in customizing lipid lowering therapy to a patient's cholesterol metabolism phenotype; etiology of diastolic heart failure. Home: 3 Sherman St 4061 Brisbane QLD Australia Office: The Aufred Hosp Dept Surgery PO Box 315 Prahran Melborne Australia Personal E-mail: drmhoenig@yahoo.com.au.

HOEPFNER, MARK THOMAS, surgeon; s. John J. and Phyllis A. Hoepfner; m. Kristina Sue Holman, Oct. 8, 1983; children: Matthew, Alicia. BS in Chemistry cum laude, Seattle U., 1977; BS in Biochemistry, U. Wash., Seattle, 1978, MD, 1982. Resident in gen. surgery Mayo Clinic, Rochester, Minn., 1982—88, fellow in gastroenterology, 1985—86; ptnr. Berliner, Rayfield, Hoepfner, Las Vegas, 1988—97; pres. Surgeons Chartered, Las Vegas, 1997—. Dir. med. adv. bd. Nev. Early Breast and Cervical Cancer Detection Program, Las Vegas, 1997—99; chief dept. gen. surgery Sunrise Hosp., Las Vegas, 1999—2005. Contbr. articles to profl. jours. Mem. Women's Health Connection, Las Vegas, 1997—2006; med. advisor Susan G. Komen Found., Las Vegas, 1998—2006. Recipient Physician's Recognition award, AMA, 1999—; named one of Our Best Doctors, Las Vegas Life Mag., 2004, Am.'s Top Surgeons, Consumers Rsch. Coun. Am., 2002—10. Fellow: ACS (licentiate; cancer liaison physician 1993—), Southwestern Surg. Congress (licentiate); mem.: Am. Bd. Surgery (licentiate; diplomate), Priestly Soc. Mayo Clinic (licentiate). Avocations: reading, languages, food and wine. Office: Surgeons Chtd 700 Shadow Ln Ste 335 Las Vegas NV 89106 Office Phone: 702-382-6591. E-mail: mhoepfner@aol.com. *

HOERSTRUP, SIMON PHILIPP, medical educator; With Tex. Heart Inst., Baylor Coll., Houston, 1992, Harvard Med. Sch., Boston, 1993; rsch. fellow Children's Hosp., Boston, 1994; cardiovascular resident Univ. Hosp., Zurich, Switzerland, 1995—98; post-doctoral rsch. fellowship Children's Hosp., Harvard Med. Sch., Boston, 1998—99; mem. Clinic for Cardiovascular Surgery, U. Hosp., Zurich, Switzerland, 2000—; asst. prof., cardiac surgery U. Hosp., Zurich, Switzerland. Spkr. in field. Contbr. articles to profl. jours.; refereed jour. publications. Mem.: Cardiothoracic Surgery Network, European Assn. for Cardio-Thoracic Surgery. Address: Raemistrasse 100 CH 8091 ZURICH 8091 Zurich CH Switzerland Office: Eindhoven Univ Tech Biomedical Engring Material Tech Po Box 513 Wh 4-145 5600 MB Eindhoven Netherlands Office Phone: 31 40 247 2920, 41 1 255 3801. Office Fax: 31 40 244 7355, 41 1 255 4369. Business E-Mail: s.p.hoerstrup@tue.nl, simon_philipp.hoerstrup@chi.usz.ch.

HOEY, HILARY MARIE CONSTANCE VICTORIA, pediatrics educator; b. Dublin, Apr. 29, 1946; d. Raphael John and Gladys Cynthia (Breen) Hoey; m. Peter Harris, Jan. 20, 1982; children: Raphline Gladys, Peter Raphael. MB, BCh, BAO, Univ. Coll., Dublin, 1971, diploma in child health, 1974; MRCPI, Royal Coll. Physicians, Dublin, 1979, FRCPI (hon.), 1992; MD, Trinity Coll., Dublin, 1988, MA (hon.), 1992, FTCD, 1994. Cert. med. pediatrician, pediatric endocrinologist. Sr. house officer Rotunda Hosp., Dublin, 1974; sr. registrar Hosp. for Sick Children, London, 1980-82; fellow in pediatric endocrinology U. Calif., San Francisco, 1982; lectr. in pediatrics Trinity Coll., 1983-87, prof. pediatrics, 1991—; cons. pediatrician Nat. Children's Hosp., Dublin, 1991—, also bd. govs.; pediatric endocrinologist Our Lady's Hosp. Crumlin, Dublin, 1991—. Mem. gov. bd. and coun. Trinity Coll., 1992—; mem. Postgrad. Med. and Dental Bd., 1992—, Tallaght Regional Hosp. Bd., 1993—; med. dir. Adelaide and Meath Hosp. Dublin, 1996—. Author, editor: Paediatric Nephro-Urology, 1989; contbr. articles to med. jours., booklets. Recipient Irish Dir. Euro Growth Study award EEC, 1991—, Best Rsch. Paper award (edn. sect.) Brit. Diabetic Assn, 1992. Fellow Royal Coll. Physicians Ireland (guest lectr. 1992), Royal Coll. Medicine, Royal Acad. Medicine (coun. mem. 1994—); mem. Brit. Pediatric Assn. (regional advisor 1991—), European Soc. for Pediatric Endocrinology, Irish Paediatric Assn. (pres. 1995—). Avocations: tennis, gardening, old masters, music, golf. Home: Ivy House Main St Leixlip Co Kildare Ireland Office: Trinity Coll Dublin Dept Pediatrics Harcourt St Dublin 2 Ireland E-mail: hhoeydge@lndigo.ie.

HOFER, SUSANNE, retired clinical nurse; b. Berne, Switzerland, Dec. 2, 1944; d. Walter and Hermine (Keller) H. RN, Lindenhof Berne, 1968; BS, Zurich U., 1981; MS, Kaderschule U., 1989. Nurse Linderhofspital, 1968—70, Inselspital, Berne, 1968-72, nurse ICU, 1972—81, nurse, sta. head, 1985-89, clin. nurse specialist, 1989—, nurse, sta. head, 1985-89, clin. nurse specialist, 1989—2006; ret., 2006. Tchg. asst. nursing sch. Lindenhof, Berne, 1982-84. Contbr. articles to profl. jours. Maj. Swiss Army Med. Corps, 1972-96. Mem. Swiss Nurses Assn. Avocations: reading, hiking, classical music.

HOFF, JAN, physiologist, educator; b. Trondheim, Norway, Oct. 28, 1949; s. William and Borghild Hoff; m. Kari Værnes, July 1, 1972; children: Thomas, Joakim. PhD, Norwegian Univ. of Sci. Tech, 2000. Rector, dean Coll. of Sports, Trondheim, Norway, 1980—90; assoc. prof. Dept. Sports Sciences, Trondheim, Norway, 1990—2000. Pres. Alpine Skiing Fedn., Norway, 1985—89. Lt. His Majesty the Kings Guard, 1972—75, Oslo, Norway. Mem.: Am. Coll. Sports Medicine (assoc.). Achievements include research in strength effects on work efficiency; training as treatment in inactivity related diseases. Office: Norwegian Univ of Sci and Tech Medicine Olav Kyrres gt 3 Trondheim NO-7489 Norway Personal E-mail: jan.hoff@ntnu.no.

HOFFER, ALMA JEANNE, nursing educator; b. Dalhart, Tex., Sept. 15, 1932; d. James A. and Mildred (Zimlich) Koehler; m. John L. Hoffer, Oct. 7, 1954; children: John Jr., James Leo, Joseph V., Jerome P. BS, Bradley U., 1970; MA, W. Va. Coll. Grad. Study Inst., 1975; EdD, Ball State U., 1981, MA, 1986. Reg. Nurse. Staff nurse St Joseph Hosp., South Bend, Ind., 1958-59, Holy Cross Cen. Sch., St Joseph Hosp., South Bend, 1959-63; sch. nurse South Bend Sch. Corp., 1970-72; faculty staff Morris Harvey Coll., Charleston, W.Va., W.Va. Inst. Tech., Montgomery, 1975-76; asst. prof. Ball State U., Ind., 1976-77, Ind. U.-Purdue U., Ft. Wayne, 1977-81; assoc. prof. U. Akron, Ohio, 1981-83, 91-95, asst. dean, grad. edn. Ohio, 1983-90, assoc. prof. Ohio, 1991-93; prof., chair Dept. of Nursing St. Francis Coll., Fort Wayne, Ind., 1993-95; prin. investigator rsch. project Well Begun is Well Done Children's Med. Ctr. Women's Bd. Akron, 1995-96; coord. parish nurse St. Hilary Ch., 2001—. Trustee Akron Child Guidance, 1983-88, 89-95, chair planning com., 1988; nursing Blick Clin., Akron, 1988; educator, coord. parish nurses Internat. Parish Nurse Resource Ctr., 2003—; rsch. cons. St. Joseph Hosp., Ohio, 1989; cons. Health Sense, 1996-98; online faculty U. Phoenix, 2005—; rschr., presenter in field. Contbg. author: Family Health Promotion Theories and Assessment, 1989, Nursing Connections, 1992. Task force mem. Gov. Celeste's Employee Assistance Program for State U. Campuses, Ohio, 1983-84, del. People to People Citizen Amb. Program to Europe, 1988; mem. health and wellness com., coord. St. Hilary Parish; parish nurse educator Internat. Parish Nurse Resource Ctr., St. Louis, 2004—. Mem. Midwest Nursing Rsch. Soc., Transcultural Nursing Soc. (chair certification and recertification com. 2006—, Leininger Leadership award 2002, 05), Cleve. Country Club, Sigma Theta Tau. Republican. Roman Catholic. Avocations: tennis, golf, skiing. Office: PO Box 794 Bath OH 44210-0794

HOFFER, JOHN LEE, anesthesiologist, medical educator and anesthesia, parioperative systems developer; BS, LeTourneau U., 1955; PhD in Biomed. Engring., U. NC, Chapel Hill; MD, U. NC, 1976. Diplomate Am. Bd. Anesthesiology, Am. Bd. Quality Assurance and Utilization Rev. Physicians. Resident anesthesiology U. N.C. Hosps.; assoc. prof. anesthesiology Ohio State U., 1979—83, assoc. prof. biomed. engring., 1979—83; assoc. prof. anesthesiology and physiology Northeastern Ohio U. Coll. Medicine, 1984—92; prof. engring. Tex. A&M U., 1992—2009; prof. anesthesiology Tex. A&M U. Health Sci. Ctr., Coll. Medicine, 1992—2009, emeritus prof., 2009—. Chmn. dept. anesthesiology libr. com., Scott & White Clinics, mem. quality assurance com., mem. instnl. rev. bd., mem. tenure and faculty promotion com. predoctoral. Predoctoral fellow, NIH. Office: Dept Anesthesiology 2401 S 31st St Temple TX 76508 Office Phone: 254-724-2407.

HOFFMAN, CHARLES LOUIS, physician; b. Dayton, Ohio, May 10, 1925; s. Hugh Holland and Ruth Louise (Thiele) H.; m. Nancy Adele Fahrendorf, June 14, 1947; children: Thomas C., Mary Lynne Hoffman Lamb, Lori Hoffman Brustkern, William Edward. Student, U. Dayton, 1943; AB, Oberlin Coll., Ohio, 1945; MD, St. Louis U., 1949. Med. intern US Marine Hosp., Balt., 1949-50, chief op. dept. Kirkwood, Mo., 1950-51; chief med. officer 2nd Coast Guard Dist., St. Louis, 1951; resident internal medicine US Marine Hosp., San Francisco, 1951-53, chief resident internal medicine, 1953-54, asst. chief internal medicine, 1954-55; pvt. practice internal medicine Marin County, Calif., 1955-92; cons. internal medicine and pulmonology Neumiller Hosp., Tamal, Calif., 1957-83; active staff Marin Gen. Hosp., 1955—92; chief of med. staff Ross Gen. Hosp., Calif., 1969. Exec. com. Ross Gen. Hosp., 1968-71, 82-88; med. dir. Rafael Convalescent Hosp., 1987—; med. coord. Regional Cancer Found., San Francisco, 1992-2004; co-founder Med. Ins. Exch. Calif., 1975. Knighted, Sovereign Mil. Order of St. John of Jerusalem, 1992. Fellow AMA, Calif. Med. Assn.; mem. Calif. Soc. Internal Medicine (bd. dirs. 1976-79), Marin Med. Soc. (pres. 1975-76, bd. dirs. 1966-69, 74-77, 88—), Calif. Acad. Medicine, Serra Club of Marin (pres. 1961), Gen. Soc. Mayflower Descendants, Calif. Soc. Mayflower Descendants, Internat. Med. Assn. Lourdes, Elks (Man of Yr. in the Healing Arts 1976). Republican. Roman Catholic. Avocations: swimming, scuba diving, bridge, backgammon. Home: 48 Junipero Serra Ave San Rafael CA 94901-2320 Home Phone: 415-456-0664. Personal E-mail: chasmd@att.net.

HOFFMAN, ELMER, surgeon; b. Balt., Sept. 5, 1921; MD, Johns Hopkins U., 1944. Diplomate Am. Bd. Surgery. Intern Sinai Hosp., Balt., 1944-45, resident in gen. surgery, 1948—52, resident in pathology, 1948, mem. staff Greater Balt. Med. Ctr., 1952—94; chief surgeon Wright Patterson Air Force Gen. Hosp., 1945—47; mem. staff Harbor Hosp., 1952-94, Johns Hopkins U., Balt., 1954-94, N.W. Hosp. Ctr., 1972-94, chief surg. surgeon, 1983-94, emeritus, 1994—; asst. prof. surgery emeritus Johns Hopkins Sch. Medicine, 1994—. Cons. quality assurance N.W. Hosp. Ctr. Capt. USAF, 1945—47. Fellow ACS, Am. Geriatric Soc., Southeastern Surg. Congress; mem. Soc. Am. Gastrointestinal Endoscopic Surgeons. Home: 41 River Oaks Cir Baltimore MD 21208-6358 Fax: 410-484-0595. *

HOFFMAN, ERIC P., medical geneticist, educator; BA in Biology, Gettysburg Coll., 1982; PhD in Biology, Johns Hopkins U., 1986. Fellow & resident Harvard Med. Sch., 1986—88, Children's Hosp., Boston, 1986—88; dir. Rsch. Ctr. Genetic Med.; prof. pediatrics George Washington U. Children's Nat. Med. Ctr. Chmn. molecular genetics Children's Rsch. Inst.

HOFFMAN, JERRY IRWIN, retired dental educator; b. Chgo., Nov. 20, 1935; s. Irwin and Luba Hoffman; m. Sharon Lynn Seaman, Aug. 25, 1963; children: Steven Abram, Rachel Irene. Student, DePaul U., 1953-56; BS in Biology and Chemistry, Roosevelt U., 1956; DDS, Loyola U., Chgo., 1960; M of Health Care Adminstrn., Baylor U., 1972. Certificate, General Practice Residency, U.S. Army, 1978. Commd. officer U.S. Army, 1960 (served to 1962, returned 1964), advanced through grades to col., 1978, hdqrs. rep. local dental tng. confs. Europe Garmisch, Fed. Republic Germany, 1965-67; cons. to Comdg. Gen. U.S. Army Med. Research and Devel. Command, Washington, 1972-76; cons. Office of Surgeon Gen. U.S. Army, Washington, 1972-76, liaison rep. to Nat. Adv. Council and Oral Biology and Medicine Study Sessions of the Nat. Inst. Dental Research and NIH, 1973-76, resident in Gen. Practice Residency, 1976-78; comdg. officer U.S. Army Dental Activity, Fort Monmouth, NJ, 1979-82; ret., 1982; pvt. practice dentistry Chgo., 1962-64; assoc. prof. operative dentistry Loyola U. Sch. Dentistry, Maywood, Ill., 1982-93, dir. gen. practice residency, 1982-85, coordinator extramural dental resources, 1983-85, assoc. dean for clin. affairs, 1985-93; dir. sci. programs Chgo. Dental Soc., 1993—2002, ret., 2002. Staff dentist Silas B. Hayes Army Hosp., Fort Ord, Calif., 1976-79, Patterson Army Hosp., Ft. Monmouth, 1979-82; lectr., presenter seminars in field. Contbr. articles to profl. jours. Decorated Legion of Merit, Meritorious Svc. Medal with oak leaf cluster. Fellow: Am. Coll. Dentists, Internat. Coll. Dentists, Odontographic Soc.; master: Acad. Gen. Dentistry; mem. ADA, Ill. Dental Soc., Chgo. Dental Soc., Am. Assn. Dental Schs., Am. Soc. Assn. Execs., Assn. Healthcare Execs., Profl. Conv. Mgmt. Assn., Omicron Kappa Upsilon. Personal E-mail: ddscds@aol.com.

HOFFMAN, JOHN P., surgeon; MD, Case Western Res. U., 1970. Diplomate Am. Bd. Surgery. Resident in gen. surgery Va. Mason Hosp., Seattle; fellow in surg. oncology Meml. Sloan-Ketterong Cancer Ctr., NY, NY; chief pancreaticobiliary svc. Fox Chase Cancer Ctr. Mem.: Am. Coll. of Surgeons, Am. Soc. of Clin. Oncology. Office: Fox Chase Cancer Center 333 Cottman Ave Philadelphia PA 19111-2497 Office Phone: 215-728-6900.

HOFFMAN, JULIEN IVOR ELLIS, pediatrician, cardiologist, educator; b. Salisbury, So. Rhodesia, July 26, 1925; arrived in U.S., 1957, naturalized, 1967; s. Bernard Isaac and Minrose (Bermant) H.; m. Kathleen (Lewis), 1986; children: Anna, Daniel. BS, U. Witwaterstrand, Johannesburg, South Africa, 1944, BSc (hon.), 1945, MB, BCh, 1949, MD, 1970. Intern, resident internal medicine, South Africa, 1950-56; rsch. asst., postgrad. Med. Sch., London, 1956-57; fellow pediatric cardiology Boston Children's Hosp., 1957-59; fellow Cardiovasc. Rsch. Inst., San Francisco, 1959-60; asst. prof. pediat., internal medicine Albert Einstein Coll., NYC, 1962-66; assoc. prof. pediat. U. Calif., San Francisco, 1966-70, prof., 1970-94, prof. physiology, 1981-88, prof. emeritus, 1994—. Sr. mem. Cardiovasc. Rsch. Inst. U. Calif., San Francisco, 1966—; mem. bd. examiners, sub-bd. pediat. cardiology Am. Bd. Pediat., 1973—78, sub-bd. pediat. intensive care, 1985—87; chmn. Louis Katz Award Com., Basic Sci. Coun., Am. Heart Assn., 1973—74, George Brown Meml. lectr., 1977; George Alexander Gibson Meml. lectr. Royal Coll. Physicians (Edinburgh), 1978; Lilly lectr. Royal Coll. Physicians (London), 1981; Isaac Starr lectr. Cardiac Systems Dynamics Soc., England, 1982, John Keith lectr., 85; Disting. Physiology lectr. Am. Coll. Chest Physicians, 1985; Nadas lectr. Am. Heart Assn., 1987; 1st Donald C. Fyler lectr. Children's Hosp., Boston, 1990; 1st MacDonald Dick lectr. U. Mich., Ann Arbor; Kreidberg lectr. Med. Sch. Tufts U., 2004; Tabatznik lectr. Mt. Sinai Hosp., Balt., 2005; Bristow lectr. Oreg. Health Scis. U., Portland, 2007. Author: Natural and Unnatural History of Congenital Heart Disease, 2009; co-editor: Rudolph's Pediatrics, 1982—96, Coronary Circulation, 1990, Recent Advances in the Coronary Circulation, 1993, Pediatric Cardiovascular Medicine, 2000. Recipient Bayer Cardiovasc. Mentor award, 1989. Fellow Royal Coll. Physicians; mem. World Congress Pediat. Cardiology and Cardiac Surgery (hon. joint pres. Paris 1993), Am. Physiol. Soc., Am. Pediatric Soc., Soc. Pediatric Rsch. Achievements include extensive research into congenital heart disease and coronary blood flow. Home: 925 Tiburon Blvd Belvedere Tiburon CA 94920-1525 Personal E-mail: jichoffmen@gmail.com Business E-Mail: julien.hoffman@ucsf.edu.

HOFFMAN, LLOYD ALAN, plastic surgeon; b. NYC, Apr. 16, 1952; MD, Northwestern U., Evanston, Ill., 1978. Diplomate Am. Bd. Plastic Surgery with subspecialty in hand surgery, Am. Bd. Surgery. Intern N.Y. Hosp., NYC, resident in gen. surgery; resident in microsurgery NYU, NYC, resident in plastic surgery, fellow in hand surgery; chief divsn. plastic surgery N.Y. Hosp./Cornell U., NYC, 1987—98; chief combined plastic surgery program Cornell and Columbia Univs., NYC, 1998—, assoc. prof. plastic surgery. Named one of Top Doctors in NY, NY mag. Achievements include targeting the interface between a limb allograft and the recipient immune system, the effect of cyclosporin A on the migration and distribution of dendritic cells in the transplanted rat limb and experiments on craniofacial synostosis. Office: 12A East 68th St New York NY 10065 Office Phone: 212-861-1640. Fax: 212-452-5125.

HOFFMAN, MARY CATHERINE, retired nurse, anesthetist; b. Winamac, Ind., July 14, 1923; d. Harmon William Whitney and Dessie Maude (Neely) Hoffman. RN, Meth. Hosp., Indpls., 1945; cert. obstet. analgesia and anesthesia, Johns Hopkins Hosp., 1949; grad., Cleve. Sch. Anesthesia, 1952. Staff nurse Meth. Hosp., 1945-49; rsch. asst., then staff anesthetist Johns Hopkins Hosp., 1949-62; staff anesthetist Meth. Hosp., 1962-64, U. Chgo. Hosps., 1964-66; chief nurse anesthetist Paris (Ill.) Cmty. Hosp., 1966-80; staff anesthetist Hendricks County Hosp., Danville, Ind., Ball Meml. Hosp., Muncie, Ind., 1981-86; ret. Mem. Am. Assn. Nurse Anesthetists, Am. Heart Assn., Ind. Fedn. Bus. and Profl. Women's Clubs (Ill. dist. chmn. 1977-78, state found. chmn. 1978-79, Found. award 1979). Republican. Presbyterian. Home: 1700 N Maddox Dr Muncie IN 47304-2674 *

HOFFMAN, PAUL JEROME, psychologist, statistician; b. San Francisco, June 25, 1923; s. Louis and Bessie (Brodofsky) H.; m. Elaine Stroll, Mar. 18, 1944; children: Valerie, Elizabeth, Jonathan. BA in Exptl. Psychology, Stanford U., 1949, PhD in Psychology and Statistics, 1954. Diplomate Am. Coll. Forensic Examiners, Am. Bd. Psychol. Specialties; lic. psychologist, Oreg., Calif. Asst. prof. Wash. State U., Pullman, 1953-57, U. Oreg., Eugene, 1957-60, adj. prof., 1967-76; prin. Paul J. Hoffman Assocs., San Carlos, Calif., 1985—; pres. Magic7 Software Co., Los Altos, Calif., 1985-98, Paul J. Hoffman Psychometrics, Inc., Los Altos, Calif., 1978-83. Cons. Am. Airlines, Dallas, 1990, 91, Nat. Heart, Lung and Blood Inst. NIH, Bethesda, Md., 1978, Am. Assn. State Psychol. Bds. Nat. Exam. Com., N.Y.C., 1972-78; prof. dept. adminstrv. sci. U.S. Naval Post-grad. Sch., Monterey, Calif., 1981-84; consulting psychologist Hewlett Packard Co., Palo Alto, Calif., 1981-83; vis. disting. prof. psychology U. Hawaii, Honolulu, 1978; testing cons. Nat. Bd. Med. Examiners and Am. Bd. Internal Medicine, Phila., 1971-72; pres., founder Oreg. Rsch. Inst., Eugene, 1960-77. Author: (with others) Decision Processes, 1954, Formal Representation of Human Judgement, 1968, Computer Aided Decision Analysis, 1993, Expert Evidence: A Practitioner's Guide to Law, Science and the FJC Manual, 1997; contbr. 53 articles to profl. jours. Chair fgn. policy Dem. Ctrl. Com., Oreg., 1960-72; advisor Sen. Wayne Morse, Oreg., 1964-70; chmn. Bob Straub for Gov. Com., Oreg., 1974. Lt. USAF, 1942-46. Grantee NIH, 1958-77, NSF, 1961-63. Fellow AAAS, APA, Psychonomic Soc., Psychometric Soc., Human Factors Soc.; mem. Am. Statis. Assn., Oreg. Psychol. Assn. (pres. 1962-63), Oreg. Inventors Coun., Am. Coll. Forensic Examiners. Achievements include copyrights for expert systems software, consensus building software. Home: 1120 Royal Ln San Carlos CA 94070-4277 E-mail: paul.hoffman@mindspring.com.

HOFFMAN, RONALD A., otolaryngologist, educator; PhD, U. Wis., 1969; MD, Jefferson Med. Coll, 1971. Diplomate Am. Bd Otolaryngology. Resident in otolaryngology NYU Med. Ctr., 1973—76; fellow in otology and neurology Lenox Hill Hosp., NYC, 1976—77; prof. otolaryngology Yeshiva Univ.; dir. rhinology and endoscopic sinus surgery Beth Israel MEd. Ctr.; chief divsn. of otology NY Eye and Ear Infirmary. Office: New York Eye and Era Infirmary 310 E 14th St New York NY 10003 Office Phone: 212-979-4000.

HOFFMAN, SEYMOUR SOL, psychologist; b. NYC, Aug. 27, 1934; s. Isidore and Gussie Hoffman; m. Betty Klarberg Hoffman, Aug. 25, 1963; children: Daniel, David, Miriam. BA, Yeshiva U., 1956, MA, 1958; PhD, Heed U., 1971. Cert. clin. psychology supr., psychotherapy and psychodiagnostics, family therapy supr. Psychology intern Cumberland Hosp., Bklyn., 1960—61, staff psychologist, 1962—66; sch. psychologist Bur. Child Guidance, Bklyn., 1961—62; sr. psychologist Kings County Hosp., Bklyn., 1966—78; clin. asst. prof. psychology Downstate Med. Sc., Bklyn., 1970—78; sr. psychologist Kaplan Med. Ctr., Rehovot, Israel, 1979—80, 1994—2000, Barzilai Hosp., Ashkelon, Israel, 1980—83, Cmty. Mental Health Ctr., Rishon Lezion, Israel, 1980—94; sr. psychologist Student Counseling Svc. Bar-Ilan U., Israel, 1983—97; sr. psychologist Cmty. Mental Health Ctr., Rehovot, 1997—2000; pvt. practice, 1994—. Instr. Moreshet Yaacov Tchr.'s Coll., Rehovot, 1999—; supervising psychologist Mayenei Hayeshua Med. Ctr., 2007—. Co-author: Cotherapy with Individuals, Families, and Groups, 1994, Innovative Intervention in Psychotherapy, 2006; editor: Issues in Psychology, Psychotherapy and Judaism, 2007; author: Two Are Better Than One: Case Studies of Brief Effective Therapy, 2011, Mental Health Psychotherapy & Judaism, 2011; contbr. articles to profl. jours. Mem.: Israel Assn. Marital and Family Therapy, Israel Psychol. Assn. Avocations: sports, music, reading. Personal E-mail: batya_ho@netvision.net.il.

HOFFMAN, TIMOTHY J., chemist, educator; b. St. Louis, Apr. 25, 1958; PhD, U. Mo., 1996. Prof. chemistry U. Mo., Columbia, 2007, nuc. sci. & engring. prof., 2004, internal medicine prof., 2001; rsch. scientist US Dept. Vet. Affairs, 1981—. Dir. Va. Biomolecular Imaging Ctr., US Dept. Veterans Affairs, 2003. Mem.: AAUP, Internat. Soc. Radiopharmaceutical Scis., Soc. Molecular Imaging, Am. Chem. Soc., Soc. Nuc. Medicine. Office: Harry S Truman Memorial VA Hosp 800 Columbia MO 65201-5275 Business E-Mail: hoffmant@health.missouri.edu.

HOFFMAN, WILLIAM YANES, plastic surgeon, educator; b. Rochester, NY, Feb. 25, 1952; MD, U. Rochester, 1977. Cert. Am. Bd. Surgery, 1985, Am. Bd. Plastic Surgery, 1987. Intern gen. surgery U. Calif. Affiliated Hosps., San Francisco, 1977—78, resident plastic surgery, 1978—80, 1981—83, resident craniofacial surgery, 1980—81, 1984—85; fellow NYU Med. Ctr., NYC, 1985—86; plastic surgeon, chief Divsn. Plastic and Reconstructive Surgery, dir. Plastic Surgery Residency Program U. Calif. San Francisco Med. Ctr.; also prof. plastic surgery U. Calif., San Francisco. Office: U Calif Med Ctr 350 Parnassus Ave, Ste 509 San Francisco CA 94143 also: 505 Parnassus Ave, Ste M-593 San Francisco CA 94143-0932 Office Phone: 415-353-4287. Office Fax: 415 353 4330. Business E-Mail: william.hoffman@ucsfmedctr.org.

HOFFMANN, INGE SCHNEIER, psychologist, educator; b. Vienna, Jan. 16, 1929; came to U.S., 1940; d. Josef Michael Schneier and Szerena Susan Löffelholz; m. Stanley Harry Hoffmann, Oct. 6, 1963. BA, Bard Coll., Annandale-on-Hudson, NY, 1950; MA, Harvard U., Cambridge, Mass., 1953. Lic. clin. psychologist, Mass. Lectr., asst. to dir. Social Sci. Found. U. Denver, 1953-54; rsch. assoc., assoc. dir. rsch. AIR, Inc., 1954-56; rsch. assoc. Ctr. for Internat. Studies, MIT, 1956-59; lectr. Harvard Coll., 1970-76; lectr. psychology, dept. psychiatry Harvard U. Med. Sch., Cambridge Hosp., 1976—. Faculty assoc. Currier House, Harvard U., 1970—, mem. group on study of violence Med. Sch., 2004— Co-author: Coercive Persuasion, 1961, DeGaulle, Artiste de la Politique, 1973; contbr. articles to profl. jours.; patentee design of art fabrics. Active in mediating Palestinian-Israeli conflict, 1976—; mem. Lifton Study Group on Mass Violence, 2004—. Recipient painting awards Mus. of Modern Art, others; Bard scholar Schepp Found., N.Y., 1947, 48, 49, 50; Radcliffe Inst. scholar Harvard U., 1970, 71, 72. Mem. Cambridge Art Assn., Harvard U. Shop Club, Boston Psychoanalytic Inst. (friend, collaborator 1972-89), Internat. Soc. Polit. Psychology (founding mem. 1987—). Avocations: lieder singing, painting. Office: 91 Washington Ave Cambridge MA 02140-2716 Personal E-mail: ingeshoffmann@gmail.com. Business E-Mail: ish1@comcast.net.

HOFFMANN, JÖRG CARL, physician; MD, U. Heidelberg, 1990. Bd. cert. for internal medicine, gastroenterology & hepatology & rheumatology. Applied Immunology rsch. fellow German Cancer Rsch. Ctr., Heidelberg, Germany, 1990—92; resident internal medicine Hannover Med. Sch., 1992—96, U. Saarland, Homburg, Germany, 1997—2001; sr. registrar for gastroenterology & hepatology Charite, Berlin, 2001—07, head ctrl. endoscopy, 2005—07; chief divsn. gastroenterology, diabetes care, rheumatology, oncology St. Mary's Hosp., Ludwigshafen, Germany, 2007—. Contbr. articles to profl. jours. Recipient IBD Rsch. award Ludwig Demling, Germany, 2000. Mem. Anglo-German Med. Soc., German Soc. Immunology, German Soc. Digestive and Metabolic Disorders, German Soc. Internal Medicine. Office: Medizinische Klinik I St Marien Krankenhaus 67067 Ludwigshafen Germany

HOFFMANN, JULES ALPHONSE, research scientist; b. Echternach, Luxembourg, Aug. 2, 1941; married; 2 children. PhD in Natural Sci., U. Strasbourg, France, 1963; MD (hon.), U. Munich, 2006. Rsch. asst. Nat. Ctr. Sci. Rsch. (CNRS), France, 1964—68, rsch. assoc., 1969—73; postdoc. tng. Inst. Physiol. Chemistry, Philipps U. Marburg, Germany, 1973—74; rsch. dir. CNRS, 1974—, dir. Lab. Gen. Biology, U. Louis Pasteur Strasbourg, 1978—2005, dir. Inst. Molecular & Cellular Biology, 1993—2005. Author: Progress in Ecdysone Research, 1980, Biosynthesis, Metabolism and Mode of Action of Invertebrate Hormones, 1985, Cellular and Molecular Aspects of Insect Immunity, 1990, Phylogenetic Perspectives in Immunity: The Insect Host Defense, 1994; co-editor: Innate Immunity, 2002; contbr. articles to profl. jours. Mem. steering com. Ctr. Excellence Insect Sci., Japan, 1996—2001. Recipient Sandoz-Wander prize, 1978, Pergamon prize, 1980, Alexander von Humboldt Found. award, Germany, 1984, William B. Coley award, Cancer Rsch. Inst., 2003, Grand prize, Found. Med. Rsch. France, 2004, Robert Koch prize for Immunology, 2004, Gairdner Internat. award, Gairdner Found., Can., 2011; co-recipient Balzan prize, Internat. Balzan Prize Found., 2007, Shaw Found. prize in Life Sci./Medicine, Hong Kong, 2011. Mem.: NAS (fgn. assoc.), Academia Europaea, American Acad. Arts. & Scis., Russian Acad. Scis., European Molecular Biology Orgn., German Acad. Scis. Leopoldina, French Nat. Acad. Scis. (pres. 2007—08, Grand Prix Joannidès 1992). Office: Institut de Biologie Moleculaire et Cellulaire 15 Rue Rene Descartes 67084 Strasbourg France Office Fax: 33+ (0)3 88 60 69 22. Business E-Mail: J.Hoffmann@ibmc.u-strasbg.fr. *

HOFFMANN, LOUIS GERHARD, immunologist, educator; b. Bloemendaal, Netherlands, July 12, 1932; arrived in U.S., 1950; s. Gerhard Hendrik and Louise Gertrude (Tobi) Hoffmann; m. Georgianna Grace Stracke, Nov. 4, 1955; children: Julianna Tobi, Eugenie Claire. BA with honors, distinction, Wesleyan U., 1953; MSc in Hygiene, Johns Hopkins U., 1958, ScD, 1960. Diplomate Am. Bd. Sexology. NSF postdoctoral fellow U. Calif., Berkeley, 1960-62; from instr. to asst. prof. microbiology Johns Hopkins U., Balt., 1962-64; asst. prof. U. Iowa, Iowa City, 1964-67, assoc. prof., 1967-74, prof., 1974-96; ret., 1997; pvt. practice sex therapy team, 1978—. Contbr. articles to profl. jours. Mem. Dem. Ctrl. Com., Johnson County, Iowa, 1966—76. Grantee, NIH, 1964—67, 1980—83, NSF, 1968—74, Iowa Heart Assn., 1969—72, 1977—79, Damon Runyon Meml. Fund, 1972—74; fellow, NIH, 1962—63. Home: 4 Timberwick Rd Santa Fe NM 87508

HOFFMANN, TORSTEN, chemist, researcher; b. Cologne, Germany, Nov. 19, 1967; s. Hans-Joachim and Gisela Hoffmann; m. Fabienne Emery, July 30, 1999; 1 child, David Jerome; 1 child, Anais Sophie. MSc in Chemistry, Heinrich Heine U., Düsseldorf, Germany, 1992; PhD, Swiss Fed. Inst. Tech., Zurich, 1996. Dir. enabling scis. F. Hoffmann-La Roche, Basel, Switzerland, 2003—04, dir. chem. rsch., 2005—. Adv. bd. mem. dept. chemistry U. Basel, Switzerland. Fellow, Studienstiftung des deutschen Volkes, Germany, 1989—92, Fonds der Chemischen Industrie, Germany, 1993—95, Alexander von Humboldt Found., Germany, 1996. Fellow: Studienstiftung des deutschen Volkes; mem.: Am. Coll. Surgeons, Elsevier Beilstein Database (adv. bd.), Swiss Chemical Soc. (assoc.). Achievements include over 60 patents and pulication in field; invention of co-inventor of befetupitant and netupitant, 2 pharmacologically active, new chemical entities which have entered human clinical trials. Home: Kleinhüninger Strasse 15 Weil am Rhein 79576 Germany Office: F Hoffmann-La Roche Grenzacherstrasse 124/92/8.88 Basel 4070 Switzerland Office Fax: 41-61-6888367. Business E-Mail: torsten.hoffmann@roche.com.

HOFFNER, PAMELA, director emergency preparedness; b. Md. BSN, U. Md., 1977; MSN, Vanderbilt U., 1988. Dir. emergency preparedness Vanderbilt U. Med. Ctr., 2003—, adj. instr. nursing, Sch. Nursing, 2007—11. Mem.: Assn. Contingency Planners, Internat. Assn. Emergency Mgrs. Office: 1161 21st Ave S B-0312 MCN Nashville TN 37232 Business E-Mail: pam.hoffner@vanderbilt.edu.

HOFKIN, GERALD ALAN, gastroenterologist; b. Balt., July 4, 1936; AB, MA, Johns Hopkins U., 1957; MD, U. Md., 1961; MBA, Johns Hopkins U., 2003. Diplomate Am. Bd. Internal Medicine, Am. Bd. Gastroenterology. Intern U. Md. Hosp., Balt., 1961, resident in medicine, 1962-63, 64-65, Sinai Hosp., Balt., 1963-64, 65-66; resident in gastroenterology Letterman Hosp., San Francisco, 1966-67; pvt. practice Balt., 1969-91, Woodholme Gastroenterology Assocs., Balt., 1999—; staff Sinai Hosp., Balt., 1991-99. Chmn. med. exec. com. Sinai Hosp. Med. Staff, Balt., 1989, pres., 1992-93; surveyor Accreditation Assn. Ambulatory Health Care, 2008-. Contbr. articles to profl. jours. Maj. US Army, 1966—69. Decorated Army Commendation medal. Fellow ACP, Am. Coll. Gastroenterology; mem. Am. Soc. Gastroenterol. Endoscopy, Md. Soc. Gastrointesinal Endoscopy (pres. 1995-97), Balt. Amateur Radio Club (v.p. 1978-79), Balt. Radio Amateur TV Soc., Alpha Omega Alpha. Avocations: amateur radio, antiques, history, computers. Office: Woodholme Gastroenterology 2411 W Belvedere Ave Ste 308 Baltimore MD 21215-5230 Home: 707 York Rd 7330 Towson MD 21204-2928 Office Phone: 410-367-9600.

HOFLING-LIMA, ANA LUISA, ophthalmologist, educator; b. Sao Paulo, Aug. 21, 1955; Doutorado, U. Fed. de São Paulo, 1989, Livre Docente, 2000. Head prof. Fed. U. São Paulo, 2004—. Bd. dirs. Internat. Coun. Ophthalmology, 2008—. Recipient Achievement award, AAO. Mem.: Pan Am. Assn. Ophthalmology (pres. elect), Am. Acad. Ophthalmology. Office: Av Ibijau 331 - 4o andar São Paulo 04524.020 Brazil Office Fax: 5511.5055.9557. Business E-Mail: coftalmo@uol.com.br.

HOFMANN, ALAN FREDERICK, biomedical researcher, educator; b. Balt., May 17, 1931; s. Joseph Enoch and Nelda Rosina (Durr) Hofmann; m. Marta Gertrud Pettersson, Aug. 15, 1959 (div. 1976); children: Anthea Karin, Cecilia Rae; m. Helga Katharina Aicher, Nov. 3, 1978. BA with honors, Johns Hopkins U., 1951, MD with honors, 1955; MD, U. Lund, Sweden, 1965; MD (hon.), U. Bologna, Italy, 1988. Intern, resident dept. medicine Columbia Presbyn. Med. Ctr., NYC, 1955-57; clin. assoc. clin. ctr. Nat. Heart Inst., NIH, Bethesda, Md., 1957-59; postdoctoral fellow, dept. physiol. chemistry U. Lund, Sweden, 1959-62; asst. physician Hosp. Rockefeller U., NYC, 1962-64, assoc. physician, 1964-66; outpatient physician N.Y. Hosp., NYC, 1963-64; cons. in medicine, assoc. dir. gastroenterology unit Mayo Clinic, Rochester, Minn., 1966-77; prof. medicine, attending physician Med. Ctr. U. Calif., San Diego, 1977-98, emeritus prof., 1998—. Asst. prof. dept. medicine Rockefeller U., NYC, 1964—66; assoc. prof. medicine and biochemistry U. Minn. Mayo Grad. Sch., 1966—69, assoc. prof. medicine and physiology, 1969—70, prof., 1970—73, Mayo Med. Sch., 1973—77; cons. physiology Mayo Clinic, Rochester, 1975—77; adj. prof. pharmacy U. Calif., San Francisco, 1986—94; vis. prof. U. Mich., Ann Arbor, 1980—85. Contbr. articles to profl. jours., chapters to books. Recipient Travel award, Wellcome Trust, 1961—63, NSF, 1964, Sr. Scientist award, Humboldt Found., Fed. Rep. Germany, 1976, 1991, Disting. Achievement award, Modern Medicine mag., 1978, Chancellor's Rsch. Excellence award, U. Calif., 1986, Disting. Alumnus award, Mayo Found., 2001, Disting. Mentor award, Found. Digestive Health Nutrition, 2004, Herbert Falk medal, Falk Found., 2010; co-recipient, 2010, Eppinger prize, 1976; Sr. fellow, NIH, 1986. Fellow: AAAS, Royal Soc. Medicine, Royal Coll. Physicians (hon.); mem.: Am. Gastroent. Assn. (Disting. Achievement award 1970, co-winner Beaumont prize 1979, Friedenwald medal 1994), Am. Physiol. Soc. (Horace Davenport medal 1996), Am. Liver Found., German Soc. Internal Medicine (hon.), German Soc. Digestive and Metabolic Disease (hon. Siegfried Thannhauser medal 1996), Brit. Soc. Gastroenterology (hon.), Gastroent. Soc. Australia (hon.), Swedish Soc. Gastroenterology (hon.), Soc. Gastrointestinal Radiology (hon.), Chilean Soc. Gastroenterology (hon.), Royal Flemish Acad. Medicine (hon.; fgn. corr. mem.), Serbian Soc. Medicine (hon.), Assn. Am. Physicians, Am. Soc. Clin. Investigation, Am. Assn. Study Liver Disease (Disting. Achievement award 1997), Sigma Xi, Phi Beta Kappa, Omicron Delta Kappa, Alpha Omega Alpha. Achievements include description and modelling of the enterohepatic circulation of bile acids; clarification of the multiple physiological roles of bile acids; conjugated bile acid replacement therapy for bile acid deficiency in short bowel syndrome; discovery of new vertebrate bile acids; structure-function relationships of bile acids; therapeutic uses of bile acids in liver, biliary and intestinal disease. Home: 5870 Cactus Way La Jolla CA 92037-7069 Personal E-mail: afhofmann@gmail.com.

HOFMANN, FRANZ, pharmacology and toxicology educator, researcher; b. Vienna, May 21, 1942; s. Ulrich and Renate (Schiebeler) H.; Heidelore Schultze, Mar. 20, 1970; 1 child, Tobias. MD, U. Heidelberg, Germany, 1968; prof. (hon.), Tongji Med. U., Wuhan, China, 1998; student, Aschoff-Preis, U. Freiburg, 2002, Max Planck-Forschungspreis, 2003, Feldberg-Forschungspreis, 2003; prof. (hon.), Chinese Acad. Scis., Shanghai, 2004. Postdoctoral fellow U. Calif., Davis, 1972-75; asst. prof. pharmacology and toxicology U. Heidelberg, 1975-80, assoc. prof., 1981-84; prof., chmn. U. Saarland, Homburg, Germany, 1985-90, Tech. U. Munich, 1990—. Prof. honoris causa Tongji Med. U., Wuhan, China, 1998, Shanghai Inst. Materia Medica, Chinese Acad. Scis., Shanghai, 2004, Aschoff-Preis, U. Freiburg, 2002, Max Planck-Forschungspreis, 2003, Feldberg-Forschungs-preis, 2003. Contbr. articles to profl. jours. Mem.: Academia Europea, LEOPOLDINA, German Acad. Natural Sci., Bavarian Acad. Scis., Pharmakologische Gesellschaft, A.S.P.E.T., N.Y. Acad. Sci., Gesellschaft fur Biol. Chemie (biochemistry, pharmacology and toxicology sect.). Avocations: skiing, bicycling. Home: Netzegaustrasse 10 81377 Munich Germany

HOFMANN, FRIEDER KARL, biotechnologist, biochemist, consultant; b. Eppstein, Hessen, Germany, June 15, 1949; came to U.S., 1984; s. Friedrich Karl and Anna Johannette (Heist) H.; m. Sigrid Marianne Thomae, Sept. 5, 1975. MS, J.W. Goethe U., Frankfurt, Germany, 1977, PhD, 1981. Staff scientist, asst. prof. J.W. Goethe U., Frankfurt, 1977-81; sci. mgr. Brunswick Corp., Eschborn, Germany, 1982-84; tech. dir. Biotechnetics, San Diego, 1984-90; pres. ProCon Internat., Vista, Calif., 1990—, Ctr. for Continuous Edn., Vista, Calif., 1992—. Author: (with others) Scale-Up and Downstream Processing of rDNA Products, 1991, GMP Production of Monoclonal Antibodies, 1991; contbr. over 40 articles to profl. jours. Recipient Senckenberg prize Senckenberg Rsch. Soc., Frankfurt, 1977; Kirkpatrick Chem. Engring. Achievement Honor award Chem. Engring., 1989, Parenteral Drug Assn. Jour. award Parenteral Drug Assn., Pa., 1985. Mem. AIChE, Am. Chem. Soc., Tissue Culture Assn., European Soc. for Animal Cell Tech. Achievements include 6 patents for bioreactor and membrane technology; invention and development of tester for membrane filters, of first scalable membrane based animal cell reactor; first integration of upstream and downstream processes in bioreactor system; invention of formulation and procedure to grow animal cells in protein-free nutrient. Office: ProCon Internat 1773 Kings Rd Vista CA 92084-3640

HOFMANN, MARY T., internist, physician; MD, Temple U., Phila.; attended, Gwynedd Mercy Coll. Diplomate Am. Bd. Internal Medicine, Am. Bd. Internal Medicine-geriatric medicine. Med. dir. Muller ctr. for sr. health Abington Meml. Hosp., chief and fellow dir. geriatric medicine divsn. Named one of the Top Doctors, Phila. Mag., 2011. Mem.: Abington Health Physicians. Office: Abington Memorial Hospital Department of Medicine 1200 Old York Rd Abington PA 19001 Office Phone: 215-481-4350. Office Fax: 215-481-4361.

HOFMANN, PAUL BERNARD, healthcare consultant; b. Portland, Oreg., July 6, 1941; s. Max and Consuelo Theresa (Bley) H.; m. Lois Bernstein, June 28, 1969; children: Julie, Jason. BS, U. Calif., Berkeley, 1963, MPH, 1965, DPH, 1994. Research assoc. in hosp. adminstrn. Lab. of Computer Sci., Mass. Gen. Hosp., Boston, 1966-68, asst. dir., 1968-69; asst. adminstr. San Antonio Community Hosp., Upland, Calif., 1969-70, assoc. adminstr., 1970-72; dep. dir. Stanford (Calif.) U. Hosp., 1972-74, dir., 1974-77; exec. dir. Emory U. Hosp., Atlanta, 1978-87; exec. v.p., chief ops. officer Alta Bates Corp., Emeryville, Calif., 1987-91, cons., 1991-92, Alexander & Alexander, San Francisco, 1992-94; disting. vis. scholar Stanford (Calif.) U. Ctr. for Biomed. Ethics, 1993-97; sr. fellow Stanford (Calif.) U. Hosp., 1993-94; sr. cons. strategic healthcare practice Alexander & Alexander Cons. Group, San Francisco, 1994-97; sr. v.p. strategic healthcare practice Aon Cons., San Francisco, 1997-99; pres. The Hofmann Healthcare Group, San Francisco, 2000-01; with Provenance Health Ptnrs., Moraga, Calif., 2001—05; pres. The Hofmann Healthcare Group, Moraga, Calif., 2005—. Instr. computer applications Harvard U., 1968-69; lectr. hosp. adminstrn. UCLA, 1970-72, Stanford U. Med. Sch., 1972-77; assoc. prof. Emory U. Sch. Medicine, Atlanta, 1978-87. Author: The Development and Application of Ethical Criteria for Use in Making Programmatic Resource Allocation Decisions in Hospitals, 1994; co-editor: Managing Ethically: A Guide for Executives, 2001, Mistakes in Healthcare Management: Identification, Prevention and Correction, 2005; Co-EDitor: Managing Healthcare Ethically: A Guide For Executives, 2nd edit., 2010; contbr. articles to profl. jours Served with U.S. Army, 1959. Fellow Am. Coll. Hosp. Adminstrs. (recipient Robert S. Hudgens meml. award 1976); mem. Am. Hosp. Assn.(award hon., 2009), U. Calif. Grad. Program in Health Mgmt. Alumni Assn. (Disting. Leadership award 2004). Office Phone: 925-247-9700. Business E-Mail: hofmann@hofmannhealthcare.com.

HOGAN, BARBARA CHRISTINE, internist, emergency physician; b. Bremen, Germany, Aug. 19, 1960; d. Ulrich and Doris Walter; m. Michael Hogan. MD, U. Leipzig, Germany, 1993. Lic. physician Germany. Resident Med. U. Hannover, Germany, 1993—95, edn. internist, 1995—99; internist Univ. Hosp., Aachen, Germany, 1999—2004; exec. physician for interdisciplinary emergency dept. Klinikum Fulda gAG, Fulda, Germany, 2004—06; dir. dept. emergency Asklepios Klinik, Hamburg, Germany, 2006—. Lectr. in field; trainer German Ultrasound Soc., 2003. Mem.: German Soc. Internal Intensive Care, German Assn. Emergency Physicians (pres. 2006—), European Soc. Emergency Medicine (v.p. 2009—), Am. Coll. Emergency Physicians, German Soc. Internal Medicine, German Ultrasound Soc., Gesellschaft der Freunde von Bayreuth e.v. Avocations: sailing, tennis, opera. Office: Asklepios Klinik Zentrale Notaufnahme Paul Ehrlich Strasse 1 22763 Hamburg Germany Business E-Mail: b.hogan@asklepios.com.

HOGAN, JAMES CARROLL, JR., retired public health administrator, research biologist; b. Milledgeville, Ga., Jan. 3, 1939; s. James C. and Leanna (Johnson) H.; m. Izola Stinson, Nov. 29, 1959; children: Pamela Renita, Gregory Karl, Jeffrey Darryl. BS, Albany State Coll., 1961; MS, Atlanta U., 1968; PhD, Brown U., 1972. Postdoc. fellow dept. biology Yale U., New Haven, 1972—73; rsch. assoc. Yale U. Sch. Medicine, New Haven, 1973-76; asst. prof. anatomy Howard U. Sch. Medicine, Washington, 1976-78; assoc. prof. U. Conn., Storrs, 1978-83; dir. minority student affairs U. Conn. Health Ctr., Farmington, 1983-87; chief clin. chemistry and hematology Conn. Dept. Health Svcs., Hartford, 1991—95, chief, dir. biochemistry and environ. chemistry, 1997—2003, divsn. dir. biomonitoring biochem. and chem. terrorism, 2003—09. Mem. Cmty. Svcs. Commn. and Bd. of Edn., 1994—, North Haven, Conn., 1989—; bd. dirs. Gateway Cmty. Coll., 1989—, A Better Chance, Glastonbury, Conn., 1990—, Hartford (Conn.) Alliance for Sci. and Math. Edn., adv. com. Math. Connections Contbr. articles to Jour. Ultrastructural Rsch., Jour. Protozoology, Jour. Embryology and Exptl. Morphology, Jour. Cell Biology, Jour. Nat. Tech. Assn., Jour. Pediat. Founder, pres. North Haven Assn. Black Citizens, 1988—, Chpt. Nat. Tech. Assn., 1990; coord. Martin Luther King Jr. annual luncheon Dept. Pub. Health, Conn., 1988—; active Dem. Town Com., North Haven, 1989—; com. chmn. Greater New Haven chpt. NAACP; mem. Bd. Edn., North Haven, 1993—. Josiah Macy Found. fellow, Marine Biol. Labs., 1978-80, Ford Found. postdoctoral fellow Marine Biol. Labs., 1980-81; vis. faculty fellow Yale U., 1984—. Mem. NAACP (life), APHA, Conn. Pub. Health Assn., Conn. Acad. Sci. and Engring., Am. Chem. Soc., Am. Soc. Cell Biology (Conn. chpt. pres.), Nat. Tech. Assn. (bd. dirs. Conn. chpt.), N.Y. Acad. Scis., Planetary Soc., Morehouse Coll. Nat. Alumni Assn. (life), Immanuel Bapt. Ch. Mens Club (pres. 1998—), Sigma Xi, Omega Psi Phi, AIDS Interfaith Network(chmn. bd. dirs.) Baptist. Achievements include first confirmation of Antigenic variation in Trypanosomes using the electron microscope, first confirmation of cytoplasmic markers in sex cells of killifishes using the electron microscope. Home: 51 Pool Rd PO Box 146 North Haven CT 06473-0146

HOGAN, MARJORIE J., pediatrician, adolescent medicine; MD, Stanford U., 1977. Diplomate Am. Bd. Pediatrics, 1982, Am. Bd. Pediatrics-adolescent medicine, 2005. Resident pediatrics Univ. Minn. Med. Ctr., Mpls., 1978—81; physician pediat. Hennepin County Med. Ctr. Recipient Gold-Headed Cane award, Univ. of Minn. Dept. of Pediat., 2009. Office: Hennepin County Medical Center Department Pediatrics 701 Pk Ave S Minneapolis MN 55415 Office Phone: 612-347-6820.

HOGAN, MICHAEL F., state official; b. 1947; married; 3 children. BS in Communication Arts, Cornell U., 1969; MS in Ednl. Adminstrn., SUNY, Brockport, 1972; PhD in Adminstrn. of Spl. Edn., Syracuse U., 1977. Tchr. NY Pub. Schools, Rochester, 1969—71; adminstrv. intern Eleanor Roosevelt Devel. Services/O.D. Heck Eleanor Devel. Ctr. NY State Dept. Mental Hygiene, 1975—76; asst. supt. planning & devel. Belchertown State Sch. Mass. Dept. Mental Health, 1976—77, Region I dir. planning, 1977—79, dist. mgr. mental health & retardation services, 1979—84; supt. Northampton State Hosp., 1982—84; dep. commr. adminstrv. services Conn. Dept. Mental Health, 1984—87, commr., 1987—91; dir. OH Dept. Mental Health, Columbus, 1991—2007; commr. NY State Office Mental Health, 2007—. Mem. Nat. Assn. State Mental Health Program Directors, 1989—2000, pres., 2003—04; mem. Nat. Assn. State Mental Health Program Directors Rsch. Inst., 1989—2004, Nat. Adv. Mental Health Coun., 1994—98; chair President's New Freedom Commn. on Mental Health, 2002—03; bd. mem. Joint Commn., 2007—10. Recipient Disting. Svc. to State Govt. award, Nat. Governors Assn, 2002, Disting. Svc. award, The Nat. Alliance for the Mentally Ill (NAMI), 2002, Spl. Leadership award, Campaign for Mental Health Reform, 2006, SPAN USA Allies for Action award, Suicide Prevention Action Network, 2006. Mem.: McArthur Found. Network on Mental Health Policy Rsch. Office: New York State Office of Mental Health 44 Holland Ave Albany NY 12229 Office Phone: 518-474-4403. Office Fax: 518-474-2149. Business E-Mail: eocomfh@omh.state.ny.us.

HOGAN, REED B., gastroenterologist; b. Clarksdale, Miss., Apr. 16, 1955; MD, U. Miss., 1980, degree in Internal Medicine, Gastroenterology, Baylor U., Tex., 1985. Physician in gastroenterology Gastrointestinal Assocs., 1985—. Mem.: Am. Coll. Gastroenterology, Am. Gastroent. Assn., Am. Soc. Gastrointestinal Endoscopy. Avocations: photography, tennis. Office: 1421 N State St Jackson MS 39202 Personal E-mail: rbhogan@comcast.net.

HOGAN, ROXANNE ARNOLD, nursing and risk management consultant, educator; b. Connellsville, Pa. d. Tyree Franklin, Sr. and Reva Gayle (Thieler) Arnold; m. Patrick B. Hogan. AAS, Gloucester County Coll., 1983; BSN, Widener U., 1989. Lic. healthcare risk mgr. Fla.; RN Fla. Staff devel. instr., nursing supr., cardiac care nurse Meth. Hosp., Phila., 1982-89; emergency nurse Underwood Meml. Hosp., Woodbury, NJ, 1988-89; critical care nurse Jupiter Hosp., Fla., 1989—92; emergency clin. nurse III Indian River Meml. Hosp., Vero Beach, Fla., 1990-92; EMT/paramedic instr. Indian River CC, Ft. Pierce, Fla., 1990-92; emergency asst. nurse mgr. Holmes Regional Med. Ctr., Melbourne, Fla., 1992-94; post anesthesia clin. nurse III Indian River Meml. Hosp., Vero Beach, 1994—98; surg. dir. Rosato Plastic Surgery Ctr., Vero Beach, Fla., 1998-99; nurse mgr. preadmissions, IV team, ambulatory infusion, spl. procedures GI lab. Ambulatory Surgery Ctr., Indian River Meml. Hosp., Vero Beach, Fla., 1999—2001; pres. Treasure Coast Cons., Inc., 2001—; risk mgmt. coord. HCA/St. Lucie Med. Ctr., Port St. Lucie, Fla., 2002—03; claims med. specialist, on-line medical tng. cons. Nationwide Ins., 2003—. Home: 5346 NW Rugby Dr Port Saint Lucie FL 34983-3384

HOGARTY, MICHAEL DAVID, pediatrician; b. July 12, 1964; MD, Columbia Univ., 1990. Cert. Am. Bd. Pediatrics, 1993, in Pediatric Hematology-Oncology Am. Bd. Pediatrics, 1998. Resident in pediatrics Children's Meml. Hosp., Northwestern Univ., Chgo.; fellowship in pediatric hematology-oncology Children's Hosp. Phila.; attending physician in pediatric oncology Stoke Rsch. Inst., Children's Hosp. Phila., 1997—. Contbr. articles to profl. jours. Office: Children's Hosp Phila 902C Abramson 34th St & Civic Ctr Blvd Philadelphia PA 19104 Office Phone: 215-590-3931. Business E-Mail: hogarty@email.chop.edu.

HOGEL, MAUREEN L., insurance company executive, lawyer; B, Wheeling Coll.; JD, U. Pitts. Labor and employment atty. Drinker, Biddle & Reath, Phila., McGlinchey, Stafford, Mintz, Cellini & Lang, PC, New Orleans; COO, chief legal officer Duquesne Light Co., Pitts; exec. v.p., chief legal officer, corp. sec. Highmark Inc. Bd. dirs. YMCA of Pitts., Three Rivers Youth Bd. Mem.: ABA, Assn. of Corp. Counsel, Allegheny County Bar Assn. Office: Highmark Fifth Avenue Place 120 Fifth Ave Pittsburgh PA 15222-3099

HOGG, RUSSELL JOHN, gynecologist, educator; b. Mt. Gambier, Australia, Oct. 7, 1957; BSc with honors, Flinders U., MBBS, 1994; PhD, Royal Australian and New Zealand Coll. Ob-Gyn., 2003. Pvt. practice, 2007—. Assoc. prof. U. Sydney, 2009. Fellow: Royal Australian and New Zealand Coll. Ob-Gyn. Office: Ste G12 Norwest Medical Ctr 11 Bella Vista NSW 2153 Australia Office Fax: 96869011. Business E-Mail: russellhogg@iprimus.com.au.

HOGIKYAN, NORMAN DERTAD, otolaryngologist; b. Detroit, Apr. 3, 1961; BS magna cum laude, U. Mich., 1982, MD cum laude, 1988. Am. Bd. Otolaryngology-Head and Neck Surgery, Nat. Bd. Med. Examiners; lic. medicine and surgery, Mich. Intern, otolaryngology William Beaumont Hosp., Royal Oak, Mich., 1988-89; resident, otolaryngology Washington U. Med. Ctr., St. Louis, 1989-94; fellow, otolaryngology Loyola U., Maywood, Ill., 1994-95; mem. staff U. Mich Hosp., Ann Arbor, 1995—; cons. physician Ann Arbor VA Med. Ctr., 1995—; asst. prof. otolaryngology U. Mich., Ann Arbor, Mich., 1995—2002, assoc. prof. otolaryngology, 2002—, med. dir. speech and lang. pathology program, 1996—, assoc. prof., music, sch. music. Dir. U. Mich. Vocal Health Ctr., Livonia, 1996—. Expert analyst, reviewer Otolaryngology Jour. Club Jour., 1996—; contbr. articles to profl. jours., chpts. to books. Grantee U. Mich., Office of V.P. for Rsch., 1996; recipient 1st prize Joseph Agura Resident Rsch. Competition, 1991, 92, award for excellence in resident tchg. Washington U. Dept. Otolaryngology, St. Louis, 1994. Fellow ACS, Am. Acad. Otolaryngology-Head and Neck Surgery; mem. AMA, Mich. Otolaryn. Soc., Walter P. Work Soc., Alpha Omega Alpha, Phi Beta Kappa. Office: U Mich A Alfred Taubman Health Care Ctr 1500 E Medical Ctr Dr Rm 1904 Ann Arbor MI 48109-0312 Mailing: Vocal Health Ctr Ctr for Specialty Care 1900 Haggerty Rd Ste 103 Livonia MI 48152 Office Phone: 734-936-9598. Office Fax: 734-936-9625.

HOHN, ARNO R., pediatric cardiologist; b. Paterson, NJ, Aug. 4, 1931; MD, NY Med. Coll., 1956. Cert. Am. Bd. Pediatrics, Am. Bd. Pediatrics, Pediatric Cardiology. Intern, pediatric cardiology Roosevelt Hosp., NYC, 1956—57; resident, pediatric cardiology Children's Hosp., Buffalo, 1957—58, fellow, pediatric cardiology, 1958—59, 1962—63, asst. chief resident, pediatric cardiology Phila., 1961—62; past head, divsn. pediatric cardiology Med. U. SC; cardiologist, clin. affiliate Children's Hosp., LA, former head, divsn. cardiology; clin. affiliate LA County and U. So. Calif. Med. Ctr.; prof. pediatrics U. So. Calif. Sch. Medicine. Mem.: Calif. Soc. Pediatric Cardiology, Southwestern Pediatric Soc., Am. Pediatric Soc., Am. Coll. Cardiology, Am. Heart Assn., Am. Acad. Pediatrics. Office: Childrens Hosp LA Divsn Cardiology 4650 Sunset Blvd M/S #34 Los Angeles CA 90027 Business E-Mail: ahohn@chla.usc.edu.

HOILE, REBECCA JANE, microbiologist, consultant; m. Richard Wood. BSc in Med. Microbiology, U. Sydney, 1997; PhD in Forensic Microbiology, U. Tech., Sydney, 2010. Molecular biologist Inst. Clin. Pathogolgy & Med. Rsch., Sydney, 1998—2003; sr. forensic microbiologist NSW Police Force, Sydney, 2003—. Cons. advisor INTERPOL, Lyon, France, 2005—. Contbr. articles to profl. jours., chapters to books. Grant, Emergency Mgmt. Australia, 2008—. Mem.: Australian and New Zealand Forensic Sci. Soc., Australian Soc. Microbiology (assoc.). Achievements include development of two biological decontamination methods for forensic evidence & crime scene processing techniques for a bioterrorism incident. Business E-Mail: hoil1reb@police.nsw.gov.au.

HOJAHMAT, MARHABA, research scientist; b. 1966; d. Hojahmat Yunus and Rehima Yusup; 1 child, Yifutehaer Nijiati. M in engring., Tokyo U. Sci., 1997, PhD, 2000. Post-doctoral rschr. U. Ky., Lexington, 2000—02, rsch. assoc., 2002; rsch. scientist Yaupon Therapeutics Inc., Lexington, 2002—. Contbr. articles to profl. jours. Japanese Govt. scholarship, Ministry of Edn., Sci. and Culture of Japan, 1996—2000, ITOCHU award, ITOCHU Co., Japan, 1995, STTR, NIH, 2002. Mem.: Soc. Silicon Chemistry, Japan, Chem. Soc. Japan, Am. Chem. Soc., Am. Assn. Pharm. Scientists. Office: Yaupon Therapeutics Inc Univ Ky A169 ASTeCC Bldg Lexington KY 40506 Office Fax: 859-257-2489. E-mail: mhoja2@uky.edu.

HOKAMA, HIROTO, psychiatrist, educator; married. MD, Sch. Medicine, U. Ryukyus, Okinawa, Japan, 1987. Med. dir. neuropsychiatry outpatient clinic Ryukyu U. Hosp., Nishihara, Okinawa, 1996—; assoc. prof., lectr., dept. neuropsychiatry, sch. medicine U. Ryukyus, 2004—. Recipient Neal Mysell award, Dept. Psychiatry, Harvard Med. Sch., 1994. Mem.: Japanese Soc. Biol. Psychiatry. Office: Univ Ryukyus 207 Uehara Nishihara Okinawa 903-0125 Japan Office Fax: 81-98-895-1419. Personal E-mail: hhokama@mac.com. Business E-Mail: hhokama@med.u-ryukyu.ac.jp.

HOK CHU, TIUNN, cultural organization administrator; b. Chiang Hoa County, Taiwan, June 30, 1951; s. Tiunn Tong Liat and Loa Kiok; m. Ko Kiu Hun, Sept. 24, 1981; children: Tiunn Eng Tek, Tiunn Hiong. B, Kaohsiung Med. Coll., 1979. Diplomate Taiwan Bd. Internal Medicine. Founder, pres. Taiwanese Romanization Assn., 2001—. Head Taiwanese lang. dept. Taiwan South Assn., Kaohsiung, 2001—05. Recipient Lai Ho Med. award on Humanity, Lai Ho Found., 2005. Achievements include first to founder of an association to promote Taiwanese languages to be national languages in Taiwan, where the ruling regime enforced it's own language policy and made native Taiwanese languages extinct. Home: Yi Hua Rd Kaohsiung Taiwan Office Fax: 886-7-3985747; Home Fax: 886-7-3958839.

HOKENSTAD, MERL CLIFFORD, JR., social work educator; b. Norfolk, Nebr., July 21, 1936; s. Merl Clifford and Flora Diane (Christian) H.; m. Dorothy Jean Tarrell, June 24, 1962; children: Alene Ann, Laura Rae, Marta Lynn. BA summa cum laude, Augustana Coll., 1958; Rotary Found. fellow, Durham U., Eng., 1958-59; MSW., Columbia U., 1962; PhD, Brandeis U., 1969, Inst. Ednl. Mgmt., Harvard U., 1977. With Lower East Side Neighborhood Assn., NYC, 1962-64; community planning assoc. United Community Services, Sioux Falls, SD, 1964-66; instr. Augustana Coll., Sioux Falls, 1964-66; research assoc. Ford Found. Project on Community Planning for Elderly, Brandeis U., Waltham, Mass., 1966-67; prof., dir. Sch. Social

Work, Western Mich. U., Kalamazoo, 1968-74; prof., dean Sch. Applied Social Scis., Case Western Res. U., Cleve., 1974-83, Ralph and Dorothy Schmitt prof., 1983—, chmn. PhD program, 1990-94; prof. internat. health Sch. of Medicine, 1994—; disting. u. prof. Case Western Reserve U., 2010—; disting. prof. Case Western Res. U., 2010—. Vis. prof. Inst. Sociology, Stockholm U., 1978, Fulbright lectr., 1980; vis. prof. Nat. Inst. Social Work, London, 1981, Sch. Social Work, Stockholm U., 1982-86, Eotvos Lorand U., Budapest, Hungary, 1992, 95-96, London Sch. Econs., 1994; Fulbright rsch. scholar Inst. Applied Social Rsch., Oslo, 1989; fellow U. Canterbury, Christchurch, New Zealand, 1994; tech. com. UN World Assembly on Aging, 2000-02, US delegation, 2002, bd. dirs. Coun. Older Persons, 1991, Ctr. Cmty. Solutions, 2010, Author: Participation in Teaching and Learning: An Idea Book for Social Work Educators; editor: Meeting Human Needs: An International Annual, Vol. V, Linking Health Care and Social Services: International Perspectives; editor-in-chief Internat. Social Work Jour., 1985-87; co-editor: Profiles in Internat. Social Work, 1992, Issues in International Social Work, 1997, Models of International Exchange, 2003, Lessons from Abroad: International Social Welfare Innovations, 2004; (internat. issue) Jour. Gerontol. Social Work, 1988, Jour. Sociology and Social Welfare, 1990, Jour. Social Policy and Administration, 1993, Jour. Aging Internat., 1994, Jour. Applied Social Scis., 1996; contbr. articles to profl. jours., chpts. to books. Mem. alcohol tng. rev. com. Nat. Inst. Alcoholism and Alcohol Abuse, 1974-78; workshop leader Am. Assn. State Colls. and Univs., 1974; chmn. U.S. com. XVIII Internat. Congress Schs. Social Work, 1976; chmn. Kalamazoo County Cmty. Mental Health Svcs. Bd., 1971, vice chmn., 1972; mem. edn. and tng. task force Mich. Office Drug Abuse and Alcoholism, 1972-73; mem. Mich. Assn. Mental Health Bds., 1972; bd. dirs. Cleve. United Way Svcs., 1982-84, del. assembly, 1974-82, mem. periodic rev. oversight com., 1982, mem. leadership devel. com., 1978, cmty. resources com., 1988—; bd. dirs. Kalamazoo United Way, 1968-72; trustee Cleve. Internat. Program for Youth Workers and Social Workers, chmn. program com., 1985-87; mem. program devel. com. Cleve. Center on Alcoholism, 1976; trustee Alcoholism Services Cleve., Inc., 1977-86, v.p., 1982-85; trustee Cmty. Info./Vol. Action Ctr., 1982-88, chmn. leadership devel. com., 1984-86, chmn. unmet needs com., 1986-88, exec. com., 1985-88, v.p., 1986-88; exec. com. Western Reserve Geriatric Edn. Ctr., 1995-2006; mem. adv. com. Coun. for Internat. Exch. Scholars, 1991-93, Ctr. Cmty. Solutions Coun. Older Persons, 1991—, bd. dirs., 2010-, vice chmn., 2005-06, chmn. 2006—, chmn. caregiver support program initiative, 1995-96; mem. Coun. on Older Persons, 1991-; mem. adv. coun. Cuyahoga County Dept. Sr. and Adult Svcs., 1998—2003, chair, 2001—03; bd. dirs. Western Res. Area Agy. on Aging, 2004—; mem. task force of social transition in Soviet Union, US State Dept. Bur. Human Rights and Humanitarian Affairs; mem. UN NGO Com. on Aging, 1996—; co-chmn. US Com. for Internat. Yr. of Older Persons, 1999. Named Outstanding Alumnus, Augustana Coll., 1980, Ohio Soc. Worker of the Yr., 1992, Columbia U. Sch. Social Work Hall of Fame, 2006; Fulbright Research fellow, NIMH trainee, 1960-61; Vocat. Rehab. trainee, 1966; Gerontology trainee, 1967; Rotary Found. fellow, 1958-59; recipient Golden Achievement Award, Golden Age Ctr., 2003. Mem. NASW (internat. com. 1989-93, chmn. 1992-93, found. pioneer 2003—, Internat. Rhoda G. Sarnat award 2006), Acad. Cert. Social Workers, Internat. Assn. Schs. Social Work (exec. bd. 1978-92, 98—, treas. 1978-86, v.p. N.Am. 1988-92, membership sec. 1996-00, Katherine Kendall award 2004), Internat. Coun. on Social Welfare (dir. U.S. com. 1982-92), Coun. on Social Work Edn. (del. 1972-75, 77-83, chmn. ann. program meeting 1973, chmn. com. on nat. legis. and adminstrv. policy 1975-79, nominating com. 1978-81, internat. com. 1980-86, 96-2006, chmn. com. 1982-84, dir. 1979-82, exec. com. 1986-89, pres. 1986-89, ptnr. Internat. Edn. award 2009, Lifetime Achievement award 2002), Nat. Conf. on Social Welfare (bd. dirs. 1978-80, chmn. sect. V program com. 1977-78), World Future Soc. (area coord. 1972-74), Fulbright Assn. (v.p. N.E. Ohio chpt. 1990-91), Nat. Coun. on Aging (bd. dirs. 1991-97, internat. com. 1991-97, pub. policy com. 1992-97), Ohio Assn. Gerontology and Edn. (Educator of Yr. 2009). Democrat. Episcopalian. Home: 2917 Weymouth Rd Cleveland OH 44120-2234 Office: Case Western Res U 10900 Euclid Ave Cleveland OH 44106-1764 Business E-Mail: mch2@cwru.edu.

HO-KYOUNG, YOON, psychiatrist; b. Seoul, Oct. 12, 1973; MD, PhD, Korea U., 2009. Intern Korea U. Med. Ctr., 1999—2000, resident, 2000—04, clin. asst. prof., 2008—; mil. physician Korean Navy Haeyang Hosp., 2004—07; clin. fellow Korea U. Ansan Hosp., 2007—08. Grant, Ministry of Health & Welfare, Republic of Korea. Mem.: Korean Acad. Sleep Medicine, Korean Acad. Anxiety Disorder, Korean Neuropsychiat. Assn., Am. Acad. Sleep Medicine. Avocations: golf, movies, music. Office: Korea University Anam Hosp Anam-dong 5 ga Seoul Seongbuk 136-705 Republic of Korea Business E-Mail: because@naver.com.

HOLDEREGGER, HANS, psychotherapist, writer, news analyst; b. Horgen, Switzerland, Nov. 24, 1942; s. Hans and Anna Holderegger; m. Susanne Zumbühl, Sept. 18, 1992; m. Johanna Aeschlimann, Jan. 7, 1970 (div.); children: Leonie Sophia, Thomas, Brigitte. PhD, U. Zurich, 1970; diploma, Höheres Lehramt U. Zürich, 1970. Cert. psychoanalyst Freud Inst. Zurich, 1983. Tchr. Kantonschule Enge, Zurich, 1970—82, prof., 1982—. Lectr. Freud Inst., Zurich, 1983, supr., 85. Contbr. scientific papers. Mem.: Swiss Assn. Psychoanalysis, Internat. Psychoanalytical Assn. Achievements include research in new theory of psychic trauma. Avocation: sailing. Office: Haldenbachstr 2 Zurich 8006 Switzerland Home: Bahnhofstrasse 108A 8803 Rüschlikon Switzerland Office Fax: 0041-44-724-06-08; Home Fax: 0041-44-724-06-08. Personal E-mail: admin@hans-holderegger.ch.

HOLDORF, HARRY HULBERT, health facility administrator; b. Jamestown, NY, May 1, 1958; s. John A. and Louise Holdorf; m. Cynthia L. Baron, Aug. 28, 1982; children: Christopher, Nicholas. AS in Radiol. Tech., Union County Coll.; BA in Environ. Scis., Stockton State Coll.; MPA, Kean U.; PhD in Health Svcs. Adminstrn., Southwest U. Lic. radiologic technologist Am. Registry Radiologic Technologists N.J., N.Y., med. sonographer Am. Registry Diagnostic Med. Sonographers. Radiol. technologist Elizabeth Gen. Med. Ctr., NJ, 1983—86, St. Barnabas Med. Ctr., NJ, 1986—87; splty. technologist Dover Hosp., NJ, 1987—88; staff ultrasonographer Overlook Hosp., NJ, 1988; staff ultrasonographer Elizabeth Gen. Med. Ctr., 1988—89, coord. ultrasound program, 1989—92, mem. faculty sch. radiol. scis., 1988—97, dir. ultrasound program, 1992—97, mgr. radiology, 1997—2000; quality assurance coord., mgr. med. imaging svcs. Irvington Gen. Hosp., NJ, 2001—. Cons. Schs. Med. Imagery and Med. Scis. Muhlenberg Regional Med. Ctr., 2000—03, adminstrv. dir. med. imaging svcs. Schs. Med. Imagery and Med. Scis., 2001—03; program dir. diagnostic med. sonography Schs. Nursing, Med. Imaging and Therapeutic Scis., 2003—; site visitor Joint Rev. Com. on Edn. in Diagnostic Med. Sonography; assoc. mem. faculty Union County Coll. Mem. Am. Coun. Edn. (mem. coll. credit recommendation svc., site visitor), Am. Soc. Diagnostic Med. Sonographers, Am. Inst. Ultrasound in Medicine, Soc. Vascular Ultrasound, Am. Soc. Radiol. Technologists, Am. Soc. Notaries, State of NJ Notary Public Commn., Pi Alpha Alpha. Home: 532 Woodland Ave Mountainside NJ 07092-2524 Office: Schs Nursing Med Imaging and Therapeutic Scis Park Ave and Randolph Rd Plainfield NJ 07062 Office Phone: 908-668-2884. Personal E-mail: keefwood@hotmail.com. Business E-Mail: hholdorf@solarishs.org, holdorf@ucc.edu. *

HOLDSWORTH, JANET NOTT, women's health nurse; b. Evanston, Ill., Dec. 25, 1941; d. William Alfred and Elizabeth Inez (Kelly) Nott; children: James William, Kelly Elizaveth, John David. BSN with high distinction, U. Iowa, 1963; M of Nursing, U. Wash., 1966. RN, Colo. Staff nurse U. Colo. Hosp., Denver, 1963-64, Presbyn. Hosp., Denver, 1964-65, Grand Canyon Hosp., Ariz., 1965; asst. prof. U. Colo. Sch. Nursing, Denver, 1966-71; counseling nurse Boulder PolyDrug Treatment Ctr., Boulder, 1971-77; pvt. duty nurse Nurses' Offcl. Registry, Denver, 1973-82; cons. nurse, tchr. parenting and child devel. Teenage Parent Program, Boulder Valley Schs., Boulder, 1980-88; bd. dirs., treas. Nott's Travel, Aurora, Colo., 1980—; nurse Rocky Mountain Surgery Ctr., 1996—. Instr., nursing coord. ARC, Boulder, 1979-90, instr., nursing tng. specialist, 1980-82. Mem. adv. bd. Boulder County Lamaze Inc., 1980-88, mem. adv. com. Child Find and Parent-Family, Boulder, 1981-89; del. Rep. County State Congl. Convs., 1972-96, sec. 17th Dist. Senatorial Com., Boulder, 1982-92; vol. Mile High ARC, 1980; vol. chmn. Mesa Sch. PTO, Boulder, 1982-92, bd. dirs., 1982-95, v.p., 1983-95; elder Presbyn. Ch. Mem. ANA, Colo. Nurses Assn. (bd. dirs. 1975-76, human rights com. 1981-83, dist. pres. 1974-76), Coun. Intracultural Nurses, Sigma Theta Tau, Alpha Lambda Delta. Republican. Home: 1550 Findlay Way Boulder CO 80305-6922 Office: Rocky Mountain Surgery Ctr 1630 30th St # 153 Boulder CO 80301-1014

HOLEN, ARE, psychiatrist; b. Oslo, July 18, 1945; s. Magnus and Anna Holen; m. Turid Suzanne Berg-Nielsen; children: Duva C., Tind A. Degree in psychology, U. Oslo, 1972, MD, 1978, PhD, 1990. Asst. prof. psychiatry U. Oslo, 1984—98, assoc. prof. psychiatry, 1990—93; rsch. scientist dept. psychiatry U. Calif., San Francisco, 1991—92; prof. behavioral medicine Norwegian U. Sci. and Tech., Trondheim, 1993—, chmn. dept. neurosci., 2002—05, vice-dean, dean of med. edn., faculty medicine, 2005—09; adj. prof. U. ND Sch. Medicine, 2009—. Vis. assoc. prof. Stanford Univ. Sch. of Medicine, 1999—2000. Author books in field; contbr. articles to profl. publs., chpts. in books. Founder ACEM, 1966, internat. head, 2001—. Lt. Norwegian Army. Mem.: Internat. Soc. Traumatic Stress Studies, Norwegian Assn. Psychiatrists.

HOLETS, JOHN ALAN, physician; MD, Temple U., 1982. Diplomate Am. Bd. of Family Medicine-family practice. Intern Sacred Heart Hosp., 1983, resident, 1985; physician Monongahela Valley Hospital, Pa. Recipient Sickman-Levin award for Dimensions In Medicine, 2008. Office: 447 W Main St Monongahela PA 15063 Address: Monongahela Valley Hospital 1163 Country Club Rd Monongahela PA 15063 Office Phone: 724-258-2070, 724-258-6019. Business E-Mail: jholets@monvalleyhospital.com.

HOLFORD, THEODORE RICHARD, biostatistician, educator; b. Columbus, Ohio, May 19, 1947; s. Charles Richard and LaVern Lucille (Lukens) H.; m. Maryellen Hutchinson Holford, Dec. 21, 1969; children: Matthew Edwin, Lesley Erin. BA in Math and Chemistry, Andrews U., 1969; PhD in Biometry, Yale U., 1973. Rsch. staff Yale U., New Haven, 1972-73, asst. prof., 1974-79, assoc. prof., 1979-89, prof., 1989—, head divsn. biostatistics, 1990-97, 2003—, dir. grad. studies, 1997—2002, acting dean pub. health, 2001. Editor: Statistical Methods in Medical Research, 1992—2005; assoc. editor Am. Jour. Epidemiology, 1989-97, Biometrics, 1984-88; contbr. articles to profl. jours. Mem. Consensus Devel. Conf. on Health Implications of Smokeless Tobacco, Washington, 1986, Epidemiology & Disease Control Study Section, Washington, 1986-89, Epidemiology Adv. Subcom. Oak Ridge (Tenn.) Assn., 1988-93, Data Safety Monitoring Bd. for Rare Disease Network, 2006-. Elinor Roosevelt Cancer fellow, 1981-82; recipient Wakeman award, 1990, numerous NIH grants. Fellow Am. Coll. Epidemiology, Am. Statis. Assn.; mem. Am. Statis. Assn., 1973—, Biometric Soc., 1973—, Soc. for Epidemiologic Rsch., 1978—. Avocations: trumpet, hiking, photography. Office Phone: 203-785-2838. Business E-Mail: theodore.holford@yale.edu.

HOLGERS-AWANA, RITA MARIE, electrodiagnosis specialist; b. Chgo., Nov. 24, 1933; d. Joseph Theodore and Kathleen (Cooney) Konecny; m. Alan Miles Holgers, Aug. 8, 1960 (div. Sept. 1986); children: Dale, Ross; m. Benedict E.C. Awana, June 13, 1989 (dec. Feb. 1995). BS, N.Am. U., 1984, M of Nutripathic Sci., 1988, D of Nutripathy, 1988, PhD in Nutritional Philosophy, 1990. Nutritional cons. Vitality Testing, Phoenix, 1982-84, pres., CEO Glendale, Ariz., 1984-86, Zac Engring. Inc., Lombard, Ill., 1986-2000; credentials coord. Prin. Health Care, Oakbrook Terrace, Ill., 1995-98; ptnr. Age-Less Group, Lombard, 2001—; team mem. Target Svc., 2008—. Spkr. women's coffee break group Harvard Ave. Free Evangelical Ch., 1997-98; spkr. Dowser's Club, 1997-98, spkr. in field; cons.; presenter 3d Whole Life Expo, Chgo., 1999, Health, Beauty and Fitness Expo, Coll. of DuPage, Glen Ellyn, Ill., 2001; bd. dirs. Global Deactivation of Radiation. Author: Me and My Non-Disease, 1983, Radiation, The Hidden Enemy, 1995; invention electronic water filter unit. Pres., v.p. S.W. Herbal Edn. Assn., Phoenix, 1984-85; sec. Better Breathers Club, Chula Vista, Calif., 1992-93, Concerned Citizens, Biggsville, Ill., 1975; co-founder, charter mem. Exec. Women's Coun., Moline, Ill., 1974; cub scout den leader Boy Scouts Am., Eldridge, Iowa, 1973; treas. food coop., Asuncion, Paraguay, 1958; bd. dirs. Unity Ctr. Light Ch., 2004—. With U.S. Fgn. Svc., 1956-61. Recipient Internat. Championship Golf Trophy, U.S. Dept. of State, 1959, Championship Golf trophy Hend-Co-Hills, 1974, 75, 77, Tai Chi Black Belt, Shingumatsu Martial Arts, 1993; named Woman of the Year, Internat. Biog. Ctr., Cambridge, Eng., 1998. Mem.: AAUW (fin. officer 2004—06, Woman of Distinction award 2007), Nat. Health Fedn., The Am. Dowsers Soc. (v.p. 1999), N.Am. Dowsers Club. Mem. Unity Ch. Avocations: golf, bowling, knitting, computers, martial arts. Home: 1315 Church Ave Lombard IL 60148 Personal E-mail: rita3holgers@aol.com.

HOLICK, MICHAEL FRANCIS, nutritionist; b. 1946; MD, U. Wis. Med. Sch., 1993, PhD, 1994. Diplomate Am. Bd. Internal Medicine, 1979. Resident Mass. Gen. Hosp., Boston, 1978; chief dept. endocrinology, metabolism and diabetes Boston U. Med. Ctr., 1993—, dir. Bone Health Care Ctr., 1993—, prof. medicine. Recipient E.V. McCollum award, Am. Soc. Clin. Nutrition, 1994, Psoriasis Rsch. Achievement award, Am. Skin Assn., 2000, Robert H. Herman Meml. award, Am. Soc. Clin. Nutrition, 2002, Excellence in Clin. Rsch. award, Nat. Ctr. Rsch. Resources, 2006, Linus Pauling Functional Medicine award, Inst. Functional Medicine, 2007, Eli Lilly Lectr. award, Can. Soc. Endocrinology & Medicine, 2007. Mem. ACI, Assn. Am. Physicians, Am. Fedn. Clin. Rsch., Am. Soc. Bone & Mineral Rsch. Office: Boston U Sch Medicine MED Endocrine Lab 85 E Newton St M-Bld Boston MA 02118 Office Phone: 617-638-4545. E-mail: mfholick@bu.edu.

HOLIFIELD-KENNEDY, LINDA R., physician; b. Johnstown, Pa., July 20, 1957; d. Cleveland, Jr. and Ruth Holifield; m. Richard O. Kennedy, Sept. 1, 1990; children: Richard O. Kennedy II, Tiffani L. Kennedy. BS, UCLA, 1982; MD, SUNY, Bklyn., 1994; MPH, Johns Hopkins U., Balt., 2000. Chem. analyst Gen. Dynamics Corp., Pomona, Calif., 1982—86; med. officer The Pentagon, Washington, 2000—. Contbr. rsch. articles to various hypertension jours. Del. leader to South Africa Nat. Physician Ambassadors Program, Vienna, Va., 2005; health ministry First Bapt. Ch. Glenarden, Upper Marlboro, Md., 2008—. Recipient Randall E. Bass award, Dept. of Environ. Health Scis., Johns Hopkins U., 1999, Cert. of Appreciation, Dept. of Army, 2002. Mem.: Am. Coll. Occupl. and Environ. Medicine (assoc.; bd. dir. Washington met. chpt. 2001—03, Resident Rsch. Presentation award 2000), Am. Coll. Physician Execs. (assoc.), Am. Coll. Preventive Medicine (assoc.). Avocations: cultural arts, travel, non-fiction. Personal E-mail: lholifieldkennedy@yahoo.com.

HOLLADAY, E. BLAIR, medical association administrator, cytologist; MD. Cert. American Soc. Clin. Pathology. Lab. profl., educator, chief dir. ctr. cytopathology and molecular diagnostics Med. Univ. SC; positions including v.p. sci. activities, exec. dir. bd. cert., acting dir. Inst. Global Outreach American Soc. Clin. Pathology, Chgo., 2005—10, exec. v.p., 2010—. Mem.: American Soc. Clin. Pathology. Office: American Soc Clin Pathology 33 W Monroe St Ste 1600 Chicago IL 60603 Office Phone: 312-541-4999. Office Fax: 312-541-4998. *

HOLLAN, IVANA, medical researcher; b. Chomutov, Czech Republic, Aug. 16, 1965; d. Jirina Stetinova and Stetina Stanislav; children: Barbora, Tomas. MD, Charles' U., Praha, 1989; PhD, 2009. Cert. cand. Med. Charles' U., 1989. Sr. resident Lillehammer Hosp. Rheumatic Diseases, 1998—2001, rsch., 2001—, Mgr. feiring heart biopsy study, 2000—, mentor psara study, 2006—; project mgr. ERAC Study, 2009—, GRAPPA, 2009—. Doctoral fellowship Feiring Heart Clinic, Norway, 2001—09; postdoc Lillemammor Hosp., 2009—. Mem.: European Vasculitis Study Group, Norwegian Society Rheumatology. Home: Gamlevegen 198 Norway Lillehammer 2615 Norway Office: Revmatismesykehuset AS M Grundtvigsv 6 Norway Lillehammer 2615 Norway Office Fax: 4761279550; Home Fax: 4761279550. Personal E-mail: i-hollan@online.no E-mail: ivana.hollan@revmatismesykehuset.no.

HOLLAND, EDWARD J., ophthalmologist, surgeon; b. Chgo., Ill., June 23, 1956; Grad., Drake U.; MD, Loyola-Stritch Sch. Medicine, Maywood, Chgo., 1981. Cert. Am. Bd. Ophthalmology, 1986. Intern Henry Ford Hosp., Detroit; resident U. Minn., Mpls., 1982—85, dir., Cornea and Refractive Surgery Svc., 1987, asst. prof. to prof., Elias Potter Lyon chair, ophthalmology; fellow, cornea and external disease U. Iowa, Iowa City, 1985—86; fellow, ocular immunology Nat. Eye Inst., NIH, Bethesda, Md., 1986—87; dir. cornea services Cin. Eye Inst.; prof. ophthalmology U. Cin. Dir. Am. Acad. Ophthalmology Skills Transfer Courses; mem. med. scientific adv. bd. OCuSoFT, Inc., 2007—; invited lectr. nationally and internationally. Contbr. articles to peer-reviewed jours.; edited (textbook) Cornea, co-edited Ocular Surface Disease: Medical and Surgical Management, guest appearance Miracle Workers (ABC), 2006. Named to Best Doctors in America. Mem.: Am. Soc. Cataract and Refractive Surgeons (chair cornea clin. com.), Min. Acad. Ophthalmology (past pres.), Am. Acad. Ophthalmology (bd. trustee 2005—, secretariat ann. mtg., sr. achievement award, honor award), Cornea Soc. (immediate past pres.), Eye Bank Assn. Am. (former chmn., med. adv. bd., chair-elect, Paton Soc. award 2002). Office: Cin Eye Laser Ctr 10700 Montgomery Rd Cincinnati OH 45242 also: Northern Kentucky Eye Laser 580 S Loop Rd Ste 200 Edgewood KY 41017 also: Cin Eye Inst 1945 Cincinnati Eye Institute Dr Cincinnati OH 45242 Office Phone: 877-984-2020, 513-984-5133. Office Fax: 513-469-2089.

HOLLAND, EDWARD JAMES, JR., (NED HOLLAND, E.J. HOLLAND JR.), federal agency administrator, former telecommunications industry executive; b. Washington, Apr. 19, 1943; s. Edward James and Jane (Murdock) Holland; m. Joyce Grandquist, Oct. 4, 1969; children: Leanne Marie, Sarah Lynn, Edward James III. BA in Philosophy, Rockhurst Coll., Kansas City, Mo., 1965; JD, Boston Coll. Law Sch., 1968. Bar: Mo. 1968, US Dist. Ct. (we. dist.) Mo. 1968, US Ct. Appeals (8th and 10th cirs.) 1968, US Supreme Ct. 1968, US Ct. Appeals (7th cir.) 1978, US Dist. Ct. (ea. dist.) Mo. 1991. Assoc. Spencer, Fane, Britt & Browne, Kansas City, 1968-74, ptnr., co-chmn. health law practice group, 1974—92; sr. v.p., chief adminstrv. officer, corp. sec. Payless Cashways, Inc., Kansas City; asst. v.p. corp. benefits Sprint Corp., Overland Park, Kans., 1999—2000, v.p. compensation, benefits, labor & employee rels., 2000—05; sr. v.p. human resources & comm. Embarq Corp., Overland Park, 2005—09; asst. sec. for adminstrn. US Dept. Health & Human Services, Washington, 2009—. Democrat. Roman Catholic. Home: 3674 Belleview Ave Kansas City MO 64111-3860 Office: US Department Health & Human Services 200 Independence Ave SW Washington DC 20201 Office Phone: 202-690-7431. E-mail: ASAStaff@hhs.gov. *

HOLLAND, ERIC CHARLES, neurosurgeon, medical educator, researcher; b. New Orleans, Feb. 7, 1959; BS in Chemistry, Miami U., 1981; PhD in Biochemistry and Molecular Biology, U. Chgo., 1985; MD, Stanford U., 1990. Intern UCLA Sch. Medicine, 1990—91, resident neurosurgery, 1992—95; fellow Nat. Cancer Inst.; asst. prof.

MD Anderson Cancer Ctr., U. Tex., Houston, 1998—2000; attending physician Depts. of Neurosurgery, Surgery, and Neurology Meml. Sloan-Kettering Cancer Ctr., NYC, lab. head Cancer Biology and Genetics Program, dir. Brain Tumor Ctr., vice chmn. translational rsch. Dept. Surgery, Emily Tow Jackson chair oncology. Recipient Peter A. Steck Meml. Award, 2000, American Brain Tumor Assn. Rsch. Award, 2000, Bressler Scholars Award, 2001, Searle Scholar Award, 2000—03, Seroussi Award, 2002, Farber Award, 2004, Voynick Award. Mem.: Inst. Medicine. Office: Memorial Sloan-Kettering Cancer Center ZRC 1304 1275 York Ave New York NY 10021 Office Phone: 646-888-2053, 212-693-3005. Fax: 646-422-0312. E-mail: hollande@mskcc.org. *

HOLLAND, JAMES F., oncologist, medical educator; b. May 16, 1925; AB, Princeton U., NJ, 1945; MD, Columbia U. Coll. Physicians & Surgeons, NYC, 1947; DSc (hon.), SUNY, Buffalo, 1997. Diplomate Am. Bd. Internal Medicine. Intern, resident Columbia-Presbyn. Med. Ctr., 1947—49; internal medicine fellowship Francis Delafield Hosp., NYC, 1951—53; dir. Derald H. Ruttenberg Cancer Ctr., chmn. dept. neoplastic diseases Mt. Sinai Sch. Medicine, NYC, 1973—94, disting. prof. neoplastic diseases, 1994—, also prof. medicine, hematology & med. oncology, prof. oncological scis. Chmn. nat. rsch. group Cancer & Leukemia Group B, 1963—81; chmn. NY State Health Rsch. Sci. Bd., 1998—2000. Editor: Cancer Medicine, 1972, 8th edit., 2010; contbr. numerous articles to med. and cancer jours. Named one of Top Doctors in NY Metro Area, Castle Connolly Med. Ltd., 1999—2009, America's Top Doctors, 2002—09, America's Top Doctors for Cancer, 2005—10. Mem.: Am. Soc. Clin. Oncology, Am. Assn. Cancer Rsch., Am. Assn. Physician. Office: Mt Sinai Med Ctr Derald H Ruttenberg Treatment Ctr 1Gustave Levy Pl PO Box1079 1190 5th Ave New York NY 10029-6500 Office Phone: 212-824-7434. Office Fax: 212-860-7186. E-mail: james.holland@mssm.edu.

HOLLAND, JIMMIE C., psychiatrist, educator; b. Forney, Tex., Apr. 9, 1928; m. James F. Holland; 5 children. BA, Baylor U., 1948, MD, 1952. Diplomate Am. Bd. Psychiatry, Am. Bd. Neurology. Instr. to prof. SUNY, Buffalo, 1956-73; assoc. prof., assoc. attending physician to asst. dir. cons.-liaison psychiatry Albert Einstein Coll. Medicine and Montefiore Med. Ctr., Bronx, 1973-77; chair dept. psychiatry and behavioral scis., Wayne E. Chapman chair in psychiat. oncology Meml. Sloan Kettering Cancer Ctr., NYC, 1997—2003. Prof. dept. psychiatry Weill Med. Coll., N.Y.C.,' 1977—; cons. NIMH-USSR joint schizophrenia study Psychiat. Rsch. Inst., Moscow, 1972-73, NIMH, Rockville, Md., 1973-75; chmn. psychiatry com. Cancer and Leukemia Group B Clin. Trials, Brookline, Mass., 1976-2001. Editor: Handbook of Psycho-oncology: Psychological Care of the Patient with Cancer, 1989, Psychooncology, 1998; co-editor Jour. Psycho-oncology; author, co-author: The Human Side of Cancer, 258 jour. articles, book chpts., monographs. Bd. dirs. Cancer Care, Inc., 1979-81. Recipient Disting. Alumna award Baylor U., Waco, Tex., 1982; Am. Cancer Soc. Medal of Honor, 1994 Fellow Inst. Medicine, Am. Coll. Psychiatrists, Am. Psychiat. Assn., Acad. Psychosomatic Medicine (founding pres.), Internat. Psycho-Oncology Soc. (founding pres.), Am. Psychosocial Oncology Soc., Am. Psychosomatic Soc., Am. Soc. Clin. Oncology. Office: Meml Sloan-Kettering Cancer Ctr 1275 York Ave New York NY 10021-6094 Home Phone: 914-725-2212; Office Phone: 646-888-0026. Business E-Mail: hollandj@mskcc.org.

HOLLAND, JOY, health care facility executive; b. NYC, Oct. 24, 1946; d. Harry Walson and Edna May (Simmons) Holland; m. Chesley Roderick Richardson, Sept.21, 1985; children: Carl Allen Fields, Craig Anthony Fields. AA in Nursing, Olive-Harvey Coll., 1972; BS, St. Joseph Coll., Bklyn., 1976; M in Health Adminstrn., C.W. Post Coll., 1978. Staff nurse U. Chgo. Hosp. and Clinics, Chgo., 1972; head nurse N.Y. Hosp., NYC, 1972; clinic adminstr. Morrisania-Montefiore Hosp., Bronx, N.Y., 1973; head nurse, supr. Pilgrim Psychiat. Hosp., Brentwood, N.Y., 1974, assoc. dir. staff devel., 1974-76, dir. nursing, 1976-78; surveyor, cons Joint Commn. on Accrediation of Hosps., Chgo., 1978-82; dir. Ypsilanti (Mich.) Regional Psychiat. Hosp., 1986-90, Clinton Valley Ctr., Pontiac, Mich., 1990-93, Huron Valley Ctr., Ypsilanti, Mich., 1993-99, Southgate Ctr., Mich., 1999-2001; CEO St. Elizabeth's Hosp., 2001—07; chief of staff to coun. mem. Muriel Bowser, Ward 4, Washington, 2007—. Dep. commr. dept. mental health State of Ohio, 1980-82; cons. Joint Commn. Accreditation of Hosps., Governing Coun. Am. Hosp. Assn. Sect. on Psychiatric and Substance Abuse; adj. lectr. Sch. Nursing, U. Mich.; cons. specialist, bd. dirs. Holland-Richardson Assocs., Detroit, bd. visitors Howard U. Contbr. author (book) Guide to J.C.A.H. Nursing Standards, 1985, 86 edits. Bd. dirs. Women in Crisis, Inc., N.Y.C., 1979-85, Washtenaw County (Mich.) ARC; bd. dirs. psychiatry dept. Chelsea (Mich.) Hosp., 1989-91. Mem. N.Y. Acad. Sci. (life), Bus. and Profl. Women, Inc., Masons, Order Ea. Star, Alpha Kappa Alpha, Sigma Theta Tau. Democrat. Avocations: chess, walking, reading.

HOLLAND, N. WILSON, geriatrician; b. Tampa, Fla., Nov. 2, 1955; MD, Bowman Gray Sch. Medicine, Wake Forest U., 1981. Geriatric fellowship program dir. dept. medicine Vets. Affairs Med. Ctr., Emory U. Sch. Medicine, 1985—. Recipient Mark Wolcott award, Dept. VA, Vets. Health Adminstrn., Sec. Health, 2010. Fellow: ACP; mem.: Am. Geriat. Soc., Alpha Omega Alpha, Phi Beta Kappa. Avocations: golf, fishing, walking. Office: 1670 Clairmont Rd Decatur GA 30033 E-mail: nwhmd@comcast.net.

HOLLEMAN, VERNON DAUGHTY, internist, educator; b. Brownwood, Tex., Oct. 1, 1931; s. Vernon Edgar and Olene Nollie (Reece) H.; m. Shirley Eyvonne Roberts, April 26, 1961; children: Richard, Joel, Douglas. BA in Chemistry and Biology, Howard Payne Coll., Brownwood, 1953; MD, Baylor U., 1958. Mem. med. staff Santa Fe Meml. Hosp, 1962-83; pres. med. staff Santa Fe Meml. Hosp., 1979-83; mem. med. staff Scott and White Hosp., 1962—; asst. chief physician Santa Fe Employees Hosp. Assn., 1962-85, med. dir., 1985—2005; intern Scott and White Clinic and Hosp., Temple, Tex., 1958-59, resident in internal medicine, 1959-62; dir., divsn. gen. internal medicine Santa Fe Ctr., Temple, Tex., 1985—, UNTL, 2005; assoc. prof. internal medicine Tex. A&M Coll. Medicine, Temple, 1982—. Adj. faculty clinician Ohio Coll. of Podiatric Medicine, Cleveland, 1982-86; med. dir. Consol. Assns. Railroad Employees, 1997—. Illustrator: Aesculapian, 1957, So. Bapt. Student Union Projects, 1954-58; illustrator ltd. edit. lithographs Baylor U. Lettermans Assn., 1994; contbr. photography to books, including Colorados Biggest Bucks and Bulls, Boone and Crocket Books, Awesome Antlers, Records of North American Mule Deer; author: articles on health, preventive medicine, and numerous others. Bd. dirs Santa Fe Meml. Found.; hon. chmn. physicians adv. bd. Tex. Nat. Rep. Congl. Com. Art Instrn., Inc. scholar, 1952; recipient Centennial award Santa Fe Meml. Found., 1991, Scott & White Pres.-Gainey Focus award, 2007, Hon. award, Santa Fe Meml. Found., 2004. Mem. AAAS, Nat. Assn. Ret. and Vet. Railway Employees (hon. life), AMA, ACP, Am. Coll. Phys. Execs., Am. Soc. Internal Medicine, Tex. Med. Assn. (Vernon D. Holleman-Lewis M. Rampy Scott and White Tex. A & M Health Sci. Ctr. Coll. Medicine Centennial chair in gerontology 1999), Tex. Med. Found., Am. Heart Assn. (cardiopulmonary coun.), Am. Assn. Ry. Physicians, Baylor B Assn. (hon.), World Med. Assn., Tex. Diabetes and Endocrine Soc., N.Y. Acad. Scis., So. Med. Assn. (life), Am. Coll. Occupl. Medicine, Am. Pain Soc., Am. Acad. Pain Mgmt. (diplomate), Am. Soc. Pain Educators (charter), Internat. Soc. Phys. Activity in Prevention of Osteoporosis (charter), Boone and Crockett Club (multiple com. mem., ofcl. measurer), Safari Club Internat. (life), Tex. Med. Assn. 50 Yr. Club, Alpha Chi, Phi Chi. Baptist. Avocations: medical history, art, hunting, photography, conservation. Office: Scott and White Clinic 1605 S 31st St Temple TX 76508-5227

HOLLENBERG, PAUL FREDERICK, pharmacology educator; b. Phila., Sept. 18, 1942; s. Frederick Henry and Catherine (Dentzer) H.; m. Emily Elizabeth Vanootighem, May 6, 1967; children: Kathryn Mary, David Paul. BS in Chemistry, Wittenberg U., 1964; MS in Biochemistry, U. Mich., 1966, PhD in Biochemistry, 1969. Postdoctoral fellow U. Mich., Ann Arbor, 1969, U. Ill., Urbana, 1969-72; asst. prof. Northwestern U., Chgo., 1972-81, assoc. prof., 1981-84, prof. pathology and molecular biology, 1984-87; prof. pharmacology, chmn. dept. Wayne State U. Sch. Medicine, Detroit, 1987-94, U. Mich. Med. Sch., Ann Arbor, 1994—. Pharmacology test com. Nat. Bd. Med. Examiners; mem. Chem. Pathology Study Sect. NIH, 1987-91. Co-founder, assoc. editor Chem. Rsch. in Toxicology, 1988—; assoc. editor Jour. Pharmacology and Exptl. Therapeutics; mem. editl. bd. Drug Metabolism and Disposition, British Jour. Pharmacology. Schweppe Found. research fellow, 1974-77; NIH research grantee, 1974—. Fellow Am. Chem. Soc.; mem. Am. Chem. Soc., Am. Soc. Biochemists and Molecular Biologists, Am. Soc. Pharmacology and Exptl. Therapeutics (sec./treas. 1998-99, pres.-elect 2001-02, pres. 2002-03), Am. Assn. for Cancer Rsch., Soc. Toxicology, Internat. Soc. Study Xenobiotics. Avocations: reading, running, golf. Home: 1968 Woodlily Ct Ann Arbor MI 48103-9728 Office: Univ Mich 2301 MSRB III Sch Medicine 1150 W Medical Center Dr Ann Arbor MI 48109-5632 Office Phone: 734-764-8166. Business E-Mail: phollen@umich.edu.

HOLLENBERG, STEVEN MICHAEL, physician, researcher; b. Alexandria, Va., May 13, 1957; s. Jack Earl and Judith Ann H. BA cum laude, Amherst Coll., Mass., 1978; MD magna cum laude, Emory U., Atlanta, 1984. Diplomate Am. Bd. Internal Medicine in Crit. Care Medicine and Cardiovasc. Disease. Intern, resident in internal medicine NY Hosp., 1984-87; fellow in critical care medicine NIH, Bethesda, Md., 1987-89; fellow in cardiology Johns Hopkins U., Balt., 1989-90; sr. staff fellow NIH, Bethesda, 1990-93; asst. prof. med. cardiology and critical care medicine Rush Med. Coll., Chgo., 1993—, assoc. dir. Med. ICU. Author: (with others) Harrison's Principles of Internal Medicine, 1996, Surgical Intensive Care, 1993, Cardiologic Shock, 2007, Cardiology in Family Practice, 2007; contbr. articles to profl. jours. Lt. comdr. USPHS, 1989-93. Recipient Career Devel. award Schweppe Found., 1995. Fellow Am. Coll. Cardiology, Am. Coll. Chest Physicians, Am. Heart Assn.; mem. ACP, Am. Heart Assn., Soc. Critical Care Medicine, Am. Fedn. Clin. Rsch., Alpha Omega Alpha. Office: One Cooper Plaza 366 Dorrance Camden NJ 08103 Office Phone: 856-342-2624. Business E-Mail: hollenberg-steven@cooperhealth.edu. *

HOLLEY, SUSAN L., psychologist; b. Coral Gables, Fla., 1951; d. Frank N. Holley III and Mary Lou Porlick, Robert A. Porlick (Stepfather) and Jean Holley (Stepmother); 1 child, H. Marie Warga. BA in Psychology, U. South Fla., Tampa, 1973; MEd in Counseling, U. Miami, Coral Gables, 1975; PhD in Clin. Psychology, Calif. Sch. Profl. Psychology, 1989. Cert. specialist in clin. psychology Am. Bd. Profl. Psychology, 2003, lic. clin. psychologist, cert. health svc. provider in psychology, profl. alcoholism specialist. Addiction counselor South Miami Hosp., Fla., 1979—81; therapist New Beginnings Chem. Dependency Program, Century City, Calif., 1983—84; employee assistance adminstr. Aero Med. Advisors, Westchester, Calif., 1984—86; psychology practicum Switzer Ctr. of Ednl. Therapy, Torrance, Calif., 1986—87; employee assistance counselor Entertainment Industry Referral and Assistance Ctr., Burbank, Calif., 1986—88; psychology intern Vets. Adminstrn. Psychology Dept., Brentwood, Calif., 1988—89; postdoctoral fellow, rsch. asst. Family Project, Psychology Dept. U. of Calif., LA, 1990—91; clin. psychologist, pvt. practice Gelbart & Assocs., Redondo Beach, Calif., 1992—94, Susan Holley, PhD A Psychology Corp., Lancaster, Calif., 1993—. Clin. psychologist Out patient Mental Health Unit, Edwards Air Force Base, Calif., 1994—95; staff psychologist Palmdale Hosp., Calif., 1993—96; chem. dependency therapist Torrance Meml. Hosp. Chem. Dependency Ctr., Torrance, 1992—93. Mem. Lancaster West Rotary Club, Calif., 2000—09. Mem.: APA, Sierra Club (bd. mem. Miami 1980), Calif. and LA Psychol. Assn., Employee Assistance Program Assn. (assoc.; treas. 1985, newsletter editor 1991, Appreciation Plaque 1991), Lancaster United Meth. Ch. Achievements include development of and presentation on the treatment of dual diagnosis patients with bipolar disorder and chemical dependency. Avocations: dressage horseback riding, photography, swimming, dance. Office: 43535 17th St W Ste 304 Lancaster CA 93534 Office Phone: 661-942-4079. Office Fax: 661-942-3887.

HOLLIDAY, ROY, radiologist, educator; MD, NYU, 1982. Diplomate Am. Bd. Radiology, 1986. Resident diagnostic radiology NYU Med. Ctr., NYC, 1983—86, fellow neuroradiology, 1986—87; clin. prof. radiology Sch. of Medicine NYU; dir. radiology NY Eye & Ear Infirmary, NYC, 2002—; diagnostic radiologist Beth Israel Med. Ctr., NYC, St. Luke's-Roosevelt Hosp. Ctr., NYC. Mem. editl. bd. (several profl. publs.). Mem.: NY Head and Neck Soc., NY Otologic Soc., Am. Soc. of Head and Neck Radiology, Am. Soc. of Neuroradiology, Radiologic Soc. of N.Am. Office: New York Eye and Ear Infirmary Radiology Department 310 E 14th St New York NY 10003 Office Phone: 212-979-4397. Office Fax: 212-353-5727.

HOLLIER, LARRY HAROLD, vascular surgeon, hospital administrator, dean; b. Crowley, La., Apr. 18, 1943; s. Villere Joseph and Agnes (Guidry) H.; m. Diana Gayle Johnson, Jan. 25, 1964; children: Larry Jr., Michelle Ann. BS, La. State U., 1965, MD, 1968. Diplomate Am. Bd. Surgery, spl. qualifications in vascular surgery. Intern Charity Hosp. La., New Orleans, 1968-69, gen. surgery resident, 1969-75; vascular surgery fellow Baylor U. Med. Ctr., Dallas, 1973-74; chief vascular surgery La. State U. Med. Sch., New Orleans, 1975-80, Mayo Clinic, Rochester, Minn., 1980-87; chmn. dept. surgery Ochsner Clnic, New Orleans, 1987-93; med. dir. HCI Internat. Med. Centre, Glasgow, Scotland, 1993—96; Julius H. Jacobson II MD prof. surgery Mount Sinai Sch. Medicine, NYC, 1996—2003, chmn. dept. surgery, 1996—2003; surgeon-in-chief Mount Sinai Med. Ctr., NYC; pres. The Mount Sinai Hosp., NYC, 2002—03; dean, Sch. Medicine La. State U. Health Sci. Ctr., New Orleans, 2004—. Founder divsn. vascular surgery Mayo Clinic, Rochester, 1983; bd. mgmt. Ochsner Clinic, New Orleans, 1989-93. Editor: Vascular Surgery - Basic Science in Clinical Correlations, 1994, Haimovici's Vascular Surgery, 1995. Maj. USAF, 1970-72. Fellow ACS (young surgeons rep. 1979, pres. La. chpt. 1989); mem. Soc. Vascular Surgery (chmn. membership com. 1985-86), Soc. Clin. Vascular Surgery (pres. 1995), So. Assn. Vascular Surgery (pres. 1995), Midwestern Vascular Soc. (pres. 1988). Avocations: sailing, scuba diving. Office: LSU Med Sch 433 Bolivar New Orleans LA 70112 Office Phone: 504-568-4800.

HOLLINGSWORTH, DONEEN B., state agency administrator; m. Rusty Hollingsworth; 2 children. BA in Polit. Sci., U. SD, Vermillion. Staff mem. SD Bur. Fin. & Mgmt.; spl. asst. to Govs. Mickelson & Miller Office of the Gov., SD; adminstr. SD Dept. Edn. & Cultural Affairs; sec. SD Dept. Health, Pierre, 1995—. Office: Dept Health 600 E Capitol Ave Pierre SD 57501-2536

HOLLINSHEAD, ARIEL CAHILL, oncologist, educator, researcher; b. Allentown, Pa., Aug. 24, 1929; d. Earl Darnell and Gertrude Loretta (Cahill) H.; m. Montgomery K. Hyun, June 12, 1957; children: William C., Christopher C. Student, Swarthmore Coll., 1947-48; AB, Ohio U., 1951, DSc (hon.), 1977; MA, George Washington U., 1955, PhD, 1957, MD, 1977. Asst. prof., fellow in virology Baylor U. Med. Ctr., 1958-59; asst. prof. pharmacology George Washington Med. Ctr., 1959-61, asst. prof. medicine, 1961-64, assoc. prof. medicine, head lab. virus and cancer rsch., 1964-73, prof., dir. lab. virus and cancer rsch., 1974-89; on sabbatical leave 1990, prof. medicine emeritus, 1991—; rschr. HI Virus and Cancer Rsch., 1991—2006. Mem. bd. Neogenix; clin. rschr. trials in oncology and virology; cons. to biotech. cos.; panelist FDA and NIH. Contbr. over 280 articles on active immunotherapy and immunochemotherapy of cancer and virus diseases to sci. jours. Bd. dirs. Nat. Women's Econ. Alliance, Ohio U., Med. Coll. Pa., 1980-2003, Women's Inst., 1995-97. Named Bicentennial Med. Woman of Yr., Joint Bd. Am. Med. Colls., 1976, one of Outstanding Woman of Am., 1987, Outstanding Alumnus of Yr., Ohio U., 1990; recipient Cert. Merit Med. Coll. Pa., 1975-76, Marion Spencer Fay Med. Woman of Year award Med. Coll. Pa.; decorated Star of Europe, 1980. Fellow AAAS (med. sci. com. 1993-96, 99—), Washington Acad. Sci. N.Y. Acad. Scis.; mem. Grad. Women in Sci. (nat. pres. 1985-86, bd. dirs. 1986-92, nat. liaison to Washington, 1992—), Internat. Soc. Preventive Oncology, Nat. Soc. Exptl. Biology and Medicine (Disting. Scientist award 1985, Disting. Scientist emeritus award for Outstanding Career in Tchg. and Rsch. in Medicine 1996, past pres. Greater Washington chpt.), Am. Soc. Microbiology, Am. Assn. Cancer Research, Am. Assn. Immunologists, Women in Cancer Rsch., Vet. Females Am., Clin. Immunology Soc., Internat. Soc. Antiviral Research, Am. Soc. Clin. Oncology, Internat. Assn. Study Lung Cancer, Internat. Union Against Cancer, Am. Med. Writers Assn., Soc. Profs. George Washington U. Emeriti, Blue Ridge Mountain Country Club, Twin Isles Country Club, Washington Forum (pres. 1987, 91), Phi Beta Kappa (Mother of Immunotherapy award 2010). Achievements include identification of antiviral drugs and vaccines; discovering resistance to antiviral drugs; being first to purify, develop and test cancer gene products, including peptides and to study activities; first to invent field called proteomics; peptides were studied and identified for the ability to induce long-lasting cell-mediated immunity; developed proteomics technology and pioneered clinical testing and monitoring epitope activity during seventeen clinical trials; patentee in field, having five volumes of medical research papers availible for review at the National Library of Medicine in Bethesda, Maryland as well as other institutions. Home: 23465 Harborview Rd #622 Punta Gorda FL 33980-2162

HOLLIS, JULIA ANN ROSHTO, critical care, medical, and surgical nurse; b. Monroe, La., June 25, 1945; d. Joseph Edward Roshto and Mary Eleanor Coverdale Larsen; m. William Davis Hollis, Mar. 2, 1964; children: David Terrel, Julia Allison. BSN, N.E. La. U., 1976. RN, La., Ala., Miss.; cert. BCLS, ACLS. Staff nurse to head nurse E.A. Conway Hosp., Monroe, 1977-84; staff nurse, charge nurse ICU, critical care North Monroe Community Hosp., Monroe, 1984-87; staff nurse neurotrama surg. ICU U. South Ala. Med. Ctr., Mobile, 1988-89; staff nurse, charge nurse Norrell Health Care, Mobile, 1990—, Medforce Internat., New Orleans; owner Resource Mgmt., 1997. Mem. AACN, AAUW, Ala. Nurses Assn., Met. Writers Guild, Baldwin County Writers Assn.

HOLLIS, RICHARD B., pharmaceutical executive; Attented, St. Mary's Coll.; BA in Psychology, San Francisco State U. Product sales position Baxter Travenol (now Baxter Internat.); divsn. mgr. Imed Corp. (acquired by Warner Lambert, now part of Pfizer Inc.); western bus. unit mgr. Genentech, Inc., 1986—89; gen. mgr., v.p., mktg. and sales Instromedix, 1989—91; COO Bioject Med., 1991—94; founder, chmn., CEO Hollis-Eden Pharmaceuticals, Inc., San Diego, 1994—. Office: Hollis-Eden Pharmaceuticals Inc 4435 Eastgate Hall Ste 400 San Diego CA 92121 Office Phone: 858-587-9333.

HOLLISTER, BROOKE ANN, sociologist, educator; b. Goleta, Calif., Sept. 13, 1981; PhD, UCSF, 2008. Asst. prof. U. Calif., San Francisco, 2009—. Dir. Students Social Security and Concerned Scientists Aging, 2004—; vice chair of nat. bd. dirs. Gray Panthers, 2009—. Grant, NIH. Mem.: Am. Sociol. Assn., Gerontol. Soc. America, Am. Soc. Aging. Avocation: swimming. Office: 3333 California St Ste 340 San Francisco CA 94118 Business E-Mail: brooke.hollister@ucsf.edu.

HOLLISTER, DICKERMAN, JR., medical oncologist; MD, U. Va., 1975. Diplomate Am. Bd. Internal Medicine, Am. Bd. Internal Medicine-med. oncology, Am. Bd. Internal Medicine-hematology. Intern NY Hosp. Med. Ctr. Queens, 1976, resident in internal medicine, 1978, fellow in hematology, 1981; hosp. affiliation includes

Greenwich Hosp., Conn. Named one of Top Doctors, NY Mag., 2010. Mem.: Greenwich Hosp. Assn. Office: Greenwich Hospital 5 Perryridge Rd Greenwich CT 06830 Office Phone: 203-863-3000.

HOLLISTER, WINSTON NED, pathologist; b. Milw., Mar. 23, 1942; s. Harold Arthur and Jeannette Clara (Gastrav) H.; m. Carol Jean Potter, Dec. 7, 1963 (div. May 1978); children: Timothy Carl, David Andrew; m. Margaret Ravenel Papen, Oct. 29, 1988; children: Charles Davis, Margaret Ravenel. BS in Physics, U. Wis., 1964; MD, Med. Coll. Wis., 1971. Diplomate Am. Bd. Internal Medicine, Am. Bd. Pathology. Staff pathologist St. Joseph's Hosp., Milw., 1976—; pres., CEO Franciscan Shared Lab, Wauwatosa, Wis., 1988-90; med. dir., chmn. bd. dirs. Med. Sci. Labs., Wauwatosa, 1989—2003. Cons. in field. Contbr. articles to profl. jours. Vestry mem. St. Paul's Episcopal Ch., Milw., 1978-83. Lt. USN, 1964-67. Recipient Houghton & Houghton award Med. Soc. Wis., 1971. Fellow Coll. Am. Pathologists (clin. practice com. 1984-87); mem. ACP, Am. Pathology Found. (pres. 1994-96), Oconomowoc Lake Club, Pine Lake Yacht Club. Republican. Episcopalian. Avocations: sailing, skiing, tennis, travel, music. Home: 4940 N Maple Lane Nashotah WI 53058 Office: 4940 N Maple Ln Nashotah WI 53058 *

HOLLMANN, WILDOR, physician; b. Menden/Westfalen, Germany, Jan. 30, 1925; s. Albert and Hetty (Bomnueter) H.; m. Inge Cuesters; children: Helmut, Ulrike. MD, U. Cologne, Germany, 1954; MD (hon.), Free U., Brussels, 1986; MD (hon.), U. Thessaloniki, Greece, 1995. Founder Inst. Cardiology and Sports Medicine, Cologne, 1958, chmn. cardiology and sport medicine, 1965; rector German Sport U., Cologne, 1969-71; pres. German Fedn. Sports Medicine, 1984-98, World Fedn. Sports Medicine, 1986-94, hon. pres., 1998—; pres. German Olympic Soc., 1994-97; hon. prof. U. Thessaloniki, 1995. Sci. com. German Def. Ministry, 1969-94. Recipient Carl-Diem award, 1961, HuFeland award, 1963, Max-Buerger award 1969, Gold medal German Med. Assn., 1976, Sir-Philip-Noel-Baker award UNESCO, 1976, Gold medal World Fedn. Sports Medicine, 1990, German Sports U., 2005, Humboldt Soc., 2008, Paracelsus medal German Med. Profession, 2002, Beckmann medal German Fedn. Prevention and Rehab. Cardiac Diseases, 2003; named Hon. Citizen german Sports U., 1995, Brueggen, 2009, Menden, 2006. Office: German Sport U 50933 Cologne NRW Germany Home Phone: 192163 5430; Office Phone: 49221498251000. E-mail: wildor.hollmann@nexgo.de.

HOLLO, GABOR, ophthalmologist; b. Budapest, Dec. 19, 1960; s. Istvan and Friderika (Hollitscher) H.; m. Marta Varga, Feb. 24, 1991; children: Hollo, Balazs. MD, Semmelweis U. Med. Sch., 1985, PhD, 1996; DSc, Semmelwies U., 2004. Resident in ophthalmology Semmelweis U. Med. Sch., Budapest, 1985-89, prof.'s asst., 1990-97, dir. glaucoma svc., 1997—, prof. ophthalmology, 2006—. Author: Practical Ophthalmology, 1995, Glaucoma: Pathophysiology and Clinics, 1997; editor: Exfoliation Syndrome and Exfoliative Glaucoma, 2008; contbr. articles to profl. jours. Mem. Soc. for Sci. Edn. Hungarian Soc. for Natural Scis., Hungarian Ophthal. Soc., European Glaucoma Soc. (travel and rsch. subcom. 1992-2000, exec. com. 2004—), Assn. for Eye Rsch., Assn. Rsch. Vision and Opthalmology. Office: Semmelweis U 1st Dept Ophthalmology Tomo Str 25/29 1083 Budapest Hungary

HOLLOWAY, EDWARD OLIN, human services manager; b. Rochester, NY, July 3, 1944; s. Charles Robert and Chrystal Gertrude (Darling) Holloway; m. Hama Elizabeth Farris, Dec. 23, 1967. AA, Palm Beach Jr. Coll., 1964; BA, Lenoir Rhyne Coll., 1967; MS in Pub. Health, U. N.C., 1975. From sanitarian I to sanitarian supr. I Palm Beach County Health Dept., West Palm Beach, Fla., 1969—73; from coord. emergency med. svcs. to exec. dir. dist. IX Health Planning Coun., Inc., West Palm Beach, 1975—89; sr. health and human svcs. planner bd. county commrs. Palm Beach County Dept. Cmty. Svcs., West Palm Beach, 1989—2000. Mem. faculty Pub. Health Physician Residency Program, 1990—2002, apptd. spl. advisor, 2002—; mem. accreditation five yrs. U. Miami, 1999—2004; mem. steering com. Fla. Atlantic U. Inst. Govt., 1992—2000, vice chmn., 1994—99, apptd. spl. adv., 2000—. Author: Our Dog Foxtrot Ans Voice Mail; contribr. (article) Alum. Profile, UNC Sch. Pub. Health Alum. News, 2010. Vol. planning staff fed. govt., 2004; chmn. dist. 9 adv. coun. Dept. Health and Rehab. Svcs., West Palm Beach, 1990—92; pres. Fla. Assn. Health Planning Agys., Inc., 1984—89; planning unit steering com. Leadership Palm Beach County, 1991; Palm Beach County data collection com. Health and Human Svcs. Planning Assn., 1992—98; mem. Interagy. Planning Group, 1994—2000; mem. sch. adv. com. Palm Beach Gardens Cmty. HS, 1994—, vice chair, 2000—03, mem. membership safety com., 2000—, mem. budget com., 2001—; appointee for customer svc. West Palm Beach VA Med. Ctr., 1997—; mem. Palm Beach County Partnership for Aging program United Way, 1998—; apptd. ex officio mem., spl. advisor Palm Beach County Citizens Adv. Com. on Health and Human Svc., 2000—, mem. planning/implementation subcom. Palm Beach County comprehensive plan, 2005—; vol. State of Fla. Dept. Health, 2000—, vol. staff, chair planning implementing and evaluation needed health and human svc. sys. improvements Guiding Principles and Ops. Comm., 2002—; vol. team to evaluate quality of care and customer svc. provided at local VA Med. Ctr. Fed. Insp. Gen.'s Office, 2002; apt. hon. co-chmn. NRA Spl. Task Force. With US Army, 1967—69, Vietnam. Decorated Bronze Star, Purple Heart, Army Commendation medal, Cross of Gallantry (Vietnam); recipient Cert. Appreciation, Wall Soc. of the Vietnam Veterans Memorial Fund, 2004, 2006, Letters of Commendation, CDC, 1980, Outstanding Svc. award, Fla. Assn. Health Planning Agys., 1989, Outstanding Achievement award, Bd. County Commrs., Palm Beach County Citizens Adv. Com. on Health and Human Svcs., 1995, Letters of Commendation, State of Fla., Lawton Chiles, 1998, Cert. of Merit, Rep. Nat. Com., 2001, Cert. Appreciation, Americans Disabled for Life Meml., 2003, Cert. Honor, Pres. 2004 Team, 2004, Cert. Commendation, Mus. US Army, 2004, Cert. of Unanimous Inclusion in Rep. Presdl. Honor Roll, Nat. Rep. Congressional Com., 2005, Congl. Order Merit, Rep. Congl. Com., 2006, 2008, Cert. Achievement, VA Med. Ctr., 2006, Cert. Appreciation, Ducks Unltd., 2007, Vietnam Vets. Meml. Fund, 2007, Cert. Appreciation award, Citizen Adv. Com. Health & Human Svcs., 2009, Recognition of Commitment in Reserving Constl. Amendment Rights, NRA; grantee State Fla. Dept. Transp. planning grantee, Regional Emergency Med. Svcs., 1975. Mem.: DAV (Comdrs. Club 2007—08), APHA, ASPA (chpt. 102 coun. 1989—98), Fla. Environ. Health Assn., Neuropathy Assn., Nat. Alliance for Mentally Ill, Nat. Environ. Health Assn., Am. Coll. Grad. Med. Edn., US Army (life; charter life mem. Army Hist. Found., decorated Mil. Order of Purple Heart 2005, decorated Sr. Freedom Team Salute Commendation 2008), Am. Legion, U. N.C. Sch. Pub. Health Alumni Assn. (bd. dirs. 1994—2001), Paralyzed Vets. Am. (life Cert. of Appreciation 2007), Vietnam Vets. Am., Silver Club. Republican. Lutheran. Avocations: reading, skeet shooting, machairology. Home and Office: 104 Vision Ct Palm Beach Gardens FL 33418-3859 Office Phone: 561-622-8495. Personal E-mail: holl1543@bellsouth.net.

HOLLOWELL, JOHN W., retired urologist; b. Norfolk County, Va., July 5, 1922; s. Edward Caleb Hollowell and Marian Louise Leggett; m. Mary Louse Akert, Jan. 17, 1953; children: Heather, Mary Louise, Lesley, John. BS, Coll. William and Mary, Williamsburg, Va., 1943; MD, U. Va., Charlottesville, 1946. Diplomate Am. Bd. Urology, 1955. Resident Roosevelt Hosp., NYC, 1949—52. Cons. urology US Naval Hosp., Portsmouth, Va., 1960—85; pres. Portsmouth Acad. Medicine, 1969—70. Contbr. scientific papers to profl. jours. Chmn. Portsmouth Planning Commn., 1982—85; bd. dirs Ea. Va. Health Sys. Agy., 1976—81, Tidewater Health Care, Va., 1988—92. Lt. USNR, 1942—49, Va. Recipient Disting. Svc. award, Gen. Assembly Va., 1993. Mem.: AMA, Med. Soc. Va. (pres. 1991—92), Rotary Club (life; pres. 1978—79, Paul Harris fellow 1988). Republican. Episcopalian. Avocations: sailing, gardening.

HOLLWEG, ARND, clergyman; b. Mar. 23, 1927; s. Ernst and Henriette (Voswinckel) Hollweg; m. Astrid Blomerius, Aug. 30, 1961; children: Heike, Uta, Karen. Student, U. Bonn, 1946—48, U. Goettingen, 1948—50, U. Tuebingen, 1952—53, U. So. Calif., 1953—54, U. Muenster, 1955—56; D of Theology, U. Bonn, 1967. Ordained to ministry United Chs. Rhineland, 1958. Tchr. religion Gymnasium and Berufsschule, Lobberich, Germany; asst. min. ch. Essen, Germany, 1955—57; lectr. Inst. Theology and Edn. of Rhineland Protestant Ch. (W.Ger.); regional pastor Rhineland Christian Edn., 1958—63; rschr. Ecumenical Inst., U. Bonn, 1964—65; pastor Bad Honnef, W.Ger., 1966—72; dept. head. hdqrs. diaconical relief ctr. German Protestant Ch., Stuttgart, 1973—76; pastor Ref. Bethlehemsgemeinde, Berlin, 1976—90; chmn. German Reformed Ch. of West Berlin, 1976—90; freelance writer and scientist, 1991—. Lectr. Free U., Berlin, 1978—79, Kirchliche Hochschule, Berlin, 1979—84. Author: Theologie und Empirie, 3d edit., 1974, Gruppe-Gesellschaft-Diakonie, 1976; author: (with others) Obdachlosenhilfe, 1981; author: (with Astrid Hollweg) Biblischer Glaube und neuzeitliches Bewusstsein, 1999; author: Die Glaubensbotschaft von Kurt Gerstein, 2002, Man in the Context of Life in his World, 2004, Ramifications of Globalizations, 2004, Dietrich Braun: Dealing with the Problem of Language for Faith, 2004, Basic Questions of Anthropological and Theological Cognition, 2005, Spirituality and Mysticism, 2006, Christian Faith, Philosophy and Science Against the Background of the Present Ecumenical Discussion, 2007, Contexts of the Global Economical Crisis in the Perspective of Empirical Theology, 2009, Work and Economy in Social Life Today, 2010, Theorie versus Lebenspraxis, 2010; editor: Innere Mission und Diakonie; contbr. numerous essays to profl. publs. With German Army, 1943—44, with German Inf., 1945. Mem.: Bibliotheque World Wide Soc. / IAPGS, Soc. Gestalt Theory and Its Applications, Soc. Protestant Educators (lectr. 1958—63), Group Dynamics and Social Psychology (founder), German Soc. Pastoral Psychology (co-founder). Achievements include discovery of theological scientific approach to social dynamics and theories of cognition and hist. of scis. in the dialogue between theology, interdisciplinary scis. and empirical thinking. Home: Hähnelstr 7 D-12159 Berlin Germany E-mail: arndastrid.hollweg@t-online.de.

HOLMAN, CHARLES RAYMOND, osteopathic physician; b. Green City, Mo., July 18, 1924; s. Squire Paul and Meeda May (Daniel). Student, N.E. Mo. State U., 1943; DO, U. Health Scis., Kansas City, 1949. Intern McDowell Hosp., Phoenix, 1949-50; practice medicine specializing in family practice Kirksville, Mo., 1950-53; Cardwell Hosp., Stella, Mo., 1957-61; resident in anesthesiology Kirksville Osteo. Hosp., 1961-63; practice medicine specializing in anesthesiology Lansing Gen. Hosp., Mich., 1963-73; gen. practice medicine VA Regional Office, Cleve., 1977-81, gen. practice Phoenix, 1981-93; pvt. practice Kirksville, 1993—. Lt. USAF, 1943-45, U.S. Army, 1953-56. Mem. AMA (life), Am. Osteopathic Assn. (life), Assn. Mil. Surgeons U.S. Home: 601 W Illinois St Kirksville MO 63501-1474

HOLMAN, HALSTED REID, physician, educator; b. Cleve., Jan. 17, 1925; s. Emile Frederic and Ann Peril (Purdy) H.; m. Barbara Marie Lucas, June 26, 1949 (div. July 9, 1982); children: Michael, Andrea, Alison; m. Diana Barbara Dutton, Aug. 10, 1985; 1 child, Geoffrey. Student, Stanford U., 1942-43, UCLA, 1943-44; MD, Yale U., 1949. Med. resident Montefiore Hosp., NYC, 1952-55; staff physician Rockefeller Inst., NYC, 1955-60; prof. medicine Stanford (Calif.) U., 1960—, chmn. dept. medicine, 1960-71, co-chief, divsn. family and cmty. medicine, 1987-2001, dir. clin. scholar program, 1969-97, dir. Multipurpose Arthritis Ctr., 1977-97, co-chief, divsn. immunology and rheumatology, 1997-2000, dir. Stanford Program for Mgmt. of Chronic Disease, 1997—2001; co chair Santa Clara Countywide Chronic Care Coalition, 2009—. Pres. Midpeninsula Health Svc., Palo Alto, Calif., 1975-80; mem. adv. bd. Calif Health Facilities Commn., Sacramento, 1978-81, Office Tech. Assessment, U.S. Congress, 1979-81, Inst. Advancement of Health, NYC, 1982-90; Guggenhime prof. medicine, 1960—; mem. steering com., Pacific Bus. Group on Health Breakthroughs in Chronic Care Program, 2005-; health adv.commn. Santa Clara County, 2006-; mem. planning com., Assn. Am. Med. Coll. Calif. Academic Chronic Care Collaborative, 2007-. Author 2 books; assoc. editor Arthritis and Rheumatism, 1995-2000; co-editor Chronic Illness, 2004—; contbr. articles to profl. jours. Recipient Bauer Meml. award, Arthritis and Rheumatism Found., N.Y., 1964, John W. Gardner Vision award, Pathways Found., 2003. Master: Am. Coll. Rheumatology (Presdl. Gold medal 2001); fellow: AAAS (coun. 1974—79), ACP (Laureate award no. Calif. chpt. 1994, John Phillips Meml. award 2004); mem.: Improving Chronic Illness Care-R.W. Johnson Found. (Vision award 2001), Arthritis Found. (Hero Overcoming Arthritis 1998, Engalitcheff award 1999, McGuire Educator award 2000), Western Assn. Physicians (pres. 1966), Am. Soc. Clin. Investigation (pres. 1970), Assn. Am. Physicians. Democrat. Home: 747 Dolores St Stanford CA 94305-8427 Office: Stanford U Divsn Immunol and Rheumatol 1000 Welch Rd Ste 203 Palo Alto CA 94304-1808 Office Fax: 650-723-9656.

HOLMAN, JAMES, allergist; b. Jacksonville, Tex., Aug. 13, 1921; MD, U. Tex. Southwest, 1945. Diplomate Am. Bd. Allergy and Immunology. Intern Parkland Meml. Hosp., Dallas, 1945-46; resident in allergy U. Va., Charlottesville, 1947-48; fellow in medicine U. Tex. Southwest, Dallas, 1946-47, 48-50; with Presbyn. Hosp., Dallas, 1966—. Asst. clin. prof. pharmacology U. Tex. Southwest Med. Sch., 1950-83, clin. assoc. prof. internal medicine, 1981-88. Fellow Am. Acad. Allergy, Asthma and Immunology, Am. Coll. Allergy, Asthma and Immunology, Am. Coll. Clin. Pharmacology and Chemotherapy. Office: 8220 Walnut Hill Ln Ste #101 Dallas TX 75231 Home Phone: 214-363-5551; Office Phone: 214-369-1901.

HOLMAN, LARRY DEAN, retired healthcare administrator; b. Adams, Nebr., Nov. 1, 1940; s. Clarence Woodford and Ethel Elizabeth (Remmenga) H.; m. Setsuko Umekawa, Dec. 5, 1960 (div. Aug. 1978); children: Lori Akiko, Yuko Donna; m. Debbie Joan Berkowitz, Dec. 8, 1980; children: Andrew Joseph, Jodi Michelle, Matthew Jacob. AA, Palomar C.C., San Marcos, Calif., 1971, C.C. of Phila., 1999; BS, George Washington U., 1974; MBA, LaSalle U., 1989, MS, 1990. Enlisted USN, 1958, advanced through grades to lt. comdr., ret., 1982, hosp. corpsman, 1958-71; with USN Med. Service Corps, 1971-82; purchasing dir. St. Francis Country House, Darby, Pa., 1982-85; bus. mgr. Stapeley Hall, Phila., 1985-86; bus., program mgr. Seaman's Ch. Inst., Phila., 1986-87; buyer Grad. Hosp., Phila., 1988-89, Grad. Health System, Phila., 1989; purchasing agt. Shriners Hosps., Phila., 1989-91; purchasing mgr. Jeanes Hosp., Phila., 1991-98; Y2K project site coord. Temple U. Health Sys., Phila., 1998-2000; asst. dir. purchasing Temple U., Phila., 2000—06; ret., 2006. Mem.: AMVETS, VFW (life), Phila. Vets. Comfort House (bd. dirs.), US Naval Inst., Nat. Mus. MC, Nat. Naval Officers Assn., CEC/Seabee Hist. Found., Nat. Assn. Medics and Corpsmen, Vets. Vietnam War, Naval. Res. Assn., Vietnam Era Seabees, Fleet Res. Assn., Non-Commd. Officers Assn., Am. Assn. Navy Hosp. Corps, Am. Soc. Mil. Compts., Marine Corps. League (assoc.), Army Navy Union (life), Phila. Vietnam Vet. Meml. Soc. (life), USN Cruiser Sailors' Assn. (life), Nat. Mus. Am. Jewish Mil. History (life), Internat. Chief Petty Officers Assn. (life), Nat. Assn. Uniformed Svcs. (life), Am. Mil. Retirees Assn. (life), Am. Mil. Soc. (life), Jewish War Vets. U.S. (life; past comdr. Phila. county coun., past comdr. dept. Pa., past comdr. Post 706), Mil. Officers Assn. Am. (life; bd. mem. chpt. 266, exec. v.p., Pa. State Coun.), Navy Seabee Vets. Am. (life), Navy League U.S. (life), Vietnam Vets. Am. (life; pres. Pa. State coun.), Assn. Mil. Surgeons U.S. (life), Hollidaysburg Veterans Home (v.p. vets. adv. coun.), Nat. World War II Mus., Friends of Pennypack Pk. (life), Nat. World War II Meml., Nat. Mus. US Army, Navy Club USA, Am. Legion. Jewish. Avocations: reading, counseling, writing. Home: 6746 Souder St Philadelphia PA 19149-2208 Personal E-mail: lholman@prodigy.net.

HOLMDAHL, JOHAN, physician; b. Gothenburg, Sweden, Feb. 17, 1955; MD, U. Gothenburg, 1982, PhD, 2001. Physician Sahlgrenska U. Hosp., 1984—. Mem. bd. Swedish Nat. Coun. on Med. Ethics, 1991—97, Halso och sjukvardsstyrelsen, Vastra Gotalandsregionen, 1998—2004. Mem.: Swedish Soc. Nephrology, Gothenburg Soc. Medicine, Swedish Soc. Medicine. Avocations: sailing, skiing. Office: Sahlgrenska University Gothenburg SE 413 45 Sweden Business E-Mail: johan.holmdahl@medicine.gu.se.

HOLMES, DAVID RICHARD, JR., cardiologist; b. Oak Park, Ill., Nov. 21, 1945; s. David R. and Ethel B. Holmes; m. Virginia Mary Zuehlke; children: David, Joshua, Nathaniel, Jessica. BA, Princeton U., 1967; MD, Marquette U., 1971. Intern Virginia Mason Hosp., Seattle, 1971-72; fellow internal medicine and cardiology Mayo Clinic, Rochester, Minn., 1972-76, physician, 1978—, dir. cardiac catheterization lab., dir. ACC/SVS renal and iliac stenting project, 2001—, Edward W. and Betty Knight Scripps prof. cardiovasc. medicine, 2003. Mem., bd, dirs. Franciscan Skemp Hospital, 2005. Capt. USN, 1976-78. Recipient Internal Medicine Achievement award Mayo Grad. Sch., 1974; Transcatheter Therapeutics Career Achievement award Wash. Cardiology Ctr., 1995, Eugene Drake award, 2006, Dist. Scientist award Am. Coll. Cardiology, 2006, Eugene Drake award, 2006. Fellow Am. Coll. Cardiology (cardiac catheterization com. 1994-96, edn. program com., co-dir. interventional symposium 1999-2000, chmn. procedures tng. work 1999, pres.-elect Minn. chpt. 2003, trustee 2004, v.p. 2009, Disting. Scientist award 2006); mem. Soc. Cardiac Angiography and Interventions, Minn. Soc. Internal Medicine, Am. Heart Assn. (James B. Herrick award, 2007), Assn. Univ. Cardiologists, Interventional Andreas Gruentzig Soc. (inaugural mem.), ACC (pres. elect, 2010), Sigma Xi, Alpha Omega Alpha. Business E-Mail: holmes.david@mayo.com.

HOLMES, DOROTHY A., psychologist; BA, Bethune-Cookman Coll., Daytona Beach, Fla.; MEd, East Carolina U., Greenville, NC; PhD, NC State U., Raleigh. Psychologist Delinquency and Dependency Ct., Fla. Mem.: Assn. Black Psychologists (past pres., treas. Fla. chpt., nat. pres. 2007—09).

HOLMES, EDWARD WARREN, academic administrator, medical educator; b. Winona, Miss., Jan. 25, 1941; s. Edward and Mary (Hart) H.; m. Judith L. Swain, Jan. 25, 1980. BS, Washington and Lee U., 1963; MD, U. Pa., 1967. Intern Hosp. of U. Pa., 1967-68; resident in medicine Duke U. Med. Ctr., Durham, NC, 1970—71, 1973—74, fellow in metabolism, 1971—73; prof. medicine and biochemistry Duke U. Sch. Medicine, Durham, NC, 1974-91, chief divsn. metabolism, endocrinology and genetics, 1983—91; investigator Howard Hughes Med. Inst., 1974-87; prof., chmn. dept. medicine U. Pa., Phila., 1991-97; sr. assoc. dean rsch. Stanford U. Sch. Medicine, 1997-2000; dean Duke U. Sch. Medicine, Durham, 1999—2000; vice chancellor academic affairs Duke U. Med. Ctr., Durham, 1999—2000; vice chancellor health scis., dean sch. medicine U. Calif., San Diego, 2000—06; exec. dep. chmn. clin.-translational scis. Biomedical Rsch. Coun. (BMRC), exec. chmn. Nat. Med. Rsch. Coun. Agency for Sci., Tech. and Rsch. (A*STAR), Singapore, 2006—; Lien Ying Chow prof. medicine Nat. U. Singapore, 2006—. Reviewer in molecular medicine. With USPHS, 1968-70. Grantee NIH. Mem. Am. Soc. Clin. Investigation, Assn. Am. Physicians. Office: Agency For Sci, Tech And Rsch 1 Fusionopolis Way 20-10 Connexis North Tower Singapore 138632 Singapore Office Phone: 858-534-1501. Office Fax: 858-822-0084. E-mail: lfelix@ucsd.edu.

HOLMES, GREGORY LAWRENCE, pediatrician, educator, neurologist; b. Toledo, Feb. 18, 1948; s. Harry and Dorothy Adeline (Wise) H.; m. Colleen Anne Reynolds, June 30, 1979; children: Marcus Christopher, Garrett Albert. BS, Washington and Lee U.,

1970; MD, U. Va., 1974. Diplomate Am. Bd. Pediatrics, 1979, Am. Bd. Psychiatry and Neurology, 1980. Intern Yale-New Haven Hosp., 1974-75, resident in pediatrics, 1975-76; resident in neurology U. Va. Sch. Medicine, Charlottesville, 1976-79; assoc. prof. pediatrics and neurology Newington (Conn.) Children's Hosp., Newington, 1979-86, Med. Coll. Ga., Augusta, 1986-88; pvt. practice specializing in pediatric neurology Farmington, Conn., 1978-86; practice medicine specializing in pediatrics Augusta, 1986-88; assoc. prof. to prof. of neurology & dir. Ctr. for Rsch, in Pediatric Epilepsy Harvard U. Med. Sch. Children's Hosp., Boston, 1988—2002; vis. rsch. scientist Institut Nat. de la Sante de la Recherche Medicale, Paris, 1996—97; prod. pediatrics Dartmouth Med. Sch., Hanover, NH, 2002—; chief, neurology sect. Dartmouth-Hitchcock Med. Ctr., Lebanon, NH, 2002—. Dir. Clin. Neurophysiology Lab. and Epilepsy Unit, Children's Hosp.; mem. speakers bur. Abbott Labs., North Chicago, Ill., 1982—, Ciba Geigy Labs., Summit, N.J., Wallace Labs., Cranbury, N.J., Parke-Davis Labs., Morris Plains, N.J.; neurol. cons. Waterbury (Conn.) Hosp., 1980-86, Southbury (Conn.) Tng. Sch., 1983-86, Mansfield (Conn.) Tng. Sch., 1983-84, VA Med. Ctr., Augusta, 1986-88. Mem. editl. bd. Brain and Devel. Jour. of Child Neurology, Pediat. Neurology, Annals of Neurology, Electroencephalography and Clin. Neurophysiology, Jour. Epilepsy; contbr. articles to profl. jours. Recipient Segawa award Japanese Child Neurology Soc., Michael Found. prize, Bonn, Germany, 1989, Basic Scientist award Milken Family Med. Found./Am. Epilepsy Soc., 1990; Sidney Farber rsch. grantee United Cerebral Palsy Assn., 1982-83. Fellow Am. Acad. Pediat.; mem. Am. Acad. Neurology (assoc.), Am. Epilepsy Soc., Am. Electroencephalographic Soc. (coun. mem. 1991-94), So. Electroencephalographic Soc., Ea. Assn. Electroencephalographers (coun. mem. 1991—), Child Neurology Soc. (exec. com. 1993-95). Presbyterian. Office: Dartmouth-Hitchcock Med Ctr 1 Med Ctr Dr Lebanon NH 03756 Office Phone: 603-650-8309. Office Fax: 603-650-6233.

HOLMES, HARRY DADISMAN, health care administrator; b. Houston, Aug. 8, 1944; s. Harry Newton and Ruth Eleanor (Dadisman) H.; children: Hillary Hunt, Ashley Elizabeth. BA, Rice U., 1966; MA, La. State U., 1968; PhD, U. Mo., 1973. Asst. prof. urban devel. U. Tenn., Knoxville, 1973—76; asst. to exec. v.p. Tex. Med. Ctr., Inc., Houston, 1976—80; dir. govt. affairs, orgnl. liaison U. Tex. System Cancer Ctr., Houston, 1980—90; asst. to pres. U. Tex. Sys. Cancer Ctr., Houston, 1981—90; v.p. govt. rels. U. Tex. M.D. Anderson Cancer Ctr., Houston, 1990—2006, pres. govt. interface strategies, 2006; sr. v.p. Tex. Med. Ctr., 2006—08; sr. policy advisor Harris County Healthcare Alliance, 2008—. Pres., bd. dirs. City of Houston Higher Edn. Fin. Corp., 1985-; mem. Cancer Ctrs. Adminstrs. Forum, 1994—; mem. select com. on pub. issues Greater Houston Hosp. Coun., 1983-94; mem. exec. adv. bd. White, Petrov and McHone, 1987-95; mem. pub. rels. adv. coun. Tex. Med. Ctr., 1985—; founder Houston Biotech. Assn., 1986; mem. exec. com. Nat. Comprehensive Cancer Networks, 1998—2006; chair public issues com. Assn. Am. Cancer Insts., 1999-2006; mem. govt. rels. com. Am. Hosp. Assn., 1999-2000; govt. rels. com., vice chmn. Tex. Healthcare and Biosci. Inst., 2005; pres. bd. dirs. City of Houston Health Facilities Corp., City of Houston Indsl. Devel. Corp., Nat. Coalition Cancer Rsch., 2005-. Mem. adminstrv. bd. St. Luke's Meth. Ch.; mem. Mayor's Task Force on Pvt. Sector Initiatives for Houston, 1981-82, Houston CC Found. Bd., 1992—, Greater Houston Partnership State and Fed. Com., 1989—; mem. U. Tex. Tex./Mex. Border Health Task Force, 1989-2003, exec. com., 1989-2001; pres. Houston Health Facilities Corp., 2000—, Houston Indsl. Devel. Corp., 2000—; mem. Rice U. Fund Coun., 1991-94, Nat. Cancer Ctrs. Task Force, 1991—; mem. steering com. Tex. Colorectal Cancer Plan; mem. exec. bd. Leadership Houston, 1983-86, Houston Ctr. for Humanities, 1983-86; mem. govt. rels. com. Greater Houston Hosp. Coun., 1985-95; mem. com. Instnl. Task Force on Oncology in Chile, 1986-87; exec. com. Instnl. Strategic Planning Com., 1986-95; divsn. chmn. United Way of Houston, 1983. Home: PO Box 1191 Houston TX 77251-1191

HOLMES, LEWIS B., pediatrician, medical geneticist; b. Memphis, Aug. 31, 1937; MD, Duke U., 1963. Cert. Pediat., Clin. Genetics. Resident in pediat. Mass. Gen. Hosp., Boston, 1963—65, fellow in pediatric endocrinology, 1965—66, chief genetics and teratology unit, dir. genetic counseling and screening services, dir. Antiepileptic Disease Pregnancy Registry; prof. pediat. Harvard Med. Sch., Boston, 1989—. Office: AED Pregnancy Registry Mass Gen Hosp 121 Innerbelt Rd Rm 220 Somerville MA 02143 also: Mass Gen Hosp for Children Warren 801 32 Fruit St Boston MA 02114 Office Phone: 617-726-1742. E-mail: holmes.lewis@mgh.harvard.edu.

HOLMES, LOUIS IRA, retired physician assistant, educator, photojournalist; b. LA, July 16, 1943; s. Louis Issac and Mabel Jane (Walsh) H.; children: Jonathan Joseph, Kimberly Ellen, Louis Boon. AA, El Camino Coll., Torrance, Calif., 1972; cert. physician asst., U. So. Calif., 1978. Cert. Nat. Commn. Cert. Physician Assts.; cert. ACLS. Resident in surgery Norwalk Hosp.-Yale U. Sch. Medicine, 1980; nursing staff emergency dept. South Bay Dist. Hosp., Redondo Beach, Calif., 1970-75; nursing staff trauma and surg. intensive care Harbor Gen. Hosp.-UCLA Med. Ctr., Torrance, 1976-77; physician asst. Gen. Med. Corp., LA, 1979; physician asst., divsn. thoracic surgery City of Hope Med. Ctr., Duarte, Calif., 1980-81; sr. physcian asst. thoracic and cardiovascular surgery Bert Meyer MD, et al, LA, 1981-91; sr. physician asst. cardiothoracic surgery, instr. postgrad. cardiothoracic surgery residency program Cedars-Sinai Med. Ctr., LA, 1991-95; asst. prof. clin. surgery and family medicine U. So. Calif., LA, 1995—2009, Keck Sch. Medicine Dept. Cardio Thoracic Surgery; phys. asst. in cardiothoracic surgery U. So. Calif., LA, 1995—2009. Vis. surg. instr., China; examiner Nat. Commn. on Cert. of Physician Assts., 1981—92; mem. program planning com. Masters Degree program in Health Sci. for Physician Assts., Calif. State U., Dominguez Hill, 1991—95; adj. faculty physician asst. program U. So. Calif., 1982—90, mem. adv. com., 1983—84, mem. long-range planning com., 1988—90; spkr., cons., expert witness in field; contbr. numerous color photographic images The Green Berets: Weapons and Equipment (Hans Halberstadt), 1999; bd. dirs. TV Parade Mag., 1991—2001; mem. adv. bd. Homeland Secuirty Policy Inst. Group, Inc., 2003—09; tactical weapons instr. Analytical Cons. for Security and Investigations, 2005—06; tactical pistol instr. Am. Def. Enterprises, 2006; NRA cert. instr., pistol and personal def., range safety officer; mil. advisor, cons. Ripple Effect-An Am. Film Inst. Movie, 2011. Contbr. articles to profl. jours. and chpts. to books; mem. editl. bd. Clinician Reviews, 1990-96, Physician Asst. Jour., 1987-90; asst. editor Family Caregiver Mag., 2005-06; med. tech. advisor, appeared in (feature film) City of Angles, TV program on History Channel, spl. ops.: Mike Force; military advisor, cons. Ripple Effect, 2011 Instr. ACLS, Am. Heart Assn., 1980-96. With Spl. Forces, US Army, 1964-70; with Calif. Army N.G., 1976-83, U.S. Army Res., 1984-91, bd. dirs. State Emergency Responces Sys. Inc., 2009-11, pres. Spl. Forces Assn., SC Recipient 21 mil. decorations, including awards from US, Vietnam, Thailand, Outstanding Svc. award Physician Asst. Jour., 1989, Outstanding Svc. award, Keck Sch. Medicine U. So. Calif., 2007, Letter Commendation, Acting Sec. Army, 2007, Cert. Appreciation, Gen. US Army Chief of Staff, 2007. Fellow Soc. Critical Care Medicine (bd. dirs. Calif. chpt. 1995), Am. Acad. Physician Assts. (ho. of dels. 1982-87, vice chair surg. coun. 1985-87, conf. planning com. 1986-88, vets. caucus chair 1986-88, advisor to bd. dirs. 1989-91), Calif. Acad. Physician Assts. (chmn. govt. affairs 1984-86, pres. 1985, Presdl. Leadership award 1986, 88), Am. Assn. Surgeons Assts. (v.p. 1988), Assn. Physician Assts. Cardiovascular Surgery (pres. 1989-91), Mil. Order World Wars (chpt. comdr. 1998-2000), Med. Reserve Corps. LA, Mil. Surgeons of the US, VFW, Spl. Forces Assn. (sec. chpt. 78 2000-01, 08-09, pres. chpt. 2010-), Spl. Ops. Assn., Chinese Nung Commando Assn., Inc. (founding v.p. 2003-06). Republican. Buddhist. Avocations: photo journalism, running, military history. Home: 24 Country Ridge Rd Pomona CA 91766-4815 Office: Special Forces Assn Chapter 78 PO Box 11927 Santa Ana CA 92711 Personal E-mail: commanderlonny@aol.com.

HOLMES, NANCY ELIZABETH, pediatrician; b. St. Louis, Aug. 3, 1950; d. David Reed and Phyllis Anne (Hunger) Holmes; m. Arthur Erwin Kramer, May 15, 1976; children: Melanie Elizabeth Kramer, Carl Edward Kramer. BA in Psychology, U. Kans., 1972; MD, U. Mo., 1976. Diplomate Am. Acad. Pediatrics. Intern., resident in pediatrics St. Louis Children's Hosp., Washington U., St. Louis, 1976-81; pediatrician Ctrl. Pediatrics, St. Louis, 1981—. Sch. physician Sch. Dist. Clayton, Mo., 1985—92; asst. prof. clin. pediats. Washington U., St. Louis, 1993—2000, assoc. prof. clin. pediats., 2000—07, prof. clin. pediat., 2007—; cons. 1st Congregational Preschool, Clayton, 1984—86, Jewish Hosp. Daycare Ctr., St. Louis, 1993—97, Flynn Park EArly Edn. Ctr., University City, Mo., 1994—; cmty. outpatient experience Preceptor Hosp., St. Louis Children's Hosp., 1991—93, 1994—; mem. med. exec. com. St. Louis Children's Hosp., 1992—94. Vol. reading tutor Flynn Park Sch., University City, 1992—98, cub scout leader, 1993—98; mem. com. Troop 493 Boy Scouts Am., 2000—; elder Trinity Presbyn. Ch., University City, 1989—92, 1996—2001, Webster Groves Presbyn. Ch., 2006—10; bd. mem. Presbyn. Children's Svcs., 2009—; bd. dirs. Children's Hosp. Care Group. Fellow Am. Acad. Pediatrics; mem. AMA, Mo. State Med. Assn., St. Louis Metro. Med. Soc, St. Louis Pediatric Soc. Presbyterian. Avocations: reading, gardening, photography, travel. Office: Ctrl Pediatrics Inc 8888 Ladue Rd Ste 130 Saint Louis MO 63124-2056 Office Phone: 314-862-4002. *

HOLMQUEST, DONALD LEE, health organization director, nuclear medicine physician, lawyer, retired aerospace engineer; b. Dallas, Apr. 7, 1939; s. Sidney Browder and Lillie Mae (Waite) H.; m. Ann Nixon James, Oct. 24, 1972. BS in Elec. Engring., So. Meth. U., 1962; MD, Baylor U., 1967, PhD in Physiology, 1968; JD, U. Houston, 1980. Student engr. Ling-Temco-Vought, Dallas, 1958-61; electronics engr. Tex. Instruments, Inc., Dallas, 1962; intern Meth. Hosp., Houston, 1967-68; pilot tng. USAF, Williams AFB, Ariz., 1968-69; scientist-astronaut NASA, Houston, 1967-73; research assoc. MIT, 1968-70; asst. prof. radiology and physiology Baylor Coll. Medicine, 1970-73; dir. nuclear medicine Eisenhower Med. Ctr., Palm Desert, Calif., 1973-74; assoc. dean medicine, assoc. prof. Tex. A&M U., College Station, 1974-76; dir. nuclear medicine Navasota (Tex.) Med. Ctr., 1976-84, Med. Arts Hosp., Houston, 1977-85; ptnr. Wood Lucksinger & Epstein, Houston, 1980-91, Holmquest & Assocs., Houston, 1991—2004; v.p. legal affairs N.Am. Med. Mgmt., Inc., Nashville, 1995-96; practice leader profl. svcs. group McKesson Info. Solutions, San Francisco, 2002—06; CEO Calif. Regional Health Info. Orgn., San Francisco, 2006—. Asst. prof. internal medicine Baylor Coll. Medicine, Houston, 1999—. Contbr. articles to med. jours. Mem. Soc. Nuclear Medicine, Am. Coll. Nuclear Physicians, Tex. Bar Assn., Am. Fighter Pilots Assn., Sigma Xi, Alpha Omega Alpha, Sigma Tau. Home and Office: 205 Princeton Rd Menlo Park CA 94025-5217 Office Phone: 415-537-6939.

HOLSINGER, JAMES WILSON, JR., cardiologist, physician; b. Kansas City, Kans., May 11, 1939; s. James Wilson and Ruth Leona (Reitz) H.; m. Barbara Jenn Craig, Dec. 28, 1963; children: Anna Elizabeth, Martha Ruth, Sarah Frances, Rachel Catherine. Student, Duke U., 1957-60, MD, 1964, PhD, 1968; MS, U. S.C., 1981; BA, U. Ky., 1997; DS (hon.), Pikeville Coll., 1996. Intern Duke U. Hosp., Durham, NC, 1964, resident in surgery, 1965, fellow in thoracic surgery, 1966, fellow in anatomy, 1966-68; resident in surgery U. Fla., Gainesville, 1968-70, fellow in cardiology, 1970-72; with VA, 1969-94; chief of staff VA Med. Ctr., Augusta, Ga., 1978-81, dir. Richmond, Va., 1981-90, Lexington, Ky., 1993-94; chief med. dir. US Dept. Vets. Affairs, Washington, 1990-93, under sec. health, 1992-93; prof. medicine and anatomy Med. Coll. Ga., Augusta, 1978-81; prof. med. and health admin. Med. Coll. of Va., Richmond, 1981-93; asst. v.p. health scis. VA Commonwealth U., Richmond, 1985-90; chancellor U. Ky. Med. Ctr., Lexington, 1994—2003, Wethington chair in health scis., 2001—, chancellor emeritus, 2003—; prof. medicine, surgery and anatomy U. Ky. Coll. Medicine, 1994—; profl. health care adminstrn. U. Ky. Coll. Allied Health Profls., 1994—2006; sr. v.p. U. Ky., Lexington, 2001—03; sec. Cabinet Health and Family Svcs. Commonwealth of Ky., Frankfort, 2003—05; prof. preventive medicine and health svcs. mgmt. U. Ky. Coll. Pub. Health, 2006—. Mem. com. evangelism N. Ga. conf. United Meth. Ch., 1980-81, com. 80, World Meth. Coun., 1981—, bd. discipleship Va. conf., 1982-86, lay mem., 1984-93, assoc. dist. lay leader, 1983-84, dist. lay leader, 1984-86, conf. lay leader, 1986-92, conf. chmn. health and welfare ministries, Ky., 1996-2000, Ky. conf. lay mem., 1996-00, del. gen. conf., 1988, 92, 96, 2000, del. S.E. jurisdictional conf., 1988, 92, 96, 2000; exec. com. World Meth. Coun., 1986—2011, order jerusalem, 2011, treas., 1993—2011, gen coun. on ministries United Meth. Ch., 1988-2000, Gen. Bd. Pubs., 1992-96, bd. dirs. United Meth. Pub. House, 1996-2000, jud. council, 2000-08, pres. 2004-08; commr. Joint Commn. on the Accreditation of Healthcare Orgns., 1996-2002. Contbr. articles to profl. jours. Major gen. M.C., Aus-Ret, 2004-. Master ACP; fellow Am. Coll. Cardiology, Am. Coll. Healthcare Execs. (Gold medal award 1993); mem. Am. Assn. Anatomists, Am. Heart Assn. (fellow clin. coun.), Soc. Med. Adminstrs., Internat. Brotherhood Magicians (order of Merlin with shield), Ky. Inst. Medicine, Ret. Officers Assn. (bd. dirs. 1998-2000), Assn. Theol. Schs. (bd. dirs. 2006—). Republican. Office: 121 Washington Ave Ste 107 Lexington KY 40506-0003

HOLT, FRIEDA M., nursing educator, retired academic administrator; BSN with honors, U. Colo., Boulder, 1956; MS in Cmty. Health Nursing, Boston U., 1969, EdD, 1973. RN, Ariz., Calif., Colo., Mass., Md., Pa., Wash., Liberia, W. Africa. Instr., dir. of nursing Cuttington Coll., Liberia, Africa, 1964-67; teaching fellow sch. of nursing Boston U., 1969, asst. prof. sch. of nursing, 1969-74; assoc. prof., assoc. dean for grad. studies sch. of nursing U. Md., 1975-77, dean's dep. sch. of nursing, 1975-86, prof., assoc. dean for grad. studies sch. of nursing, 1977-86, acting dean sch. of nursing, 1978, acting asst. dean sch. of nursing, 1981-82, acting chmn. sch. of nursing, 1983-84, acting dean sch. of nursing, 1986-87, prof., assoc. dean for grad. studies, dean's dep. sch. of nursing, 1987-88, prof., exec. assoc. dean. sch of nursing, 1988-89, acting dean, prof. sch. of nursing, 1989-90, prof. sch. of nursing, 1990-91, prof., dir. sch. of nursing, 1992—94, prof. emeritus, 2006—; dir. grad. programs Pa. State Sch. Nursing, 1994—2000; ret., 2000. Project dir. Primary Care Adult Nurse Practitioner Leadership grant, 1976-82, Preparation for Tchrs. in Maternal Child Nursing, judge U. Md. grad. sch. rsch. awards, 1979-84; author, project dir. Pa. State PhD Nursing Program Grant; NLN vis. for Accreditation of Baccalaureate and Masters Nursing Program, SREB/SCCEN Task Force on Grad. Edn., presenter seminars, confs., workshop; prof. emeritus U. Md. Sch. Nursing, 2006. Contbr. articles to profl. jours. Bd. dirs. Md. Nurses Found. (v.p., 1988—). Recipient VA Commendation award, 1990, Charter Trustee award Found. for Nursing of Md., 1990, Martin Luther King, Jr. Humanitarian award, 1990; named Pa. Nurse Educator of Yr., 1998. Mem. ANA, ANA (coun. nurse rschrs.), APHA, AAUP, Nat. League for Nursing, Am. Edn. Rsch. Assn., Am. Edn. Rsch. Assn., Md. Assn. for Higher Edn., Soc. for Rsch. in Nursing Edn., Sigma Theta Tau. Home: 151 Woodpecker Ln Port Matilda PA 16870 Personal E-mail: fmh16@hotmail.com.

HOLT, HOMER ANTHONY, JR., urologist, educator; b. Ashland, Ky., July 6, 1938; s. Homer A. Holt; m. Virginia Cayce, Nov. 22, 1962; children: Kathryn Holt Kerpestein, Kimberly Holt Cochran, Homer A. III. BA, Vanderbilt U., 1960; MD, U. Louisville, 1965. Diplomate Am. Bd. Urology. Straight surg. intern U. Louisville Sch. Medicine, 1965-66, resident in gen. surgery, 1966-68, resident in urology, 1969-72, chief resident in urology, 1971-72, clin. prof. surgery (urology), 1972—; pvt. practice, Louisville, 1972—2008. Cons. dept. surgery (urology) VA Med. Ctr., Louisville; active staff surgery(urology) Va. Med. Ctr., pres. med. staff Meth. Evang. Hosp., 1989-90 Contbr. articles to med. jours. Capt. M.C. USAF, 1967—69. Fellow ACS (com. on applicants for Ky. 1982-98, chmn. com. 1988-98); mem. Am. Urol. Assn., Southeastern Sect. Am. Urol. Assn., Am. Lithotripsy Soc., Ky. Med. Assn., Ky. Urol. Assn. (pres. 1979-80), Jefferson County Med. Soc. (editor bull. 1978-79, treas. found. bd. 1984-86, v.p., 2004-05) Home: 5808 Brittany Woods Cir Louisville KY 40222-5908 Office: VAMC Zorn Ave Louisville KY 40207

HOLT, PETER ROLF, gastroenterologist, educator; b. Berlin, Sept. 8, 1930; s. Arthur and Ruth H.; m. Joyce Weil, May 15, 1979; children: Rachel Janna, Shawn David, Tamara Naomi. BSc, U. London, 1949, MB, BS with honors, 1954. Intern London Hosp., 1954-55; asst. resident in medicine St. Luke's Hosp. Center, NYC, 1957-59; tng. fellow in medicine Mass. Gen. Hosp., Boston, 1959-61; chief gastroenterology med. Service St. Luke's Hosp. Center, NYC, 1961-96, attending physician, 1971—2008, Presbyn. Hosp., NYC, 1988; chief gastroenterology St. Luke's-Roosevelt Hosp. Ctr., NYC, 1996-2000; sr. scientist Inst. for Cancer Prevention, NYC, 2000—04, dir. James E. Olson Cancer Prevention Program, 2004—07, sr. scientist Strang Cancer Prevention Ctr., 2004—07; attending physician Rockefeller U. Hosp.; sr. rsch. assoc. Rockefeller U., 2007—. Mem. faculty dept. medicine Coll. Physicians and Surgeons Columbia U., NYC, 1961—; rsch. collaborator Brookhaven Nat. Lab., Upton, NY, 1973—79; prof. Columbia U., 1975—2000, prof. emeritus, 2000—, mem. Bio-engring. Inst., 1975—2000; mem. nat. sci. adv. com., nat. rev. com. Nat. Found. for Ileitis and Colitis, 1976—88, also chmn. rsch. tng. awards com.; mem. 12th work group on clin. rsch. Nat. Commn. on Digestive Disease, 1977—79; mem. Bio-engring. Inst. Inst. Human Nutrition, 1978—2000; vis. investigator Meml. Sloan-Kettering Cancer Ctr., 1988—89; Trevor Howell lectr. Brit. Geriat. Soc., 1992; Dorothy Ewerson lectr. U. Pisa, 1999; adj. sr. scientist Strang Cancer Ctr., NY, 2000—03; vis. assoc. physician Rockefeller U., 2001—07, adj. prof., 2004—07, sr. rsch. assoc., 2007—; mem. Bio-engring. Inst. Comprehensive Cancer Ctr.; adj. prof. medicine Weill Conell Sch. Medicine, 2010. Author, contbr. chpts. to books, articles to med. jours. Served to maj. Brit. Royal Army M.C., 1955-57. Recipient William H. Rorer award in Gastroenterology, 1965, Jannsen Lifetime Achievement award in Digestive Diseases, 2002, Internat. Solvay Nutrition award, 2002; named one of Best Doctors in Am., Castle Connoly Guide, 2002-07, Best Doctors in N.Y., N.Y. Mag., 1980-2006; NIH grantee. Fellow: ACP (gov.'s com. 1978—81); mem.: Am. Gastroenterology Assn. (pres. 1971, chmn. com. rsch. 1973—74, chmn. com. on aging 1982—86, chmn. admissions com. 1985—86, ethics com. 1997—2000, manpower and tng. com. 2001—04, internat. com. 2005—, chair 2009—), Orgn. Mondiale de Gastro-Enterologie (chair nominating com. 1990—94, nomenclature com. and rsch. com.), N.Y. Acad. Sci., Am. Soc. Cancer Rsch., Am. Soc. Clin. Investigation, Intersoc. Com. Clin. Investigation in Digestive Disease (chmn. 1975—79). Office: Rockefeller U Box 179 1230 York Ave New York NY 10065 Business E-Mail: holtp@rockefeller.edu.

HOLT, RACHAEL FRUSH, medical educator; b. Minn., Sept. 11, 1974; PhD, U. Minn., 2003. Rsch. asst. U. Minn., 1997—2003, clin. supr., audiology, 2001—02; clin. fellow, audiology Mayo Clinic, Rochester, Minn., 1999—2000; postdoc. rsch. fellow Ind. U. Sch. Medicine, 2003—05; asst. prof. Ind. U., Bloomington, 2005—. Assoc. mem. Ind. U. Cognitive Sci. Program Faculty, 2009—. Rsch. grant, NIH, Cognitive Sci. Program Faculty, Am. Hearing Rsch. Found., Ind. U. Mem.: Am. Speech-Lang. Hearing Assn., Am. Auditory Soc., Acoustical Soc. America. Avocation: running. Office: Speech and Hearing Scis 200 S Jordan Ave Bloomington IN 47405 Office Fax: 812-855-5531. Personal E-mail: rachael.frush.holt@gmail.com.

HOLTAN, TOR, foundation administrator; BS in Mktg., Wash. State U., Pullman, 1971; M in Internat. Mgmt., Thunderbird Am. Grad. Sch. Internat. Mgmt., 1975. Chief of staff to Europe, Mid. East and Africa divsn., consumer svc. group. Citibank, London; pres. Taiwan First Investment and Trust Co.; COO Strategic Rsch. Inst., v.p. ops.; v.p., chief innovation officer Kellen Co., 2007—; CEO Myasthenia Gravis Found. America, 2009—. Cons. Internat. Assn. Microfinance Investors. Mem. house of delegates US Olympic Com.; mem. exec. bd. US

Team Handball Fedn., Friends of Georgetown. Office: Kellen Co 355 Lexington Ave 15th Fl New York NY 10017 Office Phone: 212-297-2156. Office Fax: 212-370-9047. *

HÖLTERMANN, WALTER, anesthesiologist; b. Damme, Germany, Feb. 27, 1952; s. Hans and Edith (Adelmeyer) H.; m. Anna Elisabeth Krieg, Oct. 10, 1980; children: Annelen, Friederike, Clara. Dipl.Ing., U. Osnabrück, 1972; MD, U. Marburg, 1981. Resident pathology U. Dusseldorf, 1980—82; resident anesthesiology St. Marien Hosp., Hagen, Germany, 1982—85; cons. anesthesiologist U. Marburg, Germany, 1985—98; sr. physician St. Bonifatius Hosp., Lingen, Germany, 1998—; tchr. U. Marburg, 1998—. Chmn. Konvent of the U. Marburg, 1992—98, mem. senate, 1991—92; vice chmn. Christopherus-Werk Lingen, 1999—2008, chmn., 2008—; v.p. Nat. Red Cross, Dist. Lingen, 2000—. Contbr. articles to profl. jours. Mem. Korporationsring, Marburg, 1985-98. Co-recipient Edens prize Heinlich-Heine U., 1981. Mem. European Soc. Anaesthesiology, European Soc. Anaesthesiologists, European Soc. Intensive Care Medicine. Mem. Free Democracy Part of Germany. Roman Catholic. Avocations: gardening, history of 19th and 20th century in Europe. Home: Birkhuhnstr 2 D-49808 Lingen Germany Office: St Bonifatius Hosp Postfach 2040 49790 Lingen Emsland Germany Home Phone: 49 171 1936390; Office Phone: 49 591 910 1301. Business E-Mail: walter.hoeltermann@bonifatius-lingen.de.

HOLTGRAVES, THOMAS, psychology professor; b. Kans. City, Mo., July 9, 1953; BA, Marquette U., 1975; PhD, U. Nev., Reno, 1983. Prof. Ball State U., 1986—. Grant, NSF, NIH. Fellow: Soc. Exptl. Social Psychology, Midwestern Psychol. Assn.; mem.: Am. Psychol. Soc. Office: Dept Psychol Sci Ball State University Muncie IN 47306 Office Fax: 765-285-1716. Business E-Mail: 00t0holtgrav@bsu.edu.

HOLTZMAN, DAVID MICHAEL, neurologist; b. St. Louis, July 31, 1961; BS in Med. Edn., Northwestern U., 1983, MD, 1985. Bd. cert. neurology. Intern/resident U. Calif., San Francisco, 1985—89, postdoctoral rsch. tng. William C. Mobley Lab., 1989—94; lab. dir. Washington U., 1994, Charlotte and Paul Hagemann assoc. prof. neurology, 2001—, prof. molecular biology and pharmacology, 2002—; Andrew and Gretchen Jones chmn. dept. neurology Washington U. Sch. Medicine, St. Louis, 2003—. Asst. prof. U. Calif., San Francisco, 1991—94. Recipient Paul Beeson Physician Faculty Scholar award in aging rsch., MetLife award for rsch. on Alzheimer's disease, 2007, Potamkin prize, Am. Acad. Neurology, 2003, NAS, Inst. Medicine, 2008. Mem.: Inst. Medicine. Office: Washington Univ Sch Medicine Dept Neurology 660 S Euclid Ave Saint Louis MO 63110

HOLTZMAN, DEANNA, psychoanalyst, psychologist; b. Chgo. m. David B. Holtzman; children: Susan, Karen, Daniel. BA cum laude, U. Mich., 1965; MA, Wayne State U., Detroit, 1969; PhD, Wayne State U., 1975, grad., Mich. Psychoanalytic Inst., 1982. Cert. psychoanalyst Am. Psychoanalytic Assn. Assoc. in psychiatry Wayne State U., Detroit, 1975—76, dept. psychiatry, 1977—80, adj. asst. prof. dept. psychiatry, 1976—88, adj. assoc. prof., 1989—; tng. and supervising analyst Mich. Psychoanalytic Inst., 1987—. Adj. prof. psychology U. Detroit, 1980—. Author: Nevermore: The Hymen and the Loss of Virginity, 1996; contbr. articles to profl. jours. Trustee Sigmund Freud Archives, 1988—. Recipient Faculty award, Mich. Psychoanalytic Inst., 1992, Outstanding Faculty, Candidates Mich. Psychoanalytic Inst., 1996, Excellence in Tchg. award, 2002. Mem.: Mich. Psychol. Assn. (clin. essay award 1999), Am. Psychoanalytic Assn., APA. Office: 1400 Ardmoor Dr Bloomfield Hills MI 48301

HOLTZMAN, ROBERT NEIL NEHEMIAH, neurosurgeon, neurologist; b. Bklyn., Aug. 11, 1941; s. Sidney and Filia (Ravitz) H.; children: Maia Merav, Jonathan Nisson, Matthew Isaac, Sidney Isaiah. BA, Harvard U., 1964; MD, Columbia U., 1969. Diplomate Am. Bd. Psychiatry and Neurology, Am. Bd. Neurol. Surgery. Rotating intern Harlem Hosp. Ctr., NYC, 1969-70; resident in neurology Neurol. Inst. N.Y., NYC, 1970-72, resident in neurosurgery, 1973-77; resident in gen. surgery Harbor Gen. Hosp., Torrance, Calif., 1972-73; practice medicine specializing in neurosurgery and neurology, NYC, 1977—. Attending in neurosurgery Harlem Hosp., 1999—2010; attending in neurosurgery Lenox Hill Hosp., 2000; assoc. clin. prof. in neurosurgery Coll. Phys. and Surgeons, Columbia U., N.Y.C., 1996-2010; co-dir., co-founder Stonwin Med. Conf., 1983-91, attending neurosurgeon Lincoln Hosp., 2002-, chmn. NY chpt. Jackson Lab. Nat. Coun. Editor: Surgery of the Diencephalon, 1989, Endovascular Interventional Neuroradiology, 1995; editor, contbr.: The Tethered Spinal Cord, 1985, Surgery of the Spinal Cord: The Potential for Regeneration and Recovery, 1991, Spinal Instability, 1993; contbr. articles to med. jours. Mem.: N.Y. Soc. Neurol. Surgery, N.Y. State Neurosurg. Soc., Am. Assn. Neurol. Surgeons. Democrat. Jewish. Office Phone: 516-442-2250. Business E-Mail: rholtzman@nspc.com.

HOLTZMAN, STEVEN H., biotechnology and pharmaceutical company executive; BA in Philosophy, Mich. State U.; BPhil, Oxford U. Founding exec. dir. Ohio Edison Program; founder, exec. v.p., mem. exec. com. bd. dirs., pres. DNX Bio-Therapeutics, Inc. subs. DNX Corp., 1986-94; chief bus. officer Millennium Pharms., Inc., Cambridge, Mass., 1994—2001; bd. dirs. Millennium BioTherapeutics, Inc.; founder, CEO, chmn. Infinity Pharmaceuticals, 2001—09, chmn., 2009—; exec. v.p. corp. devel. Biogen Idec, 2011—. Presdl. appointee Nat. Bioethics Adv. Commn., 1996-2000; former instructor and tutor of moral philosophy and philosophy of language, Corpus Christi Coll., Oxford U., UK; bd. dirs. Archemix Corp., Anadys Pharmaceuticals; trustee Hastings Ctr. for Bioethics. Trustee Berklee Coll. of Music. Rhodes scholar. Mem. Biotech. Industry Orgn. (co-chair bioethics com.). Office: Infinity Pharmaceuticals 780 Memorial Dr Cambridge MA 02139 also: Biogen Idec 133 Boston Post Rd Weston MA 02493 *

HOLTZMAN, WAYNE HAROLD, psychologist, educator; b. Chgo., Jan. 16, 1923; s. Harold Hoover and Lillian (Manny) H.; m. Joan King, Aug. 23, 1947; children: Wayne Harold, James K., Scott E., Karl H. BS, Northwestern U., Evanston, Ill., 1944, MS, 1947; PhD, Stanford U., Calif., 1950; LHD (hon.), Southwestern U., Georgetown, Tex., 1980. Asst. prof. psychology U. Tex., Austin, 1949-53, assoc. prof., 1953-59, prof., 1959—2003, dean Coll. Edn., 1964-70, Hogg prof. psychology and edn., 1964—2003, prof. emeritus, 2003—. Assoc. dir. Hogg Found. Mental Health, 1955-64, pres., 1970-93, spl. counsel, 1993-2003; dir. Social Sci. Rsch. Coun., 1957-63, Centro de Investigationes Sociales, Mex., 1960-70; cons. USAF, sci. adv. bd., 1969-71; basic rsch. com. NRC, 1968-71; behavioral sci. study sect. USPHS, 1957-59, mem. mental health study sect., 1960, chmn. personality and cognition rsch. rev. com., 1968-72; rsch. adv. panel Soc. Security Adminstrn., 1961-62; L.Am. adv. bd. IBM, 1985-89; dir. WHO Collaborating Ctr. in Mental Health for Tex. and Mex., 1993-2003; pres. Austin Project, 2001-03; bd. dirs. Menninger Clinic, 1982-2010. Author: (with B.M. Moore) Tomorrow's Parents, 1964, Computer Assisted Instruction Testing and Guidance, 1971, (with R. Diaz-Guerrero and J. Swartz) Personality Development in Two Cultures, 1975, Introduction to Psychology, 1978; (with K.A. Heller and S. Messick) Placing Children in Special Education, 1982, (with T. Bornemann) Mental Health of Immigrants and Refugees, 1990, School of the Future, 1992, Holtzman Inkblot Technique Research Guide, 1999, (with M.R. Rozenweig, Michel Sabourin and David Belanger) History of the International Union of Psychological Science, 2000; editor: Jour. Ednl. Psychology, 1966-72. Trustee Ednl. Testing Service, Princeton, 1972-74, 77-80, 83-86, J.W. and Cornelia Scarborough Found., 1977-82, Ctr. for Applied Linguistics, 1978-80, Salado Inst. Humanities, 1980-85, Population Inst., 1979-85, Population Resource Ctr., 1980-2006, chmn. bd. dirs.; dir. Sci. Rsch. Assocs., 1975-88; pres., bd. dirs. S.W. Ednl. Devel. Lab., 1974-75; mem. adv. com. computing activities NSF, 1970-73; mem. computer sci. and engring. bd. NAS, 1971-73, chmn. panel on selection and placement of mentally retarded students, 1979-82; chmn. interdisciplinary cluster on social and behavioral devel. Pres.'s Biomed. Research Panel, 1975-76; bd. dirs. Found.'s Fund for Rsch. in Psychiatry, 1973-77, chmn., 1976-77; dir. Conf. of S.W. Found., 1976-84, pres., 1978-79; mem. nat. adv. mental health coun. Alcohol, Drug Abuse, and Mental Health Adminstrn., 1978-81; mem. acad. info. sys. adv. coun. IBM, 1982-85; bd. trustees Menninger Found., 1982-2010; bd. dirs. Menninger Clinic 1988-2010; chmn., 1994-97, dir. emeritus, 2010-. Commd. ensign USNR, 1944, Northwestern U. NROTC, anti-aircraft gunnery officer USNR, Pacific, lt. (jg.) USNR, 1945, flag lt. to admiral oscar badger to admiral roper USNR. Faculty Rsch. fellow, Social Sci. Rsch. Coun., 1953—54, Ctr. Advanced Study Behavioral Scis., 1962—63. Fellow APA, AAAS; mem. Tex. Psychol. Assn. (pres. 1957), S.W. Psychol. Assn. (pres. 1958), Am. Statis. Assn., InterAm. Soc. Psychology (pres. 1966-67), Am. Ednl. Rsch. Assn., Internat. Union Psychol. Scis. (sec.-gen. 1972-84, pres. 1984-88, exec. com. 1972-92), Philos. Soc. Tex. (pres. 1982-83), Sigma Xi. Methodist. Avocations: photography, gardening, travel, swimming. Home: 2500 Barton Creek Blvd Apt 1504 Austin TX 78735 E-mail: wayne.holtzman@mail.utexas.edu.

HOLZ, ERIC R., ophthalmologist; b. Austin, Tex., Feb. 13, 1963; BA, U. Tex., Austin, 1985; MD, Baylor Coll. Medicine, 1989. Diplomate Am. Bd. Ophthalmology. Physician Retina & Vitreous Assocs. Ky., 1994—97; asst. prof., ophthalmology Baylor Coll. Medicine, 1997—2005, assoc. prof., ophthalmology, 2005—09, clin. assoc. prof., ophthalmology, 2010, Meth. Hosp., Weill Cornell Med. Coll., 2010; ptnr. Retina & Vitreous Tex., 2010—. Recipient Fulbright & Jaworski L.L.P. Faculty Excellence award, Baylor Coll. Medicine. Mem.: Am. Soc. Retina Specialists (Hon. award), Retina Soc., Am. Ophthal. Soc., Am. Acad. Ophthalmology (Achievement award). Avocation: golf. Office: 2727 Gramercy Ste 200 Houston TX 77025 Office Fax: 713-799-1095. Business E-Mail: anitaa@retinatexas.com.

HOLZ, GEORGE G., IV, medical educator, research scientist; b. Santa Monica, Calif., May 8, 1953; s. George G. and Mignon M. (Kiproff) Holz. BS, Cornell U., 1975; PhD, U. Ill., 1984. Rsch. fellow Tufts U. Med. Sch., Boston, 1984—89; rsch. assoc. Howard Hughes Med. Inst., Boston, 1990—93; instr. medicine Mass. Gen. Hosp.-Harvard Med. Sch., Boston, 1990—93, asst. prof. medicine, 1994—98; assoc. prof. physiology and neurosci. NYU Med. Sch., NYC, 1998—2007; rsch. scientist Marine Biology Lab., Woods Hole, Mass., 2000—; prof., Medicine and Pharmacology SUNY Upstate Med. U., Syracuse, 2008—, State Med. U., Syracuse, NY, 2008—. Corp. mem. Marine Biol. Lab., Woods Hole, Mass. Mem. All-Sectional Gymnastics Team N.Y., 1971. Recipient Rsch. award, Am. Diabetes Assn., 1996, 2000; grantee rsch. grantee, NIH; scholar N.Y. State Regents scholar, Cornell U., 1971—75; Empire scholar, SUNY, 2008—. Mem.: AAAS, Am. Diabetes Assn., Soc. Gen. Physiologists, Endocrine Soc., Soc. for Neurosci. Home: PO Box 288 West Falmouth MA 02574 Office Phone: 315-464-9841. Business E-Mail: holzg@upstate.edu.

HOLZ, ROBERT KENNETH, retired geography educator; b. Kankakee, Ill., Nov. 3, 1930; s. Harry H. and Margaret (Conway) H.; m. Joyce F. Harpin, May 19, 1951; 1 child, Eric R. BA in Zoology, So. Ill. U., Carbondale, 1958, MA in Geography, 1959; PhD in Geography, Mich. State U., East Lansing, 1963. Asst. prof. U. Tex., Austin, 1962-67, assoc. prof., 1967-72, prof., 1972—, dir. ctr. for Middle Eastern Studies, 1991-99, Eric W. Zimmerman Regents prof., 1991-99, Eric W. Zimmerman Regents prof. emeritus, 1999—; ret., 1999. Cons. in field. Co-author: Mendes I, 1980; author, editor: The Surveillant Science, 2d edit., 1985. Staff sgt. USAF, 1951-55. Recipient Group Achievement award NASA, 1974, Urban Achievement award L.B.J. Sch. Pub. Affairs, 1984. Mem. Assn. Am. Geographers (chmn. remote sensing specialty group 1980-82, chmn. southwest div. 1971-72, medal for outstanding contbns. to remote sensing Remote Sensing Specialty Group 1998), Am. Soc. Photogrammetry, Tex. Assn. Coll. Tchrs., Am. Congress of Surveying and Mapping. Roman Catholic. Avocations: hunting, fishing, squash. Home: 2610 Fiset Dr Austin TX 78731-5614 Office: U Tex Dept Geography Austin TX 78712 Home Phone: 512-452-6574. Personal E-mail: holzrj@aol.com.

HOLZER, PETER, pharmacologist, neuroscientist; b. Vorau, Austria, Feb. 26, 1951; s. Peter and Maria (Wetzelberger) H.; m. Ulrike Petsche, Oct. 8, 1983; children: Veronika, Judith. MS, U. Graz, 1976, PhD, 1978. Postdoc. fellow U. Cambridge, 1980; vis. scientist UCLA, 1989; from univ. asst. to univ. docent U. Graz, 1977-85, from univ. docent to assoc. prof., 1985-90, from assoc. prof. to prof., 1990—93; head rsch. unit of translational neurogastroenterology Med. U. Graz, 2005—, chair exptl. neurogastroenterology, 2008—. Editor: Calcitonin Gene-Related Peptide, 1992, Neurogenic Inflammation, 1996, Problems of Gastrointestinal Tract in Anesthesia, 1999, Handbook of Pharmacology on Tachykinins, 2004; contbr. more than 330 articles to profl. publs. Recipient C.A. Ewald prize, German Soc. Gastroenterology, 1988, prize, Sandoz Found., Vienna, Austria, 1988, rsch. prize, Austrian Soc. Pathology, 1990, prize, Austrian Soc. Rheumatology, 1994, recognition award, Josef Krainer Found., 1997, main rsch. prize, Province of Styria, 2001, M. Jancso Meml. award, U. Szeged, Hungary, 2003, Masters award for basic rsch. in digestive scis., AGA Inst., 2006, Great Decoration for Svc. to Republic of Austria, 2006, Rsch. prize, Austrian Pain Soc., 2008; named Highly Cited Rschr. in Pharmacology, ISI Thomson, 2003, Contbr. Mem. of Faculty of 1000, 2010. Mem. European Neuropeptide Club (chmn. 1994), Austrian Neurosci. Assn. (sec. 1993), Br. Pharmacol. Soc., Internat. Union Pharmacology (sec. gastrointestinal pharmacology sect. 1994), Am. Gastroenterological Assn., German Soc. Pharmacology and Toxicology, Austrian Neuroscience Assn. (pres. 2002), Austrian Pharmacological Soc. (exec. bd. 2007-09, v.p. 2009-11). Avocations: foresting, mushrooms, classical music, history. Office: Inst Exptl Clin Pharmacol Med U Graz Universitatsplatz 4 A-8010 Graz Austria Business E-Mail: peter.holzer@medunigraz.at.

HOLZMAN, IAN RONALD, pediatrician, educator; s. Arthur and Anne Holzman; m. Ellen Dee Solow, June 17, 1967; children: Jason Dov, Benjamin Ari, Joanna Sarah. BS in Biology, U. Rochester, NY; MD, U. Pitts. Sch. Medicine, 1971. Diplomate Am. Bd. Pediat., cert. in neonatal-perinatal medicine. Resident pediat. Children's Hosp. Pitts., 1971—75; fellow perinatal medicine U. Colo. Sch. Medicine, 1975—77; asst. & assoc. prof. pediat. U. Pitts., 1977—87; prof. pediat., chief divsn. newborn medicine CUNY-Mt. Sinai Sch. Medicine, 1987—, prof. obstetrics, gynecology & reproductive sci.; chief newborn medicine Mt. Sinai Med. Ctr. Asst. surgeon USPHS, 1971—75; bd. dirs. Mt. Sinai Children's Ct.r Found. Inc., 1990—; mem. med. adv. bd. R Baby Found., 2007—. Contbr. articles to profl. jours. Recipient Dean's award, Mt. Sinai Sch. Medicine, 2008; named a Top Doc. in NY Metro Area, Castle Connolly Med. Ltd., 2009; named one of America's Top Doctors, 2009. Fellow: Am. Acad. Pediat.; mem.: Ea. Soc. Pediatric Rsch. (dir. sponsorship 2003—09), Soc. Perinatal Rsch., Am. Pediatric Soc., Soc. Pediatric Rsch. Office: Mt Sinai Sch Medicine One Gustave L Levy Pl New York NY 10029 Office Phone: 212-241-5446. Business E-Mail: ian.holzman@mssm.edu.

HOLZMAN, ROBERT STEPHEN, physician; b. NYC, Apr. 13, 1940; s. Stanford and Shiffie (Mirkin) H.; m. Clare Gottfried, June 30, 1963; children; Daniel, Diane. BA, Rutgers U., 1961; MD, Johns Hopkins U., 1965. Intern NYU Med. Ctr., NYC, 1965-66, resident, 1968-70, fellowship, 1970-73; asst. hosp. epidemiologist Bellevue Hosp., NYC, 1973-80; asst. prof. NYU Sch. Medicine, 1973—80; hosp. epidemiologist Bellevue Hosp., NYC, 1980—2007, assoc. prof., 1980—2000, prof. medicine and environ. medicine, 2000—, acting chief divsn. immunology and infectious diseases, 2000—02. Treas. Com. for the Promotion of Med. Rsch., N.Y.C., 1980—2008. Contbr. over 100 articles to profl. jours. Sr. asst. surgeon USPHS, 1966-68. Fellow ACP. Office: NYU Med Ctr 550 1st Ave New York NY 10016-6497 Office Phone: 212-263-6402.

HOM, DAVID BRIAN, surgeon; b. San Diego, 1956; s. James and Evelyn Hom; m. Lorraine Hom, 1984. BA summa cum laude, U. Calif., San Diego, 1978; MD, UCLA, 1982. Diplomate Am. Bd. Otolaryngology and Facial Plastic and Reconstructive Surgery. Gen. surg. resident U. Calif., Irvine, 1983-84; otolaryngology, head and neck surgery resident U. Mich., Ann Arbor, 1984-88; facial plastic fellow Am. Acad. Facial Plastic Surgery, Birmingham, Ala., 1988-89; asst. prof. dept. otolaryngology, head and neck surgery U. Minn., Mpls., 1989-96, assoc. prof., 1996—2007; prof. U. Cin., 2007—. Mem. otolaryngology expert adv. panel U.S. Pharmacopia Conv., Washington, 1994—; bd. dirs. Am. Bd. Facial Plastic and Reconstructive Surgery. Editor: Essential Tissue Healing of the Face & Neck, 2009; contbr. numerous articles to profl. jours., chpts. to books. Med. cons. NCAA, Mpls., 1996-97. NIH Rsch. grantee, 1996-2002. Fellow ACS, Am. Acad. Otolaryngology, Head and Neck Surgery (Nat. Percy Meml. Rsch. award 1991), Am. Acad. Facial Plastic and Reconstructive Surgery (chmn. rsch. 1997-2000, bd. dirs. 2005-08, Nat. Ben Shuster Rsch. award 1988); mem. AAAS, Minn. Acad. Otolaryngology-Head and Neck Surgery (pres. 2005). Avocations: fishing, kayaking. Office: Univ Cin 231 Albert Sabin Way Rm 6507 PO Box 670528 Cincinnati OH 45267-0528

HOMAN, RICHARD V., dean; BS in Biomedical Sci., Brown U., 1978; MD, SUNY, Buffalo, 1982. Diplomate Nat. Bd. Med. Examiners, Am. Bd. Family Practice, cert. in Geriatric Medicine Am. Bd. Family Practice, Am. Bd. Internal Medicine, in Sports Medicine Am. Bd. Family Practice, Am. Bd. Pediatrics, Am. Bd. Internal Medicine, Am. Bd. Emergency Medicine. Resident in family medicine Milton S. Hershey Med. Ctr. Pa. State U., 1982—85, chief resident Dept. Family and Cmty. Medicine, 1984—85; clin. asst. prof. Pa. State U. Sch Medicine, Hershey, 1987—89; asst. prof. Dept. Family and Cmty. Medicine Tex. Tech U. Health Sciences Ctr., Lubbock, 1989—93, assoc. prof., 1993—2001, Paul and Eva Braddock chair Dept Family and Cmty. Medicine Lubbock, El Paso, Amarillo and Odessa, 1994—2001, prof. Lubbock, 2001, assoc. dean clin. affairs and fin., 2001, dean Grad. Sch. Biomedical Sciences, 2001—03, dean Sch. Medicine, 2001—05, v.p. clin. affairs, 2003—05; dean Coll. Medicine Drexel U., Phila., 2005—, sr. v.p. health affairs, 2005—. Office: Office of Dean Drexel Univ Coll Medicine 2900 West Queen Lane Philadelphia PA 19129 Office Phone: 215-762-8900. *

HOMER, MELODIE ANTONETTE, clinical nursing instructor; b. Hamilton, Ont., Can., Aug. 29, 1966; arrived in U.S., 1989; d. Waldron Berrisford and Ena Gwendolyn Thorpe; children: Laurel, Alden. Nursing diploma, Mohawk Coll., Hamilton, 1987; BSN, Loma Linda U., 1991; MSN, Azusa Pacific U., 1995. RN Can., Calif., Pa., N.J. Staff nurse St. Josephs Hosp., Hamilton, 1988—89; pediat. staff nurse Loma Linda Children's Hosp., 1989—96, Children's Hosp. Phila., 1996—98; oncology nurse educator, cons. Marlton, NJ, 1997—2003. Nursing instr. various instns., 1994, 97; adj. prof. Burlington County Coll., Pemberton, NJ, 2007—. Author: (pediat. booklet) Sandoman Talks About ITP, 1996, Chemo Crusader and the Cancer Fighting Crew, 1999; contbr. chapters to books. Pres. LeRoy W. Homer Jr. Found., 2002—. Mem.: Sigma Theta Tau.

HOMMA, AKIHIRO, surgeon, educator; b. Furano, Hokkaido, Japan, Feb. 27, 1965; MD, Hokkaido U., 1989. Assoc. prof. dept. otolaryngology-head & neck surgery Hokkaido U. Grad. Sch. Medicine, 2010—. Named one of Eminent Scientist of Yr., Internat. Rsch. Promotion Coun., 2011. Mem.: Am. Head and Neck Soc. (corr.). Avocations: mountain climbing, skiing. Office: N15 W7 Kita-ku Sappro Hokkaido 060-8638 Japan E-mail: ak-homma@med.hokudai.ac.jp.

HOMMA, TOSHIAKI, respiratory physiologist; b. Tokyo, Oct. 2, 1954; s. Tetsuo and Yohko (Uchimura) H.; m. Fumiko Tange, June 6, 1980; children: Yuichi, Yuki, Sachi. BS, U. Tsukuba, Japan, 1980; MD, PhD, U. Tsukuba, 1984. Cert. in internal and thoracic medicine, Japan Soc. Chest Diseases. Resident trainee Gakuen Hosp., Tsukuba, 1984-85, Kekken Hosp., Tokyo, 1985-86; chief instr. Seiranso Hosp., Tohkai, Japan, 1986-88; asst. prof. Tsukuba U., 1988-93, 1996—, ward dir., 1989-93; rsch. assoc. Nat. Jewish Ctr., Denver, 1993-96. Author: Sports Medicine Guide, 1994, Laboratory Medicine, 1996, Geriatric Medicine, 1997, Practice of Internal Medicine, 1997. Exec. Onogawa Coun., Tsukuba, 1997; committeeman Prevention Disasters, Tsukuba U., 1997. Grantee in respiratory physiology, Chest Co., 1997, in physiol. technique, Teijin Co., 1997. Mem. Japanese Soc. Respiratory Care, Japanese Thoracic Soc., Japanese Internal Medicine. Avocation: model aircraft. Office: Teikyo U Chiba Med Ctr 3426-3 Anegasaki Ichihara Chiba 299-0111 Japan Home: 14-25 Onogawa Tsukuba Ibaraki 305 Japan Personal E-mail: e-toshi@hotmail.co.jp. Business E-Mail: toshi-h@med.teikyo-u.ac.jp.

HOMMEL, AMI, nursing educator; b. Borås, Sweden, May 8, 1957; RN, Lund U., 1981, PhD, 2007. Asst. prof. Lund U. Hosp., 2007—. Mem.: Swedish Soc. Nursing, Swedish Wound Nurses Assn., European Pressure Ulcer Adv. Panel, European Acad. Nursing Sci., Internat. Collaboration Orthopaedic Nursing. Avocation: sports. Office: Lund University Hospital Rörelseorg forskningsavd Lund Skåne 22185 Sweden Business E-Mail: ami.hommel@med.lu.se.

HOMOLA, SAMUEL, retired chiropractor; b. Dothan, Ala., June 10, 1929; D in Chiropractic, Lincoln Coll., 1956. Pvt. practice, 1956—98. Contbr. articles to profl. jours. & mag. Avocation: writing. Home: 1307 East Second Ct Panama City FL 32401 Personal E-mail: samhomola@comcast.net.

HON, CHUI CHAN, pediatrician; MBBS, Nat. U. of Singapore, 1990; fellowship diploma in Surgery, Royal Coll. of Surgeons, Glasgow. Cert. of Specialist Accreditation in Paediatric Surgery Ministry of Health, Singapore. Advanced surg. tng. in paediatric Acad. of Medicine, Singapore; established Children's Cancer Rsch. Lab., 2003—; head of paediatric surgery dept. KK Women's and Children's Hosp., 2005—07; past-pres. Paediatric Oncology Group, Singapore; mem. specialist tng. com. Paediatric Surgery, Singapore; instr. Advanced Trauma Life Support Course. Vis. cons. of paediatric surgery dept. KK Women's and Children's Hosp., Singapore; vis. cons. Singapore Gen. Hosp.; clin. sr. lectr. Yong Loo Lin Sch. of Medicine. Author of various publs. Recipient Health Manpower Devel. Programme (HMDP) scholarship, St Jude Children's Rsch. Hosp., 1999, Best Clin. Tchr. award, KK Women's and Children's Hosp., 2003. Mem.: Soc.of Internat. Pediatric Surg. Oncology, Chpt. of Paediatric Surgeons, Singapore (chmn.). Office: Mount Elizabeth Medical Centre 10-08 3 Mount Elizabeth 228510 Singapore Office Phone: 6567337381. Office Fax: 6567334939. *

HON, JOHN WINGSUN, physician; b. Canton, China, Aug. 21, 1947; s. Yuen-Pak and Yuk-Ying (Zhang) Hon. BA, Hunter Coll., 1972; MA, SUNY, Buffalo, 1975; DO, Kirksville Coll. Medicine, 1979. Bd. cert. emergency medicine and family practice. Enlisted U.S. Army, 1975, advanced through grades to capt., 1979; intern, resident Tripler Army Med. Ctr., Honolulu, 1979-80; gen. med. officer U.S. Army Med. Corps, Honolulu, 1979-80; intern Tripler Army Med. Ctr., Honolulu, 1979-80; gen. med. officer U.S. Army Med. Corps, Korea, Republic of Korea, 1980-81, U.S. Mil. Acad., West Point, 1981-83; attending physician Woodhull Hosp., Bklyn., 1983-86; pvt. practice Woodside, NY, 1983—2002, Elmhurst, NY, 1993—, Flushing, NY, 2002—. Attending physician Bronx Lebanon Hosp., 1987—91, Mt. Sinai Hosp., Queens, 1983—, St. John Hosp., Elmhurst, NY, 1992—, N.Y. Hosp. Dept. Medicine, 1996, Elmhurst Hosp., 1999—; clin. asst. prof. family practice N.Y. Med. Coll. Fellow: Am. Bd. Emergency Physicians, Am. Coll. Emergency Physicians; mem.: N.Y. State Osteo. Med. Soc., Chinese Am. Med. Soc. (life), Am. Osteo. Assn. Avocation: photography. Home: 10 West St Apt 33A New York NY 10004 also: 86-08 Elmhurst Ave Elmhurst NY 11373 Office: 141-05 Northern Blvd Flushing NY 11354 Office Phone: 718-424-0770. Personal E-mail: hon8song@yahoo.com.

HONAMAN, J. CRAIG, health facility administrator; b. Montclair, NJ, June 15, 1943; s. Richard Karl and Gloria (McElwain) H.; m. Dee Dee Toerpe, Dec. 31, 1971; children: Justin Craig Jr., Garman Grayson. BS, N.C. State U., 1965; MS, U. Ala., Birmingham, 1971. Sr. v.p. Bapt. Hosp., Pensacola, Fla., 1970-79; exec. v.p. Tallahassee (Fla.) Meml. Hosp., 1979-89; adminstr. Quorum Health Resources/Leesburg (Fla.) Regional Med. Ctr., 1989-91; v.p., adminstrn. home health care Meth. Med. Ctr., Jacksonville, Fla., 1991-92; pres. Kellogg Healthcare, Inc., Jacksonville, 1992-93, KNH Healthcare, Jacksonville, 1993-95; exec. dir. HomeCare Alliance of Ga., Inc., Atlanta, 1994-98; sr. v.p. Haney & Assocs., Atlanta, 1998—2001; prin. H&H Cons. Ptnrs., LLC, Atlanta, 2001—. Cons. in field, Atlanta, Ga., 1991—. Contbr. articles to profl. jours. Active Boy Scouts Am., ARC, Am. Cancer Soc., Ronald McDonald House. Capt. U.S. Army, 1966-69, Vietnam. Recipient Nat. Golden Hour award MBB Helicopter, 1988, Pub. Benefit Flying award Nat. Aeronautic Assn., 2004. Fellow Am. Coll. Healthcare Execs. (cert. health care mgr.; regent for north Ga.; cert. retirement coach), Rotary. Methodist. Avocations: golf, running. Office: H&H Cons Ptnrs LLC 560 Cambridge Way NE Ste 101 Atlanta GA 30328-1007 Personal E-mail: Careerdir1@aol.com.

HONBOLYGÓ, FERENC, psychologist, researcher, educator; b. Zirc, Hungary, Nov. 1, 1977; s. Ferenc Honbolygó and Klára Lukács; m. Nóra Nyirö. MA, U. Eötvös Lóránd, Budapest, 2002, PhD, 2010. Asst. lectr. faculty arts U. Pázmány Péter, Budapest, 2002—07; rsch. fellow Rsch. Inst. Psychology, Hungarian Acad. Scis., Budapest, Hungary, 2005—; asst. lectr. faculty pedagogy and psychology U. Eötvös Lóránd, 2006—. Contbr. articles to profl. jours., chapters to books.

HONDA, MICHIO, ophthalmologist, director; b. Takarazuka, Japan, Oct. 24, 1955; MD, Kyoto U., 1981. Dir. Honda Eye Clinic, 1990—. Avocations: music, chess, walking. Office: Wave-1 3F Nishiekimaecho 9-29 Ibaraki Osaka 567-0032 Japan Office Fax: 072-624-0678. Business E-Mail: honda.eye.clinic@mocha.ocn.ne.jp.

HONDA, YASUTOSHI, dentist, oral radiologist, researcher, educator; b. Nishio, Aichi, Japan, Mar. 17, 1965; s. Kyohei and Yasue Honda; m. Kaori Honda. BS in Engring., Kinki U., Japan, 1989; DDS, Okayama Dental U., Japan, 1996; PhD in Dentistry, Okayama U., Japan, 2001. Assoc. prof. Okayama U., 1997—98, assoc. prof., dentistry and pharm. Scis., 2001—; dental br. dir. San-ai Gen. Hosp., Fukuyama, Hiroshima, Japan, 1999—2000; vis. asst. prof. Brigham & Women's Hosp., Harvard Med. Sch., Boston, 2005—06. Contbr. articles to profl. jours. Recipient Noikura award, 2004; Grants-in-Aid, Ministry Edn., Culture, Sports, Sci. and Tech., Japan, 2001—. Avocations: swimming, beer brewing. Office: Okayama Univ 2-5-1 Shikata-cho Okayama 700-8525 Japan Office Fax: 086-235-6709. Business E-Mail: honnda@md.okayama-u.ac.jp.

HONEYCUTT, DEBORAH ANN, physician; b. Chgo., Aug. 8, 1947; m. Andrew Honeycutt. BS, Univ. Ill., 1969, MA, 1972, MD, 1991. Med. dir. Clayton State Univ. Managed Health Clinic; instr. Emory Univ. Family Practice Residency Program; physician Ga. Baptist Tenet Atlanta Med. Ctr., 1994—99; faculty mem. Atlanta Med Ctr. Family Practice Residency Program, 1994—2004; med. dir. D. Ann Travis MD LLC, 1999—; owner, physician Five Points Family Practice, 2002—05; med. dir. Good Shepherd Free Clinic, 2005—06; physician Eagle's Landing Family Practice, 2007—. Co-chair Dept. Cmty. Health Minority Health Adv. Council, 2006—. Fellow: Am. Acad. Family Physicians; mem.: Ga. Acad. Family Physicians, Nat. Med. Assn., Alpha Kappa Alpha Sorority. Republican. Christian. Mailing: 118 North Ave Jonesboro GA 30236 Office Phone: 404-895-2765.

HONG, CHI-TZONG, neurologist; b. Taipei, Apr. 13, 1953; MB, Taipei Med. Coll., 1978. Resident in neurology Chang-Gung Meml. Hosp., 1980—84; resident, fellow in neurology U. Tex. Southwestern Med. Sch., Dallas, 1984—89; dir. neurology Chi-Mei Hosp., 1989—97; dir. neurology svc. Taipei Mcpl. Wanfang Hosp., 1997—2007; supt. Taiwan Miners' Hosp., 2007—. Clin. prof. Taipei Med. U., 2006—10. Mem.: Formosan Med. Assn., Taiwan Neurol. Soc. Avocations: art, photography, history. Home: 19 NTN-SIA Rd Taipei 103 Taiwan Home Fax: 886-2-25586249. Personal E-mail: kenhong88@yahoo.com.tw.

HONG, CHUANG-YE, physician, educator, academic administrator; b. Taipei, Taiwan, Aug. 14, 1949; s. Li-Chau and Ju-Yu Hong; m. Fu-Mei Wang, June 16, 1976; children: Ann-Lee, Wan-Ching. MD, Taipei Med. Coll., 1974; PhD, U. London, 1982. Lic. Dept. of Health, Taiwan, 1974, Taiwan Soc. of Cardiology, 1979. Med. resident Taipei Med. Coll. Hosp., Taiwan, 1976—80; rsch. fellow, hon. registrar St. Bartholomew's Hosp., London, 1980—82; attending physician Vets. Gen. Hosp., Taipei, 1982—99; rsch. fellow Mass. Gen. Hosp., Harvard Med. Sch., Boston, 1987; prof. medicine Yang-Ming U., Taipei, 1986—2001, acad. dean, 1996—99; vice chmn., chief med. officer Genelabs Biotechnology Co., Taipei, 1999—2001; CEO Sinogen Internat., Ltd., Hong Kong, 2001—04; v.p. Taipei Med. U., Taiwan, 2004—08, prof., medicine, 2004—, supr., Wan Fang Hosp., 2008—11. Dir. Taipei Med. U., 1996—2004, Devel. Ctr. Biotechnology, Taipei, 1999—2002; cons. H&Q Taiwan Co. Ltd, Taipei, 2001—04; dir. Egen Corp., San Diego, 2001—04, Shenzhen Kexing Biotech Co., Ltd, Guangdong, China, 2001—04. Editor: Modernization of Traditional Chinese Medicine; contbr. articles to profl. jours. Vice chmn. Cardiovasc. Rsch. Found., Taipei, Taiwan, 2004. Lt. Army M.C., 1974—76, Taiwan. Recipient Assn. Medicial Advisors to Pharm. Industry prize, Brit. Pharmacological Soc., 1982, Med. Advancement award, Taiwan Physician's Assn., 1989, Ig Nobel prize, 2008; Studying Abroad scholar, Ministry of Edn., Taiwan, 1980. Fellow: ACP, Royal Soc. of Medicine, London; mem.: Taiwan Soc. of Internal Medicine, Taiwan Soc. of Lipid and Atherosclerosis (pres. 1997—2000). Achievements include patents for Method for protecting cells and tissues by a triacylglycerol preparation. Avocations: reading, travel. Office: Wan Fang Hospital 111 Sect 3 Hsing Long Rd Taipei 111 Taiwan Personal E-mail: hongprof@yahoo.com.

HONG, DENNIS, critical care specialist, educator; MD, Finch U. Health Scis./Chgo. Med. Sch., 1987. Diplomate Am. Bd. Internal Medicine-pulmonary disease, 1992, Am. Bd. Internal Medicine-critical care medicine, 1995. Intern Evanston Northwestern Hosp., resident in internal medicine; fellow in pulmonary critical care medicine Univ. Ill. Coll. Medicine, 1990—93, asst. clin. prof. Office: University of Illinois Medical Center 840 S Wood MC 719 Chicago IL 60612 Office Phone: 312-996-8039.

HONG, HYE-SUK, medical educator; b. Daejeon, Republic of Korea, Mar. 25, 1970; MD, Yonsei U., Seoul, Republic of Korea, 1994, M, 2000. Clin. assoc. prof. Hallym U. Coll. Medicine, Kangnam Sacred Heart Hosp., 2010—. Mem.: Korean Soc. Abdominal Radiology, Korean Radiol. Soc. Avocations: travel, photography. Office: 948-1 Daerim-1dong Yeongdeungpo-gu Seoul 150-950 Republic of Korea Office Fax: 82-2-832-1845. Business E-Mail: hshong@hallym.or.kr.

HONG, JAE-SEOK, medical researcher; b. Seoul, Republic of Korea, May 21, 1974; BS, Soon Chun Hyang U., Asan, 1999; MPH, Yonsei U., Seoul, 2001, PhD, 2004. Asst. dept. preventive medicine & pub. health, Coll. Medicine Yonsei U., 2002—04, fellow Grad. Sch. Pub. Health, 2004—06, plural prof., Grad. Sch. Pub. Health, 2008; assoc. rsch. fellow Health Ins. Rev. & Assessment Svc., Seoul, 2006. Contbr. articles to profl. jours. With Korean Army, 1996. Recipient Presdl. Citation award, Health Ins. Rev. & Assessment Svc., 2011, Great Minds award, Am. Biographical Inst., 2011, Universal Accomplishment award, 2011, Outstanding Intellectuals award, Internat. Biographical Ctr., 2011; named Man of Yr., Am. Biographical Inst., 2011. Mem.: Korea Soc. Health Policy & Adminstrn., Korean Soc. Toxicogenomics & Toxicoproteomics. Roman Catholic. Avocations: swimming, golf, baseball, skiing. Office: Health Ins Rev & Assessment Svc Peace Bldg (11F) 1451-34 Seocho-3dong Seoul Seocho-gu 137-927 Republic of Korea Office Phone: 82-2-2182-2560. Office Fax: 82-2-6710-5842. Personal E-mail: dr_hongjs@hanmail.net. Business E-Mail: jshong@hiramail.net.

HONG, JIN HWA, obstetrician, educator; b. Seoul, Republic of Korea, Nov. 2, 1974; s. Seung Il Hong and Jeong Hee Lee; m. Gee Yeun Kim, Feb. 21, 2010. MD, Coll. Medicine Korea U., 1999, PhD. Cert. Nat. Bd. Med. Doctors, 2000, Korean Bd. ob-gyn., 2004. Intern Guro Hosp. Coll. Medicine Korea U., Seoul, Republic of Korea, 1999—2000, residency dept. ob-gyn., 2000—04, fellow, 2007—08, clin. prof. dept. ob-gyn., 2008—10, Kangbuk Samsung Hosp. Coll. Medicine Sungkyunkwan U., 2010—. Contbr. articles to sci. jours. With Pub. Health Svc., 2004—07, Chungcheongnam-do, Republic of Korea. Mem.: Korean Soc. Gynecologic Oncology and Colposcopy (Achievement award 2010), Korean Soc. Ob-Gyn. Roman Catholic. Avocations: skiing, golf. Office: Kangbuk Samsung Hosp Dept Ob-Gyn 108 Pyung-dong Jongno-gu Seoul Gyeonggi-do 110746 Republic of Korea Office Phone: 82-2-2001-2552. Personal E-mail: jhblue5@naver.com.

HONG, JONG WOOK, ophthalmologist; b. Seoul, Republic of Korea, Oct. 2, 1963; s. Ki Joo Hong and Jeong Ja Lee; m. Eun Jin Park, June 16, 1990; children: Yoon Young, Yoon Jeong. MD, Korea U., 1987, PhD, 1996. Dir. ophthalmology Korea U. Med. Ctr., Ancan Hosp., 1994—96, dir. cornea, 1997—99, Korea U. Med. Ctr., Eturo Hosp., Seoul, 2001—. Mem. adv. bd. Korea Jour. Ophthalmology, Seoul, 1996—, KEEDO, 1999—; med. cons. Hyundai Ins., 1997—. Author: Cornea, 1998; editor: Korean Jour. Ophthalmology, 1996—. Lt. Korean Navy, 1991—94. Recipient Samil Rsch. award, Seoul, 1999, Gold Presentation award, Korean Ophthalmology Soc., 2001; fellow, U. Wash., Seattle, 1999—2001. Mem.: Am. Rsch. Visual Sci., Korean Soc. Cataract and Refractive Surgery, Am. Soc. Cataract and Refractive Surgery. Avocations: golf, scuba diving, swimming, skiing. Home: Mido Apt 102-1206 Daechi Dong Gang Nam Seoul 135-280 Republic of Korea Office: Korea Eye Ctr 579-2 Je-sung Bldg Shinsa Dong Kang Nam Gu Seoul 135-892 Republic of Korea Office Fax: 82-2 514 8700. E-mail: ophhong@yahoo.com.

HONG, JUN SUNG, social worker, educator; b. Seoul, Republic of Korea, May 20, 1974; MA, U. Wash., 1999; MSW, U. Mich., 2006. Rschr. U. Ill., Urbana-Champaign, 2006—. Fellowship, Coun. Social Work Edn. Avocations: reading, writing. Office: University Ill Sch Social Work Urbana IL 61801 Business E-Mail: jhong23@illinois.edu.

HONG, KEE-JONG, medical association administrator; b. Seoul, Republic of Korea, May 27, 1965; BS, Seoul Nat. U., 1988; PhD, Tex. Tech. U., 2001. Sci. dep. dir. Korea Nat. Inst. Health, 2007—. Postdoc. fellow U. Kans. Med. Ctr., 2003—06; rschr., AIDS rsch. influenza pathology vaccine devel. Korea Vaccine Rsch. Ctr. Mem.: Am. Soc. Immunologists, Korean Soc. AIDS, Korean Soc. Virology, Korean Soc. Immunologists. Office: Korea Nat Inst Health 187 Cheongwon Chungbuk 363-951 Republic of Korea Office Fax: 82-43-719-8219. Business E-Mail: khong@nih.go.kr.

HONG, KELLY, cosmetic dentist; Grad., Loma Linda U. Dentist Apple Valley Dentist; prof. Sch. of Dentistry Loma Linda U. Mem.: ADA, LA County Dental Soc., Tri-County Dental Soc., Am. Acad. of Implant Dentistry, Am. Acad. of Cosmetic Dentistry, Calif. Dental Assn. Office: Apple Valley Dentist 2080 Century Park East Suite E Los Angeles CA 90067 Office Phone: 310-553-2233.

HONG, RYOON-KI, orthodontist; b. Seoul, Korea, Mar. 20, 1961; s. Sung-Kwon Hong and In-Ae Kim; m. Jin-Sun Choi, Aug. 12, 1989; children: Hyun-Seung, Hyun-Seo. DDS, Seoul Nat. U., 1985; PhD, Tsurumi U., Yokohama, Japan, 1991. Dir. Dr. Hong's Orthodontic Office, Seoul, 1991—94; chmn. dept. orthodontics Chong-A Dental Hosp., Seoul, 1994—. Clin. prof. dept. orthodontics, Coll. Dentistry Seoul Nat. U., 1997—; clin. prof. dept. dentistry U. Ulsan, Seoul, 1997—; clin. prof. dept. orthodontics, Coll. Dentistry Dankook U., Chonan, Republic of Korea, 2001—. Author: (textbook) Mushroom Archwire Technique and the Lingual Bracket; contbr. articles to profl. jours. Consolium pastorale Nonhyun Cath. Ch., Seoul, 1996—98. Scholar Rotary Club, 1990. Fellow: World Fedn. Orthodontists; mem.: European Soc. Lingual Orthodontics, Am. Assn. Orthodontists, Korean Assn. Orthodontists, Korean Assn. Lingual Orthodontists (exec. dir. 1997—2007, v.p. 2008—). Achievements include patents for individual transfer tray in customized lingual indirect bonding system. Office: Dept Orthodontics Chong-A Dental Hosp # 648-22 Yoksam-Dong Gangnam-Gu Seoul 135-911 Republic of Korea Office Fax: 82-2-569-2812. E-mail: kloahong@naver.com.

HONG, SEONG-TSHOOL, biomedical researcher, educator; b. Unam, Chonbuk, Republic of Korea, July 10, 1965; m. Hyeon-Jin Kim, Jan. 7, 1996; children: Eugene, Eukyung. BS, Chonbuk Nat. U., Chonju, Republic of Korea, 1987; MS, Oreg. State U., 1993, PhD, 1996. Postdoctoral fellow Northwestern U. Med. Sch., Chgo., 1996—98; rsch. asst. ENH Rsch. Inst., Evanston, Ill., 1998—2000; asst. prof. Chonbuk Nat. U. Med. Sch., Chonju, 2000—. Contbr. articles to profl. jours. Recipient Hankyereh award, UTC Venture Capital, 1997, Innovation award, Merrill-Lynch and Co., 1998; scholar, Dept. Edn., Republic of Korea, 1989. Achievements include patents for methods for producing hypocholesterolemic feed. Office: Chonbuk Nat U Med Sch San 2-20 Kumam-Dong 561-712 Chonju Chonbuk Republic of Korea

HONG, SOOK HEE, medical educator; b. Seoul, Republic of Korea, Dec. 8, 1976; MD, Coll. Medicinem, Cath. U. Korea, 2000. Asst. prof. Seoul St. Mary's Hosp., 2010—. Office: # 505 Banpodogn Seochogu Seoul 137-701 Republic of Korea Business E-Mail: ssuki76@catholic.ac.kr.

HONG, SOON-KWAN, educational association administrator; b. Gangnung, Gangwon-Do, Republic of Korea, Aug. 20, 1965; MS, KNU, Republic of Korea, 1992; PhD, Tokyo U., 1996. Global edn. team mgr. Kangwon Med. Convergence Ctr., 2011—. Recipient Gold medal, Korea Red Cross. Mem.: Korean Plant Breeding, Japan Plant Breeding, Korean Biol. Engring., Korean Plant Biotech., Korean Plant Resources. Avocation: golf. Office: Dept Bio-Health Tech Chuncheon Gangwon-Do 200-701 Republic of Korea Office Phone: 82-33-250-6476. Office Fax: 82-33-250-6470. Business E-Mail: hong0820@hanmail.net, soonkwan@kangwon.ac.kr.

HONG, SUN PYO, molecular biologist, director; BS in Molecular Biology, MS in Molecular Biology, Seoul Nat. U., Republic of Korea; PhD, Seoul Nat. U., Sch. Biol. Scis. Diploma Samsung Group, 1992. Sr. rsch. scientist Biomed. Rsch. Team R & D Ctr., CJ Corp., 1992—2000; exch. rsch. scientist, dept. communicable diseases and immunity Walter Reed Army Inst. Rsch., Dept. Army, Washington, 1995—96; exec. dir. in molecular medicine, R & D Ctr. Genematrix Inc., 2000—. Editl. bd. mem. Liver Cancer Rev. Letters, Cancer Prevention Rsch., World Jour. Gastroenterology, Future Microbiology; guest scientist Cancer Rsch. Inst., Seoul Nat. U. R & D Com., Korean Soc. Cancer Prevention Project Evaluation Com., Nat. Pharmacogenomics Rsch. Network, Korean Ministry of Health and Welfare; oper. dir. Korean Clin. Bioinformatics Acad.; R & D planning and evaluation com. mem. Korean Ministry of Commerce, Industry and Energy; industry and energy new biol. project steering com. mem. Korean Ministry of Health & Welfare. Contbr. articles to numerous rsch. jours. Recipient Hepatitis Paper award, Korean Assn. Study of

Liver& GSK, 2007, Patent Tech. award, Korean Intellectual Property Office, 2007; named Korea's Glorious Scientists, Biol. Rsch. Info. Ctr., 2006, Outstanding Scientists, Internat. Biog. Ctr., 2008—09; named one of Most Prominent Tech. Innovation 100 Selections, Korean Ministry of Commerce, Industry, & Energy, 2005. Office: Genematrix Inc Yongin Gyeonggi Republic of Korea Office Fax: 031-260-9059. Business E-Mail: sunphong@genematrix.net.

HONG, SUNG KYU, urologist, educator; b. Seoul, Republic Of Korea, Aug. 23, 1970; s. Bum Pyo Hong and Ran Hur; m. Min Hee Kwon, Mar. 9, 2002; children: Yun Joe, Jeong Wook. MD, Seoul Nat. U., 1997, BS, 2000, PhD, 2006. Cert. Korean Urol. Assn., 2001, lic. physician Ministry Health and Welfare, Korea, 1996. Resident urology Seoul Nat. U. Hosp., 1997—2001, clin. fellow urology, 2004—05, asst. prof. urology, Bundang hosp. Seongnam-si, Kyunggido, 2005—, asst. prof., coll. medicine, 2007—. Vice dir. gen. affairs Korean Prostate Soc., Seoul, 2007—. Contbr. articles to profl. jours. (Best Article award, 2007, 2008). Mem. Fgn. Rels. Com., Korean Urol. Assn., Seoul, 2007—. Recipient Best Rschr. award, Seoul Nat. U. Bundang Hosp., 2007, Best Young Rschr. award, 2008. Mem.: Korean Urol. Oncology Soc. (vice chmn. fgn. rels. com. 2008—), Korean Prostate Soc. (vice dir. gen. affairs 2007—), Am. Urol. Assn., European Assn. Urology, Korean Urol. Assn. Achievements include research in genitourinary cancers in Asian population. Office: Urology Seoul Nat Univ Bundang Hosp Gumi-Dong Bundang-Gu 300 463-707 Seongnam Kyunggi-do Republic of Korea Office Phone: 82-31-787-7343. Office Fax: 82-31-787-4057. Business E-Mail: skhong@snubh.org.

HONG, SUNGWOO, medical educator; b. Busan, Republic of Korea, Feb. 28, 1973; BS, Seoul Nat. U., 1996; PhD, Pa. U., 2004. Postdoc. rsch. fellow Harvard U., 2004—06; prin. scientist GlaxoSmithKline, 2006—08; prof. KAIST, 2009—. Recipient Silver award, GlaxoSmithKline, Best Lectr. award, KAIST. Mem.: Pharm. Soc. Korea, Korean Chem. Soc., Am. Chem. Soc. Office: 291 Daehak-ro Yuseong-gu Daejeon 305-701 Republic of Korea Business E-Mail: hongorg@kaist.ac.kr.

HONG, YAN, healthcare educator; b. China, July 13, 1976; PhD, Johns Hopkins U., 2007. Asst. prof. Tex. A&M Health Sci. Ctr., 2007—. Recipient Early Career award, Am. Acad. Health Behavior. Mem.: APHA, IAS, ISSTDR, AAHB. Office: Tex A&M Sch Rural Pub Health 1266 Tex A&M University College Station TX 77843 Business E-Mail: yhong@srph.tamhsc.edu.

HONG, YOUNG JAE, ophthalmologist; b. EunyulKun, HwanghaeDo, Democratic Peoples Republic of Korea, Aug. 15, 1946; married. MD, Yonsei U. Med. Sch., Seoul, Republic of Korea, 1971, PhD, 1978. Cert. ophthalmologist Bd. Korean Acad. Ophthalmology, 1979. Intern & resident physician Yonsei U. Severance Hosp., Seoul, [illegible]—78, prof., 1979—2006, dual chair dept. ophthalmology, 1985—95, cheif office planning and mgmt., 1995—97, v.p., 1997—99, chmn. Eye-Ent Hosp., 2004; chair, lt. comdr. dept. ophthalmology Navy Base Hosp., Seoul, 1976—79; fellow Kresge Eye Inst. Wayne State U., Detroit, 1986—88; chmn. faculty coun. Yonsei U. Med. Coll., 2001—03, prof. emeritus, 2006—; chmn. 3rd Congress Asian Oceanic Glaucoma Soc., Seoul, 2001, Nune Eye Hosp., Seoul, 2006—; cheif dir. Korean Ophthal. Soc., Seoul, 2002—04; editor-in-chief Korean Jour. Ophthalmology, Seoul, 2005—. Contbr. chapters to books. Recipient Achievement award, Am. Acad. Ophthalmology, 2001, Disting. Svc. award, Asia-Pacific Acad. Ophthalmology, 2003, Jisukyoung Med. award, Whosaeng News Press, 2004. Home: #102-501 Ssanyong PlatinumValue Yuksam Seoul 135-935 Republic of Korea Office Fax: 82-2-2086-7770. Personal E-mail: youngjhong@gmail.com.

HONG, YOUNG MI, pediatrician, educator; d. Chang Yee Hong and Hyoung Sook Beun; m. Choon Ki Lee; children: Chong Yeop Lee, Hae Yeop Lee. B, Ewha Womans U., Seoul, Republic of Korea, 1980, M, 1984, D, 1988. Cert. physician Soc. Pediat., 1984. Asst. prof. Ewha Womans U., 1988—95, assoc. prof., 1995—2001, prof., 2001—, chmn. rsch. com. pediat. hypertension, 2009—. Chmn., nutrition com. Korean Pediat. Soc., Seoul, 1997—2000; chmn., editor, publ. com. Korean Pediat. Cardiology, Seoul, 2003—05; editor & chmn., publ. com. Com. Kawasaki Disease, Seoul, 2007—09, v.p., 2009—11, pres., 2011—. Contbr. articles to profl. jours. Treas. Soc. Korean Pediat. Cardiology, 2001—03. Recipient award, Korean Pediat. Soc., 2004, 2006—07, 2009—10, Korean Soc. Cardiology, 2010, Soc. Korean Pediat. Cardiology, 2006, Soc. Hypertension, 2006, Soc. Korean Pediat. Cardiology, 2008; grantee, Korean Med. Rsch. Found., 2010, Korean Hypertension Soc., Com. Pulmonary Hypertension; grant, Korean Soc. Cardiology, 2004—06, Kosef, 2008, Korean Heart Found., 2008, Korean Rsch. Found., 2008—11, Korean Soc. Cardiology, 2009, Soc. Hypertension, 2010. Mem.: Soc. Pediat. Cardiology (Seoul) (chmn. publ. com. 2003—05), Korean Pediat. Soc. (Seoul) (chmn. nutrition com. 1997—2000, grant 2007). Home: UnjungDong 379-4 Bilmot Villa C-101 Bundang-ku SeoungNam-City Republic of Korea Office: Ewha Womans Univ Hosp 911-1 MokDong YangCheon-Ku Seoul 158-710 Republic of Korea Office Fax: 82-2-2653-3718. Personal E-mail: hongym@chollian.net.

HONG, YOUNG SEOUB, medical researcher, educator; b. Busan, Republic of Korea, Nov. 15, 1965; s. Jae Sun Park; m. Keang Mie Baek; children: Sung Joo, Ji Hee. MB, Dong-A U., Busan, 1991, MS in Medicine, 1995, Dr., 1998. Cert. Korean Soc. Preventive Medicine, 1996, Korean Soc. Medicine, 1992, Korean Soc. Occupl. Medicine, 1997. Vis. scholar Baylor coll. Medicine, Huston, Tex., 1995; dir. Samsung Med. Ctr., Health Care Ctr., Seoul, Republic of Korea, 2001; prof. Dong-A U., Busan, 2003—; com. mem. bd. exam. Korean Soc. Occupl. Medicine, Seoul, 2004—07; vis. scholar Kobe U., Med. Sch., Japan, 2006, Vanderbilt U., Sch. Medicine, Nashville, 2008—. Bd. dirs. Korean Environ. Health Forum, Seoul, 2006—. Author: (books) Occupational Medicine Practice (Writing award, Busan Med. Soc., 2004), Human Ergonomics (Writing award, Busan Med. Soc., 2005); contbr. scientific papers. Med. counselor Pres. Candidate, Seoul, Republic of Korea; mgr. Korean Soc. Epidemiology, Seoul, 2004—08; gen. mgr. Korean Soc. Toxicogenomic and Proteomics, Seoul, 2005—08. Capt. Med. Comdr. Korean Army, 1998—2001, Seoul. Grantee Brain Korea 21, Dept. Edn., Korea, 2006—08; Med. Rsch. Ctr. Cancer Molecular Therapy grant, Korean Sci. and Engring. Found., 2004—08. Mem.: Korean Soc. Medicine. Achievements include research in Korean welders health problem by welding fume in 1997. Avocations: golf, soccer. Home and Office: Dong-A Univ Coll Medicine Dept Preventive Medicine Ga-1 Dongdaeshin-Dong Seo-Gu 3 602-103 Busan Busan Republic of Korea Office Phone: 82-51-240-2888. Office Fax: 82-51-253-5729. Business E-Mail: yshong@dau.ac.kr.

HONGMEI, SHEN, medical association administrator; b. Heilongjiang, China, Nov. 9, 1963; B, Harbin Med. U., 1985, D, 2007. Asst. dir. Harbin Med. U., Ctr. Endemic Disease Control, Chinese Ctr. Disease Control and Prevention, 2002. Contbr. articles to profl. med. jours. Master: Endemic Disease Br., Chinese Med. Assn.; mem.: Com. Disease Control and Prevention, Chinese MOH. Office: 157 Baojian Rd Nangang Dist Harbin Heilongjiang 150081 China Office Fax: 86-451-86657674. Personal E-mail: shenhm119@126.com.

HONG SEOK, PARK, urologist, director; b. Pusan, Republic of Korea, May 1, 1967; s. Hyun Chul Park and Kyung Ja Kim; m. Hyun Yee Cho; 1 child, Tae Young Park. MD, Seoul, Republic of Korea, 1991; PhD, Korea U. Med. Coll., Seoul, 1999. Clin. fellow Pusan Nat. U. Hosp., 1999—2000; clin. instr. Korean U. Anam Hosp., Seoul, 2000—03; asst. prof. Korea U. Med. Coll., 2003—06; postdoc. fellow MD Anderson Cancer Ctr., Houston, 2006—07; dir., urology dept. Korea U. Ansan Hosp., 2007—. Contbr. articles to profl. jours. Capt., flight surgeon ROKAF, 1996—99, Pusan. Mem.: Korean Urol. Oncology Soc., European Urol. Assn., Korean Urol. Assn. Home: 1007-104 10 Danji Shinjeong 1 Yangcheon Seoul 158-770 Republic of Korea Office: Urology Korea Univ Ansan Hosp Kojan 1-Dong Danwon-Ku 425-707 Ansan Kyunngki Republic of Korea Office Fax: 82-31-412-5194. E-mail: dr4you@korea.ac.kr.

HONIG, GEORGE RAYMOND, pediatrician; b. Chgo., May 5, 1936; s. Joseph C. and Raymonde S. (Moses) Honig; m. Karen R. Jacobson, Dec. 18, 1960 (dec.); children: Sharon, Debra, Robert; m. Olga M. Weiss, May 24, 1998. BS in Liberal Arts and Sci., U. Ill., 1959, MD, 1961, MS in Pharmacology, 1961; PhD in Biochemistry, George Washington U., 1966. Diplomate Am. Bd. Pediatrics, Nat. Bd. Med. Examiners. Intern Johns Hopkins Hosp., Balt., 1961-62, fellow in pediatrics, 1961-63, asst. resident in pediatrics, 1962-63; rsch. assoc. Nat. Cancer Inst. NIH, 1963-66; fellow in pediatric hematology U. Ill., Chgo., 1966-68, from asst. prof. to assoc. prof. pediat., 1968—74, prof., 1974-75, 1984—2003, prof. emeritus, 2004—, attending physician, 1968-75, dir. pediatric hematology svc., 1972-75, head dept. pediat. Coll. Medicine, 1984—2003. Attending physician, dir. divsn. hematology Children's Meml. Hosp., Chgo., 1975—83; prof. emeritus U. Ill. Coll. Medicine, 2004—. Contbr. articles to profl. jours. Mem.: AAUP, Soc. Pediatric Rsch., Am. Pediatric Soc., Am. Soc. Hematology, Am. Soc. Biochemistry and Molecular Biology, Am. Assn. Cancer Rsch., Am. Acad. Pediat., Alpha Omega Alpha. Office: U Ill Coll Medicine 840 S Wood St Chicago IL 60612-7317 Business E-Mail: ghonig@uic.edu.

HONKALA, EINO JUHANI, dental educator; b. Elimaki, Finland, Oct. 18, 1945; s. Mikko Frans and Mirja Serafina (Kotiranta) H.; children: Otto, Nora. LDS, U. Helsinki, 1974, D in Odontology, U. Kuopio, Finland, 1984, Docent in Preventive Dentistry, 1985; MSc, London Hosp. Med. Coll., 1986; Docent in Cariology, U. Helsinki, 1993; DDPH, Royal Coll. Surgeons Eng. Specialist in dental pub. health Nat. Bd. Health. Prof. preventive cmty. dentistry U. Dar es Salaam, Tanzania, 1986—88; assoc. prof. cariology U. Kuopio, Finland, 1986—95; assoc. prof. health edn. U. Jyvaskyla, 1990—91; prof. cariology U. Helsinki, 1995—96, assoc. prof. dental infectious diseases, 1996—98, prof. dental pub. health Kuwait U., 1999—2006, vice-dean rsch. and student affairs, 1999—2006, 2009—, prof. dental pub. health, prof. clin. odontology U. Tromsø, Norway, 2006—07; prof. cmty. dentistry U. Turku, Finland, 2007—09. Vis. prof. pediat. dentistry U. Minn., 1994; mem. senate U. Dar es Salaam, 1987—88; mem. coun. U. Kuopio, 1992—94; dir. Helsinki Internat. Inst. Oral Health; pres. European Assn. Dental Pub. Health, 2008—09. Editor: Pedodontics, 1984; mem. editl. bd.: Tanzanian Dental Jour., 1995—, Med. Prins. and Practice, 1999—2005, 2009—, Cmty. Dental Oral Epidemiology, 2002—04; mem. editl. bd. Dental Forum, 2003—, Pakistan Dental Jour., 2003—, African Jour. Oral Health, 2004—, Oral Health Dental Mgmt. in Black Sea Countries, 2007—10; assoc. editor: Cmty. Dental Health, 2001—05. Active Health Authority Bd., Kuopio, 1981-84, Finnish Bd. of Univs., Finland, 1975-80; mem. Coun. Union Univ. Rschrs., 1981. Rsch. grantee Acad. of Finland, 1985, 97. Mem.: Knight, First Class, Order of White Rose Finland, Finnish Dental Soc. (hon.). Office: Kuwait Univ P.O. Box 24923 13110 Safat Kuwait Home Phone: 965-65638738; Office Phone: 965-24986760. Business E-Mail: eino.honkala@hsc.edu.kw.

HONMA, KIRI, medical educator; b. Tokyo, July 8, 1960; MD, Sch. Medicine, Tsukuba U., 1986, PhD. Physician, dept. pediat., sch. medicine Chiba U., 1986—98; asst. prof. Nippon Med. Sch., 1998—99, Nagasaki U., 1999—2005, lectr., 2006—. Office: 1-12-4 Salamto Nagasaki Nagasaki 852-8523 Japan Office Fax: 81-95-819-7073. Business E-Mail: kiri9@me.com.

HONMA, KOICHI, pathologist, researcher; b. Shiroishi, Miyagi, Japan, Mar. 28, 1955; s. Tsuneo and Mieko (Isago) Honma; m. Kiyomi Fukuda, Nov. 27, 1986; children: Shiko, Seiji, Shino. BM, Tohoku U., 1979; MD, Dokkyo U., 1986. Instr. Dokkyo U. Sch. Medicine, Tochigi, Japan, 1981-84, asst. prof., 1984-92, assoc. prof., 1992—. Mem. sci. com. No. 9 ILO Conf., Kyoto, 1995—97; organizer internat. workshops on occupl. lung diseases, 1996—. Contbr. articles to profl. jours. Founder, diplomatic counselor London Diplomatic Acad., 2000—; mem. Asbestos Guideline Com., 2007—. Mem.: European Soc. Pathology, Pulmonary Pathology Soc., Am. Thoracic Soc., European Respiratory Soc., Deutsche Gesellschaft fur Pathologie. Avocations: music, sports. Home: Tomatsuri 3-6-45 Utsunomiya Tochigi 320-0056 Japan Office: Dokkyo University Hosp Cancer Ctr Pathology Kitakobayashi 880 Mibu Tochigi 321-0293 Japan Office Phone: 81 282 87 2129. Office Fax: 81 282 86 5171. Business E-Mail: honma@dokkyomed.ac.jp.

HONOKI, KANYA, surgeon, cancer and stem cell biology researcher; b. Osaka, Japan, Feb. 25, 1962; s. Syoichi and Harumi Honoki; m. Kumiko Yamagiwa; children: Shiho, Keigo. MD, Nara Med. U., Kashihara, Japan, 1987, PhD, 1994; MMS in Clinical Epidemiology, U. Newcastle, NSW, Australia, 2006. Resident Nara Med. U., 1987—89, post grad., 1990—94, clin. staff, 1996—2000, asst. prof., 2001—. Postdoctoral rschr. Thomas Jefferson U., Phila., 1994—95; vis. fellow St. Jude Childrens Res. Hosp., 2002. Mem.: Internat. Cell Med. Soc., European Assn. Cancer Rsch., Soc. Am. Baseball Res., Am. Assn. Cancer Rsch. Office: Nara Medical Univ 840 Shijo-cho Nara Kashihara 634-8521 Japan Office Phone: 81-744-22-3051 Ext. 2324. Office Fax: 81-744-25-6449; Home Fax: 81-742-45-6716. Personal E-mail: magnolias@kcn.jp. Business E-Mail: kahonoki@naramed-u.ac.jp.

HOOD, ANTOINETTE FOOTE, dermatologist; b. Honolulu, 1941; MD, Vanderbilt U., 1967. Cert. dermatology. Intern Vanderbilt Affiliated Hosps, 1967-68; fellow dermatology Harvard U., 1973-75, resident dermatology, 1975-76; resident dermatology-pathology Mass. Gen. Hosp., Boston, 1976-78; faculty Johns Hopkins School of Med., 1980—93; Dir. Dermatopathology Indiana Univ. School of Med., 1993—2002; exec. dir. American Board of Dermatology, Detroit, 2001—; Dir. Dermatopathology Ea. Va. School of Med, 2002—. Office: Pariser Dermatology Specialists Ltd 601 Medical Tower Norfolk VA 23507 *

HOOD, LEROY EDWARD, systems biologist, genomics, proteomics educator; b. Missoula, Mont., Oct. 10, 1938; s. Thomas Edward and Myrtle Evylan (Wadsworth) Hood; m. Valerie Anne Logan, Dec. 14, 1963; children: Eran William, Marqui Leigh, Jennifer. BS, Calif. Inst. Tech., 1960; MD, Johns Hopkins U., Balt., 1964; PhD in Biochemistry, Calif. Inst. Tech., 1968. Med. officer USPHS, 1967-70, staff scientist Bethesda, Md., 1967-70; sr. investigator Nat. Cancer Inst., 1967-70; asst. prof. biology Calif. Inst. Tech., Pasadena, 1970-73, assoc. prof., 1973-75, prof., 1975-92, Bowles prof. biology, 1977-92, chmn. divsn. biology, 1980-89; Gates prof. biomedical sci., founder & chmn. dept. molecular biotechnology University of Washington School Medicine, Seattle, 1992—2000; co-founder, pres. Institute Systems Biology, Seattle, 2000—. Dir. NSF Sci. & Tech. Ctr. Molecular Biotechnology, 1989—2001. Author (with others): Biochemistry, a Problems Approach, 1974, Molecular Biology of Eukaryotic Cells, 1975, Immunology, 1978, Essential Concepts of Immunology, 1978, The Code of Codes: Scientific and Social Issues in the Human Genome Project, 1992; co-editor: Advances in Immunology, 1987, Genetics: From Genes to Genomics, 1999; contbr. numerous articles to profl. jours. Recipient Albert Lasker Basic Med. Rsch. award, 1987, Assn. Biomolecular Resource Facilities award, 2000, Kyoto prize, Inamori Found., Japan, 2002, Lemelson-MIT prize for invention & innovation, 2003, Award for excellence in molecular diagnostics, Assn. Molecular Pathology, 2003, Biotechnology Heritage award, 2004, Heinz award for tech., economy & employment, 2006, Wharton Infosys Bus. Transformation award, U. Pa., 2006, Kistler prize, Found. for the Future, 2010; named Scientist of Yr., R&D Mag., 1993; named one of The 100 Agents of Change, Rolling Stone mag., 2009; named to Nat. Inventors Hall of Fame, 2007. Mem.: NAE (Fritz J. and Dolores H. Russ prize 2011), NAS, Inst. Medicine, Am. Philos. Soc., Am. Acad. Arts & Scis., Sigma Xi. Achievements include development of the automated DNA sequencer in 1986, the key technology enabling the Human Genome Project; invention of the protein synthesizer, an instrument that assembles long peptides from amino acid subunits; the DNA synthesizer for synthesizing DNA fragments, a key development for gene mapping and the polymerase chain reaction [illegible] reading. Office: Inst for Systems Biology 401 Terry Ave N Seattle WA 98121 Office Phone: 206-732-1201. Business E-Mail: lhood@systemsbiology.org. *

HOOD, WILLIAM BOYD, JR., cardiologist, educator; b. Sylacauga, Ala., Mar. 25, 1932; s. William Boyd and Katherine Elizabeth (Anderson) H.; m. Katherine Candace Todd, May 5, 1972; 1 son, Jefferson Boyce. BS summa cum laude, Davidson Coll., 1954, MD, Harvard U., 1958. Intern Peter Bent Brigham Hosp., Boston, 1958-59, resident in internal medicine, 1959-60, 62-63; from asst. prof. to assoc. prof. medicine Harvard U., 1967-71; from assoc. prof. to prof. medicine Boston U., 1971-82; chief cardiology Boston City Hosp., 1973-82; prof. medicine U. Rochester (N.Y.), 1982-98; head cardiology unit Strong Meml. Hosp., Rochester, 1982-98; emeritus prof. medicine U. Rochester, 1998—. Cons. NIH, 1975—, NASA, 1994—; clin. prof. medicine U. Wash. Sch. Medicine, Seattle, 2000—. Mem. editorial bd. New Eng. Jour. Medicine, 1974-81, Circulation, 1980-83, Circulation Research, 1982-89, Jour. Clin. Investigation, 1984-89, Cochrane Collaboration Heart Group, 1997—; contbr. articles, revs. and editorials on cardiovascular physiology to profl. jours., chpts. to books. Served to capt. USAF, 1963-65. Research grantee NIH, 1971-98; grantee Am. Heart Assn., 1971-76. Fellow ACP; mem. Am. Soc. Clin. Investigation, Assn. Am. Physicians, Am. Heart Assn., Am. Physiol. Soc., Assn. Profs. Cardiology (past pres.), N.Y. Cardiol. Soc. (past pres.), Phi Beta Kappa, Alpha Omega Alpha. Achievements include studies on experimental and clinical myocardial ischemia and infarction, and congestive heart failure.

HOOGENBOOM, CAROL ANNETTE, clinical neuropsychologist; b. Grand Rapids, Mich., Jan. 31; d. Cornelius Adrian and Shirley Ann (Rassi) Hoogenboom. BS, Western Mich. U., Kalamazoo, 1985, MA, 1987; PsychD, Forest Inst., Wheeling, Ill., 1993; attending, Novus Law Sch., Calif., 2007—. Lic. Clin. Psychologist Ill. Dept. Fin. & Profl. Regulation, 1995. Psychometrian Crawford Consulting Svc., Chgo., 1991—92, Behavioral Health Svcs., Chgo., 1993—94; intern, resident Cermak Hosp., Chgo., 1991—92; postdoctoral Psychealth Ltd., Evanston, Ill., 1993—95; pres., adminstr. Nat. Neuropsych. Svcs., Glenview, Ill., 1995—97, clin. psychologist, 1995—97; Neuropsychologist CAH Psychological Svcs., Chgo., 1998—. Personal injury cons. Area Personal Injury Attys., Chgo., 2003—05; domestic abuse cons. Sido's Shelter, Chgo., 2004; pro bono psychol. svcs. CAH Psychol. Svcs., Chgo., 2003—. Author: (manual) Starting a Domestic Abuse Shelter, 2004, Anti Social Personality Disorder Is Really a Delusional Disorder, 2006. AIDS speaker Area Hosps., Chgo., 2005; Provide free depression screening through local businesses, Chgo., 2003—; motivational speaker CAH Psycholog. Svcs., Chgo., 2005—. Fellow: APA; mem.: Am. Psychol Soc., Ill. Psychol. Assn., Behavior Book Club, Psi Chi. Achievements include Numerous awards in athletics: basketball, volleyball, track, softball and cycling, including All American honors; 1st female Native Am. to obtain doctoral degree in US. Avocations: coin collecting/numismatics, computers, sports, Equality and Civil Rights Issues, building trades. Office: CAH Psychol Svcs 28 E Jackson Bldg #10-H580 Chicago IL 60604 E-mail: carolhoogenboom@yahoo.com.

HOOK, JERRY B., pharmaceutical consultant; b. Elk City, Okla., Sept. 7, 1937; m. Jacqueline H. Smith; children: Bruce, Marilyn. BS, B in Pharmacy with honors, Wash. State U., Pullman, 1960; MS, U. Iowa, 1964, PhD, 1966; DSc (hon.), John Jay Coll. Criminal Justice, CUNY, 1989. Diplomate Am. Bd. Toxicology. Assoc. prof. pharmacology Mich. State U., East Lansing, 1971-75, prof. of pharmacology,

1975-78, prof. pharmacology and toxicology, 1978-83, dir. ctr. for environ. toxicology, 1980-83; v.p. preclin. R & D Smith Kline & French Labs. Phila., King of Prussia, Pa., 1983-87, v.p. preclin. R & D worldwide, 1987-88, v.p. devel., R & D, 1988-89, SmithKline Beecham Pharms., King of Prussia, 1989-90, sr. v.p., dir. devel. R & D, 1990-93; pres., chief exec. officer Lexin Pharm. Corp., Horsham, Pa., 1993-96; pres., CEO Sparta Pharm., Inc., Horsham, Pa., 1996-98, chmn., pres., CEO, 1998-99. Burroughs-Wellcome vis. prof. U. N.D., 1981; vis. scientist Fed. Am. Soc. for Exptl. Biology Vis. Scientists for Minority Instns. Program, U. P.R. Med. Sch., 1984, Herbert H. Lehman Coll. of City U., 1985, Calif. State U., 1988, Pembroke State U., 1989; mem. adv. com. to bd. sci. counselors Nat. Toxicology Program, 1982-86; chmn. peer rev. panel of experts Nat. Toxology Program; vis. scientist John Jay Coll. Criminal Justice CUNY, 1987, mem. adv. bd. Toxicology Rsch. and Tng. Ctr., 1986-93. Author 225 publs. peer-reviewed lit., 60 book chpts., published symposia, reviews, symposia presentations. Bd. dirs. Montgomery County Community Coll. Found., 1987-89. Fellow Am. Coll. Clin. Pharmacology (hon.); mem. AAAS, Am. Soc. for Pharmacology and Exptl. Therapeutics, Internat. Union of Pharmacology (vice chmn. toxicology sect. 1987-90, chmn. toxicology sect. 1990-94), Internat. Union of Toxicology (1st v.p. 1989-92), Mid-Atlantic Chpt. Soc. of Toxicology, Soc. of Toxicology (councillor 1983-85, v.p. elect 1985-86, v.p. 1986-87, pres. 1987-88, past pres. 1988-89, IUTOX councillor). Personal E-mail: jhook0937@aol.com.

HOOKER, STEVEN P., sports medicine physician, educator; Chief physical activity & health initiative Calif. Dept. Health Svcs.; dir. USC Prevention Rsch. Ctr.; rsch. assoc. prof. Arnold Sch. Pub. Health Dept. Exercise Sci. Creator Calif. Active Aging Project; prin. investigator Active Aging Cmty. Task Force; bd. mem. SC Gov. Coun. on Physical Fitness; pres. elect SC Coalition for Promoting Physical Activity. Fellow: Am. Coll. Sports Med. Office: Public Health Research Center 921 Assembly St #117 Columbia SC 29208 Office Phone: 803-777-0266. Office Fax: 803-777-9007. E-mail: shooker@mailbox.sc.edu.

HOOKS, VENDIE HUDSON, III, surgeon; b. Metter, Ga., Nov. 1, 1948; s. Vendie Hudson Jr. and May (Jones) H.; m. Carolyn Anderson Braithwaite, Nov. 1, 1974; children: Hudson, Susanna, David, Katherine. BS, U. Ga., 1970; MD, Med. Coll. Ga., 1974. Diplomate Am. Bd. Surgery, Am. Bd. Colon and Rectal Surgery. Intern surgery Med. Coll. Ga. Hosps., Augusta, 1974-75, resident gen. surgery, 1975-78, chief resident gen. surgery, 1978-79; G.I. surgery fellow gen. infirmary U. Leeds (Eng.), 1979-80; colon and rectal surgery fellow U. Minn. Hosps., 1982-83; asst. prof. surgery, asst. chief sect. GI surgery Med. Coll. Ga., Augusta, 1980-85, dir. colon/rectal surgery clinic, 1980-85; attending in surgery VA Hosp., Augusta, 1980-85; from asst. clin. prof. surgery to assoc. clin. prof. Med. Coll. Ga., Augusta, 1985-2001, clin. prof., 2001—; staff surgeon Univ. Hosp., Augusta, 1985—, St. Joseph Hosp., Augusta, 1985—; attending colon/rectal surgery endoscopy Univ. Hosp., Augusta, 1986—. Dir. Southeastern Familial Polyposis Registry; bd. dirs. Richmond-Columbia County unit Am. Cancer Soc., v.p. medicine, 1985-91; mem. Ethicon Colon and Rectal Adv. Panel, 1988, Panel Specialist-Surgery, Vocat. Rehab., 1980—; mem. interview com. for med. sch. admissions Med. Coll. Ga., 1981-82, 84-85, mem. tissue com., 1983-85; chmn. familial polyposis registry com. U. Hosp. Augusta, 1986—; assoc. examiner Am. Bd. Colon and Rectal Surgery, 1995-98, mem., 1998—2006, v.p., 2005, pres., 2006. Contbr. articles to profl. jours.; book reviewer and abstractor in field; reviewer Gastrointestinal Endoscopy, 1985-88. Pres. med. staff U. Hosp., Augusta, Ga., 1999, Richmond County Hosp. Authority, Augusta, 1998. Recipient Continuing Med. Edn. award Am. Soc. Colon and Rectal Surgeons, 1984, 87, Spl. award for colorectal cancer control Am. Cancer Soc., 1987, Cert. of Appreciation, Am. Cancer Soc., 1991-92, Award of Excellence, Am. Cancer Soc., 1992-93; grantee Am. Soc. Hosp. Pharmacists, 1981, Smith Kline & French Labs., 1981, Merck Sharp & Dohme, 1984. Fellow ACS, Southeastern Surg. Congress, Am. Soc. Colon and Rectal Surgeons; mem. AMA (Physician Recognition award 1984-89, 1990-93, 93-96, 97-2000, 04), Med. Assn. Ga., Richmond County Med. Soc. (sec.), So. Med. Assn., Moretz Surg. Soc., Assn. for Acad. Surgeons, Ga. Gastroenterologic and Endoscopy Soc., Am. Soc. for Gastrointestinal Endoscopy, Soc. Am. Gastrointestinal Endoscopic Surgeons, Ga. Surg. Soc., Piedmont Soc. Colon and Rectal Surgeons (pres. 1992-94), Soc. Surgery Alimentary Tract, Phi Beta Kappa, Alpha Omega Alpha, Phi Kappa Phi. Methodist. Avocations: golf, hunting. Office: 1348 Walton Way Ste 6500 Augusta GA 30901-5111 Office Phone: 706-722-2118.

HOON JAI, CHUN, gastroenterologist, educator; b. Seoul, Republic of Korea, Sept. 17, 1959; s. Young Ryul Chun and Hye Ja Park; m. Jung Sook Choi, Jan. 25, 1991; children: Sang Hyun Chun, So Young Chun. MD, Korea U. Coll. Medicine, Seoul, 1985; MSc, Korea U. Grad. Sch., Seoul, 1988, PhD, 1994. Lic. in med. Ministry Health & Welfare, 1985, cert. internal medicine Korean Assn. Internal Medicine, 1990, gastrointestinal endoscopy Korean Soc. Gastrointestinal Endoscopy, 1996. Guest dr. Klinikum recht der Isar Tech. U., Munchen, Germany, 1994—95, Evangelisches Krankenhaus, Dusseldorf U., Germany, 1995—96; clin. instr. Korea U. Coll. Medicine, 1992—94, asst. prof., 1996—2000, assoc. prof., 2000—04, prof., 2004—. Chief endoscopy unit Korea U. Med. Ctr., Seoul, 2005—. Contbr. articles to profl. jours. Ctrl. rev. com. mem. Health Ins. Rev. Agy., Seoul, 2005; consultation com. mem. Ministry Health & Welfare, Gwacheon-si, Gyeonngi-do, 2005, Korea FDA, Seoul. Capt. Republic Korea Army. Recipient Excellent Article award, 2001; grantee, Korean Soc. Gastroenterology: GlaxoSmithKline, 2001, Korean Soc. Gastrointestinal Endoscopy: Paul Janssen, 2002, Ministry Health & Welfare, 2003, Minstry Commerce, Industry & Energy, 2007. Fellow: Korean Soc. Gastrointestinal Cancer, Korean Gastric Cancer Assn., Am. Gastroent. Assn., Korean Coll. Helicobacter & Upper Gastrointestinal Rsch., Japan Gastroent. Endoscopy Soc., Korean Soc. Gastrointestinal Endoscopy, Korean Soc. Gastroenterology, Die Sektion gastroenterologische Endoskopie der DGVS; mem.: Korean Med. Assn., Korean Assn. Internal Medicine. Achievements include patents for bead stitching and apparatus for stitching internal organ using the same. Office: Korea Univ Coll Medicine 126-1 5-Ga Anam-Dong Seongbuk-Gu Seoul 136-705 Republic of Korea Office Fax: 82 2 953 1943. Personal E-mail: drchunhj@hanmail.net. Business E-Mail: drchunhj@chol.com.

HOOPER, ANNE DODGE, pathologist, educator; b. Groton, Mass., July 16, 1926; d. Carroll William and Bertha Sanford (Wiener) Dodge; m. William Dale Hooper, June 17, 1952; children: Elizabeth Anne, Joan Elaine, Caroline Mae. AB, Washington U., St. Louis, 1947, MD, 1952. Diplomate Am. Bd. Pathology, Pathologic Anatomy, Clin. Pathology and Forensic Pathology. Rotating intern Virginia Mason Hosp., Seattle, 1952—53; resident in internal medicine St. Francis Hosp., Hartford, Conn., 1953—54; resident in pathologic anatomy and clin. pathology New Britain Gen. Hosp., Conn., 1954—57, Presbyn. Hosp., Phila., 1957—58; resident in forensic pathology Office Med. Examiner, Phila., 1958—60; from pathologist to acting chief lab svc. VA Hosp., Coatesville, Pa., 1960—66; dir. lab. St. Albans Hosp., Vt., 1966—69, Kerbs Hosp., St. Albans, 1966—71, Williamson Appalachian Regional Hosp., South Williamson, Ky., 1971—73, Beckley Appalachian Regional Hosp., W.Va., 1974—76; asst. prof. pathology W.Va. Sch. Osteo. Medicine, Lewisburg, 1977, assoc. prof., 1978—97, cons. in pathology, 1997—. Lab. accreditation insp. CAP, 1992—, Am. Osteo. Assn., 1986—99; assoc. med. examiner State of W.Va., 1999—; med. missionary Kijabe Hosp., Kenya, 1998; med. missionary, pathologist Pathologists Overseas at SALFA Lab., Madagascar, 2000; med. missionary Glens Falls NY Med. Missionary Found., Nueva Santa Rosa, Guatemala, 2001. Contbr. articles to profl. jours. Pres. local elem. sch. PTA, St. Albans, 1967—68; mem. profl. edn. com. W.Va. divsn. Am. Cancer Soc., Charleston, 1982—94, bd. dirs. W.Va. divsn., 1987—94, pres. Greenbrier unit Lewisburg, 1989—93; bd. dirs. ARC, Greenbrier County, W.Va., 2002—. Fellow: Am. Acad. Forensic Scis., Coll. Am. Pathologists; mem.: AMA, Am. Soc. Clin. Pathologists, Raleigh County Med. Soc., W.Va. Med. Soc. Avocations: violin, viola. Office: 192 Ptarmigan Trail Estes Park CO 80517 Personal E-mail: adhooper@gmail.com.

HOOPER, MICHAEL JEFFREY, endocrinologist, educator; b. Sydney, Apr. 20, 1944; MBBS, Sydney U., 1968. Founding hon. sec., treas. Australian & New Zealand Bone & Mineral Soc., 1988—93, pres., 2001—03; pres., adult med. divsn. Royal Australasian Coll. Physicians, 2008—10, bd. mem., 2008—, hon. treas., 2009—. Jr. resident med. officer, srmo, registrar, fellow endocrinology Royal North Shore Hosp., Sydney, 1968—73; commonwealth supernumerary registrar, thomas & ethel mary ewing rsch. fellow U. Dept Medicine, Western Infirmary, Glasgow, 1973—76; dir. endocrinology Concord Repatriation Gen. Hosp., 1984—2002; clin. assoc. prof. Sydney U., 2007—; area stream head, bone & mineral stream, endocrinology CSAHS-SSWAHS, 2009. Fellow: Royal Australasian Coll. Physicians; mem.: Endocrine Soc. Australia, ASBMR. Avocation: fishing. Home: 54 St Johns Ave Gordon NSW 2072 Australia Home Fax: 61 2 94181671. Business E-Mail: mjhooper@bigpond.net.au.

HOOPS, TIMOTHY C., gastroenterologist, educator, physician; MD, U. Ill. Diplomate Am. Bd. Internal Medicine, 1985, Am. Bd. Internal Medicine-gastroenterology, 1988. Intern Univ. Colo., resident internal medicine, fellow gastrointestinal medicine; clin. prof. Medicine Univ. Pa. Health System; chief gastroenterology dept. Penn Presbyn. Med. Ctr., med. dir. endoscopy dept., dir. Gastrointestinal Cancer Risk Evaluation Program. Named recognized, Best Doctors in America, 2005—06, 2009—10; named one of the Top Doctors, Phila. Mag., 2007—11, the Top Doctors in America, 2007—08. Office: Penn Presbyterian Medical Center 218 Wright Saunders Bldg 51 N 39th St Philadelphia PA 19104 Office Phone: 215-662-8900. Office Fax: 215-662-0950.

HOOVER, PEARL ROLLINGS, nurse; b. LeSueur, Minn., Aug. 24, 1924; d. William Earl and Louisa (Schickling) Rollings; m. Roy David Hoover, June 19, 1948 (dec. Mar. 20, 1987); children: Helen Louise, William Robert(dec.). Grad. in nursing, U. Minn., 1945, BS in Nursing, 1947; MS in Health Sci., Calif. State U., Northridge, 1972. Dir. affiliate nursing sch. Mooselake State Hosp., Minn., 1948-49; nursing instr. Anchor Hosp., County Hosp., St. Paul, 1949-51; student nurse supr. and instr. Brentwood VA Hosp., LA, 1951-52; sch. nurse LA Unified City Schs., 1963-91, substitute sch. nurse, 1991-96. Camp nurse United First Meth. Ch., winter and summer past 40 yrs.; corr. sec. Reseda Women's Club, 1st v.p.; courtesy chmn. First United Meth. Women. Mem. LA Coun. Sch. Nurses, Calif. Sch. Nurses Orgn. Democrat. Methodist. Home: 17851 Lull St Reseda CA 91335-2237

HOOYENGA, JUDITH WAARA, lawyer; b. Akron, Ohio, Dec. 10, 1949; d. Dwite Allen Walker and Marian Louise Hall; m. Gerrit G. Hooyenga, Apr. 30, 1982; children: Brian Clark, Debra Sue Moody, Melanie. BA, U. Mich., Ann Arbor, 1970; JD, U. Chgo., 1991. Bar: Mich. 1991. Adminstr. Beverly Enterprises, Southgate, Mich., 1976—79, sr. adminstr. Muskegon, Mich., 1979—82; pres. Health Nursing Care Centers Mich., Inc., Grand Haven, 1982—86, Health Care Assn. Mich., Lansing, 1986—87; assoc. atty. Latham & Watkins, Washington, 1991—96, Warner Norcross & Judd LLP, Grand Rapids, Mich., 1996—97; dir. legal svcs. Priority Health, Grand Rapids, 1997—2002, gen. counsel, 2002—10, dep. gen. counsel, 2010—. Mem. adv. commn. Health Facilities Agys., Lansing, 1985—88; sec. bd. dirs. Priority Health Affiliates, Grand Rapids, 2002—10. Bd. trustees Christ Cmty. Ch., Spring Lake, Mich., 1998—2004, North Ottawa Cmty. Health Sys., Grand Haven, 2005—, sec., 2006—07, vice chair, 2007—. Recipient Pres.'s award, Healthcare Assn. Mich., 1988. Mem.: Mich. State Bar Assn., Am. Health Lawyers Assn., Mich. Assn. Health Plans (mem. legis. com. 2000—, alt. del. 2002—10). Avocations: travel, photography, reading, golf, sports. Office: Priority Health 1231 E Beltline NE Grand Rapids MI 49525 Office Fax: 616-942-0148. Personal E-mail: judyhooyenga@gmail.com. Business E-Mail: judith.hooyenga@priorityhealth.com. *

HOPF, FRANK RUDOLPH, retired dentist; b. NYC, Sept. 1, 1920; s. Rudolph Aldridge and Jennie Victoria (Fusco) Hopf; m. Elsie Hedlund, Sept. 10, 1949; children: Christine, Frank, Victoria, William, Robert. BS, Purdue U., West Lafayette, Ind., 1942; postgrad., Middlesex U. Sch. Medicine, 1943—44; DDS, NYU, 1953, postgrad., 1957—61; MA, Columbia U., NYC, 1953, MPH, 1955. Asst. dir. Bur. Dental Health, NY State Dept. Health, Albany, 1956—57, regional dental dir. White Plains, 1967—90; pvt. practice dentistry specializing in periodontics Rye, NY, 1957—2003; ret., 2003. Rsch. assoc. periodontics NYU Coll. Dentistry, 1958—61; clin. asst. prof. dept. periodontics NJ Coll. Medicine and Dentistry, Jersey City, 1962—67; adj. asst. prof. dept. cmty. dentistry Columbia Sch. Dental and Oral Surgery, NYC, 1971—76; vis. prof. dept. preventive dentistry Pitts. U. Sch. Dentistry, 1967—72. Contbr. articles to profl. publs. Pres. Country Ridge Home Owners Assn., Rye Brook, NY, 1960—62. With USNR, 1944—46. Grantee, NIH, 1957. Fellow: APHA, Am. Coll. Dentists, NY Acad. Dentistry, Am. Sch. Health Assn.; mem.: AAAS, ADA, Fedn. Dentaire Internationale, Am. Soc. Dentistry for Children, Westchester Acad. Medicine, North Eastern Soc. Periodontics, Royal Soc. Health, NY State Pub. Health Assn. (pres. 1970—72), Westchester Country Club, Westchester Shore Dental Study Club (pres. 1960—61, Rye, NY), KC (4 deg.). Roman Catholic. Home: 33 Old Field Hill Rd # 7 Southbury CT 06488

HÖPFNER, MICHAEL, physiologist, oncologist, researcher; b. Berlin, Feb. 2, 1966; s. Sigrun and Jochen Höpfner; m. Veronika Christine Dietrich, July 24, 1998; children: Marie Annika, Friederike Josephine. PhD in Biology, Free U., Berlin, 1996, diploma in sports scis., 1996; habilitation in Biomedicine, Charité, Berlin, 2007. Rschr. Charité U. Medicine Berlin, Campus Benjamin Franklin, Inst. Physiology, Berlin, 1997—; assoc. prof., pvt. docent Inst. Physiologic, Charité; group leader. Office Fax: 4930 450 528918. Business E-Mail: michael.hoepfner@charite.de.

HOPKINS, ADRIAN DENNIS, ophthalmologist, director; b. Eng., Nov. 2, 1946; MB ChB, St Andrews U., Scotland, 1971; MRCOphth, Royal Coll. London, 1988. Dist. med. officer BMS World Mission, Pimu, Democratic Republic of Congo, 1975—93; ophthalmologist, med. advisor, tech. advisor for blindness prevention and oncocerciasis control CBM, Ctrl. African Republic, 1993—99, ophthalmologist, med. advisor, dir. studies, Ophthalmology Tng. Ctr. Kinshasa, Democratic Republic of Congo, 1999—2007; dir. Mectizan Donation Program, Emory U., Task Force Global Health, 2008—. Mem., tech. consultative com. WHO African Programme for Onchocerciasis Control, 1996—2001; chairperson NGDO Coordination Group for Onchocerciasis Control, 2002—06, NTD NGDO Network, 2009; mem. WHO Africa Regional Rev. Group for Lymphatic Filariasis Elimination, 2006. Recipient Tropical Ophthalmology award, German Ophthalmology Soc., John Holt medal, Liverpool Sch. Tropical Medicine. Fellow: Royal Soc. Tropical Medicine and Hygiene; mem.: Am. Soc. Tropical Medicine and Hygiene, Royal Coll. Ophthalmologists (London). Home: Mectizan Donation Program 325 Swanton Way Decatur GA 30030 Home Fax: 1 404 371 1138. Business E-Mail: ahopkins@taskforce.org.

HOPKINS, DONALD ROSWELL, public health physician; b. Miami, Fla., Sept. 25, 1941; s. Joseph Leonard and Iva (Major) Hopkins; m. Ernestine Mathis, June 24, 1967. BS, Morehouse Coll., 1962; MD, U. Chgo., 1966; MPH, Harvard U., 1970; DSc (hon.), Morehouse Coll., 1988, Emory U., 1994; LHD (hon.), U. Mass., Lowell, 1997; DSc (hon.), Morehouse Coll., 1999. Intern San Francisco Gen. Hosp., 1966—67; resident U. Chgo. Hosps., 1970—72; med. officer program planning and evaluation Ctrs. for Disease Control, Atlanta, 1972—74, dep. chief environ. health svc. divsn., 1974, asst. dir. ops., 1977—80, asst. dir. internat. health, 1980—84, dep. dir., 1984—87; assoc. exec. dir. The Carter Ctr., Inc., 1997—2007, v.p. health, 2007—. Asst. prof. tropical pub. health Harvard U., Boston, 1974—77; chmn., advisor on internat. health rsch. Dr. Peter Bourne, White House, Washington, 1977; mem. U.S. del. World Health Assembly, Geneva, 1977—78, Geneva, 1980—86; global adv. group on immunization WHO, Geneva, 1978—79, steering com. epidemiology working group, 1980—83; cons. in field. Author: Princes and Peasants-Smallpox in History, 1983. Bd. dirs. MacArthur Found. Decorated knight Nat. Order of Mali, Order of Bifurcated Needle WHO; recipient Commd. Corps Disting. Svc. medal, USPHS, 1986, Joseph Mountin Lecture award, Ctrs. for Disease Control, 1981, John Snow award, APHA, 1997, Medal of Honor of Pub. Health, Govt. of Niger, 2004, Fries prize for improving health, 2007, Mectizan award, 2007; fellow MacArthur fellow, 1995. Fellow: Am. Acad. Arts & Scis.; mem.: Inst. Medicine NAS, Am. Soc. Tropical Medicine and Hygiene, Phi Beta Kappa. Democrat. Episcopalian. Office: Carter Presdl Ctr Inc One Copenhill Bldg 453 Freedom Pkwy NE Atlanta GA 30307-1496

HOPKINS, L. NELSON, neurosurgeon, radiologist; BA, Rutgers U., 1965; MD cum laude, Albany Med. Coll., 1969. Clin. asst. prof. neurosurgery U. Buffalo SUNY, 1975—82, clin. assoc. prof. neurosurgery, 1982—88, prof. radiology, 1989—, prof., chmn. neurosurgery, 1989—; clin. prof. neurosurgery U. Rochester, 2007—. Bd. dirs. Micrus Endovascular Corp., 1998—; dept. head Buffalo Gen. Hosp., 1989—; cons. Brooks Mem. Hosp., 2006—, Niagra Falls Meml., 2006—, Jones Meml. Hosp., 2007—, United Meml. Hosp., 2007—, others; bd. dirs. Toshiba Stroke Rsch. Ctr., 1997—. Reviewer: New England Jour. Medicine, 1999—; mem. editl. bd. STROKE, 2006—08, co-editor, 2006—, ad hoc reviewer Nature Clinical Practice Neurology, 2007—; contbr. articles to profl. jours. With USAFR, 1973. Recipient Western Neurological Soc. award, 2009, Laurel award, Congress Neurosurgeons Founders, 2009, others. Mem.: Am. Assn. Neurological Surgeons (dir.-at-large bd. dirs. 2000—). Office: State University of New York 353 Broadway Albany NY 12246 Office Phone: 518-518-5555. Office Fax: 518-443-5322. Business E-Mail: lhopkins@micrusendovascular.com. *

HOPPE, RICHARD T., oncologist, educator; b. NYC, Feb. 16, 1946; BA, Cornell U., 1967; MD, Cornell U. Med. Coll., 1971. Prof., chair, dept. radiation oncology Stanford U., 1992—. Recipient hon. Prof., Shantou U. Med. Coll., Shantou, China. Fellow: Am. Coll. Radiology, Am. Soc. Radiation Oncology (Gold medal); mem.: Radiol. Soc. N.America, Am. Soc. Clin. Oncology, Am. Radium Soc. (Janeway medal). Office: Dept Radiology 875 Blake Wilbur Dr Stanford CA 94305 Business E-Mail: rhoppe@stanford.edu.

HOPPENSTEIN, REUBEN, neurosurgeon, healthcare executive; b. Benoni, Transvaal, South Africa, Dec. 10, 1933; came to U.S., 1960; s. Charles and Rachel (Diner) H.; m. Eileen Prouser, Dec. 2, 1957 (div. 1968); children: Cheryl, Tivia, Ava, Charles; m. Raquel Shamis, July 17, 1976. MD, U. Witwatersrand, Johannesburg, South Africa, 1957. Diplomate Am. Bd. Neurol. Surgeons. Chmn. dept. neurosurgery Beekman-Downtown Hosp., NYC, 1970-80, Hosp. for Joint Diseases, NYC, 1972-80; CEO True Three Dimensional Techs., NYC, 1996—; pres. 3-D Images, London, 1996—; CEO Isle de Sol Devel. Co. Developer, CEO Yacht Club Isle De Sol, St. Martin, 2003—07; CEO Creative Carrier Corp., 2005—, 3D Virtual Lens LLC, 2009—. Prodr.: (Broadway plays) Jacques Brel Is Alive and Well and Living in Paris, 1988, (musical show) Dori, 1988; contbr. articles to med. jours. CEO Yacht Club Port De Plaisance, Saint Martin. Recipient Gerard B. Lambert award, Lambert Found., 1975; fellow, NIH, 1964—65. Fellow ACS; mem. Am. Congress Neurol. Surgeons, N.Y. State Soc. Neurol. Surgeons, N.Y.C. Soc. Neurol. Surgeons, N.Y. County Med. Soc., N.Y. State Med. Soc., Friar's Club, North Salem Golf Club (pres. 1986-90). Achievements include patents pending for building concept vehicle in England; automotive patents; patents for 3D television without using glasses. Office: 422E 72 St New York NY 10021 Office Phone: 212-628-9592. Personal E-mail: reubenmd01@aol.com, reubenmd01@gmail.com.

HOPPER, JOHN ALEXANDER, medical educator; BS, U. Mich.; MD, Wayne State U., Detroit, 1985—89. Lic. physician State of Mich., 1994. Intern, resident U. NC Hosps., 1989—93; asst. prof. Wayne State U., Detroit, 1994—2005, clin. assoc. prof., 2006—; v.p. med. affairs Brighton Hosp., Mich., 2005—07, chief med. officer, 2007—08, St. Joseph Merry Hosp., 2008—; vice-chair edn. and program dir. Dept. Internal Medicine. Med. dir. Jefferson Ave. Rsch. Clinic, Detroit, 1996—2005. Office: St Joseph Mery Hosp 5333 McAuley De Ste 309 Ypsilanti MI 48197

HOPPER, STEPHEN RODGER, hospital administrator; b. Chgo., Aug. 28, 1949; s. Rodger Patterson and Dorothy Ann (Newberg) H.; m. Janet Sue Waddill, June 10, 1972; children: Nathan John, Amanda Sue. BA, Ill. Coll., 1971; MHA, U. Minn., 1974. Adminstrv. resident Rochester (Minn.) Meth. Hosp., 1973-74; dir. support svcs. Jennie Edmundson Hosp., Council Bluffs, Iowa, 1974-78; asst. adminstr. Trinity Meml. Hosp., Cudahy, Wis., 1978-83, sr. v.p. med. svcs., 1983-84; pres., chief exec. officer McDonough Dist. Hosp., Macomb, Ill., 1985—. Bd. dirs. Midamerica Nat. Bank, Canton, Ill., chmn bd., 2004-06; bd. dirs. VHA MidAm., 2007-. Bd. dirs. Macomb Area Indsl. Devel., 1985—, Wesley Village, 2007—. Fellow Am. Coll. Healthcare Execs.; mem. Ill. Hosp. Assn. (past pres. region 1-B, bd. dirs. 1992-95, mem. venture corp. bd. 1999—), Macomb C. of C. (bd. dirs. 1990-94), Rotary (pres.-elect Macomb 1995-96, pres. 1996-97, asst. dist. gov. 2000-03). Avocations: golf, reading, computers, travel. Home: 112 W Totem Trl Macomb IL 61455-1272 Office: McDonough Dist Hosp 525 E Grant St Macomb IL 61455-3318 Office Phone: 309-836-1675. Business E-Mail: srhopper@mdh.org.

HOPPING, RICHARD LEE, retired academic administrator; b. Dayton, Ohio, July 26, 1928; s. Lavon Lee and Dorothy Marie (Anderson) H.; m. Patricia Louise Vance, June 30, 1951; children: Ronald, Debra, Jerrold. Student, Chaffey Coll., 1947-48, U. Dayton, 1948-49, Sinclair Coll., 1948-49; BS, OD, So. Coll. Optometry, 1952, DOS (hon.), 1972; DSc (hon.), SUNY, 1995; DOS (hon.), Southern Calif. Coll. Optometry, 2004. Practice optometry, Dayton, Ohio, 1953-73; pres. So. Calif. Coll. Optometry, Fullerton, 1973-97, pres. emeritus, 1997—. Mem. Nat. Acads. of Practice, 1983—; chmn. Nat. Acad. Practice in Optometry, 1985-89; vice chmn. 13th dist. med. quality rev. com., State of Calif. Bd. Med. Quality Assurance, 1985-93; mem. adv. bd. St. Jude Hosp., 1985—2000; nat. spokesperson Better Vision Inst., 1988-2000; cons. in field. Contbr. numerous articles on vision and health care to profl. publs. V.p. Orange County coun. Boy Scouts Am., Calif., 1977-79, adv. coun., 1979-94; mem. Coun. Assocs. of Red Cross, North Orange County Svc. Ctr., 1978-80; adv. coun. YWCA, North Orange County, 1984-92. Recipient Orange County Retinitis Pigmentosa award of Excellence in field of vision care, 1988, award of Excellence VisionAmerica, 1991, Dirs. Choice award Optical Labs. Assn., 1995, Leo award of Excellence in Global Eye Care Nat. Eye Rsch. Found., 1995, People of Vision award Prevent Blindness Am., 1997, Lifetime Achievement award So. Coll. Optometry, 1997; named Optimist of Yr., Dayton View Optimists, 1956; named to Nat. Optometry Hall of Fame, 2003. Fellow APHA (Vision Care Disting. Achievement award 1984), Am. Acad. Optometry (chmn. primary care optometry sect. 1973-79, chmn. awards com. 1981-90); mem. Am. Optometric Assn. (pres. 1971-72, chmn. profl. enhancement adv. com. 1982-89, Calif. Optometrist of Yr. 1988, chair industry rels. com. 1989-95, chair nat. ednl. summit conf. 1990-91, chair Nat. Optometric Edn. Summit com. 1991-92, chair centennial adv. com. 1996-98, Scope of Optometric Practice Conf. 1992, vice-chmn. Found. Optometry's Charity 2006—11, Nat. Optometrist of Yr. 1988, Dr. Raymond I. Meyers award 1990, Disting. Svc. award 1993), Calif. Optometric Assn. (hon. life, jud. coun., Optometrist of Yr. 1988, Paul Yarwood Meml. award 1997), Assn. Ind. Calif. Colls. and Univs. (trustee 1973-97), Optometric Ext. Programs Found. (hon. life), Assn. Schs. and Colls. of Optometry (pres. 1983-85), Ohio Optometric Assn. (pres. 1964-65, Ohio Optometrist of Yr. 1962, hon. life), Retinitis Pigmentosa Internat. (adv. exec. com. 1984-88), Dayton Jr. C. of C. (Man of Yr.), Lincoln Club of Orange County (chmn. ethics com. 1988-92).

HOPPMANN, RICHARD ANTHONY, dean, physician, educator; b. Charleston, SC, Aug. 20, 1950; s. Harry Joseph and Dorothy Gadsen (Couturier) H.; m. Anne Griffin Harman, May 331, 1975; children: Emily, Karla, Nicholas. BS, U. S.C., 1972; MS, U. Ga., 1978; MD, Med. U. S.C., 1982. Diplomate Am. Bd. Internal Medicine, subspeciality rheumatology. Resident internal medicine East Carolina U. Sch. Medicine, Greenville, N.C., 1982-85; rheumatology fellow Bowman Gray Sch. Medicine, Wake Forest U., Winston-Salem, N.C., 1985-87; ast. prof. medicine East Carolina U. Sch. Medicine, Greenville, 1987-90; chief rheumatology med. svcs. Dorn Vets. Hosp., Columbia, S.C., 1990—; prof. medicine, dir. divsn. allergy, immunology U. SC Sch. Medicine, Columbia, 1990—, assoc. dean med. edn. and academic affairs, 2000—06, dean, 2006—. Mem. editorial bd. Med. Problems of Performing Artists, 1992—; contbr. articles to profl. jours. Recipient VA Commendation-Profl. Leadership, 1993. Fellow ACP, Am. Coll. Rheumatology; mem. AMA, Internat. Arts Medicine Assn., Nat. Assn. VA Physicians and Dentists, Performing Arts Medicine Assn. (mem. policy com.), S.C. Rheumatology Assn. Avocations: gardening, running, music, reading. Office: University SC Sch Medicine Office of Dean Bldg 3 6311 Garners Ferry Rd Columbia SC 29209 *

HOPTMAN, MATTHEW JOSHUA, psychiatrist; b. Livonia, Mich., June 25, 1962; BS, Mich. State U., 1984; PhD, U. Chgo., 1991. Rsch. scientist Nathan S. Kline Inst. Psychiat. Rsch., 1994—. Rsch. asst. prof. NYU Sch. Medicine, 1995—2005, rsch. assoc. prof., 2005; adj. assoc. prof. City U. CCNY, 2006. Contbr. chapters to books, articles to numerous sci. profl. jours. Recipient Young Investigator award, Nat. Alliance Rsch. Schizophrenia and Depression, Joseph Kelly award, U. Chgo.; William Rainey Harper fellowship, fellowship, Irving R. Harris Ctr. Devel. Studies. Mem.: NY Acad. Scis., Assn. Psychol. Rsch., Soc. Neurosci. Avocations: hiking, music, baseball. Office: 140 Old Orangeburg Rd Bldg 35 Orangeburg NY 10962 Office Fax: 845-398-6566. Business E-Mail: hoptman@nki.rfmh.org.

HOPWOOD, DAVID ALAN, microbiologist, geneticist, educator; b. Kinver, Staffs, Eng., Aug. 19, 1933; s. Herbert Hopwood and Dora Grant; m. Joyce Lilian Bloom, 1962; 3 children. Student, St. John's Coll., Cambridge, Eng.; PhD, U. Cambridge; DSc, U. Glasgow; Dr. (hon.), ETH, Zurich, Switzerland, U. East Anglia, Norwich. John Stothert Bye fellow Magdalene Coll. U. Cambridge, 1956-58; rsch. fellow St. John's Coll., Cambridge, 1958-61; univ. demonstrator, 1957-61; lectr. genetics U. Glasgow, 1961-68; John Innes prof. U. East Anglia, Norwich, 1968-98, emeritus prof., 1998—; head genetics dept. John Innes Ctr., Norwich, 1968-98, emeritus fellow, 1998—. Hon. prof. Chinese Acad. Med. Sci., Inst. Microbiology and Plant Physiology, Chinese Acad. Scis., Huazhong Agrl. U., Wuhan, China, Shanghai Jaotong U., Guangxi U., Nanning. Author (with K.F. Chater): Genetics of Bacterial Diversity, 1989; author: Streptomyces in Nature and Medicine, 2007; contbr. chapters to books, articles to profl. jours. Fellow: Indian Nat. Sci. Acad. (corr.), Inst. Biology (hon.); mem.: Genetical Soc. Gt. Britain (former pres.), Czechoslovak Soc. Microbiology (hon.), Spanish Soc. Microbiology (hon.), Soc. Gen. Microbiology (hon.; pres. 2000—03), Hungarian Acad. Scis. (hon.). Office: John Innes Ctr Dpt Molec Microbiology Colney Lane NR4 7UH Norwich England Office Phone: 44 1603 450000. E-mail: david.hopwood@bbsrc.ac.uk.

HORACEK, JIRI, internist, educator; b. Rychnov nad Kneznou, Czech Republic, Nov. 12, 1952; MD, Charles U. Prague, 1978; PhD, Czechoslovak Acad. Scis., Inst. Pharmacology, 1982. Asst. prof., physician Postgrad. Med. Sch. Prague, Dept. Gen. Practice Hradec Kralove, 1983—87; physician Charles U. Prague, Faculty Medicine and U. Hosp. Hradec Kralove, Dept. Internal Medicine, 1982—83, asst. prof., physician, 1987—96, assoc. prof., physician, 1996—2009, prof., dep. head edn. and rsch., 2009—. Editor-in-chief Acta Medica, 2009. Mem.: Brit. Thyroid Assn., European Thyroid Assn., European Soc. Endocrinology. Avocations: travel, photography, winemaking. Office: University Hosp Hradec Kralove Dept Internal Medicine Hradec Kralove 50005 Czech Republic Office Fax: 420 495832011. Personal E-mail: horacek9@gmail.com.

HORÁNYI, JÁNOS, endocrine surgeon; b. Budapest, Hungary, Sept. 17, 1946; s. János Horányi (Hofhauser) and Éva Havel; m. Mária Sándor, Apr. 20, 1974; children: Melinda, Eszter. MD, Semmelweis U., Budapest, 1971; PhD, Semmelweis U., 1997. Lic. Surgeon Nat. Bd. Qualification, Budapest, candidate of med. scis. Bd. of Sci. Qualification, Hungary. Resident, staff mem., lectr. 1st Surg. Dept. Semmelweis U., 1971—94, assoc. prof., 1994—. Sr. cons. in endocrine surgery Semmelweis U., 1991—. Pres. Med. Assn. of Budapest Józsefváros, 1995—2002, 2006—07. Recipient Batthyány-Strattmann László prize, Ministry of Health, 1997. Mem.: Hungarian Diabetes Assn., European Fedn. Endocrine Socs., Internat. Soc. Endocrinology, European Assn. Endoscopic Surgery, Internat. Soc. Surgery, Internat. Assn. Endocrine Surgeons, Hungarian Med. Chamber (sec. 2002—03, Hippokrates Medallion 2001), Hungarian Soc. Endocrinology and Metabolism (treas. 2003—), Hungarian Soc. Gastroenterology, Hungarian Surg. Soc. (pres. monitoring com. 1999—). Achievements include discovery that injury to blood supply of the parathyroid adenomas led to the rapid and misleading intraoperative fall of intact parathyroid hormone level without removing the hyperfunctioning tumor. Office: 1st Surg Dept of Semmelweis U Üllöi út 78 H-1082 Budapest Hungary Business E-Mail: hj@seb1.sote.hu.

HORGAN, BEN ANTHONY JOHN, public relations executive; b. Sydney, July 7, 1970; s. Tony John Murc and Barbara Joan Horgan; m. Emma Jane Gooch, Mar. 23, 1996; children: Joel Benjamin Anthony, Reece William. Cert. in Comml. Radio Broadcasting, Australian Film TV and Radio Sch., 1992; cert. in Small Bus. Enterprise Mgmt., Meadowbank Coll., 2001. Prodn. mgr. Batavia Coast FM, Geraldton, Australia, 1994—98, program dir. 1071 Am, Kingaroy, Australia, 1998—99; media cons. Seekmedia, Sydney, 2000—02, patient adv. Arthritis Found. Australia, Sydney, 2002—03; coord. youth svcs. Arthritis Found. We. Australia, Perth, 2002—05; pub. rels. Combined Charities We. Australia, Perth, 2002—. Consumer rep. Bone and Joint Decade 2000-2010 Australia, Perth, 2001—05, chmn., 2005—, amb.; chmn. Juvenile Arthritis Youth Forum, Sydney, 1985. Recipient Children's Week Youth award, New South Wales, 1984; finalist Cmty. Father of Yr., 2001; nominee Children's Week Youth award. Mem.: Rotary (corr.). Office: Bone and Joint Decade Australia 17 Lemnos St Shenton Park 6025 Australia Home: 14 Tifera Cir 6025 Kallaroo WA Australia Office Fax: +61 8 9388 4488; Home Fax: +61 8 9388 4488. Personal E-mail: convenor@bjd.org.au, horgs@bigpond.net.au. Business E-Mail: benh@arthritiswa.org.au.

HORGAN, SANTIAGO, surgeon; b. Buenos Aires, Sept. 22, 1965; s. Federico Guillermo Horgan and Marta Josefina Benavides; m. Maria Natalia Presas, June 9, 1995. MD, U. Buenos Aires, Argentina, 1989. Diplomate Buenos Aires, Argentina, 1990. Asst. prof. anatomy Medicine U. Buenos Aires, 1987—89; resident in surgery Hosp. de Clinicas, U. Buenos Aires, Argentina, 1991—94, chief resident in surgery, 1994—95; acting instr. surgery U. Wash. Med. Ctr., Seattle, 1995—98, fellow laparoscopic surgery, 1995—96, fellow esophageal surgery, 1996—98; prof. surgery U. Buenos Aires, 1998—; asst. prof. surgery U. Ill., Chgo., 1999—2005, assoc. prof. surgery, 2005—06, chief minimally invasive surgery and robotic surgery, 1999—2006, co-dir. Swallowing Ctr.; dir. Minimally Invasive Bariatric Ctr., Chgo.; prof. clin. surgery U. Calif., San Diego, 2006—, dir. minimally invasive surgery, 2006—, dir. Ctr. for Treatment of Obesity, 2006—. Hon. prof. surgery U. Tucuman, Argentina, 2000—. Recipient Young Surgeon award, Surg. Soc. Alimentary Tract, 2001. Mem.: AMA, Chgo. Surg. Soc., Kansas City Surg. Soc., Warren H. Cole Soc., Chgo. Soc. Gastroenterology, Soc. Laparoendoscopic Surgeons, Ill. Surg. Soc., Henry N. Harkins Surg. Soc., Argentinian Assn. Surgery, Peruvian Colo-rectal Surg. Soc. (hon.), Guatemalan Surg. Soc. (hon.), Peruvian Surg. Soc. (hon.), Assn. Surg. Edn. (assoc.), Internat. Soc. for Diseases of the Esophagus (assoc.), Soc. Am. Gastrointestinal Endoscopic Surgeons (assoc. Rsch. Award 1999), Surg. Soc. Alimentary Tract (assoc.), Club Italo-Argentino du Chirurgia. Achievements include research and development of techniques of robotic surgery in U.S; research in surgery for morbid obesity. Office: U Calif San Diego Dept Surgery 200 W Arbor Dr San Diego CA 92103-8220 Office Phone: 619-543-6711. Office Fax: 619-543-5869. E-mail: shorgan@ucsd.edu.

HORGEN, GUNNAR, optometrist, educator; b. Oslo, Mar. 1, 1948; s. Gunvor Horgen; m. Tove Horgen, Dec. 31, 1968; children: Gro, Eirik. MS, Pa. Coll., 1999; PhD, U. Oslo, 2004. Lic. optometrist Norway, 1988. Pvt. practic Krogh Optikk Norge, Oslo, 1968—73; lectr. optics Tinius Olsen Teknical Sch., Kongsberg, Norway, 1974—87; asst. prof. optometry Buskerud Coll., Kongsberg, 1987—95; assoc. prof. optometry Buskerud College, Kongsberg, 1997—. Cons. Norwegian Optometric Assn., Oslo, 1995—. Mem.: Norwegian Optometric Assn. (sec. gen. 1995—97, Distinction Gold 1989). Office: Buskerud Coll Dept Optometry Frogs road 41 Buskerud Kongsberg 3603 Norway Office Fax: +47 32 86 96 70. E-mail: gunnar.horgen@hibu.no.

HORI, JUNICHI, computer science educator; BEng in Info. Engring., Niigata U., Japan, 1986, MEng in Info. Engring., 1988; PhD in Computer Sci., Tokyo Inst. Tech., 1996. Rsch. assoc. Niigata U., Japan, 1988—97, assoc. prof., 1997—. Mem.: IEEE (sr.). Home: 5-7-10 Mizukino Niigata 950-2264 Japan E-mail: hori@eng.niigata_u.ac.jp.

HORI, JUNKO, ophthalmologist, immunologist; b. Ojiya City, Niigata, Japan, Mar. 14, 1966; d. Kenji and Naoko Kobayashi; m. Tatsuyuki Hori; children: Sumika, Kyoka. MD, Niigata U., Sch. Medicine, Japan, 1990; PhD, U. Tokyo, Sch. Medicine, 1997. Cert. ophthalmology specialist Japanese Ophthal. Soc., 1996. Ophthalmology resident U. Tokyo Hosp., Bunkyo, Japan, 1990—92, fellow, 1992—97; postdoc. fellow Schepens Eye Rsch. Inst., Harvard Med. Sch., Boston, 1997—2000; asst. prof. Nippon Med. Sch., Bunkyo, 2001—04, assoc. prof., 2004—. Recipient Cora Verhagen prize, Immunology Sect. Assn. Rsch. in Vision and Ophthalmology, 2000, Promising Investigator award, Japan Cornea Soc., 2004, Maruyama Meml. award, Nippon Med. Sch., 2006. Mem.: Soc. Japanese Women Scientists (award 2007), Japan Cornea Soc., Japanese Soc. Immunology, Am. Uveitis Soc., Japanese Ocular Inflammation Soc. (Promising Investigator award 2005), Japanese Ophthal. Soc., Am. Assn. Immunologists, Assn. Rsch. in Vision and Ophthalmology. Achievements include research in transplantation immunology of the eye. Office: Nippon Med Sch 1-1-5 Sendagi Bunkyo Tokyo 113-8603 Japan

HORI, YASUTOMO, science educator; b. Suita, Osaka, Japan, Jan. 25, 1976; s. Taizou and Michiko Hori. PhD, Kitasato U., Aomori, 2001. Asst. prof. Kitasato U., Towada, Aomori, Japan, 2005—. Gen. Sci. Rsch. grant, Japanese Ministry Edn., Sci. and Culture, 2008. Office: Kitasato Univ 23-35-1 Higashi Towada Aomori 034-8628 Japan Office Fax: 81-176-22-3057. Business E-Mail: hori@vmas.kitasato-u.ac.jp.

HORI, YUICHI, medical educator; b. Fujiidera, Osaka, Japan, Jan. 22, 1959; s. Saburo and Eiko Hori; m. Miwa Hori; children: Yasutaka, Kanae. MD, Kobe U. Sch. Medicine, Japan, 1986; PhD, Kobe U. Grad. Sch. Medicine, 1992. Assoc. prof., dept. surgery Kobe U. Grad. Sch. Medicine, 2008—11; assoc. prof. Kobe U. Grad. Sch. Health Sci., 2011—. Grantee 21th COE project, Kobe U., 2004, Aid Sci. Rsch. grants, Ministry of Edn., Culture, Sports, Sci. and Tech., 2005, 2009; Walter V. and Idun Berry fellowship, Stanford U., 2001, Advanced Postdoc. Rsch. fellowship, Juvenile Diabetes Rsch. Found. Internat., 2002, fellowship, Kurozumi Med. Found., 2004. Mem.: Japan Diabetes Soc., Japanese Cancer Assn., Japanese Soc. Gastroenterology, Japanese Soc. Gastroent. Surgery, Japan Surg. Soc. Office: Kobe University Sch Medicine 7-10-2 Tomogaoka Suna-ku Kobe 654 0142 Japan Office Phone: 81-78-382-6302, 81 78 796 4540. Office Fax: 81-78-382-6307, 81 78 796 4540. Business E-Mail: horiy@med.kobe-u.ac.jp.

HORIO, YOSHITSUGU, oncologist; b. Kobe, Japan, July 26, 1961; MD, Nagoya U. Sch. Medicine, 1986; PhD, Nagoya U. Grad. Sch. Medicine, 1995. Chief, outpatient svcs., dept. thoracic oncology Aichi Cancer Ctr. Hosp., 2009—. Avocation: travel. Office: 1-1 Kanokoden Chikusa-ku Nagoya Aichi 464-8681 Japan Business E-Mail: yhorio@aichi-cc.jp.

HORIUCHI, AKIKO, medical educator; b. Chiba, Aug. 30, 1966; MD, Shinshu U., 1992, PhD. Assoc. prof. Sninshu U. Sch. Medicine, 2008. Office: 3-1-1 Asahi Matsumoto Nagano 3908621 Japan Business E-Mail: aki9hori@shinshu-u.ac.jp.

HORIUCHI, AKIRA, gastroenterologist; b. Nagano, Japan, Nov. 29, 1960; MD, Shinshu U., 1985, PhD, 1989. Chief Digestive Disease Ctr., Showa Inan Gen. Hosp., 2008—. Mem.: Am. Coll. Gastroenterology. Office: 3230 Akaho Nagano Komagane 399-4117 Japan Office Fax: 81265822118. Business E-Mail: horiuchi.akira@sihp.jp.

HORIUCHI, KAZUTAKA, urologist, director; b. Nagano, Japan, Aug. 9, 1957; s. Masakazu and Mieko Horiuchi; m. Maki Amemia, May 20, 1984; children: Megumi, Miwa, Seita. PhD, Nippon Med. Sch., Tokyo, 1990. Cert. urol. expert Japan Urol. Assn., urol. adv. physician Japan Urol. Assn., expert physician Japanese Soc. Dialysis Treatment, adv. physician Japanese Soc. Dialysis Treatment. With Nippon Med. Sch., Tokyo, 1984—, asst. prof., 1994—2000, assoc. prof., 2000—; dir. urology and hemodialysis treatment Nippon Med. Sch. Chiba Hokuso Hosp., 2000—; dir. urology Nippon Med. Sch. Second Hosp., 2003—. Contbr. articles to profl. jours. Recipient honors, Japan Endoscopic Promotional Found., 1998. Mem.: Japan. Endourology and ESWL Assn. (bd. dirs. 2004—), Japan Urol. Assn. (assoc.; bd. dirs. 1994—). Achievements include development of endoluminal ultrasound for urological disease. Avocations: reading, walking. Office: Nippon Med Sch Dept Urology 1-396 Kosugi-cho Nakahara-ku Kanagawa Kawasaki 211-8533 Japan Office Fax: +81-44-711-8837. Business E-Mail: kazu0809@nms.ac.jp.

HORIUCHI, NOBORU, biochemist, educator; b. Ikoma, Nara, Japan, Aug. 11, 1947; s. Shigekazu and Akiko Horiuchi; m. Mariko Tobe, July 8, 1980; children: Hanna, Isaku. DDSc, Tokyo Dental Coll., 1972; PhD, Tokyo Med. and Dental U., 1976. Rsch. assoc. Tokyo Med. and Dental U., Tokyo, 1976-77; lectr., assoc. prof. Showa U., Tokyo, 1977-86; rsch. fellow in medicine Harvard Med. Sch., Boston, 1980-83; staff scientist Helen Hayes Hosp., West Haverstraw, NY, 1986-89; rsch. scientist II Cedars-Sinai Med. Ctr., LA, 1989; prof. biochemistry Ohu U., Koriyama, Japan, 1990—2010. Contbr. articles to profl. jours. Grantee NIH/Nat. Cancer Inst. Cedars Sinai Med. Ctr., 1989-92, Ministry of Edn. Sci. and Culture Japan Ohu U., 1993-95, 1998-2000, 2003-2004. Mem. The Endocrine Soc., The Am. Soc. for Bone and Mineral Rsch., The Japanese Biochem. Soc. (councilor 1995-2010). Avocations: reading, swimming. Home: 12-17 Sugacho Shinjuku-Ku Tokyo 160-0018 Japan Business E-Mail: fwga4746@mb.infoweb.ne.jp.

HORLOCKER, TERESE TODDIE, medical educator; b. Rochester, Minn., Apr. 2, 1959; BChE, U. Minn., 1981; MD, Mayo Med. Sch., 1985. Prof., anesthesiology and orthops. Mayo Clinic, Rochester, 1989—. Recipient Disting. Svc. award, Am. Soc. Regional Anesthesia and Pain Medicine, Labat award. Office: Dept Anesthesiology Mayo Clinic Rochester MN 55905 Business E-Mail: horlocker.terese@mayo.edu.

HÖRMAN, ARI J., veterinarian, educator; b. Kaavi, Finland, June 11, 1967; s. Raili S and Vilho A Hörman. DVM, U. Helsinki, 2005; MPH, Nordic Sch. of Pub. Health, 2005; PhD. Asst. veterinarian U. Helsinki, 1995—96; rsch. veterinarian Finnish Def. Forces, Helsinki, 1996—2007, chief vet. officer, 2009—; vis. prof. Estonian U. Life Scis., Tartu, Estonia, 2005—08; legis. officer European Commn., Belgium, 2007—09. Mem.: Finnish Vet. Assn. (del. mem. 2004).

HORN, EVELYN M., cardiologist, educator; BS, Brown U., 1976; MD, Mt. Sinai Sch. of Medicine, 1980. Diplomate Am. Bd. Internal Medicine, Am. Bd. Internal Medicine-cardiovascular disease. Intern Mt. Sinai Med. Ctr., resident internal medicine, 1981—83; rsch. fellow Columbia Coll. of Physicians and Surgeons; fellow cardiovasc. disease Cedars Sinai Med. Ctr.; fellow NY-Presbyn. Hosp.; clin. prof. internal medicine Weill Cornell Med. Coll.; adj. prof. clin. medicine Columbia Univ.; dir. circulatory physiology fellowship program Columbia Univ. Med. Ctr., dir. clin. svcs. for heart failure, assoc. dir. pediatric & adult pulmonary hypertension ctr., dir. pulmonary vascular program, dir. high risk cardiac obstet. program; dir. heart failure and pulmonary hypertension Perkin Heart Failure Ctr.-Weill Cornell.; attending physician NY-Presbyn. Hosp. Co-author: (publs.) Clinical risk factors for portopulmonary hypertension, 2008, Bloodstream infections in patients given treatment with intravenous prostanoids, 2008, Plasma serotonin levels are normal in pulmonary arterial hypertension, 2008, and numerous other publications. Fellow: Internat. Pulmonary Vascular Rsch. Inst. Office: Perkins Heart Failure Center-Weill Cornell 8 Fl 1305 York Ave New York NY 10021 Office Phone: 212-746-2381. Office Fax: 212-746-6665.

HORN, JANET, physician; b. Oak Ridge, Aug. 10, 1950; d. Harry and Molly (Rich) Horn; m. Alan R. Yuspeh, June 8, 1975. BA magna cum laude, Vanderbilt U., 1972; MS in Physiology and Biophysics, Georgetown U., 1973; MD, George Washington U., 1978. Diplomate Am. Bd. Internal Medicine, also sub-bd. Infectious Diseases, Am. Bd. Med. Examiners. Intern George Washington U. Hosp., Washington, 1978-79, resident in ob-gyn., 1979-81; resident in internal medicine Georgetown U., Washington, 1981-83; fellow in infectious diseases Johns Hopkins Hosp., Balt., 1983-85, mem. med. staff, 1986—, Georgetown U. Hosp., also Sibley Meml. Hosp., Washington, 1985-86, Sinai Hosp. of Balt., 1989—, Greater Balt. Med. Ctr., 1990—, St. Joseph's Hosp., 1990—. Asst. prof. medicine Johns Hopkins U. Sch. Medicine, 1986-95, assoc. prof., 1995—. Co-author: The Smart Woman's Guide to Midlife and Beyond: A No-Nonsense Aproach to Staying Healthy After 50, 2008; mem. editl. bd. Johns Hopkins Med. Grand Rounds, Am. Jour. Gynecologic Health; contbr. articles to profl. jours., chpts. to books. Bd. dirs. Chesapeake AIDS Found., 1989-92; chair AIDS Coordinating and Adv. Coun. to Mayor, Balt., 1988-92. Recipient Pearl M. Stetler Found. Rsch. award Johns Hopkins U., 1987, Merck Found. Clinician Scientist Rsch. award Johns Hopkins U., 1988. Mem. AAAS, ACP, Am. Soc. for Microbiology, Infectious Diseases Soc. Am., Johns Hopkins Med. and Surg. Assn., Phi Beta Kappa, Alpha Omega Alpha. Home: PO Box 331728 Nashville TN 37203-7516 Office Phone: 410-367-4709. Personal E-mail: jehornmd@aol.com.

HORN, KIMBERLY, insurance company executive; b. Flint, Mich. BBA, U. Mich., Flint. Held various positions Genesee Meml. Hosp., asst. adminstr.; contr., bus. affairs dir. Physicians Health Plan, Lansing; v.p. fin. adminstrn. Health Plan of Mid America, Kansas City, Mich.; CFO Mercy Health Plan, COO; pres., CEO Priority Health, 1997—. Mem. bd. dirs. Econ. Club Grand Rapids, Bank of Holland, Davenport Univ., Tomorrow's Child/Mich. SIDS; mem. bd. dirs. Seidman Coll. of Bus. Grand Valley State Univ. Recipient TRIBUTE! award, Young Women's Christian Assn. (YWCA), 2002, Ellis J. Bonner Outstanding Achievement award, Mich. Assn. Health Plans, 2004, Women of Achievement and Courage award, Mich. Women's Found., 2006; named one of Most 50 Influential Women in West Mich., Grand Rapids Bus. Jour., 2003, 2006. Mem.: Mich. Assn. Health Plans (past pres.). Office: Priority Health 1231 E Beltline NE Grand Rapids MI 49525-4501 *

HORN, MICHAEL A., plastic surgeon; MD, Loyola U., Chgo. Diplomate Am. Bd. Plastic Surgery. Resident gen. surgery Med. Coll. Wis.; resident plastic surgery Loyola Univ., Chgo. Lectr. plastic surgery. Featured in several profl. publs. Mem.: Chgo. Soc. Plastic Surgeons, Am. Soc. Plastic Surgeons. Office: Michael Horn Center For Cosmetic Surgery 60 E Delaware Place 15th Fl Chicago IL 60611 Office Phone: 312-202-9000. Office Fax: 312-202-9002.

HORN, WADE FREDERICK, psychologist, former federal agency administrator; b. Coral Gables, Fla., Dec. 3, 1954; s. John David and Daisy (Anderson) H.; m. Claudia Blair, Jan. 7, 1977; children: Christiana Watson, Caroline Lindley. BA in Psychology, Am. U., 1975; MA in Clin. Child Psychology, So. Ill. U., 1978, PhD in Clin. Child Psychology, 1981. Rsch. asst. social skills devel. program Carbondale (Ill.) Elem. Schs., 1976-78; behavior analyst, psychol. cons. early childhood program Wabash and Ohio Valley Spl. Edn. Dist., Norris City, Ill., 1978-79; predoctoral intern dept. pediatric psychology Children's Hosp. Nat. Med. Ctr., Washington, 1980-81, postdoctoral clin. psychology fellow behavioral medicine rsch. lab., 1981-82; asst. prof. dept. psychology Mich. State U., East Lansing, 1982-86; vice chairperson dept. pediatric psychology, dir. outpatient psychol. svcs. dept. psychiatry Children's Hosp. Nat. Med. Ctr., Washington, 1987-88; dir. Pediatric Psychology Splty. Clinic, assoc. dir. Psychol. Clinic Mich. State U., East Lansing, 1984-86; attending staff child health care unit St. Lawrence Hosp., Lansing, Mich., 1983-84; assoc. prof. psychiatry, behavioral scis. and child health and devel. Sch. Medicine, George Washington U., 1986-89; mem. presdl. transition team Office of Pres. Elect, Washington, 1988-89; commr. Adminstrn. on Children, Youth & Families US Dept Health & Human Services, 1989—93, chief Children's Bur Washington, 1989—93, asst. sec. for children & families, 2001—07; dir. pub. sector practice Deloitte Consulting LLP, 2007—. Adj. faculty dept. pediatrics Coll. Human Medicine, Mich. State U., East Lansing, 1983-86, Pub. Policy Ibst., Georgetown U., 1993-2001; mem. Nat. Commn. Childhood Disability, 1994-95; mem. U.S. Adv. Bd. on Welfare Educators, 1996-97. Author: (with G. Greenberg) Attention Deficit Disorder: Questions and Answers for Parents, 1991; contbr. articles to profl. jours. Mem. Health Care Adv. Group for George Bush for Pres. campaign, 1987-88. Mem. Am. Psychol. Assn. (divs. clin. psychology and child clin. psychology), Assn. for Advancement Behavior Therapy, Phi Kappa Phi. Republican. Presbyterian.

HORNBEIN, THOMAS FREDERIC, anesthesiologist; b. St. Louis, Nov. 6, 1930; s. Leonard and Rosalie (Bernstein) Hornbein; m. Gene Schwartz (div. 1968); children: Lia, Lynn, Cari, Andrea, Robert; m. Kathryn Mikesell, Dec. 24, 1971; 1 child, Melissa. BA, U. Colo.; MD, Wash. U. Diplomate Am. Bd. Anesthesiology. Intern King County Hosp., Seattle; resident in anesthesiology Wash. U., St. Louis, USPHS postdoctoral residency, instr. anesthesiology div., 1960—61; asst. prof. U. Wash., Seattle, 1963—67, assoc. prof., 1967—70, prof. anesthesiology, physiology and biophysics, 1970—2002, prof. emeritus, 2002—. Vice chmn. dept. anesthesiology U. Wash., Seattle, 1972—74, asst. chmn. rsch., 1974—77, chmn., 1979—93, rsch. affiliate Primate Ctr., 1980; bd. dirs. Colo. Ctr. for Alternative Medicine and Physiology, 2003—. Author: Everest the West Ridge, 1966 (rated #1 Outside Mag., 2003). Mem. bd. trustees Little Sch., Bellevue, Wash., 1982—89; bd. dirs. Colorado Ctr. Alt. Medicine and Physiology, 2003. Served to lt. comdr. USN, 1961—63. Recipient George Norlin award, U. Colo., Denver, 1970, Alumni Centennial Symposium award, 1975, Disting. Tchg. award, U. Wash., 1982. Fellow: AAAS; mem.: Inst. of Medicine, Soc. Acad. Anesthesia Chmn., Assn. Univ. Anesthetists (treas. 1969—72, pres. 1974—75), Am. Soc. Anesthesiologists (Rovenstine lectr. 1989), Am. Physiol. Soc. (editor 1967—73), Alpha Omega Alpha, Phi Beta Kappa. Avocation: mountain climbing. Office: U Wash Sch Medicine Dept Anesthesiology PO Box 356540 Seattle WA 98195-6540 Business E-Mail: hornbnt@u.washington.edu.

HORNBERGER, ROBERT HOWARD, retired psychologist; b. Trenton, NJ, Jan. 26, 1933; s. Jennings Howard and Leah Margaret (Lewis) H.; m. Anne Deshon Lyman, June 11, 1958; children: Lynn Diane, Todd Lyman. BA, Amherst Coll., Mass., 1954; MA, PhD, U. Iowa, Iowa City, 1957. Instr. to assoc. in med. psychology U. Nebr. Coll. Medicine, Omaha, 1958-62; staff psychologist Nebr. Psychiat. Inst., Omaha, 1958-62; chief psychologist Drs. Young, Wigton & Aita, Omaha, 1962-65; dir. Eastern Maine Guidance Ctr., Bangor, 1965-68; assoc. dir. The Counseling Ctr., Bangor, 1968-69; lectr. in psychology U. Maine, Orono, 1966-69; dir. psychology tng. VA Med. Ctr., Gainesville, Fla., 1969-81; asst. to assoc. adj. prof. U. Fla., Gainesville, 1969-2000; staff psychologist VA Med. Ctr., Gainesville, 1981-2000; ret., 2000. Bd. advisors Fla. Mental Health Inst., Tampa, 1987-95; psychologist pvt. practice, Gainesville, 1976-85, 90-98; dir. endowment fund, The Mountain Retreat & Learning Ctrs., Highlands, N.C., 2002-07, chair 2006-07, dir. SoftRent Corp., Clearwater, Fla., 2001-04; pres. Gainesville chpt. UNA-USA, 2003-2005, 2007; pres. Fla. Dvsn. UNA-USA, 2009-10. Contbr. articles to profl. jours. Founder, 1st pres. Sugarfoot Cmty. Improvement Assn., 1972; pres. Mental Health Assn. Alachua County, Gainesville, 1981, Mental Health Assn. Fla., Tallahassee, 1987, Planned Parenthood Nebr., Omaha, 1963; comdr. Gainesville Power Squadron, 1995-96; pres. Unitarian-Universalist Chs. Omaha, 1963, Unitarian-Universalist Chs. Gainesville, 1972, 1987-88. Mem. Fla. Psychol. Assn. (pres. north ctrl. Fla. chpt. 1996). Democrat. Unitarian Universalist. Avocations: sailing, bridge, bicycling, travel, dance. Home: 4056 NW 23rd Cir Gainesville FL 32605-2683 Home Phone: 352-378-3541. Personal E-mail: bobhornberger@cox.net.

HORNE, BENJAMIN DAVIES, epidemiologist; s. David Hughes and Barbara Alice Horne; m. Carolyn Joy Waisman (div.). BSc, Brigham Young U., 1996; MPH, U. Utah, Salt Lake City, 1998, MStat, 2002, PhD, 2005. Epidemiologist, cardiovasc. dept. Intermountain Med. Ctr., Salt Lake City, 1999—2005, dir. cardiovasc. and genetic epidemiology, 2005—. Mem. Ch. Jesus Christ Latter-day Saints, Salt Lake City, 1971—. Fellow, Am. Heart Assn., 2004—06; John D. Morgan fellow, Deseret Found., 2004. Fellow: Am. Coll. Cardiology; mem.: SAR (pres. Utah soc. 2006—09). Office: Intermountain Med Ctr 5121 S Cottonwood St Salt Lake City UT 84157-7000 Office Phone: 801-507-4708. Office Fax: 801-507-4792.

HORNYKIEWICZ, OLEH, retired biochemical pharmacologist; b. Sychow, Ukraine, Nov. 17, 1926; MD, U. Vienna, 1951. Lectr. pharmacological inst. U. Vienna, 1964, head dept. biochem. pharmacology, 1976, prof. emeritus Inst. Brain Rsch., 1992—; prof. dept. pharmacology U. Toronto, 1968—76. Sci. adv. Michael J. Fox Found. Parkinson's Rsch. Author: Classics of World Science, Vol. 9, 2003; co-author: The Pharmacology of Psychotherapeutic Drugs, 1969; contbr. articles to profl. jours. Recipient Gold Medal for rsch., Canadian Parkinson's Disease Assn., 1970, Wolf Found. prize in medicine, Israel, 1979, Ludwig Wittgenstein prize, Austrian Rsch. Found., 1993, Austriam Medal Sci. & Art, 2008. Achievements include first to discover that lack of the neurotransmitter dopamine causes Parkinson's disease; development of L-dopa, a drug to treat Parkinson's disease, 1960. Office: Ctr Brain Rsch U Vienna Spitalgasse 4 A-1090 Vienna Austria Office Phone: 431 4277 62872. *

HOROHO, PATRICIA DALLAS, career military officer, nurse; b. Ft. Bragg, NC, 1960; d. F. Paul Dallas. BS, U. NC, Chapel Hill, 1982; MS, U. Pitts.; grad., Army Command and Gen. Staff Coll.; MS in Nat. Resource Strategy, Indsl. Coll. Armed Forces. RN. Advanced through ranks to lt. gen. US Army, 2011; staff nurse multi-svc. specialty ward and staff & head nurse level III emergency dept. Evans Army Cmty. Hosp., Ft. Carson, Colo.; nurse counselor 1st recruiting brigade, northeast Harrisburg and Pitts. Recruiting Batallions, Pa.; head nurse Womack Army Med. Ctr., Ft. Bragg, NC; chief nurse, hosp. comdr. 249th Gen. Hosp., Ft. Gordon, Ga.; asst. br. chief, Army Nurse Corps Br. US Total Army Pers. Command, Alexandria, Va.; asst. dep. healthcare mgmt. policy Office of Asst. Sec. of Army, Pentagon, Washington, DC; dep. comdr. nursing, comdr. Dewitt Health Care Network, Ft. Belvoir, Va., 2004—06; dep. comdr. nursing Walter Reed Army Med. Ctr. and North Atlantic Regional Med. Command, Washington; comdr. Walter Reed Health Care Sys., Washington, 2007—08, Madigan Army Med. Ctr., Tacoma, 2008—09, Western Regional Med. Command, Ft. Lewis, Wash.; dep. surgeon gen. US Army, 2010—11, surgeon gen., 2011—, chief Nurse Corps, 2010—11; comdr. US Army Medical Command, Ft. Sam Houston, Tex., 2011—. Affiliate faculty Pacific Luth. U. Sch. Nursing, Tacoma, 2009—. Decorated Disting. Svc. medal US Army, Legion Merit, Two Oak Leaf Clusters, Meritorious Svc. medal, Six Oak Leaf Clusters, Army Commendation medal, Three Oak Leaf Clusters, Army Achievement medal, One Oak Leaf Cluster, Armed Forces Expeditionary medal, Order of Mil. Med. Merit Medallion; named Ft. Bragg Supr. of Yr., 1993, U. Pitts. Legacy Laureate, 2007, Woman of Yr., USO, 2009; named a Nurse Hero, American Red Cross and Nursing Spectrum, 2002; named one of The Great 100 in the State of NC, 1993. Achievements include being the first woman to become surgeon general of the United States Army, 2011. Office: US Army Office Surgeon General 5109 Leesburg Pike Rm 682 Falls Church VA 22041-8012 *

HOROVTIZ, LEN, internist, pulmonologist; BS in Biology summa cum laude, Brown U., 1972; MD, NYU Sch. Med., 1976. Intern Mt. Sinai Med. Ctr., 1976—77, resident, Lenox Hill Hosp., 1977—80, fellow, 1980—82, attending physician, 1982—; cons. physician Manhattan Eye, Ear & Throat Hosp., 1996—. Office: 47 E 77th St Rm 201 New York NY 10021 Office Phone: 212-744-3001. Office Fax: 212-744-2303.

HOROWITZ, MARK D., rheumatologist, educator; MD, NE Ohio U., 1983. Diplomate Am. Bd. Internal Medicine, Am. Bd. Internal Medicine-rheumatology. Resident internal medicine Mt. Sinai Hosp., 1984—86, fellow internal medicine, fellow rheumatology, 1987—89; clin. instr. medicine-rheumatology Mt. Sinai Med. Ctr. Office: Mount Sinai Medical Center 21 E 90th St New York NY 10128-0654 Office Phone: 212-860-3077. Office Fax: 212-410-7410. E-mail: mark.horowitz@mssm.edu.

HOROWITZ, STEVEN F., cardiologist; MD, NY Med. Coll., 1972. Diplomate in internal medicine and cardiovasc. disease Am. Bd. Internal Medicine. Resident in medicine Beth Israel Med. Ctr., 1972—76; resident in cardiology, fellow in medicine Mt. Sinai Hosp., NYC, 1976—79; attending physician cardiovasc. disease Beth Israel Med. Ctr., NYC, 1988—2002; dir. cardiology Stamford Hosp., Conn., 2003—. Clin. prof. medicine and nuc. medicine Albert Einstein Coll. Medicine. Home: 250 Rosedale Ave White Plains NY 10605 Office: PO Box 9317 Shelburne and W Broad St Stamford CT 06904-9317 E-mail: shorowitz@stamhealth.org. *

HORTOBÁGYI, TIBOR, neuropathologist; b. Budapest, Hungary, Sept. 25, 1965; s. Tibor Hortobágyi and Éva Görög; m. Julianna Molnar, June 28, 1997; children: Tibor, Julianna, Katica, Piroska, Csenge, Viola. MD, Albert Szent-Györgyi Med. U., Szeged, Hungary, 1991; PhD, Semmelweis U. Budapest, 2001. Rsch. fellow Ludwig Maximillians U., Munich, 1998—2001; sr. lectr. U. Szeged, 2001—02; specialist registrar King's Coll. Hosp. & Inst. of Psychiatry, London, 2003—08, vis. sr. rsch. fellow, 2007—08; sr. clin. lectr. Inst. Psychiatry, London, 2008—; assoc. prof. dept. pathology U. Debrecen, Hungary, 2010—. Fellow: Royal Coll. Pathologists (Eng.); mem.: European Neuropathological Soc. (EFN 2007). Achievements include research in mechanisms of secondary injury in brain trauma and stroke; neuronal death in neurodegenerative disorders; characterization and description of novel brain tumor subtypes. Office: Dept Pathology University Debrecen Debrecen H 4032 Hungary Office Fax: 02078480988. Business E-Mail: tibor.hortobagyi@kcl.ac.uk, hortobagyi@med.unideb.hu.

HORTOLÀ, POLICARP, biologist, researcher; b. Badalona, Catalonia, Spain, Sept. 13, 1958; m. Consol Bàdenas, Jan. 25, 1986; 1 child, Conrad. MSc in Biol. Scis., U. Barcelona, Spain, 1987; PhD, Rovira i Virgili U., Tarragona, Spain, 2001. Herbarium asst. Bot. Inst. Barcelona, 1989—90; asst. biologist biochemistry svc. of the clinic hosp. U. Barcelona, 1990—92, lab. technician dept. cell biology and path. anatomy, 1992—94, lab. technician dept. stratigraphy and palaeontology, 1997—99; freelance sci. cons. biomolecular archeology Barcelona, 1995—97; CSIC fellow prehistory Rovira i Virgili U., Tarragona, Catalonia, Spain, 2000—01, sr. rschr., lectr. prehistory, 2002—. Author: (non-fiction book) Datación por Racemización de Aminoácidos, 1998; author: (with others) Hominidos: las primeras ocupaciones de los continentes, 2005, Entendre la ciència des de dins o si més no intentar-ho, 2006; contbr. chapters to books, articles to profl. jours. With artillery corps bugler Spanish Army, 1979—80. Recipient Doctorate Special Prize, Rovira i Virgili U., 2002. Achievements include research in erythrocyte morphology in bloodstains; discovery of erythrocyte morphologies in mammalian bloodstains; founded science of haemotaphonomy. Office: Rovira i Virgili Univ Prehistory 35 Catalunya Ave Tarragona Catalonia ES-43002 Spain Office Phone: 34 977 558 648. Office Fax: 34 977 558 386. Business E-Mail: policarp.hortola@urv.cat.

HORTON, PAUL CHESTER, psychiatrist; b. Cin., Jan. 29, 1942; s. Paul Chester, Sr. and Elizabeth Pauline (Rice) Horton; children: Paul Andrey, Alexander Robert. BA, U. Minn., 1964, MD, 1968. Diplomate Am. Bd. Psychiatry and Neurology. Rotating intern U. Cin., 1969; resident in psychiatry Yale U., New Haven, 1972; staff psychiatrist Guidance Clinic of Camden County, West Collingswood, NJ, 1972-74, Milford (Conn.) Family and Child Guidance Clinic, 1974-77; mem. faculty Sch. Medicine Yale U., New Haven, 1974-76; pvt. practice Meriden, Conn., 1974—; cons. psychiatrist Child Guidance Clinic Cen. Conn., Meriden, 1980—94, med. dir., 1994—99. Mem. faculty U. Conn. Sch. Medicine, Farmington, 1978—79; cons. Caring for Children, San Francisco, 1989—; psychiat. cons. schs. including Bristol Meriden Pub. Schs., 1999—; reviewer Am. Jour. Psychiatry, 1980—; assoc. dir., divsn. psychiatry Midstate Hosp., Meriden, Conn. Author: Solace, 1981, paperback edit., 1983, Japanese edit., 1985; sr. editor: The Solace Paradigm, 1988; contbr. articles to profl. jours. Active Big Bros. Orgn., Mpls., 1964—68. Lt. comdr. USN, 1972—74. Mem.: Meriden Wallingford Med. Assn., Am. Psychiat. Assn. (life), Gridiron Club. Office: 240 Pomeroy Ave Ste 205 Meriden CT 06450 Office Phone: 203-235-2505. Personal E-mail: phortonmd@aol.com.

HORTOVA, KATERINA, cell biologist, educator; b. Pelhrimov, Czech Republic, Feb. 17, 1974; d. Tomas Komrska and Zdenka Komrskova; m. Timothy Paul Hort; 1 child, Catherine Elizabeth Hort. RNDr, Charles U., Prague, PhD, 2001. Cert. in biology Charles U., 2000, in devel. biology Charles U., 2001. Lab technician Jessop Hosp., IVF Clinic, Sheffield, England, 2000—01; postdoc. fellow, dept. immunology U. Buffalo, 2001—02, postdoc. assoc., dept. microbiology, 2001—02; asst. prof., dept. cell biology, faculty sci. Charles U., Prague, Czech Republic, 2002—, rsch. asst. Mem. dept. zoology Internat. Soc. Behaviour Ecology. Recipient K. Bratanov Family award, Varna, Bulgaria, 2000, Best Abstract award, Congress on Reproductive Immunology, Rhodes, Greece, 2003, Best Poster award, European Congress Reproductive Immunology, Plzen, Czech Republic, 2004; grants, Grant Agy. Czech Republic, 2002—04, 2004—06, 2006—10, Ministry Edn. Czech Republic, 2004—, 2006. Mem.: Internat. Soc. Behavioral Ecology, European Soc. Reproductive Immunology, Internat. Soc. Andrology. Achievements include research in unique sperm behaviour of Rodents, dynamics of cytoskeleton in sperm and influence of environmental factors on reproduction of mammals, esp. sparm capacitation. Office Phone: 00420221951852. Business E-Mail: hortova@natur.cuni.cz.

HORUZSKO, ANATOLIJ, medical researcher; b. Pinsk, Belarus, Oct. 10, 1953; s. Pavel Horuzsko and Anna Juskevich; m. Vera Portik-Dobos, Mar. 30, 1981; children: Julia Szonja, Daniel David. MD (hon.), Pediat. Med. Sch., Leningrad, Russia, 1976; PhD in immunology and allergy, Inst. of Exptl. Medicine, Russian Acad. of Sci., Leningrad, Russia, 1980; MD, Semmelweis U. of Medicine, Budapest, Hungary, 1986; PhD in clin. immunology and allergy, Hungarian Acad. of Sci., Budapest, Hungary, 1987. Lectr., sr. lectr. Pediatric Med. Sch., Leningrad, Russia, 1979—86; sr. lectr. Nat. Inst. of Hematology and Blood Transfusion, Budapest, Hungary, 1986—92; non-clin. scientist, grade 1 Nat. Inst. for Med. Rsch., London, 1992—95; sr. rsch. scientist Med. Coll. of Ga., Augusta, 1995—98, instr., 1998—2002, asst. prof., 2002—06, assoc. prof., 2006—. Author: (over 40 studies) Dealing With Issues In Transplantation Medicine And Immunobiology. Recipient Prize of George Soros, George Soros Found., 1988, Internat. Rsch. award, Wellcome Trust, U.K., 1992—95, Internat. Human Frontier Sci. Program Orgn., Strasbourg, France, 1998, Internat. Union Against Cancer, Geneva, Switzerland, 1999, Roche Organ Transplantation Rsch. Found., Switzerland, 2001. Mem.: European Fedn. for Immunogenetics (assoc.), Hungarian Soc. for Immunology (assoc.), Brit. Soc. for Immunology (assoc.), AAAS (assoc.), Am. Assn. of Immunologists (assoc.). Office: Med Coll of Ga 1410 Laney Walker Blvd Augusta GA 30912-2615 Personal E-mail: horuzsko@netzero.net. Business E-Mail: ahoruzsko@mcg.edu.

HORVITZ, HOWARD ROBERT, biologist, educator; b. Chgo., May 8, 1947; s. Oscar and Mary Horvitz; m. Martha Constantine-Paton, May 2, 1993; 1 child, Alexandra. BS in Math. and Economics, MIT, 1968; MA in Biology, Harvard U., 1972, PhD in Biology, 1974; MD (hon.), U. Rome, 2004. Postdoc. fellow MRC Lab. Molecular Biology, Cambridge, England; asst. prof. biology MIT, Cambridge, Mass., 1978—81, assoc. prof., 1981—86, prof., 1986—, career devel. assoc. prof. biology, Whitehead Inst., 1982-85, Whitehead prof. biology, 1999-2000, David H. Koch prof. biology, 2000—, founding mem. McGovern Inst. Brain Rsch., 2001—. Advisor dept. biochemistry and molecular biology Harvard U., 1984—90; co-organizer Gordon Conf. Devel. Biology, 1985; mem. sci. adv. bd. Hereditary Disease Found., 1987—93; investigator Howard Hughes Med Inst., 1988—; neurobiologist, geneticist Mass. Gen. Hosp., Boston, 1989—; mem. sci. adv. bd. Jane Coffin Childs Meml. Fund for Med. Rsch., 1989—97; mem. sci. rev. com. Amyotrophic Lateral Sclerosis (ALS) Assn., 1990—95; mem. adv. bd. Umea Ctr. Molecular Pathogenesis, Sweden, 1993—96, WHO Spl. Programme Rsch. & Tng. in Tropical Diseases; chair devel. biology rev. com. Swedish Found. Strategic Rsch., 1996; cons. sci. adv. bd. Idun Pharms., Inc., 1993—, Anyo Pharms. Inc., 1998—2002, GenPath Pharms., 2003—, Novartis Inst. Biomed. Rsch., 2003—; mem. med. adv. bd. Gairdner Found., 2007—; mem. adv. coun. Nat. Ctr. Human Genome Rsch., NIH. Author (with others): The Role of Intercellular Signals: Nav., Encounter, Outcome, 1979, Genetic Maps, 1980, Nematodes as Biol. Models, 1980, Devel. of the Nervous Sys., 1981, Repair and Regeneration of the Nervous Sys., 1982, The Nematode Caenorhabditis elegans, 1988; mem. editl. bd.. Jour. Neurogenetics, 1982—88, Jour. Neurosci., 1984—89, Devel. Biology, 1985—95, Devel., 1986—93, Genes and Devel., 1986—98, Cell, 1987—99, Trends in Genetics, 1987—, Neuron, 1987—90, The New Biologist, 1989—92, Genetic Analysis: Techniques and Applications, 1990—95, Current Opinion in Neurobiology, 1990—, Current Biol., 1992—95, Annual Rev. Genetics, 1993—97, Cell Death & Differentiation, 1994—, Invertebrate Neurosci., 1994—, Neurobiology of Disease, 1994—2000, Jour. Exptl. Therapeutics and Oncology, 1995—, Cancer Rsch., 1995—2000, Procs. of the NAS, 1997—2001, Jour. Cell Biology, 1997—2000, Genome Biology, 1999—; contbr. articles to profl. jours. Recipient Rsch. Career Devel. award, NIH, 1981—86, Spencer award in neurobiology, Columbia U., 1986, Louisa Gross Horwitz prize, 2000, Warren Triennial prize, Mass. Gen. Hosp., 1986, US Steel Found. award in molecular biology, 1988, Method to Extend Rsch. in Time award, NIH, 1991, V.D. Mattia award, Roche Inst. Molecular Biology, 1993, Hans Sigrist award, 1994, Charles A. Dana award for pioneering achievements in health and edn., Inst. Medicine NAS, 1995, Ciba-Drew award for biomed. sci., 1996, Rosenstiel award, Brandeis U., 1998, Passano award for the advancement med. sci., 1998, Alfred P. Sloan Jr. prize, GM Cancer Rsch. Found., 1998, Gairdner Found. Internat. award, 1999, Paul Ehrlich & Ludwig Darmstaedter prize, Germany, 2000, Segerfalk award, 2000, March of Dimes prize in devel. biology, 2000, Charles-Leopold Mayer prize, French Acad. Scis., 2000, Bristol-Myers Squibb award for Disting. Achievement in Neuroscience, 2001, Genetics prize, Peter Gruber Found., 2002, Am. Cancer Soc. medal of honor, 2002, Wiley prize in biomed. scis., 2002, Nobel Prize in physiology/medicine, 2002, Alfred G. Knudson award, Nat. Cancer Inst., 2005, Centennial medal, Harvard U., 2005, Killian Faculty Achievement award, MIT, 2006; Woodrow Wilson fellow, 1968. Fellow: AAAS, Am. Acad. Microbiology, Am. Acad. Arts & Scis.; mem.: NAS, Am. Philos. Soc., Physiological Soc. London, Helminthological Soc. Washington, Am. Soc. Cell Biology (mem. exec. com.), Soc. Neurosci., Soc. Nematologists, Soc. Devel. Biology, Genetics Soc. America (membership com. 1984—86, bd. dirs. 1990—96, v.p. 1994, pres. 1995), Am. Assn. Cancer Rsch., Inst. Medicine. Jewish. Achievements include patents in field. Office: MIT Dept Biology Rm 68 425 77 Massachusetts Ave Cambridge MA 02139-4307 Office Phone: 617-253-4671. Office Fax: 617-253-8126. Business E-Mail: horvitz@mit.edu. *

HORWICH, ARTHUR L., biologist, educator; b. 1951; AB in Biomed. Scis., Brown U., Providence, 1972, MD, 1975. Postdoc. molecular biology/virology Salk Inst. Biol. Studies, La Jolla, Calif.; intern, resident pediat. Yale U. Sch. Medicine, dir. Horwich Lab, 1984—, now Sterling Prof. genetics and pediat.; attending physician, med. genetics and pediat. Yale-New Haven Hosp., 1988—; investigator Howard Hughes Med. Inst., Chevy Chase, Md., 1990—. Assoc. editor Cell, Molecular Cell, mem. edit. bd. Jour. Cell Biology, Structure. Recipient Hans Neurath award, Protein Soc., 2001, Stein & Moore award, 2006, Basil O'Connor Rsch. award, Albert Lasker Basic Med. Rsch. award, Lasker Found., 2011; co-recipient (with Franz-Ulrich Hartl) Gairdner Found. Internat. award, 2004, (with Franz-Ulrich Hartl) Wiley prize in biomedical sci., 2007, (with Franz-Ulrich Hartl) Lewis S. Rosenstiel award for disting. work in basic med. sci., 2008, (with Franz-Ulrich Hartl) Louisa Gross Horwitz prize, Columbia U., 2008; John A. Hartford Found. fellow, 1981. Mem.: NAS, Inst. Medicine. Office: Yale U Sch Medicine 145 Boyer Ctr Molecular Medicine 295 Congress Ave New Haven CT 06520 Office Phone: 203-737-4431. Office Fax: 203-737-1761. Business E-Mail: arthur.horwich@yale.edu. *

HORWITZ, JILL R., law educator; b. Conn., June 6, 1966; BA, Northwestern U., 1988; PhD, JD, MPP, Harvard U., 2002. Prof. law U. Mich. Law Sch., 2003—. Office: University Mich Law Sch Ann Arbor MI 48109 Business E-Mail: jrhorwit@umich.edu.

HORWITZ, MARCUS AARON, microbiologist, immunologist; b. Elmira, NY, May 3, 1946; s. Abraham and Rose (Hirsch) H.; m. Helene L. DesRuisseaux, Nov. 27, 1981; children: Joshua, Daniel. AB in Physics, Cornell U., 1968; MD, Columbia U., 1972. Diplomate Am. Bd. Internal Medicine, Am. Bd. Infectious Diseases. Resident in medicine Albert Einstein Coll. Medicine, Bronx, NY, 1972-74, fellow in infectious diseases, 1976-77; epidemic intelligence svc. officer Ctrs. for Disease Control and Prevention, Atlanta, 1974-76; NIH postdoctoral fellow The Rockefeller U., NYC, 1977-80, asst. prof., 1980-84, assoc. physician, 1980-84; chief infectious diseases UCLA Sch. Medicine, 1985-92, prof. medicine, microbiology, immunology, molecular genetics, 1985—; pres., CEO Keystone Biomedical, Inc., 1996—2003. Chmn. sci. adv. bd. Am. Leprosy Found., Rockville, Md., 1990-2003; trustee Trudeau Inst., Saranac Lake, N.Y., 1994-97; mem. tuberculosis panel U.S. - Japan Coop. Med. Scis. Program, 1991-95. Mem. editl. bd., guest editor: Jour. of Clin. Investigation, 1989-96; editor: (book) Bacteria - Host Cell Interaction, 1988; patentee vaccine for Legionnaires' Disease, vaccine for tuberculosis, Exochelins. Cmdr. USPHS 1974-76. Recipient Alexander Langmuir award Ctrs. for Disease Control, Atlanta, 1976, Faculty Rsch. award Am. Cancer Soc., 1985. Fellow AAAS, Infectious Diseases Soc. Am. (Squibb award for Outstanding Rsch. 1991), Am. Soc. Clin. Investigation. Office: UCLA/Dept Medicine CHS 37-121 10833 Le Conte Ave Los Angeles CA 90095-1688 E-mail: MHorwitz@mednet.ucla.edu.

HORWITZ, RALPH IRVING, internist, epidemiologist, educator, former dean; b. Phila., June 25, 1947; s. Sidney and Sara (Altus) H.; m. Sarah McCue, Aug. 5, 1970; 1 child, Rebecca Margaret Taylor. BS, Albright Coll., 1969; MD, Pa. State U., 1973. Diplomate Am. Bd. Internal Medicine. Intern McGill U., Royal Victoria Hosp., Montreal, Que., Canada, 1973-75; postdoctoral tng. in epidemiology, clin. scholars program Yale U. Sch. Medicine, New Haven, 1975; sr. resident Harvard U., Mass. Gen. Hosp., Boston, 1977-78; co-dir. clin. scholars program Yale U. Sch. Medicine, New Haven, 1978—2003, asst. prof. medicine, 1978-82, assoc. prof. medicine and epidemiology, 1982-88, prof., 1988—2003, chief gen. internal medicine, 1982-94, vice chmn. internal medicine, 1993-94, chmn. internal medicine, 1994—2003, Harold H. Hines Jr. Prof. Medicine and Epidemiology, 1991—2003; chief Beeson Med. Svc. Yale-New Haven Hosp., 1993—2003; v.p. med. affairs Case Western Res. U., Cleveland, Ohio, 2003—06, dean sch. medicine, 2003—06; dir. Case Rsch. Inst., 2003—06; Arthur Bloomfield prof., chmn. dept. medicine Stanford U. Sch. Medicine, Calif., 2006—. Mem. nat. selection com. faculty scholar program Henry J. Kaiser Family Found., Menlo Park, Calif., 1987-90; mem. com. allocating resources in biomed. rsch. Inst. Medicine, Washington, 1988-89; mem. profl. standards rev. orgn., Woodbridge, Conn., 1980-82; editorial bd. The Lancet, 1991-96; past chmn. bd. dirs. Am. Bd. Internal Medicine. Contbr. over 200 articles to profl. jours. Trustee Am. Bd. Internal Medicine Found. Recipient Faculty Scholar award Kaiser Family Found., 1981-86 Fellow ACP, AAAS, Am. Coll. Epidemiology, Pa. State U. Alumni Assn.; mem. Am. Soc. Clin. Investigation, Assn. Am. Physicians, Am. Epidemiol. Soc., Inst. Medicine. Jewish. Office: Stanford Univ Sch Medicine 300 Pasteur Dr S-102 Stanford CA 94305 Office Phone: 650-736-1484. Business E-Mail: ralph.horwitz@stanford.edu.

HOSGOR, IZZET, medical writer, researcher; b. Ankara, Turkey, Mar. 1, 1946; s. Emin and Zuhre Sati Ebem; m. Ayse Kadriye Orhon, May 10, 1982; children: Enes, Ezel Bersu. MD, Hacettepe U. Med. Sch., 1976; Physiologist, Istanbul U. Cerrahpasa Med. Sch., 1983; Internal Medicine, Cardiologist, Istanbul U., Inst. of Cardiology, 1988. Electrical and Electronical Technician, Ankara Inst. of Art, 1963. Author: (abstract book) VIII. Electronmicroscopy Congress, From the World of Osteoporosis, XX e Semaine Medicale Balcanique, 6th Meeting of the Danubian League Against Thrombosis and Haemorragic Disorders, International Symposium Pulmonary Circulation V, XII. Congress of the International Abstracts Society on Thrombosis and Haemostasis, 2nd Mediterranean Congress of Angiology, 12th International Congress on Thrombosis in Florence, (book) Thrombosis and Hemorrhagic Disorders, Recent Advances in Blood Coagulation; contbr. articles to profl. jours. Lt. Gendermarie, 1977—79, Bilecik. Mem.: Red Crescent, Org. of Electronmicroscopy (assoc.), Istanbul Org. of Physicians (assoc.). Islam. Achievements include research in role of lung in fibrinolyitic activity; role of fibrinolytic system in pulmonary emphysema (injury) and pulmonary fibrosis (repair); role of fibrinolytic system in pathogenesis of atherosiclerosis; role of fibrinolytic system in cardiomyopathic pathogenesis; low fibrinolytic activity independent of lipids in hypertensive patients; low fibrinolytic activity in degenerative arthritis (injury-repair process); role of ACE inhibitors in fibrinolytic activity. Avocations: reading, poetry, history, travel. Home: Atakoy 7-8 Kisim Baris Sitesi I1a/1 34750 Istanbul Istanbul Turkey Personal E-mail: atherom@superonline.com.

HOSHIDA, SHIRO, health facility administrator; s. Michio and Hisae Hoshida; m. Noriko Hoshida, Apr. 28; children: Keita, Yuta. MD, PhD, Osaka U., Suita, Japan, 1978. Physician Sakurabashi Watanabe Hosp., Osaka, 1979—82; asst. prof. Osaka U. Med. Sch., Suita, 1991—97; dir. dvisn. cardiology Osaka Rosai Hosp., Sakai, 1997—2002; v.p. Yao (Japan) Mcpl. Hosp., 2002—. Office: Yao Mcpl Hosp 1-3-1 Ryuge-Cho Yao Osaka 581-0069 Japan Office Phone: 81 72 922 0881.

HOSHINO, SHIMPEI, dermatologist; b. Tokyo, June 17, 1942; s. Junichi and Hoshino; m. Mikiko Yamamoto, Sept. 11, 1945; children: Kei, Koji, Mari Asaoka. MD, Sch. of Medicine Nagoya U., 1967, PhD, 1976. Diplomate Ministry of Health, Labour and Welfare, Japan, 1968, Ednl. Coun. for Fgn. Med. Graduates, U.S. Asst. prof., dept. dermatology Sch. of Medicine, Nagoya U., 1973—80; rsch. fellow, dept. dermatology U. Calif., San Francisco, 1977—80; mem. staff Hoshimo Clinic of Dermatology, Nagoya, 1981—. Practitioner of dermatology Hoshino Clinic of Dermatology, Nagoya, Japan, 1981—. Fellow: Am. Acad. Dermatology (life); mem.: Japanese Dermatol. Assn. (licentiate). Home: 1-1905 Horagai Midori-ku Aichi Nagoya 458-0013 Japan Office: Hoshino Clinic of Dermatology 1-1905 Hara Tenpaku-ku Aichi Nagoya 468-0015 Japan Office Fax: 81-528052650. Business E-Mail: mld43104@nifty.com.

HOSKINS, IFFATH ABBASI, obstetrician, gynecologist; b. Karachi, Pakistan, June 18, 1951; arrived in US, 1977; d. Mohd Assan and Mehru Kazi Abbasi; m. William John Hoskins, Nov. 9, 1985; 1 child, Ahad Jamie; 1 child, Maria Aisha. MD, Dow Med. Coll., Karachi, 1975. Diplomate Am. Bd. Ob-Gyn. Intern St. Elizabeth Hosp., Washington, 1977—78, psychology resident, 1978—79; ob-gyn. resident Nat. Naval Med. Ctr., Bethesda, Md., 1979—82; fellow high risk obstetrics Walter Reed Army Hosp., Washington, 1983-85, attending physician high risk obstetrics, 1985-87; dir. rsch. Bellevue Hosp., NYC, 1987-90, chief obstetrics, 1990-97; dir. residency program, chief dept. ob-gyn. NYU Downtown Hosp., NYC, 1997—2002; exec. dir. Women's Health Inst., Meml. Health Univ. Med. Ctr., Savannah, Ga., 2001—05; sr. v.p., chair, residency dir. dept. ob-gyn. Luth. Med. Ctr., Bklyn., 2005—. Contbr. articles to profl. jours. Bd. trustees March of Dimes, NYC. Capt. Med. Corps USNR, 1979—. Fellow: ACS; mem.: Wash. Soc. Pathology, Am. Coll. Ob-Gyn. (v.p. 2008, past sec. NY chpt., chair com. for underserved women, Cmty. Svc. award 1999, Dist. Outstanding Svc. award 2001). Republican. Muslim. Avocation: reading. Office: Lutheran Med Ctr 150 55th St Brooklyn NY 11220 Office Fax: 718-630-6375, 718-630-6322. Business E-Mail: ihoskins@lmcmc.com. *

HOSKINS, WILLIAM JOHN, obstetrician, educator, gynecologist; b. Harlan, Ky., May 10, 1940; s. Lonnie S. and Joanne (Huff) Hoskins; m. Betty Jean Gay, Sept. 10, 1960 (div. 1985); children: Tonya J., William John Jr.; m. Iffath Abbasi Ahson, Nov. 9, 1985; children: Ahad A., Mariya A. BA, U. Tenn., Knoxville, 1962; MD, U. Tenn., Memphis, 1965. Diplomate Am. Bd. Ob-Gyn., Am. Bd. Gynecol. Oncology. Commd. lt. USN, 1966, advanced through grades to capt.; intern Jacksonville Naval Hosp., Fla., 1966-67; med. officer Destroyer Squadron 8 USN, Mayport, Fla., 1967-68; resident in ob-gyn Oakland Naval Hosp., Calif., 1968-71; staff dept. ob -gyn Pensacola Naval Hosp., 1971—74; fellow in gynecol. oncology U. Miami, Fla., 1974-76; dir. gynecol. oncology Nat. Naval Med. Ctr., Bethesda, Md., 1976—86; assoc. prof. ob-gyn Uniformed Svcs. U., Bethesda, 1976-86; ret. USN, 1986; assoc. chief gynecology svc. Meml. Sloan-Kettering Cancer Ctr., NYC, 1988-90, chief gynecology svc., 1990—, 1990—, exec. dir. surg. activities dept. surgery, 2007—, assoc. prof. ob-gyn Cornell U. Med. Ctr., NYC, 1986—90; prof. ob-gyn Cornell U. Med. Coll., 1990—2001, vice chmn. protocol com. gynecol. oncology group, 1993-94, vice chmn. gynecologic oncology group, 1993—2002; Avon chair gynecologic oncology rsch. Meml. Sloan-Kettering Cancer Ctr., NYC, 1995-96, dep. physician in chief disease mgmt. teams, 1996—2001, dir. Curtis & Elizabeth Anderson Cancer Ctr. at Memorial Health U. Med. Ctr., Savannah, Ga., 2001—07; prof. ob-gyn. Mercer Med. Coll., Macon, Ga., 2001—07, sr. assoc. dean Sch. Medicine Savannah, 2004—05; mem., exec. dir. surg. activities, dept. surgery Meml. Sloan Kettering Cancer Ctr., 2008—; prof. ob-gyn Cornell U. Sch. Medicine, 2008—. Chmn. ovarian com. Gynecol. Oncology Group, Phila., 1984-89; disting. Ga. Cancer scholar, 2001—; co-chair NCI Cancer Steering Com., 2006—10. Editor: Principles and Practice of Gynecology and Oncology, 1992, 4th edit., 2000, 4th edit., 2004, Cancer of the Ovary, 1993, Cervical Cancer and Perinvasive Peoplasia, 1996, Cancer Management: A Multidisciplinary Approach, 1996, Handbook of Gynecologic Oncology, 2000, 8th edit., 2002, Atlas of Procedures in Gynecologic Oncology, 2003; contbr. over 224 articles to profl. jours., chpts. to books. Fellow Am. Coll. Obstetricians and Gynecologists (v.p. Navy sect. 1982-83), ACS; mem. Am. Gynecol. and Obstet. Soc., Soc. Gynecol. Oncologists (sec.-treas. elect 1992, sec.-treas. 1994—, coun. mem. 1988-91, pres. 1999), Soc. Gynecol. Surgeons, Am. Radium Soc., Am. Assn Cancer Rsch., Internat. Gyn. Cancer Soc. (v.p. 2004—), Exec. Bd. Am. Coll. Ob-Gyn. Republican. Muslim. Office: Meml Sloan-Kettering Cancer Ctr 1275 York Ave New York NY 10065 Office Phone: 212-639-2994. Business E-Mail: hoskinsw@mskcc.org.

HOSKINS, WILLIAM KELLER, pharmaceutical executive, lawyer, mediator, arbitrator; b. Cin., Feb. 22, 1935; s. John Hobart and Gertrude Louise (Keller) H.; m. Elizabeth Ann Grimm, Aug. 5, 1961; children: Bruce, Andrew, John, Elizabeth, Allison. BA, Yale U., 1956; LLB, Harvard U., 1962. Bar: Ohio 1962, N.Y. 1982, Mo. 1983, U.S. Dist. Ct. (so. dist.) Ohio 1963, U.S. Tax Ct. 1963, U.S. Ct. Appeals (6th cir.) 1964. Assoc. Frost & Jacobs, Cin., 1962-68; gen. counsel Drackett Co., Cin., 1968-71, v.p., gen. counsel, 1971-81; assoc. gen. counsel Bristol Myers Co., NYC, 1981, spl. counsel, 1982; v.p. gen. counsel Marion Merrell Dow (formerly Marion Labs. Inc.), 1982—95; gen counsel sec. Hozchst Marion Roussel, 1995—97; mgr. ptnr. Hoskins Group, Boston, 1998—; pres. Hoskins & Associates, Boston, 1998—; mng. ptnr. Resolution Coun., LLP, Portland, Oreg., 2002—07; ptnr. Resolution Strategies, LLP, Portland, 2008—. Chmn. household div. Soap and Detergent Assn., NYC, 1978-79, chmn. Chem. Spltys. Mfg. Assn., Washington, 1982; bd. dirs. Ferrrellgas, Inc., Kansas City, Mo., 2003-11. Mem. Hamilton County Rep. Ctrl. Com., Ohio, 1970-81; sec.-treas. Marion Labs. Polit. Action Com., 1982-89; sec.-treas. polit. action com. Mid-Am. Com. Sound Govt., Lake Quivira, Kans., 1982-86; bd. dirs. Landmark Legal Found., Kansas City, 1995-2003, vice chmn., 2001-2003. Lt. (j.g.) USN, 1956-59. Mem. Mo. Bar, Ohio Bar, NY Bar, Cin. Bar Assn., Harvard Law Sch. Alumni Assn. (bd. dirs. 1991-95). Roman Catholic. Home: 85 E India Row Apt 20B Boston MA 02110-3397 Home Phone: 617-742-4172; Office Phone: 617-742-8191. Business E-Mail: hoskins@resolutionstrategies.com. E-mail: Bhoskins98@aol.com.

HOSKOVA, LENKA, cardiologist; MD, Charles U., Prague, 1990. Cert. in internal medicine 1994, cardiologist 2000. Internal medicine physician Hosp. Slany, Czech Republic, 1990—94; cardiologist, heart failure, transplantologist Inst. Clin. and Postgrad. Medicine (IKEM), Prague, Czech Republic, 1996—. Contbr. articles to med. jours., chapters to books. Mem.: European Soc. Heart Failure, European Soc. Cardiology, Internat. Soc. Heart and Lung Transnplantation, Czech Soc. Transplantology, Czech Soc. Cardilogy. Office: IKEM Dept Cardiology Videnska 1958/9 Prague 14021 Czech Republic Office Phone: 420 605222868. Office Fax: 420 2 236053016. Business E-Mail: leho@ikem.cz.

HOSTETTER, MARGARET K., pediatrician, medical educator; children: Mayme Kendrick, John Heard. BA summa cum laude, Denison U., Granville, Ohio, 1970; MD magna cum laude, Baylor Coll. Medicine, Houston, 1975. Diplomate Am. Bd. Pediatrics with subspecialty in pediat. infectious diseases. Resident Children's Hosp., Boston; fellow in pediat. infectious disease Harvard Med. Sch./Beth Israel Hosp., Boston; mem. faculty U. Minn., Mpls., 1982—98, Am. Legion Heart Rsch. prof., endowed chair, 1992—98; prof. pediats., sect. chief pediat. immunology Yale U., New Haven, 1998, founder Yale Internat. Adoption Clinic, 1998, dir. Yale Child Health Rsch. Ctr., 1998—2002; chair pediatrics, physician-in-chief Yale-New Haven Children's Hosp., 2002—; Jean McLean Wallace prof. pediat., endowed chair Yale U., New Haven, 2004—. Program dir. Pediat. Scientist Devel. Program, 1996—. Editor: Ruldoph's Textbook of Pediatrics. Co-chair Success by Six Initiative United Way of Greater New Haven, 2004—05; mem. adv. coun. Nat. Inst. Child Health and Human Devel., chair of public policy and planning sub-com.; chair, co-chair grant rev. panels Veterans Adminstrn., March of Dimes, NIH, Burroughs Welcome Fund; sci. adv. bd. Howard Hughes Med. Inst., 2008—. Recipient Am. Acad. Pediatrics award for Excellence in Rsch., Samuel Rosenthal award, E. Mead Johnson award, Soc. Pediat. Rsch., Maxwell Finland award, Infectious Diseases Soc. Am.; named Nat. Merit Scholar; named to Best Doctors in Am.; John A. and George N. Hartford fellow, 1984—87. Mem.: Pediat. Infectious Diseases Soc., Infectious Diseases Soc. Am. (elected to Inst. Medicine 2001), Soc. Pediat. Rsch., Am. Pediat. Sco., Assn. Am. Physicians, Am. Soc. Clin. Investigation, Inst. of Medicine of NAS, Alpha Omega Alpha, Phi Beta Kappa. Achievements include 5 patents in field. Office: Yale Univ Sch Medicine 333 Cedar St LMP 4085 PO Box 208064 New Haven CT 06520-8064

HOSTLER, SHARON LEE, pediatrician, educator; b. Rutland, Vt., Oct. 24, 1939; d. John Gerald and Irene Adelaide (Whitney) H.; m. Alan Duane Dimock, Dec. 29, 1965 (dec. Sept. 1974); children: Kathleen Ann Dimock, Dylan Alan Dimock; stepchildren: Timothy Dimock, Gioia L. Dimock, Dorothy Dimock McNamara, Adam Dimock; m. Joseph Boardman, May 17, 1987. AB, Middlebury Coll., 1961; MD, U. Vt., 1965. Intern pediatrics U. Va., Charlottesville, 1965—66, resident pediatric hematology, 1966—68, fellow, 1967—69; co-dir. Kluge Children's Rehab. Ctr., U. Va. Sch. Medicine, Charlottesville, 1972—78, chief Divsn. Devel. Pediatrics, med. dir., 1978—; asst. prof. pediat. U. Va. Sch. Medicine, Charlottesville, 1970—76, assoc. prof., 1976—87, prof., 1986—98, McLemore Birdsong prof. pediat., 1998—, assoc. chair dept. pediat., 1999, sr. assoc. dean faculty devel., 2005—07, interim v.p., dean, 2007—08. Vis. prof. Hadassah Hosp. Ben Gurion U., Jerusalem, 1983-84; cons. Project Hope, Krakow, Poland, 1981-83; active Kluge/UCP Rsch. Project, Family Autonomy Project, MCH; mem. exec. com. U. Va. Health Svcs. Found. Contbr. articles to profl. jours. Bd. dirs. Ctrl. Va. Child Devel. Assn., Charlottesville, 1972-76; mem. Gov.'s Com. on Handicapped Child, Richmond, Va., 1972-78; founder Task Force on Ventilator Dependent Children, Richmond, 1986-89; cons. pub. schs., 1972-78; mem. Children's Med. Ctr. Cmty. Bd.; chmn. bldg. com. Kluge Children's Rehab. Ctr.'s Outpatient Dept., chair com. on women Sch. Medicine; mem. task force on women U. Va., mem. permanent com. on women's concerns. Recipient Innovative Project award Am. Assn. Children's Health, 1986, Outstanding Alumni award U. Vt., 1993, Outstanding Women of Yr. award U. Va., Women's Profl. and Leadership Assn., 1993, Lectr. award Am. Assn. Children's Health, 1994, Leadership Devel. award Women in Medicine, 1995, Middlebury Coll. Alumni Achievement award, 1999; Gould Found. scholar, 1957-61. Fellow Am. Acad. Pediatrics (sect. adolescent medicine); mem. Am. Acad. Cerebral Palsy/Devel. Neurology, Soc. Adolescent Medicine, Am. Med. Women's Assn. (bd. dirs., chpt. pres. 1987, regional gov. 1988-90), Assn. Am. Med. Colls., Boars Head Sports Club, Alpha Omega Alpha. Home: 1340 Wendover Dr Charlottesville VA 22901-7713 Office: U Va Sch Medicine McKim Hall, Rm 3028 PO Box 800793 Charlottesville VA 22908 Office Phone: 434-982-3353, 434-924-8178. Office Fax: 434-982-0874. E-mail: slh2m@virginia.edu.

HOTCHKISS, ROBERT N., orthopedist, surgeon, educator; MD, Johns Hopkins Univ., 1980. Diplomate Am. Bd. of Orthopaedic Surgery, Am. Bd. of Orthopaedic Surgery-hand surgery. Resident Johns Hopkins Hosp., 1981—82, orthopedic rsch. fellow, 1982—85; orthopedic biomechanics vis. fellow Mayo Clinic; hand and microvascular fellow Raymond M. Curtis Hand Ctr., Union Memorial Hosp., 1986—87; assoc. prof. orthopaedic surgery Weill Med. Coll.; with NY-Presbyn. Hosp.; cons. orthopedic surgery Burke Rehab. Hosp.; assoc. attending orthopaedic surgeon Hosp. for Spl. Surgery, dir. of translational and external initiatives, dir. rsch., hand & upper extremity svc., med. dir. of clin. rsch. Author: (publs.) Clinical Trials at HSS, 2010, Basal Thumb Arthritis: An Overview, 2010, Tennis Elbow: An Overview, 2010. Named one of Best Doctors in NY, NY Mag., 2009—11. Achievements include research in Removal of Volar Plates after Distal Radius Fracture; Open Label Trial for Treating Carpometacarpal Osteoarthritis: PILOT STUDY - Sub-study on Normal Controls; A Study of Hyaluronan (Synvisc) for the Treatment of Osteoarthritis in the Thumb: Randomized Control Trial. Office: Hospital for Special Surgery E River Professional Bldg 4th Fl 523 E 72nd St New York NY 10021 Office Phone: 212-606-1964. Office Fax: 212-288-8260.

HOTEZ, PETER JAY, medical and molecular parasitologist, pediatrician, educator; b. Hartford, Conn., May 5, 1958; s. Edward Joseph and Jean (Goldberg) H.; m. Ann Elizabeth Frifield, Sept. 14, 1987; children: Matthew, Emily, Rachel, Daniel. BA in Molecular Biophysics and Biochemistry, Yale U., 1980; PhD, Rockefeller U., 1986; MD, Weill Cornell Med. Coll, 1987. Cert. DC, Pediatrics. Resident pediatric Mass. Gen. Hosp., Boston, 1987-89; Pfizer postdoctoral fellow in infectious diseases Yale U., New Haven, 1989-91, instr., 1991-92, asst. prof., 1992-95, assoc. prof., 1995—2000; with George Washington U., 2000—, disting. rsch. prof. dept. microbiology, immunology, & tropical med., 2008—; Walter G. Ross prof. and chair, microbiology, immunology and tropical medicine George Washington U. Med. Ctr.; pres. Sabin Vaccine Inst. Principal scientist, founding dir. Human Hookworm Vaccine Initiative, Sabin Vaccine Inst.; cofounder Global Network for Tropical Neglected Diseases Control; vis. prof. Chinese Acad. Preventive Med.; adv. bd. Congas Memorial Inst.; amb. Paul G. Rogers Soc. for Global Health Rsch. for Research America, 2006; sci. adv. bd. March of Dimes, Albert B. Sabin Vaccine Found., Charles H. Hood Found.; mem. WHO Scientific and Technical Adv. Group for Neglected Tropical Diseases, 2010. Author Forgotten People, Forgotten Diseases: The Neglected Tropical Diseases and Their Impact on Global Health and Development; co-author: Parasitic Diseases, 5th edit., 1995;co-editor Krugman's Infectious Diseases of Children, 11th edit.; founding editor-in-chief of PLoS Neglected Tropical Diseases;contbr. of several articles to profl. publications; contbr. chapters in books; has been cited in nat. newspapers and magazines regarding his hookworm rsch.; patentee in field. Recipient Young Investigator award, Pediatric Infectious Diseases Soc., Henry Baldwin Ward medal, Am. Soc. Parasitologists, 1999, Baily K. Ashford medal, Am. Soc. Tropical Med. & Hygiene, 2003, Leverhulme medal, Liverpool Sch. Tropical Med., 2006. Fellow: Am. Acad. Pediatrics; mem.: Am. Soc. of Tropical Medicine and Hygiene (coun. mem., pres.-elect), Soc. Pediatric Rsch., Pediatric Infectious Disease Soc. (adv. bd. jour., Young Investigator award 1993), Inst. Med., Phi Beta Kappa. Office: Ross Hall 736 2300 I St NW Washington DC 20052 Home: 5213 Portsmouth Rd Bethesda MD 20816-2928 Office: Albert B Sabin Vaccine Inst 1889 F St NW Ste 200S Washington DC 20006-4400 Home Phone: 301-570-7611; Office Phone: 202-994-3532, 202-842-5025. Office Fax: 202-994-2913, 202-842-7689. Business E-Mail: mtmpjh@gwumc.edu. E-mail: photez@gwu.edu.

HOTTA, MASATO, dental educator; b. Unomachi, Japan, Jan. 18, 1954; s. Shigeo and Miyoko (Yamaguchi) H.; m. Mayumi Takada, May 12, 1985; 1 child, Akiyuki. DDS, Gifu Dental Coll., 1982; PhD in Dental Sci., Asahi U., 1988. Instr. Gifu Dental Coll., Hozumi, Japan, 1982-85, Asahi Univ., Hozumi, 1985-90, asst. prof., 1990—2006, assoc. prof., 2006—09, prof. & chmn., 2009—. Vis. scientist Baylor Coll. Dentistry, 1995-96. Author: New Functionality Materials, 1993; contbr. articles to profl. jours. Grantee, Japanese Ministry Edn., 1993—95, Japanese Ministry Edn., 2000—. Mem. Internat. Assn. Dental Rsch., Internat. Acad. Periodontology (cert. of achievement 1995), Japanese Soc. Conservative Dentistry (cons. 1991—), Japan Acad. Color for Dentistry (cons. 1995-98, dir. 1999—), Japanese Soc. Dental Materials and Devices. Avocations: golf, tennis, baseball. Home: 566-9 Kamijuku Sunomata-cho 503-0103 Japan Office: Asahi Univ Sch Dentistry 1851 Hozumi Hozumi 501-0296 Japan Office Phone: +81-58-329-1442. Business E-Mail: w7mhotta@dent.asahi-u.ac.jp.

HOU, CHARLES JIA YIN, cardiologist, director; b. Ping Tung, Taiwan, Dec. 9, 1957; s. Irene Wen Yin Hsu; m. Virginia Wan Chun Hsieh, Dec. 12, 1992; 1 child, Allison Yee Chuen. MD, Taipei Med. U., 1983. Cert. Nat. Inst. Health, Bd. Internal Medicine, 1989, in cardiology Taiwan Soc. Cardiology, 1990, in interventional electrophysiology Taiwan Soc. Cardiology, 2008. Dir. cardiac ICU Mackay Meml. Hosp., Taipei, Taiwan, 2001—, dir., cardiovasc. medicine, 2001—. Sec. gen. Taiwan Soc. Cardiology, Taipei, 2005—07, standing mem. exec. coun., 2007—; trustee Taiwan Heart Found., Taipei, 2007—. Contbr. articles to profl. jours. Recipient Distinguished Contbn. award, 16th Asian Pacific Congress Cardiology, 2007, Contbn. award, Taiwan Soc. Cardiology, 2007. Fellow: Heart Rhythm Soc., Coll. Asian Pacific Soc. Cardiology.

HOU, DONGMING, research scientist; b. Hebei, June 6, 1966; MD, BMU, PhD, 1996; MBA, UT, 2010. Sr. scientist SJTRI, 2007. Home: 5626 Princeton Run Trail Tucker GA 30084 Business E-Mail: dhou@sjha.org.

HOU, JUN STEVE, medical educator; s. Yuanyao Hou and Xiuying Song; m. Yan Liu, 1987; children: Kevin, Kristy. MD, Weifang Med. Coll., Shandong, China, 1982. Diplomate in anatomic & clin. pathology Am. Bd. Pathology, 1998, in hematology 2006. Asst. prof. Tianjin Med. U., China, 1986—88; rsch. asst. Dept. Health, Albany, NY, 1989—93; resident pathology Albany Med. Coll., NY, 1993—97; prof. Drexel U. Coll. Medicine, Phila., 1997—, prof., dir. surg. pathology & hematopathology, 2005—. Mem.: US & Can. Acad. Pathology. Office: Drexel University Coll Medicine 245 N 15th St Philadelphia PA 19102 Business E-Mail: jhou@drexelmed.edu.

HOU, SHIWANG, engineering educator; b. Wenshui, China, Aug. 16, 1978; PhD, Northwestern Poly. U., 2010. Assoc. prof. North U. China, 2005—. Office: Xueyuan Rd 3 Taiyuan Shanxi 030051 China Personal E-mail: houshiwan@163.com.

HOU, YI-PING, medical educator; b. Shanxi, Mar. 27, 1957; MD, 1983. Prof. Lanzhou U., 1999—. Office: 199 Donggangxi Rd Lanzhou Gansu 730000 China Business E-Mail: houyiping@lzu.edu.cn.

HOUGH, SIGMUND, neuropsychologist; BA in Psychology, Columbia Coll., NYC, 1978; MA in Devel. Psychology, Columbia U., NYC, 1981; PhD in Clin. Psychology, Boston U., 1987. Diplomate Am. Acad. Pain Mgmt., 1991, lic. in rehab. psychology Am. Bd. Profl. Psychology, 2003, cert. sex therapist Am. Assn. Sexuality Educators, Counselors and Therapists, 2006. Clin. neuropsychologist spinal cord injury program, VA Boston Healthcare Sys., West Roxbury, Mass., 1995—; adj. asst. prof. psychiatry Boston U. Sch. Medicine; asst. prof. psychology Harvard Med. Sch., Boston; CARF surveyor Commn. Accreditation Rehab. Facilities, Tucson; site visitor Com. Accreditation, APA, DC. Tng. dir. Boston Consortium Psychology Postdoctoral Program., Boston, 2004—07. Co-author (with Brian Hough): (book) Wisdom of a Parent Through the Eyes of a Child (Excellence in Postdoctoral Tng. award, Assn. Psychology Postdoctoral and Internship Ctrs., 2005); editor-in-chief: Sexuality and Disability (Clin. Performance award, Am. Assn. Spinal Cord Injury Psychologists and Social Workers, 2004), editl. bd. mem.: PsycCRITIQUES (Faculty of Yr. award, Boston Consortium Psychology Internship Program, 2006, 2009); contbr. articles to profl. jours. Recipient Cert. Appreciation award, VA Boston Healthcare Sys. Fellow: Nat. Acad. Neuropsychology; mem.: Acad. Spinal Cord Injury Profls. (pres. PSW sect.), Mass. Neuropsychol. Soc. (bd. dirs. 2008), Am. Assn. Spinal Cord Injury Psychologists and Social Workers. Achievements include research in co-PI sleep disorders in Gulf War veterans project. Office: 396 Washington St Ste 211 Wellesley MA 02481

HOUGHTON, IVAN TIMOTHY, anesthesiologist; b. Leamington, England, Feb. 23, 1942; s. Arnold Cecil and Enid (Cyriax) H.; m. Teresa Wan, June 17, 1978. BA with honors, Cambridge U., 1963, MB BChir, 1966, MA, 1967; LLB with honors, London U., 1987; MD, Chinese U. Hong Kong, 1993; LLM, U. Wales, 2000; BSc with honors, London Met. U., 2005. Cons. anesthesiologist British Mil. Hosp., Munster, 1980-81, Hong Kong, 1982-85, sr. cons. anesthesiologist Munster, 1985-87, Hong Kong, 1987-94, Rinteln, 1994-97; comdg. officer BMH Rinteln, 1996-97; clin. dir. critical care, cons. advisor in anesthesia Royal Hosp., Haslar, Eng., 1997-98; def. advisor anesthesia and resuscitation Surgeon Gen., 1998—2002; Queen's Hon. Surgeon, 1999—2002; vis. rsch. fellow Sir John Cass Dept. Art, Media and Design, London Met. U., 2007—; rschr. Frame Conservation Sect., Tate, 2007—. Hon. lectr. Chinese U. Hong Kong, 1982-85, 87-94; clin. tutor British Mil. Hosp., Hong Kong, 1992-94; councilor Med. Soc. London. Editor: European Jour. Anesthesiology, 2002—06. Mem. Territorial Army Vol. Res., 1960-72. Brig. Royal Army Med. Corps, 1972—2002. Recipient Charles Box surgery prize, St. Thomas Hosp., London, 1964, Marshall Webb Mil. Adminstrn. prize and medal, 1973, Alexander prize and Gilt medal, 1989. Fellow Hong Kong Coll. Anesthesiologists, Royal Soc. Medicine; mem. British Med. Assn., Assn. Anesthesiologists, Gt. Britain and Ireland, Soc. Anesthesiologists Hong Kong, Army and Navy Club, Inst. Conservation. Avocations: music, restoration and conservation of decorative hard surfaces, history of anaesthesia.

HOUGHTON, MICHAEL, geneticist; PhD, U. London, 1976. Sr. rsch. investigator human interferon genetics Searle Rsch. Labs., Buckinghamshire, England; with Chiron Corp., Emeryville, Calif., 1982—2006, dir. non-A non-B hepatitis rsch., v.p. hepatitis rsch.; chief sci. officer Epiphany Biosciences, Calif., 2007—10; Can. excellence rsch. chair in virology U. Alta., Canada, 2010—. Contbr. articles to profl. jours. Recipient Karl Landsteiner Meml. award, Am. Assn. Blood Banks, 1992, Lasker-DeBakey Clin. Med. Rsch. award, Lasker Found., 2000. Achievements include first to conduct work leading to the discovery of the virus that causes hepatitis C; development of screening methods that reduce the risk of blood transfusion-associated hepatitis in the U.S. from 30% in 1970 to virtually zero in 2000. Office: Dept Med Microbiology & Immunology University Alta Faculty Medicine & Dentistry 6010 Katz Group Rexqall Ctr Health Rsch Edmonton AB Canada T6G 2E1 Office Phone: 780-248-1888. Office Fax: 780-492-7521. Business E-Mail: michael.houghton@ualberta.ca. *

HOUK, IRENE MILLER, dentist; b. Columbiana, Ohio, Aug. 1, 1921; d. Josiah Ellsworth and Ada Isophene (Rupert) Miller; m. George Albertus Houk, Mar. 23, 1949; children: Martha Helle, George. DDS, U. Pitts., 1944. Lic. dentist, Ohio. Gen. practice dentistry, Poland, Ohio. Sunday sch. tchr. 1st Presbyn. Ch., Columbiana, 1935-49, Emmanuel Luth. Ch., New Springfield, Ohio, 1951-2003; bd. dirs. Springfield Local Sch., New Middletown, Ohio, 1960-81, past v.p., past pres.; bd. dirs. Wittenberg U., 1962-70. Mem. ADA, Ohio Dental Assn., Corydon Palmer Dental Soc.

HOUMES, BLAINE V., emergency physician; b. Sept. 13, 1952; MD, U. N.D., 1988. Diplomate Am. Bd. Emergency Medicine. Intern Cook County Hosp., Chgo., 1988-89, resident, 1989-92; mem. staff Mercy Med. Ctr., Cedar Rapids, Iowa, 1992—; med. examiner Linn County, Cedar Rapids, 1992—2004. Mem. Iowa Bd. Med. Examiners, 2004—08. Mem. Am. Coll. Emergency Physicians, Am. Acad. Emergency Medicine, Iowa Med. Soc., Am. Acad. Forensic Scis. Office: Linn County Emergency Med 701 10th St SE Cedar Rapids IA 52403-1251

HOUSE, JAMES STEPHEN, social psychologist, educator; b. Phila., Jan. 27, 1944; s. James Jr. and Virginia Miller (Sturgis) H.; m. Wendy Fisher, May 13, 1967; children: Jeff, Erin. BA, Haverford Coll., 1965; PhD, U. Mich., 1972. From. instr. to assoc. prof. sociology Duke U., Durham, NC, 1970-78; assoc. prof. sociology/assoc. rsch. scientist Survey Rsch. U. Mich., Ann Arbor, 1978-82, assoc. chair dept. sociology, 1981-84, prof. sociology, 1982—2005, chair dept. sociology, 1986-90, dir. Survey Rsch. Ctr., Inst. Social Rsch., 1991-2001, Angus Campbell disting. prof., survey rsch. pub. rsch. and sociology, prof. Survey Rsch. Ctr, 2005—. Author: Work Stress and Social Support, 1981; co-editor: Sociological Perspectives on Social Psychology, 1995, A Telescope on Society, 2004; Making Americans Healthier: Social and Economic Policy as Health Policy, 2008; assoc. editor Social Psychology Quar., 1988-91, Jour. Health & Social Behavior, 1997-2000, Internat. Ency. of the Social and Behavioral Scis., 2001; contbr. chpts. to books and articles to profl. jours. Guggenheim fellow, 1986-87, Ctr. for Advanced Study in the Behavioral Scis. fellow, 2005-06, vis. scholar Rusell Soge Found., 2010- Fellow: AAAS, Soc. Behavioral Medicine, Am. Acad. Arts and Scis.; mem.: NAS, Soc. for Epidemiol. Rsch., Soc. for Psychol. Study of Social Issues, Acad. Behavioral Medicine Rsch., Am. Sociol. Assn., Inst. Medicine of NAS. Office: Univ Mich Inst Social Rsch PO Box 1248 Ann Arbor MI 48106-1248 Office Phone: 734-764-6526. Business E-Mail: jimhouse@umich.edu.

HOUSE, JOHN WILLIAM, otolaryngologist; b. LA, July 12, 1941; s. Howard and Helen House; m. Barbara Breithaupt, Mar. 28, 1993; children: Hans, Chris, Kurt, Steven, Kevin. BS, U. So. Calif., 1964, MD, 1967. Bd. cert. otolaryngologist Am. Bd. Otolaryngology - Head & Neck Surgery, 1974, bd. cert. neurologist 2004. Intern L.A. County-U. So. Calif. Med. Ctr., 1967-68; resident Glendale (Calif.) Adventist Hosp., 1971-72, L.A. County Med. Ctr., 1972-74; fellow Otologic Med. Group, LA, 1974, pvt. practice, 1975—; pres. House Ear Inst., LA, 1987—. Mem. editorial bd. Am. J. Otology, 1986—; contbr. articles to jours. in field. Admissions com. interviewer, U. So. Calif. Sch. Medicine, Los Angeles, 1976—; Capt. U.S. Army, 1969-71. Recipient Hocks Meml. award Am. Tinnitus Assn., 1988; named Tchr. of Yr., U. So. Calif. Family Practice Dept., 1987. Fellow Am. Acad. Otolaryngology/Head and Neck Surgery (bd. dirs. 2005-08); mem. AMA, Am. Neurotology Soc. (past resident, pres. 1998-99), Am. Otol. Soc., Triologic Soc. (asst. via pres.), Pan-Am. Assn. Otorhinolaryngology Broncho Esophagology, Jonathan Club (Los Angeles). Avocations: skiing, computers, running, swimming, travel. Office: House Ear Clinic Inc 2100 W 3rd St Fl 1 Los Angeles CA 90057-1922 Office Phone: 213-483-9930.

HOUSER, HAROLD BYRON, epidemiologist; b. North Liberty, Ind., Nov. 22, 1921; s. Edgar Allen and Gladys Chloe (Stillson) H.; m. Clara Jane Goin, Sept. 18, 1944; children: Cristene, Edgar, John, Susan, James. AB, Ind. U., 1942, MD, 1944. Intern U.S. Marine Hosp., New Orleans, 1944-45; resident Crile VA Hosp., Cleve., 1947-49; asst. prof. medicine SUNY, Syracuse, 1952-58; asst. prof. medicine and community health Case Western Res. U., 1958-64, assoc. prof., 1965-74, prof. epidemiology, 1974-92, prof. emeritus, 1992—, chmn. dept. biometry, 1975-85, chmn. dept. epidemiology and biostats., 1985-92; cons. in field. Contbr. numerous articles to profl. jours. Served with U.S. Army, 1945-47, 49-52. Recipient Group Lasker award Am. Pub. Health Assn., 1954, Disting. Civilian award

Dept. Def., 1973 Fellow Infectious Diseases Soc.; mem. Am. Epidemiol. Soc. (pres. 1991). Home: 6300 E Speed Way Blvd Apt 1160 Tucson AZ 85710 Personal E-mail: halhous@aol.com.

HOUSTON, FRANK MATT, dermatologist; b. New Orleans, Dec. 15, 1939; s. Matt Francis and Amanda Vallie (Welch) H.; m. Helen Butler, Apr. 24, 1965; children: F. Matt, Catherine E.C., Amanda J.B. BS, La. State U., 1960, MD, 1964. Diplomate Am. Bd. Dermatology. Intern Johns Hopkins U., Balt., resident, fellow; physician, dermatologist Greensboro Dermatology Assocs., NC, 1970—. Cons. Moses H. Cone Hosp. Sys., Greensboro, NC, 1970—; adj. asst. clin. prof. dermatology U. NC Sch. Medicine, Chapel Hill, 1980—. Bd. dirs. Greensboro Hist. Mus., Greensboro Preservation Soc., Greensboro Symphony Soc., Greensboro Opera Co. Capt. U.S. Army, 1965-71. Fellow: Am. Acad. Dermatology; mem.: Pennybyrn Maryfield High Point, NC (adv. bd.), Friends Homes Inc. (bd. visitors), Am. Skin Assn. (sci. adv. com. to bd. dirs.), Royal Society Medicine, NC Soc. Medicine, Surf Club (Wrightsville Beach, NC), Greensboro Country Club. Republican. Episcopalian. Avocations: travel, aerobics, music. Office: Greensboro Dermatology 2704 Saint Jude St Greensboro NC 27405-3670 Office Phone: 336-954-7546. Personal E-mail: f_houston@bellsouth.net.

HOUSTON, JOSEPH BRANTLEY, JR., optical instrument company executive; b. Birmingham, Ala., June 15, 1934; s. Joseph Brantley and Inez (Graben) H.; m. Elizabeth Reece Manasco; 1 child, J. Brantley III. AB in Astronomy, U. Tex., Austin, 1956; MS, Northeastern U., Boston, 1969. Commd. 2d lt. C.E., US Army, 1956, advanced through grades to capt., 1968; optical engr. Perkin-Elmer, Wilton, Conn., 1961-64; mgr. massive optics, chief engr. underwater optical sys. Itek Corp., Lexington, Mass., 1964-71; asst. to pres. Kollmorgen E-O Divsn., Northampton, Mass., 1971-73; v.p. advanced devel. and spl. projects Itek Corp., Sunnyvale, Calif., 1973-81; founder Houston Rsch. Assocs., Saratoga, Calif., 1981—, Houston Tech. Internat., Inc., San Jose, Calif., 1991-97; founder, exec. dir. Forum for Mil. Applications of Directed Energy, Huntsville, Ala., 1989-96. Contbr. articles to profl. jours.; inventor. Recipient Outstanding Civilian Svc. medal U.S. Army, 1987. Fellow Internat. Soc. Optical Engring. (life; pres. 1977-78, advanced tech. advisor 1981-2004, Goddard award 1982); mem. Optical Soc. Am. (pres. New Eng. sect., chmn. Fabrication and Testing Tech. Group, editor Optical Workshop Notebook). Home and Office: 12150 Country Squire Ln Saratoga CA 95070-3444

HOUTZ, DUANE TALBOTT, hospital administrator; b. Kansas City, Mo., Apr. 28, 1933; s. Dudley and Helen (Talbott) H.; m. Margaret McNiel; children: Erik Siegfried, Jamie Houtz Harvey. BS, U. Kans., 1955; MHA, Washington U., St. Louis, 1960. Asst. dir. Shands Teaching Hosp. and Clinics, Gainesville, Fla., 1961-65; asst. prof. Ctr. for Health and Hosp. Adminstrn., U. Fla., Gainesville, 1964-65; adminstr., exec. v.p. Baptist Med. Ctr., Montclair-Birmingham, Ala., 1965-75; hosp. dir. Alton Ochsner Med. Found., New Orleans, 1975-77; pres. Morton F. Plant Hosp., Clearwater, Fla., 1977-92, pres. emeritus, 1992—; nat. advisor to the health care industry Pershing Yoakley & Assocs., P.C., 1995-99; ptnr. Corrigo Health Care Solutions, 2000—. Chmn. Southeastern Hosp. Conf., 1986-87; chmn., pres. SunHealth Care Plans Fla., 1986-87, bd. dirs. SunHealth Enterprises Inc., SunHealth Corp.; advisor Corrigo Health Care Solutions, LLC, 1998—; bd. mem. Madonna Ptak Alzheimer's Rsch. Ctr., 2007-. Contbr. articles to profl. jours. Bd. dirs. Cmty. Svc. Coun., Birmingham, 1972-75, United Way of Pinellas County, 1987-93, campaign chmn. med. divsn., 1992-94; bd. dirs. Fla. League for Nursing, 1989-98, Bay Area Hosp. Coun./Tampa Bay Hosp. Coun., 1990-95, Morton Plant Found., 1990-96; mem. Fla. Geriatric Rsch. Bd., 1993-98; adv. bd. Jr. League Pinellas County, 1993-94; active Vets. Affairs Mgmt. Assistance Coun., 1996—2010; vice-chmn. Sun Coast Health Coun., 1998-2003; mem. fundraising bd. Magic Found., 2005. Capt. USAF, 1955-58. Recipient Acad. award USAF Basic Flight Sch., 1956, award of merit Fla. Hosp. Rsch. and Edn. Found., 1993, Washington U. Hosp. Adminstrn. Program Alumni of Yr. award, 1996; fellow Birmingham Bapt. Hosp. Found., 1985. Fellow Am. Coll. Healthcare Execs. (Regents award 1992); mem. Nat. League Nursing (bd. dirs.), Am. Hosp. Assn. (vice-chmn. council nursing 1983, rsch. com.), Assn. Voluntary Hosps. Fla. (bd. dirs. 1979-83, pres. 1979-80), Fla. Hosp. Assn. (trustee, bd. dirs. 1979-82), Greater Clearwater C. of C. (Outstanding Citizen selection com. 1982, bd. govs. 1984-87, bd. govs. 1987-88), Pinellas Suncoast C. of C. (adv. coun. 1984-87), Kiwanis (pres. Birmingham chpt. 1970-71), Phi Delta Theta. Office Phone: 727-631-0110. Personal E-mail: dhoutz1@tampabay.rr.com.

HOUTZ, ROBERT LEWIS, agricultural studies educator, researcher; b. Princeton, W.Va., Jan. 31, 1955; MS, Mich. State U., 1980, PhD, 1985. Prof., chair U. Ky., 1985—. Recipient Thomas Poe Cooper award, U. Ky., Coll. Agr. Avocations: astronomy, fishing, hunting, woodworking. Office: University Ky N318 Ag Sci North Lexington KY 40546-0091 Office Fax: 859-257-2859. Business E-Mail: rhoutz@uky.edu.

HOVEE, MARK JOHN, psychologist; b. Portland, Oreg., Feb. 20, 1954; s. Harry Juel and Janene Arden Hovee; m. Judy Lynn Pratt, Sept. 23, 2005; children: Nathanael James, Maris Alise, Claire Marie. BA in Polit. Sci., Seattle U., 1979; MA in Political Philosophy, Boston Coll., 1983; MA in Clin. Psychology, George Fox U., 1994, PsyD in Clin. Psychology, 1997; advanced cert. in peace studies, European Peace U., Stadtschlaining, Austria, 2007. Lic. psychologist Ky. Pvt. practice psychologist, Paintsville, Ky., 2002—; psychologist ARH Psych. Ctr., Hazard, Ky., 2003—04. Adj. faculty Union Inst., Cin., 1999—2003, Morehead State U., Prestonsburg, Ky., 2005—05; supr. U. Ky., Prestonsburg, 2001—04; psychologist Highlands Regional Hosp., Prestonsburg, 2001—04, 2007—, Corrections Corp. Am., Wheelwright, Ky., 2002—04, 2005—07, 2008—, US Penitentiary Big Sandy, Ky.; psychologist Landstuhl (Germany) Reg. Med. Ctr. U.S. Army, 2004—05; presenter Transylvania U., Lexington, 2005. Contbr. articles to profl. jours.; author: Wayward Soldier: A Reserve Psychologist's Memoir and Analysis During the Second American-Iraqi War, 2007. Sgt. US Army, 1973—76, sgt. USAR, 1983—2001, capt. USAR, 2001—. Mem.: APA, Assn. Conflict Resolution, Brit. Psychol. Soc., Internat. Soc. Polit. Psychology (presenter 2004), Ky. Psychol. Assn. (presenter 2005), Rotary (presenter 2005, 2007). Democrat. Methodist. Achievements include development of cross-border food supply deliveries at Thai-Cambodian border; lobbied on behalf of Cambodian refugees with US congressional members and Geneva Conference on Refugees. Avocations: skiing, swimming, tennis, boating, travel. Home and Office: PO Box 51 Paintsville KY 41240 Office Phone: 606-297-7315. Personal E-mail: markhovee@yahoo.com.

HOVEN, ARDIS DEE, epidemiologist, medical educator; b. Cin., Aug. 1, 1944; m. Ronald L. Sanders. BS in Microbiology, U. Ky., Lexington, 1966; MD, U. Ky. Coll. Medicine, 1970. Diplomate American Bd. Internal Medicine, cert. in pediatric infectious diseases. Internal medicine intern U. NC, Chapel Hill, 1970-71, infectious disease resident, 1971-73, fellow, 1973-75; prof. medicine, divsn. infectious diseases U. Ky. Coll. Medicine, med. dir. Bluegrass Care Clinic. Apptd. Nat. Adv. Coun. Healthcare Rsch. & Quality. Recipient Alumni Svc. award, U. Ky. Coll. Medicine, 1993, Bluegrass Health Heroes award, 1994, Physician Hero award, American Coll. Med. Staff Devel., 1995. Fellow: ACP, Infectious Disease Soc. America; mem.: AMA (bd. trustees 2005—, sec. 2009—10, chair bd. trustees 2010—11, immediate past chair 2011—), Ky. Med. Assn. (pres. 1993—94, Ednl. Achievement award 1991, Disting. Svc. award), American Soc. Internal Medicine, Alpha Omega Alpha. Republican. Christian. Mailing: Univ Kentucky Chandler Med Ctr Office MN668 A 138 Leader Ave Lexington KY 40506 Office Phone: 859-323-8178. Office Fax: 859-323-8926. E-mail: adhove2@uky.edu. *

HOWANITZ, E. PAUL, thoracic surgeon; b. Wilkes-Barre, Pa., Jan. 15, 1950; s. Emil Paul Howanitz and Florence Schmick; m. Patricia Ann Denham, Mar. 14, 1980; children: Paul, Lauren. BS in Biology, Kings Coll., Wilkes-Barre, 1974; MD, Jefferson Med. Coll., Phila., 1978. Diplomate Am. Bd. Surgery, Am. Bd. Thoracic Surgery. Internship Thomas Jefferson U. Hosp., Phila.; gen. surgery residency Jefferson U. Hosp.; thoracic surgery residency Ohio State U. Hosp., asst. prof. thoracic surgery Columbus, 1986—92; vascular surgery fellowship U. Kans. Med. Ctr.; cardiothoracic surgeon St. Lukes Hosp., Duluth, Minn., 1992—93; chief cardiothoracic surgery St. Joseph Med. Ctr., Reading, Pa., 1993—2005, also bd. dirs.; chief cardiothoracic surgery Reid Hosp., Richmond, Ind., 2005—. Contbr. articles to profl. jours. Fellow: ACS, Am. Coll. Cardiology; mem.: Soc. Thoracic Surgeons, Am. Coll. Chest Physicians. Avocations: skiing, travel. Office: Reid Hosp Chief Cardiothoracic Surgery 1100 Reid Pky Richmond IN 47374

HOWARD, BETTIE JEAN, retired surgical nurse; b. Balt., Sept. 26, 1926; d. Milton James and Elizabeth Maria (Morgan) Knight; m. Stanley Lewis Howard; children: Amanda J. Scott, Sarah L. Howard, Mary McK. Strobel, Elizabeth M. Shaner, Roderick S. Diploma, Ch. Home and Hosp., Balt., 1947. RN, Md.; cert. bd. gastroenterology nurse. Head nurse med.-surg. unit Ch. Home & Hosp., Balt., 1947-48; surg. pediat. staff nurse Johns Hopkins Hosp., Balt., 1948-51, surg. pediat. acting head nurse, 1951-52, otolaryngology endoscopy head nurse, 1952-56; pediat. emergency rm. triage nurse U. Md. Hosp., Balt., 1966-68; head nurse surg. endoscopy nurse U. Md. Med. Ctr., Balt., 1968—2002, endofiberscope team coord. perioperative trauma, 2002—08. Adv. bd. Astra Merck for Patient Self Mgmt. Programs; spkr. in field. Contbr.: (book chpt. sect.) Policy and Politics for Nurses, 1993; contbr. articles to profl. jours. Chmn. Digestive Disease Nat. Coalition, Washington, 1993-95; coord. exec. panel Nat. Digestive Disease Info. Clearinghouse, NIH, Bethesda, Md., 1992-2002; adminstrv. bd. Grace United Meth. Ch., Balt., 1993-95. Recipient Woman of Yr. award, Am. Biog. Inst., 2010, Lifetime Achievement award, Dir. Gen. Internat. Biog. Ctr., Cambridge, Eng., 2010. Mem. Soc. Gastroenterology Nurses and Assocs., Inc. (pres. 1988-89, Gabriele Schindler award 1991), Soc. Internat. Gastroent. Nurses and Endoscopy Assocs.(charter, spkr. 1998, newsletter com. mem. 2008), Chesapeake Soc. Gastroenterology Nurses and Assocs. (charter, pres. 1981-83), Certifying Bd. Gastroenterology Nurses and Assocs. Inc. (pres. 1992-93). Republican. Avocations: reading, interior decorating, sewing, native-american collection. Home: 905 Saxon Hill Dr Cockeysville MD 21030-2905 Personal E-mail: bettiejhoward@comcast.net.

HOWARD, CECIL BYRON, retired pediatrician; b. Wallins, Ky., Apr. 16, 1927; s. William Knott and Maggie (Cawood) H.; m. Rebekah Ann Buckley, Mar. 4, 1931; children: Mark Byron, Sally Ann Howard Truxal, Maggie Elizabeth Howard Ray. BA, Vanderbilt U., 1949, MD, 1953. Intern U. Va. Hosp., Charlottesville, 1953-54; resident U. Tex. Med. Br., Galveston, 1954-56; pediatrician pvt. practice, Maryville, Tenn., 1956—2006. Dir. Christian Ch. Found. Handicapped, 1983—; elder 1st Christian Ch., Maryville, 1961-2003; scoutmaster Boy Scouts Am., 1964-79, chmn. Tuckaleechee Dist. Great Smoky Mountain Coun., 1973-75; mem. Blount County D.H.S. Child Abuse Rev. Team, 1965-2002. With U.S. Army, 1945-47. Fellow Am. Acad. Pediatrics; mem. Blount County Med. Soc. (pres. 1973), Maryville Optimist Club (pres. 1973). Republican. Avocations: hiking, piano, reading. Office: 1220 S Dogwood Dr Maryville TN 37804-5214

HOWARD, GRAHAME CHARLES WILLIAM, oncologist, director, consultant; b. London, May 15, 1953; s. William Titchmarsh and Shirley Warren (Parkinson) Howard; m. Andrea Mary North, 1978 (div. 2001); children: Richard, Michael, Charles. BSc London U., 1973; MB BS, London U., 1976; MD, 1986. Cert. Registrar The Royal Free Hosp., London, 1980—82; clin. scientist Addenbrookes Hosp., Cambridge, England, 1982—85, sr. registrar, 1985—87; cons. oncologist Edinburgh Cancer Ctr., 1987—2011, clin. dir., 1999—2005, clin. dir. cancer svcs., 2005—07. Chmn. house com. Sue Ryder Found. Home, Edinburgh, 1993—99; vice chmn. Scottish Intercoll. Guideline Network, 1996—2001; ex. chmn. S.E. Scotland Urological Oncology Cancer Network, SIGNmethodolgy Review Group. Co-editor (asst.): (med. jour.) Clinical Oncology, 2000—11; author: (clin. guidelines) Clinical Guidelines for Various Cancers, 1997—2011, The Tales of Dod; contbr. articles profl. jours., 1980. Avocations: music, sailing, walking.

HOWARD, JOHN JACKSON, federal agency administrator; MD, Loyola U., 1974; MS in Occupational Health, Harvard Sch. Pub. Health, 1982; JD, UCLA, 1986; LLM, George Washington U., 1987. Bd. Certified Occupational Physician. Internist UCLA Sch. Medicine Pulmonary Fellowship Program, Cedars-Sinai Med. Ctr., LA; med. dir. and chief clinician Philip Mandelker AIDS Prevention Clinic; asst. counselor to under sec. US Dept. Health & Human Services.; asst. prof. environmental and occupational medicine U. Calif., Irvine; chief Divsn. Occupational Safety and Health, State of Calif. Dept. Indsl. Rels., 1991—2002; dir. Nat. Inst. for Occupational Safety & Health (NIOSH), 2002—08, 2009—; prof. George Washington U. Sch. Medicine, 2003—08; sr. adv. to dir. Centers for Disease Control & Prevention (CDC), US Dept. Health & Human Services, 2008—09. Spl. coord. for response to health effects of Sept. 11th US Dept. Health & Human Services, 2006. Office: Nat Inst Ocupational Safety Hubert H Humphrey Bldg 200 Independence SW Rm 715H Washington DC 20201 *

HOWARD, JOHN W.S., mental health services professional, alcohol and drug abuse services professional, theology studies educator; b. Burlington, Nc, Mar. 11, 1956; s. John Henry and Nancy Marie (Watlington) Howard; m. Judy Carol Mayhand, Apr. 19, 1997; children: Trina Michelle Goins, Myra Helena Mayhand. Diploma in Bibl. Studies, Greensboro Bible Inst., 1988; BA, Shaw U., 1992; MDiv, Shaw U. Div. Sch., 1996; PhD in Philosophy, Atlantic Nat. U., 2005; PhD in Clin. Psychology, Windsor U., London, 2007. Lic. clin. addictions specialist 2009, cert. master addiction counselor 2009. Adj. prof. Guilford Coll., Greensboro, NC, 2004, Barton Coll. (Lay Acad.), Wilson, NC, 2005; pres., prof. theology Guilford Sch. Theol., Greensboro, 2006—. Author: What is Faith ? (Bronze Medal for Higher Academic Achievement, 1991). Office Phone: 336-202-5542. Business E-Mail: zorro123@triod.rr.com.

HOWARD, MARY TATUM, psychologist; b. San Francisco; d. Archibald and Mattie (Ross) Tatum; m. Robert M. Howard, Sept. 1951 (div. Sept. 1963). BA, W.Va. State Coll., 1948; MA, U. Mo., Kansas City, 1952; PhD, U. Minn., 1967. Tchr. Bd. of Edn., Kansas City, Kans., 1948-51; faculty Miles Coll., Birmingham, Ala., 1952-57; psychologist and dir. psychol. svc. Kenny Rehab. Inst., Mpls., 1963-68; prof. and dir. counseling ctr. U. D.C., 1968-73; prof. and dean student svcs. Hostos C.C./CUNY, Bronx, 1973-77; dean Kerney campus and urban affairs Mercer County C.C., Trenton, N.J., 1977-79; assoc. dir. Commn. on Higher Edn. Middle States Assn., Phila., 1979-80; psychologist and coord. of counseling Vets. Affairs Med. Ctr., St. Cloud, Minn., 1980—; adj. faculty St. Cloud State U., 1983—2010, St. Cloud Tech. Coll., 2002—. Asst. prof. Augsburg Coll., Mpls., 1963—68; cons. VISTA, 1965, Peace Corps, 1971, Washburn Clinic, Mpls., 1993—98; mem. State Operated Svcs. Bd., 2004—, State Colo. U. Diversity Coun., 2006—, MNSC U., Cin. State Coll. Contbr. articles to profl. jours. Bd. dirs., treas. Minn. Civil Liberties Union, Mpls.; treas. Minn., Dakota Conf., NAACP, 1992-95, v.p. St. Cloud br., 1990—; past pres. and mem. St. Cloud Symphony Orch. Bd., 1983-1990; bd. dirs. Girl Scouts U.S., St. Cloud, 1993-98, Boy Scouts, 1998—, United Way, 1998—2002; bd. dirs., sec. Jacob Wetterling Found., St. Cloud, 1991-95; mem. Dist. 742 Sch. Bd., treas., 2000—, bd. chmn., 2003. Fellow APA (divsn. 17, bd. dirs. 1988-89), Am. Psychol. Soc.; mem. AAUW, ACPA (pres. 1977-78), Minn. Psychol. Assn. (past bd. dirs.), Zonta, Ctrl. Minn. Psychology Assn. Avocations: bridge, reading, travel, writing. Home: 110 32nd Ave N Saint Cloud MN 56303-4140 E-mail: mthoward@cloudnet.com.

HOWARD, RICHARD RALSTON, II, medical health advisor, researcher, financial consultant; b. Winnfield, Kans., May 26, 1948; s. Richard Ralston and Ione (Mayer) H. BBA, Loyola U., New Orleans, 1970, MPH, Tulane U., 1977, MS, 1984, DrPH, 1988. Researcher Loyola U., 1973; educator Dominican Coll., New Orleans, 1977; educator Sch. Pub. Health Tulane U., New Orleans, 1978-82, researcher Sch. Medicine, 1979-88; med. health advisor Howard Med. Clinic, Slidell, La., 1982-91; founder The Inst. Econ. Tech. Rsch., New Orleans, 1993—, NIH grantee, 1979; VA grantee, 1984. Mem. Internat. Platform Assn., Am. Assn. Individual Investors, Beta Beta Beta. Achievements include research on the impact of the health food industry on nutrition awareness, cocaine testing through quantitative tear analysis, vitamin C and ophthalmic wound healing. Home: 3531 Nashville Ave New Orleans LA 70125-4339 Personal E-mail: rhoward787@aol.com.

HOWARD, SALLY, federal agency administrator; BA in History and English, Kans. State U., 1988; JD, U. Kans. Sch. Law, 1993. Assoc. Holbrook, Heaven & Fay, P.A., 1993—98; assoc. counsel Stevens & Brand, L.L.P, Topeka, 1998—2001; ptnr. Parkinson, Foth, Orrick & Brown, L.L.P., Lenexa, Kans., 2001—03; counsel Kans. Dept. Transp., 2001—03, chief counsel, 2003—07; chief counsel to Gov. Kathleen Sebelius State of Kans., 2007—09; dep. gen. counsel/acting gen. counsel US Dept. Health & Human Services, Washington, 2009—11, chief of staff, 2011—. Office: US Department Health & Human Services 200 Independence Ave SW Washington DC 20201 Office Fax: 202-690-8157. E-mail: COS_info@hhs.gov. *

HOWARD, TERRY THOMAS, obstetrician, gynecologist; b. Cleve., May 14, 1943; s. Henry and Paula H.; m. Phyllis C. Schaevitz, Aug. 21, 1965; children: Jennifer, Jason, Brian. AB magna cum laude, Columbia U., 1965; MD, Harvard Med. Sch., 1969. Diplomate Am. Bd. Ob-Gyn. Intern, resident gen. surgery Beth Israel Hosp., Boston, 1969-71; resident ob-gyn Boston Hosp. for Women (now named Brigham & Womens Hosp.), 1971-74; physician Chelmsford (Mass.) Med. Assocs., 1974-88, Harvard Cmty. Health Plan, Chelmsford, 1988-97, Harvard Vanguard Med. Assocs. (formerly Harvard Cmty. Health Plan), Chelmsford, 1998-2000; pvt. practice Chelmsford, 2000—. Trustee Lowell (Mass.) Gen. Hosp., 1987-2003, trustee emeritus, 2003—. Bd. dirs. Friends of the Children Concert Band, Chelmsford, 1981—, Lowell Cmty. Health Ctr., 2002-; trustee Congregation Shalom, Chelmsford, 1993-96; bd. trustees Merrimack Repertory Theatre, 2006-. Fellow Am. Coll. Obstetrics & Gynecology, Am. Coll. Surgeons; mem. Am. Soc. Reproductive Medicine.

HOWARD-PEEBLES, PATRICIA N., clinical cytogeneticist; b. Lawton, Okla., Nov. 24, 1941; d. J. Marion and R. Leona (prestidge) Howard; m. Thomas M. Peebles, Aug. 16, 1975. BSEd, U. Ctrl. Okla., 1963; student, Randolph-Macon Coll. Women, 1964; PhD in Zoology (Genetics), U Tex. at Austin, 1969. Diplomate Am. Bd. Med. Genetics; cert. clin. cytogeneticist, med. geneticist. Sci. and history tchr. Piedmont (Okla.) Pub. Schs., 1963-64; biochem. technician biochemistry sect. biology divsn. Oak Ridge (Tenn.) Nat. Lab., 1964-66; instr. rsch. pediatrics dept. pediatrics, instr. cytotech. U. Okla. Health Scis. Ctr., Oklahoma City, 1971-72; asst. prof., dir. Cytogenetics Lab. U. So. Miss., Hattiesburg, 1973-77, assoc. prof., dir. Cytogenetics Lab., 1977-80; assoc. prof. dept. pub. health, staff Lab. Med. Genetics U. Ala., Birmingham, 1980-81; assoc. prof., dir. Cytogenetics Lab. dept. pathology U. Tex. Health Sci. Ctr., Dallas, 1981-85, prof., dir. Cytogenetics Lab., 1985-87; prof. dept. human genetics Med. Coll. Va., Richmond, 1987—; clin. cytogeneticist, dir. postnatal lab. Genetics & IVF Inst., Fairfax, Va., 1987-98, co-dir. cytogenetics lab., 1998-2000; genetic, cytogenetic cons., 2000—. Am.

Cancer Soc. postdoctoral fellow dept. human genetics U. Mich. Med. Sch., Ann Arbor, 1969-70, dept. human genetics and devel. Coll. Physicians and Surgeons, Columbia U., N.Y.C., 1970-71; genetic cons. Ellisville (Miss.) State Sch., 1973-80; attending staff dept. pathology Parkland Meml. Hosp., Dallas County Hosp. Dist., 1981-87; mem. sci. adv. com. Fragile X Found., 1985-2002; mem. Internat. Standing Com. on Human Cytogenetic Nomenclature, 1991-96. Contbr. articles to profl. jours., chpts. to books; reviewer Am. Jour. Human Genetics, Am. Jour. Med. Genetics, Clin. Genetics, Human Genetics. Fellow Am. Coll. Med. Genetics (founding mem.); mem. Am. Soc. Human Genetics, Assn. Genetic Technologists, Tex. Genetics Soc. (chmn. planning com. ann. meeting 1984), Am. Cytogenetics Conf., Delta Kappa Gamma, Sigma Xi. Bapt. Office Phone: 214-893-8635. Personal E-mail: phpeebles@yahoo.com.

HOWARDS, STUART S., pediatric urologist; b. Milw., Mar. 29, 1937; s. Harvey H. and Anne (Levin) H.; m. Carter N. Howards, Aug. 20, 1966; children: Penelope P., Hugh N. BA, Yale U., 1959; MD, Columbia U., 1963. Cert. Am. Bd. Urology, 1975. Intern in surgery Peter Bent Brigham Hosp., Boston, 1963-64, resident in urology, 1968-71; resident in surgery Childrens Hosp., Boston, 1964-65; rsch. assoc. NIH, Bethesda, Md., 1965-68; asst. prof. urology and physiology U. Va., Charlotteville, 1971-74, assoc. prof., 1974-76, prof., 1976—, chief divsn. pediat. urology, 1986—. Chmn. exam com. Am. Bd. Urology, 1985-91, trustee, 1986-92, pres., 1992-93, exec. sec., 1997—; sr. sci. advisor to the dir. of urology. NIDDK/NIH, 2002—. Editor: Infertility in the Male, 1991, 3d edit., 1997, Adult and Pediatric Urology, 1991, 3d edit., 1995; editor Jour. Urology, 1983-2000. Maj. USPHS, 1965-68. Recipient Career Investigation award NIH, 1973-78. Fellow Am. Acad. Pediats.; mem. Am. Urol. Assn. (Golden Cystoscope award 1981, Scott award 1990, Hugh Young award 1991, Disting. Svc. award 2001), Clin. Soc. Genitourinary Surgeons, Am. Soc. Reproductive Medicine (bd. dirs. 1994-96, treas. 1996—), Soc. Andrology, Genitourinary Surgeons, Am. Assn. Genito-Urinary Surgeons (sec.-treas. 1992-97), Nat. Bd. Med. Examiners. Office Phone: 434-924-9559. Business E-Mail: ssh4e@virginia.edu. *

HOWATT, SISTER HELEN CLARE, human services administrator, director, retired school librarian; b. San Francisco, Apr. 5, 1927; d. Edward Bell and Helen Margaret (Kenney) H. BA, Holy Names Coll., 1949; MS in Libr. Sci., U. So. Calif., 1972; cert. advanced studies, Our Lady of Lake U., 1966. Joined Order Sisters of the Holy Names, Roman Cath. Ch., 1945. Life tchg. credential, life spl. svcs. credential, prin. St. Monica Sch., Santa Monica, Calif., 1957-60, St. Mary Sch., LA, 1960-63; tchr. jr. high sch. St. Augustine Sch., Oakland, Calif., 1964-69; tchr. jr. high math St. Monica Sch., San Francisco, 1969-71, St. Cecilia Sch., San Francisco, 1971-77; libr. dir. Holy Names U., Oakland, Calif., 1977-94; Spanish instr. Collins Ctr. Sr. Svcs., 1994-99; acct. St. Monica Sch., San Francisco, 1999—2002; libr. St. Martin de Porres Sch., Oakland, 2003—04; tutor Aurora Sch., Oakland, Calif., 2004—. Contbr. math. curriculum San Francisco Unified Sch. Dist., Cum Notis Variorum, publ. Music Libr., U. Calif., Berkeley. Contbr. articles to profl. jours. Needlecraft instr. Mercy Retirement Ctr., 2005—. Grantee, NSF, 1966, NDEA, 1966. Mem. Cath. Libr. Assn. (chmn. No. Calif. elem. schs. 1971-72). Home and Office: PO Box 907 Los Gatos CA 95031 *

HOWE, JOHN PRENTICE, III, health foundation president, physician; b. Jackson, Tenn., Mar. 7, 1943; s. John Prentice and Phyllis (MacDonald) H.; m. Tyrrell Flawn; children: Lindsey Warren, Brooke Olmsted, John Prentice IV. BA, Amherst Coll., 1965; MD, Boston U., 1969. Diplomate Am. Bd. Internal Medicine, internal medicine and cardiovascular disease. Research assoc. cellular physiology Amherst Coll., 1963-64; research assoc. cardiovascular physiology Boston U. Sch. of Medicine, 1966-67; lectr. medicine Boston U. Sch. Medicine, 1972-73; intern Boston City Hosp., 1969-70, asst. resident, 1970-71; rsch. fellow in medicine Harvard U., 1971-73, Peter Bent Brigham Hosp., 1971-73; survey physician Framingham Cardiovascular Disease Study, Nat. Heart and Lung Inst., 1971; asst. clin. prof. medicine U. Hawaii, 1973-75; from asst. prof. medicine to assoc. prof. U. Mass., 1975-85, assoc. prof., 1977-85, vice-chmn. dept. medicine, 1975-78, asst. dean continuing edn. for physicians, 1976-78, assoc. dean profl. affairs and continuing edn., 1978-80, acad. dean, 1980-85, vice chancellor, 1980-85, acting chmn. dept. anatomy, 1982-85; pres. U. Tex. Health Scis. Ctr., San Antonio, 1985-2000; pres., CEO Project HOPE, Millwood, Va., 2001—. Prof. medicine, U. Tex. Health Sci. Ctr., San Antonio, 1985-2005; chief of staff, U. Mass. Hosp., 1978-80. Mem. editl. bd. Archives Internal Medicine, 1991—2004; contbr. articles to profl. jours., chpts. to books. Trustee S.W. Found. for Biomed. Rsch., S.W. Rsch. Inst. Maj. M.C, U.S. Army, 1973-75; bd. trustees, Boston U., 2007. Alfred P. Sloan scholar Amherst Coll., 1962-65; recipient Ruth Hunter Johnson award Boston U. Sch. of Medicine, 1969 Fellow: Am. Coll. Chest Physicians, Am. Coll. Cardiology, ACP; mem.: Bexar County Med. Soc. (exec. com. 1985—2000, 1985—2000, pres. 1996), Tex. Soc. Biomed. Rsch. (past pres.), Tex. Med. Soc. (coun. med. edn. 1986—2001, ho. of dels. 1989—2001, pres.-elect 1997—98, pres. 1998—99), Am. Heart Assn. (fellow coun. clin. cardiology), AMA (coun. on sci. affairs 1993—2001, del. ho. dels. 1995—2001), Omicron Kappa Epsilon, Alpha Omega Alpha. Avocations: tennis, skiing. Business E-Mail: jhowe@projecthope.org.

HOWE, MARTHA MORGAN, microbiologist, educator; b. NYC, Sept. 29, 1945; d. Charles Hermann and Miriam Hudson (Wagner) M.; m. Terrance Gary Cooper. AB, Bryn Mawr Coll., 1966; PhD, MIT, 1972. Postdoctoral fellow Cold Spring Harbor Lab, NY, 1972-74; asst. prof. bacteriology U. Wis., Madison, 1975-77, assoc. prof., 1977-81, prof., 1981-84, Vilas prof., 1984-86; Van Vleet prof. virology U. Tenn., Memphis, 1986—. Mem. genetic biology rev. panel NSF, 1980-82, adv. panel prokaryotic biology, 2004—; mem. gen. rsch. support rev. com. NIH, Bethesda, 1982-86, mem. microbial physiology and genetics 2 study sec., 1997-2001; mem. sci. adv. com. instnl. rsch. grants Am. Cancer Soc., 1991-94. Assoc. editor Virology, 1983-92, Genetics, 1994; mem. editorial bd. Jour. Bacteriology, 1985-90; contbr. articles to profl. jours. and books. Recipient Rsch. Career Devel. award NIH, 1978; H.I. Romnes Faculty fellow U. Wis., 1981; Amoco Teaching award U. Wis., 1981. Fellow Am. Acad. Microbiology (bd. govs. 1991-99); mem. Am. Soc. Microbiology (chmn. divsn. H 1983, councillor divsn. H 1989-91, chmn. com. on awards 1990-96, pres.-elect 1999-2000, pres. 2000-2001, past pres. 2001-2002, Eli Lilly award 1985, ASM Founders Disting. Svc. award 1999, Alice C. Evans award 2007), Am. Soc. Biochemistry and Molecular Biology, Genetics Soc. Am. (bd. dirs. 1989-91, program com. 1989-90). Office: U Tenn Dept Molecular Scis 858 Madison Ave Memphis TN 38163-0001 Office Phone: 901-448-8215. Business E-Mail: mhowe@utmem.edu.

HOWE, WARREN BILLINGS, physician; b. Jackson Heights, NY, Oct. 25, 1940; s. John Hanna and Francelia (Rose) H.; m. Hedwig Neslanik, Aug. 7, 1971; children: Elizabeth Rose, Sarah Billings. BA, U. Rochester, 1962; MD, Washington U., St. Louis, 1965. Diplomate in family medicine and sports medicine Am. Bd. Family Practice, Nat. Bd. Med. Examiners. Intern Phila. Gen. Hosp., 1965-66; resident physician Highland Hosp./U. Rochester, 1969-71; family physician Family Medicine Clinic of Oak Harbor (Wash.), Inc., PS, 1971-92; student health physician, univ. team physician We. Wash. U., Bellingham, 1992—2011; ret., 2011. Team physician Oak Harbor HS, 1972-92; head tournament physician Wash. State HS Wrestling Championships, Tacoma, 1989-2006; attending physician Seattle Goodwill Games, 1990; clin. asst. prof. U. Wash. Sch. Medicine, 1975-82; bd. dirs. Nat. Operating Com. on Stds. for Athletic Equipment. Contbr. articles to profl. jours. and chpts. to books; editl. bd. The Physician and Sports Medicine Jour., 1984—2005. Bd. dirs. Oak Harbor Sch. Dist. #201, 1975-87; chmn. Oak Harbor Citizen's Com. for Sch. Support, 1988-90. Lt. comdr. USN, 1966-69, Vietnam. Recipient Disting. Svc. award City of Oak Harbor, 1984; named to Nat. Wrestling Hall of Fame, 2003; Paul Harris fellowship Oak Harbor Rotary Club. Fellow: Am. Acad. Family Physicians, Am. Coll. Sports Medicine (chair membership com. 1986—95, Citation award 2005); mem.: Am. Med. Soc. for Sports Medicine (Humanitarian award 2002), Wash. State Med. Assn. Episcopalian. Home: 4222 Northridge Way Bellingham WA 98226-7804 Office: WWU Student Health Ctr 2001 Bill McDonald Pkwy Bellingham WA 98225-9132 Office Phone: 360-650-3400.

HOWELL, DAVID D., oncologist, educator; b. Dec. 31, 1956; MD, U. Mich., 1983. Bd. cert. in radiation oncology, hospice and palliative medicine, cert. radiation oncologist. Ptnr., physician Clin. Assocs. Erie, 1987—2000; physician Cancer Care Group, 2000—03; asst. prof., dept. radiation oncology Case Western Res. U., 2003—04, Wayne State U., 2004—05, U. Mich., 2005—. Adj. asst. prof. Ctrl. Mich. U., 2006—11. Fellow: Am. Acad. Hospice and Palliative Medicine; mem.: Radiologic Soc. N.Am., Am. Coll. Radiology, Am. Soc. Clin. Oncology, Am. Soc. Radiation Oncology. Avocation: art. Office: 1500 E Medical Center Dr UH B2C 490/0010 Ann Arbor MI 48109 Business E-Mail: dhowell@umich.edu.

HOWELL, EMBRY MARTIN, researcher; b. Bethesda, Md., Nov. 18, 1945; d. David Grier and Louise Martin; m. Joseph Toy Howell III, Dec. 28, 1965; children: Andrew Martin, Jessica Ramsey. AB, Barnard Coll., 1968; MSPH, U. NC, 1972; PhD, George Washington U., 1991. Computer programmer Corp. Trust Co., NYC, 1968; computer programmer dept. city and regional planning U. NC, Chapel Hill, 1969—70; summer intern State Bd. Health, Raleigh, NC, 1972; rsch. asst. dept. ob-gyn Georgetown U. Hosp., Washington, 1972-73; health planner, biostatistician Health Systems Agy. No. Va., Falls Church, 1973-75; biostatistician Nat. Capital Med. Found., Washington, 1975-79; dir. SysteMetrics, Inc., Washington, 1979-92; v.p. Mathematica Policy Rsch., Washington, 1992—2000; prin. rsch. assoc. The Urban Inst., Washington, 2001—. Dir. Nat. Evaluation Healthy Start Evaluation; sprk. in field. Contbr. numerous articles to profl. jours. Vol. Children's Hosp. Hospice. USPHS trainee, 1971-72; recipient Agy. for Health Care Policy and Rsch. Dissertation Rsch. grant, 1990-91. Mem. Am. Pub. Health Assn., Acad. Health, Am. Evaluation Assn., Phi Beta Kappa. Avocations: singing, tennis, swimming.

HOWELL, JOEL DUBOSE, internist, educator; b. Tex., May 11, 1953; s. Wilson and Nora (Levitas) Howell; m. Linda C. Samuelson, June 26, 1976; children: Jonathan Samuelson, Benjamin Samuelson. BS, Mich. State U., 1975; MD, U. Chgo., 1979; PhD in History and Sociology of Sci., U. Pa., 1987. Intern, resident in internal medicine U. Chgo., 1979-82; Robert Wood Johnson clin. scholar U. Pa., Phila., 1982-84; instr. U. Mich., Ann Arbor, 1984-86, asst. prof., 1986-90, assoc. prof., 1990-97, prof., 1997—, Victor Vaughan prof. history medicine, 2001—. Editor: (book) Technology and American Medicine Practice: 1880-1930, 1988, Medical Lives and Scientific Medicine at Michigan; author: Technology in the Hospital, 1995. Scholar Henry J. Kaiser Family Fedn. Faculty, 1989—92, Charles E. Culpeper Found. Med. Humanities, 1992—96. Fellow: ACP, Am. Osler Soc., Am. Assn. History Medicine. Business E-Mail: jhowell@umich.edu.

HOWELL, RALPH RODNEY, pediatrician, geneticist, educator; b. Concord, NC, June 10, 1931; s. Fred Lee and Grace Mary (Blackwelder) H.; m. Sarah Vosburg Esselstyn, Nov. 19, 1960 (dec.); children: Grace Meyer, Elizabeth Eriksson, John Esselstyn. BS, Davidson Coll., 1953; MD, Duke U., 1957. Cert. Am. Bd. Pediatrics, Am. Bd. Med. Genetics/Clin. Biochem. Genetics. Intern Duke U., 1957—58, resident in pediat., 1958—59, rsch. fellow in pediat. and medicine, 1959—60; clin. assoc. and staff NIH, Bethesda, Md., 1960—64; assoc. prof. pediat. Johns Hopkins U., Balt., 1964—72; pediatrician-in-chief U. Children's Hosp. at Hermann, Houston, 1972—87, chmn. med. bd., 1972—87; David Park prof. U. Tex. Med. Sch., Houston, 1972—89, chmn. dept. pediat., 1972—87; prof., chmn. dept. pediat. U. Miami Sch. Medicine, 1989—2003, chmn. emeritus, prof., 2003—; sec. med. staff Jackson Meml. Hosp., Miami, 1992—93; sr. advisor dir. Eunice Kennedy Shriver Nat. Inst. Child Health & Human Devel., Bethesda, Md., 2003—11; v.p. med. staff Jackson Meml. Hosp., Miami, 1993—97, pres. med. staff, 1997—99. Cons. pediat. M.D. Anderson Hosp. and Tumor Inst., 1972-89; metabolism study sect. NIH, 1973-77, chmn. maternal and child health adv. com., 1983-86; exec. com. Nat. Practitioner Data Bank, 1995-98; nat. clin. adv. com. Nat. Found. March of Dimes, 1973-79; chmn. sci. adv. bd. Muscular Dystrophy Assn., 1989-2007, bd. dirs. chmn., 2007-; vis. prof. Inst. Molecular Genetics, Baylor Coll. Medicine, Houston, 1988; chief pediat. Holtz Childrens Hosp., U. Miami-Jackson Meml. Med. Ctr., 1989-2003; nat. adv. coun. Nat. Inst. Child Health and Human Devel., 1999-2003; chair HHS Sec.'s Adv. Com. on Hereditary Disorders in Children and Newborns, 2004—; Butterfield lectr. NICHD, U. Colo. Annual Meeting, Japan, 2009. Author: (with G.H. Thomas) Selected Screening Tests for Genetic Metabolic Diseases, 1973, (with F.H. Morriss, L.K. Pickering) Role of Human Milk in Infant Nutrition, 1986; contbr. articles to profl. jours. Trustee Jackson Lab. Bar Harbor, Maine, 1985-2003; dir. Rip van Winkle Found., Claverack, N.Y., 1987-92, pres., 1992—; bd. dirs. Congl. Ch. Found., Coconut Grove, Fla., 2003-2005, Dr. John T. Macdonald Found., Coral Gables, Fla., 2003-. Served to sr. surgeon, 1960—64, USPHS. Recipient Klauber Lectureship, Greenwood Genetic Ctr., 2004, Lifetime Achievement award, Duke Med. Sch., 2007, Butterfield Lectr. award, NICHD, U. Colo., 2009; named Jimmy Simon Hon. Lectr., Wake Forest U., 2005; Joseph P. Kenedy Jr. Sr. Rsch. scholar in Mental Retardation. Fellow AAAS, Am. Acad. Pediat. (com. on genetics); mem. AMA (ho. of dels. 1998—), Am. Pediat. Soc., Soc. Pediat. Rsch., Houston Pediat. Soc. (pres. 1978-79), Tex. Med. Assn., Soc. Inborn Errors of Metabolism (pres. 1981), Miami Pediat. Soc., Fla. Med. Assn., Am. Coll. Med. Genetics (bd. dirs., treas. 1995-96, pres.-elect 1997-98, pres. 1999—2000), Am. Coll. Med. Genetics (found. pres. 2003—), Nat. Adv. Coun. (liaison mem. 2006-), Nat. Human Genome Rsch. Inst. (chmn. ethical, social and legal issues rev. group 1996-2003), Pi Kappa Alpha, Cosmos Club (Washington). Congregationalist. Avocations: flying, classic auto collector. Office: U Miami Sch Medicine Dept Pediatrics D-820 PO Box 16820 Miami FL 33101-6820 Office Phone: 304-243-3985. Business E-Mail: rhowell@miami.edu.

HOWINGTON, JOHN, thoracic surgeon, educator; b. Nashville, Sept. 16, 1963; m. Anne Levans; children: George, Grace. MD, U. Tenn., Memphis, 1985—89. Chief thoracic surgery U. Hosp., Cin., 1999—. Assoc. prof. surgery U. Cin., 1999—. Mem. class XXVII Leadership Cin. Fellow: ACS (Ohio chpt., sec. 2004—), Am. Coll. Chest Physicians. Office: Univ Cin 231 Albert Sabin Way Cincinnati OH 45267-0558

HOWLAND, WILLARD J., radiologist, educator; b. Neosho, Mo., Aug. 28, 1927; s. Willard Jay and Grace Darlene (Murphy) H.; m. Kathleen V. Jones, July 28, 1945; children: Wyck, Candice, Charles, Thomas, Heather AB, U. Kans., 1948, MD, 1950; MA, U. Minn., 1958; DSc (hon.), Coll. Med. N.E. Ohio, 1990. Intern U.S. Naval Hosp., Newport, RI, 1950-51; pvt. practice medicine Kans., 1951-55; resident Mayo Clinic, Rochester, Minn., 1955-58; radiologist Ohio Valley Gen. Hosp., Wheeling, W.Va., 1959-67; prof., dir. diagnostic radiology Med. Units U. Tenn., Memphis, 1967-68; dir., chmn. dept. radiology Aultman Hosp., Canton, Ohio, 1968-87, pres. med. staff, 1978; prof., chmn. radiology coun. Coll. Medicine N.E. Ohio U., Rootstown, 1976-87, program dir. integrated radiology residency, 1976-87. Author, co-author three books and rsch. papers in field. With U.S. Army, 1945-46, USN, 1950-51. Fellow Am. Coll. Radiology; mem. AMA, Radiol. Soc. N.Am., Am. Roentgen Ray Soc., Ohio State Radiol. Soc. (pres. 1980-81), Masons. Democrat. Presbyterian. Home and Office: 4525 St James Cir NW Canton OH 44708 Home: 4525 Saint James Cir Nw Canton OH 44708-8902 Office Phone: 330-479-1046. Personal E-mail: whowland1@neo.rr.com.

HOWLETT, CAMERON ROLFE, pathologist, educator; b. Rotorua, New Zealand, June 3, 1940; s. Henry William and Beatrice Mary (Keane) H.; m. Annette Elizabeth Thomas, June 25, 1971; children: Andrew Cameron, Angus James. B Vet. Sci., U. Sydney, Australia, 1963, PhD, 1973. Comparative pathologist; registered specialist histopathologist Bd. Vet. Surgeons NSW. Pvt. practice vet. surgeon, Sydney, 1963-65, Eng., 1965-66; postgrad. scholar U. Sydney, 1967-71; lectr. Sch. Pathology U. NSW, Sydney, 1972-76, sr. lectr., 1976-86, assoc. prof., 1987-94, prof., 1995—. Australian del. Internat. Liaison Com. World Biomaterial Socs., 1993—; fellow biomaterials sci. and engring. Internat. Com. World Biomaterial Socs., 1996; hon. assoc. faculty vet. sci. U. Sydney, 1981—; cons. pathologist HCOA Profls., Sydney, 1987—; assessor rsch. groups issued by Australian Rsch. Coun. and Nat. Health & Med. Rsch., 1982—; vis. fellow Oxford (Eng.) U., 1987-88, 00; vis. prof. London U., 2000-01; mem. sci. and organizing coms. World Biomaterial, 1996, 00; chmn. World Biomed. Congress, 2004; chmn. 8th Internat. Meeting Ceramics, Cells and Tissues, Italy, 2003, 06; exec. mem. Internat. Union Biomaterial Sci. and Engring.; cons. vet. morbid pathologist Australian Phenomics Network, Histopathology & Organ Pathology; cons. in field. Contbr. articles to profl. jours.; editl. bd. Jour. of Biomed. Materials Rsch., Vet. and Comparative Orthopaedics and Traumatology Jour., Clin. Implant Dentistry and Related Rsch., Jour. Biomaterial Sci. Mem. therapeutic devices evaluation com. Fed. Govt., Canberra, 1989—2004, chmn. biomaterials panel, 1989—2004, mem. cardiovascular device panel, 1992—2000, mem. tracking device panel, 1995—2004. Travel grant Brit. Coun., Oxford U., 1979, 81; vis. fellow London U., 2000—03. Mem. Royal Coll. Vet. Surgeons, Coll. Vet. Scientists Australia, Australian Soc. Exptl. Pathology (treas., coun. mem. 1985-89), Australian Soc. Biomaterials (found. mem., pres., v.p., coun. mem. 1989—), Australian Vet. Assn. (life), Australian Soc. Vet. Pathology. Mem. Democratic Labour party. Avocations: dixieland jazz, reading, fishing, surfing. Office Phone: 61405139857. Business E-Mail: r.howlett@unsw.edu.au.

HOWSE, JENNIFER LOUISE, foundation administrator; b. Glendale, Calif., Jan. 31, 1945; d. Benjamin McCausland and Patricia Louise (Naylor) H. BA, Fla. State U., 1966, MA, 1968, PhD in Child Lang. Devel., 1973; LHD (hon.), SUNY, Bklyn., 1990. Rsch. asst., instr. Inst. Human Devel. Coll. Edn., Fla. State U., Tallahassee, 1967-69; dir. planning and evaluation Wakulla County Sch. System, Fla., 1969-72; dir. NARC/HEW Liaison Project Nat. Assn. for Retarded Citizens, Govtl. Affairs Office, Washington, 1972-73; dir. Developmental Disabilities Bur., dir. Bur. Tech. Assistance and Regulation Fla. Dept. Health and Rehab. Svcs., Tallahassee, 1973-75; exec. dir. Willowbrook Rev. Panel, NYC, 1975-78; assoc. commr. NY State Office Mental Retardation and Devel. Disabilities, NYC, 1978-80; state commr. mental retardation Dept. Pub. Welfare, Harrisburg, Pa., 1980-85; exec. dir. Greater NY chpt. March of Dimes Found., NYC, 1985-89, pres. White Plains, NY, 1990—. Advisor Ctr. for Family Life in Sunset Park, Bklyn., 1992—. Bd. dirs. Salk Inst., La Jolla, Calif.; active Pew Environ. Health Commn. Office: March of Dimes Found Nat Office 1275 Mamaroneck Ave White Plains NY 10605-5298 *

HOXIE, JAMES A., virologist, educator; BS in Biology, Wesleyan U., 1972; MD, U. Pa., 1976. Prof. cellular & microbiology U. Pa. Sch. Med.; dir. Penn Ctr. for AIDS Rsch. Office: Biomedical Rsch Bldg 421 Curie Blvd Rm 356 Philadelphia PA 19104 Office Phone: 215-898-0261, 215-989-0263. Office Fax: 215-573-7356. E-mail: hoxie@mail.med.upenn.edu.

HOY, MARJORIE ANN, entomology educator; b. Kansas City, Kans., May 19, 1941; d. Dayton J. and Marjorie Jean (Acker) Wolf; m. James B. Hoy; 1 child, Benjamin Lee AB, U. Kans., 1963; MS, U. Calif., Berkeley, 1966, PhD, 1972. Asst. entomologist Conn. Agrl. Expt. Sta., New Haven, 1973-75; rsch. entomologist U.S. Forest Svc.,

Hamden, Conn., 1975-76; asst. prof. entomology U. Calif., Berkeley, 1976-80, assoc. prof. entomology, 1980-82, prof. entomology, 1982-92, prof. emeritus, 1992—; Fischer, Davies and Eckes prof., dept. entomology and nematology U. Fla., Gainesville, 1992—; chmn. Calif. Gypsy Moth Sci. Adv. Panel, 1982—; mem. genetics resources adv. com. USDA, 1992—, mem. adv. com. agrl. biotech., 2000—02; mem. com. on biol. threats to agrl. plants and animals NRC and NAS, 2001—02. Chmn. Calif. Gypsy Moth Sci. Adv. Panel, 1982—; mem. genetics resources adv. com. USDA, 1992—, mem. adv. com. agrl. biotech., 2000—01; F.E. Guyton disting. lectr. Auburn (Ala.) U., 1997; mem. com. on biol. threats to agrl. plants and animals NRC and NAS, 2001—02; sci. cons. transgenic insects Pew Initiative Food and Biotech. Editor, co-editor: Genetics in Relation to Insect Managment, 1979, Recent Advances in Knowledge of the Phytoseiidae, 1982, Biological Control of Pests by Mites, 1983, Biological Control in Agricultural IPM Systems, 1985, Insect Molecular Genetics, 1994, 2d edit., 2003, The Phytoseiidae as Biological Control Agents of Pest Mites and Insects: A Bibliography, 1996, Managing the Citrus Leafminer, 1996; mem. editl. bd. Internat. Jour. Pest Mgmt., Biol. Control, Biocontrol Sci. and Tech., Environ. Biosafety Rsch.; contbr. articles to profl. jours. Mem. Sec. Agr.'s adv. com. agrl. biotech.; cons. Pew Charitable Trust. Recipient citation for outstanding achievments in regulatory entomology Fla. Divsn. Plant Industry, 1995, USDA honor award Sec. of Agr., 1996, award for sci. Nat. Agri-Mktg. Assn., 1998, sr. faculty award U. Fla. chpt. Gamma Sigma Delta, 1998, Biol. Control Scientist of Yr., Internat. Orgn. Biol. Control, 2004. Fellow AAAS, Royal Entomol. Soc. London, Entomol. Soc. Am. (mem. Pacific br. governing bd. 1985, Bussart award 1986, Founder's Meml. award 1992), Coun. Agr. Sci. and Tech. (Charles Black award 2004); mem. Nat. Acad. Scis. (com. on biol. threats to agr. plants and animals), NY Acad. Scis., Am. Genetic Assn., Internat. Orgn. Biol. Control (v.p. 1984-85, Disting. Scientist award 2004), Am. Inst. Biol. Scis. (adv. coun. 1996-98, governing bd. 1999-2001), Acarological Soc. Am. (governing bd. 1980-84, pres. 1992), Soc. for Study of Evolution, Fla. Entomological Soc. (Team Rsch. award 1997, Outstanding Tchg. award 1999), Phi Beta Kappa, Sigma Xi (chpt. sec. 1979-81, Sr. Faculty Rsch. award 1996). Avocations: hiking, gardening, snorkeling. Home: 4320 SW 83rd Way Gainesville FL 32608-4131 Office: U Fla Dept Entomology and Nematology PO Box 110620 Gainesville FL 32611-0620 Home Phone: 352-335-7839; Office Phone: 352-273-3961. Business E-Mail: mahoy@ifas.ufl.edu.

HOYE, ROBERT EARL, systems science educator; b. Warwick, RI, Jan. 12, 1931; s. S. Earl and Alice (Landry) H.; m. Patricia Buswell, Aug. 20, 1955 (dec. May 22, 2002); children: Robert Earl Jr., Joanne D., Peter M., Kathleen B. BA, Providence Coll., 1953; MS, St. John's U., NYC, 1955; PhD, U. Wis., Madison, 1973. Instr. St. John's U., 1953-55; dir. guidance Middleboro (Mass.) Pub. Schs., 1955-56, Rutland (Vt.) Pub. Schs., 1956-57; dean Champlain (Vt.) Coll., 1957-58; supt. Frontier Regional Sch. Dist., Deerfield, Mass., 1958-60; New Eng. dir. Sci. Rsch. Assocs. subs. IBM, Chgo., 1960-65; nat. dir. Learning Systems div. Xerox Corp., NYC, 1965-66, dir. Instrnl. Media Lab. U. Wis., Milw., 1966-73; asst. v.p. U. Louisville, 1974-81, prof. cmty. health Sch. Medicine, 1981-92, prof. urban policy, coord. grad. program in health systems, 1981-95, prof. edn., 1992-95, prof. emeritus, 1995—. Cons. to mgmt., Louisville, 1966—; mem. faculty health svcs. Walden U., 1988—; vis. prof. exec. leadership U. Sarasota, 1995-2001 Author: Index to Computer Based Learning, 1973; co-author: Home Health, 1996; editor Edn. Jour., 1968-73; also articles. Recipient cert. of merit San Diego State U., 1983, Grad. Teaching Excellence award U. Louisville, 1984, gold medal Project Innovation, 1984, Outstanding Faculty Mem. award Walden U., 2000. Fellow Am. Acad. Med. Adminstrs. (diplomate, chmn. editl. bd. 1986-94, dir. Ky. chpt. 2006—), Royal Soc. Health (Statesman in Healthcare Adminstrn. award 1992). Democrat. Roman Catholic. Personal E-mail: rehoye@att.net.

HOYER, STENY HAMILTON, United States Representative from Maryland; b. NYC, June 14, 1939; s. Steen T. and Jean Baldwin (Slade) H.; m. Judith Elaine Pickett, June 17, 1961 (dec. Feb. 1997); children: Susan, Stefany, Anne. BS in Polit. Sci., U. Md., 1963; LLB, Georgetown U., 1966. Bar: Md. 1966. Exec. asst. to Senator Daniel B. Brewster US Senate, 1962-66; assoc. Haislip & Yewell, Marlow Heights, Md., 1966-69; mem. Md. State Senate, 1966—79, pres., 1975—79; assoc. Hoyer & Fannon, District Heights, Md., 1969-81; pvt. law practice, 1981-89; mem. US Congress from 5th Md. Dist., 1981—, dep. majority leader (dep. majority whip), 1987—89, asst. minority leader (minority whip), 2003—07, 2011—, majority leader, 2007—11; chmn. US House Democratic Caucus, 1989—95. Mem. Md. Bd. Higher Edn., 1979-81; mem. Balt. Council Fgn. Rels.; bd. visitors U. Md. Sch. Pub. Affairs Recipient Excellence in Pub. Svc. award, Am. Acad. Pediatrics, 1991, Pub. Svc. award, Am. Assn. Pub. Health Dentistry, 1997, Jack Niles Medal of Honor, Pub. Employees Roundtable, 1999, Excellence in Immunization award, Nat. Partnership for Immunization, 2001, Freedom award, Nat. Assn. Secretaries of State, 2003, Nathan Davis award for Outstanding Govt. Svc., AMA, 2008, Leadership award, Nat. Org. on Fetal Alcohol Syndrome, 2005; named State Official of Yr., Md. Mcpl. League, 1971, Washingtonian of Yr., Washington mag., 1988, Champion of Pediatric Rsch., Children's Nat. Med. Ctr., 1995; named an Outstanding Young man, Md. Jaycees, 1975. Mem. U. Md. Alumni Assn. (trustee), Phi Sigma Alpha, Omicron Delta Kappa, Delta Theta Phi, Sigma Chi. Democrat. Baptist. Office: US Congress 1705 Longworth House Office Bldg Washington DC 20515-2005 also: 401 Post Office Rd Ste 202 Waldorf MD 20602 *

HOYME, ROGER, medical association administrator; b. Dell Rapids, SD, May 22, 1959; BA, Augustana Coll., Sioux Falls, SD, 1981. Bus. office & health info. dir. Brown Clinic, P.L.L.P., 2006—. Office: 506 1st Ave SE Watertown SD 57201 Business E-Mail: roger.hoyme@brownclinic.org.

HOYME, UDO ALBERT BRUNO, gynecologist, obstetrician; b. Kyritz, Germany, Apr. 25, 1948; s. Siegfried and Ursula Hoyme; m. Helga Marion Hoess, Apr. 25, 1980; children: Joanna Katharina, Justus Karl, Julian Klemens. Dr. med. Dr. med. habil. (hon.), U. Med. Sch., Berlin, 1970, U. Med. Sch., Hamburg, 1973. Specialist in ob-gyn. Med. Bd. Germany, 1979. Resident ob-gyn. Auguste-Viktoria-Krankenhaus, Berlin, 1975—76; rsch. fellow urology Veterans Adminstrn. Hosp., Madison, 1976—77; resident, staff ob-gyn. U. Hosp., Tuebingen, Germany, 1977—87, staff ob-gyn. Essen, Germany, 1987—93; chmn. Med. Acad. - Helios Klinikum, Erfurt, Germany, 1993—. Vis. prof. U. Wash., Seattle, 1982—83. Contbr. articles to profl. jours. Pres. Rotary Internat., Erfurt. Lutheran. Achievements include research in prevention of prematurity; nosocomial infections, urinary tract infections, sexually transmitted diseases, salpingitis, oncology-breast surgery. Avocations: reading, travel, aviation. Office: Dept Ob Gyn Helios Klinikum Nordhäuser St 74 Erfurt D 99089 Germany Office Fax: 49 361 7814002. Business E-Mail: udo.hoyme@helios-kliniken.de.

HOYOS CAMPILLO, JAIRO ENRIQUE, ophthalmologist, director; b. Cartagena de Indias, Colombia, Sept. 21, 1942; MD, U. Zaragoza, Spain, 1969; PhD, U. Autonoma Barcelona, 1993. Med. dir. Inst. Oftalmologico Hoyos, 1972—; surg. team boss Hosp. San Felix, Sabadell, 1975—77; ophthalmic cons. Clínica Infantil del Niño Jesus, Sabadell, 1975—82; ophthalmologist Ciudad Sanitaria Valle de Hebron, Barcelona, 1977—83, chief cornea and external disease, 1983—84. Founder, pres. Keratomileusis Study Group, 1993—2010. Contbr. articles to profl. publs. Recipient Gold medal, Indian Intraocular Implant & Refractive Surgery Conv., 2001; Prof. Ramon Castroviejo fellow, NY, 1974, fellow, Cirugía Refractiva en el Shepard Eye Inst., Santa María, Calif., 1985. Mem.: SECOIR, SEO, Keratomileusis Study Group (Barraquer award 2009), AAO, ASCRS. Avocations: sailing, travel, scuba diving. Office: Rambla 62 Sabadell Barcelona 08201 Spain Office Fax: 0034937276359. Business E-Mail: jairoca@iohoyos.com.

HOZAWA, KOJI, otolaryngologist; b. Morioka, Iwate, Japan, Aug. 8, 1956; s. Jiro and Miyako Hozawa; m. Hiromi Kikuchi, Aug. 1, 2000; children: Saharu, Ayano, Kaisei. MD, Tohoku U., Sendai, Japan, 1980, DSc, 1987. Diplomate. Rsch. fellow Harvard Med. Sch., Boston, 1986—88; vis. scholar Wash. U., Seattle, 1992; asst. prof. Tohoku U. Sch. Medicine, Sendai, 1995—2001, assoc. prof., 2001—02; chief dir. Sendai Shakai Hoken Hosp., 2002—10; clin. prof. Tohoku U. Hosp., 2009—; chief med. sect. Japanese Physicians Soc. Homeopathy, 2009—, chief med. Spection, 2009—; clin. prof. Tohoku U. Hosp., 2008—; chief med. sect. Japanese Physicians Soc. Homeopathy, 2009—; dir. Hozawa ENT Clinic, 2011—, Holistic Med. Ctr. Tree of Life, 2011—. Vis. lectr. Chinese Med. Sch., Shengyang, China, 1997—2000; lectr. Japan Internat. Coop. Agy., Tokyo, 1997—2000; sec. gen. Otological Soc. Japan, Sendai, 1997—98, Internat. Symposium on Recent Advances in Otitis Media, Sendai, 1998—2000; authorized rschr. Ministry Health and Welfare, Tokyo, 1999—2001. Editor: Recent Advances in Otitis Media, 2001; contbr. articles to profl. jours. Named one of Best Drs. in Japan, 2008—09. Mem.: Japan Broncho-Esophageal Soc. (coun. mem. 2005—), Internat. Otopathology Soc., Otolaryngol. Soc. Japan (mem. pub. rels. sect. 1997—2002). Avocations: golf, saxophone, reading, theater, travel. Home: 1-1-13-1301 Katahira Aoba-ku Sendai 980-0812 Japan Office: Hozawa ENT Clinic 2-14-18-303 Kokubuncho Aoba-Ku Sendai 980 0803 Japan Office Phone: 81 22 397 8338.

HOZUMI, MOTOO, medical educator, researcher; b. Fukushima, Japan, Mar. 12, 1933; s. Akiine and Fumi Hozumi; m. Sakiko Wakabayashi, May 4, 1963; children: Yuko, Masamichi, Ayako. BSc, Tokyo U. Edn., 1956, MSc, 1958, DSc, 1961. Rsch. mem. Nat. Cancer Ctr. Rsch. Inst., Tokyo, 1962-64, chief ctrl. lab., 1964-75; dir. dept. chemotherapy Saitama (Japan) Cancer Ctr. Rsch. Inst., 1975-93, dir., 1990-93; spl. rsch. Saitama (Japan) Cancer Ctr., 1993-96. Rsch. mem. Roswell Park Meml. Inst., Buffalo, N.Y., 1965-67; vis. prof. Showa U. Med. Sch., Tokyo, 1988-2001; cons. Japan Immunoresearch Inst., Takasaki, Japan, 1993-98. Author: Advances in Cancer Research, 1983, Ciba Foundation Symposium, 1990, Status of Differentiation Therapy, 1991, (rev. jour.) CRC Critical Rev. Oncol./Hematol., 1985, Internat. Jour. Hematology, 1998. Recipient Princess Takamatsu Cancer Rsch. Found. prize, 1974. Mem. AAAS, Japanese Cancer Assn. (councilor 1973-98, emeritus mem. 1999—), Japan Hematol. Soc. (councilor 1992-98, meritorious mem. 1999—), Am. Assn. for Cancer Rsch. (emeritus). Avocation: music. Home: 12-288 Fukasaku Minuma Saitama 337-0003 Japan Personal E-mail: hozumim@olive.ocn.ne.jp.

HRABAL, ANTONIN, physician, educator; b. Prilepy, Kromeriz, Czech Republic, May 21, 1957; s. Bedrich and Stepanka (Von Larisch) H. MD, Charles U., Prague, Czech Republic, 1982, PhD, 1992; DSc, U. San Jose, Costa Rica, 1998. Med. diplomate. Rschr. Charles U., Prague, 1976-88, physician, tchr., 1985-92; physician, rschr. Inst. Hippokrates, 1992-99; tchr. Palacki U., Olomouc, Czech Republic, 1989-97, 99, U. Ctr. Inst. Hippokrates, 1997—2000; prof. Hippokrates U., 2000—, Cosmopolitan U., 2000—. Chmn. Inst. Hippokrates, 1992-99; head physician U. Hosp., 1995-99; founder Found. Nadace Hippokrates, 1997-99; head rsch. Univ. Ctr., 1998-99. Mem. N.Y. Acad. Scis. Achievements include inventor of regeneration of tissues by deep stimulation through interference of electric and magnetic fields; deep brain stimulation; special immunomodulation diagnostic and therapeutic methodology therapy of autoimmune diseases, anti-aging methodology/telomeraza and hormone replacement. Home: 2F-113 5516 BOULDER HWY STE 2F Las Vegas NV 89122-6000 Personal E-mail: professorhrabal@yahoo.com.

HRABEC, GEORGE B., microbiologist; b. Hrubeshiv, Ukraine, June 19, 1941; arrived in U.S., 1949; s. Roman O. and Mera Hrabec; m. Vera M. Baranowskyj, Jan. 20, 1968; children: Taras, Larissa. BS, Ohio State U., 1966; MS, U. S.W. La., 1968. Asst. chief microbiology Salem (Mass.) Hosp., 1969—84; microbiology-serology supr. Widden Meml. Hosp., Everett, Mass., 1984—97; microbiology technologist Winchester (Mass.) Hosp., 1998; microbiol. supr. Diagnostic Lab. Medicine, Bedford, Mass., 2002—; pvt. practice adolescent medicine Peabody, Mass. Indsl. microbiol. cons. Eastman Gelatine Corp., Peabody, Mass., 1979—82; adj. prof. Northeastern U., Boston, 1985—; clin. microbiology technologist Melrose-Wakefield Hosp., 1993—96; chief microbiologist Sunny Acres Hosp., Cleve., 1966—67; chief food microbiologist Seacoast Products, Inc., Lafayette, La., 1968—70; microbiologist Washington Hosp. Ctr., 1967—68; lectr. in microbiology Salem Hosp. Sch. Nursing, 1975—76; sales rep., med. tng. coord. Northshore Products, Beverly, Mass., 1985—93. Mem.: Coll. Am. Pathologist Surveyor, Engr. Soc. (pres./treas. Boston chpt.), Nat. Am. Soc. Microbiologists, Phi Sigma. Greek Catholic. Avocations: tennis, reading, gardening. Home: 19 Trinity St Danvers MA 01923 Office: Diagnostic Lab Medicine 14 Crosby Dr Bedford MA 01730 Office Phone: 781-275-0855 124. E-mail: bibi4@prodigy.net.

HRADÍLEK, PAVEL, neurologist; b. Ostrava, Czech Republic, Mar. 17, 1970; s. Zdenek Hradílek and Zdenka Hradílková. MD, Med. Faculty, Olomouc, Czech Republic, 1994, PhD, 2008. Neurologist Dpt. Neurology, U. Hosp., Ostrava, 1994—, ms specialist, 1994—. Contbr. scientific papers. Home: Dolní Domaslavice 349 739 38 Czech Republic

HRADSKY, ONDREJ, physician; b. Olomouc, Nov. 4, 1980; MD, 2005. Physician U. Hosp. Motol, 2005—. Office: V Uvalu 84 Prague 15002 Czech Republic Business E-Mail: ondrej.hradsky@email.cz.

HREBINKO, RONALD L., urologist; MD, U. Pitts. Diplomate Am. Bd. Urology. Resident surgery dept. Univ. Pitts. Med. Ctr.; fellow Roswell Pk. Cancer Inst., Buffalo; hosp. affiliations include Univ. Pitts. Med. Ctr. Magee-Womens Hosp., Pa., Univ. Pitts. Med. Ctr. Mercy, Univ. Pitts. Med. Ctr. Shadyside, Univ. Pitts. Med. Ctr. Presbyn. Office: University of Pittsburgh Medical Center Shadyside Medical Bldg 5200 Centre Ave Ste 209 Pittsburgh PA 15232 Office Phone: 412-605-3000.

HRICAK, HEDVIG, radiologist; arrived in US, 1972; MD, U. Zagreb, 1970; DMS, Karolinska Inst., 1992; Dr. (hon.), Ludwig Maximilion U., 2005. Diplomate Am. Bd. Radiology 1978. Intern in radiology Hosp. M. Stojanovic, Zagreb, 1971—72; resident in radiology St. Joseph Mercy Hosp., Pontiac, Mich., 1974—77; fellow in diagnostic radiology Henry Ford Hosp., Detroit, sr. staff diagnostic radiology, 1978—81; asst. clin. prof. diagnostic radiology U. Mich., Ann Arbor, 1979—81; from asst. prof. to assoc. prof. U. Calif., San Francisco, 1982—86, prof. radiology, urology, radiation oncology, ob-gyn., 1986—99; chief abdominal sect. dept. radiology U. Calif. Med Ctr., San Francisco, 1982—2000; chmn. dept. radiology Meml. Sloan-Kettering Cancer Ctr., NY, 1999—; prof. radiology Weill Med. Coll. Cornell U., NY, 2000—. Hon. prof. U. Zagreb, 1997; vis. prof. ovr 30 instns. Author more than 20 books in field; assoc. editor, Jour. of Magnetic Resonance Imaging, 2001—, Radiology, 1998—, Jour. of Women's Imaging, 1996—, others; contbr. more than 315 articles to sci. and profl. jours. Decorated Order of Croatian Morning Star Katarina Zrinska, Presdl. award; recipient Marie Curie award, Soc. Women in Radiology, 2002, Beclere medal, 2005, Gold medal, Assn. U. Radiologists, 2007, Moroccan Merit medal, International Soc. Radiology, 2008; grantee numerous grants in field, including NIH, Nat. Cancer Inst., Am. Cancer Soc., Dept. of Def.; numerous hon. lectureships. Fellow Am. Coll. Radiology, Internat. Soc. Magnetic Resonance in Medicine (gold medal 2003), Soc. Uroradiology (corrs. mem., pres. 2001-03); mem. Acad. Radiology Rsch. (bd. dirs. 1997—), Radiol. Soc. N.Am. (chmn. pub. info. adv. bd. 1997-2002, pres. 2009-10), Soc. for the Advancement of Women's Imaging (pres. 1997-99), Calif. Acad. Medicine (pres. 1999), Croation Acad. Sci. and Art (hon.), German, Radiol. Soc. (hon.), Chinese Radiol. Soc. (hon.), Japanese Radiol. Soc. (hon.), Austrian Roentgen Soc. (hon.) Brit. Inst. Radiology (hon.), Inst. of Medicine, Royal Coll. Radiologists (hon.), Swedish Soc. Medicine (hon.), Journees Francaises de Radiologie (hon.), Israel Radiol. Assn. (hon.) Italian Radiol. & Imaging Assn. (hon). Business E-Mail: hricakh@mskcc.org.

HRINCZENKO, BORYS WALTER, oncologist, hematologist, medical educator, medical researcher, consultant; s. Walter and Maria Hrinczenko; m. Helena Teresa Marcyniak, Sept. 5, 1992; 1 child, Nicholas. BA magna cum laude, NYU, 1975; PhD, U. Kans., 1983; MD, SUNY, Bklyn., 1992. Diplomate Nat. Bd. Med. Examiners, in internal medicine and in hematology and oncology Am. Bd. Internal Medicine. Rsch. assoc. U. Chgo., 1983—85; project supr. Nat. Starch & Chem. Co., Bridgewater, NJ, 1985—88; med. intern and resident Mayo Clinic, Rochester, Minn., 1992—95; hematology/oncology fellow NIH, Bethesda, Md., 1995—98, clin. rsch. assoc., 1998—2000; asst. prof. medicine U. Ala., Birmingham, 2000—04; staff physician MetroHealth Med. Ctr., Cleve., 2004—; asst. prof. medicine Case We. Res. U., Cleve., 2005—. Cons. TheraMed, Inc., Rockville, Md., 2000, Network for Oncology Comm. and Rsch., Atlanta, 2003; oncology investigator rsch. adv. bd. Amgen, Inc., Thousand Oaks, Calif., 2003; mem. editl. bd., sci. manuscript reviewer Foxwell Davies & Co., London, 2003; med. adv. bd. Physicians Consulting Network, Mt. Arlington, NJ, 2003; spkr. rep. Millennium Pharms., Inc., Boston, 2003, Pfizer, 2004—05; mem. Clin. Adv. Panel, West Orange, NJ, 2003. Contbr. articles to profl. jours. Recipient Caducean Soc., NYU, 1973, NYU Coat of Arms Soc., 1974, Founder's Day award, 1975; named one of America's Top Physicians, Consumer's Rsch. Coun. of Am., 2003, America's Top Oncologists, 2007—09; NY State Regents scholarship, NY Bd. of Edn., 1971, Berger Scholarship in Chemistry, U. Kans., 1978. Mem.: ACP, AMA, Eastern Coop. Oncology Group, Am. Chem. Soc., N.Y. Acad. Sci., Am. Soc. Clin. Oncology, Am. Soc. Hematology, Phi Lambda Upsilon. Achievements include the first to discover anomalous dendritic cell function in sickle cell disease; the first to outline the increased purine biochemical catabolic process in sickle cell disease and explored potential therpeutic targets; the first to show that platelets from sickle cell disease patients display an atypical response to nitric oxide drugs; research in applied biomedical imaging techniques and discovered abnormal mitochondrial function in the skeletal muscle of sickle cell disease patients; discovered useful biomarkers of oxidative stress in sickle cell disease that assessed disease severity and response to therapy. Avocations: photography, chess, piano, ping pong/table tennis. Home: 434 Tulip Tree Ln East Lansing MI 48823-2511

HRUZA, GEORGE J., dermatologist, educator; MD, NYU, 1982. Diplomate Am. Bd. Dermatology, 1986. Resident dermatology NYU Med Ctr.-Skin Cancer Unit, NYC, 1983—86; fellow laser surgery Mass Gen. Hosp.-Harvard, Boston, 1986—87; fellow mohs surgery Univ. Wis. Affiliated Hosp., Madison, Wis., 1987—88; dir. Laser & Dermatologic Surgery Ctr.; bd. dirs. Am. Coll. of Mohs Micrographic Surgery and Cutaneous Oncology; clin. prof. dermatology, otolaryngology St. Loius Univ., hosp. affiliation includes, St. Luke's Hosp. Writer (jour.) Jour. Watch Dermatology, 1993—, assoc. editor, bd. mem., 2007. Mem.: Am. Soc. of Laser Medicine and Surgery (chair 2003). Office: Laser & Dermatologic Surgery Center Ste 101 1001 Chesterfield Pkwy E Chesterfield MO 63017 Office Phone: 314-878-3839.

HRYNKOW, SHARON HEMOND, federal agency administrator, neuroscientist, researcher; BA in Biology, RI Coll., 1983; PhD in Neurosci., U. Conn., 1990; student, U. Oslo, Norway. Health/sci. officer Bur. Oceans, Internat. Environ. & Sci. Affairs, US Dept. State, Washington, 1992-95; sci. policy analyst Fogarty Internat. Ctr. (FIC), NIH, Bethesda, Md., 1995-97, spl. asst. FIC office of dir., 1997-99, dep. dir. FIC, 2000—07, acting dir., 2004—06, assoc. dir. Nat. Inst. Environ. Health Scis. (NIEHS), 2007—. Mem. adv. bd. Nat. Coun. Internat. Health, Washington, 1997. Contbr. articles to profl. jours. Recipient Order of Merit, King of Norway, 2008, Presdl. Rank award for outstanding efforts in sr. exec. svc., US Dept. State. Mem.: APHA, AAAS (mem. com. on sci., engring. & pub. policy), Coun. Fgn. Rels., Women in Neurosci., Soc. Neurosci. (mem. internat. affairs com.), Norwegian Soc. Washington, Am. Scandinavian Assn. Home: Apt T3 3940 Persimmon DR Fairfax VA 22031-4165 Office Phone: 301-496-3511. Office Fax: 301-402-0563. Business E-Mail: hrynkows@niehs.nih.gov.

HSEU, YOU CHENG, nutritionist, researcher; b. Taipei, Taiwan, July 30, 1962; s. Chung Lung Hseu and Yu Chung Fan; m. Hsin Ling Yang; children: Chih Shuan, Chih Ko. PhD, Nat. Tsing Hua U., Hsinchu, Taiwan. Cert. nutritionist Taiwan, 1989. Asst. prof. Fooyin U., Kaoshiung, Taiwan; assoc. prof. Chungtai Inst. Health Sci. and Tech., Taichung, Taiwan; prof. Ctrl. Taiwan U. Sci. and Tech., Taichung, China Med. U., Taichung. Contbr. articles to profl. jours. Cons. Fooyin U. Hosp., Kaohsiung, Taiwan. Lt. US Army, 1987—88, Taiwan. Recipient, Dr. Hsu Chien-tien Found., 1995. Mem.: Nutrition Soc. Taiwan. Achievements include research in etiology of humic acid-induced vascular disorders associated with blackfoot diseases for humans in Taiwan; antrodia camphorata as a traditional Chinese medicine has been shown to exhibit antioxidant and anticancer properties valuable for application in drug products in Taiwan. Office: China Med U 91 Hsueh Shih Rd Taishung 40421 Taiwan

HSIAO, KWANG-JEN, genetics and biochemistry educator; b. Canton, Guangdong, China, Dec. 14, 1948; s. Mong-Neng and Wan-Chieng (Chu) H.; m. Yuh-Yeh Yang, Jan. 20, 1973; children: Hann C., Yi-Ching. BSc in Chemistry, Chung-Yuan U., Republic of China, 1971; PhD in Biomed. Scis., CUNY, 1978. Assoc. prof. biochemistry Nat. Yang Ming U. (formerly Nat. Yang Ming Med. Coll.), Taipei, Taiwan, 1979-80, prof. Inst. of Genetics, 1989—2004; chmn. Inst. Genetics, Taipei, 2000—03; dean gen. affairs Nat. Yang Ming U. (formerly Nat. Yang Ming Med. Coll.), Taipei, Taiwan, 1990-93, dir. Genome Rsch. Ctr., 2000—04; vis. assoc. investigator Vets. Gen. Hosp., Taipei, 1980-81, assoc. investigator, 1981-83, investigator dept. med. rsch., 1983—90, dir. biochem. genetic lab., 1984—2004, adj. investigator, 1990—; dir. dept. rsch. resources Nat. Health Rsch. Insts., 1996-98; vice chancellor U. Sys. Taiwan, 2003—04. Cons. in clin. biochemistry Cancer Soc. Republic of China, Taipei, 1985-87; dep. sec. 4th Asian Pacific Congress of Clin. Biochemistry, Hong Kong, 1985-88; mem. internat. organizing com. 5th and 6th Internat. Congress of Inborn Errors of Metabolism, Asilomar, Calif., 1989-90, Milan, Italy, 1993-94; cons. Neonatal Screening Ctr. Maternal and Child Health Assn., Taipei, 1993-2000, Neonatal Screening Ctr., Guangzhou, Canton, 1994—, Neonatal Screening Ctr., Chinese Found. Health, 2000—, Taipei Inst. Pathology, 2005—; vis. prof. Shanghai Second Med. U., 1995—; hon. prof. Rsch. Inst. Clin. Med., China-Japan Friendship Hosp., Beijing, 1995—, guest prof., Peiking U. Health Sci. Ctr., 2006-08, mem., Genetic Health Advisory Com., Dept. Health Taiwan, 2002-, cons., Ctr. Disease Control, Dept. Health Taiwan, 2007-10, Dept. Med. Edn. & Rsch. Taipei City Hosp., 2008-. Mem. editorial bd. Advances in Clin. Chemistry, 1992-2003; contbr. articles to profl. publs. Named Outstanding Svcs. Pers. VA, Republic of China, 1986, Outstanding Rsch. Scientist, Nat. Sci. Coun., 1989, 90, 91, Outstanding Edn. Pers., Ministry of Edn., 1993; recipient Health Medal of 2d Order, Dept. Health, Republic of China, 1998. Fellow: Nat. Acad. Clin. Biochemistry; mem.: Human Genome Variation Soc., Human Genome Orgn., Soc. Study Inborn Errors Metabolism, Nat. Pub. Health Assn., Endocrine Soc. Rep. of China, Chinese Soc. Microbiology, Chinese Chem. Soc., Chinese Biochem. Soc., Internat. Soc. for Neonatal Screening, Asian Pacific Fedn. Clin. Biochemistry (sci. com. 1988—95), Internat. Soc. Clin. Enzymology, Internat. Fedn. Clin. Chem. (awards com. 1997—99), Assn. Lab. Medicine (exec. dir. 1991—97), Chinese Assn. Clin. Biochemistry (pres. 1992—94), Preventive Medicine Found. (pres. 1987—). Avocations: classical chinese furniture, classical chinese folk arts and works of art.

HSIAO, LIANG-TSAI, hematologist; s. Cheng-zhou Hsiao and Ahe Hsiao-Tsai; m. Hsin-Jung Hao; 1 child, Tzu-Yun. MD, Nat. Yang-Ming Coll., Taipei, Taiwan, 1994. Cert. internal medicine specialist Taiwan Soc. Internal Medicine, 1999, hematology specialist Hematology Soc. Taiwan, 2001, med. oncology specialist Chinese Oncology Soc., 2002, cancer palliative medicine specialist Taiwan Soc. Cancer Palliative Medicine, 2007. Attending physician Taipei Vets. Gen. Hosp., 2002—; sec. gen. Hematology Soc. Taiwan, 2008—; hematopoietic stem cell transplantation specialist Soc. Blood & Marrow Transplantation, China, 2008. Cons. Taiwan Clin. Oncology Rsch. Found., Taipei, 1999—. Contbr. articles to profl. jours. Recipient Travel award, 29th World Congress Internat. Soc. Hematology, 2002, Young Travel award, 3rd Ann. Meeting Asian Hematology Assn., 2005. Mem.: Am. Soc. Hematology. Office: Taipei Veterans Gen Hosp No 201 Sec 2 Shipai Rd Taipei 112 Taiwan Office Phone: 886-2-28757529, 886-2-28712121 ext. 2507. Office Fax: 886-2-28732184. Business E-Mail: lthsiao@vghtpe.gov.tw. E-mail: hs1085@ms9.hinet.net.

HSIAO, PEI-WEN, medical researcher; b. Kauhsiung, Taiwan, Aug. 7, 1967; PhD, U. Wis., Madison, 1999. Vis. fellow NIEHS, NIH, 1999—2002; asst. rsch. fellow Acad. Sinica, 2002—10, assoc. rsch. fellow, 2010—. Recipient Career Devel. award, Acad. Sinica, 2011, Travel award, Golden Rsch. Conf. Hormonal Carcinogenesis; Travel grant, Endocrine Soc. Avocations: jogging, gardening, hiking. Office: 128 Academia Rd Sec 2 Nan-Kang Taipei 11529 Taiwan Business E-Mail: pwhsiao@gate.sinica.edu.tw.

HSIAO, TZU-YU, surgeon, researcher; b. Tainan, Taiwan, Nov. 25, 1955; s. Jin-Jer and Lin-Jih Hsiao; m. Mei-Ling Chiu, Nov. 5, 1956; children: Ya-Wen, Ching-Wen. MB, Nat. Taiwan U., 1980, PhD, 1994. Dir., divsn. laryngology Nat. Taiwan U. Hosp., Taipei, 1999—; prof. dept. of speech and hearing scis. and disorders Taipei Nursing Coll., 2000—; prof. dept. otolaryngology Nat. Taiwan U., 2003—. Recipient Dr. Tu Publ. award, Formosan Med. Assn., 1995, Publ. award, Taiwan Otolaryngology-Head and Neck Surgery Soc., 1994. Mem.: Taiwan Otolaryngology-Head and Neck Surgery Soc. (corr.). Achievements include research in fields of Phonosurgery and Voice science. Avocations: travel, jogging, swimming. Office: National Taiwan Univ Hosp #7 Chung-Sun S Rd Taipei 100 Taiwan Office Fax: 886-2-23410905. Business E-Mail: tyhsiao@ntu.edu.tw.

HSIAO-MING, CHAO, ophthalmologist, consultant; b. Kaohsiung, June 25, 1960; PhD, U. Oxford, 2001. Cons. ophthalmologist Cheng Hsin Gen. Hosp., 2009—. Office: 45 Cheng-Hsin St Bei-Tou Taipei 112 Taiwan E-mail: ox_drchao@yahoo.ca.

HSIEH, CHEN-HSI, oncologist; b. Taiwan, Apr. 28, 1970; MD, Sch. Chinese Medicine China Med. U., 2002; PhD, Nat. Yang-Ming U. Attending oncologist Far Eastern Meml. Hosp., 2008—. Office: 21 Nan-Ya S Rd Sect 2 Pan-Chiao Taipei 220 Taiwan Personal E-mail: chenci28@ms49.hinet.net.

HSIEH, CHING HSIU, educator; b. Taiwan, Oct. 22, 1973; EDD, Spalding U., 2005. Asst. prof. Chang Gung Inst. Tech., 2009—. Scholar Internat. award, U. New South. Office: 2 Chia-Po Rd West Sec Putz Chiayi 613 Taiwan Personal E-mail: chinghsiuh@yahoo.com.

HSIEH, HSING MEI, molecular biologist, educator; b. Changhua, Taiwan, Nov. 23, 1965; d. Shui-Chiao Hsieh and Ling-Yueh Chang. B, Nat. Taiwan U., 1988, M, 1990, PhD, 1996. Instr. Chungtai Inst. Med. Tech., Taiwan, 1990-91; assoc. prof. Yuanpei Inst. Med. Tech., Taiwan, 1996, Natiol Ctrl. Police Univ., Taiwan, 1999. Rschr. Nat. Univ. Singapore, 1993. Contbr. articles to profl. jours. Scholar Tein Chiabing Culture Found., scholar Changhua Rotary Ednl. Found. Mem. Cellular and Molecular Biology Assn., Botany Assn. Avocations: music, movie, reading. Business E-Mail: mei@mail.cpu.edu.tw.

HSIEH, JU-TON, urologist, educator; b. Taipei, Taiwan, Oct. 6, 1951; s. Yu-Fu Hsieh and Lang-Ying Wu; m. Ming-Hsiu Lu, Mar. 29, 1983; children: J-Chun, Ping-Hsun, Ping-Han, I-Chen. MD, NAt. Taiwan U., 1978. Chief urologic dept. Provincial Tao-Yuan Gen. Hosp., Taiwan, 1984—91; asst. prof. Nat. Taiwan U. Hosp., Taipei, 1991—2001, assoc. prof., 2001—. Editor: World Jour. Urology, 2001; contbr. scientific papers to profl. jours. Fellow, U. Calif., San Francisco, 1985—86. Mem.: Internat. Soc. Impotence Rsch., Asia Pacific Soc. Impotence Rsch., Am. Urology Assn., Taiwan Urol. Assn. (mem. adv. bd. 1996—2000, bd. dirs. 2000—), Taiwan Assn. Andrology (bd. dirs. 1994—, pres. 2004—06). Achievements include invention of in field. Office: Nat Taiwan U Hosp 7 Chung-Shan S Rd Taipei 100 Taiwan Office Fax: 886-2 23219145. Business E-Mail: jthsieh@ha.mc.ntu.edu.tw.

HSIEH, PETER C. C., medical educator; b. Taipei, Taiwan, Nov. 30, 1955; MD, Taipei Med. U., 1980. Assoc. prof. Chnag Gung Meml. Hosp., 2000—. Office: 199 Tun Hwa North Rd Taipei 105 Taiwan Personal E-mail: doctor717@gmail.com.

HSIEH, SHENG-HWU, endocrinologist and diabetologist; b. Zhang Hwa, Taiwan, Feb. 1, 1959; s. Jin-Yi Hsieh and Zhi-Tu Song; m. Hsiu-Ying Cheng, Apr. 2, 1977; children: Chia-Chen, Chia-Yun, Chia-Han. MD, Kaoshiung Med. U., 1985. Internal Medicine Taiwan Internal Medicine Soc., 1991, cert. Endocrine and Metabolism Taiwan Endocrine, 1993. Resident, Dept. Medicine Chang- Gung Meml. Hosp., Kwei-Shan, Taoyuan, Taiwan, 1987—90, fellow, Divsn. Endocrinology and Metabolism, 1990—92, mem. Med. Edn. Com. Internal Medicine, mem. Med. Quality Com. Internal Medicine, attending physician, Divsn. Endocrinology and Metabolism, Divsn. Taipei Internal Medicine, 1992—, chief Taipei Internal Medicine, 1999—2007, chief Taipei Internal Medicine Ward, mem. Med. Record Com., mem. Safe & Health Com. Recipient Efforts Against SARS Exploit, Dept. Health, Taiwan, 2004. Mem.: Diabetes Educator Soc (represent mem.), Internal Medicine Soc. (represent mem.), Diabetes Educator Assn., Formosan Med. Assn., Internal Medicine Assn. R.O.C, Endocrine Assn. R.O.C, Diabetes Assn. R.O.C, Am. Diabetes Assn. Office: Chang Gung Memorial Hosp 199 Tung-Hwa N Rd Taipei Taiwan Office Fax: 886-3-3288257.

HSIEH, SHENG-YI See SHAI, SEN-EI

HSIEH, WING CHEONG, optometrist, educator; b. Hong Kong, May 2, 1956; s. Chao Joseph and Nancy Kwok Hsieh; m. Sharon Kay Tharp, Sept. 29, 1984; children: Eric, Suzanne, Sierra. BA in Biophysics, U. Calif., Berkeley, 1978; OD, Ind. U., 1982. Pvt. practice, San Francisco, 1982—84; optometrist Kaiser Med. Ctr., Hayward, Calif., 1984—85; pvt. practice Muncie, Ind., 1985—87; resident in ocular disease Vision Ednl. Found., Northeastern State U., Oklahoma City, 1987—88; optometrist, dir. clinic Jones Eye Clinic, Sioux City, Iowa, 1989—. Clin. examiner Nat. Bds. Examiners Optometry, 1990—; adj. clin. faculty U. Montreal, 1995—97, So. Coll. Optometry, Memphis, 2002—. Author: Jones Eye Clinic Optometric Training Manual, Cornea Research Foundation Optometric Educational Manual; author, editor, publisher: mag. CyberVision; contbr. articles ato profl. jours. Recipient Presdl. citation, Nebr. Optometric Assn., 1995; named Optometrist of Yr., Iowa Optometric Assn., 2005. Fellow: Am. Acad. Optometry; mem.: Am. Optometric Assn. Office: Jones Eye Clinic 4405 Hamilton Blvd Sioux City IA 51104 E-mail: wing.hsieh@joneseyeclinic.com.

HSIEH, YU-HSI, gastroenterologist; b. Taiwan, Aug. 26, 1966; MD, Nat. Yang-Ming U., 1992. Chief, dept. gastroenterology Buddhist Dalin Tzu-Chi Gen. Hosp., 2008—. Office: 2 Min-Sheng Rd Dalin Chia-Yi 622 Taiwan Business E-Mail: hsieh.yuhsi@msa.hinet.net.

HSIN, YUE-LOONG, neurologist, department chairman; b. Taiwan, June 11, 1967; MD, Kaohsiung Med. U., 1982. Chair, neurology Hualien Tzu Chi Med. Ctr., 2007—. Mem.: Internat. Brain Mapping & Intraoperative Surg. Planning Soc., Taiwan Epilepsy Soc. Office: 707 Sect 3 Chung-Yan Rd Hualien 970 Taiwan Personal E-mail: hsin.yloong@msa.hinet.net.

HSU, ANNE ANN LING, physician, researcher; d. John Tsu Ter Hsu and Cheng Hwa Lim; m. Kok Jin Foo, Aug. 24, 1996; children: Andrea Foo, Shawn Foo. MBBS, Nat. U. Singapore, 1986, M of Medicine, 1991. Ho. officer Tan Tock Seng Hosp., Singapore, 1986—87, Singapore Gen. Hosp., 1987—90; med. officer Nat. Skin Ctr., 1990—91; registrar Singapore Gen. Hosp., 1991—94, sr. registrar, 1995—97, cons., 1997—2002; clin. tchr. Nat. U. Singapore, 1998—; sr. cons. Singapore Gen. Hosp., 2002—, dir. sleep disorders unit, 2002—04, 2006—. Vis. cons. Nat. Lung Cancer Ctr., Singapore, 2000—; program leader SingHealth, 2004—. Contbr. articles to profl. jours. and books. Recipient Svc. Heart award, Singapore Gen. Hosp., 1998; grantee, Nat. Med. Rsch. Coun., Singapore, 1998, 2001, 2004, SingHealth Cluster, 2002; fellow, Min. Health, Singapore, 1994—95, Mayo Clinic Found., Rochester, Minn., 1994—95, St. Marguerite Hosp., Marsielle, France, 1995; scholar, Min. Health, 1981—86. Fellow: Acad. Medicine Singapore, Am. Coll. Chest Physicians, Royal Coll. Physicians; mem.: Singapore Sleep Soc., Singapore Thoracic Soc., World Assn. Bronchology. Roman Catholic. Avocations: swimming, scuba diving, tennis, piano, violin. Business E-Mail: anne-hsu.a.l@sgh.com.

HSU, CHI-YUAN, nephrologist, researcher; b. Hong Kong, Mar. 5, 1967; arrived in U.S., 1985; s. Kwan-san and Wendy Hsu; m. Sandra Young; children: Sophia Rochelle Ming-xi, Theodore Cole Ming-ang, Isabelle Auden Ming-ying. BS, MS, Yale U., 1989; MSc, Harvard U., 1999, MD, 1993. Instr. medicine Harvard Med. Sch., Boston, 1998—99; asst. prof. U. Calif., San Francisco, 1999—2006, assoc. prof., 2006—09, chief, nephrology divsn., 2008—, prof., 2009—. Fellow: ACP; mem.: Am. Soc. Clin. Investigation. Office: U Calif San Francisco Box 0532 521 Parnassus Ave San Francisco CA 94143-0532 Office Phone: 415-476-2172. Office Fax: 415-476-3381.

HSU, CHRISTOPHE FRANÇOIS, dermatologist; s. Francisco and Marie-Claude Hsu. MD, Geneva U., 2004. Cert. in pvt. practice in dermatology Geneva, 2010. Resident, pathology Geneva U. Hosp., 2006—07, resident, clin. dermatology, 2004—06, Nat. Skin Ctr., Singapore, 2007—09. Contbr. scientific papers to profl. publs. Advanced Dermatology fellowship, Nat. Skin Ctr., Singapore. Mem.: Am. Acad. Dermatology, European Acad. Dermatology and Venerology, Dermatol. Soc. Singapore, Singapore Med. Assn., Swiss Med. Assn. (Dermatology Specialist 2009). Avocations: golf, travel, languages. Office: boulevard James-Fazy 4 1201 Geneva Switzerland Personal E-mail: watashimoi@yahoo.com.

HSU, CHUNG Y., healthcare system administrator; b. Taipei, Taiwan, Taiwan, Oct. 14, 1944; s. Huo and Jane (Wu) H.; m. Amy Yang, Sept. 27, 1974; children: Alice L., Virginia, Charles Y. PhD in Neuropharmacology, Va., 1975; MD in Medicine, Nat. Taiwan U., Taiwan, 1970. Diplomate Am. Bd. Psychiatry and Neurology. Prof. and head, cerebrovascular disease sec. Dept. Neurology, Washington U. Sch. Med., St. Louis, 1993—2002; dir. Stroke Ctr., Washington U., St. Louis, 1994—2002, Barnes-Jewish Hosp. Washington U. Med. Ctr., St. Louis, 1994—2002, Elliot H. Stein prof. neurology, 2001—02; pres. Taipei Med. U., Taiwan, 2002—08; ceo China Med. U. Healthcare Sys., Taichung, Taiwan, 2008—; chair prof. China Med. U., 2008—. Mem. adv. panel on drug info. U.S. Pharmacopeial Conv., Rockville, Md., 1985-90; mem. Nat. Inst. Neurol. Disease and Stroke, NIH, 1988-97, mem. nat. adv. bd. on med. rehab. rsch. Nat. Inst. Child Health and Human Devel., NIH, 1997-2001; mem. merit rev. com. neurobiology C, VA, 2000—. Mem. editl. bd. Stroke, Jour. Cerebral Blood Flow and Metabolism, Brain Rsch., Jour. Neurotrauma, Clin. Neuropharmacology, Jour. Med. Ethics and Humanities, Taiwan, Acta Neurologica Taiwanica; mem. guest editl. bd. Jour. Formosan Med. Assn.; editor 4 monographs; contbr. articles to profl. jours. Mem. rsch. and program evaluation com. Am. Heart Assn., 1998—; chair Bugher Found. award rev. com., 1999, 2000, 01. 2d lt. Taiwan Navy, 1970-71. Mil. ship physician Republic of China Navy, 1970—71. Grad fellow U.Va. Sch. Medicine, Charlottesville, 1971-75; recipient Nat. Rsch. Svc. award USPHS, 1977, 81, NIH Tchr. Investigator Devel. award 1983-88, NIH Javits Neurosci. Investigator award, 1991-2001, Disting. Rschr. award Vivian L. Smith Found., 1993-94, Taiwanese Am. Found. award, 1997. Fellow Am. Acad. Neurology; mem. Am. Heart Assn. (fellow stroke coun., chair brain rev. com. 1996-97, rsch. program and devel. com. 1998—), Am. Neurol. Assn., Taiwan Stroke Soc., Taiwan Neurol. Soc., Internat. Soc. Cerebral Blood Flow and Metabolism, Neurotrauma Soc. (pres. 1992-93), N.Am. Taiwanese Prof. Assn. (pres. 1995-96), Taiwanese Assn. Charleston (pres. 1984-85), Dana Alliance for Brain Initiatives. Achievements include research in a nation-wide collection of data on stroke prevention and treatment. Avocation: literature. Office: 21st fl 2 Yuh-Der Rd Taichung 40447 Taiwan Office Phone: 886-4-2206-5299. Office Fax: 886-4-2206-4888. Business E-Mail: hsuc@mail.cmuh.org.tw.

HSU, CHUNG-HUEI, medical educator; b. Tainan, Taiwan, Mar. 10, 1951; s. Yi-Fa Hsu and Yu-Ying Liu; life ptnr. Hsueh-Chin Jean Lee; m. Yun-Ying Chang; children: Min-Mi Vivian, Chen-Hsuan Sean, Su-Han Sarah. MD, China Med. U., Taichung, Taiwan, 1977. Dir. dept. nuc. medicine Taipei Mcpl. Jen-Ai Hosp., Taiwan, 1986—98, Taipei Med. U. Hosp., 1998—2008, assoc. prof. sch. medicine, 2003—. Rsch. fellow Berson Rsch. Lab. VA Med. Ctr., NYC, 1986—87; reviewer med. jour. Contbr. articles to profl. jours. Recipient award, Nat. Academic Coun., 1992. Mem.: Soc. Nuc. Medicine. Office: Taipei Med Univ Hosp Wu-Shing St Taipei 110 Taiwan Office Fax: 886-2-27395749; Home Fax: 886-2-23963863. Business E-Mail: chhsu@tmu.edu.tw.

HSU, DAPHNE T., pediatrician, educator; d. Roger Yk and Evangeline C. Hsu; m. Jeffrey B. Rosen, May 15, 1982; children: Robert H Rosen, Michael H Rosen. AB, Harvard U., 1978; MD, Yale U., 1982. Cert. Am. Bd. Pediatrics, 1988, in Pediatric Cardiology Am. Bd. Pediatrics, 1988. Resident in pediat. N.Y. Presbyn. Hosp., NYC, 1985, fellow in pediatric cardiology, 1988; from asst. prof. to assoc. prof. pediat. Columbia U., NYC, 1988—2003, prof., 2003—; attending physician Morgan Stanley Children's Hosp. N.Y. Presbyn., NYC, 2003—. Pres. Pediatric Heart Transplant Study Group, Birmingham, Ala., 2006—. Cardiologist, med. missionary HeartCare Internat., Greenwich, Conn., 1993—2005., NHLBI-NIH Pediatric Heart Network grantee. Mem.: Pediatric Cardiology Soc. Greater N.Y. (pres. 2005—), Soc. Cardiac Angiography and Intervention (life), Internat. Soc. Heart and Lung Transplantation (life), Am. Coll. Cardiology (life), Am. Heart Assn. (life; exec. com., coun. cardiovasc. diseases of young 2002—04, com. congenital heart disease). Office: Children's Hospital at Montefiore 3415 Bainbridge Ave Bronx NY 10467 Office Fax: 212-342-1563. Business E-Mail: dh17@columbia.edu, dhsu@montefiore.org.

HSU, GENG-LONG, urologist, researcher; b. Taipei, Taiwan, Aug. 2, 1953; s. Neng-Chang Hsu and Kua Hsu-Chen; m. Yung-Chun Tung, Nov. 1, 1983; children: Tan-Ling, Chih-Yuan, Chih-Chia. B of Bus., Nat. Cheng-Kung U., Tainan, Taiwan, 1978; BM, Nat. Taiwan U., Taipei, 1985. Postdoctoral rsch. fellow U. Calif.-San Francisco Sch. Medicine, 1992; mechanic, lectr. Chinese Army Aviation, Tainan, 1971—77; head dept. quality control I-Teh Lock Corp., Tainan, 1977; urol. resident Nat. Taiwan Univ. Hosp., Taipei, 1985—89; chief urology dept. Min-Shen Gen. Hosp., Taipei, 1989—91, Taiwan Adventist Hosp., Taipei, 1993—97, chief Microsurg. Potency Reconstrn. Ctr., 2002—; v.p. Po-Jen Gen. Hosp., Taipei, 1998—2002. Contbr. articles to profl. jours. Recipient Jean-Paul Ginestie prize, Internat. Soc. Impotence Rsch., 1992, Herbert Newman prize. Mem.:

Am. Soc. Andrology, Taipei Med. Assn. (editor 2002—), Am. Urol. Assn. (corr. mem.), Soc. Urol. Assn. Taiwan, Rotary. Achievements include research in penile tunica albuginea: anatomical and clinical application; penile venous anatomy: anatomical revolution and its application; penile anatomy. Avocations: badminton, ping pong/table tennis, hiking, Chinese poetry. Home: 7th Fl No 170 Chih-Shan Rd Sect 2 Shih-Lin Dist Taipei 111 Taiwan Office: Taiwan Adventist Hosp 424 Pa-Te Rd Sec 2 Taipei 105 Taiwan Office Phone: 8862-28807287. Personal E-mail: hsu6411@ms38.hinet.net. Business E-Mail: glhsu@tahsda.org.tw.

HSU, JEFFREY H., vascular surgeon; b. Cleve., Feb. 15, 1969; BS, Stanford U., 1991; MD, NY Med. Coll., 1997. Resident surgery, critical care, vascular surgery U. Rochester Med. Ctr., 2000—05; vascular surgeon Kaiser Permanente - Southern Calif., 2005—. Assoc. program dir., surgery resident Arrowhead-Kaiser Surg. Residency, 2009—. Fellow: ACS; mem.: Soc. Vascular Surgery. Office: 9985 Sierra Ave Fontana CA 92335 E-mail: jhsu1234@gmail.com.

HSU, KWAN-LIH, physician, educator; b. Pinton County, Taiwan, Sept. 7, 1951; MD, Nat. Taiwan U., 1977; PhD, Postgrad. Sch. Clin. Medicine, Nat. Taiwan U. Chief dept. internal medicine E-Da Hosp., 2008; asst. prof. Nat. Taiwan U. Hosp., Med. Coll. Nat. Taiwan U.; assoc. prof. I-Shou U. Office: 1 Yida Rd Jiaosu Village Yanchao Kaohsiung City 82445 Taiwan Office Fax: 886-7-615-0940. Business E-Mail: ed103914@edah.org.tw.

HSU, NANLY, nursing educator; b. Ponghu, Taiwan, Dec. 17, 1948; PhD, U. Il., Chgo., 1989. Cert. profl. nurse, Dept. Health, 2009. Dep. dir., supr. Taipei Veterans Gen. Hosp., Taiwan, 1983—2001; dean, sch. nursing Tzu-chi U., Hualien, Taiwan, 2001—07; prof. Yuan-pei U., Hsin-chu, Taiwan, 2007—11; maj. Taiwan Air Force, 1970—83. Editor Veterans Gen. Hosp. Nursing, Taipei, 1984—2001; cons. Venus Breast cancer club, Taipei, 1998—2009, Hualien Tzu-chi Hosp., 2001—07; chief editor Tzu-chi Nursing Jour., Hualien, 2001—07. Author: (textbook) Nursing Administration And Management, Introduction of nursing research, (novel) Positive Thinking; contbr. articles to profl. jours. Bd. dir. Hualien Nurses' Assn., 2001—07. Recipient Nat. Heroine award, Dept. Nat. Def., 1975; named Ten Outstanding Women in Taiwan, Ten Outstanding Women Found., 1976; Rsch. Grants, Nat. Sci. Coun., Taiwan, 1986. Mem.: Taiwan Nurses' Assn. Buddhist. Avocations: travel, music, dance, swimming. Home: Hoping East Rd Sec 3 223 Fl12-1 Taipei 110 Taiwan Office: Yuan-pei University No 306 Yuan-pei St Hsin -Chu 30015 Taiwan Office Fax: 88635381183-8575; Home Fax: 00886227396242. Personal E-mail: nanly.hsu@msa.hinet.net. Business E-Mail: nlhsu1217@mail.ypu.edu.tw.

HSU, PING-I, gastroenterologist, educator; b. Nan-Tong, Taiwan, Sept. 17, 1961; s. Kuei-Lin Hsu and In-Chao Ho; m. Hui-Chun Chen, May 4, 1990, children: Ruei-Ting, Ruei Je. MD, Taipei Med. Coll., Taiwan, 1986. Cert. physician internal medicine Taiwan, specialist gastroenterology Taiwan. Resident Nat. Chung-Kung U. Hosp., Tainan, Taiwan, 1989—93, chief resident Kaohsiung Vets Gen. Hosp., Taiwan, 1993—94, attending physician, 2004—. Assoc. prof. Nat. Yang-Ming U., Taipei, 2001—, Chia-Nan U. Pharmacy and Sci. Contbr. articles to profl. jours. Recipient Rsch. prize, Nat. Sci. Coun., Taipei, 1995, 2000, Best Paper prize, Chung-Kung Liver Found., Tainan, 2001. Mem.: Gastroenterol. Soc. Taiwan. Avocations: bowling, baseball, travel, reading, singing. Office: Kaohsiung Vets Gen Hosp Dept Medicine 386 Tai-Chung 1st Rd Kaohsiung 813 Taiwan Office Phone: 886-7-3422121 ext. 2075. E-mail: williamhsup@yahoo.com.tw.

HSU, S. DANA, technologist; b. Tainan, Taiwan, Apr. 7, 1956; arrived in U.S., 1964; BS, George Washington U., 1978; MS, Hood Coll., Frederick, Md., 1986; JD, Am. U., Washington, DC, 1994. Bar: Md. 1995, D.C. 1996, U.S. Patent and Trademark Office 1998. Biologist NIH, Bethesda, Md., 1977—2005, technology transfer assoc., 2005—. Contbr. articles to profl. jours. Mem.: Am. Intellectual Property Law Assn. Avocations: gardening, crafts, reading. Office: NIH 6610 Rockledge Dr Rm 4076 MSC 6606 Bethesda MD 20892

HSU, STEPHEN DE, medical educator; b. Tianjin, China, June 11, 1955; arrived in US, 1982, naturalized, 2000; s. Xukai Hsu and YunLian Qian; m. Yan Ping Wang, Dec. 5, 1995; children: Alexander, Andrew. BS, Wuhan U., China, 1982; MA, Montclair State U., 1985; PhD, U. Cinn., 1990. Fellow Sloan-Kettering Inst., NYC, 1991—95; sports anchor ESPN Internat., Bristol, Conn., 1995—98; asst. prof. Nat. U. Singapore, Singapore, 1997—98; rsch. fellow N.Y. U., NYC, 1998—99; asst. prof. Med. Coll. Ga., Augusta, 1999—2004, assoc. prof., 2004—, rschr., 2007—. Contbr. articles to profl. jours. Recipient Ruth L. Kirstein Rsch. Svc. award, Nat. Cancer Inst., 1998, innovation award, 2006; Rsch. grant, Nat. Cancer Inst., 2003. Mem.: Soc. Investigative Dermatology, Am. Assn. Dental Rsch., Am. Assn. Cancer Rsch. Independent. Buddhist. Achievements include invention of mega-t green tea chewing gum and mints; green tea skin care and nail care lines; helped train military dentists. Avocations: travel, sports, history. Home: 4476 Woodberry Ct Evans GA 30809 Office: Med Coll Ga AD1443 Sch Dentistry Augusta GA 30912 Office Phone: 706-721-2317.

HSU, SYLVIA, dermatologist, educator; arrived in US, 1968; d. Mao Yang and Chih Jean Hsu; m. Tien Pei Wong, Dec. 27, 1986; children: Michael Gregory Wong, Kenneth Jason Wong. BA, Rice U., 1985; MD, Baylor Coll. Medicine, Houston, 1989. Cert. Am. Bd. Dermatology, 1994. Clin. asst. prof. dermatology Jefferson Med. Coll., Phila., 1994—97; asst. prof. dermatology Baylor Coll. Medicine, Houston, 1997—2000, assoc. prof. dermatology, 2000—05, prof. dermatology, 2005—. Chief dermatology Ben Taub Gen. Hosp., Houston, 2000—. Mem.: Houston Dermatol. Soc. (pres. 2006), Phi Beta Kappa. Office: Baylor College of Medicine 6620 Main St Ste 1425 Houston TX 77030 Office Fax: 713-798-3250. Business E-Mail: shsu@bcm.edu. *

HSU, TUN-YEN, otolaryngologist; b. Taipei, Taiwan, Mar. 31, 1974; MD, Nat. Taiwan U., 2000. Vis. staff E-da Hosp. I-Shou U., 2004—. Office: 1 Yida Rd Yanchao Dist Kaohsiung City 824 Taiwan Personal E-mail: dunyen@yahoo.com.tw.

HSU, WEI, medical educator; PhD, Mt. Sinai Med. Ctr., 1994. Asst. prof. U. Rochester Med. Ctr., 2002—06, assoc. prof., 2006—. Office: Box 611 601 Elmwood Ave Rochester NY 14642 Office Fax: 585-276-0190. Business E-Mail: wei_hsu@urmc.rochester.edu.

HSU, WEI-CHERNG, ophthalmologist, educator; b. Taipei, Taiwan, Oct. 2, 1963; s. George Hsu and Ran-Ying Ou; m. Carol Yao, June 7, 1997; children: Julian, Nicole. MD, Coll. Medicine, Chang Gung U., Taoyuan, Taiwan, 1994. Rsch. fellow Harvard Med. Sch, Boston, 1999; chief dept. ophthalmology Buddhist Tzu Chi Gen. Hosp. Taipei Br., Taipei, 2007—; asst. prof. Dept. Ophthalmology, Tzu Chi U., Hualien, Taiwan, 2007—. Cons. Life-Spring Bio-Tech. Inc., Taipei. Contbr. scientific papers (Gold Medal of City of Bio-driven, Taipei, 2006). Recipient Outstanding Publ. award, Alcon, 2007. Mem.: Glaucoma Found. Achievements include application of tissue engineering in filtering surgery (glaucoma); patents for conjunctival wound healing modified by 3-D collagen GAG scaffold in filtering surgery; research in biodegradable sclera buckling for retina detachment surgery; application of 3-D collagen GAG matrix in MMC affected poor conjunctival wound healing and corneal stromal regeneration. Office: Buddhist Tzu Chi Hosp No 289 Jianguo Rd Xindian City Taipei 231 Taiwan Office Fax: 886-2-66289009. Business E-Mail: cyao@seed.net.tw.

HSU, WEI-CHIH, engineering educator; b. Nantou, Taiwan, Feb. 21, 1963; PhD, Nat. Taiwan U., 1984. Assoc. prof. Nat. Kaoshiung First U. Sci. and Tech., 1986—. Cons. Chunghwa Telecom, Taiwan, 1984—85. Mem.: Taiwan Project Mgmt. Assn. Avocations: ping pong/table tennis, swimming, hiking. Home: 1 Daxue Rd Yanchao Dist Kaohsiung 82445 Taiwan Home Fax: 886-7-6011012. Business E-Mail: weichih@ccms.nkfust.edu.tw.

HSU, WEN-MING, ophthalmologist; b. Tainan, Taiwan, July 10, 1948; s. Yung-Chiuan and Chuen-Tz (Chen) H.; m. Bi-Yu Huang, Apr. 3, 1975; children: Han-Pu (Henry), Chi-Hsin (Gregory), Shih-Ju (Jeff). MD, Tapei Med. Coll., 1973. Diplomate Nat. Health Dept., Taiwan. Resident dep. ophthalmology Vets. Gen. Hosp., Taipei, 1974-78, attending physician ophthalmology, 1978-83; chief, dept. of ophthalmology Vets. Gen. Hosp. Taichung, Taiwan, 1983-89; dir. oculoplastic section Vets. Gen. Hosp., Taipei, Taiwan, 1989-97; vice-dir. Yung-Kang Vets. Hosp., Tainan, Taiwan, 1997-98; chmn. Dept. Opthalmology Vets. Gen. Hosp., Taipei, Taiwan, 1998—2007; prof., chmn. dept. ophthalmology sch. medicine Nat. Yang-Ming U., Taiwan, 1999—2007; prof., assoc. dean Taipei Med. U., Med. Coll., Taiwan, 2008 . Fellow N.Y. Eye & Ear Infirmary, 1982, Pacific Med. Ctr., San Francisco, 1983, Moorfields Eye Hosp., London, 1989; assoc. prof. Nat. Yang-Ming U., Taipei, 1987-2002; clin. prof. Nat. Def. Med. Coll., 1996—. Author: Mini-Encyclopedia in Ophthalmology, 1993, Practical Ophthalmology, 2003, Total Eye Care, 2005, Clinical Ophthalmology, 2007; editor Jour. Ophthal. Soc. Republic of China, 1994-2006, Chinese Med. Jour., 1999-2007. Fellow Internat. Coll. Surgeons; mem. Am. Acad. Aesthetic Restorative Surgery, Am. Acad. Ophthalmology, Ophthal. Soc. Republic of China (v.p. 1993 96, dir. adv. bd. 1996-99, pres. 2003-06, hon. pres. 2006—), Taiwan Acad. Ophthamology (v.p. 2005—08), Taiwan Agy. Prevention of Blindness (v.p. 2005-08) Avocations: golf, writing, stamp collecting/philately. Office: Vets Gen Hosp Dept Ophthal 201 Sect 2 Shih Pai Rd Taipei Taiwan Office Phone: 886-2-2875-7325. Business E-Mail: wmhsu@vghtpe.gov.tw.

HSU, WU-HUEI, medical educator, educator; m. Hsiu-Fen Yu. MD, China Med. Coll., Taichung, 1985. Dep. dir. and assoc. prof. China Med. U. Hosp., Taichung, 2002—08, dir. and prof., 2008—. Achievements include development of lung ultrasound in clinical practice. Office: China Med Univ Hosp Yuh-Der Rd Taichung 40447 Taiwan Office Phone: 886-4-22052121 ext. 2011. Business E-Mail: hsuwh@mail.cmuh.org.tw.

HSU, YUNG-TSUNG, dentist, director; b. Taiwan, Sept. 10, 1963; DDS, Chung-shan Med. U., 1988; MS, U. Ala., Birmingham, 2001, DMD, 2010. Dir., removable prosthodontics U. Ala., 2005—. Recipient Disting. Alumni award, NYU Coll. Dentistry, Pres.'s award, U. Ala. Fellow: Acad. Dentistry Internat.; mem.: ADA, Acad. Osseointegration, Am. Coll. Prosthodontists. Office: 1919 7th Ave S RM 534 Birmingham AL 35294 Business E-Mail: ythsu@uab.edu.

HSU, ZUEY-SHIN, physiologist, educator; b. Shining, Taiwan, Dec. 13, 1930; s. Kua and Mun Mei (Kuo) Hsu; m. Pan Tsu Wu, Feb. 1, 1964; 1 child, Sheng Chin. MD, Nat. Taiwan U., 1956; D in Physiology (hon.), London Inst. Applied Rsch., 1991. Internal medicine intern Nat. Taiwan U., 1956-57; asst. Kaohsiung Med. Coll. Taiwan, 1957-59, instr., 1959-62, assoc. prof. legal medicine, 1962-68, assoc. prof. physiology, 1968-72, prof., 1972—, dir. dept. physiology, 1972-85, dir. dept. pharmacology, 1973-74; prof. HS Rsch. Alliance Universelle pour la Paix par la Connaissance, 1991—. Grantee, Nat. Sci. Coun. Taipei, 1967. Fellow: Inst. Med. Sci. Tokyo U.; mem.: London Diplomatic Acad. (founder), Pharmacol. Soc. Taiwan, Endocrine Soc. Republic of China, Chinese Soc. Immunology, Chinese Physiol. Soc., Formosan Med. Assn., Maison Internationale des Intellectuels and Academi Midi, Internat. Parliament for Safety and Peace. Achievements include invention of a method of detoxicating heterologous blood for transfusion; new immunological method for desensitizing allergic individuals; preparation of tumor vaccine. Home: 8F-1 No 153 Min Tsu Rd Taichung Taiwan Office: HS Rsch Alliance Universelle pour la Paix par la Connaissance 8F-1 No 153 Min Tsu Rd Taichung Taiwan

HSUEH, CHUNG-TSEN, oncologist, educator; b. Taichung, Taiwan, Nov. 27, 1961; MD, Taipei Med. U., 1986; PhD, SUNY, Buffalo, 1993. Intern, resident, clin. asst. instr., dept. medicine SUNY, 1993—96; med. oncology, hematology fellow Meml. Sloan-Kettering Cancer Ctr., 1996—99; asst. prof. medicine China Med. U., 1999—2004; assoc. prof. medicine U. Kans. Med. Ctr., 2004—07, Loma Linda U., 2007—. Cons. Bio-Cancer Treatment Internat. Ltd., Hong Kong, 2004—11, Novartis, 2007—11, R&G PharmaStudies Co., Ltd., Beijing, 2009—11; assoc. editor Jour. Hematology & Oncology, 2009—11; editl. bd. mem. Jour. Gastrointestinal Oncology, 2010—11; chair Clin. Rsch. Oversight Com. Loma Linda U. Cancer Ctr., medical dir. Ctrs. Excellence-Gastrointestinal & Head/Neck Cancers. Contbr. articles to profl. publs. Recipient Nat. Rsch. Svc. award, Nat. Cancer Inst.; Travel fellowship, NY Soc. Med. Oncologists and Hematologists, Inc. (Downstate Divsn.). Fellow: ACP, Am. Assn. Cancer Rsch. (Translation Cancer Rsch. fellow); mem.: Am. Soc. Hematology, Am. Soc. Clin. Oncology (Merit award). Avocations: reading, cooking, travel. Office: Loma Linda University 11175 Campus St CSP 11015 Loma Linda CA 92354 Business E-Mail: chsueh@llu.edu.

HSUEH, PO-REN, medical educator; b. Tainan, Taiwan, June 7, 1958; s. Na-Chun Hsueh and Bu-Chu Wu; m. Huei-Huei Wu, Nov. 15, 1962; children: Chun-Chung, Shun-Chung. MD, Nat. Taiwan U., Taipei, 1988. Cert. internal medicine Dept. Health, Taiwan, 1988. Lectr. Nat. Taiwan U., Taipei, 1998—2000, asst. prof., 2000—03, assoc. prof., 2003—. Lt. Army, 1982—83, Tao-Yuan. Recipient SARS Task Force award, Dept. Health, Taiwan, 2003. Mem.: Taiwan Soc. Microbiology (pres.), Soc. Infectious Diseases (dir. 2002—, Rsch. award 1999, 2000, 2003). Achievements include research in antimicrobial resistance field; emerging infections (SARS). Home: No 7 Chung-Shan South Rd Taipei 100 Taiwan Office: Nat Taiwan Univ Hosp No 7 Chung-Shan South Rd Taipei 100 Taiwan Office Fax: 886-2-23224263; Home Fax: 886-2-23224263. Business E-Mail: hsporen@ha.mc.ntu.edu.tw.

HSUEH, WILLA, endocrinologist, educator; b. Ind., Mar. 3, 1948; MD, Ohio State U., 1973. Dir., Meth. Diabetes and Metabolism Inst. Weill Cornell Meth. Hosp., RI, head, sect. diabetes, obesity and lipids, dept. medicine, prof., 2008—. Adv. coun. mem. Nat. Heart Lung and Blood Inst., NIH. Named Chinese Am. Physician of Yr., Outstanding Alumni Endeavors, John Hopkins Soc. Fellow: Coun. High Blood Pressure Rsch.; mem.: Endocrine Soc. (named one of Best Drs. in America, Edwin B. Astwood award), Am. Assn. Physicians, Am. Soc. Clin. Investigation, Western Soc. Clin. Investigation. Office: 6565 Fannin St F8-060 Houston TX 77030 Office Fax: 713-793-7162. Business E-Mail: wahsueh@tmhs.org.

HU, CHAOSU, medical educator; b. Jiangxi, China, Dec. 6, 1962; PhD, Shanghai Med. U., 1992. Prof. Shanghai Cancer Ctr., Fudan U., 2000—. Office: 270 Dong An Rd Shanghai 200032 China Personal E-mail: hucsu62@yahoo.com.

HU, CHAUR-JONG, neurologist, researcher; b. Yun-Lin, Taiwan, Dec. 21, 1963; s. Way-Kong Hu and Su-Rer Lin; m. Chang, Jan. 16, 1992; children: Jane, Grace. MD, Taipei Med. U., Taiwan, 1990. Cert. neurologist Dept. Health, Taiwan. Dir. dept. rsch. Taipei Mcpl. Jen-Ai Hosp., 2001—05; asst. prof. Taipei Med. U., 2005—. Grantee, NSC, Taiwan, 1995—2005. Achievements include research in neuroscience. Office: Taipei Med Univ 252 Wu-Hsing St Taipei 110 Taiwan Personal E-mail: mimin@seed.net.tw. E-mail: chaurjongh@tmu.edu.tw.

HU, DEYU, medical association administrator; b. Chongqing, China, Jan. 9, 1950; DDS, West China U. Med. Scis., 1983, MS, 1986. Prof., chmn., dept. preventive dentistry Chinese Stomatological Assn.; pres. Chinese Assn. Preventive Dentistry, 2006—, Chinese Assn. Dental Pub. Health, 2008—. Mem.: Internat. Assn. Dental Rsch. Office: 14 Sect 3 Ren Min Nan Rd Chengdu Sichuan 610041 China Office Fax: 86-28-85501457. E-mail: hudeyu@vip.sina.com.

HU, FRANK B., epidemiologist, educator; b. Hubei Province, China; MD, Tongji Med. U., Wuhan, China, 1988; MPH, U. Ill., Chgo., 1994, PhD, 1996. Rsch. assoc. Nat. Inst. Health Edn., Beijing, 1988—91, Prevention Rsch. Ctr., U. Ill., 1995—96; rsch. fellow nutritional epidemiology Harvard Sch. Pub. Health, Boston, 1996—98, rsch. assoc. dept. nutrition, 1998—99, asst. prof. dept. nutrition, 1999—2002, assoc. prof. nutrition & epidemiology, 2002—08, co dir. Donald and Sue Pritzker Nutrition & Fitness Initiative, 2006—, prof. nutrition & epidemiology, 2008—. Vis. scholar U. Hong Kong, 1991, Dutch Ctr. Health Promotion & Disease Prevention, Netherlands, 1991, Karolinska Inst., Sweden, 1998, 2000; asst. prof. medicine Harvard Med. Sch./Channing Lab., Brigham & Women's Hosp., 2001—06, assoc. prof. medicine, 2006—; dir. epidemiology & genetics core Boston Obesity Nutrition Rsch. Ctr., 2003—; mem. sci. adv. bd. Harvard Prevention Rsch. Ctr., 2007—; med. dir., consulting clin. epidemiologist Mass. Dept. Pub. Health, 2007 ; mem. kidney, nutrition, obesity & diabetes epidemiology study sect. NIH, 2007—. Author: (textbooks) Obesity Epidemiology, 2008; assoc. editor Obesity Rsch., 2005—, mem. editl. bd. Jour. Metabolic Syndrome & Related Disorders, 2003—, Current Diabetes Rev., 2004 , Diabetes Care, 2007—; contbr. articles to profl. jours. Recipient Outstanding Young Scientist award, Nat. Natural Sci. Found. China, 2001, Yangtze Scholar Professorship award, Chinese Ministry Edn., 2005. Fellow: American Heart Assn. (Established Investigator award 2002); mem.: American Epidemiologic Soc., American Soc. Clin. Nutrition, American Soc. Nutritional Scis., Soc. Epidemiologic Rsch., American Diabetes Assn. (Rsch. award 1999), Delta Omega. Achievements include research in epidemiology and prevention of type 2 diabetes and metabolic diseases through diet and lifestyle; gene-environment interactions in relation to type 2 diabetes and cardiovascular complications; obesity, metabolic syndrome, and cardiovascular disease in Chinese populations. Office: Harvard Sch Public Health Dept Nutrition Bldg 2 Rm 323 665 Huntington Ave Boston MA 02115 Office Phone: 617-432-0113. Office Fax: 617-432-2435. Business E-Mail: frank.hu@channing.harvard.edu. *

HU, FUNG-RONG, ophthalmologist, medical researcher, educator; b. Taichung, Taiwan, Sept. 1, 1956; s. Hui-Te and Chan-Chin (Chan) H.; m. Shan-Chwen Chang; children: Hao-Chun Chang, Hao-Yun Chang. MD, Nat. Taiwan U., Taipei, 1981. Intern Nat. Taiwan U. Hosp., Taipei, 1980-81, resident, 1981-85, attending staff, 1985—, chief. corneal sect., chmn. dept. ophthalmology, 1996—; postdoctoral fellow Harvard Med. Sch., Boston, 1988-89; fellow in ophthalmology Mass. Eye & Ear Infirmary, Boston, 1985—93, lectr. ophthalmology; assoc. prof. ophthalmology Nat. Taiwan U., Taipei, 1993-98, prof., 1998—. Cons. Lo-Ton (Taiwan) Po-Ai Hosp., 1985—, Cathay Gen. Hosp., Taipei, 1990—. Contbr. articles to profl. jours. Mem. Ophthalmol. Soc. of Republic of China (supr. 1994—, exec. gen. acad. com. 1991-93, exec. gen. fin. com. 1991-93), Formosan Med. Assn., Am. Acad. Ophthalmology. Avocations: music, playing piano, hiking, tennis, ping pong/table tennis. Office: Nat Taiwan Univ Hosp No 7 Chung-Shan South Rd Taipei Taiwan Office Phone: 886-2-23123456 Ext. 62130. Business E-Mail: fungronghu@ntu.edu.tw.

HU, HAI, medical association administrator; b. Zhejiang, Dec. 24, 1960; MD, Shanghai Jiaotong U., 1992, PhD. Dir. Shanghai East Hosp., 2004—. Vice chmn. Nat. Evaluation Com. Endoscopic Skills & Minimally Invasive Surg. Tech., 2011—, Chinese Endoscopy Doctors Assn., 2011—, World Endoscopy Doctors Assn. China Chpt., 2011—. Recipient Endos award, Evaluation Com. Mem.: Chinese Med. Assn. Avocation: golf. Office: 150 Jimo Rd Shanghai Pudong 200120 China Office Fax: 86 21 58798999. Personal E-mail: huhailc@hotmail.com.

HU, HOWARD, occupational medicine physician, educator; b. NYC, June 12, 1956; s. Henry Hung-Yuan and Mabel (Liang) H.; m. Sudha

Kotha Hu, June 30, 1993; 1 child, Krishna. BSc in Biology, Brown U., 1976; MD, Albert Einstein Coll. Medicine, 1982; MPH, Harvard Sch. Pub. Health, 1982, MS in Epidemiology, 1986, DSc in Epidemiology, 1990. Lic. Mass., 1984, Mich., 2006, diplomate Am. Bd. Internal Medicine, 1985, Am. Bd. Preventive Medicine, Occupl. Medicine, 1987. Intern in medicine Boston City Hosp., 1982-83, jr. asst. resident, internal medicine, 1983—84, sr. asst resident internal medicine, 1984—85; resident, occupl. medicine Harvard Sch. Pub. Health, 1985-87, occupl. health rsch. fellow dept. environ. health, 1987-88, asst. prof. occupl. medicine, dept. environ. health, 1990-94, assoc. prof. occupl. medicine, dept. environ. health, 1994—2002, prof. occupl. and environ. medicine, dept. environ. health, 2002—06, adj. prof. occupl. and environ. medicine, dept. environ. health, 2006—, dir. residency program in occupl. and environ. medicine, 1996—2006, dir., occupl. and environ. medicine core, Nat. Inst. for Occupl. Safety and Health Ednl. Resource Ctr., 1996—2006; instr. in medicine, dept. medicine Harvard Med. Sch., 1988-92, asst. prof. medicine, dept. medicine, 1992—97, assoc. prof. medicine, dept. medicine, 1997—2006; attending physician, emergency dept. Whidden Meml. Hosp., 1985-87; attending physician occpl. medicine Mass. Respiratory Hosp., 1985—; attending physician occupl. health program U. Hosp./Boston U. Med. Ctr., 1987; assoc. physician (clin. and rsch.), Channing Lab., Dept. Medicine Brigham and Women's Hosp., 1988—2006, rsch. assoc. physician, Channing Lab., dept. medicine, 2006—; occpl./environ. medicine cons. Brigham and Women's Hosp. Employee Health Svcs., 1990-95; chair, dept. environ. health scis. U. Mich. Sch. Pub. Health, 2006—, prof. environ. health scis., dept. environ. health scis., 2006—, NSF Internat. Endowed Chair environ. health scis., 2007—, prof. epidemiology, 2007—; prof. medicine U. Mich. Sch. Medicine, 2007—. Asst. vis. physician, dept. medicine, Boston City Hosp., 1985-88; vis. physician South Cove Health Ctr., Boston, 1987-90; assoc., Ctr. for Health and the Global Environ., Harvard Med. Sch., 1996-2006; Alice Hamilton vis. prof., divsn. occupl. and environ. medicine, dept. medicine, U. Calif. San Francisco, 1997; dir., metals epidemiology rsch. group, Channing Lab., dept. medicine, Brigham and Women's Hosp., Harvard Med. Sch., and dept. environ. health, Harvard Sch. Pub. Health, 1991-2006; dir., Commn. to Investigate the Health and Environ. Effects of Nuclear Weapons Production, Internat. Physicians for the Prevention of Nuclear War, 1992-95; assoc. dir. and dir. metals core, Harvard Nat. Inst. Environ. Health Scis., Environ. Scis. Ctr., Harvard Sch. Pub. Health, 2000-06; prin. investigator, dir., Harvard Ctr. for Children's Environ. Health and Disease Prevention Rsch., 2004-; co-dir., Mich./Harvard-Harvard/Mich. Metals Epidemiology Rsch. Group., 2006-; cons. in occupl. and environ. medicine, Ctr. for Occupl. and Environ. Medicine, Northeast Specialty, 1985-2006; cons. in field; vis. scientist, Sri Ramachandra Med. Coll. and Rsch. Inst., Chennai, India, 2000-, vis. prof. 2000-01; vis. prof., dept. environ. medicine, U. Rochester, 2004; mem. numerous task forces in field; guest lectr. in field. Editl. bd. Einstein Comm. Health Newsletter, 1977-82, Jour. of Health and Human Rights, 1993-, Environ. Health Perspective, 1998-, Am. Jour. Insdl. Medicine, 2004-, Harvard Jour. of Minority Pub. Health, 1995—; book rev. co-editor: sect. on occupl. safety and health, Am. Pub. Health Assn., 1988-92; med. editor, Environ. Health Perspectives, 1998-2004; contbr. articles to profl. jours. and publs.; contbr. chpts. to books; peer-reviewer for several profl. jours. Recipient Nat. Health Svc. Corp. scholarship, 1978-82, Nat. Rsch. Svc. award 1985-88, Agy. for Toxic Substances and Disease Registry Clin. Environ. Medicine award 1990-92, Will Solimene award of excellence Am. Med. Writers Assn., 1994, Nat. Inst. for Environ. Health Scis. Progress and Achievement of the Yr. award, 1998-99, Harriett Hardy award, New England Coll. Occupl. and Environ. Medicine, 2006; Sr. Fulbright Scholar in India, 2000-01; grantee in field. Mem. APHA(program com., occupl. safety and health sect. 1981-82, mem. program com., Asian-Am. caucus, 1987-88), ACP, Mass. Coalition for Occupl. Safety and Health, Physicians for Social Responsibility, Physicians for Human Rights, Internat. Soc. for Environ. Epidemiology(mem. com. 1992-98), AAAS, Assn. Occupl. and Environ. Clinics (mem. quality assurance com. 1995-98), Soc. for Occupl. and Environ. Health, Am. Coll. Occupl. and Environ. Medicine, Sigma Xi. Office: Dept Environ Health Scis Bldg 1 Rm 6667 U Mich Sch Pub Health 109 S Observatory St Ann Arbor MI 48109-2029 Office Phone: 734-764-3188. Office Fax: 734-936-7283. Business E-Mail: howardhu@umich.edu.

HU, JIM C., surgeon, educator, urologist; BA, Johns Hopkins U., Balt., 1993; MPH, Johns Hopkins Sch. Pub. Health, Balt., 1994; MD, Baylor Coll. Medicine, Houston, 1998. Lic. Med. Bd. Calif., in fluorocopy Calif., diplomate Am. bd. Urology; lic. Commonwealth Mass. Bd. Registration Medicine. Resident gen. surgery UCLA, 1998—2000, resident urology, 2000—04; health svc. rsch. fellow UCLA Dept. Urology, LA, 2001—02; fellow robotic & laparoscopic urology City Hope Cancer Ctr., Duarte, Calif., 2004—05; instr. Harvard Med. Sch., Boston, 2005—07, asst. prof., 2007—; assoc. surgeon Brigham & Women's Hosp., Boston, 2005—, dir. minimally invasive urologic oncology, 2007—, Dana Farber Cancer Inst., Boston, 2007—. Vis. lectr. Taipei City Hosp., 2005; presenter in field. Recipient 2nd Pl. award, Joseph F McCarthy Physician Eassy Contest Western Sect. Am. Urological Assn., 2005, Lance Armstrong Young Investigator award, 2006, Exellence (SPORE) Devel. award, Dana Farber Harvard Cancer Ctr. Prostate Cancer Specialized Program Rsch., 2006, Prostate Cancer Physician Tng. award, Dept. Def., 2007, 1st Pl. Poster, Am. Urologic Assn. General & Epidemiological Trends & Socieoeconomics: Evidence Based Medicine and Outcome Analysis Session, 2008, Brigham & Women's Physician Orgn. Clin. Innovation award, 2008; Am. Found. for Urologic Disease Med. Student Summer Fellowship, 1997, Am. Cancer Soc. Med. Student Fellowship, 1998, U. Calif. San Francisco CaPSURE Scholar, 2002—04. Office: Brigham & Women's Hosp Divsn Urologic Surgery 45 Francis St ASBII 3rd Fl Boston MA 02115 *

HU, KE-QIN, medical educator; b. Wuhan, 1957; MD, Tongji Med. Coll., 1982. Prof. clin. medicine U. Calif., Irvine, 2003. Office: 101 City DR Bldg 56 Ste 231 Orange CA 92868 Business E-Mail: kqhu@uci.edu.

HU, MARY X., medical association administrator; b. China, Jan. 01; MD, Xian Med. Coll., 1983; MS, Hunter Coll., 1993. Med. dir. Flushing Imaging Ctr., 2003—. Office: Flushing Imaging Ctr 137-10 Northern Blvd Flushing NY 11354

HU, RONG, medical educator; b. Beijing, Jan. 1, 1970; D, Capital Med. U., Beijing, 2003. Prof. Beijing Anzhen Hosp., 2008—. Office: 2 Anzhen Rd Beijing 100029 China E-mail: hurongg@sina.com.

HU, SHILIAN, hospital administrator; b. Feb. 1955; Chief physician Anhui Med. Univ., prof.; dir. evidence based medicine Anhui Provincial Univ.; v.p. Anhui Provincial Hosp. Dir. inst. health Min. Health; mem. Nat. Nutrition Inst. Editor: Clin. Health Mag.; assoc. editor China Grassroots Med. Jour., Chinese Jour. of Geriat., Chinese Med. Jour. Named Outstanding Provincial Party Sec. Gen. Hosp., Party Sec. Excellence, 5th Ideological & Polit. Work award, Min. Health; named one of Nat. Health System Outstanding Ideological & Polit. workers, Nat. Hosp. Outstanding Newspaper Editors. Mem.: Hosp. Mgmt. Assn., Anhui Geriat. Soc. (chmn.), Chinese Hosp. Mgmt. Assn., Chinese Med. Assn., Polit. Assn. (v.p.). Office: Anhui Provincial Hospital Number 17 Lujiang Road Hefei Anhui 230001 China Office Phone: 8605512283114. Business E-Mail: ahslyyxcb@163.com. *

HU, XIAOHAN (HENRY HU), epidemiologist; b. Hefei, Anhui, China, Dec. 27, 1956; came to U.S., 1984; s. Jun and Min (Liu) H.; m. Erluo Chen, July 13, 1986; children: Malin, Irene. MD, Shanghai First Med. Coll., 1983; MPH, UCLA, 1986; PhD, U. Mass., 1990. Cert. Ednl. Commr. for Fgn. Med. Grads. Rsch. scientist Hosp. for Sick Children, Toronto, Ont., Can., 1990-93; lectr. U. Toronto, 1990-91, asst. prof., 1992-96; assoc. dir. Ciba-Geigy Can. Ltd., Mississauga, Ont., 1994-96, Merck & Co., Inc., Whitehouse Sta., NJ, 1997-98, dir., 1999—2002, sr. dir., 2003—. Mem. med./legal bd. U.S. Human Health, 1997-98. Contbr. articles to profl. jours. Mem. trauma adv. com. Ont. Min. of Health, Toronto, 1992-94; lobbist for children bicycle helmet law HSC and Kiwanis Injury Prevention Program, Toronto, 1993. Recipient 8 rsch. grants from various funding agencies, 1991-96; Min. of Edn. (China) Nat. scholar, 1984. Mem.: Assn. for Health Svcs. Rsch., Assn. Pharmacoecon. and Outcomes Rsch. Avocations: tennis, swimming. Home: 125 Bay Hill Dr Blue Bell PA 19422-3264 Business E-Mail: henry_hu@merck.com.

HU, YUH-JYH, computer scientist, educator; s. Ying-Chin Hu and Mei-Er Liao; m. Ching-Fen Hsieh, Oct. 20, 1970. BS, Nat. Chiao Tung U., Hsinchu, 1987; MS, U. of So. Calif., LA, 1992, U. of Calif., Irvine, 1994, PhD, 1999. Asst. prof. Tatung U., Taipei, Taiwan, 1999—2000, Nat. Chiao Tung U., Hsinchu, Taiwan, 2000—, dir. of computer and info. sci. dept. computer ctr., 2001—. Rsch. asst. U. of Calif., Irvine, 1997—99, tchg. asst., 1993—96; database designer Shen Tzu-Hai Architecture Co., Taipei, Taiwan, 1992; reviewer IEEE Trans. on Neural Networks, Jour. of Bioinformatics, Jour. of Info. Sci. and Engring.; chair of undergrad recruitment com. Dept. of Computer and Info. Sci. Dept., Nat. Chiao Tung U., Hsinchu, Taiwan, 2003—. Contbr. articles to profl. jours. 2d lt. 319 Divsn., Army of Taiwan, 1987—89, Kin-Men. Recipient Rsch. award, Nat. Sci. Coun. of Taiwan, 2000; grantee, Nat. Sci. Coun., 2000—03. Achievements include design of NCTU BioInfo Data Archive: the world's first data archive for experiments of bioinformatics analysis tools; GPRM: a genetic programming approach to RNA secondary structure prediction. Office: Nat Chiao Tung Univ 1001 Ta Hsueh Road Hsinchu 300 Taiwan Business E-Mail: yhu@cis.nctu.edu.tw.

HUA, KUO-FENG, biotechnologist, educator; b. Taipei, Taiwan, Jan. 28, 1977; PhD, Inst. Biotech. Medicine, Nat. Yang Ming U., 2006. Postdoc. fellow Inst. Biophotonics, Nat. Yang Ming U., 2006—07, Inst. Biol. Chemistry, Academia Sinica, 2007—08; asst. prof. Grad. Inst. Drug Safety, China Med. U., 2008—09, Inst. Biotech., Nat. Ilan U., 2009—. Cons. Wei-Cheng Biotech Co., Ltd., 2007—11, Jr-Bau Biotech Co., Ltd., 2010—11. Avocation: travel. Office: 1 Sect 1 Shen-Lung Rd Ilan 260 Taiwan Personal E-mail: kuofenghua@gmail.com.

HUAHAO, SHEN, medical educator; b. Datong, China, Jan. 4, 1963; D, Zhejiang U., 1999. Cert. physician Ministry of Health People's Republic of China. Dir., dept. respiratory medicine 2nd Affiliated Hosp. Zhejiang U. Med. Sch., Hangzhou, 2001—; prof. Zhejiang U., Hangzhou, 2001—; dean Inst. Respiratory Medicine Zhejiang U., Hangzhou, 2003—. Mem. Asian Pacific Soc. Respirology, 1997—, Chinese Thoracic Soc., 2000—, Am. Thoracic Soc., 2002—; fellow Am. Coll. Chest Physician, 2003—; chmn. Zhejiang Respiratory Medicine Assn. CMA, China, 2005—; chief Asthma Alliance Zhejiang Respiratory Medicine Assn. CMA, 2005, COPD Alliance Zhejiang Respiratory Medicine Assn. CMA, 2002—; vis. scientist Mayo Clinic, Phoenix, 2006—; standing com. mem. Asthma Group Chinese Thoracic Soc., 2007—; temp. advisor WHO Alliance against Chronic Respiratory Diseases, 2007—; fellow, chinese soc. respiratory diseases, 2008; assoc. editor Therapeutic Advances in Respiratory Disease, 2008—; adj. prof. dept. microbiology and immunology U. Rochester Ctr., NYC, 2008—. Co-editor: (book) SARS; contbr. articles to numerous med. jours. Recipient Outstanding Teaching award, Zhejiang U. and Zhejiang Province Govt. Office: 2nd Affiliated Hosp Zhejiang Univ 88 Jiefang Rd Hangzhou Zhejiang 310009 China Office Fax: 86-571-87767122. Personal E-mail: hh_shen@yahoo.com.cn.

HUAIJUN, LIU, radiologist, educator; b. Tian jin, China, Nov. 10, 1953; BM, Hebei Med. U., 1975. Prof. Second Hosp. Hebei Med. U., 1998, dept. head med. imaging, 2000. Dept. head of med. imaging Hebei Med. U., 2000. Recipient Nat. award, Nat. Office Sci. and Tech. Progress, Advanced Individual Earthquake Relief award, Chinese Ministry Health. Mem.: Chinese Soc. Radiology. Avocations: art, painting, philosophy. Office: 215 West Heping Rd Shijiazhuang Hebei 050000 China Office Phone: 86 311 6600 2088. Office Fax: 86 311 6600 2088. Personal E-mail: huaijun_hb@yahoo.comm.cn.

HUANG, ALICE SHIH-HOU, virologist, microbiologist, educator; b. Nanchang, Jiangxi, China, Mar. 22, 1939; arrived in US, 1949; d. Quentin K.Y. and Grace Betty (Soong) Huang; m. David Baltimore, 1968. BA in Human Biology, Johns Hopkins U., Balt., 1961, MA in Microbiology, 1963, PhD in Microbiology, 1966; MA (hon.), Harvard U., 1980; DSc (hon.), Wheaton Coll., Mass., 1982, Mt. Holyoke Coll., 1987, Med. Coll. Pa., Phila., 1991. Postdoc. fellow Salk Inst. Biol. Studies, San Diego, 1967, MIT, 1968-69, rsch. assoc. dept. biology, 1969-70; asst. prof. microbiology and molecular genetics Harvard Med. Sch., Boston, 1971-73, assoc. prof., 1973-78, prof., 1979-91; prof. biology, dean Faculty of Sci. NYU, 1991—97; faculty assoc. biology, sr. councilor external rels. Calif. Inst. Tech., 1997—2006, sr. faculty assoc. biology, 2007—. Dir. Labs. Infectious Diseases, Children's Hosp., Boston, 1979—91; mem. sci. adv. bd. Inst. Molecular Cell Biology, Nat. U. Singapore, 1985—2003; apptd. mem. Calif. Coun. Sci. & Tech., 2004—07. Assoc. editor Rev. Infectious Diseases, 1978—89, mem. editl. bd. Intervirology, 1973—90, Archive of Virology, 1975—78, Jour. Virology, 1976—93; contbr. articles to profl. jours. Bd. trustees Waksman Found. Microbiology, 1986—, U. Mass., 1987—91, Johns Hopkins U., 1992—2004, Keystone Ctr., Colo., 1993—98, Keck Grad. Inst. Applied Life Scis., Claremont, Calif., 1998—2006, Pub. Agenda, NY, 2001—, Rockefeller Found., 2004—. Fellow: AAAS (bd. dirs. 1997—2001, pres. 2010—11, chair, bd. dirs. 2011—), Assn. Women in Sci. (Outstanding Woman Scientist award 1994), Infectious Diseases Soc. America; mem.: Acad. Sinica, Soc. Chinese Bioscientists America, Am. Acad. Microbiology, Am. Soc. Virology, Am. Soc. Biochemistry & Molecular Biology, Am. Soc. Microbiology (pres. 1988—89, Eli Lilly award 1977, Alice C. Evans award 2001). Office: Calif Inst Tech Mail Code 156 29 Pasadena CA 91125 Office Phone: 626-395-3446.

HUANG, CHANG-QUAN, physician; b. China, July 7, 1974; MD, SiChuan U., 2009. Physician Third Hosp. Mianyang, 1998—. Home: Jian Nan Lu 190 Mianyang Sichuan 621000 China Personal E-mail: huangshan319@yahoo.com.cn.

HUANG, CHAO-CHENG, pathologist; b. Tainan, Taiwan, Aug. 17, 1963; s. Ting-Chia Huang and Jui-Ching Huang-Wan; m. Chao-Min Chiu, Jan. 26, 1991; children: Po-Yuan, Po-Chun. MD, Kaohsiung Med. U., Taiwan, 1988. Registered in anatomic pathology Bd. Pathology Dept. Health, Exec. Yuan, Taiwan, 1994, lic. physician Dept. Health, Exec. Yuan, Taiwan, 1988. Resident dept. pathology Chang Gung Meml. Hosp., Kaohsiung, 1990—94, attending physician dept. pathology, 1994—, chief anatomic pathology, dept. pathology, 2002—10, asst. prof. dept. pathology, 2000—05, assoc. prof. dept. pathology, 2005—. Rsch. fellow Johns Hopkins U. Sch. Medicine, Balt., 1997—98; asst. prof. Chang Gung U. Sch. Medicine, Taoyuan, Taiwan, 2003—07, assoc. prof., 2007—; editl. bd. mem. Jour. Clin. Pathology, 2010—; rschr. in field; presenter in field. Second lt. Marine Corps, 1988—90, Taiwan. Grantee, Chang Gung Med. Rsch., 2000—02, 2003—04, 2005—06, 2008—, Nat. Sci. Coun., 2000—02, 2003—. Mem.: Taiwan Soc. Pathology (licentiate), U.S. and Can. Acad. Pathology (life), Chinese Soc. Genetics (life), Formosan Med. Assn. (life), Chinese Soc. Clin. Pathology (life). Achievements include research in liver fibrosis associated with biliary atresia and in oncogenesis of head and neck cancers. Office: Chang Gung Meml Hosp Dept Pathology 123 Ta-Pei Rd Niao Sung Dist Kaohsiung 833 Taiwan Office Fax: 886-7-7333198. Business E-Mail: huangcc@adm.cgmh.org.tw.

HUANG, CHAO-CHING, pediatrician; b. Chai-Yi, Taiwan, Jan. 1, 1954; s. Kun-Tsan and Wan-Tsui (Lee) H.; m. Ling-Ling Pan, Nov. 27, 1982; children: Po-Hsiang, Po-Yin, Kevin. MD, Taipei Med. Coll., 1980. Resident Taipei Mackay Meml. Hosp., Taiwan, 1980—84, rsch. fellow in pediat. neurology, 1984—86, vis. staff in pediats., 1986—88; pediats. instr. Coll. Medicine Nat. Cheng Kung U., Tainan, Taiwan, 1988—91, assoc. prof. pediats. Coll. Medicine, 1991—98, prof. pediats., 1998—, dir. Inst. Clin. Medicine, Coll. Medicine, 2005—; rsch. fellow in physiology and pediats. U. Pa., Phila., 1991—92. Mem. editl. bd.: Taiwan Pediat. Assn., 1998; contbr. articles to profl. jours. including New Eng. Jour. Medicine, Neurosci. and Ann. Neurology. Recipient Taiwan Pediat. Assn. award, 2001, Disting. Rsch. award Taiwan Nat. Sci. Coun., 2000, 02. Office: Nat Cheng Kung U Hosp 138 Sheng-Li Rd Tainan 704 Taiwan Office Phone: 886-6-2353535 ext. 5287. Business E-Mail: huangped@mail.ncku.edu.tw.

HUANG, CHIH-KUN, medical association administrator; b. Taiwan, Sept. 16, 1970; MD, Kaohsiung Med. Coll., 1995. Dir. Bariatric & Metabolic Internat. Surgery Ctr. E-Da Hosp., Taiwan, 2007—. Pres. Taiwan Obesity Support Assn., 2008; editl. bd. mem. Global Jour. Surgery, 2010. Recipient award, Obesity Surgery Jour., 2008, Surg. Rev. Corp., 2009, Endos award, Dept. Health and Govt. Ofcls. China, 2010. Mem.: Taiwan Surg. Soc. Gastroenterology, Taiwan Surg. Assn., Asia-Pacific Bariatric Soc., Internat. Fedn. Surgery Obesity, Am. Soc. Metabolic and Bariatric Surgery. Avocations: swimming, badminton, mountain climbing. Office: 5 F 1 E-Da Rd Kaohsiung Yan-Chao 824 Taiwan Personal E-mail: dr.ckhuang@hotmail.com.

HUANG, CHING-SHUI, hospital administrator; MD, Nat. Taiwan U., 1971. Internship Nat. Taiwan Univ. Hosp., 1970—71, residency surgery dept., 1972—76; fellowship surgery dept. Cornell-NY Med. Ctr., 1988; clin. prof. Taipei Med. Univ., Taiwan, 2000—; vice supt. Cathay Gen. Hosp., Taiwan, 2000—06, supt., 2006—; clin. prof. Fu Jen Cath. Univ., Taiwan, 2002—. Bd. of gov. Pediatric Surgery Assn., 1980—90, The Digestine Endoscopy Soc., 1991—2003, Chinese Assn. of Endocrine Surgery, 1995—96, pres., 1995—96; bd. of gov. Breast disease Assn., 1995—2001, Taipei Med. Assn., 1996—98, Taiwan Surg. Assn., 2000—; pres. Surg. Soc. of Gastro-enterology, 2004—06, Taiwanese Hernia Soc., 2007—08; exec. com. mem. Asia-Pacific Hernia Soc., 2007—. Achievements include research in Hepatobiliary Surgery; Hernia Surgery; Endoscopic Surgery; Surgical Oncology. Office: Cathay General Hospital 280 Sect 4 Jen-Ai Rd Taipei Taiwan Office Phone: 0227082121. E-mail: cshuang@cgh.org.tw. *

HUANG, CHIN-WEI, physician, researcher; b. Tainan, Taiwan, Dec. 26, 1969; s. Tung Yang and An-An (Lee) Huang; m. Yi Jung Hsieh, July 25, 2000; children: Huai Ying, Huai Hsien, Huai Chun. MD, Kaohsiung Med. U., Taiwan, 1996; PhD in Clin. Medicine, Nat. Cheng Kung U., Tainan, Taiwan, 2009. Lic. neurologist Taiwan. Attending physician Nat. Cheng Kung U. Med. Ctr., Tainan, Taiwan, 2001—; asst. prof. Nat. Cheng Kung U., Tainan, 2006—. Contbr. articles to profl. jours. Recipient Outstanding Rsch. award, Nat. Cheng Kung U., 2006, 2007; grantee, Nat. Sci. Coun. Taiwan, 2003, 2005—, Nat. Cheng Kung U. Med. Ctr., 2003, 2005—08, Japan Epilepsy Found., 2005; scholar, Fujisawa Pharm. Found., 2004. Mem.: Taiwan Neurol. Soc. (Best Poster Presentation award 2006), Japan Pharmacological Soc., Soc. Neurosci., Taiwan Neurol. Soc. (licentiate), Taiwan Epilepsy Soc. (licentiate Best Oral Presentation 2007, Best Poster Presentation award 2008), Japan Epilepsy Soc. (corr.). Achievements include discovery of mechanism of anti-epileptic drugs; research in pathophysiology in epileptic seizures. Avocation: music. Home: No23 Alley 18 Ln 21 Hua-Ping Rd Tainan 708 Taiwan Office: Dept Neurology Nat Cheng Kung U Hosp No138 Sheng-Li Rd Tainan 701 Taiwan Office Fax: 886-6-2374285; Home Fax: 886-6-2958631. Personal E-mail: ht996@ms18.hinet.net. Business E-Mail: huangcw@mail.ncku.edu.tw.

HUANG, CHI-YING F., education educator, researcher; b. Chang-Hwa, Taiwan, Aug. 9, 1963; m. Jin-Mei Lai, July 10, 2005. BSc in Chemistry, Tunghai U., Taiwan; PhD, Iowa State U., 1994. Postdoctoral fellow Stanford U., Palo Alto, Calif., 1994—98; asst. investigator Nat. Health Rsch. Inst., Taipei, Taiwan, 1998—2003, assoc. investigator, 2003—; assoc. prof. Nat. Taiwan U., Taipei, 2003—, Nat. Yang-Ming U., Taipei, 2003—, Nat. Def. Med. Ctr., Taipei, 2003—. Recipient The Honor Soc. of Agr., Gamma Sigma Delta, 1989, Grad. Rsch. Excellence award, Iowa State U., 1994; Stanford Dean's Postdoctoral Fellowship, Stanford U., 1994—95, Leukemia Soc. of Am. Fellowship, 1996—98. Achievements include patents pending for identifying several markers for liver fibrosis; research in identifying a Chinese herb for treatment of liver fibrosis; building a website (POINT) for the prediction of protein-protein interactions; building a website (Encyclopedia of Hepatocellular Carcinoma, EHCO) for hepatocellular carcinoma; identifying a novel oncogene, HURP, from hepatocellular carcinoma. Office: Nat Health Rsch Inst 7F No 161 Sec 6 Min Chuan East Road Taipei 114 Taiwan Office Fax: (886)-2-2792-9654. Business E-Mail: chiying@nhri.org.tw.

HUANG, CHRISTOPHER LI-HUR, physiology educator; b. Singapore, Dec. 28, 1951; arrived in Eng., 1971; s. Rayson Lisung and Grace Wei-Li (Lee) H. BA, U. Oxford, Eng., 1974, B of Medicine and Surgery, 1976, MA, 1979, DM, 1985; DSc, U. Oxford, England, 1995; MA, U. Cambridge, Eng., 1979, PhD, 1980, MD, 1986; ScD, U. Cambridge, England, 1995. House physician and surgeon Nuffield dept. medicine U. Oxford, Eng., 1977-78; med. rsch. coun. scholar U. Cambridge, 1978-79, asst. lectr., 1979-84, fellow, lectr. New Hall, 1979—, dir. studies in medicine, 1981—, lectr., 1984-96, reader in cellular physiology, 1996—2002, prof. cell physiology, 2002—; ind. nonexec. dir. Hutchison Chi-Med, 2006—; dir. Cambridge Cardiac Sys., 2009—. Hon. sr. rsch. fellow St. George's Hosp. Med. Sch., London, 1991—; vis. prof. U. Debrecen, Hungary, 1996, Mt. Sinai Med. Sch., N.Y., 2001. Author: Research in Medicine, 1991, 1999, 2011, Intramembrane Charge Movements in Striated Muscle, 1993, Applied Physiology for Surgery and Critical Care, 1995, Molecular and Cellular Biology of Bone, 1998, Translational Models for Cardiac Arrhythmogeness, 2008, Nerve and Muscle, 2011; editor: The Jour. of Physiology, 1990—99; chmn. editl. bd.: Monographs of the Physiol. Soc., 1994—99, Biol. Reviews, 2000—; contbr. articles to profl. jours. Mgr. Prince Philip scholar fund, U. Cambridge, 1986—. Recipient Benefactors prize The Queen's Coll., Oxford, 1973, Brian Johnson prize, U. Oxford, 1976, Rolleston Meml. prize, 1980; Gedge prize, 1981, Lepra award Bris. Leprosy Relief Assn., London, 1977; presdl. scholar Republic of Singapore, 1971-76, Florence Heale scholar 1971-76. Mem. Am. Soc. Gen. Physiologists, Biophys. Soc., Physiol. Soc. U.K., Cambridge Philos. Soc. (coun. 1994—, biol. sec. 2000-08, v.p., 2010-), Royal Coll. Surgeons of Edinburgh (ct. examiner 1999—); Fellow Soc. Biology Avocation: music.

HUANG, HAICHANG, biomedical researcher, physician; b. Ningdu, Jiang-Xi, China, Sept. 28, 1966; s. Yiwei Huang and Jinxiu He; m. Jinxia Peng; 1 child, Shengjie. MD, PhD, Peking U. Health Sci. Ctr., Beijing, 1997. Rsch. fellow U. Tex. Southwestern Med. Ctr., Dallas, 1997—2000; physician Peking U. Inst. of Nephrology, Beijing, 2001—. Grantee, Nat. Natural Sci. Found. China. Office: First Hosp Peking U # 8 Xi-Shi-Ku St Beijing 100034 China Office Fax: +86-10-66551055. Business E-Mail: haichang@bjmu.edu.cn.

HUANG, HUANG-WEN, biomedical engineer, educator; b. Taiwan, Jan. 17, 1965; PhD, U. Ariz., 1996. Assoc. prof. Tamkang U., 2006—. Grant, Nat. Sci. Coun. Mem.: Taiwanese Soc. Biomed. Engring. Avocations: ping pong/table tennis, walking. Office: 180 Linwei Rd Jiaoxi Twp Yilan 26247 Taiwan Business E-Mail: hlm402@mail.tku.edu.tw.

HUANG, HUI-TING, hospital administrator; Grad., Taipei Med. U. Pres. Taiwan Adventist Hosp. Office: Taiwan Adventist Hospital No 424 Sec 2 Bade Rd Songshan Dist Taipei 10556 Taiwan Office Fax: 886227775623. *

HUANG, I-SHUN, physician, researcher; MD, Kaohsiung Med. U., Taiwan, 1996; PhD student, U. Pitts., 2006—. Cert. otolaryngologist specialist Dept. Health, Exec. Yuan, Taiwan, 2001. Attending physician Chang Gung Meml. Hosp., Kaohsiung, 2001—. Grant, Chang Gung Meml. Hosp., 2004, 2005. Mem.: Taiwan Otolaryn. Soc. Achievements include invention of the theory of phase-time conversion; patents for methods and modules to introduce phase information into cochlear implants and retinal implants. Office: Univ Pittsburgh 4020 Forbes Tower Pittsburgh PA 15260 Personal E-mail: huangishun@gmail.com.

HUANG, JACOB CHEN-YA, physician, educator, city health official; b. Chia-Yi, Taiwan, Dec. 25, 1937; came to U.S., 1966; naturalized, 1974; s. Chang-Chiang and Agenes Cheng-Jen H.; m. Vivian Lin; children: Phyllis, Albert, Edward. Diplomate Am. Bd. Family Practice. Intern Taipei City Hosp., 1964-65, house officer pediatrics, 1965-66; fellow clin. pathology Albert Einstein Coll. Medicine-Lincoln Hosp., 1968-70; dir. pub. health N.Y.C. Health Dept., 1971—77; sr. pub. health officer N.Y. State Dept. Health, 1970—76, chief drug diagnostic sect. N.Y.C. chief med. examiner, 1968—70; resident family medicine Lutheran Med. Ctr., NYC, 1970-71; clin. assoc. prof. N.Y. U., 1972-76; med. dir. Paterson City (N.J.) Health Dept., 1977—. Chmn. dept. family practice Dover (N.J.) Gen. Hosp. Med. Center, 1980-88; trustee N.J. Passaic PRO, 1987—; ambulatory care adv. bd. Beth Israel Hosp., N.Y.C., 1972-76; cmty. adv. bd. ambulatory svcs. St. Vincent Med. Ctr., N.Y.C., 1972-76, COMED-IPA Inc., NJ, 1980— N.J. hon. chmn. physician adv. bd. Nat. Rep. Com., 2001; hon. chmn. bus. adv. coun., mem. Presdl. Healthcare Commn., 2002. Recipient Physician's Recognition award AMA, Ronald Reagan Golden award Rep. Congress Nat. Com., 2004 Fellow Am. Coll. Preventive Medicine, Am. Acad. Family Physicians; mem. APHA, Am. Chinese Med. Assn. N.J. (pres., founder), N.J. Am. Acad. Family Physicians (trustee 1994—, bd. dirs. 1993-96, exec. bd. dirs. 1995—), Chinese Am. Med. Soc. (bd. dirs.), Chinese Am. Physicians Network NJ (pres. 1997—), Columbia U. Sch. Pub. Health Alumni Assn. (exec. bd. 1992). Achievements include discovery of a single reagent for wide screening of abused drugs. Avocations: golf, travel. Home: 3 Walnut Hill Dr Chester NJ 07930-3006 Office: Bartley Sq Rte 206 Flanders NJ 07836 Home Phone: 908-234-0519; Office Phone: 973-584-0233. Personal E-mail: drcyhuang@yahoo.com.

HUANG, JIANZHONG, biomedical researcher; s. Longhe Huang and Yinzhu Xu; m. Shan Zeng, Feb. 11, 2002; children: Mary, Jason Z. MD, Tongji Med. U., Wuhan, China, 1980—85; Postdoctoral, Med. Coll. of Ga., Augusta, 1995—98, Columbia U., NYC, 1998—2001. Attending surgeon Health Dept. of Jiangsu, 1991; cert. in ECFMG 2010. Resident in surgery Nanjing Children's Hosp., Nanjing, Jiangsu, China, 1985—91, attending surgeon, 1991—94; assoc. rsch. scientist Columbia U. Med. Ctr., NYC, 2001—. Chief divsn. neonatal surgery Nanjing Children's Hosp., China, 1992—94; chair oral session of urology, Symposium of Pediatric Surgery 23rd Internat. Congress of Pediat., 2001. Contbr. articles to profl. jours. Recipient Aventis Young Investigator award, Eastern Coop. Oncology Group, 2003; grantee, NIH, 2003—08, Nat. Cancer Inst. NIH, 2005—10; fellow, Nat. Cancer Ctr., 2002—04. Fellow: AMA, Am. Chinese Med. Assn., Southeastern Pharmacology Soc., Chinese Med. Assn.; mem.: Am. Assn. Cancer Rsch., Chinese Pediatric Surg. Assn. Achievements include invention of tumor model used to investigate effects of antitumor agents on large, metastatic tumors; discovery of regression of established tumors and metastases by a potent antiangiogenic agent. Home: 1042 Harvard Pl Fort Lee NJ 07024 Personal E-mail: jzh611@gmail.com.

HUANG, JIUN-HAU, behavioral scientist, researcher, educator; b. Taipei, Taiwan, 1969; SM, Harvard Sch. Pub. Health, 1998, ScD, 2003. Rsch. fellow Harvard U., 2004—06; postdoc. rsch. fellow Fernand-Seguin Rsch. Ctr. Louis-H. Lafontaine Hosp., 2005—06, U. Montreal, 2005—06, McGill U., 2006—08; asst. prof. Nat. Taiwan U. Coll. Pub. Health, 2008—. Jour. reviewer Can. Med. Assn. Jour., 2007, Psychoneuroendocrinology, 2007, Am. Jour. Pub. Health, 2008, European Jour. Psychiatry, 2008, Psychiatry Rsch., 2010, Addiction, 2011, Sexual Health, 2011. Recipient Academic Achievement award, Nat. Taiwan U., Pres.'s award. Mem.: Taiwan Pub. Health Assn., Taiwan Soc. Adolescent Medicine and Health. Avocations: yoga, tennis, swimming. Office: 17 Xu-Zhou Rd Rm 616 Taipei 10055 Taiwan Business E-Mail: jhuang@ntu.edu.tw.

HUANG, JUI-CHEN, public health service officer, educator; b. Taiwan, Oct. 8, 1971; BSN, Taipei Medical U., Taiwan, 1994; MS in Pub. Health, Kaohsiung Med. U., Taiwan, 1997; PhD in Tech. Mgmt. Adminstrn., Chung-Hua U., Hsin-Chu, Taiwan, 2009. Cert. asst. prof., health exec. Commr. divsn. R & D Landseed Hosp., 1997—98; lectr. dept. healthcare adminstrn. and hosp. mgmt. Meiho U., 1994—2004; assoc. rschr. Taiwan, 2005—06; asst. prof. dept. health bus. adminstrn. Hungkuang U., Taiwan, 2009—. Lectr. Kaohsiung and Paingtung Br. Nat. Health Ins. Bur., Taiwan, 1997; part time lectr. Yuanpei U., 2006—07; part time lectr., dept. sr. citizen svc. mgmt. Must U., Taiwan, 2008; part time lectr., dept. deotech. care mgmt. Chang Gung Inst. Tech., 2008—09; invited spkr. Chuanghua Annual Symposium, spkr., 2009; instr., sr. resources Ctr. Hsinchu County Chubei CC, instr., Taiwan, 2009, Sr. Resources Ctr., Taiwan, 2009; spkr. EPS Global Medical Devel. Inc. Hangzhou and Shanghai; reviewer Jour. SCI, 2009—, 7th Symposium on Corp. Operation Mgmt. Cases Cheng Gung U., Taiwan, 2004; proposal reviewer, 09; profl. cons., 10. Contbr. numerous article and sci. papers to profl. jours.; author: (book) The Innovative Adoption Model of Home Telehealth, 2009, Prevention of Chronic Disease and Cancer. Public Health Introduction, 2009, Social Transformation and Future Prospects of Public Health. Public Health Introduction, 2009. Vol. Social Welfare Promotion Com., Taiwan. Scholar 2010 Outstanding Paper Award of 2010 Internaitonal Joint Conf. in Helathcare, Taiwan Coll. of Healthcare Executives. Mem.: Taiwan Pub. Health Assn., Chinese Health Svcs. Mgmt. Assn., Taiwan TRIZ Assn., Long-term Care Mgmt. Assn., Taiwan Pub. Health Assn., Chinese Health Svc. Mgmt. Assn., Soc. Adaptive Sci. Taiwan, Taiwan TRIZ Assn., Taiwan Long-term Care Mgmt. Assn., Taiwan Assn. Gerontology and Geriat., Taiwan Hosp. Assn., Taiwan Coll. Healthcare Execs. Achievements include patents for wheelchair with self-luminous apparatus; research in grey system theory to explore the effect of RFID on the quality of life among older adult users; remote health monitoring adoption model based on artificial neural networks; exploring the key factors in the choice of home telehealth by using the health belief mode; patents for self-lighting footwear, healthcare wristband. Avocations: swimming, running. Office: Hungkuang University Dept Health Bus Adminstrn 34 Chung-Chie Rd Sha Lu Dist Taichung City 43302 Taiwan Home: 4F No 42 Jhuangjing 3rd Rd Jhubei City Hsin Chu 302 Taiwan Personal E-mail: juichen@ms17.hinet.net.

HUANG, JYH-HSIUNG, immunologist, virologist, epidemiologist, researcher; b. Tainan, Taiwan, Dec. 16, 1950; s. Guo-liang Huang and Yen-Bi Hur; m. Ai-Chu Lu; children: Grace, KerBin. PhD, SUNY Buffalo, 1986. Divsn. dir. dept. biochemistry Nat. Def. Med. Ctr., Taipei, Taipei city, Taiwan, 1983—86; rschr. Ctr. Disease Control, Taipei, Taipei city, Taiwan, 1987—. Lt. Republic of China Army, 1973—75. Dengue rsch. grantee, Nat. Sci. Coun., 1997-2000. Mem.: Am. Soc. Microbiology. Independent Thinkers. Avocations: travel, music, gardening. Office: Center for Disease Control #161 Kun-Yang St Taipei city Taipei 115 Taiwan Home Phone: 886-3-4097984; Office Phone: 886-2-26531374. Office Fax: 886-2-27883992. Business E-Mail: jhhuang@cdc.gov.tw.

HUANG, MING SHYAN, medical educator; b. Taiwan, Mar. 10, 1952; MD, Koahsiung Med. Coll., 1977; PhD, Tokyo Med. U., 1984. Prof. Kaohsiung Med. U. Hosp., 1999—. Office: Kaohsiung Med Univeristy Hosp Kaohsiung 80756 Taiwan Office Phone: 886-7-3208159. Office Fax: 886-7-3161201. Business E-Mail: shyang@kmu.edu.tw.

HUANG, MIN-HO, hospital administrator; b. Mar. 1, 1940; married. MD, Nat. Taiwan U. Med. Coll., 1958—65; PhD, Tokyo Women's Med. Coll., 1987; MPH, Johns Hopkins U., 1996. Intern Nat. Taiwan Univ. Hosp., Taipei, Taiwan, 1964—65; chief surg. dept. Provincial Changhua Hosp., 1970—72; supt. Maywa's Surg. Clinic, Changhua, Taiwan, 1972—80, Show Chwan Meml. Hosp., Changhua, Taiwan, 1980—; instr. China Med. Coll., 1981—82, clin. assoc. prof., 1985—; instr. Nat. Cheng Kung Univ. Med. Coll., 1985—; legislator Legislative Yuan, 1987—89, 1990—92, 1999—2001; clin. assoc. prof. Nat. Taiwan Univ. Med. Coll., 1994—; pres. Show Chwan Health Care System, 1997—; com. chmn. Health, Welfare & Environment Sci. & Tech. Foreign Affairs, 1989—2001. Author various publs. Founder Health and Welfare Found., 1990—. Gen. practice army doctor Chinese Army Force, 1965—66. Mem.: World Assn. of Hepato Pancreato Biliary Surgery, American Inst. of Ultrasound in Medicine, Internat. Biliary Assn., Assn. of Surgeons of SE Asia, Western Pacific Assn. of Critical Care Medicine, Internat. Coll. of Surgeons, Ultrasound in Medicine Soc., Chinese Bd. of Orthopaedic Surgery, Japanese Soc. of Ultrasound in Medicine. Address: 542 Sec 1 Chung Shang Rd Changhua Taiwan Business E-Mail: minho@show.org.tw. *

HUANG, PAI-TSANG, internist; b. Taipei, Taiwan, Apr. 28, 1960; m. Shu-Ru Chen; children: Chiao-Yi, Chiao-En. MD, Taipei Med. Coll., 1985; MS, U. Cin., 1993. Internal Medicine Specialist Dept. Health, Taiwan, 1991, Occupl. Medicine Specialist Dept. Health, Taiwan, 2002, Coun. Physicians, Berlin, 1995. Med. intern Chang Gung Meml. Hosp., Taoyuen, Taiwan, 1984—85, med. resident, 1987—91; asst. Inst. Occupl. Medicine, Free U. Berlin, 1993—95; attending physician Changhua Christian Hosp., Taiwan, 1995—2003; physician Dr. Lin's Clinic, Taipei, 2003—; lectr. Nat. Cheng Kung U., Tainan, Taiwan, 2002, Chang Jung Christian U., Kwayjen, Taiwan, 2002. Dept. dir., dept. med. screening Changhua Christian Hosp., 1996—2001; cons. physician Taiwan Semiconductor Mfg. Co., 2004—, Bur. Labor Ins., Taiwan, 2000—; com. mem. Adjudication Com. Occupl. Disease, Coun. Labor Affairs, Exec. Yuen, Taiwan, 1995—2005, Adjudication Com. Occupl. Disease, Taipei City Govt., 1997—2005; co. physician Grand Hyatt Taipei, 2003—; attending physician dept. occupl. medicine Wanfang Mcpl. Hosp., Taiwan, 2007—; bd. mem. Taiwan Environ. & Occupl. Medicine Assn., 1996—. Contbr. articles to profl.jours. Recipient Pub. Health Contbn., Changhua Precinct Govt., Taiwan, 2000. Home: 7F No3 Lane 323 Jia Hsin St Taipei 10675 Taiwan Office: Dr Lin's Clinic No2-1 Section 1 Da-An Rd Taipei 10675 Taiwan Office Fax: 011886-2-27402105. Business E-Mail: ptsr.huang@msa.hinet.net.

HUANG, PO-HAN, dermatologist, educator; b. Kaohsiung, Taiwan, May 21, 1968; s. Chao-chun Huang and Chin-hsiang Huang-Chen; m. Chia-Chen Lu, Oct. 20, 1997; 1 child, Derek Yu-Chien. MD, China Med. U., Taichung, Taiwan, 1993. Bd. cert. dermatologist Chinese Dermatol. Soc., Tapei, 1997. Resident Chang Gung Meml. Hospital-Taipei, Taiwan, 1993—97; attending dermatologist Chang Gung Meml. Hospital-Kaohsing, 1997—; lectr. Su-Ren Inst. Medicine, Nursing and Mgmt., 2001—02, Nat. Kaohsiung U. Marine Tech., 2002—03, Chang Gung U., Taoyuen, 2003—. Chmn. dept. dermatology Chang Gung Meml. Hospital-Kaohsing, 2002—04, dir. psoriasis treatment ctr., 2002—. Contbr. articles to profl. jours. Recipient Intern of Yr. award, Chang Gung Meml. Hospital-Taipei, 1992, Outstanding Educator award by Interns, Chang Gung Meml. Hospital-Kaohsiung, 2005. Fellow: Am. Acad. Dermatology; mem.: Soc. Pediatric Dermatology, Phi Beta Kappa. Achievements include first to Establishment of the first and only psoriasis treatment center in Taiwan; research in Clinical Trials of Antipsoriatic Biologic; Coordination Reseach of Dermatology and Engineering; discovery of Pediatric varient of papulopurpuric glove and sock syndrome; research in Pediatric onychomycosis. Office: Chang Gung Meml Hosp-Kaohsiung No 123 Ta-pei road Niao-sung Hsiang Kaohsiung 833 Taiwan Office Fax: 886-7-7317123 ext 2421. Personal E-mail: michelle.lu@seed.net.tw. E-mail: dermahuang@cgmh.org.tw.

HUANG, POR JAU, cardiologist, educator; b. Tainan, Taiwan, Oct. 30, 1939; s. King Tau and Wu Mee (Tsai) Huang; m. Su-Fen Jung, Jan. 15, 1968; children: Irene Y., James C., Brian C. MD, Nat. Taiwan U., 1960. Intern, then resident in cardiology Nat. Taiwan U. Hosp., 1966—71; fellow cardiology Osaka (Japan) City U. Med. Coll. and Hosp., 1972; mem. faculty Nat. Taiwan U. Coll. Medicine and Hosp., 1973—, assoc. prof. medicine, 1980—85, prof., 1985—, nuclear cardiology sect., 1980—; fellow nuclear cardiology Columbia U.-St. Luke's Hosp. Ctr., NYC, 1978—79. Contbr. articles to profl. jours. Fellow, Am. Buf. Med. Advancement China, 1978—79. Mem.: Republic China Soc. Cardiology, Am. Soc. Nuclear Cardiology, Formosan Med. Assn. Home: 20 Lane 127, Sect 2 Sien-Sun N Rd Taipei 104 Taiwan Office: 1 Chang Te St Taipei 100 Taiwan also: Nat Taiwan U Hosp 7 Chung Shan South Rd Taiwan 100 Taipei Taiwan Office Phone: 886-2-23711306. Business E-Mail: porjau@ntuh.gov.tw.

HUANG, QIANG-MING QIMIN, physician, educator; b. Kunming, Mar. 13, 1956; MS, Hunan med. U., 1988; PhD, Karolinska Inst., 2001. Lectr. Dali Med. Coll., 1985—92; chief physician, vice dir. Yuxi Renming Hosp., Yuxi City, Yunnan Province, 2001—05; prof., chief physician Shanghai Sports U., Shanghai Shangde Hosp., 2006—. Recipient award, Adminstrn. Office of Sports Medicine Sweden; grant, Govt. of Yunnan Province. Office: Hengren Rd 200 Shanghai 200438 China E-mail: huaqia404@yahoo.com.cn.

HUANG, RONG-NAN, medical educator; b. Taiwan, Sept. 18, 1960; PhD, Nat. Taiwan U., 1992. Prof. Nat. Taiwan U., 2006—. Prof. Nat. Ctrl. U., 1995—2006. Mem.: Entomol. Soc. Taiwan. Avocation: jogging. Office: 27 Ln 113 Sec 4 Roosevelt Rd Taipei 106 Taiwan Office Fax: 27325017. Business E-Mail: rongent@ntu.edu.tw.

HUANG, SHERRY C., gastroenterologist, educator; b. Taiwan, July 24, 1968; SB, MIT, 1990; MD, Albert Einstein Coll. Medicine, 1994. Assoc. prof., dir. residency tng. U. Calif., San Diego Sch. Medicine, 2000—. Grant, NIH DDK, Found. Digestive Diseases, Am. Gastroenterology Assn. Fellow: Am. Acad. Pediat.; mem.: N.Am. Soc. Pediat. Gastroenterology and Nutrition. Office: 3030 Children's Way 5124 San Diego CA 92131 Office Fax: 858-966-7966. Business E-Mail: shuang@ucsd.edu.

HUANG, SONG-YUAN, health educator; b. Miaoli County, Taiwan, China, Aug. 19, 1942; s. Liang-Hsing Huang and San-Mei Chiu; m. Chia-Chin Chiu, Apr. 22, 1969; children: Hui-Chun, Yi-Chun. BEd, Nat. Taiwan Normal U., Taipei, 1965; MEd, U. Toledo, 1979, PhD, 1988. Cert. health edn specialist. Lectr. Nat. Taiwan Normal U., 1970—80, assoc. prof., 1980—88, prof., 1988—, chmn. dept. health edn., 1991—97, dean Office Internship, Supervision and Placement, 1997—2000. Sr. advisor John Tung Found., Taiwan, 1988—, Soc. Red Cross, 1989—; vis. scholar Chinese U. Hong Kong, 2001. Author: Health Promotion & Health Education, 1990; contbr. articles to profl. jours. Chair health edn. textbook com. for jr. h.s. Nat. Inst. Compilation and Transl., Taipei, 1995—2002. Recipient Biennial Disting. Scholar, Internat. Coun. Health, Phys. Edn., Recreation, Sport and Dance, 2002, Outstanding Contbn. award, Taiwan Health Promotion and Edn. Assocs., 2007; scholar, Nat. Sci. Coun., 1984—85, 1989—90. Mem.: Am. Assn. Health Edn., Am. Sch. Health Assn., Internat. Union Health Promotion and Edn., Nat. Health Promotion and Health Edn. Assn. (bd. dirs. 1982—), Nat. Sch. Health Assn. (pres. 1990—94, 1996—2000, 2004—), Phi Tau Phi (hon.). Avocations: reading, travel, writing, bicycling. Home: 5th Flr 2 Ln 5 Lung Chuan St Taipei Taiwan Office: Nat Taiwan Normal Univ 162 Hoping E Rd Sec 1 Taipei Taiwan

HUANG, WEI-SHENG, chemist, director; b. Gaoan, Jiangxi, China, Nov. 12, 1969; PhD, Shanghai Inst. Organic Chemistry, 1995. Assoc. dir. chemistry ARIAD Pharmaceuticals, 2011—. Mem.: Am. Chem. Soc. Avocations: badminton, soccer, singing. Office: 26 Landsdowne St Cambridge MA 02139 Business E-Mail: wei-sheng.huang@ariad.com.

HUANG, WEN-CHEN, gynecologist, educator; b. Kaoshiung, Taiwan, Apr. 13, 1970; MD, Nat. Cheng Kung U., 1997. Vis. staff Cathay Gen. Hosp., 2000—. Asst. prof. Taipei Med. U., 1998. Avocation: piano. Home: 280 Sec 4 Ren-Ai Rd Taipei 106 Taiwan Home Fax: 886-2-27094693. Personal E-mail: huangwc0413@hotmail.com.

HUANG, WENWEI, medical educator, integrative medicine doctor; b. Shantou, China, Mar. 15, 1979; s. Yongming Huang and Chujun Chen. B in Health care & rehab., Guangzhou U. Chinese Medicine, 2003, B in Traditional Chinese Medicine, 2004, M in Integrated Chinese Medicine & Western Medicine, 2006, PhD in Integrative Medicine, 2007; PhD diploma in Integrative Medicine, 2008; PhD candidate in Family Medicine & Quality Life, U. Hong Kong, 2008—. Cert. Internat. Soc. Quality Life, 2006, chinese medicine practitioner Ministry Health People's Republic China, 2005, in irritable bowel syndrome-quality life MAPI, France, 2006. Integrative medicine dr. Guangzhou U. Chinese Medicine, 2004—07; rschr. Family Medicine Unit, U. Hong Kong, Hong Kong, 2008—; academic tutor St. John's Coll., Hong Kong, 2008—; integrative medicine dr. Ministry Medicine Health Peoples Republic of Chaina, 2005; chinese medicine practitioner HKSAR, Hong Kong, 2009; chinese medicine physician PRC, 2005. Translator Internat. Coll. Guangzhou U. Chinese Medicine, 2002; integrative medicine dr. Guangzhou U. Chinese Medicine, 2004—07; rsch. project cons. Health Rsch. Assocs. Inc., Seattle, 2005—07; reviewer Elite Jour. Quality Life Rsch., Los Angeles, 2006—; reviewer Jour. Pain, NYC, 2007—; peer reviewer Jour. Quality Life Rsch., LA, 2007—, Jour. Assessment SAGE. Contbr. articles to profl. jours. Conf. organizing com. mem. Internat. Soc. Quality Life, Lisbon, Portugal, 2005—06; assoc. dir. Chinese Calligraphy & Painting Inst. GZUCM, Guangzhou, 1999; rep. Shantou TV Channel, 1999; mem. Guangzhou U. Chinese Medicine, 2004—04. Recipient First prize, Chinese Calligraphy Competition, 1994, Excellent Postgrad., GZUCM, 2006, Excellence award, Shanzhang Mid. Sch. Shantou, 1992, 1993, 1994, award, Shanzhang Mid. Sch., 1995, Tri-Good Quintessence Student award, Shantou, 1995, First prize, Nat. Chemistry Olympic Competition, 1995, Chinese Calligraphy, 1998, 2000; ISOQOL scholarship, USA, 2006. Fellow: IBA Cambridge (life); mem.: MRC (Poster Presentation award 2009), ISOQOL (Oral Presentation award 2006, Poster Presentation award 2009), Hong Kong Soc. Quality Life, Internat. Soc. Quality Life. Achievements include development of Chinese irritable bowel syndrome-quality of life (IBS-QOL) questionnaire & sub-health questionnarie (SHQ). Office: St John Coll HKU Rm 3003 New Wing 82 Pokfulam Hong Kong China Office Phone: 00852-98041597. Business E-Mail: puppy88@gmail.com.

HUANG, WU-JANG, chemistry professor, materials scientist; s. Chiu-Chalg and Hsia (Wang) Huang; m. Suey-Chun Chu, Feb. 18, 2001; 1 child, Magin. PhD in Polymer Sci., Nat. Chaio-Tun U., Taiwan, 2000. Rschr. Formosa Plastic Co., Taipei County, Taiwan, 2000; asst. prof. Nat. Pingtung U. Sci. and Tech., 2000—04, assoc. prof., 2004—. Bd. mem Bioassy Testing Assn. in Taiwan, Pingtung, Taiwan, 2004—. Recipient Rsch. award, Nat. Pingtung U. Sci. and Tech., 2003. Mem.: Chinese Chem. Soc. (Taiwan). Office: Nat Pingtung U Sci & Tech EP 107 Rm 1 Hseuh Rd Neipu Pingtung 91201 Taiwan Office Fax: 886-8-7740256. Business E-Mail: wjhuang@mail.npust.edu.tw.

HUANG, XIAOZHEN, cardiologist, educator; b. Jinan, China, Mar. 17, 1970; MD, Shandong U., 2011. Assoc. prof. Jinan Huaiyin Hosp., China, 1991—. Office: Jing 4 Rd 589# Jinan Shandong 250021 China Business E-Mail: huangxiaozhen2@sina.com.

HUANG, YING CHIEH, emergency physician; b. Kaohsiung, Taiwan, Nov. 27, 1962; s. Chun-Jen Huang and Shiow-Jy Chen; m. Cristina Yang, Oct. 25, 1991; children: Eric, Eddie. MD, Kaohsiung Med. U., 1987. Diplomate Nat. Bd. Med. Examiners. Chief dept. emergency medicine Kaohsiung Med. U. Hosp., 1994—97, Chiayi Christian Hosp., Chiayi City, Taiwan, 1997—. Mem.: Taiwan Soc. Emergency Medicine (dir. clin. policy 1997—2004), Am. Coll. Emergency Medicine. Personal E-mail: galaxy.bear@msa.hinet.net.

HUANG, YU-CHUAN, medical researcher; b. Taiwan, Feb. 28, 1974; PhD, Nat. Def. Med. Ctr., 2009. Asst. rsch. fellow Inst. Preventive Medicine, 2008—. Office: Minquan E Rd Taipei Neihu 114 Taiwan Business E-Mail: alexha@mail.ndmctsgh.edu.tw.

HUARD, DONALD V., psychologist, educator; b. Dearborn, Mich., May 9, 1932; s. George Raymond and Viola Margaret Huard; m. Marie Darlene Fournier, June 13, 1957 (dec. Nov. 2, 1981); children: Christopher Leon, Theresa Anne, David Donald, Gregory George; m. Margaret Eugenia Russell, July 2, 1982. AA, Phoenix C.C., Ariz., 1955; BS, Ariz State U., Tempe, 1957; MA, Ariz.State U., 1959, PhD, 1971. Lectr. in psychology Ariz. State U., 1960—62; prof. psychology and stats. Phoenix C.C., 1963—98, prof. emeritus. Emphasis editl. writer The Phoenix Gazette, 1980—81; assoc. editor The Maricopa County C.C. Jour., Phoenix, 1982—83. Author: (books) Behavioral Statistics, 1992, The Violence That Prevails, 1996, Teen Agers: What Will Drugs, Safe Sex Do to You?, 1997, Where Grandpa's Been: An Autobiography, 1999, Youth Deficit Disorder, 2001, You Need a Red Hat, 2002, America's Guns & the Second Amendment, 2009; contbr. Mem., contbr. Brady Campaign to Prevent Gun Violence, Wash. Cpl. US Army, 1952—54, Alaska. Avocations: photography, travel, writing. Home: 7305 E Goodnight Ln Prescott Valley AZ 86314 Personal E-mail: donderhead@juno.com.

HUBBARD, LINCOLN BEALS, medical physicist, consultant; b. Hawkesbury, Ontario, Sept. 8, 1940; arrived in U.S., 1957; s. Carroll Chauncey and Mary Lunn (Beals) Hubbard; m. Nancy Ann Krieger, Apr. 3, 1961; children: Jill, Katrina. BS in Physics, U. NH, 1961; PhD, MIT, 1967. Diplomate Am. Bd. Radiology, cert. health physicist Am. Bd. Health Physics. Postdoctoral appointee Argonne Nat. Lab., 1966—68; asst. prof. math. and physics Knoxville (Tenn.) Coll., 1968—70; asst. prof. physics Furman U., Greenville, SC, 1970—74; chief physicist Mt. Sinai Hosp., Chgo., 1974—75, 1979—2002, Cook County Hosp., Chgo., 1975—88; prof. med. physics Rush U., 1986—; ptnr. Fields, Griffith, Hubbard & Assoc., Ltd., 1978—93; pres. Hubbard, Zickgraf & Broadbent, Inc., 1993—. Author (with S.S. Stefani): Mathematics for Technologists, 1979; author: (with G.B. Greenfield) Computers in Radiology, 1984. Fellow: Am. Coll. Radiology, Am. Assn. Physicists in Medicine. Home and Office: 4113 W End Rd Downers Grove IL 60515-2307 Home Phone: 630-963-2913; Office Phone: 630-963-2913.

HUBBELL, FLOYD ALLAN, internist, educator; b. Waco, Tex., Nov. 13, 1948; s. F.E. and Margaret (Fraser) H.; m. Nancy Cooper, May 23, 1975; 1 child, Andrew Allan. BA, Baylor U., 1971, MD, 1974; MS in Pub. Health, UCLA, 1983. Diplomate Am. Bd. Internal Medicine. Intern, then resident Long Beach med. program U. Calif., Irvine, 1975-78, asst. prof. medicine, 1981-89, assoc. prof. medicine and social ecology, 1989-97, prof. medicine, 1997—, dir. primary care internal medicine residency, 1992-97, chief divsn. gen. internal medicine and primary care, 1992—2002, dir. Ctr. for Health Policy and Rsch., 1993—2003, chair dept. medicine, 2001—08, sr. assoc. dean, academic affairs, 2008—, prof. pub. health, 2007—, prof. nursing sci., 2010—, exec. vice dean, 2010—. Contbr. articles to profl. jours. Fellow ACP; mem. APHA, Soc. Gen. Internal Medicine, Physicians for Social Responsibility, Assn. Profs. Medicine. Democrat. Avocations: reading, skiing, water sports. Office: U Calif 264 Irvine Hall 1001 Health Scis Rd Irvine CA 92697-395 E-mail: fahubbel@uci.edu.

HUBEL, DAVID HUNTER, physiologist, science educator; b. Windsor, Ont., Can., Feb. 27, 1926; s. Jesse Hervey and Elsie (Hunter) Hubel; m. Shirley Ruth Izzard, June 20, 1953; children: Carl Andrew, Eric David, Paul Matthew. BSc, McGill U., Montreal, Que., Can., 1947, MD, 1951, DSc (hon.), 1978, U. Man., 1983, U. Western Ont., 1993, Oxford U., 1994, Gustavus Adolphus Coll., 1994, Ohio State U., 1995; D (hon.), U. Madrid, 1997, U. Miguel, 1998, U. Toronto, 2002, SUNY, 2004, McMaster U., 2005; DHL (hon.), Johns Hopkins U., 1990; JD (hon.), Dalhousie U., 1998. Intern Montreal Gen. Hosp., 1951—52; asst. resident neurology Montreal Neurol. Inst., 1952—53, fellow clin. neurophysiology, 1953—54; asst. resident neurology Johns Hopkins Hosp., Balt., 1954—55; rsch. fellow Walter Reed Army Inst. Rsch., Washington, 1955—58; sr. fellow neurol. scis. group Johns Hopkins U., 1958—59; faculty Harvard Med. Sch., Boston, 1959—, George Packer Berry prof. physiology, chmn. dept., 1967—68, George Packer Berry prof. neurobiology, 1968—82, John Franklin Enders Univ. prof., 1982—2004, John Franklin Enders prof. neurobiology emeritus, 2004—. George Eastman prof., Oxford, England, 1991—92. Contbr. articles to profl. jours. With AUS, 1955—58. Recipient Trustees award, Rsch. Prevent Blindness, 1971, Lewis S. Rosentiel award for disting. work in basic med. rsch., 1972, Karl Lashley prize, Am. Philos. Soc., 1977, Louisa Gross Horwitz prize, Columbia U., 1978, Dickson prize in medicine, U. Pitts., 1979, Ledile prize, Harvard U., 1980, Nobel prize in physiology/medicine, 1981, Outstanding Sci. Leadership award, Nat. Assn. Biomed. Rsch., 1990, Glen A. Fry medal, Coll. Optometry, Ohio State U., 1991, Helen Keller award, Helen Keller Eye Rsch. Found., 1995. Fellow: AAAS, Am. Acad. Arts & Scis.; mem.: NAS, Acadmica Europaea (fgn. mem.), Royal Soc. London, Am. Philos. Soc. (Karl Spencer Lashley prize 1977), Johns Hopkins U. Soc. Scholars, Spanish Soc. Ophthalmology (hon.), Assn. Rsch. Vision & Ophthalmology (Friedenwald award 1975), Soc. Neurosci. (Bwditch lectr. 1966), German Acad. Scis. (Grass lectr. 1976, Gerard award 1993), Am. Physiol. Soc., Sigma Xi. Office: Harvard Med Sch Dept Neurobiology 220 Longwood Ave Goldenson Bldg Rm 420 Boston MA 02115-5701 *

HUBER, DONALD SIMON, physician; b. Clarendon, Pa., Apr. 18, 1929; s. Walter Casper and Mary Agnes (Earley) H.; m. Mary Hanks, Sept. 6, 1958; children: Donald Scott, Mark Walter, Mary Lisa. BA, Duke U., 1951, MD, 1954. Diplomate Am. Bd. Internal Medicine, Am. Bd. Allergy and Immunology. Intern Charity Hosp., New Orleans, 1954-55; resident internal medicine Tulane U. Hosp., New Orleans, 1955-56, 58-60; pvt. practice Huntsville, Ala., 1960-96 (ret. 1996); clin. assoc. prof. medicine Sch. Primary Med. Care, Huntsville, 1985—. Med. dir. Cmty. Free Clinic., 1998—. Lt. commdr. USN, 1956-58, USNR, 1958-60. Fellow Am. Coll. Allergists; mem. AMA, Am. Acad. Allergy and Immunology, Ala. Soc. Allergy and Immunology (pres. 1985), Huntsville Rotary Club (bd. dirs. 1978). Republican. Methodist. Avocation: travel. Home: 507 Holmes Ave Huntsville AL 35801 E-mail: donhuber@comcast.net.

HUBERFELD, NICOLE LAUREN, healthcare educator; b. Balt. m. David Treacy, July 2, 2004. BA, U. Pa., 1995; JD, Seton Hall U., 1998. Assoc. healthcare team Wilentz, Goldman and Spitzer, Woodbridge, NJ, 1998—2000; assoc. health law group Gibbons Del Deo, Newark, 2000—02; assoc. healthcare group Wolff and Samson, West Orange, 2002—03; dir. healthcare compliance cert. program Law Sch. Seton Hall U., Newark, 2003—05, health law faculty fellow Law Sch., 2003—05; asst. prof. Coll. Law U. Ky., Lexington, 2005—08; Willbunt D. Ham assoc. prof. law UK Coll. Law, 2008—. Contbr. articles to profl. jours. Team leader Komen Race for Cure, NYC, 2000—02, Lexington, 2005, Revlon Run/Walk Women's Cancers, NYC, 2000—02; vol. Habitat for Humanity, Newark, 2000—05, Lexington, 2005—, fundraiser, 2000—05. Recipient award, Trustees Coun. Pa. Women, 1994, Raymond DelTufo Constl. Law award, Seton Hall Law Sch., 1998; named Outstanding Woman Law Grad., Nat. Assn. Women Lawyers, 1998. Mem.: Am. Health Lawyers Assn. (mem. fraud and abuse practice group enforcement panel 2005—), Am. Soc. Law, Medicine and Ethics. Avocations: scuba diving, yoga, travel, hiking, cooking. Office: U Ky Coll Law 258 Law Bldg Lexington KY 40506 Business E-Mail: nicole.huberfeld@uky.edu.

HUBERT, HELEN BETTY, epidemiologist; b. NYC, Jan. 22, 1950; d. Leo and Ruth (Rosenbaum) H.; m. Carlos Barbaro Arostegui, Sept. 11, 1976 (div. May 1987); 1 child, Joshua Daniel Hubert. BA magna cum laude, Barnard Coll., 1970; MPH, Yale U., 1973, MPhil, 1976, PhD, 1978. Rsch. assoc. Yale U., New Haven, 1977-78; rsch. epidemiologist Nat. Heart, Lung and Blood Inst., Bethesda, Md., 1978-84; rsch. dir. Gen. Health, Inc., Washington, 1984-87; sr. rsch. scientist Stanford (Calif.) U., 1988—2007, cons. epidemiologist, 2007—. Peer rev. Am. Jour. Epidemiology, Am. Jour. Pub. Health, Chest, Jour. AMA (JAMA), Archives Internal Medicine; contbr. articles to profl. jours., chpts. to books. NIH grantee, 1997-2007. Mem. Am. Coll. Epidemiology, Soc. Epidemiol. Rsch., Phi Beta Kappa, Sigma Xi (grant-in-aid for rsch. 1978). Home: 1043 Oakland Ave Menlo Park CA 94025-2205 Home Phone: 650-323-4744. Personal E-mail: helen.hubert@sbcglobal.net.

HUBERT, LAWRENCE J., psychology professor; PhD, Stanford U. Prof. stats. and ednl. psychology U. Ill., Champaign, Lyle H. Lanier prof. psychology, former head psychology dept. Contbr. articles to profl. jours. Office: Dept Psychology 433 Pscyhology Bldg 603 East Daniel St MC 716 Champaign IL 61820 Office Phone: 217-333-6593. Office Fax: 217-244-5876. E-mail: lhubert@uiuc.edu.

HUCK, JOHN LLOYD, pharmaceutical executive; b. Bklyn., July 17, 1922; s. John Lloyd and Adrienne (Warner) H.; m. Dorothy Bertha Foehr, Nov. 20, 1943; children: Lloyd E., Jeanne Huck Leslie-Hughes, Virginia Huck Stalcup. BS in Chemistry, Pa. State U., 1946. Research chemist Hoffmann-LaRoche, Nutley, NJ, 1946, sales rep., 1948, dir. sales tng., 1951, asst. gen. sales mgr., 1955, dir. product devel., 1958; dir. mktg. Merck Sharp & Dohme Div., West Point, Pa., 1958; v.p. mktg. planning MSD div., 1966, v.p. sales and mktg., 1968, exec. v.p., 1969, exec. v.p., gen. mgr., 1972, pres., 1973; sr. v.p. Merck & Co., Rahway, NJ, 1975, exec. v.p., 1977, dir., 1977-86, pres., chief operating officer, 1978-85, chmn. bd., 1985-86; chmn. bd., chief exec. officer Nova Pharm. Corp., Morristown, NJ, 1986-88, chmn. bd., 1988-91; dir. Found. Mt. Nittany Med. Ctr., 2008—. Patentee in field. Trustee Pa. State U., 1977-92, v.p., 1985-88, pres. bd., 1988-91; trustee Morristown Meml. Health Found., Inc., N.J., 1979-96, chmn. bd., 1986-88; trustee Geraldine R. Dodge Found., 1987-2003. 1st lt. USAAF, 1942-46. Alumni fellow Coll. Medicine Pa. State U., 1980, Coll. of Sci., 1983; named to Nutley Hall of Fame, 2003. Mem. Centre Hills Country Club. Home: 233 Lion's Hill Rd State College PA 16803

HUCKMAN, MICHAEL SAUL, neuroradiologist, educator; b. Newark, Aug. 20, 1936; s. Louis Fillmore and Mollie (Lehman) H.; m. Beverly Joy Blachman, Aug. 2, 1964; children: Andrew Garfield, Robert Steven. AB, Princeton U., 1958; MD, St. Louis U., 1962. Rotating intern, then resident in radiology Phila. Gen. Hosp., 1962-63, 65-68; fellow in neuroradiology Edward Mallinckrodt Inst. Radiology, Washington U., St. Louis, also univ. instr. radiology, 1968-70; mem. faculty Rush Med. Coll., Chgo., 1970—, prof. radiology, 1978—; dir. sect. neuroradiology Rush U. Med. Ctr., 1970—; mem. faculty Cook County Grad. Sch. Medicine, 1972-91. Cons. Nat. Ctr. for Health Care Tech., 1980-81; sec.-gen. XVI Symposium Neuroradiologicum, 1994-98. Editor-in-chief: Am. Jour. Neuroradiology, 1989-97; mem. editorial bd. Jour. Computer Assisted Tomography, 1976-94, Radiographics, 1983-87, Applied Radiology, 1987-89; cons. editor Am. Jour. Roentgenology, 1990-91; contbr. articles to med. jours. Served with USNR, 1963-65. Spl. fellow Nat. Inst. Neurol. Diseases and Blindness, 1968-70 Fellow Am. Coll. Radiology, Coll. Physicians of Phila.; mem. AMA, Am. Soc. Neuroradiology (sec. 1980-83, pres. elect 1986-87, pres. 1987-88, editor emeritus 1998—, archivist 1998—, Gold medal 1999), Radiol. Soc. N.Am. (Gold medal 2002), Am. Soc. Head and Neck Radiology, Am. Roentgen Ray Soc., Assn. Univ. Radiologists, Am. Soc. Pediatric Neuroradiology, World Fedn. Neuroradiol. Socs. (historian 1993-97, v.p. 1997—, pres.-elect 1998, pres. 2002—2006), European Soc. Neuroradiology (hon.), Ill. Med. Soc., Ill. Radiol. Soc., Chgo. Med. Soc., Blockley Radiol. Soc., Soc. for Scholarly Publ., Japanese Soc. Neuroradiology (hon.), Coun. Biology Editors, Soc. Fifth Line, Indian Soc. Neuroradiology (hon. life), Sigma Xi, Phi Delta Epsilon. Clubs: Princeton Alumni of Chgo. (trustee 1982-84), Caxton. Jewish. Office: 1653 W Congress Pky Chicago IL 60612-3809 E-mail: m.huckman@comcast.net.

HUCKSTEP, RONALD LAWRIE, traumatic and orthopaedic surgery educator, consultant; b. Chefoo, China, July 22, 1926; (parents English citizens), arrived in Australia, 1972; s. Herbert George and Agnes (Lawrie-Smith) H.; m. Margaret Ann Macbeth, Jan. 2, 1960; children: Susan, Michael, Nigel. MA, MB BChir, Cambridge U., Eng., 1952, MD, 1957; MD (hon.), U. New South Wales, Australia, 1988. Chief asst. orthopaedic dept. St. Bartholomews Hosp., London, 1959-60; prof. orthopaedic surgery Makerere U., Kampala, Uganda, 1960-71; found. prof., head dept. traumatic and orthopaedic surgery U. New South Wales, Sydney, Australia, 1972-92, chmn. sch. surgery, 1972-92, emeritus prof., 1993—; dir. accident svcs., chmn. orthopaedic surgery Prince of Wales Hosp., Sydney, Australia, 1972-92. Hon. cons. orthopaedic surgeon Mulago and Mengo Hosps. and Round Table Polio Clinic, Kampala, 1960—72; hon. orthopaedic surgeon to all govt. and mission hosps., Uganda, 1960—72; hon. adviser to Rotary Internat., The Commonwealth Found., WHO, UN, 1970—; sr. med. disaster comdr., chmn. various disaster and emergency coms. Dept. Health, New South Wales, Australia, 1972; founder, hon. mem. World Orthopaedic Concern, 1973—2002; cons. orthopaedic surgeon Royal S. Sydney and Sutherland Hosps., Sydney, 1974—92; hon. prof. dept. surgery U. Sydney, 1995—; vis. prof. surgery Sydney U., 1995—. Author: (Book) Typhoid Fever and Other Salmonella Infections, 1962, A Simple Guide to Trauma, 5th edit., 1995, A Simple Guide to Trauma, Italian edit., 1978, A Simple Guide to Trauma, Japanese edit., 1982, Poliomyelitis Including Appliances and Rehabilitation, 1975, A Simple Guide to Orthopaedics, 1993, Picture Tests orthopaedics and Trauma, 1994; contbr. chapters to books Brit. Jour. Bone and Joint Surgery, 1965—72. Recipient Melsome Meml. prize, 1948, Raymond Horton Smith prize, 1957, Irving Geist award Internat. Soc. for Rehab. of Disabled, 1969, James Cook medal Royal Soc. New South Wales, 1984, Humanitarian award Orthopaedics Overseas, 1991, Centenary medal Australia, 2003, Eyre-Brook medal, World Orthop. Concern, 2009; Paul Harris fellow and medal Rotary Internat. and Rotary Found., 1987. Fellow Royal Coll. Surgeons Edinburgh, Royal Coll. Surgeons Eng., Royal Australasian Coll. Surgeons Australia, Australian Acad. Technol. Scis. and Engring. (K.L. Sutherland medal 1986), Australian Orthopaedic Assn. (v.p. 1982, Betts Meml. medal 1983), Brit. Orthopaedic Assn., Western Pacific Orthopaedic Assn. (hon.), Assn. Surgeons Uganda (hon.); mem. Coast Med. Assn. (pres. 1986), Med. Soc. U. New South Wales (patron), Australian Club. Achievements include invention of Huckstep locking nail and hip plus calipers and wheelchairs for developing countries. Home and Office: 108 Sugarloaf Crescent Castlecrag Sydney NSW 2068 Australia Business E-Mail: rlh333@optusnet.com.au.

HUCUMENOGLU, SEMA, medical educator; b. Yesilhisar, Turkey, Sept. 9, 1961; Degree, Hacettepe U., 1985. Assoc. prof. & chief, pathology dept. Etlik Ihtisas Edn. and Rsch. Hosp., 1985—. Home: Hosdere 164/3 Ankara 06550 Turkey Personal E-mail: semah3@gmail.com.

HUDAK, CHRISTINE ANGELA, health informatics educator, specialist; b. Cleve., Dec. 13, 1950; d. Ernest J. and Helen M. (Orovets) H. BSN, Case Western Res. U., 1974; MEd in Post-

Secondary Edn., Cleve. State U., 1980, PhD, 1998. Cert. informatics nurse, Am. Nurses Credentialing Ctr.; profl. health info. mgmt. sys. Healthcare Info. Mgmt. Sys. Soc., CPHIMS, 2006. Pub. health nurse Vis. Nurse Assn. of Cleve., 1974-75; clin. preceptor physician's asst. program Cuyahoga Community Coll., Cleve., 1975-77; staff nurse MetroHealth Ctr. for Skilled Nursing Care, Cleve., 1977-78; staff devel. instr. The MetroHealth System, Cleve., 1978-82, instr. in continuing edn., 1982-85, health care analyst, info. specialist, 1985-87; coord. clin. info. systems tng. Metro Health System, Cleve., 1987-90, mgr. specialized instnl. progs., 1990-94; mgr. user support svcs. Metro Health Sys., Cleve., 1994-95; lectr., lead instr. nursing informatics Case Western Res. U., Cleve., 1995-98, asst. prof. nursing informatics and mgmt., 1998—, dir. Nurse Web, 2002—, assoc. prof., 2006—. Dir. MS in nursing informatics program Case-Western Res. U., 2002—; instr. in health care info. systems adult degree program Capital U., Cleve.; instr. div. continuing edn. Cleve. State U.; clin. instr. nursing info. systems Case Western Res. U., 1990, part-time instr. nursing info. systems, 1990-95. Mem. Am. Assn. Artificial Intelligence, Am. Med. Informatics Assn., Am. Soc. Health Info. Mgrs., Ctr. Profl. Ethics (charter), Ednl. Computer Consortium Ohio, Midwest Alliance for Nursing Informatics, Am. Nursing Informatics Assn., Hosp. Info. and Mgmt. Systems Soc., Nat. League for Nursing, Phi Delta Kappa, Pi Lambda Theta, Sigma Theta Tau, Midwest Nursing Rsch. Soc. Office: Case Western Res U Frances Payne Bolton Sch Nursing 10900 Euclid Ave Cleveland OH 44106-4904 Home Phone: 216-371-4639; Office Phone: 216-368-6315. Business E-Mail: cah16@case.edu.

HUDD, NICHOLAS PAYNE, retired physician; b. Romford, Essex, Eng., Oct. 11, 1945; s. Harold Payne and Marguerita Eva (Clarke) H.; m. Gwendeleen Mary Johnstone, Oct. 11, 1969; children: Alastair Payne, Anne Marguerita Jane, Robert Nicholas Harold. BA, Sidney Sussex Coll., Cambridge, Eng., 1967, MB, BChir, Sidney Sussex Coll., Cambridge, Eng., 1970, MA, 1971. House surgeon Westminster Children's Hosp., 1970; house physician Princess Alexandra Hosp., Harlow, Essex, Eng., 1971; sr. house officer Orsett Hosp., Grays, Essex, Eng., 1972; med. registrar Basildon (Eng.) Hosp., 1972-74; pathology registrar Orsett Hosp., Grays, 1974-76; sr. med. registrar Manchester Royal Infirmary, Eng., 1976-78, Benenden Hosp., 1978-79, cons. physician, 1980—2003. Chmn. Romney Marsh Hist. Chs. Trust, 1988-96; pres. The Rising Mercury Soc., 1994-2004, churchwarden St. Mildred's Ch., Tenterden, 1983-88; condr. Benenden Hosp. Choir. Fellow Royal Soc. Medicine, Royal Coll. Physicians; mem. Brit. Diabetic Assn. Kent County Cricket Club, Tenterden Golf Club, Royal Nat. Rose Soc. Anglican. Avocations: golf, gardening, singing, history, pontificating. Home: 13 Elmfield Tenterden TN30 6RE England

HUDDER, ALICE MARY, toxicologist, educator; d. Phyllis R. and Paul R. Hudder. BA, Hofstra U., Hempstead, NY, 1981; MA, 1987; PhD, U. Miami, Fla., 2000. Naturalist Hofstra U. Marine Lab., Priory, St. Ann's, Jamaica, 1981—85; rsch. specialist U. Miami Sch. Medicine, 1985—89, rsch. specialist II, 1989—91, rsch. assoc., 1991—93, sr. rsch. assoc., 1993—95, postdoc. rsch. assoc., 2000—03; adj. faculty St. Thomas U., Miami, 1988—89; asst. scientist U. Miami Rosenstiel Sch. Marine & Atmospheric Sci., Virginia Key, 2003—07; asst. prof. Wayne State U. IEHS, Detroit, 2007—. Editl. assoc. IUBMB Life, Miami, 2000—03. Contbr. articles to profl. jours. Recipient Margaret Whelan Travel award, U. Miami Sch. Medicine Med. Faculty, 1998, Nancy Noble award, U. Miami Dept. Biochemistry & Molecular Biology, 1997, 1999, named Scholar, State Fla., 1999—2000; grantee, NIH SBIR, 2010—11; Fellowship, U. Miami, 1995—98, Pilot Project grant, NIH, NIEHS Marine & Freshwater Biomedical Scis. Ctr., 2006—07, Rsch. grant, Korein Found., 2005—07. Mem.: IAGLR, Soc. Toxicology. Avocations: bicycling, rock climbing, travel. Office: Wayne State University 259 Mack Ave Detroit MI 48201 Office Phone: 313-577-6578. Business E-Mail: alice.hudder@wayne.edu.

HUDES, GARY R., oncologist, educator; BEE, Rutgers U.; MD, SUNY. Diplomate Am. Bd. Internal Medicine-med. oncology. Resident internal medicine Grad. Hosp., Phila.; fellow hematology-oncology Presbyterian-Univ. of Pa. Med. Ctr., Phila.; prof. Rsch. at Fox Chase; dir. genitourinary malignancies Fox Chase Cancer Ctr., 1985—. Co-author: (publs.) New paradigm in dose-finding trials: Patient-specific dosing and beyond phase I, 2005, Impact of zoledronic acid on renal function in patients with cancer: Clinical significance and development of a predictive model, 2006, Phase II study of KOS-862 in patients with metastatic androgen independent prostate cancer previously treated with docetaxel, 2007, NCCN Task Force Report: mTOR inhibition in solid tumors, 2008, Effect of temsirolimus versus interferon-alpha on outcome of patients with advanced renal cell carcinoma of different tumor histologies, 2009, Global Reactivation of Epigenetically Silenced Genes in Prostate Cancer, 2010, and numerous other publs. Mem.: ACP, Radiation Therapy Oncology Group, Pa. Soc. of Oncology and Hematology, Am. Assn. for the Advancement of Sci., Am. Soc. for Clin. Oncology, Am. Assn. for Cancer Rsch. Office: Fox Chase Cancer Center 333 Cottman Ave Philadelphia PA 19111 Office Phone: 215-728-6900.

HUDIK, MARTIN FRANCIS, hospital administrator, educator, consultant, writer; b. Chgo., Mar. 27, 1949; s. Joseph and Rose H.; m. Eileen Hudik; 1 child, Theresa Margaret Hudik Gisseler. AAS in Engring., Morton Coll., 1969; BSMAE in Mech. and Aerospace Engring., Ill. Inst. Tech., 1971; BPA, Jackson State U., 1974; MBA, Loyola U., 1975; postgrad., U. Sarasota, 1975-76. Cert. health care safety mgr., hazard control mgr., hazardous materials mgr., OSHA hazardous materials response instr., hazardous materials incident comdr., disaster coord., police instr., Ill., security cert. instr., Ill. With Ill. Masonic Med. Ctr., Chgo., 1969-94, dir. risk mgmt., 1974-79, asst. adminstr., 1979-94; facilities engring. mgr. Bethany/Adv. Hosp., 1997-98; health care cons., 1995—2005; bus. mgr. St. Bernadine Parish, 2001—11. Capt. tng. divsn. Cicero (Ill.) Police Dept., tng. and internal affairs divsn., aux. divsn., 1971-99, U.S. Dept. Commerce, 2000, ind. cons., 2000; instr. Nat. Safety Coun. Safety Tng. Inst., Chgo., 1977-85; cons. Coun. Tech. users Consumer Products, Underwriters Labs., Chgo., 1977-96; instr., lt. U.S. Def. Civil Preparedness Agy. Staff Coll., Battle Creek, Mich., 1977-85; liaison officer to Cook County Emergency Svcs.; asst. dir. Emergency Svcs. and disaster Agy. Town of Cicero, 1988-97; founding pres. Cook County Emergency Mgmt. Coun., 1991-92; exec. bd., pres. U.S. Postal Svc. Postal Customer Adv. Coun., Cicero, 1996-99, sec., v.p., exec. bd., 2003—; mem. exec. bd. Chicagoland Postal Adv. Coun., 1994-2006, 2008-; exec. bd. advisor Cicero PCAC, 1998—. Co-chmn. Archdiocese of Chicago Deanery IV-C, 1999—2003; active Cath. Edn. Com., 2000—03; pastoral coun. Archdiocese Chgo., 2000—03; pres. sch. bd. Mary Queen of Heaven Sch., Cicero, 1977—79, 1984—86, Mary Queen of Heaven Ch. Coun., 1979—81, 1983—86, St. Leonard Parish Coun., 1998—2001, St. Bernardine Parish Coun., 2001—05, St. Bernardine Fin. Coun., 2001—, I.M.M.C. Employee Club, 1983—86. Recipient Presdl. Sports award, Amateur Athletic Union, 1978, 1980—81, Spl. Svc. award Underwriters Lab., 1992, Presdl. Sports award, Amateur Athletic Union, 2000, Meritorious Svc. award, Town of Cicero, 1990, medal of Merit, 1996, Emergency Svcs. Achievement award, 1997, Police Achievement award, 1998, Spl. Svc. award, Cook County Sheriffs Dept., 1993, Excellence in Svc. award, U.S. Postal Svc., 1997, Outstanding Effort award, 1998, Outstanding Svcs. award, Cicero Postal Coun., 1998, Svc. Recognition award, 1999, Outstanding Performance award, 2001, Volunteerism award, U.S. Postal Svc., 2002, Svc. Recognition award, Archdiocese of Chgo., 2003; scholar state scholar, Ill., 1969—71. Mem. Am. Coll. Healthcare Execs., Am. Soc. Hosp. Risk Mgmt., Nat. Fire Protection Assn., Am. Soc. SafetyEngrs. (profl.), Am. Soc. Law and Medicine, Ill. Hosp. Security and Safety Assn. (co-founder 1976, founding pres. 1976-77, hon. dir. 1977-82), Cath. Alumni Club Chgo. (bd. dirs. 1983-84, 86), Mensa, KC (mem. 4th degree cardinal coun., 25 Yr. Svc. award 2002), Pi Tau Sigma, Tau Beta Pi, Alpha Sigma Nu. Democrat. Roman Catholic. Home: 7246 W Harrison St Forest Park IL 60130-2345 Office: 6845 Riverside Dr Berwyn IL 60402-2231

HUDIS, CLIFFORD ALAN, internist, oncologist; b. Phila., 1959; m. Jane Hertzmark, Nov. 2003. BA, Lehigh U.; MD, Med. Coll. Pa., 1983. Diplomate Am. Bd. Internal Medicine, Am. Bd. Oncology. Intern, internal medicine Med. Coll. Pa., Phila., 1983-84, resident, internal medicine, 1983—87, chief med. Resident, 1986—87; fellow, med. oncology and hematology Meml. Sloan-Kettering Cancer Ctr., NYC, 1988-91, chief, breast cancer medicine svc., 1998—; clin. asst. Meml. Hosp., NYC, 1991—94, asst. attending physician, 1994—2000, assoc. attending physician, 2000—07, attending, 2007—; instr. Weill Med. Coll. Cornell U., NYC, 1991-94, asst. prof. medicine, 1994—2000, assoc. prof. medicine, 2000—07, prof. medicine, 2007—. Co-leader, breast disease mgmt. team Meml. Sloan-Kettering Cancer Ctr.; co-chair Breast Com. Cancer and Leukemia Group B; mem. Breast Com. Radiation Therapy Oncology Group, Nat. Comprehensive Cancer Network. Contbr. numerous articles to profl. publs., chpts. to books; editl. bd. mem. Journal of Clinical Oncology, Clinical Cancer Research, Cancer Investigation. Mem. ACP, Am. Soc. Clin. Oncology (past chair internet svcs. com., info. technol. treas 2009-), Am. Assn. Cancer Rsch. Office: Meml Sloan Kettering 1275 York Ave New York NY 10065 Office Phone: 212-639-5449, 646-888-4551. Business E-Mail: hudisc@mskcc.org.

HUDSON, JOEL EDWARD, former state legislator, pharmacist; b. Lamar County, Miss., May 26, 1939; m. Kathy Hatten; children: Jolynn, Christopher Lee. Student, U. So. Miss., Samford U. Pharmacist Hattiesburg, Miss., owner Hudson Pharmacy; state legislator Miss. Ho. of Reps., Jackson, 1996—2008, mem. agrl., game and fish com., mem. judiciary B com., mem. juvenile justice com., mem. pub. health com., mem. appropriations com., mem. transp. com., mem. PEER com., mem. Medicaid com., mem. pub. health and welfare com., mem. wildlife fishers and pks., univs., and colls. Mem. Miss. Pharmacy Assn., Nat. Assn. of Retail Druggists, Farm Bur., C. of C. Democrat. Baptist. Home: RR 1 Box 4B Monticello MS 39654-9801 Office: State Capitol Bldg PO Box 1018 Jackson MS 39215-1018 Office Phone: 601-455-0294.

HUDSON, KATHY, microbiologist, geneticist, educator; BA in Biology, Carleton Coll., MS in Microbiology, U. Chgo.; PhD in Molecular Biology, U. Calif., Berkeley. Asst. dir. Nat. Human Genome Rsch. Inst.; founder & dir. Genetics & Pub. Policy Ctr. Johns Hopkins U., assoc. prof. dept. pediatrics; assoc. prof. Berman Inst. Bioethics, Inst. Genetic Medicine. Sr. policy analyst US Dept. Health & Human Svcs.; bd. dirs. Guttmacher Inst.; editorial bd. Ann. Rev. Genomics & Human Genetics. Mem.: AAAS, Inst. Medicine, Am. Soc. Human Genetics. Office: The Genetics and Public Policy Center Johns Hopkins University 1717 Massachusetts Ave NW Ste 530 Washington DC 20036 E-mail: khudson5@jhu.edu.

HUDSON, ROBERT PAUL, medical educator; b. Kansas City, Kans., Feb. 23, 1926; s. Chester Lloyd and Jean (Emerson) H.; m. Olive Jean Grimes, Aug. 1, 1948 (div. 1963); children: Robert E., Donald K., Timothy M.; m. Martha Isabelle Holter, July 10, 1965; children: Stephen, Laurel. BA, U. Kans., 1949, MD, 1952; MA, Johns Hopkins U., 1966. Instr. U. Kans., Kansas City, 1958-59, assoc. in medicine, 1959-63, asst. prof., 1964-69, assoc. prof., 1969—, prof., chmn. history of medicine, 1969-95, ret. Author: Disease and Its Control, 1983; mem. editl. bd. Bull. History of Medicine, Balt., 1981-94; contbr. articles to profl. jours. 1st lt. U.S. Army, 1953-55. Master ACP; mem. Am. Assn. for History of Medicine (pres. 1984-86), Am. Osler Soc. (bd. govs., pres. 1987-88). Home: 12925 S Frontier Rd Olathe KS 66061-8647 Office: Kans U Med Ctr 39th And Rainbow Blvd Kansas City KS 66160-0001

HUDSON, ROY DAVAGE, retired pharmaceutical executive; b. Chattanooga, June 30, 1930; s. Roy and Everence (Wilkerson) H.; m. Constance Joan Taylor, Aug. 31, 1956; children: Hollye Lynne, David Kendall. BS, Livingstone Coll., 1955; MS, U. Mich., 1957, PhD, 1962; MA, Brown U., 1968; LL.D., Lehigh U., 1974, Princeton, 1975. Asst. prof. pharmacology U. Mich. Sch. Medicine, 1961-66; assoc. prof. med. sci. Brown U. Sch. Medicine, 1966-70, assoc. dean grad. sch., 1966-69; pres. Hampton U., 1970-76; dir. rsch. planning and coordination Parke, Davis Pharm. Co., Ann Arbor, Mich., 1976; v.p. rsch. planning Warner Lambert/Parke-Davis Pharm. Rsch. Divsn., Ann Arbor, 1977-79; mgr. sci. liaison Upjohn Co., Kalamazoo, 1979-81, mgr. CNS diseases rsch., 1981—85, dir. CNS diseases rsch., 1985-87; v.p. pharm. rsch. divsn. Europe Upjohn Co., Brussels, 1987-90; corp. v.p. pub. rels. Upjohn Co., Kalamazoo, 1990-92, ret., 1992. Adj. prof. Black Americana studies Western Mich. U., Kalamazoo, 1993; interim exec. dir., CEO Guidance Clinic, Kalamazoo, 1993; interim pres. Livingstone Coll., Salisbury, N.C., 1995-96; dir. Parke-Davis & Co., United Va. Bank-Citizens and Marine, United Va. Bankshares, Comerica Bank-Mich., Chesapeake and Potomac Telephone Co. of Va. Contbr. articles to profl. jours., chpts. to books. Mem. screening com. Danforth Grad. Fellowships, 1962-78; mem. adv. council Danforth Grad. Fellows program Danforth Found., 1972-79; chmn. Va. Com. on Selection Rhodes Scholars, 1973; mem. Commn. on Fed. Relations, Am. Council on Edn., 1972-76, bd. dirs., 1973-76; mem. adv. council to dir. NIH, 1974—; Mem. R.I. Commn. Econ. Devel., 1967-69, R.I. Urban League scholarship com., 1966-70; mem. inst. policy commn. So. Regional Edn. Bd.; bd. dirs. Afro-Am. Soc. Conn. Coll., Kalamazoo Area Math and Sci. Ctr., Kalamazoo Area Academic Achievement Program, ARC; bd. dirs., v.p. Nat. Assn. Equal Opportunity in Higher Edn.; trustee Brown U., Livingstone Coll., Peninsula United Community Services, Spelman Coll. Served with USAF, 1948-52. Recipient Disting. Alumni award Livingstone Coll.; Outstanding Civilian Service award U.S. Army.; Danforth Grad. fellow, 1955-61 Mem. Am. Soc. Pharmacology and Exptl. Therapeutics, Peninsula C. of C., NAACP (life, 1st v.p., Golden Heritage), AAAS, N.Y. Acad. Scis., Sigma Xi, Phi Kappa Phi, Phi Sigma, Beta Kappa Chi, Kappa Delta Pi, Omega Psi Phi, Gamma Alpha, Alpha Kappa Mu. Home: 201 Brookview Pl Woodstock GA 30188 Personal E-mail: r.d.hudson@att.net.

HUDSON, STEVEN J., surgeon; b. Wilkinsburg, Pa., Dec. 27, 1968; m. Lori Hudson; children: Alaina, Brennan, Chloe, Avery. BS in Neuroscience, U. Pa., 1990; MD in Medicine and Surgery, Uniformed Svcs. U. Sch. Medicine, 1994; JD in Law and Health Care, U. Md., 2001; MPA, Marist Coll., 2008. Med. officer USN Res. Med. Corps, 1990—; eye surgeon Willis-Falkenberg Eye Care, Fredericksburg, Va. Mem.: AMA. Republican. Home: 13253 Blue Heron Hills Dr King George VA 22485-2433 Office Phone: 540-371-2777. Office Fax: 703-666-9143. Business E-Mail: steven.hudson@williseye.com. *

HUDSON-ZONN, ELIZA, nurse, psychologist; b. Monrovia, Liberia, Dec. 12, 1956; arrived in U.S., 1978; d. Hartzell Gleh and Joan Eliza (Roberts) Killen; m. Henry Clay Hudson, July 28, 1979 (div. Apr. 1985); 1 child, Kimberly Clayde; m. Mawuli Sonny Zonn, July 31, 1988; 1 child, Jewel Lorraine. BA in Psychology, BSC in Nursing, U. So. Miss., 1984. RN, N.J., Tex. Pvt. duty nurse Maxim Healthcare, Inc., South Orange, NJ, 1990—; critical care nurse Midpoint Profl. Agy., East Orange, NJ, 1988; supervising nurse Interim Healthcare, Inc., Morristown, NJ, 1990—; staff nurse Montclair Gen. Hosp., NJ, 1989—91; pvt. nurse Beth-Israel Med. Ctr., Newark, 1988—92; staff nurse United Children's Hosp., Newark, 1989—92; critical care nurse Nat. Staffing Assn. Inc., East Orange, 1988—2004; DON Med. Day Care Ctr., New Cmty. Extended Care, Newark, 2003—; supr. St. Mary's Life Ctr./Pope John Paul II Pavilion, Orange, NJ, 2007; DON Better Care Nursing Health Svcs., Bloomfield, NJ, 2007—08. Charge nurse Cmty. Psychiat. Ctr., Houston, 1993. Rural health vol. Red Cross Liberia, Monrovia, 1973—74; women's refugees health adv. Union Sierra Leone for Liberia, 1990—95; human rights adv. Movement for Justice in Africa, 1975—; coord., health svcs. dir. Liberian Cmty. Assn. N.J., 2001; mem. leadership counsel Southern Poverty Law Ctr., 2003; membership recruiter Student Unification Party, Monrovia, 1975—76; counselor Providence Bapt. Ch., 1975, St. Elmo Bapt. Ch., 1982. Recipient Pub. Svc. award East Miss. Bapt. Women Conv., 1972; So. Bapt. Conv. scholar, 1978-84, Nat. Bapt. Conv. scholar, 1972-84. Mem.: NAACP, Nat. Assn. Profl. Women, Nat. Staffing Assn. Skilled Home Care Nursing, Suehn Acad. Alumni Assn. (founding mem. 1995). Democrat. Avocations: reading, writing, sports, decoration, antiques. Home: 64 Hillyer St Orange NJ 07050 Office: Nat Staffing Assocs Inc 134 Evergreen Pl East Orange NJ 07018 Office Phone: 973-985-4233.

HUDZINSKI, LEONARD GERARD, social sciences educator, researcher; b. Aug. 14, 1946; BA in Psychology and Sociology, Findlay Coll., Ohio, 1968; MSW, U. Mich., 1971; PhD, U. Pitts., 1975. Diplomate Clin. Social Work Examiners. Tchg. asst. dept. sociology Findlay Coll., 1966-68; psychology specialist Lyster Army Hosp., Ft. Rucker, Ala., 1969-70; psychiat. social worker Toledo (Ohio) Mental Health Ctr., 1972; instr. in applied social rsch. and social work Med. Coll. Ohio, 1974-77; head divsn. clin. social work Ochsner Med. Instns., New Orleans, 1977—2001; ret., 2001. Dir. Ochsner Ctr. for Elimination of Smoking; asst. clin. prof. psychiatry La. State U. Med. Ctr.; asst. clin. prof. Tulane Med. Ctr.; instr., social scis. dept., Tahoe Coll. South Lake Tahoe, Calif.; psychology and sociology faculty Lake Tahoe C.C., 2002-; program dir., adminstr. State of Ohio Epilepsy Deinstitutionalization Assistance Program, 1976-77. Contbr. articles to profl. jours.; mem. editorial bd. Headache Quar., 1989—. Bd. dirs. Biofeedback Certification Inst. Am., Wheat Ridge, Colo., 1995. With U.S. Army, 1968-70. Fellow Am. Assn. for Study of Headache; mem. Assn. for Advancement of Behavior Therapy, Assn. Applied Psychophysiology and Biofeedback, La. Assn. Applied Psychophysiology and Biofeedback (past pres.), Am. Assn. for Study of Headache, NASW, La. Assn. for Clin. Social Work Vendorship (bd. dirs., treas., pres.), ACSW, Am. Fedn. for Clin. Rsch. Home: 700 West E St #3902 San Diego CA 92101 Personal E-mail: lhudzinski@att.net.

HUEB, MARCELO M., otolaryngologist, educator; b. Uberaba, Minas Gerais, Brazil, Sept. 10, 1962; s. Aziz Miguel and Dalal Helou Hueb; m. Flávia Barbosa Rocha, Apr. 14, 2000; children: Marcela Rocha, Fernanda Rocha, Lara Rocha. Degree in Med., Fed. U. Triângulo Mineiro at Uberaba, 1985; MSc, U. São Paulo, Ribeirão Preto, Brazil, 1991, PhD, 1997. Cert. specialist in otorhinolaryngology Ministry of Edn., 1988, specialist Brazilian Traffic Medicine Assn., 1999. Resident otorhinolaryngology U. São Paulo, 1986—87; fellow U. Minn., 1989—90; prof., head otorhinolaryngology Fed. U. Triângulo Mineiro, 1993—; dir. phonoaudiology sch. U. Uberaba, 1997—2004. State coord. Minas Gerais nat. week voice campaign Brazilian Assn. Laryngology and Voice, 2003; adminstrv. dir. Brazilian Assn. Otorhinolaryngology, São Paulo, 2005—08, v.p., 2008—11; sec. Ctrl. Brazilian Assn. Otorhinolaryngology, 2003—05, pres., 2005—07, treas., 2007—09, Brazilian Soc. Otology, São Paulo, 2009—11, v.p. SE Brazil, 2005—07, coord. nat. hearing health campaign, 2007; state dir. Minas Gerais Otorhinolaryngology Found., São Paulo, 2005—, editor in chief, 2006—08, Internat. Archieves Otolaryngology Jour.; treas. Brazilian Ctrl. Cochlear Implants, Brazil, 2009—. Recipient Maj. Eustáqio medal, Twp. of Uberaba, 2004. Fellow: Internat. Hearing Found. (Mpls.); mem.: Collegium ORL Amicitiae Sacrum. Office: Hosp Santa Lúcia Avenida Santos Dumont 409 Uberaba Minas Gerais 38060-600 Brazil Office Fax: 34-3332-4759. Business E-Mail: mmhueb@terra.com.br.

HUECHTKER, EDWARD DARRELL, professor; b. Louisville, May 24, 1937; s. Charles Edward and Hazel Irene (Munkers) H.; m. Sandra Wallace Dunning, Apr. 16, 1960 (dec. Feb. 23, 2006); children: Tracie, Tara, Edward, Trent; m. Betty Gravitt Holcomb, Oct. 25, 2008. Cert. physician assoc., Duke U., 1975; BA, Marymount Coll., 1979; MPA, L.I. U., 1981; cert. physician asst. leadership tng., St. Francis Coll., 1994; PhD, Kennedy We. U., 2004. Cert. Nat. Commn. Physician Assts. With USN, 1955—71, USCG, 1971—87, physician asst., 1975—87; assoc. dean Tampa Coll., Clearwater, Fla., 1982—87, dean, 1987—88; internat. recruiter Sperry Internat., Clearwater, 1988—90; asst. prof., assoc. dir. physician asst. program Med. Coll. Ga., Augusta, 1990—96; chair, dir. physician asst. program East Caroline U., Greenville, NC, 1996—2002; assoc. prof. U. Ala., Birmingham, 2002—, chmn. Depts. Critical Care and Diagnostic and Therapeutic Sci., 2002—10. Med. examiner Phys. Measurements, Inc., Newport News, Va., 1975-78, Tricorps of Tenn., Spring, 1990-94; physician asst. Med. Ctr. Ctrl. Ga., Macon, 1992-96, various hosps. and clinics, Ga. and N.C., 1990—; sec., bd. dirs. Ala. Grief Support Svcs., 2006-10, bd. dir., chmn., 2010-. Contbr. articles to profl. jours., chpts. to books. Chair adv. com. VA Hosp., Bay Pines, Fla., 1988-90; chair adv. bd. A.R. Johnson Med. H.S., Augusta, 1991-96; deacon 1st Bapt. Ch., Seminole, fla., 1984-90. Fellow Am. Acad. Physician Assts.; mem. Assn. Physician Asst. Programs (co-chair conf. planning), Ala. Soc. Physician Assts., N.C. Acad. Physician Assts., Ret. Officers Assn. Republican. Avocations: travel, reading, motorcycling. Office: Univ Alabama Birmingham Health Professions Clin and Diagnostic Scis SHPB 431 1530 3rd Ave S Birmingham AL 35294-1212 Office Phone: 205-934-9134. Business E-Mail: huechtke@uab.edu.

HUEMER, GEORG MICHAEL, plastic surgeon, researcher; b. Linz, Austria, July 29, 1976; s. Alfred and Ulrike Huemer. MD, Med. Sch., Innsbruck, 2000. Rsch. fellow Mayo Clinic, Scottsdale, Ariz., 2001—02; resident Dept. Plastic Surgery, Innsbruck, Austria, 2002—. Consulting rsch. co-worker Microsurgical Tng. Ctr., Linz, Austria, 2002—04. Contbr. articles to profl. jours., chapters to books. Home: Gruentalerstrasse 58 Linz 4020 Austria Office: Dept Plastic Surgery Anichstrasse 35 Innsbruck 6020 Austria E-mail: georg.huemer@uibk.ac.at.

HUET, JEAN-MARC, former pharmaceutical executive; married; 2 children. BA, Dartmouth Coll., Hanover, NH; MBA, INSEAD, Fontainebleau, France. Comml. mgr. Clement Trading, Milan, 1991—93; exec. dir., investment banking svcs. Goldman Sachs Internat., London, 1993—2003; CFO Royal Numico, NV, Amsterdam, 2003—07; sr. v.p., CFO Bristol-Myers Squibb Co., NYC, 2008—09, mem. exec. com., 2009. Bd. dirs. Mead Johnson Nutrition Co., 2008—.

HUET, RAUL, psychiatrist; b. Mexico City, Jan. 25, 1953; arrived in US, 1954; s. Raul Huet Sobrado and Yolanda Juan Franco de Huet. MD, Kans. U. Sch. Medicine, 1982. Cert. diplomate Psychiatry Am. Bd. Psychiatry and Neurology. Rschr. asst. Kans. U. Sch. Medicine, Dept. Physiology, Kans. City, 1985—87; psychiatrist Labette Ctr. for Mental Health Svcs., Inc., Parsons, Kans., 1997—2004, Wyandot Ctr. for Cmty. Behavioral Healthcare, Inc., Kans. City, 2004—. Psychiatric cons. Labette County Med. Ctr., Parsons, Kans., 2002—04, Providence Med. Ctr., Kansas City, Kans., 2004—; clin. asst. prof. psychiatry Kans. U. Sch. Medicine, Dept. Psychiatry, 2005—. Author: Ischemic Colitis - Digestive Diseases, 1987. Fellow: Am Psychiat. Assn., Kans. Psychiat. Soc.; mem.: AMA, Med. Soc. Johnson and Wyandotte Counties, Kans. Med. Soc., Hispanic C. of C. Republican. Roman Catholic. Avocations: tennis, movie videos and DVDs, spy novels. Office: Wyandot Ctr for Cmty Behavioral Healthcare Inc 7840 Wash Ave Kansas City KS 66112 Home: 9536 Horton Overland Park KS 66207 Office Phone: 913-328-4600. Office Fax: 913-328-4604. Personal E-mail: rahuet@sbcglobal.net.

HUFF, SARA DAVIS, retired nursing manager; b. Moundville, Ala., May 16, 1935; d. George W. and Maggie A. (Callahan) Davis; m. Eugene H. Huff, May 21, 1956 (div. June 1992); children: John Davis Huff, Timothy Eugene Huff. RN, Druid City Hosp. Sch. Nursing, Tuscaloosa, Ala., 1956; BS, Oglethorpe U., 1980. CNOR. RN oper. rm. Druid City Hosp., Tuscaloosa, 1956-58; asst. head nurse thoracic cardiovascular St. Joseph's Hosp., Atlanta, 1958-60; charge nurse open heart thoracic Emory U. Hosp., Atlanta, 1960-64, edn. coord. oper. room, 1974-75; oper. rm. supr. H. Egleston Hosp. for Children, Atlanta, 1964-73; nurse cons. Cons. Surg. Svcs., Atlanta, 1986-92; dir. surg. svcs. Northside Hosp., Atlanta, 1975-86; staff nurse oper. rm. Northlake Hosp., Atlanta, 1990-92; dir. surg. svcs. Atlanta Hosp., 1989-90, Newton Gen. Hosp., Covington, Ga., 1992—98; clin. resource mgr. Emory Dunwoody Med. Ctr., Atlanta, 2002—06; ret., 2006. Spkr. in field. Mem. AORN (nat. bd. dirs. 1980-84, gen. AORN nat. congress 1980, other coms.), ANA, Assn. of Oper. Rm. Nurses of Atlanta (Nurse of Yr. 1975), Atlanta Area Oper. Rm. Suprs. (chmn. 1973-75). Home: 2534 Warwick Cir NE Atlanta GA 30345-1632

HUFFMAN, DAVID MICHAEL, endocrinologist; b. Hickory, NC, Apr. 28, 1956; MS, NC State U., 1979; MD, U. NC, 1982. Dir. U. Diabetes & Endocrine Cons., 2003—. Head, endocrinology U. Tenn. Sch. Med., Chattanooga Br., 2003—. Melvin Jones fellowship, Lions Clubs Internat. Mem.: ADA, AACE, Am. Coll. Endocrinology, FACE. Avocation: woodworking. Office: 823 McCallie Ave Chattanooga TN 37403 Office Fax: 423-265-1364. E-mail: dhuffman@drhuffman.com.

HUFFMAN, DELTON CLEON, JR., pharmacy association executive; b. St. Louis, Feb. 18, 1943; s. Delton Cleon and Kathryn (Saegesser) H.; m. Judy Hill, Aug. 11, 1962; children: Kimberly Lea, Jeffrey Keith. BS in Pharmacy, U. Ark., 1966; PhD, U. Miss., 1971. Pharmacist Crank Drug Co., Inc., Little Rock, 1966—67; asst. prof., dir. divsn. pharmacy adminstrn. U. Tenn. Coll. Pharmacy, Memphis, 1970—73, asso. prof., chmn. dept. pharmaceutics, 1973—2010; exec. v.p. Am. Coll. Apothecaries, 1971—2010, also prof., chmn. dept. pharmacy, 1974—89, vice chancellor adminstrn., 1984—89; exec. dir. Nat. Cmty. Pharmacists Assn. Mgmt. Inst., Alexandria, Va., 1989—99, sr. v.p. practice and mgmt., 1992—99. Contbr. articles to profl. lit. Recipient Lederle Faculty award, 1971; NDEA fellow, 1967-70; Am. Found. for Pharm. Edn. fellow, 1967-70; Archer Drug Co. scholar, 1966. Fellow Am. Coll. Apothecaries; mem. AAAS, Am. Assn. Colls. Pharmacy, Am. Pharm. Assn., Nat. Cmty. Pharmacists Assn., Tenn. Pharm. Assn., Okla. Pharm. Assn. (hon.), Ark. Pharm. Assn. (hon., life), Am. Soc. Assn. Execs., Kappa Psi, Rho Chi. Home: 240 Lewis Fairway Cir Oakland TN 38060 Office: 2830 Summer Oaks Dr Bartlett TN 38134-3811

HUG, CARL CASIMIR, JR., pharmacology and anesthesiology educator, medical ethics educator; b. Canton, Ohio, Dec. 20, 1936; s. Carl Casimir and Aimee Cecelia (McArdle) H.; m. Marilyn Ann France, May 12, 1956; children: Patricia Ann DeStephano, Michael Stephen, Joan Marie Daniel, Mary Lynn Higgins, Lori Renee Mauldin. BS in Pharmacy summa cum laude, Duquesne U., 1958; PhD in Pharmacology, U. Mich., 1963, MD with distinction, 1967. Diplomate Am. Bd. Anesthesiology 1975, recert., 1993. From instr. to assoc. prof. pharmacology U. Mich., Ann Arbor, 1963-71; from assoc. prof. anesthesiology and pharmacology to emeritus prof. Emory U. Sch. Medicine, Atlanta, 1972—, dir. cardiothoracic anesthesiology, 1982—98, dep. chmn. for rsch., 1987-95, dep. chmn. for acad. affairs, 1995—2001; faculty affiliate Emory U. Ctr. for Ethics, 1999—. Vis. rsch. prof. U. Leiden, The Netherlands, 1982, dir. Am. Bd. Anesthesiology, 1984-96, v.p. 1990-92, pres. 1992-93; bd. dirs. Found. Anesthesia Edn. Rsch. 1993-2002, v.p. 1995-98, pres. 1998-2001; councilor-at-large Assn. U. Anesthesiologists 1980-83, pres. 1984-86; vis. prof., lectr. in field, grantee in field. Author: Alfentanil: Pharmacology and Uses in Anesthesia, 1984; New Developments in Drugs Used in Anaesthesia, 1991; editor Pharmacokinetics of Anaesthesia, 1984; editor Anesthesiology, 1979-88; contbr. articles to profl. jours. Chmn. St. Francis Sch. Bd., Ann Arbor, Mich., 1967—71; coach Little League, Ann Arbor, 1967—71; active Corpus Christi Cath. Ch., Stone Mountain, Ga., 1972—96, St. John Neumann Cath. Ch., Liburn, Ga., 1997—. Recipient Lifetime Achievement award Am. Soc. Critical Care Anesthesiologists, 2002; Ralph M. Waters, MD award Ill. Soc. Anesthesiologists, 2004; named Tchr. of Yr. Emory U. Anesthesiology, 1989, Excellence in Cardiothoracic Anesthesiology award, 1998. Fellow Royal Coll. Anaesthetists (Eng., hon.), Australian and New Zealand Coll. Anaesthetists (hon.), Am. Coll. Anesthesiologists; mem. Belgian Soc. Anesthesia and Reanimation (hon.), Am. Soc. Anesthesiologists (chmn. various coms. 1976—, named Emery A. Rovenstine lectr. 1999, Disting. Svc. award 2006), Assn. Cardiac Anesthesiologists, Soc. Cardiovasc. Anesthesiologists, Am. Soc. Clin. Pharmacology and Therapeutics, Am. Soc. Pharmacology and Expl. Therapeutics. Roman Catholic. Avocations: bicycling, walking, racquetball, piano. Office: Emory Univ Hosp Dept Anesthesiology 1364 Clifton Rd NE Atlanta GA 30322-1104 Office Phone: 404-778-3917. Business E-Mail: chug@emory.edu.

HUGGER, ERIN DENISE, science association director; b. Milw., Feb. 1, 1975; BS in Chemistry, U. Tulsa, 1997; PhD in Pharm. Chemistry, U. Kans., 2001. Prin. scientist pharm. devel. GlaxoSmithKline, 2001—03, prin. investigator microbial, musculoskeletal & proliferative diseases DMPK, 2003—05, mgr. oncology drug metabolism & pharmacokinetic, 2005—08, mgr. sci. licensing world-wide bus. devel., 2008—10, dir. sci. licensing rare diseases world-wide bus. devel., 2010—. Biotech. Tng. grant, NIGMS, 1999—2000, fellowship, U. Kans., 1997—98. Mem.: Am. Assn. Pharm. Scientists, Healthcare Businesswomen's Assn., Delta Delta Delta (Phila. main line alumnae chpt.). Office: GlaxoSmithKline 709 Swedeland Rd King Of Prussia PA 19406 Business E-Mail: erin.d.hugger@gsk.com.

HUGGINS, CHARLES EDWARD, obstetrician, gynecologist, educator; b. Hartsville, SC, Nov. 16, 1944; s. Charles Witherspoon Huggins and Frances Sue (Fountain) Evans; m. Mary Ellen Esto, May 29, 1966; children: Chadwick Edward, Laura Ruth, Mary Elizabeth. BS, Wofford Coll., 1965; MD, Med. U. S.C., 1969. Diplomate Am. Bd. Ob-Gyn. Intern Strong Meml. Hosp., Rochester, 1969-70; resident in ob-gyn. Med. U. S.C. Hosp., Charleston, 1970-74; chief of ob-gyn. Roper Hosp., Charleston; chmn. ob-gyn. dept. Bon Secours St. Francis Hosp., Charleston, 1999—. Clin. assoc. prof. Med. U. S.C.; mem. exec. bd. Roper Hosp., Charleston,1992-95, perinatal adv. bd., Charleston, 1992-95. Leader Boy Scouts Am., Mt. Pleasant, S.C., 1978-88; coach Hungry Neck Internat. Soccer, Mt. Pleasant, 1978-88. Lt. comdr. USN, 1974-76. Fellow ACOG, South Atlantic Assn. Ob-Gyn. (chair state com. 1995-98); mem. AMA, Am. Fertility Soc., NYAS, S.C. Med. Assn., Charleston County Med. Soc., Pi Kappa Phi (archon 1962—), Phi Rho Sigma. Presbyterian. Home: 2145 Henry Tecklenberg Dr Ste 270 Charleston SC 29414-5893 Office Phone: 843-577-0220. Fax: 843-577-4193.

HUGHES, A. N., retired psychotherapist; b. Ft. Meade, Md. d. G.M. and G.T. Nolen; m. E.L. Hughes, Oct. 21, 1961; 1 child, Andrew G. BS in Psychology, Rollins Coll., 1985, MA in Counseling, 1986; student in pub. speaking and human rels., Dale Carnegie Inst., 1981; student, Duke U., 1950-52. Lic. mental health counselor Nat. Bd. Cert. Counselors, nat. cert. counselor, nat. cert. gerontol. counselor. Supr. top secret control, audio/visual and small parts supply U.S. Army, Continental U.S. and Tokyo; adminstrv. sec. Sys. Devel. Corp., Rand Corp., Santa Monica, Calif.; adminstrv. asst., editor, exec. sec., adminstrv. sec. Aerospace Corp., El Segundo, Calif.; staff therapist Circles of Care, Melbourne, Fla. Developer program for leading divorce support groups for Brevard Women's Ctr. Various leadership positions PTA, Pittsford, NY, Brookfield, Wis., 1968—81; mem. Brevard Cmty. Chorus, 1991—, adv. bd., 1997; mem. Citizen's Emergency Response Team (CERT), 1999—2001; various vol. positions in several organizations in Brevard County, 1991—. Mem. DAR, Space Coast PC Users Group, South Brevard, Suntree Country Club, Suntree Master Homeowners Assn. (Twin Lakes rep. 1997—), Brevard County Alumnae Assn. of Kappa Kappa Gamma, Kappa Kappa Gamma. Avocations: photoimaging, fitness, genealogy, choral singing, growing orchids. Office: PO Box 410162 Melbourne FL 32941-0162

HUGHES, BARBARA ANN, dietitian, public health administrator; b. McMinn County, Tenn., July 22, 1938; d. Cecil Earl and Hannah Ruth (Moss) Farmer; m. Carl Clifford Hughes, Oct. 13, 1962. BS in Home Econs. cum laude, Carson Newman Coll., Jefferson City, Tenn., 1960; MS in Instl. Mgmt., Ohio State U., Columbus, 1963; MA (Adonarium Judson scholar), So. Bapt. Theol. Sem., 1968; MPH, U. N.C., Chapel Hill, 1972; postgrad. in nutrition, U. Iowa, 1974, U. N.C., 1975-85, Case Western Res. U., 1979, Walden U.; PhD, 1988; grad, Inst. Polit., NC, 1994. Registered, lic. nutritionist, dietitian, cert. Tng. adult weight mgmt., 2004, in child & adlecent weight mgmt, 2010. Instr., clin. dietitian Riverside Meth. Hosp., Riverside Whitecross Sch. Nursing, Columbus, Ohio, 1963-66; consulting dietitian Mount Holly Nursing Home, Ky. Dept. Mental Health, 1966-68, Eastern Region N.C. Bd. Health, Raleigh, 1968-73; dir. Nutrition and Dietary Svcs. br. Divsn. Health Svcs. N.C. Dept. Human Resources, Raleigh, 1973-89, also dir. Women-Infants-Children Program; pres. B.A. Hughes and Assocs., 1990—; dir. adult nutrition Inst. Lifestyle and Weight Mgmt., 2006—07. Instr. Wake Tech. C.C., 1996—97; med. nutrition therapist CIGNA Health Care of N.C., Inc., United Behavioral Health, Blue Cross, Blue Shield N.C., NC State Health Plan, Aetna Ins., Medicaire Ins.; asst. to rep. Karen Gottovi 14th dist. N.C. Ho. of Reps., Gen. Assembly N.C., 1994; adj. instr. Case Western Res. U., Cleve., 1988—89; adj. asst. prof. dept. nutrition Sch. Public Health U. N.C., Chapel Hill, 1975—89; adv. bd. Hospitality Edn. program NC Dept. Cmty. Colls., 1974—80; adv. com. Ret. Senior Vol. Program, Raleigh and Wake County, NC, 1975—79, N.C. Network Coordinating Coun. for End-Stage Renal Disease, 1975, Nat. Adv. Coun. on Maternal, Infant and Fetal Nutrition, Spl. Supplemental Food Program for Women, Infants and Children, Dept. Agr., 1976—79; adv. com. Nutrition Edn. and Tng. program N.C. Dept. Pub. Instrn., 1978—80; chmn. adv. leadership coun. N.C. Cooperative Ext. Svc., 1997—99, advisor com. to Wake County, 1992—, chair adv. coun., 1994—96; coord. undergrad. program in gen. dietetics East Carolina U.; apptd. rep. Coll. of Agrl. and Life Scis. N.C. State U. to Nat. Coun. for Agrl. Rsch. Extension and Tchg., 1996—2000; apptd. mem. strategic planning and new directions com. Wake County Bd. Commrs. to Wake County Human Svcs. Bd., 1996—2006, new dirs. strategic planning com., children's com., bd. liaison, partnership com., 2001—04, agy. performance com., 1998—2000; chmn. agy. svcs. com., exec. com. Wake County Human Svcs. Bd., 2004, cmty. health comm., 2005—; apptd. to adv. bd. Agromedicine Program East Carolina and N.C. State Univs., 1996—99; apptd. N.C. Dept. Human Resources Sec.'s Adv. Coun. Alternative/Contemporary Medicine Consortium Natural Medicine and Pub. Health, 2000; adv. coun. N.C. Gov.'s Office Citizen Affairs; cons. dietitian Augusta Victoria Hosp. and Jerusalem (Israel) Crippled Childrens Ctr., 1968; witness U.S. congressional and Senate hearings in field; mem. planning com. NC Summit on Natural Med. Products, 2002; dietitian, dir. food svcs. archaeol. expedition, Israel, 1968. Co-author: Diet and Kidney Disease, Assn. for N.C. Regional Med. program, 1969, Ohio State U., Alumni Assoc., sec. Triangle chpt.; contbr. numerous papers, articles to symposia, periodicals in field, vol. areas. Trustee Gardner-Webb Coll., Boiling Springs, NC, 1978—82, chmn. curriculum com., 1981—82; chmn. adv. bd. dept. home econ. Carson-Newman Coll., 1975—78; chmn. Edn. and Cmty. Com., 1992; pres. NC Coun. on Spl. Teens, 1993—94; appt. mem. Raleigh Human Rels. Commn., 2006, NC Dept. Health & Human Svc. Accreditation Bd., 2010; mem. Race Rels. Commn.; chair Bylaws, Police Affairs & Awards & Celebrations Commn., 2011; v.p. Wake County Literacy Coun., 1986—87, bd. dirs., 2004; nat. assoc. local bd. health assn. NC Local Bd. Health Reps. SA & BOH; del. various Dem. Convs., 1981—, precinct sec.-treas., 1981—, 1st vice chmn., 1983—85, 2nd vice chmn., 1993—96, 1998—, chair, 1985—87, 1998—2000, 2005—; adv. bd., del. NC Dem. Party Exec. Com., 1998—2002, 2008—; active edn. program Pullen Meml. Bapt. Ch., Raleigh; area ministry capt. Pullen Meml. Bapt. Ch., Raleigh, Raleigh, 1977—78, personnel com., 1978—80; elected mem. NC Dem. Party Coun. Review Representing 4th Congl. Dist.; bd. dirs. Cmty. Outreach, 1989—92, futuring com., 1995—96, coordinating coun. vice-chair, 1996—97, chmn., 1997—98; bd. dirs. NC Literacy Assn., 1978—83, 1993, 1995, pres., 1981—83. Named Woman of Yr., Wake County, 1975, N.C. Outstanding Dietitian of Yr., 1976, N.C. Outstanding Dietitian, Southeastern Hosp. Conf. Dietitians, 1978; recipient Disting. Alumna award Carson-Newman Coll., 1983, Eleanor Roosevelt Humanitarian award Altrusa Internat., 1995, S.E. Trustee award Nat. Assn. Local Bd. Health, 2002, Women in Bus. award Triangle Bus. Jour., 2002, Power of Prevention award, NC Health and Wellness Trust Fund leadership in Obesity award, 2007, Nutrition-Entrepreneurs DPG, 2006, Excellence Practice award, 2005, 08 Fellow: Am. Dietetic Assn. (mem., commn. on dietetic registration), N.C. Inst. Polit. Leadership; mem.: APHA (mem. nutrition sect. 1969—, chmn. nominating com. 1975—77, chair pub. policy com. 1977—79, mem. pub. policy com. 1977—79, chair award com. food and nutrition sect., other offices 1995—96, Catherine Cowell award 1994), AAUW (life; pres. Raleigh/Wake County br. 1971—75, pres. N.C. divsn. 1978—80, area rep. 1980—82, mem. Program Com. Legis./Pub. Policy Com. 1980—82, ednl. founder 1980—82, nat. bd. dirs. 1980—92, nat. edn. found. bd. dirs. 1987—91, mem. found. 1987—91, pres. Raleigh/Wake County br. 1991—93, ednl. equity roundtable 1992, coord. Wake Women Celebrate 1995, coord. ptnrs. for heart disease and stroke prevention 1995), Nat. Assn. Local Board of Health (State Assn. Comm. 2010, mem. representating NC to state assn.), Interfaith Food Shuttle, Raleigh (bd. mem. 2007—08, mem. bd. affiliate 2009—10), Women's Forum N.C. (young leadership award com. 1989—90, 1992—, newsletter editor bd. dirs. 1992—, adminstr. 1995—2003), N.C. Acad. Pub. Health (pres.-elect 2001, pres. 2002), Nutrition Today Soc., Soc. Nutrition Edn., Am. Acad. Health Adminstrn., N.C. Coun. Women's Orgns. (Wellness in State Employees adv. bd. 1989—91, mem. at large bd. dirs. 1989—92, leadership com. 1991—, chair nutrition subcom.), N.C. Coun. Foods and Nutrition (chmn. membership 1975, dir. 1976—78, nominating com. 1979), N.C. Assn. Bds. of Health (dir. 1994—98, nominating com. 1998—2000, treas. 1999—2000, mem. com. 1999—2005, awards com. 1999—2006, pres. 2002—03, immediate past pres. 2004—06), Assn. State and Territorial Pub. Health Nutrition Dirs. (pres. 1977—79, dir. 1981—89, chair legis. and pub. policy com. 1984—89, liaison to Assn. Faculties Grad. Program in Pub. Health Nutrition, Commendation award 1989), So. Health Assn. (pres. 1982—83, chair nominating com. 1985—86, 1991—92, awards com. 1992—93, Spl. Meritorious award 1989), Greater Raleigh C. of C. (mem. Alumni Assn. 1995, mem. west area bus. coun., chair legis. com. rep. leadership Raleigh Alumni Assn.), Altrusa Internat. Found. (1st v.p. 1985—87, chmn.-elect 1990—92, chmn. 1992—, bd. dirs. 1993—97), U.N.C. Pub. Health Alumni Assn. (life), U.N.C. Gen. Alumni Assn. (life), Ohio State U. Alumni Assn. (life), Altrusa Internat. (pres. Raleigh club 1973—74, 1973—74, dir. 1976—78, Internat. vocat. svcs. chmn. 1977—79, 1st vice gov. 1978—79, dist. Three gov. 1979—81, chmn. nomination com. 1980—82, 1st v.p. 1985—87, Ist v.p. 1985—87, pres.-elect 1987—89, pres. 1989—91, 1989—91, past pres. 1991—92, pres. 1991—93, pres. Raleigh club 2005—08, chmn. nomination com. 2010—, pres. Raleigh club 2010—11, chmn. nomination com. 2010—11, Triangle Bus. Jour. Women in Bus. award 2002), Kappa Omicron Nu. Achievements include olympic torchbearer, 1996. Home and Office: 4208 Galax Dr Raleigh NC 27612-3714 Home Phone: 919-787-2949. Business E-Mail: barbara-ann@bahughes.com. *

HUGHES, CHARLES E., III, plastic surgeon; b. Chgo., Mar. 19, 1943; s. Charles E. and Jane Wittig (McClintock) H.; m. Ellen Alice Schowe, Nov. 1, 1963; children: Kristian, Chad, Adnrew, Polly. BS, Northwestern U., Chgo., 1966, MD, 1969. Diploamte Am. Bd. Plastic Surgery. Fellow in surg. oncology Am. Cancer Soc., Chgo., 1973-74; resident Northwestern U., 1974-76; asst. prof. plastic surgery Ind. U., Inspls., 1976-82; pvt. practice Geech Grove, Ind., 1983—. Contbr. articles to profl. jours. Fellow ACS (fgn. lang. editor jour. 1974-88); mem. Lipoplasty Soc. (pres. 1995—), Am. Soc. Plastic and Reconstructive Surgeons, Am. Soc. Aesthetic Plastic Surgery, Cleft Palate Soc. Avocations: exercise, sailing, reading, travel. Office: 8051 S Emerson Ave Indianapolis IN 46237

HUGHES, EDWARD F. X., healthcare educator, preventive medicine physician; b. Boston, Jan. 10, 1942; s. Joseph Daniel and Elizabeth (Dempsey) Hughes; m. Susan Lane Mooney, Feb. 11, 1967; children: Edward Francis, John Patrick, Dempsey Lane. BA in Philosophy, Amherst Coll., Mass., 1962; MD, Harvard U., Cambridge, Mass., 1966; MPH, Columbia U., NYC, 1969. Intern, resident surg. Columbia-Presbyn. Med. Ctr., NYC, 1966-68; instr. to assoc. prof. Mt. Sinai Sch. Medicine, NYC, 1969-77; rsch. assoc. Nat. Bur. Econ. Rsch., NYC, 1970-77; prof. prevention medicine Northwestern U. Med. Sch., Chgo., 1977—, founder, dir. ctr. health svc. policy rsch., 1977-94; prof. health enterprise mgmt. and mgmt. & strategy J. L. Kellogg Grad. Sch. Mgmt., Northwestern U., Evanston, Ill., 1977—, dir. health enterprise mgmt. program, 1980—83, co-dir. biotech. program, 2001—08. Cons. Nat. Ctr. Health Svcs. Rsch., Rockville, Md., 1975-82, AMA, Chgo., 1981-83, Midwest Bus. Group on Health, Chgo., 1983-85; expert witness for providers, health Plans and pharm. firms, 1993—. Editor: Hospital Cost Containment: A Policy Analysis, 1979, A Perspective on Quality in American health Care, 1988 (Bradley award 1962, Health Career Scientist award 1973-75); mem. editl. bd. Managed Care Interface (Latiolias Honor medal 1999, Beta Gamma Sigma award), Jour. Clin. Outcomes, Group Health News, Counseline; contbr. articles to profl. jours. Health Care Financing Adminstrn. grantee, Washington, 1978-84, Ford Found., 1983-86, Robert Wood Johnson Found, 1978-82, NIH, 1983-95, Pew Charitable Trusts, 1990-92, Baxter Found., 1991-96. Fellow N.Y. Acad. Medicine, Am. Coll. Physician Execs.; mem. APHA, Americas Health Ins. Plans (acad. dir. exec. leadership program), Assn. Health Svcs. Rsch. (co-founder, v.p. 1981-83, bd. dirs. 1981-84), Assn. Tchrs. Preventive Medicine (bd. dirs. 1973-76), Med. Adminstrs. Conf., Nat. Assn. Managed Care Physicians (med. adv. bd.), Boston Latin Sch. Chgo. Club (bd. dirs. 1983-86), Chapoquoit Yacht Club (West Famouth, Mass.) Home: 810 Lincoln St Evanston IL 60201-2405 Office: Kellogg Sch Mgmt 2001 Sheridan Rd Evanston IL 60208-0814 Office Phone: 847-491-8384. Business E-Mail: efx-hughes@kellogg.northwestern.edu.

HUGHES, LAUREN, physician; b. Iowa; BS, BA Zoology, Spanish, Iowa State U., Ames, 2002; MPH, George Wash. U., Washington, 2007; MD, U. Iowa, Iowa City, 2009. Rsch. asst. George Wash. U., 2006—07; MPH practicum intern Nat. Assn. Cmty Health Centers, 2007; health policy intern to Tom Harkin US Senate, 2007; resident physician dept. family medicine U. Wash., 2010—. Mem. Beyond Flexner Adv. Coun., 2010—; resident trustee Wash. Acad. Family Physicians, 2011—; resident rep. Annals of Family Medicine Editl. Bd., 2011—. Vol. Iowa City Free Med. Clin.; AmeriCorps vol. LifeLong Med. Care, Berkeley, Calif., 2002—03; CPR & first aid instr. Fast Response, Inc., 2002—03. Vis. scholar Robert Graham Ctr. Mem.: Am. Med. Student Assn. (nat. pres. 2009—10, nat. v.p. internal affairs), Am. Coll. Preventive Medicine (pres. med. student sect. 2006). Office: c/o University Wash Dept Family Medicine 1959 NE Pacific St Box 356390 Seattle WA 98195-6390 Office Phone: 703-620-6600 ext. 202. E-mail: pres@amsa.org. *

HUGHES, MARTIN P., insurance company executive; Chmn. Assurex Internat.; from mem. staff to pres. Mack and Parker, Inc., 1973—90, pres., 1990—99, chmn., 1999—2001, HUB Internat. Ltd., Chgo., 1999—, CEO, 1999—. Bd. dir. Assurex Mktg. Group, Coun. Ins. Agents and Brokers. Office: HUB International Ltd 55 East Jackson Blvd Chicago IL 60604 *

HUGHES, STEPHEN H., virologist, researcher; PhD, Harvard U. Postdoctoral rsch. with Dr. J. Michael Bishop and Harold Varmus U. Calif., San Francisco; sr. staff investigator Cold Spring Harbor Lab.; founder gene expression in eukaryotes sect., ABL Rsch. Program Ctr. Cancer Rsch., Nat. Cancer Inst., NIH, Frederick, Md., 1984—88, dep. dir. ABL Rsch. Program, 1988—95, dir. Molecular Basis of Carcinogenesis Lab., 1995—99, chief Retroviral Replication Lab., HIV Drug Resistance Program, 1999—2006, dir. HIV drug resistance program, 2006—, dir. HIV DRP host-virus interaction br., head in vivo virology sect., chief HIV DRP Retroviral Replication Lab., head vector design and replication sect. Rschr. Rutgers U., Ctr. of Advanced Biotechnology and Medicine, Piscataway, NJ, 1987—; co-organizer, retroviruses and viral vectors mtgs. Cold Spring Harbor Lab.; co-organizer, annual meeting on Oncogenes. Named one of Most Frequently Cited AIDS Researchers, Science Watch, 1996. Achievements include partnering with Edward Arnold at Rutgers University Laboratory, Center of Advanced Biotechnology and Medicine, to develop a trio of drugs believed to destroy HIV, the virus that causes AIDS, tenifovir, or the DAPY (diarylpyrimidine), 1987. Office: Nat Cancer Inst HIV Drug Resistance Program NCI-Frederick PO Box B Bldg 539 Frederick MD 21702-1201 Office Phone: 301-846-1619. Office Fax: 301-846-6966. Business E-Mail: hughesst@mail.nih.gov. *

HUGHES, SUSAN L., gerontologist, researcher; b. Boston, Feb. 2, 1943; d. John Joseph and Agnes Thomasine Mooney; m. Edward Francis Xavier Hughes, Feb. 11, 1967; children: Edward Francis, John Patrick, Dempsey Lane. DSW, Columbia U., New York, NY, 1981; MSW, Simmons Coll., Boston, MA, 1966; BA, Manhattanville Coll., Purchase, NY, 1964. Certified Social Worker IL. Post-doctoral fellow instr., asst. prof. Northwestern U. Med. Sch., Chicago, Ill., 1977—87, assoc. prof., 1987—94, prof., 1994—96; dir. program in long-term care Inst. Health Svcs. & Policy Rsch., Northwestern U., Evanston, Ill., 1981—96; assoc. rsch. career scientist Hines VA Hosp., Hines, Ill., 1991—97; prof. Sch. Pub. Health U. Ill., Chicago, 1997—, co-director Ctr. Rsch. on Health & Aging, 1997—. Nat. rsch. mentor, geriatric social work faculty scholar, Hartford Found., NY, 2001—03; expert panel mem. Adminstrn. on Aging, DHHS, Washington, DC, 1999—2000; editl. bd. mem. Health Services Rsch., Chicago, Ill., 1987—98; chair, gerontol. health sect. APHA, Washington, DC, 1994—95; mem. Inst. of Medicine Com. to plan maj. study of long-term care reform, Washington, DC, 1985—86; mem. editl. adv. bd. Long Term Care Interface, NY, 2000—. Lead author (24), co-author (34) (scientific journal articles), co-author (book) Living at Home Program; author: (book) Long Term Care: Options in an Expanding Market. Mem. Ill. Disabilities Services Adv. Com., Springfield, Ill., 2002—03; founding chair Ill. Medicaid Adv. Com., Subcommittee on Long Term Care, Springfield, Ill., 1994—; mem. Cmty. Based Long Term Care Reform Com., Ill. Dept. on Aging, Springfield, Ill., 1995—96, Long Term Care Committe, Ill. Health Care Reform Task Force, Springfield, Ill., 1993—94. Recipient Mem. of Delta Omega Honor Soc., ASPH, 1991-1997, Assoc. Rsch. Career Scientist, DVA, 1979, Dissertation Support Award, NCHSR, 1978; fellow HRET/Kellogg Found. Fellowship, Kellogg Found., 1979. Fellow: Gerontol. Soc. of Am.; mem.: Am. Geriat. Soc., APHA (sect. chair 1994—95). Home: 810 Lincoln Evanston IL 60201 Office Phone: 312-996-1473. Business E-Mail: shughes@uic.edu.

HUGHES, SUSAN MARIE, statistician, educator; b. Sacramento, June 8, 1957; BA, Calif. State U., Fresno, 1979; MS, UCLA, 1980. Rsch. liaison U. Calif., San Francisco Fresno Family & Cmty. Medicine, 1997—2000, instr., 2001—05, rsch. coord., 2001—04, rsch. dir., 2004—, asst. adj. prof., 2005. Rsch. grant, U. Calif., San Francisco Fresno Med. Edn. Program. Mem.: N. Am. Primary Care Rsch. Group, Soc. Tchrs. Family Medicine. Avocations: scuba diving, cello, knitting, crocheting, sewing. Office: Family & Community Medicine 155 N Fresno St Fresno CA 93701 Office Fax: 559-499-6451. Business E-Mail: shughes@fresno.ucsf.edu.

HUGHES, W. JAMES, optometrist; b. Shawnee, Okla., Oct. 15, 1944; s. Willis J. and Elizabeth Alice (Nimohoyah) Hughes. BA in Anthropology, U. Okla., 1966, MA in Anthropology, 1972; OD, U. Houston, 1976; MPH, U. Tex., 1977. Lic. optometrist Okla., Tex., W.Va. Commd. med. officer USPHS, 1966, advanced through grades to capt./optometrist, 1993; physician's asst. Houston, Dallas, 1969-70; teaching asst. in clin optics U. Houston, 1973-74; contact lens rsch. asst., 1974; Wesley Jessen Contact Lens Rep., 1974-76; extern eye clinic Tuba City Indian Hosp., 1975; Indian Health Svc. optometrist Eagle Butte, S.D., 1976; optometrist vision care project Crockett Ind. Sch. Dist., 1977; vision care program dir. Bemidj Area Indian Health Svc., 1977-78; optometrist Navajo Area Indian Health Svc., Chinle Health Ctr., 1978-79, Shiprock USPHS Indian Hosp., 1979—; chief vision care program No. Navajo Med. Ctr., 1994—; dir. eye clinic USPHS No. Navajo Med. Ctr., Shiprock, N.Mex. Adj. prof. So. Calif. Coll. Optometry, L.A., U. Houston Coll. Optometry, 1978—, So. Coll. Optometry, Memphis, 1980—; Navajo area Indian Health Svc. rep. to optometry career devel. com. USPHS. Contbr. articles to profl. jours. Sgt. U.S. Army, 1966-69, Capt, USPHS, 1993—. Decorated Bronze Star, Purple Heart; recipient House of Vision award, 1974, Cmty. Health Optometry award, 1976; Better Vision scholar, 1973-76. Mem. Am. Pub. Health Assn., Am. Optometric Assn., Tex. Optometric Assn. Commd. Officers Soc., Assn. Am. Indian Physicians, Beta Sigma Kappa. Democrat. Roman Catholic. Home: 350 N Guadalupe St STE 140 San Marcos TX 78666-5692 Home Phone: 512-667-0865; Office Phone: 505-828-0928. Business E-Mail: jhughes.1976@alumni.opt.uh.edu. E-mail: jim.hughes@shiprock.ihs.gov.

HUGHES, WALTER THOMPSON, pediatrician, educator; b. Cleve., May 16, 1930; s. Walter Thompson and Millie Hasentine (Collette) H.; m. Frances J. Skinner, Nov. 24, 1957; children: Carla, Gregory, Christopher. MD, U. Tenn., 1954. Diplomate Am. Bd. Pediatrics. Resident in pediatrics U. Tenn. Coll. Medicine, Memphis, 1955-57, prof. pediatrics and microbiology, 1969-77, prof. pediatrics, 1981—, mem. St. Jude Children's Rsch. Hosp., Memphis, 1969-77, mem., chair dept. infectious diseases, 1981-95; mem. staff Walter Reed Army Med. Ctr., Ft. Detrick, Md., 1957-59; pvt. practice pediatrics Cleve., 1959-61; instr. to prof. U. Louisville Sch. Medicine, 1961-69, Eudowood prof. pediatrics, dir. div. infectious diseases Johns Hopkins U. Sch. Medicine, Balt., 1977-81; Arthur Ashe chair in pediat. AIDS rsch. St. Jude Children's Rsch. Hosp., Memphis, 1993-98, emeritus mem., 1998—. Capt. U.S. Army, 1957-59. Fellow Am. Acad. Pediatrics; mem. Am. Pediatric Soc., Infectious Diseases Soc. Am., Soc. Pediatric Rsch., Pediatric Infectious Diseases Soc. (pres. 1983-85). Republican. Methodist. Home: 854 River Park Dr Memphis TN 38103-0804 Office: Saint Jude Childrens Rsch Hosp 262 Danny Thomas Pl Memphis TN 38105-3678 Home Phone: 901-528-9460; Office Phone: 901-495-3485. Personal E-mail: fhu5774238@aol.com. Business E-Mail: walter.hughes@stjude.org.

HUGHES-AYANRU, GRACE, retired geriatrician; d. Roy Eldon and Thelma Ruth (Clark) H.; m. Hilary Oni Ayanru, May 24, 1969 (dec. 1984); 1 child, Hilary Oni II. BS, Hampton Inst., Va., 1954; MD, Meharry Med Coll., 1962. Lic. physician N.Y., 1963. Intern. Bklyn. Jewish Hosp., NY, 1962—63; medicine resident Brooklyn Jewish Hosp., 1963—65; fellow rheumatology Med. Sch. NYU, 1965—67; med. dir. Charles Drew Neighborhood H C, Bklyn., 1969—71; physician-in-chief geriatrics Queens Hosp. Ctr., NYC, 1972—98, ret., 1998. Lectr. scientist in sch. program N.Y. Acad. Scis.; clin. asst. prof. medicine NYU Sch. Medicine, N.Y.C.; adj. clin. asst. prof. medicine Mt. Sinai Sch. Medicine. Contbr. articles to newspapers. Participant in pub. svc. programs on health of elderly. Fellow Am. Coll. Rheumatology; mem. AAAS, Am. Med. Womens Assn., Am. Lung Assn. Queens (bd. dirs. 1988—, pres. bd. dirs. 1996—), N.Y. Rheumatism Assn. (exec. com. 1984—), N.Y. Acad. Scis., Nat. Med. Assn. Avocations: dance, reading, music, travel.

HUGO, NORMAN ELIOT, retired plastic surgeon, educator; b. Beverly, Mass., Sept. 23, 1933; s. Victor Joseph and Helen Bernadette (Box) Hugo; m. Geraldine P Tonry, Oct. 10, 1959; children: Helen, William, Geraldine, Norman, Catherine. BA, Williams Coll., Williamstown, Mass., 1955, DSc (hon.), 1989; MD, Cornell U. Med. Coll., Ithaca, NY, 1959. Diplomate (dir 1982-88, vice chmn 1987-88, residency rev comt, accreditation coun, grad med educ, 1994-98) Am Bd Plastic Surg. Intern, resident Cornell U. Surg. Svc., Bellevue Hosp., NYC, 1959-63; resident NY Hosp.-Cornell Med. Ctr., 1963-65, univ. instr. surgery, 1966-65; asst. prof. Ind. U.; asst. chief plastic surgeon Walter Reed Army Med. Ctr., 1967-69; assoc. prof. U. Chgo., 1969-71; chief plastic and reconstructive surgery Michael Reese Hosp., Chgo., 1969-71, Passavant Hosp., Chgo., 1971-79; assoc. prof. Northwestern U., Chgo., 1971-82; dir. plastic surgery Lakeside VA Hosp., 1971-77; chief plastic and reconstructive surgery Columbia U.-Presbyn. Med. Ctr., NYC, 1982-95; prof. Columbia U. Coll. Physicians & Surgeons, 1982-98, prof. emeritus, 1998—; ret., 1998. Maj MC AUS, 1967—69. Mem.: AMA (del. 1983—88), ACS, Am. Burn Soc., NY Acad. Sci., Soc. Head and Neck Surgeons, Assn. Acad. Surgery, Am. Cleft Palate Soc., Plastic Surg Rsch. Coun., Chgo. Soc Plastic Surg (sec. 1979—81, v.p. 1981—82), Am. Soc. Aesthetic Plastic Surgery (sec. 1979—82), Am. Assn. Plastic and Reconstructive Surgery (trustee 1982—84), Am. Soc. Plastic and Reconstructive Surgeons (trustee 1981—84, historian 1982—84, v.p. 1985—86, pres.-elect 1986—87, pres. 1987—88, bd. dirs. edn. found.), Touchdown Club Am. (dir. 2002—06), Union Club (gov. 2002—08, NYC). Home and Office: 37 Carriage Ln New Canaan CT 06840-4401 Office Phone: 203-966-2434. Personal E-mail: normanehugo@optonline.net.

HUH, BONG-YUL, physician; b. Taegu City, Republic of Korea, Mar. 2, 1942; s. Dong and Cha-Kyu (Kim) Huh; m. Ran-Young Shim, Oct. 14, 1971; children: Kyu-Ha, Kyu-Yeon. MD, Seoul Nat. U., Republic of Korea, 1967, MSc in Med. Sci., 1977, PhD, 1980. Lic. Korean Ministry Health and Welfare, 1967, cert. in internal medicine Korean Ministry Health and Welfare, 1976, family medicine Korean Ministry Health and Welfare, 1986. With Seoul Nat. U. Hosp., 2006—. Capt. Korean Army, 1969—72. Recipient award, Korean Ministry Health and Welfare, 1993, Healthy Family Movement award, Pres. Korean Govt., 1996. Mem.: Korean Soc. Stress Medicine (pres. 2003—), Korean Soc. Hospice and Palliative Care (pres.), Korean Soc. Health Promotion and Disease Prevention (pres. 2000—02), Asia Pacific World Orgn. Family Doctors (mem. conf. organizing com. 1994—97, vice chmn. 2001—04), Korean Acad. Family Medicine (pres. 1991—99), Korean Healthy Family Movement (pres. 1995—2005).

HUH, PIL WOO, neurosurgeon, educator; s. Myoun-Goo Huh and Kyu-Bong Kim; m. Kwang-Soon Kim, May 20, 1959; children: Sun-Young, Hye-Young. MD, Cath. U. Korea Coll. Medicine, Seoul, 1984; PhD, PhD, Cath. U. Korea Grad. Sch. Medicine, Seoul, 1995. Medical diplomate Korea(South), 1984. Assoc. prof. Cath. U. Korea, Seoul, 1992—; dir. dept. neurosurgery Uijeongbu St. Mary's Hosp., Cath U., Korea U. Medicine, Republic of Korea, 2006—; dir. clin. rsch. ctr. Uijeongbu St. Mary's Hosp., dir. stroke ctr., 2009—; prof. dept. neurosurgery Cath. U. Korea Coll. Medicine, 2005—. Contbr. chapters to books. Mentor Onuri ch., Seoul, Korea (South), 1999—2004. Capt. mil. svc., 1989—92, Seoul. Grantee, Health Tech. Planning and Evaluation Bd., 2002-2005, Korea sci. and engring. found., 2001-2003, Health Tech. Planning and Evaluation Bd., 1999-2001. Mem.: Korean Neurosurgical Soc., Korean Soc. Cerbrovascular Surgery, Soc. for Neuroscience, World Fed. Neurosurgery. Office Fax: 82-31-846-3117. Business E-Mail: pilbrain@catholic.ac.kr.

HUHEEY, MARILYN JANE, ophthalmologist, educator; b. Cin., Aug. 31, 1935; d. George Mercer and Mary Jane (Weaver) Huheey. BS in Math., Ohio U., Athens, 1958; MS in Physiology, U. Okla., 1966; MD, U. Ky., 1970. Diplomate Am. Bd. Ophthalmology. Tchr. math. James Ford Rhodes H.S., Cleve., 1956-58; biostatistician Nat. Jewish Hosp., Denver, 1958-60; life sci. engr. Stanley Aviation Corp., Denver, 1960-63, N.Am. Aviation Co., LA, 1963-67; intern U. Ky. Hosp., 1970-71; emergency room physician Jewish Hosp., Mercy Hosp., Bethesda Hosp., Cin., 1971-72; ship's doctor, 1972; resident in ophthalmology Ohio State U. Hosp., Columbus, 1972-75; practice medicine specializing in ophthalmology Columbus, 1975—. Mem. staff Univ. Hosp., Grant Hosp., St. Anthony Hosp., 1975—79; clin. asst. prof. Ohio State U. Med. Sch., 1976—, dir. course ophthalmologic receptionist/aides, 1976; mem. Peer Rev. Sys. Bd., 1986—92, mem. exec. com., 1988—92; mem. Ohio Optical Dispensers Bd., 1986—91; bd. dirs. Ctrl. Ohio Radio Reading Svc., 1997—2003; mem. Ohio Bd. Cosmetology, 1999—. Mem. United Way, mem. planning com., 1992—93; Dem. candidate Ohio Senate, 1982. Fellow: Am. Acad. Ophthalmology; mem.: LWVMC (bd. dirs. 2010—), AAUP, Herb Soc., Grandview Area Bus. Assn., Columbus Coun. World Affairs, Life Care Alliance (pres. sustaining bd. 1987—88), Am. Coun. the Blind (bd. dirs. 1995—96), Columbus EENT Soc., Ohio State Med. Assn. (dr.-nurse liaison com. 1983—87), Ohio Soc. Prevent Blindness (chmn. med. adv. bd. 1978—80), Franklin County Acad. Medicine (mem. profl. rels. com. 1979—82, mem. edn. and program com. 1981—88, mem. legis. com. 1981—89, chmn. 1982—85, chmn. cmty. rels. com. 1987—90, chmn. resolution com. 1987—92, mem. fin. com. 1988—92), Ohio Ophthalmol. Soc. (del. to Ohio State Med. Assn. 1984—88, bd. govs. 1984—89), Am. Assn. Ophthalmologists, Columbus Area Women's Polit. Caucus, Federated Dem. Women Ohio, Columbus C. of C., Mercedes Benz Club (bd. dirs. 1981—83), Wicked Investment Club (pres. 1999—2004, treas. 2005—), Columbus Met. Club (mem. forum com. 1982—85, mem. fundraising com. 1983—84, chmn. 10th anniversary com. 1986), Colubmus Bus. and Profl. Women's Club, Zonta (chmn. internat. com. 1983, mem. program com. 1984—86), Phi Mu. Home: 2396 Northwest Blvd Columbus OH 43221-3829 Office: 1335 Dublin Rd Ste 25A Columbus OH 43215-1000 Office Phone: 614-488-8836. E-mail: mhuheey.1@yahoo.com. *

HUI, STANLEY SAI-CHUEN, physical education educator; b. Hong Kong, Aug. 26, 1962; s. Yuk Hui and Yee-mui Lam; m. Ruth Siu-king Chung, Mar. 27, 1988; 1 child, Emmanuel Andrew. Cert. in Advanced Tchg., Grantham Coll. Edn., 1989; BS in Phys. Edn., Springfield Coll., Mass., 1991, MS, 1992; EdD, U. Houston, 1995. Tchr. phys. edn., math. Pentecostal Lam Hon Kwong Secondary Sch., Shatin, Hong Kong, 1985—90; exercise test technologist Cardiology Dept. Kelsey Seybold Clinic, Houston, 1994—95; phys. edn. officer Lingnan U., Tuen Mun, Hong Kong, 1995—97; asst. prof. Dept. Sports Sci. and Phys. Edn. The Chinese U. Hong Kong, Shatin, Hong Kong, 1997—2002, assoc. prof. Dept. Sports Sci. and Phys. Edn., 2002—07, prof. Dept. Sports Sci. and Phys. Edn., 2007—. Cons. in field. Author: Wellness: The Key to Quality Life, 2000, One-minute Office Stretching Exercise, 2001, Aquatic Exercise for Fitness and Health, 2002, Manual of Health-Related Physical Fitness Assessment for Hong Kong Students, 2005; dir.: PE-WEB: An Interactive Web-based Program in Physical Education, 2002, Virtual Trainer: An Interactive Web-based Program for Exercise Promotion, 2006; prodr.: (video) Low-impact Aerobic Exercise for Children Series I, II, 1999, On-line Health-related Physical Fitness Evaluation Softwares, 2004; contbr. (video) Healthy Exercise with Kid's Songs for Children, 1999, Exercise for Health Videos; contbr. research reviews (Reviewer of the Yr. award, 2005), articles to profl. jours. Subject expert Hong Kong Coun.Academic Accreditation, 2002—. Recipient Outstanding Tchg. award, Faculty Edn., The Chinese U. Hong Kong, 1998—, Exemplary Tchg. award, 2000—02; grantee, U. Grant Coun., Hong Kong, 1999—2000, 2003—, Hong Kong Sports Devel. Bd., 1999—2000, Edn. Dept., Hong Kong, 2000—02, Edn. and Manpower Bur., Hong Kong, 2003—, Health, Welfare and Food Bur., Hong Kong, 2004—; fellow, Springfield (Mass.) Coll., 1992, U. Houston, Tex., 1992—95. Fellow: Am. Coll. Sports Medicine (instr. health fitness 1998, dir. health fitness 2000); mem.: Am. Alliance Health, Phys. Edn., Recreation and Dance (Highest Rated Rsch. Abstract award 2005), Hong Kong Profl. Tchrs. Union, Hong Kong Assn. Study Obesity (mem. coun. 2005—), The Asian Assn. Aerobic Fitness Health and Wellness, Phys. Fitness Assn. Hong Kong (vice chmn. 1997—), Internat. Fedn. Sports Medicine. Achievements include development of stretch reminder software. Office: Dept of Sports Science & PE The Chinese University of Hong Kong Shatin 00000 Hong Kong Office Fax: 852-26035781. Business E-Mail: hui2162@cuhk.edu.hk.

HUIQI, LI, research scientist; b. Harbin, China, June 13, 1972; PhD, Nanyang Technol. U., 2003. Engr. Beijing Inst. Control Device, 1995—99; rsch. fellow Nat. U. Singapore, 2002—04; rsch. scientist Inst. Inforcomm Rsch., Singapore, 2004—; prof. Beijing Inst. Tech., 2011. Adj. rsch. fellow Singapore Eye Rsch. Inst., 2007—. Recipient Young Inventor' award, Tan Kan Kee Found.; Rsch. grant, Nanyang Technol. U. Mem.: IEEE (sr.), Pattern Recognition & Machine Intelligence Assn., Med. Image Computing & Computer Assisted Intervention Soc., Assn. Rsch. Vision & Ophthalmology. Home: Toh Guan Rd BLK 286D 14-12 Singapore 604286 Singapore Personal E-mail: li_huiqi@yahoo.com.

HUIS IN 'T VELD, DIANA, medical researcher; b. Novi Sad, Serbia, Jan. 10, 1979; Degree in Internal Medicine, Infectious Diseases, UMCN; MD, Katholieke U. Nijmegen, 2004; PhD, U. Limpopo, 2011; attending, U. Antwerp, 2010—. Rschr. Welcome Trust Bangkok, 2004—05; resident internal medicine Slingeland Hosp. Doetinchem, 2005—08, UMCN, 2008—09; rschr. U. Antwerp, 2010—. Home: 134 Annie Botha Ave Pretoria Gauteng 0084 South Africa Personal E-mail: dhuisintveld@itg.be.

HUISMAN, ALBERT, biochemist, pharmacist; b. Avereest, Overijssel, Netherlands, Dec. 30, 1967; s. Jacob Huisman and Jacoba Wilkina ter Veen; m. Helen Elizabeth Clayton, June 29, 2006; children: Sarah Sophie Elisabeth, Annabel Neeltje Jacoba, Joris Jacob John. MSc, Utrecht U., Netherlands, 1992, PharmD, 1994, PhD, 2003. Cert. clin. chemist Nederlandse Vereniging voor Klinische Chemie & Laboratoriumgeneeskunde, 2003. Capt., pharmacist Royal Netherlands Army, 1994—96; pharmacist Pub. Pharmacy, Utrecht, 1996—98; rsch. fellow U. Med. Ctr. Utrecht, 1998—99, trainee clin. chemistry, 1999—2003, clin. chemist, 2003—. Mem.: Netherlands Pharm. Soc., Am. Soc. Hematology, Internat. Soc. Lab. Hematology (treas.), Netherlands Soc. Clin. Chemistry and Lab. Medicine. Office: Univ Med Ctr Utrecht Heidelberglaan 100 Utrecht 3584CX Netherlands Office Fax: 3188 7555418. Personal E-mail: alberthuisman@yahoo.com. Business E-Mail: a.huisman@umcutrecht.nl.

HULKA, JAROSLAV FABIAN, obstetrician, gynecologist; b. NYC, Sept. 29, 1930; s. Jaroslav Hugo and Milada (Touskova) H.; m. Barbara E. Sorenson, Nov. 13, 1954; children— Carol Ann, Gregory Fabian, Bryan Herbert. BA, Harvard U., 1952; MD, Columbia U., 1956. Diplomate: Am. Bd. Ob-Gyn. Intern Roosevelt Hosp., NYC, 1956-57; resident Sloane Hosp. for Women, Columbia-Presbyn. Med. Center, NYC, 1957-60; Josiah Macy, Jr. fellow Columbia-Presbyn. Med. Center, 1960-61; practice medicine specializing in Ob-Gyn, 1961—; asst. prof. Ob-Gyn U. Pitts. Sch. Medicine, 1961-66, asso. mem. grad. faculty, 1962-66, acting chmn. dept. ob-Gyn, 1963-64; assoc. prof. dept. ob-Gyn Sch. Medicine, U. N.C., Chapel Hill, 1967-76, prof. dept. ob-Gyn and dept. maternal and child health, 1976-96, prof. emeritus dept. ob-gyn.; prof. emeritus dept. maternal and child health U. N.C. Sch. Pub. Health, Chapel Hill. Author: Textbook of Laparoscopy, 1985, 3d edit., 1997; patentee in field. Assoc. dir. Carolina Population Center, 1967-74. Recipient Excel award Soc. of Laparoendoscopic Surgeons, 1994. Fellow ACOG; mem. Soc. for Gynecol. Investigation, Am. Assn. Gynecol. Laparoscopists (pres. 1980), Am. Fertility Soc., Soc. Reproductive Surgeons (founding), N.C. State Bar (bd. legal specialization 1990-96), Planned Parenthood Fed. Am. (chair nat. med. com. 1991-94), Soc. Physicians for Reproductive Choice and Health (founding). Achievements include development of and teaching of worldwide use of clips for female sterilization by laparoscopy; demonstration of local anesthesia for safer procedures. Home: 2317 Honeysuckle Rd Chapel Hill NC 27514-1716 Personal E-mail: jhulka@unc.edu.

HULL, DAVID HUGILL, retired internist; b. London, Aug. 21, 1931; s. Thomas Edward and Marjorie Ethel Hull; m. Ann Thornton-Symington, Sept. 28, 1957; children: Diana Clare, Jennifer Sarah. MA with 1st class honors, Cambridge U., Eng., 1953; MB, St. Thomas Hosp. Med. Sch., Eng., 1956. Commd. RAF, 1957, advanced through grades to air vice marshal; intern St. Thomas Hosp., London, 1956—57, Kingston Hosp., Kingston-on-Thames, England, 1956—57; cons. internal medicine Princess Mary's RAF Hosp., Akrotiri, Cyprus, 1966—67, RAF Hosp., Cosford, England, 1968—74; RAF exch. officer USAF Sch. Aerospace Medicine, San Antonio, 1974—77; cons. internal medicine Princess Alexandra's RAF Hosp., Wroughton, England, 1977—82; cons. advisor medicine RAF Ctrl. Med. Establishment, London, 1982—93, clin. dir. RAF, tri-svc. med. dean, 1993—96; ret., 1996. Reader aviation medicine London U., 1978—93. Contbr. chapters to books, scientific papers to profl. publs. Mem. working group Adv. Group for Aerospace R&D, NATO, 1988—93. Fellow: Aerospace Med. Assn., Royal Coll. Physicians; mem.: Order St. John Jerusalem. Avocations: gardening, boating, languages, fitness.

HULL, MICHAEL ALAN, behavioral scientist; b. Melbourne, Victoria, Australia, Jan. 26, 1944; s. William Peter and Rae Marie (Neale) H. BA, Flinders U. South Australia, Adelaide, 1973, BA with honors, 1974; MA, Victoria U. Wellington, New Zealand, 1977. Cert. Victoria U., Melbourne, 2007, TESOL Victoria U., Melbourne, 2008. Rsch. officer Ministry of Transport, Wellington, 1980-81, Melbourne, 1983-85; rsch. officer accident rsch. unit U. Adelaide, 1981-82; spl. projects mgr. Technisearch Royal Melbourne Inst. Tech., 1985-87; head tng. and licensing Road Traffic Authority, Melbourne, 1987-89; prin. behavioral scientist Roads Corp., Melbourne, 1989—; dir. Rsch. Australia, Melbourne, 1985-2000; mng. dir. Pan Pacific Rsch. Pty Ltd., 2000—. Demonstrator Victoria U. Wellington, 1975-77; occasional lectr. Royal Melbourne Inst. Tech., 1985-88, Swinburne U., Melbourne, 1997-99; rd. safety coord. Hobsons Bay City Coun, Australia, 2003-. Contbr. articles to profl. jours.; patentee hazard perception test. Hon. ESL tutor Swinburne U., 1997-99; fitness to drive project mgr. Austroads, Melbourne, 1997-99; road safety expert witness Victoria State Ct., Melbourne, 1995-99. Recipient Innovation award Roads Corp. Victoria, 1991; named Justice of the Peace, Victoria, 2003-. Mem. Internat. Assn. Applied Psychology, Australian Sociol. Assn. Office Phone: 61 403 180842. Business E-Mail: mike@panfacificresearch.net.

HÜLLEMANN, KLAUS-DIETHART, health consultant, internist, psychotherapist, sports medicine physician; b. Eisenach, Germany, Apr. 5, 1938; s. Siegfried and Thekla H.; m. Brigitte Schube, May 16, 1975; children: Mirko, Niko, Philipp. BS, Frankfurt U., Fed. Republic Germany, 1958; MD, Heidelberg U., Fed. Republic Germany, 1964. Intern Psychiat. Hosp. Heidelberg, 1964-65; resident Gen. Hosp. Konstanz, 1966-67; with Ludolf-Krehl-Klinik, Heidelberg, 1968-75; dir. dept. medicine Höhenried (Fed. Republic Germany) Hosp., 1975-77; med. dir. St. Irmingard Hosp., European Pilot Hosp., WHO, Prien, Germany, 1977—2004; pvt. practice Unterwoessen, 2004—. Prin. investigator German Cardiovasc. Prevention Study, Bergen, 1979-91; prof. internal medicine, 1975, Munich U., 1978—; dir., prof. Dr. med. Klaus-D, Hüllemann GmbH; pres. Managementakademic Chiemsee GmbH; chmn. bd. dirs., 2010, German Network of Health Promoting Hosps., WHO, 1995—; spkr. sci. coun. HPH Network/WHO, chair, bd. dirs., chief exec., bd. trustees, U. Applied Scis. Hamburg, 2010. Author, editor: Quo Vadis Medicine?, 1989; author: Fitness and Wellbeing, 1992, German Cardiovascular Preventive Study-GCP, 1998, The Idea of Man in Medicine, Medicine in the Idea of Man, 1999; contbr. more than 300 articles to profl. jours. Trustee U. Applied Scis., Hamburg, 2010. Mem. AAAS, NY Acad. Scis., German Chinese Med. Assn., German Assn. Internal Medicine, German Assn. Oncology, German Milton Erickson Soc. Clin. Hypnosis (sci. coun.), Mgmt. Acad. Chiemsee GmbH (pres. 2007). Avocations: cross country skiing, hiking, piano, skiing. Office: Quellstr 16 83346 Bergen Germany also: Lerchnauer Str 34 80809 Munich Germany Office Phone: 8662 6653 558. Office Fax: 8662 6653 557. Business E-Mail: klaus-d@huellemann.net.

HULME, MARY ANN PRIM KUMM, women's health nurse, administrator; b. Galion, Ohio, July 25, 1952; d. Walter Herman and Mary Elizabeth (Prim) Kumm; m. Roy Allan Hulme, Jan. 8, 1977; children: Eric A., Ann E. BSN, Capital U., 1974; MSN, Case Western Res. U., 1993. RN, Ohio; cert. in ob-gyn., inpatient ob-gyn., neonatal nursing ANCC, NEBC. Staff and charge nurse, labor and delivery St. Ann's Hosp., Columbus, Ohio, 1974-76, head nurse, dir. ob-gyn. outpatient clinic, 1976-77; clin. nurse, sr. clin. nurse, head nurse mgr. labor/delivery Univ. Hosps., Cleve., 1977-94; head nurse mgr. labor/delivery antepartum U. Hosps. Cleve., Cleve., 1994-98, head nurse mgr. labor and delivery, 1998—2003, adminstr. risk prevention, quality and accreditation dept. ob-gyn., 2003—07, prin. advisor accreditation dept. of nursing adminstrn., 2006—07; dir., prin. advisor Magnet Appraiser Anu, 2007. Clin. instr. maternity and gynecology nursing Case Western Res. U., Cleve., 1986—, Kent State U., 1995—, leader magnet force 6, 2004, coord. magnet accreditation, 2005, magnet appraiser ANCC, 2007-; cons. in field Contbr. articles to profl. jours. With United Way Svcs., 1998. Recipient Pre Gold medal U.S. Figure Skating Assn. Mem. Ohio Orgn. Nurse Execs. (past program chair, past bd. dirs., program com. mem.), Assn. Womens Health, Obstet. and Neonatal Nursing, Assn. Oper. Room Nurses, Greater Cleve. Orgn. Nurse Execs. (planning com.), Cleve. Skating Club (past bd. dirs., past co-chmn. skating com., curling com.), ANA, ONA, GCNA (nominating com.), AONE Sigma Theta Tau. Lutheran. Avocations: ice dancing, curling. Home: 16070 S Park Blvd Cleveland OH 44120-1673 Home Phone: 216-991-0110; Office Phone: 216-844-1659. Business E-Mail: maryann.hulme@uhhospitals.org.

HULOT, JEAN-SEBASTIEN, cardiologist, pharmacologist, educator; b. Lille, France, Aug. 16, 1973; s. Michel and Danièle Hulot; m. Sylvie Lorand; 1 child, Camille. MD, Paris 5 U., 2001, PhD, 2005. Cert. clin. pharmacologist Paris 5 U., 2002. Assoc. prof. Pitie-Salpetriere U. Hosp., Paris, 2006—; assoc. prof. medicine Mt. Sinai Sch. Medicine, NYC, 2010—. Med. rschr. INSERM Unit, Paris, 2004—. Contbr. articles to profl. jours. Transatlantic fellow, Leducq Found., 2007—08. Achievements include patents for new therapeutic target in cardiovascular disease; first to pharmacogenetics of antiplatelet agents. Office: Mount Sinai Sch Med Cardiovasc Rsch Ctr Gustave L Levy Pl New York NY 10029 Office Fax: 33142161688, 212-241-4080. Business E-Mail: jean-sebastien.hulot@psl.aphp.fr, jean.hulot@mssm.edu.

HULSEY, THOMAS C., epidemiologist, researcher; BS in Biology, Bapt. Coll., Charleston, SC, 1975; MPH, U. SC, 1977; DSc, Johns Hopkins U., Balt., 1988. Prof. Med. U. SC, Charleston, 1987—. Fellow: Am. Coll. Epidemiology; mem.: Am. Pediatric Soc., Soc. Pediatric Rsch. Lutheran. Office: Med Univ South Carolina PO Box 250566 135 Ashley Ave Charleston SC 29425 Home: 424 Rice Hope Dr Mount Pleasant SC 29464 Business E-Mail: hulseytc@musc.edu.

HULTBORN, RAGNAR, oncologist, educator; b. Stockholm, Oct. 31, 1946; MD, U. Gothenburg, PhD, 1974. Prof. U. Gothenburg Sahlgrenska Acad., 2005—. Head, dept. oncology Sahlgrenska Acad., 2005—. Mem.: European Soc. Therapeutic Radiology & Oncology. Office: Sahlgrenska University Hosp Gothenburg S 41345 Sweden Business E-Mail: ragnar.hultborn@oncology.gu.se.

HUMAYUN, MARK S., ophthalmologist, educator, medical researcher; BS, Georgetown U., Washington, 1984; MD, Duke U. Med. Sch., Durham. NC, 1989; PhD in Biomedical Engring., U. NC, Chapel Hill, 1994. Diplomate Am. Bd. Ophthalmology, lic. Calif., Md., Fla. Intern Roanoke Meml. Hosp., Va., 1990; resident Duke Eye Ctr., 1990—93, clin. preceptor, 1993—95; fellow Wilmer Opthalmological Inst., John Hopkins U., Balt., 1994—95, asst. prof., 1995—99, assoc. prof., dir. Intraocular Retinal Prothesis Lab., 2000—01; prof. ophthalmology and biomed. engring. U. So. Calif. Keck Sch. Medicine, 2001—, assoc. dir. rsch. Doheny Retina Inst., 2001—, dir. Biomimetic MicroElectronic Systems Engring. Rsch. Ctr., Cornelius J. Pings chair biomed. scis., 2009—. Retinal cons. Columbia Med. Plan, Md., 1996—97; vis. prof. Kresge Eye Inst., Detroit, 1998, Oakland Eye Inst., Rochester, Mich., 1998; bd. mem. Springer Serres BMP-BME, Calif., 2001—; dir. Artificial Retina Project, US Dept. Energy. Contbr. numerous articles to profl. jours., chapters to books. Recipient William & Mary Greve Scholars award, Rsch. to Prevent Blindness, 1997, Richard S. Ross Clin. Scientist award, 1998, Jules Stein Living Tribute award, 2002; named Innovator of Yr., R&D Mag., 2005. Mem.: NAE, IEEE Engring. in Medicine & Biology Soc., Inst. Medicine, American Inst. Med. & Biological Engring., Biomedical Engring. Soc., Retina Soc., American Acad. Ophthalmology, American Soc. Retinal Specialists (Sr. Honor award 2004), Assn. Rsch. in Vision & Ophthalmology, American Ophthal. Soc., Pacific Coast Oto-Ophthalmological Soc. (hon.). Achievements include patents for retinal prostheses, retinal microstimulation, intraocular drug delivery, opthalmic surgical devices (cannulas), implantable retinal electrode arrays, and methods for training visual prosthesis. Office: Doheny Eye Institute DVRC 119 1355 San Pablo St Los Angeles CA 90033 Office Phone: 323-442-6523. Office Fax: 323-442-6755. Business E-Mail: humayun@usc.edu. *

HUMBLE, WILLIAM, state agency administrator, public health service officer; Dir., office risk assessment and investigations Ariz. Dept. Health Services, chief, epidemiology and disease control bur., dep. dir., interim dir., 2009—. Office: Ariz Dept Health Services 150 N 18th Ave Phoenix AZ 85007 Office Phone: 602-542-1025. Office Fax: 602-542-1062. Business E-Mail: will.humble@azdhs.gov.

HUMER, FRANZ B., pharmaceutical executive; JD, MBA, U. Innsbruck; PhD (hon.), U. Basel. With ICME, Zurich, Switzerland, 1971—73; gen. mgr. of Ecuador, UK, Portugal Schering Plough Corp., 1973—81; area mgr., So. Europe, dir. of mktg. develop. and product licensing, then chief operating dir. Glaxo Holdings plc, 1981—95; head, pharmaceuticals div. F. Hoffmann-La Roche Ltd., 1995—, COO, 1996; CEO Roche Holding Ltd., 1998, chmn., CEO, 2001—08, chmn., 2008—. Chmn. European Federation of Pharmaceutical Industries and Assns.; mem. European Round Table of Industrialists, JPMorgan Internat. Council, Internat. Bus. Leaders' Adv. Council for Mayor of Shanghai; bd. mem. Diageo Plc, Allianz AG. Chmn. Friends of Phelophepa Found.; mem. Internat. Adv. Bd. of Nat. Ctr. for Missing and Exploited Children. Office: F Hoffmann-La Roche Ltd Grenzacherstrasse 124 4058 Basel Switzerland *

HUMES, HARVEY DAVID, nephrologist, educator, director; b. Honolulu, Nov. 20, 1947; s. William and Nancy Humes; m. Dolores Humes; 1 child, Michael David. BA, U. Calif., Berkeley, 1969; MD, U. Calif., San Francisco, 1973. Diplomate Am. Bd. Internal Medicine. Intern Moffit Hosp. and U. Calif. Hosps., San Francisco, 1973—74; resident U. Calif. Hosps., San Francisco, 1974—75; clin. fellow nephrology U. Pa. Hosp., Phila., 1975—76; rsch. fellow lab. kidney & electrolyte physiology Peter Bent Brigham Hosp., Boston, 1976—77; from instr. to asst. prof. medicine Peter Bent Brigham Hosp./Harvard Med. Sch., Boston, 1977—79; from asst. prof. to assoc. prof. internal medicine U. Mich., Ann Arbor, 1979—86, prof. internal medicine, 1986—, John G. Searle prof., chmn. internal medicine, 1996—2000; founder, gen. ptnr., mgr. EpiGenesis, LLC; founder Nephros Therapeutics, Inc.; founder, chair sci. adv. bd. RenaMed Biologics, Inc.; founder, pres., dir. Chelux Medica, Inc.; founder, pres., chief sci. officer Innovative BioTherapies; founder, chief sci. officer, dir. Cytopherex Inc. Mem. sci. adv. bd. NephRx, Renal Solutions, Inc.; cons. Dow Chem.; chmn. Mich. regenerative Medicine Ctr.; sr. advisor Phoenix Venture Ptnrs.; dir., chief Nephrology Rsch. Labs., U. Mich., Ann Arbor, 1980-81; chief med. svc. VA Med. Ctr., Ann Arbor, 1983-96. Editor: Current Opinion in Internal Medicine, 2001—10; editor-in-chief: Kelley's Textbook of Internal Medicine, 1997—2001; mem. editl. bd. Am. Jour. Medicine, 1997—2006; mem. editl. bd.: Seminars in Nephrology, 1993—2007, Internat. Yearbook of Nephrology, 1989—2005; contbr. articles to profl. jours. Grantee Nat. Kidney Found., 1981-85, 87-88, PHS, 1987—, Am. Heart Assn., 1982-87, 94-95. Fellow: AAAS, ACP; mem.: Am. Soc. Artificial Internal Organs (trustee, pres.), Ctrl. Soc. Clin. Rsch. (past pres.), Nat. Kidney Found. Mich., Nat. Kidney Found. (Pres. award), Internat. Soc. Nephrology, Am. Fedn. Clin. Rsch., Am. Soc. Nephrology (sec.), Am. Heart Assn., Am. Soc. Clin. Investigation, Assn. Prof. Medicine, Am. Physiol. Soc., Phi Beta Kappa, Alpha Omega Alpha. Achievements include development of bioartificial kidney; research in cellular basis of acute renal failure, biochemical basis of aminoglycoside-induced acute renal failure, cyclosporine nephrotoxicity, lipid alterations in ischemic acute renal failure, free-radical-induced mitochondrial injury, molecular basis of renal repair in acute renal failure, molecular basis of kidney tubulogenesis, biometric selective cytopheretic device to treat accute and chronic inflamation. Office: U Mich Med Sch SPC 5651 4520 MSRB I, 1150 W Medical Ctr Ann Arbor MI 48109 Office Phone: 734-647-8018. Business E-Mail: dhumes@umich.edu.

HUMPHREY, CHESTER BOWDEN, cardiothoracic surgeon; b. Marblehead, Mass., July 29, 1939; s. Leonard Graves and Mary Louise (Bowden) H.; m. Joyce Claire Jazwinski, Mar. 20, 1971; 1 child, Andrew Bowden. BS, Dickinson Coll., 1961; MD, Temple U., 1965. Diplomate Am. Bd. Thoracic Surgery, Am. Bd. Surgery. Intern Hartford Hosp., 1965-66, resident in gen. surgery, 1966-71; resident in thoracic and cardiovascular surgery Naval Regional Med. Ctr., San Diego, 1973-75; cardio-thoracic surgeon Cardiothoracic and Vascular Surgeons, P.C., 1976—. Adv. com. Town of West Hartford (Conn.) Paramedics, 1989—. Comdr. USN, 1970-76. Fellow Am. Coll. Surgeons, Am. Coll. Cardiology, Am. Coll. Chest Physicians; mem. Soc. for Thoracic Surgeons, Denton Cooley Surg. Soc., New England Soc. for Vascular Surgery. Office: Cardiothoracic & Vascular Surgeons PC 85 Seymour St Ste 325 Hartford CT 06106-5522 Office Phone: 860-527-8201.

HUMPHREY, HOLLY J., dean, medical educator; MD with honors, Univ. Chgo. Cert. Internal Medicine, Nat. Bd. Med. Examiners. Internship and residency U. Chgo. Hosps., fellow in pulmonary & critical care medicine; chief med. resident U. Chgo. Med. Ctr., med. doctor dept. pulmonary & critical care medicine, 1986—; asst. prof., dir. internal med. residency program U. Chgo. Pritzker Sch. Medicine, 1989—2003, prof. medicine, dean med. edn., 2003—, founding dean Acad. Disting. Med. Educators, 2006—. Recipient Hilger Pretty Jenkins Tchg. award, Univ. Chgo., Laureate award, Am. Coll. Physicians, 1999, Dema C. Daley Founders award, Assn. Program Dirs. in Internal Medicine, 2005; named a Woman to Watch, Crain's Chgo. Bus., 2009. Mem.: Am. Thoracic Soc., Assn. Program Dirs. in Internal Medicine (former pres.), Am. Bd. Internal Medicine (chmn. 2006—07). Office: 5841 S Maryland Ave MC6091 Chicago IL 60637 Office Phone: 773-834-2138. Office Fax: 773-702-2598. *

HUMPHRIES, JOHN O'NEAL, cardiologist, educator, dean; b. Columbia, SC, Oct. 22, 1931; s. Arthur Lee and Helen Elliott (O'Neal) H.; m. Mary Ellen Cregan, Mar. 13, 1954; children: Arthur Thomas, Ellen Cregan, John Elliott. BS, Duke U., 1952; MD, Johns Hopkins U., 1956. Diplomate Am. Bd. Internal Medicine (mem. bd. subsplty. cardiovascular disease 1974-79). Intern Johns Hopkins Hosp., 1957; asst. resident Osler Med. Service, Osler Med. Svc., 1958-60, resident physician pvt. med. svc., 1962-64, staff physician, 1962-79; rsch. fellow in cardiology U. London, St. George's Hosp., 1960-61, Johns Hopkins U. Med. Sch., 1956-57, 61-62, mem. faculty, 1964-79, Robert L. Levy prof. cardiology, 1975-79, prof. medicine, 1976-79; O.B. Mayer Sr. and Jr. prof. medicine U. S.C., Columbia, 1979-86, prof. medicine, 1979-96; disting. prof. medicine, dean emeritus, 1997—; chmn. dept. medicine U. S.C., Columbia, 1979-87, dean Sch. Medicine, 1983-94. Contbr. articles to med. publs.; mem. editl. bd. various jours. Bd. dirs. Md. Ballet, Balt., 1975-78. Master ACP (bd. govs. for S.C. chpt. 1986-90), Am. Coll. Cardiology (bd. govs. for

Md. chpt. 1973-76); mem. Am. Fedn. Clin. Rsch., Am. Heart Assn. (fellow coun. clin. cardiology, chmn. postgrad. edn. com., exec. com. 1972-75), Cen. Md. Heart Assn. (pres. 1972-73), Md. Heart Assn. (pres. 1976-77), Assn. Univ. Cardiologists, Am. Clin. and Climatol. Assn., Alpha Omega Alpha. Office: U SC Sch Medicine Columbia SC 29208-0001

HUNG, CHAO CHIA, nursing educator; b. Kaohsiung, Jan. 17, 1965; PhD, Nat. Taiwan U., 2009. Asst. prof. Yuanpei U., 1997—. Mem.: Taiwan Nurses Assn. Office: 306 Yuanpei St HsinChu 30015 Taiwan Business E-Mail: hungcc0117@yahoo.com.tw.

HUNG, CHI-FENG, medical researcher; BS, Kaoshiung Med. U.; MS, PhD, Taiwan U. Cert. Pharmacist Taiwan. Prof. Fu-Jen Cath. U., Taipei County, Taiwan, 2009. Office: Sch Medicine Rm 518-2 510 Chung Cheng Rd Hsinchuang Taipei 242 Taiwan Office Fax: 886-2-29052096. E-mail: skin@mails.fju.edu.tw.

HUNG, GUANG-UEI, nuclear medicine physician, educator; s. Chin-Ming Hung and Tsui-Yen Hsiao; married. Degree in medicine, Kaohsiung Med. U., 1986, MD, 1989. Diplomate Dept. Health, Exec. Yuan, 1996, cert. nuc. medicine Dept. Health, Exec. Yuan, 2001, diplomate Dept. Health, Exec. Yuan, 2001, cert. nuc. medicine specialist Taichung Vets. Gen. Hosp., 2001. Attending physician Changhua Christian Hosp., Taiwan, 2003—08; dir. nuc. medicine dept. Chang-Bing Show-Chwan Hosp., Lukong, Changhua, Taiwan, 2008—; rsch. fellow Taichung Vets. Gen. Hosp. Contbr. scientific papers to profl. jours. Lt. Matine Corp, 1996—98, Kaohsiung. Recipient Asia and Oceania Disting. Young Investigator Award, Japanese Soc. Nuc. Medicine, 2006. Office: Chang Bing Show Chwan Hosp 6 Lukon Rd Lukong Changhua 505 Taiwan Office Fax: 886-7-7073299.

HUNG, IOU-JIH, pediatrician; d. Hsun-Hsin Hung and Twey-Fong Lin; m. Delon Wu, Oct. 19, 1968; 1 child, Lawrence Wu. MD, Nat. Taiwan U. Coll. Medicine, 1966. Diplomate Am. Bd. Pediat., 1972, in pediatric hematology, oncology Am. Bd. Ped. hematooncology, 1984. Head, dept. pediatrics Chang Gung Meml. Hosp., Taipei, Taiwan, 1979—82, clin. prof., 2004—, cons. physician, 2007—; head, divsn. hematology oncology Chang Gung Children's Hosp., Taoyuan, 1984—2006; assoc. prof. Chang Gung U. Coll. Medicine, Taoyuan, 1987—. Fellow: Am. Acad. Pediat.; mem.: Taiwan Pediatric Assn., Taiwan Med. Assn., Am. Acad. Pediatric Hematology Oncology, Internat. Soc. Pediatric Oncology. Office: Chang Gung Memorial Hosp 5 Fu-Hsin St KueiShan Hsiang Taoyuan 333 Taiwan

HUNG, KUN-LONG, pediatric neurologist, educator, researcher; b. Changhwa, Taiwan, Feb. 28, 1952; s. Sui-Fa Hung and Hwa-Chung Hung-Lee; m. Chu-Hui Susan Su, Feb. 22, 1981; children: Joseph, Jonathan, Jeff. MD, Nat. Taiwan U., Taipei, 1977, PhD, Tokyo Women's Med. Coll., 1994. Diplomate in pediatrics, pediatric neurologist. Fellow in pediatric neurology U. Mich. Med. Ctr., Ann Arbor, 1987, Tokyo Women's Med. Coll., 1986; resident in pediatrics Cathay Gen. Hosp., Taipei, 1977-81, mem. vis. staff, 1981—, chmn., 1992-2000, supt. Neihu, 2000—04, Sijhih, 2005—08, vice supt., 2008—; fellow in pediat. neurology Nat. Taiwan U., 1981, lectr., 1987-94, assoc. prof., 1994—2002, prof., 2002—. Cons. Taipei Mcpl. Yung Ming Rehab. Ctr., 1985-87, Taipei Mcpl. Chung-Hsiao Hosp., 1990-91; coord. acute flaccid paralysis com. Dept. Health, Exec. Yuan, Taipei, 1994—. Contbr. articles to pediat., & neonatology, Jour. Formosa Med. Assn., Brain and Devel., Sci. Recipient Takeda prize Takeda Sci. Co., 1986, Nestle prize Taiwan Pediat. Assn., 1991, Taiwan Pediat. Assn. prize, 2008. Mem. Formosan Med. Assn., Am. Acad. Neurology, Internat. Child Neurology Assn., Taiwan Child Neurology Soc. Avocations: swimming, music. Office: Cathay Gen Hosp 280 Sec 4 Jen-Ai Rd Taipei Taiwan Office Phone: 886-2-27082121. Office Fax: 886-2-7082423. Personal E-mail: klhung@ms10.hinet.net

HUNG, MEI-JONG CHOW, social worker; b. Taipei, Taiwan, Republic China, Oct. 7, 1937; s. Wen-tung Yeh Chow; m. Chao-huang Hung, Mar. 24, 1964; children: Jennifer Ching-yi, John Ching-tsung. BS, Nat. Taiwan U., 1960; MSW, Simmons Coll. Sch. Social Work, 1963. Cert. hypnotherapist; social worker. Mental health counselor Taipei Pub. Health Teaching Demonstration, 1963-66; asst. prof. Taiwan U., 1964-66; social work supr. Johns Hopkins Hosp., Balt., 1969-71; pvt. practice social work Columbia, Md., 1972—. Vol. cmty. recreational social work, 1988—; co-prodr. Opera Internat., Washington, 1999—, prodr., 2002—. Fellow, WHO. Mem.: NASW, Acad. Cert. Social Workers. Home and Office: 7255 Meadow Wood Way Clarksville MD 21029-1714 Address: PO Box 140 Fulton MD 20759-0140

HUNG, MING-YOW, physician; b. Taichung, Taiwan, Feb. 15, 1969; MD, Chang Gung U., 1996. Lic. specialist in internal medicine & chinese physician 2001, in cardiology 2004, cert. in ultrasound medicine 2007, lic. in coronary intervention 2008, in echocardiography 2009. Resident internal medicine Chang Gung Meml. Hosp., Taoyuan, Taiwan, 1998—2001, fellow divsn. cardiology, 2001—03, attending divsn. cardiology, 2003—08; dir. ICU divsn. cardiology Taipei Med. U.-Shuang Ho Hosp., Taiwan, 2008—; asst. prof. Taipei Med. U., 2011—. Ad hoc reviewer Acta Cardiologica Sinica, 2009—. Lt. mil. physician Taiwan Navy, 1996—98. Named one of Best Resident, Chang Gung Meml. Hosp. Mem.: Coun. Arteriosclerosis, Thrombosis & Vascular Biology (premium profl. mem.), Am. Stroke Assn., Am. Heart Assn., Taiwan Soc. Cardiovasc. Interventions, Taiwan Soc. Echocardiography, Soc. Ultrasound Medicine, Taiwan Soc. Cardiology, Taiwan Soc. Internal Medicine. Avocations: fishing, jogging, basketball, movies. Office: No291 Zhongzheng Rd None Zhonghe City 235 Taiwan Office Phone: 886-2-22490088. Personal E-mail: myhung6@ms77.hinet.net.

HUNG, TERRY CHE WAI, medical educator; b. Hong Kong, Aug. 31, 1969; BA, U. Cambridge, UK, 1991, MBBChir, 1993, MA, 1995. Specialist registrar Medway NHS Trust, England, Frimley Pk. Hosp., Surrey, England, St George's Hosp., London, Kent & Canterbury Hosp., Kent, England, Royal Surrey County Hosp., Guildford, England; house officer Peterborough Dist. Hosp., Peterborough, England, 1994—95, Addenbrooke's Hosp., Cambridge, England, 1994—95; sr. house officer Princess Margaret Hosp., Swindon, England, 1995—99, Royal Infirmary Edinburgh City Hosp., 1995—99, Charing Cross Hosp., London, 1995—99, Hammersmith Hosp., London, 1995—99, St George's Hosp., 1995—99, Royal Free Hampstead NHS Trust Royal Nat. Throat Nose & Ear Hosp., London, 1995—99; acting cons. St George's Hosp., 2005; asst. prof. Chinese U. Hong Kong, 2005—, dir. undergrad. tchg. dept. otorhinolaryngology, 2007—. Hon. editl. bd. mem. Clin. Medicine Cases Report, 2008—; invited reviewer Laryngoscope, 2007—, Jour. Plastic Reconstructive & Aesthetic Surgery, 2007—. Recipient Beargle Crawford Travel award, Trinity Coll. U. Cambridge, 1990, Academic Travel award, Pfizer Pharm., 2001; AJ Pressland studentship, U. Cambridge, 1989, Spl. Trustees grant, St George's Hosp., 1999, grant, St George's Charitable Found., 2002, Travel fellowship, Harvenian Soc. London, 2003. Master: Royal Coll. Surgeons and Physicians Glasgow; fellow: CCT Postgrad. Med. Edn. and Tng. Bd., UK, Assn. Facial Plastic Surgeon, European Acad. Facial Plastic Surgeons, Royal Soc. Medicine, Royal Coll. Surgeons Edinburgh; mem.: Hong Kong Med. Assn., Med. Protection Soc., Brit. Med. Assn., Brit. Assn. Paediatric Otolaryngology, Brit. Assn. Otolaryngology Head and Neck Surgeons. Home: Flat C 11F Block 5 Skylodge Dynasty Heig Kowloon Hong Kong Office: Chinese Univ Hong Kong Dept Otorhinolaryngology Head and Neck Surgery Prince Wales Hosp Shatin Hong Kong Office Fax: (852) 26466312. Personal E-mail: hterryhung@aol.com, drterryhung@hotmail.com. Business E-Mail: terryhung@ent.cuhk.edu.hk.

HUNGENBERG, THOMAS, radiologist; b. Cologne, Germany, July 23, 1955; s. Paul and Hedwig (Schiefer) H. MD, U. Cologne, 1982. Bd. cert. radiologist. Resident St. Katharinen Hosp., Frechen, Germany, 1981-83, Univ. Hosp., Cologne, 1983-88, Duesseldorf, Germany, 1989-90; dept. head Eduardus Hosp., Cologne, 1990—, hosp. head, 1995—. Tchr. Teleradiologic Consulting Ctr., 1998—, Deutsche Gesellschaft für Ultraschall in der Medizin, Boeblingen, 1995—. Mem. Deutsche Roentgengesellschaft, Deutsche Gesellschaft für Ultraschall in der Medizin, Radiol. Soc. N.Am. Roman Catholic. Avocations: skiing, swimming. E-mail: th_hungenberg@yahoo.de.

HUNGERFORD, DAVID SAMUEL, orthopedic surgeon, educator; b. Rochester, NY, May 4, 1938; s. Francis Samuel and Marjorie Ellen (Wilson) H.; m. Uta-Heide Jung, July 20, 1962; children: Marc Wilson, Kyle Sasha, Lars Daniel. BA, Colgate U., 1960; MD, U. Rochester, 1964. Diplomate Am. Bd. Orthopaedic Surgery. Asst. prof. orthopaedic surgery Johns Hopkins U., Balt., 1972-78; chief orthopaedic surgery VA Hosp., Balt., 1975-80, Good Samaritan Hosp., Balt., 1972—, chief div. arthritis surgery, 1979—2001; assoc. prof. orthopaedic surgery Johns Hopkins U. Sch. Medicine, Balt., 1978-86, prof. orthopaedic surgery, 1987—. Cons. Balt. City Hosp., 1972-85, Children's Hosp., 1972-80, East Balt. Med. Ctr., 1972-78; co-dir. Johns Hopkins U. Ctr. for Osteonecrosis Rsch. and Edn., 1995—; bd. dirs. Nat. Osteonecrosis Found. Author: Progress in Orthopaedics, 1977, Ischemia and Necroses of Bone, 1980, Total Knee Arthroplasty: A Comprehensive Approach, 1984, Total Hip Arthroplasty: A New Approach, 1984, Bone Circulation, 1984, Disorders of the Patello Femoral Joint, 1990, Videobook of Total Knee Arthroplasty, 1994; founding editor Jour. Arthroplasty, 1985-93. Elder Cen. Presbyn. Ch., Balt., 1974-83; dir. Crippled Children's United Rehab. Effort, 1997—, Christian Orthopaedic Ptrs., 1997—; chmn. bd. Med. Assistance Program Internat., 1998—. Maj. U.S. Army, 1969. Recipient George Hoyt Whipple award, 1965; named Disting. So. Orthopedist, So. Orthopedic Assn., 2002; Colgate U. scholar, 1956-59, GM scholar, 1956-59, U. Rochester scholar, 1959-61, Girdlestone Meml. scholar Oxford U., Eng., 1969-70; fellow USPHS, Paris, 1961-62, Carl Berg traveling fellow, 1973. Mem. Johns Hopkins Med. and Surg. Soc., Md. Orthopaedic Soc., Arthritis Found., Hip Soc., Am. Assn. Orthopaedic Surgeons, Am. Assn. Hip Knee Surgeons, Soc. Internat. de Chirurgie Orthopedique et de Traumatologie, Knee Soc. (pres. 1994), Girdlestone Orthopaedic Soc. (chmn. 2005-). Republican. Home: 10715 Pot Spring Rd Cockeysville Hunt Valley MD 21030-3019 Office: Good Samaritan Hosp Profl Office Bldg G-1 5601 Loch Raven Blvd Baltimore MD 21239-2991 also: Johns Hopkins U Sch Medicine Dept Orthopaedic Surgery Baltimore MD 21205 Business E-Mail: dhunger@jhmi.edu.

HUNLEY, TRACY EARL, pediatrician, educator; b. Nashville, Mar. 10, 1965; BA, Vanderbilt U., 1987; MD, U. Tenn., Memphis, 1991. Asst. prof., pediat. Vanderbilt Children's Hosp., 1997—. Office: 11133 Doctors Office Tower 2200 Children Nashville TN 37232-9560 Office Fax: 615-322-7929. Business E-Mail: tray.hunley@vanderbilt.edu.

HUNOLD, PETER, diagnostic and international radiologist; b. Goettingen, Germany, Sept. 29, 1972; s. Winfried and Irmgard Hunold; m. Anja Brondics; 2 children. MD, U. Essen, Germany, 1998. Cert. in diagnostic radiology North Rhine Chamber Physicians, 2005. Resident in cardiology Univ. Hosp., Essen, Germany, 1998—2000; resident and rschr. U. Essen Radiology, 2000—05; sr. staff, cons. and rschr. U. Hosp. Essen, 2005—08; asst. prof., vice chmn. U. Hosp. Schleswig-Holstein, Campus Lubeck, Germany, 2008—. Avocation: sports. Home: Carl Muehlenpfordt Strasse 16 Lubeck 23562 Germany Office: Univ Hosp Dept Radiology & Nuc Medicine Ratzeburger Allee 160 23538 Lubeck Germany Office Phone: 49-4515006552. Office Fax: 494515006497. Business E-Mail: peter.hunold@uk-sh.de.

HUNSTAD, JOSEPH PAUL, plastic surgeon, educator; b. Detroit, Mar. 14, 1955; s. Norman Allan and Freda Mae Hunstad; m. Sherry Sue Sietsema, July 11, 1987; children: Lauren Grace Marie, Megan Alexandra Ann. MD, Mich. State U., East Lansing, Michigan, 1981. Diplomate The Am. Bd. Plastic Surgery, 1989. Intern gen. surgery Butterworth Hosp., Grand Rapids, Mich., 1981—82, resident plastic surgery, 1982—84, Grand Rapids Area Med. Edn. Ctr., 1984—86, resident, 1985—86; fellowship reconstructive microsurgery MECOM Microsurgical Inst., Baylor Dept. Plastic Surgery, Houston, 1986—87; staff mem. Carolinas Med. Ctr U., 1987—95, Presbyn. Hosp., U. Hosp., Charlotte, 1995—; asst. clin. prof. Sch. Medicine Dept. Surgery U. NC, Chapel Hill, NC, 1987—95; asst. consulting prof. plastic surgery Med. Ctr. Dept. Surgery Duke U., Durham, NC, 2001—; pvt. practice Charlotte. Contbr. chapters to books. Mem. bd. dirs. Team Staffing Internat., Charlotte, NC, 2001—06. Named one of Charlotte Top Doctors, Charlotte Mag., 2005, America's Top Physicians, Consumer Rsch. Coun. Am., 2005, 2006. Fellow: ACS; mem.: Internat. Soc. Asthetic Plastic Surgery, Southeastern Soc. Plastic and Reconstructive Surgeons, Mecklenburg County Med. Soc., Lipoplasty Soc. N.Am. (bd. dirs. 1992—2001), NC Med. Soc., NC Soc. Plastic Surgeons (pres. 2004—05, Presdl. award 2005), Am. Soc. Aesthetic Plastic Surgery, Am. Soc. Plastic Surgeons. Independent. Presbyn. Avocations: woodworking, hunting, water sports, skiing, tennis. Office: 8605 Cliff Cameron Dr Suite # 100 Charlotte NC 28269 Office Fax: 704-549-1511, 704-549-1511. E-mail: jph1@hunstad.com.

HUNT, ANDREA WHEATON, nurse; b. Cin., Mar. 31, 1955; d. Harlan Richard Wheaton and Geraldine Meade Smithers; m. David Ralph Hunt, June 4, 1999; children: Kristopher W. Stafford, Laura Ann Elizabeth Bolling. Studied, Marshall U., Huntington, W.Va., 1973—76. LPN Roanoke Meml. Hosp., Va., 1981—92; paralegal Law Office of Marc James Small, Roanoke, Va., 1983—91; LPN Cmty. Hospice, Ashland, Ky., 1999—2001; adminstrv. dir. Med. Res. Corps., Ashland, Ky., 2003—07. Health officer ABC Emergency Mag., Ashland, Ky., 2004—. Sec. Catlettsburg Cemetary Corp., Ky., 2002—; mass care coord. ARC, Ashland, Ky., 2002—04, disaster com. chmn., 2004—. 1st lt. Tenn. Def. Force, 1987—91. Republican. Methodist. Office Phone: 606-571-4223. Business E-Mail: andiofthehunt@windstream.net.

HUNT, DANIEL PAYSON, internist; b. Knoxville, Tenn., Apr. 1, 1956; BS in Math., Frostburg State U., 1977; MD, Vanderbilt U., 1981. Practicing internal medicine physician Kelsey-Seybold Clinic, Houston, 1984—88, Med. Clinic Houston, 1988—95; clinician educator Baylor Coll. Medicine, 1995—2005; dir., inpatient clinician educator svc., dept. medicine Mass. Gen. Hosp., 2005, chief, hosp. medicine unit, divsn. gen. internal medicine, 2010—. Assoc. prof. medicine Harvard Med. Sch., 2005; dep. editor Jour. Hosp. Medicine, 2007. Recipient Excellence in Tchg. award, Soc. Hosp. Medicine, Best Clin. Instr. award, Harvard Med. Sch., 2008, Alfred Kranes award, Mass. Gen. Hosp., Dept. Medicine, 2006, 2011. Fellow: ACP; mem.: Mass. Med. Soc., Soc. Gen. Internal Medicine, Soc. Hosp. Medicine. Avocations: bicycling, reading, writing. Office: 50 Staniford St Ste 503B Inpatie Boston MA 02114 Business E-Mail: dphunt@partners.org.

HUNT, ELIZABETH HOPE, psychologist; b. Hattiesburg, Miss., Oct. 14, 1943; d. Emory Spear and I. Elizabeth (Burkett) Hunt; m. John Volney Allcott, III, Sept. 9, 1978; children: Hunt Volney Allcott, Elizabeth Hunt Allcott. AB, Sweet Briar Coll., 1965; MSW, U. Pa., 1971; PhD, U. Oreg., 1980. Lic. psychologist Oreg. Peace Corps vol., Santiago, Chile, 1967—69; civil rights specialist Region III HEW, Phila., 1971—74; doctoral fellow Rehab. Rsch. and Tng. Ctr., U. Oreg., Eugene, 1974—77; intern Phila. Child Guidance Ctr., U. Pa., 1977—78; psychologist in pvt. practice Eugene, 1980—. Rschr., civic activist. Contbr. articles to profl. jours. Bd. dirs. Lane County Relief Nursery for Abused and Neglected Children, 1981—84; activist, bd. dirs. Eugene Edn. Found., 1993—2002; vol. psychologist Friends of Torture Survivors, 1993—2004; founder Allcott/Hunt Scholarship for Recent Immigrants; philanthroper Wellsprings Quaker Friends Sch., Eugene; steering com. clerk Quaker North Pacific Yearly Meeting Religious Soc. of Friends, 2003—05. Grantee, Nat. Inst. Handicapped Rsch., 1977—79. Mem.: Lane County Psychologists Assn., Oreg. Psychol. Assn., APA. Home: 2650 Cresta De Ruta St Eugene OR 97403-1849 E-mail: bhunt5425@comcast.net.

HUNT, JAMES CALVIN, physician, academic administrator; b. Lexington, NC, Sept. 11, 1925; s. James Lee and Sarah Della (Frank) Hunt; m. Irene [illegible], Sept. 17, 1949; children: James Calvin, Michael S., Cynthia Irene. AB, Catawba Coll., 1949; MD, Bowman Gray Sch. Medicine, 1953; MS, U. Minn., 1958; ScD, Wake Forest U., 1992. Diplomate Am. Bd. Internal Medicine. Intern N.C. Bapt. Hosp., Winston-Salem, 1953-54; resident, fellow Mayo Grad Sch. Medicine, Rochester, Minn., 1954-58; practice medicine, specializing in internal medicine (cardiovasc.-renal diseases) Rochester, 1958-78; cons., instr. to asst. prof. dept. medicine Mayo Clinic and Mayo Med. Sch., 1958-63, assoc. prof., chmn. divsn. nephrology, 1963-72, prof., chmn. dept. medicine, 1973-78; prof., assoc. dean clin. ednl. programs Mayo Med. Sch., 1972-74; prof. medicine U. Tenn., Memphis, 1978—, dean Coll. Medicine, 1978-81, v.p. health affairs, chancellor Univ. Health Scis. Ctr., 1981-93, univ. disting. prof., dir. clin. scholars program, 1993—2001, v.p. health affairs, chancellor emeritus, 2001—. Adv. coun. Nat. Heart, Lung and Blood Inst. NIH, 1976—81. Contbr. articles to profl. jours. Pres. Nat. Kidney Found., 1973—76; mem. Congl. Tech. Adv. Coun., 1987—96; bd. dirs. Memphis Downtown Neighbors Assn., 1995—99, pres., 1997—98; mem. adv. bd. Goals for Memphis, 1987—95; bd. dirs. YMCA, Memphis, Memphis Riverfront Devel. Corp., 1999—, sec., 2000—02; trustee Le Bonheur Children's Med. Ctr., 1981—93, Christian Bros. Coll., 1983—96; mem. cmty. adv. bd. Bapt. Meml. Hosp., 1986—; bd. dirs. Bapt. Meml. Coll. Health Scis., 1995—2005, chair acad. affairs com., 1998—2005; mem. adv. bd. Rhodes Coll. With USAAF, 1943—46, ETO. Recipient Disting. Svc. award, Bowman Gray Sch. Medicine, Wake Forest U., 1975, Disting. Alumnus award, Catawba Coll., 1974, Educator of the Yr. award, Memphis State U., 1986, Outstanding Alumnus award, Mayo Found., 1991, Gift of Life award, Nat. Kidney Found., 1991. Fellow: ACP, Am. Heart Assn. (mem. coun. circulation), Am. Coll. Cardiology; mem.: AMA, Am. Soc. Clin. Pharmacology and Therapeutics, Am. Soc. Internal Medicine, Coun. High Blood Pressure Rsch., Soc. Nuc. Medicine, Internat. Soc. Hypertension, Internat. Am. Socs. Nephrology, Sigma Xi, Phi Rho Sigma, Alpha Omega Alpha. Home: 504 Shannondale Way Maryville TN 37803-5967

HUNT, LINDA, hospital administrator; BS in nursing, William Carey Coll.; MS in nursing adminstrn., Univ. Colo. Health Sciences Ctr. Faculty mem. U. Colo. Health Sci. Ctr., Regis U., Denver; pres., CEO St. Joseph's Hosp. and Med. Ctr., Phoenix. Named Bus. Leader, Tribute to Women Awards, Maricopa County YWCA, 2001. Mem.: Am. Assn. of Med. Colleges (rep.). Office: St Joseph's Hosp and Med Ctr 350 W Thomas Rd Phoenix AZ 85013 *

HUNT, ROGER SCHERMERHORN, healthcare administrator; b. White Plains, NY, Mar. 7, 1943; s. Charles Howland and Mildred Russell (Schermerhorn) H.; m. Mary Adams Libby, June 19, 1965; children: Christina Markle, David. BA, DePauw U., 1965; MBA, George Washington U., 1968. Adminstrv. resident Lankenau Hosp., Phila., 1966-68; asst. adminstr. Hahnemann Med. Coll. and Hosp., Phila., 1968-71, hosp. dir., 1971-74, assoc. v.p., hosp. adminstr., 1974-77; dir. Ind. U. Hosp., Indpls., 1977-84; pres. Luth. Gen. Hosp., Pk. Ridge, Ill., 1984-90; pres., CEO Fontbonne Health Sys., Toronto, Canada, 1990-92; sr. v.p. Northwestern Healthcare Network, Chgo., 1993-96; pres., CEO ViaHealth, Rochester, NY, 1996-99; prin. Hunt Healthcare, Deerfield, Ill., 1999—2002; CEO, BroMenn Healthcare Sys., Bloomington, Ill., 2002—09; pres. Adv. BroMenn Med. Ctr.-Adv. Eureka Hosp., 2010; sr. cons. Advocate Healthcare Sys., 2011—. Chmn. Alliance of Indpls. Hosp., 1981; pres. United Hosp. Services, 1979-81; assoc. prof. hosp. adminstrn. Ind. U. Sch. Medicine, 1977-84; vice chmn. Pa. Emergency Health Services Council, 1975-77; pres. Chester County Emergency Med. Service Council, 1971-77.

Pres. Wayne Area Jr. C. of C., 1970-71, state dir., 1971-72; bd. dir. Rochester Philharm. Orch., 1998-99. Fellow Am. Coll. Healthcare Exec. (regent for Ind. 1984, Ill. 1988-90, Postgrad. tng. award 1968); mem. Am. Hosp. Assn., Hosp. Assn. of NY State (bd. dir. 1998-99), Ind. Hosp. Assn. (bd. dir. 1982-84), Met. Chgo. Healthcare Coun. (bd. dirs. 1986-95), DePauw U. Alumni Assn. (bd. dir. 1988-94), Greater Rochester Metro C. of C. (bd. dir. 1998-99), Comm. Cancer Ctr. (bd. dir. 2002—, chmn. 2004—06), Ill. Symphony Orch. (bd. dir. 2003—), McLean C. of C. (bd. dirs. 2005—), Ill. Symphony Orchestra(pres. 2011-) Office: Adv BroMenn Med Ctr PO Box 2850 Bloomington IL 61702-2850 Office Phone: 309-268-5676. Business E-Mail: roger.hunt@advocatehealth.com.

HUNT, RONALD J., dean, dental educator; DDS, U. Iowa, 1973, MS in Dental Pub. Health, 1982. Diplomate Am. Bd. Dental Pub. Health. Assoc. prof. dental ecology U. NC Sch. Dentistry, Chapel Hill, 1986—88, prof. dental ecology, 1990—92, asst. dean, 1992—98, assoc. dean academic affairs, 1992—98; Harry Lyons Prof., dean Va. Commonwealth U. Sch. Dentistry, Richmond, Va., 1999—. Disting. vis. scholar U. Adelaide, Australia, 1990. Fellow: Am. Coll. Dentists, Am. Assn. Dental Schools; mem.: Va. Dental Saan., Am. Ass. Dental Rsch., Am. Dental Edn. Assn. (pres.-elect 2008—09, pres. 2009—10, William J. Gies Ednl. Fellowship 1997). Office: VCU Sch Dentistry 520 N 12th St Box 980566 Richmond VA 23298 Office Phone: 804-827-2077. Business E-Mail: rjhunt@vcu.edu. *

HUNT, SIR TIM (RICHARD TIMOTHY HUNT), retired biomedical researcher; b. Neston, Cheshire, Eng., Feb. 19, 1943; s. Richard William Hunt and Kit Rowland. BA, U. Cambridge, 1964, PhD, 1968. Prin. scientist, head cell cycle control lab. Cancer Rsch. UK (formerly Imperial Cancer Rsch. Fund), London, 1991—2011; ret., 2011. Mem. sci. coun. European Commn., 2011—. Recipient Abraham White Scientific Achievement award, George Washington U., 1993, Nobel prize in physiology/medicine, 2001. Fellow: Royal Soc.; mem.: NAS (fgn. assoc.). Achievements include discovery of cell cycle regulation by cyclin and cyclin-dependent kinases. Office: Clare Hall Laboratories Blance Ln South Mimms Potters Bar Herts EN6 3LD England Office Phone: 020 7269 3981. Business E-Mail: tim.hunt@cancer.org.uk. *

HUNT, WILLIAM B., pulmonologist; b. Lexington, NC, Sept. 27, 1927; s. William B. and Maxine (Cox) H.; married; children: William B., III, Anne, Alex, Sarah. BS, Wake Forest U., 1948; MD, Bowman Gray Sch. Medicine, Winston Salem, NC, 1953. Diplomate Am. Bd. Internal Medicine, Am. Bd. Allergy and Immunology. Intern, resident U. Va., Charlottesville, 1953-55, resident, fellow, 1957-59, assoc. prof., 1960-75, asst. dean Sch. Medicine, 1972-75; fellow gastroenterology Bowman Gray Sch. Medicine, Winston Salem, 1959-60; instr. internal medicine N.Y. Med. Coll., NYC, 1959-60; from clin. assoc. prof. medicine to clin. prof. medicine East Carolina Sch. Medicine, Greenville, NC, 1975—; staff physician Craven Regional Med. Ctr., New Bern, NC, 1975—, med. dir. cardiopulmonary svcs., 1975-95. Cons. N.C. Health Dept., TB Control Br., 1997-2000; TB control physician Craven County Health Dept., 1999—; mem. N.C. TB Peer Rev. Com., 1996-2000. Pres. Ea. Area Health Edn. Ctr., 1990-95. Recipient Douglas Southhall Freeman award Va. Lung Assn., 1975, Disting. Alumnus award Bowman Gray Sch. Medicine, 1973, Robert Bageant award Va. Soc. Respiratory Care, 1987. Fellow Am. Coll. Chest Physicians, Am. Thoracic Soc., Am. Coll. Physicians; mem. N.C. Med. Soc. (councillor 1978, exec. com. 1981), Va. Thoracic Soc. (pres. 1974), N.C. Thoracic Soc. (pres. 1984), N.C. Lung Assn. (pres. 1986), Craven Pamlico Jones Med. Soc. (pres. 1984). Democrat. Episcopalian. Avocations: skiing, golf, flying, sailing, tennis. Home: 80 Bishops Ridge Dr Charlottesville VA 22901

HUNTER, C. EARL, state agency administrator, environmental services administrator; BS in Marine Biology, U. SC, 1979; MBA, Webster U., St. Louis, 1985. District water quality inspector S.C. Dept. Health & Environmental Control, 1980—84, environmental technician, 1984—88, mgr. facilities compliance, 1988—91, dir. water quality assessment & enforcement, 1991—93, asst. to commr., 1993—2001, commr., 2001—. Fellow, EPA, 1983—85. Office: Dept Health & Environmental Control 2600 Bull St Columbia SC 29201

HUNTER, DANIEL A., medical researcher; b. Toronto, Ont., Can., July 20, 1951; s. Arthur Hunter and Lillian Varga. Cert. technologist Can. Soc. Med. Lab. Sci., 1975. Sr. scientist Wash. U. Sch. Medicine, St. Louis, 1991—; sr. assoc. mem. Plastics Surgery Rsch. Coun. Contbr. articles to profl. jours. Mem.: Am. Soc. Peripheral Nerve. Achievements include contibution to research that led to the first peripheral nerve transplantation; development of comprehensive computer macros for peripheral nerve histomorphometry. Office: Washington University Sch Medicine WOHL Clinic Rm 9937 660 South Euclid Box 8238 Saint Louis MO 63110 Office Phone: 314-362-8080. Office Fax: 314-747-0579. Business E-Mail: hunterd@wustl.edu.

HUNTER, DAVID JAMES, health policy and management educator, researcher, analyst; b. Irvine, Scotland, Apr. 17, 1950; s. Thomas Drummond and Peggie Eileen (Scotcher) H.; m. Mairi Christine Hunter (div.); m. Jacqueline Floyd, Mar. 31, 1994; children: Eve Floyd, Miles Cameron. MA with honors, U. Edinburgh, Scotland, 1974, PhD, 1979. Rsch. officer Outer Circle Policy Unit, London, 1977-80; health studies officer Royal Inst. Pub. Adminstrn., London, 1980-82; dir. Unit for Study of Elderly U. Aberdeen, Scotland, 1982-87; policy analyst King's Fund Inst., London, 1987-88; dir. Nuffield Inst. for Health, U. Leeds, Eng., 1989-97, prof. health policy and mgmt., 1989-99, U. Durham, England, 1999—. Trustee Dementia Svcs. Devel. Ctr., Stirling, Scotland, 1988-94; adviser WHO, Copenhagen, 1989—; non-exec. dir. Leeds Healthcare, Eng., 1990-99; adviser House of Commons Social Svcs. Com., London, 1990-91; co-chair Assn. Pub. Health, 1998-2000; advisor health com. Ho. of Commons, 2000-01; dep. dir. Ctr. Translational Rsch. in Pub. Health, 2008-. Contbr. articles to profl. jours.; editor Jour. Mgmt. in Medicine, 1997-99. Fellow Royal Coll. Physicians Edinburgh; mem. Faculty of Pub. Health (hon.), European Health Mgmt. Assn. (bd. dirs. 1990-95, 97-98, pres. 1995-97), UK Pub. Health Assn. (coun. mem. 1999-, chair 2004-2009), South Tees Hosps. NHS Trust (gov.), Nat. Inst. Health & Clin. Excellence(non exec. dir. 2009-). Avocations: jazz, swimming, reading, walking, films. Office: U Durham Sch Medicine Health Wolfson Rsch Inst Queen's Campus University Boulevard TS17 6BH Thornaby Stockton-on-Tees England Office Phone: 44 191 334 0362. Business E-Mail: d.j.hunter@durham.ac.uk.

HUNTER, JAMES EDWARD, chemist, consultant; b. Phila., May 4, 1945; s. James Bruce and Ruth Moyer (Lenker) H.; m. Marilyn Kay Jones, Aug. 24, 1968; children: Melanie Kay, Timothy Edward. BS in Chemistry, Lehigh U., 1967; MS in Biochemistry, U. Wis., 1969, PhD in Biochemistry, 1974. Staff nutritionist Procter & Gamble Co., Cin., 1974-92, staff toxicologist, 1992-95, staff toxicologist regulatory affairs, 1995-96; adj. prof. chemistry Cin. State Tech. and Cmty. Coll., 1997-98, U. Cin., 1998—2008, Xavier U., 2010—. Mem. biol. subcom. of tech. com. Inst. of Shortening and Edible Oils, Inc., Washington, 1981-93, chmn. biol. subcom., 1985-93; mem. human nutrition bd. of sci. counselors USDA, Washington, 1990-92; mem. oral health com. and subcom. on fatty acids and health Internat. Life Scis. Inst., Washington, 1985-92. Editor: (booklet) Food Fats and Oils, 5th edit., 1982, 6th edit., 1988, 7th edit., 1994; contbr. numerous articles to profl. jours. including Jour. Am. Oil Chemists Soc., Am. Jour. Clin. Nutrition. V.p., chmn. fundraisers St. Xavier H.S. Music Promoters Bd., Cin., 1992-94; mem., mem. com. mgmt. Powel Crosley Jr. YMCA, Cin., 1980-86, sec., 1982-86; cubmaster Boy Scouts Am., Cin., 1985-87. With U.S. Army, 1969-71. Mem.: Am. Soc. for Nutrition, Am. Chem. Soc. (chair various local coms., treas. local chpt. 2009—), Am. Oil Chemists Soc. (treas. local chpt. 1990—93, bd. dirs.), Runners Club Greater Cin. (v.p. 1994—95, sec. 1995—), Tau Beta Pi, Sigma Xi, Phi Beta Kappa. Avocations: ragtime piano, running, swimming, photography, woodworking. Office Phone: 513-745-3605. Business E-Mail: hunterj3@xavier.edu.

HUNTER, JILL VANESSA, physician, researcher; b. Eng., Aug. 7, 1952; MBBS, St Bartholomew's Hosp. Med. Coll., London, 1975. Sr. registrar Nat. Hosp. Neurology And Neurosurgery, Queen Sq., London, 1988—; instr. Mass. Gen. Hosp., Harvard U., 1992—93; assoc. prof. Children's Sch. Phila., U Pa., 1993—2001; prof. Tex. Children's Hosp., Baylor Coll. Medicine, 2001. Dir. DI rsch. lab. Feigin Ctr., Tex. Children's Hosp., 2001—11. Award, Mike Hogg Found., Houston. Fellow: Royal Coll. Radiologists (London), Royal Soc. Medicine (London). Avocations: scuba diving, singing, sailing. Home: 6725 Westchester Houston TX 77005 Personal E-mail: jhunter@bcm.tmc.edu.

HUNTER, JOHN OAKLEY, medical educator, researcher; s. Harry and Hilda Gertrude Hunter; m. Mary (Maureen) Leonard, Oct. 2, 1965; children: Catherine Mary Calder, John Patrick, Joanna Elisabeth. MBBChir, St Mary's Hosp. Med. Sch., London, 1964; MA, U. Cambridge, Eng., 1961, MD, 1974. Fellow Royal Coll. Physicians London, 1981, Am. Coll. Gastroenterology, 1992, Am. Gastroent. Assn., 2006. Hon. lectr. medicine U. Cambridge, 1976—2002; cons. physician and gastroenterologist Addenbrooke's Hosp., Cambridge, 1975—2002, dir. gastroenterology, 1995—2002; vis. prof. medicine U. Cranfield, Bedfordshire, England, 2002—. Cons. Shell Rsch., Sittingbourne, Kent, England, 1973—78, Unilever Rsch. and Engring., Vlaardingen, Netherlands, 1988—93, Sci. Hosp. Supplies Internat., Liverpool, Merseyside, England, 1992—. Author: (nonfiction book) The Allergy Diet, 1984, (textbook) Food and the Gut, 1985, (non-fiction books) Irritable Bowel Solutions, 2007, Inflammatory Bowel Disease, 2010; contbr.: textbook Human Nutrition, 12th edit., 2011, med. textbook Clinical Gastroenterology and Hepatology, 2005. Recipient Geraldine Harmsworth Entrance scholarship, St. Mary's Hosp. Med. Sch., London, 1961—64. Mem.: Newmarket Med. Soc. (pres. 2005—06), Yorkshire County Cricket Club, Scarborough Club (chmn. 1996—99), Jockey Club Rooms, Newmarket, Scarborough Cricket Club (life). Church Of England. Achievements include discovery of dietary treatment of Crohn's Disease; role of food intolerance as a cause of irritable bowel syndrome; role of intestinal bacteria in causing food intolerance; value of 1-alpha-hydroxycholecalciferol in renal osteodystrophy; hepatic enzymes by occupational exposure to organochlorine pesticides; role of intestinal bacteria in the development of disease; research in effects of sucrose polyester on the gut, preventing its use in European Union. Avocations: horse racing, skiing, fishing, literature, walking. Home: Bridge House Hildersham Cambridgeshire Cambridge CB1 6BU England Office: Addenbrookes Hosp Hills Rd Cambridgeshire Cambridge CB2 2QQ England Home Fax: +44 1223 890377. Personal E-mail: johunter@uk-consultants.co.uk. Business E-Mail: john.hunter@addenbrookes.nhs.uk.

HUNTER, RICHARD EDWARD, retired physician; b. Worcester, Mass., May 30, 1919; s. William and Catherine (Powers) H.; m. M. Minta Shaw, Jan. 30, 1993 (dec.); children: Todd Wayne, Elayne Cheryl, Jill Elizabeth, Amy Louise. AB, Clark U., 1941; MD, Boston U., 1944. Diplomate Am. Bd. Ob-Gyn. Intern Worcester City Hosp., 1944-45; resident gen. surgery Framingham (Mass.) Union Hosp., 1947; resident ob-gyn Mercy Hosp., Balt., 1947-49; practice medicine specializing ob-gyn Worcester, 1949—; prof. dept. ob-gyn U. Mass., Worcester, 1976—, chmn. dept. ob-gyn, 1976-89, emeritus prof., 1989—; ret., 1999. Contbr. articles to med. jours. Served with US Army, 1945-47. Mem. ACS, ACOG, New Eng. Assn. Gynecologic Oncologists, Soc. Gynecologic Oncology, Boston Obstetric Soc., New Eng. Cancer Soc., Am. Soc. Clin. Oncology, Soc. Gynecologic Surgeons, Royal Soc. Medicine. Republican. Home: 406 Browning Ln Worcester MA 01609 Office: 55 Lake Ave N Worcester MA 01655-0002 *

HUNTER, ROBERT PAUL, pharmacologist, senior research scientist; s. Raymond Paul and Hazel Merle (Blackmer) H.; m. Trisha Ann Turk, May 21, 1988; children: Mark Andrew, Brandon Paul, Logan James. BS, Angelo State U., San Angelo, Tex., 1987; MS, Tex. A&M U., College Station, 1989; PhD, Louisana State U., Baton Rouge, 2000. Asst. prof. Kans. State U., Manhattan, 2000—04; sr. rsch. scientist Elanco Animal Health, Greenfield, Ind., 2004—. Contbr. articles to profl. jours. Fellow, Pfizer Inc, 1995—99. Fellow: Am. Acad. Vet. Pharmacology and Therapeutics (exec. councilor 2003—06); mem.: Am. Zoo and Aquarium Assn., Euro Assoc. Vet. Pharmacology Toxicology. Lutheran. Office: Elanco Animal Health 2500 Innovation Way Greenfield IN 46140

HUNTER, STEVEN L., medical center administrator; b. Alton, Ill., Oct. 3, 1953; s. Samuel and Harriet (Wetstein) H.; children: Ryan, Jeff, Victoria. BS in Med. Tech. summa cum laude, Ea. Ill. U., Charleston, 1975; cert. in med. tech., Carle Found. Hosp., Urbana, Ill., 1975; MHA, St. Louis U., 1978. Cert. med. technologist Am. Soc. Clin. Pathologists. Various staff and mgmt. positions Cardinal Glennon Hosp. and Christian Hosp. N.E., St. Louis, 1975-78; asst. adminstr. St. Elizabeth Med. Ctr., Granite City, Ill., 1978-81, v.p. corp. planning & mktg., 1981-87; COO Incarnate Word Hosp., St. Louis, 1987-90; pres., CEO St. Mary's Health Ctr., Jefferson City, Mo., 1990—93; pres. St. Anthony's Hosp., Oklahoma City, 1993—98; regional pres. SSM Healthcare, Oklahoma City, 1998—2005; CEO Covenant Health Sys., Lubbock, Tex., 2005—07, Provena Health, Mokena, Ill., 2007—. Mem. faculty dept. human resource mgmt. Webster U., St. ZLouis; bd. dirs. Missouri River Home Health Agy., 1991—. Bd. dirs. ARC, 1992—, Lincoln U. Found., 1991—, Tri-City YMCA; mem. governing body Jefferson City Area United Way, 1991—. Recipient Malclom Baldridge Nat. Quality award, 2002. Fellow Am. Coll. Health Care Execs.; mem. Mo. Hosp. Assn. (by-laws com. 1991—, medicaid com. 1991—).

HUNTER, TONY (ANTHONY REX), molecular biologist, educator; b. Ashford, Kent, Eng., Aug. 23, 1943; arrived in US, 1971; s. Ranulph Rex and Nellie Ruby Elsie (Hitchcock) Hunter; m. Philippa Charlotte Marrack, July 19, 1969 (div. 1974); m. Jennifer Ann Maureen Price, June 8, 1992; children: Sean Alexander Brocas, James Samuel Alan. BA, U. Cambridge, Eng., 1965, MA, 1966. Rsch. fellow Christ's Coll., U. Cambridge, 1968-71, 73-75; rsch. assoc. Salk Inst. Biol. Studies, U. Calif., San Diego, 1971-73, asst. prof., 1975-78, assoc. prof., 1978-82, prof., 1982—, rsch. prof., Am. Cancer Soc., 1992—2008; dir. Salk Inst. Cancer Ctr., 2008—. Contbr. articles to sci. jours. Recipient Katharine Berkan Judd award, Meml. Sloan-Kettering Cancer Ctr., 1992, Gairdner Found. Internat. award, 1994, Hopkins Meml. award, Gairdner Found., 1994, Charles S. Mott prize, GM Cancer Rsch. Found., 1994, Feodor Lynen medal, 1999, J. Allyn Taylor Internat. prize in medicine, John P. Robarts Rsch. Inst./C.H. Stiller Meml. Found., 2000, Keio Med. Sci. prize, Tokyo, 2001, Sergio Lombroso award for cancer rsch., Weizmann Inst. Sci., 2003, Medal of Honor, Am. Cancer Soc., 2004, Kirk A. Landon prize, Am. Assn. Cancer Rsch., 2004, Prince of Asturias award for sci./tech. rsch., 2004, Louisa Gross Horwitz prize, Columbia U., 2004, Wolf Found. prize in medicine, Israel, 2005, Daniel Nathans Meml. award, Van Andel Inst., 2005, Herbert Taylor award, Am. Soc. Biochemistry & Molecular Biology, 2007, Pasarow award in cancer rsch., Robert J. & Claire Pasarow Found., 2006, Clifford prize, Inst. Med. Vet. Sci., Adelaide, 2007. Fellow: Am. Acad. Arts & Scis., Royal Soc. Arts, Royal Soc. London; mem.: NAS, Am. Philos. Soc., Inst. Medicine, European Molecular Biology Orgn. (assoc.). Avocations: white water rafting, desert camping. Home: 4578 Vista de la Patria Del Mar CA 92014-4150 Office: Salk Inst Biol Studies Molecular-Cell Biology Lab 10010 N Torrey Pines Rd La Jolla CA 92037-1099 Office Phone: 858-453-4100 1385. *

HUNTER, TRUDY PEARL, surgical nurse; b. Beaver, Ky., Apr. 8, 1950; d. Charlie Hatler and Goldie Edith (Hall) Hamilton; m. James Norman Hunter; 1 child, James Randall. ADN, U. Ky., Prestonsburg, 1986. LPN 1979; RN, Ky.; cert. nurse oper. room Assn. Oper. Room Nurses; ACLS; Circulator Open Heart Surgery and Neurosurgery, 2005, cert. in laser tng., arthroscopy, mgmt. and care of anesthetized patient, advance EKG interpretation. Scrub nurse Meth. Hosp. Ky., Pikeville, Ky., 1979-82; scrub nurse/circulator Pikeville Surg. Ctr., Pikeville, Ky., 1982-88; circulator/scrub nurse Meth. Hosp. Ky., Pikeville, Ky., 1988-94, OR charge nurse, 1995-96, O.R. supr., 1996—. Avocations: reading, camping, travel, woodworking. Home: 104 Lower Hollow Rd Betsy Layne KY 41605-7020 Office: Pikerville Med Hosp 911 Bypass Rd Pikeville KY 41501-1689

HUNTER, WILLIAM JOHN, public health service officer, director; b. London, Apr. 5, 1937; s. William George and Margaret (Beattie) H.; m. Estelle Edwards. MB, BS, U. London, 1961. Cert. occupl. health specialist. Casualty officer Westminster Hosp., London, 1962; house surgeon Gordon Hosp., London, 1962; house physician Brook Hosp., London, 1961; asst. pathologist Deptford Seaman's Hosp. Group, London, 1963-64; occupl. health physician Vauxhall Motors (GM Corp.), UK, 1964-65, Gen. Foods Ltd., UK, 1965-72; European dir. Gen. Foods Corp., UK, 1972-74; prin. adminstr. European Commn., Brussels, 1974-82, head divsn.-occupl. health and hygiene Luxembourg, 1982-87, dir. pub. health and safety at work directorate, 1987-99, dir. pub. health, 1999-2000, hon. dir. gen.; ret., 2000. Chmn. Com. Sr. Ofcls. Pub. Health, Brussels, 1987-2000, High Level Com. on Health, 1993-2000; jury mem. Europe et Medicine, 1993-2005; advisor Drugs for Neglected Diseases, 2005; mem. adminstrv. bd. Riberac Local Hosp., 2006-. Policy editor: Internat. Jour. Integrated Care, 1999—2002. Decorated Officer Brother, Order of St. John of Jerusalem, 1996. Fellow Royal Coll. Physicians (internat. advisor), Faculty Pub. Health (hon.); mem. Royal Coll. Surgeons, Internat. Assn. Former Ofcls. European Cmtys. (bd. dirs. French sect. 2001-), Ensemble Vocal Arnaut de Mareuil (admin. bd. 2002-06), Cercle de généalogie et de l'histoire de Perigord (adminstrv. bd. 1995-2005), Inst. des Sci. de la Sante (mem. adv. bd., 2004-06), European Inst. for Health (mem. peer adv. bd. 2006). Avocations: swimming, scuba diving, photography, painting.

HUNTLEY, BRENDA K., research scientist; b. Rochester, Minn., 1960; BS, Viterbo Coll., 1982. Software and hardware engr. Metafile, 1982—84; rsch. scientist Mayo Clinic, 1984—95, sr. rsch. scientist, 1996—; chem. engr. U. Karlsruhe, 1995—96. Grant, Nile Therapeutics. Office: 200 1st St SW Guggenheim 915 Rochester MN 55905 Office Fax: 507-266-1470. Business E-Mail: huntley.brenda@mayo.edu.

HUNTSMAN, ANNE, health consultant; b. Melbourne, Australia, May 28, 1954; BA, 1975; MS in Environ. Sci., Monash U., 1984; PhD in Biol. Scis., La Trobe U., 2002. Diploma in edn. 1976. NAPLAN marker, cons. internat. devel. VCAA, 2009—. Part time lectr. La Trobe U., 2001—06; cons. Sagric Internat., Indonesia, 2003; cons., Timor Leste Oxfam Australia, 2006; data analyst Burnet Inst., Melbourne, 2006; vol. cons. IWDA, 2007. Avocations: travel, writing, swimming. Home: 10 Reserve St Carlton North Victoria 3054 Australia Office Phone: 0403494477. Personal E-mail: a.huntsman@optusnet.com.au.

HUOT, RACHEL IRENE, biomedical educator, research scientist, physician; b. Manchester, NH, Oct. 16, 1950; d. Omer Joseph and Irene Alice (Girard) Huot. BA in Biology cum laude, Rivier Coll., 1972; MS in Biology, Cath. U. Am., 1976, PhD in Biology, 1980; MD, La. State U. Health Sci. Ctr., Shreveport, 2000. Cert. in family medicine 2008, lic. State Va., 2007. Sr. technician Microbiol. Assocs., Bethesda, Md., 1974-77; chemist Uniformed Svcs. Univ. of Health Scis., Bethesda, 1977-79; biologist Nat. Cancer Inst., Bethesda, 1979-82; postdoctoral fellow S.W. Found. for Biomed. Rsch., San Antonio, 1982-85, asst. scientist, 1985-87, staff scientist, 1987-88; instr. U. Tex. Health Sci. Ctr., San Antonio, 1988-89; asst. prof., dir. basic urologic rsch. La. State U., New Orleans, 1990-96; resident in family practice Aultman Hosp., Canton, Ohio, 2001—02; resident in family practice Mayo Clinic U. Minn., Waseca, 2002—05; resident in family practice Ea. Va. Med. Sch., 2005—07; family medicine physician Health Care on the Sq. Boydton Med. Ctr., 2008—. Judge sr. divsn. Alamo Regional Sci. Fair, San Antonio, 1989—90. Contbr. Vol. ARC, Christus Schumpert Hosp., Shreveport; patient educator vol. Martin Luther King Clinic, Shreveport, 1996—2000; choir Good Shepherd Ch. Recipient Young Investigator award, Searle, 1994; grantee, NSF, 1972—74, NIH, 1983—86. Mem.: AMA, AAUW, LWV, AAAS, Va. Acad. Family Practice, Med. Soc. Va., Am. Acad. Family Practice, Am. Soc. Experiment Biology, St. Vincent De Paul Soc., N.Y. Acad. Scis., Soc. In Vitro Biology, Fedn. Am. Scientists, Am. Soc. Cell Biology, Am. Assn. Cancer Rsch., Am. Soc. Microbiology, Sierra Club, Sigma Xi, Delta Epsilon Sigma, Iota Sigma Pi. Democrat. Roman Catholic. Avocations: drawing, painting, reading, cooking, stamp collecting/philately. Home: 112 N Walker St South Hill VA 23970 Office Phone: 434-738-6102.

HUPPERT, STACEY S., medical educator; b. Ft. Wayne, Ind., July 29, 1969; BS, Purdue U., 1992; PhD, Ind. U., 1998. Postdoc. fellow, instr. Wash. U. Med. Sch., 1998—2005; asst. prof. Vanderbilt U. Med. Ctr., 2005—. Mem.: ISHSR, SDB, AASLD. Office: 2213 Garland Ave Nashville TN 37232-0494 Business E-Mail: stacey.huppert@vanderbilt.edu.

HUR, JIN-WOO, neurosurgeon; b. Hamyang, Kyungnam, Republic Of Korea, Sept. 15, 1967; s. Soon-Gob Hur and Seon-Yi Rho; m. Hyeon-Mee Park, Aug. 7, 1994; children: Tae-Kyum, Soo-Min. Cert. neurosurgeon Korean Neurosurg. Soc., 2000. Dir. dept. neurosurgery Cheongju St. Mary Hosp., Cheongju, Chungbuk, Republic of Korea, 2005—. Cons. Korea Labor Welfare Corp., Cheongju, 2007. Lt. US Army. Mem.: Korean Soc. Geriatric Neurosurgery, Korean Neurotraumatology Soc., Korean Soc. Cerebrovascular Surgery (Seoul) (exec. com. mem. 2008—), Korean Spinal Neurosurg.Soc.(Seoul), Koren Neurosurg.Soc. (Seoul). Avocations: golf, swimming, tennis. Home: 909-1802 Jueun Apt Bunpyeong-dong Cheongju Chungbuk 361 853 Republic of Korea Office: Cheongju Saint Mary Hosp 589-5 Jujung-dong Cheongju Chungbuk 360 568 Republic of Korea Office Phone: 82-43-219-8152. Office Fax: 82-43-211-7925. Business E-Mail: somalh@nate.com, somalh@naver.com.

HUR, MINA, medical educator, researcher; b. Jeonju, Jeon-Ra, Republic of Korea, Jan. 2, 1970; d. Weenam Hur and Gangsun Lee; m. Byung Soon Park, Dec. 17, 1995; 1 child, Dohyun Park. MD, Seoul Nat. U., Republic of Korea, 1994, MS, 2000, PhD, 2005. Cert. in clin. pathology Ministry Health Welfare, 2000. Intern Seoul Nat. U. Hosp., 1994—95, resident, 1996—2000, fellow, 2000—01; instr. Hangang Sacred Heart Hosp., Seoul, 2001—05, asst. prof., 2005—, dir., 2007—; assoc. prof. Konkuk U., Sch. Medicine, 2009—. Author: (book) Diagnostic Laboratory Medicine, 2009; contbr. articles to profl. jours. Recipient Academic award, Asian Pacific Orthop. Assn., Seoul, 2007. Mem.: Internat. Soc. Lab. Hematology, Korean Soc. Hematology, Korean Soc. Lab. Medicine (sec. tng. com., Academic award 2001), Korean Ctr. Disease Control Prevention (Seoul) (adv. bd. mem. 2007—).

HUR, SEUNG-HO, medical educator; b. Daegu, Republic Of Korea, Oct. 12, 1965; s. Kyu-Kab Hur and Hee-Jun Choi; m. Jung-Hyang Park, Apr. 11, 1992; 1 child, Young-Jun. MD, PhD, Keimyung U., Daegu, 1990. Diplomate Korean Med. Assn., 1990. Clin. instr. Keimyung U. Dongsan Med. Ctr., Daegu, Republic of Korea, 2001—07, asst. prof., 2008—, assoc. prof. Postdoctoral rsch. fellow Stanford U. Sch. Medicine, Calif., 2005—06. Contbr. chapters to books. Capt. Korean Army, 1997—2000. Mem.: Korean Soc. Interventional Cardiology, Korean Soc. Internal Medicine, Korean Soc. Hypertension, Korean Soc. Echocardiography, Korean Soc. Circulation, Korean Med. Assn., Am. Coll. Cardiology. Avocations: movies, jogging. Home: 1205/1002 Hwanggeum-dong Suseong-gu Daegu 706932 Republic of Korea Office: Keimyung U Dongsan-Dong Jung-Gu 194 700-712 Daegu Daegu Republic of Korea Office Fax: 82-53-250-7034. Personal E-mail: shur@dsmc.or.kr.

HUR, SU-RYONG, physician, anesthesiologist; b. Korea, Feb. 8, 1942; arrived in US, 1966; s. Hyung Keun and JaeKyung (Kim) H.; m. Myung Ja; children: Jennifer, Steven, Michelle. MD, Seoul Nat. U., 1966. Diplomate Am. Bd. Anesthesiology. Intern Union Hosp., Fall River, Mass., 1966-67; resident St. Vincent's Hosp, Worcester, Mass., 1967-68, Mass. Gen. Hosp., Boston, 1968-71; staff anesthesiologist St. Michael's Hosp., 1975—; asst. prof. anesthesiology Med. Coll. Wis., 1971-75, mem. clin. faculty anesthesiology, 1976—, asst. prof. anesthesiology Milw., 2005—, assoc. prof. anesthesiology, 2009—; staff anesthesiologist Froedtert Meml. Luth. Hosp., 2004—. Contbr. articles to profl. jours. Fellow Am. Coll. Anesthesiologists; mem. AMA, Internat. Anesthesia Rsch. Soc., Am. Soc. Anesthesiologists, Korean Am. Med. Assn., Wis. Soc. Anesthesiologists, State Med. Soc. of Wis., Med. Soc. of Milw. County, Milw. Soc. of Anesthesiologists. Office: Froedtert Lutheran Memorial Hosp Anesthesia Dept 9200 W Wisconsin Ave Milwaukee WI 53226-3596 Office Phone: 414-805-6100. Office Fax: 414-805-6147, 414-805-6147; Home Fax: 262-241-3415.

HURD, ERIC RAY, rheumatologist, internist, educator; b. Columbus, Kans., July 5, 1936; s. Myron Alexander and Isobel (Moore) H.; m. Beverly Jean Button, June 14, 1962; children: Sherryl Lynn, Susan Rae, Brent Eric. BS, U. Tulsa, 1958; MD, U. Okla., Norman, 1962. Intern St. John's Hosp., Tulsa, 1962-63, resident in internal medicine, 1963-65; rsch. fellow U. Tex., Dallas, 1965-67, instr. internal medicine, 1967-68, asst. prof., 1968-73, assoc. prof., 1973-80, prof., 1980—. Cons. rheumatologist, attending physician Parkland, VA Hosps.; dir. John Peter Smith Hosp. Arthritis Clinic, Ft. Worth; chief rheumatology VA Hosp., 1982—, mem. immunology research merit rev. bd.; assoc. Baylor Arthritis Ctr., 1981—; mem. med. and sci. com. North Tex. Arthritis Found., bd. med. dirs., 1988—, chmn. profl. edn. com.; traveling guest lectr. Tex. Med. Assn., Belgium and Fed. Republic Germany, 1990. Contbr. articles to profl. jours. Served to maj. US Army, 1963-74. Recipient Clin. Scholar award Arthritis Found., 1975-77; named Outstanding Cons. Faculty Mem. John Peter Smith Hosp., 1983-84, Outstanding Part-time Clin. Prof. John Peter Smith Hosp., 1989-90. Mem. ACP, Am. Assn. Immunologists, Am. Fedn. Clin. Research, Am. Rheumatism Assn. (cooperating clinics com. 1968-74, Founding Fellow 1986), Tex. Rheumatism Assn. (sec.-treas. 1976-79, 2d v.p. 1979-80), Tex. Med. Soc., Dallas County Med. Soc., Phi Eta Sigma. Democrat. Methodist. Office: Arthritis Ctrs Tex Ste 300 712 N Washington Ave Dallas TX 75246-1632 Office Phone: 214-823-6503.

HURD, JOSEPH KINDALL, JR., obstetrician, gynecologist; b. Hoisington, Kans., Feb. 12, 1938; MD, Harvard U., 1964. Cert. ob.-gyn. Intern Boston City Hosp., 1964-65, resident in surgery, 1965-66; resident in ob.-gyn. Bronx Mcpl. Hosp. Ctr., NY, 1966-70; with Walson Army Hosp., Ft. Dix, NJ, 1970—72, Lahey Clinic Med. Ctr., Burlington, Mass., 1972—, chair dept. gynecology, 1988—2000. Clin. instr. surgery Harvard U., 1972—; clin. asst. prof. Tufts U. Sch. Medicine, Boston, 1996—. Named one of Top 100 Black Physicians in Am., Black Enterprise Mag., 2001. Fellow Am. Coll. Ob.-Gyn., ACS; mem. AMA, Nat. Med. Assn. Office: Lahey Med Ctr 41 Mall Rd Burlington MA 01805-0001 Home Phone: 781-235-5912; Office Phone: 781-744-8495. Business E-Mail: jkhurd@massmed.org.

HURD, RICHARD NELSON, pharmaceutical executive; b. Evanston, Ill., Feb. 25, 1926; s. Charles DeWitt and Mary Ormsby (Nelson) H.; m. Jocelyn Fillmore Martin, Dec. 22, 1950; children: Melanie Gray, Suzanne Dewitt. BS, U. Mich., 1946; PhD U. Minn., 1956. Chemist Gen. Electric Co., Schenectady, NY, 1948-49; R&D group leader Koppers Co., Pitts., 1956-57; rsch. chemist Mallinckrodt Chem. Works, St. Louis, 1957-63, group leader, 1963-66, Comml. Solvents Corp., Terre Haute, Ind., 1966-68, sect. head, 1968-71; mgr. sci. affairs G. D. Searle Internat. Co., Skokie, Ill., 1972-73, dir. mfg. and tech. affairs, 1973-77; rep. to internat. tech com. Pharm. Mfrs. Assn., Skokie, Ill., 1973-77; v.p. tech. affairs Elder Pharms., Bryan, Ohio, 1977-81; v.p. rsch. & devel. U.S. Proprietary Drugs & Toiletries div. Schering-Plough Corp., Memphis, 1981-83; v.p. sci affairs Moleculon, Inc., Cambridge, Mass., 1984-88; v.p. regulatory affairs Pharmaco-LSR, Inc., Austin, Tex., 1989-94; prin. Hurd & Assocs., Inc., Evanston, Ill., 1994—. Contbr. articles to profl. jours.; patentee in field. Mem. Ferguson-Florissant (Mo.) Sch. Bd., 1964-66; bd. dirs. United Fund of Wabash Valley (Ind.), 1969-71. With USN, 1943-46, 53-55. E.I. DuPont de Nemours & Co., Inc. fellow, 1956. Fellow AAAS; mem. Am. Acad. Dermatology (life), Am. Soc. Photobiology, Am. Chem. Soc., N.Y. Acad. Sci., Am. Pharm. Assn., Am. Assn. Pharm. Scientists, Food and Drug Law Inst., Drug Info. Assn., Sigma XI, Mich. Shores Club (Wilmette, Ill.). Presbyterian. Achievements include codevelopment of Ralgro and Oxsoralen; research in thioamides as a class of organic compounds; development of macrocyclic synthetic routes for natural products; development of psoralens for photochemotherapy of dermatologic disorders. Home Phone: 847-864-9773. Personal E-mail: hurdreg@earthlink.net.

HURET, JEAN-LOUP MARIE, geneticist, educator; b. France, 1951; MD, Necker U. Hosp., Paris, 1981; PhD, Poitiers U., 1991. Head cytogenetics lab., hematology dept. Univ. Hosp. of Poitiers, France, 1986—96; founder, editor in chief Atlas of Genetics and Cytogenetics in Oncology and Hemagology, 1997—. Recipient Knight of the French, Nat. Order of Merit. Achievements include discovery of first case of Down syndrome with a normal karyotype. Avocation: painting. Office: Univ Hosp Dept Medical Info/Genetics 86021 Poitiers France E-mail: j.l.huret@chu-poitiers.fr.

HURLBURT, WARD B., public health service officer, state official; MD, George Washington U.; MPH, Johns Hopkins U. Hospital adminstr. US Pub. Health Svc., Dillingham, Alaska, hospital adminstr., chief of surgery Alaska Native Med. Ctr., dep. dir. Alaska Area Native Health Svc.; divisional med. dir. Group Health Cooperative; med. dir., treas. Warm Beach Health Care Ctr.; chief med. officer Molina Healthcare of Wash., Inc.; chief med. officer, dir. Divsn. Pub. Health Alaska Dept. Health and Social Services, 2009—. Office: Alaska Department Health and Social Services Chief Medical Officer 3601 C St, Suite 756 Anchorage AK 99503 Office Phone: 907-269-8126. Office Fax: 907-269-2048. *

HURLBUT, ROBERT HAROLD, health care services executive; b. Rochester, NY, Mar. 9, 1935; s. Harold Leroy and Martha Irene (Fincher) H.; m. Barbara Cox, June 14, 1958; children: Robert W., Christine A. Hurlbut. Student, Coll. Hotel Adminstrn., Cornell U., 1953-56; PhD (hon.), St. John Fisher Coll., NY, 2005. Lic. health care adminstr. Adminstr. and dir. Pillars Nursing Home, Rochester, 1956—80, Elmcrest Nursing Home, Churchville, NY, 1960—75, Elm Manor Nursing Home, Canandaigua, NY, 1960—75, Penfield Nursing Home, Rochester, 1963—75, Avon Nursing Home, NY, 1964—75, Newark Nursing Home, NY, 1965—75, Lakeshore Nursing Home, Rochester, 1972—75; adminstrv. cons. Hale Nani Nursing Home, Honolulu, 1975—76, Forest Green Nursing Home, Phila., 1976—78, Batavia Nursing Home, 1975—78, MT Zion Nursing Home, 1979—81. Bd. dir. St. Marys Hosp., 1960—66, HSBC Bank, 1990—2007; organizer, adminstrv. dir. hdqrs. Rohm Svcs. Corp., Rochester, 1964—; organizer, pres. hdqrs. Vari-Care Inc., Rochester, 1969—93; hon. commr. NY State Ins. Fund, 1982—, chmn. bd., 2006—, Rochester Area Found., 1986—90; adv. bd. mem. Cornell Hotel Sch., NY, 2003—. Trustee St. John Fisher Coll., 1983—98, trustee emeritus; trustee U. Rochester, 2001—11, Eastman Dental Ctr. Found., 1975—2011, Roberts Wesleyan Coll., 1960—66, Adv. Com. Cornell U., Coll. Human Ecology, 1990—95; mem. U. Rochester, sch. nursing adv. bd., 2004—11, grad. sch. academic health care bd. mem., 2005—11; bd. mem. Sheriffs Found., 1995—; pres. Hurlbut Trust, 1994—; mem. bd. dir. Strong Meml. Hosp., 1984—2011, chmn. bd. dir., 2004—06; life coun. mem. Cornell U., 2003—; mem. Lifespan Cmty. Orgn., 1995—, WXXI Pub, TV, 1973—; chmn. bd. Rochester Philharmonic Orch., 1985—88, mem. hon. bd., 1988—, United Way Comm., 1985—89; spl. monroe county dep. sheriff pres. Hurlbut Found., 1993—, pres. Hattie Harris Found., 2000—07; co-chair, Capital Campaign U. Rochester, 1988—2000, chmn., Capital Campaign, Sch. Nursing, 2005—07; mem. Nat. Nursing Coun., 2008—11; founding mem. Mus. Am. Indians. Recipient Boy Scout Cmty. award, 1990, Hon. Trooper, Ala., 1990, NY, Hon. Lt. award, Ala., 1990, Life Span Cmty. Leadership award, 1998, Compeer award, Compeer Inc., 2001, George Eastman Medal award, U. Rochester, 2006, Jr. Achievement award, Bus. Hall of Fame, 2008, Rotary Annual award, 2011. Fellow Am. Coll. Health Care Adminstrs.; mem. Greater Met. C. of C. (past chmn. bd. dirs., Rochester Rotary Ann. award 2011), George Eastman Soc., Audubon Soc., World Wildlife Fund, Nat. Geographic Soc., Genesee Valley Club, Oak Hill Country Club, Cornell Soc. Hotelmen, Meml. Art Gallery, NY State Sheriff's Assn., Senela Zoo. Soc. (life), Smithsonian, Rochester MUs. and Sci. Ctr., Lambda Chi Alpha,Rochester Area Found.; Rochester Police Lucust Club, NRA (life, pub. channel XXI mem.), Rochester Rotary Club, Nat. Mus. Am. Indian. Home: 200 Sheldon Rd Honeoye Falls NY 14472-9316 Office: Hurlbut Trust 740 East Ave Rochester NY 14607-2107 Office Phone: 585-271-1650.

HURLEY, JAMES ROBERT (BOB HURLEY), medical products executive; BA in Polit. Sci., U. Ga., 1971. Joined Baxter / American Hosp. Supply Corp., 1980; v.p. human resources, global businesses Baxter Internat., Inc., 1987, corp. v.p., pres. Baxter Japan/China, 1992, corp. v.p. restructuring; v.p., human resources Beckman Coulter, Inc., 2005, sr. v.p. human resources and comm., 2005—, chmn. Beckman Coulter Japan, interim pres., CEO, 2010—. Capt. US Army, 1971—80. Office: Beckman Coulter Inc 4300 N Harbor Blvd Fullerton CA 92834-3100 Office Phone: 714-871-4848. Office Fax: 714-773-8111. Business E-Mail: jhurley@beckmancoulter.com. *

HURST, DEBORAH, pediatric hematologist; b. Washington, May 9, 1946; d. Willard and Frances (Wilson) H.; m. Stephen Mershon Senter, June 14, 1970; children: Carlin, Daniel. BA, Harvard U., 1968; MD, Med. Coll. Pa., 1974. Diplomate Nat. Bd. Med. Examiners, Am. Bd. Pediatrics, Am. Bd. Pediatric Hematology-Oncology. Intern Bellevue Hosp., NYU Hosp., NYC, 1974-75, resident in pediatrics, 1975-76; ambulatory pediatric fellow Bellevue Hosp., NYC, 1976-77; hematology, oncology fellow Bellevue Hosp., Columbia U., NYC, 1977-80; assoc. hematologist Childrens Hosp. Oakland, Calif., 1980-92; asst. clin. prof. U. Calif. San Francisco Med. Ctr., 1992—2004; med. dir. Bayer Corp., Berkeley, Calif., 1992-98; sr. dir. clin. devel. Chiron Corp., Emeryville, Calif., 1998—2006; sr. director bio-oncology devel. Genentech, Inc., South San Francisco, Calif., 2006—. Hematology cons. Assn. Asian/Pacific Community Health Orgns., Oakland; dir. Satellite Hematology Clinic/Valley Childrens Hosp., Fresno, Calif., 1984-92; cons. state dept. epidemiology Calif. State Dept. Health, Berkeley, 1992; chelation cons. lead poisoning program Childrens Hosp., Oakland, 1986-92. Contbr. articles to profl. jours. Vol. cons. lead poisoning State Dept. Epidemiology and Toxicology, Berkeley, 1986-92. Fellow Am. Acad. Pediatrics; mem. Am. Soc. Hematology, Am. Soc. Gene Therapy, Am. Soc. Clin. Oncology, Am. Soc. Pediat. Hematology/Oncology. Office: Genentech Inc 1 DNA Way South San Francisco CA 94080-4990 Personal E-mail: hurst.deborah@gene.com.

HURST, ROBERT W., interventional neuroradiologist, educator; BS, US Mil. Acad., West Point, NY, 1972; MD, U. Tex., 1981. Diplomate Am. Bd. Psychiatry and Neurology, 1986, Am. Bd. Radiology, 1989, Am. Bd. Radiology-neuroradiology, 2005. Intern internal medicine Univ. Va., Charlottesville, Va., 1981—82, resident neurology, 1982—85, resident radiology Charlottesville, Va., 1985—89, fellow neuroradiology Hosp. of the Univ. of Penn., Phila., 1989—91, interventional neuroradiologist, prof. radiology. Named one of Best Doctors in America, 2003—04, 2005—06, 2007—08, 2009—10, Top Docs, Phila. Mag., 2004—11, America's Best Doctors, 2007, 2008, 2010. Office: Hospital of the University of Pennsylvania 3400 Spruce St Philadelphia PA 19104 Office Phone: 215-662-3083 E-mail: robert.hurst@uphs.upenn.edu.

HURTEAU, GILLES DAVID, retired obstetrician, gynecologist, educator, dean; b. Cornwall, Ont., Can., Nov. 28, 1928; s. Joseph A. and Antoinette (St-Laurent) H.; m. Janine Anita Carriere, June 16, 1956; children: Michele, Jean, Louise, Pierre, Gilles Andre. BA, U. Ottawa, 1951; MDCM, McGill U., 1955. Licentiate, Med. Council Can., 1956; cert. postgrad. tng. in surg. Case Western Res. U. 1956-58, in ob gyn. Yale U., New Haven, 1958-61. Instr. and clin. asst. Yale U. Med. Sch., New Haven, 1961-62; asst. prof. U. Ottawa Med. Sch., Ont., 1963-66, assoc. prof., 1966, prof. and chmn. dept. ob-gyn, 1967-76, dean Sch. Medicine, 1976-89, dean faculty health scis., 1978-89, emeritus prof., 1990—; exec. dir./registrar Royal Coll. Physicians and Surgeons Can., Ottawa, 1990-95. Trustee Children's Hosp. East Ont., 1977-89, bd. govs. U. Ottawa, 1995-2008, vice chmn. bd., chmn. exec. bd. govs. 2003-08, emeritus mb. bd. govs. 2008-; bd. dirs. Assoc. Med. Svcs. Inc., 2000-05, chmn., 2004-05. Contbr. articles to profl. jours., chpts to books. Mem. coun. Ottawa-Carleton Dist. Health Coun., 1970-78; bd. dirs. Ont. Cancer Treatment and Rsch. Found., 1983-92, Physicians Svcs. Inc. Found. Ont., 1984-86, 95-2001. Fellow Royal Coll. Physicians and Surgeons Can. (coun. 1970-78, v.p. 1976-78), Royal Coll. Physicians Ireland, Am. Coll. Ob-gyn.; mem. Coun. Ont. Faculty Medicine, Assn. Can. Med. Colls. (pres. 1981-82), Soc. Ob-gyn. Can., Alpha Omega Alpha Honor Med. Soc. (faculty mem.). Home: 203-31 Durham (Pvt) Ottawa ON Canada K1M 2J1 Personal E-mail: gilles.hurteau@sympatico.ca. *

HURTIG, HOWARD I., neurologist, educator; BA in English, Tulane U., New Orleans, 1962, MD, 1966. Diplomate Am. Bd. Psychiatry and Neurology, 1976. Intern medicine NY Hosp-Cornell Med. Ctr., 1966—67, resident medicine, 1967—68; resident neurology Hosp. of the Univ. Pa., 1970—73; Elliott prof. neurology Univ. Pa. Named one of Top Docs, Phila. Mag., 2004—05, 2007—08, 2010—11, Best Doctors in America, 2005—06, 2007—08, 2009—10, America's Top Doctors, 2007, 2008, 2010. Office: Pennsylvania Hospital 8th & Spruce Streets Philadelphia PA 19104 Office Phone: 215-829-8407. Office Fax: 215-829-6606.

HURVITZ, EDWARD A., physiatrist; MD, Wayne State Coll. Medicine, Detroit, Mich., 1984. Cert. Physical Medicine and Rehab. 1989, Adolescent and Young Adult Rehab.Electroneuromyography Laboratory 1989. Joined faculty U. Mich., 1988, assoc. prof. dept. physical rehab., chair, dept. physical rehab., 2006—. Reviewer Archives of Physical Medicine and Rehab.; national lecturer in field. Office: U Michigan 325 E Eisenhower Pkwy Ann Arbor MI 48108-5032

HURWITZ, SHEPARD RAPHAEL, orthopaedic surgeon, educator, medical association administrator; b. NYC, Aug. 19, 1950; s. Paul A. and Beatrice T. H.; m. Margretta Kristine Manser, Apr. 11, 1992; children: Zoe, Leah. BA, Columbia Coll., 1972; MD, Columbia U., 1976. Internship U. Va., 1976—77, residency, 1977—78, N.Y. Orthopaedic Hosp., 1978—81; asst. prof. George Washington U., Washington, 1984-88; assoc. prof. U. Rochester, NY, 1989-94; assoc. prof. orthop. surgery U. Va., Charlottesville, 1994—2000, prof. orthop. surgery, 2000—08, S. Ward Casscells prof. orthop. surgery, 2001—08; exec. dir. American Bd. Orthop. Surgeons, 2008—; prof. orthop. surgery U. NC Sch. Medicine, 2008—. Cons. NIH Clin. Ctr., Bethesda, Md., 1983-2001. Author, editor: Foot and Ankle Pain, 2nd edit., 2000. Mem. American Orthopaedic Assn. (mem. nominating com. 1997-98), American Assn. Orthop. Surgeons (leadership devel.

com., dir. 2005). Jewish. Avocations: fishing, hunting, tennis. Office: American Bd Orthop Surgery 400 Silver Cedar Ct Chapel Hill NC 27514 Office Phone: 919-929-7103. Business E-Mail: shurwitz@abos.org. *

HUSBY, PAUL J.A., medical educator, researcher; s. Torfinn and Else Margrethe Husby; m. Joanna Spruyt, Dec. 2, 1944; children: Lars Andre, Carl Fredrik, Else Margrethe, Pal Jeroen. MD, U. Kiel, Germany, 1971; PhD, U. Bergen, Norway, 1982. Bd. cert. specialist anesthesiology and intensive care Norway, 1982. Cons. U. Med. Ctr., U. Hosp., Bergen, Norway, 1982—; prof. U. Bergen, Sch. Medicine, 1996—. Acad. head dept. anesthesia, intensive care U. Bergen, 1999—2004; cons. cardiac anesthesia, intensive care Haukeland U. Hosp., 1982—; prof., rschr. U. Bergen, Faculty Medicine, 1996—; vis. prof. U. Vienna Med. Ctr., 2001—02. Contbr. about 80 articles to profl. jours. Lt. Norwegian Air Force. Grantee, Norwegian Rsch. Coun., Norwegian Coun. on Cardiovascular Diseases, Lordal Found. for Acute Medicine, Univ. Bergen, Frank Mohn Found., European Union. Mem.: Scandinavian Soc. Anesthesiology and Intensive Care, Soc. Cardiac Anesthesiologists. Achievements include research in hypothermia with special focus on fluid physiology and cellular metabolism in relation to extracorporeal circulation. Office: Univ Bergen Haukeland Univ Hosp Bergen N-5021 Norway Office Fax: 47+ 55976898. E-mail: paul.husby@kir.uib.no.

HUSKEY, HARRY DOUGLAS, information and computer science educator; b. Whittier, NC, Jan. 19, 1916; s. Cornelius and Myrtle (Cunningham) H.; m. Velma Elizabeth Roeth, Jan. 2, 1939 (dec. Jan. 1991); children: Carolyn, Roxanne, Harry Douglas, Linda; m. Nancy Grindstaff, Sept. 10, 1994. BS, U. Idaho, 1937; student, Ohio U., 1937—38; MA, Ohio State U., 1940, PhD, 1943. Temp. prin. sci. officer Nat. Phys. Labs., England, 1947; head machine devel. lab. Nat. Bur. Stds., 1948; asst. dir. Inst. Numerical Analysis, 1948-54; assoc. dir. computation lab. Wayne U., Detroit, 1952-53; assoc. prof. U. Calif., Berkeley, 1954-58, prof., 1958-68, vice chmn. elec. engring., 1965-66, prof. info. and computer sci. Santa Cruz, 1968-85, prof. emeritus, 1985—, dir. Computer Ctr., 1968-77, chmn. bd. info. sci., 1976-79, 82-83. Vis. prof. Indian Inst. Tech., Kanpur; (Indo-Am. program), 1963-64, 71, Delhi U., 1971; cons. computer divsn. Bendix, 1954-63; vis. prof. MIT, 1966; mem. computer sci. panel NSF, Naval Rsch. Adv. Com.; cons. on computers for developing countries UN, 1969-71; chmn. com. to advise Brazil on computer sci. edn. NAS, 1970-72; project coord. UNESCO/Burma contract, 1973-79; mem. adv. com. on use microcomputers in developing countries NRC, 1983-85. Co-editor: Computer Handbook, 1962. Recipient Disting. Alumni award Idaho State U., 1978, Pioneer award Nat. Computer Conf., 1978, IEEE Computer Soc., 1982; named U.S. sr.scientist award Fulbright-Alexander von Humboldt Found., Mathematisches Institut der Tech. U. Munich, 1974-75, 25th Ann. medal ENIAC; named to U. Idaho Alumni Hall of Fame, 1989. Fellow AAAS, IEEE (edit. bd., editor-in-chief computer group 1965-71, Centennial award 1984), Brit. Computer Soc.Computer Soc. India; mem. Am. Math. Soc., Math. Assn. Am., Assn. Computing Machinery (pres. 1960-62), Am. Fedn. Info. Processing Socs. (governing bd. 1961-63), Sigma Xi. Achievements include designing SWAC computer, Bendix G-15 and G-20 computers. Office: U Calif Computer & Info Sci Santa Cruz CA 95064 Home: 23 Eastridge Dr Santa Cruz CA 95060-1803 Personal E-mail: harryhuskey@gmail.com.

HUSSAIN, ALTAF, orthopedist, consultant; s. M. and A. Saiyed; m. Khalida Sultan; children: H. H. Syed, S. A. Syed. MBBS, Med. Coll. Srinagar, Kashmir, India, 1966, MS, 1973; MChOrth, Liverpool U., UK, 1982. Resident SMHS Hosp. & Med. Coll., Srinagar, 1967—70, registrar orthops., 1970—74, lectr. orthops., 1974—81; dep. chmn. Bridgend Conservative Assn., 2011—. Resident to registrar Royal Liverpool Hosp., 1979—83; cons. orthop. surgeon Al Zulfi Hosp., Riyadh, Saudi Arabia, 1983—86, Prince Salman Hosp., Riyadh, 1986—92, NHS, 1992—2000, Prince Charles Hosp., Merthyr Tydfil, 2000—10; cons. editor Internat. J&K Practitioner; cons.; tutor Royal Coll. Surgeon, 2004—. Contbr. numerous articles to internat. profl. jours. Recipient Best Practice Team award, 2007, Glory of India, 2008, Bharat Gaurav award, 2009, Life Time Achievement award, 2010. Fellow: Internat. Coll. Surgeons, Brit. Orthop. Assn.; mem.: Brit. Med. Assn., Indian Orthop. Soc.(UK) (life), Indian Orthop. Assn. (life). Achievements include invention of notch trial in total knee replacement and thumb index reference in total hip replacement. Personal E-mail: altafhussain_uk@hotmail.com. Business E-Mail: altaf.hussain@talktomeclinic.com, admin@bridgendconservatives.net.

HUSSAIN, MAHA, oncologist, educator; b. Iraq, June 2, 1956; MD, Baghdad U. Sch. Medicine, 1980. Prof. medicine U. Mich., 2002—. Office: 1500 E Med Ctr Dr 7314 Cancer Ctr Ann Arbor MI 48109 Business E-Mail: mahahuss@umich.edu.

HUSSAIN, SYED A., oncologist, educator; b. Pakistan, Aug. 14, 1970; arrived in Eng., 1997; s. Arshad Hussain and Siddiqua Arshad; m. Arfeen Fatima, Dec. 22, 2002. MB, BS, U. Karachi, Pakistan, 1994; MSc, U. Birmingham, Eng., 2000, MD, 2003. Clin. rsch. fellow/registrar U. Hosp. Birmingham, 1999—2002; clin. lectr. oncology U. Birmingham /U. Hosp. Birmingham, 2002—. Contbr. articles to profl. jours. Mem.: European Soc. Med. Oncology, Am. Soc. Clin. Oncology (Merit award 2002, 2003). Office: Cancer Rsch UK Institute for cancer studies Vincent Dr B15 2TT Birmingham England Office Fax: + 44 (0)121 414 3263. E-mail: hussainsa@cancer.bham.ac.uk.

HUSSAIN, SYED TASEER, biomedical researcher, educator; b. Lahore, Pakistan, Sept. 18, 1943; came to U.S., 1970; s. S. Fayyaz and Riaz (Fatima) H. BS, Punjab U., Pakistan, 1963, BS with honors, 1964, MS, 1965; PhD, U. Utrecht, Netherlands, 1969. Postdoct. fellow Am. Mus. Natural History, NYC, 1970—72; instr. Howard U. Coll. Medicine, Washington, 1972-73, asst. prof., 1973-76, assoc. prof., 1977-85, prof. anatomy, 1985—. Dir. gen. Pakistan Mus. of Natural History, Pakistan Sci. Found., Islamabad, 1985-87; grants reveiwer NSF, 1980—, NATO, 1987—, Nat. Geog. Soc., 1985—; frequent invited spkr. on evolutionary processes, biological changes, climate change and human health. Author, co-author over 60 publs. and several book chpts., contbr. articles to profl. jours. Grantee Smithsonian Instn., 1974-94, NSF, 1977—, Nat. Inst. Environ. Health Scis., 1994. Fellow Pakistan Acad. Geol. Scis.; mem. AAAS, Am. Assn. Anatomy, Soc. Vertebrate Paleontology. Achievements include research in evolution in locomotion and hearing mechanism in mammals; human health and forced climate change; influence of increased temperatures on diseases. Office: Howard Univ Coll Medicine 520 W St NW Washington DC 20001-2337

HUSSAR, PIRET, science educator; b. Tartu, Estonia, Mar. 9, 1971; d. Ülo and Viive Hussar. MD in Histology, U. Tartu, 1997, DMSc. Lab. technician U. Tartu, 1995—97, 2002, asst., 1997—2004, sr. asst., 2004—08, assoc. prof., 2008—; monbusho rsch. fellow Gunma U., Maebashi, Japan, 1999—2000; postdoc. fellow Tsurumi U., Yokohama, Japan, 2005—06. Author: (books for medical students) Textbooks of Histology; contbr. articles to profl. jours. Recipient award, Japan Soc. Promotion Sci., 2005—06, Archimedes Found., Estonia, 2007; fellowship, Estonian Sci. Found., 1997—2000, Ministry Edn., Sci., Sports, and Culture of Japan, 1998—2000, grant, Europian Union (EU) publ., 2005, 2007. Mem.: European Assn. Vet. Anatomists, Internat. Soc. Vertebrate Morphologists, Soc. Ecology and Toxicology St-Petersburg, Assn. Estonian Scientists, Assn. Estonian Doctors, Assn. Estonian Morphologists. Lutherian. Achievements include first to importance of perichonder in post-traumatic bone repair; GLUT1 may serve as a part of the machinery for the specific transfer of glucose in the olfactory system. Avocations: music, languages. Home: Leevikese 1A-12 Tartu 50413 Estonia Office: Univ of Tartu Ravila 19 Tartu 50411 Estonia Home: Arhitekti 28 Tartu 50408 Estonia Business E-Mail: piret.hussar@ut.ee.

HUSSEIN, AHMED ABBAS, surgeon, orthopedist; b. Khartoum, Sudan, Mar. 24, 1951; s. Abbas Hussein and Afia Abdella; married, July 19, 1986; children: Ramiz, Afia, Reem, Mazin. MBBS with honors, U. Buckarest, 1974; MD in Orthops., U. Budapest, 1982. Lic. Gen. Med. Coun., UK. Fellow paediat. orthops. Inst. Orthops., Oswostry, England, 1990, fellow spinal surgery, 1992; cons. Frenchy Hosp., Bristol, England, 1992—94, Cheltenham (England) Gen. Hosp., 1994—96; cons. orthops. and spinal surgeon Princess Alexandera Hosp., Harlow, England, 1996—. Contbr. articles to profl. jours. Fellow: Royal Coll. Surgeons Edinburgh, Royal Coll. Surgeons Eng.; mem.: Brit. Orthop. Assn., Spinal Arthoplasty Soc., European Spinal Soc., Soc. for Back Pain and Related Rsch., Brit. Cervical Spinal Soc., Brit. Spinal Soc., Amnesty Internat., Physician for Human Rights. Office: Princess Alexandera Hosp Harlow CM20 1GX England Home: 125 River Meads SG12 8EL Stanstead Abbotts England Office Phone: 0044 1279 827405. Personal E-mail: aah.spine@btinternet.com.

HUSSEIN, HASSAN ABDELSABOUR, veterinarian, educator; b. Assiut, Egypt, May 31, 1969; BVSc in Vet. Medicine, Assiut U., 1992; PhD, Giessen U., Germany, 2003. Assoc. prof. U., 2008—. Recipient Best Rsch. award, Egyptian Soc. Cattle Disease; scholarship, Egyptian Govt. Office: El Gamaah St Dept Theriogenology Assiut 71526 Egypt Office Fax: 2 088 2322564. E-mail: hassansabour69@yahoo.com.

HUSSEIN, MOHAMMED ABDALLA, chemistry professor; b. Egypt, 1973; PhD, 2006. Lectr., biochemistry Faculty Pharmacy U., Egypt, 1996—. Office: Pharmacy University Cairo 002 Egypt Office Fax: 0020238353270. Personal E-mail: abdallamohammed_304@hotamil.com.

HUSSEIN SALEH, KAMAL, plastic surgeon; b. Baghdad, Iraq, 1961; MD, U. Baghdad, Iraq, 1985. Lic. cons. plastic surgeon Qatar Nat. Health, 2006. Plastic-cosmetic surgeon Med. City Hosp., Baghdad, Iraq, 1998—2005; cons. cosmetic surgeon Al Emadi Hospital, Doha, Qatar, 2006; cons. cosmetic & plastic surgeon Dr. Kamal Hussein Saleh Cosmetic Clinic, Qatar, 2006—. Lectr. Al Kofa Med. Coll., Iraq, 1997, tng. postgrad. students burn surgery, Iraq, 97; lectr. Baghdad Med. Coll., Iraq, 2000; tng. postgrad. plastic bd. Med. City Hosp., Iraq, 2000. Author: (articles) Reconstruction of nasal defect following excision of basal cell carcinoma of the nose., 1994, Baldness in Iraqi people., 1998, Management of obesity., 2000, Hair transplantation comparative study., 2001, Treatment of hemangioma by local injection of triamcilonone., 2007, Letter A mastopexy-breast augmentation., 2009. Mem.: Qatar Nat. Health, Jordanian Med. Assn., Nat. Arab-Am. Med. Assn., Pan Arab Assn. of Plastic Surgeons, Iraqi Assn. of Plastic Surgeons, Iraqi Med. Assn., Internat. Plastic & Reconstructive Surgery. Office: Al Emadi Hospital PO Box 5804 Doha Qatar Office Phone: 97455742973. Personal E-mail: drkhsh2001@yahoo.com. *

HUSSEY, JOHN FRANCIS, physician, geriatrician; b. Richmond Hill, NY, Jan. 6, 1951; BS in Biology, St. Johns U., 1972; MD, Creighton U., 1976. Family practice resident St. Joseph's Hosp., Omaha; pvt. practice, Augusta, Maine, 1982-90; med. cons. Augusta Mental Health Inst., 1990-95; geriatrician, psychiatry cons. Togus (Maine) VA Hosp., 1995—. Capt. USPHS, 1979-82. Fellow Am. Acad. Family Physicians; mem. Am. Geriat. Soc., Kennebec County Med. Assn. (treas. 1995-96, pres. 1996-97), Am. Heart Assn. Office: VA Hosp 1 VA Ctr Sta 171 Augusta ME 04330-6795 E-mail: jfhmd@msn.com.

HUSTED, RUSSELL FOREST, research scientist; b. Lafayette, Ind., Apr. 4, 1950; s. Robert Forest and Miriam Ruth (Jackson) H.; m. Nancy Lee Driscoll, Oct. 25, 1969 (div. Feb. 1986); children: Jacqueline Marie, Randall Forest; m. Ruth Elaine Hurlburt, Nov. 12, 1988. BS in Chemistry with highest distinction, Colo. State U., 1972; PhD in Pharmacology, U. Utah, 1976. Post-doctoral fellow dept. medicine U. Iowa, Iowa City, 1976-79, rsch. scientist dept. medicine, 1979-81, 1982—; asst. prof. U. Conn. Sch. Medicine, Farmington, 1981-82. Contbr. articles to profl. jours. Mallinckrodt scholar Colo. State U., 1968. Mem. AAAS, Am. Soc. Nephrology, Am. Physiol. Soc., Soc. Gen. Physiology, N.Y. Acad. Sci., Sigma Xi. Democrat. Methodist. Office: Univ Iowa 3180 Medical Labs Iowa City IA 52242 Business E-Mail: russell-husted@uiowa.edu.

HUSTON, JANIS LYNNE, medical educator, consultant; b. Napoleon, Ohio, Sept. 14, 1952; d. Walter Ray and Betty Irene Huston. BS, Ohio State U., 1975; MEd, Bowling Green State U., 1983; PhD, U. Ky., 1997. Asst. dir. med. records Providence Hosp., Anchorage, 1976-79; dir. med. record adminstrn. program Bowling Green State U., Ohio, 1979-84; dir. med. records Crestview Hosp., Casper, Wyo., 1985-86; prof. Ea. Ky. U., Richmond, 1987-94; telemedicine rsch. assoc. U. Ky., Lexington, 1995-97; data accreditation assessor, telemedicine cons. Histopathol. Lab., Wiesbaden, Germany, 1998-99; EPR facilitator North London Cancer Network, 2001—02; med. record and data quality mgr. Univ. Coll., London, 2002; clin. dataset rschr. Royal Coll. Physicians, London, 2002—03; clin. coding advisor S.E. London Strategic Health Authority, 2003—04; health info. mgmt. cons. Nat. Health Svc., London, 2000—, EHR sr. tng. and devel. cons. NHS Capital Care Alliance, 2004—05; coding cons. Salford Royal NHS Trust, Manchester, England, 2008, SNOMED Ct Course Development, Ohio Health Info. Mgmt. Assn., 2007; coding mgr. Royal Marsden NHS Trust, London, 2009; dir. svcs. NWOREC Hosp. Coun. Northwest Ohio, Toledo, 2011—. Cons. Williams County Nursing Home, Bryan, Ohio, 1980-81, Henry County Hosp., Napoleon, Ohio, 1980-84, Midway (Ky.) Coll., 1990, Nat. City Bank, Lexington, 1990-91; vis. prof. Ohio State U., Columbus, 1997-98, reviewer Brit. Med. Jour., 2008, 10. Contbr. articles to profl. jours. Mem. Am. Health Info. Mgmt. Assn. (registered health info. adminstr.), Royal Soc. Medicine (mem. telemedicine forum 1999, fellow, 2008), Brit. Med. Informatics Soc., Brit. Computer Soc., Internat. Fedn. Health Records Orgn., Ins. Healthcare Mgrs. Avocations: sports, music, art. Home: Flat 3 The Argyll 25 The Esplanade Scarborough Y011 2AQ England E-mail: jangeorg@yahoo.com.

HUSZAR, GABOR BELA, obstetrician, gynecologist, andrologist; b. Budapest, Hungary, Nov. 3, 1938; m. Theresa Gal Huszar, July 20, 1966; children: Thomas, Andrew. MD, Med. Sch. Budapest, Hungary, 1963. Resident physician U. Budapest Sch. Medicine, 1963—66; rsch. fellow Retina Found., Boston, 1967—71; spl. rsch. fellow Harvard U., Cambridge, Mass., 1971—74; asst. prof. dept. ob-gyn. Yale U. Sch. Medicine, New Haven, 1974—80, dir. uterine physiol. lab. dept. ob-gyn., 1978—86, assoc. prof., 1986—90, sr. rsch. scientist, 1991—. Mem. reprodn. biology study sect. NIH, 1991—95; invited spkr. Nobel Conf., Stockholm, 1995; dir. sperm physiology lab., 1983—; cons. in field; mem. editorial bd. Jour. Andrology, Basic and Applied Myology, Hungarian Jour. Ob-gyn., Mediterranean Jour. Gynecology, Reproductive Technology Update; mem. Hungarian Nat. Acad. Scis., 1998, Conn. Acad. Scis. & Engring., 2000. Contbr. articles numerous profl. jours., chapters to books; editor: The Physiology and Biochemistry of the Uterus, 1986. Grantee, NIH. Mem.: AAAS, Soc. Study Reproduction, Soc. Wine Educators (bd. dirs.), Am. Soc. Gyn. Med., Am. Soc. Andrology, Soc. Gynecologic Investigation, Am. Soc. Biol. Chemists, Soc. Hungarian Ob-gyns. (hon.). Democrat. Roman Catholic. Achievements include patents for ob-gyn diagnostic instruments and fertility diagnostic procedures. Office: Yale University Sch Medicine Dept Ob-gyn 333 Cedar St New Haven CT 06510-3289

HUTCHESON, JACK ROBERT, hematologist, medical oncologist; b. Rock Hill, SC, Dec. 26, 1946; s. Jack Robert and Lillian Massey (Dunlap) H.; m. Charlene Marie Dixon, Sept. 14, 1974; children: Gregory Allen, Julia Lynn. BS in Biology, Wake Forest U., 1969; MD, Med. U. S.C., 1973. Diplomate in internal medicine, hematology, oncology Am. Bd. Internal Medicine. Straight med. intern U. Md. Hosp., Balt., 1973-74, resident in medicine, 1974-76; fellow in hematology Med. U. S.C., Charleston, 1976-78; fellow in oncology Emory U., Atlanta, 1978-79; oncologist, hematologist Oncology and Hematology Assocs. SW Va. Inc., Roanoke, 1979—2007; med. dir. Carilion Health Sys. Oncology Svc. Line, Roanoke, 1996—2003. Instr., assoc. investigator in hematology Med. U. S.C./VA Hosp., Charleston, 1977-78; assoc. prof. medicine U. Va., Roanoke. Contbr. articles to med. jours. Pres. Scottish Soc. Va. Highlands, Roanoke, 1996, 2000, 01; chair com. on smoking cessation Va. br. Am. Cancer Soc., Roanoke, 1980; mem. Vets. Corps. of Artillary, N.Y. Decorated officer brother with Commander Most Venerable Order of Hosp. of St. John of Jerusalem, Caballero Grand Cruz Order Don Carlos I (Portugal); recipient Berson Yalow award, Soc. Nuclear Medicine, 1977; grantee for hematology, VA Career Devel., 1977—78. Fellow ACP; mem. Am. Soc. Clin. Oncology, Am. Soc. Hematology, St. Andrews Soc. Presbyterian. Avocations: Jaguar auto restoration, genealogy, Scottish/Celtic activities, bagpipes. Home: 2860 S Jefferson St Roanoke VA 24014-3320 Personal E-mail: auldpyper@aol.com.

HUTCHESON, JAMES STERLING, retired physician, allergist; b. Richmond, Va., Apr. 17, 1936; s. James P. and Daisy-Clarke (Lorentz) H.; m. Nancy Montgomery Sanders, May 20, 1961; children: Anne Farrar McCausland, Betsy Dulaney Hutcheson Harvey. Student, Roanoke Coll., Va., 1953-55; BA, U. Va., 1955-57; MD, The Johns Hopkins U., 1957-61. Diplomate Am. Bd. Allergy and Clin. Immunology. Intern in medicine U. Va., Charlottesville, Va., 1961-62; resident in medicine Med. Coll. Va., Richmond, Va., 1962-64; fellow in allergy and immunology U. Va., Charlottesville, Va., 1964-65; asst. prof. medicine Med. Coll. Va., 1967-68; staff Nalle Clinic, Charlotte, 1968-89; pvt. practice Carolina Asthma and Allergy Ctr., 1990—2005, ret., 2005. Founder Allergy Clinic USAF Acad. Hosp., Colo., 1965-67; cons. Blue Cross/Blue Shield of NC, 1985-2002; adj. assoc. prof. pediats. U. NC Sch. Medicine, Carolinas Med. Ctr., Charlotte, 1997-2000. Bd. trustees Charlotte County Day Sch., 1974-85; bd. dirs. Friends of Music Queens Coll., 1994-96. Capt. USAF M.C. Fellow Am. Acad. Allergy, Asthma and Immunology, Am. Coll. Allergy, Asthma and Immunology; mem. Southeastern Allergy Assn., NC Soc. Allergy and Clin. Immunology (former pres.). Episcopalian. Avocations: gardening, hiking, classical music, reading. Home: 334 Green Cove Rd Sugar Mountain Banner Elk NC 28604 Personal E-mail: sthutch@skybest.com.

HUTCHESON, KELLY, medical educator; b. Va., Jan. 1, 1965; MD, U. Va. Sch. Medicine, 1992; MBA, George Wash. U., 2010. Assoc. prof. Children's Nat. Med. Ctr., 2001—. Fellow: AAO; mem.: WIO, ACHE, ACPE, AAOE. Office: 111 Michigan Ave NW Dept Ophthalmology Washington DC 20010 Business E-Mail: khutches@cnmc.org.

HUTCHINS, JEFF T., medical association administrator; b. Pontiac, Mich., Oct. 13, 1958; BSc, Oral Roberts U., 1981; PhD, U. Tex. Health Sci. Ctr, Houston, 1986. V.p. preclin. devel. Inhibitex, Inc., 2001—. Vis. prof. Rush Coll. Medicine, 1999—2001. Home: 1120 Quail Run Ln Cumming GA 30041 Office Phone: 678-746-1141. Home Fax: 678-746-0617. Personal E-mail: jhutchins@inhibitex.com.

HUTCHINSON, EDNA M., home care nurse; d. William Henry and Mary L. Hutchinson; children: Wendell, Antoinette, Lynette, Mary Maxine. Cert., San Diego C.C., 1981, Grossmont C.C., El Cajon, Calif., 1988. Cert. electrocardiographic technologist, Calif.; sec. sci. lab. Calif., in tng. developmental disabilities 2009, in tng. devel. disabilities 09. Nurse asst., Phoenix, 1965—66, San Diego, 1966—69; med. asst. Med. Clinic, San Diego, 1980—85; electrocardiogram tech. Maricopa County Hosp., Phoenix, 1989—91; home care nurse Home Health Care, San Diego, 1991—. Songwriter Hill Top Records, Hollywood, Calif., 2000—. Author: (book) Inspiration Songs and

Poems, 2000; songwriter In the Beginning, 2000, Jesus in the Inside, 2000; author: Etches in Time, 1997, (songs) God Creation, 2000; co-author: Best Poems and Poets, 2000, Poetry's Elite's Best Poets of 2001, 2001; contbr. over 400 songs & poems copyrights, poems to anthology. Daycare provider County of Riverside, Calif., 2001. Recipient Editor's Choice award for Outstanding Achievement in Poetry, State of Md., 1997, Poet of Merit award, Internat. Soc. Poets, 1997, Achievement award, Creative Writing Skills, 1999, Cert., Wall of Tolerance Nat. Campaign, 2001; named Ten Best Dressed, 1983; finalist Top Model, San Diego, Calif., 1976. Avocations: reading, music, songwriting.

HUTCHINSON, RAYMOND JOSEPH, pediatrician, educator; b. Washington, Sept. 23, 1947; MD, Harvard Med. Sch., 1973; MS, U. Mich., 1989. Prof. pediat. U. Mich., Med. Sch., 1978—2011, assoc. dean, regulatory affairs, 2006—. Bd. dirs. Gerber Found., 2007—11. Mem.: Soc. Pediatric Rsch., Am. Soc. Clin. Oncology, Am. Soc. Hematology. Avocation: fly fishing. Office: 1301 Catherine St MS I Room 3109 Ann Arbor MI 48109 Business E-Mail: rhutchin@umich.edu.

HUTCHISON, VICTOR HOBBS, biologist, educator; b. Blakely, Ga., June 15, 1931; s. Joseph Victor and Veva (Hobbs) H.; m. Theresa Dokos, Dec. 14, 1952; children: Victoria Ann, John Christopher, David Michael, Kenneth Hobbs. BS, N. Ga. Coll., 1952; MA, Duke U., 1956, PhD, 1959; grad., U.S. Army Command and Gen. Staff Coll. Instr. Duke U., 1957-58, faculty fellow, So. Fellowship Fund fellow, 1958-59; mem. faculty U. R.I., 1959-70, prof. biology, 1968-70; dir. Inst. Environ. Biology, 1966—70; prof., chmn. dept. zoology U. Okla., Norman, 1970-80, George Lynn Cross rsch. prof. zoology, 1979-2001, rsch. prof. emeritus, 2001—. Rsch. prof. Universidad de Los Andes, Bogotá, Colombia, 1965-66; prin. investigator Nat. Geog. Soc.-U. R.I. herpetological expdn. to Colombia, 1964-65, Nat. Geog. Soc.-U. Okla. expdns. to Lake Titicaca, 1975, Cameroon, 1981. Editor Animal Natural History series, 1991—; rsch. and articles on heat tolerances of lower vertebrates, effects of day-length on metabolism and temperature tolerance of lower vertebrates, physiology of lower vertebrates, physiol. ecology of amphibians and reptiles, respiration in amphibians, behavioral thermoregulation. With US Army, 1952—54, col. med. svc. corp. USAR. Decorated Army Commendation medal, Meritorious Svc. medal; Guggenheim fellow, 1965-66; Friend of Darwin award Nat. Ctr. Sci. Edn., 2008, Constl. Heritage award, Okla. Chpt., Ams. United Chpt. & State, 2000. Fellow AAAS; mem. Am. Inst. Biol. Sci., Am. Soc. Ichthyologists and Herpetologists (pres. 1988), Am. Physiol. Soc., Ecol. Soc. Am., Herpetologists League (exe. com. 1968-71), Soc. Study Amphibians and Reptiles (bd. govs. 1986-88, pres. 1998-99), Explorers Club, Sigma Xi, Phi Sigma, Phi Kappa Phi, Oklahomans for Excellence in Sci. Edn.(founder, 2002). Achievements include demonstration of facultative endothermy in brooding pythons; research on role of skin in amphibian respiration; development of standardized method for determination of critical thermal maximum in animals. Home: 2010 Crestmont Ave Norman OK 73069-6414

HUTH, EDWARD JANAVEL, internist, educator, editor; b. Phila., May 15, 1923; s. Edward Gaston and Suzanne Madeleine (Janavel) H.; m. Carol Elizabeth Monnik, Apr. 6, 1957; children: John Edward, James Janavel. BA, Wesleyan U., Middletown, Conn., 1945; MD, U. Pa., 1947. Diplomate Am. Bd. Internal Medicine, Nat. Bd. Med. Examiners. Intern Hosp. of U. Pa., 1947-48, resident medicine, 1949-51, ward physician, 1951-61; mem. Diagnostic Clinic, 1959-61; postdoctoral fellow Life Ins. Med. Research Fund, 1952-53; spl. research fellow USPHS, Univ. Coll. Hosp., London, Eng., 1957-58. Asst. instr. pharmacology U. Pa. Sch. Medicine, Phila., 1948-49, assoc. in medicine, 1951-58, asst. prof. medicine, 1958-61; assoc. prof. comparative medicine Sch. Vet. Medicine, 1963-68; adj. asst. prof. medicine U. Pa. Sch. Medicine, 1966-71, assoc. prof. clin. medicine, 1971-74, adj. clin. prof. medicine, 1974-78, adj. prof. medicine dept. medicine Assoc. Faculty, 1978-91; asst. prof. medicine Woman's Med. Coll., Phila., 1961-62, assoc. prof., 1962-65; chmn. com. on 4th edit. CBE Style Manual Coun. Biology Editors, 1971-78, chmn. com. on 6th edit., 1990-95; biomed. comms. study sect. NIH, 1972-76; chmn. subcom. 10 of Com. Z39 Am. Nat. Stds. Inst., 1974-77; mem. UNISIST Working Group on Primary Sources of Info., UNESCO, Paris, 1973-74; bd. regents Nat. Libr. Medicine, 1979-83; office med. applications of rsch. NIH, 2001—; expert com. on info. devel. and dissemination US Pharmacopeia, 2002-05. Author: Medical Style and Format, 1987, How to Write and Publish Papers in the Medical Sciences, 1990, Writing and Publishing in Medicine, 1998, SI Units for Clinical Medicine, 1998, Medicine in Quotations, 2000, 2d edit., 2006, Landmark Papers in Internal Medicine; asst. editor Annals of Internal Medicine, 1960-63, assoc. editor, 1963-71, editor, 1971-90, editor emeritus, 1990-93, 95—, book rev. editor, 1990-93, 95-96, interim editor, 1994-95; editor Online Jour. Current Clin. Trials, 1991-94, also articles; mem. editl. bd. Nat. Med. Jour. India, 1991—, Transactions and Studies of the Coll. Physicians Phila., 2002—04; mem. adv. bd. Croatian Med. Jour., 1998—; rev. editor Pa. Geneal. Mag., 2003; contbr. sci. papers. Sec. Harriton Assoc., Bryn Mawr PA, 1991-2005. With AUS, 1943—46. Fellow ACP, AAAS (coun. 1968, editor Online Jour. Current Clin. Trials 1991-94), Royal Coll. Physicians (London), Am. Med. Writers Assn. (pres. 1967-68); mem. Coun. Biology Editors (dir. 1970-75, chmn. 1973-74), European Assn. Sci. Editors, Coll. Physicians Phila. (chmn. Wood Inst., Libr. and Mus. com. 2004-06, chmn, sect. on med. history 2005—06), Soc. for Scholarly Pub. (dir. 1988-92), Phi Beta Kappa, Sigma Xi, Alpha Omega Alpha, Zeta Phi. Democrat. Home and Office: 1124 Morris Ave Bryn Mawr PA 19010-1712

HUTSON, THOMAS E., oncologist, director; b. Warren, Ohio, Sept. 26, 1970; PharmD, Ohio Northern U., 1993; DO, Ohio U., 1997. Dir., Genito-urinary Oncology Program Tex. Oncology Baylor Sammons Cancer Ctr., 2003—. Co-chair, genito-urinary oncology rsch. US Oncology, 2003. Fellow: ACP. Home: 3212 Coventry Ln Plano TX 75093 Home Fax: 214-370-1925. Personal E-mail: thomas.hutson@usoncology.com.

HUTT, CAROLYN MARIE, practice administrator; b. Lincoln, Nebr., Aug. 25, 1963; Grad., Omaha Coll. Health Careers, 1995. Reimbursement coord. Oncology Hematology West PC, 2001—07; faculty Iowa Western CC, 2001—07; assoc. dir. reimbursement US Oncology, 2006—10; practice adminstr. Tex. Oncology, 2010. Adj. faculty IWCC, 1999—2007; cons. Coding Inst., 2002—05, Amgen, 2003—06, Ortho Biotech, 2004—06, Novartis, 2005—06. Recipient 21st Century award, Am. Biog. Inst.; named Woman of Yr. Mem.: AAMA, AHIMA, AAPC. Avocations: running, reading, singing. Home: 1218 Crawford Court Apt 106 Granbury TX 76048 Home Phone: 817-559-9446. Personal E-mail: carolyn.hutt@usoncology.com, carolyn.hutt@gmail.com.

HUTT, PETER BARTON, lawyer; b. Buffalo, Nov. 16, 1934; s. Lester Ralph and Louise Rich (Fraser) H.; children: Katherine Zurn, Peter Barton, Sarah Henderson, Everett Fraser. BA magma cum laude, Yale U., 1956; LLB, Harvard U., 1959; LLM, NYU, 1960. Bar: N.Y. 1959, D.C. 1961, U.S. Supreme Ct. 1967. Assoc. Covington & Burling, Washington, 1960-68, ptnr., 1968—71, 1975—2004, sr. counsel, 2004—; chief counsel FDA, Washington, 1971-75. Bd. dir. Living Proof, Cambridge, Mass., 2007—, CV Therapeutics Inc., Palo Alto, Calif., 2000—08, Favrille, Inc., San Diego, 2003—08, Momenta, Inc., Cambridge, Mass., 2001—, Q Therapeutics, Salt Lake City, 2002—, Ista Pharms., Inc., Irvine, Calif., 2002—, Pervasis Therapeutics, Inc., Boston, 2004—, Introgen Therapeutics, Inc., Houston, 2004—08, Xoma, Inc., Berkeley, Calif., 2005—, Calif. HealthCare Inst., San Diego, 1996—, Life Line Screening, Cleve., 2006—, Concert Pharms., Inc., Lexington, Mass., 2006—, Endotis Pharma, Romainville, France, 2008—, Bind Bioscis. Inc., Cambridge, 2008—, Seventh Sense Inc., Cambridge, Mass., 2008—, Celera Corp., Alameda, Calif., 2008—11, Nano Med. Sys., Austin, Tex., 2008—, Keck Grad. Inst. Applied Life Sci., Claremont, Calif., 2007—, Aeras Global TB Vaccine Found., Rockville, Md., 2006—, DBV Techs., Paris, 2009—, Selecta Bioscis., Inc., Watertown, Mass., 2010—; adv. com. to dir. NIH, 1976—81; com. on rsch. tng. NAS, 1976—80; counsel to Alcoholic Beverage Med. Rsch. Found., 1984—85, chmn. bd. dir., 1986—92; mem. Nat. Com. to Rev. Current Proc. for Approval of New Drugs for Cancer and AIDS, Nat. Cancer Inst., 1988—90; mem. nat. bd. Scripps Clinic and Rsch. Found., La Jolla, 1977—85, mem. adv. bd., 1990—95; mem. internat. bd. Scripps Instns. of Medicine and Sci., 1995—2002, Ctr. for Study Drug Devel., Tufts U. Ctr., 1976—99, Ctr. for Advanced Studies, U.Va., 1982—2002, Inst. for Health Policy Analysis, 1982—, Am. Coun. Sci. and Health, 2006—, Am. Pharm. Inst., Washington, 1988—92; com. on food laws and regulations Inst. Food Tech.; adv. com. Progress and Freedom Found., 1994—97; adv. bd. Frazier Healthcare Investments, Seattle, 1993—99, Sprout Group, NY and Menlo Park, 1993—, Polaris Venture Ptnrs., Waltham, 1995—, Kearny Venture Partners, San Francisco, 2006 , Vanguard Medica Ltd., Guildford, England, 1993—99, Columbia U. Sch. Pub. Health, 1997—2004, Sherbrook Capital Health & Wellness Fund, Lexington, Mass., 1999—, Burrill Neutraceuticals, San Francisco, 2000—, New Leaf Venture Ptnrs., NY, Menlo Park, Calif., 2005—, Sirtris Phrams., Inc., Cambridge, Mass., 2006—09, Magen BioScis., Inc., Cambridge, 2006—09, Aretais, Inc., 2008—, Gelesis Inc., 2008—, Yale Sch. Pub. Health, New Haven, 2011—; panel mem. US Congl. Office Tech. Assessment; lectr. on food and drug law Harvard U., 1994—, Stanford U., 1998; adv. com. to dir. NIH, 1978—81; panel on adminstrv. restructuring NIH, Nat. Acad. Pub. Adminstrn., 2004—06; mem. working group AIDS divsn. Nat. Inst. Allergy and Infectious Diseases, 2005—06; mem. sci. bd. subcom. on state of FDA sci. FDA, 2006—07. Author: (with Patricia Wald) Dealing with Drug Abuse, 1972, (with Richard Merrill, Lewis Grossman) Food and Drug Law, 2007, (with Bruce Kuhlik) Understanding Export Law, 1998; editor-in-chief U.S. Food Labeling Law, 1991—; contbg. editor: Legal Times of Washington, 1978-86; mem. editl. bd. various jours.; editor: Food and Drug Law. An Electronic Book of Harvard Law School Student Papers, 1994-. Bd. dirs. Sidwell Friends Sch., Washington, 1976-84; bd. dirs. Legal Action Ctr., N.Y.C., 1976 2003, vice-chmn., 1984-98; bd. dirs. Found. for Biomed. Rsch., 1976-, vice chmn., 1989—; trustee Washington Lawyers Com. for Civil Rights and Urban Affairs, 1976—, Food and Drug Law Inst., 2001-05, bd. dirs. Soc. Risk Analysis, 1985-88, 89-92, counsel, 1992—; mem. vis. com. Harvard Sch. Pub. Health, 1980-86, Columbia Sch. Pub. Health, 97-84. Recipient award of merit FDA, 1972, 75, Disting. Svc. award HEW, 1974, Underwood-Prescott award MIT, 1977, Disting. Alumni award FDA, 2005, Lifetime Achievement award Found. Biomed. Rsch., 2005; named Leading Food and Drug Lawyer Legal Times, 2005. Fellow: Soc. Risk Analysis; mem.: Inst. Medicine of NAS (Devel. of Drugs and Vaccines Against AIDS roundtable 1988—94, bd. on health care svcs. 1998—2002). Episcopalian. Home: 124 S Fairfax St Alexandria VA 22314 Office: Covington & Burling 1201 Pennsylvania Ave NW Washington DC 20004-2401 Office Phone: 202-662-5522. Business E-Mail: phutt@cov.com.

HUTTER, ADOLPH MATTHEW, JR., cardiologist, educator; b. Fond du Lac, Wis., Feb. 22, 1937; s. Adolph Matthew and Janet (Kay) H.; m. Sylvia H. Murray, June 18, 1960; children: Janice Marie, Adolph Joseph, Elizabeth Kay, Matthew Murray, Jonathan James. BS summa cum laude, Georgetown U., 1959; MD, U. Wis., 1963. Diplomate Am. Bd. Internal Medicine, Am. Bd. Cardiovascular Diseases; lic. physician, Mass. Med. intern Strong Meml. Hosp., Rochester, N.Y., 1963-64; clin. assoc. Nat. Cancer Inst., Bethesda, Md., 1964-66; asst. resident Strong Meml. Hosp., 1966-67, assoc. resident, 1967-68; fellow in medicine (oncology) Georgetown U. Sch. Medicine, Washington, 1965-66; clin. and rsch. fellow in cardiology Mass. Gen. Hosp., Boston, 1968-70; instr. medicine Harvard U. Med. Sch., Boston, 1970-72, asst. prof., 1972-76, assoc. prof., 1976-99, prof., 1999—. Vis. prof. 100 univs. and med. ctrs., 1979-96; asst. in medicine Mass. Gen. Hosp., 1970-72, asst. physician, 1972-76, assoc. physician, 1976-84, physician, 1984—, assoc. dir. CCU, 1970-81, dir., 1981-86, chmn. med. intensive care coord. com., 1986-94; dir., Cardiac Performance Program, 2009-, cardiologist Boston Bruins Hockey Team, 1972—, New Eng. Patriots Football Team, 1982—, New Eng. Revolution Soccer Team, 2007-. Contbr. over 150 articles to med. jours. Trustee The Roxbury Latin Sch., 1988-90, mem. soc. of fellows, 1995—. Recipient Howard H. Blakeslee award, Am. Heart Assn., 1974; fellow, Roxbury Latin Sch. Fellow: AAAS, ACP, European Soc. Cardiology, Am. Coll. Cardiology (mem. program com. on sci. sessions 1975—76, mem. credentials com. 1976—83, asst. sec. 1981—82, chmn. 1981—83, mem. long-range planning com. 1981—83, trustee 1981—85, mem. ACCEL com. 1982—90, sec. 1984—85, chmn. 1987—90, mem. ACCEL edn. bd. 1987—90, trustee 1987—95, mem. strategic planning com. 1988—92, v.p. 1990—91, mem. exec. com. 1990—94, pres. 1992—93, past pres. 1993—94, mem. chmn. award com. 1994—96, mem. ACCEL edn. bd. 1993—, chmn. chpt. rels. com. 1993—99, mem. tech. and practice exec. com. 1994—, moderator, convs. expert 2004—10, editl. bd. 2004—, govt. rehab. com. mem. 1984—90, chmn. 1988—90), CLin Coun. Am. Heart Assn. (mem. com. on postgrad. edn. 1972—75, mem. com. on sci. sessions program 1973—75, mem. sci. sessions com. 1979—81, vice chmn. com. on cardiovasc. disease of elderly 1987—90); mem.: Mass. Med. Soc., Am. Clin. and Climatol. Assn., U. Wis. Med. Alumni Assn., Alpha Omega Alpha. Roman Catholic. Avocations: golf, gardening. Business E-Mail: ahutter@partners.org. *

HUTTON, JOHN EVANS, JR., surgeon, educator, retired military officer; b. NYC, Sept. 9, 1931; s. John Evans and Antoinette (Abbott) H.; m. Barbara Seward Joyce, Apr. 15, 1961; children: John III, Wendy, James, Elizabeth. BA, Wesleyan U., 1953; MD, George Washington U., 1963. Diplomate: Am. Bd. Surgery, Am. Bd. Med. Examiners. Commd. 2d lt. USMC, 1953, advanced through grades to capt., 1962; discharged USMCR; commd. capt. U.S. Army, 1963, advanced through grades to brig. gen., 1989, intern, resident in gen. surgery Walter Reed Army Med. Ctr. Washington, 1963-68, fellow vascular surgery, 1969-70, asst. chief vascular surgery, 1970-71, mem. staff gen. surgery svcs., 1969-71, chief dept. surgery, 1981-84, White House physician, 1984-86, physician to the Pres. Ronald Reagan, 1987—88, chief surgeon 91st Evacuation Hosp., Republic of Vietnam, 1968—69, chief vascular surgery, asst. chief gen. surgery Letterman Army Med. Ctr., 1971-74, chief gen. and vascular surgery, program dir., gen. surgery residency Letterman Army Med. Ctr. San Francisco, 1975-81; comdr. 47th Field Hosp., Honduras, 1984; commanding gen. Madigan Army Med. Ctr. U.S. Army, Tacoma, 1989-92; ret., 1992; prof. surgery, chief div. gen. surgery, dept. surg. Uniformed Svcs. U. Sch. Medicine, Bethesda, Md., 1992—, mem. faculty senate, 1996—99, mem. students promotion com., 1993-96, 2002—05, mem. instl. rev. bd., 1993-96, mem. com. appointments, promotion and tenure, 1998-99, pres. elect faculty senate, 1997; pres. faculty senate Uniformed Svcs. U. Health Scis., Bethesda, 1998. Assoc. clin. prof. surgery U. Calif., San Francisco, 1978-81, mem. dean's adv. group Uniformed Svc. U. Health Sci., 1998-99; assoc. prof. surgery, vice chmn. dept. surgery Uniformed Svcs. U. Health Scis., Bethesda, 1981-84, prof. surgery, 1985—; clin. prof. surgery Tulane U. Sch. Medicine, 1988—, George Washington Sch. Medicine, Washington, 1985—. Contbr. articles, photographs to profl. publs., chpts. to books. Mem. men and boys choir Grace Cathedral, San Francisco, 1971-75. Decorated D.S.M., Bronze Star, Meritorious Svcs. medal with oak leaf cluster, Army Commendation Medal, Navy Commendation Medal, Joint Svc. Commendation Medal, Vietnam Svc. medal with four bronze svc. stars, Nat. DSM with two bronze svc. stars, Naval Occupation medal, WWII, Vietnam Honor medal 1st class, Vietnam Cross of Gallantry; recipient Barron Dominique Larrey award for excellence in surgery, Disting. Svc. medal, Uniformed Svcs. U. Sch. Medicine, 2000. Fellow: ACS; mem.: Internat. Soc. Vascular Surgery, Soc. Vascular Surgery, Soc. Med. Cons. Armed Forces (councilor 1988—89, v.p. 2000, pres. 2001), Acad. Medicine Washington D.C., Chesapeake Vascular Soc., Soc. Mil. Vascular Surgery, Am. Assn. Surgery of Trauma, Soc. Clin. Vascular Surgery, Bay Surg. Soc. (hon.), U.S. Naval Acad. Sailing Squadron, Severn Sailing Assn., St. Francis Yacht Club (membership com. 1978—81). Republican. Episcopalian. Avocations: music, photography, sailing, sports. Home: 1707 Priscilla Dr Silver Spring MD 20904 1610 Office: Uniformed Svcs U Health Scis Dept Surgery 4301 Jones Bridge Rd Bethesda MD 20814-4712 Office Phone: 301-295-9822.

HUURMAN, WALTER WILLIAM, pediatric orthopaedic surgeon, educator; b. Rochester, NY, Mar. 16, 1936; s. Walter U. and Anna Mae (Lennon) H., m. Lindsay Ann McGuiness, Dec. 16, 1967; children: Sean Patrick, Anne Lindsay. BS, U. Notre Dame, 1958; MD, Northwestern U., 1962. Diplomate Am. Bd. Orthop. Surgery. Intern Cook County Hosp., Chgo., 1962—63; flight surgeon USS Hornet, San Diego and Vietnam, 1964—66, NAS Miramar, San Diego, 1966—68; resident in orthop. surgery Naval Regional Med. Ctr., Oakland, Calif., 1968 71; dir. pediat. orthop. USN, Oakland, 1973—77; prof. pediat. and orthop. U. Nebr., Omaha, 1977—, prof. emeritus, 2006—; dir. pediat. orthop. U. Nebr./Children's Meml. Hosp., Omaha, 1977. Bd. dirs. Nat. Alumni, Northwestern U. Mem. editl. bd. Jour. Pediat. Orthop., 1981-83, Jour. Bone and Joint Surgery, 1983-87, Pediat. in Rev., 1995-2000; reviewer Clin. Orthop. and Related Rsch., 1985—, Jour. Am. Acad. Orthop. Surgeons, 1998—; contbr. articles to sci. and profl. jours Pres., chmn. bd. dirs. Nebr. Arthritis Found., 1984. Capt. USN, 1963-77; res., 1980-95, ret. Fellow ACS, Am. Acad. Orthop. Surgery, Am. Acad. Pediat. (chmn. orthop. sect. 1986-89, mem. exec. com. sect. on sports medicine, 1992-2000); mem. AMA, Am. Orthop. Assn., Omaha Midwest Clin. Soc. (pres. 1994), Nebr. Orthop. Soc. (pres. 2000-07), Pediat. Orthop. Soc. N.Am.(bd. dirs. 1994-2000), Acad. Orthop. Soc., Northwestern U. Feinberg Sch. Medicine Alumni Assn. (pres. 2005-07), Soc. Med. Cons. to Armed Forces. Roman Catholic. Office: U Nebr Med Ctr 600 S 42d St Omaha NE 68198-1002 Personal E-mail: whuurman@ix.netcom.com.

HUVOS, ANDREW, internist, cardiologist, educator; b. Budapest, Hungary, Apr. 23, 1930; came to U.S., 1950; s. Julian Gyula and Magdolna (Matyas) H.; m. Monique Chatriot, June 8, 1959; children: Christine, Anne, Philip. Student, Free U. Brussels, 1948-50, Harvard U., 1951; MD, Boston U., 1955. Diplomate Am. Bd. Internal Medicine, Am. Bd. Cardiovasc. Disease. Resident in medicine Yale-New Haven Med. Ctr., 1955-59; fellow in cardiology Mass. Gen. Hosp., Boston, 1961-63; physician-in-charge cardiac catheterization lab. Univ. Hosp., Boston, 1963-70; chief cardiology Faulkner Hosp., Boston, 1970-74, chief medicine, 1974-95, hon. staff, 2005—; lectr. medicine Harvard Med. Sch., Boston, 1974-86; lectr. medicine and physiology Boston U. Sch. Medicine, 1976—95; prof. medicine Tufts U. Sch. Medicine, Boston, 1985-97, prof. emeritus, 1997—. Dir. Tufts Assoc. Health Plan, 1979-81. Contbr. articles to med. jours., chpts. to books. Chmn. bd. trustees Ecole Bilingue, Inc., Arlington, Mass., 1970-74; trustee Boston Med. Libr., 1981-85. Capt. M.C., U.S. Army, 1959-61. Recipient Excellence in Teaching award Boston U. Sch. Medicine, 1974; USPHS grantee, 1977-83. Fellow: ACP, Mass. Med. Soc. (del., mem. com. on med. edn. 1981—95), Am. Heart Assn., Am. Coll. Chest Physicians (pres. New Eng. States chpt. 1981—83), Am. Coll. Cardiology; mem.: Roxbury Clin. Record Club, Dorchester Med. Club, Alpha Omega Alpha. Presbyterian. Avocations: opera, classical music.

HUWEZ, FARHAD UMER, cardiologist, consultant, educator; b. Koysinjaq, Arbil, Iraq, Jan. 1, 1952; s. Umer Huwez and Najiya Haini; m. Abeer Al-Hassani, May 14, 1999; children: Tara, Mustafa. BS in Medicine and Surgery, U. Mosul, Iraq, 1975; PhD in Cardiovasc. Medicine, U. Glasgow, Scotland, 1990. Physician, hon. lectr. Sch. Medicine, Arbil, Iraq, 1983—85; rsch. fellow in cardiology St. Bartholomew's Hosp., London, 1985—86, Glasgow U., Scotland, 1986—90; staff cardiologist Scottish Cardiac Transplant Ctr., Glasgow, Scotland, 1994—95; sr. med. registrar Chelsea and Westminster Hosps., London, 1998—99; cons. physician Basildon and Thurrock NHS Trust, Essex, England, 1999—; prof. internal medicine Sint Eustatius Sch. Medicine, 2007—. Hon. clin. tchr. U. Coll. London U.; past examiner Gen. Med. Coun. UK. Author: Case Histories and Data Interpretations for Medical Examinations, 2003, Stroke Care: A Practical Manual, 2005, rev. edit., 2007. Fellow: Royal Coll. Physicians London (author part 2 revision for new format of the written sect. 2007, examiner U. Coll. London), Royal Coll. Physicians Glasgow; mem.: Royal Coll. Physicians Ireland. Achievements include development of point scoring system for electrocardiographic left ventricular hypertrophy; research in echocardiographic left ventricular hypertrophy based on LV Geometry; left ventricular strain; normal echocardiographic measurements in adults and children; original studies on medicinal effects of mastic gum; PTO studies on mastic gum. Office: Basildon and Thurrock NHS Trust Nethermayne Essex Basildon SS16 5NL England Office Fax: 01268-598897; Home Fax: 01708-224727. Personal E-mail: farhad.huwez@hotmail.com. Business E-Mail: farhad.huwez@btuh.nhs.uk.

HUXLEY, SIR ANDREW (FIELDING), physiologist, educator; b. London, Eng., Nov. 22, 1917; s. Leonard and Rosalind (Bruce) H.; m. Jocelyn Richenda Gammell Pease, July 5, 1947 (dec. Mar. 2003); children: Janet Rachel, Stewart Leonard, Camilla Rosalind, Eleanor Bruce, Henrietta Catherine, Clare Marjory Pease. BA, Cambridge U., Eng., 1938, MA, 1941, ScD (hon.), 1978; MD (hon.), U. Saar, 1964, Marseille U., 1979, Humboldt U., Berlin, 1985, Ulm U., 1993, Charles U., Prague, 1998; DSc (hon.), U. Sheffield, Eng., 1964, U. Leicester, 1967, London U., 1973, U. St. Andrews, Scotland, 1974, U. Aston, Birmingham, Eng., 1977, U. Western Australia, 1982, Oxford U., 1983, U. Pa., 1984, Harvard U., 1984, U. Keele, 1985, East Anglia U., 1985, U. Md., 1987, Brunel U., 1988, U. Hyderabad, 1991, Glasgow U., 1993, Witwatersrand U., 1998; LLD (hon.), U. Birmingham, 1979, Dundee U., 1984; Dr (hon.), York U., 1981, Toyama Med. and Pharm. U., 1995; DHL (hon.), NYU, 1982. Mem. rsch. staff Anti-Aircraft Command, 1940-42, Admiralty, 1942-45; fellow Trinity Coll., Cambridge, 1941-60, 90—, hon. fellow, 1967-90, master, 1984-90, dir. studies, 1952-60, Tarner lectr., 1988. Demonstrator dept. physiology Cambridge U., 1946—50, asst. dir. rsch. dept. physiology, 1951—59, reader exptl. biophysics, 1959—60; Jodrell prof. physiology U. Coll. London, 1960—69, Royal Soc. rsch. prof., 1969—83; emeritus prof. London U., 1983—, hon. fellow, 1980—; fellow Royal Soc. London, 1955—, Croonian lectr., 1967, mem. coun., 1960—62, 1977—79, pres., 1980—85; Herter lectr. Johns Hopkins U., 1959; Jesup lectr. Columbia U., 1964; Forbes lectr., 66; Florey lectr., 82; Blackett Meml. lectr., 84; Fullerian prof. Royal Inst., London, 1967—73; Hans Hecht lectr., Chgo., 1975; Sherrington lectr Liverpool U., 1976—77; Centenary Colloquium lectr. Berlin Inst. Physiology, 1977; Cecil H. and Ida Green vis. prof. U. B.C., 1980; 6th ann. Darwin lectr., 82; Romanes lectr. Oxford U., 1983; Tarner lectrs. Trinity Coll., Cambridge, 1988; Maulana Abul Kalam Azad Meml. lectr., New Delhi, 91; C.G. Bernhard lectr. Stockholm, 1993; Davson lectr. Am. Physiol. Soc., 1998; Wartenweiler lectr. Internat. Soc. Biomechanics, Calgary, 1999. Author: Reflections on Muscle, 1980; editor Jour. Physiology, 1950-57, chmn. bd. Publs. on analysis of nerve conduction (with Hodgkin), physiology of striated muscle, devel. of interference microscope and ultramicrotome. Trustee Brit. Mus. (Natural History), 1981-90, Sci. Mus., 1984-88; mem. Agrl. Rsch. Coun., 1977-80, Nature Conservancy Coun., 1985-88, Animal Procedures Com., 1987-95. Decorated knight bachelor, Order of Merit, Grand Cordon of Sacred Treasure Japan; recipient (with A.L. Hodgkin and J.C. Eccles), Nobel Prize for physiology or medicine, 1963, Swammerdam medal, Soc. for Advancement of Natural Scis., Medicine and Surgery, Amsterdam, 1997, Copley medal, Royal Soc., 1973; fellow, Imperial Coll. Sci., Tech. and Medicine, 1980, Queen Mary and Westfield Coll., 1987, Royal Holloway and Bedford New Coll., 1994. Fellow Royal Acad. Engring. (hon.), Inst. Biology (hon.), Royal Soc. Can. (hon.), Royal Soc. Edinburgh (hon.), Royal Coll. Physicians (hon.), Acad. Med. Sci. (hon.), Indian Nat. Sci. Acad. (fgn.); mem. Physiol. Soc. (hon., rev. lectr. on muscular contraction 1973), Internat. Union Physiol. Scis. (pres. 1986-93), Brit. Biophys. Soc., Found. for Sci. and Tech., Royal Acad. Scis., Letters and Fine Arts Belgium (assoc.), Muscular Dystrophy Campaign (chmn. med. research com. 1974-81, v.p., 1981—), Royal Instn. Gt. Britain (hon.), Anat. Soc. Gt. Britain and Ireland (hon.), Am. Acad. Arts and Scis. (hon.), Am. Philos. Soc. (Penrose lectr. 1986), Brit. Assn. Advancement Sci. (pres. 1976-77), Leopoldina Acad. (hon.), NAS (U.S.) (fgn. assoc.), Royal Acad. Medicine Belgium (assoc.), Dutch Soc. Scis. (fgn.), Royal Danish Acad. Sci. (hon.), Am. Soc. Zoologists (hon.), Royal Irish Acad. (hon.), Japan Acad. (hon.). Home and Office: Dr Grantchester Manor Field 1 Vicarage Drive CB3 9NG Cambridge England *

HUXLEY, HUGH ESMOR, molecular biologist, educator; b. Birkenhead, Eng., Feb. 25, 1924; s. Thomas Hugh and Olwen (Roberst) H.; m. Frances Fripp; 1 child, 3 stepchildren. BA, Cambridge U., Eng., 1948, MA, 1950, PhD, 1952, ScD, 1964; DSc (hon.), Harvard U., 1969, U. Chgo., 1974, U. Pa., 1975, U. Leicester, 1989. Rsch. student molecular biology unit Med. Rsch. Coun., Cavendish Lab., Cambridge, 1948-52, sci. staff, 1954-55; external staff dept. biophysics Med. Rsch. Coun., U. Coll., London, 1956-61, Med. Rsch. Coun. Lab. Molecular Biology, London, 1962-87, joint head structural studies divsn., 1974—87, dep. dir., 1977-87; prof. biology rosenteil Basic Med. Scis. Rsch. Ctr., Brandeis U., Waltham, Mass., 1987-97, dir., 1988-94, prof. emeritus, 1997—. Editor: Progress in Biophysics and Molecular Biology, 1960-66; mem. editl. bd. Jour. Cell Biology, 1959-63, Jour. Molecular Biology, 1962-70, 79-86, 90-93, Jour. Cell Sci., 1966-70; contbr. articles to profl. jours. Officer RAF, 1943-47. Decorated Mem. Order Brit. Empire; recipient Feldberg prize, 1963, Hardy prize, 1965, Louisa Gross Hurwitz prize, 1971, Internat. Feltrinelli prize, 1974, Gairdner award, 1975, Baly medal Royal Coll. Physicians, 1975, E.B. Wilson medal Am. Soc. Cell Biology, 1983, Albert Einstein award World Cultural Coun., 1987, Franklin medal, 1990, Disting. Scientist award Electron Microscopy Soc. Am., 1991; Commonwealth Fund fellow Mass. Inst. Tech., 1952-54, Christ's Coll. fellow Cambridge U., 1954-56, hon. fellow, 1981, King's Coll. fellow, 1961-67, Churchill Coll. fellow, 1967-87. Fellow Royal Soc. (Royal medal 1977, Copley medal 1997), Am. Biophysical Soc.; mem. NAS (hon. fgn. assoc.), Physiol. Soc., Brit. Biophys. Soc., European Molecular Biology Orgn., Am. Acad. Arts and Scis. (hon. fgn.), Danish Acad. Scis., Leopoldina Acad. Home: 349 Nashawtuc Rd Concord MA 01742-1616 Business E-Mail: huxley@brandeis.edu.

HUY, TRAN QUANG, nurse; b. Namdinh, Oct. 2, 1960; BSN, Hanoi Med. U., 1998; PhD, Karolinska Inst., 2007. Expert nursing Ministry Health, 2010—. Adj. prof. Nursing Sch. Queensland U. Tech., 2009—. Named Outstanding Health Worker, Nation Pres. Mem.: Vietnam Nurses Assn. Avocation: gardening. Office: Giangvo N Hanoi 04 Vietnam Office Fax: 84462732101. E-mail: huyub@yahoo.com.

HWANG, CHANG HO, physician; b. Republic Of Korea; MD, Korean Med. Assn., 1997. Cert. medical specialist and physiatrist Korean Acad. Rehab. Medicine, 2005, med. lic. Ednl. Commn. Fgn. Med. Graduates, 1999. Chief mgr. Puyo Pub. Health Ctr., 1997—2000; internship, asan med. ctr. U. Ulsan Coll. Medicine, Seoul, Republic of Korea, 2000—01, resident, dept. rehab. medicine, Asan Med. Ctr., 2001—05, med. tchg. staff dept. rehab. medicine Ulsan, 2005—. Consulting mem. com. Korea Employment Promotion Agy. Disabled, Seoul, 2007—; cons. dr. Nat. Pension Svc., Seoul, 2007—. Contbr. articles to profl. jours. Voluntary svc. dr., Ulsan, 2005—08. Soldier Korean Mil. Mem.: Korean Dysphagia Soc., World Fedn. Neurorehab., Korean Soc. Pediat. Rehab. & Devel. Medicine, Korean Soc. Sport Medicine, Korean Soc. Neurorehabilitation, Korean Med. Assn., Korean Assn. Electrodiagnostic Medicine, Korean Acad. Rehab. Medicine. Office: Ulsan Univ Hosp 290-3 Jeonha-Dong Dong-Gu 682-714 Ulsan Republic of Korea Office Fax: 82-052-250-7211. Business E-Mail: chhwang1220ciba@yahoo.co.kr.

HWANG, CHUN, cardiologist; b. South Korea, June 10, 1955; Grad., U. Brasilia, Brazil, 1976—82, U. Hosp., Brasilia, 1983—84. Cert. Am. Bd. Internal Medicine, subspecialty cardiovasc. disease, clinical cardiac electrophysiology. Intern straight medicine King-Drew LA County Med. Ctr., 1987—88, resident jr. asst., 1988—89, resident sr. asst., 1989—90; fellow King-Drew/UCLA Hypertension Rsch. Ctr., LA, 1985—87; fellow cardiology & electrophysiology Cedars-Sinai Med. Ctr./UCLA, LA, 1990—93; cardiologist Ctrl. Utah Clinic, Provo; asst. prof. medicine UCLA. Mem.: Utah Med. Assn., Am. Coll. Cardiology, Electrophysiology Soc., North Am. Soc. Pacing and Electrophysiology, Am. Heart Assn. Office: Central Utah Clinic Heart Ctr 1055 N 500 W Ste 100 Provo UT 84604 Office Phone: 801-373-4366. Office Fax: 801-429-8191.

HWANG, DAE YONG, oncologist, surgeon; b. Seoul, Republic Of Korea, Jan. 18, 1960; s. Sang Jin Hwang and Choon Sam Kim; m. Hyun Jae Chang; 1 child, Jin Young. MD, Seoul Nat. U., 1984, MS in Medicine, 1994, PhD, 1996. Cert. physician Ministry Health & Welfare, 1984, surgeon 1992. Intern Seoul Nat. U., 1987—88; clin. instr.-gi surgery Seoul Assn. Med. Ctr., 1992—93; staff surgeon-chief colorectal sect. Korea Cancer Ctr. Hosp., Seoul, 1993—2008, dir. pub. rels., 2007, chief clin. affairs, 2008, dir. planning, 2007—08; rsch. fellow-colorectal surgery-colorectal rsch. lab Cleve. Clinic Found., 1997—98; resident, surgery Seoul Nat. U., 1998; rsch. fellow-colon & rectal surgery Lahey Clinic, Burlington, Mass., 2002—03; assoc. prof. U. Sci. and Tech., Daejeon, Republic of Korea, 2005—08; prof., dept. surgery Konkuk U., Med. Ctr., Seoul, 2008—, chief colorectal cancer ctr., 2009—, dir. pub. rels., 2009—10, mgr. dept. surgery, 2010—. Mem., cancer rev. and evaluation com. Helath Insurancer Rev. and Assessment Svc., Seoul, Republic Of Korea, 2007—09. Author (representative traslator): (cancer textbook) Colorectal Cancer; author: (books) Secret of 1.5 meter (Colorectal cancer guide book for general polulation), (coloproctology) Textbook of Coloproctology, (chemotherapy texbook) Colorectal Cancer Chmeotherapy; contbr. articles to profl. jours. (Young Investigator award, 03). 1st lt. Korean Army, 1984—87. Recipient award, Ministry Sci. Tech., 2003; named Chief of Inst., Korea Atomic Energy Rsch. Inst., 2002. Mem.: Korean Soc. Clin. Oncology, Korean Soc. Gastrointestinal Endoscopy, Korean Cancer Soc., Korean Soc. Coloproctology (editior-in-chief 2006—, publ. 2007—10), Korean Surg. Soc. (exam.-ins. 2008—10), Korean Med. Assn., Am. Soc. Colon and Rectal Surgeons, Am. Soc. Clin. Oncology. Avocations: travel, photography. Office: Konkuk University Med Ctr Colorectal Cancer Ctr Dept Surgery 4-12 Hwayang-dong Gwangjin-gu Seoul 143-729 Republic of Korea Home Phone: 82-2-514-9461; Office Phone: 82-2-2030-5111. Office Fax: 82-2-2030-5112. Personal E-mail: hwangcrc@gmail.com. Business E-Mail: hwangcrc@kuh.ac.kr.

HWANG, DEUK-SOO, biology professor, department chairman; b. Daejeon, Republic Of Korea, Feb. 12, 1956; m. Choon-Jung Lee; children: Ju-Tae, Ju-Il. Lic. physician Chungnam Nat. U., Daejeon, 1980, cert. orthopedic surgery Korea Orthop. Assn. Soc., 1985. Chmn. Dept. Orthop. Surgery, Chungnam Nat. U. Hosp., Daejeon, 1998—, prof., 1998—. Capt. Army, 1995—98, Seoul. Recipient Academic Promote, Korea Hip Soc., 1999, Korea Soc. Fracture, 1992, Academic Gold, 1999, Academic Best award, AAC, 2010. Mem.: Korea Orthop. Assn. Soc. (Seoul) (dir. 2002—, Academic Promote 2003, 2010). Office: Chungnam Nat Univ Hosp 640 Daesa-dong Jung-ku Daejeon 301-721 Republic of Korea Office Phone: 82-42-280-7345. Office Fax: 82-42-252-7098. Business E-Mail: dshwang@cnu.ac.kr.

HWANG, HYEON-SHIK, orthodontist, educator, dean; b. Bonghwa, Republic of Korea, July 13, 1959; s. Eui-Sun Hwang and Ki-Nam Kim; m. Jung-Un Park, May 23, 1987; children: Ji-Sup, Joon-Sup. DDS, Yonsei U., Seoul, Republic of Korea, 1983, MSD, 1989, PhD, 1992. Cert. Dentist 1983. Instr. Yonsei U., 1990; prof. orthodontics Chonnam Nat. U., Gwangju, Republic of Korea, 1990—; chmn., dept. orthodontics Chonnam U. Hosp., Gwangju, Republic of Korea, 1994—; dir. Dental Sci. Rsch. Inst., Gwangju, Republic of Korea, 2000—; dean Coll. Dentistry Chonnam Nat. U., Gwangju, Republic of Korea, 2001—. Dir. Korean Adult Orthodontic Rsch. Inst., Seoul, 1993—, Korean Adult Occlusion Study Ctr., Seoul, 1996—; mem. coun. Chonnam U. Hosp., 2001—; vis. prof. U. Pa., Phila., 1993—94, U. Tenn., Memphis, 1995. Author: Adult Orthodontics, 1995, Lingual Orthodontics, 2000; editor: Clinical Orthodontics Year Book 99, 1999, Clinical Orthodontics Year Book 2001, 2001; contbr. chapters to books. Fellow: World Fedn. Orthodontists; mem.: Korean Assn. Orthodontists (mem. coun. 1996, Young Scientist Rsch. award 1996, Outstanding Rsch. award 2000, Outstanding Table Clinic award 2001), Internat. Assn. Dental Rsch., European Orthodontic Soc. (assoc.), Japan Orthodontic Soc., Am. Assn. Orthodontists. Home: 203-1002 Hyundai Apt Yongbong-Dong Pukgu Gwangju 500-070 Republic of Korea Office: Chonnam Univ Hosp Dept Orthodontics Yongbong-Ro 77 Buk-Gu 500-757 Gwangju Republic of Korea Office Fax: 82 62 530-0393. Business E-Mail: hhwang@chonnam.ac.kr.

HWANG, JEE-IN, nursing educator; b. Busan, Republic of Korea, Nov. 29, 1969; PhD, Seoul Nat. U., 2000. Prof. Kyung Hee U., 2005. Bd. dirs. Korean Quality Improvement Nurses Soc., 2002, Korean Soc. Quality Assurance Health Care, 2008. Recipient President's award, Korean Nurses Assn.; rsch. grants, Nat. Rsch. Found. Korea. Fellow: East-West Nursing Rsch. Inst. Office: Med Sci Bldg Dongdaemoon-Gu Hoegi-Dong 1 Seoul 130-701 Republic of Korea Office Phone: 82-2-961-9145. Office Fax: 82-2-961-9398. E-mail: jihwang@khv.ac.kr.

HWANG, JIN SOON, medical educator; b. Masan, Gyeongsangnam-do, Republic Of Korea, Apr. 20, 1964; m. Jung Won Ha, May 25, 1993; children: June Young, Ho Young. MD, PhD, Seoul Nat. U., 1989. Cert. in Med. diplomate Republic Of Korea, 1989. Assoc. prof. Ajou U. Sch. Medicine, Suwon, Gyeonggi-do, Republic of Korea, 2003—. Office: Ajou Univ Sch Medicine San 5 Wonchon-dong Yeongtong-gu Suwon Gyeonggi-do 443-721 Republic of Korea Office Phone: 82-31-219-5166. Office Fax: 82-31-219-5169. Business E-Mail: pedhwang@ajou.ac.kr.

HWANG, JING-MIN, physician, researcher; s. Cheng-Biao Hwang and A-Mei Shen; m. Sheau-Huey Liang, Mar. 27, 1984; children: Gwo-Yang, Cheau-Shing. MD, Nat. Def. Med. Ctr., Taipei, 1983, DMS, 1989. Cert. bd. radiation oncology Chinese Soc. Therapeutic Radiation Oncology, 1993. Dir. divsn. radiation oncology Nat. Def. Med. Ctr., Taipei, Taiwan, 2002—05; dir. dept. radiation oncology Tri-Svc. Gen. Hosp., Taipei, 2002—05, Buddhist Tzu Chi Gen. Hosp., Xindian City, Taipei County, Taiwan, 2005—; assoc. prof. divsn. radiology Tzu Chi U., Hualien County, Taiwan, 2005—. Deputy editor-in-chief Therapeutic Radiological Oncology. Rsch. Fellowship, UCSF, Taiwan, 1995. Mem.: Chinese Soc. Therapeutic Radiation Oncology (assoc.). Achievements include research in combined modality treatment of cancer. Office: Tzu Chi Gen Hosp Taipei Branch No289 Jianguo Rd Taipei County Xindian City 231 Taiwan E-mail: jm195711@ms19.hinet.net.

HWANG, JINKYUNG, medical researcher, director; b. Seoul, Nov. 20, 1965; PhD, Korea U., 2002. Rschr. ETRI, 1991—93; dir. KT, 1996—. Rapporteur ITU-T, 2008—; vice chair IEEE, 2009—. Recipient Best standardization expert 2010, TTA. Mem.: IEEE Comm. Soc. Avocation: reading. Office: 17 Woomyun-dong Seoucho-gu Seoul 137-792 Republic of Korea Business E-Mail: jkhwang@kt.com.

HWANG, JUNG HWA, medical educator; b. Gwangju, Republic of Korea, Feb. 26, 1967; B, Soonchunhyang U., 1992, D, 2003. Fellowship, thoracic and body imaging Samsung Med. Ctr. Sch. Medicine Sungkyunkwan U., Seoul, Republic of Korea, 1997—99; fellowship, thoracic radiology Asan Med. Ctr. U. Ulsan, Seoul, 1999—2000; instr., thoracic radiology Mok-Dong Hosp. Ewha Womens U., Seoul, 2000—01; asst. prof., radiology Sch. Medicine Soonchunhyang U., Seoul, 2001—05, dir., radiology dept., 2007—10, assoc. prof., radiology, 2008—; postdoc. fellowship Nat. Jewish Health, Denver, 2005—07. Mem.: Radiology Soc. N.Am., Korean Assn. Study of Lung Cancer, Korean Soc. Thoracic Radiology, Korean Radiol. Soc. Avocations: swimming, skiing. Office: 59 Daesagwan-gil Yongsan-gu Seoul 140-743 Republic of Korea Office Phone: 82-2-709-9396. Office Fax: 82-2-709-9066. Business E-Mail: jhhwang@schmc.ac.kr.

HWANG, KWANG YEON, microbiologist, educator; b. Seoul, June 27, 1966; PhD, Seoul Nat. U., 1994. Postdoc. fellow U. Alta., 1995—97; prin. scientist LG Biotech. & Crystal Genomics, 1999—2003; sr. scientist Korea Inst. Sci. and Tech., 2003—05; prof. Korea U., 2005—. Mem.: Am. Microbiology. Achievements include X-ray crystallography, structural biology and structural proteomics. Avocations: hiking, fishing, chess. Office: Coll Life Sci Anam-dong 5 Seongbuk-gu Seoul 136-791 Republic of Korea Office Fax: 82-2-923-3229. Business E-Mail: chahong@korea.ac.kr.

HWANG, KWANG-KUO, psychology educator; b. Taipei, Taiwan, Nov. 6, 1945; s. Tze-Tzeng Hwang and Chong-Yin Hong; m. Feng-Ying Yang, Sept. 18, 1974; children: James Yen-Juin, Allen Yen-Shyang. BA in Psychology, Nat. Taiwan U., 1969, MS in Psychology, 1971; PhD, U. Hawaii, 1976. Lectr. Nat. Taiwan U., Taipei, 1976—77, assoc. prof., 1977—81, prof. dept. psychology, 1981—; nat. chair prof. Ministry Edn., 1997—; invited rschr. Nat. Sci. Coun., 1977—, principle investigator, 2000—, pres.'s nat. policy adv., 2009—. Editor Indigenous Psychol. Rsch. Chinese Socs., Taipei, 1993—, Asian Jour. Social Psychology, 1997—; external reviewer Jour. Cross-Cultural Psychology; exec. editor Chinese Jour. Psychology, Taiwan, 1974—76. Exec. editor Chinese Jour. Psychology, 1974—76, consulting editor Indigenous Psychol. Rsch. Chinese Socs., 1993—, Asian Jour. Social Psychology, 1997—, external reviewer Jour. Cross-Cultural Psychology, Jour. Personality, Jour. Theory Social Behavior, Internat. Jour. Leadership in Edn., MIS Quar., Human Rels., The China Jour., Mgmt. and Orgn. Rev., Asia Pacific Jour. Mgmt.; contbr. articles to profl. jours. Recipient Gen. Rsch. award, Nat. Sci. Coun., China, 1977—87, Outstanding Rsch. award, 1985—87, 1987—89, 1992—94, Outstanding Alumni award, East West Ctr., 1999, Outstanding Rschr. award, Nat. Sci. Coun., China, 2002, Outstanding Sci. and Technol. Worker award, Ministry Adminstrn., China, 2003, Outstanding Scholar awards, 2006; fellow, East West Ctr., 1986; Found. Advancement Outstanding scholar, 2006—. Mem.: Chinese Psychol. Assn., Taiwanese Sociol. Assn., Asian Assn. Indigeneus and Cultural Psychology (pres.), Asian Assn. Social Psychology (pres. 2003—05), Mental Health Assn. Taiwan (nat. policy adv. to the pres.). Buddhist. Achievements include Indigenization Movement of Psychology and Social Sciences in Chinese Society. Avocation: swimming. Office: Nat Taiwan U 1 Roosevelt Rd Sec 4 Taipei 106 Taiwan Office Phone: 886 2 3366 3081. Office Fax: 886 2 83691590. Business E-Mail: kkhwang@ntu.edu.tw.

HWANG, SAMUEL SUK-HYUN, psychologist; b. Seoul, Republic of Korea, Nov. 22, 1971; BA in Psychology, U. Calif., Berkeley, 1994; MA in Psychology, Seoul Nat. U., 1998. Rschr. Inst. Human Behavioral Medicine, Seoul Nat. U. Hosp., 2005—. Mem.: Korean Soc. Social and Personality Psychology, Korean Academic Soc. Clin. Psychology, Korean Psychol. Assn. Avocations: travel, movies, sports. Home: Sungdong-gu Sungsoo-1-ga 2-dong 668 Seoul 133-824 Republic of Korea Personal E-mail: hwansama@hanmail.net.

HWANG, SANG-GU, medical researcher; b. Masan, Republic of Korea, Jan. 28, 1964; BS, Pusan Nat. U., 1986, PhD, 1994. Tchr. Ulsan First HS, 1990—92; instr. Pusan Nat. U., 1992—97; vis. fellow NIH, 1997—2000; rsch. assoc. prof. Gwangju Inst. Sci. and Tech., 2002—06; sr. investigator Korea Inst. Radiol. and Med. Scis., 2006—.

Dir. Lab. Radiation Tumor Biology, 2007—11. Master: Korean Soc. Radiation Biology; mem.: Korean Soc. Cell Biology, Korean Soc. Biochemical and Molecular Biology. Avocations: mountain climbing, guitar. Office: 215-4 Gongneung Nowon KIRAMS Seoul 139-706 Republic of Korea Office Phone: 82-2-970-1353. Office Fax: 82-2-970-2417. Business E-Mail: sgh63@kcch.re.kr.

HWANG, SEUNG YONG, molecular biologist, statistician, educator; b. Yeosu, Chunranam-do, Republic of Korea, Nov. 17, 1965; s. Woon Taeg Hwang and Mae Sil Jung; m. Eun-Ah Lee, Dec. 9, 1995; 1 child, Do Won. BS, Hanyang U., 1989; PhD, Monash U., Melbourne, Australia, 1995. Assoc. prof. Hanyang U., Ansan, Gyeonggi-do, Republic of Korea, 1997—; CEO GenoCheck Co. Ltd., Ansan, 2000—. Adv. Nat. Agrl. Products Quality Mgmt Svc., 2005—; adj. prof. dept. bio nanotechnology Hanyang U., Republic of Korea, 2005—. Contbr. articles to profl. jours. Recipient Young Investigator award, Asian-Pacific Orgn. Cell Biology, 1994; grantee, Korean Govt., 1997—. Mem.: Korean BioChip Soc. (editor-in-chief 2006—), Korean Soc. Bioinformatics (chmn. subcom. DNA chip 1999—2002, chmn. bd. edn. 2002—04), Korean Soc. Toxicogenomics and Toxicoproteomics (chmn. bd. edn. 2004—, Becton Dickinson Sci. award 2006), Korean Soc. Biochemical and Molecular Biology (life). Achievements include patents for diagnostic DNA chips and Lab-on-a-chips. Office: Hanyang Univ Divsn Molecular and Life Scis Sa-dong Sangrok-gu Ansan Gyeonggi 426-791 Republic of Korea Home: Gojan-dong Danwon-gu Hosugongwon Apt 116-1202 Ansan Gyeonggi 425-882 Republic of Korea Office Fax: +82-31-502-5518. Business E-Mail: syhwang@hanyang.ac.kr.

HWANG, SHIN, surgeon, educator; b. Masan, Kyeongsangnam-do, Republic of Korea, Oct. 13, 1963; s. Hae-Soo Hwang and Hyeong-Soon Kim; m. Ji-Won Kim, July 5, 1994; children: Seung-Ouk, Min-Young. MD, Coll. Medicine, Busan Nat. U., Republic of Korea, 1987; PhD, Coll. Medicine, U. Ulsan, Seoul, Republic of Korea, 1997. Cert. med. dr. Korean Med. Assn., 1988, in surgery Bd. Korean Soc. Surgery, 1996. Asst. prof. surgery Asan Med. Ctr., U. Ulsan, 1998—2003, assoc. prof. surgery, 2004—08, dir. tissue bank, 2007—, prof. surgery, 2009—. Contbr. chapters to books, more than 110 articles to profl. jours. Mem. Korean Network Organ Sharing, Seoul, 2006—08. 1st lt. Korean Army, 1988—91, Masan. Recipient Investigator award, IHPBA, 1998, ILTS, 2004—05, ATC, 2008. Office: Asan Med Ctr 388-1 Poongap-dong Songpa-gu Seoul 138-736 Republic of Korea Office Phone: 82-2-3010-3930. Office Fax: 82-2-474-9027. Personal E-mail: hskjw@chol.com. Business E-Mail: shwang@amc.seoul.kr.

HWANG, SUNG KYOO, medical educator; b. Yeongju, Kyungpook, Republic of Korea, July 13, 1953; s. Byung Soo Hwang and Bok Kyoo Kim; m. Hyun Sook Woo, July 6, 1980; children: Sun Young, Jong Won, Jong Ho. MD, Kyungpook Nat. U., Daegu, Korea, 1977; MSc in Medicine, Kyungpook U., Daegu, Korea, 1981; PhD in Med. Sci., Chunbuk U., Cheonju, Korea, 1991. Bd. cert. neurosurgery Ministry Health, 1982. Intern Kyungpook U. Hosp., Daegu, 1977—78, resident neurosurgery, 1978—82; chmn. St. Luke's Hosp., Yeonju, Kyungpook, Republic of Korea, 1985—86; instr. Kyungpook U. Med. Sch., Daegu, 1986—89, asst. prof., 1989—93, assoc. prof., 1993—98, prof., 1998—. Dir. Office of Edn. and Rsch. Kyungpook U. Hosp., Daegu, 2001—03, dir. Clin. Trial Ctr., 2005—10; vis. rschr. NYU Med. Ctr., NYC, 1989—90. Capt. Korean Mil., 1982—85. Mem.: Korean Soc. Spina Bifida, Am. Assn. Neurosurgeons (assoc.), World Soc. for Stereotactic and Functional Neurosurgery (life), Korean Soc. for Neurotraumatology (life), Korean Soc. for Pediatric Neurosurgery (life; pres. 2000—02), World Fedn. for Neurosurgery (life), Internat. Soc. for Pediatric Neurosurgery (life), Korean Neurosurgical Soc. (life), Korean Med. Assn. (life). Home: 1402 House 105 dong Lotte Castle Apt Suseong-3-ga Daegu 706-948 Republic of Korea Office: Neurosurgery Kyungpook University Hospital 50 Samdeokdong Jung-gu Daegu 700-721 Daegu Republic of Korea Office Phone: 82-10-7288-9392. Office Fax: 82-53-423-0504. Business E-Mail: shwang@knu.ac.kr.

HWANG, SUNG OH, emergency physician, educator; b. JeCheon, Republic of Korea, July 25, 1959; s. Dal Soon Hwang and Soon Young Park-Hwang; m. Hyun Sil Joo; children: Hee Won, Hee Yon. MD, Yonsei U., Seoul, Republic of Korea, 1984; PhD, Korea U., Seoul, Republic of Korea, 1995. Diplomate Korean Bd. Internal Medicine 1991, Korean Bd. Circulatory Medicine 1994, Korean Bd. Emergency Medicine 1996. Vis. prof. Med. Coll. Va., Commonwealth U., Richmond, 1995—96; prof. Wonju (Republic of Korea) Coll. Medicine, Yonsei U., 1997—. Editor-in-chief Jour. Korean Soc. Emergency Medicine, 2004—. Author: Cardiopulmonary resuscitation and ACLS, 2001. Com. chmn. Kangwon Province Fire Dept., ChoonCheon, Republic of Korea, 2000—. Capt., 1985—88, Republic of Korea Mil. Mem.: Wonju Christian Hosp., South Korea (exec. dir. fin. and planning), Korean Assn. CPR (chmn. planning and coordination 2004—, sec. gen. 2004—, chmn., bd. dir. 2007—), Asian Soc. Emergency Medicine (Hong Kong) (sci. com. 2002—, bd. mem. 2004—, v.p. 2007—, pres. 2009—), Am. Coll. Emergency Medicine, Korean Soc. Internal Medicine (life), Korean Soc. Emergency Medicine (life; peer reviewer 1999—, chmn. com. planning and coord., Seoul 2001—, chmn. CPR subcom. 2001—, editor-in-chief 2003—05, bd. dirs. 2007—, 2007—, chmn.,), Korean Circulation Soc. (life; peer reviewer 2001—). Achievements include invention of simultaneous sternothoracic cardiopulmonary resuscitation, 2000. Home: 102-505 Taejangdong Wonju 220-110 Republic of Korea Office: Yonsei U Wonju Coll Medicine Ilsandong 164 220-701 Wonju Gangwon-do Republic of Korea Home Phone: 82-33-743-1209. Office Fax: 82-33-742-3030; Home Fax: 82-33-741-3030. E-mail: shwang@yonsei.ac.kr.

HWANG, TAE HO, pharmacologist, researcher; b. Busan, Republic of Korea, Apr. 18, 1963; s. Joo Won Hwang and Kyeong Seon Lee; m. Seon Im Kang, Sept. 27, 1998; children: Hae Sook, Min Su, Isu. PhD, Pusan Nat. U., 1982—89. Cert. dentist Korean Dental Assn., 1989. Postdoctoral fellow Johns Hopkins U., Balt., 1987—89; prof. Dong-A Med. Coll., Busan, Republic of Korea, 1996—; asst. prof. Baylor Coll. Medicine, Houston, 1998—99. Achievements include patents for the virus development for tumor treatment. Home: SeoGu Dongdaeshin Dong Pusan 602-714 Republic of Korea Office: Dept Pharmacology SeoGu Dongdaeshin Dong Pusan 602-714 Republic of Korea Office Fax: 82-51-241-0778. E-mail: thhwang@daunet.donga.ac.kr.

HWU, PATRICK, oncologist; BA, Lehigh U., 1983; MD, Med. Coll. Pa., 1987. Cert. med. oncology 1993. House officer Johns Hopkins Hosp., 1987—89; fellow & clinical assoc. Nat. Inst. Health, 1989—93; chmn. dept. melanoma med. oncology U. Tex. MD Anderson Cancer Ctr., 2003—, assoc. dir. Ctr. for Cancer Immunology Rsch. Office: MD Anderson Cancer Center Dept of Melanoma Medical Oncology 1515 Holcombe Blvd #207 Houston TX 77030-4017 Office Phone: 713-563-1728. Office Fax: 713-745-1046. E-mail: phwu@mdanderson.org.

HYANEK, JOSEF, physician, medical educator; b. Velikova, Moravia, Czech Republic, July 27, 1933; s. Josef and Frantiska Hyanek; m. Milena Hyanek; children: Milena, Thomas. MD, Charles U., Prague, Czech Republic, 1957; PhD, Charles U., 1975; DSc, Czech Acad. Scis., 1984. Resident Hradiště Hosp.; specialist in clin. biochemistry Med. Faculty Hosp., Prague, 1961-68; assoc. prof. Clin. Biochemistry Inst., Prague, 1984-88, prof., 1988; head dept. clin. biochemistry Med. Sch. Charles U., Prague; head metab. lab. Inherited Disorders Faculty Hosp., Prague, 1968; head. reference control lab. clin. biochemistry; head depts. clin. biochemistry, hematology and immunology Homolka Hosp., Prague, 1991; ret., 2006; cons. in metabolic unit, 2006—09, 2011—. Cons. WHO, 1980-84; lectr. in field clin. biochemistry, med. biochemistry genetics, pediatric biochemistry, biochemical screening. Author: (textbooks) Clinical Metabolic Bases Inherited Disorders, 1975, 90, Clinical Biochemistry for Medical Students, 1990; contbr. over 225 articles to profl. publs. on clin. biochemistry, biochem. genetics, pediat. and nutrition. Capt. med. svc., Czech Mil., ret. Mem. Am. Assn. Clin. Chemistry, Soc. Study Inborn Errors, Fed. Clin. Biochemistry Soc., Internat. Soc. Athrosclerosis, Internat. Soc. Newborns Screening, European Soc. Human Genetics, Hunting Club. Achievements include research in amino acids, cholesterol and lipids in children and pregnant women. Office Phone: 420252273229. Business E-Mail: josef.hyanek@homolka.cz.

HYDE, JANET SHIBLEY, psychology professor; b. Akron, Ohio, Aug. 17, 1948; d. Grant O. and Dorothy Mae Shilbey; m. John DeLamater; children: Margaret, Luke. BA in Math., Oberlin Coll., Ohio, 1969; PhD in Psychology, U. Calif., Berkeley, 1972; DSc (hon.), Denison U., 1996. Asst. prof. psychology Bowling Green State U., Ohio, 1972—76, assoc. prof. Ohio, 1976—79, Denison U., Granville, Ohio, 1979—83, prof., 1983—86, acting provost, 1985—86; prof. psychology and women's studies U. Wis., Madison, 1986—, dir. Women's Studies Rsch. Ctr., 1986—90, assoc. vice chancellor academic affairs, 1990—92, Evjue-Bascom prof. women's studies, 1996—2001, chair dept. psychology, 1998—2001, Helen Thompson Woolley prof. psychology & women's studies, 1999—. Author: (book) Half the Human Experience: The Psychology of Women, 1976, Understanding Human Sexuality, 1979; editor: Psychology Women Quarterly, 1986—89; assoc. editor Jour. Sex Rsch., 1991—97, mem. editl. bd. Sex Roles, 1996—, Sexuality Rsch. & Sexual Policy, 2008—; contbr. articles to profl. jours. Bd. dirs. Nat. Coun. Rsch. Women, 1988—90, Found. Sci. Study of Sexuality, 2000—01. Fellow: AAAS, APA (pres. 1993—94, mem. com. women in psychology 2003—05, chair 2005, Heritage award 1996, Award for Disting. Svc. to Psychological Sci. 2008), Soc. Sci. Study of Sexuality (bd. dirs. 1991—94, pres. 1999—2000, Kinsey award 1992), American Ednl. Rsch. Assn. (Women Educators award 1988), Assn. Psychol. Sci.; mem.: Internat. Acad. Sex Rsrch., Soc. Rsch. in Adolescence, Soc. Rsch. in Child Devel. Democrat. Episcopalian. Office: U Wis Dept Psychology 1202 W Johnson St Madison WI 53706 Office Phone: 608-262-9522. Office Fax: 608-262-4029. E-mail: JSHyde@wisc.edu. *

HYDE, PAMELA SUZON, federal agency administrator; b. Thayer, Mo., Nov. 7, 1950; d. Gaston Clark Hyde and Leta Vineta (Crass) Sponsler. BA, Southwest Mo. State U., 1972; JD, U. Mich. Law Sch., 1976. Law clk. Vedder, Price, Kaufman, Kammholz, Chgo., 1975; VISTA atty. Ohio State Legal Services Assn., Columbus, 1976-77; atty. Ohio Legal Rights Svc., Columbus, 1977-78, chief mental health unit, 1978-80, dir., 1980-83, Ohio Dept. Mental Health, 1983-90, Ohio Dept. Human Services, 1990-91, Seattle Dept. Housing & Human Services, 1992—93; pres., CEO Comcare-Cmty. Partnership Behavioral Health Care, Phoenix, 1994—96; sr. cons. Tech. Assistance Collaborative, Inc., Boston, 1996—2003; sec. N.Mex. Human Services Dept., 2003—09; adminstr. Substance Abuse & Mental Health Services Adminstrn. (SAMHSA), US Dept. Health & Human Services, Rockville, Md., 2009—. Mem. editl. bd. Jour. Mental Health Policy Adminstrn., 1988—2003. Recipient Disting. Svc. to State Govt. award, Nat. Govs.' Assn., 1987, Excellence in Case Mgmt. award, Nat. Case Mgmt. Conf., Cin., 1990, Dr. Nathan Davis award for outstanding govt. svc., AMA, 2009. Mem.: Women Execs. in State Govt. (founding mem.), Nat. Assn. State Mental Health Program Directors (pres. 1989—90). Democrat. Avocations: hiking, golden retrievers, music. Office: Substance Abuse & Mental Health Services Adminstrn 1 Choke Cherry Rd Rockville MD 20857 *

HYDE, PATRICE M., dermatologist; MD, Jefferson Med. Coll., 1980. Diplomate Am. Bd. Pediatrics, Am. Bd. Dermatology. Intern Children's Hosp. of Wash., resident; intern Sinai Hosp. of Balt., Thomas Jefferson Univ. Hosp., with. Named one of Top Docs, Phila. Mag., 2010. Office: Jefferson University Hospitals Ste 740 833 Chestnut St Philadelphia PA 19107 Mailing: Nemours 1600 Rockland Rd Wilmington DE 19803-3607 Office Phone: 215-955-6680, 302-651-4200. Office Fax: 215-503-5333, 302-651-5844.

HYMAN, ABRAHAM, electrical engineer; b. Bklyn., Mar. 8, 1934; s. Rubin and Regina (Holzman) H.; m. Marianne Daniel, June 19, 1955; children: Debra Hyman Rathauser, Lori Hyman Rones, Karen Hyman Cantor. BEE, Poly. Inst. Bklyn., 1952; MS, Newark Coll. Engring., 1954. Registered profl. engr., N.Y. Chief elec. engr. Med. Equipment R&D Lab., Fort Totten, NY, 1955-64; head lab. Office Naval Rsch., Port Washington, NY, 1964-66; tech. adminstr. AEC, Upton, NY, 1966-71; supr. indsl. hygienist Dept. Labor, Westbury, NY, 1971-80, regional indsl. hygienist NYC, 1980-84; mgr. health and safety Unisys Corp., Great Neck, NY, 1984-95; safety and health cons. New Hyde Park, NY, 1995—. Adj. prof. York Coll., Queens, NY, 1974—78; cons. Poison Control Ctr., Mineola, NY, 1981—; adj. assoc. prof. Staten Island Coll., NY, 1983—95; lectr. Queensboro C.C., Queens, NY, 1994—96. Patentee in field. Bd. dirs. Am. Lung Assn., East Meadow, 1974-99. Mem. IEEE, Am. Acad. Environ. Engrs. (diplomate), NSPE, Am. Conf. Indsl. Hygienists, Sci. Rsch. Soc. Am., Sigma Xi. Avocations: photography, swimming, bicycling. Home and Office: 142 Claudy Ln New Hyde Park NY 11040-1635

HYMAN, ALBERT LEWIS, cardiologist, educator; b. New Orleans, Nov. 10, 1923; s. David and Mary (Newstadt) Hyman; m. Neil Steiner, Mar. 27, 1964; 1 child, Albert Arthur. BS, La. State U., 1943; MD, 1945; postgrad., U. Cin., U. Paris, U. London. Diplomate Am. Bd. Internal Medicine. Intern Charity Hosp., 1945-46, resident, 1947-49, sr. vis. physician, 1959-63; resident Cin. Gen. Hosp., 1946-47; instr. medicine La. State U., 1950-56, asst. prof. medicine, 1956-57; asst. prof. Tulane U., 1957-59, assoc. prof., 1959-63, assoc. prof. surgery, 1963-70, prof. rsch. surgery in cardiology, 1970—, prof. clin. medicine Med. Sch., 1983—, adj. prof. pharmacology Med. Sch., 1974—, dir. Cardiac Catheterization Lab., 1957—, Mayerson meml. lectr. in physiology, 2000; prof. medicine in cardiology La. State U. Sch. Medicine; physician in cardiology, dept. medicine Brigham and Women's Hosp. Harvard Med. Sch., Boston, 2007—; rschr., pulmonary circulation, dept. pharmacology & physiology NY Med. Coll., 2009. Vis. physician Touro Hosp., Touro Infirmary, electrocardiographer; vis. physician Hotel Dieu Hosp., Brigham & Women's Hosp.; chief cardiology Sara Mayo Hosp., electrocardiographer, Metairie Hosp., St. Tammany Hosp.; internat. sci. com. IV Internat. Symposium Pulmonary Circulation Charles U., Prague; vis. prof. SUNY, Stony Brook, 2001, U. South Ala. Med. Sch., 2001; Mayerson meml. lectr. Tulam Medivial Sch., 2001; vis. prof. medicine Harvard Med. Sch., Boston, 2006; lectr. in field; cons. in field; computting physician Mass. Gen. Hosp., 2002. Mem. editl. bd. Jour. Applied Physiology; contbr. articles to profl. jours. Recipient Rsch. award, Hadassah, 1980, Vis. Scientist award, Wellcome Found., U. Coll., London, 1991, Albert Hyman award for excellence in cardiology, Tulane U. Med. Sch., 1997, Disting. Achievement award in sci. and rsch., Orlean Parish Med. Soc., 2001, Seminal Rsch. award, NY Med. Coll., 2009; Tulane Med. Sch. Sect. on Cardiology fellow, 1997. Fellow: ACP, Am. Fedn. Clin. Rsch., Am. Coll. Cardiology, Am. Coll. Chest Physicians; mem.: AAUP, Am. Physiologic Soc., N.Y. Acad. Scis., N.Am. Soc. Pacing and Electrophysiology, Am. Physiol. Soc., New Orleans Surg. Soc. (hon.), So. Med. Soc. (Seale-Harris award 1988), So. Soc. Clin. Investigation (chmn. membership com.), Am. Soc. Pharmacology and Exptl. Therapeutics, La. Heart Assn. (v.p. 1974, Albert L. Hyman Ann. Rsch. award, Wellcome Rsch. Found. Vis. Scientist award U. Coll. London 1992, Disting. Achievement award for outstanding sci. contbns. to cardiopulmonary medicine), Am. Heart Assn. (chmn. sci. com. cardiopulmonary coun. 1981, fellow coun. circulation, fellow coun. clin. cardiology, chmn. cardiopulmonary coun., mem. editl. bd. Circulation Rsch., Jour. Applied Physiology, Am. Jour. Physiology, Heart Disease and Stroke, mem. rsch. com. bd. dirs., mem. coun. cardiopulmonary medicine, regional rep. coun. clin. cardiology, vice-chmn. rsch. com., Dickinson Richards Meml. lectr. 1986, Disting. Sci. Achievement award 1990, Dickinson Richards Meml. lectr. 1992, Disting. Achievement award 1992, Disting. Sci. Achievement award 1993, Disting. Achievement award 1993), Alpha Omega Alpha. Achievements include research in cardiopulmonary circulation. Office: 2400 Beacon St PH608 Chestnut Hill MA 02467 Business E-Mail: aahyman@tulane.edu.

HYMAN, BRUCE MALCOLM, ophthalmologist; b. NYC, May 22, 1943; s. Malcolm A. and Sylvia S. Hyman. AB, Columbia U., 1964; MD, NYU, 1968. Diplomate Am. Bd. Ophthalmology. Intern surgery Albert Einstein Coll. Medicine-Bronx Mcpl. Hosp., 1968—69; pvt. practice NYC, 1974—; resident ophthalmology Manhattan Eye, Ear and Throat Hosp., NYC, 1971—74, tchr. attending surgeon, 1974—; med. cons. US Seaplane Pilots Assn., 1975—, Health Ins. Plan Greater NY, 1977—; ophthalmologist Hotel Trades Coun., Hotel Assn, NYC, 1974—; attending ophthalmologist Roosevelt Hosp., NYC, 1979—, dir. adult outpatient ophthalmology, 1980—, 1977—, dep. chief police surgeon, 1978—; attending ophthalmologist Doctors Hosp., 1979—, Le Roy Hosp., 1979—, St. Luke's Hosp., 1980—. Outpatient ophthalmologist NY Hosp., 1975—77; clin. ophthalmologist Columbia Coll. Physicians and Surgeons, 1981—. Contbr. articles to profl. jours. With USPHS, 1969—71. Mem.: ACS, Am. Acad. Ophthalmology and Otolaryngology, NY County Med. Soc. Office: 133 E 64th St New York NY 10065-7045

HYMAN, JEFFREY, internist; MD, U. Guadalajara. Diplomate Am. Bd. Internal Medicine. Intern Maimonides Med. Ctr., Bklyn., resident, 1981—84, Staten Island Univ. Hosp., NY, assoc. med. dir. NY. Office: Staten Island University Hospital 1 Edgewater St Staten Island NY 10305-4900 Home: 8012 Third Ave Brooklyn NY 11209 Office Phone: 718-745-5600. Office Fax: 718-745-8860.

HYMAN, JOSHUA E., pediatric orthopaedic surgeon; b. NYC, Sept. 14, 1963; s. Allen I. Hyman; m. Elizabeth Corsini, Sept. 4, 1994; children: Jacob, Julia, Zoe. MD, Columbia U., 1990—90, BA, 1985. Diplomate Am. Bd. of Orthop. Surgery. Fellow in orthop. surgery U. Toronto/Hosp. for Sick Children; instr. orthop. surgery Harvard U., Boston, 1997—98; asst. to assoc. prof. orthop. surgery Columbia U., NYC, 1999—; attending surgeon N.Y. Presbyn. Hosp., NYC, 1999—; resident in orthop. surgery Harvard U., Boston; dir.; pediat. Orthop. fellowship. Dir. pediat. orthop. trauma svc. Children's Hosp. Of N.Y., NYC, 2001—; assoc. med. dir. Children of China Pediat. Found. Bd. mem. Cmty. Partnership Network, Englewood, NJ, 2001; pres. Palisades Parks Conservancy, NJ, 2007—; assoc. med. dir. CCPF, 2007—. Recipient 1st pl. rsch. award, Am. Acad. Pediat., 1999, Sci. Presentation award, European Pediat. Orthop. Soc., 2000. Fellow: Am. Acad. Cerebral Palsy and Devel. Medicine; mem.: Am. Orthop. Assn., Pediat. Orthop. Soc. N.Am., Am. Acad. Orthop. Surgeons. Office: Children's Hosp of NY 3959 Broadway 8N New York NY 10032

HYMAN, LAWRENCE ROBERT, psychiatrist; b. Amsterdam, NY, Dec. 7, 1940; s. Morris Arthur and Bertha (Berkman) H.; m. Lois Armstrong Wilson, June 27, 1978; children: Elyse Michelle, Michael Louis, Joshua William. BA, Ohio Wesleyan U., 1963; MD, Chgo. Med. Sch., 1968. Intern then resident U. Wis., Madison, 1968-72; guest worker NIH, Bethesda, Md., 1973-76; asst. prof. Johns Hopkins Sch. Medicine, Balt., 1976-78; resident George Washington U., Washington, 1978-80; asst. clin. prof. U. Md., Balt., 1981-84; pvt. practice Columbia, Md., 1981—; active staff dept. psychiatry Howard County Gen. Hosp., Columbia, Md., 1981—; CEO Orchard Hill Treatment Ctr. for Chem. Dependency, Columbia, 1987-93; pvt. practice gen. psychiatry Columbia; CEO, med. dir. Howard Behavioral Health, Inc., 2003—; med. dir. Lawrence R. Hyman MD and Assocs., 1993—, Vis. Speakers Bureau, Lilly, Forest, Wyeth & Janssen Pharm. Cos., 2003—. Cons. Family Therapy Inst., Rockville, Md., Pfizer Pharma, 2004, others; bd. dirs. Closecall Am., Inc. Contbg. editor Gould Med. Dictionary, 1979; contbr. articles to profl. jours. Adv. bd. Nat. Kidney Found., Balt., 1971. Maj. M.C., AUS, 1972-76. Recipient USPHS Rsch. Career Devel. award, 1977; NIH fellow, 1972; NIH grantee. Mem. Am. Psychiat. Assn., Md. Psychiat. Soc., Med. and Chirurgical Faculty State of Md., Howard County Med. Soc., Am. Orthopsychiat. Assn. Avocations: sailing, marathons. Home: 3681 Folly Quarter Rd Ellicott City MD 21042-1452 Office: # 201 11055 Little Patuxent Pky Columbia MD 21044 Home Phone: 410-531-2638; Office Phone: 301-997-8847. E-mail: lrhymanmd@aol.com.

HYNES, MARTIN DENNIS, III, pharmacologist, toxicologist; b. Albany, NY, Dec. 23, 1949; s. Martin Dennis Hynes, Jr. and Mary Lynch Hynes; m. Lynn Williams Miller, Apr. 17, 1982; children: Amy Guilfoil, Kathleen Owen. BA in Psychology, Providence Coll., 1972; MS in Pharmacology and Toxicology, U. RI, Kingston, 1975; PhD in Pharmacology and Toxicology, U. RI, 1978. Postdoctoral fellow, dept. physiol. chemistry and pharmacology Roche Inst. Molecular Biology, Nutley, NJ, 1977—79; sr. pharmacologist Lilly Rsch. Labs., Indpls., 1979—84, head ctrl. nervous sys. and endocrinology rsch., 1984—86, mgr. pharm. products and product mgmt., 1986—87; dir. clin. rsch. Eli Lilly Japan K.K., Kobe, Japan, 1987—90; dir. quality assurance rsch. and devel. Eli Lilly and Co., 1990—93, dir. product rsch. and devel., 2001—, sr. dir. product rsch. and devel., 2009—; adj. prof. Coll. Bus. Administrn. Butler U., Indpls., 2010—. Editor: (books) Preparing for FDA Pre-Approval Inspections, 1998, Pharmaceutical Pre-Approval Inspections: A Guide to Regulatory Succes, 2008; contbr. articles to profl. jours. Dir. Sister City, Carmel, Ind., 1993—2001. Mem.: Drug Info. Assn. (steering com. 2000—08, Outstanding Svc. award 2006). Achievements include patents in field. Home: 744 Mayfair Ln Carmel IN 46032 Office: Eli Lilly and Co Lilly Corp Ctr Indianapolis IN 46285 Office Phone: 317-276-4034. Office Fax: 317-997-5581. Business E-Mail: mdh@lilly.com.

HYNES, RICHARD OLDING, biology researcher, educator; b. Nairobi, Kenya, Nov. 29, 1944; s. Hugh Bernard Noel and Mary Elizabeth (Hinks) Hynes; m. Fleur Marshall, July 29, 1966; children: Hugh Jonathan, Colin Anthony. BA with honors, U. Cambridge, Eng., 1966, MA, 1970; PhD, MIT, 1971. Asst. prof. biology MIT, Cambridge, 1975-78, assoc. prof., 1978-83, prof. dept. biology, 1983—, assoc. head dept. biology, 1985-89, head, 1989-91, dir. Ctr. for Cancer Rsch., 1991-2001, Daniel K. Ludwig prof. cancer rsch., 1999—; investigator Howard Hughes Med. Inst., Chevy Chase, Md., 1988—. Gov. Wellcome Trust, 2007—. Author: Fibronectins, 1990; editor: Tumor Cell Surfaces and Malignancy, 1979; contbr. articles to profl. jours. Recipient Gairdner Found. Internat. award, 1997, E.B. Wilson medal, 2007, Pasarow award, 2008; Guggenheim Found. fellow, 1982. Fellow: AAAS, Royal Soc. London, Am. Acad. Arts and Scis.; mem.: NAS, Inst. Medicine NAS (co-chair adv. com. Human Embryonic Stem Cell Rsch. 2006—10). Office: MIT Ctr Cancer Rsch EI7-227 77 Massachusetts Ave Cambridge MA 02139-4307 Office Phone: 617-253-6422. Business E-Mail: rohynes@mit.edu. *

HYNES, VIRTNER GILMORE, retired rehabilitation services professional; b. Phila., Nov. 24, 1943; s. George Marcus and Virginia Pauline Hynes. BA, Rowan U., Glassboro, NJ, 1979. Tchr. Sch. Dist. Phila., 1985—90; vocat. rehab. counselor Office Vocat. Rehab., Phila., 1990—; singer Ctr. in Pk., Phila., 2010—; music tchr. Ctr. Pk. Phila., Pa., 2010. Organist St. Peters Hope Luth. Ch., Phila., 1995—; singer Ctr. Pk., Phila., sing-along leader, 2010—. Singer: Delaware Valley Opera Co., 1993. With US Army, 1965—67. Recipient Svc. award, African Am. Luth. Assn., Phila., 1996, Customer Svc. award, Office Vocat. Rehab., 2004, Svc. award, St. Michael's Luth. Ch., Phila., 2004. Mem.: Am. Guild Organists. Avocations: languages, theater. Home: 6312 Ross St Philadelphia PA 19144 Office: Office Vocat Rehab 444 N 3d St 5th Fl Philadelphia PA 19123

HYODO, HARUO, radiologist, educator; b. Honai-cho, Japan, Mar. 3, 1928; B of Medicine, Tokushuma U., 1959, MD, 1966. Chief clinic of radiology Nat. Kochi Hosp., 1963-65; chief divsn. of radiology Ehime Prefectural Ctrl. Hosp., 1970-77; prof. dept. radiology Dokkyo U. Sch. Medicine, Mibu, Japan, 1977—90; dir. emeritus Ikeda Meml. Hosp., Sukagawa, Japan, 1990—; asst. dir. Fukuda Meml. Hosp., Mooka, 1993—2006. Guest prof. Dokkyo U. Sch. Medicine, 1994-2006, Tenjin (China) 2d Med. Coll., 1986-2006. With Japanese Navy, 1944—45. Mem. Japanese Radiol. Soc. (cert. radiologist), Japanese Soc. Med. Imaging Tech. (pres. ann. gen. mtg. 1989-90), Japan Biliary Assn. (hon.; pres. ann. congress 1987-88), Japanese Med. Imaging Tech. Assn. (councilor 1980-95), Japanese Soc. Interventional Radiology (hon.). Achievements include patents in field. Avocations: photography, motoring, bowling, fishing. Home: 1-9-3 Saiwai-chou Mib-machi Shimotsuga-gun Tochigi 321-0203 Japan Office: Fukuda Meml Hosp 3-10 Namiki-chou Mooka Tochigi 321-43 Japan Business E-Mail: hyodo283@green.ocn.ne.jp.

HYOUNG DOO, SHIN, medical association administrator, educator; b. Andong, Republic Of Korea, Feb. 7, 1963; married. PhD, Seoul Nat. U., 1992. CEO SNP Genetics, Inc., Seoul, Republic of Korea, 2000—; prof. Sogang U., Seoul, 2008—. With, 1985—87, Mil. Svc. ROTC. Office: Sogang Univ 1 Shinsu-dong Mapo-Gu Seoul 121-742 Republic of Korea

HYPPOLITO, SILVIA BOMFIM, science educator, director; b. Fortaleza, Ceara, Brazil, Jan. 10, 1941; d. Jorge de Castro and Gisela Targino Bomfim; m. Archimedes Memoria Hyppolito, May 29, 1965; children: Karen Bomfim, Elodie Bomfim, Archimedes Memoria Hyppolito Filho. Degree in Medicine, Fed. U. Ceara, 1978; D in Ob-Gyn., U. Campinas, Sao Paulo, Brazil, 2002; MS in Pub. Health, Fed. U. Ceara, 1997. Cert. physician Fed. U. Ceara, 1978, human reproduction specialist U. Geneva, 1998. Med. resident Fed. U. Ceara, 1978—80, prof. sch. medicine, 1988—, head maternal and neonatal health dept., 2003—05, vice-dir. sch. medicine, 2007—; mem. bd. trustees Johns'Hopkins U., Baltimore, 1994—2002; acad. program coord., vice dean Sch. Medicine, Fed. U. Ceara, 2007—. Contbr. scientific papers. Recipient Zayra Cintra Vidal award, B. Braun S/A Lab., 2001, Prof. Galba Araujo award, Gynecology & Obstetrics Assn., 2008, 2009. Office: Fed Univ Ceara Rua Alexandre Baraúna 949 - Porangabusu Fortaleza Ceara 60430-160 Brazil Home: Nunes Valente - 3041- Dionisio Torres 60125-071 Fortaleza Cearß Brazil Office Phone: 55-85-3226-8569. Office Fax: 55-85-3366-8515; Home Fax: 55-85-3226-5444. Personal E-mail: facmed@ufc.br. Business E-Mail: silviabh@secrel.com.br.

HYSLOP, NEWTON EVERETT, JR., infectious disease specialist; b. Newton, Mass., 1935; AB, Harvard U., 1957, MD, 1961. Diplomate Am. Bd. Allergy and Immunology, Am. Bd. Internal Medicine, Am. Bd. Infectious Disease. Intern Mass. Gen. Hosp., Boston, 1961-62, resident in medicine, 1962—63, fellow in infectious disease, 1966—68; rsch. assoc. lab. immunology Nat. Inst. Allergy and Immunology, Bethesda, Md., 1963—65; resident in medicine Peter Bent Brigham Hosp., Boston, 1965—66; with Tulane U. Med. Ctr., New Orleans, 1984—; prof. medicine Tulane U., 1984—2006, prof. emeritus, 2006—. Instr. to asst. prof. Harvard Med. Sch., 1965—85; asst. to assoc. physician Mass. Gen. Hosp., 1965—85; Moseley traveling fellow and vis. scientist dept. biochemistry U. Oxford, 1968—69; chief infectious disease sect. Tulane Sch. Medicine, 1984—2006; founder and prin. investigator Tulane-La. State U. AIDS Clin. Trials unit, 1987—96, co-prin. investigator, 1996—2006; med. dir. HIV/AIDS/TB In-Patient unit, Charity Hosp., 1991—2006; clin. head HIV disease mgmt. initiative, health care svcs. divsn. La. State U. Health Scis. Ctr., 1999—2007. Fellow ACP, Infectious Dis. Soc.; mem. Am. Assn. Immunologists, Am. Soc. Microbiology, Assn. Subspecialty Professors. Office: Tulane U Sch Medicine Infectious Diseases Sect SL87 1430 Tulane Ave New Orleans LA 70112-2699 Home Phone: 504-891-1541; Office Phone: 504-988-7316. Business E-Mail: nhyslop@tulane.edu.

HYUN, INGYU, pulmonologist, educator; b. Seoul, Republic of Korea, Mar. 21, 1958; s. Kwangchul Hyun and Sookhee Choi; m. Jinsook Choi, June 12, 1987; children: Seokmin, Sooyoun. MD, Seoul Nat. U. Med. Coll., 1984, PhD, 1995; MS, Seoul Nat. U. Grad. Sch., 1990. Cert. Korean Med. Assn., 1984, Korean Assn. Internal Medicine Bd., 1991, Bd. Pulmonary Medicine, Korean Acad. Tb and Respiratory Diseases, 1995. Clin. rsch. fellow, dept. internal medicine Seoul Nat. U. Hosp., 1991—92; instr. Hangang Sacred Heart Hosp., Hallym U. Med. Coll., Seoul, 1992—95, asst. prof., 1995—98, assoc. prof., 1997—2004, chief planning dept., 1998, assoc. dir., 1998—2004, dir., 2004—08, prof., 2005—, chief pulmonary, allergy and critical care divsn., 2007—; postdoc. fellow Pulmonary and Critical Care Unit, Mass. Gen. Hosp., Boston, 1996—97. Dir. sci. com. Seoul Hosp. Assn., 2004—08. Mem. trustee Korean Multicultural Assn., Seoul. Maj. Korean Army Physician, 1985—88, Anyang, Gyeonggi-do, Republic of Korea. Home: #27-303 Woosung Apt Samsil-dong Songpa-gu Seoul 138-798 Republic of Korea Office: Hangang Sacred Heart Hosp Hallym Univ 94-200 Youngdeungpo-dong Youngdeungpo-gu Seoul 150-030 Republic of Korea Office Fax: 822-2677-9756. Business E-Mail: ighyun@hallym.ac.kr.

HYUN MEE, RYU, medical educator; b. Seoul, Republic of Korea, Dec. 25, 1963; MD, Ewha Women's U., 1988, PhD, 1997. Resident dept. ob-gyn, Ewha Women's U. Hosp., 1989—93; faculty Samsung Cheil Hosp., 1993—96; instr. Divsn. Maternal Fetal Medicine, Coll. Medicine, Samsung Cheil Hosp., Sungkyunkwan U., 1997—99, prof., 1999—2007, Dept. Ob-Gyn., Coll. Medicine, Cheil Gen. Hosp., Kwandong U., 2007—. Dir. Lab. Med. Genetics, Med. Rsch. Inst., Cheil Gen. Hosp. and Women's Healthcare Ctr., 2001; dir. publ. Korean Soc. Med. Genetics, 2008; editor-in-chief Jour. Med. Genetics, 2008. Recipient Academic awards, Cheil Gen. Hosp. and Women's Healthcare Ctr.; Rsch. grant, Life Ins. Philanthropy Found., grant, Ministry Edn., Sci. and Tech., Nat. Rsch. Found. Korea, Korean Govt., Korean Rsch. Found. Mem.: Korean Soc. Perinatology, Korean Assn. Ob-Gyn., Korean Med. Assn. Office: Cheil General Hosp 1-19 Mookjung-do Seoul 100-380 Republic of Korea Office Fax: 82-2-2278-4574. E-mail: hmryu@yahoo.com.

IACOBELLIS, GIANLUCA, physician; b. Rome, May 6, 1970; s. Gianfranco Iacobellis and Maria Luisa Santi. MD, La Sapienza U., 1994, PhD, 2003. Cert. endocrinology and diabetology specialist La Sapienza U., 2000. Intern La Sapienza U., Rome, 1994—2000, cons. phys.; research fellow Huddinge U. Hosp., Stockholm, 1999; physician dept. clin. scis. La Sapienza U., Rome; postdoctoral fellow, ctr. for human nutrition U. Texas Southwestern Med Ctr., 2004—. Recipient Doxazosin award, Pfizer Program Cardiovascular Proposals, 2003. Mem.: Diabetology Med. Assn. (assoc.), European Group for Study Insulin Resistance (assoc.), Italian Soc Diabetology (assoc.), Italian Soc. Endocrinology (assoc.). Achievements include research in New Imaging Method For Fat Tissue Detection. Avocations: soccer, running, water sports, driving sport cars, reading. Home: Via Ravenna 7a Rome 00161 Italy Office: Dipart Scienze Cliniche Pol Umberto I Viale del Policlinico 155 Rome 00161 Italy Office Fax: +39649970524; Home Fax: +39649970524. Personal E-mail: gianluca.iaco@tin.it.

IACONETTA, GIORGIO, neurosurgeon, researcher; b. Cosenza, Italy, Feb. 1, 1962; d. Pasquale Iaconetta and Aida Covello; m. Giosetta DeSimone, June 22, 1991; children: Giorgia, Gianmarco. MD, U. Naples, Italy, 1986. Resident Sch. Neurosurgery, Naples, 1986—91; asst. neurosurgery dept. Naples, 1991—2000; asst. prof. neurosurgery dept., 2001—. Tchr. Sch. Gen. Surgery, Naples, 1995—2000, Med. Sch., Naples, 1997—, Sch. Neurosurgery, Naples, 2000—. Author: Anatomical Variants of Cerebral Arteries, Idee E Confronti in Chirurgia; contbr. over 70 papers to internat. jours. Mem.: Italian Soc. Computer Assisted Surgery, Italian Soc. Skull Base Surgery, Italian Soc. Neurosurgery. Avocations: skiing, tennis, diving, motor sports. Home: Via Gravina 2 80055 Portici Italy

IACOVELLI, ROBERTO, oncologist; b. Rome, Sept. 1, 1981; MD, U. Rome, 2006. Physician Sapienza U. Rome, 2007—. Recipient Merit award, Am. Soc. Clin. Oncology, 2011; fellow award, Italian Assn. Med. Oncology, 2009, 2010. Home: Via Monte Gennaro 25 Marcellina 00010 Italy Personal E-mail: roberto.iacovelli@alice.it.

IAFRATE, FRANCO, radiologist, consultant; b. Rome, Oct. 10, 1976; s. Cesare Iafrate and Carla Vivarelli; m. Antonella Spagnuolo. Diploma in Medicine, Rome, 2001; degree, Sapienza U., Rome, 2001. Cons. radiologist Sapienza U. Rome, 2005—; cons. ct colonography Rome, 2007—. Liberal. Roman Catholic. Achievements include research in radiology, ct colonography. Avocations: football, travel, photography. Office: Sapienza Univ Rome Viale Regina Elena 324 161 Rome RM Italy Office Fax: 39 06490243. Business E-Mail: francoiafrate@gmail.com, franco.iafrate@uniroma1.it.

IAKOBISHVILI, ZAZA, cardiologist, director; b. Kutaisi, Georgia, Sept. 18, 1964; MD, Tbilisi State Med. U., PhD, 1988. Cons. cardiologist Meuhedet Health Fund, 2002—; dir., emergency cardiology svcs. Rabin Med. Ctr., 2009—. Mem.: Israel Heart Assn. Office: 39 Jabotinsky Petah Tikva 49100 Israel Personal E-mail: zaza@013.net.il.

IASIELLO, DOROTHY BARBARA, clinical social worker, former brokerage company executive; b. Bklyn., Oct. 6, 1949; d. Albert William and Josephine (Accardo) Rehorn; m. John Joseph Iasiello Jr., May 5, 1974 AAS Mktg., NYCCC, 1969; BS Econs., Coll. S.I., 1978; MSW, Columbia U., 2000. With J.P. Morgan Securities, NYC, 1978-81, asst. treas. sales, 1981-84, asst. v.p. sales, 1984-88, v.p. sales adminstrn. mgmt., 1988-91, v.p. sales, 1991-95; bus. cons., 1996—98; clin. social work practitioner, 2000—. Roman Catholic. Avocations: reading, foreign and domestic travel. E-mail: dbil@columbia.edu.

IAVAZZO, CHRISTOS R., gynecologist; b. Athens, Attica, Greece, June 19, 1977; MD, Med. Sch. U. Athens, 2002, PhD, 2010. Physician dept gynecology Metaxa Meml. Cancer Hosp., 2003—07, Vougiouklakeio Hosp., 2007—09; physician 2nd dept ob-gyn. Aretaieion Hosp. U. Athens, 2009—. Home: 38 Seizani St Nea Ionia Athens Attica 14231 Greece Personal E-mail: christosiavazzo@hotmail.com.

IBANEZ-NOLLA, JORDI, emergency physician, consultant; b. Barcelona, Spain, Apr. 13, 1961; s. Teresa Nolla and Enric Ibanez; m. Aurora Navarro, Oct. 9, 2002; m. Cristina Gonzalez, Jan. 20, 1992 (div. Sept. 1, 2001); children: Carmen Ibanez, Jordi Ibanez, Maria Ibanez. PhD, U. Ctrl. Barcelona, 1985, MD, 1998. Med. staff from icu Hosp. Gen. de Catalunya, Sant Cugat del Valles, Barcelona, Spain, 1991—2003, chief emergency dept. Office: Hosp Gen de Catalunya Pedro Pons 1 Sant Cugat del Valles 8195 Barcelona Spain Business E-Mail: jibanyez@hgc.es.

IBARRA, PEDRO F., anesthesiologist; b. Bogota, Jan. 1, 1963; MD, U. Javeriana, 1990; degree in Trauma Anesthesia & Critical Care, NY U., 1996. Attending anesthesiologist Clinicas Colsanitas, 1992—. Mem., edn. com. World Fedn. Socs. Anesthesia, 2004; chair, anesthesia residency program Fundacion U. Sanitas, 2007; chair, safety com. L.Am. Confederation Socs. Anesthesia, 2007. Recipient 1st Nat. Medicine award, COLSANITAS. Mem.: Internat. Anesthesia Rsch. Soc., Internat. Trauma Anesthesia & Critical Care, Colombian Soc. Anesthesiologists (chair, safety com. 2007, 1st prize), European Soc. Anesthesiologists, Am. Soc. Anesthesiologists. Avocations: tennis, astronomy. Office: Ave Calle 127 21-60 C 218 Bogota DC Colombia Personal E-mail: pfibarra@yahoo.com.

IBBOTSON, PATRICIA ANN, occupational health nurse, writer; b. Detroit, Nov. 17, 1940; d. Russell and Sophia (Nigbor) I. Diploma in nursing, Mercy Sch. Nursing, Detroit, 1961. RN, Mich. From staff nurse to clin. nursing supervisor Wayne County Gen. Hosp., Westland, Mich., 1961-84; corp. screening nurse Fairlane Health Sys., Birmingham, Mich., 1986-91; occupl. health nurse Ford Motor Co., Dearborn, Mich., 1990—99. Author: Eloise Poorhouse, Farm, Asylum and Hospital 1839-1984, 2002, Detroit's Hospitals, Healers, and Helpers, 2004, Detroit's Hist. Hotels Res., 2007. Avocations: genealogy, travel. Home: 36021 Abbey Dr Westland MI 48185-8520

IBBOTT, GEOFFREY STEPHEN, physicist; b. London, Mar. 23, 1949; s. Frank Alfred and Gladys Josephine (Gilbert) I.; m. Suzan Helen Doro, Feb. 14, 1969 (div. 1971); 1 child, Brian Richard; m. Diane Lorraine McCollum, Dec. 2, 1989. BA, U. Colo., 1979; MS, U. Colo. Health Sci., 1981; PhD, Colo. State U., 1993. Cert. radiol. physics Am. Bd. Radiology. Sr. instr., med. physicist U. Colo. Health Scis. Ctr., Denver, 1974-90; lectr., med. physicist Yale-New Haven Hosp., 1990-94; assoc. prof., dir. physics U. Ky. Med. Ctr., Lexington, 1994—2000; prof., chief outreach physics, dir. radiol. physics ctr. U. Tex. M.D. Anderson Cancer Ctr., Houston, 2001—10; prof., chmn. dept. radiation physics U. Tex. MD Anderson Cancer Ctr, Houston, 2010—. Trustee Am. Bd. Radiology, 2007—; pres. Coun. Ionizing Radiation Measurements and Stds., 2002—03. Assoc. editor Jour. Med. Physics, 1982-99, sr. assoc. editor Internat. Jour. Radiation Oncology, Biology and Physics, 2005—; contbg. author: The Selection and Performance of Radiologic Equipment, 1985: author: (booklet) Performance Evaluation of Hyperthermia Equipment, 1989; co-author: Radiation Therapy Physics, 1995, 3d edit., 2004; contbr. articles to profl. jours. Recipient Meml. award for profl. achievement Rocky Mountain chpt., Health Physics Soc., 1973, Farrington Daniels award, Med. Physics Jour., 1996. Fellow Am. Assn. Physicists in Medicine (pres. 1999), Am. Coll. Radiology, Am. Soc. Therapeutic Radiology and Oncology. Achievements include research on radiation response of mouse taste organ, development of polymer-gel dosimeter. Office: Dept Radiation Physics UT MD Anderson Cancer Ctr 1515 Holcombe Blvd Unit 94 Houston TX 77030 Business E-Mail: gibbott@mdanderson.org.

IBE, ELENA G., physician; b. Manila, May 12, 1961; MD, U. Toronto, 1985. Pamily physician Novant Health, 1997—. Office: 200 Greenwich Rd Charlotte NC 28211 Office Fax: 704-384-8684. Business E-Mail: egibe@novanthealth.org.

IBRAHIM, ASHRAF S., medical educator; b. Kuwait, Jan. 13, 1965; PhD, Loughbourough U. Tech., 1992. Prof., medicine David Geffen Sch. Medicine UCLA LA Biomed. Rsch. Inst. Harbor UCLA Med. Ctr., 1992—. Mem.: Internat. Soc. Human and Animal Mycology, Am. Soc. Advancement Sci., Genetics Soc. America, Am. Soc. Microbiology. Office: 1124 W Carson St LA Biomed Rsch Inst Torrance CA 90502 Office Fax: 310-782-2016. Business E-Mail: ibrahim@labiomed.org.

IBRAHIM, HASSAN N., nephrologist, educator; Resident Wayne State U. St. John Hosp. Med. Ctr.; assoc. prof. med. U. Minn. Div. Renal Diseases & Hypertension, 1998—; dir. U. Minn. Renal Fellowship Program, 2005—. Office: Division of Renal Diseases and Hypertension 717 Delaware St SE Ste 353 MDC 1932 Minneapolis MN 55414 Office Phone: 612-626-7002.

IBRAHIM, MAZEN MOHAMED, surgeon; b. Algeria, June 17, 1979; MBBCh, Med. Sch. Mansoura, 2002, MS in Orthop., 2008. Resident orthop. surgeon Mansoura U. Hosp., 2004—08; registrar orthop. surgeon Dar Al Foad Hosp., Cairo, 2008—09, Al Razi Hosp. Kuwait, 2009—. Fellow: AO Trauma Instn. Avocations: football, volleyball, painting. Home: PO BOX 18927 Reggee Farwaneya 81010 Kuwait Personal E-mail: mazenabdallah79@yahoo.com.

ICHIHARA, KIYOSHI, medical educator; b. Osaka, Japan, May 5, 1950; MD, Yamaguchi U., 1975; PhD, Osaka U., 1979. Prof. Yamaguchi U. Grad. Sch. Medicine, 2002—. Assoc. editor Annals Clin. Biochemistry, 2007; chair, com. evidence based lab. medicine Japan Soc. Lab. Medicine, 2007; chair, sci. com. Asia-Pacific Fedn. Clin. Biochemistry, 2007—; chair, com. reference intervals and decision limits Internat. Fedn. Clin. Chemistry and Lab. Medicine, 2010—. Avocations: running, skiing. Office: Yamaguchi University Med Sch Minami Kogush Ube Yamaguchi 755-8505 Japan Office Fax: 81-836-35-5213. Business E-Mail: ichihara@yamaguchi-u.ac.jp.

ICHIJIMA, HIDEJI, pharmaceutical executive; b. Tokyo, Oct. 18, 1959; MS in Pharm. Scis., Meijo U., 1985. Sr. mgr. Menicon Co. Ltd., 2008—. Rsch. fellow ophthalmology U. Tex., Southwestern Med. Ctr. Dallas, 1991—92, Ctr. Sight Georgetown U. Med. Ctr., Washington, 1990—91. Avocations: swimming, skiing. Office: 3-21-19 Aoi Naka-ku Nagoya Aichi 460-0006 Japan Office Fax: 81-52-935-1121. Business E-Mail: h-ichijima@menicon-net.co.jp.

ICHIKAWA, MAKOTO, psychology professor; b. Miyazaki, Japan, May 5, 1965; PhD, Osaka City U., 1994. Postdoc. rsch. fellow York U., 1994—97; lectr. Yamaguchi U., 1997—2000; assoc. prof. Chiba U., 2000—06. Recipient Grand prize, Visual Illusion Contest Japanese Psychonomic Soc. Mem.: Vision Scis. Soc., Japanese Psychol. Assn. Office: Chiba University Faculty Letters 1-33 Yayoicho Chiba 2638522 Japan Office Fax: 81-43-290-2356. Business E-Mail: ichikawa@l.chiba-u.ac.jp.

ICHISE, MASANORI, radiologist, educator; b. Japan, Jan. 24, 1948; MD, U. Toronto, 1979. Cert. specialist in nuc. medicine Harvard Med. Sch., 1986. Assoc. prof. radiology U. Toronto, 1986—2001; prin. investigator NIH, 2001—05; assoc. prof. radiology Harvard Med. Sch., 2005—06; prof. radiology Columbia U., 2006—. Recipient Sadek K. Hilal Faculty Rsch. award, Columbia U., Spl. Act award, NIH. Mem.: Radiol. Soc. N.Am., Soc. Nuc. Medicine (Brain Imaging Coun. award). Avocation: photography. Office: Neurological Inst Rm B04L 710 W New York NY 10032 Business E-Mail: mi2193@columbia.edu.

ICHORD, REBECCA N., child neurologist; BS in Biology, magna cum laude, U. Hawaii, 1975; MD, NY Med. Coll., 1977, George Wash. U., 1979. Diplomate Am. Bd. Pediat., 1984, Am. Bd. Psychiatry and Neurology-child neurology, 1992. Resident and chief resident pediat. dept. Children's Nat. Med. Ctr., Wash., DC, 1979—83; fellow devel. pediat. J.F.Kennedy Inst. Johns Hopkins Hosp., Baltimore, 1983—85; resident and chief resident child neurology dept. Johns Hopkins Med. Institutions, Baltimore, 1988—91. Co-author: (publs.) Electroencephalographic monitoring during hypothermia after pediatric cardiac arrest, 2009, Use of tPA in childhood arterial ischemic stroke: A multicenter observational cohort study, 2009, Neuron Specific Enolase and S 100B are Associated with Neurologic Outcome after Pediatric Cardiac Arrest, 2009, Perioperative stroke in infants undergoing open heart surgery for congenital heart disease, 2009, and several others. Named one of the Top Doctors, Phila. Mag., 2011. Office: Children's Hospital of Philadelphia Department of Neurology Wood Ctr 6th Fl 34th & Civic Ctr Blvd Philadelphia PA 19104-4318 Office Phone: 215-590-4142. Office Fax: 215-590-5120. E-mail: ichord@email.chop.edu.

ICKENSTEIN, GUNTRAM W., neurologist, researcher; MD, U. Würzburg, Germany, 1994; PhD, Havard U., Boston, Tech. U. Dresden, Germany, 2009. Cert. in neurology State Examination, Frankfurt, 2000. Stroke fellow MGH, Harvard U., Boston, 2000—02; attending stroke neurology U. Regensburg, Bavaria, Germany, 2002—05; dir. dept. neurology Tech. U. Dresden, Helios Gen. Hosp. Aue, Saxony, Germany. Achievements include patents for stroke lysis box. Office: Tech Univ Dresden HELIOS Gen Hosp Aue Gartenstr 6 Saxony Aue 08280 Germany

IDE, JUNJI, orthopaedic surgeon; b. Japan, Dec. 4, 1958; MD, Miyazaki Med. Coll., 1984; PhD, Kumamoto U., 1992. Rsch. ministry edn., sci. and culture Royal Nat. Orthops. Hosp., Shoulder Unit, London, 2001—02; assoc. prof., faculty life scis., dept. orthop. surgery Kumamoto U., 2006—. Sci. Rsch. grant, Ministry Edn., Culture, Sports, Sci. and Tech. Mem.: Internat. Soc. Orthop. Surgery Traumatology. Avocation: golf. Office: 1-1-1 Honjo Kumamoto 860-8556 Japan Office Phone: 81-96-373-5226. Office Fax: 81-96-373-5228. Business E-Mail: ide@kumamoto-u.ac.jp.

IDE, TAKESHI, ophthalmologist; b. Japan, Sept. 25, 1972; MD, Osaka U. Med. Sch., 1999, PhD, 2006. Vice dir. Minamiaoyama Eye Clin., 2009—. Office: 3-3-11 Renai Aoyama Bldg 4F Minato-ku Tokyo 107-0061 Japan Office Phone: 81-3-5772-1440. Business E-Mail: teyede@minamiaoyama.or.jp.

IDEGUCHI, MAKOTO, medical educator; b. Japan, Sept. 16, 1970; PhD in Med., 2000. Asst. prof. Yamaguchi U. Med. Sch. Hosp., 2008—. Avocation: biking. Office: 1-1-1 Minamikogushi Ube Yamaguchi 7558505 Japan Business E-Mail: ideguchi@yamaguchi-u.ac.jp.

IDRIS, AYMEN I., pharmacologist, researcher; s. Ibrahim Idris and Amal Hassan Abdoun; m. Rasha Abbas; 1 child, Samer. BSc (hon.), U. Sunderland, 1999; MSc, U. Aberdeen, Scotland, 2001; PhD (hon.), U. Aberdeen, Scotland, England, 2004. Postdoc. rschr. Inst. Biol. Scis., Aberdeen, 2004—05; rsch. fellow Inst. Genetics and Molecular Medicine, Edinburgh, 2005—. Recipient Young Investigator award, Internat. Bone and Mineral Soc., 2002, European Calcified Tissue Soc., 2004—07; fellow Bone Biology fellowship, ECTS/ AMGEN, 2006. Independent Thinkers. Office: Univ Edinburgh Crewe Road South EH4 2XU Edinburgh England Business E-Mail: aymen.idris@ed.ac.uk.

IDRIZBEGOVIC, ESMA, physician; d. Azaudin and Ulfeta Aganovic; m. Enes Idrizbegovic, Apr. 23, 1977; 1 child, Selma. MD, U. of Sarajevo, 1975; specialist in ENT, Huddinge U. Hosp., Stockholm, 1991; specialist in Audiology, Huddinge U. Hosp., 1994; specialist in ENT, U. of Sarajevo, Sarajevo, 1985; PhD, Karolinska Inst., 2001. Physician Health Care Ctr., Sarajevo, Bosnia-Herzegovina, 1975—81, ENT clinic, Huddinge U. Hosp., Stockholm, 1989—91; specialist in ENT Clinic Huddinge U. Hosp., Stockholm, 1991, specialist in audiology, 1991—, sr. specialist, chief sect. for auditory rehab., 2000—05. Mem.: Assn. of Drs. in Audiology, Internat. Tinnitus Orgn. (assoc.). Achievements include research in The effects of noise and aging on the expression of calcium binding proteins in the central auditory system in mice and the correlation with the auditory periphery. Office: Karolinska Univ Hosp Dept Audiology Stockholm Sweden Office Fax: +46 8 711 62 88. Personal E-mail: esmaidr@hotmailcom. Business E-Mail: esma.idrizbegovic@karolinska.se.

IDROVO, ALVARO JAVIER, epidemiologist, educator; b. Bogotá, Colombia, July 8, 1871; MD, Nat. U. Colombia, 1996; PhD, Nat. Inst. Pub. Health - Mex., 2006. Rschr., prof. Nat. Inst. Pub. Health, 2007—. Office: Avenida Universidad 655 Cuernavaca Morelos 62100 Mexico Business E-Mail: javier.idrovo@insp.mx.

IDSTAD, MARIANN, medical researcher; b. Norway, Mar. 5, 1978; MS in Psychology, Norwegian U. Sci. and Tech., 2007. Rschr. Norwegian Inst. Pub. Health, 2007—. Mem.: Norwegian Assn. Rschrs. Office: PB 4404 Nydalen Oslo 0403 Norway Business E-Mail: mariann.idstad@fhi.no.

IEZZI, MANUELA, medical researcher; b. Chieti, Italy, Dec. 19, 1971; Degree in Medicine and Surgery, G. d'Annunzio U., 1998, degree in Surg. Pathology, 2003. Rschr. G. d'Annunzio U., 2008—. Avocations: cooking, dance. Office: CESI Via Colle dell'Ara Chieti Scalo CH 66100 Italy Office Fax: 390871541545. Business E-Mail: m.iezzi@unich.it.

IEZZONI, LISA I., medical educator, researcher; MSc, Harvard U., 1978; MD, Harvard U., Boston, 1984. Sr. rschr. health care rsch. unit Boston U., 1984—85, asst. rsch. prof. dept. medicine, 1985—90, dir. health svcs. rsch. Health Policy Inst., 1988—90, asst. prof. health svcs., 1989—90; asst. prof. medicine Harvard Med. Sch., Boston, 1990—93, prof. medicine, 1993—; co-dir. rsch. divsn. gen. medicine and primary care Beth Israel Deaconess Med. Ctr., Boston. Mem. Nat. Com. on Vital and Health Stats.; bd. dirs. Nat. Forum for Health Care Quality Measurement and Reporting. Contbr. articles to profl. jours.; mem. editl. bds of maj. med. and health svcs. rsch. jours.; author (and editor): Risk Adjustment for Measuring Healthcare Outcomes; author: When Walking Fails: Mobility Problems of Adults with Chronic Conditions, 2003. Recipient Investigator Award in Health Policy Rsch., The Robert Wood Johnson Found., 1996, Founder's award for Outstanding Contbns. to Field, Am. Coll. Med. Quality. Mem.: Inst. of Medicine of NAS. Avocations: gardening, painting, reading. Office: Beth Israel Deaconess Med Ctr Divsn Gen Medicine Libby 326 330 Brookline Ave Boston MA 02215

IFFY, LESLIE, retired medical educator; b. Budapest, Hungary, May 17, 1925; arrived in U.S., 1969; s. Zoltan and Rozsa (Lantos) Iffy; m. Margaret Lesniak. MD, U. Budapest, Hungary, 1949; MD (hon.), U. Budapest, 1993. Diplomate Am. Bd. Ob-Gyn., 1970, Am. Bd. Maternal-Fetal Medicine, 1977. Resident, fellow Országos Testnevelési és Sportegészségügyi Intézet Hosp. Ministry of Health, Budapest, 1951-56; fellow U. Wash., Seattle, 1964; asst. prof. Temple U., Phila., 1969-70; assoc. prof. U. Ill., Chgo., 1971-72, Jefferson Med. Coll., Phila., 1972-73; prof. U. Medicine and Dentistry of N.J., Newark, 1974—2011; dir. obstetrics U. Hosp., Newark, 1974—2011. Editor: Perinatology Case Studies, 1978, 1985, Obstetrics and Perinatology, 1981, Operative Perinatology, 1984, Operative Obstetrics, 1992, 3d edit., 2006; contbr. articles to profl. jours. Recipient Dr. Robert Jardine Rsch. prize, U. Glasgow, 1963, award, U. Medicine and Dentistry NJ, 1984, 2005, Semmelweis Meml. award, U. Budapest, 1993, 2005; rsch. fellow, Ford Found., Seattle, 1964, hon. fellow, Hungarian Obstet. Soc., 1986. Fellow: Am. Coll. Legal Medicine (bd. dirs. 1989—95), Royal Coll. Surgeons Can., Royal Faculty Physicians and Surgeons (licentiate), Romanian Soc. Obstetricians and Gynecologists (hon.), Ctrl. Assn. Ob Gyn. (life). Avocations: music, chess, literature, art. Home: 5 Robin Hood Rd Summit NJ 07901 Personal E-mail: liffy@comcast.net.

IFRIM-CHEN, FENG, medical educator, researcher; b. Hefei, Anhui, China, Jan. 16, 1962; arrived in Romania, 1997; d. Yi ping Gong and Yu-lan Chen; m. Mircea Ifrim, July 1997. B in Medicine, Tech. U., Huaibei, China, 1986; MS, East China Normal U., Shanghai, China, 1995; PhD, U. Oradea, Romania, 2002; DSc (hon.), China Med. U., Taiwan, 2006, Asia U., 2006. Lic. rschr. Romania Med. Acad. Sci., 2002. Tchr. math. Coal Vocat. Sch., Huaibei, China, 1979—82; physician Coal Worker's Hosp. Gen., Huaibei, 1986—92; rschr. China Nat. Inst. Edn. Rsch., Beijing, 1995—97; adj. staff China Nat. Commn. United Nations Ednl. Sci. Cultural Orgn., Beijing, 1996—97; prof. U. Oradea, Romania, 1998—2009, dep. dean faculty medicine, 2004—08; chief & assoc. prof. U. Medicine & Pharmacy, Bucharest, Romania, 2008—. Cons. Taiwan Nat. Dr. Union, Taipei, 2003—06; hon. investigator Taiwan Nat. Rsch. Inst., Taipei, 2003; advisor min. Romania Health Ministry, 2006—08. Author: A Regulation System of the Body - The Meridians and Acupoints, 2003, Health Education & Health Promotion, 2003, The Basic Theories of Traditional Chinese Medicine, 2005, Psychology and Health Education, 2007, Medical Pedogogy-Health Education, 2009, Pedagogy General for the Teacher in High Education, 2011; contbr. scientific papers. Recipient Diploma of Excellence in Contbn., Hon. Mem., Mediterranean Med. Union, 2004, Balkan Med. Union, 2004, Am. medal, Am. Biog. Inst., 2009, World medal of Freedom, 2009, Internat. Order of Merit, 2009, Internat. Peace prize, Am. Biog. Inst., 2010; named Hon. Prof., China Med. U., Taiwan, 2006, World Leading Scientist, Internat. Biog. Ctr., Cambridge, 2008, 500 Great Leaders, 2010, Woman of Yr., 2010; named one of Top 100 Scientists, 2009; named to America Hall of Fame, Great Minds 21st Century, 2010. Mem.: Internat. Soc. Oriental Medicine (bd. dirs. 2005—), NY Acad. Sci. (licentiate), Mediterranean Med. Union (hon. Excellence diploma 2004), Balkan Med. Union (hon. Excellence diploma 2004), Am. Anatomists. Soc. (assoc.), Am. Chem. Soc. (assoc.), Am. Soc. Cell Biology (assoc.), Internat. Soc. Med. Pedagogy (assoc.). Achievements include research in the fields of health education, modern and traditional medicine, pedagogy, psychology, physical education and sports science; contributions to improve the standard of educational level and health systems. Avocations: poetry, music, sports.

IGARASHI, HIROKO TAKEUCHI, dentist, researcher; b. Tokyo, Mar. 24, 1980; DDS, Nippon Dental U., 2004, PhD, 2009. Rsch. fellow, dept. periodontology Nippon Dental U., 2009—. Recipient Academic Rsch. Incentive awards, Nippon Dental U. Gen. Session, 2010, Incentive awards, Japanese Soc. Periodontology. Avocations: travel, diving. Office: 1-9-20 Fujimi Chiyoda-ku Tokyo 102-8159 Japan Office Fax: 81-3-3261-5937. Personal E-mail: hiroko.p0324@gmail.com.

IGARASHI, KAZUEI, biochemist; b. Shirone, Niigata, Japan, July 7, 1941; s. Kyushirou and Fuyo (Ichikawa) I.; m. Kiyoko Kadota, May 29, 1969; children: Kazutsugu, Keiko. B in Pharm. Scis., Chiba U., 1963, M in Pharm. Scis., 1965; D in Pharm. Sci., U. Tokyo, 1970. Rsch. assoc. Chiba U., 1970-74, asst. prof., 1975-79, assoc. prof., 1980-83, prof., 1984—2007, dean, 1999—2001, v.p., 2002—03; pres. Amine Pharma Rsch. Inst., Chiba, Japan, 2007—. Cons. Environtl. Conservation, Kisarazu, Japan, 1996—. Editl. bd. Internat. Jour. Biochemistry and Cell Biology, 1997; author: Physiological Functions of Polyamines (in Japanese), 1993. Mem. Am. Soc. for Biochemistry and Molecular Biology, The Japanese Biochem. Soc., Molecular Biology Soc. Japan, Pharm. Soc. Japan (hon., Abbott prize 1979, PSJ award 2006) Avocations: reading, travel. Home: 3-12 C-1102 Ichikawaminami Ichikawa 272-0033 Japan Office Phone: 81-43-224-7500. Business E-Mail: iga16077@faculty.chiba-u.jp.

IGEL, GERARD J., pediatrician, educator; MD, Hadassah Med. Sch. Hebrew U., 1981. Diplomate Am. Bd. Pediatrics. Asst. clin. prof. pediat. Albert Einstein Coll. Med.; resident in pediat. Jacobi Med. Ctr., Bronx, NY, 1982—84, with; pediatrician Henry and Lucy Moses divsn. Montefiore Med. Ctr. Office: Montefiore Medical Center 1613 Tenbroeck Ave Bronx NY 10461 Office Phone: 718-828-9060. Office Fax: 718-828-9845.

IGIETSEME, JOSEPH UGBODAGA, biomedical researcher, educator; b. Agenebode, Edo State, Nigeria, Feb. 17, 1955; s. Igietseme Omogbako Ugbodaga and Adishetu Omosi Igietseme; m. Veronica Emeke Onwude; children: Gabriel Ugbodaga, Nene Veronica, Jojackson Ugbodaga. PhD, Georgetown U., Washington, 1988. Chief molecular pathogenesis lab. Ctrs. Disease Control and Prevention, Atlanta, 2002—. Prof. Morehouse Sch. Medicine, Atlanta, 2002—. Scholar, NIH, 1996—. Mem.: Am. Assn. Immunologists (life), Nigerians in the Diaspora Orgn. (gen. sec. 2005). Achievements include research in immunology, infectious disease and vaccines. Home: 982 Carlisle Rd Stone Mountain GA 30083 Office: Ctrs Disease Control C 17 1600 Clifton Rd Atlanta GA 30333 Office Fax: 404-639-3199; Home Fax: 404-343-6571. E-mail: jigietseme@cdc.gov.

IGLARZ, MARC, pharmaceutical executive; b. Paris, Feb. 5, 1970; married. PhD, U. Paris VI, 2001; PharmD, U. Paris XI, 2001. Pharmacist resident C.H.U. X. Bichat-Cl. Bernard, Paris, 1995—2001, biochemist asst., 2001—02; postdoc. fellow Clin. Rsch. Inst. Montreal, Can., Québec, 2002—04; sr. lab. head Actelion Pharms. Ltd., Allschwil, Switzerland, 2004—. Lt. USN, 1998, Toulon. Mem.: Am. Heart Assn.

IGNAGNI, KAREN MARIE, lobbyist; b. 1953; BA in Polit. Sci., Providence Coll., 1975; MBA, Loyola U., 1985. With US Dept. Health & Human Services, 1975—77, Com. for Nat. Health Ins., 1977—79; policy aide to Sen. Claiborne Pell US Senate Labor & Human Resources Com., 1979—82; dir. Dept. Employee Benefits AFL-CIO, 1990—93; pres., CEO Group Health Assn. America, 1993—95, American Assn. Health Plans, 1995—2003, America's Health Ins. Plans, Washington, 2003—. Contbr. articles pub. in newspapers, journals and mags. Named one of The 100 Most Powerful Women in DC, Washingtonian Mag., 2009, Top Guns, The 10 Most Powerful Women in Washington, Fortune mag., 2009, 50 Most Powerful People in DC, GQ mag., 2009, The Top 25 Women in Healthcare, Modern Healthcare Mag., 2011, 50 Most Powerful People in Politics, George Mag. Roman Cath. Office: Americas Health Insurance Plans 601 Pennsylvania Ave NW S Bldg Ste 500 Washington DC 20004 Office Phone: 202-778-3200. Office Fax: 202-331-7487. *

IGNARRO, LOUIS J., pharmacology educator; b. Bklyn., May 31, 1941; m. Sharon Elizabeth Williams, July 1997; 1 child from previous marriage. BS in Pharmacy, Columbia U., NYC, 1962; PhD in Pharmacology, U. Minn., Mpls., 1966. Postdoc. fellowship chem. pharmacology Nat. Heart, Lung & Blood Inst., NIH, 1968; staff scientist pharm. divsn. Ciba-Geigy Corp., Ardsley, NY, 1968—72; asst. prof. pharmacology Tulane U. Sch. Medicine, New Orleans, 1973, assoc. prof., 1973—78, prof., 1979—85; prof. dept. pharmacology UCLA Sch. Medicine, 1985—, acting chmn. dept. pharmacology, 1989—90, asst. dean student rsch., 1990—93, Jerome J. Belzer, MD disting. prof. pharmacology, 1993—. Founder, editor-in-chief Nitric Oxide Biology and Chemistry, 1996; founder, bd. dirs. Nitric Oxide Soc., 1996—; mem. sci. adv. bd. Herbalife Internat., Inc. Author: NO More Heart Disease: How Nitric Oxide Can Prevent - Even Reverse - Heart Disease and Strokes, 2005, Health Is Wealth: 10 Power Nutrients That Increase Your Odds Of Living To 100, 2009; contbr. articles to profl. jours. Recipient Edward G. Schlieder Found. award, 1973, Merck Rsch. award, 1974, Rsch. Career Devel. award, USPHS, 1975—80, Roussel Uclaf prize for cell comm. and signaling, 1994, Nobel prize in physiology/medicine, 1998, Can. Medal of Merit, 2008. Mem.: NAS, Am. Acad. Arts & Scis., Inst. Medicine, Soc. Exptl. Biology & Medicine, Am. Heart Assn., Am. Soc. Hematology, Am. Rheumatism Assn., Am. Soc. Cell Biology, Am. Physiol. Soc., Am. Soc. Biochemistry & Molecular Biology, Am. Soc. Pharmacology & Exptl. Therapeutics, Alpha Omega Alpha (hon.). Achievements include research in the mechanisms of regulation and modulation of nitric oxide (NO) production and cytotoxicity in macrophages, vascular cells, and tumor cells. Office: UCLA Sch Medicine Dept Molecular & Med Pharmacology Office CHS 10833 Leconte Ave Los Angeles CA 90095-1735 Office Phone: 310-825-5159, 310-825-9930. E-mail: lignarro@mednet.ucla.edu. *

IGNATOV, DMITRY YURIEVICH, research scientist; b. Kramatorsk, Ukraine, Nov. 17, 1971; m. Tatiana Georgievna Ignatova; 1 child, Andrey Dmitrievich. Rsch. asst. Rsch. Inst. Family Med. Problems of Donets Nat. Med. U., Donetsk, Ukraine, 1998—; sr. Java developer M9 Ukraine, Donetsk, 2007—. Achievements include patents for the method of determining the state of immunity by metabolic activity of neutrophils, and apoptosis and necrosis of lymphocytes in venous blood; research in functional heterogenicity of human blood neutrophils. Office: Donetsk National Med Univ Levitskogo 4 Donetsk 83048 Ukraine Office Phone: 38 050 610-9208. Personal E-mail: dmitri.ignatov@gmail.com.

IGNOTZ, RONALD ALAN, medical researcher, educator; b. July 8, 1953; BA, Wash. and Jefferson Coll., Pa., 1975; PhD in Medicine, U. Pitts., 1984. Sr. rsch. scientist, asst. prof. surgery U. Mass. Med. Sch., 1989—. Adj. asst. prof. biomed. engring. Worcester Poly. Inst., 2009—. Owens fellowship, U. Pitts. Achievements include research in wound healing. Avocations: running, bicycling, horseback riding. Office: 55 Lake Ave N Worcester MA 01655 Office Fax: 508-856-5250. Business E-Mail: ronald.ignotz@umassmed.edu.

IGUCHI, TAISEN, biology educator; b. Okayama, Japan, Mar. 17, 1951; s. Tohru and Yukiko (Hashimoto) Iguchi; m. Setsuko Katoh, Jan. 2, 1982; children: Lisa, Mona. BSc, Okayama U., 1974, MSc, 1976; PhD, U. Tokyo, 1981. Rschr. Shigei Med. Inst., Okayama, 1978-79; asst. prof. Yokohama City U., Japan, 1979—87, assoc. prof., 1987-91, prof., 1992-2000; postdoctoral fellow U. Calif., Berkeley, 1981-83; prof. Ctr. Integrative Biosci. Okazaki Nat. Rsch. Inst., Japan, 2000—03; prof. Okazaki Inst. Integrative Biosci., Nat. Inst. Basic Biology, Nat. Inst. Natural Sci., Japan, 2004—. Vis. endocrinologist

U. Calif., Berkeley, 1989, 91; vis. prof. U. Fla., 2008-. Mem. NY Acad. Scis., Endocrine Soc., Sigma Xi. Home: Tatsumiminami 2-4-1 2-43 Okazaki 444-0874 Japan Office: 5-1 Higashiyama Myodaijii Okazaki 444-8787 Japan Office Phone: 81-564-59-5235. Business E-Mail: taisen@nibb.ac.jp.

IGWE, SAMUEL AGINA, pharmacologist, educator, researcher; b. Port Harcourt, Nigeria, Mar. 18, 1953; s. Isaiah Okike and Esther Ekodu (Princess Okafor) I.; m. Julie Ijeoma Okorie, Nov. 2, 1990; children: Chibuzor, Chimamaka, Chikezie. BSc in Pharmacology, U. Ibadan, Nigeria, 1980; MS in Pharmacology and Therapeutics, U. Nigeria, Nsukka, 1983; PhD in Biochem. Pharmacology, Nnamdi Azikiwe U., Awka, 1995. Cert. in in vivo/in vitro testing technique for P Falciparum sensitivity WHO, 1985, cert. in computer proficiency, 1994. With Nat. Youth Svc. Gen. Hosp., Macurdi, Nigeria, 1981-82; rsch. asst. Tchg. Hosp., Enugu, Nigeria, 1983-88; lectr. Imo State U., Okigwe, Nigeria, 1988-94, Abia State U., Uturu, Nigeria, 1994—2002, head ocular pharmacology Sch. Optometry, 1988—2002, head dept. pharmacology, 1994—2002, dir. malaria control, 1996—2002. Mem. Univ. Senate Abia State U., 1994-2002; external examiner U. Nigeria, U. Port Harcourt, Nnamdi Azikiwe U., U. Benin; reader in pharmacology Ebonyi State U., Abakaliki, 1998. Editor: Perspectives in Visual Sciences, 1996, Jour. Health/Visual Scis., 1998; mem. editl. bd. EbonyiMed Jour., 2001; author: Textbook of Ocular Pharmacology, 1999, Handbook of Ophthalmic Drugs, 1996; contbr. articles to profl. jours. Sec. Ndiuche Youth Movement, Arondizuogu, Nigeria, 1985-98; mem. coll. bd. medicine Coll. Medicine Abia State U., 1993-2002. Mem. African Soc. for Pharmacologists, West African Soc. Pharmacology, N.Y. Acad. Sci. Anglican. Avocations: tennis, badminton, walking, photography. Office: Dept Pharmacology & Therapeutics Ebonyi State U Tchg Hosp CollHealth Scis Abakaliki Nigeria E-mail: jovel@infoweb.abs.net, nwosuigwe@yahoo.com.

IHM, CHUN-GYOO, nephrologist, educator; b. Kunsan, Republic of Korea, Oct. 15, 1953; MD, Kyung-Hee U., Seoul, 1978, PhD, 1985. Specialist in internal medicine, nephrology. Rsch. fellow UCLA Med. Ctr., Torrence, 1988—89; prof. Kyung-Hee U. Med. Coll., Seoul, 1998—. Mgr. 9th Asian Colloquim in Nephrology, Seoul, 1992, chair dept. internal medicine, Kyung Hee Med. Ctr. Contbr. articles to profl. jours Recipient Dongsin-SKB Sci. award Korean Med. Assn., 1995 Mem. Korean Soc. Nephrology (dir. sci. program 2004-06), Am. Soc. Nephrology, Korean Soc. Hypertension(dir. at large). Avocations: soccer, skiing, writing. Office: Dept Internal Med Kyung-Hee Univ Med Ctr 1 Seoul 130 702 Republic of Korea Office Phone: 822-958-8188. Office Fax: 822-968-1848. E-mail: cgihm@yahoo.co.kr.

IIDA, NOBUTOSHI, medical educator; b. Sapporo, Hokkaido, Japan, Nov. 14, 1928; m. Yuri Iida, June 15, 1952. MD, Hokkaido U., 1952, PhD, 1957. Chief med. dept. Yodogawa Christian Hosp., Osaka, Japan, 1960—72; chief nephrology Osaka Prefectural Gen. Hosp., 1972—92; prof. Aino Gakuin Coll., 1992—96; med. advisor Yodogawa Christian Hosp., 1996—2004, Shirasagi Hosp., 2004—. Cons. in field. Author: Illustrated Water and Electrolytes, 1969, Standard Dialysis Therapy, 1981, Illustrated Diagnosis of Renal and Urological Diseases, 1986, Management of Renal Diseases, 1991, Dilemma in the Management of Renal Diseases, 1998, EBM Blood Purification Therapy, 2000, Risk Management of Dialysis Therapy, 2002, Diabetic Nephropathy, 2003, Dialysis Therapy, 2007. Trustee Osaka Kidney Found., 2003—06. Mem.: Europe Renal Assn.-Europe Dialysis Transplant Assn., Am. Soc. Nephrology, Internat. Soc. Nephrology. Avocations: travel, classical music. Office: Shirasagi Hosp 7-11-23 Kumata Higashisumiyoshi Osaka 546 Japan Office Phone: 06-6714-1661.

IIDA, NORIHIKO, psychiatrist, educator; b. Ogaki, Japan, Feb. 24, 1947; s. Koichi and Tsuya (Ohta) I.; m. Hatsuko Kuriyama, June 10, 1974; children: Tomoko, Masahiko, Nobuko. MD, Osaka Med. Coll., Japan, 1971. Instr. psychiatry Osaka Med. Coll., 1972-76, 78-81; rschr. Tokyo Met. Neurosci. Inst., 1976-78; v.p. Shin-Abuyma Hosp., Osaka, 1981-86; dir. Med. Ctr. Kansai U., Osaka, 1986—, prof., 1991—, dean, prof. clin. psychology, 2009, trustee, 2009; prof. emeritus, 2011. Contbr. articles to profl. jours. Pres. com. health promotion planning Taito City, Tokyo, 1995-2000; pres. 4th Congress of Japan Assn. Sch. Mental Health; counsilor, Com. of Social Welfare, Takatsuki City, counsilor Com. Psychiatric Svc., Osaka Prefecture, 2005, pres., 32th Congress Japan Assn. Coll. Mental Health. Recipient Kashida prize, Japan Jour. Multiphasic Health Testing and Svc., 1997. Mem.: AAAS, Japan Assn. Coll. Mental Health (pres., 32th congress 2011), NY Acad. Scis., Japanese Soc. Psychosomatic Medicine (councilor), Japan Assn. Sch. Mental Health (councilor, editor), Japanese Assn. Univ. Mental Health (councilor), Japanese Assn. of Univ. Health Adminstrn. (supr.), World Psychiatry Assn., World Fedn. Mental Health (gold sponsor 2002). Avocations: piano, playing flute, skiing, billiards. Office: Kansai Univ Yamate Cho 3 3 35 5648680 Suita Japan Office Phone: 6-6368-1121. Business E-Mail: v862264@kansai-u.ac.jp.

IIMURA, OSAMU, cardiologist, nephrologist, endocrinologist; b. Ochiai town, Karafuto, Japan, Jan. 28, 1931; s. Hachiro and Sotoe (Watanabe) I.; m. Kyoko Kudo, Feb. 2, 1964; 2 children. BSc, Hokkaido U., Sapporo, Japan, 1953; MD, Sapporo Med. U., 1958, PhD, 1963. From asst. prof. to prof. Sapporo Med. U., 1963—96; prof. emeritus Sapporo Med U., 1996—, pres. U. Hosp., 1992—96; chief med. cons. Hokkaido JR Sapporo Hosp., 1996—. Editor-in-chief: Hypertension research - Clinical and Experimental, 1996-99; editor Jour. Hypertens, 1990-92, Clin. and Exptl. Pharmaco and Physiol, 1986-2003, Clin. autonom Rsch., 1990-96. Recipient Hokkaido Med. Assn. award, 1981, Hokkaido Gov. award, 1981, Hokkaido Sci. and Tech. award, 1994. Fellow Am. Heart Assn.; mem. Japan Circulation Soc. (dir. 1983-94), Japan Soc. Hypertension (dir. 1981-96), Japan Soc. Preventive Cardiology (pres. 1992-99), Japan Soc. Gerontology (dir. 1988-2000), European Soc. Cardiology, Internat. Soc. Hypertension, Am. Heart Assn., Am. Soc. Hypertension, European Soc. Hypertension. Avocations: classical music, travel, reading. Office: Hokkaido Rwy Co Sapporo Hos N-3 E-1 Chuo-ku Sapporo 060-0033 Japan Office Phone: 81-241-0457.

IINO, YUICHI, scientist, educator; b. Ohmuta, Japan, Oct. 21, 1958; s. Fujio and Chikako (Ueda) I. BS, U. Tokyo, 1982, MS, 1984, D, 1987. Fellow Japan Soc. Promotion Sci., Tokyo, 1987-88, Columbia U., NYC, 1988-90; researcher U. Tokyo, 1990-93, lectr., 1993—. Mem. Japanese Soc. Molecular Biology, Soc. Neurosci. Avocations: tennis, skiing, mountain climbing. Office: U Tokyo 7-3-1 Hongo Bunkyo-ku 113 Japan

IINUMA, GEN, physician, radiologist, medical researcher, medical educator; b. Gifu, Gifu, Japan, Apr. 9, 1960; s. Touichi and Misako Iinuma; m. Yumi Fuseya, Feb. 8, 1961; children: Masataka, Tomohiro. MD, Dept. of Radiology, Gifu U. Sch. of Medicine, Gifu, 1980—86. Corresponding Membership Radiol. Soc. N.Am., 1998, Japanese Bd. Radiology Japan Radiol. Soc., 1992. Resident Dept. Radiology, Gifu U. Sch. Medicine, Gifu, Gifu, Japan, 1986—88, instr., 1988—90, asst. prof., 1990—92; med. staff Akita Red Cross Hosp., Akita, Akita, Japan, 1992—94, Dept. Diagnostic Radiology, Nat. Cancer Ctr. Hosp., 1994—2003; head staff Research Ctr. for Cancer Prevention and Screening, Nat. Cancer Ctr., Tokyo, Tokyo, 2004—. Head investigator (performance) Development of Digital radiography using 4 million pixel charge coupled device (Grants for Sci. Rsch. Expenses for Health and Welfare Programs from the Ministry of Health, Labor and Welfare, 1997), Development of Flat Panel Digital radiography (Grants for Sci. Rsch. Expenses for Health and Welfare Programs from the Ministry of Health, Labor and Welfare, 2002), Virtual endoscopy for the diagnosis of colorectal carcinomas using multi-detector row CT (Grants for Sci. Rsch. Expenses for Health and Welfare Programs from the Ministry of Health, Labor and Welfare, 2002). Avocations: scuba diving, travel, drive, listening to classical music. Home: 2-31-16 Kairaku Chiba Urayasu 279-0003 Japan Office: Nat Cancer Ctr Hosp 5-1-1 Tsukiji Tokyo Chuo-ku 104-0045 Japan Office Fax: 81-3-3542-3815. Personal E-mail: giinuma@jcom.home.ne.jp. Business E-Mail: giinuma@ncc.go.jp.

IINUMA, YASUSHI, emergency physician, pediatric surgeon; b. Niigata, Japan, Nov. 20, 1958; s. Hiroshi and Reiko Iinuma; m. Shyoko Kobayashi, Sept. 25, 1993; children: Akiko, Tomoko. MD, Niigata U., 1984. Diplomate Japan Bd. Pediat. Surgeons, 2003, Japan Bd. Emergency Physicians, 2008. Resident Niigata U., Japan, 1984—86, staff dir. dept. pediat. surgery, asst. prof. Divsn. of Pediatric Surgery, 2002—03; vice-dir. Emergency and Critical Care Med. Ctr. Niigata City Gen. Hosp., 2003—. Contbr. articles to profl. jours. Office: Niigata City Gen Hosp 463-7 Shumoku Chuo-ku Niigata Japan Office Phone: 81-25-281-5151. Office Fax: 81-25-281-5169. Business E-Mail: iinuma@hosp.niigata.niigata.jp.

IIZUKA, TOSHIRO, gastroenterologist; b. Japan, Oct. 14, 1968; MD, Nagasaki U., 1996. Physician, dept. gastroenterollogy Toranomon Hosp., 2002—. Mem.: ASGE, ASCO. Avocation: travel. Office: 2-2-2 Toranomon Mitato-ku Tokyo 105-8470 Japan Business E-Mail: t-iizuka@toranomon.gr.jp.

IKARI, KATSUNORI, geneticist, rheumatologist, orthopedic surgeon; s. Makoto and Masako Ikari; m. Eriko Nakayama, Sept. 5, 1998. MD, Hirosaki U., 1996, PhD, 2001. Rsch. asst. Gunma U., Maebashi, Japan, 1998—2000, U. Tokyo, Minato, 2000—00; instr. Tokyo Women's Med. U., Shinjuku, 2001—08, asst. prof., 2008—. Contbr. scientific papers. Recipient Young Investigator award, Japan Coll. Rheumotology, 2010; grantee, Internat. Bone and Mineral Soc. and European Soc. Calcified Tissue, 2001, Ichiro Kanehara Found., 2002, Japanese Ministry Edn., Sci., Sports and Culture, 2002—04, Japan Rheumatism Found., 2004, Japan Orthopaedics and Traumatology Found., Inc., 2006, Japanese Ministry Edn., Sci., Sports and Culture, 2006—, Takeda Sci. Found., 2007; fellow, Inst. Phys. and Chem. Rsch., Tokyo, 2003—04. Mem.: Japanese Orthopaedic Assn., Japan Coll. Rheumatology, Japanese Soc. Human Genetics, Am. Soc. Human Genetics. Office: Tokyo Women's Med U 10-22 Kawada Shinjuku 162-0054 Japan Business E-Mail: kikari@ior.twmu.ac.jp.

IKEDA, CLYDE JUNICHI, plastic and reconstructive surgeon; b. Kobe, Japan, 1951; s. Paul Tamotsu and Kazu Ikeda. BA, SUNY, Binghamton, 1973; MD, N.Y. Med. Coll., Valhalla, 1979. Resident St. Vincent Hosp., NYC, 1979-83, Francis Meml. Hosp., San Francisco, 1983-86; med. dir. Burn Ctr. St. Francis Meml. Hosp., San Francisco, 1992—2001, 2007—, med. examiner, 1993—, med. dir. Wound Healing Ctr., 1994—2001; dir. Hosp. de la Familie, 2000—06, v.p., med. dir., 2006—. Asst. clin. prof. plastic surgery U. Calif., San Francisco, 1998-2003, assoc. clin. prof. plastic surgery, 2003—; adj. clin. prof. surgery Stanford Sch. Medicine, 2004—. Recipient Edward Weisband Disting. Alumni award, Binghamton U., 2003, medal of honor, Alumni Assn. N.Y. Med. Coll., 2004, Outstanding Physician award, Med. Bd. Calif., 2007. Fellow ACS. Office: 1199 Bush St Ste 640 San Francisco CA 94109-5977

IKEDA, HIDETOSHI, neurosurgeon, neuropathological researcher; b. Ueda City, Nagano, Japan, Nov. 7, 1952; s. Makoto and Teruko (Takei) I.; 2 children. MD, Tohoku U., Sendai, Japan, 1981, PhD, 1987. Cert. specialist in neurosurg. diseases. Clin. resident Mito Nat. Hosp., Japan, 1981-83; asst. prof. dept. neurosurgery Tohoku U., 1988-96, instr. dept. neurosurgery, 1998—. Vis. scientist dept. neuropathology U. Zürich, 1992, Harvard U., Boston, 1992-93; spl. rschr. for incurable disease Ministry and Welfare, Tokyo, 1997-98; head rsch. inst. pituitory diesease Southern Tohoku Gen. Hosp., 2008-. Contbr. articles to Anatomy and Embryology, Acta Neuropathologica, Cell and Tissue Rsch., Cancer, Brit. Jour. Cancer, Am. Jour. Human Genetics, Jour. Neurosurgery, Cytokine, Jour. Neurosurgery, others. Grantee Japan Brain Found., 1993, Ministry of Edn., 1994, 96-98. Mem. AAAS, Japan Neurosurg. Com. (councilor 1987), Internat. Soc. Neuropathology. Avocations: kyu-do (Japanese archery), jogging. Office: Southern Tohoku Gen Hosp Rsch Inst for Pituitary Disease 7-115 Yatsuyamada Koriyama Fukushima 963 8563 Japan Office Phone: 024-934-5322. Business E-Mail: ikeda@nsg.med.tohoku.ac.jp, hidetoshi.ikeda@int.strins.or.jp.

IKEDA, KIYOSHI, orthopaedic surgeon; b. Omi-Hachiman, Shiga, Japan, May 24, 1939; s. Nobuo and Naka (Kurosawa) I.; m. Reiko Kitazume, Nov. 23, 1965; children: Eiko, Ken, Mitsuko, Koh, Yuriko. MD, Kyoto U., Japan, 1964; PhD, Gifu U., Japan, 1978. Med. diplomate. Intern Maebashi Red Cross Hosp., 1964; resident Kyoto (Japan) U. Hosp., 1965-68; chief orthopedic surgeon Kohga Hosp., Minakuchi, Japan, 1970-72, Fukui (Japan) Red Cross Hosp., 1972-74; asst. prof. Gifu (Japan) U., 1974-87, assoc. prof., 1987-90; chief orthopedic surgeon Kansai Denryoku Hosp., Osaka, Japan, 1990-2001; pres. Kakamigahara Meml. Clinic, 2001—03, Ikeda Seikei Clinic, 2004—; clin. advisor Gifu Ctrl. Hosp., 2009—. Mem.: AAAS, Japanese Orthop. Assn. Avocations: soccer, mountain climbing. Home: 2-187 Sohara Higashijima Kakamigahara 504-0816 Japan Office: Ikeda Seikei Clinic 2-187 Sohara Higashijima Kakamigahara 504-0816 Japan Office Phone: 8158-371-3346. Personal E-mail: ike-orthop@hi-ho.ne.jp.

IKEDA, MASAFUMI, physician; b. Fukuoka, Japan, Jan. 30, 1969; MD, Kumamoto U., 1994. Physician Nat. Cancer Ctr. Hosp. East, 2008. Office: 6-5-1 Kashiwanoha Kashiwa Chiba 277-8577 Japan Business E-Mail: masikeda@east.ncc.go.jp.

IKEDA, MASAYOSHI, orthopedist, surgeon, educator; b. Higashi-osaka, Japan, Jan. 9, 1958; m. Naoko Ikeda, May 3, 1997; children: Hirotaka, Alisa. MD, PhD, Tokai U., Kanagawa, Japan, 1984. Diplomate Japanese Orthop. Assn., 1991. Assoc. prof. medicine Tokai U., Isehara, Kanagawa, 2001—04. Office: Tokai Univ Oiso Hosp 21-1 Gakkyo Kanagawa Oiso 259-0198 Japan Office Fax: +81-463-72-2256. Business E-Mail: zenryo@oiso.u-tokai.ac.jp.

IKEDA, ROBIN M., public health service officer; BA, Stanford U., Calif.; MD, Cornell U. Med. Coll., NY; MPH in Epidemiology, Emory U., Ga. Cert. in internal medicine, in preventive medicine. Epidemic intelligence officer NY State Dept. Health Bur. Communicable Disease Control; various positions including team leader and staff epidemiologist Centers Disease Control and Prevention, Atlanta, 1993—2006, assoc. dir. sci. Nat. Ctr. Injury Prevention and Control, 2003—06, acting dir. Nat. Ctr. Injury Prevention and Control, 2010, dep. dir., 2010—, dir. Office Communicable Diseases, Injury and Environ. Health, 2010—. Capt. US Pub. Health Svc. Office: Centers Disease Control and Prevention Office NC Diseases Injury Environ Health 1600 Clifton Rd Atlanta GA 30333 *

IKEDA, SHINSUKE, economics professor; b. Osaka, Japan, Oct. 20, 1957; BS, Kobe U., 1980; PhD, Osaka U. Prof. Osaka U., 1984—. Office: 6-1 Mihogaoka Ibaraki Osaka 567-0047 Japan Business E-Mail: ikeda@iser.osaka-u.ac.jp.

IKEDIOBI, OGECHI, medical educator; b. Tallahassee, Nov. 27, 1981; PharmD, Fla. A&M U., 2003; PhD, U. Cambridge, 2007. Asst. prof. U. Calif., San Francisco, 2007. Office: 521 Parnassus Ave San Francisco CA 94143 Business E-Mail: ikediobio@pharmacy.ucsf.edu.

IKEGAMI, KAZUNORI, physician; b. Japan, Mar. 26, 1978; MD, U. Occupl. and Environ. Health, Japan, 2003, PhD, 2010. Occupl. physician Stanley Electric Co., Ltd., 2008—. Home: Imaizumi 78-4-201 Hadano Kanagawa 2570014 Japan Business E-Mail: kikegami@med.uoeh-u.ac.jp.

IKEGAMI, TOSHIHIKO, medical educator; b. Nagano, Nov. 11, 1959; MD, Tohoku U., 1984; PhD, Shinshu U., 1998. Assoc. prof. Shinshu U., Sch. Medicine, 2009—. Office: Asahi 3-1-1 Matsumoto Nagano 390-8621 Japan Business E-Mail: tikegami@shinshu-u.ac.jp.

IKEMOTO, MASAKI, medical educator; b. Kyoto, Sept. 3, 1951; s. Sohichi and Michiyo Ikemoto; m. Machiko Sawada; children: Madoka, Kohki, Saki. PhD, Kyoto, 1990. Cert. in med. transcription SCC. Med. technologist Dept. San., Kyoto, 1975—80; asst. Kyoto U., 1980—90, assoc. prof., 1990—. Dir.: (novel) Development of ELISA for Liver Arginase (Tomio Ogata prize, 1992, Saburo Kojima prize, 2000). Avocations: fishing, baseball, classical music. Home: 28-63 Tanai Ao Nagaokakyo Kyoto 617-0811 Japan Office: Kyoto Univ 53 Kawahara-cho Shogoin Sakyo-ku Kyoto 606-8507 Japan Home Phone: 81-75-954-6610; Office Phone: 81-75-751-3945. Office Fax: 81-75-751-3945; Home Fax: 81-75-954-6610. Personal E-mail: i_masaki@gaia.eonet.ne.jp. Business E-Mail: mmas@kuhp.kyoto-u.ac.jp.

IKONOMIDOU, CHRYSANTHY, pediatric neurologist, researcher; b. Thessaloniki, Greece, May 18, 1962; arrived in Germany, 1980; d. Nikolaos and Anastasia (Gutsidou) I.; m. Lechoslaw Adam Turski; children: Christopher Turski, Gabrielle Turski, Jennifer Turski. MD, Georg-August U., Goettingen, Germany, 1986, PhD, 1987. Resident Free U. Berlin, 1989-90; rsch. assoc. Washington U., St. Louis, 1987-88, resident in pediatrics, 1990-92, resident in neurology, 1992-93, fellow in pediatric neurology, 1993-95; attending in pediatric neurology, asst. prof. Humboldt U., Berlin, 1995-97, assoc. prof., 1997—2004; prof., head Dept. Pediatric Neurology, U. Tech., Dresden, Germany, 2004—09; prof. child neurology U. Wis., 2009—. Contbr. articles to profl. jours. German Acad. Austauschdienst scholar, 1980-86. Mem. Soc. for Neurosci. Office: Dept Neurology H 6/574 CSC 1685 Highland Ave Madison WI 53705 also: 4929 Gilkeson Rd Westport WI 53597 Office Phone: 608-263-5421. Business E-Mail: ikonomidou@neurology.wisc.edu. E-mail: ikonomidou@aol.com.

ILDSTAD, SUZANNE T., transplant surgeon, immunologist, educator; b. Mpls., May 20, 1952; m. David J. Tollerud, Dec. 19, 1971; children: David J. II, Suzanne K. BS in Biology summa cum laude, U. Minn., 1974; MD, Mayo Med. Sch., 1978. Diplomate Am. Bd. Surgery. Resident in gen. surgery Mass. Gen. Hosp., Boston, 1978-82, 85-86; med. staff fellow, immunology Nat. Cancer Inst., NIH, Bethesda, Md., 1982-85; clin. fellow pediatric surgery Children's Hosp. Med. Ctr., Cin., 1986-88, prof., chief dept. surgery, 1994; asst. prof. dept. surgery U. Pitts., 1988—92, assoc. prof. dept. surgery, 1992—95, prof., chief, divsn. cellular therapeutics, 1995—96; dir., Inst. for Cellular Therapeutics, prof. surgery, dept. surgery Allegheny U. Health Scis., Phila., 1996—98; Jewish Hosp. Disting. Prof. Transplantation, prof. surgery U. Louisville, Ky., 1998—, dir., Inst. for Cellular Therapeutics Ky., 1998—. Mem. Affirmative Action com., resident adv. com. dept. surgery U. Pitts., 1988-91; mem. instl. animal care and use com., 1991-94; mem. coord. com. rsch. integrity, 1992; mem. lab. usage com., oncology com., GCRC adv. com., residency coord. dept. surgery Children's Hosp., Pitts., 1988-91; vis. prof. U. Minn., 1991, Children's Meml. Hosp., U. Chgo., 1992; mem. various coms. Children's Cancer Study Group; founder, Med. Sch. Sickle Cell Project, 1999; lectr., rschr. in field. Mem. editorial bd. Jour. Transplantation, 1992, Transplantation Sci., 1992, Jour. ACS and others; mem. adv. bd. Clin. Transplantation Procs., 1992; editor Chimerism and Tolerance; contbr. articles to profl. jours., also numerous abstracts, letters and presentations in field, chpts. to books; work has been covered by CNN, CBS, Time Mag., US News and World Report, Discover, People, NY Times, Washington Post and USA Today. Recipient James A. Shannon Dirs.'s award for rsch. excellence, NIH, 1991; Instl. grantee Am. Cancer Soc., 1990-91; grantee U. Pitts., 1989-90, 91-92, Children's Hosp. Pitts. Rsch. Adv. Com., 1990-91, NIH - RO1, 1991-96, 92-95, U. Pitts. Med. Ctr., 1991-92, Juvenile Diabetes Found., 1991-92, Nat. Kidney Found., 1991-92, Am. Heart

Assn., 1992-95, Am. Diabetes Assn., 1992-94, E. Donnall Thomas Lectr. award for rsch. contbn. to the field of bone marrow transplantation; named Mayo Med. Sch. Alumnus of the Decade, 2001. Fellow ACS (Pediatric Surg. Forum award 1990, Young Investigator award 1990-92, fellowship award 1990-92, sec. Pediatric Surgery Biology Club 1989-91); mem. AAAS, AMA, Inst. Medicine, Am. Acad. Pediatrics, Am. Assn. Cancer Rsch., Am. Assn. Immunologists, Am. Fedn. Clin. Rsch., Am. Soc. Clin. Rsch., Am. Soc. Transplant Surgeons (program com. 1991-94), Am. Soc. Transplant Physicians, Mass. Med. Soc., Pediatric Transplant Study Group, Soc. Clin. Immunology, Soc. Head and Neck Surgeons (Resident/Fellow award 1983), Soc. Univ. Surgeons, Surg. Infection Soc. (travel grantee XII Internat. Congress, Sydney, Australia, 1988), Assn. Acad. Surgeons (program com. 1989-91), Cell Transplant Soc. (adv. bd. 1991, counselor-at-large 1992—), Internat. Soc. for Hematotherapy and Graft Engrng., Internat. Soc. for Heart and Lung Transplantation, Pa. Med. Soc., Phila. County Med. Soc., Transplantion Soc., NY Acad. Scis., Am. Soc. for Blood and Marrow Transplantation. Achievements include discovery of the facilitating cell in bone marrow, which allows marrow transplants to take hold and grow, even when donor and recipient are poorly matched; one of only 5 women pediatric transplant surgeons in the US; first women to ever receive a Mayo Clinic Distinguished Alumnus award; patents in field. Office: U Louisville 570 S Preston St Baxter Bldg Ste 404 Louisville KY 40202 Office Phone: 502-852-2080. Office Fax: 502-852-2085. E-mail: stild01@gwise.louisville.edu.

ILES, WARTHELL BROWNE, retired nursing educator, consultant; b. Smithfield, Va., Apr. 6, 1931; m. Comet Iles Jr.; 1 child, Comet III. Diploma, Howard U., 1952; BSN, NYU, 1969; MS in Nursing, Adelphi U., 1971; postgraduate study, NYU, 1972, Med. Coll. Va., 1984; postgrad., Old Dominion U., 1988; PhD, Columbia Pacific U., 1994; BA in Theology, Richmond Va. Sem., 1997. Cert. family nurse practitioner, clin. nurse specialist. Asst. prof. A&M U. Prairie View, Tex.; assoc. prof. U. Hampton, Va.; asst. prof. Med. Coll. Va., Richmond, Rutgers U., NJ; asst. prof. clin. chair U. Texas, Austin; cons. long and home care Met. Health Agy., Oren Hill, Md. Pre-clin. chairperson preclin. studies Prairie View A&M U., psychiatric counselor Lee Army Hosp., supr. Eastern State Psychiatric Hosp., Va., counselor Outreach Evangelistic Ministry. Author: Autonomy in Nursing Practice by USE of the Nursing Process, 1994, Imagery: It's Affect on Black Male Female Relation, 1994. Counselor outreach Holistic Out-Reach Health Program. Major USAF, 1954-74, lt. col. ret. Mem. ANA, APHA (CHP com.), Sigma Theta Tau, Chi Eta Phi. Personal E-mail: warthe7@aol.com.

ILGNER, JUSTUS FRIEDRICH RUDOLF, otorhinlarynologist, medical researcher; b. Bochum, Germany, Dec. 9, 1965; s. Martin Otto Hermann and Isolde Gertrud Ilgner. Diploma, U. Aachen Med. Sch., 1985—92; MD, Manchester U. Med. Sch., 1990—91. Bd. Cert. Med. Practitioner Chief Dist. Adminstr. Cologne / Germany, 1992, Specialization in Oto Rhino Laryngology North Rhine Gen. Med. Coun. Dusseldorf / Germany, 1997. Resident asst. Dept. Oto-Rhino-Laryngology, Head and Neck Surgery, Aachen U. Hosp., Germany, 1992—98, registrar (oberarzt), 1998—, dep. head dept., 2005—. Expert med. ins. reports Dept. Oto-Rhino-Laryngology, Head and Neck Surgery, Aachen U. Hosp., 1996—; dep. chmn. Dept. Oto-Rhino Laryngology U. Hosp. Aachen, 2005—. Contbr. articles to profl. jours. Bd. mem. Med. Students' Rep. Coun., U. of Aachen Med. Sch., 1985—90. Sr. pvt. (compulsory mil. duty) Telecom., 1984—85, Koblenz / Germany. Mem.: Am. Soc. Lasers in Surgery and Medicine, German Soc. Ultrasound in Medicine, European Rhinologic Soc., German Soc. Oto Rhino Laryngology, Head and Neck Surgery. Protestant. Achievements include patents for electro-mechanic steering device for head-lamp mounted miniature video cameras; advanced lighting for nystagmus glasses. Avocations: photography, rail travel, bicycling, sailing. Home: Am Weissenberg 8 North Rhine - Westfalia Aachen 52074 Germany Office: Univ Hosp Aachen (HNO-Klinik) Pauwelsstrasse 30 North Rhine - Westfalia Aachen 52057 Germany Office Fax: +49-241-8082523; Home Fax: +49-241-8942527. Personal E-mail: justus.ilgner@t-online.de. Business E-Mail: jilgner@ukaachen.de.

ILIADES, THEOFILOS TH, otolaryngologist, educator; s. Theodoros Kostas Iliades and Vassiliki Dimitrios Stilianidis; m. Lena Vassilios Balta, Dec. 17, 1967; children: Vassiliki Theofilos Iliadou, Asimakis Theofilos. MD, U. Thessaloniki, 1964. Diplomate Bd. Otolaryngologists, 1964. Prof. Aristotele U., Thessaloniki, Greece, 2002—, assoc. prof., 1993—2002. Dir. AXEPA Hosp., Thessaloniki, 1977—. Home: Agias Sofias 23 54623 Thessaloniki Greece Office: Univ Aristotele Filellininon 8 55236 Thessaloniki Greece Home Fax: +2310240776. E-mail: tiliades@med.auth.gr.

ILIADOU, ANASTASIA NYMAN, medical educator; b. Gothenberg, Nov. 17, 1972; MSc, U. Stockholm, 1998; PhD, Karolinska Inst., 2003. Assoc. prof. Karolinska Inst., 2009—. Mem.: SPER. Office: Nobels väg 12A Stockholm 17177 Sweden Business E-Mail: anastasia.iliadou@ki.se.

ILIC, NENAD, surgeon; b. Split, Croatia, Oct. 3, 1955; MD, Zagreb Med. Sch., 1979, PhD, 1999. Head thoracic surg. Dept. U. Surg. Hosp., 2005—. Prof. surgery Split Med. Sch., 2007. Recipient Golden Ring, Silver Star, Croatian Med. Bd., Croatian Internal Affair. Mem.: EACTS, IASLC, ESSO, ESTS, STS, Rotary Internat. Avocation: sports, music. Office: University Surg Hosp Spinciceva 1 Split 21000 Croatia E-mail: n_ilic_hr@yahoo.com.

ILIEVA, ILIYANA, ophthalmologist; b. Sofia, Bulgaria, June 7, 1970; d. Bozhidar Iliev and Anna Ilieva; m. Philip Petrov; 1 child, Boris Petrov. MD, Sofia Med. U., Bulgaria, 1995, ophthalmology specialist, 2003; PhD, Hokkaido U., Japan, 2007. Cert. ophthalmology specialist Sofia, 2004. Ophthalmologist 30 Polyclinic, Sofia, 1996—97, Third City Hosp., Sofia, 1998—2003, First City Hosp., Sofia, 2003—. Scholar, Japanese Govt., 2002—07. Achievements include research in the effects of GBE, captopril and other agents on uveitis models. Home Fax: 359 2 885 5050. Personal E-mail: achibobo@yahoo.com.

ILIOPOULOU, EVGHENIA, plastic surgeon; b. Tirgoviste, Romania, Sept. 20, 1952; d. Athanasios and Vasiliki (Vafiadou) I. Degree, Bucharest Med. U., Romania, 1979. Sr. house officer, gen. surgeon U. Alex-Polis, 1982-84; registrar plastic surgeon Kat. Hosp., Athens, 1984-87; registrar NTL clinic Gen. Hosp., Athens, registrar urology clinic; specialist in plastic surgery, 1988; jr. cons. dept. plastic surgery K.A.T. Gen. Hosp., Athens, 1989-97, sr. cons. dept. plastic surgery, 1997—. Clin. observer Shriners Burns Hosp., Boston, 2000, East Grinstead Hosp., England, 2003. Author: Burn—What Next, 1997; contbr. articles to profl. jours. Mem. Am. Burn Assn., Med. Burn Assn., Internat. Soc. Burn Injuries, European Burn Assn., IPRAS. Avocation: writing articles for newspapers. Home: 3is Septembriu 119 112 51 Athens Greece E-mail: tzenilio@gmail.com.

ILKGUL, OZER, surgeon; b. Antalya, Turkey, Sept. 29, 1971; Degree in Surgery, Ege U., 2000. Med. staff surgeon Celal Bayar U., 2000—05; staff surgeon Pvt. Anadolu Hosp., 2005—. Mem.: European Soc. Surg. Rsch. Avocation: water sports. Office: 1352 Sokak Antalya 07100 Turkey Business E-Mail: ilkgul@doctor.com.

ILLANES, DIEGO SEBASTIAN, obstetrician, gynecologist, urogynecologist; naturalized, 2010; s. Luis Eduardo Illanes and Marta Lucia Vidal; m. Katarina Muckova, Feb. 25, 2005; 1 child, Julia. MD, Cath. U., Cordoba, 1999. Diplomate Am. Bd. Obstetrics and Gynecology. Rsch. assoc. in medicine Brigham and Womens Hosp., Harvard Med. Sch., Boston, 2001—04; gross anatomy instr. Harvard Med. Sch., Boston, 2003—04; ob-gyn. intern physician Albany Med. Coll., NY, 2004—05; ob-gyn. resident physician U. Mass. Med. Sch., Worcester, 2005—08, female pelvic medicine and reconstructive surgery fellow, 2008—11. Contbr. articles to profl. jours. Capt. USAR. Recipient Gross Anatomy award, Cordoba Nat. U., 1995; named Best Gross Anatomy Lab Instr. of Yr., Harvard Med. Sch., 2004, Berlex Tchg. award, U. Mass., 2006. Mem.: AMA, Am. Assn. Gyn. Laparoscopists (resident mem. 2005), Am. Coll. Ob-Gyn. (jr. fellow 2004). Roman Catholic. Office: University Mass Meml Med Ctr Women's Health Ctrl Mass 100 MLK Jr Blvd Ste 300 Worcester MA 01608 Office Phone: 508-755-4861.

ILLGEN-WILCKE, BRUNHILDE, biologist; b. Zagreb, Yugoslavia, Apr. 14, 1950; d. Werner and Nada (Sušić) I.; m. Wilko Wilcke, Mar. 26, 1990. Dipl.Biol., U. Tubingen, Tubingen, Germany, 1975, Dr. rer.nat., 1983; MD, U. Zagreb, Zagreb, 1985, D in Med. Sci., 1986. Clin. rschr. Merz & Co., Frankfurt, Germany, 1986; head microbiology, lab. animal breeding Ciba, Stein, Switzerland, 1986—96, head lab. animal breeding, 1995-96; head microbiology, lab animal svcs. Novartis, Basle, Switzerland, 1997-2000; head microbiol. svcs. MicroBioS, Reinach, Switzerland, 2000—. Mem. German Assn. Lab. Animal Sci., Am. Assn. Lab. Animal Sci., Swiss Assn. Lab. Animal Sci., Com. Hygiene, Swiss Assn. Tropical Medicine and Parasitology. Office: MicroBioS GmbH 4153 Reinach Switzerland

ILLIDGE, TIMOTHY MARTIN, oncologist, researcher; b. Wallasey, Eng., July 29, 1964; s. John James and Dorothy Illidge; m. Elizabeth Frances Jane Coningsby, Apr. 11, 1987; children: Benjamin Charles James, Laura Alice Elizabeth, Rebecca Charlotte Kate. BSc in Biochemistry with honors, U. London, 1985, MB, BChir, 1988; PhD, U. Southampton, Eng., 1998. Sr. lectr. Southampton U., 1998—2004; prof. targeted therapy and oncology Manchester U., 2004—. Contbr. articles to profl. jours. Chmn. clin. rsch. tng. fellowship com. Cancer Rsch. UK. Named Investigator of Yr., Brit. Oncol. Assn./Royal Coll. Radiologists, 1997, Brit. Nuc. Medicine Soc., 1998; Sr. Fulbright scholar, Fulbright Commn., 1998, Karol Sicher Cancer scholar, 1998, Winston Churchill fellow for medicine, 1998, Sr. Clin. Rsch. fellow, Cancer Rsch. UK, 1998. Fellow: Royal Coll. Pathologists, Royal Coll. Radiologists (life; chmn. rsch. com. 2004—, fellow 2010—, FRCR 1998, Frank Ellis Gold medal 1998); mem.: Royal Coll. Physicians (life). Achievements include research in antibody targeted therapies. Office: Christie Hospital 550 Wilmslow Road M20 4BX Manchester England Personal E-mail: tmi@manchester.ac.uk.

ILOGU, NOEL OBIAJULU, physician; b. Ibadan, Oyo, Nigeria, Dec. 15, 1961; came to U.S., 1994; s. Edmund Christopher and Elizabeth Chineze (Obiago) I.; m. Sandra Nneka Ike, July 15, 1995; children: Chudi, Chisom, Tobenna. MD, U. Benin, Nigeria, 1985. Diplomate Am. Bd. Internal Medicine, Am. Bd. Addiction Medicine. Sr. house officer NHS Hosps., U.K., 1988-92; career registrar Burnley Gen. Hosp., England, 1992-94; resident St. Peter's U. Hosp., New Brunswick, NJ, 1994—97; pvt. practice Somerset, NJ, 1997—. Cons. on tobacco issues in Africa, Lagos, Nigeria, 1997—; attending physician Robert Wood Johnson U. Hosp., St. Peters U. Hosp., New Brunswick. Contbr. articles to profl. jours. Mem. ACP, Am. Soc. Addiction Medicine, Med. Soc. NJ, Royal Coll. Physicians (Edinburgh), NAACP. Office: 81 Veronica Ave Ste 204 Somerset NJ 08873 Office Phone: 732-247-9001. Personal E-mail: nilogu@pol.net.

ILUNGA, TSHINKO BONGO, chief health expert; b. Kananga, Zaire, July 28, 1950; s. Ladislas and Muadi Adolphine (Kasonga) I.; m. Ntumba Cathy Kabamba, Apr. 11, 1975; children: Kasonga, Muadi, Ilunga, Kanyeba. BA, U. Zaire, 1972; MPH, Tulane U., 1977; PhD, U. Montreal, 1992. Adminstr. Mama Yemo Hosp., Kinshasa, Zaire, 1972-75; asst. prof. U. Zaire, Kinshasa, 1978-81; health sys. analyst African Devel. Bank, Abidjan, Côte d'Ivoire, 1981—89, cons., 1989-90, chief health expert, officer-in-charge human devel., divsn. mgr. OSHD3 Madagascar. Lectr. U. Montreal, Can., 1990-91. Author: Health Systems- The Challenge of Change, 1992. Internat. Devel. Rsch. Ctr. grantee U. Montreal, 1990; U.S. Aid scholar Tulane U., 1975, United Nations U. scholar U. Philippines, 1981. Mem. APHA, Nat. Coun. for Internat. Health, N.Y. Acad. Scis. Roman Catholic. Avocations: lawn tennis, biking, movies, music. Office: c/o African Devel Bank 15 Ave du Ghana PO Box 323 1002 Tunis Tunisia *

ILYIN, VICTOR IVANOVITCH, molecular biologist, researcher; b. Kazan, Russia, Mar. 5, 1950; MS in Bionics, Kazan State U., 1972; PhD in Cell Biophysics, Inst. Biol. Physics, USSR Acad. Sci., 1977. Head Lab. Nerve Cell Biophysics, Inst. Cell Biophysics, Russian Acad. Scis., 1989—96; postdoc. rschr., sr. scientist I ACEA Pharms., Inc., 1993—95; sr. scientist I, II, rsch. fellow CoCensys, Inc., 1995—99; rsch. fellow Purdue Neurosci., Discovery Rsch., 1999—2001; assoc. dir., molecular pharmacology Purdue Pharma., L.P., Discovery Rsch., 2002—. Sci. coun. bd. mem. Inst. Biophysics, Inst. Cell Biophysics, 1986—92. Grants, Small Bus. Innovative Rsch., 1999—2000. Mem.: Biophys. Soc., Soc. Neurosci. Avocations: tennis, fishing, gymnastics. Home: 308 Bridgepoint Rd Belle Mead NJ 08502 Personal E-mail: victor.ilyin@pharma.com.

IM, JEEAEE, medical researcher; b. Busan, Republic of Korea, Mar. 1, 1966; d. BulEe Im and OkHee Kim; m. DongJu Lee; 1 child, MinYoung Lee. PhD, Yonsei U., Seoul, Republic of Korea, 2003. Cert. clin. lab. technologist Ministry Health Welfare, 1989. Lab. supr. Mizmedi Hosp., Seoul, 1994—2008; CEO INTOTO Co., Seoul, 2008—, head rschr., dept. sport medicine rsch. ctr., 2008—. Prof. Yonsei U., Wonju, Republic of Korea, 1999—2003, consulting, Seoul, 2004—. Translator: (text book) Essential Hematology; author: Clinical Hematology; contbr. scientific papers. Grant, Korean Acad. Famliy Medicine, 2006, 2008, Prof. grant, Yonsei U., 2006, 2008, Base Sci. Rsch. grant, Sci. Found., 2007, grant, Korean Acad. Clin. Geriat., 2007, Health Promotion grant, Mgmt. Ctr. Health Promotion, 2008, grant, Small and Medium Bus. Adminstrn., 2006. Fellow: J. Exp. Biomed. Sci. (corr.). Achievements include research in relationship between osteocalcin and glucose metabolism in postmenopausal women; visceral adiposity is associated with serum retinol binding protein-4 levels in healthy women; insulin resistance is associated with arterial stiffness independent of obesity in male adolescents; differential immune profiles following experimental echinostoma hortense infection in BALB/c and C3H/HeN mice; different levels of platelet activation in normal pregnancy and pregnancy-induced hypertension (PIH); the relationship between fitness and insulin resistance and cardiovascular risk factors; circulating levels of chemokine. Avocations: classical music, travel. Home: 201-1004 Raemian Tower Bangbae-Dong Seoul 137-935 Republic of Korea Office: Intoto Co 1304 ACE High-End Tower 2 Guro3-Dong Seoul 157-280 Republic of Korea Personal E-mail: jeaeim@hanmail.net.

IM, MOON WHAN, obstetrician, professor; s. Km Sang Chung. MD, Seoul Nat. U., 1980, PhD, 1992. Cert. ob-gyn. specialist Ministry Health, Welfare & Family Affairs, 1990, E.C.F.M.G., 1980, specialist Korean Soc. Menopause, 2008. Resident, ob-gyn. Seoul Nat. U. Hosp., 1985—90; asst. prof., ob-gyn. Dongguk U., Kyung Ju, Republic of Korea, 1990—96; prof., ob-gyn. Inha U., Incheon, 1996—; vis. prof. Stanford U. Sch. Medicine, Palo Alto, Calif., 2001, Harvard U. Sch. Medicine, Boston, 2002; postdoc. fellow Yale U. Sch. Medicine, New Haven, 2001—02. Mem., transfusion, med. ins. & proper treatment com. Dongguk U. Hosp., Pohang, 1991—94, mem., emergency com., 1991—94, mem., oper. rm. com., 1991—94, mem., pharmacy com., 1991—94, chmn., dept. ob-gyn., 1992—94; mem. Ob-Gyn. Specialist Qualifying Exam. Com., Seoul, 1996; mem., nutrition com. Inha U. Hosp., Incheon, 1998—2002, mem., med. svc. mgmt. com., 1998—2004, mem., med. emergency com., 1998—2002, mem., med. libr. com., 2000—, mem., oper. rm. com., 2000—04, mem., med. edn. com., 2000—06; mem. Entrance Exam. Com. Residency Tng., Seoul, 2000, Com. Specialist Qualifying Exam., Seoul, 2001, Organizing Com. 8th Internat. Congress Andrology, Seoul, 2004—05, Com. Med. Info. Svc. Korean Med. Assn., Seoul, 2006—, Rsch. Achievement Assessment Com. Korea Food & Drug Adminstrn., Seoul, 2007—, Exam. Com. Korea Rsch. Found., Seoul, 2007; mem., planning com. Korean Soc. Gynecologic Endoscopy, Seoul, 1996—98; exec. sec. Exam. Com. Korean Soc. Complementary, Seoul, 2004—; dir. Korean Birth Defect Forum, Seoul, 2004—05; chair person XIXth Asian & Oceanic Congress Ob-Gyn., Seoul, 2005, 11th Congress World Fedn. Ultrasound Medicine & Biology, Seoul, 2006; consultation com. mem. Ministry Environment, Seoul, 2006—; editl. bd. mem. Jour. Infectious Diseases & Immunity, 2009—; reviewer Jour. Perinatal Medicine, 2010; editl. bd. mem. Open Jour. Ob-gyn., 2011—; mem. scoring panel Korean Health Industry Devel. Inst., 2011. Contbr. numerous sci. papers & articles to profl. jours. and numerous publs. Capt. Army Physician, 1982—85, Incheon, Republic of Korea. Recipient Citation for Best Clin. Trainee award, Seoul Nat. U., 1986. Mem.: Korean Soc. Ob-gyn. (mem, Legis. and Judiciary Com. 2010—), Internat. Biog. Ctr. (dep. dir. gen. 2011—, hon. dir. gen. 2011—), Am. Biog. Inst. (dep. gov. 2010—), World Congress Arts, Scis. and Comms. (amb. 2010—, v.p. 2010—), Nat. Rsch. Found. (assessor 2010), Korean Soc. Reproductive Medicine, Am. Soc. Reproductive Medicine, Korean Assn. Gynecologic Endoscopy, Korean Soc. Menopause, Korean Soc. Complementary & Integrative Medicine (dir. exam bd. 2004—), Korean Assn. Genetics, Korean Soc. Perinatology, Korean Assn. Ob-Gyn. (academic rsch. dir. 1999—2001, Citation for Best Dr. award 1997), Korean Soc. Gynecologic Oncology & Colposcopy (mem., judging com. 2000—02), Korean Soc. Fetal Medicine, Korean Acad. Anti-Aging Medicine, Korean Assn. Voluntary Sterilization, World Assn. Perinatal Medicine, Am. Acad. Anti-Aging Medicine, Korean Soc. Ultrasound Obstetrics (mem., exhbn. com. 1997—99), Korean Med. Assn. (expert advisor 2006—). Home: Unit 1-2106 1st World Apt Songdo-dong Yeonsu-gu Incheon 406-743 Republic of Korea Office: Inha Univ Sch Medicine Dept Ob & Gyn 7-206 3-Ga Shinheung-Dong Jung-Gu 400-711 Incheon Incheon Republic of Korea Home Phone: 82-10-3250-2331; Office Phone: 82-32-890-3427. Business E-Mail: mwim@inha.ac.kr.

IM, SANGHEE, medical educator; b. Inchon, May 9, 1976; MD, Kwandong U., 2001; PhD, Yonsei U., 2010. Asst. prof. Jeju Nat. U. Hosp., 2008—11, MyongJi Hosp., Kwandong U. Coll. Medicine, 2011—. Dir. Regional Cerebrovascular Rehab. Ctr., Jeju, 2008—11. Recipient Pres. Rsch. Initiative awards, AANEM. Mem.: Korean Soc. Musculoskeletal Medicine, Korean Acad. Gereat. Rehab. Medicine, Korean Assn. EMG-Electrodiagnostic Medicine, Korean Acad. Rehab. Medicine. Office: MyongJi Hosp Dept Rehabilitation Goyang Gyeonggi 412-270 Republic of Korea E-mail: dongin32@yahoo.com.

IM, SIN-HYEOG, immunologist, educator; b. Gwangju, Republic of Korea, Mar. 1, 1964; s. Kim; m. Geong-Ok Hong; children: Chang-Rok, Chang-Kyun. PhD, Weizmann Inst. Sci., Rehovot, Israel, 2001. Sr. rschr. CKD Pharm. Co., Seoul, Republic of Korea, 1991—96; rsch. fellow Harvard Med. Sch., Boston, 2001—03; prof. Gwangju Inst. Sci. and Tech., 2004—. Recipient Young Investigator award, Soc. Biol. Rsch., 2003. Fellow: Am. Assn. Immunologists. Office: Gwangju Inst Sci and Tech Oryong-Dong Buk-Gu 1 500-712 Gwangju Republic of Korea Office Fax: 82629702484. Business E-Mail: imsh@gist.ac.kr.

IM, SOOKBIN, nursing educator; d. Yisoo Im and Minja Park. BS in Nursing, Seoul Nat. U., 1979, MS in Nursing, 1988, PhD in Nursing, 1997. Cert. health tchr., Ministry Edn., 1979; youth counseler(1st level) Ministry Culture and Tourism, 2003, counseling profl. (2nd level) Assn. Korean Counseling Profls., 2006. Child-psychiatry nurse intern Children's Meml. Hosp., Chgo., 1984—85; nurse Seoul Nat. U. Hosp., 1979—85, headnurse, 1985—92; fulltime lectr. Seoul Health Jr. Coll., Sungnam City, Kyungi-Do, Republic of Korea, 1992—95, asst. prof., 1995—98; vis. scholar U. Wash., Sch. Nursing, Seatle, 1997—97; assoc. prof., dir. nursing dept. Eulji U., Daejeon Metropolitan City, Republic of Korea, 1998—2002, prof., dean sch. nursing, 2002—05, prof., dean grad. sch. advanced practice nursing, 2003—07, prof., dir. edn. ctr., 2007—. Dir. academia Korean Assn. Persons with Autism, Seoul, 1996—98, bd. mem., 2006—; mem. consulting com. Sungnam Childabuse Counseling Ctr., Republic of

Korea, 1996—98; bd. mem. Korea Assn. Prevention Child Abuse, Neglect, Seoul, 1998—; mem. examinational com. tchr. mid. sch. Korean Ednl. Devel. Inst., Seoul, 1998; v.p. Korean Soc. Stress Medicine, Seoul, 1999—2001, cons., 2006—; cmty. bd. mem. Korean Coun. Dir. Nursing Coll., Seoul, 2000—01; mem. com. devel. test items nurses licensing exam. Nat. Health Pers. Licensing Exam. Bd., Seoul, 2000; lectr. Daejeon Ednl. Tng. Inst., 2000; mem. of oper. com. Daeduk-Gu Mental Health Ctr., Daejeon Metropolitan City, 2001—; mem. com. devel. test items nurses licensing exam. Nat. Health Pers. Licensing Exam. Bd., Seoul, 2002; v.p. Korean Assn. Woman Faculty, Daejeon-Chungnam Br., 2005—07, Coun. Nursing Faculty Chungchyung Area, Daejeon Metropolitan City, 2005—07, pres., 2007—. Contbr. articles to profl. jours. Profl. vol. Narrative Rsch. Ctr., Seoul, 2007—08, Nat. Emergency Mgmt. Agy., Seoul, 2008. Recipient award, Mayor Daejeon Met. City, 1999, Excellent paper, Korean Acad. Nursing, 2001—02, Ofcl award, Pres. Daejeon Met. City Nurses Assn.-, 2006, Min. Edn., Sci., and Tech., 2007; grantee, Seoul Nat. U. Hosp., 1985, Hosp. Mgmt. Rsch. Ctr., 1994, Seoul Health Jr. Coll., 1994, 1997, Korea Rsch. Found., 1997, 2002, Eulji U., 2003, Korea Rsch. Found., 2007. Mem.: Internat. Soc. Psychiatric-Mental Health Nurses, Sigma Theta Tau Internat. Honor Soc. Nursing, Korean Acad. Nursing (mem. academic com. 2000—02, article reviewer 2000—, 2000—, mem. ednl. com. 2002—03, mem. academic com. 2002—03, mem. ednl. com. 2002—03), Korean Soc. Stress Medicine, Korean Acad. Psychiat. Mental Health Nursing (treas. 1994—95, dir. academia 1999—2001, article reviewer 1999—, cmty. bd. mem. 2001—03, v.p. 2008—), Korean Psychiat. Mental Health Nurses Assn. (academia, rsch. bd. 2005—07, v.p. 2007—), Korean Nurses Assn. Buddhist. Achievements include development of multi-agent weight-control camp program consisted exercise, cognitive therapy, and aroma therapy; return-to-work program for off-work nurses; first to establishing nursing care svc. System for child-adolescent psychiatric inpatient program. Avocations: travel, walking, writing, flower arranging. Office: Sch Nursing Eulji Univ 143-5 Yongdu-Dong Joong-Gu 301-832 Daejeon Daejeon Republic of Korea Office Fax: 82-42-259-1709. Personal E-mail: imsb550901@hanmail.net. Business E-Mail: imsb@eulji.ac.kr.

IMAGAWA, SHIGEHIKO, hematologist, molecular biologist; b. Tokyo, Apr. 26, 1955; d. Uzuhiko and Miyuki Imagawa; m. Yoshiko Imagawa, May 12, 1984; children: Takahiko, Ayako. MD, U. Tsukuba, 1980, PhD in Med. Sci., 1984. Bd. cert. physician Japan. Med. resident Tsukuba U. Hosp., 1984—86; assoc. investigator Harvard Med. Sch., Boston, 1986—89; asst. prof. Jichi Med. Sch., Tochigi, 1989—2000, Jichi Med. Sch., Grad. Sch., 1996—2000, U. Tsukuba, 2000—. Program com. Kidney and Erythropoietin Forum, Tokyo, 2001—. Author: (books) Molecular Biology of Erythropoietin, 1989, Molecular Medicine, 2001, Molecular Biology and Clinical Use of Erythropoietin, 2002. Mem.: Am. Soc. Clin. Oncology, Japanese Soc. Hematology (mem. editl. bd. 1998—2000, Young Investigator award 1998), Am. Soc. Hematology. Avocations: baseball, music, golf. Office: Doctoral Program Sports Medicine Grad Sch Comprehensive U Tsukuba Tennoudai 1-1-1 Ibaraki Tsukuba 305-8577 Japan Home Phone: 81 29 836 7638; Office Phone: 81 29 853 3045. Office Fax: 81 29 853 3045. Business E-Mail: simagawa@md.tsukuba.ac.jp.

IMAI, HIROYUKI, pediatrician; b. Kyoto, Apr. 11, 1957; s. Ei-ichi and Masako Imai; m. Yoshiko Hori; children: Shoutaro, Koutaro, Kentaro, Rintaro. MD, Kanazawa U., Japan, 1982. With Japan Red Cross Med. Ctr., Tokyo, 1982—84; resident Mastudo (Japan) Mcpl. Hosp., 1984—85; fellow Kyoto Min-iren Ctrl. Hosp., 1986—99; dir. Kishoin Children's Clinic, Kyoto, 2000—. Author: Children and the Car-Dominated Society, 1998; translator: Saving Children (Japanese edit.), 1998. Adviser People Before Cars, Tokyo, 1995; dir. Safekids Network Japan, Kyoto, 1997. Avocations: fossil collecting, entomology. Home: 222 Nishinokyo-SH 16-44 Nishinokyo-Kasuga Kyoto 604-8453 Japan Office: Kishoin Children's Clinic 23 Kishoin-Nishiura-cho Minami-ku Kyoto 601-8352 Japan Office Fax: +81-75-693-1601. Personal E-mail: imaih@gold.ocn.ne.jp. Business E-Mail: dkaly304@kyoto.zaq.ne.jp.

IMAI, ITSUKI, physical therapist; b. Yamagata, Yamagata, Japan, Jan. 12, 1978; s. Emiko Imai; m. Hiromi Imai. Master's degree, Internat. U. of Health and Welfare Grad. Sch., Japan, 2003. Lic. phys. therapist Ministry of Health, Labour and Welfare. Technol. asst. Basic Med. Rsch. Ctr., Internat. U. of Health and Welfare, Otawara, Tochigi, Japan, 2001—03; phys. therapist Kawagoe Rehab. Ctr., 2003—04, Nasu Neurosurg. Ctr., Nasushiobara, 2004—. Mem.: The World Fed. for Neurorehabilitation, Japanese Soc. Neural Repair & Neurorehabilitation, Soc. Phys. Therapy Sci., Japanese Phys. Therapy Assn. (assoc.). Avocations: reading, tea drinking, walking. Office: Nasu Neurosurg Ctr 453-14 Nomaazakaminuma Nasushiobara 325-0014 Japan Office Phone: 81 287-62-5500. Office Fax: +81 287-62-5505. Personal E-mail: itsuki_i@hotmail.com.

IMAI, KAZUSHI, dentist, educator; b. Kushiro, Hokkaido, Japan, June 16, 1964; s. Tsuneo and Junko Imai; m. Yumi Kanehira, June 16, 1991; 1 child, Lisa. DDS, PhD, Kanazawa U., Japan, 1994. Cert. dentist Japanese Govt., 1989. Postdoctoral fellow Kanazawa U., 1995—97, Columbia U., NYC, 1997—2000; asst. prof. Nippon Dental U., Chiyoda-ku, Tokyo, Japan, 2000—02, assoc. prof., 2003—. Fellow, Japan Soc. for Promotion Sci., 1997—2000; Postdoctoral fellow, 1995—97. Office: Dept Biochemistry Nippon Dental Univ 1-9-20 Fujimi Tokyo 102-8159 Japan Office Fax: 81.3.3261.8875. E-mail: kimai@tky.ndu.ac.jp.

IMAI, MASAHITO, ophthalmologist, educator; b. Tokyo, Feb. 28, 1959; MD, Yamanashi Med. Coll., 1986. Assoc. prof., dept. ophthalmology U. Yamanashi, Japan, 2006—. Mem.: Assn. Rsch. Vision & Ophthalmology. Office: Shimokato 1110 Chuo Yamanashi 409-3898 Japan Office Fax: 81-552-73-6757. E-mail: mimai@yamanashi.ac.jp.

IMAI, YASUO, pathologist, researcher; b. Imabari, Ehime, Japan, July 22, 1963; married. M. D., Ph. D., Faculty of Medicine, U. of Tokyo, Tokyo, Japan, 1982—88. Lic. Japanese Govt., 1988, cert. Japanese Soc. Pathology, 1999. Trainee dr. Tokyo U. Hosp., Bunkyo-ku, 1988—90, staff dr., 1992—94, 1998—2000, Mitsui Meml. Hosp., Chiyoda-ku, 1990—92, Grad. Sch. Medicine U. Tokyo, 1994—98; assoc. Japanese Found. Cancer Rsch., Toshima-ku, Tokyo, 2001—04; assoc. prof. Dokkyo Med. U., Koshigaya, Saitama, Japan, 2005—. Recipient Seki Minato award, Dokkyo Med. U., 2005, Rsch. award, Japanese Soc. Pathology, 2005; grantee, Pub. Trust Haraguchi Meml. Cancer Rsch. Fund, 1999, Pub. Trust Hishinomi Cancer Rsch. Fund, 2002; Rsch. grant, Ministry of Edn., Sci., Sports, and Culture Japan, 2006—07, Ministry of Edn., Sci., Sports, and Culture of Japan, 2008—10. Fellow: Japanese Soc. Internal Medicine. Achievements include patents for circumvention of ABC transporter-mediated anti-cancer drug resistance; method for detecting cells sensitive to anti-cancer drugs. Office: Dokkyo Med Univ 2-1-50 Minami-Koshigaya Koshigaya Saitama 343-8555 Japan Office Phone: 81-48-965-8869. Office Fax: 81-48-965-9326. Personal E-mail: yimai@sepia.ocn.ne.jp. Business E-Mail: ya-imai@dokkyomed.ac.jp.

IMAMURA, ATSUSHI, pediatrician; b. Ogaki, Gifu Prefecture, Japan, July 11, 1961; s. Masayoshi and Mariko Imamura; m. Kiyomi Tanase, Jan. 27, 1991; children: Eiji, Jun, Takashi. MD, Gifu U., 1987. Resident pediats. Gifu (Japan) Hosp., 1988, Takayama Red Cross Hosp., Japan, 1989—91; resident neuropediatrics Nat. Ctr. Hosp. Mental Nervous and Muscular Disorders, Japan, 1991—93; mem. staff pediats. Gifu (Japan) U. Hosp., 1993—97, Toyohashi-Higashi Nat. Hosp., Japan, 1997—2000, Ogaki Mcpl. Hosp., Japan, 2000—02; chief pediatrician Gifu (Japan) Gen. Med. Ctr., 2002—. Contbr. articles to profl. jours. Recipient prize, Japanese Soc. Inborn Error of Metabolism, 1999. Home: 2-2 Wakafuku-cho Gifu 502-0811 Japan Office: Gifu Gen Med Ctr 4-6-1 Noishiki Gifu 500-8717 Japan Office Fax: 81-58-248-3805. E-mail: aimamura30@hotmail.com.

IMANISHI, YOSHIMASA, medical educator; b. Hiki-gun, Saitama, Japan, Feb. 14, 1949; s. Manji and Kaku; m. Yoshida Imanishi Kazuyo; 1 child, Hiroharu. BS in Pharmacy, Tokyo Coll. Pharmacy, Hachioji, 1975; MB, St. Marianna U. Sch. Medicine, Kawasaki, Kanagawa, Japan, 1979, MD, 1986. Cert. pharmacist. Vis. prof. St. Marianna U. Sch. Medicine, 1986—90, asst. prof., 1991—94, assoc. prof., 1994—2009, vis. prof., 2009—; fellow Johns Hopkins Med. Inst., Balt., 1990—91. Home: 694-14 Miyazaki Miyamae-ku Kawasaki 2160033 Japan Business E-Mail: y-imanishi@e04.itscom.net.

IMBASCIATI, ANTONIO, psychologist, educator; b. Pisa, Italy, May 9, 1936; Degree in Medicine & Surgery, U. Milan, 1961, M in Psychotechnics, 1964, M in Clin. Psychology, 1965; M in Infant Neuropsychiatry, U. Milan, Pisa, 1967; student, Italian Psychoanalytical Soc., 1968. Cert. univ. prof. 1961, lic. lectr. 1970. Prof., faculty medicine U. Brescia, 1971—; tng. psychoanalyst Internat. Psychoanalytical Assn., 1980—2011; assoc. prof. psychology U. Turin, 1971; assoc. mem. Italical Psychoanalytical Soc. & Internat. Psychoanalytical Assn., 1980—; prof. psychology Turin, 1975—; prof. clin. psychology U. Brescia, 1986—; tng. analyst Italian Psychoanalytical Soc., 1994—. Office: Viale Europa 11 Brescia 25123 Italy Business E-Mail: imbascia@med.unibs.it, antonio@imbasciati.it.

IMBER, GERALD, plastic surgeon; b. NYC, Jan. 9, 1941; s. George Howard and Rose (Weiss) I.; children: Peter, Jason, Gregory. MD, SUNY, 1966. Diplomate Am. Bd. Plastic Surgery. Intern LI Jewish Med. Ctr., 1966-67; resident Kaiser Hosp., LA, 1970-72, USAF Griffiss AFB Hosp., Rome, NY, 1970-72, NY Presbyn. Hosp.-Cornell Med. Ctr., NYC, 1972-74, attending surgeon, 1974—, clin. asst., prof. surgery; dir. Imber Clinic, NYC, 1982—. Author: Youth Corridor, 1997, For Men Only, 1998, Absolute Beauty, 2005. Trustee Inwood House, NYC, 1998—. Capt. USAF, 1968—70. Mem. Am. Soc. Plastic Surgeons, NE Soc. Plastic Surgeons, NY State Med. Soc., NY County Med. Soc. Avocations: polo, sailing. Office: Imber Clinic 1009 5th Ave New York NY 10028-0155 Office Phone: 212-472-1800. Business E-Mail: drimber@drimber.com.

IMMEL, BARBARA KAY KEPHART, management consultant; b. Bakersfield, Calif., July 31, 1956; m. Joseph Herbert Immel, Jr., Aug. 31, 1979; children: Joseph Herbert Immel, III, Elizabeth Logan. BA in English, U. Calif., Santa Barbara, 1978, single subject tchg. credential, 1979; grad., Stanford Profl. Pub. Course, 1981, Stanford U. Exec. Pub. Course, 1982, grad., 2002, Buckley Sch. Pub. Speaking, 2000, grad., 2001, Stanford Writer's Workshop, 2009. Asst. to pres. Vet. Practice Pub. Co., Santa Barbara, 1980—81; tech. editor I-III Syva Co., Palo Alto, Calif., 1982—86; adminstr. Syntex Corp., Palo Alto, 1986—92; compliance mgr. Chiron Corp., Emeryville, Calif., 1993—95; cons. pres. Immel Resources, LLC, Petaluma, Calif., 1995—. Vol. libr. Career Action Ctr., Palo Alto, Calif., 1982—86; instr. U. Calif. Berkeley Ext., 1995—2000, co-dir. drug devel. course, 1998—2000; guest lectr. undergrad. pharmacology course U. Calif., Berkeley, 1999—; cons. in field. Columnist: Biopharm mag., 1996—2007; contbr. articles to profl. jours., Dekker's Ency. of Pharm. Tech.; editor-in-chief Immel Report, 2004—. Scholar Pres. scholar, U. Calif. Santa Barbara, 1974—78. Mem.: Med. Device Planning Com., Food & Drug Adminstrn. Inspections Summit (chair person 2006—), Pharm. Rschrs. and Mfrs. Am. (tng. com. 1988—92), Parenteral Drug Assn. (tng. com. 1993—96). Avocations: reading, travel. Office Phone: 707-778-7222. Personal E-mail: immel@immel.com.

IMPARATO, ANTHONY MICHAEL, vascular surgeon, educator, researcher; b. NYC, July 29, 1922; s. Silverio and Olga (Santilli) I.; m. Agatha Maria Petriccione, Dec. 19, 1943; children: Maria April Imparato, Karen Elsa Imparato Cotton. AB, Columbia U., 1943; MD, NYU, 1946. Diplomate Am. Bd. Surgery; cert. spl. qualifications in gen. vascular surgery. Intern U.S. Naval Hosp., Bklyn., 1946-47; fellow in anatomy NYU Med. Sch., 1949-50; successively intern, asst. resident in surgery, resident, chief resident in surgery NYU Med. Center Bellevue Hosp., 1950-56; mem. faculty NYU Med. Center, 1956—, dir. div. vascular surgery, 1975-92, prof. surgery, 1975—2000, prof. emeritus surgery, 2000—. Leader People-to-People delegation in vascular surgery: western Europe 1982, Soviet Union, 1985; ops. com. "Cooperative VA Study on Asymptomatic Carotid Stenosis", 1983-87 and Nascet, 1987-92; hon. pres. Societa Italiana Prevenzione Ictus Cerebrale, 1997, 98; lectr. in field. Contbr. over 175 articles in field, over 35 chpts. to textbooks. Served as officer M.C. USNR, 46-49, 50. Recepient Jerome S. Cole Honoree award, NYU Med. Sch., 2001; grantee NIH, 1976-81. Fellow ACS, Am. Coll. Cardiology, Acad. Sr. Profl. Eckerd Coll.; mem. Am. Heart Assn. (fellow Stroke Coun.), Am. Surg. Assn., Soc. Vascular Surgery (pres. 1984-85, Disting. Svc. award, 1983, 2003), Internat. Cardiovascular Soc., Soc. Clin. Vascular Surgery, Soc. Angiologia Uruguay, Royal Australasian Coll. Surgeons (hon.), Soc. Internat. Chirurgie, N.Y. Regional Vascular Soc. (co-founder, pres. 1982-84), N.Am. Soc. Pacing and Electrophysiology (founding mem.), James IV Assn. Surgeons (dir., treas.), Lithuanian Vascular Soc. (hon.), Alpha Omega Alpha. Office: NYU Faculty Practice Area 530 1st Ave Ste 6-f New York NY 10016-6402 Business E-Mail: amimparatomdprnj@aol.com.

IMPERATO, PASCAL JAMES, physician, healthcare administrator, writer, historian; b. NYC; s. James Anthony and Madalynne Marguerite (Insante) Imperato; m. Eleanor Anne Maiella; children: Alison Madalynne, Gavin Humbert, Austin Clement. BS, St. John's U., 1958, DSc (hon.), 1977; MD, SUNY, Downstate Med. Ctr., 1962; M in Pub. Health and Tropical Medicine, Tulane U., 1966, DSc (hon.), 1996. Diplomate Am. Bd. Preventive Medicine, Nat. Bd. Med. Examiners. Fgn. fellow Assn. Am. Med. Colls., Kenya, Tanzania, Uganda, 1961; intern in internal medicine LI Coll. Hosp., 1962-63, resident in medicine, 1963-65; fgn. rsch. fellow Tulane Univ.-U. del Valle, Cali, Colombia, 1965; N.Y. Acad. Medicine/Glorney Raisebeck fellow Tulane U., New Orleans, 1965-66; med. epidemiologist smallpox eradication-measles control program Ctrs. Disease Control/USPHS, Mali, 1966-72; dir. Bur. Infectious Disease Control, NYC Dept. Health, 1972-74, prin. epidemiologist, dir. immunization program, 1972-74, 1st dep. commr., 1974-77, dir. pub. health residency tng. program, 1974-77; chmn. NYC Swine Influenza Immunization Task Force, 1976-77; commr. health NYC, 1977-78; chmn. NYC Bd. Health, 1977-78; chmn. bd. NYC Health and Hosps. Corp., 1977-78; chmn. exec. com. NYC Health Systems Agy., 1977-78; acting health services adminstr. NYC, 1977-78; clin. instr. dept. medicine Cornell U. Med. Coll., NYC, 1972-74, asst. clin. prof., 1974-78, asst. clin. prof. dept. pub. health, 1974-77, assoc. clin. prof., 1977-78, adj. prof., 1979-2000; clin. assoc. prof. dept. preventive medicine and cmty. health SUNY Health Sci. Ctr., Bklyn., 1974-77, lectr., 1977-78, prof., chmn., 1978-94, disting. svc. prof. and chmn., 1994-2001, disting. svc. prof., chmn., dir. master pub. health program, 2001—08, disting. svc. prof., dean pub. health grad. program, 2008—09, disting. svc. prof., dean sch. pub. health, 2009—, disting. svc. prof., dean sch. pub. health, dir. ctr. global health, 2011—. Mem. staff NY Hosp. 1972-78, LI Coll. Hosp., 1973—, State U. Hosp., 1978—, Kings County Hosp., 1978—; lectr. dept. cmty. medicine Mt. Sinai Sch. Medicine, CUNY, 1974-90; lectr. dept. health adminstrn. Sch. Pub. Health, Columbia U., 1982-89; cons. NY State Dept. Edn., 1982-87, NAS, 1985; med. cons. Africa bur. US AID, 1974; med. dir. R&D and Epidemiology Island Peer Rev. Orgn., 1991—2005. Author: Doctor in The Land of the Lion, 1964, (with Osa Johnson) Last Adventure, 1966, Bwana Doctor, 1967, The Treatment and Control of Infectious Diseases in Man, 1974, The Cultural Heritage of Africa, 1974, A Wind in Africa: A Story of Modern Medicine in Mali, 1975, What To Do About the Flu, 1976, African Folk Medicine, 1977, Historical Dictionary of Mali, 1977, (with Gavin H. Imperato) 4th edit., 2008, Dogon Cliff Dwellers: The Art of Mali's Mountain People, 1978, Medical Detective, 1979, (with Eleanor Imperato) Mali: A Handbook of Historical Statistics, 1982, The Administration of a Public Health Agency: A Case Study of the New York City Department of Health, 1983, Buffoons, Queens and Wooden Horsemen, 1983, (with Greg Mitchell) Acceptable Risks, 1985, (with Robert I. Goler) Early American Medicine, 1987, Arthur Donaldson Smith and the Exploration of Lake Rudolf, 1987, Mali: A Search for Direction, 1989, (with Eleanor Imperato) They Married Adventure: The Wandering Lives of Martin and Osa Johnson, 1992, Quest for the Jade Sea: Colonial Competition Around an East African Lake, 1998, Legends, Sorcerers, and Enchanted Lizards: Door Locks of the Bamana of Mali, 2001, Tudor Village: The History of a Unique Community in Queens County, New York, 2004, African Mud Cloth: The Bogolanfini Art Tradition of Gneli Traoré of Mali, 2006; editor: Acquired Immunodeficiency Syndrome: Current Issues and Scientific Studies, 1989; Historical and Contemporary Aspects of Communicable Disease Control, 1996, (with Ronald E. Coons and J. Winthrop Aldrich) Over Land and Sea: Memoir of an Austrian Rear Admiral's Life in Europe and Africa, 1857-1909 (Ludwig Ritter von Höhnel), 2000, (with Leonard Kahan and Donna Page) Surfaces. Color, Substances and Ritual Applications on African Sculpture, 2009; contbr. articles to profl. jours.; cons. editor NY State Jour. Medicine, 1983, dep. editor, 1983-86, editor, 1986-93; editor Jour. Cmty. Health, 1985—; mem. editl. bd. Explorers Jour., 1979-88, Am. Jour. Chinese Medicine, 1985-2001, The Pharos, 1995—; med. adv. bd. Med. Herald, 1992—2003; chmn. publs. com. Annals of Epidemiology, 1996-99. Bd. trustees Milton Helpern Libr. Legal Medicine, 1977—89; hon. trustee Martin & Osa Johnson Safari Mus., 1964—; mem. adv. bd. Physicians for Social Responsibility, 1983—; mem. NY State Bd. Medicine, 1985—95, vice chmn., 1990—93, chmn., 1993—95; mem. bd. zoning & appeals Village of Plandome Heights, NY, 1986—90, trustee, 1990—92; mem. sci. adv. bd. Explorers Club, 1988—93; chmn. NYC Met. Area Task Force on Syphilis, 1990—91; mem. bd. regents LI Coll. Hosp., 1992—2000; mem. NY State Coun. on Grad. Med. Edn., 1994—98; co-chmn. adv. commn. on pub. health NYC Coun., 1994—2001; mem. NY State Bd. Profl. Med. Conduct, 1994—2008, Fulbright Selection Com. for Africa, 1999—2002, NYC Mayor Elect Giuliani's Health Care Adv. Group, 1993; bd. dir. numerous orgs., 1977—78; mem. Adv. Coun., NYC Dept. Health & Mental Hygiene, 2010—. Lt. comdr. USPHS, 1966—69. Recipient Meritorious Honor award Dept. State, 1971, US AID Meritorious Honor award, 1970, Outstanding Alumnus award Tulane U., 1978, Delta Omega Nat. Merit award, 1978, Frank Babbot award SUNY, 1980, Disting. Alumni Achievement award SUNY, 1987, Spl. Svc. award USPHS, 1987, Pub. Health Achievement award NYC Dept. Health, 1999, Nat. Acads. Practice Interdisciplinary Creativity award, 2000, Clark-Curran award SUNY, 2002, Haven Emerson award Pub. Health Assn. NYC, 2008; Fulbright scholar, North Yemen, 1985. Master: ACP (James D. Bruce Meml. award 2003); fellow: Am. Coll. Preventive Medicine, Am. Coll. Epidemiology, Royal Soc. Tropical Medicine & Hygiene; mem.: African Studies Assn., NY Soc. Tropical Medicine (v.p. 1976—77, pres. 1989—90), Am. Soc. Tropical Medicine & Hygiene, Author's Guild, Explorers Club, Alpha Omega Alpha, Delta Omega. Business E-Mail: pascal.imperato@downstate.edu.

IMRAN, HAMAYUN, medical educator; b. Peshawar, Pakistan, Feb. 11, 1972; MBBS, Khyber Med. Coll., 1995; MSc, Mayo Grad. Sch., 2006. Cert. pediatric hematology & oncology specialist Am. Bd. Pediat. Instr., pediat. Mayo Clinic, 2004—06; med. dir. U. South Ala., 2006—11, asst. prof., 2006—. Mem.: Am. Soc. Pediatric Hematology & Oncology, Am. Acad. Pediat. Avocations: tennis, ping pong/table tennis, cricket. Office: 1504 Springhill Ave Mobile AL 36695 Office Fax: 251-405-5120. Business E-Mail: imran@usouthal.edu.

IMRAY, THOMAS JOHN, retired radiologist, educator; b. Milw., Nov. 11, 1939; s. George William and Genevieve (Bresnehan) I.; m. Carla Marie Rake, Aug. 17, 1963; children: John Scott, Jean Ann, Jeff William. BA, Marquette U., 1961, MD, 1965. Diplomate Nat. Bd. Med. Examiners, Am. Bd. Radiology (guest examiner 1975-76, 79, 85-2002). Intern St. Mary's Hosp., San Francisco, 1965-66; resident in radiology U. Minn., Mpls., 1966-70, instr., 1969-70; asst. prof.

Med. Coll. of Wis., Milw., 1973-77, assoc. prof., 1977-80, U. Calif., Irvine, 1980-82; prof. and chmn. dept. radiology U. Nebr. Med. Ctr., Omaha, 1982-96, prof. dept. radiology, 1996—2005, prof. emeritus radiology, 2005—10. Vis. prof. Vanderbilt U., Nashville, 1976, 82, U. Wis., Madison, 1978, SUNY Downstate Med. Ctr., Bklyn., 1978, Harvard Med. Sch., Boston, 1980, Loyola U. Sch. Medicine, Maywood, Ill., 1980, UCLA-Wadsworth VA Hosp., 1981, UCLA, 1982 Northwestern U. Sch. Medicine, Chgo., 1984, Meth. Hosp., Indpls., 1984, U. Mo., Kans. City, 1985, U. Iowa, Iowa City, 1986, U. Ark., Little Rock, 1987, Keio U. Sch. Medicine, Tokyo, 1989, Mich. State U., 1993. Contbr. articles to profl. jours. Mem. Tech. Task Force on Diagnostic Radiology Nebr. Dept. Health, 1983-84; Major U.S. Army M.C., 1970-73. Co-recipient Magna Cum Laude in Sci. Exhibits award Am. Soc. Neuroradiology, 1987; GE grantee, 1985-87. Fellow Am. Coll. Radiology; mem. AMA (rep. to radiology residency rev. com., 1987), Radiol. Soc. N. Am. (award 1981, 82), Am. Coll. Radiology (com. on satellite communications 1981-83), Am. Roentgen Ray Soc. (award 1986), Assn. Univ. Radiologists, Soc. Chmn. Acad. Radiology Depts., Am. Soc. Uroradiology, Nebr. State Radiol. Soc., Nebr. State Med. Assn., Omaha Metro Med. Soc., Omaha Mid-West Clin. Soc. (hosp. and svc. exhibits com. 1984, award 1986), Omaha C. of C. (task force on edn. 1983-85, edn. coun. steering com. 1984, edn. coun. 1985), Rotary Internat. (program com. 1986), Marquette U. Club (bd. dirs. Omaha chpt., 1987), Alpha Omega Alpha (alumni and faculty mems. com., 1986). Roman Catholic. Avocation: swimming.

IMRE, ZS NAGY, retired medical educator; b. Balassagyarmat, Hungary, Oct. 28, 1936; MD, U. Debrecen, 1961; DSc, Hungarian Acad. Scis., 1978. Sen. sci. coworker Biol. Rsch. Inst., Hungarian Acad. Scis., Tihany, Hungary, 1963—73; sci. coord., dipartimento di ricerche gerontologiche INRCA, Ancona, Italy, 1973—95; prof., head chair Med. & Health Sci. Ctr., U. Debrecen, Hungary, 1997—2006, prof., emeritus, 2006—. Editor-in-chief archives gerontology & geriatrics ELSEVIER, 1982. Recipient Monte Carlo award, Monte Carlo Congress Anti-Aging Medicine, 2002, Infinity award, Am. Acad. Anti-Aing Medicine, Pres. A4M, 2009. Avocation: stamp collecting/philately. Home: Komlóssy u 28 Debrecen H-4032 Hungary Personal E-mail: izsnagy@dote.hu

IMRIE, CLEMENT WILLIAM, retired surgeon, medical educator; BSc, Glasgow, Scotland, MBChB, 1967. Pres. European Pancreatic Club, 1989—90, Internat. Pancreatic Assn., 1994—96; prof., surgery U. Glasgow, 1996—2007. Co-author (with Colin D Johnson): (book) Pancreatic Disease (Basic Science & Clinical Management). Recipient Lifetime Achievement award, European Pancreatic Club, 2008; Fellowship, German Soc. Visceral Surgery, 2002. Fellow: Royal Coll. Physicians & Surgeons; mem.: Pancreatic Soc. Gt. Britain & Ireland (pres. 1990—91). Achievements include clinical grading of disease severity in acute pancreatitis; research in role of systematic inflammation in cancer outcomes. Home: 11 Penrith Avenue G46 6LU Glasgow Scotland

INABA, TOSHIO, veterinarian, educator; b. Amagasaki, Hyogo, Japan, Jan. 9, 1952; s. Inaba Nobuyoshi and Inaba Sueko; m. Mikiko Kawabe, May 2, 1982; children: Inaba Tetsushi, Inaba Natsuki. BS, Osaka Prefecture U., Japan, 1974; DVM, Ministry of Agr., Forestry and Fisheries, Japan, 1974; MSc, Osaka Prefecture U., Japan, 1976, PhD, 1982. Rsch. fellow Wash. U, St. Louis, 1978—80; rsch. assoc. Osaka Prefecture U, Sakai, Osaka, 1980—91; asst. prof. Osaka Prefecture U, 1992—95, assoc. prof, 1996—2001, prof, 2001—. Author: (book) Endocrinological Examinations in Obstetrics and Gynecology, 1978, Veterinary Dictionary, 1989, Reproduction in the Dog and Cat, 1989, Dictionary of Dairy Terminology, 1993, Textbook of Theriogenology, 1995, 2d edit., 2001, Seventh Lake Shirakaba Conference, 1996, Manual of Small Animal Reproduction and Neonatology, 2000, Clone Animals and Placentation, 2000, Mauual of Theriogenology, 2002, Textbook of Veterinary Internal Medicine, 2005; contbr. numerous aticles to profl. jours. Grantee, Ito Found., 2001, 2002; Sci. Rsch. grant, Japan Soc. Promotion Sci., 1981, 1983—84, 1987—93, 1995—2000, 2002—. Fellow: Jananese Soc. Vet. Sci. (assoc. Acad. Theriogenology award 2003, 2007); mem.: Japanese Soc. Farm Animal Vet. Medicine (assoc. Acad. award 1992, 2003), Japanese Soc. Animal Reproduction (assoc. Shimamura prize 1989), Osaka Vet. Med. Assn. (assoc. Pres. award 2003). Avocation: bicycling. Office: Osaka Prefecture Univ Dept Advanced Pathobiology 1-58 Rinku Ourai Kita Izumisano Osaka 5988531 Japan E-mail: inaba@vet.osakafu-u.ac.jp.

INABINETT, CURTIS BANJAMIN, JR., medical technician, director; b. Charleston, SC, Feb. 5, 1959; s. Curtis Benjamin and Ethel Mae Joy Inabinett. BS in Health Adminstrn., Kennedy Western U., Cheyenne, Wyo., 2006. Cert. echocardiographer Ariz. Heart Assn., Phoenix, 1989, echocardiography. Owner Cardiac Imaging & Sound Mobile Cardiac Ultrasound Svc., Ravenel, SC, 1991—; exec. dir., co-owner Ravenel Med. Ctr., Ravenel. Cardiac outreach technician Med. U. SC, Charleston, 1991—2005; writer Dispatch News. Author: Curtis' Poems, 1985; jazz saxophonist with appearances on BET and PBS-TV. Bd. dirs. Clemson Extension, Charleston, 2002—03; active Coun. Town Ravenel; exec. mem. Charleston, SC Dem. Party; dean U. Marching Band Dir. Dr. William P. Foster Fla. A & M U. Kennedy Centers Honor Program. Recipient Honor Award, SC Vision Bus. Mag., 1996, Trailblazer award, Charleston Br. NAACP, 1998, BET Jazz Discovery Winner award, Life Time Achievement award, Coll. Band Dir. Nat. Assn., 2009; grantee, Charleston County Arts Commn., 2002. Mem.: Am. Inst. Ultrasound Medicine. Prince Hall, Am. Soc. Echocardiography, Nat. Soc. Cardiac Sonographers, Med. U. SC Stroke Belt Initiative Leadership Team, Soc. Cardiac Sonographers, Am. Soc. Echocardiography, Am. Inst. Ultrasound, Masonic Lodge (Charleston). Democrat. Achievements include patents pending in field. Avocations: fishing, saxophone, writing, poetry. Home: PO Box 188 Ravenel SC 29470 Office: Ravenel Med Ctr 5531 Savannah Hwy PO Box 188 Ravenel SC 29470 Home Phone: 843-889-8302; Office Phone: 843-475-2660. Office Fax: 843-889-8302. Business E-Mail: inabinett1@aol.com.

INAGAKI, HITOSHI, surgeon; b. Japan, Aug. 19, 1960; MD, Nagoya U., PhD, 1988. Chief dept. surgery Yokoyama Hosp., 2004—. Mem.: SAGES. Office: 3-11-20 Chiyoda Naka-ku Nagoya Aichi 460-0012 Japan Business E-Mail: h.inagaki@yokoyama-hospital.or.jp.

INAGAKI, TAKUJI, psychiatrist, educator; b. Shimane, Japan, July 18, 1958; MD, Shimane U., PhD, 1985. Prof., spl. support edn. Shimane U., Faculty Edn., 2009—. Office: Nishikawatsu 1060 Matsue Shimane 690-8504 Japan Office Fax: 81-852-32-6362. Business E-Mail: inagaki@edu.shimane-u.ac.jp.

INAGAMI, TADASHI, biochemistry professor; b. Kobe, Japan, Feb. 20, 1931; m. Masako Araki, Nov. 12, 1961 BS, Kyoto U., 1953, DSc, 1963; MS, Yale U., 1955, PhD, 1958. Rsch. staff Yale U., New Haven, 1958—59, rsch. assoc., 1962—66; rsch. staff Kyoto U., Japan, 1959—62; instr. biochemistry Nagoya City U., Japan, 1962; asst. prof. biochemistry Vanderbilt U., Nashville, 1966—69, assoc. prof., 1969—74, prof. biochemistry, 1975—91, dir. hypertension rsch. ctr., 1979—95, Stanford Moore prof. biochemistry, 1991—, prof. medicine, 1992—. Contbr. numerous articles to profl. jours. Fulbright fellow, 1954-55; recipient Roche Vis. Prof. award, 1980, Humboldt Found. award, 1981, Spa award Belgium Nat. Funds Sci. Rsch., 1985, Ciba award High Blood Pressure Res Coun., 1986, Sutherland prize Vanderbilt U., 1990, Charles Park award for Excellence in Rsch., 2002, Okamoto Internat. award Japan Vascular Disease Rsch. Found., 1994. Res Achievement award Am. Heart Assn., 1995, award for excellence in cardiovascular rsch. Bristol Meyers Squibb, 1996, award Japan Acad., 1996, Jokichi Takamine award Japan Cardiovasc. Endocrine-Metabolism Soc., 1998, Merit award NHLBI, 2000, Distng. Scientist award, Am. Heart Assn., 2009 Mem.: Am. Soc. Advancement Sci., Japan Soc. Cardiovascular Endocrinol. Metabolism, Japan Soc. Biochemistry, Japan Soc. Hypertension, Internat. Soc. Hypertension, Am. Soc. Hypertension, Soc. Neurosci., Am. Soc. Cell Biology, Am. Heart Assn. (Rsch. Achievement award 1994, Disting. Scientist award 2009), Am. Soc. Pharmacology and Therapeutics, Am. Chem. Soc., Endocrine Soc., Am. Physiol. Soc., Am. Soc. Biol. Chemists and Molecular Biologists, Japan Soc. Agrl. Chemistry (hon.), Japan Endocrine Soc. (hon.). Office: Vanderbilt U Sch Medicine Dept Biochemistry 23D Ave S And Pierce Ave Nashville TN 37232-0146 Office Phone: 615-322-4347. Business E-Mail: tadashi.inagami@vanderbilt.edu.

INDIG, GUILHERME LUIZ, chemistry professor; b. Sao Paulo, June 28, 1958; BS, Unicamp, 1979; PhD, U. Sao Paulo, 1988. Asst. prof. U. Wis., Madison, 1995—2003, assoc. prof. Milw., 2003—. Recipient Rsch. Excellence award, U. Wis. Madison. Mem.: Am. Chem. Soc. Avocation: soccer. Office: University Wis Madison Dept Chemistry & Biochemisty Milwaukee WI 53211 Office Fax: 414-229-5530. Business E-Mail: glindig@uwm.edu.

INDOREWALA, SHABBIR TASSADUQUEHUSAIN, surgeon, researcher; b. Nashik, Maharashtra, India, Oct. 13, 1953; MS, Grant Med. Coll., Mumbai, 1972—83; DORL, Coll. Physicians and Surgeons, Mumbai, 1982; MS, Bombay U., 1982. Hon. ear, nose, throat surgeon Govt. Dist. Hosp., Nashik, Maharashtra, India, 1982—88; hon. ear, nose, throat cons. Nagjee Meml. Hosp., Nashik, Maharashtra, 1985—90; head dept. Nasik Dist. Maratha Vidya Prasarak Samaj's Med. Coll., Nashik, 1990—, prof., 1995—. Dir. Indorewala ENT Hosp., Nashik, 1997—. Indorewala ENT Hosp. Bldg.; contbr. rsch. articles to profl. publs. (AOI-E. Merck award, 97, R.A.F. Cooper award, 98). Mem. Adhar Ashram, Nashik, 1999—2003. Mem.: Indian Med. Assn. (life), Assn. Otolaryngologists India (life). Achievements include development of remote controlled hydraulic operation table; temperature controlled foot controlled ear syringe; automatic, conceptualize, perform and popularize autoclave; foot controlled pressurized cannula (tube) cleaner; control panel for generator starting; research in dimensional stability of the free fascal grafts; anterior tympanoplasty and endomeatal tymanoplasty; patents for surgical instrument combining suction, cautery, and mechanized cutting for endoscopic surgery. Office: Indorewala ENT Hospital Behind Mahamarg Busstand Maharashtra Nashik 422 002 India E-mail: stindorewala@yahoo.com.

INFANTOLINO, ANTHONY, gastroenterologist, educator, physician; MD, U. Medicine and Dentistry of NJ, 1985. Diplomate Am. Bd. Internal Medicine, Am. Bd. Internal Medicine-gastroenterology. Hospital affiliation includes Meth. Hosp. divsn. Thomas Jefferson Univ. Hosp., intern, resident, dir. endoscopy dept.; clin. assoc. prof. Medicine Thomas Jefferson Univ.; fellow Grad. Hosp., Phila.; co-dir. Jefferson Gastrointestinal Bleeding Ctr.; coord. continuing med. edn. gastrointestinal/hepatology divsn.; rep. trainer. Named one of the Top Doctors, Phila. Mag., 2002, 2010. Fellow: ACP; mem.: Am. Gastrointestinal Assn., Am. Coll. of Gastroenterology. Office: Thomas Jefferson University Hospital Ste 480 132 S 10th St Philadelphia PA 19107 Office Phone: 215-995-9397. Office Fax: 215-503-6678. Business E-Mail: Anthony.Infantolino@jefferson.edu.

INGALLS, CHRIS, physical education educator; b. Williamsville, Feb. 29, 1964; PhD, Tex. A&M U., 1994. Assoc. prof. Ga. State U., 1999—. Fellowship, Am. Coll. Sports Medicine. Office: Ga State University PO Box 3975 Atlanta GA 30302-3975 Business E-Mail: cingalls@gsu.edu.

INGBAR, DAVID H., physician, researcher; b. Boston, Aug. 1, 1953; s. Sidney H. and Mary Lee Ingbar; m. Mary E. Meighan, Oct. 14, 1991. BA, Reed Coll., 1974; MD, Harvard Med. Coll., 1978. Diplomate Am. Bd. Internal Medicine. Intern then resident U. Wash., Seattle, chief resident; pulmonary fellow Yale U., New Haven, 1982-85, asst. prof. medicine, 1985-91; assoc. prof. medicine U. Minn., Mpls., 1991-98, prof. medicine, physiology and pediat., 1998—, dir. pulmonary, allergy and critical care divsn., 2001—. Dir. med. ICU and respiratory care Yale New Haven Hosp., 1986-91, U. Minn., 1991—; pres. Assn. Pulmonary and Crit. Care Medicine Program Dir., 2003-04. Mem.: Am. Thoracic Soc. (pres. 2007—08). Office: U MN Pulmonary & Critical Care Dept Medicine MMC 276 UMMC 420 Delaware St SE Minneapolis MN 55455-0374 Office Phone: 612-624-0999. Business E-Mail: ingba001@umn.edu.

INGE, THOMAS, pediatric surgeon; BS, Coll. William and Mary, Williamsburg, Va., 1987; PhD, MD, Va. Commonwealth U., Richmond, 1993. Lic. Calif., Ala., Ohio, Ind., diplomate Am. Bd. Surgery, 1999, cert. in pediat. surgery Am. Bd. Surgery, 2002, DEA. Internship and residency, gen. surgery Stanford U. Med. Ctr., Calif., 1993—98; pediat. surgery fellowship U. Ala. Children's Hosp., Birmingham, 1998—2000; asst. prof. surgery & pediat. U. Cin. Children's Hosp. Med. Ctr., 2000—06, dir. pediat. surg. oncology lab., 2000—03, dir. ctr. bariatric rsch. and innovation, 2003—, surg. dir., comprehensive weight mgmt. ctr., 2004—, assoc. prof. surgery, 2006—. Cons. FDA, 2005—; invited panelist, spkr. and faculty in field. Ad hoc editl. reviewer: Jour. Pediat., Jour. Pediat. Surgery, Am. Jour. Surgery, Pediat., others, mem. editl. bd.: Jour. Laparoendoscopic & Advanced Surg. Techniques, 2005—; contbr. articles articles to profl. jours., chapters to books. Treas. Internat. Pediatric Endosurg. Group, 2005—08, mem. exec. com., 2005—08, mem. devel. com., 2005—, mem. program com., 2005—, co-chair, program com., 2007—08. Fellow: ACS, Am. Acad. Pediat.; mem.: North Am. Assn. the Study of Obesity, Am. Pediat. Surgery Assn., ACS Commn. on Cancer, Internat. Pediatric Endosurgery Group, Soc. Am. Gastrointestinal Endoscopic Surgeons, Am. Soc. Bariatric Surgery, Phi Sigma. Office: Cin Childrens Hosp Med Ctr Dept Pediatric Surgery 3333 Burnet Ave Cincinnati OH 45229-3039 Office Fax: 859-422-8444. Business E-Mail: Thomas.inge@cchmc.org.

INGERMAN, MARK J., infectious disease physician; MD, Jefferson Med. Coll. Diplomate Am. Bd. Internal Medicine, 1984, Am. Bd. Internal Medicine-infectious disease, 1987. Intern Lankenau Hosp., resident; fellow Med. Coll. of Pa.; with Lankenau Med. Ctr., 1986, Paoli Hosp., 1998, Bryn Mawr Hosp., 1998; clin. assoc. prof. medicine Thomas Jefferson Univ. Hosp. Chmn. infection ctrl. com. Lankenau Hosp., Chestnut Hill Hosp., chief infectious diseases, Mainline Hosp. System. Mem.: AMA, ACP, Phila. County Med. Soc., Pa. Med. Soc., Infectious Disease Soc. of America. Office: Lankenau Medical Center MOB E Ste 164 100 Lancaster Ave Wynnewood PA 19096 Office Phone: 610-896-0210. Office Fax: 610-896-5101.

INGLE, JAMES NEWELL, oncologist, consultant; b. Iowa City, Iowa, Sept. 21, 1944; s. Newell George and Lorraine Jessie (McNamara) I.; m. Mary Alice Sahs, Aug. 3, 1968; children: William James, Peter Newell. AB, Cornell Coll., 1966; MD, Johns Hopkins U., 1971. Diplomate Am. Bd. Med. Examiners, Am. Bd. Internal Medicine, Am. Bd. Medical Oncology. Cons. Mayo Clinic, Rochester, Minn., 1976—. Foust prof. oncology Mayo Med. Sch., Rochester, 1992—. Contbr. numerous articles to profl. jours. With USPHS, 1973-75. Business E-Mail: ingle.james@mayo.edu.

INGLE, JOHN IDE, dental educator; b. Colville, Wash., Jan. 19, 1919; s. John James and Jessie Belle (Ide) I.; m. Joyce Ledgerwood, July 11, 1940; children: John Geoffrey, Leslie Ide Ingle Moxley, Schuyler Neal. Student, Wash. State U., 1936 38; D.D.S., Northwestern U., 1942; MSD., U. Mich., 1948. Diplomate: Am. Bd. Endodontics, Am. Bd. Periodontology. Asst. Northwestern U., 1942-43; asst. prof. endodontics and periodontology Sch. Dentistry, U. Wash., 1948-51, assoc. prof., 1951-59, prof., 1959-64, exec. officer dept., 1956-64; dean Sch. Dentistry, U. So. Calif., Los Angeles, 1964-72; dir. div. internat. health, sr. profl. asso. Inst. Medicine Nat. Acad. Scis., 1973-78; pres. Palm Springs Seminars, 1978-92; sr. lectr. UCLA, 1979; vis. lectr. Loma Linda U., 1983. Attending staff exec. com. Los Angeles County/U. So. Calif. Med. Center, 1964-72; cons. Nat. Bd. Dental Examiners, 1964-68; endodontics, asst. surgeon gen. U.S. Army, 1969-70, Nat. Naval Med. Center, 1973, mem. adv. com. dental health Office Sec. HEW, 1970-72; mem. rev. com. on dental edn. NIH, 1970; mem. adv. panel on nat. health ins. U.S. Ho. of Reps. Ways and Means Com., 1975 Author: (with others) Endodontics, 1965, 5th edit. (with L.K. Bakland), 2002, (with L.K. Bakland and J.Craig Baumgartner), Ingle's Endodontics, 2008, PDQ Endodontics, 2nd edit., 2009; editor: (with P. Blair) International Dental Care Delivery Systems, 1978. Bd. dirs. Los Angeles United Way Crusade, 1967-69. Served with Dental Corps AUS, 1943-46. Recipient Northwestern U. Alumni Merit award, 1966 Fellow AAAS, Internat., Am. colls. dentists; mem. Internat. Assn. Dental Research, Am. Assn. Endodontists (past pres., Ralph F. Sommer research award 1987, Edgar D. Coolidge Leadership award 1999), Am. Acad. Periodontology, Am. Dental Assn. (cons. dental therapeutics), Los Angeles Dental Soc. (sec. 1968-71), Am. Assn. Dental Schs., Alpha Omega (hon. mem., Achievement medal 1985) Clubs: Cosmos (Washington). Mailing: 18755 W Bernardo Dr Ste 1231 San Diego CA 92127 Office Phone: 858-673-4136. Business E-Mail: johningle@sprintmail.com. *

INGLIS, STEVEN R., obstetrician-gynecologist, educator; b. NYC, Oct. 28, 1959; BS, Tulane U., New Orleans, Louisiana, 1978—82; MD, NY Med. Coll., Valhalla, 1982—86. Diplomate Am. Bd. Ob-Gyn, cert. maternal and fetal medicine. Rsch. asst. Hosp. for Spl. Surgery, 1982—83; intern ob-gyn. and medicine Albany Med. Ctr. Hosp., NY, 1986—87, resident ob-gyn., 1987—89, chief resident ob-gyn., 1989—90; fellow maternal-fetal medicine The NY Hosp.-Cornell Univ. Med. Coll., 1990—92; dir. fetal transfusion svc. divsn. of maternal-fetal medicine The NY Hosp.-Cornell Med. Ctr., 1992—, dir. infectious diseases divsn. of maternal-fetal medicine, 1995—97; instr. ob-gyn. Cornell Univ. Med. Coll., 1990—92, asst. prof. ob-gyn., 1992—99; assoc. prof. clin. ob-gyn. Weill Med. Coll. Cornell Univ., 1999—2005; chief maternal-fetal medicine dept. of ob-gyn. Jersey City Med. Ctr., Jersey City, 1992—97, chief obstetrics dept. of ob-gyn, 1997; acting chmn. dept. of ob-gyn. Lincoln Med. and Mental Health Ctr., Bronx, NY, 1997—98, dir. residency program dept. of ob-gyn., 1997—98; asst. dir. residency program dept. of ob-gyn. Jamaica Hosp. Med. Ctr., NY, 2006—07, vice chmn., dir. of obstetrics dept. of ob-gyn., 2006—07, dir. residency program dept. of ob-gyn., 2007—, chmn. dept. of Jamaica, 2008—; instr. ob-gyn. Albany Med. Coll., NY, 1988—90; clin. asst. dept. of ob-gyn. Elmhurst Hosp., Queens, 1992—95; assoc. dir. maternal-fetal medicine NY Presbyn. Hosp.-Cornell Med. Ctr., 1998—2005; network chief of ob-gyn. St. Barnabas Hosp. and Affiliates, Bronx, 1998—2005. Co-author: (articles) Labor Associated Problems: A New Diagnosis for Primary Cesarean Section, 1990, Predictive Reliability of Normal Biophysical Profile (BPP) Following Vibroacoustic Stimulation (VAS) is Equivalent to Normal BBP Without VAS, 1991, Meconium Stained Amniotic Fluid (MSAF) 32 Weeks Predicts Poor Perinatal Outcome, 1991, and numerous others. Recipient Bachelor of Sci. with distinction in Biology, Tulane Univ., 1986, Ann. Resident Rsch. award, Albany Med. Ctr. Hosp., 1989, Clinical Meeting Award: Am. Coll. of Obstetricians and Gynecologists Burroughs- Welcome Jr. fellow chmn., 1989, NY's Top Doctors: 6th Edit. Castle Connolly Guide, 2001, 2002, 2003, 2004, The Best Doctors in NY, NY mag., 2005; named, 2001, 2006; fellow Sect. chmn., Dist. II Am. Coll. of Obstetricians and Gynecologists Jr. Fellows, 1988, Vice chmn., 1989, chmn., 1990; Summer Rsch. Fellowship: Biochemistry Rsch. Lab. Hosp. for Spl. Surgery, NY, 1982, Legis. Com., Dist. II Am. Coll. of Obstetricians and Gynecologists, 2004. Fellow: Am. Coll. of Obstetrics and Gynecologists; mem.: Internat. Fetal Medicine and Surgery Soc., Soc. for Maternal Fetal Medicine, NY Obstetrical Soc., Nat. Bd. of Medicine Examiners (diplomate), AMA. Office: Jamaica Hospital Medical Center Department of Obstetrics & Gynecology 8900 Van Wyck Expy Jamaica NY 11418 Office Phone: 917-309-6774.

INGRAM, DONALD KEITH, psychologist; b. Bogalusa, La., Oct. 17, 1948; s. John H. and Jocelyn P. (Mann) Ingram; m. Cathline Singleton Cole, Dec. 30, 1972; children: Eric Cole, Kyle Singleton. BA, La. State U., 1970; MS, U. Ga., 1977, PhD, 1978. Health statistician Nat. Ctr. Health Stats., Rockville, Md., 1970—74; postdoc. assoc. Jackson Lab., Bar Harbor, Maine, 1978—80; staff fellow Gerontology Rsch. Ctr., Nat. Inst. Aging, Balt., 1980—85, rsch. psychologist, 1985—; adj. asst. prof. psychology Johns Hopkins U., Balt., 1993—; prof. Pennington Biomed. Rsch. Ctr.; adj. prof. Sch. Human Ecology, LSU, 2007—. Editorial bd. Jour. Gerontology, 1984—88, Neurobiology of Aging, 1988—; cons. editor Exptl. Aging Rsch., 1985—; editor N. Am. Geronology, 1999—2007. Contbr. 350 chpts. and articles to sci. jours. Mem.: Am. Aging Assn. (bd. dirs. 1995—, editor in chief 1997—2007, pres. 1998—99), Gerontol. Soc. (sec., treas. biology sect. 1996—, pres. 2010—), Psi Chi, Phi Kappa Phi, Sigma Xi. Achievements include patents for methods for treating cognitive disorders with phenserine. Office: Louisiana State Univ System Pennington Biomedical Rsch Ctr 6400 Perkins Rd Baton Rouge LA 70808

INGRAM, ROBERT ALEXANDER, pharmaceutical executive; b. Dec. 6, 1942; BS in Bus. Adminstrn., Ea. Ill. U., 1965. Various positions including sales rep., sales mgr. and v.p. pub. affairs Merrell Dow Pharms.; v.p. govt. affairs Merck & Co., Inc. (formerly Schering-Plough Corp.), 1985—88, pres. Merck Frosst Can. Inc., 1988-90; exec. v.p. adminstrv. and regulatory affairs Glaxo Inc., 1990—93, exec. v.p., 1993, pres., COO, 1993—94, pres., CEO, 1994—97; CEO Glaxo Wellcome plc, 1997—2000; chmn. Glaxo Wellcome Inc., 1999—2000; pres., COO pharm. ops. GlaxoSmithKline plc, 2001—03, vice chmn. pharmaceuticals, 2003—09, advisor to CEO, 2010—; gen. ptnr. Hatteras Venture Partners, 2007—. Bd. dirs. Lowe's Companies, Inc., 2001—, Edwards Lifesciences Corp., 2003—, Valeant Pharmaceuticals Inc., 2003—, chmn., 2010—; bd. dirs. Allergan, Inc., 2005—, Cree, Inc., 2008—, Elan Corp. plc, 2010—, chmn., 2011—, OSI Pharmaceuticals, Inc., 2003—. Mailing: Hatteras Venture Partners 280 S Mangum St Ste 350 Durham NC 27701 also: OSI Pharmaceuticals Inc 41 Pinelawn Rd Melville NY 11747 Office Phone: 631-962-2000. Office Fax: 631-752-3880. Personal E-mail: ringram@osip.com. *

IN HO, CHANG, urologist, educator; b. Seoul, Sept. 30, 1972; MD, Coll. Medicine, Chung-Ang U., 1997, PhD, 2005. Assoc. prof. dept. urology Chung-Ang U. Hosp., 2010—. Grant, Ministry of Edn. Sci. and Tech. Mem.: Korean Urologic Assn. Avocation: exercise. Office: 224-1 Heuksuk-dong Dongjak-gu Seoul 156-755 Republic of Korea Office Fax: 82-2-6294-1406. Business E-Mail: caucih@caumc.or.kr.

INIESTA LOPEZ, IVAN, neurologist, consultant; b. Madrid, Nov. 19, 1971; s. Pascual Iniesta Quintero and Mariana Lopez Mora; m. Marta Rodriguez Pena-Marin, Apr. 21, 2007; 1 child, Pascual Iniesta. Degree in Medicine and Surgery, Facultad de Medicina, U. Complutense de Madrid, Ministerio de Edn., 1996, MD Morphology Temporal Lobe, Facultad de Medicina U. Complutense de Madrid, 1997; PhD in Medicine cum laude, U. Complutense Madrid, 2004; diploma in History Medicine Soc. Apothecaries, Apothecaries' Hall, London, 2009. Lms Ministerio de Educacion/Madrid, 1996, Suficiencia Investigadora - MD Thesis: Morfologia del Lobulo Temporal Universidad Complutense de Madrid, 1997, PhD Thesis - La enfermedad en la literatura de Dostoyevski Universidad Complutense Madrid, 2004. Cons. neurologist Walton Ctr., Liverpool, Merseyside, England, 2005—; neurosci. physician U. Complutense de Madrid, 1997, medical humanities physician, 2001; physician Med. History DHMSA, London, 2009—. Med. history DHMSA, London, 2009—. Author: (definition and clin. description) Don Quixote Syndrome, (book) Disease in Dostoevsky's literature, (poetry) La Montana Rusa, 2002 (Alonso Quijano Poesia, 2009), (book) Amputacion, Exilio, 2004, 2009, Cuidados Paliativos, 2003, Cenicienta Encuentra a Dulcinea, 2008, (poetry) Consulta a Orillas del Azahar, 2010, Accesit Asemeya. Mem. Liverpool Medical History Soc. Com.; active mem. British Epilepsy Assn.; coun. mem. Liverpool Med. Instn., Merseyside, England, 2008—. Fellow FRCP, Royal Coll. of Physicians of London, 2009. Mem.: Epilepsy Action (corr.; uk 2007), Internat. League Against Epilepsy - Spanish Chpt. (LECE) (corr.), Sociedad Espanola de Neurologia (corr.; barcelona 2002), Assn. Brit. Neurologists (corr.; london 2006), ASEMEYA (life; madrid 2007—10, Assn. de Medicos Escritores y Artistas 2007). Achievements include don quixote syndrome; guadiana syndrome; dostoevsky's epilepsy: pathography, disease experience and literary recreation; iatroversalia with pascual iniesta quintero. Avocations: tennis, football, writing, reading, coin collecting/numismatics. Office: Walton Ctr NHS Found Trust Lower Ln Fazakerley L9 7LJ Liverpool England Home Phone: 01513361829; Office Phone: 01515298844. Personal E-mail: iniesta.ivan@gmail.com. Business E-mail: ivan.iniesta@thewaltoncentre.nhs.uk.

INOGUCHI, TOYOSHI, medical educator; b. Fukuoka, Mar. 23, 1953; MD, Kyushu U., PhD, 1981. Prof. Innovation Ctr. Med. Redox Nav., Kyushu U., 2009. Office: Higasi-ku Maidashi 3-1-1 Fukuoka Kyushu 812-8582 Japan Business E-Mail: toyoshi@intmed3.med.kyushu-u.ac.jp.

INOUE, KEN, neurologist, researcher; s. Shunichiro and adopted s. Satsuki Inoue; m. Julia Jarzembowski; children: Kai, Erika, Mia. MD, U. Tokushimma, Japan, PhD, 1990. Asst. prof. Kawasaki Med. Sch., Kurashiki, Okayama, Japan, 2005—07; sub-chief Hiroshima Prefectural Hosp., Japan, 2007—. Internist Hiroshima U., 1991—94, asst. prof., 1998—2005; internist Kamo Nat. Hosp., Hiroshima 1994—95; vis. rsch. fellow U. Iowa, 1995—98. Recipient Best Rsch. award, Japanese Clin. Neurophysiology Assn., 2008. Mem.: Am. Clin. Neurophysiology. Achievements include research in somatosensory pathway.

INOUÉ, SHINYA, microscopy and cell biology scientist, educator; b. London, Jan. 5, 1921; came to US, 1948, naturalized, 1989; s. Kojiro and Hideko I.; m. Sylvia McCandless, July 18, 1952; children: Heather C., Jonathan H., Christopher W., Stephen K., Theodore D. Rigakushi, Tokyo U., 1944; MA, Princeton U., 1950, PhD, 1951; MA (hon.), Dartmouth Coll., 1959, U. Pa., 1966. Instr. U. Wash. Med. Sch., Seattle, 1951-53; asst. prof. Tokyo Met. U., 1953-54; rsch. assoc., assoc. prof. U. Rochester, NY, 1954-59; instr. Marine Biol. Lab., Woods Hole, Mass., 1961—, NATO Summer Sch., Cannes, Stressa, Szeged, 1967, 70, 75; prof., chmn. Dartmouth Med. Sch., Hanover, NH, 1959-66, U. Pa., Phila., 1966-89; disting. scientist Marine Biol. Lab., Woods Hole, 1980—. Cons. Am. Optical Co.,

1954-60, NSF, 1962-65, NIH, 1965-70, Hamamatsu Photonics K.K., Hamamatsu City, Japan, 1988-2002, Nikon Corp., Tokyo, 1994—, Olympus Optical Co. Ltd., Tokyo, 1994-2001, Yokogawa Elec. Corp., Tokyo, 1997—, AutoQuant Imaging Inc., Watervliet, NY, 2000—, Universal Imaging Corp., Downington, Pa., 1984-2002; bd. dir. 1987-2002, Author: Video Microscopy, 2d edit., 1997, Collected Works of Shinya Inoué, 2008; co-editor: Molecules and Cell Movement, 1975; contbr. articles to profl. jours.; mem. editl. bd. several sci. jours., ad hoc reviewer, advisor on sci. and tech. NSF, NIH, many Univ., founds. Trustee Marine Biol. Lab., 1970-77, 81-85, 92-96, mem. sci. coun., 1993-98. Recipient Rosenstiel award Brandeis U., 1988, Brown-Hazen award State of NY, 1988; Guggenheim Found. fellow, 1971-72; cancer rsch. scholar Am. Cancer Soc., NYC, 1955-58. Fellow Am. Acad. Arts and Scis., Royal Microscopial Soc. (hon.); mem. NAS, Biophys. Soc. (coun. 1968-71), Soc. Gen. Physiologists (coun., pres. 1962-65, 69-70), Am. Soc. Cell Biology (coun. 1970-73, E.B. Wilson award 1992), Optical Soc. Am., Microscopy Soc. Am. (Disting. Scientist award 1995), N.Y. Microscopical Soc. (Ernst Abbe award 1997), Japan Soc. Promotion of Sci. (Internat. Prize Biology, 2003). Achievements include 4 patents in optics. Avocations: reading, photography. Home: 40 Shore St Falmouth MA 02540-3146 Office: Marine Biol Lab 7 M B L St Woods Hole MA 02543-1015

INOUE, TAKESHI, psychiatrist, educator; b. Iwamizawa, Hokkaido, Japan, June 2, 1959; MD, Hokkaido U. Sch. Medicine, PhD, 1984. Lectr. Hokkaido U. Hosp., 2000—. Office: N15 W 7 Kita-ku Sapporo Hokkaido 060-8638 Japan Office Fax: 81-11-706-5081. Business E-Mail: tinoue@med.hokudai.ac.jp.

INOUE, YOJIRO, plastic surgeon; b. Kitakyuusyuu, Japan; MD, Kurume U., Japan, 1981, PhD, 1985. Asst. prof. Kurume U., 1990—2000, assoc. prof., 2001—. Contbr. articles to profl. jours. Mem.: Am. Soc. Plastic Surgeons, Japan Esophageal Soc. (councilor 2005—), Japan Soc. Plastic and Reconstructive Surgery (councilor 1987—), Japanese Soc. Reconstructive Microsurgery (councilor 2000—). Home: # 1303 13-22 Chuou-machi Kurume Fukuoka 830-0023 Japan Office: Kurume U Dept Plastic Surgery 67 Asahi-machi Kurume Fukuoka 830-0011 Japan Office Phone: 81-942-31-7569.

INOUYE, YOSHIO, pharmacist, educator; b. Yamanashi, Jan. 4, 1950; BS, Tokyo U., 1972, PhD, 1977. Asst. prof. Hiroshima U., Faculty Medicine, 1980—85, assoc. prof., 1985—95; prof., pharm. scis. Toho U., 1995—, bd. dirs., 2009. Master: Japanese Soc. Toxicology; mem.: Pharm. Soc. Japan. Avocation: gardening. Office: 2-2-1 Miyama Funabashi Chiba 274-8510 Japan Office Fax: 81-47-472-1188. E-mail: yinouye@phar.toho-u.ac.jp.

INOZEMTSEV, ANATOLY, research scientist; b. Lipetskaya obi, Dec. 31, 1937; MS, Moscow Lomonosov State U., 1966, postgrad, 1969; PhD, MLSU, 1978. Prof. Ctrl. U. Venezuela, 1969—72; head lab. Moscow Lomonosov State U., 2008—. Avocation: music. Home: iCirovogradskaya 6-1-2 Moscow 117208 Russia Personal E-mail: A_Inozemtsev@neurobiology.ru.

INRA, LAWRENCE A., cardiologist, educator; Attended, Johns Hopkins U. Sch. Medicine, 1976. Diplomate Am. Bd. Cardiology-cardiovascular disease, Am. Bd. Internal Medicine. Intern NY Hosp. - Cornell Med. Ctr., resident in internal medicine, 1976—79; fellow in cardiovascular disease Mt. Sinai Hosp., NY, 1979—81; assoc. clin. prof. medicine Cornell Univ. - Weill Med. Coll; with Hosp. Spl. Surgery; cardiologist NY Presbyn Hosp. Office: NY Presbyterian Hospital 407 E 70th St New York NY 10021 Office Phone: 212-249-1011.

INRIG, JULA K., nephrologist, researcher; d. Charles Henry and Deborah Jean Kern; m. Stephen Inrig; children: Evan Thornton, McKenna Karyn. BA, Calif. State U., Sacramento, 1996; MD, Loma Linda U. Sch. Medicine, Calif., 2000; MHS, Duke U., Durham, NC, 2006. Lic. ABIM, 2004. Internal medicine resident Duke U., 2000—03, nephrology fellow, 2003—06, instl. rev. bd. mem., 2006—08; instr. medicine Duke U. and Duke Clin. Rsch. Inst., 2006—. Contbr. scientific papers to profl. pubs. Recipient Young Investigators award; Mentored Clin. Rsch. grant, NIH, 2005—08. Mem.: Am. Soc. Nephrology, Alpha Omega Alpha. Office: Duke Univ Med Ctr DUMC Box 3646 Durham NC 27710 Office Fax: 214-645-8903. Business E-Mail: jula.inrig@utsw.edu.

INSCHO, JEAN ANDERSON, retired social worker, landscape artist; b. Camden, NJ, Oct. 31, 1936; d. George Myrick and Alfrida Elizabeth (Anderson) Hewitt; m. James Ronald Inscho, June 4, 1955 (div. Mar. 1982); children: James Ronald Jr., Cynthia Ann, Michael Merrick. BA, Fla. Atlantic U., 1971; MA in Coll. Teaching, Auburn U., 1974, postgrad., 1998-99. Instr. So. Union State Jr. Coll., Wadley, Ala., 1973-75; social worker Jefferson County Dept. Human Resources, Birmingham, Ala., 1976-77, Shelby County Dept. Human Resources, Columbiana, Ala., 1977-78, Houston County Dept. Human Resources, Dothan, Ala., 1978-98. Adj. instr. Troy State U., Dothan, 1984-97. Bd. dir., v.p. Adolescent Resource Ctr., 1992-93, sec., 1993-95; mem. Alzheimer's Assn. EPDA fellow Auburn U., 1973, 74. Mem.: Am. Horticultural Therapy Assn. (Ga.-Ala. chpt.), Wiregrass Master Gardeners (pres. 1994—95), Ala. Master Gardeners Assn. (bd. dir., sec. 2003—, sec. 2003, recipient award 2004, Outstanding Svc. and Dedication award 2004), Dist. 7 State Employees Assn. (polit. action com. rep. 1994—98), Ala. State Employees Assn. (bd. dir.), Am. Daffodil Soc. Episcopalian. Avocations: gardening, needlecrafts, church activities.

INSEL, RICHARD A., medical facility administrator/pediatrics educator; Dir. Strong Children's Rsch. Ctr., Richester, NY; with U. Rochester Med. Ctr., 1977—2003; prof. pediatrics, microbiology and immunology U. Rochester Med. Sch., NY; acting chair pediat. U. Rochester Med. Ctr., assoc. chair for pediat. rsch., chief, divsn. pediat. immunology, allergy and rheumatology, dir., Strong Children's Rsch. Ctr., dir., Ctr. for Human Genetics and Molecular Pediat. Disease; exec. v.p., rsch. Juvenile Diabetes Rsch. Found. Internat. (JDRF), 2003—. Founding dir. Ctr. for Human Genetics and Molecular Pediat. Disease, 2000—; serves on Nat. Adv. Allergy and Infectious Diseases Coun., NIH; scientific co-founder Praxis Biologics, 1983; vis. assoc. prof., biochemistry and biophysics Coll. Physicians and Surgeons, Columbia U.; fellow in pediat. rsch. Harvard Med. Sch.; fellow in medicine (immunology) Children's Hosp. Med. Ctr., Boston; fellow Lab. Parasitic Immunochemistry, Ctr. for Disease Control, Atlanta. Office: Juvenile Diabetes Rsch Found Internat 120 Wall St New York NY 10005-4001

INSEL, THOMAS R., federal agency administrator, psychiatrist; m. Deborah Insel; 2 children. BA, Boston U., 1971, MD, 1974. Intern Berkshire Med. Ctr., Pittsfield, Mass.; resident Langley Porter Neuropsychiatric Inst., U. Calif., San Francisco; assoc. clin. neuropharmacology br. Nat. Inst. Mental Health (NIMH), NIH, Bethesda, Md., 1979, various adminstrv. and leadership positions including head sect. comparative studies of brain & behavior, Lab. Clin. Sci., 1979—94, dir. NIMH, 2002—; prof. psychiatry Emory U., Atlanta, 1994—2002, dir. Yerkes Regional Primate Rsch. Ctr., dir. Ctr. Autism Rsch., 1994—99, dir. Ctr. Behavioral Neurosci., 1999—2002. Recipient A.E. Bennett award, Soc. Biol. Psychiatry, 1986, Curt Richter prize, Internat. Soc. Psychoneuroendocrinology, 1991, Outstanding Svc. Medal, USPHS, 1993, Disting. Alumnus award, Boston U. Sch. Medicine, 1997, Disting. Investigator award, Nat. Alliance Rsch. of Schizophrenia & Depression. Fellow: Am. Coll. Neuropsychopharmacology; mem.: Inst. Medicine. Achievements include initiating and developing the first program for study of adults with obsessive-compulsive disorder in the US. Office: NIMH 15K 107 15K North Dr Bethesda MD 20892 Office Phone: 301-443-3673. Business E-Mail: thomas.insel@nih.gov. *

INSELMAN, LAURA SUE, pediatrician, educator; b. Bklyn., Nov. 2, 1944; d. Alexander M. and Rae (Bloom) Inselman. BA, Barnard Coll., 1966; MD, Med. Coll. Pa., 1970. Diplomate Am. Bd. Pediatrics, Am. Bd. Pediatric Pulmonology. Intern and resident St. Lukes Hosp. Ctr., NYC, 1970-73; fellow in pediatric pulmonary disease Babies Hosp., NYC, 1973-76; chief pediatric pulmonary divsn. Interfaith Med. Ctr., Bklyn., 1976-81, Newington Con. Children's Hosp., 1987-92; pulmunologist, med. dir. dept. respiratory care duPont Hosp. for Children, Wilmington, Del., 1992-99, med. dir. pulmonary function lab., 1992—2011. Asst. prof. pediatrics Cornell U. Med. Coll., NYC, 1981-86; mem. staff Good Samaritan Hosp., West Islip, NY, 1982-87; asst. clin. prof. pediatrics, Yale U. Sch. Medicine, New Haven, 1987-92; asst. prof. pediatrics, U. Conn. Health Ctr., Farmington, 1987-92; assoc. prof. pediatrics, Jefferson Med. Coll. Thomas Jefferson U. Hosp., Phila., 1992-2007, prof. pediats., 2007-. Bd. dirs. Am. Lung Assn. Nassau-Suffolk, East Meadow, N.Y., 1983-86, Del., 1992—. Fellow Am. Acad. Pediatrics, Am. Coll. Chest Physicians; mem. Am. Thoracic Soc., Am. Fedn. Med. Rsch., N.Y. Acad. Medicine, Soc. Pediatric Rsch. Office: duPont Hospital for Children 1600 Rockland Rd Wilmington DE 19803-3607

INTERIAN, ALBERTO, JR., cardiac electrophysiologist, educator; MD, U. Miami, 1982. Diplomate Am. Bd. Internal Medicine, 1985, Am. Bd. Internal Medicine-cardiovasc. disease, 1987, Am. Bd. Internal Medicine-clin. cardiac electrophysiology, 2000. Resident internal medicine Jackson Meml. Hosp., 1983—85, fellow cardiovasc. disease, 1986—88; prof. medicine and cardiology Univ. of Miami; med. dir. Arrhythmia Syncope Ctr.; hosp. affiliations include Mercy Hosp., Jackson Meml. Hosp. Author numerous book chapters, co-author more than 50 articles. Recipient numerous honors and awards. Office: Mercy Arryhthmia and Syncope Center 3641 S Miami Ave Ste 221 Bayside Pavillion Bldg Miami FL 33133 Office Phone: 305-285-2685.

INTUWONGSE, CHAI-SIT, orthopedist, consultant; b. Nakornpanom, Thailand, Feb. 4, 1935; s. Doom and Nian (Ku-Si) Intuwongse; m. Siriporn Nipatsat Intuwongse, Mar. 9, 1966; 3 children. MD, Siriraj, Mahidol U., Bangkok, 1959. Diplomate Thailand Bd. Orthopaedics. Intern Siriraj, Mahidol U., Bangkok, 1959-60, resident, 1960-61; instr. Chiangmai U., Thailand, 1961-64; surg. staff Prae Provincial Hosp., Thailand, 1964-65, Pa-Yao Provincial Hosp., Thailand, 1965-66; orthopaedist Lerd-Sin Gen. Hosp., Bangkok, 1966-96, head orthopaedic dept., 1981-91, cons., 1991-96; sr. supr. dept. med. svcs. Ministry Pub. Health, Bangkok, 1996—; cons. Sports Authority Thailand, Bangkok, 1996—2009; sr. supr. sports medicine Royal Coll. Orthop. Surgeons Thailand, Thai Orthop. Assn. Editor: Lerd-Sin Bull., 1976; contbr. articles to profl. jours. Grantee, Singapore U., 1965, WHO, 1985, 1989. Fellow: Internat. Coll. Surgeons Thailand; mem.: Thai Orthopedic Assn., Psychol. Security Assn. Thailand, Royal Coll. Surgeons Thailand. Avocations: golf, tennis, ping pong/table tennis, bowling, football. Office: Lerd Sin Gen Hosp Dept Orthopaedic Surgery Bangkapi Bangkok 10250 Thailand Home Phone: 662 02 719 0435; Office Phone: 662 02 314 6458. Personal E-mail: geennikul@yahoo.com. Business E-Mail: intuwongse@hotmail.com.

INUI, MAKOTO, medical educator, researcher; b. Hyogo, Japan, June 7, 1953; MD, Osaka U., 1979, PhD, 1983. Assoc. prof. Osaka U. Sch. Medicine, 1994—96; prof. Yamaguchi U. Grad. Sch. Medicine, 1996—. Recipient Louis Katz award, Am. Heart Assn. Office: Yamaguchi University 1-1-1 Minamikogushi Ube Yamaguchi 755-8505 Japan Business E-Mail: minui@yamaguchi-u.ac.jp.

INVERNIZZI, MARCO, physician; b. Magenta, Dec. 25, 1981; MD, U. Ea. Piedmont, 2006. Physician U. Ea. Piedmont 'A. Avogadro', 2006—. Mem.: Società Italiana di Medicina Fisica e Riabilitativa, Am. Soc. Bone & Mineral Rsch. Office: Viale Piazza D'Armi 1 Novara 28100 Italy Office Fax: 3903213734870. E-mail: marco.invernizzi@med.unipmn.it.

INWARDS, DAVID JAMES, hematologist, educator; b. Parkers Prairie, Minn., Mar. 10, 1958; s. Gene and Mary Inwards; m. Carrie Young, June 26, 1989; children: Sarah, Ryan. BA summa cum laude, Carleton Coll., Northfield, Minn., 1980; MD, Mayo Med. Sch., Rochester, Minn., 1984. Diplomate Am. Bd. Internal Medicine, 1987, in internal medicine, hematology 1990. Internal medicine resident Mass. Gen. Hosp., Harvard U., Boston, 1984—87; hematology fellow Mayo Grad. Sch. Medicine, Rochester, Minn., 1988—90; oncology, hematology fellow U. Nebr. Med. Ctr., Omaha, 1990—91; cons., divsn. hematology Mayo Clinic, 1991—, pres. voting staff, 2008—09. Med. dir. Gift Life Transplant House, Rochester, 1996—2003. Recipient Laureate award, Dept. Medicine, Mayo Clinic, 2003, Excellence Through Teamwork award, 2004; named one of Top Physicians, Consumer's Rsch. Coun. America, 2008. Mem.: AMA, Lymphoma Rsch. Found. (mem., mantle cell lymphoma consortium 2006—), Ctr. Internat. Blood and Marrow Transplant Rsch. (lymphoma working com. mem. 2004—), Eastern Coop. Oncology Group, North Ctrl. Cancer Treatment Group, Am. Soc. Clin. Oncology, Am. Soc. Hematology, Sigma Xi, Phi Beta Kappa Honor Soc. Avocations: running, skiing, bicycling. Home: 1331 19th Ave SW Rochester MN 55902 Office: Mayo Clinic 200 1st St SW Rochester MN 55905 Office Fax: 507-266-4972.

INZELBERG, RIVKA, neurologist, educator; b. Istanbul, Turkey, May 10, 1959; MD, Istanbul U., 1982. Prof. Sheba Med. Ctr., Tel Aviv U., 2007—, prof., Sackler Faculty Medicine, 2009. Mem.: Movement Disorders Soc., Am. Acad. Neurology, Am. Neurol. Assn. Home: Mordechai 8 Ramat Hasharon 47441 Israel Personal E-mail: inzelber@post.tau.ac.il.

INZUCCHI, SILVIO E., endocrinologist, educator; MD, Harvard U., 1985; postdoc., Yale New Haven Hosp., 1994. Diplomate Am. Bd. of Internal Medicine, 1988, Am. Bd. of Internal Medicine-endocrinology, diabetes & metabolism, 2006. Intern Yale New Haven Hosp., 1986, resident, 1988; assoc. prof. medicine Yale Univ. Sch. of Medicine, clin. dir. endocrinology; dir. endocrinology & metabolism fellowship Yale Med. Group; dir. Yale Diabetes Ctr. Office: Yale-New Haven Hospital 20 York St New Haven CT 06510 Office Phone: 203-688-4242.

IOANNIDI-KAPOLOU, ELIZABETH, sociologist, research scientist; b. Chios, Greece, Apr. 25, 1955; BA, City Coll., NY, 1978; PhD, Pantion U., Athens, 1996. Sr. rschr. Nat. Sch. Pub. Health, 1988—. Rschr. Sextant Rsch. Group, 1991—2000. Mem.: Hellenic Assn. Study And Control Aids, Hellenic Soc. Assn., Internat. Soc. Assn., European Soc. Assn. Avocations: poetry, music, gardening. Office: 196 Alexandras Ave Athens 11521 Greece Office Fax: 302102850818. Business E-Mail: ioanel@otenet.gr.

IOANNIDIS, JOHN P.A., internist, researcher, educator; b. NYC, Aug. 21, 1965; s. Paul J. Ioannidis, Angeliki D. Katrachoura; m. Despina G. Contopoulos, Sept. 2, 1993; 1 child, Angeliki. Lykeion, Athens Coll., Greece, 1984; MD, U. Athens, Greece, 1990, D in Pathobiology, 1996. Diplomate Am. Bd. Internal Medicine, Am. Bd. Infectious Diseases. Intern, resident in internal medicine New Eng. Deaconess Hosp., Harvard Med. Sch., Boston, 1990—93; clin. fellow in medicine Harvard Med. Sch., Boston, 1990—93; fellow in infectious diseases New Eng. Med. Ctr., Boston, 1993—96; asst. prof. Johns Hopkins U. Sch. Medicine, Balt., 1996—98; med. officer NIAID, NIH, Bethesda, Md., 1996—98; assoc. prof., chmn. dept. hygiene and epidemiology U. Ioannina Sch. Medicine, Epirus, Greece, 1998—2003, prof., chmn. dept. hygiene and epidemiology, 2004—10; prof. medicine, CF Rehnborg prof. in disease prevention, dir. Stanford Prevention Rsch. Ctr. Stanford U. Sch. Medicine, Calif., 2010—, prof. health rsch. and policy, 2011—. V.p. Hellenic Ctr. Infectious Disease Control, Athens, 2000—01; adj. prof. Tufts-New Eng. Med. Ctr., Boston, 2002—; ctr. dir., exec. bd. mem. Human Genome Epidemiology Network, 2004—; pres. Soc. Rsch. Synthesis Methodology, 2009—10; adj. prof. Harvard U. Sch. Pub. Health, 2010—. Editor: HIV/AIDS CRG, Internat. Cochrane Collaboration. Mem.: European Acad. Cancer Sciences, Assn. American Physicians. Office: Stanford Prevention Rsch Ctr Med Sch Office Bldg 1265 Welch Rd Mailcode 5411 Stanford CA 94305-5411 Office Phone: 650-725-5465. Business E-Mail: jioannid@stanford.edu. *

IOANNIDIS, ORESTIS, physician; b. Thessaloniki, Greece, Nov. 20, 1980; s. Ioanndis Markellos and Anni (Vatseri) Ioannidou. MD, Aristotle U., 2005; MSC, U. Thessaloniki, 2008, PhD candidate in Surgery, 2009—. Resident Gen. Hosp. Papanikolaou, 2007—. Contbr. articles to jours. Recipient 1st Pl. award, Med. Sch. Aristotle U. Thessaloniki. Home: Alexandrou Mihailidi 13 Macedonia Thessaloniki 54640 Greece Personal E-mail: telonakos@hotmail.com.

IOANNOU, YIANNIS P., surgeon; MD, Vienna U., Austria, 1980—87. Diplomate Am. Bd. Surgery, 2011, cert. ACLS, Fgn. Med. Graduates Examinations (ECFMG), 1989, Fed. Lic. Exam. (FLEX) NY, 1992, lic. Republic of Cyprus. Fellow Am. Coll. of Surgeons; resident pediat. dept. NY Univ. Med. Ctr., 1989—90, resident surgery dept., 1990—94, chief resident surgery dept., 1994—95; cons. surgeon Ygia Polyclinic, Limassol, Cyprus, 1995—. Fellow: Am. Soc. of Metabolic and Bariatric Surgery; mem.: Cyprus Surg. Soc. (bd. mem.), European Surgical Soc., Soc. of Am. Gastointestinal Endoscopic Surgeons. Achievements include One of Cyprus top minimally invasive surgeons specialized in Laparoscopic and Bariatric Surgery. Office: Ygia Polyclinic Medical Court 401 28 Naupliou St 3025 Limassol Cyprus Office Phone: 35725346410. Office Fax: 35725748056. *

IODICE, ARTHUR ALFONSO, biochemist; b. Rome, NY, Nov. 7, 1928; s. Gaetano and Loretta (Pace) Iodice. AB, Columbia U., 1950; PhD, SUNY, Syracuse, 1958. Postdoctoral fellow U. Calif., Berkeley, 1958-60, rsch. assoc., 1960-62, Inst. Muscle Disease, NYC, 1962-65, asst. mem., 1965-69, assoc. mem., 1969-74; rsch. scientist Masonic Med. Rsch. Lab., Utica, N.Y., 1975—. Contbr. articles to profl. jours. Jane Coffin Childs Meml. Fund med. rsch., postdoctoral fellow U. Calif., 1958-60. Mem. AAAS, Electrophysiol. Soc., Am. Heart Assn., N.Y. Acad. Scis. Home: PO Box 663 Rome NY 13442-0663 Office: Masonic Med Rsch Lab 2150 Bleecker St Utica NY 13501-1738 Office Phone: 315-735-2217.

IOI, HIDEKI, orthodontist; PhD, Kyushu U., 1995. Japanese Orthodontic Soc. Splty. Cert. Japanese Orthodontic Soc., 1998. Asst. prof. Kyushu U., Fukuoka, Japan, 1995—2004, lectr., 2004—. Recipient 18th Ann. Meeting, Japanese Soc. for the Temporomandibular Joint, 2005. Mem.: Japanese Orthodontic Soc., Am. Assn. of Orthodontists. Office: Kyushu Univ Dentistry 3 1 1 Maidashi Higashi ku Fukuoka 812-8582 Japan Home: 4-1-7-304 Kashiihama Higashi-ku Fukuoka 813-0016 Japan Office Fax: 81-92-642-6398. Business E-Mail: ioi@dent.kyushu-u.ac.jp.

IONESCU, GABRIEL, paediatric surgeon; b. Bucharest, Ilfov, Romania, Jan. 21, 1943; s. Octavian and Rica-Cecilia (Voisin) Ionescu; m. Dorina Stan, July 1, 1973; children: Octavian, Carin. Med. Diplomate, Faculty of Medicine, Iasi, Romania, 1966, PhD, 1980. Clin. asst. Paediatric Surgery Dept., Iasi, Romania, 1966-73, lectr., 1973-83, asst. prof., 1983-89, prof., dept. head, 1990-91; cons. Surg. Dept., Pretoria, South Africa, 1991-96; prof., chief surgeon Paediatric Surgery Dept., South Africa, 1996—2003; cons. pediatric surgery Tawam Hosp., Al Ain, United Arab Emirates, 2003—. Dean faculty medicine, Iasi, 1990—91. Author (with others): Surgical Oncology, Vol. 12, 1983, Paediatric Surgical Oncology, Vol. 1, 1987; contbr. articles to profl. jours.; co-author (with D. K. Gupta): Pediatric Surgery, 2008. Capt. Romanian Mil. Force, 1966. Mem.: European Soc. Surg. Oncology (founding mem.), Swiss Soc. Paediatric Surgeons, French Soc. Paediatric Surgeons, Romanian Soc. Paediatric Surgeons (v.p. 1988—). Mem. Eastern Orthodox Ch. Achievements include 3 unique operations to separate Siamese Twins. Avocations: classical music, skiing, literature, tennis, swimming. Home: 284 Malherbe St Capital Pk Pretoria 0084 South Africa Office: Dept Surgery Divsn Pediat Surgery Tawam Hosp PO Box 15258 Al Ain United Arab Emirates Home Phone: 971-3-763-0585; Office Phone: 971-50-3317141, 971-3-7677 444. Personal E-mail: gabnescu@yahoo.com.

IONESCU, MARIUS ANTON, dermatologist, researcher; MD, U. Medicine Carol Davila, Bucharest, 1985; PhD in Biology and Pharmacology of the Skin, U. Paris, 2003. Dermatologist Sait-Louis Hosp., Paris, 1995—; dermatologist, head of pediatric dermatology unit U. Hosp. Colentina, Bucharest, 1996—99. Cons. dermatologist dept. rsch. & devel. Laboratoire dermatologique Bioderma, Lyon, France, 2000—04, Laboratoires Dermatologiques Uriage, 2004—; psoriasis cons. and prospective trials unit Saint-Louis Hosp., 2004—. Contbr. articles to profl. jours. Co-founder Psoriasis Patients Organisation, Bucharest, Romania, 1990; co-founder mem. Esthetic Medicine Soc., Bucharest, Romania, 1997. Grantee, French Govt., 1999—2003; fellow, Saint-Louis Hosp., 1999—2003. Mem.: Romanian Soc. Dermatology (assoc.), European Soc. Photobiology (assoc.), French Soc. Dermatology (assoc.), Am. Acad. Dermatology (assoc.). Christian. Achievements include research in Eosinophilic activation in Cutaneous T cell lymphomas; Topical Genistein role in sun-induced damage prevention; Topical Ectoin and Manitol in sun-induced damage prevention; development of Use of topical polymers in contact dermatitis treatment; SPF 100 sunscreen for the prevention of UV-induced skin cancers (model: xeroderma pigmentosum patients). Avocations: painting, history of art, tennis. Home: 57 Cours Albert Thomas Lyon 69003 France Office: St Louis Hosp 1 Avenue Claude Vellefaux Paris 75010 France Office Fax: 33-1-55-70-19-51. Personal E-mail: marius.ionescu@club-internet.fr. Business E-Mail: t.ionescu@uriage.tm.fr.

IP, DAVID, orthopaedic surgeon; b. Hong Kong, Aug. 21, 1960; s. Kout Yee Wong; m. Nga Yue Fu, June 14, 1997. MB, Med. Sch., Hong Kong U., 1981, MBBS, 1985. Deputy dir. gen. Internat. Biographical Ctr., sci. advisor to dir. gen.; sci. advisor Am. Biog. Inst., Lehrman Group; deputy gov. Am. Biog. Inst. Rsch. Assn. Author: Orthopedic Principles-A Resident's Guide, 2005, Orthopaedic Traumatology-A Resident's Guide, 2006, Orthopedic Rehabilitation, Assessment, and Enablement, 2007, Casebook of Orthopedic Rehabilitation, 2008; contbr. articles articles to profl. jours. Recipient Internat. Peace Prize, United Cultural Conventions of USA. Fellow: Hong Kong Acad. Medicine, Hong Kong Coll. Orthop. Surgeons, Royal Coll. Surgeons Edinburgh; mem.: Am. Acad. Orthopaedic Surgeons, Order Internat. Ambs., World Peace & Diplomacy Forum, Order of Distinction, Internat. Order Merit, Order Internat. Fellowship. Achievements include discovery of method to retrieve bent broken screws in IM nailing; pathogenesis of early screw failure in tibial IC nail; method of managing broken medullary tube in IM nailing; research in pathogenesis of patella clunk syndrome in TKR; management of forearm deformities in Multiple Exostosis; management of infected total joint replacement by multi-resistant bacteria and prevention of serial fragility hip fractures in the elderly population. Avocations: reading, swimming, bicycling, ping pong/table tennis, badminton. Personal E-mail: sartorius86@hotmail.com.

IQBAL, ZAFAR, neuroscientist, biochemist, educator; b. Lucknow, India, July 12, 1946; came to U.S., 1972, naturalized, 1979; s. Shujaat Ali and Saleha (Begum) Siddiqui. Cert. proficiency in French, Lucknow U., 1965; PhD, All India Inst. Med. Scis., New Delhi, 1971. Jr. research fellow Council Sci. and Indsl. Research, India, 1963-66, research fellow, 1967-68; research scholar Directorate Gen. Health Services, India, 1966-67; asst. research officer Indian Council Med. Research, 1968-71; research assoc. in physiology, investigator Ind. U. Sch. Medicine, Indpls., 1972-82, asst. prof. med. biophysics, 1977-82, asst. prof. biochemistry, 1979-82; asst. prof. neurology and neurosci. Northwestern U. Sch. Medicine, Chgo., 1982-85; assoc. prof. pharmacology Chgo. Med. Sch., 1985-88; assoc. prof. neurology Northwestern U. Inst. for Neuroscience, Chgo., 1989-95; adj. prof. neurology and neurosci. Northwestern U. Med. Sch., 1995—; mem. Northwestern U. Ctr. Devel. Biology, Chgo., 1989—; health sci. specialist VA Cen. Office Med. Rsch. Svc., Washington, 1995—. Contbg. author: Macromolecules in Storage and Transfer of Biological Information, 1969, Macromolecules and Behavior, 1972, Growth and Development of the Brain, 1975, Mechanism, Regulation and Special Function of Protein Synthesis in the Brain, 1977, Peripheral Neuropathies, 1978, Neurochemistry and Clinical Neurology, 1980, Calcium-Binding Proteins, 1980, Axoplasmic Transport, 1981, Calcium and Cell Function, 1982; editor: Axoplasmic Transport, 1986, Recent Progress in Polyamine Research, 1986, The Physiology of Polyamines, 1987; mem. editorial bd. Neurochem. Rsch.; contbr. articles to profl. jours. Bd. dirs. India Cultural Coord. Cmty. Rsch. grantee NIH, 1973-77, Muscular Dystrophy Assn. Am., 1975-77, 94-97, Am. Cancer Soc., 1979-80, NSF, 1981, 84, Juvenile Diabetes Found., 1981, Am. Diabetes Assn., 1980; recipient internat. travel award NSF, 1984, Fidia Rsch. Found. award, 1987, UN Devel. Program Internat. Expert award, 1987, 93, award Am. Soc. for Biochemistry and Molecular Biology, 1994. Mem. AAAS, Am. Physiol. Soc., Indian Acad. Neuroscis., Soc. Biol. Chemists (India), Internat. Brain Rsch. Orgn., Internat. Soc. Neurochemistry (award 1994), Soc. Neurosci., Am. Soc. Neurochemistry, Ind. Acad. Sci. (chmn. cell biology 1982-83), N.Y. Acad. Scis., Biophys. Soc., Soc. Exptl. Biology and Medicine, Assn. Scientists of Indian Origin Am. (counselor 1986—), Ameer Khusro Soc. Am. (v.p.), Lucknow Rschrs. Assn. in Am., All-Indian Inst. Med. Scis. Assn., Assn. of Communal Harmony in Asia, Orgn. of Univ. Communal Harmony, Aligarh Alumni Assn. Mct. Washington (sec. 2007-), Fedn Aligarh Alumni Assn. (councelor), India Culture Coordination Com., Lucknow U. Alumni Assn., Global Orgn. People of Indian Origin (sec.-gen. 2003-, v.p. 2010-, pres. Met. Wash. Chpt.), Nat. Coun. Indian Orgns. (sec. gen., pres., 2011-). Home: 19105 Warrior Brook Dr Germantown MD 20874 Personal E-mail: z_iqbal_19105@yahoo.com. Business E-Mail: zafar.iqbal@va.gov. E-mail: raabta_india@gmail.com.

IRACE, GREGORY, pharmaceutical executive; BS in Acctg., Albany State U. CPA 1982. With Price Waterhouse, 1980, sr. audit mgr., 1988—89, sr. mgr. corp. fin. dept., 1989—91; regional contr. Sterling Winthrop Inc., 1991—93; dir. fin. planning and analysis Sanofi Winthrop LP, 1993, sr. v.p. fin. and adminstrn., CFO US & Can., 1994—2007; sr. v.p. pharm. ops. US & Can. Sanofi-Avenits US, 2007—11, sr. v.p. global services, 2011—. Office: Sanofi-Aventis 55 Corporate Dr Bridgewater NJ 08807 *

IRANI, MINOCHER, pediatrician, consultant; b. Mumbai, Maharashtra, India, Mar. 8, 1965; m. Gulnar Irani; children: Ava children: Neville. MBBS, Gordhandas Sunderdas Med. Coll., Mumbai, India, 1989; MD in Pediats., Bombay U., India, 1992; MSc in Pediats., U. London, 2000, MSc in Health Mgmt., 2004. Specialist registrar Oxford Deanery, England, 1997—2000; cons. pediatrician Upton Hosp., Slough, Berkshire, England, 2001—. Expert Berkshire Rsch. Ethics Com., England, 2002—. Network lead for specialists NHS Alliance, Nottingham, England, 2005. Recipient Dr. A.R.Normand Comm. prize, Wilson Coll., Mumbai, 1982—83. Fellow: Royal Coll. Pediats. & Child Health; mem.: Royal Coll. Physicians, Brit. Assn. Cmty. Child Health, Brit. Med. Assn. Office: Upton Hosp Upton Hospital Albert Street SL1 2BJ Slough SL1 2BJ England Office Phone: 441753635537. Office Fax: 441753635536. Business E-Mail: m.irani@virgin.net.

IRIE, MASACHIKA, microbiologist, educator; b. Tokyo, July 10, 1931; s. Biho and Moto (Shimomura) I.; m. Reiko Ohta, Nov. 15, 1959; children: Nobuko, Atsusi. B of Pharmacy, U. Tokyo, 1953, PharmD, 1958. Rsch. asst. U. Tokyo, 1959-67; asst. prof. Kyoto U., 1967-74; prof. Hoshi Coll. Pharmacy, Tokyo, 1974-97, prof. emeritus, 1997—. Guest prof. Showa U. Sch. Pharm. Scis., 2000—. Recipient award for advanced rsch. Pharm. Soc., 1967, Miyata award Miyata Found., 1974. Mem. Pharm. Soc. Japan (award for divsnl. sci. contbn. 1997), Biochem. Soc. Japan. Home: Akazutsumi 2-50-3 Setagaya-ku 156-0044 Japan Office: Hoshi Coll of Pharmacy Ebara 2-4-41 Shinagawa-ku 142 Japan E-mail: iriechica@muc.biglobe.ne.jp.

IRIGARAY, PHILIPPE, biomedical researcher; b. Laxou, Lorraine, France, Aug. 17, 1974; s. Jean-Paul and Anne-Marie Irigaray; life ptnr. Stephanie Lacomme. Degree in Sci., Henri Poincaré U., Vandoeuvre, France, 1997; MS, Henri Poincaré U., Vandoeuvre, 1999, INPL Inst. Nat. Polytech. Lorraine, 2000; PhD (hon.), INPL, Vandoeuvre, 2005. Lab. technician during mil. nat. svc. Legouest Hosp., Metz, France, 1999—2000; rsch. engr. Genclis, Vandoeuvre, 2004—05; sci. rsch. coord. ARTAC Assn. Rsch. Treatments Against Cancer, Paris, 2005—. Sci. com. mem. Second Internat. Congress Paris Appeal UNESCO, Paris, 2006, Third Internat. Congress Paris Appeal UNESCO, Paris, 2011; gen. sec. ISDE, France. Contbr. articles to profl. jours. Achievements include research in benzo pyrene impairs beta-adrenergic stimulation of adipose tissue lipolysis and causes weight gain in mice basic properties and molecular mechanisms of Exogenous chemical carcinogens. Office: Assn ARTAC 57/59 Rue De La Convention Paris 75015 France Office Fax: 331 45 78 53 50. Business E-Mail: philippei.artac@gmail.com.

IRONS, SONYA L., physical therapist, educator; b. Bozeman, Mont., May 18, 1979; d. Charles Dean and Wanda Lou Anderson. BS, SD State U., Brookings, 2001; M in Phys. Therapy, Mayo Sch. Health Scis., Rochester, Minn., 2003; specialization, Acad. Content Experts, 2008 ; D in Phys. Therapy, Temple U., Phila., 2010. Cert. in cardiopulmonary physical therapy Am. Phys. Therapy Assn., 2007, bd. cert. cardiopulmonary specialist; lic. phys. therapist SD, 2003, Nebr., 2004. Rsch. assoc. U. SD, Vermillion, 2004, adj. faculty, 2010—; staff phys. therapist Madonna Rehab. Hosp., Lincoln, Nebr., 2004—. Adj. faculty SE CC, Lincoln, 2006—; clin. instr. internat. Creighton U., Santiago, Dominican Republic, 2006, guest lectr., Omaha, 2006—08, U. SD, Vermillion, 2006—08; clin. asst. prof. phys. therapy Creighton U., 2009—; co-chair Eastern Dist. Nebr. Physical Therapy Assn., 2007—09; exec. com. Nebr. Physical Therapy Assn.; coord. clin. edn. Madonna Rehab. Hosp. Ctr., 2009—. Contbr. articles to profl. jours. Vol. track coach Spl. Olympics, Rochester, 2002; vol. Mayo Outreach for Students and Tchrs., Rochester, 2002; vol. sci. judge St. Joseph Sch., Lincoln, 2005. Recipient Youth Svc. award, La Sertoma, 1997, Disting. Young Alumna award, SD State U., 2009; scholar, Treacy Corp., 1997—2001, Marine Corps, Tylenol, 1998—2000, Datatel, 1999—2001, Circle K, 2000—01. Mem.: Nebr. Phys. Therapy Assn., Am. Phys. Therapy Assn. (cardiopulmonary sect.), Mensa Soc., Mayo Clinic Alumni Assn., U. Nebr. Med. Ctr. Jour. Club, Golden Key (grad. scholar 2001), Alpha Lambda, Mortar Bd., Phi Kappa Phi. Avocations: running, exercise, travel, reading. Office: Madonna Rehab Hosp 5401 South St Lincoln NE 68506 Home: 2316 S 61St Lincoln NE 68506

IRSCH, KRISTINA, medical researcher; MS in Med. Physics, U. Heidelberg & U. Hosp. Mannheim, Germany, 2006; diploma in Physics, U. Heidelberg, Germany, 2007, PhD in Physics, 2008. Asst. Max Planck Inst. Nuc. Physics, Heidelberg, 2004—05; rsch. assoc. Sch. Medicine U. Heidelberg Mannheim, 2007, rsch. assoc. tchg. asst., 2008; rsch. fellow Wilmer Ophthal. Inst., Johns Hopkins U. Sch. Medicine, Balt., 2009—10, asst. prof. ophthalmology, 2010—. Recipient award, NASA Tech Briefs Mag. & Dassault Sys. Solid Works, 2009, Knights Templar Eye Found. Young Investigator award, 2009, Rsch. award, Pediat. Ophthalmology & Strabismus Wilmer, 2009. Mem.: AAAS, European Neuro Ophthalmology Soc., European Optical Soc., German Soc. Applied Optics, SPIE Internat. Soc. Optical Engring., Optical Soc. Am., Assn. Rsch. Vision & Ophthalmology, German Phys. Soc. Office: Johns Hopkins Wilmer Eye Inst 600 N Wolfe St Wilmer 233 Baltimore MD 21287-9028

IRSHAID, YACOUB MAHMOUD, physician, pharmacologist; b. Seir, Jordan, Aug. 10, 1954; s. Mahmoud Fahad and Wedad Hafez Irshaid; m. Hala Hisham Zalatimo, June 1981; children: Mustafa Yacoub, Zainab Yacoub, Wedad Yacoub, Aya Yacoub. MD, U. Jordan, Amman, Jordan, 1980; PhD, U. Iowa, Iowa City, Iowa, 1986. Lic. Abcp Am. Bd. of Clin. Pharmacology, 1994. Prof. dept. Clin. Pharmacology Coll. of Medicine, Abha, Saudi Arabia, 1999—2005; prof. dept. Pharmacology U. Jordan, Amman, Jordan, 2005—. Office: Dept Pharmacology Coll. of Medici Amman Jordan Personal E-mail: yacoubmf@yahoo.com.

IRVINE, ALAN DAVID, dermatologist, researcher; b. Enniskillen, Northern Ireland, Oct. 29, 1967; s. Ronald Cecil and Mary Edith Irvine; m. Michele Barbara Falls, Sept. 20, 1997; children: Steffi Naimh, Zara Kathryn Beatrice, Conal David William. B Medicine B Surgery BA Obstetrics, Queen's U. Belfast, Northern Ireland, 1991, MD, 1998. Pre-registration ho. officer Royal Victoria Hosp., Belfast, 1991—92; sr. ho. officer dept. dermatology Royal Hosps. Trust, Belfast, 1992—93, 1993—94, sr. ho. officer gen. medicine and hepatology, 1994, in-lieu registrar detp. dermatology, 1994—95; divsn. molecular medicine Queen's U., 1995—96; HMT dept. dermatology Belfast City Hosp. Trust, 1996—97; specialist clin. fellow in pediat. dermatology Gt. Ormond St. Hosp. Children, London,

1999—2001; clinician, scientist fellow pediat. dermatology Children's Meml. Hosp., Northwestern U., Chgo., 2000—01; sr. lectr. human genetics, hon. cons. dermatologist Ninewells Hosp. and Med. Sch., Dundee, Scotland, 2001; cons. pediat. dermatologist Our Lady's Hosp. for Sick Children, Dublin, 2002—; cons. dermatologist St. James' Hosp., Dublin, 2000—. Hon. cons. Coombe Women's Hosp., Nat. Maternity Hosp., Dublin, Children's U. Hosp., Dublin; assoc. prof. dermatology Trinity Coll. Contbr. more than 100 articles to profl. jours., chapters to books. Recipient Paul Gerson Unna prize, 2007; Fulbright scholar, Northwestern U., Chgo., 2000—01. Fellow: Royal Coll. Physicians London, Royal Coll. Physicians Ireland. Achievements include research in eczema and related allergic diseases. Avocations: rugby, reading, mountain walking. Office: Our Lady's Children's Hosp Crumlin Dublin D12 Ireland Office Phone: 3531 428 2532.

IRWIN, DAVID E., psychology professor, department chairman; PhD in Exptl. Psychology, U. Mich., Ann Arbor, 1983. Faculty mem. Cornell U., Ithaca, NY, Mass. Inst. Tech., Cambridge, Mich. State U., East Lansing, U. Ill., Urbana-Champaign, 1991—, prof. psychology, visual cognition and human performance divsn., affiliate faculty, Beckman Inst. Advanced Sci. and Tech., head psychology dept. Contbr. articles to profl. jours. Recipient James McKean Cattell Sabbatical award, 1991—92; fellow, John Simon Guggenheim Meml. Found., 1991—92. Office: Univ Ill Psychology Dept 315 Psychology Bldg 603 E Daniel St Champaign IL 61820 Office Phone: 217-333-0632. Office Fax: 217-244-5876. Business E-Mail: irwin@uiuc.edu.

IRWIN, GERALD PORT, physician; b. Muncie, Ind., July 11, 1945; s. Francis Inlow and Helen Marcella I.; m. Martha Sue Vincent, Mar. 10, 1946; 1 child, Tamara Suzette. AB in Biol. Sci., Ind. U., 1968; MD, Ind. U., Indpls., 1972. Diplomate Am. Bd. Family Physicians. Intern and resident Ball Meml. Hosp., Muncie, Ind., 1972-73; pvt. practice Alexandria, Ind., 1973—. Mem. AMA (Physician Recognition award 1992-95, 98-2001, 2007—), Am. Acad. Family Physicians,Ind. State Med. Assn., Ind. Assn. Family Physicians, Elks. Methodist. Avocations: computers, backpacking. Office: PO Box 124 Alexandria IN 46001-0124 Office Phone: 765-724-7711.

IRWIN, GLENN WARD, JR., medical educator, physician, academic administrator; b. Roachdale, Ind., July 18, 1920; s. Glenn Ward and Elsie (Browning) I.; m. Marianna Ashby; children: Ann Graybill Irwin Warden, William Browning, Elizabeth Ashby Irwin Schiffli. BS, Ind. U., Bloomington, 1942; MD, Ind. U., Indpls., 1944; LLD (hon.), Ind. U., 1986, Marian Coll., 1987. Diplomate: Am. Bd. Internal Medicine. Intern Meth. Hosp., Indpls., 1944-45; resident in internal medicine Ind. U. Med. Ctr., Indpls., 1945-46, 48-50; mem. faculty Ind. U., Indpls., 1950—, instr., asst. prof. then assoc. prof., 1950-61, prof. medicine, 1961-86, prof. emeritus, 1986, dean Sch. Medicine, 1965-73, dean emeritus, 1986, v.p., 1974-86; chancellor Ind. U.-Purdue U., Indpls., 1973-74, chancellor emeritus, 1989. Sr. assoc. Ind. U. Found. Bd. dirs. Goodwill Industries of Ctrl. Ind., Indpls., Greater Indpls. Progress Com., Greater Indpls. YMCA, Walther Med. Rsch. Inst., Walther Oncology Ctr., Indpls. Health Inst., Eiteljorg Mus. Western Art and the Am. Indian; elder 2d Presbyn. Ch. Served to capt. M.C. U.S. Army, 1946-48. Recipient Disting. Alumnus award Ind. U. Sch. Medicine, 1972, Otis R. Bowen Physician County Service award, Benjamin Harrison award, Ind. Acad. award; named Sagamore of the Wabash, Gov. of Ind., 1961, 79, 86. Fellow ACP (gov. for Ind. 1964-70); mem. AMA, Ind. State Med. Assn., Marion County Med. Soc., Ind. Soc. of Chgo., 500 Festival Assn., James Whitcomb Riley Meml. Assn. (bd. govs. 1986—), Newcomen Soc., Sigma Xi, Alpha Omega Alpha, Beta Gamma Sigma, Sigma Theta Tau. Clubs: Columbia (Indpls.), Contemporary (Indpls.), Meridian Hills Country, Skyline (bd. dirs.). Lodges: Masons (33 degree), Rotary. Home: 8025 N Illinois St Indianapolis IN 46260-2938 Office: Ind U-Purdue U at Indpls 1120 South Dr Indianapolis IN 46202-5135 Home Phone: 317-255-7445; Office Phone: 317-274-5160. E-mail: drglenni@aol.com.

IRWIN, MICHAEL RAY, psychology professor, researcher; b. Casper, Wyo., May 25, 1954; s. Donald Charles and Carolyn Irwin; m. Jennifer Len Pike, Dec. 30, 1988. AB in Biophysics, magna cum laude, U. Pa., 1976; student, U. Colo. Sch. Medicine; MD, U. Calif., San Diego, 1981. Lic. Calif., diplomate Am. Bd. Psychiatry. Intern internal medicine U. Calif., San Diego, 1981—82, resident psychiatry LA, 1982—85, asst. prof. psychiatry San Diego, 1985—91, assoc. prof., 1991—95, prof., 1995—2001, dir. Psychopharmacology Rsch. Fellowship Training Prog., 1991—2001; Norman Cousins prof., chair psychoneuroimmunology UCLA Semel Inst. Neurosoci. & Human Behavior, 2001—, dir. Cousins Ctr. for Psychoneuroimmunology, 2001—; disting. prof. psychiatry and biobehavioral scis. UCLA David Geffen Sch. Medicine, 2001—. Chief resident Clin. Rsch. Ctr. on Schizophrenia, VA Med. Ctr., LA, 1984—85; assoc. dir. Clin. Ctr. Rsch. on Alcoholism, VA Med. Ctr., San Diego, 1985—91, staff psychiatrist, 1985—2001; assoc. med. dir. Scripps McDonald Ctr. Alcohol & Drug Treatment, 1992—97; mem. mental health, AIDS, and immunology II review panel Nat. Inst. Mental Health, Bethesda, Md., 1995—98; mem. adv. coun. Nat. Ctr. Complementary & Alternative Medicine, Washington, 2001—05. Cons. editor Annals of Behavioral Medicine, 1993—98, mem. editl. bd. Psychosomatic Medicine, 1995—, Brain, Behavior and Immunity, 1995—, Sleep, 2006—, assoc. editor Psychosomatic Medicine, 1998—2001, Brain, Behavior and Immunity, 2002—; contbr. articles to profl. jours., chapters to books. Recipient Faculty Rsch. Mentor award, UCLA Sch. Medicine, 2005; grantee NIH; fellow NSF, 1974, Boettcher Found., 1977. Fellow: Am. Psychiatric Assn., Soc. Behavioral Medicine, Acad. Behavioral Medicine Rsch. (pres. 2002—04); mem.: ACP (Laughlin Fellow 1985), Am. Psychosomatic Soc. (adv. coun. 2001—04, Early Career award 1995), Pschoneuroimmunology Rsch. Soc. (pres. 1999—2001, Norman Cousins Rsch. award 2007). Office: Cousins Ctr Psychoneuroimmunology 300 UCLA Med Plz Ste 3109 Los Angeles CA 90095 Office Phone: 310-825-8281. Office Fax: 310-794-9247. E-mail: mirwin1@ucla.edu.

IRWIN, PETER JOHN, orthopaedic surgeon; b. East St. Louis, Ill., July 7, 1934; s. Peter and Anne (Sokalski) Iwasyszyn; m. Kathryn Swanson, June 15, 1960; children: Kathryn Linda, Mary Elizabeth, Amy Marie, Kenneth John, James Patrick. BS in Biology, St. Louis U., 1955; MD, 1959. Diplomate Am. Bd. Orthopedic Surgery. Intern Creighton Meml. St. Joseph Hosp., Omaha, 1959-60; resident in orthop. surgery U. Ark. Med. Ctr., Little Rock, 1961-65, tchg. staff, 1965—77; pvt. practice Fort Smith, Ark., 1965-97; mem. staff St. Edward Mercy Med. Ctr., 1965-97; ret., 1997. Mem. staff Sparks Regional Med. Ctr., 1965—97, chief staff, 1979, bd. dirs., 1980—87. Lt. comdr. M.C. USN, 1966—68. Fellow: ACS, Am. Acad. Orthop. Surgeons (councillor 1983—89); mem.: AMA, Am. Soc. Sports Medicine, Am. Orthop. Soc. Sports Medicine, So. Orthop. Assn., Mid-Ctrl. States Orthop. Soc. (pres. 1979—80), Clin. Orthop. Soc., Mid-Am. Orthop. Assn. (founding mem., pres. 1993—94), Ark. Orthop. Assn. (pres. 1976—77), Sebastian County Med. Soc. (pres. 1997), So. Med. Assn., Ark. Hand Club.

IRWIN, RICHARD STEPHEN, physician, scientist, educator; b. New London, Conn., Nov. 15, 1942; s. Harold H. and Sylvia Rowena (Hendel) I.; m. Diane Hazel Northrop, June 21, 1969; children: Rachel Helen, Sara Beth, Catherine Jamie, Rebecca Susan. BS, Tufts U., 1964, MD, 1968. Diplomate Am. Bd. Med. Examiners, Am. Bd. Internal Medicine, Am. Bd. Pulmonary Disease, Am. Bd. Critical Care Medicine. Intern Tufts New England Med. Ctr., Boston, 1968-69, jr. asst. resident in medicine, 1969-70; fellow in pulmonary disease Columbia-Presbyn. Hosp., NYC, 1970-72; dir. med. ICU R.I. Hosp., Providence, 1974-79; asst. prof. medicine Brown U., Providence, 1974-79; assoc. prof. medicine U. Mass. Med. Sch., Worcester, 1979-82, prof. medicine, 1982—; dir. pulmonary, allergy and critical care medicine U. Mass. Meml. Health Care, Worcester, 1979—2005. Dir. Respiratory Care Dept., U. Mass. Med. Ctr., Worcester, 1979-2005, Pulmonary Nursing Svc., 1989-2005, Pulmonary Rehab., 1986-2005, Asthma Co-Mgmt. Program, 1990—, chair critical care ops. U. Mass. Meml. Med. Ctr., 2004—. Co-editor: (textbook) Intensive Care Medicine, Diagnosis and Treatment of Symptoms of the Respiratory Tract, 1997; co-editor Jour. Intensive Care Medicine, 1986-2005; editor in chief CHEST, 2005—; contbr. over 250 articles to profl. jours., over 260 chpts. to books and 43 textbooks. Maj. USAF, 1972-74. Fellow Am. Coll. Physicians, Am. Coll. Chest Physicians (regent, pres. 2003-04); mem. Am. Thoracic Soc. (ea. sect. pres. 1980-81), Nat. Assn. Med. Dirs. Respiratory Care, Soc. Critical Care Medicine. Avocations: physical fitness, writing. Office: University Mass Meml Med Ctr 55 Lake Ave N Worcester MA 01655-0001 Business E-Mail: richard.irwin@umassmemorial.org. *

ISAACS, CLAUDINE JANET DIANA, internist; b. Montreal, Que., Can., June 22, 1962; BSc, McGill U., Montreal, 1983, MD, 1987. Cert. in internal medicine Am. Bd. Internal Medicine, 1990, Royal College of Physicians, 1991, in hematology Royal College of Physicians, 1992, in oncology Am. Bd. Internal Medicine, 1993. Internal medicine intern Montreal Gen. Hosp., 1987-88, hematologic oncology resident, 1988-90; oncology resident McGill U., 1990-92; resident Georgetown U., Washington, 1992-93, assoc. prof. oncology and medicine, 1998—, dir. clin. breast cancer program, 2001—, dir. cancer assessment and risk evaluation program, Lombardi Cancer Ctr., 2002—. Fellow Royal Coll. Physicians; mem. Am. Soc. Clin. Oncology, Surgeons Can. Office: Georgetown Univ Hosp 3800 Reservoir Rd NW Washington DC 20007-2196 Office Phone: 202-444-3677. Business E-Mail: isaacsc@georgetown.edu.

ISAACSON, ROBERT LEE, neurobehavioral scientist, educator; b. Detroit, Sept. 26, 1928; s. Emil Alfred and Evelyn (Johnson) I.; m. Susan Doherty, Dec. 16, 1956 (div. 1972); children: Gunnar, Lars, Mary Ingrid, Mary Christina; m. Ann W. Braden, Dec. 31, 1974; stepchildren: Richard, Milly Braden AB Psychology, U. Mich., 1950, MS Psychology, 1954, PhD Psychology, 1958. Co-dir. U. Fla. Ctr. for Neurobiol. Sci., Gainesville, 1970—78; grad. rsch. prof. U. Fla., Gainesville, 1977—78; disting. prof. psychology SUNY, Binghamton, 1978—, dir. Ctr. Neurobehavioral Sci., 1978—88, Bartle prof., 1998—; prof. U. Cordoba, 2002; hon. prof. Nat. U. Cordoba, Argentina, 2000. Author: Limbic System, 2d edit., 1982; co-author: Fluoride in the Drinking Water, 2006; deditor: (with others) Expression of Knowledge, 1982, The Hippocampus, vols. 3-4, 1986, The Vulnerable Brain and Environmental Risks, vols. 1-2, 1992, vol. 3, 1994; contbr. articles to profl. sci. jours. Pres. Alachua County Assn. for Retarded Children, Gainesville, 1973-75; chmn. dist. III Human Rights Advocacy Com., Gainesville, 1975-77. Served with USN, 1950-53, Korea Holloway fellow U.S. Navy, 1946-50; grantee NSF, NIH, U.S. Army Surgeon Gen., NIMH. Fellow APA, AAAS; mem. Internat. Behavioral Neurosci. Soc. (councilor 1991-95, pres. 1999, Myers Lifetime Achievement award 2002), Soc. for Neurosci. (pres. ctrl. N.Y. chpt. 1982-84), Assn. Neurosci. Depts. Programs, Am. Physiol. Soc., Sec. Health Rehab. Svcs. State of Fla. (Blue Ribbon com. 1976), Nat. Rsch. Coun. (subcom. on fluoride in drinking water, 2003-06) Office: SUNY Dept Psychology Binghamton NY 13902-6000 Office Phone: 607-777-6764.

ISAACSON, STEVEN ROBERT, surgeon; b. Bronx, NY, 1947; BS, Pa. State U., 1969; MD, Thomas Jefferson U., Phila., 1973. Bd. cert. radiation oncology Am. Bd. Radiology, bd. cert. otolaryngology Am. Bd. Otolaryngology. Attending physician Columbia Presbyn. Med. Ctr., 1988—; intern surgery Abington Meml. Hosp., 1973—74, resident surgery, 1974—75; resident otolaryngology U. Pa., 1975—78; resident radiation oncology SUNY Health Sci. Ctr., Bklyn., 1985—88; co-dir. Ctr. for Radiosurgery Columbia Presbyn. Med. Ctr., 1998—. Asst. prof. radiation oncology and otolaryngology Columbia Coll. Physicians and Surgeons Columbia U., NYC, 1990—94, assoc. clin. prof. radiation oncology and clin. otolaryngology, 1994—98, assoc. clin. prof. head and neck surgery in dentistry, 1998—2005, clin. prof. radiation oncology (in neurol. surgery), 2005—. Office: Columbia Presbyn Med Ctr BHN-Bll Dept Rad Oncol 115 Central Park W New York NY 10023-4198

ISABELL, LINDA MARSH, nursing administrator; b. Tyler, Tex., June 15, 1953; BSN, U. Tex., Tyler, 1987; MBA, LeTourneau U., 2004. Charge nurse Trinity Mother Frances Hosps. and Clinics, 1978—88, unit mgr., 1988—99, clin. site mgr., 2000—. Named Gen. Duty Nurse of Yr., Tex. Nurses Assn. Dist. 19, 1985, Minority Nurse of Yr., Mother Frances Hosp., 1998; nominee Daisy award, TMFHC, 2011. Mem.: Tyler Ind. Sch. Dist. Vol. and Mentor, Greater East Tex. Black Nurses Assn. NBNA (charter mem. 1991—2011, v.p., sec. 1994—98, pres. 1998—2002), Delta Sigma Theta Sorority Inc., Top Ladies of Distinction Inc. Avocations: reading, scrapbooks, music, singing. Office: 214 E Houston St Tyler TX 75702 Office Fax: 903-533-0726. Business E-Mail: isabell@tmfhs.org.

ISAKOW, WARREN, medical educator; b. South Africa, Oct. 24, 1974; MD, U. Witwatersrand, 1998. Asst. prof., medicine Wash. U., St. Louis, 2006—. ICU dir. Barnes Jewish Hosp., 2006. Recipient Robert Sr. award, Wash. U.; named Internal Medicine Tchg. Physician of Yr. Fellow: Am. Coll. Chest Physicians; mem.: Soc. Critical Care Medicine, Am. Thoracic Soc. Office: Campus Box 8052 660 S Euclid Ave Saint Louis MO 63110 Business E-Mail: wisakow@dom.wustl.edu.

ISAYAMA, HIROYUKI, gastroenterologist, oncologist; b. Tokyo, June 27, 1967; s. Shinichi and Kaoru Isayama; m. Noriko Inoue; 1 child, Ryuusei. MD, Jikei U., 1992; PhD, Tokyo U., 2001. Intern Japanese Red Cross Med. Ctr., 1992—93, resident dept. internal medicine, 1993—94, fellow dept. gastroenterology, 1994—97; asst. prof. Tokyo U. Hosp., Tokyo, 1997—. Contbr. articles to profl. jours. Mem.: Am. Soc. Gastrointestinal Endoscopy, Japanese Soc. Gastroenterology, Japanese Soc. Internal Medicine, Japan Gastroent. Endoscopy Soc. Achievements include research in biliary stenting; pancreato-biliary intervention and endoscopy. Office: Tokyo Univ Hosp Dept Gastroent 7-3-1 Hongou Bunkyou-ku Tokyo 113-8655 Japan also: Japanese Red Cross Med Ctr 4-1-22 Hiroo Shibaya-ku Tokyo 150 8935 Japan Office Fax: 81-3-3814-0021. Personal E-mail: isayama-tky@umin.ac.jp. Business E-Mail: isayama-2im@h.u-tokyo.ac.jp.

ISBERG, RALPH R., medical educator; b. Detroit, Jan. 3, 1955; AB, Oberlin Coll., 1977; PhD, Harvard U., 1984. Investigator, prof. Howard Hughes Med. Inst., Tufts Med. Sch., 1986—. Recipient Eli Lilly award, Am. Soc. Microbiology, Presdl. Young Investigator award, NSF, Disting. Faculty award, Tufts U. Sch. Medicine. Fellow: Am. Acad. Microbiology; mem.: NAS. Office: 150 Harrison Ave Boston MA 02111 Business E-Mail: ralph.isberg@tufts.edu.

ISENBERG, SHERWIN JAY, pediatric ophthalmologist; b. Chgo., Feb. 1, 1948; MD, UCLA, 1973. Cert. Am. Bd. Ophthalmology, 1978. Intern LA County Univ. So. Calif. Med. Ctr., 1973—74; resident in ophthalmology Chgo. Med. Ctr., Univ. Ill., 1974—77, Children's Hosp., Nat. Med. Ctr., Washington, 1977—78; prof. of surgery, chief ophthalmology div. Harbor UCLA Med. Ctr., physician, pediatric ophthalmology & strabismus. Contbr. articles to profl. jours. Office: Harbor UCLA Med Ctr 21840 Normandie Ave Torrance CA 90502 Office Phone: 310-794-9770.

ISERSON, KENNETH VICTOR, bioethicist, writer, medical educator; b. Washington, Apr. 8, 1949; s. Isadore I. and Edith (Swedlow) I.; m. Mary Lou Sherk, June 16, 1973. BS, U. Md., 1971, MD, 1975; MBA, U. Phoenix, 1987. Diplomate Am. Bd. Emergency Medicine, Nat. Bd. Med. Examiners; cert. in Thanatology: Death, Dying and Bereavement, Assn. Death, Dying and Counseling, 2003. Intern surgery Mayo Clinic, Rochester, Minn., 1975; resident emergency medicine Cin. Gen. Hosp., 1976-78; capt. USAF, 1978-80; chmn. emergency dept. Tex. A&M Coll. Medicine, Temple, 1980-81; asst. prof. surgery U. Ariz. Coll. Medicine, Tucson, 1981-84, residency dir. emergency medicine, 1981-91, assoc. prof. surgery, 1984-92; dir. Ariz. Bioethics Program U. Ariz., Tucson, 1991—2008, prof. surgery, 1992—2001, prof. emergency medicine, 2001—08; supervisory med. officer Disaster Med. Assistance Team AZ-1 Dept. Health and Human Svcs., 2002—; chief med. officer Project HOPE Continuing Promise Mission Carribean, 2009; prof. emeritus emergency medicine U. Ariz. Coll. Medicine, Tucson, 2008—; lead physician McMurdo Sta., Antarctica, 2009—10; HVO physician Peru & Bhutan, 2009—10. Pres. Iserson Assocs. Ltd., Tucson, 1984—; vis. scholar Ctr. Clin. Med. Ethics U. Chgo., Pritzker Sch. Medicine, 1990-91. Author: Iserson's Getting Into a Residency: A Guide for Medical Students, 1988, 7th edit., 2006, Death to Dust: What Happens to Dead Bodies?, 1994, 2nd edit., 2001, Non-Standard Medical Electives in the U.S. and Canada, 1997, 2nd edit., 1998, Get Into Medical School! A Guide for the Perplexed, 1997, 2nd. edit., 2004, Grave Words: Notifying Survivors About Sudden Unexpected Death, 1999, (video and slide sets) The Gravest Words, 2000, Demon Doctors: Physicians as Serial Killers, 2002; sr. editor: Ethics in Emergency Medicine, 1986, 2nd edit., 1995; mem. editl. bd. Cambridge Quar., 1991—, Jour. Emergency Medicine, 1985—; contbr. sci. articles to profl. jours. Med. dir. So. Ariz. Rescue Assn., Pima County, 1983—. Fellow Am. Coll. Emergency Physicians (life): mem. AMA, Med. Soc. US and Mex. (treas. 2002-03, v.p. 2003-04, pres. 2004-06), Soc. Acad. Emergency Medicine (pres. 1984-85), Wilderness Med. Soc. (bd. dir. 1987-91). E-mail: kvi@u.arizona.edu.

ISGRÒ, ANTONELLA, medical researcher; b. Salerno, Italy, Sept. 23, 1970; MD in Medicine, 1995. Rschr. Mediterranean Inst. Hematology, 2005—. Mem.: ASH. Office: Viale Oxford 81 Rome 00133 Italy Business E-Mail: a.isgro@fondazioneime.org.

ISHAK, SITI RAIHAN, ophthalmologist; b. Malaysia, May 14, 1974; MD in Med. Scis., 1999; MS in Ophthalmology, Med. Scis., U. Sains Malaysia, 2008. Med. officer Ministry of Health, 1999—2003; specialist U. Sains Malaysia, 2008—, cons. ophthalmologist, 2008—. Recipient Young Traveller award, Asia Assn. Rsch. Vision and Ophthalmology, 2009. Mem.: Malaysian Soc. Ophthalmologist, Assn. Alumni USM Drs. PADU (life; treas.). Office: Sch Med Scis Universiti Sains Malaysia Kota Bharu Kelantan 16150 Malaysia Office Fax: 6097653370. Business E-Mail: sitiraihan@kb.usm.my.

ISHAK, WAGUIH WILLIAM, psychiatrist; b. Port Said, Egypt, Oct. 16, 1964; s. William Makram IsHak and Nawara Yacoub Dawoud; m. Asbasia A Mikhail-IsHak, M.D.; children: William Waguih, Michael Waguih. MD, Cairo U., 1987. Dir., psychiatry residency tng. program Cedars-Sinai Med. Ctr., LA, 2001—, med. dir., adult outpatient psychiatry, 2003—, dir. med. student edn. psychiatry, 2008—; assoc. prof. psychiatry UCLA, USC & CSMC. Assoc. dir., psychiatry residency program NYU Sch. of Medicine, NYC, 1998—2001. Editor: (book) Outcome Measurement in Psychiatry: A Critical Review (Reviews in the Am. Jour. of Psychiatry and Psychiat. Services, 2003); editor, author (book) The Guidebook of Sexual Medicine, A&W Pub., 2008. Fellow: Am. Psychiat. Assn. (disting. 2008). Achievements include development of online screening tests for psychiatric disorders. Office: Cedars-Sinai Med Ctr 8730 Alden Dr Thalians W-157 Los Angeles CA 90048 Office Fax: 310-423-3497.

ISHAY, JACOB SCHECTMANN, biologist; b. Podul Iloaiei, Romania, Jan. 13, 1931; arrived in Israel, 1947; s. Israel and Debora (Schapira) Schechtmann; m. Ada Brizel, children: Isac, Michal. BSc, Tel-Aviv Univ., Tel-Aviv, Israel, 1959, postgrad. studies, 1959-60, MSc, 1960; PhD, The Hebrew Univ., 1967. Asst. Sackler Sch. Medicine, Tel-Aviv, 1966-67; instr. Tel-Aviv Univ., 1967-69, lectr., 1969-74, sr. lectr., 1974-81, assoc. prof., 1981-87, prof., 1987—. Chairperson Assn. Sr. Staff, Tel-Aviv, 1987-91; 1st Israeli Space experiment with NASA, 1992. Contbr. over 300 articles to profl. jours. Honorary Texan, 1996. Jewish. Achievements include research in hornet and wasp toxins and semiconductive properties of their silk and cuticle; the presence of some quantitative liver functions in the hornet yellow cuticle; the microstructure of yellow granules; the possible contribution of sunlight in the various metabolic processes of the yellow granules. Avocations: bee-keeping, literature. Home: Bd Emanuel 15 Tel Aviv Israel Office: Sackler Medical Sch Levanon St 69978 Tel Aviv Israel Office Phone: 972-3-6409138. E-mail: physio7@post.tau.ac.il.

ISHIBASHI, HIROMI, medical educator, researcher; b. Nagasaki, Japan, Oct. 4, 1946; MD, Kyushu U., Fukuoka, Japan, 1971, PhD, 1980. Med. diplomate internal medicine. Resident Kyushu U. Hosp., Fukuoka, Japan, 1971-73, sr. resident, 1974-76; biochemistry rsch. fellow U. Tex. Health Sci. Ctr., Dallas, 1976-78; rsch. assoc. internal medicine Kyushu U. Faculty of Medicine, Fukuoka, Japan, 1979-91, asst. prof. internal medicine, 1991—2001, assoc. prof. internal medicine, 1995—2001; gen. dir. Nat. Nagasaki Med. Ctr. Clin. Rsch., 2002—; prof. dept. hepatology Nagasaki Univ. Grad, Sch. of Biomedical Sci., 2004—. Gen. sec. 95th gen. meeting Japanese Soc. Internal Medicine, Fukuoka, Japan, 1998. Contbr. articles to profl. jours. Grantee Ministry of Health and Welfare of Japan. Master ACP (Laureate award, Japan chpt. 2010); fellow Am. Coll. Gastroentrology, Japanese Soc. Internal Medicine, Japanese Soc. Gastroentrology, Japan Soc. Hepatology, Japanese Soc. Ultrasonics in Medicine; mem. Internat. Assn. for Study of the Liver, Asian-Pacific Assn. for Study of the Liver, Am. Assn. for Study of the Liver. Office: Nat Nagasaki Med Ctr Clin Rsch Ctr 2-1001-1 Kubara Omura Nagasaki 856-8562 Japan Business E-Mail: hiishibashi-gi@umin.ac.jp.

ISHIDA, HAJIME, anatomist, educator; b. Sapporo, Japan, Dec. 28, 1956; PhD, Sapporo Med. Coll., 1988. Assoc. prof. Sapporo Med. Coll., 1991—98; prof. U. Ryukyus, 1998—. Mem.: Anthrop. Soc. Nippon. Avocation: walking. Office: Uehara 207 Nishihara Okinawa 903-0215 Japan Office Fax: 81-98-895-1100. Business E-Mail: ishidaha@med.u-ryukyu.ac.jp.

ISHIDA, KAZUYOSHI, medical educator; b. Japan, July 1, 1964; MD, Yamaguchi U., 1989, PhD, 1999. Asst. prof. Yamaguchi U. Grad. Sch. Medicine, 2003—11, assoc. prof., 2011—. Avocations: travel, movies, swimming. Office: Yamaguchi University Dept Anesthesiology Ube Yamaguchi 7558505 Japan Office Fax: 81836222292. Business E-Mail: ishid002@yamaguchi-u.ac.jp.

ISHIDA, KEIICHI, cardiologist; b. Ibaraki, Japan, May 12, 1971; MD, Chiba U., 1997, PhD, 2005. Cardiovascular surgeon Dept. Cardiovascular Surgery Chiba U. Grad. Sch. Medicine, 2009—, asst. prof. Achievements include research in surgical treatment for chronic thromboembolic pulmonary hypertension. Office: 1 8 1 Inohana Chuo Ku Chiba 260 8670 Japan

ISHIDA, MARI, physician, director; b. kanagawa Pref, Japan, Oct. 12, 1961; MD, Kitasatwo U. Med., 1986. Asst. dir. Kitasaito Hosp., 2005. Mem.: ASN, JSPD, JSDT. Avocations: reading, cooking. Office: 4153-12 9 choume Miyashita-Dori Asahikawa Hokkaido 070-0030 Japan Office Fax: 8-166-26-1047. Business E-Mail: mari@kitasaitohospital.or.jp.

ISHIDA, MICHIYO, research scientist, educator; b. Japan, May 29, 1973; PhD, Meiji U., 2004. Asst. prof. Meiji U., 2008—11. Office: 1-1-1 Higashimita Tama-ku Kawasaki Kanagawa 214-8571 Japan Office Fax: 81 44 934 7819. Business E-Mail: michi@isc.meiji.ac.jp.

ISHIDA, RIICHIRO, medical educator; b. Japan, Jan. 13, 1948; EdB, Niigata U., 1972, MD, 2001. Tchr. Elem. Sch., 1972—2008; part-time lectr. Niigata U., 2006—. Avocations: music, walking, reading, painting. Home: 321-8-Akasabi Nishikan-ku Niigata 953-0042 Japan Personal E-mail: ishida-riichiro@hh.tp1.jp.

ISHIDA, TAKAFUMI, biology professor; b. Japan, May 15, 1955; BSc, U. Tokyo, 1980, DSc, 1986. Assoc. prof. U. Tokyo, 1994—. Office: 7-3-1 Hongo Bunkyo Tokyo 113-0033 Japan Business E-Mail: tishida@biol.s.u-tokyo.ac.jp.

ISHIDA (NAKAJIMA), WAKO, pediatrician; d. Hisamichi and Keiko Nakajima; m. Akira Ishida; children: Lisa Ishida, Sarah Ishida. MD, Akita U. Sch. Medicine, 1992, PhD, 1997. Resident in pediats. Akita U. Sch. Medicine, 1992—93, Yamamoto Nokyo Gen. Hosp., Noshiro, Japan, 1993—94, Yuri Nokyo Gen. Hosp., Honjyo, Japan, 1994, Kanagawa Children's Med. Ctr., Yokohama, Japan, 1994; postdoc. fellow Kennedy Krieger Inst./Johns Hopkins U., Balt., 1998—2000; attending Akita Nokyo Gen. Hosp., 2000—01; asst. in pediats. Akita U. Sch. Medicine, 1997—2000, staff pediats., 2001—04, asst. prof., 2006—; attending Akita Red Cross Hosp., 2005—. Asst. prof. Akitu U. Sch. Medicine, 2005—. Contbr. articles to profl. jours. Recipient Yamashita Taro prize, 2004; Nakayama grantee, 2002. Office: Akita U Sch Medicine Hondo 1-1-1 Akita 010-8543 Japan Office Fax: 81-18-836-2620. Personal E-mail: wakonakajima@hotmail.com. E-mail: wako@doc.akita-u.ac.jp.

ISHIDA, YASUSHI, pediatrician; b. Japan, Aug. 24, 1957; MD, PhD, Ehime Grad. Sch. Medicine, 1983. Assoc. prof. dept. pediat. Ehime Grad. Sch. Medicine, 2004—08; chief dept. pediat. St. Luke's Internat. Hosp., 2008—. Chief med. rsch. St. Luke's Life Sci. Inst., 2008—11. Recipient Otani award, Japanese Soc. Pediat. Hematology. Mem.: Japanese Soc. Hematology, Japanese Cancer Assn., Children's Oncology Group, Internat. Berlin-Frankfurt-Munstar, Internat. Orgn. Pediat. Oncology. Avocation: golf. Office: 10-1 Akashi-cho Chuo-ku Tokyo 104-0044 Japan Office Phone: 81-3-5550-2426. Office Fax: 81-3-5550-2426. Business E-Mail: yaishida@luke.or.jp.

ISHIHARA, OSAMU, gynecologist, educator; b. Tokyo, Nov. 11, 1954; MD, Gunma U., PhD, 1980. Prof., chair Dept. Ob-Gyn., Saitama Med. U., 2002—. Office: 38 Morohongo Moroyama Saitama 350-0495 Japan Office Fax: 81 49 294 8305. Business E-Mail: osamishr@saitama-med.ac.jp.

ISHII, ITSUKO, medical educator; b. Chiba, Aug. 25, 1964; BS, Chiba U., 1988, PhD, 1995. Assoc. prof. Grad. Sch. Pharm. Scis., Chiba U., 2003—. Mem.: Japan Atherosclerosis Soc., Japanese Biochem. Soc., Pharm. Soc. Japan. Office: 1-8-1 Inohana Chuo-ku Chiba 260-8675 Japan Office Phone: 81-43-226-2889. Business E-Mail: iishii@faculty.chiba-u.jp.

ISHII, KENICHIRO, medical educator; b. Nagoya, Japan, July 4, 1973; PhD, Gifu Pharm. U., 2001. Asst. prof. Mie U. Grad. Sch. Medicine, 2011—. Mem.: Am. Assn. Cancer Rsch. Avocation: drums. Office: 2-174 Edobashi Tsu Mie 514-8507 Japan Office Fax: 81-59-231-5010. Business E-Mail: kenishii@clin.medic.mie-u.ac.jp.

ISHII, KUNIO, pharmacologist, educator; b. Tokyo, Dec. 21, 1950; MS, U. Tokyo Sch. Pharm. Scis., 1977, PhD, 1980. Asst. prof. Keio U. Sch. Medicine, 1980—90; sr. lectr. U. Shizuoka Sch. Pharm. Scis., 1990—91, assoc. prof., 1991—97; prof. Kitasato U. Sch. Pharm. Scis., 1997—. Postdoc. fellow Stanford U. Sch. Medicine, 1987—88, Northwestern U. Sch. Medicine, 1988—90. Mem.: Assn. Rsch. Vision and Ophthalmology, Pharm. Soc. Japan, Japanese Pharmacological Soc. Avocations: mountain climbing, photography, reading. Office: Dept Molecular Pharmacology Kitasato University Sch Pharmaceutical Scis 5-9-1 Shirokane Minato-Ku Tokyo 108-8641 Japan Office Fax: 81-3-3444-3233. Business E-Mail: ishiik@pharm.kitasato-u.ac.jp.

ISHII, NORIYUKI, research scientist; b. Japan, Sept. 1963; PhD, Tokyo Inst. Tech., 1992. Sr. rsch. scientist Nat. Inst. Advanced Indsl. Sci. & Tech., 1995—. Lectr. Chuo U., 1993—95; vis. rschr. U. Calif., Berkeley, 1997—99, Lawrence Berkeley Nat. Lab., 1997—99; rsch. assoc. NYU Med. Ctr., 1997; adj. prof. Tokyo U. Agr. & Tech., 2009. Overseas' Rsch. fellowship, Japan Sci. & Tech. Agy., Rsch. grant, Sci. & Tech. Agy., Inst. Phys. & Chem. Rsch. Mem.: Protein Sci. Soc. Japan, Japanese Biochemical Soc., Biophysical Soc. Japan. Avocation: reading. Office: Tsukuba Ctrl-6 1-1-1 Higashi Tsukuba Ibaraki 305-8566 Japan E-mail: ishii@ni.aist.go.jp.

ISHII, YOSHIKI, thoracic surgeon, educator; b. Japan, June 12, 1957; MD, Jichi Med. Sch., 1982, PhD, 1992. Prof. Dokkyo Med. U. Sch. Medicine, 2007—. Mem.: European Respiratory Soc., Am. Thoracic Soc., Japanese Respiratory Soc. (Kumagaya award). Office: 880 Kitakobayashi Mibu Tochigi 321-0293 Japan Office Fax: 81-282-86-7780. Business E-Mail: ishiiysk@dokkyomed.ac.jp.

ISHIJIMA, TOSHIMICHI, biotechnologist, educator; b. Tokyo, Feb. 2, 1983; PhD, Waseda U., 2009. Asst. prof. Tokyo U. Agr. and Tech., 2011—. Mem.: Japan Soc. Phys. Fitness and Sports Medicine, European Coll. Sport Sci. Avocation: sports. Office: 2-24-16 Naka-cho Koganei Tokyo 1848588 Japan Business E-Mail: toshi.51@toki.waseda.jp.

ISHIKADO, ATSUSHI, medical researcher; b. Shiga, Japan, Feb. 27, 1972; M, Kyoto Pharm. U., 1996; PhD, Shiga U. Med. Sci., 2011. Rschr. Sunstr Inc., 1996—. Office: 3-1 Asahi-machi Takatsuki Osaka 569-1195 Japan Office Fax: 81-72-681-8202. Business E-Mail: atsushi.ishikado@jp.sunstar.com.

ISHIKAWA, HAJIME, orthopaedic surgeon; b. Niigata City, Mar. 17, 1958; MD, Yamagata U., Sch. Medicine, 1982. Med. mgr. Niigata Rheumatic Ctr., 2006—. Office: Niigata Rheumatic Ctr 1 2 8 Honcho Shibata city Niigata Prefecture 957-0054 Japan Office Fax: 81-254-23-7763. Business E-Mail: med@ra-center.com.

ISHIKAWA, HIDEAKI, medical educator; b. Japan, Mar. 30, 1963; PhD in Med. Sci., Hiroshima U., 1990. Postdoc. rschr. Inst. Virus Rsch. Kyoto U., 1990—94; postdoc. fellow Bristol-Myers Squibb Pharm. Rsch. Inst., 1994—97; assoc. prof. Grad. Sch. Medicine Yamaguchi U., 1997—. Recipient Aki's Memory award, Internat. Myeloma Found., 21st Kojinkai award, Hiroshima U. Sch. Medicine, Nakamura award, Yamaguchi U. Sch. Medicine; Rsch. grant, Japanese Leukemia Rsch. Fund. Mem.: Japanese Soc. Immunology, Molecular Biology Soc. Japan, Japanese Cancer Assn., Japanese Soc. Hematology, Am. Soc. Hematology. Office: 1-1-1 Minami-kogushi Ube Yamaguchi 755-8505 Japan Office Fax: 81-836-22-2237. Business E-Mail: hishika@yamaguchi-u.ac.jp.

ISHIKAWA, MASAHITO, medical technologist; b. Bihoro-cho, Hokkaido, Japan, Aug. 5, 1966; s. Masao and Kumiko Ishikawa; m. Akemi Akita, Sept. 26, 1993; 1 child, Sena. Degree in med. tech., Kitasato Gakuen Coll. of Hygienic Sci., Aomori, Japan, 1988. Med. technologist dept. microbiology Ogyu Clin. Testing Lab., Hokkaido, Japan, 1988—92; med. technologist dept. clin. lab. Sapporo Teishin Hosp., 1992—. Contbr. reports to profl. publs. Mem.: Japanese Assn. Med. Technologists, Japanese Soc. Sonographers, Japan Soc. Ultrasonics in Medicine (registered med. sonographer, gastroenterology, cardiology). Office: Sapporo Teishin Hosp Clin Lab 14-1-5 Kawazoe Minami-ku Hokkaido Sapporo 005-8798 Japan Business E-Mail: zen_ji@me.com.

ISHIKAWA-FULLMER, JANET SATOMI, psychologist, educator; b. Hilo, Hawaii, Oct. 17, 1925; d. Shinichi and Onao (Kurisu) Saito; m. Calvin Y. Ishikawa, Aug. 15, 1950; 1 child, James A. Ishikawa; m. Daniel W. Fullmer, June 11, 1980. B of Edn., U. Hawaii, 1950, MEd, 1967, MEd, 1969, PhD, 1976; postgrad., Queen's Med. Ctr., 1980—82. Diplomate Am. Acad. Pain Mgmt. Postdoctoral trainee Queen's Med. Ctr., intern pain diagnosis tng., biofeedback/self-hypnosis tng.; prof. Honolulu Bus. Coll., 1953-59; prof., counselor Kapiolani C.C., Honolulu, 1959-73; prof., dir. counseling Honolulu C.C., 1973-74, dean of students, 1974-77; psychologist, pres., treas. Human Resources Devel. Ctr., Inc., Honolulu, 1977—. Cons. United Specialties Co., Tokyo, 1979, Filipino Immigrants in Kalihi, Honolulu, 1979—84, Grambling State U., La., 1980, La., 81, Legis. Ref. Bur., Honolulu, 1984—85, Honolulu Police Dept., 1985; co-founder Waianae Child and Family Ctr., Hawaii, 1979—92. Co-author: Family Therapy Dictionary, 1991, Manabu: The Diagnosis and Treatment of a Japanese Boy with a Visual Anomaly, 1991; contbr. articles to profl. jours. Commr. Bd. Psychology, Honolulu, 1979—85; co-founder Kilohana United Meth. Ch. Family Ctr., 1993—. Recipient Outstanding Educator award, Grambling State U., 1977, Pres.'s award, 1984, Disting. Benefactor award, U. Hawaii Coll. Edn., 2004, Disting. Alumna award, 2005. Mem.: ACA, APA, Hawaii Psychol. Assn., Delta Kappa Gamma (sec., v.p. scholarship 1975, Outstanding Educator award 1975, Thomas Jefferson award 1993, Francis Clark award 1993, Donor Recognition award 2004), Pi Lambda Theta (sec. 1967—68, v.p. 1968—69, pres. 1969—70, 1996—98, Disting. Pi Lambda Theta award 2007). Avocations: jogging, tennis, dance. Office: Human Resources Devel Ctr 1750 Kalakaua Ave Apt 809 Honolulu HI 96826-3725 Office Phone: 808-942-2072.

ISHIKURA, FUMINOBU, cardiologist, educator; b. Kyoto, Oct. 27, 1955; MD, Mie U., 1982. Assoc. prof. Osaka U., 2004—. Fellow: Am. Coll. Cardiology. Office: 1-7 Yamadaoka Suita Osaka 565-0871 Japan Business E-Mail: ishikura@sahs.med.osaka-u.ac.jp.

ISHIMORI, YOSHIYUKI, radiologist, educator; b. Fukui, Japan, Apr. 20, 1964; A, Nagoya U., 1986; PhD, Fukui U. Radiol. technologist Fukui U., 1987—2005; lectr. Ibaraki Prefectural U. Health Scis., 2005—10, assoc. prof., 2010—. Office: Ami 4669-2 Ami-machi Inashiki-gun Ibaraki 300-0394 Japan Business E-Mail: ishimori@ipu.ac.jp.

ISHIZAKA, HIROSHI, radiologist; b. Toyama, Nov. 7, 1956; MD, Kanazawa Med. Coll., 1956. Physician, radiology Maeebashi Red Cross Hosp., 2001—. Avocation: swimming. Home: 1-8-11 903 Maebashi Gunma 371-0021 Japan Personal E-mail: hirishi@jcom.home.ne.jp.

ISHLER, HAROLD LEROY, JR., retired physician; b. Lock Haven, Pa., Mar. 16, 1941; s. Harold and Marqueta (Guiser) I.; m. Suzanne McNeilly, July 17, 1965; children: Stephanie, Stephen. BS, Pa. State U., 1963; MD, Jefferson Med. Coll., 1967. Diplomate Am. Bd. Family Practice. Pres. East Baton Rouge Parish Med. Soc., 2000, La. Acad. Family Physicians, 2000—01; physician Ochsner Clinic Found., Baton Rouge; ret., 2007. Home: 11414 Copperwood Dr Denham Springs LA 70726-6083

ISHRAK, OMAR S., medical products company executive; b. 1955; BS, U. London, King's Coll., PhD in Elec. Engring. Sr. v.p. worldwide mktg. and product devel. Elbit Ultrasound Group; product devel. Philips Ultrasound; sr. v.p., worldwide mktg. and product devel. General Electric Co., 1995, v.p., 1999; pres., CEO clin. sys. divsn. GE Healthcare Systems, 2005—09, pres., CEO, 2009—11; chmn., CEO Medtronic Inc., Mpls., 2011—. Bd. dirs. Medtronic Inc., 2011—. Mem. Blood Ctr. of Wis.; health leadership coun. Save the Children Found. Office: Medtronic Inc 710 Medtronic Pkwy Minneapolis MN 55432 Office Phone: 763-514-4000. *

ISIK, AHMET TURAN, physician, director; b. Turkey, Apr. 27, 1972; Degree in Geriat. Medicine, Gulhane Sch. Medicine, 2007. Assoc. prof. Gulhane Sch. Medicine, 1995, dir., 2010—. Avocations: motorcycling, tennis. Office: Vatan Istanbul 34093 Turkey Personal E-mail: atisik@yahoo.com.

ISIK, FRANK, plastic surgeon; b. Izmir, Turkey, Nov. 20, 1960; married. MD, Mt. Sinai U., 1985. Diplomate Am. Bd. Plastic and Gen. Surgeon, cert. Am. Bd. Surgery. Assoc. prof. U. Wash., Seattle, 1995—2003, prof. plastic surgery, 2003—07; with Polyclinic, Seattle, 2007—. Examiner Am. Bd. Plastic Surgery. Assoc. editor Jour. Plastic & Reconstructive Surgery. Named one of Seattle's Top Doctors, Seattle mag. Mem.: Am. Soc. Plastic Surgery. Office: Polyclinic 1145 Broadway Seattle WA 98122 Office Phone: 206-860-4566. Office Fax: 206-860-4750. Business E-Mail: frankisik@polyclinic.com.

ISIKLI, BURHANETTIN, physician, educator; b. Kayseri, Turkey, Aug. 18, 1960; MD, Ankara U., 1985, Osmangazi U., 1994. Prof., physician Eskisehir Osmangazi U., 1994—. Office: Eskisehir Osmangazi University Eskisehir 26480 Turkey Business E-Mail: burhan@ogu.edu.tr.

ISLAM, MUHAMMAD NURUL, pathologist; b. BeaniBazar, Sylhet, Bangladesh, Jan. 1, 1959; s. Feroze Ali and Hurun Nessa; m. Mahbuba Mali - Zabeen, Mar. 1, 1992; children: Muhammad Raiyanul, Muhammad Rafsanul. Diploma in Forensic Medicine, U. Dhaka, Bangladesh, 2000; MBChB, U. Dhaka, 1984. Registered physician Bangladesh Med. & Dental Coun., 1985. Asst. surgeon Mymensingh (Bangladesh) Med. Coll. Hosp., 1984—85; med. officer KurarBazar Union Health Ctr., BeaniBazar, Sylhet, Bangladesh, 1985—88, Companigonj (Bangladesh) Thana Health Complex, 1988—90, MoulviBazar (Bangladesh) Dist. Hosp., 1990—92, Nat. Inst. Cardiovasc. Disease Hosp., Dhaka, 1992—93, Baniachang Thana Helath Complex, Hobigonj, Sylhet, Bangladesh, 1993—94; indoor med. officer Dhaka Med. Coll. Hosp., 1994—96; med. officer dept. forensic medicine Sir Salimullah Med. Coll., Dhaka, 1996—97, lectr., 1997—2000; asst. prof. Dhaka Med. Coll., 2000—02; forensic pathologist serious crimes unit UN Mission of Support in East Timor, Dili, 2002—. Trainer Health Complex, Sylhet, Bangladesh, 1985—90, MoulviBazar Dist. Hosp., 1990—92, Dhaka Med. Coll., 2000—02, coord. med.-legal activities dept. forensic medicine, 2000—02; examiner U. Dhaka, 2000—02; mgr. epidemic outbreaks of diseases Union Health Ctr., KurarBazar, Bangladesh, 1985—88; cons., presenter in field. Mem. editl. bd. A Handbook On Forensic Management Of Sexual Violence; contbr. articles to profl. jours. Vol. physician Free Friday Clinic, Dhaka, 1994—2002. Mem.: Bangladesh Coll. Pysician and Surgeons, Bangladesh Med. and Dental Coun. (licentiate), Bangladesh Civil Svc. (life), Medicolegal Soc. Bangladesh (life), Bangladesh Med. Assn. (life). Achievements include research in trauma from sharp and blunt force instruments; design of ideal practical format on forensic medicine for management sexual violence victims in Bangladesh; research in medicolegal death investigation; motor vehicle accidents; suicide and sexual violence in Bangladesh. Avocations: travel, music, movies, internet, literature. Home: 86 / 2 - B Zigatola Dhaka 1209 Bangladesh Office: Serious Crimes Unit UNMISET P O Box 2436 Darwin 0801 Australia Office Fax: 212-963-2180 Ext. 6460. Personal E-mail: mnirunu@yahoo.com. E-mail: islam23@un.org.

ISLAM, NURUL, medical educator; b. Chittagong, Bangladesh, Apr. 1, 1928; s. Syedur Rahman and Gulmeher; m. Anwara Begum, Dec. 26, 1962; children: Dina, Iftekhar, Neena. MBBS, Calcutta Med. Coll., India, 1951; diploma in tubercular diseases, U. Wales, 1955; DSc (hon.), Internat. U. Alt. Medicine, Sri Lanka, 1999. Assoc. prof. medicine Dhaka (Bangladesh) Med. Coll., 1956-62; prof. medicine Chittagong Med. Coll., 1962-64; dir., prof. Inst. Posgrad. Medicine and Rsch., Dhaka, 1965-87; physician to Founding Father of Bangladesh, Bangabandhu Sheikh Mujibur Rahman, 1971-75; internat. adv. Madinat-al-Hikmah City Edn. Sci. and Culture, Karachi, Pakistan, 1996—. Vis. prof. Royal Free Med. Coll., London, 1962-63; chmn. Med. Rsch. Coun., Bangladesh, 1975-96; mem. expert adv. panel health manpower devel. WHO, 1976-90, expert adv. panel tobacco health, 1992; founder, chmn. Alliance Prudent Use Antibiotics, 1987—, Inst. Applied Health Scis., Bangladesh, 1989—, Janasheba Found., 1991—; founder, pres., vice-chancellor U. Sci. Tech., Chittagong, 1992—; vice-chmn. Hammond Found. Author: New Disease Esoniophils Lung Abcess, 1962, Tropical Eosinophilia, 1964

(Nat. Book award 1967), Prescriptions, 1985, Finger Method for Examining Pharynx, 1986 (Nat. Acad. award), In the Stream of Life, 1991, Some Thoughts, 1993, (in Bengali) Kichu Bhabna, 1995, Bangabanhu, 1997, (Bengali), English version, 2001, Essential Drugs for Village Practice, 1998. Founder Islamic Med. Mission, Bangladesh, 1981; mng. trustee Anwara-Nur Welfare Trust, Bangladesh, 1985—; bd. govs. Islamic Found. Recipient Gold medal Pres., 1963, Nat. Acad. Scis., 1982, WHO Commemorative Medal on Tobacco and Health, 1990, 92, Golden Grahak Sewa award, 1993, Ibn Sina medal, 1995, M. K. Ghandi Peace award, 1996, Independence Day award, 1997, Swamaj Sheba Padak medal Govt. Bangladesh, 1999, B.C. Roy award Kalkata, 2003, Spl. Tobacco Control award WHO, 2005; named Nat. Prof. Bangladesh, Govt. Bangladesh, 1987. Fellow: Pakistan Acad. Scis., Coll. Gen. Practitioners, Royal Coll. Physicians (Edinburgh and London, emeritus regional adviser 1998), Acad. Scis.; mem.: Bangladesh Soc. Allergy and Immunology, Bangladesh Assn. Advancement Med. Scis. (founder, pres. 1986), Nat. Anti-Tobacco Orgn. ADHUNIK (founder, pres. 1987—). Avocations: travel, reading, writing. Home: Gulmeher 63 Ctrl Rd Dhaka 1205 Bangladesh Office: U Sci Tech Chittagong Gulmeher 63 Ctrl Rd Dhaka 1205 Bangladesh E-mail: ustcbd@bangla.net.

ISLAM, SALEEM, pediatric surgeon, researcher; b. NYC, Nov. 25, 1967; s. Naseem and Swaleha Islam; m. Shehla P. Peshimam, Feb. 14, 1993; children: Rubab, Nazli, Feryal. MD, Aga Khan U., Karachi, Pakistan, 1992; MPH, U. Mass., Amherst, 2006. Diplomate Am. Bd. of Surgery, spl. cert. in pediat. surgery Am. Bd. of Surgery. Intern U. Mass., Worcester, 1995—96, resident, 1995—2001; fellow U. Mich., Ann Arbor, 2001—03; assoc. prof. surgery U. Fla., Gainsville, 2003—, dir. pediat. minimal invasive surgery. Dir. extracorporeal membraine oxygenation U. Miss. Med. Ctr., Jackson, 2004—06. Contbr. scientific papers to profl. jours. Mem.: Assn. of Acad. Surgeons, Assn. of Surg. Edn., Children's Oncology Group, Internat. Pediat. Endosurgery Group, Am. Acad. of Pediats., Am. Pediat. Surg. Assn, Mass. Med. Soc. Office Phone: 352-273-8800.

ISLA PERA, PILAR, nurse; b. Huesca, Spain, Aug. 7, 1947; Degree in Anthropology, U. Barcelona, 1968; PhD in Nursing, U. Alicante, 2006. Nurse Hosp. Clínico Barcelona, 1965—90. Recipient Stern' award, U. Hogeschool Zeeland Vlissingen, Netherlands. Master: Spanish Sci. Soc. Nursing; mem.: Catalan Soc. Pub. Health, Catalan Soc. Diabetes, Adv. Coun. Diabetes Catalonia, Spanish Diabetes Soc. Avocations: reading, travel, art. Office: Campus Ciències de la Salut de Bellvitge L'Hospitalet de Llobregat Barcelona 08907 Spain Office Fax: 34934024297. Business E-Mail: pisla@ub.edu.

ISMAIL, FYAZ MAHMOOD DAUD, chemist, researcher; b. Kampala, Uganda, Dec. 29, 1961; s. Mohammed Daud and Mohtrim Khanum Ismail. BSc in Biochemistry, Monsanto, Salford; PhD in Biochemistry, Nat. Health Svc., Salford, 1989. Lectr. Salford (Eng.) U., Lancashire, 1983—89; dir., sr. lectr. U. Hertfordshire, Hatfield, England, 1991—2001; sr. lectr., program leader, dir. Liverpool John Moores Univ. Pharmacy, Merseyside L3 3AF, England, 2001—. Dir. Medicinal Chemistry Rsch. Group, Liverpool, Merseyside, England, 1983—. Air tng. core cadet Ickneild U.K. Mil., 1973—76, Luton. Recipient Nuc. Magnetic Resonance Discussion Group award, Royal Soc. Chemistry, 1996. Mem.: Soc. Chemistry Industry (Liverpool sect. comittee mem. 2001—), Am. Chem. Soc. (life). Muslim. Achievements include research in synthesis of enodogenous hypertension inducing substance in humans; invention of flow process for MBT production; patents for transplant rejection and anticancer agents; antioxidant therapy for Parkinsons disease; research in novel antimalarials active in vivo; first to correction of errors in Semenov's theory of antioxidant action (Nobel Laureate); discovery of cheap industrial synthesis of vitamin E. Avocations: photography, history of science. Office: Liverpool John Moores Univ 221 C Byrom St Merseyside Liverpool L3 3AF England Office Fax: UK: +440151 231 2170; Home Fax: uk +(44)0151 231 2170. Business E-Mail: f.m.ismail@livjm.ac.uk.

ISMAIL, SHATRIAH, ophthalmologist, educator; b. Baling, Kedah, Malaysia, Aug. 15, 1970; d. Ismail Daud and Saadiah Abdul Hameed; m. Nik Ahmad Zuky; children: Nik Luqmanul Hakim, Nik Syamim Firdaus, Nik Zahid Asyraf, Nik Aimi Munirah. MD, U. Sains Malaysia, 1995, MSc in Medicine, 2004. Med. officer Hosp. Alor Setar, Kedah, 1996—2000, Hosp. Kota Bharu, Kelantan, 2000—02; house officer U. Sains Malaysia, 2002—04, med. lectr. & ophthalmologist, 2004—07, academician, 2004—08, sr. med. lectr., 2007—, cons. ophthalmologist, 2007—. Vis. cons. ophthalmologist Hosp. Tengku Anis, Kelantan, Kota Bharu Med. Ctr., 2007—. Contbr. articles to numerous profl. jours., to numerous presentations (Best Poster Presentation award, 2004). Recipient Best Clin. Lectr. award, U. Sains Malaysia, 2007; Short Term grant, 2002—04, Sydney Programme fellowship, 2007. Mem.: Alumni USM Med. Drs. Home: PT 248 Lorong Taman Sri Mawar Kubang Kerian Kelantan 16150 Malaysia Office: Univ Sains Malaysia Health Campus 16150 Kubang Kerian Malaysia Office Fax: 6097653370. Business E-Mail: shatriah@kck.usm.my.

ISMAILOV, ROVSHAN M., biomedical researcher; b. Uzbekistan, May 6, 1975; MPH, Boston U., 2001; PhD, U. Pitts., 2005. Postdoc. rsch. assoc. Brown U., 2006—08; editl. bd. mem. Biomed. Engring. Online, 2005—. Contbr. articles to profl. jours. Avocations: tennis, reading. Home: 157 Adelaide St W #275 Toronto ON Canada M5H 4E7 Personal E-mail: rovshani@yahoo.com.

ISOBE, KAZUTOSHI, physician; b. Japan, May 1, 1972; MD, Toho U., PhD, 1998. Physician, dept. respiratory medicine Toho U. Omori Med. Ctr., 2006—. Office: 6-11-1 Omori-Nishi Ota-ku Tokyo 143-8541 Japan Office Fax: 81-3-3766-3551. Personal E-mail: kazutoshiisobe@aol.com.

ISODA, KIKUO, cardiologist, researcher; s. Masahiro and Setsuko Isoda; m. Naoko Jo, Oct. 24, 1998; children: Sachiho children: Mitsuaki, Narumi. MD, PhD, Nat. Def. Med. Coll., Tokorozawa, 1991. Asst. Nat. Def. Med. Coll., Tokorozawa, Saitama, Japan, 1999—2003, instr., 2009—; post doctoral fellow Brigham Women's Hosp., Harvard Med. Sch., 2003—05. Physician Self Defense Force, Tokyo, 1985—99. Fellow: Japanese Circulation Soc. (life; cert. interventional cardiologist, Young Investigator's award 2004); mem.: AHA, Assn. Nat. Def. Med. Coll., Coun. Arteriosclerosis, Thrombosis, Vascular Biology (Merit award for Young Investigators 2006), Japanese Soc. Interventional Cardiology (Intervention Rsch. award 2004), Japanese Soc. Echocardiography (Young Investigator's award 2000), Japan Atherosolerosis Soc. (Young Investigator's award 2005). Office: Nat Def Med Coll 3-2 Namiki Saitama Tokorozawa 359-8513 Japan Office Fax: +81-4-2996-5200. Business E-Mail: isoda@ndmc.ac.jp.

ISOM, OTTIS WAYNE (WAYNE ISOM), thoracic surgeon, educator; b. Lubbock, Tex., Feb. 9, 1940; m. Pat Isom; 5 children. Undergraduate studies, Tex. Tech; MD, U. Tex. Southwestern Med. Sch., 1965. Cert. Surgery, Thoracic Surgery. Med. intern Parkland Hosp., Dallas, 1965—66, gen. surgery resident, 1966—70; cardiothoracic resident NYU Med. Ctr., 1970—72; with faculty NYU Sch. Medicine, prof. surgery, dir. cardiothoracic tng. prog., 1978—85; chmn. dept. cardiothoracic surgery NY-Cornell Med. Ctr. (before the NY Hosp. and Presbyn. Hosp. merged to become NY Presbyn. Hosp.), 1985; Terry Allen Kramer prof of cardiothoracic surgery NY Presbyn.-Weill Cornell Med. Ctr., chmn., dept. cardiothoracic surgery, cardiothoracic surgeon-in-chief. Spkr. in field. Contbr. articles to profl. jours., chapters to books. Recipient Bugher Found. award for Achievement in Cardiovascular Sci. and Medicine, Hero With a Heart award, Nat. Marfan Found., 2000, Humanitarian award, Larry King Cardiac Found. & NYSAE Edn. Rsch. Found. Mem.: Am. Heart Assn. (bd. mem., NYC), Am. Coll. Surgeons, Am. Assn. for Thoracic Surgery. Office: 525 E 68th St M-404 New York NY 10065 Office Phone: 212-746-5151. Office Fax: 212-746-8388. Business E-Mail: owisom@med.cornell.edu.

ISOMURA, EMIKO TANAKA, dentist; b. Japan, Aug. 2, 1975; DDS, Osaka U., 2000, PhD, 2004. Oral surgery specialist first dept. oral and maxillofacial surgery Osaka U., Grad. Sch. Dentistry, 2004—. Mem.: Japanese Soc. Oral and Maxillofacial Surgeons (6th Academic Encouraging prize). Office: 1-8 Yamadaoka Suita Osaka 565-0871 Japan Business E-Mail: tanaemi@dent.osaka-u.ac.jp.

ISRAEL, CARSTEN WALTER, cardiologist, researcher; b. Hagen, Germany, Feb. 20, 1967; s. Walter Paul Rudolf and Halina Richarda (Goldner) Israel. MD, Ruhr U., Bochum, Germany, 1994, D in Internal Medicine, 1999. Intern Ruhr U. Hosp., Bochum, 1991—92, med. resident, 1992—99; fellow clin. cardiology J.W. Goethe U. Hosp., Frankfurt, 1999—2003, assoc. prof. internal medicine, 2003—; head, dept. internal medicine - cardiology Ev. Hosp. Bielefeld, 2009—. Cons., tchr. on pacemaker functions., 1995—; adv. bd. Medtronic Inc., Mpls., 1999. Editor, author: Advances in the Treatment of Atrial Tachyarrhythmias, 2002; editor: Herzschrittmacher, 1999—2002, Herzschrittmachertherapie & Elekrophysiologie, 2004—; mem. editl. bd.: Pacing Clin. Electrophysiology, 2006—, PACE, 2006—; assoc. editor EUROPACE, 2007—; contbr. articles to profl. jours. Mem.: German Pacing Group (mem. bd.), Heart Rhythm Soc., Deutsche Ärztekammer, German Cardiac Soc. Protestant. Avocations: reading, history, classical music, art. Home: Klaberkampweg 4 Bielefeld Germany Office: Ev Hosp Bielefeld Dept Medicine - Cardiology Burgsteig 13 Bielefeld 33617 Germany Office Fax: 49-69-6301-6341. Business E-Mail: c.w.israel@em.uni-frankfurt.de.

ISRAELI, DAVID, molecular biologist; b. Beer sheva, Israel, Jan. 7, 1961; s. Eli and Hana Israeli; m. Florence Levy, Sept. 10, 1995; children: Daniel, Mathy, Yael. BSc (hon.), Hebrew U., Jerusalem, Israel, 1991; MSc, Weizmann Inst Sci., Rehovet, Israel, 1992, PhD, 1998; postdoc. degree, Genethon, Evry, 2000. Maintenance mgr. Dairy Farm, Kibbutz Revivim, Israel, 1983—86; employer, dept. maintenance Raviv Plastic Industry, Kibbutz Revivim, 1986—88; project mgr. Genethon, Evry, France, 2000—. Sgt. Parachutist Land Army IDF, 1980—83, Israel. Marie Curie grant, 5th European Framework Program, 1999—2000. Achievements include research in stem cells, cell and gene therapy and regenerative therapy with a particular focus on the neuromuscular system.

ISRAELITE, CRAIG LANE, orthopaedic surgeon, educator; MD, Hahnemann Univ., 1987. Lic. Pa., 1991, NJ, 1992, diplomate Am. Bd. Orthopaedic Surgery, 1994. Intern gen. surgery Hahnemann Univ. Hosp., 1988, resident orthop. surgery, 1992; hosp. affiliations include Univ. Pa. Hosp., Clin. Health Care Assoc., NJ; asst. prof. orthop. surgery Pa. Presbyn. Med. Ctr., surgeon. Named one of the Top Doctors, Phila. Mag., 2002, 2010—11. Office: Pennsylvania Presbyterian Medical Center 1 Cupp Pavilion 51 N 39th St Philadelphia PA 19104 Office Phone: 215-662-3340.

ISRAELSSON, LEIF ANDERS, surgeon; b. Umea, Sweden, Jan. 4, 1954; children: Anders, Maria. MD, 1980, PhD, 1995. Surgeon cons. Kirurgkliniken, Sundsvall, Sweden, 1992—, head emergency unit, 1995—2005, assoc. prof., 2001—, head dept. surgery, 2004—. Office: Kirurgkliniken 851 86 Sundsvall Sweden Home Phone: 4660174251; Office Phone: 4660181459.

ISRAILI, ZAFAR HASAN, pharmacologist, educator; came to U.S., 1961, naturalized, 1977; s. Siddiq Hasan and Zahida Khatun I.; m. Sally Jean Smith, Oct. 24, 1970; children: Shahnaz Joy, Taj Hasan, Rana Shereen. BSc, Aligarh M. U., 1951, MSc, 1953; PhD, U. Kans., 1968. Lectr. chemistry Aligarh M. U., 1953-54, sr. rsch. scholar, 1954-57; rsch. asst., jr. sci. officer AEC India, 1957-61; rsch. assoc. U. Kans., 1968-69; sr. rsch. chemist Alza Corp., Lawrence, Kans., 1969-70; asst. prof. medicine and chemistry Emory U., Atlanta, 1970-75, assoc. prof. chemistry, 1975-78, assoc. prof. medicine, 1975—, prof. chemistry, 1978—. Rsch. pharmacologist Atlanta VA Med. Ctr., Decatur, 1979-87; sci. staff Grady Hosp., Atlanta, 1974—; adj. prof. chemistry Ga. Perimeter Coll., 2004—. Editor Ethnicity and Disease, 1997—; assoc. editor Drug Metabolism Revs., 1974—, Venezuelan Jour. Hypertension, 2005-, Revista Latino Americana Hipertension, 2006—; guest editor Internat. Jour. Hypertension, 2010-; mem. editl. bd. Drug Devel. Rsch., 1979—, Archives Venezuelan Pharm. Ter., 1983—, Am. Jour. Ther., 2003-, Diabetes Internat., 2009-; contbr. articles to profl. jours., chpts. to books. Recipient Asia Found. award, 1962; Merit scholar Aligarh M. U., 1953; Merck Sharpe & Dohm grantee, 1977, 85, 87, NIH grantee, 1978-83, VA grantee, 1979-87, Am. Heart Assn. grantee, 1989-91. Mem. Am. Soc. Clin. Pharmacology and Therapeutics, Am. Soc. Pharmacology and Exptl. Therapeutics, Soc. Exptl. Biology and Medicine, Am. Assn. Cancer Rsch., Am. Aging Assn., Am. Chem. Soc., Am. Soc. Hypertension, Chem. Soc. London, Internat. Soc. for Study Xenobiotics, Interam. Soc. Clin. Pharm. Therapeutics (pres.-elect 1997-2000, pres. 2000—), Internat. Soc. on Hypertension in Blacks, Am. Heart Assn., Sigma Xi, Rho Chi, Phi Lambda Upsilon. Independent. Muslim. Home: 3567 Cloudland Dr Stone Mountain GA 30083-4005 Office: Emory Univ Sch Medicine Dept Medicine 69 Jesse Hill Jr Dr Atlanta GA 30303-2607 Office Phone: 404-616-5176. Personal E-mail: israiligpc@yahoo.com.

ISSELBACHER, KURT JULIUS, internist, educator; b. Wirges, Germany, Sept. 12, 1925; arrived in U.S., 1936, naturalized, 1945; s. Albert and Flori (Strauss) Isselbacher; m. Rhoda Solin, June 22, 1955; children: Lisa, Karen, Jody, Eric. AB, Harvard U., 1946, MD cum laude, 1950; ScD (hon.), Northwestern U., 2001. Intern, then resident Mass. Gen. Hosp., Boston, 1950—53, chief gastrointestinal unit, 1957—89, chmn. com. rsch., 1967, dir. Cancer Ctr., 1987—2003, dir. emeritus, 2003—; investigator NIH, 1953—56; prof. medicine Harvard Med. Sch., 1966—, chmn. exec. com. depts. medicine, 1968—97, Mallinckrodt prof. medicine, 1972—97, disting. Mallinckrodt prof. medicine, 1998—, chmn. univ. cancer com., 1972—87. Mem. governing bd. NRC, 1987—90; mem. sci. bd. FDA, 1993; acad. liaison Novartis Biomed. Rsch. Inst., 2002—; trustee Marine Biol. Labs., 2004—; editor Harrison's-on-line, 1999—. Editor-in-chief (Harrison): Principles of Internal Medicine, 1976, 1991—99. Recipient award for disting. achievement in nutrition, Bristol-Myers Squibb, 1991, Sci. Bd. FDA, 1993—97, Tree of Life award, Jewish Nat. Fund, 2001. Fellow: ACP (John Phillips award for disting. achievement in clin. medicine 1989); mem.: NAS (chmn. food and nutrition bd. 1983—88, mem. exec. com., mem. coun. 1987—90, chmn. com. on risk assessment of hazardous air pollutants 1991—94), Inst. Medicine of NAS, Assn. Am. Physicians (pres. 1977—78, Kober medal 2001), Am. Gastroenterology Assn. (pres. 1974—75, Julius Friedenwald medal for outstanding achievement in gastroenterology 1985), Am. Acad. Arts and Scis. Achievements include research in molecular and genetic changes in malignant cells, metastasis in breast and colon cancer. Home: 20 Nobscot Rd Newton MA 02459-1323 Office: Cancer Ctr Mass Gen Hosp 149 13th St Charlestown MA 02129-2023 Office Phone: 617-726-5610. E-mail: KIsselbacher@partners.org.

ISTANBULLUOGLU, MUSTAFA OKAN, urologist, educator; b. Turkey, Jan. 30, 1977; MD, Istanbul U., 1999. Assoc. prof. urology, 2008—. Office: Baskent University Konya Hosp Hocac Selçuklu Konya 42060 Turkey Personal E-mail: drokanist@hotmail.com.

ITAH, REFAEL, physician; b. Haifa, Israel, Jan. 25, 1971; MD, Ben-Gurion U., Negev, 2005; PhD student, Ben Gurion U., Kreitman Sch. Advanced Grad. Studies. Intern-gen. surgery Tel Aviv Sourasky Med. Ctr., Ichilov, 2005—11. Physician, clin. devel. specialist Biosense-Webster Johnson & Johnson, Israel, 2010. Home: Eli Cohen 7/46 Tel-Aviv 69630 Israel

ITAMI, JUN, oncologist; b. Kanagawa, Japan, Feb. 17, 1957; MD, Chiba U., PhD, 1981. Chmn. Nat. Cancer Ctr. Hosp., Dept. Radiation Oncology, 2008—. Mem.: European Soc. Med. Oncology, Am. Soc. Clin. Oncology, Am. Brachytherapy Soc., European Soc. Therapeutic Radiology and Oncology, Japanese Soc. Therapeutic Radiology and Oncology. Office: Tsukiji 5-1-1 Chuo-ku Tokyo 104-0045 Japan Business E-Mail: jitami@ncc.go.jp.

ITELD, LAWRENCE H., plastic surgeon; b. NJ; married. BA in Biological Sci. and Economics, Rutgers Coll.; MD with distinction in rsch., U. Mich. Diplomate Am. Bd. Plastic Surgery. Trainee plastic surgery Univ. Chgo. Hosps., 1998, resident dept. gen. surgery, resident dept. plastic and reconstructive surgery, chief resident plastic and reconstructive surgery; fellow microsurgery and oncologic reconstruction Univ. Tex. MD Anderson Cancer Ctr.; asst. prof. plastic surgery Univ. Miami; chief plastic surgery Adv. Ill. Masonic Hosp., Mercy Hosp.; hosp. affiliations include St. Joseph Hosp., Chgo., Adventsit Hinsdale, Adventist LaGrange Hosps.; plastic surgeon The Geldner Ctr. Author: various jour. articles; featured in Chgo. Tribune, the RedEye, WGN-TV. Named one of America's Top Surgeons, 2009, America's Top Plastic Surgeons, 2009. Mem.: Am. Soc. Plastic Surgery. Office: The Geldner Center 680 N Lake Shore Dr Ste 1325 Chicago IL 60611 Office Phone: 312-981-4440. Office Fax: 312-981-4441.

ITEN, PETER XAVER, retired toxicologist, chemist; b. Zug, Switzerland, July 22, 1944; s. Xaver Johann Iten and Erna Meyer; children: Mirjam Francine, Christian Peter. PhD, U. Zurich, Switzerland, 1973. Chem. diplomate, U. Zurich, 1969. Head asst. dept. organic chemistry U. Zurich, 1973—77, head dept. forensic chemistry, toxicology, Inst. Legal Medicine, 1986—2009, analyst, 2009; dir. dept. criminal investigation Zurich State Police, 1977—86. Author: (books) Driving Under The Influence Of Drugs, Forensic Interpretation; contbr. articles to profl. jours. Mem.: Soc. Toxicology and Forensic Chemistry, Internat. Assn. Forensic Toxicology, Am. Acad. Forensic Scis., Swiss Soc. Legal Medicine. Home: Greifenseestr 39A Schwerzenbach CH-8603 Switzerland Home Phone: 41 76 559 77 11, 0041 44 82550 86. E-mail: peter.iten@ggaweb.ch.

ITO, MASAO, neuroscience researcher; b. Nagoya, Aichi, Japan, Dec. 4, 1928; s. Rikuo and Chiyo (Inagaki) I.; m. Midori Watanabe, May 29, 1931; children: Minami, Yukari. MD, U. Tokyo Med. Sch., 1953, DMS, 1959. Asst. prof. med. faculty Kumamoto (Japan) U., 1954-57, U. Tokyo, 1958-62, assoc. prof. med. faculty, 1963-70, prof. med. faculty, 1970-86, dean med. faculty, 1986-88; dir. gen. Frontier Rsch. Sys. Inst. Phys. and Chem. Rsch., Wako, Japan, 1991—; dir. RIKEN Brain Sci. Inst., Wako, Japan, 1997—2003, sr. advisor, 2003—. Emeritus prof. U. Tokyo, 1989—. Co-author: (book) The Cerebellum as a Neuronal Machine, 1967; author: The Cerebellum and Neural Control, 1984-2000; editor-in-chief Neuroscience Rsch. Decorated chevalier Legion d'Honneur (France), Order of Culture (Japan); recipient Fujiwara Found. prize, 1981, Imperial prize Japan Acad., 1986, Neural Plasticity prize IPSEN Found., 1993, Person of Cultural Merit award Japanese Govt., 1994, Japan prize The Sci. and Tech. Found. Japan, 1996, The Order of Culture, 1996, Neurosci. prize Peter Gruber Found., 2006. Mem. NAS, Royal Swedish Acad. Scis., Royal Soc. London, Russian Acad. Scis., French Acad. Scis., Armenian Acad. Scis., Japan Acad., Hungarian Acad. Scis., Indian Acad. Scis., European Acad. Scis., Nat. Acad. Scis. (fgn. assoc.), Internat. Brain Rsch. Orgn. (pres. 1980-86), Internat. Union Physiol. Scis. (pres. 1993-97), Sci. Coun. Japan (pres. 1994-97), Human Frontier Sci. Program (pres. 2000—), Sci. and Tech. Found. of Japan (pres. 2005—). Avocations: travel, book reading. Office: RIKEN Brain Sci Inst Wako Saitama 351-0198 Japan Office Phone: 048462-1111. E-mail: ito-bsi@brain.riken.jp.

ITO, MITSUHIRO, medical educator; b. Nagoya, Aichi, Japan, Mar. 25, 1963; s. Kiyoji and Masako Ito; m. Michiko Kadoya; children:

Chihiro, Shun. MD, Kobe U. Sch. Medicine, Hyogo, Japan, 1987; PhD, Kobe U., 1994. Bd. cert. hematologist Japanese Soc. Hematology, 1994. Resident internal medicine Kobe U. Sch. Medicine, 1987—90, lectr., 3rd divsn., dept. medicine, 1994—95, rsch. fellow Japan Soc. Promotion Sci., 1995—97, prof., divsn. hematology, dept. medicine, 2008—09, physician, divsn. hematology-oncology, dept. medicine, 2002—03, asst. prof., divsn. hematology-Oncology, dept. medicine, 2003—06, prof., 2006—08, lectr. civic health promotion, 2007, project mem., global ctr. excellence, 2008—; postdoc. fellow Lab. Biochemistry and Molecular Biology, Rockefeller U., NYC, 1996—2001, rsch. assoc., 2001—02; prof. Lab. Hematology, Divsn. Med. Biophysics, Kobe U. Grad. Sch. Health Scis., 2008—; prof. dept. family & cmty medicine; adj. faculty Rockefeller U., 2010—. Com. mem. Kobe Med. Industry Devel. Project, 2007—08; lectr. med. assn. Kakogawa City Med. Assn., Hyogo, 2007. Rsch. fellowship, Japan Soc. Promotion Sci., 1995—97, Cancer Rsch. grant, Hyogo Prefecture Health Promotion Assn., 1995, Osaka Cancer Found., 2004, Sagawa Found. Promotion Cancer Rsch., 2006, Sci. Rsch. grant, Ministry of Edn., Culture, Sports, Sci. and Tech., 1996—98, 2004—, Long-term fellowship, Human Frontier Sci. Program, 1997—99, Med. Rsch. grant, Kanae Found. Promotion Med. Sci., 1995, Takeda Sci. Found., 2006, Ono Med. Rsch. Found., 2005, Suzuken Meml. Found., 2006. Mem.: Japan Human Care Soc., Molecular Biology Soc. Japan, Japanese Cancer Assn., Japan Soc. Transfusion Medicine and Cell Therapy, Japan Soc. Hematopoietic Cell Transplantation, Japanese Soc. Internal Medicine (faculty 1995), Japanese Soc. Clin. Oncology (faculty, tentative, Subspecialty Bd. Med. Oncology, JSMO 2005), Japanese Soc. Hematology (faculty, councilor 1996, councilor 2008—), Am. Soc. Hematology. Avocations: philosophy, languages. Office: Kobe Univ Grad Sch Medicine Dept Family & Cmty Medicine 7-5-1 Kusunoki-cho Chuo-ku Kobe Hyogo 650-0017 Japan Office Phone: 81-78-796-4546. Business E-Mail: itomi@med.kobe-u.ac.jp.

ITO, SHIGENORI, cardiologist; b. Fukui, Japan, June 23, 1957; MD, Nagoya City U., 1984, PhD. Dir. divsn. cardiology Nagoya City East Med. Ctr., 2007—. Dir. Cardiovasc. Imaging Core Lab., 2007—11. Office: 1-2-13 Wakamizu-cho Chikusa-ku Nagoya Aichi 464-8547 Japan Office Fax: 81-52-721-1308. Business E-Mail: sito@higashi-hosp.jp.

ITO, YOSHIAKI, research scientist; b. Iwate Prefecture, Japan, Jan. 7, 1939; arrived in Singapore, 2002; MD, PhD, Tohoku U., Sendai, Japan, 1968. Rsch. fellow Imperial Cancer Rsch. Fund Labs., London, 1972—74, scientist, 1975—79; vis. scientist NIH, Bethesda, Md., 1979—83; head cell transformation sect. Nat. Cancer Inst., NIH, Frederick, Md., 1983—84; prof. dept. viral oncology Inst. for Virus Rsch., Kyoto, 1984—2002, dir., 1995—2001; prof., prin. investigator Inst. Molecular and Cell Biology, Singapore, 2002—; dir. Oncology Rsch. Inst., Nat. U. Singapore, 2002—. Recipient Kuroya award, Japanese Virology Soc., 1968, Princess Takamatsu Cancer Rsch. award, Princess Takamatsu Found., 1995, Tomizo Yoshida prize, Japan Cancer Assn., 2003. Office: Inst Molecular & Cell Biology 61 Biopolis Dr Proteos #06 16B Singapore 138673 Singapore Office Fax: 65-6873 9664. Personal E-mail: itoy@imcb.a-star.edu.sg.

ITO, YUJI, engineering educator; b. Fukuoka, Japan, Jan. 9, 1962; PhD, Kyushu U., 1990. Prof. Kagoshima U., 1997—. Office: Korimoto 1-21-35 Kagoshima 890-0065 Japan Business E-Mail: yito@be.kagoshima-u.ac.jp.

ITOH, ROICHI, biochemistry educator, researcher; b. Tokyo, Nov. 1, 1938; MD, Yokohama City U., 1963, PhD, 1971. Assoc. prof. Yokohama City U., 1972—82; chief Nat. Inst. Health and Nutrition, Tokyo, 1982—94, rschr. emeritus, 1996—; prof. biochemistry Tokyo Kasei Gakuin U., Tokyo, 1994—2009, vis. prof., 2009—, acting. pres. Vis. assoc. prof. Duke U. Med. Ctr., Durham, N.C., 1974-75, Northwestern U., Evanston, Ill., 1975-76. Contbr. articles to sci. jours., including Jour. Biol. Chemistry, Jour. Cytochemistry and Histochemistry, Biochem. Jour., Am. Jour. Clin. Nutrition, others. Recipient Japan nutrition promotion award Japanese Soc. Nutrition and Dietetics, 1985. Office: Tokyo Kasei Gakuin U 2600 Aiharamachi, Machida Tokyo 194-0292 Japan Office Fax: 81-42-782-9880. Business E-Mail: roytoh@kasei-gakuin.ac.jp.

ITOH, ZEN, physiology researcher, physician; b. Tokyo, Oct. 9, 1931; s. Toshio and Chika (Nakao) I.; m. Fumiko Ishii, May 10, 1964; children: Haruna, Nanae, Momoyo. MD, Gunma U., Maebashi, Japan, 1960, PhD, 1965. Instr. Tulane U. Sch. of Medicine, New Orleans, 1965-68; asst. prof. Gunma U. Sch. of Medicine, Maebashi, Japan, 1980-89; prof. Inst. Endocrinology Gunma U., Maebashi, 1989-94; dir. Inst. for Molecular and Cellular Regulation Gunma U., Maebashi, 1994-97; prof. emeritus Grumna U., 1997—. Chmn. Internat. Symposium on Gastrointestinal Motility, Kobe, Japan, 1989-91, chmn. emeritus, 1991-93. Author: (book) Gut Endocrinology (Japanese), 1979; editor Gastroprokinetics (Japanese), 1985, Motilin, 1990. Recipient Janssen awards for lifetime achievement in digestive sci. Janssen Pharmaceutica Rsch. Found., 1999. Mem. Am. Gastroenterology Assn. (sr. mem.), Japanese Soc. Smooth Muscle Rsch. (pres., chmn. Karuizawa, Japan 1989), Japanese Soc. Gastroenterology (exec. mem.), Japanese Soc. Physiology (exec. mem.), Internat. Union of Physiol. Scis. (gastrointestinal commn.) Avocations: mountain climbing, classical music. Home: 188-3 Kogure Yoshii-machi Takasaki 370-2102 Japan Office Phone: 81-27-320-4412. Office Fax: 81-27-320-4413.

ITSCOITZ, SAMUEL, cardiologist; Attended, Harvard U.; MD, George Wash. U. Diplomate Am. Bd. Internal Medicine, Am. Bd. Internal Medicine-cardiovasc. disease. Resident internal medicine Peter Bent Brigham Hosp., fellow cardiology, Brigham and Womens Hosp., Nat. Insts. of Health; med. staff Md. Heart P.C. Named one of Top Doctors, Washingtonian Mag., 2011. Office: Maryland Heart PC Ste 200 6410 Rockledge Dr Bethesda MD 20817 Office Phone: 301-897-5301.

ITTHAGARUN, ANUT, dental educator; b. Thailand, Aug. 20, 1965; PhD, U. Hong Kong, 1999. Asst. prof. U. Hong Kong, 1998—2003, assoc. prof., 2003—07; prof., paediatric dentistry Griffith U., 2008—. Office: 16-30 High St Southport Gold Coast Queensland 4215 Australia Business E-Mail: a.itthagarun@griffith.edu.au.

IVAN, MIRCEA, medical educator; b. Brasov, Romania, Nov. 10, 1967; MD, Carol Davila U. Medicine and Pharmacy, Bucharest, Romania, 1993; PhD, Cardiff U., Eng., 1998. Postdoc. fellow Dana Farber Cancer Inst., 1998—2002; instr. medicine Harvard Med. Sch., 1998—2002; asst. prof. medicine Tufts U., 2003—08, Ind. U., 2008—. Grant, Am. Cancer Soc. Mem.: Am. Assn. Cancer Rsch. (Career Devel. award). Achievements include discovery of oxygen dependent HIF hydroxylation; key mechanism for Oxygen sensing. Office: 980 W Walnut St R3-C225 Indianapolis IN 46202 Business E-Mail: mivan@iupui.edu.

IVANCEVIC, VELIMIR, physician; b. Zagreb, Croatia, Aug. 18, 1958; s. Zeljko and Vesna (Vrkljan) Ivancevic; m. Birgit Stuwe; 1 child, Janko. MD, U. Zagreb, 1986, PhD, 1993. Diplomate German Bd. Nuclear Physicians. Intern Univ. Hosp., Zagreb, 1985-86, resident, 1987-90; rschr. U. Zagreb, 1989-90; resident Bethesda Hosp., Duisburg, Germany, 1990-91, Univ. Hosp., Göttingen, Germany, 1991-94; head physician Univ. Hosp. Charité, Berlin, 1994—2001; pvt. practice Gen. Hosp., Celle, Germany, 2002—. Contbr. chpts. to books and articles to profl. jours. IAEA grantee, Moscow, St. Petersburg and Kiev, 1987; Familie Gerhard Wuth-Stiftung rsch. grantee, Phila., 1996. Mem. European Assn. Nuclear Medicine, German Assn. Nuclear Medicine. Office: Gen Hosp Siemensplatz 4 29223 Celle Germany Office Phone: 49-5141-721601. E-mail: info@nuklearmedizin-am-akh.de.

IVANCEVIC, VLADIMIR G., mathematical physiologist, researcher; b. Belgrade, Serbia, May 12, 1955; m. Tijana T. Jovanovic; children: Nitya Nick, Atma Maria, Kali Rebekha. PhD in Biomechanics, U. Belgrade, 1986. Chief scientist Torson, Int. CG Co., Adelaide, Australia, 2000—02; sr. rsch. scientist Def. Sci. & Tech. Orgn. Australia, Adelaide, 2002—. Author (with Tijana T. Ivancevic): Human-Like Biomechanics, 2006, Natural Biodynamics, 2006, Geometrical Dynamics of Complex Systems, 2006, Neuro-Fuzzy Associative Machinery for Comprehensive Brain and Cognition Modelling, 2007, Computational Mind: A Complex Dynamics Perspective, 2007, High-Dimensional Chaotic and Attractor Systems, 2007, Applied Differential Geometry, 2007, Complex Dynamics: Advanced System Dynamics in Complex Variables, 2007; author: Complex Nonlinearity: Chaos, Topology Change and Path Integrals, 2008, Quantum Leap: From Diric and Feyaman Across the Universe to Human Body and Mind, 2008, Quantum Neural Computation, 2009. Recipient Excellence in Sci. and Tech. award, Def. Sci., 2005. Achievements include development of human biodynamics engine, a world-class human neuro-musculo-skeletal simulator with 270 DOF, muscular excitation-contraction dynamics and hierarchical neural control. Office: Def Sci & Tech Orgn Australia PO Box 1500 5111 Adelaide SA Australia Home Phone: 61 8 8285 4019; Office Phone: 61 8 7389 7337. Office Fax: 61 8 7389 4193. E-mail: vladimir.ivancevic@dsto.defence.gov.au.

IVANEK-MIOJEVIC, RENATA, medical educator; b. Zabok, Croatia, Oct. 17, 1971; DVM, U. Zagreb, Croatia, 1997; PhD in Comparative Biomedical Scis., Epidemiology, Coll. Vet. Medicine, Cornell U., 2008. Asst. prof., epidemiology Tex. A&M U., 2009—. Office: Tex A&M University VMA Bldg Rm 107 4458 College Station TX 77843 Business E-Mail: rivanek@cvm.tamu.edu.

IVANKOVICH, ANTHONY D., anesthesiologist, educator; b. Debeljaca, Yugoslavia, Mar. 25, 1939; came to U.S., 1965; m. Olga Ivankovich. MD, U. Zagreb, Croatia, 1963. Lic. physician, Ill.; diplomate Am. Bd. Anesthesiology. Resident in internal medicine County Hosp. Nurnberg, Fed. Republic Germany, 1963-65; rotating intern Edgewater Hosp., Chgo., 1966; resident in anesthesiology U. of Chgo. Hosps., 1967-68; asst. prof. anesthesiology Stritch Sch. Medicine Loyola U., Maywood, Ill., 1970-71; instr. anesthesiology Pritzker Sch. Medicine U. Chgo., 1969, assoc. prof. anesthesiology, 1972-74; faculy Sch. Medicine Cook County Postgrad., Chgo., 1975—85; prof. anesthesiology Rush Med. Coll. Rush Univ. Med. Ctr., 1980; dir. Rush Pain Ctr., chmn. anesthesiology Rush U. Med. Ctr., Chgo., 1980—2006. Dir. anesthesia rsch. Michael Reese Med. Ctr., Chgo., 1971—74, attending anesthesiologist, 1971—74, Stritch Sch. Medicine, Loyola U., Chgo., 1970—71, lectr. in anesthesiology, 1971—81; cons. anesthesiology Suburban TB Sanatorium, Hinsdale, Ill., 1970—71, Shriners Hosp. for Crippled Children, Chgo., 1977—82; chief oper. rm. svcs. 801st Gen. Hosp., USAR, Lincolnwood, Ill., 1971—73, chief surgery, 1973—74, assoc. chief profl. svcs., 1974—76; chmn. anesthesiology Ill. Masonic Med. Ctr., Chgo., 1974—80, Rush U. Med. Ctr., Chgo., 1980—2006, chmn. coun. surg. chmn. divsn. surg. scis. and svcs., 1992—94, dir. Surg. Svcs., assoc. v.p., 1993—2007, dir. Women & Children's Hosp., assoc. v.p., 1994—2007, pres. med. staff, trustee, 2005—; assoc. examiner Am. Bd. Anesthesiology, 1978; presenter in field. Author: (books) Nitroprusside and Other Short-Acting Hypotensive Agents, 1978, (book chpts. with others) Perspective in High Frequency Ventilation, 1983, Current Controversies in Thoracic Surgery, 1986, Anesthesia and ENT Surgery, 1987, Liposomes as Drug Carriers, 1987, Effective Hemostasis in Cardiac Surgery, 1988, Adjuncts to Cancer Therapy, 1989, Advances in Anesthesia, 1990, Cardiothoracic and Vascular Anesthesia Update, 1991, Cardiothoracic and Vascular Anesthesia Update, 1991, Clinical Anesthesia, 1992, Clinical Anesthesia Updates, 1992, Liposomes in Drug Delivery, 1992; contbr. articles and abstracts to profl. jours. Fellow Am. Coll. Anesthesiologists; mem. AMA, Internat. Assn. for Study of Pain, Internat. Anesthesia Rsch. Soc., Am. Soc. Anesthesiologists, Am. Heart Assn., Am. Coll. Chest Physicians, Am. Pain Soc., Pan Am. Med. Assn., Soc. for Intravenous Anesthesia, Ill. Med. Soc., Ill. Soc. Anesthesiologists, Soc. Neurosurg. Anesthesia and Neurologic Supporting Care, Midwest Pain Soc., Chgo. Med. Soc., Chgo. Soc. Anesthesiologists, Inst. of Medicine of Chgo., Chgo. Heart Assn., Sigma Xi. Office: Rush Univ Med Ctr Dept Anesthesiology 1653 W Congress Pkwy Chicago IL 60612-3833 Home Phone: 847-770-0600; Office Phone: 312-942-3137. Business E-Mail: anthony_ivankovich@rush.edu. E-mail: aivankov@rush.edu.

IVANOV, DMITRY, medical educator, researcher; b. Smolensk, Russia, June 24, 1973; PhD, Vavilov Inst. Gen. Genetics, 2003. Rsch. asst. prof. U. Miami Miller Sch. Medicine, 2011. Rsch. grant, NIH. Mem.: AAAS, Am. Heart Assn. (Scientist Devel. award), Assn. Rsch. Vision & Ophthalmology. Office: 1638 NW 10th Ave Rm 614 Miami FL 33136 Business E-Mail: divanov@med.miami.edu.

IVANOV, RADA IVANOVA, critical care specialist; MD, Med. Acad. Sofia, Bulgaria, 1990. Diplomate Am. Bd. Internal Medicine, 1995, Am. Bd. Internal Medicine- critical care medicine, 1998, Am. Bd. Internal Medicine- pulmonary disease, 1999. Intern Ill. Masonic Hosp., Chgo., resident in internal medicine, 1993—95; fellow in pulmonary critical care medicine Rush- Presbyn. St. Luke's Med. Ctr., Chgo.; hosp. affiliation include Our Lady of the Resurrestion Medical Center, Advocate Ill. Masonic Med. Ctr. Office: Advocate Illinois Masonic Medical Center 5600 W Addison Chicago IL 60634 Office Phone: 773-481-1570. Office Fax: 773-481-0547.

IVANOVA, ELENA PETER, medical educator; arrived in Australia, 2001; d. Peter P. Semenov and Polina P. Semenova; 1 child, Anna P. MSc, Irkutsk Far-East State U., 1979; PhD, Inst. Virology and Microbiology, 1991; ScD, Pacific Inst. Bio-organic Chemistry, 1999. Sr. scientist Pacific Inst. Bioorganic Chemistry, Vadivostok, Russia, 1985—2000; assoc. prof. Swinburne U. Tech., Melbourne, Australia, 2001—. Advanced tech. rschr. Agy. of Indsl. Sci. Osaka (Japan) Nat. Rsch. Inst., 1994—97; vis. scientist Ctr. Marine Biotech. U. Md., Balt., 1997—98. Recipient Morrison Rogosa award, Am. Soc. for Microbiology, 2002;, UNESCO fellow, 1997. Mem.: Australian Soc. Microbiology (bd. dirs. Victorian Br. 2002—). Office: Swinburne University of Technology Burwood Road 3122 Melbourne VIC Australia Fax: 908-673-1179.

IVANUSA, MARIO, cardiologist; b. Bjelovar, Croatia, Mar. 11, 1967; s. Vladimir and Ljubica Ivanusa; m. Zrinka Hecimovic, Oct. 14, 1966; 1 child, Domagoj. Med. tech., Bjelovar Secondary Sch., 1985; MD, Med. Faculty Zagreb, 1990, PhD, 2007. Resident Bjelovar Gen. Hosp. & Clin. Hosp., Zagreb, 1993—97, Bjelovar Gen. Hosp., 1997—2009, head lab. cardiovasc. diagnostics, 2001—09; resident Inst. Cardiovasc. Diseases Prevention & Rehab. Zagreb, 2009—; primarius Ministry Health and Social Welfare, Croatia, 2007; rsch. assoc. Ministry Sci. Edn. & Sports, Croatia, 2010. Author: Laboratory for Cardiovascular Diagnostics at Bjelovar General Hospital, 2004; author: (with M. Bergovec) Cardiopulmonary Resuscitation: Handbook for Medical Staff, 2006; contbr. articles to profl. jours. Decorated Meml. Fatherland War 1990-1992 Republic of Croatia. Fellow: European Soc. Cardiology; mem.: European Assn. Echocardiography, Croatian Cardiac Soc., Croatian Med. Chamber, Croatian Med. Assn. Home: Zlatarska 14A Zagreb HR-10000 Croatia Office: Inst Cardiovasc Diseases Prevention & Rehab Draskoviceva 13 Zagreb HR-10000 Croatia Home: Naselje Kr.Zvonimira I 4/1 NULL Bjelovar Croatia Office Phone: 385-43-279-228. Office Fax: 385-1-4612-343. Personal E-mail: mivanusa@vip.hr.

IVARSSON, KJELL IVAR, physician; b. Hässleholm, Skåne, Apr. 11, 1960; Degree, U. Lund, 1995, PhD, 2003. Head emergency Gen. Hosp. Helsingborg, 2009. Home: Barsebäcksvägen 107A Löddeköpinge Skåne SE24632 Sweden Personal E-mail: kjell.i.ivarsson@gmail.com.

IVASHKIN, VLADIMIR TROFIMOVITCH, physical therapist, researcher; b. Rjazan, Russia, Mar. 24, 1939; s. Trofim Petrovitch Ivashkin and Nina Ivanovna Ivashkina; m. Galina Konstantinovna Novikova, Nov. 8, 1953; 1 child, Konstantin Vladimirovitch. Resident clinic and internal medicine, Med. Mil. Acad., 1967—70; MD, St. Petersburg Mil. Med. Acad., 1970, PhD, 1976. Dir. clinic internal medicine Sechenov Med. Acad., Moscow, 1995—. Chief editor Russian Jour. Gastroenterology, Hepatology. Major-general Med. Svc., 1989, Russian Federation. Recipient Reknowned Person of Sci., Russian Fedn., 1994. Mem.: Russian Gastroenterol. Assn. (pres. 1993), Russian Soc. Study Liver (pres.), Russian Acad. Med. Sci. (moscow 1996). Office: Sechenov Moscow Med Acad Pogodinskaya str 1 bldg 1 Moscow 119435 Russia Office Fax: (007)(095) 2483610; Home Fax: (007)(095) 248 3610. Personal E-mail: liver@orc.ru.

IVER, ROBERT DREW, dentist; b. Miami, Fla., Feb. 6, 1947; s. William Henry and Jeanette (Minden) I.; m. Lisa Marie Stettner-Iver, May 5, 1974. Student, Ohio State U., Columbus, 1965-66, U. Miami, 1966-68; DDS, Georgetown U., Washington, DC, 1972. Lic. yachtsmaster USCG Approved Capts. Pvt. practice dentistry, Miami Beach, Fla., 1974—; with Dade County Med. Examiners Dept. Bd. dirs. Cmty. Svc. Sunset Islands. Lt. USNR, 1968-81. Fellow ADA, Gold Coast Dist. Dental Soc.; mem. Fla. Dental Assn., East Coast Dist. Dental Soc., Acad. Gen. Dentistry, Miami Beach Dental Soc., Gold Coast Acad. Gen. Dentistry, South Fla. Dist. Dental Soc., Esthetic Dental Assn., Nature Conservancy, Am. Radio Relay League, K4pbf, N.Am. Fishing Club, Dade Radio Club Miami, Everglades Amateur Radio Club, Miami Rod and Reel Club, Meml. Dental Study Club, Nova U. Sch. Dental Medicine. Avocations: sports fishing, ham radio operating. Office: 1205 Lincoln Rd Ste 207 Miami FL 33139-2365 Home Phone: 305-538-1505; Office Phone: 305-672-8894. Personal E-mail: robertiver@bellsouth.net.

IVERSON, ROBERT LOUIS, JR., retired internist, physician; b. Borden, Ind., Sept. 3, 1944; s. Robert L. and Agnes Maxine (Knight) Iverson; m. Elsa Maschmeyer, Sept. 9, 1967 (div. 1982); children: Nathan, Kirsten; m. Deborah A. Budd, June 16, 1984 (dec. May 1996); children: Richard, Colin; m. Amy M. Neidert, May 9, 1998. Student, Wabash Coll., 1962-64; BA, Ind. U., 1970, MD, 1974, Intern, 1974-75. Diplomate Am. Bd. Internal Med., diplomate in critical care medicine, Am. Bd. Internal Med. Intern Ind. U., Indpls., 1974-75; resident (internal med.) Methodist Hosp., Indpls, 1975-77, co-dir. critical care, mem. tchg. staff dept. medicine, 1977-84; fellow in critical care med. U. So. Calif. Shock Rsch. Unit, Ctr. for Critically Ill, LA, 1977; vis. lectr. U. So. Calif., LA, 1977; co-dir. critical care, teaching staff, Dept. of Med. Methodist Hosp., 1977-84; asst. prof. medicine Wayne State U., Detroit, 1984-96, assoc. prof. clin. medicine, 1996-2000; dir. med. affairs Hutzel Hosp., Detroit, 1996-97, vice chief med. staff, 1995-97, dir. ICU, 1986-2000, chief critical care medicine, 1988-2000; chief critical care svcs. Vassar Bros. Hosp., Poughkeepsie, NY, 2000—02; ret., 2002. Mem. bd. Rudgate Neighborhood Assocs., Bloomfield Hills, Mich. 1996-98; mem. physician leadership coun. Detroit Med. Ctr., 1996-2000; participant Ind. Malpractice Rev. Panels, 1981-85; chief med. officer Oakland County (Mich.) Sheriff's Dept., 1997-2000, tactical med. officer Spl. Response Team (SWAT), 1997-2000. Author: (with others) Respiratory Care of the Neurosurgical Patient, 1983, Septic Shock in Critical Care Clinics, 1988, established adminstrv. core curriculum for intensivists Critical Care Clinics, 1993; contbr. abstracts and articles to profl. jours. Med. advisor to Ind. Coun. Emergency Response Teams, 1980—85; mem. Ind. Symphonic Choir, 1970—84, trustee, 1983—84; hon. dep. sheriff Marion County Sheriff's Dept., 1982—84; bd. dirs. City of Bloomfield Hills, Mich., Rudgate Neighborhood Assn., 1996—98; pres. Ashley Homeowners Assn., Inc., 2004—07. With US Army, 1964—67, Vietnam. Fellow: ACP, Am. Coll. Chest Physicians; mem.: AMA (Physicians Recognition award 2002—05, 2006—), Sarasota County Med. Soc., Fla. State Med. Soc., Wayne County Med. Soc. (elected del. 1990—91), Soc. Critical Care

Medicine, Fla. Sheriffs Assn., Phi Beta Kappa. Avocations: music, shortwave radio communications, sailing, astronomy, astrophotography. Home: 4845 Sawyer Rd Sarasota FL 34233 Personal E-mail: robertive@msn.com.

IVES, JEFFREY C., physical education educator; b. San Diego, Dec. 29, 1959; PhD, U. Mass., 1994. Prof., grad. program chair Ithaca Coll., 1996—. Mem.: N.Am. Soc. Psychology Phys. Activity, Am. Coll. Sports Medicine. Office: Ctr Health Scis Ithaca Coll Ithaca NY 14850 Business E-Mail: jives@ithaca.edu.

IVEY, FREDERICK M., medical educator; b. NYC, Mar. 31, 1964; PhD, U. Md., Coll. Pk., 1998. Assoc. prof. U. Md. Sch. Medicine, 1998—. Mem.: Am. Coll. Sports Medicine. Office: Baltimore VA Med Ctr 10 N Greene St 4B-193A Baltimore MD 21201 Office Fax: 410-605-7913. Business E-Mail: fivey@grecc.umaryland.edu.

IVEY, SUSAN LEE, health services researcher, educator; b. Newport News, Va., Jan. 2, 1955; d. Henry and Margaret (Farmer) Ivey; m. Peter Berl Bernhard, May 18, 1985; children: Rachel, Lauren, Daniel. BA in Psychology, U. So. Calif., 1975; BS in Biol. Sci., BA in Chemistry, U. Calif., Irvine, 1977; MD, St. George U., Grenada, 1981; M in Health Svcs. Adminstrn., George Washington U., 1995. Diplomate Am. Bd. Family Practice, Am. Bd. Emergency Medicine. Intern internal medicine Mt. Sinai Hosp., Hartford, Conn., 1981—82; resident dept. family practice U. Conn., Farmington, 1982—84; physician Manchester Meml. Hosp., Conn., 1984—85, LDS Hosp., Salt Lake City, 1985-88, 95-97, Jordan Valley Hosp., West Jordan, Utah, 1985—89, Potomac Hosp., Woodbridge, Va., 1990—94, Urgent Med. Care, Lakeridge, Va., 1990—94, Calif. Emergency Physicians/Delta Meml. Hosp., Antioch, 1996—98; NIMH rsch. fellowship U. Calif., Berkeley, 1995—97; asst. clin. prof. joint med. program U. Calif. Berkeley Sch. Pub. Health, 2000—03, assoc. adj. prof., 2003—. Assoc. adj. prof. U. Calif. San Francisco Sch. Nursing. Contbr. articles to profl. jours. Mem. Teen Pregnancy Prevention Better Beginnings Coalition, Woodbridge, 1993—94, Calif. Cardiovasc. Disease Prevention Coalition, 1998—; physician Prince William Free Clinic, Manassas, Va., 1994. Fellow: Am. Acad. Family Practice, Am. Coll. Emergency Physicians; mem.: Am. Med. Women's Assn. (state dir. Calif. chpt. 1995—99, chmn. govt. affairs 1996—98, publs. com. 1998, prog. chair 1999, v.p. prog. 2002—04, v.p. comm. 2004, pres.-elect 2005, pres. 2006). Democrat. Unitarian Universalist. Avocations: walking, dance, reading, movies, skiing. Office: U Calif Sch Pub Health 513 Univ Hall Berkeley CA 94720-7360 Business E-Mail: sivey@berkeley.edu.

IVY, DAVID DUNBAR, cardiologist, educator; BS, Davidson Coll., New Orleans, 1984; MD, Tulane U. Sch. Medicine, La., 1988. Cert. Pediat., Pediat. Cardiology. Intern pediat. U. Colo. Sch. Medicine, Denver, 1988—89, resident pediat., 1989—91, fellow pediat. cardiology, 1991—94, instr. pediat. cardiology, 1994—96, asst. prof. pediat. cardiology, 1996—2001, assoc. prof. pediat., 2001—07, prof. pediat., 2007—; chief, pediat. cardiology U. Colo at Denver and Health Scis. Ctr., Denver, 2003—, Selby's endowed chair, pediat. cardiology, 2003, dir., pulmonary hypertension program, 2003—, sect. head, cardiology, 2003—. Invited spkr. in field. Mem. review boards of several med. jours., editl. bd. mem. American Thoracic Soc., Congenital Heart Disease: Clinical Studies from Fetus to Adulthood; contbr. several articles to profl. jours., chapters to books. Recipient Heart Who Cares award, Children's Hosp. Heart Inst., 2008; named one of Top Docs, 5280 Mags. Fellow: Am. Coll. Cardiology; mem.: Assn. for European Paediatric Cardiology, Soc. For Pediatric Rsch., Am. Physiological Soc., Pediatric Cardiac Intensive Care Soc., Am. Heart Assn., Am. Coll. Chest Physicians, Am. Acad. Pediatrics, Pulmonary Hypertension Assn. *

IWAHASHI, HIDEHIKO, medical educator; b. Miyazaki, Japan, June 9, 1967; s. Takehiko and Masuko Iwahashi; m. Mitsue Fukami, Sept. 18, 1999; children: Iwahashi Hakuei, Iwahashi Ogyoku. MD, Fukuoka U., Nanakuma, 1994, PhD, 2001. Diplomate Ministry Health, Labour and Welfare, Tokyo, 1994, Master of Artificial Organist Baylor Coll. Medicine, Tex., 2004, bd. cert. surgery Japan Surg. Soc., 2006, cert. bd. balneotherapy physician Japanese Soc. Balneology, Climatology and Phys. Medicine, 2005. Instr. cardiovasc. surgery Fukuoka U., Japan, 2001—03, 2004—05, sr. asst. prof. cardiovasc. surgery, 2005—09; adj. instr. dept. surgery Baylor Coll. Medicine, Houston, 2003—04; dir. Abies Clinic, Fukuoka, 2009—. Mem.: Asian Soc. Cardiovasc. Surgery. Achievements include research in new monitoring method for anticoagulant therapy. Avocations: travel, hot spring. Office: Abies Clinic Canal City Bus Ctr Bldg 1F 1-2-25 Sumiyoshi Hakata-ku Fukuoka 812 0018 Japan Business E-Mail: hiwahasi@siren.ocn.ne.jp.

IWAI, KAZUNORI, physical education educator, researcher, trainer; b. Kishiwada, Japan, Feb. 18, 1978; s. Sumio and Kazuyo Iwai; m. Misao Shigyo, May 15, 2007; 1 child, Ippei. BSc, Nippon Sport Sci. U., 2000, MS, 2002; PhD in Health Scis., Hiroshima U., 2009. Instr. Kure Nat. Coll. Tech., Hiroshima, Japan, 2002—04; rschr. Nippon Sport Sci. U., Tokyo, 2002—06; instr. Onomichi U., 2002—04, Hiroshima Nat. Coll. Maritime Tech., Hiroshima, 2002—08, assoc. prof., 2009—. Instr. Higashihiroshima Jr. Wrestling Club, Hiroshima, 2002—. Contbr. articles to profl. jours. Named 8th Greco-Roman Style Wrestling, 3d World U. Wrestling Championship, 1998, 3d Greco-Roman Style Wrestling, U. Wrestling Championship, Japan, 1999. Mem.: Japanese Soc. Phys. Fitness and Sports Medicine, Am. Coll. Sports Medicine. Office: Hiroshima Nat Coll Maritime Tech 4272-1 Higashino Osakikamijima-cho Hiroshima 725-0231 Japan Home: 3467-2-203 Shimono-cho Takehara Hiroshima 725-0012 Japan Office Phone: 81-846-67-3185. Office Fax: 81-846-67-3185. Personal E-mail: rockwellone@nifty.com. E-mail: iwai@hiroshima-cmt.ac.jp.

IWAI, KAZURO, physician, research consultant; b. Tokyo, Mar. 8, 1927; s. Shosaburo and Yoshi (Okanoya) I.; m. Yoshiko Kimura, Oct. 23, 1955; children: Akiko Asakura, Yukiko Tabata, Setsuko Iwai. Diploma, Kyoto U. Med. Sch., Japan, 1949; MD (hon.), Kyoto U., 1959. Chief pathology sect. Rsch. Inst. Tuberculosis, Kiyose, Tokyo, 1959-76, head dept. rsch., 1977-79, vice-dir., 1980-83, dir., 1984-87, cons., 1987—. Rsch. com. intractable disease Ministry Health and Welfare, Japan, 1970-; chmn. rsch. com. diesel exhaust health effect Environ. Agy., Japan, 1986-98. Chief editor (computer program): Respiro-Navi, 1998; contbr. articles to profl. jours. Mem. Japanese Soc. Tuberculosis (hon.), Japanese Soc. Sarcoidosis (hon.), Japan Antituberculosis Assn., Japanese Air and Environ. Soc. Avocation: sailing by cruiser. Home: 2-4-16 hibarigaoka-kita Nishitokyo-shi Tokyo 202-0002 Japan Office: Rsch Inst Tuberculosis Japan Antituberculosis Assn 3-1-24 Matsuyama Kiyose-shi Tokyo 204-0022 Japan E-mail: iwai@jata.or.jp.

IWAI, YOSHIYASU, neurosurgeon; b. Sakurai, Japan, Jan. 9, 1956; s. Seiji and Kayoko Iwai; m. Junko Iwai, Dec. 16, 1984; children: Kenji, Hiroko, Takato. MD, Osaka City Med. Sch., 1974—80. Diplomate Neurosurgery Tokyo, 1986. Neurosurgeon Osaka City Gen. Hosp., 1994—. Office: Osaka City Gen Hosp 2-13-22 Miyakojima-hondohri Miyakojima Osaka 534-0021 Japan Office Fax: 81-6-6929-1091.

IWAMI, TAKU, medical educator; b. Tokyo, Jan. 22, 1972; MD, Gunma U., 1996; PhD, Osaka U. Grad. Sch. Medicine, 2005. Physician, divsn. cardiology Tomioka Gen. Hosp., 1998—2000, Motojima Gen. Hosp., 2000—01; rsch. resident, divsn. cardiology Nat. Cardiovasc. Ctr., 2005—06; asst. prof. Kyoto U. Health Svc., 2006—. Sub-chief dir. Nonprofit Orgn. Osaka Life Support Assn., 2005. Recipient Young Investigator award, Am. Heart Assn., Resuscitation Sci. Symposium, 2007; named Best investigator, Kyoto U., 2006; vis. scholar, U. Wash., Harborview Ctr. Prehospital Emergency Care, 2007—08; PUSH Project grant, Medtronic Found., grant, Pfizer Health Rsch. Found. Mem.: Japanese Soc. Internal Medicine, Japanese Circulation Soc., Japanese Assn. Acute Medicine, Am. Heart Assn. Avocations: skiing, bicycling. Office: Yoshidahonmachi Sakyo-ku Kyoto 606-8501 Japan Business E-Mail: iwamit@e-mail.jp.

IWAMOTO, SHOZO, medical association administrator; b. Osaka, Japan, Aug. 4, 1950; MD, Kumamoto U. Sch. Medicine, 1977. Dir. Iwamoto Hosp., 1990—. Mem.: Asian Pacific Assn. Study of Liver, Internat. Liver Cancer Assn., Japanese Soc. Hepatology, Japanese Soc. Gastroenterlogy, Japanese Soc. Internal Medicine. Avocations: reading, cooking. Office: 1-2-8 Shimoishida Kokuraminami-ku Japan Kitakyushu-shi Fukuoka 8020832 Japan Office Fax: 0939611942. Business E-Mail: iwamotos@orion.ocn.ne.jp.

IWAMURA, MASATSUGU, physician, educator; b. Tottori, May 30, 1958; MD, PhD, Kitasato U. Sch. Medicine, 1983. Asst. prof. U. Rochester Med. Ctr., 1992—94; assoc. prof. Kitasato U. Sch. Medicine, 2004—. Mem.: Japanese Soc. Endourology & ESWL, Japan Urol. Assn., Am. Assn. Cancer Rsch., Am. Urol. Assn. Avocations: golf, mountain climbing, skiing. Home: 2-17-8 Unomori Minami-ku Sagamihara Kanagawa 252-0301 Japan Business E-Mail: miwamura@med.kitasato-u.ac.jp.

IWARSON, STEN AXEL, infectious diseases physician educator; b. Svenljunga, Sweden, Apr. 28, 1940; s. Stig L. and Elsa C. (Lind) I.; m. Birgitta R. Rennerfelt, Nov. 14, 1964; children: Matts, Pelle, Charlotte, Susanne. MD, U. Göteborg, 1967, PhD, 1973. Head dept. infectious diseases Sahlgrenska U. Hosp., Göteborg, Sweden, 1980—97. Vis. scientist Office Biologies, FDA, Bethesda, Md., 1983-84; prof. Infectious Diseases, Göteborg U.; med. advisor Nat. Bd. Health, Sweden, 1980—96; med. expert Med. Products Agy., Sweden, 1990-00. Author, editor: (textbooks) Infectious Diseases; contbr. articles to profl. jours. Fellow Infectious Diseases Soc. Am., Royal Coll. Physicians Edinburgh, Royal coll. Physicians London (hon.). Avocation: collecting swedish glass art. Office: Sahlgrenska U Hosp Ostra Dept Infectious Diseases S-41685 Göteborg Sweden Home: Mimersvagen 47 433 64 Partille Sweden Office Phone: 0047313434242.

IWASAKI, KOHICHIRO, cardiologist; b. Okayama, Japan, Oct. 16, 1955; s. Yoshisuke and Mieko Iwasaki; m. Shoko Komiyama; children: Keiichiro, Iori. MD, Okayama U. Grad. Sch. Medicine and Dentistry, 1980. Dir. dept. cardiology Sakakibara Hosp. Cardiovasc. Ctr., Okayama, 1992—2005, Okayama Kyokuto Hosp., 2010—; chmn. Okayama Ctrl. Hosp. Dept. Cardiovasc. Medicine, 2005—10. Clin. assoc. prof. Okayama U. Grads. Sch. Medicine and Dentistry, 2000—05. Contbr. articles to profl. jour. Mem.: Japanese Soc. Cardiovasc. Imaging and Dynamics, Japanese Coll. Cardiology, Japanese Soc. Internal Medicine, Japanese Assn. Cardiovasc. Intervention Therapeutics, Japanese Circulation Soc. Buddhist. Achievements include research in coronary pressure measurement and coronary intervention, cardiac computed tomography. Avocations: jazz, stamp collecting/philately. Office: Okayama Kyokuto Hosp 567-1 Kurata Naka-ku Okayama 703-8265 Japan Office Fax: 81-86-274-1028.

IWASE, TAKESHI, ophthalmologist, researcher; b. Oyama, Japan, Nov. 19, 1966; s. Yoshimi Iwase and Michiko; m. Chie Hounoki, Apr. 4, 1999; children: Takashi children: Aya, Tsuyoshi. MD, Kanazawa U., Japan, 1992; PhD, Kanazawa U., 2001. Lic. physician Japan, 1992. Resident Dept. Ophthalmology Kanazawa (Japan) U. Hosp., 1992—95; chief Dept. Ophthalmology Himi City Hosp., Toyama, Japan, 1995—2000, Toyama (Japan) Red Cross Hosp., 2000—03, Toyama (Japan) Prefectural Ctrl. Hosp., 2003—. Mem.: Am. Acad. Ophthalmology (assoc.). Avocations: golf, skiing, travel, swimming. Office Fax: +81-76-422-0667.

IWASHITA, SHINTARO, biochemistry professor; b. Tokyo, Oct. 25, 1946; BSc, U. Tokyo, 1970, PhD, 1975. Rschr. Tokyo Met. Inst. Med. Sci., 1977—80; postdoc. fellow MBI, UCLA, 1981—83, Japan Found. Cancer Rsch., 1984—85; sr. rschr., group head, dir. Mitsubishi Kagaku Inst. Life Sci., 1986—2006; prof. Iwaki Meisei U., 2007—. Mem. editl. adv. bd. Open Evolution Jour., 2007. Overseas Rsch. grant, Yoshida Found. Sci. and Tech., Tokyo. Mem.: Japanese Biochem. Soc. Office: 5-5-1 Chuodai Iino Iwaki City Fukushima 970-8551 Japan Office Fax: 81-246-29-5394. Business E-Mail: siwast@iwakimu.ac.jp.

IWATSUKI, KOICHI, surgeon, educator; b. Japan, Feb. 12, 1962; MD, Tokushima U., PhD, 2007. Assoc. prof. Osaka U. Med. Sch., 1992—2011, U. Tsukuba, 2008—11. Physician Japanese Soc. Spinal Surgery, 2009—11. Office: 2-2 Yamadaoka Suita Osaka 565-0871 Japan Business E-Mail: ytakahashi@nsurg.med.osaka-u.ac.jp.

IWAZAKI, MASAYUKI, thoracic surgeon; b. Shizuoka, Japan, Feb. 7, 1960; MD, Tokai U., 1984, PhD, 1990. Staff surgeon Sasaki Inst. Medicine, 1986—, Nat. Kanagawa Hosp., 1988; faculty surgery Tokai U. Sch. Medicine, 1990, asst. prof. surgery, 1995, assoc. prof. surgery, 2001, chair thoracic surgery, prof. surgery, 2009. Mem.: Japanese Soc. Chest Surgery, Am. Assn. Clin. Oncology, Soc. Thoracic Surgeon. Avocation: skiing. Office: 143 Shimokasuya Isehara Kanagawa 2591193 Japan Office Fax: 81463957567. Business E-Mail: iwasaki@is.icc.u-tokai.ac.jp.

IYER, KRISHNA S., pediatric cardiac surgeon; b. Ahmedabad, India, May 8, 1956; MBBS, All India Inst. Med. Scis., 1978, MCh in Cardiothoracic Surgery, 1984. Faculty mem. dept. cardiothoracic surgery All India Inst. Med. Scis., New Delhi, 1985—95; sr. cons., head dept. Fortis-Escorts Heart Inst., New Delhi, 1995—2004, dir., 2004—. Founder, pres. APPCS; mem. steering com. World Congress Pediat. Cardiology and Cardiac Surgery. Recipient Sardari Lal Kalra Gold medal, All India Inst. Med. Scis., Hira Lal Gold medal, Med. award, Pfizer Pharms. Fellow: Indian Assn. Cardiothoracic & Vascular Surgeons; mem.: Asian Soc. Cardiovasc. & Thoracic Surgery, Pediat. Cardiac Soc. India (past pres.). Achievements include development of pediatric cardiac surgery in India and South- East Asia. Avocations: reading, music, photography. Home: C-773 2nd Fl New Friends Colony New Delhi 110065 India Office Phone: 91-11-47134540. Fax: 91 11 26825013. Personal E-mail: iyerks_ehirc@yahoo.com.

IZAWA, KAZUHIRO, physical therapist; b. Ogi-City, Saga Prefecture, Japan, Dec. 22, 1970; s. Kazuyoshi and Emiko Izawa; m. Sachiko Tsuji Izawa, Sept. 20, 2003. Degree in phys. therapy, Japanese Sch. Tech. for Social Medicine, Koganei City, Tokyo, 1994; BSc in Econs., Komazawa U., Setagaya-ku, Tokyo, 2000; MSc in Rehab. Scis., U. Tsukuba, Bunkyo-ku, Tokyo, 2003; PhD in Human Scis., Waseda U., Tokorozawa City, Saitama, Japan, 2006. With dept. of rehab. medicine St. Marianna U. Sch. of Medicine Hosp., Kawasaki-City, Kanagawa Prefecture, Japan, 1994—. Contbr. articles to profl. jours. Mem.: Japanese Soc. Phys. Fitness and Sports Medicine, Japanese Circulation Soc., Japanese Phys. Therapy Assn., Japanese Assn. Cardiac Rehab. (mem. editl. bd. 2003—, Young Investigator award 2004), Japan Heart Club (trustee 2005—). Avocations: travel, reading, tennis. Office: St Marianna U Sch of Medicine Hosp Kawasaki Kanagawa 2168511 Japan Office Phone: 81-44-977-8111. Office Fax: 81-44-977-9486.

IZEGBU, VICTOR AMECHI EDOZIE, urological surgeon; arrived in Eng., 1980; s. Benedict Robert Onochie Izegbu and Beatrice Umeadi Isichei; m. Antonia Rosalind Therese Izegbu, May 16, 1992; 1 child, Edozle Anthony Isichei. MB BChir, U. Benin Med. Sch., Benin City, Nigeria, 1977. Lead surgeon urol. oncology N.W. London Hosps. Trust, London, 2002—. Vis. fellow urology Cleve. Clinic, 2003; cons. urol. surgeon Chelsea and Westminster Hosp., London, 2000—01. Contbr. articles to profl. jours. Founder, chmn. Onochie Izegbu Found., London, 2000. Recipient Top Surgeon award, World Assn. Black Surgeons, 2002. Fellow: European Bd. Urology, Royal Coll. Surgeons Scotland, Royal Coll. Surgeons Edinburgh; mem.: Brit. Assn. urol. Surgeons, Brit. Med. Assn., Med. Profl. Soc. Achievements include development of Izegbu's method of orthotopic bladder after radical cystectomy; research in various treatment methods in urological oncology. Avocations: music, golf. Office: Cen Middlesex Hosp Dept Urology Acton Ln London NW10 7NS England Office Fax: 44 20884532439. E-mail: vizegbu@aol.com.

IZENBERG, PAUL HERBERT, plastic surgeon, educator; married; 3 children. MD. Diplomate Am. Bd. Plastic Surgery. Intern in surgery Univ. Mich. Med. Ctr., resident in gen. surgery, Beth Israel Med. Ctr., NYC; resident in plastic surgery Univ. Mich. Med. Ctr.; fellow in head and neck surgery Beth Israel Med. Ctr., 1976; clin. tchg. staff Univ. Mich. Med. Ctr.; plastic surgeon Ctr. for Plastic and Reconstructive Surgery, Mich., 1978—. Author: various publs. Office: Center for Plastic and Reconstructive Surgery PO Box 994 5333 McAuley Dr Suites 5001 and 5008 Ann Arbor MI 48106 Office Phone: 734-712-2323. Office Fax: 734-712-2312.

IZNAK, EKATERINA, research scientist; b. Moscow, Aug. 20, 1973; MS, M.V.Lomonosov Moscow State U., 1996, PhD, 1999. Sr. rschr. Mental Health Rsch. Ctr. Russian Acad. Med. Scis., Lab. Neurophysiology, 2001—. Docent dept. psychology Moscow State U. Design and Tech., 2009—. Recipient Young Scientists award, Russian Acad. Med. Scis., 2004—06. Mem.: Internat. Neuropsychiat. Assn. Avocation: travel. Office: Kashirskoye Shausse 34 Moscow 115522 Russia Office Fax: 7 (499) 614-4925. Business E-Mail: iznak@inbox.ru.

IZUMI, MIKI, physician, educator; b. Yamaguchi, July 5, 1963; MD, Kawasaki Med. Sch., 1988; PhD, U. Tokyo. Prof. dept. med. edn. Tokyo Med. U., 2009—. Recipient Best Poster award. Avocation: ping pong/table tennis. Office: Tokyo Med University Dept Med Education Nishi-Shinjuku 6-7-1 Shinjuku Tokyo 1600023 Japan Office Fax: 81-3-5339-3785. Business E-Mail: mizumi@tokyo-med.ac.jp.

IZUMO, TSUYOSHI, neurosurgeon; b. Sasebo, Nagasaki, Japan, Feb. 7, 1971; s. Shinobu and Toshiko Izumo. PhD in Medicine, Nagasaki U. Grad. Sch. Medicine, Japan, 2007. Lic. med. dr. Ministry of Welfare, Japan, 1995. Dir. 1st. dept. neurosurgery Nagasaki Rosai Hosp., Sasebo, Japan, 2006—. Quest Diagnostics Young Investigator Travel grant, Endocrine Soc. Ann. Meeting, 2002. Buddhism. Avocations: running, fishing. Office: Nagasaki Rosai Hosp 2-12-5 Setogoe Sasebo-Shi 857-0134 Japan

IZUTSU, TAKASHI, psychologist, researcher; b. Tokyo, June 25, 1975; s. Mutsumu and Akiko Izutsu. BA in Liberal Arts, Internat. Christian U., Tokyo, 1998; MA in Health Sci., U. Tokyo, 2001, PhD in Health Sci., 2004. Cert. psychiatric social worker Ministry of Health, Labour and Welfare, Tokyo, 2004; clin. psychologist Japanese Cert. Bd. Clin. Psychologist, 2005. Counselor Fujitsu Ltd., Tokyo, 1998—2004, Tokyo Met. Mental Health and Welfare Ctr., Tokyo, 2000—04; tech. ofcl. Nat. Inst. Mental Health, Nat. Inst. Neurology and Psychiatry Ministry of Health Labour and Welfare, Tokyo, 2004—06; tech. analyst UN Population Fund, NYC, 2006—. Adv. staff Tokyo Met. Govt., 1999—2001; asst. prof. Tokyo Gakugei U., 2003—04; advisor rsch. on mental health of atomic bomb survivors Nagasaki Prefecture and Nagasaki City, Nagasaki, Japan, 2003—04; psychol. counselor for abductees and their families Cabinet Secretariat, Tokyo, 2004; asst. to dir. joint grad. courses UN U., Tokyo, 2004; temp. advisor WHO, Kobe, Japan, 2005. Translator: (books) A Rorschach Workbook for the Comprehensive System, 2003; author: Mental Health Care Handbook for Collective Emergency Situations in Foreign Countries, 2004; translator: Betrayed as Boys: Psychodynamic Treatment of Sexually Abused Men, 2005; author: Textbook for Forensic Psychiatry Training, 2005; contbr. articles to profl. jours. Grantee, Mitsubishi Found., 2004. Mem.: Internat. Soc. Traumatic

Stress Studies, Internat. Rorschach Soc., Gakushikai. Avocation: travel. Office: UN Population Fund 220 East 42nd St New York NY 10017 Personal E-mail: izutsu@gakushikai.jp.

IZZETTIN, FIKRET VEHBI, pharmacist, educator; b. Kerkuk, Iraq, Mar. 23, 1951; s. Vehbi Izzettin Muhammed Said and Sabriye Sukur Namik; m. Nese Sevket, June 18, 1995; 1 child, Can. BSc in Pharmacy, Baghdad U., Iraq, 1973, MSc in Pharm. Sci., 1976; PhD, U. Nebr., 1983. Asst. prof. Baghdad U., Coll. Pharmacy, 1983—88, assoc. prof., 1988—91, Marmara U., Faculty Pharmacy, Istanbul, 1991—94, prof. clin. pharmacy, 1994—, head clin. pharmacy dept., 1996—. Founding mem., clin. coord. Marmara U. Pharm. Care Unit, Istanbul, Turkey, 2004—. Translator: (book) Chemotherapy Protocols in Cancer; contbr. chapters to books, articles to profl. jour. Recipient, Ministry of Higher Edn. and Rsch., Iraq, Baghdad U. Coll. Pharmacy, 1986, Higher Achievement award, Marmara U., 2000. Master: Soc. Clin. Pharmacy (founding mem., head 1996—); fellow: Iraqi Pharm. Assn. (gen com. mem. 1986—90, registered); mem.: European Soc. Clin. Pharmacy. Achievements include initiated and introduced the clinical pharmacy concept in Iraq and in Turkey; initiated the clinical pharmacy undergraduate and/or graduate courses in Iraq and Turkey. Avocations: soccer, swimming, tennis, jogging, travel. Office: Marmara Univ Faculty Pharmacy Clinical Pharmacy Dept Hydarpasa Istanbul 34817 Turkey Office Fax: +90.216.346 40 60. E-mail: fvizzetin@hotmail.com.

JAARIN, KAMSIAH, pharmacologist, educator; b. Kuala Lumpur, Malaysia, June 24, 1953; d. Jaarin Liujud and Salmah Sain; m. Masbah Omar, Aug. 4, 1976; children: Dani Irwan Masbah, Safin Darlina Masbah, Norliana Masbah. MD with honors, U. Kebangsaan, Kuala Lumpur, 1979; MSc in Pharmacology, U. Kebangsaan, 1985. House officer Ministry of Health, Kuala Lampur, Malaysia, 1979—80; trainee lectr. U. Kebangsaan, Kuala Lampur, 1980—85, assoc. prof., 1996—2002, prof., 2003—. Chair Asian course on problem based pharmacotherapy WHO/U. Kebangsaan, Kuala Lumpur, 2003. Author: You and Hypertension DBP, 1999, Pharmacology of Antibiotic DBP, 2000, You and Antibiotics, 2001, Cardiovascular Pharmacology DBP, 2005; mem. editl. bd.: Malaysian Jour. Biochemistry, Pharmacol. Rsch. Jour., Jour. Pharmacol. Recipient Best Presentation award, U. Malaysia, 1999, Best Svc. award, U. Kebangsaan, 1994, 1999, 2003. Mem.: Malaysia Med. Assn., Malaysian Soc. Pharmacology. Avocations: gardening, interior decorating. Home: 29 Jln Au 2A/6 Taman sri Keramai Kuala Lumpur 54200 Malaysia Office: Univ Kebangsaan Dept Pharmacology Jalan Raja Muda 50300 Kuala Lumpur Malaysia Business E-Mail: kamsiah@medic.ukm.my.

JAASKELAINEN (NEE LAURONEN), ERIKA, physician; b. Oulu, Finland, Apr. 18, 1980; d. Hannu Matias and Sinikka Mirjami (Heikkinen) Lauronen; m. Juha Matti Ilmari Jääskeläinen, Sept. 15, 2007; 1 child. Licentiate in Medicine, U. Oulu, 2005, PhD, 2007, MD; MPhil in Epidemiology, U. Cambridge, Eng., 2006; BMed, 2001. Rschr. dept. psychiatry U. Oulu, 2001—, clin. lectr. dept. psychiatry, 2007—09; physician tng. dept. psychiatry Oulu U. Hosp., 2005—. Presenter in field. Contbr. articles to profl. jours. Recipient Young Investigator award, NARSAD, 2008; grantee, Oy H. Lundbeck Ab Finland, 2002, 2004—05, Pharmacy Found. U. Oulu, 2002, U. Oulu, 2003, 2005, Rsch. Found. Orion Pharma Corp., 2003—04, 2011, Med. Drs. Assn. Duodecim, 2004, 2010, Finnish Med. Found., 2008, 2010; scholar, Jalmari and Rauha Ahokas Found., 2006; GlaxoSmithKline scholar, 2005. Mem.: Finnish Psychiat. Assn. (mem. tng. com. 2010—), Acta Psychiat. Scandinavica (mem. tng. bd. 2007—09), Oulu Psychiat. Epidemiology Soc. (founding mem. 2007, sec.), Coun. No. Ostrobothnia Med. Assn. Avocations: sports, dance. Office: Univ Oulu Dept Psychiatry PO Box 5000 90014 Oulu Finland Business E-Mail: erika.jaaskelainen@oulu.fi.

JABBAR, ABDUL, physician, educator, gastroenterologist; b. Multan, Punjab, Pakistan, Oct. 14, 1968; s. Muhammad Sharif and Hajira Bibi; m. Nosheen Jabbar, Nov. 12, 2000; 1 child, Ayyan. MD, Nishtar Med. Coll., Pakistan, 1992. Clin. instr. U. Louisville, 2002—03, asst. prof., 2003—. Consulting gastroenterologist Gastroenterologist Group U. Louisville, 2002—; staff attendant VA Hosp. Contbr. rsch. and med. lit. revs. Gastroenterology/Hepatology fellow, Am. Bd. Internal Medicine, 2002. Mem.: Am. Coll. Gastroenterology. Achievements include research in guidelines for intagastric versus intrajejunal feeding. Home: 9911 Fringe Tree Ct Louisville KY 40241 Office: 530 S Jackson St Louisville KS 40202 Office Fax: 502-852-0846. Personal E-mail: ajh5@hotmail.com.

JABBARI, BAHMAN, neurologist, educator; b. ZanJan, Iran, Jan. 22, 1942; came to U.S., 1968; s. Taghi Jabbari and Fatemeh Golzar-Jabbari; m. Fattaneh Tavassoli, Dec. 30, 1949. Student, Tehran Med. Sch., Iran; MD, Tehran U. Sch. Medicine, Iran, 1966. Diplomate in neurology and in clin. neurophysiology Am. Bd. Psychiatry and Neurology; lic. physician, Md., D.C. Intern Martland Med. Ctr., Newark, 1968-69; resident in neurology Albany (N.Y.) Med. Ctr., 1969-72; fellow Tulane Med. Sch., New Orleans, 1972-73, asst. prof., 1974-76; from assoc. prof. neurology to prof., chair Uniformed Svcs. U., Bethesda, Md., 1978-98, prof., chair neurology, 1998—; prof. neurology Yale U., New Haven, 2004—. Adj. prof. George Washington U., 1985—, Georgetown U., 1986—; dir. clin. neurophysiology Walter Reed Army Med. Ctr., 1977—2000; prof. neurology Yale U., 2004—. Col. U.S. Army, 1986-2004. Recipient VA Superior Performance award. Mem. Internat. Movement Disorder Soc., Am. Epilepsy Soc., Am. Acad. Neurology, Am. Neurol. Assn., Am. Soc. Clin. Neurophysiology. Office: Dept Neurology LCI 708 Yale Univ 15 York St New Haven CT 06520 Office Phone: 203-785-4085. Business E-Mail: bahman.jabbari@yale.edu.

JABER, WAEL A., cardiologist; b. Lebanon, May 3, 1967; BS, Am. U. Beirut, 1988, MD, 1992. Staff cardiologist Cleve. Clinic, 2000—. Fellow: Am. Soc. Nuc. Cardiology, Am. Soc. Echocardiography, Am. Heart Assn., Am. Coll. Cardiology. Office: 9500 Euclid Ave J1-5 Cleveland OH 44195 Business E-Mail: jaberw@ccf.org.

JABLON, LISA K., surgeon; MD, Temple U., 1985. Diplomate Am. Bd. Surgery-gen surgery, Am. Bd. Surgery-breast sugery. Intern Albert Einstein Med. Ctr, resident; hosp. affiliation includes: Albert Einstein Med. Ctr.; tchg. appointment sch. of medicine Temple Univ. Office: Albert Einstein Medical Center 5501 Old York Rd Philadelphia PA 19141 Office Phone: 215-456-7890.

JABS, DOUGLAS ALAN, ophthalmology professor, chairman, dean; b. Hartford, Conn., Oct. 2, 1951; m. Ethylin Wang, 1977; 1 child, Alexandra Wang. AB, Dartmouth Coll., 1973; MD, Johns Hopkins U., 1977, MBA, 2000. Diplomate Am. Bd. Ophthalmology, Am. Bd. Internal Medicine, Nat. Bd. Med. Examiners. Intern Cornell-N.Y. Med. Ctr., NYC, 1977-78; resident in ophthalmology Johns Hopkins Hosp., Balt., 1978-81, resident in internal medicine, 1981-83; fellow in rheumatology Johns Hopkins Med. Instns., Balt., 1983-84; asst. prof. ophthalmology Johns Hopkins U. Sch. Medicine, Balt., 1984-88, assoc. prof., 1988-93, asst. prof. medicine, 1987-89, assoc. prof., 1989-93, prof. ophthalmology & medicine, 1993—2007, prof. epidemiology, 2000—07; prof. & chair, dept. opthalmology Mt. Sinai Sch. Medicine, 2007—, chief exec. officer, faculty practice assocs. dean clin. affairs. Cons. FDA, Rockville, Md., 1994-2000. Recipient Sr. Scientist award, Rsch. to Prevent Blindness, 2002; Lew R. Wasserman merit award, Rsch. To Prevent Blindness, 1997; Olga Keith Weiss scholar award Rsch. to Prevent Blindness, 1991, Ethel Baxter-Sjogren Syndrome Found., 1995. Fellow Am. Acad. Ophthalmology, Am. Coll. Rheumatology; mem. Am. Uveitis Soc. Office: Mt Sinai Sch Medicine One Gustave L Levy Pl PO Box 1183 New York NY 10029 Office Phone: 212-241-6752.

JACINTO, SYLVIA S., dermatologist; b. Manila, Nov. 5, 1939; d. Carmelo Pongco and Concepcion (Sayoc) Jacinto; children: Marie Therese, Gary, Maria Jasmin, Jennifer, Marietta. MD, U. Philippines, 1962; grad., Sheffield Sch. Interior Design, 1990. Adj. resident dept. internal medicine Philippine Gen. Hosp., Manila, 1962-63, asst. resident dept. internal medicine, 1963-64, instr. dept. internal medicine, 1967-72; resident dept. dermatology NYU-Bellevue Med. Ctr., NYC, 1964-67; dir. Philippine Dermatol. Soc., Inc., Manila, 1970-74, 79-84, 2000—02, founding dir., 1974, pres., 1975-78; founder, treas. J&J Med. Clinics, Inc., Makati, 1976—, Gary's Corp., Manila, 1989; clin. prof., chmn. dept. dermatology Skin and Cancer Found., Inc., 1984—2006, emeritus, 2006—; chmn. dept. dermatology Quirino Meml. Med. Ctr., 2001—07; head sect. dermatology Ospital ng Makati, Makati City, 2000—. Cons. dermatologist Med. Ctr. Manila, 1967-87, U.S. Embassy, 1968—2009, Cardinal Santos Med. Ctr., Mandaluyong, 1975-92, 96—2007, St. Martin de Porres Charity Hosp., San Juan, 1980-92, Ctrl. Bank Philippines, 1972—86, U.S. Peace Corps., 1968-86, Can. Embassy, 1986—2006. Contbg. author Diseases of the Skin, Textbook of Pediatrics and Child Health, 1976, 1982, 1990, 1995, editor, founder Philippine Jour. Dermatology and Dermatologic Surgery, 1979—95, mem. editl. bd. Jour. Philippine Dermatol. Soc., 1993—98; author: Clinical Atlas of Dermatology of Brown Skin; contbr. articles to profl. jours.; one-woman shows include Ayala Mus., Makati, 1993, Gallery Y, Mandaluyong, 1995, 2-woman show, 2002, 2008. Pres. White Plains Ladies' Assn., Quezon City, 1976—77, White Plains Homeowner's Assn., Inc., 1995—96; mem. Manila chpt. Zonta Internat., 1976—84, Manila Mahikari Okiyomesho Ctr., 1984—88; founding pres. Hospice Philippines Found., Inc., 1997 ; trustee Christian Parenting for Peace and Justice Found., Inc., 1995—97; bd. dirs. White Plains Homeowner's Assn., Inc., 2006—08. Recipient Enrile Award of Distinction Philippine Bd. Med. Examiners, 1962. Fellow: Am. Coll. Cryosurgery (corr. mem. 1986—), Am. Acad. Dermatology (life; internat.); mem.: Photomedicine Soc., Philippine Acad. Cutaneous Surgery (founding pres. 2001—), Am.Acad. Cosmetic Surgery, Nat. Rsch. Coun. of The Philippines, Internat. Sheng Zhen Soc., Skin Cancer Found. (adv. bd. Philippines 1995—), Internat. Soc. Pediatric Dermatology, Dermatology Found. (Century mem. 1988—92, 1993), Hwy. to Health, Skin and Cancer Found. Inc. (exec. dir. 1984—, pres., co-founder), Am. Holistic Med. Assn., Am. Soc. for Hair Restorative Surgery, Venous Forum of The Philippines, Soc. Investigative Dermatology, Nail Disorders (charter), Am. Soc. Dermatol. Surgery, Internat. Soc. Dermatology, Pacific Dermatol. Assn., Am. Contact Dermatitis Soc., U. Philippines Med. Alumni Soc. (life), Philippine Med. Assn. (life Outstanding Physician award 2002), Philippine Dermatologic Soc. (life), Internat. Soc. Dermatol. Surgery (adv. bd. Philippines 1978—95), Tagaytay Midlands Country Club, White Plains Country Club. Avocations: Qigong, interior design, pottery, painting, Flamenco. Office: Skin Clinic 1311 Batangas St Makati 1234 Philippines Office Phone: 6328943952. Personal E-mail: vijacinto@yahoo.com.

JACK, MICHELLE MARION, endocrinologist; b. Brisbane, Australia, Nov. 6, 1968; MB BChir with first class honors, U. Queensland, 1991, PhD, 2003. Head dept. paediat. endocrinology Royal North Shore Hosp., 2004—. Chair adolescent subcom. Northern Sydney Paediat. Network, 2010—11. Recipient Gold medal, U. Queensland; fellowship, Juvenile Diabetes Rsch. Found. Fellow: Royal Australasian Coll. Physicians; mem.: Australasian Paediat. Endocrine Group. Office: Royal North Shore Hosp Level 5 Douglas Bldg St Leonards NSW 2065 Australia Business E-Mail: mjack@nsccahs.health.nsw.gov.au.

JACKMAN, STEPHEN V., urologist; MD, Yale U., New Haven. Diplomate Am. Bd. Urology. Resident Johns Hopkins Univ.; hosp. affiliations include Univ. Pitts. Med. Ctr. Magee-Womens Hosp., Pa., Univ. Pitts. Med. Ctr. Presbyn., Univ. Pitts. Med. Ctr. Mercy, Univ. Pitts. Med. Ctr. Shadyside, Univ. Pitts. Med. Ctr. Kidney Stone Ctr. Office: University of Pittsburgh Medical Center Kidney Stone Center 3471 5th Ave Ste 801 Pittsburgh PA 15213 Office Phone: 412-692-4100.

JACKSON, BENJAMIN TAYLOR, retired surgeon, educator, health facility administrator; b. Jacksonville, Fla., Apr. 28, 1929; s. Julian Harold and Helen Louise (Blasingame) J.; m. Alda Jean Davis, June 18, 1953; children: Benjamin Taylor Jr., Jean Leigh, Kimberly Louise, Jillian Davis. MD, Duke U., 1954; MS, Brown U., 1982. Diplomate Am. Bd. Surgery. Instr. Med. Coll. of Va., Richmond, 1963-64; asst. prof. Boston U. Sch. Medicine, 1964-67, assoc. prof., 1967-75, prof., 1975-80; vis. surgeon U. Hosp., Boston, 1975-80; prof. Brown U. Sch. Medicine, Providence, 1980-97, prof. in surgery emeritus, 1997—; chief surg. svc. VA Med. Ctr., Providence, 1980-97, cons. in surgery, 1997—; prof. surgery, rschr. Brown U., Providence, 1999—2002. Contbr. articles to profl. jours. Capt. U.S. Army, 1955-57. Mem. ACS, Soc. Univ. Surgeons, Soc. for Gynecologic Investigation. Methodist. Home: 11 October Ln Weston MA 02493-1724 Office: VA Med Ctr Davis Pk Providence RI 02908

JACKSON, CYNTHIA ANN, medical association administrator, health consultant; b. Hornell, NY, Feb. 13, 1960; d. William Thompson and Carol Ann (Dailey) Moss; m. Robert Dale Jackson, Dec. 2, 2000; m. Clinton Newell Colvin, Mar. 3, 1984 (div. Oct. 10, 1994); stepchildren: Brandi Louise Moss, Robert Dale II children: Christopher David Colvin, Cassandra Lynn Colvin. Assocs. in Environ. Health Tech., Merritt Coll., Oakland, Calif., 1985; B of Occupl. Health and Safety magna cum laude, Nat. U., San Diego, 1987, M of Forensic Sci., 1989. Lic. practical nurse, U. of N.Y.; registered environ. health secialist, ServSafe instr. Nat. Restaurant Assn., cert. pest control applicator Va. Dept. of Agr. and Consumer Svcs., food safety mgr. Nat. Registry of Food Safety Profls., spl. conservator of the peace Commonwealth of Va. Dept. of Criminal Justice Svcs. Cook Coachlight Steakhouse, Hornell, 1978—79; head preventive medicine dept. Naval Med. Clinic, Phila., 1992—94, Naval Hosp. Camp Pendleton, Calif., 1995—98, 1st Med. Bn., Camp Pendleton, 1998—2001, Mil. Sealift Command, Norfolk, Va., 2001—04; environ. health specialist Chesapeake Health Dept., Va., 2004—06, environ. health tech. specialist, 2007—09, environ. health supr., 2010—; hosp. corpsman Naval Regional Med. Ctr., Bremerton, Wash., 1980—81; preventive medicine technician U.S. Naval Hosp., Yokosuka, Japan, 1982—84, Naval Hosp. San Diego, 1984—89; surface force ind. duty corpsmen instr. Naval Sch. of Health Scis., San Diego, 1989—92; officer recruit Officer Indoctrination Sch., Newport News, RI, 1992. Mgr. bio-hazardous waste Naval Hosp. Camp Pendleton Marine Corps Base, 1995—98; legal officer 1st Med. Bn., Camp Pendleton, 1998—2001, equal opportunity officer, 1998—2001, mem. awards bd., 1998—2001; environ. health cons. Miliatry Sealift Command, Norfolk, 2001—04; health promotion mgr. Mil. Sealift Command, Norfolk, 2001—04, inspector shipboard material assessments and readiness team, 2001—04, mem. awards bd., 2001—04; environ. health cons. Chesapeake Health Dept., Va., 2004—, epidemiology rep., 2004—; chmn. rabies control bd. Naval Hosp. Camp Pendleton Marine Corps Base, Camp Pendleton, 1995—98, mem. infection control com., 1995—98, mem. base water steering com., 1995—98, mem. quality rev. bd. for child care, 1995—98, mem. hazardous material control mgmt., 1995—98, mem. wellness adv. com., 1995—98; environ. health officer cons. 1st Med. Bn., Camp Pendleton, 1998—2001, health promotion mgr., Semper Fi fit coord., 1998—2001. Co-author: Field Biomedical Waste Program; author, exhibitor: poster bd. Med Cap Results in Kenya, Africa. Decorated Navy Marine Corps Commendation Medals (3) USN, Navy Achievement Medals (2), Good Conduct Medals (3), Rifle and Pistol Expert Medals (2), Seven Letters of Commendation, Thirty-five Letters of Appreciation, Twenty Certs. of Recognition; recipient Four Certs. of Appreciation, Chesapeake Health Dept., 2004—05; named Employee of the Quar., 2005. Mem.: Va. Environ. Health Assn., Tidewater Environ. Health Assn., Nat. Environ. Health Assn., U.S. Naval Inst., Women's Meml. (chartered mem.). Methodist. Avocations: bass fishing, camping, arts and crafts, sewing. Home: 1129 Cherrytree Ln Chesapeake VA 23320 Office: Chesapeake Health Dept 748 N Battlefield Blvd Chesapeake VA 23320 Office Phone: 757-382-8661. Personal E-mail: chscynthia@yahoo.com. Business E-Mail: cynthia.jackson@vdh.virginia.gov.

JACKSON, DONALD F., medical technician; b. Arab, Ala., Jan. 20, 1967; AAS, CC Air Force, 2003. Mem. USAF, 1985—2005, shift supr., Gulf War, 1991, sonographer, 1991—, ultrasound supr., 1993—2000, diagnostic ultrasound instr., phase II, 2000—05, ultrasound career field mgr., 2003—05; ultrasound mgr. Women and Infants Hosp., 2011—. Decorated Air Combat Command Reall Pro award USAF, Achievement medal (3), Commendation medal (2), Humanitarian Svc. medal, Good Conduct medal (4). Master: Free and Accepted Masons; mem.: Am. Soc. Radiologic Technologists, Soc. Diagnostic Med. Sonographers, Am. Registry Radiology Technologists, Am. Registry Diagnostic Med. Sonographers. Avocation: sports. Office: 101 Dudley St Providence RI 02905 Personal E-mail: sonoteacher@cox.net

JACKSON, EARL, JR., retired medical technician, microbiologist; b. Paris, Ky., Sept. 4, 1938; s. Earl Sr. and Margaret Elizabeth (Cummins) J. BA, Ky. State U., 1960; postgrad., U. Paris, 1978. Clin. rsch. coord. Harvard U., Boston, 1962-64; chem. devel. specialist Electro-Power Pacs, Corp., Cambridge, Mass., 1964-67; sr. rsch. tech. Mass. Gen. Hosp., Boston, 1967-81, med. tech. specialist, 1981-95; ret., 1995. Contbr. articles to profl. jours. Named to, Hall of Fame of Disting. Alumni, Ky. State U., 1988. Mem.: N.E. Assn. for Microbiology and Infectious Disease, Am. Soc. Clin. Microbiology, Am. Assn. Clin. Chemistry, N.Y. Acad. Sciences, AAAS, Boston Mus. of Fine Arts, N.Y. Met. Mus. of Art. Democrat. Home: 501 Fenwick Dr San Antonio TX 78239-2532 Personal E-mail: EJR29@aol.com, ejr29@att.net.

JACKSON, GEORGE LYMAN, retired nuclear medicine physician; b. Arlington, Mass., Dec. 17, 1923; s. William and Alice (Tenney) J.; m. Alyce Verne Yeager, Sept. 7, 1946; children: Scott Douglas, Carole Elizabeth, Diane Priscilla, Richard Lee. BS cum laude, Franklin and Marshall Coll., 1944; MD, U. Pa., 1948. Diplomate: Am. Bd. Internal Medicine, Am. Bd. Nuclear Medicine. Intern Hosp. U. Pa., 1948-49, resident, 1949-52; practice medicine specializing in internal medicine Harrisburg, Pa., 1952-63; dir. med. edn., acting med. dir. Harrisburg Hosp., 1963-68, dir. undergrad. fellowships, 1968-69, head sect. nuclear medicine, 1965-75, med. dir. dept. nuclear medicine, 1975-89. Asst. prof. medicine Hahnemann Med. Coll., 1963-68, assoc. prof., 1968-70; clin. assoc. prof. M.S. Hershey Med. Centre, Pa. State U., 1970-76, clin. prof., 1976-90; dir. Harrisburg Hosp. Sch. Nuclear Medicine Tech.; adj. faculty Harrisburg Area Community Coll., Millersville State Coll.; cons., chmn. med. adv. com. Lebanon (Pa.) VA Hosp., 1968-75; nuclear medicine adv. Pa. Dept. Edn., Pa. Med. Soc., Pa. Blue Shield. Author: Of Thee I Sing, 1993, The Eclectic Club of Harrisburg, 1997, 150th Anniversary of St. Paul's Lutheran Church, 2005, Ebenezer Tolman & Benedict Arnold's Canadian Expectation 1775-1776, 2006, Matthew Stanley Quay-Scoundrel or Statesman, 2007; contbr. articles to profl. jours. & publs. Mem. Cen. Dauphin Sch. Bd., 1971-73; bd. dirs. Bethesda Mission, Harrisburg Hosp. Med. Edn. and Rsch. Found.; bd. dirs. New Hope Ministries, 1987-93, pres. 1988-93; chmn. archives and collections com. No. York County Hist. and Preservation Soc., 1998-2000. With USN, 1942-45. Fellow ACP (govs. com. for coll. affairs 1969-76, gov. 1976-80, laureate 1985), Soc. Nuclear Medicine, Am. Coll. Nuclear Physicians (bd. regents), Am. Coll. Nuclear Medicine; mem. Am. Thyroid Assn., Pa. Soc. Internal Medicine (past pres.; chmn. liaison com.), Pa. Coll. Nuclear Medicine (pres.), Joint Rev. Com. Nuclear Medicine Tech., Phi Beta Kappa, Alpha Omega Alpha. Lutheran. Home: 22 N Baltimore St Dillsburg PA 17019-1210

JACKSON, GREGORY WAYNE, orthodontist; b. Chgo., Sept. 4, 1950; s. Wayne Eldon and Marilyn Frances (Anderson) J.; m. Nora Ann Echtner, Mar. 17, 1973; children: Eric, David. Student, U. Ill., 1968-70; DDS with honors, U. Ill., Chgo., 1974; MSD, U. Wash., 1978. Practice dentistry specializing in orthodontics, Chgo., 1978—. Instr. orthodontic dept. U. Ill. Coll. Dentistry, Chgo., 1978-81. Coach

Little League Baseball, Oak Brook, Ill., 1986-89. Served to lt. USN, 1974-76. Mem. ADA, Ill. State Dental Soc., Chgo. Dental Soc., Am. Assn. Orthodontists, Midwestern Soc. Orthodontists, Ill. Soc. Orthodontists, Omicron Kappa Upsilon. Evangelical. Avocations: golf, tennis, skiing. Office: 6435 S Pulaski Rd Chicago IL 60629-5148

JACKSON, JAMES SIDNEY, psychologist, educator; b. Detroit, July 30, 1944; s. Pete James and Johnnie Mae (Wilson) J. BS, Mich. State U., 1966; MA, U. Toledo, 1970; PhD, Wayne State U., 1972. Probation counselor Lucas County Juvenile Ct., Toledo, 1967-68; tchg. and rsch. asst. Wayne State U., Detroit, 1968-71; from asst. prof. to prof. psychology U. Mich., Ann Arbor, 1971—, faculty assoc. Rsch. Ctr. Group Dynamics, 1971—86, dir. Rsch. Ctr. Group Dynamics, 1996—2005, faculty assoc. Inst. Gerontology, 1976—, dir. program rsch. on Black Ams., 1976—2005, faculty assoc. Ctr. Afro-Am. and African Studies, 1982—, rsch. prof., 1986—, assoc. dean Rackham Sch. Grad. Studies, 1987-92, prof. pub. health, 1990—, Daniel Katz Collegiate prof., 1994-95, Daniel Katz Disting. Univ. prof. psychology, 1995—; Hill Disting. vis. prof. U. Minn., Ann Arbor, 1995; dir. Ctr. Afro-Am. and African Studies U. Mich., Ann Arbor, 1998—2005, dir. Inst. Social Rsch., 2005—. Chair sociol. psychology tng. program U. Mich., 1980-86, 93-96; cons. Emergency Sch. Aid Project, 1973-74, Commn. on Equal Opportunity in Psychology, 1970, Project to Provide Psychol. Svcs. to Head Start Programs, 1973-74, European Econ. Commn. Project on Racism, Xenophobia and Immigration, 1989—; mem. com. on aging and com. on status of Black Ams., panel on race, ethnicity and health in later life, Nat. Acad. of Scis.; mem. com. on African Am. Population Year 2000 and 2010 U.S. Census Bur.; mem. nat. adv. com. Boston Mus. Sci., 1998-2002; mem. Nat. Adv. Coun. on Aging, NIH, 1996-99; mem. bd. sci. counselors, Nat. Inst. Aging; invited rschr. Ecole des Hautes Etudes en Scis. Sociales, Paris, 1992-2004; disting. lectr. gerontology UCLA, 1992; mem. steering com. Nat. Acad. Aging Soc., 1995—; co-chair Ford Found. Fellow's Conf., Washington, 2006-07; mem., bd. dirs. Mich. Aerospace Found., Inc., 2007-, Shelter Assn. Washtenaw County, 2007-; mem. Nat. Rsch. Coun., Inst. Medicine Com. Effects HIPPA Regulations Rsch., 2007-08, Aging Soc. Network, MacArthur Found., 2008-, Nat. Rsch. Coun. Com. Underrepresented Groups, 2008-, Review Com., Intramural Dir., NIA, Nat. Rsch. Coun. Com. Biomed. Tng. Needs, 2008-, Associateship and Fellowship Programs Adv. Com., Nat. Rsch. Coun., 2008-; mem. adv. com. to dir. NIH, 2009-. Author: The Black American Elderly: Research on Physical and Psychosocial Health, 1988, African American Elderly, 2d edit., 1997, (with Gurin P., Hatchett S.) Hope and Independence: Blacks Response to Electoral and Party Politics, 1989, Life in Black America, 1991, (with Chatters L., Taylor R.) Aging in Black America, 1993, (with H. Neighbors) Mental Health in Black America, 1996, (with R. Taylor and L. Clatters) Family Life in Black America, 1997, (with Antonucci, T.C.) Life-Course Perspectives on Late Life Health Inequalities, 2009, (with Caldwell, C.H. & Sellers, S.) Survey Research Methodology in African American Communities, 2010; editor: New Directions: African Americans in a Diversifying Nation, 2000; editl. cons. Jour. Behavioral and Social Scientists; editl. bd. Jour. Gerontology, Applied Social Psychology Ann., Psychol. Bull., Jour. Social Issues; cons. editor Psychology and Aging; contbr. articles to profl. jours. Bd. dirs. Pub. Commn. on Mental Health, Ronald McDonald House, Ann Arbor, 1993—; bd. trustees Greenhills Sch., Ann Arbor, 1997-2003, v.p., 2002-03. Recipient Disting. Faculty Svc. award U. Mich., 1976, Harold R. Johnson Diversity Svc. award U. Mich., 2000, Orgn. Black Alumni Achievement award Wayne State U., 2005, James McKeen Cattell Fellow award Assn. for Psychol. Sci., 2005, Health Disparities Innovation award Nat. Ctr. Minority Health & Health Disparities, NIH, 2008, medal NY Acad. Medicine, 2010, Pearmain prize Edward R. Roybal Inst., U. Southern Calif., 2011; Urban Studies fellow Wayne State U., 1969-70; NSF fellow, 1969; Sr. Postdoctoral fellow Groupe d'Études et de Recherches sur la Science, École des Hautes Études en Sciences Sociales, 1986-87; Sr. Ford Found. Minority Postdoctoral fellow, 1986-87; Fogarty Sr. Internat. fellow, 1993-94; Robert W. Kleemeier award for rsch., Gerontol. Soc. Am. Fellow APA (divs. 9-20, policy and planning bd., fin. com. 1984-86, award for early contbns. 1983, Tenth Anniversary Peace and Social Justice award Soc. for the Study of Peace, Conflict and Violence, Peace Psychology divsn. 2000, com. on internat. rels., 1999-02, chair 2001-02, Disting. Career Contbns. ro Rsch. award Divsn. 45, 2001, Presdl. Citation award 2008), AAAS (past chmn. sect. social, econ. and polit. scis.), Am. Acad. Arts & Scis., Gerontol. Soc. Am. (task force on minority issues in gerontology, chmn. 1988-92, ann. sci. conv. program com., Minority Task Force Mentoring award 2003, Disting. Mentorship in Gerontology award behavioral and social sci. sect. 2004), Internat. Demographic Assn. (St. Gallens, Switzerland), Soc. Exptl. Social Psychology; mem. Assn. Advancement of Psychology (trustee 1973-89, chmn. 1978-80), Inst. of Medicine, Nat. Acad. Scis., Black Students Psychol. Assn. (nat. chmn. 1970-71), Assn. Black Psychologists (nat. chmn. 1972-73), Soc. Psychol. Study of Social Issues (pres. elect, pres., past pres. 2009-), World Future Soc., Assn. Behavioral and Social Scientists, Gerontol. Soc. Am. (chair behavioral and social scis. sect. 1997-98), Internat. Platform Assn., NIMH (nat. mental health coun. 1989-93, panel on equal access com. on instl. cooperation 1989-92), Psi Chi, Alpha Phi Alpha., Aging Soc. Network Home: 340 Orchard Hills Dr Ann Arbor MI 48104-1832 Office: U Mich 5110 Inst Social Rsch 426 Thompson St Ann Arbor MI 48104-2321 Home Phone: 734-623-7783; Office Phone: 734-763-2491. Business E-Mail: jamessj@umich.edu.

JACKSON, JON, medical educator, consultant; s. Dale and Marlys Alice Jackson; m. Margaret Ellen Moore, May 1, 1999; children: Maia, Finn. BA, Luther Coll., 1983; PhD, U. ND, 1989. Post-doctoral fellow Vanderbilt U., Nashville, 1990—93; asst. prof. Vanderbilt U. Sch. Medicine, 1993—96, U. ND, Grand Forks, 1998—; prin. med. tech. writer Daedalus Consulting, Oakland, Calif., 1996—98; prin., account exec. Jensen, Ramsey and Jackson, San Ramon, 1996—97; cons. Inst. Natural Resources, Berkeley, 1998—2000, Pearson Christensen, Grand Forks, 2002—04. Med. tech. writer Daedalus Consulting, Grand Forks, 1998—; med. writer MedCo Comm., Evergreen, Colo., 1998—2004; faculty advisor Coun. Coll. Faculty, 2004—08, ND State Bd. Higher Edn., 2008—10. Author: Corpus: A User's Guide to the Human Body; musician: (musical performance, acappella quartet) 4 Blow Zero. Vol. ND Mus. Art, 1999—; vol. educator Dakota Sci. Ctr., 2003—05; pres. Grand Forks Master Chorale, 1998—2004; mem. North Valley Arts Coun., 2000—. Scholar, Archibald Bush Found., 2001—02. Mem.: AAAS, Am. Physiologic Soc., Am. Assn. Clin. Anatomists (anatomic svcs. com. 2007—11), ND Acad. Sci. (sec., treas. 1999—2006, coun. mem. 2006—09), ND Funeral Dir.'s Assn., Am. Med. Writers Assn., Human Anatomy and Physiology Soc. (co-chair membership 2005—09), Am. Assn. Anatomists (terminology com. mem. 2008—11, pub. affairs com. mem. 2009—, mem. ednl. affairs com. 2011—), Grand Forks C. of C., Sigma Xi. Democrat-Npl. Avocations: music, rugby, travel, running, handball. Office: U ND Dept Anatomy and Cell Biology Grand Forks ND 58202-9037 Office Fax: 701-777-2477. Personal E-mail: jcksn@mac.com. Business E-Mail: jon.jackson@med.und.edu.

JACKSON, LAIRD GRAY, geneticist, internist, educator; b. Seattle, Oct. 10, 1930; married. BA, Pomona Coll., 1951; MD, U. Cin., 1955. Diplomate Am. Bd. Internal Medicine, Am. Bd. Med. Genetics (bd. dirs.). Rotating gen. intern Sacramento County (Calif.) Hosp., 1955-56; resident in internal medicine Jefferson Med. Coll., Phila., 1959-61, NIH postdoctoral fellow med. oncology, 1961-62, instr. medicine, 1962-64, asst. prof. medicine, 1964-66, assoc. prof., 1966-69, assoc. prof. medicine, pediatrics and ob-gyn, 1969-78, prof., 1978—, dir. div. med. genetics, 1969-98. Founder, bd. dirs., treas. Am. Coll. Med. Genetics, 1991-95. Mem. editorial bd. Am. Jour. Med. Genetics, Prenatal Diagnosis, Repository of Human Chromosomal Variants. Capt. USAF, 1956—59. Leukemia Soc. fellow, 1963-65, Leukemia Soc. scholar 1965-70. Fellow ACP; mem. Am. Soc. Human Genetics (social issues com. 1976-80, bd. dirs.). Independent. Home and Office: 245 N 15th St Philadelphia PA 19102-1192 Office Phone: 215-762-3155. Business E-Mail: ljackson@drexelmed.edu.

JACKSON, MARY L., health services executive; b. Phila., June 25, 1938; d. John Francis and Helen Catherine (Peranteau) Martin; m. Howard Clark Jackson III, Dec. 17, 1954; children: Michael, Mark, Brian, Bert. Student, Bucks County C.C., 1977-83. Asst. mgr. retail divsn. Sears Roebuck & Co., Bensalem, Pa., 1972-77; educator, adminstr., dir. Trevose Behavior Modification Program, Pa., 1975—, leadership tng. workshops, 1979—. Participant rsch. studies in field; salesman Makefield Real Estate, Morrisville, Pa., 1977-78; mortgage fin. cons. Tom Dunphy Real Estate, Feasterville, Pa., 1978-81; weight loss cons., Hulmeville, Pa., 1984—, also TV and radio appearances on behavior modification for weight loss and maintenance. Co-author: The Official Calorie Book; pub., columnist monthly newsletter The Modifier, 1977—; pub. several studies in weight loss field; pub. co-author multi-studies in field. Recipient Chapel of Four Chaplain award, 1977. Mem. Assn. Advancement Behavior Therapy, Bucks County Bd. Realtors, Hulmeville Hist. Soc. (founder, charter mem.). Democrat. Roman Catholic. Avocations: reading, classical music, speed walking, knitting, fishing. Address: 800 Trenton Rd Apt 144 Langhorne PA 19047

JACKSON, RICHARD JOSEPH, epidemiologist, educator, pediatrician, preventive medicine physician; b. Newark, Oct. 23, 1945; s. Robert Joseph Jackson and Dorothy C. (Devine) Connolly; m. Joan M. Guilford, June 21, 1975; children: Brendan, Devin, Galen. AB in Biology, St. Peter's Coll., Jersey City, 1969; M in Med. Sci., Rutgers U., 1971; MD, U. Calif. San Francisco, San Francisco, 1973; MPH in Epidemiology, U. Calif. Berkeley, Berkeley, 1979. Diplomate Am. Bd. Pediatrics, Am. Bd. Preventive Medicine; lic. physician, Calif. Intern, resident U. Calif., San Francisco, 1973-74, 77-78, resident San Francisco Gen. Hosp., 1974-75; officer Epidemic Intelligence Svc. U.S. Pub. Health Svc., Albany, N.Y., 1975-77; spl. epidemiologist World Health Orgn., Bihar State, India, 1976; med. officer Epidemiol. Studies Sect. Calif. State Dept. Health Svcs., Berkeley, 1979-88, acting chief Office Environ. Health Hazard Aassessment Sacramento, 1988-90, chief hazard identification and risk assessment br. Berkeley, 1990-91; chief hazard identification and risk assessment br. office environ. health hazard assessment Calif. EPA, Berkeley, 1991-92; chief divsn. communicable disease control Calif. State Dept. Health Svcs., 1992-94; dir. Nat. Ctr. Environ. Health, Ctrs. Disease Control and Prevention, Atlanta, 1994—2003; sr. advisor to dir. Ctr. Disease Control, Atlanta, 2003—04; state pub. health officer State of Calif., Sacremento, 2004—. Adj. lectr. U. Calif. San Francisco, 1980—, asst. clin. prof., 1986—; adj. prof. Emory U. Rollins Sch. Pub. Health, 1998—. Lt. comdr. USPHS, 1975-77. Office: Ca Dept Of Health Services PO Box 997413 Sacramento CA 95899-7413 Home Phone: 925-837-7890. E-mail: RJJackson@cdc.gov, rjackso6@dhs.ca.gov.

JACKSON, THAD MARSHALL, health services administrator, medical educator; b. Dallas, May 21, 1933; d. Thad M. and Opal P. (Miller) J.; m. Linda Susan Pfeiffer. BA, San Francisco State U., 1951; MS, U. San Francisco, 1968; PhD, U. Calif., Berkeley, 1974. Lectr. med. microbiology U. Calif., Berkeley, 1971; assoc. prof. dept. pathology Johns Hopkins U. Sch. Hygiene and Pub. Health; v.p. Nestle Coordination Ctr. for Nutrition, 1981—85; owner, dir. Geriatric Retirement Ctr., Norwich, England, 1985—86; dir. issues mgmt. Nestle USA, 1986—96; exec. v.p. Internat. Med. Svcs. for Health, 1996—. Dir. Johns Hopkins U. Internat. Ctr. Med. Rsch. and Tng., Nepal, India, Bangladesh, 1972—79, dir. children's nutrition rsch. unit, Bangladesh, 1972—79; condr. tng. programs in nutrition and primary health care; developer village outreach programs for mothers and children; owner, dir. two nursing homes, 1977—80; cons. Clintec (joint venture Nestle/Baxter Travenol), 1985—86, Save the Children Fedn., 1973—78; adj. prof. dept. pediats. Georgetown U. Sch. Medicine, 1981—; del. Internat. Women's Forum, Beijing, 1995; organizer, dir. Woemn's Forum, Washington; organizer various confs. on nutrition and the elderly; researcher on nutrition; mem. adv. bd. League of Women Voters, 1991—93, Bus. and Profl. Women's Assn., 1991—95; advisor to rsch. protocol com. Cholera Rsch. Labs., Dhaka, 1974—76; advisor Netherlands Embassy, 1976; ad hoc advisor UNICEF, 1972—77. Contbr. articles. Mem. bd. regents Cath. U. Am., 1992—. Grantee, NIH, 1972—74, UN Devel. Programme, 1977, USAID, 1976—77; fellow U.S. Pub. Health fellowship, 1968—72. Mem.: Royal Soc. Tropical Medicine, Am. Soc. Tropical Medicine and Hygiene. Home: PO Box 413 Upperville VA 20185

JACKSON, WILLIAM RICHARD, entrepreneur; b. Nampa, Idaho, Aug. 23, 1936; s. Richard W. and Josie P. (Mulder) J.; m. Marilyn Kay Samp, June 10, 1956 (div. 1975); children: James Lee, Robbi Jo, Jolynn Kay. BA in Secondary Edn., N.W. Nazarene Coll., Nampa, 1957; MA in Secondary Edn. Adminstrn., U. No. Colo., 1961; EdM, U. Denver, 1964, PhD in Higher Edn. Adminstrn. and Rsch., 1991; PhD in, Stanford U., 1991. Owner, operator Janitorial Svc., Walla Walla, Wash., 1950-54; account mgr., collection contractor Montgomery Ward, Walla Walla, Wash., 1953-57; exec. ins. dir. edn. svcs. Idaho Sch. Employment, Boise, 1957-58; sch. tchr., football coach Humanities, Speech & Art, Caldwell, Idaho, 1958-60; tchr. psychology and econs. Englewood (Colo.) Sch. Dist., 1961-64; dir. student coun. Brook Forest Leadership Inst., Evergreen, Colo., 1961-64; co-owner, operator Jackson Bros. Investments, Englewood, 1970-84; co-owner, pres. Internat. Bell Mus., Inc., Evergreen, 1978-86; pres. Jackson Bros. Industries, Evergreen, 1984—, Jackson Internat., Inc., Evergreen, 1984—. Chmn. bd. Petro Silver, Inc., Denver, 1979-83; rsch. cons. in agr., toxic waste remediation and hyperbaric oxygenation medicine; sr. cons. Envrion. Health Found., San Francisco; mem. staff Southwest Rsch. Inst., San Antonio, Tex. Co-author: Brook Forest Leadership Curriculum, 1964, Disciplining Curriculum, 1978; author: Hyperbaric Oxygenation Effects on the Cognitive Function of Memory, Barter, The History, Mystery and Mastery of Mutual Exchange, Humic, Fulvic and Micorbial Balance: Organic Soil Conditioning, Environmental Care & Share, 1995, The Arthritis, Osteoporosis and Silica Link, The Calcium Deception, Fabulous Fulvic Electrolyte, 1995. Co-founder Benevolent Brotherhood Found., Denver, 1971—; bd. dirs. Ch. of the Nazarene, past chmn. bd. edn. Grantee Denver Presbyn. Med. Ctr., 1991, Hyperbaric Oxygen Therapy System, San Diego, 1991, Denver, 1991; recipient 1st Pl. Nat. Self-Publishing award Writer's Digest, 1993. Mem. Internat. Found. Hyperbaric Medicine, Undersea and Hyperbaric Med. Soc. (rsch. cons. 1990—), Stanford U. Alumni Assn., Phi Delta Kappa. Republican. Avocation: bartering. Office: Jackson Internat Rsch Ctr PO Box 1749 Evergreen CO 80437-1749 Office Phone: 303-674-7351. Personal E-mail: wirjak@jps.net.

JACOB, FRANÇOIS, biologist, educator; b. Nancy, France, June 17, 1920; s. Simon and Therese (Franck) Jacob; m. Lysiane Bloch, Nov. 27, 1947 (dec. 1984); children: Pierre, Laurent, Odile, Henri; m. Geneviève Barrier, 1999. MD, Faculty of Medicine, Paris, 1947; DSc, Faculty of Scis., Paris, 1954; DSc (hon.), U. Chgo., 1965; Dr (hon.), various univs. Asst. Pasteur Inst., 1950—56, head dept. cellular genetics, 1960—92, pres., 1982—88; prof. cellular genetics Coll. of France, 1964—92; prof. emeritus Coll. of France and Inst. Pasteur, 1992—. Author: (books) The Logic of Life, 1970, The Possible and the Actual, 1981, The Statue Within, 1987, Of Flies, Mice and Men, 1997. Recipient Charles Leopold Mayer prize, 1962, Nobel prize in physiology and medicine (with A. Lwoff and J. Monod), 1965. Mem.: Royal Acad. Scis. Madrid, Acad. Scis. Hungary, Royal Acad. Medicine Belgique, Royal Soc. (London), Am. Philos Soc., Nat. Acad. Scis., Am. Acad. Arts and Scis. (fgn.), Royal Danish Acad. Scis. and Letters (fgn.), Acad. Française Paris, Acad. Sci. (Paris). Achievements include research in on genetics bacterial cells and viruses; contbr. to mechanisms of information transfer (messenger RNA) and genetic basis of regulatory circuits, early stages of the mouse embryo. Office: Pasteur Inst 25 Rue du Dr Roux 75724 Paris Cedex 15 France Office Phone: 0145688487. Business E-Mail: fjacob@pasteur.fr. *

JACOB, STANLEY WALLACE, surgeon, educator; b. Phila., 1924; s. Abraham and Belle (Shulman) J.; m. Marilyn Peters; 1 son, Stephen; m. Beverly Swarts; children: Jeffrey, Darren, Robert; m. Gail Brandis; 1 dau., Elyse. BA, Ohio State U., Columbus, 1945; MD cum laude, Ohio State U. Med. Sch., Columbus, 1948. Diplomate Am. Bd. Surgery. Intern Beth Israel Hosp., Boston, 1948-49, resident surgery, 1949-52, 54-56; chief resident surg. svc. Harvard Med. Sch., 1956-57, instr., 1958-59; assoc. vis. surgeon Boston City Hosp., 1958-59; Kemper Found. rsch. scholar ACS, 1957-60; asst. prof. surgery U. Oreg. Med. Sch., Portland, 1959-66, assoc. prof., 1966—; Gerlinger prof. surgery Oreg. Health Scis. U., 1981—. Author: Structure and Function in Man, 5th edit, 1982, Laboratory Guide for Structure and Function in Man, 1982, Dimethyl Sulfoxide Basic Concepts, 1971, Biological Actions of DMSO, 1975, Elements of Anatomy and Physiology, 1989; contbr.: Ency. Britanica. Served to capt. M.C. AUS, 1952-54; col. Res. ret. Recipient Gov.'s award Outstanding N.W. Scientist, 1965; 1st pl. German Sci. award, 1960; Markle scholar med. scis., 1960. Mem. Phi Beta Kappa, Sigma Xi, Alpha Omega Alpha. Achievements include co-discovery of therapeutic usefulness of dimethyl sulfoxide and MSM. Home: 1055 SW Westwood Ct Portland OR 97239-2708 Office: Oreg Health Scis U Dept Surgery 3181 SW Sam Jackson Park Rd Portland OR 97239 Business E-Mail: jacobs@ohsu.edu.

JACOBE, HEIDI, dermatologist, director; b. Berea, Ohio, Feb. 18, 1970; MD with Honors, Baylor Coll. Medicine, Houston, 1996; M in Clin. Sci. with distinction, U. Tex. Southwestern Med. Ctr., Dallas, 2008. Asst. prof. dept. dermatology, dir., phototherapy U. Tex. Southwestern Med. Ctr., 2002—, assoc. residency dir., 2007—. Dir., phototherapy unit North Tex. Vets. Adminstrn. Med. Ctr., Dallas, 2002—. Named Teacher of the Yr., Dept. Dermatology, U. Tex. Southwestern Med. Ctr., 2003—04; grantee Faculty Mentor award, Women Dermatology Soc., 2009, grant, NIH, 2008, Clinically Oriented Rsch. award, Dermatology Found., 2008—09. Mem.: AMA, SCD, Soc. Investigative Dermatology, Nat. Psoriasis Found., Med. Dermatology Soc., Am. Skin Cancer Found., Dallas Dermatol. Soc., Am. Acad. Dermatology, Photomedicine Soc. Avocations: travel, gardening. Office: UT Southwestern Med Ctr 5323 Harry Hines Blvd Dallas TX 75390-9069 Office Phone: 214-648-2985. Office Fax: 214-648-9292. Business E-Mail: heidi_jacobe@utsouthwestern.edu.

JACOBOWITZ, ISRAEL JACOB, cardiothoracic surgeon; b. Lanzberg, Germany, Nov. 8, 1947; came to U.S., 1949; MD, SUNY, Buffalo, 1973. Diplomate Am. Bd. Thoracic Surgery. Attending surgeon in cardiothoracic surgery Maimonides Med. Ctr., Bklyn., 1982—, Brookdale Med. Ctr. SUNY, Downstate Med. Ctr. Prof. surgery SUNY, Bklyn., 1991—. Fellow ACS, Am. Coll. Chest Physicians, Am. Coll. Cardiology. Office: 984 50th St Brooklyn NY 11219

JACOBS, ALICE KAUFMAN, cardiologist, educator; b. Apr. 16, 1949; MD, St. Louis U., 1971. Cert. internal medicine, cardiovasc. disease, endocrinology and metabolism, interventional cardiology. Resident St. Louis U. Sch. Medicine, 1977; fellow metabolism and endocrinology U. Calif. San Diego, 1980; fellow cardiology Boston Med. Ctr., 1982; prof. medicine Boston U. Sch. Medicine; dir. cardiac catheterization lab. and interventional cardiology Boston Med. Ctr. Mem.: Am. Heart Assn. (pres. 2004—05, vol., Disting. Nat. Leadership award 2004). Office: Cardiac Catheterization Lab Newton Pavilion 88 E Newton St 3rd Fl Boston MA 02118 Office Phone: 617-638-8702. Office Fax: 617-638-8770.

JACOBS, ARTHUR DIETRICH, health services executive, educator, researcher; b. Bklyn., Feb. 4, 1933; s. Lambert Dietrich and Paula Sophia (Knissel) Jacobs; m. Viva Jane Sims, Mar. 24, 1952; children: Archie(dec.), David L., Dwayne C., Dianna K. Hatfield. BBA, Ariz. State U., 1962, MBA, 1966. Enlisted USAF, 1951, commd. 2d lt., 1962, advanced through grades to maj., 1972, ret., 1973; indsl. engr. Motorola, Phoenix, 1973-74; mgmt. cons. State of Ariz., 1974-76,

Productivity Internat., Tempe, Ariz., 1976-79; faculty assoc. Coll. Bus. Adminstrn. Ariz. State U., Tempe, 1977-94, sr. lectr., 1995, ret., 1996. Productivity advisor Scottsdale Meml. Health Svcs. Co., Ariz., 1979—84; rschr. U.S. Internment of European-Am. Aliens and Citizens of European Ancestry during World War II. Author: (book) The Prison Called Hohenasperg: An American Boy Betrayed by His Government During World War II, 1999; editor, pub.: Freedom of Information Times; co-editor: The World War Two Experience - The Interment of German-Americans, Documents, vol. IV (now in spl. collections of USAF Acad.); contbr. Bd. dirs. United Way of Tempe, 1979—85. Recipient Meritorious Svc. award, Coll. Ozarks, Mo., 2000. Mem.: Ops. Rsch. Soc. Am., Inst. Indsl. Engrs. (pres.ctrl. Ariz. chpt. 1984—85), Am. Soc. Quality Control, Ariz. State U. Alumni Assn. (bd. dirs. 1973—79), Optimist (life), Delta Sigma Pi, Beta Gamma Sigma, Sigma Iota Epsilon. Achievements include research in the special collections of the United States Air Force Academy. Personal E-mail: adjacobs@cox.net.

JACOBS, BENJAMIN FRANKLIN, cardiologist; b. St. Louis, Oct. 2, 1942; MD, Tulane U., 1968. Intern Barnes Hosp., St. Louis, 1968-69, resident, 1969-70, VA Hosp., St. Louis, 1972-73; fellow in cardiology Ochsner Found. Hosp., New Orleans, 1973-75, staff cardiologist, 1975—78; with East Jefferson Gen. Hosp., Metairie, La., 1978—. Fellow Am. Coll. Cardiology. Office: 4200 Houma Blvd Metairie LA 70006-2970 Office Phone: 504-454-4102. E-mail: bfj3@aol.com.

JACOBS, ERIC J., epidemiologist, researcher; PhD in Epidemiology, U. Wash., 1996. Strategic dir. & sr. epidemiologist Am. Cancer Soc.

JACOBS, FRED M., hospital administrator, former state agency administrator; AB, Colgate U.; MD, U. Miami; JD, Rutgers U. Bar: N.J., Fla.; cert. internal medicine, pulmonary disease. Residency Maimonides Med. Ctr., Mt. Sinai Hosp., NYC; fellowship Univ. Calif. San Francisco Med. Ctr.; chief residency Kings County Hosp. Ctr., Bklyn.; chief pulmonary disease St. Barnabas Med. Ctr., NJ, pres. med. staff, sr. v.p. med. affairs; exec. v.p. med. affairs St. Barnabas Health Care Sys., NJ, exec. v.p., dir. quality inst., 2008—; commr. NJ Dept. Health & Sr. Svc., Trenton, 2004—08. Clinical assoc. prof. UMDNJ; mem. N.J. Bd. Med. Examiners; pres. N.J. Med. Examiners, 1993—95. Fellow: Am. Coll. Physicians, Am. Coll. Chest Physicians, Am. Coll. Legal Medicine; mem.: Alpha Omega Alpha. Office: St Barnabas Health Care Sys 95 Old Short Hills Rd West Orange NJ 07052

JACOBS, GEORGE BRAUN, neurosurgeon; b. Poland, Jan. 9, 1934; naturalized US citizen, 1954; s. Maurice and Lena J.; m. Rosanne Wille, 1980; children: Leigh, Steven, Alec. Jeffrey. Student, NYU, 1952-54; MD, SUNY, Syracuse, 1958; postgrad. in general surgery, Bronx Mcpl. Hosp., 1958-59; postgrad. in neurological surgery, Albert Einstein Coll. of Medicine, 1959-61. Cert. airline transport pilot, flight instr., sr. aviation med. examiner, FAA accident counselor. Attending neurosurgeon Hackensack Med. Ctr., NJ, 1965-86, sr. attending neurosurgeon, 1986—, chief neurosurgery sect., 1981-86; attending surgeon Holy Name Hosp., Teaneck, NJ, 1965, chief neurosurgery, 1976-81, 90-94; chief sect. neurosurgery Hackensack U. Med. Ctr., 1970-86, chief spine surgery, 1986—2001, chmn. dept. neurosurgery, chief spine surgery, 1986—2001; dir. spine svcs. Montefiore Med. Ctr. Albert Einstein Coll. Medicine, Bronx, 1992-93; prof. neurological surgery U. Pitts. Sch. Medicine, 1993-94, dir. spine ctr., spine surgery U. Pitts., 1993-94; prof. neurosurgery U. Medicine and Dentistry NJ, Newark, 1994—. Vis. prof. neurosurgery, U. Saigon, Vietnam, 1965-66; clin. asst. prof. neurosurgery, NJ Coll. Medicine, Newark, 1970-73; asst. prof. clin. neurosurgery, Albert Einstein Coll. Medicine, 1973-75; assoc. prof. clin. neurosurgery, 1975-89; prof. clin. neurosurgery, 1989-92, prof. neurosurgery, 1992-93; prof. neurosurgery, 1993-1994, prof. surgery NJ Med. Sch., UMDNJ, 1994-; spkr. numerous convs./cons. in field. Author: (novels) A Simple Twist of Fate, Freedom Quest, (textbooks) Medical Malpractice: A Guide to Medical Issues, 1986, Textbook of Operatives Spine Surgery, 1999; contbr. numerous articles to profl. jours. and publs. Fellow US Public Health Svc., 1959-60; bd. trustees Lehman Coll. Art Gallery, 1986-87; bd. dirs. Hackensack U. Med. Ctr. Found., 1997-2003, gov. bd. govs., 1979-2002; mem. Hillcrest Found. Bd., 1980-2002; bd. dirs. Lehman Coll. Art Gallery, 1986-87; hon. surgeon Police Dept. City of NY Decorated Army Commendation medal for Vietnam Svc., 1966; Disting. Svc. cert. of Merit Bd. of Chosen Freeholders of Bergen County, 1971. Fellow USPHS, Am. Coll. Surgeons, Am. Coll. Angiology, Internat. Coll. Angiology, Internat. Coll. Surgeons, Scoliosis Rsch. Soc., Cervical Spine Rsch. Soc., N.Am. Spine Soc.; mem. AMA, Internat. Soc. Pediatric Neurosurgery, Internat. Health Policy and Mgmt. Inst., Am. Pain Soc., Am. Assn. Neurol. Surgeons (chmn. liaison com. 1976-78), Bergen County Med. Soc. (trustee 1976, mem. judicial com. 1977-82, chmn. legis. com. 1980), Congress of Neurol. Surgeons, Assn. of Mil. Surgeons of US, NY Soc. Neurosurgery, Acad. Medicine NJ, NJ Neurosurg. Soc. (mem. exec. com. 1973, chmn. peer review com., 1974, pres. 1989-90), Fla. Med. Assn., Fla. Physicians Assn., Soc. Surgeons of NJ, Med. Soc. NJ, San Francisco Neurosurg. Soc. (corr.), others. Avocations: golf, aviation, boating, cooking. Address: 5506 Harbour Preserve Cir Cape Coral FL 33914

JACOBS, GORDON WALDEMAR, surgeon, educator; b. Cuero, Tex., May 30, 1933; s. Elmer Waldemar and Clara Esther Jacobs; m. Lorraine Maria Maguire, Oct. 24, 1970; children: Mary Lou Baker, Kristen Clara Goodman, Damien Gordon, Melanie Anne. BA, U. Iowa, 1955, MD, 1958; diploma in Tropical Medicine and Hygiene, U. Liverpool, 1983; diploma in French, Tng. Inst. for Execs., 1984. Diplomate Am. Bd. Surgery, 1972. Resident in surgery Loma Linda U., Riverside, Calif., 1959; intern U. Calif., Sacramento, 1958—59; locum tenens family practice Santa Barbara County Hosp., Calif., 1962; locum tenens gen. surgery Kaiser Permanente Hosp., Santa Clara, Calif., 1966, 1969; resident gen. surgery U. Calif., Oakland-Martinez, Calif., 1962—66; fellow gen. surgery Lahey Clinic, Boston, 1969—70; gen. surgeon Somerville (Mass.) Surg. Assocs., 1970—75; pvt. practice gen. surgeon Gordon W. Jacobs, Md, Vallejo, Calif., 1975, Berkeley, Calif., 1975—83, Lancaster, SC, 1986—88, Gordon W. Jacobs, Md Facs Pa, Charlotte, NC, 1989—2003, gen. surgeon locum tenens, 2003—. Missionary gen. surgeon Evang. Covenant Mission Hosp., Karawa, 1984—86; missionary gen. surgeon, instr. in surgery Evangelical Covenant Mission Hosp. & N.W. Teams Internat., Karawa, 2005, Bongolo Hosp., Pan African Acad. Christian Surgeons and N.W. Med. Teams Internat., Lebamba, Gabon, 2005—08, Bongolo Hosp., Pan African Acad. Christian Surgeons Cameroon, 2008—09; missionary gen. surgeon Luth. Mission Hosp., Madang, Papua New Guinea, 1966—69; missionary surgeon, instr. surgery Haile Selassie U. Med. Sch., Addis Ababa, Ethiopia, 1973—74, Pan African Acad. Christian Surgeons Ngaoundéré Protestant Hosp., Cameroon, 2009—10; with SIM, 2008—10. Contbr. articles to profl. jours. Pres. Oakland (Calif.) Uptown Toastmasters, 1980—81; active Big Bros., Boston, 1970—73; vol, med. dir. SIM (Serving in Missions); with Kibogora Hosp. Cyangugu Rwanda World med. Mission, 2010; vol. missionary surgeon Kibogora Hosp., 2010, Ngaoundere Protestant Hospital, 2010—; pres. Trinity Luth. Ch., Oakland, 1979—81; troop physician Boy Scouts Am., Charlotte, Calif., 1995. Capt. med. corp. US Army, 1960—62, Germany. Recipient Vol. Presdl. Svc. award, Northwest Med. Teams, 2007; named Presdl. Vol., 2009; named one of Notable Americans, Am. Biog. Inst., 1978, Cmty. Leaders & Noteworthy Americans, 1978, Personalities Of West & Midwest, 1978; named to Book Of Honor, 1978, Personalities Of Am., 1978, Men Of Achievement, Internat. Biog. Centre, 1979. Fellow: ACS, Am. Soc. Gen. Surgeons, S.E. Surg. Congress; mem.: AMA (chmn. com. medicine and religion Calif. chpt. 1980—81), Christian Med. & Dental Assn., Mecklenburg County Med. Soc., Charlotte Surg. Soc., N.C. Med. Soc. Republican. Avocations: woodworking, french studies, flying, exercise, gardening. Home and Office: Gordon W Jacobs Md Facs Pa 14920 Wyndham Oaks Drive Charlotte NC 28277 Business E-Mail: gordonjacobsmd@pol.net.

JACOBS, JOSHUA J., orthopaedic surgeon; b. Chgo., Apr. 6, 1956; s. Abraham F. and Bernice J.; m. Faye Robbins. BS in Material Sci. and Engring., Northwestern U., 1977; MD with hon., U. Ill., Chgo., 1981. Diplomate Am. Bd. Orthopaedic Surgery. Adj. attending Rush Med. Coll., Chgo., 1987—94, assoc. attending, 1994—97, sr. attending, prof. orthopaedic surgery, 1997—. Adj. prof. Northwestern U., Chgo., 1992—. Recipient Career Devel. award Orthopaedic Rsch. & Edn. Found. Fellow Am. Acad. Orthopaedic Surgery, Hip Soc. (Otto award); mem. ASTM (vice chmn.), Soc. Biomaterials. Office: Midwest Orthopaedics At Rush # 300 1611 W Harrison St Chicago IL 60612-4861

JACOBS, LAURENCE STANTON, physician, educator; b. Boston, Mar. 24, 1940; s. David W. and Sylvia Dorothea (Berenson) J.; m. Katherine Elizabeth Meyerand, Mar. 24, 1963; children: Karen Emily, Pamela Susan. AB magna cum laude, Harvard U., 1960; MD, U. Rochester, 1965. Diplomate Am. Bd. Internal. Medicine. Intern Barnes Hosp., St. Louis, 1965, resident, 1966-67; research fellow Washington U. Med. Sch., St. Louis, 1967-68, 70-72, asst. prof., 1972-77; assoc. prof. U. Rochester, 1977-82, prof., 1982-2000, prof. emeritus, 2000—, dir. Clin. Research Ctr., 1977-91, assoc. dean Sch. Medicine and Dentistry N.Y., 1990-94; dir. residency edn. Strong Meml. Hosp., 1990-94; researcher in field; prof. medicine emeritus U. Rochester Sch. of Medicine and Dentistry. Chmn. merit rev. bd. in endocrinology VA, Washington, 1983-86; mem. study sect. NIH, 1987-91. Contbr. articles to profl. publs., chpts. to books Served to lt. comdr. USPHS, 1968-70 Mem. Assn. Am. Medical Colls. (northeast group on student affairs), Assn. Clin. Research Ctr. Dirs. (treas., bd. dirs., pres.-elect, pres. 1987-89), Endocrine Soc. (sci. program com. 1983-85), Am. Fedn. for Clin. Research, Am. Soc. for Clin. Investigation, Internat. Soc. for Neuroendocrinology, N.Y. Acad. Scis., Am. Diabetes Assn., Am. Soc. Biochem. and Molecular Biol., Alpha Omega Alpha. Avocations: skiing, ice skating, sailing. E-mail: lsjacobsnynm@msn.com.

JACOBS, MICHAEL JOHN, surgeon; b. Feb. 17, 1969; MD, St. George, 1996. Pvt. practice, 2001—. Named one of America's Top Surgeons, 2010. Fellow: ACS; mem.: AMA. Office: 26850 Providence Pky Ste 504 Novi MI 48374 Office Fax: 248-662-3022. Business E-Mail: brandy.lapko@stjohn.org.

JACOBS, RICHARD FULLER, pediatrics and pediatric infectious disease educator; b. Arkadelphia, Ark., May 1, 1952; s. Robert Earl and Addye Lou (Fuller) J.; m. Margaret Ann Pennington; 1 child, Robert Fuller. BS, Henderson State U., 1973; MD, U. Ark., 1977. Cert. Am. Bd. Pediatrics, 1982, Ark., Am. Bd. Pediatric Infectious Diseases, 1994. Asst. prof. pediatrics U. Ark. Med. Sci., Little Rock, 1982-85, assoc. prof. pediatrics, 1985-92, prof. pediatrics, 1992—, Horace C. Cabe prof. pediatrics, 1993—. Editl. bd. mem. Infectious Diseases Newsletter, 1989, The Pediatric Infectious Diseases Jour., 1992, Seminars in Respiratory Infections, 1992, Report on Pediatric Infectious Diseases, 1993. Bd. dirs. KLRE Radio Sta., Little Rock, 1985-91, St. James United Meth. Ch., Little Rock, 1986-90; mem. Ark. Advs. for Children, Little Rock, 1986—. Fellow Royal Soc. Pediatrics of the Philippines (hon.); mem. So. Soc. for Pediatric Rsch. (pres./councillor 1985—, instnl. rep. 1988—, Young Investigator award 1982), Am. Acad. Pediatrics (spkr., com. mem. 1989—), Am. Thoracic Soc. (sec./liaison 1984—, nat. nominating com. 1990-93), Pediatric Infectious Diseases Soc. (councillor 1993—, treas. 1994—), Soc. for Pediatric Rsch. Avocations: golf, fishing, hunting, travel. Office: Ark Childrens Hosp 800 Marshall St Little Rock AR 72202-3591 *

JACOBS, STEFAN, psychology professor; b. Magdeburg, Germany, Apr. 4, 1943; s. Kurt and Eva Jacobs; m. Brigitte Ritter, Aug. 30, 1974; 1 child, Raoul Stephan. Diploma in psychology, U. Cologne, 1969; PhD, U. Bonn, 1973. Asst. prof. U. Cologne, Germany, 1970—72; clin. psychologist U. Hannover, 1972—74; prof. U. Goettingen, 1974—2008. Co-author (with J. Bosse-Düker) Behavior Modification Hypnosis: A Short Time Program for the Treatment of Chronic Pain, 2005; co-author: (with A. de jong) EMDR and Biofeedback in the Treatment of Posttraumatic Stress Disorder, 2007; editor: Neuroscience and the Treatment of PTSD, 2009. Recipient Rsch. prize, NSF, 2004. Mem.: German Soc. Client-Centered Psychotherapy, German Soc. Behavior Modification, German Psychol. Assn. (v.p. 1990—92). Office: Pain Ctr Weenderstr 27 Goettingen 37073 Germany Office Phone: 049551 40144002. Business E-Mail: sjacobs@uni-goettingen.de.

JACOBS, TIMOTHY ANDREW, epidemiologist, consultant; b. St. Petersburg, Fla., Nov. 5, 1944; s. W. Andrew and Virginia (Ott) J.; m. Carolyn Martin, Nov. 4, 1972; 1 child, Jenny Thuy Ha. BSN, U. Fla., 1970; MS, PNP, U. Utah, 1976; PhD, Internat. Inst. Advanced Studies, 1979; C.T.M., Liverpool Sch. Medicine, Eng., 1982; cert. hosp. epidemiology, U. Iowa, 1985; MPH, Yale U., 1991. Nat. design and media cons. Nat. Assn. Pediatric Nurse Assocs. and Practitioners, Cherry Hill, NJ, 1977-83; asst. prof., co-coord. community health nursing U. N.D., Grand Forks, 1980; vol. epidemiologist, pub. health specialist Vinh Children's Hosp., Vinh City, Vietnam, 1989; pediatric staff nurse I U. Fla. Pediatric Svc., Shands Teaching Hosp., Gainesville, 1970; instr. pediatric nursing U. Utah Coll. Nursing, Salt Lake City, 1976-77; pvt. cons. Internat. Cmty. Health and Epidemiology, New Haven, 1990-94; med. supr., health svcs. mgr. Brown & Root Logcap Med. Clinic, Port-au-Prince, Haiti, 1994-95; med. tech. proposal cons. UN, Rwanda, Angola, 1995; specialist Home Health Care, Tampa, Fla., 1996—. Vol. pub. health scientist, cons. Hanoi (Vietnam) Sch. Pub. Health; cons. epidemiologist Vinh and Huong Son, Vietnam, 1993; internat. edn. cons. U. Am., New Orleans, 1994; cons. infectious disease epidemiology, consulate of Nicaragua, Miami, Health for Health Svcs. Hurricane Mitch, 1998; cons. Christian Haitian Outreach Clinics and Orphanages, Jeremie and Mariani, Haiti, 1998—; pediatric clin. planner and designer, Carrafour, Haiti, 2002; prin. designer Ambulatory Primary Care Clinic, Mariani, Haiti, 2002; trustee and dean academic affairs and prof. pub. health Burnett Internat. U. Sch. Medicine and Health Scis., Port-au-Prince, 2004, St. Kitts, BWI, 2009. Contbg. editor Episource, 1991, 97, Resources in Epidemiology; contbr. articles to profl. jours.; contbr. to poetry jours.; anthologies Daybreak on the Land, 1997, Audiotape Sounds of Poetry, 1997, Archive of the Vietnam Conflict, Personal Papers Collection, 1999. Donor, contbr. Asian Family and Comty. Empowerment Ctr., St. Petersburg, Fla., Caribbean Mercy, Mercy Ships, Garden Valley, Tex., 2001, Love a Child Orphanage and Med. Clinic, Fond Parisien, Haiti, 2001-02. Capt. Nurse Corps, U.S. Army, 1968-73, Vietnam. Recipient Cert. of Achievement in HIV-AIDS Edn., AIDS Project, New Haven, Conn., 1994, Editor's Choice award for outstanding achievement in poetry Nat. Libr. Poetry, 1997. Fellow Royal Soc. Tropical Medicine and Hygiene (London), Am. Biog. Inst. (advisor, rsch. adv. bd.); mem. AMA, VFW, Am. Legion, Vietnam Vets. Am., Nat. Assn. Pediatric Nurse Assocs. and Practitioners (com. dir. graphics & logos mil. chpt., former chmn. nat. art and exhibits subcom., former mem. pub. rels. com., Cert. Recognition 1983), Am. Pub. Health Assn. (epidemiology sect., internat. healthsect., mem. caucus pub. health and faith cmty.), Internat. Assn. Med. Assistance to Travellers, Fla. Pub. Health Assn., Nat. Adolescent Health Promotion Network, Assn. Mil. Surgeons U.S., Ret. Army Nurse Corps Assn., Liverpool Tropical Sch. Assn. (Eng.), Assn. Yale Alumni in Pub. Health, Consortium for Internat. Nursing Edn., Rsch. & Practice, U.S.-Vietnam Friendship Assn., Doctorate Assn. N.Y. Educators, Fleet Marine Force Corpsman Assn. (former Conn. rep., charter mem.), U.S. Navy Corpsmen United Assn., Am. Assn. Navy Hosp. Corpsmen, U.S. Army (Vietnam) 24th Evacuation Hosp. Assn. (com. asv. reunion 1993), Vets. Vietnam Restoration Project, U.S. Com. Scientific Cooperation with Vietnam, N.Y. Acad. of Sci., Walter Reed Army Med. Ctr. Soc. (charter), Spl. Ops. Med. Assn., Soaring Soc. Am., Tampa Bay Soaring Soc. (student pvt. pilot), Sigma Xi, Sigma Theta Tau (charter mem. Gamma Rho chpt.), Phi Kappa Phi. Avocations: racewalking, fishing, travel. Home: 11333 Calgary Cir Tampa FL 33624-4804 Home Phone: 813-269-9094; Office Phone: 813-269-9094. Personal E-mail: cpidoc91@tampabay.rr.com.

JACOBSEN, KLAUS, retired orthopaedic surgeon, consultant, researcher; b. Frederiksberg, Copenhagen, Denmark, Mar. 23, 1939; s. Christian and Signe Henriette Margrethe (Skjold) J.; m. Kirsten Klinge Sørensen, Oct. 14, 1961; children: Jørgen Henrik, Jacob, Mår MD, U. Copenhagen, 1965, PhD in Surgery, 1981. Diplomate in. gen practice, orthop. surgery. Sr. registrar Orthop. Hosp., Copenhagen, 1979—80; sr. registrar neurosurgery dept. Glostrup Hosp., Copenhagen, 1980—81; sr. registrar orthop. surgery Rigshosp., Copenhagen, 1981—83, Frederiksberg Hosp., 1984, head dept. orthop., sr. cons., 1986—97; asst. cons. dept. orthop. Gentofte Hosp., Denmark, 1985; chief arctic Inuit Hosp in Qaanaaq, Thule, Greenland, 1997—2006; ret., 2006. Lectr. Copenhagen U., 1984—85, Danish Orthop. Soc., 1973—97. Author: Klaus Jacobsen: Stress Radiography of the Human Knee, 1981, (with others) Danish Textbooks of Surgery, 1987, 96, 99, Of Alsian Peasant Stock, 2002, The Time of our Fathers, 2004; contbr. articles to profl. jours Grantee Danish Med. Rsch. Coun., 1972-74, Danish Coun. for Sports Rsch., 1974, Found. for the Handicapped, 1974, Poul Guildahl Found., 1981 Mem. Danish Orthop. Soc. (exec. com. 1986-90, chmn. 1988-90), Danish Surg. Soc., Scandinavian Orthop. Soc., European Soc. Knee Surgery and Arthroscopy Avocations: drawing, wood carving, sailing, skiing, husky dogs. Home: Hegnstoften 10 DK 2630 Taastrup Denmark

JACOBSON, BARRY FRANK, hematologist, consultant; s. Marx and Hilda Jacobson; m. Deborah Shapiro, Dec. 16, 1999; 1 child, Sarah Danielle. MB, BChir, U. Pretoria, 1980; MMed in Haematology, U. Witwatersrand, Johannesburg, 1992, PhD, 1992. Head clin. haematology Nat. Health Lab. Svc., Johannesburg, Gauteng, 1998—; head surg. rsch. unit U. Witwatersrand, Johannesburg, Gauteng, 1998—. Med. chmn. Jewish Helping Hand, Johannesburg, 2000—05. Lt., 1982—84, South African Med. Def. Recipient Protea Holding prize, U. Pretoria, 1980. Fellow: Royal Coll. Surgeons Glasgow; mem.: South African Soc. Haemostasis and Thrombosis (pres. 2003—05), South African Soc. Haematology (assoc.), South African Soc. Aviation Medcine (life), Surg. Rsch. Soc. So. African (pres. 2003—05, Davis and Geck Rsch. award 1986). Jewish. Achievements include research in aviation and thrombosis, sclerotherapy of esophageal varices, asprin resistence, deep vein thrombosis. Office: Univ Witwatersrand Rm 21 Area 454 Jhb Hosp Gauteng Johannesburg 2193 South Africa Home: 406 Houghton Heights 56 Second Ave 2198 Lower Houghton, Johannesburg 2198 South Africa Office Fax: +27114898513. Business E-Mail: clot@nhls.ac.za.

JACOBSON, HARRY RUDOLF, hospital administrator, physician; MD, U. Ill., 1972. Resident, internal medicine Johns Hopkins University; resident, nephrology U. Tex. Health Sci. Ctr.; chief, nephrology U.S. Army Surg. Rsch. Ctr., Brooke Army Med. Ctr., 1976—78; faculty mem. U. Tex. Southwestern Med. Sch., Dallas, 1978—81; prof., medicine, dir., nephrology divsn. Vanderbilt Med. Sch., 1981—97, CEO, vice chancellor, health affairs, 1997—. Bd. dirs. Nashville Health Care Coun., Mid. Tenn. Coun., Boy Scouts Am., Health Gate, Inc., CSA, Inc., Renal Care Group, Kinetic Concepts, Inc. Contbr. articles to profl. jours.; co-editor: The Principles and Practice of Nephrology. Mem.: Inst. Medicine, Soc. Med. Adminstrs. (pres.), Assn. Am. Physicians, Am. Soc. Clin. Investigation. Office: Vanderbilt University Medical Center 21st Ave S and Medical Center Dr Nashville TN 37232 Office Phone: 615-322-5000. Business E-Mail: hjacobson@vanderbilt.edu. *

JACOBSON, HOWARD NEWMAN, obstetrics and gynecology educator, researcher; b. St. Paul, Aug. 13, 1923; s. Irvin Oliver and Nora Henrietta (Olson) J.; m. Barbara Jane Dinger, Aug. 20,1961. BSc in Medicine, Northwestern U., Chgo., 1947, BM, 1950, MD, 1951. Intern Presbyn. Hosp., Chgo., 1950-51, resident in ob-gyn, 1951-52; fellow, rsch. fellow in obstetrics, mem. family clinic Harvard Sch. Pub. Health, Boston, 1952-55; resident Boston Lying-In Hosp. and Free Hosp. for Women, Brookline, Mass., 1955-58; obstetrician, physiologist Lab. Neuroanat. Scis., Nat. Inst. Nervous Disease and Blindness, NIH, Bethesda, Md., 1958-60; instr., asst. prof. Harvard Med. Sch., Boston, 1960-65; assoc. prof. U. Calif., San Francisco, Berkeley, 1965-69; dir. Macy program Med. Sch. Harvard U., 1969-74; prof. dept. cmty. medicine Coll. Medicine and Dentistry NJ, Piscataway, NJ, 1974-78; dir. Inst. Nutrition, clin. prof. U. NC, Chapel Hill, 1978-88; rsch. prof. Coll. Pub. Health U. So. Fla., 1988—2003; prof. dept. ob-gyn U. South Fla. Med. Sch., Tampa, 1990-96, facilitator spl. programs Health Sci. Ctr., 1996—2003. Cons. Children's Bur., HEW, Washington, 1964-73, GAO, Washington, 1974-83, AMA, 1980-82, 88—; mem. food and nutrition bd. NRC/NAS, Washington, 1971-74; prof. dept. biology and Sch. Home Econs., U. N.C., Greensboro, 1978-88, Ellen Swallow Richards lectr., 1978; cons. pregnancy and nutrition study U. Minn., Mpls., 1979—; adj. prof. dept. food, nutrition and instn. mgmt. East Carolina U. Sch. Home Econs., Greenville, 1981-88; mem. nutrition grad. faculty N.C. State U., Raleigh, 1979-88. Contbr. over 130 articles and abstracts to FMA Today, Jour. Nurse-Midwifery, Clin. Nutrition, Contemporary Internal Medicine, Food and Nutrition News, Nutrition Today, New Eng. Jour. Medicine, chpt. to books. Panel vice chmn. White House Conf. on Food, Nutrition and Health, Washington, 1969; chmn. Quality of Life Conf., Mass. Med. Soc., Boston, 1972; mem. hunger com. Episcopal Ch. S.W. Fla., 1990-94; mem. Fla. Health Start Initiative working Group, 1991—. Lt. (j.g.) USNR, 1943-46, PTO. Recipient Agnes Higgins award March of Dimes and APHA, 1987; recipient Career Devel. award NIH, 1963-65. Fellow Am. Coll. Ob-Gyn (assoc.); mem. Am. Soc. Clin. Nutrition, Am. Physiol. Soc., Mass. Med. Soc. (chmn. commn. 1972-74), Fla. Pub. Health Assn. (chmn. sect. 1990-91), Am. Dietetic Assn. (hon.). Democrat. Achievements include co-develop. of guides for clin. nutrition studies, portable ultrasound for body composition; co-determination of nature of cardiovasc. changes at birth; co-intro. of computer assisted methodology in nutrition; co-initiation of modern nutrition standards for healthy pregnancy. Office: U South Fla Coll Pub Health 13201 Bruce B Downs Blvd Tampa FL 33612-3805

JACOBSON, IRA M., gastroenterologist, educator; BS summa cum laude, Yale U., 1975; MD, Columbia U., 1979. Diplomate Am. Bd. Internal Medicine, Am. Bd. Internal Medicine-gastroenterology, Am. Bd. Internal Medicine-transplant hepatology. Intern internal medicine Univ. of Calif., San Francisco, resident internal medicine, 1980—82; fellow gastroenterology Mass. Gen. Hosp., Boston, 1982—84; prof. medicine Weill Cornell Med. Coll., NYC; attending physician NY-Presbyn. Hosp. Author (books): ERCP: Its Application, 1998, ERCP: Diagnostic and Therapeutic Applications, 1989, and numerous others. Recipient award for Excellence in Clin. Medicine, Herbert J. Bartelsone Award in Pharmacology, Urology prize, Dr. Harold B. Stevelman Award in Cardiology, and numerous others. Mem.: NY Gastroenterological Assn. (pres.), NY Soc. for Gastrointestinal Endoscopy (pres.). Office: New York Presbyterian 1305 York Ave 4th Fl New York NY 10021 Office Phone: 646-962-4040. Office Fax: 646-962-0433.

JACOBSON, JULIUS H., II, vascular surgeon, writer; m. Joan Jacobson. AS, U. Toledo, 1947; MS in Cell Physiology, U. Pa.; MD, John Hopkins Sch. Medicine, 1952. Resident, gen. and thoracic surgery Columbia-Presbyn. Hosp., NY; dir. surg. rsch. U. Vt.; dir. emeritus, vascular surgery Mt. Sinai Med. Ctr., NY, disting. svc. prof. surgery. Established Joan L. and Julius H. Jacobson II Professorship Pub. Health Harvard Sch. Pub. Health. Author: (Book) The Classical Music Experience, 2001. Named in his honor, Julius H. Jacobson, II award, Vascular Disease Found., 2004. Fellow: Am. Coll. Surgeons. Preeminent pioneer in microsurgery; first surgeon to bring a microscope into the operating room for the entire range of surgery beyond the eye and ear; developed the first microscope "diploscope" that allowed the surgeon and first assistant to view the operative field simutaneously (now in a collection at the Smithsonian Institution); widely renowned as the inventor of microsurgery, the technique that accounts for half of all neurosurgeries performed in the US; established professorships in vascular surgery(with wife) at John Hopkins University, Hadassah-Hebrew University School of Medicine, Jerusalem, Mount Sinai Medical Center, NY, and (endowed professorship in Biomedical Research) University of Toledo. Address: 1125 Fifth Ave New York NY 10128 Home Phone: 212-289-1417; Office Phone: 212-289-1417. E-mail: jhjdoc@pipeline.com.

JACOBSON, MARC STEPHEN, pediatrician, educator; b. June 25, 1947; BA, U. Kans., 1969, MD, 1973. Diplomate Am. Bd. Pediatrics; lic. physician, Kans., Mo., Md., N.Y. Resident in pediatrics U. Kans., Kansas City, 1973-77; fellow in adolescent medicine U. Md., Balt., 1977-79, asst. prof. pediatrics, 1979-85, dir. adolescent ambulatory clinic, 1980-85, asst. dir. adolescent medicine div., 1981-85, dir. nutrition lab., 1981-85; attending physician Schneider Children's Hosp., New Hyde Park, N.Y., 1985—, dir. atherosclerosis prevention ctr., 1986—. Asst. prof. pediat. SUNY, Stony Brook, 1985-89; asst. prof. Albert Einstein Coll. Medicine, Bronx, N.Y., 1989, assoc. prof., 1991—; lectr., cons. in field. Ad hoc reviewer Annals of Internal Medicine, 1992—; contbr. abstracts and articles to profl. jours. Mem. women's, infants and children nutrition adv. bd. Md. Dept. Mental Health and Hygiene, Balt., 1982-84; bd. dirs. L.I. Heart Coun., 1986, mem. exec. com., 1989-92, pres., 1993—. Grantee Bressler Fund, 1983-85, HHS Materna and Child Health, 1984-87, L.I. Jewish Med. Ctr., 1986, 88-92, Am. Heart Asn. Nassau County, 1986-87, S.L.E. Found., 1986-88, Merck Sharpe and Dohme, 1990-91. Fellow Am. Acad. Pediatrics (nutrition com. 1985—, chmn. 1987—); mem. AAAC, Am. Heart Assn., Queens Pediatric Soc., N.Y. Acad. Sci., Soc. Adolescent Medicine (jour. adv. com. 1993—), Nassau County Pediatric Soc., Soc. Pediatric Rsch. Office: 833 Northern Blvd Ste 230 Great Neck NY 11021 Home Fax: 516-558-1120.

JACOBSON, STANLEY, biologist, educator; b. Chgo., Aug. 24, 1937; BS in Zoology, U. Ill., 1959; PhD in Anatomy, Northwestern U., 1963. Rsch. biologist NIH Divsn. Neuroanat. Scis., 1963—65, VA Rsch. Hosp. Chgo., 1965—67; prof. anatomy & cellular biology dept. anatomy Tufts U. Health Scis. Campus, 1967—. Fulbright fellow, US Dept. of State. Mem.: AAAS, Am. Assn. U. Profs., Assn. Med. Edn. in Europe, Am. Assn. Anatomists, Soc. Neurosci. Avocations: hiking, motorcycling, golf, travel, photography. Office: 136 Harrison Ave Boston MA 02111 Office Fax: 617-636-6536. Business E-Mail: stan.jacobson@tufts.edu.

JACOBSON, SUSAN BOGEN, psychotherapist; b. Far Rockaway, NY, June 19, 1957; d. Paul and Blanche (Itzkowitz) Bogen; m. Adam Hartley Jacobson. BS in Bus. Adminstrn., SUNY, Albany, 1977; MS in Mental Health Counseling, Nova U., Ft. Lauderdale, Fla., 1992. Nat. cert. counselor; lic. mental health counselor, Fla., Diplomate profl. counseling, 2008. Pvt. pactice psychotherapist, Boca Raton, Fla., 1992—; instr. CCM Partnerships, Inc., Delray Beach, Fla., 1995—. Officer Coun. for Marriage Preservation and Divorce Resolution, Boca Raton, 1995; mem. 15th Judicial Cir. Ctl Arbitration Com. for Fla. Bar, 1999-2000. Bd. dirs. Aid for Victims of Domestic Assault, 1998. Mem.: ACA. Avocations: swimming, boating, gourmet cooking. Office: 23123 State Rd 7 ste 305C Boca Raton FL 33428 Office Phone: 561-912-0190. Personal E-mail: sueshrink1@aol.com, sueshrink1@gmail.com.

JACOBY, IRVING, physician; b. NYC, Sept. 30, 1947; s. Philip Aaron and Sylvia Jacoby; m. Sara Kay Vartanian; children: James Tyler, Kathryn Aaryn. BS magna cum laude, U. Miami, Coral Gables, Fla., 1969; MD, Johns Hopkins U., 1973. Diplomate Am. Bd. Internal Medicine, Am. Bd. Infectious Diseases, Am. Bd. Emergency Medicine, Am. Bd. Preventive Medicine (undersea and hyperbaric medicine). Intern Boston City Hosp., 1973-74, resident in medicine, 1974-75, chief resident, 1978-79; resident in medicine Peter Bent Brigham Hosp., Boston, 1975-76, fellow in infectious diseases, 1976-78; asst. dir. emergency med. svcs. U. Mass. Med. Ctr., Worcester, 1979-84; attending physician dept. emergency med. U. Calif., San Diego Med. Ctr., 1984—, assoc. prof. med. surgery, 1988-94, hosp. dir. for emergency preparedness and response, 2003—10, prof. med. surgery, 1994—2010, emeritus prof., 2010—; with Disaster Deployments Northridge EQ, 1984, Centennial Olympics Atlanta, Ga., 1986, Floods, Grand Forks, ND, 1998, Terrorist Attack WTC NY, 2001, Supertyphoon Pongsona Guam, 2002, Hurricane Katrina, 2005, Hurricanes Gustav Ikc, La., 2008. Attending physician Hyperbaric Med. Ctr., 1985—; vis. physician, cons. infectious diseases Soroka Med. Ctr., Ben Gurion U., Beer-Sheva, Israel, 1980; flight physician New Eng. Life Flight, Worcester, 1982-84, Life Flight Aeromed. Program U. Calif., 1984-87. Sect. editor for disaster medicine Jour. Emergency Medicine, 1996—; assoc. editor Undersea and Hyperbaric Medicine, 1996-2002. Comdr. Disaster Med. Assistance Team CA-4, 1991-. Fellow ACP, Am. Coll. Emergency Physicians, Am. Acad. Emergency Medicine; mem. Am. Soc. Microbiology, Infectious Diseases Soc. Am., Nat. Assn. Disaster Med. Assistance Teams (vice chair 1999, chmn. 2000-01), Soc. Acad. Emergency Medicine, Undersea and Hyperbaric Med. Soc., World Assn. for Disaster and Emergency Medicine, Disaster Emergency Response Assn., Johns Hopkins Med. and Surg. Assn., Iron Arrow Leadership Soc., Omicron Delta Kappa, Phi Kappa Phi, Alpha Epsilon Delta, Phi Eta Sigma. Office: U Calif Med Ctr 200 W Arbor Dr San Diego CA 92103-8676 Office Phone: 619-543-6216.

JACOBY, WILLIAM JEROME, JR., retired military officer, internist; b. Mt. Carmel, Pa., Aug. 9, 1925; s. William Jerome and Florence Marie Jacoby; m. Joeann J. Powroznick, May 5, 1956; children: William Jerome, Teresa Marie. AB, Emory U., 1946; MD, Jefferson Med. Coll., 1950. Diplomate Am. Bd. Internal Medicine. Commd. lt. (j.g.) M.C., USN, 1950, advanced through grades to rear adm., 1972; intern Jefferson Med. Coll. Hosp., Phila., 1950-51, resident in internal medicine, 1951-52, 55-56; Am. Heart Assn. fellow, 1956-57; chmn. dept. medicine U.S. Naval Hosps. Gt. Lakes, Ill., 1964-69, Phila., 1969-72; chmn. dept. medicine, dir. edn. and rsch. Nat. Naval Med. Ctr., Bethesda, Md., 1972-75; comdg. officer Naval Regional Med. Ctr., Portsmouth, Va., 1975-78; dir. med. svcs. VA Cen. Office, Washington, 1978-80, dep. chief med. dir., 1980-83. Assoc. clin. prof. Jefferson Med. Coll., 1969—; prof. medicine George Washington U. Med. Sch., 1972, Eastern Va. Sch. Medicine, Norfolk, 1976-78; mem. adv. coun. Nat. Heart, Lung and Blood Inst., NIH, 1972-75. Contbr. articles to profl. jours. Decorated Legion of Merit, Meritorious Svc. medal. Fellow ACP (Laureate award 1996); mem. Assn. Mil. Surgeons (Founders medal 1974), Alpha Omega Alpha, Phi Beta Pi. Roman Catholic. Home: 737 E Tazewells Way Williamsburg VA 23185-6521

JACONO, ANDREW A., facial plastic surgeon; MD Otorhinolaryngology, Albert Einstein Coll. of Medicine, NYC. Cert. American Bd. of Facial Plastic and Reconstructive Surgery, Am. Bd. Otolaryngology. Intern St. Vincent's Hosp. and Med. Ctr., New York City; surgical resident New York Eye and Ear Infirmary, New York City, chief adminstr. resident; asst. prof. facial plastic and reconstructive surgery NY Eye and Ear Infirmary, NYC; asst. prof. head and neck surgery Albert Einstein Coll. Medicine, NYC. Sect. head facial plastic & reconstructive surgery North Shore U. Hosp., Manhasset, NY, 2007—. Author: (medical lit.) topics including minimal incision eyelid surgery, endoscopic (telescopic) minimally invasive brow lifting, endoscopic midface and face lifting surgery, rhinoplasty and revision rhinoplasty, lip augmentation, orbital reconstruction, Face the Facts the truth About Facial Surgery Procedures that Do & Dont Work, 2006. Volunteer surgeon Beyond Our Borders; nat. chmn. Face to Face Charity Domestic Violence Am. Acad. Facial Plastic and Reconstructive Surgery; chair About Face: Making Changes, 2003—11; vol. Surgeon Healing the Children. Recipient William H. Turner, excellence in surgical and patient care skills, Ten Leaders in Plastic Surgery in Long Island, The New York Times, One of America's Top Plastic Surgeons, The Consumer Rsch. Coun. of America, 2007, Good Guy, Ctr. for the Women of New York, 2006; fellow American Academy of Facial Plastic and Reconstructive Surgery, American Coll. of Surgeons. Achievements include He is one of a small group of surgeons that has achieved Dual Board Certification in Facial Plastic and Reconstructive Surgery as well as Head and Neck Surgery; has appeared on ABC's Good Morning America, Inside Edition, CNN, CNBC and WB 11 News and he has conducted radio interviews on NPR, 1010 Wins and WCBS Radio. Office: NY Ctr for Facial Plastic and Laser Surgery 440 Northern Blvd Great Neck NY 11021 Office Phone: 516-773-4646. Business E-Mail: drjacono@newyorkfacialplasticsurgery.com.

JACQUOT, SERGE E., medical researcher; b. Dijon, France, Nov. 18, 1959; s. Bernard Lucien Jacquot and Colette Fanny Picard. MD, Paris U., 1989, PhD, 1998. Asst. prof. Paris U., 1989—94; rsch. assoc. Dana Farber Cancer Inst., Harvard U., Boston, 1994—99; assoc. prof. Rouen U. Med. Sch., 1999—. Capt. French Mil. Mem.: Am. Assn. Immunologists. Home: 8 rue Perciere 76000 Rouen France Office: Rouen U Sch Medicine 22 Blvd Gambetta 76183 Rouen France Home Phone: 33 2 35 98 1732; Office Phone: 33 2 3288 8071. Business E-Mail: serge.jacquot@chu-rouen.fr.

JADAON, MEHREZ MAHFOOD, medical researcher, educator; b. Kuwait, Aug. 18, 1969; s. Mahfood Mehrez Jadaon and Nadia Ibrahim Nasrallah; m. Hend Lewis Lewis, July 24, 2004; children: Stephanie Mehrez, Mahfooz Mehrez. MSc in Patholgy, Haematology, Faculty Medicine, Kuwait U., Jabriya, 1998; BSc in Med. Lab. Scis., Faculty Allied Health Scis. Kuwait U., Jabriya, 2004. Med. lab. technologist Farwaniya Govt. Hosp. Ministry Health, Kuwait, 1994—95; tchg. asst. pathology Faculty Medicine, Kuwait U., 1995—2004; lectr. Med. Lab. Scis. Dept. Faculty of Allied Health Scis. Kuwait U., 2004—. Secondment Haematology Lab. Mubarak Al-Kabeer Govt. Hosp. Ministry Health, Jabriya, Kuwait, 2000—. Contbr. scientific papers to profl. jours. Rsch. grant, Kuwait U., 2007—09. Mem.: Assoc. Molecular Pathology, Internat. Soc. Lab. Haematology, Internat. Soc. Fibrinolysis and Proteolysis, Internat. Soc. Thrombosis and Haemostasis. Achievements include development of simple whole blood PCR method, factor V Kuwait, origin of factor V Leiden in Kuwait, SHV-112 & SHV-122 mutations. Avocations: reading, writing, swimming. Office: Allied Health Kuwait Univ MLS PO Box 31470 Sulaibekhat 90805 Kuwait Office Fax: 00965-24983835. Personal E-mail: al3adawia@yahoo.com. Business E-Mail: mehrez@hsc.edu.kw.

JADVAR, HOSSEIN, nuclear radiologist, biomedical engineer; b. Tehran, Iran, Apr. 6, 1961; arrived in U.S., 1978, naturalized, 1995; s. Ramezan Ali and Fatemeh (Afzal) Jadvar; m. Mojgan Maher, 1995; children: Donya S., Delara A. BS, Iowa State U., Ames, 1982; MS, U. Wis., Madison, 1984, U. Mich., Ann Arbor, 1986, PhD, 1988; MD, U. Chgo., 1993; MPH, Harvard U., Boston, 2005; MBA, U. So. Calif., LA, 2007; student, U. Cambridge, Eng., 2007, U. Oxford, 2008, U. Pa., Wharton, 2009. Diplomate Am. Bd. Nuc. Medicine, Bd. Nuc. Cardiology. Rsch. asst. dept. human oncology U. Wis., Madison, 1983-84; rsch. asst. dept. elec. engring. U. Mich., Ann Arbor, 1984-88; sr. rsch. engr. Arzco Med. Electronics, Inc., Chgo., 1988-89; sr. rsch. assoc. Pritzker Inst., Ill. Inst. Tech., Chgo., 1989-92; med. intern U. Calif., San Francisco, 1993-94; resident in radiology Stanford (Calif.) U., 1994-96, resident in nuclear medicine, 1996-98, chief resident in nucelar medicine, 1997-98; clin. fellow in radiology (positron emission tomography) Harvard Med. Sch., Boston, 1998-99; asst. prof. radiology and biomed. engring. U. So. Calif., LA, 1999—2005, assoc. prof. radiology and biomed. engring., 2005—, dir. rsch. radiology, 2006—. Reviewer study sect. small bus innovative rsch. program NIH, 1989, med. imaging, 2005—, In Vivo Cellular and Molecular Imaging Ctrs., 2007—; vis. assoc. bioengring. Calif. Inst. Tech., Pasadena, 2001—; fellow clin. effectiveness program Sch. Pub. Health Harvard U., Boston, 2003; mem. radioactive drug rsch. com. FDA, 2003—; faculty fellow Ctr. Excellence in Rsch. U. So. Calif., 2007—10; guest editor Molecular Imaging Prostate Cancer, 2009, Pet Clinic. Author (with J.A. Parker): Clinical PET and PET-CT, 2005; mem. editl. bd. Clin. Nuc. Medicine, 2007—; asst. editor sect. nuc. medicine and molecular imaging: Am. Jour. Roentgenology, 2008—; contbr. chapters to books, articles to profl. jours. Recipient Resident Rsch. award, NIH, 1994, Best Drs. America, 2011—; named Top Dr., Pasedena Mag., 2010; grantee, Am. Cancer Soc., The Wright Found., NIH/Nat. Cancer Inst. Fellow: Am. Coll. Nuc. Medicine (faculty New Orleans 2000, faculty Tampa 2001, faculty Scottsdale 2002, faculty San Antonio 2006, sci. sessions chmn. 2008, bd. reps.), Am. Coll. Nuc. Physicians (bd. regents); mem.: IEEE (sr.), Pet Ctr. Excellence (v.p. 2011—), Annual SNM Sci. Meeting (vice chair 2011—), LA Radiol. Soc. (faculty 2002, pres. nuc. medicine sect. 2007—11, sci. program chmn. 2010, sci. chmn. Nuc. Med. Update 2010), Calif. Med. Assn. (nuc. med. sci. com. 2002—05), Computers in Cardiology (local organizing com. 1990), Acad. Molecular Imaging (mem. editl. bd. Molecular Imaging and Biology 2004—), Soc. Nuc. Medicine (mem. editl. bd. Jour. Nuc. Medicine 2006—, mem. house of delegates 2009—, pres., Pacific SW Chpt. 2009—11, sci. program chmn. western regional 2010, bd. dirs. 2010—, v.p. 2011—, mem. pub. and govt. rels. com., Tetalman Young Investigator award 2000, seed grant award 2000, Disting. Scientist award Western Regional 2010), Radiol. Soc. N.Am. (Resident Rsch. award 1997, seed grant award 2002), Eta Kappa Nu, Sigma Xi, Tau Beta Pi (assoc. editor in radiology 2010—). Achievements include patents for esophgeal catheters and method and apparatus for detection of posterior ischemia. Office: U So Calif Divsn Nuc Medicine Dept Radiology Keck Sch Medicine 2250 Alcazar St CSC Ste 102 Los Angeles CA 90033

JAEGER, MARCOS RICARDO DE OLIVEIRA, plastic surgeon, consultant; s. Geraldo Elio Jaeger and Shirley Celina de Oliveira Jaeger; m. Adriana Elnecave Herscovitz, July 6, 1996; children: Eduarda Herscovitz, Bruna Herscovitz. PhD, Pucrs U., Av Ipiranga, 2008. Cons. staff plastic surgery Pucrs U., Porto Alegre, RS, Brazil, 2008—. Dir. NOVAplastia, Porto Alegre, 2008—. Contbr. articles to profl. jours. Surgeon Operation Smiles Project, Rio de Janeiro, 2003—08. 2nd tenant Policlinica Militar, 1999—2002, Porto Alegre, Brazil. Fellow, U. Toronto, 2002—03. Mem.: Brazilian Soc. Plastic Surgery, Internat. Soc. Aesthetic Plastic Surgery, Am. Soc. Reconstructive Microsurgery. Office: NOVAplastiacom Rua Mostardeiro 780 - 502 Porto Alegre Rio Grande do Sul 90430-000 Brazil Office Phone: 55-51-30288738. Personal E-mail: marcosjaeger@hotmail.com. Business E-Mail: novaplastia@novaplastia.com.

JAEHO, BYUN, oncologist; b. Seoul, Republic of Korea, Mar. 7, 1964; MD, Soon Chun Hyang U., 1990, PhD, 2002. Assoc. prof. Divsn. Oncology, Incheon St. Mary's Hosp., Cath. U. Korea, 2002—. Mem.: Korean Assn. Clin. Oncology, Am. Soc. Clin. Oncology. Home: 1-209 HanKang Apt Jamwondong Seocho-Gu Seoul 137-798 Republic of Korea Personal E-mail: jhbyun37@catholic.ac.kr.

JAENISCH, RUDOLF, biology professor; b. Wolfeslgrund, Germany, 1942; arrived in U.S.A., 1984; MD, U. Munich, 1967. Postdoctoral fellow Max Planck Inst. Biochemistry, Munich, 1967; vis. fellow Inst. Cancer Rsch., Phila.; from asst. prof. to assoc. prof. Salk Inst., La Jolla, Calif., 1972—77; head Dept. Tumor Virology, Heinrich Pette Inst. Exptl. Virology and Immunology U. Hamburg, Germany, 1977—84; founding mem. Whitehead Inst. Biomedical Rsch. MIT, Cambridge, Mass., 1984—, prof. biology, 1984—. Contbr. articles to profl. jours. Recipient Boehringer Mannheim Molecular Bioanalytics prize, 1996, Award in Genetics, Peter Gruber Found., 2001, Robert Koch prize for Excellence in Scientific Achievement, 2002, Max Delbruck medal, 2006, Wolf prize in Medicine, The Wolf Found., 2011. Fellow: American Acad. Microbiology; mem.: AAAS, NAS. Achievements include creating first transgenic animal model; development of first experiment showing therapeutic cloning could correct genetic defects in mice. Office: Massachusetts Inst Tech 77

Massachusetts Ave 68 132 Cambridge MA 02142 Address: Whitehead Inst Nine Cambridge Center Cambridge MA 02142-1479 Office Phone: 617-258-5186. Office Fax: 617-258-6505. E-mail: jaenisch@wi.mit.edu. *

JAFFE, BERNARD MICHAEL, surgeon; b. NYC; s. Abner I. and Sylvia (Rothman) J.; m. Marlene Lambert, June 4, 1961; children: Mark Allen, Debra Lynn. BA, U. Rochester, 1961; MD, NYU, 1964. Diplomate Am. Bd. Surgery (dir. 1982-88, sr. dir. 1988—, exec. com. 1987-88, rep. to Am. Bd. Med. Specialists 1986-89). Asst. prof. surgery Washington U., St. Louis, 1971-75, assoc. prof., 1975—77, prof., 1977—79; prof., chmn. dept. surgery SUNY Health Sci. Ctr., Bklyn., 1979-92, vice-chmn. dept. surgery, chief divsn. surg. rsch., 1992-2000; prof. surgery Tulane U., New Orleans, 2000—. Author: (with Behrman) Methods of Hormone Radioimmunoassay, 1980; editor-in-chief: Surgical Rounds, 1989—. Med. dir. Trauma Edn., Operation Smile; pres. Southern Rep; Devel. Officer, New Orleans Opera Assn.; v.p. Touro Synagogue. Lt. col. USAF, 1972—74. James IV traveling surg. fellow. Mem. ACS, Assn. Acad. Surgery (pres. 1978-79), Soc. Univ. Surgeons (sec. 1979-82, pres. 1983-84), Am. Surg. Assn., Soc. Clin. Surgery, Surg. Biol. Club I (sec. 1982-85), Am. Soc. Clin. Investigation, Soc. for Surgery Alimentary Tract (pres. 1987-88), So. Surg. Assn., Halsted Soc., Transplant Soc., Soc. for Surg. Oncology, Soc. Exptl. Biology Medicine (councillor 2002-2006), Phi Beta Kappa, Alpha Omega Alpha. *

JAFFE, ELAINE SARKIN, pathologist, researcher; b. NYC, Aug. 27, 1943; d. David and Mona (Shane) Sarkin; m. Michael Evan Jaffe, July 22, 1967; children: Gregory, Caleb. AB, Cornell U., 1965, MD, U. Pa., 1969; Dr. Honoris Causa, U. Barcelona, 2008. Cert. Am. Bd. Pathology. Intern in pathology Georgetown U. Hosp., 1969; resident anatomic pathology Clin. Ctr. NIH, Bethesda, Md., 1970-72; sr. investigator Lab. Pathology Nat. Cancer Inst., NIH, Bethesda, Md., 1974—, chief hematopathology sect., Lab. Pathology, 1980—, dep. chief Lab. Pathology, 1982—2005, acting chief Lab Pathology, 2005—08. Lectr. in field; elected mem. Inst. Medicine, 2008. Assoc. editor: Cancer Rsch.; mem. editl. bd. Am. Jour. Pathology, Blood; mem. editl. bd.: Clin. Lymphoma; mem. editl. bd. Am. Jour. Surg. Pathology; editor: Surgical Pathology of the Lymph Nodes and Related Organs, 1984, 2d edit., 1996, WHO Classification of Hematopoietic and Lymphoid Neoplasms, 2001, 4th Series, 2008; contbr. articles to New Eng. Jour. Medicine, Blood; editor: (journ.) Hematopathology, 2010. Recipient Fred W. Stewart award, Meml. Sloan Kettering Cancer Ctr., 2002, Walter Putscher Lectureship, Harvard U., 2003, Dir.'s award, NIH, 2005, Disting. Tchr. award, 2006, Anita B. Roberts Disting. Women Scientist award, 2006, Lennert prize, European Assn. for Haematopathology, 2006, Chugai award, Am. Soc. Investigative Pathology, 2008, Mostofi Award, USCAP, 2003, Dir.'s award, NIH, 2010, Maude Abbott Lecturer United States & Canadian Acad. Pathology Inst. Med., 2000, 2011. Fellow AAAS (clin. med. scis. sect. 2004-2005); mem. Inst. Medicine, Am. Soc. Hematology (exec. coun. 1988-91), U.S.-Can. Acad. Pathology (pres. 1998-99), Am. Soc. Investigative Pathology (Meritorious awards), Soc. for Hematopathology (pres. 1994-96). Office Phone: 301-496-0183. Business E-Mail: ejaffe@mail.nih.gov. *

JAFFE, JAMISON S., urologist; married; 2 children. BA in Biology, Pa. State U., Phila., 1995; D in Osteopathic Medicine, Phila Coll. Osteopathic Medicine, 2000. Intern Albert Einstein Med. Ctr., Phila., 2003, resident, 2006; fellow Minimally Invasive Urologic Surgery L'Institut Mutualiste Montsouris, Paris, 2006; urologist Hahnemann Univ. Hosp., Urologic Consultants of Southeastern Pa. Named Recognized Dr., HealthGrades; named one of the Top Doctors, Phila. Mag., 2011. Avocations: golf, hockey, running. Office: hahnemann University Hospital Broad and Vine Philadelphia PA 19102 Office Phone: 215-762-7000. Office Fax: 215-762-8109.

JAFFE, MURRAY SHERWOOD, retired surgeon; b. Sept. 29, 1926; s. Lester A. and Rosa (Shor) J.; m. Margery Blum Jaffe, Mar. 26, 1951 (dec.) Oct. 16 2010; children— Emily, Margaret, Dan BS, MD, U. Cin., 1948. Diplomate Am. Bd. Surgery. Intern Barnes Hosp., St. Louis, 1948-49; resident Cin. Gen. Hosp., 1949-50, 52-56, Cin. VA Hosp., 1949-50, 52-56, Dayton VA Hosp., Ohio, 1949-50, 52-56; practice medicine specializing in surgery Cin., 1958-98; asst. chief surgery VA Hosp., Cin., 1958-82; pres. med. staff Jewish Hosp., Cin., 1978-80; pres. Medco Peer Rev., 1981-84; retired surgeon, 1996; assoc. clin. prof. surgery emeritus U. Cin. Pres. Ohio div. Am. Cancer Soc., 1970-71. Served with USN, 1945, 50-52 Mem. ACS, Cin. Surg. Soc., U. Cin. Grad. Surg. Soc., Shriners, Phi Beta Kappa, Alpha Omega Alpha Republican. Jewish. Home: 1775 E Mcmillan St Cincinnati OH 45206 Business E-Mail: jaffems@ucmail.uc.edu.

JAFFE, ROBERT BENTON, obstetrician, gynecologist, endocrinologist; b. Detroit, Feb. 18, 1933; s. Jacob and Shirley (Robins) J.; m. Evelyn Grossman, Aug. 29, 1954; children: Glenn, Terri. MS, U. Colo., 1966; MD, U. Mich., 1957. Intern U. Colo. Med. Ctr., Denver, 1957-58, resident, 1959-63; asst. prof. Ob-Gyn. U. Mich. Med. Ctr., 1964-68, assoc. prof., 1968-72, prof., 1972-74, dir. steroid rsch. unit, 1964-74; prof. U. Calif., San Francisco, 1974—, chmn. dept. ob-gyn and reproductive scis., 1974-96, dir. reproductive endocrinology ctr., ctr. reproductive scis., 1977-2000. Mem. nat. adv. council, mem. human embryology and devel. and reproductive biology study sect. Nat. Inst. Child Health and Human Devel.; bd. dirs. Population Resource Center. Author: Reproductive Endocrinology: Physiology, Pathophysiology and Clinical Management, 1978, 4th edit., 1999, Prolactin, 1981, The Peripartal Period, 1985; contbr. numerous articles to profl. jours.; mem. editorial bd. Jour. Clin. Endocrinology and Metabolism, 1971-75, Fertility and Sterility, 1972-78; editor-in-chief Obstetric and Gynecologic Survey, 1991—. Josiah Macy Found. faculty fellow, 1967-70, 81; USPHS postdoctoral fellow, 1958-59, 63-64; Rockefeller Found. grantee, 1974-78; Andrew Mellon Found. grantee, 1978-81 Mem. Endocrine Soc. (coun. 1985-86, sec.-treas. 1994-99), Soc. Gynecologic Investigation (pres. 1975-76, Pres.'s Disting. Scientist award 1993, Pres.'s Mentorship award 2000), Perinatal Rsch. Soc. (pres. 1973-74), Am. Coll. Obstetricians and Gynecologists (awards), Assn. Am. Physicians, Inst. Medicine Nat. Acad. Scis., Royal Coll. Obstetricians and Gynaecologists, The Hormone Found. (pres. 1999—2005). Democrat. Jewish. Home: 90 Mt Tiburon Rd Belvedere Tiburon CA 94920-1512 Office: U Calif Med Sch OB Gyn & Reproductive Sci San Francisco CA 94143-0556 Office Phone: 415-476-6130. Business E-Mail: jaffer@obgyn.vesf.edu.

JAFFE, RUSSELL MERRITT, pathologist, research director; b. Albany, NY, Jan. 1, 1947; AB cum laude, Boston U., 1972, MD with honors, 1972, PhD in Biochemistry, 1972. Diplomate Am. Bd. Pathology (clin., chem.), Nat. Bd. Med. Examiners. Med. intern Boston U. Med. Ctr., 1972-73; resident in clin. pathology NIH, Bethesda, Md., 1973-75, sr. staff physician clin. pathology dept., 1973-79, chief resident tng. program clin. chemistry sect., 1976-79; fellow health rsch., practice, policy devel. Health Studies Collegium, 1979—; dir. ELISA/ACT Biotech., Sterling, Va., 1987—, Princeton BioCenter, 1989-92. Prin. faculty Oriental Med. Strategy in Western Med. Practice, HSC, N.Y.C., 1980-85. Assoc. editor The New Physician, 1971-72, sr. assoc. editor, 1972-73. Bd. govs. Light Found., 1980-99. Comdr. USPHS, 1973-79. Recipient Nat. Rsch. award Am. Acad. Med. Preventics, 1979, J.D. Lane award USPHS, 1975, Excellence in Rsch. award Mead Johnson, 1969, Man of Yr. award Hillel Found., 1967. Fellow Am. Coll. Nutrition, Am. In-Vitro Allergy/Immunology Soc., Am. Soc. Clin. Pathologists; mem. APHA, Am. Assn. Clin. Chemists. Achievements include patent in field. Home: 300 Amwell Rd Hopewell NJ 08525-3116

JAFFE, STEPHEN L., neurologist, educator, researcher; b. NYC; s. Walter and Pearl Jaffe; m. Nancy Marie Holman; children: Adam Byron, Emily Blythe. BA in Philosophy, Purdue U., W. Lafayette, Ind., 1964; MD, Cornell U. Méd. Coll., NY, 1968. Lic. Va. Bd. Med. Examiners, 1969, Ill. Dept. Registration & Edn., 1972, diplomate Nat. Bd. Med. Examiners, 1969, Am. Bd. Psychiatry & Neurolgy, 1974, cert. Fed. State Méd. Bbs. US, 2001; lic. La. State Bd. Med. Examiners, 2001. Externship neurology Inst. Neurology, Queen Square, London, 1967; externship psychiatry Payne Whitney Clinic, Cornell U. Méd. Coll., 1968; intern straight medicine U. Va. Hosp., Charlottesville, 1969, house staff executive, 1970, v.p., 1971, resident neurology, 1972; asst. prof. medicine neurology, neurosci. curriculum coord. Southern Ill. U. Sch. Medicine, 1972—75, acting dir., family practice residency program, 1974—75; clin. prof. neurology Méd. Coll. Va., 1999—2001; Joanna Gunning Magale prof. neurology La. State U., Sch. Medicine-Shreveport, 2001—; course dir., active staff La. State U., Health Sci. Ctr., 2003—. Clin. practice, 1972—; internat. lectr. US Army, 1994—2006; editl. bd. mem. J. Pédiatrie Neurology, Turkey, J. Pediatric Epilepsy, Turkey. Contbr. articles to profl. jours. & publs. With 29th Inf. Divsn., 94th Combat Support Hosp. Col. RC US Army, 2002—06. Decorated Meritorious Svc. medal, 2 Army Commendation medals. Fellow: Am. Acad. Neurology; mem.: N.Am. Ménopause Soc., Am. Clin. Neurophysiology Soc., Internat. Brain Rsch. Orgn., Am. Epilepsy Soc., Soc. Neuroscie., Delta Rho Kappa. Achievements include research in neurophysiologic correlates of behavior, neurotransmission/neuromodulation; neuromuscular disease, headache, epilepsy, stroke, MS, clinical/basic neurophysiology, molecular genetics, médical éducation, curriculum development. Avocations: languages, horseback riding. Office: La State University Health Sci Ctr Dept Neurology 1501 Kings Hwy PO Box 33932 Shreveport LA 71103 Office Phone: 318-675-4241. Office Fax: 318-675-6382. Business E-Mail: sjaffe1@lsuhsc.edu.

JAFFREY, IRA, oncologist, educator; b. NYC, July 28, 1939; s. Mack and Elaine (Schneider) J.; m. June Sharon Friedman, Dec. 26, 1964 (div. Mar. 1979); children: Jonathan David, Marc Jason; m. Sandra Read, June 17, 1979 (div. Mar. 2008); 1 child, Marc Read. AB, Columbia Coll., NYC, 1960; MD, SUNY, Bklyn., 1965. Intern Jewish Hosp., Bklyn., 1965-66; chief resident Elmhurst Gen. Hosp., NYC, 1970; asst. resident Mt. Sinai Hosp., NYC, 1968-69, resident, 1969-70, chief resident, 1970, ednl. fellow dept. hematology, 1970-71, asst. clin. prof. dept. medicine divsn. neoplastic disease, 1980—99; pres. Palisades Oncology Assocs. P.C., Pomona, 1972—; asst. clin. prof. dept. medicine U. Colo. Health Scis., Denver, 2000—. Lt. USNR, 1961-65. Oak Ridge (Tenn.) Inst. fellow, 1965. Fellow ACP, Am. Cancer Soc. (pres. Rockland City unit 1973-74), Rockland City Med. Soc. (v.p. 1992, pres. 1993-94), Mt. Sopris County Med. Soc. (pres. 2002-03, 2006-), Colo. Med. Soc. (bd. dirs. 2004—08). Office: Western SLOPE Oncology Assoc PC 622 19th St Ste 301 Glenwood Springs CO 81601 Office Phone: 970-384-2274. Personal E-mail: dr.jaffrey@aol.com.

JAGDALE, SWATI C., pharmacist, educator; b. Pune, June 15, 1977; PharmM, PhD, MBA, 1998. Prof. Maharashtra Inst. Pharmacy, 2000. Home: Plot 42 Shitolenagar Sangavi Pune Maharashtra 411027 India Personal E-mail: jagdaleswati@rediffmail.com.

JAGTAP, SURESH DNYANDEO, physician; b. Saswad, May 6, 1975; MSc, Pune U., 1998, PhD, 2005. Physician Interactive Rsch. Sch. Health Affairs, 2008—. Sr. taxonomist Medicinal Plants Conservation Centre, 2000—07. Postdoc. fellowship, Dept. Biotech. Mem.: IAAT. Office: Pune Satara Rd Pune Maharashtra 411043 India Office Fax: 91 020 24266929. Personal E-mail: chiritatml@rediffmail.com.

JAGUSZTYN-KRYNICKA, ELZBIETA KATARZYNA, microbiologist, director; b. Milanówek, Poland, Mar. 1, 1947; D, Warsaw U., 1974. Adj. prof. Warsaw U., 1994—2004, prof., 2004, dir., Inst. Microbiology, 2005. Mem., sci. bd. Inst. Biophysics and Biochemistry PAS, 2010. Recipient award, Polish Soc. Genetics, 2002, Polish Agy. Enterprise Devel., 2005, Gold medal, 54th World Exhbn. Innovation, Rsch. and New Tech., Brussels EUREKA, 2005, Achievement award, Rector U. Warsaw, 1983, 1989, 1990, 2000, 2003, 2004, 2007, 2010. Mem.: Polish Acad. Scis. (microbiology com.), Polish Soc. Genetics, Polish Soc. Microbiologists, Am. Soc. Microbiology. Avocations: hiking, theater. Office: Miecznikowa Warsaw 02-096 Poland Office Fax: 4822-5541402. Business E-Mail: kjkryn@biol.uw.edu.pl.

JAHAN, ISRAT, medical researcher; b. Bangladesh, Sept. 13, 1976; MBBS, Dhaka U., Bangladesh, 2000; PhD, Gifu U., Japan, 2007. Postdoc. rschr. U. Iowa, 2008. Monbukagakusho scholarship, Japanese Govt. Mem.: ARO. Avocation: music. Home: 210 6th St Coralville IA 52241 Personal E-mail: israt1317@yahoo.com.

JAHIEL, RENE INO, physician; b. Boulogne, Seine, France, Mar. 29, 1928; s. Richard and Cecile (Lwovsky) J.; m. Deborah Berg, May 8, 1955; children: Abigail, Richard, Beth. BA, NYU, 1946; MD, SUNY, Bklyn., 1950; PhD, Columbia U., 1957. Intern Montefiore Hosp., NYC, 1950-51; resident Mt. Sinai Hosp., NYC, 1951—52, fellow in virology, 1952-55; exptl. immunologist Nat. Jewish Hosp., Denver, 1957-59; asst. attending pathologist, exptl. pathology Mt. Sinai Hosp., 1959-61; asst. prof. pub. health Cornell U. Med. Coll., NYC, 1961-66; rsch. assoc. prof. preventive medicine NYU, NYC, 1967-70, rsch. prof., 1970-76, rsch. prof. medicine, Sch. Medicine, 1976-88. Cons. health svcs. rsch., policy and planning, 1989—; adj. prof. health svcs., rsch. and policy New Sch. for Social Rsch., 1991-96; dean faculty of sci. and pub. health, Ecole Libre des Hautes Etudes of N.Y., 1991-94, v.p. scis., 1994—, acting pres., 2003-06, pres. 2006—; vis. prof. dept. cmty. medicine and healthcare U. Conn. Health Ctr., 1995-98, lectr., 1999—2010; pres. Internat. Health Policy Rsch. Corp., Hartford, Conn., 1995—; med. dir. Southbury (Conn.) Tng. Sch., 1993-95; med. cons. State of Conn. Dept. Mental Retardation, 1996-97; tchr. met. leadership program, U. Coll., NYU, 1969-73; physician Assn. for Help for Retarded Children, 1982-88, Young Adult Inst., 1984-89, Assn. for Children with Retarded Mental Devel., 1988-93; cons. Nat. Ctr. for Health Svcs. Rsch., 1983-85; bd. dirs. N.Y. Scientists Com. Pub. Info., 1974-79, Physicians Forum, 1975-84; cons. Yale U Primary Care Tng. Program at Waterbury (Conn.) Hosp., 2000-04. Editor: Homelessness: A Prevention-Oriented Approach, 1992; contbr. articles to profl. jours.; mem. editl. bd. European Jour. Disability Rsch., 2007—. Mem. interferon adv. com. Am. Cancer Soc., 1984-93; mem. nat. bd. Com. for Nat. Health Svc., 1976-79, coalition, 1980-85. Lt. USNR, 1955-57. Recipient Daring to Dream award, U. Maine, 2005; grantee, USPHS, 1966—79. Mem.: APHA (chmn. com. health svcs. rsch. 1980—87, governing com. 1983—85, chmn. homelessness study group 1984—90, chmn. policy com. caucus on disablement 1989—92, founding chmn. caucus on homelessness 1990—91, chmn. membership com. spl. interest group on disability 1993—97, chair 1998—99, governing com. 1999—2007, edn. bd. 2000—01, pres. conf. emeritus mem. 2009—, Med. Care sect. award 1985, Lifetime Achievement award disability sect. 2011), Am. Assn. Psychol. Rehab., Acad. Health, Internat. Soc. for Equity in Health (founding), World Assn. Psychosocial Rehab. (chmn. com. on mental handicaps 1992—94), Assn. Health Svcs. Rsch. (Spl. Recognition award 1986), Physicians for Social Responsibility, Internat. Assn. Health Policy (bd. dirs. 1998—2000). Achievements include research in tissue culture, virology, interferon, preventive medicine, health policy, health svcs. rsch., disability, homelessness, social epidemiology and sociology of knowledge. Office: 2600 Netherland Ave Unit 1605 Bronx NY 10463-4818

JAHNKE, KRISTOPH, internist, hematologist, oncologist, researcher; b. Halle, Germany, Apr. 13, 1973; s. Hans-Otto and Monika Jahnke. RN, Franziskus Hosp., Bielefeld, Germany, 1995; MD, Martin Luther Univ., Halle-Wittenberg, Germany, 2001. Lic. Oreg. Bd. Med. Examiners, 2005. Resident and fellow dept. hematology, oncology and transfusion medicine Charité Univ. Medicine, Berlin, 2002—08; rsch. instr. and vis. instr. dept. neurology, blood-brain barrier and neuro-oncology program and dept. medicine Oreg. Health and Sci. U., Portland, 2005—07; bd. exam. internal medicine, 2008; assoc. prof. Internal Medicine, Charite U. Medicine, Berlin, 2009, Bd. Exam. Hematology & Med. Oncology, 2010. Contbr. articles to profl. jours. Mem.: German Soc. Hematology and Oncology, German Soc. Internal Medicine, German Cancer Soc., European Soc. Med. Oncology, Am. Soc. Clin. Oncology, German Child Welfare Orgn. (assoc.), Fedn. for Environment and Nature Protection Germany (assoc.), Marburger Fedn. (assoc.), German Child Def. Assn. (assoc.). Office: Charité Univ Medicine Campus Benjamin Franklin Dept Hematol Oncol and Transfusion Med Hindenburgdamm 30 D-12200 Berlin Germany

JAHNKE, SARA ANNE, research scientist; b. Kansas City, Mo., Oct. 24, 1978; PhD, U. Mo., Kansas City, 2006. Prin. investigator Nat. Devel. & Rsch. Insts., 2009—. Office: 1920 W 143rd St Ste 120 Leawood KS 66204 Business E-Mail: jahnke@ndri.org.

JAILE-MARTI, JESUS CARLOS, neonatal-perinatal physician; m. Diane Jaile-Marti; 4 children. Grad., Manhattan Coll., 1983; MD, Columbia U., 1987. Diplomate Am. Bd. Pediatrics, Am. Bd. Medical Specialties. Resident pediat. Columbia-Presbyn. Med. Ctr., NY, 1988—90, fellow neonatolgy NY, 1990—93; joined White Plains Hosp., 1993, physician neonatology; dir. neonatology dept. of pediat. Nyack Hosp., 2004. Named one of Top Doctors, NY Mag., 2010. Office: White Plains Hospital Center 41 Ease Post Rd White Plains NY 10601 Office Phone: 914-681-2282. *

JAIME, THAIS JEREZ, dermatologist; b. Sao Paulo, Brazil, Apr. 10, 1983; D, Pontifícia U. Católica de São Paulo, 2008. Resident dermatologist Hosp. Naval Marcílio Dias, 2009—. Home: Honduras Barueri Sao Paulo 0647130 Brazil Personal E-mail: thaisjerez@yahoo.com.br.

JAIN, ANIL KUMAR, medical professor, consultant; b. Village Parson, Madhya Pradesh, India, Apr. 14, 1957; s. Kapoor Chand and Sumantra Devi Jain; m. Shashi Prabha Jain, Nov. 24, 1984; children: Pragya Blank, Aayush Blank. MBBS, Gandhi Med. Coll., Bhopal, 1980; MS, Gandhi Med. Coll., 1984; MAMS, Nat. Acad. Med. Scis., 1999. Sr. registrar Ctrl. Inst. Orthops. Safdarjang Hosp., New Delhi, 1985—88; lectr. in orthopaedics U. Coll. Med. Scis, U. Delhi, 1988—92, reader orthops., 1992—97, prof. orthops., 1997—. Sr. cons. orthops. Guru Tegh Bahadur Hosp., Delhi, 1988—; head dept. orthops. Faculty Medicine, U. Delhi, 1997—2000, New Delhi, 2003—06, U. Coll. Med. Scis., 1998—2001. Editor: Indian Jour. Orthops.; guest editor: Clinical Orthops. and Related Rsch., 2005, 2007; contbr. articles to profl. pubs. Pub. health edn. programme and rehab. Shri Anandpur Charitable Trust Hosp., Sukhpur, India, 1991—2008. Recipient SN Buxi Publ. award, Indian Jour. Orthops., 2005, Publ. award, Assn. Spinal Surgeons India, 2005; fellow, WHO, 1993, AO, 2001. Mem.: SICOT (hon.; mem. 2008—08, commonwealth fellow in spine surgery 2010, XIII World Congress Best Poster award 2005, XIII World Congress Best Oral Presentation award 2005), Indian Orthop. Assn. (life; chmn. implant and superspeciality tng. 2001—05, Silver Jubilee Lecture award 1994). Home: A-10 Ashok Nagar Uttar Pradesh Ghaziabad 201002 India Office: U Coll Med Scis Dilshad Garden Delhi 110095 India Office Fax: 0091-11-22590495. Home Fax: 0091-11-22590495. Personal E-mail: dranilkjain@gmail.com.

JAIN, KEWAL KRISHAN, neurosurgeon, biotechnology consultant; b. Dec. 7, 1937; arrived in Can, 1957, arrived in Switzerland, 1986; s. Bans Raj and Malavi (Devi) Jain; m. Verena Johanna Pulver, Sept. 29, 1976; children: Eric, Adrian, Vivien. MD, Medical Coll., Amritsar, 1957. Neurosurgeon Lion's Gate Hosp., U. B.C., Vancouver, Can., 1964-74; prof. neurosurgery Sri Chitra Tirunal Med. Ctr. and Hosp., Trivandrum, India, 1976, U. Shiraz, Iran, 1977; scientist GSF, Munich, 1978-79, Huntington Inst., Pasadena, Calif., 1978-79; chief neurosurgery Letterman Army Med. Ctr., Francisco, 1979-80; rsch. neurosurgeon, pvt. practice UCLA, 1981-86; cons. in neurosurgery and hyperbaric medicine Fachclinic Klausenbach, Nordach,

Germany, 1986-89; cons. in neurosurgery and biotech., Basel, Switzerland, 1989-97; pres. Jain PharmaBiotech, Basel, Switzerland, 1996—. Author: Health Care in New China, 1973, Handbook of Laser Neurosurgery, 1983, Oxygen in Physiology and Medicine, 1989, Textbook of Hyperbaric Medicine 5th edit., 2005, Carbon Monoxide Poisoning, 1990, Cerebral Insufficiency: Pathophysiology and Management, 1990, Textbook of Gene Therapy, 1998, Drug-Induced Neurological Disorders: Pathophysiology and Management 3rd edit., 2010, Nanobiotechnology in Molecular Diagnostics, 2006, Neuroprotection, 2009, Proteomics, 2009, Biomarkers, 2009, Handbook of Nanomedicine, 2008, Textbook of Personalized Medicine, 2009, Applications of Biotechnology in Cardiovascular Therapeutics, 2011; contbr. chapters to books, articles to profl jours. Lt col MC US Army, 1979—80. Fellow: RCP (UK) (faculty pharm. medicine), Int Col Surgeons, Royal Australasian Col Surgeons, Royal Col Surgeons (Can); mem.: Am Col Hyperbaric Med (European bd govs 1989—, diplomate), Int Soc Hyberbaric Med (secy-gen 1990—). Avocations: philosophy, skiing, long-distance running, writing. Office Phone: +4161-692-4461. E-mail: jain@pharmabiotech.ch.

JAIN, MANU, physician, educator; b. Ludihana, Punjab, India, Mar. 26, 1963; BA, Northwestern U., 1985, MSc, 1989; MD, U. Chgo., 1989. Assoc. prof. medicine, pediat. Northwestern U., 1996—. Office: 240 E Huron Ave M-332 Chicago IL 60611 Business E-Mail: m-jain@northwestern.edu.

JAIN, RAKESH K., chemical engineering and tumor biology educator; b. Lalitpur, India, Dec. 18, 1950; came to U.S., 1972; s. Sanat Kumar and Kailash W. Jain; m. Janet Carrick. BTech in Chem. Engring., Indian Inst. Tech., Kanpur, 1972; MS in Chem. Engring., U. Del., 1974, PhD in Chem. Engring., 1975. Asst. prof. chem. and biomed. engring. Columbia U., NYC, 1976-78; from asst. to assoc. prof. chem. and biomed. engring. Garnegie Mellon U., Pitts., 1978-83, prof., 1983-91; Andrew Werk Cook prof. tumor biology dept. radiation oncology Harvard Med. Sch., Boston, 1991—; dir. Edwin L. Steele Lab. for Tumor Biology MGH Cancer Ctr. Mass. Gen. Hosp., Boston, 1991—; prof. Harvard-MIT divsn. health scis. and tech. MIT, Cambridge, Mass., 1991—. Vis. prof. chem. engring. MIT, 1983; vis. prof. bioengring. U. Calif., San Diego, LaJolla, 1984; vis. prof. radiology Stanford (Calif.) U. Med. Sch., 1984; vis. prof. pathophysiology, U. Mainz, Germany, 1990-91; vis. prof. surg. rsch. U. Munich, 1991; vice chmn. Gordon Conf. Microcirculation, 1993; cons. Lab. Pathophysiology, NCI, 1976-84, DuPont Merck Pharm., Wilmington, Del., 1988-90, Hybritech-Lily, San Diego, 1988-93; mem. adv. bd. Pitts. Biomed. Devel. Corp., 1989-91; mem. radiation study sect. NIH, 1991-94; bd. dirs. Am. Cancer Soc.; B.F. Ruth lectr. Iowa State U., Ames, 1983; Allan P. Colburn lectr. U. Del., Newark, 1983; Hugh C. Muldoon lectr. Duquesne U., Pitts., 1986; Kurt Wohl lectr. U. Del., 1992. Mem. edit. bd. Biotech. Progress, 1985—, Microvascular Rsch., 1985—, CRC Crit. Revs. in Biomed. Engring., 1986-95, Cancer Rsch., 1987—, Drug Targeting and Delivery, 1991—, Microcirculation, 1994-2001, Angiogenesis, 1997-, British Journal of Cancer, 1997-, Internat. Journal of Oncology, 1997-, Journal of Theoretical Medicine, 1997-2005, Molecular Imaging, 2002-, Clinical Cancer Rsch., 2003-, Nature Reviews Cancer (Highlights Section), 2004-, Molecular Cancer Rsch., 2004-, Computational and Mathematical Methods in Medicine, 2005-, Nature Clin. Practice Oncology, 2008-. Recipient Rsch. Career Devel. award Nat. Cancer Inst., 1980-85, Abbott Microcirculation award European Soc. Microcirculation, 1990, Sr. Scientist award Alexander von Humboldt Found., 1990-91, Instrumentation for Physiology and Medicine award Am. Microcirculation Soc., 1993, 94, Disting. Alumnus award Indian Inst. Tech., 1994; Outstanding Investigator grantee Nat. Cancer Inst., 1993—; John Simon Guggenheim Meml. Found. fellow, 1983-84. Fellow Am. Acad. Arts and Sciences, Am. Inst. Biol. and Med. Engrs. (founder); mem. AICE (chmn. nat. planning com. area 15e-engring. fundamentals in life scis. 1981-84, chmn. tech. sects. life scis. area 1976-82, 84-86, co-editor AIChE Symposium Series 1983, 86), AAAS, NAE, Am. Assn. Cancer Rsch., N.Am. Soc. Biorheology (chmn. membership com. 1988-90), N.Am. Hyperthermia Soc., N.Y. Acad. Scis. (chmn. thermal characteristics of tumors conf. 1979, guest editor Annals N.Y. Acad. Scis. 1980), Internat. Inst. Microcirculation (bd. dirs. 1987-91, co-chmn. cancer cells and tumor microcirculation conf. 1989, Rsch. award 1984), Microcirculation Soc. (chmn. membership com. 1986-88, nomination com. 1993—), Biomed. Engring. Soc. (conf. chmn. ann. meeting 1987, chmn. meeting programming com. 1987-90), Radiation Rsch. Soc., Sigma Xi, Inst. Medicine. Avocations: swimming, classical music, jazz. Office: Edwin L Steele Lab Dept Radiation Oncology, Cox 7 Mass Gen Hosp Boston MA 02114 Office Phone: 617-726-4083. Office Fax: 617-724-1819. E-mail: jain@steele.mgh.harvard.edu.

JAIN, REEMA, pharmacist, pharmaceutical executive; d. Ashok and Kusum Jain. BS, PharmD, Ernest Mario Sch. Pharmacy, New Brunswick, NJ, 2003. Cert. pharmacist NJ. Bd. Pharmacy, 2002. Pharmacist CVS Pharmacy, Plainfield, NJ, 1998—2006, Mandell's Pharmacy, New Brunswick, NJ, 2002—08, Target Pharmacy, 2008—; assoc. dir. Johnson & Johnson PRD, Titusville, NJ, 2003—08; med. pharmacovigilance Johnson Johnson PRD, 2008—. Office: Johnson & Johnson PRD 1125 Trenton Harbourton Road Titusville NJ 08560 also: Johnson & Johnson PRD 920 Route 202 South Raritan Raritan NJ 08869 Business E-Mail: rjain@brmus.jnj.com.

JAIN, SAURABH, surgeon; b. Kota, Rajasthan, India, July 29, 1975; s. Vinod and Sudha Jain; l child, Olesya. MD, Vinnitsa State Med. U., Ukraine, 2000. Cert. ECFMG, 2003. House staff physician Tufts U., Boston, 2003—04; gen. surgery house staff Med. U. SC, Charleston, 2004—05, USC Huntington Meml. Hosp., Pasadena, Calif., 2005—06; rsch. fellow, dept. surgery U. Southern Calif., LA, 2006—07; clin. fellow, trauma & critical care surgery, surg. critical care program Cedars-Sinai Med. Ctr., LA, 2007—08; trauma and critical care specialist Colusa Regional Med. Ctr., Calif., 2008, trauma and critical care surgeon, 2008—. Contbr. scientific papers to med. jours. Med. dir. Anesthesia IAG Svcs. Ltd., Victorville, Calif., 2008. Surg. Critical Care fellowship, Cedars-Sinai Med. Ctr., 2008, Travel grants, Cedars-Sinai Med. Ctr., LA, 2008. Mem.: ACS, AMA, Southwestern Surg. Congress, Soc. Am. Gastrointestinal and Endoscopic Surgeons, Soc. Critical Care Medicine, Assn. Academic Surgeons, Panamerican Trauma Soc., Am. Trauma Soc. Achievements include research in validated ultrasound cardiac output monitor, which can replace swan ganz catheter in ICU practice; in videolaryngoscopic intubation as a teaching tool for surgical residents for airway control; first to develop blood management program to conserve blood in hospitals and moving towards transfusion free surgery. Office: Colusa Regional Med Ctr 199 E Webster St Colusa CA 95932 Home: 350 S San Fernando Blvd Apt 321 Burbank CA 91502-1371 Personal E-mail: jainsx@gmail.com.

JAIN, SHRUTI, engineering educator; b. Ambala, June 15, 1983; PhD, SD Pub. Sch., 2004. Sr. lectr. Jaypee U. Info. Tech., 2004—. Mem.: IEEE, Internat. Assn. Engrs. Office: Jaypee University Info Tech Solan Waknaghat Himachal Pradesh 173234 India Office Fax: 01792245362. E-mail: jain.shruti15@gmail.com.

JAIN, SUDHIR KUMAR, medical educator, surgeon; b. Delhi, India, Mar. 26, 1959; s. Rajendra and Sarla Jain; m. Deepti Jain, May 11; 1 child, Anuj. MBBS, Maulana Azad Med. Coll., New Delhi, 1981; MS, Lady Hardinge Med. Coll., New Delhi, 1985. Cert. Med. Coun. India, Gen. Med. Coun., USMLE. Surg. specialist Anand Hosp. Preet Vihar, New Delhi, 1990—2000; asst. prof. Maulana Azad Med. Coll., 2001—02, assoc. prof., 2003—06, prof., 2007—. Author: (book) Basic Surgical Skills and Techniques, 2008; contbr. articles to 60 profl. jours. Fellow: RCS(Edinburgh); mem.: Internat. Coll. Surgeons, Assn. Surgeon's India (life), Indian Med. Assn. (life). Personal E-mail: sudhirkumar11@gmail.com.

JAINGUE, MAMERTO PEÑEDA, internist, gastroenterologist, physician; b. Tacloban City, Leyte, Philippines, May 3, 1947; s. Vicente Ortigosa and Felipa Peñeda Jaingue; m. Isabelita Aglugub, Dec. 28, 1978; 4 children. Degree in liberal arts, Divine Word U., Tacloban, 1967; MD, Cebu Inst. Medicine, Cebu, The Philippines, 1972. Diplomate Bd. Internal Medicine, Bd. Gastroenterology, 1991. Resident physician Tacloban City Hosp., 1972-76; gen. med. practitioner Iran Ministry of Health, 1976-79, Riyadh, Saudi Arabia, 1980-81; resident physician East Ave Med Ctr., Quezon City, Philippines, 1983—87, fellow in gastroenterology, 1988-90, cons., 1993—. Tchg. cons. Internal Med., Philippines, 1991—; head sect. gastroenterology and endoscopy unit East Ave. Med. Ctr., Quezon City, Philippines, 1991—2006, chmn., internal medicine, 2008—; asst. prof. Manilla Ctrl. U., Caloocan City, Philippines, 1992—94; head health program com. Diocese of Cubao Phillipines, 2003—05. Contbr. articles to med. jours., including Gastroenterology Jour. Head coord. svc. ministry Our Lady of Perpetual Help, Cubao, The Philippines, 2000-2003, editor in chief of Kalinga Newsletter, 2000-06; lay minister, Our Lady of Perpetual Help Parish, Quezon City, 2000-2003. Fellow Philippine Coll. Physicians, Philippine Soc. Gastroenterology; mem. Philippine Med. Assn. (life), Rotary (dir. cmty. svc. 1997-2000, Outstanding Cmty. Svc. award 2000, pres.-elect Uptown Cubao 2001-02), Gastro-Intestinal Fellows Alumni Assn. Inc., Internal Med. Alumni Assn. Inc. (pres. 2002-04), Rotary Internat. (asst. gov. dist. 3780, 2005-06, 08-10, 11-), Parish Pastoral Coun. Our Lady Perpetual Help Parish(chmn., 2009-). Roman Catholic. Avocations: bowling, dance, singing, reading, writing. Home: No 19 9th Ave Cubao Quezon City 1109 Philippines Home Phone: 632-911-6850; Office Phone: 632-4372977. Fax: 632 4372979. E-mail: mel_jaingue@yahoo.com.

JAISWAL, VIJAYA, pharmaceutical executive; b. New Delhi, Nov. 12, 1959; MD, Govt. Med. Coll. Nagpur India, 1983. V.p. med. svcs. Troikaa Pharms. Ltd., 2007. Home: Row House B/12 Someshwara-2 Satellite Ahmedabad Gujarat 380015 India

JAITIN, ROSA ELSA, psychologist, professor; b. Buenos Aires, Aug. 17, 1947; m. Bruno Rene De Carlo, Feb. 22, 1997; children: Maximo Langer, Maria Andrea Langer, Marcela Amalia Langer; m. Martin Alfredo Langer, Jan. 30, 1970 (div. 1990). Ms in Edn. Sci., Buenos Aires U., Argentina, 1970, MS in Psychology, 1975; D in Psychology, U. Lyon France, 1995. Specialized in edn.; cert. in social psychology Pichon Riviere Sch., 1972, prof. tenure Psychology Dept. Buenos Aires U., 1987. Sci. coun. mem. Pichon Riviere Sch., 1983—91; counceling mem. bd. dir. Psychology Dept. U. Buenos Aires, 1986—89, pedagogical dir., 1986—89. Author: (sci. book) Clinique de l'inceste fraternel, la psicología de la educación: el educador y la institucion- Buenos Aires, Los apoyos grupales en la crianza infantil - (Les appuis groupaux dans le développement de l'enfant), Buenos Aires, Ediciones Cinco., Aprendizaje, juego y placer (Sobre el tratamiento de los problemas de aprendizaje) - (Apprentissage, jeu et plaisir - Sur le traitement des troubles de l'apprentissage), Buenos Aires, Búsqueda., Aprendizaje, juego y placer (Sobre el diagnóstico de los problemas de aprendizaje) - (Apprentissage, jeu et plaisir - Sur un diagnostic d'apprentissage), Buenos Aires, Búsqueda., Clínica Grupal de Niños - (Clinique groupale d'enfants), Buenos Aires, Trieb. Psychology supr. children's groups Mental Health Solidarity Group, Buenos Aires, 1976—80; mental health counselor Mental Health Com. To Help Ex Soldiers In The Folklands, Buenos Aires, 1983—86. Mem.: Soc. Française Thérapie Familiale Psychanalytique. (sec. 1997—2010), Assn. Française de Psychothérapie Psychanalytique de Groupe. Achievements include research in notion of proto-rhythms as forms of initial representation of the epistemic and family links. Avocations: swimming, horse riding., travelling, museums, music. Home: 24 Rue Auguste Comte Lyon 69002 France Office: Inst Psychologie Paris Descartes 71 avenue E Vaillant Boulogne-Billancourt 92774 France Office Fax: 01 55 20 55 20; Home Fax: 33 4 72 41 01 77. Personal E-mail: rosajaitin@wanadoo.fr. Business E-Mail: rosa.jaitin@parisdescartes.fr.

JAJOO, MAMTA, medical educator; b. Madhya Pradesh, India, May 27, 1969; MBBS, Gajra Raja Med. Coll., Gwalior, Madhya Pradesh, 1994; DNB, Nat. Bd. Edn., 1999. With Maulana Azad Med. Coll. Chacha Nehru Bal Chikitsalaya, Delhi, 2000—, asst. prof., 2007—. Recipient Best Poster Paper award, Nat. Neonatology Forum. Mem.: Indian Acad. Pediat., Nat. Neonatology Forum. Avocation: reading. Office: Chacha Nehru Bal Chikitsalaya Maulana Azad Med Coll Geeta Colony New Delhi 100031 India E-mail: jajoomamta@yahoo.co.in.

JAKAB, IRENE, psychiatrist; b. Oradea, Romania; came to US, 1961, naturalized, 1966; d. Odon and Rosa A. (Riedl) J. MD, Ferencz József U., Kolozsvar, Hungary, 1944; lic. in psychology, pedagogy, philosophy cum laude, Hungarian U., Cluj, Rumania, 1947; PhD summa cum laude, Pazmany Peter U., Budapest, 1948; Dr honoris causa, U. Besançon, France, 1982, U. Pécs, Hungary, 1999. Diplomate Am. Bd. Psychiatry, Am. Bd. Pediatric Neuropsychology. Rotating intern Ferencz József U., 1943-44; resident in psychiatry Univ. Hosp., Kolozsvar, 1944-47, resident in neurology, 1947-50; resident internal medicine Univ. Hosp. for Internal Medicine, Pécs, Hungary, 1950-51; chief physician Univ. Hosp. for Neurology and Psychiatry, Pécs, 1951-59; staff neuropathol. rsch. lab. Neurol. Univ. Clinic, Zurich, 1959-61; sect. chief Kans. Neurol. Inst., Topeka, 1961-63; dir. rsch. and edn., 1966; resident psychiatry Topeka State Hosp., 1963-66; asst. psychiatrist McLean Hosp., Belmont, Mass., 1966-67, assoc. psychiatrist, 1967-74; prof. psychiatry U. Pitts. Med. Sch., 1974-89, prof. emerita, 1989—, co-dir. med. student edn. in psychiatry, 1981-89. Dir. John Merck Program, 1974-81; faculty dept. psychiatry Med. Sch., Pecs, 1951-59; asst. Univ. Hosp. Neurology, Zurich, 1959-61; assoc. psychiatry Harvard U., Boston, 1966-69, asst. prof. psychiatry, 1969-74, program dir. grad course mental retardation, 1970-87; lectr. psychiatry, 1974—; editor in chief newsletter Am. Bd. Pediatric Neuropsychiatry. Author: Dessins et Peintures des Aliénés, 1956, Zeichnungen und Gemälde der Geisteskranken, 1956, Pictorial Expression in Psychiatry, 1998; editor: Psychiatry and Art, 1968, Art Interpretation and Art Therapy, 1969, Conscious and Unconscious Expressive Art, 1971, Transcultural Aspects of Psychiatric Art, 1975; co-editor: Dynamische Psychiatrie, 1974; mem. editl. bd. Confinia Psychiatrica, 1975-99; contbr. articles to profl. jours. Recipient 1st prize Benjamin Rush Gold medal award for sci. exhibit, 1980, Bronze Chris plaque Columbus Film Festival, 1980, Leadership award Am. Assn. on Mental Deficiency, 1980; Menninger Sch. Psychiatry fellow, Topeka, 1963-66. Mem. AMA, Am. Psychol. Assn., Am. Psychiat. Assn., Société Medico Psychologique de Paris, Internat. Rorschach Soc., NY Acad. Scis., Internat. Soc. Psychopathology of Expression (v.p. 1959—), Am. Soc. Psychopathology of Expression (chmn. 1965—, Ernst Kris Gold Medal award 1988), Royal Soc. of Medicine (overseas fellow), Internat. Soc. Child Psychiatry and Allied Professions, Internat. Assn. Knowledge Engrs. (v.p. for medicine 1988-95), Deutschsprachige Gesellschaft für Psychopathologie des Ausdruckes (hon. Prinzhorn prize 1967), Hungarian Psychiat. Assn. (hon. 1992), World Psychiat. Assn. (co-chmn. sect. on mass and media and mental health). Home and Office: 74 Lawton St Brookline MA 02446-5801 Office Phone: 617-738-9821.

JAKAB, ZSUZSANNA, international organization administrator; b. Hungary, 1951; M, Eötvös Lóránd U., Budapest, Hungary; postgrad. degree, U. Polit. Sciences, Budapest; diploma in pub. health, Nordic Sch. Pub. Health, Gothenburg, Sweden; postgrad. diploma, Nat. Inst. Pub. Adminstrn. and Mgmt., Hungary. Joined external affairs Ministry Health and Social Welfare, Hungary, 1975; various positions including dir. divsn. info., evidence & comm., coord. EUROHEALTH program, dir. country devel. and dir. adminstrn. & mgmt. support WHO Europe, 1991—2002; state sec. Ministry Health, Social and Family Affairs, Hungary, 2002—05; founding dir. European Union European Ctr. Disease Prevention and Control, Stockholm, 2005—10; regional dir. Europe WHO, Copenhagen, 2010—. Office: WHO Regional Office Europe Scherfigsvej 8 2100 Copenhagen Denmark *

JAKACKI, REGINA I., pediatric oncologist, educator; MD, U. Pa., 1985. Diplomate Am. Bd. Pediatrics, Am. Bd. Pediatrics-pediatric hematology-oncology, cert. am. bd. of hospice and palliative medicine. Resident Children's Hosp. of Phila., 1988, fellow, 1991; hosp. affiliation include/s Magee-Womens Hospital of UPMC, Children's Hosp. of Pitts. of UPMC, dir. neuro-oncology program, med. dir. supportive care program; assoc. prof. Univ. of Pitts. Fellow: Am. Acad. of Pediatrics; mem.: Am. Acad. of Hospice and Palliative Medicine, Soc. for Pediatric Rsch., Soc. for Neuro-Oncology, Am. Soc of Pediatric Hematology/Oncology, Am. Soc. of Clin. Oncology. Office: Childrens Hospital of Pittsburgh of UPMC 4401 Penn Ave Fl 9 Pittsburgh PA 15224 Office Phone: 412-692-5055. Office Fax: 412-692-7693. E-mail: regina.jakacki@chp.edu.

JAKOBSEN, LINDA PLOVMAND, plastic surgeon; b. Elsinore, Denmark, May 25, 1972; MD, PhD, U. Copenhagen, 1999. Physician, dept. plastic surgery U. Copenhagen, 2001. Home: Solsortvej 85 Frederiksberg 2000 Denmark Personal E-mail: lindapjakobsen@gmail.com.

JAKŠIC, ŽELIMIR, retired medical educator; b. Zagreb, Croatia, May 23, 1930; s. Djuro Jakšic and Ljerka Bošnjak; m. Darinka Gašparic, May 25, 1963; children: Ranko Jakšic, Mirka Jakšic. MD, Med. Sch., Zagreb, 1955. Dr. of scis. U. Zagreb, 1965, Diploma in Public Health A Stampar Sch. of Pub. Health, U. of Zagreb, 1958, Specialist in social medicine and organization of health care Croatia, Yugoslavia, 1960. Asst. prof. Stampar Sch. Pub. Health, Zagreb, Croatia, 1957—71; leader Iran/who rsch. team World Health Orgn., Geneva, 1971—74. Head of dept. for orgn. of health care, and sequentially dir. A Stampar Sch. of Pub. Health, Zagreb, Croatia, 1975—87; vice-dean for edn. Med. Sch., U. of Zagreb, Zagreb, Croatia, 1987—89, dean, 1989—90; head of deparment of ednl. tech. A Stampar Sch. of Pub. Health, Zagreb, Croatia, 1990—95; prof. emeritus U. of Zagreb, Zagreb, Croatia. Fellow: Royal Coll. Gen. Practitioners (hon. Ad Eundem 1983); mem.: Croatian Med. Acad. (mem. senate 2003—08). Achievements include development of general/family practice and primary health care; research in epidemiology of diabetes and other non-communicable chronic diseases, evaluation of medical education, health services development (West Azerbaijan Project), continuous education using new techniques; development of WHO collaborating centre for primary health care. Office: A Stampar School of Public Health Rockefellerova 4 Zagreb 10000 Croatia Home: DeÀmanova 2 10-000 Zagreb Croatia Personal E-mail: zelimir.jaksic@zg.t-com.hr.

JALALI, BEHNAZ, psychiatrist, educator; b. Mashad, Iran, Jan. 26, 1944; came to U.S., 1968; d. Badiolah and Bahieh (Shahidi) Samimy; m. Mehrdad Jalali, Sept. 18, 1968. MD, Tehran U., Iran, 1968. Rotating intern Burlington County Meml. Hosp., Mt. Holly, NJ, 1968—69; resident in psychiatry U. Md. Hosp., Balt., 1970—73; asst. prof. psychiatry dept. psychiatry Sch. Medicine Rutgers U., Piscataway, NJ, 1973—76, Yale U., New Haven, 1976—81, assoc. clin. prof. psychiatry, 1981—85; assoc. clin. prof. psychiatry dept. psychiatry UCLA, 1985—94, clin. prof. psychiatry dept. psychiatry Sch. Medicine, 1994—. Dir. psychotherapy Sch. Medicine Rutgers U., Piscataway, 1973-76; dir. family therapy unit dept. psychiatry Yale U., New Haven, 1976-85; chief clin. med. svcs. Mental Health Clinic, 1987-96; coord. med. student edn. in psychiatry West LA VA Hosp., 1985—2000; dir. family therapy clinic W.Va. VA Hosp., 1991—, co-dir. Schozophrenia Clinic, Mental Health Clinic, West LA VA Med. Ctr., 1996—; med. dir. Mental Health Clinic, West LA VA Med. Ctr., 2004-08; dir. recovery program West LA VA Med. Ctr., 2008-. Author: (with others) Ethnicity and Family Therapy, 1982, Clinical Guidlines in Cross-Cultural Mental Health, 1988; contbr. articles to profl. jours. Fellow Am. Psychiatric Assn., Am. Orthopsychiatry Assn., Am. Assn. Social Psychiatry; mem. Am. Family Therapy Assn., So. Calif. Psychiatric Assn. (chair com. for women 1992), World Fedn. Mental Health. Avocations: photography, hiking, cinema, painting. Home:

1203 Roberto Ln Los Angeles CA 90077-2304 Office: UCLA Dept Psychiatry West LA VA Med Ctr B116aa Los Angeles CA 90073-1003 Office Phone: 310-268-4651. Business E-Mail: behnaz.jalali@med.va.gov.

JALBA, MIHAI SERGIU, epidemiologist, pulmonologist, physician, researcher; b. Tecuci, Moldova, Romania, May 28, 1953; arrived in US, 1995; s. Teodor and Olimpia Jalba; children: Theodor Lucian, Heliodor Ioan. MD, Carol Davila U. Medicine, 1980, PhD in Clin. Med. Scis., 2001; MPH in Epidemiology, U. Medicine Dentistry, NJ, 2006. Cert. pulmonologist Ministry of Health, Romania, 1994. Intern Nat. Inst. Endocrinology, Bucharest, 1980—83; gen. practitioner Barlad City Hosp., Perieni, Romania, 1984—87, Ialomitza County Hosp., Milosesti, Romania, 1987—91; sci. rschr. Nat. Inst. Pulmonology, Bucharest, 1991—95; assoc. sci. rschr. Bklyn. Hosp., 1996—2001; epidemiologist Dept. of Health, NYC, 2002—03; post-doc. rsch. fellow Robert Wood Johnson Med. Sch., NB, NJ, 2004—06; sr. scientist Respharma Alpha Corp, NY, 2006—. Contbr. articles to profl. jours. Mem.: N. am. Primary Care Rsch. Group, Am. Thoracic Soc., Romanian Soc. Pulmonology (sec. (exec. bd. nat. com.) 1992—95), So. Med. Assn. Achievements include breakthroughs in tuberculosis epidemiology, adult respiratory distress syndrome and asthma research. Avocations: chess, opera, violin. Personal E-mail: drmjalba@netzero.net.

JAMA, MOHAMED ABDI, international organization administrator; b. Somalia; Grad. in medicine, Somali Nat. U., Mogadishu, Somalia, postgrad. tng. in paediatrics; med. tng., Italy, US. Program mgr. child health Govt. of Somalia; lectr. in paediatrics Somali Nat. U.; head paediatrics dept. Banadir Hosp., Somalia; project officer for primary care devel. Somalia, Djibouti; med. officer for primary health care devel. WHO, Afghanistan, 1991—98, rep. for Afghanistan, 1998—2000, acting rep. for Pakistan, 1999—2000, regional advisor for program devel., 2000—01, asst. regional dir., regional coord. for Afghan crisis, 2001—02, dep. regional dir., dir. programme mgmt. of regional office for Ea. Mediterranean, 2002—09, asst. dir.-gen. gen. mgmt. Geneva, 2009—. Office: WHO avenue Appia 20 1211 Geneva Switzerland *

JAMADAR, DAVID A., radiologist, educator; b. San Fernando, Trinidad, West Indies, Sept. 7, 1957; MBBS, U. West Indies, 1982. Clin. prof. U. Mich. Med. Ctr., 1994—. Office: University Mich Med Ctr Dept Radiology 1500 E Med Ctr Dr TC 2910 Ann Arbor MI 48109 Business E-Mail: djamadar@umich.edu.

JAMEMA, SWAMIDAS V., biophysicist; b. Vandavasi, Tamilnadu, India, May 31, 1972; MSc in Physics, Loyola Coll., Chennai, 1994; Dip.R.P, BARC, Mumbai, 1996. Med. physicist Tata Meml. Hosp., 2001—. Postgrad. tchr. Homi Bhabha Nat. Inst., 2008. Resident Travel grant, Am. Brachytherapy Soc. Mem.: European Soc. Therapeutic Radiation Oncology (Best Poster award), Assn. Radiation Oncologists India, Assn. Med. Physicists India. Avocations: music, travel. Office: Tata Memorial Hosp Parel Mumbai Maharashtra 400012 India E-mail: svjamema@gmail.com.

JAMES, ELIZABETH JOAN PLOGSTED, pediatrician, educator; b. Jefferson City, Mo., Jan. 15, 1939; d. Joseph Matthew Plogsted and Maxie Pearl (Manford) Plogsted Acuff; m. Ronald Carney James, Aug. 25, 1962; children: Susan Elizabeth, Jason Michael. BS in Chemistry, Lincoln U., 1960; MD, U. Mo., 1965. Diplomate Am. Bd. Pediat., Am. Bd. Neonatal-Perinatal Medicine. Resident in pediat. U. Mo. Hosps. & Clinics, Columbia, 1965-68, fellow in neonatology, 1968-69, dir. neonatal-perinatal medicine Children's Hosp., 1971—2007; fellow in neonatal-perinatal medicine U. Colo. Hosps., Denver, 1969-71; from asst. to assoc. prof. pediatrics and obstetrics sch. medicine U. Mo., 1971-83, prof. child health and obstetrics, 1983—2007, prof. emeritus, 2007—. Dir. pediatric edn. program dept. child health sch. medicine U. Mo., Columbia, 1989-98. Mem. editl. bd. Mo. Medicine, 1983—; contbr. chpts. to books and articles to profl. jours. Fellow Am. Acad. Pediat. (sect. neonatal-perinatal medicine); mem. Mo. State Med. Assn., Boone County Med. Soc., Alpha Omega Alpha. Roman Catholic. Avocations: classical music, bicycling, gardening. Office: U Mo Hosps & Clinics Childrens Hosp 1 Hospital Dr Columbia MO 65201-5276 Office Phone: 573-882-7919. Business E-Mail: jamese@health.missouri.edu.

JAMES, EVERETTE (ALTON EVERETTE JAMES III), academic administrator; b. 1961; m. Gretchen James; 2 children. BA in Art History, U. NC, Chapel Hill, 1985; JD, MBA, Ill. Inst. Tech., Chgo., 1990. Gen. counsel United Med. Internat. (UMI), 1990—95; sr. advisor, dep. asst. sec. US Dept. Commerce, Washington, 1996—97; ptnr. LeBoeuf, Lamb, Greene & MacRae, Washington, 2000—06; sr. advisor to Gov. Edward G. Rendell State of Pa., Harrisburg, Pa., 2006—08; sec. Pa. Dept. Health, Harrisburg, 2008—10; assoc. chancellor for health policy & planning U. Pitts., 2010—; prof. health policy & mgmt. Graduate Sch. U. Pitts. Grad. Sch. Pub. Health, 2010—. Trustee Pub. Employee Benefits Trust Fund, Pa.; gov. designated bd. mem. Ben Franklin Tech. Devel. Authority, Pa., Pub. Sch. Employees Retirement Sys., Pa. Contbr. articles to profl. jours. Founding chmn. Orgn. Econ. Cooperation and Devel. Working Party on Pvt. Pensions. Office: Graduate School Public Health 130 Desoto St A619 Crabtree Hall Pittsburgh PA 15261 Office Phone: 412-383-7049. Office Fax: 412-624-3146. E-mail: aejames@pitt.edu. *

JAMES, FRANCIS MARSHALL, III, anesthesiologist; b. Phila., Dec. 22, 1935; MD, Hahnemann U., 1961. Intern Phila. Gen. Hosp., 1961—62; resident Hosp. U. Pa., Phila., 1964—67, attending anesthesiologist, 1967—68, NC Bapt. Hosp., Winston-Salem, 1968—2000; assoc. dean grad. med. edn. Wake Forest U., NC, 1999-2000, faculty Sch. Medicine NC, 1968—2000, chair dept. anesthesiology NC, 1983—98, prof. emeritus NC, 2001—. Dir. Am. Bd. Anesthesiology, 1988-2000, pres., 1999-2000. Office: Wake Forest U Sch Medicine Dept Anesthesiology Medical Ctr Blvd Winston Salem NC 27157-1009 Personal E-mail: fmj111@aol.com.

JAMES, GARY DOUGLAS, biological anthropologist, educator, researcher; b. Norwich, Conn., Dec. 6, 1954; s. Godfrey Merchant and Joan (McIlwaine) J.; m. Kathleen Louise Wilson, July 28, 1979. BA, Wake Forest U., 1976; MA, Pa. State U., 1980, PhD, 1984. Part-time instr. Pa. State U., University Park, 1982-84; postdoctoral assoc. Cornell U. Med. Coll., NYC, 1984-86; asst. prof., assoc. rsch. prof. physiology medicine biophysics Med. Coll. Cornell U., NYC, 1991—98; rsch. prof. Decker Sch. Nursing SUNY, Binghamton, 1998—2003, dir. Inst. Primary Preventive Health Care, 1998—, adj. prof. anthropology, 1999—2003, prof. anthropology, 2003—, prof. nursing, 2003—, prof. bioengring., 2006—. Adj. prof. dept. psychology SUNY, Binghamton, NY, 2000—. Contbr. chapters to books, articles to profl. jours. Recipient New Investigator Rsch. award NIH, 1986, Internat. Man of Yr. award Internat. Biog. Ctr., 1993; NIH postdoctoral trainee, 1984, SUNY Chancellors award, 2008-09. Fellow Human Biol. Assn. (sec.-treas. 1992-96, exec. com. 1996-2000, pres. 2008-09), Soc. Behavioral Medicine, AAAS; mem. Am. Assn. Phys. Anthropologists, Internat. Platform Assn., Soc. Study Social Biology, Am. Soc. Hypertension, Am. Anthrop. Assn., Am. Dermatologlyphics Assn. (exec. com. 1996-98, sec. 1998-99, editor newsletter 2001-07, pres. 2004-05), Harvey Soc. Lutheran. Office: Decker Sch of Nursing Binghamton Univ SUNY Box 6000 Binghamton NY 13902-6000 Business E-Mail: gdjames@binghamton.edu.

JAMES, SHERMAN ATHONIA, epidemiologist, educator; b. Hartsville, SC, Oct. 25, 1943; s. Jerome and Helen Genese (Bachus) J.; m. Vera Lucia Moura; children: Sherman Alexander, Scott Anthony. AB, Talladega Coll., 1964; PhD, Washington U., 1973. Prof. epidemiology U. N.C., Chapel Hill, 1973-89, U. Mich., Ann Arbor, 1989—2003, assoc. dean acad. affairs Sch. Pub. Health; prof. pub. policy Duke U., Durham, NC, 2003—. Cons. NIMH, NIH, Bethesda, Md., 1979-83, Nat. Heart, Lung and Blood Inst., 1985—, Nat. Inst. Environ. Health Sci., 1990—; cons. NAS, Washington, 1994—. Contbr. articles to profl. jours. Capt. USAF, 1964-69. Fellow Soc. of Fellows, U. Mich., 1993—. Fellow Am. Heart Assn., Acad. Behavioral Medicine Rsch., Soc. Behavioral Medicine, Am. Coll. Epidemiology; mem. Am. Men and Women of Sci. Inst. Medicine. Avocations: travel, photography, tennis, nature walks. Office: Duke Univ 213 Sanford Inst 90245 Durham NC 27708

JAMES, WILLIAM D., dermatologist, educator; BS, US Mil. Acad., 1972; MD, Ind. U., 1977. Diplomate Am. Bd. Dermatology, 1981, cert. immunodermatology 1985. Intern Walter Reed Army Med. Ctr.; resident Letterman Army Med. Ctr.; vice chair dept. of dermatology Univ. of Pa. Health System, dir. clin. practices and tng. program dept. dermatology; prof. dermatology Univ. of Pa. Named one of Top Docs, Phila. Mag., 2002, 2005, 2009—11. Mem.: Assn. of Mil. Derrmatology, Am. Dermatol. Soc. for Allergy and Immunology, Alpha Omega Alpha Med. Honors Soc., West Point Med. Officers Soc., Assn. of Profs. of Dermatology, Am. Dermatol. Assn. Office: Penn Medicine Radnor 250 King of Prussia Rd Wayne PA 19087 Mailing: Perelman Center for Advanced Medicine S Pavilion 1st Fl 3400 Civic Center Blvd Philadelphia PA 19104 Office Phone: 800-789-7366.

JAMESON, JAMES LARRY, dean, educator, internist, endocrinologist; b. Fort Benning, Georgia, June 21, 1954; MD, U. North Carolina, Chapel Hill, 1981. Cert. NBME, 1982, Am. Bd. Internal Medicine, 1985, Endocrinology & Metabolism, 1987. Intern Mass. Gen. Hosp., Boston, 1981—82, resident, 1982—83, fellow, 1983—85, asst. physician, 1987—92, chief thyroid unit, 1987—93, dir. molecular biology, 1991—93, assoc. physician, 1992—93; rsch. assoc. Howard Hughes Medical Inst., Boston, 1985—87; asst. prof. Harvard Med. Sch., Boston, 1987—92, assoc. prof., 1992—93; chief divsn. endocrinology, metabolism and molecular medicine Feinberg Sch. Medicine, Northwestern U., 1993—2000, Irving S. Cutter prof. medicine, chair dept. medicine, 2000—07, v.p. med. affairs, Lewis Landsberg dean, 2007—11; Robert G. Gunlop prof. medicine, dean Perelman Sch. Medicine at the U. Pa., Phila., 2011—; exec. v.p. U. Pa. for the Health Sys., 2011—. Fellow: Am. Acad. Arts & Sciences; mem.: Inst. Medicine. Office: Perelman Sch Medicine at the University Pa 295 John Morgan Bldg 3620 Hamilton Walk Philadelphia PA 19104-6055 Office Phone: 215-898-6796. Office Fax: 215-573-2030. Business E-Mail: evpdean@mail.med.upenn.edu. *

JAMESON, JULIE, immunologist, educator; b. Calif., 1972; BA, U. Calif., Santa Barbara, 1994; PhD, U. Mass. Med. Ctr., 1999. Asst. prof. Scripps Rsch. Inst., 2005—. Fellowship, Leukemia & Lymphoma Soc. Mem.: Am. Assn. Immunologists, Am. Diabetes Assn. Office: 10550 N Torrey Pines Rd La Jolla CA 92037 Business E-Mail: jamesonj@scripps.edu.

JAMIESON, STUART WILLIAM, surgeon, educator; b. Bulawayo, Rhodesia, July 30, 1947; came to U.S., 1977; MB, BS, U. London, 1971. Intern St. Mary's Hosp., London, 1971; resident St. Mary's Hosp., Northwick Park Hosp., Brompton Hosp., London, 1972-77; asst. prof. Stanford U., Calif., 1980-83, assoc. prof. Calif., 1983-86; prof., head cardiac surgery U. Minn., Mpls., 1986-89, U. Calif., San Diego, 1989—. Dir. Minn. Heart and Lung Inst., Mpls., 1986-89; pres. Calif. Heart and Lung Inst., San Diego, 1991-95. Co-author: Heart and Heart-Lung Transplantation, 1989; editor: Heart Surgery, 1987; contbr. over 600 papers to med. jours. Recipient Brit. Heart Found. Fellowship award, 1978, Irvine H. Page award Am. Heart Found., 1979, Silver medal Danish Surg. Soc., 1986. Fellow ACS, Royal Coll. Surgeons, Royal Soc. Medicine, Am. Coll. Chest Physicians, Am. Coll. Cardiology; mem. Royal Coll. Physicians (licentiate), Internat. Soc. for Heart Transplantation (pres. 1986-88), Calif. Heart and Lung Inst. (pres. 1991—), Internat. Soc. Cardiothoracic Surgery (pres. 2003-.). Office: U Calif Divsn Cardiothoracic Surgery 200 W Arbor Dr San Diego CA 92103-8892 Office Phone: 619-543-7777. E-mail: sjamieson@ucsd.edu.

JAMISON, DEAN TECUMSEH, economist; b. Springfield, Mo., Oct. 10, 1943; s. Marshall Verdine and Mary Dell (Temple) J.; m. Joanne Leslie, Sept. 14, 1971 (div. 1995); children: Julian C., Eliot A., Leslie S.; m. Kin Bing Wu, Jan. 19, 1997. AB in Philosophy, Stanford U., 1966, MS in Engring. Sci., 1967; PhD in Econs., Harvard U., 1970. Asst. prof. grad. sch. bus. Stanford U., Palo Alto, Calif., 1970-73; economist World Bank, Washington, 1976-88, dir., 1992-93, advisor, 1993-98; dir. Ctr. for Pacific Rim Studies UCLA, 1993-2000, prof. Sch. Pub. Health, Grad. Sch. Edn. and Info. Studies, 1988—2006; dir. econs. adv. svc. WHO, Geneva, 1998-2000; fellow Fogarty Internat. Ctr., NIH, 2002—06; prof. U. Calif, San Francisco, 2006—. Chmn. ad hoc com. on health R&D for developing countries WHO, Geneva, 1996-97; trustee Drug Strategies, 1994—; chmn. bd. on global health Inst. Medicine NAS, 2000-05; vis. prof. Harvard U., 2006—; chmn. expert group econs., fin., and impact Malaria control programs WHO, 2006—. Author: Farmer Education and Farm Efficiency, 1982, (with L. J. Lau) Disease Control Priorities in Developing Countries, 2006, World Bank World Development Report 1993: Investing in Health, 1993, WHO World Health Report 1999: Making a Difference, 1999; cons. editor AERA Ency. Rsch., 6th edit., 1992. Fellow Woodrow Wilson Found., 1967, NSF, 1968, Bill and Melinda Gates Found. fellow, 2001. Mem. Inst. Medicine Nat. Acad. Scis. Avocation: tennis. Office: UCSF Global Health Sci 50 Beale St 12th Fl San Francisco CA 94105 Business E-Mail: djamison@globalhealth.ucsf.edu.

JAMPOLIS, MELINA BETH, internist, physician nutrition specialist; b. Chgo., Ill., Apr. 8, 1970; BA, Tufts Univ.; MD, Tufts Sch. Med., 1996. Intern, internal medicine Santa Clara Valley Med. Ctr., San Jose, Calif., 1996—97, resident, 1997—99; private practice internist San Francisco, Burlingame; founder, pres. Amarna Medical Ctr., San Francisco. Lectr. throughout the country on nutrition for weight loss and optimal health; lauched own line protein bars, 2007. Host (10 episode diet program, Discovery Network, FIT TV) Fit TV Diet Doctor, 2005; author: The No-Time-to-Lose-Diet, 2007, Busy Person's Guide to Permanent Weight Loss, 2008; mem. adv. bd., regular contbr. vivmag.com, interviewed by USA Weekend, First for Women, Women's World, Alternative Medicine Mag., Women's Health, San Francisco Mag., Quick and Simple Mag., and more on nutrition and weight loss related topics, guest appearances Regis and Kelly, View from the Bay, NBC-11, & KRON-4. Mem.: Am. Coll. Physicians, Am. Coll. Sports Med., No. Am. Assn. Study Obesity. Achievements include being one of only 200 physician nutrition specialist in the country. Address: 3580 California St Ste 201 San Francisco CA 94118-1717 Office Phone: 415-885-6474. E-mail: info@amarnamedical.com.

JAN, CHUNG-REN, pharmacologist, educator; b. Taiwan, Oct. 23, 1961; PhD, Albany Med. Coll., NY, 1992. Postdoc. rschr. Duke Med. Ctr., Durham, NC, 1994; prof. Kaohsiung Vets. Gen. Hosp., 1994—. Recipient ISI Citation Classic award, Thomson Sci. Avocation: gardening. Office: 386 Ta Chung 1st Rd Kaohsiung 813 Taiwan Business E-Mail: crjan@isca.vghks.gov.tw.

JAN, DOMINIQUE MICHEL, surgeon, educator; b. Villeneuve St. Georges, France, Jan. 8, 1953; s. Robert Jan and Yvette Bezou-Jan; m. Claire Anita Marie Guilhamon, June 17, 1986; children: Mathilde, Etienne, Antoine, Lucile. MD, Paris 6 U., France, 1978. Cert. Surgeon Paris 6 U., 1984. Prof. pediat. surgery Necker U. Hosp., Paris, 1984—. Bd. mem. Surgeons of Hope Fund, NYC; prof. clin. surgery Columbia U., NYC, 2003; prof. Surgery Albert Einstein Coll., Bronx, NY; divsn chief, pediat. surgery Montefiore Children's Hosp., Bronx. Rep. pediat. surgeon Chaine de L'espoir, Paris, 1992—2003. Mem.: Intestinal Transplantation Soc., Am. Soc. Pediat. Surgeons, Am. Soc. Transplant Surgeons. Achievements include first to accomplish intestinal transplantation in children. Home: 601 W 113 St New York NY 10025 Office: Columbia Univ Med Ctr 622 W 168 St New York NY 10032 Business E-Mail: dj2107@columbia.edu, djan@montefiore.org.

JAN, MEEI-LING, research scientist, director; married; children: Lisa Wang, Jason Wang. Leader imaging physics group Inst. Nuc. Energy Rsch., Longtan, Taoyuan County, Taiwan, 2003—, dep. dir. physics divsn., 2008—. Avocations: travel, reading, swimming. Office: Inst Nuclear Energy Rsch Wenhua Rd Jiaan Village Longtan Taoyuan County 32546 Taiwan Office Fax: 886-3-4711408. Business E-Mail: mljan@iner.gov.tw.

JAN, MEI-HWA, physical therapist, educator; b. Taipei, Taiwan, Jan. 3, 1950; d. Shui-Pou and Yuh-Ying Jan; married, Dec. 16, 1973; children: Da Hon Lin, Janice Chien-Ho Lin. BS, Nat. Taiwan U., 1972; MS, Nat. Yang-Ming U., 1999. Registered phys. therapist. Instr. Sch. Phys. Therapy Nat. Taiwan U., 1976—91, assoc. prof. Sch. and Grad. Inst. Phys. Therapy, 1991—, chmn. Sch. Phys. Therapy, 1991. Chmn. dept. phys. therapy Nat. Taiwan U. Hosp., Taipei, 1987. Supporter Dem. Progressive Party, Taipei, 2000, 2004. Mem.: Taiwan Orthopaedic Rsch. Soc. (bd. dirs.), Phys. Therapy Assn. (chmn. bd. dirs. 1992, bd. dirs.). Achievements include patents in field. Avocations: golf, mountain climbing, jogging, travel. Home: 11F 283 Sec 1 Dun-Hwa South Rd Taipei 106 Taiwan Office: Sch Grad Inst Phys Therapy NTU 7 Chung-Shan S Rd Taipei 100 Taiwan

JAN, YA-TING, radiologist; b. Taipei, Taiwan; MD, Nat. Yang-Ming U., Taipei, Taiwan, 2002. Intern Taichung (Taiwan) Vets. Gen. Hosp., 2000—02; resident Dept. Radiology Macky Meml. Hosp., Taipei, Taiwan, 2002—06, attending, 2006—. Contbr. articles to profl. jours. Office: Radiology Dept Mackay Meml Hosp No 92 Sec 2 Chung-Shan N Rd Taipei 10449 Taiwan Office Fax: 886-2-25239437. E-mail: gracilis0328@pchome.com.tw.

JANASZEK-SEYDLITZ, WIESLAWA, microbiologist, researcher; d. Katarzyna and Boleslaw Makosa; m. Maciej Janaszek-Seydlitz, Feb. 11, 1943; children: Piotr, Joanna. MSc in Biology, Warsaw U., 1970; PhD in Microbiology, Nat. Inst. Hygiene Warsaw, 1981, habilitation, 2001. I st specialist of epidemiology & hygiene Warsaw Health Dept., 1994. Rsch. asst. Nat. Inst. Hygiene, Warsaw, 1972—80, adjunkt, 1981—2002, head lab. vaccines control, dept. sera and vaccines evaluation, 2003—. Med. expert Registration Office for Pharm. Products, Warsaw, 1990—; lectr. Specialization Courses for Physicians, Warsaw, 1991—. Sec. Com. of Epidemiology of Infection Diseases, Warsaw, 1993—2003. Recipient Award Minister's of Health, Min. of Health, 1987, Rajchman's Award, Sci. Coun. of Nat. Inst. of Hygiene, 2002; grantee Rsch. project VRD/V28/181/39, Who & Phls, 1997—98, Rsch. project 6P05D05720, Polish Com. of Rsch. Investigations, 2001—02. Mem.: Polish Soc. of Epidemiologists and Physicians of Infection Diseases (life), Polish Soc. (life), Polish Soc. of Microbiologists (life). Roman Catholic. Achievements include invention of intro. of seed lot sys. to prodn. of BCG vaccine in Poland; intro. of new methods for evaluation of onco-BCG products used in immunotherapy of bladder cancer in human beings; research in characterisation of BCG Moreau substrain; evaluation of immunological status of Polish population against measles, mumps, rubella, pertussis and varicella infections. Avocations: poetry, classic music, painting, swimming, travel. Home: 24 Kochanowskiego St Apt 12 Warsaw 01-864 Poland Office: Nat Inst Hygiene 24 Chocimska St Warsaw 00-791 Poland Office Fax: +48 (22) 8497484. E-mail: wjanaszek@pzh.gov.pl.

JANATOVA, JARMILA, biomedical investigator, educator; b. Pisek, Czech Republic, Jan. 9, 1939; naturalized, 1983; d. Jan Kovarik (killed May 8, 1945) and Jarmila Blechova-Kovarikova-Ticha, Josef Tichy (Stepfather); m. Jiri Janata, 1962 (div. 1992); children: Petr Janata, Hana Janatova. MSc in Chemistry, Charles U., Prague, 1961; PhD in Biochemistry, Czechoslovak Acad. Scis., Prague, 1965. Lectr. in phys. chemistry Charles U., 1965—66; postdoc. rsch. assoc. biophysics U. Mich., Ann Arbor, 1966—67; postdoc. rsch. assoc., dept. biology U. Utah, Salt Lake City, 1973—75, postdoc. rsch. assoc., dept. pathology, 1977—79, rsch. instr., asst. prof. pathology, 1979—85, rsch. assoc. prof. pathology, 1985—92, rsch. assoc. prof. bioengring., 1991—2004, dir. bioprocessing facility, Huntsman Cancer Inst., 1997—2000, adj. prof. bioengring., 2004—11, prof. emeritus bioengring., 2011—; sr. exptl. officer U. Liverpool, 1975—76; sr. academic visitor, immunochemistry unit U. Oxford, England, 1986—87; guest prof. U. Innsbruck, Austria, 1991. Sec. Internat. Complement Workshop, Salt Lake City, 1997—2000; sci. reviewer Miscellaneous Biochemical Journals, Salt Lake City, 1985. Contbr. articles, reviews to profl. jours.; presenter (nat. and internat. confs.). Grantee Rsch. grants, NIH, NSF, 1979—91. Mem.: Am. Soc. Biochemistry Molecular Biology, Surfaces in Biomaterials, Internat. Complement Soc., Am. Chem. Soc., Soc. Biomaterials. Achievements include elucidation of the heterogeneity of serum albumin; discovery of the presence of thiolester in the third and fourth components of complement (plays pivotal role in defense against infection); study of structure and function of several complement proteins; development of procedures for purification and analyses of a variety of plasma proteins; an immunochip prototype for simultaneous detection of AEDs using an enhanced one step homogenous immunoassay; research in biocompatibility of biomaterials and their potential to activate complement; study of coating inhibitory activity in human tears that interfere with the formation of immune complexes at polymer surfaces; patent for apo-transferrin as a potent inhibitor of bacterial adhesion to biomaterials. Office: Univ Utah Dept Bioengring 50 S Central Campus Dr Rm 2440 Salt Lake City UT 84112-9202 Business E-Mail: jarmila.janatova@utah.edu.

JANELLE, GREGORY M., anesthesiologist; b. Kans. City, Kans., June 9, 1970; BA, Boston U., 1994; MD, Boston U. Sch. Medicine, 1994. Chief, divsn. cardiothoracic anesthesia U. Fla. Coll. Medicine, 1999—. Mem.: Soc. NASA Flight Surgeons, Congenital Cardiac Anesthesiology Soc., Internat. Anesthesia Rsch. Soc., Am. Soc. Anesthesiology, Soc. Cardiovasc. Anesthesiologists. Avocations: travel, scuba diving, hunting. Office: PO Box 100254 Gainesville FL 32610-0254 Office Fax: 352-392-7029. Business E-Mail: gjanelle@anest.ufl.edu.

JANES, DONALD WALLACE, biologist, educator, academic administrator, consultant; b. Kans. City, Mo., June 12, 1929; s. H. Wallace and Leila G. (Duncan) Janes; m. Norma Marie Lee, Feb. 21, 1953 (dec. 1978); children: Todd Allan, Jeffrey Wallace, Scott Lee Duncan, Nancy Marie; m. Janina Z. Piorkowska, Nov. 14, 1981. BA, Baker U., Baldwin City, Kans., 1951; MS, U. Kans., Lawrence, 1956; PhD, Kans. State U., Manhattan, 1962. Instr. biology Washburn U., Topeka, 1957-61; asst. prof. biology Parsons Coll., Fairfield, Iowa, 1962-63; postdoctoral research assoc. Ind. U., Bloomington, 1963, Baylor Coll. Medicine, Houston, 1964, 66, Iowa State U., Ames, 1965; assoc. prof. and dean Colo. State U., Pueblo, 1963—78; prof. biology U. So. Colo., Pueblo, 1978-92; ret., 1992; microbiology cons., 1992—. Cons., examiner North Ctrl. Assn. Colls. and Schs., Chgo., 1969-90; vis. prof. U. Colo., Boulder, 1978-79; ski guide Over the Hill Gang, Keystone Resort, Colo., mem. Mountain Responsibility Team, 1998-2002. People to People amb. People's Republic of China, 1989, Program in Understanding to the Middle East, 1997, Program in Understanding to Israel and Egypt, 1999; vice-chair, sec. bd. dirs. Breckenridge Music Inst., 1990-99, pres., 1999-2001; vol. Vail Music Festival, 1990-, Vail Internat. Dance Festival, 1998-, Vail Valley Jazz Festival, World Cup Ski Championships. Fulbright fellow U. Graz, Austria, 1956-57; Acad. Adminstrn. fellow Am. Council on Edn., Washington, 1968-69. Mem. Audubon Club, Pueblo (organizer 1968); Pueblo C. of C. 1968-78; Am. Soc. Microbiology, Soc. for Indsl. Microbiology, Sigma Xi (pres. 1986-88), Breckenridge Ski Touring Soc. (pres. 1993-96), Colo. Mountain (Pueblo, chmn. 1973-74), Breckenridge Music Inst. (pres., bd. dirs.). Clubs: Colo. Mountain (Pueblo) (chmn. 1973-74). Avocations: mountain climbing, skiing, bicycling, music, reading. Home: 52 Aspen Dr PO Box 2434 Frisco CO 80443 Personal E-mail: donaldwjanes@gmail.com.

JANEWAY, RICHARD, retired academic administrator; b. LA, Feb. 12, 1933; s. VanZandt and Grace Ellen (Bell) Janeway; m. Katherine Esmond Pillsbury, Dec. 23, 1955 (dec. Jan. 7, 2010); children: Susan Kent, David VanZandt, Elizabeth Anne; m. Nancy Hirsman Harper Janeway, May 28, 2011. AB, Colgate U., 1954; MD, U. Pa., 1958. Diplomate Am. Bd. Psychiatry and Neurology. Intern Hosp. U. Pa., 1958—59; resident N.C. Baptist Hosp., Winston-Salem, 1963—66; mem. faculty Bowman Gray Sch. Medicine (now Wake Forest U. Sch. Medicine), Winston-Salem, 1966—; prof. neurology Wake Forest U., Winston-Salem, 1971—2003, prof. medicine and mgmt., 1997—2003, prof. emeritus, 2003—, dir. Cerebral Vascular Rsch. Ctr., Bowman Gray Sch. Medicine, 1969—71; dean Bowman Gray Sch. Medicine,(now Wake Forest U. Sch. Medicine), Winston-Salem, 1971—85, exec. dean, 1985—94, v.p. health affairs, 1983—90, exec. v.p. health affairs, 1990—97, ret., 1997—. Mem. exec. com. So. Nat. Bank, Winston-Salem, NC, 1982—95; dir. BB&T Corp., 1995—2003, bd. dirs., mem. exec. com., chmn., 2001—03; mem. nat. adv coun. regional med. programs HEW, 1974—77; mem. -at-large Nat. Bd. Med. Examiners, 1979—87; mem. N.C. Joint Conf. Com. on Med. Care, Inc., 1983—2003; dir. N.C. Inst. Medicine. Mem. Winston-Salem Forsyth Co. Bd. Edn., 1970—73; trustee Winston-Salem State U., 1991—95, Colgate U., 1988—95, Sr. Svcs. Inc., 2007—; mem. investment com. Episcopal Diocese NC, 2000—06, chmn., 2004, 2005; bd. dirs. Nat. Assn. for Biomed. Rsch., 1993—96, Ams. for Med. Progress, Inc., 1993—97, Winston-Salem Found., 1994—2002, chmn., 1997, 1998. Capt. USAF, 1959—63, flight surgeon, 1962—63. Recipient fellow, USPHS, 1956, Markle scholar, 1968—73, Medallion of Merit, Wake Forest U., 1998, Maroon citation, Colgate U., 2004. Fellow: ACP, Am. Heart Assn. (coun. on stroke), Am. Acad. Neurology; mem.: AMA, Soc. Med. Adminstrs., Greater Winston-Salem C. of C. (bd. dirs. 1985—89, 1991—95, chmn. 1992), Inst. Medicine of NAS, Am. Clin. and Climatol. Assn., Assn. Am. Med. Colls. (exec. coun. 1977—86, mem. accreditation coun. on grad med. edn. 1981—85, chmn. coun. of deans 1982—83, exec. com. 1982—86, chmn. 1984—85), Am. Neurol. Assn., Rotary (dir. 1977—80, v.p. 1981—82, pres. 1982—83), Alpha Omega Alpha, Sigma Xi, Phi Beta Kappa. Republican. Episcopalian. Avocations: photography, golf, flower arranging, reading, gardening. Personal E-mail: rjaneway@triad.rr.com.

JANG, BYUNG IK, internist, educator; b. Daegu, Republic Of Korea, June 17, 1964; s. Hak Yul Jang and Ok Ja Jung; m. Jung A. Chae; children: Mu Kyung, Hwan Jun. PhD, Yeungnam Med. Sch., Deagu, 1996. Diplomate in med. Deagu, 1996. Assoc. prof. Yeungnam U. Coll. Medicine, Daegu, Republic of Korea, 1998—; dr. Yeungnam U. Med. Ctr., Daegu, 1998—. Rschr. U. NC, Chapel Hill, 2003—05. Fund mem. Yeungnam Med. Ctr., 2007. Capt. Army, 1996—99, Daegu. Recipient Disting. Investigator award, 2006. Office: Yeungnam Med Ctr Internal Medicine Deamyung Dong 705-030 Daegu Daegu Republic of Korea Office Fax: 053-654-8386; Home Fax: 82-53-654-8386. Business E-Mail: jbi@med.yu.ac.kr.

JANG, GI YOUNG, pediatric cardiologist; b. Gwang Ju, Jeon la nam Do, Republic of Korea, Dec. 24, 1965; s. Sang Soo Jang and Ssang Soon Bong; m. Hye Kyung Noh, Oct. 12, 1994; children: Min Woo, Jin Woo. PhD in medicine, Korea U., Seoul, 2005. Diplomate Korean Bd. Pediats., Korean Bd. Pediat. Heart Assn. Staff pediat. cardiology Sejong Heart Inst., Bucheon, Kyunggi Do, Republic of Korea, 2003—06; prof. pediatric cardiology Korea U. Hosp., Ansan, Kyunggi Do, 2006—. Contbr. articles to profl. jours. Presbyn. Rodem Tree Ch., Seoul, 2004—08. Mem.: Korean Pediatric Soc., Korean Pediatric Heart Assn. (diplomate pediatric cardiology). Mem. Christian Ch. (Disciples Of Christ). Achievements include research in cardiac intervention in congenital heart disease; renin-angiotensin-aldosterone system in cardiac development. Avocation: swimming. Office: Korea Univ Hosp Gojan 1-Dong Dan Won-Gu 516 425-707 Ansan Kyunggi-do Republic of Korea Office Fax: 82-31-405-8591. Personal E-mail: jgynhg@dreamwiz.com, jgynhg@yahoo.co.kr.

JANG, GUNJA, nursing educator; b. Republic of Korea, Mar. 20, 1970; PhD, Kyungpook Nat. U., 2004. Full-time instr. Daegu U., 2010—, dir., dept. nursing, 2010—. Cons. Shelter Victims Domestic Violence, 2003—, Shelter Sexually Abused Children, 2005—. Recipient Commendation medal, Korean Ministry of Health and Welfare; grant, Nat. Rsch. Found. Korea. Mem.: Korea Nurse Assn. Avocations: mountain climbing, swimming, reading. Office: 2288 Daemyeong 3-dong Nam-gu Daegu 705-714 Republic of Korea Office Fax: 82-53-650-8389. Business E-Mail: kjjang14@daegu.ac.kr.

JANG, HONGSEOK, medical educator; b. Kwnagju, Nov. 4, 1959; MD, Cath. Med. Sch., 1985. Prof. Radiation Oncology, Cath. Med. Sch., 1994—; dir. gen. affairs com. Korean Soc. Therapeutic Radiology and Oncology, 2001—04, dir. info. & communication com., 2001—07, dir. ins. com., 2007. Editl. bd. Jour. Korean Soc. Complementary and Interrogative Medicine, 2006; dir. Ins. Com. Korean Photodynamic Assn., 2007, Panel Com., Health Ins. Rev. and Assessment Svc., 2008, Soc. Gastrointestinal Intervention, 2009. Mem.: Korean Cancer Assn., Korean Soc. Hyperthermia and Oncology, Am. Soc. Therapeutic Radiology and Oncology, Am. Assn. Cancer Rsch., Korean Liver Cancer Study Group. Avocations: photography, travel. Office: #505 Banpo-Dong Seocho-Gu Seoul St Mary Seoul 138-200 Republic of Korea Business E-Mail: hsjang11@catholic.ac.kr.

JANG, HYE RYOUN, medical educator; b. Daegu, Republic of Korea, Sept. 23, 1974; MD, Seoul Nat. U., PhD, 2000. Asst. prof. Samsung Med. Ctr., Sungkyunkwan U. Sch. Medicine, 2010—. Grant, NKF Md. Office: 50 Irwon-dong Gangnam-gu Seoul Kyunggi-do 135-710 Republic of Korea Office Fax: 82-2-3410-0064. Personal E-mail: shinehr@gmail.com.

JANG, HYUK JAI, surgeon, department chairman; b. Seoul, Kangwon Do, Republic Of Korea, Apr. 28, 1964; PhD, U. Ulasn, 2006. Cert. surgeon Korea Med. Assn., 1994. Assoc. prof. U. Ulsan Coll. Medicine, Kyung Sang Nam Do, 2001—; chmn. surgery ICU Gangneung Asan Hosp., 2002—08, chmn. dept. surgery, 2006—. Contbr. articles to profl. jours. Lt. Med. army, 1994—97, Kangwon do. Home: Apt 101-402 415 Sachyun Myon Bangdong Ri Kang won Do Gangneung 241-711 Republic of Korea Office: Gangneung Asan Hosp Surgery Sachyun Myon Bangdong Ri 415 210-711 Gangneung Gangwon-do Republic of Korea Office Fax: 82336413218. Business E-Mail: jhj@gnah.co.kr.

JANG, JEONG WON, hepatologist; b. Seoul, Republic of Korea, May 23, 1971; s. Ik Soo Jang and Young Ja Lee; m. Ji Young Kwon, Aug. 24, 2002; children: Ho Jun, Eun Jun. MD, Cath. U. Korea, Seoul, 1996. Cert. dr. Korean Med. Assn., 1997. Residency Kangnam St. Mary's Hosp., Seoul, 1998—2001, fellowship, 2002—04; asst. prof. Incheon St. Mary's Hosp., Republic of Korea, 2005—. Contbr. articles to med. jours. Recipient Young Investigator award, Cath. U. Korea, 2006, Best Poster prize, Seoul Internat. Liver Symposium, 2007. Fellow: Korean Assn. for Study of Liver; mem.: Korean Soc. Gastroenterology. Achievements include research in liver diseases. Avocations: piano, jazz. Office: Incheon St Marys Hosp Bupyeongdong Bupyeonggu 665 403-720 Incheon Incheon Republic of Korea Office Fax: 82 32 510 5683. Business E-Mail: garden@catholic.ac.kr.

JANG, JIN-YOUNG, medical educator; m. Yunjo Park, Feb. 16, 1997; children: Jaehyuk, Junhyuck. MD, Seoul Nat. U., Korea, 1992; PhD, Seoul Nat. U. Prof. Seoul Nat. U. Hosp., 2002—. Office: Seoul Nat Univ Hosp Surgery Yongon-dong 28 Chongno-gu Seoul 110-744 Republic of Korea Office Fax: 82-2-766-3975. Business E-Mail: jangjy4@snu.ac.kr.

JANG, KYOUNG-AE, dermatologist; b. Suwon, Gyeonggi-Do, Republic of Korea, Apr. 8, 1968; d. Pil-Su Jang and In-Hee Lee; m. Sung-Sik Yoo, Aug. 28, 1999; children: Ji-Ho Yoo, Jay Yoo. MD, Seoul Nat. U., Republic of Korea, 1994; M in Med. Sci., Ulsan U., Republic of Korea, 2000, PhD, 2003. Lic. physician Health and Social Affairs, Republic of Korea, 1994, dermatologist Health and Social Affairs, Republic of Korea, 1999. Intern Asan Med. Ctr., Seoul, 1994—95, resident, 1995—99, fellow, 1999—2000; asst. prof. Seoul Paik Hosp., 2000—01; dir. Leaders Clinic, Seoul, 2001—. Cons. physician Seoul Nat. Hosp., 2003—05. Mem.: Korean Hair Rsch. Soc., Assn. Korean Dermatologists, Korean Dermatol. Assn. Office: Leaders Clinic Yeounyi Blg 71-1 Mia 4-Dong Gangbuk-Gu Seoul 142-804 Republic of Korea Office Phone: (02)-945-7070. Office Fax: (02)-986-3517. Personal E-mail: jang722@netsgo.com.

JANG, SEON, medical educator; b. Jeonju, Republic of Korea, June 19, 1961; parents Tae and Soon Lim Park; m. Poo Ok Chung, Jan. 14, 1984; 1 child, Hoon Dow. PhD, Chunbuk Nat. U., Jeonju, 1992. Postdoc. rschr., dept. immunology Aberdeen U., 1993—94; lectr. Chunbuk Nat. U., 1994—97; sr. rschr. Nat. Fisheries Rsch. and Devel. Inst., Pusan, 1994—97, ABI Corp., Jeonju, 1998—2001, Immunopia, Iksan, 2002—03, Lab. Immunology Med. Sch. Wonkwang U., Iskan, 2002—03; asst. prof. Seojeung Coll., Yangju, 2004—07; prof. Jeonju U., 2007—, chief, Atopy Care Inst., 2010—. Mem., adv. com., Jeonbuk, 2009—. Contbr. articles to profl. publs. Dir. Atopy Cluster Project, Jinan, 2008—; mem. Edn. Chronic Diseases Care & Health Promotion, 2008—, Devel. & Mgmt. Atopic Care Program, 2009—10, Atopic Children Care Cmty. Investment Svcs., 2010—. Recipient Excellence award, Jeonju U., 2009; named Respected Person of Yr., SiSa Today Media, 2010. Mem.: Korean Soc. Applied Biol. Chemistry, Korean Soc. Food and Nutrition, Korean Soc. Molecular and Cellular Biology, Korean Assn. Immunologists. Democrat. Office: 1200 3-GA Hyoja-dong Wansan-gu Jeonju 560-759 Republic of Korea also: Sch Alternative Medicine & Health Sci Coll Medicine Jeonju University 116 Chunjum Jeonju Republic of Korea

JANG, SUNG HO, rehabilitative medicine physician, researcher; b. Jinchun, Republic of Korea, Aug. 18, 1964; s. Dae Kwon Jang and Jung Hee Park; m. Sook Ja Back, Feb. 28, 1992; children: Han Jae, Chae Woon. MSc, Kyungbook U. Med. Coll., 2002; MD, Yonsei U. Med. Coll., 1990. Cert. gen. physician Republic of Korea, specialist in phys. medicine and rehab. Republic of Korea. Intern Yonsei Med. Ctr., Seoul, Republic of Korea, 1990—91, resident, 1994—98; rsch. fellow Yeungham Med. Ctr., 1998—99; instr. Yeungham U. Med. Coll., Taegu, 1999—2001, asst. prof., 2001—. Dept. chief Yeungham U. Hosp. Dept. Rehab., Taegu, Republic of Korea, 2001—03, Yeungham U. Hosp. Dept Quality Assessment, 2003—. With Korean Army, 1991—94. Mem.: Internat. Soc. Physical Rehab. Med., Korean Acad. Human Brain Mapping, Korean Acad. Rehab. Med. (Acad. award 2000). Office: Yeungham U Coll Medicine Dept Phys Medicine and Rehab 317-1 Daemyungdong Namku Daegu 707-717 Republic of Korea Business E-Mail: strokerehab@hanmail.net, belado@med.yu.ac.kr.

JANG, SUNG SOO, plastic surgeon; Grad., Seoul Nat. U. Med. Coll. Bd. cert. tng. palstic surgery dept. Seoul Nat. Univ. Hosp., fellowship plastic surgery dept; dir. Dream Plastic Surgery Clinic. Mem.: Internat. Confederation Plastic reconstructive and Aesthetic Surgery, Korean Cleft-Palate-Craniofacial Assn., Korean Microsurgical Soc., Korean Soc. Reconstructive Hand Surgery, Korean Med. Assn., Korean Soc. Aesthetic Plastic Surgery, Korean Soc. Plastic and Reconstructive Surgeons. Office: Dream Plastic Surgery Clinic Apkujung Subway Sta Seoul Republic of Korea Office Phone: 8225461616. Office Fax: 8225461614. *

JANG, TAE YOUNG, medical educator; b. Republic of Korea, Apr. 24, 1954; MD, Yonsei U., 1979, PhD, 1991. Prof., dept. otorhinolaryngology, head & neck surgery Inha U. Hosp., 1996—. Chmn. Korean Academic Soc., 2008—09, Korean Acad. Facial Plastic and Reconstructive Surgery, 2010. Recipient Academic award, Korean Rhinologic Soc. Office: Inha University Hosp Shin-heung Dong 3-Ga Incheon Jung-gu 400-711 Republic of Korea Business E-Mail: jangty@inha.ac.kr.

JANG, YANGSOO, cardiologist, educator; b. Republic of Korea, Dec. 12, 1957; BS in Med. Sci., Yonsei U., Seoul, Republic of Korea, 1982, PhD in Med. Physiology, 1991. Instr., internal medicine Yonsei U. Coll. Medicine, 1991—92, asst. prof., 1992—98, assoc. prof., 1998—2004, physician, Severance Cardiovasc. Hosp., 2004—, chmn., cardiology divsn., 2008—, dir., Yonsei Cardiovasc. Rsch. Inst., 2008—; clin. rsch. fellow, dept. cardiology Cleve. Clinic, 1993—95. Dir., cardiovasc. genome ctr. Severance Cardiovasc. Hosp., Yonsei U. Health Sys., Seoul, 2001—, clin. dir., 2004—, dir., cardiovasc. product evaluation ctr., 2010—. Recipient First Med. award, Korean Med. Assn., prize, Best Achievement prize, Yonsei U., Best Prof. prize, First prize, Korean Intellectual Property Office. Fellow: ACC, Soc. Cardiovasc. Angiography and Interventions, Asian Pacific Soc. Interventional Cardiology, Am. Heart Assn., Am. Coll. Cardiology; mem.: Korean Soc. Circulation. Avocation: golf. Office: 250 Sungsanno Seoul Seodaemun 120-752 Republic of Korea Office Fax: 82-2-365-1878. Business E-Mail: jangys1212@yuhs.ac.

JANGID, ARVIND, research scientist; b. Nagaur, Rajasthan, India, Nov. 8, 1978; MSc, M.S. U., Baroda, 2000. Gen. mgr. Accutest Rsch. Lab (I) Pvt. Ltd., 2005; scientist-ii Torrent Rsch. Ctr., 2000—. Office: Accutest Research Lab (I) Pvt Ltd Ahmedabad Gujarat 380015 India E-mail: jangid_arvind@rediffmail.com.

JANI, HITESH ISHWARLAL, physician, educator; b. Mundra, India, Apr. 6, 1960; BAMS, Gujarat Ayurved U., MCS, 1982; ND, Mahatma Gandhi Naturopathy Inst. Sr. lectr. & panchakarma physician Gujarat Ayurved U., 2010—. Recipient Internat. Excellency Ayurved award, Tathagat Found. Office: 105 Sidhivinayak Apts Limda Jamnagar Gujarat 361008 India Office Fax: 91-2559292. Personal E-mail: dr_hitesh_jani2000@yahoo.com.

JANI, KALPESH, gastroenterologist, consultant; s. Vinodrai and Madhu Jani; m. Sadhna Hukku, Dec. 3, 1994; 1 child, Kashish Hukku-Jani. MS, Baroda Med. Coll., Gujrat, India, 1995; MS, DNB, FNB in Surgery, Baroda Med. Coll., 1994. Asst. prof. Baroda Med. Coll., 1995—96; cons. gen. surgeon Manjalpur Hosp., Baroda, 1996—2004; sr. registar Gem Hosp., Coimbatore, Tamil Nadu, India, 2004—06; cons. surg. gastroenterologist SIGMA, Baroda, 2006—. Contbr. articles to profl. jours. Fellow: ACS, Internat. Coll. Surgeons; mem.: Nat. Acad. Med. Scis., New Delhi, Assn. Minimal Access Surgeons (cons. 2006—), Indian Assn. Surgeon, Indian Med. Assn. Achievements include research in various aspects of minimal access surgery. Office Fax: 912652637515. E-mail: kvjani@gmail.com.

JANI, SUSHMA NIRANJAN, pediatric psychiatrist; b. Gwalior, Madhya, Pradesh, India, Sept. 26, 1959; arrived in U.S., 1983; d. Kirty Ambalal and Purnima Kirty (Bhatt) Dave; m. Niranjan Natwerial Jani, Mar. 30, 1983; children: Suni Jani, Raja Jani, Roma Jani. Intern Sci., Mithibai Coll., Bombay, India; MB, BS, B.J. Med. Coll., Ahmedabad, India; MD in Adult Psychiatry, Ind. U., 1984; MD in Child Psychiatry, Johns Hopkins U., 1987. Diplomate Am. Bd. Psychiatry and Neurology, sub-bd. Child Psychiatry, Am. Bd. Pediat., Am. Bd. Forensic Examiners; cert. in addiction medicine Am. Soc. Addiction Medicine; cert. med. review officer Med. Rev. Officer Cert. Courell. Pediat. emergency physician Mercey Hosp., Balt., 1997—99; child psychiatrist Johns Hopkins Univ. Hosp., Balt.; asst. clin. prof., mem. faculty dept. pediats. and psychiatry Georgetown U. Med. Ctr., Balt., assoc. prof. pediat. and psychiatry; assoc. prof. psychiatry Georgetown U.; med. dir. Chesapeake network Devereux Found., Md., Va., W.Va., Washington and Del., 1998-99; med. dir. Riverside Hosp., Washington, 1999—2005; pediat. emergency physician Howard County Hosp., 1999—; chief med. officer Maple Shade Youth and Family Svcs., Mardela Springs, Md., 2005—; assoc. clin. prof. U. Md., Balt.; subject matter expert Def. Ctrs. Excellence. Chief cons. psychiatrist Balt. Detention Ctr., 1988-89, cons. psychiatrist Vets. Hosp., Indpls., 1986-87. Vol. Radha-Krishna Leporsy Camp, Bombay, 1981—83.

Mem. AMA, Am. Acad. Child & Adolescent Psychiatry, Am. Psychiatry Assn., Md. Psychiat. Soc., Columbia Assn., India Assn., Am. Acad. Podiatrics, Am. Soc. Addiction Medicine (cert.). Hindu. Avocations: reading, knitting, sewing, letter-writing. Home and Office: 10810 Hickory Ridge Rd Columbia MD 21044 Office Phone: 410-997-5500.

JANICAK, PHILIP GREGORY, psychiatrist, educator; b. Chgo., Aug. 2, 1946; s. Edward and Josephine (Raskauskas) J.; m. Mary Judith Cray, Oct. 16, 1976; 1 child, Matthew Cray. BS in Psychology with honors, Loyola U., Chgo., 1969, MD, 1973. Diplomate Am. Bd. Psychiatry and Neurology. Asst. clin. prof. dept. psychiatry Loyola U., Maywood, Ill., 1976-78; rsch. assoc. U. Chgo., 1979-81; asst. prof. U. Ill., Chgo., 1982-85, assoc. prof., 1986-92, prof., 1992—2004, Rush U., 2004—. Chief rsch. unit Ill. State Psychiat. Inst., Chgo., 1984-96; med. dir. psychiat. clin. rsch. ctr. U. Ill., 1996-2004, Rush U., 2004-. First author: Principles and Practice of Psychopharmacotherapy, 1993, 5th edit., 2011. NIMH grant co-investigator, 1986, 91, 93; NIMH grant prin. investigator, 1990; NIH grant assoc. program dir. 2000-2004. Fellow Am. Psychiat. Assn. (disting. life fellow). Roman Catholic. Business E-Mail: pjanicak@rush.edu.

JANICKI, ROBERT STEPHEN, retired pharmaceutical executive; b. Manette, Wash., Dec. 7, 1934; s. Stephen Walter and Elizabeth Caroline (Gorman) J.; m. I. Jane Betcher, Aug. 18, 1956; children: Robert, Beth, David. BS, Grove City Coll., 1956; MD, Temple U., 1961. Diplomate Nat. Bd. Med. Examiners. Intern U.S. Naval Hosp., Phila., 1961-62; resident in occupl. medicine USN, 1962-63; assoc. dir. clin. rsch. Dow Pharms., Indpls., 1966-68; assoc. med. dir. Neisler divsn. Union Carbide Corp., Sterling Forest, NY, 1968-69; assoc. med. dir. regulatory affairs Abbott Labs., North Chicago, Ill., 1969-70, dir. clin. rsch. pharm. products divsn., 1970-71, v.p. med. affairs pharm. products divsn., 1971-79, v.p. research pharm. products divsn., 1979-83, corp. v.p. R & D pharm. products divsn., 1983-89, sr. v.p., 1989-90. Bd. dirs. Osprey Pharms., Jacksonville, Fla.; cons. New Drug Devel Contbr. articles to profl. jours. Trustee Grove City (Pa.) Coll., 1995-99. Lt. comdr. M.C., USN, 1961-66. Fellow Am. Coll. Clin. Pharmacology; mem. Am. Soc. Clin. Pharmacology and Therapeutics, Sigma Xi, Alpha Omega Alpha. Home: 138 Anchor Dr Vero Beach FL 32963-2941 Personal E-mail: rsjanicki@aol.com.

JANIER, MARC F., nuclear medicine physician, researcher; b. Lyon, France, June 10, 1962; MD, Lyon U., PhD, 1990. Physician, rschr. Lyon U., 1993 , head, nuc. medicine unit, Hospices Civils de Lyon, 2000. Office: Hôsp Edouard Herriot 5 Pl d'Arson Lyon 69437 France Business E-Mail: marc.janier@univ-lyon1.fr.

JANIS, JEFFERY E., plastic surgeon, educator; b. Cleve., May 6, 1971; BSBA magna cum laude, Washington U., St. Louis, 1993; MD, Case Western Res. U. Sch. Medicine, Cleve., 1998. Lic. Tex., 2000, Ohio, 2006, diplomate Am. Bd. Plastic Surgery, 2004. Resident, gen surgery U. Tex. Southwestern Med. Ctr., Dallas, 1998—2001, resident, plastic surgery, 2001—03, asst. instr. dept. plastic surgery, 2003—04, asst. prof. dept. plastic surgery, 2004—08, assoc. prof. dept. plastic surgery, 2008—; chief plastic surgery Parkland Health and Hosp Sys., Dallas, 2006—, chief wound care, 2008—, pres. elect med. staff, 2010—, mem. OR com., 2006—, chmn., 2009—, with med. adv. com., 2006—, sec., 2010—. Dir. adminstrv. coord. dept. plastic surgery U. Tex. Southwestern, 2003—, admissions interviewer, med. sch., 2004—, faculty senate, med. ctr., 2005—, chmn. health info. mgmt. com., 2005—, dir. integrated residents, dept. plastic surgery, 2005—06, assoc. program dir. residency program, dept. plastic surgery, 2006—07, dir. resident cosmetic clinic, dept. plastic surgery, 2006—, mem. clin. info. svcs. steering com. med. ctr., 2006—, mem. performance improvement com., 2006—, program dir. residency program, dept. plastic surgery, 2007—; OR com. Parkland Health and Hosp. Sys., 2006—, med. adv. com., 2006—, performance improvement com., 2006, chmn. health info. mgmt. com., 2007—. Contbr. articles to profl. jours., chapters to books. Attending staff Parkland Meml. Hosp., Dallas, Zale Lipshy U. Hosp., Dallas, Baylor U. Med. Ctr., Dallas, VA Med. Ctr., Dallas, St. Paul Med. Ctr., Dallas, Children's Med. Ctr., Dallas. Recipient William D. Holden award, Case Western Res. U., 1998, Cert. Achievement, Surg. Edn., U Tex. Southwestern Med. Ctr., 1998—99, 1999—2000, Excellence in Tchg. award, 2002—03, Dept. Plastic Surgery Mr. Chip's award, 2003, Clinician the Yr. award, 2003—04, Special Achievement award, 2007. Mem.: ACS, AMA, Dallas County Med. Soc., Tex. Med. Assn. (membership com. 2007—), Dallas County Med. Soc. (membership com. 2003—, mediations com. 2007—, alt. del. 2007—), Wound Healing Soc., Assn. Acad. Chairmen Plastic Surgery (residency model assessment project com. 2007—, Website redesign com. 2007—, taskforce on establishment of policy and guidelines 2007—), Am. Soc. Aesthetic Plastic Surgery (CME com. 2007—), Dallas Soc. Plastic Surgeons, Tex. Soc. Plastic Surgeons, Am. Soc. Plastic Surgeons (membership stategies taskforce 2003—, membership com. 2006—, program evaluation com. 2006—, in-svc. exam writing com. 2006—, product adv. com. 2007—, instructional course com. 2007—, feasibility study oversight com. 2007—, editl. adv. bd. 2006—), Alpha Omega Alpha, Beta Gamma Sigma. Office: Dept Plastic Surgery Univ Tex SW Med Ctr Dallas TX 75390-9132

JANKOVIC, JOSEPH, neurologist, educator; b. Teplice, Czechoslovakia, Mar. 1, 1948; came to U.S., 1965; m. Cathy Sue Inselberg, May 26, 1973; children: Jason, Daniel, Zachary. MD, U. Ariz., 1973. Diplomate Am. Bd. Neurology. Med. intern Baylor Coll. Medicine, Houston, 1973-74, asst. prof. neurology, 1977-84, assoc. prof., 1984-88, prof., 1988—; resident in neurology Columbia U., NYC, 1974-76, chief resident in neurology, 1976-77. Dir. Parkinson's Disease Ctr. and Movement Disorder Clinic, Houston, 1977—; sr. attending physician Meth. Hosp., Houston, 1988—. Author over 700 articles and book chpts. in field; editor/co-editor 40 med. books; mem. editorial bd. jours. Movement Disorders, Clin. Neuropharmacology, Neurology Jour., Jour. Neurology Psychiatry. Chmn. sci. adv. bd. Blepharospasm Rsch. Found.; mem. adv. bd. Dystonia Med. Rsch. Found., Internat. Tremor Found., Tourette's Syndrome Med. Adv. Bd. Grantee disease rsch. founds., pharmaceutical cos., NIH Fellow Am. Acad. Neurology (Rsch. award); mem. AMA, Am. Neurol. Assn. (hon.), Soc. for Neurosci., Movement Disorders Soc. (pres.-elect 1991-94, pres. 1994-96). Avocations: tennis, music. Office: Baylor Coll Medicine 6550 Fannin St Ste 1801 Houston TX 77030-2744

JANNE, PASI ANTERO, oncologist, educator; b. Helsinki, Finland, Dec. 20, 1967; MD, PhD, U. Pa. Sch. Medicine, 1996. Diplomate Am. Bd. Internal Medicine, cert. in med. oncology. Intern, resident internal medicine Brigham & Women's Hosp., Boston, 1996—98; fellow med. onclogy Dana-Farber Cancer Inst., Harvard Med. Sch., Boston, 1998—2001, asst. prof. medicine, 2001—. Contbr. articles to profl. jours. Mem.: Am. Soc. Clin. Oncology (Merit award 2001). Achievements include research in mechanisms of sensitivity and resistance to kinase inhibitors, translating laboratory-based observations into therapeutic treatments for patients with cancer. Office: Harvard Med Sch Dana Farber Cancer Inst Lowe Ctr Thoracic Oncology 44 Binney St D820B Boston MA 02115 Office Phone: 617-632-6036. Office Fax: 617-632-7683. E-mail: pjanne@partners.org. *

JANNE D'OTHEE, BERTRAND, radiologist, researcher; b. Verviers, Belgium, June 27, 1966; s. Charles Janne d'Othee and Anne Dessain. MD, Cath. U. Louvain, Belgium, 1992. Cert. radiologist, Belgium. Clin. fellow in interventional radiology U. Med. Ctr., Toulouse, 1997—98, attending interventional radiologist, 1998—99; rschr. in interventional radiology Dartmouth Coll., Lebanon, NH, 1999—2000; attending interventional radiologist Beth Israel Deaconess Med. Ctr., Boston, 2001—07, Mass. Gen. Hosp., 2007—09; assoc. prof. radiology U. Md. Sch. Medicine, 2009—. Contbr. articles to profl. jours. Mem. Am. Heart Assn. (coun. on cardiovasc. radiology), Am. Assn. Univ. Radiologists, Cardiovasc. and Interventional Radiology Soc. Europe, French Soc. Radiology (grantee 1999). Office: University Md Med Ctr Dept Radiology N2W74 22 S Greene St Baltimore MD 21201 Office Phone: 410-328-3631. Personal E-mail: bjanne@yahoo.com.

JANOSKO, RUDOLPH E.M., psychiatrist; b. Munhall, Pa., Apr. 30, 1930; s. Rudolph E. and Anne (Gerek) J.; m. Audrey M. Nemeth, May 18, 1932; children: Beth, Gwen, Ellen. BS, U. Pitts., 1952, MD, 1956. Cert. in psychiatry Am. Bd. Psychiatry and Neurology. Intern Easton Hosp., Pa., 1956—57; resident psychiatry U. Pitts., 1957—59, 1961—62, instr. psychiatry Sch. Medicine, 1962—65, lectr. Grad. Sch. Dept. Spl. Edn., 1966—70; faculty Pitts. Psychoanalytic Inst., 1970—. Clin. assoc. prof. psychiatry Sch. Medicine U. Pitts., 1965-75, 1975—; mem. attending staff Presbyn.-Univ. Hosp., Pitts., 1962—; pres. Pitts. Psychoanalytic Inst., 1979—; dir. Pitts. Psychoanalytic Inst., 1985-86, tng. and supervising analyst, 1979—; med. dir. Family Svcs. We. Pa., Pitts., 1988-99; cons. Greater Pitts. Guild for Blind, Bridgeville, Pa., 1964—, Social Security Adminstrn., HHS, Pitts., 1979—, Pitts. Pastoral Inst., 1999—. Author in field. Capt. USAF, 1959—61. Recipient Meritorious Distinction award Greater Pitts. Guild for Blind, 1967, Outstanding Tchr. award We. Psychiat. Inst., 1981. Fellow Am Psychiat. Assn (disting. life); mem. AMA, Am. Psychoanalytic Assn. (tng. and supervising analyst 1979—), Pitts. Acad. Medicine, Pitts. Psychoanalytic Soc. (pres. 1983-85). Republican. Roman Catholic. Avocation: running. Office: 161 N Dithridge St Pittsburgh PA 15213-2646 Home: 5859 Beacon St Pittsburgh PA 15217-2542 Office Phone: 412-682-7652.

JANOSSY, GEORGE, immunologist, educator; b. Debrecen, Hungary, May 22, 1940; MD in Medicine, Med. Sch., Budapest, Hungary, 1964; PhD in Immunology, Univ. Coll., London, 1974; DSc in Medicine/Immunology, U. London, 1986. Med. scientist Inst. Radiology, Semelweiss U., Budapest, 1964—68, Inst. Haematology, Budapest, 1968—70; Royal Soc. scholar Nat. Inst. for Med. Rsch., London, 1970, Wellcome Trust scholar, 1971; rsch. scientist Clin. Rsch. Ctr., Harrow, England, 1971—74; postdoctoral rsch. fellow tumor immunology Univ. Coll. London and Imperial Cancer Rsch. Fund, 1974—78; sr. lectr., reader Royal Free Hosp. Sch. Medicine, London, 1978—83, prof. immunology, 1983—99, Royal Free and Univ. Coll. Med. Sch., London, 1999—. Cons. immunologist Royal Free NHS Trust, Hampstead, England, 1978—; advisor strategies for HIV/AIDS diagnostic support in resource poor countries WHO, 2001—. Named Hon. Prof., Witwatersrand U., Johannesburg, South Africa, 1999—. Fellow: Royal Coll. Pathologists London; mem.: European Flow Cytometry Soc. (founding mem.), Brit. Soc. for Histocompatibility, Hungarian Immunologist Soc. (hon.), Hungarian Pathology Soc. (hon. sci. excellence in clin. diagnosis award 1995, award for helping immunology edn. in Hungary 1990, award for recognition of original leukemia rsch. 1986), Hungarian Hematologist Soc. (hon.), Brit. Haematology Soc. Achievements include research in lymphocyte activation; use of antibodies to characterize markers for haemopoietic precursors and leukemia and HIV diagnosis; immunohistology and FACS analysis, including cell sorting, to delineate the tissue distribution and differentiation pathways of lymphocyte lineages in man. Office: Royal Free and Univ Coll Med Sch HIV Immunol Dept Immunol/Molecular Path Royal Free Hospital Pond Street NW3 2QG London England

JANSEN, G. THOMAS, dermatologist; b. Manitowoc, Wis., July 16, 1926; s. Gerald M. and Sarah (Grady) J.; m. Frances Bovick, Sept. 6, 1952; children: Mark, Kurt, Anne, Drew, Fran. BS, U. Wis., Madison, 1948, MD, 1950. Diplomate: Am. Bd. Dermatology (pres. 1985-86). Intern Med. Coll. of Va., 1950-51; resident in dermatology U. Wis., 1953-54, U. Mich., 1954-56; practice medicine specializing in dermatology Little Rock, 1956—2004; pres. Little Rock Dermatology Clinic, 1968—2004; ret., 2004. Mem. faculty U. Ark. Med. Center, 1956—2004, prof. dermatology, 1965—2004, prof. emeritus, 2004—, chmn. dept., 1965-82; mem. staff Doctors Hosp., U. Ark. Hosp., St. Vincent Infirmary, Bapt. Hosp.; pres. Am. Dermatology Found., 1980-81 Served as officer M.C. USNR, 1951-54. Recipient Disting. Svc. award, Am. Bd. Dermatologists, 1987, Finnerud award, 1996, Alumni citation, U. Wis. Med. Sch., 2002. Mem. AMA, Am. Dermatol. Assn. (pres. 1993), Am. Acad. Dermatology (asst. sec.-treas. 1980-83, sec.-treas. 1983-85, pres.-elect 1987, pres. 1988, hon. 1991, Master in Dermatology 1991, Everett C. Fox Lectureship award 1995, Gold medal 1997), Soc. Investigative Dermatology, Nat. Program Dermatology, Am. Coll. Chemosurgery, So. Med. Assn. (pres. 1976-77, Disting. Svc. award 1991), Ark. Med. Soc., Ark. Dermatol. Soc., Pulaski County Med. Soc. (A Lifetime of Outstanding Contbns. to Medicine award 2004), Alpha Omega Alpha. Roman Catholic. Home: 6601 Pleasant Pl Little Rock AR 72205-2868 Office: 500 S University Ave Ste 501 Little Rock AR 72205-5307 *

JANSEN, MICHAEL JOHN, health facility administrator; b. Swannanoa, NC, July 24, 1945; s. Edward John and Mary Bernadette (Haughian) J.; m. Roxanne Shellenberger, June 27, 1970 (div. May 1992); m. Linda Kathryn Hughes, Aug. 21, 1993; children: Kathryn Anne, Victoria Elizabeth. BS in BA, U. S.C., 1967; M. Health Adminstrn., Duke U., 1976. Adminstrv. asst. Watts Hosp., Durham, NC, 1976-77; asst. dir. Durham County Gen. Hosp., 1977-80; asst. adminstr. St. Joseph's Hosp., Atlanta, 1980-83, sr. v.p., COO, 1983-89; group v.p. SunHealth, Charlotte, NC, 1989-90; sr. assoc. adminstr., COO Cape Fear Valley Health Sys., Fayetteville, NC, 1991-2001; CEO MedAccom, Research Triangle Park, NC, 2001—03; adminstr. Breezewood Family Healthcare, Fayetteville, NC, 2003—08, Linda K. Hughes MD, PA, Fayetteville, 2008—. Bd. dirs. St. Joseph's Hosp., Atlanta, 1985-89, Fayetteville Symphony Orch., 1993-95, United Way of Cumberland County, Fayetteville, 1993-95; chmn. bd. dirs. Shared Svcs. for So. Hosps., Atlanta, 1986-87. Capt. USAF, 1967-72, Col. USAFR, 1990-96. Recipient Falcon award/Spaatz award Civil Air Patrol, 1967. Fellow Am. Coll. Healthcare Execs. Office: Linda K Hughes MD PA 2149 Valleygate Dr Ste 001 Fayetteville NC 28304-3666

JANSEN VAN RENSBURG, DIRKIE JOHANNA, physician, medical researcher; b. Stellenbosch, Western Cape, South Africa, Oct. 9, 1951; d. Jurgens Antonie Jansen van Rensburg and Elizabeth Catherine Simpson, William Simpson (Stepfather); m. Pieter Johannes Lodewikus Venter, Apr. 6, 1974; children: Johan Venter, Willem Venter, Lize Venter, Annemarie Venter. MBChB, U. Pretoria, South Africa, 1974, MPraxMed, 1996; postgrad. in Diabetes, Cardiff U. Lic. gen. practitioner Brit. Gen. Med. Coun., 1981, family physician Health Professions Coun. South Africa, 1997, accredited Ctrs. Diabetes and Endocrinology, 2004, cert. advanced life support Trauma Soc. South Africa, 2005, advanced cardiac life support Am. Heart Assn., 2005. Med. intern Dept. Health, Witbank, Mpumalanga, South Africa, 1974—75; med. officer Provincial Hosp., 1976—79, sr. med. officer, 1979—81, acting supt., 1980—81; gen. practitioner Drs. Joynt, Venter and Assoc., 1982—97, asst. dist. surgeon, 1984—97, family physician, 1997—; med. rschr. Pk. Med. Ctr., 1996—. Nat. prin. investigator Multinational Cmty. Acquired Pneumonia Trial Abbot Pharmaceuticals, Witbank, South Africa, 2002; nat. prin. investigator - multinational cmty. acquired pneumonia trial Sanofi-Aventis, 2005—; bd. dirs. Rhodes Street Properties, Joynt Venter and Assocs.; presenter to profl. confs. Contbr. scientific papers, articles to profl. jours. Bd. mem. Whitbank Soc. Aged, South Africa, 1993—94. Recipient Posters of Distinction Authors, Am. Coll. Chest Physicians, 2003. Mem.: Super Divers Scuba Diving Club, Lissataba Pvt. Game Res. Reformed Ch. Achievements include research in infectious diseases. Avocations: scuba diving, nature conservation, gardening, reading, art. Office: Drs Joynt Venter and Assoc Park Med Ctr 19 Rhodes St 1035 Witbank 1035 South Africa Office Phone: 27 1365 66512. Office Fax: 27 1369 02808. Personal E-mail: dirkieventer@gmail.com. Business E-Mail: jp-ass@mweb.co.za.

JANSMAN, FRANK, clinical pharmacologist; married. PhD, State U. Groningen, 1991. Cert. hosp. pharmacist NVZA, 1991. Dir. pharmacy Deventer Ziekenhuis, Netherlands, 2008—. Office: Deventer Ziekenhuis Nico Bolkesteinlaan 75 Deventer 7416 SE Netherlands Office Phone: 31 (0)570 536002. Business E-Mail: f.g.a.jansman@dz.nl.

JANSON, VERONICA, veterinarian; b. Stockholm, May 12, 1974; MS in Vet. Medicine, Swedish U. Agrl. Scis., Uppsala, 2002, PhD in Medicine, Umeå U., Sweden, 2008. Jr. rschr., lab. vet. officer dept. pathology and wildlife disease Nat. Vet. Inst., 2009—. Rsch. asst. Swedish Rsch. Coun. (Vetenskapsrådet),, Stockholm. Mem.: European Assn. Cancer Rsch., Swedish Vet. Assn. Office: Nat Veterinary Inst Uppsala SE 75189 Sweden Business E-Mail: veronica.janson@sva.se.

JANSSEN, ROB PAULUS AUGUSTINUS, orthopedic surgeon, researcher; b. Heerlen, Netherlands, Apr. 19, 1968; s. Martin J. Janssen and Annemie S.E. Janssen-Smeets. PCEM 1, Caen U., France, 1987, Internship, Brown U. Med. Sch., Providence, 1993; MD, Maastricht U., Netherlands, 1994. Cert. ATLS instr. Advanced Trauma Life Support, 2003. Orthop. surgeon Maxima Med. Ctr., Veldhoven, Netherlands, 2002—, Maxima Sports Medicine and Orthop. Ctr., Eindhoven, Netherlands, 2004—; pres. Dutch Arthroscopy Soc., 2011—. Treas. Orthop. Rsch. Soc., Eindhoven, 2003—; ATLS instr. Advanced Trauma Life Support, Riel, 2003—, bd. dirs., 2007—, dep. head, orthop. residency program, 2008—, instr. yearly internat. ISAKOS/ESSKA advanced knee course, 2008—. Contbr. chapters to books, articles to peer-reviewed jours. Mem.: Dutch Med. Assn., Dutch Orthop. Trauma Soc., Dutch Arthroscopy Soc. (pres. 2011—), Dutch Orthop. Soc., ISAKOS, ESSKA 2000. Office: Maxima Med Ctr Postbus 7777 5500 MB Veldhoven Netherlands Office Fax: 0031408888609. Business E-Mail: r.janssen@mmc.nl.

JAO, YEUN TARL FRESNER NG, cardiologist, intensivist; b. Manila, Nov. 25, 1970; s. Simon Yeunche and Lilian Ng; m. Chiung-Chi Geraldene Chiu. BS in Biology, U. Santo Tomas, Manila, 1990, MD, 1994. Cert. in physician Philippine Regulatory Commn., 1995, lic. US Med. Licensing Exam., 1997, cert. Taiwan Dept. Health, Exec. Yuan, 2000. Attending physician, internal med. Tainan Mcpl. Hosp., 2004—06, attending physician, critical care medicine, 2007—, dept. head, critical care medicine, 2007—, attending physician, cardiology, 2008—. Vis. physician Yuan Da-Hsiang Hemodialysis Ctr., Tainan, 2002—04, Huai-An Hemodialysis Ctr., Tainan, 2002—. Contbr. articles to profl. sci. jours. Fellow: European Soc. Cardiology, Am. Soc. Angiology; mem.: ACP, Taiwan Soc. Critical Care Medicine, Taiwan Soc. Cardiology, U. Santo Tomas Med. Alumni Assn. (life), Taiwan Soc. Internal Medicine, Formosan Med. Assn., Phi Sigma Gamma Fraternity (life; lord keeper 1991—92, lord grand tribunal 1992—93). Office: Tainan Mcpl Hosp No 670 Chung-De Rd E Dist Tainan 70120 Taiwan Office Fax: 886-6-2606351. Personal E-mail: pogibomb@hotmail.com.

JAQUA, RICHARD ALLEN, pathologist; b. Fort Dodge, Iowa, Apr. 15, 1938; s. John Franklin and Esther J.; m. Mary Joanne Stewart, Dec. 29, 1969 BA magna cum laude, Yale U., 1960; MD, Harvard U., 1965. Diplomate: Am. Bd. Pathology, Am. Bd. Nuclear Medicine. Teaching fellow pathology Harvard Med. Sch., 1965-67; resident clin. pathology NIH, 1967-69; intern pathology Mass. Gen. Hosp., Boston, 1965-66; fellow tumor pathology Meml.-Sloane Kettering Cancer Center, NYC, 1969-70; asst. prof. pathology U. S.D. Sch. Medicine, Vermillion, 1970-73, asso. prof., 1973-74, asso. prof., acting chmn. dept. lab. medicine, 1974-77, prof., chmn. dept. lab. medicine, 1977—2002, dir. Electron Microscopy Lab. and Clin. Virology Lab., 1979—2002; pathologist VA Hosp., Sioux Falls, SD, 1978—2002; physician Lab. Clin. Medicine, Sioux Falls, 1970—2002. Part-time prof. pathology Sch. Medicine U. S.D., 2003—; prof. emeritus U. S.D. Sch. Medicine. Served with USPHS, 1967-69. Recipient Outstanding Prof. awards U. SD Med. Students, 1971, 75, 77, U. SD Faculty Recogition award, 1986, U. SD Sci. Faculty award, Student Am. Med. Assn., 1992, Lifetime Achievement award, 2002, U. SD

Centennial Tchg. award, 2007; VA grantee, 1980-82. Fellow Coll. Am. Pathologists, Am. Soc. Clin. Pathologists; mem. AAAS, Sigma Xi, Alpha Omega Alpha. Home: 27546 483rd Ave Canton SD 57013-5511 Office: USD Health Sci Ctr 1400 W 22nd St Sioux Falls SD 57105-1505

JAQUET, KAI, biologist; b. Kiel, Germany, Mar. 9, 1960; s. Günter Hubertus and Ellen Jaquet; m. Andrea Jaquet, Aug. 16, 1991; children: Amelie, Finja Paulina. Degree in Natural Scis., Kiel U., 1988, PhD, 1991. Lab. dir. Kiel U., 1991—93, Duesseldorf U., Germany, 1993—98, Asklepios Klinik St. Georg, Hamburg, Germany, 1999—. Editl. bd. mem. Open Stem Cell Jour. Contbr. articles to profl. sci. jours. Sgt. Med. Svc., 1979—81, Rendsburg Germany. Mem.: Clin. Rehabilitative Tissue Engring. Rsch. Office: Asklepios Klinik St Georg Lohmuehlenstrasse 5 Hamburg 20099 Germany Office Fax: 49401818853989. Business E-Mail: k.jaquet@asklepios.com.

JARA, RAUL DIAZ, cardiologist, educator, researcher, lab administrator; b. Manila, Dec. 4, 1948; s. Trinidad Zarzuela and Felicidad (Diaz) Jara; m. Eleanor Castro Aquino, July 3, 1977; children: Paolo Cecilio, Monica Felise, Rouwella Elinor, Mikaela Nikkola, Christina Elize. BS, Pre-Med. U. Philippines, Quezon City, 1971, MD, 1975. Cert. Philippine Med. Bd. Resident in internal medicine Philippine Gen. Hosp., Manila, 1977—79, instr., 1977—87, fellow in cardiology, 1980—81, clin. asst. prof., 1988—98, clin. assoc. prof., 1999—; chairperson non-invasive lab. Philippine Heart Ctr., Quezon City, 1999—. Cons. Sandoz-Phils, Makati, 1981—86. Dir. Philippine Heart Assn., Quezon City, 1994—2000; organizer Drs. for Pres. Corazon Aquino Movement, Quezon City, 1983—86. Fellow: Philippine Coll. Cardiology (pres. 1999—2000), Am. Coll. Cardiology, Philippine Coll. Physician and Cardiology, Philippine Coll. Physicians (life); mem.: Asia Pacific Soc. Cardiology (chmn. edn. com. 1996—2004), U. The Philippines Alumni Soc. (pres. 2000). Avocations: singing, swimming, bicycling, tennis, golf. Office: Philippine Heart Ctr Mab Hall East Ave Ste 608 0850 Quezon City Philippines Office Fax: (632) 9220551. Personal E-mail: rdjaramdcg@yahoo.com.

JARAMILLO, DIEGO, pediatric radiologist, educator; b. Cali, Colombia, Nov. 4, 1957; MD, U. Javeriana, 1981; MPH, Harvard U., 2002. Radiologist-in-chief Children's Hosp. Phila., 2004—. Prof. U. Pa., 2004—. Recipient Caffey award, Soc. Pediat. Radiology. Mem.: Soc. Chairpersons Academic Radiology Depts. Avocation: literature. Office: Children's Hosp Dept Radiology Philadelphia PA 19104 Office Fax: 215-590-5797. Business E-Mail: jaramillo@email.chop.edu.

JARDETZKY, OLEG, retired medical educator, researcher; b. Yugoslavia, Feb. 11, 1929; came to U.S., 1949, naturalized, 1955; s. Wenceslas Sigismund and Tatiana (Taranovsky) J.; m. Erika Albensberg, July 21, 1975; children by previous marriage: Alexander, Theodore, Paul. BA, Macalester Coll., 1950, D.Sc. (hon.), 1974; MD, U. Minn., 1954, PhD (Am. Heart Assn. fellow), 1956; postgrad., U. Cambridge, Eng., 1965-66; LL.D. (hon.), Calif. Western U., 1978; MD (hon.), U. Graz, Austria, 1994; Doctorate (hon.), U. Aix-Marseille II, 1998. Rsch. fellow U. Minn., 1954-56; NRC fellow Calif. Inst. Tech., 1956-57; assoc. Harvard U., 1957-59, asst. prof. pharmacology, 1959-66; dir. biophysics and pharmacology Merck & Co., 1966-68, exec. dir., 1968-69; prof. Stanford U., 1969—2006, prof. emeritus, 2006—, dir. Stanford Magnetic Resonance Lab., 1975-97, dir. NMR Ctr. Sch. Medicine, 1983-84, dir. emeritus, 1998—. Vis. fellow Merton Coll., Oxford (Eng.) U., 1976; cons., vis. prof., lectr. in field; chmn. Internat. Coun. on Magnetic Resonance in Biology, 1972-74; dir. Internat Sch. on Magnetic Resonance in Biology, 1993—; mem. adv. bd. Ettore Majorana, 2006—; chmn. biotech. panel World Fedn. Scientists, 1998-2003. Contbr. articles to profl. jours.; mem. editorial bd. Jour. Theoretical Biology, 1961-88, Molecular Pharmacology, 1965-75, Jour. Medicinal Chemsitry, 1970-78, Biochimica Biophypica Acta, 1970-86, Revs. on Bioenergetics, 1972-89, Biomembrane Revs., 1972-80, Jour. Magnetic Resonance in Biology and Medicine, 1986—2000, Jour. Magnetic Resonance, 1993—2000. Recipient Career Devel. award USPHS, 1959-66, Kaiser award, 1973, Von Humboldt award, 1977, Pauling medal, 1984, Grand Gold Honor insignia, Austria, 1993, Founder's Gold medal Internat. Coun. Magnetic Resonance in Biology, 1994, Prix Marianne Dessewffy Internat. Conf. of Genealogy and Heraldry, 1998; grantee NSF, 1957-2001, NIH, 1957-2006; travel fellow Am. Physiol. Soc., 1959. Fellow AAAS; mem. Am. Chem. Soc., Am. Soc. Biol. Chemistry and Molecular Biology, Biophys. Soc., Assn. Advanced Tech. in Biomed. Scis. (pres. 1981-88), Internat. Soc. Magnetic Resonance (chmn. divns. of biology and Medicine 1986-89, fellow 2008-), Phi Beta Kappa, Sigma Xi, Alpha Omega Alpha. Home: 950 Casanueva Pl Stanford CA 94305-1068 Office: Stanford U CCSR 269 Campus Dr Rm 4155 Stanford CA 94305-5174 Office Phone: 650-723-6153. Business E-Mail: jardetzky@stanford.edu.

JARECKI, HENRY GEORGE, physician, financial planner; b. Stettin, Germany, Apr. 15, 1933; s. Max Jarecki and Gerda Kunstmann; m. Gloria Friedland, 1957; children: Andrew, Thomas, Eugene, Nicholas. MD, U. Heidelberg, Germany, 1957. Diplomate Am. Bd. Psychiatry and Neurology. Dir. Mocatta Metals Corp., NYC, 1970-89, Mocatta & Goldsmid Ltd., London, 1973-89, Mocatta Hong Kong Ltd., 1975-89; chmn. Brody, White & Co. Inc., NYC, 1971-95, Brody White Ltd, London, 1989-95, Guana Island Hotel Corp., British Virgin Islands, 1975—, Falconwood Corp., NYC, 1976—, Gresham Investment Mgmt., LLC, NYC, 1992—, The Programming Corp., NYC, 1999—, MovieFone, Inc., NYC, 1989-99, PsychoGenics, Inc., Tarrytown, NY, 1998—. Bd. dirs. Classical Theatre Harlem; gov. Brit. Virgin Islands CC, 1989—; dir. Caribbean Cellular Telephone, Brit. V.I., 1993-; dir. Tourist Bd. Brit. V.I., 2003-; trustee Inst. Internat. Edn., 2000-, vice-chmn., 2003—; chmn. Scholar Rescue Fund, 2002-; clin. prof. psychiatry Yale U. Sch. Medicine, New Haven, 2007-. Author: Modern Psychiatric Treatment, 1971; dir. (film) Gardeners of Eden, 1997, Cuba, Island of Music, 2000; exec. prod. (film) The Third Wave, 2007, Tyson, 2009; prod. Cat on a Hot Tin Roof, London; contbr. articles to profl. jours. Adv. coun. Princeton U., Yale U. Sch. Medicine Dept. Psychiatry, 1992—; trustee Am. Mus. Natural History, 1991-99; bd. dirs. Botanic Soc. Brit. V.I., 1986—, Chgo. Bd. Trade, 1993-96; internat. liaison com. Food Corps Program, 1987-95, Island Resources Found., Tortola, Brit. Virgin Is., 1988— Mem. Nat. Futures Assn. (bd. dirs. 1979-93), Am. Psychiat. Assn. (Presdl. Commendation 1984). Office: Falconwood Corp 67 Irving Pl 12th Fl New York NY 10003 Office Phone: 212-984-1440. Business E-Mail: hj@jarecki.com.

JARHULT, SUSANN J., physician; b. Vasteras, Sweden, Sept. 18, 1971; MD, PhD, Uppsala U., 2000. Physician Uppsala U. Hosp., 2000—. Avocations: music, sports. Office: Akademiska Sjukhuset Sjukhusvagen Uppsala 75185 Sweden

JARNAGIN, BARRY K., physician, educator; b. Union City, Tenn., Jan. 3, 1958; BS in Chemistry, Union U., 1980; MD, U. Tenn. Ctr. Health Scis., 1984. Dir. womens health care program Horizon Med. Ctr. Jackson Clinic, 1994—96; med. dir. Vanderbilt U. Med. Ctr., 1994—96, asst. prof., 1996—2004, clin. assoc. prof., 2004—, gynecology divsn. dir., 2005—06; med. dir. Ctr. Pelvic Health, 2008—. Mem. Coun. Stewards Bethlehem Methodist Ch. Recipient Chemistry Rsch. award, Dept. Chemistry Physics Faculty Union U., Disting. Sci. Alumnus award, Union U., 2006. Mem.: Internat. Pelvic Pain Soc., Am. Assn. Gynecologic Laparoscopists, Am. Urogynecology Soc., Am. Coll. Obstetrics & Gynecology. Avocations: baseball, basketball. Office: 4601 Carothers Pky Ste 350 Franklin TN 37067 Office Fax: 615-284-4668. Business E-Mail: jessica.mathews@baptisthospital.com.

JARON, DOV, biomedical engineer, educator; b. Tel Aviv, Oct. 29, 1935; came to U.S., 1958, naturalized, 1972; s. Meir and Sara (Levit) Yarovsky; m. Brooke E. Boberg, Sept. 16, 1978; children: Shulamit, Tamara. BS magna cum laude, U. Denver, 1961; PhD, U. Pa., 1967. Sr. research asso. Maimonides Med. Center, Bklyn., 1967-70; dir. surg. research Sinai Hosp. of Detroit, 1970-73; asso. prof. elec. engring. U. R.I., Kingston, 1973-77, prof., 1977-79, coordinator biomed. engring., 1973-79; prof. biomend. engring. and sci. Drexel U., Phila., 1979—, dir. Biomed. Engring. and Sci. Inst., 1979-96. Calhoun disting. prof., 1998—; vis. prof. elec. engring. Rutgers U., New Brunswick, N.J., 1968-73; adj. prof. biomed. engring. Wayne State U., 1971-73; adj. prof. physiology Temple U. Sch. Medicine, 1980—; adj. prof. radiology Jefferson Med. Coll., 1983—; dir. Div. Biol. and Critical Systems, NSF, 1991-93; assoc. dir. Nat. Ctr. Rsch. Resources, dir. biomedical tech. NIH, 1996-98. Contbr. articles to sci. jours. NSF, NIH, Office Naval Research, pvt. founds. research grantee. Fellow AAAS, IEEE, Am. Inst. for Med. and Biol. Engring., World Acad. Biomed. Tech., Internat. Acad. for Med. and Biol. Engring., Biomed. Engring. Soc.; mem. Internat. Fedn. for Med. and Biol. Engring. (pres. 2000-03), Internat. Union for Phys. and Engring. Scis. in Medicine (v.p. 2003-06), Am. Soc. for Engring. Edn., Assn. for Advancement Med. Instrumentation, Internat. Soc. Artificial Organs, ICSU(exec. bd. 2008-), Am. Soc. for Artificial Internal Organs, Biophys. Soc., Engring. in Medicine and Biology of IEEE (pres. 1986-87), Internat. Coun. Sci. (mem. exec. bd. 2008-), Sigma Xi, Tau Beta Pi, Eta Kappa Nu, Polish Acad. Scis. (fgn. mem.). Achievements include research of cardiac assist devices, cardiovascular dynamics and modeling, microcirculation, biomed. instrumentation. Home: 122 Bethlehem Pike Philadelphia PA 19118-2815 Office: Drexel U Sch Biomed Engring Sci and Health Systems 32nd and Chestnut St Philadelphia PA 19104

JARQUIN VALDIVIA, ADRIAN ALBERTO, internist, neurologist, researcher; b. Jinotepe, Nicaragua, June 16, 1966; s. Alberto Jarquin Bonilla and Yolanda Valdivia Quijano; m. Tonya Jarquin Valdivia, May 1, 2004; 1 child, Isabella G. Jarquin-Valdivia. MD, Universidad Nacional Autonoma de Honduras, 1993. Diplomate Am. Bd. Internal Medicine, 1997, Neurology ABPN, 2004, Critical Care Am. Bd. Internal Medicine, 2005, Vascular Neurology ABPN, 2005, ARDMS, 2003, Ct/Mri ASN, 2004, Neurosonology ASN, 2002. Asst. prof. neurology, anesthesiology and internal medicine Vanderbilt U. Med. Ctr., Nashville, 2002—. Dir., neurology clerkship Vanderbilt U. Med. Ctr., Nashville, 2004—. Recipient CANDLE Tchg. Award, Vanderbilt Med. Sch., 2004. Mem.: AMA. Achievements include research in new ultrasound sign for non-invasive intracranial pressure determination - the angle of deceleration. *

JARRAHNEJAD, PAYAM, plastic surgeon; m. Amy Yaghmai. MD, Med. Sch. Resident gen. surgery North Shore U., NYU, Manhasset, 2000—02, Morristown Meml. Hosp., 2002—05, chief resident surgery, 2004—05; fellow, hand surgery Beth Israel Med. Ctr., NYC, 2005—06; resident plastic and re constructive surgery Wayne State U. & Detroit Med. Ctr., Detroit, 2006—08. Named Americas Top Surgeon, Consumers Rsch. Coun. America. Mem.: ACS, AMA, LA Med. Assn., Calif. Med. Assn. Office: 9025 Wilshire Blvd Ste 202 Beverly Hills CA 90211

JARRARD, LEONARD EVERETT, psychologist, educator; b. Waco, Tex., Oct. 23, 1930; s. Thomas Ivan and Levis Everett (Lasswell) J.; m. Janet Grier Shoop, Aug. 16, 1958; children: Alice Grier, David Frazier, Hugh Everett. BA, Baylor U., Waco, 1955; MS, Carnegie Inst. Tech., Pitts., 1957, PhD, 1959. Asst. to asso. prof. psychology Washington and Lee U., 1959-66; assoc. prof. to prof. psychology Carnegie-Mellon U., 1966-71; Robert L. Telford prof. psychology Washington and Lee U., Lexington, Va., 1971-2001, prof. emeritus, 2001—. Vis. lectr., prof. exptl. psychology U. Oxford, Eng., 1975-76; interim assoc. prof. anatomy U. Fla., 1965-66; acad. visitor Inst. Psychiatry, U. London, 1988-89. Editor: Cognitive Processes of Nonhuman Primates, 1971; cons. editor: Jour. Comparative and Physiol. Psychology, 1970-75, Behavioral Neurosci. Psychology, 1995-2001, Hippocampus, 03-. Served with USAF, 1952-54. Officer USAF, 1952—54. Fellow AAAS, APA, APS; mem. Soc. for Neurosci., Psychonomics Soc., Va. Acad. Sci. So. Soc. Philosophy and Psychology, Phi Beta Kappa, Omicron Delta Kappa, Sigma Xi. Home: PO Box 5 1067 Lexington VA 24450 Office: Washington and Lee U Dept Psychology Lexington VA 24450 Business E-Mail: jarrardl@wlu.edu.

JARRETT, FREDRIC, surgeon, educator; s. Julian Everett and Melba Jarrett; m. Esther Kathleen Szeolleosy-Toth, June 26, 1972; children: James Alexander, Julia Nicole Reid, Andrew Whitney. AB, Dartmouth Coll., Hanover, NH, 1963, B Med. Sci., 1965; MD cum laude, Harvard U., Boston, 1967. Diplomate Am. Bd. Surgery. Intern then resident in surgery Mass. Gen. Hosp., Boston, 1967—71, 1974—75; chief resident Sint Lucas Ziekenheis, Amsterdam, 1971—72; surg. cons. US-UN Forces, Republic of Korea, 1972—74; asst. prof. U. Wis., Madison, 1975—81; adj. prof. surgery Temple U. Sch. Medicine, 2000—; clin. prof. surgery U. Pitts., 1981—. Cons. vascular surgery Blue Cross/Blue Shield Pa., 1983—. Editor: (textbook) Vascular Surgery of the Lower Extremity, 1985; contbr. numerous sci. papers to profl. publs. (Nat. Leadership award, 2002, Physician of Yr., 2003). Bd. dirs. Three Rivers Shakespeare Festival, Pitts., 1989—95; parents rep. St. Paul's Sch., 2007—. 1st lt. to col. US Army, 1967—90, USA. Fellow: ACS (pres. SW Pa. chpt. 2005—06), Royal Soc. Medicine Gt. Britain, Royal Coll. Surgeons Can. (cert.); mem.: Ctrl. Surg. Assn., Soc. Vascular Surgery, Dutch Surg. Soc., Ea. VascularSociety (pres. 1998—99), Harvard Club Boston. Office: Shadyside Med Ctr 5200 Centre Ave Ste 705 Pittsburgh PA 15232 Office Fax: 412-681-8713. Business E-Mail: jarrettf@upmc.edu.

JARRIS, PAUL, medical association administrator, former state agency administrator, physician; BS, Univ. Vt.; MD, Univ. Pa., 1984; MBA, Univ. Wash., 1989. Cert. Am. Bd. Family Med., Am. Bd. Med. Mgmt. Internship Duke Watts Family Residency prog., Durham, NC; residency Swedish Family Practice Residency prog., Seattle, 1987; fellowship Univ. Wash.; med. dir. Cmty. Health Plan, Vt., 1992—96; pres., CEO Vt. Permanente Med. Group, 1998—2000; CEO Primary Care Health Partners, Vt.; commr. Vt. Dept. Health, Burlington, 2003—06; exec. dir. Assn. State and Territorial Health Officials, 2006—. Co-founder Catamount Trail. Office: Assn State and Territorial Health Officials 2231 Crystal Dr Ste 450 Arlington VA 22202

JARUKAMJORN, KANOKWAN, medical educator; b. Bangkok, Oct. 9, 1967; B in Pharm. Sci. with honors, Khon Kaen U., Thailand; PhD in Pharm. Sci., U. Toyama, Japan, 2004. Assoc. prof. Khon Kaen U., 1993—. Postdoc. fellowship, Tokyo Biochem. Rsch. Found. Mem.: Royal Pratonage Pharmacy Coun. Thailand. Office: Khon Kaen University Mitraparb Rd Muang Khon Kaen 40002 Thailand Office Fax: 66-43-202379. Business E-Mail: kanok_ja@kku.ac.th.

JARUZELSKA, JADWIGA MARIA, biology professor; b. Krakow, Poland, May 12, 1954; PhD, A. Mickiewicz U. Poznan, 1977. Prof. biology Polish Acad. Scis., 2004—. Recipient Established Scientist award, European Soc. Embryology and Reproduction. Mem.: Polish Soc. Genetics. Office: 32 Strzeszynska Poznan Wielkopolska 60-479 Poland Business E-Mail: jaruzjad@man.poznan.pl.

JARVIK, ROBERT KOFFLER, biomedical research scientist; b. Midland, Mich., May 11, 1946; s. Norman Eugene and Edythe (Koffler) Jarvik; m. Elaine Levin, 1968 (div. 1985); m. Marilyn vos Savant, 1987. BA, Syracuse U., NY, 1968; Ms in Med. Engring., NYU, 1971; MD, U. Utah, 1976; DSc (hon.), Syracuse U., 1983; DSc (hon.), Hahnemann U., 1985. Rsch. asst. divsn. artificial organs U. Utah, Salt Lake City, 1971-76, asst. dir. exptl. labs., 1976-82, asst. rsch. prof. surgery, 1979-87; pres. Symbion, Inc., Salt Lake City, 1978—87; founder, pres., CEO Jarvik Heart Inc., NYC, 1988—. Sect. editor Internat. Jour. Artificial Organs, 1979—88. Recipient John W. Hyatt award, Soc. Plastics Engineers, 1983, Gold Heart award, Utah Heart Assn., 1983, Golden Plate award, American Acad. Achievement, 1983; named Inventor of Yr., Intellectual Property Owners Assn., 1983. Achievements include invention of the first permanently-implantable artificial heart, the Jarvik-7; development of a highly reliable innovative left ventricular assist system, the Jarvik 2000 FlowMaker, a thumb sized battery operated pump that fits directly into the left ventricle and pushes oxygenated blood throughout the body. Office: Jarvik Heart Inc 333 W 52d St New York NY 10019 *

JARVIS, DAPHNE ELOISE, laboratory administrator; b. Lithia, Fla., Feb. 18, 1945; d. Grady Edwin and Vera Eloise (Smith) Smith; m. Hubert E. Jarvis, Aug. 1, 1964; 1 child, Jessica Ellen. BS, Blue Mountain Coll., 1966; MA, Spalding U., 1972. Cert. med. technologist with specialist in blood bank. Med. technologist St. Anthony's Hosp., Louisville, 1968-69, Clark County Meml. Hosp., Jeffersonville, Ind., 1969-73; asst. to edn. coord. ARC, Washington, 1973-75; dir. Grace Bapt. Ch. Sch., Bryans Rd., Md., 1978-83; sect. chief blood bank Physicians Meml. Hosp., LaPlata, Md., 1975-76, 83-84; supr. donor blood labs. Southwest Fla. Blood Bank, Tampa, 1984-87, dir., 1987-89; asst. dir. tech. svcs. Ark. Region ARC, Little Rock, 1989-93, dir. tech. svcs./hosp. svcs. Ark. Regional Blood Svcs., 1993-95; mfg. team leader Lifeblood-Midsouth Regional Blood Ctr., Memphis, 1995-2000, tech. mgr., 2000—06, project mgr., tech. svcs. specialist, 2006—09, quality assurance dir., 2009—. Lectr. UAMS Sch. Med. Tech., Little Rock, 1989-95. Vol. coord. Playhouse Sq., 2005. Recipient Vol. of Yr. award, Playhouse Sq., 2007. Mem. Am. Assn. Blood Banks, Am. Soc. Quality, South Ctr. Assn. Blood Banks (membership com. 1989-95). Office: Lifeblood Midsouth Reg Blood Ctr 1040 Madison Ave Memphis TN 38104-2198 Office Phone: 901-529-6336.

JARVIS, WILLIAM ROBERT, epidemiologist, educator; s. John James and Mattie Belle (Steele) J.; m. Janine M. Jason, July 4, 1982; children: Danielle Kristin, Ashley Alana. BS in Psychology with honors, U. Calif., Davis, 1970; MD, U. Tex., Houston, 1974. Intern U. Tex. Med. Ctr., Houston, 1974-75; resident in pediat. Children's Hosp., LA, 1975-77; pediatric infectious disease fellow Toronto Hosp. for Sick Children, 1977-78; fellow pediat. infectious diseases, virology, pub. health Yale U. Sch. Med., 1978-80; commd. med. officer USPHS, 1980, advanced through grades to capt., 1990, ret., 2003; asst. chief Nat. Nosocomial Infections Surveillance Systems Ctrs. for Disease Control, Atlanta, 1981-90, asst. chief epidemiology br., 1984-87, chief epidemiology br. hosp. infections program, 1987-91, chief investigation, prevention br. hosp. infections program, 1991-2000, acting dir. hosp. infections program, 1996-98, assoc. dir. program devel. Divsn. Healthcare Quality Promotion, 2001—02; dir. Office Extramural Rsch. Nat. Ctr. for Infectious Diseases, Atlanta, 2002—03; pres. Jason and Jarvis Assoc., LLC, 2003—. Asst. prof. pediat. infectious disease and immunology Emory U., Atlanta, 1985-96, assoc. prof., 1996-2009; asst. prof. Rollins Sch. Pub. Health, 1999-2003, pvt. cons., 2003-2004; pres Jason & Jarvis Assocs., 2003—. Editor: ICHE, 2004—07, Hosp. Infections Book, 2005—; contbr. articles to profl. jours., chapters to books. Capt. Commn. Corps, US Public Health Service. Mem. Infectious Diseases Soc. Am., Am. Soc. Microbiology, Soc. Hosp. Epidemiologists Am. (pres. 2001-02). Roman Catholic. Avocations: stock market, gardening, tennis, travel. Office: Jason &Jarvis Assoc 135 Dune Ln Hilton Head Island SC 29928 Home: 135 Dune Ln Hilton Head Island SC 29928-6527 Office Phone: 404-512-4777. Personal E-mail: wrjmj@aol.com.

JASEMIAN, YOUSEF, physical therapist, educator; b. Abadan, Iran, Dec. 20, 1954; s. Nasser Jasemian and Kolsom Assadi. BSc in Engring., Engring. Coll., Iran, 1975; BSc in Biomed. Engring., Aarjus Engring. Sch., 1991; MS in Biomed. Engring., Denmark Tech. U., 1998; PhD in Health Sci. and Tech., Aalborg U., 2005. Leader Iranian Oil Refinery and Nat. Iranian Petroleum, Abadan, 1975—83, Iranian Offshore Oil Co., Dep. Telecomm., Lavan Island, Parsian Gulf, 1983—85; lectr. project devel., communication, mktg. and promotion Fedn. Free Info., Aarhus, Denmark, 1992—94; rsch. asst. Royal Dental Coll., 1992—94; rsch. asst. prof. Dep. Info. Tech., Denmark

Tech. U., Lyngby, 1998—99; software designer Ericsson Mobile Co., Aalborg, 1999—2002, project mgr., 2002—05; sport injury therapist pvt. practice, 2002—, acupuncturist, 2004—; asst. rsch. prof. Ctr. Sensory-Motor Interaction, Dept. Health Sci. & Tech., Aalborg U., 2005—. Expert reviewer Rsch. Grants Com., South Africa, 2005—. Author: (booklet) Exercises Handbook in Electronic Circuits for Second Semester Students; contbr. articles to profl. jours. Mem.: IEEE, Danish Med. Acupuncture Soc., Scandinavian Assn. for Study of Pain, Internat. Brain Rsch. Orgn., Internat. Assn. for Study of Pain, Assn. Natural Medicine Pharmacists, Danish Soc. Sports Injury Therapists, Danish Soc. Clin. Telemedicine, Assn. Danish Massure & Sport Therapist (assoc.), Danish Med. Telemedicine Assn. (assoc.). Achievements include invention of Wireless Telemedicine System applying Bluetooth technology & Cellular Communication Network: New Approach for Real-time Remote Patient Monitoring. Office: Dept Health Sci & Tech Fredrik Bajers Vej 7 D-3 Aalborg 9220 Denmark Office Fax: +45 9815 4008. Personal E-mail: yj@effektivterapi.dk. E-mail: yj@hst.aau.dk.

JASIEWICZ, RONALD CLARENCE, anesthesiologist, educator, osteopath; b. Suffern, NY, June 8, 1964; s. Clarence William and Adele Helen (Rucki) J. AAS in Sci. and Math., SUNY, Rockland, 1984; BS in Life Sci., N.Y. Inst. Tech., 1987; DO, N.Y. Coll. Osteo. Medicine, 1992; AAS in Emergency Med. Tech., SUNY, Rockland, 1993. Diplomate Am. Bd. Anesthesiology, Am. Osteo. Bd. Anesthesiology, Nat. Bd. Osteo. Med. Examiners. Unit asst. Good Samaritan Hosp., Suffern, 1980-87; paramedic Empress Ambulance Svc., Yonkers, NY, 1985-86, Nyack (N.Y.) E.M.S., 1986-87; intern in medicine and surgery Wilson Meml. Regional Med. Ctr., Johnson City, NY, 1992-93; asst. clin. instr. Stony Brook (N.Y.) Med. Sch., 1993-96; resident in anesthesiology Univ. Med. Ctr., 1993-96; fellow pediatric anesthesiology Children's Hosp. of Buffalo, 1996-97; clin. instr. Buffalo Med. Sch., 1996-97; pediatric anesthesiologist U. Med. Ctr. Stony Brook, NY, 1997—; asst. prof. anesthesiology SUNY Sch. Medicine, Stony Brook, 1997—. Mem. admission com. SUNY Stony Brook Med. Sch., 1998-2001, mem. cirriculum com., 2001-. Bd. mgrs., treas. Stonington at Port Jefferson-Condominium II, 1998—2001; bd. dirs. Stonington at Port Jefferson HOA, 1998—2001. Med. corps. USNR, 1998—. Am. Osteo. Coll. Anesthesiologists, Am. Osteo. Assn., Sigma Omicron. Roman Catholic. Avocations: downhill skiing, travel, kayaking, physical fitness, the arts. Office: U Med Ctr at Stony Brook Dept Pediatric Anes Stony Brook NY 11794-0001

JASINSKAS, VYTAUTAS, ophthalmologist, educator; b. Lithuania, June 8, 1951; MD, Kaunas Inst. Medicine, 1974. Prof., head eye dept., Nat. Ctr. Ophthalmology Lithuanian U. Health Scis., 1991—. V.p., chmn. residency exch. com. European Bd. Ophthalmology, 2009—. Named Hon. Lithuanian Dr., Lithuanian Health Care Ministry. Mem.: European Soc. Cataract and Refractive Surgeons, Lithuanian Soc. Ophthalmologists, ESCRS. Office: 9 Mickeviciaus St Kaunas LT 44307 Lithuania Office Fax: 370 37 326146. Business E-Mail: vytautas.jasinskas@kaunoklinikos.lt.

JASKULA, JANET, pediatrics nurse, educator; b. Chgo., Mar. 9, 1951; d. John J. and Katheryn O. (Cheatham) J. Diploma, Ill. Masonic Med. Ctr., Chgo., 1973; BSN cum laude, Sonoma State U., Rohnert Park, Calif., 1983; MS, U. Calif., San Francisco, 1986. Cert. pub. health nurse. Staff nurse Rush Med. Ctr., Chgo., 1973-75, Kentfield (Calif.) Hosp., 1976-78, R.K. Davies Hosp., San Francisco, 1978-80, Marin Gen. Hosp., Greenbrae, Calif., 1983-86; clin. nurse in pediatrics U. Calif., San Francisco, 1980-86, clin. nurse III, in pediatric surgery, 1986-94, asst. clin. prof. dept. family health care nursing; pediatric clin. instr. Coll. San Mateo, Calif., 1994-96; clin. specialist pediatric nephrology U. Calif., San Francisco, 1995—. Mem. ethics com. U. Calif., San Francisco, 2002—. Mem. ANA, Calif. Nurses Assn., U. Calif. San Francisco Nursing Alumni Assn., Sigma Theta Tau. Office Phone: 415-476-2423. Business E-Mail: jjaskula@peds.ucsf.edu.

JASMIN, DIDI, medical association administrator; b. Vancouver, Can., Sept. 27, 1951; Licence, U. Paris 8, 1985, M, DESS, DEA, U. Paris 8. Exec. dir. European Sch. Haematology, 1988—. Avocations: reading, theater, dance. Office: European Sch Haematology IUH Hôp Paris 75010 France E-mail: didi.jasmin@univ-paris-diderot.fr.

JASONNI, VALERIO-MARIA, obstetrician, gynecologist, educator; b. Bologna, Italy, Nov. 2, 1944; d. Dario M. Jasonni and Paola M. Cheli. MD cum laude, U. Bologna, 1969. Fellow dept. ob-gyn. U. Bologna, 1974—80, asst. prof., 1980—89, assoc. prof., 1989—94; chair dept. ob-gyn. U. Messina, 1994—97; chair, chief med. sch. U. Modena, 1997—. Dir. gynecology Modena Gen. Hosp., 1997—; referee Ministry for Rsch., Italy, 2000—. Editor: Endometrial Cancer, 1985, Manuale Per Il Medico Pratico, 2000; contbr. articles to profl. jours. With Italian Army, 1969—70. Grantee Rsch. grantee, CNR, 1985—94. Fellow: Am. Assn. for Cancer Rsch.; mem.: Rotary. Avocation: fishing. Office: Univ Modena Cargo Del Pozzo 41100 Modena Italy Home: Via Santo Stefano 29 40125 Bologna BO Italy

JATLOW, PETER I., pathologist, medical educator, researcher; b. New Brunswick, NJ, Feb. 12, 1936; s. Daniel and Anne (Davis) J.; m. Stephanie Bea Yager, Dec. 22, 1959; children: Allison, Julia. BS, Union Coll., Schenectady, NY, 1957; MD, SUNY Downstate Med. Ctr., Bklyn., 1961; MS (hon.), Yale U., 1976. Cert. in pathology 1967. Intern Montefiore Hosp., Bronx, NY, 1961-62; resident Yale-New Haven Hosp., 1962-66; asst. prof. lab. medicine Yale U., New Haven, 1968-73, assoc. prof. lab. medicine, 1973-76, prof. lab. medicine, 1976—, chmn. dept. lab. medicine, 1984—2006. Cons. FDA, Washington, 1978-82; mem. biomed. rsch. rev. com. USPHS, Nat. Inst. Drug Abuse, Rockville, Md., 1982-86; mem. test material devel. subcom. FLEX Program Nat. Bd. Med. Exam., Phila., 1990-91. Editor: Methodology in Analytical Toxicology, vol. II, 1982; editl. bd. Clin. Chemistry, 1973-83, Selected methods in Clin. Chemistry, 1976-79, Jour. Analytical Toxicology, 1978-79, Therapeutic Drug Monitoring, 1979-86, 90—, Clinica Chimica Acta, 1984-90, Am. Jour. Clin. Pathology, 1988—; co-editor The Yale University School of Medicine Patient's Guide To Medical Tests, 1998; contbr. numerous articles to profl. jours. Served to surgeon USPHS, 1966-68. Recipient Irving Sunshine award in clin. toxicology Internat. Assn. Therapeutic Drug Monitoring and Toxicology, 1993, Jean R. Oliver award/Master Tchr. in Pathology, Alumni Assn., SUNY Health Sci. Ctr., Bklyn., 2001. Fellow AAAS (award for rsch. and leadership in lab. medicine 1997), Coll. Am. Pathologists; mem. Acad. Clin. Lab. Physicians and Scientists (pres. 1983-84, Gerald T. Evans award 1988), Am. Soc. Clin. Pathology, Am. Assn. Clin. Chemistry (award for outstanding contbns. to clin. chemistry in selected area of rsch. 1985, award for outstanding contbns. in edn. 1995). Home: 617 Saddle Ridge Rd Orange CT 06477-2024 Office: Yale U Sch Medicine Dept Lab Medicine PO Box 208035 New Haven CT 06520-8035

JAUHAR, SANDEEP, cardiologist, educator; b. New Delhi, Dec. 16, 1968; s. Prem Prakash and Raj Jauhar; m. Sonia Jauhar, Apr. 24, 1999; children: Mohan, Pia. BA in Physics, U. Calif., Berkeley, 1989, MA in Physics, 1991, PhD in Physics, 1995; MD, Wash. U. Sch. Medicine, St. Louis, 1998. Diplomate Am. Bd. Internal Medicine, cert. Bd. Nuc. Cardiology. Internal medicine intern NY Weill-Cornell Med. Ctr., 1998—99, internal medicine resident, 1999—2001; cardiology fellowship NYU Med. Ctr., 2001—04; dir. heart failure program LI Jewish Med. Ctr., New Hyde Park, NY, 2004—, co-chair ethics com., 2007—08. Instr. phys. diagnosis NYU Sch. Medicine, 2001—03; asst. prof. medicine Albert Einstein Coll. Medicine, NYC, 2004—. Author: (memoir) Intern: A Doctor's Initiation, 2007; reg. contbr., med. writer NY Times, 1998—, mem. editl bd. Am. Assn. Physicians of Indian Origin Jour., 2003—05, reviewer Jour. Am. Bd. Family Medicine, 2006, Mt. Sinai Jour. Medicine, 2009; contbr. numerous artles to profl. jours., chapters to books; broadcast appearances include NPR, CNN, Am. Pub. Radio, Fox 5 News, ABC News, Bloomberg News Sunday. Recipient Spl. Recognition award for outstanding contbn. of med. articles to NY Times, South Asian Journalists Assn., 2004; grantee Grad. Fellowship, NSF, 1989—92, Dr. Lee B. & Virginia G. Harrison scholarship in internal medicine, Washington U. Sch. Medicine, 1997. Fellow: Am. Coll. Cardiology; mem.: ACP, Phi Beta Kappa. Office: LI Jewish Med Ctr 270 05 76th Ave New Hyde Park NY 11040 Office Phone: 718-470-7732. Business E-Mail: sjauhar@lij.edu. *

JAUREGUI, CONNIE LEE, internist; b. Cin., Apr. 3, 1962; d. James Harold and Joan Lee (Marston) Senour; Luis Jauregui, Sept. 16, 2000. BS in Biology cum laude, U. Cin., 1984; MD with honors in Psychiatry, Med. Coll. Ohio, 1991. Histocompatibility technologist Hoxworth Blood Ctr., Cin., 1985-87; intern in internal medicine Pa. State U. Hershey Med. Ctr., 1991-92; resident in internal medicine Med. Coll. Ohio, Toledo, 1992-94; pvt. practice Toledo, 1994—2003. Contbg. author: Diagnosis and Management of Bone Infections, 1995. Mem. AMA. Lutheran. Avocations: swimming, travel to exotic locations.

JAVER, AMIN HASSANALI, aircraft production inspector, medical facility executive, aeronautical engineer; b. Nairobi, Oct. 2, 1960; s. Hassanali Hasham and Zubeda Hassanali Javer; m. Nasrine Husein Premji Nov. 21, 1987; children: Aliya Teja, Farah Teja, Alif Javer. Diploma in aero. engring., Chelsea Coll. Aero. & Auto Engring., 1985; MBA in publ. health adminstrn., Nottingham U., Eng., 2002. Engring. supr. and Boeing Fleet engr. Kenya Airways, Nairobi, 1986-97; asst. dir. hotel & support svcs. Aga Khan Hosp., Nairobi, 1997-98, CEO Kisumu, 1998-2000, dir. facilities mgmt. Nairobi, 2001—; exec. dir., COO Alvik Prestige Ltd., Nairobi, Kenya, 2003—; CEO Rwandair Express, Rwanda, 2004—05; aircraft prodn. inspector (Toulouse) Emirates Airline, 2008—. Chmn. Aga Khan 1st aid com., 1988-94, hon. mgr. biomed. engr., Aga Khan Hosp., 1994-96; sec. Kisumu Dist. Hosps.' Adminstrs. com., 1999-2000, vice chmn. Kisumu Dist. Disaster Mgmt. com., 2000. Officer, St. John's Ambulance Brigade, Shoreham-by-Sea, Eng., 1982-86, Nairobi, 1986-97; chmn. Nairobi Health com. of Aga Khan Health Svc., 1993-96, mem. risk mgmt. com., 1988-96, mem. for health, Aga Khan Coun. for Nairobi, 1993-96, mem. without portfolio, Aga Khan Coun. for Nairobi, 1996-99. Recipient Mollison Amy Johnson Challenge trophy, 1985; named Wakefield Meml. scholar, 1984. Fellow Internat. Biog. Assn. (life, dep. dir. gen., 2003—); mem. Royal Aero. Soc. (assoc.), Assn. MBAs, Am. Biog. Assn. (dep. gov., 2003—), Nottingham U. Alumni Assn. Avocations: photography, travel, stamps, reading. Home: #46 Blvd Matabiau Apt 16 31000 Toulouse France Office Phone: 33-6-45-47-91-22. Personal E-mail: aminjaver@yahoo.co.uk. Business E-Mail: aminjaver@gmail.com.

JAVID, MANUCHER J., retired neurosurgeon, educator; b. Tehran, Iran, Jan. 11, 1922; came to U.S., 1944, naturalized, 1957; s. Asdolah and Touba (Ahdiyeh) J.; m. Lida Emma Fabbri, Oct. 19, 1951; children— Roxane, Daria, Jeffrey, Claudia. MD, U. Ill., 1946. Diplomate: Am. Bd. Neurosurgery. Intern Augustana Hosp., Chgo., 1946-47, resident gen. surgery, 1947-48, resident neurosurgery, 1948-49; asst. in neuropathology Ill. Neuropsychiat. Inst., Chgo., 1948-49; fellow in neurosurgery Lahey Clinic, Boston, 1949; resident neurosurgery New Eng. Med. Center, Boston, 1950; clin. research fellow neurosurgery Mass. Gen. Hosp., Boston, 1950, asst. resident, 1951, chief resident neurosurgery, 1952; teaching fellow in surgery Harvard, 1952; instr. Med. Sch. U. Wis., Madison, 1953—54, asst. prof., 1954—57, assoc. prof., 1957—62, prof. neurosurgery, 1962—98, chmn. dept. neurosurgery, 1962—95, endowed named prof. neurol. surgery, 1998, emeritus prof., 1998—; ret., 1998. Cons. neurosurgeon VA Hosp., Madison, 1956-98. Contbr. articles profl. jours. Mem. AMA, ACS, AAUP, AANS, Soc. Neurol. Surgeons, Am. Assn. Neurol. Surgeons, Am. Assn. Med. Colls., Soc. for Neurosci., Central Neurosurg. Soc. (pres. 1964), Internat. Intradiscal Therapy Soc. (hon., treas. 1987-90, pres.-elect 1990—, pres. 1991), NY Acad. Scis., Xeiron, Sigma Xi, Phi Beta Pi, Alpha Omega Alpha. Mem. Baha'i Faith. Club: Rotarian. Achievements include introduction of osmotherapy in neurosurgery and ophthalmology by the clin. use of urea for reduction intracranial and intraocular pressure. Home: 4750 Lafayette Dr Madison WI 53705-4865 Business E-Mail: mjavid@wise.edu.

JAVID, NIKZAD SABET, dentist, prosthodontist educator; b. May 24, 1934; s. Salam and Pika (Farhang) Javid-S; m. Mahnaz Zolfaghari, Oct. 22, 1942; children: Nikrooz, Behrooz, Farnaz. DMD, U. Tehran, Iran, 1958; cert., U. Chgo., 1970; MSc, Ohio State U., 1971; MEd, U. Fla., 1981. Asst. prof. U. Tehran, 1959-69; prof., dean, 1975-79; asst. prof. Ohio State U., 1971-73; assoc. prof., 1973-74; assoc. prof. removable prosthodontics U. Fla., 1974-75; prof., 1982; pvt. practice dentistry specializing in prosthodontics Gainesville, Fla., 1980—; mng. dentist Dental Group with CLOIS. Cons., lectr. in field. Author books, including: Stress Breaker in partial Denture, 1966, Cleft Palate Prosthetics, 1968, Complete Denture Construction, 1974 (with Sara Nawab) Essentials of Complete Denture Prosthodocntics, 1988; contbr. numerous articles to profl. jours. Named Outstanding Clin. Instr. of Yr., Student Dental Coun., Columbus, Ohio, 1973, Outstanding Tchr. of Yr., 1990, Excellent Clin. Prof., U. Fla., 1994, Most Outstanding Prof. of Yr., 1996, Disting. Prof. of Yr., 1998, 2000, 2001, 2002, Tchr. of Yr., Class of 2001, 2001, Prof. of Yr., Class of 2002, 2002. Fellow Internat. Coll. Dentists, Internat. Coll. Prosthodontics, Am. Coll. Prosthodontics, Am. Acad. Maxillofacial Prosthetics, Royal Soc. Health (Eng.); mem. Iranian Dental Assn. (dir. 1975-78), ADA, Internat. Assn. Dental Rsch. (sec.-treas. Iran div. 1978), Iranian Am. Dental Assn. Calif. (hon. life, award 2000), Lions. Home: 800 Minnewawa Ave Apt 123 Clovis CA 93612-1783 Office Phone: 352-318-4018. Personal E-mail: nikzadjavid@yahoo.com.

JAVIER, AILEEN RIEGO, pathologist, educator; b. Fabrica, Philippines, Apr. 4, 1948; d. Filemon Yanson Riego and Alicia Vazquez (Alteros) R.; m. Mark Anthony Navarro Javier, July 15, 1972; children: Martha Francesca, Nadine Ruth. BS, U. Philippines, 1967, MD, 1972; Cert. Completion Hosp. Adminstrn., Ateneo de Manila U., 1989. Diplomate Philippine Bd. Pathology. Instr. pathology U. Philippines, Manila, 1972-76, asst. prof., 1976-80, sr. lectr., 1987-94, med. specialist, chmn. dept. Lung Ctr. Philippines Quezon City, 1987-91; cons., 1991—98; lectr. Ateneo de Manila Grad. Sch., Makati City, 1989—2002. Med. specialist Philippine Children's Ctr., Quezon City, 1981-82, cons., 1986; cons. VRP Med. Ctr., Rizal, Philippines, 1984-86, 95-, dept. chmn., 1987-94, 2009-10; med. specialist Nat. Kidney and Transplant Inst., Quezon City, 1984-87, 91-93, cons., 1987-91, dep. dir., 1994-2000, chair lab. dept., 2001-04, exec. dir., 2010-; cons. Bur. Rsch. and Labs, Manila, 1987—93; cons. Cardinal Santos Med. Ctr., 1986-98; v.p. Philippine Blood Coordinating Coun., 1987-88, pres., 1990; bd. dirs. Fetus as a Patient Inst., Philippines, 1990—. Active Goodwill Industries, Quezon City, 1981; bd. dir. Rizal chpt. Phillipine Nat. Red Cross, 1994—2003. Fellow Philippine Soc. Oncologists (sec.-treas. 1990-91); mem. Philippine Med. Assn. (life), Transplantation Soc. of the Philippines (life), Internat. Acad. Pathology, Philippine Soc. Pathologists (treas. 1985-87, pres. 1987-89, bd. pathology, 1994-96), Philippine Soc. for Quality in Health Care (bd. dir. 1997-2000, 2002-06, pres. 2004), Philippine Bible Soc. (life). Baptist. Avocation: playing piano. Office: Nat Kidney & Transplant Inst East Ave 1100 Quezon City Philippines Office Phone: 632-9240135. Business E-Mail: aileen.javier@nkti.gov.ph.

JAVIER, SATURNINO PEREZ, cardiologist; b. Tanauan, Batangas, Philippines, Nov. 29, 1958; s. Victorio Opulencia and Perfecta Perez Javier; m. Ma. Angela Navato Javier, Nov. 30, 1995; children: Luis Gabriel, Franco Andre, Sofia Alessandra. BS in Biochemistry magna cum laude, U. Santo Tomas, Sampaloc, Manila, Philippines, 1981; MD, U. Santo Tomas, Manila, Philippines, 1984. Lic. physician Profl. Regulations Commn., 1986, Foreign Medical Graduates Examinations 1989, US Medical Licensure Examinations, Federal Licensure Examinations 1993. Chief resident dept. internal medicine Santo Tomas U. Hosp., Manila, 1988—89; asst. tchg. fellow faculty medicine and surgery U. Santo Tomas, 1988—89; fellow adult clin. cardiology dept. medicine sect. cardiology Makati Med. Ctr., 1992; fellow interventional cardiology Washington Hosp. Ctr., 1994, fellow intravascular ultrasound, 1994. Chair rsch. com. for residents Makati Med. Ctr., Makati City, Philippines, 2000—, chair rsch. com. for fellows, 2000—, chair instl. rev. bd., 2005—; clin. faculty U. Santo Tomas, 2000—04; head sect. interventional cardiology Asian Hosp. and Med. Ctr., Metro Manila, 2002—, adminstrv. officer in charge of fellows, 2005—. Editor: (book) Escape Beat, (newsletter) Philippine Heart Assn. Newsbriefs; columnist: Health and Lifestyle Magazine, Manila Times, Prime Angle. Vol. Philippine Nat. Red Cross, Metro Manila, 1977—78; founding pres. Cath. Student Press, Metro Manila, 1980; bd. mem. Cath. Press Assn. of the Philippines, Metro Manila, 1980; dep. bd. mem. Movie and TV Rev. and Classification Bd., Metro Manila, 1996—97. Recipient Gerry Roxas Leadership award, 1975, Insular Life Gold Eagle award, 1975, Benavides award of Merit for Civic Achievement, 1980, Francisco F. Tangco Young Investigator's award, Philippine Heart Assn., 1988, Golden Scroll award for Medicine and Allied Sciences; scholar, U. Santo Tomas, 1975—81, Japan Air Lines, 1979; Nat. State scholar, 1975—80. Fellow: Am. Coll. Cardiology, Philippine Soc. Cardiovasc. Catheterizations and Interventions (pres. 2005—06, Presdl. Award of Merit 2003, 2004), Philippine Coll. Cardiology (co-chair com. on media affairs 2005—), Philippine Coll. Physicians (life); mem.: Makati Med. Soc., Philippine Soc. Echocardiography, Cardiac Rehab. Soc. Philippines, U. Santo Tomas Med. Alumni Assn. (life), Internat. Bd. Internal Medicine, PHA Coun. on Cardiac Catheterization and Interventions, Regional Atherothrombosis Collaborative Group, Philippine Med. Assn. Roman Catholic. Avocations: writing, photography, swimming. Office: Asian Hosp and Med Ctr Ste 520 Fillinvest City Alabang Philippines Personal E-mail: spjavier@yahoo.com.

JAVITT, DANIEL C., psychiatrist, researcher; b. NYC, Nov. 16, 1958; s. Norman and Suzanne Javitt; m. Reba Kizner, Oct. 20, 1957; children: Solomon, Michael, Sarah, Gabriel. BA, Princeton U., 1979; MD, Albert Einstein Coll. of Medicine, 1983, PhD, 1990. Lic. Md., diplomate Am. Bd. of Psychiatry and Neurology. Intern in gen. medicine Albert Einstein Coll. of Medicine, Montefiore Med. Ctr., Bronx, NY, 1983—84; resident in psychiatry Albert Einstein Coll. of Medicine, Bronx, 1984—87, asst. prof., 1990—95; assoc. prof. NYU Sch. of Medicine, NYC, 1995—2000, prof. of psychiatry and neuroscience, 2001—11, Columbia U., Coll. Physicians & Surgeons, 2011—. Dir. schizophrenia rsch. unit Bronx Psychiat. Ctr., 1992—95; dir. program in cognitive neurosci. and schizophrenia Nathan Kline Inst. for Psychiat. Rsch., Orangeburg, NY, 1995—; dir. brain stimulation & exptl. therapeutics NY State Psychiat. Inst. Contbr. papers to med. jours. (Milton Rosenbaum award, 1986, Hillside Jour. of Psychiatry Resident Rsch. award, 1986, Am. Psychiat. Assn. Kempf Fund award, 1992, MA Brazier award 14th Internat. Congress of EEG and Clin. Neurophysiology, 1997, A.E. Bennet award Soc. for Biol. Psychiatry, 1998, Joel Elkes Rsch. award Am. Coll. of Neuropsychopharmacology, 2002). Recipient Young Investigator award, Internat. Congress of Schizophrenia Rsch., 1987, merit scholarship, N.Y. State, 1979—83, Physician Scientist award, NIMH, 1986—91, FIRST award, 1992—97, Ind. Invsigator award, Nat. Alliance for Rsch. on Schizophrenia and Affective Disorders, 1995—97, Rsch. award, McDonnell-Pew Found., 1995, Nat. Inst. on Drug Abuse, 1998—2006, Clin. Rsch. award, Stanley Found., 2000, Ind. Scientist award, NIMH, 1997—2006, Young Investigator award, Nat. Alliance for Rsch. on Schizophrenia and Affective Disorders, 1990, Lieber Investigator award, 1995, Dozor vis. prof., Ben-Gurion U. of the Negev, 1995, N.Y. State Rsch. Award, N.Y. State Office of Mental Health, 1998, Sr. Investigator award, Winter Workshop of Schizophrenia Rsch., 1998, Clin. Scientist award, Burroughs Wellcome Fund, 2000; fellow Joels vis. prof., Hebrew U. Med. Ctr., 2001. Fellow: Am. Coll. of Neuropsychopharmacology (mem. credentials com. 2004—06); mem.: Soc. for Neuroscience, Soc. for Biol. Psychiatry. Independent. Jewish. Achievements include patents for Treatment of negative and cognitive symptoms of schizophrenia with glycine and its precursors; Treatment of negative and cognitive symptoms of schizophrenia with glycine uptake antagonists; Treatment of negative and cognitive symptoms of schizophrenia with glycine uptake antagonists; Treatment of negative and cognitive symptoms of schizophrenia with D-serine; Glycine substitutes and precursors for treating a psychosis; Assay for D-serine transport antagonist and use for treating psychosis. Avocations: scuba diving, sailing, skiing, hiking, travel. Office Fax: 834-398-6546. Business E-Mail: javitt@nki.rfmh.org.

JAVITT, JONATHAN C., physician, health information technology executive, presidential appointee; b. NYC, Nov. 7, 1956; s. Norman B. and Suzanne (Markovits) J.; m. Marcia C. Fishman, June 29, 1986; children: Zachary, Matthew, Gabrielle. AB with honors, Princeton U., 1978; MD, Cornell U., 1982; MPH, Harvard U., 1984. Diplomate Am. Bd. Ophthalmology. Sr. fellow Potomac Inst. Policy Studies, 1991—; instr. Johns Hopkins U., 1987—88, asst. prof., 1989—93, assoc. prof., 1994—96, adj. prof. Balt., 1996—; asst. prof. Georgetown U., Washington, 1990-93, assoc. prof., 1993-96, prof. Sch. Medicine, prof. sch. Pub. Policy, 1996—; founder, chmn. Certitude, Inc., Mpls., 1994—; sr. v.p., nat. med. dir. United Health Care/Applied Health Care Informatics, Mpls., 1997-98; chmn. Health Directions LLC, Bethesda, 1998—; founder, pres., vice chmn. EMEDX, Inc., 1999—; founder Coderyte, Inc., 2000; chief sci. officer Active Health Mgmt., 2000—05; exec. v.p. FCG, Inc., 2005—06; mng dir. BTI, 2007—08; founder, CEO, vice chmn. Telcare, Inc., 2008—. Resident medicine Lenox Hill Hosp., NY, 1982—1983; resident surgeon Wills Eye Hosp., Thomas Jefferson U., Phila., 1984—1987,expert cons. Health Care Fin. Adminstrn., Balt., 1987—; spl. employee The White House Health Reform Task Force, Washington, 1992; cons. Nat. Eye Inst./NIH, 1990—, Nat. Inst. Diabetes Digestive and Kidney Disease/NIH, 1991—, Agy. for Health Care Policy Rsch., 1994—, The World Bank, Washington, 1993—2000, Swedish Coun. on Tech. Improvement, 1997, Japanese Min. of Health, 1993, Australia Min. of Health, 1994; bd. dirs, chief med. officer, Acad. Homeland Security 2001-2002, chair, Health Subcom., Pres.'s Info. Tech. Adv. Com., 2003—2005,White House Exec. Office pres. presidl. del. White House Conf. Aging, 2005. Sect. editor Archives of Ophthalmology, 1993—, Ophthalmology Times, 1993—; author more than 200 sci. books, chpts., articles to profl. jours., to profl. publs. Princeton Alumni Schs. Com., 1990-, chair Nat. Health Policy Coun., Washington, 1992—; cmty. spkr. on health care The White House, 1992—; trustee Md. Rep. Party, 2000—; mem. campaign com. Bush for Pres., 2000, 04; mem. Rep. Regents Roundtable; bd. dirs. Washington Jewish Fedn., Brookdale Inst., Am. Joint Distbn. Com.; active Johns Hopkins Pres.'s Club, Weill Cornell Med. Coll. Deans Cir., Rep. Senatorial Trust; fin. cmty. Erlich for Gov., 2002, presdl. appointee, spl. employee, Office Undersecretary Def. (ATL), 2003-2005. Recipient Cert. of Appreciation, USAF, 1991, Physician Scientist award Nat. Eye Inst., 1988; Kellogg Found. fellow, 1983; Prevention of Blindness Lectr. award, Ill. Eye Soc., 1995; named guest of honor Japanese Glaucoma Soc., 1996, New England Ophthalmologic Soc., 1997.; CTIA, People's Choice award 2009, Leopold Lectr., Wills Eye Hosp., 2010, CTIA, Emerging Tech. award 2010; Ophthalmology fellowship Wilmer Ophthalmological Inst., Johns Hopkins U., 1987-88. Fellow Am. Acad. Ophthalmology (Honor award 1990, Sr. Recognition award 2000, Secretariat award 2006), Am. Glaucoma Soc.; mem. AMA, AOPA, NBAA, Assn. for Rsch. in Vision and Ophthalmology, Assn. for Health Svc. Rsch., Am. Glaucoma Soc., Kehilath Jeshurun, Royal Ocean Racing Club, Princeton Club, Harvard Club, Cosmos Club. Republican. Jewish. Achievements include leading the White House policy initiative to foster universal adoption of electronic medical records and health information technology; invention of use of information technology to improve the delivery and outcomes of healthcare, ranging from early applications in use of electronic medical records; use of electronic decisionmaking systems to identify medical errors, use of natural language processing to interpret electronic records, and use of wireless technology in medical monitoring devices; patents for ovel compounds for treatment of glaucoma and vehicles for enhancing effectiveness of ophthalmologic drugs. Avocations: sailing, aviation.

JAVITT, NORMAN B., medical educator, researcher; b. NYC, Mar. 9, 1928; s. Bernard and Zara (Hillman) Jakubovitz; m. Suzanne Markovits, June 5, 1955; children: Jonathan Chaim, Daniel Coleman, Joel Israel, Gail Hannah. AB cum laude, Syracuse U., 1947; PhD in Physiology, U. N.C., 1951; MD, Duke U., 1954. Diplomate Am. Bd. Internal Medicine; lic. physician, N.Y. Predoctoral fellow USPHS, Chapel Hill, NC, 1949-51; intern Mt. Sinai Hosp., NYC, 1954-55, asst. resident, 1957-58, chief resident, 1959-60, Sara Welt fellow in medicine, spl. USPHS, 1961-62; asst. physician, advanced fellow Am. Heart Assn. Vanderbilt Clinic, Columbia Coll. Physicians and Surgeons, NYC, 1957-58; instr. dept. medicine NYU Sch. Medicine, 1962-64, asst. prof., 1964-68; assoc. prof. Cornell U.Med. Coll., NYC, 1968-73, prof., 1973-83; assoc. attending physician N.Y. Hosp., NYC, 1968-73, attending physician, 1973-83; prof. medicine, prof. pediatrics NYU Med. Ctr., NYC, 1983—, dir. divsn. hepatic diseases, 1983-2000; guest investigator Nat. Inst. Child Health and Development, Nat. Insts. of Health, Bethesda, Md., 2000—; assoc. dir. clin. rsch. unit NYU Med. Ctr., NYC, 1985-90. Cons. Meml. Sloan-Kettering Cancer Ctr., N.Y.C., 1970-83; vis. prof. Rockefeller U. Hosp., 1970-76; cons. medicine VA Hosp., Bklyn., 1977-83; chief divsn. gastroenterology Cornell-N.Y. Hosp. Med. Ctr., 1973-81, chief divsn. hepatic diseases, acting chief divsn. gastroenterology, 1981-83; cons. Tisch Hosp., NYU Med. Ctr., 1983—; mem. tng. grant study sect. Nat. Inst. Arthritis, Metabolic & Digestive Diseases, NIH, 1978-85; mem. steering com. Nat. Cooperative Gallstone Study, 1973-80, chmn. clin. mgmt. com., 1974-78; gen. medicine study Section A, NIH, 1976-80. Mem. editl. adv. bd. Hosp. Practice, 1969-93; assoc. editor Jour. Lipid Rsch., 1977-78, 86—, editl. bd., 1983—; author, editor 2 books; contbr. articles to profl. jours. Capt., M.C., U.S. Army, 1955-57. Fellow ACP; mem. Am. Physiol. Soc., Am. Soc. Pharmacology and Exptl. Therapeutics, Am. Fedn. Clin. Rsch., Am. Soc. Clin. Investigation, Am. Assn. Study of Liver Disease, Am. Gastroenterol. Assn., Am. Soc. Clin. Pharmacology and Therapeutics, Am. Soc. Biol. Chemists, Am. Pediatric Soc., Am. Soc. Parenteral and Enteral Nutrition, Harvey Soc., Sigma Xi, Alpha Omega Alpha. Jewish. Home: 501 E 79th St New York NY 10021-0735 Office: NYU Med Ctr Divsn Hepatic Disease New York NY 10016 Business E-Mail: norman.javitt@med.nyu.edu.

JAVLE, MILIND, physician, educator; b. India, Sept. 5, 1964; MD, Grant Med. Coll., 1991. Assoc. prof. MD Anderson Cancer Ctr., Houston, 2001—. Grant, NIH. Mem.: AACR, ASCO. Office: 1515 Holcombe Blvd Houston TX 77030 Business E-Mail: mjavle@mdanderson.org.

JAWALI, VIVEK, surgeon; MS in Gen. Surgery, Nat. Acad. Med. Sci.; MCh in Cardio-Thoracic Surgery. With Dudley Johnson MD St. Mary's Hosp., Milwaukee, Wis.; with John Wright London Chest Hosp., The Princess Grace Hosp., England; with Steven J. Westbay, John Radcliff Oxford Hosp., England; with Steven J. Philips MD Mercy Hosp., Des Moines; with Prof. Calafiore Univ. Hosp., Chieti, Italy, with Dr. Erick Jansen Utrecht, Netherlands, with Dr. Urbon Lonn Linchoping, Sweden; chief cardio-thoracic and vascular surgeon Wockhardt Super Speciality Hosp., Banglore, India, 1992—. Fellow: Indian Assn. of Cardiovasc. and Thoracic Surgeons (pres., vice chmn. organizing com. 2005); mem.: Indian Med. Assn. (exec. com. Karnataka chpt. 2001), Jour. of Indian Assn. of Cardio-Thoracic Surgery (editor 2001), Banglore Surg. Soc. (hon. sec. 1992), Cardiology Soc. of India (hon. sec. Banglore chpt. 1987), Indian Coll. of Cardiology (v.p. 1999—2002), Indian Assn. of Cardio-Thoracic Surgeons (exec. coun. 1995), Internat. Soc. of Minimally Invasive Cardiac Surgeons (founder). Achievements include performing India's first minimally invasive bypass surgery (MIDCAB) and also minimally invasive valve replacement; performed the world's first awake open heart surgery (Aortic valve replacement with triple bypass); first to movement of minimally invasive heart surgery in India. Office: Wockhardt Super Speciality Hospital 1643 N Ambazari Rd Nagpur 440033 India Office Phone: 917126624289. *

JAWORSKA, MALGORZATA DOROTA, pharmacist; b. Warsaw, Oct. 21, 1967; MS in Pharmacy, Warsaw Med. U., 1991, PharmD, 2011. Specialist pharm. analysis Drug Inst., 1991—2002; asst. scientist Nat. Inst. Pub. Health, 2002—06, Nat. Medicines Inst., 2006—11, mem. sci. bd., 2008—11, adj., 2011—; sci. dir. European Directorate Quality Medicines & Healthcare, 2008—09. Mem.: CASSS. Avocations: hiking, horseback riding, ballroom dancing. Office: Chelmska St 30/34 Warsaw 00-725 Poland Business E-Mail: m-jaworska@il.waw.pl.

JAYAWEERA, DUSHYANTHA T., medical educator; b. Sri Lanka, May 3, 1951; MD, U. Colombo, 1976. Prof., medicine U. Miami, 1992—. Fellow: ACP; mem.: Royal Coll. Obstetricians and Gynaecologists, Rotary Club Pinecrest and Dadeland (Fla.). Home: 7925 SW 195th St Cutler Bay FL 33157 Home Phone: 305-253-0553. E-mail: jayaweeramd@gmail.com.

JAZIREHI, ALI, medical educator; b. Iran, 1968; CLS, UCLA, PhD, 2003. Asst. prof., dept. surgery UCLA Sch. Medicine, 2009—. Career Devel. grant, Melanoma Rsch. Found. Mem.: Am. Assn. Cancer Rsch. Avocations: hiking, gardening. Office: 10833 LeConte Ave CHS 54-140 Los Angeles CA 90095-1782 Business E-Mail: ajazirehi@mednet.ucla.edu.

JEA, SEUNG YOUN, ophthalmologist, director; b. Seoul, Republic of Korea, Nov. 8, 1973; MD, Busan Nat. U., 1998, PhD, 2007. Glaucoma fellow Pusan Nat. U. Hosp., Republic of Korea, 2003—04, instr., 2004—06, asst. prof., 2006—07; postdoc. rsch. fellow, glaucoma svc. Harvard Med. Sch., Mass. Eye and Ear Infirmary, Boston, 2008—09; dir. glaucoma Goodmorning St. Mary's Eye Clinic, Republic of Korea, 2010—. Fellowship, Taejoon-Santen Com. Mem.: Am. Acad. Ophthalmology, Assn. Rsch. Vision and Ophthalmology, Korean Ophthal. Soc., Korean Glaucoma Soc. Avocation: golf. Office: Goodmorning Saint Mary's Eye Clinic 260-5 Busan 614-030 Republic of Korea Personal E-mail: jeasy2@gmail.com.

JEAN, YEN-HSUAN, surgeon; b. Taiwan, Oct. 20, 1965; PhD, Nat. Def. Med. Ctr., 2006. Attending physician, dept. orthop. surgery Pingtung Christian Hosp., 1999—. Rsch. grant, Nat. Sci. Coun. Mem.: Taiwan Orthop. Assn. Avocations: singing, golf. Home: 8 Alley 30 Chung-Der I Rd Pingtung 900 Taiwan Home Fax: 886-8-7338536. Business E-Mail: jean.tang@msa.hinet.net.

JEANNET, MICHEL, retired transplantation immunology unit head; b. Geneva, Apr. 22, 1932; s. Paul Constant and Helene-Alice (Veinie) J.; m. Marie-Claire Mermod, Jan. 31, 1979; children: Nathalie, Pierre-Yves. MD, U. Geneva, 1956; pvt. docent, Faculty of Medicine, Geneva, 1972. Intern in surgery U. Geneva Med. Sch., 1957, intern in medicine, 1957-60, 63-65; intern in hematology Hôpital St. Louis, Paris, 1960-61; rsch. fellow Ctrl. Lab. Swiss Red Cross, Berne, 1961-63; clin. and rsch. fellow depts. surgery and medicine Harvard Med. Sch., Boston, 1966-68; head transplantation immunology unit Hôpital Cantonal Universitaire, Geneva, 1968-97; ret., 1997. Mem. sci. com. J. Carreras Found., Barcelona, 1994. Contbr. articles to profl. jours.; mem. editl. bd. Transplantation, Bone Marrow Transplantation. Fellow Swiss Acad. Sci., Basel, 1966; Chevalier Légion d'Honneur, 1998. Mem. Swiss Soc. Immunology and Allergology (pres. 1978-80), Swiss Soc. Hematology (pres. 1984-86), European Found. Immunogenetics (bd. dirs. 1985), Transplantation Soc. Business E-Mail: micheljeannet@bluewin.ch.

JEE, WON-HEE, radiologist, educator; b. Seoul, Republic of Korea, Oct. 4, 1960; d. Chung Jee and Hong-Suk Yoon; 1 child, Gyu-Won Eo. BS, Kyung-Hee U., 1986. Intern Kyung-Hee U. Hosp., Seoul, 1986—87; resident radiology, fellow, then instr. to asst. prof. Cath. U. Korea, Seoul, 1989—99, asst. prof., 2000—04; assoc. prof. Kangnam St. Mary's Hosp. Cath. U. Korea, Seoul, 2005—. Vis. assoc. Yale U. Hosp., New Haven, 1999—2000. Contbr. articles to profl. jours. Mem.: Asian Musculoskeletal Soc., Internat. Skeletal Soc., Radiol. Soc. N.Am., Korean Radiol. Soc. Avocations: music, movies, travel. Office: Kangnam St Marys Hosp Cath Univ Korea 505 Banpo-dong Seocho-gu Seoul 137 701 Republic of Korea Office Phone: 82-2-590-2784. Business E-Mail: whjee@catholic.ac.kr.

JEE, YOUNGHEUN, immunologist, researcher; b. Pohang, Kyoungsangbook-do, South of Korea, Dec. 5, 1970; d. Dooha Jee and Chuja Park; m. Taehoon Chung, May 6, 2001; 1 child, Eunsuh Chung. DVM, Republic of Korea, 1993; PhD, Kyoungsangbook-do, Daegu City, 1998. Cert. Korean Coll. Vet. Pathologists, 2003. Postdoctoral rsch. fellow Korea Inst. Radiological and Med. Sci., Seoul, Republic of Korea, 1997—98; postdoctoral rsch. fellow Tokyo Met. Inst. Neurosci., Tokyo, 1998—2001; asst. prof. Cheju Nat. U., Jeju, Jeju, Republic of the Congo, 2002—; rsch. fellow Barrow Neurol. Inst., Phoenix, 2005—. Contbr. numerous articles to profl. jours. Grantee, Japan Multiple Sclerosis Soc., 2000, Nat. Multiple Sclerosis Soc., 2006; fellow, Hob Family Found., 2005. Mem.: Korean Coll. Vet. Pathologists (licentiate). Home: Odeung-dong 1352 Jeju 690-121 Republic of Korea Office: Cheju Nati Univ Ara 1-dong Jeju 690-756 Republic of the Congo Office Fax: 82-64-756-3354; Home Fax: 82-64-756-3354. Personal E-mail: yhjee@cheju.ac.kr.

JEEN, YOONTAE, gastroenterologist; b. Seoul, Republic of Korea, June 24, 1963; s. Chulhyun Jeen and Hyesoon Yoon; m. Namyoung Huh, Nov. 7, 1992; children: Hyunkyung, Chandong. BA in Medicine, Korea U., Seoul, 1988, MD in Gastroenterology, 1991, PhD in Gastroenterology, 1997. Intern Korea U. Hosp., Seoul, 1988—89, resident, 1989—92, clin. fellow, 1995—98, asst. prof., 1998—2001, assoc. prof., 2001—06, prof., 2006—. Gastroenterological cons. Joongang Daily Newspaper, 1999—; dir. quality improvement com. Korea U. Hosp., Seoul, 2006—, exec. com. mem., 2006—. Editor: Korean Jour. Gastrointestinal Endoscopy, 2000—, Korean Jour. Gastroenterology, 2006—; contbr. articles to profl. jours. Capt. Korean Mil., 1992—95. Recipient Young Clinician award, Asian-Pacific Congress Gastroenterology, 2000. Mem.: Am. Pancreatic Assn., Korean Assn. for the Study of Intestinal Disease (com. dir. 2005—, dir. sci. com. 2007—), Korean Soc. Gastrointestinal Motility, Korean Assn. for the Study of Pancreas and Biliary Tract, Korean Soc. Gastrointestinal Endoscopy (mem. examination bd. for qualification of endoscopy), Korean Assn. Internal Medicine, Korean Soc. Gastroenterology (scientific com. mem. 2006—), Am. Gastroenterology Assn. Avocations: golf, tennis. Office: Korea Univ Hosp Dept Gastroenterology 126-1 5-Ga Anam Dong Sungbuk-ku Seoul 136-705 Republic of Korea Home: Gaepo Woosung Apt 8-101 Daechi-dong 503 Gangnam-gu Seoul 135 280 Republic of Korea Home Phone: 82-2-2051-6049; Office Phone: 82-2920-6555. Personal E-mail: ytjeen@korea.ac.kr.

JEFFCOAT, MARJORIE K., dean emeritus, professor, dental educator, researcher; Degree, MIT; DMD, Harvard U. Sch. Dental Med., 1976. Faculty mem. Harvard U. Sch. Dental Med.; asst. dean rsch. U. Ala. Sch. Dentistry, prof., chair dept. periodontics, prof. biomedical engring., James Rosen Endowed chair of dental rsch., interim chair dept. oral biology; dean U. Penn. Sch. Dental Med., 2003—. Mem. adv. com. rsch. on women's health Nat. Inst. Dental and Craniofacial Rsch., NIH; dir. Friends of the Nat. Inst. of Dental and Craniofacial Rsch., 2005—. Editor-in-chief: Journal of the American Dental Assoication, 2001—. Recipient President's Achievement award, U. Ala., Birmingham Inst. Med. Mem.: Inst. Medicine, Acad. of Osseointegration (pres.), Am. Acad. Periodontology (Clin. Rsch. award, Gies award), Internat. Assn. Dental Rsch. (past pres.), Am. Assn. Dental Rsch. (past pres.). Office: U Penn Sch Dental Med Robert Shattner Ctr 240 S 40th St Philadelphia PA 19104-6030 Office Phone: 215-898-8941. Office Fax: 215-573-4075. Business E-Mail: jeffcoat@dental.upenn.edu.

JEFFCOAT, SALLY, hospital administrator; B in Nursing, M in Nursing, U. Tex. CEO Christus Health; pres., CEO St. Joseph Hosp. Carondelet Health Network, Tucson, 2003—07; exec. v.p. Healthcare Ops. Ascension Health, St. Louis, CEO Healthcare Ops.; pres., CEO St. Alphonsus Med. Ctr., Boise, Idaho, 2009—. Named one of Top 25 Women, Modern Healthcare mag. Fellow: American Coll. Healthcare Execs. Office: Saint Alphonsus Regional Medical Center 1055 N Curtis Rd Boise ID 83706 Office Phone: 208-367-2121.

JEFFERS, VICTORIA WILKINSON, psychologist; b. Orange, NJ, Feb. 20, 1939; d. John Whitmore and Marian Lorene (Vaughan) Wilkinson; m. Richard S. Smith, div. June 1965; children: Lisa Bonsall, Richard S. Jr.; m. Albert Brown Jeffers, Aug. 10, 1968; children: Albert III, James Wilkinson. AAS, Briarcliff Coll., 1959; AB, Rutgers U., 1970, MS, 1974, PhD, 1976. Cert. sch. psychologist, N.J. Adj. asst. prof. pscyhology County Coll. Morris, Randolph, N.J., 1976-77, Coll. of St. Elizabeth, Convent Station, N.J., 1976-83, Rutgers U., Newark and New Brunswick, N.J., 1976-80; sch. psychologist Morris County Edn. Svc. Commn., N.J., 1980-84; pvt. practice Morristown, NJ, 1980—2006, Calif., 2006—. Cons. Cheshire Home, Florham Park, NJ, 1990-92; faculty Psychoanalytic Ctr. No. NJ, 1997-2003; mem. NJ Bd. Psychol. Examiners, 1995-2007, chair, 2002-07. Mem.: APA. Avocations: guitar, breeding cats. Home and Office: 670 Winding Brook Rd Califon NJ 07830 Office Phone: 908-832-6683. Personal E-mail: vj4467@earthlink.net.

JEFFERSON, JAMES WALTER, psychiatrist, educator; b. Mineola, NY, Aug. 14, 1937; s. Thomas Hutton and Alice (Withers) J.; m. Susan Mary Cole, June 25, 1965; children: Lara, Shawn, James C. BS, Bucknell U., Lewisburg, Pa., 1958; MD, U. Wis., 1964. Diplomate Am. Bd. Psychiatry and Neurology, Am. Bd. Internal Medicine. Asst. prof. psychiatry U. Wis. Med. Sch., Madison, 1974-78, assoc. prof., 1978-81, prof., 1981-92; disting. sr. scientist Dean Found. for Health, Rsch. and Edn., Madison, 1992-98; clin. prof. psychiatry U. Wis. Med. Sch., Madison, 1992—; disting. sr. scientist Madison Inst. Medicine, 1998—. Pres. Healthcare Tech. Sys., Madison, 1998-2005; co-dir. Lithium Info. Ctr., Madison, 1975—, Obsessive Compulsive Info. Ctr., Madison, 1990—; dir. Ctr. Affective Disorders, Madison, 1983-92. Co-author: Neuropsychiatric Features of Medical Disorders, 1981, Lithium Encyclopedia for Clinical Practice, 1983, 2nd edit., 1987, Depression and Its Treatment, 1984, 2d edit., 1992, Anxiety and Its Treatment, 1986, Handbook of Medical Psychiatry, 1996, 2nd edit., 2004. Served to maj. US Army, 1968-71. Fellow ACP, Am. Psychiat. Assn.; mem. Collegium Internat. Neuropsychopharmacologium, Am. Soc. Clin. Psychopharmacology (nat. bd. trustees 1996—). Avocations: bicycling, travel. Office: Madison Inst Medicine 6515 Grand Teton Plz Ste 100 Madison WI 53719-1048 Office Phone: 608-827-2451. Business E-Mail: jjefferson@healthtechsys.com.

JEFFERY, GEOFFREY MARRON, medical parasitologist; b. Dundee, NY, May 13, 1919; s. Joseph Ewart and Augusta (Knapp) J.; m. Jane Wicker, Aug. 16, 1941; children: Janet A. Harrison, Thomas W., Sarah V. Houghton, Susan E. Tosh. AB, Hobart Coll., 1940; MA, Syracuse U., 1942; ScD, Johns Hopkins U., 1944; MPH, Yale U., 1961. Biol. aide health and safety dept. TVA, 1944; commd. officer USPHS, 1944, scientist dir., 1960; tech. aid, cons. malaria control in war areas TVA, 1944-45; assigned divsn. lab. svcs. Communicable Disease Ctr., 1945-46, charge br. lab. Sch. Tropical Medicine San Juan, 1946-47; asst. prof. biology U. Bridgeport, Conn., 1947-48; charge Malaria Rsch. Lab., NIH, Milledgeville, Ga., 1948-54; mem. staff Lab. Tropical Diseases-Lab. Parasite Chemotherapy, NIAID, NIH, Columbia, SC, 1954-63, head sect. epidemiology, 1961-63; asst. chief Lab. Parasite Chemotherapy, NIAID, NIH, Bethesda, 1963-66, acting chief, 1966, chief, 1967-69, C.Am. Malaria Rsch. Sta., San

Salvador, El Salvador, 1969-74; asst. dir. Bur. Tropical Diseases, Ctr. Disease Control, Atlanta, 1974-75; dir. vector biology and control div. Bur. Tropical Diseases, 1975-81; asst. dir. divsn. parasitic diseases Ctr. for Infectious Diseases, Ctrs. for Disease Control, 1982-84. Mem. expert adv. panel on malaria WHO, 1963—99; assoc. mem. commn. malaria Armed Forces Epidemiol. Bd., 1965-69, mem., 1969-73; Del. Internat. Congress Tropical Medicine and Malaria, Lisbon, 1958, Rio de Janeiro, 1963, Teheran, Iran, 1968; Del. Internat. Congress Parasitology, Rome, Italy, 1964, Washington, 1969; Del. Internat. Conf. on Protozoology, London, 1965, Latin Am. Congress Parasitology, Medellin, Colombia, 1973; mem. sci. group on chemotherapy of malaria WHO, Geneva, 1967, mem. sci. group on parasitology, Teheran, 1968; cons. on status of malaria in Africa AID, 1979; mem. sci. working group on applied field rsch. in malaria WHO, Geneva, 1979, mem. steering com., 1981-86; cons. on malaria U.S.-China Health Agreement, 1980; del. Asia and Pacific Conf. on Malaria, Honolulu, 1985; temp. advisor meetings WHO, Kuala Lumpur, 1981, Albuquerque, 1982, Nairobi, 1983, Bangkok, 1984; invited participant concerted action 1st plenary meeting on malaria modelling European Union, Tuebingen, Germany, 1998. Contbr. numerous articles to sci. jours. tropical medicine and parasitology. Recipient Pub. Health Svc. Commendation medal, 1966, Dept. Army cert. of appreciation patriotic civilian svc., 1973 Fellow Royal Soc. Tropical Medicine (local sec. 1984-89); mem. Am. Soc. Tropical Medicine and Hygiene (sec.-treas. 1961-67, v.p. 1971, pres. 1975, Bailey K. Ashford award 1959), Am. Soc. Parasitologists, Assn. Southea. Biologists (editor bull. 1959-60, exec. com. 1962-66), Tropical Medicine Assn. Washington, Southea. Soc. Parasitologists, S.C. Acad. Sci. (mem. council 1960, 62, Jefferson award 1952, 56, 60), Commd. Officers Assn. USPHS, Sigma Xi, Kappa Sigma. Presbyterian. Home: 1085 Blackshear Dr Apt B Decatur GA 30033-2626 Personal E-mail: gjeffery2@comcast.net.

JEFFREYS, SIR ALEC JOHN, geneticist, educator; b. Oxford, Eng., Jan. 9, 1950; s. Sidney Victor and Joan Jeffreys; m. Susan Miles, 1971; 2 children. BA in Biochemistry, Merton Coll., U. Oxford, 1972, MA, PhD, 1975; DSc (hon.), U. Leicester, 2004, U. Liverpool, 2006, King's Coll., London, 2007, U. Huddersfield, 2009. Postdoc. rschr., dept. med. enzymology and molecular biology U. Amsterdam, 1975—77; lectr. dept. genetics U. Leicester, 1977—84, Lister Inst. rsch. fellow, dept. genetics, 1982—91, reader in genetics, 1984—87, prof., 1987—, Royal Soc. Wolfson rsch. prof., 1991—. Contbr. articles to prof. jours. Recipient Allen award, Am. Soc. Human Genetics, 1992, Albert Einstein World of Sci. award, World Cultural Coun., 1993, Australia prize, 1998, Pride of Britain Lifetime Achievement award, The Daily Mirror, 2004, Louis Jeantet prize for medicine, Geneva, 2004, Albert Lasker award for clin. med. rsch., 2005, H.P. Heineken prize for biochemistry, Royal Netherlands Acad. Arts & Scis., 2006, Millennium Tech. prizr, Tech. Acad. Finland, 2008, Graham medal, Glasgow Philos. Soc., 2008, Edinburgh medal, 2010; named an Hon. Freeman City of Leicester, 1993; named to Nat. Inventors Hall of Fame, 2005. Fellow: Royal Coll. Pathologists, Royal Soc. (Davy medal 1987, Royal medal 2004), Royal Coll. Physicians (hon.); mem.: NAS (fgn. assoc.), Am. Acad. Forensic Sciences, Academia Europaea, European Molecular Biology Orgn. Achievements include discovery of a method of showing variations between individual's DNA; invention of genetic fingerprinting, a technique employed by forensic scientists to assist in the identification of individuals on the basis of their respective DNA profiles. Office: Univ Leicester Dept Genetics Rm G19 University Road LE1 7RH Leicester England Office Phone: 44 0 116 252 3435. Office Fax: 44 0 116 252 3378. Business E-Mail: ajj@leicester.ac.uk. *

JEFFRIES, CHARLES DEAN, microbiology educator, research scientist, dean; b. Rome, Ga., Apr. 9, 1929; s. Andrew Jones and Rachel Lucinda (Ringer) J.; m. Virginia Mac Alford, Sept. 6, 1953 BS, N. Ga. Coll., 1950; MS, U. Tenn., 1955, PhD, 1958; postgrad., Purdue U., 1955-56. Technician Ga. Pub. Health Dept., Rome, 1950-51; instr. microbiology Wayne State U., Detroit, 1958-60, asst. prof., 1960-65, assoc. prof., 1965-70, prof., 1970-96, prof. emeritus, 1996, acting chmn. dept., 1972-73, assoc. dermatology, 1968—96, asst. dean for curriculum affairs, dir. grad. programs Sch. Medicine, 1975-80, prof. (voluntary) dept. biol. scis., 1990—96; prof., chair dept. microbiology and immunology Ross U. Sch. of Medicine, Roseau, Commonwealth of Dominica, West Indies, 1996—2000, dean basic scis., 1997-98, dean, 1998—2000; guest lectr., 2000—03; adj. instr. Sch. Heatlh Professions Davenport U., 2005. Guest researcher Ctr. for Disease Control, USPHS, Dept. HHS, Atlanta, 1980-81; Fulbright-Hays lectr., Cairo, 1965-66; examiner bacteriology Bd. Basic Scis., State of Mich., 1967-72; v.p., 1970-72; cons. VA Med. Ctr., Allen Park, Mich., 1989-92. Contbr. articles to profl. jours. Councilor Am. Assn. Basic Sci. Bds., 1970-72; mem. sci. adv. bd. Mich. Cancer Found., 1970-79; mem. Am. Inst. Biol. Scis.-EPA adv. panel, 1979-80; pres. acad. senate Wayne State U., 1989-92. Served with AUS, 1951-53, pres., Saline Area Sr. Coun., Mich., 2009-. Grantee NIH, 1958-70, NSF, 1959-69 Fellow Am. Acad. Microbiology; mem. Am. Soc. for Microbiology (councilor 1976-78, chmn. med. mycology div. 1977-78), Nat. Registry Microbiologists, Internat. Soc. Human and Animal Mycology, Sigma Xi Address: 590 Berkshire Drive Saline MI 48176 Personal E-mail: cjeffries235196mi@comcast.net.

JEFFRIES, RICHARD HALEY, physician, broadcasting company executive; b. Harrisburg, Pa., June 7, 1941; s. Richard Lawrence and Jeanette Ruth (Haley) J.; 1 child, Richard Straley. BS, Pa. State U., 1963; DO, Kirksville Coll. Osteo. Medici, 1968. Diplomate Am. Coll. Osteo. Internists. Intern Cmty. Gen. Osteo. Hosp., Harrisburg, 1968-69, resident in internal medicine, 1969-72, attending staff dept. internal medicine, 1972—, dir. coronary and intensive care units, 1983-86, chmn. dept. medicine, 1986-98, v.p. med. staff, 1977-79, pres., chief of staff, 1979-82; pvt. practice Harrisburg, 1972—; founder, pres. Quaker State Broadcasting, Inc., WTPA-FM, Mechanicsburg, Pa., 1982-99; founder, sec. Midstate Comm., Inc., 1990-97; vice chmn. dept. medicine Pinnacle Health Sys., 1998—2002, chief internal medicine, 2000—, chmn. dept. medicine, 2002—. Sr. clin. instr. Phila. Coll. Osteo. Medicine, 1977-81, clin. asst. prof., 1981—; clin. asst. prof. Hahnemann Med. Coll., Phila., 1977—, N.Y. Coll. Osteo. Medicine, N.Y.C., 1981-84; adj. asst. prof. U. Osteo. Medicine and Health Scis., Des Moines, 1990—; regional clin. faculty Kirksville (Mo.) Coll. Osteo. Medicine, 1993; trustee Cmty. Gen. Osteo. Hosp., Harrisburg, 1979-84, mem. staff exec. com., 1974-84, 86-2000, chmn. staff exec. com., 1979-82; sr. flight surgeon FAA, 1975—; med. dir. Ecumenical Home of Harrisburg, Beverly Preferred Choice Hospice Program, Harrisburg, 1995-2004, Blue Ridge Haven East Nursing Home, Harrisburg. Contbr. articles to profl. jours. Chmn. fundraising dr. Dauphin County Retarded Citizens Assn., 1984; founding mem., bd. dirs., past pres. Dauphin Residences, Inc., 1974-81; mem. Allied Arts Fund, Physicians Divsn., 1992, 93, 94; alumni bd. Kirksville Coll. Osteo. Medicine, 1997-2006. Mem. Am. Osteo. Assn., Pa. Osteo. Med. Assn., Am. Coll. Osteo. Internists, Am. Heart Assn. (bd. dirs. South Ctrl. Pa. chpt. 1976-79), Daguerreian Soc., Alpha Chi Sigma. Republican. Methodist. Avocations: photography, photographic collection, fly fishing, travel. Home: 516 Halyard Way Enola PA 17025 Office: Bronstein-Jeffries PA 4830 Londonderry Rd Harrisburg PA 17109-5207 Personal E-mail: rjeff588@aol.com.

JELINEK, FRANTISEK, pathologist; s. Frantisek Jelinek and Ruzena Jelinkova; m. Marie Hojkova, Oct. 12, 1973; children: Jana, Pavel, Eva. MDV, Vet. U., Brno, Czech Republic, 1962—68. Cert. vet. surgeon Vet. U., 1968, vet. pathologist Inst. for postgraduate edn., 1974, Univ. lectr., Habilitation Vet. and Pharm. U., Brno, 1981, prof. Faculty of Agr., South Bohemia U., 2001. Head of dept. exptl. animals Inst. for Sera and Vaccines, Prague, Czech Republic, 1969—72, head of histo-logical lab., 1972—83, State Inst. for Drug Control, 1983—92; rsch. worker Inst. of Path. Anatomy, First Med. Faculty, Charles U., 1992—94; sr. lectr. Vet. and Pharm. U., Brno, Czech Republic, 1995—95; pvt. vet. pathologist Vet. Histo-pathological Lab., Prague, Czech Republic, 1996—. Prof. Faculty of Agr., Ceske Budejovice, Czech Republic, 2000—06. Author sci. and profl. articles. Mem.: European Soc. of Toxicological Pathology (assoc.), European Coll. of Vet. Pathologists (assoc.), European Soc. of Vet. Pathologists (assoc.). Achievements include research in malignant lymphoma in golden hamsters, campylobacteriosis in golden hamsters, adenocarcinoma of the intestine in hamsters; myocardial lesion in cercopithecus aethiops; pathogenesis of parvovirosis of dogs; clostridial enterotoxaemia in rabbits; multiple osteomas in mice; application of lectin histochemistry in histology; acidophilic macrophage pneumonia in mice; postinflammatory sarcoma in cats; and tumours in guinea pigs; cutaneous papillomalosis in cattle; immuno deficiency in Fell pony; gastrointestinal stromal tumour in a guinea pig. Avocations: classical music, travel, breeding domestic animals. Home and Office: Vet Histopathological Lab Sojovicka 16 197 00 Prague Czech Republic

JELINEK, JOSEF EMIL, dermatologist; b. Prague, Czechoslovakia, Feb. 12, 1928; came to U.S., 1958, naturalized, 1964; s. Frank and Olga (Frankl) J.; m. Vera Adrienne Schnitzer, June 19, 1960; children— David Frank, Paul William. M.B., BS, U. London, 1951; postgrad., U. London Postgrad. Sch., 1956, NYU, 1963—. Diplomate Am. Bd. Dermatology. Intern, house surgeon in orthopedics St. Mary's Hosp., London, 1951-52; house physician in internal medicine Harold Wood Hosp., Essex, Eng., 1952, Princess Beatrice Hosp., London, 1955; registrar in internal medicine Royal Victoria Hosp., Bournemouth, Eng., 1955-57, Dulwich Hosp., London, 1957-58; precepteeship in dermatology with Norman B. Kanof, NYC, 1961-62; chief resident dermatology Bellevue Hosp., NYC, 1962-63, chief resident Univ. Hosp., NYC, 1963; cons. VA Hosp., NYC, 1965—, asst. attending physician Bellevue Hosp., NYC, 1965—; attending physician Univ. Hosp., NYC, 1976—, chief skin and cancer unit, 1973; clin. prof. dermatology N.Y. U. Sch. Medicine, 1976—; practice medicine specializing in dermatology, 1963—. Cons. AMA Council on Drugs and the Dept. of Drugs, 1972. Author: The Skin in Diabetes, 1985; contbr. articles to profl. jours, also chpts. to textbooks. Served to flight lt. RAF, 1952-54. Fellow ACP, Am. Acad. Dermatology; mem. Atlantic Dermatologic Conf. (past chmn.), Dermatologic Soc. Greater N.Y. (past pres.), N.Y. Acad. Medicine (past chmn.), Manhattan Dermatol. Soc. (past pres.), Am. Folk Art Soc. (pres. 1986-91). Office: NYU Med Offices Ste 351 726 Broadway New York NY 10003-6947 Office Phone: 212-992-9180.

JELKS, GLENN WILLIAM, plastic surgeon; b. South Gate, Calif., Oct. 21, 1943; s. William Harry and Parthena Imogene Jelks; m. Elizabeth Anne Brady, Sept. 4, 1965; children: Jennifer, Deborah, Michael. BA, U. Calif., Berkeley, 1965; MS, Mich. State U. Coll., 1973; MD, Mich. State U. Coll. Human Medicine, 1973. Diplomate Am. Bd. Ophthalmology, 1979, Am. Bd. Plastic and Reconstructive Surgery, 1982, Nat. Bd. Med. Examiners. With med. edn., mktg. and sales dept. Merck, Sharp and Dohme divsn. Merck and Co., Inc., San Francisco, 1965-69; med. rsch. fellow dept. interdepartmental curriculum Mich. State U.-Biomed. Comm. Ctr., East Lansing, 1971-73; grad. asst., clin. sci. instr. Mich. State U., East Lansing, 1973; intern straight surgery UCLA, 1973-74, resident gen./orthopaedic surgery, 1974-75; resident ophthalmology UCLA-Jules Stein Eye Inst., 1975-78; resident Inst. Reconstructive Plastic Surgery, NYU Med. Ctr., NYC, 1978-80. Assoc. prof. ophthalmology, assoc. prof. plastic surgery NYU Med. Ctr., NYC, 1980-; attending plastic surgeon NYU Med. Ctr., NY, 1980-, Bellevue Hosp., NYC, 1980-, Manhattan Eye, Ear and Throat Hosp., NYC, 1980-, The Valley Hosp., Ridgewood, NJ, 1991-; adj. attending in ophthalmology and plastic surgery NY Eye and Ear Infirmary-Lenox Hill Hosp., NYC, 1995-; examiner Am. Bd. Plastic Surgeons, 1995, 96; mem. continuing med. edn. adv. com., surg. case rev. com., oper. rm. com. NY Eye and Ear Infirmary; mem. laser com. NYU Med. Ctr.; mem. audiovisual com. Manhattan Eye, Ear and Throat Hosp.; vis. prof. Mass. Eye and Ear Infirmary, Boston, 1989, Robert H. Ivy Soc., Phila., 1990, UCLA, 1992, Yale U., New Haven, Conn., 1992. Consulting editor Ophthalmic Plastic and Reconstructive Surgery, Plastic Surgery Outlook, Ophthalmic Plastic and Reconstructive Surgery Jour; assoc. editor Annals of Plastic Surgery, 1995-96. Recipient Rsch. Travel award Am. Coll. Cardiology, 1970, Sci. Exhibit award AMA Conv., San Francisco, 1972, Lester T. Jones award for excellence in surg. anatomy Am. Soc. Ophthalmic Plastic and Reconstructive Plastic Surgeons 1986, Arthur L. Garnes Lectr. award Harlem Hosp., NY, 1987; NIH Cardiovas. trainee Mich. State U., 1969; Student Rsch. fellow Mich. Heart Assn., 1970, 71; Plastic Surgery Ednl. Found. traveling prof., 2000-01, named one of Best Doctors in NY, NY mag., 2002, named to The List for eyelid lifts, NY Times mag., 2005. Fellow Am. Acad. Ophthalmology; mem. AMA (Continuing Edn. award 1976, 79, 82, 85, 88), Internat. Soc. Craniofacial Surgeons, European Soc. Opthalmic Plastic and Reconstructive Surgery, Am. Acad. Ophthalmology, Am. Soc. Plastic and Reconstructive Surgeons, Am. Coll. Surgeons, Am. Soc. Maxillofacial Surgeons (mem. continuing med. edn. com. 1995-96), Am. Soc. Aesthetic Plastic and Reconstructive Surgery (mem. edn. commn. 1994, traveling prof. 1995), Am. Assn. Plastic Surgeons (mem. time and place com. 1995-96), Northeastern Soc. Plastic Surgeons (chmn. membership com. 1994-95, mem. nominating com. 1994-95, sec. 1995-99, pres. 1999-2000), NY State Med. Soc., NY County Med. Soc., NY Regional Soc. Plastic and Reconstructive Surgeons, NY Acad. Medicine, NY Orbit Soc. Avocations: boating, fishing, golf, skiing, tennis. Office: 875 Park Ave New York NY 10021-0341 also: NYU Langone Med Ctr 8 8V 550 First Ave New York NY 10016 Office Phone: 212-988-3303, 212-263-7300. E-mail: gwj@jelksmedical.com.

JELKS, MARY LARSON, retired pediatrician; b. Galva, Ill., 1929; MD, U. Nebr., 1955. Diplomate Am. Bd. Pediats., Am. Bd. Allergy and Immunology. Intern Johns Hopkins Hosp., Balt., 1955-56, resident, 1956-57, 58-60, Grace-New Haven Hosp., 1957; fellow U. Fla. Tchg. Hosp., 1960-61; clin. asst. prof. U. South Fla.; ret.; active aerobiology, 1985—. Fellow Am. Acad. Allery and Immunology, Am. Acad. Pediats.; mem. AMA. Achievements include active research in aerobiology. Home: 1930 Clematis St Sarasota FL 34239-3813

JELSKI, WOJCIECH JOZEF, biochemist; b. Bialystok, Poland, Dec. 14, 1970; MD, Med. U. Bialystok, 2003, PhD, 2009. Asst. Dept. Biochemical Diagnostics, 1997—. Mem.: PTDL. Avocations: history, sports. Office: Waszyngtona 15A Bialystok Podlasie 15-269 Poland Business E-Mail: wjelski@umwb.edu.pl.

JEMISON, MAE CAROL, physician, engineer, entrepreneur, philanthropist, educator, former astronaut; b. Decatur, Ala., Oct. 17, 1956; d. Charlie and Dorothy (Green) J. BS in ChemE, BA in African-Am. Studies, Stanford U., 1977; MD, Cornell U., 1981. Physician Peace Corps, Sierra Leone, Western Africa, 1983—85; pvt. practice LA; mission specialist NASA, Houston, 1987—93, astronaut on space shuttle Endeavor, 1992; prof. Dartmouth Coll., 1995—2002. Founder, pres. The Earth We Share Internat. Sci. Camp; A.D. White prof.-at-large Cornell U.; bd. dirs. Valspar Corp.; founder, pres. BioSentient Corp.; bd. dirs. Kimberly-Clark Corp.; mem., bd. dirs. Scholastic, Inc., 1993—; founder, pres. The Jemison Group, Inc., 1993—, The Dorothy Jemison Foundation for Excellence, 1994—; national sci. literary advocate Bayer Corp., 1995—. Author: Find Where The Wind Goes, 2001; TV host Discovery Channel, World of Wonder, 1994—95. Named one of World's 50 Most Beautiful People, People Mag., 1993. Mem.: NAS Inst. Medicine. Achievements include being first woman of color to fly in space. Office: Jemison Group Inc PO Box 591455 Houston TX 77259 Business E-Mail: mae.jemison@scholastic.com.

JEN, TIEN MING, microbiology educator; b. Wanhsien, China, Dec. 19, 1927; s. Sou Koun and Chi Yui (Hsun) J.; m. Hua Chuan Wang, Apr. 12, 1959; children: Kai-li, Kai-chen. Degree in Medicine, Nat. Def. Med. Ctr., Taipei, Taiwan, 1952; MD, Duke U., 1961. Mil. surgeon Chinese Army, Quemoy, 1952-54; asst., instr., assoc. prof. Nat. Def. Med. Ctr., 1954-75, prof., dept. microbiology and immunology, 1975—; vis. physician, lab. dept. Vets. Gen. Hosp., Taipei, 1963-73, dir. bacteriology and serology sect., 1973-83, med. rschr., mycosis rsch. lab., pathology dept., 1983-92. Sect. chief bacterioloy and serology Tri-Svc. Gen. Hosp., Taipei, 1955-60; cons. dept. dermatology Vets. Gen. Hosp., 1992-2000. Author textbooks on mycoses, mycology The Essentials of Clinical Mycology Study-NDMC, 2000, contbr. articles to profl. jours. Mem. Am. [illegible], Taipei, 1984. Col. M.C. Chinese Army, 1979-83. Recipient Model of Faithfulness and Honesty award Ministry of Nat. Def., 1980, Model of Disting. Svc. award Adminstrv. Yuan, 1990, Excellent Physician award Mayor of Taipei City, 1992. Mem. Mycological Soc., R.O.C. (Taiwan), Taiwan Soc. Microbiology, Infectious Diseases Soc. of Taiwan. Avocations: travel, reading. Home: 24 5 3rd Fl Ln 24 Kinmen St 100-17 Taipei Taiwan Office: Clinical Mycology Study PO Box 30-167 100 Taipei Taiwan

JENICEK, ALICIA JOANNE, nursing consultant; d. John Andrew and Alice Jeanette Jenicek; children: James Josef Wong, John Daniel Wong. BS in Biology, Tex. A&M U., 1982; BSN, U. Tex. Med. Br., 1984. Cert. legal nurse cons., Med.-Legal Consulting Inst., Inc., RN Tex.; cert. massage therapist Dept. Health, Tex., massage therapy instr. Dept. of Health, Tex. Staff nurse U. Tex. Med. Br., Galveston, 1984—85, La. State U. Med. Ctr., Shreveport, 1986, Hosp. Corps. Am. Highland Hosp., Shreveport, 1986—87, Highland Clinic, Shreveport, 1987, Schumpert Med. Ctr., Shreveport, 1987—92; tchr. San Jacinto Med. Ctr., Baytown, Tex., 1992—2001; massage therapist Healing With Feeling, Taylor Lake Village, 1997—, massage therapy instr., 1998—; legal nurse cons. Med.-Legal Consulting, Taylor Lake Village, 2001—; paramed. technician Exam One, Houston, 2004—11. Instr. European Massage Therapy Inst., Houston, 1999—2001; cons. James M. Andersen, Esquire, Houston, 2002—, Sanes, Matthews and Forester, Houston, 2004—; admission nurse Compassionate Care Hospice, Houston, 2006—07; case mgr. Encompass Home Health, Houston, 2007—08, Access Home Care, Pasadena, Tex., 2008—. Editor: (newsletter) Medical-Legal Consulting. Mem. St. Paul Cath. Cmty., Houston, 1992. Mem.: Tex. A&M Assn. Former Students, Friendswood-Clear-Creek Aggie Moms (historian 2010—11, parliamentarian 2011—), U. Tex. Med. Br. Aux., Internat. Massage Assn., Healing Arts Network, Am. Specialty Health Networks, Am. Assn. Legal Nurse Cons., Nat. Alliance Cert. Legal Nurse Cons., Bay Area Aggies Former Student Assn. (scholarship reviewer 2003—04), Massage and Bodywork Educators Alliance. Roman Catholic. Avocations: art, crafts, reading. Home and Office: Med-Legal Consulting 1126 Live Oak Ln Taylor Lake Village TX 77586 Personal E-mail: ajajenicek@cs.com. Business E-Mail: ajenicekwongclnc@cs.com.

JENKINS, DENNIS L., archaeologist, educator; BA, U. Nev., 1977, MA, 1981; PhD, U. Ore., 1991. Sr. staff archaeologist U. Ore. Mus. Natural & Cultural Hist.; rsch. archaeologist Ore. Dept. Transp., 1987—; supr. & dir. Northern Great Basin Archaeological Field Sch., 1989—. Lectr. Ore. Coun. for the Humanities, 2000—. Achievements include discovery of oldest directly dated human DNA in the Americas. Office: University of Oregon Museum of Natural & Cultural History Rm 1224 Eugene OR 97403-1224 Office Phone: 541-346-3026. E-mail: djenkins@uoregon.edu.

JENKINS, EVAN H., state legislator; b. Huntington, W.Va., Sept. 12, 1960; s. John E. and Dorothy C. Jenkins; m. Elizabeth Weiler; children: Evan Jr., Charles, Olivia. Atty. Jenkins Fenstermaker PLLC, 1987—92; with W. Va. State C. of C., 1992—99; exec. dir. W. Va. Med. Assn., 1999—; mem. W. Va. House of Dels., 1994—98; mem. Dist. 5 W. Va. State Senate, 2002—. Former bus. law instr. Marshall U.; mem. US Delegation to Taiwan, Am. Coun. Young Polit. Leaders. Past pres. Big Brothers/Big Sisters of the Tri-State; bd. dir. Cabell County Cmty. Svcs. Orgn., Huntington Main St., Riverview Manor, W. Va.Coun. on Economics in Edn., W. Va. EPSCORE; pres. bd. dir. Leadership W. Va., Operation Bus. and Edn. Succeeding Together; past. mem., bd. dirs. Western W. Va. Chpt. Am. Red Cross; organizer W. Va. Health Initiative Inc. and W. Va. Ctr. for Patent Safety; mem.

cmty. adv. com. YMCA Activate America. Recipient Med. Exec. Meritorious Achievement award, AMA, 2006. Mem.: W. Va. Bar Assn., Cabell County Bar Assn., ABA, Dem. Leadership Coun. (adv. bd.). Democrat. Presbyterian. Office: State Capitol, Rm 216 W Bldg 1 Charleston WV 25305 Mailing: 306 Holswade Dr Huntington WV 25701 Office Phone: 304-357-7956. E-mail: evan.jenkins@wvsenate.gov.

JENKINS, HERMAN ARTHUR, otolaryngologist, educator; b. Glenwood, W.Va., Apr. 24, 1945; s. Melva Winson and Sarah (Qualls) J.; m. Karen Hull Jenkins, June 22, 1974; children: Lee Vincent, Kelly Hull. BS in Zoology, Marshall U., 1966; MD, Vanderbilt U., 1970. Diploma Am. Bd. Otolaryngology (assoc. examiner 1994), Nat. Bd. Med. Examiners. Straight surg. intern UCLA Ctr. for Health Scis., 1970-71, resident in surgery, 1971-72, resident in otolaryngology, 1974-77, asst. prof., 1977-81; clin. and rsch. fellow in neurotology U. Hosp. Zurich, Switzerland, 1979-80; prof. otolaryngology Baylor Coll. Medicine, Houston, 1981—2000, vice chmn. dept. otorhinolaryngology and communicative scis., 1989—2000; active staff Meth. Hosp., Houston, 1981—2000, Harris County Hosp. Dist., Houston, 1981—2000; attending physician VA Med. Ctr., Houston, 1981—2000; prof., chmn. dept. otolaryngology U. Colo. Sch. Medicine, Denver, 2000—. Mem. courtesy staff Meml. Med. Ctr., Corpus Christi, Tex., 1981-2000, St. Luke's Epis. Hosp., Houston, 1981-2000; sci. exhibitor; frequent presenter in field; lectr., guest spkr. in field, 1978—; reviewer med. jours., 1986—; mem. sci. rev. com. Deafness Rsch. Found., 1985-88; cons. panel on devices in otolaryngology FDA, 1985-89, mem., 1989—; mem. task force Nat. Inst. on Deafness and Other Communication Disorders, 1989; mem. CDRC; cons. Nat. Inst. for Aging, NIH, 1985—, Nat. Eye Inst., 1986—, others. Mem. editl. bd. Microsurgery, 1986—, Internat. Jour. Base of Skull Surgery, 1989—, Skull Base Surgery, 1989—; contbr. numerous articles and abstracts to med. jours., chpts. to books. Maj. M.C., USAF, 1972-74. Named one of Best Doctors in America, 1994-2011, America's Top Doctors Castle Connolly Guide, 2000-11; I.N.C.O. scholar, 1961-66; grantee Nat. Inst. Neurol. and Communicative Disorders and Stroke, NIH, 1977-81, 84—, Clayton Found. for Rsch. Neurotology, 1981—, Union Pacific Found., 1985-89. Mem. AMA, ACS, Am. Acad. Otolaryngology-Head and Neck Surgery, honor award 1986, award for exhibits 1986, 87, 91), Am. Laryngol., Rhinol. and Otol. Soc., Barany Soc., Am. Neurotology Soc., Am. Otol. Soc. (pres. 2011—), Assn. for Rsch. in Otolaryngology, Internat. Skull Base Soc., Soc. Univ. Otolaryngologists-Head and Neck Surgeons, Acoustic Neuroma Assn., Am. Auditory Soc., Internat. Soc. Posturography, Tex. Med. Assn. (best sci. exhibit award 1987), Harris County Med. Soc., also others. Office: University Colo Denver Sch Medicine 12631 E 17th Ave B205 Aurora CO 80045 Office Fax: 303-724-1961. Business E-Mail: herman.jenkins@ucdenver.edu. *

JENKINS, JAMES STEPHEN, internist; b. Little Rock, Jan. 24, 1961; MD, U. Ark., 1987. Diplomate Am. Bd. Internal Medicine. Intern U. Mo. Hosp., Columbia, 1987-88, resident in medicine, 1988-90, fellow in cardiology, 1991-93; fellow in interventional cardiology Oschner Clin., New Orleans, 1993-94; assoc. sect. head, interventional cardiol. Ochsner Med. Inst., New Orleans, and dir. interventional cardiology rsch. Named one of Top Doctors La., La. Life mag., 2007. Fellow Am. Coll. Cardiology (La. chpt.), mem. Coll. Physicians. Office: Ochsner Med Inst 1514 Jefferson Hwy New Orleans LA 70121-2429 Office Phone: 504-842-3786.

JENKINS, LOUISE SHERMAN, nursing researcher, professor; b. Normal, Ill., Jan. 19, 1943; d. Fred and Zylpha Louise (Garrett) Sherman; m. Gary L. Jenkins, Oct. 30, 1965 (div. July 1976). Diploma, Evanston Hosp. Sch. Nursing, 1963; BS, No. Ill. U., 1979; MS, U. Md., Balt., 1982, PhD, 1985. Asst. head nurse intensive care Cmty. Meml. Hosp., LaGrange, Ill., 1963—65; head nurse coronary care Luth. Gen. Hosp., Park Ridge, Ill., 1965—69; nurse clinician hemodialysis unit Evanston Hosp., 1969—74; head nurse Skokie Valley Cmty. Hosp., 1974—75; faculty dept. continuing edn. N.W. Cmty. Hosp., Arlington Heights, Ill., 1975—80; Walter Schoeder chair nursing rsch. U. Wis. Milw. Sch. Nursing and St. Luke's Med. Ctr., Milw., 1987—96; faculty Sch. Nursing U. Md., Balt., 1996—, acting dir. grad. studies, 1997—98, dir. grad. studies, 1998—2003, co-dir. clin. edn. and evaluation lab., 2000—, dir. tchg., nursing and health professions postgrad. cert. program, 2004—; interim co-dir. Inst. for Nurse Educators, 2004—05; co-dir. Inst. for Educators in Nursing and Health Professions, 2005—. Mem. editl. bd. Jour. Cardiopulmonary Rehab., Jour. Hispanic Health Care, Am. Jour. Health Behavior, 2010—, mem. rev. panel, Nursing Rsch., Heart & Lung. Bd. dirs. Am. Heart Assn., Milw., 1988—95, exec. bd. dirs. Wis. affiliate, 1995—96, fellow, 2001, chair coun. cardiovasc. nursing Dallas, 1995—97, fellow coun. cardiovasc. nursing. Fellow, Am. Heart Assn., 2001; fellow, Clin. Nurse scholar, Robert Wood Johnson Found., U. Calif., San Francisco, 1985—87. Mem.: Heart Rhythm Soc., N.Am. Soc. Pacing and Electrophysiology, Coun. Nursing Rsch., Midwest Nursing Rsch. Soc. (gov. bd. 1993—95), Wis. Nurses Assn. (bd. dirs. 1988—90, Excellence in Nursing Rsch. award 1995), Am. Assn. Cardiovasc. and Pulmonary Rehab. (bd. dirs.-at-large 1993—95), Sigma Xi, Sigma Theta Tau (past pres. Pi chpt.). Office: Sch Nursing U Md 655 W Lombard St Ste 311 Baltimore MD 21201-1512 Business E-Mail: jenkins@son.umaryland.edu. *

JENKINS, MICHAEL B., microbiologist; b. Long Beach, Calif., Jan. 17, 1944; BA, U. Calif., Berkeley, 1966; MS, Oreg. State U., PhD, 1984. Rsch. microbiologist USDA Agr. Rsch. Svc., 1999—. Adj. prof. U. Ga., 2001—11. Grant, USDA Nat. Rsch. Initiative Competitive Grants Program. Mem.: AAAS, Agronomy Soc. America, Am. Soc. Microbiology, Sigma Xi. Avocations: backpacking, camping, running. Office: 1420 Experiment Sta Rd Watkinsville GA 30677 Office Fax: 706-769-8962. Business E-Mail: michael.jenkins@ars.usda.gov.

JENKINS, RENEE R., pediatrician, educator; b. Phila., Jan. 16, 1947; m. Charles Woodard Jenkins; 1 child, Kristinza. MD, Wayne State U. Diplomate Am. Bd. Pediatrics. Intern Jacobi/Albert Einstein Hosp., Bronx, 1971—72, resident in pediats., 1972—74; fellow in adolescent medicine Montefiore Hosp. Ctr., Bronx, 1974—75; prof., chmn. dept. pediats. Howard U., Washington, 1994—2007; staff pediatrician Howard U. Hosp., Washington. Adj. prof. George Washington U. Mem.: SAM, NMA, APS, Am. Acad. Pediats. (pres.-elect 2006—08), Inst. Medicine of NAS. Office: Howard Univ Coll of Medicine Dept Pediatrics and Child Health 1840 Seventh St NM HURB 1, Rm 214 Washington DC 20001

JENKINS, SHEILA ALNITA, psychologist; b. Inverness, Fla., Sept. 28, 1963; d. Peggy Ann Gary. BS, U. Houston, 1985, MEd, 1987; PhD, U. Ga., 1992. Psychologist Tex., registered Nat. Register Health Svc. Providers in Psychology. Psychologist Houston Ind. Sch. Dist., 1992—2003; psychologist, owner Sheila A. Jenkins, PhD & Associates, Houston, 1993—. Bd. dirs. Tex. Psychol. Found., 2004—08, pres., 2007, Houston Psychol. Found., 2004—; active Delta Academic, Artistic, and Philanthropic Found., Inc., Houston, 2004—08. Named Leadership Honoree, Heman Sweat Found., 2004; grad. scholar, U. Ga., 1989. Mem.: APA, Houston Psychol. Assn. (pres. 1999—2000, President's award 1997, 2004), Tex. Psychol. Assn. (trustee 2000—01), Delta Sigma Theta (chpt. pres. 2004—06). Office: 2630 Fountain View Dr Ste 350 Houston TX 77057 Business E-Mail: drjenkins@drsheilajenkins.com.

JENNER, PETER GEORGE, pharmacology educator; b. Gravesend, Eng., July 6, 1946; s. George Edwin and Edith (Hallett) J.; m. Katherine Mary Philomena (Snell), Dec. 1, 1973(div. 2003); 1 child, Terence. BPharm with honors, U. London, 1967, PhD, 1970, DSc, 1987. Postdoctoral fellow Chelsea Coll., U. London, 1970-72; lectr. in biochemistry dept. neurology Inst. Psychiatry, U. London, 1972-78, sr. lectr. in biochemistry dept. neurology, 1978-85, reader in neurochem. pharmacology, 1985-89; hon. sr. lectr. Inst. of Neurology, London, 1988—2000; prof. pharmacology, head dept. King's Coll., London, 1989-98, co-dir. neurodegenerative diseases rsch. ctr., 1993—, prof. pharmacology; head divsn. pharmacology and therapeutics Guys, Kings and St. Thomas' Sch. Biomed. Sci., Kings Coll., London, 1998—2004; prof. pharmacology GKT Sch. Biomed. Sci. King's Coll. London, 2005; dir. Proximagen Ltd., 2005—10; emeritus professor pharmacology Kings Coll. London, 2008. Cons. to pharm. industry. Editl. bds.,Jour. Pharmacy and Pharmacology, Polish Jour. Pharmacology, editor. Neuropharmacology; European editor Synapse; series editor Internat. Review Neurobiology; handling editor Jour. Neural Transmission, fellow, Kings Coll London. Fellow Royal Pharm. Soc., Brit. Pharm. Soc.; mem. European Soc. Clin. Pharmacology (v.p. 2001-08), Royal Pharm. Soc. Great Britain, Kings Coll. London, Royal Soc. Medicine Office: Kings Coll London Sch Biomedical Scis Guys Campus Hodgkin Bldg SE1 1UL London England

JENNETT, SHIRLEY SHIMMICK, health home administrator; b. Jennings, Kans., May 1, 1937; d. William and Mabel C. (Mowry) Shimmick; m. Nelson K. Jennett, Aug. 20, 1960 (div. 1972); children: Jon W., Cheryl L.; m. Albert J. Kukral, Apr. 16, 1977 (div. 1990) Diploma, Rsch. Hosp. Sch. Nursing, Kansas City, Mo., 1958. RN, Mo., Colo., Tex., Ill.,cert. geriat. care mgr., 2009-. Staff nurse, head nurse Rsch. Hosp., 1958-60; head nurse Penrose Hosp., Colorado Springs, Colo., 1960-62, Hotel Dieu Hosp., El Paso, Tex., 1962-63; staff nurse Oak Park (Ill.) Hosp., 1963-64, NcNeal Hosp., Berwyn, Ill., 1964-65, St. Anthony Hosp., Denver, 1968-69; staff nurse, head nurse, nurse recruiter Luth. Hosp., Wheat Ridge, Colo., 1969-79; owner, mgr. Med. Placement Svcs., Lakewood, Colo., 1980-84; vol., primary care nurse, admissions coord., team mgr. Hospice of Metro Denver, 1984-88, dir. patient and family svcs., 1988, exec. dir., 1988-94; pres., profl. geriatric care mgr. Care Mgmt. & Resources, Inc., Denver, 1996—. Mem. NAFE, Nat. Women Bus. Owners Assn., Nat. Hospice Orgn. (mem., bd. dirs. 1992-95, coun. former bd. mems. 1995—), Nat. Orgn. Profl. Geriatric Care Mgrs.(cert care mgr.), Denver Bus. Women's Network, Home Care Resources. Mem. Ch. of Religious Sci. Avocations: reading, walking, golf. Office: Care Mgmt & Resources Inc 900 S Dexter St Denver CO 80246 Home Phone: 303-757-6988; Office Phone: 303-639-5455. Business E-Mail: shirleyj@denvercmr.com.

JENNIFER, DOMM ANN, medical educator; b. NY, Dec. 13, 1974; MD, Vanderbilt U., 2000. Asst. prof. Vanderbilt U., 2006. Office: 397 PRBII 2220 Pierce Ave Nashville TN 37232 Office Fax: 615-936-1767. Business E-Mail: jennifer.domm@vanderbilt.edu.

JENNINGS, BRUCE, research institute director; b. Ft. Wayne, Ind., Apr. 27, 1949; s. Hugh Jack and Margaret Evangeline (Wisman) J.; m. Margaret Ann Machulis, May 26, 1972; 1 child, Andrew. BA in Polit. Sci. (magna cum laude), Yale U., 1971; MA in Polit. Sci., Princeton U., 1973. Asst. instr., dept. polit. sci. Princeton U., NJ, 1973—74; asst. prof., polit. sci. and philosophy Stockton State Coll., Pomona, NJ, 1975-80; rsch. assoc. Hastings Ctr., Briarcliff Manor, NY, 1980-83, assoc. for policy studies, 1983-91, exec. dir., 1991—96, exec. vp, 1996—99, sr. rsch. scholar, 1999—2006, sr. cons., 2006—, fellow, 2007; lectr., sch. medicine, dept. epidemiology and pub. health Yale U., NY, 1995—; dir. Ctr. Humans and Nature, NY, 2006—; lectr. Weill Cornell Med. Coll., NY, 2010—. Cons. U.S. Senate Select Com. on Ethics, Washington, 1980, W.K. Kellogg Found., 1993-94, Eli Lilly and Co., 1996-98, Robert Wood Johnson Found., Last Acts Campaign mem. standards com., 1996-, NY State Partnership to Improve End of Life Care, steering com. 1998-, AMA Expert Adv. Panel on Health Care Priorities, 1999-, Montefiore Med. Ctr., Rsch. Group Mem., Rethinking Dependency Project, 2004-, Huntington's Disease Soc. America Edn. Com., NY, 2004-, and several others; adj. lectr., sch. journalism, Columbia U., 1984-90; adj. prof., humanities divsn. SUNY-Purchase, 1985, dept. polit. sci., Vassar Coll., 1989,; treas., bd. dirs. Am. Health Decisions, Atlanta, Ga. 1988—; mem. ethics com. N.Y. Hosp./Cornell Med. Ctr., N.Y.C., 1989—; ethics adv. subcommittee, CDC, 2005-; mem. adv. bd., Sarah Lawrence Coll., Health Adv. Program, 1996-97, Genetic Counseling and Health Advocacy Programs, 2004-, NY Citizens Com. on Health Care Decisions, 1992-, NY Acad.Medicine, Ctr. for Urban Bioethics, NY 1998-; bd. dirs. Am. Assn. Bioethics 1994-97, Hosp. and Palliative Care Assn. NY State, 1996-2004, Nat. Hospice and Palliative Care Orgn., Arlington, Va., 1999-2003, Assn. for Politics and Life Scis., 1998-2001, Andrus-on-Hudson, NY 2004-; cons. ethics com., Sound Shore Med. Ctr., New Rochelle, NY, 1996-, Visiting Nurses Assn. Hudson Valley, Mt. Kisco, NY 1998-, Aging in America/Morningside House, Bronx, NY, 1998-; ethics cons. St. Cabrini Nursing Home, Dobbs Ferry, NY, 1990-, Beth Abraham Health Sys., NYC, 2000-01; hosp. ethics com. NY Presbyterian Hosp., 1989-; lectr. and presenter in field; cons. in field. Co-author: On the Uses of the Humanities: Vision and Application, 1984, Ethics of Legislative Life, 1985, Congress and the Media: The Ethical Connection, 1985, Guidelines on the Termination of Life-Sustaining Treatment and the Care of the Dying, 1987, The Perversion of Autonomy: the Proper Uses of Coercion and Constraints in a Liberal Soc., 1996, 2nd edit. 2003; Faithful Living, Faithful Dying: Anglican Reflections on End of Life Care, 2000, Access to Hospice Care: Expanding Boundaries, Overcoming Barriers, 2003, Public Health Ethics: Theory, Policy and Practices, 2006; adv. editor Hastings Ctr. Report, 1997-, Jour. Health Politics and Law, 2002-; co-edtior of several books; contbr. articles to profl. jours. and chapters to books. Advisor Josephson Inst. Ethics, Marina del Rey, Calif., 1990-; chair Westchester Fair Campaign Com., White Plains, N.Y., 1991-2000, chair 1992, 1997; mem. task force on sexual exploitaion and the clergy, Episcopal Diocese N.Y., N.Y.C., 1992-93; task force on End-of-Life Care, Episcopal Ch. US, NY, 1998-2000, working group on sci., tech. and faith, NY, 2000-03; mem. Am. Hosp. Assn. Bioethics Adv. Panel, 1993-94; mem. ethics adv. bd. March of Dimes Birth Defects Found., White Plains, NY, 1995-; police commr. Village of Hastings-on-Hudson, NY 1998-2000; elected village trustee Hastings-on-Hudson, NY, 2006-06, 09. Nat. Merit Scholar, 1967, Jack M. Griffin Meml. scholar Yale U., 1967-71; U. Fellowship, Princeton U., 1971-75, Andrew B. Weiss Vis. Fellowship, Williams Coll., 1987; recipient Leadership award, Prudential Found., 1987, Nat. Hospice and Palliative Care Orgn., Spl. Recognition award, 2004, Yale Westchester Alumni Assn. Cmty. Svc. award, 2005. Mem. Am. Polit. Sci. Assn., Columbia Seminar Social Thought (assoc.), Assn. Pub. Policy and Mgmt., Alzheimer's Assn. (mem. ethics adv. com., Chgo. Ill., 1993-), Conf. Polit. Thought, Conf. Polit. Thought, Yale Club N.Y., Yale Westchester Alumni Assn. (pres. 2007—). Democrat. Episcopalian. Avocations: swimming, bicycling, poetry. Office: Ctr Humans and Nature 109 W 77th St Ste 2 New York NY 10024 Office Phone: 212-362-7170. Office Fax: 212-362-9592. Business E-Mail: brucejennings@humansandnature.org.

JENNINGS, GARRY, medical association administrator, cardiologist; MD, Monash U., Australia, 1984. Former dir. cardiology, chair divsn. medicine Alfred Hosp., Melbourne, Australia; prof. Baker Heart Rsch. Inst., Melbourne, dep. dir., 1996—2001, dir., 2001—08, merger with Internat. Diabetes Inst., 2008; exec. dir., CEO Baker IDI Heart & Diabetes Inst., 2008—. Founder, chmn. bd. dirs. Nucleus Network, Melbourne, 2002—; bd. dirs. Nat. Heart Found. Australia, 2004—; pres. High Blood Pressure Rsch. Coun. Australia, 2001—04, Australian Assn. Med. Rsch. Institutes, 2006—08. Mem. editl. bd. Jour. Hypertension, Clin. Sci., Cardiovasc. Guidelines, Jour. Clin. & Exptl. Hypertension, Australian Prescriber, Clin. & Exptl. Pharmacology & Physiology, Nutrition, Metabolism & Cardiovasc. Diseases; contbr. articles to profl. jours. Recipient Kempson Maddox award, World Congress Cardiology, 2004. Fellow: Am. Heart Assn., Cardiac Soc. Australia & New Zealand, Royal Coll. Physicians London, Royal Australasian Coll. Physicians. Achievements include research in the role and mechanisms of exercise in cardiovascular disease and metabolism and the sympathetic pathophysiology of hypertension and heart failure. Office: Baker IDI Heart & Diabetes Institute PO Box 6492 8008 Victoria VIC Australia Office Phone: 61 03 8532 1111. Office Fax: 61 03 8532 1100. Business E-Mail: garry.jennings@baker.edu.au. *

JENNINGS, HENRY SMITH, III, cardiologist; b. Atlanta, May 16, 1951; s. Henry Smith Jr. and Elizabeth (Martin) J.; m. Polly Cooper; 1 child, Mary Bailey. BS summa cum laude, Davidson Coll., 1973; MD, Vanderbilt U., 1977. Diplomate Am. Bd. Internal Medicine, subspecialty cardiovascular diseases and interventional cardiology, Nat. Bd. Med. Examiners; lic. physician and surgeon, Tenn., Ky. Intern internal medicine Vanderbilt U. Affiliated Hosps., Nashville, 1977-78, resident internal medicine, 1978-80; fellow clin. cardiology divsn. cardiology dept. medicine Vanderbilt U., 1980-82; clin. instr. medicine Vanderbilt U. Sch. Medicine, 1982-89, asst. clin. prof. medicine, 1989-97, assoc. clin. prof. medicine, 1997—2007, asst. prof. medicine, 2007—; med. dir. Cardiac Rehab. Ctr. St. Thomas Hosp., Nashville, 1984—2001, assoc. chief cardiac scis., 2001—05, pres.-elect med. staff, 2005—06; chmn. steering com. St. Thomas Heart Inst., 2002—04; med. dir. Network Develop. Vanderbilt Heart & Vascular Inst., 2007—10. Mem. active staff Vanderbilt U. Med. Ctr.; mem. courtesy staff Centennial Med. Ctr., Nashville, St. Thomas Hosp.; mem. cons. staff Bapt. Hosp., Nashville. Contbr. articles to profl. jours. Bd. dirs. Heart Inst., St. Thomas Hosp., Nashvile, 1992-94, Tenn. Heart Inst., 1989-91. Justin Potter med. scholar Vanderbilt U. Sch. Medicine, Nashville, 1973-77. Fellow ACP, Am. Coll. Cardiology, Am. Coll. Chest Physicians, Coun. Clin. Cardiology Am. Heart Assn., Soc. Cardiac Angiography and Interventions; mem. AMA, Am. Assn. Cardiovasc. and Pulmonary Rehab., Internat. Soc. Heart Transplantation, Am. Heart Assn., So. Med. Assn., Tenn. Med. Assn., Nashville Acad. Medicine, Gottlieb Friesinger Soc. (pres.-elect 2001, pres. 2002), Canby Robinson Soc. Bd. Methodist. Home: Northumberland 3 Castle Rising Nashville TN 37215-4126 Office: Vanderbilt Heart and Vascular Inst Ste 5209 MCE South Tower 1215 21st Ave S Nashville TN 37232-8802 Home Phone: 615-665-0860; Office Phone: 615-322-2318. Office Fax: 615-936-7365. Business E-Mail: henry.jennings@vanderbilt.edu.

JENNINGS, REBA MAXINE, retired critical care nurse; b. Gainesville, Mo., Oct. 28, 1936; d. William Claude and Osa Marie (Whillock) Loftis; m. Robert Wayne Jennings, Nov. 10, 1953; children: Sherry Anita, Robert Allen, Lalia Marie. Diploma, Burge Sch. Nursing, Springfield, Mo., 1983. ACLS, RN Mo. Med-surg. staff nurse AMI-Springfield Community Hosp., 1983-84; pvt. duty nurse Western Med. Svcs., Springfield, 1984; staff nurse in CCU, ICU, emergency dept. Tri-County Sisters of Mercy Hosp., Mansfield, Mo., 1984-85; cardiac telemetry staff nurse St. John's Regional Health Ctr., Springfield, 1985-93; nurse obs. unit Valley Hosp., Palmer, Alaska, 1993-94; nurse PCU Alaska Regional Hosp., Anchorage, 1994; PCU nurse Providence Alaska Med. Ctr., Anchorage, 1995-98; ret., 1998. Personal E-mail: sleepyheadcharly2@yahoo.com.

JENNINGS, ROBERT BURGESS, experimental pathologist, medical educator; b. Balt., Dec. 14, 1926; s. Burgess Hill and Etta (Crout) J.; m. Linda Lee Sheffield, June 28, 1952; children: Carol L., Mary G., John B., Anne E., James R. BS, Northwestern U., 1947, MS, B.M., 1949, MD, 1950. Diplomate Am. Bd. Pathology (trustee 1976-87, pres. 1986-87). Intern Passavant Meml. Hosp., Chgo., 1949—50, resident pathology, 1950—51; mem. faculty Northwestern U. Med. Sch., 1953—75, prof. pathology, 1963—75, chmn. dept., 1969—75, Magerstadt prof., 1969—75; prof., chmn. dept. pathology Duke U. Med. Sch., Durham, NC, 1975—89, James B. Duke prof., 1980—2003, prof. emeritus, 2003—. Vis. scientist Middlesex Hosp. Med. Sch., London, 1961-62; cons. VA Rsch. Hosp., Chgo.; mem. attending staff Northwestern Meml. Hosp., Chgo., 1963-75; mem. pathology A Study sect. USPHS, 1960-65; mem. clin. cardiology adv. com. NIH, 1976-80, mem. cardiovasc. and renal study sect., 1992-95. Mem. editl. bd. Lab. Investigation, 1967-95, Archives Pathology, 1970-80, Jour. Molecular and Cellular Cardiology, 1972-89, Exptl. and Molecular Pathology, 1973-99, Circulation, 1988-91, 93-96,

Circulation Rsch., 1976-82, Histopathology, 1977-92, Am. Jour. Pathology, 1983-92, Jour. Applied Cardiology, 1986-90, Cardiosci., 1990-95, Trends in Cardiovasc. Medicine, 1991-92, Cardiovasc. Pathology, 1991-95, Heart Failure Revs., 1996-. Served as lt. (j.g.) USNR, 1951—53. Recipient Peter Harris award, Internat. Soc. Heart Rsch., 1992, Disting. Leader award, 2009, Disting. Achievement award, Soc. Cardiovasc. Pathology, 1996, Discovery Health Channel Am. Med. Honors award, AHA, 2004, Medal of Merit award, Internat. Acad. Cardiovasc. Scis., 2005, Gold-Headed Cane award, Am. Soc. Investigative Pathology, 2007; Markle scholar med. scis., 1958—63. Office: Duke U Med Ctr Dept Pathology Durham NC 27710-0001 Home: 7 Silver Maple Ct Durham NC 27705-5642 Office Phone: 919-684-3776. Business E-Mail: jenni004@mc.duke.edu.

JENNY, CAROLE, physician, researcher; b. St. Louis, June 4, 1946; d. Vance Buescher and Alice Emelie Jenny; m. Thomas Allen Roesler, Mar. 16, 1974; children: Laura Alice Roesler, Amelia Martha Roesler. BA, U. Mo., 1968; BMS, Dartmouth Med. Sch., 1970; MD, U. Wash., 1972; MBA, Wharton Sch., U. of Pa, 1976. Pediatrics Am. Bd. of Pediat., NC, 1977. Prof. of pediat. Brown Med. Sch., Providence, 1996—; dir., child protection team Hasbro Children's Hosp., Providence. Chair, com. on child abuse and neglect Am. Acad. of Pediat., Elk Grove Village, Ill. Mem. Am. Profl. Soc. on the Abuse of Children, Chgo., 1991—. Recipient Outstanding Svc. to Maltreated Children, Am. Acad. of Pediat., 1999, Ray Helfer award, Nat. Coalition of Children's Trust Funds, 2002. Achievements include research in child abuse, head trauma, sexual abuse. Office: Brown Medical School 593 Eddy St Potter-005 Providence RI 02903 Personal E-mail: cjenny@lifspan.org. Business E-Mail: cjenny@brown.edu. *

JENSEN, DORTE MØLLER, endocrinologist; b. Bedsted Thy, Denmark, Apr. 4, 1964; MD, Aarhus U., 1991; PhD, U. Southern Denmark, 2002. Cons. Dept. Endocrinology, Odense U. Hosp., 2008—. Office: Kløverævænget 6 Odense 5000 Denmark Business E-Mail: dortemj@dadlnet.dk.

JENSEN, ELWOOD VERNON, biochemist; b. Fargo, ND, Jan. 13, 1920; s. Eli A. and Vera (Morris) J.; m. Mary Welmoth Collette, June 17, 1941 (dec. Nov. 1982); children: Karen Collette, Thomas Eli; m. Hiltrud Herborg, Dec. 21, 1983 AB, Wittenberg U., 1940, DSc (hon.), 1963; PhD, U. Chgo., 1944; DSc (hon.), Acadia U., 1976, Med. Coll. Ohio, 1991; MD (hon.), U. Hamburg, 1994, U. Athens, 2005. Faculty U. Chgo., 1947-90, assoc. prof. biochemistry Ben May Inst. Cancer Rsch., 1954-60, prof., 1960-63, Am. Cancer Soc. rsch. prof. physiology, 1963-69, dir. Ben May Inst., 1969-82, dir. Biomed. Ctr. Population Research, 1972-75, prof. physiology, 1969-73, 77-84, prof. biophysics, 1973-84, prof. biochemistry, 1980-90, Charles B. Huggins disting. svc. prof., 1981-90, emeritus prof., 1990—; rsch. dir. Ludwig Inst. for Cancer Rsch., 1983-87; scholar-in-residence Fogarty Internat. Ctr. NIH, 1988, Cornell U. Med. Coll., 1990—91, prof. Inst. for Hormone and Fertility Rsch. U. Hamburg, Germany, 1992—97. Vis. prof. Max Planck Inst. for Biochemie, Munich, 1958; chemotherapy rev. bd. Nat. Cancer Inst., 1960—62, bd. sci. counselors, 1969—72; mem. adv. com. biochemistry and chm. carcinogenesis Am. Cancer Soc., 1968—72, coun. for rsch. and clin. investigation, 1974—77; mem. assembly life scis. NRC, 1975—78; mem. Nat. Adv. Coun. Child Health and Human Devel., 1976—80; com. on sci., engring. and pub. policy NAS, 1981—82; rsch. adv. bd. Clin. Rsch. Inst. Montreal, 1987—96, Klinik for Tumor Biologie, Freiburg, 1993—2002, Strang Cancer Prevention Ctr., 1994—98; cons. Rockefeller U. Hosp., 1990—92; Nobel vis. prof. Karolinska Inst., Huddinge, Sweden, 1998, STINT vis. scientist, 1998—99, prof. emeritus, 1999—2001; vis. scientist NICHD/NIH, 2001; internat. adv. bd. Fundazione Giovanni Lorenzini, Milan, 2001—; John and Gladys chmn. for cancer rsch. U. Cin. Med. Ctr., 2002—03, George and Elizabeth Wile chmn. in cancer rsch. and disting. univ. prof. dept. cancer and cell biology, 2004—. Mem. editl. bd. Perspectives in Biology and Medicine, 1966—, Archives of Biochemistry and Biophysics, 1979-84, Biochemistry, 1969-72, Life Scis., 1973-78, Breast Cancer Rsch. and Treatment, 1980—, Endocrine-Related Cancer, 1994-2004, Jour. Biol. Markers, 1998—, Internat. Jour. Oncology, 2004-; assoc. editor: Jour. Steroid Biochemistry, 1974-94; contbr. articles to profl. jours. Recipient D.R. Edwards medal, 1970, La Madonnina prize, 1973, Pap award, 1975, prix Roussel, 1976, Nat. award Am. Cancer Soc., 1976, Gregory Pincus Meml. award, 1978, Gairdner Found. award, 1979, Lucy Wortham James award, 1980, Charles F. Kettering prize, 1980, Golden Plate award, 1980, Nat. Acad. Clin. Biochemistry award, 1981, Scientist of Yr. award Achievement Rewards for Coll. Scientists Found., 1981, Pharmacia award, 1982, Hubert H. Humphrey award, 1983, Rolf Luft medal, 1983, Renzo Grattarola medal, 1984, Fred C. Koch award, 1984, Axel Munthe award, 1985, Humboldt Sr. Rsch. prize, 1992, Joseph Bolivar DeLee award Chgo. Lying-In Hosp., 1995, Brinker Internat. award for breast cancer rsch. Susan G. Komen Found., 2002, Albert Lasker award for Basic Med. Rsch., Lasker Found., 2004; Thomson Sci. laureate in physiology/medicine, 2006; citations: Ohio State Senate and Ho. Reps., 2004; Guggenheim fellow, 1946-47. Mem. NAS (coun. 1981-84), AAAS (Amory prize 1977), Am. Soc. Biochemistry and Molecular Biology, Am. Chem. Soc., Am. Assn. Cancer Rsch. (G.H.A. Clowes award 1975, Dorothy P. Landon prize 2002), Endocrine Soc. (pres. 1980-81), Am. Gyn/Ob Soc. (hon.), St. Paul Surg. Soc. (hon.), EORTC Receptor and Biomarker Group (hon.), Honorable Order Ky. Cols. Office: University Cin Dept Cancer & Cell Biology Vontz Ctr Molecular Studies 3125 Eden Ave Cincinnati OH 45267-0521 Office Phone: 513-558-5750. Business E-Mail: elwood.jensen@uc.edu. *

JENSEN, EVA MARIE, medical/surgical nurse; b. Santa Maria, Calif., Sept. 2, 1956; d. Paul Cabello and Dolores Margaret Gutierrez; m. Royal George Jensen, Mar. 22, 1986 (div. Mar. 15, 1993). AA, Cuesta Coll., Calif., 1977; lic. vocation nurse, Hartnell Coll., Salinas, Calif., 1980. RN Calif., 1982, cert. psychiat. and mental health nurse, Calif., 1995. Nurse Atascadero State Hosp., Calif., 1986—2003, Twin Cities Hosp., Templeton, 1982—86, 2003—. Participant nurses' health study Harvard Med. Sch., Boston, 1992—. Democrat. Roman Catholic.

JENSEN, HANNE MARGRETE, pathologist, educator; b. Copenhagen, Dec. 9, 1935; came to US, 1957; d. Niels Peter Evald and Else Signe Agnete (Rasmussen) Damgaard; m. July 21, 1957 (div. Apr. 1987); children: Peter Albert, Dorte Marie, Gordon Kristian, Sabrina Elisabeth. Student, U. Copenhagen, 1954—57; MD, U. Wash., 1961. Resident and fellow in pathology U. Wash., Seattle, 1963-68; asst. prof. dept. pathology U. Calif. Sch. Medicine, Davis, 1969-79, assoc. prof., 1979—2001, dir. transfusion svc., 1973—, prof., 2001—. McFarlane prof. exptl. medicine U. Glasgow, Scotland, 1983. Fellow Pacific Coast Ob-Gyn. Soc., Coll. Am. Pathologists; mem. U.S. and Can. Acad. Pathology, Am. Soc. Clin. Pathologists, AAAS, Am. Assn. Blood Banks, Calif. Blood Bank Sys. Office: U Calif Sch Medicine Dept Pathology Davis CA 95616 Office Phone: 530-752-7229. Business E-Mail: hmjensen@ucdavis.edu.

JENSEN, HELENE WICKSTROM, retired nutritionist, educator; b. Carthage, Mo., Mar. 3, 1929; d. Frank Emil and Lois (Stroup) Wickstrom; m. Robert Gordon Jensen, Dec. 20, 1947; children: Gordon Lee, Jeffrey Alan. BS, U. Mo., 1951; MS, U. Conn., 1983; PhD, Century U., 1996. Registered dietitian; cert. dietitian/nutritionist. Dietitian-in-charge U. Mo., Columbia, 1952-56; therapeutic dietitian Windham Community Meml. Hosp., Willimantic, Conn., 1967, dir. food service, 1967-72; dir. sch. lunch program Windham Pub. Schs., Willimantic, 1963-66; lectr. U. Conn., Storrs, 1972-78, leader ednl. outreach program, 1979-92; ret., 1992. Recipient award Met. Life Ins. Co., 1985, Czajowski Nutrition award U. Conn., 1989, Disting. Alumna award U. Conn. Agr. and Natural Resources Alumni Assn., 1989. Mem. Am. Dietetic Assn. (presenter 50 yr. membership recognition, 2005), Am. Sch. Food Svc. Assn. (exec. bd. 1989-91, presenter), Soc. Nutrition Edn., Conn. Sch. Food Svc. Assn., Conn. Nutrition Coun. (presenter), Conn. Dietetic Assn. (presenter, Dietitian of Yr. 1987), Phi Kappa Phi, Gamma Sigma Delta.

JENSEN, IRENE BOTILDE, psychologist, researcher; b. Hasseris, Denmark, Dec. 31, 1955; d. Egon Peder and Siv Elisabeth (Roman) J.; m. Bjorn Urban Holmgren; children: Christian, Sebastian. BSc in Behavioral Sci., U. Orebro, 1985; PhD, Karolinska Inst., Stockholm, 1993, postgrad., 1993—. Psychologist Orebro (Sweden) Med. Ctr., 1985-88, Åre (Sweden) Hosp., 1988-90; psychologist, rschr. Karolinska Inst., Stockholm, 1989—; rschr., project adminstrs. Inst. for Futures Studies, Stockholm, 1995—. Cons. Hälsolnuest, Sweden, 1994—; presenter in field. Contbr. articles to profl. jours. Mem. Internat. Assn. for the Study of Pain (task force mem. 1993—), Internat. Soc. Hypnosis, Internat. Soc. Behaviour Medicine. Avocations: cross country skiing, painting. Office: Dept Clin Neurosci Karolinska Inst 171 76 Stockholm Sweden

JENSEN, JEFFREY T., obstetrician, researcher, gynecologist, educator; b. Seattle, May 29, 1958; BS, Stanford U., 1980; MD, Emory U., 1984. Prof. Oreg. Health & Sci. U., 1992—. Office: Oreg Health & Sci University Dept Obstetrics & Gynecology Portland OR 97239 Business E-Mail: jensenje@ohsu.edu.

JENSEN, MICHAEL DENNIS, endocrinologist, researcher; b. San Angelo, Tex., May 3, 1955; BA in Biology, U. Mo., Kansas City; MD, U. Mo. Sch. Medicine, 1979. Diplomate Am. Bd. Internal Medicine, cert. in pediatric endocrinology, diplomate Am. Bd. Nutrition. Internal medicine intern St. Lukes Hosp., Kansas City, 1979—80; endocrinology resident Mayo Grad. Sch. Medicine, Mayo Clinic, Rochester, Minn., 1980—82, W. L. Stevenson fellow clin. nutrition, 1982—85, prof. medicine, 1985—. Vice chair Integrative Physiology Obesity & Diabetes Study Sect., NIH, 2004—05, chair, 2005—06. Contbr. articles to profl. jours. Pres. Shaping America's Health: Assn. Weight Mgmt. & Obesity Prevention, 2005—07. Mem.: N.Am. Assn. Study of Obesity (sec./treas. 1995—98), Am. Soc. Clin. Nutrition, Am. Soc. Clin. Investigation, Am. Diabetes Assn., Assn. Am. Physicians. Achievements include research in the effects of obesity and how body fat and body-fat distribution influence health. Office: Mayo Clinic Dept Endocrinology 200 First St SW Rochester MN 55905 E-mail: jensen@mayo.edu. *

JENSEN, RONALD D., podiatrist; DPM, Calif. Coll. Podiatric Medicine, San Francisco, 1984. Diplomate Am. Bd. Podiatric Surgery, Am. Bd. Podiatric Orthopedics & Primary Podiatric Medicine. Postgrad. microbiology Brigham Young U., Provo, Utah; resident Circle City Hosp., Corona, Calif.; podiatrist Gould Med. Group, Inc., Modesto, Calif. Bd. trustees Sutter Gould Med. Found.; bd. dirs. Meml. Med. Ctr., Modesto; past bd. dirs. Podiatry Ins. Corp. America. Contbr. articles to profl. jours. Named Calif. Podiatric Physician of Yr., 1999. Mem.: Am. Podiatric Med. Assn. (bd. dirs. 1998—, pres. 2009—10), Calif. Podiatric Med. Assn. (former pres.). Office: Sutter Gould Med Found 600 Coffee Rd Modesto CA 95355 Office Fax: 209-544-6088. *

JENSSEN, TROND GEIR, nephrologist, educator; b. Tromsoe, Norway, June 5, 1955; s. Werner Johan and Gerd (Johannessen) J. MD, U. Tromsoe, 1980, PhD, 1986. Specialist internal medicine, renal diseases. Trainee Rana (Norway) Hosp., 1980-82; rsch. fellow U. Hosp. Tromsoe, 1982-84, clin. fellow, resident dept. medicine, 1984-87, resident dept. medicine, 1988-91, cons. divsn. nephrology, 1991—94, 1996—97, cons. divsn. endocrinology, metabolism, 1994-96, prof. medicine, 1995—; cons. divsn. nephrology Nat. Hosp. Norway, 1997—; med. advisor Norwegian Diabetes Assn., 2004—. Contbr. over 130 articles to profl. jours. Spkr. in field. Pitts. U. fellow, 1987-88; recipient Ednl. Fogarty, 1987. Mem.: N.Y. Acad. Sci., European Assn. Study Diabetes, Norwegian Rsch. Coun. (chmn. bd. clin. rsch.), Am. Diabetes Soc., Am. Soc. Nephrology, Norwegian Soc. Nephrology (bd. dirs. 1994—2001, sec. 1998—2001, pres. 1999—2001), Norwegian Diabetes Assn. (chmn. med. adv. bd. 1998—2000, med. advisor 2005—, diabetes coord., Nordic Network Islet Transplantation 2006—), Scandinavian Soc. Study Diabetes (bd. dirs. 1993—2001, pres. 1995—96). Office: Nat Hosp Norway Dept Medicine 27 Oslo Norway Business E-Mail: trond.jenssen@rikshospitalet.no.

JENSSEN, WARREN DONALD, microbiologist, consultant; b. Woodbridge, NJ, Aug. 23, 1942; s. Joseph and Lillian (Anderson) J.; m. Donna M. Larson; children: Kirsten E., Erik C. BA, Rutgers U., 1965, PhD, 1970; MS, Purdue U., 1966. Diplomate Am. Acad. Microbiology, Am. Bd. Bioanalysis. Tchg. fellow Purdue U., W. Lafayette, Ind., 1965-66; rsch. fellow Rutgers U., New Brunswick, N.J., 1966-70; postdoctoral fellow Rutgers Med. Sch., New Brunswick, N.J., 1983-84; rsch. fellow Robert Wood Johnson Med. Sch., 1984-87; adj. prof. Union County Coll., Cranford, N.J., 1969-70, asst. prof., 1970-74, assoc. prof., 1974-79, prof., 1979-85, sr. prof., 1985—; adj. prof. Kean Coll., Union, N.J., 1972-75. Clin. microbiology cons. JFK Med. Ctr., Edison, N.J., 1973-76, Raritan Bay Med. Ctr., Perth Amboy, N.J., 1976-98, VA Med. Ctr., Lyons, N.J., 1989-96; dir. health svcs. lab. Union County Coll., 1974-82; dir. Union County Pub. Health Lab., 1977-82; pub. health bacteriologist N.J. Dept. Environ. Protection, 1973—; assoc. med. staff Raritan Bay Med. Ctr., 1985—; clin. lab. dir. N.J. Bd. Med. Examiners, 1985—; adj. clin. instr. Robert Wood Johnson Med. Sch., 1985-91; adj. prof. biomed. careers program Univ. Medicine and Dentistry of N.J., 1999—2002; recycling coord., Califon, 1988-92, Hunterdon County Health Adv. Com., 1985-88, Hunterdon County Mcpl. Officers Assn., 1987-89. Contbr. articles to profl. jours. Den leader, asst. scoutmaster Boy Scouts Am., Califon, N.J., 1980-84; vice chmn. Bd. Health, Califon, 1983-89; mem. Environ. Comm., Califon, 1985-89. Mem. Theobald Smith Soc., Am. Soc. Microbiology, N.J. Link for Microbiology (program chair 1983-85), AAUP (exec. bd. 1973-98). Avocations: boating, fishing, hiking, camping. Home: 83 River Rd Califon NJ 07830-4371 Office: Union County Coll 1033 Springfield Ave Cranford NJ 07016-1528 Office Phone: 908-709-7562. Business E-Mail: jenssen@ucc.edu.

JEON, BYEONG HWA, physiologist; s. Sangsoon Park; m. Wonsoon Ryoo, May 30, 1993; children: Sungho, Hyunkyung. BA in Medicine, Chungnam Nat. U., Daejeon, Republic of Korea, 1989, MS in Physiology, 1991, PhD in Physiology, 1996. MD Ministry Health Welfare Korea, 1989. Asst. prof. Chungnam Nat. U. Coll. Medicine, 2000—04, assoc. prof., 2004—; post-doctoral fellowship Johns Hopkins U., Balt., 2001—03. Lectr. Chungnam Nat. U. Coll. Medicine, 1998—2000, chmn. dept. physiology, 2004—08, dir. divsn. med. sci., 2009—. Contbr. articles to profl. jours. Capt. Korean Army Forces, 1995—98, Daejeon. Mem.: Am. Heart Assn., Korean Physiol. Soc. Achievements include patents in field. Office: Chungnam Nat Univ Munhwa-Dong Jung-Gu 6 301-131 Daejeon Daejeon Republic of Korea Office Fax: 82-42-585-8440. Business E-Mail: bhjeon@cnu.ac.kr.

JEON, CHANGHO, internist, chemistry professor, molecular biologist, director; b. Daegu, Republic of Korea, Sept. 12, 1960; s. Byungheon Jeon and Youngja Yoon; m. Eunkyung Jo, Dec. 15, 1993; children: Hajin, Gaeun, Gyungjin. MD, Keimyung U., 1985; MD in Clin. Pathology, Yeungnam U., 1989, DSc in Clin. Pathology, 1993. Diplomate Ministry of Health & Welfare/Korea, 1985. Asst. prof. Dongguk U., Seoul, 1989—95; prof. Cath. U. Daegu, 1995—, dir. adult stem cell therapy ctr., 2005—. Dir. Cath. Med. Ctr. Daegu, 2002—, Adult Cell Therapy Ctr., 2005—. Com. mem. CDR Ctr. Keimyung U., Daegu, 2005—. Grantee, Leading Indsl. Tech. R&D Project, 2003—. Mem.: Am. Assn. Cancer Rsch. Roman Catholic. Achievements include patents for Primer for diagnosis of one or more kinds of cancer. Avocation: vocalist. Office: Catholic Medical Center of Daegu 3056-6 Daemyung 4 Dong 705-718 Daegu Daegu Republic of Korea Office Phone: 82-53-650-4144. Office Fax: 82-53-653-8672. Business E-Mail: chjeon@cu.ac.kr.

JEON, HAN-YONG, engineering educator, researcher; b. Jeonju, Republic of Korea, Sept. 4, 1955; s. Dong-Joo Kim; m. Gyeong-Hye Jin, Aug. 25, 1958; children: A-Ram, Woo-Ram. BS in Textile Engring., Hanyang U., Seoul, 1979, MEng in Dyeing Chemistry, 1981, PhD in Textile Physics, 1989. Cert. engr., Republic of Korea, 1979. Prof. Chonnam Nat. U., Gwangju, Republic of Korea, 1992—2004, INHA U., Republic of Korea, 2005—. Dir. Geosynthetic Inst., Seoul, 1998—; mem. internat. tech. adv. com. Geotech. Fabric Report; internat. rschr. CTT Group, Canada; mem. adv. com. Environ. Mgmt. Corp., Republic of Korea, FITI Testing and Rsch. Inst., Republic of Korea. Author: Guidebook of Design and Installation of Geosynthetics, 1998, 2d edit., 1999, Polymeric Materials for Civil Engineering, 1999, Mechanics of Textile Materials, 2001, Geosynthetic Reinforcement Materials, 2002, High-Tech Textile Materials, 2003, Practice of Geosynthetics, 2004, Geosynthetics, 2004. Mem. adv. com. Ministry of Environment, Republic of Korea, Ministry of Commerce, Industry and Energy, Republic of Korea. Pvt. first class US Army, 1981—82, Jeonju. Mem.: ASTM (D35 com.), Internat. Geosynthetics Soc. (WG3 and WG4 com.), Korean Geosynthetic Application Tech. Rsch. Assn. (chmn.), Korean Geosynthetic Soc. (mgmt. dir., v.p.), Korean Fiber Soc. (bus. dir.), Soc. for Rsch. Geosynthetics (chmn.). Democrat. Methodist. Achievements include 17 geosynthetic-related patents. Office: INHA Univ Younghyun-Dong 253 402-751 Incheon Incheon Republic of Korea Office Fax: 82-32-872-1426. Business E-Mail: hyjeon@inha.ac.kr.

JEON, HUI-KYUNG, cardiologist, director; b. Pusan, Republic of Korea, Apr. 2, 1964; MD, PhD, Cath. Med. Coll., 1988. Dir. med. ins. com. Korean Soc. Echocardiography, 2009—. Office: Kumoh-dong 65-1 Uijeongbu Kyeongki 480-821 Republic of Korea E-mail: jhkmht@gmail.com.

JEON, HYO SUNG, medical educator; b. Deagu, Republic of Korea, Oct. 15, 1970; PhD, Kyungpook Nat. U., 2003. Prof. Sch. Medicine Kyungpook Nat. U., 2008. Office: 101 Dongin-dong Jung-gu Daegu 700422 Republic of Korea Business E-Mail: jeonh@knu.ac.kr.

JEON, KYEONGMAN, physician, researcher; b. Jeju, Republic Of Korea, Mar. 13, 1974; s. Yeong-Cheon Jeon and Ok-Sang Han; m. Young Oh, Oct. 22, 2005; children: Sinu, Nayoung. MD, Korean Med. Assn., 1999; MS in Medicine, Sungkyunkwan U., Seoul, Republic Of Korea, 2003. Cert. Bd. Korean Assn. Internal Medicine, 2004, in pulmonary medicine 2006. Clin. fellow Samsung Med. Ctr., Seoul, 2004—, asst. prof., 2010—. Capt. Armed Forces Med. Command Korean Army, 2005—07, Seongnam. Office: Samsung Med Ctr 50 Ilwon-dong Kangnam-ku Seoul 135-710 Republic of Korea Business E-Mail: kjeon@skku.edu. E-mail: kyeongman.jeon@samsung.com.

JEON, SEONG WOO, medical educator; b. Busan, Republic of Korea, Dec. 29, 1971; PhD, Kyungpook Nat. U. Sch. Medicine, 1996. Prof. Kyungpook Nat. U. Sch. Medicine, 2008. Mem.: Am. Gastroenterology Assn. Office: 50 Samduk 2Ga Chung-gu Daegu Kyungpook 700-721 Republic of Korea Office Fax: 82-53-426-8773. Business E-Mail: sw-jeon@hanmail.net.

JEON, TAECK JOONG, biology professor; b. Wooljin-gun, Kyungbuk, Republic of Korea, Jan. 1, 1968; PhD, U. Tenn., Knoxville, 2003. Asst. prof. Chosun U., Gwangju, Republic of Korea, 2011—. Office: Chosun University 375 Seosuk-dong Dong-gu Gwangju 501-759 Republic of Korea Office Fax: 82-62-230-6654. Business E-Mail: tjeon@chosun.ac.kr.

JEON, WOO KYU, medical educator; b. Kangneung-Si, Korea, Jan. 9, 1962; s. Ik Chan Jeon and Seung Chul Won; m. Jee Seon Kim; children: Ihn Wung, Ihn Seung. MD, Chungang U., Seoul, 1986, PhD, 1996. Exch. prof. Mass. Gen. Hosp., Harvard Med. Sch., Boston, 1996—2001; asst. prof. Kangbuk Samsung Hosp., Sungkyunkwan U.

Sch. Medicine, Seoul, 2001—06, assoc. prof., 2006—09, prof., chmn. gastroenterology divsn., 2007—. Dir. endoscopy ctr. Kangbuk Samsung Hosp., Sungkyunkwan U. Sch. Medicine, 1997—. Home: Tower Palace E-1106 Dogok-Dong Kangnam-Ku Seoul Republic of Korea Office: Kangbuk Samsung Hosp 108 Pyung-Dong Jongno-Ku Seoul 110-746 Republic of Korea Home Phone: (82)-2-576-3955; Office Phone: (82)-2-2001-2056. Office Fax: (82)-2-2001-2049. Personal E-mail: jeonwk2056@naver.com. Business E-Mail: wookyu.jeon@samsung.com.

JEON, YANG-WHAN, psychiatrist, educator; b. Seoul, Sept. 28, 1959; s. Chang-Seo Jeon and Bong-Seon Jang; m. Yoon-Kyung Jang; children: Young-Hoon, Young-Chan, Young-Eun. MD, Cath. U. Korea, Seoul, 1985, PhD, 1998. Cert. Bd. Psychiatry Republic of Korea, 1995. Vis. scientist Scripps Rsch. Inst., San Diego, 1999—2001; assoc. prof. Cath. U. Korea, Seoul, 2002—07. Dir. dept. neuropsychiatry Our Lady of Mercy Hosp., Inchon, Republic of Korea, 2003—08. Contbr. articles to profl. jours. Lt. Republic Of Korean Navy, 1986—88. Grantee, Ministry Health Welfare, Republic of Korea, 2004—06, 2007—08. Mem.: Korean Academic Assn. Schizophrenia (life; v.p. 2006—). Roman Catholic. Avocation: travel. Office: Incheon St Mary's Hospital Bupyung-Gu Bupyung-Dong 403-720 Incheon Incheon Republic of Korea Office Fax: +82-32-505-8994. Business E-Mail: jeonleo@olmh.cuk.ac.kr.

JEON, YONG SUN, radiologist, educator; s. Young Jin Jeon and Kyung Heui Kim; m. Hye Jin Yang, Oct. 28, 1995; children: Jung Won, Hee Won. MD, Inha U., Incheon, Republic of Korea, 1993; PhD in Medicine, Kangwon, Choonchun, Republic of Korea, 2007. Lic. MD Korean Med. Assn., 1994, radiologist Korea Med. Assn., 1999. Trainee dept. radiology Inha U. Hosp., 1995—98, physician dept. radiology, 2002—03; pub. health dir. Korean Assn. Health Promotion, Suwon, 1999—2001; instr. med. sch. Inha U., 2003—05, asst. prof. med. sch., 2005—. Contbr. articles to profl. jours. Grantee, Korea Industry-Sch. Assn., Yulchon Chemistry, 2004—07. Mem.: Korean Soc. Molecular Imaging, Korean Soc. MRI, Korean Soc. Abdominal Radiology, Korean Soc. Interventioanl Radiololgy. Office: Inha Univ Hosp Dept Radiology 7-206 3rd St Shinheung-Dong Choong-Gu 400-711 Incheon Incheon Republic of Korea Office Fax: 8232-890-2743. Business E-Mail: radjeon@korea.com.

JEON, YOU-JIN, medical educator; b. Busan, Busan, Republic of Korea, July 16, 1964; s. Yeon-Hee Ko; m. Eun-Suck Park, July 29, 1964; children: Min-Gi, Da-Bin, Eun-Gi. BS, Pukyung Nat. U., 1990; PhD, Pukyong Nat. U., Busan, 1998. Rschr. Meml. U. Nfld., St. John's, Newfoundland, Canada, 1998—99; prof. Cheju Nat. U., Jeju, Jeju-Do, Republic of Korea, 2002—. Contbr. articles to profl. jours. Home: Wonsin Apt 101-601 1718-3 Ara-1 Dong Jeju-Do Jeju 690-756 Republic of Korea Office: Cheju Nat Univ Ara-1 Dong 1 690-756 Jeju Jeju-do Republic of Korea Office Fax: 82-64-756-3493; Home Fax: 82-64-756-3493.

JEONG, BI O., medical educator; b. Seoul, Republic of Korea, Nov. 8, 1971; Degree in Medicine, Kyung Hee U., 1998; MD, Ul Ji U., 2010. Instr., dept. orthop. surgery Coll. Medicine Kyung Hee U., Seoul, Republic of Korea, 2007—09, asst. prof., dept. orthop. surgery, 2009—. Orthop. surgeon Kyung Hee U. Med. Ctr., 2007. Mem.: Korean Arthroscope Soc., Korean Fracture Soc., Korean Foot and Ankle Soc., Korean Orthop. Assn. Avocations: skiing, golf, classical music. Office: 1 Hoegi-dong Dongdaemun-gu Seoul 130-702 Republic of Korea Office Phone: 82-2-958-9488. Office Fax: 82-2-964-3865. Business E-Mail: biojeong@khmc.or.kr.

JEONG, BYUNG-HOON, research scientist; b. Naju, Republic of Korea, Nov. 7, 1968; PhD, Kangwon Nat. U., 2002. Sect. chief, rschr. Ilsong Inst. Life Sci., Hallym U., 1995—. Editl. bd. mem. World Jour. Med. Genetics. Korea Rsch. Found. grant, Korean Govt., 2008—, grant, Korea Healthcare Tech. R&D Project, Ministry Health, Welfare & Family Affairs, 2008—. Fellow: Korean Soc. Virus (mgr. neurologic virus). Avocations: drums, ping pong/table tennis. Office: 1605-4 Gwanyang-dong Dongan-Gu Anyang Gyeonggi-do 431-060 Republic of Korea Office Phone: 82-31-380-1981. Office Fax: 82-31-388-3427. Business E-Mail: bhjeong@hallym.ac.kr.

JEONG, CHANGHOON, orthopedist, educator; b. Jeju, Republic of Korea, Aug. 4, 1963; MD, Cath. U. Korea, 1988, PhD, 2000. Prof. Buchon St. Mary's Hosp., Cath. U. Korea, 1996—, orthop. dept. chief, 2009—. Mem.: Korean Shoulder and Elbow Soc., Korean Pediat. Orthop. Soc., Korean Orthop. Assn. Avocations: golf, fishing, tennis. Office: 2 Sosa-Dong Wonmi-Gu Bucheon Kyunggi 420-717 Republic of Korea Office Fax: 82323402671. Business E-Mail: changhoonj@naver.com. E-mail: changhoonj@yahoo.com.

JEONG, CHOON-SIK, medical educator; b. Jin Ju, Republic Of Korea, Feb. 4, 1953; m. Kyu-jung Lee; children: Jae-pyo Lee, Jun-pyo Lee. PharmD, Duksung Women's U., Seoul, Republic Of Korea, 1991. Prof. Duksung Women's U., 1996, dean, Coll. Pharmacy, 2007—. Contbr. articles to profl. jour. Office: Duksung Women's Univ Kunhwakhogil 19 Do Bong Gu Seoul 132-714 Republic of Korea Office Phone: 82-2-901-8382. Office Fax: 82-2-901-8386. Business E-Mail: choonsik@duksung.ac.kr.

JEONG, HYUN CHUL, gynecologist, educator; b. Republic of Korea, June 17, 1968; BPharm, Chung-Ang U., 1997, PharmM, 2000; MD, Korea U., 2004. Clin. instr. dept. ob-gyn. Korea U. Ansan Hosp., 2009—11; clin. asst. prof. dept. ob-gyn. Chung-Ang U. Hosp., 2011—. Mem.: Korean Soc. Ultrasound in Ob-gyn., Korean Soc. Ob-gyn. Office: Chung-Ang University Hosp Dept Obstetrics & Gynecology Seoul Dongjakgu 156-755 Republic of Korea Business E-Mail: pierremr@medimail.co.kr.

JEONG, IL YUN, research scientist; b. Jinju, Gyeongsangnam, Republic of Korea, Oct. 16, 1963; B, Gyeongsang U., 1990; PhD, Tokushima U., 1999. With dept. radiation machinery rsch. Korea Atomic Rsch. Inst., 2005—. Cons. Korea Food & Drug Adminstrn., 2007—09. Scholarship, Ministry of Edn., Culture, Sports, Sci. & Tech., Japan. Mem.: Korean Soc. Radiation Industry, Korean Soc. Food Sci. & Nutrition, Pharm. Soc. Korea. Avocation: golf. Office: 1266 Sinjeong-dong Jeongup Jeollabuk-do 580-185 Republic of Korea Office Fax: 82-63-570-3159. Business E-Mail: iyjeong@kaeri.re.kr.

JEONG, IN-HO, medical educator; b. Republic of Korea, Feb. 26, 1971; BA, Chonnam Nat. U., 1995; PhD, Ajou U., 2006. Assoc. prof. Jeju Nat. U., Sch. Medicine, 2005—. Adj. prof. Jeju Nat. U. Hosp., 2005. Office: Jeju Daehangno102 Ara 1-Dong Jeju nati Jeju 690-121 Republic of Korea E-mail: 41056@naver.com.

JEONG, JE HOON, neurosurgeon educator; b. Jeju-si, Jeju-do, Republic of Korea, Aug. 27, 1971; MD, Kyung Hee U., 1996, PhD, 2001. Asst. prof. Dept. Neurol. Surgery, U. Hallym, Coll. Medicine, Hangang Sacred Heart Hosp., 2007—. Recipient Medtronic Spine award; grant, Ministry of Edn., Sci. and Tech., Hallym U. Med. Ctr. Mem.: Asia Pacific Cervical Spine Soc., North Am. Spine Soc., Korean Neurol. Soc., Korean Spinal Neurosurgery Soc. (life), Korean Neurotraumatology Soc. (life; sci. program exec. sec. 2008—10, exec. sec. 2008—). Office: 94-195 Yeongdeungpo-dong Yeongdeungpo-gu Seoul 150-030 Republic of Korea Office Phone: 82-2- 2639-5650, 82 2 2639 5184. Office Fax: 82-2-2676-7020. Business E-Mail: neuri71@gmail.com.

JEONG, JI HOON, pharmacist, educator; b. Seoul, Republic Of Korea, June 13, 1970; s. Il Joo Jeong and Soon Sik Choi; m. Suk Hee Yun; children: Da Eun, Won Joon. MS, Chung-ang U., Seoul, 1999; PhD, Chung-ang U., 2003. Cert. pharmacist Ministry Of Health And Welfare, 1993. Rmgr. Ildong Pharm. Co., Seoul, 1993—97; dir. Genome And Medicine Co., Seoul, 2003—04; rsch. prof. Inje Univ., Busan, Kyungsangnam-Do, Republic of Korea, 2004—05; mem. Central Pharm. Affairs Coun., Seoul, 2008—. Recipient Best Presentation of Yr., Kyunggi Pharm. Assn. Mem.: Korean Soc. Gerontology, Korean Pharm. Assn. Achievements include patents for composition of natural ingredent for hangover. Home: 118-1201 Moraksan Hyundai Apt Kyunggi-Do Euwang-Si 437-770 Republic of Korea Office: Sch Of Medicine Chng-Ang Univ 221 Heuksuk-Dong Dongjak-Gu Seoul 156-756 Republic of Korea Office Fax: 82-2-826-8752.

JEONG, JINYOUNG, medical educator; b. Seoul, Republic of Korea, Nov. 13, 1965; MD, Cath. U. Korea, 1991, PhD, MPH, 2005. Vol. Korea Internat. Cooperation Agy., 1996—99; clin. fellow tumor surgery Seoul Nat. U. Hosp., 1999—2000; clin. fellow shoulder surgery Cleve. Clinic, 2006—08; asst. prof. dept. orthopaedic surgery St. Vincent's Hosp., Cath. U. Korea, 2004—09, assoc. prof. dept. orthop. surgery, 2010—. Recipient Best Oral Presentation award, 6th Ann. Conf. St. Vincent's Hosp., 2005, Japan Orthopaedics & Traumatology Found. (JOTF) Travel award, Japanese Orthopaedic Assn., 2006, Best Rsch. award, Orthopaedic and Rheumatology Inst., Cleve. Clin., 2008. Office: Orthopaedic Surgery St Vincent's Hosp Suwon Gyeonggi-do 442723 Republic of Korea Office Fax: 82-2-6008-0587. Personal E-mail: osjeong@hotmail.com.

JEONG, JOON-HOON, physician; b. Jinju, Republic of Korea, Feb. 11, 1969; s. Gi-Dong Jeong and Phil-Sook Lee. MD, Pusan Nat. U., Busan, Republic of Korea, 1993; PhD, Pusan Nat. U., 2005. Intern, residency Pusan Nat. U. Hosp., Busan, Republic of Korea, 1993—98, fellow cardiology, 2003—04; dir. Wallace Meml. Bapt. Hosp., Busan, 2004—. Office: Wallace Meml Bapt Hosp 374-75 Namsan-Dong Geumjung-gu 609-728 Busan Busan Republic of Korea Office Fax: 82-51-583-6200. Business E-Mail: jjhoon69@yahoo.co.kr.

JEONG, KEUNHONG, chemistry professor; b. Chonan, Chungnam, Republic of Korea, Aug. 11, 1979; BS, Korea Mil. Acad., 2003; MS, Seoul Nat. U., 2007. Platoon leader 5th Maneuver Divsn., 2003—04; instr. Korea Mil. Acad., 2007—10, asst. prof., 2011—; instr. Seoul Women's U., Samyook U., 2009—10, vis. rsch. assoc., 2009—. Vis. rsch. assoc. Seoul Nat. U., 2007—11; adv. bd. mem. Sci. Adv. Bd., 2010—. Recipient Honor prize, Hdqs. Army, Lt. Gen. Honor prize, ROK Pers. Command, Korea Mil. Acad., Tng. and Doctrine Command, Maj. Gen. Honor prize, 5th Maneuver Divsn. Mem.: Korean Soc. Indsl. & Engring. Chemistry, Korean Chem. Soc., Royal Soc. Chemistry. Avocations: horseback riding, swimming. Office: Korea Military Acad Dept Chemistry Seoul 139-799 Republic of Korea Business E-Mail: doas1mind@kma.ac.kr.

JEONG, KYU-SHIK, veterinarian, pathologist, educator; b. Po-Hang, Kyung Sang Buk Do, Republic of Korea, Oct. 16, 1959; s. Man-Hee and Tae-Soon (Won) Jeong; m. Mi-Kyung Kim, Jan. 21, 1990; children: Yoo-Jin, Jae Yeop. DVM, Kyungpook Nat. U., Daegu, Korea, 1988, MS, 1990, PhD, 1997. Rsch. scientist Korea Rsch. Inst. Chem. Tech., Daejon, 1988—91; postdoctoral staff NIH, Bethesda, Md., 1991—95, prin. investigator, 1998—2000; sr. rsch. scientist Korea Rsch. Inst. Biosci. and Biotech., Daejon, 1995—98, 2000—01; resident Armed Forces Inst. Pathology, Washington, 1998—2000; prof. Coll. Vet. Medicine, Kyungpook Nat. U., Daegu, 2001—, vice dean, 2007—08. Author: Large Dictionary Veterinary Medicine, 2004, Color Atlas of Surgical Diagnostic Pathology of Animals, 2007; mem. editl. bd.: In Vivo, 2005—, reviewer: Jour. Pathology, 2005. Spl. com. mem. Ctrl. Environ. Adjustment, Ministry Environ. Adminstrn., Seoul, 2001—. Sgt. Korean Army, 1981—83. Recipient Top prize, Advances in Molecular Medicine, 2005, Academic award, Kyungpook Nat. U., 2009. Mem.: Korean Soc. Vet. Pathology (acad. affairs 2003—05, v.p. 2006—07), Korean Coll. Vet. Pathologists (gen. affairs 2002—04), Asian Soc. Vet. Pathology (gen. sec. 2005—06). Avocations: tennis, golf, walking, swimming, reading. Office: Coll Vet Medicine Kyungpook Nat Univ Daegu 702-701 Republic of Korea Office Phone: 053 950 5975. Business E-Mail: jeongks@knu.ac.kr.

JEONG, MOON-JIN, cell biologist, educator; b. Seoul, Republic of Korea, Aug. 27, 1968; s. Kyu-Bum Jeong and Ai-Ja Huh; m. Soon-Jeong Jeong, Aug. 22, 1999; 1 child, John Seung-Min. BS in Biology, Dankook U., Cheonan, Republic of Korea, 1991, MS in Biology, 1991—93, MD, 1998. Cert. clin. pathologist Korean Ministry Health and Welfare. Rschr. clin. pathology Seoul Nat. U. Hosp., 1991—93; clin. rschr. dept. clin. pathology Dankook U. Hosp., Cheonan, 1994—96; rschr. dept. biology Dankook U., 1995—98; postdoctoral fellow Korea Rsch. Inst. Bioscience and Biotech., Daejon, Republic of Korea, 1998—2001; vis. fellow NIDCR/NIH, Bethesda, Md., 2001—03; prof. Coll. Dentistry Chosun U., Kwangju, Cheonnam, Republic of Korea, 2003—. Grantee Young Rschr. Project, Korea Rsch. Found., 1997, Young Scientist Project, Korea Sci. and Engring. Found., 2003—; vis. fellow, NIH, 2001—03, Postdoctoral fellow, Korea Rsch. Inst. Biosci. and Biotech., 1998—2001. Mem.: Soc. Korea Entomology, Korea Soc. Anatomy, Wound Healing Soc., Soc. Korea Electromicroscopy, Zoologica Soc. Korea, Soc. Conservation Nature. Achievements include research in wound healing, ultrastructural cell migration. Home: LineDongSan Apt 105-1410 Bukgu Dooam Cheonnam Kwangju Republic of Korea Office: College of Dentistry Chosun University Seosuk-Dong Dong-Gu 501-825 Gwangju Cheonnam Republic of Korea Office Fax: 82-62-224-3706. E-mail: mjjeong@mail.chosun.ac.kr.

JEONG, MYEONG JA, radiologist; b. Pusan, Republic Of Korea, Aug. 8, 1969; d. Gap Chun Jeong and Sook Ja Kim; m. Seung Chan Paik, June 6, 1997; children: Isaac Paik, Irene Paik. MD, Inje U., Coll. Medicine, Pusan, Korea, 1993; MS in Medicine, Kangwon U., Coll. Medicine, Korea, 2006. Diplomate Korean Bd. Diagnostic Radiology, 1998. Intern Inje U. Sanggyepaik Hosp., Seoul, Republic of Korea, 1993—94, resident diagnostic radiology, 1994—98, instr. dept. diagnostic radiology, 2004—06, asst. prof. dept. diagnostic radiology, 2006—; physician diagnostic radiology Uijeongbu Sunchunhyang Hosp., Republic of Korea, 1998—2000; med. practitioner Jeong's Radiol. Clinic, Seoul, 2000—02; physician Health Screening Ctr., Sanggyepaik Hosp., 2002—04. Contbr. articles to profl. med. jour. Sponcer Campus Crusade for Christr, Seoul, 1997—, ChildFund, Seoul, 2006—. Mem.: Korean Soc. Abdominal Radiology (Seoul), Korean Soc. Radiology (Seoul), Korean Med. Assn. (Seoul) (licentiate). Avocations: travel, reading. Office: Sanggye Paik Hosp Inje Univ 761-1 Sanggye 7-dong Nowon-gu Seoul 139-707 Republic of Korea Office Fax: 82-2-950-1220. Business E-Mail: 1969j@paik.ac.kr.

JEONG, MYUNG HO, cardiologist, educator; b. Nam Won, Jeon Buk, Korea, Oct. 25, 1958; s. Jeong Jae Wan and Lee Jung Suk; m. Jeong Jin Suk Dec. 11, 1983; children: Chan Yong, Chan Uk. MD, Chonnam Nat. U., Gwang Ju, Republic of Korea, 1983, PhD, 1989. Fellow in cardiology Chonnam Nat. U. Hosp., Gwang Ju, 1989; instr. Chonnam Nat. U., Gwang Ju, 1992-94, asst. prof., 1994-98, assoc. prof., 1998—2003, prof., 2003—; fellow in cardiology Mayo Clinic, Rochester, Minn., 1994-95; chief cardiovasc. medicine Chonnam Nat. U. Hosp., 2001—07, dir. cardiovascular rsch. inst., 2007—, dir. med. ICU, 2002—04, dir. foreigner's clin., 1998, dir., Heart Rsch. Ctr., dir., dept. edn. and rsch., 2011—; dir. Heart Rsch. Ctr., Korea Ministry Health Welfare & Home Affairs, 2008—, Korea Cardiovascular Stent Rsch. Inst., 2010—; prof. Gwangju Inst. Sci. & Tech., 2011—. Dir. Health Screening Ctr., Foreigners Clinic Chonnam Nat. U. Hosp., 1998—, dir. Cardiac Catheterization Lab., 2000—05, dir. basic and clin. rsch. lab., head of tng. and edn. of clin. trial ctr., 2005—08; dir. Korea Cardiovascular Stent Rsch. Inst., 2010—. Contbr. articles to profl. jours. Capt., med. officer Korean Army, Korea, 1989-92. Recipient Rsch. award Korean Soc. Circulation, 1996, Rsch. award Korean Soc. Internal Medicine, 1998, The Best Acad. Rsch. award Korean Soc. Hypertension, 2001, Excellant Acad. Rsch. award Korean Soc. Hypertension, 2002, Acad. Rsch. award Chonnam Nat. U., 2004, 09, Rsch. award Korean Soc. Internal Med., 2005, Rsch. award Korean Lipidology and Soc. Atheroselerosis, 2005, Best Editor award Korean Soc. Circulation, 2005, Rsch. award Chonnam Nat. U. Med. Sch., 2006, Cardiovasc. Dir. award, Rsch. Inst. Chonnam Nat. U., 2009, Acad Med. Rsch. award Chonnam Nat. U. Hosp, 2009; named Prof. of Yr., 2008, 09, Excellent rschr. Korean Med. Assn., 2009; grantee Korean Ministry Health and Welfare, 1998-2001, Korean Min. Nat. Health and Welfare, 2001-03, Korean Sci. and Engring. Found., 2003-05, Korean Rsch. Found., 2005-, Korean Circulation Soc., 2006, rsch. grant Min. Industry and Resources, 2007, Korean Min. Health and Welfare, 2008, Academic Rsch. award, Korean Soc. Cardiology, 2010. Fellow: Soc. of Asia Pacific Interventional Cardiology, European Soc. Cardiology, Am. Coll. Cardiology, Am. Heart Assn., Soc. Cardiac Angiography Intervention; mem.: NY Acad. Scis., Korean Acad. Sci. and Tech., Am. Soc. Nuc. Cardiology. Home: 104-1903 Hyunjin Everville 933 Suwan-dong Gwaogsan-Ku Gwangju 504-833 Republic of Korea Office: Chonnam Nat U Hosp Jaebangro 671 501-757 Gwangju Dong-Ku Republic of Korea Office Phone: 82-62-220-6243. Personal E-mail: myungho@chollian.net, mhjeong@chommam.ac.kr.

JEONG, OK CHAN, biomedical engineer; b. Cheju, Republic of Korea, June 28, 1972; s. Jung Sam Jeong and Jung Sun Kim; m. Hye Ja Koh, Sept. 22, 2003; children: Sung Soo children: Sung Hee. BS in Control and Instrumentation Engring., Ajou U., Suwon, Republic of Korea, 1995, MS in Control and Instrumentation Engring., 1997, PhD, 2004. Sr. rschr. Rsch. Inst. Sci. and Engring. Ajou U., Republic of Korea, 2002—04; postdoctoral fellow Ctr. Promotion COE Program Ritsumeikan U., Japan, 2004—06; lectr. dept. biomed. engring. Inje U., Gimhae, Gyengnam, 2007—08, asst. prof., 2009—. Gen. mgr. MEMS/NANO Febrication Ctr., Republic of Korea, 2007—. Contbr. articles to profl. jours. With Korean Army, 1999—2002. Recipient Paper award, Japan Soc. Computer Aided Surgery, 2005. Mem.: IEEE (Best Paper award 2005). Achievements include patents pending for polymeric micro hand with pneumatic balloon actuators. Avocation: soccer. Office: Inje U Dept Biomedical Eng Obang-Dong 607 621-749 Gimhae Gyeongsangnam-do Republic of Korea Office Fax: +82-55-327-3292. Business E-Mail: memsoku@inje.ac.kr.

JEONG, SEO YOUNG, engineering educator; b. Seoul, Republic Of Korea, Mar. 10, 1956; PhD, U. Utah, Salt Lake City, 1984. Cert. R.Ph Korea, 1979. Prin. rsch. scientist Korea Inst. Sci. and Tech., Seoul, 1986—2005; prof. Kyung Hee U., Seoul, 2005—. Recipient New Korea award, Pres. Korea, 1997. Fellow: Biomaterials Sci. and Engring.; mem.: Korea Acad. Sci. and Tech. Achievements include research in oral insulin delivery system. Office: Kyung Hee Univ 1 Hoegi-dong Dongdaemoon-Ku Seoul 130-701 Republic of Korea Office Fax: 82-2-962-0222. Business E-Mail: syjeong@khu.ac.kr.

JEONG, SUNG-WOOK, medical educator; b. Busan, Republic of Korea, Mar. 5, 1974; MD, Dong-A U., PhD, 2004. Asst. prof. Coll. Medicine, Dong-A U., 2009—. Mem.: Korean Audiological Soc., Korean Otologic Soc., Korean Soc. Otolaryngology-Head & Neck Surgery. Office: 3-1 Dongdaeshin-dong Seo-gu Busan 602-715 Republic of Korea Office Fax: 82-51-253-0712. Business E-Mail: su0305@lycos.co.kr.

JEONG, TAESUNG, dentist, educator; DDS, Pusan Nat. U., Republic of Korea, 1986; MSD, Pusan Nat. U., 1990, PhD, 1997. Lic. dental surgeon Ministry of Health, 1987. Vis. asst. prof. U. Mich. Dental Sch., Ann Arbor, 2000—01; dept. chair pediat. dentistry Pusan Nat. U. Hosp., Busan, 2002—04, 2009—; prof. Pusan Nat. U., 2003—08, vice dean Dental Profl. Sch., 2009—. Capt., 1990—93, Republic of Korea. Fellow: Korean Assn. Disability and Oral Health (life; editor 2004—05); mem.: Korean Assn. Pediat. Dentistry (life; editl. bd. 2003—05). Office: Dental Profl Sch PNU 3-3 Beomeo-Ri Mulgeum-Eup 626-870 Yangsan Gyeongsangnam-do Republic of Korea

JERABEK, JAROSLAV, neurologist; b. Prague, Czech Republic, Dec. 19, 1951; m. Alena Pathova, Sept. 18, 1975; children: Petra Jerabkova, Veronika Jerabkova. MD, Charles U., Prague, 1976. Diplomate 1976. Assoc. prof. neurology Charles U., Prague, 2002—; resident Neurol Clinic of Pediat. Faculty, Prague, Czech Republic. Author: The Vertigo and Loalauce Disorders in the Elderly, 2000, Differential Diagnosis of Vertigo, 2001. Recipient rsch. prize, Czech Neurol. Soc.; grantee, Czech Grant Agy., 1999. Mem.: European Fed. Neurological Soc. Office: Neurologic Clinic Charles Univ V uvalu 84 150 00 Prague Czech Republic

JERJES-SANCHEZ DIAZ, CARLOS, medical association administrator; b. Mexico City, Jan. 30, 1950; Degree in Pulmonology, U. Nat. Autonoma de Mex., 1980, degree in Cardiology, 1982. Cardiologist, emergency rm. dept. Hosp. de Cardiologia Cr. Medico Nat. Siglo XXI Ciudad de Mex., 1982—95, Hosp. de Cardiologia, Monterrey, Mexico, 1996—97, head, emergency rm. dept., 1997—2010; clin. rsch. dir. Inst. de Cardiologia y Medicina Vascultar TEC de Monterrey, 2010—. Sec. Soc. Mexicana de Neumologia y Cirugia de Torax, 1987—89, Mexican Pulmonology Bd., 1990—91, pres., 1991—92, Exam. Mexican Pulmonology Bd., 1992—94. Master: Soc. Mexicana de Cardiologia (Manuel Vaquero fellow 2003, Ignacio Chavez fellow 2006, 2009, Arturo Rosenbluth fellow 2007, Felipe Mendoza fellow 2007); fellow: Soc. Mexicana de Neumologia y Cirugia de Torax, Am. Coll. Cardiology, Am. Coll. Chest Physicians; mem.: Acad. Nat. de Medicina. Avocations: swimming, exercise. Office: Ave Morones Prieto 3000 CITES 2 Nivel Ote Monterrey Nuevo Leon 64710 Mexico E-mail: jerjes@prodigy.net.mx.

JERNDAL, SIR JENS, futurist, consultant; b. Goteborg, Sweden, Jan. 5, 1934; s. Ebbe and Ingrid M. (Forsberg) J.; children: C. Patrick, J.O. Mathias, J.T. Christofer. MS, Stockholm U., 1958; BA, Uppsala U., 1959; Diploma, Internat. Coll. Acupuncture, Colombo, Sri Lanka, 1982; MD, 1987; DSc (hon.), World U. Roundtable, 1988. Attaché Royal Swedish Ministry Fgn. Affairs, 1960-62; embassy sec. Royal Swedish Embassy, Copenhagen, 1962, 1st sec., chargé d'affaires Karachi, Pakistan, 1964; 1st sec. Royal Swedish Ministry Fgn. Affairs, 1965-68. Expert del. UN High Commr. for Refugees, Geneva, 1966—67; investment broker Real Lanzarote SA, Las Palmas, Spain, 1968—79; pres. Cosmosophical Found., Stockholm, 1977—88, vis. prof., internat. coord. The Open Internat. U. for Complementary Medicines, Colombo, Sri Lanka, 1988, prof. holistic medicine, 91; pres. Life Expansion U. Author: Indonesien, 1958, Vakna Sverige, 1997, The Secret Key, 2004, Cracking the Rainbow-Code, 2009, Paradigm Pulse-Sensing The Surge of Change, 2010; contbr. articles to profl. jours. Fgn. lang. transmission mgr., broadcaster for Radio Sweden, 1956-57; rep. Assn. Swedish Citizens Residing Abroad, Canary Islands, 1972-75. Decorated knight Royal Order Dannebrog (Denmark), knight grand cross of justice Sovereign Order of St. John of Jerusalem (Knights of Malta); recipient Albert Schweitzer Prize for Medicine, 1990 Fellow: World Assn. Integrated Medicine; mem.: World Future Soc. (profl.), Inst. Noetic Scis., Sci. and Med. Network, Cosmosophical Found. (chmn.). Home: Edificio Malta Avenida Rivadavia 1352 1033 Buenos Aires Argentina Home Phone: 011541150328573; Office Phone: 541150328570. Office Fax: 1530 239 3504. Personal E-mail: jerndal@iplanmail.com.ar.

JERNIGAN, DONALD, hospital administrator; BS in chemistry, U. Tex., Arlington; PhD, Baylor U. Former pres. Metroplex Hosp., Killeen, Tex., Tennessee Christian Med. Ctr.; CEO, Multi-State Hosp. Divsn. Adventist Health Sys., sr. v.p.; CEO, pres. Fla. Hosp. Ctr., 1999—2006; exec. v.p. Adventist Health Sys., pres., CEO, 2006—. Diplomat Am. Coll. Healthcare Execs. Office: 111 N Orlando Ave Winter Park FL 32789 *

JÉRÔME, BOURSIER, gastroenterologist, researcher; b. Lille, France, Dec. 2, 1978; MD, U. d'Angers, 2006. Physician, rsch. scientist Ctr. Hosp. d'Angers, 2006—11. Mem.: European Assn. Study of Liver, Assn. Française pour l'Etude du Foie. Office: CHU - 4 rue Larrey Angers Pays de la Loire 49000 France Business E-Mail: jeboursier@chu-angers.fr.

JEROME, NORGE WINIFRED, nutritionist, anthropologist, educator; b. Grenada, Nov. 3, 1930; arrived in U.S.A., 1956, naturalized, 1973; d. McManus Israel and Evelyn Mary (Grant) Jerome. BS magna cum laude (hon.), Howard U., 1960; MS, U. Wis., 1962, PhD, 1967. Cert. nutrition splty.; fellow Am. Coll. Nutrition. Asst. prof. U. Kans. Med. Sch., Kans. City, 1967—72, assoc. prof., 1972—78, prof., 1978—95, dir. cmty. nutrition divsn., 1981—95; dir. Office of Nutrition, AID, Washington, 1988—91; sr. rsch. fellow Univ. Ctr., AID, Washington, 1991—92; interim assoc. dean minority affairs U. Kans. Med. Sch., Kans. City, 1996—98, prof. emerita, 1996—; v.p. AARP Chpt. Johnson County, Kans. City, 2011—. Tech. adv. group The Nat. Ctr. for Minority Health; dir. ednl. resource centers U. Kans. Med. Center, 1974-77, head cmty. nutrition lab., 1978-95; cons. Children's TV Workshop, 1974-77; chair adv. bd. Teenage Parents Ctr., 1971-75, Urban League Greater Kans. City; planning and budget coun., children and family svc. United Cmty. Svc. Greater Kans. City, 1971-80; panel on nutrition edn. White House Conf. on Food, Nutrition and Health, 1969; bd. dir., health care com. Prime Health, 1976-79; bd. dir. Coun. on Children, Media and Merchandising; consumer edn. task force Mid Am. Health Systems Agy., 1977-79; commr. N. Am. working group Commn. Anthropology Food and Food Habits, Internat. Union Anthrop. and Ethnol. Sci., 1979-80; chmn. com. nutritional anthropology Internat. Union Nutritional Sci., 1979-80; lipid metabolism adv. com. NIH, 1978-80; nat. adv. panel multi-media campaign to improve children's diet U.S. Dept. Agrl., 1979-81; bd. advisers Am. Coun. on Sci. and Health, 1985-88; cons. in field. Sr. author: Nutritional Anthropology, 1980; asso. editor: Jour. Nutrition Edn., 1971-77; adv. council, 1977-80; editor: Nutritional Anthropology Communicator, 1974-77; mem. editl. bd.: Med. Anthropology: Cross Cultural Studies in Health and Illness, 1976-88, Internat. Jour. Nutrition Planning, 1977-88, Nutrition and Cancer: An Internat. Jour, 1978-2000, Jour. Nutrition and Behavior, 1981-86; contbr. articles to profl. journals. Mem. com. man food sys. NRC, 1980-83; bd. dirs. Kans. City Urban League, 1969-77, Crittenton Ctr., Kans. City, Mo., 1979-80, 2008-, Johnson County Kans. Libr. Found., 2004—09, exec. com., 2005-08; mem. awards com. in nutrition edn. Met. Life Found., 1983-85; pres. Assn. for Women in Devel., 1991-93; trustee U. Bridgeport, Conn., 1992—; trustee Child Health Found., 1992-2000, chmn. bd. dirs., 1996-98; v.p., bd. trustees U. Bridgeport, Conn., 1997—; bd. dirs. Black Health Care Coalition of Kansas City, 1993-2002, Solar Cookers Internat., 1992-2000, pres., 1998-2000, Johnson County, Kans. Found. on Aging, 2001-04, Health Care Found. Greater Kansas City, 2004-06; mem. Commn. on Aging, Johnson County, Kans., 1997-2007; bd. dirs., vice chair cmty. adv. com. Health Care Found., Greater Kans. City, 2003-09. Decorated Dau. Brit. Empire; recipient First Higuchi Irvin Youngberg Rsch. Achievement award U. Kans., 1982, Excellence in Academia award Inst. Caribbean Studies, 2002, Disting. Svc. award NAACP, 2005, Johnson County Trailblazer award, 2006. Fellow Am. Soc. for Nutritional Sci., Am. Anthrop. Assn. (chair com. nutritional anthropology 1974-77, founder com. nutritional anthropology 1974), Soc. Applied Anthropology, Am. Coll. Nutrition, Soc. Med. Anthropology, Am. Soc. Nutritional Sci., 1998; mem. Am. Public Health Assn. (food and nutrition coun. 1975-78, governing coun. 1982-85), Am. Inst. Nutrition (program com. 1983-86), Am. Soc. Clin. Nutrition, Am. Men and Women of Sci., Nat. Acad. Sci. (world food and nutrition study panel), N.Y. Acad. Sci., Inst. Food Technologists, Am. Dietetic Assn., Assn. for Women in Devel. (pres. 1991-93), Soc. Behavioral Medicine, Club of Rome (U.S. assoc.). Office: U Kans Med Ctr 3901 Rainbow Blvd Mail Stop 1008 Kansas City KS 66160 Office Phone: 913-588-2775.

JERUSHALMI, JACQUELINE, nuclear medicine physician; b. Congo, Mar. 17, 1954; Maturita classica, A. D'oria Genova, 1973; degree in Medicine, U. Genova, 1983. Dept. head, nuc. medicine Western Galilee Hosp. Nahariya, 1988—. Mem.: Israeli Med. Assn. Avocations: music, singing. Home: Rehov Havazelet 35/1 Nesher 36780 Israel Home Fax: 0972-4-901529. Business E-Mail: jacqueline.jerushalmi@naharia.health.gov.il.

JESKE, HANS-CHRISTIAN CLAUS, orthopedist, educator; b. Stockholm, Dec. 24, 1972; s. Hans and Jeske (Elisabeth); m. Martina Alexandra Wieser, Mar. 5, 2005; children: Helena Sophia, Valentina Sophia. MD, Franz Leopold U., Innsbruck, Austria, 2001. Anesthesiologist, dept. anesthesiology and intensive Care Med. U. Innsbruck, 2001—04; anesthesiologist, dept. gastroenterology Med. Hosp. St. Gallen, Switzerland, 2003; gen. surgeon, dept. gen. surgery U. Tübingen, Germany, 2005—06; orthop. surgeon, trauma surgeon, dept. trauma surgery and sports medicine, assoc. prof. Med. U. Innsbruck, 2006—. Mem.: SECEC, Am. Gastroent. Assn., OGU. Office: Univ Innsbruck Anichstrasse 35 Innsbruck Tirol 6020 Austria Office Phone: 43-512-504-82166. Personal E-mail: hans.jeske@i-med.ac.at.

JESKY, T. J., pharmaceutical products executive; b. Chgo., Feb. 15, 1947; s. Henry J. and Joan F. (Lalko) J.; m. Jackeline Vasquez, Feb. 28, 2004; 1 child, Julia Alexandra. Lic. in derecho, Nat. U. Autónoma Mexico, Mexico City, 1967—70; BA Mktg. and Retailing, Bradley U., 1969. Field rep. Morton Norwich, Chgo., 1973-76, major account rep., 1976-79; Chgo. dist. mgr. Norwich Eaton Pharms., NY, 1979-80; NYC dist mgr. Norwich Eaton (A Procter & Gamble Co.), NY, 1980-83; mgr. Midwest and P.R. divsn. Norwich Eaton, Oak Brook, Ill., 1983-90; mgr. P.R. divsn. nat. accounts, mgr. nat. hosp. divsn. Procter & Gamble Pharms., Norwich, NY, 1990-93, mgr. divsn. Cin., 1994-95; pres., CEO Studebaker's, Inc., Scottsdale, Ariz., 1995-97, Ionosphere, Inc., Scottsdale, 1997-98, Barrington Labs., Inc., Las Vegas, 1998-2000, CEO Eaton Labs., Inc., Las Vegas, 2000—07, EZJR Inc., Las Vegas, 2006—. Contbr. articles to profl. jours. Mem. Pharm. Mfr. Assn., Am. Mgmt. Assn., Nat. Pharm. Coun. Home: PO Box 2742 Scottsdale AZ 85252-2742

JESSE, ROBERT L., federal agency administrator, cardiologist; BS in Biochemistry, U. NH, Durham, 1974; PhD in Biophysics, Med. Coll. Va., 1980, MD, 1984. Diplomate American Bd. Internal Medicine. Rsch. assoc. Harvard U. Sch. Pub. Health, Mass.; residency and fellowship in cardiology Med. Coll. Va.; dir. of acute cardiac care program Va. Commonwealth U. Health Sys., tenured prof. internal medicine/cardiology; chief cardiology sect. Richmond Veterans Affairs Med. Ctr., Va.; chief cons. med. surg. services, office patient care services US Dept. Veterans Affairs, Washington, nat. program dir. cardiology, acting prin. dep. undersec. health, 2010, prin. dep. undersec. health, 2010—. Contbr. articles to profl. jours. Fellow: American Heart Assn., American Coll. Cardiology (former gov., pres. Richmond metro chpt.). Office: US Dept Veterans Affairs 810 Vermont Ave NW Washington DC 20420 *

JESSE, SANDRA L., lawyer, health care supplies company executive; BA in Journalism, Ind. U.; JD, Boston Coll.; completed Advanced Mgmt. Program, Harvard Bus. Sch. Newspaper reporter Journal Gazette; congl. legis. asst.; press sec. to Congressman Lee Hamilton; exec. v.p., chief legal officer Blue Cross Blue Shield Mass., 1995—2011; ptnr. Choate Hall & Stewart LLP; assoc. Bingham, Dana & Gould; v.p., chief legal officer exec. coun. oper. com. Haemonetics Corp., 2011—. Commr. Mass. Commn. on Status of Women. Pres. Boston Bar Found.; bd. dirs. New Eng. Legal Found., Alliance for Non-Profit Health Care. Mem.: Boston Bar Assn. (trustee). Office: Haemonetics Corp 400 Wood Rd Braintree MA 02184 Office Phone: 800-225-5242. *

JESSELL, THOMAS M., biochemist, medical educator; b. 1951; B, U. London; PhD in Neurobiology, Cambridge U., Eng., 1977; DPhil (hon.), Umea U., Sweden, 1998. Rsch. fellow Trinity Coll., Cambridge U., England; postdoctoral fellow Gerald Fishbach Lab. Harvard Med. Sch., Boston, asst. prof. neurobiology; prof. biochemistry and molecular biophysics and mem. Ctr. for Neurobiology and Behavior Columbia U. Coll. Physicians and Surgeons, 1985—; investigator Howard Hughes Med. Inst., 1985—. Contbr. articles to profl. jours.; co-editor (with others): Principles of Neural Science; mem. editl. bd. several jours. Decorated (with Corey S. Goodman) J. Allyn Taylor Internat. prize for medicine; recipient Ameritec Found. prize, 1998, Jansen prize in advanced biotech. and medicine, 2000, Disting. Neurosci. Rsch. Achievement award, Bristol-Myers Squibb, 2000; co-recipient (with Corey Goodman) Devel. Biology prize, March of Dimes, 2001, Kavli prize for neuroscience, Norwegian Acad. Sci. and Letters in partnership with the Kavli Found. and the Norwegian Ministry of Edn. and Rsch., 2008. Fellow: cad. Arts and Scis., Royal Soc. London; mem.: NAS (foreign assoc.), Inst. Medicine. Achievements include research in on early development of the vertebrate central nervous system; the molecular mechanisms that determine the identities of neurons generated in the spinal cord; on the guide the axons of sensory and motor neurons to their targets that permit them to form functional neuronal circuits; how nerve cells in the developing spinal cord assemble into functional circuits that control sensory perception and motor actions. Office: Columbia Univ Med Ctr Haener Health Sci Ctr 701 W 168 St 1013 New York NY 10032 Office Phone: 212-305-1531. Office Fax: 212-568-8473. Business E-Mail: tmj1@columbia.edu. *

JESSER, STEVEN H., attorney; b. Chgo., Feb. 29, 1948; BA, Northwestern U., Evanston, Ill., 1970; JD, Ill. Inst. Tech., Chgo. Kent Coll. Law, 1974. Bar: NY 2003, Tex. 2005, Wis. 2005, Armed Forces, Washington 2005, Ga. 2006, Minn. 2007, Nebr. 2008, US Ct. Internat. Trade 2008, Ark.-Eastern and Western 2009, Colo. 2009, Ill. 2009, Fla. 2009, Mich. 2009, Boston 2009, Atlanta 2009, Fed. Circuit, Washington 2009, Vets. Claims, Washington 2009, US Cts. Criminal Appeals Air Force, Army, and Navy-Marine Corps 2009, US Bankruptcy Appellate Panels 2009, US Ct. Fed. Claims 2009, Ariz. 2010, Mass. 2010, US Dist. and Bankruptcy Cts. Dists. Ariz. 2010, ND 2010, Ohio 2010, Bankruptcy Ct. Dist. Mass. Mediation Register 2010, Phila. 2011, Richmond 2011, mediator: Circuit Ct. Cook County, Ill. Law Divsn. Major Case Ct.-Annexed Mediation Program 2005, Circuit Ct. Cook County, Ill. Chancery Divsn. Mediation Program 2007, cert.: Eighteenth Jud. Circuit, DuPage County, Ill., Ct.-Annexed Alternative Dispute Resolution Program (arbitrator) 2010, Nineteenth Jud. Circuit, Lake County, Ill., Mandatory Arbitration Program 2010. Assoc. gen. counsel Northwestern Meml. Hosp. and Northwestern Meml. Health Care, Chgo., 1981—95; prin. Steven H. Jesser, Attorney Law, P.C., 1995—. Contbr. chapters to books, articles to profl. publs. Named one of Ill. Super Lawyers, 2010—. Mem.: ABA, Ill. Assn. Healthcare Attys., Am. Assn. Nurse Attys., Internat. Trade Commn. Trial Lawyers Assn. (Washington), Dane County Bar Assn. (Madison), Milw. Bar Assn., Racine County Bar Assn., State Bar Wis., Chgo. Bar Assn. (past chair, Health and Hospital Law Com), Ill. State Bar Assn. (past chair, Health and Hospital Law Com). Office: 790 Frontage Rd Ste 110 Northfield IL 60093 Office Phone: 800-424-0060, 847-424-0200. Office Fax: 800-330-9710. Business E-Mail: shj@sjesser.com.

JESSOR, RICHARD, psychologist, educator, director; b. Bklyn., Nov. 24, 1924; s. Thomas and Clara (Merkin) J.; m. Shirley Glasser, Sept. 27, 1948 (div. 1982); children: Kim, Tom; m. Jane Ava Menken, Nov. 13, 1992. Student, CCNY, 1941-43; BA, Yale U., 1946; MA, Columbia U., 1947; PhD, Ohio State U., 1951. Intern, clin. psychology trainee VA, Ohio State U., Columbus, 1947-50; asst. prof. psychology U. Colo., Boulder, 1951-56, assoc. prof., 1956-61, prof., 1961—, disting. prof. behavioral sci., 2005—, emeritus prof. psychology, 2009—, dir. rsch. program problem behavior Inst. Behavioral Sci., 1966-97, dir. Inst. Behavioral Sci., 1980—2001, dir. health and soc. program Inst. Behavioral Sci., 2001—. Dir. MacArthur Found. Rsch. Network on Successful Adolescent Devel. Among Youth in High Risk Settings, 1987-96; cons. Nat. Inst. on Drug Abuse, 1975-76, Nat. Inst. on Alcohol Abuse and Alcoholism, 1976-80, WHO, Geneva, 1976-80; cons. in field. Author: (with T.D. Graves, R.C. Hanson & S.L. Jessor) Society, Personality, and Deviant Behavior: A Study of a Tri-Ethnic Community, 1968, (with S.L. Jessor) Problem Behavior and Psychosocial Development: A Longitudinal Study of Youth, 1977, (with J.E. Donovan and F. Costa) Beyond Adolescence: Problem Behavior and Young Adult Development, 1991; co-editor: Contemporary Approaches to Cognition, 1957, Cognition, Personality and Clinical Psychology, 1967, Ethnography and Human Development: Context and Meaning in Social Inquiry, 1996; editor: New Perspectives on Adolescent Risk Behavior, 1998, Perspectives on Behavioral Science: the Colorado Lectures, 1991; cons. editor Jour. Cons. and Clin. Psychology, 1975-77, Cmty. Mental Health Jour., 1974-78, Alcohol Health and Rsch. World, 1981-90, Alcohol, Drugs and Driving, 1985-92, Adolescent Medicine: State of the Art Revs., 1989—; mem. editl. bd. Prevention Sci., 1999—; cons. editor Sociometry, 1964-66, assoc. editor, 1966-69, contbr. articles to profl. jours. Served with USMC, 1943-46, PTO. Decorated Purple Heart; Social Sci. Rsch. Coun. pre-doctoral fellow Ohio State and Yale U., 1950-51; Social Sci. Rsch. Coun. fellow Ohio State U., 1954, Social Sci. Rsch. Coun. postdoctoral fellow U. Calif.-Berkeley, 1956-57, NIMH spl. rsch. fellow Harvard-Florence Rsch. Project, Italy, 1965-66, Ctr. for Advanced Study in the Behavioral Scis. fellow Stanford U., 1995-96; recipient Faculty Rsch. Lectureship award U. Colo., 1981-82; Gallagher lectr. Soc. Adolescent Medicine, 1987, Outstanding Achievement in Adolescent Medicine award, 2005; named Highly Cited Rsch. in Social Scis., Inst. for Sci. Inf., 2003. Fellow APA, Am. Psychol. Soc. (charter fellow); mem. Soc. for Psychol. Study of Social Issues, Soc. for Study of Social Problems. Avocations: mountain climbing, running marathons. Home: 1303 Marshall St Boulder CO 80302-5803 Office: U Colo Inst Behavioral Sci Cb 483 Boulder CO 80309-0001 Home Phone: 303-440-4024; Office Phone: 303-492-8148. Business E-Mail: jessor@colorado.edu.

JESSUP, MARIELL L., cardiologist, educator; d. Mary Badger Jessup; 1 child, Mary Parker. MD, Hahnemann U., 1972. Cert. internal medicine 1980, cardiovasc. medicine 1984. Intern. Hahnemann U. Hosp., resident; fellow U. Pa. Hosp., Phila., med. dir. heart failure & cardiac transplantation, 2001—, prof. medicine, 2003—. Named to Best Doctors in America, 2003—08. Office: U Pa Hosp 6 Penn Tower 3400 Spruce St Philadelphia PA 19104 Home: 1101 Brynlawn Rd Villanova PA 19085-2101 Office Fax: 215-615-0828. Business E-Mail: mariell.jessup@uphs.upenn.edu.

JESTE, DILIP VISHWANATH, psychiatrist, researcher; b. Pimpalagaon, India, Dec. 23, 1944; came to U.S., 1974; naturalized Feb., 1980; m. Sonali D. Jeste, Dec. 5, 1971; children: Shafali, Neelum. B in Medicine & Surgery, U. Poona, India, 1966; D. Psychiat. Medicine, Coll. Physicians and Surgeons, 1970; MD, U. Bombay, 1970. Cer. Am. Bd. Psychiatry and Neurology, 1979; lic. physician, D.C., Md., Calif. Hon. asst. prof. KEM Hosp., G.S. Med. Coll., Bombay, 1971-74; staff psychiatrist St. Elizabeth's Hosp., Washington, 1977-82, chief movement disorder unit, 1982-86; clin. assoc. prof. psychiatry Walter Reed Med. Ctr., Bethesda, Md., 1981-84; assoc. clin. prof. psychiatry and neurology George Washington U., Washington, 1984-86; prof. psychiatry and neurosciences U. Calif., San Diego, 1986—; chief psychiatry svc. San Diego VA Med. Ctr., San Diego, 1989-92; dir. geriatric psychiatry clin rsch ctr. U. Calif. and VA Med. Ctr., San Diego, 1992—, disting. prof. psychiatry and neurosciences, chief, geriatric psychiatry divsn., dir. Sam and Rose Stein Inst. for Rsch. on Aging. Vis. scientist dept. neuropathology Armed Forces Inst. of Pathology, Washington, 1984-86; co-dir. Med. Students' Psychiatry Clerkship Program, 1987-91; ad-hoc mem. Vets. Adminstrn. Neurobiology Grant Rev. Bd., 1984—; participant numerous meeting and confs.; lectr. in field. Co-author: Understanding and Treating Tardive Dyskinesia, 1982; editor: Neuropsychiatric Movement Disorders, 1984, Neurpsychiatric Dementias, 1986, Psychosis and Depression in the Elderly, 1988; editor-in-chief: Am. Jour. Geriatric Psychiatry; contbr. articles to numerous profl. jours, reviewer numerous profl. jours. Mem. Acad. Geriatric Resource Com., U. Calif., 1986-87, mem. com. on joint doctoral program in clin. psychology, 1986-87, mgmt. com. faculty compensation fund com., 1988-89, chmn. Psychiat. Undergrad. Edn. Com., 1987. Recipient Merit award NIMH, 1988, Disting. Svc. commendation, Am. Legion, VA and Rehab. Commn., Calif., 1991, Disting. Investigator award, Nat. Alliance Rsch in Schizophrenia and Affective Disorders, 2002, Committed Svc. to Aging Population award, San Diego County Med. Soc., 2002, C. Charles Burlingame award, Inst. Living, Hartford, 2003, Asian Heritage award, Asia Jour. Culture and Commerce, 2004, Internat. Psychogeriatric Assn. award, 2005, Recovery Rsch. Inspiration award, Nat. Alliance on Mental Illness, San Diego chapt., 2006; named one of World's Most Cited Authors, Inst. Sci. Info., 2002; recipient numerous grants in field. Fellow Indian Psychiatric Soc. (recipient Sandoz award 1973), Am. Psychiatric Assn. (disting. fellow; co-chmn. Tardive Dyskinesia task force 1984-92; Rsch. award, 2005, George Tarjan award, 2006), Am. Coll. Neuropsychopharm. (co-chmn. fin. com. 1988-89), San Diego Soc. Psychiatric Physicians,; mem. NIH (nat. adv. mental health coun., 2006), Inst. Medicine of NAS, Soc. for Neurosci., Internat. Brain Rsch. Orgn., Soc. Biolog. Psychiatry (A.E. Bennett Neuropsychiatric Rsch. award 1981), Am. Acad. Neurology, Am. Geriatrics Soc., Calif. Psychiatric Soc., Am. Assn. Geriatric Psychiatry (pres., 1998-99, prs. edn. and rsch found., 1999-2000; Sr. Investigator award, 1996), West Coast Coll. Biolog. Psychiatry (pres., 1999-2000; Warren B. Smith award, 2004), Assn. Scientists of Indian Origin in Am. (pres. neurosci. chpt. 1988-89, named Outstanding Neuroscientist 1988, Disting. Physician Tchr./Rschr. award, 2004), Internat. Coll. Geriatric Psychoneuropharmacology (founding pres., 2001-03), Collegium Internationale Neuro-psychopharmacologicum, Am. Coll. Psychiatrists (Geriatric Rsch. award, 2005). Avocations: tennis, reading. Office: VA San Diego Healthcare System Psychiatry Svc 116A-1 3350 La Jolla Village Dr # 16A San Diego CA 92161-0002 also: Dept Psychiatry 0603 Univ Calif San Diego La Jolla CA 92093-0603 E-mail: djeste@ucsd.edu.

JETER, WAYBURN STEWART, retired microbiologist, educator; b. Cooper, Tex., Feb. 16, 1926; s. Joseph Plato and Beulah (Stewart) J.; m. Margaret Ann McDonald, May 30, 1947; children— Randall Mark, Monette Ann, Marcus Kent. BS, U. Okla., 1948, MS, 1949; PhD, U. Wis., 1950. Diplomate: Am. Bd. Microbiology. Mem. faculty U. Iowa, 1950-63, assoc. prof., 1958-63; prof. microbiology U. Ariz., Tucson, 1963-89, prof. microbiology emeritus, 1989—, prof. pharmacology and toxicology, 1983-91, prof. pharmacology and toxicology emeritus, 1991—, head dept. microbiology and med. tech., 1967-83, dir. lab. cellular immunology, 1976-91, dir. med. tech. program, 1976-79. Vis. prof. immunology and med. microbiology U. Fla., 1980; pres. Scientific Rels. Svcs., Inc., 1988—99. Contbr. articles profl. jours. Served with USNR, 1943-46. Fellow AAAS; mem. Am. Acad. Microbiology, Am. Assn. Immunologists, Ariz. Acad. Sci., Am. Soc. Microbiology (mem. council 1975-77), Soc. Exptl. Biology and Medicine, Sigma Xi. Democrat. Presbyterian. Home: 5140 N Via Sempreverde Tucson AZ 85750-5966 Personal E-mail: wsjeter@hotmail.com.

JETTER, ROBERT BRUCE, plastic surgeon; b. July 2, 1953; s. Harold Jetter and Pearl Hoenig-Jetter; m. Rochelle N. Sharfman, June 22, 1981. B magna cum laude, Yeshiva Univ.; MD, Albert Einstein Med. Coll., Yeshiva Univ., Bronx, NY, 1979. Cert. Am. Bd. Plastic Surgery, 2000. Intern Bronx Mcpl. Hosp. Ctr., 1979—80; resident in surgery Montefiore Hosp. & Med. Ctr., Bronx, NY, 1980—82; fellowship in plastic surgery Westchester County Med. Ctr., 1982—83; resident in plastic surgery Lenox Hill Hosp., NYC, 1983—85; private practice in plastic surgery NYC; prog. dir. plastic & reconstructive surgery Lenox Hill Hosp., NYC.

JEUN, YONGCHULL, plant pathologist, researcher; b. Seoul, Republic of Korea, Apr. 1, 1964; s. Loijin Jeun and Hanjung Kim; m. Yeonhwa Jang, June 5, 1964; children: Jisu, Changsu. PhD, Hohenheim U., Germany, 1999. Rschr. Rural Devel. Adminstrn., Suwon, Kyunggido, Republic of Korea, 1999—2000; scientist Seoul Nat. U., Suwon, 2000—01; permanent lectr. Cheju Nat. U., Jeju, Jejudo, Republic of Korea, 2001—04, asst. prof., 2004—08, assoc. prof., 2008—. Collaborative rschr. Rural Devel. Adminstrn., Suwon, 2003—; temporary lectr. Korea U., Seoul, 2000—01. Translator: (text book) How Plants Defend Themselves Against Pathogens. Fellow, Orgn. Econ. Coop. and Devel. 2003, 2003. Mem.: Korean Soc. Plant Pathology. Office: Jeju Nat University Jejudaehakno 66 690-756 Jeju Jeju-do Republic of Korea Home Phone: 82 64 713 8684; Office Phone: 82 64 754 3319. Office Fax: 82 64 725 2351. Business E-Mail: ycjeun@jejunu.ac.kr.

JEUNG, KYUNG WOON, emergency physician; b. Gwangju, Republic of Korea, Nov. 18, 1972; s. Jae Yu Jeung and Bang Lim Park; m. Jun A. Cho. MD, Chonnam Nat. U., Gwangju. Bd. cert. emergency physician Ministry for Health, Welfare and Family Affairs, Republic of Korea, cert. basic life support instr. Am. Heart Assn., advanced cardiac life support instr. Clin. instr. Chonnam Nat. U. Hosp., Gwangju, 2005—07; dir. dept. emergency medicine Chonnam Nat. U. Hwasun Hosp., Hwasungun, Republic of Korea, 2008—. Mem.: Korean Soc. Clin. Toxicology, Korean Soc. Critical Care Medicine, Korean Soc. Emergency Medicine. Achievements include research in rapidly induced selective cerebral hypothermia using a cold carotid arterial flush during cardiac arrest in a dog model. Office: Chonnam Nat Univ Hosp Jebongno Donggu 671 501-757 Gwangju Republic of Korea Office Phone: 82-62-220-6809. Office Fax: 82-62-228-7417. Personal E-mail: neoneti@hanmail.net.

JEVTOVIC-TODOROVIC, VESNA, physician, researcher; d. Dragomir Jeftimije and Milka Radisav Jevtovic; m. Slobodan Milenko Todorovic, Oct. 6, 1984; children: Marko Slobodan Todorovic, Nikola Slobodan Todorovic, Katarina Vesna Todorovic. MD, U. Belgrade Sch. Medicine, Yugoslavia, 1980—85; PhD, U. Ill. Sch. Medicine, Chgo., 1986—2000. Cert. Mo., 1992, Va., 2001. Asst. prof., anesthesiology Wash. U. Sch. Medicine, St. Louis, 1998—2001; assoc. prof. U. Va., Dept. Anesthesiology, Charlottesville, 2001—. Grantee, NIH, 2000—. Mem.: Va. Soc. Anesthesiology (life), Assn. U. Anesthesiologists (life), Soc. for Neuroscience (life), Mo. Soc. Anesthesiologists (life), Am. Soc. Anesthesiologists (life). Achievements include patents for the role of NMDA antagonists in the management of chronic painful conditions. Avocations: piano, needlepoint, gardening. Office: U Va Dept Anesthesiology PO Box 800710 Charlottesville VA 22908-0710 Business E-Mail: vj3w@virginia.edu.

JEWELEWICZ, RAPHAEL, obstetrician, gynecologist, educator; b. Nowogrodek, Poland, Dec. 26, 1932; arrived in US, 1963; s. Chaim and Chaia (Tawricki) J.; m. Ronnie Oved, July 3, 1955; children: Rachel, Dov, Daniel, Dory. MD, Hebrew U., Jerusalem, 1961. Cert. Am. Bd. Ob-gyn. 1971, 89, reproductive endocrinology, 1974. Intern Hadassah Hebrew U. Hosp., Jerusalem; resident NYU Med. Ctr., Bellevue Hosp., NYC; assoc. prof. ob-gyn. Columbia U., NYC, 1975-92; prof. ob-gyn. SUNY, 1992—; chair. dept. ob-gyn. Memonides Medical Ctr., Bklyn. Bd. dirs. divsn. reproductive endocrinology Columbia U. Coll. Physicians and Surgeons, N.Y.C.; chmn. ob-gyn. Maimonides Med. Ctr.; prof. ob-gyn. SUNY, Bklyn. Author: Clinical Aspects of Cervical Incompetence, 1989, The Menstrual Cycle: Physiology, Reproductive Disorders and Infertility, 1993; editor ob-gyn. investigation: mem. editorial bd. several sci. jours.; contbr. over 100 articles to profl. jours. Mem. Am. Coll. Ob-gyn., Am. Coll. Surgeons, Am. Fertility Soc., Am. Gynecol. & Obstet. Soc., N.Y. Obstet. Soc., N.Y. Gynecol. Soc. (pres. 1994-95), Soc. for Gynecol. Jewish. Avocations: opera, ballet, theater, travel. Home: Church St Alpine NJ 07620 Office: Memonides Med Ctr Dept Ob-gyn 4802 10th Ave Brooklyn NY 11219-2844 Personal E-mail: ronijewel@msn.com.

JEWELL, MARK LAURENCE, plastic surgeon; b. Kansas City, Mo., Oct. 26, 1947; s. James Lemley and Martha (Bullock) Jewell; m. Mary Rita Lind, Nov. 30, 1975; children: Mark II, James, Hillary. BS in Zoology, U. Kans., 1969, MD, 1973; postgrad., UCLA, 1977, U. Tenn., 1979. Cert. Am. Bd. Plastic Surgery, 1981. Resident in surgery UCLA, 1973—76; fellow, burn surgery U. So. Calif., LA, 1976—77; resident, plastic surgery U. Tenn., Chattanooga, 1977—79; practice medicine specializing in plastic surgery Eugene, Oreg., 1979—; plastic surgeon Inamed Aesthetics; asst. clin. prof. plastic surgery Oreg. Health Sci. U., Portland. Pres. Aesthetic Surgery Jour.; contbr. articles to profl. jours. Lt. USNR, 1970—79. Recipient Rsch. award, Am. Soc. Clin. Pathologists, 1972, U. Kans. Sch. Medicine, 1973; Joyce Kaye Lectureship, 1998—2004. Mem.: Nat. Endowment for Plastic Surgery (gov.), Aesthetic Soc. Edn. and Rsch. Found. (treas.), Oreg. Soc. Plastic Surgery, Am. Soc. for Aesthetic Plastic Surgery (pres. 2005—06, Tiffany award 2003), Am. Med. Joggers Soc., Lane County Med. Soc., Oreg. Med. Assn., Am. Soc. Plastic Surgeons (former mem. bd. dirs.). Episcopalian. Avocations: helicopter skiing, marathons, art, cooking, computers. Office: 10 Coburg Rd Ste 300 Eugene OR 97401-7481 Office Phone: 541-683-3234. Office Fax: 541-683-8610. E-mail: mljmd@teleport.com.

JEYAKUMAR, SHANMUGAM MURUGAIHA, biochemist; b. India, Apr. 5, 1974; PhD, Nat. Inst. Nutrition, Osmania U., 2005. Scientist B Nat. Inst. Nutrition, Hyderabad, Andhra Pradesh, India, 2006—. Recipient Jr. Young Scientist award, Nutrition Soc. India; Internat. fellowship, Indian Coun. Med. Rsch., Jr. Rsch. fellowship, Nat. Inst. Nutrition-Indian Coun. Med. Rsch., Sr. Rsch. fellowship. Avocation: music. Office: National Inst Nutrition Jamai Hyderabad Andhra Pradesh 500 604 India Office Phone: 9104027017341. Personal E-mail: smjkumar@yahoo.com.

JEYAPALAN, SURIYA, neurooncologist; b. England; Neurology instr. Beth Israel Deaconess Med. Ctr. Office: Beth Israel Deaconess Medical Center Harvard Medical School 330 Brookline Ave TCC-867 Boston MA 02215 Office Phone: 617-667-1665. Office Fax: 617-667-1664.

JEZDINSKÝ, JAROSLAV, pharmacologist, consultant, educator, researcher; b. Dolni Cermna, Czech Republic, May 11, 1933; s. Karel Jezdinsky and Lidmila Jezdinska (Kuzelova); m. Vera Frimlova, June 15, 1963; 1 child, Hana Jezdinský Klesnasta; 1 child, Karolina Jezdinska-Hrbkova, Mgr. MD, Palacky U., Olomouc, Czech Republic, 1957; PhD, Czechoslovak Acad. Scis., 1968. House physician Dist. Hosp., Prostejov, Czech Republic, 1957—58; lectr. pharmacology Palacky U., Olomouc, 1958—60, asst. prof. pharmacology, 1961—89, assoc. prof. pharmacology, 1990—91, prof., head dept. pharmacology, 1991—99, process cons., 1999; head divsn. clin. pharmacology U. Hosp., 1991—2001. Fellow mem. ethical com. Med. Faculty and U. Hosp., 1991—. Editor: (sci. jour.) Clin. Pharmacology and Pharmacy in Czech, 1995—2002; co-author: (textbook) Basic and Applied Pharmacology in Czech, 2002, 2007; contbr. articles to profl. pubs. Mem.: Czech Pharmacology Soc. (hon.; Prague 1958, Hon. Membership 1993), Czech Med. Soc. J.E.Purkynje (hon.; Prague 1957, Hon. Membership 2006). Achievements include patents for a device for measuring a nociceptive reaction of laboratory animals. Home: Hranicni 5 Olomouc 77900 Czech Republic Office: Dept Pharmacology Fac Med Hnevotinska 3 Olomouc 77515 Czech Republic

JHANG, KYUNG-YOUNG, mechanical engineer, biotechnologist, educator; b. Seoul, Korea, Nov. 10, 1960; s. Ki-Yeoul Jhang and Byung-Ok So; m. Hyo-Sook Hwang; children: Jin-Ho, Hye-Jin. PhD, Tokyo Inst. Tech., 1991. Prof. Hanyang U., Seoul, Republic of Korea, 1992—; vis. prof. Johns Hopkins U., Balt., 1999—2000; rsch. assoc. Tokyo Inst. Tech., 1991—92. Author: (research) High-Order Correlation Analysis (Best Paper, 1992). Mgr. Reliability Analysis Rsch. Ctr., Seoul, 2002—04. Grantee, Korean Orgn. Sci. and Engring. Found., 1997—2000, Korean Ministry Edn., 1995—2000, Korean Ministry Industry and Commerce, 2002—, Korean Ministry Agr. and Forestry, 2001—04; scholar, Japanese Ministry Edn., 1987—91. Mem.: Japanese Soc. Nondestructive Inspection, Am. Soc. Nondestructive Testing, IEEE Ultrasonics, Ferroelectronics, and Frequency Control, Korean Soc. Mech. Engring. (life), Korean Soc. Nondestructive Testing (life). Achievements include patents for Ultrasonic Quality Evaluation System for Agricultural Product; research in Diagnosis of Blood Vessel using Ultrasonic Nonliear Effect; Health Monitoring Techniques using Ultrasound and Laser; Diagnosis of Soft Tissue using Nonlinear Propagation of Vibration; Reliability Evaluation Techniques using Ultrasonic Wave and Optical Technologies Machine Vision Techniques; Visualization of Velocity Field by using High Order Correlation Analysis; development of Nondestructive evaluation techniques using Nonlinear Ultrasonic Waves.

JHEON, SANGHOON, thoracic surgeon, medical educator, medical researcher; b. Daegu, Daegu, S. Korea, Nov. 14, 1959; s. Heewon and Sookhee Jheon; m. Hyunmin Lee, Apr. 12, 1987; children: Kevin, Tim. B, Kyungpook Nat. U., Daegu, 1984; MD, Ministry of Health and Welfare, Korea, 1984; M of Medicine, Keimyung U., Daegu, 1989; PhD, Keimyung U., Deagu, 1994. Diplomate Bd. Thoracic and Cardiovasc. Surgery Ministry Health and Welfare, Korea. Instr. Kyungpook Nat. U. Hosp., Daegu, 1994—95; asst. prof. Sch. Medicine Kyungpook Nat. U., Daegu, 1996—99, assoc. prof. Sch. Medicine, 2000; rsch. fellow Massachussets Gen. Hosp. and Harvard Med. Sch., Boston, 1997—98; assoc. prof. Cath. U. Daegu, 2001—02; assoc. prof. Coll. Medicine Seoul Nat. U., Republic of Korea, 2003—06; prof. Coll. Medicine Seoul Nat. U., 2007—; dir. respiratory ctr. Seoul Nat. U. Bundang Hosp., 2009—. Vis. surgeon Nat. Cancer Ctr., Tokyo, Meml. Sloan Kettering Cancer Ctr., NYC. Contbr. articles to profl. jours. Capt. Korean Army, 1990—93. Mem.: Korean Soc. Thoracic and Cardiovasc. Surgery, Internat. Assn. Heart and Lung Transplantation, Internat. Assn. Study Lung Cancer, Asian Thoracic Surg. Club. Office: Seoul Nat Univ Hosp Gumi-Dong Bundang 300 462-707 Seongnam Gyeonggi-do Republic of Korea Office Phone: 82-31-787-7133. Office Fax: +82-31-787-4050. Business E-Mail: jheon@snu.ac.kr.

JHUN, HYUNG-JOON, medical educator; b. Jeong-up City, Jeonrabuk-Do, Republic Of Korea, June 18, 1965; s. Yang-Kwon Jhun and Gong-Rye Lee; m. Young-Mi Seo, Nov. 11, 1995; 1 child, Min-Ki. MD, PhD, Seoul Nat. U., Republic of Korea. Lic. dr. Min. Health & Welfare, 1991. Asst. prof. dept. preventive medicine Gachon Med. Sch., Incheon, Republic of Korea, 2002—04; asst. prof. dept. occupl. & environ. medicine Hallym U. Coll. Medicine, Seoul, 2004—; clin. prof. dept. occupl. & environ. medicine Korea U. Coll. Medicine, Ansan, Kyeonggi-Do, Republic of Korea, 2007—. Mem.: Korean Soc. Occupl. & Environ. Medicine. Achievements include research in health of Korean atomic-bomb survivors and health promotion. Office: Korea Univ Coll Medicine Gojan-dong Danwon-Gu Kyeonggi-Do Ansan 425-707 Republic of Korea Office Fax: 82 31 412 5394. Personal E-mail: occenvmed@yahoo.co.kr. Business E-Mail: oemdoc21@yahoo.co.kr.

JI, HEE CHUNG, medical educator, researcher; s. Hyun Byung Ji and Dong Whan Lim; m. Young Hee Yoon; children: Hyung Gyu, Yun Ah. PhD, Chungnam Nat. U., Daejeon, 1997. Prof. U. Hawaii, Honolulu, 2001—05, rschr.; prof. Chungnam Nat. U., Daejeon, 2006. Sgt. MEDIC, 1988—90, Chungnam province. Decorated Comdr. award. Mem.: Korean Jour. Breeding (mem. 1991—). Avocation: fishing. Home: 104-502 Eunhasu Apt Dunsan-dong Seo-gu Chungnam Daejeon 302-120 Republic of Korea Office: Grassland & Flora Divsn Nat Inst Animal Sci Rural Devel Adminstrn 29 Sinbang-ri Seonghwan-eup Chungnam Cheonan 331-808 Republic of Korea Office Fax: 82-41-580-6779. Personal E-mail: cornhc@hanmail.net. Business E-Mail: cornhc@korea.kr. E-mail: cornhc@rda.go.kr.

JI, HO SEONG, engineering educator; b. South Korea, Apr. 20, 1960; BS, Pusan Nat. U., 1986, PhD, 2001. Rschr. RIMT at Pusan Nat. U., 2000—04, U. Tokyo, 2004—05; sr. rschr. POSTECH, 2005—08; asst. prof. Pusan Nat. U., 2008—. Recipient Best Paper awards, Cross Straits in Symposium. Mem.: Korean Soc. Med. Biol. and Engring., Korean Soc. Cardiology, Korea Soc. Mech. Engrs., WSEAS, European Soc. Biomechanics. Office: Sch Mech Engineering Jang Jeon 2 Dong Guem Jeong Gu Busan 609-735 Republic of Korea Office Fax: 82-51-518-2430. Business E-Mail: hsji@pusan.ac.kr.

JI, SEUNG-CHUL, research scientist; b. Jeju, June 28, 1971; D, Yeosu U., Republic of Korea, 2002. Asst. Yeosu U., 1998—99, lectr., 2003—03; sr. rschr. EOSIMGA Ltd., 2002—03, Nat. Fisheries R & D Inst., 2007; rschr. Fisheries Lab., Kinki U., Japan, 2004—07. Mem. Jour. Fisheries and Aquatic Sci., Aquaculture Sci., Fisheries Sci. Avocations: badminton, fishing, hiking. Office: Oedo 2-dong Jeju 690-192 Republic of Korea Office Fax: 82-64-743-5883. Business E-Mail: jsc0414@nfrdi.go.kr.

JI, ZHEN-LING, medical educator, department chairman; b. China, May 10, 1961; MD, SE U., 1982; PhD, Zhejiang U., 2005. Prof., chmn., dept. gen. surgery Zhongda Hosp. SE U., 1997—. Recipient Sci. and Tech. Progress award, Jiangsu Provincial Govt., Model Worker award, Taizhou City Govt., Outstanding Expert award, State Coun. China; Govt. grant. Mem.: European Soc. Digestive Surgery, Internat. Colon and Rectal Cancer Club, Chinese Med. Assn. Jiangsu Surg. Br., ASCRS, SAGES. Avocations: photography, travel. Office: 87 Ding Jia Qiao Nanjing Jiangsu 210009 China Office Fax: 86-25-83272011. E-mail: zlji@vip.sina.com.

JIA, ZHENG, chemistry professor; b. Harbin, July 8, 1972; PhD, Harbin Inst. Tech., 2004. Assoc. prof. Harbin Inst. Tech., 2006—. Vis. scholar Oxford U., Nat. Comm. Vis. Scholarship China. Mem.: Internat. Soc. Electrochemistry. Avocations: exercise, swimming, travel. Office: Harbin Inst Tech Rm 907 Sci Bldg 92 XiDaZhi St Harbin Heilongjiang 150001 China E-mail: jiazjiazjz@yahoo.com.cn.

JIA, ZHENQUAN, medical educator; b. China, Apr. 15, 1972; PhD, Va. Poly. Inst. & State U., 2006. Asst. prof. Edward Via Coll. Osteo. Medicine, 2009—. Grant, NIH. Mem.: Am. Soc. Nutrition, Soc. Free Radical Biology & Medicine, Soc. Neurosci., Soc. Toxicology. Office: 1861 Pratt Dr Rd Blacksburg VA 24060 Business E-Mail: zjia@t.edu.

JIANG, BING-HUA, science educator; arrived in U.S., 1991; s. Guilin Jiang and Yueying Zheng; m. Jenny Z. Zheng, Jan. 21, 1986; children: Lisa L., Rena Z. PhD, Miss. State U., 1994; BS in Tropical Crops, S. China U. Postdoctoral rsch. assoc. Johns Hopkins U. Sch. Medicine, Balt., 1994—97; rsch. assoc. Scripps Rsch. Inst., La Jolla, Calif., 1997—2000; asst. prof. cell signaling W.Va. U., Morgantown, 2000—. Mng. editor Frontiers in Bioscience, Albertson, NY, 2000—; prof. Chinese Acad. of Sci., Shanghai, 2003—. Contbr. articles to profl. jours. Grantee, Am. Heart Assn., Am. Cancer Soc., NIH, 2000—. Mem.: Am. Assn. for Cancer Rsch. (life). Achievements include patents in field. Office: Cancer Ctr W Virginia Univ 1801 Health Sciences South Morgantown WV 26506 E-mail: bhjiang@hsc.wvu.edu.

JIANG, CHING CHUAN, orthopedic surgeon, educator; b. Chang-Hwa, Taiwan, Republic of China, Aug. 5, 1951; s. Tsu-Tsuan and Lou I (Huang) J.; m. Carol Guey-Yue Chen; children: David Churng Wei, Gina Yi Jen. MD, Nat. Taiwan U., Taipei, 1977, PhD, 1989, MBA, 2002. Orthopaedic specialist King Fahad Hofuf (Saudi Arabia) Hosp., 1982-84; resident and chief resident dept. orthopaedic surgery Nat. Taiwan Univ. Hosp., Taipei, 1978-82, orthopaedic attending physician, 1984—; lectr. Nat. Taiwan U., Sch. Medicine, Taipei, 1985-89, assoc. prof., 1989-94, prof., 1994—; dir. Divsn. Sports Medicine Dept. Orthop. Surgery Nat. Taiwan U. Hosp., Taipei, 1995—2005, chmn. Dept. Orthop. Surgery, 2005—11. Chmn. dept. out-patient clinic, 1999-2005; pres. Arthroscopic Assn. Republic of China, Taipei, 1998-2000; vice gen. sec. Formosan Med. Assn., Taipei, 1996-2001, pres. Taiwan Orthop. Assn., 2008-10 Contbr. articles to profl. jours; editor: Jour. Arthroplasty, Tech. in Knee Surgery, Jour. Formosan

Med. Assn., BMC Musculosketletal Disorders. Mission leader Sino-Saudi Med. Mission, Hofuf, 1983-84. Recipient Medicine award Formosan Med. Assn., Taipei, 1990; Rsch. grantee Nat. Sci. Coun., Taipei, 1989-2006, Dept. of Health, Taipei, 1991-92, 95-96, 98-2003. Mem. Orthopaedic Assn. Republic of China (coun. mem. 1993-95, Best Article award 1994, 98), Orthopaedic Rsch. Soc., Am. Soc. Biomechanics Am. Orthopaedic Soc. Sports Medicine, Internat. Coll. Surgeons, Soc. Internat. de Chirurgie Orthopedique et de Traumatologie, Sports Medicine Assn. (gen. sec. 1993-95, 97-99, pres. 2005—07), Am. Assn. Hip and Knee Surgeons, Asian Insall Club (chmn. 2000—), Am. Orthop. Assn. Avocations: tennis, photography, travel. Home: No 2 9-F 192 Section 2 Nan-Chang Rd Taipei Taiwan Office: Nat Taiwan U Hosp 7 Chung-San South Rd Taipei 10016 Taiwan Office Phone: 886 2 23123456 ext. 65273.

JIANG, MING, medical educator; b. China, June 6, 1963; MD, Nantong Med. Coll., 1986; PhD, Shanghai Med. U., 1997. Rsch. asst. prof. Vanderbilt U. Med. Ctr., 2002—. Postdoc. fellow IGBMC, France, 1999—2002. Mem.: AACR. Office: A-1302 MCN 1161 21st Ave S Nashville TN 37232 Office Fax: 615-322-8990. Business E-Mail: ming.jiang.1@vanderbilt.edu.

JIANG, RULANG, biomedical researcher, educator; PhD, Wesleyan U., 1995. Assoc. prof. biomedical genetics Ctr. Oral Biology; assoc. prof. biology U. Rochester Med. Ctr., assoc. prof. dentistry. Office: University of Rochester Medical Center KMRB G-9633 601 Elmwood Ave Box 611 Rochester NY 14642 Office Phone: 585-273-1426, 585-273-1422. E-mail: rulang_jiang@urmc.rochester.edu.

JIANG, SHI-YUN, engineering educator; b. Guilin, Guangxi, China, Jan. 16, 1964; D, Huazhong U. Sci. & Tech., 2008. Prof., biotech. dept. Guangxi U. Tech., 2008—. Office: 268 Dong Huan Dadao Liuzhou Guangxi 545006 China

JIANG, WEIBO, agricultural studies educator; b. China, Apr. 18, 1963; PhD, Hebrew U., 1994. Prof. China Agrl. U., 1987—. Mem.: Inst. Food Technologists. Office: Hai-dian Qing Hua Dong Lu 17 Beijing 100083 China Business E-Mail: jwb@cau.edu.cn.

JIANG, WEN G., medical educator; b. Zhaoyuan, Shangdong, China, July 20, 1962; came to UK, 1989; s. Yuan X. and Meiying (Wan) J.; m. Ling Guoyan Guo, Oct. 26, 1987; children: David, Amy. M.B.B.Sc., Beijing Med. U., 1984; MD, U. Wales, 1995. Chief resident Beijing Med. U., 1987-89; rsch. fellow U. Wales Coll. Medicine, Cardiff, 1989-96, sr. rsch. fellow, 1996-97, sr. lectr., 1997—2003, reader surgery and tumor biology, 2003—04, prof. surgery and tumour biology, 2004—. Editor: Cancer Metastasis, 1999, Growth Factor and Receptor in Cancer Metastasis, 2001, Metastasis of Breast Cancer, 2007; exec. prodr.: (book series) Cancer Metastasis, Biology and Treatment; mem. editl. bd.: Internat. Jour. Molecular Medicine, Internat. Seminars of Surg. Oncology, Current Opinion in Oncology, Advances in Therapies, Current Oncology; contbr. articles to profl. jours. Brit. Coun. Vis. fellow, 1998. Mem. Am. Assn. for Cancer Rsch., Brit. Assn. for Cancer Rsch., European Assn. for Cancer Rsch. Achievements include patents in field. Avocations: reading, sports, travel. Office: Cardiff U Med Sch Heath Park Cardiff CF14 4XN Wales Office Phone: 44 (0) 29-20-74-2895. E-mail: jiangw@cf.ac.uk.

JIANG, ZHI-GANG, neuroscientist; b. Changchun, Jilin, China; s. Hong Jiang and Zhujun Gao; m. Jie Wang, 1987; 1 child, Hao. MD, Norman Bethune U. Med. Scis., Changchun, China, 1982, MSc, 1987; PhD, U. Glasgow, Scotland, 1994. Postdoc. rschr. Ohio State U. Med. Ctr., Columbus, 1994—97; rsch. fellow lab. neurotoxicology NIMH, NIH, Bethesda, Md., 1997—2002; acting chief, lab. cell biology China Rehab. Rsch. Ctr., Beijing, 1987—91; dir., neurodegenerative diseases Panacea Pharm., Inc., Gaithersburg, Md., 2002—09; adj. prof. Inner Mongolia U. Nationalities, China, 2008—; contractor specialist Lab. Molecular Medicine & Virology NINDS NIH, 2009—. Editor: Frontiers in Biosciences, 2008—, Current Neurobiology, 2009—; reviewer Alzheimer's Assn. jour., 2008, Nat. Natural Found. China, 2008; contbr. sci. reports to profl. jours. Recipient Found. award, Henry Lester Trust, 1991, scholar, U. Glasgow, 1992—94, Intramural Rsch. Tng. award, NIMH, NIH, 1997—2000, Spl. Act Svc. award, 2002, 2006; grantee, Nat. Inst. Neurol. Disorders and Stroke, NIH, 2004, Nat. Lung, Heart and Blood Inst., NIH, 2006—08. Mem.: Soc. Neurosci. Achievements include patents for novel neuroprotectant PAN-811, which efficiently suppress ischemic neurodegeneration; five patens pending in field. Avocations: drawing, music, travel, ping pong/table tennis, martial arts. Office: Bldg 10 Rm 3B07 10 Ctr Dr Bethesda MD 20892-1296 Office Phone: 301-594-3248. Office Fax: 240-465-0198. Personal E-mail: zgjiang2002@yahoo.com. Business E-Mail: zgjiang@mail.nih.gov.

JIANG, ZHIYONG, medical educator; b. Hangzhou, Zhejiang, China, Aug. 25, 1974; PhD, Zhejiang U., 2004. Prof. Henan U., 2009. Rsch. grant, Nat. Natural Sci. Found. China, Excellent Youth Found., Henan Sci. Com., Internat. Cooperation Found., Henan Sci. Com. Avocations: basketball, ping pong/table tennis. Office: Jinming Campus Henan University Kaifeng Henan 475004 China Business E-Mail: chmjzy@henu.edu.cn.

JIAN-JUN, LI, medical educator; b. Wuhan, China, Aug. 1, 1957; s. Li Chang-Qing and Chen Hui-Yun; m. Fang Chun-Hong; 1 child, Li Hao. MD, Kyushu U., Fukuoka, 1995, PhD. Cert. in nat. China, 1957. Prof. Wuhan U. Hosp., 1997—2003, assoc. dir.; prof. Dept. Cardiology, Beijing, 2004—08, assoc. dir. Consulting nat. healthy bur. Nat. Healthy Bur., Beijing, 2004—08. Contbr. articles to profl. sci. jours. Disease rsch. and prevention Chinese Med. Assn., China, 1997—2008. Recipient Nat. Sci. award, 2000. Mem.: Chines Cardiovasc. Assn. Office: Fu Wai Hosp CAMS Bei Li Shi Rd 167 Beijing 100037 China Personal E-mail: lijnjn@yahoo.com.cn.

JIBRIN, ISMAIL MUSA, hospital administrator; b. Nigeria, Dec. 12, 1966; MD, Ahmadu Bello U., Zaria, Nigeria, 1990; PG Dip (ID), London Sch. Hygiene & Tropical Medicine, 2001. Sr. med. officer Jan Med. Clinic, Makkah, Saudi Arabia, 1995—2004; resident St. Agnes Healthcare, Balt., 2004—07; hospitalist, faculty, chief resident Yale Griffin Hosp., Derby, Conn., 2007—08; hospitalist Apogee Physicians, 2008—10; hospitalist, site med. dir. Verde Valley Med. Ctr., Cottonwood, Ariz., 2010—. Asst. med. dir. Apogee Physicians, Phoenix, 2007—10; clin. asst. prof. medicine Mid Western U., Glendale, 2010. Fellow: ACP; mem.: London Sch. Hygiene & Tropical Medicine Alumni, Soc. Hosp. Medicine. Avocations: travel, computers. Office: 269 S Candy Ln Divsn Hosp Cottonwood AZ 86325 Personal E-mail: imjibrin@yahoo.com.

JIBUIKE, OKECHUKWU OGBONNA, emergency physician, surgeon; b. Umuahia -Ibeku, Abia State, Nigeria, Dec. 17, 1960; s. Jonah Ogbonna and Cecelia Janet Jibuike; m. Louisa Onyenonachi Ononiwu, Apr. 3, 1994; children: Chimaobi Fortune, Adaeze Blessing, Chioma Joy. MBBS, U. Nigeria, 1987; diploma, Royal Coll. Surgeons, Edinburgh, 1996, U. Glamorgan, 2001. Cert. pediatric advanced life support Resuscitation Coun. UK, 1997, advanced life support provider 1998, advanced trauma life support 1998, diplomate Am. Bd. Emergency Medicine, 2001, Royal Coll. Surgeons, Edinburgh. Rotating ho. officer U. Port Harcourt Tchg. Hosp., Port Harcourt, Nigeria, 1988; resident Dr. gen. medicine St. Mary's Hosp., Ihiala, Nigeria, 1989; chief resident Dr. gen. medicine St. Patrick's Hosp., Port Harcourt, Nigeria, 1990—92; sr. ho. officer gen. surgery Sconthrope Gen. Hosp., England, 1993; rotating sr. ho. officer in surg. specialties Scarborough (Eng.) Hosp., 1993—96; specialist registrar in emergency medicine Morriston Hosp., Swansea, Wales, 2001—02, U. Hosp. of Wales, Cardiff, Wales, 2000—04. Contbr. articles to profl. jours. (First Prize award for essay, 1985). Recipient Fed. Merit award, Fed. Republic of Nigeria, 1986. Fellow: Royal Coll. Surgeons, Royal Soc. Medicine; mem.: Brit. Med. Assn., Nigerian med. Assn., Brit. Assn. Accident and Emergency Medicine, Am. Coll. Emergency Medicine. Office: Univ Hosp Wales Heath Park Cardiff CF14 4XW Wales E-mail: ojibuike@hotmail.com.

JIE, YOU, physician; b. Shandong, China, July 4, 1962; MD, Shanghai U. Traditional Chinese Medicine, 2004. Physician, tumor dept. Shanghai Longhua Hosp., 1984—, bd. dirs., 2005—. Rsch. grant, Chinese Sci. Found., Shanghai Sci. Com. Avocations: music, travel. Home: 22-101 125 Nong Zhanghong Rd Shanghai 200032 China Personal E-mail: yooujieyj@163.com.

JILHEWAR, ASHOK, gastroenterologist; b. Nanded, Maharashtra, India, Jan. 30, 1947; arrived in US, 1977, naturalized, 1987; BS, MB, Marathwada U., 1970; MD, Govt. Med. Coll., Aurangabad, 1970. Diplomate Am. Bd. Internal Medicine, Am. Bd. Gastroenterology, Am. Bd. Geriatric Medicine, Am. Bd. Quality Assurance and Utilization Rev. Physicians. Rotating intern Med. Coll. Hosp., Aurangabad, India, 1968—70; resident St. Luke's Hosp. and Royal infirmary, Huddersfeild, Bolton, England, 1970—72; med. registrar internal medicine Gen. Hosp., Sligo, Ireland, 1973—77; chief resident PG1 and internal medicine U. Health Scis.-Chgo. Med. Sch. and VA Hosp., 1977—79; clin. instr. U. Health Scis.-Chgo. Med. Sch., 1978—79; fellow in gastroenterology Michael Reese Hosp., Chgo., 1980—81; mem. exec. com. Meth. Hosp., Chgo., 1985—90, chmn. med. dept., 1988—90; mem. staff dept. medicine Grant Hosp., Chgo., 1986—. Lectr. preventive and social medicine Med. Coll., Aurangabad, 1970; mem. exec. com. Meth. Hosp. Chgo., 1985-90, v.p. med. staff, 1987-88, treas., sec. 1985-87, chmn. dept. medicine, 1988-90; med. dir. approved home for intermediate care nursing home, 1986-95; med. advisor Office Hearings and Appeals, HHS, 1985—; med. reviewer Ill. Med. Rev. Orgn., 1993—, Crescent Cmty. Found. for Med. Care, 1994—. Fellow Royal Coll. Physicians Can., Am. Coll. Internat. Physicians; mem. AMA, Am. Gastroenterol. Assn., Royal Coll. Physicians U.K., Royal Coll. Physicians Ireland, Ill. State Med. Assn., Chgo. Med. Soc. (PRO study com., fee mediation subcom. 1992) Office: North Park Stomach Clinic 5393 N Milwaukee Ave Chicago IL 60630-1251 Office Phone: 773-775-9500. Personal E-mail: ajilhewar@hotmail.com.

JIMBA, MASAMINE, medical educator, researcher; b. Omagoshi, Aomori, Japan, Nov. 17, 1957; s. Kei Jimba; m. Kazuko Kondo, Mar. 30, 1986; children: Koji, Shinji. MD, Hamamatsu U. Sch. Medicine, Shizuoka, Japan, 1979—85, PhD, 1987—95; MPH, Nat. Inst. Pub. Health, Tokyo, 1987—89. Resident, physician Takayama Red Cross Hosp., Takayama, Gifu, Japan, 1985—87; rsch. assoc. Nat. Inst. of Pub. Health, Minato-ku, Tokyo, Japan, 1987—94; vis. scientist Harvard Sch. of Pub. Health, Boston, 1991—92; cons. WHO, Geneve, Switzerland, 1994—96; pub. health expert Japan Internat. Cooperation Agy., Shibuya-ku, Tokyo, Japan, 1996—2001; takemi rsch. fellow Harvard Sch. of Pub. Health, Boston, 2001—02; prof. Grad. Sch. Medicine, U. Tokyo, Bunkyo-ku. Health coord. for the Gaza Strip WHO, Gaza, Gaza Strip, 1994—95, health coord. for the Gaza Strip and West Bank, Jerusalem, 1995—96; team leader of the Nepal Sch. and Cmty. Health Project Japan Internat. Cooperation Agy. Nepal Office, Kathmandu, Nepal, 1996—2001. Author: (non document book) Palestinian days, (academic journals) Lancet, Tropical Doctor, Tropical Medicine and International Health, etc. Mem. Campaign for Palestinian children, Shinjuku-ku, Tokyo, Japan, 1994—2003, Japan Overseas Christian Med. Coop. Svc., Shinjuku-ku, Tokyo, Japan, 1983—2005, Asian Health Inst., Nisshin, Aichi, Japan, 1985—2005. Fellow Takemi program at Harvard Sch. of Pub. Health, Japan Med. Assn., 2001—02; scholar Long-term studies in the overseas, Sci. and Tech. Agy., Japan, 1991—92. Mem.: Japan Assn. for Internat. Health (tokyo 1986—2005). Achievements include research in HIV/AIDS in Nepal, Traditional healers in Nepal, Health Promotion in Nepal; consultancy in making Nat. Sch. Health Policy in Lao PDR. Office: Univ Tokyo School of Medicine 7-3-1 Hongo Tokyo Bunkyo-ku 113-0033 Japan Office Fax: +81-3-5841-3422.

JIMENEZ, JOSEPH, pharmaceutical company executive; BA, Stanford U., 1982; MBA, U. Calif., Berkeley, 1984. With Clorox Co.; held positions including pres. of two divisions ConAgra Grocery Products; pres., CEO H.J. Heinz Co., N.Am., 1998—2002; pres, CEO H.J. Heinz Co., Europe, 2002—06; non-exec. dir. AstraZeneca PLC, 2002—07; advisor Blackstone Group; head consumer health divsn. Novartis AG, Basel, Switzerland, 2007, head pharmaceuticals divsn., 2007—10; mem. exec. com. Novartis; CEO Novartis Pharma AG, Basel, Switzerland, 2010—. Bd. dirs. Colgate-Palmolive. Office: Novartis International AG Novartis Campus Forum 1 4002 Basel Switzerland Office Phone: 41 61 324 0770. Office Fax: 41 61 324 6677. Business E-Mail: joe.jimenez@novartis.com. *

JIMÉNEZ, RAIMUNDO, optometrist, educator; b. Granada, Spain, Dec. 20, 1965; Grad., U. Granada, 1989, PhD, 2000. Prof. in biology U. Granada, 1983—89, prof., rschr. in optometry, 1990—93. Avocation: sports. Office: Facultad de Ciencias Fuentenueva Granada 18071 Spain Office Fax: 958243387. Business E-Mail: raimundo@ugr.es.

JIMENEZ, SERGIO A., internist, educator, rheumatologist; b. Cuzco, Peru, Feb. 21, 1942; s. Julio Alexandre and Bertha Margarite (Astete) J. BS, Nat. U. San Marcos, Lima, Peru, 1959, MD, 1964; MS, U. Pa., 1984. Diplomate Am. Bd. Internal Medicine. Asst. prof. dept. medicine U. Pa., Phila., 1974-80, asst. prof. dept. orthop. surgery, 1978-80, assoc. prof. medicine and orthop. surgery, 1980-86, prof., 1986-87; prof. medicine, dir. rheumatology rsch. Thomas Jefferson U., Phila., 1987-92, prof. biochemistry and molecular biology, 1987—, dir. divsn. rheumatology, 1992—2007, Dorrance H. Hamilton prof. medicine, 1992—2007, vice-chmn. rsch. dept. medicine, 1999—2003; dir. divsn. connective tissue diseases, co-dir. Jefferson Inst. Molecular Medicine, 2007—. Hon. adj. fellow Benjamin Franklin Inst., Phila., 1981-85; chmn. med. adv. bd. Scleroderma Rsch. Found., Mid-Atlantic Chpt., 1979—; mem. rsch. scholarships com., Ea. Pa. chpt. Arthritis Found., 1981-84; mem. med./sci. bd. Scleroderma Fedn., 1994—; mem. Nat. Inst. Health Gen. Medicine A Study Sect., 1990-94, mem. spl. rev. com., 1995-2000; mem. NIH Peer Review Oversight Group, 1998-2000; bd. sci. councellors Nat. Inst. Arthritis Musculoskeletal Diseases, NIH, 1999-2000; acting chmn., bd. councellors Nat. Inst. Arthritis Musculoskeletal Diseases NIH, 2000-02; chmn. bd. sci. councellors Nat. Inst. Arthritis Musculoskeletal Disease, NIH, 2002-05. Author over 300 articles to med. jours., 515 abstracts in procs. worldwide sci. jours., 97 editls., revs., and chpts. to jours. and books. Bd. dirs. Washington Square West Civic Assn., Phila., 1978-82, v.p., 1981-82, trustee, 1988—; mem. Phila. Hispanic C. of C., 1990—. Capt. Peruvian Army Res., 1964-65. Recipient Gerald P. Rodnan award for excellence in scleroderma rsch., U. Pitts., 1986, Joseph Lee Hollander award for excellence in rheumatology Ea. Pa. Arthritis Found., 2000,Hero award, Arthritis Found., 2000, Basic Rsch. award, Osteoarthritis Rsch. Internat., 2005. Master Am. Coll. Rheumatology; fellow Soc. for Molecular Medicine; mem. Am. Soc. Biol. Chemistry and Molecular Biology, Osteoarthritis Rsch. Soc. (exec. bd. 1994—, pres.-elect 1997-2000, pres. 2000-02), Internat. Soc. for Matrix Biology (founding mem.), Am. Soc. Matrix Biology; fellow RCP (Eng.). Republican. Roman Catholic. Avocations: sculpture, opera, archaeology. Home: 900 Spruce St Philadelphia PA 19107-6131 Office: Thomas Jefferson Univ 233 S 10th St Ste 509 Philadelphia PA 19107-5541 Office Phone: 215-503-5042.

JIMENEZ-HEFFERNAN, JOSE ANTONIO, pathologist; b. NYC, Apr. 6, 1966; arrived in Spain, 1969; s. Jose Antonio Jimenez and Margaret Heffernan; m. Gloria Del Peso, June 4, 1999; children: Blanca, Gloria. Degree in medicine, Faculty Medicine, Cordoba, Spain, 1991. Diplomate European Bd. Pathology. Pathologist Hosp. La Paz, Madrid, 1993-96, staff pathologist, 1997, Hosp. La Zarzuela, Madrid, 1998-99, Hosp. Gral, Guadalajara, Spain, 2000—. Asst. prof. U. Altonso X, Madrid, 1998—2000, U., Alcala, Spain, 2000—; cons. pathologist Hosp. La Zarzuela, Madrid, 2000—. Contbr. articles to profl. jours. Mem.: Royal Coll. Pathologists. Achievements include research in cytopathology. Office: Hosp Universitario Donantes de Sangre 19002 Guadalajara Spain E mail: jjheffernan@yahoo.com

JIMENEZ-QUEVEDO, PILAR, cardiologist; b. Madrid, Sept. 22, 1973; MD, Navarra U., PhD, 1997; MD, Computense U., 2008. Interventional cardiologist Hosp. Clin. San Carlos, 2006—. Mem.: European Soc. Cardiology, Spanish Soc. Cardiology. Avocations: music, sports. Office: Hosp Clinico San Carlos Martin la Madrid 28040 Spain Office Fax: 34913303289. Business E-Mail: patrop@telefonica.net.

JIMENEZ-VAZQUEZ, OSCAR HUMBERTO, neurosurgeon, researcher; s. Oscar Humberto Jimenez-Sosa and Alicia Vazquez-Acevedo; m. Norma Enriqueta Nagore-Robles, July 6, 1979; children: Norma Jimenez-Nagore, Oscar Jimenez-Nagore. MD, La Salle Med. Sch., Mexico City, 1979. Cert. neurosurgeon Nat. Health Svc., 1986. Jr. staff in neurosurgery Oil Co., Mexico City, 1986—87; staff neurosurgeon and rschr. State Health Svc., Morelia, Michoacan, Mexico, 1989—. Lectr. in neuroscience State U., Morelia, 2000—. Fellow, U. London, 1986—89. Mem.: State Neuroscience Assn. (life). Avocations: travel, photography, crafts. Office: Health Service Hospitales # 235 58230 Morelia MICH Mexico Business E-Mail: ohjv@yahoo.com.mx.

JIN, GUOHUA, medical educator; b. Nantong, Jiangsu, China, Oct. 1, 1947; PhD, Southern Med. U., 1997. Prof. dept anatomy Nantong U., 1982—. Rsch. grant, Nat. Natural Sci. Found. China. Avocation: writing. Office: Nantong University 19 Qixiu Rd Nantong Jiangsu 226001 China Office Fax: 86-513-85051718. Business E-Mail: jguohua@ntu.edu.cn.

JIN, HOON, plastic surgeon; b. Seoul, Republic of Korea, Dec. 1, 1966; s. Soo Il Jin and Young Jo Choi; m. Youn Jung Shin, Nov. 2, 1996; 1 child, Se Eun. PhD, Yonsie U., Seoul, 1999. Diplomate South Korean Bd. Plastic Surgery. Dir. Dept. of Plastic Surgery of Daejeon Mil. Hosp., Daejeon, Korea (South), 1996—99, Bon Plastic Surgery Clinic, Sungnam-shi, Republic of Korea, 1999—2000, BK Plastic Surgery Clinic, Seoul, 2000—07; clin. prof. Inje U. Med. Coll., Busan, Republic of Korea, 2000—, Ye Plastic Surgery Clinic, Seoul, 2008—11, IDEA Plastic Surgery Clinic, Seoul, 2011—. Bd. dirs. Plastic Surgeon Orthognathic Initiatives, Seoul, 2003—; dir. Workshop on Facial Contouring Surgeries, Seoul, Republic of Korea, 2004—. Contbr. articles to profl. jours. Violist Drs.' Quartet, Seoul, 2003—; violinist, violist Korean Amateur Festival Ensemble, Seoul, 1990—; violist Made For Quartet, Seoul, 2000. Capt. Republic of Korea Army, 1996—99. Home: 203-1202 Olympic Family Town Apartment Munjung-dong, Songpa-gu, Seoul 138-202 Republic of Korea Office: IDEA Plastic Surgeon Clinic Daekwang Bldg 27 3-15 Nonhyum dong Goadnam-gu Seoul 135 010 Republic of Korea Office Phone: 82-2-541-9500, 82-2-1600-0602. Office Fax: 82-2-6200-5200. Personal E-mail: jinhoon@mac.com. Business E-Mail: jinhoonps@hotmail.com, jinhoon@me.com.

JIN, JONG-YOUL, medical educator; b. Chil-Seo, Ham-an, Korea, Sept. 15, 1958; s. Jin Pan-Seok and Joo Jung-Soon; m. Kim Ki-Sook; children: Jin Joon-Ho, Jin Hey-Young. MD, Cath. U. Korea, Seoul, 1983, PhD, 1994. Cert. med. dr. Ministry of Health and Welfare, Korea, specialist in internal medicine Ministry of Health and Welfare, Korea, subspecialist in hemato-oncology Korean Assn. Internal Medicine. Intern St. Mary's Hosp., Seoul, 1983—84, resident in internal medicine, 1983—87, fellow, 1991—92, Kang-Nam St. Mary's Hosp., Seoul, 1990—91; instr. Dae-Jun St. Mary's Hosp., Cath. U. of Korea, Dae-Jun, 1992—93, Holy Family Hosp., Cath. U. of Korea, Bucheon, 1993—94, asst. prof., 1994—97, assoc. prof., 1997—2002, prof., 2002—; sr. registrar, vis. rsch. scientist St.George's Hosp. Med. Sch.,

U. London, 1995—96. Dir. hematology-oncology Bucheon St. Mary's Hosp., Cath. U. Korea, 1992—. Capt. Korean mil., 1987—91. Recipient Best Prof. award, Cath. U. of Korea, 2003; scholar, Ministry Sci. and Tech. Korea and Fgn. and Commonwealth Office, UK, 1995. Mem.: Korean Cancer Assn. (life), Korean Soc. Hematology (life), Korean Assn. Internal Medicine (life Acad. awarad 1995, Best Jour. award 1995, Acad. awarad 1996), Korean Med. Assn. (life Best Jour. award). Roman Catholic. Home: #512-501 Mok-Dong Yang-Chun Seoul 158-050 Republic of Korea Office: Bucheon St Mary's Hosp Sosa Wonmi Bucheon 420-717 Republic of Korea Office Fax: 82-2-340-2669.

JIN, PENGFEI, pharmacist; b. Zhejiang, China, Dec. 12, 1978; PhD, Shenyang Pharm. U., 2005. Dean drug QC Beijing Hosp., 2005—. Office: #1 Dahua Rd Dongcheng Dist Beijing 100730 China Business E-Mail: j790101@sohu.com.

JIN, SUNG-CHUL, physician, educator; b. Seoul, Aug. 17, 1974; MD, Korea U., 2001, MS, 2006. Resident Mokdong Hosp., Ewha Med. Ctr., 2002—06, clin. fellow, 2006—07, Asan Med. Ctr., 2007—09, Seoul Nat. U., Bundang Hosp., 2009—10; asst. prof. Inje U. Coll. Medicine, Haeundae Paik Hosp., 2010—. Editor Jour. Neurology Rsch., 2011, Jour. Korean Soc. Cerebrovas. Surgeons, 2010; reivewer Jour. Korean Med. Sci., 2010. Mem.: Korean Soc. Interventional Neuroradiology, Korean Soc. Cerebrovascular Surgery, Korean Neurosurg. Soc. Office: 1435 Jwa 4-dong Busan Haeundae 612-862 Republic of Korea E-mail: kusmal@hanmail.net.

JIN, SUNG-HO, surgeon; b. Pyeongtaek, GyeongGi-Do, June 2, 1971; MD, Sch. Medicine, Ajou U., Suwon, Republic of Korea, 1997; MS, Grad. Sch. Medicine, Ajou U., Suwon, Republic of Korea, 2004. Pub. health physician Republic of Korea Army, 1997—2000; intern Ajou U. Hosp., Republic of Korea, 2000—01, residency, dept. surgery, 2001—05, fellow, upper gastrointestinal, laparoscopic surgery divsn. dept. surgery, 2005—06; surg. oncologist, divsn. gastric cancer dept. surgery Korea Cancer Ctr. Hosp., Korea Inst. Radiol. & Med. Scis., 2006—. Sr. rsch. engr., translational rsch. dept. Rsch. Inst. Radiol. & Med. Scis., Korea Inst. Radiol. & Med. Scis., 2011. Mem.: Korean Surg. Soc., Korean Soc. Peritoneal Surface Malignancy, Korean Soc. Clin. Oncology, Internat. Gastric Cancer Assn., Korean Gastric Cancer Assn. Avocations: reading, soccer, snorkeling. Office: 75 Nowon-gil Nowon-Gu Seoul 139-606 Republic of Korea Office Fax: 82-2-970-2419. E-mail: shjin@kcch.re.kr.

JIN, XIAOTAO, medical educator; b. China, Nov. 24, 1959; PhD, Boston Coll., 1996. Instr. Emory U., 2002—. Pioneer fellowship, Salk Inst., 2000—01. Home: 710 Potters Bar Ln Suwanee GA 30024 Home Fax: 404-727-7306. Business E-Mail: xjin@rmy.emory.edu.

JIN, YONG-JIU, medical educator; b. Jiangsu, China, July 4, 1944; PhD, U. Calif., Berkeley, 1987. Instr. Dana-Farber Cancer Inst., Havard Med. Sch., 1988—99; asst. prof. NYU, Med. Sch., 2000—07, Mt. Sinai Med. Sch., 2007—. Home: 22 Melendy Ave Watertown MA 02472 Business E-Mail: yong-jiu.jin@mssm.edu.

JIN, YOUNG-HO, medical educator; b. Jeonju, Jeonbuk, Sept. 17, 1960; s. Jin Soo-Dong and Cha Nam-Soon; m. Kim Kyoung-Suk; children: Jin Hyonseo, Jin Yunseo. MD, Chonbuk Nat. U., Jeonju, Republic of Korea, 1985, M, 1988; PhD, Chungbuk Nat. U., Cheongju, 2001. Cert. in anesthesiology & pain medicine Korean Soc. Anesthesiologists, 1989, in emergency medicine Korean Soc. Emergency Medicine, 2000, in critical care medicine Korean Soc. Critical Care Medicine, 2009. Resident Chonbuk Nat. U. Hosp., 1985—89, clin. fellow, 1995—96, prof., 1996—, dir., 2004—. Chmn., exam. com. Korean Soc. Emergency Medicine, Seoul, Republic of Korea, 2005—07, chmn., resident tng. com., 2007—09, chmn., edn. com., 2009—. Contbr. scientific papers (young investigator award, 2008). Chief, sci sect. Rschr. Future Soc., Jeonju, 2003. Lt. Kunsan Airbase, 1989—92. Christian Ch. Home: 202-1303 Ctrl Pk Apt Jeonju Jeonbuk 561-300 Republic of Korea Office: Chonbuk Nat Univ Hosp 634-18 Keumam-Dong 561-712 Jeonju Jeonbuk Republic of Korea Office Fax: 82-63-250-1075. Business E-Mail: emjin@chonbuk.ac.kr, emjin@jnbu.ac.kr.

JINDADAMRONGWECH, SUMALEE, medical educator; b. Surin, Thailand, Apr. 26, 1963; BS in Med. Tech., Chiang Mai U., Thailand, 1983; PhD, Mahidol U., Thailand, 2005. Lectr. faculty medicine Srinakharinwirot U., Thailand, 1993—94; med. technologist Faculty Medicine, Ramathibodi Hosp., Mahidol U., 1994—2007, lectr., 2007—. Rsch. grant, Mahidol U., 2008—11, Ramathibodi Hosp. Mem.: Assn. Med. Technologists Thailand. Office: Rama VI Rd Bangkok 10400 Thailand Business E-Mail: tesjd@mahidol.ac.th.

JING, ZHI-CHENG, pulmonologist, educator; b. Wannan, Anhui, China, Aug. 4, 1971; s. Ke-Qin Jing and Dai-Fen Wang; m. Zhi-Yan Han; 1 child, Yue-Qian. MD, Pekin Union Med. Coll., Beijing, 1998. Cert. Cardiologist Ministry of Health China, 1999. Attending physician Fu Wai Hosp., Beijing, 2006—08; head dept. pulmonary circulation Shanghai Pulmonary Hosp., 2008—. Dir. Chinese Pulmonary Hypertension Assn., Beijing, 2005, Shanghai, 2005. Recipient Sci. Star, Beijing; fellowship, Govt. Mem.: PHA. Avocations: travel, running, reading, music, films. Office: Shanghai Pulmonary Hosp 507 Zhengmin Rd Shanghai 200433 China Office Fax: 86-21-55662767. Personal E-mail: jingzhicheng@gmail.com.

JINGA, MARIANA R., gastroenterologist; b. Stefanesti, Arges, Romania, Feb. 1, 1963; d. Radu I. and Stela S. Stefan; m. Viorel G. Jinga, Apr. 20, 1985; 1 child, Oana-Andreea. MD, Univ. Medicine and Pharmacy, Bucharest, Romania, 1988; specialization in internal medicine, 1994, specialization in ultrasonography, 1996, specialization in gastroenterology, 1999, specialization in digestive endoscopy, 2000, PhD, 2000. Clin. practice in medicine Ctrl. Clin. Emergency Mil. Hosp., Bucharest, 1988—90, specialist in internal medicine, rschr., 1994—96, specialist in internal medicine, gastroenterologist 2d Internal Medicine and Gastroenterology Clinic, 1996—2002; resident in internal medicine, rschr. Prof. Dr. N. Gh. Lupu Inst., Army Ctr. Med. Rsch., Bucharest, 1990—94. Maj., 2000—02, Bucharest, Romania. Mem.: Romanian Soc. Gastrointestinal Endoscopy, Romanian Soc. Ultrasound in Medicine and Biology, Romanian Soc. Gastroenterology, Am. Gastroent. Assn., Balkanic Med. Union, European Assn. Gastroenterology and Endoscopy, Internat. Assn. Surgeons and Gastroenterologists, European Assn. Study of Liver Disease, Am. Soc. Gastrointestinal Endoscopy. Home: PO BOX 4-16 13 Decebal Av Bl S15 Sc 2 Ap 31 743313 Bucharest Sector 3 Romania Office: Ctrl Clin Mil Emergency Hosp PO Box 4-16 88 Mircea Vulcanescu St Sector 1 Bucharest Romania Home Phone: +40213236475. E-mail: mariana_jinga@hotmail.com.

JIN HYEOK, JEONG, otolaryngologist, educator; b. Korea, Nov. 1, 1970; MD, Hanyang U., Seoul, Republic of Korea, 1996, PhD, 2005. Physician dept. otolaryngology-head and neck surgery Hanyang U. Guri Hosp., 2003—; assoc. prof. dept. otolaryngology Hanyang U., Sch. Medicine, 2011—. Mem.: Korean Soc. Facial Plastic and Reconstructive Surgery, Korean Acadey Asthma, Allergy and Clin. Immunology, Korean Soc. Rhinology, Korean Soc. Otorhinolaryngology - Head and Neck Surgery. Office: 249-1 Hanyang University Guri Hosp Gyomun Guri Gyunggi 471-701 Republic of Korea Office Fax: 82-31-566-4884. Business E-Mail: ent@hanyang.ac.kr.

JINNO, SATOSHI, dental educator; b. Aichi, Japan, Dec. 4, 1979; Degree in Periodontology Dentistry; PhD, Aichi Gakuin U., 2008. Affiliate rschr. MIT, 2007; postdoc. fellow Brigham and Women's Hosp., 2007; instr. Aichi Gakuin U. Sch. Dentistry, 2008—. Office: 1-100 Kusumoto-cho Chikusa-ku Nagoya Aichi 464-8650 Japan Business E-Mail: sjin@sdent.agu.ac.jp.

JINXIANG, FU, hematologist, educator; b. Suzhou, Oct. 18, 1960; MD, Suzhou Med Coll., 1984; PhD, Soochow U., 2001. Chair dept. hematology, prof., chief physician No.2 Affiliated Hosp. Soochow U., 2001, prof., 2005. Mem.: Chinese Med. Assn. Office: No 2 Affiliate Hosp Soochow University Hematology Dept Suzhou Jiangsu 215004 China Office Fax: 086-512-67784066. Business E-Mail: uufjxly@public1.sz.js.cn.

JIQUN, CAI, pharmacologist, educator; b. Liaoning, China, Aug. 28, 1949; MD, China Med. U., 1973; PhD, Niigata U., Japan, 1991. Prof. China Med. U., 2000—. Head Sch. Pharm. Sci., 2003. Recipient PBL Tchg. award. Mem.: Chinese Pharmacology Soc. Avocation: music. Home: 92 Bei-er Rd Heping Dist Shenyang Liaoning 110001 China Home Fax: 86-24-23255471. E-mail: jqcai@mail.cmu.edu.cn.

JIRASIRITHAM, SOPON, surgeon, educator; s. Pote Jirasiritham; m. Siriwan Umpornpukdi, Aug. 12, 1982; children: Jakrapan, Pachariya Kate, Jakrapong, Surapat. BSc, Mahidol U., Bangkok, 1975, MD, 1977, Diploma in Clin. Sci., 1979. Diploma in surgery. Bd. Thai Med. Coun., 1981, cert. in vascular surgery 2005. Gen. and vascular surgeon Faculty Medicine Ramathibodi Hosp. Mahidol U., 1985—, transplantation surgeon, 1986—, prof., surgery, 2005—. Pres. Thai Transplantation Soc., Bangkok, 2004—, Thai Vascular Assn., Bangkok, 2004—, Asian Soc. Vascular Surgery, Bangkok, 2007—. Contbg. editor profl. jours. Fellow: ACS, Internat. Coll. Surgeons, Royal Coll. Surgeons Thailand. Office: Ramathibodi Hosp Dept Surgery Pra Ram 6 Bangkok 10400 Thailand Office Fax: 662-2011316. Business E-Mail: rasja@mahidol.ac.th.

JIRASKOVA, NADA, ophthalmologist, educator; b. Usti nad Labem, Czech Republic, Feb. 18, 1965; d. Stanislav Jirasek and Jaroslava Jiraskova. MD, Charles U., Med. Faculty, Prague, 1986; PhD, Charles U., Prague. Clin. prof. and cons. ophthalmologist Charles U., Med. Faculty and Hosp., Hradec Kralove, Czech Republic, 1993—; prof. Charles U., Prague. Office: Charles Univ Hosp Sokolska 581 Hradec Kralove 500 05 Czech Republic

JITTPOONKUSON, TEERAPAT, ophthalmologist; b. Bangkok, Mar. 10, 1970; MD, Chulalongkorn U., 1993; degree in Retina and Vitreous, NY Eye and Ear Infirmary, 2009. Chief, retina svc., dept. ophthalmology Bangkok Met. Adminstrn. Gen. Hosp., 2004—, chmn., bd. occupl. medicine, 2010. Mem.: Thai MD Soc., Thai Retina Soc., Am. Acad. Ophthalmology. Avocations: tennis, swimming. Home: 55/5 Sinbodi Pk 4 Village Prachautid 72 Thungkru 10140 Thailand Personal E-mail: dr.teerapat@yahoo.com.

JNEID, HANI, interventional cardiologist, researcher; BS, Am. U. Beirut, 1994, MD, 1998. Diplomate in internal medicine Am. Bd. Medicine, 2002, Am. Soc. Nuc. Cardiology, 2004, Am. Bd. Cardiovasc. Medicine, 2006, Am. Bd. Interventional Cardiology, 2008. Intern Cleveland Clinic Found.; fellow in cardiology U. Louisville; fellow in interventional cardiology Mass. Gen. Hosp. Harvard Med. Sch.; asst. prof. medicine Baylor Coll. Medicine, Houston, 2008—; asst. dir. interventional cardiology Michael E. DeBakey VA Med. Ctr., Houston. Mem. leadership com. Nat. Am. Heart Assn., Dallas. Recipient Fellow of Yr. Award, Divsn. Cardiology-U. Louisville, 2004; named Sr. Med. Resident of Yr., Cleve. Clinic Found., 2002. Fellow: Am. Coll. Cardiology; mem.: Am. Heart Assn. Office: Micheal E DeBakey Med Ctr 2002 Holcombe Blvd Houston TX 77030 Office Phone: 713-794-7300. Office Fax: 713-794-7134.

JO, BYUNG WOOK, science educator; b. Gwang Ju, Republic Of Korea, July 13, 1948; m. Kyung Shim Jo; children: Jie Woon, Sueng Hwan, Hie Myung, Jong Jin. PhD in Chemistry, Dankook U., Seoul, Republic Of Korea, 1988. Prof. Chosun U., Seosuk-dong, Gwang Ju, Republic of Korea, 1975—; vis. scientist Nat. Polymer Lab., Amherst, 1988—90; rsch. assoc. U. Mass., Amherst, 1996—97, vis. prof., 1996—98, U. Duisburg, Germany, 1999—2000; v.p. Polymer Soc. Korea, Seoul, 2002—03; provost, v.p. Chosun U., Seosuk-dong, 2004—06; dir. BK21 MFM Ctr., Seosuk-dong, 2006—; exch. scientist E.S.P.C.I. CNRS, Paris. Sci. com. mem. Polychar World Forum, Tex., 2002—. Mem. Nat. Sci. Coun., Seoul, 2007—08. Achievements include patents for water soluble taxol prodrugs; research in syntheses of liquid crystal polymers; flame retarding polymeric foams; binders based on polyoxetane; LM silver alginates. Home: 209-1306 Gumho-Ssangyong Apt Chipyung-dong Gwang Ju 502-430 Republic of Korea Office: Chosun Univ Chem Engring Dept Seosuk-Dong 375 501-759 Gwang Ju Republic of Korea Office Phone: 82-62-230-7214, 82-11-9474-7214. Office Fax: 82-62-230-7214. Business E-Mail: bwjo@chosun.ac.kr.

JO, DEOG-YEON, hematologist, researcher; b. Seosan, Chungcheongnamdo, Republic of Korea, Dec. 1, 1962; s. Nam-Bok Jo and Yeon-Dong Jeong; m. Chun-Young Lee, Sept. 20, 1987; children: Seong-Min, Seong-Jun. MD, Chungnam Nat. U., 1985, MSc, 1988, PhD, 1995. Lic. physician Korean Ministry Health & Wellfare, 1985, cert. Internal Medicine Bd. Korean Ministry Health & Wellfare, 1989, Hematology/Oncology Bd. Korean Assn. Internal Medicine, 1999. Clin. fellow Chungnam Nat. U. Hosp., Daejon, Republic of Korea, 1992—93; rsch. fellow Meml. Sloan-Kettering Cancer Ctr., NYC, 1997—99; assoc. prof. Coll. Medicine Chungnam Nat. U., Daejon, 1999—2004, prof., 2004—. Chief divsn. hematology/oncology dept. internal medicine Chungnam U. Hosp., 2000—. Contbr. scientific papers, articles to profl. jours. Capt. MC Korean Army, 1989—92. Recipient Eudang Scholar award, Korean Dr.'s Assn., 1993, LG Hematology Scholar award, Korean Acad. Med. Sci., 2004. Mem.: Korean Assn. Internal Medicine, Korean Cancer Assn., Korean Soc. Hematopoietic Stem Cell Transplantion, Korean Soc. Hematology, Am. Soc. Hematology. Home: Saerom Apt 103-1203 420-1 Taepyung-dong Jung-gu Daejeon Republic of Korea Office: Chungnam Univ Hosp Daesa-Dong Jung-Gu 640 301-721 Daejeon Daejeon Republic of Korea Office Fax: 82-42-257-5753. E-mail: deogyeon@cnu.ac.kr.

JO, KIHYUN, surgeon; b. Pusan, Republic of Korea, July 22, 1973; B, Inje Med. U., 1998. Chief, orthop. surgery Yang-Ju Mil. Hosp. Svc., Republic of Korea, 2003—06; lectr. Seoul Nat. U., Bundang Hosp., 2007—08; chief, shoulder surgery divsn. Seoul Med. Ctr., Citizen Hosp., 2008—09; chief, joint surgery ctr. Himchan Hosp., 2010—. Cons. Korean Worker's Compensation and Welfare Svc., 2008. Mem.: Korean Soc. Surgery Hand, Korean Soc. Ultrasound Medicine, Korea Knee Soc., Korean Shoulder and Elbow Soc., Korean Orthop. Assn. Avocations: golf, saxophone, fishing. Office: 20-8 Songpa-dong Songpa-gu Seoul 138-170 Republic of Korea Business E-Mail: haikan@naver.com.

JO, SUNGHO, medical educator; b. Gangneung, Republic Korea, Dec. 20, 1969; B, Chung-Ang U. Coll. Medicine, 1996; D, Ulsan U. Coll. Medicine, 2006. Prof. Dankook U., 2008—. Cons. Dankook U. Hosp., 2008. Mem.: Korean Assn. Hepato-Biliary-Pancreatic Surgery, Korean Surg. Soc. Avocation: soccer. Office: Dankook University Coll Medicine 201 Manghyang-ro San 29 Anseo-dong Dongnam-gu Cheonan Chungnam 330-714 Republic of Korea Office Fax: 82-41-556-3878. Business E-Mail: agapejsh@dankook.ac.kr.

JO, WON-MIN, cardiothoracic surgeon, vascular surgeon, educator; b. Seoul, Republic of Korea, Jan. 22, 1968; s. Kwan-Ho Jo and Sung-Sun Sim; m. Jungin Choi, Oct. 25, 1997; children: Eu-Gene, Eu-Kyung. BA, MD, Korea U. Medicine, Seoul, 1993, PhD, 2004. Lic. thoracic and cardiovasc. surgeon Seoul, 1998. Asst. prof. Korea U. Coll. Medicine, Seoul, 2004—07, assoc. prof., 2007—; exchange scholar Cleve. Clinic, Ohio; assoc. prof. Korea U. Med. Coll. Cardiothoracic surgeon Ansan Hosp., Korea U., Kyonggi-do, Ansansi, Republic of Korea, 2003—. Contbr. scientific papers to profl. pubs. Capt. surgeon Korean Military, 1998—2001, Chunnanam-do, Republic of Korea. Mem.: Korean Soc. Thoracic and Cardiovasc. Surgery, Cardiothoracic Surgery Network (assoc.), Acad. Minimally Invasive Surgery (assoc.). Achievements include development of advanced techniques of surgery. Avocations: travel, reading, music, mountain climbing. Office: Ansan Hosp Korea Univ Kyunggi-do 425-707 Ansan Republic of Korea Home Phone: 82-31-412-5060; Office Phone: 82-31-412-4977. Office Fax: 82-31-414-3249. Business E-Mail: jowonmin@korea.ac.kr.

JOB, RAYMOND FRANKLIN SOAMES, psychologist; b. Dubbo, Australia, July 13, 1954; s. Raymond Wallace and Nancy Colleen (Cook) J.; m. Mai Peedo, Oct. 4, 1986 (separated 1999); children: Shannon, Lara, Lawson. BA with honors, U. Sydney, 1977, PhD, 1986. Tutor U. Sydney, 1977-80, lectr., sr. lectr. then assoc. prof., 1986—2003; sr. behavioral scientist Roads and Traffic Authority, Sydney, 1980-82; sr. behavioural scientist Nat. Acoustic Labs., Sydney, 1982-85; gen. mgr. road and safety strategy Roads and Traffic Authority, Surry Hills, Australia, 2003—. Dir. Fleming Job & Assocs., 1988-93, Soames Job & Assocs., 1995—; cons. Roads and Traffic Authority of N.S.W., 1989—. Author: (with D. Kenny) Australia's Adolescents: A Health Psychology Perspective, 1995; contbr. numerous articles to profl. jours. Mem. New South Wales Rd. Safety Task Force, 2001-03. Recipient Tasman Lovell Meml. medallion U. Sydney, 1986; large grants scheme Australian Rsch. Coun., 1992-98, 2004, Australian Rsch. Coun. Infrastructure grant, 1997, Fed. Office of Road Safety grants, 1993-94, 96-97, 99-2000, grantee Motor Accidents Authority, 2001—; Commonwealth scholar 1971-72, 73, 1977-80. Fellow Australian Coll. of Road Safety (assoc., v.p. 1998-2001, pres. 2001-03); mem. Internat. Commn. Biol. Effects of Noise (sec. 1998-2003, chmn. 2003—). Avocations: scuba diving, surfing. Home Phone: +61-2-99386699. Business E-Mail: soames_job@rta.nsw.gov.au.

JOBE, ALAN HALL, pediatrician, educator; b. LA, July 5, 1944; MD, PhD, U. Calif., San Diego, 1973. Cert. Pediat., 1978, Neonatal-Perinatal Medicine. Resident in pediat. U. Calif., San Diego, 1974—75, fellow in neonatology, 1975—77; asst. prof. pediat. Harbor-UCLA Med. Ctr., 1977—80, assoc. prof. pediat., 1980—83, dir. neonatal ICU and pulmonary rsch. lab., 1980—86, prof. pediat., 1983—97; dir. perinatal rsch. laboratories Walter P. Martin Rsch. Ctr., 1991—97; Joseph W. St. Geme, Jr. prof. pediat. UCLA Sch. Medicine, 1995—97; prof. pediat. U. Cin. Coll. Medicine, 1997—; dir. perinatal biology Cin. Children's Hosp. Med. Ctr. Adj. clin. prof. U. Western Australia, 2007. Recipient Richard E. Weitzman award, Harbor-UCLA Faculty Soc., 1982, Ross award, Western Soc. Pediat. Rsch., 1984, E. Mead Johnson Rsch. award, Am. Acad. Pediat., 1986, Mead Johnson Excellence in Tchg. award, Cin. Children's Hosp. Med. Ctr., 1999, 2000, Alvo Yippo medal, Finnish Pediatric Soc., 2002. Mem.: Inst. Medicine, Am. Pediat. Soc. (sec.-treas. 2003—09), Phi Beta Kappa. Office: Cin Childrens Hosp Med Ctr 3333 Burnet Ave Cincinnati OH 45229-3039 Office Phone: 513-636-8691. Office Fax: 513-636-8691. E-mail: alan.jobe@cchmc.org.

JOBE, FRANK WILSON, orthopedic surgeon; b. Greensboro, NC, July 16, 1925; MD, Loma Linda U., Calif., 1956; PhD (hon.), U. Tokushima, Japan. Diplomate Am. Bd. Orthop. Surgery. Intern LA County Gen. Hosp., 1956-57, resident, orthop. surgery, 1960-64; staff Centinela Hosp. Med. Ctr., Inglewood, Calif., med. dir., bio mechanics; staff LA County U. So. Calif. Med. Ctr., LA; clin. prof. dept. orthopedics U. So. Calif. Sch. Medicine. Orthop. cons. LA Dodgers Baseball Team, PGA Tour, Sr. PGA Tour, LOA Lakers Basketball Team, LA Kings Hockey Team, Calif. Angels Baseball Team; cons. President's Coun. on Phys. Fitness and Sports; mem., sponsor Neufeld Chair, orthop. surgery, Loma. Authored several med. publications, books and chapters to books. With AUS, 1943-46. Fellow ACS, Am. Acad. Orthop. Surgeons (past mem., com. on sports medicine, chmn., com. on shoulder, 1982-87); mem. Western Orthop. Assn., LA Chpt. (program chmn., 1978-79), Internat. Soc. of the Knee (founding mem.), Am. Orthop. Assn., Major League Baseball Physicians Assn. (pres. 1976-77, sec. 1977-79), Am. Shoulder and Elbow Surgeons (founding mem., pres. 1985-86, Charles S. Near award, 1987, 1997),

Am. Orthop. Soc. for Sports Medicine (founding mem., chmn. membership com., 1978-79, O'Donohue award, 1984). Achievements include being responsible for the procedure known as Tommy John surgery (LA Dodgers pitcher Tommy John, diagnosed with a career-threatening torn ulnar collateral ligament was repaired by this procedure). Office: Kerlan-Jobe Orthop Clinic 6801 Park Ter Dr Fl 5 Los Angeles CA 90045 Office Phone: 310-665-7200. Office Fax: 310-665-7215.

JOE, KEITH J., orthopedist; b. Anaheim, Calif., Nov. 6, 1974; BS, UCLA, 1996; MD, USUHS, 2002. Chmn., orthops. Malcolm Grow Med. Ctr., Joint Base Andrews, MD, 2008—. Named Ams. Top Orthopedist, SLD Industries, 2011. Fellow: Am. Bd. Orthop. Surgeons; mem.: Soc. Mil. Orthop. Surgeons, Am. Acad. Orthop. Surgeons. Avocations: bicycling, rock climbing, mountain climbing. Home: 259 S Pickett St #201 Alexandria VA 22304 Personal E-mail: dyno_kjoe@hotmail.com.

JOE, SOOK-HAENG, medical educator, psychiatrist; s. Byung-jae Joe and Hyung-gi Kim; m. Seung-duk Ko, June 14, 1983; 1 child, Sung-jun. MD, PhD, Korea U., Seoul, Republic Of Korea, 1976. Cert. in neuropsychiatry Korean Neuropsychiatric Assn., 1981. Staff psychiatrist Nat. Seoul Mental Hosp., 1984—85; asst. prof., dept. neuropsychiatry Korea U. Guro Hosp., Seoul, 1986—90, assoc. prof., dept. neuropsychiatry, 1990—95, chmn., dept. psychiatry, 1999—, prof., dept. neuropsychiatry, 1995—; vis. prof., dept. psychiatry SUNY, Buffalo, 1991—92; v.p. Korean Neuropsychiatric Assn., 2002—03, pres., Seoul SW regional soc., 2000—01; editor chief, Korean jour. psychosomatic medicine Korean Psychosomatic Soc., Seoul, 1996—2000, pres., 2006—08. Cons. J Healthcare, Women Mental Health, Joongang Daily, Seoul, 1999—; dir. Rsch. Inst. Mental Health, Korea U., Seoul, 2007—, Guro Cmty. Mental Health Ctr., Seoul, 2007—10. Contbr. articles to sci. rsch. jours. Capt. Army, Dept. Psychiatry, Mil. Cheongpyeong, 1981—84, Gyung-Gi Province. Mem.: Korean Acad. Sleep Medicine and Psychophysiology, Korean Psychopharmacology Soc., Korean Psychosomatic Soc., Am. Psychosomatic Soc., Soc. Light Treatment Biol. Rhythms, Edn. Rsch. Com., Korean Neuropsychiatric Assn., Korean Bd. Neuropsychiatric Com. Avocations: painting, checkers. Office: Korea Univ Guro Hosp Guro-dong Seoul Guro-gu 152-703 Republic of Korea Office Fax: 82-2-852-1937. Business E-Mail: shaeng@korea.ac.kr.

JOENSEN, JÓN, psychotherapist, educator; b. Vágur, Faroe Islands, Sept. 8, 1961; Degree in Physiotherapy, Sch. Health Scis., Aarhus, Denmark, 1990; MS, U. Bergen, Norway, 2006. Assoc. prof. Dept. Physiotherapy, Faculty Health & Social Scis., Bergen U. Coll., Norway, 2006—. Office: Möllendalsveien 6 Bergen Hordaland N-5009 Norway Business E-Mail: jon.joensen@hib.no.

JOERGER, JAY HERMAN, psychologist, entrepreneur; b. Freeport, NY, Sept. 23, 1957; s. Herman Alexander and Ellen Rose (Becker) J.; m. Diana Botero, Mar. 27, 1993; children: Nicholas Alexander, Richard Andrew. BS, Union U., 1980, MA, Colgate U., 1981; EdD, Columbia U., 1987. Diplomate Am. Bd. Profl. Disability Consultants, Substance Abuse Psychology, Clin. Psychology, Psychology Assessment, Evaluation and Testing, Child Custody Evaluation, lic. psychologist N.Y., Pa., bd. cert. forensic examiner, bd. cert. in forensic medicine, cert. homeland security, registered hypnotherapist, cert. med. examiner, registered psychologist NY State Workers Compensation Bd. Drug abuse counselor Drug Abuse Coun., Norwich, NY, 1980-81; vocat. rehab. counselor Community Workshop, Glens Falls, NY, 1981-83; assoc. psychologist N.Y. State, Wingdale, NY, 1986-96; pres. Mentors Resource and Devel. Corp., 1991—; mem. group practice Ctr. Stress Reduction, 1993-97, Carmel Psychol. Assocs., 1993-94. Admission and hosp. privileges Four Winds Hosp., Katonah, N.Y., 1995—; cons., Somers, N.Y., 1988—; adj. asst. prof. Iona Coll., 1993-95; adj. prof. Lehman Coll., 1994-97; founding coord. Alcoholism and Drug Abuse Counselor Tng. Program Lehman Coll., 1996; bd. dirs. Rapid Rabbit, Inc., 2004-08; forensic psychol. cons. and expert witness. Author: A Participant Manual for Mentally Ill Chemical Abusers, 1989, Living Successfully: A Self-Study Guide, 1993; co-author: The Physical, Psychological and Social Effects of Chemical Abuse - A Clinician's Workbook, 1994, 2d edit., 1995, Substance Abuse: Evaluation and Treatment Training Program, 1995; (book, audio tape) Living Successfully: Relax and Enhance Your Life, 1996. Amateur radio operator USAF; mil. affiliate radio operator Westchester Emergency Comm. Assn., Westchester County, 1983-99; bd. dirs. Hudson Valley Fedn., Clintondale, N.Y., 1987-88, physical injury specialist, 2002-, leader BSA, 2001-06, scout master, 2006-, merit badge counselor. Recipient Excellence in Psychology award Med. Staff Orgn., Harlem Valley Psychologists, 1990. Mem. Am. Coll. Forensic Examiners (life), Am. Bd. Profl. Disability Cons., N.Y. State Psychol. Assn. (sec.-treas. addiction divsn. 1993-95, liaison managed care task force 1994-95), Westchester County Psychol. Assn. (pres. indsl. orgn. divsn. 1992-95). Achievements include design of audio production studio. Avocation: amateur radio. Home and Office: RR 2 1016C Dingmans Ferry PA 18328-9613 Office: 758 E Main St Middletown NY 10940 Home: 102 Joergers Ln Dingmans Ferry PA 18328-9613 Home Phone: 570-828-6664; Office Phone: 570-828-6444. Personal E-mail: mentors@ptd.net.

JOFFE, JOHNATHAN KEITH, medical oncologist, consultant; b. Johannesburg, Sept. 23, 1958; s. Walter Gerald and Rosalie Sylvia Joffe; m. Claire Elizabeth Fisher, July 23, 1998; children: William Barney, Ruby Elizabeth, Grace Eleanor. MBBS, U. London, 1984, MD, 1994. Mem. Royal Coll. Physicians (U.K.)., 1987, Fellow Royal Coll. Physicians, 1999. Clin. rsch. fellow Royal Marsden Hosp., London, 1989-92; sr. registrar St. James U. Hosp., Leeds, Eng., 1992-95; sr. clin. scientist ICRF Cancer Medicine Rsch. Unit, Leeds, Eng., 1995-96; Macmillan cons. in med. oncology Calderdale and Hudderfiled NHS Trust, 1996—2006, clin. dir. oncology, hematology, 2001—06, divsn. dir. med. and elderly svcs., 2006—11. Mem. Joint Collegiate Coun. for Oncology, London, Great Britain and No. Ireland, 1996-99, 2011-; mem. NCRI Testis Clin. Studies Group, 2003—, chmn., 2009, Nat. Chemotherapy Adv. Group, Eng., 2006-. Mem. editl. bd. (jour.) Clin. Oncology, 1998-2003; contbr. articles on biology and treatment of cancer to profl. jours. Mem. Am. Soc. Clin. Oncology, Assn. Cancer Physicians (exec. com. 1997-2000, chmn. 2011-), Brit. Assn. Cancer Rsch., European Soc. for Med. Oncology., Royal Coll. Physicians(London)(Joint Soc. com. chmn., 2011-) Office: Huddersfield Royal Inf Acre St Lindley Huddersfield HD3 3EA England Business E-Mail: jk.joffe@cht.nhs.uk.

JOFFE, RUSSELL, psychiatrist, educator; b. South Africa, Feb. 25, 1954; MD, U. Witwatersrand, Johannesburg, 1977; DSc, Stellenbosch U., 2008. Prof., psychiatry Boston U., 2010—. Dean, v.p. McMaster U., 1997—2000; dean NJ Med. Sch., 2001—05. Recipient Heinz Lehman award, Can. Coll. Neuropsychopharmacology. Fellow: Am. Psychiat. Assn. Avocations: reading, travel, sports. Home: 24 Sherwood Rd Short Hills NJ 07078 Personal E-mail: rjoffe51@verizon.net.

JOHANNING, GARY LEE, medical educator; b. Boonville, Mo., Sept. 29, 1950; s. Leon Fredrick Johanning and Evelyn Marie Brucks; m. Feng Wang, Apr. 24, 1993; children: Tony Xiao Meng, Emily Marie. BS, U. Mo., Columbia, 1973, MS, 1976; PhD, U. of Mo., Columbia, 1978. Assoc. prof. U. of Ala., Birmingham, 1993—2003, M.D. Anderson Cancer Ctr., Bastrop, Tex., 2003—. Asst. prof. Armstrong Atlantic State U., Savannah, Ga., 1981—86; postdoctoral fellow U. of Mo., Columbia, 1987—89, Case Western Res. U., Cleve., 1989—93; spkr. and lectr. in field; jour. reviewer. Author: (book chpt.) Annual Review of Nutrition, Methods of Molecular Biology; contbr. articles to profl. jours. Recipient Cancer CAM Vitamins and Cancer Chemotherapy Resistance grant, NIH, 2003—06, Vitamins and Prevention of Cancer Progression grant, 2003—06, Epigenetic Changes and Vitamin Status in Breast Cancer grant, 2000—03, HPV Oncoprotein Expression in Cervical Cancer grant, 1999—2001, HPV Oncoprotein Ablation via Single-Chain Antibodies grant, 1998—2000, Folic Acid and Antigen-Specific Cellular Immunity grant, Cattlemen for Cancer Rsch., 2006—07, Acyl Co-A Binding Protein Expression in Cancer grant, 2004—06. Mem.: AAAS, Am. Assn. for Cancer Rsch., Am. Soc. for Nutrition, Sigma Xi. Achievements include patents for animal feedstuffs and process; research in cellular vitamins, DNA methylation and cancer risk; DNA methylation and diet in cancer; Timecourse of Cisplatin Resistance in Tumor Cells; Cellular Vitamins and DNA Methylation in Cancer; HPV 16 Oncogene Variant Expression in Cervical Cancer; Role of Environmental Factors in Epigenetic Cancer Therapy. Home: 128 Musket Dr Bastrop TX 78602 Office: 650 Cool Water Dr Bastrop TX 78602 Office Phone: 512-332-5211. Office Fax: 512-332-5218. Business E-Mail: gljohann@mdanderson.org.

JOHANSEN, ODDMUND JOHANNES, orthopedist, educator; s. Erling and Klara Antonette Johansen; m. Toril Olsen, July 15, 1972; children: Eline, Maren Marie, Johan Markus. MD, Tromsø U., Norway, 1979, PhD, 1995. Cert.; in gen. and ortopaedic surgeon Norwegian Med. Assn., 1995. Prof. U. Tromsø, 2005—; consulting surgeon U. Hosp., Tromsø, 1995—. Contbr. articles to profl. jours. Mem.: AAOS. Achievements include research in ethiology of osteoarthritis and finding optimal repair techniques for damaged cartilage. Office: Tromsø Univ Breivika Tromsø 9038 Norway Office Phone: 0047 77626000.

JOHANSON, JOHN F., gastroenterologist, researcher; s. John R. Johanson MD, U. Ill., Rockford, 1985; MSc, Med. Coll. Wis., 1991. Diplomate Am. Bd. Internal Medicine, 1991. Ptnr. Rockford (Ill.) Gastroenterology Assocs., 1991—, dir. rsch., 1991—2005. Cons. in field; presenter in field. Editor: (med. jour.) Evidence Based Gastroenterology; contbr. articles to profl. jours. Bd. dirs. Joseph's Walk Ministries, Rockford, 2003—05; physician advisor Americas Dr., Gurnee, Ill., 2003—05; mem. Rockford Christian Schools, 2005. Recipient Excellence in Clin. Rsch., Americas Dr., 1997, 1998, 2000. Fellow: Am. Coll. Gastroenterology; mem.: Am. Soc. Gastrointestinal Endoscopy, Am. Gastroenterologic Assn. Office: Rockford Gastroenterology Associates 401 Roxbury Rd Rockford IL 61107

JOHANSON, NORMAN A., othopaedic surgeon; MD, Cornell U., Ithaca, NY, 1978. Diplomate Am. Bd. Orthopaedic Surgery, lic. Pa., 1990. Resident orthop. surgery Hospital for Spl. Surgery, 1984, fellow orthop. surgery; physician Hahnemann Univ. Hosp. Recipient Best Dr., Best Doctors in America, 2010; named one of the Top Doctors, Phila. Mag., 2010—11. Office: Hahnemann University Hospital Pennwood Bldg Ste 131 2500 Maryland Rd Willow Grove PA 19090 Office Phone: 215-830-9255.

JOHANSON, PER-ERIK, orthopedist; b. Boras, July 29, 1966; MD, U. Gothenburg, 1997. Orthop. specialist Sahlgrenska U. Hosp., 2008—. Mem.: Swedish Orthop. Assn. Achievements include research in hip arthroplasty radiostereometry, wear assessment, register studies. Office: Sahlgrenska University Hosp Dept Orthop Gothenburg Vastra Gotaland 41345 Sweden Business E-Mail: per-erik.johanson@vgregion.se.

JOHANSON, WANDA L., medical association administrator, critical care nurse; married. Grad., Holy Cross Sch. Nursing; BS in Nursing, M in Nursing, Univ. Wash. Registered profl. nurse, Wash., Calif., NC. Dir., profl. devel./ethics AACN, 1993—97; v.p. ops. InnoVision Group (AACN subs.), 1998; assoc. operating officer, med./surg./critical care svcs. Duke Univ. Health Sys., Durham, NC, 1998—99; now CEO AACN, Aliso Viejo, Calif. Office: AACN 101 Columbia Aliso Viejo CA 92656-4109 Office Phone: 949-362-2020. *

JOHANSSON, BENGT WILHELM, cardiologist, educator; b. Lund, Sweden, Feb. 28, 1930; s. Nils V. and Ulla E. (Karlsson) J.; m. Ulla Margareta Petersson, June 5, 1954; 1 child, Anita Christin Olsson MB, U. Lund, 1957, MD, 1966. Intern Malmo Gen. Hosp., Sweden, 1957—59, resident, asst. med. officer, 1957—67, mem. med. staff, 1957—, registrar, 1967—74, head sect. cardiology, 1974—90; practice medicine specializing in cardiology Lund, 1957—, Malmo, 1957—. Former dist. med. officer Limmared, Sweden; mem. faculty dept. medicine U. Lund, 1967— Contbr. numerous articles on cardiovascular physiology and rsch. to sci. jours Lt. M.C., Swedish Army, 1948-66 Mem. AAAS, Am. Coll. Cardiology, Swedish Soc. Cardiology (hon.), Am. Coll. Angiology, Swedish Soc. Internal Medicine, Royal Physiographic Assn. Lund, Internat. Hibernation Soc., Am. Geriat. Soc., Swedish Assn. Med. Physics and Technics, Swedish Soc. Med. Scis., Malmo Assn. Head Physicians, Swedish Med. Assn., Lund Med. Assn., Malmo Med. Assn., Travellers' Club Malmö, Rotary, Masons. Office: Malm Univ Hosp Heart Clinic 205 02 Malmö Sweden

JOHANSSON, BJÖRN AXEL, psychiatrist; b. Malmö, Sweden, Jan. 30, 1959; s. Lennart and Alli Johansson; life ptnr. Pia Håkansson, Mar. 23, 1989; children: Julia, Laura Håkansson, August, Maja Håkansson, Villiam Håkansson, Johan Håkansson. BSc, Lund U., Malmö, 1984, MD, 1993, PhD, 2006. Cert. specialist in child and adolescent psychiatry Malmö, 2004. Intern U. Hosp. Malmö, Sweden, 1996—97, resident, dept. child and adolescent psychiatry, 1998—2003, sr. physician, dept child and adolescent psychiatry, 2005—. Office: Psychiatry Skåne Dept Child and Adolescent Psychiatry Malmö 205 02 Sweden

JOHANSSON, PETER, hematologist, educator; b. Uppsala, Sweden, Mar. 3, 1958; MD, U. Gothenburg, 1987, PhD, 2004. Hematology cons. Uddevalla Hosp., 1996—. Assoc. prof. Sahlgrenska U. Hosp. Office: Fjallvagen 8 Uddevalla 45180 Sweden Business E-Mail: peter.l.johansson@vgregion.se.

JOHANSSON, ROLF NILS, physician, educator; b. Osby, Sweden, Aug. 17, 1953; s. Arvid Ingemar and Birgit Elisabet Johansson; m. Boel Margareta Ahnberg, 1987; children: Helena, Hillevi, Vibeke. MSc, Lund Inst. Tech., Sweden, 1977, PhD, 1983; BMed, Lund U., 1980, MD, 1986. Tchg. asst. automata theory Lund Inst. Tech., 1976-80; tchg. asst. control theory Lund U., 1979-83, tchg. asst. math. stats., 1979-80; rsch. assoc. CNRS Laboratoire d'Automatique, Grenoble, France, 1985-86; docent Uppsala (Sweden) U., 1985; asst. prof. Lund Inst. Tech., 1983-85, assoc. prof., 1986—, prof. control sci., 1999—. Coord. dir. program in robotics Lund Inst. Tech., 1993. Author: System Modeling and Identification, 1993. Recipient Innovation Cup award, 1988, Ebeling prize Swedish Soc. Medicine, 1995, Russell S. Springer Prof. award U. Calif. Berkeley, 2004; fellow Royal Physiographic Soc., 2007. Avocations: private aviation, forestry, language study. Office: Lund Inst Tech Dept Automatic Control S22100 Lund Sweden E-mail: rolf.johansson@control.lth.se.

JOHKURA, KEN, neurologist, researcher; b. Yokohama, Kanagawa, Japan, Oct. 23, 1964; MD, Yokohama City U., 1990, PhD, 1998. Med. practitioner, rschr. Yokohama City U. Med. Ctr., Kanagawa, Japan, 2000—02, Hiratsuka Kyosai Hosp., Hiratsuka, 2002—. Dir., dept. neurology Hiratsuka Kyosai Hosp., 2002—, dir., stroke ctr., 2005—. Recipient Acad. award Excellence, Japanese Neuro-ophthalmology Soc., 1999; grantee, Fedn. Nat. Pub. Svc. Pers. Mut. Aid Assns., 2003—05, Okinaka Meml. Inst., 2003, 2005. Fellow: Japanese Neuro-ophthalmology Soc. (licentiate); mem.: Japan Stroke Soc. (licentiate), Societas Neurologia Japonica (licentiate). Home: 2-7-5-501 Mori Isogo-ku Yokohama 235-0023 Japan Office: Hiratsuka Kyosai Hosp 9-11 Oiwake Hiratsuka 254-8502 Japan Office Fax: +81-463-31-1865. Business E-Mail: johkura-k@kkr.hiratsuka.kanagawa.jp.

JOHN, ESTHER M., research scientist, educator; DES in Secondary Edn., U. Fribourg, Switzerland, 1980; MA in Geography, U. NC, Chapel Hill, 1986, MSPH in Epidemiology, 1987, PhD in Epidemiology, 1990. Rsch. scientist III Northern Calif. Cancer Ctr., 2000—; co-leader, cancer epidemiology Stanford Cancer Ctr., 2005—; Consulting assoc. prof. Dept. Health Rsch. & Policy, 2004—. Contbr. several articles to profl. jours. Achievements include research that focuses on the epidemiology of breast, prostate and ovarian cancer, particularly in Hispanic and African-American populations.

JOHN, GERALD WARREN, pharmacist, educator; b. Salem, Ohio, Feb. 16, 1947; s. Harold Elba and Ruth Springer (Pike) J.; m. Jean Ann Marie Orris, Nov. 5, 1977; children: Patrick Warren, Jeanette Lynn. BS in Pharmacy, Ohio No. U., 1970; MS, U. Md., 1974. Registered pharmacist, Ohio, S.C. Staff pharmacist North Columbiana County Cmty. Hosp., Salem, 1970-72; asst. resident in hosp. pharmacy U. Md. Hosp., Balt., 1972-73, sr. resident, 1973-74, clinn. patient care pharmacies, 1974-76; dir. pharmacy Ohio Valley Hosp., Steubenville, 1976-97; exec. dir. Tri State Health Svcs., Inc., 1997—. Mem. adv. bd. Contemporary Pharmacy Practice, 1977-83; preceptor profl. externship program Ohio No. U. Sch. Pharmacy, 1977—, adj. clin. instr. practical experience program Duquesne U. Sch. Pharmacy, 1976—; dir. pharmacy Trinity Med. Ctr., Steubenville, 1997—. Columnist Weirton Daily Times, 1990-94. Trustee, v.p. Valley Hospice Inc., 1985-98, 2000-05. Named Hosp. Pharmacist of Yr., Md. Soc. Hosp. Pharmacists, 1976, Outstanding Young Man of Am., U.S. Jaycees, 1977. Fellow Am. Soc. Con. Pharmacists; mem. Am. Soc. Hosp. Pharmacists, Ohio Soc. Hosp. Pharmacists, Jefferson County Acad. Pharmacy, Southeastern Ohio Soc. Hosp. Pharmacists (pres. 1985-87), Rho Chi, Phi Eta Sigma, Soc. Martial Arts(bd. dirs., 2009-), West Karate Inc.(bd. dirs.) Methodist. Avocation: Karate (black belt). Office: 4000 Johnson Rd Steubenville OH 43953 Home Phone: 740-264-2058. Personal E-mail: gwjohn47@yahoo.com. Business E-Mail: gjohn@trinityhealth.com.

JOHNS, HARRY, medical association administrator; B, Eckerd Coll., St. Petersburg, Fla.; MBA, Northwestern U. J.L. Kellogg Sch. Mgmt., Evanston, Ill. Joined American Cancer Soc., 1983, sr. mgmt. positions including exec. v.p. strategic initiatives, 1994—2005; pres., CEO Alzheimer's Assn., Chgo., 2005—. Bd. mem. Rsch. America, Nat. Health Coun. Office: Alzheimers Assn Nat Office 225 N Michigan Ave Fl 17 Chicago IL 60601-7633 Office Phone: 312-335-8700. Office Fax: 312-335-5886. *

JOHNS, MICHAEL DOUGLAS, healthcare executive, medical device executive, former federal government official, writer; b. Allentown, Pa., Sept. 8, 1964; s. Glenn Franklin and Nancy Louise (Hummel) J.; m. Nicole Denise Miles, Sept. 30, 1995 (div. 1999); 1 child, Michael Douglas Jr. Student, Cambridge U., Eng., 1984; BBA in Econs., U. Miami, 1986. Asst. editor Policy Rev. Mag. The Heritage Found., Washington, 1986-88, policy analyst, 1988-91; spl. asst. to pres. Drew U., Madison, NJ, 1991-92; speechwriter to Pres. of U.S. The White House, Washington, 1992; speechwriter to U.S. Sec. Commerce U.S. Dept. Commerce, Washington, 1992-93; dir. rsch. Internat. Rep. Inst., Washington, 1993-94; mgr. corp. comm., sr. writer Eli Lilly and Co., Indpls., 1994-95; aide to U.S. Senator Olympia J. Snowe U.S. Senate, Washington, 1996-97; sr. assoc. S.R. Wojdak & Assocs., Phila., 1997-2000; v.p. Gentiva Health Svcs., Melville, NY, 2000—03; divisional head & corp. v.p. Electric Mobility Corp., Sewell, NJ, 2003—09. Fgn. policy group advisor Dole for Pres., Inc., Washington, 1996; sr. advisor to global devel. projects Internat. Rep. Inst., Kuwait, Turkey, other nations, 1993-94; mgr. mktg., promotion and communication strategies cancer, cardiovasc., endocrine, infectious and ctrl. nervous sys. pharm. products Eli Lilly and Co., 1994-95; guest polit. and pub. policy analyst MacNeil/Lehrer News Hour, C-SPAN, CNBC, PBS Nightly Bus. Report, Al Jazeeva, Fox Morning News, Voice of Am., BBC, others; sr. mgmt. and mgr. mktg., comms. and investor rels. for Fortune 1000 health svcs. co., 2000-03; guest lectr. UN, Vassar Coll., U. N.C., Chapel Hill, Sirins Satellite, others. Author: Seventy Years of Evil in the Soviet Union, 1988, U.S. and Africa Statistical Handbook, 1990, U.S. and Africa Statistical Handbook, 2d edit., 1991; co-author: Freedom in the World: The

Annual Survey of Political Rights and Civil Liberties, 1993, Finding Our Roots, Facing Our Future: America in the 21st Century, 1997; contbg. editor: USSR Monitor newsletter, The Heritage Found., 1989—91; contbr. articles to Wall St. Jour., Christian Sci. Monitor, Nat. Rev., others. Active Luth. Ch. of the Holy Spirit, Emmaus, Pa. Recipient Century III Leadership award, Shell Oil Co., 1981, Svc. award, Kiwanis, 1982, Cert. appreciation, Spl. Olympics, 1983, award of appreciation, Lao Vets Am., 1995, numerous citations, Congl. Record, U.S. Congress, First Pl. Health and Sci. awards, LI Web, 2001. Mem.: Case Mgmt. Soc. Am., Bush/Quayle Alumni Assn., Reagan Alumni Assn., Nat. Journalism Ctr. Alumni Coun., Am. Assn. Homecare (pub. affairs com.), Am. Med. Writing Assn., Nat. Investor Rels. Inst., Assn. on Third World Affairs, Iron Arrow Honor Soc. of U. Miami, Lambda Chi Alpha (Internat. Hall of Fame 1996). Republican. Lutheran. Home: 219 Cabot Ct Deptford NJ 08096-5114 Home Phone: 610-967-5689.

JOHNS, RICHARD JAMES, physician, educator; b. Pendleton, Oreg., Aug. 19, 1925; s. James Shanard and Pearl (McKenna) Johns; m. Carol Greacen Johnson; children: Richard Clark, Robert Shanard, James Ashmore. BS, U. Oreg., 1947; MD, Johns Hopkins U., 1948, DHL (hon.), 2009. Diplomate Am. Bd. Internal Medicine. Intern Johns Hopkins Hosp., Balt., 1948—49, asst. resident, 1951—53, fellow in medicine, 1953—55, resident, 1955—56, instr., 1955—57, physician, 1956—, asst. prof., 1957—61, assoc. prof., 1961—66, asst. dean admissions, 1962—66, prof. medicine, 1966—, dir. subdept. biomed. engring., 1966—70, mem. adv. bd., prin. profl. staff Applied Physics Lab., 1967—, prof., dir. dept. biomed. engring., 1970—91, disting. svc. prof., 1991—. Bd. dirs. Sparton Corp. Bd. visitors Sch. Engring., Duke U., 1986—; chmn. adv. com. Divsnl. Health Scis. and Tech., Harvard-MIT, 1987—92; mem. com. sci., engring. and pub. policy NAS, 1988—90; mem. sci. adv. com. GM, 1991—97; sec., vice chmn., chmn. med. bd. Myasthenia Gravis Found.; trustee Am. Bd. Clin. Engring., pres., 1976—83; bd. dirs. Whitaker Found., 1991—94. Capt. M.C. US Army, 1949—51. Fellow: Royal Soc. Medicine, Am. Inst. for Biol. and Med. Engring. (founding), AAAS, ACP; mem.: Inst. Medicine-NAS (coun. 1987—90), IEEE (pres. group on engring. in medicine and biology 1970—72), Biomed. Engring. Soc. (bd. dirs. 1972—75, pres. 1978—79), Assn. Am. Physicians, Am. Soc. Clin. Investigation, Am. Clin. and Climatol. Assn. (v.p. 1977—78, sec.-treas. 1979—85, pres. 1986—87), Sparton Corp. (dir. 2002—07), Annapolis Yacht Club, Caduceus Club, Elkridge Club, Johns Hopkins Club (v.p. 1969—70), Peripatetic Club, Interurban Clin. Club (pres. 1980—81), Johns Hopkins Med. Soc. (pres. 1968—69), Tau Beta Pi, Nu Sigma Nu, Phi Kappa Psi, Alpha Omega Alpha, Sigma Xi. Home: 203 E Highfield Rd Baltimore MD 21218-1105 Office: Johns Hopkins U Sch Med 1830 E Monument St Ste 501 Baltimore MD 21287 E-mail: rjohns@jhmi.edu.

JOHNS, ROGER ANTHONY, anesthesiologist, educator; m. Lisa Kolp; children: Brian, Matthew, Jessica. BS in Biol. Scis., Stanford U., Palo Alto, Calif., 1977; MD, Wayne State U. Sch. Medicine, Detroit, 1981; M of Health Sci., Johns Hopkins U. Bloomberg Sch. Pub. Health, Balt., 2005. Diplomate American Bd. Anesthesiology, Nat. Bd. Med. Examiners. Intern internal medicine/anesthesiology U. Va., Charlottesville, 1982—83, resident anesthesiology, 1983—85, fellow cardiac anesthesia, dept. anesthesiology, 1985—86, rsch. fellow pharmacology, 1985—87, asst. prof. anesthesiology, 1987—91, assoc. prof., 1991—95, prof., 1995—99, vice chair dept. anesthesiology, 1997—98, chair, 1998—99; prof. dept. anesthesiology & critical care medicine Johns Hopkins Sch. Medicine, Balt., 1999—, Mark C. Rogers prof. and chmn. dept. anesthesiology & critical care medicine, 1999—2003, prof. medicine, 2006—. Assoc. examiner American Bd. Anesthesiology, 1997—2001; Robert Wood Johnson Health Policy fellow Inst. Medicine, NAS, 2005—08; mem. Nat. Coalition Health Care, 2008—. Editor: Intelligence Reports in Anesthesia, 1986—87, Jour. Cardiothoracic & Vascular Anesthesia, 1992—2000, Jour. Vascular Rsch., 1995—, American Jour. Physiology: Lung, Cellular & Molecular Biology, 2000—, Anesthesiology, 1996—2006; contbr. articles to profl. jour. Mem.: AMA, AAAS, Soc. Neuroscience, Johns Hopkins Med.-Surg. Assn., Balt. County Med. Soc., American Physiol. Soc., American Soc. Echocardiography, Va. Soc. Anesthesiologists, Albemarle County Med. Soc., Va. State Med. Soc., American Thoracic Soc., Fedn. American Societies Exptl. Biology, Assn. Cardiac Anesthesiologists, Soc. Cardiovasc. Anesthesiologists, Internat. Anesthesia Rsch. Soc., American Soc. Anesthesiologists, Inst. Medicine, Nat. Acad. Scis., Assn. Univ. Anesthesiologists, American Soc. Pharmacology & Exptl. Therapeutics, Assn. Cardiovasc. Anesthesiologists. Achievements include research in the molecular mechanisms that underlie the onset and maintenance of chronic pain, particularly neuropathic pain; the mechanism of inhalational anesthetics; patents in field. Avocations: hiking, bicycling, soccer, outdoor activities. Office: Dept Anesthesiology/Critical Care Medicine Johns Hopkins U Sch Medicine 720 Rutland Ave Ross 361 Baltimore MD 21205 Office Phone: 410-614-1810. Office Fax: 410-614-7711. E-mail: rajohns@jhmi.edu.

JOHNSEN, ERIK LISBJERG, physician; b. Vejle, Denmark, Nov. 4, 1981; MD, Aarhus U., 2009, PhD, 2010. Physician Aarhus U. Hosp., 2010—. Office: Aarhus University Hosp Nørrebrogade Aarhus Midtjylland 8000 Denmark Business E-Mail: erik.johnsen@ki.au.dk.

JOHNSON, (MARY) ANITA, physician, medical association administrator; b. (Clarksburg, W.Va., Oct. 18, 1926; d. Paul F. and Mary Elizabeth (Harris) Johnson; m. Lawrence J. Ciessau, Aug. 22, 1959 (div. 1974); children: Matthew A., Susan E., Sharon L., Mark A.; m. Ralph Allen Fretwell, Dec. 18, 1976 (dec. Aug. 18, 2001). BS, North Tex. U., 1946; MD, Woman's Med. Coll. Pa., 1950. Intern Baylor U. Hosp., Dallas, 1950-51, resident, 1951-54; practice medicine specializing in internal medicine Dallas, 1954-58, Chgo., 1958—; instr. internal medicine Southwestern Med. Coll., U. Tex., Dallas, 1954-58; med. dir. YWCA, Dallas, 1955-58; physician for infant welfare Chgo. Bd. Health, 1960-63; house physician, emergency physician St. Mary of Nazareth Hosp. Ctr., Chgo., 1963-81, instr. nurses ICU, 1963-80, asst. cardiologist, 1963-86, sec. med. staff, 1974-75, treas. med. staff, 1980, pres. med. staff, 1982, 84; med. dir. Family Care Ctr., 1973-74, chief med. clinics, 1977-78, chmn. credentials com., 1982-92, chief internal medicine, 1983-92; clin. instr. medicine U. Health Scis., Chgo. Med. Sch., North Chicago, Ill., 1982-95; nat. med. dir. Nat. Cath. Soc. Foresters Ins. Co., Chgo., 1975-77. Chmn. ann. benefit com. St. Mary of Nazareth Hosp. Ctr., 1992; cons. internal medicine Lisbon VA Hosp., Dallas, 1955-56; lectr. to cmty. elem. sch. students on opportunities in health field, 1967—; gov. bd. St. Mary Nazareth Hosp. Ctr., 1991-94, life trustee, 1994—. Disaster vol. Lyons Twp. Pharm. Distbn. Team, 2006—. Named Med. Woman of Yr., St. Mary of Nazareth Hosp. Ctr., 1973. Mem. ACP, AMA (del. hosp. med. staff sect. 1980-92), Ill. Soc. Internal Medicine (councillor 1990-93), Am. Soc. Internal Medicine, Am. Coll. Angiology, Am. Med. Women's Assn. (S.W. regional dir. 1955-58, nat. chmn. publicity and pub. rels. 1991-93, pres.-elect br. 2, 1981, 82, 89, 90, pres. 1983-85, 91-94, regional gov. Midwest sect. 1985-91, bd. dirs. 1985-91, 92-98, v.p. fin. 1997-98, cmty. svc. award 1991, nat. chmn. retirement issues com. 1993-2000, nat. pres.-elect 1998-99, Pres.'s Recognition award 1998, Bertha Van Hoosen Nat. award 1999, found. bd. dirs. 1999-05), Ill. State Med. Soc. (trustee 1987-90, com. on CME accreditation 1987-96, coun. on pub. rels. on membership svcs 1992, govt. affairs com. 1991-05, jud. panel mem. 2003-08, site accreditation surveyor), Chgo. Med. Soc. (councillor 1980—, chmn. malpractice ins. com., del. to Ill. Med. Soc. 1981—, pres. Northside br. 1985-87, chmn. practice mgmt. com. 1990-93, nominating com., Midwest Clin. Conf. 1991—2008, Cook County jud. panel 1995-2000, chmn. sr. physicians com. 1997-99, chmn. subcom. continuing med. edn. 1997-98, chmn. continuing med. edn. com. 1998-2004, chmn. election com. 2002-07, created M. Anita Johnson award 1999—), Zeta Phi. Home and Office: 6226 Edgebrook Ln W Indian Head Park IL 60525-6983 Personal E-mail: ajohnsonmd@sbcglobal.net.

JOHNSON, ANNETTE J., medical educator; b. Hampton, Va., May 27, 1965; MD, Med. Coll. Va., 1992; MS in Clin. Rsch., Ind. U., 2005. Asst. prof. U. Ala. Birmingham, 1999—2000, Ind. U., 2001—07, tenure assoc. prof., 2007; assoc. prof. Wake Forest U. Sch. Medicine, 2007—. Faculty Wake Forest U. Brain Tumor Ctr. Excellence, 2009—; chair, bd. exam com. critical thinking Am. Bd. Radiology, 2010—11; editl. bd. mem. Jour. Am. Coll. Radiology, 2010—; pres. Radiology Alliance Health Svcs. Rsch., 2011—. Named to America's Top Drs., Castle Connolly, 2010—11; fellowship, Gen. Electric Assn. U. Radiologists. Mem.: Radiology Alliance Health Svcs. Rsch., Assn. U. Radiologists, Am. Soc. Neuroradiology, Radiol. Soc. N.Am., Am. Coll. Radiology. Office: WFU Sch Medicine Dept Radiology Winston Salem NC 27157 Office Fax: 336-716-0555. Business E-Mail: anjohnso@wfubmc.edu.

JOHNSON, ARTHUR GILBERT, microbiology educator; b. Eveleth, Minn., Feb. 1, 1926; s. Arthur Gilbert and Selma (Niemi) J.; m. Mildred Louise Anderson, June 15, 1951; children: Susan, Sally, Gary, Peter. BA, U. Minn., 1950, M.Sc., 1951; PhD, U. Md., 1955. Biochemist Walter Reed Army Inst. Rsch., Washington, 1952-55; asst. prof. U. Mich., 1956-62, asso. prof., 1962-66, prof. microbiology, 1966-78; prof., head dept. med. microbiology/immunology U. Minn. Sch. Medicine, Duluth, 1978-99, prof. emeritus, 1999—. Mem. pre, postdoctoral and spl. fellowships study sect. NIH, 1968-70; mem. nat. adv. dental rsch. coun. NIH, 1972-75; mem. Nat. Bd. Med. Examiners, 1980-84; mem. bacteriology and mycology study sect. NIH, 1983-87, chmn., 1986-87; cons. microbiology. Editor Infection and Immunity, 1977-86. Served with US Merchant Marine, 1943-46. Mem. Am. Assn. Immunologists, Am. Soc. Microbiology, Infectious Diseases Soc. Am., Soc. Biol. Therapy, Immunocomprised Host Soc., Internat. Endotoxin Soc., Assn. Med. Sch. Microbiology and Immunology Chairs (pres. 1991-92). Achievements include research on immunology. Home: 4001 Glacier Hills Dr #327 Ann Arbor MI 48105 Personal E-mail: agjohnson99@yahoo.com.

JOHNSON, CAGE SAUL, hematologist, educator; b. New Orleans, Mar. 31, 1941; s. Cage Spooner and Esther Georgianna (Saul) J.; m. Shirley Lee O'Neal, Feb. 22, 1968; children: Stephanie, Michelle. Student, Creighton U., 1958-61, MD, 1965. Cert. Am. Bd. Internal Medicine, 1972, Am. Bd. Hematology, 1974. Intern U. Cin., 1965-66, resident, 1966-67, U. So. Calif., 1969-71, instr. LA, 1971-74, asst. prof., 1974-80, assoc. prof., 1980-88, dir. Comprehensive Sickle Cell Ctr., 1991—, prof., 1988—. Chmn. adv. com. Calif. Dept. Health Svcs., Sacramento, 1977—; dir. Hemoglobinopathy Lab., L.A., 1976—; bd. dirs. Sicke Cell Self-Help Assn., L.A., 1982-86, Team HEAL, 2002-. Contbr. numerous articles to profl. jours. Dir. Sickle Cell Disease Rsch. Found., L.A., 1986-94; active Nat. Med. Fellowships, Inc., Chgo., 1979—; chmn. rev. com. NIH, Washington, 1986-91; chmn. adv. com., 1995-97, mem. adv. coun., 1997-2002. Major U.S. Army, 1967-69, Vietnam. Fellow N.Y. Acad. Scis., Am. Coll. Angiology; mem. Am. Soc. Hematology, Am. Fedn. Clin. Rsch., Western Soc. Clin. Investigation, Internat. Soc. Biorheology, E.E. Just Soc. (sec.-treas. 1985-93, pres. 1994-95, sec. 1996—). Avocation: restoring antique automobiles. Office: 2025 Zonal Ave Rm R304 Los Angeles CA 90089-0110 Office Phone: 323-442-1259.

JOHNSON, CALVIN B., academic administrator, former state agency administrator, pediatrician; m. Pamela Johnson; 4 children. BS, Morehouse Coll.; MD, MPH, Johns Hopkins Univ., 1993. Cert. pediatrics. Residency Children's Hosp., Phila.; med. dir. divsn. family health NYC Dept. Health; asst. prof. pediat. Temple Univ. Sch. Medicine; staff pediatrician Temple Univ. Children's Med. Ctr.; sec. Pa. Dept. Health, Harrisburg, 2003—08; v.p., chief med. officer Temple Univ. Health Sys., Phila., 2008—. Bd. dir. Phila. Health Mgmt. Corp., Physicians for Social Responsibility; mem. Phila. Interdisciplinary Youth Fatality Review Com. Physician for 12 yrs. USAR. Named one of 40 Under 40, Phila. Bus. Jour., 2006. Office: Temple Univ Health Sys 3420 N Broad St Philadelphia PA 19140 Office Phone: 215-707-7000.

JOHNSON, CANDICE ELAINE BROWN, pediatrician, educator; b. Cin., Mar. 21, 1946; d. Paul Preston and Naomi Elizabeth Brown; m. Thomas Raymond Johnson, June 30, 1973; children: Andrea Eleanor, Erik Albert. BS, U. Mich., 1968; PhD Microbiology, Case Western Reserve U., 1973, MD, 1976. Diplomate Am. Bd. Pediat., 1981. Intern, resident in pediat. Rainbow Babies and Children's Hosp./Met. Gen. Hosp., Cleve., 1976-78; fellow in ambulatory pediatrics Met. Gen. Hosp., 1978-79; asst. prof. pediat. Case Western Res. U., Cleve., 1980-90, assoc. prof., 1990-97; prof. pediat. U. Colo., Denver, 1997—; pediatrician Children's Hosp., Denver, 1997—2006. Mem. rev. panel NIH, Washington, 1993; faculty sen. Case Western Res. U., 1988-91; mem. spkrs. bur. Merck, GlaxoSmithKline, Abbott Labs., 1998-2007; CME spkr. Outcomes Mgmt. Edn. Workshops, 2000-11. Contbr. articles profl. jours. Mem. Pediat. Infectious Disease Soc., Soc. Pediat. Rsch., Infectious Disease Soc. Am., So. Utah Wilderness Alliance, Sierra Club. Home: 2290 Locust St Denver CO 80207-3943

JOHNSON, CHARLES DANIEL, radiologist; b. Boise, Idaho, Oct. 7, 1952; m. Therese Ann Petsche; 1 child, Kristina. BS, Coll. Idaho, 1975; MD, Mayo Med. Sch., 1979; MS, U. Minn., 1984. Resident in internal medicine Mayo Clinic, Rochester, Minn., 1979-81, resident in diagnostic radiology, 1979-84, sr. assoc. cons., 1986-90, from asst. to prof. radiology, 1990-97, prof. radiology, 1997—; assoc. diagnostic radiology Duke U., Durham, NC, 1984-86. Cons. virtual colonoscopy Nat. Cancer Inst., 1995, 96; corp. advisor radiography and fluoroscopy equipment GE, 1991-96, 98; prin. investigator Am. Coll. Radiology Imaging Network, NIH, 2000-; head sect. GI radiology, 1991-99, head body MRI, 2001-2003, chair quarterly oversight com. radiology dept., co-chair safety leadership com. Mayo Rochester, 2005-. Grantee, NIH, 1997—. Mem. Am. Coll. Radiology (chair colon cancer con. 1996, 97), Am. Roentgen Ray Soc., Radiol. Soc. N.Am., Soc. Gastrointestinal Radiologist (Traveling Fellowship award 1997). Office: Mayo Clinic 200 1st St SW Rochester MN 55905-0002

JOHNSON, CHARLES FELZEN, retired medical educator; b. Chgo., Aug. 23, 1935; BA with honors, U. Calif., Santa Barbara, 1957; MD, UCLA, 1961. Lic. physician. Asst. prof. pediatrics U. Iowa, Iowa City, 1967, 72, prof. pediatrics, 1977; asst. dean continuing edn. Ea. Tenn. State U., 1977-81; prof. pediatrics Coll. Medicine Ea. Tenn. State U., 1977-81; dir. child abuse program Children's Hosp., Columbus, 1981—2002; attending physician autism clinic Ohio State U. Coll. Medicine, 2002—05; prof. pediatrics Ohio State U., Columbus, 1981—2005, prof. emeritus pediatrics, 2005. Adj. prof. pediat. North East Ohio U. Coll. Medicine, 2010—. Contbr. chpts. to books and articles to profl. jours. Capt. M.C. U.S. Army, 1964-67. Recipient Cert. Achievement, USA Europe, 1967, Cert. Appreciation, Assn. for Retarded Citizens, 1978, 1979, Tenn. State Assn. for Retarded Citizens, 1980, Child Advocacy award, Ohio State Atty. Gen., 1998, Lifetime Achievement award, Christopher Columbus Soc., 2002, Disting. Educator award, Ohio State U. Coll. Medicine, 2003. Fellow Am. Acad. Pediats.; mem. Rubber City Artists Group, Akron Toastmasters. Avocations: woodworking, gardening, painting. *

JOHNSON, CHARLES MCCOY, III, otolaryngologist, educator; b. Coronado, Calif., May 31, 1947; BS, Am. U., 1968; MD, Johns Hopkins U., 1972. Vice-chairman otolayngology dept. US Navy Oakland Naval Hosp., 1978—80; asst prof. U. Chgo. Dept Surgery, 1980—84; asst prof. otolaryngology U. Va., 1984—86; ptnr. ENT Cons. VA, PC, Charlottesville, 1986—2007; prof., pediat., anesthesia chief, pediatric otolaryngology Va. Commonwealth U. Dept Otolaryngology, 2007—. Pres. Va Soc. Otogaryngology, 1995—96, Assn Med. Officers Navy, 1996—97; mem. chair v.p. Med Soc. VA, 1996—2003; sci. cons. Cosmos Group, 2001—09; pres. Albemarle County Med. Soc., 2001—02. Decorated Legion of Merit US Navy, Meritorious Svc. medal, Navy Commendation medal; recipient Top Doc award, Richmond Mag., 2011. Fellow: ACS, Am. Acad. Piedat., Am. Acad. Otolayngology; mem.: Am. Med. Assn, Am. Soc. Pediat. Otolarngology (charter mem.). Avocations: cooking, history. Office: Dept Otolaryngology VCU Med Ctr Richmond VA 23219 Office Phone: 804-828-3966. Office Fax: 804-828-3495. Business E-Mail: cjohnsoniii@mcvh-vcu.edu.

JOHNSON, CRYSTAL DUANE, psychologist; b. Houston, Mar. 2, 1954; d. Alton Floyd and Duane (Mullican) J. BA, U. Tex., 1983, MS, 1985. Lic. profl. counselor, psychol. assoc., marriage and family therapist, specialist in sch. psychology, cert. chem. dependency specialist. Student devel. specialist U. Tex., Tyler, 1985-86, intake counselor, 1986-88; staff psychologist Sabine Valley Ctr., Longview, Tex., 1987-88, Mental Health/Mental Retardation Ctr. of East Tex., Tyler, 1988-89; pvt. practice psychologist Tyler, 1989—. Counselor Juvenile and Adult Probation Depts., 1988—, ICF/MR Resdl. Homes, 1991—, Children's Advocacy Ctr., 2000—; spl. edn. counselor, 1990—. Mem. Smith County Humane Soc., Tyler, 1985—, Humane Soc. of the U.S., Washington, 1987—, Am. Soc. Prevention Cruelty to Animals, 1987—, Nat. Wildlife Fedn., 1986—, World Wildlife Fedn., 1986—. Avocations: horticulture, oil and watercolor painting, travel.

JOHNSON, CYNDA ANN, physician, educator; b. Girard, Kans., July 16, 1951; BA in Biology and German with honors, Stanford U., 1973; MD, UCLA, 1977; MBA, U. Mo., Kansas City, 1999. Diplomate Am. Bd. Family Medicine (bd. dirs., pres. 1999-2000). Tchg. fellow U. N.C., Chapel Hill, 1980-81; intern U. Kans. Med. Ctr., Kansas City, 1977-78, 1978-80, prof., acting chair dept. family medicine, 1998—99; prof., head dept. family medicine U. Iowa Coll. Medicine, Iowa City, 1999—2003; dean Brody Sch. Medicine East Carolina U., Greenville, NC, 2003—06, sr. assoc. vice chancellor for clin. and translational rsch., 2007—08; pres. and dean Va. Tech. Carilion Sch. Medicine, 2008—. Mem. Am. Acad. Family Physicians, Soc. Tchrs. Family Medicine, Va. Acad. Family Physicians, Va. Med. Soc. Office: Va Tech Carilion Sch Medicine PO Box 13727 Roanoke VA 24036 Office Phone: 540-853-0432. Office Fax: 540-983-1190. E-mail: cajohnson@carilion.com.

JOHNSON, DAVID HORTON, oncologist; b. Dalton, Ga., Apr. 19, 1948; BS in Zoology, U. Kentucky, MS in Physiology; MD, Med. Coll. Ga., 1976. Intern, medicine U. South Ala. Med. Ctr., Mobile, Ala., 1977, resident, medicine, 1977—79; resident Med. Coll. Ga. Hosp., Augsuta, Ga., 1979—80, Vanderbilt U. Med. Ctr.; dir. divsn. oncology, hematology Vanderbilt U., Nashville, Cornelius Abernathy Craig Prof. Med. and Surgical Oncology; dep. dir. Vanderbilt-Ingram Cancer Ctr., Nashville. Investigator in field. Contbr. articles to profl. publications. Recipient Frank Moran Clinical Leadership award, U. Mich., 2000. Mem.: Am. Soc. Clinical Oncology. Office: Vanderbilt U 777 Preston Research Bldg Hematology/Oncology Nashville TN 37232-6307 also: 1903 The Vanderbilt Clinic Nashville TN 37232-5536 Office Phone: 615-343-9454, 615-322-6053. Office Fax: 615-343-8668.

JOHNSON, DAVID WOLCOTT, psychologist, educator; b. Muncie, Ind., Feb. 7, 1940; s. Roger Winfield and Frances Elizabeth (Pierce) J.; m. Linda Mulholland, July 7, 1973; children: James, David, Catherine, Margaret, Jeremiah. BS, Ball State U., Muncie, Ind., 1962; MA, Columbia U., NYC, 1964, EdD, 1966. Asst. prof. ednl. psychology U. Minn., Mpls., 1966-69, assoc. prof., 1969-73, prof., 1973—, Emma Birkmaier prof. in ednl. leadership, 1994—. Bd. dirs. Infrared Solutions, Inc.; orgnl. cons., psychotherapist. Author: Social Psychology of Education, 1970; (with Goodwin Watson) Social Psychology: Issues and Insights, 1972, Reaching Out, 1972, 9th edit., 2005, Contemporary Social Psychology, 1973; (with F. Johnson) Joining Together, 1975, 9th edit., 2005; (with D. Tjosvold) Porductive Conflict Management, 1983, Circles of Learning, 1984, 4th edit., 2002; (with R. Johnson) Learning Together and Alone, 1975, 5th edit., 1999, Human Relations and Your Career, 1978, 3d Edit., 1991, Educational Psychology, 1979, Structuring Cooperative Learning,

1987, Creative Conflict, 1987, Leading the Cooperative School, 1989, 2d edit., 1994, Cooperation and Competition: Theory and Research, 1989, Teaching Students to be Peacemakers, 1991, 4th edit., 2005, video, 1991, Learning Mathematics and Cooperative Learning, 1991, Creative Controversy, 1992, 4th Edit. 2007, Positive Interdependence, 1992, (video) 1992, Meaningful and Manageable Assessment Through Cooperative Learning, 1996, Learning to Lead Teams, 1997, Human Relations: Valuing Diversity, 1999, Meaningful Assessment, 2002, Multicultural Education and Human Relations, 2002, Constructive Controversy, 4th edit., 2007; (with R. Johnson, E. Holubec) Cooperative Learning, 1984, 7th edit., 1998, Cooperation in the Classroom, 1984, 7th edit., 1998, Advanced Cooperative Learning, 1988, 3d edit., 1998, Cooperative Learning: Increasing College Faculty Instructional Productivity, 1991, The Nuts and Bolts of Cooperative Learning, 1994, Academic Controversy, 1997, (with R. Johnson, K. Smith) Active Learning: Cooperative Learning in the College Classroom, 1991, 3d edit., 2006, (with R. Johnson) Assessing Students in Groups, 2004; editor Am. Ednl. Rsch. Jour., 1981-83; contbr. over 500 articles to profl. jours. and edited books Bd. dirs. Walk-In Counseling Ctr., 1971-74. Recipient Gordon Allport award Soc. for Psychol. Study of Social Issues, 1981, Helen Plante award Am. Soc. Engring. Edn., 1984, Outstanding Rsch. award Am. Pers. and Guidance Assn., 1972, Nat. Coun. for the Social Studies Rsch. award, 1986, Outstanding Rsch. award AACD, 1988, award for Outstanding Contbn. Am. Edn. Minn. ASCD, 1990, Outstanding Alumni of Yr. award Ball State U., 1990, Rsch. and Practice award S.W. Ohio Planning Coun. for Insvc. Edn., 1990, Excellence in Tchg. award Dept. Def. Schs., Panama, 1994, Emma Birkmaier Prof. in Ednl. Leadership Coll. Edn. U. Minn., 1994-97, Disting. Contbns. Applications Psych. award, 2003, Brock Internat. prize in Edn., 2007, Disting. Contbns. Rsch. in Edn. award, 2008. Fellow APA (Disting. Contbns. Applications of Psychology to Edn. and Tng. award 2003); mem. Am. Sociol. Assn., Am. Ednl. Rsch. Assn. (award for Outstanding Contbn. to Coop. Learning 1996, Disting. Scholar award 2001, Disting. Contbn. to Rsch. in Edn. award 2008), Am. Mgmt. Assn., Am. Assn. for Counseling and Devel., Nat. Rsch. Coun. Office: U Minn 330 Burton Hall Minneapolis MN 55455 Address: 5028 Halifax Ave S Edina MN 55424 Home: 5028 Halifax Ave S Minneapolis MN 55424-1417

JOHNSON, DEWEY, JR., retired biochemist; b. Sapulpa, Okla., Sept. 23, 1926; s. Dewey and Maude (Hickey) Johnson; m. Patricia R. Rodgers, Feb. 14, 1953 (dec. Mar. 1997); children: Joseph D., Paul D., Mary Ann, Richard E.; m. Carol S. Martin, Sept. 25, 1999. BS, Colo. State U., 1950; MS, U. Conn., 1955; PhD, Rutgers State U., 1958. Nutritionist Limecrest Rsch. Lab., Newton, NJ, 1958-63; biochemist Equitable Life, NYC, 1963-79, Met. Life, NYC, 1980-90, disability underwriter, 1990-92; chemist EPA, Edison, NJ, 1993—2001; ret., 2001—. Contbr. Avocations: gardening, woodworking. Home: 59 Dunnell Rd Maplewood NJ 07040-1333

JOHNSON, DORIS JEAN, social worker; b. Raymond, Miss., July 16, 1946; AA, Wayne County C.C., Detroit, 1986; BSW, U. Detroit, 1989; MSW, Wayne State U., 1993. Supr. Ren, Detroit, 1993—94; psychiat. social worker Aurora Healthcare, Inc., Detroit, 1994—2001, Detroit Cmty. Health Connection, 2002—; clin. social worker Psychiat. and Behavioral Medicine Profls., 2003—. Author: (novel) A Reflection of Memories, 2003. Pres. Slum Lord Fighters, Detroit, 1981, Human Svcs. Orgn./Wayne County C.C., 1984; v.p. social work orgn./Univ. Detroit, 1988. Recipient cert. Appreciation, Detroit Police Athletic League, 1989, award of Recognition, Detroit City Coun., 1989, cert. appreciation, 36th Dist. Ct., Detroit, 1997; named to Wall of Tolerance, Civil Rights Meml. Ctr., 2005. Mem.. Black Expression Club. E-mail: doris0716@aol.com.

JOHNSON, DOUGLAS WILLIAM, radiologist; b. Westpoint, NY; s. Andrew Larson and Barbara Joan (Rosborough) J.; m. Susan Mary Friedman, July 23, 1977; children: Danielle, Michael. BS in Biology, Va. Tech., Blacksburg, Va., 1976; MD, Med. Coll. Va., Richmond, 1979. Chmn. radiation oncology David Grant USAF Med. Ctr., Travis AFB, Calif., 1983-87; ptnr. Fla. Radiation Oncology Group, Jacksonville, Fla., 1987—. Asst. prof. radiation-oncology Stanford Med. Ctr., Stanford U., Calif., 1983-87; asst. prof. oncology Mayo Clinic Med. Sch., Rochester, Minn., 1995—; fellow Am. Coll. Radiology, Phila., 1995. Patentee in field. Col. USAF, 1975-. Fellow Am. Coll. Radiology; mem. Am. Soc. Therapeutic Radiology & Oncology. Avocation: aviation. Office: Baptist Cancer Inst 1235 San Marco Blvd Ste 100 Jacksonville FL 32207-8560 Office Phone: 904-202-7020.

JOHNSON, EDGAR MCCARTHY, psychologist; b. Jacksonville, Fla., Oct. 29, 1941; s. James Mack and Dorothy (Vickers) Johnson; m. Fatima Nunes, Sept. 9, 1967; children: Victoria C., David M. BS in Applied Psychology, Ga. Inst. Tech., 1964; MS in Exptl. Psychology, Tufts U., 1967, PhD in Exptl. Psychology, 1969. Rsch. psychologist U.S. Army Rsch. Inst., Alexandria, Va., 1970-78, chief human factors sect., 1978-80, dir. systems rsch. lab., 1980-82, tech. dir., 1982-93, dir., 1993—2002; chief psychologist U.S. Army, 1982—2002; mem. rsch. staff Inst. Def. Analyses, Alexandria, Va., 2002—. Bd. trustees Amelia Island Mus. History, 2007—. Served to capt. US Army, 1968—70. NDEA fellow, 1965—67. Fellow: APA, Washington Acad. Sci. (Sci. Achievement award 1980), Human Factors and Ergonomics Soc., Am. Psychol. Soc.; mem.: Cosmos Club (Washington), Sigma Xi. Home: 1384 Mission San Carlos Dr Amelia Island FL 32034 Personal E-mail: emj1@sigmaxi.net.

JOHNSON, EDWARD ELEMUEL, psychologist, educator; b. Jamaica, B.W.I., July 25, 1926; came to U.S., 1941, naturalized, 1948; s. Edward and Mary Elizabeth (Blake) J.; m. Beverley Jean Morris, Jan. 26, 1955; children— Edward Elemuel, Lawrence Palmer, Robin Jeannine, Nathan Jerome, Cyril Ulric. BS, Howard U., 1947, MS, 1948; PhD, U. Colo., 1952. Assoc. prof. psychology Grambling Coll., La., 1954-55; prof. So. U., Baton Rouge, 1955-60, prof., head dept. psychology, 1960-69, assoc. dean univ., 1969-72, dir. Regional Head Start Evaluation and Research Ctr.; clin. prof. La. State U. Med. Sch., New Orleans, 1969-72; dir. United Bd. for Coll. Devel., 1972-74; dir. 13 coll. curriculum program So. U., Baton Rouge; clin. prof. psychiatry Emory U. Med. Sch., Atlanta, 1973-74; prof. psychiatry Robert Wood Johnson Med. Sch., Piscataway, NJ, 1974—2003, clin. prof. psychiatry, 2003—; pres. Limited Liability Corp. in Forensic Psychology, 2002—; pvt. practice, 2003—. Cons. collaborative child devel. project; cons. State Indsl. Sch. Scotlandville, La., 1973-74, VA Hosp., Lyons, N.J., 1987; mem. Med. Rev. Panel, State of N.J., 1976-2006, chmn., 1993; vocat. cons. HEW; mem. mental health adv. group Westinghouse Health Systems, 1978-82; region II mental health coordinator Head Start Program, 1978—; mem. gen. research support rev. com. NIH, 1980—; mem. acad. council Thomas A. Edison Coll. NJ, 1978-83; mem. adv. bd. Office Pub. Guardian, State of N.J., 1988—; chmn. minority and cultural concerns com. div. Mental Health and Hosps. State of N.J., 1989—; psychol. evaluator Superior Ct. NJ Middlesex Vicinage, 1996—; lectr. forensic psychology U. V.I., St. Croix; cons. forensic psychology. Contbr. articles to profl. jours.; Lectr. Drugs & Drug User Stress & Forensic Psychology, 2008—. Bd. dir. Crossroads Theatre Co., New Brunswick, N.J. Served to 1st lt. AUS, 1951-53. Fellow AAAS; mem. Am. Psychol. Assn. (com. on adv. svcs. for edn. and tng. 1968-69, task group on faculty devel. for minority and non-minority faculty to implement culturally relevant curriculum 1992), N.Y. Acad. Scis. (life), Masons, Sigma Xi, Sigma Pi Phi, Alpha Phi Alpha, Beta Beta Beta, Pi Gamma Mu, Psi Chi. Home: PO Box 597 East Brunswick NJ 08816-0597 Home Phone: 732-257-4885.

JOHNSON, ELIZABETH MISNER, health services executive; d. Gervase Arthur and Blenda N. (Westerlund) Misner; m. Dohn Robert Johnson, Oct. 13, 1962; children: Dohn Robert Jr., Kevin Arthur. BS in Acctg., U. Idaho, 1961. CPA, Calif., Wash. Audit staff Randall, Emery, Campbell & Parker (now Pricewaterhouse Coopers), Spokane, Wash., 1961—62; audit staff, sr. Price Waterhouse, LA, 1962-65; CPA LA, 1966-73; CFO KLP, Inc. dba Call-America, Mesa, Ariz., 1995-98; gen. mgr. Life Line Screening, Phoenix, 2001—02; contr. Martin Park Ranch Homeowners Assn., Phoenix, 2002—. Treas., pres., hon. life mem. Arts Coun. Calif. State U., Northridge, 1975—; internat. dir. alumnae devel. Alpha Gamma Delta (recipient unusually outstanding svc. award, 1993), U.S. and Can., 1988-98; chmn. bd. trustees Alpha Gamma Delta Found., 1998-2001, trustee, 1998—2004. Pres. Soroptimist Internat., Coeur d'Alene, Idaho, 1991-92, regional nominating com., 1993-. Mem. Ariz. Soc. of CPAs. Home: 14839 S 47th Way Phoenix AZ 85044-6881 Office: MPR Home Owners Assn 15425 S 40th St Ste 4 Phoenix AZ 85044 Personal E-mail: liz@mtparkranch.org.

JOHNSON, EVAN KENNETH, physical therapist, educator; b. NYC, Feb. 14, 1960; m. Wendy Haberman, Aug. 21, 1993; children: Jared Ian, Ethan Francis. BA in Psychology and Biology, Hunter Coll., CUNY, NYC, 1992; MS in Phys. Therapy, Columbia U., NYC, 1994; PhD in Phys. Therapy, U. St. Augustine, Fla., 2006. Cert. manual therapist U. St. Augustine. Phys. therapist Ball Meml. Hosp., Muncie, Ind., 1994-96; asst. chief phys. therapist Phys. Medicine and Rehab. Ctr., Englewood, N.J., 1996-98; site coord. St. Charles Hosp. Rehab. Network, Bronx/Queens, NY, 1998-2000; phys. therapy coord. Phys. Medicine and Rehab. Ctr., Bardonia, N.Y., 2000-2001; sr. therapist advanced clinician N.Y. Presbyn. Hosp.: Columbia Presbyn. Spine Ctr., 2001—. Clin. instr., lectr. Columbia U., NYC, 1996-2003, asst. prof. clin. phys. therapy, 2003—, dir., Spine Ctr., dept. neurol. surgery, 2006-, with rehab. medicine, anestheology and neurol. surgery, 2007-; clin. faculty assoc. N.Y. Med. Coll., 1998-2003; phys. therapy coord. clin. pathways com., Ball Meml. Hosp., 1994, 95, mem. Bottom Line Com. Phys. Therapy Jour., 2007-. Contbr. articles to Jour. Orthopaedic and Sports Phys. Therapy, Neurosurgery. Recipient J and W Freedman award Hunter Coll., 1992, Phys. Therapy Alumni award Columbia U., 1992, 93, Mary E. Callahan award Columbia U., 1994; Paul Brachfeld grantee CUNY, 1991, 92. Mem. Am. Phys. Therapy Assn. (cert. othopedist specialist, platform presenter, Reno, 1995, performing arts spl. interest group, orthopaedic sect.), Internat. Assn. Dance Medicine and Sci., Am. Acad. Orthopaedic Manual Phys. Therapists, Phi Beta Kappa. Office: Columbia Univ Spine Ctr 710 W 168th St 5th Floor New York NY 10032 Office Phone: 212-305-9625.

JOHNSON, FRANK EDWARD, surgeon educator; b. Evanston, Ill., Oct. 28, 1943; s. Frank E. and Beryl Madeline (Johnson) J.; m. Tamiko Asato, Jan. 24, 1976; children: Mariko, Michael, Eric, David. BA, U. Minn., 1964, MD, 1967. Diplomate Am. Bd. Surgery. Intern UCLA affiliated hosps., 1967-78; resident in surgery U. Wash., Seattle, 1972-74, U. Colo., 1974-77; rsch. fellow U. Calif., San Francisco, 1975-76; fellow in surg. oncology Meml. Sloan-Kettering Cancer Ctr., NYC, 1977-79; rsch. prof. Guy's Hosp., London, 1986-87; clin. instr. surgery Cornell U., NYC, 1977-79; asst. prof. St. Louis U. Med. Ctr., 1979-84, assoc. prof., 1984-89, prof., 1989—. Editor: Cancer Patient Follow-up, 1997, The Bionic Human, 2005, author 16 med. films; contbr. articles to profl. jours. Co-founder Children's Heart Link, Mpls., 1969. Lt. comdr. USN, 1969-71, Vietnam. Decorated Bronze Star; grantee NIH, Am. Cancer Soc., Royal Coll. Surgeons Found., VA Merit Rev. Mem. ACS, Am. Gastroent. Assn., AMA, Soc. Surg. Oncology, Am. Soc. Clin. Oncology, Am. Assn. Cancer Edn., Am. Paraplegia Soc., Am. Assn. Cancer Rsch., Am. Soc. Preventive Oncology, Ctrl. Surg. Assn. (grantee), Southwestern Surg. Congress, Am. Head and Neck Soc., Am. Physiol. Soc., Soc. Univ. Surgeons, Soc. Surgery of the Alimentary Tract, Assn. Acad. Surgeons, Assn. Surgeons of Gt. Britain and Ireland, Am. Surg. Assn. Office Phone: 314-577-8316. Business E-Mail: frank.johnson1@va.gov. *

JOHNSON, HAZEL WINIFRED, retired army officer, nurse; b. West Chester, Pa., Oct. 10, 1927; d. Clarence Lemont and Garnett J. RN diploma, Harlem Hosp., NYC, 1950; BSN, Villanova U., 1959; MSN, Tchr.'s Coll., Columbia U., 1963; PhD in Ednl. Adminstrn., Cath. U. Am., 1978. 1st lt. U.S. Army Nurse Corps, 1955, advanced through grades to brig. gen., 1979; mem. staff U.S. Army Med. R&D Command, Washington, 1967-73; dir. Walter Reed Army Inst. Nursing, Washington, 1976-78; asst. for nursing Office of Surgeon Med. Command, Korea, 1979-83; chief Army Nurse Corps Office of Surgeon Gen. Dept. of the Army, Washington, 1983-86; dir. govtl. affairs office Am. Nurses Assn., 1986-96; prof. Coll. Nursing and Health Sci. George Mason U., 1989-96; dir. Ctr. for Health Policy George Mason U., 1996—. Cons. Nursing Edn. Health Policy, Health Adminstrn. Decorated Disting. Svc. medal, Legion of merit, Meritorious Svc. medal, Army Commendation medal; recipient Evangeline G. Bovard Army Nurse of Yr. award Letterman Army Med. Ctr., San Francisco, 1964, Dr. Anita Newcomb McGee award DAR, Washington, 1971. Mem. Assn. Balck Nursing Faculty, Black Women United for Action, Assn. U.S. Army, Nat. Assn. Military Family, Am. Nurses Assn., Nat. League Nursing, Sigma Theta Tau.

JOHNSON, HOPE L., epidemiologist, educator; b. Caribou, Maine, Mar. 21, 1977; d. Frank B. and Nanette A. Johnson; m. Ruben H. Schurman, Aug. 4, 2004; 1 child, Suriyanah E. Schurman. BA, U. Wash., Seattle, 1999; MPH, Johns Hopkins Bloomberg Sch. Pub. Health, Balt., 2003, PhD, 2007. Health & nutrition ext. vol. Peace Corps, Paramaribo, Suriname, 1999—2001; epidemiology & health info. sys. cons. Pan Am. Health Orgn., Paramaribo, 2001—02; grad. rsch. asst. Johns Hopkins Bloomberg Sch. Pub. Health, Balt., 2003—07, faculty, 2007—, epidemiologist, 2007—; program asst./rsch. project interviewer Fred Hutchinson Cancer Rsch. Ctr., Seattle, 1998—99. Cons. PATH, Washington, 2007. Contbr. articles to profl. jours. Predoc. fellowship, Nat. Inst. Allergy and Infectious Diseases, 2004—07, Edward T. Conroy State scholarship, Md. State, 2006—07, Dean's Alumni Adv. Coun. scholarship, Johns Hopkins Bloomberg Sch. Pub. Health, 2006—07, Rsch. grant, Bill & Melinda Gates Found., 2008—. Mem.: APHA, Global Health Coun., Am. Sexually Transmitted Diseases Assn., Alpha Delta Pi. Roman Catholic. Achievements include research in Pneumococcal Global Serotype Project; Pneumococcal Global Disease Burden; Epidemiology of sexually transmitted infections and adverse pregnancy outcomes among pregnant STD clinic attendees. Business E-Mail: hjohnson@jhsph.edu.

JOHNSON, IRVING STANLEY, pharmaceutical executive, biomedical research consultant; b. Grand Junction, Colo., June 30, 1925; s. Walter Glen and Frances Lucetta (Tuttle) J.; m. Alwyn Neville Ginther, Jan. 29, 1949; children: Rebecca Lyn, Bryan Glenn, Kirsten Shawn, Kevin Bruce. BS, Washburn U., Topeka, 1948; PhD in Devel. Biology, U. Kans., Lawrence, 1953; student, Cornell U., Duke U., Harvard U. With Lilly Rsch. Labs., Indpls., 1953-88, v.p. rsch., 1973-88; mem. profl. edn. com. Am. Cancer Soc., 1972-82. Rschr. cancer, virus, genetic engring.; mem. UCLA Symposia Bd., 1988-; bd. dirs. Allelix Biopharms., Ligand Pharms.; sci. adv. bd. Elan Corp., 1996-; cons., Swedish Govt. & European Pharma Co., trustee La Jolla Cancer Rsch. Found., 1990-93; advisor to biomed. rsch. cos., venture capital groups; mem. Recombinant Adv. Com., NIH; indep. biomedical rsch. cons. Editor: Biology and Medicine in the 21st Century, 2007; mem. sci. adv. bd. Biotech., 1986—; mem. editorial bd. Chemico-Biol. Interactions, 1968-73; contbr. articles to profl. publs.; patentee in field. Industry spkr. NAS Open Forum. With USNR, 1943—46. Named Ten Outstanding Young Men, US C.of C., 1960; recipient 1st ann. Congl. award for sci. and tech., 1984, Alumni Disting. Achievement award U. Kans., 2005, Disting. Svc. Citation award U. Kans., 2006, Recognition award, US Congress State Legis. Coms. Fellow AAAS; mem. Am. Assn. Cancer Rsch. (emeritus mem; Cain Meml. award for outstanding preclin. rsch. in cancer chemotherapy 1986), Am. Soc. Cell Biology (mem. pub. policy com.), Environ. Mutagen Soc., Internat. Soc. Chemotherapy, NY Acad. Scis., Soc. Exptl. Biology and Medicine, Am. Soc. Immunologists (mem. sci. adv. bd. biotech), Soc. for Neurosci., NSF (del. mem.), Sigma Xi, Phi Sigma. Episcopalian. Achievements include being widely acknowledged for leadership team which led to the production and approval of the first health care product manufactured by recombinant DNA/genetic engineering techniques, ie human insulin. Home Phone: 239-472-4782, 207-367-2667. Personal E-mail: alwynjohnson@comcast.net.

JOHNSON, JAMES D., researcher; b. San Diego, Oct. 1, 1954; MS, FSU, 1987; JD, U. SD, 1993. Rsch. collaborator Auburn U., 2007—. Adj. prof. numerous cmty. colls., 1990—2009. Mem.: AAAS. Achievements include research in biochemistry of carotenoids in tetrapods. Avocation: music. Home: 4720 SW Elim Ch Rd Fort White FL 32038 Personal E-mail: jdj@3dbiochem.com.

JOHNSON, JEAN ELAINE, nursing educator; b. Wilsey, Kans., Mar. 11, 1925; d. William H. and Rosa L. (Welty) Irwin. BS, Kans. State U., 1948; MS in Nursing, Yale U., 1965; MS, U. Wis., 1969, PhD, 1971; DS (hon.), Univ. Wis., 1998. Instr. nursing, Iowa, 1948—58; staff nurse Swedish Hosp., Englewood, Colo., 1958—60; in-svc. edn. coord. Gen. Rose Hosp., Denver, 1960—63; rsch. asst. Yale U., New Haven, 1965—67; assoc. prof. nursing Wayne State U., Detroit, 1971—74, prof., 1974—79; dir. Ctr. for Health Rsch., 1974—79; assoc. dir. oncology nursing Cancer Ctr. U. Rochester, NY, 1979—93, prof. nursing, 1979—95, prof. emerita, 1995—. Rosenstadt prof. health rsch. Faculty Nursing, U. Toronto, 1985; vis. prof. U. Utah Coll. Nursing, 1996—97, U. Wis., Madison, 1998. Author: Self-Regulation Theory: Applying Theory to Your Practice, 1997; contbg. author Handbook of Psychology and Health, vol. 5, 1984; contbr. articles to profl. jours. Recipient Bd. Govs. Faculty Recognition award, Wayne State U., 1975, award for disting. contbn. to nursing sci., Am. Nurses Found. and ANA Coun. for Nurse Rschrs., 1983, Grad. Tchg. award, U. Rochester, 1991, Disting. Rschr. award, Oncology Nursing Soc., 1992, Outstanding Contbns. to Nursing and Psychology award, divsn. of health psychology APA, 1993, recognized as a Living Legend, Am. Acad. Nursing, 2005; grantee, NIH, 1972—95. Fellow: AAAS, Am. Psychol. Soc., Acad. for Behavioral Medicine Rsch.; mem.: ANA (chmn. coun. for nurse rschrs. 1976—78, commn. for rsch. 1978—82), Inst. Medicine of NAS (com. on patient injury compensation 1976—77, membership com. 1981—86, gov. coun. 1987—89), Phi Kappa Phi, Omicron Nu, Sigma Xi. Home: 4924 Whitecomb Dr Apt 15 Madison WI 53711-2661 Personal E-mail: jean_joh@msn.com.

JOHNSON, JOHN H., pharmaceutical executive; BS, U. Pa. Pres. Ortho Biotech Products; group chmn. worldwide biopharmaceuticals unit Johnson & Johnson; CEO, Med. Info. Sys. Parkstone; various positions, sales, sales mgmt. Pfizer; CEO ImClone Systems, Inc., NYC, 2007—09; sr. v.p., pres. oncology bus. unit Eli Lilly and Co., 2009—11; CEO, bd. dirs. Savient Pharmaceuticals Inc., 2011—. Bd. dirs. BioNJ, ImClone Sys., Cempra Pharmaceuticals, 2009—. Office: Savient Pharmaceuticals Inc One Tower Ctr 14th Fl East Brunswick NJ 08816 *

JOHNSON, JOHNNY, research psychologist, consultant; b. Clarksdale, Miss., Jan. 10, 1938; s. Eddie B. and Elizabeth (Ousley) J.; children: Tonya, Anita. Student, Coahoma Jr. Coll., 1957, Hunter Coll., 1964, N.Y.U., 1963; BS, Tenn. State U., 1970, MS, 1974; postgrad., Saybrook Inst., 1987-89. Instr. Dept. of the Navy, Millington, Tenn., 1976-80, edn. specialist, 1980-87, curriculum advisor, 1987-88; prof. human resources mgmt. Pepperdine U., LA, 1975-77; prof. psychology Shelby State C.C., Memphis, Tenn., 1985—. Actor: (films) Elvis, 1989, Memphis, 1990, The Firm, 1993, A Family Thing, 1995; recording artist with releases in jazz, blues and Latino. With USN, 1957-63. Mem. APA (assoc.), Am. Psychol. Soc., Soc. Psychol. Study of Social Issues, Assn. Black Psychologists, Soc. Psychol. Study Gay and Lesbian Issues, Internat. Platform Assn. Avocations: golf, dog breeding, music, foreign languages, pocket billiards. Home: 773 Margie Dr Memphis TN 38127-2727 Office Phone: 901-357-5613. E-mail: CoolJuanJohnny@yahoo.com.

JOHNSON, JOYCE MARIE, psychiatrist, epidemiologist, public health officer; b. Baton Rouge, Jan. 30, 1952; d. Gene Addison and Helen Marie (Kalcik) Johnson; m. James Albert Calderwood, Mar. 28, 1987; 1 child, James. BA, Luther Coll., Decorah, Iowa, 1972; MA, U. Iowa, 1974; DO, Mich. State U., 1980; DFA (hon.), NY Inst. Tech., 2001. Cert. in psychiatry, pub. health and preventive medicine, and clin. pharmacology. Cooking instr. Kirkwood CC, Iowa City, 1974—76; health planner Iowa Regional Med. Program, Iowa City, 1974—76; commd. USPHS, rear adm./asst. surgeon gen.; intern USPHS Hosp., Balt., 1980—81; med. epidemiologist Hepatitis Labs., Ctrs. Disease Control, Phoenix, 1981—83, AIDS, Ctrs. Disease Control, Atlanta, 1983—84; resident psychiatry NIMH, 1984—87, staff psychiatrist, 1987—88; epidemiologist, divsn. dir. FDA, 1995—2003; dir. divsn. nat. treatment demonstrations Substance Abuse and Mental Health Svcs. Adminstrn., 1993—97; chief med. officer USCG, 1997—2003; v.p. health scis. Battelle Meml. Inst., 2004—. Clin. faculty mem. Mich. State U., 1983—93, Georgetown U. Med. Ctr., 1988—2009. Recipient Dr. Nathan Davis award Outstanding Work Govt. Svc., 2001; Med. Perspectives fellowship, New Guinea and Thailand, 1978—79. Mem.: Cosmos Club, Mensa, Explorers Club. Office: 5518 Western Ave Bethesda MD 20815-7122

JOHNSON, KAREN C., physician, epidemiologist, researcher; MD, U. Tenn., Memphis, 1985; MPH, Johns Hopkins U., Baltimore, 1989. Prof. Dept. Preventive Medicine, Memphis, 1990—, vice chair, 1996—2010, interim chair, 2010—. Office: Univ Tennessee Health Sci C 66 N Pauline Ste 633 Memphis TN 38163 *

JOHNSON, KAREN L., nursing researcher; b. Corning, NY, May 14, 1958; MSN, U. Rochester, 1986; PhD, U. Ky., 1999. Assoc. prof. Sch. Nursing U. Md., 2001—, don, rsch. and evidence-based practice Med. Ctr., 2003—. Nominating com. AACN, 2011—, chair, evidence-based practice work group, 2009—10. Mem.: AACN (Outstanding Advanced Practice Nurse award), Soc. Critical Care Medicine. Office: University Md Med Ctr Baltimore MD 21201 Business E-Mail: kjohnson8@umm.edu.

JOHNSON, KEN B., anesthesiologist, educator; b. Oakland, July 23, 1962; BS, U. Calif., Berkeley, 1987; MD, Tulane U., 1991. Prof. dept. anestheisology U. Utah, 1999—. Office: 30 N 1900 E Rm 3C444 Salt Lake City UT 84132 Office Fax: 801-581-4367. Business E-Mail: ken.b.johnson@hsc.utah.edu.

JOHNSON, KENNETH PETER, neurologist, researcher; b. Jamestown, NY, Mar. 12, 1932; s. Kenneth Peter and Nina (Bengtson) Johnson; m. Jacquelyn Johnson, June 23, 1956; children: Peter, Thomas, Diane, Douglas. BA, Upsala Coll., East Orange, NJ, 1955; MD, Jefferson Med. Coll., Phila., 1959. Diplomate: Am. Bd. Psychiatry and Neurology. Intern Buffalo Gen. Hosp., 1959-60; resident Hosp. of Cleve., 1963-65; asst. prof. neurology Case Western Res. U., Cleve., 1968-71, assoc. prof., 1971-74; prof. U. Calif., San Francisco, 1974-81; prof., chmn. U. Md., Balt., 1981—2009, prof. emeritus, 2009, chmn., 1981—2002; chief neurology VA Hosp., Balt., 1981-83. Editor: Neurovirology, 1984; contbr. numerous articles in field to profl. jours. Served to lt. U.S. Navy, 1961-63. Recipient Weil award Am. Assn. Neuropathology, 1967, Research Ctr. Devel. award NIH, 1968-73, John J. Dystal prize, 2000; Zimmerman lectr. Stanford U., 1981 Fellow Am. Neurol. Assn.; mem. Am. Acad. Neurology, Am. Soc. Virology, Am. Congress Rehab. Medicine, Am. Soc. Neurorehab., Internat. Soc. for Neuroimmunology, America's Com. Treatment & Rsch. Multiple Sclerosis (founder). Lutheran. Office: Md Ctr for MS 110 S Paca St 3rd Fl Baltimore MD 21201

JOHNSON, KEVIN B., pediatrician, biomedical researcher; BS in Biology, Dickinson Coll., Carlisle, Pa.; MS in Med. Informatics, Stanford U. Sch. Medicine, Calif.; MD, Johns Hopkins U. Sch. Medicine, Balt. Diplomate American Bd. Pediat. Resident dept. pediat. Johns Hopkins Hosp.; postdoc. rsch. fellowship U. Calif., San Diego; mgmt. of perioperative services fellowship Stanford U.; faculty pediat. and biomedical info. scis. Johns Hopkins U. Sch. Medicine, 1992—2002; pediatric chief resident Johns Hopkins Hosp., 1992—2002; faculty Vanderbilt U. Sch. Medicine, Nashville, 2002—, prof. pediat., vice chair biomedical informatics. Mem. med. adv. bd. PatientKeeper, Inc., 2001—. Asst. editor JAMIA-Jour. American Med. Informatics Assn., mem. editl. bd. Ambulatory Pediat.; contbr. numerous articles to profl. jours., chapters to books. Harold Amos Med. Faculty Devel. Program scholar, Robert Wood Johnson Found., 1998—2002. Mem.: American Pediatric Soc., Inst. Medicine, American Acad. Pediat., American Med. Informatics Assn. Achievements include research in the uses of advanced computer technologies, including the Worldwide Web, personal digital assistants, and pen-based computers in medicine; development of computer-based documentation systems for the point of care. Office: Vanderbilt U Rm 428 Eskind Biomedical Library 2209 Garland Ave Nashville TN 37232 Office Phone: 615-936-3596. Office Fax: 615-936-1427. E-mail: kevin.b.johnson@vanderbilt.edu. *

JOHNSON, LENORA, federal agency administrator, public health service officer; BA in Biology, Lafayette Coll., 1981; MPH, Emory U., 1989. Sci. tchr.; with Am. Cancer Soc., Pub. Health Assn.; dir. office edn. and spl. initiatives Nat. Cancer Inst., NIH, 2002—, dir. office comm. and edn. Rockville, Md., 2007—. Office: Office of Comm and Edn Nat Cancer Inst 6116 Executive Blvd, Ste 407 Rockville MD 20852 *

JOHNSON, LEONARD MORRIS, retired pediatric surgeon; b. Gowanda, NY, June 11, 1931; s. Leonard Brynolf and Helen Berdena (Morris) J.; m. Ann Marie Homer, Mar. 30, 1968; children: H. Leif B. Johnson, Nils A.C. Johnson. BA, Haverford Coll., 1954; MD, U. Pa., 1958; MS in Surgery, U. Minn., Mayo Grad. Sch., Rochester, 1966. Diplomate in surgery and in pediat. surgery Am. Bd. Surgery. Intern Colo. Gen. Hosp., Denver, 1958—59; fellow in gen. surgery Mayo Clinic, Rochester, 1959—63; fellow in pediat. surgery Children's Mercy Hosp., Kansas City, Mo., 1964—65; vis. pediat. surgeon Acad. Hosp., Uppsala, Sweden, 1967; registrar in pediat. urology Alder Hey Children's Hosp., Liverpool, England, 1967—68; gen. surgeon SS Hope (Project Hope), Guayaquil, Ecuador, 1964, gen. and pediat. surgeon Conakry, Guinea, 1965, Nicaragua, Colombia, Sri Lanka, 1965—68; pediat. surgeon Children's Hosp., Oakland, Calif., 1969—97, ret., 1997, chief surgery dept., 1989—92. Bd. dirs. Children's Hosp., Oakland, Calif., 1982-91; trustee Children's Hosp. Found., Oakland, 1986-95; mem. exec. bd. Mt. Diablo-Silverado Coun. Boy Scouts Am., 1996—2010. Decorated Order Ruben Dario (Nicaragua), 1966; recipient Bronze Bambino award Children's Hosp., Oakland, 1990, Silver Beaver award Boy Scouts Am., 2005. Fellow ACS, Am. Acad. Pediat.; mem. Am. Trauma Soc. (founder), Am. Pediat.-Surg. Assn., Pacific Assn. Pediat. Surgeons, Brit. Assn. Pediat. Surgeons, Alameda-Contra Costa Med. Assn. Avocations: photography, hiking, skiing, travel, music. Personal E-mail: lmorrisjohnson@me.com.

JOHNSON, MALCOLM, pharmacologist, researcher; b. Middlesbrough, Eng., Sept. 23, 1946; s. Bernard and Edna Mary Johnson; children: Daniel William, Christopher Malcolm. BSc, Sch. Pharmacy, Sunderland, Eng., 1968; PhD, U. Newcastle-Upon-Tyne, Eng., 1971. Rsch. assoc. Stanford U., Palo Alto, Calif., 1971—73; sr. rsch. assoc. Georgetown U., Washington, 1973—75; sr. scientist ICI Pharms., Macclesfield, England, 1975—85; head rsch. dept. Glaxo Group, Ware, England, 1985—90, head rsch., 1990—93; dir. respiratory sci. Glaxo Wellcome, Uxbridge, England, 1993—2000; global dir. respiratory sci. GlaxoSmithKline, Uxbridge, 2000—. External examiner U. London, 1995—; vis. prof. Nat. Heart and Lung Inst. Imperial Coll., London, 2002—; rsch. reviewer Nat. Asthma Campaign, England, 2001—. Office: GlaxoSmithKline Stockley Pk W UB11 1BT Uxbridge England Home Phone: (44)1223-207978; Office Phone: 44(0)2089902357. E-mail: malcolm.w.johnson@gsk.com.

JOHNSON, MARCIA K., psychology professor, department chairman; BA in Psychology, U. Calif., Berkeley, 1965, PhD in Exptl. Psychology, 1971. Asst. to full prof. dept. psychology SUNY, Stony Brook, 1970—85; prof. dept. psychology Princeton U., NJ, 1985—2000, Yale U., New Haven, 2000—, prof. dept. psychiatry, 2000—, mem. interdepartmental neuroscience program, 2000—, acting chair dept. psychology, 2003, dir. grad. studies, 2004—06, Charles C. & Dorathea S. Dilley prof. psychology, 2004—, chair dept. psychology, 2006—. Co-author (with R.M. Liebert): Statistics: Tool of the Behavioral Sciences, 1977; co-author: (with S.P. Springer and S.H. Sternglanz) How to Succeed in College, 1982; contbr. articles to profl. jours., chapters to books. Fellow: APA, Assn. Psychol. Sci.; mem.: Psychonomic Soc., Cognitive Neuroscience Soc., Soc. Exptl. Psychologists, Memory Disorders Rsch. Soc., Eastern Psychol. Assn., Midwestern Psychol. Assn., Soc. Applied Rsch. in Memory and Cognition, Sigma Xi. Office: Dept Psychology Yale Univ PO Box 298205 New Haven CT 06520-8205 Office Phone: 203-432-6761. Office Fax: 203-436-4617. Business E-Mail: marcia.johnson@yale.edu.

JOHNSON, MARGARET M., critical care specialist; MD, Thomas Jefferson U., 1990. Diplomate Am. Bd. Internal Medicine, 2003, Am. Bd. Internal Medicine- pulmonary disease, 2006, Am. Bd. Internal Medicine- critical care medicine, 2007. Intern Thomas Jefferson Univ., Phila., resident in internal medicine; fellow in pulmonary critical care medicine Wake Forest Baptist Hosp., Winston- Salem, NC, 1993; asst. prof. Bowman Gray; chair allergy and pulmonary medicine Mayo Clinic. Co-author: Amoxicillin therapy of poultry flocks: effect upon the selection of amoxicillin-resistant commensal Campylobacter spp, 2009, Predictors of poor neurologic outcome after induced mild hypothermia following cardiac arrest, 2009, Postmenopausal estrogen and progestin effects on the serum proteome, 2009, Upfront, randomized, phase 2 trial of sorafenib versus sorafenib and low-dose interferon alfa in patients with advanced renal cell carcinoma: clinical and biomarker analysis, 2010, Bordetella bronchiseptica pneumonia in a kidney-pancreas transplant patient after exposure to recently vaccinated dogs, 2010, 73-year-old woman with progressive shortness of breath, 2010, Distribution and abundance of anthropogenic marine debris along the shelf and slope of the US West Coast, 2010, Facial nerve hemangiomas: vascular tumors or malformations?, 2010, Case records of the Massachusetts General Hospital. Case 6-2010. A 37-year-old man with a lesion on the tongue, 2010, Use of electron microscopy in core biopsy diagnosis of oncocytic renal tumors, 2010, Single-dose palifermin prevents severe oral mucositis during multicycle chemotherapy in patients with cancer: a randomized trial, 2010, Detection of elevated plasma levels of epidermal growth factor receptor before breast cancer diagnosis among hormone therapy users, 2010, Clinical correlates of NRAS and BRAF mutations in primary human melanoma, 2011, CAN-mediated oxidations for the synthesis of xanthones and related products, 2010, various publs. Office: Mayo Clinic 4500 San Pablo Rd S Jacksonville FL 32224 Office Phone: 904-953-7290.

JOHNSON, MARIE-LOUISE TULLY, dermatologist, educator; b. NYC, July 26, 1927; d. James Henry and Mary Frances (Dobbins) Tully; m. Kenneth Gerald Johnson, June 10, 1950. AB, Manhattanville Coll., 1948; PhD, Yale U., 1954, MD, 1956. Intern, then resident Yale-New Haven Med. Ctr., 1956-59; asst. prof. medicine, dermatology Yale U., 1961-67, clin. prof. dermatology, 1980—; chief dermatologist med. svc. Atomic Bomb Casualty Commn., Hiroshima, Japan, 1964-67; assoc. prof. dermatology NYU, 1967-70, 74-76, prof. dermatology, 1976-80; assoc. prof. dermatology, coord. continuing med. edn. Dartmouth Coll., Hanover, NH, 1971-74; chief dermatology Bellevue Hosp., NYC, 1974-80; dir. med. edn. Benedictine Hosp., Kingston, NY, 1980-93. Cons. Health and Nutrition Exam. Survey I, II, Health Stats., Washington, 1967-84. Contbg. author: Cecil's Textbook of Medicine, 15th edit., 1979, 16th edit., 1982, 17th edit., 1985, Dermatology in General Medicine, 2d edit., 1979. Mem. Cardinal Cooke Pro-Life Commn., Albany, N.Y., 1986-87; bd. dirs. Maternity and Early Childhood Found., Albany, 1984-2001, pres., 1987-2001; bd. dirs. Sulzberger Inst. for Dermatologic Edn., 1986-93; pres. Mid-Hudson Consortium for the Advancement of Edn. for Health Professions, 1989-92; bd. govs. Yale U. Alumni Assn., 1991-94; v.p. Assn. Yale U. Alumni in Medicine, 1991-93, pres., 1993-95. Named Disting. Alumna, Manhattanville Coll., 1977, Rose Hirschler award Women's Dermatologic Soc., 1993, Papal Cross Pro Ecclesia et Pontifice Pope John Paul II, 1994, Clark W. Finnerud award Dermatology Found., 1997. Fellow Am. Acad. Dermatology (master 1995, bd. dirs. 1976-80, Presdl. citation 1999); mem. Am. Dermatol. Assn. (bd. dirs. 1986-92, v.p. 1991-92, pres. 2000-01), Inst. Medicine of NAS, Internat. Physicians for Prevention of Nuc. War (del. 1982, 83, 87, 88, 89). Roman Catholic. Home: 15 Strawberry Bank Rd High Falls NY 12440-5128 Office: Kingston Hosp Med Arts Bldg Ste 202 368 Broadway Kingston NY 12401-5159 Home Phone: 845-687-0404; Office Phone: 845-338-7472.

JOHNSON, MARILYN, retired obstetrician, gynecologist; b. Houston, May 7, 1925; d. William Walton and Marilyn (Henderson) J. BA, Rice Inst., 1945; MD, Baylor U., Houston, 1950. Intern New Eng. Hosp. Women and Children, Boston, 1950—51; resident Meth. Hosp., Houston, 1951—53; fellow in gynecol. pathology Harvard Med. Sch., 1952—53; resident in gynecology M.D. Anderson Tumor Inst., Houston, 1954, fellow, 1955; practice medicine specializing in ob-gyn. Houston, 1954—81, Fredericksburg, Tex., 1981—97; ret., 1997. Mem. staffs St. Joseph's, Meml., Meth., Park Plaza, Hill Country Meml. Rosewood, South Austin Cmty., Comfort Cmty. hosps., Tex.; clin. instr. ob-gyn Coll. Medicine, Baylor U., 1954—, Postgrad. Sch. Medicine, U. Tex., 1954—; gynecologist De Pelchin Faith Home, Houston, 1954—, also Rice U., Richmond State Sch.; med. dirs. Birthright, Inc., Houston, 1973—; chief med. staff Hill Country Meml. Hosp., Fredericksburg, Tex., 1990-92; cons. Tex. bd. Blue Cross Blue Shield; pro-life public spkr. Bd. dirs. Right to Life, Houston, Found. for Life, amb medicine World Forum Internat. Biographical Congress, 2009 Recipient Amb. US to World Forum IBS, 2009, Grantee Sandoz Labs., 1973, 75, Delbay Pharm. Co., 1977; named Internat. Women of Yr. in Medicine IBC, Cambridge, Ing., 1992, San Francisco, 1995, Great Women of 21st Century ABI, 2004-2005, AVVO Rating, 2011, Superb ABI, 2011, Greatest Mind of 21st Century. Fellow Am. Coll. Obstetricians and Gynecologists; mem. AMA, Am. Soc. Colposcopic Pathologists, Tex. Med. Assn., Am. Med. Women's Assn., Internat. Infertility Assn., Harris County Med. Soc., Postgrad. Med. Assembly South Tex., Houston Ob-Gyn. Soc., Tex. Folklore Soc., Zonta, Fredericksburg Rockhounds. Republican. Baptist. Home: 606 Silverado Rockport TX 78382

JOHNSON, MARTIN CLIFTON, SR., retired physician; b. Santa Fe, Nov. 16, 1933; s. Henry J. and Dorothy (Clifton) J.; m. Priscilla Bollam, June 13, 1959; children: Martin Clifton II, Kurt B., Kirsten L. Ustach, Katharine E. AB, Stanford U., 1955, MD, 1959. Diplomate Am. Bd. Neurol. Surgery, Am. Bd. Pediat. Neurosurgery, Am. Bd. Forensic Examiners, Am. Bd. Forensic Medicine; cert. Homeland Security Level III. Intern in surgery Palo Alto (Calif.) Stanford U. Hosp., 1959-60; fellow in neurosurgery Mayo Found., Rochester, Minn., 1960-61; asst. resident gen. surgery Presbyn. Med. Ctr., San Francisco, 1963-64; asst. resident, sr. resident, chief resident in neurosurgery U. Cin., 1964-68; pvt. practice neurosurgery/pediat. neurosurgery Portland, Oreg., 1968-99. Lt. comdr. M.C. USNR, 1960-69; col. M.C. AUS, 1988-99, ret. Fellow ACS, Am. Acad. Pediats.; mem. AMA, Portland Met. Med. Soc.,Oreg. Neurosurg. Soc., Oreg. Med. Soc., Congress Neurol. Surgeons, Am. Assn. Neurol. Surgeons, Am. Assn. Pediatric Neurosurgery, Internat. Pediat. Soc. Neurological Surgery, Multnomah Athletic Club, Columbia Aviation Club.

JOHNSON, MARYL RAE, cardiologist; b. Ft. Dodge, Iowa, Apr. 15, 1951; d. Marvin George and Beryl Evelyn (White) Johnson. BS, Iowa State U., 1973; MD, U. Iowa, 1977. Diplomate Am. Bd. Internal Medicine, Am. Bd. Cardiovasc. Diseases. Intern U. Iowa Hosps., Iowa City, 1977-78, resident, 1978-81, fellow, 1979-82; assoc. in cardiology U. Iowa Hosps. and Clins., Iowa City, 1982-86, asst. prof. medicine cardiovasc. divsn., 1986-88; asst. prof. medicine Med. Ctr. Loyola U., 1988-92, assoc. prof., 1992-94, Rush. U., 1994-97, Northwestern U. Med. Sch., 1998—2002; prof. medicine U. Wis. Med. Sch., Madison, 2002—. Med. dir. cardiac transplantation U. Iowa Hosp., 1986—88; assoc. med. dir. cardiac transplantation Loyola U., 1988—94, assoc. med. dir. Rush Heart Failure and Cardiac Transplant Program, 1994—97; dir. heart failure cardiac transplant program Northwestern U. Med. Sch., 1998—2001, dir. heart failure program, 2001—02; med. dir. heart failure and transplantation U. Wis. Hosp. and Clinics, 2002—. Assoc. editor: Jour. Heart and Lung Transplantation, 1995—99, 2007—09, mem. editl. bd.:, 2000—06, 2009—. Mem. Nat. Heart Lung and Blood Adv. Coun., Bethesda, Md., 1979—83; mem. biomed. rsch. tech. rev. com. NIH, 1990—93, chairperson, 1992—93, chair biomed. rsch. tech. spl. emphasis panel, 1999—2002. Recipient Jane Leinfelder Meml. award, U. Iowa Coll. Medicine, 1977, Clin. Investigator award, NIH, 1981, New Investigator Rsch. award, 1981, 1986; Barry Freeman scholar, 1974. Mem.: ACP, AAAS, AMA, United Network Organ Sharing (thoracic organ com. 2005—, vice chair 2006—08, chair 2008—10), Am. Soc. Transplantation (chair membership com. 2003—04, bd. dirs. 2004—06, sec.-treas. 2006—09, pres. elect. 2009—10, pres. 2010—), Am. Coll. Cardiology (heart failure and cardiac transplant com. 2002—07, chair 2004—07), Am. Heart Assn., Ctrl. Soc. Clin. Rsch., Internat. Soc. Heart and Lung Transplantation (mem. program com. 2005, chair, communication com. 2008—10), Order of Rose, Alpha Omega Alpha, Iota Sigma Pi, Phi Kappa Phi, Alpha Lambda Delta. Office: U Wis Madison E5/582D CSC 5710 600 Highland Ave Madison WI 53792 Office Phone: 608-263-0080. Business E-Mail: mrj@medicine.wisc.edu.

JOHNSON, NEAL FREDERICK, psychologist, educator; b. Willmar, Minn., May 1, 1934; s. Malcolm Ruben and Helen Laura Johnson; m. Kathleen A. Crimmins, Sept. 9, 1960 (dec. Jan. 2000); children: Neal, Margaret (dec. Sept. 1999), Elizabeth, Michael. PhD, U. Minn., 1961. Prof. psychology Ohio State U., Columbus, 1961—. Vis. prof. U. Calif., Berkeley, 1965, Berkeley, 74, Berkeley, 75, Berkeley, 77, Berkeley, 78, Berkeley, 83. Contbr. articles to profl. jours.; assoc. editor Jour. Memory and Lang., 1984-88; consulting editor Jour. Verbal Learning and Verbal Behavior, 1965-84, Memory & Cognition, 1972-82, Jour. Exptl. Psychology: Human Perception and Performance, 1978-82, Jour. Exptl. Psychology: Learning, Memory and Cognition, 1982-89, Jour. Memory and Lang., 1988-94, Gen. Psychology Rev., 1996—. Troop com. Boy Scouts Am., Columbus, 1974-81. Rsch. scholar Tozer Found., Stillwater, Minn., 1959; grantee U.S. Office Edn., NIH, NSF. Fellow APA (pres. Soc. Gen. Psychology 1995, pres. divsn. exptl. psychology 1996), AAAS (governing coun. 1998-2000, presiding officer psychology sect. 2002-04); mem. Psychonomic Soc. (pres. 1997), Coun. Sci. Soc. Presidents, Midwestern Psychol. Assn. (pres. 1987). Presbyterian. Avocations: fencing, skiing. Home: 5478 Rockwood Rd Columbus OH 43229-4324 Office: Dept Psychology Ohio State U Columbus OH 43210 Home Phone: 614-885-6686. Business E-Mail: johnson.64@osu.edu.

JOHNSON, NOEL LARS, biomedical engineer; b. Palo Alto, Calif., Nov. 11, 1957; s. LeRoy Franklin and Margaret Louise (Lindsley) J.; children: Margaret Elizabeth, Kent Daniel. BSEE, U. Calif., Berkeley, 1979; M of Engring., U. Va., 1982, PhD, 1990. Mgr. R & D Hosp. Products divsn. Abbott Labs., Mountain View, Calif., 1986-99; founder HealtheTech., Inc., 1999—2004; pres., CEO NovaShunt, Inc., Saratoga, Calif., 2004—; CEO NovaShunt, AG, Zurich, 2006—. Contbr. articles to profl. jours. Fellowship NIH 1980-85; rsch. grantee Abbott Labs. 1989. Mem. IEEE, Biomed. Engring. Soc., Delta Chi (founder, 1st pres. chpt. U. Calif. at Berkeley). Achievements include invention of metabolic monitor, patented automated drug delivery system, pharmacokinetic drug infusion, and critical care disposables. Business E-Mail: noel.johnson@novashunt.com.

JOHNSON, PAUL ROBERT VELLACOTT, pediatric surgeon; b. London, Aug. 5, 1964; s. Alan and Esther Johnson; m. Hilary Joy Ellacott, July 21, 1990; children: Thomas David, Abigail Tilly. MBChB, U. Leicester, Eng., 1988, MD, 2001; MA (hon.), U. Oxford, 2002. House officer Leicester Royal infirmary, England, 1988—99; lectr. in surgery U. Leicester, 1993—96, demonstrator in anatomy, 1999—2000; sr. ho. officer Leicester and Derby Hospitals, 1990—93; specialist registrar in pediat. surgery John Radcliffe Hosp., Oxford, 1996—98; chief registrar pediat. surgery Royal Children's Hosp., Melbourne, Australia, 1998—99; sr. registrar in pediat. surgery Gt. Ormond St. Hosp. Children, London, 1999—2000; dir. islet transplant program U. Oxford, England, 2002—, reader in pediat. surgery, 2001—; cons. pediat. surgery John Radcliffe Hosp., Oxford, 2001—. Fellow St. Edmund Hall Oxford U. Contbr. articles to profl. jours., chpts. to books. Recipient Peter-Paul Rickham Prize, Bitish Assn. of Paedaitric Surgeons, 1997; grantee, Diabetes Rsch. and Wellness Found., Eng., 2004. Fellow: Royal Coll. Surgeons Edinburgh (life), Royal Coll. Surgeons Eng. (life; mem. specialist adv. com. in pediatric surgery 2001—04, Hunterian professorship 1998); mem.: Pancreatic Soc. Gt. Britain and Ireland (licentiate), Internat. Pancreas and Islet Transplant Assn. (life; co-secretary 2004—), Brit. Assn. Pediat. Surgeons (life; chmn. rsch. com. 2003—). Achievements include Performed first islet autotransplant in UK.

JOHNSON, PHILIP RUDOLPH, JR., pediatrician, epidemiologist; b. Goldsboro, NC, July 15, 1954; BA U. NC, Chapel Hill, 1976; MD, U. NC Sch. Medicine, 1980. Cert. Gen. Pediat., 1985, Pediatric Infectious Diseases, 1994, Pediatric Infectious Diseases, 2002, lic. NC, 1985, Ohio, 1991. Resident in pediat. Vanderbilt U., Nashville, 1980—83, fellow in pediatric infectious diseases, 1983—85; instr. pediat. Vanderbilt U. Hosp., Nashville, 1985—87; med. staff fellow, lab. infectious diseases Nat. Inst. Allergy and Infectious Diseases, NIH, Bethesda, Md., 1983—85, guest worker, lab. infectious diseases, 1985—91; rsch. asst. prof. molecular virology and immunology Georgetown U. Sch. Medicine, Washington, 1987—89, rsch. asst. prof. molecular virology and immunology, head retroviral pathogenesis sect., 1989—91; attending physician Children's Hosp., Columbus, Ohio, 1991—2004; prof. pediat. and medical microbiology and immunology, Henry G. Cramblett chair medicine Ohio State U. Coll. Medicine and Pub. Health, Columbus, Ohio, 1991—2004, dir. molecular medicine divsn., 1995—2004, vice-chair rsch., dept. pediat., 1996—2004; prof. vet. biosciences Ohio State U. Coll. Vet. Medicine, Columbus, Ohio, 1995—2004; pres. Columbus Children's Rsch. Inst. Columbus Children's Hosp., Inc., 1996—2004, dir. Ctr. for Gene Therapy, Columbus Children's Rsch. Inst., 2002—04; chief sci. officer and sr. v.p. Children's Hosp. Phila., 2005—07, dir. Joseph Stokes Rsch. Inst. and Edmond Notebaert chair in pediatric rsch., 2005—, chief sci. officer and exec. v.p., 2007—; prof. pediat. U. Pa. Sch. Medicine, Phila., 2005—. Sci. adv. bd. U. Sci. Ctr., Phila., 2007—, bd. dirs., Cangene Corp., Winnipeg, Canada; mem. Greater Phila. Life Sciences Congress, 2007—. Fellow: AAAS, Am. Soc. Microbiology, Am. Acad. Pediat.; mem.: Am. Soc. Virology, Pediatric Infectious Diseases Soc., Infectious Diseases Soc. Am., Am. Soc. Gene Therapy, Molecular Medicine Soc., Phi Beta Kappa, Phi Eta Sigma. Office: Childrens Hosp Phila Abramson Rsch Ctr Rm 1216D 3615 Civic Ctr Blvd Philadelphia PA 19104-4318 Office Phone: 267-426-0351. Office Fax: 267-426-0363. E-mail: johnsonphi@chop.edu.

JOHNSON, REBECCA L., pathologist; B, Illinois State U.; MD, South Illinois Sch. Medicine. Resident Hartford Hosp.; fellowship NIH Clinical Ctr., Bethesda, Md.; pathologist Berkshire Health Systems, 1990—, chair dept. pathology and clinical laboratories; clinical prof. pathology U. Mass. Medical Sch., Worchester, Mass. Fellow: Coll. American Pathologists (Outstanding Communicator award 2003); mem.: American Bd. Medical Specialites (bd. dirs. 2009—), American Bd. Pathology (pres. 2009), Mass. Medical Soc. (trustee, Committee Chair Service award 2009). Office: Berkshire Health Systems 725 North St Pittsfield MA 01201

JOHNSON, RICHARD DEAN, pharmaceutical consultant, educator; b. DeKalb, Ill., July 8, 1936; s. Arthur Dean Johnson and Evelyn Alice (Telford) Williams; m. Paula Marcellus Jennings, Nov. 3, 1942; children: Janet Telford Bijur, Julie Johnson McVeigh, Richard Dean Jr., Jennings Brodie. BS, U. Calif., Berkeley, 1960; PharmD, U. Calif., San Francisco, 1961, MS, 1962, PhD, 1965; MBA, Rockhurst U., 1984. Cert. tchr. Calif., lic. pharmacist Calif. Sect. head R&D Allergan Inc., Irvine, Calif., 1965—67; dir. regulatory affairs Syntex Labs., Inc., Palo Alto, Calif., 1967—73; mng. dir. licensing Marion Labs., Inc., Kansas City, Mo., 1973—79, v.p. licensing, 1980—82, v.p. corp. devel., 1983—87, v.p. bus. alliances, 1987—88; corp. v.p. Marion Merrell Dow, Inc., Kansas City, 1989—91, ret., 1991; prin., owner KC Pharma, LLC, Kansas City, 1991—. Adj. prof. Sch. Pharmacy, U. Mo., Kansas City, 1991-95, R&D coun., 1993—, adj. grad. prof., 1995—; bd. dirs. Dey Labs., Inc., Concord, Calif., Tanabe-Marion Labs., Kansas City, U.S. Biosci., Inc., Blue Bell, Pa., ImmunoPharmaceutics, Inc., San Diego, Lovelace Respiratory Rsch. Inst., Albuquerque, Micrologix Biotech Inc., Vancouver, B.C.; comp. and audit coms., AusAm Biotech., Inc., Santa Monica, Calif.; comp. and intellectual property coms. Sober Rovers, LLC, Bellingham, Wash.; guest lectr. U. SC Sch. Bus. Adminstrn., Columbia, 1975-79; pharm. analyst SunTrust Robinson Humphrey, 2002, Cottonwood Capital Mgmt., LLC, 2002-04; med. analyst Reynders, McVeigh Capital Mgmt. LLC, Boston, 2005—, NanoCell Biotech, LLC, San Francisco, 2008-10. Contbr. articles to profl. jours. Presdl. exch. exec. White House, Washington, 1970-71, U.S. Pharmacopeia Com. of Rev., 1990-2001; trustee U. Mo., Kansas City Pharmacy Found., 1993-07, v.p., 1994-96, pres., 1996-98, fin. com., 1996—2000, pres. emeritus, 1998—, chmn. devel. com., 1994-96, chmn. exec. and fin. coms., 1996-98, dean's adv. bd., 1995—; trustee Johnson Family Fund, Kansas City Cmty. Found., 1993—, U. Kansas City Bd., Mo., 1996-2001, U. Mo., Kansas City, 2001—; fin., real estate and life scis. coms., 1998—; mem. Kansas City Life Sci. Initiative and Undergrad. Rsch. coms., 2001—, mem. dev. com., 2010-; dean's adv. bd. Sch. Pharmacy U. Calif., San Francisco, 1994-97, bd. counsellors, 1997-2001, deans dev. com., 2010-; dean's adv. bd. Sch. Pharmacy U. Mo., Kansas City, 1995-2001, 2003—, dean's res. coun., 2010-; trustee Conservatory of Music, U. Mo., Kansas City, 1998-2002; Henry W. Bloch Sch. Bus. and Pub. Adminstrn. exec. roundtable U. Mo., Kansas City, 1998-2003; active Internat. Rels. Coun., Kansas City, 1998-2008; active De La Salle Sch. Devel. Com., 1993-2001, St. Lukes Hosp. Stroke Com., 1993—2006, U.S. Pharmacopeia Drug Nomenclature Com., 1990-2001, vet. drug com., 1998-2001, ARC; mem. State of Mo. Life Sci. Rsch. Bd., Jefferson City, 2005-08. Recipient Grad. award Borden Co., 1962; NIH Pub. Health Svc. Tng. grant, 1962-65; Am. Found. for Pharm. Edn. fellow, 1962-65, Sir Henry S. Wellcome Meml. fellow, 1962-63, Am. Inst. Chemists fellow, 1965-70; named to FBI Citizens' Acad., Kansas City, 2007-, 50 Yrs. Recognition award, Calif. St. Bd. Mem.: Am. Chem. Soc., Am. Assn. Pharm. Scis., Am. Found. for Pharm. Edn. Centurion, ARC Kirkwood Soc., Kans. City Country Club (Shawnee Mission, Kans.), River Club (Kansas City), Carriage Club (Kansas City, Mo.), La Jolla (Calif.) Beach and Tennis Club, La Jolla Country Club, Sigma Xi, Theta Delta Chi, Phi Lambda Sigma, Rho Chi. Home: 5330 Ward Pky Kansas City MO 64112-2369 Office: KC Pharma LLC 222 W Gregory Blvd Kansas City MO 64114-1110 also: 8486 El Paseo Grande La Jolla CA 92037-3013 Address: 4000 N Lake Blvd Tahoe City CA 96145-5303 Office Phone: 816-444-5556. Business E-Mail: kcpharma@webtv.net.

JOHNSON, ROBERT LEE, dean, physician, educator; b. Spartanburg, SC, Aug. 7, 1946; s. Robert and Clalice (Brewton) J.; m. Maxine Johnson, June 1972. BA, Alfred U., NY, 1968; MD, Coll. Medicine. Dentistry NJ, Newark, 1968—72. Pediat. intern Martland Hosp., Newark, 1972-73, resident in pediats., 1973-74; asst. prof. pediats. Univ. Medicine and Dentistry NJ-Medical Sch., Newark, 1976-83, assoc. prof. clin. pediats., 1983-89, assoc. prof. clin. psychiatry, 1989, prof. clin. pediats., 1989-95, prof. pediats., 1995—, vice chair pediats., 1996, chmn. pediats., prof. psychiatry, dir. adolescent and young adult medicine, interim dean, 2005—11, Sharon and Joseph L. Muscarelle endowed dean, 2011—. Chmn. credentials com. Bd. Med. Examiners, N.J., 1990-97, pres., 1995-97; IOM com. mem., Immunization Fin. Dissemination Workshop; mem. Health Care Svcs. Bd.; chmn. Governor's adv. coun., AIDS/HIV and Related Blood Borne Pathogens; mem. planning bd., U.S. Surgeon General Report on Youth Violence; lectr./spkr. in field in the media and at workshops. Contbr. articles to prof. jours.; guest appearances 20/20, The O' Reilly Factor, med. and cultural advisor (TV series) ER. Recipient NJ Pride in Health award State of NJ, 1989, Richard J. Cross award, 1993, Hyacinth AIDS Found. award, 1994. Fellow Am. Acad. Pediats. Democrat. Baptist. Office: UMDNJ-NJ Med Sch 185 S Orange Ave MSB C671 Newark NJ 07103 Office Phone: 973-972-4538. Business E-Mail: rjohnson@umdnj.edu. *

JOHNSON, ROBERT WILLIAM GREENWOOD, transplant surgeon; b. Reigate, Surrey, Eng., Mar. 15, 1942; s. Robert William and Suzanne (Mills) J.; m. Carolyn Mary Vooght, July 23, 1942; children: Melanie Jane Johnson, Julian Robert Greenwood Johnson B Medicine, Durham U., 1965, B Surgery, 1965; M Surgery with distinction, U. Newcastle on Tyne, 1973. Reg. GMS, gen. surgery. House surgeon Royal Victoria Infirmary, Newcastle Upon Tyne, 1965—66; sr house officer, registrar Newcastle Gen. Hosp., Royal Victoria Infirmary, 1966—70; sr. rsch. fellow Newcastle U., 1970—71; sr. registrar Royal Victoria Infirmary, Newcastle, 1971—74; vis. asst. prof. U. Calif.-Moffat Hosp., San Francisco, 1974; cons. surgeon, reader in surgery Manchester Royal Infirmary Manchester U., 1974—2004. Dir. N.W. Regional Transplant Svc., 1976-2002, med. dir., Ctrl. Manchester Healthcare Trust, 2000-02; hon. cons. surgeon Ctrl. Man and Manchester Childrens Trust Author: Scientific Foundations of Urology, 1990 Fullbright scholar, 1973—74; Hunterian Prof. Royal Coll. Surgeons, 1981; recipient Pybus medal North Eng. Surg. Soc., 1991 Fellow Royal Coll. Surgeons London and Edinburgh (coun.); mem. Royal Coll. Physicians and Surgeons Glasgow (coun.), Royal Coll. Surgeons Gt. Britain and Ireland (senate), Fedn. Surg. Splty. Assns. (pres. 2003—06), Am. Soc. Transplant Surgeons, Assn. Surgeons Gt. Britain and Ireland (pres. 2002-03), Brit. Transplantation Soc. (pres. 1995-98), Internat. Transplant Soc Avocations: golf, tennis, skiing. Office: Anson Med Ctr 23/25 Anson Rd Manchester M14 5BZ England Home Phone: 44 161 980 8840; Office Phone: 44 161 248 2038. Business E-Mail: rwgj@hotmail.com.

JOHNSON, SHELLY, trade association administrator; Exec. dir. American Soc. Healthcare Materials Mgmt. for American Hosp. Assn., Neuroscience Nursing Found., American Bd. Neuroscience Nursing, American Soc. Neuroscience Nurses, American Soc. Quality; dep. dir. American Message Therapy Assn., 2002—10, interim exec. dir., 2010—11; exec. dir. American Message Therapy Assn. and the Message Therapy Found., 2011—. Office: American Message Therapy Assn 500 Davis St Evanston IL 60201 Office Phone: 847-864-0123. Office Fax: 847-864-5196. *

JOHNSON, SHERI, medical educator, former state agency administrator; d. Roland Pattillo. BA, Brown Univ.; MA, Boston Univ., PhD in clinical psychology. Clinical fellowsip Harvard Med. Sch.; dir. Behavioral Health Svcs. Ctr. Isaac Coggs Health Connection; core scientist, Ctr. AIDS Intervention Rsch. Med. Coll. Wis., 2004—, asst. prof. pediat., divsn. cmty. medicine, 2008—; adminstr., state health officer, Divsn. Pub. Health State of Wis., Madison, 2005—08. Recipient June Dobbs award, Children's Hosp. Wis., 2000; Martin Luther King Jr. fellow, 1987, Mass. Commonwealth fellow, 1988, Minority fellow, APA, 1988—91. Office: Med Coll Wis 8701 Watertown Plank Rd Milwaukee WI 53226

JOHNSON, TIMOTHY M., dermatologist, educator; BA in Biology, U. Tex., Austin, Tex., 1980; MD, U. Tex., Houston, 1984. Diplomate Am. Bd. Dermatology, 1988, cert. Am. Coll. of Mohs Micrographic Surgery & Cutaneous Oncology, 1990. Intern transitional St. Joseph Hosp., Houston, 1984—85; resident dermatology dept. Univ. of Tex. Health Sci. Ctr., Houston, 1985—88, chief resident dermatology, 1987; external cons. M.D. Anderson Cancer Ctr. Univ. of Tex. Health Sci. Ctr. — Devel. of a Mohs Surgery Program, Houston, 1994, 2001; fellow mohs micrographic surgery and cutaneous oncology dermatology dept. Univ. Oreg., Portland, Oreg., 1989—90; lectr. dermatology dept. Univ. of Oreg. Health Sci. Ctr., Portland, Oreg., 1989—90; fellow mohs micrographic surgery and cutaneous oncology dermatology dept. Univ. of Mich., Ann Arbor, Mich., 1988—89, lectr. dermatology dept., 1988—89, asst. prof. dermatology dept., otolaryngology head and neck surgery and surgery dept., 1990—96, assoc. prof. dermatology dept., otolaryngology head and neck surgery and surgery dept., 1996—2003, prof. dermatology dept., otolaryngology head and neck surgery and surgery dept., 2003—, William B. Taylor collegiate prof. dermatology, 1999—2005, Lewis and Lillian Becker prof. dermatology, 2005—, dir. cutaneous surgery and oncology program (Mohs Surgery Program, Melanoma Program, Cosmetic Dermatology and Laser Ctr.) dermatology dept., 1990—; dir. multidisciplinary melanoma program Univ. of Mich. Comprehensive Cancer Ctr., 1990—, clin. dir. cutaneous oncology program, 1990—, mem., 1990—, clin. dir. team 7 melanoma, 1998—; hosp. affiliation include Univ. of Mich. Hosps. and Health Centers; mem. adv. bd. Berlex Dermatology, 2000. Editl. bd. (jour.) Jour. of the Am. Acad. of Dermatology, 1998—2005, surgery adv. bd. Archives of Dermatology, 1999—2005, mem. editl. bd., 2001—05, assoc. editor Jour. of the Am. Acad. of Dermatology, 2005—08; contbg. editor: (jour.) Dermatologic Surgery, 1997—2005. Recipient Outstanding Resident Tchr. of the Year, Univ. of Tex. Med. Sch., 1987, William B. Taylor Resident Tchg.award, Univ. of Mich., 1994, Metro Detroit's Best Doctors, Hour Detroit Mag., 2002, 2005—10, Soc. of Surgical Oncology publ. impact award, 2007, AAD Model State award, Mich. Dermatol. Soc., 2007; named one of America's Top Doctors, 2001—07, The Best Doctors in America, 1993—, America's Top Doctors for Cancer, 2005—08; named to Guide to Top Doctors, 2002—04, Guide to America's Top Physicians, Consumer's Rsch. Coun. of America, 2004—05. Mem.: Dermatology Found., Assn. of Academic Dermatologic Surgeons (bd. dirs. 2003—06), Assn. of Academic Dermatologic Surgeons, Am. Soc. of Mohs Histotechnologists (bd. dirs. 1998—2000), Mich. Dermatol. Soc., SW Oncology Group, Assn. of Academic Dermatologic Surgeons, Am. Soc. for Dermatologic Surgery (bd. dirs. 1998—2000), Am. Acad. of Dermatology, Am. Coll. of Mohs Micrographic Surgery and Cutaneous Oncology (bd. dir. 1998—2000), Am. Acad.of Facial Plastic and Reconstructive Surgery, Iowa Dermatol. Soc. (hon.), Alpha Omega Alpha, Phi Beta Kappa. Office: University MI Dermatology 1910 Taubman Center 1500 E Medical Center Dr Ann Arbor MI 48109-5314 Office Phone: 734-936-4190. Office Fax: 734-936-6395.

JOHNSON, TIMOTHY PATRICK, health and social researcher; b. Batavia, NY, July 14, 1954; s. Elmore Thomas and Sara (McKinsey) J.; m. LuEllen Doty, June 20, 1988; children: Sara Elizabeth, Elliott William. BA, Western Ky. U., 1977; MA, U. Wis., Milw., 1978; PhD, U. Ky., 1988. Rsch. analyst dept. medicine U. Ky., Lexington, 1980-82, rsch. coord. survey rsch. ctr., 1982-88; staff assoc. for psychometrics Am. Bd. Family Practice, Lexington, 1988-89; asst. rsch. prof. epidemiology and biostatistics sch. pub. health U. Ill., Chgo., 1991—2002, project coord. survey rsch. lab., 1989-91, asst. dir. survey rsch. lab., 1991-93, assoc. dir., 1993-96, acting dir., 1996-98, dir., 1998—, assoc. prof. pub. adminstrn., 1996—2003, prof. pub. adminstrn., 2003—, assoc. rsch. prof. pub. health, 2002—03, rsch. prof. public health, 2003—; dep. dir. Ctr. Clin. & Translational Sci., 2008—. Contbr. chpts. to books, articles to profl. jours. Mem. APHA, Am. Sociol. Assn., Am. Assn. Pub. Opinion Rsch., Am. Statis. Assn., Am. Coll. Epidemiology, Am. Assn. for the Advancement of Sci. Roman Catholic. Office: U Ill Survey Rsch Lab 412 S Peoria St Chicago IL 60607-7063 Office Phone: 312-996-5310. Business E-Mail: timj@uic.edu.

JOHNSON, TIMOTHY R. B., obstetrician, gynecologist, educator; b. Duluth, Jan. 13, 1950; s. Timothy and Myra Johnson; m. Jo Wiese, June 17, 1972; children: Bradley, Clark, Anna. AB, AM, U. Mich., 1971; MD, U. Va., 1975. Diplomate Am. Bd. Ob-gyn., Am. Bd. Maternal-Fetal Medicine. Asst. prof. Uniformed Svcs. U., Bethesda, Md., 1983-85; assoc. prof. gynecol. obstetrics, pediats., dir. pediats. Johns Hopkins U. Hosp., Balt., 1985-93; prof., chair dept. ob-gyn. U. Mich., Ann Arbor, 1993—, prof. women's studies, 1995—, chmn. med. sch. rev., 1997. Bd. dirs. Ann Arbor Art Ctr., 1994—; bd. dirs. S.E. Mich. March of Dimes, 1998—. Fellow Am. Coll. Ob-Gyn. (chair internat. com. 1991-95), West African Coll. Surgeons (hon.); mem. Soc. for Maternal and Fetal Medicine (bd. dirs. 1993-97), Am. Assn. Med. Colls. (com. on advancing women in the acad.), Inst. Medicine NAS, Alpha Omega Alpha. Office: 1500 East Med Ctr Dr Ann Arbor MI 48109 Home Phone: 734-662-4918; Office Phone: 734-764-8123. Business E-Mail: trbj@umich.edu.

JOHNSON, VALERIE LYNNE, pediatric nephrologist, educator; b. Sacremento, May 2, 1949; d. Norman Stanley and Della Mae Noreen (Wanek) Johnson; m. James Joseph Zazra, Aug. 1, 1975. BS, U. Calif., Davis, 1971; PhD, Cornell U. Med. Coll., NYC, 1976, MD, 1977. Diplomate Am. Bd. Pediat., Pediat. Nephrology. Resident pediat. Mt. Sinai Hosp., NYC, 1977—79; clin. fellow, divsn. pediat. nephrology Albert Einstein Coll. Medicine, Bronx, NY, 1979—82; asst. prof. NY Med. Coll., Valhalla, 1982-85, Cornell U. Med. Coll., 1985-90, assoc. prof. clin. pediat., assoc. attending pediatrician, 1990—. Med. adv. bd. Nat. Kidney Found., NYC, 1988—. Contbr. articles to profl. jours. Recipient Outstanding Tchr. award, Cornell U. Med. Coll., 1988, 1989, Nat. Med. award in pediat. nephrology, Nat. Kidney Found., 1997; named one of Best Dr.'s in NY, NY Mag., 1992—2007, Best Doctors in America, Woodward/White, Inc., 1998—2008, Top Pediatricians in the City, NY Family Guide, 2007; named to, Castle, Connolly Guide to top Dr.'s, 1996—2007. Mem.: NY Soc. Nephrology, Am. Soc. Nephrology, Am. Soc. Pediat. Nephrology, Internat. Soc. Nephrology, Internat. Pediat. Nephrology Assn. Office: NY Presbyn Hosp Pediat Nephrology Dept 525 E 68th St New York NY 10065-4870 Office Phone: 212-746-3260. Office Fax: 212-746-8861.

JOHNSON, VAN R., retired healthcare executive; b. Idaho; BS, Brigham Young U., Provo, Utah; MS in Healthcare Adminstrn., U. Minn. Sr. mgr. Intermountain Healthcare Corp., Salt Lake City; pres., CEO Sutter Cmty. Hospitals, Sacramento, 1990—95; sr. v.p., COO Sutter Health, Sacramento, 1990—95, pres., CEO, 1995—2005, ret., 2005. Bd. dirs. VISICU Inc., 2007—08, The Ensign Group Inc., 2009—. Office: The Ensign Group Inc Ste 450 27101 Puerta Real Mission Viejo CA 92691 Office Phone: 949-487-9500.

JOHNSON, WAINE CECIL, dermatologist, educator; b. Mt. Vernon, Tex., Sept. 30, 1928; s. Tulley Bell and Lizzie J.; m. Deanna Glutz, Dec. 1973; children: Susan Lynn, Carol Ann, Sandra Kay. BS, East Tex. State U., 1949; MD, U. Tex., 1953. Intern Brooke Army Hosp., 1953-54; resident in dermatology Walter Reed Army Hosp., 1955-58; fellow in dermal pathology Armed Forces Inst. Pathology, 1960-61; mem. staff Skin and Cancer Hosp., Phila., 1962-78, asst. dir. lab., 1962, dir., 1970-78; mem. faculty Temple U. Med. Sch., Phila., 1962-78, prof. dermatology, 1970-78; clin. prof. U. Pa. Med. Sch., 1978—; chmn. dept. dermatology Grad. Hosp. U. Pa., 1978-98; mng. ptnr. Delaware Valley Dermatopathology LLP, 1998—2000; co-mng. dir. Delaware Valley Dermatopathology divsn. Inst. Dermatopathology, Conshohocken, Pa., 2001—05; with dept. dermatology U. Pa., Phila., 2006—. Author numerous papers in field.; Co-editor: Dermal Pathology, 1974. Served to maj. M.C. USAR, 1953-62. Recipient Gold medal sci. exhibit Am. Soc. Clin. Pathologists-Coll. Am. Pathologists, 1962 Mem.: ACP, AMA, Coll. Physicians of Phila.

(chmn. dermatology sect. 1994—97), Atlantic Dermatol. Conf. (pres. 1979—80), Phila. Dermatol. Soc. (pres. 1979—80), Histochem. Soc., Soc. Investigative Dermatology, Am. Soc. Dermatopathology (pres. 1988), Am. Registry Pathology (pres. 2003—05), Internat. Acad. Pathology, Am. Dermatol. Assn., Am. Acad. Dermatology (chmn. pathology com. 1976—80). Home: 744 Crosswicks Rd Rydal PA 19046-3004 Personal E-mail: wainejohnson@comcast.net.

JOHNSON, WILLIAM GESSNER, neurologist, educator; s. Hugh Johnson; m. Sandra Johnson. AB summa cum laude, Princeton U., NJ; MD, Columbia Med. Sch., NYC. Cert. in neurology Am. Bd. Psychiatry & Neurology, in clin. genetics Am. Bd. Med. Genetics, in clin. biochem. genetics Am. Bd. Med. Genetics. Prof. neurology Robert Wood Johnson Med. Sch. U. Medicine and Dentistry NJ, Piscataway, 1991—; asst. prof., assoc. prof. clin. neurology Columbia Med. Sch., NYC. Rsch. assoc. US Pub. Health Svc., Bethesda, Md. Contbr. scientific papers to profl. pubs. Achievements include discovery of first gene for Parkinson disease; maternal genes contributing to autism; patents pending for human genetic disorders; research in late-onset Tay-Sachs disease. Office: U Medicine and Dentistry NJ Robert Wood Johnson Med Sch 675 Hoes Ln Piscataway NJ 07078 Office Phone: 732-235-4508. Business E-Mail: wjohnson@umdnj.edu.

JOHNSON EFFINGER, NAOMI BOWERS, nursing and health facility administrator; b. Ft. Benning, Ga., Aug. 17, 1954; d. Bob and Henrietta Violet (Hoomalu) Bowers; m. James William Johnson, Dec. 7, 1973 (div.); children: Amelia, Melissa, Charity, James-William; m. Bobby L. Effinger, Mar. 19, 2005; stepchildren: Wilson, Margaret, Gloria. ADN, Troy State U., Montgomery, Ala., 1974. Office supr., lab. supr., nursing coord. physician's office, Selma, Ala.; patients care coord. West. Ala. Home Health Agy., Selma; discharge planning/social svcs., SOBRA and clin. case mgmt. coord. Vaughan Regional Med. Ctr. Hosp., Selma; DON Dunn Nursing Home, Selma, Capitol Hill Health Care Ctr.; dir. mktg. and admissions Mariner Post Acute Health Care Network, Montgomery, Ala.; DON Ball Healthcare-Lighthouse, Selma. Author (poet): Publish America/International Poet Society, 2002—03. Personal E-mail: hoomalu@bellsouth.net, nululani@yahoo.com.

JOHNSTON, COLIN IVOR, medical educator, researcher; b. Hong Kong, May 28, 1934; s. James Hamilton and Dorothy Eleanor (Shields) J.; m. Susan Bailhache, June 12, 1959; children: Sam, Anna, Amy. MB BS, U. Sydney, Australia, 1957; MD (hon.), Melb U., 2000. Residency Royal Prince Alfred Hosp., Sydney, Australia, 1958-64; prof. medicine Monash U., 1973-86, hon. prof. medicine, 2000—; reader dept. medicine U. Melbourne, Australia, 1971-72, prof. medicine, chmn., 1986-99, emeritus prof., 2000—; v.p. Austin & Repatriation Med. Ctr., Melbourne; v.p. bd. mgmt. Prince Henry's Hosp., Melbourne, 1982-86; sr. prin. rsch. fellow Baker Med. Rsch. Inst., Melbourne, 1999—. Mem. sci. and edn. com. Nat. Heart Found. Australia, 1990-97; chmn. trustees Found. for High Blood Pressure Rsch., 1994—. Fellow Royal Australasian Coll. Physicians (Gold medal 1995); mem. Am. Soc. Hypertension (exec. coun. 1988-2000, Richard Bright award 1995), Internat. Soc. Nephrology (coun. 1978-86), High Blood Pressure Rsch. Coun. Australia (chmn. 1990-93, treas. 1993-95), Internat. Soc. Hypertension (v.p. 1985-90, Franz Volhard award 1992). Avocations: fly fishing, collecting, horticulture. Home: 6 Berkeley St Hawthorn Melbourne VIC 3122 Australia Office: Baker Med Rsch Inst Alfred Ln Prahran Victoria 3181 Australia

JOHNSTON, CYRUS CONRAD, JR., medical educator; b. Statesville, NC, July 16, 1929; m. Marjorie Tarkington, Feb. 20, 1960; 2 children. BA, Duke U., 1951, MD, 1955. Diplomate Am. Bd. Internal Medicine. Intern Duke Hosp., Durham, NC, 1955-56; resident in medicine Barnes Hosp., St. Louis, 1956-57; rsch. fellow in endocrinology and metabolism Ind. U., Indpls., 1959-61, instr. medicine, 1961-63, asst. prof., 1963-67, assoc. prof., 1967-69, prof. medicine, 1969-97, disting. prof. medicine, 1997—2002, disting. prof. emeritus, 2002—; assoc. dir. Gen. Clin. Rsch. Ctr. Ind. U. Med. Ctr., Indpls., 1962-67, program dir., 1967-72, prin. investigator, 1968-88, dir. divsn. endocrinology and metabolism, 1968-94. Mem. aging rev. com. Nat. Inst. Aging, 1982-85, chmn. geriatrics rev. com., 1985-86; mem. nursing sci. rev. com. NIH, 1988-89; mem. com. for protection of human subjects Ind. U.-Purdue U., Indpls., 1966—, chmn., 1978—; chmn. Nat. Osteoporosis Found. Sci. Adv. Bd., 1992-96; med. adv. panel Paget's Disease Found., 1989—; bd. trustees Nat. Osteoporosis Found., 1992—, pres., 1996-2001; mem. Nat. Adv. Coun. on Aging, 1992-95. Assoc. editor Bone and Mineral, 1985-94, Bone, 1995-2004; editl. bd. Jour. Bone and Mineral Rsch., Jour. Clin. Endocrinology and Metabolism, 1988-91. Capt. USAF, 1957-59. Recipient Career Rsch. Devel. award USPHS, 1963-68, Sandoz prize Internat. Assn. Gerontology, 1993, Experience Excellence Recognition award Glenn W. Irwin, Jr., MD, 2001. Mem. ACP, AAAS, AMA, Am. Assn. Clin. Endocrinologists (Yank D. Coble, Jr. M.D. Disting. Svc. award 1998), Am. Fedn. Clin. Rsch., Am. Soc. for Bone and Mineral Rsch. (Frederic C. Bartter award 1996), Am. Clin. and Climatological Soc., Ctrl. Soc. for Clin. Rsch., Endocrine Soc. Office: Indiana Univ Dept Medicine 541 N Clinical Dr CL 459 Indianapolis IN 46202-5124 E-mail: cjohnsto@iupui.edu.

JOHNSTON, DENNIS GEORGE, pharmacologist, consultant; b. Belfast, No. Ireland, Sept. 9, 1946; s. George and Catherine (Stewart) Johnston; m. Barbara Agnes Hawkins, July 15, 1971; children: Gail, David, Kate. MB, BChir, Queens U., Belfast, 1971, MD, 1978, PhD, 1985, DSc, 1996. Internat. rsch. fellow, Denver, 1979—80; cons. physician, sr. lectr. Belfast City Hosp., Queens U., Whitla prof. therapeutics and pharmacology. Chmn. Regional Group for Prescribing Specialist Drugs, 2000—; cons. in field. Author: Fundamentals of Cardiovascular Pharmacology, 1999; contbr. articles to profl. jours. Exec. com. British Pharm. Soc., 1991—94, British Hypertension Soc., 1997—2000. Named Graves lectr., Royal Irish Acad. Medicine, 1988; fellow Internat. fellow, 1979—80. Fellow: Royal Coll. Physicians (Edinburgh, Ireland and London); mem.: European Assn. Poisons Ctrs., Assn. Physicians, Irish Assn. Pharmacologists (chmn. 2001—). Avocations: music, painting, walking. Home: 12 Ormiston Park Belfast BT4 3JT Northern Ireland Office: Dept Therapeutics Pharmacology 97 Lisburn Rd Belfast BT9 7BL Northern Ireland Office Phone: 02890 975770. Personal E-mail: g.d.johnston@qub.ac.uk.

JOHNSTON, FRANK C., psychologist; b. West Hartford, Conn., June 21, 1955; s. Frank C. and Chris (Butler) J.; m. Susan H. Leffert, July 26, 1981; 1 child, Daniel Frank. BA, Fairfield U., 1977; MEd, MA, Columbia U., 1979; PhD, SUNY, Albany, 1984. Sch. psychologist bd. coop. ednl. svcs. Herkimer, NY, 1979—80; intern Counseling Ctr., SUNY, Buffalo, 1983—84; psychologist Family Svc. Rochester, NY, 1985—87, Child and Youth divsn. Rochester Mental Health Ctr., 1988; pvt. practice Rochester, 1988—; co-founder Flow Productivity Consumers, 2010—. Cons. Brockport (N.Y.) Day Care Ctr., 1989-90, Learning Devel. Ctr., Rochester Inst. Tech., 1989-90; co-founder Behavioral Health Consortium Rochester, 1993-96. Mem. APA, N.Y. State Psychol. Assn., Genesee Valley Psychol. Assn. (mem. legal legis com. 1988-90, mem. ins. com. 1990-92, chmn. ins. com. 1990-93, pres. 1994, past pres. 1995), Rochester Cmty. Individual Practice Assn. (mem. psychology subcom. 1988-98, mem. mental health task force Preferred Care 1999-2000), Rochester Area Assn. Clin. Psychologists, Nat. Register Health Svc. Providers in Psychology. Office: 160 Allens Creek Rd Rochester NY 14618 Home Phone: 585-442-4992; Office Phone: 585-427-7800. Office Fax: 585-427-7817. Personal E-mail: jpsych2@frontiernet.net.

JOHNSTON, GERALD SAMUEL, physician, educator; b. Johnstown, Pa., Aug. 4, 1930; s. Fleurence Gerald and Lorna Freda (Lawhead) J.; m. Dorothy Anna Jones, June 18, 1956; children: Joy Johnston Biciocchi, Jill A. Verna, Jana S. Moritzkat, Gerald S. Jr., Amy L. Tapparo, Douglas S. BS, U. Pitts., 1952, MD, 1956. Diplomate Am. Bd. Internal Medicine, Am. Bd. Nuclear Medicine. Intern Walter Reed Gen. Hosp., Washington, 1956-57; resident in internal medicine Brooke Gen. Hosp., San Antonio, 1958-61; commd. med. officer U.S. Army, 1955-71, advanced through grades to col., 1971; capt. USPHS, 1971-82; surgeon 358 Gen. dispensary, Seoul, Korea, 1961-62; chief nuclear medicine Walter Reed Gen. Hosp., Washington, Md., 1963-69, Letterman Gen. Hosp., San Francisco, 1969-71, NIH, Bethesda, Md., 1971-82, U. Md., Balt., 1982-93, acting chmn. dept. radiology, 1989-92, prof. medicine, radiology and oncology, 1982-93; chmn. dept. nuclear medicine Washington Hosp. Ctr., 1993-99, staff nuclear med. physician, 1999—2009; established nuclear medicine svc. Royal Hobart Hosp., Tasmania, Australia, 1999. Author two books; contbr. over 250 articles to profl. jours. Decorated Legion of Merit, 1970. Fellow ACP, Am. Coll. Radiology; mem. AMA, AAUP, Am. Coll. Nuclear Medicine (pres. 2002-03), Soc. Nuclear Medicine. Republican. Avocations: history, running, carpentry, philosophy. Business E-Mail: docgsj@starpower.net.

JOHNSTON, JAMES R., internist, educator; BS, Pa. State U., 1975; MD, U. Pitts., 1979. Diplomate Am. Bd. Internal Medicine, Am. Bd. Internal Medicine-nephrology. Chief resident Montefiore Hosp., Pitts., 1982; fellow Brigham & Women's Hosp., Boston; rsch./clin. fellow Harvard Univ., 1986; prof. medicine, dept. medicine and renal-electrolyte divsn. Univ. of Pitts. Med. Ctr. Presbyterian, dir. renal fellowship tng. program, dir. clin. svcs., renal-electrolyte divsn., dir. acute dialysis unit; hosp. affiliation includes Magee-Womens Hospital of UPMC. Recipient Nat. Golden Apple Tchg. Excellence award, Am. Med. Student Assn., The Dean's Master Educator award, Chancellor's Tchg. award, Univ. of Pitts., Excellence in Edn. awards, Golden Apple award, Univ. of Pitts. Sch. of Medicine (UPSOM) Med. Students. Office: University of Pittsburgh Presbyterian Renal-Electrolyte Division Ste 300 120 Lytton Ave Pittsburgh PA 15213 Office Phone: 412-802-3043. Office Fax: 412-647-6222. E-mail: Jamiej@pitt.edu.

JOHNSTON, LLOYD DOUGLAS, social sciences educator; b. Boston, Apr. 18, 1940; s. Leslie D. and Madeline B. (Irvin) Johnston; m. Janet Wilson, Nov. 13, 2004; 1 stepchild, Leah Wilson Brown; 1 child from previous marriage, Douglas Leslie. BA in Econs., Williams Coll., 1962; MBA, Harvard U., 1965, postgrad., 1965—66; MA in Social Psychology, U. Mich., 1971, PhD, 1973. Research asst. Grad. Sch. Bus. Adminstrn., Harvard U., Boston, 1965-66; asst. study dir. Inst. Social Research, U. Mich., Ann Arbor, 1966-73, asst. research scientist, 1973-75, assoc. rsch. scientist, 1975-78, sr. rsch. scientist and program dir., 1978-98; disting. sr. rsch. scientist, rsch. prof. Inst. Social Rsch., U. Mich., Ann Arbor, 1998—; chmn. exec. com. U. Mich. Substance Abuse Rsch. Ctr. Excellence, 1990-95, acting dir., 1994-95. Prin. investigator Monitoring the Future: A Continuing Study of Lifestyles and Values of Am. Youth, 1975—, Youth, Education and Society, 1996—, also other nat. and internat. survey studies; cons. to WHO, UN, EEC, Coun. of Europe, Pan Am. Health Orgn., White House, U.S. Congress, various founds., numerous fgn. govts., fed. agys., univs., rsch. insts., TV networks, Nat. Partnership for Drug Free Am., 1978—; chmn. tech. planning group; mem. Resource Group for Goal Seven, Nat. Ednl. Goals Panel, 1991-2002; mem. extramural sci. adv. bd. Nat. Inst. on Drug Abuse, 1990-94; mem., also chmn. prevention subcom., Nat. Adv. Coun. on Drug Abuse, 1982-86, Presdl. appointee White House Conf. for a Drug-Free Am., 1987-88, Presdl. appointee Nat. Commn. for Drug Free Schs., 1989-90; chmn. drug epidemiology sect. Internat. Coun. on Alcohol and Addictions, 1982-2002; mem. Com. on Problems of Drug Dependence, 1982-86; mem. or chmn. various adv. coms. various univs., founds.; mem. various working groups NAS; mem. various coms. and adv. groups Nat. Inst. Drug Abuse, 1975—; mem. or chmn. 7 working groups WHO, 1975—; invited lectr. nat. and internat. confs. and convs.; testimony before Congress and fed. regulatory agys. Author: Drugs and American Youth, 1973, Student Drug Use in America, 1975-81, 82, Monitoring the Future Nat. Survey Results on Drug Use 1975-2006, vol. 1 and 2, 2007, over 66 other books and monographs on drug use and lifestyles of Am. Secondary Sch. Am. Coll. Students and Young Adults, 1972—, 32 reference vols.; editor: Conducting Follow Up Research on Drug Treatment Programs, 1977; contbr. more than 153 chpts. to books, articles to profl. jours. Recipient Nat. Pacesetter award in rsch. Nat. Inst. on Drug Abuse, 1982, 1st Sr. Rsch. Scientist award and lectureship U. Mich., 1987, Regents award for disting. pub. svc., 1998, Disting. Rsch. Scientist award, 1998. Fellow Coll. on Problems of Drug Dependence; mem. APA, Soc. for Psychol. Study Social Issues (sec.-treas. 1976-79), Am. Sociol. Assn., Am. Pub. Health Assn. Home: 5538 Lawrence Ct Pinckney MI 48169-9257 Office: U Mich Inst Social Rsch Ann Arbor MI 48109 Business E-Mail: lloydj@umich.edu.

JOHNSTON, NICKLETT ROSE, research nurse, clinical perfusionist; d. Robert Nick Moriana and Melba Grohe, Roger E. Grohe (Stepfather); m. Roy Edwin Johnston, Aug. 5, 1995; m. Michael Minnella, 1979 (div. 1992); children: Michael Paul Minnella, Anita Marie Minnella. ADN, Cochise Coll., Douglas, AZ, 1979; BSN, U. Phoenix, 2002; MSN, Graceland U., 2005. Cert. clin. perfusionist Tex., 1989, ACLS, Tex., 2002. RN Tucson Med. Ctr., 1982—87; clin. perfusionist, RN, Cardiovasc. Support Svcs., Dallas, 1988—89; clin. perfusionist, RN dept. cardiovascular and thoracic surgery U. Tex. Southwestern Med. Ctr., Dallas, 1989—2003, sr. rsch. nurse dept. cardiovascular and thoracic surgery, 2003—. Mem. ANA, Washington, 1979—90, Am. Soc. for Extra Corporeal Tech., Hattiesburg, Miss., 1989—, knowledge base com., 1999—2000; instr. Am. Heart Assn., Dallas, 1994—95. Author: The Emergency use of Recombinant Hirudin in Cardiopulmonary Bypass (Am. Soc. for Extra Corporeal Tech. Case Report award, 2000), Argatroban in Adult Extracorporeal Membrane Oxygenation, Simplified Solution to Eliminating Electrical Noise During Cardiac Surgery. Mem.: Am. Bd. Perfusionists, Am. Bd. Nursing (licentiate), Theta Tau. Home: 324 Harbor Landing Dr Rockwall TX 75032 Personal E-mail: johnstonr@sbcglobal.net.

JOHNSTON, NIKKI, otolaryngologist, educator; b. Dundee, Scotland, July 10, 1977; BSc with honors, U. Dundee, 1999, PhD, 2003. Rsch. fellow Wake Forest U. Sch. Medicine, 2003, rsch. asst. prof., 2003—06; dir., airway digestive and voice rsch. Med. Coll. Wis., Dept. Otolaryngology, 2010, asst. prof., dir., translational rsch. scientist, 2006—, edn. coord., 2009, chair, resident rsch. com., 2009. Cons. Koufman Diagnostics LLC, 2010; vice chair otolaryngology com. World Orgn. Specialized Studies on Diseases of Esophagus, 2011. Recipient Travel award, Am. Cancer Soc., MCW Cancer Ctr., 2011. Mem.: Am. Broncho-Esophagological Assn. (Broyles-Maloney award 2008—09), Assn. Rsch. Otolaryngoloy, Soc. Biomolecular Scis., Am. Assn. Cancer Rsch., Med. Coll. Wis. Admissions Com. Faculty Coun., Internat. Scholarly Rsch. Network (editl. bd. mem., Otolaryngology Jour.). Avocations: walking, travel, hiking. Office: Med Coll Wis 9200 W Wisconsin Ave Milwaukee WI 53226 Business E-Mail: njohnsto@mcw.edu.

JOHNSTON, PAUL WARREN, retired surgeon; b. Kingsburg, Calif. s. Karl Gunnar and Ester Matilda Johnston; m. Lillian Ruby Rogstad, Nov. 25, 1949; children: Mark, Anne, Gail. BA, U. So. Calif., LA, 1944, MD, 1947. Intern LA County Hosp., LA, 1947; resident VA Hosp., Long Beach, Calif., 1949—53, surgeon, 1953—56; pvt. practice surgeon Burbank, Calif., 1957, Pasadena, Calif., 1957—95; ret., 1995. Pres. med. staff Huntington Hosp., Pasadena, 1979, chair instnl. rev. bd., 1985—2000, dir. surg. residency program, 1990—95. Contbr. articles to profl. jours. Lt. (j.g.) USNR, 1947—49. Mem.: ACS, Western Surg. Assn., Pacific Coast Surg. Assn. Avocations: golf, reading, travel. Personal E-mail: pwjlrj@msn.com.

JOHNSTON, RICHARD BOLES, JR., pediatrician, educator, biomedical researcher; b. Atlanta, Aug. 23, 1935; s. Richard Boles and Jane (Dillon) Johnston; m. Mary Anne Claiborne, Aug. 13, 1960; children: Richard B. III, S. Claiborne, Kristin M. BA, Vanderbilt U., 1957, MD, 1961; MS (hon.), U. Pa., 1986. Diplomate Am. Bd. Pediat. Resident in pediat. Vanderbilt U., 1961-63, Harvard U., 1963-64, fellow pediat. immunology, 1967-70; asst. prof., assoc. prof. depts. pediat. and microbiology U. Ala. Med. Ctr., Birmingham, 1970-76; vis. assoc. prof. Rockefeller U., NYC, 1976-77, vis. prof., 1983-84; prof. pediat. U. Colo. Sch. Medicine, Denver, 1977-86; chmn. dept. pediat. Nat. Jewish Ctr. Immunology and Respiratory Medicine, Denver, 1977-86, U. Pa. Sch. Medicine, Phila., 1986-90, Wm. H. Bennett prof. pediat., 1986-92; physician-in-chief Children's Hosp. of Phila., 1986—90; med. dir. March of Dimes Birth Defects Found., White Plains, NY, 1992-98. Adj. prof. pediat., chief sec. pediat. immunology Yale U. Sch. Medicine, 1992—98; prof. pediat. Sch. Medicine U. Colo., Denver, 1999—, assoc. dean rsch. devel., 2001—; trustee Internat. Pediat. Rsch. Found., 1983—87, 1995—98, chmn., 1984—87, 1997—98; chmn. adv. bd. for vaccines and related biols. FDA, Bethesda, Md., 1990—93, chmn. com. vaccine safety, Inst. Medicine, 1992—93, chmn. com. new rsch. in vaccines, 1993—94, chmn. forum vaccine safety, 1995—98, chmn. com. asthma and indoor air, 1998—99, bd. health promotion disease prevention, 1994—2001, chmn. com. rsch. in multiple sclerosis, 1999—2001, chmn. com. health implications of perchlorate, 2003—05, chmn. com. tng. physicians for pub. health careers, 2006—07, review coord., 2005, 11; exec. v.p. acad. affairs Nat. Jewish Med. & Rsch. Ctr., 2004—07, v.p. rsch. affairs, 2007—08. Mem. editl. bd. 8 profl. jours., 1978—; contbr. 280 scholarly publs.; editor Current Opinion in Pediatrics, 1997—. Mem. med. ctr. adv. com. Vanderbilt U. Bd. Trust, 2011-. Capt. M.C., U.S. Army, 1964-66. Faculty scholar Josiah Macy Jr. Found., 1976-77; recipient Commr. citation and Wiley medal FDA, 1994, John Howland medal, Am. Pediat Soc., 2008, Disting. Alumnus Vanderbilt Sch. Med., 2008. Fellow AAAS; mem. Inst. Medicine NAS, Am. Soc. Clin. Investigation, Am. Pediat. Soc. (pres. 1996-97), Assn. Am. Physicians, Soc. Pediat. Rsch. (pres. 1980-81). Office: Univ Colo Sch Medicine Dean's Office C-290 13001 E 17th Pl Aurora CO 80045 Office Phone: 303-724-5365. Business E-Mail: richard.johnston@ucdenver.edu.

JOHNSTON, WILLIAM WEBB, pathologist, educator; b. Statesville, NC, Aug. 26, 1933; s. Jesse Clyde and Pauline Elizabeth (Massey) J. BS, Davidson Coll., 1954; MD, Duke U., 1959. Diplomate Am. Bd. Pathology, Am. Bd. Cytopathology, Internat. Bd. Cytopathology. Intern Duke U., 1959-60, resident in pathology, 1960-63, mem. faculty, 1963—, prof. pathology, 1972-97, dir. div. cytopathology and cytotechnology tng. program, 1966—; ret., 1996. Bd. dirs. Anatomical Pathology Svc.; cons. pathologist Durham VA Hosp., Duncan County Hosp.; chmn. Internat. Bd. Cytopathology, 1992-98. Author: (with W.J. Frable) Respiratory Cytopathology, 1974; Diagnostic Respiratory Cytopathology, 1979; (with S.H. Bigner) The Cytopathology of the Central Nervous System, 1981, 2d edit., 1994, Pulmonary Cytology (with James Linder), 1992; assoc. editor Acta Cytologica, 1978—, sr. mem. editorial bd., 1992; editor: Masson Monographs in Cytopathology; mem. editorial bd. Am. Jour. Clin. Pathology, 1986; editorial cons. Masson Publs., N.Y.C.; mem. editorial adv. bd. Jour. Nat. Cancer Inst. Fellow Internat. Acad. Cytology (Maurice Goldblatt award 1995), Am. Soc. Clin. Pathologists, Coll. Am. Pathologists, Royal Soc. Medicine; mem. AMA (del. 1982-96), Am. Soc. Cytology (rev. bd., pres. 1981-82, Papanicolaou award 1986), Am. Assn. Pathologists, Arthur Purdy Stout Soc. Surg. Pathology, Internat. Acad. Pathology, Am. Assn. for Cancer Rsch. Republican. Presbyterian (organist). Home: 8200 Bromley Rd Hillsborough NC 27278-9709

JOINER, KEITH A., medical educator, epidemiologist; BA in Biology, U. Chgo., 1970; MD cum laude, U. Colo., 1974; MPH, Yale U., 2003. Cert. American Bd. Internal Medicine, 1977, in infectious diseases American Bd. Internal Medicine, 1980. Intern in medicine Royal Victoria Hosp., McGill U., Montreal, Canada, 1974—75, jr. asst. resident, 1975—76; sr. asst. resident in medicine Mary Hitchcock Hosp., Dartmouth Med. Sch., Hanover, NH, 1976—77; clin. and rsch.

fellow in infectious diseases Tufts-New Eng. Med. Ctr., Boston, 1977—80; asst. prof. medicine Tufts U. Sch. Medicine, Boston, 1980; sr. investigator lab. clin. investigation NIAID NIH, 1980—87, sr. investigator, head unit microbial pathogenesis lab. parasitic diseses, 1987—89; prof. medicine, cell biology and epidemiology Yale U. Sch. Medicine, 1989—2004, chief infectious disease sect., 1989—2004, Waldemar von Zedtwitz prof. medicine, assoc. chmn. dept. medicine, 1999—2004, founder, dir. investigative medicine program, 1999—2004; prof. medicine, cell biology and health promotions sci. U. Ariz. Coll. Medicine, Tucson, 2004—, dean, 2004—08, vice provost med. affairs, 2007—08; co-dir. Center Mgmt. Innovations in Healthcare U. Ariz. Eller Coll. Mgmt., 2010—. Lectr. in field. Monitoring editor Jour. Cell Biology, editl. bd. Cellular Microbiology, Current Drug Targets Infectious Disorders, Parasite Cell Biology; contbr. articles to profl. jours. Recipient Burroughs Wellcome Fund New Initiatives in Malaria Rsch. award; Sr. Scholar in Global Infectious Diseases, Ellison Found. Fellow: Infectious Disease Soc. America, Am. Assn. for Advancement Sci.; mem.: Am. Soc. Clin. Investigation, Assn. Am. Physicians. Office: Ctr Mgmt Innovations in Healthcare University Ariz Eller Coll Mgmt 1130 E Helen St McClelland Hall 411 Tucson AZ 85721 Office Phone: 520-626-4655. Office Fax: 520-621-4171. Business E-Mail: kjoiner@email.arizona.edu. *

JOKLIK, WOLFGANG KARL, biochemist, virologist, educator; b. Vienna, Nov. 16, 1926; s. Karl F. and Helene (Giessl) J.; m. Judith Vivien Nicholas, Apr. 9, 1955 (dec. Apr. 1975); children: Richard G., Vivien H.; m. Patricia Hunter Downey, Apr. 23, 1977. B.Sc. with 1st class honors, U. Sydney, Australia, 1948, M.Sc., 1949, D.Phil. (Australian Nat. U. scholar), U. Oxford, Eng., 1952. Australian Nat. U. research fellow, Copenhagen, 1953, Canberra, Australia, 1954-56; fellow, 1957-62; assoc. prof. cell biology Albert Einstein Coll. Medicine, Bronx, NY, 1962-65, prof. cell biology, 1965-68, Siegfried Ullmann prof. biochem. virology, 1966-68; prof., chmn. dept. microbiology and immunology Duke U. Med. Ctr., Durham, NC, 1968-92, James B. Duke Disting. prof. microbiology and immunology, 1972-92, James B. Duke prof. microbiology, 1992-96, James B. Duke prof. emeritus, 1996—. Sr. author: Zinsser Microbiology, 15th, 16th, 17th, 18th, 19th, 20th edits.; editor-in-chief Virology, 1975-93, Microbiological Rev., 1991-95; contbr. articles to profl. jours. Recipient Sr. US award Alexander Humboldt Found., 1985, ICN Internat. prize for virology, 1991. Mem. NAS, Inst. Medicine of NAS, Am. Soc. Virology (pres. 1982-83), Am. Soc. Microbiology, Am. Soc. Biol. Chemists. Address: Duke U Med Ctr Dept Molecular Genetics and Microbiology PO Box 3020 Durham NC 27710-0001 Office Fax: 919-489-4433. Personal E-mail: joklikb@aol.com.

JOLLEY, WELDON BOSEN, surgery educator, research executive; b. Gunnison, Utah, Sept. 8, 1926; s. Edward Mckinley Jolley and Rosella (Elvira) Bosen; m. Dorathy Timms, Dec. 21, 1954 (dec. Jan. 1983); children: Elizabeth Price, Kathleen Cope, Phillip Jolley; m. JoLane Laycock, Aug. 20, 1983; children: Jessica, Brian. BA, Brigham Young U., 1952; PhD, U. So. Calif., 1959; postdoctoral, UCLA, 1960. Prof. surgery, physiology and biophysics Loma Linda (Calif.) U., 1969—, assoc. dir. surg. research lab., 1969—; dir. surg. research VA Hosp., Loma Linda, 1979-85; pres. Nucleic Acid Research Inst., Costa Mesa, Calif., 1985—95. Bd. dirs. SPI Pharms., Inc.; sr. v.p., bd. dirs. ICN Pharms., Inc.; sci. adv. Viratek, Inc. Contbr. tech. articles to publs. Named McPherson Soc. Clin. Prof. of Yr., 1982. Home: 4493 Pepper Creek Ln Anaheim CA 92807 *

JOLLY, DANIEL EHS, dental educator; b. St. Louis, Aug. 25, 1952; s. Melvin Joseph and Betty Ehs (Koehler) Jolly; 1 child, Farrell. BA in Biology and Chemistry, U. Mo., Kansas City, 1974, DDS, 1977. Diplomate Am. Bd. Special Care Dentistry. Resident in hosp. dentistry VA Med. Ctr., Leavenworth, Kans., 1977-78; pvt. practice Newcastle, Wyo., 1978-79; asst. prof. U. Mo., Kansas City, 1979-87; chief restorative dentistry Truman Med. Ctr., Kansas City, 1979-87; dir. dental oncology Trinity Luth. Hosp., 1982-87; assoc. prof., dir. gen. practice residency program Ohio State U., Columbus, 1987—, prof., dir. gen. practice residency program, 1993—2008; pres. Immediadent of Ohio, 2008—. Dir. Honduras Clinic Project, 1992—; bd. dirs. Rinehart Found. U. Mo. Dental Sch., Kansas City, 1985—87; cons. Lee's Summit (Mo.) Care Ctr., 1984—87, Longview Nursing Ctr., Grandview, 1986—87; sec. Combined Hosp. Dental Staff, Columbus, 1989—90, v.p., 1990—91, pres., 1991—92. Author: (manual) Hospital Dental Hygiene, 1984, Hospital Dentistry, 1985, OSU Manual Hospital Dentistry, 1989—, (booklet) Nursing Home Dentistry, 1986, Dental Oncology, 1986. Mem. profl. adv. coun. Easter Seal Soc., 1986—92, sec. bd. dirs. Easter Seal Rehab. Ctr. Columbus, 1990—93, mem. regional coun. Kansas City, 1985—87; pres. Health Profls. Serving Humanity. With U.S. Naval Sea Cadet Corps, 1998—99. Recipient Alumni Achievement award in dentistry, U. Mo., Kansas City, 1995. Fellow: Pierre Fauchard Acad., Am. Coll. Dentistry, Acad. Dentistry Handicapped (pres. 1992), Am. Soc. Geriatric Dentistry, Acad. Dentistry Internat., Am. Soc. Dentistry Children, Am. Assn. Hosp. Dentists (regional v.p. 1993—, sec., pres.-elect 2002—03, pres. 2003—), Acad. Gen. Dentistry; mem.: ADA, Immedia Dent Ohio (pres. 2008—), Am. Bd. Special Care Dentistry (diplomate 2004, pres. 2004—), Ohio Dental Assn. (Humanitarian award 1998), Internat. Soc. Oral Oncology, S.W. Oncology Group, Fedn. Spl Care Orgns. Dentistry (chmn. 1992—93), Greater Kansas City Dental Soc., Internat. Assn. Dentistry handicapped (pres. 1994—96, past pres. 1996—98, editor 1998—), Magna Charta Barons Club. Avocations: photography, scuba diving, swimming, horses. Office: Immediadent 4044 Morse Rd Columbus OH 43230 Home: 5991 Outville Rd SW Pataskala OH 43062-8434 Home Phone: 614-329-4178. E-mail: djolly82552@cs.com.

JOMEEN, JULIE, social sciences educator, director; b. Scarborough, Eng., May 26, 1967; m. Omar Jomeen, Feb. 18, 1995; children: Ellie Grace, Aaron Jack. MA in Health Svc. Studies, Nuffield Inst. Health, U. Leeds, 2001; PhD, Sch. Medcine, U. Leeds, 2005. Cert. RGN, Nursing & Midwifery Coun., 1992, RM, Nursing & Midwifery Coun., 1994. Staff nurse Royal Hull Hosps., Hull, England, 1992—93; midwife Hull & East Yorkshire NHSTrust, 1995—2002, practice devel. midwife, 2002—06; sr. lectr. midwifery & women's health U. Hull, 2006—, assoc. dean rsch. & scholarship faculty health & social Care, 2007—. Com. mem. Soc. Reproductive & Infant Psychology; editl. bd. mem. Brit. Jour. Midwifery, Jour. Health Orgn. & Mgmt.; mem. rsch. adv. network Internat. Confederation Midwives; chair Hull & East Yorkshire Maternal Mental Health Strategy Group. Author: Choice, Control & Contemporary Childbirth; contbr. articles to professional journals and books. Recipient Radcliffe Writing award, 2007. Mem.: Royal Coll. Midwives. Office: Univ Hull Cottingham Rd Hull HU6 7RX England Business E-Mail: j.jomeen@hull.ac.uk.

JONAS, ADAM J., clinical geneticist, educator; MD, U. Calif., San Diego, 1976. Lic. Calif., 1979, diplomate Am. Bd. Pediatrics, 1982, cert. Am. Bd. Clin. Biochemical Genetics-Med. Genetics, 1987, Am. Bd. Clin. Genetics-Med. Genetics, 1990. Resident pediat. Children's Orthop. Hosp., 1977—78, Univ. Hosp., San Diego, 1978—79; fellow genetics and metabolism U. Calif., San Diego, 1979—82; prof. pediat. UCLA; hosp. affiliation includes Mary Med. Ctr., Torrance, San Pedro, UCLA Med. Ctr., Harbor. Office: University California Los Angeles Medical Center Medical Genetics Division 1000 W Carson St Box 17 Torrance CA 90509-2910 Office Phone: 310-222-2301.

JONAS, GARY FRED, healthcare executive; b. NYC, Apr. 26, 1945; s. Otto and Hilde (Levy) Jonas; m. Rosalyn Ethel Levy; children: Lauren, Rachel. BS in Ops. Rsch., Columbia U., 1966; MBA, Harvard U., 1968. Mgmt. cons. Fry Cons., Washington, 1968-69; divsn. dir. Univ. Rsch. Corp. Ctr. Human Svcs., Chevy Chase, Md., 1970-73, exec. v.p., 1973-75, pres., CEO, 1975-85, chmn., CEO, 1985-88, also bd. dirs.; pres., COO The Earle Palmer Brown Cos., Bethesda, Md., 1988-93, also bd. dirs.; pres., CEO 20/20 Laser Ctrs., Inc., Bethesda, 1993-97, also bd. dirs.; exec. v.p., dir. TLC Laser Eye Ctrs., Inc., Bethesda, 1997-2000; mng. ptnr. Venture Philanthropy Ptnrs., Inc., Reston, Va., 2000—02; CEO Strategic Planning Advisors, Inc., 2002—; pres. Alase Laser Hair Removal Ctrs., 2002—05; CEO Med. Body Sculpting, 2006—07. Faculty assoc. Johns Hopkins U., 1999—; adj. faculty Am. U., Washington. Contbr. articles to profl. jours. Mem.: Young Pres.'s Orgn. (exec. com., chmn. Washington metro chpt. 1987—88), Washington Bd. Trade, Am. Soc. Tng. and Devel., Conf. Bd., Nat. Contract Mgmt. Assn., Profl. Svcs. Coun. (past bd. dirs., v.p.), Inst. Mgmt. Cons. (cert.), Woodmont Country Club, Harvard Club. Home: 6716 Melody Ln Bethesda MD 20817-3115 Office Phone: 301-529-2020. Personal E-mail: gary@jonas.com.

JONAS, RUTH HABER, psychologist; b. Tel Aviv, Aug. 24, 1935; d. Fred S. and Dorothy Judith (Bernstein) Haber; m. Saran Jonas, Sept. 16, 1956; children: Elizabeth, Frederick. AB, Barnard Coll., 1957; MA, New Sch. for Social Rsch., 1977, PhD, 1987; grad. psychotherapy and psychoanalysis, NYU, 1996. Lic. psychologist, NY. 1st and 2d yr. intern clin. psychology NYU Med. Ctr.-Bellevue Hosp., NYC, 1985-87; postdoctoral rsch. fellow NYU Med. Ctr., NYC, 1987-88; clin. instr. psychiatry NYU Sch. Medicine, NYC, 1987, clin. asst. prof. psychiatry, 1991; sr. psychologist forensic svc. Bellevue Hosp., NYC, 1988—; pvt. practice psychotherapy NYC, 1988—. Fellow Am. Orthopsychiat. Assn.; mem. APA, NY State Psychol. Soc., Manhattan Psychol. Assn., Am. Heart Assn. (fellow stroke coun.). Office: 200 E 33d St Ste 2J New York NY 10016-4827 Office Phone: 212-684-2721.

JONAS, SARAN, neurologist, educator; b. NYC, June 24, 1931; s. Myron and Margaret (Wurmfeld) J.; m. Ruth Haber, Sept. 16, 1956; children: Elizabeth Ann, Frederick Jonathan. BS, Yale U., 1952; MD, Columbia U., 1956. Diplomate Am. Bd. Psychiatry and Neurology, Am. Bd. Internal Medicine. Intern Bellevue Hosp., NYC, 1956-57, resident and fellow in medicine and neurology, 1957-62; practice medicine specializing in neurology NYC, 1964—; from clin. instr. to assoc. prof. clin. neurology NYU Sch. Medicine, 1964-77, prof. clin. neurology, 1977—2000, acting chmn. dept. neurology, 1987-91, prof. neurology, 2000—. Dir. electroencephalography NYU Hosp., 1969-94, assoc. dir. neurology, 1970-87, dir., 1987-91; acting dir. neurology Bellevue Hosp., NYC, 1987-91, assoc. dir., 1991—, dir. electroencephalography, 1994—, co-founder, Com. Enterns & Cender NYC, Dept. Hosp., 1958, chmn., 1959-60, CIR SEIU Svc. Employment Internat. Union. Served with USN, 1962-64. NY State fellow in rheumatic diseases, 1962-64. Mem. Am. Acad. Neurology, Assn. for Rsch. in Nervous and Mental Diseases, Am. Heart Assn. (Stroke Coun., Epidemiology Coun.), Am. Epilepsy Soc. Office: 530 1st Ave New York NY 10016-6402

JONAS, STEVEN, preventive medicine physician, author; b. NYC, Nov. 22, 1936; s. Harold Jacob and Florence Jane (Kyzor) J.; m. Josephine Gear, June 19, 1964 (div.); m. Linda Sue Friedman, Nov. 23, 1971 (div.); children: Jacob Henry, Lillian Sara. BA cum laude, Columbia Coll., 1958; MD, Harvard U., 1962; MPH, Yale U., 1967; MS, NYU, 1997. Diplomate Am. Bd. Preventive Medicine-Pub. Health. Intern Lenox Hill Hosp., NYC, 1962—63; postdoctoral rschr. Univ. Coll. London and London Sch. Econs., 1963—65, resident in preventive medicine and pub. health, 1965—67; dist. health officer NYC Dept. Health, 1967—68, dir. ambulatory care planning and devel., 1969; dir. dept. social medicine Morrisania City Hosp., Bronx, NY, 1969—71; asst. prof. Albert Einstein Coll. Medicine, Bronx, 1969—71; lectr. Mt. Sinai Sch. Medicine, NYC, 1969—89; asst. prof., dept. cmty. medicine Stony Brook U. Sch. Medicine, 1971—74, coord. ambulatory svcs., 1971—74, assoc. prof., dept. cmty. and preventive medicine, 1974—83, prof., dept. preventive medicine, 1983, prof., grad. program pub. health, 2004—; attending physician Nassau County Med. Ctr., East Meadow, NY, 1973—86. Adj. assoc. prof. Columbia U. Sch. Architecture, 1977-79; cons. dept. medicine Winthrop-U. Hosp., Mineola, NY, 1979-93; mem. NY State Bd. Medicine, 1979-88; adj. assoc. prof. med. edn. Tex. Coll. Osteo. Medicine, Ft. Worth, 1980-85; adj. prof. legal edn. Touro Coll. Sch. of Law, Huntington, NY, 1998—2006. Author: Quality Control of Ambulatory Care: A Task for Health Departments, 1977, Medical Mystery: The Training of Doctors in the United States, 1978, Triathloning for Ordinary Mortals, 1986, rev., 1999, 2d edit, 2006, An Introduction to the U.S. Health Care System, 5th edit., 2003, The New Americanism, 1992, Take Control of Your Weight, 1993, Regular Exercise: A Handbook for Clinical Practice, 1995, The Essential Triathlete, 1996, Talking About Health and Wellness with Patients, 2000, 101 Ideas and Insights for Triathletes & Duathletes, 2011; editor, co-author: Health Care Delivery in the United States, 1977, 2d edit. 1981 (Book of Yr. award Am. Jour. Nursing 1982), 3rd edit., 1986, co-editor, 1999, 2002, Health Promotion and Disease Prevention in Clinical Practice, 1996, 2008; co-author: Pacewalking: The Balanced Way to Aerobic Health, 1988, The "I Don't Eat (But I Can't Lose)" Weight-Loss Program, 1989, Just the Weigh You Are, 1997, Help Your Man Get Healthy, 1999, 30 Secrets of the World's Healthiest Cuisines, 2000, An Introduction to the US Health Care System, 6th Edit, 2007, Championship Triathlon Training, 2008, Italian Translation Triathlon da Campioni, 2009, Am. Coll. Sports Medicine's Excercise is Medicine: A Clinician's Guide to Exercise Presciption, 2009; chief editor: (Springer series) Health Care and Society, 1976-79, Medical Education, 1978-2000; assoc. editor Preventive Medicine, 1983-2005; mem. editl. bd. ACSM's Health & Fitness Jour., 1999—, Am. Jour. Preventive Medicine, 1987-99; book rev. editor Am. Jour. Preventive Medicine, 1991-92; mem. editl. bd. Am. Med. Athletic Assn. Quarterly, 1988—, columnist, 1999—, editor-in-chief (J), 2002—; staff writer, Am. TRI, 2002-04; columnist USA Triathlon Life, 2006—; contbr. articles to profl. jours.; reviewer in field. Sr. advisor US Preventive Svcs. Task Force, 1984-89. Recipient Founder's medal, Tex. Coll. Osteo. Medicine, 1982, Duncan Clark Lifetime Achievement award, Assn. Prevention Tchg. and Rsch., 2006, Faculty Recognition award, Grad. Program Pub. Health, Stony Brook U., 2008, Disting. Alumni award, Yale Sch. Pub. Health, 2010, Top Ten Most Influential Pub. Health Prof. award, Health Hawk, 2010, Outstanding Svc. Recognition award, United University Professions, 2011, World Forum Spoken award, San Francisco, Calif., 2011. Fellow APHA, Am. Coll. Preventive Medicine (com. chmn. 1979-82), NY Acad. Medicine (med. edn. com. 1983-92), NY Acad. Scis. (elected), Royal Soc. Medicine (Eng.); mem. AMA, Am. Hosp. Assn. (life), Profl. Ski Instrs. Am. (cert. level I), Assn. Prevention Tchg. and Rsch. (pres. 1977-78), Am. Mensa, Phi Beta Kappa. Democrat. Jewish. Avocations: bicycling, pacewalking and running, weightlifting, triathlon competition, skiing. Home: 105 Washington Ave Port Jefferson Station NY 11777-2003 Office: Stony Brook U Sch Med Stony Brook NY 11794 Office Phone: 631-444-2147. Business E-Mail: steven.jonas@stonybrook.edu, smulkey1@aol.com.

JONATHAN, NTEIMAM, medical microbiologist; b. Ikuru Town, Rivers State, Nigeria, Oct. 10, 1970; s. Jonathan and Regina Ofor; m. Mary Owonte, Oct. 7, 1999; children: Adrienne Ama, Ibelek Benjamin, Crystal Awajiony. MBBCh, U. Calabar, 1994; DTM, Royal Coll. of Surgeons in Ireland, 2002; postgraduate diploma in mgmt. studies, Edexcel, UK, 2007. House officer U. Port Harcourt Tchg. Hosp., Nigeria, 1994—95, registrar in pathology, 1997—2000, sr. registrar, chief resident in med. microbiology, 2000—02; med. officer Nat. Youth Svc. Corps, Port Harcourt, 1995—96; specialist registrar in virology St. Bartholomew's Hosp., London, 2002—03, Health Protection Agy., Birmingham Heartlands Hosp., 2003—07; cons. in med. microbiology Wrexham Maelor Hosp., 2007—. Editl. referee Jour. Hosp. Infection, Drug, and Therapeutic Bulletin. Fellow: Royal Coll. Pathologists, Royal Soc. Medicine, Faculty of Pathology, Nat. Postgraduate Med. Coll. of Nigeria (assoc.); mem.: AAAS, Welsh Microbiological Assn., Chartered Mgmt. Inst., Soc. for Gen. Microbiology, Am. Soc. for Microbiology, Brit. Med. Assn. Office: Dept Pathology Wrexham Maelor Hosp North East Wales NHS Trust Wrexham LL13 7TD Wales Home: 4 Sheppard Street LL11 5FF Wrexham Wales Personal E-mail: drntejonathan@yahoo.com. Business E-Mail: nteimam.jonathan@new-tr.wales.nhs.uk.

JONES, BRUCE HOVEY, physician, researcher; b. St. Paul, Apr. 2, 1947; s. H. Ivor and Jean Elizabeth (Berger) J.; m. Gail Schneider, Dec. 28, 1978 (div. Mar. 1985); m. Tanya Eyre Morgan, Oct. 28, 1989; children: Ian Fisher, Aaron Grayson. BA in History and Sci. cum laude, Harvard U., 1970, MPH, 1986; MA in Biology, Kans. U., 1974; MD, Kans. U., Kansas City, 1977. Diplomate Am. Bd. Preventive Medicine. Intern Winter Gen. VA Hosp., Stormont Vail Hosp., Topeka, 1979-80; resident in preventive medicine Walter Reed Army Inst. Rsch., 1986; commd. capt. U.S. Army, 1977, advanced through grades to col., 1995, gen. med. officer Ft. Jackson, S.C., 1977-79; med. officer, investigator U.S. Army Rsch. Inst. of Environ. Medicine, Natick, Mass., 1980-84, 90-94, chief occupl. medicine rsch. divsn., 1986—90; chief divsn. occupl. illness and injury control Aberdeen Proving Ground, Md., 1994-96; dir. epidemiology and disease surveillance U.S. Army Ctr. Health Promotion and Preventive Medicine, 1996—98, program mgr. Aberdeen, 2002—; team leader Motor Vehicle Injury Prevention, Nat. Ctr. Injury Prevention and Control, CDC, Atlanta, 1998—2002. DOD rep. to DHHS, CDC Adv. Com. on Injury Prevention and Control, chmn, DOD Work Group on Injury Surveillance and Prevention, mem. DOD Mil., Tng. Task Force. Author, contbr. chpts. in books, articles to jours. in field. Hon. freshman scholar Harvard U., 1965, CHPPM's Lovell award, 2008, Outstanding Supr. award Bronz Balt. Fed. Exec. Bd., 2008; decorated Meritorious Svc. medal, Army Commendation medal with 2nd oak leaf clusters, Army Achievement medal with 2 oak leaf clusters, Legion of Merit, Outstanding Rsch. award Assn. Mil. Surgeons US, 1988. Fellow Am. Coll. Preventive Medicine, Am. Coll. Sports Medicine; mem. Am. Pub. Health Assn., Sigma Xi. Office: US Army Pub Health Command Aberdeen Proving Ground MD 21010-5422

JONES, CHRISTINA, critical care nurse, consultant; b. York, Eng., June 2, 1956; d. Edward and Kathleen Newall; m. Frederick Malcolm Jones, Sept. 27, 1975 (div. Apr. 8, 2001); children: Simon, Edward; m. John Bell, Sept. 1, 2003. BSN, Cape Town U., 1987; MPhil, U. Liverpool, 1994, PhD in Medicine and Clin. Psychology, 2001. Rsch. and audit fellow Whiston Hosp., Prescot, Merseyside, England, 2000—03, nurse cons. critical care follow-up, 2003—; hon. reader, chair nursing and allied health prof. com. U. Liverpool, 2010—. Fellow: European Acad. Nursing Sci.; mem.: European Soc. Critical Illness Medicine (assoc.; mem. nursing and allied health profl. com. 2007—), Brit. Assn. Counsellors and Psychotherapists (assoc.), Brit. Psychol. Soc. (assoc.), Intensive Care Soc. (assoc.), Brit. Assn. Critical Care Nurses (assoc.), European Soc. Traumatic Stress (assoc.). Achievements include design of and testing of rehabilitation program following critical illness; research in the importance of memories for intensive care unit in developing post traumatic stress disorder. Avocations: painting, travel, walking. Office: Whiston Hosp Intensive Care Unit Whiston Hospital Warrington Road L35 5DR Prescot England Office Phone: 00441514302382.

JONES, CLEOPATRA CELESTE, retired gerontologist, sociologist, educator; d. Dock Thomas and Georgia Ann Davis; m. Julian Thomas Jones, Aug. 19, 1939 (dec. 2001); children: Camille Jeannette Jones-Hanna, Brenda (Naima) Carol Jones-Shamborguer. MA, U. Mich., Ann Arbor, 1976; PhD, Mich. State U., Lansing, 1991; postdoc in Ednl. Gerontology, U. North Tex., Denton, 1996. Cert. specialist in gerontology U. Mich., 1976, specialist in curiculum devel. adult edn. Wayne State U., 1990. Procurement analyst Fed. Govt., Detroit, 1953—71; tchr. adult edn. Detroit Pub. Schs., 1977—96; adult edn. tchr. Ferndale Adult Edn., 1977—96; prof. sociology Wayne County C.C., Detroit, 2005—06; ret.; with Intergenerational Reading Program Nat. Conf. Chpt. Daughters Union St. Louis, Reading Program African Am. History, 2010. Adv. coun. on aging State of Mich., Lansing, 1996—2006; adv. bd. Wayne County C.C., Detroit, 1993—96; minority tng. program adminstrn. on aging Fed. Govt., Washington, 1987—88. Author: Special Women On The Move, 1999.

Active People's Cmty. Ch., Detroit; parliamentarion Zeta Phi Beta, Detroit, 1989—90; with union heritage chpt. Nat. Congress Daughter Period 1961 to 1965, 2010. Civil war sgt. Recipient Howard Mc Clusky award, Howard McClusky Symposium Kansas City, Mo., 1995, Intergenerational Edn. for Aging award, Citizens Amb. Com. Washington, 1995, Cert. Appreciation award, Mich. State U., 2009, award, St. Louis Mo., Nat. Conf. Daughters Union, 2010, Wayne County CC, 2011; grantee, U. North Tex., 1996. Mem.: NAACP, Daughters of the Civil War, Nat. Soc. Union Heritage (life; vice regent 1998—2006).

JONES, CLYDE WILLIAM, anesthesiologist; b. Barbados, West Indies, Sept. 29, 1929; came to U.S., 1947; s. Lewis F. and Albertha B. (Lewis) J.; m. Norma Anita, Sept. 14, 1963; children: Michael W., Ronald C., Stephen T. BS, City Coll., NYC, 1954; MD, Howard U., 1958. Diplomate Am. Bd. Anesthesiology. Capt. U.S. Navy, 1959-79, med. officer, 1959-63; resident in anesthesiology U.S. Naval Hosp., San Diego, 1963-66, staff anesthesiologist Camp Pendleton, Calif., 1966-67, chief of anesthesiology, 1967-69, 1st Hosp. Co., Danang, Vietman, 1968, U.S. Naval Hosp., Marianas Island, Guam, 1969-71; staff anesthesiologist Naval Regional Med. Ctr., San Diego, 1971-73, chief of anesthesiology, 1973-79, Kaiser Permanente Med. Ctr., San Diego, 1981-87, staff anesthesiologist, 1979—81, 1987—2001. Contbr. articles to profl. jours. Acolyte lay reader, sub Deacon All Sts. Episc. Ch., San Diego, 1971—2001; acolyte, chalice bearer, lay eucharistic min. St. Dunstan's Episco. Ch., San Diego; pres. standing com. Episc. Diocese, San Diego, 2007; bd. dirs. Bishop's Sch., San Diego, 1980—81, San Diego Civic Light Opera, Inc., 1980—83. Recipient Meritorious Svc. medal, certificate of merit Surgeon Gen. U.S. Navy, 1979. Fellow Am. Coll. Anesthesiologists; mem.Am. Soc. Anesthesiologists (delegate), Assn. Mil. Surgeons of U.S., Am. Soc. Clin. Hypnosis, Internat. Anesthesia Rsch. Soc., Naval Inst., Sigma Pi Phi. Democrat. Avocations: hypnosis, coin collecting/numismatics, medical volunteer. Home: 5201 Countryside Dr San Diego CA 92115-2136 Personal E-mail: cwjretired@yahoo.com.

JONES, DAN BRIGMAN, ophthalmologist, educator; b. Raleigh, NC, June 12, 1936; m. Marilyn Woodall; children: Danny Brigman Jr., Allen Walker. BA, Duke U., 1958, MD, 1962. Diplomate Am. Bd. Ophthalmology. Intern Duke Hosp., Durham, NC, 1962-63; resident in ophthalmology Bascom Palmer Eye Inst., U. Miami (Fla.) Sch. Medicine, 1965-69; fellow in cornea and external disease Moorfields Eye Hosp., Inst. Ophthalmology, London, 1967-68; asst. prof. then assoc. prof. ophthalmology dept. surgery Vanderbilt U. Sch. Medicine, Nashville, 1969-71; assoc. prof. then prof. ophthalmology Cullen Eye Inst., Baylor Coll. Medicine, Houston, 1972-78, Sid W. Richardson prof., chmn. dept. ophthalmology, 1981—, Margarett Root Brown chair ophthalmology, 1991—, Disting. Svc. prof., 2003—; mem. staff, then chief ophthalmology svc. Ben Taub Gen. Hosp., 1972—; mem. staff, then chief ophthalmology Meth. Hosp., Houston, 1972—2009; mem. staff St. Luke's Episcopal Hosp., Houston, 1973—. Chief ophthalmology sect. VA Hosp., Houston, 1973-78; mem. sci. adv. com. Knights Templar Eye Found., Inc., 1984-2002; mem. various coms. and couns. Nat. Eye Inst., 1975-76; mem. adv. panel on ophthalmology U.S. Pharmacopeial Conv., 1980-84; mem. ophthalmic drugs adv. com. FDA, 1975-78; cons. in field; vis. prof. to numerous schs., including Johns Hopkins U., Balt., 1975, 79, Washington U., St. Louis, 1975, Tipler Army Hosp., Honolulu, 1974, Yale U., New Haven, 1988, others; lectr. in field. Contbr. numerous articles to profl. jours. Bd. dirs. William C. Connor Found., Tex. Christian U., 1981—, Tex. Soc. to Prevent Blindness, 1981—; bd. dirs. The Lighthouse of Houston, 1981-89, mem. adv. coun., 1989—; mem. exec. med. com. Lions Eye Bank of Tex., 1981—, bd. dirs., 1989—. Epidemic intelligence officer USPHS, 1963-65. Recipient Honor award in Edn. Am. Acad. Ophthalmology and Otolaryngology, 1976; grantee NIH, 1978—, Sid W. Richardson Found., 1977-82. Mem. AMA (mem. program com. sect. ophthalmology 1970-73), Am. Acad. Ophthalmology (mem. faculty of basic and clin. sci. course 1970-76, mem. ophthalmology knowledge assessment com. 1972-80, mem. adv. com. 1973-77, mem. long range planning com. 1976-80, mem. program adv. com. 1986-89, sec. instrn. 1989—, trustee 1989-93, Sr. Honor award 1986, Life Achievement award, 2003, Spl. Recognition award, 2003), Am. Ophthalmol. Soc., Am. Soc. for Microbiology, Assn. for Rsch. in Vision and Ophthalmology, Assn. Univ. Profs. Ophthalmology (chmn. resident and fellowship edn. com. 1986-88, chmn. edn. com. 1988-93, trustee 1988-93, pres. bd. trustees 1993-94), Harris County Med. Soc., Houston Ophthal. Soc. (pres. 1979-80), Ocular Microbiology and Immunology Group, Inc. (exec. sec. 1973-89, bd. dirs. 1989-93), Pan Am. Assn. Ophthalmology, Tex. Ophthal. Assn. (mem. bd. councillors 1982-85), Tex. Soc. Infectious Diseases, Baylor Ophthalmology Alumni Assn., Inc., Bascom Palmer Alumni Assn., Phi Beta Kappa, Phi Eta Sigma, Alpha Omega Alpha. Office: Cullen Eye Inst 6565 Fannin NC 205 Houston TX 77030 Home Phone: 713-668-0219; Office Phone: 713-798-5951. Business E-Mail: dbj@bcm.tmc.edu.

JONES, DAVID A., JR., venture capital firm executive, former insurance company executive; s. David A. Jones. BA in History magna cum laude, Yale U., 1980, JD, 1988. English tchr. Hunan Med. Coll., Changsha, China; with internat. divsn. First Nat. Bank Boston; atty.-adviser Bur. East Asian and Pacific Affairs U.S. Dept. State, 1988-92; assoc. Hirn Reed & Harper, Louisville; chmn., mng. dir. Chrysalis Ventures, LLC, Louisville, 1993—; vice chmn. Humana, Inc., Louisville, 1996—2005, chmn., 2005—10. Bd. dir. Humana, Inc., 1993-; adj. prof. Georgetown U. Law Ctr., Washington; former chmn. Greater Louisville Health Enterprises Network; mem. adv. com. Brookings Ctr. on Health Policy; bd. mem. Nat. Com. on US-China Relations. Office: Chrysalis Ventures LLC 1650 Nat City Tower 101 S Fifth St Louisville KY 40202 also: Humana Inc 500 W Main St Louisville KY 40202 *

JONES, DAVID ALLEN, retired health benefits company executive; b. Louisville, Aug. 1931; m. Betty L. Ashbury, July 24, 1954. BS, U. Louisville, 1954; JD, Yale U., 1960. Bar: Ky. 1960. Founder Humana Inc. (formerly Extendicare Inc.), Louisville, 1961, CEO, 1961—97, chmn., dir. Louisville, 1997—; ptnr. Greenebaum, Doll and McDonald and predecessor, Louisville, 1965—69, of counsel, 1969—74; ret. Lt. (j.g.) USN, 1954—57.

JONES, DAVID ALWYN, retired geneticist, botanist, educator; b. Colliers Wood, Surrey, Eng., June 23, 1934; s. Trefor and Marion Edna Jones; m. Hazel Cordelia Lewis, Aug. 29, 1959; children: Catherine Susan, Edmund Meredith, Hugh Francis. BA, MA in Natural Scis., U. Cambridge, Eng., 1957; DPhil in Genetics, U. Oxford, Eng., 1963. Chartered biologist, UK. Lectr. genetics U. Birmingham, Eng., 1961-73; prof. genetics U. Hull, Eng., 1973-89, head dept. plant biology and genetics, 1983-88; prof. botany U. Fla., Gainesville, 1989—2003, prof. emeritus., 2003—, chmn. dept. botany, 1989—98. Chmn. membership com. Inst. of Biology, London, 1982-87. Co-author: Variation and Adaptation in Plant Species, 1971, Analysis of Populations, 1976, What is Genetics?, 1976, Zmiennosc i przystosowanie roslin, 1977; contbr. over 100 articles to profl. jours. Fellow Linnean Soc. Biology; mem. AAAS, Internat. Soc. Chem. Ecology (coun. 1983-84, 89-91, keynote spkr. ann. meeting 1984, pres. elect 1986-87, pres. 1987-88, past pres. 1988-89, co-editor Jour. Chem. Ecology 1994-2000, Outstanding Svc. award 2001), Brit. Assn. Advancement of Sci. (chmn. coord. com. for cytology and genetics 1974-87), Genetical Soc. Gt. Britain (convenor ann. meetings profs. of genetics 1983-88), Ecol. Genetics Group, Population Genetics Group, Soc. for Study of Evolution, Rotary Club Bicester, Gamma Sigma Delta, Sigma Xi (pres. U. Fla. chpt. 2000-01). Achievements include research in practical population biology especially in ecological genetics and chemical ecology of cyanogenic plants. Address: The Gatehouse Bignell Park OX26 1UE Oxfordshire England Personal E-mail: david_jones@his-locker.net.

JONES, DERYK GERARD, sports medicine physician; b. Detroit, July 25, 1964; BA, Emory U., BS, 1986; degree in Medicine, Stanford U., 1991. Sect. head, sports medicine & cartilage restoration Ochsner Health Sys., 2004—. Prof. U. Queensland Ochsner Clin. Sch., Brisbane, Australia, 2009—11. Recipient Deans award, Stanford U. Med. Sch., Stanford, Calif., 1991, William H. Thomas award, Harvard Combined Residency Program, 1996, 1997; named Outstanding Physician of Yr., Ochsner Clinic Found., 2005. Mem.: Am. Acad. Orthop. Surgeons, Am. Orthop. Soc. Sports Medicine, Arthroscopy Assn. N.Am., Biha'i Faith, Phi Sigma Tau. Avocations: golf, bicycling. Office: 1201 S Clearview Pky Ste 104 Jefferson LA 70121 Office Fax: 504-736-4810. Business E-Mail: djones@ochsner.org.

JONES, EDITH IRBY, internist; b. Conway, Ark., Dec. 23, 1927; d. Robert and Mattie (Buice) Irby; m. James Beauregard Jones, Apr. 16, 1950 (dec. Oct. 1989); children: Gary Ivan, Myra Vonceil Jones Romain, Keith Irby. BS, Knoxville Coll., 1948; MD, U. Ark., 1952; Doctorate (hon.), Mo. Valley Coll., Mary Holmes Coll., Knoxville Coll. Intern Univ. Hosp., Little Rock, 1952-53; gen. practice medicine Hot Springs, Ark., 1953-59; resident in internal medicine Baylor Coll. Medicine, Houston, 1959-62; pvt. practice medicine specializing in internal medicine Houston, 1962—; mem. staff Meth. Hosp., Houston, Hermann Hosp., Houston, St. Elizabeth Hosp., Houston, St. Anthony Ctr., Houston, St. Joseph Hosp., Houston, Thomas Care Ctr., Houston, Town Pk., Houston, chief of staff; chief med. staff Riverside Gen. Hosp., Houston, 2006—. Clin. asst. prof. medicine Baylor Coll. Medicine, U. Tex. Sch. Medicine, Houston; dir. Prospect Med. Lab.; bd. dirs., sec. Mercy Hosp. Comprehensive Health Care Group; ptnr. Jones, Coleman and Whitfield; grad. med. examiner Ct. Calanthe Jurisdiction, Tex.; cons. Social Security Agy., Tex. Pub. Welfare Dept., Vocat. Rehab. Assn., Tex. Rehab. Commn.; bd. dirs. Std. Savs. Assn., others. Contbr. articles to profl. jours. Bd. dirs. Drug Addiction Rehab. Enterprise, March of Dimes, Houston, Odessey House, Houston; adv. bd. Houston Coun. Alcoholism; mem. com. revising justice code Harris County, Tex.; impartial hearing officer Houston Ind. Sch. Dist.; mem. Cmty. Welfare Planning Assn., Friends of Youth, Human Svcs. Adv. Coun., Houston, PTA, YMCA; founder Edith Irby Jones Found.; bd. dirs. Houston Internat. U.; chmn. bd. trustees Knoxville Coll.; trustee Must. Assn. Profl. Svc.; bd. visitors U. Houston, others. Recipient proclamation, Houston City Coun., 1985, Mayor of Houston, 1986, cert. of citation, Tex. Ho. of Reps., 1986, commendation, Calif. Senate, 1989, Volunteerism and Cmty. Svc. award, Tex. Acad. internal Medicine, 2000, Scroll of Merit award, Nat. Med. Assn., 2001, Silas Hunt Legacy award, U. Ark., Fayetteville, 2006; named Dr. Edith Irby Jones Day in her honor, State of Ark., 1985, NYC, 1986, Disting. Alumna, J. William Fulbright Coll. Arts and Scis., 2005, a clinic in her honor, Veracruz, Mex., Most Influential People of 1986, Ebony mag.; named one of 30 Most Influential Black Women Houston, 1984, 100 Leading Black Physicians, Black Enterprise mag., 2001; named to Tex. Black Women's Hall of Fame, 1986, Hall of Fame, U. Ark. Sch. Med. Scis., 2004. Master: ACP; fellow: Am. Soc. Internal Medicine (Oscar E. Edward award 2001), Am. Coll. Medicine; mem.: NAACP, AMA, Physicians for Human Rights, Bus. and Profl. Women, Tex. Assn. Disability Examiners, Houston Med. Forum, Harris County Med. Assn., Lone Star Med. Assn., Nat. Med. Assn. (first female past pres., Scroll of Merit 2001, Living Legend), Am. Med. Women's Assn. (v.p. Houston chpt.), Nat. Coun. Negro Women (v.p. Dorothy Height chpt.), Women of Achievement (Hall of Fame 1985), Girl Friends, Tops Ladies of Distinction, Links, Order Eastern Star, Eta Phi Beta, Delta Sigma Theta, Alpha Kappa Mu. Democrat. Achievements include being first African American to graduate from the University of Arkansas School for Medicine Sciences. Avocations: travel, walking, swimming. Home: 3402 S Parkwood Houston TX 77021 Office: 2601 Prospect St Houston TX 77004-7737 Home Phone: 713-747-5116; Office Phone: 713-529-3145. Business E-Mail: eijones@advmed.com.

JONES, GENIA KAY, critical care nurse, consultant; b. Dallas, Dec. 21, 1954; d. Joe and Juanita Sue (White) Self; m. Paul L. Jones, June 1, 1986. ADN, Tarrant County Jr. Coll., 1976; mgmt. cert., Cedar Valley Coll., 1980; postgrad., Mountain View Coll., Dallas, 1984—85; BSN, Regent's U., 2001. RN; cert. emergency nurse; cert. BLS, ACLS, pediat. advanced life support, trauma nurse core curriculum, ACLS instr. Instr. Steven's Pk. Hosp., Dallas, 1972-77; asst. dir. nursing svcs. Four Season's Conv. Ctr., Dallas, 1977-78; nurse surgery dept. Dallas/Ft. Worth Med. Ctr., 1978-80; dir. nursing Med. Staffing Svcs., Dallas, 1980, Reproductive Svcs., Inc., Dallas, 1981; adminstrv. supr. Dallas Family Hosp., 1982-85; patient care coord., emergency dept. Dallas S.W. Med. Ctr., 1985-90, staff nurse, emergency dept., 1990-99; medical consultant Needham, Johnson, Lovelace, and Johnson, 1992—2002; emergency nurse dir. Rockwall Minor Emergency Ctr., 1999—2001; emergency nurse Virtual Healthcare Svcs. Meth. Med. Ctrs. Dallas, 2001—03; emergency nurse Virtual Healthcare Svcs. emergency dept. Med. Ctr. Arlington, 2002—. Internat. flight nurse Air Ambulance Network, Inc., Dallas, 1987—92; instr. intravenous therapy, 1980—; cons., adv., 1980—; medico-legal cons., 1990—; clin. instr. Edn. Am., 1999—2001. Recipient Citizens award, Certs. Apprecition, HOSA Nat. Leadership Conf., Silver medal of Honor; Internat. Biog. Assn. fellow, 1990. Mem. NAFE, Am. Heart Assnb., Nurses' Svc. Orgn., Tex. Nurses' Assn., Emergency Nurses' Assn. Home: 108 Burkett Ln Red Oak TX 75154-7602 Home Phone: 972-617-3618; Office Phone: 214-803-4903. Personal E-mail: jgeniak@aol.com. E-mail: genia.jones@worldnet.att.net.

JONES, GEOFFREY MELVILL, physiology research educator; b. Cambridge, Eng., Jan. 14, 1923; s. Benett and Dorothy Laxton (Jotham) J.; m. Jenny Marigold Burnaby, June 21, 1953; children: Katharine, Francis, Andrew, Dorothy. BA, Cambridge U., 1944, MA, 1947, MB, BCh, 1949. House surgeon Middlesex Hosp., London, 1949-50; sr. house surgeon Addenbrookes Hosp., Cambridge, England, 1950-51; sci. med. officer Royal Air Force Inst. Aviation Medicine, Farnborough, England, 1951-55; sci. officer Med. Rsch. Coun., England, 1955-61; assoc. prof. physiology, dir. aviation med. rsch. unit McGill U., Montreal, Que., Canada, 1961-68, prof., dir., 1968-88, Hosmer rsch. prof., 1978-91, emeritus prof. physiology, 1991—. Rsch. prof. clin. neuroscis. U. Calgary, Alta., Can., 1991—, Coll. France, 1979, 95; vis. prof. Stanford U., 1971-72. Author: (with another) Mammalian Vestibular Physiology, 1979; editor: (with another) Adaptive Mechanisms in Gaze Control, 1985; contbr. numerous articles to profl. jours. Served to squadron leader Royal Air Force, 1951-55. Sr. rsch. assoc. Nat. Acad. Sci., 1971-72; recipient Skylab Achievement award NASA, 1974, 1st recipient Dohlman medal Dohlman Soc. Toronto U., 1987, Quinquennial Gold medal Barany Soc. Internat., 1988, Ashton Graybiel award U.S. Naval Aerospace Labs., 1989, Wilbur Franks Annual award Can. Soc. Aerospace Medicine, Buchanan-Barbour award Royal Aeronautical Soc., 1991, Mc Laughlin Medal, 1991, Royal Soc. Can. Fellow Can. Aeronautics and Space Inst., Aerospace Med. Assn. (Harry Armstrong award 1968, Arnold D. Tuttle award 1971), Royal Soc. Can. (McLaughlin medal 1991), Royal Soc. London, Royal Aeronautical Soc. London (Stewart Meml. award 1989, Buchanan Barbour award 1990); mem. U.K. Physiol. Soc., Can. Physiol. Soc., Can. Soc. Aerospace Med. Soc., Internat. Collegium Otolaryngology, Soc. Neurosci. Avocations: tennis, sailing, outdoor activities, reading, piano and violin playing/composition. Office: U Calgary Dept Clin Neurosci 3330 Hospital Dr NW Calgary AB Canada T2N 4N1 Office Phone: 403-220-4307.

JONES, HARVEY ROYDEN, JR., neurologist; b. Plainfield, NJ, Nov. 18, 1936; m. Mary Elizabeth Norman, Mar. 18, 1961; children: Roy, Kathryn, Frederick, David. BS, Tufts U., 1958; MD, Northwestern U., 1962. Diplomate in neurology, clin. neurophysiology and neuromuscular medicine Am. Bd. Psychiatry and Neurology, bd. dirs., 1997-2004 Am. Bd. Psychiatry and Neurology, diplomate Am. Bd. Electroencephalography, Am. Bd. Electrodiagnostic Medicine. Intern Phila. Gen. Hosp., 1962-63; resident in internal medicine Mayo Grad. Sch. Medicine, Rochester, Minn., 1963-65; resident in neurology Mayo Grad. Sch. medicine, Rochester, Minn., 1965-66; chief neurology svc. U.S. Army Hosp., Bad Cannstatt, Germany, 1966-70; resident in neurology/clin. neurophysiology Mayo Grad. Sch. medicine, Rochester, Minn., 1970-72; from clin. instr. to clin. prof. neurology Harvard Med. Sch., Boston, 1973—; staff neurologist, Jaime Ortiz-Patino chair neurology, chair divsn. of med. specialties, emeritus chair Lahey Clinic, Burlington, Mass., 1972—; assoc. in neurology, assoc. divsn. neurophysiology, dir. emeritus electromyography lab. Children's Hosp., Boston, 1977—; assoc. in neurology, assoc. divsn. neurophysiology Brigham Women's Hosp., Boston, 2001—09. Editor, author: CIBA Collection, Nervous System Part II, 1986, Pediatric Clinical Electromyography, 1996, Neuromuscular Disorders of Infancy, Childhood and Adolescence, A Clinician's Approach, 2003, Netter's Neurology, 2005, CLinical Neurophysiology of Infancy, Childhood & Adolscence, 2006; contbr. numerous articles to profl. jours. Fellow Am. Acad. Neurology; mem. Am. Neurol. Assn. Office: Lahey Clinic 41 Mall Rd Burlington MA 01805-0002 Office Phone: 781-744-5126. E-mail: royden.jones@lahey.org.

JONES, IAN STUART CRAWFORD, obstetrician, educator; b. Romford, Essex, Eng., Oct. 3, 1942; MBChB, Otago U., New Zealand, 1969, ChM, 1977; PhD, U. Queensland, MEd, 2004; MHA, U. NSW, 1992. Prof. U. Queensland, 1991—2005, Queensland Health, Royal Brisbane and Women's Hosp., 2006—. Decorated Res. Force Decoration Australian Defence Force; recipient Queen Australia award, Order of Australia. Fellow: RCOG, RANZCOG. Avocation: history. Office: Royal Brisbane Hosp Butterfield St Herston Brisbane Queensland 4029 Australia Office Fax: 3636 7798. Business E-Mail: ian_jones@health.qld.gov.au.

JONES, JACQUELINE ELEANOR, otolaryngologist; b. NYC, Mar. 11, 1958; d. Farrell and Audrey Jones; m. John Wilfred Gassett, Sept. 20, 1986; children: David Scott Gassett, Peter Wilfred Gassett. BA in Biochemistry, Smith Coll., Northampton, Mass., 1980; MD, Cornell U. Med. Coll., NYC, 1984. Lic. physician Pa., 1985, Mass., 1989, NY, 1990, cert. Am. Bd. Otolaryngology, 1989, diplomate Nat. Bd. Med. Examiners, 1985. Intern surgery U. Pa., Phila., 1984—85, resident surgery, 1985—86, resident otolaryngology, 1986—89; asst. instr. otorhinolaryngology, human comm. U. Pa. Sch. Medicine, Phila., 1986—89; fellow pediatric otolaryngology Harvard Med. Sch. Children's Hosp. Boston, 1989—90; asst. prof. clin. otolaryngology Cornell U. Med. Coll., NYC, 1990—96, assoc. prof. clin. otolaryngology, 1996—; pvt. practice Park Ave. ENT, NYC, 2003—. Clin. instr. Harvard U. Med. Coll., Boston U., 1989—90; attending physician otolaryngologist dept. otolaryngology NY Hosp., NYC, 1990—; attending dept. otolaryngology Lenox Hill Hosp., NYC, 1990—, Manhattan Eye, Ear and Throat Hosp., NYC, 1990—; mem. clearinghouse adv. bd. Nat. Inst. Deafness Other Communicative Disorders NIH, Washington, 1991—94, mem. voice, voice disorders panel, 1992—98, panel mem. consensus conf. on cochlear implants, 1995; alt. rep. med. bd., exec. faculty coun. NY Hosp., Cornell U. Med. Coll., NYC, 1992—2003; participant shadow program minority pre-med. students Cornell U. Med. Coll., NYC, 1991—2003, mem. curriculum com., 1992—, 2003, mem. admissions com., 1992—2003, mem. affirmative action com., 1994—2003, chair affirmative action com., 1997—2000, resident coord. dept. otolaryngology, 1996—2000; dir. pediat. otolaryngology NY Hosp., NYC, 1996—2003; chair phenylephrine adv. panel NY State Dept. Health, 1997—98; mem. nat. deafness and other communicative disorders adv. coun. NIH, Bethesda, Md., 1998—2002; cons. health and human svcs. NY Presbyn. Hosp., NYC, 2002—03; mem. joint com. physician health NY State Med. Soc, NY State Bd. Profl. Conduct, 2002—07; spr., lectr. in field. Contbr. scientific papers, chapters to books, articles to profl. jours. Participant Mentor Program NY Pub. Schs., NYC, 1982—84, Health Alert Seminars Lenox Hill Hosp., NYC, 1991—; recruiter Smith Coll. Minority Recruitment Program, 1991—; participant quality assurance com. Blue Cross-Blue Shield of NY, 1992—2003; bd. trustees The Episcopal Sch., NYC, 1998—2004; pres. St. Bernard's Sch. Parents Assn., NYC, 2003—04; bd. trustees Kieve Affective Edn., Nobleboro, Maine, 2004—. Named Tchr. of Yr., Dept. Otolaryngology Cornell U. Med. Coll., 1998, Top 100 Black Doctors Am.; named one of Best Doctors in NY, Castle Connolly Med., Inc., 1999—2009. Fellow: ACS, Am. Acad. Otolaryngology (head and neck surgery - pediat. otolaryngology com. 1992—99, head & neck surgery comm. polysomnography 2010), Am. Acad. Pediat. (exec. com. broncheosophagolgy sect. 1995—97, com. obstructive sleep apnea 2009—); mem.: AMA, AAOHNI (mem. plan on polysomnography obstructive sleep apnea in children 2010—), NY Bronchoscopic Soc., Am. Acad. Pediat. (mem. panel on obstructive sleep apnea in children 2009—), Am. Soc. Pediat. Otolaryngology (exec. bd. 2000—04). Office: Park Ave ENT Ste 1A 1175 Park Ave New York NY 10128-1211 Office Phone: 212-996-2559.

JONES, JAMES WILSON, physician, cell biologist, ethicist; b. Muskogee, Okla., Oct. 13, 1941; s. James C. and Hildred L. Jones; m. Joan Wachna, Aug. 24, 1983; children: James A., Misty A., Cyndra L., Jena S., Hayden E. Student, U. Tulsa, 1959-62; MD, Tulane U., 1966, PhD, 1979, postgrad., 1981-82; MHA, Mo. Diplomate Am. Bd. Surgery, Am. Bd. Thoracic Surgery, Am. Bd. Critical Care. Intern Phila. Gen. Hosp., 1966-67; resident in surgery Mayo Grad. Sch. Medicine, 1969-70; resident in gen. surgery Charity Hosp. La., 1971-73, 74-75, resident in thoracic surgery, 1973-74, 75-76, asst. clin. dir., co-dir. surg. intensive care unit, 1976-83; resident in thoracic surgery Ochsner Clinic, 1976; asst. prof. surgery sch. medicine Tulane U., New Orleans, 1976-83; chief surg. svc. VA Med. Ctr., Houston, 1983-85, 89-98; prof. surgery, cell biology and med. ethics Baylor Coll. Medicine, Houston, 1983-85, 89-98; surg. dir. Ritter Heart Inst., Toledo, 1985-89; W. Alton Jones Disting. prof. Columbia Hosp.-U. Mo., 1998—2003, Hugh E. Stephenson chair surgery, 1998—2003; vis. prof. Medicine & Med. Ethics; asst. editor Jour. Vascular Surgery. Mem. student affairs com. med. sch. Tulane U., 1977-82; mem. hosp. bylaws com. Tulane Med. Ctr., 1978-79, mem. transfusion com., 1980-81; mem. transfusion com. Charity Hosp. La., 1978-80, mem. tracheotomy audit, 1980-81; mem. clin. exec. bd. VA Med. Ctr., 1983-85, 89-98, mem. various coms.; sr. cardiac surgeon King Faisal Hosp., Riyadh, Saudi Arabia, 1984; mem. med. ethics com. St. Mary Hosp., Port Arthur, Tex., 1987; mem. trustee's cardiovascular com. Toledo Hosp., mem. critical care com.; mem. high sch. adv. com. health care professions Baylor Coll. Medicine, 1990-92, chmn. allied health com., 1992-97; mem. Regional Cardiology Adv. Com., 1993-94; mem. sub-com. indsl. rels. Annals Thoracic Surgery; cons., presenter in field, asst. editor, journal Vascular Surgery, Ethics Com. AAIS, 2006-. Author: Autotransfusion: Therapeutic Principles & Trends, 1993, Surgical: The Ethics of Manage the Ethics of surgery, Surgical Ethics, The Ethics of Managed Care, The Ethics of Surgical Practice; mem. editorial bd. Internat. Rev. Anesthesiology, 1990-94; contbr. articles to profl. jours.; patentee in field. Lt. comdr. M.C., USNR, 1967-69. Recipient anni. svc. award, Mended Hearts, grantee NIH, 1963, 64, New Orleans Cancer Soc., 1965, Haemonetics Corp., 1988, Ortho Pharm., 1989, Berlex, 1990, Baxter-Edwards, 1991, 93, Sandoz Pharms., 1992, Cardiogenesis, 1996, VA Merit Rev., 1997; rsch. fellow Am. Cancer Soc., 1975-76, 77-78, Soc. Surg. Oncology, 1977; Hawthorne scholar, 1964-65, 65-66. Fellow ACS; mem. Am. Assn. Thoracic Surgery, NASA IRB, Am. Assn. Thoracic Surg., Cntl. Surg., Assn., Am. Surg. Assn., Soc. Yascular Surgery, James Assn. Surgeons, So. Thoracic Surg. Assn., Soc. Vascular, Michael E. DeBakey Internat. Surg. Soc., Soc. Thoracic Surgeons, So. Surg. Assn., Tex. Surg. Assn., Houston Surg. Soc., Mayo Alumni Assn., Sigma Xi, Alpha Kappa Kappa, Alpha Omega Alpha. Avocation: diving. Office: Baylor College of Medicine 1 Baylor Plaza Houston TX 77030 Home Fax: 936-582-1493. Business E-Mail: jwjones@bcm.tmc.edu.

JONES, JUDITH MILLER, director; BA, George Washington U., 1965; student, Georgetown U. Law Sch., 1965—67; MA in Edn. Tech., Cath. U., 1969. With IBM, 1965—69; legis. asst. Sen. Winston L. Prouty Vt., 1969—71; spl. asst. Office Dep. Asst. Sec. Legis. Dept. HEW, Washington, 1971—72; dir. Nat. Health Policy Forum The George Washington U., Washington, 1972—. Mem. Nat. Com. Vital and Health Stats., 1988—91, chmn., 1991—96; profl. lectr. health policy The George Washington U.; former chmn. Ctr. for Advancement of Health. Chair Healthier Jefferson County. Office: National Health Policy Forum 2131 K Street NW Ste 500 Washington DC 20037 Office Phone: 202-872-1469. Business E-Mail: jmjones@gwu.edu.

JONES, JULIAN R., engineering educator; b. Hastings, Eng., Mar. 2, 1977; M Engring., U. Oxford, Eng., 1999; PhD, Imperial Coll. London, 2002. Lloyds tercentenary fellow Imperial Coll. London, 2002—04, Royal Acad. Engring., Engring. and Phys. Scis. Rsch. Coun. rsch. fellow, 2004—09, sr. lectr., 2009—. Cons. Novathera Fourth Med. Bioscis., Cambridge, England, 2005—. Editor, author (textbook) Biomaterials, Artificial Organs and Tissue Engineering, 2005; contbr. articles to profl. publs. Recipient Philip Leverhulme prize, 2007, Early Investigator award, Tissue and Cell Engring. Soc., 2008, Robert L. Coble award, Am. Ceramics Soc., 2010. Mem.: Inst. Materials, Mining and Minerals (Silver medal 2004). Achievements include development of bioactive glass foaming process toward making a scaffold for bone regeneration. Avocation: cricket. Office: Dept Materials Imperial College SW7 2AZ London England Home: 139 Elgar Ave Surray England Business E-Mail: julian.r.jones@imperial.ac.uk.

JONES, KENNETH B., JR., retired surgeon; b. Shreveport, La., 1940; MD, Tulane U., 1966. Diplomate Am. Bd. Surgery. Intern Confederate Meml. Med. Ctr., Shreveport, 1966—67; resident gen. surgery La. State U. and affiliated Hosp., Shreveport, 1969—73; fellow pediat. surgery Ala. Children's Hosp., 1973; chief staff Christus Schumpert Med. Ctr., Shreveport, 1999—2001; clin. asst. prof. surgery La. State U. Med. Ctr., 1984—; assoc. editor Obesity Surgery, 2010—. Presenter, lectr. in field; assoc. editor, obesity surgeon Jour. Metabolic Surgery & Allied Care, 2009—, 2010—. Co-author: Obesity Surgery: Principles and Practice, 2008; contbr. articles to profl. med. jours., chapters to books; edtl. bd. mem. Obesity Surgery and Surgery Obesity and related Diseases, 2007—, assoc. editor Obesity Surgery, 2010—. Fellow: ACS, Am. Soc. Metabolic and Bariatric Surgery (chmn. surg. access com. 1997—2000, sec. treas. 1998—2000, pres. 2001—02, chmn. surg. access com. 2002—06); mem.: AMA, Internat. Fedn. Surgery Obesity, Surg. Assn. La., Brazilian Soc. Bariatric Surgery (hon.), Am. Soc. Gen. Surgeons (nomination com. 2004), Southeastern Surg. Congress. Achievements include research in bariatric surgery. Home and Office: 6121 Fern Ave #112 Shreveport LA 71105 Personal E-mail: pbsurgkj@aol.com.

JONES, KENNETH BRUCE, surgeon; b. Scottsville, Ky., Apr. 17, 1953; s. Kenneth C. and Betty (Miller) J.; m. Carol Jean Munger, June 28, 1980; children: Daniel, Christopher, Elizabeth. BS, U. Ky., 1974; MD, Vanderbilt U., Nashville, 1978. Diplomate Am. Bd. Surgery; cert. advanced trauma life saving. Surg. intern and resident U. Louisville Med. Sch., 1978-80; resident in surgery East Tenn. U. Med. Sch., Johnson City, 1980-82, chief resident, 1983; surgeon Claiborne Surg. Group, Tazewell, Tenn., 1983-84, N.E. Ark. Surg. Clinic, Jonesboro, Ark., 1984—; sec. med. staff Meth. Hosp., 1986-87, chief of surgery, 1988-90, vice chief of staff, 1989-91, chief of staff, 1992-94; chief of surgery St. Bernard's Regional Med. Ctr., 1996-97; mem. hosp. bd. Regional Med. Ctr. N.E., 1997, NEA Baptist Hosp. Bd. & Clinic Bd., 2010—. Asst. clin. prof. surgery U. Ark. Area Health Edn. Ctr., Jonesboro, 1985—; cancer liaison of ACS Commn. on Cancer to St. Bernard's, 1996-2006; alumni bd. Vanderbilt Med. Sch., 2005—; cons. Am. Bd. Surgery, 2005-07; pres. Ark. chpt. Am. Coll. Surgeons, 2009-10. Contbr. articles to profl. jours. Active sch. bd., 1993-98; deacon So. Bapt. Ch.; bd. dirs. N.E. Ark. Clinc Found, 2005-08, mem. bd. NEA Baptist Med. Clinic, bd. mem., Operation New Life Surg. Missions to Honduras. Justin Potter med. scholar, 1974-78. Fellow: ACS (pres., Ark. chpt. 2009—10); mem.: NRA, Am. Soc. Bariatric and Metabolic Surgery, Soc. Am. Gastrointestinal Endoscopic Surgeons, Am. Soc. Gen. Surgery, Am. Cancer Soc. (pres. Craighead County unit 2000—01), Nat. Wild Turkey Fedn., QUAIL Unlimited, Ducks Unltd., Phi Beta Kappa. Baptist. Avocations: hunting, jogging, toy trains, target shooting. Home: 2600 Nix Lake Dr Jonesboro AR 72404-0917 Office: NE Ark Surg Clinic 800 S Church St Ste 104 Jonesboro AR 72401-4154 Home Phone: 870-972-6895; Office Phone: 870-932-4875.

JONES, KENNETH LYONS, pediatrician, birth defects researcher; b. Phila., Dec. 10, 1939; MD, Hahnemann U., 1966. Cert. Pediat., 1971. Intern pediat. Phila. Gen. Hosp., 1966—67; resident Children's Orthop. Hosp., U. Wash., Seattle, 1967—69, resident pediat., 1971—72; staff mem. Children's Hosp. U. Calif. San Diego, chief Divsn. Dysmorphology/Teratology, Dept. Pediat., founder, med. dir. Calif. Teratogen Info. Svc. (CTIS), prof. pediat. Co-chair Sci. Working Group on Diagnostic Guidelines for Fetal Alcohol Syndrome Disorder, Nat. Ctr. Birth Defects & Devel. Disabilities. Contbr. articles to med. jours. Recipient March of Dimes/Colonel Harland Sanders Award, 2007; named one of Am.'s Top Doctors, Castle Connolly Medical Ltd., 2002; Hartwell Biomedical Rsch. Award, 2008. Mem.: Teratology Soc. (pres. 2004—05), Western Soc. Pediat. Rsch. (past pres.). Achievements include being one of two doctors who identified fetal alcohol syndrome (FAS), 1973. Office: 9500 Gilman Dr # 0828 La Jolla CA 92093-0828 also: U Calif San Diego 200 W Arbor Dr San Diego CA 92103 Office Phone: 619-294-6460, 858-246-0047. Office Fax: 858-246-0014. E-mail: klyons@ucsd.edu.

JONES, LAWRENCE WAGER, physician, researcher; b. Ithaca, NY, July 16, 1940; s. Charles Williams and Sarah Bosworth Jones; m. Mireya Francesca Asturias, Apr. 21, 1962; children: Shannon Tucker, Erin Bouquin, Alison Kelly, Lawrence, Charles. BS, Univ. Calif., Berkeley, Calif., 1962; MD, Yale Coll., New Haven, Conn., 1965. Lic. A21999 Calif., diplomate Am. Bd. Urology, 1974. Internship L.A. County/USC Med. Ctr., 1965—66, residency, 1966—70; fellowship Rsch. Fellowship. Divsn. of Urology U.C.S.F., 1973—74; clin. prof. surgery/urology Univ. So. Calif. Sch. of Medicine; attending physician Hungtington Meml. Hosp., Pasadena, Calif. Clin. collaborator, dir. of prostate rsch. program Huntington Med. Rsch. Inst., 1974—, bd. mem., 1993—; pres. Dona Mireya Inc., 1992—; bd. dirs. Guided Discoveries, Inc., 1980—. Editor: American Urological Association Centennial History, 2002; contbr. over 40 articles to profl. jours. Chief urology svc. US Army, 1970—73, Bad Cannstatt, Germany. Mem.: Pasadena Med. Soc. (pres. 1983—84), L.A. Urol. Soc. (pres. 1989), Calif. Urol. Assn. (pres. 1991—93), Western Section Am. Urol. Assn. (pres. 1992—93), Western Urol. Forum (sec. 1993—98), Am. Urol. Assn., Am. Found. for Urol. Disease (bd. dirs. 2000—05), Am. Assn. Clin. Urologists (pres. 2000—01), Soc. Internat. Urology, Am. Assn. Cancer Rsch. Office: Hungtington Med Rsch Inst 99 N El Molino Ave Pasadena CA 91101-1830 Office Phone: 626-796-8102.

JONES, LEANNE, biomedical researcher, educator; BS, Wash. and Lee U.; PhD, Harvard Coll.; postdoc. fellow, U. Sheffield, UK, Stanford U. Mem. Lab. of Genetics; assoc. prof. The Salk Inst. for Biol. Studies, 2011—. Co-author: (publs.) Orientation of asymmetric stem cell division by the APC tumor suppressor and centrosome, 2003, Decline in self-renewal factors leads to aging of the stem cell niche in the Drosophila testis, 2007, Multipotent somatic stem cells contribute to the niche in the Drosophila testis, 2008, Stem cell dynamics in response to nutrient availability, 2010. Recipient Rhône Poulenc Young Investigator award, 1997, New Scholar in Aging award, Ellison Med. Found., 2005—09, New Faculty awar, Calif. Inst. of Regenerative Medicine, 2008—13; fellow postdoc. fellowship, Human Frontiers Sci. Program (HFSP), 1999—2000, Lilly Fellow, Life Sciences Rsch. Found., 2001—04; scholar Cancer Rsch., AACR-AFLAC, 1998, Am. Cancer Soc. Rsch. Scholar, 2007—11. Achievements include discovery of stem cells adjust their numbers depending on the availability of nutrients to coordinate tissue maintenance with environmental conditions. Office: The Salk Institute for Biological Studies UC San Diego 9500 Gilman Dr La Jolla CA 92093 Office Phone: 858-534-2230. E-mail: ljones@salk.edu.

JONES, M. DOUGLAS, JR., pediatrician, educator; b. San Antonio, Apr. 22, 1943; BA, Rice U., 1964; MD, U. Tex., 1968. Diplomate Am. Bd. Pediat. Intern U. Colo. Sch. Medicine, Denver, 1968-69, resident, 1969-71, fellow neonatal-perinatal medicine, 1973-75, prof. pediatrics, 1990—; faculty John Hopkins U. Sch. Medicine, 1977—90; dir. neonatal Intensive care John Hopkins Hosp. Mem. Am. Bd. Pediat.(chair, 2009), Am. Acad. Pediat., Am. Pediat. Soc., Soc. for Pediat. Rsch. Office: Children's Hospital Mail Stop 8402 PO Box 6508 Education 2 S Room 4304 13121 E 17th Ave Aurora CO 80045 Office Phone: 303-724-2851. Office Fax: 303-777-7323. Business E-Mail: jones.doug@fchden.org.

JONES, MARILYN C., clinical geneticist, educator; BA, Wellesley Coll., Mass., 1970; MD, Columbia U., NY, 1974. Lic. Calif., 1975, diplomate Am. Bd. Pediatrics, 1979, cert. Am. Bd. Clin. Genetics-Med. Genetics, 2006. Med. dir. Bernardy Ctr., San Diego, 1980—; dir. dysmorphology and genetics Rady Children's Hosp., San Diego, 1979—, dir. cleft palate program, 1980—, dir. sharp/children's prenatal diagnostic ctr., 1990—2007, dir. craniofacial defects program, 1993—; intern Univ. Calif. San Diego Med. Ctr., 1975, resident internal medicine, 1975—77, chief resident pediat., 1977—78, fellow divsn. dysmorphology, 1978—79, asst. adjunct prof. pediat., 1979—95, dir. craniofacial defects program, 1988—93, dir. prenatal diagnostic ctr., 2006—. Editl. bd. Cleft Palate Jour., 1986—92; adjunct prof. pediat. Univ. Calif. San Diego Med. Ctr., 1995—. Fellow: Am. Coll. Med. Genetics (bd. dirs. 1995—2000, sec. 1997—2000, pres. elect 2003—05, pres. 2005—07, past pres. 2007—); mem.: Western Soc. for Pediatric Rsch. (sec.-treas. 1990—95, pres. elect 2003—04, pres. 2004—05, past pres. 2005—06, of coun. 2006—), Soc. Pediat. Rsch., Am. Acad. Pediat., Am. Pediat. Soc., Am. Cleft Palate-Craniofacial Assn. (coun. 1992—95, v.p. 1995—97, pres. elect. 1997—99, pres. 1999—2000, past pres. 2000—01, Disting. Svc. award 2003), Am. Soc. Human Genetics, Soc. of Craniofacial Genetics, Western Assn. of Physician, AMA, Calif. Med. Assn., San Diego County Med. Soc., Am. Med. Dirs. Assn. Office: Rady Children's Hospital 7920 Frost St Ste 200 San Diego CA 92123 Office Phone: 858-966-5840. Office Fax: 858-966-8550.

JONES, MORRIS S., medical association administrator; b. San Francisco, Mar. 29, 1973; BS, U. Calif. Davis, 1996; PhD, NYU, 2002. Dir., rsch. & devel. David Grant Med. Ctr., 2008—10; chief, viral immunoserology and molecular diagnostics Calif. Dept. Pub. Health, 2010—. Adj. prof. Pacific Union Coll., 2004—11; mem. Instl. Rev. Bd. David Grant Med. Ctr., 2009—10, Internat. Com. Taxonomy of Viruses Adenovirus Study Group, 2010—11, Enteric Surveillance Steering Com. DoD-Global Emerging Infections Surveillance, 2010, Human Adenovirus Genome Working Group NIH, 2011. Recipient Sci. Excellence award, David Grant Med. Ctr.; named US Pioneer Rschr. of Yr., Blastocystis Rsch. Found. Avocation: photography. Office: 850 Marina Bay Pky Richmond CA 94804

JONES, NEIL FORD, surgeon, educator; b. Merthyr Tydvil, Wales, Nov. 30, 1947; s. John Robert and Kathleen Mary (Ford) J.; m. Barbara Rose Unterman, Feb. 18, 1978; 1 child, Nicholas Huw. MA, Oxford U., Eng., 1971; MD Oxford U., Eng., 1974. Registrar N.E. Thames Regional Plastic Surgery Centre, Billericay, Eng., 1982; fellow in hand surgery and microsurgery, dept. orthopaedic surgery Mass. Gen. Hosp. Harvard U., Boston, 1983; asst. prof. surgery U. Pitts., 1984-89, assoc. prof. surgery, 1989-93, dir. hand and microsurgery, 1987-93; chief hand surgery UCLA Sch. Medicine, 1993—2008, prof. orthop. surgery, prof. plastic and reconstructive surgery; chief of hand surgery U. Calif. Irvine Sch. Med., 2008—. Contbr. articles to profl. jours. Fellow ACS, Royal Coll. Surgeons Eng.; mem. Am. Assn. Plastic Surgeons, Am. Soc. Surgery of Hand (mem. coun. 2000-03), Am. Soc. Reconstructive Microsurgery (pres. 2008-2009), World Soc. Reconstructive Microsurgery. Avocations: travel, antiques. Home: 532 N Bonhill Rd Los Angeles CA 90049-2326 Office Phone: 714-456-5759.

JONES, PETER B., psychiatrist, educator; s. Owen Trevor and Amy Mary Anita Jones; m. Caroline M. Lea-Cox; children: Hugo Owen, Oliver Thomas. BSc, U. London, 1981, MBBS, Westminster Med. Sch., 1984; MSc in Epidemiology, London Sch. Hygiene Tropical Medicine, 1992; PhD, Inst. Psychiatry, 1997; MA, U. Cambridge, 2004; MD (hon.), U. Oulu, 2006. Registrar internal medicine King's Coll. Hosp., London, 1986—87; registrar psychiatry Maudsley Hosp., London, 1987—90; hon. lectr. Inst. Psychiatry, London, 1991—93, sr. lectr. psychiatry, 1993—95; sr. lectr. psychiat. epidemiology U. Nottingham, England, 1995—97, prof. psychiatry, cmty. mental health, 1997—2000; prof. psychiatry U. Cambridge, England, 2000—, chair dept. psychiatry, 2000—. Non-exec. dir. Cambrideshire and Peterborough Found. Trust, Cambridge, 2002—05; dir. NIHR CLAHRC Region, Cambridge, Peterborough, Cambridge U. Health Ptnrs., 2009—. Contbr. articles. Fellow: Acad. Med. Sci., Royal Coll. Psychiatrists, Royal Coll. Physicians London. Avocations: fishing, hiking. Office: Univ Cambridge Dept Psychiatry Herchel Smith Bldg Brain & Mind Scis Forvie Site Robinson Way CambBiomed Camp Cambridge CB2 0S2 England

JONES, PHILIP NEWTON, internist, educator; b. Billings, Mont., May 27, 1924; s. Robert Newton and Edith (Woodbury) J.; m. Rebecca Ann Means, June 13, 1948; children: Robert Newton II, Rebecca Ann, Margaret Jane. Student, Stanford, 1942-43, U. Wis., 1944; MD, Washington U., St. Louis, 1948. Diplomate Am. Bd. Internal Medicine. Intern St. Luke's Hosp., Chgo., 1948-49, resident in internal medicine, 1949-51; rssch. fellow internal medicine Northwestern U., Chgo., 1953, clin. asst. medicine, 1954-57; practice medicine, specializing in internal medicine and hepatology Chgo., 1954-94; clin. asst. medicine U. Ill., Chgo., 1957-58, from clin. instr. to clin. assoc. prof. medicine, 1958-71; assoc. prof. medicine Rush Coll. Medicine Chgo., 1971-75, prof. medicine, 1975-94, prof. emeritus, 1994—. Sr. attending physician Presbyn.-St. Luke's Hosp., Chgo., 1954-94, treas. med. staff, 1960-62, mem. exec. com., med. staff, 1960-62, 72-77, sec. med. staff, 1972-73, pres. med. staff, 1973-75; mem. exec. bd. Rush-Presbyn.-St. Luke's Med. Ctr., Chgo., 1973-75, trustee, 1973-77. Contbr. articles to books and profl. jours. Mem. bd. edn., Kenilworth, Ill., 1962-68, pres., 1965; mem. Welfare Council Met., Chgo., 1965-66; bd. dirs. Presbyn. Home, Evanston, Ill., 1978-88, 93-2009. Served with AUS, 1943-46, to capt. USAF, 1951-53. Fellow Am. Coll. Physicians, Inst. Medicine Chgo.; mem. Am. Assn. Study Liver Disease, Chgo. Soc. Internal Medicine, Am. Fedn. Clin. Research, AMA, Ill. Med. Assn., Chgo. Med. Soc., Nu Sigma Nu. Republican. Congregationalist (pres. bd. trustees). Home: 868 Pembridge Dr Lake Forest IL 60045-4200 Personal E-mail: pnjrmj1@yahoo.com.

JONES, ROBERT NEIL, biology educator, university administrator; b. Shrewsbury, Shropshire, U.K., Aug. 30, 1939; s. Geoffrey James and Sarah Jones; m. Dorothy Oswald, July 18, 1964 (div. Feb. 2006); children: Alexandra Elizabeth, Robin Neil. BSc, U. Wales, Aberystwyth, UK, 1963, PhD, 1967, DSc, 1987. Lectr. genetics Queen's U., Belfast, UK, 1967-69; lectr. U. Wales, Aberystwyth, 1969-82, sr. lectr., 1982—88, reader, 1988—91, prof. genetics, 1991—2004, dean of sci., 1997—2002. Hon. prof. faculty of biology St. Petersburg State U., 2000; mem. adv. bd. Internat. Soc. Cytogenetics and Genomics; emeritus fellow Leverhulme Trust, 2004; adv. Third World Acad. Scis., 2004; emeritus prof. U. Wales, 2007. Co-author: Chromosome Genetics, 1977, B-Chromosomes, 1982, Introducing Genetics, 1986, Practical Genetics, 1991, The Essentials of Genetics, 2001; mem. editl. bd. Heredity, 1988-98, Cytogenetics and Genome Rsch.,

2002—; assoc. editor Jour. of Chromosome Research, 1997—. Mem. adv. bd. Rsch. Ctr. Botany and Applied Agr. Tech. U. Lisbon, 2005—. Fellow Inst. of Biology; mem. Genetical Soc. UK (com. 1984-87, jr. sec. 1987-90, sr. sec. 1990-93, v.p. 1993-96), Fedn. European Genetical Socs. (pres. 1993-98), Spanish Genetical Soc. (hon.), Soc. Geneticist and Breeders (hon.), European Ctr. Excellence (adv. bd.), Inst. Plant Genetics, Polish Acad. Scis., Internat. Cytogenetics and Genomics Soc., Lithuanian Acad. Scis. (foreign mem.), Russian Soc. Naturalists.(Hon.) Avocations: birdwatching, growing orchids, travel, movies. Office: Aberystwuth U Inst Biol Environ and Rural Scis Edward Llwyd Bldg Penglais Campus Aberystwyth SY23 3DA Wales Home: 94 Rhoshendre SY23 3PX Aberystwyth Wales Office Fax: 4401970622307. Business E-Mail: rnj@aber.ac.uk.

JONES, RONALD CHARLES, hospital administrator; b. Panaca, Nev., Jan. 20, 1937; s. Charles Russell and Margaret Leona (Heaps) J.; m. Nancy Christensen, Dec. 23, 1955; children: Linda Diane, Jackie Lynn, Karen Kaye, Ronald Brent, Patricia Marie, Bryan David, Brandon Lee. BS, U. nev., Reno, 1955; M in Healthcare Adminstrn., Baylor U., 1970. Commd. 2d lt. U.S. Army, 1959, advanced through grades to col., 1980; comdr. 47th Field Hosp., Ft. Sill, Okla., 1979; dep. comdr. for adminstrn. MEDDAC and Reynolds Army Hosp., Ft. Sill, 1979-84, 2d Gen. Hosp., Langstuhl, Germany, 1984-87; dep. post comdr., chief staff, dep. comdr. for adminstrn. Fitzsimmons Army Med. Ctr., 1987-89; ret. U.S. Army, 1989; dir. mil. rels. LDS Ch., 1989-91; asst. adminstr. Utah Valley Regional Med. Ctr., Provo, 1991—. Decorated Silver Star, Legion of Merit with oakleaf cluster, Disting. Flying Cross, Bronze Star, Meritorious Svc. medal with 3 oakleaf clusters, Air medal with 30 oak leaf clusters, Army Commendation medal with oakleaf cluster, others. Fellow Am. Coll. Healthcare Execs.; mem. Am. Hosp. Assn., Assn. U.S. Army, Utah Hosp. Assn. Avocations: coin collecting/numismatics, boating, hunting, fishing, gardening. Home: 2636 Jody St West Jordan UT 84088-8506 Office: Utah Valley Regional MC Ste 500 1055 N 300 W Provo UT 84604-3312 *

JONES, STANLEY BOYD, retired researcher; b. Balt., July 27, 1938; s. Arthur Boyd and Lillian Ailene (Powell) J.; m. Judith K. Miller, Mar. 9, 1981; children— Andrew, Jeffrey, Lisa, Julia. BA, Dartmouth Coll., 1960; postgrad., Yale U., 1960-63. Ordained Episc. priest., 1992. Mem. profl. staff Subcom. on Health, U.S. Senate, Washington, 1970-76; program devel. officer Inst. of Medicine, Nat. Acad. Scis., Washington, 1976-78; v.p. Fullerton, Jones & Wollkstein (Health Policy Alternatives), Washington, 1978-80; v.p. for Washington representation Nat. Assns. Blue Cross and Blue Shield Plans, 1980-83; prin. Health Policy Alternatives, 1983-86; pres. Consol. Healthcare, 1986-89; ind. cons. on health policy Washington, 1989—; clergyman Diocese of W.Va., 1992—2004; dir. Health Ins. Reform Project George Washington U., 1994-99. Commr. D.C. Gen. Hosp. Mem. Inst. of Medicine of Nat. Acad. Scis. Office: 2021 K St NW Washington DC 20006-1003 Personal E-mail: stan@stanjudyjones.com.

JONES, STEPHANIE LEE, biologist, ornithologist, botanist; b. Salt Lake City, Nov. 17, 1948; d. Lamar Spenser Jones and Marian Frances (Schoular) Robinson; Richard L. Robinson (stepfather). BA, San Francisco State U., 1978; MA, San Jose State U., Calif., 1989. Clk. U.S. Geol. Survey, Menlo Pk., Calif., 1985-88; dist. biologist U.S. Forest Svc., Weaverville, Calif., 1989-91; nongame bird biologist U.S. Fish and Wildlife Svc., Denver, 1992—. Author: Canyon Wren, 1995; contbr. articles to profl. publs. Recipient Merit Achievement award Ptnrs. in Flight, Estes Pk., Colo., 1992. Mem. Am. Ornithol. Soc., Wilson Ornithol. Soc.(life), Cooper Ornithol. Soc. (life; mem. membership com. 1988—). Avocations: hiking, backpacking, silkscreening, quilting. Office: US Fish and Wildlife Svc PO Box 25486 Denver CO 80225-0486 Office Phone: 303-236-4409. Business E-Mail: stephanie_jones@fws.gov.

JONES, STEPHEN G., geriatrician; Grad., State U. of NY Coll. of Medicine. Diplomate Am. Bd. of Internal Medicine, Am. Bd. of Internal Medicine-geriatric medicine. Internship Univ. Hosp. of Stony Brook; assoc. clin. prof. medicine Yale Univ.; with Greenwich Hosp. Office: Greenwich Hospital 5 Perryridge Rd Greenwich CT 06830 Office Phone: 203-863-3000.

JONES, TREVOR OWEN, biomedical industry executive, management consultant; b. Maidstone, Kent, Eng., Nov. 3, 1930; came to U.S., 1957, naturalized, 1971; s. Richard Owen and Ruby Edith (Martin) J.; m. Jennie Lou Singleton, Sept. 12, 1959; children: Pembroke Robinson (dec.), Bronwyn Elizabeth. Higher Nat. Cert. in Elec. Engring., Aston Tech. Coll., Birmingham, Eng., 1952; Ordinary Nat. Cert. in Mech. Engring., Liverpool Tech. Coll., Eng., 1957; DSc (hon.), Cleve. State U., 2006. Registered profl. engr., Wis.; chartered engr., U.K. Student engr., elec. machine design engr. Brit. Gen. Electric Co., 1950-57; project engr., project mgr. Nuc. Ship Savannah, Allis-Chalmers Mfg. Co., 1957-59; with GM, 1959-78, staff engr. in charge Apollo computers, 1967, dir. electronic control sys., 1970-72, dir. advanced product engring., 1972-74; dir. GM Proving Grounds, 1974-78; v.p. engring., automotive worldwide TRW Inc., Cleve., 1978-80, v.p. transp. electronics group, 1980-87; chmn. bd. dirs. Libbey-Owens-Ford Inc., 1987-94; chmn., CEO Internat. Devel. Corp., 1987—; from vice chmn. to chmn. Echlin Inc., 1995-98, chmn. bd. dir., interim pres. and CEO, 1997; chmn., founder, CEO Biomec Inc., 1998—2007; chmn. Electrosonics Med., Inc., 2007—, CEO, 2007—. Chmn. emeritus Ohio Fuel Cell Coalition; vice chmn. Nat. Motor Vehicle Safety Adv. Coun., 1971; chmn. Nat. Hwy. Safety Adv. Com., 1976; assoc. NRC, 2002. Author, patentee automotive safety and electronics. Trustee Lawrence Inst. Tech., 1973-76; exec. bd. Clinton Valley coun. Boy Scouts Am., 1975; bd. govs. Cranbrook Inst. Sci., 1977; mem. Sec. of Def. Def. Sci. Bd. Task Force on Internat. Arms Devel. Cooperation, 1995-98; chmn. Nat. Rsch. Coun. Com. Partnership for a New Generation Vehicle, 1994-2001; vice chair bd. trustees Cleve. State U., 2001-06, mem., 2007; trustee Cleve. Orch., 2003—. Officer Brit. Army, 1955-57. Recipient Safety award, US Dept. Transp., 1978, Ellis Island Medal of Honor, 2008, Life Time Achievement award, Ohio Fuel Cell Coalition, 2010. Fellow Brit. Instn. Mechanical Engrs. (hon.), Brit. Instn. Elec. Engrs. (Hooper Mem. prize 1950), IEEE (life, exec. com. vehicle tech. soc. 1977-81), Royal Soc. of the Arts, Mfg. and Commerce, Soc. Automotive Engrs. (Arch T. Colwell paper award 1974-75, Vincent Bendix Automotive Electronics award 1976, Edward N. Cole award 1988), Engring. Soc. Detroit, Engring. Soc. Cleve., Instn. Mech. Engrs. (hon.); mem. NAE (Einstein Soc.), Ohio Fuel Cell Coalition (chmn. emeritus; Lifetime Achievement award 2010), Shoreby Club, Union Club Episcopalian. Home: Two Bratenahl Pl Ste 9EF Bratenahl OH 44108 Office Phone: 216-357-3310 ext. 1003. Business E-Mail: tojones@elecsonmed.com.

JONES, WILLIAM LEE, JR., psychologist, educator; b. Electra, Tex., Jan. 4, 1944; s. William Lee Jones Sr. and Mamie Kathryn Baker. BA, U. Ariz., Tucson, 1966; cert., Def. Lang. Inst./Yale U., Monterey, Calif./New Haven, 1969; MA cum laude, U. Sorbonne, Paris, 1974; MA, Ariz. State U., Tempe, 1986, PhD in Clin. Psychology, 1986. Psychologist, outpatient coord. St. Luke's Hosp., Phoenix, 1985—91; psychologist Tex. State Hosp., Wichita Falls, 1991—96; pvt. practice psychologist, psychotherapist Hemet, Calif., 1995—; psychology clin. cons. Riverside County, Riverside and Hemet, 1996—2004. Instr. Phoenix Coll., 1988, Rio Sala de Coll., Ariz., 1989—91, Midwestern State Coll., Wichita Falls, Tex., 1993, Mt. San Jacinto Coll., Calif., 2002—03; family advocate Valley Wide Svcs., Hemet and San Jacinto, Calif., 2002—. Author: Rites of Passage, 1996, Group Therapy: Manual for Clinicians, 1987. Recipient Fiction Divsn. 1st Pl. award, Mensa Writing Contest, 1995. Mem.: Mensa (1st pl. regional award for fiction 1993), Phi Delta Theta. Mailing: PO Box 3556 Idyllwild CA 92549 E-mail: wljones4@verizon.net.

JONES-LUKÁCS, ELIZABETH LUCILLE, physician; b. Norfolk, Va. d. Oliver C. and Gertrude (Layden) Jones; m. Michel J. Lukacs (dec.); children: Amanda, Laurel, Angelique, Klara. BS, Oglethorpe U., 1955; MD, Downstate Med. Ctr., 1964. Diplomate Am. Bd. Family Practice. Intern Beth Israel Hosp., NYC, 1964-65; family practice medicine Goshen, NY, 1965-73, Buckingham, Va., 1973-78; commd. maj. U.S. Air Force, 1978; flight surgeon Andrews AFB, Md., 1978-85, chief exec. med. program Md., 1991-2000; med. dir. Armed Forces Benefit Assn., Alexandria, Va., 2000—06. Unit charge physician Student Health Ctr., U. Md., College Park, 1985—91; bd. dirs. Falcon's Landing Mil. Officers Retirement Home. Author: The Curies Radium & Radioactivity, 1962, The Golden Stamp Book of Flying Animals, 1963. Col. USAFR, commd. 459th USAF Clinic. Mem. ACP, Am. Med. Womens Assn. (pres. Br. I). Episcopalian. Home: 15430 Mount Calvert Rd Upper Marlboro MD 20772-9616 Personal E-mail: ejlukacs@verizon.net.

JONIAU, SANDER HUGO KORNEEL, otolaryngologist; b. Kortrijk, West-Vlaanderen, Belgium, Apr. 9, 1976; s. Marcel Joniau and Rita Hens; m. Bénédicte Elisabeth H. G. Denys, Aug. 24, 2002; 1 child, Tomas Joniav. MD, Cath. U., Leuven, 2006. Cert. otorhinolaryngologist, head and neck surgeon Cath. U. Leuven, 2006. Lectr. Cath. U. Coll. Bruges-Ostend, West-Vlaanderen, 2001—03; vis. fellow U. Adelaide-Flinders U., Australia, 2005; otorhinolaryngologist, head and neck surgeon OLV Van Lourdes Ziekenhuis, Waregem, West-Vlaanderen, 2007—. Ink drawings; contbr. med. articles. Mem.: European Acad. Allergology and Clin. Immunology, Royal Belgian Soc. ENT, Head and Neck Surgery. Achievements include research in role of gastro-pharyngeal reflux on upper airway symptoms; surgical techniques for improving nasal breathing; microbiology of acute rhinosinusitis. Personal E-mail: sanderjoniau@hotmail.com.

JONIKIS, ARVIDAS ANTHONY, psychologist; b. Bad Aibling, Bavaria, Germany, July 21, 1945; arrived in Australia, 1949; s. Antanas and Bronislava (Grinkevičius) J.; m. Helene Ilze Pudovskis, Jan. 28, 1967; children: Martin Anthony, Simon Alexander. BA, U. Western Australia, Perth, 1971, diploma in Edn., 1972, B in Psychology, 1976, M in Psychology, 1983; grad. diploma in Psychol. Counselling, Curtin U. of Tech., Perth, 1980. Registered clin. psychologist specialist, Australia. Counselling psychologist Tech. and Further Edn., Perth, 1974-82, clin. psychologist, 1983-87; sr. clin. psychologist Corrective Svcs. Dept., Perth, 1987-89, Graylands Hosp., Perth, 1989—, specialist clin. psychologist, 2002—. Mem. West Australian Ice Skating Assn. (judge, referee, hon. life mem., councillor 1979-82), Ice Skating Australia (championship judge, referee, councillor 1980-2001), Internat. Skating Union (championship judge, referee), Personal Construct Psychology Assn. West Australia (chair 1990-92, hon. treas. 1992—, lectr. 1992—), Australian Psychol. Soc. (hon. treas. West Australian Bd. Clin. Psychologists 1986-87). Avocations: amateur astronomy, computing, science fiction. Home: 73 Williams Rd Nedlands 6009 Australia Office: Graylands Hosp Brockway Rd Mount Claremont 6010 Australia E-mail: Tony.Jonikis@health.wa.gov.au.

JONSEN, ALBERT R(UPERT), medical ethics educator; b. San Francisco, Apr. 4, 1931; s. Albert R. and Helen (Sweigert) Jonsen; m. Mary Elizabeth Carolan. BA, Gonzaga U., 1955, MA, 1956; STM, U. Santa Clara, 1963; PhD, Yale U., 1967. Mem. S.J., 1949—76; ordained priest Roman Cath. Ch.; instr. philosophy Loyola U., LA, 1956—59; asst. in instrn. Yale Div. Sch., 1966—67; asst. prof. theology and philosophy U. San Francisco, 1967—72, pres., 1969—72; prof. med. ethics Sch. Medicine, U. Calif.-San Francisco, 1972—87; adj. assoc. prof. dept. community medicine and internat. health Sch. Medicine, Georgetown U., 1977; prof. med. ethics, chmn. dept. med. history and ethics Sch. Medicine U. Wash., Seattle, 1987—99, prof. emeritus; faculty Fromm Inst. for Life-Long Learning, U. San Francisco, 2000—, dean faculty, 2009—; co-dir. and sr. ethics scholar in residence, Program in Medicine and Human Values, Calif. Pacific Med. Ctr., San Francisco, 2004—. Vis. prof. Yale U., 1999—2000; mem. artificial heart assessment panel Nat. Heart and Lung Inst., 1972—73, 1984—86; mem. Am. Bd. Med. Spltys., 1978—81; cons. Am. Bd. Internal Medicine, 1978—82, ACOG, 1983—88; mem. Pres.'s Commn. for Study of Ethical Problems in Medicine, 1979—82, Nat. Commn. for Protection Human Subjects of Biomed. and Behavioral Rsch., HEW, 1974—78, Nat. Bd. Med. Examiners, 1985—87, Commn. on AIDS Rsch., NRC, 1986—92, Panel on Social Impact of AIDS (chmn.), 1989—91; chmn. nat. adv. bd. Ethics and Reprodn., 1991—96; mem. ethics adv. bd. GERON Corp., 2000—; vis. prof. Stanford U. Sch. Medicine, 2002, U. Va. Law Sch., 2002; vis. prof. dept. surgery U. Calif., San Francisco, 2004. Author: Responsibility in Modern Religious Ethics, 1968, Patterns of Moral Responsibility, 1969, Christian Decision and Action, 1970, Ethics of Newborn Intensive Care, 1976, Clin. Ethics, 1982, 6th edit., 2005, The Abuse of Casuistry: A History of Moral Reasoning, 1987, The New Medicine and the Old Ethics, 1990, The Social Impact of AIDS in the United States, 1993, Bioethics, 1997, The Birth of Bioethics, 1998, A Short History of Medical Ethics, 2000, Bioethics Beyond the Headlines, 2005; mem. editl. bd. Jour. Philosophy and Medicine, Jour. Clin. Ethics. Bd. trustees Inst. Ednl. Mgmt., Harvard U., 1971—74, Ploughshares Found., 1980—84; mem. San Francisco Crime Com., 1969—71; bd. dirs. Found. Critical Care Medicine, 1983—86, Sierra Health Found., 1987—. Fellow, Guggenheim, 1995—96. Fellow: The Hastings Ctr.; mem.: Am. Osler Soc. (McGovern award 1986), Am. Coll. Cardiology (Convocation Medal 1996), Am. Soc. for Bioethics and Humanities (Lifetime Achievement award 1999), Blue Cross and Blue Shield Assn. (tech. assessment program 1985—2003, med. adv. panel), Instituto de Bioetica (Madrid), Inst. Medicine (com. human values 1973, coun. 1983—85, 1990—92), Soc. Christian Ethics, Am. Soc. Law and Medicine (bd. dirs. 1986—88), Soc. Health and Human Values (pres. 1986—87). Home: 3400 Laguna St Apt 412 San Francisco CA 94123-7219 E-mail: arjonsen@aol.com.

JÖNSSON, BODIL E., physician; b. Stockholm, Jan. 22, 1959; d. Ann-Margret and Torsten K. Jönsson; 1 child, Niklas O. MD, U. Gothenburg, Sweden, 1988; PhD in Medicine, 2009. Registered physician Socialstyrelsen, 1991. Head physician Sahlgrenska U. Hosp., Gothenburg, 2007—. Lutheran. Avocations: swimming, exercise, reading, travel. Office: Sahlgrenska Univ Hosp Bact Lab Guldhedsgatan 10A 413 46 Gothenburg Sweden

JONSSON, KJELL, hospital administrator; b. Hammeldal, Sweden, Oct. 18, 1955; s. Gunnar and Wanja Jonsson; m. Nina Jonsson; children: Gunnar, Erik, Nora. Degree, U. Karlberg, Stockholm, 1977, Militarhogskolan, 1985. Platoon comdr. Faltjagarregementet, Estersund, Sweden, 1977—80, co. comdr., 1980—85; head sect. Def. Staff, Stockholm, 1987—95; batallion comdr. Lappland Ranger, Kiruna, 1995—98; mng. dir. Ostersund (Sweden) Hosp., 2000—05; CEO, Swedish Rett Ctr., 2005—. Mem.: KSSS, Rotary.

JONSSON, OLOF KNUT, urologist; b. Torsby, Varmland, Sweden, May 12, 1941; s. Knut Theodor and Doris Elisabeth Jonsson; m. Marianne Ingrid Hulten, Oct. 25, 1969; children: Ann, Martin, Karin. PhD in Physiology, U. Göteborg, 1971, MD, 1971, PhD in Surgery, 1980, PhD in Urology, 1986. Gen. surgeon Sahlgrenska Hosp., Göteborg, Sweden, 1972-84, sr. urologist, 1984—, prof. urology, 2001—. Contbr. articles to profl. jours. Home: Gertruds Gata 25 42167 Västra Frölunda Sweden Office: Dept Urology Sahlgrenska Hosp 41345 Göteborg Sweden E-mail: olof.jonsson@vgregion.se.

JOO, SEONG SOO, medical educator; b. Republic of Korea, Nov. 16, 1966; PhD, Chung-Ang U., Seoul, Republic of Korea, 2003. Clin. rsch. mgr. GlaxoSmithKlien Korea, 1999—2001; devel. mgr. Handok Pharm. Co., 2001—02; rsch. prof. Chung-Ang U., Coll. Pharmacy, 2004—07, Chungbuk Nat. U., Coll. Vet. Medicine, 2007—10; prof. Gangneung-Wonju Nat. U., Coll. Life Sci., 2010—. Office: 120 Gangneung Daehangno Gangneung Gangwon 210-702 Republic of Korea Business E-Mail: ssj66@gwnu.ac.kr.

JOO, WON IL, medical educator; b. Seoul, Republic Of Korea, Mar. 24, 1969; s. Dae Pyung Joo and Hee Ja Seo; m. Su Mee Kim, Oct. 25, 2002; children: Seo Yeon, Hyeun Jun. MD, PhD, The Cath. U. Korea, Seoul, Republic of Korea, 1994. Cert. in med. practioner Ministry for Health and Welfare, 1994, in neurol. surgery The Korean Neurol. Soc., 1999. Clin. fellow St. Mary's Hosp., Seoul, Republic of Korea, 2002—03; instr. The Cath. U. Korea, Seoul, Republic of Korea, 2003—04, asst. prof., 2005—. Mem. Korean Neurol. Soc., Seoul, 1999—. Contbr. scientific papers to profl. jours. Vol., Seoul, Republic Of Korea, 2002—08. Capt. the army, 1999—2002. Mem.: Korean Neurol. Soc. Sect. Brain Tumor. Achievements include research in Study of characteristics of adipose derived stem cell. Avocations: golf, jogging. Home: Yongsangu ichondong Seoul Republic of Korea Office: The Cath Univ Korea #62 Youido-dong Yeongdeungpo-gu Seoul 150-713 Republic of Korea Office Fax: 82-2-786-5809. Business E-Mail: jwi@catholic.ac.kr.

JOOS, ULRICH KLAUS, oral and maxillofacial surgeon, educator; b. Wangen, Germany, Dec. 26, 1947; s. Alois and Alice (Vollmer) J.; m. Regine Joos. DDS, U. Freiburg, Germany, 1972, MD, 1974, DSc, 1978, DSc, 1992; DSc (hon.), U. Budapest, Hungary, 1994. Diplomate German Bd. Maxillofacial Surgery, Bd. Plastic and Reconstructive Surgery. Assoc. prof. U. Nantes, France, 1979-80, U. Freiburg, 1980-83, prof., 1983-92; chmn., prof. U. Muenster, Germany, 1992—; chair Muenster Dental Sch., 2006—. V.p. German Coun. Cleft, Lip and Palate Contbr. articles to profl. jours., chapters to books. Med. Adv. Orgn. Parents of Children with Congenital Craniofacial Malformations. Mem. European Assn. Cranio-Maxillofacial Surgery (pres. 2000-02), French Cranio-Maxillofacial Surgery Assn. (hon.), Hungarian Cranio-Maxillofacial Surgery Assn. (hon.), Chilean Cranio-Maxillofacial Surgery Assn. (hon.), Spanish Cranio-Maxillofacial Surgery Assn. (hon.), Hyderabad Cleft Soc. (hon.; internat. adv. com.). Roman Catholic. Address: Albert Schweitzer Campus 1 Geb W 30 Munster Germany Business E-Mail: joos@uni-muenster.de.

JORDAN, BARBARA MOORE, retired psychiatrist; b. Petersburg, Va., June 5, 1928; d. Carlisle Seward and Bertha Edna (Beasley) Moore; m. Harmon Geiger Jordan, Oct. 28, 1960; children: Jon David, Lisa Anne, Monica Leigh, Robert Bruce. AB, U. N.C., Greensboro, 1949; MD, U. N.C., 1954. Diplomate Am. Bd. Psychiatry and Neurology. Intern Queens Hosp., Honolulu, 1954-55; resident in psychiatry U. N.C. Med. Sch., Chapel Hill, 1955-57, Dorothea Dix Hosp., Raleigh, N.C., 1957-58, chief of female service, 1958-60; clin. dir. Dorothea Dix, Raleigh, 1966-71, asst. supt., 1971-73; gen. practice psychiatry, 1960-66; mem. attending staff Rex Hosp., Raleigh, 1960-66; med. cons. disability determination div. N.C. Dept. Pub. Welfare, Raleigh, 1961-66; project physician NIMH, Raleigh, 1965-66; psychiatrist Southeastern Regional Area Program, Lumberton, N.C., 1973-91; mem. staff Southeastern Gen. Hosp., Lumberton, 1973-91; ret., 1991. Clin. instr. U. N.C. Med. Sch., 1958-61; bd. dirs. United Way, 2001-04, Juvenile Crime Prevention Coun., 2003-06. Organizer Drug Action Com. Wake County, Raleigh, 1968. Fellow Am. Psychiat. Assn.; mem. Robeson County Med. Soc. (pres. 1986), N.C. Med. Soc. (del. 1984, 85), N.C. Neuropsychiat. Assn., AMA. Episcopalian. Avocations: swimming, sailing. Home: 972 Rockridge Rd Murphy NC 28906-6210 Personal E-mail: barbara972@verzon.net.

JORDAN, BARRY D., neurologist, educator; BA, U. Pa., 1977; MD, Harvard U., 1981; PhD, Columbia U., 1997. Diplomate Am. Bd. Psychiatry and Neurology. Intern UCLA, 1982; resident neurology NY Hosp., 1982—86; clin. fellow Meml. Sloan- Kettering Cancer Ctr., NYC, 1986; fellow Cornell Univ., 1987, Hosp. for Spl. Surgery, 1987; assoc. prof. clin. neurology Weill Cornell Med. Coll.; chief med. officer NY State Athletic Commn.; dir. brain injury program

Burke Rehab. Hosp., dir. memory evaluation and treatment svc., attending neurologist. Office: Burke Rehabilitation Hospital 785 Mamaroneck Ave White Plains NY 10605 Office Phone: 914-597-2500.

JORDAN, DEOVINA NASIS, nursing researcher, author, administrator, educator; b. Bangued, Abra, Philippines, May 7, 1960; d. Demetrio Villamor Nacis and Franisca Bicarme Baptista; m. James Lowell Jordan, July 25, 1992. BS in Nursing, U. Perpetual Help, Rizal, Philippines, 1980; MD in Surgery, U. Santo Tomas, Philippines, 1985; M in Pub. Health, Loma Linda U., 2001; MS in Nursing, UCLA, 2004, PhD in Nursing, 2008. Cert. Ednl. Comm. for Foreign Med. Grads. Phila., Pa.; Ped. Nursing, Am. Nursing Credentialing Ctr., Wash. DC. Clin. nurse Hosp. for Joint Dis. Ortho. Inst., NYC, 1987—88; clin. nurse III Mattel Children's Hosp, UCLA, LA, 1988—; admin. nurse IV UCLA Med. Ctr., LA, 2002—; v.p., founder Jordan Rsch. Inst., Murietta, Calif., 1994—; pres Fil-Am Assoc., Murietta, 1994—; prof. West Coast U., LA, 2006—, Calif. State U., Fullerton, 2009—. Rsch. adv. bd. Am. Biographical Inst., 2002—. Contbr. articles various prof. jours. Recipient Outstanding Profl. Woman award, Am. Biographical Inst., 2001. Mem.: Nat. Coalition Ethnic Minority Nurses Assn., Philippine Nurses Assn. Am., Philippine Nurses Assn. So. Calif., Assn. Calif. Nurse Leaders, Am. Assn. Critical Care Nurses, Calif. Nurses Assn., Am. Coll. Healthcare Execs., Alpha Tau Delta, Sigma Theta Tau. Personal E-mail: djjords@verizon.net. Business E-Mail: dnjordan@ucla.edu.

JORDAN, DESMOND ARTHUR, anesthesiologist, educator; b. Englewood, NJ, June 9, 1955; BS, Cornell U., 1975; MD, Brown U. Program Medicine, 1979. Assoc. prof. anesthesia NY Hosp., Columbia Presbyn. Campus, 1986—. Anesthesiologist NYPH. Office: Columbia University Med Ctr 177 New York NY 10032 Business E-Mail: daj3@columbia.edu.

JORDAN, JUDITH VICTORIA, clinical psychologist, educator; b. Milw., July 28, 1943; d. Claus and Charlotte (Backus) J.; m. William M. Redpath, Aug. 11, 1973. AB, Brown U., 1965; MA, Harvard U., 1968, PhD, 1973; DHL (hon.) (hon.), New Eng. Coll., 2001. Diplomate Am. Bd. Profl. Psychology. Psychologist Human Relations Service, Wellesley, Mass., 1971-73; assoc. psychologist McLean Hosp., Belmont, Mass., 1978-93, psychologist, 1993—, dir. women's studies program, 1988—, dir. tng. in psychology, 1991, dir. Women's Treatment Network, 1992—. Vis. scholar Stone Ctr. Wellesley Coll., 1985—; asst. prof. psychiatry Harvard Med. Sch., 1988—; co-dir. Jean Baker Miller Tng. Inst., dir., 2006, Wellesley Coll. 1998; adv. bd Fox TV Network, Women First healthcare., 1998; disting. prof. Menninger Clinic, 1999; dir. Jean Baker Miller Tng. Inst., 2006. Author: Relational-Cultural Therapy, Empathy and Self Boundries, 1984, Women's Growth in Connection, 1991, (with others) The Self in Relation, 1986; editor, author: Relational Self in Women; editor: Women's Growth in Diversity, 1997, editor: The Complexity of Connection, 2004, The Power of Connection, 2009, Relational Cultural Therapy. Recipient Outstanding Contbn. award, Feminist Therapy Inst., 2002, Disting. Psychol. award, Am. Psychology Assn., 2010. Fellow Am. Psychol. Assn.; mem. Mass. Psychol. Assn. (bd. dirs. 1983-85, Career Achievement award for outstanding contbns. to advancement of psychology as a sci. and a profession), Phi Beta Kappa. Office: McLean Hosp 114 Waltham St Lexington MA 02421-5415

JORDAN, LYNDON KIRKMAN, physician; b. Mount Olive, NC, Jan. 6, 1935; s. Lyndon Kirkman and Rachael Loucille (Hazelton) J.; m. Beverly Hayes Brooks, Aug. 19, 1961; children: Lyndon III, Christopher, Patrick. BA, Duke U., 1957, MD, 1961. Diplomate Am. Bd. Family Practice. Intern Watts Hosp., Durham, NC, 1961—62; flight surgeon Beale AFB, Marysville, Calif., 1962—64; pvt. practice Smithfield, NC, 1964—2001; dir. family medicine residency program Duke U. Sch. Medicine, Durham, 1972—74. Cons. Roche Biomed. Labs., Burlington, NC, 1987-92, Pfizer Pharms. Co., Mahwah, NJ, 1994-92; bd. dirs. Bank of Four Oaks of Smithfield, NC; chmn. bd. dirs. Millennium Healthczre Network of N.C. and S.C., 1997-99; chmn. Johnston County Bd. Health, Smithfield, 1998-2000, Vis. prof. Duke U. Sch. Medicine, 2004-09; lectr. in field. Capt. USAF, 1962-64, mem. diocesan coun. Episcopal DIocesa NC, 2006-09, sr. warden St. Pauls Episcopal Ch. Smithfields NC, 2006 Named family physician of Yr. N.C. Acad. Family Physicians, 1982, N.C. Tarheel of the Week, News & Observer Newspaper, Raleigh, 1983; Paul Harris fellow Rotary Internat., 1989. Fellow Am. Acad. Family Physicians. Episcopalian. Avocations: flying, hunting, fishing, painting. Home: 105 Mariah Dr Four Oaks NC 27524-8433

JORDAN, RANDALL WARREN, optometrist; b. Camilla, Ga., May 19, 1952; s. Billie Howard and Sara Ann (Richards) Jordan; m. Angela Marie Farmer, May 15, 1982; 1 child, Samantha Marie. BS in Biology, So. Coll. Optometry, 1987, OD, 1989. Diplomate So. Coun. Optometrists. Supply and distbn. mgr. Phoebe Putney Meml. Hosp., Albany, Ga., 1981-85; ophthalmic technician Omni Eye Svcs., Memphis, 1987; optometrist Albany Retinal-Eye Ctr., Albany, 1989-90, Eyecare Assocs. Ga., Brunswick, 1990-91, Eye Med, Chamblee, 1992-95, Drs. Shelton, Spooner, and Jordan, 1995-2000, Jordan Eye Care, 2000—. Optometrist Dougherty County Health Dept., Albany, 1989-90, Dept. Children's Med. Svcs., Albany, 1989-90, Lion's Club Vision Screening, Montezuma, Ga., 1989; mem. Emory Vision Correction Ctr. With U.S. Army, 1972-74. Mem. Am. Optometric Assn., Ga. Optometric Assn., Kiwanis, Beta Sigma Kappa, Omega Delta, Phi Theta Upsilon. Avocations: water-skiing, scuba diving, photography, reading, music. Home: PO Box 5103 Cordele GA 31010-5103 Office: PO Box 5103 Cordele GA 31010-5103 Home Phone: 229-271-0347; Office Phone: 229-273-0018.

JORDAN, RUTH ANN, retired physician; b. Oct. 12, 1928; d. Willard and Esther (Fouts) J.; children: Diane J., Linda J. AB, Ind. U., 1950; MD, Columbia U., 1957. Intern St. Luke's Hosp., NYC, 1957—58, asst. resident, 1958—59; physician Met. Life Ins. Co., NYC, 1960—62, Standard Oil Co. of N.J., NYC, 1962, MIT, Cambridge, Mass., 1963—71, New Eng. Mut. Life Ins. Co., Boston, 1963—66, asst. med. dir., 1971—74; fellow internal medicine Mass. Gen. Hosp., Boston, 1974—75; physician Simmons Coll., Boston, 1975—78, Northeastern U., Boston, 1976—78; assoc. med. dir. New Eng. Telephone Co., Boston, 1978, med. dir. clin. svcs., 1978—86; dir. occupl. medicine Gen. Med. Assn./Harvard Cmty. Health Plan, Boston, 1986—91; assoc. med. dir. Allmerica, Worcester, Mass., 1991—97; plant med. dir. GM, Westwood, Mass., 1995—2005; physician Health Resource, Woburn, Mass., 1996—2005; ret., 2005. Therapeutic dietitian Meth. Hosp., Indpls., 1951-53, Presbyn. Hosp., N.Y.C., part-time 1954-57; nat. coord. com. on cholesterol, 1986-2005, Mass. Adv. Coun. for Workers Compensation, 1986-89; bd. Coll. Arts and Sci., Ind. U., 2003—. Dean's advisory coun. Ind. U. Coll. Arts and Scis., 2004—. Fellow: Am. Coll. Occupl. and Environ. Medicine (health edn. com. 1984—, membership com. 1985—88, bd. dirs. 1986—92); mem.: PEO, DAR, AMA, Mass. Med. Soc. (ho. of dels. 1984—2001, chmn. environ. and occupl. health com. 1985—88, interspity. com. 1985—88, nutrition com. 2001—05, bylaws com. 2001—05, bd. trustees 2001—05), Norfolk Dist. Med. Soc. (v.p. 1998—99, edn. com. 1998—2005, exec. com. 1998—2005, pres. 1999—2001, bd. trustees 2000—03), New Eng. Occupl. Med. Assn. (bd. dirs. 1980—89, pres. 1981—84), The Country Club, Columbia U. Club of New Eng. (v.p. 1981—84, bd. dirs. 1981—91, pres. 1989—91), Alpha Chi Omega. Home: 2618 N Terrace Ave Milwaukee WI 53211 Home Phone: 414-962-4002.

JORDAN, SARA MELTZER, gynecologic oncology fellow; b. Rotterdam, Netherlands, Apr. 16, 1980; d. Richard Stuart and Colette Haesaerts Meltzer; m. Roberto Fernando Jordan, Aug. 30, 2008; 1 child, Sophia Isabella Jordon. BS, Cornell U., Ithaca, NY, 2002; MD, U. N.Mex., Sch. Medicine, Albuquerque, 2006; degree in Ob-gyn., U. Calif. Irvine, Orange, 2010, attending in Gynecologic Oncology, 2010—. Cert. in biol. engring., Cornell U., 2006; lic. in medicine and surgery Med. Bd. Calif., 2008. Ob-gyn. resident U. Calif. Irvine, 2006—10, gynecologic oncology fellow, 2010—. Recipient Cmty. Svc. award, U. N.Mex., Sch. Medicine, 2006, Resident Tchg. award, U. Calif., 2008, 2010, Resident Rsch. award, 2010, Chief Resident Humanitarian award, 2010; Perinatal Rsch. grant, 2009. Fellow: Am. Coll. Ob-gyn.; mem.: AMA. Achievements include research in gynecologic oncology and orthopedics. Avocations: travel, skiing, backpacking. Office: University Calif Irvine Ob-gyn Dept 101 The City Dr Bldg 56 Rm 260 Orange CA 92868

JORDAN, V. CRAIG, endocrine pharmacologist, educator; b. New Braunfels, Tex., July 25, 1947; s. Geoffry Webster and Sybil Cynthia (Mottram) Jordan; m. Monica Morrow, Apr. 17, 1993; children: Helen Melissa Yvonne, Alexandra Katherine Louise. BSc in Pharmacology, U. Leeds, Eng., 1969, PhD in Pharmacology, 1972, DSc in Pharmacology, 1985, MD (hon.), 2001; DSc (hon.), U. Mass., 2001, U. Bradford; MD (hon.), U. Crete, 2008. Rsch. assoc. Worcester Found. Exptl. Biology, Shrewsbury, Mass., 1972—73, vis. scientist, 1973—74; lectr. pharmacology Leeds U., 1973—79; head endocrine unit Ludwig Inst. Cancer Rsch., Bern, Switzerland, 1979—80; asst. prof. human oncology and pharmacology U. Wis., Madison, 1980—81, assoc. prof., 1981—85, leader pharmacology group, Wis. Clin. Cancer Ctr., 1981—85, prof., 1985—93, dir., Breast Cancer Program, 1987—92, vis. prof. human oncology, 1993—95; Diana, Princess of Wales prof. cancer rsch. Northwestern U., Chgo., 1993—2004, prof. cancer pharmacology Cancer Ctr., 1993—2004, assoc. dir. cancer control, 1993—96, dir. Lynn Sage breast cancer rsch. program Robert H. Lurie Comprehensive Ctr., 1993—2004, prof. molecular pharmacology and biol. chemistry Feinberg Sch. Medicine, 1994—2004; Alfred Knutdson chair cancer rsch. Fox Chase Cancer Ctr., Phila., 2005—; sci. dir. Lombardi Cancer Ctr., Georgetown U., Washington, 2009—; vice chair, dept. oncology Vincent T. Lombardi; chair Pittarslatcorld Cancer Rsch. Trustee Worcester Found./U. Mass., 1996—2005, hon. trustee, 2005—; adj. prof. cancer cell biology U. Pa., Phila., 2004—; hon. prof. Leeds Inst. Molecular Medicine, England, 2007. Mem. editl. bd.: Breast Cancer Rsch. Treatment, Clin. Cancer Rsch., European Jour. Cancer, Jour. Steroid Biochemistry, Jour. Nat. Cancer Inst., Molecular Cell Endocrinology, Receptor, Molecular Aspect Med., mem. editl. bd, mng. editor: Cancer Letters, mem. editl. bd, assoc. editor: Endocrine Related Cancer, editor 8 books; contbr. more than 600 articles to profl. jours. Served to capt. Intelligent Corps. Brit. Army, 1971—76, served to capt. Spl. Air Svc., 1976—79. Recipient Brinker Internat. Breast Cancer award, Susan G. Komen Found., 1992, Cameron prize, U. Edinburgh, 1993, WL McGuire Meml. award, 1994, Herbert J. Block Meml. award Dist. Achievement in Cancer, Ohio State U., 1996, Strang award, Cornell Med. Sch., 2000, Hon. Fellowship award and medal, U. Coll., Dublin, 2000, Disting. Achievement in Cancer Rsch. award and medal, Bristol Myers Squibb, 2001, Third Annual Breast Cancer award, European Inst. Oncology, Milan, Italy, 2001, Vivian and Meyer P. Potamkin found. award Breast Cancer Rsch., Pa. Breast Cancer Coalition, 2001, Med. Advancement award, Avon Found., 2002, Medal of Honor, Am. Cancer Soc., 2002, Officer Most Excellent Order of the British Empire for Services to Internat. Breast Cancer Rsch., Queen Elizabeth II, 2002, Charles F. Kettering award, GM Cancer Rsch. Found., 2003, Excellence award, Miami Breast Cancer Conf., 2003, 3rd George & Christine Sosnovsky award in Cancer Therapy, 2003—04, Rsch. award, N. Am. Menopause Soc./Eli Lilly SERM, 2003, Gregory Pincus award, U. Mass. Worcester Found. Exptl. Biology, 2007; co-recipient prize, Boston Obstet. Soc., 1974; named hon. prof., Iguca U., Brazil, 2005; scholar, Med. Rsch. Coun., 1969—72; Internat. Cancer Research Tech. Transfer grantee, UICC, 1981, Faculty fellow, Romnes, 1984—85. Fellow: Acad. Med. Sci. (UK), Am. Soc. Clin. Oncology (ACS award 2006, Karnofsky award 2008), Am. Inst. Chemists, Royal Soc. Medicine (hon. Jephcott award 2009, fellowship 2008), Brit. Pharmacol. Soc. (Sir John Gaddum Meml. award 1993), Royal Soc. Chemistry (Sosnovsky award 2004); mem.: NAS, Inst. Biology (UK), Y-ME Chgo. (hon.; nat. bd. dir.), Biochem. Soc., Endocrinse Soc., Am. Soc. Pharmacology and Exptl. Therapeutics (award 1993), Am. Assn. Cancer Rsch. (chair Pres. Circ. 2002—, pres. cir. 2004—, bd. dirs. 2007—, bd. trustee Found., 8th Cain Meml. award 1989, Inaugural Dorothy P. Landon prize Translational Rsch. 2002). Avocations: antique weapons, history. Office: 3970 Reservoir Rd NW Washington DC 20057 Business E-Mail: vcj2@georgetown.edu.

JORDAN, WILLIAM REYNIER, SR., retired therapist, poet; s. Russell Clinger and Lois Eleanor (Van Evera) J.; m. Ruth Corrigan Frauenheim, 1949 (dec. Mar. 2005); children: William (dec. 2001), Michael, Paul. BS in Journalism cum laude, U. Fla., 1956; South Asia area specialist, U. Pa., 1960-62; grad., Strategic Intelligence Sch., 1962, Gen. Staff Coll., 1968, Def. Lang. Inst., 1970; MA in Psychology, U. No. Colo., 1979; postgrad., U. So. Fla., 1986-87; PhD in Psychology, Calif. Coast U., 1989. Cpl. U.S. Army, 1947-48, with Mil. Intelligence Res., 1948-51, to 1st lt. inf., 1951-54, re-entered, 1957, fgn. area specialist Pakistan, 1962—64, co. comdr., dep. bn. comdr. Vietnam, 1966, advanced through grades to lt. col., 1968; chief of plans and analysis psychol. ops. divsn. Mil. Assistance Command, Vietnam, 1970-71; group ops. officer, later spl. asst. to comdg. officer 902d Mil. Intelligence Group, Washington, 1971-72; ret., 1972; vol. psychotherapist Juvenile Detention, Pensacola, Fla., 1976-77, Colorado Springs (Colo.) Social Svcs. Dept., 1977-78; psychotherapist Med. Clinic, St. Petersburg, Fla., 1980-84, Epilepsy Found., St. Petersburg, 1984-88; vol. VA Mental Health Clinic, Bay Pines, Fla., 1985-99; ret., 1999. Author: Darkness and Shadows, 1975, More Than Friends, 1978, Heat Lightning, 1984, Shrapnel, 2011. Leader Rawalpindi coun. Boy Scouts Am., Pakistan, 1960-62, also troops at Ft. Bragg. N.C., Ft. Leavenworth, Kans., Ft. Holabird, Md., 1964-70; bd. dirs. YMCA, Dundalk, Md., 1969-71, Epilepsy Assn., Pensacola, 1975-77. Decorated Legion of Merit with oak leaf cluster, Cross of Gallantry with Palm (Republic of Vietnam), Meritorious Svc. medal, Joint Svcs. Commendation medal, Army Commendation medal, Navy Unit Commendation, Army Valorous Unit Citation, Army Meritorious Unit Citation with oak leaf cluster; named Vol. of Yr., Colorado Springs Social Svcs. Dept., 1978. Mem. APA (assoc.), DAV, Epilepsy Assn. Am. (pres.'s club). Democrat. Congregationalist. Avocation: photography. Address: 1051 79th Ave N Apt 111 Saint Petersburg FL 33702-1127

JORDON, ROBERT EARL, physician; b. Buffalo, May 7, 1938; s. James Wallace and Helen Viola (Sampson) J.; m. Mary Ann Michels, July 12, 1969; children: James H., Kathryn L., Marie H. BA, Hamilton Coll., 1960; MD, SUNY-Buffalo, 1965; MS, U. Minn., 1970. Diplomate: Am. Bd. Dermatology, Dermatological Immunology Diagnostic and Laboratory Immunology. Intern straight medicine Buffalo Gen. Hosp., 1965-66; resident, fellow in dermatology Mayo Clinic and Mayo Found., Rochester, Minn., 1966-69, asso. cons., 1971-73, cons. dermatology, 1973-77; instr. pathology U. Minn. Hosps., Mpls., 1971-73; Nat. Inst. Arthritis and Metabolic Diseases spl. research fellow U. Minn., Mpls., 1972-73; asst. prof. dermatology Mayo Grad. Sch. Medicine, Rochester, 1971-73, Mayo Sch. Medicine, Rochester, 1973-76, asst. prof. immunology, 1974-77, asso. prof. dermatology, 1976-77; prof. medicine, chmn. dermatology Med. Coll. Wis., Milw., 1977-82; med. career investigator VA, 1978-82; chief dermatology Froedtert Meml. Luth. Hosp., Milw., 1980-82; chmn. dept. dermatology U. Tex. Health Sci. Ctr., Houston, prof., 1983—; chief dermatology Hermann Hosp., Houston, 1983—2003; mem. study sect. NIH, 1983-86. Mem. nat. arthritis adv. bd. Nat. Inst. aRthritis and Metabolic Diseases, NIH; mem. nat. adv. bd. Arthritis, Musculoskeletal and Skin Diseases, 1989-91, chmn. 1992-93. Mem. editl. bd. Jour. Investigative Dermatology, 1977-82, Jour. Clin. and Lab. Immunology, 1977—, Archives of Dermatology, 1978-87, sect. editor Am. Jour. Dermatopathology, 1981-83, Clin. Aspects Autoimmunity, 1989-92. Elder Grace Presbyn. Ch., Houston, 1987—; bd. dirs. CAnCare of Houston, 1991-2001, pres. bd. dirs., 1997-99, chmn. bd., 1999-2001. Lt. comdr. M.C., USN, 1965-71. Recipient Bacelli Research award SUNY, Buffalo, 1965, Med. Spltys. Outstanding Achievement award Mayo Found., 1969, Marion B. Sulzberger award Am. Soc. Dermatologic Allergy and Immunology, 1983, award Am. Skin Assn., 1999, JB & Blanche Earthman award 2002. Mem. AAAS, AMA, Soc. Investigative Dermatology (com. nominations 1986—, dir. 1977-82, v.p. 1993-94), Am. Acad. Dermatology (co-chmn. com. lab. proficiency and quality control in immunodermatology 1980-83, dir. Immunopathology Symposium 1981-86, bd. dirs. 1993-98), Am. Assn. Immunologists, Am. Dermatol. Assn., Am. Fedn. Clin. Research, Am. Soc. Clin. Investigation, Assn. Profs. Dermatology (bd. dirs. 1987-89), Central Soc. Clin. Research, Dermatology Found. (chmn. med. and sci. com. 1980-81, trustee 1993-98, discovery award 2000), Soc. Exptl. Biology and Medicine, Lupus Erythematosus Soc. Wis. (mem. med. adv. bd. 1977-83), Wis. Dermatol. Soc. (pres. 1979-80), Wis. State Med. Soc., Chgo. Dermatol. Soc., Tex. Med. Assn., Houston Dermatol. Soc., Lupus Soc. Houston (adv. bd. 1986—90), Sigma Xi. Home: 376 Green Cove Dr Montgomery TX 77356-8267 Office: U Tex Health Sci Ctr Houston TX 77030 Office Phone: 713-500-8336. Business E-Mail: robertejordon@uth.tmc.edu. *

JORDT, SVEN-ERIC, pharmacologist, researcher; BS in Biochemistry, Free U. Berlin, 1993, PhD, 1997. Fellow U. Calif., San Francisco, 1998, German Acad. Natural Sciences, 1998—2001; asst. prof. dept. pharmacology Yale U. Sch. Medicine, principal investigator Jordt Lab. Recipient Outstanding New Environmental Scientist award, Nat. Inst. Environ. Health Sciences, 2006, Early Excellence award, Sandler Found. for Asthma Rsch., 2007. Office: Yale University School of Medicine Dept Pharmacology 333 Cedar St PO Box 208066 New Haven CT 06520-8066 Office Phone: 203-785-2159. E-mail: sven.jordt@yale.edu.

JORFELDT, LENNART SVEN, retired physiologist, educator; b. Stockholm, June 18, 1936; MD, Karolinska Inst., 1964, PhD, 1970. Prof., ad interem Karolinska Inst., Huddinge Hosp., Dept. Clin. Physiology, 1973—76; sr. lectr., dept. clin. physiology Linköping U., 1976—85, vice chmn., dept. medicine, study programs bd., 1980—84, head and vice head, dept. pharmacology and physiology, 1980—86, mem., rsch. programme bd., 1984—91, prof., dept. clin. physiology, 1985—91; emeritus prof., dept. clin. physiology Karolinska Hosp., 1991—2001. Recipient Lectr. award, Linköping U. Mem.: Swedish Soc. Cardiology, Swedish Soc. Pulmonary Medicine, Swedish Soc. Nuc. Medicine, Swedish Soc. Clin. Physiology (chmn., tech. and quality assurance bd. 1973—80, chmn., vice chmn. 1990—96). Avocation: history. Home: Bromma Kyrkväg 461A Bromma Stockholm 168 58 Sweden Personal E-mail: lennart.jorfeldt@ki.se.

JORGE, TEREZA CRISTINA MARINHO, medical educator; b. Rio de Janeiro, Apr. 27, 1955; M, IME, 1981; D, UEM, 2005. Prof. U. Estadual do Oeste do Paraná, 1988—. Office: Rua Universitária 2069 Cascavel Paraná 85919110 Brazil Office Fax: 45 3220 3280. Business E-Mail: tcmjorge@unioeste.br.

JORGENSEN, GERALD THOMAS, psychologist, educator, lawyer; b. Mason City, Iowa, Jan. 15, 1947; s. Harry Grover and Mary Jo (Kollasch) J.; m. Mary Ann Reiter, Aug. 30, 1969; children: Amy Lynn, Sarah Kay, Jill Kathryn. BA maxima cum laude with honors, Loras Coll., 1969; MS in Psychology, Colo. State U., 1970, PhD in Psychology, 1973; JCL in Canon Law, Cath. U. Am., 1998. Lic. psychologist, Iowa; lic. canonist Cath. Ch.; cert. health svc. provider Nat. Register, Iowa; ordained to ministry Roman Cath. Ch. as deacon, 1979. Psychology intern Counseling Ctr., Colo. State U., Ft. Collins, 1971—72, VA Hosp., Palo Alto, Calif., 1972—73; psychologist Loras Coll., Clarke Coll., Dubuque, Iowa, 1973—76; asst. prof. psychology Loras Coll., 1976—80, assoc. prof., 1981—93, dir. Ctr. for Counseling and Student Devel., 1977—86, assoc. dean of students, 1985—86, dean students, v.p. student devel., 1986—93; cons., supervising psychologist Gannon Ctr. for Cmty. Mental Health, 1977—2006. Assoc. med. staff Mercy Med. Ctr., 1989—, mem. credentials com.,

1992—, chmn. credentials com. 2007-; asst. dir. for formation Office of Permanent Diaconate, Archdiocese of Dubuque, 1979-93, 96—, dir., 1993-96; auditor Met. Tribunal, 1993-98, cons. psychologist, 1993—, judge, 1998—, promoter of justice, 2009-; promoter justice Archdiocese of Dubuque, 2009-; mem. Iowa Bd. Psychology Examiners, Des Moines, chair, 1984-90, coord. continuing edn., 1983, mem., 2003-08, vice-chmn., 2005-08, chmn. 2008; sec.-gen. First Internat. Congress on Licensure, Cert. and Credentialing of Psychologists, New Orleans, 1995. Contbr. articles to profl. jours. Treas. Dubuque County Assn. Mental Health Inc., 1975-82, v.p., 2002—. NDEA fellow, 1969-72. Fellow Assn. State and Provincial Psychology Bds. (exec. com. 1986-89, pres. 1989-92, Morton Berger award 1996); mem. APA, ACA, Am. Coll. Pers. Assn. (chmn. com. VII 1980-82), Iowa Psychol. Assn. (treas. 1976-80, exec. coun. 1980-83, highest honors 1990), Nat. Assn. Diaconate Dirs. (sec. 1983-85, treas. 1985-90, award 1991), Canon Law Soc. Am. (sec. 2002—04), Iowa Student Pers. Assn., Fedn. Assns. Reg. Bds. (v.p. 1993-94, 96-97, pres. 1994-96), Delta Epsilon Sigma, Phi Kappa Phi, Sigma Tau Phi. Democrat. Roman Catholic. Avocations: walking, reading. Office: Archdiocesan Ctr 1229 Mount Loretta Ave Dubuque IA 52003-7826 Home Phone: 563-556-7239; Office Phone: 563-556-2580. Business E-Mail: dbqcmtaud@arch.pvt.k12.ia.us.

JORGENSEN, JUDITH ANN, psychiatrist, educator; b. Parris Island, SC; d. George Emil and Margaret Georgia Jorgensen; m. Ronald Francis Crown, July 11, 1970 (dec. Oct. 1996). BA, Stanford U., 1963; MD, U. Calif., 1968. Cert. sex therapist Am. Assn. Sexuality Educators, Counselors and Therapists. Intern Meml. Hosp., Long Beach, Calif., 1969-70; resident County Mental Health Svcs., San Diego, 1970-73; staff psychiatrist Children and Adolescent Svcs., San Diego, 1973-78; practice medicine specializing in psychiatry La Jolla, Calif., 1973—. Staff psychiatrist County Mental Health Svcs. San Diego, 1973—78, San Diego State U. Health Svcs., 1985—87; psychiat. cons. San Diego City Coll., 1973—78, 1985—86; asst. prof. dept. psychiatry U. Calif., 1978—91, assoc. prof., 1991—96; chmn. med. quality rev. com. Dist. XIV, State of Calif., 1982—83. Fellow: Am. Soc. Adolescent Psychiatry, Am. Psychiat. Assn. (disting. life fellow); mem.: Sex Therapy and Edn., Soc. Sci. Study of Sexuality, San Diego Soc. Adolescent Psychiatry (pres. 1981—82), San Diego Psychiat. Soc. (chmn. membership com. 1976—78, v.p. 1978—80, fed. legis. rep. 1985—87, fellowship com. 1989—), Rowing Club. Office: 470 Nautilus St Ste 211 La Jolla CA 92037-5981 Office Phone: 858-459-1140. Office Fax: 858-551-0964.

JORGOVA-MAKEDONSKA, JULIA BORISSOVA, cardiologist, consultant; b. Sofia, Bulgaria, June 24, 1952; m. Krum Iordanov Makedonski; 1 child, Boris Krumov Makedonski. MD, Med. U., Sofia, 1977, PhD, 1997. Diplomate Bulgarian Bd. Internal Medicine, Bulgarian Bd. Cardiology, Bulgarian Bd. Invasive and Interventional Cardiology. Gen. practitioner Out Patient Dept., Studena, Pernic, Bulgaria, 1977—79; resident in internal medicine and cardiology Med. U., Sofia, 1979—84, head ICU, CCU, 1984—87, staff, cons. cardiologist, 1987—89, head cardiology clinic, 1990—2005, 2005—. Named Dr. of Yr., Bulgarian Med. Assn., 2004. Fellow: Am. Coll. Cardiology, European Soc. Cardiology; mem.: Bulgarian Soc. Interventional Cardiology (pres. 2000—05), Bulgarian Soc. Cardiology (pres. 2004—). Home: Nicola Mirchev 27 G Ap32 Sofia 1113 Bulgaria Office: Univ Hosp St Ekaterina P Slavenkov 52A 1431 Sofia Bulgaria Personal E-mail: jorgova@yahoo.com.

JORIZZO, JOSEPH L., dermatology educator; b. Rochester, NY, Oct. 6, 1951; s. Joseph Lucius and Margaret R. (Volpe) J.; m. Susan MacLeod, Aug. 23, 1975 (div.); children: John Joseph, Michael Wesley; m. Irene Carros, Dec. 30, 1995; 1 child, Melina Margaret. AB, Boston U., 1972, MD magna cum laude, 1975. Diplomate Am. Bd. Dermatology. Intern in internal medicine N.C. Meml. Hosp., Chapel Hill, 1975-76, resident in dermatology, 1976-78, chief resident, 1978-79; overseas registrar Dermatology Inst. St. John's Hosp. for Diseases of the Skin, London, 1979-80; clin. asst. prof. dept. dermatology U. Tex. Med. Br., Galveston, 1979-80, from asst. prof. dept. dermatology to assoc. prof. dept. dermatology, 1980-86; prof. Sch. Medicine of Wake Forest U., Winston-Salem, NC, 1986—, prof. and founding chair dept. dermatology, 1986—2002. Cons. VA Clinic, Winston-Salem, 1986—, Forsyth Meml. Hosp., Winston-Salem, 1989—, VA Hosp., Salisbury, N.C., 1991—; mem. med. adv. bd. Am. Behcet's Disease Assn., 1988—, Winston-Salem/Forsyth County Lupus Found., 1989—; co-chmn. Southeastern Consortium for Dermatology, 1990, steering com., 1987—; mem. internat. steering com. Bechet's Disease, 1989—; mem. adv. com. Nat. Student Rsch. Forum, 1981-86; speaker more than 100 meetings, symposia, U.S. and Europe; vis. prof. Cath. U. Rome Med. Sch., 1981, U. Ark. Med. Scis., Little Rock, 1982, Brooke Army Med. Ctr., San Antonio, 1982, U. Louisville, 1982, U. N.Mex., Albuquerque, 1985, U. Mich., Ann Arbor, 1985, Duke U. Med. Ctr., 1986, U.Va., Charlottesville, 1986, Emory U., Atlanta, 1986, 92, U. South Fla., Tampa, 1987, Brown U. Med. Ctr., Providence, R.I., 1990, U. Ind., Indpls., 1991, NYU Med. Ctr., 1991, Columbia U., N.Y.C., 1993, U. Pitts., 1993, many others; invited speaker numerous meetings including Chapel Hill Alumni Dermatology Conf., 1981, Immunology Club Meeting, Galveston, 1984, Fla. Dermatol. Soc. Ann. Meeting, Ft. Lauderdale, 1984, Stetson lectr. N.Mex. Dermatol. Soc., Albuquerque, 1985, Mich. Dermatological Soc., Shanty Creek, 1985, Charlotte Dermatol. Soc., 1986, Greensboro Dermatopathology/Dermatology Semiann. Meeting, 1987, N.C. Med. Soc., 1987, Richmond-Tidewater Dermatologic Soc., Williamsburg, Va., 1988, AARP, Winston-Salem, 1988, No. Calif. Dermatologic Assn., North Lake Tahoe, Calif., 1989, Stiefel Can. Symposium, Key Biscayne, Fla., 1990, Dermatologic Soc. Greater N.Y., 1990, Westwood Conf. Clin. Dermatology, Hilton Head, S.C., 1990, Westwood Conf., Charleston, S.C., 1991, Charlotte Dermatol. Soc. Meeting, 1992, N.C. Med. Soc. Dermatology Sect., 1992, Charlotte Family Practice Soc., 1993. Co-author: Dermatological Signs of Internal Disease, 1988; contbr. chpts. to books, more than 90 articles to profl. jours.; author abstracts in field; reviewer Archives of Dermatology, 1981—, Jour. Am. Acad. Dermatology, 1981—, Pediatric Dermatology, 1986—, Jour. Investigative Dermatology, 1986—, Internat. Jour. Dermatology, 1984—, JAMA, 1988—, others; mem. editorial bd. Clin. and Exptl. Dermatology, 1988—, Jour. Am. Acad. Dermatology, 1988-93, Archives of Dermatology, 1990—, Jour. European Acad. of Dermatology and Venereology, 1992—, Current Problems in Dermatology, 1992—, Practical Cases in Dermatology, 1993—, others. Trustee Forsyth County Day Sch., Winston-Salem, 1990-94, chmn. devel. com., 1991-92, coord. new parent's bldg. fund, 1987-88; participant med bowl fund raiser for Crisis Control, Winston-Salem, 1990. William Reed traveling fellow, 1979, Am. Acad. Dermatology fellow, 1982, 84, Dermatology Found. fellow, 1983, Upjohn Pharm. Co. Spl. grantee, 1982, Ital. Dermatology Soc. grantee, 1981, Italian Found. Rsch. Dermatology grantee, 1981, Wellcome Trust/Royal Soc. Medicine grantee, 1993, Dermatology Found. grantee, 1984, 86, 87, Noah Worcester Dermatologic Soc. grantee, 1986, Nat. Inst. Dental Rsch. grantee, 1985-86, Neutrogena grantee, 1986, Am. Cyanamid Co. grantee, 1987, Hoechst-Roussel grantee, 1988, numerous other grants including Herbert Labs., Genderm, Dermik Labs., R.W. Johnson Pharms., Stiefel Labs., Pfizer Labs., Curatek Pharms., Allergan Herbert, Bristol-Myers Squibb, Hoffman LaRoche Dermatologics, Glaxo Pharm. Co., RJR Nabisco, Ortho-McNeil Pharms. Fellow ACP; mem. AMA, Soc. Investigative Dermatology (sec.-treas. So. sect. 1984-85, v.p. So. sect. 1985-86, pres. So. sect. 1986-87, membership com. 1987-90, chmn. membership com. 1989-90), Am. Acad. Dermatology (mem. numerous coms. including internat. affairs 1981-84, summer session com. 1989—, chmn. clin. studies session 1990, nominating com. 1993—, v.p.-elect 2002--, chmn. various awards coms., media tng. recipient 1984), Am. Coll. Cyrosurgery, Dermatology Found. (dir. membership subcom. 1983-85, devel. com. 1983-86), So. Med. Assn., Forsyth County Med. Soc. (Membership Task Force 1989-90), N.C. Med. Soc., N.C. Dermatology Soc., Am. Fedn. Clin. Rsch., Psoriasis Found., Noah Worcester Dermatologic Soc., N.Am. Clin. Dermatological Soc., Pacific Dermatologic Assn. (hon.), Am. Dermatologic Assn., Am. Bd. Dermatology (Part I test com.), Societe Francaise de Dermatologie et de Venereologie, Am. Skin Assn., Internat. Soc. Tropical Dermatology, St. John's Dermatological Soc. (U.K.), Sir James Saunders Soc., Academia Medicorum Litteratorum (Italy), South Ctrl. Dermatological Soc. (organizing com. 1981-84, program com. 1984-86),Italian Soc. Dermatology and Venereology (corr.), Brit. Assn. Dermatologists (overseas mem.), Assn. Profs. Dermatology (internal medicine com. 1984-86), Dowling Club (U.K.), Phi Beta Kappa, Sigma Chi Rsch. Soc., Alpha Omega Alpha. Home: 4424 Bent Tree Farm Rd Winston Salem NC 27106-4252 Office: Wake Forest U Sch Med Dept Dermatology Med Ctr Blvd Winston Salem NC 27157-0001

JOSEHART, CARL, rehabilitation hospital administrator; BA in psychology, Washington U. St. Louis, MSW George Warren Brown Sch. Social Work. Clinician then moved into leadership positions in acute care hospitals, rehab. and ambulatory care; sr. v.p., COO Schwab Rehab. Hosp., Chgo., 2002—07; CEO Memorial Hermann The Inst. Rehab. and Rsch., Houston, 2007—. Mem.: American Hosp. Assn. (governing coun. long-term care and rehab. 2009). Office: TIRR 1333 Moursund St Houston TX 77030

JOSEPH, JOHN H., facial plastic surgeon, educator; Grad. in Biology, U. Ill., MD. Diplomate Am. Bd. Otolaryngology, cert. facial plastic and reconstructive surgery. Med. sch. tng. and gen. surgery intern Univ. Ill., Chgo.; resident head and neck surgery Univ. Iowa Hosps.; fellow with Dr. Frank Kramer in facial plastic and reconstructive surgery; attending physician UCLA; asst. clin. prof. UCLA David Geffen Sch. of Medicine; founder and dir. Brighton Med. Corp. Author many rsch. papers. Recipient UCLA Tchg. award; named Top Plastic Surgeons, LA Mag.; named one of the Leading Surgeons in the US, Harper's Bazaar and W Mags. Office: Brighton Medical Corporation Ste 203 9400 Brighton Way Beverly Hills CA 90210 Office Phone: 310-859-7139. Office Fax: 310-859-9241.

JOSEPH, MARIES, pediatrician, consultant; b. Trichur, Kerala, India, Sept. 29, 1956; arrived in UAE, 2000; d. Rappai Kochappu Malliakkal and Mariam Mathew Kaitharath; m. Jose Joseph, May 4, 1980; children: Claire Ann, Eugene Michael. MBBS, Bangalore U., India, 1980; DCH, St. Johns Med. Sch., Bangalore, 1985. Diplomate Am. Bd. Pediatrics. Resident Vimal Hosp. and Damien Inst., Trichur, 1980—82; resident in pediat. St. Johns Med. Coll. Hosp., Karnataka, India, 1982—85, Children's Hosp. Med. U. S.C., Charleston, 1992—93, fellow, clin. genetics, 1993—95; sr. ho. officer Barnsley Gen. Hosp., S. Yorkshire, England, 1988—89, Rotherham Gen. Hosp., S. Yorkshire, 1990—91; cons. pediatrician Amala Hosp., Trichur, 1996—97, Social Ins. Hosp., Riyadh, Saudi Arabia, 1997—99, Al Ain (United Arab Emirates) Hosp., United Arab Emirates, 2000—. Adj. asst. prof. United Arab Emirates U., Al Ain, 2000—. Contbr. articles to profl. jours. Scholar, Countess Dufferin Fund, 1980—96, Nat. Merit Scholarship Fund India, 1980—94. Fellow: Am. Acad. Pediat., Royal Coll. Pediat. and Child Health; mem.: Royal Coll. Physicians. Roman Catholic. Avocations: gardening, sewing, crafts, travel. Office: UCSF 155 N Fresno St Fresno CA 93701 Personal E-mail: mariesjoseph@yahoo.com. Business E-Mail: mjoseph@fresno.ucsf.edu.

JOSEPH, MARILYN SUSAN, gynecologist; b. Aug. 18, 1946; BA, Smith Coll., 1968; MD cum laude, SUNY Downstate Med. Ctr., Bklyn., 1972. Diplomate Am. Bd. Ob-Gyn, Nat. Bd. Med. Examiners. Intern U. Minn. Hosps., 1972-73, resident in ob-gyn, 1972-76; med. fellow specialist U. Minn., 1972-76, asst. prof. ob-gyn, 1976—, dir. women's clinic, 1984—. Med. dir. Boynton Health Svc., 1993-2007; asoc. med. dir. Boynton Health Svc., 2007-. Author: Differential Diagnosis Obstetrics, 1978. Fellow Am. Coll. Ob-Gyn (best paper dist. VI meeting 1981); mem. West Metro Med. Soc., Minn. State Med. Assn., Minn. State Ob-Gyn Soc. Avocations: cooking, bird watching, travel. Office: Boynton Health Svc 410 Church St SE Minneapolis MN 55455-0346 Office Phone: 612-626-5422. Business E-Mail: mjoseph@bhs.umn.edu.

JOSEPH, RAMON RAFAEL, internist, educator; b. NYC, May 17, 1930; s. Felix R. and Helen Joseph; m. Mary Ann Kowalchik, June 16, 1956 (dec. Jan 25, 2006), m. Karen Marie Moran, Feb 18, 2010; children: Ricardo George, Maria Ann Thompson, Lisa Marie Benson. BS, Manhattan Coll., 1952; MD, Cornell U., 1956. Diplomate Nat. Bd. Med. Examiners, Am. Bd. Internal Medicine. Intern Meadowbrook Hosp., Hempstead, NY, 1956-57, resident, 1957, Wayne County Gen. Hosp., Westland, Mich., 1959-62, dir. gastroenterology, 1962-84, asst. dir. internal medicine, 1964-73, dir., chmn., 1973-84, pres. med. staff, 1971-72; cons. internal medicine and gastroenterology Annapolis Hosp., 1962-87; from instr. internal medicine to prof. U. Mich., 1962-85, prof. emeritus, 1998—; asst. dean U. Mich. Med. Sch., 1973-84; 1st v.p., dir. Univ. Med. Affiliates PC, 1981-84; pres., CEO Univ. Med. Affiliates (P.C.), 1985-87; med. dir. Henry Ford Hosp. Westland (Mich.) Ctr., 1987-94; sr. attending physician Henry Ford Hosp., Detroit, 1987-95. Cons. gastroenterology St. Mary Hosp., Livonia, Mich., 1966—95, chmn. divsn. of gastroenterology, 1987-93. Contbr. articles to profl. jours. Mem. Community Commn. on Drug Abuse, Livonia and Westland, Mich., 1970-73; mem. Mich. Dept. Edn. Council on Drug Abuse, cons. on drug abuse public schs., Livonia, 1968-74; pres. Livonia Sch. Bd. Adv. Council, 1970-71. Capt. US Army, 1957—59. Fellow ACP; mem. Am. Fedn. Clin. Research, Am. Gastroent., Assn., AAAS, Assn. Am. Med. Colls., AMA, N.Y. Acad. Sci., Detroit Gastroent. Soc. (pres. 1969-70), Mich., Wayne County Med. Socs., Am. Assn. Lab. Animal Sci., Am. Soc. Gastrointestinal Endoscopy, Am. Soc. Internal Medicine, Mich. Soc. Gastrointestinal Endoscopy (pres. 1982-86), Mich. Soc. Internal Medicine, Assn. Program Dirs. in Internal Medicine. Personal E-mail: rjoseph517@gmail.com. Business E-Mail: rrj22@cornell.edu.

JOSEPH, RICHARD SAUL, cardiologist, educator; b. NYC, Mar. 27, 1937; s. Charles Irving and Lillian (Horowitz) J.; m. Frances B. Rappaport, Jan. 27, 1963; children: Lauryl, James, Alisa, Jennifer. BA magna cum laude, Hofstra Coll., 1958; MD, Albert Einstein U., 1962. Intern U. Utah Affiliated Hosp., Salt Lake City, 1962-63; resident in chest medicine Bronx (N.Y.) Mcpl. Hosp., 1963-64; resident in internal medicine Mt. Sinai Hosp., NYC, 1966-68; fellow in cardiology Nassau County Med. Ctr., East Meadow, N.Y., 1968-69; pvt. practice cardiology Huntington (N.Y.) Hosp., 1969—, chief cardiology, 1981-90, attending cardiology, 1973—; asst. prof. clin. medicine cardiology SUNY, Stony Brook, 1973—74. Cons. in cardiology Kings Park Hosp., N.Y., 1971—; electro cardiographer Huntington Hosp., 1971—, co-dir. cardiac stress lab., 1975—; dir. Huntington Cardiac Rehab., 1977-94; adj. attending cardiologist St. Francis Hosp., Roslyn, N.Y., 1993-2000. Contbr. articles to profl. jours. Speaker med. adv. bd. Suffolk County Heart Assn., Blue Point, N.Y., 1971-73; speaker med. dir. Huntington (N.Y.) YMCA, 1973-77. Lt. USN, 1964-66. Recipient Pres. prize Hofstra Coll., Uniondale, N.Y., 1954; named Valedictorian Hofstra Coll., Uniondale, N.Y., 1958. Fellow Am. Coll. Cardiology; mem. Alpha Omega Alpha. Jewish. Avocations: jogging, piano. Office: 205 E Main St Huntington NY 11743-2923

JOSEPHA, JOSEPH, nursing educator; b. Jaffna, Apr. 14, 1955; BSN, Bangalore U., India, MSN, 2002; PhD in Cmty. Medicine, Tromso U., Norway, 2011. Adminstr. and tchr. Faculty Health Care Scis., Eastern U., Sri Lanka, 2006, sr. lectr., head, dept. supplementary health scis., 2006—. Mem.: Rsch. Com. and Publ. (faculty bd. mem., senate mem.). Avocations: singing, reading. Home: Holy Cross Convent Trinco Rd Batticoloa Sri Lanka Office Phone: 94 65 3642326. Home Fax: 94 65 2227286. Personal E-mail: josepha_joseph@yahoo.com.

JOSEPHBERG, ROBERT GARY, ophthalmologist, consultant, retina and vitreous surgeon; b. NYC, Oct. 22, 1950; s. Sol and Sally (Lampert) J.; m. Lisa Monique Harth, Sept. 18, 1958; children: Sari, Daniel. BS, U. Wis., 1972; MD, Albany Med. Coll., NY, 1976. Diplomate Am. Bd. Ophthalmology. Intern in medicine Meml. Hosp., Worcester, Mass., 1976-77; resident in ophthalmology U. Medicine and Dentistry, NJ, 1977-80; fellow in retina and vitreous surgery Baylor U., Houston, 1980-82. Asst. clin. prof. NY Med. Coll., Valhalla, 1985—, NJ Coll. Medicine, Newark, 1985—, NJ Coll. Medicine, New Brunswick, 1982—; chief of retina Westchester Med. Ctr.-NY Med. Coll. Vol. surgeon Project Orbis, 1982, 85, 87. Mem. AMA, Fla. Med. Assn., Assn. Rsch. and Vision in Ophthalmology, Am. Acad. Ophthalmology, NY State Med. Soc, NY State Ophthal. Soc., NJ Retina Soc., Atlantic Coast Retina Group, NJ Ophthal. Soc., Am. Soc. Retinal Specialists(nominating com. 1996-98), Aspen Retinal Detachment Soc., Westchester County Med. Soc., Phi Kappa Phi. Achievements include patents for portable vitrectomy machine for endophthalmitis (Visitrec). Avocation: skiing. Office: 984 N Broadway Ste 511 Yonkers NY 10701-1308 Office Phone: 914-965-2526. Personal E-mail: rj2526@aol.com.

JOSEPHSON, JORDAN STUART, otolaryngologist; b. Dec. 15, 1957; BS in Chemistry, SUNY, Albany, 1979; MD, SUNY Downstate Med. Sch., Bklyn., 1983. Intern gen. surgery Long Island Jewish Hosp., 1983-84, chief resident otolaygoly, 1984-88; fellow in endoscopic sinus surgery Johns Hopkins Med. Sch., Balt., 1989; otolaryngologist N.Y. Nasal and Sinus Ctr., NYC, 1994—. Author, editor: Medical Clinics of North America, 1991, 2d edit., 1993; author: Sinus Relief Now, 2006; contbr. articles to profl. jours., chpt. to book. Recipient Functional Endoscopic Sinus Surgery Tchg. award, 1989, NIH Recognition for Svc. and Dedication award, 1989-94, cert. of recognition Best Drs. N.Y. Metro Area, 1994—, N.Y. Magazine Best Doctors in NY, 2004, Honors award by the American Academy of Otolaryngology-Head and Neck Surgery, 2004. Mem. AMA, Am. Rhinologic Soc., Am. Acad. Otolaryngology, Head and Neck Surgery, N.Y. State County Med. Soc. Avocations: skiing, music, reading, writing. Office: NY Nasal and Sinus Ctr 111 E 77th St New York NY 10021-1802 Office Phone: 212-717-1773.

JOSEPHSON, STEPHEN C., psychiatrist, educator; Diplomate cognitive behavior therapy, behavioral psychology, cert. sex therapist AASECT. Coord Rutgers Med. Sch. Sleep Disorders Lab.; sr. cons. Beth Israel Hosp. Stroke Prevention Clinic; sr. supr. Cornell Med. Ctr. Inpatient Obsessive-Compulsive Disorders unit; dir. Internat. Ctr. Disabled Hypertension Program, Behavior Med. Assocs.; assoc. prof. dept. psychiatry Cornell U. Med. Sch.; assoc. prof. Columbia U. Coll. Physicians & Surgeons. Office: 815 5th Ave Ste 1A New York NY 10065 Office Phone: 212-888-2777. Office Fax: 212-888-4888.

JOSHI, ANIL KUMAR, orthopedist, educator; b. Lucknow, India, May 11, 1975; MBBS, GSVM Med. Coll., Kanpur, India, MS in Orthops., 1999, Allahabad U., 2004. Rsch. assoc., sr. resident All India Inst. Med. Scis. New Delhi, India, 2005—08; asst. prof. Med. Coll., 2009—. Asst. prof. V.C.S.G. Govt. Med. Scis. & Rsch. Inst., Srinagar, Uttarakhand, India, 2008—. Mem.: Ao Spine, Indian Orthop. Assn. Avocations: cricket, football. Home: Type IV/10 HNB Base Hosp Campus PO Sriko Pauri Garhwal Uttarakhand 246174 India Personal E-mail: draniljoshi75@rediffmail.com.

JOSHI, AVNI Y., pediatrician, researcher; b. India, Sept. 13, 1976; MB, BChir, MD, B.J. Med. Coll., Gurjarat U., Ahmedabad, Gurjarat, India. Diplomate Am. Bd. Pediat. Grad. edn. in pediat. B.J. Med. Coll., U. Buffalo Sch. Medicine & Biomedical Scis.; fellow in allergy, immunology & infectious diseases Mayo Clinic, Rochester, Minn., 2006—10; instr. pediatric medicine, divsn. pediatric infectious disease & allergy/immunology, dept. pediatric & adolescent medicine Mayo Clinic Coll. Medicine. Contbr. articles to profl. jours. Office: Mayo Med Labs 3050 Superior Dr NW Rochester MN 55901 Business E-Mail: joshi.avni@mayo.edu. *

JOSHI, C.S., research and development company executive; b. India, June 15, 1968; PhD in Phytochemistry, DSB Campus, Nainital, 2000.

Head, R & D divsn. Sanat Products Ltd., gen. mgr., R & D, 2010—. Recipient Technologist award, Dept. Sci., New Delhi; Rsch. Assoc. fellowship, ICMR, New Delhi. Avocation: reading. Home: HS Kuti Deshraj Colony Pilikothi Haldwani Uttarakhand 263001 India Personal E-mail: drcsjoshi19@yahoo.com.

JOSHI, MAHESH, biochemist, educator; b. India, May 15, 1962; PhD, Mysore U., 1992. Prin. investigator Fla. Internat. U., 2008, rsch. asst. prof., 2008—. Office: 10555 W Flagler St Miami FL 33174 Personal E-mail: mjoshi20@yahoo.com.

JOSHI, SUDHA KIRAN, research scientist; b. Chandigarh, India, June 15, 1979; MSc in Microbiology with honors, Punjab U., Chandigarh, 2004, PhD in Molecular Biology, 2011. Rsch. fellow PGIMER Hosp. Punjab U., Chandigarh, 2006. Mem.: European Microbiologists Assn. Avocations: painting, poetry, music, interior decorating. Office: Dept Biotechnology Punjab University Chandigarh 160014 India Personal E-mail: d_susiin@yahoo.com.

JOSIFOVA, TATJANA, ophthalmologist; b. Skopje, Macedonia, Aug. 9, 1962; d. Tomislav Petreski and Snezana Petreska; 1 child, Martin Josifov. MD, U. Medicine, Skopje, Macedonia, 1986, PhD, 2005. Registered Macedonian and Switzerland Chamber Ophthalmology, ct. expert ophthalmology Macedonia. Fellow Medicine U., Munster, Germany, 1984, ophthalmologist; sci. investigator U. Eye Clinic, Skopje, 1988—2007, chief Dept. Retinal Vascular Disorders, 1992—2007, retinologist Nürnberg, Germany, 1994—95, vitreoretinal surg. edn. Würzburg, Germany, 1999—2000, vitreoretinal surgeon Skopje, 2002—07, chief vitreoretinal surgery Basel, Switzerland, 2007. Cons. United Nations devel. programe project DEUS Ophthalmology Clinic, Skopje, 2002—04; supervisory phisican Eye Clinic, Stip and Tetovo, Macedonia, 2004—07; study investigator Bayer Pharma, Germany, 2007, Novartis, Switzerland, 2008; spkr. in fields. Contbr. articles to med. jours. & books. Mem. German-Macedonian Assn., Skopje, 1996—2007, Orgn. Com. Deutscher Akademischer Austausch Dienst and Hombold grants, Skopje, 2006—07; humanitary activities Lions Club, Skopje, 2005—06. Grant, Deutscher Akademischer Austausch Dienst, Germany, 1994, Phare, Belgium, 1999, Orbis Internat., USA, 2000. Mem.: European Assn. Predictive Preventive & Personalised Medicine (Nat. Swiss rep. 2008), Internat. Soc. Ocular Trauma, Macedonian, German and Switzerland Ophthalmology Soc., Assn. Rsch. Vision Ophthalmology (guest editor, med. jours. & articles rev.). Achievements include development of vitreoretinal surgery and retinal research. Avocations: travel, skiing, reading. Office: Univ Ophthalmology Clinic Mittlere Strasse 91 4031 Basel Switzerland Office Fax: 41 61 265 86 19. Business E-Mail: tjosifova@uhbs.ch.

JOSIPOVIC JELIC, ZELJKA, neurologist; b. Vares, Bosnia and Herzegovina, May 27, 1956; MD, U. Medicine, 1981. Head neurology dept. Polyclinic Medikol, 2005—. Home: Novakova 26 Zagreb 10000 Croatia Personal E-mail: zeljka.josipovic-jelic@si.t-com.hr.

JOSLOFF, ROBERT K., surgeon; BS magna cum laude, Muhlenberg Coll., 1981—85; MD, Thomas Jefferson U., 1985—89. Diplomate Am. Bd. Surgery. Resident gen. surgery Abington Meml. Hosp., 1989—94; fellow in advanced laparoscopic & endoscopic surgery Univ. N.Mex., 1994—95; instr. dept. of surgery Univ. N.Mex. Sch. of Medicine, 1994—95, asst prof. dept. of surgery, 1995, instr. dept. of surgery Veteran's Adminstrn. Med. Ctr., 1994—95, asst prof dept of surgery, 1995; clin. asst. prof. surgery Temple Univ. Sch. of Medicine, 1995—; pres. med. staff Abington Meml. Hosp., 2006—08, with exec. com., 2008—, attending surgeon, 1995—. Named Top Docs, Phila. Mag., 2011. Office: Abington Memorial Hospital 1200 Old York Rd Abington PA 19001 Office Phone: 215-481-2000.

JOST, WOLFGANG HEINZ, neurologist; b. Landau id Pfalz, Germany, Aug. 15, 1959; s. Heinz and Waldetrudis Agnes Katharina (Scheibenreif) J.; children: Caroline M., Anna-Theresa L., Leonard H., Clava S. Physician, J.W. Goethe U., Frankfurt, Germany, 1985; Med. Registration/MD, Dr.med., J. Gutenberg U., Mainz, 1989. Intern U. Mainz, 1988; resident dept. neurology U. Saarland, 1989, physician in practice dept. neurology Homburg, 1989-91, physician, 1991-93, physician dept. psychiatry, 1994, cons. dept. neurology, 1995; chief neurologist dept. neurology/clin. neurophysiology German Diagnostic Clinic, Wiesbaden, 1995; habilitation U. Saarland, 1995, asst. prof. neurology, 1996-2000, prof., 2000—; dean Europa Fachhochschule Idstein, 2001—02. Editor: Diagnosis of Parkinson's Diseases, 2006, Therapy of Parkinson's Disease, 16th edit., 2011, Neurology of the Pelvic Floor, Treatment of Advanced Parkinson's Diseases, 2008, Pictorial Atlas of Botulinum Toxin Injection, others; editor-in-chief Jour. Kontinenz, 1991-95, Jour. Neurodate, Basel Ganglia, 2011; mem. editl. bd. Jour. Coloproctology, 1998; contbr. 180 articles to profl. jours. Mem. Movement Disorder Soc., European and Germany Soc. Neurology (Parkinson award 1996), German Continence Soc. (bd. dirs.), Am. Autonomic Soc., German Autonomic Soc. (bd. mem.), German Botulinumtoxin Group (vice-chmn.), German Parkinson Soc. (chair) Roman Catholic. Office: German Diagnostic Clinic Aukammallee 33 D-65191 Wiesbaden Hessen Germany Home Phone: 0049-611-509643; Office Phone: 0049-611-577430. E-mail: jost.neuro@dhd-wiesbaden.de.

JOU, HEI-JEN, obstetrician, gynecologist, researcher; b. Chung-Hwa, Taiwan, Republic of China, Mar. 26, 1960; s. Yung-Tien Chow, Hsien-Nu Chou Chen; m. I-Ping Hsu; children: Te-Chuan, Pei-Lin, Te-Yuan. MD, National Taiwan U., Taipei, 1985, MBA, 2001. Resident Nat. Taiwan U. Hosp., 1987—91, Provincial Tao-Yuan Gen. Hosp., Tao-Yuan, Taiwan, 1991—92, vis. ob-gyn., 1992, Nat. Taipei Nursing Coll. Hosp., Taipei, Taiwan, 1994—96, Nat Taiwan U. Hosp., Taipei, Taiwan, 1992—, Taiwan Adventist Hosp., Taipei, Taiwan, 1996—, head women's weight control, 2001—06, head perinatology, 2001—, chief ob-gyn., 2006—. V.p. of Retirement Found. Taiwan Adventist Hosp., 2001—; lectr. Coll. Medicine Nat. Taiwan U. Hosp., Taipei, 1996—2004; lectr. Ministry Edn., Taipei, 1997—2006, asst. prof., 2006—. Editor: (jour.) Advanced Ob-Gyn., 1994; translator: Celestial Lancets: A History & Rational of Acupuncture & Moxa, 1995; author: Pregnancy Book (by Chinese), 1996, Menopause Book (by Chinese), 1997, Youth, Happiness and Climacterism (by Chinese), 2001. Profl. peer rev. doctor Bur. Nat. Health Ins., Taipei, 2001—; chmn. Taipei Women Health Promotion Assn, Taipei, 1998—. Recipient Gold prize for poster, 1st Internat. Congress of Perinatal Medicine, 1991. Mem.: Soc. Menopause of Republic of China, Soc. Infertility and Endocrinology of Republic of China, Soc. Perinatology of Republic of China, Soc. Ob-Gyn of Republic of China, Soc. Ultrasound in Medicine of Republic of China, Formosan Med. Assn. Achievements include research in antenatal diagnosis; antenatal sonographic findings of fetuses with chromosmoal aberratoins. Avocations: travel, reading. Office: Taiwan Adventist Hosp 424, Sec 2, Ba-De Rd Taipei 105 Taiwan Office Phone: 886-2-8773 2205. Business E-Mail: jouhj@ms12.hinet.net.

JOUNG-HYUN, PARK, food scientist, educator; b. Busan, Republic of Korea, Feb. 22, 1969; MS, Pukyoung Nat. U., 1997, PhD, 2000. Marine bio-resources rsch. team mem. Korea Food Inst., 2001—04; with, biobusiness divsn. Hit Co. Ltd., 2004—05; mem., product planning team Dongwoo Indsl. Co. Ltd., 2006—10; rsch. prof., dept. food sci. and nutrition Dankook U., 2011—. Mem.: Korean Soc. Food Sci. and Tech. Avocation: swimming. Office: 126 Jukjeon-Dong Suji-Gu Yongin Gyeonggi 448-701 Republic of Korea Office Fax: 083180053170. Personal E-mail: pdc327@hanmail.net.

JOVANOVIC, ALEKSANDRA, healthcare educator; b. Belgrade, Serbia, June 24, 1964; BSc with honors, Belgrade, Serbia, 1998, MSc, 2007. Lectr. Faculty Health Scis., 2007—. Avocations: painting, interior decorating. Office: 7 York Rd Parktown 2193 Johannesburg Gauteng 2193 South Africa Office Fax: 27117172422. Business E-Mail: aleksandra.jovanovic@wits.ac.za.

JOVANOVIC, GORAN, genetics educator; b. Belgrade, Yugoslavia, May 18, 1961; s. Branislav and Jelena (Djukic) Jovanovic; m. Ljiljana Martinovic, Nov. 5, 1987 (div. May 1998); 1 child, Milica; m. Milija Jovicic, Aug. 15, 1998; children: Visnja, Anka. BS, Faculty Biology, Belgrade, 1986, MS, 1990; PhD, The Rockefeller U., 1997. Rsch. asst. Inst. Molecular Genetics, Belgrade, 1988-93; tchg. asst. Faculty Biology, Belgrade, 1989-97; ind. rschr. Inst. Molecular Genetics, Belgrade, 1997-98; asst. prof. Faculty Biology, Belgrade, 1997-99, assoc. prof., 1999—; rsch. assoc. U. Geneva, Switzerland, 1998—2000; sr. rsch. assoc. Inst. Molecular Genetics and Genetic Engring., Belgrade, 1999—2004, sci. counselor, 2004—; sr. rsch. assoc. Imperial Coll., London, 2004—. Inventor in field. Rsch. fellow Beckman Fund Biomed. Rsch., 1994-97, Rockefeller U., 1993-97, Nat. Fund for Sci., 1998-2000, Wellcome Trust, 2004-10, Biotech. Biol. Sci. Rsch. Coun., 2009-. Mem. AAAS, Am. Soc. for Microbiology, Biochem. Soc.-UK. Office: Imperial Coll London Divsn Biology Faculty Sci Saf Bldg Imperial College SW7 2AZ London England Office Phone: 44 (0)2075045366. E-mail: g.jovanovic@imperial.ac.uk.

JOVANOVIČ, LOIS, medical researcher; b. Mpls. BS in Biology, Columbia U., NYC, 1969; B in Hebrew Lit., Jewish Theol. Seminary, NYC, 1968, M in Hebrew Lit., 1970; MD, Albert Einstein Coll. Medicine, Bronx, NY, 1973. Intern, resident NY Hosp./Cornell U. Med. Coll., 1973—76; endocrinology & metabolism fellow Cornell U. Med. Coll., 1976—78, instr., asst. then assoc. prof., 1978—86; assoc. adj. prof. U. Calif., Irvine, 1986—88; sr. scientist Sansum Diabetes Rsch. Inst., Santa Barbara, Calif., 1985—96, CEO, chief sci. officer, 1996—; clin. assoc. prof. medicine U. So. Calif.- LA Med. Ctr., 1986—89, prof., 1989—; rsch. biologist U. Calif., Santa Barbara, 1990—, adj. prof. biomolecular sci. & engring. Asst. attending physician NY Hosp., 1978—85; asst. adj. prof. Rockefeller U., NYC, 1979—85; physician Rockefeller U. Hosp., 1979—85. Author numerous books and articles on diabetes and women's health. Recipient Robert & Ray Kroc award for excellence in diabetology, Sweden, 2002, Agnes Higgins award for disting. achievement in maternal-fetal nutrition, March of Dimes, 2003, Louis Izenstein award for excellence in diabetes care, Tufts U. Baystate Med. Ctr., 2009; named a Health Hero, Santa Barbara Neighborhood Clinics, 2009. Fellow. ACP, NY Acad. Medicine, Am. Coll. Endocrinology (Clintec award for excellence in clin. nutrition), Am. Coll. Nutrition. Office: Sansum Diabetes Research Institute 2219 Bath St Santa Barbara CA 93105 Office Phone: 805-682-7638. Office Fax: 805-682-3332. *

JOWERS, RONNIE LEE, university health sciences center executive; b. Columbia, SC, July 4, 1951; s. Talbert Joseph and Mary Helen (Reed) J.; m. Kay Byars, July 6, 1974; children: C. Ryan, Ivey Amanda. BA, Furman U., 1973; MBA, Clemson U., 1984. Acct., mortgage banker First Piedmont Mortgage Co., Greenville, S.C., 1972-76; fin. mgr. Greenville Hosp. System, 1976-80; bus. mgr. Greenville Gen. Hosp., 1980-81; adminstr., med. edn. Greenville Hosp. System, 1981-87; adminstrv. dept. medicine Emory U., Atlanta, 1987-91, assoc. v.p. for health affairs, 1991-2000, v.p. for health affairs, 2000—, CFO, Woodruff Health Scis. Ctr., 2003—; CFO Emory Healthcare, 1995—2004. Bd. dirs. Clifton Casualty Ins. Co., 2003—08; co-mgr. Emory Med. Care Found., Atlanta, 1989—90; chmn. adv. coun. S.C. Consortium of Cmty. Tchg. Hosps., Charleston, SC, 1982—86; adj. asst. prof. Med. U. S.C.; bd. dirs. Emory Adventist Hosp., 2002—, vice chmn. bd. dirs., 2003—. Transp. chmn. Beat Leukemia Celebrity Classic, 1988—97; vice chair, fin. com. and deacon 1st Bapt. Ch. Decatur, 2011—; mem. nat. planning com. Sr. Adminstrn. Acad. Health Ctr. Meetings, program chmn., 1997, 2011; treas. Greenville Hosp. Sys. Credit Union, 1980—84, pres., 1985; bd. trustee Devel. Disabilities Ministries, Pathways Success Inc. Mem. Am. Coll. Healthcare Execs. (assoc.), Acad. Health Ctrs. Assn., mem. of Ways and Means Com., Emory Univ., Beta Gamma Sigma. Baptist. Avocations: autograph collecting, magic. Home: 1980 Grace Arbor Ct NE Atlanta GA 30329 Home Phone: 404-315-4861; Office Phone: 404-727-4360. Business E-Mail: rjowers@emory.edu.

JOX, RALF J., physician, educator; b. Weingarten, Baden-Württemberg, Germany, July 9, 1974; s. Rainer Rudolf and Angela Jox; m. Lucia Bodyová, Sept. 3, 2005; children: Jakob Adam, Julia Clara. MD, Ludwig-Maximilians U., Munich, Germany, 2002; MA, King's Coll., London, 2003; Bakk. in Phil., Sch. Philosophy, Munich, 2001. Resident physician and postdoctoral rschr. U. Hosp. Munich, Interdisciplinary Ctr. for Palliative Medicine (IZP), Munich, 2003—; rsch. fellow Inst. Applied Ethics and Med. Ethics, Basel, Switzerland, 2005—06; resident physician U. Hosp. Psychiatry and Psychotherapy, Klinikum Rechts Der Isar, Tech. U. Munich, Munich, 2007—08; asst. prof. Inst. Ethics, History and Theory of Medicine, U. Munich. Reviewer Sci. Jours. Recipient German acad. award, 2004; Internat. Rsch. fellowship, Bavarian Rsch. Trust, 2005—06, Rsch. grant, German Ministry Edn. and Rsch. (BMBF), 2008—. Mem.: German Soc. Neurology (DGN), Munich Competence Ctr. Ethics (MKE) (mem. ethics working group), German Soc. Palliative Medicine, German Acad. Ethics Medicine. Office: Univ Hosp Munich IZP Marchioninistrasse 15 Munich Bavaria D-81377 Germany Business E-Mail: ralf.jox@med.uni-muenchen.de.

JOY, ROBERT JOHN THOMAS, medical educator; b. South Kingstown, RI, Apr. 5, 1929; s. Angelo Francois and Mary Frances (Egan) Joy; m. Beverly June Boxer, July 5, 1952 (div. May 1984); children: Robert L.F., Lisa; m. Janet Lucille Brady, July 12, 1985. BS, U. RI, Kingston, 1950; MD, Yale U., New Haven, Conn., 1954; MA, Harvard Coll., Cambridge, Mass., 1965; cert., Armed Forces Staff Coll., 1968; D in Mil. Medicine (hon.), U. Health Scis., 2009. Commd. 1st lt. US Army, 1954, advanced through grades to col., 1970; intern, resident Walter Reed Army Med. Ctr., Washington, 1954-58; asst. dir. environ. medicine USA Med. Rsch. Lab., Fort Knox, Ky., 1959-61; comdr. USA Rsch. Inst. Environ. Medicine, Natick, Mass., 1961-62; chief comdr. USA Med. Rsch. Team, Saigon, Vietnam, 1965-66; chief med. rsch. div. Office Surgeon Gen., US Army, Washington, 1968-69; dep. med. life scis. Office Dir. Def. Rsch. Engring., Washington, 1969-71; dep. dir., dir. Walter Reed Inst. Rsch., Washington, 1971-76; prof., chmn. mil. medicine Uniformed Svcs. U. Health Scis., Washington, 1976-81, prof., chmn. med. history, 1981-96, prof. emeritus, 1996—; ret. US Army, 1981. Hon. mem. faculty Indsl. Coll. Armed Forces, Washington, 1990; faculty mem. USAF Sch. Aerospace Medicine, 1992—. Editor: Jour. History Medicine and Allied Scis., 1983—87; contbr. articles to profl. jours. Decorated DSM, Legion Merit (4); recipient John Shaw Billings award, Am. Mil. Surgeons of US, 1986, William P. Clements award Uniformed Svcs., U. Health Scis., 1980. Fellow: Coll. Physicians Phila., AAAS, ACP (Davies award Med. Humanism 2002); mem.: Am. Physiol. Soc., Am. Assn. History Medicine (coun. 1979-81) (William Osler medal 1954), Osler Soc. (bd. govs. 1986-89). Home: 5821 Highland Dr Bethesda MD 20815-5531 Office: Uniformed Svcs U Dept Med History 4301 Jones Bridge Rd Bethesda MD 20814-4712 Home Phone: 301-654-2965.

JOYCE, DIANA, psychologist, education educator; d. Donald Ray and Caroline Ann Joyce. PhD, U. Fla., Gainesville, 2000. Cert. clin. educator Dept. Edn., Fla., 2002, lic. school psychologist 2003, psychologist 2004. Outside examiner Psychol. Corp., Orlando, Fla., 2001—03; sch. psychologist Hillsborough County Schools, Tampa, Fla., 2000—03; faculty spl. ednl. Sch. Psychology & Early Childhood Studies U. Fla., 2003—. Author: Essentials of Temperament Assessment. Mem.: APA, Nat. Assn. Sch. Psychologists (nat. cert. sch. psychologist 2001), Fla. Assn. Sch. Psychologists. Methodist. Achievements include research in temperament-based preferences of students with oppositional defiant disorder and conduct disorder; social-emotional assessment for behavior disorders & behavioural Response-to-Intervention. Avocations: travel, art. Business E-Mail: djoyce@coe.ufl.edu.

JOYCE, JUDITH MARIE, radiologist; d. William Charles and Janet Margaret Hugenberg; m. Edward James Joyce, Aug. 16, 1975; children: Janet Margaret, Molly Sandra. BSN, U. Tex., San Antonio, 1977, MD, 1983. Bd. cert. radiologist Am. Bd. Radiology, 1987, bd. cert. in nuc. medicine Am. Bd. Nuc. Medicine, 1988; RN Ohio, 1974. Asst. prof. U. Ky., Lexington, 1988—89; chief and assoc. chief nuc. medicine The Western Pa. Hosp., Pitts., 1989—2003; assoc. prof. Temple Med. Sch., Pitts., 2001—03, U. Pitts. Med. Ctr., 2003—. Radiology residency program dir. The Western Pa. Hosp., Pittsburgh, Pa., 2002—03. Contbr. articles to profl. jours. Recipient Radiology Resident Tchg. award, Western Pa. Hosp. Radiology Residents, 2000—01, Ronald J. Hoy Excellence in Tchg. award, U. Pitts. Med. Ctr. Radiology Residents, 2004—05. Mem.: Am. Coll. Radiology, Soc. Nuc. Medicine (pres. Pitts. chpt. 1995—2002). Home: 103 Downing Dr Pittsburgh PA 15238 Office: Univ Pitts Med Ctr 200 Lothrop St Pittsburgh PA 15213 Business E-Mail: joycejm@upmc.edu.

JOYCE, MICHAEL DANIEL, neuro technology consultant; b. St. Cloud, Minn., June 8, 1948; s. Francis Daniel and Bernadette (Ferkinhoff) J.; m. Patricia Mary Boom, July 7, 1969. BA in Psychology and Sociology, St. Cloud State U., 1973, postgrad., 1977, Moorhead State U., 1993, Atwood Inst., 1993, Biofeedback Tng. and Treatment Ctr., 1994. Cert. behavior analyst, rsch. analyst, Minn., master practitioner of neuro-linguistic programming, Colo.; cert. hypnotherapist, neurolearning therapist; cert. in hemisphere specific auditory stimulation; cert. to practice hemisphere specific auditory stimulation; cert. in biofeedback; cert in EEG neurofeedback. Resident mgr. Dan J. Brutger, Inc., St. Cloud, 1969-71; rsch. analyst Faribault (Minn.) State Hosp., 1974-75, behavior analyst, 1975-76; therapist/behavior analyst Ctrl. Minn. Mental Health Ctr., St. Cloud, 1977-78; emotional/behavior disabled facilitator, chpt. 1 tutor Perham (Minn.) Dent Schs., 1978-92, dir. neurofeedback svcs. Tech. cons. Inclusive Edn. Tech. Assistance Team, Region IV, State of Minn., Perham, 1991-93, Personal Resource Strategies, Vergas, Minn., 1994-99; dir. neurotechnology svcs. A Chance To Grow, Mpls., 1999-2004, Personal Resource Strategies, Roseville, Minn., 2004-; trainer and mentor Minn. Learning Resource Ctr., Mpls., 1999—. Co-author: Life-Threatening Behavior: Analysis and Intervention, 1982, Audio-Visual Entrainment Program as a Treatment for Behavior Disorders in a School Setting—Journal of Neurotherapy, 2001. Coord. Youth Assn. for Retarded Citizens, St. Cloud, 1977-78; developer propritory protocols to accompany launch new model, Audio Visual Entrainment Device, respite care provider Ctrl. Minn. Mental Health Ctr., St. Cloud and Perham, 1977-78, 79-86; vol. Perham Schs., 1978—, Spl. Olympics - Winter Games, Duluth, Minn., 1980, 81. Named Mem. of Yr. Minn. Sch. Employees Assn., 1989. Mem. Neuro-Linguistic Programming (cert. master level), Internat. Med. and Dental Hypnotherapy Assn. (cert. neurolearning therapist). Avocations: organic gardening and orcharding, tree farming, basketball, computers, psycho-technology hardware and software. Home: 1749 Roselawn Ave W Saint Paul MN 55113-5757 Office Phone: 651-647-0490. Personal E-mail: mdmjoyce@hotmail.com.

JOYNT, ROBERT JAMES, academic administrator, physician; b. Le Mars, Iowa, Dec. 22, 1925; MD, 1952, PhD, 1963. Diplomate Am. Bd. Psychiatry and Neurology. Intern Royal Victoria Hosp., Montreal, Que., Canada, 1952—53; chief neurology Strong Meml. Hosp., Rochester, NY, 1966—84; assoc. U. Iowa, Iowa City, 1957—58, asst. prof. neurology, 1958—61, assoc. prof., 1961-66; prof. neurology U. Rochester, 1966—, chmn. dept., 1966—84, Disting. Univ. prof., 1997; dean U. Rochester Sch. Medicine and Dentistry, 1984—89, v.p., vice provost for health affairs, 1989—94. Fulbright scholar, Cambridge U., 1953—54, USPHS fellow, 1954—57. Fellow: AAAS; mem.: AMA (chief editor Arch Neurology 1982—97), Am. Bd. Psychiatry and Neurology (dir. 1973—80, v.p. 1978, pres. 1979), Am. Acad. Neurology (past pres.), Am. Neurol. Assn. (past pres.), Inst. Medicine, Royal

Soc. Medicine, Am. Electroencephalographic Soc. Office: U Rochester Sch Medicine and Dentistry PO Box 673 Rochester NY 14642-0001 Business E-Mail: robert_joynt@urmc.rochester.edu.

JÓZSEF, SÓKI, molecular biologist; b. Makó, Csonrád, Hungary, May 16, 1965; s. József Antal Sóki and Rozália Kresztúri. PhD, U. Szeged, Hungary, 2000. Cert. in molecular biology and biotechnology Attila József U., Szeged, 1989. R & D scientist Biotechnika Ltd., Szeged, 1989—90; asst. rschr. Albert Szent-Györgyi Med. U., Szeged, 1990—93; rsch. assoc. U. Szeged, 1998—. Contbr. 30 sci. papers. Rsch. grant, Hungarian Nat. Rsch. Fund, 2002—05. Mem.: European Soc. Clin. Microbiology and Infectious Diseases (Rsch. grant 2003), Am. Soc. Microbiology, Hungarian Soc. Microbiolgy. Office: Univ Szeged Semmelweis U 6 Szeged Csongrád H-6725 Hungary Home: Hargitai Utca 58/A 6726 Szeged Hungary Office Fax: 36 62 545712. Personal E-mail: dr.soki.jozsef@invitel.hu. Business E-Mail: soki@mlab.szote.u-szeged.hu.

JUAN, ANTONIO AGUERO, retired medical educator; b. Almeria, Spain, May 29, 1941; Degree in Psychiatry Medicine, 1965; MD, Facultad Medicina, 1968. Adj. prof. Medicine Sch., 1968—2010; rschr., psychiatry medicine, 1968—2011. Mem.: Soc. Española De Psiquiatria. Avocation: golf. Home: Baron De Carcer 24 PTA 21 Valencia 46001 Spain Personal E-mail: antonio.aguero@uv.es.

JUAN, CHI WEN, hospital administrator, consultant; b. Changhua County, Taiwan, May 18, 1962; s. Feng Yen Juan and Chin Yeh Yeh; m. Hsiu Lan Chen; children: Yu Chung, Yu Tang, Tzu Ming. PhD, Chung Shan Med. Coll., Taichung, Taiwan, 1989. Cert. in internal medicine Dept. Health Exec. Yuan, Taiwan, 1995, in family medicine 1997, in emergency medicine 1995, 1997, Soc. Emergency & Critical Care Medicine, Taiwan, 1999, Soc. Ultrasound Medicine, 2006, instr. advanced hazmat life support AHLS Internat. Office, 2006, EMS med. dir. Justice Inst. BC, 2006, incident comdr. hazardous materials course Govt. Office Emergency Svcs., Calif. Specialzed Trainin, 2006. Resident, emergency medicine Changhua Christian Hosp., 1991—95, attending physician, emergency medicine, 1995—2002, attending physician, family medicine, 1997—2002, dir., acute care unit, 1995—2001, dep. dir., emergency medicine, 2001—02; dir., emergency medicine Show Chwan Meml. Hosp., Changhua, 2002—07, vice supt., emergency critical care and cmty. medicine, 2007—09; supt. Lee's Hosp., Taichung, 2009—. Cons. Fire Bur. Changhua County, 2003—, Shinchu County Club Red Cross Soc., Taiwan, 2004—, Emergency Operation Ctr., Ctrl. Taiwan Region Dept. Health Exec. Yuan, Taichung, 2005—. Editor jours. Lt. Army, 1989—91, Taiwan. Recipient Honor forensic physician, Changhua Dist. Prosecutors Office, 1996. Fellow: Changhua Med. Assn. (supr. 2003), Taiwan Assn. Family Medicine. (trustee bd. 2006), European Soc. Intensive Care Medicine, Taiwan Soc. Emergency Medicine (trustee bd. 1998), Soc. Emergency & Critical Care Medicine (trustee bd. 1998), Changhua County Club (trustee bd. 2005). Buddhism. Avocation: travel. Home: No 216 Chien Kuo N Rd Changhua Taiwan 500 Taiwan Office: Show Chwan Meml Hosp No 542 Sect 1 Chung-Shang Rd Changhua Taiwan 500 Taiwan Office Phone: 886-4-7256166, 886-4-26862288. Office Fax: 886-4-26883978. Personal E-mail: juanchiwen@yahoo.com.tw.

JUAREZ, ANTONIO, psychotherapist, counselor, consultant, educator; b. El Paso, Tex., Nov. 6, 1952; s. Juan Antonio and Amelia (Rivas) J. BS in Psychology, U. Tex.-El Paso, 1976, MA in Clin. Psychology, 1982; postgrad., N.Mex. State U., 1987—, Calif. Coast U., 1990—. Cert. counselor; cert. diplomate, Am. Psychotherapy Assn., lic. profl. counselor, Tex., PhD of Martial Arts, Ea. USA Internat. Coll. Martial Arts, Pittsburgh, 2000. Caseworker asst. El Paso Mental Health Ctr., 1978-79, caseworker III, 1982-83; clin. specialist S.W. Mental Health Ctr., Las Cruces, N.Mex., 1979-80; therapist, trainer S.W. Cmty. House, El Paso, 1980-81; psychol. cons. El Paso Guidance Ctr., 1981-82, psychotherapist, 1983—, dir. N.E. svcs.; pvt. practice El Paso, 1987—. Mem. Nat. Bd. for Cert. Counselors; dir. Cross-Cultural Counseling Ctr., 1988-04; asst. prof. psychology El Paso C.C., 1988-90, faculty coord. social scis., counselor, cons.; cons. Citizens and Students Together, El Paso, 1983—; group facilitator, Tai Chi Chuan instr. Sun Valley Regional Hosp., El Paso, Tex., 1988; psychotherapist, treatment team coord. El Paso State Ctr., 1997—; adj. prof. counseling Webster U., Ft. Bliss, Tex., 1995—. Mem. Latin Am. com. N.Mex. State U., 1985. Served with USAF, 1972-76. Recipient Faculty Achievement award, El Paso CC, 2007, CC Disting. Svc. award, Tex. Assoc. Chicanos Higher Edn., 2009. Fellow Am. Assn. Integrative Medicine, US-Mex. Border Health Assn., El Paso Psychol. Assn., Tex. Assn. Counseling and Devel., Tex. Assn. Children of Alcoholics, Nat. Acad. Clin. Mental Health Counselors, Nat. Istn. Staff and Orgnl. Devel, Ea. US Martial Arts Assn. (Black Belt Hall of Fame 1996, Master of Wushu 2000), Ea. US Internat. Martial Arts Assn. (named Man of Yr. 2003, Black Belt Hall of Fame 2003, Grandmaster of Yr. Eastern US Internat., 2008), Golden Key. Democrat. Roman Catholic. Avocations: martial arts, playing stringed instruments. Office: Cross-Cultural Counseling Ctr PO Box 20500 El Paso TX 79935 Business E-Mail: antonioj@epcc.edu.

JUAREZ, FERNANDO, psychologist; PhD in Health Psychology cum laude, Autonoma U. Madrid, 1997. Lic. psychologist Psychology Ofcl. Coll. of Madrid, Spain, 1993, Health Sec., Boyaca, Colombia, 2005, Health Sec., Cundinamarca, Colombia, 2006. Prof. El Bosque U., Bogota, Colombia, 1997—2005, rschr., 1997—. Rschr. Cath. U. Colombia, Bogota, 1997—2006, Ctrl. Mil. Hosp., 1998—2000, Pedagogic and Technologic U. Colombia, Tunja, 2004—05, La Sabana U., 2006—07, San Buenaventura U., 2007; prof. Pedagogic and Technologic U. Colombia, 2003—05. Contbr. articles to profl. jours. Mem.: APA, Assn. Coll. of Psychology, Health Psychology Latin Am. Assn. Achievements include research in Neuromuscular Rehabilitation Methodology; violent behavior patterns. Home: Avenida Carrera 45 No 94-27 apt 301 Bogotá Colombia Personal E-mail: fernando_juarez2@yahoo.com.

JUAREZ OLGUIN, HUGO, pharmaceutics educator; b. Mexico City, Sept. 21, 1959; s. Gervacio Juarez Palafox and Julia Olguin Monroy; m. Graciela Tapia Reyes, Mar. 9, 1991; children: Belen, Victor. Student, Colegio de Bachilleres, Mex., 1978; MS, U. Autonoma Met. Mex., 1983. Paramedic coord Inst. Nat. Perinatologia, Mexico City, 1987-91; assoc. prof. U. Nacional Autonoma Mex., Mexico City, 1988—; assoc. rschr. Inst. Nacional Pediatria, Mexico City, 1991—, chief dept. pharmacology, 1998—. Contbr. articles to profl. jours. Recipient award Inst. Nat. Perinatology, 1988-90, 93-99, U. Nat. Autonoma Mex., 1996-99. Mem. N.Y. Acad. Scis., Assn. Mex. Pharm., Assn. Mex. Med. Inst. Nat. Avocations: family, concerts, soccer, travel. Home: Emiliano Zapata No 25 Col Malinche Mexico City 10310 Mexico Office: Inst Nacional Pediatra Av Iman No 1 Col Cuicuilco Mexico City 04530 Mexico Fax: 525 606 8058. E-mail: juarezol@yahoo.com.

JUDE, EDWARD, endocrinologist, consultant; b. Mumbai; MBBS, MD, St Johns Med. Coll., Bangalore, 2003. Registered DNB, doctorate in medicine Eng., 1994. Cons. diabetes and endocrinology Tameside Gen. Hosp., Ashton-under-Lyne, Lancashire, England, cons. physician, 2001—, reader medicine, 2011—. Master: RCP. Achievements include research in treatment for charcot neuroarthropathy, first RCT. Office: Tameside Hosp NHS Found Trust Fountain St Ashton-under-Lyne Lancashire OL6 9RW England Office Phone: 00441613316964. Business E-Mail: edward.jude@tgh.nhs.uk.

JUDELSON, DANIEL A., medical educator; b. New Haven, May 13, 1977; PhD, U. Conn., 2006. Asst. prof. Calif. State U., Fullerton, 2006—. Fellow: Am. Coll. Sports Medicine; mem.: Nat. Strength and Conditioning Assn., Am. Physiol. Soc. Office: 800 N State College Blvd Fullerton CA 92834 Office Fax: 657-278-5317. Business E-Mail: djudelson@fullerton.edu.

JUDGE, KATHLEEN W., dermatologist; MD, La. State U. Med. Ctr. Diplomate Am. Bd. Dermatology. Resident La. State Univ. Med. Ctr.; hosp. affiliations include Orlando Regional Healthcare, Fla. Hosp., Health Ctrl. Mem.: AMA, Leader Soc. Dermatology Found., Am. Acad. of Anti-Aging Medicine, Am. Soc. for Dermatologic Surgery, Fla. Med. Assn., Am. Soc.of Cosmetic Dermatology & Aesthetic Surgery, Orange County Med. Soc., Am. Soc. for Laser Medicine & Surgery, Women's Dermatologic Surgeon's Interest Group, Women's Dermatology Soc., Fla. Soc. of Dermatology and Dermatologic Surgeons, Ctrl. Fla. Soc. of Dermatology, Am. Acad. of Dermatology. Office: Central Florida Dermatology Associates 700 E Michigan St Orlando FL 32806 Office Phone: 407-481-2620.

JUDSON, PATRICIA LYNN, obstetrician, gynecologist, oncologist; 2 children. BS, Hamline U., St. Paul, 1987; MD, U. Minn., 1998. Assoc. prof. U. Minn., Mpls., 1999—2011, dir. gyn. oncology, 2011—, fellowship dir. Mpls., 2003—11; dir. gyn. oncology North Meml. Med. Ctr., Robbinsdale, Minn., 1999—2009; assoc. prof. Moffitt Cancer Ctr., 2011—. Med. adv. bd. Minn. Ovarian Cancer Alliance, St. Louis Park, 1999—. Reviewer: Jour. Ob-Gyn., 1987—, Jour. Gyn. Oncology, 2000—; contbr. articles to profl. jours., chapters to books. Sci. adv. com. Gyn. Oncology Group, 2005—06. Named one of America's Top Obstetricians and Gynecologists, Consumers' Rsch. Coun. of Am., 2004—10, Top Twin Cities Doctors for Women, Minn. Monthly Mag., 2006—10. Fellow: ACS (life); mem.: Soc. Gynecol. Oncologist (edn. com. 2006), Minn. Women Physicians, Minn. Soc. Clin. Oncology, Deborah E. Powell Ctr. for Women's Health, Am. Coll. Ob-Gyn. (life; program com. 2001—05). Lutheran. Office: Moffitt Cancer Ctr MOF-SOU 12902 Magnolia Dr Tampa FL 33612

JUDY, KEVIN D., neurosurgeon; MD, Pittsburgh U., 1984. Diplomate Am. Bd. Neurol. Surgery, lic. Pa., 1985. Intern in gen. surgery Mercy Hosp. Pitts., 1985, resident in gen. surgery, 1986; fellow in neurology Johns Hopkins Hosp., 1991, resident in neurology, 1992; hosp. affiliations include Hosp. Univ. Pa., Thomas Jefferson Univ. Hosp., Pa., Meth. Hosp. divsn. Named one of Top Doctors, Phila. Mag., 2009—10, Best Doctors in America, 2009—10, America's Top Doctors, 2010. Fellow: Am. Coll. of Surgeons; mem.: Congress of Neurol. Surgeons, Am. Assn. of Neurol. Surgeons. Office: Thomas Jefferson University Hospital Methodist Hospital Division 2nd Fl 909 Walnut St Philadelphia PA 19107 Office Phone: 215-955-7000. Office Fax: 215-503-9170.

JUERGENS, STEVEN MANLEY, psychiatrist; MD, Mayo Med. Sch., 1979. Lic. Wash., 1981, diplomate Am. Bd. Psychiatry and Neurology-psychiatry, 1986, Am. Bd. Psychiatry and Neurology-addiction psychiatry, 2003. Intern Hennepin County Med. Ctr., 1980; resident psychiatry Univ. Wash. Med. Ctr., 1981—83, Mayo Clinic Health System, Rochester, Minn., 1983—85; hosp. affiliations includes Overlake Hosp. Med. Ctr. Named one of Top Doctors, Seattle Mag., 2010—. Office: Overlake Hospital Medical Center Overlake Psychiatry Department 11201 SE 8th St Ste 105 Bellevue WA 98004 Office Phone: 425-454-0255. Office Fax: 425-454-3066.

JUERGENS, UWE ROLF, internist, pneumologist, allergist; s. Rolf and Liselotte Juergens; m. Heike Greiner, Aug. 19, 1988; children: Lisa Joy, Anna Mai Joy, Marie Joy, Julia Joy. MD, Med. Sch., U. Bonn, Med. Clin. II, Dept. Pneumology, Germany, 1982; Habilitation in Internal Medicine, Med. Sch.,U. Bonn, 1999. Cert. in internal medicine Ärztekammer Nordrhein Düsseldorf, 1994, prof. respiratory medicine Med. Faculty U. Bonn, 2005, in respiratory medicine Ärztekammer Nordrhein, Düsseldorf, 2002, in allergology Ärztekammer Nordrhein, Düsseldorf, 2004. Postdoc. dept. exptl. medicine Scripps Clinic & Rsch. Found., La Jolla, Calif., 1989—91; head dept. pneumology, allergology, sleepmedicine U. Hosp. Bonn, Med. Clinic and Outpatient Clinic II, Bonn, Germany, 1985—. Rschr. dept. pneumology-allergology-sleepmedicine U. Hosp. Bonn, 1992—2008; coordinate rschr. Actelion Inc, Freiburg, Germany. Contbr. to profl. journals (Wollheim award, German Soc. Internal Medicine, 1989). Mem.: Am. Biographical Inst., Deutscher Hochschulverband, European Respiratory Soc., German Soc. Internal Medicine, German Soc. Pneumology, Am. Thoracic Soc., Alexander von Humboldt Found. Achievements include discovery of mechanism aspirin desensitization,aspirin intolerance; mechanism anti inflammatoy and anti-oxidative activities monoterpenes; development of clinical use 1.8-cineol as co-medication in asthma, COPD and sinusitis; clinical and an in vitvo research on the antioxident activity of the monoterpense 1.8-cineol to improve steroid resistance in COPD and asthma; research in perpetuation systemic inflammation following long-term smoking cessation in COPD; characterization pro-inflammatory function endothelin B-receptor. Avocations: boating, travel, golf. Home: Rheinallee 2 Niederkassel 53859 Germany Office: Univ Hosp Bonn Med Clin Outpatient Clin II Sigmund Freud St 25 Bonn D 53105 Germany Office Phone: 49-228-287-15052. Office Fax: 0049 228 287 4983; Home Fax: 0049 228 455192. Personal E-mail: juergens_uwe@t-online.de. Business E-Mail: uwe.juergens@ukb.uni-bonn.de.

JUHASZ, ISTVAN, dermatologist, surgeon; b. Sajoszentpeter, Hungary, June 19, 1956; s. Istvan Juhasz and Iren Szabo; m. Eszter Csanky, Feb. 12, 1985; children: Lili, Levente. MD, U. Med. Sch. Debrecen, Hungary, 1981, PhD, 1994. Bd. cert. surgeon Hungary, bd. cert. dermatologist Hungary, bd. cert. oncologist Hungary. Asst. prof. dept. dermatology U. Med. Sch. Debrecen, 1981—89, assoc. prof., head dermatol. surgery, burn and dermatosurgery unit dept. dermatology, 1994—, head coordinating dept. surg. techniques, Dental Sch., 2001—; vis. scientist Wistar Inst. Anatomy and Biology, Phila., 1989—92; Szechenyi prof. Ministry of Edn., Budapest, 1999—2003. Mem. ethical com. Hungarian Med. Chamber, Debrecen, 1998—2003; sec.-gen. Hungarian Dermatol. Soc., Budapest, 2001—04; mem. exec. bd. Med. Coll. Hungarian Dermatologists, Budapest, 2004—. Contbr. articles to profl. jours. Dir. bd. curators Found. for Burn Victims, Debrecen, 1997—. Recipient Fekete Zoltan award, Hungarian Dermatol. Soc., 1994, Kaposi Mor award, 2005, Stefan G. Nicolau award, Romanian Dermatol. Soc., 2002. Mem.: Hungarian Burn Assn. (pres. 2004—), European Burn Assn. (ex-officio mem. exec. bd. 2005), European Acad. Dermatology and Venerology, European Soc. Dermatol. Rsch. Roman Catholic. Office: U Debrecen Med and Health Sci Ctr Nagyerdei Krt 98 H-4032 Debrecen Hungary Office Phone: 36 52 425 285. Office Fax: 36 52 414 632. Business E-Mail: ji@dote.hu.

JU-HYUNG, LEE, physician, educator; b. Republic of Korea, Oct. 13, 1977; MD, Chonbuk Nat. U., 2009, PhD. Assoc. prof. Chonbuk Nat. U. Med. Sch., 2009—. Home: San 2-20 Geumam-dong Jeonju Jeonbuk 561-180 Republic of Korea Personal E-mail: premd77@jbnu.ac.kr.

JUKIC, DRAZEN MARIJAN, dermatologist; b. Zagreb, Croatia, Nov. 4, 1968; MD, U. Zagreb Sch. Medicine, 1993, PhD, 1998. Vis. asst. prof. U. Zagreb Sch. Medicine, 2004; asst. prof., dermatology and pathology U. Pitts. Sch. Medicine, 2001—11; assoc. prof., pathology, cell biology and dermatology U. South Fla., Sch. Medicine, 2011; chief, dermatopathology and telepathology James A. Haley Veterans Adminstrn. Med. Ctr., 2010—. Spokesperson Coll. Am. Pathologists, 2002; adv. mem. Intel, 2004—07; dir., quality assurance program Am. Soc. Dermatopathology, 2007. Recipient award, Sulzberger Inst. Dermatol. Rsch.; grant, Veterans Adminstrn., NIH, Agy. Healthcare Rsch. and Quality. Mem.: Am. Acad. Dermatology, Coll. Am. Pathologists, Internat. Soc. Dermatopathology, Am. Soc. Dermatopathology. Avocations: history, martial arts. Office: 13000 Bruce B Downs Blvd PLMS 113 Tampa FL 33647 Business E-Mail: jukicdm@ovi.com.

JULHAKYAN, HUNAN, hematologist, researcher; b. Yerevan, Armenia, June 15, 1980; PhD, Med. U., MD, 2003. Oncohematologist, fellow Hematology Sci. Ctr., 2003—. Office: Noviy Zikpvskiy proezd 4 Moscow 127165 Russia Business E-Mail: hunan_julhakyan@mail.ru.

JULIÁ-MOLLÁ, M. DOLORES, gynecologist; b. Valencia, Spain, Apr. 25, 1950; Degree in Medicine and Surgery, Valencia U., 1973, PhD in Reproductive Endocrinology, 1985. Residency endocrinology and nutrition La Fe U. Hosp., 1978—82, gynecologic endocrinology asst., 1977—93, gynecologic endocrinology chief, 1993—. Doctoral thesis supr. Sch. Medicine, U. Valencia, 1962—66, 1998—2002, adj. prof., ob-gyn. dept., 2009—11. Grant, Social Security San. Rsch. Fund., Work and Social Affairs Ministery, Woman's Inst., Valencian Inst. Health Studies. Mem.: Spanish Soc. Menopause Study, Phytotherapy Rsch. Group, Spanish Fertility Soc., Ob-Gyn. Spanish Soc. Avocations: reading, travel, sailing. Office: La Fe Hosp Blvd Sur S/N Piso 3 Torre C Valencia 46026 Spain Office Phone: 34-961411120. Business E-Mail: ljulia@ono.com.

JULIAN, THOMAS B., surgeon, educator; Attended, U. Pitts. Diplomate Am. Bd. Surgery, lic. Pa. Intern Univ. Pitts. Med. Ctr., 1977, resident, 1982; assoc dir. Breast Cancer Ctr. Allegheny Gen. Hosp.; assoc. prof. Human Oncology Drexel Univ. Named one of the Top Doctors, Pitts. Mag., 2011. Fellow: ACS; mem.: Pa. Med. Soc., Inst. for the Study of Natural Sys., Am. Soc. for Bariatic Surgery, Am. Soc. of Breast Disease, AMA. Office: Allegheny General Hospital Allegheny Cancer Center 320 E N Ave Pittsburgh PA 15212 Office Phone: 412-359-8229. Office Fax: 412-359-6263.

JULIAN, THOMAS MICHAEL, gynecologic surgeon, educator; b. Mpls., June 30, 1949; s. Earl Eugene and Pearl Louise (Passi) J.; m. Kathryn Ann Chalupsky, June 12, 1971; children: Christine, Andrew, Matthew. BA, St. Cloud State Coll., Minn., 1971; MD, U. Minn., 1978. Diplomate Am. Bd. Ob-Gyn. Intern U. Minn., Mpls., 1978-79, resident, 1979-82, assoc. prof., program dir. dept. ob-gyn., 1982-88; prof., program dir. dept. ob-gyn. U. Wis., Madison, 1988-99; ret., 1999—. Invited instr. Internat. Vaginal Surgery Conf., St. Louis, 1994, 95; mem. step 2 com. Nat. Bd. Med. Examiners, 1996-2000. Author: Review of Obstetrics and Gynecology, 1994, Manual of Colposcopy, 1996; editor Jour. of Lower Genital Tract Disease, 1994-present; contbr. numerous articles to profl. jour. Recipient Outstanding Med. Writing award Minn. State Med. Soc., 1985, Teaching award Assn. Profs. Ob-Gyn., 1995. Mem. Am. Soc. Colposcopy and Cervical Pathology (bd. dir. 1992-98, Meritorious Svc. award 2000, Meritorious Sci. Achievement award 2004), Soc. Gynecologic Surgeons, Minn. Ob-Gyn. Soc. (sec.-treas. 1984-88, pres.-elect 1988), Vaginal Surgeons' Life time acheivement Award from Society of Pelvic Reconstructive surgeons. Roman Catholic. Home: 4892 Foxfire Trl Middleton WI 53562-1104 Office: U Wis 600 Highland Ave Madison WI 53792-3284 Office Phone: 608-263-5573. Business E-Mail: tmjulian@wisc.edu.

JULIANA, FIGUEIRÊDO DA COSTA LIMA, medical researcher; b. Brazil, July 27, 1982; Degree in Biomedicine, Fed. U. Pernambuco, 2006; M, Ageu Magalhães Rsch. Ctr., FIOCRUZ, 2009. Rschr. Rsch. Ctr. Ageu Magalhães, FIOCRUZ, 2003—. Recipient award, ICOHRTA/NIH. Home: Rua Mamanguape 59 Apt 2001 Boa Viagem Recife Pernambuco 51020250 British Indian Ocean Territories Personal E-mail: jujufig@hotmail.com.

JULIANOV, ALEXANDER EMILOV, surgeon, educator; s. Yousseinov and Yousseinova; life ptnr. Aneliya Kaneva. MD, Higher Med. Inst., Stara Zagora, 1994; attended, Thracian U. Hosp., Stara Zagora, Nat. Cancer Ctr., Bulgaria. Board certifications in Surgery, Board certifications in Oncology Thracian U., Stara Zagora, Bulgaria. Sr. asst. prof. surgery Thracian U., Stara Zagora, Bulgaria, 1995—; cons. surgeon Thracian U. Hosp. Contbr. articles. Mem.: Bulgarian Surgical Soc., Bulgarian Assn. Surgeons and Gastroenterologists,

Internat. Soc. Surgery, Societe Internat. de Chirurgie (Travel scholar 2001). Achievements include research in treatment of liver metastases. Office: Tracian Univ Hosp 11 Armeiska Stara Zagora 6000 Bulgaria

JULIEN, TERRENCE DARRYL, neurosurgeon, researcher; b. Washington, Oct. 12, 1966; s. Selwyn McGregor and Thelma Sally J.; m. Thuy-An H., June 23, 1990(div.). BA, U. Del., 1988; MD, Howard U., 1993. Intern Med. Ctr. Del., Newark, 1993-94; fellow in neurosurgery NYU Med. Ctr., NYC, 1994-95, resident in neurosurgery, 1995-96, SUNY, Syracuse, 1996-2001, asst. chief resident neurosurgery, 1999-2000, chief resident in neurosurgery, 2000-01; fellow in neurosurg. oncology Meml. Sloan-Kettering Cancer Ctr., NYC, 2001—02; instr. neurosurgery H. Lee Moffitt Cancer Ctr., Tampa, Fla., 2002—03; staff physician Togus VA Med. Ctr., Augusta, Maine, 2005—06; asst. prof. neurosurgery, dir. surg. neuro-oncology Robert C. Byrd Health Sci. Ctr., W.Va. U. Sch. Medicine, Morgantown, 2007—; attending physician Kings Ct. Hosp. Ctr., Dept. Neurosurgery; dir. surg. Minimally Invensive Spine Surgery. Recipient cancer rsch. scholarship, AACR, 2001; fellow, Mitchel Found., Howard U., 1991. Mem.: AMA, Soc. Minimally Invasive Spine Surgery, Soc. Neuro-Oncology, West. Va. State Neurusurgery Soc., Nat. Med. Assn., Soc. Minimally Invasive Spine Surgery, Soc. Neurooncology, Congress Neurol. Surgeons, Am. Assn. Cancer Rsch. (Minority Scholar in Cancer Rsch. 2001), Am. Asn. Neurolog. Surgeons (joint sect. tumors 1988, joint sect. spine guidelines com. 1998—2001, Preuss award 1999). Office: W Va Univ Dept Neurosurgery 1 Medical Center Dr Morgantown WV 26506 Office Phone: 304-293-5041. Personal E-mail: julient@mac.com, tjulien@gmail.com. Business E-Mail: tjulien@hsc.wvu.edu.

JULL, GWENDOLEN ANNE, physical therapist, educator; b. Brisbane, Sept. 23, 1948; Diploma in Physiotherapy, U. Queensland, 1968, PhD, 2001. Physiotherapist Hosps., 1969—86; lectr., sr. lectr. U. Queensland, 1987—2002, assoc. prof., 1996—2003, prof., 2004—. Specialist musculoskeletal physiotherapist Chapel Hill Physiotherapy, 1989—. Recipient Internat. Svc. award, World Confederation Phys. Therapists; Hon. fellowship, Am. Acad. Orthop. Manipulative Phys. Therapists. Fellow: Australian Coll. Physiotherapists; mem.: Australian Pain Soc., Australian Physiotherapy Assn. (hon.), Internat. Assn. Study Pain. Avocations: travel, gardening. Office: Divsn Physiotherapy University Queensland Brisbane Queensland 4072 Australia Office Fax: 61 7 3365 1622. Business E-Mail: g.jull@uq.edu.au.

JUN, CUI, dentist; b. Shaanxi, China, Dec. 16, 1979; PhD, Sichuan U., 2007. Physician Peking U. Shenzhen Hosp., 2007—. Mem.: Chinese Stomatology Acad. Office: 1120 Lianhua Shenzhen Guangdong 518036 China Personal E-mail: 1979boy1216@163.com

JUN, JAE-HOON, biomedical engineer, educator; b. Seoul, Republic Of Korea, Jan. 30, 1963; s. Yonghan Jun and Eunsook Kim; m. Kyung Lee, Dec. 20, 1989; children: Alice Yehjin, William Jongwon. BS (hon.), Korea U., Seoul, 1986; MS, Tex. A&M, College Station, 1993, PhD, 2001. Rsch. asst. Va. Commonwealth U., Richmond, 2001—04; asst. prof. Konkuk U., Chungju Si, Chungcheongbuk Do, Republic of Korea, 2004—08, assoc. prof., 2008—; sr. rschr. Rsch. Inst. Biomedical Engrng., Chungju-Si, 2004—. Editor Korean Soc. Indsl. Chemistry, Seoul, 2008—. Contbr. articles to engrng. jours. Mem.: Korean Soc. Biomedical Engrng. Achievements include patents pending for optical goneometer development. Office: Konkuk University Dept Biomed Engrng Danwol-Dong 322 Chungju Chungchongbuk 380-701 Republic of Korea Office Phone: 82438403799. Office Fax: 82438510620. Business E-Mail: jjun81@kku.ac.kr.

JUN, JIN HYUN, biology professor; b. Gwangju-si, Apr. 12, 1967; PhD, Hanyang U., 1999. Dir. Lab. Reproductive Biology & Infertility, Cheil Gen. Hosp., 1993—2008; asst. prof., dept. bio-med. lab. sci. Eulji U., 2008—. Mem.: Am. Soc. Cell Biology, Korean Soc. Reproductive Medicine. Avocation: fishing. Office: 212 Yangji dong Sujeong-gu Seongnam-si Gyeonggi-do 461-713 Republic of Korea Business E-Mail: junjh55@hanmail.net.

JUN, TAE-YOUN, psychiatrist, neurologist, educator; b. Jinhae, Republic of Korea, Jan. 9, 1954; s. Sang-Yeop Jun and Seung-Ran Jun(Yang); m. Hye-Jung Lee, May 4, 1960; children: Min-Hee, Min-Kyu. PhD in Medicine, The Cath. U. of Korea, 1987—90. Lic. physician Ministry Health & Welfare, Republic of Korea, 1978, cert. specialist in psychiatry Korean Neuropsychiatric Assn., 1983, specialist in neurology Korean Neurol. Assn., 1983. Prof. Coll. Medicine The Cath. U. Korea, Seoul, Republic of Korea, 2001—09; dir. Dept. Psychiatry St. Mary's Hosp., Seoul, Republic of Korea, 2001—; dir., sci. com. Korean Neuropsychiatric Assn., Seoul, Republic of Korea, 2003—05; dir. Clin. Rsch. Ctr. for Depression, 2005—, Yeongeungpo-gu Cmty. Mental Health Ctr., 2006—. Contbr. articles to profl. jours. Cons. Ministry of Justice, Republic of Korea, Seoul, 1996—2004. Recipient Dr. Paul Janssen Schizaphrenii Rsch. award, 2004, Rsch. prize, World Fed. Socs. Biol. Psychiatry, 2007, GSK Sci. award, 2009. Mem.: Nat. Gaming Control Commn. (Republic of Korea), Nat. Acad. Medicine Korea, Korean Neurol. Assn. (licentiate), Korean Neuropsychiatric Assn. (licentiate). Office: St Mary's Hosp The Cath U 62 Yeouido-dong Yeongdeungpo-gu Seoul 150-713 Republic of Korea Office Phone: 82-2-3779-1250. Office Fax: 82-2-780-6577. Business E-Mail: tyjun@catholic.ac.kr.

JUNE, CARL HOWARD, immunologist; b. July 13, 1953; m. Cynthia June (dec. 2001). BS in Biology, Naval Acad., Annapolis, Md., 1971; MD, Baylor Coll. Medicine, Houston, 1979. Diplomate American Bd. Internal Medicine, cert. in Med. Oncology. Grad. tng. in immunology & malaria WHO, Geneva, 1978—79; postdoc. tng. in transplantation biology Fred Hutchinson Cancer Rsch. Ctr., Seattle, 1983—86; head dept. immunology, founder immune cell biology program Naval Med. Rsch. Inst., Md., 1990—95; prof. dept. medicine, dept. cell & molecular biology Uniformed Services Univ. Health Sciences, Bethesda, Md., 1995—99; prof. pathology & lab. medicine U. Pa., Phila., 1999—, dir. Translational Rsch. Programs Abramson Cancer Ctr., 1999—. Investigator Abramson Family Cancer Rsch. Inst., 1999—. Contbr. articles to profl. jours. Mem.: American Assn. Clin. Oncology. Achievements include research in various mechanisms of lymphocyte activation that relate to immune tolerance and adoptive immunotherapy. Office: June Lab Rm 554 BRB II/III 421 Curie Blvd Philadelphia PA 19104-6160 Office Phone: 215-573-5745. Office Fax: 215-573-8590. Business E-Mail: cjune@mail.med.upenn.edu. *

JUNG, BETTY CHIN, adjunct lecturer, epidemiologist, nurse, educator; b. Bklyn., Nov. 28, 1948; d. Han You and Bo Ngan (Moy) Chin; m. Lee Jung, Oct. 1, 1972; children: Daniel, Stephanie. AA, King's Coll., Briarcliff Manor, NY, 1968; BS, Columbia U., NYC, 1971; MPH, So. Conn. State U., New Haven, 1993. RN, Conn., Miss., N.Y.; cert. health edn. specialist master, 2011; credentialed health info. web site rater; notary pub., Conn., 2004. Adminstrv. asst. Columbia U., NYC, 1968-69; practical nurse Babies Hosp., NYC, 1969-70, charge nurse, 1974-76; staff nurse Columbia-Presbyn. Hosp., NYC, 1971-73; sch. nurse Nassau County Sch. System, Long Island, NY, 1984-85; grad. asst. So. Conn. State U., New Haven, 1991-92; coop. edn. intern Conn. Dept. Health Svcs., Hartford, 1991-92; intern North Ctrl. Dist. Health Dept., Enfield, Conn., 1992; epidemiologist Conn. Dept. Pub. Health, Hartford, Conn., 1992-98, health program assoc., 1998-2001, cardiovascular epidemiologist, 2003—05, cardiovascular and diabetes epidemiologist, 2005—09, hepatitis program evaluator, 2007; staff nurse Quinnipiac Coll. Student Health Svcs., 1998; mem. multicultural adv. coun. Conn. Dept. Children and Families, assoc. rsch. analyst, 2001—03. Instr. Albertus Magnus Coll., 1995—96; health columnist Baldwin Newcomers Club, NY, 1977—78; coord. Dept. Pub. Health and Svcs./Conn. EPI Info. Network, Hartford, 1994—2001; mem. Nat. Lead Info. Ctr. Spkrs. Bur., 1997—98; vol. scientist Sci.-By-Mail, 1997—98; mem. Nat. Safety Coun. Environ. Health Ctr. Spkrs. Referral Bur., 1998—2001; mem. affirmative action employee adv. com. Conn. Dept. Pub. Health, 1998—2001, mem. diabetes planning com., 2004—09, mem. genetics edn. and workforce devel. work group, 2006—09, mem. connectifit adv. com., 2006—07, mem. connectifit survey subcommittee, 2006—07; mem. Permanent Commn. Status of Women Talent Network, 1996—, chair news subcom., editor affirmative action newsletter, 2001, Nat. Commn. Health Edn. Credentialing, 2009—, elected divsn. bd. for cert. health edn. specialists; apptd. mem. multicultural adv. coun. Conn. Dept. Children and Families, 2002—03; pilot reviewer CDC Pub. Health Tng. Network, 2002—; assoc. NIH, 2004—09; mem. functions workgroup EPI; dir.'s coun. pub. reps. NIH, 2004—09; mem. CDC CVH Inst. planning com. Conn. Dept. Pub. Health, 2005—09, lead cardiovasc. epidemiology work group, 2005—09, mem. genetics edn. nurse edn. subcom., 2005—09, lead diabetes data and surveillance work group, 2007—09; numerous positions So. Conn. State U., 1991—, adj. prof., 1998—, apptd. CDC cardiovascular health and bus. work group, 2005—09; cons. in field; mem. grants and contracts working group Status of Women Talent Network, 2005, mem. cardiovas. state plan exec. com., 2005—09; mem. adv. coun. So. Conn. State U. Dept. Pub. Health, 2007—; book proposal reviewer in field; co-chair Stroke Rehab. Working Group, CT Stroke Plan, 2008—09. Mem. editl. bd.: Data Quality, 1994—98, mem. manuscript rev. bd.: Jour. Clin. Outcomes Mgmt., 1995—2010, Pub. Health Reports, 1997—98; contbg. editor: Episource, A Guide to Resources in Epidemiology, 1998—99; editor/web pub.: SCSU Pub. Health E-News Bull., 2000—01, Public Health E-news, 2001—, Public Health Jobs Electronic Newsletter, 2000—; contbr. articles to profl. jours. Vol. nurse health educator, coord. Chinatown's First Ann. Health Fair, 1971-72; treas. Tenant Assn., Bronx, N.Y., 1976-77; pre-confirmation tchr. Bethlehem Luth. Ch., Baldwin, N.Y., 1981-85. Recipient Disting. Alumni Neighbours award, Columbia U. Presbyn. Hosp. Sch. Nursing, 2011, Outstanding Alumni award, SCSU, 2011; grantee, USPHS, 1992—98, Fed. HUD, 1995—98, U.S. Preventive Health and Health Svcs., 1998, CDC Cardiovasc. Health Program, 2003—07, CDC Diabetes Prevention and Control Program, 2005—09, others; Merit scholar, Kings Coll., 1968, Columbia U. scholar, 1968—69, Women's Florist Assn. scholar, 1968, Bessie Lee Gambrill scholar, So. Alumni Assn., 1992, block grantee, Maternal Child Health, 1998—2001, Adult Blood Lead Epidemiology and Surveillance Program grantee, CDC/Nat. Inst. Occupl. Safety and Health, 1992—98. Fellow: Soc. for Pub. Health Edn.; mem.: APHA (health care reform activist network, peer assistance the model stds. project), Columbia U. Presbyn. Hosp. Sch. Nursing Alumni Assn. (survey cons. 1994—95, Disting. Alumni award 2011), Cardiovascular Health Coun., Nat. Assn. Chronic Disease Dirs., Sci. and Epidemiology (com. mem. 2007—09), Pub. Health Expertise Network of Mentors (program dir. 2002—), Internat. Assn. Webmasters and Designers (web site rater Health Improvement Inst. 2006—), Boston Mus. Sci., Internat. Assn. IT Trainers (assoc.), Nat. Acad. Sci. (mentor career planning ctr. beginning scientists & engrs. 1997—98), So. Conn. State U. Alumni Assn. (founder pub. health chpt. 1994, interim pres, then pres. 1994—98, founder, coord. pub. health alumni mentor program 1994—2002, chair coms. 1994—, numerous other positions 1994—, editor MPH Alumni Record 1995—, founder, dir., coord. pub. health alumni spkrs. bur. 1997—, founder, program dir. pub. health expertise network of mentors 2002—, alumni surveys program dir. 2007—, Alumni Appreciation award 1998), Conn. Pub. Health Assn., Nat. Lead Info. Ctr. Spkrs. Bur., Conn. State and Territorial Epidemiologists (alternate cons. 1996—, co-leader Healthy People 2010 1999—2001, lead cardiovasc. disease 2002—09), Am. Statis. Assn. (OSPA media experts list 1997—2000). Avocations: reading, writing, research, web development and design, bicycling. Home: 25 Driftwood Ln Guilford CT 06437-1929 Office: Conn Dept Pub Health 410 Capitol Ave Hartford CT 06106 Personal E-mail: bettycjung@yahoo.com.

JUNG, CHAN-KWON, medical educator; b. Hadong-gun, Republic of Korea, June 25, 1972; MD, Coll. Medicine, Gyeongsang Nat. U., 1997; PhD, Cath. U. Korea, 2007. Intern St. Mary's Hosp., Cath. U. Korea, Uijeongbu, 1997—98, resident, anatomic pathology, 1998—2002; flight surgeon Aeromedical Ctr., Republic of Korea Air Force, 2002—05; instr. Coll. Medicine, Cath. U. Korea, 2005—07, asst. prof., 2007—. Recipient Acad. Rsch. award, Aerospace Med. Assn. Korea, 2007. Mem.: Endocrine Pathology Soc., Gastrointestinal Pathology Soc., Korean Soc. Cytopathology, Korean Soc. Pathologists, Korean Med. Assn. Avocations: hiking, skateboarding. Office: 505 Banpo-dong Seocho-gu Seoul 137-701 Republic of Korea Business E-Mail: ckjung@catholic.ac.kr.

JUNG, EUI, medical educator; b. Republic of Korea, Sept. 24, 1973; MD, Ulsan U., PhD, 2003. Asst. prof. ob-gyn. Kyung Hee U. Med. Ctr., 2006—. Office: Kyung Hee University Dong-Dae-Moon-Gu Hoi-Gi-Dong Seoul 130-702 Republic of Korea E-mail: eui2536@hotmail.com.

JUNG, GYOO-SIK, radiologist, educator; b. Daegu, Republic Of Korea, June 6, 1691; m. Sung-Jin Park; children: Hye-Jung, Eun-Jung. PhD, Busan Nat. U., Republic of Korea, 2000. Cert. Korean Soc. Radiology, 1990, lic. Korean Med. Assn., 1986. Chief, dept. radiology Ulsan Hosp., Republic of Korea, 2004—06; assoc. prof. Dankook U. Coll. Medicine, Cheonan, Chungnam, Republic of Korea, 2006—07, Kosin U. Coll. Medicine, Busan, 2000—04, asst. prof., 1996—2000, instr., 1993—96, prof., 2007—, chief, interventional medicine sect., 2007—. Contbr. articles to numerous profl. jours. Capt. US Army, 1990—93, Eonyang. Recipient Cert. Merit Pub. Svc., Korean Soc. Radiology, 2003. Mem.: Cardiovasc. and Interventional Radiol. Soc. Europe, Radiol. Soc. N.Am., Korean Soc. Interventional Radiology, Korean Soc. Radiology. Avocation: mountain climbing. Office: Kosin Univ Coll Medicine Amnam-Dong Seo-Gu 34 602-702 Busan Busan Republic of Korea Office Fax: 82-51-255-2764. Personal E-mail: gsjung@medimail.co.kr. E-mail: gsjung240@hanmail.net.

JUNG, HWOON-YONG, gastroenterologist, medical educator; s. Munki Jung and Se-Gyung Kim; m. Jee-Yeon Min, Sept. 25, 1993; children: Jaehee, Da-Kyung. BS, Seoul Nat. U., Republic Of Korea, 1988; MS, U. Ulsan, Seoul, 2000; PhD, Hanyang U., Seoul, 2005. Diplomate Korean bd. Internal Medicine, 1992. Internship Seoul Nat. U. Hosp., 1988—89, residency, internal medicine, 1989—92; mil. svc. physician Korean Army, Seoul, 1992—95; clin. instr. Asan Med. Ctr., Seoul, 1997—2001; instr. U. Ulsan, Asan Med. Ctr., 1998—2000, asst. prof., 2000—05, assoc. prof., 2005—. Vis. scholar U. Calif., San Diego, La Jolla, 2002—04. Recipient Young Clinician award, Asia-Pacific Congress of Gastroenterology, 1998; fellowship, Asan Med. Ctr., 1995—97. Office: Univ Ulsan Coll Medicine Asan Med Ctr 388-1 Pungnap-Dong Seoul 138-736 Republic of Korea Office Fax: 02-485-5782. Business E-Mail: hyjung@amc.seoul.kr.

JUNG, JI-WON, research scientist, director; b. Kyeonggi-do, Jan. 30, 1977; PhD, Seoul Nat. U., 2005. Postdoc. rsch. fellow Japan Nat. Inst. Health Sci., 2005—06; rsch. asst. prof. Seoul Nat. U., 2006—09; dep. sci. dir. Korea Nat. Inst. Health, 2009—. Editl. bd. mem. Korean Jour. Food Hygiene, 2007, World Jour. Stem Cell, 2011; profl. assessor Korea Evaluation Inst. Indsl. Tech., 2010. Mem.: Korean Soc. Biochemistry & Molecular Biology. Avocation: music. Office: KNIH 643 Yeonje-ri Gangoe-myun Cheongwon-gun Chungbuk 363-951 Republic of Korea Personal E-mail: infranova@gmail.com.

JUNG, KWANG AM, orthopaedic surgeon; b. Chang Won, Kyung Sang Nam-do, Republic Of Korea, Feb. 27, 1970; s. Mal Deuk Koo; m. Su Jeong Song, Jan. 25, 1998; children: Jae Hong, Jae Min. MB, Yeung Nam U. Med. Sch., Republic of Korea, 1996, MS in Orthopaedics, 2001—01. Chief orthopadic surgery The 16th Air forces Base Hosp., Yecheon, Republic of Korea, 2001—03, Armed Forces Daegu Hosp., Republic of Korea, 2003—04, Himchan Hosp., Republic of Korea, 2005—; fellow in arthroscopy and sports medicine Yonsei U. Med. Sch., Seoul, 2004—05. Instr. Yonsei U. Arthroscopy & Joint Rsch. Inst., 2004—, com. mem., 2004. Contbr. articles to profl. jours. Mem.: Internat. Soc. Arthroscopy, Knee and Orthopaedic Sports, Arthroscopy Assn. of N.Am. (internat. mem.), Korean Shoulder and Elbow Soc., Korean Knee Soc., Korean Arthroscopy Soc., Korean Orthop. Assn., Korean Fracture Soc., Korean Med. Assn. Office: Himchan Hosp 404-3 Mok-dong Yangcheon-gu Seoul 158-806 Republic of Korea Home: 136-1601 Banpo Xi Apt Banpodong Seoul 137-041 Republic of Korea Office Phone: 822 3219 9114. Office Fax: 822 3219 9347. Personal E-mail: osjka@dreamwiz.com. Business E-Mail: osika@dreamwiz.com.

JUNG, KYUNG HAE, oncologist, educator; b. Seoul, Feb. 17, 1964; MD, Seoul Nat. U., 1988, PhD, 2005. Med. oncologist Seoul Mcpl. Boramae Hosp., 1994—2002, Nat. Cancer Ctr., 2003—08; instr. Seoul Nat. U. Coll. Medicine, 1997—2002; assoc. prof. U. Ulsan Coll. Medicine, Asan Med. Ctr., 2008—. Cons. Ctrl. Pharmaceutic Affairs Coun., Korea Food & Drug Adminstrn., 2010—11. Mem.: Korean Cancer Assn. (Best reviewer award), Korean Soc. Coloproctology, Korean Breast Cancer Soc., Am. Soc. Clin. Oncology, Am. Assn. Cancer Rsch. Avocation: swimming. Office: 88 Olympic-ro 43-gil Songpa-gu Seoul 138-736 Republic of Korea Office Fax: 82-2-3010-6961. Business E-Mail: khjung@amc.seoul.kr.

JUNG, MIN-HO, orthodontist, educator; b. Seoul, Republic of Korea, Sept. 19, 1969; PhD, Seoul Nat. U., 2003. Dir. SNU Honors Orthodontic Clinic, 2001—; clin. prof. Seoul Nat. U., 2004—, Sungkyunkwan U., 2007—, Kyung-Hee U., 2009—, Cath. U., 2010—. Dir. Seoul Orthodontic Forum, 2003—. Fellow: World Fedn. Orthodontists; mem.: Korean Assn. Orthodontists (bd. trustees, bd. dirs. 2008—, Best Table Clinic award), Am. Assn. Orthodontists. Avocations: exercise, golf, reading. Office: 3rd Fl Tae-nam Bldg 72-3 Chamwon Dong Seoul 137909 Republic of Korea Office Fax: 8225994002. Business E-Mail: fortit@chol.com.

JUNG, RODNEY C., internist, academic administrator; b. New Orleans, Oct. 9, 1920; s. Frederick Charles and Clara (Cuevas) J. BS in Zoology with honors, Tulane U., 1941, MD, 1945, MS in Parasitology and Microbiology, 1950, PhD, 1953. Diplomate: Am. Bd. Internal Medicine. Intern Charity Hosp. La., New Orleans, 1945-46; dir. Hutchinson Meml. Clinic, 1948; asst. parasitology Tulane U., 1948-50, instr. tropical medicine, 1950-53, asst. prof., 1953-57, assoc. prof. tropical medicine, 1957-63, prof. tropical medicine, 1963-73, clin. prof. internal medicine, 1973-91, clin. prof. tropical medicine, 1983-92, prof. emeritus tropical medicine, 1992—, head div. tropical medicine, 1960-63; health dir. City of New Orleans, 1963-70, 79-82; internist in charge Ill. Central Hosp., New Orleans, 1956-70. Sr. vis. physician Charity Hosp., 1959—; mem. study sect. on tropical medicine and parasitology Nat. Inst. Allergy and Infectious Disease, 1963-67; mem. Commn. on Parasitic Diseases Armed Forces Epidemiol. Bd., 1967-73; chief communicable disease control, City of New Orleans, 1978; sr. in internal medicine Touro Infirmary. Co-author: Animal Agents and Vectors of Disease and Clinical Parasitology; editl. bd. Am. Jour. Tropical Medicine and Hygiene, 1972-94; contbr. articles to profl. jours. Pres. Irish Cultural Soc. New Orleans, 1980-92, pres. emeritus 1992—; officer res. div. New Orleans Police Dept., 1977-84; chmn. New Orleans Mosquito and Termite Control Bd. John and Mary Markle Scholar in med. sci. Fellow ACP; hon. fellow Brazilian Soc. Tropical Medicine; mem. Am., Royal socs. tropical medicine and hygiene, Am. Soc. Parasitologists, La. State Med. Soc., Orleans Parish Med. Soc., Nat. Rifle Assn., Irish Georgian Soc., La. Mosquito and Termite Control Assn., La. Soc. Internal Medicine, Am. Soc. Internal Medicine, New Orleans Acad. Internal Medicine, Am. Def. Preparedness Assn., Irish-Am. Cultural Inst., Nat. Trust. Historic Preservation, La. Landmarks Soc., Naval Inst., New Orleans Mus. Art, New Orleans Opera Assn., La. Wildlife Fedn., Phi Beta Kappa, Sigma Xi, Delta Omega, Alpha Omega Alpha. Presbyterian.

JUNG, SEUNG-IL, urologist, educator; b. Gwangju, Oct. 17, 1973; BS, Chonnam Nat. U., 1998, MD, 2010. Asst. prof. Chonnam Nat. U. Hosp., 2008—09, Hwasun Chonnam Nat. U. Hosp., 2009—. Mem., pub. com. Korean Prostate Soc., 2009—. Mem.: Korean Endourol. Soc., Korean Urol. Oncology Soc., Korean Urol. Assn. (mem., ins. com. 2010—), Korea Assn. Urogenital Tract Infection and Inflammation (ins. dir. 2010—), Am. Urol. Assn. Avocation: art. Office: 160 Ilsimri Hwasuneup Hwasungun Jeollanamdo 519-809 Republic of Korea Office Phone: 82-379-7749, 82-61-379-8160. Personal E-mail: drjsi@yahoo.co.kr.

JUNG, SOON-HEE, pathologist, educator; b. Wonju, Gangwon, Republic of Korea, Mar. 28, 1960; B, Yonsei U. Wonju Coll. Medicine, 1992; PhD, Yonsei U., 1992. Assoc. prof. Yonsei U. Wonju Coll. Medicine, 1998—2002, prof., 2002; com. mem. Korean Assn. Study Lung Cancer, 2006; rep. Korean Soc. Pathologists Korean Cardiopulmonary Soc., 2011—. Editl. bd. Korean Jour. Pathology, 2008, Korean Assn. Study Lung Cancer, 2011. Mem.: Korean Soc. Cytopathologists, Internat. Acad. Pathologists, US and Can. Acad. Pathologists, Korean Assn. Study Lung Cancer, Korean Soc. Pathologists. Avocations: reading, music, piano. Office: Ilsan-Dong Wonju Gangwon-Do 220-701 Republic of Korea Office Phone: 82-33-741-1551. Office Fax: 82-33-731-6590. E-mail: soonheej@yonsei.ac.kr.

JUNG, TIMOTHY TAE KUN, otolaryngologist; b. Seoul, Republic of Korea, Dec. 1, 1943; came to U.S., 1969; s. Yoon Yong and Helen Chung-Hyuk (Im) J.; m. Lucy Moon Young, Sept. 10, 1972; children: David, Michael, Karen. BS, Seoul Nat. U., 1966, Loma Linda U., 1971, MD, 1974; PhD, U. Minn., 1980. Diplomate Am. Bd. Otolaryngology. Med. intern Loma Linda U. Med. Ctr., Calif., 1974—75; resident in surgery U. Minn. Med. Sch., Mpls., 1975—76, resident in otolaryngology, 1976—80, asst. prof. otolaryngology, 1980—84, clin. asst. prof., dir. prostaglandin lab., 1984—85; assoc. prof., dir. otolaryngology rsch. Loma Linda U., 1985—90, prof., dir. otolaryngology rsch., 1990—92, clin. prof., dir. otolaryngology rsch., 1992—. Mem. deafness and communications disroders rev. com. Nat. Inst. Deafness and Communications, NIH, 1989-92. Mem. editl. bd. Annals of Otology, Rhinology & Laryngology, 1994-2004, Acta Otolaryngologica, 1999—; contbr. chpts. to books, over 100 articles to profl. jours. Pres. Korean-Am. Otolaryngcology Soc., 2010—. Sgt. Korean Army, 1966—69. Recipient Edmund Price Fowler award. Fellow ACS, Triological Soc., Am. Acad. Otolaryngology (honor award 1990), Am. Acad. Surgeons; mem. AMA, Am. Otol. Soc., Am. Neurotol. Soc., Assn. Rsch. in Otolaryngology, Centurions, Collegium Otorhinolaryngogicum Amicetiae Sacrum, Alpha Omega Alpha. Seventh-day Adventist. Avocations: horticulture, photography, hiking, running. Home: 11790 Pecan Way Loma Linda CA 92354-3452 Office: 3975 Jackson St Ste 202 Riverside CA 92503-3947 Office Phone: 951-352-7920. Personal E-mail: jungstaff@sbcglobal.net.

JUNG, WOO SANG, medical educator; b. Seoul, Republic of Korea, June 7, 1971; m. Jung Min Woo. Grad, Coll. Orental Medicine, Seoul, 1996; MD, Kyung Hee U., Coll. Oriental Medicine, Seoul, 2001. Cert. in Oriental internal medicine. Prof. CHA U., Pochon, Kyunggi-do, Republic of Korea, 1999—2000, Kyung Hee U., Seoul, 2000—. Editor: Jour. Korean Oriental Internal Medicine, 2005—, Jour. Korean Oriental Med. Soc., 2005—; contbr. articles to profl. jours. Recipient acad. award, Korean Oriental Med. Soc., 2008. Mem.: Soc. Joong-Poong, Soc. Korean Internal Medicine, Korean Med. Soc. Avocation: travel. Office: Kyung Hee Medical Ctr Kyung Hee Univ Hoegi-dong Dongdaemu-gu Seoul 130-702 Republic of Korea Office Phone: 82-2-958-9289. Office Fax: 82-2-958-9132. Business E-Mail: wsjung@khu.ac.kr.

JUNG, YOUNG BOK, orthopedist, educator; b. Kyungpook, Cheong-do gun, Republic of Korea, Jan. 16, 1946; s. Dong Bong Jung and Cha Soon Park; m. Hae Ran Kim, Mar. 1, 1977; children: Eun Kyung, Eun Jin, Ji Ho. BS, Coll. Medicine, Kyungpook U., Daegu, 1970; MS, Coll. Medicine, Cath. U., Seoul, Republic of Korea, 1978; PhD in Orthopedics, Seoul, 1982. Orthop. surgeon specialist Republic of Korea, 1978. Trained resident course Cath. U. Coll. Medicine, Dept. Orthop. Surgery, Seoul, 1974—78, lectr., 1978—79; asst. prof. Chung-Ang U. Coll. Medicine, Dept. Orthop. Surgery, Seoul, 1979—84, assoc. prof., 1984—89, chmn. Yong-San Hosp., 1984—2001, prof., 1989—, chmn., 1994—2001; clin. fellow Toronto U. Arthroscopic Surgery, Orthop. & Arthritic Hosp., Canada, 1986—87. Editor in chief Jour. Korean Orthop. Assn., 2001—04; adv. bd. Archives Orthop. Trauma Surgery, 2003—. Contbr. articles to profl. jours. Surgeon, capt. Korean Army, 1970—73. Recipient Good Paper, Chung-Ang U. Med. Ctr., 2006. Mem.: Asia-Pacific Knee Surgery Soc., Asia-Pacific Orthop. Surgery Assn., Internat. Soc. Arthroscopy Knee Surgery Orthopedic Sports Medicine, Korean Orthop. Sport Medicine Soc. (pres. 2002—03), Korean Knee Soc. (pres. 1999—2000), Korean Arthroscopic Soc. (pres. 1996—97), Korean Orthop. Assn (dir. 1994—2000, pres. 2010, Good Paper 2002, 2005). Avocation: golf. Home: 4-505 Sang-A Apt Samsung 2 Dong Kang-Nam Gu Seoul Republic of Korea Office: 663 Janghyeon-Yi Jinjeop-eup Namyangju Gyeonggi 472-865 Republic of Korea Office Phone: 82-2-6299-1587.

JUNGCHUL, SEO, medical educator; b. Dangjin, Kyungbuk, Republic of Korea, June 16, 1970; s. Seo Sejoong and Kim Youngsun; m. Oh Hyunjoo, Sept. 23, 1970; children: Seo Youngsuk, Seo Yoonsuk. PhD, Kyunghee U., Seoul, 2001. Prof. Dongeui U., Busan, Republic of Korea, 2001—02, Daegu Haany U., Republic of Korea, 2002—. Physician Gumi Hosp. Traditional Medicine, Daegu Haany U., Republic of Korea, 2002—. Grantee, Korean Rsch. Found., 2005. Mem.: Korean Acupuncture & Moxibustion Soc. (life Award for good articles in Acupuncture & Moxibustion 2003). Achievements include patents for genetical identification of gingseng by using pyrosequencing. Avocations: skiing, mountain climbing. Home: 5-107 Woobang 1st APT Songjeong-dong Gumi 730-090 Republic of Korea Office: Daegu Haany University 458-7 Songjeong-Dong 730-090 Gumi Gyeongsangbuk-do Republic of Korea Office Fax: 82-505-245-9279; Home Fax: 82-54-452-2219. E-mail: acumox@hanmail.net.

JUNG DUG, YANG, medical educator; b. Daegu, Republic of Korea, Aug. 15, 1970; s. Sung Ki Yang and Jung Ja Park; m. Gyung Jin Song, Oct. 18, 1998; children: Seung Hun Yang, Seung Hyuk Yang. PhD, Kyungpook Nat. U., Daegu. Diplomate Bd. Korea. Clin. prof. Kyungpook Nat. U. Hosp., Daegu, 2006—07, asst. prof., 2007—11, assoc. prof., dept. plastic & reconstructive surgery, Grad. Sch. Medicine, 2011—; head, info. & communication Kyungpook Nat. U. Med. Ctr. Home and Office: Kyungpook Nat University Med Ctr 807 Hogukno Buk-gu Daegu 702-210 Republic of Korea Office Fax: 82-53-200-2149. Business E-Mail: lambyang@knu.ac.kr.

JUNGER, MIGUEL CHAPERO, retired acoustics researcher; b. Dresden, Germany, Jan. 29, 1923; came to U.S., 1941, naturalized, 1946; s. José and Adrienne (Junger) Chapiro; m. Ellen Sinclair, 1960; children: M. Sebastian, A. Carlotta. BS, MIT, 1944, SM, 1946; ScD (Gordon McKay scholar), Harvard U., 1951. Postdoctoral rsch. fellow in acoustics Harvard U., 1951-55; partner Cambridge Acoustical Assocs., Inc., 1955-59, pres., 1959-89, chmn. bd. dirs., 1989-97; ret. Sr. vis. lectr. ocean engring. dept. MIT, Cambridge, 1968-78; vis. prof. U. Technologie de Compiègne, 1975, 77-82 Author: Sound, Structures and Their Interaction, 1972, 2d edit., 1986, rev. edit., 1993, Eléments d'Acoustique Physique, 1978, Handbook of Acoustic Characteristics of Turbomachinery Cavities, 1997; guest editor, author: Structural Acoustics, 1997; contbr. articles to profl. jours. Fellow ASME (Rayleigh lectr., Per Bruel Noise Control and Acoustics Gold medal 1992), Acoustical Soc. Am. (Trent-Crede medal 1987). Achievements include patents in field. Home: 32 Lake St Arlington MA 02474 Personal E-mail: ellenandmiguel@earthlink.net. *

JUNG SOOK, HA, medical educator; b. Daegu, Republic of Korea, Apr. 13, 1971; MB, Keimyung U. Sch. Medicine, 1996, M, 2003. Fellow, clin. faculty Keimyung U. Sch. Medicine, 2001—03, lectr., 2004—05, asst. prof., 2006—10, assoc. prof., 2011—. Rsch. fellow, dept. pathology Charles Lee's Cytogenetic Lab. Brigham and Women's Hosp., 2008—09. Mem.: Korean Med. Assn., Korean Soc. Hematology, Korean Soc. Lab. Medicine. Avocations: travel, movies. Office: 56 Dalsung-ro Jung-gu Dongsan Med Ctr Daegu 700-712 Republic of Korea Office Phone: 82-53-250-7266. Office Fax: 82-53-250-7275. Business E-Mail: ksksmom@dsmc.or.kr.

JUN HUA, PENG, physician; b. Qidong, Hunan, June 6, 1966; D, Third Mil. Med. U., 2005. Resident physician Lanzhou Gen. Hosp., 1990—96, attending physician, 1997—2001, assoc. chief physician, dep. dir., 2002—. Recipient 3rd prize, Gen. Logistics Dept., Gansu Provincial Com. Challenges Sci. Mem.: Chinese Nutrition Soc., Gansu Provincial Clin. Virologica Com., Chinese Soc. Microbiology, Gansu Provincial Clin. Chemistry and Lab. Medicine. Avocations: music, singing, mountain climbing, jogging, cooking. Office: 333 Southern Binhe Rd Lanzhou Gansu 730050 China Business E-Mail: junhua_p@sohu.com.

JUNKER, ANNETTE MARTINA, pharmacist; b. Wermelskirchen, Germany, Nov. 16, 1962; d. Siegfried and Elizabeth Hackenberg; m. Uwe Junker; children: Britta, Sonja. Degree in Pharmacy, Friedrich-Wilhelm-Universität, Bonn, 1987. Lic. pharmacist 1987. Clin. pharmacist Sana Klinikum Remscheid, Remscheid, NRW, Germany, 1987—; chief editor OnkoNet, Hamburg, Germany, 1999—. Editor (author): articles to profl. jours. Mem.: Internat. Soc. Oncology Pharmacy Practitioners. Home: Sellscheid 100 NRW Wermelskirchen 42929 Germany Office: Sana Klinikum Remscheid Burger Straße 211 NRW Remscheid 42859 Germany Home Phone: 0049 2196 95795; Office Phone: 0049 2191 133031.

JUNKER, UWE, anesthesiologist; b. Remscheid, Germany, Aug. 2, 1959; s. Hans-Gerd and Hannelore Junker; m. Annette Hackenberg Junker, Nov. 16, 1962; children: Britta, Sonja. MD, U. Cologne, 1984; grad., U. Bonn, 1984. Anesthesiologist Hosp. Luedenscheid, Germany, 1986, Hosp. Sanaklinikum, Remscheid, 1986—2004; chief pain therapy, 2002—04; chief anaesthesiology, intensive care and pain therapy St. Mary's Hosp., Ratingen, 2004—. Spkr. Opioids/Pfizer, Germany, 2001—; mem. adv. bd. Coxibs/Pfizer, 2002—, Life Quality, 2003—. Mem.: Deutsche Gesellschaft Anasthesiologie Intensivmedizin, Deutsche Gesellschaft Palliativmedizin, Deutsche Gesellschaft zum Studium des Schmerzes, Deutsche Gesellschaft fuer Schmerztherapie. Avocations: tennis, jogging, travel. Home: Sellscheid 100 42929 Wermelskirchen Germany Office Phone: 02102-8510. E-mail: u.junker@smkr.de.

JUNOD, DANIEL AUGUST, retired podiatrist; b. Vandalia, Ill., Sept. 12, 1928; s. Louis August and Nettie Louise (Martin) J.; m. Joanne Alice Denton, Mar. 29, 1952; children: Paul, John, Timothy, David, Stephen. Student, Greenville Coll., Ill., 1946-48; DPM, Scholl Coll. Podiatric Med., Chgo., 1952. Pvt. practice podiatrist, Greenville, 1952—2011; staff podiatrist Fair Oaks Nursing Home, Greenville, 1970—2003, Brauns Terrace, Greenville, 1989—2011, Woodlawn Ct., Greenville, 1999—2011, Faith Countryside Homes Nursing Ctr., Highland, Ill., 1992—2003, Highland (Ill.) Health Care Ctr., 1993-2000. Contbr. articles to profl. jours. Avocations: photography, volksmarching, video photography, photography and artwork. Home: 511 S 2nd St Greenville IL 62246-1742

JUN SEOK, KOH, medical educator; PhD, Kyung Hee U. Grad. Sch. Medicine, Seoul, Republic Of Korea, 2002. Cert. in neurosurgery Ministry of Korean Health & Welfare, 1996. Asst. prof. neurosurgery Kyung Hee U. Sch. Medicine, 2003—07, assoc. prof. neurosurgery, 2007—; chief endovascular neurointerventional divsn., dept. nuerosurgery, stroke & neurol. disorders ctrs. East-West Neo Med. Hosp. Kyung-Hee U., 2006—, dir. stroke & neurol. disordrs ctrs., 2009. Rev. bd. mem. Jour. Korean Neurosurg. Soc., Seoul, 2006—, Jour. Korean Soc. Intravascular Neurosurgery, Seoul, 2006—; com. mem. Korean Neurosurg. Soc. Acute Ischemic Stroke, 2009—. Contbr. articles to profl. jours. Capt., med. officer Korean Army, 1996—99. Achievements include research in bilateral vertebral artery dissecting aneurysm causing subarachnoid hemorrhage cured by staged endovascular reconstruction following occlusion; carotid artery stenting in a patient with spontaneous recanalization of a proximal internal carotid artery occlusion; three-dimensional angiographic demonstration of plexiform fenestrations of the proximal anterior cerebral artery associated with a ruptured aneurysm; less invasive approach for rupture aneurysm with intracranial hemato: coil embolization followed by clot evacuation; serial angiographic evolution and regrassion of traumatic aneurysm of the internal carotid artery associated with a carotid-cavernous fistula; management and clinical outcome of acute basilar artey dissection; ruptured aneurysm arising form the distal end of a proximal A1 fenestration: case report and review of the literature. Office: East-West Neo Med Ctr Sangil-dong 149 Gandong-gu Seoul 134-090 Republic of Korea Office Phone: 822-440-6145. Office Fax: 822-440-7171. Personal E-mail: neurokoh@khu.ac.kr. Business E-Mail: neurokoh@hanmail.net.

JUNZHAO, ZHAO, medical educator; b. Zhejiang, China, Nov. 28, 1967; D, Wenzhou Med. Coll., 2011. Assoc. prof. 1st Affiliated Hosp. Wenzhou Med. Coll., 2004—09, prof., 2010—. Office: 2 Fuxue Ln Wenzhou Zhejiang 325000 China Personal E-mail: z.joyce08@163.com.

JUOCEVICIUS, ALVYDAS, physiatrist, educator; b. Prienai, Lithuania, May 19, 1951; M, Tartu U., Estonia, 1976; PhD, Inst. Exptl. and Clin. Medicine, Vilnius, Lithuania, 1986. Rschr., dept. rehab. Inst. Exptl. and clin. Medicine, Health Ministry Republic of Lithuania, 1980—89; cons. rehab. field Health Ministry Republic of Lithuania, 1989—; med. dir. Ctr. Rehab., Phys. and Sports Medicine, Vilnius U. Hosp. Santariskiu klinikos, 1991—; head prof., dept. rehab., phys. and sports medicine, faculty medicine Vilnius U., 1991—, mem. coun., faculty medicine, 2007—. Recipient prize, Govt. Republic of Lithuania, award, Olimpic Com. Lithuania. Mem.: Baltic Nordic Sea Forum Phys. and Rehab. Medicine, European Soc. Phys. and Rehab. Medicine (exec. com.), UEMS Phys. and Rehab. Medicine Sect. and Bd. Avocations: sailing, sports, reading. Office: Santariskiu 2 Vilnius LT 08661 Lithuania Office Fax: 37052365173. Business E-Mail: alvydas.juocevicius@santa.lt.

JURADO-PALOMO, JESUS, physician, allergist; b. Cordoba, Spain, July 30, 1979; s. Jesus Jurado Fernandez and Dolores Palomo Toledano. Degree in Medicine, U. Cordoba, Spain, 2003; degree in Clin. Rsch., Autonomous U. Madrid, Spain, 2006; specialist in Allergology, U. Hosp. La Paz, Madrid, 2008; graduate in Clin. Genetics, U. Alcala de Henares, Spain, 2010. Cert. in allergology and clin. immunology European Acad. Allergology and Clin. Immunology, Barcelona, 2008, London, 2010. Dept. cellular biology, physiology and immunology U. Cordoba, Spain, 1998—2003; allergology specialist U. Hosp. La Paz, Madrid, 2004—08, Complexo Hosp. U. A Coruña, 2008—09, Hosp. General Nuestra Señora del Prado, Talavera de la Reina, 2009—. Contbr. scientific papers to profl. publ. jours., chapters to books, clin. assays in Spanish and English. Mem.: European Respiratory Soc., Madrid-Castille La Mancha Soc. Allergology & Clin. Immunology, European Acad. Allergology and Clin. Immunology (Cert. Excellence Barcelona 2008, Cert. Excellence London 2010, Cert. Excellence Istanbul 2011), Spanish Soc. Allergology and Clin. Immunology, Spanish Group for the study of Bradykinin induced Angioedema. Office: Dept Allergology Hosp General Ntra Sra del Prado Planta Baja Consultas Externas Carretera de Madrid Km 114 Talavera de la Reina Toledo 45600 Spain Personal E-mail: h72jupaj@yahoo.es.

JURECKA, TOMAS, ophthalmologist, educator; b. Kyjov, Czech Republic, Nov. 20, 1972; s. Jiri Jurecka and Drahomira Jureckova; m. Andrea Vecerova, June 24, 2000; children: Adela Jureckova, Nikol Jureckova. MD, Masaryk U., Brno, 1997, PhD, 2007. Cert. ophthalmologist Ministry of Health, Czech Republic, 2005. Ho. officer St. Ann Tchg. Hosp., Brno, 1999—2001, sr. ho. officer, 2001—02; asst. prof. Masaryk U. Med. Sch, Brno, 2002—09, NeoVize Eye Clinic, Brno, 2009—. Grantee, Soc. European Ophthalmologists, 2002. Mem.: Czech Ophthal. Soc. Avocations: photography, skiing, hiking, volleyball. Home: Pavlovska 12 Brno Kohoutovice 623 00 Czech Republic Office: NeoVize Eye Clinic Vinicni 235 615 00 Brno Czech Republic Office Phone: 420517070707, 420517070700. Business E-Mail: jurecka@neovize.cz.

JURENKA, JULIE SHALEEN, research scientist; b. Mont., May 27, 1959; BS in Microbiology, Mont. State U., 1982; postgrad., Meth. Hosp. Sch. Med. Tech., 1983. Cert. med. tachnologist Am. Assn. Clin. Pathology. Lab. supr. Vets. Adminstrn. Med. Ctr., 1987—90; asst. lab. supr. Winslow Clinic - Va. Mason Med. Ctr., 1990—93; rsch. asst., event mgr. Thorne Rsch., Inc., 1997—. Assoc. editor Alternative Medicine Rev., 2006—11. Mem.: Am. Assn. Clin. Pathology. Avocations: skiing, bicycling, travel. Office: PO Box 25 Dover ID 83825 Business E-Mail: jjurenka@thorne.com.

JUREVICIUS, JONAS, medical researcher; b. Siauliai, Lithuania, Aug. 21, 1946; PhD, Lithuanian U. Health Scis., 1992. Head lab. Lithuanian U. Health Scis., 1987—. Recipient Lithuanian Sci. award, 2008. Mem.: Biophys. Soc. Office: Sukileliu 17 Kaunas LT-50009 Lithuania Business E-Mail: jonas.jurevicius@lsmuni.lt.

JURGENSEN, MONSERRATE, clinical nurse, consultant; b. Guyanailla, PR, Oct. 25, 1945; d. Francisco and Felicita (Feliciano) Muniz; m. Timothy J. Jurgensen, Dec. 1, 1978; children: Timothy J. Jr., Jeremy J. Diploma, Presbyn. Hosp. Sch. Nursing, San Juan, PR, 1967; BSN, Barry U., 1990; postgrad., Webster U., 1992—, U. Phoenix. RN, Fla. Surg. unit and surg. ICU staff nurse U. Hosp., PR, 1967-69; commd. 2d lt. USAF, 1969, advanced through grades to maj., 1986; pediat. unit staff nurse USAF Hosp., Sheppard AFB, Tex., 1969-70, orthopedic and psychiat. unit staff nurse Cam Ranh Bay, Vietnam, 1970-71, staff nurse obstetrics unit Torrejon AFB, Spain, 1971-74, obstetrics head nurse K.I. Sawyer AFB, Mich., 1974-78, staff nurse obstetrics unit, head nurse pediatric clinic Langley AFB, Va., 1978-81; med.-surg. nurse USAFR, Langley AFB, Va., 1984-86, staff nurse Primary Care Clinics Norfolk, Va., 1985-86; staff nurse Cigna HMO, Miami, Fla., 1986-87; staff nurse long-term care unit VA Hosp., Miami, 1988-90, med.-surg. nurse psychiat. unit, 1990-91; quality control nurse, infection control Immunization Clinic, Duke Field, Fla., 1989-91; evening-night supr., mgr. med.-surg. unit same day surgery Army Hosp., Ft. Jackson, SC, 1991-94; mgr. same day surgery med.-surg. unit Reynolds Army Cmty. Hosp., Ft. Sill, Okla., 1994—96; registered nurse Primary Care Clinics Vet. Adminstrn., 1997—. Ret. maj. Mem. Soc. Presbyn. Hosp. Sch. Nursing, Sigma Theta Tau, Nursing Orgn. Veterans Affairs. Republican. Avocations: tennis, cooking, sewing. Office: US Army VA Adminstn Tulsa Outpatient Clinic Tulsa OK 74145 Office Phone: 918-628-2513.

JURGENSEN, WARREN PETER, retired psychiatrist, educator; b. Sioux City, Iowa, June 30, 1921; s. Matthias Peter and Dagmar J.; m. Gwenda Doris Downey, Mar. 30, 1946; children— Gail, Karen, Timothy BS, Northwestern U., 1945; MD, Creighton U., 1950. Diplomate: Am. Bd. Psychiatry and Neurology. Intern Edward W. Sparrow Hosp., Lansing, Mich., 1950—51; regional health dir., then asst. chief U.S. Health Mission to Iran, 1951—54; psychiat. resident USPHS Hosp., Lexington, Ky., 1955—57, Cin. Gen. Hosp., 1957—58; with USPHS, 1951—70; chief Clin. Research Center, NIMH, Ft. Worth, 1969-70; dir. student health services U. Tex.-Arlington, 1970-77, also adj. prof. biology; psychiatrist Tarrant County Mental Health Mental Retardation Services, Ft. Worth, 1977-86; psychiat. cons., 1984—96; ret., 1996. Clin. asst. prof. U. Ky. Med. Sch., 1962—66; clin. asst. prof. psychiatry U. Tex. Southwestern Med. Sch., 1966—72; vis. rsch. scientist Inst. Behavorial Rsch.

Tex. Christian U., 1967—72; vis. lectr. Regional Tng. Ctr. North Ctrl. Tex. Council Govts., 1967—77; cons. Alive and Well Program U. Tex. Southwestern Med. Sch., 1974—79. Mem. Gov.'s Adv. Council on Drug Abuse, 1973-79. Served with USNR, 1942-45. Fellow Am. Pub. Health Assn.; mem. Am. Psychiat. Assn. (Disting. Life fellow) Episcopalian. Office: Warren & Gwenda Jurgensen 5100 Randoll Mill Rd Apr 1116 Fort Worth TX 76112-1523

JURKIEWICZ, MAURICE JOHN, surgeon, educator; b. Claremont, NH, Sept. 24, 1923; s. Charles B. and Mary (Ostrowska) J.; m. Mary de Forest Freeman, July 7, 1951; children— Elizabeth de Forest, John Christopher. D.D.S. magna cum laude, U. Md., 1946; MD, Harvard U., 1952. Diplomate: Am. Bd. Surgery, Am. Bd. Plastic Surgery (mem. bd. 1971-77, chmn. 1977-78). Intern Barnes Hosp., Washington U., St. Louis, 1952-53, resident, 1953-58, clin. fellow, 1958-59, instr. surgery, 1957-59; mem. staff U. Fla. Hosp., Gainesville; asst. prof. surgery U. Fla., 1959-64, assoc. prof., 1964-67, prof., 1967-71, chief div. plastic and reconstructive surgery, 1959-71; chief of surgery VA Hosp., Gainesville, 1968-71; prof. surgery, chief of plastic and reconstructive surgery Emory Affiliated Hosps., Atlanta, 1971-92; chief surg. services Grady Meml. Hosp., Atlanta, 1972-77; chief of surgery VAMC, Atlanta, 1989-93. Cons. plastic surgery Walter Reed Gen. Hosp., Washington, 1971-91; sci. counselor Nat. Inst. Dental Rsch., 1966-71; chmn. com. on study of evaluation procedures Am. Bd. Med. Spltys., 1979-81; mem. at large Nat. Bd. Med. Exams., 1985-93; commr. Joint Commn. on Accreditation of Health Care Orgns., 1985-94 (sec. 1989-90, treas. 1990-91, vice chmn. 1991-92); nat. Ccns. plastic surgery Shriners Hosp., 1995-2000. Editor: Operative Techniques in Plastic Surgery, 1994-99; assoc. editor: Plastic and Reconstructive Surgery, 1972-78, 79-83, co-editor, 1985-89; assoc. editor Am. Surgeon, 1977-87. Served to lt. (j.g.) USNR, 1946-48. Fellow Royal Australasian Coll. Surgeons (hon.); mem. AMA, Am. Cancer Soc., Am. Cleft Palate Assn., ACS (bd. regents 1979-88, vice chmn. 1985-88, pres.-elect 1988, pres. 1989-90), Am. Soc. Plastic and Reconstructive Surgeons, Southeastern Soc. Plastic and Reconstructive Surgeons, Ga, Soc. Plastic and Reconstructive Surgeons, Southeastern Surg. Congress (hon. fellow), Am. Soc. Head and Neck Surgeons (pres. 1989), Ednl. Founds. Plastic Surgery Coun., Am. Assn. Plastic Surgeons (pres. 1980, dist. fellow), Am. So. Surg Assns. (1st v.p. 1993-94, hon. fellow), Med. Assn. Ga. Home: 715 Old Post Rd NW Atlanta GA 30328-4758 Office: Emory U Clinic 550 Peachtree St 8th Fl Ste 4300 Atlanta GA 30308

JUROWSKI, PIOTR, ophthalmologist, researcher; b. Lódz, Poland, Aug. 23, 1965; s. Wladyslaw Jurowski and Dorota (Berlinska) Jurowska; m. Maja Beata Sobczyk, Oct. 25, 1990; children: Iga Joanna Jurowska, Julia Wiktoria Jurowska. MD, Mil. Med. U. Lódz, 1990. Asst. dept. physiology Med. U., Lódz, 1991, mem. staff dept. ophthalmology and visual rehab., 2002—; mem. staff dept. ophthalmology Mil. Med. U., Lódz, 1992—2002. Grantee, Polish Sci. Rsch. Com., 2002. Achievements include research in nitric oxide function in ophthalmology. Avocations: geography, sports, literature. Home: Ul. Mimozy 35A 91-864 Lodz Poland Fax: +48 (42) 616 83 92. E-mail: p.jurowski@poczta.wprost.pl.

JURTSHUK, PETER, JR., microbiologist, educator; b. NYC, July 28, 1929; s. Peter and Mary (Ferens) J.; m. Rebecca Jones, Jan. 2, 1971; children: Peter, Larissa. AB, NYU, 1951; MS, Creighton U., 1953; PhD, U. Md., 1957. Asst. prof. pharmacology Bklyn. Coll. Pharmacy, L.I. U., 1957-59; asst. prof. enzyme chemistry U. Wis.-Madison, 1962-63; asst. prof. microbiology U. Tex., Austin, 1963-69; assoc. prof. biology and biochemistry U. Houston, 1970-76, prof., 1976—, undergrad. chmn., 1976—80, dir. program in microbiology, 1990—2004. Mem. vis. biol. program Am. Inst. Biol. Scis., 1969-72. Contbr. chpts. to books. Recipient Disting. Svc. award Tex. br. Am. Soc. Microbiology, 1982; NIH grantee, 1964-75; NSF grantee, 1986-89. Fellow Am. Acad. Microbiology; mem. Am. Soc. Microbiology (pres. Tex. br. 1972-74), N.Y. Acad. Scis., Am. Soc. Biochemistry and Molecular Biology, Am. Chem. Soc., Sigma Xi (pres. U. Houston chpt. 1979-80). Russian Orthodox. Home: 879 Ramada Dr Houston TX 77062-5607 Office: U Houston Biology and Biochemistry Dept Houston TX 77204-5001 Home Phone: 281-280-8457; Office Phone: 713-743-2668. Business E-Mail: jurtshuk@uh.edu.

JURUKOVA, ZANKA BORISSOVA, pathologist, educator; b. Plovdiv, Bulgaria, Mar. 18, 1931; d. Boris Vassilev Jurukov and Rouja Todorova Jurukova; m. Peter Georgiev, Apr. 4, 1969; children: Nijagul, Ava. MD, H.S. Medicine, Sofia, Bulgaria, 1957; PhD, Med. Acad., Sofia, Bulgaria, 1968, DSc, 1978. Med. diplomate. Rsch. fellow Bulgarian Acad. Scis., Sofia, 1964-73; assoc. prof. pathology Med. Acad., Sofia, 1974-85, prof. pathology, 1986—. Cons. pathologist State Hosp., Blagoevgrad, Bulgaria, 1981-88; mem. Superior Med. Certifying Commn., Sofia, 1987-92; pres. Sci. Coun. Morphology, Sofia, 1992-97; prof. cardiac pathology U. Hosp. St. Ekatherina, Sofia, 2000-06. Author: Cellular Pathology of the Arterial Wall, 1981; mem. adv. bd. Gen. Pathology/Pathol. Anatomy, 1990—95. Active Union Bulgarian Women. Recipient Best Monography of the Yr., Med. Acad. Sofia, Bulgaria, 1981. Mem.: Internat. Soc. Artherosclerosis, European Soc. Pathology, Bulgarian Soc. Pathology (bd. mem. 1993—), N.Y. Acad. Scis. Roman Catholic. Avocations: classical music, skiing. Home: Boul Vitosha 28 1000 Sofia Bulgaria Office: Med Acad Dept Pathology G Sofiiski str 1 BG-1431 Sofia Bulgaria Office Phone: 359-2-9159465. Personal E-mail: zankajurukova@yahoo.com.

JUSKOWA, JOANNA TERESA, medical educator; b. Wola Zbrozkowa, Poland, Apr. 21, 1935; d. Wacław Padzik and Euzebia Halina Kazanecka-Padzik; m. Dionizy Marcin Juska, June 29, 1957; 1 child, Margaret-Catherine (dec.). Diploma, Med. U., Warsaw, Poland, 1958; degree in Internal Medicine, Med. U., 1966, degree in Cardiology, 1971, degree in Nephrology, 1987, MD, 1969, PhD, 1981. Vice-dir. transplantation inst. Med. U., Warsaw, 1984—87, head dept. immunotherapy transplantation, 1986—91, prof., organizer new physiotherapy faculty, 2000—02, head dept. rehab., dean physiotherapy faculty, 2002—05. Tchr. Med. U., Warsaw, 1960—75, tchr. internal medicine, dental faculty, 1986—2003. Contbr. articles to profl. jours., chapters to books. Decorated Knight of Polish Renaissance; recipient 10 awards, Med. U. Warsaw, 1966—2002, Golden Cross award, 1984, award, Polish Acad. Scis., 1987, Very Good Healthcare award, 1988, awards, Ministry of Health, Ministry Higher Edn., 1988, 1991. Mem.: Polish Soc. Transplantation, Internat. Soc. Nephrology, Polish Soc. Nephrology, European Soc. Cardiology, Polish Soc. Cardiology. Avocations: theater, opera, gardening, walking. Office: Transplantation Inst 59 Nowogrodzka St 02-006 Warsaw Poland Home: 7 Wańkowicza St m 57 02-798 Warsaw Poland Fax: 04822 502 2127. Personal E-mail: nasilowska@poczta.onet.pl.

JUSTINIANI, FEDERICO ROBERTO, retired internist, educator; b. Havana, Cuba, Aug. 15, 1929; came to U.S., 1964, naturalized, 1969; s. Federico Luis and Margarita (Longa) J.; m. Maria Suarez, Nov. 29, 1955. BS, De La Salle Coll., Havana, 1947; MD, Havana U., 1954. Diplomate Am. Bd. Internal Medicine (recognized for advanced achievement 1987). Intern, resident in internal medicine Havana U. Hosp., 1955-61; practice medicine Havana, 1961-64; intern St. Francis Hosp., Miami Beach, Fla., 1965; resident in internal medicine Mt. Sinai Hosp., Miami Beach, 1966-69, program coord. residency in internal medicine, 1969-74; dir. med. edn. Mt. Sinai Med. Ctr., Miami Beach, 1974—2002; instr. medicine U. Miami, 1969-72, asst. prof., 1972-82, assoc. prof., 1982-90, prof., 1990—2010. Contbr. articles to profl. jours. Master ACP; mem. AMA (Physicians Recognition awards), Fla. Med. Assn., So. Med. Assn., Dade County Med. Assn., Am. Geriatrics Soc., Cuban Med. Assn. in Exile, Nat. Assn. Cuban-Am. Educators (pres. 2004—08). Home Phone: 305-444-6845. Personal E-mail: fjustin@bellsouth.net.

JUVONEN, TATU, cardiologist, educator; b. Finland, Oct. 6, 1960; MD, U. Oulu, 1984, PhD, 1993, MBA, 2009. Prof. surgery U. Oulu, 2000—. Avocations: cross country skiing, hunting. Office: Kajaanintie 52 Oulu 90029 Finland Office Phone: 35883152092. E-mail: tatu.juvonen@oulu.fi.

KAAKAJI, WAYEL, neurosurgeon, educator; b. Aleppo, Syria, May 19, 1967; s. Mohamed Kaakaji and Souna Nasri. BS, McGill U., 1989; MD, U. Tex., San Antonio, 1993. Surg. intern Cleve. Clinic Found., 1993—94, neurosurg. resident, 1994—99; staff neurosurgeon Neurol. and Spinal Surgery, Inc., Merrillville, Ind., 1999—2002, St. John Hosp., Detroit, 2002—. Adv. cons. EPS Pharms., Detroit. Contbr. articles to profl. jours., chapters to books. Fellow: ACS; mem.: Asian Am. Med. Soc. (bd. dirs.), Nat. Assn. Spine Specialists (congl. liaison), Congress of Neurol. Surgeons, Am. Assn. Neurol. Surgeons (Dewey Penehouse award 1999), Alpha Omega Alpha. Avocations: tennis, rowing, hiking.

KABALA-DZIK, AGATA BEATA, pharmacist, educator; b. Sosnowiec, Poland, July 7, 1969; MS in Lab. Medicine, Med. U. Silesia, 1994, PhD in Med. Sci., 2003. Rsch. scientist, adj. prof., faculty pharmacy Med. U. Silesia, 1998—. Asst. Inst. Occupl. Medicine and Environ. Health, 1995—98. Recipient Didactic award, Med. U. Silesia. Mem.: Polish Soc. Exptl. and Clin. Immunology, Polish Pharmacy Assn., Polish Med. Diagnostics Assn. Avocations: music, travel, mountain climbing. Office: Ul Ostrogórska 30 Sosnowiec Slaskie 41-200 Poland Business E-Mail: adzik@sum.edu.pl.

KABALIN, JOHN NICHOLAS, urologist; b. LA, Dec. 23, 1958; s. Nicholas Augustin and Mary Jane (Engleman) Kabalin; m. Pamela Grace White, July 11, 1981. BS, Stanford U., 1980; MD, Johns Hopkins U., 1984. Diplomate Am. Bd. Urology. Intern in surgery Stanford U. Med. Ctr., 1984-85, resident in surgery, 1985-86, resident in urology, 1986-90, chief resident in urology, 1989-90; chief urology sect. Va Med. Ctr., Palo Alto, Calif., 1990-97; asst. prof. urology Stanford (Calif.) U., 1990-97; asst. prof. surgery U. Nebr. Coll. Medicine, 1999—. Contbr. over 100 articles to profl. jours., over 20 chpts. in books. Fellow: ACS, Am. Coll. Forensic Examiners, Sexual Medicine Soc. of N. Am., Am. Soc. for Laser Medicine and Surgery, Internat. Coll. Surgeons; mem.: AAAS, AMA, Soc. Urology & Engring., Soc. Urologic Prosthetic Surgeons, Soc. Laparoendoscopic Surgeons, Am Inst. Ultrasound Medicine, Am. Bd. Forensic Medicine, NY Acad. Scis., Internat. Soc. Urology, Biomed. Optics Soc., Am. Lithotripsy Soc., Endourol. Soc., Soc. Univ. Urologists, Soc. Urol. Oncology, Am. Soc. Clin. Oncology, Am. Urol. Assn., Am. Assn. Clin. Urologists, Alpha Omega Alpha, Phi Beta Kappa. Roman Catholic. Achievements include adaptation and clinical development of Holmium laser sources for soft tissue and prostatic surgery. Office: Ste 2200 3911 Ave B Scottsbluff NE 69361-4669 Home Phone: 308-632-2552; Office Phone: 308-632-5315. Business E-Mail: kabalij@rwmc.net.

KABIR, JAHANGIR, urologist; MBBS, Fairfax County Pub. Sch., 1983; short course, Inst. of Urology and Nephrology, London, Bristol Urological Inst., Glan Clawyd Hosp., UK. Fellowship Bangladesh Coll. of Physicians and Surgeons, Royal Coll. of Physician and Surgeons, Glasgow, England; urol. intern Bangabandhu Sheikh Mujib Med. Univ., Dhaka, Bangladesh, St. Mary's Hosp., Isle of Wight, England, Univ. Hosp. Aintree, Liverpool, England; sr. cons. & head urology dept. Lab Aid Specialized Hosp., Dhaka, Bangladesh, 2001—. Prof. health and sci. faculty State Univ. of Bangladesh; head academic affairs Lab Aid Specialized Hosp., Dhaka, Bangladesh. Mem.: Soc. of Surgeons of Bangladesh (life), Bangladesh Assn. Urol. Surgeons (life). Office: Lab Aid Specialized Hospital House Number 6 Road Number 4 Dhanmondi Dhaka Bangladesh Office Phone: 88028610793. Office Fax: 88028617372. *

KABIR, ZARINA NAHAR, research scientist, educator; b. Dhaka, Bangladesh, Sept. 30, 1964; MA, U. Sussex, 1990; PhD, Karolinska Inst., 2001. Assoc. prof. Karolinska Inst., 2001. Dir. BRAC, 2007—09. Mem.: Swedish South Asian Studies Network. Office: Alfred Nobels Allé 23 Stockholm Huddinge 14183 Sweden

KACAR KOCAK, MEHTAP, physiologist; b. Elazig, Aug. 29, 1969; Degree in Medicine, Firat U. Medicine Sch., 1991; PhD, Ankara U. Medicine Sch., 2004. Pathophysiologist Yeditepe U. Medicine Sch., 2007—. Mem.: Turkish Thoracic Soc. Avocations: tennis, golf. Office: EPDK Muhsin Yazicioglu C 51/C Ankara 06520 Turkey Business E-Mail: mkocak@epdk.org.tr.

KACHNOWSKI, STAN, medical educator, researcher; s. Robert Kachnowski and Winnie McCarthy; m. Jennifer Kachnowski; 1 child, Katherine. Bachelors, Masters, U. of Vt., Burlington, Vermont. Senior Fellow Health Informatics Lab, 2002, Fellow Royal Med. Soc., 2003. Prof. Columbia U., New York, NY, 1997—, Pace U. Sch. of Bus., New York, NY, 1995—97. Bd. mem. Medem, Inc., San Francisco, 2002—03, PGMSi.com, New York, NY, 2002—03. Advisor Can. Govt., Toronto, Ontrario, Canada, 2003—03. Grantee Many, Many, 1991 to 2003. Achievements include research in eClinical Trials; Online Physician Patient Messaging; Bioterrorism; Bioinformatics; Electronic Medical Records. Home: 182 Riverview Ave Tarrytown NY 10591 Office: Columbia Univ 3960 Broadway 4th Fl Informatics New York NY 10032 Business E-Mail: swk16@hitlab.org.

KACHROO, PRADEEP, biology professor; b. Kashmir, India, Sept. 3, 1966; PhD, M. S. U., India, 1995. Assoc. prof. U. Ky., 2003—. Mem.: Internat. Soc. Plant-Microbe Interactions, Am. Phytopathol. Soc., Am. Soc. Plant Biologist. Office: Plant Sci Bldg 1405 Veterans Dr 201F Lexington KY 40546 Office Fax: 859-323-1961. Business E-Mail: pk62@uky.edu.

KACKER, ASHUTOSH, medical educator; m. Maneesha Sharma, Nov. 21, 1966; children: Ila Nikki, Avi. MBBS, All India Inst. of Med. Scis., New Delhi India, 1989; MS, All India Inst. Med. Scis., New Delhi, 1992. Intern internal medicine St. Peters Med. Ctr., New Brunswick, NY, 1993; fellowship ENT Lenox Hill Hosp., 1993—95, intern surgery, 1995—96, resident surgery, 1996—97; resident ENT Manhattan Eye Ear and Throat Hosp., 1997—99, NY Presbyn. Hosp., 1999—2001; fellow ENT/rhinology Weill Coll. Medicine Cornell U., 2001—; asst. prof. Weill Med. Coll., NYC, 2001—05, assoc. prof., 2005—. Fellow: Am. Acad. Otolaryngology Head and Neck Surgery. Office: Weil Med Coll Cornell 1305 York Ave 5th Fl New York NY 10021 Office Fax: 640-962-0100. Business E-Mail: ask9001@med.cornell.edu.

KACZMARZYK, TOMASZ, oral surgeon, educator; b. Czestochowa, Poland, Oct. 11, 1975; s. Tadeusz and Maria Kaczmarzyk. DDS, Jagiellonian U., Krakow, Poland, 1999, PhD, 2004. Sr. asst. dept. oral surgery Jagiellonian U., Krakow, 2001—. Sec. mgmt. Polish Dental Assn., Krakow, 2005—. Editor, author (textbook) Contemporary pharmacotherapy in oral and maxillofacial surgery, 2006; contbr. articles to profl. jours. Grantee, State Com. for Sci. Rsch., 2003—04, Jagiellonian U., 2002—05. Mem.: Polish Assn. Oral and Maxillofacial Surgery (assoc.), Polish Dental Assn. (assoc.), Brit. Assn. Oral and Maxillofacial Surgery (assoc.), Internat. Assn. Oral and Maxillofacial Surgery (assoc.). Achievements include research in peripheral morphine administration in inflamed oral and maxillofacial tissues; efficacy of one-shot antibiotic therapy in oral surgery; interactions of drugs used in oral and maxillofacial surgery; efficacy of azithromycin in oral and maxillofacial surgery. Avocations: travel, sight-seeing, swimming, cinema, jazz music. Office: Jagiellonian Univ Montelupich 4 Cracow 31-155 Poland Office Fax: +48 12 4245499. E-mail: tomkaczm@cm-uj.krakow.pl.

KADER, NANCY STOWE, nursing consultant, bioethicist, philosopher; b. Ogden, Utah, May 29, 1945; d. William Hessel and Mildred (Madsen) Stowe; m. Omar Kader, Jan. 25, 1967; children: Tarik, Gabriel, Aron, Jacob. BSN, Brigham Young U., 1967; PhD, U. Md., 2005. RN. Nurse ICU Glendale (Calif.) Adventist Hosp., 1970-75, Utah Valley Hosp., Provo, 1975-83; campaign coord. Matheson for Gov., Salt Lake City, 1976-85, Wilson for Senate, Salt Lake City, 1980; nurse cons. MESA Corp., Reston, Va., 1984—85; mgr. cost containment Health Mgmt. Strategies, Washington, 1985-88; nurse cons. Birch & Davis, Washington, 1988-90; cons. Inst. Medicine NAS, Washington, 1990-92; cons. Pal-Tech Inc., Arlington, Va., 1992—. Vice chmn. Utah State Bd. Nursing, Salt Lake City, 1977—83; adj. prof. Hood Coll., Md., 2000; ethics cons. to Healthcare Systems, Washington; cons. in field. Contbr. articles various profl. jours. Dem. county chmn., Utah, 1977-79; del. Dem. Nat. Conv., 1980, Va. State Dem. Conv., 1984-95; vice chmn. Gov.'s Commn. on Status of Women, Salt Lake City, 1975-78; bd. dirs. Health Sys. Agy. No. Va., 2000-. Democrat. Home: 10301 Dunfries Rd Vienna VA 22181 Business E-Mail: nkader@cox.net.

KADIR, REZAN A., obstetrician, gynecologist, educator; b. Erbil, Iraq, Nov. 18, 1962; d. Ahmed and Samaa Abdul Kadir; m. Zaid T. Dabbagh; children: Cameron Adam Dabbagh, Alan Eamonn Dabbagh. MBChB, Baghdad U.; MD, U. London, 2000. Cert. in ob-gyn. Arab Bd., Jordan, 1990, in obstetric ultrasound Royal Coll. Radilogists, 1998, specialist in ob-gyn. 2002. Postgrad. trainee Royal Free Hosp., London, 1995—97, postgrad. rsch. fellow, 1995—98, cons., fetal medicine, ob-gyn. & women with bleeding disorders, 2002—, sr. lectr., ob-gyn., 2002—; postgrad. trainee, ob-gyn. North Thames Deanery, London, 1998—2002. Chair, women bd. Haemophilia Soc., London, 2004—; editl. bd. mem. Jour. Haemophilia; mem Internat. Adv. Bd. Women Issues Thrombosis & Haemostasis. Editor: (book) Inherited Bleeding Diosrders in Women; contbr. scientific papers (Fondazione Angelo Biancho Bonomi prize, 1998). Fellow: Royal Coll. Surgeons; mem.: Brit. Maternal and Fetal Medicine Soc., World Fedn. Haemophilia, Internat. Soc. Thrombosis and Haemostasis, Royal Coll. Ostetrician & Gynecologists (cert. in obstetric ultrasound 1998). Achievements include research in field of women and inherited bleeding disorders; development of multidsicplinary medical care provision for women. Office: Royal Free Hosp Hampstead London NW3 2QG England

KADOSH, DAVID, medical educator; b. Calif., Feb. 12, 1969; BS in Biol. Scis., Cornell U., Ithaca, NY, 1991; PhD in Molecular Pharmacology, Harvard U., Cambridge, Mass., 1998. Postdoc. fellow U. Calif., San Francisco, 1998—2003, rschr., 2003—05; asst. prof. dept. medicine, divsn. infectious diseases U. Tex. Health Sci. Ctr., San Antonio, 2006—. Contbr. articles to profl. jours. Office: University Tex Health Sci Ctr Dept Microbiology and Immunology 7703 Floyd Curl Dr San Antonio TX 78229-3900 Office Fax: 210-567-6612. Business E-Mail: kadosh@uthscsa.edu.

KADOWAKI, KOZO, medical researcher; b. Yachiyo-cho, Hyogo prefecture, Japan, Dec. 23, 1953; s. Kiyoshi and Kinue Kadowaki; m. Yukari Yoshida; 1 child, Aya. MD, Osaka U. Med. Sch., 1980, PhD, 1990. Asst prof. Osaka U. Med. Sch., Suita, Osaka, Japan, 1987—90; rsch. officer AFRC Babraham Inst., Cambridge, England, 1990—93; chief dept. obstetrics and gynecology Aizenbashi Hosp., Osaka, 1993—99, Yao Mcpl. Hosp., 1999—2001, Kawachi Gen. Hosp., Higashi-Osaka, 2007—; asst chief dept. obstetrics Osaka Med. Ctr. and Rsch. Inst. Maternal and Child Health, Izumi, 2001—06. Author: (journals) J Clin Endocrinol Metab; contbr. articles to profl. jours. Home: 5-1 Kitashinmachi Ikoma Nara 6300245 Japan Office: Kawachi Gen Hosp 1-31 Yokomakura Higashi Osaka 578-0954 Japan Home Phone: 0743756879; Office Phone: 0729650731. Office Fax: 0729652022; Home Fax: 0743756879. Personal E-mail: kozo1223@aol.com.

KAELIN, WILLIAM GEORGE, JR., oncologist, educator; b. Jamaica, NY, Nov. 23, 1957; BA, Duke U., Durham, NC, 1979, MD, 1982. Diplomate Am. Bd. Internal Medicine, cert. in med. oncology. Intern, resident John Hopkins Hosp., Balt., 1983—86; clin. fellow med. oncology Dana-Farber Cancer Inst., Boston, 1987—92; asst. prof. medicine Harvard Med. Sch., Boston, 1992—97, assoc. prof.,

1997—2002, prof., 2002—, assoc. dir. basic sci. Dana-Farber/Harvard Cancer Ctr. Investigator Howard Hughes Med. Inst., 1998—; attending physician medicine Brigham & Women's Hosp., Boston; attending physician adult oncology Dana-Farber Cancer Inst. Contbr. articles in profl. jours. Recipient Richard A. Smith prize, Dana-Farber Cancer Inst., 1996—97, Paul Marks prize for Cancer Rsch., Meml. Sloan-Kettering Cancer Ctr., 2001, Gairdner Found. Internat. award, Can., 2010, Richard & Hinda Rosenthal prize, Am. Assn. Cancer Rsch., Doris Duke Disting. Clin. Scientist award. Mem.: NAS, ACP, Am. Soc. Clin. Investigation, Inst. Medicine. Achievements include identification of molecular mechanisms of oxygen sensing in the cell. Office: Dana Farber Cancer Inst 44 Binney St Mayer 457 Boston MA 02115 Office Phone: 617-632-3975. Office Fax: 617-632-4760. Business E-Mail: william_kaelin@dfci.harvard.edu. *

KAESEMEYER, WAYNE HARRY, vascular medicine and hypertension specialist; b. Cincinatti, Ohio, Oct. 12, 1947; s. Harry and Grace (Sanker) K.; m. Dorothy Jean Kaesemeyer, Nov. 3, 1978 (div. Feb. 1984); 1 child Kelly Ann. BS, BA, Wilmington Coll., 1969; MD, Wake Forest U., 1978. Diplomate Nat. Bd. Med. Examiners, Am. Bd. Internal Medicine. Intern in internal medicine N.C. Baptist Hosp., Winston Salem, N.C., 1978-79; residency internal medicine Washington (D.C.) Hosp. Ctr., 1979-80, Med. Coll. Ga., Augusta, 1980-81, chief resident, 1981-82; clinical attending, internal medicine Med. U. S.C., Charleston, 1983-86, Univ. Hosp., Augusta, Ga., 1987-90, clinical attending, Hypertension Clinic, 1987-94, Summerville Profl. Ctr. St. Joseph Hosp., Augusta, 1993—; pres., sr. sci. officer NitroSys. Inc., Augusta. Hosp. appts. Talmadge Hosp., Augusta, 1981-82, VA Hosp., Augusta, 1981-82, Univ. Hosp., Augusta, 1987—, St. Joseph Hosp., Augusta, 1987—, Humana Hosp., Augusta, 1990—; speaker Pfizer Pharms., Calcium Antagonists in Hypertension, Cardiovascular Diseases, 1988—, speaker Knoll Pharms., Calcium Antagonists in Hypertension Cardiovascular diseases, 1989—, speaker for Parke Davis, Med. Edn. programs on Angiotensin Mediated Hypertension and cardiovascular diseases, 1991-92, speaker Hoechst Pharms. ACE Inhibition in Hypertensive and Cardiovascular diseases, 1993— speaker Bristol Myers Squibb Pharms ACE Inhibition in Hypertensive and Cardiovasculardiseases, 1993—; organic chemist Richardson Merrill Pharms., Phillipsburg, N.J., 1970-73; prin. investigator Parke-Davis ADPOt1, 2 segments, Hoechst Pharms, Altace Care Program, Pfizer Pharms., Abbott Labs. Renin inhibitor, Sankyo U.S.A. Corp., Temocapril alone or in combination with hydrochlorothiazide, 1987—. Inventor: Method and Formulation of Stimulating Nitric Oxide Synthesis, U.S. patent, 1994, Method and Formulation for Treating Vascular Disease, patent pending, applied 04/05/97; contbr. more than 15 articles to profl. jours. including New Eng. Jour. Medicine, Am. Jour. Hypertension, Archives Internal Medicine and others. With U.S. Army Reserves, 1969-75. Grantee: Bristol Myers Squibb, Merck & Co., Pfizer. Mem. ACP, Richmond County Med. Soc., Med. Assn. Ga., Am. Soc. Hypertension, Am. Coll. Clin. Pharmacology, Am. Heart Assn., Inter-Am. Soc. Hypertension. Office: NitroSys Inc 512 Telfair St Augusta GA 30901-5863 Home: 106 Mallard Ct Chapel Hill NC 27517-9150 E-mail: htn007@mindspring.com.

KAFKA, MARIAN STERN, neuroscientist; b. Richmond, Va., Mar. 30, 1927; d. Henry Sycle and Adele (Lewit) Stern; m. John S. Kafka, Oct. 3, 1952; children: David Egon, Paul Henry, Alexander Charles. AB in Zoology, Conn. Coll., 1948; PhD in Physiology, U. Chgo., 1952. Rsch. asst. dept. physiol. chemistry Emory U. Sch. Medicine, Atlanta, 1952-53; rsch. assoc. Ill. Neuropsychiat. Inst., U. Ill. Sch. Medicine, Chgo., 1953-54; rsch. asst. dept. internal medicine Yale U. Sch. Medicine, New Haven, 1954-57; USPHS postdoctoral fellow endocrinology br. Nat. Heart, Lung and Blood Inst. NIH, Bethesda, Md., 1965-68, physiologist hypertention-endocrine br., 1968-74, physiologist sect. biochemistry and pharmacology Biol. Psychiatry Br., 1974-82; physiologist Clin. Neurosci. Br. NIMH, Bethesda, 1982-86, exec. sec. neurobehavioral rsch. rev. subcom., neuroscis. rsch. rev. com. Rockville, Md., 1986, exec. sec. cellular neurobiology & psychopharmacology com., 1986-90, chief clin. rev. br. divsn. extramural activities, 1990. Contbr. articles, revs. to sci. publs. Recipient Adminstr.'s award for Meritorious Achievement, ADAMHA, 1989; Marie J. Mergler fellow in physiology, 1950. Mem. AAAS, Am. Physiol. Soc. (mem. pub. affairs and pub. info. com. 1974-79, chair pub. info. com. 1980-84, centennial com. 1979-85), Soc. for Neurosci., Endocrine Soc., Biophys. Soc., Internat. Soc. Chronobiology, Fedn. Am. Soc. for Exptl. Biology (pub. info. com. 1977-82), Phi Beta Kappa, Sigma Xi. Achievements include research in neurotransmitter receptors in animals and humans, molecular interactions between neurotransmitters, receptors and cell membranes, central nervous system control of circadian rhythms. Home: 7834 Aberdeen Rd Bethesda MD 20814-1102 Office: NIMH Parklawn Bldg 5600 Fishers Ln Rm 902C Rockville MD 20852-1750

KAGAN, JEROME, psychologist, educator; b. Newark, Feb. 25, 1929; s. Joseph and Myrtle (Liebermann) K. BS, Rutgers U., 1950; PhD, Yale, 1954. Instr. psychology Ohio State U., 1954-55; research assoc. Fels Research Inst., Yellow Springs, Ohio, 1957-59, chmn. dept. psychology, 1959-64; assoc. prof. psychology Antioch Coll., 1959-64; rsch. prof. psychology Harvard U., 1964-2000, dir. Mind Brain Behavior Initiative, 1996-2000, rsch. prof., 2000—05, prof. emeritus, 2005—. Adv. com. Nat. Inst. Child Health and Devel. Author (with G.S. Lesser): Contemporary Issues in Thematic Apperceptive Methods, 1961; author: (with Moss) Birth to Maturity, 1962; author: (with Mussen, Conger and Huston) Child Development and Personality, 7th edit., 1990; author: (with Segal) Psychology, 7th edit., 1991; author: (with Janis, Mahl and Holt) Personality, 1969, Understanding Children, 1971, Change and Continuity in Infancy, 1971; author: (with Kearsley and Zelazo) Infancy, 1978; author: (with Brim) Constancy and Change, 1980, The Second Year, 1981, The Nature of the Child, 1984; author: Unstable Ideas, 1989, Galen's Prophecy, 1994, Three Seductive Ideas, 1998, Surprise, Uncertainty and Mental Structures, 2002; author: (with Snidman) The Long Shadow of Temperament, 2004; author: (with Norbert Herschkovitz) A Young Mind in a Growing Brain, 2005; author: An Argument for Mind, 2006, What is Emotion?, 2007, The Three Cultures, 2009. Served with AUS, 1955-57. Recipient Lucius Cross medal Yale U., 1981; Phi Beta Kappa scholar, 1988-89. Fellow AAAS, APA (Disting. Sci. Contbn. award 1987, G. Stanley Hall award 1995), Am. Acad. Arts and Scis., Soc. Rsch. Child Devel. (Disting. Sci. Contbn. award 1989); mem. NAS, Inst. Medicine, Ea. Psychol. Assn. Home: 210 Clifton St Belmont MA 02478-2605 Office: Harvard U Dept Psychology William James Hall 33 Kirkland Hl Cambridge MA 02138 Business E-Mail: jk@wjh.harvard.edu.

KAGAN, MIKHAIL YUDOVICH, pediatrician; b. Orenburg, Russia, Dec. 13, 1959; MD, Orenburg State Med. Inst., 1982. Diplomate Bd. Moscow State Medico-Stomatologist U., 2008. Gen. pediatrician Orenburg Regional Children's Hosp., 1988—93, nephrologist, 1993—. Contbr. articles to profl. jour. Grant, Internat. Soc. Nephrology, 2002. Mem.: Russian Dialysis Soc. Avocation: chess. Office: Orenburg Regional Children's Hosp Rybakovskaya 3 Orenburg 460006 Russia Home: Turkestanskaya 15 a-37 460024 Orenburg Russia Office Fax: 7 3532 572008. Personal E-mail: mkaganorenburg@yahoo.com. Business E-Mail: odkb@yandex.ru.

KAGAWA, SUSUMU, hospital administrator; b. 1944; Grad., U. Tokushima, Japan, 1969, MD, 1977, PhD. Asst. prof. faculty medicine Univ. of Tokushima, Japan, 1971, lectr. faculty medicine, 1976, assoc. prof. faculty medicine, 1987, prof. faculty medicine, 1988, pres., 2010; vice dir. Tokushima Univ. Hosp., Japan, 1997, dir., 1999, Tokushima Univ. Med. and Dental Hosp., Japan, 2003—. Co-author: (journals) CD7 and CD29 mediate galectin-3 induced T cell apoptosis, 2003, The t(1;3) breakpoint-spanning genes LSAMP and NORE1 are involved in clear cell renal cell carcinomas, 2003, cDNA microarray analysis assists in diagnosis of malignant intrarenal pheochromocytoma originally masquerading as a renal cell carcinoma, 2005. Recipient The Shigematsu prize, Japanese Urol. Assn., 1977, 1996. Mem.: Japan Soc. of Clin. Oncology (meritorious mem. 2010—), The Japanese Urol. Assn. (hon.), Am. Urol. Assn. (sr.), Société Internationale d'Urologie (sr.). Office: Tokushima University Hospital 3-18-15 Kuramoto Tokushima 770-8503 Japan Office Phone: 81886337143. *

KAGEN, STEVEN LESLIE, former United States Representative from Wisconsin, physician; b. Appleton, Wis., Dec. 12, 1949; s. Marv Kagen; m. Gayle Kagen; 4 children. BS in Molecular Biology, with honors, U. Wis., Madison, 1972, MD, 1976. Diplomate Am. Bd. Internal Medicine, Am. Bd. Allergy & Immunology, cert. in diagnostic lab. immunology. Teamster Foremost Dairy; intern, then resident internal medicine Northwestern U. Sch. Medicine, Chgo., 1976—79; fellow allergy/immunology Med. Coll. Wis., Milw., 1979—81; founder Kagen Allergy Clinics, Appleton, Wis., 1981, Oshkosh, Wis., 1981, Green Bay, Wis., 1986, Fond du Lac, Wis., 1990; asst. clin. prof. allergy & clin. immunology Med. Coll. Wis.; mem. US Congress from 8th Wis. Dist., Washington, 2007—11. Consulting staff HCA Med. Ctr., Port St. Lucie, Fla., 1986—93; bd. dirs. Joint Coun. Allergy, Asthma and Immunology, Palatine, Ill., 1988—92; staff dept. medicine Mercy Med. Ctr., Oshkosh, Appleton Med. Ctr.; affiliate staff dept. medicine Bellin Hosp., Green Bay. Allergy cons. CNN, CNN Airport News, CNN Headline News, CNN Interactive, 1995—2002; contbr. articles to med. jours. Recipient Founder's award, Fox Cities Children's Mus., 1996, Children's Environ. Health Recognition award, EPA, 2005. Mem.: AMA, State Med. Soc. Wis., Wis. Allergy Soc., American Coll. Allergy, Asthma & Immunology, American Acad. Allergy, Asthma & Immunology (Pub. Outreach award 2004), American Meteorol. Soc. (assoc.). Democrat. Jewish. *

KAHAN, BARRY DONALD, surgeon, educator; b. Cleve., July 25, 1939; s. Jacob Marvin and Pearl (Schultz) Kahan; m. Rochelle Liebling, Sept. 22, 1963 (dec.); 1 child, Kara; m. Marsha Capen, Dec. 3, 2005. BS, U. Chgo., 1960, PhD, 1964, MD, 1965. Intern Mass. Gen. Hosp., Boston, 1965-66, resident in surgery, 1968-72; staff asso. in immunology NIH, 1966-68; asst. prof. surgery and physiology Northwestern U. Sch. Medicine, Chgo., 1972-74, asso. prof., 1975-76; prof. surgery U. Tex. Med. Sch., Houston, 1977—2008, emeritus dir., divs. organ transplantation dept. surgery, dir. program immunology, grad. sch., 1998—2008. Editor in chief Transplantation Proceedings, 2002—. Bd. dirs. Ill. Kidney Found., 1974—76. Mem. ACS, AAAS, Soc. Univ. Surgeons, Am. Soc. Clin. Investigation, Am. Soc. Transplant Surgeons (pres. 1989—), Am. Surg. Assn., Internat. Transplantation Soc. (charter, treas. 1990—), Am. Surg. Assn., Am. Assn. Immunologists, Am. Assn. Cancer Rsch., Am. Physiol. Soc.

KAHANA, MADELYN D., pediatric anesthesiologist; MD, U. South Fl., Tampa. Diplomate Am. Bd. Pediat., Am. Bd. Anesthesiology. Resident Children's Hosp. Med. Ctr., Cin., Michael Reese Hosp., Chgo.; fellowship Children's Hosp. Seattle; prof. pediat. U. Chgo. Med. Ctr. Med. dir. pediat. intensive care unit U. Chgo. Med. Ctr. Contbr. articles to profl. jours. Mem.: Soc. Critical Care Med., Soc. Cardiovascular Anesthesiologists, Soc. Pediat. Anesthesia, Internat. Anesthesia Rsch. Soc., Ill. Soc. Anesthesia, Am. Thoracic Soc., Am. Soc. Anesthesiologists, Am. Acad. Pediat. Office: U Chgo Hosp 5841 S Maryland Ave MC 6380 Chicago IL 60637 Office Phone: 773-702-5019. Office Fax: 773-702-5019. Business E-Mail: mkahana@uchicago.edu.

KAHANA, MICHAEL JACOB, cognitive neuroscientist, educator; b. St. Louis, May 7, 1969; s. Boaz and Eva (Frost) Kahana; m. Jessica A. Wachter; children: Nathan Abraham, Joseph Morris. BA, Case Western Res. U., 1989; PhD in Psychology, U. Toronto, 1993. Postdoctoral fellow, psychology Harvard U., Cambridge, Mass., 1993-94; asst. prof. Brandeis U., Dept. Psychology and Nat. Ctr. for Complex Systems, Waltham, Mass., 1994—2000, assoc. prof., 2000—04; prof., dept. psychology U Pa., 2004—. Mem. BBBP-4 (Cognition and Perception) study sect., Centers for Scientific Review, NIH, 2003—07; founder, organizer 1st, 2nd, 3rd & 5th Ann. Meetings of the Context and Episodic Memory Symposium. Mem. editl. bd. Memory and Cognition, 1997, cons. editor 1997-2001, assoc. editor 2001-05; assoc. editor Cognitive Psychology, 2005-09; cons. editor Journal of Experimental Psychology: Learning, Memory and Cognition, 1999-2001, Psychonomic Bulletin & Review 2005-07, Journal of Experimental Psychology: General, 2008-; Ad Hoc revieer; contbr. of several articles to profl. publications. Mem. adv. panel Doris Duke Charitable Found. Recipient 1st award NIH, 1997-2002; co-recipient Troland Rsch., award, NAS, 2010; Bernstein fellow, Brandeis U., 1998-99. Mem. APA, Psychonomic Soc., Soc. for Neuroscience, Memory Disorders Rsch. Soc., Soc. for Cognitive Neuroscience, Soc. for Math. Psychology; fellow Soc. Exptl. Psychologists Office: Dept Psychology U Pennsylvania Ste 302C 3401 Walnut St Philadelphia PA 19104 Office Phone: 215-746-3500, 215-746-3501. Office Fax: 215-746-6848. Business E-Mail: kahana@sas.upenn.edu. *

KAH BIK, CHEONG, internist, researcher; b. Ipoh, Perak, Malaysia, Oct. 24, 1969; d. Cheong Chan Hon and Wong Wei Cheng. BSc with honours, Nat. U. Malaysia, Kuala Lumpur, 1994, MMedSc, 1996; diploma, Internat. Med. U., Malaysia, 1999, MBBS, 2002; MPhil, U. Hong Kong, 2009. Registered internist Malaysian Med. Coun., 2002. Rsch. asst. Nat. U. Malaysia, 1994—96, internist, 2002—07, rschr., 2002—07; rsch. asst. U. Hong Kong, 2007—. Home: 35 Hala Rapat Baru 16 Taman Seri Rapat Ipoh Perak 31350 Malaysia Office: University Hong Kong Pokfulam Hong Kong China E-mail: cheong_kah_bik@yahoo.com.sg.

KAHL, LESLEY PATRICIA, research scientist; d. John Neville Ball and Patricia Marie Kahl; 1 child, Rebecca Claire Thorne. BSc with honors I, U. Newcastle, Australia, 1979; PhD in Med. Biology, U. Melbourne, Australia, 1983. Fogarty NIH postdoctoral rsch. fellow Dept. Medicine Harvard Med. Sch., Boston, 1983—86; postdoctoral rsch. fellow Wellcome Labs., London, 1986—92; clin. rsch. scientist Wellcome/Glaxo Wellcome, London, 1992—2004; sr. mgr., mgr. clin. devel. GlaxoSmithKline, London, 2005—. Contbr. articles to profl. jours. Recipient Univ. Gold medal, U. Newcastle, 1979, CSci. award, Sci. Coun., Eng. Mem.: Inst. Clin. Rsch., Royal Soc. Medicine(London) (assoc.). Avocations: the arts, singing, gardening, cooking, fitness. Office: GlaxoSmithKline R&D and Respiratory Immuno Inflammation CCSE Stockley Pk W Middlesex Uxbridge UB111BT England Office Phone: 4402089902187. Business E-Mail: lesley.p.kahl@gsk.com.

KAHLERT, PHILIPP, physician; b. Hannover, Lower-Saxony, Germany, Dec. 9, 1976; s. Reiner and Gabriele Kahlert; life ptnr. Anne-Christina Schulze. MD, Albert-Ludwigs-U., Freiburg, Germany, 2003. Cons., dept. cardiology West German Heart Ctr. Essen, U. Duisburg-Essen, NRW, 2010—. Contbr. to profl. pubs. Recipient award, Gesellschaft zur Förderung der Herz- und Kreislaufforschung Essen e.V., 2008, AGIK-Publikationspreis, 2010; Travel grant, European Assn. Echocardiography, 2008, Rsch. grant, U. Duisburg-Essen, 2009. Mem.: European Assn. Percutaneous Cardiovasc. Interventions, European Assn. Echocardiography, European Soc. Cardiology, German Cardiac Soc. Office: West German Heart Ctr Essen Hufelandstr 55 Essen NRW 45122 Germany Office Phone: 4920172384805. Office Fax: 492017235837. Business E-Mail: philipp.kahlert@uk-essen.de.

KAHN, BRUCE S., obstetrician, gynecologist; BS in Biology, U. Calif., Irvine, 1984; MS in Physiology, Georgetown U., Washington, 1986, MD, 1990. Diplomate Am. Bd. Ob-gyn., 1999. Intern, dept. medicine St. Joseph Hosp. & Health Care Ctr., Chgo., 1990—91; resident, divsn. radiation oncology George Washington U. Med. Ctr., 1991—92; intern, dept. ob-gyn. Cedars-Sinai Med. Ctr., LA, 1992—93; resident, dept. ob-gyn. Abington Meml. Hosp., Pa., 1993—96; dir., chronic pelvic pain clinic Naval Med. Ctr., San Diego, 1996—98; clin. instr., dept. reproductive medicine U. Calif., San Diego, 1997—2000, dir. ambulatory gynecology, hillcrest, 1998—99, asst. clin. prof., dept. reproductive medicine, 2000—05; dir. grad. med. edn. Scripps Clinic Med. Group, La Jolla, Calif., 2001—; chmn. grad. med. edn., dir. Scripps Meml. Hosp., La Jolla, 2008—; adj. prof. ob-gyn. Uniformed Svcs. U. Health Scis, Bethesda, Md., 2003—09, adj. assoc. prof. ob-gyn., 2009—. Lcdr USN, 1996—98, San Diego. Recipient Resident Tchg. award, Abington Meml. Hosp., 1994—95, Naval Med. Ctr. Scripps Clinic, 2001. Fellow: Am. Coll. Ob-gyn. Office: Scripps Clinic Medical Group 3811 Valley Center Dr S99 San Diego CA 92130 Office Fax: 858-764-9097. Business E-Mail: bkahn@scrippsclinic.com. *

KAHN, C. RONALD, research laboratory administrator; b. Louisville, Jan. 14, 1944; s. David L. and Reva W. (Waldman) K.; m. Susan Becker; children: Stacy, Jeffrey. BA in Chemistry with high honors, U. Louisville, 1964, MD with high honors, 1968, MS in Chemistry, 1984; MA (hon.), Harvard U., 1984; DSc (honoris causa), U. Louisville, 1984, U. Paris-Pierre and Marie Curie, 1990, U. Geneva, 2000. Diplomate Am. Bd. Internal Medicine, Am. Bd. Endocrinology and Metabolism.; Lic. Mass., Ky. State Bd. Med. Examiners. Intern and resident in ward medicine Barnes Hosp., St. Louis, 1968-70; clin. assoc., sr. clin. assoc., clin. endocrinology br. Nat. Inst. Arthritis, Metabolism and Digestive Diseases, NIH, Bethesda, Md., 1970-73; sr. investigator Diabetes Br. NIH, Bethesda, Md., 1973-78, chief diabetes br., 1979-81; rsch. dir., Elliot P. Joslin Rsch. Lab. Joslin Diabetes Ctr., Boston, 1981-2000, sr. staff, Joslin Clinic, 1985—, dir., 1997—, exec. v.p., 1997—2000, pres., 2000—07, vice chmn., 2007—; assoc. prof. medicine Harvard Med. Sch., Boston, 1981-84, prof. medicine, 1984—, Mary K. Iacocca prof. medicine, 1986—. Lectr. symposia, meetings, thesis supr., course dir. and devel. numerous med. instns.; admitting and attending physician NIH Clin. Ctr., 1972-81; sr. investigator, diabetes br., Nat. Inst. Arthritis, Metabolism and Diestive Diseases, NIH, 1973-78; physician Brigham and Women's Hosp., Boston, 1981-91, chief div. Diabetes and Metabolism, Dept. Medicine, 1981-92, sr. physician 1986-92, sr. cons. Diabetes and Metabolism, 1993-; assoc. staff Endocrinology/Internal Medicine, New Eng. Deaconess Hospital, Boston, 1981-85, active staff, 1986-95; active staff, dept. medicine, Beth Israel Deaconess Hosp., Boston, Mass., 1995-; mem. scientific adv. com., Boston Obesity Ctr., New England Med. Ctr., 1996-; adv. coun. mem., Nat. Diabetes and Digestive and Kidney Diseases, NIH, 1998-2002; clin. assoc. prof. medicine, Uniformed Svcs. U. Health Scis, Bethesda, Md., 1979-81; vis. scientist Centre de Moleculaire, Centre National de la Recherche Scientifique, Gif-sur-Yvette, France, 1979-80; adj. prof. genetics George Washington U., 1980-81; overseas vis. prof. Royal Melbourne Hosp., Australia, 1985; vis. prof. Royal Postgrad. Hosp., London, 1985; Rosemary Sarver vis. prof. in endocrinology and metabolism, The Hosp. of the Good Samaritan, L.A., 1985; Roerig vis. professorship in diabetes, U. Colo. Health Scis., Denver, Colo., 1990; vis. scientist, dept. cellular and molecular biology, Dana Farber Cancer Inst., Boston, Mass., 1990-91; vis. rsch. scientist, Brandeis U., Waltham, Mass., 1998-99; hon. dir. and prof., Diabetes Ctr. Beijing U., China, 2005; bd. dir. Care Group, Health Care Sys., 2000-03. Author or co-author of several articles in publs. in field; mem. editl. bds. Jour. Clin. Endocrinology and Metabolism, 1977-80, Diabetes, 1977-84, Am. Jour. Medicine, 1979-84, Jour. Clin. Investigation, 1979-84, Jour. Receptor Rsch., 1980-83, Hormone and Metabolic Rsch., 1980-83, Endocrinology, 1981-85, Jour. Biol. Chemistry, 1983-88, Diabetes and Metabolism Revs., 1984, Receptor, 1989-, Trends in Endocrinology and Metabolism, 1991-, Jour. Receptor Rsch., 1992-, Proceedings of the Assn. Am. Physicians, 1997-, Am. Jour. Medicine, 1998-, Am. Jour. Physiology, 2001-; exec. editor Trends in Endocrinology and Metabolism, 1989-90; cons. editor Jour. Clin. Investigation, 1992-96, 1998-; bd. editor Endoctine, 1993-94; assoc. editor Diabetes, 1996-2001, Endocrine Reviews, 2000-, Cell Metabolism, 2004-; mem. adv. bd. Endocrine Reviews, 1996-97. Mem. Nat. Diabetes Adv. Bd., 1981-85, co-chmn. rsch. com., 1982-85. Recipient David Rumbough Meml award for Sci. Achievement Juvenile Diabetes Found., 1977, CIBA-Geigy Drew award for biochem. rsch., 1981, Mary Jane Kugel award Juvenile Diabetes Found., 1982, Sol Berson Meml. lectureship NIH,

1983, Hehnemann Lectr. in Pharmacology U. Calif.,1984, Pfizer Biomed. Rsch. award, Pfizer inc., 1986, Cristobal Diaz award Internat. Diabetes Fedn., 1988, Banting award for Disting. Scietific Achievement, 1993, Disting. Scientist award, Clin. Ligand Assay Soc., 1997, Dorothy Hodgkin award, British Diabetes Assn., 1999, Hamden award U.A.E., 2000, Naomi Berrie award for Outstanding Achievement in Diabetes Rsch., Columbia U., NYC, 2001, Societa'Italiana Di Diabetologia Mentor award, Italy, 2002, Steven C. Beering award for Advancement of Biomedical Sci., 2002, J. Allyn Taylor Internat. prize in Medicine for Diabetes, 2002, Claude Bernard medal, European Assn. for the Study of Diabetes, Munich, Germany, 2004, Freedom to Discover Achievement Award for Metabolic Disease, Bristol-Myers Squibb, 2004, Dale medal, British Soc. for Endocrinology, 2005; named Top 100 Most-Cited Scientist for 1973-84 and 1981-88, The Scientist 1990. Fellow AAAS, Am. Acad. Microbiology; mem. NAS, Inst. Medicine, Am. Acad. Arts & Scis., Am. Fedn. Clin. Rsch. (Award for Outstanding Clin. Rsch. under Age 40, 1983), The Endocrine Soc. (Edwin B. Astwood lectr. 1987, Fred Conrad Koch award for Disting. Contributions to Endocrinology, 2000), Am. Diabetes Assn. (Eli Lilly award for rsch. 1981, Otto Brandman award N.J. affiliate 1989, Elliott P. Joslin medal Mass. affiliate, 1989, Albert Renold award 1998), Am. Soc. Clin. Investigation (nat. coun. 1986—, pres. elect 1987-88, pres. 1988-89), Am. Soc. Biol. Chemistry, Assn. Am. Physicians, Sigma Xi, Alpha Epsilon Delta, Phi Kappa Phi, Alpha Omega Alpha. Achievements include rsch. in insulin receptors and insulin action, insulin-like growth factors, diabetes mellitus, hypoglycemia, immunity, autoimmunity and viruses in endocrine disorders; patents in field. Office: Joslin Diabetes Ctr Dept Medicine One Joslin Pl Boston MA 02215 Office Phone: 617-732-2635. Office Fax: 617-732-2593. E-mail: c.ronald.kahn@joshn.harvard.edu.

KAHN, CHARLES N., III, (CHIP KAHN), lobbyist; b. New Orleans, Jan. 4, 1952; m. Joanne Willis. BA in Social & Behavioral Sciences, Johns Hopkins U., 1974; MPH, Tulane U., 1980. Adminstrv. resident with Tchg. Hosp. Dept. Assn. Am. Med. Colls.; dir. Office Fin. Mgmt. Edn. Assn. Univ. Programs in Health Adminstrn., 1980—83; legis. asst. of health to Senator Dan Quayle US Senate, 1983—84, former sr. health policy advisor to Senator David Durenberger, 1984—86; minority health counsel health subcommittee US House Ways & Means Com., Washington, 1986—93, staff dir. health subcommittee, 1995—98; exec. v.p. Health Ins. Assn. America (HIAA), Washington, 1993—94, pres., 1998—2001; pres., CEO Fedn. Am. Hospitals, Washington, 2001—. Chmn. Econ. Rsch. Initiative on the Uninsured U. Mich.; mem. adv. com. Ctr. for Studying Health Sys. Change; mem. program adv. bd. Robert Wood Johnson Health Fellowships Program; mem. Medicare Competitive Pricing Adv. Com.; instr. health policy Johns Hopkins U., George Washington U., Tulane U.; adj. clin. prof. Tulane U. Sch. Pub. Health and Tropical Medicine; bd. dirs. Zix Corp.; commr. Am. Health Info. Cmty.; prin. Hosp. Quality Alliance; mem. Quality Alliance Steering Com. US Dept. Health & Human Services (HHS), 2009—. Contbr. articles to profl. jours. Named one of The 100 Most Powerful People in Healthcare, Modern Healthcare mag. Mem.: Delta Omega. Republican. Office: Fedn Am Hosps Ste 245 801 Pennsylvania Ave NW Washington DC 20004-2604 Office Phone: 202-624-1500. Business E-Mail: ckahn@fah.org. *

KAHN, CYRIL JEAN-FRANÇOIS, research scientist; b. Paris, Jan. 19, 1981; MSc, ENSEM, 2005; PhD, Nancy-U., 2009. Rsch. engr. CNRS LEMTA - UMR 7563, 2005; fellow Nancy-U. INPL, 2005—09; postdoc. rschr. Nancy-U. UHP Nancy 1, 2009—. Rsch. grant, French Ministry of Sci. Avocation: tennis. Office: 2 Ave de la Forêt de Haye Vandoeuvre-Lès-Nancy Lorraine 54504 France Business E-Mail: cyril.kahn@ensem.inpl-nancy.fr.

KAHN, DAVID M., medical educator; b. NYC, Apr. 1, 1965; BS, Tufts U., 1987; MD, Albany Med. Coll., 1991. Resident, gen. surgery U. Medicine and Dentistry NJ Med. Sch., 1991—96; fellowship, plastic surgery U. Calif., San Francisco, 1996—98; fellowship NYU Inst. Reconstructive Plastic Surgery, 1998—99; fellow, craniofacial surgery Stanford U. Med. Sch., 1999—2000; clin. assoc. prof. Stanford U. Divsn. Plastic Surgery, 2000—. Mem.: Am. Cleft Palate-Craniofacial Assn., Am. Assn. Plastic Surgeons, Am. Soc. Maxillofacial Surgeons, Am. Soc. Aesthetic Plastic Surgery, Am. Soc. Plastic Surgeons. Avocations: reading, music, photography. Home: 814 Clark Way Palo Alto CA 94304 Home Fax: 650-498-8667. Business E-Mail: david.kahn@stanford.edu.

KAHN, MARC LESLIE, orthopedic surgeon; b. Phila., Mar. 12, 1956; s. Sigmund and Joanne (Pokras) K.; m. Cynthia Petrowsky; 5 children. AB, Lafayette Coll., 1978; MD, Hahnemann Med. Coll., 1982. Resident in orthopedics Monmouth Med. Ctr., Long Branch, NJ, 1987; surgeon, maj. U.S. Army, Ft. Dix, NJ, 1987-91; orthop. surgeon Garden State Orthopedics, Cherry Hill, NJ, 1991—2008, Regional Orthop., 2008—. Clin. instr. N.J. Sch. Osteo. Medicine. Contbr. articles to profl. jours. Decorated Army Achievement medal with 2 oak leaf clusters, Meritorious Svc. medal. Fellow: Arthroscopy Assn. N.Am., Am. Acad. Orthop. Surgeons; mem.: AMA, South Jersey Surg. Ctr. (founder and past pres.), N.J. Med. Soc., Camden County Med. Soc, Orthop. Surgeons of N.J. (bd. dirs., vice chmn., past pres.), N.J. Orthop. Soc. (bd. dirs., past pres.), N.J. Med. Soc. Home: Regional Orthopedic Pa 2201 Chapel Ave West Cherry Hill NJ 08002 Office Phone: 856-663-7080. Personal E-mail: mmkabn03@comcast.net.

KAHN, NORMAN, dental educator, pharmacologist; b. NYC, Dec. 28, 1932; s. Louis Meyer and Dorothy (Simon) Kohn; m. Dale Krasnow, Mar. 30, 1958 AB, Columbia U., 1954, D.D.S., 1958, PhD, 1964. Lic. dentist, N.Y. State. Dental intern Montefiore Hosp., Bronx, NY, 1958-59; instr. Coll. Physicians and Surgeons, Columbia U., NYC, 1962-65, asst. prof., 1965-72, assoc. prof., 1972-80, prof. pharmacology, 1980-99, prof. dentistry, 1980-92, Edwin S. Robinson prof. dentistry, 1992-99; assoc. dean acad. affairs Sch. Dental and Oral Surgery, Columbia U., 1989-94, acting dean, 1994-95; attending dentist Presbyn. Hosp., NYC, 1985-99, Robinson prof. dentistry & pharm. emeritus, spl. lectr., 1999—, cons. dentist, 1999—. Vis. assoc. prof. UCLA, 1978; chair instl. rev. bd. Columbia-Presbyn. Med. Ctr., N.Y.C., 1981-91; cons. pharmacologist Harlem Hosp., N.Y.C., 1966-80; vis. scientist U. Pisa, Italy, 1965-66. Contbr. chpts. to books, articles to profl. jours. NIH grantee, 1969-75, Nat. Fund Med. Edn. grantee, 1973; recipient Outstanding Contbn. to Teaching award Columbia U. Coll. Physicians and Surgeons, 1980, Physicians & surgeons Disting. Svc. award in Pre-Clinical Yrs., 2001; hon. research fellow Univ. Coll., London, 1986. Mem. Am. Physiol. Soc., ADA, Am. Assn. Dental Schs., Confrerie des Chevaliers du Tastevin, Alpha Omega Alpha, Omicron Kappa Upsilon Jewish. Avocation: oenology. Office: Columbia U 630 W 168th St New York NY 10032-3795 E-mail: n.k5@att.net.

KAHN, RICHARD L., anesthesiologist; b. Balt., July 15, 1953; ScB, Brown U., 1975; MD, Boston U., 1981. Anesthesiologist Hosp. Spl. Surgery, 1987—. Asst. clin. prof. Weill Cornell Coll. Medicine, 1987—. Office: 535 E 70th St New York NY 10021 Business E-Mail: kahnr@hss.edu.

KAHN, SANDRA S., psychotherapist; b. Chgo., June 24, 1942; d. Chester and Ruth Sutker; m. Jack Murry Kahn, June 1, 1965; children: Erick, Jennifer. BA, U. Miami, 1964; MA, Roosevelt U., 1976. Tchr. Chgo. Pub. Schs., 1965—67; pvt. practice psychotherapy Northbrook, Ill., 1976—. Host Shared Feelings, Sta. WEEF-AM, Highland Park, Ill., 1983—. Author: The Kahn Report on Sexual Preferences, 1981, The Ex Wife Syndrome Cutting The Cord and Breaking Free After The Marriage Is Over, 1990; contbr. columnist Single Again mag. Mem.: Chgo. Psychol. Assn. (past pres. 1990), Ill. Psychol. Assn. Jewish. Office: 790 Frontage Rd Northfield IL 60093

KAHN, SIGMUND BENHAM, retired internist, dean; b. Phila., May 18, 1933; s. Maxwell Louis and Clara (Parris) K.; m. Joanne Pokras, June 11, 1955; children: Marc L., Elissa Kahn Petrosky, Hillary Kahn Roth, Lauren B. Westlake. BA, U. Pa., Phila., 1954, MD, 1958. Diplomate Am. Bd. Internal Medicine; cert. hematology and med. oncology. Rotating intern Albert Einstein Med. Ctr., Phila., 1958-59; resident in internal medicine Hosp. of U. Pa., Phila., 1959-61, fellow in hematology, 1961-62, USPHS rsch. fellow dept. hematology, 1962-63; assoc. in hematology medicine Hahnemann U. Hosp., Phila., 1963-66, asst., assoc., then prof. medicine, 1966-99; prof. dept. neoplastic disease Hahnemann Univ. Hosp., Phila., 1978-99, dir. edn., vice chmn. dept., 1978-94; assoc. dean Hahnemann U., Phila., 1986-94; prof. emeritus, 1999—2002; prof. dept. medicine divsn. hematology/ med. oncology Med. Coll. Pa./Hahnemann U., Phila., 1992-94, assoc. dean edn., 1992-94, prof. emeritus, 1999—2002, Drexel U. Coll. of Med., 2002—. Cons., chmn. dean's com. Wilkes-Barre (Pa.) VA Hosp., 1987-92. Mem. editl. bd. Jour. Cancer Edn., 1985-95, Am. Jour. Clin. Oncology; contbr. articles to profl. jours. Instl. rep. Boy Scouts Am., 1970-75; pres. Temple Beth Sholom, Cherry Hill, N.J., 1977-80; mem. med. bd. Lupus Found., Delaware Valley, 1977-79. Mem. AMA, ACP, Phila. County Med. Soc., Phila. Hematology Soc., Pa. Med. Soc., Am. Fedn. Clin. Rsch., Am. Hematology Soc., Am. Assn. Cancer Rsch., Am. Soc. Clin. Oncology, Am. Assn. Cancer Edn., Am. Cancer Soc. (chmn. patient svc. com. Phila. divsn. 1981-83, chmn. med. subcom. profl. cdn. com. 1979-81, fin. com. 1981), Phi beta Kappa, Alpha Omega Alpha. Jewish. Home: 2307 Sagemore Dr Marlton NJ 08053-4315 Personal E-mail: kahnsb@msn.com.

KAHN, THOMAS, medical educator; b. Offenburg, Germany, June 23, 1938; s. Ludwig and Ellen (Kaufman) K.; m. Si Mi Pak, Nov. 7, 1968; children: Diana, David, Philip. BA, NYU, 1958, MD, 1962. Intern medicine Balt. City Hosps., 1962 63, U. Pitts. Hosps., 1963 64, Mt. Sinai, NYC, 1964-65, resident in nephrology, 1965-67; chief renal sect. Bronx VA Med. Ctr., 1979-96, prof. medicine Mt. Sinai Sch. Medicine, NYC, 1988 . Maj. US Army, 1967—69. Office: VA Med Ctr 130 W Kingsbridge Rd Bronx NY 10468-3904 Office Phone: 718 584 9000.

KAHNEMAN, DANIEL, psychology professor; b. Tel Aviv, Mar. 5, 1934; BA in Psychology and Math., Hebrew U., Jerusalem, 1954; PhD in Psychology, U. Calif., Berkeley, 1961; DSc (hon.), U. Pa., 2001; D (hon.), U. Trento, 2002, Ben-Gurion U., 2003, The New Sch., NYC, 2003, U. BC, 2004, Harvard U., 2004, U. East Anglia, 2004, U. Wurzburg, 2004, U. Milan, 2005, U. Paris, 2006, U.Alberta, 2006, U. Rome, 2007. Lectr. psychology Hebrew U., 1961—66, sr. lectr., 1966 70, assoc. prof., 1970 73, prof., 1973—78, fellow Ctr. for Rationality, 2000—; prof. psychology U. BC, Canada, 1978—86, U. Calif., Berkeley, 1986—94; Eugene Higgins prof. psychology, prof. pub. affairs Princeton U., NJ, 1993—2007, Eugene Higgins prof. psychology emeritus, 2007—, prof. pub. affairs emeritus, sr. scholar Woodrow Wilson Sch., 2007—. Vis. scientist dept. psychology U. Mich., 1965—66; lectr. psychology, fellow Ctr. Cognitive Studies, Harvard U., 1966—67; vis. scientist Applied Psychol. Rsch. Unit, U. Cambridge, England, 1968—69; fellow Ctr. Advanced Studies in Behavioral Scis., Stanford, Calif., 1977—78; assoc. fellow Canadian Inst. Advanced Rsch., 1984—86; vis. scholar Russell Sage Found., 1991—92. Mem. editl. bd. Thinking and Reasoning, Environ. and Resource Economics; contbr. articles to profl. jours. Second lt. to lt. Israel Defence Forces, 1954. Recipient Disting. Scientific Contbn. award, Soc. Consumer Psychology, 1992, Hilgard award for lifetime contbn. to gen. psychology, 1995, Nobel prize in economics, 2002, Grawemeyer prize in psychology, 2002, Career Achievement award, Soc. Med. Decision Making, 2002, Thomas Schelling prize, 2006, Frank P. Ramsey medal, Decision Analysis Soc., 2006. Fellow: Econometric Soc., Can. Psychol. Assn., Am. Psychol. Assn., Am. Psychol. Soc. (Disting. Scientific Contbn. award 1982, William James Fellow), Am. Acad. Arts & Scis.; mem.: NAS, Soc. Judgment & Decision Making (pres. 1992—93), Soc. Econ. Sci., Psychonomic Soc., Brit. Acad. (corr.), Soc. Exptl. Psychologists (pres. 1992—93, Warren medal 1995). Office: Princeton U Woodrow Wilson Sch 322 Wallace Hall Princeton NJ 08544-1010 Office Phone: 609-258-2280. Home Fax: 609-258-5974. E-mail: kahneman@princeton.edu. *

KAHOLOKULA, JOSEPH KEAWEAIMOKU, psychologist, health disparities researcher, behavioral scientist; b. Honolulu, Nov. 11, 1969; s. Lawrence Pauahi and Beverly Leilani (Lyons) Kaholokula. BA in Psychology, U. Hawaii, 1996, MA in Psychology, 2001, PhD in Psychology, 2003. Rsch. specialist Native Hawaiian Health Rsch. Project, Honolulu, 1994—2001; resident dept. psychology Tripler Army Med. Ctr., 2002—03, postdoc. fellow in behavioral medicine, 2003—04; assoc. chmn., asst. rschr., faculty dept. Native Hawaiian health John A. Burns Sch. Medicine, Honolulu, 2004—, dep. dir. ctr. Native and Pacific health disparities rsch., 2007—, chair, assoc. prof., dept. Native Hawaiian Health, 2011—. Instl. rev. bd. chair Native Hawaiian Health Care Sys., Honolulu, 2005—; adj. faculty Argosy U. Am. Sch Profl. Psychology, 2005—; co-dir. PILI Ohana Project, 2006—. Contbr. articles to profl. jours., chapters to books. Sr. mem. Halemua o Kuali'i, Honolulu, 1999—; bd. dirs., past pres., co-founder I Ola Lahui: Hawaii Rural Behavioral Health Tng. Program, Honolulu, 2007—. Recipient Student Rsch. award, Hawaii Psychol. Assn., 2001, Judy E. Hall, PhD Early Career Psychologist award, 2007; named Outstanding New Program Vol., Am. Diabetes Assn., Hawaii, 2002;, APA Minority fellow, 1998—2001, Kamehameha Schools/Bishop Estate scholar, 1994—2001, U.S. Achievement Acad. scholar, 1995, Honolulu Hawaiian Civic Club scholar, 1996, NIMH-COR scholar, 1996, J. Watumull scholar, Sch. Social Scis., U. Hawaii at Manoa, 1996, Pacific-Asian scholar, U. Hawaii, Manoa, 1998—2001, Dr. Hans & Clara Zimmerman Found. scholar, Hawaii Cmty. Found., 1999—2003, Native Hawaiian Leadership Project, U. Hawaii scholar, 2000—03, Na Liko Noelo scholar, 'Imi Hale, Native Hawaiian Cancer Network, 2002—05. Mem.: APA, Hawaii Psychological Assn., Golden Key Nat. Honor Soc. (life). Achievements include research in ethnic-by-gender interactions in cigarette smoking behavior among Asian and Pacific Islanders; the relationship between acculturation and depression among Native Hawaiians; the relationship between acculturation and diabetes in Native Hawaiians; the relationship between cigarette smoking and depression among Native Hawaiians; ethnic differences in the relationship between health-related quality of life and depression in people with type 2 diabetes. Avocations: Native Hawaiian cultural activities, travel, volleyball, wood carving. Office: Dept Native Hawaiian Health 651 Ilalo St MEB 307L Honolulu HI 96813 Office Fax: 808-692-1255. Business E-Mail: kaholoku@hawaii.edu.

KAHRILAS, PETER JAMES, medical educator, researcher; b. Culver City, Calif., June 9, 1953; s. Peter Jerome and Leticia (Llorett) K.; m. Elyse Anne Lambiase, Mar. 30, 1984; children: Genevieve Anne, Ian James, Miranda Elyse. Student, Yale U., 1971-75, U. Rochester, NYC, 1975-79. Resident in medicine U. Hosp. of Cleve., 1979-82; fellow in gastroenterology Northwestern U., Chgo., 1982-84; rsch. fellow Med. Coll. of Wis., Milw., 1984-86; asst. prof. medicine Med. Coll. Wis., Milw., 1986—90, assoc. prof. medicine, 1990—95, prof. medicine, 1995—; chief gastroenterology Northwestrn U. Feinberg Sch. Medicine, Chgo., 1999—2006. Contbr. articles to profl. jours. NIH grantee, 1990—. Fellow ACP, Ctrl. Soc. for Clin. Rsch., Am. Coll. Gastroenterology; mem. Am. Gastroenterol. Assn., Am. Fedn. for Clin. Rsch., Am. Soc. for Clin. Investigation, Am. Motility Soc. Democrat. Home: 203 Columbia Ave Park Ridge IL 60068-4923 Office: Northwestern U 676 N St Clair Ste 1400 Chicago IL 60611 Home Phone: 847-823-4799; Office Phone: 312-695-4016. Business E-Mail: p-kahrilas@northwestern.edu. *

KAHVECI, NEVZAT, medical educator; b. Konya, Turkey, Jan. 3, 1963; Md, Uludag U. Sch. Medicine, PhD, 1993. Asst. prof. Uludag U. Sch. Medicine, 2003—. Office: Uludag University School of Medicine Bursa Gorukle 16059 Turkey Personal E-mail: nevzatkahveci62@gmail.com. Business E-Mail: nevka@uludag.edu.tr.

KAI, JOSEPH PETER, physician, academic; b. London, 1965; s. Marianne Joy Naidoo and Peter Kai; m. Sophia Rachel Christie; children: Isobel, Felix. MB BS, U. Newcastle upon Tyne, 1987, MD with distinction. Gen. practitioner, lectr. in primary care U. Newcastle, Newcastle upon Tyne, Tyne and Wear, England, 1992 98; clin. sr. lectr. U. Birmingham, England, 1998—2002; prof. gen. practice and primary care U. Nottingham, England, 2002—. Dir. Midlands Rsch. Practice NHS R&D Consortium, Birmingham, West Midlands, 1998—2002; gen. practitioner Ridgacre House Surgery, Birmingham, 1999—2003; chair Primary Care Orgn. and Devel. Newcastle and North Tyneside Health Authority, Newcastle upon Tyne, England, 1996—98. Editor (book and DVD): Valuing Diversity: A training resource for effective health care of ethnically diverse communities-actitioners, 1999, 2nd edit., 2006; editor: (book) Ethnicity, Health and Primary Care, 2003, Primary Care in Urban Disadvantaged Communities, 2004; contbr. more than 50 peer reviewed research articles to profl. jours. in health services research, ethnic diversity, applied genetics. Mem.: Royal Coll. General Practitioners (distinction 1991). Office: U Nottingham Divsn Primary Care Grad Med Sch DE22 3DT Derby England Office Phone: 44(0)1332 724606.

KAI, KEITA, medical educator; b. Kumamoto, Japan, June 3, 1974; s. Tamihiko and Suzuyo Kai; m. Miki Kai, Dec. 24, 2002; children: Hikaru, Hina, Yohta. MD, Saga U., Japan, 2008, PhD. Cert. med. dr. Japan, 2000. Asst. prof. Saga U., 2007—. Office: Saga University Dept Pathology & Biodefense Faculty Medicine Nabesima 5-1-1 Saga 849-8501 Japan Office Fax: 81-952-34-2055. Business E-Mail: kaikeit@cc.saga-u.ac.jp.

KAI, KENTARO, gynecologist; b. Oita, Japan, Oct. 12, 1977; MD, Oita U., 2005. Physician dept. ob-gyn. Oita U. Faculty Medicine, 2005—. Grant, Meiji Co., Ltd., 2011. Fellow: Japan Soc. Ob-gyn. Office: 1-1 Idaigaoka Hasama-cho Yuhu Oita 879-5593 Japan Office Fax: 81 97 586 6687. Business E-Mail: kenta9sp@oita-u.ac.jp.

KAILAS, ARAVIND, engineering educator; b. Trichy, July 24, 1980; PhD, Ga. Inst. Tech., 2010. Engr. QUALCOMM, 2004—06; vis. rsch. scientist DOCOMO USA Labs., 2010—; affiliate rschr. Ctr. Biomed. Engring. Sys., 2011, Charlotte Rsch. Inst., 2011; asst. prof. U. NC, Charlotte, 2011—. Vis. rsch. scientist Docomo USA Labs., 2010; adv. bd. mem. Acad. Engring., East Mecklenberg, 2011; faculty mem. U. Phoenix, 2011; instr. ITT Tech. Inst., 2011; affiliate rschr. Charlotte Rsch. Inst., 2011—. Contbr. articles to sci. profl. jours. Recipient Grad. Rsch. Asst. Excellence award, Ga. Inst. Tech., Col. Oscar P. Cleaver award; Williams States Lee Coll. Engring. Faculty grant, U. NC, Faculty Excellence fellowship, Wachovia Found. Mem.: IEEE, INRIA, ICST, SIAM, IETE. Avocations: stamp collecting/philately, painting. Office: 9201 University City Bvd Woodward Hall Charlotte NC 28223 Business E-Mail: aravind.kailas@uncc.edu, aravindk@ieee.org.

KAIM, SAMUEL C., retired psychiatrist; b. NYC, Nov. 24, 1911; s. Adolph and Nettie Kaim; m. Joan P. Kaim, Jan. 25, 1992; 1 child, Edward H. BA, Case We. U., Cleve., 1928—31; MD, U. Zwrich, Switzerland, 1931—37. Resident in psychiatry U. Zurich, Switzerland, 1937—38; pvt. practice Rock Island, Ill., 1938—50. Med. dir. Nat. Pharm. Coun., DC, 1972—75; com. head Nat. Acad. Sci., DC, 1975—80. Contbr. articles to profl. jours. Maj.1946 US Army, 1942. Mem.: NIH (mem. study sections), Am. Coll. Neuropsycho Pharmacology, Am. Psychiat. Assn. Avocation: golf.

KAISER, ALLEN BERNARD, health facility administrator; b. Columbia, SC, 1942; BA, MD, Vanderbilt U., 1967. Intern Johns Hopkins Hosp., Balt., 1967—68, resident internal medicine, 1968—69, Vanderbilt U. Hosp., 1971—72, fellow, 1972—74; (former) hosp. epidemiologist St. Thomas Hosp., chief divsn. infectious diseases, chief dept. medicine; vice-chmn. clin. affairs Vanderbilt

U. Hosp., prof. medicine, chief of staff, 2004—, vice chair med. affairs; assoc. chief med. officer Vanderbilt U. Med. Ctr., 2004—. Mem.: Soc. Healthcare Epidemiology Am. (past pres.). Office: Vanderbilt Med Ctr D 3100 Med Ctr N Nashville TN 37232 *

KAISER, FRAN ELIZABETH, endocrinologist, gerontologist; b. NYC, Dec. 6, 1949; d. Philip Francis and Bronia (Weiss) K. BS, CCNY, 1970; MD, N.Y. Med. Coll., NYC, 1974. Diplomate Am. Bd. Internal Medicine, Am. Bd. Geriat. Intern Beth Israel Med. Ctr., NYC, 1974-75, resident to chief resident, 1975-78; fellow in endocrinology and metabolism U. Minn., Mpls., 1978-81, instr. dept. medicine, 1980-81, asst. prof., 1981-86; asst. prof. in residence UCLA Sch. Medicine, 1986-89; assoc. prof. medicine St. Louis U., 1989-94, prof., 1994-97, assoc. dir. divsn. geriatric medicine, 1989-97, prof., 1994-97; sr. regional med. dir. Merck & Co., Inc., Irving, Tex., 1997—2003, exec. med. dir., 2003, 2005—; CEO, Kaiser and Assocs. Cons., 2004—05. Adj. prof. medicine St. Louis U, 1997-; chief sect. endocrinology and metabolism Dept. Internal Medicine, St. Paul Ramsey Med. Ctr./U. Minn. Hosps., St. Paul, 1981-86; John A. Hartford Geriatric Faculty Devel. award scholar Hartford Found., NYC/UCLA Sch. Medicine, 1986-87; chief geriatric medicine Olive View Med. Ctr./UCLA San Fernando Valley Program, Sylmar, Calif., 1987-89; med. dir. Hosp. Based Home Care, VA Med. Ctr., Sepulveda, 1987-89; clin. prof. medicine U. Tex. Southwestern Med. Sch., Dallas, 1999-2008. Former mem. editl. bd.: Jour. Clin. Endocrinology and Metabolism, ad hoc reviewer: Endocrinology, Jour. AMA, Jour. Am. Geriatrics Soc., past mem. editl. bd.: Am. Geriatric Soc., Internat. Medicine Bull., cons. editor: Am. Health Mag.; contbr. articles to profl. jours. Grantee NIH, 1980-81, 97, Genetech, 1987-89, Syntex Corp. 1990-92, Hoechst-Roussel, 1992-94, Bur. Health Professions, 1991-97, VIVUS, 1993-97, Merck, 1994-97, Upjohn, 1995-97. Fellow: Am. Geriatrics Soc. (past mem. editl. bd. Internal Medicine Bull., Jour. Geriatric Nephrology & Urology), Gerontol. Soc. Am.; mem.: AAAS, Am. Assn. Home Care Physicians, N.Y. Acad. Sci., Am. Fedn.Clin. Rsch., Endocrine Soc., Am. Diabetes Assn., Alpha Omega Alpha. Achievements include research in hormonal changes with aging, studies of therapy of erectile dysfunction, testosterone, estrogen and frailty and women's health and sexuality. Office: 3510 Edgewater Dr Dallas TX 75205 Office Phone: 214-686-6008. Personal E-mail: Kaiserf@sbcglobal.net.

KAISER, LARRY ROBERT, dean, thoracic surgeon; b. St. Louis, Aug. 31, 1952; s. Patricia Glaser; m. Lindy Snider; children: Jonathan, Jeffrey, Daniel. BS, Tulane U., 1973, MD, 1977. Diplomate Am. Bd. Thoracic Surgery, Am. Bd. Surgery. Resident in surgery UCLA, 1977—83, fellow in surg. oncology, 1979—81; resident in thoracic and cardiovasc. surgery U. Toronto, Ont., Canada, 1983—85; asst. attending surgeon Meml. Sloan-Kettering Cancer Ctr., 1985—88; asst. and assoc. prof. surgery Washington U. Sch. Medicine, 1988—91; prof. and chief thoracic surgery U. Pa. Sch. Medicine, Phila., 1991—2001, John Rhea Barton prof. & chmn. dept. surgery, 2001—08; surgeon-in-chief U. Pa. Health Sys., Phila., 2006—08; pres. U. Tex. Health Sci. Ctr., Houston, 2008—11; Alkek Williams chair U. Tex. Med. Sch., Houston, 2008—11; sr. exec. v.p. health sciences, dean Temple U. Sch. Medicine, 2011—; CEO Temple U. Health Sys., Phila., 2011—. Elected mem. Inst. Medicine, Nat. Acad. Sci., 2005. Bd. dir. Thoracic Surgery Found. for Edn. and Rsch. Fellow: Am. Coll. Surgeons; mem.: Am. Bd. Thoracic Surgery (dir.), Am. Bd. Surgery (dir.,), Soc. Thoracic Surgeons, Am. Assn. for Thoracic Surgery, Soc. Clinical Surgery, Halsted Soc., Fleischner Soc., Soc. Univ. Surgeons, Am. Surgical Assn. Office: Temple University Sch Medicine Office of Dean 3500 N Broad St 11th Fl Philadelphia PA 19140 Office Phone: 215-707-7000. *

KAISER, NINA IRENE, quality director; b. San Diego, Nov. 29, 1953; d. Louis Frederick and Mary Elizabeth (Wright) K.; children: Kellen Anne Kaiser, Ethan Andrew Kaiser-Klimist. BSN, BA in Women Studies, San Francisco State U., 1980; MBA, U. Phoenix, 2001. RN, Calif. RN Calif. Pacific Med. Ctr., San Francisco, 1980-81, Ralph K. Davies Med. Ctr., San Francisco, 1982-85, Planned Parenthood, San Francisco, 1985-86, Visiting Nurses and Hospice, San Francisco, 1986-88; RN supr. St. Mary's Home Care, San Francisco, 1991-93; RN dir. St. Vincent's Homecare and Hospice, Fremont, Calif., 1993-94; aux. dir. Home Health Link, San Leandro, Calif., 1994-99; mgmt. cons. Kaiser Home Health, Calif., 1999—2002, mgr., 2003—. Regional coun. chair San Francisco Bay Area, 1999. Pres. Daus. of Bilitis, San Francisco, 1977-78; founding mem. Buena Vista Lesbian and Gay Parents Assn., San Francisco, 1985; treas., bd. dirs. Holladay Ave. Homeowners Assn., San Francisco, 1984-96; bd. dirs. Midrasha High Sch., Berkeley, Calif., 1996. With USN, 1971-74.

KAISER, PAUL, psychotherapist; MSW. Diplomate in clin. social work Am. Bd. Examiners, cert. psychoanalyst Nat. Assn. the Advancement Psychoanalysis. Pvt. practice psychoanalyst, psychotherapist; tng. analyst and supr. Nat. Psychol. Assn. Psychoanalysis, Inc., sr. mem., bd. dirs., former pres. bd. dirs., treas. Fellow: NY Soc. Clin. Social Work. Office: Nat Psychol Assn Psychoanalysis 40 W 13th St Lbby 1 New York NY 10011-7940 Office Phone: 212-924-7440. Office Fax: 212-989-7543. *

KAISER, SANJA, physician; b. Split, Croatia, Apr. 18, 1965; m. Peter John Kaiser, Aug. 4, 2000; children: F. L., F. C. Dr. med., Faculty Medicine, Zagreb, Croatia, 1989; MPH, Netherlands Inst. Health Scis., Rotterdam, 2004. Specialist in gen. medicine Med. Assn. State Hesse, Germany, 2004. Intern U. Hosp., Split, 1990—91, Zagreb; resident internal medicine Hosp., Winterberg, Germany, 1992—95, Duesseldorf, Germany; pvt. practice Frankfurt am Main, Germany, 1995—2001; sr. rschr. and content coord. European Pub. Health Info. Sys., RIVM-Nat. Inst. Pub. Health and Environment, Bilthoven, Netherlands, 2005—07; dir. Sunce Internat. Health Ctr., Zagreb, 2007—08; gen. practitioner and coord. preventive medicine Internat. Health Ctr., The Hague, Netherlands, 2007; ind. cons. pub. health & gen. practitioner Split, 2008—. Cons. EUGLOREH-Global Report on the Health Status in European Union, 2007—08. Contbr. articles to profl. jour. Mem.: European Pub. Health Assn., Croatian Med. Assn., Dutch Med. Assn., German Med. Assn. Avocations: reading, writing.

KAITHWAS, GAURAV, pharmacist, educator; b. New Delhi, Dec. 1, 1980; B in Pharmacy, Delhi Inst. Pharm. Scis. & Rsch., U. Delhi, 2003; PharmM, Jamia Hamdard U., New Delhi; PhD, Sam Higginbottom Inst. Agrl. Tech. & Sci.-Deemed U., Allahabad, 2010. Asst. prof. dept. pharm. scis. Sam Higginbottom Inst. Agrl. Tech. & Sci.-Deemed U., 2005—10, Assam U., 2010—. Reviewer Jour. Pharmacy and Bioallied Scis., Silchar, 2010. Sr. Rsch. fellowship, Indian Acad. Sci., Bangalore, India, 2011. Mem.: Delhi Pharmacy Coun., Assn. Pharmacy Tchrs. India, Sci. Adv. Bd. Avocations: reading, writing. Office: Assam University Dept Pharmaceutical Sci Silchar Assam 788011 India

KAIZHENG, GONG, medical researcher, cardiologist; b. Qujing, Oct. 11, 1976; MD, Dali Med. Coll., 1999; PhD, Peking U., 2008. Assoc. dir. dept. cardiology Second Clin. Med. Sch. Yangzhou U., 2009; dir. Care Lab. Contbr. articles to profl. jours. Recipient Young Investigator award, Am. Fedn. Med. Rsch./Southern Soc. Clin. Investigation, award, Nat. Natural and Sci. Found. of China; named Young Expert of Yangzhou, Govt. of Jiangsu Province. Master: Chinese Med. Assn. (Yangzhou Cardiology Br.); mem.: American Heart Assn. (SE Postdoc. fellowship). Achievements include research in immune activation mechanism of congestive heart failure and molecular mechanism of p 38 biphasic activation by beta 2 Abrenergic receptor. Avocations: sports, music. Office: Taizhou Rd 45 Yangzhou Jiangsu 225001 China Office Phone: 8651487907309. Personal E-mail: kzgong@hotmail.com. Business E-Mail: yungkzh@163.com.

KAJANDER, JOHN, hospital administrator; BA, Mich. State U. Exec. dir. Tex. Bus. Group on Health, Houston Area Health Care Coalition; exec. v.p., chief adminstrv. officer Inst. Rehab. and Rsch/TIRR Systems, Houston, 1999—2001, pres., CEO, 2003—06; sr. v.p. Texas Medical Ctr., 2007—. Bd. dirs. Houston Achievement Place, Child Devel. Ctr.; mem. med. advisory bd. Southwest Bancorp. of Tex., Inc.; mem. tech. advisory com. Tex. Health Care Info. Coun. Office: Texas Medical Ctr 2450 Holcombe Blvd Ste 1 Houston TX 77021

KAJI, AKIRA, microbiology scientist, educator; b. Tokyo, Jan. 13, 1930; arrived in U.S., 1954; s. Kiichi and Chiyo (Hanai) K.; m. Hideko Katayama, Aug. 22, 1958; children: Kenneth, Eugene, Naomi, Amy. BS, Tokyo U., 1953; PhD, Johns Hopkins U., 1958; MS (hon.), U. Pa., 1973. Rsch. fellow Johns Hopkins Hosp., Balt., 1958-59; guest investigator Rockefeller U., NYC, 1959; rsch. assoc. microbiology Vanderbilt Med. Sch., Nashville, 1959-62; vis. scientist Oak Ridge (Tenn.) Nat. Lab., 1962-63; assoc. U. Pa. Med. Sch., Phila., 1963-64, asst. prof. microbiology, 1964-67, assoc. prof., 1967-72, prof., 1972—. Permanent mem. bd. sci. councilors Nat. Eye Inst., Bethesda, Md., 1987-92; prof., chair Tokyo U. Faculty Pharm. Scis., 1972-73; vis. prof. Kyoto U. Virus Rsch. Inst., 1985. Contbr. scientific papers over 200 articles to profl. jours. Recipient Fulbright-Smith-Mundt award, 1954, Helen Hay Whitney award, 1964-69, John Simmon Guggenheim award, 1972-73, Fogarty Internat. Sr. award, 1985-86. Mem. Am. Soc. Biol. Chemistry and Molecular Biology, Am. Soc. Cell Biology, Am. Soc. Microbiology, Am. Soc. Chemistry. Avocations: ice dancing, swimming. Office: U Pa Sch Medicine Dept Microbiology Johnson Pavilion Philadelphia PA 19104 Business E-Mail: kaji@mail.med.upenn.edu.

KAJI, HIDEKO, pharmacology educator; b. Tokyo, Jan. 1, 1932; arrived in U.S., 1954; d. Sakae and Tsuneko Katayama; m. Akira Kaji, Aug. 23, 1958; children: Kenneth, Eugene, Naomi, Amy. BS, Tokyo U. Pharm. Scis., 1954; MS, U. Nebr., 1956; PhD, Purdue U., 1958. Vis. scientist Oak Ridge (Tenn.) Nat. Lab., 1962-63; assoc. U. Pa., Phila., 1963-64; rsch. assoc. The Inst. Cancer Rsch., Phila., 1965-66, asst. mem., 1966-76; vis. mem. Max Planck Inst. Molek. Gen., Berlin, 1972-73, Nat. Inst. Med. Rsch., London, 1973; assoc. prof. Jefferson Med. Coll., Phila., 1976-82, prof. biochemistry and molecular biology, 1983—, Kimmel Cancer Ctr., 2005—; vis. prof. Wistar Inst., Phila., 1984-85. Cons. Nippon Paint Co., Ltd., Tokyo, 1990—, Coatesville (Pa.) VA Hosp., 1982-84. Contbr. articles to profl. jours. Fellow NIH (bd. dirs. 1986-89); mem. Am. Soc. Biochemistry and Molecular Biology, Am. Soc. Pharmacol. and Exptl. Therapeutics, Am. Soc. Microbiology, Am. Chem. Soc., Sigma Xi. Home: 334 Fillmore St Jenkintown PA 19046-4328 Office: Jefferson Med Coll 1020 Locust St Philadelphia PA 19107-6731 Office Phone: 215-503-6547. Business E-Mail: hideko.kaji@jefferson.edu.

KAJITA, YASUKAZU, neurosurgeon, educator; b. Ehime, Dec. 13, 1954; MD, Nagoya U., 1984, PhD. Assoc. prof. Nagoya U., Postgrad. Sch. Medicine, 2001—. Mem.: Japanese Stereotactic and Functional Neurosurgery (bd. dirs. 2008—), Japanese Neuromodulation Soc. (bd. dirs. 2005—). Office: 65 Tsurumai Showa Nagoya Aichi 466-8550 Japan Office Fax: 052 744 2360. Business E-Mail: ykajita@med.nagoya-u.ac.jp.

KAJIYA, KENTARO, research scientist; b. Japan, Mar. 28, 1977; MS, Tokyo U., 2001; PhD, Tokyo U. Agr. and Tech., 2008. Rsch. scientist Shiseido, 2001—. Office: 2-12-1 Fukuura Yokohama Kanagawa 236-8643 Japan Business E-Mail: kentaro.kajiya@to.shiseido.co.jp.

KAKATI, DINESH CHANDRA, physician; b. Gauhati, India, Feb. 1, 1941; arrived in Eng., 1969; s. Nara Kanta and Subhadra (Baishya) Kakati; m. Bhabani Medhi, Mar. 27, 1974; children: Rita, Rishi. MBBS with distinction, Gauhati Med. Sch., 1967; Diploma in Tropical Medicine and Hygiene, Liverpool U., Eng., 1970; Diploma in Thoracic Medicine, London U., 1984, Diploma in Cardiac Medicine, 1984; Diploma in Geriatric Medicine, Royal Coll. Physicians, 1985. Sr. house officer Sunderland (Eng.) Health Authority, 1969-70, med. registrar, 1970-72, Addinbrook Hosp., Cambridge, Eng., 1972-74, London Hosp., 1974-77; assoc. specialist N.E. Thames region, Hornchurch, Eng., 1977-84, asst. physician in medicine, 1984—; coronary heart disease lead Havering Primary Care Trust, Hornchurch, Essex, England. Pres. Sankar Jayanty Com., U.K.; gen. sec. London Bihu Com., London. Recipient Glory of India award, Indian Internat, Friendship Soc., London, 2008. Fellow Royal Soc. Health Eng.; mem. Brit. Med. Assn., Royal Coll. Gen. Practitioners (assoc.), Cultural Assn. of Assam in England (pres.). Office: St Georges Hosp Suttons Ln London RM12 6RS England Home: Ardleigh Green Road RM11 2LE Essex RM11 2LE England Office Phone: 01708-520830. Business E-Mail: dinesh.kakati@nhs.net.

KAKIYAMA, TETSUJI, sports medicine physician, educator; b. Yamaga, Kumamoto, Japan, Nov. 25, 1966; s. Kouji and Etsuko Kakiyama; m. Yukie Aoki, Mar. 30, 1996; children: Tetsuto, Ryutoshi, Saeko. D of Sport Sci., U. Tsukuba, Japan, 1999. Rsch. assoc. Otsuma Women's U., Chiyoda-ku, Tokyo, 1995—98; lectr. Kyushu U. Health and Welfare, Nobeoka, Miyazaki, Japan, 1999—2003; assoc. prof. Kwassui Women's Coll., Nagasaki, Japan, 2004—05. Recipient Young Investigators award, Second Ann. Congress European Coll. Sport Sci., 1997. Home: Takashirodai 1-25-2 Nagasaki 851-0137 Japan Office: Kwassui Women's Coll 1-50 Higashiyamate-machi Nagasaki 850-8515 Japan Office Fax: +81-95-828-3702. Business E-Mail: kakiyama@kwassui.ac.jp.

KAKUGAWA, YASUO, gastroenterologist; b. Hiroshima, Japan, Apr. 6, 1967; s. Masahiro and Yoko Kakugawa; m. Takemi Nakada, May 5, 1999; 1 child, Koki. MD, Kurume U., Fukuoka, Japan, 1995. Cert. Japanese Ministry Welfare, 1995. Internal medicine resident Doai Meml. Hosp., Tokyo, 1995—98, St. Luke's Internat. Hosp., Tokyo, 1998—99; resident endoscopy divsn. Nat. Cancer Ctr. Hosp., Tokyo, 1999—2002, chief resident endoscopy divsn., 2002—04, staff endoscopist, 2004—, Rsch. Ctr. Cancer Prevention and Screening, Tokyo, 2004—. Contbr. scientific papers to profl. jours. Mem.: Japanese Soc. Gastroent. Cancer Screening, Japanese Soc. Gastroenterology, Japanese Soc. Internal Medicine, Japan Gastroent. Endoscopy Soc. Avocations: travel, golf, tennis, Japanese cuisine. Office: Nat Cancer Ctr Hosp 5-1-1 Tsukiji Chuo-ku Tokyo 104-0045 Japan Office Phone: 81-3-3542-2511. Office Fax: 81-3-3542-3815. Business E-Mail: yakakuga@ncc.go.jp.

KAKULAS, BYRON ARTHUR, neuropathologist, neurologist; b. Mar. 29, 1932; s. Arthur Bartholomew and Phyllis (Dimantis) K.; m. Valerie Anne Patsoyannis, Feb. 5, 1961; children: Arthur Phillip, Felice Anne, Carolyn Rose. MB, St. Mark's Coll., 1956; BS, U. Adelaide, 1956; MD, U. Western Australia, 1964; Didaktora h.c., U. Athens, 1979. Intern, resident Royal Perth Hosp., 1957—60, med. officer, 1957—63, dept. head neuropathology, 1967—2002, prof. emeritus, 2007; mem. staff Mass. Gen. Hosp., Boston, 1963—65; prof. neuropathology U. We. Australia, 1971—2006, dean medicine, 1977—78; med. dir. Australian Neuromuscular Rsch. Inst., 1982—. Lectr. U. W. Australian Faculty Med., 1960-71; bd. dirs. Muscular Dystrophy Rsch. Assn., Australian Neurological Found.; sci. com. Internat. Spinal Rsch. Trust, 1983-1998; bd. mgmt. Sir Charles Gairdner Hosp., 1977-80, Good Samaritan Industries Inc., 1972-85; pres. XIIIth Internat. Congress Neuropathology, 1997; pres. (hon.) IXth Congr. on Neuromuscular Disroders, 1998; Sir Ludwig Cottmann lectr. Internat. Spinal Cord Soc., 2004. Author: Man Marsupials & Muscle, 1982, (with R.D. Adams) Diseases of Muscle, Pathological Foundations of Clinical Myology, 4th edit., 1985; editor: Basic and Clinical Research in Myology, 1973, (with M.R. Dimitrijevic, G. Vrbova) Recent Achievements in Restorative Neurology 2 Progressive Neuromuscular Diseases, 1986; co-editor: Pathogenesis & Therapy of Duchenne & Becker Muscular Dystrophy, 1990, Duchenne Muscular Dystrophy Animal Models and Genetic Manipulation, 1992; contbr. articles to med. jours. Decorated officer Order Australia; recipient Citation award Rotary, 1987, Advance Australia award, 1989, Hellenism award Greek Australian Businessmen's Assn., 1989, Medicus Hippocraticus prize 1996, Gaetano Conte prize, 2000, Gaetano Conte Gold Medal for clin. rsch., 2000, Lifetime Achievement award World Fedn. Neurology, 2002; Eli Lilly fellow 1963-64, C.J. Martin fellow 1964-65, Fulbright fellow 1969, Anzaas fellow 1987, Paul Harris fellow Rotary Internat. Found., 1990, Centenial of Federation medal Australia, 2003 Fellow Royal Australiasian Coll. Physicians (Rennie Meml. lectr., Bronze medal 1972), Royal Coll. Pathologists Australia and U.K.; mem. Australian and N.Z. Soc. Neuropathology (pres. 1996-98), Internat. Soc. Neuropathology (v.p. 1997-98), Internat. Congress Neuropathology (pres. 1997), Internat. Soc. Neuropathology (v.p. 1997-2000), Soc. Belge de Neurologie (hon.), Asian and Oceanian Myology Ctr. (v.p. 2001-, pres. 2005). Home: 59 Dampier Ave City Beach Western Australia 6015 Australia Office: Australian Neuromuscular Rsch Inst 4th Flr A Block QEII Med Ctr Verdun St Nedlands WA 6009 Australia Office Phone: 61-8-9346-3944. Personal E-mail: bkakulas@gmail.com. Business E-Mail: bkakulas@meddent.uwa.edu.au.

KALABOKA, SOFIA, pediatrician, allergist; b. Athens, Greece, Apr. 2, 1972; d. Kosmas Kalabokas and Kalliopi Kalaboka. Degree in Med., U. Athens, Greece, 1998, Splty. in Pediat., 2002; Splty. in Allergology, U. René Descartes - Paris 5, 2007, DU in Immunotherapy, 2007, DU in Nutrition, 2008, DU in Chronobiology, 2008; DU in Stress Trauma, 2008. Cert. Basic Life Support Greek Nat. Ctr. Emergency Med., 1997, lic. Physician Greek Ministry Health, 1998, Pediatrician Greek Ministry Health, 2003, cert. APLS Johns Hopkins Hosp. Pediatric Trauma Care, 2001, lic. Physician Gen. Med. Coun., UK, 2004, Pediatrician Gen. Med. Coun., UK, 2004, Physician Ordre des Méd., 2004, Pediatrician Ordre des Méd., 2004, allergist Ordre des Méd., 2007, cert. Surgery Primary Care Physicians Ecole Européenne Chirurgie U. René Descartes - Paris 5, 2006, Cardio-respiratory emergencies Ecole Européenne Chirurgie U. René Descartes - Paris 5, 2007, European Acad. Allergy and Clin. Immunology, 2008. Child health clerkship Children's Meml. Hosp., Chgo., 1996; internal medicine clerkship Rush-Presbyterian - St Luke's Med. Ctr., Chgo., 1996; primary care clerk Karpathos Med. Ctr., Greece, 1997; pediat. clerkship St. Orsola Hops., 1998; resident pediat. Gen. Hosp. Asclepieion, Voula, Greece, 1998—99, Gen. Pediatric hosp. Agia Sofia, Athens, 1999—2002; cons. pediat. Iatriko Athinon hosp., Athens, 2003—04, Greek Cmty. and Preventive Pediat., Nissyros, Kassos, Kimolos, Antiparos, Donoussa, Heraclia, Schinoussa, 2000—02; fellow St. Vincent de Paul Hosp., Pediatric Allergology Svc., Paris, 2004; fellow epidemiology allergic and respiratory diseases INSERM (French Nat. Inst. Health and Med. Rsch.) Unité 472, Villejuif, France, 2004—05; fellow Necker - Enfants Malades hosp., Pediatric Pulmonology and Allergology Svc., Paris, 2005—06, Inst. Pasteur, Dermatology/Allergology Svc., Paris, 2006; fellow epidemiology allergic and respiratory diseases INSERM (French Nat. Inst. Health and Med. Rsch.) Unité 707, Paris, 2006, investigator clin. and epidemiol. rsch. allergic and respiratory diseases, 2006—; rsch. fellow U. Pierre Marie Curie - Paris 6, Med. Sch. St Antoine, 2006—; clin. assoc. Pediatric Med. Ctr., Argenteuil, France, 2007—08; cons. Inst. Pasteur, Clin. Allergology Svc., Paris, 2008—, Necker-Enfants Malades Hosp., Anesthesiology Svc., Paris, 2008—, Mairie de Paris, Children's Health Sch., DASES, 2008—. Transl. med. articles Brit. Med. Jour. Greek Edit., Athens, Greece, 1997—2003, Brit. Med. Jour. French Edit., Paris, 2005—06; specialist on tv programs for children's health, breastfeeding and nutrition, vaccine expert. Editl. bd.: Jour. Allergy and Asthma; contbr. articles to numerous profl. jours. Recipient 12 Ann. awards for Highest Marks And Best Rank, Greek Ministry Edn., 1985—90, Best student award, Rotary Club, 1990, First woman in Med. Sch., Social and Ednl. Ctr. Hollargos City, 1991, Excellence Med. Studies, J Sp Latsis Found., 1991—97; scholarship, Nat. Scholarship Found. Greece, 2004—06. Mem.: European Acad. Allergy and Clin. Immunology, European Soc. Cancer Immunology and Immunotherapy, Soc. Francaise Pédiatrie, Soc. Pédiatrique Pneumologie et d'Allergologie, Soc. Francaise d'Allergologie et d'Immunologie

Clinique, Ordre des Médecins (French Med. Coun.), Gen. Med. Coun., UK, Greek Pediatric Soc., Athens Med. Coun. Avocations: sailing, chess, photography, ecology. Personal E-mail: sofiakalaboka@yahoo.com. Business E-Mail: sofia.kalaboka@paris.fr.

KALASHNIKOVA, LIUDMILA ANDREEVNA, neurologist; b. Moscow, Dec. 30, 1948; MD, 1st Moscow Med. Inst., 1972. Rsch. Inst. Neurology, 1975—, PH prof., 1989. Mem.: Russian Soc. Neurologists. Avocation: theater. Office: Volokolamskoye shosse Moscow 125367 Russia E-mail: kalashnikovancn@yandex.ru.

KALAVAGUNTA, SUDHAKIRAN BHASKARARAO, surgeon; b. Eluru, India, May 16, 1966; s. Suguna Bhaskararao and Rajeswari Kalavagunta; m. Sailaja Mopidevi, Mar. 23, 2000. MBBS, B J Med. Coll., Pune, Maharashtra, 1988, MS (ENT), 1992. Fellow (Surgery) Royal Coll. of Surgeons of Glasgow, 1999, Fellow (Ent) Royal Coll. of Surgeons of Eng., 2000. Ho. officer B J Med. Coll., Pune, India, 1987—88, sr. ho. officer ent surgery, 1990—91, sr. ho. officer gen. surgery, 1991, specialist registrar ent surgery, 1991—92; sr. ho. officer accident and emergency Pune Mcpl. Corp. Hosps., Pune, India, 1989; sr. ho. officer in ent surgery Al Nahda Hosp., Ministry of Health, Muscat, Oman, 1995—97, specialist registrar in ent surgery, 1997—2000, The Royal Liverpool U. Hosp., England, 2000—01; specialist registrar ent surgery Warrington Gen. Hosp., England, 2002, U. Hosp. Aintree, Liverpool, England, 2002—03, Leeds Gen. Infirmary, England, 2003—04; specialist registrar ENT surgery Bradford Royal Infirmary, England, 2004—. Lectr. B J Med. Coll., Pune, India, 1993—95; consulting surgeon Ministry of Health, Muscat, Oman, 1995—2000, NHS, Liverpool, 2000—03, Leeds, 2003—, Bradford, 2004—. Author: (rsch. article) The Turkish Jour. of Ear Nose & Throat, (internat. presentation) Proceedings of Fourth Internat. Conf. on Vestibular Schwannomas and Other CPA Lesions, (editl.) Pakistan Jour. of Otolaryngology, (nat. presentation) Proceeding of Brit. Soc. of Neuro-otology. Fellow: Royal Coll. of Surgeons of Glasgow, Royal Coll. of Surgeons of Eng.; mem.: Indian Med. Coun., Gen. Med. Coun. Achievements include research in Classification of extensively pneumatized maxillary sinuses. Office: Bradford Royal Infirmary Duckworth Ln Bradford BD9 6RJ England Home: A1/101 Aundh D P Road 411 007 Pune 411 007 India Fax: 0044 113 2777162; Office Fax: 00441133923165. Personal E-mail: sudhakiran7@yahoo.com.

KALBFLEISCH, JOHN MCDOWELL, retired cardiologist; b. Lawton, Okla., Nov. 15, 1930; s. George and Etta Lillian (McDowell) K.; m. Jolie Harper, Dec. 30, 1961. AS, Cameron A&M U., Lawton, 1950; BS, U. Okla., 1952, MD, 1957. Diplomate Am. Bd. Internal Medicine, Am. Bd. Cardiovascular Disease. Intern U. Va. Hosp., 1957-58; resident and fellow U. Okla. Med. Ctr., 1958-62, instr. medicine, 1964-66, asst. prof., 1966-69, assoc. clin. prof., 1970-78, clin. prof. Tulsa br., 1978—2007; pvt. practice Tulsa, 1969—2007; founder, chmn. bd., CEO Cardiology of Tulsa, Inc., 1969—2007; dir. cardiovascular svcs. St. Francis Hosp., Tulsa, 1975—2005. Physician adv. bd. City of Tulsa, 1978-81; bd. dirs. St. Francis Hosp., exec. com., 1987-97, 2001-06; exec. v.p., chief med. officer St. Francis Health Sys., 1998-99; treas. Tulsa Med. Edn. Found., 1988-89, v.p., 1990-92, pres., 1992-94; med. dir., chmn. bd. Warren Clinics, 1990-97; mem. Okla. Ctr. for Advancement of Sci. and Tech., 1989-95; mem. adv. com. Ctr. for Laser Devel. and Applications Okla. State U. Contbr. articles to profl. jours. With USPHS, 1962-64. Recipient Lifelong Svc. award, Tulsa Med. Edn. Found./U. Okla. Coll. Medicine, 2002; named Okla. Profl. Health Care Champion, Partnership Blue Cross Blue Shield Okla., Okla. State Dept. Health, Okla. Hosp. Assn., Okla. Osteo. Assn., 2005; named to, St. Francis Health Sys. Hall of Fame, 2003. Fellow ACP (gov.-elect Okla. 1990-91, gov. 1991-95, Okla. Laureate award 1995), Am. Coll. Cardiology (gov. Okla. 1978-81); mem. AMA, AAAS, Tulsa County Med. Soc., Okla. State Med. Assn., Am. Heart Assn. (Fellow coun. on clin. cardiology), tchg. scholar 1967-69), Okla. Soc. Internal Medicine v.p., pres.-elect 1983-84, pres. 1985-86), Am. Soc. Internal Medicine, Am. Fedn. Clin. Rsch., Am. Inst. Nutrition, U. Okla. Med. Alumni Assn. (Physician of Yr. in Pvt. Practice 1999), Delta Upsilon. Republican. Presbyterian. Home: 6528 E 101st St Ste D-1 # 254 Tulsa OK 74133 Personal E-mail: jmkalbfleisch@aol.com.

KALDARI, SAED M., plastic surgeon; Grad., Royal Coll., Ireland, 1997. Cert. Plastic and Reconstructive Surgery Swedish Bd., 2005. Cons. plastic surgeon Malmo Univ. Hosp., Sweden, affiliate, Lund Univ. Hosp.; cons. plastic surgeon Scandinavian Outer Ear Reconstruction Centre; clin. surg. affiliate Weill Cornel Med. Coll., Qatar; cons. plastic and reconstructive surgeon Rumailah Hosp.; cons. and dir. Dr. Saed Kaldari Plastic Surgery Clinic (Pvt. Practice). Mem.: GCC Plastic Surgery Assn., Pan ARAB Plastic Surgery Assn., IPRAS internat. Plastic & reconstructive Surgery Assn., SWEDISH Plastic Surgery Assn. Office: Dr Saed Kaldari Plastic Surgery Clinic PO Box 31431 Doha Qatar Office Phone: 9744515177. Office Fax: 9744515188. *

KALE, AHMET, medical educator; b. Adana, Turkey, June 26, 1974; Assoc. prof. Ankara U., 1998—. Office: Kurttepe Adana Seyhan 21280 Turkey Personal E-mail: ahmetkale5@yahoo.com.

KALE, GAUTAM, physician, educator; b. Mumbai, June 22, 1977; MD, BJ Med. Coll., 2002; MS in Biomedical Engring., U. Tenn. Health Sci. Ctr., 2004. Rsch. asst. U. Tenn. Health Sci. Ctr., 2001—04; resident physician Albert Einstein Coll. Medicine, Bronx Lebanon Hosp. Ctr., 2004—07; academic hospitalist Healthpartner Med. Group, 2007—11; asst. prof. medicine U. Minn., 2010—. Contbr. scientific papers to profl. publs. Mem.: ACP, Am. Soc. Hosp. Medicine, Internat. Soc. Travel medicine, Am. Bd. Internat. Medicine. Avocations: meditation, travel, cricket. Home: 1353 Sumner St Saint Paul MN 55116

KALEMKERIAN, GREGORY PETER, oncologist, educator; b. Bronx, NY, Feb. 9, 1961; MD, Northwestern U., 1985. Diplomate Am. Bd. Oncology. Clin. fellow oncology Johns Hopkins U., Balt., 1989-93; asst. prof. Wayne State U., Detroit, 1993-99; assoc. prof. U. Mich., 1999—2005, prof., 2005—, dir. thoracic oncology. Mem. ACP, Am. Assn. Cancer Rsch., Am. Soc. Clin. Oncology. Office: C350 Med Inn 1500 E Med Ctr Dr Ann Arbor MI 48109-0848 Office Phone: 734-615-4762. Office Fax: 734-647-8792. Business E-Mail: kalemker@umich.edu.

KALENIKOVA, ELENA IGOREVNA, pharmacologist, educator; b. Kursk, Russia, June 1, 1957; d. Igor Vitaljevitch Loktev and Elena Ivanovna Lokteva; m. Eugeny Andreevitch Sjutkin, Aug. 21, 1987; 1 child, Darja Eugenjevna Sjutkina; m. Alexandr Vasiljevitch Kalenikov, July 23, 1980 (div. Feb. 21, 1987); 1 child, Egor Alexandrovitch Kalenikov. Degree in Pharmacy, First Moscow Med. Inst., 1979, PhD in Pharmacy, 1984; Sci.D in Pharmacy, 2009. Rschr. ctrl. sci. rsch. lab. 4th main dept. Ministry Health of USSR, Moscow, 1984—85; sr. rschr. All-Union Cardiology Rsch. Ctr., Moscow, 1985—90, Lomonosov Moscow State U., Moscow, 1993—2004; assoc. prof. Moscow State U., 2005—, dep. dean edn. faculty basic medicine, 2004—, head chair pharmacy, 2010—. Achievements include research in pharmacokinetics of bioactive peptides; central mechanisms of blood pressure regulation during acute stress; the role of oxidative stress in pathogenesis of ischemia-induced myocardial remodelling and cardioprotective effects of coenzyme Q10. Home: Tokmakov St 12/20 ap 55 Moscow 105066 Russia Office: Faculty Medicine Lomonosov Moscow State Univ Lomonosovskiy Pr-Kt 31/5 119192 Moscow Moskva Russia Business E-Mail: eikaleni@fbm.msu.ru.

KALESNIKOFF, JANET, research scientist; b. Canada, May 12, 1975; BSc, U. BC, 1997, PhD, 2003. Sr. rsch. scientist Stanford U., 2007—. Instr. U. Calif. Berkeley Ext., 2010. Office: 269 Campus Dr CCSR Rm 3250 Stanford CA 94305 Business E-Mail: jkalesni@stanford.edu.

KALEV-ZYLINSKA, MAGGIE LUCY, pathologist; b. Sulecin, Poland, Oct. 13, 1963; d. Edwarda and Czeslaw Zylinski; life ptnr. Vincent John Matheson Stewart; m. Dimtcho Iordanov Kalev, May 25, 1994 (div. 1999). MD with honors, U. Szczecin, Poland, 1988; FRCPA, Groote Schuur Hosp., Cape Town, South Africa, 1994, Auckland U., New Zealand, 2000; PhD, U. Auckland, 2003. Cert. med. practitioner New Zealand, 1996, South Africa, 1990. Lab. asst. U. Szczecin, Szczecin, 1987—88; intern Military Hosp., Cracow, Poland, 1988—89; Medical Registrar - Cardiology Cracow Hospital, Cracow, Poland, 1989—91; sr. house officer bone marrow transplantation Groote Schuur Hosp., Cape Town, 1991—92, sr. house officer cardiology, 1992—93, sr, house officer hematology, 1993—94, registrar hematopathology, 1994—95; registrar pathology Auckland Hosp., 1996—97; registrar hematology Auckland Hosp. and Middlemore Hosp., Auckland, 1997—98; sr. registrar hematopathology Auckland Hosp., 1998—99; rsch. fellow U. Auckland, 2003—. Tutor lab. medicine U. Auckland, 1999—; cons. Diagnostic Lab., 2000; presenter at confs. in field. Contbr. articles, confs. procs. in field (best paper Zebrafish workshop, 2001). Student mediator U. Szczecin, 1983—88. Recipient Registrar in Rsch. award, Royal Coll. Pathologists of Australasia, 2000, Ruth Spencer Med. Rsch. fellowship, Med. Rsch. Found. of New Zealand and New Zealand Guardian Trust, 1999, Neil Prentice Memorial prize, Royal Coll. Pathologists of Australasia, 1998, Scholarship Talent-Promotion-Progress, Polish Ministry of Health, 1988, travel grants, Leukemia and Blood Found., Cancer Soc., Med. Rsch. Found., 1998—2001; grantee Graduate Rsch. Fund, U. Auckland, 2000—01. Mem.: NY Acad. Scis., Hematology Soc. of Australia and New Zealand. Avocations: exercise, reading, travel. Office: Univ Auckland 85 Park Rd Auckland 1001 New Zealand Home Phone: 64 9 5754572; Office Phone: 64 9 373 7599. Office Fax: + 64 9 373 7492. Business E-Mail: m.kalev@auckland.ac.nz.

KALIA, AWDHESH, microbiologist, educator; b. New Delhi, Oct. 8, 1969; PhD, All India Inst. Med. Scis., 2000. Postdoc. fellow Yale U., 1999—2002; rsch. assoc. Wash. U. Sch. Medicine, 2002—04; assoc. prof. U. Louisville, 2004—. Recipient Young Investigator award, Internat. Soc. Chemotherapy, Ralph E. Powe Jr. Faulty Enhancement award, Oak Ridge Associated U.; James Hudson Brown Alexander Brown-Coxe fellowship, Yale U. Mem.: Am. Soc. Microbiology. Avocations: reading, gardening. Home: 5727 Innsbruck St Bellaire TX 77401 Personal E-mail: awdhesh.kalia@gmail.com.

KALICHMAN, MICHAEL, neuropathologist; BS in Applied Mechanical & Engring. Sci., U. Calif., San Diego, 1975; M.Ap.Sc. in Biomedical Engring., U. Toronto, 1980, PhD in Pharmacology, 1980. Co-founder Ctr. for Ethics in Sci. & Technol.; prof. Divsn. Neuropathology Dept. Pathology U. Calif., San Diego, dir. Rsch. Ethics Program. Office: University of California 9500 Gilman Dr Mail Code 0612 La Jolla CA 92093-0612 Office Phone: 858-822-2027. Office Fax: 858-822-5765. E-mail: kalichman@ucsd.edu.

KALIMI, ROBERT, cardiovascular surgeon; b. Tehran, Iran; BA magna cum laude, NYU; MD, Sackler Sch. Medicine, NYC, 1996. Cert. Am. Bd. Surgery, 2002, Am. Bd. Thoracic Surgery, 2004. Intern LI Jewish Med. Ctr., New Hyde Park, NY, 1996—97, resident, 1997—2001; fellow Rush-Presbyn. St. Luke's Med. Ctr., Chgo., 2001—03; clin. instr. surgery Columbia-Presbyn. Coll. Physicians and Surgeons, NYC, 2003—04; surgeon North Shore Univ. Hosp., Manhasset, NY, 2004—. Presenter in field. Contbr. articles to profl. jours.; co-editor: Clin. Scenarios in Thoracic Surgery, 2004. Office: North Shore Univ Hosp 300 Community Dr Manhasset NY 11030 Office Phone: 516-562-4970. Office Fax: 516-562-3786. Business E-Mail: kalimi@nshs.edu.

KALIMULLINA, LILIJA BARIEVNA, medical educator; b. Ufa, Russia, Oct. 19, 1941; D, Bashkir Med. Inst., 1964, D in Biol. Sci., 1967. Prof. Bashkir State U., 1971—. Mem.: Internat. Agademija Sci., Internat. Brain Rsch. Orgn. Home: Revolutionaja 60 Flat 70 Ufa Bashkortostan 450005 Russia Personal E-mail: mpha@ufanet.ru.

KALINA, IVAN, pediatrician; b. Kosice, Slovak Republic, May 22, 1932; came to US, 1965; s. Geza and Helen (Fedorak) K.; m. Vera M., July 1, 1956; children: Peter, Yvette. MD, Charles U., Prague, Czechoslovakia, 1956. Diplomate Am. Bd. of Pediats. Pediatrician Children's Univ. Hosp., Kosice, Slovak Republic, 1956-65; resident NYU Hosp., 1965-68; pvt. practice pediats. Rocky Point, N.Y., 1968—, assoc. clin. prof. pediats. SUNY, Stony Brook. Attending physician St. Charles Hosp., Port Jefferson, Mather Meml. Hosp., Port Jefferson, Stony Brook U. Hosp. Fellow Am. Acad. Pediats.; mem. AMA (Physician Recognition award), Suffolk County Med. Soc., Suffolk County Pediat. Scc., N.Y. State Med. Soc. Republican. Avocations: skiing, tennis. Office: 81 Broadway Rocky Point NY 11778-9723

KALINA, ROBERT EDWARD, ophthalmologist, educator; b. New Prague, Minn., Nov. 13, 1936; s. Edward Robert and Grace Susan (Hess) K.; m. Janet Jessie Larsen, July 18, 1959; children: Paul Edward, Lynne Janet. BA magna cum laude, U. Minn., 1957, BS, MD, U. Minn., 1960. Diplomate Am. Bd. Ophthalmology (dir. 1981-89). Intern U. Oreg. Med. Sch. Hosp., Portland, 1960-61, resident in ophthalmology, 1961-62, 63-66; asst. in retina surgery Children's Hosp., San Francisco, 1966-67; Nat. Inst. Neurol. Diseases and Blindness Spl. fellow Mass. Eye and Ear Infirmary, Boston, 1967; instr. ophthalmology U. Wash., 1967-69, asst. prof., 1969-71, acting chmn. dept. ophthalmology, 1970-71, assoc. prof., 1971-72, chmn. dept. ophthalmology, 1971-96, prof., 1972—. Mem. staffs Univ. Hosp., Harborview Hosp.; assoc. head divsn. ophthalmology dept. surgery Children's Hosp., Seattle, 1975-86; pres. U. Wash. Physicians, 1990-93. Contbg. author: Introduction to Clinical Pediatrics, 1972, Ophthalmology Study Guide for Medical Students, 1975; contbr. numerous articles to profl. publs. Served to capt., M.C. USAF, 1962-63. Recipient Outstanding Achievement award, Nat. Eye Inst., 2003. Fellow ACS, Am. Acad. Ophthalmology (Life Achievement Honor award 1989); mem., Assn. Univ. Profs. Ophthalmology (pres. 1983-84, exec. v.p. 1989-94), Assn. Rsch. in Vision and Ophthalmology, Pacific Coast Oto-Ophthalmol. Soc. (councilor 1972-74), King County Med. Soc., Wash. State Acad. Ophthalmology, Phi Beta Kappa.

KALINICH, LILA JOYCE, psychiatrist, educator; BA, Northwestern U., Chgo., 1966, MD, 1969. Clin. prof. psychiatry Columbia U., NYC; tng. and supervising analyst Columbia Psychoanalytic Ctr. for Tng. and Rsch., NYC. Mem.: Assn. Psychoanalytic Medicine (pres. 2005—07). Office Phone: 212-866-0200.

KALININ, VLADIMIR VENIAMINOVICH, psychiatrist, researcher; b. Orenburg, Russia, Mar. 15, 1952; s. Lydia Kalinina; m. Elena Korovina, Aug. 2, 1980; 1 child, Anna Kalinina. MD, PhD, Moscow Med. Stomatological Inst., 1976. Lic. psychiatrist Sechenov's Moscow (Russua) Acad., 1977. Sr. rschr. Dept. Therapy Mental Disorders Moscow (Russia) Rsch. Inst. Psychiatry Ministry Health and Social Devel., 1978—2002, head Dept. Brain Organic Disorders and Epilepsy Moscow (Russia) Rsch. Inst. Psychiatry, 2002—. Contbr. articles to profl. jours. Mem.: Russian Psychiatric Assn., Russian League Against Epilepsy. Office: Moscow Research Institute of Psychiatry 3 Poteshnaya str Moscow 107076 Russia Personal E-mail: doct.kalinin@mail.ru.

KALISCH, BEATRICE JEAN, nursing educator, consultant; b. Tellahoma, Tenn., Oct. 15, 1943; d. Peter and Margaret Ruth Petersen; children— Philip P., Melanie J. BS, U. Nebr., 1965; MS, U. Md., 1967, PhD, 1970. Pediatric staff nurse Centre County Hosp., Belle fonte, Pa., 1965-66; instr. nursing Philipsburg (Pa.) Gen. Hosp. Sch. Nursing, 1966; pediatric staff nurse Greater Balt. Med. Center, Towson, Md., 1967; asst. prof. maternal-child nursing Am. U., 1967-68; clin. nurse specialist N.W. Tex. Hosp., Amarillo, 1970; assoc. prof. maternal-child nursing, curriculum coordinator nursing Amarillo Coll., 1970-71; chmn. baccalaureate nursing program, asso. prof. nursing U. So. Miss., 1971-74; prof. nursing, chmn. dept. parent child nursing U. Mich. Sch. Nursing, Ann Arbor, 1974-86, Shirley C. Titus Disting. prof., 1977—, Titus Disting. prof. nursing mgmt., 1989—, chair nursing bus. and health sys. program, 2000—; prin., chair, nursing consultation svcs. Ernst & Young, Detroit, 1986-89. Prin. investigator USPH grant to study image of nurses in mass media and the informational quality nursing news, U. Mich., 1977-86, prin. investigator to study intrahosp. transport of critically ill patients, 1991—; prin. investigator to study use of HIA nurse in N.Y.C. labor market, U. Mich.; prin. investigator to study the impact of managed care on critical care, U. Mich.; vis. Disting. prof. U. Ala., 1979, U. Tex., 1981, Tex. Christian U., 1983; prin. investigator Med. Nursing Care and Nurse Staffing, staff nurse investigator. Author: Child Abuse and Neglect: An Annotated Bibliography, 1978; co-author: Nursing Involvement in Health Planning, 1978, Politics of Nursing, 1982, Images of Nurses on Television, 1983, The Advance of American Nursing, 1986, revised, 1994, The Changing Image of the Nurse, 1987; co-editor: Studies in Nursing Mgmt.; contbr. articles to profl. jours. Recipient Joseph L. Andrews Bibliog. award Am. Assn. Law Libraries, 1979; Book of Yr. award Am. Jour. Nursing, 1978, 83, 86, 87, Outstanding Achievement award U. Md., 1987, Distinguished Alumni award U. Nebr., 1985, Shaw medal Boston Coll., 1986; USPHS fellow. Fellow: Am. Acad. Nursing; mem.: ANA, APHA, Am. Coll. Healthcare Execs., Am. Orgn. Nurse Execs., Sigma Theta Tau, Phi Kappa Phi. Presbyterian. Office: U Mich Sch Nursing 400 N Ingalls St Ann Arbor MI 48109-0482 Business E-Mail: bkalisch@umich.edu.

KALLAND, KARL-HENNING, education educator; b. Hareid, Norway, Sept. 6, 1955; s. Jorunn Mork and Kåre Hilmar Kalland; life ptnr. Anne Margrete Oyan; 1 child, Unn Merete Oyan Kalland. MD, U. Bergen, Norway, 1984, PhD, 1989. Lic. Medical Practice Norwegian Med. Assn., 1984. Post doctoral Harvard Med. Sch., Boston, 1989—91; prof. U. of Bergen, Bergen, Norway, 1993—2005; dir. U. of Bergen, Gade Inst., 2005—. Mem.: Norwegian Med. Assn. (life). Achievements include discovery of signal mediated nuclear export of proteins; nucleocytoplasmic shuttling of HIV-1; development of cDNA macroarray hybridization. Office: Gade Inst Bergen Univ Jonas Lies Vei 91 5009 Bergen Norway Office Fax: 47 55584512; Home Fax: 47 55584512. Business E-Mail: kalland@gades.uib.no.

KALLEE, EKKEHARD ALBERT HERMANN, medical researcher, educator; b. Stuttgart-Feuerbach, Germany, Jan. 30, 1922; s. Albert and Helene (Schmolz) K.; m. Barbara Weigmann, Sept. 23, 1941; 1 child: Stephan. MD, U. Tuebingen, Germany, 1950. Asst. prof., dozent U. Tuebingen, 1961, assoc. prof., 1967, prof. emeritus, 1987; fellow Max Kade Found., NYC, 1955-56; with dept. radiology Strong Meml. Hosp., U. Rochester, NY, 1955-56; with Med. U. Klinik, Tuebingen, Germany. Founder, chief Med. Radioisotope Lab., U. Tuebingen, 1951. Inventor direct detection of protein traces (e.g. insulin) using paper electrophoresis, 1952; first descriptions of (a) some details of Bennhold's analbuminemia, (b) passive transport of protein-bound substances by means of adsorptive distribution equilibria (transport chains), (c) binding ability of subcellular proteins, (d) disruption of antigen-antibody bonds by antirheumatics, (e) pyramidal lobe in hyperthyroidism, coincidence of TBG deficiency with HOCM; contbr. over 150 articles to profl. jours. Mem. Student Fraternity Tuebinger Königsgesellschaft "Roigel", European Thyroid Assn. (emeritus), Deutsche Gesellschaft fuer Endokrinologie, Deutsche Gesellschaft fuer Innere Medizin. Avocations: gardening, foreign languages.

KÄLLÉN, BENGT ANDERS JAN, embryology educator, consultant; b. Kristianstad, Sweden, June 1, 1929; s. A.O. Yngve and Karin S.M. (Redin) K.; m. O. Ingegerd Mörck, June 14, 1951(dec. Feb. 27, 2011); children: Anders, Ragnar, Rune, Barbro. PhD, Med. Faculty, Lund, Sweden, 1952, MD, 1958. Assoc. prof. Med. Faculty, Lund,

1952-64, prof. embryology, 1965-94, prof. emeritus, head of Tornblad Inst., 1994—. Rsch. fellow Med. Rsch. Coun. Sweden, 1964-65, Univ. Coll., London, 1953; Rockefeller fellow Washington U., St. Louis, 1954-55; cons. Nat. Bd. Health, Stockholm, 1964—. Contbr. articles on teratology, embryology, reprodn. epidemiology, immunobiology, and cancer rsch. to profl. jours. Home: Galjevangsv 26 S-22465 Lund Sweden Office: U Lund Tornblad Inst Biskopsgatan 7 S-22362 Lund Sweden Office Phone: 46-46-222 7536. Business E-Mail: bengt.kallen@med.lu.se.

KALLIAKMANIS, IOANNIS, gastroenterologist; b. Athens, Apr. 10, 1974; Degree, U. Athens, 2000. Asst., gastroenterology dept. Hygeia Med. Hosp., 2010—. Office: 108 Dodekanisou & 21 Anapafseos Athens 12135 Greece Office Fax: 0030 2105744232. E-mail: ikalliak@yahoo.gr.

KALLOO, ANTHONY, gastroenterologist, educator; MB, BS in Medicine, Surgery, U. West Indies Med. Sch., 1979. Rotating intern, medicine and surgery Port of Spain Gen. Hosp., Trinidad, West Indies, 1979—80, house officer, dept. medicine, 1980—81; rsch. assoc. prevalence of Hepatitis B in Trinidad and Tobago Rsch. U. West Indies, Trinidad, West Indies, 1981—82; intern, internal medicine Howard U. Hosp., 1982—83, resident, internal medicine, 1983—85; fellow, gastroenterology/hepatology combined Vet. Adminstrn. Med. Ctr. Georgetown, U. Hosp. and NIH, 1985—87; instr., medicine, gastroenterology Georgetown U. Hosp., Washington, 1987—88; asst. prof., medicine, divsn. gastroenterology John Hopkins U. Sch. Medicine, Balt., 1988—94, assoc. prof., medicine, 1994, prof., medicine, dir. therapeutic endoscopy, divsn. gastroenterology, 1992—95; clin. dir., divsn. gastroenterology John Hopkins Hosp., 1999—2001, dir., gastrointestinal endoscopy, divsn. gastroenterology, 1995—2005, dir., divsn. gastroenterology and hepatology, 2005—. Past panel med. dir. Hopkins Gastroenterology and Hepatology Resource Ctr.; past panel chair for gastroenterology and urology devices with the US FDA; mem. Apollo Group. Contbr. several articles to profl. jours., scientific papers, chapters to books; assoc. editor Gastrointestinal Endoscopy. Named Best Gastroenterology, Balt. Mag., 2002; named one of Best Doctors in America, 2001. Mem.: Am. Coll. Gastroenterology (chair, Am. Soc. Gastrointestinal Endoscopy by-laws com. 1992—93, chair, rsch. com. 1993—95, chair, program com. 1993—95, com. on minority affairs 1995—98, rsch. com. 1995—98, chair, com. on minority affairs 1998—2000, chair, standard care 2000—01, chair, task force on pub. edn. 2000—01). Achievements include being the pioneer of the surgery method using natural orfices for organ removal; part of team that removed a donor kidney through the vagina for the first time in 2009; patents in field. Office: John Hopkins Liver Cancer Ctr Cancer Research Bldg II 1550 Orleans St 1M 12 Baltimore MD 21231 Office Phone: 410-955-9697. Office Fax: 410-614-7340.

KALMAN, LISA VIVIAN, geneticist; b. Allentown, Pa., May 24, 1961; BS, U. Calif., 1984, PhD, 1990. Health scientist Ctrs. Disease Control and Prevention, 2001—. Coord. Genetic Testing Reference Material Coordination Program (GeT-RM), 2005; mem. area com. Clin. and Lab. Standards Inst. (CLSI), 2008. Mem.: Assn. Molecular Pathology. Office: 1600 Clifton Rd MS G-23 Atlanta GA 30333 Business E-Mail: ljk0@cdc.gov.

KALNICKI, SHALOM, radiologist, educator; b. Tel Aviv, July 18, 1951; s. Samuel and Dina Kalnicki; m. Rachel Leia Cukier, May 20, 1975; children: Miriam, Michael, Dina, Eva. MD, U. Sao Paulo, Brazil, 1974. Diplomate Am. Bd. Radiology, cert. in Therapeutic Radiology, Radiation Oncology, diplomate Am. Bd. Internal Medicine, cert. in Med. Oncology. Intern radiology U. Sao Paulo, 1973—74; resident in radiology Montefiore Hosp. Med. Ctr., Bronx, 1975-78, chief resident, fellow, 1978-79; med. instr. U. Sao Paulo Med. Sch., 1979-83; asst. prof., dir. radiotherapy dept. Albert Einstein Hosp., 1983-84; asst. prof. clin. radiotherapy Mt. Sinai Med. Ctr., NYC, 1984-88; faculty U. Pitts. Sch. Medicine, 1988—, prof., 2000—; dir radiation oncology Magee Women's Hosp. and Shadyside Hosp. U. Pitts. Med. Ctr., 1988—93, vice chmn. clin. affairs, dept. radiation oncology, 2000—04; prof., chmn. dept. radiation oncology Albert Einstein Coll. Medicine., Montefiore Med. Ctr., Bronx, NY, 2004—. Prof. Hahnemann Med. Sch., Med. Coll. of Pa., 1993—99; chmn. dept. radiation oncology Allegheny Gen. Hosp., Pitts., 1993—2000. Contbr. articles to profl. jours. Named an Outstanding House Officer, Montefiore Hosp. Med. Ctr. Alumni Assn., 1979; grantee Sao Paulo Rsch. Found., 1972. Fellow: Am. Coll. Radiation Oncology; mem.: Am. Coll. Radiology, NY Roentgen Ray Soc., NY Cancer Soc., NY Acad. Sci., Am. Soc. Clin. Oncology, Am. Soc. Therapeutic Radiology & Oncology. Office: Montefiore Med Ctr 111 E 210th St Klau Rm 3rd Fl Bronx NY 10467 Home: 5220 Independence Ave Bronx NY 10471-2826 Office Phone: 718-980-5280. Business E-Mail: skalnicki@montefiore.org.

KALOGJERA, IKAR JAKSA, psychiatrist, educator; b. Zagreb, Croatia, Aug. 30, 1945; arrived in U.S., 1972; s. Jaksa Jakov and Biserka Erak Kalogjera; m. Araceli Colina Cabaron, July 15, 1976; 1 child, Liliana Marie. MD, U. Zagreb, Croatia, 1970. Diplomate in psychiatry and child and adolescent psychiatry Am. Bd. Psychiatry and Neurology. Intern U. Zagreb, 1970—71; resident in psychiatry Med. Coll. Wis., Wauwatosa, 1972—74; fellow in child and adolescent psychiatry U. Cin., 1974—76; pvt. practice Rockford, Ill., 1976—79; dir. adolescent in-patient unit Med. Coll. Wis., 1979—80, dir. adolescent in-patient svc., 1980—81; pvt. practice adult, child and adolescent psychiatry Wauwatosa, 1981—. Asst. clin. prof. Med. Coll. Wis., 1981—87, assoc. clin. prof., 1987—2001, clin. prof. psychiatry, 2001—; mem. hon. staff Aurora Psychiat. Hosp., Wauwatosa, 1999—; founder, leader Milw. Group for the Advancement of Self Psychology, 1991—. Co-author: (article) Am. Jour. Psychotherapy, 1988; author: Hosp. and Cmty. Psychiatry, 1989, (book chpt.) Disordered Couple, 1998. Cons. Family Svc., Milw., 1982—89, Lutheran Social Svcs., Milw., 1984—90, Jewish Family Svc., Milw., 1979—; contbr. Croatian Cmty., Milw., 1979—. Recipient Outstanding Therapists, Town and Country Mag., 1988, Tchg. award, Dept. Psychiatry and Behavioral Medicine, Med. Coll. Wis., 1992, award for Excellence in Tchg., 1992, Top Psychiatrists, Psychotherapists, Milw. Mag., 1996, 2001, Marvin Wagner Clin. Preceptor award, Med. Coll. Wis., 1999, Golden Apple Tchg. award, 1996, 2000, Give a Damn award, 1991, 2003, Cmty. Svc. honor, Jewish Family Svcs. Milw., 2003, Excellence award, Child & Adolescent Psychiatry Tng. Program, 2010, Irma Bland award, Am. Psychiat. Assn., 2006, Svc. award, Jewish Family Svc., 2010; named one of Ams. Top Psychiatrists, Consumer Rsch. Coun. America, 2002—11; named to Top Psychiatrists, Psychotherapists, Milw. Mag., 1994; Disting. Life fellow, Am. Psychiat. Assn. Fellow: Acad. Cognitive Therapy, Am. Acad. Child Psychiatry; mem.: Wisc. Psychoanalytic Soc. (spl. mem.), Med. Soc. Milw. County, Alumni Assn. of Family Inst. Northwestern U., Am. Soc. Addiction Medicine, Am. Group Psychotherapy Assn., Wis. Psychiat. Assn., AMA, Wis. State Med. Soc. Avocations: boating, photography, movies, theater, travel. Office: 1220 Dewey Ave Wauwatosa WI 53213 Office Phone: 414-454-6630.

KALOS, ALAN V., health planning administrator; b. NYC, July 10, 1946; s. Sol and Anne Kalos; m. Mary F. Brogan, Nov. 23, 1977; children: James A., Elizabeth A. BA in Psychology, U. Fla., Gainesville, 1969; MEd, U. Cin., 1982. Health planning adminstr. Northern Ky. Health Dept., Edgewood, 1987—; with process devel. com. Pub. Helath Accreditation Bd., 2009, site reviewer, 2010. Com. mem. Nat. Assn. County and City Health Ofcls., Washington, 1997—; co-developer Protocol for Assessing Cmty. Excellence in Environ. Health, 1997—2000, Mobilizing for Action through Planning and Partnerships, 2000—08; reviewer NACCHO Project Pub. Health Ready, Nat. Assn. County & City Health Offcls., 2010. Contbr. article to Pub. Health Mgmt. and Practice, chapters to books. Participant Nat. Pub. Health Performance Standards, 2006—07. Mem.: Ky. Pub. Health Assn. Avocation: stamp collecting/philately. Office: Northern Kentucky Health Department 610 Medical Village Dr Edgewood KY 41017-3416 Office Fax: 859-578-3689. Business E-Mail: alan.kalos@nkyhealth.org.

KALOUSOVÁ, MARTA, medical educator; b. Vsetín, Czech Republic, Sept. 26, 1974; d. Miroslav Janeba and Milada Janebová; m. Jan Kalous, Sept. 22, 2000; 1 child, Hana. MD, 1st Faculty of Medicine Charles U., Prague, Czech Republic, 1998, PhD in Biochemistry and Pathobiochemistry, 2002. Specialization in internal medicine, clin. chemistry and nephrology Czech Republic. Med. doctor Gen. U. Hosp., Prague, Czech Republic, 1998—; asst. prof. Faculty of Medicine, Charles U., Prague, Czech Republic, 1999—2005, scientific worker, 1999, assoc. prof. med. chemistry and biochemistry, 2005, prof. med. chemistry and biochemistry, 2010. Contbr. articles and scientific papers to profl. jours. and publs. Recipient Josef Hlavka prize, Assn. Josef, Marie and Zdenek Hlavka, Czech Republic, 1997, 2003, Bruno Watschinger award for best poster, 16th Danube Symposium on Nephrology, Bled, Slovenia, 2002, Jan Brod Price award, Assn. Paul Janssen, 2004, others; fellow, L'Oréal CZ for Women Scis., 2008;, Assn. Olga Havel France Paris Hosps. fellow, 1999. Fellow: German Soc. Nephrology; mem.: Czech Soc. Clin. Chemistry, Czech Soc. Nephrology, Czech Med. Soc. Avocations: travel, theater, music, sightseeing. Office: Inst Clin Chem Lab Med Karlovo Nam 32 Prague 12111 Czech Republic

KALPATTHI, RAM, pediatrician, educator; b. India, Mar. 13, 1972; MD, Thanjavur Med. Coll., India, 1994. Asst. prof. pediat. Med. U. SC., 2006—09, Children's Mercy Hosp., 2009—. Recipient Young Investigator Travel award, Am. Pediat. Soc. - Soc. Pediat. Rsch.; William Kennedy Rsch. fellowship, Nat. Childhood Cancer Found. Mem.: Am. Acad. Pediat., Am. Soc. Pediat. Hematology & Oncology, Am. Soc. Hematology. Office: 2401 Gillham Rd Kansas City MO 64108 Business E-Mail: kalpatthi.1@osu.edu.

KALSNER, STANLEY, pharmacologist, physiologist, educator; b. NYC, Aug. 21, 1936; s. William Louis and Sadie (Feldman) K.; m. Jenny Book, Aug. 4, 1963; children— Lydia, Pamela, Louisa. AB, NYU, 1958; postgrad., SUNY Downstate Med. Ctr., 1959—62; PhD, U. Man., Can., 1966; postgrad., Cambridge U., Eng., 1966—67. Asst. prof. pharmacology U. Ottawa, Ont., Canada, 1967-72, assoc. prof. Ont., 1972-77, prof. Ont., 1977-85; prof., chmn. joint dept. physiology and pharmacology CUNY, 1985—2003. Med. rsch. scientist on heart disease and blood vessel function; sci. referee Med. Rsch. Coun. Can., Can. Heart Found. Editor, contbr. chpts. to books, articles to jours.; asso. editor Can. Jour. Physiology and Pharmacology, until 1985; mem. editorial bd.: Jour. Autonomic Pharmacology, Blood Vessels. USPHS fellow, 1960-67; Med. Rsch. Coun.-NRC and Ont. Heart Found. grantee; Am. Heart Assn. grantee, 1987—. Mem. AAAS, AAUP, Can. Pharmacology Soc., Am. Soc. Pharmacology and Therapeutics. Home: 21 Hillcrest Rd Suffern NY 10901-6834 Office: CUNY Med Sch 138th St and Convent Ave New York NY 10031 Home Phone: 845-368-1983. Personal E-mail: jskalsner@optonline.net.

KALUS, RAM HANAN, plastic surgeon; b. Tel Aviv, Aug. 30, 1957; BA cum laude, Boston U., 1982, MD, 1982. Founder, owner Plastic Surgery of Carolinas PA, 1997. Traveling fellowship, Internat. Coll. Surgeons. Fellow: ACS, Am. Acad. Pediat.; mem.: Am. Soc. Aesthetic Plastic Surgery, Am. Soc. Plastic Surgeons. Avocations: photography, woodworking, travel. Office: 578 Lone Tree Dr Ste 102 Mount Pleasant SC 29464 Office Fax: 843-881-3814. E-mail: rkalus1@mac.com.

KALYANPUR, ARJUN, radiologist; b. Beijing, June 27, 1965; s. Bhaskar Ramkrishna and Leela Rao Kalyanpurkar; m. Sunita Maheshwari, Sept. 24, 1994; children: Alisha, Adil Bharat. MBBS, All India Inst. Med. Scis., New Delhi, 1983—88, MD, 1989—92. Diplomate Am. Bd. Radiology, 1998. Asst. clin. prof. Yale U. Sch. Medicine, New Haven, 1998—. Contbr. articles to profl. jours. Trustee People for People, Bangalore, India, 2003—04. Mem.: Radiologic Soc. N.Am. Avocations: travel, reading, music, theater. Home: Villa 19 Regent Pl Whitefield Mn Rd Bangalore 560066 India Office: Teleradiology Solutions 205 Church St 3rd Fl New Haven CT 06510 Office Fax: 775-860-2508; Home Fax: 91 80 41103411. E-mail: arjun.kalyanpur@telradsol.com.

KALYONCU, ALI FUAT, chest physician, allergist, educator; b. Eskisehir, Anatolia, Turkey, Mar. 20, 1959; s. Berki Özdemir and Fatma Gülsen (Bora) K.; m. Alev Köker, Mar. 16, 1985; 1 child, Zeynep Begüm. Medicine Faculty, Istanbul U., 1982. Staff physician Malaria Fighting Svc., Erzincan, Turkey, 1982-84; asst. Dept. Chest Diseases Hacettepe U. Hosp., Ankara, Turkey, 1984-88; asst. allergic diseases sect. Uppsala (Sweden) U. Hosp., 1989-90; asst. prof., assoc. prof. dept. chest diseases Hacettepe U. Hosp., Ankara, 1991-92, assoc. prof., head adult allergy unit, 1993—. With Turkish Army, 1993. UCB Inst. Allergy scholar, 1994. Mem. European Acad. Allergology and Clin. Immunology, Turkish Allergy Soc., Turkish Thoracic Soc., Nordic Club. Avocations: history, music, coin collecting/numismatics. Office: Hacettepe U Hosp Dept Chest Diseases Adult Allergy Unit Sihhiye Ankara 06100 Turkey

KAMAKURA, MITSUHIRO, epidemiologist researcher, educator; b. Tokyo, Feb. 15, 1954; s. Nakanari and Sachiko (Wada) K. MD, Keio U., Tokyo, 1979; PhD, Keio U., 1984. Trainee in surgery Keio U. Hosp., Tokyo, 1979-80, asst. dept. preventive medicine and pub. health, 1984-88, asst. prof., 1988-01, assoc. prof. faculty of nursing and med. care and sch. of medicine, 2001—, prof. grad. sch. health mgmt., 2005—, vice dean faculty of nursing and med. care, 2005—07, councilor, 2007—08. Steering com. Clinic for Infectious Diseases, Keio U. Hosp., 1995—; rsch. group HIV epidemiology Min. Health, Labour and Welfare, Japan, 1992—2007; AIDS panel Japan-U.S. coop. med. sci. program Min. Fgn. Affairs, 1995—; AIDS task force overseas med. coop. com. Japan Internat. Coop., 1995; mem. Monitoring the AIDS Pandemic Network, 1996—, AIDS Ann. Report Drafting Com., Japan, 1997—98; chief rschr. Internat. Epidemiology HIV Infection, Min. Health, Labor and Welfare, Japan, 1998—2000, group leader internat. epidemiology The Study Group for HIV/AIDS Epidemiology, Japan, 2000—03, prin. investigator, study group for HIV/AIDS epidemiology, Japan, 2004—07; mem. Japan-Germany AIDS Panel, 2005—; expert com. mem. Tokyo Met. AIDS. Author: AIDS-A Basic Guide, 1987; editor: (Japanese edit.) The Status and Trends of the Global HIV/AIDS Pandemic, 1996; mem. editl. staff (Japanese edit.) AIDS in the World II, 1997. Grantee, Uehara Fund, 1987. Avocations: classical music, painting, travel. Office: Grad Sch Health Mgmt 4411 Endoh Fujisawa 252-0883 Japan

KAMAKURA, SHINJI, dentist, educator; b. Shizuoka, Japan, Feb. 1, 1958; DDS, Tohoku U. Grad. Sch. Dentistry, 1983, PhD, 1987. Resident Sendai Nat. Hosp., 1987—90; asst. prof. Tohoku U. Sch. Dentistry, 1990—2002; assoc. prof. Tohoku U. Sch. Medicine, 2002—08; vis. scholar U. Iowa, 1999—2000; prof. Grad. Sch. Biomed. Engring., Tohoku U., 2008—. Assoc. editor Tohoku U. Dental Jour., 2005. Mem.: Japanese Soc. Biomaterials, Japanese Soc. Regenerative Medicine (councilor 2006), Internat. Assn. Oral and Maxillofacial Surgeons. Office: 2-1 Seiryo-Machi Aoba-Ku Sendai Miyagi 980-8574 Japan Office Fax: 81-22-717-8235. Business E-Mail: kamakura@bme.tohoku.ac.jp.

KAMANGAR, NADER, physician, pulmonologist, director, researcher, educator; b. Tehran, Iran, June 21, 1970; s. Fereidoun and Fari Kamangar; m. Goli Khodadad, Dec. 22, 2001; children: Maya, Mina. MD, St. George's U., 1997. Diplomate Am. Bd. Internal Medicine, 2001, Am. Bd. Internal Medicine-Pulmonary Disease, 2002, Am. Bd. Internal Medicine-Critical Care, 2003, Am. Bd. Sleep Medicine, 2005. Resident in internal medicine Highland Gen. Hosp., Oakalnd, Calif., 1997—2000; pulmonary, critical care and sleep medicine fellow Cedars-Sinai Med. Ctr., LA, 2000—03; dir. Olive View-UCLA Med. Ctr. Sleep Medicine Lab., dir., intensivist hospitalist program, site dir., pulmonary/critical care fellowship program; assoc. prof. medicine UCLA Sch. Medicine, 2009—. Edn. dir. pulmonary/critical care medicine Olive View-UCLA Med. Ctr., Sylmar, 2003—; dir. Hospitalist/Intensivist program, 2007—. Contbr. articles to profl. publ., chapters to books. Recipient Golden Apple award Best Sub-Specialist, UCLA, 2003, 2004, 2005, 2009—11. Fellow: Coll. Critical Care Medicare, Am. Acad. Sleep Medicine, Am. Coll. Physicians, Am. Coll. of Chest Physicians; mem.: Golden Key Nat. Honor Soc. Office: Olive View-UCLA Med Ctr 14445 Olive View Dr 2B-182 Sylmar CA 91342-1495 Home: 4637 Noeline Ave Encino CA 91436 Office Phone: 818-364-3205, 818-364-4509. Office Fax: 818-364-4573. Business E-Mail: kamangar@ucla.edu.

KAMAT, UMESH SUBHASH, physician, educator; b. Kudal, Maharashtra, Oct. 17, 1979; MBBS, MD, Goa Med. Coll., DNB in Pub. Health, 2003. Cons. physician Goa Med. Coll. Hosp., 2004—, asst. prof., 2006—. Mem.: Rsch. Soc Study Diabetes (India). Avocations: music, travel. Home: St Caitan Merces Tiswadi Panjim Goa 403005 India Personal E-mail: neetumesh@rediffmail.com.

KAMBAM, PRAVEEN, psychiatrist, educator; b. Nashville, May 18, 1977; BA, Emory U., 1999; MD, U. Tenn., Memphis, 2004. Pres. Praveen Kambam, M.D., PC, 2010—. Asst. clin. prof., dept. psychiatry UCLA Sch. Medicine, 2011; adj. prof. Grad. Sch. Edn. & Psychology, Pepperdine U., 2011. Mem.: So. Calif. Soc. Child & Adolescent Psychiatry, Am. Acad. Child & Adolescent Psychiatry, Am. Acad. Psychiatry & Law, Am. Psychiat. Assn. Office: 10850 Wilshire Blvd Ste 850 Los Angeles CA 90024 Business E-Mail: pkambam@ucla.edu.

KAMBARA, HIROFUMI, cardiologist; b. Kagawa, Japan, June 1941; married, Apr. 17, 1968; 2 children. MD, Kyoto U., 1966, PhD, 1982. Med. intern U.S. Army Hosp., Camp Zama, Kanagawa, Japan, 1966-67; med. resident Kyoto U. Hosp., 1967-68, asst. physician, 1975-84, asst. prof. medicine, 1984-85, assoc. prof. medicine, 1985-88; straight med. intern St. Louis City Hosp., 1968-69; med. resident VA Hosp., New Orleans, 1969-72, chief resident in cardiology, 1972-73; fellow in cardiology Sch. Medicine, Tulane U., New Orleans, 1973-74, lectr., 1974-75; dir. of cardiology Osaka Red Cross Hosp., Japan, 1992-94, dir. Cardiovasc. Ctr., 1994—2003, vice-dir., 1996—2003; dir. Shizuoka Gen. Hosp., 2003—. Expert advisor WHO, Geneva, 1985—97; mem. adv. bd. Internat. Symposium Cardiovascular Pharmacotherapy, 1988—95. Author: Tissue Plasminogen Activator in Thrombolytic Therapy, 1987; mem. editl. cons. Jour. Interventional Cardiology, 1987—. Fellow: Am. Coll. Cardiology; mem.: Japanese Col. Cardiology, Japanese Coronary Assn. (hon.; dir. 1997, trustee), Japanese Circulation Soc. Avocations: golf, flute, computers. Home: 16-2 Naka-Osagi-cho Kyoto 606-0002 Japan Office: Shizuoka Gen Hosp 4-27 Kita-andou Shizuoka 420-8527 Japan Office Phone: 81 54 247 6111.

KAMBAS, ANTONIS, psychomotor therapist, researcher; b. Athens, Greece, Mar. 5, 1963; s. John and Kalliope Kambas; m. Zoe Gavriilidou, Apr. 29, 1971; children: Evita, Katerina. Msc, U. Maarburg, Germany, 1993; MSc, U. Thrace, Greece, 1998; PhD, Democritus U., Thrace, 2000. Cert. psychomotor therapist Sci. Psychomotor Assn. Hellas, 1999. Pres. Sci. Psychomotor Assn., Komotini, Greece, 1999—; ass. prof. Democritus U., Komotini, Greece, 2000—; vis. prof. U. Osnabrueck, Germany. Author: (books) Motor Development, 2001, The Development of Motor Coordination, 2002. Bd. dirs. Nat. Assn. U. Tchg. and Rsch. Stuff, Alexandroupolis, Greece, 2003—05. Mem.: Psychomotor Action (assoc.). Liberal. Orthodox. Achievements include research in accidents in schools and playgrounds and physical activity in youth. Avocations: hunting, fishing. Home: Ekavis 30 Kavala 65201 Greece Office: Dep Phys Edn Spl Sci Democritus U University Campus Komotini 69100 Greece Office Fax: 00302531039623. Personal E-mail: akambas@otenet.gr. Business E-Mail: akampas@phyed.duth.gr.

KAMBHAMPATI, SRINIVAS BHASKARA SESHACHALA, orthopedist, registrar; b. Kakinada, Andhra Pradesh, India, Sept. 1, 1971; s. Prabhakara Rao Venkata Ramakrishna and Satya Kumari Naga Venkata Kambhampati; m. Lalitha Madhavi Avva, Aug. 16, 1998; children: Anirudh, Anupama. MBBS, Pondicherry U., 1993, MS in Orthop., 1998. Jr. resident orthop. Jawaharlal Inst. Postgrad. Med. Edn. & Rsch., Pondicherry, India, 1994—97, sr. resident orthop., 1997—2000; sr. house officer in trauma & orthop. Oldchurch Hosp., Romford, Essex, England, 2002—03; hon. fellow Royal Nat. Orthop. Hosp., Stanmore, Middlesex, England, 2004—05; specialist registrar in trauma & orthop. Hillingdon Hosp., Uxbridge, England, 2005—06, Leicester Gen. Hosp., Leicestershire, England, 2006—08. Contbr. articles to profl. jours. Master: Orthop. Surgery; fellow: Royal Coll. Physicians and Surgeons (Glasgow); mem.: Indian Orthop. Assn., Brit. Orthop. Assn., Am. Acad. Orthop. Surgeons. Hindu. Achievements include design of constructing pedotti diagram using excel charts; research in posterior subluxation and dislocation of shoulder in obstetric brachial plexus palsy; development of orthopaedic associations meetings and journals webpage; design of database for shoulder subluxation and dislocation in obstetric brachial plexus palsy; database for metal on metal total hip replacement. Home: 9 Rushden Gardens London NW7 2PA England Personal E-mail: kbssrinivas@gmail.com.

KAMBLE, RAVINDRA RAMAPPA, chemistry professor; b. Hukeri, Apr. 15, 1975; MSc, PG Dept. Studies in Chemistry, 1995, PhD, 1997. Reader Karnatak U. Dharwad, 2008—, assoc. prof., 2011. Fellow: Indian Chem. Soc.; mem.: Indian Coun. Chemists. Avocations: cricket, reading. Office: PG Dept Studies In Chemistry Dharwad Karnataka 580003 India Office Phone: 91-9449264997. Office Fax: 91-836247886. E-mail: kamchem9@gmail.com.

KAMEL, EHAB MOHAMED, nuclear medicine physician, researcher; b. Cairo, Apr. 14, 1969; s. Kamel and Fatemah; m. Amany Shawky Hassanein, July 30, 1995; children: Basel Ehab-Mohamed, Arij Ehab-Mohamed. MBBCh, Assiut U. Sch. Medicine, Egypt, 1992, MS in Nuc. Medicine, 1998. Bd. cert. nuc. medicine Swiss Soc. Nuc. Medicine, 2003. Ho. officer Assiut U. Hosp., Egypt, 1993—94, resident, 1994—98; registrar Assiut U. Sch. Medicine, 1998—2000; sr. fellow nuc. medicine Lausanne U. Hosp., Switzerland, 2003—. Contbr. articles to profl. jours., chapters to books. Fellow, Zurich U. Hosp., 2000—03. Peace And Freedom. Muslim. Avocations: music, fishing, reading. Office: Lausanne U Hosp Chuv Lausanne 1011 Switzerland Office Fax: 0041 21 314 44 43. Business E-Mail: mohamed-ehab.kamel@chuv.ch.

KAMEL, HOSAM KAMAL, medical educator, researcher, geriatrician; b. Cairo, May 18, 1965; married; 1 child. MB, BChir, Kuwait U., 1989; MPH, Med. Coll. Wis., 2004. Cert. Am. Bd. Internal Medicine, Am. Bd. Geriatric Medicine, Cert. Bd. Nutrition Specialists, Nat. Bd. Wound Mgmt. Asst. prof. medicine SUNY, Stony Brook, 1998—99; chief divsn. geriatric medicine Nassau U. Med. Ctr., East Meadow, NY, 1999—2001; asst. prof. medicine St. Louis U. Sch. Medicine, 1999—; asst. prof. geriatrics Med. Coll. Wis., 2001—03; dir. geriatrics and extended care St. Joseph's Mercy Health Ctr., Hot Springs, Ark., 2003—; asst., assoc. clin. prof. geriatric U. Ark. Med. Sci., 2004—. Dir. edn. and rsch., geriatrics Nassau U. Med. Ctr., East Meadow, 1999; mem. physician adv. panel Divsn. Aging, Dept. Social Svcs., Jefferson City, Mo., 2000—; pres. Ark. Med. Dirs. Assn., 2006—; bd. dirs. Mo. Assn. Long-Term Physicians, Mo. Fellow: Am. Coll. Nutrition; mem.: ACP, Gerontol. Soc. Am., Am. Geriatric Soc., Ctrl. Soc. for Clin. Rsch. Democrat. Muslim. Home: 162 Trabecca Cir Hot Springs AR 71913-8149 Office: Mission Clin Svc 1 Mecy Ln Ste 405 Hot Springs AR 71913 Personal E-mail: kamel@pol.net.

KAMEN, DEAN, entrepreneur, inventor; b. Rockville Centre, NY, Apr. 5, 1951; s. Jack Kamen. Attended, Worcester Poly. Inst., Mass.; Deng (hon.), Kettering U., 2001; D (hon.), Wentworth Inst. Tech., Boston, 2004, Bates Coll., 2007, Ga. Inst. Tech., 2008, Ill. Inst. Tech., 2008, Plymouth State U., 2008; DSc (hon.), U. Ariz., 2009. Founder, pres. AutoSyringe, Inc., 1976—82, DEKA R&D Corp., Manchester, NH, 1982—. Co-founderfounder, bd. dirs. FIRST (For Inspiration & Recognition of Sci. & Tech.), 1989—; bd. dirs. Segway LLC, 2001—. Co-host of Planet Green show Dean of Invention, 2010—. Recipient Med. Product of Yr. award, Design News Mag., 1993, Engr. of the Yr. award, 1994, Kilby Internat. award, 1994, Hoover medal, 1995, Edwin Church medal, Am. Soc. Mech. Engineers, 1997, Heinz award in Tech., Heinz Family Found., 1998, Nat. Medal Tech., 2000, Lemelson-MIT prize, 2002, Rockwell medal, Internat. Tech. Inst., 2002, UN Global Humanitarian Action award, 2006, Benjamin Franklin Medal in Mechanical Engineering, Franklin Inst., 2011; named NH Bus. Leader of Yr., 1996, Person of Yr., Juvenile Diabetes Rsch. Found., 2002, Innovator of Yr., R&D Mag., 2006; named to Nat. Inventors Hall of Fame, 2005. Mem.: NAE. Achievements include invention of the AutoSyringe, a class of automatic, self contained, ambulatory infusion pumps designed to free patients from round-the-clock injections, delivering precise doses of medication to diabetics and other patients with a variety of medical conditions, 1978; a portable dialysis machine, 1993; development of the iBot mobility system, an all-terrain electric wheelchair made to help people with severe mobility problems; invention of the Segway PT, an electric, self-balancing human transporter with a complex, computer-controlled gyroscopic stabilization and control system; holds more than 440 US and foreign patents. Office: DEKA R&D 340 Commercial St Manchester NH 03101-1121 *

KAMIMURA, KENYA, medical researcher; b. Japan, Nov. 16, 1974; MD, Niigata U., 1999, PhD, 2007. Postdoc. clin. fellow, divsn. gastroenterology & hepatology Niigata U. Grad. Sch. Med. and Dental Scis., 2010—. Grant, Japan Soc. Promotion Scis., Rsch. grant, Sumitomo Found., Yokoyama Found. Mem.: Japanese Cancer Assn., Japanese Soc. Internal Medicine, Japan Soc. Hepatology, Japanese Soc. Gastroenterology, Am. Soc. Gene and Cell Therapy (Excellence Rsch. award 2008). Office: 1-757 Asahimachidori Niigata 9518510 Japan Office Phone: 81252272207. Office Fax: 81252270776. Business E-Mail: kenya-k@med.niigata-u.ac.jp.

KAMIMURA, MITSUHIRO, pulmonologist; b. Osaka, Japan, Apr. 17, 1962; MD, Tokushima U., 1989. Chief pulmonology dept. Nat. Hosp. Orgn. Disaster Med. Ctr., 2004—. Avocation: travel. Office: Midorimachi 3256 Tachikawa Tokyo 190-0014 Japan Office Fax: 042-526-5535. Business E-Mail: kamimura@tdmc.hosp.go.jp.

KAMINKER, MARCIA KAHN, physical therapist; b. Phila., Mar. 11, 1955; d. Alan and Norma Bernstein Kahn; m. Martin Alan Kaminker, Dec. 28, 1975; children: Jacob, David, Eva. BS in Phys. Therapy, U. Pa., 1976; MS in Pediat. Phys. Therapy, with distinction, Drexel U., Phila., 2003, DPT in Phys. Therapy, with distinction, 2007. Cert. sch. based therapy MCP Hahnemann U., 2000, pediat. specialist Am. Bd. Phys. Therapy Specialties, 2004. Phys. therapist Moss Rehab. Hosp., Phila., 1976—79, Cleve. Met. Gen. Hosp., 1979—80, John F. Kennedy Med. Ctr., Edison, NJ, 1984—85, Bayshore Cmty. Hosp., Holmdel, NJ, 1990—91, Robert Wood Johnson U. Hosp., New Brunswick, NJ, 1990—96, Piscataway Regional Day Sch., NJ, 1993—96, South Brunswick Twp. Pub. Schs., Monmouth Junction, NJ, 1995—; chair Sch. Based Physical Therapy Spl Interest Group, APTA Section Pediat., 2009—. Mentor entry-level doctors of phys. therapy students Drexel U., Phila., 2003—04, NY Med. Coll., Valhalla, 2004—06; NJ rep. to sect. pediats. Am. Phys. Therapy Assn., 2006—11, northeastern region rep. sch.-based spl. interest group sect. pediats., 2007—09, chair com. awareness sub com. of pub. rels. com.pediats. section, 2008—09. Contbr. articles to profl. jours. Pres. South Brunswick Bd. Edn., Monmouth Junction, NJ, 1993—95, v.p., 1991—93, bd. mem., 1989—95; leader Girl Scouts of Am., South Brunswick, NJ, 1993—97. Recipient Class of 1958 Award for Scholarship and Svc., U. of Pa., 1976, Evelyn B. Noyovitz award, 2004, Leadership in Phys. Therapy Practice award, Drexel U., 2007; grantee Maternal and Child Health Leadership Tng. grantee, US Dept. of Edn., 1998—2000. Mem.: Am. Acad. for Cerebral Palsy and Devel. Medicine, Am. Phys. Therapy Assn., Phila. HS for Girls Alumnae Assn. (life), Alpha Eta Soc., Friars Sr. Honor Soc. (life). Home: 81 Davidson's Mill Rd North Brunswick NJ 08902 Office: South Brunswick Pub Schs PO Box 181 Monmouth Junction NJ 08852 Office Fax: 732-297-1997. Personal E-mail: mkkaminker@aol.com. Business E-Mail: marcia.kaminker@sbschools.org.

KAMINSKY, BEN, chemist; Grad., Faculte de Pharmacie de l'Universite de Montreal. Founder Odan Labs., 1974—, B. Kamins. Author: Beyond Botox: 7 Strategies for Sexy, Ageless Skin Without Needles or Surgery. Recipient Canadian Ingenuity award, Spa Life. Office: 325 Stillview Ave Pointe-Claire PQ Canada H9R 2Y6 also: 32 Union Sq Ste #414 New York NY 10003 Office Phone: 212-253-7126. Office Fax: 212-253-7469. E-mail: info@beyondbotox.com.

KAMIYA, NOBUHIRO, orthopedist, educator; b. Nagoya, Japan, May 12, 1970; MD, Gifu U. Sch. Medicine, Japan, 1996; PhD, Gifu Grad. Sch. Medicine, Japan, 2003. Rsch. scientist Tex. Scottish Rite Hosp. Children, 2009; asst. prof. dept. orthop. surgery U. Tex. Southwestern Med. Ctr., 2010—. Adj. grad. faculty Tex. A & M Health Sci. Ctr., 2011. Fellow, NIH, grant, Scoliosis Rsch. Soc. Mem.: Japanese Soc. Bone and Mineral Rsch. (Abstract award), Japanese Soc. Cartilage Metabolism, Japanese Orthop. Assn., Am. Soc. Bone and Mineral Rsch. (Young Investigator award), Orthop. Rsch. Soc. Avocation: tennis. Office: 2222 Welborn St Dallas TX 75219 E-mail: nkamiya1@hotmail.com.

KAMIYA, TAKESHI, medical educator; b. Nagoya, Japan, Dec. 23, 1959; PhD, Nagoya City U. Grad. Sch. Med. Scis., 1993. Assoc. prof. Nagoya City U. Grad. Sch. Med. Scis., 2007. Mem.: Am. Gastroenterology Assn. Avocations: travel, photography. Office: 1 Kawasumi Mizuho-ku Mizuho cho Nagoya Aichi 467 8601 Japan Office Fax: 81-52-852-0952. Business E-Mail: kamitake@med.nagoya-cu.ac.jp.

KAMLER, KENNETH MARK, microsurgeon; b. NYC, Oct. 4, 1947; s. William and Ethel Kamler; children: Jonathan, Jennifer. BA in Biology, CUNY, NYC, 1968; MD, U. Marseille, France, 1975. Resident orthoped. surgery L.I. Jewish Med. Ctr., NYC, 1980; fellow hand and microsurgery Columbia-Presbyn. Med. Ctr., NYC, 1981; microsurgeon specializing in hand surgery New Hyde Park, N.Y., 1981—. Mt. Everest (Nepal) expdn. doctor Nat. Geog., 1992-93, 95-96; chief high altitude physician NASA/Yale Comml. Space Ctr., Mt. Everest, 1998, 99; expdn. doctor Andes, Amazon, Arctic, Galapagos, Antarctica, Peru, Ecuador, Tanzania; tech. advisor IMAX Movie Everest, 1997; lectr. in field. Author: Doctor on Everest, 2000, Surviving the Extremes, 2004; contbg. author: Everest: Mountain Without Mercy, 1997; former columnist Nat. Geographic Adventure, Popular Mechanics, editl. bd. advisors. Fellow Explorers Club (dir. 1995-2001, 03-09, 11, sci. adv. bd. 1996-2008, v.p. membership 1996-99, v.p. rsch. and edn. 1999-2008, dir., heroism and altruism on Everest award 1999, Sci. Achievement award 2002, named one of NY Mag. Top Dr. 2002, Newsday Long Island Top Dr. 2010, US News & World Report Top Dr. 2011); mem. Sigma Xi. Jewish. Avocations: sailing, scuba diving, mountain climbing, drawing. Office: 410 Lakeville Rd Ste 303 New Hyde Park NY 11042-1101 Home Phone: 516-728-4308; Office Phone: 516-326-2266. E-mail: kenkamler@yahoo.com.

KAMM, ROGER DALE, biomedical engineer, educator; b. Ashland, Wis., Oct. 10, 1950; s. Rudolph Wilhelm and Betty Jane (White) Kamm; life ptnr. Judith Mary Brown, Sept. 1, 1974; 1 child, Peter Martin. BS in Mech. Engring., Northwestern U., Evanston, Ill., 1972; MS in Mech. Engring., MIT, Cambridge, Mass., 1973, PhD in Mech. Engring., 1977. Lectr. MIT, 1977-78, asst. prof. mech. engring., 1978-81, assoc. prof. mech. engring., 1981—88, prof. mech. engring. and bioengineering, 1988—, assoc. dir. Ctr. Biomedical Engring., 1994—, Germeshausen prof. mech. & biol. engring., assoc. chair. mech. engring., 2005—. Mem. World Coun. Biomechanics, 1998—, vice chair, 2002—06, chair, 2006—; sec. US Nat. Com. Biomechanics, 2000—03, vice chair, 2003—06, chair, 2006—; disting. lectr. biomechanics Stanford U., 2004. Assoc. editor Jour. Fluids & Structures, 1993—2004, mem. editl. bd. Methods in Cell Sci., 1995—2004, Biomechanics & Modeling in Mechanobiology, 2001—, Mechanics & Chemistry of Biosystems, 2003—; contbr. articles to profl. jours. Recipient Everett Moore Baker Meml. award for excellence in undergrad. tchg., MIT, 2001, Eschbach Disting. Vis. Scholar award, Northwestern U., 2002. Fellow: ASME (H.R. Lissner Medal 2010), Internat. Acad. Med. & Biol. Engring., American Inst. Med. & Biol. Engring., Biomedical Engring. Soc. (bd. dirs. 2003—06, chair publs. bd. 2003—06); mem.: Biophysical Soc., Inst. Medicine. Achievements include research in the fundamental nature of how cells sense and respond to mechanical stimuli, and to employ the principles revealed by these studies to seek new treatments for vascular disease and to develop tissue constructs for drug and toxicity screening; patents in field. Office: MIT 77 Massachusetts Ave Rm NE47 321 Cambridge MA 02139-4307 Home: 71 Fox Rd Unit 816 Waltham MA 02451-0204 Home Phone: 781-431-2283; Office Phone: 617-253-5330. *

KAMOLZ, LARS PETER, plastic surgeon; b. Berlin, Mar. 11, 1972; s. Wolfgang Klaus and Heidi Elke Kamolz; life ptnr. Birgit Kruse. MD, U. Vienna, Austria, 1998. M.D. U. of Vienna, Med. Sch., 1998. Univ. asst. dept. anatomy U. Vienna, 1997—98, univ. asst. divsn. plastic and reconstructive surgery, 1998—. Rschr. Div. of Plastic and Reconstructive Surgery, Vienna, 1998—2002. Contbr. articles to profl. jours. Mem.: European Burn Assn., Internat. Soc. Burn Injuries, Austrian Soc. Plastic and Reconstructive Surgery (assoc.). Achievements include research in See Medline. Office: Divsn Plastic & Reconstructive Surgery Waehringer Guertel 18-20 1090 Vienna Austria Home Phone: +43 1 367 9943; Office Phone: +43 1 40400 6860. Business E-Mail: lars.peter.kamolz@univie.ac.at.

KAMPMAN, KYLE M., psychiatrist, educator; BA in Chemistry, Northwestern U., 1981; MD, Tulane U. Diplomate Am. Bd. of Psychiatry and Neurology, Am. Bd. of Psychiatry and Neurology-addiction psychiatry. Resident Hosp. of the Univ. of Pa., fellow, assoc. prof. psychiatry. Named one of Top Docs, Phila. Mags., 2007—08, 2010—11, Best Doctors in America, 2005—10, America's Top Doctors, 2007—08, 2010. Office: Hospital of the University of Pennsylvania 3400 Spruce St Philadelphia PA 19104 Office Phone: 215-662-4000. E-mail: kampman_k@mail.trc.upenn.edu.

KAMRAVA, MICHAEL M., reproductive endocrinologist; Grad., U. Ill.; MD, Case Western Reserve U. Sch. Medicine. Resident Cleveland Mt. Sinai Hosp.; med. dir. West Coast In Vitro Fertilization Clinic, Inc. (formally known as the West Coast Infertility Med. Clinic), Beverly Hills. Mem.: Phi Beta Kappa. Mailing: West Coast IVF Clinic Inc 9730 Wilshire Blvd Ste 211 Beverly Hills CA 90212

KAMRIN, MICHAEL ARNOLD, toxicology educator; b. Bklyn., Aug. 5, 1940; s. Benjamin Barnett and Bessie (Bloom) K.; m. Ritva Anneli Nieminen, July 19, 1964 (dec. Oct. 2002); children: Kari and Edward (twins); m. Katherine O'Sullivan See, Nov 6, 2004. BA in Chemistry, Cornell U., 1960; MS in Biophys. Chemistry, Yale, 1962, PhD in Biophys. Chemistry, 1965. Teaching asst. then rsch. asst. dept. chemistry Yale U., New Haven, 1960-63; rsch. assoc. biology div. Oak Ridge (Tenn.) Nat. Lab., 1963-66; NIH postdoctoral trainee Hopkins Marine Sta. Stanford (Calif.) U., 1966-67; asst. prof. natural sci. Mich. State U., East Lansing, 1967-72, assoc. prof., 1972-79, prof., 1979-89, prof. Inst. for Environ. Toxicology, 1982-2000, prof. resource devel., 1990-2000, prof. emeritus, 2000—. Vis. lectr. dept. zoology U. Turku, Finland, 1973-74, docent, 1996—; vis. scientist Legis. Office Sci. Advisor, State of Mich., 1980-81; participant numerous confs. and workshops, 1965—; mem. internat. evaluation team on environ. toxicology Acad. Finland, Helsinki, 1988; expert Media Resource Ctr., Scientists' Inst. for Pub. Info.; mem. risk comm. project planning group, grant reviewer USDA; peer reviewer for agy.-sponsored rsch. projects Agy. for Toxic Substances and Disease Registry, HHS; numerous others. Author: Toxicology: A Primer on Toxicology Principles and Applications, 1988, (with D.J. Katz and M.L. Walter) Reporting on Risk: A Journalist's Handbook, 1995, Is it Safe: Evaluating Chemical Risks, 2011; also others; editor: (with [illegible]) PCBs: Human and Environmental Hazards, 1983, (with P. Rodgers) Dioxins inthe Environment, 1985; editor: Pesticide Profiles, 1997, Environmental Risk Harmonization, 1997; contbr. numerous articles and abstracts to sci. jours. Numerous presentations to Rotary, Consumers Coun., LWV, county commrs., Ch. Women United, sch. dists., Mich. Med. Soc.; participant in news broadcasts, radio call-in shows and interview programs. Recipient Meml. medal U. Turku, 1974; grantee USDA, 1983-84, 86-87, 88-89, 91-98, All-Univ. Rsch. Initation grantee, 1989, All-Univ. Outreach grantee, 1995-96, EPA, 1992-95, Agy. for Toxic Substances and Disease Registry, 1992-2000, Nat. Food Safety and Toxicology Ctr., 1993-94, grantee Nat. Inst. Environ. Health Scis., 1995-2000. Fellow AAAS; mem. Am. Chem. Soc., Soc. Toxicology (editor newsletter Mich. chpt. 1984-87, chmn. nominating com. 1986, pres.-elect 1992-93, pres. 1993-94; nat. pub. comm. com. 1987-90, Nat. Pub. Comm. award 1994), Soc. Environ. Toxicology and Chemistry (bd. dirs. Ctrl. Gt. Lakes chpt. 1985-87, v.p. 1988, pres. 1989-90, Disting. Svc. award 1993; nat. govt. affairs com. 1986-2000), Soc. for Risk Analysis. Office Phone: 517-655-1896. Business E-Mail: kamrin@msu.edu.

KAN, YUET WAI, hematologist, educator; b. Hong Kong, China, June 11, 1936; arrived in US, 1960; s. Tong-Po and Lai-Wan (Li) Kan; m. Alvera Lorraine Limauro, May 10, 1964; children: Susan Jennifer, Deborah Ann. BS, MB, U. Hong Kong, China, 1958, DSc, 1980, DSc (hon.), 1987, Chinese U., Hong Kong, 1981; MD (hon.), U. Cagliari, Sardinia, Italy, 1981; degree (hon.), Open U. Hong Kong. Investigator Howard Hughes Med. Inst., San Francisco, 1976—2003; prof. lab. medicine U. Calif., San Francisco, 1977—, Louis K. Diamond prof. hematology, 1991—. Mem. Nat. Inst. Diabetes Digestive Kidney Dieseases adv. coun. NIH, 1991—95; trustee Croucher Found., Hong Kong, 1992—, chmn., 1997—; mem. bd. adjudicators The Shaw prize, Hong Kong, 2005—, chmn. selection com., life sci. and medicine, 2005—. Contbr. chapters to books, over 250 articles to med. jours. Recipient Dameshek award, Am. Soc. Hematology, 1980, George Thorn award, Howard Hughes Med. Inst., 1980, Gairdner Found. Internat. award, 1984, Allan award, Am. Soc. Human Genetics, 1984, Lita Annenberg Hazen award for Excellence in Clin. Rsch., 1984, Waterford award, 1987, ACP's award, 1988, Genetic Rsch. award, Sanremo Internat., 1989, Warren Alpert Found. prize, 1989, Lasker-DeBakey Clin. Med. Rsch. award, Lasker Found., 1991, Christopher Columbus Discovery award, 1992, City of Medicine award, 1992, Excellence 200 award, 1993, Helmut Horten Rsch. award, 1995, Shaw prize in Life Sci. & Medicine, Shaw Found., Hong Kong, 2004. Fellow: AAAS, Am. Acad. Arts and Scis., Third World Acad. Scis., Royal Soc. (London), Royal Coll. Physicians (London); mem.: NAS, Acad. Sinica Taiwan, Soc. Chinese Bioscientists in Am. (pres. 1998—99), Am. Soc. Hematology (pres. 1990), Assn. Am. Physicians, Chinese Acad. Scis. (fgn. mem.). Office: University Calif HSW 901E Box 0793 513 Parnassus Ave San Francisco CA 94143 Office Fax: 415-476-2956.

KANAKOUDI-TSAKALIDOU, FLORENCE, pediatrician, immunologist, educator; b. Thessaloniki, Greece, Jan. 27, 1940; d. Sterianos and Hellen (Kouyoumtzi) Kanakoudi; m. Dimitrios Tsakalides, Apr. 24, 1971; children: Maria, Venetia. DCH, Thessaloniki U., Greece, 1968, MD, 1970, PhD, 1980. Lectr. Aristotle U., Thessaloniki, Greece, 1970-80, sr. lectr., 1980-86, assoc. prof., 1986-2000, prof., 2000—; rsch. fellow Royal Infirmary, Edinburgh, 1970-71; head 1st dept. pediats. Aristotle U./Ippokration Hosp., 2002—. Head immunology lab. Hippokration Hosp., U. Thessaloniki, 1972—, cons. for chronic rheumatic diseases, 1982—; dir. child health sect. of med.

faculty Aristotle U., 2000-02, 06-07; chair Nat. Com. on Vaccinations in Greece, 2003-2005 Organizer, leader League Against Pediatric Rheumatism in No. Greece, Thessaloniki, 1989—; mem. Nat. Com. on Vaccinations in Greece, 2006—. Recipient Rotary Club award, 1990, 95, Internat. Women's Orgn. of Greece award, 1991, Acad. of Athens award, 1998. Mem.: Pediat. Rheumatology Internat. Trial Orgn. (nat. coord. 1998—), Friends Assn. Children with Rheumatic Diseases (pres. 1989—, rep. of Greece in European League against rheumatism standing com. on 1990—99), Brit. Soc. Immunology, Greek Soc. Immunology (v.p. 1988—91), Med. Soc. No. Greece, Greek Soc. Pediats. (adminstrv. bd. 1996—98), Pediat. Soc. No. Greece (v.p. 1982—84, pres. 1998—2000), Lions Club (award). Greek Orthodox. Avocation: supporting financially and socially children with rheumatic diseases. Office: Hippokration Hosp 49 Konstantinoupoleos 1st Dept of Pediatrics 546 42 Thessaloniki Greece Business E-Mail: flkan@med.auth.gr, flkan@auth.gr.

KANAT-PEKTAS, MINE, medical researcher; b. Izmir, Turkey, Aug. 6, 1978; d. Yilmaz Halil and Mediha Kanat; m. Ayhan Pektas, June 3, 2006; 1 child, Efe Nazim Pektas. MD, Hacettepe U., Ankara, Turkey, 2002. Rsch. asst. Dr. Zekai Tahir Burak Women Hosp., Ankara, 2003—. Contbr. articles to profl. med. jours. Mem.: Turkish Assn. Physicians. Home: Kutlugun Sok 37/14 Iccebeci Ankara 06590 Turkey Office: Dr Zekai Tahir Burak Women Hosp Talatpasa Cad Samanpazari Ankara 06230 Turkey Office Fax: +903123124931. Personal E-mail: minekanat@hotmail.com.

KANAZAWA, OSAMU, physician, researcher; b. Tokamachi, Japan, Jan. 29, 1951; s. Kaneji and Masako Kanazawa; m. Ayako Tamura, Apr. 20, 1981; children: Ikuko, Suzuko, Eiko, Akiko. MB, Kyoto U., Japan, 1977. Lic. Ministry of Pub. Welfare and Labor, 1977. Mem. med. staff dept. pediat. Nat. Epilepsy Ctr., Shizuoka Med. Inst. of Epilepsy and Neurol. Disorders, Japan, 1982—83, Regional Epilepsy Ctr., Utano Nat. Hosp., Kyoto, 1983—90; asst. dept. pediat. Kyoto U. Hosp., 1990—91; rsch. fellow dept. Neurology, epilepsy unit U. Hosp. of Western Ont., London, Canada, 1991—93; vice-head dept. pediat. Kitano Hosp., Osaka, Japan, 1993—95; chief dept. pediat. Epilepsy Ctr., Chuo Nat. Nishi-Niigata Hosp., Japan, 1995—. Clin. asst. prof. Niigata U., Japan, 2000—. Author: (book) Epilepsia, Pediatric Neurology, Brain & Development, Epilepsy-A Hidden Sickness with a Milloin Sufferers (in Japanese), Epilepsy Should Be Suspected in Case of Fits Convulsions in Children (in Japanese), A book being never hasty, when children under 3 years having fever or sudden turn (in Japanese), Are LD and ADHD real sicknesses? (in Japanese); mem. editl. bd. Jour. of Japan Epilepsy Soc., 2000—. Grantee, Japan Epilepsy Rsch. Found., 1996. Mem.: Japanese Soc. of Clin. Neurophysiology, Japan Epilepsy Soc., Japanese Soc. of Child Neurology, Japan Pediatric Soc., Internat. Child Neurology Assn. Office: Chuo Nat Nishi-Niigatal Hosp 1-14-1 Masago Niigata 950-2085 Japan Office Fax: 81-25-231-2831. Personal E-mail: kaos@pavc.ne.jp. E-mail: kaz@masa.go.jp.

KANBAYASHI, YUKO, pharmacist; b. Kyoto, May 14, 1957; Grad, Gifu Pharm. U., 1980; PhD, Osaka U., 2011. Bd. cert. oncology pharmacy specialist dept. hosp. pharmacy, pain treatment & palliative care unit Kyoto Prefectural U. Medicine, 1980—. Avocation: piano. Office: Dept Hosp Pharmacy Kyoto Pref University Medicine Kawaramachi Hirokoji Kamigyo-ku Kyoto 602 8566 Japan Office Phone: 81-75-251-5865. Office Fax: 81-75-251-5863. Business E-Mail: ykokanba@koto.kpu.m.ac.jp.

KANBAYASHI, YUKO, pharmacist; b. Kyoto, May 14, 1957; Grad., Gifu Pharm. U., 1980; PhD, Osaka U., 2011. Bd. cert. oncology pharmacy specialist Dept. Hosp. Pharmacy, Pain Treatment & Palliative Care Unit, Kyoto Prefectural U. Medicine, 1980—. Avocation: piano. Office: Kawaramachi Hirokoji Kamigyo-ku Kyoto 602-8566 Japan Office Fax: 81-75-251-5863. Business E-Mail: ykokanba@koto.kpu-m.ac.jp.

KANDA, TATSUO, physician, surgeon; b. Tagami, Japan, Aug. 20, 1960; s. Takuji and Fumie (Hirota) K.; m. Eriko Nakano Kanda, Apr. 14, 1991; children: Mutsuo, Marie. MD, Niigata U. Sch. Medicine, Japan, 1985; PhD, Grad. Sch. Niigata U., Japan, 1991. Cert. Nat. Bd. for Med. Lic. Resident U. Hosp. Niigata U., Japan, 1985-86; jr. surgeon Prefectual Cancer Ctr., Niigata, Japan, 1991-92; postdoctoral fellow Nat. Superior Biology Application and Nutrition, Dijon, France, 1992-93; rsch. fellow Japan Soc. for Promotion of Sci., Niigata, 1993-94; assoc. dept. surgery Niigata U. Sch. Medicine, 1997—; asst. prof. Niigata U. Grad. Sch. Med. Dental Sci., 2002—. Contbr. articles to profl. jours. Mem. Japan Surgical Soc., The Japanese Soc. for Gastroenterology, The Japanese Soc. Gastroent. Surgery. Buddhism. Avocation: japanese chess. Home: 202 President-Yorii Niigata 951-8113 Japan Office: Niigata Sch Medicine 1 Asahimachi-dori Niigata 951-8510 Japan Home Phone: 25-229-1543; Office Phone: 25-227-2228. Business E-Mail: kandat@med.nagata-u.ac.jp.

KANDA, TATSUO, physician, educator; b. Japan, Dec. 18, 1965; MD, Niigata U., Japan, 1991; PhD, Chiba U., Japan, 1999. Assoc. prof. Dept. Medicine and Clin. Oncology, Chiba U., Grad. Sch. Medicine, 2008—. Office: 1-8-1 Inohana Chuo-ku Chiba 260-8677 Japan E-mail: kandat@aol.com.

KANDARAKIS, ARTEMIOS S., ophthalmologist; b. Piraeus, Greece, Nov. 18, 1947; MD, U. Athens, 1972. Cons. Ophthalmiatreion Eye Hosp., 1986—97, chmn., 2001—; head Dept. Ophthalmology, Polikliniki Gen. Hosp., 1997—2001. Glaucoma and Cornea fellowship, La. State U., 1984. Master: Hellenic Ophthal. Soc. (pres. 2009); fellow: ACS; mem.: Am. Acad. Ophthalmology. Home: 1A Zefyrou St Ekali Attiki 14578 Greece Home Fax: 30 210 8130031. Personal E-mail: kandarte@gmail.com.

KANDEL, ERIC RICHARD, neuroscientist, educator; b. Vienna, Nov. 7, 1929; arrived in U.S., 1939; s. Herman and Charlotte (Zimels) Kandel; 2 children. BA, Harvard Coll., 1952; MD, NYU Sch. Medicine, 1956. Intern Montefiore Hosp., NYC, 1956—57; rsch. assoc. neurophysiology lab. NIH, Bethesda, 1957—60; resident in psychiatry Harvard Med. Sch., Boston, 1960—64, staff psychiatrist, 1964—65; assoc. prof. dept. physiology and psychiatry NYU Sch. Medicine, 1965—74; prof. dept. physiology and psychiatry Columbia U. Coll. Physicians & Surgeons, NYC, 1974—, founding dir. Ctr. Neurobiology & Behavior, 1974—83, Univ. prof., 1983—, prof. dept. biochemistry and molecular biophysics, 1992—. Sr. investigator Howard Hughes Med. Inst., Chevy Chase, Md., 1984—. Author: Cellular Basis of Behavior: An Introduction to Behavioral Neurobiology, 1976, Cellular Biology of Neurons, 1977, A Cell Biological Approach to Learning, 1978, Behavioral Biology of Aplysia: A Contribution to the Comparative Study of Opisthobranch Molluscs, 1979, Essentials of Neural Science Value Pack, 1995, Psychiatry, Psychoanalysis, and the New Biology of Mind, 2005, (autobiography) In Search of Memory: The Emergence of a New Science of Mind, 2006 (LA Times Book award for sci. & tech., 2006); co-author (with James H. Schwartz & Thomas M. Jessell): Essentials of Neural Science and Behavior, 1995; editor: Molecular Neurobiology in Neurology and Pschiatry, 1987; co-editor: Molecular Aspects of Neurobiology, 1986, Principles of Neural Science, 2000; contbr. articles to profl. jours. Recipient Henry L. Moses award, Montefiore Hosp., 1959, Lester N. Hofheimer prize for rsch., 1977, Lucy G. Moses prize for rsch. in basic neurology, 1977, Solomon A. Berson Med. Alumni Achievement award, 1979, Karl Spencer Lashley prize in neurobiology, 1981, Dickson prize in biology & medicine, 1982, Albert Lasker award for Basic Medical Rsch., 1983, Howard Crosby Warren medal, Soc. Exptl. Psychologists, 1984, Gairdner Found. Internat. award, 1987, Nat. Medal Sci., The White House, 1988, Disting. Svc. award, American Psychiatric Assn., 1989, Robert J. & Clarie Pasarow Found. award in neurosci., 1989, Bristol-Myers Squibb award for disting. achievement in neurosci. rsch., 1991, Warren Triennial prize, 1992, Jean-Louis Signoret's prize, 1992, Harvey prize, Technion-Israel Inst. Tech., 1993, FO Schmitt medal in neurosci., 1993, NYC Mayor's award for excellence in sci. and tech., 1994, Charles A. Dana award for pioneering achievement in health, 1997, Wolf Found. Prize in Medicine, Israel, 1999, Heineken prize, 2000, Nobel Prize in Physiology/Medicine, The Nobel Found., 2000, Viktor Frankl award, Vienna, 2008. Fellow: AAAS; mem.: NAS, Acad. Scis. France, Am. Philos. Soc., NY Acad. Scis., Internat. Brain Rsch. Orgn., Soc. Neuroscis. (pres. 1980—81). Achievements include patents in field. Office: Columbia U NYSPI Unit 25 1051 Riverside Dr New York NY 10032 also: Howard Hughes Med Inst 4000 Jones Bridge Rd Chevy Chase MD 20815-6789 Office Phone: 212-543-5204. Office Fax: 212-543-5474. Business E-Mail: erk5@columbia.edu. *

KANDIL, MANAL ESSAM, pediatrician, educator; b. Cairo, July 8, 1961; MBBCh, Cairo U., 1985, MD in Pediat., 1999. Rschr. Dept. Pediat., NRC, 1999—2004, asst. prof., 2004—09, prof., 2009—, cons.; trainer clin. courses NRC. Reviewer rsch. papers Several Internat. Med. Jours. Contbr. scientific papers. Mem.: Egyptian Soc. Pediatric Allergy and Immunology, Egyptian Soc. Pediat., Internat. Soc. Nephrology. Avocations: drawing, music. Office: NRC Dept Pediatrics El-Tahreer St Dokki Giza 12622 Egypt Personal E-mail: manalkandil2001@yahoo.com.

KANDT, RAYMOND S., neurologist; b. Rochester, NY, July 8, 1950; m. Irene Kandt; children: Melanie, Lauren. AB cum laude, U. Va., 1972; MD, U. Va. Sch. Medicine, 1976. Diplomate Am. Bd. Med. Examiners, Am. Bd. Pediatrics, Am. Bd. Psychiatry & Neurology with spl. competence in child neurology and with added qualifications in clin. neurophysiology; cert. neurovascular & pediat. neurosonologist; cert. MRI/CT. Intern, resident in pediatrics Johns Hopkins Hosp., Balt., 1976-78, resident in pediatric neurology, fellow in devel. pediatrics, 1978-81; instr. depts. neurology, pediatrics U. Mich., Ann Arbor, 1981-82, asst. prof. depts. neurology & pediatrics, 1982-84; asst. prof. pediatrics div. pediatric neurology Duke U. Med. Ctr., Durham, NC, 1984-89, assoc. prof. pediatrics div. pediatric neurology, 1989-92, asst. prof. medicine div. neurology, 1990-92; assoc. prof. neurology, pediatrics Bowman Gray Sch. Medicine, Winston-Salem, NC, 1992-97; clin. assoc. prof. pediatrics Wake Forest U./Bapt. Med. Ctr., Winston-Salem, 1997—. Chief sect. child neurology Bowman Gray Sch. Medicine, 1992-97, grad. med. edn. com. 1993-97, clin. faculty adv. coun., 1993-97; faculty advisor pediatric house staff U. Mich., 1981-84, faculty advisor med. students, 1983-84, com. on edn., 1982-84; pediatric rep. continuing med. edn. com. Duke U. Med. Ctr., 1985-92; mem. gen. clin. rsch. ctrs. com. nat. ctr. for rsch. resources NIH, 1991-95; cons. in field. Reviewer: Am. Jour. Human Genetics, 1995, Jour. Neurol. Scis., 1993—97, Nature Genetics, 1993, Annals of Neurology, 1998—2002; contbg. editor: Annals of Behavioral Medicine, 1991—93. Adv. bd. My Father's House Group Homes, 1993; med. adv. com. Children's Ctr. for the Physically Handicapped, Winston-Salem, N.C., 1993—. Grantee NIH, 1986-91, 89-92, Nat. Tuberous Sclerosis Assn., 1992-93, grantee Glaxo, 1995-96; recipient Merck award, 1976. Mem.: Profs. Child Neurology, Tuberous Sclerosis Alliance (mem. profl. adv. bd. 1990—, scientific adv. bd. 1995—, chmn. clin. care adv. bd. 1995—97, scientific grant rev. com. 1995—, chmn. med. adv. com. N.C. chpt. 1988—), Child Neurology Soc., N.C. Med. Soc., Am. Neurol. Assn., Phi Sigma, Alpha Omega Alpha. Home: 3428 Jameson Ln Winston Salem NC 27106-4771 Office: Johnson Neurologic Clinic 606 N Elm St High Point NC 27262-4336 Office Phone: 336-889-8877.

KANE, AGNES BREZAK, pathologist, educator; b. Danbury, Conn., Nov. 3, 1946; d. John Edward and Mary Elizabeth (Hatfield) Brezak; m. David E. Kane, June 22, 1970. BA, Swarthmore Coll., 1968; MD, Temple U., 1974, PhD, 1976. Diplomate Am. Bd. Pathology. Resident Temple U. Hosp., Phila., 1975-76, 77-78; postdoctoral fellow Karolinska Inst., Stockholm, 1976-77; asst. prof. Temple U. Sch. Medicine, Phila., 1977-82, Brown U., Providence, 1982-87, assoc. prof. pathology, 1987-95, prof. pathology, 1995-96, chair dept. pathology and lab. medicine, 1996—. Mem. merit rev. bd. for basic scis. VA, Washington, 1984-86; cons. R.I. Commn. for Safety and Occupational Health, Providence, 1986—; commr. Commn. to Identify Occupational Diseases, Providence, 1987-88; mem. rev. com. Nat. Inst. Environ. Health Scis., Research Triangle Park, N.C., 1988—. Assoc. editor Am. Jour. of Pathology, 1992—; contbr. articles on exptl. pathology to sci. publs. Lucretia Mott fellow Swarthmore Coll., 1969-71; recipient Rsch. Career Devel. award NIH, 1981-86. Mem. Am. Assn. Pathologists (women's com. 1987—, program com. 1990—), Assn. Women Med. Faculty Brown U. (founder, coord.), Women in Medicine (faculty advisor Brown U. chpt.; Mary Putnam Jacobi award 1986), Phi Kappa, Sigma Xi. Avocation: gardening. Office: Brown Univ Box G Providence RI 02912 Business E-Mail: agnes_kane@brown.edu.

KANE, FRANK LESTER, physician; b. Passaic, NJ, July 21, 1951; s. Frank L. and Eunice (Zank) K.; m. Patricia L. Brantigan, May 16, 1981; children: Frank L., Michael A. BA, U. Conn., 1974; BS, Rutgers U., Livingston, NJ, 1977; MD, N.J. Med. Sch., Newark, 1982. Resident Mountainside Hosp., Montclair, N.J., 1982-85; pvt. practice specializing in family practice Cedar Grove, N.J., 1985-87, Newton, N.J., 1987—. Bd. dirs. Am. Bd. Family Medicine, 2000—05, chmn., 2005. Fellow Am. Acad. Family Practice; mem. N.J. Acad. Family Practice (past pres.), Nat. Commn. Cert. Physician Assts.(bd. dir. 2006-). Roman Catholic.

KANE, GRACE MCNELLY, retired women's health and pediatrics nurse; b. Auburn, Ill., Mar. 31, 1939; d. Irving Benjamin and Ruby Louise (Stinnett) McNelly; m. Robert John Kane, July 23, 1960 (dec. 1994); children: Scott Robert, Timothy Phillip, Pamela Collette, Glenn Randall, Andrew Keith, Bruce Ryan. Diploma, Mem. Hosp. Sch. Nursing, Springfield, Ill., 1960; BS in Profl. Arts, St. Joseph's Coll., North Windham, Maine, 1985. RN Ill. Ariz., cert. in occpl. hearing conservation, fetal monitoring I and II, ACLS. Staff nurse nursery-newborn units Walther Meml. Hosp., Chgo., 1962-67; staff nurse rooming-in nursery Luth. Gen. Hosp., Park Ridge, Ill., 1977-85; staff nurse med.-surg. unit Swedish Covenant Hosp., Chgo., 1989; staff nurse occpl. clinic Rush-Presbyn-St. Luke's, Elk Grove Village, Ill., 1988; nurse various hosps., Chgo., 1989-93; staff nurse couplet care St. Joseph's Hosp., Phoenix, 1997—2004; ret., 2004—08. Ob-gyn. staff nurse Casa Grande Regional Med. Ctr., Ariz., 2004—06; staff nurse Dependable Staffing, Ariz., 2006—07, Readylink Healthcare, 2007—, Mollen Immunization Clinics, 2009—10, Kenwood-Kenmont Campus, Kent, Conn., 2010; readylink travel nurse Northern Novado Med. Ctr., 2010. Personal E-mail: gracelane39@yahoo.com.

KANE, KAY SHOU-MEI, dermatologist, educator; MD, Harvard U., 1993; grad., Williams Coll., Williamstown, Mass. Diplomate Am. Bd. Dermatology, 2005. Tchg. fellow, pre-medical advisor and residential tutor Harvard Coll.; Harvard combined dermatology tng. program Mass. Gen. Hosp., Brigham and Women's Hosp., active staff; Harvard combined dermatology tng. program Beth Israel Deaconess Med. Ctr., staff mem.; Harvard combined dermatology tng. program The Dana Farber Cancer Inst., Cambridge City Hosp., Harvard Vanguard Group, VA Hosps., Boston Children's Hosp., intern, active staff, Mt. Auburn Hosp.; instr. dermatology dept. Harvard Med. Sch.; with SkinCare Physicians; asst. prof. dermatology Hardvard Med. Sch. Author: (textbook) Color Atlas and Synopsis of Pediatric Dermatology; co-author: (CD-Rom) The Oral and Cutaneous Manifestations of HIV Disease. Mem.: New Eng. Dermatology Soc., Dermatology Found., Soc. for Pediatric Dermatology, Am. Acad. of Dermatology. Office: SkinCare Physicians 1244 Boylston St Rt 9 Chestnut Hill MA 02467 Office Phone: 617-731-1600.

KANE, MICHAEL JOEL, physician; b. Erie, Pa., July 2, 1951; BS, US Naval Acad., 1973; MD, NJ Med. Sch., 1983. Diplomate Am. Bd. Internal Medicine. Med. intern Thomas Jefferson U. Hosp., Phila., 1983—84, resident medicine, 1984—86; fellow neoplastic diseases Mt. Sinai Med. Ctr., NYC, 1986—88; attending physician Jefferson Med. Coll., Phila., 1988—91, Med. Ctr. Princeton, NJ, 1991—96, Cancer Inst. N.J., Hamilton, 1996—2004, Cancer Ctr. Mountainside, Montclair, NJ, 2004—06, Cancer Ctr. Bayshore Hosp., Holmdel, NJ, 2007—. Served to lt. US Navy, 1969-79. Decorated Navy Achievement medal. Fellow ACP, Am. Soc. Clin. Oncology, Am. Assn. Cancer Rsch., Am. Soc. Hematology, Oncology Soc. NJ. Office: Bayshore Hosp 668 N Beers St Holmdel NJ 07733 Office Phone: 732-888-1345.

KANE, PETER BAYARD, physician; b. Bryn Mawr, Pa., Apr. 3, 1938; MD, U. Pa., 1964. Diplomate Am. Bd. Anesthesiology. Intern Wis. Hosps., Madison, 1964-65; resident Hosp. U. Pa., Phila., 1965-67, fellow in rsch., 1967-69; mem. staff SUNY Hosp., Syracuse; prof. SUNY Upstate Med. U., Syracuse. V.p., treas. Academic Solutions, 2002—. Recipient Disting. Svc. Nina Mitchell award, United U. Professions, 1999. Mem. AMA, Am. Soc. Anesthesiology, Internat. Anesthesia Rsch. Soc., NY State Soc. Anesthesia (Disting. Svc. award 2009), Academic Health Profls. Ins. Assn. (treas. 1992-). Office: SUNY Upstate Med U 750 E Adams St Syracuse NY 13210-2306

KANE, ROBERT CHARLES, physician, director; b. Pa., Nov. 4, 1947; MD, Jefferson Med. Coll. Phila, 1970. Dep. dir. safety, hematology products CDER, FDA, 2010—. Fellow: ACP. Office: 10903 New Hampshire Ave Silver Spring MD 20993-0002 Business E-Mail: robert.kane@fda.hhs.gov.

KANE, ROBERT LEWIS, public health service officer, educator; b. NYC, Jan. 18, 1940; m. Rosalie Smolkin, June 17, 1962; children: Miranda, Ingrid, Kate AB, Columbia Coll., NYC, 1961; MD, Harvard U., 1965. Acting coordinator sr. clerkship program dept. community medicine U. Ky., Lexington, 1968-69; svc. unit dir. USPHS Indian Hosp., Shiprock, N.Mex., 1969-70; spl. asst. to regional health dir. USPHS HEW Region VIII, Denver, 1970-71; from asst. to assoc. prof. family and community medicine U. Utah Sch. Medicine, Salt Lake City, 1970-77; sr. researcher The Rand Corp., Santa Monica, Calif., 1977-85; from assoc. prof. to prof. medicine UCLA Sch. Medicine, 1978-85; prof. Sch. Pub. Health UCLA, 1980-85, U. Minn., 1985—, dean, 1985-90; intern U. Ky. Med. Ctr., Lexington, 1965-66, resident in community medicine, 1966-69. Adj. prof. Leonard Davis Sch. Gerontology, U. So. Calif., 1982-85; mem. expert com. on aging WHO, 1986-2002; Minn. endowed chair in long-term care and aging, 1989—; mem. adv. com. on Alzheimer's Disease, Washington, 1988-96; mem. com. on quality Inst. Medicine, 1988-90. Co-author: A Will and A Way, 1985, Long-term Care: Principles, Programs, and Policies, 1987, Essentials of Clinical Geriatrics, 9th edit., 2009, Understanding Health Care Outcomes Research, 2nd edit., 2005, The Heart of Long Term Care, 1998, Assessing Older Persons, 2000, It Shouldn't Be This Way, 2005, Meeting the Challenge of Chronic Illness, 2005. With USPHS, 1969-70. Home: 2715 E Lake Of The Isles Pky Minneapolis MN 55408-1053 Office Phone: 612-624-1185. Business E-Mail: kanex001@umn.edu.

KANE, THOMAS JAY, III, surgeon, educator; b. Merced, Calif., Sept. 2, 1951; s. Thomas J., Jr. and Kathryn (Hassler) Kane; m. Marle Rose Van Emmerik, Oct. 10, 1987; children: Thomas Keola, Travis Reid, Samantha Marie. BA in History, U. Santa Clara, 1973; MD, U. Calif., Davis, 1977; grad., FBI Citizen's Acad., 2009. Diplomate Am. Bd. Orthopaedic Surgery. Intern U. Calif. Davis Sacramento Med. Ctr., 1977-78, resident in surgery, 1978-81; resident in orthopaedic surgery U. Hawaii, 1987-91; fellowship adult joint reconstruction U. SC, Rancho Los Amigos Med. Ctr., 1991-92; ptnr. Orthop. Assocs. Hawaii, Inc., Honolulu, 1992—; asst. prof. surgery U. Hawaii, Honolulu, 1993—, chief divsn. implant surgery, 1993—, asst. chief orthopedics, 2003—04; dir. joint reconstruction Inst. Pacific, 2008—; med. dir. Queen's Joint Ctr., 2009—; founder & dir. Kane Orthop. Inst., 2010—. Contbr. articles to profl. jours. Mem.: AMA, Fed. Law

Enforcement Found., Am. Coll. Sports Medicine, Western Orthop. Assn., Am. Acad. Orthop. Surgery, Hawaii Orthop. Assn. (v.p. 2003—04, pres. 2004—), Hawaii Med. Assn., Am. Assn. Hip and Knee Surgeons, Phi Kappa Phi, Alpha Omega Alpha. Avocations: tennis, golf, skiing, music, surfing. Office: Kane Orthop Inst 550 S Beretania St Ste 402 Honolulu HI 96813 Office Phone: 808-521-2233.

KANE, WILLIAM HARRISON, hematologist, educator; b. Glen Cove, NY, Oct. 24, 1955; BS, U. Iowa, 1976; MD, Wash. U., St. Louis, PhD, 1982. Intern, resident, internal medicine Barnes Hosp., St. Louis, 1982—84, fellow, hematology-oncology, 1984—85; sr. fellow, biochemistry U. Wash., Seattle, 1985—88; assoc. prof. medicine & pathology Duke U. Med. Ctr., 1988—; dir. hematology-oncology fellowship program, Duke U., 2004—10. Mem. Am. Heart Assn. Thrombosis Study Sect., 1988—91, Am. Soc. Hematology Subcom. Hemostasis, 1995—99, Nat. Hemophilia Found. Rsch. Com., 1997—2002; regular mem. NIH Hematology, HEM1 Study Sect., 1997—2001. Recipient Established Investigator award, Am. Heart Assn.; grant, Med. Scientist Tng. Program, Wash. U., St. Louis, Chgo. Cmty. Trust, NIH. Mem.: Am. Soc. Clin. Investigation, Am. Soc. Hematology, Phi Beta Kappa. Avocations: running, cooking, genealogy. Office: Duke Clinic 100 Trent Dr Durham NC 27710

KANEDA, YASUHIRO, neuropsychiatrist; b. Marugame-shi, Japan, Apr. 5, 1963; s. Nobuharu and Aiko (Sako) K.; children: Makito, Taiki. MD, U. Tokushima, Japan, 1992, PhD, 1997. Lic. physician, Japan; qualified psychiatrist, Japan; European cert. anxiety mood disorders. Intern, resident U. Tokushima Sch. Medicine, 1992-93, lectr., 1997-99, med. dir., 2000—02, 2004—06, asst. prof., 2000—06, Iwaki Clinic, 2006—; neuropsychiatrist Pvt. Health Facility Old Men, Komatsushima, Japan, 1996—2002, 2004—, Pvt. Psychiat. Hosp., Anan, Japan, 1997—2002, 2004—. Cons. Pub. Psychiat. Hosp., Tokushima, 1993—97, Pub. Health Care Ctr., Tokushima, 1995—97, 2000—02, 2004—06, 2007—11; with Coll. Welfare, Tokushima, 1998—2002, 2004—, U. Tokushima Sch. Med. Sci., 2000—02; vis. rsch. fellow U. Vanderbilt Sch. Medicine, 2002—04. Recipient award Tokushima Med. Assn., 1999, European Cert. award World Fedn. Soc. Biol. Psychiatry, 2000, World Assn. Social Psychiatry award, 2004. Mem.: Am. Psychiat. Assn., Internat. Neuropsychiatric Assn., Japanese Coll. Neuropsychopharmacology, Coll. Internat. Neuropsychopharmacology, German Soc. Biol. Psychiatry, Soc. Biol. Psychiatry, Japanese Soc. Psychiatric Diagnosis, Japan Psychogeriatric Soc. (cert. specialist in geriat. psychiatry), Japanese Soc. Clin. Neuropsychopharmacology (cert. specialist clin. neuropsychopharmacology, councilor 2006—, Lilly fellow 2001), Japanese Soc. Biol. Psychiatry, Japanese Soc. Psychosomatic Medicine (councilor 2002—04), Japanese Soc. Psychiatry Neurology, Internat. Brain Rsch. Orgn., Internat. Psychogeriatric Assn. Avocations: watching movies, listening to music, travel, reading books. Office: Dept Psychiatry Iwaki Clinic 11-1 Kamimizuta Gakubara Anan tokushima 774-0014 Japan Home Phone: 08035083163; Office Phone: 81-884-23-5600. Business E-Mail: kaneday-tsh@umin.ac.jp.

KANEKO, MASAO, radiology educator, researcher, specialist; b. Nagoya, Japan, May 6, 1933; s. Gensaku and Kaneko (Kitagawa) K.; m. Sachiko Yamazaki, May 11, 1961; children: Tomoo, Akio, Takeo. MD, Nagoya U., 1958, PhD, 1965. Intern St. Luke's Internat. Hosp., Tokyo, 1958-59; rsch. asst. Nagoya U., 1964, asst. prof., 1971-74; sect. chief Aichi Cancer Ctr., Nagoya, 1965-71; rsch. fellow UCLA, 1960-61; assoc. prof. radiology Hamamatsu U. Sch. Medicine, Japan, 1974-76, prof., 1976—99. Head radiology Hamamatsu U. Hosp., 1977-99; dir. Hamamatsu Red Cross Blood Ctr., 1999-2003, Tokoha Rehab. Hosp., 2003 . Author: Radiological Protection, 1982, Medical Optical Tomography, 1993. Recipient discovery promotion award Japan Discovery Assn., 1980. Mem. Japan Radiol. Soc. (emeritus; councilor), Radiol. Soc. N.Am. (corr.), Assn. Univ. Radiologists. Avocation: listening to classical music. Home: 347-5 Hatsuoi-cho Kita-ku Hamamatsu 433-8112 Japan Office: Tokoha Rehab Hosp 130 Nearai-Cho Kita-ku Hamamatsu 433-8108 Japan Home Phone: 81 53 436 7571. Home Fax: 81 53 436 7571. Personal E-mail: m.kaneko@oboe.ocn.ne.jp. Business E-Mail: d-tokoha-r-h@mail.wbs.ne.jp.

KANEKO, NAOYUKI, medical educator, medical association administrator; b. Arakawa, Tokyo, July 30, 1960; s. Yoshihiro and Hatsue Kaneko; married; 1 child, Shoki. Dr., Nagoya U., Japan, 1987. Cert. Japan Surg. Soc., 1993, Japanese Assn. Acute Medicine, 1994, Japanese Soc. Gastroent. Surgery, 1997, Japanese Soc. Burn Injuries, 2002. Mem., dept. surg. oncology Grad. Sch. Medicine, Nagoya U., 1987; super-rotator Kamo Hosp., Toyota, Aichi, Japan, 1987—88, resident gen. surgery, 1988—91, instr. gen. surgery, 1991—93; instr. trauma surgery Dept. Traumatology, CCM, Nat. Def. Med. Coll., Tokorozawa, Saitama, Japan, 1993—, asst. prof., instr. trauma surgery, 1996—. Mem., exec. com. Japanese Soc. Abdominal Emergency Medicine, 1998—, Japanese Assn. Surgery Trauma, 2000—, mem., gen. planning com., 2005—; active fellow Am. Assn. Surgery Trauma, 2006—; mem., exec. com. Japan Surg. Assn., 2001—; bd. cert. sr. mem. Japanese Assn. Acute Medicine, 2002—, mem., exec. com., 2005—; instr., dir. Japan Pre-hosp. Trauma Evaluation and Care, 2003—; instr. Internat. Trauma Life Support Internat., 2003—; bd. cert. sr. mem. Japan Surg. Soc., 2003—; instr. Immediate Cardiac Life Support, Japan, 2004—; mem., dirs. Japanese Soc. Trauma Surg. Techniques, 2004—. Office: Nat Def Med Coll Namiki Tokorozawa Saitama 359-8513 Japan Office Fax: 81-4-2996-5221. Business E-Mail: nk8639@ndmc.ac.jp.

KANEKO, SUNAO, psychiatrist, educator; b. Otaru, Hokkaido, Apr. 4, 1946; MD, Hirosaki U., 1972, PhD, 1976. Prof. Hirosaki U., 1995—. Pres. Japanese Soc. Clin. Neuropsychopharmacology, 2006; hon. prof Chine Med. Sch., 2006; pres. Japan Epilepsy Soc., 2009; bd. dirs. CAOA-ILAE, 2009. Master: Japan Neuropsychiatry Soc. (Paul Janssen prize). Avocation: stamp collecting/philately. Office: Zafiu Chou 5 Hirosaki Aomori 036-8562 Japan Office Fax: 172-39-5067. Business E-Mail: sk@cc.hirosaki-u.ac.jp.

KANELLOS, IOANNIS DIMITRIOS, surgeon, educator; b. Volos, Greece, Nov. 19, 1953; s. Dimitrios Ioannis Kanellos and Vasiliki Dimitriou Moutou; m. Kalliopi Alexandros Galovatsea, July 7, 1953; children: Vasiliki, Dimitrios, Alexandra. MD, Aristotle U., 1977; PhD in Surgery, U. Berlin, 1984. From lectr. to assoc. prof. surgery Aristotle U., Thessaloniki, Greece, 1989—2001, assoc. prof. surgery, 2001—; pvt. practice surgeon Thessaloniki, 1990—. Rschr. U. Berlin, 1980—. Author (editor): General Surgery, 2001, Haemorrhoidopexy with PPH, 2004, Colorectal Cancer, 2004; contbr. over 320 articles to profl. jours. Physician Greek Army, 1977—79. Scholar, Artistotle U. Mem.: Internat. Soc. Surgery. Avocations: swimming, football. Personal E-mail: ik@hol.gr.

KANENGISER, STEVEN, pediatrician, pulmonologist; Attended, Yale U., U. Calif. Diplomate Am. Bd. of Pediatrics, pediatric pulmonary medicine. Resident Children's Hosp., Boston; fellow NY Hosp. Cornell Med. Ctr., Westchester County Med. Ctr. Office: The Valley Hospital 223 N Van Dien Ave Ridgewood NJ 07450 Office Phone: 201-447-8000.

KANERVISTO, MERJA, healthcare educator, researcher; b. Tampere, Finland, Mar. 17, 1954; d. Pertti and Leila Järvinen; m. Kari Kanervisto, Aug. 18, 1979; children: Tarja, Mikko. RN, Health Care Sch. Tampere, 1993; M in Nursing Sci., U. Tampere, 2000; PhD, 2008. Nurse Tampere City Hosp., Finland, 1986—2000, head nurse, 2001—02; nurse Pirkanmaa Hosp. Dist., Tampere U. Hosp., 2000—01; health care tchr. Tampere Inst. Social and Health Care Studies, 2002—03, 2005—; rsch. asst., dept. nursing sci. U. Tampere, 2003—04, rschr., dept. nursing sci., 2003—04, postdoc. rschr., dept. nursing sci., 2009—; rschr. Inst. Occupl. Health, 2007—08. Vice councillor Tampere Mcpl. Coun., 2005—08; coun. mem. Joint Mcpl. Authority for Social Svcs. Pirkanmaa, Tampere, 2005—08; bd. mem. Womens' Def. House, Tampere, 2006—; bd. chair person Dementia Soc. Tampere, 2006. Mem.: Finnish Assn. Nursing Rsch. Conservative. Lutheran. Avocations: dogs, rollerskating, movies, reading, politics. Home: Kohmankaari 33310 Tampere Finland Home Phone: 35840-5129590. Personal E-mail: mkanervisto@hotmail.fl.

KANEYAMA, KAZUHIRO, pediatric surgeon; b. Tajimi, Gifu, Japan, Sept. 11, 1974; s. Taiichi and Miyoko Kaneyama; m. Aiko Hiraga, Sept. 3, 1975; 1 child, Kouki. MD, Juntendo U., 1999, PhD, 2005. Lic. Japanese Ministry of Health Labor and Welfare, 1999. Resident in gen. surgery Juntendo U., Sch. Medicine, Bunkyo, Tokyo, 1999—2001, trainee in pediatric surgery, 2001—05, fellow in pediatric surgery, 2005—. Office Fax: 81-3-5802-2033. Business E-Mail: kaneyama@med.juntendo.ac.jp.

KANG, BYUNG-UK, hospital administrator; b. Seoul, Republic Of Korea, Apr. 3, 1969; s. Gun Kang and Hyo-Sook Lee; m. Na Ri Kim; 1 child, Ye Ah. MD, KonKuk U., Seoul, 1997. Diplomate Korean Med. Assn., 1997. Rsch. fellowship Wooridul Spine Hosp., Seoul, 2003—04, dir., neurosurgery, 2005—06, dir., med. neurosurgery Daegu, Republic of Korea, 2007—; adj. prof., neurosurgery Cath U., Seoul. Contbr. scientific papers to profl. jours. Lt. sr. South Korean Army, 1997—2000. Recipient Excellence Rsch. Paper award, Wooridul Spine Hosp., 1st prize, 2006—07. Fellow: Asian Acad. Minimally Invasive Spinal Surgery, Royal Coll. Physician & Surgeon, Royal Coll. Surgeon, Am. Bd. Minimally Invasive Spinal Surgery. Office: Wooridul Spine Hosp 50-3 Dongin-Dong Jung-Gu 700-732 Daegu Daegu Republic of Korea Office Fax: 82-53-212-3068. Personal E-mail: skulspine@hanmail.net.

KANG, CHIL-YONG, virologist, immunology educator; arrived in Can., 1966, naturalized, 1971; s. Whashik and Ungee (Song) K.; m. Myung-Ja Oh (Kang), Dec. 17, 1966; children: Julie, Rosanne, Matthew. Diploma in Vet. Sci., Malling Agrl. Coll., Denmark, 1965; BSA, Kon-Kuk U., Korea, 1965; PhD, McMaster U., Hamilton, Ont., 1971; DSc, Carleton U., 1991. Postdoctoral fellow U. Wis., Madison, 1971—74; asst. prof. Southwestern Med. Sch. U. Tex., Dallas, 1974—78, assoc. prof. Southwestern Med. Sch., 1978—82; prof., chmn. dept. microbiology, immunology U. Ottawa, Ont., Canada, 1982—92; dir. U. Ottawa Biotech. Inst., Ont., 1987—92; dean sci., prof. medicine U. Western Ont., Canada, 1992—99, prof. virology, 1992—. Contbr. articles to profl. jours. Office: Univ Western Ont Siebens-Drake Inst 1400 Western Rd Rm 129 London ON Canada N6G 2V4 Office Phone: 519-661-3226. Personal E-mail: chilyongkang@gmail.com. Business E-Mail: cykang@uwo.ca.

KANG, CHONG MYUNG, internist, nephrologist; b. Seoul, Republic of Korea, Dec. 19, 1947; s. Eui Jun Lee; m. So Sung Kim, Nov. 15, 1972; children: Hyo Jin, Hyo Eun, Hyo Min. MD, Seoul Nat. U., 1972, PhD, 1979. Lic. MD Ministry of Welfare, 1972, Certified Board of Internal Medicine Ministry of Welfare, 1977, Subspecialty Board of Nephrology Korean Soc. of Internal Medicine, 1992. Prof. Hanyang U. Hosp., Seoul, Republic of Korea, 1978—, dir., dept of internal medicne, 2001—03, dir., hemodialysis unit, 1988—. Recipient Gi Suk Young Med. award, Glaxo SmithKline Co., 2002. Mem.: Nat. Acad. Medicine of Korea, Korean Soc. Transplantation (v.p.), Korean Soc. Nephrology, Korean Soc. Internal Medicine (auditor), Transplantation Soc., Internat. Soc. Nephrology, European Soc. Nephrology (corr.), Am. Soc. Nephrology (corr.). Achievements include research in renal toxicity of immunosuppressive agents; renal transplantation. Home: 513-101 Samick Park Apt Kildong Seoul 134-010 Republic of Korea Office: Hanyang Univ Hosp 17 Haengdang Dong Sungdong Ku Seoul 133-792 Republic of Korea Office Fax: (02)2298-9183. Business E-Mail: kangjm@hanyang.ac.kr.

KANG, DAE YOUNG, medical educator; b. Daejeon, Republic of Korea, Apr. 21, 1948; s. Myung Sik Kang and Nak Soon Seong; m. Jeong Hee Lee; children: Gu Hyun, Gu Heum. MD, Chungnam Nat. U., Daejeon, 1979, PhD in Med. Sci., 1981. Prof. Chungnam Nat. U. Coll. Medicine, 1982—, dean, 1994—96. Dean Grad. Sch. Pub. Health & Biotech., Daejeon, 1995—96. Maj. chmn. Korean Army Capital Hosp., 1979—82, Seoul, Republic of Korea. Mem.: Korean Soc. Toxicologic Pathology (pres. 2006—08), Korean Soc. Pathologists (pres. 2008), Korean Soc. Med. Edn. Avocations: travel, mountain climbing, golf. Office: Coll Medicine Dept Pathology Moonwha-1-Dong Jung-Gu 6 301-747 Daejeon Daejeon Republic of Korea Home: 115-1504 SooMokTo Apt Doan-dong 16th Block Seo-Gu Daejeon 302-318 Republic of Korea Office Phone: 82-62-580-8232. Office Fax: 82-42-581-5233. Business E-Mail: dykang@cnu.ac.kr.

KANG, DAE-JUNG, research scientist; b. Sacheon, Gyeongnam, Republic of Korea, May 5, 1964; M in Engring., Konkuk U., 1993, D, 2011—. Prin. rsch. scientist Ildong Pharm. Co., Ltd., Rsch. Labs., 1993—, team head Bioprocess Engring. Team, 2007; rschr. Korea U. Grad. Sch., 2011. Office: Seogu-Dong 23-9 Hwaseong Gyeonggi 445-170 Republic of Korea

KANG, DO-HYUNG, psychiatrist, educator; b. Daejeon, Nov. 3, 1972; PhD, Seoul Nat. U., 2009. Clin. instr. Dept. Neuropsychiatry, Seoul Nat. U. Hosp., 2006—08, clin. asst. prof., 2008—. Chief psychiatry dept. Daejeon Mil. Hosp., 2003—06. Recipient Sci. award, Korean Pain Soc. Fellow: Korean Pain Rsch. Soc.; mem.: Korean Soc. Schizophrenia Rsch. (Rschr. award), Korean Soc. Human Brain Mapping, Korean Neuropsychiatric Assn. Avocation: meditation. Office: 101 Daehak-No Chongno Seoul 110-744 Republic of Korea Business E-Mail: basuare@paran.com.

KANG, DONGMUG, medical educator; b. Busan, Kyong-Buk, Republic Of Korea, Oct. 18, 1964; s. Byung Yoon Kang and Sun-Ja Sin; m. Euna Kim; 1 child, Jee-Hyun. MD, Pusan Med. Sch., Busan, 1992; MPH, Harvard Sch. Pub. Health, Boston, 1997; PhD, Kosin Med. Sch., Busan, 2003. Cert. in occupl. & environ. medicine Korea, 2000. Assoc. prof. Pusan Med. Sch., Busan, Republic of Korea, 2002—; vis. scholar U. Mass., Lowell, 2006; vis. scientist Dept. Health, Boston, 2006; sec. gen. Korean Soc. Occupl. & Environ. Medicine, Busan, 2006—; chief Asbestos Mesothelioma Rsch. Ctr. Instr. Pusan Paik Hosp., Busan, 2000—02; asst. prof. Busan Nat. U., 2002—07; sci. com. mem. Musculo-skeletal Disease, ICOH, Boston, 2006; vis. scientist Dept. Work Environment, Lowell, Mass., 2006, Dept. Pub. Health, Boston, 2006. Mem. Steering Com. Workers' Ins., Seoul, 2003. Lt. Mcpl. Health Ctr., 1993—96, Sacheon, Republic Of Korea. Recipient Citizen's Broadcasting award, MBC, 2008. Mem.: Korean Soc. Occupl. & Environ. Medicine (sec. gen. 2006—08). Achievements include research in relationship between firefighter and cancer; distribution and determinant of maximal physical work capacity. Avocation: travel. Office: Yangsan Pusan Univ Hosp Dept Occupl & Environ Medicine Pusan Med Yangsan Si Gyeongnam 626770 Republic of Korea Office Phone: 82553601281. Office Fax: 82-51-243-1925. Personal E-mail: kangdm@dreamwiz.com. Business E-Mail: kangdm@pusan.ac.kr.

KANG, DONG-WHA, neurologist; b. Daegu, Republic of Korea, Apr. 6, 1967; s. Do-Jin Kang and Jeong-Ja Kim; m. In-Kyong Jeong, May 17, 1997; 1 child, Astrid Eunjee. MD, Seoul Nat. U., 1991, MS in Neuroscience, 1999, PhD in Neuroscience, 2001. Diplomate Ministry Health and Welfare, Republic of Korea, 1991. Intern Seoul Nat. U. Hosp., 1994—95, resident, 1995—99, fellow dept. neurology, 1999—2001; with stroke br. Nat. Inst. Neurol. Disorders and Stroke, NIH, Bethesda, Md., 2001—03; asst. prof. Asan Med. Ctr., U. Ulsan, Seoul, 2003—08, assoc. prof., 2008—. Vis. assoc. prof. Harvard Med. Sch., 2010—; vis. assoc. neuro scientist Mass. gen. Hosp., 2010—. Contbr. articles to profl. jours. With Korean Mil., 1991—94. Recipient Med. Coll. Grad. Student Excellence award, Seoul Nat. U., 1991, Young Investigator award, Korean Neurol. Assn., 2006, Excellent Rschr. award, Korea Health Industry Devel. Inst., 2009, Stroke Care in Emergency Medicine award, Am. Stroke Assn., 2011; grantee, Korea Sci. & Engring. Found., 2001, Korean Ministry Health & Welfare, 2004—07, Asan Inst. Life Sciences, Seoul, 2004—05, Korea Health 21 R&D Project, Korean Ministry Health & Welfare, 2005—07; fellow, Nat. Rsch. Found. Republic of Korea, 2011—, Vision Scis. Soc. Mem.: Soc. Neuroscience Vision Sciences Soc., Vision Scis. Soc., Soc. Neurosci., Am. Heart Assn. Stroke Coun., Korean Soc. Human Brain Mapping (assoc.), Korean Stroke Soc. (assoc.), Korean Soc. Clin. Neurophysiology (assoc.), Korean Neurol. Assn. (assoc. Young Investigator Award 2006), Korean Med. Assn. (assoc.). Presbyterian. Achievements include research in investigation of stroke mechanism with stroke lesion patterns on diffusion-weighted imaging; validation of silent ischemic lession recurrence on MRI; application of MRI criteria to acute stroke treatment. Office: Dept of Neurology Asan Medical Center 388 1 Pungnap 2 dong Songpa-gu Seoul 138-736 Republic of Korea Office Phone: 82-2-3010-3440. Office Fax: 82-2-474-4691. Personal E-mail: ffdongwha@gmail.com. Business E-Mail: dwkang@amc.seoul.kr.

KANG, DOO KYOUNG, radiologist, educator; b. Incheon, Gyeonggi-do, Republic of Korea, Mar. 15, 1968; s. Yeong Gap Kang and Won Ja Lee; m. Sun Mi Lee, July 6, 1998; children: Mo Hyeon, Mo Rin. MD, Wonju Coll. Medicine, Yonsei U., MS, 1994. Asst. prof. Ajou U. Sch. Medicine, Suwon, Gyonggi-do, Republic of Korea, 2003—. Mem.: Korean Radiol. Soc. Home: Mactan-dong Yeongtong-gu Suwon Gyeonggi-do 443-721 Republic of Korea Office: Ajou University Sch Medicine Dept Radiology San-5 Wonchon-dong Yeongtong-gu Suwon Gyeonggi-do 443-721 Republic of Korea Office Fax: 82-31-219-5862. Business E-Mail: kdklsm@ajou.ac.kr.

KANG, DO-YOUNG, physician, education educator; s. Ji-Seon Kang and Yeon-Seob Han; m. Soo-Jeong Lee, Dec. 4, 1971; children: Seo-Young, Seo-Eun. PhD, Dong-A U., 1991; MD, Ministry of Health and Welfare, Korea, 1991. Specialist of internal medicine Ministry Health and Welfare, Korea, 1996, specialist of nuclear medicine Ministry Health and Welfare, Korea, 1999, lic. mgmt. radioisotope Ministry Sci. and Tech., Korea, 1998. Intern Dong-A U. Med. Ctr., Busan, Republic of Korea, 1991—92, resident in internal medicine, 1992—96, fellow dept. endocrine and metablism of internal medicine, 1996—97; fellow dept. nuc. medicine Asan Med. Ctr., Seoul, Republic of Korea, 1997—98; instr. dept. nuc. medicine Kyungpook Nat. U. Coll. of Medicine, Kyungpook Nat. U. Hosp., Daegu, Republic of Korea, 1998—2000, Dong-A U. Coll. of Medicine, Dong-A U. Med. Ctr., Busan, Republic of Korea, 2000—02, asst. prof., dept. of nuc. medicine, 2002—06, assoc. prof., dir dept. nuc. medicine, 2006—. Author: (book) Nuc. Medicine-Molecular Imaging Medicine. Tchr. Sooyoungro Ch., Busan, Korea (South), 2001—03. Mem.: Am. Thyroid Assn. (assoc.), Am. Soc. Nuc. Medicne (assoc.), European Soc. of Nuc. Medicine (assoc.), Soc. Nuc. Medicine (assoc.), Korean Soc. Nuc. Medicine (assoc. Daiichi 1999). Office: Dong-A Univ Med Ctr Seo-gu Dongdaesin-dong 3-ga 1 Pusan 602-715 Republic of Korea Office Fax: +82-51-242-7237. Business E-Mail: dykang@dau.ac.kr.

KANG, GYEONG HOON, pathologist; b. Masan, Korea, Jan. 3, 1964; s. Se Gu Kang and Ju Yon Choi; m. Ho Kyeong Rhee, June 19, 1966; children: Kyuwon, Curie. PhD, Seoul Nat. U., Korea, 1997. Asst. prof. Asan Med. Ctr., Seoul, Korea, 1996-2000, Seoul Nat. U. Hosp., 2000—. Capt. Korean Mil., 1992-95. Mem. U.S. and Can. Acad. Pathologists. Home: 74-2 Chamwon-dong Seoul 137-043 Republic of Korea Office: Seoul Nat U Hosp 28 Yongon-dong Seoul 110-744 Republic of Korea Office Phone: 82-2-2072-3312. Business E-Mail: ghkang@snu.ac.kr.

KANG, HEE GYUNG, medical educator; b. Seoul, Republic of Korea, Mar. 11, 1971; MD, Seoul Nat. U., PhD, 1996. Asst. prof. Seoul Nat. U. Children's Hosp., 2008—. Recipient Young Investigator award, Korean Soc. Transplantation, Am. Transplant Congress, 2004. Mem.: Korean Pediatric Soc. (Kuhnil Rsch. grant), Korean Soc. Nephrology, Internat. Pediatric Transplant Assn., Korean Soc. Pediatric Nephrology, Am. Soc. Nephrology. Avocation: cello. Office: Seoul Nat University Childrens Hosp 101 Daehang-Ro Jongno-Gu Seoul 110-744 Republic of Korea Business E-Mail: kanghg@snu.ac.kr.

KANG, HEE YOUNG, nursing educator, consultant; d. Young Soo Kang and Hwa Soon Lee; m. Geon Moo Lee, Nov. 28, 1992; children: In Seong Lee, June Seong Lee. B, Chosun U., Gwangju, 1989, M, 1993; PhD, Cath. U., Seoul, 2006. RN Korean Nurses Assn., 1989, NY State Edn. Dept., 2001; cert. in aromatherapist Korean Nurses Assn., 2003, healthcare provider Am. Heart Assn., 2007. Staff nurse Chosun U. Hosp., Gwangju, Republic of Korea, 1989—91; instr. Christian Coll. Nursing, Gwangju, 1992—95, lectr., 1995—2000, assoc. prof., 2007—08, asst. prof., 2000—07, Chosun U., Gwangju, 2008—. Cons. com. mem. Kwangju Christian Hosp., Gwangju, 2004—, Keumho Welfare Ctr., Gwangju, 2008—, Donggu Sr. Welfare Ctr., Gwangju, 2008—, YWCA, Gwangju, 2008—; editl. bd. mem. Med. Jours. Chosun U. Mem. Goyang Women Minwoo Orgn., 2006—08; supporting mem. Korea Campus Crusade Christ, 2002—08; deacon, tchr. Dail Ch., Gwangju, 2004—08. Mem.: Korean Soc. Nursing Sci. Achievements include research in Effects of EMLAcream intradarnal skin test of ampicillin sodium antibiotics; Health habits and obesity by Sasang constitution among female college students; art integrated dementia intervention for Korean -older adults; Effects of an aquarobic exercise program for osteoarthritis patients; the effects of preoperative PCA education, with multimedia and brochure on pain management in surgical patients; effects of oral care with essential oil on improvement in orai health status of hospice patients; factors influencing loneliness in elderly living in nursing homes; effect of obesity control program in obese elementary school children, Chi exercise program on physical health, well-being and self-efficacy of the women; relationship among life style, body composition, and Bone Mineral Density (BMD) in female college students; development of web-based multimedia contents for the critical t&r® practice of nursing students through inter-college collaboration; effects of a bereavement intervention program in middle aged widows in Korea; the effects of web-based multimedia contents for the critical care practice of nursing students; effects of a bereavement intervention program on depression and life satisfaction in middle aged widows in Korea. Office Fax: 82-62-230-6329. Business E-Mail: moohykang@naver.com.

KANG, HO-CHEOL, endocrinologist, researcher; b. Suncheon, Jeollanamdo, Republic Of Korea, July 7, 1966; s. Sun-Ku and Pil-Rye (Kim) Kang; m. Jee-Hyun Park, Aug. 20, 1967; children: Myung-Hoon, Myung-Seo, Si-Hoon. MD in Medicine, Chonnam U., Gwangju, Republic of Korea, 1991, PhD, 2002. Cert. med. specialist Ministry of Health and Welfare of Korea, 1996, lic. physician Ministry of Health and Welfare of Korea, 1991. Resident in internal medicine Chonnam U. Hosp., Gwangju, Republic of Korea, 1992—96; freign rschr. Yamanashi Med. U., Tamaho, Yamanashi, Japan, 1999—2000; instr. dept. internal medicine Chonnam U. Med. Sch., Gwangju, Republic of Korea, 2001—03, asst. prof. dept. internal medicine, 2003—07, assoc. prof. dept. internal medicine, 2007—; chief dept. internal medicine Chonnam U. Hwasun Hosp., Jeollanamdo, Republic of Korea, 2004—. Dir. med. support Chonnam U. Hwasun Hosp., 2006—. Contbr. articles to profl. jours. Lt. sr. Korean mil., 1996—99. Named Man of the Yr., Am. Biog. Inst., 2004; named one of Gt. Minds of 21st Century, 2005. Mem.: US Endocrine Soc., Korean Geriat. Soc., Korean Med. Assn., Korean Assn. Internal Medicine, Korean Diabetes Assn., Korean Endocrine Soc. (bd. dirs. med. ins. 2005—07). Achievements include research in regulatory role of iodine in VEGF expression in Graves' disease; molecular thyroidology; Hypokalemic paralysis and rhabdomyolysis in distal renal tubular acidosis; calcinosis cutis universalis in juvenile dermatomyositis; thyroid ultrasonography and fine-needle aspiration cytology; medical photography. Avocations: photography, music. Home: 501 1602 Kumho Apt Pungam-dong Seo-ku Gwangju 502 776 Republic of Korea Office: Chonnam U Med Sch Dept Internal Medicine Hak-Dong 5 Dong-Ku 501-757 Gwangju Republic of Korea Office Phone: 82-61-379-7620. Office Fax: 82-61-379-7628. Business E-Mail: drkang@chonnam.ac.kr.

KANG, HONG, dentist, educator; s. Chengxue Kang and Xiangjun Li; m. Guangjie Bao, Feb. 14, 1998. MB in Medicine, Lanzhou Med. Coll., China, 1986; MB in Stomatology, Xi 'An Med. U., China, 1988; MS in Stomatology, West China U. Med. Scis., Chengdu, 1997, PhD in Stomatology, 2000. Diplomate Chinese Med. Assn., 1988. Asst. prof. dept. oral anatomy and physiology, Lanzhou Med. Coll., 1988—94, lectr., 1994—2000; assoc. prof. dept. prosthodontics, Lanzhou Med. Coll., 2001—04; assoc. prof., sch. stomatology dept. prosthodontics, Lanzhou U., 2004—06, prof., sch. stomatology, 2007—. Assoc. dean, faculty stomatology Lanzhou Med. Coll., 2000—01, dean, faculty stomatology, 2001—04; dean, sch. stomatology Lanzhou U., 2004—05, dir. dept. temporomandibular joint and occlusion, sch. stomatology, 2005—; mem. editl. com. Yearbook of Chinese Stomatology, Chengdu, Sichuan, 2005—. Editor: Jour. Stomatology, 2002—; contbr. articles to profl. jours. Commissary Com. Chronic Disease Control of Gansu Province, Lanzhou, 2002—08. Recipient 1st Prize award, Bayer Dental Co., Ltd., 1996, Sci.-Tech. Progress award, Gansu Province, 2003, 2005; scholar 1st Prize award, Heraeus-Kulzer Dental Co., 1998. Mem.: Chinese Stomatological Assn., Internat. Assn. Dental Rsch. (licentiate), Soc. Temporomandibular Disorders and Occlusion (licentiate). Avocations: swimming, bicycling. Home: Dong Gang Xi Rd #199 Lanzhou 730000 China Office: Lanzhou Univ Sch Stomatology Dong Gang Xi Rd #199 Lanzhou 730000 China Office Fax: 86 931 8915051. Personal E-mail: kanghong@lzu.edu.cn.

KANG, HYUN-SIK, physiologist; b. Jin-Ju, Republic of Korea, Mar. 3, 1964; s. Namsuon Kim and Ubong Kang; m. Shinuk Kim, July 8, 1989; children: Seamon, Unhae. PhD, Kent State U., 2000. Teaching Certificate Korean Ednl. Bd., 1987. Phys. edn. tchr. Kyongwon Mid. Sch., Changwon, Republic of Korea, 1989—90; tchr. (phys. edn.) Bansong Mid. Sch., Changwon, Republic of Korea, 1990—94; instr. Kent Sate U., Kent, 1995—2000; post-doctoral fellow Med. Coll. of Ga., 2000—02; asst. prof. Sungkyunkwan U., Suwon, Republic of Korea, 2003—. Exec. bd. Korean Exercise Sci. Acad., 2004—; profl. mem. Am. Coll. of Sports Medicine, Indpls., 1996—, North Am. Assn. for the Study of Obesity, Silver Spring, Md., 2001—03; profl. mem. and reviewer Korean Soc. for Exercise Nutrition, 2003—; exec. bd. mem. Korean Soc. for the Study of Obesity, 2003—; profl. mem. Korean Soc. of Sports Medicine, 2004—, Korean AAHPERD, 2003—. Contbr. scientific papers. Organizer Hypokinetic Diseases Prevention Program for Mid. Aged Women, Suwon, Republic of Korea, 2003—05. Rsch. Funding, Ohio Assn. of Health, Phys. Edn., Recreation and Dance, 1999. Office: Sungkyunkwan Univ 300 chunchun-dong Jangan-gu Kyonggi-do Suwon 440-746 Republic of Korea

KANG, INSUG, medical educator; b. Wonju, Republic Korea, Jan. 25, 1965; BS, Seoul Nat. U., 1987; PhD, SUNY, 1994. Rsch. asst. SUNY, Buffalo, 1989—93, postdoc. rsch. assoc., 1993—95; prof. biochemistry & molecular biology Kyung Hee U. Med. Sch., 1996—. Recipient Kohwang Med. Rsch. award, Kyung Hee U. Mem.: Korean Cancer Assn., Korean Chem. Soc., Korea Soc. Molecular Cell Biology, Korean Soc. Biochemistry and Molecular Biology. Avocation: tennis. Office: 1 Hoegi-dong Dongdaemun Seoul 130-701 Republic of Korea Office Fax: 82-2-965-6349. Business E-Mail: iskang@khu.ac.kr.

KANG, ISAMU YONG, retired nuclear medicine physician; b. Osaka, Japan, Aug. 27, 1939; came to U.S., 1966; s. Chi-Chieh and Ichi (Morita) K.; m. Midori Ishibashi, Mar. 15, 1971; children: Rika Florence, Hiroshi Frederick. MD, Kyushu U., Fukuoka, Japan, 1965. Diplomate Am. Bd. Pathology, Am. Bd. Nuc. Medicine. Intern Grad. Hosp. U. Pa., Phila., 1967-68; resident in pathology U. Calif., San Diego, 1972-74, Letterman Army Med. Ctr., San Francisco, 1974-76; resident in nuclear medicine Walter Reed Army Med Ctr., Washington, 1976-78; asst. chief nuclear medicine Walter Reed Army Med. Ctr., Washington, 1978-80; co-dir. clin. lab., nuclear med. staff physician Kaiser Permanente Med. Ctr., Oakland, Calif., 1980-86, dir. clin. lab. Richmond, Calif., 1980—86, chief nuclear medicine Walnut Creek, Calif., 1986—2000, radiation safety officer, 1986—2006; ret., 2006. Lt. col. U.S. Army, 1969-80, Vietnam; col. USAR, 1980-97, ret. With US Army, 1969—71, South Vietnam. Mem. Soc. Nuc. Medicine, Calif. Med. Assn. Buddhist. Avocations: jogging, golf, tennis, carpentry, reading. Home: 3554 Via Los Colorados Lafayette CA 94549-5332 Personal E-mail: i-kang@sbcglobal.net.

KANG, JAE GOO, otolaryngologist; b. Seoul, Republic of Korea, Aug. 2, 1967; s. Seok Ryul Kang and Il Nam Bang; m. Myung Hye Shin, May 8, 1999; children: Min Ji, Min Seo. BS, Seoul Nat. U., 1992, MS in Physiology, 1996; PhD, Chung-Buk Nat. U., 2002. Diplomate in med. Korean Bd. Med. Assn., 1992, in otolaryngology 1997. Internship Seoul Nat. U. Hosp., 1993, resident, 1994—97, instr. and fellow, 2000; head dept. Nat. Med. Ctr., Seoul, 2001—. Sci. dirs. Korean Soc. Aesthetic Surgery, Seoul, 2002—; mem. med. adv. bd. Korea Consumer Agy., Seoul, 2003—; manuscript reviewer Laryngoscope, Phila., 2005—. Contbr. articles to profl. jours. Lt. comdr. head dept. otolaryngology Ednl. Hdqs. Korean Navy, 1997—99, Jin Hae. Fellow: Korean Soc. Rhinology; mem.: Korean Acad. Otolaryngology-Head and Neck Surgery. Achievements include custom made osteotomy for deviated nose in Asians; endonasal application of modified septal extension graft for Asian tip surgery. Office: Nat Med Ctr Eulgiro 6-ga Jung-gu Seoul 100799 Republic of Korea Office Fax: 82222760534. E-mail: kwilly@paran.com.

KANG, JI HOON, neurologist, researcher; b. Jeju, Jeju-do, Republic of Korea, Feb. 18, 1968; s. Dae Won Kang and In Soon Moon; m. Yeon Soo Bae, Oct. 16, 1993; children: Min Ji, Na Yun. MD, Coll. Medicine, Seoul Nat. U., South Korea, 1992; PhD, Coll. Medicine, U. Ulsan, South Korea, 2003. Cert. microsoft sys. engr. 1999; neurology bd. Ministry Health & Welfare, Seoul, 2001, lic. neurology specialist. Neurology resident Asan Med. Ctr., Seoul, 1997—2001, fellow movement disorders, 2001—02; full time instr. Coll. Medicine, Cheju Nat. U., Jeju, 2002—04, prof., 2004—; fellow neuro-ophthalmology & neuro-otology Toronto We. Hosp., Ontario, Canada, 2005—06. Dir., Hosp. info. team Cheju Nat. U. Hosp., 2002—07, dir., ICU, 2003—04, dir., planning & control team, 2004—05, dir., Dept. Neurology, 2003—, head, Dept. Neurology, 2003—. Contbr. articles to profl. jours. Lt. Capital Armed Forces Combined Hosp., 1993—96, Seoul. Recipient award, Min. Edn. and Human Resources Devel., 2005. Mem.: Am. Acad. Neurology, Korean Stroke Soc., Korean Neurol. Assn. Buddhist. Avocations: travel, golf. Office: Cheju Nat Univ Hosp Ara1-Dong 1953-3 690-121 Jeju Jeju-do Republic of Korea Business E-Mail: jhkang@cheju.ac.kr.

KANG, JOON-SOON, orthopedist; b. Seoul, Republic Of Korea, Aug. 16, 1958; s. Nam-Chae Cho; m. Young-Sook Park, Oct. 25, 1986; children: Dong-Kwan, Dong-Hoon. PhD, Yonsei U. Med. Coll., Seoul, 1994. Cert. bd. dr. Korean Orthopaedic Assn., Seoul, 1988. Rsch. fellow JVL Orthopaedic Rsch. Ctr., LA, 1998—99; clin. fellow Centinela Hosp., LA, 1998—99; exec. sec. Korean Hip Soc., Seoul, 2002—04, editl. bd., 2001—; cons. Korean FDA Med. Device Divsn., Seoul, 2006—; bd. editor Korean Orthopaedic Assn., 2006—08. Contbr. articles to profl. jours. Capt. Korean Army, 1988—91, Seoul. Home: Bangpagu Bangii Dong 89 Olympic Apt 250 306 Songpagu Seoul 138 882 Republic of Korea Office: Inha Univ Hosp 3ga 7 206 400-711 Incheon Incheon Republic of Korea Office Phone: 82-32 890 2380. Office Fax: 032 890 3047. Business E-Mail: kangjoon@inha.ac.kr.

KANG, JU-SEOP, medical educator, consultant, medical researcher; b. Cheju, Republic of Korea, Feb. 2, 1961; s. Yong-Hee Lee; m. Tae-Eun Kim; children: Ji-Sook, Mina, Ryun. PhD, Hanyang U., Seoul, 1993. Diplomate Korea Food and Drug Adminstrn., Korea Rsch. Found. Rsch. and tchg. asst. Hanyang U., Republic of Korea, 1988—92, asst. prof. Seoul, 1993—2002, assoc. prof., 2003—04; vis. scholar Hosp. U. Pa., Phila., 2000—08, assoc. prof., 2004—06, prof., 2009—, mem. edn. com., 2005—, chief sec. Inst. Biomed. Scis., 2005—, chief dept. pharmacology, new drug devel., head Hanyang Food and Drug Adminstrn. Ctr., 2005—; CEO Pharmbrain Co., 2008—09. Dir. Mil. Gen. Lab., Republic of Korea, 1994—97; mem. drug rev. com. Korean Food and Drug Adminstrn., Seoul, 2000—11; mem. com. office rsch. integrity Hanyang U., Republic of Korea, 2007—. Author: Pharmacokinetic Books, Applied Pharmacokinetics, 2001; contbr. articles to profl. jours. Capt. Korean Mil., 1994—97. Mem.: Korean Soc. Food Sci. and Tech., Internat. Assn. Therapeutic Drug Monitoring and Clin. Toxicology, Korean Assn. Clin. Pharmacology and Therapeutics, Korean Assn. Pharmacology, Korean Assn. Applied Pharmacology. Avocation: golf. Office: Hosp Univ Pa Spruce St Philadelphia PA 19104 also: Hanyang Univ Pharmacology Coll Medicine 17 Haengdang Dong Sungdong Ku Seoul 133791 Republic of Korea Home: Hyundai Apt 106-301 Ungbong-dong Sungdong-ku Seoul 133-797 Republic of Korea Office Phone: 82-2-2220-0652. Business E-Mail: jskang@hanyang.ac.kr.

KANG, LIQING, medical association administrator; b. Huanghua, Hebei, China, Nov. 25, 1964; D, Tinanjin Med. U., 2005. Chief, dept. med. imaging Cangzhou Ctrl. Hosp., 2005—. Adj. prof. Hebei Med. U., 2008—10, prof., 2011. Recipient Sci. and Technol. Progress 1st prize, People's Govt. Cangzhou City, Sci. and Technol. Progress 2nd prize. Mem.: Chinese Med. Assn. Avocation: opera. Office: 16 W Xinhua Rd Yunhe Dist Cangzhou Hebei 061001 China Office Fax: 0086-317-2075763. E-mail: kangliqing168@vip.sohu.com.

KANG, SEONG-KYU, occupational health physician; s. Hee Sung Kang and Myung Soon Ryu; m. Soonie Chung, Jan. 10, 1961; children: Laura, Noorie. BS in Medicine, ChungNam Nat. U., Daejeon, 1983, MS in Medicine, 1985, PhD, 1993. Cert. occupl. physician Ministry Health, Republic of Korea, 1997, family physician Ministry Health, Republic of Korea, 1986, med. doctor Ministry Health, Republic of Korea, 1983. Resident physician Severance Hosp., Yonsei U., Seoul, Republic of Korea, 1983—86; mgr. dept. famly medicine Sun's Gen. Hosp., Daejeon, 1986—89; chief rschr. Inst. Occupl. Disease, Korea Labor Welfare Corp., Incheon, Republic of Korea, 1989—91; dir. Ctr. for Occupl. Disease Rsch. Korea Occupl. Safety and Health Agy., Incheon, 1992—2005, dir. dept. occupl. health, 2005—08; dir. gen. Occupl. Safety & Health Rsch. Inst., 2009—; bd. mem. Internat. Commn. on Occupl. Health, 2009—; editor-in-chief Safety and Health at Work, 2010—. Epidemic intelligence svc. officer Nat. Inst. Occupl. Safety and Health, CDC, Cin., 1995—97; sec. 9th Internat. Symposium on Neurobehavioral Methods and Effects in Occupl. and Envrionmental Health, Gyeongju, 2002—05, Sci. Com. Neurotoxicology, Internat. Commn. Occupl. Health, Milan, 2006—; advisor Ministry Labor and Invalids, Hochimin City, Vietnam, 2003. Author: The Origins of Occupational Health Associations; editor: (jour.) Jour. Occupl. Health, Indsl. Health, Korean Jour. Occupl. and Environ. Medicine; guest editor: jour. Neurotoxicology; contbr. articles to profl. jours. Capt. Korean Army, 1986—89. Recipient Excellence award, Pres. Rep. Of Korea, 2008. Achievements include patents for standard sample for analysing metablites of organic solvents; standard sample for analysing heavy metals in blood. Office: KOSHA 478 Munemi-ro Bupyeong-Gu 403-711 Incheon Incheon Republic of Korea Office Fax: 82-32-518-0863. Business E-Mail: skk@kosha.net.

KANG, SEONG-WOONG, physiatrist, educator; b. Jinzu, Republic of Korea, Oct. 11, 1959; s. Cha-Man Kang and Ok-Su Hwang; m. Hyun-Sook Kim, Nov. 7, 1987; children: Won-Suk, You-Suk. PhD, Yonsei U., Seoul, Republic of Korea, 1996. Intern Yongdong Severance Hosp, Seoul, 1985—86, resident, 1989—92; assoc. prof. medicine Yonsei U. Coll. Medicine, 2000—06, prof. medicine, 2006—; dir. Pulmonary Rehab. Ctr., Gangnam Severance Hosp., 2009—; chmn. Korean Acad. Rehab. Medicine, 2010—. Chmn. dept. rehab. medicine Gangnam Severance Hosp., Seoul, 2004—. Capt. South Korean armed forces, 1986—89. Mem.: Nat. Pension Corp. (advisory dr. 2004—), Korean Assn. Amyoprophy Lateral Sclerosis (bd. dirs. 2003—), Korean Orgn. Rare Diseases (bd. dirs. 2005—), Internat. Soc. Phys. and Rehab. Medicine (corr.), Korean Acad. Rehab. Medicine (life; bd. dirs. 2005—, Best Paper award 2002). Achievements include patents for device for pulmonary rehabilitation. Office: Gangnam Severance Hosp Gangnam PO Box 1217 Seoul 135-720 Republic of Korea Office Fax: 82-2-3463-7585. Business E-Mail: kswoong@yuhs.ac.

KANG, SEUNG-BAIK, physician; b. Seoul, Republic of Korea, May 28, 1959; MD, Seoul Nat. U., 1986, PhD, 1998. V.p. Boramae Med. Ctr., 2009—. Gender verification comdr. '88 Seoul Olympic Games Orgn. Com., 1987—89; prof. Chungbuk Nat. U. Coll. Medicine, 1995—96, prof. orthop. Seoul Nat. U., 1998; rsch. scientist Korean Inst. Sci. & Tech., 1996—97; vis. prof. Scripps Clinic, San Diego, 2001—02. Mem.: Korean Hip Soc. (Yr. Best Paper award 1995), Korean Knee Soc., Am. Orthop. Rsch. Soc., Korean Orthop. Assn. Avocation: golf. Office: 39 Boramae-Gil Dongjak-Gu Seoul 156-707 Republic of Korea Office Fax: 82-2-870-2709. E-mail: ossbkang@gmail.com.

KANG, SHIN-SUNG, biologist, educator; b. Seoul, Republic of Korea, Feb. 11, 1945; m. Young-Hee Min, Nov. 11, 1969; children: Min-Suk, Yoo-Lee. BS, Seoul Nat. U., 1969, MS, 1971; PhD, Cath. Med. Coll., Seoul, 1976; postgrad., Med. U. S.C., 1980-81. From lectr. to assoc. prof. Kyungpook Nat. U., Daegu, Republic of Korea, 1976-90, prof. Taegu, 1990—2010, prof. emeritus, 2010—, chmn. dept. premedicine Taegu, 1990-92, chmn. dept. biology, 1993-96, dir. rsch. inst. genetic engring., 1996-97, vice-dean acad. affairs, 1997-98, dean, planning coord., 1998—99; dir. Daegu Ctr., Korea Basic Sci. Inst., 2001—07. Asst., lectr. Cath. Med. Coll., Seoul, 1971-76; rsch. assoc. U. Ky., Lexington, 1982-84; vis. scientist Nat. Cancer Inst., Frederick, Md., 1995. Author: Biological Sciences, 1987, College Biology, 1991; contbr. articles to profl. jours. Mem. Zool. Soc. Korea (bd. dirs., editor 1988—2002, v.p. 1998-99, pres. 2003-04), Korean Soc. Molecular Biology (dir. 1991—, v.p. 2000), Genetic Soc. Koea (v.p. 1997-99, pres. 1999-2000), Korean Assn. Biol. Scis. (bd. dirs. 1984—, v.p. 2004-05, pres. 2006-07). Avocations: swimming, tennis, golf. Office: Kyungpook Nat U 702-701 Daegu Daegu Republic of Korea Office Phone: 82 16 504-5349. Business E-Mail: kangss@knu.ac.kr.

KANG, SUNG-DON, neurosurgeon, educator; b. Gwang-Ju, Jeonnam, Republic Of Korea, Oct. 12, 1957; s. So-Won Kang and Sang-Eui Kim; m. Mee-Sook Choi; children: Min-Ku, Hong-Ku. PhD, Jeonnam Grad. Sch., Gwang-Ju, 1992. Cert. neurosurgeon Korean Neurosurgical Soc., 1990. Physician Min. Health and Cmty., Seoul, 1982—, with, korean bd. neurosurgery, 1990—; intern Presbyn. Med. Ctr., Jeonju, Jeonbuk, Republic of Korea, 1982—83, resident, neurosurgery, 1986—90; instr. to assoc. prof. Wonkwang U., Iksan, Jeonbuk, 1990—2001, prof., 2001—, chmn., 2007—; rsch. fellowship Dept. Neurol. Surgery U. Va., Charlottesville, 1993—94. Com. mem. Korean Soc. Cerebrovascular Surgery, Seoul, 1990—, chmn., planning and pub. rels. com., 2006—07, editor, jour., 2007—08, sci. com. chmn., 2008—; bd. mem. dirs. Korean Neurosurgical Soc., Seoul, 2007—. Contbr. numerous articles to profl. jours. (Academic award, 2004). Surgeon Korean Army, 1983—86, Yangpyung, Gyunggi. Office: Wonkwang Univ Hosp Dept Neurosurgery Sinyongdong Iksan Jeonbuk 570-711 Republic of Korea Office Fax: 82-63-852-2606. Business E-Mail: kangsd@wonkwang.ac.kr.

KANG, YIBIN, medical educator, researcher; s. Haigen and Yapeng Kang; m. Ling Yun Lin, Jan. 3, 2000; 1 child, Michelle Z. BS in Genetics, Fudan U., Shanghai, China, 1995; PhD cand. in Genetics,

Mich. State U., East Lansing, Mich., 1995—96; PhD in Genetics, Duke U., Durham, NC, 2000. Grad. rsch. asst., Dept. Genetics and Howard Hughes Med. Inst. Duke U. Med. Ctr., Durham, NC, 1996—2000; postdoctoral rsch. assoc., Cell Biology Program and Howard Hughes Med. Inst. Meml. Sloan-Kettering Cancer Ctr., NYC, 2000—04; asst. prof., molecular biology Princeton U., NJ, 2004—; undergraduate rsch. asst., Dept. Genetics Fudan U., Shanghai, 1993—95. V.p. Duke U. Chinese Student and Scholar Assn., 1998—99; mem. Meml. Sloan-Kettering Cancer Ctr. Rsch. Fellow Adv. Group, 2001—; Meml. Sloan-Kettering Cancer Ctr. Campus rep. Science Next Wave, 2002—04; invited presenter/lectr. in field. Contbr. several articles to profl. jours. Recipient Advances in Mineral Metabolism-ASBMR John Haddad Young Investigator award, 2004, Meml. Sloan-Kettering Cancer Ctr. Ann. Postdoctoral Rsch. award, 2004, Era of Hope Scholar award, Dept. Def., 2006; Irvington Inst. Postdoctoral Fellowship in Immunological Rsch., 2001—04. Mem.: Metastasis Rsch. Soc., Chinese Biol. Investigator Soc., Am. Soc. Biochemistry & Molecular Biology, AAAS, Am. Assn. Cancer Rsch. (assoc.). Office: Princeton Univ Dept Molecular Biology Lewis Thomas Lab-255 Washington Rd Princeton NJ 08544 Office Fax: 609-258-2340. E-mail: ykang@molbio.princeton.edu.

KANG, YOOGOO, anesthesiologist, educator; b. Seoul, Apr. 10, 1946; s. Kiduk and Samkum (Koh) K.; m. Young H. Kim, Nov. 9, 1972; children: Michael N., David H. BS, Seoul U., Republic of, 1967, MD, 1971. Diplomate Am. Bd. Anesthesiology. Intern St. Raphael Hosp., New Haven, Conn., 1974-75; resident in surgery Albert Einstein Med. Ctr., Phila., 1975-76; resident in anesthesiology Thomas Jefferson U. Hosp., Phila., 1976-78; fellow in obstetric anesthesia Magee Women's Hosp., Pitts., 1978-79; asst. prof. U. Pitts., 1979-88, dir. hepatic transplantation anesthesiology, 1984-98, assoc. prof., 1989-93, prof., 1994-98; prof., chmn. dept. anesthesiology Tulane U. Med. Ctr., New Orleans, 1998-2000; prof. vice chmn. dept. anesthesiology Thomas Jefferson U., Phila., 2000—. Head Internat. Symposium in Liver Transplantation, Pitts., 1984-88. Editor: Hepatic Transplantation: Anesthetic Management and Perioperative Care, 1985, Anesthesia and Intensive Care for Patients with Liver Diseasae, 1995; assoc. editor Liver Surgery and Transplantation, 1993—; mem. editl. bd. Current Opinions in Organ Transplantation, 1996—. Med. officer Korean Army, 1971-74. Mem. Am. Soc. Anesthesiologists, Internat. Soc. Rsch. In Anesthesiology, Internat. Liver Transplantation Soc. (pres. 1989-93, mem. exec. coun. 1993-95, adv. bd. 1995—), Liver Intensive Care Group Europe. Avocations: woodwork, photography. Office: Thomas Jefferson U Dept Anesthesiology 111 S 11th St Ste 5480 Gibb Philadelphia PA 19107 5092 Business E-Mail: yoogoo.kang@jefferson.edu.

KANG, YOON KYOO, medical educator; b. Seoul, Republic of Korea, Nov. 16, 1957; m. Mi Kyung Park; 1 child, Tae Wook. MD, PhD, Korea U., 1993. Diplomate The Ministry of Health and Welfare, Republic of Korea, 1989. Prof. Coll. Medicine Korea U., Seoul, Republic of Korea, 1989—. Capt. Korean Army, 1983—86. Recipient President's Rsch. Initiative award, Am Acad. Electrodiagnostic Medicine, 2002, Med. Sci. award, Korean Med. Assn., 2005. Home: Hyundae Apartment 52-301 Apgujung-dong Seoul Republic of Korea Office: Anam Hospital 5-1 Anam dong Sungbuk gu Seoul 136 701 Republic of Korea Business E-Mail: yoonkang@korea.ac.kr.

KANG, YOON-KOO, oncologist, educator; b. Seoul, Korea, Mar. 18, 1957; s. Jung-Sik Kang; m. Young-Hee Lee, Oct. 10, 1987; children: Hyo-Min, Yurie, June-Mo. MD, Seoul Nat. U., 1981—81, PhD, 1992. Cert. Ministry Health and Welfare, diplomate in hematology/oncology Korean Soc. Internal Medicine. Chief hematology/oncology divsn. Korea Cancer Ctr. Hosp., Seoul, 1989—99, chief Exptl. Therapeutics Lab., 1995—99; rsch. fellow Nat. Cancer Inst., Bethesda, Md., 1992—93; prof. medicine Asan Med. Ctr. U. Ulsan, Seoul, 1999—; chief oncology/hematology divsn. Asan Med. Ctr., Seoul, 2003—05, dir. Clin. Rsch. Ctr., 2006—. Chmn. lymphoma com. Korean Cancer Study Group, Seoul, 2002—03. Capt. Army Dr., Spl. Forces, 1982—85, Bucheon, Korea. Mem.: Korean Med. Assn. (corr.), Korean Cancer Soc. (corr.), Am. Assn. Cancer Rsch. (corr.), European Soc. Med. Oncology (corr.), Am. Soc. Clin. Oncology (corr.). Office: Asan Med Ctr Univ Ulsan 388-1 Poongnap-dong Songpa-gu Seoul 138-736 Republic of Korea Office Fax: 82-2-3010-6961. Business E-Mail: ykkang@amc.seoul.kr.

KANG, YOUNG-HEE, nutritionist, educator; PhD, Rutgers U., NJ, 1988. Prof. Hallym U., Chuncheon, Kangwon-do, Republic of Korea, 1990—. Vis. scholar Klinikum Grossharden, Munich, 1995—96; chief editor Nutrition Rsch. and Practice. Recipient Prize for Ilsong paper publ., Hallym U., 2004, 2005, Outstanding Rsch. Paper award, KOFST, 2006. Mem.: Am. Physiol. Soc., Korea Nutrition Soc. Office: Hallym Univ Ockchon-Dong 200-702 Chuncheon Gangwon-do Republic of Korea Office Fax: 82332541475. E-mail: yhkang@hallym.ac.kr.

KANG, YOUNGMI, nursing educator; b. Republic of Korea, Sept. 22, 1971; PhD, U. Ariz., 2007. Asst. prof. U. Ark. Ft. Smith, 2009—. Rsch. assoc. U. Ariz., 2002—07; peer reviewer Geriatric Nursing, 2009. Recipient award, Asian Am. Faculty Alumni Assn., Judith Brain award, Nat. Gerontol. Nursing Assn. Mem.: Asian Am. Faculty, Staff, and Alumni Assn., Western Inst. Nursing, Nat. Gerontol. Nursing Assn. (Judith Braun award), Nat. League Nursing, Ark. Nursing Assn. Avocations: hiking, kabuki, knitting. Office: 5201 Grand Ave Fort Smith AR 72903 Office Fax: 479-424-6817. Business E-Mail: youngini.kang@uafs.edu.

KANG, YOUNG-SOOK, medical educator; b. Republic of Korea, Oct. 18, 1958; PhD in Pharmacy, Kanazawa U. Japan, 1990; Postdoc., UCLA Sch. Medicine, 1994. Prof. Sookmyung Women's U., 1994—. Rsch. fellow Alexander Von Humboldt Found. Germany, 1995—96. Recipient Academic Rsch. award, Korean Soc. Applied Pharmacology. Master: Pharm. Soc. Korea. Avocation: climbing. Office: 52 Hyochangwon-Gil Yongsan-Gu Seoul 140-742 Republic of Korea Office Phone: 82-2-710-9562. Office Fax: 82-2-710-9871. Business E-Mail: yskang@sm.ac.kr.

KANGAS, EDWARD A., healthcare company executive; b. 1942; m. Catherine Elizabeth Stephens, Sept. 17, 1994. BBA, U. Kansas, 1967, MBA. CPA NY, Conn. CPA, staff acct. Touche Ross & Co., Kansas City, 1967-74, ptnr., 1975-76, dir. mgmt. consulting ops., 1976-81, nat. dir. mgmt. consulting, 1981-85, mng. ptnr., CEO NYC, 1985-89; mng. ptnr. Deloitte and Touche USA LLP, NYC, 1989-94; global chmn, chief exec. Deloitte Touche Tohmatsu International, 1989—2000; cons. Deloitte Touche, Wilton, Conn., 2000—; non-exec. chmn. Tenet Healthcare Corp., Dallas, 2003—. Bd. dirs. Electric Data Systems Corp., 2004—, Intuit Inc., 2007—, United Technologies Corp., 2008—, Eclipsys Corp., Hovnanian Enterprises, Inc., Com. for Econ. Develop.; chmn. Oncology Therapeutics Networks. Bd. dirs., mem. fin. com., mem. and chmn. fund raising com. Nat. Multiple Sclerosis Soc.; trustee Com. Econ. Devel., U. Kansas Endowment Assn.; bd. overseers The Wharton Sch.; mem. U. Kansas Bus. Sch. Advisors Office: Tenet Healthcare Corp 13737 Noel Rd Dallas TX 75240 *

KANGO GOPAL, GOPINATH, physician; b. Vellore, India, Dec. 18, 1977; MBBS, Christian Med. Coll., 1999; MD in Geriat., Madras Med. Coll., 2006. Asst. prof. Christian Med. Coll., 2006—11; advanced trainee Queen Elizabeth Hosp., 2011—. Home: 5/7 Findon Rd Woodville Adelaide South Australia 5011 Australia Personal E-mail: gops95@yahoo.com.

KANG-SEUK, CHOI, veterinarian, researcher; b. Uiryeong, Kyoung-Sang-Nam-Do, Republic of Korea, Nov. 13, 1967; s. Choi Choeng-Ju and Lim Seong-Yeon; m. Kim Sang-Ae, June 8, 1969; children: Choi Dong-Hyun, Choi So-Yeon. DVM, Seoul Nat. U., 1991, MS, 1993; PhD, Chung-Buk Nat. U., 2003. Lic. vet. medicine Ministry Agr. & Forestry, 1991. Chief lab. Rinderepst and Other Diseases Nat. Vet. Res. and Quar. Svc., Anyang, Gyeonggi, Republic of Korea, 2001—05, chief lab. TSE Rsch., 2005—; lectr. Chung-Buk Nat. U., Cheongju, Chung-Chung-Nam-Do, 2004—. Expert dispatched Mongolia Korea Internat. Cooperation Agy., Seoul, 2003. Contbr. articles to profl. jours. Mem.: Korea Vet. Assn., Microbiological Soc. Korea, Korean Soc. Vet. Sci. Achievements include research in diagnostics of foreign animal diseases. Office: Nat Vet RES & QUAR Svc Anyang-6 Dong 480 430-824 Anyang Gyeonggi-do Republic of Korea Office Fax: (+82) 31 467 1814. Business E-Mail: choiks@nvrqs.go.kr.

KANICK, VIRGINIA, retired radiologist; b. Coaldale, Pa., Nov. 10, 1925; d. Martin and Anna (Pisklak) K. BA, Barnard Coll., 1947; MD, Columbia U., 1951. Diplomate Am. Bd. Radiology. Intern Western Reserve U. Hosps., Cleve., 1951-52; resident in radiology St. Luke's Hosp., NYC, 1952-55, attending radiologist, 1955-74; acting dir. radiology St. Luke's Roosevelt Hosp., NYC, 1981-84, dep. dir. of radiology, 1984-89; ptnr. West Side Radiology, NYC, 1989—2003; ret., 2003. Clin. prof. radiology Coll. Physicians and Surgeons Columbia U., N.Y.C., 1975—; pres. Med. Bd. St. Luke's Roosevelt Hosp., 1980-82. Contbr. articles to profl. jours. Bd. dirs. Health System Agy. of N.Y.C., 1978-81. Fellow Am. Cancer Soc., 1955. Fellow Am. Coll. Radiology; mem. Am. Roentgen Ray Soc., Radiol. Soc. N.Am., N.Y. County Med. Soc. (sec., dir. 1978—), N.Y. State Radiol. Soc. (bd. dirs. 1975—). Independent. Avocations: skiing, travel, archaeology. Home: 560 Riverside Dr Apt 14B New York NY 10027-3240 Office Phone: 212-666-7258. Business E-Mail: vk3@columbia.edu.

KANKAANRANTA, HANNU ILMARI, pulmonologist; b. Tampere, Finland, Apr. 4, 1967; m. Terhi Karttunen, Sept. 1995. MD, Med. Sch. U. Tampere, 1993, PhD, 1995. Cert. specialist in respiratory medicine and allergology U. Tampere, 2004, specialist in clin. pharmacology and drug treatment 2007. Acad. rschr. Acad. Finland, Tampere, 1995—97, sr. acad. scientist, 2005—07; rschr. Nat. Heart and Lung Inst., Imperial Coll., London, 1996—97; physician, specialization tng. dept. respiratory medicine and internal medicine Tampere U. Hosp., 1997—2004; assoc. prof. pharmacology U. Helsinki, Finland, 1998; assoc. prof. respiratory medicine & allegologgy U. Tampere, Finland, 2011, head, rsch. prof., 2004—05, prin. investigator, 2007; head, respiratory medicine Seinäjoki Ctrl. Hosp., Finland, 2007—. Bd. dirs. Finnish Med. Soc. Duodecim, Finland, 1992—93; advisor Nat. Agy. Medicines, Helsinki, Finland, 2000—06; advisor, several pharm. cos., 2000—; sec. gen. Finnish Pharm. Soc., Finland, 2004—06; pvt. practice, Tampere, 2005—09. Contbr. scientific papers (Young Scientist award, San Diego, 2000). Sgt. Med., 1986—87, Kankaanpää, Finland.

KANKARE, JYRKI HEIKKI ANTERO, orthopedic and trauma surgeon, spine consultant; b. Helsinki, Finland, Mar. 29, 1959; s. Antero and Tuulikki Kankare; m. Susanna Virrankoski; children: Vilja, Markus, Matti;children from previous marriage: Lotta, Johannes, Tuomas, Reetta, Sora. MD, U. Helsinki, 1986, Specialty Gen. Surgery, 1992, Specialty in Orthopedics and Traumatology, 1994, PhD, 1999. Med. diplomate. Asst. surgeon City Hosp., Helsinki, 1987-90, cons. in orthopedics and traumatology, 1994-95; asst. surgeon U. Hosp., Helsinki, 1990-94, cons. in orthopedics and traumatology, 1995—, head orthop. spine dept., 2001—. Med. cons. Ins. Co. Ilmarinen, Helsinki, 1994-96. Contbr. articles to profl. jours. Mem. Finnish Med. Assn., Finnish Surg. Soc., Finnish Orthopedic Assn., Finnish Soc. of Spine Surgery (pres., 2004—08), Spine Soc. Europe Eurospine Lutheran. Office: Ctrl Hosp PO Box 266 Helsinki 00029 Finland

KANKI, PHYLLIS JEAN, pathobiology educator; b. Chgo., Mar. 16, 1956; s. Mamoru and Mary Fuji (Okamoto) K. BS, Tufts U., 1978; DVM, U. Minn., 1982; DS, Harvard U., 1985; DSc (hon.), U. Ibadan, Nigeria, 2008. Lic. veterinarian, Minn. Pathology rsch. fellow Med. Sch. Harvard U., Boston, 1982-85, rsch. fellow Sch. Pub. Health, 1983-87, rsch. assoc. Sch. Pub. Health, 1987-89, rsch. scientist AIDS Inst. Cambridge, Mass., 1988—, asst. prof. pathobiology Sch. Pub. Health Boston, 1989-93, assoc. prof. pathobiology Sch. Pub. Health, 1993; prof. immunology and infectious diseases Harvard Sch. Pub. Health, Boston, dir. AIDS Prevention Initiative in Nigeria. Cons. on HIV-related viruses, simian retroviruses and AIDS, WHO, 1987—; mem. orgn. com. Internat. Conf. on AIDS in Africa and Related Cancers, 1987—; co-chair track C VIII Internat. Conf. on AIDS, Amsterdam, The Netherlands, 1992. Co-editor: AIDS in Africa, AIDS in Nigeria; mem. editorial bd. Jour. AIDS, 1988—; reviewer publs. in field; contbr. articles, revs. to profl. publs., chpts. to books. Recipient Instnl. Rsch. Svc. award NIH, award Am. Found. for AIDS Rsch., award for small animal medicine Mpls. Kennel Club; grantee U.S. Army, 1987—, NIH, 1990—. Fellow Leukemia Soc. Am.; mem. AAAS, Inst. Medicine, Am. Vet. Med. Assn., Infect Disease Soc. Am., Phi Zeta. Office: Dept Immunology and Infectious Diseases FXB Bldg 4th Fl 653 Huntington Ave Boston MA 02115 Office Phone: 617-432-1267. E-mail: pkanki@hsph.harvard.edu.

KANNO, MANABU, cardiologist, researcher; b. Sapporo, Hokkaido, Japan, Nov. 14, 1964; m. Chisato Kanno, Nov. 15, 1998; 1 child, Mizuki. MD, Sapporo Med. U., 1990; PhD, Hokkaido U., 2004. Med. staff Asahikawa Med. Coll., 1995—97, Hokkaido U. Med. Hosp., Sapporo, 1999—2004; sr. investigator Hokkaido U. Grad. Sch. Medicine, Sapporo, 2004—. Grantee, Akiyama Found., 2004—05;, CASIO Sci. Promotion Found. grantee, 2002—03. Fellow: Japanese Pharm. Soc., Japanese Soc. Internal Medicine; mem.: Japanese Circulation Soc. (bd. cert. mem. cardiology 2000). Office: Hokkaido U Grad Sch Medicine Dept Neuropharmacology Nish 7 Kita 15 Kita-ku Sapporo 060-8638 Japan Home Phone: 81-11-552-2518; Office Phone: 81-11-716-2111. E-mail: m-kanno@umin.ac.jp.

KANORIA, SANJEEV, medical educator; b. India, Sept. 18, 1963; MBA, La Martiniere Boys, PhD, 1988, U. Coll. London, 2009. Sr. lectr. Royal Free Hosp. and Med. Sch., 2010. Mng. dir. Asthaa Heatlh Care Ltd., 2006. Peter Samuel Royal Free Grant. Fellow: Royal Soc. Medicine, Royal Coll. Surgeons (Eng.). Avocations: squash, skiing. Home: 19 Hendon Ave London N3 1UJ England Personal E-mail: sanjkan@gmail.com.

KANSAKU, KENJI, neuroscientist; MD, Chiba U. Sch. Medicine, Japan, 1995; PhD, Chiba U. Grad. Sch. Medicine, 2000. Diplomate Japan, 1995. Resident Dept. Neurosurgery, Chiba U. Hosp., 1995—96; med. staff Dept. Neurosurgery, Kimitsu Ctrl. Hosp., Kisarazu, Chiba, 1996—97; rschr. Sys. Neurosci. Group, Neurosci. Rsch. Inst., Nat. Inst. Advanced Indsl. Sci. & Tech., Tsukuba, Ibaraki, Japan, 2000—01; vis. assoc., human motor control sect. Nat. inst. Neurol. Disorders Stroke-NIH, Bethesda, Md., 2001—04; asst. prof. Divsn. Cerebral Integration, Nat. Inst. Natural Scis., Okazaki, Aichi, Japan, 2004—06; chief Cognitive Functions Sect., Rsch. Inst. Nat. Rehab. Ctr. Persons with Disabilities, Tokorozawa, Saitama, Japan, 2006—10; chief sys. neurosci. sect. Rsch. Inst. Nat. Rehab. Ctr. Persons with Disabilities, Tokorozawa, Saitama, Japan, 2010—. Contbr. articles to profl. jours. Recipient NINDS Competitive Fellowship award, 2001. Office: Research Inst NRCD 4-1 Namiki Tokorozawa Saitama 359-8555 Japan

KANSU, EMIN, internist, hematologist, oncologist, educator; b. Istanbul, Turkey, Sept. 9, 1947; s. Tugrul Atuf and Rasende (Altmisdört) Kansu; m. Tulay Adile Sunman, Dec. 17, 1971; 1 child, Cem. MD, Hacettepe U., Ankara, Turkey, 1970. Bd. cert. internist Thomas Jefferson U. Coll. Medicine, Phila., 1974, bd. cert. hematologist Thomas Jefferson U. Coll. Medicine, Phila., 1978. Med. intern N.J. Med. Coll.-Jersey City Med. Ctr., 1971—72; resident internal medicine Thomas Jefferson U., Phila., 1972—74, chief fellow, instr., 1977—79; assoc. prof. Hacettepe U., Ankara, 1980—88, prof. medicine, 1988—, dep. dir. Inst. Oncology, 1982—99, chmn. dept. basic oncology Inst. Oncology, 1982—2009, dir. Hematopoietic Stem Cell Transplantation Unit, 2000—; dir. Inst. Oncology, 2009—. Lt. Turkish Air Force, 1976. Recipient Sci. Merit award, Turkish Sci. and Tech. Rsch. Coun., 1997, Eczacibasi Sci. Merit award, Istanbul, 1987. Fellow: ACP; mem.: Internat. Soc. Hematology (sec. gen. 2000—, v.p. 2009—), Am. Soc. Hematology, Alpha Omega Alpha. Avocations: tennis, jogging, bicycling. Office: Inst Oncology Hacettepe U Faculty Medicine 06100 Ankara Turkey Home Phone: +90-312-2666290; Office Phone: +90 312 3052994. Personal E-mail: eminkansu47@gmail.com.

KANT, SURYA, medical educator; b. Etawah, Jan. 1, 1965; MBBS, King George's Med. Coll., 1988, MD, 1992. Physician King George's Med. U. CSMMU, Lucknow, 1996—, prof., 2004. Recipient Charu Chandra Das Meml. award, TB Assn. Fellow: Nat. Coll. Chest Physician, Internat. Academic Med. Scis., Am. Coll. Physician. Office: CSMMU Dept Pulmonary Medicine Lucknow Uttar Pradesh 226003 India Office Fax: 00915222255167. E-mail: kant_skt@rediffmail.com.

KANTACHUVESIRI, ARREE, cardiologist, consultant; b. Bangkok, May 8, 1960; s. Bancha and Vimon Kantachuvesiri. MD with second class honors, Mahidol U., Bangkok, 1984, PhD in Tropical Medicine, 2005. Diplomate Thai Med. Bd. Internal Medicine, 1990, Thai Med. Bd. Cardiovasc. Medicine, 1992, Thai Med. Bd. Family Medicine, 2003. Instr. biochemistry dept. faculty medicine Siriraj Hosp., Mahidol U., Bangkok, 1985—87, resident internal medicine, 1987—90, fellow cardiovasc. medicine, 1990—92; staff cardiovasc. medicine Rajvithi Hosp., Bangkok, 1992—94, Vachira Hosp., Srinakharinwirot U., Bangkok, 1995—97; physician, cons. Phyathai 3 Hosp., Bangkok, 1998—; fellow interventional cardiology Phramongkut Hosp., Bangkok, 2003—. Mem. editl. bd.: S.E. Asian Jour. Tropical Medicine and Pub. Health, 2002—05, Thai Jour. Epidemiology, 2003, Jour. Med. Assn. Thai, 2005; contbr. articles to profl. jours. Mem.: Endocrine Assn. Thailand, Heart Assn. Thailand, Royal Coll. Physicians Thailand. Avocations: reading, exercise, bicycling, travel, television. Office: Phyathai 3 Hosp Petkasem Rd Bangkok 10160 Thailand Home: 37/74-75 Petkasem Rd 10160 Bangkok Bangkok Thailand Office Phone: 662 869 1111. Personal E-mail: akanta@medscape.com.

KANTARCI, KEJAL, radiologist, researcher; b. Istanbul, Turkey, Dec. 1, 1969; arrived in U.S., 1998; d. Vehbi and Gülseren Aydin; m. Orhun H. Kantarci, Nov. 25, 1994. Degree, Am. Acad. Girls, Istanbul, 1987; MD, Marmara U., Istanbul, 1993; MSc in Clin. and Translational Rsch., Mayo Grad. Sch., 2009. Resident Istanbul U., 1993—97; radiologist pvt. practice, 1997—98; asst. prof., assoc. cons. Mayo Clinic, Rochester, Minn., 2004—, assoc. prof., 2009. Contbr. chapters to books; mem. editl. bd.: Neurosci. Imaging, 2004—. Recipient Paul Beeson Career Devel. in Aging award, Nat. Inst. on Aging, 2007; fellow, Mayo Clinic, 1998—2004; scholar, NIH, 2005—. Mem.: Internat. Soc. Magnetic Resonance Medicine, Radiol. Soc. N.Am. Avocations: mountain climbing, scuba diving, bicycling. Office: Mayo Clinic 200 First St Rochester MN 55905 Office Phone: 507-284-9770. E-mail: kantarci.kejal@mayo.edu.

KANTER, JOLIE LYNN, psychologist; 1 child, Ariel Simone Mydlo. PhD, Yeshiva U. Assoc. dir. Psychotherapy Resources, PLLC, NYC. Contbr. articles to profl. jours. Activities cons. for cmty. garden and bird sanctuary Green Thumb, Bronx. Mem.: Am. Bd. Hypnotherapy, Am. Acad. Experts in Traumatic Stress, Acad. Cert. Expressive Therapists, Nat. Inst. Expressive Therapy (cert.), Nat. Expressive Therapy Assn., Assn. for Integrative Medicine, Phi Eta, Psi Chi. Achievements include research in obesity and cancer.

KANTOR, HARVEY SHERWIN, medical educator; b. NYC, Apr. 30, 1938; s. Jack and Henrietta (Feingold) K.; m. Elvia Frostick, Nov.

8, 1992; stepchildren: Harold, Eric Frostick. Student, U. Miami, 1955-58; MD, Washington U., 1962; postgrad., MIT, 1967-69. Diplomate Am. Bd. Internal Medicine, Am. Bd. Pathology certification in Medical Microbiology, Am. Bd. Infectious Diseases. Instr. U. Miami Sch. Medicine, 1969-71; asst. prof. medicine and microbiology U. Ill. Sch. Medicine, Chgo., 1971-75; assoc. prof. medicine and pathology Chgo. Med. Sch., North Chgo., Ill., 1975—93; dir. divsn. infectious diseases VA Med. Ctr., North Chicago, 1975-85, chief med. microbiology, 1985-92; prof. internal medicine Tex. Tech. U. Health Sci. Ctr., Odessa, 1993—2002, dir. divsn. infectious diseases, 1993—2002, interim chmn. dept. internal medicine, 2000—02; clin. prof., dept. medicine Rosalind Franklin U. Medicine and Sci./Chgo. Med. Sch., 2005—. Contbr. chpts. to textbooks, articles to profl. jours. Capt. U.S. Army, 1964-66. Recipient NIH postdoctoral fellowship in infectious diseases New Eng. Med. Ctr. Hosp., Boston, 1966-69, U. Health Scis./Chgo. Med. Sch. Bd. Trustees Rsch. award, 1977, Master Educator award Rosalind Franklin U. Medicine, Chgo. Med. Sch., 2010. Fellow ACP, Infectious Diseases Soc. Am.; mem. Am. Soc. Microbiology, Soc. Hosp. Epidemiology in Am. Avocations: cooking, photography, computers.

KANTOR, STEPHEN RICHARD, orthopedic surgeon; b. Montreal, Que., Canada, Dec. 10, 1969; s. Jonathan Kantor and Joyce Kramer, Beatrice Kantor (Stepmother); m. Kimberly Jagodnik, May 30, 1999; children: Drew Rhyan children: Avery Brooke; 1 child, Morgan Lily. BSc, McGill U., Montreal, 1992, Master of Surgery, 1996, MD, 1996. Cert. physician and surgeon NH. Med. Bd. Orthop. surgery resident McGill U., Montreal, 1996—2002; clin. instr. U. So. Calif., LA, 2002—03; vol. faculty U. Calif., San Diego, 2003—04; assoc. physician Orthop. Med. Group San Diego, 2003—04; asst. prof. orthop. surgery Dartmouth Med. Sch., Hanover, NH, 2004—; attending orthop. surgeron Dartmouth-Hitchcock Med. Ctr., Lebanon, NH, 2004—. Contbr. articles to profl. jours. Mem. univ. senate McGill U., Montreal, 1992—94. Recipient Joseph Sugar award for orthop., McGill U. Faculty Medicine, 1996, Eugene Rogala prize in orthop., 2000, 2001, 2002; Arthritis and Jt. Reconstrn. fellow, U. So. Calif., Keck Sch. Medicine, 2003, U. Calif., San Diego and San Diego Arthritis Surgery Ctr., 2004. Mem.: NH. Med. Soc., Calif. Orthop. Assn., Internat. Soc. for Tech. in Arthroplasty, Med. Coun. Can. (licentiate), Am. Acad. Orthop. Surgeons (assoc.), Can. Orthop. Assn. (assoc.). Achievements include multiple published research projects relating to the design and function of orthopaedic joint replacement implants. Office: Dartmouth-Hitchcock Med Ctr One Medical Ctr Dr Lebanon NH 03756 Office Fax: 603-650-2097. E-mail: kantormd@yahoo.com.

KANY, JUDY C(ASPERSON), retired state senator; b. Ill., June 29, 1937; d. Helmer C. and Florence P. Casperson; m. Robert Kany, Aug. 16, 1958; children: Kristin, Geoffrey, Daniel. BBA, U. Mich., 1959; MPA, U. Maine, Orono, 1976. Mem. Maine Ho. of Reps., 1975-82, Maine Senate, 1982-92; project dir. for health professions regulation Med. Care Devel., Augusta, Maine, 1993—; mem. task force on health workforce regulation Pew Health Professions Commn., 1994-97; mayor Waterville, Maine, 1988-89; mem. issues and policy adv. com. Citizens Advocacy Ctr., Washington, 1994—2000; cmty. liaison Amity Circle Tree Ranch, Tucson, 2003—. Chmn. Maine's Adv. Commn. on Radioactive Waste, 1981-87, Joint Standing Com. Legal Affairs, 1987-88, Joint Standing Com. on State Govt., 1979-82, Joint Standing Com. Energy and Natural Resources, 1983-84, 89-90, Joint Standing Com. Banking and Ins., 1991-92, com. Maine Lakes, 1990-92, adv. com. on accountability to the Maine Health Care Reform Commn., 1994-95; mem. Commn. on Maine's Future, 1976, 87-89; project coord. Amity Found.'s Ariz Gov.'s Innovative Domestic Violence Prevention Grant, Amity, 2004-06. Democrat. Home: 36832 S Stoney Flower Dr Tucson AZ 85739 Business E-Mail: jkany@amityfdn.org.

KAO, CHENG HSING, physician, educator; b. Kaohsiung City, Taiwan, Mar. 10, 1953; B, Nat. Def. Med. Ctr., 1979. Dir. Chi Mei Med. Ctr., 1980—; clin. prof. Nat. Def. Med. Ctr., 2007—; asst. prof. Southern Taiwan U. Tech., 2008—. Pres. Taiwan Soc. Minimally Invasive Spine Surgery, 2007—09, Taiwan Neurospinal Soc., 2005—07; co-chmn., exec. mem. AP Cervical Spine Soc., 2009; rep. Internat. SAS-Taiwan Chpt.; chmn. Chinese Conf. Spine. Fellow: Internat. Coll. Surgeons; mem.: North Am. Spine Soc., Spine Soc. Europe. Office: 901 Zhonghua Rd Yungkang Dist Tainan 710 Taiwan Office Phone: 886-6-2812811, 886-6-2812811. Office Fax: 886-6-2824178. Personal E-mail: georgekao10@hotmail.com. Business E-Mail: spine@mail.chimei.org.tw.

KAO, CHIA-HUNG, nuclear medicine researcher; b. Taipei, Taiwan, Aug. 8, 1963; s. San-Lang and Yang-Hsiu-Jen Kao; m. Mei-Chi Wang. B in Medicine, China Med. U., 1988. Resident Taichung Veterans Gen. Hosp., 1988-92, chief resident, 1992-93, attending physician, 1993—; asst. prof. China Med. U., Taichung, 1996—2000, assoc. prof., 2000—; chief, dept. nuc. medicine China Med. U. Hosp., 2000—. Contbr. more than 260 sci. papers to profl. jours. Recipient rsch. award Nat. Sci. Coun., Taiwan, 1991-96, Excellent Med. Paper award Chen-Hsing Found. of Taiwan Medicine, 1992, Important Contbn. to Rsch. award Kaohsiung Jour. Med. Scis., 1993, Rsch. award for clin. physician Inst. Biomed. Scis., Sinica Acad., Taiwan, 1995, Excellent Med. Paper award Chinese Med. Assn., Taipei, 1995, Excellent contbn. award Taichung Vets. Gen. Hosp., 1992, 95, 96, 97, Prof. Chen-Fang-Wu award of excellent paper Soc. Endocrinology, Taipei, 1995, Award of Disting. Young Investigators of 6th Asia and Oceania Congress of Nuc. Medicine and Biology, Young award Medal, Republic of China, 1997, Excellent Young Medal award, Spl. Contbn. Doctor, Taichung, 1997. Mem. Soc. Nuc. Medicine, European Assn. Nuc. Medicine, Am. Soc. Nuc. Medicine. Avocations: golf, bowling, reading, singing, movies. Office: China Med Univ Hosp 2 Yuh Der Rd Taichung 404 Taiwan Personal E-mail: kaoch5288@kimo.com.tw.

KAO, LEE C., physician; b. Dec. 20, 1958; MD, Taipei Med. U., 1983; PhD, U. Pa., 1991. Physician Laurel Fertility Care, 2007—. Office: 1700 Calif St Ste 570 San Francisco CA 94109 E-mail: drkao@laurelfertility.com.

KAO, RUEY HO, hematologist, oncologist; b. Taipei, Taiwan, June 21, 1959; s. Ho Hsiong Kao and Su Mei Jen; m. Ying Shen Wu, Sept. 29, 1990; children: Yun Chi, Yun Ya, Yun Shuo. B of Medicine, Taipei Med. Coll., 1986; PhD, King's Coll.U. London, 1999. Clin. instr. Tzu Chi Med. Sch., Hualien, Taiwan, 1994—95, assoc. prof., 2004—, dir. dept. oncology, 2000—; dir. hematology-oncology Tzu Chi Gen. Hosp., 2000—. Vis. physician Fred Hutchinson Cancer Rsch. Ctr., Seattle, 2003; dir. dept. med. edn. Inst. Rev. Bd., Tzu. Chi Gen. Hosp., Hualien, 2005—08; dir. Tzu Chi Cancer Ctr., 2008—; vice supt. Tzu Chi Gen. Hosp., 2008—. Author: Metastasis Research Protocol, 2001. Scholar, King's Coll. U. London, 1997. Mem.: Nat. Health Rsch. Inst. (breast cancer com. 1999—), Chinese Bone Marrow Transplantation Soc., Chinese Oncology Soc. Achievements include discovery of differential expression of heat shock cognate 70 gene between human mammary carcinoma and normal mammary glandular cells. Avocations: travel, reading, hiking, china collecting, movies. Office: Tzu Chi Gen Hosp 707 Sect 3 Chung Yang Rd Hualien 970 Taiwan Office Phone: 886-3-8561825. Office Fax: 03 8577161. Business E-Mail: rueykao@tzuchi.com.tw.

KAO, SHANG-JYH, internist; b. Taiwan, Aug. 5, 1950; MD, Nat. Def. Med. Ctr. Sch. Medicine, 1975. Chair, dept. internal medicine Shin Kong Wu Ho-Su Meml. Hosp., 2003—07, chair, dept. health mgmt., 2011—. Prof. medicine Taipei Med. U., 2007—11. Recipient Outstanding Physician award, Taipei Assn. Physicians and Surgeons. Mem.: Taiwan Soc. Pulmonary and Critical Care Medicine. Avocations: golf, music, motorcycling. Office: 95 WenChang Rd ShiLin Dist Taipei 11101 Taiwan Office Fax: 886-2-28389335. Business E-Mail: m001002@ms.skh.org.tw.

KAORU, ONO, medical researcher; b. Hiroshima, Japan, May 18, 1971; PhD, Hiroshima U., 2010. Chief med. physicist Hiroshima Heiwa Clinic, 2008—. Office: 1-31 Kawaramachi Naka-ku Hiroshima 730-0856 Japan Business E-Mail: koukun@ms4.megaegg.ne.jp.

KAOUK, JIHAD H., urologist; m. Rula Hajj-Ali; children: Sahar, Reem, Reda. BS, Am. U. Beirut, 1989, MD, 1993. Intern and resident in urology and surgery Am. U. Beirut, 1993—99; fellow in advanced laparoscopic surgery Rsch. Urol. Inst., Cleve. Clinic Found., 1999—2002; dir. Ctr. for Advanced Laparoscopic and Robotic Surgery, Glickman Urological & Kidney Inst., Cleve. Clinic, 2002—; assoc. prof. surgery Cleve. Clinic., 2002—. Cons., spkr. Endocare, Inc., Intuitive Surgical Inc. Contbr. articles to profl. jours. Recipient First prize in the 18th World Congress on Endourology and Shockwave, Sao Paulo, Brazil, 2000, Coun. America, 2005-2006 Recognition award, ACS, Lebanon Chpt. XIth Clin. Congress, 2005; named one of America's Top Physicians in Urology, Consumers' Rsch. Coun., 2005—07. Mem.: Endourological Soc., Am. Urol. Assn. (assoc.). Achievements include research in surgical techniques in urology such as Laparoscopic and minimally invasive surgery for bladder cancer, prostate cancer, and kidney diseases; performed initial lab work that helped in development of laparoscopic radical cystectomy & urinary diversion that is widely performed at present; developed a technique for robotic radical prostatectomy and sural nerve grafting. This technique allows the surgeon to graft a nerve from the patient's leg to the area of excised prostate to restore continuity of nerves responsible for potency in men; developed a technique of nerve-sparing robotic radical prostatectomy that uses laser energy to dissect tissue with minimal collateral damage; pioneered single-port laparoscopic surgery in urology. Laparoscopic surgery usually requires several small incisions. With single-port surgery, was able to perform various laparoscopic procedures through a single incision. Most of these procedures were first ever done in urology such as single-port laparoscopic nephrectomy, cryoablation, renal cyst excision, sacrocolpopexy, varicocelectomy, radical prostatectomy and radical cystectomy; designed an instrument that can be used to perform laparoscopic partial nephrectomy with minimal risk of bleeding and without the need for advanced laparoscopic skills. The device uses radiofrequency ablation to create a bloodless zone around kidney tumor, then one can pass a knife to cut the tumor (patented device, received the Innovator Award for this device in 2006); development of new robotic urologic surgery techniques, pioneered lopanscopic single port surgery that leaves no visible scan after surgery, performed first in the world kidney surgery through the original approach. Office: Cleve Clinic Found Robotic Laparoscopic Single Port Surgery 9500 Euclid Ave Mail Code Q10-1 Cleveland OH 44195 Office Phone: 216-444-2976.

KAPADIA, SAMIR R., cardiologist, educator; b. Ahmedabad, India, Nov. 15, 1966; MBBS, Smt NHLM Med. Coll. Gujarat U., India, 1989. Cert. Internal Medicine, Cardiology, Interventional Cardiology. Intern, internal medicine Smt NHLM Med. Coll. Gujarat U., India, 1989—90, Baylor Coll. Medicine, Houston, 1991—92, resident, internal medicine, 1992—93, rsch., cardiology, 1993—95; fellow Cleve. Clinic Found., Ohio, 1995—2000, staff interventional cardiologist, dept. cardiovascular medicine Ohio, 2003—; cardiac. dir. Catherization Lab.; assoc. prof. Cleve. Clin. Sch. Medicine, Ohio, 2003—; former interventional cardiologist Puget Sound Health Care Sys., Vet. Adminstrn. Hosp., Seattle, Ohio; former acting asst. prof. medicine, dept. medicine U. Wash., Seattle. Contbr. chapters to books, several articles to peer-reviewed jours.; editl. reviewer Circulation, Jour. Am. Coll. Cardiology, Cytokine, Jour. AMA. Named one of Top Doctors, Cleve. Mag., 2004—10. Fellow: Am. Coll. Cardiology; mem.: Am. Heart Assn. Office: Cleveland Clinic Dept Cardiovascular Medicine 9500 Euclid Ave J2-3 Cleveland OH 44195 Office Phone: 216-444-6735. Office Fax: 216-445-6176.

KAPALE, SADHANA DILIP, medical laboratory technician; b. Mumbai, Jan. 12, 1958; d. Bhagawan Dinkar Kale; m. Dilip Trimbak Kapale, May 22, 1979; children: Deepti Amit Kulkarni, Saurabh Dilip. BSc, L.A.D. Coll., Nagpur, 1976; Diploma in Med. Lab. Tech., Govt. Med. Coll., Nagpur, 1993. Lab. technician Microbiology Dept. Govt. Med. Coll., Maharashtra, 1977—. Sec. Maharashtra State Unit Lab. Technician's Assn., Nagpur, 1997—2000; with USAID, India CLEN, IIDI, ICMR. Contbr. to profl publs. (1st prize All India med. Lab. Technologist Assn., 2005, 2nd prize Lab. Technician Assoc. Maharashtra State, 1995, 2nd prize state Conf. AIMLTA Nagpur, 1986). Recipient Letter of Appreciation, Dean Govt. Med. Coll., Nagpur. Office: Govt Med Coll Med Sq Hanumannagar Nagpur Maharashtra 440003 India

KAPAMAJIAN, MICHAEL ALEXAN, ophthalmologist; b. LA, Feb. 17, 1979; BS, UCLA, 2001, MD, 2005. Svc. asst. chief Doheny Eye Inst., 2010—. Attending resident, clinic adminstrn. LAC-USC Med. Ctr., 2010—. Mem.: Am. Gloucoma Soc., Am. Uveitis Soc., Am. Acad. Ophthalmology. Avocations: bowling, poetry, astronomy. Home: 115 E Del Mar Blvd #402 Pasadena CA 91105 Personal E-mail: mkapa17@yahoo.com.

KAPELMAN, BARBARA ANN, hepatologist, gastroenterologist, educator, medical informaticist; b. NYC, Apr. 30, 1949; d. Leonard A. and Helen (Hass) K.; m. Lawrence William Koblenz, Mar. 24, 1979; 1 child, Adam. BA, Barnard Coll., 1970; MS in Microbiology, Yale U., 1972; MD, Albert Einstein Coll. Medicine, 1975; MS in Med. Informatics, Northwestern U., 2011. Diplomate Am. Bd. Internal Medicine, Am. Bd. Gastroenterology. Clin. asst. prof. hepatology and gastroenterology Mt. Sinai Sch. Medicine Mt. Sinai Hosp., 1981—82; intern Roosevelt Hosp.-Columbia U., NYC, 1975-76, resident, 1976-78, fellow gastroenterology, 1978-80; fellow liver diseases Mt. Sinai Sch. Medicine-CUNY, NYC, 1980-81; attending physician liver diseases Mt. Sinai Hosp., NYC, 1981—82; asst. attending physician in gastroenterology Beth Israel Hosp., NYC, 1982-88, assoc. attending physician in medicine and gastroenterology, 1988-96, attending physician in medicine and gastroenterology, 1996—2008, Montefiore Med. Ctr., 2008—10; clin. instr. in medicine Mt. Sinai Sch. of Medicine, NYC, 1981-87, asst. clin. prof. medicine, 1987-94; bd. dirs. Beth Israel Med. Ctr., NYC, 1984—, trustee, med. liaison, 1996-97; asst. clin. prof. medicine Albert Einstein Coll. Medicine, NYC, 1994—; dir., clin. content Cath. Health East, 2010—. Trustee Med. Bd. Liaison, 1996-97; attending physician Beth Israel North, Beth Israel Med. Ctr., N.Y.C., 1982—2008, Hosp. for Joint Diseases-Orthopedic Inst., N.Y.C., 1982—2008, Montefiore Med. Ctr., 2008-; vis. clin. fellow Columbia U. Coll. Physicians and Surgeons, N.Y.C., 1975-80; cons. gastroenterology and hepatology, 2004—. Co-author: Gastroenterology for the House Officer, 1989; contbr. articles to profl. jours. Fellow ACP, Am. Coll. Gastroenterology; mem. AMA, Am. Women's Med. Assn., Women's Med. Assn. NYC (officer), Am. Gastroent. Assn., Am. Assn. for Study of Liver Diseases, Am. Soc. for Gastrointestinal Endoscopy, Am. Med. Informatics Assn., NY Acad. Gastroenterology, NY Soc. for Gastrointestinal Endoscopy. Home: 630 W 246th St Ste 1024 Bronx NY 10471-3644

KAPIKIAN, ALBERT ZAVEN, physician, epidemiologist; b. NYC, May 9, 1930; s. Zareh Kaloust and Baizar (Bazikian) K.; m. Catherine Firth Andrews, Feb. 27, 1960; children: Albert Kaloust, Thomas Firth, Gregory Baird. BS cum laude, Queens Coll., 1952; MD, Cornell U., 1956; postgrad., Johns Hopkins U. Sch. Hygiene and Pub. Health, 1961-62, Royal Postgrad. Med. Sch. U. London, 1970; DSc (hon.), CUNY, Queens, 1999. Intern Meadowbrook Hosp., Hempstead, NY, 1956-57; with epidemiology sect. Lab. Infectious Diseases, Nat. Inst. Allergy and Infectious Diseases, NIH, Bethesda, Md., 1957—, Lab. Viral Diseases, 1967—68; asst. chief, head epidemiology sect. Lab. Infectious Diseases, Nat. Inst. Allergy and Infectious Diseases, NIAID, NIH, 1967—2010; commd. med. officer USPHS, 1957, advanced through grades to capt., ret., 1988, with civil svc., 1988-90, with sr. exec. svc., 1990-2000, with sr. biomed. rsch. svc., 2000—01, sr. investigator, 2001—; rsch. prof. child health and devel. George Washington U. Sch. Medicine and Health Svcs., 1977—2006. Temporary advisor WHO, 1980-88, 91, 2006, 2007 Contbr. articles to profl. jours. Recipient Meritorious Svc. medal USPHS, 1970, 74, Disting. Svc. medal USPHS, 1983, Disting. Alumnus award Queens Coll., 1974, Stitt award Assn. Mil. Surgeons, 1974, Kabakjian award Armenian Students Assn. Am., 1974, Diagnostic Virology award (Murex) Pan Am. Soc. for Clin. Virology, 1993, joint recipient Pasteur award Children's Vaccine Initiative, 1998; invited to deliver Theobold Smith Lectr., 1995, Kinyoun Lectr., 1999, NIH Dirs. Lectr., 2000, Wyeth-Ayerst Rhesus Rotavirus Project Team award, 1995, Queens Coll Alumni Star award, 1998, Presdl. Disting. Exec. Rank award, 2000, award of distinction Cornell U. Weill Med. Coll. Alumni Assn., 2001, Butantan medal, Sao Paulo, Brazil, 2005, Albert B. Sabin Gold medal, Sabin Vaccine Inst., 2005, Disting. Svc. award Dept. Health & Human Svc., Rotavirus Rsch. Team, 2006, Merit award NIAID, 2008; named to Leon G. Smith Infectious Disease Hall of Fame, St. Michael's Med. Ctr., 2000. Fellow AAAS, Infectious Disease Soc.; mem. APHA, Am. Epidemiol. Soc. (pres. 1996-97), Am. Soc. Microbiology (Behring Diagnostics award 1987), Am. Soc. Virology, Phi Beta Kappa. Mem. Armenian Apostolic Ch. Home: 11201 Marcliff Rd Rockville MD 20852-3631 Office: NIH Lab Infectious Diseases Bethesda MD 20892-0001

KAPLAN, ALAN LESLIE, gynecology educator, oncologist, department chairman; b. Atlanta, Sept. 10, 1930; children: John, Robert; m. Cissie Rauch Kaplan, Feb. 13, 2004. AB, Washington and Lee U., 1951; MD, Columbia U., 1955. Diplomate Am. Bd. Ob-Gyn. Intern Jackson Meml. Hosp., Miami, Fla., 1955-56; resident in ob-gyn Columbia-Presbyn. Med. Ctr., NYC, 1956-59, 61-63; prof. dept. ob-gyn, dir. divsn. gynecologic oncology Baylor Coll. Medicine, Houston, 1963—2005; prof. dept. ob-gyn Cornell U., 2005—; chmn. dept. ob-gyn The Meth. Hosp., Houston, 2005—. Med. dir. gynecologic oncology program Meth. Hosp., Houston, 1989—. Capt. M.C., U.S. Army, 1959-61. Mem. ACS, AMA, Am. Coll. Obstetricians and Gynecologists, Am. Cancer Soc., Am. Soc. Clin. Oncology, Soc. Gynecol. Oncology, Houston Gynecol. and Obstet. Soc. Office: Smith Tower Ste 901 6550 Fannin Houston TX 77030 Office Phone: 713-441-3193. Business E-Mail: akaplan@tmhs.org.

KAPLAN, BARRY HUBERT, physician; b. Bklyn., Nov. 16, 1938; s. Samuel and Mildred (Rabiner) K.; m. Rosalind Perlow Kaplan, June 23, 1962; children: Andrew, Scott. BA summa cum laude, NYU, 1958; MD, Johns Hopkins U., 1962, PhD, 1967. Diplomate Am. Bd. Internal Medicine, Am. Bd. Hematology, Am. Bd. Med. Oncology. Intern in medicine Johns Hopkins Hosp., 1962-63; fellow dept. physiol. chem. Johns Hopkins Sch. of Medicine, 1963-64; rsch. assoc. NIH, 1964-66; resident in medicine Bronx Mcpl. Hosp. Ctr., 1966-67; assoc. in medicine Albert Einstein Coll. Medicine, 1967-70, asst. prof. medicine, 1970-75, asst. prof. biochemistry, 1973-82, acting dir., divsn. med. oncology, 1974-81, acting assoc. dir. clin. rsch., Cancer Ctr. to assoc. dir., 1975-82, assoc. prof. medicine, 1975-82, assoc. clin. prof. medicine, 1982-93, vis. clin. assoc. prof. of medicine, 1993-95; clin. assoc. prof. of medicine Cornell Med. Coll., 1995—. Dir. divsn. med. oncology Albert Einstein Coll. Medicine, 1981-82, vis. asst. prof. biochemistry, 1982-87; physician in charge med. oncology Booth Meml. Med. Ctr., 1985-91, physician in charge med. oncology/hematology N.Y. Hosp. Med. Ctr. of Queens, 1991—; pres. Queens Med. Assocs., 2001—; asst. attending physician Bronx Mcpl. Hosp. Ctr., 1967-71; attending physician The Weiler Hosp. of the Albert Einstein Coll. of Medicine, 1972-93, Bronx Mcpl. Hosp. Ctr., 1972-93, Westchester Square Hosp., Bronx, 1982-93, Union Hosp., 1983-91, N.Y. Hosp. Med. Ctr. of Queens, 1983—. Contbr. articles to profl. jours. Mem. Am. Assn. for Cancer Rsch., Am. Soc. for Clin. Oncology, Am. Soc. Hematology, N.Y. Cancer Soc. (pres. 1981-82), Am. Cancer Soc. (N.Y.C. divsn. bd. dirs. 1981-84, steering com. profl. ednl. and grants com. 1981-83), Queens County Med. Soc., Phi Beta

Kappa (Edward J. Noble Found. fellowship student leadership 1958-62). Home: 17660 Union Tpke Ste 360 Fresh Meadows NY 11366-1531 Office Phone: 718-460-2300. Personal E-mail: bhkaplan@aol.com. Business E-Mail: bhakap@nyc.rr.com.

KAPLAN, BERNARD S., pediatric nephrologist; MD, U. of Witwatersrand, 1964. Diplomate Am. Bd. of Pediatrics-pediatric nephrology. Intern pediatrics Coronation Hosp., 1967; resident pediatrics Transvaal Meml. Hosp., 1970; fellow nephrology Montreal Children's Hosp., 1972; resident nephrology Royal Victoria Hosp., 1973. Named top doc., Phila. Mag., 2007, 2010. Office: Children's Hospital Nephrology S 34th St and Civic Ctr Blvd Philadelphia PA 19104 Office Phone: 215-590-2449.

KAPLAN, EUGENE ALKEN, psychiatry professor, department chairman; b. Syracuse, NY, Dec. 24, 1933; s. David S. and Florence F. Kaplan; m. Sandra Ecker Kaplan, May 14, 1961; children: Susan Beth Kaplan Lue, Karen Lynn. BA magna cum laude, Syracuse U., 1954; MD, SUNY, Syracuse, 1957. Diplomate Nat. Bd. Med. Examiners, cert. Am. Bd. Psychiatry and Neurology. Med. intern Albert Einstein Med. Ctr., NYC, 1957—58; psychiatry resident, chief resident SUNY Upstate Med. U., Syracuse, 1958—61, from instr. to prof., 1961—, prof., chair dept. psychiatry, 1987—99, prof., chair emeritus dept. psychiatry, 1999—. Cons. Peace Corps tng. programs Syracuse U., 1962—66; vis. prof. Sloan Sch. Cornell U., Ithaca, NY, 1967—82; lectr. Washington Sch. Psychiatry, 1967—69; vis. scientist The Tavistock Psychiat. Ctr., London, 1981; cons. psychiatrist Syracuse U. Health Svc., 1982—87. Co-editor: International Psychiatric Clinics, vol. 2 & 3, 1965; contbr. articles to profl. jours. Bd. dirs. Transitional Living Svc., Syracuse, 1975—82, Syracuse Opera, Syracuse, 1990—98, Syracuse Symphony, Syracuse, 1999—. Comdr. Med. Corps USN, 1967—69. Fellow: Am. Psychiat. Assn. (Disting. Life fellow); mem.: Am. Bd. Psychiatry and Neurology (sr. examiner 1974—98), Phi Kappa Alpha, Phi Beta Kappa. Avocations: sailing, piano. Home: 2804 West Lake Rd Cazenovia NY 13035 Office: SUNY Upstate Med Univ Dept Psychiatry 750 E Adams St Syracuse NY 13210 Home Phone: 315-655-8589; Office Phone: 315-464-3105. Business E-Mail: kaplane@upstate.edu.

KAPLAN, GABRIELA DIANA, radiologist; arrived in U.S., 1963; d. Isidor and Rosa Kaplan. MD, U. Autonoma Guadalajara, 1972; BA, Whittier Coll. Diplomate Am. Bd. Radiology. Asst. prof. Columbia U., Presbyn. Hosp., NYC, 1979; lectr. diagnostic radiology Johns Hopkins Hosp., Balt., 1980—82; fellow in body imaging Johns Hopkins U., Balt., 1980, fellow in neuroradiology, 1982; fellow in whole body magnetic resonance U. Mich., Ann Arbor, 1989, asst. prof. radiology Med. Ctr., 1978—79; pres. Lifewatch Group Ltd., Cleve., 1990—; lectr. impact population growth on health, hunger and peace in USA, S. Am., France, 2009—11. Lectr. in health and enbiron. sustainability in Europe, S.Am. & US. Author: Say I Promise-Health, Population, Economy, Energy, Hunger and Peace, 1989—, Aquarelles, 2007, Reflections, 2007, Earth; contbr. articles to profl. jours. including Radiology Jour., Jour. Magnetic Resonance Imaging. Recipient Presdl. Rep. award of merit, Ptnrs. in Conservation award, World Wildlife Fund, 1999, Amb. Internat. award of Merit, Internat. Soc. Poetry, 2005; named Amb. Poetry, Internat. Poetry, 2006. Mem.: Radiology Soc. N.A., P.I.B. Yacht Club (fleet surgeon). Republican. Roman Catholic. Achievements include invention of device to aid women in family planning. Avocations: poetry, gardening. Personal E-mail: life_watch@msn.com. Business E-Mail: life@lifewatchgroup.org.

KAPLAN, GARY S., hospital administrator, internist; MD, U. Mich., Ann Arbor, 1978. Cert. American Bd. Internal Medicine, 1981. Residency in internal medicine Virginia Mason Med. Ctr., Seattle, 1981; section head Virginia Mason East, Kirkland, Oreg., 1982—86, dep. chief medicine, 1984—86, chief dept. satellites, 1986—2000, med. dir., 1996—2000; chmn., CEO Virginia Mason Health Sys., Seattle, 2000—. Bd. dirs. Virginia Mason Health Sys./Med. Ctr., 1987—, co-chmn. ops. com., 1996—2000; mem. Virginia Mason Rsch. Ctr./Benaroya Rsch. Inst. Virginia Mason Bd., 2000—. Recipient John M. Eisenberg award, Nat. Quality Forum and Joint Commn. Individual Achievement, 2009; named one of Most Powerful Physician Executives, Modern Physician Mag., 2005, 100 Most Powerful People in Healthcare, Modern Healthcare, 2008, 2011, Most Influential Us Physician Leader in Healthcare, 2009—11. Fellow: American Coll. Physicians Executives, American Coll. Physicians, American Coll. Med. Practice Executives; mem.: Med. Group Mgmt. Assn. (chmn. 2001—02, Harry J. Harwick Lifetime Achievement award 2009). Office: Virginia Mason Med Ctr 1100 Ninth Ave Seattle WA 98101 also: Virginia Mason Kirkland Evergreen Plz Bldg 11800 NE 128th St Ste 300 Kirkland WA 98034 Office Phone: 206-223-6955. *

KAPLAN, GEORGE WILLARD, urologist; b. Brownsville, Tex., Aug. 24, 1935; s. Hyman J. and Lillian (Bennett) Kaplan; m. Susan Gail Solof, Dec. 17, 1961; children: Paula, Elizabeth, Julie, Alan. BA, U. Tex., Austin, 1955; MD, Northwestern U., Evanston, Ill., 1959, MS, 1966. Diplomate Am. Bd. Urology, 1971; cert. sub-splty. in pediat. urology, 2008. Intern Charity Hosp. of La. at New Orleans, 1959-60; resident Northwestern U., 1963-68, instr. Med. Sch. Chgo., 1968-69; clin. prof. U. Calif., San Diego, 1970—, chief pediatric urology, 1970—98. Trustee Children's Hosp. and Health Ctr., San Diego, 1978-90, Am. Bd. Urology, Bingham Farms, Mich., 1991-96; del. Am. Bd. Med. Specialties, Evanston, Ill., 1992-96. Author: Genitourinary Problems in Pediatrics; asst. editor Jour. Urology, Balt., 1982-89, 98-2002; assoc. editor Child Nephrology and Urology, Milan, Italy, 1988-94; contbr. articles to profl. publs. Pres. med. staff Children's Hosp., San Diego, 1980-82. Lt. USN, 1960-63. Recipient Joseph Capps prize Inst. of Medicine, 1967. Fellow ACS (pres. San Diego chpt. 1980-82), Am. Acad. Pediat. (chmn. sect. on urology 1986, Urology medal 2007); mem. AMA, Soc. for Pediatric Urology (pres. 1993), Am. Urol. Assn., Soc. Internat. Urologie, Soc. Univ. Urologists, Am. Assn. Genito-Urin. Surgeons. Independent. Jewish. Avocation: rare books. Office: 7930 Frost St Ste 300 San Diego CA 92123-2740 Business E-Mail: gkaplan@rcns.org, gkaplan@rchsd.org.

KAPLAN, HENRY JERROLD, ophthalmologist, educator; b. NYC, Dec. 29, 1942; s. Ralph and Henrietta (Davis) K.; m. Adele Lotner, June 26, 1966; children: Wendi Suzanne, Todd Daniel, Ariane Dev. AB, Columbia U., 1964; MD, Cornell U., 1968. Diplomate Am. Bd. Ophthalmology. Intern in medicine Lakeside Hosp., Univ. Hosps. Cleve., Case-Western Res. U., 1968-69; surg. resident Bellevue Hosp., NYU Med. Ctr., 1969-70; NIH rsch. fellow in immunology U. Tex. (Southwestern) Med. Sch., Dallas, 1972-74, asst. prof. dept. cell biology, 1974-75; resident in ophthalmology U. Iowa Hosps. and Clinics, Iowa City, 1975-78; retina-vitreous fellow dept. ophthalmology Med. Coll. Wis., Milw., 1978-79; assoc. prof. dept. ophthalmology Emory U. Sch. Medicine, Atlanta, 1979-84, prof., dir. rsch., 1984-88, assoc. prof. dept. microbiology, 1985-88; prof. dept. ophthalmology and visual scis. Washington U. Sch. Medicine, St. Louis, 1988-2000, chmn. dept. ophthalmology and visual scis., 1988-98; prof., chmn. dept. opthalmology and visual scis. U. Louisville (Ky.) Sch. Medicine, 2000—, William H. and Blondina F. Evans Prof. Ophthalmology, 2000—. Ophthalmologist in chief Barnes-Jewish Hosp., Washington U. Med. Ctr., 1988-98; affiliate scientist in pathology and immunology Yerkes Regional Primate Rsch. Ctr., Atlanta, 1981—; adj. prof. dept. small animal medicine U. Ga., Athens, 1985—; assoc. chief ophthalmology Emory U. Hosp., 1985-88; mem. visual scis. study sect. A-1 NIH, Bethesda, Md., 1985-89, chmn., 1987-89; pres. Barnes Eye Care Network, 1994-98; dir. Ky. Lions Eye Ctr., Louisville, 2000—; pres. Eye Specialists Louisville, Ky.,2000—; chmn. U. Physician Assocs., 2004—06. Author, coauthor or editor, co-editor more than 250 med. textbooks, chpts. and articles on uveitis and macular degeneration and retinal degeneration pub. in refereed sci. and med. jours., 1974—; mem. sci. jour. rev. bds. Archives Ophthalmology, 1978—, Retina, 1982—, Am. Jour. Ophthalmology, 1983—, Ophthalmology, 1983—, Current Eye Rsch., 1986—, Exptl. Eye Rsch., 1986—; mem. sci. rev. bd. Investigative Ophthalmology and Visual Sci., 1983—, mem. editorial bd., 1990-92; co-editor Ocular Immunology and Inflammation, 1994-98; editor: Ocular Immunology and Inflammation, 1999—2009. Maj. M.C., USAF, 1970-72. Recipient sci. award Alcon Rsch. Inst., 1987; Olga Keith Weiss rsch. scholar to Prevent Blindness, Inc., N.Y.C., 1984. Fellow ACS, Am. Acad. Ophthalmology (Honor award 1984, Sr. Honor award 1994); mem. AMA, Assn. for Rsch. in Vision and Ophthalmology, Am. Assn. Immunologists, Macula Soc., Am. Uveitis Soc. (pres. 1997-99), Retina Soc., Louisville Ophthal. Soc., Ky. Acad. Eye Physicians and Surgeons. Jewish. Office: U Louisville Sch Medicine Dept Opthalmol & Visual Sci 301 E Muhammad Ali Blvd Louisville KY 40202-1511 Office Phone: 502-852-3716. Business E-Mail: hank.kaplan@louisville.edu.

KAPLAN, JOSHUA M., medical educator; b. July 19, 1969; BS, Yale U., 1990; MD, Cornell U., 1995. Asst prof. NJ Med. Sch., 2002—. Mem.: Am. Soc. Nephrology. Office: 185 South Orange Ave Newark NJ 07103 Office Fax: 973-972-3578. Business E-Mail: kaplanjm@umdnj.edu.

KAPLAN, JULIUS ALLAN (JAY KAPLAN), physician, director; b. New Orleans, Jan. 28, 1949; AB, Harvard Coll., 1971; MD, Harvard Med. Sch., 1975. Dir., svc. & operational excellence CEP Am. Emergency Physician Ptnrs., 2003—. Cons., spkr., coach MDRN Assocs., 1999. Recipient Physician Firestarter award, Studer Group, Gracec Humanitarian award, Thomas Jefferson U. Hosp. Dept. Emergency Medicine. Fellow: Am. Coll. Emergency Physicians (bd. dirs. 2009, Outstanding Spkr. of Yr. 2003). Avocations: hiking, skiing, poetry. Home: 300 Oak Ave San Anselmo CA 94960 Home Fax: 415-460-6221. Business E-Mail: jaykaplan@cep.com.

KAPLAN, MARK J., surgeon; MD, Temple U. Diplomate Am. Bd. Surgery, Am. Bd. Surgery-surg. critical care. Intern Albert Einstein med. Ctr., resident; tchg. appointment sch. of medicine Temple Univ. Office: Albert Einstein Medical Center 5501 Old York Rd Philadelphia PA 19141 Office Phone: 215-456-7890.

KAPLAN, MARK S., healthcare educator; BA in Sociology, U. Miami, Coral Gables, 1975; MSW, Ariz. State U., Tempe, 1977; MPH in Behavioral Sciences, U. Calif., Berkeley, 1978, DPH in Behavioral Sciences, 1984. Cons. Ariz. Dept. Health Svcs., Divsn. Behavioral Health Sciences, 1976—77; rsch. specialist, mental health and social welfare rsch. group U. Calif., Sch. Social Welfare, Berkeley, 1979—85; asst. prof., dept. sch. and cmty. health U. Oreg., 1985—87; prof., cmty. health-urban & pub. affairs Portland State U., Oreg.; cons., Making Risky Decisions Eugene Rsch. Inst., Oreg., 1988; postdoctoral fellow Inst. for Health Promotion and Disease Prevention Rsch., Dept. Preventative Medicine, U. So. Calif., 1988—90; asst. prof., Sch. Social Work U. Ill., Urbana-Champaign, 1990—97, chair, mental health specialization, Sch. Social Work, 1992—97; assoc. prof., Sch. Cmty. Health, Coll. Urban and Pub. Affairs Portland State U., Oreg., 1997—2003, prof., Sch. Cmty. Health, Coll. Urban and Pub. Affairs Oreg., 2003—. Adj. assoc. prof., psychiatry Oreg. Health Sciences U., 1999—; mem. NIMH/NIH Spl. Emphasis Panel, 2004; vis. prof., dept. epidemiology & cmty. medicine U. Ottawa, 2004; contbr. to state and fed. suicide prevention initiatives; participated on review panels for the NIH, Canadian Social Sci. and Humanities Rsch. Coun. & Coun. for Internat. Exchange of Scholars.; mem. scientific adv. coun. Suicide Prevention Action Network (SPAN USA). Editl. bd. mem., book review editor Internat. Jour. Men's Health, 2002—, peer reviewer for several profl. jours. Recipient US Pub. Health Svc. Nat. Rsch. award, 1977—81, AAAS (Pacific Divsn.) award for Excellence for the best paper presented at the 65th Ann. Mtg. on the program sect. L, History of Sci., 1984; fellow NIMH Summer Rsch. Inst. in Geriatric Psychiatry, 1999; Nat. Inst. Alcohol Abuse and Alcoholism Pre-Doctoral Rsch. Traineeship, 1977—79, J. William Fulbright Scholar to Can., 2004. Mem.: Am. Assn. Suicidology (mem. strategic planning com. 1998—, serves on Coun. Delegates). Office: Portland State U Sch Cmty Health-SCH PO Box 751 Office 450J URBN Portland OR 97207-0751 Office Phone: 503-725-8588. Office Fax: 503-725-5100. Business E-Mail: kaplanm@pdx.edu.

KAPLAN, MARSHALL MYLES, medical educator, researcher, gastroenterologist; b. Boston, Feb. 20, 1935; s. Harold and Ginda (Braverman) K.; m. Nancy Proger, June 5, 1960; children: Ginda, William, Thomas, Deborah. BS summa cum laude, Yale U., 1956; MD cum laude, Harvard U., 1960. Intern, resident Columbia-Presbyn., NYC, 1960-62; clin. assoc. NIH, Bethesda, Md., 1962-65; trainee liver disease Yale U., New Haven, 1965-66; asst. prof. medicine Tufts-New England Med. Ctr., Boston, 1966-69, assoc. prof. medicine, 1969-75, prof. medicine, 1975—, chief divsn. gastroenterology, 1972—2002. Chmn. merit rev. com. VA Hosps., Washington, 1975-77; mem. gastroenterology bd. Am. Bd. Internal Medicine, 1983-89, chmn., 1987-89, bd. govs., 1987-89, trustee, Tufts-New England Med. Ctr., 201-05; manuscript reviewer Annals Internal Medicine, Am. Jour. Medicine, Archives of Internal Medicine, Gastroenterology, Hepatology, Digestive Diseases and Sci., Am. Jour. Gastroenterology, Jour. Hepatology Assoc. editor New Eng. Jour. Medicine, 1993-2001; editor Tufts Family Health Guides, 1979-82; mem. editl. bd. Hepatology, 1988-92; sect. editor Up to Date in Medicine, 2006—; contbr. over 300 articles to med. jours., chpts. to books. Lt. comdr. USPHS, 1962-65. Recipient Mentor Rsch. Scholar award, AGA Found., 2005. Master ACP (chair sci. program com. 1990-93, gastroenterology med. knowledge self-assessment program); mem. Assn. Am. Physicians, Am. Soc. Clin. Investigation, Am. Gastroenterology Assn., Am. Assn. for Study of Liver Disease (com. chair 1984-86), Am. Gastroenterology Assn. (Mentors award Am. Gastroenterology Assn. Found. 2005), Phi Beta Kappa, Alpha Omega Alpha (dir. 1983-89). Democrat. Jewish. Avocations: tennis, bridge, golf, gardening, music. Home: 75 Grove St Unit 426 Wellesley MA 02482-7830 Office: Tufts Med Ctr 800 Washington St Boston MA 02111-1526 Office Phone: 617-636-5877.

KAPLAN, MARTIN P., retired allergist, retired immunologist, retired pediatrician; b. Bklyn., Oct. 28, 1928; MD, SUNY Downstate Med. Ctr. Diplomate Am. Bd. Allergy & Immunology, Am. Bd. Pediat. Resident Jewish Hosp., Bklyn., 1954-55, SUNY Upstate Med. Ctr., Syracuse, 1957-58; fellow Children's Hosp., Washington, 1958-59; active staff mem. dept. medicine St. Joseph Hosp., Lexington, Ky., 1959—2009; clin. assoc. prof. pediatrics and medicine U. Ky. Coll. Medicine, 1982-97. Mem. Am. Acad. Allergy and Clin. Immuniology, Am. Coll. Allergy, Asthma, and Immunology, AMA, Ky. Med. Assn.

KAPLAN, PETER W., neurologist, director; b. NYC, Aug. 20, 1951; MBBS, St. Bartholomew's Med. Coll., 1977. Dir., EEG and Epilepsy, JHBMC Johns Hopkins U. Sch. Medicine, 1987—, prof., neurology, 2005. Fellow: ACNS, ANA, AAN, Royal Coll. Physicians (London). Home: Neurology Johns Hopkins Bayview Med Ctr Baltimore MD 21224 Business E-Mail: pkaplan@jhmi.edu.

KAPLAN, ROBERT MALCOLM, federal agency administrator, health researcher, educator; b. San Diego, Oct. 26, 1947; s. Oscar Joel and Rose (Zankan) K.; children: Cameron Maxwell, Seth William AB in Psychology, San Diego State U., 1969; MA, U. Calif., Riverside, 1970, PhD, 1972. Lic. psychologist Calif., cert. Calif. Bd. Med. Quality Assurance. Tchg. asst. dept. psychology U. Calif., Riverside, 1969—72; sr. rsch. assoc. Am. Inst. for Rsch., Palo Alto, Calif., 1972-73; from asst. prof. to prof. U. Calif., San Diego, 1973—2004, chief health care svcs. divsn., 1989—96, chmn. health care svcs. divsn., 1997—2004, prof. dept. family and preventive medicine, 2004; from asst. prof. to prof. psychology San Diego State U., 1974-88, dir., Ctr. Behavioral Medicine; prof. medicine UCLA, 2004—10; dir. office behavioral and social sciences rsch., assoc. dir. behavioral and social sciences rsch. NIH, Bethesda, Md., 2011—. Mem. health svcs. rsch. study sect. Nat. Ctr. Health Svcs. Rsch., 1981-85, 88-92, VA Sci. Rev. and Evaluations Bd. Health Svcs., 1989-91, chair 1991-92; cons., lectr. in field. Faculty fellow San Diego State U., 1977, epidemiology fellow Am. Heart Assn., 1983; recipient Career Rsch. Devel. award NIH, 1981-86, Alumni and Assocs. Disting. Faculty award San Diego State U., 1982, Exceptional Merit Svc. award, 1984. Fellow APA (bd. dirs., Outstanding Sci. Achievement award health psychology divsn. 1987, 2001, pres. 1992-93); mem. AAAS (exec. com. Pacific divsn. 1978-82), Soc. Behavioral Medicine (bd. dirs., pres. 1996-97, pres. elect 2001—, editor-in-chief Annals of Behavioral Medicine, 2000 05, Health Psychology, 2005—), Inst. Medicine NAS. Office: NIH Office Behavioral and Social Sciences Rsch Bldg 31 Claude D Pepper Bldg B1C19 31 Center Dr Bethesda MD 20892 Office Phone: 301-402-1146. Business E-Mail: robert.kaplan@nih.gov. *

KAPLAN, SADI, cardiothoracic and vascular surgeon; b. Konya, Kulu, Turkey, Feb. 10, 1966; s. Mehmet and Esma Kaplan; m. Muzeyyen Ozlem Sokmen, Aug. 11, 1992; 1 child, Guven Ozan. MD, Hacettepe U., Ankara, 1992. Resident in thoracic and cardiovasc. surgery Hacettepe U., Ankara, 1993—97, chief resident in thoracic and cardiovasc. surgery, 1997—2000; vice dir. cardiothoracic surgery Sevgi Millennium Hosp., Ankara, 2000—01; attending in cardiovasc. surgery Yuksek Ihtisas Hosp. of Turkey, Ankara, 2001—; cardiothoracic surgery postdoc. rsch. fellow Columbia U. Coll. Phys. and Surg./N.Y. Presbyn. Hosp., NYC, 2002—. Reviewer Med. Sci. Monitor Jour., NYC, 2003—; chmn. in valve disease sci. session European Soc. for Cardiovasc. Surgey, Istanbul, 2003—. Contbr. articles to profl. jours. Exec. mem. Konya Platform, Ankara, 2000; mem. The Am. Turkish Soc., Ankara, 2002. Recipient First Degree in Chemistry Contest, Turkish Sci. and Tech. Rsch. Assn., 1984;, Turkish Ministry of Health grantee, 2002. Mem.: Am. Stroke Assn., Am. Heart Assn., Am. Assn. Turkish Scientists, N.Y. Acad. Scis., European Assn. for Cardiovasc. Surgery (chmn. valve disease sci. session 2003—), European Assn. for Vascular Surgery. Avocations: chess, fishing, tennis, mountain climbing, basketball. Home: 2Dedeefendi Altay Sokak 4/11 Kurtulus/Cankaya Ankara 06600 Turkey Office: Yuksek Ihtisas Hospital Turkey Sihhiye Ankara 06100 Turkey Personal E-mail: skaplan@bir.net.tr. E-mail: skpn1966@hotmail.com.

KAPLITT, MICHAEL GORDON, neurosurgeon, medical educator; b. Bklyn., Sept. 1, 1965; m. Melissa Beth Rutkin. AB magna cum laude in Molecular Biology, Princeton U., 1987; MD, Cornell Med. Coll., 1995; PhD in Molecular Neurobiology, Rockefeller U., 1993. Bd. cert. neurological surgery. Resident neurosurgery, chief resident Cornell; fellow in stereotactic and functional neurosurgery U. Toronto; asst. prof. then assoc. prof. neurosurgery Weill Med. Coll., Cornell U., N.Y. Presbyn. Hosp., NYC, 2001—, assoc. attending neurosurgeon, dir. Ctr. for Stereotactic and Molecular Neurosurgery, 2001—. Clin. asst. attending divsn. neurosurgery dept. surgery Meml.-Sloan Kettering Cancer Ctr., NYC; adj. asst. prof. Lab. Neurobiology and Behavior The Rockefeller U., NYC; mem. admissions com. Weill Cornell Med. Sch., NYC. Editor: (web site) World Soc. for Stereotactic and Functional Neurosurgery; co-editor: Viral Vectors: Gene Therapy and Neuroscience Applications, 1995, Gene Therapy in the Brain: From Bench to Bedside, 2005; contbr. scientific papers. Recipient Albert Cass Traveling Fellowship, 1992, Saul R. Korey award for exptl. neurology, Am. Acad. Neurology, 1994, Fellowship award, Med. Rsch. Coun. Can., 2000, Young Investigator Award, Am. Soc. for Gene Therapy, 2005, Disting. Housestaff Award, NY Hospital-Cornell Med. Ctr.; named a Victor and Tara Menezes Clinical Scholar; named one of "Best Doctors in NY, NY Mag., 2004; named to, Crain's N.Y. Bus. "40 under 40", 2004; Charles Elsberg fellow in neurol. surgery, N.Y. Acad. Medicine, 2002, New Scholar award in aging rsch., Ellison Med. Found., 2002. Office: Weill-Cornell Med Coll Dept Neurosurgery 525 E 68th St New York NY 10065 Office Phone: 212-746-4966. Office Fax: 212-746-5592.

KAPLOW, JULIE B., psychologist, educator; d. Lois S. and Robert D. Kaplow; m. Alan R. Prossin, June 25, 2005. BA, U. Mich., Ann Arbor, 1997; MA, Duke U., Durham, NC, 2000, PhD, 2002. Lic. psychologist NY State Edn. Dept., 2005, Mass. Bd. Registration Psychologists, 2003; registered nat. health svc. provider Nat. Register Health Svc. Providers. Asst. prof. Boston U., 2004, U. Medicine Dentistry NJ, Newark, 2004—06; assoc. prof. John Jay Coll. of Criminal Justice, CUNY, NYC, 2006—; asst. prof. Boston U. Med. Ctr., Boston, 2003—04, U. Mich. Med. Sch., 2007—. Dir. psychology tng. Boston U. Med. Ctr., Dept. Child and Adolescent Psychiatry, Boston, 2003—04; cons. Nat. Child Traumatic Stress Network, Traumatic Grief Task Force, Durham, NC, 2002—05. Author: (book) Samantha Jane's Missing Smile: A Story for Children Who Have Lost a Parent, Collaborative Treatment of Traumatized Children and Teens: A Trauma Systems Therapy Approach; contbr. articles to profl. and med. jours. Recipient J. P. Guilford Undergraduate Rsch. award, Psi Chi, 1997, Psychology award, Psi Chi Nat. Honor Soc., U. Mich., 1995—99; grantee Mentored Clin. Scientist Devel. award, NIMH, 2006—; fellow, Terry Sanford Ctr. for Child and Family Policy, Duke U., 1999—2000; Alcohol and Substance Abuse grant, NC Gov.'s Inst., 2000—02, Clin. Psychology fellow, Harvard Med. Sch., 2001—02, Carolina Consortium on Human Devel. Predoctoral fellow, NIMH, 2000—01, James B. Angell scholar, U. Mich., 1997. Mem.: APA, Soc. Prevention Rsch., Internat. Soc.Traumatic Stress Studies, Soc. for Rsch. in Child Devel., Am. Psychopathological Assn., Phi Beta Kappa. Achievements include research in discovered link between different forms of anxiety and the initiation of adolescent alcohol use; Found link between children's coping strategies in immediate aftermath of sexual abuse and later post-traumatic stress symptoms; Identified various risk factors for the development of early-onset substance use in children. Office: Univ Mich Med Sch Dept Psychiatry Rachel Upajhn Bldg 4250 Plymouth Rd Rm 2117 Ann Arbor MI 48109 Office Phone: 734-615-1641. Business E-Mail: julieb@med.umich.edu.

KAPNICK, S. JASON, oncologist; b. Providence, Mar. 28, 1949; s. I.H. and Martha (Shaulson) K.; children: Senta Marie-Rose, Isrel Berndt-Stefan, Sesselja Edda, Finn MacComaill. BLS summa cum laude, boston U., 1974; MD, Harvard Med. Sch., 1981. Surg. rsch. assoc. Harvard Med. Sch., Boston, 1976—79, assoc. in ob/gyn., lectr., 1981-85; intern, resident in ob-gyn. Brigham & Women's Mass. Gen. Hosp., Boston, 1981—85; adminstrv. chief resident Mass. Gen. Hosp./Brigham Hosps., 1985; instr. in gynecology, fellow tumor surgery Harvard Med. Sch., Boston, 1985—87; cons. in gynecologic oncology Dana Farber Cancer Inst., Boston, 1985-87; clin. fellow Am. Cancer Soc., Boston, 1985-87; attending gynecologic oncologist West Palm Beach, Fla., 1989—; cert. gynecologic oncologist, 1991—. Asst. cons. prof. Duke U. Med. Ctr., Durham, NC, 1994—; reviewer rsch. submissions Cancer med. jour., Bethesda, Md., 1995—; invited lectr. Am. Cancer Soc., Bethesda, 1995, also Switzerland, Germany, France and Eng., 1990-, bus. advisory bd. Admiralty Bank 1992-99. Contbr. articles to profl. jours. Vol., contbr. Ctr. for Family Svcs., West Palm Beach, 1992—; mem. Mass. Gen. Hosp., Bulfinch Soc.; trustee, founder Helga Helgason BSRN Meml. Fund; dean's coun. and John Warren Fellow Med. Sch., Harvard U.; donor Covenant House Children's Shelter, 2004—; founder, dir. Kapnick Meml. Cancer Ctrl. Consortium, 2006; founder clinical care initiative Theresa Pratt RN Meml., 2006; active Cath. Diocese children's programs, 1998—; mem., donor First Unitarian Ch., North Palm Beach, Fla.; bd. dirs. Palm Beach Opera, 1992—. Henry Merritt Wriston scholarship Brown U. Mem. Ezekial Hersey Soc., Harvard Med. Sch., Legacy Soc., Brigham Women's Hosp., Harvard Club of Palm Beach. Achievements include research in colon, breast, and pelvic cancers. Avocations: philosophy, music. Address: PO Box 30053 Palm Beach Gardens FL 33420-0053 Office: 335 Leeward Dr Jupiter FL 33477 Office Phone: 561-622-3810, 561-622-3810. Personal E-mail: jasonkapnicknwd@gmail.com.

KAPOOR, ATUL, radiologist, director; b. Amritsar, India, May 18, 1962; MBBS, Med. Coll. Amritsar, 1984; MD, Med. Coll. Patiala, 1989. Dir. Advanced Diagnostics and Inst. Imaging, 1993—. Recipient Rotary Vocat. award. Mem.: Nat. Acad. Med. Scis. Avocation: golf. Office: 17/8 Kennedy Ave Amritsar Punjab 143001 India Personal E-mail: advanced@sancharnet.in.

KAPOOR, JOHN N., venture capitalist, management consultant; b. Amristar, India; m. Editha Kapoor. BS in Pharmacy, Bombay U., India; PhD, SUNY, Buffalo, 1972; doctorate (hon.), SUNY. Plant mgr. Invenex Laboratories, Grand Island, NY, 1972—78; pres., CEO LyphoMed, 1978—83, chmn., 1983—90; founder, pres., chmn EJ Fin. Enterprises, Inc., 1990—; CEO Option Care, 1993—96, chmn. of bd.; CEO Akorn, 1996—98, 2001—02, chmn. of bd.; mng. ptnr. Kapoor-Pharma Investments, 2000—; co-founder, chmn. of bd. Insys Therapeutics, Inc.; chmn. of bd. NEO Pharm. Bd. dirs. Introgen Therapeutics. Founder John and Editha Kapoor Charitable Found. Recipient Disting. Alumni award, UB Alumni Assn., Chakra award, San Diego Indian American Soc., American Cancer Soc. Internat. Achievement award. Office: EJ Fin Enterprises Inc 225 E Deerpath #250 Lake Forest IL 60045-5302 *

KAPOOR, KAPIL, research scientist; s. Kamal Kumar and Asha Kapoor; m. Nidhi Kapoor, Nov. 19, 1995; 1 child, Saumya. MBBS, KGMC, India, 1985; MD, KGMC, 1987, PhD, 1997. Scientist CDRI, Lucknow, Up, India. Fellow, Ibro, Insa, Csir, 1996-1999. Mem.: IPS (life). Achievements include research in cardiovascular pharmacology. Home: C-11/4 River Bk Colony Up Lucknow 226018 India Office: Ctrl Drug Rsch Inst MG Rd Uttar Pradesh Lucknow 226001 India

KAPOOR, KAPIL G., ophthalmologist; b. Parma, Ohio, Jan. 8, 1982; s. Gopal Ragunathrai and Neerja Kapoor; m. Elleni Kaur Kapoor, Sept. 27, 2007. MD, Ohio State U., Columbus, 2007. Internship preliminary medicine U. Tex. Med. Br., Galveston, 2007—08, ophthalmology resident, 2008—. Ophthalmology resident, 2008—11; fellow Mayo Clinic Vitreoretical Surgery, 2011—. Contbr. articles to profl. jours., chapters to books. Mem.: Am. Acad. Ophthalmology. Office: University Tex Med Br 301 University Blvd Galveston TX 77555 also: Mayo Clinic 200 First St SW Rochester MN 55905 Personal E-mail: kaps2003@gmail.com.

KAPOOR, NEERA, optometrist, research scientist; b. Melfort, Sask., Can., June 25, 1966; arrived in U.S., 1990; d. Ajit and Prem Kapoor. BSc, U. Toronto, 1989; MS, SUNY, NYC, 1993; OD, SUNY, 1994. Asst. clin. prof. optometry SUNY, NYC, 1995—2002, assoc. clin. prof., 2002—, dir. head trauma vision rehab. unit., 1996—2002, dir. Raymond J. Greenwald Rehab. Ctr., 2002—10, chief, Vision Rehab. Svcs., 2010—. Cons. neuro-optometry JFK Med. Ctr., NJ Neuro Sci. Inst., Edison, 2001—05. Co-author, co-editor: Visual & Vestibular Consequences of Acquired Brain Injury, 2001. Recipient Founder's award, Brain Injury Assn. NY State, 2002, Disting. Achievement award, NY State Optometric Assn., 2003, Chancellor's award, SUNY, 2005. Fellow: Am. Acad. Optometry; mem.: Assn. Rsch. in Vision and Ophthalmology, Coll. Optometrists in Vision Devel. (assoc.). Office: SUNY 5th Fl 33 W 42nd St New York NY 10036 Business E-Mail: nkapoor@sunyopt.edu.

KAPPAS, ATTALLAH, physician; b. Union City, NJ, Nov. 4, 1926; m. Oct. 26, 1963; children: Peter, Michael, Nicholas. AB, Columbia U., 1947; MD with honors, U. Chgo., 1950; ScD, N.Y. Med. Coll., 1978. Diplomate: Am. Bd. Internal Medicine. Med. intern Univ. Service, Kings County Hosp., NYC, 1950-51; ACS rsch. fellow Sloan Kettering Inst., NYC, 1951-54; asst. resident physician and sr. asst. resident physician Peter Bent Brigham Hosp. Harvard Med. Sch., Boston, 1954-56; assoc. div. steroid biochemistry and metabolism Sloan Kettering Inst., NYC, 1956—57; from asst. prof. to assoc. prof. dept. medicine, head divsn. metabolism and arthritis U. Chgo. Med. Sch., 1957—67; Guggenheim fellow, guest investigator Rockefeller U., NYC, 1966—67, assoc. prof., physician, 1967—71, sr. physician, 1971—74, prof., 1971—91, physician-in-chief, 1974—91, physician-in-chief emeritus, 1991—, Sherman Fairchild prof., 1991—2004, Sherman Fairchild prof. emeritus, 2004—. Prof. medicine Cornell U., NYC, 1972—2002, emeritus prof., 2002; Vincent Astor prof. clin. sci. Cornell U. Meml. Hosp. Sloan Kettering Inst., NYC, 1979—81; v.p. Rockefeller U., NYC, 1983—91; mem. coun. SUNY Health Scis. Ctr., Bklyn., 1998—2004; dir. Theresa and Eugene Lang Ctr. Rsch. & Edn. NY Hosp. Queens Med. Ctr. Weill-Cornell Med. Coll., NYC, 1998—2002, emeritus, 2002; mem. dean's coun. U. Vt. Coll. Medicine, Burlington, 2000—04; prof. medicine emeritus Weill Cornell Med. Coll., NYC, 2002; mem. vis. com. divsn. biol. sci. and Pritlker Sch. Medicine U. Chgo., 2003—09; life mem. vis. com. U. Chgo. Med. Ctr., 2009. Contbr. articles to profl. jours. Bd. dir. Vis. Nurse Service N.Y., 1982-86, 98—2011, emeritus dir., 2011, Scenic Hudson, Inc., 2002-2007; mem. gov.'s com. on rev. sci. studies and devel. pub. policy on problems resulting from hazardous wastes N.Y. State, 1980; bd. dir. Beatrice Renfield Found., N.Y.C., 2003—. Served with U.S. Army, 1945-46. Recipient Spl. award in clin. pharmacology, Burroughs Wellcome Fund, 1973, Disting. Svc. award in med. scis., U. Chgo. Sch. Medicine, 1975, Citation for profl. achievement, U. Chgo. Alumni Assn., 1995, 1st Ann. award for excellence in clin. rsch., NIH, 1989, Lilian D. Wald award, Vis. Nurse Svc. NY, 2010; named named Sr. Henry Hallet Dale Meml. lectr. and vis. prof., Johns Hopkins Hosp., 1975, Pfizer lectr. clin. pharmacology, Peter Bent Brigham Hosp., Harvard Med. Sch., 1977, Pfizer lectr., Pa. State U., 1980, first Rolf Blomstrand lectr., Karolinska Inst., 1988, first Glaxo lectr., Cornell U. Med. Sch., Gunner and Lillian Nicholson Found. exch. prof., Karolinska Inst., Stockholm, 1985—86, Barowsky Meml. lectr., N.Y. Med. Coll., 1986, First Annual Lang Rsch. lectr., N.Y. Hosp. Med. Ctr., Queens, 2000; fellow Commonwealth Fund, 1961—62, Guggenheim fellow, 1966—67. Fellow ACP; mem. Assn. Am. Physicians, Am. Soc. Clin. Investigation, Am. Clin. and Climatol. Assn., Am. Soc. Pharmacology and Exptl. Therapeutics (pub. affairs com., award for exptl. therapeutics 1978), Practitioners Soc. N.Y., Harvey Soc., Endocrine Soc., Interurban Clin. Club, Cosmos Club (Washington), Lotos Club, Univ. Club (NY). Office: Rockefeller U Hosp 1230 York Ave New York NY 10065-6307 Office Phone: 212-327-8494. Office Fax: 212-327-8690. Business E-Mail: kappas@rockefeller.edu.

KAPPLER, JOHN W., microbiology educator; m. Philippa Marrack, 1974; children: Kate, Jim. BS in Chemistry, Lehigh U.; PhD in bioChemistry, Brandeis U. Postdoctoral work with Richard Dutton U. of Calif. San Diego; faculty U. Rochester Medical Sch.; prof. microbiology and immunology U. Colo., Denver; investigator Marrack and Kappler Rsch. Lab. Howard Hughes Med. Inst., 1986—; integrated dept. immunology Nat. Jewish Health, Denver. Recipient Wellcome Found. prize, Royal Society, Paul Ehrlich and Ludwig Darmstädter award, Paul Erhlich Found., Louisa Gross Horwitz prize, Columbia U., 1994, William B. Coley award, Cancer Rsch. Inst. Mem.: NAS, Inst. Medicine, Am. Assn. Immunologists. Office: Howard Hughes Med Inst H1400 Jackson St 5th fl Goodman Bldg Denver CO 80206

KAPPY, MICHAEL STEVEN, pediatrics educator; b. Bklyn., Feb. 8, 1940; s. Jack and Lilyan (Banchefsky) K.; m. Peggy Markson; children: Douglas Bruce, Gregory Louis. BA, Johns Hopkins U., 1961; MD, PhD, U. Wis., 1967. Asst. prof. U. Ariz. Med. Sch., Tucson, 1975-78; fellow pediatric endocrinology Johns Hopkins Hosp., Balt., 1978-80; assoc. prof. U. Fla. Med. Sch., Gainesville, 1980-85; clin. prof. U. Ariz. Med. Sch., Tucson, 1985-94; med. dir. Children's Health Ctr., Phoenix, 1985-94; prof. pediatrics U. Colo. Health Sci. Ctr., Denver, 1994—; chief pediatric endocrinology The Children's Hosp., Denver, 1994—. Editor: (jour.) Today's Child, 1985, Advances in Pediatrics, 2004, (book) Wilkins-The Diagnosis and Treatment of Endocrine Disorders in Childhood and Adolescence, 1994, Principles and Practice of Pediatric Endocrinology, 2005. Med. advisor Am. Diabetes Assn., Phoenix, 1985-94; bd. dirs. Ronald McDonald House, Phoenix, 1987-94. Named Tchr. of Yr., St. Joseph's Hosp., Phoenix, 1993, Disting. Alumni award, Johns Hopkins U., 1994, Med. Alumnus award, U. Wis., 2004. Mem. Assn. Pediatric Program Dirs. (pres. 1992-94), Soc. for Pediatric Rsch., Endocrine Soc., Am. Acad. Pediatrics, Physicians for Social Responsibility, Alpha Omega Alpha. Avocations: photography, cooking, four-wheel drive touring. Home: 460 S Marion Pkwy Apt 1706c Denver CO 80209-5547 Office: Childrens Hosp 13 23 E 16th Ave B-265 Aurora CO 80045

KAPRAL, FRANK ALBERT, microbiologist and immunology educator; b. Phila., Mar. 12, 1928; s. John and Erna Louise (Melching) K.; m. Marina Garay, Nov. 22, 1951; children: Gloria, Robert; m. Esther McKenzie, May 10, 2003. BS, U. of the Scis. in Phila., 1952; PhD, U. Pa., 1956. With U. Pa., Phila., 1952-66, assoc. in microbiology, 1958-66; assoc. microbiologist Phila Gen. Hosp., 1962-64, chief microbiology research, 1964-66, chief microbiology, 1965-66; asst. chief microbiol. research VA Hosp., Phila, 1962-66; assoc. prof. med. microbiology Ohio State U., Columbus, 1966-69, prof. med. virology, immunology and med. genetics, 1969—95, prof. emeritus dept. molecular virology, immunology and med. genetics, 1995—. Cons. Ctr. Disease Control, Atlanta, 1980, Proctor and Gamble Co., 1981-87. Contbr. articles to profl. jours. Active Ctrl. Ohio Diabetes Assn., 1992-93. With AUS, 1946-47. Grantee, Ctrl. Ohio Diabetes Assn., 1992—93; Rsch. grant, NIH, 1959—95. Fellow Am. Acad. Microbiology, Infectious Diseases Soc. Am.; mem. AAAS, Am. Soc. for Microbiology, Am. Assn. for Immunologists, Sigma Xi. Democrat. Roman Catholic. Achievements include patents for implant chamber. Home: 873 Clubview Blvd S Columbus OH 43235-1771 Home Phone: 614-885-1795. Personal E-mail: elaureo2@yahoo.com.

KAPRIELIAN, VICTORIA SUSAN, medical educator; b. Bronx, NY, June 30, 1959; d. Walter and Julia (Hachigian) Kaprielian. BA, Brown U., 1981; MD, UCLA, 1985. Diplomate Am. Bd. Family Practice. Resident Duke-Watts Family Medicine, Durham, NC, 1985-88; fellow UCLA Family Medicine, LA, 1988-89; asst. clin. prof. Duke U. Med. Ctr., Durham, NC, 1989-98, chief, divsn. predoctoral edn. and faculty devel., dept cmty and family medicine, 1994-96, assoc. clin. prof., 1998—2003, clin. prof., 2003—06, prof., 2006—; fellowship dir., dept. cmty. and family medicine Duke U., Durham, NC, 1994—99, 2000—04, dir. predoctoral edn. and faculty devel., 1996-99, vice chair for edn., dept. cmty. and family medicine, 2006—; interim chief Phys. Therapy Program, 2009—11; fellow Am. Coun. Edn., 2009—10. Dir. inpatient svc. divsn. cmty. medicine Duke U., 1989-90, dir. sports medicine, 1989-94, dir. arts medicine, 1989-95, dir. predoctoral edn., 1990-2000; dir. quality improvement and continuing med. edn. dept. cmty. and family medicine, 1996—2009; dir. faculty devel. dept. cmty. and family medicine, Duke U., 2000-04; dir. clin. core program Duke U. Sch. Medicine, 2004—. Fellow Am. Acad. Family Physicians (pub. com. 1985, mental health com. 1986-88); mem. NC Acad. Family Physicians (bd. dirs. 1998-2002, 2005—09 edn. com. 1989-90, med. sch. affairs 1990—2001, chair of com. 1991-97), Soc. Tchrs. Family Medicine (steering com., predoc. dir. working group 1995-98, chair 1998, Bishop fellow 2009-10), Nat. Commn. Certification Physician Assts. (bd. dirs. 2008-). Avocations: singing, cooking. Office: Duke U Dept Cmty and Family Medicine Box 2914 Durham NC 27710-0001

KAPTAN, GULBANU, research scientist; b. Turkey, July 7, 1971; MS in Food Engring., 2002, PhD in Mgmt., 2008. Food engr. Turkish Standards Instn., 1995—2003; Marie Curie rsch. fellow Carnegie Mellon U., 2009—, Wageningen U., 2009—. Recipient Prof. Dr. Orhan Karacadag award, Bilkent U.; fellow Marie Curie Internat. Outgoing fellowship, Rsch. Exec. Agy. European Commn.; Süleyman Demirel Rsch. grant, Tel Aviv U. Mem.: Soc. Judgment and Decision Making, Soc. Risk Analysis. Avocations: travel, walking. Office: 5000 Forbes Ave 208 Porter Hall Pittsburgh PA 15213 Personal E-mail: gulbanug@hotmail.com.

KAPUR, GAURAV, nephrologist; b. India, Oct. 7, 1977; MD in Pediat., Wayne State U., 2008. Staff, pediat. nephrologist Children's Hosp. Mich., 2007—. Home: 3901 Beaubien Blvd Detroit MI 48201 Home Fax: 313-966-0039. Business E-Mail: gkapur@med.wayne.edu.

KAPUR, REUBEN, medical educator; b. India, Mar. 30, 1966; PhD, U. Ariz., 1994. Prof. pediat. Ind. U. Sch. Medicine, 1999—. Office: 1044 W Walnut St R4 168 Indianapolis IN 46202 Business E-Mail: rkapur@iupui.edu.

KAPUR, SUMAN, biology professor, researcher; b. New Delhi, Sept. 23, 1956; MSc, AIIMS, New Delhi, 1980, PhD, 1987. Prof., biol. scis. dept. Birla Inst. Tech. and Sci., Pilani, 2005—11, prof., chief cmty. welfare and internat. rels. unit, 2007—10, prof., dean rsch. and consultancy Hyderabad, 2010—. Adj. prof. Albert Eisenstein Med. Ctr., 2006—11; mem. selection com. Commonwealth Fellowship Doctoral Rsch., 2005—11, King Faizal Internat. Prize Scis., 2008—11; mem., steering com. nat. guidelines on, minimum standards sanitation disaster relief and nat. guidelines minimum stds Nat. Disaster Mgmt. Authority, 2008—10. Mem.: Assn. Clin. Biochemist India, Soc. Biol. Chemists, Indian Immunological Soc., Internat. Soc. Biomedical Rsch. Alcoholism, Soc. Neurosci. Avocations: reading, writing, travel. Office: Birla Inst Tech and Sci Pilani Dean Research and Consultancy Hyderabad Andhra Pradesh 500078 India Office Fax: 91-40-66303998. Personal E-mail: mssuman@gmail.com.

KAR, MOUSUMI, education educator; b. Parasia, Madhya Pradesh, India, Mar. 21, 1977; d. Shanti Charan and Bula Rani Kar; m. Sujit Pillai, Jan. 8, 2000. MS in Pharmaceutics, Manipal Coll. Pharmaceutical Sci., India, 2002; post-grad student in Pharmacy, Mohanlal Sukhadia U., India, 2004—. Asst. prof. Smriti Coll. Pharm. Edn., Indore, Madhya Pradesh, India, 2002—04, Mohanlal Sukhadia U., Udaipur, Rajasthan, India, 2004—. Warden Kamla Nehru Girls Hostel, Mohanlal Sukhadia U., Udaipur, 2005—. Contbr. articles to profl. jours. Mem.: Assn. Pharmaceutical Tchrs., Canadian Soc. Pharmaceutical Sci. (assoc.). Achievements include development of and evaluation of microspheres for antidiabetic drugs. Home: Hiran Magri Rajasthan Udaipur 313001 India Office: Mohanlal Sukhadia Univ Rajasthan Udaipur 313001 India

KAR, RAKHEE, medical educator; b. Cuttack, Orissa, India, Oct. 20, 1976; MD in Pathology, Post Grad. Inst. Med. Edn. and Rsch., Chandigarh, India, 2005; DM in Hematopathology, All India Inst. Med. Scis., New Delhi, 2009. Asst. prof. Inst. Liver and Biliary Scis., New Delhi, 2009—10, Jawaharlal Inst. Med. Edn. and Rsch., Puducherry, India, 2010—. Recipient Bronze medal, PGIMER, Chandigarh, Gold medal, Utkal U., Orissa, Prof. Banbehari Patnaik Meml. award, Indian Assn. Pathologists and Microbiologists-Orissa chpt., award, Dr Gopal Chandra Pattanayak Meml. Trust. Mem.: Indian Assn. Pathologists & Microbiologists, Indian Med. Assn., Delhi Soc. Hematology, Indian Soc. Hematology & Transfusion Medicine. Avocations: music, painting, reading. Home: 26 JJ House 3rd Cross St Priyadarshini Nagar Puducherry 605006 India Office Phone: 91-9487896560. Personal E-mail: rakhee_kar@rediffmail.com.

KAR, SAIBAL, cardiologist; b. Sept. 15, 1960; MD, Nil Ratan Sircar Med. Coll., Calcutta, 1986. Cert. internal medicine 1998, cardiovasc. disease 2000, interventional cardiology 2001. Resident in medicine Postgrad. Inst. Med. Edn. and Rsch., Chandigarh, India, fellow in cardiology, asst. prof.; fellow in interventional cardiology Epworth Hosp., Melbourne, Australia; resident in medicine West LA Veterans Adminstrn. Hosp.; fellow in cardiology Cedars-Sinai Med. Ctr., fellow in interventional cardiology, interventional cardiologist dept. medicine, dir. interventional cardiac rsch.; asst. prof. David Geffen Sch. Medicine, UCLA. Mem. sic. adv. com. World Congress Heart Failure. Fellow: Am. Heart Assn., Am. Coll. Cardiology; mem.: Cardiology Soc. India, AMA, Am. Coll. Physicians, Soc. Coronary Angiography and Intervention, Am. Heart Assn., Am. Coll. Cardiology. Home: 2783 Hollyview Ct Los Angeles CA 90068 Office: Cedars-Sinai Med Ctr 8700 Beverly Blvd Los Angeles CA 90048

KARABÖRKLÜ, SALIH, research scientist; b. Sariz, Kayseri, Jan. 1, 1982; Grad, Erciyes U., 2005, MS, 2008. Rsch. asst. Osmaniye Korkut Ata U., 2009—. Avocations: football, travel. Office: Osmaniye Korkut Ata University Faculty Arts& Sci Osmaniye 80000 Turkey Office Fax: 903288271030. Business E-Mail: skaraborklu@osmaniye.edu.tr.

KARADENIZ, TURAN, agricultural studies educator; b. Tirebolu, Mar. 3, 1964; D, Ondokuzmayis U., 1987; PhD, Yüzüncü Yil U., 1993. Assoc. prof. Ordu U., 1997. Dirs., dean, 2009. Recipient Encouragement award, Tübitak. Mem.: ISHS. Avocation: travel. Office: Cumhuriyet Campüs Ordu 52200 Turkey Office Fax: 904522346632. Business E-Mail: turankaradeniz@hotmail.com.

KARAKI, MASAYUKI, otorhinolaryngologist; b. Miki-cho, Kita-Gun, Japan, Aug. 21, 1965; s. Katsuyuki and Noriko Karaki; m. Rie Karaki, Apr. 15, 2001; children: Hana, Mao. MD, Kagawa Med. Sch., Miko-Cho, Kita-Gun, 1993, Kagawa U., 2005. Resident Kagawa Med. Sch. Hosp., Miko-Cho, 1993—96; med. dr. Eikou Hosp., Takima-Cho, Mitoya-Gun, Japan, 1996—97; staff mem. Kagawa Med. Sch., Miko-Chi, Kita-Gun, 1996—2005; asst. prof. Kagawa U., Miko-Chi, Kita-Gun, 2005—. Avocations: triathlon, marathon. Home: 1080-2 Tahishim-Machi Takamatsu Kagawa 761-8075 Japan Office: Kagawa U 1750-1 Ikenobe Miki-Cho Kagawa 761-0793 Japan Office Phone: 81 87 891 2214. Business E-Mail: ironman@med.kagawa-u.ac.jp.

KARAKLA, DANIEL W., otolaryngologist, surgeon; b. Springfield, Mass., Mar. 7, 1957; AS in Bus. Adminstrn., Holyoke C.C., 1978; BS in Zoology, U. Mass., 1981; MD, Uniformed Svcs. U. Health Scis., Bethesda, Md., 1986. Diplomate Am. Bd. Otolaryngology, Head and Neck Surgery, 1994. Intern Nat. Naval Med. Ctr., Bethesda, 1987, resident, 1993; clin. instr. surgery Uniformed Svcs. U. Health Scis., 1993—96; dir. residency edn. Naval Med. Ctr., Portsmouth, Va., 1995—99; asst. clin. prof. Ea. Va. Med. Sch., Norfolk, Va., 1996—2000, assoc. prof., 2000—, dir. med. edn., 2002—. Adj. asst. prof. surgery Uniformed Svcs. U. Health Scis., 1996—2002; dir. head and neck surgery Ea. Va. Med. Sch., Norfolk, 2002—; presenter in field. Contbr. articles to profl. jours., chapters to books. Advisor Head and Neck Cancer Patient Support Group, Norfolk, 2004—; mem. med. adv. coun. Am. Cancer Soc., Norfolk, 2000—. With USN, 1982—2000. Fellow, Meth. Hosp. Ind., Indpls., 1995. Fellow: Am. Head and Neck Soc., Am. Acad. Otolaryngology, Head & Neck Surgery, Am. Coll. Surgeons; mem.: Tidewater Otolaryngology and Ophthalmology Soc., Va. Soc. Otolaryngology, Head and Neck Surgery, Med. Soc.Va., Norfolk Acad. Medicine, Soc. U. Otolaryngologists, Assn. Mil. Surgeons US, Alpha Omega Alpha. Office: Ea Va Med Sch Dept Otolaryngology Head & Neck Surgery 600 Gresham Ave Norfolk VA 23507

KARAM, ALLAN, dermatologist; b. Tartous, Syria, June 23, 1967; s. Youssef Karam and Najibet Vizmensky; life ptnr. Maela Perrot, May 17, 1977. MD, Alepo U., 1984—90; diploma in dermatology, Montpellier U., France, 1997, diploma in oncology, 1996, diploma in photodermatology, 1998, diploma in cutaneous surgery, 1999, diploma in med. and surg. laser, 2000. Physician dermatology dept. U. Hosp., Montpellier, 1991—99, Brest, France, 1999—. Contbr. articles to profl. jours. Orthodox Christian. Avocations: travel, swimming. Home: 40 Rue Lino Ventura Brest 29200 France Office: U Hosp avenue Marechal Foch 29200 Brest France Office Phone: 33298443316. Office Fax: 0033298223382. Business E-Mail: allan.karam@chu-brest.fr.

KARAMAN, FERYAL, forensic dentist; d. Nazmiye Karaman. DDS, Istanbul U., Turkey, 1981; PhD, Istanbul U., 1999. Gen. dentist Istanbul State Tng. Hosp., 1982—2001; forensic dentist Istanbul U. Inst. Forensic Scis., 2001—, expert, 2001—. Mem.: Istanbul Chamber Dentistry, Turkish Dental Assn., Balcan Acad. Forensic Scis., Am. Soc. Forensic Odontology. Muslim. Avocations: travel, painting. Office: Istanbul Univ Inst Forensic Scis Cerrahpasa Istanbul 34098 Turkey Home: Oguzhan Cad 21/A Aras Apt D5 Findikzade 34093 Istanbul Istanbul Turkey Office Phone: 905323263190. Personal E-mail: feryalkaraman@hotmail.com, feryalkaraman@gmail.com.

KARAMAN, KSENIJA, ophthalmologist, educator; b. Split, Croatia, Feb. 5, 1951; MD, Sch. Medicine, Zagreb, 1975, PhD, 1993. Ophthalmologist, prof. U. Hosp. Ctr. Split, 1978—. Recipient Achievement award, Croatian Med. Bd. Mem.: Croatian Ophthal. Soc., Internat. Soc. Intraocular Inflammation. Avocations: music, walking, swimming. Office: Zoraniceva 4 Split Dalmatia 21000 Croatia Office Fax: 38521556407. E-mail: ksenija.karaman@kbsplit.hr.

KARAMEHIC, JASENKO, immunologist, educator; b. Banovici, Bosnia-Herzegovina, Feb. 18, 1953; MD, Med. U. Sarajevo, PhD, 1977, Med. U. Tuzla, 1993. Gen. dir. Hosp. City Vares, 1987—93; chief dept. pharmacology & toxicology Med. Faculty Tuzla, 1993—2002; academician, tenured prof. pharmacology & immunology Clin. Ctr. Sarajevo U., 1993—; vice-rector sci. U. Tuzla, 1998—2002. Recipient Golden Excellence award, Municipality Tuzla, Bosnia-Herzegovina. Mem.: Am. Biog. Inst., J.William Fulbright Fgn. Scholarship Bd. (Fulbright Internat. Scholarship), Acad. Med. Scis. Bosnia and Herzegovina. Avocations: soccer, ping pong/table tennis, tennis, running, bicycling. Office: University Clin Cr Sarajevo Bolnicka 25 Sarajevo 71000 Bosnia-Herzegovina Home Fax: 387297839. Personal E-mail: karamehicjasenko@hotmail.com.

KARANDE, SUNIL, pediatrician, researcher, educator; b. Bombay, July 29, 1961; s. Chandrakant and Swarooprani (Bhatt) Karande. MBBS, Seth GS Med. Coll., Bombay, 1984, DCH, 1988, MD Pediat., 1989. House physician pediat. Seth GS Med. Coll. and Bai Jerbai Wadia Hosp. for Children, Bombay, 1986—87, Seth GS Med. Coll. and Dr. RN Cooper Hosp., Bombay, 1987—88; registrar pediat. Seth GS Med. Coll. and KEM Hosp., Bombay, 1988—90, med. officer adverse drug reaction monitoring project, 1990—91, lectr. pediat., 1992—98; assoc. prof. pediat. Lokmanya Tilak Mcpl. Med. Coll., Bombay, 1998—2009; prof. pediat. Seth G.S. Med. Coll., Mumbai, 2009—. Med. tchr. U. Bombay, 1988—; expert for essential drug list Indian Pharmacol. Soc. Clinicians & Pharmacologists, 1994; tech. com. WHO, 1997—99; examiner pediat. 3d MBBS exam., 1998—; postgrad. guide Diplomate Nat. Bd. Pediat. Dissertation Nat. Bd. Exams., New Delhi, 1999—2004; steering com, facilitator Mother and Child Friendly Hosp. Initiative, UNICEF, 2000—07; mem. com., master trainer HIV seminars Greater Bombay Mcpl. Corp. and UNICEF, 2000—02; examiner pediat. DCH exam, 2001—; examiner MD Pediat. exam, 2006—; cons. in field. Joint editor Pediatric Pulmonology Update, 1993-97; reviewer profl. jours.; contbr. chpts. to books and articles to profl. jours. Trainer, breastfeeding mgmt. course, Maharashtra State Breastfeeding Promotion Initiative, Bombay, 1994-2007; nodal person for surveillance of acute flaccid paralysis cases, Greater Bombay Mcpl. Corp., 1996-98. Surgeon lt., Indian Navy, 1991-92, INHS Asvin Indian Acad. Pediat., 2009, Fellow Internat. Acad. Rsch. Learning Disabilities; mem. NY Acad. Scis., Indian Acad. Pediat. (life), Indian Acad. Pediat. Respiratory Chpt. (life., treas. 1997, coord. seminars, confs. and continuing med. edn. 1993-99). Avocations: swimming, music, computers, novels, cricket. Home: Fl 24 5th fl Joothica 22A Naushir Bharucha Rd Mumbai 400 007 India Office: Seth G S Medical College & KEM Hospital Department Pediatrics Mumbai 400 012 India Office Phone: 91-22-24107559. Personal E-mail: karandesunil@yahoo.com.

KARANFILIAN, RICHARD, vascular surgeon educator; Grad., U. of Bologna, 1977. Diplomate Am. Bd. Surgery, Am. Bd. Surgery-vascular surgery. Residency gen. surgery Rutgers Med. Sch., 1978—83, fellowship vascular surgery, 1983—85; chief vascular surgery Sound Shore Med. Ctr.; assoc. clin. prof. surgery NY Med. Coll. Named Best Dr., NY Mag., 2008—09, 2010 Top Doc. Office: Sound Shore Medical Center Ste 14 150 Lockwood Ave New Rochelle NY 10801 Office Phone: 914-636-1700.

KARANJIA, NARIMAN DADY, hepatobiliary surgery professor; b. Bombay, India, Apr. 2, 1959; s. Khorshed Dady and Dady Nariman Karanjia; m. Caroline Rosemary Cooper, June 2, 1984; children: Rustam Nariman, Delna Nariman. MBBS, Guys Hosp. Med. Sch., London, 1983; MS, U. London, 1990. Cons. surgeon Mt. Alvernia Hosp., Guildford, England, 1995—, Royal Surrey County Hosp., Guildford, England, 1995—, Guildford Nuffield Hosp., Guildford, England, 1999—; prof. hepato-pancertio biliary surgery Surrey U., 2005. Hunterian prof. Royal Coll. of Surgeons of Eng., London; surg. advisor Mt. Alvernia Hosp., Guildford, England, 1999—2003; program dir. gen. surgery South Thames KSS Deanery, London, 2004—08. Author: (sci. articles) Brit. Jour. of Surgery, World Jour. of Surgery, Annals of The Royal Coll. of Surgeons of Eng. Recipient Ross Residents prize, Soc. for Surgery of the Alimentary Tract, 1990; scholar Conjoined War Meml. Clin. Exhbn., Guys Hosp. Spl. Trustees, 1980—83, Robert Schumann Found. Scholarship, European Inst. of Telesurgery, 1994. Fellow: Royal Coll. Surgeons Edinburgh, Royal Coll. Surgeons Eng. (fellow intercoll. bd.); mem.: Assn. Endoscopic Surgeons of Gt. Britain and Ireland (assoc.), Royal Soc. Medicine (assoc. Norman Tanner medal 1992), Brit. Soc. Gastroenterology (assoc.), Internat. Hepato-Pancreato-Biliary Assn. (assoc.), Assn. Surgeons of Gt. Britain and Ireland (assoc.). Zoroastrian. Avocations: digital photography, travel, squash. Office: Guildford Nuffield Hosp Stirling Road GU2 7RF Guildford GU2 7RF England Office Phone: 0044-1483-569947. Office Fax: 0044-1483-575029.

KARANTANIS, DIMITRIOS, nuclear medicine physician, educator; b. Mytilini, Lesvos, Greece, Feb. 26, 1972; MD, Aristotle U. Thessaloniki, Greece, 1997; PhD, Nat. and Kapodistrian U. Athens, Greece, 2009. Cons., nuc. medicine Greek Air Force Hosp., 2007—10; asst. prof., nuc. medicine David Geffen Sch. Medicine UCLA, 2010—. Home: 827 Levering Ave Apt 713 Los Angeles CA 90024 Personal E-mail: dkarantanis@nuclmed.net.

KARASU, T(OKSOZ) BYRAM, psychiatrist, educator, writer; b. Feb. 11, 1935; MD, U. Istanbul, Turkey, 1959. Jr. intern St. Jeanne D'Arc Hosp., Montreal, Canada, 1963; resident in psychiatry Yale U., New Haven, 1969; prof. psychiatry Albert Einstein Coll. Medicine, Bronx, NY, 1981—, Silverman prof., chmn. psychiatry, 1993—, univ. chmn., 1998—. Chmn. Albert Einstein Coll. Medicine, 1993—; psychiatrist-in-chief Montefiore Med. Ctr., 1993—. Author: Wisdom in the Practice of Psychotherapy, 1992, Deconstruction of Psychotherapy, 1996, The Psychotherapists's Interventions, 1998, The Psychotherapist as Healer, 2001, The Art of Serenity, 2003, Of God and Madness, 2006, The Spirit of Happiness, 2006, Rags of My Soul, 2009, The Gravity of Weight, 2010, Gothan Chronicles: The Culture of Sociopathy, 2011; editor: Psychotherapy Research, 1982, The Psychiatric Therapies, 1984, Treatments of Psychiatric Disorders, 1989, others; editor-in-chief: Am. Jour. Psychotherapy, 1994—; contbr. articles to profl. jours. Recipient Sigmund Freud award, 1997. Mem.: Am. Psychiat. Assn. (chmn. commn. 1979—83, task force 1981—90, practice guidelines in major depression 1993, revised 2000, Disting. Svc. award 1983, Spl. Presdl. award 1988, Disting. Life fellow). Office: 2 E 88th St New York NY 10128-0555 Also: Albert Einstein Coll Medicine 1300 Morris Park Ave Bronx NY 10461-1975

KARAYAN-TAPON, LUCIE, physician; b. Istanbul, May 19, 1962; MD, Montpellier Med. Sch., 1992; PhD, Poitiers U., 2009. MCU-PH Poitiers U., Med. Sch. & U. Hosp., 2003—. Avocation: diving. Office: CHU de Poitiers UM Oncologie Biologique Poitiers Vienne 86000 France E-mail: l.karayan-tapon@chu-poitiers.fr.

KARCZMARCZYK, URSZULA, medical researcher; b. Otwock, Sept. 21, 1973; PhD in Engring., Warsaw U. Tech., 2003. Specialist Nat. Medicines Inst., 2004. Rschr. Inst. Atomic Energy POLATOM Radioisotope Ctr., 2001—04. Mem.: Polish Soc. Nuc. Medicines. Avocations: sailing, cooking. Home: Stefana Okrzei Otwock Woj Mazowieckie 05-400 Poland Personal E-mail: ukarczmarczyk@o2.pl.

KARDORFF, BERND, dermatologist, laser specialist, writer, allergist; s. Dr. med. Thea and Dr. med. Ulrich Kardorff; m. Dr. med. dent. Maria Kardorff; children: Simon, Johanna. MD, Heinrich-Heine U., Duesseldorf; diploma in Reflectance Confocal Microscopy, Modena, 2011. Lic. specialist in dermatology Aerztekammer Nordrhein, specialist in allergology Aerztekammer Nordrhein, specialist in environmental medicine Aerztekammer Nordrhein, 2000, specialist in acupuncture Aerztekammer Nordrhein, 2006, skin cancer trainer KV Nordrhein, 2008. Head physician in laser medicine St. Barbara Hosp., Duisburg, Germany, 1996—99, registrar, 1998—99; vice head physician Rhein-Klinik St. Joseph, Duisburg-Beeckerwerth, Germany, 1996—99; chief dermatologist and allergologist Kardorff & Dorittke Out Patients Clinic, Moenchengladbach, Germany, 1999—; head dermatologist, allergologist, environ. and acupuncture physician Skin, Allergy, and Venous Diseases Clinic, Korschenbroich, 2007—. Pres. Umbrella Assn. Neighborhood Dermatol. Rehab. and Therapy of Chronic Skin Disorders, Moenchengladbach, Germany, 2000—; adv. bd. mem. DERM Specialist periodical, Omnimed-Verlag, Hamburg, Germany, 2001—, Cosmetic Medicine Specialists Periodical, Grosse-Verlag, Berlin, 2008. Author: (book) Allergic Diseases in Practice, Gesunde Haut - Encyclopaedia of the Skin, (specialist book) Self-Payment Therapies in Dermatology and Aesthetic Medicine, (book) Patient's Guidebook and Short Encyclopedia of Skin Diseases, Venous Diseases, Allergies and Cosmetic Medicine; inventor (invention to improve skin diseases) Atopic Eczema Skin Model of Kardorff, Schnelle-Parker (Hautmodell nach Kardorff, Schnelle-Parker) (Med. Inventors Award, 2001). Head med. cons Bellheim Network, Willich, Germany, 2004; initiator and founder Northrhine-Westphalia Psoriasis Day, Duisburg,), Germany, 1996—2005; originator Dermatologic Neighbourhood Rehab. in Germany, Duisburg, Northrine-Westphalia (NRW), 1996; initiator VDL awards Assn. Aesthetic Dermatology and Laser Medicine, Kempen, Germany, 2000, 2002, 2005, 2010. Recipient Award for pediat. dermatology, Hans Karrer GmbH, 1999, Lit. award, Georg Thieme Pub. Co. Stuttgart, 1995, 1998, 2002, Fed. Republic of Germany Order of Merit, Fed. Pres. Horst Köhler, 2009. Master: Dachverband für Wohnortnahe Dermatologische rehab. und Therapie chronischer Hautkrankheiten (DWDR e.V.) (hon.; pres. 2000); mem.: German Acad. Acupunture and Auricular Medicine, Assn. Operative and Surg. Dermatology, Working Group Cosmetology and Dermatology, VDL e.V. (innovation commisioner 2000, VDL-Förderpreis), German Dermatology Assn., NVV Lions Mönchengladbach (coach, trainer, player, Westgerman Basketball Mastership, Third Pl. All German Basketball Sr. Mastership 2000). Achievements include patents for atopic eczema skin model, Hautmodell nach Kardorff, Schnelle-Parker; implementation of 308nm Excimer laser therapy of chronic skin diseases in Germany. Avocations: basketball, skiing, piano, Ju Jitsu, water polo. Office: Dermatology & Laser Out Patients Clinic Marktstrasse 31 Moenchengladbach 41236 Germany E-mail: drkardorff@hotmail.com.

KARGANOV, MIKHAIL YURIEVICH, pathologist; b. Odessa, Nov. 13, 1956; Degree in Engring., Moscow Mendeleev Inst. Chem. Tech., 1980; PhD, Inst. Gen. Pathology and Pathophysiology, Russian Acad. Med. Scis., 1986. Head Lab. Med.-Ednl. Diagnostics Moscow Inst. Open Edn., 1997—; head Polysystemic Investigations Lab. Inst. Gen. Pathology and Pathophysiology, Russian Acad. Med. Scis., 2001—. Recipient Lenin Komsomol prize; grant, Moscow Govt. Mem.: Internat. Rsch. Soc. Spinal Deformities, European Cell Death Orgn. Avocation: diving. Office: 8 Baltiiskaya Moscow 125315 Russia Office Fax: 7(495)601 21 83. Business E-Mail: mkarganov@mail.ru.

KARIM, AHMED A., neuroscientist, psychotherapist; s. Rahmi A. and Agathe A. Karim. MS in Psychology and Neuropsychiatry, Freie Universität Berlin, Germany; PhD in Neurosci., Med. Faculty U. Tuebingen, Germany, 2009. Rsch. asst. Charité-Clinic Psychiatry, Psychotherapy and Psychosomatic, Berlin, 1997—99, Max Planck Inst. Human Devel., Berlin, 1999—2000; rsch. scientist Inst. Med. Psychology and Behavioral Neurobiology, U. Tuebingen, Germany, 2001—09; lectr. cognitive neuroscience and perceptual psychology U. Schwäbisch Gmuend, Germany, 2003—; asst. prof., med. psychology and clin. neuropsychology U. Tuebingen, Germany, 2010—. Students spokesperson inst. coun. for psychology U. Potsdam, Germany, 1995—96, mem. DSc com. for psychology, 1995—96; mem. Internat. Max Planck Rsch. Sch. of Neural and Behavioral Scis. U. Tuebingen, 2002—. Recipient 1st prize, German Senate Adminstrn. for Edn., Berlin, 1994, Poster award, 2d Internat. Brain-Computer Interface Meeting, NY, 2002; grantee, German Rsch. Soc., 2004. Mem.: Volkswagen Found. (European Platform Life Scis., Mind Scis., and the Humanities, recipient 2 rsch. grants 2007, grantee 2004), German Neurosci. Soc., Soc. Psychophysiological Rsch. (assoc. Tursky award 2005). Achievements include development of brain-computer interface for paralyzed patients; neural internet system for paralyzed patients to surf the World Wide Web; research in therapeutic applications of transcranial magnetic stimulation and transcranial direct current stimulation; neural foundation of deception and moral cognition, neuroplasticity and learning. Office: Inst Med Psychology Gartenstr 29 Tübingen 72074 Germany Business E-Mail: ahmed.karim@uni-tuebingen.de.

KARL, THOMAS HELMUT, surgeon; b. Aachen, Nordrhein-Westfalen, Germany, Jan. 18, 1967; s. Helmut Friedrich and Emmy Karl; Cert. vascular surgeon Landesärztekammer Baden, Württemberg, 2005. Oberarzt Klinikum der Johann Wolfgang Goethe U., Frankfurt Am Main, Hessen, Germany, 2007—08, Klinikum Karlsruhe, Baden- Württemberg, Germany, 1997—2006; leitender oberarzt Klinikum Offenbach, Offenbach Am Main, Hessen, Germany, 2008—. Dir.: (wundhealing orgn.) Wundverbund- Südwest E.V. Grant, Siebold Soc., 2007. Mem.: German Vascular Soc. (grant). Office: Klinikum Offenbach Starkenburgring 66 Offenbach Am Main Hessen 63069 Germany Personal E-mail: dr.t.karl@web.de. Business E-Mail: thomas.karl@klinikum-offenbach.de.

KARLAN, BETH YOUNG, gynecologic oncologist; b. NYC, May 8, 1957; Grad. magna cum laude, Harvard-Radcliffe Coll.; MD, Harvard Med. Sch. and Harvard-Mass. Inst. Tech. Program in Health Scis. and Tech., 1982. Cert. obstetrics, gynecology, gynecologic oncology, diplomate Am. Bd. Ob.-Gyn. Intern Yale-New Haven Hosp., 1982-83, resident in ob-gyn., 1983-86; fellow molecular biology Yale U. Sch. Medicine; dir., Women's Cancer Rsch. Inst. Cedars-Sinai Medical Center, LA, dir., divsn. gynecologic-oncology, dir., Gilda Radner Cancer Detection Program, fellow gynecologic oncology, 1987—; fellow gynecologic oncology, sch. medicine UCLA, 1995—, prof. ob-gyn., David Geffen Sch. Medicine, 2001—. Spkr. in field; bd. gov. endowed chmn. in gynecologic oncology Cedars Sinai; editorial bd. mem. Obstetrics & Gynecology, Jour. of Clinical Oncology, Gynecologic Oncology; editor-in-chief Gynecological Oncology Jour.; bd. dirs. Iris Internat. Inc., 2009—. Contbr. several articles to profl. jours. Named one of America's Top Doctors in Cancer; awarded grants from Dept. Def., NIH and Ahmanson Found. Mem.: AMA, ACS (Early Detection Prof. award 2006), Soc. for Gynecologic Investigation, Internat. Gynecologic Cancer Soc., Am. Soc. of Clin. Oncology, Am. Assn. for Cancer Rsch., Am. Coll. Ob-Gyn., Am. Coll. Surgeons (bd. govs.), Am. Bd. Obstetrics & Gynecology, Soc. Gynecologic Oncologists (pres. 2005—06). Office: Cedars Sinai Med Ctr 8700 Beverly Blvd Ste 290-W Los Angeles CA 90048 Office Phone: 310-423-3302. Office Fax: 310-423-9753. *

KARLOV, VLADIMIR, neurologist, educator; b. Or'el, Russia, Jan. 5, 1926; s. Alexey and Berta (Farber) K.; children: Lidiya, Alexey; m. Cathrin. MD, 1st Med. Inst., Moscow, 1946; PhD, Inst. Pediat., Moscow, 1961; DMS, Moscow Stomatological Inst., 1970. Tng. Acad.

Postgrad. Edn., Moscow; practical physician Mcpl. Hosp., Malo-Arhangelsk, Russia, 1952-57; chief neurology dept. Ramenskoye, Moscow, 1960-63; asst. prof. neurology Moscow Stomatological Inst., 1963-70, prof. neurology and neurosurgery, 1971—, head dept., 1973—2001. Dir. neurology clinic Mcpl. Hosp., Moscow, 1982—2001; prof. neurology Moscow State Medico-Stomatology U., 2001-. Author: Epilepsy, 1990, Facial Neurology, 1991, Therapy of Nervous Diseases, 1996, Neurology, 2002;, Convulsive Status Epilepticus, 2003, Absence Epilepsy of Childhood and Adolescence, 2005, Stimalsensitivity Epilepsy, 2006, Temporal Epilepsy, 2008; contbr. articles to med. jours. Sgt. Soviet Army, 1943-45. Named Meritorious Sci. Worker, Russia, 1997. Fellow: Royal Soc. Medicine UK; mem.: NY Acad. Scis., Cochrane Epilepsy Group (expert), Russian Acad. Med. Scis. (corr.), European Fedn. Neurol. Socs., European Acad. Epileptologists. Office: Moscow State Med Stomatological U Neur Novaya Basmannaya 26 107078 Moscow Russia Home: Lyeningradskoye Sh 29-34 125212 Moscow Moskva Russia Office Phone: 7(499)261-10-67. Personal E-mail: v_karlov@barnsly.ru.

KARLSBERG, RONALD P., cardiologist, educator; b. Syracuse, NY, July 24, 1947; BA in Psychology with honors, U. Calif., Berkeley, 1969; MD, U. Calif., San Francisco, 1973. Intern-resident U. Colo., 1973—75; instr. medicine Wash. U.-Barnes Hosp., 1975—78; asst. prof. medicine U. Calif. Irvine, 1978—81; clin. prof. medicine, David Geffen Sch. Medicine Cardiovasc. Med. Group Southern Calif., Cedars Sinai Heart Inst., UCLA, 1981—. Pres. Cardiovasc. Rsch. Found. Southern Calif., 1981; v.p. Southern Calif. U. San Francisco Alumni Assn., 1998—2011. Recipient Commendation medal, City of LA, Culver City, Calif., County of LA; named Tchr. of Yr., Cedars Sinai Med. Ctr., 2011. Fellow: ACP, Soc. Cardiac Computed Tomography, Am. Heart Assn., Am. Coll. Cardiology; mem.: Internat. Commn. Accreditation Computed Tomographic Labs. (bd. mem.). Avocations: skiing, golf, motorcycling. Office: 414 North Camden Dr Ste 1100 Beverly Hills CA 90210 Business E-Mail: karlsberg@cvmg.com.

KARLSSON, JAN OLOF GUSTAV, research scientist, educator; b. Finspång, Sweden, Oct. 5, 1951; s. Karl Gustav Åke and Dagny Viola Karlsson; m. Eva Christina Tuner; 1 child, Enoka Terese. MSc in Biology, Linköping U., Sweden, 1982, PhD, 1988. Rsch. fellow Linköping U., 1988—89; vis. scientist Dept. Neurosci., U. Calif., San Diego, 1989—90; rsch. fellow Swedish Med. Rsch. Coun., Linköping, 1990—93; sr. rsch. scientist GE Healthcare R&D, Oslo, 1992—. Contbr. over 70 articles to sci. pubs. Achievements include inventing four world-wide patents describing therapeutic use of a contrast agent, including cancer treatment; discovery of superoxide dismutase activity of the MRI contrast agent MnDPDP 1994-1999; cellular mechanism behind photorelaxation 1983-1985. Office: GE Healthcare R&D Nycoveien 2 485 Oslo Norway Personal E-mail: janolof.karlsson@c2i.net.

KARMACHARYA, JAGAJAN, surgeon, educator; b. Nepal, Oct. 10, 1965; MD, Nilrattan Sircar Med. Sch., 1990. Assoc. prof. surgery U. Miami Miller Sch. Medicine, 2008—. Recipient Clin. Rsch. award, Del. Valleu Vascular Surgery, Young Investigator award, Wound Healing Soc., Basic Sci. award, Robert H. Ivy Soc., Phila. Fellow: ACS; mem.: South Fla. Soc. Vascular Surgery, Internat. Soc. Endovascular Specialist, Soc. Vascular Surgery, Am. Soc. Gene Therapy. Avocations: fishing, reading, bicycling. Office: Divsn Vascular Surgery 3016 Holtz Miami FL 33136 Office Fax: 305-585-8569. Business E-Mail: whenry@med.miami.edu.

KARMALI, RASHIDA A., lawyer; b. Uganda, May 12, 1948; arrived in US, 1978; BSc, Makerere U., Kampala, Uganda, 1971; MSc, Aberdeen U., Scotland, 1973; PhD, U. Newcastle Upon Tyne, Eng., 1976; JD, Rutgers U., New Brunswick. NJ, 1993; MBA, Rutgers U., Newark, NJ, 2007. Bar: NY 1994, US Patent Office; Cert. Lionsing Profl. Fellow Clin. Rsch. Inst., Montreal, 1976-78; rsch. assoc. E. Carolina U., Greenville, NC, 1978-80, Meml. Sloan-Kettering Inst., NYC, 1980-84; adj. assoc. prof. Cook Coll., New Brunswick, NJ, 1984-90; practice in tech. law NYC, 1991—; CEO Tactical Therapeutics Inc., NYC. Mem. ABA, Am. Soc. Clin. Oncology (assoc.), Am. Intellectual Property Law Assn., Licensing Execs. Soc. Office: 99 Wall St 23rd Fl New York NY 10005 Office Phone: 212-651-9653. Personal E-mail: karmali@aol.com.

KARMOWSKI, ANDRZEJ, medical educator, researcher; b. Pilica, Poland, Jan. 2, 1943; s. Jan and Genowefa Karmowski; m. Barbara Marek; children: Agata Karmowska Myslakowska, Mikolaj. MS in Medicine, Wroclaw Med. U., Poland, 1968, PhD, 1976, habilitation, 1989. Asst. Wroclaw Med. U., 1968—75, tutorial, 1976—89, prof., 2002—. Cons. in field. Recipient Golden Cross of Honor, Pres. of Poland, 2003, medal, The Commitee of The Nat. Edn., 2004. Mem.: NY Acad. Sci., Polish Med. Assn., Polish Gynecol. Assn. (v.p.). Roman Catholic. Achievements include patents for anty-haemorrhagic patent medicine hemorigen; research in anomalities of mesonefritic carcinoform structures in Wolff - Gaertner tract; Colostrum Milk Way for cotinine, nicotine metabolite. Avocations: sports, painting, music. Office: Wroclaw Med Univ Chalubinskiego 6a Wroclaw 50-368 Poland Home: Ul. Poziomkowa 22 53-007 Wroclaw Poland Office Fax: 48717840111. Business E-Mail: ed@adm.am.wroc.pl.

KARMY-JONES, RIYAD CARADOG, surgeon, educator; b. London, Oct. 27, 1959; s. William John and Leila Jones; m. Lorie Thomas, May 12, 1984; children: Safiya Meredith, Tala Nuran, Tariq Raymond. MD, U. Alta., Edmonton, Can., 1983. Cert. general surgery Am. Bd. of Surgeons, 1990, critical care Am. Bd. of Surgeons, 1991, Am. Bd. Thoracic Surgeons, 1994. Chief thoracic surgery Harborview Med. Ctr., Seattle, 1998—; assoc. prof. U. Wash., 2001—06; med. dir. thoracic and vascular surgery Southwest Wash. Med. Ctr., Vancouver, 2006—, chief surgery, 2010—. Author: (textbook) Thoracic Trauma and Critical Care, 2002. Mem.: ACS, Am. Coll. Chest Physicians, Royal Coll. Surgeons Can. Office: Southwest Med Ctr 200 NE Mother Joseph Pl Ste 300 Vancouver WA 98664

KARNAHL, HUBERT MARTIN, medical researcher; b. Wangen im Allgau, Germany, July 20, 1944; s. Helmut and Hanna Karnahl; m. Sabine Cornelia Sonnenkalb, Sept. 12, 1947; 1 child, Navina Tatjana; 1 child, Sophie Jeannette. Dr.med., 1971. Asst. U. Zurich, Switzerland, 1964—66, U. Berlin, 1967—71, U. Nantes, France, 1971, U. Salzburg, Austria, 1972; asst. dir. Prof. Hoeffken, Cologne, Germany, 1973—87; chief Klinikum Heide (Germany)/Holstein, 1988—92, Outstanding Patients, Eisenhuttenstadt, Germany, 1992—. Leading bd. mem. Deutsche Gesesllschaft Magnetresonanz, Munich, 1973—87; fellow Arbeits Gemeinschaft Interventionelle Radiologie inder Dsutschen Rontgen Gesellschaft, Bonn, 1980—2003. Assoc. editor: Rofo, 1975—87; contbr. articles to profl. jours. Fellow: Cardiovascular and Interventional Radiology Soc. Europe, Soc. Vascular and Interventional Radiology; mem.: Deutsche Rontgen Gesellschaft. Achievements include patents for interventional catheters. Avocations: gardening, sports, photography, history.

KARNAUKHOVA, ELENA, chemist; b. Moscow, Nov. 22, 1952; PhD, Lomonosov Acad. Fine Chem. Tech., 1979. Asst. prof. dept. biologically active compounds Lomonosov Acad. Fine Chem. Tech., Moscow, 1988—91, assoc. prof. dept. biotechnology, 1991—94; sr. rsch. scientist dept. chemistry Columbia U., NY, 1994—98; prin. scientist Starzent, Inc., Manassas, Va., 1998—2002; staff scientist, regulatory reviewer Ctr. Biologics Evaluation and Rsch., US FDA, 2002—. Vis. scientist CNRS, France. Recipient prize, Internat. Sci. Found., Sci. Achievement award, Ctr. Biologics Evaluation and Rsch., US FDA. Avocation: literature. Office: 8800 Rockville Pike NIH Bldg 29 Bethesda MD 20892 Office Fax: 301-402-2780. Business E-Mail: elena.karnaukhova@fda.hhs.gov.

KARNES, ROBERT JEFFREY, urologist, educator; b. Du Quoin, Ill., Apr. 29, 1970; BA, Brown U., 1992; MD, SIU Sch. Medicine, 1997. Cons., assoc. prof. Mayo Clinic, 2006—. Bd. pres. TeamWinter, 2011. Fellow: ACS. Avocations: bicycling, fishing. Office: Mayo Clinic 200 1st St SW Rochester MN 55905 Business E-Mail: karnes.r@mayo.edu.

KARNIK, NIRANJAN SUBHASH, psychiatrist, consultant, sociologist; b. Phila. BA, U. Pa., Phila., 1993; MA, U. Ill., Urbana, 1995, MD, 2002, PhD, 2003. Cert. physician surgeon Med. Bd. Calif., 2003, diplomate in psychiatry Am. Bd. Psychiatry & Neurology, 2009, cert. physician Ill. Dept. Prof. Reg., 2009. Resident gen. psychiatry Stanford U., Palo Alto, Calif., 2002—05, fellow child & adolescent psychiatry, 2005—07; asst. adj. prof. U. Calif., San Francisco, 2005—09; staff physician Palo Alto Found. Med. Group, Fremont, Calif., 2007—09; cons. psychiatrist Larkin St. Youth Svcs., San Francisco, 2007—09; asst. prof. U. Chgo., 2009—. Achievements include research in mental health problems among underserved and vulnerable youth. Office: University Chgo 5841 S Maryland Ave MC 3077 Chicago IL 60637 Business E-Mail: nskarnik@uchicago.edu.

KARNIOL, RACHEL, psychology educator; b. Haifa, Israel, July 23, 1950; d. Eugene and Irene (Deutsch) K.; m. Yoram Tambour, Mar. 24, 1983; children: Karen, Orren. BS, U. Toronto, Can., 1973; MA, U. Waterloo, Can., 1975, PhD, 1977. Lectr. Tel Aviv (Israel) U., 1977-81, sr. lectr., 1982-90, assoc. prof., 1991—, prof., 1999—. Vis. asst. prof. U. Toronto, 1976-77; vis. prof. U. Fla., 1986, Princeton U., 1995-96, Carnegie Mellon U., 1996-97, 2003-04. Contbr. articles to profl. jours. including Jour. Personality and Social Psychology, Ann. Rev. Psychology, others; author. Social Development as Preference Management: How Infants Children & Parents Get What They Want from One Another, 2010. Fellow APA; mem. Soc. Rsch. Child Devel. Office: Tel Aviv U Dept Psychology Ramat Aviv Israel

KARNSAKUL, WIKROM, medical educator; b. Thailand, Sept. 9, 1968; MD, Mahidol U., 1992. Asst. prof. Johns Hopkins U. Sch. Medicine, 2008—. Recipient Clin. Rsch. award, Pediat. Soc. Mem.: Am. Assn. Study Liver Diseases. Office: 600 N Wolfe St Baltimore MD 21287 Business E-Mail: wkarnsa1@jhmi.edu.

KARP, ADAM, geriatrician, educator; Attended, Albert Einstein Coll. of Medicine, 1987. Diplomate Am. Bd. of Internal Medicine, Am. Bd, Internal Medicine-geriatric medicine. Residency tng. Maimonides Med. Ctr., 1987—90, internship; clin. asst. prof. dept. of medicine and hosp. for joint diseases NYU Langone Med. Ctr. Clin. fellow NYU Med. Ctr., 1990—92. Contbr. (jour.) Thromboprophylaxis after hip fracture: evaluation of 3 pharmacologic agents, Predictive value of preoperative arterial blood gas evaluation for geriatric patients with hip fractures, Effect of postoperative delirium on outcome after hip fracture, Calcium channel blockers in systemic hypertension, Calcium-channel blockers in systemic hypertension. Office: NYU Langone Medical Center and School of Medicine 550 1st Ave New York NY 10016 Office Phone: 212-263-7300.

KARP, GERALD CHARLES, biologist, educator, writer; b. LA, Dec. 24, 1942; s. Harry and Sally Karp; m. Patrice Marie Patrick, Nov. 21, 1973; 1 child, Jennifer. BS, UCLA, 1964; PhD, U. Wash., 1970. Postdoctoral rschr. U. Colo. Med. Ctr., Denver, 1970—71; prof. biology U. Fla., Gainesville, 1971—84; vis. scientist U. Iowa, Iowa City, 1984, U. Calif., San Francisco, 1988—89; freelance writer Cin., 1990—. Ad hoc com. med. grants rsch. NIH, Bethesda, Md., 1976; cons. Morrison and Foerster, San Francisco, 1988, Wiley and Sons Publs., NYC, 1990— Author: Development, 1976, 2d edit., 1981, Cell Biology, 1979, 2d edit., 1984, Cell and Molecular Biology, 1996, 6th edit., 2010. Predoctoral fellow NSF, 1964-69, Postdoctoral fellow NIH, 1970-71. Mem. AAAS, Phi Beta Kappa.

KARP, HARVEY NEIL, pediatrician; b. NY, 1951; married; 1 child. MD, Albert Einstein Coll. Medicine, 1976. Intern, pediat. Children's Hosp., LA, 1976—77, resident, ambulatory pediat., 1977—79; fellow, child develop. UCLA Sch. Medicine, 1980—82, asst. prof. pediatrics, 1989—; pvt. practice Santa Monica, Calif., 1982—2005. Invited lectr. in field. Author: Happiest Baby on the Block, 2002, Happiest Toddler on the Block, 2004; guest appearances on Good Morning America, Dr. Phil Show, ABC World News Tonight, CNN, Lifetime Channel, numerous nat. radio programs, AP, Time, Newsweek, and People mag. Office: 12300 Wilshire Bvld Ste 320 Los Angeles CA 90025 Office Phone: 310-207-1111. Office Fax: 310-207-1221. E-mail: info@thehappiestbaby.com.

KARP, HERBERT RUBIN, neurologist, educator, geriatrician; b. Atlanta, Apr. 13, 1921; s. Louis and Sadie (Fischer) K.; m. Hazel Berman, June 16, 1948; children: Eleanor Beth, Miriam Sarah, Benjamin Chaim. BA, Emory U., Atlanta, 1943, MD, 1951. Diplomate Am. Bd. Psychiatry and Neurology. Intern then resident in internal medicine Grady Meml. Hosp., 1951-54; resident in neurology Duke U. Med. Ctr., 1954-56; clin. and rsch. fellow in neurology and neuropathology Harvard U.-Mass. Gen. Hosp., 1956-58; asst. prof. neurology Emory U., Atlanta, 1958-63, prof., 1963-91, prof. emeritus, 1991—, disting. emeritus prof., 2006—, prof. medicine, 1983-91, chmn. dept. neurology, 1974-83, dir. geriat. program dept. medicine, 1983-90; dir. med. svcs. Wesley Woods Geriatric Ctr., 1983-91, med. dir. emeritus, 1991—. Med. dir. medicare svcs. Ga. Med. Care Found.; med. dir. for Medicare quality improvement, 2005-11; trustee Atlanta Symphony Orch., 1975-95, bd. counselors 1996—, sec., 1979-80; pres. Ahavath Achim Synagogue, 1980-82; trustee Nat. Found. Jewish Culture, 1976-84, mem. bd. overseers, 1984-90. With USNR, 1943—46, with U.S. Public Health Svc. Reserve, 1946—. Recipient Thomas Jefferson award Emory U., 1984, Outstanding Med. Alumnus award, 1986, Disting. Med. Achievement award, 2001; Eternal Light award Jewish Theol. Sem. Am., 1985, Civic Endeavor award Med. Assn. Ga., 1989, Myrtle Wreath award Hadassah, 1990, Wakeman award Duke U., 1990; spl. fellow Nat. Inst. Neurol. Diseases, 1956-58; Herbert R. Karp Leadership award established in his name Dept. of Neurology, Emory U., 1999. Fellow Am. Acad. Neurology; mem. Am. Neurol. Assn. (mem. coun.), Assn. Univ. Profs, Neurology, Atlanta Interfaith Broadcasters (bd. dirs. 1991—2009, sec. 1997-2005, chair 2005-08), Alpha Omega Alpha. Democrat. Jewish. Home: 880 Somerset Dr NW Atlanta GA 30327-3732 Personal E-mail: hkarp02@emory.edu.

KARP, NOLAN SERGE, plastic surgeon; b. NYC, July 26, 1959; BS, Northwestern U., 1979, MD, 1983. Diplomate Am. Bd. Surgery, Am. Bd. Plastic Surgery. Resident in gen. surgery NYU Med. Ctr., 1983—88; resident in plastic surgery Inst. Reconstructive Plastic Surgery, NYU Med. Ctr., 1989—91, exec. chief resident, 1990—91, fellow in microsurgery, 1991—92, craniofacial rsch. fellow, 1988—89; asst. prof. plastic surgery NYU Sch. Medicine, 1992—99, assoc. prof. clin. plastic surgery, 1999—; attending physician Tisch Hosp., 1992—, NY VA Hosp., NYC, 1992—; asst. attending physician Bellevue Hosp. Ctr., NYC, 1992—; attending physician Manhattan Eye, Ear, Throat Hosp., NYC, 1992—. Contbr. articles to profl. jours. Recipient Award for best clin. paper, Am. Soc. Maxilofacial Surgery, 1990, 1st place for outstanding paper, NY Acad. Medicine, 1990. Mem.: Am. Soc. Breast Disease, Tissue Engring. Soc., Am. Soc. for Laser Medicine and Surgery, Am. Soc. Plastic and Reconstructive Surgery, Plastic Surgery Rsch. Coun., NY County Med. Soc., Med. Soc. State NY. Office: NYU Med Ctr 530 First Ave Ste 8Y New York NY 10016 also: 305 E 47th St, Ste 1A New York NY 10017 Office Phone: 212-355-5779. Office Fax: 212-486-7166.

KARPEH, MARTIN S., JR., surgeon, educator; MD, Pa. State U., 1983. Diplomate Am. Bd. Surgery, 1990. Resident in surgery Hosp. Univ. Pa., 1984—89; fellow in surgical oncology Meml. Sloan-Kettering Cancer Ctr., 1989—91, attending surgeon dept. surgery; assoc. prof. clin. surgery Cornell Univ.; prof. surgery Stony Brook Univ. Cancer Ctr., chief surgical oncology, dir.; assoc. dir. Continuum Cancer Ctrs. of NY; dir. surgical oncology St. Luke's Med. Ctr.; chmn. dept. surgery Beth Israel Med. Ctr., 2007—, dir. surgical oncology. Co-author: A phase I/pilot study of sequential doxorubicin/vinorelbine: effects on p53 and microtubule-associated protein 4, 2002, Improvement in inter-observer accuracy in delineation of the lumpectomy cavity using fiducial markers, 2009. Named one of Best Doctors, NY mag., 2008. Office: Beth Israel Medical Center 1st Ave at 16th St New York NY 10003 Office Phone: 212-420-4044.

KARPMAN, HAROLD LEW, cardiologist, educator, writer; b. Belvedere, Calif., Aug. 23, 1927; s. Samuel and Dora (Kastleman) K.; m. Molinda Karpman. Student, UCLA, 1945-46; BA, U. Calif., Berkeley, 1950; MD, U. Calif., San Francisco, 1954. Diplomate Am. Bd. Internal Medicine. Rotating intern L.A. County Gen. Hosp., LA, 1954-55; cardiovascular trainee Nat. Heart Inst., LA, 1957-58; asst. resident Beth Israel Hosp., Boston, 1955-57; fellow Wyley Winsor Rsch. Found., LA, 1958-59; pvt. practice Beverly Hills, Calif., 1958—; clin. instr. medicine U. So. Calif., LA, 1958-64, asst. clin. prof., 1964-71, assoc. clin. prof., 1971-72; assoc. clin. prof. medicine David Geffen Sch. Medicine, UCLA, 1972—92, clin. prof. medicine, 1992—, attending physician. Bd. govs. Cedars-Sinai Med. Ctr., L.A., 1958-, UCLA Med. Ctr., 1958-04, Brotman Med. Ctr., 1958-04, Culver City, Calif.; founder, chmn., CEO Cardiovasc. Rsch. Found. Southern Calif., 2007-; examiner in cardiovascular diseases Calif. Indsl. Accident Commn., Calif. Dept. Vocat. Rehab.; founder, bd. dirs., chmn. bd. Cardio-Dynamics Labs., Inc., 1969-82; gen. ptnr. Camden Med. Bldg., L.A., 1970-86; bd. dirs. Mcht. Bank Calif.; bd. dirs. med. rsch. Faberge, Inc., N.Y.C., 1980-84; cardiovascular cons. Delta Air Lines, 1992-94; founder, bd. dirs., chmn. bd., chief med. officer CORDA Med. Care, Inc., 1995-2000; chmn., founder, dir. Integrated Diagnostic Ctrs., Inc., 2000-07. Author: Your Second Life, 1979, Preventing Silent Heart Disease, 1989; assoc. editor Internal Medicine Alert, 1992—; contbr. numerous articles to med. jours. Fellow ACP, Am. Coll. Cardiology, Am. Coll. Chest Physicians, Internat. Cardiovascular Soc., Am. Coll. Angiology, Internat. Coll. Angiology, Am. Thermographic Soc. (charter, pres. 1971-72), Am. Acad. Thermology; mem. AMA, Calif. Med. Assn., L.A. Med. Assn., Nat. Cardiovascular Network (exec. com., bd. dirs. 1994-98), Western Cardiovascular Network (chmn., med. dir. 1993-96), Am. Soc. Internal Medicine, Am. Heart Assn., Calif. Heart Assn., L.A. County Heart Assn. Office: 414 N Camden Dr 1100 Beverly Hills CA 90210-4532 Office Phone: 310-278-3400.

KARRAZ, MAZEN ABDUL MASIH, anesthesiologist; b. Sednaya, Syria, July 7, 1964; s. Abdul Masih Tawfiq Karraz and Jerjet Elias AL Chaghouri. MD, U. Damascus, 1987. Cert. anesthesia specialist, acupuncture specialist. Anesthesiologist Bicetre U. Hosp., Paris, 1994—95, Beauvais Hosp., 1996—2001, Evry Hosp., 2001—02, Verdun Hosp., 2003—; cons. pain mgmt. Polyclinique Beauvaisis, Beauvais, 2003—. Cons. Coun. Helthcare Advisors, 2003—. Columnist Soc. Iberoamericana Sci. Info.; contbr. articles to profl. jours. Mem.: European Anesthesia Assn. (assoc.), French Pain Mgmt. Assn. (assoc.), French Anesthesia Assn. (assoc.). Roman Catholic. Achievements include invention of score predicting the difficulty of neuraxial block; development of method of epidural ambulatory labor analgesia for parturient which allowed all parturients to walk during labor. Avocations: travel, pétanque. Office: Verdun Hosp Anesthesia Dept Verdun 55107 France Home: 57 Rue Planchat 75020 Paris France Home Phone: 0033143717508; Office Phone: 0033329838485. Office Fax: 0033329838356. Personal E-mail: mazenkarraz@hotmail.com.

KARSENTY, GERARD, genetics educator; m. Patricia Ducy; children: Antoine, Cecile. MD, PhD in Endocrine Physiology, U. Paris V, France, 1984. Postdoctoral fellowship NIH, Bethesda, Md., 1987; postdoctoral fellowship, gene regulation Nat. Cancer Inst.; postdoctoral fellowship, faculty mem. molecular genetics U. Tex., MD Anderson Cancer Ctr., 1987—97; prof., dept. molecular & human genetics and program develop. biology Baylor Coll. Medicine, Houston, 1998—2006; prof., chair, genetics & develop. Columbia U. Med.

Ctr., 2006—. Scientific dir. The Bone Disease Program Tex. Contbr. articles to profl. jours.; editor: Jour. Cell Biology, Developmental Cell and Cell Metabolism. Recipient Richard Lounsbery award, NAS, 2010. Office: Columbia U Med Ctr 701 W 168th St Rm 1602A New York NY 10032 Office Phone: 212-305-6398. Office Fax: 212-923-2090. Business E-Mail: gk2172@columbia.edu. *

KARSLIGIL, TEKIN, medical educator; b. Gaziantep, Feb. 3, 1959; AA, Gazi Ü., 1995. Prof. Gaziantep U., 1996—. Office: Gaziantep Üniversitesi Tip Fakültes Gaziantep Türkiye 27300 Turkey Business E-Mail: karsligil@gantep.edu.tr.

KARST, GREGORY MARK, physical therapist, educator; b. Great Bend, Kans., Aug. 14, 1954; s. Ralph Lawrence and Esther Marie K.; m. Melanie Jo, Sept. 25, 1993. BS in Phys. Therapy cum laude, Wichita State U., 1976; MS in Animal Physiology, U. Ariz., 1984, PhD in Physiology, 1989. Cert. phys. therapist, Ariz., Nebr. Phys. therapist St. Mary's Hosp., Tucson, 1976-78, Tucson Gen. Hosp., 1978-79; phys. therapist in pvt. practice Tucson, 1979-84; rsch. asst. NASA-Ames Rsch. Ctr., Moffett Field, Calif., 1983-84; grad. teaching asst. U. Ariz., Tucson, 1984-89; asst. prof. U. Wis., Madison, 1989-92; assoc. prof. U. Nebr. Med. Ctr., Omaha, 1992—2006, prof., 2006—, asst. dean Sch. Allied Health Professions, 2007—. Instr. Pima C.C., Tucson, 1987-88. Contbr. chpt. to book, articles to profl. jours.; editl. bd. Phys. Therapy jour., 2000—. Mem. Am. Phys. Therapy Assn., Soc. for Neurosci. Office: U Nebr Med Ctr 984000 Nebr Med Ctr Omaha NE 68198-4000 Office Phone: 402-559-6596. Business E-Mail: gmkarst@unmc.edu.

KARSTEN, UWE RAINER, biologist; b. Breslau, Germany, Oct. 23, 1934; s. Ernst Eberhard and Charlotte (Heilmann) K.; m. Helga Hintz, June 4, 1960 (dec. Dec. 1997); children: Peter, Christine, Stefan; m. Christel Kemsies, Aug. 21, 2004. Diploma in biology, Humboldt U., Berlin, 1958, D Natural Sci., 1964, D habil, 1993. Asst. Humboldt U., Berlin, 1959-67; head rsch. group Inst. Cardiology Acad. Scis., Berlin, 1967-76, head rsch. group Inst. Cancer Rsch., 1976-84, head rsch. group Inst. Molecular Biology, 1985-91; head rsch. group Max Delbrück Ctr. for Molecular Medicine, Berlin, 1992-2001. Cons. Glycotope GmbH. Contbr. articles to sci. jours. Study grant WHO, 1981; recipient Nat award German govt., 1985. Mem. European Assn. Cancer Rsch., Soc. Biochem. Molecular Biology, European Tissue Culture Soc., European Soc. Cancer, Immunology and Immunotherapy, N.Y. Acad. Scis., Internat. Soc. Oncodevelopmental Biology and Medicine. Achievements include patents in field. Avocation: painting. Office: Glycotope GmbH Robert-Rössle-St 10 Berlin D-13125 Germany Office Phone: 493094892613. Business E-Mail: uwe.karsten@glycotope.com.

KARTAVTSEV, YURI PHEDOROVICH, geneticist, professor; b. Vladivostok, Russia, May 11, 1948; s. Fedor Evtekhovich Kartavtsev and Olga Nikiforovna Filipas; m. Irina Vasilievna Kartavtseva, May 20, 1971; children: Eugeny Yurievich, Margarita Yurievna Suvorova. Degree in Biology, Far Ea. State U., Vladivostok, 1971; DSc in Biology, 1995. Metal-worker Locomotive Depot, Vladivostok, Russia, 1963—65; sr. lab. asst. Pacific Rsch. Inst. Fishery and Oceanography, Vladivostok, 1965; rsch. probationer to leading sci. rschr. A.V. Zhirmunsky Inst. Marine Biology, Vladivostok, 1973; dir. Vostok Marine Biol. Sta., 1995—2002; head Group of Genetic Resources, 2005—. Contbr. articles to profl. jours. Chmn. Vladivostok Pub. Found. Devel. Genetics, 1992—; working group chmn. Fish BOL NE Asia. Capt. Russian Army, 1971—73. Grantee, Russian Govt., 1997; grant, RFBR, 2002. Mem.: Russian Acad. Sci. (award 1999), Sci. Coun. Far Ea. Fed. U. (assoc.). Avocations: home made wine, poetry, sports. Office: A V Zhirmunsky Inst Marine Biology ul Pal'chyevskogo 17 690041 Vladivostok Primorskiy Kray Russia Office Phone: 7-4232-311138. Office Fax: 7-4232-310900.

KARTEN, HARVEY JULES, neurosciences educator; b. NYC, July 13, 1935; s. Ernest and Esther (Wacks) K.; m. Elizabeth Bunim, Mar. 22, 1964; children: Joseph Thomas, Seth David, Daniel Evan. BA, Yeshiva U., NYC, 1955; MD, Albert Einstein Coll. Medicine, Bronx, NY, 1959. Diplomate Nat. Bd. Med. Examiners. Intern in medicine U. Utah, Salt Lake City, 1959-60; resident in psychiatry U. Colo., Denver, 1960-61; rsch. assoc. Walter Reed Army Inst. Rsch., Washington, 1961-65, Washington Sch. Psychiatry, 1961-65, MIT, Cambridge, 1965-72, sr. rsch. assoc., 1972-74; prof. psychiatry SUNY, Stony Brook, 1974-86; prof. neurosci. U. Calif. San Diego, La Jolla, 1986—, prof. psychiatry, disting. prof., 2004. Vis. prof. Calif. Inst. Tech., Pasadena, 1972; adj. prof. Salk Inst., La Jolla, Calif., Scripps Rsch. Inst.; vis. disting. Wiersma prof. Calif. Tech. Inst., 2003; sci. editl. bd. Jour. Comparative Neurology. Author: Stereotaxic Atlas, 1967; mem. editl. bd. Jour. Comparative Neurology, 1974-88, 95—, Jour. Neurosci., 1984-86, Visual Neurosci., 1988-91, Brain Behavior and Evolution, 1970—, NeuroImage, 1991-94; also over 175 articles. Lt. comdr. USPHS, 1961-65. Recipient J. Javits award, Nat. Inst. Neurol. Disease and Stroke, 1988, Krieg Cortical Discoverer award, Cajal Club, 2005, Sanford Palay award, 2008 Fellow Am. Acad. Arts and Scis.; mem. Am. Assn. Anatomists (C.J. Herrick award 1968), Soc. Neurosci., Winter Conf. on Brain Rsch., Soc. for Neurosci. Jewish. Avocations: hiking, skiing, kayaking. Home: 4678 Sun Valley Rd Del Mar CA 92014-4115 Office: Sch Medicine Basic Sci Bldg Rm 3009 U Calif San Diego La Jolla CA 92093 Office Phone: 619-534-4938. Office Fax: 858-534-6602. E-mail: hjkarten@ucsd.edu.

KARTSIOS, CHARALAMPOS (HARIS), hematologist, consultant; s. Christos Kartsios and Anastassia Kartsiou. MD, Aristotle U., Thessaloniki, 1995. Cert. in hematology Gen. Med. Coun. Eng., 2007, Nat. Coun. Health, Greece, 2005. Internal medicine fellow Theagenion Cancer Ctr., Thessaloniki, 1998—2000, locum cons. hematologist, 2005—07; hematology fellow Papanicolaou Gen. Hosp., Thessaloniki, 2001—05; hon. cons. hematologist Hematological Malignancy Diagnostic Svc., Leeds, England, 2007—08; locum cons. hematologist Hull Royal Infirmary, England, 2007—08; chronic lymphocytic leukemia rsch. fellow St James U. Hosp., Leeds, England, 2007—08; cons. hematologist Papageorgiou Gen. Hosp., Thessaloniki, 2008—. Lt. Med. Dept. Greek Army, 1995—97. Grant, Inst. Hellenic Soc. Hematology, 2006. Mem.: European Rsch. Initiative CLL, Med. Soc. Thessaloniki, Hellenic Soc. Hematology, Am. Soc. Hematology. Avocations: basketball, reading, cooking. Office: Hematology Papageorgiou General Hosp Periferiaki Odos Nea Efkarpia Thessaloniki GR-56403 Greece Home Fax: 0030-2310673521. Personal E-mail: hariskartsios@gmail.com.

KASAHARA, KAZUO, hematologist, educator; b. Fukui, May 1, 1961; MD, Kanazawa U., 1986, PhD, 1991. Hosp. clin. prof. Kanazawa U. Hosp., 2007—. Office: Takara-machi 13-1 Kanazawa Ishikawa 920-8641 Japan Office Fax: 81-76-234-4252. Business E-Mail: kasa1237@med3.m.kanazawa-u.ac.jp.

KASAI, HIROSHI, medical educator; b. Tokyo, Mar. 31, 1947; s. Ken and Uta Yanagisawa; m. Miwako Kasai, Mar. 17, 1974; 1 child, Jun. Degree in Chemistry, Gakushuin U., Tokyo, 1974. Postdoc. fellow Dept. Chemistry, Columbia U., NYC, 1975—77; sr. rsch. assoc. Nat. Cancer Ctr. Rsch. Inst., Tokyo; prof. U. Occupl. Environ. Health, Kitakyushu, Japan, 1993—; dir. OHG Inst. Co., Ltd., Kitakyushu, 2005—. Contbr. scientific papers. Recipient Japanese Environ. Mutagen Soc. award, 2007. Achievements include research in discovery of 8-hydroxydeoxyguanosine as an oxidative DNA damage. Office: Univ Occupl Environ Health 1-1 Iseigaoka Yahatanishi-ku Kitakyushu 807-8555 Japan

KASAI, KOHEI, surgeon; b. Sapporo, Hokkaido, Japan, Nov. 26, 1937; s. Takemi and Suzu (Isobe) K.; m. Haruko Fujimura, Oct. 30, 1972 (div. Oct. 1995); children: Takatoshi, Aki. MB, Showa Med. Coll., Tokyo. Surgeon Maruyama Meml. Hosp., Saitama-Ken, Japan, 1946, Tokyo Isuzumorter Hosp., Tokyo, 1947, Oomiya Cen. Hosp., Saitama-Ken, 1948; cardiologist Hakodate Mcpl. Hosp., Hokkaido, Japan, 1949-53; surgeon Orissa State U. Host, India, 1946. Mem. Hakodate Unesco Assn. (v.p. 1975), Lions (41st pres. Hakodate Higasi club). Japan Democratic Party. Avocations: mountain climbing, philatelist. Home: 5-10 Honcho 0400011 Hokkaido Japan Office: 5-10 Honcho Hakodate Hokkaido 0400011 Japan E-mail: dr-kasai@siren.ocn.ne.jp.

KASAI, TOKUO, physician, researcher; b. Shibuya-ku, Tokyo, Kazakhstan, Aug. 25, 1965; s. Takayoshi and Kiyoko Kasai; m. Megumu Amino. MD, PhD, Jikei U. Sch. of Medicine, Tokyo, Japan, 1984—2000. Cbnc Am. Soc. of Nuc. Cardiology, 2002, Fjsim Japanese Soc. of Internal medicine, 1999, Fjcs Japanese Circulation Soc., 1999, Fjsnm Japanese Soc. of Nuc. Medicine, 1997, BLS Instr. Am. Heart Assn., 2003, ACLS Instr. Am. Heart Assn., 2004, Japanese Assn. for Acute Medicine, 2004, Japanese Circulation Soc., 2004, ACLS Course Dir. Japanese Assn. for Acute Medicine, 2005. Fellow St. Luke's-Roosevelt Hosp. Ctr., NY, 2001—03; asst. prof. Jikei U. Sch. of Medicine, Minato-ku, Tokyo, Japan, 2003—. Asst. prof. Jikei U. Sch. of Medicine, Minato-ku, Tokyo, Japan, 1999—2001. Contbr. articles pub. to profl. jour. (Am. Soc. of Nuc. Cardiology/Fujisawa Award, 2002). Bls/acls instr. Am. Med. Responce, Honolulu, Hawaii, 2003—05. Fellow: Japanese Soc. of Internal medicine (licentiate). Citizens. Achievements include patents for PTCA guide wire. Avocations: cpr education, widespread use of nuclear cardiology. Office: Jikei Univ Sch of Medicine 3 25 8 Nishishinbashi Minato ku Tokyo 105 8471 Japan Office Fax: +81-3-3459-6043; Home Fax: +81-3-3603-2234. Personal E-mail: tk_kasai@yahoo.co.jp. E-mail: tkkasai@jikei.ac.jp.

KASAJ, ADRIAN, medical researcher, periodontist; b. Gross-Gerau, Germany, Sept. 26, 1974; s. Branko and Jadranka Kasaj; m. Aristea Gortan-Kasaj. DDS, Sch. Dentistry, U. Zagreb, Croatia, 2000; DMD, Dept. Operative Dentistry, U. Mainz, Germany, 2001; Dr.med.dent. habil., U. Mainz, 2009. Cert. in periodontology LZK Rhineland-Palatinate, 2005, specialist in periodontology German Soc. Periodontology, 2006, European Dental Assn., 2007. Dentist pvt. practice, Neustadt, Weinstraße, Germany, 2000—01; rsch. assoc., dept. operative dentistry Johannes Gutenberg U., Mainz, 2002—. Vis. rschr., dept. periodontology Goldman Dental Sch., Boston U., 2006, Ohio State U., Columbus, 2007. Contbr. articles to numerous sci. jours. Mem.: Working Group Basic Sci., German Soc. Dentistry and Oral Medicine, German Soc. Periodontology (Best prize 2007). Office: Johannes Gutenberg-Univ Augustusplatz 2 Mainz 55131 Germany Office Fax: 49-6131-17-3406. Business E-Mail: kasaj@gmx.de.

KASANA, RAMESH CHAND, biotechnologist; b. Chilt, NY, Sept. 1, 1974; PhD, PAU, Ludhiana, 1996. Rschr. Inst. Himalayan Bioresource Tech., Palampur, 2004—. Mem.: Biotech Rsch. Soc. India, Assn. Microbiologists India. Home: Ihbt Palampur Himachal Pradesh 176061 India Personal E-mail: rameshkasana@yahoo.co.in.

KASARSKY, JASON S., cosmetic dentist; Grad., NYU; attended, Cornell U. Tchr. Coll. of Dentistry NYU. Lectr. Biolase Inc.; vis. faculty Spear Inst. Scottsdale Center for Dentistry; tchr. Coll. of Dentistry NYU. Mem.: Crown Coun. of Dentistry, Internat. Congress of Oral Implantology, Am. Acad. of Implant Prosthodontics, Am. Acad. of Cosmetic Dentistry, Dental Soc. of NY, Am. Acad. of Implant Dentistry. Office: Jason S Kasarsky DDS 530 Park Ave New York NY 10021 Mailing: Jason S Kasarsky DDS 137 Maple Ave White Plains NY 10605 Office Phone: 212-838-8230 212.838.8230, 212-838-8230 212.838.8230.

KASASHIMA, SATOMI, pathologist; b. Kanazawa, Ishikawa, Japan, Aug. 24, 1968; PhD, Kanazawa U. Grad. Sch. Medicine, 1995, MD, 1999. Dir. pathology, clin. lab. Nat. Hosp. Orgn., Kanazawa Med. Ctr., 2007—. With pathology sect. Kanazawa U. Hosp., 2004—06. Mem.: Japanese Soc. Clin. Cytology, Japanese Soc. Lab. & Medicine, Japanese Soc. Pathology. Avocation: gardening. Office: Shimoishibikimachi 1 1 Kanazawa Ishikawa 920-8650 Japan Office Fax: 81-76-222-2758. E-mail: sato-kasa@kinbyou.hosp.go.jp.

KASCH, MARY COURTEOL, occupational therapist; b. Chgo., Feb. 15, 1947; d. Paul and Bernice Zimmerman Courteol; children: Elizabeth Kasch Peter, David Michael. BS, Tufts U., 1970. Registered occupl. therapist, lic., cert. hand therapist. Pres. Hand Therapy Certification Commn., Sacramento, 2000—, exec. dir.; hand therapist Campus Commons Phys. Therapy, Sacramento, 1997—2001. Author: Rehabilitation of the Hand, 1979, 1985, 1991, 1996, 2001, Occupational Therapy: Practice Skills for Physical Dysfunction; mem. editl. rev. bd.: Jour. Hand Therapy, 1998—2005. Sec. Sacramento Choral Soc. Orch., Sacramento, 1998—2006. Recipient Award of Excellence, Occupl. Therapy Assn. Calif., 1986, Lillian Terris award, Profl. Exam. Svc., 1997, Nat. Svc. award, Arthritis Found., 1985, Pres.'s Gold award, Am. Soc. Hand Therapists, 1992. Fellow: Am. Occupl. Therapy Assn. Achievements include development of Certified Hand Therapist Credential. Avocations: singing, sewing. Office: Hand Therapy Certification Commission 1337 Howe Ave Ste 230 Sacramento CA 95825 Business E-Mail: mkasch@htcc.org.

KASCHINA, ELENA, pharmacologist, researcher; b. St. Petersburg, Russia, Sept. 10, 1961; d. Galina Kaschina-Linde and Andrej Kaschin-Linde; m. Andrej Spiegel, Apr. 23, 1987; 1 child, Olga. MD, Mil. Med. Acad., Russia, 1995. Diplomate in internal medicine St. Petersburg Pavlov State Med. U., 1984. Physician Hosp. 144, St. Petersburg, 1984—87; rsch. fellow Mil. Med. Acad., Dept. Pharmacology, St. Petersburg, 1987—92, asst. prof., 1992—97; rsch. assoc. Inst. Pharmacology, Christian Albrechts U. Zu Kiel, Germany, 1999—2001; rsch. assoc., group leader Ctr. Cardiovasc. Rsch., Inst. Pharmacology, Charité U., Berlin, 2002—. Translator: (book) Color Atlas of Pharmacology; contbr. chapters to books. Recipient Young Investigator award, Hypertension Congress, 2001; Fellowship, Otto Benecke Fund, 1999—2000, grant, German Ministry Edn. Rsch., 2000—08. Russian Orthodox. Achievements include research in new drugs for treatment of aortic aneurysm and myocardial infarction; role of kininogen in vascular remodeling, molecular mechanisms of aneurysm formation. Avocation: photography. Office: Ctr Cardiovascular Rsch Hessische Strasse 3-4 Berlin 10115 Germany Office Fax: 49 30450525901.

KASCHKE, MICHAEL, medical products executive; b. June 18, 1957; married; 2 children. PhD in Physics, U. Jena; degree in mktg. and fin., Grad. Bus. Sch. Zurich. Lab. mgr. Max Born Inst., Berlin, 1989—90; vis. scientist IBM T.J. Watson Rsch. Ctr., Yorktown Heights, NY, 1990—92; staff mem. and leader devel. operation microscopes Carl Zeiss, Germany, 1992—95, head geodesy, 1995—98, head surg. products, 1998—99, dir. med. divsn., 1999—2002; bd. dirs. Carl Zeiss AG, 2000—10, CEO, 2011—; chmn. Carl Zeiss Meditec AG, 2002—08, 2010—, CEO, 2008—10. Hon. prof. U. Karlsruhe and the Karlsruhe Inst. Tech., Germany, 2009—; chmn. supervisory bd. Carl Zeiss Meditec AG; mem. supervisory bd. Henkel KGaA; mem. adv. bd. Karlsruhe Sch. Optics & Photonics. Bd. trustees Max Planck Inst. Astronomy. Office: Carl Zeiss AG Carl Zeiss Strasse 1 73446 Oberkochen Germany Office Phone: 49 7364 20 8221. Office Fax: 49 7364 20 8220. Business E-Mail: kaschke@zeiss.de. *

KASCHULA, RONALD OTTO CHRISTIAN, retired pathologist; b. Gweru, Midlands, Zimbabwe, Nov. 11, 1935; arrived in South Africa, 1960; s. Frederich Otto Robert and Anna Johanna Maria (Pretorius) K.; m. Sheila Roberta Darby, Oct. 19, 1963; children: Andrew Russell, Marion Jean, Wendy Anne. M.B.Ch.B., U. Cape Town, South Africa, 1959, M.Med. in Pathology, 1964. Cert. pathologist, South Africa; cert. med. practitioner, Gt. Britain. Intern Groote Schuur Hosp., Cape Town, 1960, registrar/resident, 1961-65; med. officer Cape Town City Hosp., 1961; lectr. U. Cape Town, 1965-67, sr. lectr., 1967-78, assoc. prof., 1978—2000; paediatric pathologist Red Cross War Meml. Children's Hosp., Cape Town; emeritus assoc. prof., 2000—. Dir. St. Luke's Hospice, Cape Town, 1982-84; external examiner Nairobi U., Kenya, 1993-95, Makarere U., Uganda, 1998, Stellenbosch U., 1995—2001, fellow, Royal Coll. Pathologists, 1997—, S. African Coll. Pathologists, 2000—. Author: Infectious Diseases and AIDS in Paediatric Pathology, 1995; contbr. articles to profl. jours. Chmn. group and divsn. coun. Boy Scouts Assn. South Africa, Cape Town, 1974-80; treas., chmn. Christian Med. Fellowship of South Africa, Cape Town, 1983-91; mem. mgmt. com. Rustenburg H.S. for Girls, Cape Town, 1979-85; lay minister Christ Ch., Kenilworth, South Africa, 1984—. Rsch. grantee Med. Rsch. Coun. South Africa, 1983—2005, Nat. Cancer Assn. South Africa, 1983-96. Fellow Internat. Paediatric Pathology Assn. (life, sec. 1984-92, pres. 1992-94), Royal Coll. Pathology, Fedn. South African Socs. of Pathology (pres. 1988-90), Internat. Coun. of Socs. Pathology (councillor 1989—), Internat. Acad. Pathology (v.p. 1984-2000, Gold medal 2004), Chilian Soc. Pathology (hon. life), Paediatric Pathology Soc. (acting chmn. 1984, pres.-elect 1998-2000, pres. 2000—03), Pathol. Soc. Gt. Britain and Ireland, Kenya Assn. Clin. Pathologists (hon. life), Soc. Pediatric Pathology, Internat. Paediatric Assn., World Assn. Socs. Pathology. Avocations: hiking, gardening, woodworking, cricket, rugby. Office: Forensic Pathology UCT Med Sch Anzio Rd, Observatory 7925 Cape Town South Africa

KASE, NATHAN GINDEN, dean; b. NYC, Apr. 6, 1930; s. Joseph and Flora (Ginden) Kosovsky; m. Judith Caryl Glass, July 8, 1956; children: Deborah Lillian, James, Nancy Kase O'Brasky. AB, Columbia U., 1951, MD, 1955; MA (hon.), Yale U., 1969; LHD honoris causa, Mt. Sinai Sch. Medicine, 2004. Instr. dept. ob-gyn. Yale U. Med. Sch., New Haven, 1962-63, asst. prof., 1963-66, assoc. prof., 1966-69, prof., chmn., 1969-78, prof., 1978-81; prof. ob-gyn. Mt. Sinai Sch. Medicine, 1981—, dean, 1984-98, acting chief exec. officer, 1986-88, emeritus dean, 1998—, interim dean, 2001—03, interim pres., CEO, 2001—02, prof. dept. medicine, 2005—. Chmn. adv. bd. Gateway Inst. Pre-Coll. Edn., NYC, 2002—05; pres., chair NY State Dept. Edn. Bd. for Medicine, 2007—09. Co-author: Clinical Gynecologic Endocrinology and Infertility, Advances in Obstetrics/Gynecology, Principles and Practice of Gynecology, Medical Surgical and Obstetrical Complications of Pregnancy, Diagnosis and Management of Ovarian Disorders. Served to capt. USAF, 1957-59. Recipient Francis Gilman Blake award Yale U. Sch. Medicine, 1967. Fellow Am. Coll. Obstetricians and Gynecologists; mem. Am. Fertility Soc., Endocrine Soc., Associated Med. Schs. N.Y. (pres. 1989-91). Office: Mt Sinai Med Ctr Box 1025 One Gustave Levy Pl New York NY 10029 Home Phone: 914-232-8769; Office Phone: 212-659-9760. Business E-Mail: nathan.kase@mssm.edu.

KASEDA, SHUNICHI, cardiologist; b. Kagoshima, Japan, July 24, 1953; s. Shigeo and Kyoko Kaseda; m. Yumiko Hashiba Kaseda, Oct. 28, 1984; 1 child, Ken. MD, Kyushu U. Sch. Medicine, Fukuoka, 1978; PhD, Kyushu U., 1985. Resident Kyushu U. Hosp., Fukuoka, 1978—85, fellow, 1988—89, asst. prof., 1992—; fellow Krannert Inst. Cardiology, Ind. U., Indpls., 1985—88; asst. prof. Rhyukyu U. Hosp., Okinawa, Japan, 1989—91; chief dept. cardiology Hiroshima Red Cross Hosp., Atomic Bomb Survivors Hosp., 1992—. Medtronic Japan fellowship for Young Japanese Investigator, Japanese Soc. Cardiac Pacing and Electrophysiology, 1985—86. Mem.: Hiroshima City Med. Assn. (dir. 2006—), Japanese Soc. Cardiac Pacing and Electrophysiology, Japanese Circulation Soc., Japanese Soc. Internal Medicine. Avocations: astronomy, skiing, tennis. Home: 4-50-101 Furue-Higashi Nishi-ku Hiroshima 733-0872 Japan Office: Hiroshima Red Cross Hosp 1-9-6 Sandamochi Naka-ku Hiroshima 730-8619 Japan Office Phone: 81-82-241-3111. Personal E-mail: c8i6r1c9@hiroshima-med.jrc.or.jp.

KASHGARIAN, MICHAEL, pathologist, educator; b. NYC, Sept. 20, 1933; s. Toros and Arax K.; m. Jean Gaylor Caldwell, July 2, 1960; children: Michaele, Thea. AB, N.Y. U., 1954; MD, Yale U., 1958. Diplomate: Am. Bd. Pathology. Intern Barnes Hosp., St. Louis,

1958-59; asst. in medicine Washington U., St. Louis, 1958-59; asst. resident in pathology Yale New Haven Med. Center, 1959-61, resident in pathology, 1962-63; rsch. fellow in renal physiology U. Goettingen, Germany, 1961-62; practice medicine specializing in pathology New Haven, 1962—. Instr. Yale U., 1962-64, asst. prof., 1964-67, asso. prof., 1967-74, prof., 1974-2008, porf. emeritus, 2008, vice chmn. dept., 1976-89, chmn., 1990— assoc. pathologist Yale New Haven Hosp., 1964-66, asst. attending pathologist, 1966-69, attending pathologist, 1969—, pres. med. staff, 1983-84; cons. in pathology, 1962—. Author: (with J.P. Hayslett, B.H. Spargo) Renal Disease, 1974, (with G.N. Burrow) The Endocrine Glands; co-author (with A. Fogo) Diagnostic Atlas of Renal Pathology, 2005; editor: Yearbook of Nephrology, Yale Medicine, Current Opinion in Nephrology; mem. editorial bd. Nephron, 1970—, Am. Jour. Pathology, 1975—, Am. Jour. Kidney Diseases; contbr. articles to med. jours. Chmn. ednl. adv. council North Haven Bd. Edn., 1971; chmn. Christian edn. com. Ch. of Christ, Yale, 1970; bd. dirs. New Haven Symphony Orch.; v.p. Conn. Fund for Environ. 1st lt., M.C. USAR, 1954-65. USPHS fellow, 1963-65; research career devel. awardee, 1965-75. Fellow AAAS, Am. Soc. Clin. Pathologists, Coll. Am. Pathologists, Am. Soc. Nephrology, Am. Heart Assn.; mem. AMA, Internat. Acad. Pathology, Conn. State Med. Soc. (chmn. com. on organ and tissue transfer), New Haven County Med. Assn. (pres. bd. govs.), Am. Soc. Investigative Pathologists, Conn. Soc. Pathologists (pres. 1975), Am. Physiol. Soc., Gesellshaft Nephrologie (hon.), Renal Pathology Soc. (Jacob Churg award), Nat. Kidney Found. (Disting. Achievement award), Sigma Xi, Alpha Omega Alpha, Alpha Kappa Kappa. Home: 22 Old Orchard Rd North Haven CT 06473-3022 Office: 310 Cedar St PO Box 208023 New Haven CT 06520-8023 Home Phone: 203-248-9208; Office Phone: 203-785-2750. Business E-Mail: michael.kashgarian@yale.edu.

KASINATH, BALAKUNTALAM S., medical researcher; b. Nov. 9, 1951; m. Uma Kasinath; children: Manasa, Vivek. MBBS in Medicine, Bangalore Med. Coll., India, 1975. With internal medicine Ill. Masonic Med. Ctr., Chgo., 1977-80; with nephrology U. Chgo. Hosps. and Clinics, 1980-83; asst prof. Rush-Presbyn.-St. Luke's Med. Ctr., Chgo., 1983-90; assoc. prof. dept. medicine divsn. nephrology U. Tex. Health Sci. Ctr., San Antonio, 1990-98; chief renal sect. Audie Murphy Meml. VA Hosp., San Antonio, 1991—2005, staff physician, 1991—. Prof. dept. medicine U. Tex. Health Sci. Ctr., San Antonio, 1998—. Contbr. articles to profl. jours., chpts in books; lectr. in field. Recipient Henry Christian award for excellence in rsch. Am. Fedn. for Clin. Rsch., 1994, Rsch. award Am. Diabetes Assn., 1995, 99, 2002, 05, Rsch. award VA, 1993, 97, 2002, 07, Rsch. award NIH, 1986, 90, 2003, 07. Mem. AAAS, Am. Soc. Nephrology, Internat. Soc. Nephrology, Indian Soc. Nephrology. Achievements include research in metabolic regulation of extracellular matrix molecules in diabetic renal disease. Office: U Tex Health Sci Ctr Dept Medicine-Nephrology Mail Code 7882 7703 Floyd Curl Dr San Antonio TX 78229-3900 Office Phone: 210-567-4707. Business E-Mail: kasinath@uthscsa.edu.

KASLICK, RALPH SIDNEY, dentist, educator; b. Bklyn., Oct. 17, 1935; s. John J. and Dorothy K.; m. Jessica Hellinger, Oct. 24, 1976; 1 child, Andrew AB, Columbia U., 1956, D.D.S., 1959, cert. in periodontology, 1962. Instr. Fairleigh Dickinson U., Coll. Dental Medicine, Hackensack, NJ, 1965-67, asst. prof., 1967-70, assoc. prof., 1970-74, prof., 1974-88, asst. dean for acad. affairs, 1973-75, acting dean, 1975-76, dean, 1976-88, acting provost, Teaneck-Hackensack campus, 1983-85, sr. dean Teaneck-Hackensack campus, 1985-88; chief dentistry Coler-Goldwater Splty. Hosp., Roosevelt Island, NY, 1988—2003, pres. med. staff, 1992-94, 97-99, dir. consultative svcs., 1995—2003; chmn., Percy T. Phillips Vis. Prof. Program Columbia U. Coll. Dental Medicine, 2007—. Clin. prof. periodontics Coll. Dentistry, NYU, 1988—; cons. in field. Contbr. chpts. to textbooks, articles to profl. jours. Served to capt. U.S. Army, 1962-64. Recipient Journalism award of the Internat. Coll. of Dentists, 1972, medal of Japan Stomatological Soc., 1977, Stanley S. Bergen award for contbn. to dental edn. Seton Hall U., 1982, Disting. Alumnus award Columbia U. Periodontal Alumni Assn., 1984, Achievement award Fairleigh Dickinson U. Periodontal Alumni Assn., 1984, Hirschfeld Meml. medal and cert. Northeastern Soc. Periodontists, 1987, Disting. Practitioner medallion Nat. Acad. Practice, 1999, Disting. Alumni award Columbia U. Coll. Dental Medicine, 2007. Mem., Heritage Hall Induction Fairleigh Dickinson U., 2007; fellow Am. Coll. Dentists, N.Y. Acad. Dentistry; mem. ADA, AMA, Am. Dental Edn. Assn., Internat. Assn. Dental Rsch. (past pres. N.J. sect.), Am. Acad. Periodontology, Fedn. Spl. Care Orgns. in Dentistry, NY Acad. Scis., Sigma Xi, Omicron Kappa Upsilon.

KASLOW, FLORENCE WHITEMAN, psychologist, educator, family business consultant, executive, life transitions and relationship coach; b. Phila., Jan. 06; d. Irving and Rose (Tarin) Whiteman; m. Solis Kaslow; children: Nadine Joy, Howard Ian. AB in Sociology with distinction, Temple U., 1952; MA, Ohio State U., 1954; PhD, Bryn Mawr Coll., 1969. Lic. psychologist, Fla.; bd. cert. psychologist Am. Bd. Clin. Psychology, Am. Bd. Forensic Psychology, Am. Bd. Couple & Family Psychology, Am. Bd. Profl. Psychology. Pvt. practice, Palm Beach Gardens, Fla., 1964—; dir. Fla. Couples and Family Inst., Palm Beach Gardens, 1982—2009; pres. Kaslow Assoc., Palm Beach Gardens, 1985—2011. Cons. USN Dept. Psychiatry Residency Tng. Programs, San Diego, Portsmouth, Va., Phila., 1976-88, Palm Beach Inst., 1983-90; adj. prof. med. psychology Duke U. Med. Ctr., Durham, N.C., 1982-2002; disting. vis. prof. psychology Fla. Inst. Tech., Melbourne, 1985-; disting. vis. prof. Calif. Grad. Sch. Family Psychology, 1989-92; vis. prof. psychiatry & behavioral sci. Mercer Med. Coll., Macon, Ga., 2007-10; weekly radio guest Voice of Am., Focus on Families, 1993-2003; pres. Am. Bd. Forensic Psychology, 1977-80, Am. Bd. Family Psychology, 1996-2000. Editor: Voices in Family Psychology, 1990, The Military Family in Peace and War, 1993, Handbook of Relational Diagnoses and Dysfunctional Family Patterns, 1996, Handbook of Family Business and Family Business Consultation: A Global Perspective, 2006; editor: (with F. Shapiro and L. Maxfield) EMDR & Family Therapy Processes, 2007; editor: (with L.L. Schwartz) Dynamics of Divorce: A Life Cycle Perspective, 1987; editor: Painful Partings: Divorce and Its Aftermath, 1997, Handbook of Couple and Family Forensics, 2000, Comprehensive Handbook of Psychotherapy, 4 vols., 2002; author (with L.L. Schwartz): Welcome Home: an International and Non Traditional Adoption Reader, 2004; mem. editl. bd. Jour. Marital and Family Therapy, 1976—, Jour. Family Psychology, 1987—, Jour. Sex and Marital Therapy, 1984—2002, Jour. Clin. Child Psychology, 1986—2002, Jour. Psychotherapy, 1988—2004, Profl. Psychology, 2002—07, Jours. Couple Family Psychology, 2011—, assoc. editor Jour. Family Psychotherapy, 1990—; contbr. chapters to books, articles to profl. jours. Recipient Outstanding Family Therapy Contbn. award, Am. Assn. Marriage and Family Therapy, 1991, NIMH trainee, 1969, Interdisciplinary Achievement award, Family Firm Inst., 2007, Life Achievement award in Practice of Psychology, Am. Psychol. Found., 2008. Mem. APA (divsn. family psychology pres. 1987, sec. 1983-85, com. mem. 1987—, pres. divsn. media psychology 1993, coun. rep. 2002-08, co-chair, Com. on Internat. Rels. in Psychology 2011, Disting. Lifetime Contbn. to Media Psychology award, 2000, Outstanding Conbtn. Internat. Advancement Psychology, 2002), Internat. Acad. Family Psychology (pres. 1998-2002), Am. Assn. Marital and Family Therapy, Am. Bd. Profl. Psychologists (trustee 2002-, Disting. Psychology Contbn. award 1994, Russell Bent award 2010), Am. Family Therapy Acad., Coalition Family Diagnosis (chmn. 1989-93), Am. Assn. Sex Educators, Counselors and Therapists, Internat. Family Therapy Assn. (founding pres. 1987-90), Acad. Family Mediators (bd. dir. 1982-88, treas. 1985-87), Family Therapists Without Borders (hon. chair 2007-10). Office Phone: 561-625-0288. Personal E-mail: drfkaslow@bellsouth.net.

KASMAR, MARILYN WALSH, health facility administrator, nurse; d. Leo A. and Beverly J. Walsh; m. Charles Donald Kasmar, Dec. 30, 1983; children: Eric Charles, Jayne C. BSN, Seattle U., 1981; MBA, Alaska Pacific U., Anchorage, 1995. Lic. Nursing Certification Corp., 1985. Clin. staff nurse, nurse mgr. Providence Med. Ctr., Anchorage, 1982—95; chief ops. officer Anchorage Neighborhood Health Ctr., 1991—96; CEO Alaska Primary Care Assn., Anchorage, 1996—. Office: Alaska Primary Care Assn 903 W Northern Lights Blvd Ste 200 Anchorage AK 99503 Home: 334 11th Ave Unit B Anchorage AK 99501 Office Fax: 907-929-2734. Business E-Mail: marilyn@alaskapca.org. *

KASNER, SCOTT E., neurologist, educator; BS in Physics & Zoology, Duke U., Durham, NC, 1988; MD, Yale U., New Haven, 1992; MSCE in Clin. Epidemiology, U. Pa., Phila., 2007. Diplomate Am. Bd. Psychiatry and Neurology-neuology, 1997, Am. Bd. Psychiatry and Neurology-neurology, 2007, Am. Bd. Psychiatry and Neurology-vascular neurology, 2006. Fellow stroke and neurocritical care Univ. Tex. Health Sci. Ctr., Houston, 1996—97; intern medicine Hosp. of the Univ. Pa., 1992—93, resident neurology, 1993—96, prof. neurology. Co-author: Predictors of ischemic stroke in the territory of a symptomatic intracranial arterial stenosis, 2006, Antiplatelet medications and hemorrhage growth after intracerebral, 2008, Who will participate in acute stroke trials?, 2009, Community views on neurologic emergency treatment trials, 2011, Guidelines for the prevention of stroke in patients with stroke or transient ischemic attack: a guideline for healthcare professionals from the american heart association/american stroke association, 2011, various others. Named one of Best Doctors in America, 2003—04, 2005—06, 2007—08, 2009—10, Top Docs, Phila. Mag., 2002, 2011. Mem.: Am. Acad. Neurology. Office: Hospital of the University of Pennsylvania Department of Neurology 3W Gates Bldg 3400 Spruce St Philadelphia PA 19104-4283 Office Phone: 215-662-3564. Office Fax: 215-614-1927. Business E-Mail: kasner@mail.med.upenn.edu.

KASPAR, SVATOPLUK, surgeon; b. Policka, Czech Republic, Dec. 12, 1952; s. Frantisek Kaspar and Marie Kasparova; m. Libuse Cajzlova; children: Martin, David. MD, PhD, Faculty Medicine, Charles U., Prague, 1978. Diplomate in medical Czech Med. Bd., 1994. Chief surgeon Flebocentrum, Hradec Kralove, Czech Republic, 1994—; chief surgeon dept. surgery U. Pardubice, Czech Republic, 1995—. Mem.: Czech Soc. Phlebology, Czech Soc. Angiology, Czech Soc. Surgery, French Soc. Phlebology. Office: Flebocentrum Liznerova 737 Hradec Králové 50009 Czech Republic Office Fax: 420495275652. Business E-Mail: kaspar@flebocentrum.cz.

KASPERSKA-ZAJAC, ALICJA EWA, allergeologist; b. Prudnik, Poland, Mar. 9, 1970; d. Edward Kasperski and Krystyna Kasperska; m. Piotr Zajac, Sept. 9, 1995; 1 child, Magdalena Zajac. MD, PhD, Med. U. Silesia, Katowice, 1995, Habil., 2009. Asst. dept. pharmacology Med. U. Silesia, Zabrze, Poland, 1995—2000, adj. chair, dept. internal diseases, allergology and clin. immunology, 2000—. Contbr. articles to profl. jours. Recipient Team Sci. award, Polish Ministry of Health, 2007. Achievements include discovery of behavior of DHEA in chronic urticaria. Office: Med Univ Silesia Poniatowskiego 15 Katowice 40-055 Poland Personal E-mail: kasperska@plusnet.pl.

KASPROW, BARBARA ANNE, biomedical researcher, writer; b. Hartford, Conn., Apr. 23, 1936; d. Stephen G. and Anna M. Kasprow. AB cum laude, Albertus Magnus Coll., 1958; postgrad., Laval U., 1958, Yale U., 1958-61; PhD, Loyola U., Chgo., 1969. Staff microbiology dept. Conn. State Dept. Health, 1957; lab. asst. dept. microbiology Yale U., New Haven, 1958—59; tng. scholar USPHS, 1959—60; asst. rsch. and editl. dept. anatomy Yale U., New Haven, 1961; rsch. assoc. N.Y. Med. Coll., 1961—62; rsch. assoc. to sr. rsch. assoc. and adminstrv. assoc. Inst. for Study Human Reprodn. St. Ann Ob-Gyn. Hosp., Cleve., 1962—67, asst. to dir. grad. med. edn., asst. dir. adminstrn. grad. rsch. endocrinology, Inst. for Study Human Reprodn., 1962—67; sr. rsch. assoc. dept. anatomy Stritch Sch. Medicine, Chgo., Hines, Ill., 1967—69; asst. prof. anatomy Loyola U., Chgo., 1969—75; asst. to v.p. University Rsch. Sys., 1975-79; v.p. med. topics Univ. Rsch. Sys., 1979—; asst. to pres. Internat. Basic and Biol.-Biomed. Curricula, Lombard, Ill., 1979—. Lectr. in field; invited U.S. del. on reprodn. to Vatican, 1964; round table leader Brazil-Israel Congress on Fertility and Sterility, Brazil Soc. Human Reprodn., São Paulo, 1972. Editl. asst. vol. VIII/3 Handbuch der Histochemie, Gustav Fischer Verlag, 1963; prodn. aide ednl. med. film The Soft Anvil, 1965-66; co-editor: Biology of Reproduction, Basic and Clinical Studies, 1973; contbr. articles to profl. jours. Recipient Certificate of Outstanding Achievement and Scholarship award Am. Assn. German Tchrs. and New Britain German Assn., 1954; named Honorary Citizen São Paulo, 1972. Mem. AAAS (life), Am. Assn. Anatomists, Am. Soc. Zoologists-The Soc. Integrative and Comparative Biology, Pan Am. Assn. Anatomy (co-organizer symposium on reproduction New Orleans 1972), Midwest Anatomists Assn. (program officer ann. meeting Chgo. 1974), Sigma Xi (life). Roman Catholic. Achievements include biological elucidation of growth horizons in uterine development, growth, and maturity; perfection of a hormonal model-system in highly controlled (surgerized) animals to ascertain quantitative relationships of purified estradiol-17beta and progesterone required for promotion of and duplication of these uterine growth horizons; development of experimental paradigms for the biomorphological elucidation of hormonally stimulated growth responses in endocrine target organs, and cyto- and histochemical elucidation of growth stimulants. Office: 607 E Wilson Ave Lombard IL 60148-4062 *

KASS, LAWRENCE, hematologist, oncologist, educator; b. Toledo, Ohio, Sept. 30, 1938; AB magna cum laude, U. Mich., 1960; MD with hons., U. Chgo., 1964, MS Anatomy, 1964. Diplomate Nat. Bd. Med. Examiners, Am. Bd. Internal Medicine/Internal Medicine and Hematology, Med. Oncology, Am. Bd. Pathology/Hematology. Intern Peter Bent Brigham Hosp., Boston, 1964-65, asst. resident internal medicine, 1965-66; sr. asst. resident internal medicine U. Hosps. of Cleve., 1966-68; Elliott Hoyt fellow in hematology Univ. Hosps. of Cleve., 1967-68; various to rsch. assoc. U. Chgo., 1968-70; asst. prof. internal medicine U. Mich. Med. Sch., Ann Arbor, 1970-73, assoc. prof. internal medicine, 1973-78; prof. path., medicine Case Western Res. U. Sch. Medicine, Cleve., 1978—; head hematopathology Metro-Health Med. Ctr., Cleve., 1978—. Cons. in medicine, VA Hosp., Ann Arbor; editorial cons. Williams and Wilkins Pubs., Balt., 1974—, Archives of Pathology and Lab. Medicine Blood, The Jour. of Hematology, The Jour. of Histochemistry and Cytochemistry, Western Jour. of Medicine, Am. Jour. of Hematology, Biotechnic & Histochemistry, 1975—, Rsch. Career Selection Rev. Com., VA, Washington, 1976—; active numerous coms. in field. Contbr. articles to profl. jours. Maj. med corps. U.S. Army, 1968-70. Recipient Internat. Giovanni DiGuglielmo prize, Giovanni DiGuglielmo Found., Accademia Nazionale Die Lincei, Rome, 1976, Diamond Cover award Nat. Soc. Histotechnologists and Jour. of Histotechnology, 1988, C.V. Mosby award, 1964, Merck award 1964. Fellow Am. Coll. Phys., Coll. Am. Pathologists; mem. AAAS, Am. Soc. Hematology, Am. Fedn. Clin. Rsch., Am. Soc. Clin. Oncology, Soc. Exptl. Biology and Medicine, Cen. Soc. Clin. Rsch., Histochem. Soc., Biol. Stain Commn., Am. Soc. Clin. Path., Phi Eta Sigma, Phi Beta Kappa, Alpha Omega Alpha. Office: MetroHealth Med Ctr 2500 Metrohealth Dr Cleveland OH 44109-1900 Office Phone: 216-778-4945. Office Fax: 216-778-5701. Business E-Mail: lkass@metrohealth.org.

KASS, LEON RICHARD, humanities educator; b. Chgo., Feb. 12, 1939; s. Samuel and Anna (Shoichet) K.; m. Amy Judith Apfel, June 22, 1961; children: Sarah, Miriam. BS, U. Chgo., 1958, MD, 1962; PhD in Biochemistry, Harvard U., 1967. Intern Beth Israel Hosp., Boston, 1962-63; staff assoc. Lab. Molecular Biology, Nat. Inst. Arthritis and Metabolic Diseases, NIH, Bethesda, Md., 1967-69, staff fellow, 1969-70, sr. staff fellow, 1970; exec. sec. com. on life scis. and social policy NRC-NAS, Washington, 1970-72; tutor St. John's Coll., Annapolis, Md., 1972-76; Joseph P. Kennedy Sr. rsch. prof. in bioethics Kennedy Inst., Georgetown U., 1974-76; Henry R. Luce prof. liberal arts of human biology in coll. U. Chgo., 1976-84, prof. com. on social thought, 1984-90, Addie Clark Harding prof. in coll. and com. on social thought, 1990—2010; Hertog fellow Am. Enterprise Inst., Washington, 2002—. Founding fellow, bd. dirs. Hastings Ctr., 1969-96; bd. govs. U.S.-Israel Binat. Sci. Found., 1982-88; mem. coun. Nat. Humanities Coun., 1984-91, vice chmn. 1987-89; mem. Pres.'s Coun. Bioethics, 2001-07, chmn. 2001-05; Jefferson lectr. Nat. Endowment Humanities, 2009. Author: Toward a More Natural Science: Biology and Human Affairs, 1985, The Hungry Soul: Eating and the Perfecting of Our Nature, 1994, (James Q. Wilson) The Ethics of Human Cloning, 1998, (Amy A. Kass) Wing to Wing, Oar to Oar: Readings on Courting and Marrying, 2000, Life, Liberty, and The Defense of Dignity: The Challenge for Bioethics, 2002, The Beginning of Wisdom: Reading Genesis, 2003; contbr. articles to profl. jours. Served with USPHS, 1967-69. NIH postdoctoral fellow, 1963-67, John Simon Guggenheim Meml. Found. fellow, 1972-73, Nat. Humanities Ctr. fellow, 1984-85, W.H. Brady, Jr. Disting. fellow Am. Enterprise Inst., 1991-92, 98-99; NEH grantee, 1973-74; recipient Bradley prize The Lynde and Harry Bradley Found., 2003. Mem. Phi Beta Kappa, Alpha Omega Alpha. Jewish. Office: American Enterprise Inst 1150 17th St NW Washington DC 20036-4603

KASS, MARY ELIZABETH, pathologist, hospital administrator; d. Gilbert Randolph and Carrie Elliot Musselman; m. Dennis Schumer, Apr. 8, 1944; children: Michael Paul, David Andrew. BA, George Wash. U., 1964, MD, 1967. Diplomate Am. Bd. Pathology, 1972. Chief resident pathology Wash. Hosp. Ctr., Washington, 1971—72, attending pathologist, 1972—83, chmn., dept. pathology, 1983—2002, dir., sch. med. tech., 1983—2000, dir., residency tng. program, 1983—2000, sec. med. bd. med. and dental staff, 1988—92, mem., bd. dirs., 1983—91, sec., found., 1991—2000; med. dir., lab. Nat. Rehab. Hosp., Washington, 1986—95; pres. Wash. Soc. Pathologists, Washington, 1987—88, Found. Coll. Am. Pathologists, Northfield, Ill., 2006—; mem., Helix bd. dirs. Medlantic Healthcare, Washington, 1998—2001. Convenor Coalition To Assre Women's Confidence In And Access To Affordable Pap Smears, Washington, 1998. Contbr. articles to profl. jours. Pres. Found., Coll. Am. Pathologists, Northfield, Ill., 2006—. Recipient award for Excellence, Pathology Residents Wash. Hosp. Ctr., 1994, Spl. award, Wash. Hosp. Ctr., 1994, Gold Headed Cane award, 1997; named Alumnus of Yr., 1996, Pathologist Yr., Coll. Am. Pathologists, 2006; grant, Ctrs. Disease Control, 1988—93, Centers Disease Control, 1993—95. Fellow: Coll. Am. Pathologists (pres. 2003—05, Pathologist of Yr.); mem.: Phi Beta Kappa. Avocations: travel, painting, swimming.

KASS, MICHAEL ALLEN, ophthalmologist, educator; b. Chgo., Dec. 24, 1941; MD, Northwestern U., Evanston, Ill., 1966. Diplomate Am. Bd. Ophthalmology. Intern Passavant Meml. Hosp., Chgo., 1966-67; asst. prof. ophthalmology Sch. Medicine Yale U., New Haven, 1973-75; resident Sch. Medicine Washington U., St. Louis, 1969-71, asst. ophthalmologist, 1972-73, asst. prof., 1975-77, assoc. prof., 1977-83, prof., 1983—, chmn., 1999—. Mem. AMA, Am. Acad. Ophthalmology, Assn. for Rsch. in Vision Ophthalmology. Office: Washington U Sch Medicine 660 S Euclid Ave # 8096 Saint Louis MO 63110-1010 Office Phone: 314-362-3724. Business E-Mail: kass@vision.wustl.edu.

KASS, NANCY, bioethicist, public health educator; BA, Stanford U.; ScD, Johns Hopkins Sch. Pub. Health. Phoebe R. Berman prof. bioethics and pub. health Johns Hopkins Bloomberg Sch. Pub. Health, Balt., prof. health policy and mgmt., dep. dir. pub. health. Faculty assoc. Kennedy Inst. Ethics, Georgetown U., Washington; cons. Pres.'s Adv. Com. on Human Radiation Experiments, 1994—95. Co-editor (with Ruth Faden): HIV, AIDS and Childbearing: Public Policy, Private Lives, 1996. Fellow Hastings Ctr. Mem.: Inst. Medicine, Delta Omega. Office: Hampton House 344 624 N Broadway

Baltimore MD 21205 also: Johns Hopkins Berman Inst Bioethics 201 N Charles Ste 1701 Baltimore MD 21201 Office Phone: 410-955-0310. Office Fax: 410-614-9567. E-mail: nkass@jhsph.edu.

KASSABIAN, GARO, plastic surgeon; BS in Biol. Sciences, U. So. Calif., MD. Diplomate Am. Bd. Surgery, Am. Bd. Plastic Surgery. Intern gen. surgery Los Angeles County + Univ. of So. Calif. Med. Ctr., resident gen. surgery; fellow cosmetic facial surgery Bruce Connell Aesthetic Surgery Inst.; rsch fellow plastic surgery Univ. of So. Calif. Sch. of Medicine; fellow plastic and reconstructive surgery Oregon Health Sciences Univ.; fellow cosmetic surgery Baker, Stuzin & Baker Inst., Miami, Fla.; fellow face/breast/body sculpturing with Dr. Lloyd Hale; laser and hair transplantation fellow with Dr. Bruce Rusell; plastic surgeon Lift MD Aesthetics, Beverly Hills, Calif. Mem.: AMA, ACS, Am. Soc. of Plastic Surgeons, Am. Soc. for Laser Medicine and Surgery. Office: Lift MD Aesthetics 436 N Bedford Dr Ste 301 Beverly Hills CA 90210 Office Phone: 301-285-0400.

KASSAM, AMIN B., neurosurgeon, educator; m. Greta Kassam; children: Armand, Mikaeel. MD, U. Toronto, Can., 1991. Vis. instr. neurol. surgery U. Pitts., Sch. Medicine, 1997—98, asst. prof. neurol. surgery, 1998—2004, assoc. prof. neurol. surgery, 2004—07, prof., 2008—. Dir. minimally invasive endoneurosurgery U. Pitts., Sch. Medicine, 1998—, co-dir., skull base surgery ctr., 1998—2008, interim chair dept. neurol. surgery, 2006—07, chair dept. neurol. surgery, 2007—09. Mem. editl. bd. Neurol. Rsch., 2007—, ad hoc reviewer Jour. Neuroimaging, 1999—, Neurology, 2000, Jour. Neurology, Neurosurgery and Psychiatry, 2005—, Surg. Neurology, 2007—, Neurosurgery, 2007—. Recipient Frederick Urghart Acad. scholarship, 1985, Aga Khan Acad. scholarship, 1985, George Brown Meml. award for rsch., U. Toronto, 1990, Track scholarship in surgery, 1991, Best Paper in eHealth award, Internat. Conf. on Telemedicine and Multi-media Comm., 2005, Endoscopics award, Beijing Neurosurg. Inst., 2006, Interurban Neurological Soc. Lectr., 2006, Top Drs., Pitts. Mag., 2009, Penfield Lectr., 2007; named honored Guest, Soc. Neurochirurgic Langue Francaise, 2007; named one of Top Drs., Pitts. Mag., 2006—07, 2008. Fellow: Royal Coll. Physicians and Surgeons Can. (life); mem.: Soc. Neuro-Oncology (life), Trigeminal Neuralgia Assn. (life), European Skull Base Soc. (life), North Am. Skull Base Soc. (life; mem. exec. bd. 2005—), Congress Neurol. Surgeons (life), Am. Assn. Neurol. Surgeons (life). Achievements include development of the Expanded Endonasal Approach (EEA) for minimally invasive brain surgery. Office: Univ Pitts Med Ctr 200 Lothrop St PUH B-400 Pittsburgh PA 15213 Office Fax: 412-647-1778. Business E-Mail: kassamab@upmc.edu.

KASSAN, STUART S., rheumatologist; b. White Plains, NY, Nov. 19, 1946; s. Robert Jacob and Rosalind (Suchin) K.; m. Gail Karesh, Apr. 4, 1971; children: Michael Andrew, Merrill Alissa. BA, Case Western Res., 1968; MD, George Washington U., 1972. Diplomate Am. Bd. Internal Medicine, Am. Bd. Rheumatology, Am. Bd. Geriatrics. Intern and resident Grady Meml. Hosp., Altanta, 1972-74; clin. fellow NIH, Bethesda, Md., 1974-76, fellow Hosp. for Spl. Surgery, Cornell Med. Ctr., NYC, 1976-78; head rheumatology clinic VA Med. Ctr., Denver, 1978-80; pvt. practice rheumatology, 1978—; asst. clin. prof. medicine U. Colo. Health Scis. Ctr., Denver, 1978-84, assoc. clin. prof. medicine, 1984-94, clin. prof. medicine, 1994—; med. dir. rehab unit. Luth. Med. Ctr., Wheatridge, Colo., 1983-87; med. dir. rehab. unit St. Anthony Hosp., Denver, 1987-93. Cons. Annals Internal Medicine, Phila., 1986—, Arthritis and Rheumatism, Atlanta, 1995—, Jour. of Rheumatology, 1996—; vis. alumni scholar George Washington U. Sch. Medicine, 1986; chmn. med. adv. bd. Sjögren's Syndrome Found., Bethesda, 1997-03, bd. dirs., 1996-03, Lupus Found. Colo., 2005-. Co-editor: Sjögren's Syndrome, 1987, contbr. over 40 articles to profl. jours. Bd. dirs. Rocky Mountain chpt. Arthritis Found., Denver, 1978-80, 03—, pres., 2007-09, Polachek fellow, 1976-77, pres.-elect, Mental Health America, Colo., 2011; bd. dirs. Lupus Found. Colo., v.p., 1995-96, pres., 1996-05; bd. dirs. Lupus Rsch. Inst., NYC, 2002-, Nat. Arthritis Found., 2006—, public policy coun., 2007-; pres. Metrowest IPA, Lakewood, Colo., 1997-03. With USPHS, 1974-76, bd. trustees, George Wash. U., 2010-. Recipient Disting. Alumni Svc. award, George Washington U., 2006; named Physician Honoree, Arthritis Found., Rocky Mt. Chpt., 2004, Annual Honoree, Lupus Found. Colo., 2005. Fellow ACP, Am. Coll. Rheumatology (regional adv. com. 2005-, corp. affairs com. 2007-, mem. bd. dirs., Rsch. and Edn. Found. 2008-10), Colo. Rheumatology Assn. (pres. 2004—), George Washington U. Sch. Medicine Alumni Assn-.(pres. 2004—, mem. bd. dirs. 2004—); mem. Harvey Soc., Rocky Mountain Rheumatism Soc. (pres. 1997—), George Washington U. Alumni Assn. (bd. dirs.), Alpha Omega Alpha Hon. Soc., Cosmos Club, Cactus Club. Jewish. Achievements include namesake for Lupus Found. of Colo. Stuart S. Kassan Humanitarian award. Office: 198 Union Blvd Lakewood CO 80228 Office Phone: 303-892-6033. Personal E-mail: skassan@earthlink.net.

KASSIRER, JEROME PAUL, medical educator; b. Buffalo, Dec. 19, 1932; Grad., U. Buffalo, 1953, MD magna cum laude, 1957; DS (hon.), U. Mass., 1992; D honoris causa, L'Universite Rene Descartes, Paris, 1992; DS (hon.), Thomas Jefferson U., 1994, SUNY, 1995. Diplomate Am. Bd. Internal Medicine (mem. certifying examination com. 1987-89, bd. dirs. 1989-96, mem. exec. com. 1993-96, chmn. 1995-96). Intern, asst. resident in medicine Buffalo Gen. Hosp., Buffalo, 1957—59; fellow in nephrology New Eng. Med. Ctr., Boston, 1959—61, sr. resident in medicine, 1961—62, asst. physician, 1961—65, physician renal svc., 1969-74, assoc. physician-in-chief, 1971—91, acting physician-in-chief, 1976—77; instr. medicine Sch. Medicine, Tufts U., Medford, Mass., 1961-65, asst. prof. medicine, 1965—69, assoc. prof., 1969—74, vice chmn. dept. medicine, 1971—91, acting chmn. dept. medicine, 1974—75, prof. medicine, 1974—, Sara Murray Jordan Prof. Medicine, 1987—91; editor in chief New Eng. Jour. Medicine, Boston, 1991—99. Lectr. in medicine Harvard U., 1991—; bd. dirs. Postgrad. Med. Inst. Mass. Med. Soc., 1988—91; vis. prof. Stanford U., 2007—. Editor in chief: Current Therapy in Internal Medicine, 1990; co-editor: Clin. Problem Solving, Hosp. Practice, 1985—91; cons. editor: Am. Jour. Medicine, 1976—86, mem. editl. bd.: New Eng. Jour. Medicine, 1972—75; co-editor: Nephrology Forum, Kidney Internat, 1978—91, ed. Decision Making, 1987—89; author: On the Take: How Medicine's Complicity with Big Business Can Endanger Your Health, 2004; editl. advisor: Outline of Knowledge, Part 4: Human Life, The New Encyclopaedia Britannica, 1989; co-author: Learning Clinical Reasoning. Recipient Ednl. Rsch. Found. award, AMA, 1993, David E. Rogers award, AAMC, 2009. Master: ACP (gov. Mass. 1985—89, mem. exec. com. bd. govs. 1988—89, mem. health and pub. policy com. 1989—91, bd. regents 1990—91, chmn. sci.); mem.: Am. Acad. Arts & Scis., Soc. Clin. Decision Making (charter mem.), Buffalo Acad. Medicine, Nat. Libr. Medicine (chmn. bd. sci. counselors 1989—90, mem. biomed. journalism award com. 1992—), Assn of Am. Physicians, Inst. Medicine NAS. Jewish. Avocation: photography. Office: Tufts U Sch Med 136 Harrison Ave Boston MA 02111 Office Phone: 617-636-6523. Personal E-mail: jpkassirer@aol.com. *

KASTANAKIS, SERAFIM, medical educator; b. Chania, Greece, Dec. 25, 1936; s. George and Ariadni (Loupasaki) K.; m. Maria Vittoraki, Nov. 5, 1978 BSc in Medicine, Athens U., Greece, 1963, spl. diploma in internal medicine, MD, 1969, specialist in infectious diseases, 1997. Cert. prof. physician. House officer in medicine Alexandra Hosp., Athens, 1967-69; registrar in medicine King Paul Hosp., Athens, 1969-74; sr. registrar in medicine Gen. Hosp., Athens, 1974-75; dir. 1st med. dept. St. George Hosp., Chania, 1976—2003, dir. medicine, 1987-93, gen. dir. med. svcs., 1999—2003, hon. med. dir. med. svcs., 2004—. Hon. registrar in cardiology Queen Elizabeth Hosp., Birmingham, 1972-73; pres. infection control com. St. George Hosp., Chania, 1987—. Contbr. numerous articles and papers to profl. jours. Pres. Julius Tsirakis Cultural Found., Crete, Greece, 1995—. Mem. Internat. Soc. Chemotherapy, Internat. Soc. for Infectious Diseases, Am. Soc. for Microbiology. Avocations: hill walking, travel, swimming. Home: Xirouhaki str 1 koube Chania 73100 Greece Office: Saint George Hosp 73300 Mournies Chania Greece

KASTE, MARKKU KAUKO ANTTI, neurologist, emeritus professor of neurology; b. Helsinki, Finland, Sept. 23, 1941; s. Kauko Igor and Eeva Maria Elisabeth (Räsänen) K.; m. Tuula Lempi Maria Järnström, May 29, 1965; children: Johanna, Janne. MD, U. Helsinki, Finland, 1968, PhD Medicine and Surgery, 1970, Docent in Neurology, 1977, Prof. in Neurology, 1980. Diplomate Bd. Neurology; lic. in medicine. Resident in neurology Helsinki U. Ctrl. Hosp., 1972—74, sr. neurologist, 1976-84, vice-chmn. dept. neurology, 1984—90, acting chmn., 1990—92, chmn., 1992—2005; asst. prof. neurology U. Helsinki, 1974—75, postdoc. neurology, 1977—93, assoc. prof. neurology, 1979—87, Finland, 1993—98, prof. health care and hosp. adminstrn., 1988-89, prof. neurology, 1998—2001, prof. neurology, chair Finland, 2001—06. Vis. prof. U. Mo., Columbia, 1981-82; chmn. sci. panel on stroke European Fedn. of Neurol. Socs., 1993—; mem. exec. com. European Stroke Coun., 1994—; chmn. Scandinavian Soc. for the Study of Cerebrovascular Diseases, 1995—; mem. steering com. numerous internat. multicenter trials in stroke prevention and treatment; founding mem. & chmn. European Stroke Initiative, 1996-2004; clin. advisor European Agy. Evaluation Medicinal Products, 1999-; mem. Task Force Improving Chain Recovery in Your Soc. NINDS 2002; fgn. expert UK Dept. Health, 2005, 2009, chmn., Finnish Stoke Soc., Divsn. Finnish Neurol. Assn., 2007-, World Stroke Day Activity World Stroke Orgn., 2009-, World Stroke Campaign WSO, 2010-. Assoc. editor Med. Jour. Duodecim, 1984—, STROKE jour. Europe, 2000-05; mem. editl. bd. Stroke, 1983-86, 95—, Acta Neurologica Scandinavica, 1994-97, European Jour. Neurology, 1994-97, contbr. chpts. to textbooks, articles to profl. jours. Permanent adv. in neurology Minister of Social Svcs. and Health Care, Helsinki, 1990—, Nat. Bd. Health, 1984-92, Mat. Authority Medicolegal Affairs, 1992-, Nat. Bd. Medicolegal Affairs, Helsinki, 1992—, Nat. Agy. for Medicines, Helsinki, 1993—, Nat. Rsch. and Devel. Ctr. for Welfare and Health, Helsinki, 1993—; temporary adv. WHO Regional Office for Europe, Copenhagen, 1993—. 2d Light Infantry, 1960-61. Decorated Cross knight 1st Class Order Lion of Finland Pres. Finland, 1991; recipient HJM Barnett Lectr. award McMaster U. Ont., 1986, Silver medal Helsinki U. Cen. Hosp., 1997, Prof. Erkki Kivalo Lectr. award Finnish Neurol. Fund, 2004, Ludvig Puusepp Hon. Lectr. award U. Tartu, Estonia, 2005, 2nd Johann Jacob Wepfer award European Stroke Conf., 2006, Stroke award Karolinska Inst., 2006, William M. Feinberg award, Am. Stroke Assn., 2010, Salus Ansvar prize, Medicine Salus Ansvar Found., Sweden, 2010. Fellow Am. Heart Assn. (mem. stroke coun., chmn. internat. trial collaboration subcom. internat. stroke liaison com. 1998-2002), European Stroke Orgn. (founding mem. & vice chmn. 2007-); mem. Am. Neurological Assn. (corresponding), Scandinavian Soc. for the Study of Cerebrovascular Diseases (founding), Finnish Med. Assn. (hon.) (Merit award 1985), Finnish Neurol. Assn. (hon.), Finnish Med. Found. (Pohjola and Suomi Mutual Medical award, 2008), Finnish Neurol. Soc. (hon.) (chmn. 2006-08, Snellman lectr. 2009), Nordic Stroke Soc. (founding mem. 1982-, chmn. 1995-99), World Stroke Orgn. (founding mem. & v.p. 2006-08, mem. 2008-), AHA's Stroke Telemedicine Policy Writing Group, Hungarian Stroke Soc. (hon.). Home: Virtapolku 3 A 4 FIN-01600 Vantaa Finland Office: Helsinki Univ Ctrl Hosp Dept Clin Neuroscis PO Box 340 Haartmaninkatu 4 FI-00290 HUS Helsinki Finland

KASTE, SUE CREVISTON, pediatric radiologist, researcher; b. Lakewood, Ohio, Feb. 25, 1952; d. Donald P. and Marion S. Creviston; m. Ronald H. Kaste, Apr. 28, 1984; children: Rebecca, Steven, Matthew. BA, Lake Erie Coll., Painesville, Ohio, 1974; AAS, Cuyahoga CC, Cleve., 1977; DO, Chgo. Coll. Osteo. Medicine, 1981. Diplomate Am. Bd. Radiology, Am. Bd. Pediat. Radiology, 2004, cert. osteopath Osteo. Nat. Bd. Med. Examiners, physicians asst. Ohio. Intern Chgo. Coll. Osteo. Medicine, Ill., 1981-82; diagnostic radiology U. Hosps. Cleve., 1982-86, fellow pediat. radiology, 1986-87; officer in charge pediat. radiology KTTCMC, Keesler AFB, Biloxi, Miss., 1987-90, chief diagnostic radiology, 1990-91; cons. dept. radiology LeBonheur Children's Med. Ctr., Memphis, 1991—; prof. dept. radiology U. Tenn. Coll. Medicine, Memphis, 1991—2003, prof., 2003—; full mem. dept. diagnostic imaging St. Jude Children's Rsch. Hosp., Memphis, 2002—; mem. bd. dirs. Soc. Pediat. Radiology, 2007—, 1st v.p., 2010—. Reviewer Am. Jour. Roentgenology, 1994—, Pediat. Radiology, 1997—, others; contbr. articles to profl. jours Leader, asst. leader Girl Scouts Am., Cordova, Tenn., 1992-99; youth club asst. Advent Presbyn. Ch., Cordova, 1993-98, ch. orch. Maj. USAF Med. Corps, 1977-91. Grantee, Soc. Pediat. Radiology, 1998. Mem. Children's Oncology Group, Am. Coll. Radiology, Radiologic Soc. N.Am., Am. Soc. Bone and Mineral Rsch., Soc. Pediat. Radiology (pres.-elect 2011-). Avocations: flute, painting, swimming, drawing, knitting. Office: St Jude Childrens Rsch Hosp Dept Diagnostic Imaging msn #220 262 Danny Thomas Pl Memphis TN 38105-2729 Office Fax: 901-495-3981.

KASTIN, ABBA JEREMIAH, endocrinologist, researcher; b. Cleve., Dec. 24, 1934; s. Isadore I. and Ruth (Urdang) K. AB, Harvard U., 1956, MD, 1960; doctorate (hon.), U. Nacional Federico Villarreal, Lima, Peru, 1980; DSc (hon.), U. New Orleans, 1984; PhD (hon.), Uppsala U., Sweden, 2008. Hon. prof. Peking U. Health Sci. Ctr., Beijing, Lanzhou U., China; intern Vanderbilt U. Hosp., Nashville, 1960-61, resident in internal medicine, 1961-62; clin. assoc. USPHS, NIH, 1962-64; clin. investigator VA Hosp., New Orleans, 1965-68; chief endocrinology sect. VA Med. Ctr., 1968—2004; prof. dept. medicine Tulane U. Sch. Medicine, New Orleans, 1974—2004; grad. faculty U. New Orleans, 1976—2006; prof. and endowed chair Pennington Biomed. Rsch. Ctr., Baton Rouge, 2004—. Cons. prof. dept. psychology U. New Orleans, 1986-2006, FDA, 1979; mem. visual arts vis. com. Loyola U., New Orleans, 2004-11; mem. med. adv. bd. Nat. Pituitary Agy., 1974-77; Wellcome vis. prof., 1990; pre-reviewer in endocrinology, mem. residency com. for internal medicine Accreditation Coun. for Grad. Med. Edn., 1984-95; vis. sr. scientist Japan Soc. Promotion Sci., 1997; spkr., lectr. in field. Editor-in-chief: Peptides, an Internat. Jour., 1980—; editor: Handbook of Biologically Active Peptides, 2006; mem. editl. bd. Jour. Clin. Endocrinology and Metabolism, 1976-80, Brain Rsch. Bull., 1986-95, Neurosci. and Biobehaviorial Rev., 1977-95, New Trends Exptl. Clin. Psychiatry, 1985-2001, Progress in Neuroendocrinimmunology, 1988-90, Pharmacology, Biochemistry and Behavior, 1989-1995, Molecular and Cellular Neuroscis., 1990-95, Physiology and Behavior, 1993-95, Endocrine Practice, 1994-2004, Neuroimmunomodulation, 1995-2000, Current pharm. Design, 2003—, Medicinal Chemistry, 2004—; contbr. more than 850 articles to profl. jours. Advisory bd. La. Philharmonic Orch., 1997—; bd. dirs. Baton Rouge Symphony Orch., Opéra Louisiane. Recipient Edward T. Tyler Fertility award Internat. Fertility Soc., 1975, Eagle award Fed. Bus. Assn., 1975, Copernicus medal Med. Faculty Krakow, Poland, 1979, William S. Middletown award VA, 1982, Strand award 2001; named in top 100 Most Cited Scientist List, Inst. for Scientific Info. Fellow Am. Coll. Endocrinology; mem. Am. Physiol. Soc., Am. Peptide Soc., Endocrine Soc., Soc. Exptl. Biol. Medicine, Soc. Neurosci., Internat. Soc. Psychoneuroendocrinology (introductory hon. scientific lectr. XVth Congress), Internat. Soc. Neuroendocrinology, Internat. Behavioral Neuroscience Soc. (keynote speaker first meeting, mem. adv. coun.), Internat. Neuropeptide Soc. (pres. 1993—) hon. mem. Brazilian Soc. Toxinology, Indian Soc. Comparative Endocrinology, La Soc. de Dermo-Chimie, Chilean Soc. Endocrinology, Phillippine Soc. Endocrinology and Metabolism, Peruvian Ob-Gyn Soc., Peruvian Endocrine Soc., Polish Endocrine Soc., Hungarian Endocrine Soc., Harvard Club La. (pres. 1991-95), Green Wave Masters Swim Club (pres. 1978-84). Jewish. Office: Pennington Biomed Rsch Ctr 6400 Perkins Rd Baton Rouge LA 70808-4124 Office Phone: 225-763-3042. Business E-Mail: peptides@pbrc.edu.

KASTNER, MICHAEL JAMES, dentist; b. Huntington, Ind., Oct. 20, 1954; s. James H. and Barbara A. (Bartrom) K.; m. Kimberly A. Ricke, June 18, 1983; children: Kevin Michael, Ryan James, Derek Edward. BS in Biology and Chemistry, Manchester Coll., 1977; DDS, Ind. U., Indpls., 1981; postgrad., Armed Forces Inst. Pathology, 1989. Gen. practice dentistry, Toledo, 1981—. Asst. dentist Toledo Zoo, 1991—; mem. Ohio Mass Disaster Team, 1995—, team capt., 2001—; with Lucas County Coroner's Office, 1987—; with N.Y. Med. Examiners Office in dental forensic identification of World Trade Ctr. victims, 2001. Contbr. articles to profl. publs., columns in newspapers. Bd. trustees Dental Ctr. Northwest Ohio, 1994-2000, nominating com., 1995-2001, long range planning com., 1999-2001, dental com., 1995-98, 2000; mem. Lucas County Oral Health Coalition. Recipent Alumni Honor award Manchester Coll., 1997, Recognition for Honor award Ohio State Senate Resolution, 1997, Honoring Am. Spirit award Gov. Ohio, 2002, cert. of recognition City of NY Office of Chief Med. Examiner, 2003, Congressman Vito Fosella, 13th Dist. NY, 2003. Fellow Pierre Fauchard Acad., Am. Coll. Dentists; mem. ADA (chmn. local chpt., chmn. area grassroots membership initiative, house of dels., alternative del., 2011, Recognition for Vol. Svc. Fgn. Country award Dominican Republic 1984, 87, Costa Rica 1990, Nepal 1994, Nicaragua 2000, 01, Mission Trip Guatemala 2009, Mission Trip Africa 2010), Ohio Dental Assn. (state del. 2002—, alt. del. 1999-01, statewide subcom. on peer rev. 2000—, chmn. 2004, dental OPTIONS program, 1999—, Give Kids A Smile program 2001-, Humanitarian of Yr. 1995, 02), Toledo Dental Soc. (bd. dirs. 1996-99, peer rev. com. 1998—, nominating com. 1999-2001, chmn. 2001, program and continuing edn. com. 1999—, relief fund subcom. 1999, fin. com. 2000, long range planning com. 2000, exec. office com. 2000-03, exec. bd. sec./treas. 2000, v.p. 2001, pres. 2002, constitution by-laws com., 2002—, scholarship com., 2007-), Am. Acad. Cosmetic Dentistry, Am. Soc. Forensic Odontology, Am. Coll. Oral Implantology, Am. Soc. Osseointegration Internat. Congress Oral Implantologists, MENSA. Roman Catholic. Avocations: photography, sports, travel, outdoor activities, oenology. Home: 6944 Hickory Ridge Rd Sylvania OH 43560

KASTOR, JOHN ALFRED, cardiologist, educator; b. NYC, Sept. 15, 1931; s. Alfred Bernard and Ellen Voigt Bentley; m. Mae Belle Eisenberg, July 4, 1954; children: Elizabeth Mae, Anne Sarah, Peter John. BA, U. Pa., 1953; MD, NYU, 1962. Diplomate Am. Bd. Cardiology. With NBC, NYC, 1956-58; intern, asst. resident in medicine Bellevue Hosp., NYC, 1962-64; chief resident physician N.Y. U. Hosp., NYC, 1964-65; clin. and research fellow in medicine Mass. Gen. Hosp., Boston, 1965-68, clin. asst. and asst. in medicine, 1968-69; instr. in medicine Harvard Med. Sch., 1968-69; dir. med. intensive care unit Hosp. U. Pa., Phila., 1969-72, assoc. chief cardiovascular sect., 1972-77, chief, 1977-81; physician-in-chief U. Md. Hosp., 1984-97; prof. medicine U. Pa. Sch. Medicine, Phila., 1976-83; Theodore E. Woodward prof. medicine U. Md. Sch. Medicine, 1984-97, chmn. dept. medicine, 1984-97, prof. medicine, 1997—. Vis. prin. fellow Nat. Heart and Lung Inst., London, 1995. Author: Arrhythmias, 1994, 2d edit., 2000, Mergers of Teaching Hospitals in Boston, New York and Northern California, 2001, Governance of Teaching Hospitals: Turmoil at Penn and Hopkins, 2003, Specialty Care in the Era of Managed Care: Cleveland Clinic versus University Hospitals of Cleveland, 2005, A Guide To Cardiac Arrhythmias For Patients And Families, 2006, Selling Tchg. Hosps. & Practice Plans, 2008—; founding editor Internat. Jour. Cardiology, 1981—84; contbr. articles to profl. jours.; editor: Health Policy Sect., The Pharos. With US Army, 1953—55. Fellow: ACP, Coun. Clin. Cardiology of Am. Heart Assn., Am. Coll. Cardiology; mem.: NIH (founding editor 1991—2008, 2010), Paul Dudley White Soc. (dir. 1977—86), Venezuelan Soc. Internal Medicine, Assn. Univ. Cardiologists, Assn. Am. Physicians, Am. Heart Assn. (bd. govs. southeaster Pa. chpt. 1975—81, bd. govs. Md. affiliate 1990—93), Am. Fedn. Clin. Rsch., Alpha Omega Alpha. Home: 2415 Boston St Baltimore MD 21224-4733 Office: University Md Med Sys 110 S Paca St Rm 2N 139 Baltimore MD 21201 *

KASUBA, PAUL, insurance company executive; Grad., Tufts U. Sch. of Medicine; AB with honors in Polit. Sci., Duke U. Med. tng. St. Elizabeth Med. Ctr., Boston, chief divsn. internal medicine, v.p., med. dir., Caritas Physician Network's cmty. practice divsn., pres. health profl. IPA; asst. clin. prof. medicine Tufts U. Sch. Medicine; chief med. officer Tufts Health Plan, 2010—; limited internal medicine practice. Mem.: Mass. Med. Soc., American Med. Assn. Office: Tufts Health Plan 705 Mt Auburn St Watertown MA 02472 *

KASUYA, HIDEKI, medical researcher, surgeon; b. Nagoya, Aichi, Japan, Aug. 27, 1961; s. Morimasa and Makiko Kasuya; m. Yoshie Kasuya, Sept. 28, 1961. PhD, Nagoya U., Japan, 2000; MD, Aichi Med. U., Nagoya, 1990. Cert. surgeon 1995. Surgery staff Holy Spirit Internat. Hosp., Nagoya, Aichi, Japan, 1990—95, Nagoya Red Cross Hosp., Kidney Transplantation Ctr., Nagoya, 1995—96; rsch. fellow Harvard Med. U., Boston, 2000—03; v.p. Kanda Hosp., Nagoya, 1998—2000, Kasuya Clinic, Nagoya, 1990—2004, exec. dir. divsn. oncolytic virus therapy, 2005—; chief of cancer gene therapy dept. surgery Nagoya U. Sch. Medicine, 2000—04, exec. dir. divsn. oncolytic virus therapy, 2004—, from asst. prof. to assoc. prof., 2010—, assoc. dean, 2010—, prof., 2010—; chief med. team Kasamatsu Women's Prison, 2004—06, Seto Juvenile Prison, 2006—07. Exec. editor Jour. Current Cancer Drug Targets, 2006—. Mem. editl. bd.: Current Cancer Drug Targets, 2006—; contbr. numerous articles to profl. jours. Mem.: ACS, Am. Assn. for Cancer Rsch., The Japan Surg. Assn., The Japan Soc. Cancer Therapy, The Japan Med. Assn., The Japan Enterol. Surgery, The Japan Pancreas Soc., The Japan Gene Therapy Assn. Buddhist. Avocation: Surfine. Home: 5-20 Auchi-dori Showa-ku Aichi Nagoya 466-0027 Japan Office: Nagoya Univ Sch Medicine Dept Surgery 65 Tsurumai-cho Showa-ku Aichi Nagoya 466-8550 Japan Home Phone: 81-52-842-2322; Office Phone: 81-052-744-2249. Office Fax: 052-744-2255; Home Fax: 81-052-842-2322. Personal E-mail: hidekikasuya@aol.com.

KASUYA, HIDETOSHI, neurosurgeon; b. Kyoto, Feb. 28, 1957; s. Toshio and Isako Kasuya; m. Chino Kasuya, Dec. 8, 1985; children: Nobuyuki, Tomoaki, Naofumi. MD, Tokushima Univ. Sch. of Medicine, Japan, 1982. Diplomate Japanese Neurosurgery Soc. Lectr. Tokyo Women's Med. Ctr., 1984, sr. lectr., 1997, asst. prof., 2002; prof. head dept. neurosurgery Med. Ctr. East. Recipient Galenus award, Japenese Neurosurgery Soc., 1995. Office: Tokyo Women's Med Univ Dept Neurosurgery Med Ctr East 2-1-10 Nishiogu Arakawaku Tokyo 1168567 Japan Office Phone: 81-3 3816-8111. Business E-Mail: kasuyane@dnh.twmu.ac.jp.

KASZNIAK, ALFRED WAYNE, neuropsychologist; b. Chgo., June 2, 1949; s. Alfred H. and Ann Virginia (Simonsen) K.; m. Mary Ellen Beaurain, Aug. 26, 1973; children: Jesse, Elizabeth. BS with honors, U. Ill., 1970, MA, 1973, PhD, 1976. Instr. dept. psychology Rush Med. Coll., Chgo., 1974-76, asst. prof. dept. psychology, 1976-79; from asst. prof. to assoc. prof. dept. psychiatry U. Ariz. Coll. Medicine, Tucson, 1979-82, assoc. prof. dept. psychology and psychiatry, 1982-87, prof. dept. psychology, neurology and psychiatry, 1987—; chmn. U. Ariz. Commn. on Gerontology, Tucson, 1990-93; acting head dept. psychology U. Ariz., 1992-93, assoc. head dept. psychology, 1999—2002, head dept. psychology, 2002—. Dir. U. Ariz. Coordinated Clin. Neuropsychology Program, dir. Ctr. Consciousness Studies, 1998-2002; staff psychologist Presbyn.-St. Luke's Hosp., Chgo., 1976-79, Univ.Hosp., Tucson, 1979—; mem. human devel. and aging study sect. divsn. rsch. grants, NIH, 1981-86. Author 6 books; mem. editl. bd. Psychology and Aging, 1984-87, The Clin. Neuropsychologist, 1986-96, Clin. Geropsychology, 1994-2003, Jour. Clin. and Exptl. Neuropsychology, 1987-90, Jour. Gerontology, 1988-92, Neuropsychology, 1992-93, Psychological Bull., 1998-2003, Aging, Neuropsychology, and Cognition, 1999—, Consciousness and Emotion, 2000—; contbr. articles to profl. jours. Trustee So. Ariz. chpt. Nat. Multiple Sclerosis Soc., 1980-82; mem. med. and sci. adv. bd. Nat. Alzheimer's Disease and Related Disorders Assn., 1981-84; mem. VA Geriatrics and Gerontology Adv. Com., 1986-89, Ariz. Gov.'s Adv. Com. on Alzheimer's Disease, 1988-92; mem. med. adv bd. Fan Kane Fund for Brain-Injured Children, Tucson, 1980-92. Grantee Nat. Inst. Aging, 1978—83, 1989—94, 2001—, NIMH, 1984—94, 2002—, Robert Wood Johnson Found., 1986—89, Fetzer Inst., 1997—, Flinn Found., 1998—99. Fellow Am. Psychol. Assn. (Disting. Contbr. award div. 20 1978, pres. clin. geropsychology sect. 1995), Am. Psychol. Soc.; mem. Internat. Neuropsychol. Soc. (bd. govs. 1994-97), Gerontol. Soc. (rsch. fellow 1980). Office: Univ Ariz Dept Psychology Psychology Bldg 312B/214 1503 E University Tucson AZ 85721-0001 E-mail: kaszniak@u.arizona.edu.

KATAI, SATOSHI, neurologist; b. Tokyo, Nov. 1, 1965; s. Taketo and Emiko Katai; m. Hiroko-Masatsuka Katai, Mar. 24, 2001; 1 child, Haruka. MD, Shinshu U., Matsumoto, Nagano, Japan, 1991, PhD of Med. Sci., 2000. Lic. Japan. Resident in internal medicine 3d Dept. Medicine, Shinshu U. Sch. Medicine, Matsumoto, 1991, Kenwakai Hosp., Ida, Nagano, Japan, 1992; med. staff internal medicine Komoro Kousei Gen. Hosp., Nagano, 1993, Fukuyama Cardiovasc. Hosp., 1994; med. staff internal medicine neurology Kakeyu Hosp., JA Nagano Koseiren Kakeyu-Misayama Rehab. Ctr., Ueda, Nagano, 1995—. Contbr. articles to profl. jours. Mem.: Soc. for Neurosci., Neuropsychology Assn. Japan, Japanese Neurosci. Soc., Japanese Soc. Neurology (cert. Bd. Clin. Neurology). Achievements include research in neuropsychological investigation of the prospective memory of patients with Parkinson's disease; neurophysiological investigation of cortical neuronal types and neuronal mechanisms involved in the generation of saccadic eye movements. Avocation: watching soccer. Office: Kakeyu Hosp JANaganoKoseiren Kakeyu-MisayamaRehabCtr 1308 Kakeyu Onsen Ueda Nagano 386-0396 Japan Office Phone: 81-268-44-2111. Business E-Mail: skatai@kakeyu-hp.com.

KATAKKAR, SURESH BALAJI, hematologist, oncologist; b. Poona, India, Feb. 9, 1944; arrived in USA, 1978, naturalized, 1985; s. Balaji Vasudeo Katakkar and Padmavati (Gangadhar) Varavandkar; m. Sunila Moghe; children: Smita, Sucheta, Swati. MB, BS, Poona U., India, 1969; grad., Ednl. Coun. Fgn. Med., 1970. Lic. Med. Coun. Can., diplomate in internal medicine and oncology Am. Bd. Internal Medicine, Am. Bd. Quality Assurance and Utilization Rev., Am. Bd. Forensic Medicine, Am. Bd. Thrombosis and Vascular Medicine, bd. cert. European Soc. Med. Oncology, Am. Bd. Oncology. Intern, then resident St. Paul's Hosp., Saskatoon, 1969-71; resident U. Hosp., Saskatoon, 1971-72; resident clin. hematology Gen. Hosp., Ottawa, 1973-74; fellow in med. oncology W.W. Cross Cancer Inst., Edmonton, Can., 1974-75; sr. cancer clin. assoc. Sasketchewan Cancer Commn., 1975-78; clin. investigator NCI, USA, 1975—; med. oncologist Madigan Army Med. Ctr., 1978-80; pvt. practice Tucson, Ariz., 1980—; med. dir., chmn. cancer com. N.W. Cancer Ctr., 1991—. Chmn. tumor bd. St. Mary's Hosp., Tucson, 1981-83, chmn. transfusion com., 1982-97; chmn. dept. med. Northwest Hosp., 1983-84, med. dir. UMC Orange Grove Hem-ONC, 2007-09, pvt. practice, 2009, lead med. oncologist hematologist BC Cancer Agy. Prince George BC, 2011-, chief of staff, 1984-86, NWH bd. trustee, 1984-96, clin. lectr. Univ. Med. Ctr., Ariz. Cancer Ctr., 1989—. Contbr. articles to profl. jours.; spkr, presenter, abstracts in field. W.W. Cross Cancer Inst. fellow, 1974-75, Patients Chiose award, 2008-10. Fellow ACP, Royal Coll. Physicians Can., Internat. Acad. Thrombosis/Hemostasis; mem. AMA, Am. Soc. Clin. Oncology, Internat. Soc. Preventive Oncology, Am. Geriatrics Soc., Am. Hosp. Assn., Am. Assn. Blood Banks, Am. Bd. Med. Dirs., Am. Coll. Med. Quality, N.Y. Acad. Scis., European Soc. Med. Oncology, European Assn. Cancer Rsch., European Hematology Assn., Am. Soc. Hematology, BC Med. Assn. Hindu. Avocations: swimming, stamp collecting/philately, coin collecting/numismatics, bicycling. Home: 1391 E Placita Mapache Tucson AZ 85718-3929 Office: Regional Cancer Care Ctr Prince George BC V2M1S2 Canada Home: AZ HEM ONC 1391 E Placita Mapache Tucson AZ 85718 Office Phone: 520-297-8429. Personal E-mail: azhemonc@aol.com.

KATAKURA, YOSHIKI, gastroenterologist; b. Sendai, Miyagi Prefecture, Japan, June 28, 1969; MD, St. Marianna U., PhD, 1996. Head gastroenterologist Seirei Yokohama Hosp., 2010—. Mem.: Japan Pancreas Soc., Japan Gastroent. Endoscopy Soc., Japan Soc. Hepatology, Japanese Soc. Gastroenterology, Japan Biliary Assn. Avocation: guitar. Office: 215 Iwai-cho Hodogaya-ku Yokohama Kanagawa 240-8521 Japan Office Fax: 81-45-715-3387. Business E-Mail: katabon@n03.itscom.net.

KATAOKA, MIKIO, biophysicist, educator; b. Nagasaki, Japan, Nov. 19, 1949; PhD, Osaka U., 1980. Prof. Nara Inst. Sci. and Tech., 1998, v.p., 2011. Mem.: Biophys. Soc. Japan. Office: 8916-5 Takayama Ikoma Nara 630-0192 Japan Office Fax: 81-743-72-6109. Business E-Mail: kataoka@ms.naist.jp.

KATARIA, TEJINDER, radiologist, oncologist, consultant; b. Shimla, Himachal Prdesh, India, Jan. 28, 1960; d. Pritam Singh and Surjit Kaur Sethi; m. Rajiv Kataria, Dec. 10, 1985; 1 child, Shruti. MB, BChir, Indira Gandhi Med. Coll., India, 1983; MD in Radiotherapy, Inst. Med. Edn. and Rsch., India, 1987; cert. in clin. oncology, Specialist Tng. Authority, U.K., 2005. Diplomate Nat. Acad. Med. Sci. Coord. dept. radiation oncology Rajiv Gandhi Cancer Inst. and Rsch. Ctr., New Delhi, 2005—07, sr. cons. dept. radiation oncology, 1996—2007; cons., head radiation oncology Artemis Health Scis. Inst., Gurgaon, 2007—09; chair Indian Breast Cancer Initiative Breast Congress, 2008; chairperson Medanta Cancer Inst., Radiation Oncology, Medanta-the Medicity, Gurgaon, 2009—. QUATRO Asia team Internat. Atomic Energy Agy., Vienna, 2005—, Asian auditor radiation oncology, 2005—07; task force com. nat. cancer control program 11th yr. plan Ministry of Health and Family Welfare, New Delhi, 2005—06; lectr., reveiwer in field. Recipient Nat. Excellence award, All India Lawyers Forum for Civil Liberties, New Delhi, 2002, Best Poster award, Dharamshila Cancer Found., 2003; fellow, Internat. Med. Sci. Acad., 2003; scholar, Commonwealth of India, 1994; Leeds U. fellow, Assn. Radiation Oncologists India, 1993, Commonwealth scholar, Ministry of Human Resources, India and Brit. Coun., 1994—95. Fellow: Assn. Radiation Oncologists India (life; joint sec. 2000—04), Internat. Med. Sci. Acad. (life; guest editor 2003); mem.: Nat. Acad. Med. Sci., European Soc. Radiation and Therapeutic Oncology, Am. Soc. Therapeutic Radiation Oncology (licentiate), Indian Coll. Radiation Oncology (life; founding mem. 1997). Avocations: reading, walking, travel, swimming, badminton. Home: R-615 New Rajinder Nagar New Delhi 110 060 India Office: Medanta-the Medicity Gurgaon 122001 India Personal E-mail: teji1960@gmail.com.

KATARIYA, KUSHAGRA, cardiothoracic surgeon, educator, healthcare developer, strategist; MBBS, U. Delhi, 1989. Cert. Am. Bd. Surgery, Am. Bd. Thoracic Surgery. Resident in gen. surgery Beth Israel Med. Ctr., Albert Einsten Coll. Medicine, NYC, 1990—95, chief resident dept. surgery, 1995—96; resident divsn. cardiothoracic surgery Jackson Meml. Med. Ctr., U. Miami Sch. Medicine, 1996—98, attending physician, 1998—; asst. prof. dept. surgery U. Miami Sch. Medicine, 1998—2004, assoc. prof., 2004—; chief sect. cardiothoracic surgery Miami VA Hosp., 2001—; attending physician cardiothoracic surgery Cedars Med. Ctr., Miami, 2006—; chief exec. officer Artemis Health Scis., Gurgaon, India, 2006—. Spkr. in field. Contbr. chapters to books, articles to profl. jours.; guest reviewer Annals Thoracic Surgery, 2000—, Asian Annals Thoracic and Cardiovasc. Surgery, 2000—. Recipient Leon Ginzburg award, Albert Einstein Coll. Medicine, 1996, Resident Achievement award, Soc. Laparoendoscopic Surgeons, 1996, Best Tchr. award, Divsn. Cardiothoracic Surgery, U. Miami Sch. Medicine, 2001—02; grantee, U. Miami, Jackson Meml. Med. Ctr., 2001—, Aventis Pharm., 2001—02, St. Jude Med., Mpls., 2002—, Dept. Vet. Affairs, 2002—, Ethicon, Inc., 2003—. Mem.: ACS, Am. Assn. Physicians from India, Internat. Soc. Minimally Invasive Cardiac Surgery, Am. Coll. Cardiology (affiliate mem.), Assn. VA Surgeons, Soc. Thoracic Surgeons, So. Thoracic Surg. Assn. Office: Artemis Health Scis 122 001 Haryana India Office Phone: +91-124-6767999. Business E-Mail: kkatariya@artemishealthsciences.com.

KATEN, KAREN L., retired pharmaceutical company executive; b. 1948; BA in Polit. Sci. and Econ., U. Chgo., 1970, MBA in Mktg. and Fin., 1974. Mktg. assoc. pharms. Pfizer, Inc., 1974, various positions Roerig divsn. product mgmt. group, 1975—78, group product mgr. Pfizer Labs., 1980, dir. product mgr. Pfizer Labs., v.p. mktg. Roerig divsn., 1983—86, v.p., dir. ops. Roerig divsn., 1986—91, v.p., gen. mgr. Roerig divsn., 1991—93, v.p., 1992—99, exec. v.p. Pfizer US Pharms. Group, 1993—95, pres. Pfizer US Pharms. Group NYC, 1995—2002, sr. v.p., 1999—2001, exec. v.p., 2001—05, vice chmn., 2005—06; exec. v.p. Pfizer Global Pharmaceuticals (formerly Pfizer Pharmaceuticals Group), 1997—2001, pres., 2001—05, Pfizer Human Health, 2005—06; adv. health policy Pfizer, Inc., 2006; chair Pfizer Foundation, 2006—08; sr. adv. Essex Woodlands Health Ventures, 2007—. Bd. dirs. Harris Corp., 1994—, Gen. Motors Corp., 1997—, Home Depot Inc., 2007—, Air Liquide, Catalyst, Nat. Alliance Hispanic Health, Am. Bur. for Med. Advancement in China; mem. internat. coun. J.P. Morgan Chase & Co.; mem. coun. U.S. and Italy, U. Chgo. Grad. Sch. Bus.; trustee U. Chgo.; nat. bd. trustees Am. Cancer Soc. Rsch. Found., NCAA Found.; health bd. advisors RAND Corp.; bd. corp. advisors Am. Diabetes Assn.; appointee US-Japan Private Sector/Govt. Commn., 2003, Nat. Infrastructure Adv. Com., 2003; bd. trustees Healthcare Leadership Coun. Recipient Salute to Women Achievers award, YMCA, Women Yr. award, Boy Scout Am. Greater N.Y. Coun., NY Women's Agenda Star award, Bus. Leadership award, Burden Ctr. Aging, Iphigene Ochs Sulzburger award, Barnard Coll., Am. Fedn. Aging Rsch. Distinction award, Woman of Yr. award, NYC Police Athletic League, 2001, Woman With Heart award, Am. Heart Assn., 2004; named one of The 50 Most Powerful Women in Bus., Fortune mag., 1998—2005, The Top 50 Women to Watch, Wall St. Jour., 2005, The Next 20 Female CEOs, Pink Mag. & Forté Found., 2006. Mem.: Nat. Pharm. Coun. (mem. bd. dirs.), Am. Diabetes Assn. (mem. bd. corp. advisors, Women of Valor award), Am. Cancer Soc. Rsch. Found. (mem. nat. bd. trustees), Nat. Alliance Hispanic Health, European Fedn. Pharm. Industry Assns. (bd. mem.), Health Leadership Coun., Pharm. Rsch. and Mfrs. Assn. Am. Office: Essex Woodlands Health Ventures 717 Fifth Ave 14th Fl Ste B New York NY 10022 Office Phone: 646-429-1251. Office Fax: 212-355-2313.

KATEN-BAHENSKY, DONNA, health facility administrator; BA in Anthropology, U. Mo., Columbia, 1980, MS in Pub. Health Adminstrn., 1982. COO, assoc. hosp. dir., acting hosp. dir. U. Nebr. Hosp., Omaha, 1991—98; vice chancellor bus. and fin. U. Nebr. Med. Ctr., Omaha, 1996—97; v.p. ambulatory care Nebr. Health Sys., Omaha, 1997—98; COO Med. Coll. Va. Hosps., Richmond, 1998—2000, exec. v.p., COO, 2000—02, Clinics of Va. Commonwealth U. Health Sys., Richmond, 2000—02; dir., CEO U. Iowa Hosps. and Cilinics, Iowa City, 2002—08; pres., CEO Univ. Wis. Hospital & Clinics, Madison, 2008—. Adj. faculty, preceptor grad. program in health adminstrn. Med. Coll. Va. Hosps.; mem. U. Health Sys. Consortium, Am. Coll. Healthcare Execs.; mem. adv. bd. Pfizer Health Solutions. Office: Univ Wis Hosp & Clinics 600 Highland Ave Madison WI 53792 *

KATES, KENNETH P., hospital administrator; BS in Bus. Adminstrn./Mktg., Phila. U.; MBA in Health Adminstrn., Temple U. V.p., dir. U. Chgo. Children's Hosp. U. Chgo. Hosps. and Health Sys., exec. v.p., COO; cons. Alvarez and Marsal, Chgo.; assoc. v.p., CEO U. Iowa Hosps. and Clinics, 2008—. Office: UI Hospitals and Clinics 200 Hawkins Dr Iowa City IA 52242 *

KATHREN, RONALD, health physicist; b. Windsor, Ont., Can., June 6, 1937; s. Ben and Sally (Forman) Kathren; m. Susan Ruth Krafft, Dec. 24, 1964; children: SallyBeth, Daniel, Elana(dec.). BS, UCLA, 1957; MSc, U. Pitts., 1962. Registered profl. engr., Calif.; diplomate Am. Bd. Health Physics, Am. Acad. Environ. Engrs. Health physicist Lawrence Radiation Lab. U. Calif., Livermore, 1962—67; mgr. external dose evaluation Battelle Pacific Northwest Labs., Richland, Wash., 1967—70, sr. rsch. scientist, 1970—72, staff scientist, program mgr., 1978—89; dir. US Transuranium and Uranium Registries Hanford Environ. Health Found., 1989—92; prof., dir. US Transuranium and Uranium Registries, Wash. State U., 1992—99, prof. emeritus, 1999—. US expert Internat. Atomic Energy Agy., Caracas, Venezuela, 1977; affiliate assoc. prof. U. Wash., 1978—94, program coord. radiol. scis., 1980—82, 1986—88, prof., 1994; cons. adv. com. Reactor Safeguards, Washington, 1979—89, Nuc. Waste, 1988—94; mem. adv. com. Richland City Schs., 1985—87; bd. dirs. Mid-Columbia Symphony, 1987—92; chmn. Nat. Coun. Radiation Protection and Measurements Sci. Com. Collective Dose, 1991—95; cons. Com. Environ. Radioactivity, 2005—09. Author: Ionizing Radiation: Tumorigenic and Tumoricidal Effects, 1983, Radioactivity in the Environment, 1984, Radiation Protection, 1985, The Plutonium Story, 1994; co-editor (with others): Health Physics: A Backward Glance, 1980, Computer Applications in Health Physics, 1984, Environmental Health Physics, 1993, Radiation Protection Dosimetry, 1990—, Internat. Jour. Low Level Radiation, 2002—; contbr. numerous articles to profl. jours., tech. reports, chapters to books. Trustee Richland Pub. Libr. Found., 2003—, pres., 2004—06, 2008—10, Herbert M. Parker Found., 1987—, Master Gardner Found., 2004—06, Richland Players, 2007—09, Nev. Test Site Hist. Found., 2008—. Recipient Arthur Humm award, Nat. Registry Radiation Protection Technologists, 1988, Radiology Centennial Hartman Orator medal, 1995; named Disting. Alumni., U. Pitts. GSPH, 2010. Fellow: Health Physics Soc. (life; pres. Columbia chpt. 1971, dir. 1973—76, pres. 1989—90, Elda E. Anderson award 1977, Founders award 1985, Disting. Sci. Achievement award 2003, G. William Morgan Lectr. award 2006); mem.: NAS (com. on film badge dosimetry in atmospheric nuclear tests 1989, subcom. health effect depleted uranium 2005), Delta Omega (Omricon chapt.), Nat. Coun. Examiners Engring. and Surveying Com. on Exams. Profl. Engrs., Am. Acad. Environ. Engrs., Am. Bd. Health Physics (bd. dirs. 1982—84, sec.-treas. 1984), Am. Acad. Health Physics (bd. dirs. 1984—86, pres. 1993—96). Home: 137 Spring St Richland WA 99354-1651 Office: Wash State Univ 137 Spring Richland WA 99354-1641 Office Phone: 509-375-5643. Personal E-mail: kathren@bmi.net. Business E-Mail: rkathren@tricity.wsu.edu.

KATIKANENI, PAVAN, cardiologist; b. Hyderabad, India, Aug. 26, 1978; MBBS, NTR U. Health Scis., India, 2002; MD, La. State U. Health Scis., 2011. Gen. physician, pvt. med. practitioner, 2002—04; grad. rsch. asst., molecular biology, microbiology and biochemistry U. Idaho, 2004—06; rsch. assoc. scientist, immunology, virology, pathology U. Mass., Med. Sch., Dept. Pathology, 2006—08; physician, internal medicine La. State U. Health Scis. Ctr., 2008—, postdoc. fellow, cardiovasc. disease, cardiology, 2011—, elected mem., Residency Coun., 2008—, mem., Professionalism Com., 2008—, mem., Pharmacy and Therapeutics Com., 2009—. Chief house staff, dept. medicine Overton Brooks VA Méd. Ctr., 2010—. Recipient Excellence award, NTR U. Health Scis., India. Mem.: AMA, ACP (award 2010, nominee Nat. Drs. Dilemma, San Diego 2011), Am. Soc. Virology, Am. Heart Assn., Coun. Clin. Cardiology. Avocations: photography, travel, theater. Home: 214 Colonel Ap Kouns Dr Shreveport LA 71115 Office: Lousiana State University Health Scis 1501 Kings Hwy Shreveport LA 71130 Personal E-mail: contactpav@yahoo.com.

KATILA, MARJA LEENA, medical educator; b. Kuopio, Finland, Oct. 26, 1939; d. Edvart and Ida Raatikainen; m. Touko Katila; m. 1963; children: Päivi, Lisbeth, Antti-Jussi. MD, Turku U., Finland, 1966; PhD, Kuopio U., Finland, 1979. Cert. respiratory diseases and clin. microbiology. Cons., asst. head dept. respiratory diseases Kuopio U. Hosp., Finland, 1972—77; asst. head. dept. clin. microbiology U.

Hosp., Kuopio, Finland, 1980-98, head dept. clin. microbiol., 1999—2003; tech. lab. expert Finnish Lung Health Assn., 1997—, coun. mem., 2008—, Finnish Antitubercular Found., 2000. Bd. dirs. TB Control Group, Finland; adv. com. communicable diseases Ministry Social Affairs and Health, Finland, 1995—2004; program sec. Internat. Union Against Tb and Lung Disease, Paris, 1994—97, chair sect. bacteriology and immunology, 1998—99; specialist respiratory diseases Med. Bd. Finland, 1972—, specialist clin. microbiology, 1980—; assoc. prof. Kuopio U., 1991—; thematic working group for TB info. network and QC WHO-Ministry Health, Russian Fedn., 1999—2002; cons. Nat. TB Programs, Estonia, 1998—2004, Karelia, Russian Fedn., 1999—2005, St. Petersburg, Russia, 2001—; mem. stop TB working group on MDR-tuberculosis WHO, 2004—08, mem. infection control sub-group, 2006—08. Nat. editor: APMIS, 1999—2003. Pres. European Soc. Mycobacteriology, 1993—94. Mem. Zonta Internat. Club, European Soc. Microbiology, Internat. Union Against TB and Lung Diseases, Am. Soc. for Microbiology, European Soc. for Clin. Microbiology and Infectious Diseases (European coun.), Coun. Finnish Lung Health Assn. Avocations: gardening, literature, history. Office: Filha Sibeliuksenkan 11A 00250 Helsinki Finland Home: Kehvolantie 20 71800 Siilinjarvi Finland Business E-Mail: marja-leena.katila@fimnet.fi.

KATIPAMULA MALISETTI, RAJINI, hematologist; MD, Andhra Med. Coll., India. Cert. internal medicine, hematology, oncology. Resident St. Vincent Hosp., Worcester, Mass.; fellow in transfusion medicine Mayo Clinic, fellow in hematology & oncology; physician Humphrey Cancer Ctr. Mem.: Am. Assn. for Cancer Rsch., Am. Soc. Clinical Oncology (Merit award 2008). Office: 200 First St SW Rochester MN 55905 E-mail: katipamula.rajini@mayo.edu.

KATO, AKIKO, medical educator; DDS, Aichi Gakuin U., 1999; PhD, Tokyo Med. Dental U., 2004. Asst. prof. Aichi Gakuin U., 2005—08, lectr., 2008—. Mem.: Japanese Assn. Anatomists, Japanese Assn. Oral Biology, Am. Assn. Phys. Anthropology, Japan Prosthodontic Soc. Office: 1-100 Kusumoto-cho Chikusa-ku Nagoya Aichi 464-8650 Japan Business E-Mail: a-kato@dpc.agu.ac.jp.

KATO, HIROTOMO, vector biologist, immunologist; b. Osaka, Osaka, Japan, Mar. 24, 1970; s. Takayasu and Hideko Kato; m. Rie Hashiguchi, Nov. 3, 1995; 1 child, Minami. BS, U. Tokyo, 1995, PhD, 1999. DVM Ministry Agr., Forestry and Fisheries, Japan, 1995. Postdoc. fellow Immunobiology Vaccine Ctr., U. Ala., Birmingham, 1999—2001; rsch. fellow Dept. Immunotherapeutics, Tokyo Med. and Dental U., 2001—02; guest rschr. Vector Molecular Biology Unit, NIAID, NIH, Rockville, Md., 2005—06; assoc. prof. Yamaguchi U., Japan, 2002—11, Hokkaido U., Japan, 2011—. Achievements include research in leishmaniasis and vector biology. Avocations: travel, crafts. Office: Hokkaido University Grad Sch Vet Medicine Lab Parasitology Dept Disease Control Kita 18 Nishi 9 Kita-ku Sapporo Hokkaido 060-0818 Japan

KATO, HIROYUKI, surgeon; MD, Hamamatsu U., Japan, 1983; PhD, Gunma U., Maebashi, Japan, 1991. Fellow surgery Fujioka Gen. Hosp., Japan, 1984—85, Saitama Red Cross Hosp., Ohmiya, Japan, 1985, Shinohara Hosp., Kiryu, Japan, 1985—86, Gunma U. Hosp., Maebashi, Japan, 1986—87, Hidaka Hosp., Takasaki, Japan, 1987—89, Miyazaki Aiwa Hosp., Japan, 1989—90; instr. dept. surgery Gunma U. Hosp., Maebashi, Japan, 1990—93, 1997—2002, asst. prof. dept. surgery, 2002—03; physician in chief divsn. surgery Fujioka Gen. Hosp., 1993—97; asst. prof. dept. gen. surg. sci. Gunma U. Grad. Sch. Medicine, Maebashi, 2003—09; prof. chmn. surg. oncology Dokkyo Med. U., 2009—. Fellow: ACS, Japanese Soc. Gastroenterology, Japanese Soc. Gastroenterol. Surgery, Japan Surg. Soc.; mem.: Japan Surg. Assn. (bd. mem. 1999—), Japan Esophageal Soc. (bd. mem. 2003—), Japan Soc. Clin. Oncology (bd. mem. 2003—), Japanese Gastric Cancer Assn. (bd. mem. 2005—), Japanese Soc. Gastroenterology, Japanese Cancer Assn., Japanese Assn. for Thoracic Surgery, Internat. Soc. Diseases of Esophagus. Home: Dept Surg Oncology Dokkyo Med Univ 880 Kttakobayashi Mrbu-mach Tochigi 321-0293 Japan Office: Dept Surg Oncology Dokkyo Med University Mibu Tochigi 321-0293 Japan Office Phone: 81-282-86-1111. Office Fax: 81-282-86-6213. Business E-Mail: hiroyuki@showa.gunma-u.ac.jp, hkato@dokkyomed.ac.jp.

KATO, HISAKAZU, plastic surgeon, consultant; s. Kenshi and Kiyoko Kato; m. Kazumi Okamoto, Aug. 10, 1968; children: Miku, Kanta. MD, PhD, U. Occupl. and Environ. Health, Kitakyusyu, Japan, 1988. Resident Kariya Gen. Hosp., Japan, 1988—89, Nagoya U., Japan, 1989—90; with Chubu Rosai Hosp., Nagoya, 1990—99; cons. plastic surgeon, 1996—; asst. dir. Aichi Cancer Ctr. Hosp., Nagoya, 1999—2001; dir. Ohgaki Mcpl. Hosp., Japan, 2001—04, Gifu Prefectural Tajimi Hosp., Japan, 2004—. Asst. dir. Aichi Cancer Ctr. Hosp., Nagoya, Japan, 1999—2001; adj. asst. prof. Nagoya U. Sch. Medicine, 2005—, Gifu U. Sch. Medicine, 2005—, Asahi U. Sch. Dentistry, 2005—. Contbr. articles to profl. jours. Mem.: Japan Soc. Plastic and Reconstructive Surgery (assoc.).

KATO, NAOKI, orthopedic surgeon; b. Osaka, Japan, Oct. 22, 1968; s. Yasuo and Mitsuko Kato; m. Momoko Kato; children: Saki, Yuki. MD, PhD, Nat. Def. Med. Coll., Saitama. Cert. Nat. Bd. Medicine, Japan, 1994, Japanese Bd. Orthop. Surgeons, 2001, qualified hand surgeon Japanese Soc. Surgery of Hand, 2008. Resident Nat. Def. Med. Coll. Hosp., Tokorozawa, Saitama, Japan, 1994—2001, orthopaedic surgeon, 2001—06, assoc. prof., 2005—06; orthopaedic surgeon Saitama Med. U. Hosp., Iruma, Saitama, 2006—, assoc. prof., 2006—. Contbr. articles to profl. jours. Grantee rsch. abroad, Nakayama Found. Human Sci., 2003, Nakatomi Found., 2004; grants-in-aid for sci. rsch., 2008—. Mem.: Brit. Soc. Surgery Hand, Japanese Elbow Soc., Japanese Shoulder Soc., Japanese Peripheral Nerve Soc., Japanese Soc. Surgery Hand, Japanese Orthopaedic Assn. Office: Saitama Med Univ 38 Morohongo Moroyamacho Iruma Saitama 350-0451 Japan Business E-Mail: drkato@saitama-med.ac.jp.

KATO, NOBUO, bacteriology educator; b. Nagoya, Aichi, Japan, Jan. 25, 1930; s. Kiyoshi and Mieko Kato; m. Shoko Kato, Nov. 18, 1958; children: Katsuhiko, Masako, Yoshiro. MD, Nagoya U., 1955, D Med. Sci., 1959. Intern Tosei Hosp., Seto City, Japan, 1954-55; assoc. prof. Aichi Gakuin U. Sch. Dentistry, Nagoya, 1963-70; rsch. assoc. dept. bacteriology Nagoya U. Sch. Medicine, 1959-63, asst. prof. to prof., 1970—, dean, 1976-78, 81-85, dir. Rsch. Inst. for Germfree Life, 1977-79, dir. Rsch. Inst. for Disease Mechanism and Control, 1983-84; pres. Nagoya U., 1992-98, Aichi Arts Ctr., Nagoya, 1998—2005, Aichi Med. U., Nagoya, 2000—. Mem.: Japanese Soc Bacteriology (bd dirs 1983—, chmn educ comt 1988—, emeritus). Home: 1-17 Shumoku-cho Higashi-ku Nagoya 461-0014 Japan Office: Aichi Med U Nagakute Aichi 480-1195 Japan Home Phone: 81-52-051-23-1; Office Phone: 81-561-63-4940. E-mail: hisho01@aichi-med-u.ac.jp.

KATO, SATOSHI, dentist; b. Japan, Nov. 30, 1957; DDS, Nippon Dental U. Tokyo, 1982. Mgr. Med. Corp. Meisinkai, Kato Dental Clinic, Implant Ctr., 1991—. Mem.: Acad. Osseointegration. Office: 4-17 Honmachi Tonadabayashi Osaka 584-0093 Japan Office Fax: 81-721-20-0721. Business E-Mail: katosika@sage.ocn.ne.jp.

KATO, TOMOAKI, surgeon; b. Tokyo, Aug. 30, 1963; came to U.S., 1995; s. Shinro and Yoko (Fujita) K.; m. Chika Shimizu, Mar. 30, 1996. BS in Biochemsitry, U. Tokyo, Japan, 1987; MD, Osaka U. Med. Sch., Japan, 1991. Cert. Japan Nat. Bd., ECFMG Crt., Japan Surgical Bd., lic. Fla. Intern gen. surgery Osaka U. Hosp., Japan, 1991-92; resident gen. surgery Itami City Hosp., Hyogo, Japan, 1992-95; clin. fellow transplant U. Miami Sch. Medicine/Jackson Meml. Hosp., Fla., 1995-97, assoc. dir., pediat. liver and GI transplant Fla., 2003—07, dir., pediat. liver and GI transplant Fla., 2007—08; assoc. prof. clin. surgery U. Miami Sch. Medicine, 1997—2003, prof. clin. surgery, 2007—08; asst. prof. surgery Osaka U. Med. Sch., Japan, 2000—02; attending surgeon NY-Presbyn. Hosp./Columbia U. Med. Ctr., 2008—, surgical dir., liver and GI transplantation, 2008—; asst. prof. surgery Columbia U. Coll. Physicians and Surgeons, NY, 2008—. Contbr. chpt. to book., more than 150 articles to profl. jours. Named Best Resident in Gen. Surgery, Osaka U. Hosp., 1992. Mem. AMA, Japan Surg. Soc., Japanese Soc. Gastroenterol. Surgery., Japan Soc. Cancer Chemotherapy, Am. Soc. for Transplant Surgeons, Am. Gastroenterol. Assn., Transplant Soc., Internat. Pediat. Transplant Assn., Soc. U. Surgeons. Office: Columbia U Med Ctr PH Room 14-105 622 W 168th St New York NY 10032 Office Phone: 212-305-5101. Office Fax: 212-305-5124.

KATO, YASUMASA, dental educator; b. Kanagawa, Japan, Jan. 18, 1967; BS, Kitasato U., 1989; PhD, Yokohama City U., 2005. Assoc. prof. Kanagawa Dental Coll., 2008—10; prof. Ohu U. Sch. Dentistry, 2010—. Vis. prof. Yokohama City U. Grad. Sch. Medicine, 2011. Mem.: Internat. Soc. Proton Dynamics Cancer, Am. Soc. Biochemistry and Molecular Biology, Japanese Soc. Connective Tissue Rsch. (Otaka prize). Avocation: camping. Office: Tomita-machi Misumido 31-1 Koriyama Fukushima 963-8876 Japan Business E-Mail: yasumasa@kdcnet.ac.jp.

KATO, YOKO, neurosurgeon; PhD, Aichi Med. U., 1978; MD, 1978. Asst. prof. Fujita Health U., Toyoake, Japan, 2000—06, prof., 2006—. Editl. bd. Perspectives Neurol. Surgery, NY; adv. bd. Minimally Invasive Neurosurgery, NYC, Japanese Soc. Neurosurgery, Neurosurgical Rev.; active mem. Acad. Neurochirurgica Eurasiana, Japan; internat. adv. bd. Pan Arab Jour. Neurosurgery, Saudi Arabia. Recipient Yayoi Yoshioka award, Japanese Med. Women's Assn., 1994, First Place Poster Competition, Fourth Internat. Conf. Cerebrovascular Surgery, 1995, Best Contbd. Paper, N. Am. Skull Base Soc., 2002, 2003. Avocations: swimming, tennis, skiing. Office: Fujita Health Univ 1-98 Dengakugakubo Kutsukake-cho Toyoake Aichi 470-1192 Japan Office Phone: 81562939253. Office Fax: 81562933118. Business E-Mail: kyoko@fujita-hu.ac.jp.

KATO, YUTAKA, pharmaceutical executive; b. Sapporo, Japan, June 21, 1963; BE, Waseda U., 1988; PhD, Hokkaido U., 2005. Assoc. mgr. Mochida Pharm. Co., Ltd., 2001—. Avocation: piano. Office: Jimba Uenohara 712 Gotemba Shizuoka 412-8524 Japan Business E-Mail: yutakato@mochida.co.jp.

KATOH, TADASHI, pharmacist, educator; b. Shibuya Tokyo, Japan, Mar. 31, 1958; s. Osamu and Kiyoko Katoh; m. Sachiko Katoh, June 27, 1999; 1 child, Eri. BSc, Hoshi U., Tokyo, 1983; MSc, Hoshi U., 1985, PhD, 1988. Cert. pharmacist. Postdoctoral fellow Ind. U., Bloomington, 1988, U. Tex., Austin, 1988—89; rsch. fellow Sagami Chem. Rsch. Ctr., Sagamihara, Japan, 1989—94, sr. rsch. fellow, 1995—2003; prof. Tohoku Pharm. U., Sendai, Japan, 2004—. Vis. prof. Tokyo Inst. Tech., Yokohama, Japan, 1997—2003; rsch. cons. Meiji Seika Kaisha, Ltd., Yokohama, 2003—, Sagami Chem. Rsch. Ctr., Ayase, Japan, 2004. Author: Studies in Natural Products Chemistry, 1977, My Favorite Organic Synthesis, 2002. Recipient Progress award, Synthetic Organic Chemistry, Japan, 1998, Pfizer award, 1999. Mem.: Am. Chem. Soc., Chem. Soc. Japan, Pharm. Soc. Japan. Office: Tohoku Pharm Univ 4-4-1 Komatsushima Aoba-ku Sendai 981-8558 Japan

KATOH, YOSHIMITSU YUKI, anatomist, educator; b. Miyoshi, Japan, Oct. 3, 1953; s. Genichiro and Yukie (Kasai) K.; m. Keiko Suzuki, Mar. 12, 1978; children: Yasuyo, Taihei. B of Health Scis., Fujita Health U., Toyoake, Japan, 1976, PhD, 1986. Med. technologist Fujita Health U. Hosp., Toyoake, 1976-78; asst. dept. anatomy Fujita Health U., 1978-88; asst. prof. physiology Albert Szent (Hungary)-Györgyi Med. U., 1988-90; asst. dept. anatomy Fujita Health U., 1990-93, asst. prof. anatomy, 1993-98, assoc. prof. anatomy, 1998—. Part-time instr. Chiiki-Iryo Acad. Nursing, Toyota, Aichi, 1985, Yokkaichi U. Jr. Coll., Yokkaichi, Japan, 1992-95, Toyota Acad. Nursing, Toyota, 1995—, Aichi Women's Jr. Coll., 1998-2001. Fujita Health U. grantee, 1994—; grantee Min. Edn., Sci., and Culture Japan, 1996-98. Buddhist. Achievements include work with staining method, distribution, and quantitative changes of nucleolus-like inclusion bodies in the mouse brain; direct projections from the cerebellar fastigial nucleus to the thalamic suprageniculate nucleus in the cat; bilateral projections from the superior colliculus to the thalamic suprageniculate nucleus in the cat. Home: 34-7 Maehara Nishiishiki Miyoshi Aichi 470-02-26 Japan Office: Fujita Health U Anatomy Dept 1-98 Dengaku-Gakubo Aichi Toyoake 470-11-92 Japan Business E-Mail: ykatoh@fujita-hu.ac.jp.

KATONA, PETER GEZA, biomedical engineer, educator; b. Budapest, Hungary, June 25, 1937; came to U.S., 1956, naturalized, 1962; s. Stephan and Irene (Renner) K.; m. Jaroslava Blanar, Aug. 27, 1966; children— Catherine Iris, Andrew George. BS in Elec. Engring, U. Mich., 1960; S.M. in Elec. Engring. (Sloan fellow, 1960-62), M.I.T., 1962, Sc.D. in Elec. Engring, 1965. Asst. prof. elec. engring. M.I.T., 1965-69; assoc. prof. biomed. engring. Case Western Res. U., Cleve., 1969-78, prof., 1978-92, chmn. dept., 1980-87. Program dir. biomed. engring. and aiding the disabled NSF, 1989—91; v.p. biomed. engring. The Whitaker Found., 1991—95, exec. v.p. biomed engring., 1995—98, pres. biomed. engring., 1998—2000, pres., CEO, 2000—06; prof. elec. and computer engring. George Mason U., 2006—. Mem. editl. bd. Am. Jour. Physiology, 1975-81; contbr. articles on cardio-respiratory control and automated drug delivery to profl. jours. Recipient Alexander von Humboldt award, 1987-88, Disting. Achievement award, BMES, 2005, Pierre Galletti award, AIMBE, 2006. Fellow AAAS, Am. Inst. Med. & Biol. Engring. (founding); sr. mem. IEEE, Am. Physiol. Soc., Biomed. Engring. Soc. (bd. dirs. 1977-80, pres. 1984-85), Am. Soc. Engring. Edn. Office Phone: 703-993-9347. Business E-Mail: pkatona@gmu.edu. E-mail: peter@katonaconsulting.org.

KATSAROS, MICHAEL G., dentist; Grad., Villanova U.; DMD, Temple U. Posturology tng.; resident gen. practice Newark Beth Israel Med. Ctr.; dentist Washington Ctr. for Dentistry. Mem.: ADA, Am. Acad. of Dental Sleep Medicine, Internat. Assn. of Comprehensive Aesthetics, Am. Acad. of Gen. Dentistry, Omicron Kappa Upsilon Dental Honor Soc. Office: Washington Center for Dentistry 8th Fl 1430 K St NW Washington DC 20005 Office Phone: 202-223-6630.

KATSENIS, DIMITRIS L., orthopedist; b. Argos, Greece, May 1, 1964; s. Labros D. and Elli E. Katsenis; m. Rene G. Fytrou, Dec. 14, 1996; children: Labros D., Grigoris D. Degree, Athens U., 1987. Diplomate Orthopaedic Bd., 1995. Registrar orthopaedics Nuffield Orthopaedic Centre, Oxford, England, 1996—99; cons. orthopaedics Argos Gen. Hosp., Greece, 1999—. Postgrad. studies dir. Patras U., Greece, 2002—. Contbr. articles to profl. jours. Rsch. scholar, Onasis Found., 1998, 1999, Trauma fellow, AO, 2001. Mem.: Panargiakos Football Club (v.p. 2004—05). Home: Zografou 21 Argos 21200 Greece Office: Argos Gen Hosp Korinthou 191 Argos 21200 Greece Home Fax: 00302751025656. Personal E-mail: katsenis@yahoo.com.

KATSOULOS, COSTAS, optometrist; b. Athens, Feb. 19, 1976; BSc, NTEI, Athens, 2000. Quality control mgr., optical sector Theon Sensors, Koropi, Greece, 2002—04; optical store dir. Optical Stores Anastasiadis, Athens, Greece, 2004—06; contact lens designer and optometrist, specializing in contact lenses Eyeart, Thessaloniki, Greece, 2006—09; founder, dir. and sr. optometrist Art In Vision, Athens, 2009—; optometrist, specializing in splty. contact lens fits and low vision Athens Vision, Athens, 2009—. Lectr. Panhellenic Assn. Opticians and Optometrists, 2004—; reveiwer Ophthalmic and Physiol. Optics Jour., 2008—; cons. Eyeart Labs., Thessaloniki, 2009—. Co-author: Optics and Supervision (in Greek), 2006; author: The Modern Refractive Examination (in Greek), 2007; editor: Contact Lenses - Science and Practice (in Greek), 2009. Mem.: Northern Assn. Opticians and Optometrists (lectr. 2004—), European Acad. Optometry and Optics (founder). Achievements include patents for an ophthalmic slit lamp with an image intensifier. Avocation: photography. Office: Alexandras Leof. 209 115 23 Athens Greece Office Phone: 0030 210 6436298. Office Fax: 0030 210 6436291. Business E-Mail: artinvision@yahoo.gr.

KATSUDA, SHIN-ICHI, research scientist; b. Osaka, Japan, Aug. 9, 1961; DVM, Osaka Prefecture U., PhD, 1986. Dept. head Japan Food Rsch. Labs., 1986—. Bd. mem. Japanese Soc. Toxicologic Pathology, 2007—10. Office: 2-3 Bunkyo Chitose Hokkaido 066-0052 Japan Office Phone: 81-123-28-5914. Office Fax: 81-123-28-5922. Business E-Mail: katudas@jfrl.or.jp.

KATSUMATA, AKITOSHI, dentist, educator; b. Japan, Aug. 20, 1958; PhD, Asahi U., 1987. Prof., chmn. Asahi U. Sch. Dentistry, 2011—. Office: 1851 Hozumi Gifu 5010296 Japan Business E-Mail: kawamata@dent.asahi-u.ac.jp.

KATSUYOSHI, TAMAKI, hepatologist; b. Sapporo, Japan, July 13, 1974; PhD, Tokushima U., 2004; MD, Tokyo U., 2005. Radiofrequency ablation therapy hepatocellular carcinoma Tokushima U., 2001—10. Office: Okubo Hosp 2-30 Omichi Tokushima 770-0023 Japan Personal E-mail: yokkun49@hotmail.com.

KATTAN, HODA ABDULLAH, pediatrician, consultant; b. Cairo, Dec. 25, 1953; d. Abdullah Abbas Kattan and Kabera Ahmed Nazer; m. Adnan Abdulsamad Ezzat, Mar. 11, 1983; children: Mai Adnan Ezzat, Daniah Adnan Ezzat, Arwa Adnan Ezzat, Loui Adnan Ezzat. MB, BcH, Cairo U., 1978. Rotating intern U. Cairo, 1978—79; pediat. resident King Faisal Specialist Hosp. and Rsch. Ctr., 1979—82; assoc. cons. King Faisal Specialist Hoep. and Rsch. Ctr., 1988—89, cons. pediatrician, 1989—, head sect. gen. pediat., 1999—; rsch. fellow nutrition svc. Children's Hosp., Ont., Canada, 1983—84, resident in pediat., 1984—88. Corr. Down Syndrome Advocacy and Edn. Com., 1999—, Nat. Genetic and Birth Defect Registry Project, 2004—. Corr. Nat. Family Safety Program, 2008, Child Advocacy Com., 1994—. Fellow: Am. Acad. Pediat.; mem.: Royal Coll. Physicians and Surgeons Can. (licentiate), Nat. Genetic and Birth Defect Registry Project (corr.), Down Syndrome Advocacy and Edn. Com. (corr.), Saudi Attention Deficit Hyperactivity Disorder Support Group (corr.), Neural Tube Defects Registry (corr.). Muslim. Achievements include development of Spina Bifida Registry in Saudi Arabia; combined Spina Bifida clinic; initiation of first child advocacy committee in Saudi Arabia. Avocation: travel. Home: Takhasusi Riyadh 11211 Saudi Arabia Office: King Faisal Specialty Hosp & Rsch Ctr Takhasusi Riyadh 11211 Saudi Arabia Office Fax: 00966-4427784. Business E-Mail: hoda@kfshrc.edu.sa.

KATTWINKEL, JOHN, pediatrician, educator; b. Newton, Mass., June 24, 1941; s. Egon Emil and Dorothy Lucile (Fish) K.; m. Phyllis Ann Denton, Sept. 14, 1963; children: Susan, Linda. BS, Rensselaer Poly. Inst., 1964; B in Med. Sci., Dartmouth Coll., 1966; MD, Harvard U., 1968. Diplomate Am. Bd. Pediatrics, Am. Bd. Neonatology (bd. dirs. 1981-86). Resident in pediatrics Duke Med. Ctr., Durham, NC, 1968-70; clin. assoc. NIH, Bethesda, Md., 1970-72; neonatology fellow Case Western Res. U., Cleve., 1972-74; asst. prof. pediatrics U. Va., Charlottesville, 1974-78, assoc. prof., 1978-84, prof., 1984—, dir. neonatology, 1974—, Charles Fuller chair in neonatology, 1998—. Founder Perinatal Edn. Ctr., Charlottesville, 1976—; Poland and China cons. Project HOPE, Milwood, Va., 1979-92; hon. prof. Zhejiang Med. U., Hangzhou, People's Republic of China, 1985. Mem. editl. bd. Pediatrics, 1999—2005; contbr. articles on newborn respiration and med. edn. to profl. jours.; inventor device for nasal ventilation of infants. Lt. comdr. USPHS, 1970-72. Recipient Discovery Health Channel Med. Honor, 2004, Outstanding Faculty award, State Coun. Higher Edn. Va., 2008; named Disting. prof., U. Va. Alumni Assn., 2007. Fellow: Am. Acad. Pediat. (fetus and newborn com. 1983—89, neonatal resuscitation program steering com. 1989—98, chair 1994—98, editor 1999—, Ross Profl. Edn. award 1989, Apgar award 2008); mem.: Am. Found. Resp. Care (Charles H. Hudson award 2009), Soc. Pediat. Rsch., Am. Pediat. Soc. Avocation:

tennis. Home: 500 Rocks Farm Dr Charlottesville VA 22901 Office: U Va Dept Pediatrics Charlottesville VA 22908-0001 Office Phone: 434-924-5428.

KATZ, AARON EDWARD, urologist, educator; b. NYC, June 30, 1960; MD, Columbia U., 1986. Prof., dir. Ctr. Holistic Urology, Columbia U., 1993—. Expert on complementary and alternative medicine, cryosugery for prostate cancer, leading expert on prostate cancer, treatment diagnosis and staging. Office: 161 Fort Washington Ave 11th Fl New York NY 10032 Business E-Mail: aek4@columbia.edn.

KATZ, ALAN CHARLES, toxicologist; b. Kearny, NJ, Nov. 10, 1946; s. Edward Myron and Margaret Ellen Katz; m. Marcia Anne Ellenwood, July 26, 1974; children: Bryan Jeffrey, Jeffrey Alan. BS in Biology, Fairleigh Dickinson U., 1970, MS in Human Physiology, 1977; Cert. in Mgmt., Ctrl. Conn. State U., 1981. Diplomate Am. Bd. Toxicology, Am. Bd. Forensic Examiners. Chemist Union Carbide Corp., Bound Brook, N.J., 1965-70; toxicologist Ortho Pharm. Corp., Raritan, N.J., 1971-74; sr. ophthalmic pharmacologist Cooper Labs., Cedar Knolls, N.J., 1974-76; sr. assoc. toxicologist J&J Rsch. Found., North Brunswick, N.J., 1976-79; study dir. Stauffer Chem. Co., Farmington, Conn., 1979-84; sr. toxicologist EPA, Washington, 1984-87; exec. dir. TAS, Inc., Washington, 1987-97; mgr. tech. affairs Sanachem USA, Inc., 1997-98; prin. Katz Assocs., 1985—, TOXCEL, LLC, 1999—; dir. TOXCEL Internat., Ltd., 2000—. Contbg. editor Acute Toxicity, 1991-97; editl. bd. Jour. Applied Toxicology. Fellow Am. Coll. Forensic Examiners; mem. N.Y. Acad. Scis., Soc. Comparative Ophthalmology (past pres.), Soc. Toxicology, Am. Coll. Toxicology, Am. Chem. Soc., Soc. Toxicologie du Can., Roundtable Toxicology Cons., Food & Drug Law Inst. Home: 16090 Simon Kenton Rd Haymarket VA 20169-2109

KATZ, ALAN ROY, medical educator; b. Pitts., Aug. 21, 1954; s. Leon B. and Bernice Sonia (Glass) Katz; m. Donna Marie Crandall, Jan. 19, 1986; 1 child, Sarah Elizabeth. BA, U. Calif., San Diego, 1976; MD, U. Calif., Irvine, 1980; MPH, U. Hawaii, 1987; postgrad., U. So. Calif., 1980-81, U. Hawaii, 1982-83. Staff physician emergency medicine Los Angeles County U. So. Calif. Med. Ctr., 1981-82; staff physician, med. dir. Waikiki Health Ctr., Honolulu, 1983-87; dir. AIDS/STD prevention program Hawaii State Dept. Health, Honolulu, 1987-88; asst. prof. dept. pub. health scis. U. Hawaii, Honolulu, 1988-94, assoc. prof., 1994—2005, prof., 2005—, dir. preventive medicine residency program, 1994—99; grad. chair Public Health Studies, 2006—. Com. mem. Chlamydia control workgroup USPHS, 1985—87; sci. adv. bd. Hawaii AIDS Clin. Trials Rsch. Program; staff physician, med. dir. Diamond Head STD Clinic Hawaii State Dept. Health, 1998—. Contbr. articles to profl. jours. Leptospirosis ad hoc com. Hawaii State Dept. Health, Honolulu, 1988—; mem. com. human subjects U. Hawaii, 1989—. Recipient Presdl. citation for meritorious tchg., U. Hawaii, 1989, Regents medal Excellence in Tchg., 1992, Disting. Grad. Mentoring award, 2008; Tuberculosis Survey grantee, U. Hawaii, 1991, USPHS Chlamydia Prevalence Survey grantee, Hawaii, 1986. Fellow: Am. Coll. Epidemiology, Am. Coll. Preventive Medicine; mem.: APHA, Soc. Epidemiologic Rsch., Delta Omega. Office: U Hawaii Medicine Dept Pub Health Sci 1960 E West Rd Honolulu HI 96822-2319 Business E-Mail: katz@hawaii.edu.

KATZ, ARNOLD MARTIN, medical educator; b. Chgo., July 30, 1932; s. Louis Nelson and Aline (Grossner) K.; m. Phyllis Beck, Apr. 18, 1959; children: Paul, Sarah, Amy, Laura. BA with honors, U. Chgo., 1952; MD cum laude, Harvard U., 1956; D.Med. (hon.), Carol Davila U., 1994. Diplomate Nat. Bd. Med. Examiners. Intern Mass. Gen. Hosp., Boston, 1956-57, asst. resident, 1959-60; rsch. assoc. NIH, Bethesda, Md., 1957-59; asst. registrar Inst. Cardiology, London, 1960-61; rsch. fellow dept. medicine UCLA, 1961-64; asst. prof. physiology Columbia U., NYC, 1963-67; assoc. prof. medicine and physiology U. Chgo., 1967-69; Philip J. and Harriet L. Goodhart prof. cardiology Mt. Sinai Sch. Medicine, NYC, 1969-77; prof. medicine U. Conn., Farmington, 1977—2000, prof. medicine emeritus, 2000—, head cardiology divsn., 1977—95; vis. prof. medicine Dartmouth Med. Sch., 1990—2001, vis. prof. medicine and physiology, 2001—; vis. prof. medicine Harvard Med. Sch., 2008—. Coord. Problem Area #3, US-USSR Collaboration in Cardiovasc. Rsch., 1983—86; mem. adv. com. Chinese Acad. Med. Sci., 1982—89; R.T. Hall lectr. Cardiac Soc., Australia, New Zealand, 1991; chair sci. bd. Stanley J. Sarnoff Endowment Cardiovasc. Sci. Inc., 1992—93; chair, sci. adv. bd. Patrick, Catherine, Weldon, Donaghue Med. Rsch. Found., 1994—97; mem. bd. sci. counsellors Nat. Heart Lung Inst., 1989—92. Author: Physiology of the Heart, 5th edit., 2011; mem. editl. bd.: Jour. Molecular and Cellular Cardiology, 1970—92, editor-in-chief:, 1986—92. Served with USPHS, 1957-59. Recipient: Lifetime Achievement award Heart Failure Soc. Am., 2007; Humboldt fellow Alexander von Humboldt Found., 1975-76, Moseley traveling fellow Harvard U., 1960-61. Fellow ACP, Am. Coll. Cardiology (gov. Conn. 1984-87); mem. Am. Heart Assn. (advanced rsch. fellow 1961-63, established investigator 1963-68, v.p. couns. 1992-94, bd. dirs. 1992-94, chmn. coun. affairs com. 1992-94, chmn. exec. com. basic sci. coun. 1990-92, Rsch. Achievement award 1989, Disting. Achievement award Basic Sci. Coun. 1991, award of Meritorious Achievement 1995, Honoree Louis N. and Arnold M. Katz prize Basic Sci. Coun. 1995), Cardiac Muscle Soc. (pres. 1969-71), Assn. Am. Physicians, Internat. Soc. Heart Rsch. (pres. Am. sect. 1985, founding fellow 2000, Peter Harris Disting. Scientist award 2004), Internat. Acad. Cardiovasc. Sci.(Medal of Merit 2010), Alpha Omega Alpha. Home: PO Box 1048 1592 New Boston Rd Norwich VT 05055-1048 E-mail: arnold.m.katz@dartmouth.edu.

KATZ, BRIAN JEFFREY, dermatologist; b. Detroit, Jan. 28, 1975; s. Gerald Alan Katz and Dianne Faye Politzer; m. Tara Lynn Harrison, Dec. 23, 2000. BS with high distinction, U. Mich., Ann Arbor, 1997; MD, Sackler Sch. Medicine Tel Aviv U., 2002. Cert. M.D. Ednl. Commn. Fgn. Med. Grads., 2002. Rsch. fellow Skin and Cancer Assoc., Plantation, Fla., 1997—98; dermatology resident Robert Wood Johnson Med. Sch., New Brunswick, NJ, 2003—06; chief resident dept. dermatology Robert Wood Johnson Med Sch., 2005—06. Consensus bd. mem. 1st World Congress Dermoscopy, Rome. Contbr. chapters to books, articles to profl. jours.; co-author: American Academy of Dermatology CD on Dermoscopy, 2000. Med. asst. Salvation Army Free Med. Clinic, Fort Lauderdale, Fla., 1997—98; co-founder cafe 88 Orchard, Manhattan, NY, 2003—05. Mem.: AMA, Internat. Soc. Dermoscopy (bd. dirs. 2003—), Am. Acad. Dermatology (maintenence of cert. com. 2004—07, bd. dirs.). Achievements include development of 3 step diagnostic algorithm used in diagnosing pigmented lesions with dermoscopy. Office: Mt Sinai Med Ctr 4302 Alton Rd Ste 960 Miami Beach FL 33140 Office Fax: 305-674-1459. Personal E-mail: briankatz88@yahoo.com.

KATZ, DAVID LAWRENCE, preventive medicine physician, researcher; b. LA, Feb. 20, 1963; s. Donald I. and Susan Gail Katz; m. Catherine Sananes; children: Rebecca Wortman, Corinda, Valerie, Natalia, Gabriel. BA in French, Dartmouth Coll., 1984; MD, Albert Einstein Coll. Medicine, 1988; MPH, Yale U., 1993. Diplomate Am. Bd. Internal Medicine, Am. Bd. Preventive Medicine; Gen. Preventive Medicine and Pub. Health, lic. Conn., cert. Advanced Trauma Life Support, ACS, Advanced Cardiopulmonary Life Support, AHA. Intern, internal medicine Norwalk Hosp., Conn., 1988—89, resident, internal medicine Conn., 1989—91; resident, preventive medicine Yale U. Sch. Medicine, Conn., 1991—93, lectr., dept. epidemiology and pub. health New Haven, 1993—, asst. clin. prof. medicine, 1994, asst. clin. prof. epidemiology and pub. health & medicine, 1996—2000, dir., med. studies (pub. health), 1997—2006, assoc. clin. prof., epidemiology & pub. health & medicine, 2000—06, assoc. prof. pub., adj. public health, 2006—; attending physician, emergency medicine St. Mary's Hosp. Emergency Dept., Waterbury, Conn., 1991—93; attending physician, internal medicine Yale U. Health Services, New Haven, 1993—96; assoc. dir. Preventive Medicine Residency Program, Griffin Hosp., Derby, Conn., 1996—99, dir., 1999—2000; founder, dir. Integrative Medicine Ctr., Griffin Hosp., Derby, Conn., 2000—; co-founder, dir. Yale-Griffin Prevention Rsch. Ctr., 1998—; nutrition columnist O, The Oprah Magazine, 2002—; med. contbr. ABC News, 2005—07; health columnist NY Times Syndicate, 2005—; dir. med. programming Stepping Stone Spa & Wellness Ctr., Lyndon, Vt., 2006—; founder, pres. Turn the Tide Found., Inc., 2007—; host, healthy living segment WTNH New Haven Your Weekend Program, 2003—. Mem. editl. adv. bd. Men's Health Mag., 2004—, Health Mag., 2004—, "O", 2004—, Alternative Medicine Mag., 2004—, Sly Mag., 2004—, Am. Jour. Preventive Medicine, 2004—, Prevention Mag., 2007; mem. expert panel on overweight/obesity Am. Assn. Med. Colleges, 2004—; lectr. Yale Sch. Nursing, 2001—; Yale U. rep., steering com. Consortium of Academic Health Centers for Integrative Medicine, 2006—; cons. Nat. Governor's Assn., 2006—, Anian Advisors; Reuters, Inc., 2007—; mem. expert panel on overweight/obesity Assn. Am. Med. Colleges, 2004—; mem. strategic plan adv. group Nat. Heart, Lung & Blood Inst., 2007—; mem. med. adv. bd. Nat. Fibromyalgia Assn., 2007—; joined Harry Walker Agy., 2005—; invited spkr. in field at several professional conferences throughout the US and abroad. Co-author: Epidemiology, Biostatistics and Preventive Medicine, 1996, Epidemiology, Biostatistics and Preventive Medicine, 2nd edit., 2001, Epidemiology, Biostatistics and Preventive Medicine, 3rd edit., 2007, The Way to Eat: A Six-Step Path to Lifelong Weight Control, 2002 (Healthy U award for Excellence, 2003), Cut Your Cholesterol, Reader's Digest, 2003, Stealth Health: How to Sneak Age-Defying, Disease-Fighting Habits Into Your Life Without Really Trying, Reader's Digest, 2005, Flavor Point Diet: The Delicious, Breakthrough Plan to Turn Off Your Hunger and Lose Weight for Good, 2005, The Flavour Point Diet: Use Great Flavours to Control Your Appetite and Reduce Your Weight-Permanently, 2006, The Flavor Full Diet: The paperback version of The Flavor Point Diet, 2007; author: Epidemiology, Biostatistics and Preventive Medicine Review, 1997 (Rising Star, American College of Preventive Medicine, 2001), Nutrition in Clinical Practice, 2000, Clinical Epidemiology and Evidence-Based Medicine, 2001, Nutrition in Clinical Practice 2nd edition, 2008; contbr. scientific papers, chapters to books; peer reviewer for many prestigious biomedical journals, health columnist New Haven Register, Valley Edition, 1997—, New Haven Register, All Editions, 2002—, numerous guest appearances on Today Show, Good Morning America, FOX Network, 20/20, World News Tonight, CNN, PBS, 48 Hours, Food Network, NiteBeat, BBC, NPR Radio, Montel Williams Show, History Channel, VH1 and others, frequent contbr. of expert opinion on nutrition & obesity to New York Times, Wall Street Journal, Washington Post, Chicago Tribune, Boston Globe, HealthDay News, AP and Reuters and others, provides daily blog to Prevention.com, mem. of grant review panels for NIH & Centers for Disease Control, work has been featured in Men's Health, three cover stories in TIME, Newsweek, Shape, Remedy, Child's Health, Modern Maturity, Fitness, Muscle & Fitness, Child, Parenting, Glamour, Women's World, Ladies Home Journal, Business Week, Economist, Marie Claire, Prevention, Better Homes & Garden, Real Simple, US News & World Report, and others, Op-Ed on obesity epidemic & related topics have appeared in Hartford Courant, Orlando Sentinel, New York Newsday, ABC.com, Houston Chronicle and Wall Street Journal, co-developer with wife (nutrition tng. program) The Nutrition Detectives Program, developer (physical activity program) ABC for Fitness. Clin. preceptor HOPE Homeless Project, New Haven, 1994—96; cons. Project CoNECT, 1997—. Recipient numerous clin. rsch. grants, CDC, NIH, DHHS, USDA, AHA, 1996—, Ricketts award, Cmty. Hosp. of the Monterey Peninsula, Calif., 2007, Pfizer, Inc. Health Literacy Rsch. Initiative award, 2002, Dream Maker award, Greater New Haven Chpt., Juvenile Diabetes Rsch. Found. Internat., 2008, Shape Up RI, Nat. Leadership award, Obesity Prevention and Edn., RI, 2008; named to America's Top Physicians, Preventive Medicine, Consumers' Rsch. Coun. America, 2003—05; Dorothy Epstein Nutrition Fellow, Hunter Coll., CUNY, 2007. Fellow: ACP, N.Am. Assn. for the Study of Obesity, Am. Coll. Preventive Medicine (vice-chair planning com. ann. meeting 2000, chair, planning com. ann. meeting 2001—02, chair, prevention practice com. 2001—, bd. dirs. 2002—, northeast regent, bd. mem. 2002—, chair, adolescent health com. 2002—, Rising Star award 2001); mem.: N.Am. Assn. for the Study of Obesity, Am. Coll. Nutrition, Soc. Behavioral Medicine, New Haven County Med. Soc., Am. Soc. for Clin. Nutrition, Am. Pub. Health Assn., Soc. Epidemiology Rsch., NY Acad. Sciences, Assn. Teachers of Preventive Medicine (chair, edn. com. 2001—, pres. 2004, mem. governing bd. 2002), American College of Nutrition. Achievements include patents in field; patents pending in field. Avocations: skiing, hiking, poetry/creative writing, carpentry, horseback riding, cooking, inventing. Office: Yale Prevention Rsch Ctr Griffin Hospital 2nd Fl 130 Division St Derby CT 06418 also: Yale U Sch Pub Health LEPH Rm 314 60 College St New Haven CT 06510 Office Phone: 203-732-1265, 203-732-7194. Office Fax: 203-732-1264. Business E-Mail: david.katz@yale.edu.

KATZ, GEORGE GERSHON, psychologist, lawyer; b. Aug. 3, 1927; s. Abraham Michael and Dora K.; 1 child, Esti Goodman. BA, Brooklyn Coll., 1950; JD with honors, Calif. Coll. Law, 1978; PhD with honors, N.Y. U., 1956. Diplomate Am. Bd. Clinical Psychology, Am. Bd. Forensic Psychology, Am. Bd. Profl. Psychology. Clin. assoc. U. So. Calif., Los Angeles, 1971-89; instr. Northwestern U., Evanston, Ill., 1960-64; assoc. prof. Calif. State U., Los Angeles, 1969-72; adj. prof. Fuller Inst., Pasadena, Calif., 1982-86; clin. prof. U. Calif., Los Angeles, 1974-94; dir. clin. tng. VAMC, Los Angeles, 1984-93, asst. chief psychology, 1984-94. Mem. pres.'s com. mental health edn., White House, Washington, 1972; cons. senate com. on Vets. Affairs, Washington, 1972-74, Hathaway Sch. for Children:, Calif., 1969-74; co-dir./cons. Project NOVA, L.A., 1971-72; author/presenter papers in field. Co-initiator of the unit system within VA; introduced the first ombudsman program in the VA. Oral commr. Bd. of Psychology, State of Calif., 1992—. With USCG, 1944-46. Grantee NIMH, Va., 1971-75; patient advocate VISTA program, 1973. Fellow: APA, Am. Acad. Forensic Psychology, Am. OrthoPsychiatric Assn., Am. Psychol. Soc.; mem.: State Bar Calif. (chair, legal profl. com. 1998—), Am. Bd. Profl. Psychology (treas. 1992—2001, v.p. 2001—), Acad. Clin. Psychology. Office: Forensic Psych Assocs 17337 Tramonto Dr Pacific Palisades CA 90272-3121 Home Phone: 310-454-6693. E-mail: psychlaw1@verizon.net.

KATZ, JEFFRY ADAM, gastroenterologist; b. Youngstown, Ohio, Mar. 15, 1961; MD, Case Western Res. U., Cleve., 1987. Cert. in internal medicine and gastroenterology 2003, diplomate Am. Bd. Internal Medicine, in gastroenterology 1993. Resident in internal medicine Columbia-Presbyn. Med. Ctr., NYC, 1987—90; chief resident Columbia Presbyn. Med. Ctr., NYC, 1990—91; gastroenterology fellow Hosp. of the U. of Pa., Phila., 1991—94; asst. prof. medicine Case Western Res. U. Sch. Medicine, Cleve., 1994—2000, assoc. prof. medicine, 2000—. Office: Univ Hosp Cleve 11100 Euclid Ave Cleveland OH 44106

KATZ, JOSE, cardiologist, sleep medicine specialist, internist, theoretical physicist, educator; b. Havana, Cuba, June 6, 1944; s. Lipa and Victoria (Masson) K.; m. Anke Ebsen; children: David, Rachel, Hannah. BS, U. Ill., 1963, MS, 1964, PhD, 1967; MD, Free U. Berlin, 1980. Rsch. assoc. physicist U. Hamburg, Germany, 1967—69; instr. physics Purdue U., West Lafayette, Ind., 1969—71; asst. prof. physics Free U., West Berlin, Germany, 1971—74, prof. physics, 1974—82; resident in internal medicine Cleve. Met. Gen. Hosp., Mt. Sinai Med. Ctr., 1982—85; cardiology fellow Southwestern Med. Sch., Dallas, 1985—88; asst. prof. medicine and radiology Columbia U. Coll. Physicians and Surgeons, NYC, 1988—94, assoc. prof. medicine and radiology, 1994—2004; dir. cardiovasc. MRI and spectroscopy Columbia-Presbyn. Med. Ctr., NYC, 1988—2004, co-dir. EKG lab., 1999—2004; pres., CEO, med. dir. Cardio-Med. Svcs., LLC, NJ, 2004—, Comprehensive Healthcare and Med. Svc. PLLC, NYC, 2004—. Sr. staff attending Columbia-Presbyn. Med. Ctr., NYC, 1988-2004, Mt. Sinai Med. Ctr., NYC, 2004-. Contbr. articles to profl. jours., chpts. to books. Fellow ACP, Am. Coll. Cardiology, Am. Coll. Chest Physicians, Am. Coll. Angiology, Am. Heart Assn. (coun. clin. cardiology, coun. on cardiovasc. radiology, coun. on basic scis.), Internat. Soc. Magnetic Resonance in Medicine; mem. AMA, Radiol. Soc. N.Am., Soc. Nuc. Medicine, N.Am. Soc. Cardiac Imaging, Sigma Xi, Phi Kappa Phi, Sigma Tau, Pi Mu Epsilon, Tau Beta Pi. Office: 425 5th Ave 4th Floor New York NY 10016 Business E-Mail: jkatz@mdadvice.com.

KATZ, JULIAN, gastroenterologist, educator; b. NYC, Apr. 3, 1937; s. Abraham M. and Fay (Sher) K.; m. Sheila Moriber, Aug. 18, 1963; children: Jonathan Peter, Sara Katherine. AB, Columbia U., 1958; MD, U. Chgo., 1962. Diplomate Am. Bd. Internal Medicine. Intern U. Chgo. Hosps., 1962-63; resident in medicine Duke U., 1963-65; fellow in gastroenterology Yale U., 1965—67; practice medicine specializing in gastroenterology, internal medicine and geriatrics Phila., 1969—; prof. medicine and lectr. physiology and biochemistry Med. Coll. Pa., 1970—. Prof. medicine Jefferson Med. Coll., Phila., 1988—2001; chief clin. gastroenterology Med. Coll. Pa.; lectr. in field. Editor profl. jours. and books; contbr. articles to profl. jours. and books. Mem. Bd. Health, City of Phila. With USN, 1967-69. Fellow ACP, Am. Coll. Gastroenterology; mem. Am. Soc. Gastrointestinal Endoscopy, Am. Soc. Study Liver Disease, Am. Gastroent. Assn., Phila. County Med. Soc. (pres. 1997-98), Pa. Soc. Gastroent. (pres. 1999-2001), Del. Valley Geeriatrics Soc. (pres. 2004), Digestive Disease Nat. Coalition (exec. com.) Home and Office: 701 Dodds Ln Gladwyne PA 19035-1516 Business E-Mail: jkatz@icdc.com.

KATZ, KENNETH DARREN, medical educator; b. Nyc, May 25, 1970; MD, SUNY, Stony Brook, 1996. Asst. prof. U. Pitts. Med. Ctr., 2004—. Home: 2830 Beechwood Blvd Pittsburgh PA 15217 Business E-Mail: katzkd@upmc.edu.

KATZ, LEONARD, psychology professor, researcher; b. Boston, 1938; s. William and Ruth K.; m. Barbara A. Mahoney, 1962; children: Nicholas, Stephen, Alexis. BS, U. Mass., 1959, PhD, 1963. Postdoctoral fellow Stanford (Calif.) U., 1963-65; prof. psychology U. Conn., Storrs, 1965—2006; researcher Haskins Labs., New Haven, 1974—. Contbr. articles to profl. jours. Fulbright fellow, Yugoslavia, 1986. Fellow Am. Psychol. Soc., Am. Assn. Advancement of Sci. Office: U Conn Dept Psychology Wab U 20 Storrs Mansfield CT 06269-1020 Business E-Mail: leonard.katz@uconn.edu.

KATZ, MICHAEL, pediatrician, educator; b. Lwow, Poland, Feb. 13, 1928; arrived in U.S., 1946, naturalized, 1951; s. Edward and Rita (Gluzman) Katz; m. Robin J. Roy, July 19, 1986; 1 child, Edward Alexander. AB, U. Pa., 1949, postgrad. (Harrison fellow), 1950—51; MD, SUNY, Bklyn., 1956; MS, Columbia U. Sch. Public Health, 1968; DMS (hon.), Med. U. Lódz, Poland, 2009. Intern UCLA Med. Ctr., 1956—57; resident Presbyn. Hosp. (Babies Hosp.), NYC, 1960—62, dir. pediatric svc., 1977—92, cons., 1992—; hon. lectr. pediat. Makerere U. Coll., Kampala, Uganda, 1963—64; instr. in pediat. Columbia U., 1964—65, prof. tropical medicine Sch. Pub. Health, 1971—92, prof. pub. health emeritus, 1992—, prof. pediat. Coll. Physicians and Surgeons, 1972—77, prof. pub. health, 1977—92, Reuben S. Carpentier prof., 1977—92, Reuben S. Carpentier prof. emeritus, 1992—; sr. v.p. for rsch. and global programs March of Dimes Found., White Plains, NY, 1992—. Assoc. mem. Wistar Inst., Phila., 1965—71; asst. prof. pediat. U. Pa., 1966—77; cons. WHO, Guatemala, Venezuela, Egypt, Yemen; mem. U.S. del. 32d World Health Assembly, Geneva, 1979; cons. UNICEF, NYC, Tokyo, USAID, Egypt, 1982, Poland, 87; mem. bd. sci. councillors Nat. Inst. Dental Rsch., 1986—90, chmn., 1990—92; vis. prof. U. Würzburg, Germany, 1988; vis. prof. pediat. U. Negev, Beer Sheva, Israel, 1996. Author (with others): Parasitic Diseases, 1982, 2d edit., 1989; editor (with Volker ter Meulen): Slow Virus Infections of the

Central Nervous System, 1977; mem. editl. bd.: Med. Microbiology and Immunology, 1975—90, Pediatric Infectious Diseases Jour., 1981—92, Vaccines, 1983—94; co-editor: Manuals in Pediatrics; contbr. articles to profl. jours, Pres. World Alliance Orgns. Prevention Birth Defects, Inc., 1995—2005. Lt. M.C. USNR, 1957—59. Recipient Jurzykowski Found. award in Medicine, 1983, Alexander von Humboldt Sr. U.S. Scientist award, 1988; grantee, NIH, 1968—76, WHO, 1972—76. Fellow: AAAS, Am. Acad. Pediat., Infectious Diseases Soc. Am.; mem.: Eastern Soc. for Pediatric Rsch., Inst. Medicine NAS, World Alliance of Orgns. for the Prevention of Birth Defects (pres. 1995—2005), Pediatric Infectious Disease Soc., Royal Soc. Tropical Medicine and Hygiene (London), Deutsche Gesellschaft für Neuropathologie und Neuroanatomie E.V. (corr.), N.Y. Soc. Tropical Medicine (pres. 1976—77), Am. Soc. Tropical Medicine and Hygiene, Am. Soc. Microbiology, Harvey Soc., Am. Pediatric Soc., Soc. Pediatric Rsch., Sigma Xi. Office: March of Dimes Found 1275 Mamaroneck Ave White Plains NY 10605-5298 Home: 200 E 57th St Apt 11K New York NY 10022-2867 Office Phone: 914-997-4555. Personal E-mail: katzfamily@optonline.net. Business E-Mail: mkatz@marchofdimes.com.

KATZ, MITCHELL H., city health department administrator; b. 1959; BS, Yale U., New Haven, Conn.; MD, Harvard U. Med. Sch., Cambridge, Mass., 1986. Attending physician San Francisco Gen. Hosp., AIDS Clinic; chief, rsch., AIDS office San Francisco Dept. Pub. Health, dir., AIDS Office, 1992—97, interim dir., health, 1997—98, dir., health, 1998—. Author: Multivariable Statistics: A Practical Guide for Clinical Researchers. Office: San Francisco Dept Health 101 Grove St Rm 308 San Francisco CA 94102

KATZ, NAFTALE, physician, researcher; b. Belo Horizonte, Brazil, June 13, 1940; s. David and Chana Katz; children: Samy, Sheila, Daniel B., Cristina B. MD, Fed. U., 1964; Phd in Health Sci. Head lab. clin. therapy Fundacaõ Oswáldo Cruz, Belo Horizonte, 1966—67, head lab. schistosomiasis, 1968—70, 1972—90, dir. Ctr. de Pesquisas Rene Rachou, 1970—71, 1985—97; scientific dir. Minas Gerais State Found. Rsch. Support, Belo Horizonte, 2000—04. ERP WHO, Geneva, 1985-, Med. Acad. Minas Gerais; expert WHO, 1985—; cons. Health Sec. Minas Gerais State, 1980-90. Contbr. more than 270 articles to profl. jours. Named Hon. Citizen of Baldim, 1972; recipient gold award Internat. Films & TV Festival of N.Y., 1976, Spl. Rsch. award Pfizer Chems., 1976, Hon. of Merit Belo Horizonte City Hall, 1988, 60 Yrs. Tropical Medicine Inst. Pedro Kouri, 1998. Mem. Cuban Soc. Microbiology and Parasitology (hon.), Helminthological Soc. Washington (hon.). Office: Rene Rachou Fundacaõ Oswáldo Cruz Av Augusto de Lima 1715 30190002 Belo Horizonte Brazil Home Phone: 55-31-32274382; Office Phone: 55-31-99490999. Business E-Mail: nkatz@cpqrr.fiocruz.br.

KATZ, ROGER, pediatrician, allergist, immunologist, educator; b. Menominee, Mich., Feb. 23, 1938; s. Peter W. and Mae C. (Chudacoff) Katz; children: Carl, Gary, Robyn. BS, U. Wis., 1960; MD, U. Louisville, 1965. Diplomate Am. Bd. Allergy and Immunology, Am. Bd. Pediatric Allergy, Am. Bd. Pediat. Clin. prof. pediat. UCLA, 1978—. Spkr. in field, expert legal evaluator. Author and editor sci. books and manuscripts. Maj. U.S. Army, 1970-72. Named One of Best Drs. in Am., 1996, 97, 2001, 02, 05. Fellow Am. Acad. Allergy, Asthma and Immunology, Am. Coll. Allergy, Asthma and Immunology (bd. regents 1990-93), Am. Acad. Pediat., Am. Coll. Chest Physicians, Joint Coun. Allergy, Asthma and Immunology (pres. 1986-90). Office: UCLA Med Ctr 11500 W Olympic Blvd 630 Los Angeles CA 90064 Office Phone: 310-393-1550. *

KATZ, RONALD ALAN, dermatologist; b. St. Joseph, Mo., July 13, 1942, s. Walter and Mildred (Talman) K.; m. Jane Ellen Markin, Dec. 26, 1968; children: Jennifer Lynn, Hilary Beth. BS, U. Cin., 1964; MD, U. Md., 1969. Diplomate Am. Bd. Dermatology. Intern Childrens Nat. Med. Ctr., Washington, 1969-70, resident Yale U., New Haven, Conn., 1972-75, chief resident in dermatology, 1974-75; pvt. practice College Park, Md., 1975—. Clin. prof. dermatology and pediats. George Washington U., 1975—. Contbr. articles to profl. jours. Founding vol. U.S. Meml. Holocaust Mus., Washington, 1993-96. Lt. comdr. USPHS, 1970-72. Named Outstanding Physician Specialist, Consumer Checkbook, 1998, 2002; named one of Top Doctors, Washingtonian, 1993, 1995, 1999, 2002, 2005, 2007—10, Top Drs., Consumer Checkbook, 2011, Best Doctors in Am., Washingtonian, 2001, 2002, 2007—08, 2008—10, Best Dr., 2011. Mem. Md. State Med. Soc., Prince George's County Med. Soc., Washington Dermatol. Soc. pres. 1990-91), Am. Acad. Dermatology, Soc. for Pediatric Dermatology, Soc. for Investigative Dermatology, Alpha Omega Alpha. Democrat. Jewish. Avocations: photography, running marathons. Home: 9304 Sprinklewood Ln Potomac MD 20854-2257 Office: 6201 Greenbelt Rd College Park MD 20740-2354 E-mail: ronaldk204@aol.com.

KATZ, SAMUEL LAWRENCE, pediatrician, researcher; b. Manchester, NH, May 29, 1927; s. Morris and Ethel (Lawrence) Katz; m. Betsy Jane Cohan, June 27, 1950; children: Samuel Lawrence Jr.(dec.), John S.L., David L., Deborah Susan, William L., Susan Johanna, Penelope Jennifer; m. Catherine Minock Wilfert, July 23, 1971; stepchildren: Rachel Ann, Katie Claiborne. AB magna cum laude, Dartmouth Coll., 1948; MD cum laude, Harvard U., 1952; DSc (hon.), Georgetown U., 1996, Dartmouth Coll., 1998. Intern Beth Israel Hosp., Boston, 1952—53; resident Children's Hosp., Boston, 1953—54, 1955—56, Mass. Gen. Hosp., 1954—55; from rsch. fellow to asst. prof. Harvard Med. Sch., 1956—68; prof., chmn. dept. pediat. Duke Med. Sch., 1968—90, Wilburt C. Davison prof., 1972—97. Mem. sci. adv. bd. Hasbro Children's Found., St. Jude Children's Rsch. Hosp.; rschr. on virology, virus vaccines and immunization NIH couns. and study sects. WHO; chmn. India-US Vaccine Action Program, 1999—2004; chmn. adv. com. immunization practice Ctrs. for Disease Control, Atlanta, 1985—93. Developer (with John F. Enders) attenuated live measles-virus vaccine; contbr. chapters to books, articles to profl. jours. Chmn. bd. trustees Internat. Vaccine Inst., Seoul, Republic of Korea, 2003—07. With USNR, 1945—46. Recipient Rsch. Career Devel. award, NIH, 1965—68, Presdl. medal of achievement, Dartmouth Coll., 1991, Sabin Gold medal, Albert Sabin Vaccine Inst., 2003, Duke U. Founder's medal, 2004, Alfred duPont award Pediat. Rsch., Nemours Found., 2006, Pollin prize Pediat. Rsch., 2007; fellow, Nat. Found., 1956—58. Mem.: APHA (Needleman medal and award 1997), Inst. Medicine NAS, Pediat. Infectious Diseases Soc. (Disting. Physician award 1991), Assn. Med. Sch. Pediat. Dept. Chmn. (pres. 1977—79), Am. Acad. Pediat. (Grulee award 1975, Jacobi award 1986), Am. Assn. Immunologists, Infectious Diseases Soc. Am. (co-chmn. vaccine initiative 1998—99, co-chmn. nat. network for immunization info. 1999—2003, Bristol award 1988, Soc. citation 1993), New Eng. Pediat. Soc., Am. Pediat. Soc. (pres. 1986—87, St. Geme award 1988, Howland award 2000), Soc. Pediat. Rsch., Am. Soc. Clin. Investigation, Am. Fedn. Clin. Rsch. Home: 1917 Wildcat Creek Rd Chapel Hill NC 27516-9786 Office: Duke U Med Ctr PO Box 2925 Durham NC 27710-0001 Office Phone: 919-668-4852, 919-684-3734. Office Fax: 919-668-4859.

KATZ, STEPHEN IRA, federal agency administrator; b. Bklyn., Jan. 26, 1941; BA in Hist., cum laude, U. Md., College Park, 1962; MD cum laude, Tulane U. Med. Sch., New Orleans, 1966; PhD in Immunology, U. London, 1974. Diplomate Am. Bd. Dermatology. Intern LA County Hosp.; dermatology resident U. Miami. Med. Ctr., Fla., 1967—70; asst. dermatology Walter Reed Army Med. Ctr., Washington, 1970-72; rsch. fellow dept. pathology Royal Coll. Surgeons of Eng., London, 1972-74; sr. investigator dermatology br. Nat. Cancer Inst., NIH, Bethesda, Md., 1974—, acting chief dermatology br., 1977-80, chief dermatology br., 1980—2001, dir. Nat. Inst. Arthritis & Musculoskeletal & Skin Diseases, 1995—. Marion B. Sulzberger prof. dermatology Uniformed Svcs. Univ. Health Scis., Bethesda, 1989—95. Mem. editl. bd. Internat. Jour. Dermatology, 1977—81, Jour. Investigative Dermatology, 1979—82, Jour. Am. Acad. Dermatology, 1979—83, Jour. Immunology, 1981—85, Am. Jour. Dermatopathology, Epithelia, 1986—88, Regional Immunology, 1988—95, Medicine, 1992—, Am. Jour. Contact Dermatitis, 1992—, Dermatology Internat., 1992—; contbr. articles to profl. jours., chapters to books. Recipient Excellence in Leadership award, Internat. Pemphigus Found., 2006, Outstanding Mentor award, Nat. Cancer Inst., Outstanding Alumnus award, Tulane U. Sch. Medicine, Stephen Rothman Meml. award, Soc. Investigative Dermatology, Messenger of Hope award, Scleroderma Found., Presdl. Exec. Meritorious Rank award, PHS Superior Svc. award, Inflammatory Skin Disorders Rsch. award, NIH Director's award, Master Dermatologist award/Sulzberger Lecture award, Am. Acad. Dermatology, Lifetime Achievement award/D. Martin Carter Mentor award, Am. Skin Assn. Mem.: Internat. League Dermatol. Societies, Clin. Immunology Soc., Assn. Professors Dermatology, Soc. Investigative Dermatology. Office: Nat Inst Arthritis & Muscoskeletal & Skin Diseases Bldg 31 Claude D Pepper Bldg Rm 4C32 31 Center Dr Bethesda MD 20892-2350 Office Phone: 301-496-4353. Office Fax: 301-402-3607. Business E-Mail: stephen.katz@nih.gov.

KATZ, STEVEN GARY, surgeon, educator; b. LA, Jan. 11, 1951; s. Herbert and Marianne Katz; m. Gail Ellen Sowsy, Oct. 16, 1983; children: Tracey Anne, Michael Lawrence. MD, U. Calif., Irvine, 1975. Cert. physician and surgeon Calif., 1976. Prof. surgery U. So. Calif., LA, 2003—; dir. vascular lab. Huntington Hosp., Pasadena, Calif., 1999—, dir. surg. edn., 2000—, bd. mem., 2007—. Recipient Phi Beta Kappa, U. So. Calif., 1971. Fellow: ACS; mem.: So. Calif. Vascular Surg. Soc. (pres. 2003—04), Western Vascular Soc. (chair mem. com. 2001—02), Western Surg. Assn., Pacific Coast Surg. Soc., Disting. Fellow Soc. Vascular Surgery. Office: USC Surgeons 50 Bellefontaine St Ste 404 Pasadena CA 91105 Office Fax: 626-792-3144. Business E-Mail: skatz@surgery.usc.edu. *

KATZ, STUART D., cardiologist, educator; Attended, SUNY Health Sci. Ctr., 1983. Diplomate Am. Bd. Internal Medicine, 1986, Am. Bd. Cardiology-cardiovascular disease, 1989. Intern in internal medicine Balt. City Hosp., 1983—84; resident in internal medicine Francis Scott Key Med. Ctr., 1984—86; clin. fellow in cardiology Albert Einstein Coll. Medicine, 1986—89; prof. NYU Sch. Medicine; cardiologist NYU Langone Med. Ctr. Co-author: (jour. articles) Insulin sensitivity, vascular function, and iron stores in voluntary blood donors, 2007, The prevalence of anemia in chronic heart failure and its impact on the clinical outcomes, 2008, Mineralocorticoid-receptor Antagonists in Heart Failure: A Tale of Serendipity and Success, 2011, numerous other jour. articles. Office: New York University Langone Medical Center 530 1st Ave Skirball 9U New York NY 10016 Office Phone: 212-263-7751. Office Fax: 212-263-7908.

KATZ-BEARNOT, SHERRY P., psychiatrist, educator; BA, Barnard Coll., 1973; MD, Mt. Sinai, 1977. Mem.: Am. Acad. Psychoanalysis and Dynamic Psychiatry (pres. 2006—08), Am. Psychiatric Assn. (dist. fellow). Office: Ctr Psychoanalytic Training & Rsch Columbia U 1051 Riverside Dr New York NY 10032 Business E-Mail: spk1@columbia.edu.

KATZIN, CAROLYN FERNANDA, nutritionist, consultant; b. London, July 21, 1946; came to US, 1983; naturalized US citizen, 1992. d. John Mourier and Shelagh B. A. (Tighe) Lade; m. Anthony Arthur Speelman, Mar. 18, 1968 (div. Dec. 1984); 1 child, Zara Jane. BS with honors, U. London, 1983; MS in Pub. Health, UCLA, 1988. Nutritionist, LA, 1985—; pres. Fountain Resources Inc., 2005—. Chair dean's adv. bd. UCLA Sch. Pub. Health, 1997-2005; mem. profl. adv. bd. The Wellness Cmty., WLA, 1998—; pres. Fountain Resources Inc., 2005—. Author: The Advanced Energy Guide, 1994, The Good Eating Guide and Cookbook, 1996, The Cancer Nutrition Ctr. Handbook, 2001, 4th edit., 2011., Everything Career Fighting Cookbook, 2011. Mem.: Am. Cancer Soc. (pres. Coastal Cities unit 1999—2002, bd. dir. Calif. divsn. 2002—, chair 2011—). Democrat. Office: Fountain Resources Inc 12011 San Vicente Blvd Ste 402 Los Angeles CA 90049-4946 Personal E-mail: cfk@aol.com. Business E-Mail: carolyn@carolynkatzin.com.

KATZIN, WILLIAM E., pathologist, director; b. Litchfield, Conn., Mar. 28, 1952; PhD, Case Western Res. U., 1980, MD, 1983. Lab. med. dir. AmeriPath-Cleve., 2005—. Clin. assoc. prof. Case Western Res. U. Sch. Medicine, 1989. Fellow: US and Can. Acad. Pathology (The Stowell-Orbison award), Am. Soc. Clin. Pathologists, Coll. Am. Pathologists. Office: 7730 First Pl Ste A Oakwood Village OH 44146 Business E-Mail: wkatzin@ameripath.com.

KATZMAN, MERLE HERSHEL, retired orthopaedic surgeon; b. Hartford, Conn., Aug. 28, 1928; s. Samuel Sidney and Bertha (Hirshberg) K.; m. Charna Lytell, June 26, 1955; children: Beth, Amy, Sam, Robert. BS, Trinity Coll., 1950; MD, Jefferson Med. Coll., 1954. Diplomate Am. Bd. Orthop. Surgery. Intern Hartford (Conn.) Hosp., 1954-55, resident in surgery, 1957-58; surgeon N.Y. Orthop. Hosp., 1958-61; attending orthop. surgeon, chief orthop. dept. Englewood Hosp., 1965-94, attending orthop. surgeon, 1980-94; asst. attending orthopedic surgeon Presbyn. Hosp., NYC, 1963-94; asst. clin. prof. orthopedic surgery Columbia U. Med. Sch., 1975-94; pres. Katzman, Tarsney & Feldman, Tenafly, N.J., 1994; ret., 1994. Mem. credentials com., exec. com., chmn. future devel. com., Englewood Hosp.; asst. attending orthopedic surgeon Presbyn. Hosp., N.Y.C., until 1994; asst. clin. prof. orthopedic surgery Columbia U. Coll. Physicians & Surgeons, N.Y.C., until 1994. Lt. USNR, 1955-57. Fellow ACS, Am. Acad. Orthopaedic Surgeons, Bergen County Med. Soc. (del., health ins. review com. mem.), N.J. State Med. Soc., N.J. Orthopaedic Soc. (exec. com. pres. 1977-78), Stannard Beach Assn. (exec. com. mem., pres. 1996-98). Personal E-mail: gonce28@gmail.com.

KATZNELSON, ALEXANDER M., orthopedist, retired surgeon; b. Tomsk, Siberia, Russia, Sept. 23, 1919; arrived in Israel, 1949; s. Michael Mordechai and Rebecca (Senderson) K.; m. Judith Radom, June 20, 1948 (dec. 1967); children: David, Jonathan; m. Mariassa Bat Miriam, Dec. 26, 1968. BS, St. John's U., Shanghai, 1942, MD, 1946. Diplomate Israeli Bd. Orthop. Surgery. 2d lt. Israel Def. Forces, 1949-70, advanced through grades to lt. col., 1965; resident in surgery Chinese Gen. Hosp., Shanghai, 1945-48; resident Tel Hashomer Hosp., Ramat Gan, Israel, 1949-55, asst. dir. orthopedics, 1957-66; fellow in orthopedics Hosp. Joint Diseases, NYC, 1956; fellow in spinal surgery Baylor U., Houston, 1966; dir. orthop. surgery Sheba Med. Ctr., Israel, 1966—84; orthop. cons. Laniado Hosp., Nethania, Israel, 1985—. Chmn. bd. examiners Orthop. Scientific Coun. Israel Med. Assn.; assoc. emeritus clin. prof. orthop. Sackler Sch. Medicine, Tel Aviv, 1980; med. dir. Laniado Hosp., Nethania, 1990-94. Author: Craftsmanship and Art in Walking Sticks. Contbr. articles to profl. jours. Recipient Meritorius Citizen of City of Ramat Gan, Israel, 1998, Legion of Hon. United Cultural Conv., 2005, Genious Laureate of Isreal in Orthopaedics, 2005 Fellow Internat. Coll. Surgeons; mem. Soc. Internat. Orthop. Surgery Trauma (emeritus), Internat. Coll. Surgeons, Israel Med. Assn., Israel Soc. Orthopaedic Surgeons (chmn. 1968-70), Spinal Deformities Soc., Civil Guard Ramat Gam, Shanghai Vol. Corps. Jewish Company. Avocations: coin collecting/numismatics, gardening, photography. Office Phone: 0505 266 744. Personal E-mail: alexkat@bezeqint.net.

KAUFFMAN, GORDON LEE, JR., surgeon, educator; b. Grand Rapids, Mich., Mar. 30, 1946; s. Gordon Lee Sr. and Jeanne (Klunder) K.; m. Christie Lyn VanSweden, June 28, 1969; children: Gordon Lee III, Christian Anthony. BS, Wheaton Coll., 1968; MD, U. Mich., 1972. Diplomate Nat. Bd. Med. Examiners, Am. Bd. Surgery. Resident in surgery U. Mich., Ann Arbor, 1972-77; rsch. assoc. VA Wadsworth, LA, 1977-80, staff surgeon, 1977-85; asst. prof. surgery UCLA Sch. Medicine, 1979-83, assoc. prof., 1983-85; prof. surgery and physiology, chief div. gen. surgery Pa. State U., Hershey, 1985—2005, vice chmn. dept. surgery, 1994—2005, head surg. oncology. Investigator Ctr. for Ulcer Rsch. and Edn., L.A., 1979-81, key investigator, 1981-85; cons. City of Hope Nat. Med. Ctr., Duarte, Calif., 1982-85, Harbor Gen. Hosp., Torrance, Calif., 1983-85; mem. surgery and bioengring. study sect. NIH, 1990-94, mem. consensus devel. panel on helicobacterpylori, 1994. Mem. editl. bd. Surgery, 1988—, Jour. Gastrointestinal Surg., 1997—, Jour. Surg. Rsch., 1990-97, Am. Jour. Surgery, 1994-97; contbr. chpts. to books, numerous articles to profl. jours. Grantee Coun. Tobacco Rsch., 1969, VA, 1980-85; Galens Fgn. fellow, 1971, Med. Assistance Program Fgn. fellow, 1971, Frederick Coller resident fellow, 1976, James IV fellow, 1991. Mem. ACS (sec.-treas. cen. Pa. chpt. 1990-96), Assn. Acad. Surgery (chmn. edn. com. 1985-87), Am. Fedn. for Clin. Rsch., Soc. for Exptl. Biology and Medicine, Am. Gastroenterol. Assn. (chmn. abstract rev. com. 1986-87, 95-96), Soc. Univ. Surgeons (chmn. com. on publs.), Soc. Surgery of Alimentary Tract (nominating com. 1990, publ. com. 1991-93, chmn. 1994, recorder 1994-97), Frederick A. Coller Surg. Soc. (counsilor 2007-), Collegium Internat. Chirurgiae Digestivae, Surg. Biology Club I, Soc. Clin. Surgery (membership com. 1992-95, chmn. 1995-96), Cent. Surg. Soc. (councilman at large 1995-96), Am. Surg. Assn. (membership adv. com. 1993-97). Office: Milton S Hershey Med Ctr H149 500 University Dr Hershey PA 17033-2391 Office Fax: 717-531-4335. Business E-Mail: gkauffman@psu.edu.

KAUFFMAN, SCOT R., medical supply company executive; b. Windham, Conn., May 31, 1971; s. Richard R. and Susan Kauffman. BA in English, U. Conn., 1993. Cert. pharmacy technician. Pharmacy clk. Hebron (Conn.) Pharmacy Inc., 1985-96, cert. pharmacy technician, 1997-98; stock broker Olde Discount Corp., White Plains, N.Y., 1996-97; mng. ptnr., CFO, Americare Med. Supply, Hebron, 1998—. Mem. Inland Wetland and Conservation Commn., Town Bd., Hebron, 1997-2001; mem. Bd. of Selectmen, Hebron, 2001--; town rep. to Catch 15 coun. Regional Health Commn., Rockville, Conn., 1995. Recipient Provider Svc. award Conn. Cmty. Care Inc., Norwich, Conn., 1999. Republican. Avocations: financial planning, investment strategizing. Office: Americare Med Supply 103 Main St Hebron CT 06248-1519 Office Phone: 860-228-0606. Personal E-mail: scotkauffman@comcast.net.

KAUFFOLD, RUTH ELIZABETH, psychologist; b. Decatur, Ill., Sept. 5, 1946; d. James Henry and Elizabeth Opal Kauffold; m. Paul Dwight Entner, Aug. 23, 1968; 1 child, James Paul. BA, Cedarville Coll., Ohio, 1968; MEd, Wright State U., 1972; MS, U. Dayton, 1986; PhD, The Union Inst., 1997. Tchr. Springfield Pub. Schs., Ohio, 1968—72, Pomona Unified Sch. Dist., Calif., 1973—76, Bethel Sch. Dist., New Carlisle, Ohio, 1977—81; practicum Sycamore Hosp., Miamisburg, Ohio, 1994; intern, resident clin. psychology Agape Counseling Ctr., Centerville, 1995—2000. Co-hostess talk show Radio Sta. WHIO, Dayton, 1998; guest speaker Think TV, 2005—; lectr., spkr. in field. Active Missionary Project Ptnr., Lima, Peru, 1986; tchr. Far Hills Bapt. Ch., Dayton, Ohio, 1997, Fair Haven Ch., 2000-04 Jennings scholar Martha Holden Jennings Found., 1972. Mem. APA, Dayton Area Psychol. Assn. Avocations: interior design, architecture, gardening, reading, walking. Office Phone: 937-434-0540.

KAUFMAN, DAVID MARC, pediatric neurologist; b. Bronx, NY, July 10, 1945; s. Harold M. and Edna M. (Markowitz) K.; m. Harriet B. Kaufman, June 30, 1968; 1 child, Jill R. BS, Union Coll., 1967; MD, Boston U. Sch. of Medicine, 1975. Diplomate Am. Bd. Pediatrics. Intern-resident N.Y. Hosp., NYC, 1975-77; resident-fellow Mt. Sinai Med. Ctr., NYC, 1977-80, assoc. clin. prof. pediat., asst. clin. prof. neurology; pvt. practice in pediatric neurology NYC, 1980—; med. dir. Premier Health Care / YAI Nat. Inst. for People with Disabilities, 1997—. Mem. admissions com. Mt. Sinai Sch. of Medicine, N.Y.C., 1992—, ethics com. Child Neurology Soc., Mpls., 1995—; adv. bd. Winston Prep Sch. Spl. Edn. Sch., N.Y.C., 1990, Young Adult Inst., N.Y.C., 1995—. Author: (with others) The

Founders of Child Neurology, 1990. Fellow Am. Acad. Pediatrics; mem. Am. Acad. Neurology, Child Neurology Soc. Office: 3 E 83d St New York NY 10028 Office Phone: 212-737-4911. Personal E-mail: davidneuro@aol.com.

KAUFMAN, FRANCINE R., pediatric endocrinologist; m. Neal Kaufman; children: Adam, Jonah. B., Northwestern U., 1972; MD, Chgo. Med. Sch., 1976. Cert. pediatric endocrinology & metabolism. Intern Childrens Hosp. Los Angeles, 1976—77, resident, 1977—78, fellow, 1978—80, attending physician, head of Ctr. for Endocrinology, Diabetes & Metabolism; dir. Comprehensive Childhood Diabetes Ctr., Los Angeles; prof. pediatrics Univ. So. Calif. Keck Sch. Medicine. Diplomat Am. Bd. Pediatrics; co-principal investigator Keck Diabetes Prevention Initiative, Los Angeles; med. adv. bd. Mini-Med Technologies, 1993—2001, 2003—, Eli Lilly Corp., 1998—, Novo Nordisk, 1999—, Life Scan, Inc., 2000—01, 2003—; editorial bd. Internat. Diabetes Monitor, 1994—95, 1998—, Diabetes Forecast, 1998—, Diabetes Reviews, 1998—, Current Diabetes Reports, 2001—, Pediatric Diabetes, 2002—, DOC News, 2004—. Author: Diabesity, 2005; contbr. scientific papers, chapters to books. Del. WHO Assembly, Geneva, 2002, Calif. Task Force on Childhood Obesity; chair Los Angeles County Task Force on Children & Youth Physical Fitness, 2002; Calif. del. to Healthy Sch. Summit in Washington DC, 2003; chair Studies to Treat or Prevent Type 2 Diabetes in Youth (STOPP-T2); sci. adv. group Am. Diabetes Assn., 1997—, programs com., 1997—, bd. dirs., 1993—96, 2000, chair, Task Force on Health Care Reform, 1993—95, chair, Task Force on Signature Advocacy, 1993—94, chair, Pub. Policy Leadership Forum, 1995—96, Profl. Ed. Project Team, 1999—, Task Force on Schools, 2002—03, nominating com., 2003—04, pres., 2002—03; active Juvenile Diabetes Assn., Nat. Diabetes Ed. Program, Internat. Diabetes Fedn., Ctr. Disease Control & Prevention, UNESCO, NIH; profl. & patient ed. com. Am. Diabetes Assn. Los Angeles Chpt., 1985—, bd. dirs., 1986—, pres, 1988—90, caper com., 1986—, fundraising com., 1990—; pub. seminar com. Am. Diabetes Assn. Calif. Affiliate, 1985—, bd. dirs., 1988—, exec. com., 1991—, pres., 1996—97. Recipient Woman of Valor award, Am. Diabetes Assn., 2003, Banting Medal, 2003, Albert Renold award, European Assn. for the Study of Diabetes, 2003. Mem.: AAP (Endocrine exec. com. 1998—, Task Force on Obesity), Inst. Medicine. Achievements include invention of Extend Bar. Office: Childrens Hospital Los Angeles MS #1 4650 Sunset Blvd Los Angeles CA 90027 E-mail: fkaufman@chla.usc.edu.

KAUFMAN, JEROME BENZION, retired neurosurgeon; b. Waterloo, Iowa, July 22, 1934; s. Louis and Dorothy (Rosenbloom) K.; m. Judith Ellen Lasker, June 29, 1967; children: David, Jonathan, Jefferey. BA, Wayne State U., 1955, MD, 1961; postgrad., U. Madrid. Diplomate Am. Bd. Neurol. Surgery 1975. Rotating intern Michael Reese Hosp. and Med. Ctr., Chgo., 1961-62; resident in internal med. Michael Reese Hosp. and Med. Ctr., Chgo., 1962-63; resident in gen. surgery VA Hosp., Bronx, 1965-66, resident in neurology, 1966, resident in neurosurgery, 1967, from sr. to chief resident neurosurgery, 1969-70; resident neurosurgery Neurol. Inst. NY, Columbia Presbyn. Hosp., 1968; resident neuropathology Mt. Sinai Hosp. and Med. Sch., NYC, 1968; chief resident neurosurgery City Hosp., Elmhurst, NY, 1969; chmn. dept. neurosurgery Carle Clinic Assn. and Found. Hosp., Urbana, Ill., 1972—96, prof. emeritus, 1997—, U. Ill. Coll. medicine, Champaign-Urbana. Cons. neurosurgery McKinley Hosp., Urbana, Covenant Hosp., Urbana; asst. instr. internal medicine Chgo. Med. Sch., 1963; clin. assoc. prof. neurosurgery U. Ill. Coll. Medicine, Urbana, 1982-96, clin. prof., chmn. neurosurgery. Contbr. chapters to books to profl. jours. Capt. USAF, 1963—65. Named One of Best Drs. in Am.- Midwest, Ill. Fellow ACS, Am. Assn. Neurol. Surgeons (Continuing Edn. award in neurosurgery 1980, 83, 85, 87, 89, 93, 96), Internat. Coll. Surgeons (vice regent) NY Acad. Scis.; mem. AMA (Physicians Recognition award 1980, 82, 85, 89, 93), Ill. Med. Soc., Champaign County Med. Soc., Congress Neurol. Surgeons, Ctrl. Neurosurg. Soc., Assn. Mil. Surgeons US, Chgo. Neurol. Soc. (Best Doctors in Am. Midwest). Home: 2104 Zuppke Dr Urbana IL 61801-6706 Personal E-mail: j-kauf@uiuc.edu. Business E-Mail: j-kauf@illinois.edu.

KAUFMAN, LARRY J., critical care specialist; MD, Wayne State U., 1981. Diplomate Am. Bd. Internal Medicine, 1984, Am. Bd. Internal Medicine- critical care medicine, 1999. Resident in internal medicine Boston VA Med. Ctr., Boston, 1982—84; fellow in critical care medicine Univ. Pitts. Med. Ctr., Pitts., 1985—87; asst. prof. Univ. Hawaii; hosp. affiliation includes Hawaii Medical Center East. Office: Hawaii Medical Center 2230 liliha St Honolulu HI 96817 Office Phone: 808-547-6204.

KAUFMAN, MATTHEW, plastic surgeon; b. Oct. 29, 1972; Grad. with honors, SUNY, Binghamton; MD, SUNY, Syracuse, 1998. Cert. Plastic Surgeon and Otolaryngologist-Head and Neck Surgeon. Surgical tng., otolaryngology-Head and Neck Surgery Mt. Sinai Hosp., Manhattan; tng., plastic and reconstructive surgery UCLA Med. Ctr. Cancer reconstruction and microsurgery cons., Head and Neck Oncology Group of Ctrl. NJ St. Peter's Univ. Hosp., New Brunswick, NJ; lectr. in field both nationally and internationally. Contbr. articles to publications on plastic surgery, chapters to books; featured in Cosmetic Surgery Times, med. cons. Untold Stories in the ER. Mem. adv. bd. FM World Charities. Mem.: Alpha Omega Alpha, Phi Beta Kappa Soc. Office: Plastic Surgery Ctr 561 Cranbury Rd East Brunswick NJ 08816 Address: Plastic Surgery Ctr 111E 59th St New York NY 10022

KAUFMAN, MICHELE BETH, clinical pharmacist, educator, writer, editor, consultant; b. Perth Amboy, NJ, May 13, 1963; d. Harold Alexander and Elaine Sue (Sommers) K; m. Jo E. Fusio (Feb. 2011). BS in Pharmacy, U. R.I., 1986; PharmD, Mass. Coll. Pharmacy, 1991. RPh, Mass., N.J., N.Y. Staff pharmacist Robert Wood Johnson U. Hosp., New Brunswick, N.J., 1986-91; product devel. pharmacist Reed & Carnrick Pharm. Co., Piscataway, N.J., 1987-89; poison info. specialist Mass. Poison Control System Children's Hosp., Boston, 1990-92; drug info. specialist U. R.I. Drug Info. Ctr., Providence, 1991-92; asst. clin. prof. pharmacy St. John's U., Jamaica, NY, 1992-96; owner, pres. PRN Commn. Inc., 2006—; sr. med. writer Prime Inc., Tamarac, Fla., 2006—08; freelance writer & editor Prime, 2001—06, pharmacy planner, 2008—; asst. clin. prof. UF Coll. Pharmacy, 2007—08. Clin. coord. internal medicine, drug info. specialist L.I. Jewish Med. Ctr., New Hyde Park, N.Y., 1992-96; clin. pharmacy coord., drug info. specialist HIP Health Plan of N.Y., N.Y.C., 1996-2001, project leader clin. pharmacy programs, 2001-06; drug info. cons. PDHI, Inc., 1998-2008; freelance med. writer, 1996—, cons., 2006-; reviewer Formulary Jours. Drug Topics, Pharmacotherapy; St. Johns U. Coll. Pharmacy, 2005-2006, adj. faculty U. Fla. Coll. Pharmacy, 2007-08; clin. pharmacist NY Downtown Hosp., 2009-; adj. clin. prof. Touro Coll. Pharmacy, 2010-. Contbg. editor: Formulary Jour.; contbr. articles and revs. to profl. jours., editl. bd. mem., speciality Pharm. Jour., 2011-; patent pending for pineapple colon electrolyte lavage solution. Player tenor sax St. John's Univ. Jazz Ensemble, 1992-97, player alto, tenor and baritone sax Lesbian and Gay Big Apple Corps Band, N.Y.C., 1997—; player, Bariton Sax Tribattery Pops, NYC, 2011-, capt. team Tour de Cure Am. Diabetes Assn., 2002-05, Susan G. Komen Race for Cure, 2000-05. Fellow Drug Info., 1992; recipient Harold Neham Meml. award, NYC Soc. Health Sys., 2006, Joel Yellin Merit award, NYC Soc. Health Sys. Pharmacists, 2011. Mem. Acad. Managed Care Pharmacy (NY met. chpt., ednl. affairs com. 2010-), Am. Soc. Health Sys. Pharmacists, Am. Coll. Clin. Pharmacy, Am. Diabetes Assn. (profl. divsn. 1999—), Am. Coll. Rheumatology, Am. Med. Writers Assn.(mem. chair 2011-), N.Y. State Coun. Health Sys. Pharmacists, N.Y.C. Soc. Health Sys. Pharmacists (membership chair 1998-99, bull. editor 1999-2003, grants com. 2009-, del. ann. assembly 2008-09, 2011-), Lesbian and Gay Band Assn. (exec. com. 2004-06), Sci. Writers NY, Editl. Freelancers Assn., Authors Guild. Avocations: travel, saxophone, music, reading. Home and Office: 445 W 23rd St Apt 14E New York NY 10011-1450 Personal E-mail: michekauf@yahoo.com.

KAUFMAN, NATHAN, retired pathologist, educator; b. Lachine, Que., Can., Aug. 3, 1915; s. Solomon and Anna (Sabesinsky) K.; m. Rita Friendly, Sept. 10, 1946 (dec.); children: Naomi, Michael, Miriam, Hannah, Judith. B.Sc., McGill U., Montreal, 1937, MD, C.M., 1941. Mem. faculty Western Res. U. Med. Sch., 1948-60, asst. prof., 1952-54, asso. prof., 1954-60; pathologist-in-charge Cleve. Met. Gen. Hosp., 1952-60; prof. pathology Duke Sch. Medicine, 1960-67; prof. dept. pathology Queen's U. Med. Sch., Kingston, Ont., Canada, 1967-81, prof. emeritus, 1981—, head dept., 1967-79; clin. prof. office of humanities Med. Coll. Ga., Augusta, 1980-85. Pathologist-in-chief Kingston Gen. Hosp., 1967-79; past cons. Hotel Dieu Hosp., St. Mary's of the Lake Hosp., Kingston Clinic, Ont. Cancer Treatment and Rsch. Found.; asso. editor Lab. Investigation Jour., 1952-66, editor, 1972-75, mem. editorial bd., 1975—; assoc. editor Am. Jour. Pathology, 1967, mem. editl. bd., 1967-71; Mem. grants panel Med. Rsch. Coun. Can., 1970-74, mem. coun., 1971-77, exec. com., 1971-74; active coms. Ont. Coun. Health, 1968-79, chmn. provinical rev. ednl. subcom., 1972-75 Found. editor Modern Pathology, 1988, mem. editl. bd., 1989—95. Served to capt. M.C., Royal Can. Army, 1942-46. Decorated Mem. Brit. Empire; recipient Disting. Alumni award Duke U., 1975, Internat. Acad. Pathology Gold medal, 1996, Disting. Pathologist award, US & Canadian Acad. Pathology, 2008. Mem. Internat. Acad. Pathology (v.p. 1972-74, pres. elect 1974, pres. 1976-78, pres. U.S.-Can. div. 1973-75, sec.-treas. 1979-91, F.K. Mostofi Disting. Svc. award U.S.-Can. div. 1990), US and Canadian Acad. Pathology (Disting. Pathologist award 2008), Royal Coll. Physicians and Surgeons Can. (com. on exams. 1972), Cleve. Soc. Pathologists (past pres.), Am. Assn. Pathologists (editor Symposium series 1970-71), Am. Soc. for Investigative Pathology, Am. Soc. Clin. Pathologists, Am. Assn. Cancer Research, Am. Soc. Cytology, Coll. Am. Pathologists, Canadian Med. Assn., Can., Ont. assns. pathologists, Ont. Med. Assn., Can. Soc. Cytology. Home: 111 Avenue Rd # 603 Toronto ON M5R_3J8 Canada

KAUFMAN, RUSSEL EUGENE, hematologist, oncologist; b. Kenton, Ohio, Mar. 7, 1946; s. George W. and Eileen M. (Risner) K.; m. Jane Ann Steinman; children: Jonathon R., Emily J. BS, Ohio State U., 1969, MD cum laude, 1973. Diplomate Am. Bd. Internal Medicine. Resident in medicine Duke U. Med. Ctr., Durham, NC, 1973-77, chief resident in medicine, 1977; rsch. hematologist NIH, Bethesda, Md., 1978-80; asst. prof. medicine Duke U. Med. Ctr., Durham, 1980-86, from asst. prof. to assoc. prof. biochemistry, 1985—2001, from assoc. prof. to prof. medicine, 1986—, prof. dept. biochemistry, 2000—02, prof. emeritus, 2002—, chief divsn. hematology and oncology, 1989-96, chief divsn. med. oncology & transplantation, 1996-98, vice chair dept. medicine, 1995-99, assoc. dean Sch. of Medicine, 1998-99, vice dean for edn. and acad. affairs, 1999—2002, assoc. vice chancellor acad. affairs, 2000—02; dir., CEO Wistar Inst., Phila., 2002—03, pres., CEO, 2004—; dir. Wistar NCI Cancer Ctr., Phila. Mem. sci. adv. com. Am. Cancer Soc., Atlanta, NYC, 1987—; mem. com. NAS, Washington, 1983-86; mem. sci. rev. coms. NIH, Bethesda, Md., 1985—; assoc. chief of staff edn. Durham VA Med. Ctr., 1998-99; Wistar prof. medicine Sch. Medicine U. Pa. Health Sys., 2003-; bd. dirs. U. City Sci. Ctr., 2002-, BioAdvance, 2004-06, chmn. 2006-, bd. advisors Osage Venture Ptnrs., 2005—, founding bd. mem. Pharm. Safety Inst. 2006—,sci. adv. bd. A.M. pappaas & Assocs. LLC, health & Sci. desk adv. com, mem. WHYY Inc. Contbr. articles to profl. jours., chpts. to books. Mem. Pa. Cancer Ctr. Alliance, 2002—; bd. dirs., CEO Coun. for Growth Greater Phila. C. of C., 2003—; mem. coun. for extramural grants Am. Cancer Soc., 2004—07, chair, 2007—. Searle Found. scholar, 1983-86, Leukemia Soc. scholar, NYC, 1986-90, Cancer Control award, Am. Cancer Soc. Southeast Region, award, Coll. Physicians Phila. Fellow ACP; mem. AAAS, Am. Soc. Biochemistry, Am. Soc. Hematology (head subcom. on red cell 1985-88, chmn. com. on tng. programs 1995-98), Assn. Subsplty. Profs. (exec. coun. 1994, treas. 1997-98, pres.-elect 1998-99, pres. 1999-2000, past pres. 2000-01), Assn. Hematology/Oncology Program Dirs. (chair 1997-98), U. the Arts (bd. mem. 2004-), Neuland Labs. (bd. mem. 2007—), Pa. Cancer Ctr. Alliance, Am. Assn. Cancer Rsch., Coun. Am. Med. Innovation(adv. bd. mem., 2009-) Presbyn. Avocations: golf, tennis. Office: The Wistar Institute 3601 Spruce St Philadelphia PA 19104-4265 Office Phone: 215-898-3926. Office Fax: 215-573-2097. Business E-Mail: kaufman@wistar.org. *

KAUFMAN, STEPHEN CHARLES, ophthalmologist, clinician, surgeon; b. Boston, Apr. 14, 1960; s. Herbert Edward and Eleanor (Schmidt) K.; m. Valette Kaufman; children: Benjamin, Alexander. BS, Dickinson Coll., 1982; MD, La. State U., New Orleans, 1988, PhD, 1997; PhD h.c., U. Alicante, Spain, 1998. Diplomate Am. Bd. Ophthalmology. Intern St. John Hosp., Detroit, 1988-89; resident in ophthalmology Henry Ford Hosp., Detroit, 1989-92; cornea fellow La. State U. Eye Ctr., New Orleans, 1992-94; cornea rsch. fellow La. State U. Med. Ctr., New Orleans, 1994-97, asst. prof., 1997—99; sr. staff Henry Ford Health Sys., 2000—07; prof., Lyon chair, dept. ophthalmology U. Minn., 2007—. Cons. Akorn, Lincoln, Ill., 1994—, Advanced Scanning, New Orleans, 1996—. Editor: Cornea Handbook; author book chpt. Recipient Rsch. prize CIBA, 1998; grantee NIH, 1995. Fellow HEED, Am. Acad. Ophthalmology (compass com., OTAC com., media com., Achievement award), Am. Soc. Cataract and Refractive Surgeons, Contact Lens Assn. Ophthalmologists (Young Investigators award 1996); mem. Internat. Soc. Refractive Surgeons, Eye Bank Assn. America (chmn. sci. sessions 2010-, dir. sci. program.) Achievements include a patent for confocal microscopy application. Office: Univ Minn Dept Ophthalmology 420 Delaware St SE 493 Minneapolis MN 55455

KAUFMAN, STEPHEN LAWRENCE, radiologist, educator; b. Phila., Nov. 7, 1942; s. Abraham S. and Genevieve (Finestone) Kaufman. BA, U. Pa., 1963, MD, 1967. Resident in radiology, then fellow cardiovasc. radiology Johns Hopkins Med. Ctr., Balt., 1970-75, asst. prof. radiology, 1975-79, assoc. prof., 1980-88; prof. radiology, dir. cardiovasc. and interventional radiology Emory U., Atlanta, 1988—2003, prof. emeritus radiology, 2003—; attending radiologist Asheville VA Med. Ctr., 2003—, 2003—. Author: Techniques in Interventional Radiology, 1982; editor: Billiary Radiology, 1992; contbr. articles to profl. jours. Lt. comdr. USPHS, 1968—70. Fellow: Am. Heart Assn., Soc. Interventional Radiology; mem.: Am. Coll. Radiology, Radiol. Soc. N.Am. Avocations: hiking, white-water rafting, golf, computers. Personal E-mail: kauf8727@bellsouth.net.

KAUFMANN, MICHAEL, health products executive; BBA, Ohio No. U., Ada. CPA. Auditor, cons. Arthur Andersen; joined as a controller and held various sr. operational, sales and fin. positions primarily in pharms. Cardinal Health, head pharm. repackaging operation, head retail sales and mktg., pharm. distbn., exec. v.p. supply chain svcs.; CFO Cardinal Health Healthcare Supply Chain Services, group pres., med. segment, 2007—08, group pres.,pharm. segment, 2008, CEO, pharm. segment, 2008—. Bd. trustees Ohio No. U. Office: Cardinal Health 7000 Cardinal Pl Dublin OH 43017 Office Phone: 614-757-5000. *

KAUFMANN, STEFAN HUGO ERNST, immunologist; b. Ludwigshafen, Germany, June 8, 1948; s. Otto and Annelore (Niemeyer) K.; m. Elke Pamp, Dec. 18, 1980; children: Moritz, Felix. Diploma in Biology, U. Mainz, Germany, 1973, PhD, 1977; Habilitation, U. Berlin, 1981; Dr. honoris causa (hon.), U. de la Mediterranée, Marseille, France, 2007. Sci. asst. U. Bochum, Germany, 1976-78; asst. prof. U. Berlin, 1978-81, docent, 1981-87; staff scientist Max-Planck Inst., Freiburg, Germany, 1982-87; prof. U. Ulm, Germany, 1987-91, full prof. and chair dept. immunology, 1991-98, chair Collaborative Rsch. Ctr., 1992-97; dir. Max-Planck Inst., Berlin, 1993—. Advisor German Rsch. Soc., Bonn, 1992-99, WHO, Geneva, 1992-95; E. Neter Meml. lectr. ASM, 1996; alt. bd. mem. Global Alliance Vaccination & Immuzation, 2010-. Mem. editl. bd. more than 20 sci. jours.; contbr. some 600 articles to jours. Recipient Sasse prize, 1981, Krupp Found. prize, 1987, Aronson prize, State of Berlin, 1988, Smith Kline Beecham prize, 1991, Merckle prize, 1991, Pettenkofer prize, City of Munich, 1992, Pfleger prize, 1992; named Highly Cited Rschr., Inst. for Sci. Info., 2001. Mem. European Fedn. Immunol. Socs. (sec.-gen. 1992-95, pres. 2006-09), German Soc. Med. Microbiology and Hygiene (Ann. award 1983, 93), Internat. Union Immunological Socs. (pres. 2010-), German Soc. Immunology (mem. sci. bd. dirs. 1999-02, pres. 2002-04), Am. Acad. Microbiology, Am. Soc. Microbiology, Berlin-Brandenburg Acad. Sci., German Acad. Naturforscher, Leopoldina. Office: Max-Planck Inst Infect Biol Charitéplatz 1 10117 Berlin Germany Home Phone: 49/30-4017336; Office Phone: 0049/30-28460-502. Business E-Mail: kaufmann@mpiib-berlin.mpg.de.

KAUL, SANJAY, cardiologist; b. India, Dec. 31, 1960; MD, Govt. Med. Coll., Srinagar, Kashmir, India, 1986. Cert. internal medicine 1990, cardiovasc. disease 1993. Resident in internal medicine Cedars-Sinai Med. Ctr.; fellow in cardiovasc. diseases U. Iowa Hospitals & Clinics; dir. vascular physiology and thrombosis rsch. lab., Burns and Allen Rsch. Inst. Cedars-Sinai Med. Ctr., dir. cardiology fellowship tng. program, dir. cardiology consult svc. Recipient Trainee Investigator award, Am. Fedn. Clinical Rsch. Fellow: Am. Heart Assn. (Postdoctoral Rsch. Fellowship award, Young Investigator award); mem.: Internat. Soc. Heart Failure (mem. sci. adv. bd.), Internat. Congress on Coronary Artery Disease (mem. sci. adv. bd.). Office: Cedars-Sinai Heart Inst Cedars-Sinai Med Ctr 8700 Beverly Blvd Los Angeles CA 90048 Business E-Mail: kaul@cshs.org.

KAUL, VINOD RADHENATH, health facility administrator; b. Srinagar, India, Feb. 2, 1953; s. Radhey Nath and Mohini Kaul; m. Asha Ganjoo, May 19, 1993; children: Chanakya, Chaitanya. BSc, U. Jammu & Kashmir, India, 1973; MSc in Microbiology, M.S U. Baroda, India, 1975; PhD in Microbiology, U. Bombay, 1985. Jr. sci. officer microbiology Bhagwati Hosp., Bombay, 1980—81; head dept microbiology Sir Ganga Ram Hosp., New Delhi, 1981—97; med. dir., founder Vibles Biotech, Faridabad, Haryana, India, 1993—. Cons. microbiologist Metro Hosp., Faridabad, Haryana, India, 2001—, Nobel Hosp., Faridabad, 2000—. Social work Chetana, New Delhi, 2000. Rsch. fellow, Shushrusha Hosp., 1975—80. Mem.: Am. Soc. Microbiology (assoc.). Achievements include first to Development of ready to use, room temprature stable, economically priced culture media for clinical microbiology work. Avocations: travel, reading. Office: Vibles Biotech 28/63 West Patel Nagar New Delhi 110008 India Home: 297 121 006 Faridabad 121007 India Office Fax: +91-129-2226708; Home Fax: +91-129-2265805. Personal E-mail: vibles_biotech@yahoo.com.

KAUNITZ, JONATHAN DAVIDSON, physician; b. NYC, Nov. 6, 1950; s. Paul Ehrlich and Rita (Davidson) K.; m. Christine Lee, July 31, 1983; children: Justin Lee, Genevieve Jung. BA in Molecular Biology, Columbia Coll., 1972, MD, 1976. Diplomate Am. Bd. Internal Medicine, Am. Bd. Gastroenterology. Intern medicine Presbyn. Hosp., NYC, 1976—77, resident medicine, 1977—79; gastroenterology fellow U. Calif., San Francisco, 1979—80, gastrointestinal rsch. fellow, 1980—81, UCLA, 1981—82; asst. prof. medicine UCLA Sch. Medicine, 1983—91; assoc. investigator VA Career Devel. Series, 1984—85, rsch. assoc., 1985—88, clin. investigator, 1990—95; assoc. dir. UCLA Integrated Tng. Program in Digestive Diseases, 1986—90, co-dir., 1996—98, dir., 1998—2001; assoc. prof. dept. medicine Sch. Medicine UCLA, 1991—97, prof. dept. medicine Sch. Medicine, 1997—. Assoc. chief med. svc. gastrointestinal sect. Wadsworth VA Med. Ctr., 1993—; mem. legis. assembly UCLA, 1991-94, com. on appts. and promotions, 1991-2005; mem. gastrointestinal bd. Med. Rsch. Svc., Dept. VA, 1993-96, chair, 1995, mem. coun., 1996; mem. NIH study sects., chmn., 2006—; vis. lectr. Keio U. Med. Soc., Tokyo, 1994, 97, 2000, 05, 08; vis. prof. Asahi (Japan) Gen. Hosp., 2003—, Hamamatsu Seirei Med. Ctr., 2003—sr. assoc. editor Digestive Diseases & Scis., 2009-. Mem. editl. bd. Am.

Jour. Physiology. Bd. dirs. Cure Found., 2002—. Recipient numerous rsch. grants. Fellow Am. Coll. Gastroenterology; mem. Am. Gastroenterol. Assn., Am. Physiol. Soc., Columbia Coll. Physicians and Surgeons (alumni dir. 1976-86, dir. emeritus 1986—), Cure Autism Now (bd. dirs., sci. adv. group 1995-2004, chair 1996, sci. rsch. coun. 2000-06), Brentwood Biomed. Rsch. Inst. (bd. dirs., chair, 2003-06), Gastrointestinal Rsch. Group (pres.2006-10), West Coast Salt and Water Club (program chmn. 1989, treas. 1989-98, pres. 1998—), Western Assn. Physicians, Alpha Omega Alpha. Avocations: soccer, bicycling, travel, collecting books. Office: CURE Wadsworth VA Med Ctr Los Angeles CA 90073 Home Phone: 310-450-4564. E-mail: jake@ucla.edu.

KAUR, HARPREET, physician, researcher; b. Punjab, India, Apr. 7, 1979; MBBS, MD, Govt. Med. Coll, Patiala, DNB, 2000; FNB, Delhi U., New Delhi, 2011. Rsch. fellow Bangalore Assisted Conception Ctr., 2009—. Faculty mem. Postgrad. Inst. Med. Edn. & Rsch., Chandigarh, 2006—09. Mem.: ISAR (India). Home: H 1178 Aryans Enclave Sector 51B Chandigarh 160047 India Personal E-mail: drharpreet_sidhu@hotmail.com.

KAUR, JASBIR, biochemist, educator; b. Delhi, India, Oct. 8, 1967; MS in Biochemistry, Madras U., India, 1990; PhD, All India Inst. Med. Scis., New Delhi, 1996. Asst. prof. ocular biochemistry Dr. R.P. Ctr. Ophthalmic Scis., All India Inst. Med. Scis., 2003—07, assoc. prof. ocular biochemistry, 2007—10, prof. ocular biochemistry, 2010—. Recipient Indo-German award, UICC; fellow Cert. of Merit, Coun. Sci. and Indsl. Rsch., India., 1990. Avocation: reading. Office: R P Ctr Ophthalmic Scis All India Inst Med Scis Ocular Biochemistry New Delhi Delhi 110029 India Office Fax: 11-26588919. E-mail: kaurjasbir@rediffmail.com.

KAUR, KANWAL JEET, immunologist; b. New Delhi, Jan. 14, 1959; PhD, U. Lucknow, India, 1988. Rsch. scientist Nat. Inst. Immunology, 1991. Office: Nat Inst Immunology Aruna New Delhi Delhi 100067 India Business E-Mail: kanwal@nii.res.in.

KAUR, PRITINDER, medical researcher; b. Kanpur, India, Jan. 14, 1960; BSc with honors, U. London, 1981; PhD, U. Manchester, 1984. Group leader Peter MacCallum Cancer Ctr., 1999—. Sr. rsch. fellow Nat. Health & Med. Rsch. Coun. Australia, 2008—; fellow U. Melbourne. Office: St Andrew's Pl Melbourne Victoria 3101 Australia Business E-Mail: pritinder.kaur@petermac.org.

KAUSHIK, MANU, cardiologist, educator; b. Patiala, India, Sept. 28, 1979; MBBS, Govt Med. Coll., Patiala, 2002; MD, PGIMER, 2006. Cardiology fellow, resident clin. instr. Crighton U. Med. Ctr., 2010—. Nominee Golden Apple, Creighton Sch. Medicine; scholarship, Govt. of India. Mem.: AMA, Am. Coll. Cardiology. Avocations: photography, travel, sports. Office: 3006 Webster St Omaha NE 68131 Personal E-mail: drmanukaushik@gmail.com.

KAUTEN, JAMES RICHARD, cardiothoracic surgeon; b. Neosho, Mo., Nov. 26, 1952; MD, U. Health Scis. Chgo. Med. Sch., 1978. Cert. Am. Bd. Thoracic Surgery, Am. Bd. Surgery. Intern, gen. surgery So. Ill. Sch. Medicine, Springfield, Ill., 1978—79, resident, cardiothoracic surgery, 1979—83; fellow Emory U., Atlanta, 1983—86, mem. chief surgical donor cardiectomy team, 1984—85, mem., cardiac transplant team, surgery, 1984—85; clin. assoc. prof., surgery So. Ill. U., 1987—88; asst. prof. Emory U., Ga., 1988—90, with Peachtree Cardiovasc and Thoracic Surgeons, PA, Ga., 1986—. Hosp. appointments include St. Joseph's Hosp., Atlanta, Northeast Ga. Med. Ctr., Gainesville. Office: Peachtree Cardiovasc and Thoracic Surgeons 95 Collier Rd NW Ste 2055 Atlanta GA 30309 Address: 5665 Peachtree Dunwoody Rd Ste 150 Atlanta GA 30342 Office Phone: 404-252-6104, 404-355-9515. Office Fax: 404-257-1808, 404-355-9537.

KAUTZ, STEVEN A., biomedical engineer, educator; b. Detroit, July 19, 1961; MA, U. Tex., 1987; PhD, U. Calif., Davis, 1992. Biomed. engr. VA Rehab. Rsch. and Devel. Ctr., Palo Alto, Calif., 1992—2002, VA Brain Rehab. Rsch. Ctr., 2002—10, Ralph H. Johnson VA Med. Ctr., Charleston, SC, 2010—11; prof. U. Fla., 2002—10; chair, prof. Med. U. SC, 2010—. Adj. assoc. prof., dept. functional restoration Stanford U., 1996—2002; adj. prof., dept. biomed. engring. Clemson U., 2011. Rsch. Career Scientist grant, VA Rehab. R & D Svc. Mem.: Am. Phys. Therapy Assn., Neural Control Movement Soc., Soc. Neurosci., Am. Physiol. Soc. Office: Dept Heath Scis and Rsch Charleston SC 29425 Office Fax: 843-792-1358. Business E-Mail: kautz@musc.edu.

KAVA, BRUCE RICHARD, urologist, educator; b. Bklyn., Oct. 16, 1963; BA, SUNY Binghamton, 1985; MD, Albert Einstein Coll. Medicine, 1989. Diplomate Am. Bd. Urology. Chief, urology Dept. Vets. Affairs Med. Ctr., 2001; interim chair, urology, assoc. prof. U. Miami Miller Sch. Medicine, 2010—. Fellow: ACS; mem.: SE Sect. Am. Urol. Assn., Sexual Medicine Soc. N.Am., Internat. Soc. Sexual Medicine, Am. Urol. Assn. Office: 1150 NW 14th St Ste 309 Miami FL 33136 Office Fax: 305-243-3396. Business E-Mail: bkava@med.miami.edu.

KAVALALI, GULSEL MALKOC, pharmacist, consultant, researcher; d. Ahmet Hamdi and Zehra Malkoc; m. Gulsel Malkoc Kavalali, Sept. 24, 1968; 1 child, Ege Taner. BSc in Pharmacy, U. Istanbul, 1961, PhD in Pharmacognosy, 1965; post-doctoral, U. Purdue, 1965—67. Lectr. Faculty Pharmacy U. Istanbul, assoc. prof. Cerrahpasa Faculty Medicine, Dept. Pharmacology, 1985, head Herbal Medicines R&D Ctr., 1985, prof., 1996—. FIP mem. natural substances spl. interest group, sec. Internat. Fedn. Pharmaceutics, De-Haggen, Netherlands, 1967. Contbr. articles to profl. jours. Mem., v.p., pres. Turkish Am. Univs. Assn., Istanbul, 1967—. Scholar, AAUW, 1965—67. Mem.: Turkish Pharmacology Soc., Turkish Soc. History of Medicine, Internat. Soc. for History of Medicine, Am. Soc. Pharmacognosy, Internat. Soc. Ethnopharmacology (referee sci. articles 1998—). Islamic. Achievements include research in pharmacological investigations, isolating and identifying medically active compounds from the natural sources. Avocations: reading, classical music, travel. Office: Univ Istanbul Cerrahpasa Faculty of Medicine 34303 Istanbul Turkey Home: Haci Emin Efendi Sknr 16/2-Nisantasi 34365 Istanbul Istanbul Turkey Home Fax: 90.212.2480737. Personal E-mail: gulsel.kavalali@isbank.net.tr.

KAVALER-ADLER, SUSAN, clinical psychologist, psychoanalyst; b. NYC, Jan. 31, 1950; d. Solomon and Alice (Zelikow) Weiss; m. Thomas Kavaler, July 12, 1970; m. Saul Michael Adler, Aug. 14, 1983. PhD in Clin. Psychology, Adelphi U., 1974; ABPP in Psychology, 2002; LittD (hon.), Ignatius U., 2008. Cert. in clin psychotherapy, NY, 1975, psychoanalysis supr., Nat. Inst. Psychotherapies 1981, psychoanalysis, 1987, NCPsyA psychologist, Nat. Assn. Advancement Psychoanalysis; diplomate in psychoanalysis, 1998, APA, 2002, psychology, 2002. Psychologist Beth Israel Hosp., NYC, 1974-76, Manhattan Psychiat. Children's Ctr., NYC, 1977-80; pvt. practice psychotherapy-psychoanalysis NYC, 1976—; founder, exec. dir. Object Rels. Inst. Psychotherapy and Psychoanalysis, 1991—. Condr. writing and mourning groups; founding dir., supr., faculty, founder, exec. dir., faculty, tng. analyst Object Rels. Inst. for Psychotherapy and Psychoanalysis, 1991—; mem. faculty Postgrad. Ctr. Mental Health, N.Y.C., 1984-86, 90; mem. faculty, supr. Nat. Inst. Psychotherapies, N.Y.C., 1985-91; bd. dirs., supr. Bklyn. Inst. Psychotherapy and Psychoanalysis; adj. prof. Fordham U.; founding exec. dir. Object Rels. Inst. Psychotherapy and Psychoanalysis, 1991-; spkr pvt. seminars, writing groups. Author: The Compulsion to Create, 1993, 2d edit., 2000, Women Writers and Their Demon Lovers, 1993, rev. edit., 2000, The Creative Mystique: From Red Shoes Frenzy to Love and Creativity, 1996, International Forum of Psychoanalysis, 1999, The Divine, the Deviant and the Diabolical: A Female Artist's Developmental Journey from Self Fragmentation to Self Integration in a Creative Process Group, 2000, Mourning, Spirituality and Psychic Change, 2003 (Nat. Gradiva award Nat. Assn. Advancement Psychoanalysis, 2004), Object Relations Perspectives On, The Phantom of the Opera, Seduction, Date Rape, and Aborted Surrender, 2010; editor: book chpts.; contbr. chapters to books, 60 articles to profl. jours., scientific papers. Recipient 11 writing awards, Postgrad. Ctr. for Mental Health, Gradiva award, Nat. Assn. for Advancement of Psychoanalysis. Mem.: Acad. Psychoanalysis. Office: 115 E 9th St Apt 12P New York NY 10003-5420 also: 41 Central Park W New York NY 10023 Office Phone: 212-674-5425. Personal E-mail: suska674@aol.com, susan@kavaleradler.com, drkavaleradler@gmail.com.

KAVATKAR, ANITA NEELKANTH, pathologist, researcher; d. Suresh Narayan and Vasudha Suresh Kale; m. Neelkanth Chandrakant Kavatkar, Dec. 2, 1990. MB, BChir, MD, Byramjee Jeejeebhoy Med. Coll., Pune, India, 1994, MD in Pathology. Lectr. B. J. Med. Coll., Pune, India, 1995—2004, assoc. prof., 2004—. Contbr. articles to profl. journals. Internat. fellow, indian Coun. Med. Rsch., 2004. Mem.: Rsch. Soc. B.J. Med. Coll., Indian Acad. Cytologists (life), Indian Assn. Pathologists and Microbiologists (life SMT. Kuntidevi Mehrotra award 2004). Avocation: reading. Office: B J Med Coll Dept Pathology Sassoon Rd Maharashtra Pune 411001 India Personal E-mail: kavatkaranita@rediffmail.com.

KAVISHE, FESTO PATRICK, nutritionist; b. Mkuu-Rombo, Tanzania, May 5, 1951; s. Patrick Lemama and Celina Ali-Maskoi (Swai) K.; m. Mwagombeani Juma, Dec. 18, 1982; children: Patrick, Lulu-Lucy. MD, U. Dar Es Salaam, Tanzania, 1978, MSc, U. London, 1982, postgrad. cert., U. Brussels, 1987, U. Lubeck, Germany, 1991. Registered gen. med. practitioner. Dist. med. officer Ministry of Health, Mafinga, Tanzania, 1979-80; head med. nutrition Tanzania Food and Nutrition Ctr., Dar-Es-Slaam, 1980-85, dir. med. nutrition, 1985-89, mng. dir., 1989-93, regional nutrition advisor UNICEF Eastern and Southern Africa Regional Office, Nairobi, Kenya, 1993-96; chief of Cmty. Action for Social Devel. Program UNICEF, Phnom Penh, Cambodia, 1996-99, rep. Asmara, Eritrea, 1999—2001, Harare, Zimbabwe, 2001—. Bd. dirs., sr. advisor Internat. Coun. Control of Iodine Deficiency Disorders, Adelaide, Australia, Brussels, 1986-98; rsch. attachment U. Uppsalla, Sweden, 1989-93; cons. WHO, UNICEF, FAO, World Bank, USAID, UN-Administv. Coordinating Com./Sub-Com. on Nutrition, various cities, 1985-93; v.p., bd. dirs. Ctr. Biol. and Oncol. Studies, Lyon, France, 1991-95; rep. Internat. Vitamin A Consultative Group, 1992-93. Contbr. articles to profl. jours. Recipient Med. Assn. Tanzania award, 1978, Hecht prize, U. London, 1982, Intl. Peace Prize United Cultural Convention, USA, 2003, Min. Culture Am. Biographical Inst., 2003, World Lifetime Achievement Award Am. Biographical Inst, 2003; UN Univ. fellow, 1981; Named one of 2000 Outstanding Intellectuals 21st Century Intl. Biographical Ctr, 2002. Mem. British Nutrition Soc., UNICEF Staff Assn. (1st dep. chair 1997, chair Cambodia and the East Asia and Pacific region 1999), Am. Inst. Cancer Rsch./World Cancer Rsch. Fund (mem. internat. panel), Opportunities for Micronutrient Intervention (tech. adv. group 1993-99), World Health Policy Forum. Roman Catholic. Avocations: ping pong/table tennis, basketball, writing, photography, reading. Home: PO Box 621 Dar-Es-Salaam Tanzania Office: UNICEF No 6 Fairbridge Belgravia PO Box 1250 Harare Zimbabwe Home Phone: +263-4-369095; Office Phone: +263-4-704276. E-mail: fkavishe@unicef.org.

KAVOUSSI, LOUIS RAPHAEL, urologist; b. NYC, Oct. 24, 1957; s. James P. and Margaret Kavoussi; m. Julie Kavoussi; children: Nicholas, Rebecca, Andrianna. BS, Columbia U., 1979; MD, SUNY, Buffalo, 1983. Resident in surgery and urology Washington U., St. Louis, 1991-93, asst. prof.; chief urology Jewish Hosp., St. Louis, 1989-91; asst. prof. Harvard Med. Sch., Boston, 1991-93; chief urology, assoc. prof. urology Johns Hopkins Bayview Med. Ctr., Balt., 1993—2006; prof. of urology NYU Sch. of Medicine, 2006—. Mem. med. bd. Johns Hopkins Bayview Med. Ctr., 1993—2006; dir. Stone Ctr. Johns Hopkins U., 1991—2006, Patrick C. Walsh Disting. prof. urologic surgery; cons., dept. of urology, Johns Hopkins U.; chmn. of urology, the N. Shore—LI Jewish Health System, Manhasset, NY Fellow Am. Urologic Assn., Endourology Soc. Achievements include first to perform laparoscopic nephrectomy, laparoscopic donor nephrectytor transplant; development of first clinical telesurgical system.

KAVUNKAL, ALPHA MATHEW, surgeon, consultant; b. Obomosho, Oyo State, Nigeria, Mar. 22, 1971; s. Kavunkal Mathias and Saramma Mathew; m. Kavitha Abraham, Apr. 29, 2001; children: Anton Alpha Mathew, Adrien Alpha Abraham. MBBS, MS, Christian Med. Coll. and Hosp., Vellore, India, 2004, MCh in Cardiothoracic Surgery. Cardiothoracic Surgery Dr.M.G.R.Medical U., Tamilnadu, 2004, General Surgery Dr.M.G.R.Medical U., Tamilnadu, 2000, Mbbs Dr.M.G.R.Medical U., Tamilnadu, 1994. Dr. Christian Med. Coll. and Hosp., 1994—97, registrar, gen. surgery, 1997—2000, sr. registrar-,cardiothoracic surgery, 2001—04, sr. lectr., cardiothoracic surgery, 2004—. Cons. Christian Med. Coll. and Hosp., Vellore, Tamilnadu State, India, 2004—08. Contbr. articles to profl. jours. (Marquis who's who in the world, 2008). Life mem. Indian Assn. of Cardiothoracic Surgery, Delhi, New Delhi, India, 2006. Mem.: Cardiothoracic Surgeons Network, Indian Assn. Cardiothoracic Surgeons (life mem. 2006). Achievements include research in cardiovascular. Avocations: football, swimming, music, tennis. Office: Cardiothoracic Surgery Unit 1 CMCHosp Vellore Tamilnadu 632004 India

KAWACHI, YOSHIO, urologist, educator; s. Hiroshi and Michiko Ushizima; m. Keiko Sato; children: Takahiro Sato, Anna. MD, Juntendo U., Tokyo, 1974. Urologist Juntendo U., 1977—, prof., 2000—. Chief urologist Juntendo U. Urayasu Hosp., 1987—; dir. med. practice Urology Dept. Mem.: Soc. Internat. Urology. Office: Juntendo Univ Urayasu Hosp 2-1-1 Tomioka Urayasu Chiba Pref 279-0021 Japan Office Phone: 047-353-3111. Office Fax: 047-353-3138.

KAWAGUCHI, KOJI, dental educator; b. Fukuoka, Japan, June 26, 1961; DMD, Tsurumi U., 1990, PhD, 1995. Asst. prof. Tsurumi U. Sch. Dental Medicine, 1997—. Mem.: ASCO. Avocation: yachting. Office: 2-1-3 Tsurumi Tsurumi-ku Yokohama Kanagawa 2308501 Japan Office Fax: 81455810024. Business E-Mail: kawaguchi-k@tsurumi-u.ac.jp.

KAWAGUCHI, MIO, medical educator; b. Setagaya-ku, Tokyo, June 19, 1970; MD, Showa U., Tokyo, 1995; PhD, Tokyo, 1999. Rsch. fellow Johns Hopkins U., Balt., 1999—2001; asst. prof. Showa U. Hosp., Shinagawa-ku, Tokyo, 2006—; asst. prof. dept. pulmonary medicine Inst. Clin. Medicine, U. Tsukuba, Japan, 2008—. Achievements include discovery of human interleukin (IL)-17F gene in 2001; found mouse IL-17F gene (mIL-17Ftv) and listed in GenBank (GenBank#:AF332389 and AB116259). Office: Dept Pulmonary Medicine Tsukuba Univ Hosp Inst Clin Medicine 1-1-1 Tennodai Tsukuba Ibaraki 3058575 Japan Office Phone: 81-298533144. E-mail: mkawguchi@md.tsukuba.ac.jp.

KAWAHARA, HIROYUKI, molecular cell biologist, professor; b. Takada-city, Japan, Sept. 15, 1965; s. Hidenori Kawahara and Setsuko Kawahara (Wobara); m. Masumi Shimada, June 1, 2002; 1 child, Naohito. BS, Hokkaido U., Sapporo, 1989, M in Pharm. Scis., 1991, PhD, 1994. Postdoctoral fellow U. Coll. London, 1994—95; lectr. U. Tsukuba, Ibaraki, Japan, 2006—; postdoctoral fellow U. Newcastle Med. Sch., Newcastle, 1995—96; rsch. fellow Tokyo Met. Inst. Med. Sci., 1996—98; asst. prof. U. Tokyo, 1998—2000; assoc. prof. Hokkaido U., Sapporo, 2000—08; prof. Tokyo Met. U., 2008—. Contbr. scientific papers. Recipient Subsidy for Med. Rsch., Akiyama Found., 2006; fellowship for Young Scientists, Uehara Meml. Found., 1994, grant-in-aid for Young Scientists, Ministry Edn., Culture, Sci. and Tech. Japan, 2002—04, grant in aid for Specific Area, 2006—, 2001—05. Mem.: Japanese Cancer Assn., Japanese Biochemical Soc., Molecular Biology Soc. Japan, Am. Soc. Cell Biology, Genetic Soc. Am. Achievements include research in understanding the mechanism of cell growth and differentiation. Avocations: travel, wine, baseball, piano. Office: Tokyo Met Univ Dept Biol Scis 1-1 Minami-Osawa Tokyo Hachioji 192-0397 Japan Home: Tama City Tokyo 206-0034 Japan Business E-Mail: hkawa@tmu.ac.jp.

KAWAI, KEIICHI, medical educator; b. Tokyo, Apr. 29, 1959; PhD, Kyoto U., 1988. Asst. Sci. U. Tokyo, 1988—96; assoc. prof. Miyazaki Med. Coll., 1996—2001; vis. prof. Fukui U., 2001; prof. Kanazawa U., 2001—. Vis. fellow NIH, 1992—93, rsch. cons., 1995. Recipient 36th award, Japanese Soc. Nuc. Medicine, Young Scientist award, Inoue Rsch. Found. Mem.: Japanese Soc. Xenobiotics, Pharm. Soc. Japan, Japanese Soc. Nuc. Medicine, Soc. Radiopharm. Scis., Soc. Nuc. Medicine. Office: 5-11-80 Kodatsuno Kanazawa Ishikawa 920-0942 Japan Office Fax: 81-76-234-4366. Business E-Mail: kei@mhs.mp.kanazawa-u.ac.jp.

KAWAI, NAOKI, internist; b. Gifu City, Japan, Feb. 7, 1951; MD, Hokkaido U., Sapporo, Japan, 1975. Physician Nat. Hosp. Orgn. Nagoya Med. Ctr., Aichi Pref, Japan, 1975—79; physician 1st dept. internal medicine Nagoya Sch. Medicine, 1979—85; dir. Kawai Clinic, Gifu City, 1985—. Bd. dir. Influenza Study Group, Japan Physicians Assn., Tokyo, 2005—. Office: Kawai Clinic 4-9 Tonomachi Gifu City Gifu Pref 500-8116 Japan Business E-Mail: nkawai@city.gifu.med.or.jp.

KAWAI, TOSHIAKI, pathologist, educator; b. Tokyo, Jan. 5, 1949; s. Masatoshi and Ikuko Kawai; m. Noriko Kida, Sept. 21, 1950; children: Ryoji, Yoko, Yuko. MD, Tokyo Med. U., 1973, Keio U., Tokyo, 1977. Cert. pathologist Japan Soc. Pathology, 1981, cytopathologist Japanese Soc. Clin. Cytology, 1989. Instr. Keio U., Tokyo, 1977—79; asst. prof. Nat. Def. Med. Coll., Tokorozawa, Saitama, Japan, 1979—87, assoc. prof., 1987—97, prof., 1998—. Vis. asst. prof. Baylor Coll. Medicine, Houston, 1985—86. Home: Hibarigaoka-kita 4-8-24 Nishi-Tokyo 202-0002 Japan Office: Nat Def Med Coll Dept Pathology and Lab Medicine Namiki 3-2 Tokorozawa 359-8513 Japan Office Phone: 42-995-1505. Office Fax: 42-996-5192; Home Fax: 424-38-7717. E-mail: tkawai@ndmc.ac.jp.

KAWAKAMI, MASAYA, medical educator; b. Tokyo, Apr. 27, 1929; s. Shoichiroh and Kimiko (Hasegawa) K.; m. Noriko Tsuchida, Oct. 1, 1957; children: Kyoko, Toshiya, Eriko. MB, Hokkaido U., Sapporo, Japan, 1953; D of Med. Sci., Gunma U., Maebashi, Japan, 1960. Diplomate Med. Bd. Japan. Lectr. Gunma U., Maebashi, 1958-60; rsch. assoc. Georgetown U., Washington, 1964-66; assoc. prof. Gunma U., Maebashi, 1960-72; prof. Kitsako U., Sagamihara, Japan, 1972-96, dir. dept. molecular biology, 1972—95. Dir. Future Med. Lab., Tokyo, 2001-, tech. advisor SRL Inc., Tokyo, 1996—. Author: Immune Response, 1978; editor, author: Genetic Engineering in Medicine, 1992; (textbooks) Medical Molecular Biology, 1984, Human Medical Genetics, 1991, Bactericidal Lectin Conserved by Veterbrates for 300 Million Years, 1984, Complement Activating-lectin, RaRF, 1999, Gene Stucture of protease Component of the Human RaPF, 1999, Role of the Complement Lectin Pathway in Anaphlyactoid Reaction, 2003, Effectiveness of Finasteride and Androgen Receptor Gene Polymorphism, 2005, Complement Activating Lectin and Hereditary Angioedema, 2008, MASP-2 in Neonates and its Clinical Associations, 2009. Mem. com. of Bioethics Japan Med. Assn., Tokyo, 1986-92, Gene Therapy, Japan. Govt.; bacteriology divsn. Japan del. Internat. Union of Microbiol. Socs., Washington, 1991—. Recipient Asahi Sci. award Asahi Co., Tokyo, 1959, Naito award Naito Meml. Found., Tokyo, 1975, award Internat. Hair Rsch. Soc., 2004; grantee: Japanese Govt., Tokyo, 1960-92. Mem. Japanese Soc. Bacteriology (hon.; trustee, Asakawa award 1999), Molecular Biology Soc. Japan, Japanese Biochem. Soc., Am. Soc. Microbiology. Avocations: painting, rose culture. Home: 2-3-3 Kamitsuruma Sagamihara Kanagawa 252-0302 Japan Office: Future Med Lab 14F San-eh Bldg 1-22-2 Nishishinjuku Shinjuku Tokyo 160-0023 Japan also: Kitasato U Sch Medicine 1-15 Kitasato Sagamihara Kanagawa 252-0329 Japan also: Kitasato Inst 5-9-1 Shirokane Minato Tokyo 108-8642 Japan Office Phone: 813 5250 7333. Personal E-mail: qwe02046@nifty.com.

KAWAKAMI, NORIAKI, surgeon, educator; b. Nagoya, Japan, May 11, 1956; MD, Nagoya U., 1981; DMSc. Clin. prof. Nagoya U., Sch. Medicine, 2004—; guest prof. Jiji Med. U., 2010—. Bd. dirs. Japanese Scoliosis Soc., 1997—, Japanese Spinal Instrumentation Soc., 1997—, Japanese Soc. Spine Surgery and Related Rsch., 2010—. Mem.: Chest Wall & Spinal Deformity Study Group, Japanese Rehab. Soc., Japanese Orthop. Assn., Scoliosis Rsch. Soc. Avocation: tennis. Office: Meijo Hosp 1-3-1 Sannomaru Naka-ku Nagoya Aichi Prefecture 460-0001 Japan Office Fax: 81522015318. Business E-Mail: meijo.kawakami@gmail.com.

KAWAMOTO, HENRY KATSUMI, JR., plastic surgeon; b. Long Beach, Calif., Jan. 19, 1937; AA, East LA Coll., 1956; DDS, U. So. Calif., 1960, MD, 1964. Cert. Am. Bd. Surgery, 1972, Am. Bd. Plastic Surgery, 1976. Intern U. Calif. Hosp., LA, 1964—65; resident gen. surgery Columbia Presbyn. Med. Ctr., NYC, 1965—71; resident plastic surgery Inst. Reconstructive Plastic Surgery, NYU, 1971—73; fellow crano-facial surgery Dr. Paul Tessier, L' Hôpital Foch and Clinique Belvédère, Paris, 1973—74; joined divsn. plastic surgery UCLA, 1975, dir., chief craniofacial surgery emeritus, clin. prof. plastic and reconstructive surgery LA; chief plastic surgery So. Calif. Sys. Clinics (formerly Sepulveda VA Hosp.). Spkr. in field. Contbr. articles to med. jours. Fellow: ACS; mem.: Childrens Craniofacial Assn. (med. adv. bd.), Am. Bd. Plastic Surgery (mem. Com. on Credential and Requirements, Com. on Rectification, past dir., chmn. Com. on Rectification), Am. Soc. Plastic and Reconstructive Surgeons (past historian and chmn. bd. trustees), Internat. Soc. Craniofacial Surgeons (founding mem.), Am. Cleft Palate Assn., Calif. State Dental Assn., Calif. Soc. Plastic Surgeons (past pres.), Am. Soc. Craniofacial Surgeons (founding mem. past pres.), Am. Soc. Maxillofacial Surgeons (past pres.), Am. Assn. Plastic Surgeons. Office: 1301 20th St Ste 460 Santa Monica CA 90404-2054 Office Phone: 310-829-0391.

KAWAMOTO, HIROSHI, pharmaceutical executive; b. Yokohama, Japan, May 23, 1965; MSc in Pharm. Scis., Chiba U., 1991, PhD in Pharm. Scis., 2001. Mgr. Banyu Pharm. Co. Ltd. Tsukuba Rsch. Inst. Merck Rsch. Labs., 1991—2009, Taisho Pharm. Co. Ltd. Medicinal Chemistry Labs., 2009—. Avocation: jogging. Office: 1-403 Yoshino-cho Kita-ku Saitama 331-9530 Japan Office Fax: 81-48-652-7254. Business E-Mail: hiroshi.kawamoto@po.rd.taisho.co.jp.

KAWAMURA, AKIO, cardiologist, educator; b. Toronto, Can., Sept. 1, 1968; MD, Keio U. Sch. Medicine, 1994, PhD. Asst. prof. Keio U. Sch. Medicine, Japan, 2007—. Fellowship, Keio U. Hosp., Lahey Clinic. Mass. Mem.: Am. Coll. Cardiology. Achievements include patents for ovale, valvular heart diseas. Avocation: languages. Office: 35 Shinanomachi Shinjuku-ku Tokyo 160-8582 Japan Business E-Mail: kawamura@cpnet.med.keio.ac.jp.

KAWAMURA, YUSUKE, hospital administrator; b. Minato-ku, Japan, Oct. 17, 1974; MD, Saitama Med. U., Japan, 2001. Diplomate Japan. Resident physician Toranomon Hosp., Minato-ku, Tokyo, 2001—06, attending staff, dept. hepatology, 2006—. Contbr. articles to clin. rsch. publs. Achievements include research in viral elimination reduces incidence of malignant lymphoma in patients with hepatitis. Office: Toranomon Hosp 2-2-2 Toranomon Minato-ku Tokyo 105-8470 Japan Office Phone: 81-3-3588-1111. Office Fax: 81-3-3582-7068. Personal E-mail: k_yusuke@mub.biglobe.ne.jp. Business E-Mail: k-yusuke@toranomon.gr.jp.

KAWASAKI, HIROHIDE, pediatrician, hematologist, oncologist, immunologist; b. Nishinomiya, Hyogo, Japan, Apr. 21, 1960; s. Shunzo and Ikuko Kawasaki; m. Miyako Sakamoto, Mar. 30, 1991; 1 child, Risa. MS, MD, Kansai Med. U., Osaka, Japan, 1988, PhD, 1995. Resident Kansai Med. U., 1988-90, instr., 1993-96; sr. resident Nat. Cancer Ctr., Tokyo, 1990-93; postdoctoral fellow Ctr. for Human Genetics, Boston U. Sch. Medicine, 1996-98; instr. Kansai Med. U., 1998—2003, asst. prof., 2006—11, assoc. prof., 2011—; instr. Inst. Med. Sci. U. Tokyo, 2003—05. Author: Minor Pediatrics, 1996, 2008, Workbook in Practical Neonatology, 1996. Office: Kansai Med U Dept Pediat 2-3-1 Shinmachi Hirahata Osaka 573-1191 Japan Business E-Mail: kawasaki@hirakata.kmu.ac.jp.

KAWASAKI, KOZO, medical educator; b. Japan, May 25, 1963; s. Shizue and Shozo Kawasaki; m. Miho Kawasaki, Mar. 1, 1992; children: Takamasa, Naho, Toshimasa. MD, Yamaguchi U. Diplomate in med. Japan, 1989. Assoc. prof. Kawasaki Med. Sch., Matsushima, Kurashiki, Japan, 2005—. Office: Kawasaki Med Sch Matsushima 577 Kurashiki Okayama 701-0192 Japan Business E-Mail: kozok@med.kawasaki-m.ac.jp.

KAWASAKI, MASANORI, medical educator; MD, Gifu U., Japan, 1988, PhD in Medicine, 2002. Resident cardiology Gifu U., 1988—89; asst. prof. Asahi U., Japan, 1989—91; cardiologist Matsunami Gen. Hosp., Japan, 1991—94, chief cardiology, 1994—97; rsch. fellow Gifu U. Grad. Sch. Medicine, 1997—2000, asst. prof., 2000—03, assoc. prof., 2005—; postdoc. rschr. Harverd Med. Sch., Boston, 2003—05. Contbr. scientific papers. Cardiovasc. Disease Rsch. grant, Japan Heart Found., Pfizer Pharms. Inc., 2001, Banyu fellowship in Cardiovasc. Medicine, 2003, Rsch. grant, Japan Soc. Promotion Sci., 2007. Mem.: Japanese Soc. Cardiovasc. Imaging & Dynamics (mem. coun. 2006—), Japanese Interventional Cardiology Soc., Japanese Soc. Echocardiography (award 2000), Japanese Internal Medicine Soc., Am. Heart Assn., Japanese Circulation Soc. Achievements include development of integrated backscatter intravascular ultrasound. Office: Gifu Univ Grad Sch Medicine 1-1 Yanagido Gifu Japan Office Phone: 81-58-230-6523. Office Fax: 81-58-230-6524. Business E-Mail: mkawa@gifu-u.ac.jp.

KAWASHIMA, HIROTO, biology professor; b. Japan, 1965; PhD, U. Tokyo, 1988. Assoc. prof. U. Shizuoka, 2005—. Mem.: Soc. Glycobiology, ASBMB. Office: University Shizuoka 52-1 Yada Shizuoka 422-8526 Japan Business E-Mail: kawashih@u-shizuoka-ken.ac.jp.

KAWASHIMA, MASATOU, neurosurgeon, educator; b. Kyoto, Mar. 14, 1967; s. Kumiko Kawashima; m. Azusa Takahira, July 3, 1974. MD, Kyushu U., Fukuoka, Japan, 1994, PhD, 2001. Cert. neurosurgery Japan Neurosurg. Soc., 2000. Basic surg. tng., Dept. Surgery Kyushu U. Hosp., Fukuoka, 1994, resident, Dept. Neurosurgery, 1995—96, Nat. Kyushu Med. Ctr., Fukuoka, 1996—97, Baba Meml. Hosp., Osaka, 1997—98; staff neurosurgeon Chidoribashi Hosp., Fukuoka, 2001; clin. rsch. fellow U. Fla., 2001—03; asst. prof. Kyushu U. Hosp.; staff neurosurgeon, vice dir. Yamaguchi Red Cross Hosp., Japan, 2003—04; asst. prof. Kitasato U. Hosp., Kanagawa, Japan, 2004—. Mem.: Mt. Fuji Workshop, Japan Stroke Soc., Japanese Soc. on Surgery for Cerebral Stroke, Japan Soc. Brain Tumor Pathology, Japan Neurosurg. Soc. Achievements include research in microneurosurgical anatomy.

KAWATA, SHUICHI, physician; b. Yonago, Japan, Aug. 3, 1951; s. Iwao and Takako Kawata; m. Keiko Nakamoto, Apr. 21, 1981; children: Souichiro, Miyuki, Riichiro. MD, Tottori U., Yonago, 1977, PhD in Med. Sci., 1981. Med. staff Tottori U. Sch. Medicine, Yonago, 1977-82; rsch. assoc. Ariz. U. Sch. Medicine, Tucson, 1982-83; med. staff Mimasaku Chuoh Hosp., Mimasaka, 1983-85; dir. Kawata Naika Iin (Kawata Med. Clinic), Yonago, 1985—. Author: Cardiology, 1983, Clinical Cardiology, 1985; contbr. articles to profl. jours. Fellow Japanese Soc. Internal Medicine (bd. cert.), ACP, Japanese Circulation Soc. (bd. cert.); mem. N.Y. Acad. Scis. Avocations: fishing, driving. Office: Kawata Naika Iin 4-1 Kaikeonsen 1 Chyome Yonago 683-0001 Japan Business E-Mail: kawatas@apionet.or.jp.

KAWAUCHI, KIYOTAKA, physician, researcher; b. Takashima, Shiga, Japan, Jan. 14, 1957; MD, Kyorin U. Sch. Medicine, 1981; PhD in Medicine, Tokyo Women's Med. U., 1988. Physician, rsch. scientist, dept. medicine Tokyo Women's Med. U., 1981—, assoc. prof., 2000—; physician, rsch. scientist, dept. immunology Best Inst. U. Toronto, 1991—97. Editl. bd. mem. Case Report Hematology, 2011. Leukemia Rsch. Fund grant, grant, Aid for Sci. Rsch. Japan. Fellow: Japanese Soc. Hematology, Japanese Soc. Internal Medicine; mem.: Japanese Soc. Immunology. Avocation: reading. Office: 2-1-10 Nishiogu Arakawa-ku Tokyo Arakawa-ku 116-8567 Japan Office Fax: 03-3894-0282. Business E-Mail: ochamegm@dnh.twmu.ac.jp.

KAWESKI, SUSAN, plastic surgeon, naval officer; b. Oil City, Pa., Jan. 27, 1955; d. Richard Francis and Lottie Ann (Malek) K.; m. Henry Nicholas Ernecoff, Aug. 7, 1983. BA, Washington and Jefferson Coll., 1976; MA, SUNY, Buffalo, 1979; MD, Pa. State U., 1983. Diplomate Am. Bd. Surgery, Am. Bd. Plastic Surgery. Commd. lt. USN, 1983, advanced through grades to capt., 1993; intern Naval Hosp., San Diego, 1983-84; head med. dept. USN, 1984-85; resident in gen. surgery Naval Hosp., San Diego, 1985-89; resident in plastic surgery Pa. State U., Hershey, 1989-91; staff plastic surgeon Naval Med. Ctr., San Diego, 1991-95; head divsn. plastic surgery, surgeon gen. advisor USN, 1994-95; craniofacial fellow Dr. Ian T. Jackson, Mich., 1995-96; head cleft palate/craniofacial team Naval Med. Ctr., 1996-98; resigned, 1998; pvt. practice, San Diego, 1998—. Chmn. Cleft Palate/Craniofacial Bd., San Diego; plastic surgery advisor to surgeon gen. USN, 1994-95; presenter in field. Author chpt. to book. Recipient Ernest Witebsky Meml. award for proficiency in microbiology SUNY at Buffalo, 1978. Fellow ACS (assoc., 1st Place Rsch. award 1991); mem. Am. Assn. Plastic and Reconstructive Surgeons, Am. Cleft Palate Assn., Am. Assn. Women Surgeons, Am. Med. Women's Assn., Assn. Mil. Surgeons U.S., Univ. Club. Republican. Roman Catholic. Avocations: skiing, tennis, swimming, painting, playing piano. Home: 1158 Barcelona Dr San Diego CA 92107-4151 Office: Craniofacial Reconstructive 8415 Grant Ave La Mesa CA 91941-5303 E-mail: skaweski@pacbell.net.

KAWEWE, SALIWE MOYO, social work educator, researcher; children: Neo, Rujeko, Godfrey, Kudakwashe. BSW, U. Zambia, Lusaka, 1974; MSW, Washington U., St. Louis, 1979; PhD, St. Louis U., 1985. Cert. edn. accreditation reaffirmation Coun. on Social Work, 2001. Adminstrv. asst. U. Zambia, Lusaka, 1974—77; social svcs. officer, probation officer Dept. Social Svcs., Bulawayo, Zimbabwe, 1979—81; instr. St. Louis Pub. Schs., 1981—83; social svc. worker II Mo. Divsn. Family Svcs., St. Louis, 1984—85; asst. prof. Southea. La. U., Hammond, 1985—88, Ctrl. State U., Wilberforce, Ohio, 1989, James Madison U., Harrisonburg, Va., 1989—91, Wichita State U., 1991—96; assoc. prof. So. Ill. U., Carbondale, 1996—2001, dir. grad. program, 1996—98, prof., 2002—. Contbr. chapters to books; mem. editl. bd.: Social Devel. Issues, Jour. Social Work Edn., Jour. African Policy Studies, Jour. Immigrant and Refugee Svcs., Jour. Women and Lang., 1998—, mem. guest editl. bd.: Nat. Women Studies Jour., 1997—98; contbr. articles to profl. jours. and publs. Mem. Nat. Assn. Social Workers, Bulawayo, Matabeleland, Zimbabwe, 1980—82; Africa regional rep. Inter-Univ. Consortium for Internat. Social Devel., Wichita, 1992—94; mem. Tangipohoa Parish Mayor's commn. on Needs of Women, Hammond, 1985—88, Inter-Univ. Consortium for Internat. Social Devel., Carbondale, 1995—, Ill. Hunger Coalition, Chgo., 1998—; sec. Kans. Coun. on Social Work Edn., Topeka, 1992—93; mem. Com. to Enhance Minority, Human and Civil Rights, Springfield, 2000—; pres. Delmo Housing Corp., 2006—. Recipient Outstanding Scholastic Achievement award, George Warren Brown Sch. of Social Work, Wash. U., 1979, Superior Acad. Achievement award, St. Louis U. Internat. Student Assn., 1984, Appreciation for Continuing Svc. as a Faculty Advisor, Nat. Assn. Black Social Workers, 2001, Appreciation as Faculty Advisor, 2000, certificate of Dedication, African Student Coun. So. Ill. U. at Carbondale, 2001, Internat. Student Coun So. Ill. U. at Carbondale, 2001, Award of Appreciation of Svc., Nat. Assn. Black Social Workers, 2000, Recognition of Dedicated Svc., African Student Coun. So. Ill. U. at Carbondale, 1998, Dedication of Svc., African Student Coun., So. Ill. U. at Carbondale, 1997, Outstanding Leadership and Guidance, Student Orgn. of Social Work, Wichita State U., 1996, Outstanding Multilateral Study Del. award, World Congress on the Family, 1992; grantee Summer Rsch. Travel Grant, Wichita State U., 1994. Mem.: NASW (asst. dist. chair 1997—99), Internat. Coun. Social Welfare, Internat. Assn. for Schs. of Social Work, Soc. for Study of Social Problems, Peace and Social Justice Ctr. of So. Ctrl. Kans., Coun. on Social Work Edn., Internat. Assn. Feminist Econs., So. Ill. U. Women's Caucus, Nat. Women Studies Assn., So. Ill. HIV Care Consortium (bd. mem. 1997—2001), Internat. Fedn. Social Workers (life), Phi Alpha (hon.). Office: So Ill U Sch Of Social Work Mailcode 4329 Carbondale IL 62901 Office Phone: 618-453-3359. Business E-Mail: smkawewe@siu.edu.

KAWOOSA, ALTAF AHMAD, orthopedist, educator; b. Srinagar, Feb. 22, 1968; MBBS, Govt. Med. Coll. Srinagar, 1993, MS in Orthop., 2000. Cons. dept. orthop. Govt Med. Coll. Srinagar, 2005, lectr. dept. orthop., 2005—09, asst. prof., 2009—. Recipient Best Paper award, SKIMS. Mem.: Arthroscopic Soc. India, Indian Orthop. Assn. Avocation: cricket. Home: Bazaz Manzil Near Old Post Office Nows Srinagar Jammu & Kashmir 190011 India Home Fax: 0194 2433730. Personal E-mail: draltafk@yahoo.com.

KAY, CHRISTOPHER K., nonprofit organization executive, lawyer; b. Cin., Jan. 5, 1953; s. Robert and Joan Kay; m. Kristine Kenney, 1977; 1 child, Lauren. BA in Polit. Sci. and History, with honors, U. Mo., 1975; JD, Duke U. Sch. Law, Durham, NC, 1978. Bar: 1978. Atty. Shughart, Thomson & Kilroy, Kansas City, Mo., 1978—84; chmn. litig. dept. Swann & Haddock, Orlando, Fla., 1984—90; ptnr. Foley & Lardner, Orlando, 1990—96; founding ptnr. Kay, Panzl & Latham, Orlando, Fla., 1996—98, Kay, Gronek & Latham, Orlando, Fla., 1998—2000; exec. v.p. ops., gen. counsel Toys "R" Us, Inc., Wayne, NJ, 2000—05, corp. sec., then COO, 2002—05; mng. dir. internat. bus. devel. Universal Parks & Resorts; COO Trust for Pub. Land, 2010—. Mem. US-Japan Pvt. Sector/Govt. Commn., 2002. Presbyn. Fellow: American Bar Found.; mem.: AMA (pub. mem. bd. trustees 2008—), ABA (vice chmn. antitrust sect. bus. torts and unfair competition com. 2000—), American Bd. Trial Advocates, Fla. State Bar. Office: Trust for Public Land National Office 101 Montgomery St Ste 900 San Francisco CA 94104 *

KAY, MARK ALLAN, medical educator; BS in Phys. Sciences, Mich. State U., 1980; PhD in Develop. Genetics, Case Western Reserve U., 1986, MD, 1987. Diplomate Am. Bd. Pediat., Am. Bd. Med. Genetics in Clin. Biochemical Genetics and clin. genetics. Intern. resident, dept. pediat. Baylor Coll. Medicine, Houston, 1987—90, clin. fellow, med. genetics, 1990—93; acting asst. prof., dept. medicine U. Wash., 1993, asst. prof., dept medicine, investor. Molecular Medicine Ctr., 1993—94, adj. asst. prof., dept. pediat., 1994, adj. asst. prof., dept. biochemistry, 1995, adj. asst. prof., dept. pathology, 1995, assoc. prof. medicine with adjuncts in pediat., biochemistry and pathology, 1997—98; assoc. prof., dept. pediat. and genetics Stanford U. Sch. Medicine, 1998, dir., program in human gene therapy, 1998—, prof., dept. pediat. and genetics, 2001—. Invited spkr. in field; mem. scientific review bd. Nat. Gene Vector Lab., 1996—; ad-hoc reviewer NIH, 1997—2000; mem. scientific planning bd. German-Am. Frontiers of Sci. sponsored by Nat. Acad. Sci., 1997—98; NIH Study Sect. mem.-med. biochemistry, 2000—04; mem. com. on gene therapy for genetic diseases European Soc. for Gene Therapy, 2000—01; chair, organizing com. Gordon Conf. on Viral Vectors for Gene Therapy, 2003—04; co-founder, chief scientific advisor Avocel, 2003—. Mem. editl. bd. Gene Therapy, 1995—, Human Gene Therapy, 1995—, assoc. editor, 2000—, mem. editl. bd. Molecular Therapy, 1999—2003; contbr. several articles to profl. jours. Recipient Arthur F. Hughes Meml. award for Outstanding Rsch. in Develop. Biology, 1986, Upjohn Achievement award-Excellence in Clin. Pharmacology, 1987, Henry Christian award for Excellence in Rsch., Am. Fedn. for Clin. Rsch., 1992, Student award for best paper in category of post-doctoral-basic sciences, Am. Soc. Human Genetics, 1992, E. Mead Johnson award for Pediat. Researcher of the Yr., 2000, Nat. Hemophilia Found. Researcher of the Yr., 2000. Mem.: Am. Soc. for Clin. Investigation, Am. Soc. Microbiology, Am. Soc. Gene Therapy (bd. dirs. 1997—2000, founding bd. dirs. 1997—2000, chair. com. on genetic diseases 2001—03, v.p. 2003—04, pres.-elect 2004—05), Western Soc. for Clin. Investigation, AAAS, Am. Acad. Pediat., Am. Soc. Human Genetics, Japanese Soc. Inherited Metabolic Disease (hon.), Phi Kappa Phi. Office: Dept Pediat and Genetics Stanford U Sch Medicine 300 Pasteur Dr Rm G-305A Stanford CA 94305-5208 Office Phone: 650-498-6531. Office Fax: 650-498-6540. Business E-Mail: markay@stanford.edu.

KAY, STEPHEN, computer scientist, educator; b. Farnborough, England, Mar. 31, 1954; s. Thomas and Doreen Kay; m. Lindsey Ann Bate, June 10, 1978; children: Sarah Rachel, Laura Ruth. BSc, U. Stafford, Eng., 1976; MSc, U. Wales, 1981, PhD, 1995. Chartered engr., Brit. Computer Soc./Inst. Elec. Engrs., 1990. Rsch. assoc. Welsh Nat. Sch. Medicine, Cardiff, Wales, 1976—81; analyst/programmer U. Wales Coll. Medicine, Cardiff, 1982—87; lectr. dept. computer sci. U. Manchester, England, 1987—95, sr. lectr. computer sci., 1996—99; prof. health informatics U. Salford, England, 2000—. Dir. Salford Health Informatics Rsch. Environment, 2000—; coun. mem. U.K.Coun. Health Informatics Professions, 2005—; rsch. mem. senate U. Salford, 2005—; bd. mem. NHS Faculty of Health Informatics, 2006—. Contbr. articles to profl. jours.; mem. editl. bd., editor: Internat. Jour. Med. Informatics and the Internet in Medicine, 2006—. Grantee, Med. Rsch. Coun./Dept. Health, 1988—90, Sci. and Engring. Rsch. Coun., 1990—92, Dept. Health, 1992—94, 1995—97, Engring. and Physical Sci. Rsch. Coun., 1996—98, European Standardisation, 1998—2000, Sci. Rsch. Investment Fund, 2002—04, Nat. Health Svc., 2004—05, Econ. and Social Rsch. Coun., 2005—. Fellow: Am. Coll. Med. Informatics; mem.: Com. European Normalization (convenor of working group on info. models and messaging 2006—), Brit. Computer Soc. (sci. program conf. chair 2000—, coun. mem. 2002—05). Achievements include co-inventor of the clinical workstation prototype; European project team leader of the extended electronic health record architecture; established health informatics research at the university of Salford. Office: Salford Health Informatics Rsch Envi Univ Salford Blatchford Building Salford M6 6PU England Business E-Mail: s.kay@salford.ac.uk.

KAY, STEPHEN R., surgeon; b. Washington; MD, Cornell Med. Coll., NYC, 1978. Diplomate Am. Bd. Plastic Surgery, 1991. Plastic surgeon Chevy Chase Plastic Surgery, Md., 1986—; faculty George Washington U. Med. Sch. Pres. Nat. Capital Soc. Plastic Surgeons, Washington, 1995—96. Fellow: ACS; mem.: Am. Soc. Maxillofacial Surgeons, Am. Soc. Plastic Surgeons. Office: Stephen R Kay 5530 Wisconsin Ave #1510 Chevy Chase MD 20815

KAYA, KAAN, cardiologist; b. Turkey, Sept. 24, 1970; Degree, Ankara U., 2003. Cardiovasc. surgeon Kavaklidere Umut Hosp., Ankara, Turkey, 2003—11. Office: Buklum Sokak 72 Kavaklidere Dist Ankara 06500 Turkey Personal E-mail: drkaankaya@yahoo.com.

KAYA, OSKAY, physician, educator; b. Tekirdag, Turkey, Mar. 1, 1960; MD, Ankara U., 1984. Assoc. prof. gen. surgery Diskapi Yildirim Beyazit Tchg. and Rsch. Hosp., 2010—. Office: Diskapi Yildirim Beyazit Tchg & Rsch Hos Ankara Altindag 06010 Turkey E-mail: oskaykaya@yahoo.com.

KAYA, ZIYA, medical researcher; b. Gemerek, Turkey, Oct. 10, 1971; s. Kazim and Nursel Kaya; m. Özay Özkalp Kaya, Mar. 2, 2002. MD, U. Ulm, Germany, 1997. Resident cardiology U. Ulm, Germany,

1997—99; postdoc. fellow Johns Hopkins U., Balt., 1999—2001; resident cardiology U. Heidelberg, Germany, 2001—, rsch. group leader, 2001—. Recipient Young Investigators award, Johns Hopkins U., 2001; grantee, Deutsche Forschungs Gemeinschaft, 2003—05, 2006—, Deutsche Herzstiftung, 2004—, Ernst und Berta Grimmke Stiftung, 2006—; fellow, Deutsche Herzstiftung, 1999—2001. Office: U of Heidelberg Im Neuenheimer Feld 410 Baden-Württemberg Heidelberg 69120 Germany E-mail: ziya.kaya@med.uni-heidelberg.de.

KAYABASOGLU, FURKAN, gynecologist; b. Sakarya, Turkey, Sept. 25, 1978; Degree, Istanbul U., 2002. Physician, mgr. Kosuyolu Women Health Ctr., 2010—. Master: Turkish Minimal Invasive Gynecologic Surgery; mem.: Turkish Soc. Gynecology And Obstetrics, Turkish Soc. Gynecologic Endoscopy. Office: Kosuyolu Women Health Ctr Kadikoy Istanbul 34718 Turkey Office Fax: 0090 216 339 9002. E-mail: furkankayabasoglu@yahoo.com.

KAYA BICER, ELCIL, orthopedist; b. Jan. 1, 1980; MD, Hacettepe U., 2003; specialist in Orthopaedics, Ege U., 2010. Specialist under obligatory svc. Van Ipekyolu Pub. Hosp., 2010—. Mem.: Turkish Assn. Sports Traumatology, Arthroscopy & Knee Surgery. Avocations: skiing, rowing, dance. Office: Ipekyolu Cd Ipekyolu Pub H Van 65200 Turkey Personal E-mail: elcil@yahoo.com.

KAYAL, SAMER, physician, educator; b. Prague, Czech Republic, Dec. 1, 1961; MD, U. Lille, 1992; PhD, U. Paris Descartes, 1998. Prof. U. Rennes1, 2009—. Assoc. prof. U. Paris Descartes, 2001—09. Mem.: Am. Soc. Microbiology. Avocation: scuba diving. Office: CHU Pontchaillou 2 rue Henri le Guillou Rennes Bretagne 35000 France E-mail: kayal.samer@gmail.com.

KAYAMA, TAKAMASA, hospital administrator; b. 1950; Grad., Tohoku U., Japan, 1975. Lectr. Tohoku Univ.; asst. prof. Yamagata Uiv., prof.; dir. Yamagata Univ. Hosp.; dean Yamagata Univ.; chief dir. Nat. Cancer Ctr. Mem.: Min. Health, Labour & Welfare (Ctrl. Social Ins. Med. Coun.). Office: National Cancer Center 5-1-1 Tsukiji Chuo-ku Tokyo 104-0045 Japan also: National Cancer Center 6-5-1 Kashiwanoha Kashiwa Chiba 277-8577 Japan Office Phone: 81335422511. Business E-Mail: www-admin@ncc.go.jp. *

KAYE, ALAN DAVID, anesthesiologist, interventional pain practitioner, researcher; b. LI, NY, Mar. 21, 1962; s. Joel and Florence Susan (Feldman) K.; m. Kim Sutker, May 26, 1990; children: Aaron, Rachel. BS in Biology, U. Ariz., 1984, BS in Psychology, 1985, MD, 1989; PhD in Pharmacology, Tulane U., 1997. Diplomate Am. Bd. Anesthesiology, Nat. Bd. Med. Examiners, Am. Bd. Pain Medicine; lic. physician, La.; cert. ACLS. Intern Alton Ochsner Med. Found. and Clinic, New Orleans, 1989-90; resident in anesthesiology Mass. Gen. Hosp., Boston, 1990-91, Tulane Med. Ctr., New Orleans, 1991-93, asst. prof. anesthesiology/attending staff, 1993-97, assoc. prof., 1997-99, attending staff/vice med. dir. Greater New Orleans Surg. Ctr., 1995-97, med. dir., 1997-2000; chmn., prof. dept. of anesthesia Tex. Tech U. Med. Ctr., Lubbock, 1999—2005, prof. dept. pharmacology, 1999—2005; dir., anesthesia U. Hosp., 2005, charity, 2005; with Ochsner Hosp. Kenner, 2005 , North Shore Surgi Ctr., 2005 09; chair, dept. anesthesia LSU, 2005 , dir., pain svcs.; founder, program dir. Independent LSU Anesthesia Residency, 2008. Lectr. in field. Contbr. articles and abstracts to profl. jours., chpts. to books; mem. editl. adv. bd. OR Reports, 1997-2004; co-editor: Moderate & Deep Sedation, regional Anesthesia Understanding pain Leadership, mem. editl. bd. Current Drugs, Anesthesia News; editor: Current Opinion in Anesthology, 2007-09. Adv. bd. mem. Baselor; capt. U.S. Army Med. Res., 1990—, maj., 1997. Named Consumer Rsch. Outstanding Anesthesia Dr. USA, 2006-07, Outstanding Leader, LSU Anesthesia; named one of 500 Leaders Influence, 2001-, Best Drs. New Orleans, 2009; recipient Nat. Student Rsch. Forum 1st place Roche Labs. award for excellence in basic sci. rsch., 1992, Baxter Clin. Rsch. award of Excellence, 1999, Spl. Cert. in Pain, Am. Bd. Anesthesia, 2003; Ariz. Med. Assn. scholar, 1987-89, U. Utah Joshua Millbank Scholars Program scholar, 1987, E. Blois du Bois scholar, 1981-89; Tulane Sch. Medicine grantee, 1993-94, 94, 95—, 97—; Pain fellow Tex. Tech. U.-Lubbock, 2001-03, Man of Yr. 2009-, Super Doctors; named to Hall of Fame Tex. Tech. Anesthology, 2004, New Orleans Anesthology, 2007, Sahaano HS Hall of Fame, 2011. Fellow N.Y. Acad. Sci., Am. Physiol. Soc.; mem. Bd. Examiners in Anesthesia (nat. assoc.), Am. Soc. Anesthesiology (pres. 1992-93), Am. Heart Assn., Mass. Gen. Hosp. Anesthesia Alumni Assn., Soc. Critical Care Medicine, Soc. Cardiovascular Anesthesiologists, Internat. Anesthesia Rsch. Soc., La. Soc. Anesthesiologists, New Orleans Anesthesia Soc., Tulane Med. Ctr. Anesthesia Alumni Assn., Golden Key, Blue Key, Phi Beta Kappa, Phi Eta Sigma (pres. 1982-83, Baxter award of appreciation 1999), Mensa, A. Soc. Critical Care Anesthologists (keynote spkr. 2009). Home Phone: 504-715-0888; Office Phone: 504-568-2319, 504-568-2315. Personal E-mail: alankaye44@hotmail.com, akaye@isuhsc.edu.

KAYE, DONALD, internist, educator; b. NYC, Aug. 12, 1931; s. Morris and Rose (Hirschtritt) K.; m. Janet Miriam Sovitsky, June 26, 1955; children: Kenneth Marc, Karen Lynne, Kendra Beth, Keith Steven. AB, Yale, 1953; MD, NYU, 1957. Diplomate Am. Bd. Internal Medicine, Am. Bd. Infectious Disease. Intern N.Y. Hosp., 1957-58, resident, 1958-60, fellow infectious diseases, 1960—63, asso. attending physician, 1961-69; physician-in-chief Hosp. Med. Coll. Pa., 1969-95; instr. medicine Cornell U. Med. Coll., 1961-63, asst. prof., 1963-66, asso. prof., 1966-69; prof., chmn. dept. medicine Med. Coll. Pa., Phila., 1969-94, Med. Coll. Pa. and Hahnemann U. Sch. Medicine, 1994-95, prof., 1995-96, Allegheny U. of Health Scis., 1996-98, MCP Hahnemann Sch. Medicine, 1998—2002, Drexel U., Coll. Medicine, 2002—. Cons. Phila. VA Hosp., 1969-95; CEO, pres. Med. Coll. Hosp., 1991-94, Med. Coll. Pa. and Hahnemann U. Hosp. Sys., 1994-96, Allegheny U. Hosps., 1996-98, Allegheny Integrated Health Group, 1996-97, Allegheny U. Health Scis., 1998; revision com. U.S. Pharmacopeia, 1975-95; mem. VA Merit Rev. Bd. in Infectious Diseases, 1976-78; com. on infectious diseases Am. Bd. Internal Medicine, 1976-84, cons., 1984-86. Author: Urinary Tract Infection and Its Management, 1972, Infective Endocarditis, 1976, Fundamentals of Internal Medicine, 1983, Internal Medicine for Dentists, 1983, 2d edit., 1990, Endocarditis, 1984, Infective Endocarditis, 1992; mem. editorial bd. Aging: Immunology and Infectious Diseases, Gerontology: Med. Sci., 1987-98, Antimicrobial Agts. Chemotherapy, 1972-98, Clinical Infectious Diseases, 2001-; contbr. articles to med. jours. Recipient Disting. Tchg. award Lindback Found., 1972; NIH grantee, 1967-76, 82-96; Pharm. Industry grantee, 1965-96, Emilio Ribas medal for disting svc. Brazilian Soc. of Infectious Diseases, 1994, Disting. Achievement award N.Y. Hosp.-Cornell Med. Ctr. Alumni Coun., 1994, Solomon A. Berson Alumni Achievement award NYU Sch. Medicine, 1996, Strittmatter award Philadelphia County Med. Soc., 1997. Master ACP (gov. Ea. Pa. region 1983-88, pres. Pa. chpt. 1987); fellow Gerontol. Soc. Am., Infectious Disease Soc. Am. (Mentor award 2005); mem. AMA, Pa. Med. Soc. (alt. del to AMA 1991-92), Phila. County Med. Soc. (pres. 1991-92), Am. Soc. for Microbiology, Am. Fedn. for Clin. Rsch., Am. Soc. for Clin. Investigation, Assn. Am. Physicians, Am. Clin. and Climatol. Assn., Phi Beta Kappa, Alpha Omega Alpha, Sigma Xi. Home: 1535 Sweet Briar Rd Gladwyne PA 19035-1216 Personal E-mail: donjank@aol.com.

KAYE, GORDON ISRAEL, pathologist, educator, waste management consultant; b. NYC, Aug. 13, 1935; s. Oscar Swarz and Rebecca (Schachman) K.; m. Nancy Elizabeth Weber, June 4, 1956; children: Jacqueline Elizabeth, Vivienne Rebecca. AB, Columbia U., 1955, AM, 1957, PhD, 1961. From rsch. asst. cytology to dir. Columbia U., NYC, 1953—63, dir. F. Higginson Cabot Lab. Electron Microscopy, 1963—76; rsch. and tchg. asst. cytology Rockefeller Inst., NYC, 1957-58; from Alden March prof. to prof. emeritus Albany (N.Y.) Med. Coll., 1976—99, prof. emeritus pathology, 1999—; prof. biomed. sci. SUNY Sch. Pub. Health, 1986-99; pres., CEO Waste Reduction by Waste Reduction, Inc., Troy, NY, 1993-98, chmn., 1998—2007, exec. v.p., 2002—06, acting CEO, 2006—07, waste mgmt. cons., em conss., 2007—. Mem. seminar on creative process Wenner-Gren Found., 1964-65; cons. electron microscopy dept. pathology N.Y. VA Hosp., 1965—99; Raymond C. Truex Disting. lectr. Hahnemann U., 1987, adj. prof. anatomy, Med. Coll. Wis., 1982-85. Co-author: Key Facts in Histology, 1985, Histology. A Text and Atlas, 1995, 4th edit., 2003; co-author: (in German) Atlas der Histologie, 1995; co-author: Histology, nat. med. series rev. series, 1997; editor: Current Topics in Cellular Anatomy, 1981; assoc. editor The Anat. Reocrd, 1972—98, editl. reviewer Exptl. Eye Rsch., 1964, Cancer, 1972—2007, Investigative Ophthalmology, 1973—2006, Gastroenterology, 1969—2006, Jour. Morphology, 1999—2008. Trustee Palisades free Libr., 1965-71; mem. Citizens Adv. Com., Sparkill Palisades Fire Dist., 1968-69; pres. Palisades Free Libr., 1969-71; trustee Orangetown Pub. Libr., 1971-73, Friends of Chamber Music, Troy, N.Y., 1988—; mem. citizens adv. com. Title III Program, S. Orangetown Ctrl. Sch. Dist., 1972-75; chmn. N.Y. State Low Level Waste Group, 1986-95; trustee Rockland Country Day Sch., 1974-78. Recipient Charles Huebschman prize in zoology Columbia U., 1954, Career Scientist award Health Rsch. Coun. N.Y.C., 1963 72, Rsch. Career Devel. award Nat. Inst. Arthritis and Metabolic Diseases, NIH, USPHS, 1972-76, Tousimis prize in biology, 1984; Ford Found. scholar, 1951-55; NSF predoctoral fellow, 1955-56, Nat. Inst. Neurol. Diseases and Blindness predoctoral fellow, 1959-61 Mem.: EM Cons. Svc. (pres.), N.Y. Soc. Electron Microscopists (dir. 1964—67), Assn. Career Scientists Health Rsch. Coun., Harvey Soc., Am. Soc. Cell Biology, Am. Assn. Anatomists, Assn. Am. Med. Colls. (rep. coun. acad. socs. 1979—2002, mem. adminstrn. bd. CAS 1985—86), Assn. Anatomy Chmn. (pres. 1980—81), Arthur Purdy Stout Soc. Surg. Pathologists (hon.), Waquoit Bay Yacht Club, Sigma Xi. Achievements include research in disposal of radioactively labeled animal carcasses; patents for methods for treatment and disposal of regulated medical waste; patents in field. Office: EM Consultant Svc 212 Pinewoods Ave Troy NY 12180-7244 Home Phone: 518-273-0292; Office Phone: 518-369-6399. Business E-Mail: em1gkaye@aol.com.

KAYE, KENNETH MARC, physician, educator, scientist; b. NYC, Feb. 5, 1960, s. Donald and Janet Kaye, m. Elaine Tracy, Jul. 4, 1985, 3 children. AB summa cum laude, Harvard U., 1982, MD, 1986. Diplomate Am. Bd. Internal Medicine, also sub-bd. Infectious Disease. Resident in internal medicine Mass. Gen. Hosp., Boston, 1986-89; fellow in infectious disease Dana Farber Cancer Inst. Brigham & Women's Hosp., Beth Israel Hosp., Boston, 1989—91; assoc. physician Brigham & Women's Hosp., 1991—; instr. Harvard Med. Sch., Boston, 1991—95, asst. prof. medicine, 1995—2007, assoc. prof. medicine, 2007—. Contbr. articles to profl. jours. Recipient Edward H. Kass award for Clin. Excellence, Mass. Infectious Diseases Soc., 1991; Howard Hughes Med. Inst. postdoctoral fellow, 1991-92, Physician Scientist awardee NIH, 1992-97. Fellow ACP, IDSA; mem. AAAS, Am. Soc. Clin. Investigation, Phi Beta Kappa. Office: Brigham & Womens Hosp Divsn Infectious Diseases 75 Francis St Boston MA 02115-6106

KAYE, ROBIN D., pediatric radiologist, educator; MD, U. Colo. Health Scis. Ctr. Sch. Med. Lic. Pa. Resident diagnostic radiology Denver Children's Hosp., 1991, fellowship pediat. radiology, 1992; fellowship pediat. interventional radiology Children's Hosp. Pitts., 1992—93, asst. prof. radiology. Staff Pediat. Diagnostic Imaging, Milw. Contbr. articles to profl. jours.

KAYIGIL, ONDER, urologist, educator; b. Ankara, Turkey, Mar. 30, 1964; PhD, Ankara U. Med. Sch., 1987. Cert. assoc. prof. in urology Gazi U. Sch. Medicine, 1998. Urology resident Gazi U. Sch. Medicine, 1987—92; cons. urologist Türkish State and Rlwys. Hosp., 1992—2003, assoc. prof., 1998—2003; chief in 2nd urology clinic, assoc. prof. Atatürk Tng. and Rsch. Hosp., 2003—. Recipient Exptl. Animal Study 1st prize, Turkish Urologic Assn. Marmaris Meeting, 1996, Sedat Tellaloglu award, Turkish Urol. Assn. Antalya Meeting, 2008. Master: Ankara Urologic Assn.; mem.: Urologic Surgery Assn., European Soc. Sexual Medicine, European Urologic Assn., Türkish Urologic Assn. Achievements include development of double forced sling technique; the longitudinal imbrication technique in complex curvature patients. Avocations: violin, jogging, history, tennis, archaeology, bodybuilding. Home: 596 St 45/3 Ilkbahar Dist Ankara Cankaya 06550 Turkey Home Fax: 00903124426646. Personal E-mail: kayigilo@yahoo.com.tr.

KAYIRAN, SINAN MAHIR, pediatrician; b. Kahramanmaras, Feb. 19, 1970; MD, Istanbul U., 1994. Cert. pediatrician Baskent U., 2001. Pediatrician Meml. Hosp., 2002—07. Pediatrician Am. Hosp., 2007. Mem.: Turkish Nat. Pediat. Orgn. Avocations: reading, music. Office: Guzelbahce sk 20 Nisantasi Istanbul 34450 Turkey E-mail: sinanmahir@gmail.com.

KAYMEN, AMELIA, dermatologist; Graduate, Vassar Coll., Rush Univ. Med. Sch. Cert. Internal Med., Dermatology. With Dermatology Med. Group, San Francisco, 1989, ptnr., 1991—98; found., private practice dermatologist Presidio Dermatology, 2002—. Chief, dermatology divsn. Calif. Pacific Med. Ctr.; staff CPMC, UCSF; spkr. in field. Office: Presidio Dermatology 3905 Sacramento St No 303 San Francisco CA 94118 Office Fax: 415-933-8491, 415-933-8490.

KAYNAK, KAMIL, cardiothoracic surgeon, consultant; b. Manisa, Turkey, Aug. 23, 1962; s. Halil Behic and Sabiha Kaynak; m. Yildiz Titiz, Dec. 8, 1996; 1 child, Enis. MD, Istanbul U., Istanbul, Turkey, 1985. Resident thoracic and cardiovasc. surgery Istanbul U. Cerrahpasa Faculty Medicine, 1986—93, fellow, 1993—97, assoc. prof., 1997—2003, prof. and dir. thoracic surgery dept., 2001—. Pres. Rotary club, Istanbul Taksim, 1994—95. Fellow: European Bd. Thoracic and Cardiovasc. Surgery; mem.: Nat. Bd. Cardiothoracic Surgeons Turkish Health Ministry. Office: Istanbul U Cerrahpasa Med Sch Cerrahpasa Cd 34300 Istanbul Istanbul Turkey Office Fax: +90212 632 8474. E-mail: kamil@istanbul.edu.tr.

KAYNE, JON BARRY, industrial psychologist; b. Sioux City, Iowa, Oct. 20, 1943; s. Harry Aaron and Barbara Valentine (Daniel) Kayne; m. Bunee Ellen Price Kayne, July 25, 1965; children: Nika Jenine, Abraham; m. Sandra Kay Fossbender Kayne, Jan. 5, 1985; 1 child, Shay-Marie Kathryn. BA, U. Colo., 1973; MSW, U. Denver, 1975; PhD, U. Northern Colo., 1978. With spl. svcs. Weld County Sch. Dist. 6, Greeley, Colo., 1975—77; forensic diagnostician Jefferson County Diagnostic Unit, Colo., 1977—78; assoc., dir. mktg. 1 Dow Ctr.; assoc. prof. psychology Hillsdale Coll., Mich., 1978—87; pres. Jon B. Kayne, PC, Hillsdale, 1980—87; pres. bd. dirs. Lang. Learners Partnership Omaha, 1989—93; chmn. bd. dirs., CEO Am. Internat. Mgmt. Assocs. Ltd., Denver, 1984—87; prof. bus. adminstrn. & psychology Bellevue U., Nebr., 1987—, v.p. profl. & continuing edn. studies, 1987—93, v.p. acad. affairs, 1993. Candidate sheriff Boulder County, 1974; bd. dir. religious sch., Greeley, 1975—77; chmn. bd. dirs. Domestic Harmony, 1979—82. With USAR, 1962. Mem.: NY Acad. Scis., Mich. Soc. Investigative & Forensic Hypnosis (chmn. bd., pres. 1982), Internat. Neuropsychol. Soc., Am. Statis. Assn., Am. Soc. Clin. Hypnosis, Am. Psychol. Assn., Alpha Gamma Sigma, Psi Chi, Phi Delta Kappa. Office: Bellevue U 1000 Galvin Rd S Bellevue NE 68005-3098

KAZACHKOV, MIKHAIL, pediatric pulmonologist; b. Lenengrad, Russia, July 16, 1961; s. Yuriy Kazachkov and Elizabeth Kazachkova; m. Irina Sotnikova, Nov. 6, 1983; children: Andrey, Alexandra Kazachkova. MD, Pediatric Med. Inst., St. Petersburg, Russia, 1984. Lic. pediatrician, pediatric pulmonologist Am. Bd. of Pediat., 1998. Attending physician in pediat. City Hosp. of Kondopoga, Kondopoga, Russia, 1987—88; fellow in pediat. pulmonology State Inst. of Postgrad. Med. Edn., St. Petersburg, 1988—90; attending physician in pediat. pulmonology City Hosp. #19, St. Petersburg, Russia, 1992—94; resident in pediat. Albany Med. Ctr., NY, 1995—97; fellow in pediat. pulmonology U. N.C., Chapel Hill, 1997—2000, attending physician dept. pediats., divsn. pediat. pulmonology Maimonides Infants and Children's Hosp., Bklyn., 2000—. Reviewer: Chest jour., 2005—. Recipient Best Investigator award, Internat. Pediat. Pulmonology Assn., 2000, Thomas Boat Scholarship award, 1999. Fellow: Am. Coll. Chest Physicians. Achievements include research in lipid laden macrophages and respiratory symptoms; mycoplasma pneumonia infection in epithelial cells; gastroesophageal reflux and respiratory diseases. Office: Maimonides Infants and Children's Hospi 4802 10th Ave Brooklyn NY 11219 Office Fax: 718-635-6331. Personal E-mail: mkazachkov@maimonidesmed.org.

KAZAK, ILKAY, otolaryngologist; b. Torbali, Turkey, Nov. 26, 1972; MD, Free U., Berlin, 1999. Sr. physician Free U. Berlin, Charité Campus Benjamin Frankli, 2006—09; ENT specialist, plastic ops. HNO-Praxis, 2009—. Office: Innsbrucker Str 58 Berlin 10825 Germany Business E-Mail: ilkay.kazak@t-online.de.

KAZARYAN, AIRAZAT MISHIKOVICH, surgeon, researcher; b. Yerevan, Armenia, Nov. 27, 1977; s. Mishik Airazatovich Kazaryan and Arpik Ashotovna Asratyan. MD, PhD, Moscow Secondary Sch., 1994. Diplomate I.M.Sechenov Moscow (Russia) Med. Acad., 2001. Rsch. fellow Interventional Ctr., Rikshopitalet U. Hosp., Oslo, 1999—2000, rschr., 2007—; fellow, clin. resident Dept. Faculty Surgery Moscow Med. Acad., 2001—04, attending surgeon, sr. lab. asst. Dept. Faculty Surgery, 2004, attending surgeon Dept. Faculty Surgery, 2004—07, rsch. fellow, 2004—07. Cons. First Moscow Hospice, 2002—03, Am. Med. Ctr., Moscow, 2005—07. Contbr. Recipient award, Ministry Edn. Russian Fedn., 1999; scholar, Ministry Edn. Russian Fedn. and Adminstrn. Pres. Russian Fedn., 1999. Mem.: Russian Assn. Endoscopic Surgery, Soc. Laparoendoscopic Surgeons. Office: Rikshopitalet Univ Hosp Interventional Ctr Oslo 0027 Norway Business E-Mail: airazat.kazaryan@rikshospitalet.no.

KAZAZIAN, HAIG HAGOP, JR., pediatrician, researcher, educator; b. Toledo, July 30, 1937; s. Haig Hagop and Hermine Adriene (Papelian) K.; m. Lillian Agnes Cleaver, Oct. 13, 1962; children: Haig Hagop III, Sonya Elizabeth. AB, Dartmouth Coll., 1959; MD, Johns Hopkins U., 1962. Diplomate Am. Bd. Pediatrics, Am. Bd. Medical Genetics (pres. 2000). Asst. prof. pediatrics Johns Hopkins U., Balt., 1969-74, assoc. prof. pediatrics, 1974-77, prof. pediats., 1977-94, prof. biology, 1979-94, prof. ob-gyn., 1985-94, prof. medicine, 1989-94, dir. Ctr. Med. Genetics, 1989-94, Sutland prof. pediat. genetics, 1991-94; prof., chmn. dept. genetics U. Pa. Sch. Medicine, Phila., 1994—2006. Mem. mammalian genetics study sect. NIH, Bethesda, Md., 1981-85; pres. bd. dirs. Citizens for Good Govt., Balt., 1973-75; bd. dirs. Am. Bd. Med. Genetics. Author more than 350 sci. papers; editor jour. Human Mutation, 1992-2007. Sr. surgeon USPHS, 1966-68. Grantee NIH, 1968—; recipient Mead Johnson award Am. Acad. Pediatrics, 1976. Fellow Am. Acad. Arts & Scis. (mem.); mem. Inst. of Medicine, Am. Pediat. Soc., Am. Soc. Human Genetics (bd. dirs. 1982-85), Am. Soc. Clin. Investigation, Assn. Am. Physicians, Alpha Omega Alpha. Democrat. Episcopalian. Avocations: jogging, tennis, classical music. Office: U Pa Sch Medicine 475 Clinical Research Bldg 415 Curie Blvd Philadelphia PA 19104-4218

KAZDIN, ALAN E., psychology professor; b. Cin., Jan. 24, 1945; s. Leon Nathan Kazdin and Eva Edith Shapira; children: Nicole, Michelle. BA, San Jose State U., 1967; MA, Northwestern U., 1968, PhD, 1970. Diplomate Am. Bd. Profl. Psychology, Am. Bd. Assessment Psychology. Asst. prof. psychology Northwestern U., Evanston, Ill., 1971; from asst. prof. to assoc. prof. Pa. State U., University Park, 1971-77, prof. psychology, 1977-81; vis. prof. U. Pitts. Sch. Medicine, 1979-80, prof. psychiatry and psychology, 1981-89; program/rsch. dir. Children's Psychiat. Intensive Care Svc. Western Psychiat. Inst. and Clinic, 1981-89; dir. clin. tng. dept. psychology Yale U., New Haven,

1991-95, chmn. dept. psychology, 1997—2000; chmn. child study ctr. and dept. child psychiatry Yale U. Sch. Medicine, New Haven, 2000—. Author: Psychotherapy for Children and Adolescents: Directions for Research and Practice, 2000, The Encyclopedia of Psychology, Vols. 1-8, 2000, Behavior Modification in Applied Settings, 6th edit., 2001, The Kazdin Method for Parenting the Defiant Child, 2008; editor: (jours.) Behavior Therapy, 1979-83, Jour. Consulting and Clin. Psychology, 1985-90, Psychol. Assessment, 1989-91, Clin. Psychology: Sci. and Practice, 1994-98, Current Directions in Psychol. Sci., 1999-2004. Recipient Nat. Inst. Mental Health MERIT Award, 1987, award for disting. profl. contbn. to clin. child psychology divsn. 12 APA, 1995, Outstanding Rsch. Contbn. by an Individual award Assn. for Advancement of Behavior Therapy, 1998, Disting. Scientist award Soc. for Sci. of Clin. Psychology, divsn. 12 APA, 1999, Outstanding Lifetime Contribution award, APA, 2009; fellow Ctr. for Advanced Study in Behavioral Scis., 1976-77; grantee Leon Lowenstein Found., Nat. Inst. Mental Health, State of Conn., Dept. Social Svcs., Behavioral Mental Health Outcomes of Psychotherapy for Children and Adolescents. Mem.: APA (pres. elect 2007, pres. 2008, James McKean Cuttell award 2010). Office: Dept Psychology Yale Univ PO Box 208205 New Haven CT 06520-8205

KAZLOW, PHILIP, pediatric gastroenterologist, educator; BA, Yeshiva U., 1976; MD, Mt. Sinai Sch. of Medicine, 1980. Diplomate Am. Bd. Pediatrics-pediatric gastroenterology, Am. Bd. Pediatrics. Resident in pediat. Mt. Sinai Med. Ctr., NY, 1981—83, chief resident dept. of pediat. NY, 1983—84, fellow in pediatric gastroenterology NY, 1984—86; clin. prof. in pediat. Columbia Univ. Med. Ctr. Co-author: (publs.) Percutaneous endoscopic gastrostomies in children, 1986, Identical twins concordant for Crohn's disease, 1986, Eikenella corrodens: a rare pathogen in a polymicrobial hepatic abscess in an adolescent, 1999, Celiac Disease in Children with Normal Weight and Overweight: Clinical Features and Growth Outcomes Following a Gluten-Free Diet, 2011, numerous publs. Fellow Cystic Fibrosis Clinical Fellow, 1985—86. Office: Columbia University Medical Center 630 West 168th St New York NY 10032

KAZUHIKO, NATORI, medical educator; b. Tokyo, May 10, 1963; MD, Toho U., 1995, MD in Philosophy, 2005. Assoc. prof. Toho U. Med. Ctr. Oomori Hosp., 2008—. Avocation: mountain climbing. Office: 6-1-1 Oomorinishi Oota Tokyo 143-8541 Japan Office Fax: 81 03 3763 8298. Business E-Mail: natori@med.toho-u.ac.jp.

KAZUMI, MASUDA, exercise physiologist; b. Toyama-city, Japan, Aug. 1970; PhD, U. Tsukuba, 1989—99. Rsch. assoc. U. of Tsukuba, Japan, 1999—2002; assoc. prof. Kanazawa U., Japan, 2003—. Office: Kanazawa Univ Faculty Human Scis Kakuma-machi Kanazawa-city 920-1192 Japan Office Fax: +81-76-234-4117. Business E-Mail: masuda@ed.kanazawa-u.ac.jp.

KAZUMI, SANO, pharmacologist, educator; b. Tokyo, July 1, 1959; PhD, Kitasato U., 1982. Lectr., rschr. Meiji Pharm. U., 1982. Mem.: Japanese Soc. Study Xenobiotics, Japanese Cancer Assn. Avocation: gardening. Office: 5-522-8 Noshio Kiyose Tokyo 204-8588 Japan

KAZUO, HAYAKAWA, epidemiologist, nursing educator; b. Kariya, Aichi-Ken, Japan, Nov. 25, 1951; PhD, Kinki U., Osaka, Japan, 1979. RN Ministry Health and Welfare, Japan, 1975. Assoc. prof. Kinki U., 1982—94. Editor of sci. jours. Planning rsch. activity Japan Soc. Nursing Rsch., Chiba City, Chiba-Ken, Japan, 1989—2006. Grant, Ministry Sci. and Edn., Japan, 2008. Fellow: Japan Soc. Nursing Rsch. (Young Rschr. award 1982). Office: Osaka Univ 1-7 Yamadaoka Suita City Osaka-Fu 565-0871 Japan Office Fax: 06-6879-2550. Business E-Mail: hayakawa@sahs.med.osaka-u.ac.jp.

KAZUO, YAO, otolaryngologist; b. Tokyo, Jan. 1, 1949; MD, Kitasato U., 1976. Vis. prof. Kitasato U., Sch. Medicine, 2005; chair person dept. otorhinolaryngology Kanagawa Dental Coll., 2005. Mem.: Japan Soc. Immunology & Allergology Otorinolaryngology, Japanese Soc. Stomato-pharyngology, Japanese Soc. Allergology, Japan Rhinology Soc., Otorhinolaryngology Japan. Avocation: coin collecting/numismatics. Office: 3-31-6 Tsuruya-cho Kanagawa-ku Yokohama 221-0835 Japan Office Fax: 81-45-313-0027. Business E-Mail: ytaokazuo@kdcnet.ac.jp.

KAZUSHI, OKAMOTO, epidemiologist, researcher; MD, Aichi Med. U., Japan, 1981, PhD, 1987. Asst. prof. Aichii Prefectura Coll. of Nursing and Health, Nagoya, Japan, 1995—2001, prof., 2003—, dir. epidemiology rsch. Achievements include research in Clarification of risk factor for subarachnoid hemorrhage using case-control study; Clarification factors associated with the development of dementia using nested case-control study. Office: Aichi Prefectural Coll Nursing and Healt Togoku Kamishidami Moriyama-ku Nagoya 463-8502 Japan Office Fax: +81-52-736-1401; Home Fax: +81-52-753-2010. E-mail: okamoto@aichi-nurs.ac.jp.

KAZUYA, TANIMURA, physician; b. Hyogo, Japan, Aug. 27, 1981; MD, Kyoto U., 2006. Physician Dept. Respiratory Medicine, Takatsuki Red Cross Hosp., 2006. Office: Abuno 1-1-1 Takatsuki City Osaka 569-1096 Japan Office Phone: 072-696-0571. E-mail: tanigue1981@yahoo.co.jp.

KE, YUNBO, medical educator, researcher; b. Hubei, China, Aug. 18, 1960; s. Yuchao Ke and Shiying Qi; m. Grace X. Peng, Mar. 5, 1987; children: Joyce W., Andrew. PhD, Ohio State U., Columbus, 1995. Postdoc. fellow, rsch. assoc. U. Chgo., 1995—98; rsch. assoc., asst. prof. U. Ill., Chgo., 1998—, rsch. asst. prof., 2003—08. Contbr. scientific papers. Rsch. grant, NIH, 1999—2002. Achievements include discovery of signal transduction pathway and a novel molecular mechanism involving p21 activated kinase-1 that regulate mammalian heart rate and other functions. Home: 1513 W Polk St Chicago IL 60607 Office: Univ Ill Chgo 909 S Wolcott Ave Chicago IL 60612 Office Fax: 312-996-1414. Business E-Mail: yke@uic.edu.

KEALY, WILLIAM FRANCIS, cytologist, histopathologist; b. Dublin, July 27, 1940; s. John Laurence Kealy and Annie Finlay; m. Mary Olivia Howley, Sept. 4, 1974; children: David, Ruth, Brendan, John. B Medicine B Surgery, BAO, Univ. Coll., Dublin, 1964, MD, 1976. Cert. Med. Coun. Ireland. Intern Mater Hosp., Dublin, 1964—65, registrar, 1966—70; sr. house officer City Hosp., Belfast, Northern Ireland, 1965—66; registrar King's Coll. Hosp., London, 1970—72; sr. registrar King's Coll. Hosp./Kingston Hosp., London, 1972—75; cons. histopathologist/cytopathologist Kingston Hosp., London, 1975—79, Univ. Hosp., Cork, Ireland, 1979—, chmn. divsn. pathology, 1996—2001, rotational head dept. histopathology, 1996—99. Contbr. articles to med. jours. Grantee, S.W. Thames Regional Health Authority, London, 1973. Fellow: Royal Coll. Pathology; mem.: Internat. Acad. Pathology, Irish Assn. Clin. Cytology (sec. 1987—91), Assn. Clin. Pathologists (pres. Irish br. 1998—2001). Avocations: reading, music, angling, cinema, theater. Office: Univ Hosp Dept Pathology Cork Ireland E-mail: kealy@shb.ie.

KEAM, BHUMSUK, physician, researcher; b. Seoul, Republic Of Korea, Apr. 26, 1977; married. MD, Seoul Nat. U., 2002. Lic. in med. Min. Health and Welfare, Korea, 2002. Rschr. Seoul Nat. U. Hosp., 2002—; pub. health physician Korean Nat. Inst. Health, Seoul, 2008—. Recipient Young Investigator award, Asian Pacific Cancer Conf., 2005. Mem.: Korean Soc. Hospice and Palliative Care, Korean Cancer Study Group, Korean Assn. Clin. Oncology, European Soc. Med. Oncology, Am. Soc. Clin. Oncology. Office: Seoul Nat Univ Hosp 28 Yongon-dong Chongno-gu Seoul 110-740 Republic of Korea Personal E-mail: bhumsuk@hanmail.net. E-mail: bhumsuk@medimail.co.kr.

KEAN, THOMAS HOWARD, retired academic administrator, former Governor of New Jersey; b. NYC, Apr. 21, 1935; s. Robert W. and Elizabeth (Stuyvesant) Kean; m. Deborah Bye; children: Thomas Jr., Reed, Alexandra. AB, Princeton U., NJ, 1957; MA, Columbia U. Tchrs. Coll., NYC, 1963; LLD (hon.), Dartmouth Coll., Hanover, NH, 2005. Mem. NJ Gen. Assembly, 1967-77, asst. majority leader, 1970—71, majority leader, 1971—72, spkr., 1972—74, minority leader, 1974; acting gov. State of NJ, Trenton, 1973, gov., 1982—89; pres. Drew U., Madison, NJ, 1990—2005, ret., 2005. Bd. trustees Robert Wood Johnson Found., 1990—, chmn. bd. trustees, 2005—; bd. dirs. Hess Corp., 1990—, UnitedHealth Group, 1993—, Aramark Ltd., 1994—, Franklin Resources Inc., 2003—, Pepsi Bottling Group, 1999—2007, CIT Group Inc., 1999—2007; gen. ptnr. Quad Partners, NYC, 2000—; chmn. Nat. Commn. Terrorist Attacks Upon US (The 9-11 Commn.), 2002—04. Author: The Politics of Inclusion, 1988; co-author (with Lee H. Hamilton): Without Precedent: The Inside Story of the 9/11 Commission, 2006. Bd. dirs. World Wildlife Fund/Conservation Found. Served in 50th Armored Divsn. US Army. Recipient Pub. Svc. award, Rutgers U., NJ, 2006. Fellow: Am. Acad. Arts & Scis.; mem.: NJ Audubon Soc., NJ Hist. Soc., Alpha Phi Omega. Republican. Episcopalian. Office: Quad Partners 21 Penn Plaza Ste 1501 New York NY 10001 also: RWJ Found PO Box 2316 Rte 1 & College Rd E Princeton NJ 08543 *

KEANE, WILLIAM M., otolaryngologist; MD, Harvard U., 1970. Diplomate Am. Bd. Otolaryngology. Intern Univ. of Rochester Medicine & Dentistry, NY, Strong Meml. Hosp., Rochester, NY; resident Hosp. of Univ. of Pa.; chief otolaryngology dept.-head and neck surgery Thomas Jefferson Univ. Hosp., physician Meth. Hosp. divsn. Named one of the Top Docs, Phila. Mag., 2010—11. Office: Jefferson University Hospitals 925 Chestnut St 6th Fl Philadelphia PA 19107 Office Phone: 215-955-6760. Office Fax: 215-503-3736.

KEARNEY, THOMAS J., surgeon, educator; MD, Georgetown U., 1984. Diplomate Am. Bd. Surgery. Intern Univ. Southern Calif. Med. Ctr.; resident in surgery Cedar Sinai Med. Ctr., 1988—92; fellow in surgical oncology Univ. Chgo. Hosps., 1992—95; assoc. prof. surgery Univ. Medicine and Dentistry in NJ; physician Robert Wood Johnson Univ. Hosp. Office: Robert Wood Johnson University Hospital 195 Little Albany St New Brunswick NJ 08903 Office Phone: 732-235-8524. Office Fax: 732-235-8098.

KEARNEY-NUNNERY, ROSE, nursing administrator, educator, consultant; b. Glen Falls, NY, July 8, 1951; d. James J. and Helen F. (Oprandy) K.; m. Jimmie E. Nunnery (dec.). BS, Keuka Coll., 1973; M of Nursing, U. Fla., 1976, PhD, 1987. Asst. prof. La. State U. Med. Ctr., New Orleans, 1976-87; project coord., indigent health care U. Fla., Gainesville, 1984-85; asst. prof. U. South Fla., Tampa, 1987-88; dir. nursing programs SUNY, New Paltz, NY, 1988-94; project dir. MS in gerontol. nursing advanced nursing edn. grant U.S. Health Resources and Svc. Adminstrn. Div. Nursing, 1992-94; head nursing dept. Tech. Coll. of the Low Country, Beaufort, SC, 1995-97, v.p. acad. affairs, 1997—2005, cons., adj. instr., 2005—08, interim v.p. acad. affairs, 2007; dean Coll. Nursing South U., 2009—10; adj. prof. Armsstong Alantic State U., 2010. Author: Advancing Your Profession Concepts for Profl. Nursing, 4th edit., 2008, Making the Transition from LPN to RN, 2010. Bd. dirs. Beaufort Co. First Steps, 2000-01; Ulster County unit Am. Cancer Soc., 1991-94; nursing edn. com., 1990-92; bd. dir. Mid-Hudson Consortium for Advancement Edn. for Health Profl., 1988-94; nursing edn. com., 1988-92; scholarship com., 1989-93; com. chmn., 1990-93, treas., 1992-94; prof. devel. program SUNY, Albany, 1989-92; adv. coun. Ulster CC, 1989-94; adv. regional planning group for early intervention svc. United Cerebral Palsy Ulster County Inc., Children's Rehab. Ctr., 1989-91; mem. Ulster County adv. com. Office for Aging, 1991-94; state del. S.C. Conf. on Aging, 1995; bd. dir. Beaufort County Coun. on Aging, 1995; cmty. adv. bd. Hilton Head Med. Ctr. and Clinics, 1996-2000; mem. SC Bd. Nursing, 2000—, pres. 2001-03; accreditation evaluator So. Assn. Coll. and Sch. Commn. on Coll., 2000-05. Mem. ANA, Nat. League Nursing, S.C. Nurses Assn. (editl. bd. 1994-99, chair 1996-99), Nat. Coun. State Bds. of Nursing (mem. practice, regulation and edn. com. 2001-05, area III dir. 2005-07, chair Nodel Act & Rules Comm., 2010-), Sigma Theta Tau. Roman Catholic. Home: 80 Peninsula Dr Hilton Head Island SC 29926-1119 Personal E-mail: rosekn@hargray.com.

KEATHLEY, WAYNE E., hospital administrator; b. 1950; married; 2 children. BS in Healthcare Adminstrn., Wayne State U., Detroit; M in Healthcare Adminstrn., Columbia U., NYC. Adminstrv. positions Mt. Auburn Hosp., Cambridge, Mass., Luth. Med. Ctr., Bklyn.; various positions including dir. profl. svcs. Bklyn. Hosp. Ctr., 1981—91; v.p. ops. Lenox Hill Hosp., NYC, 1991—2000; exec. v.p., COO St. Peter's Health Care Svcs., Albany, NY, 2000—03; COO Mt. Sinai Hosp., 2003—, pres., 2008—; exec. v.p. bus. devel. Mt. Sinai Med. Ctr., Inc., 2008—. Office: Mt Sinai Med Ctr Inc 1 Gustave L Levy Pl New York NY 10029 Office Phone: 212-241-6403. Business E-Mail: wayne.keathley@mtsinai.org.

KEATING, DOMINIC T., physician; b. Tipperary, Ireland, Feb. 22, 1971; MB, BAO, NUI Galway, BCh, 1995; MD, 2007. Cons. physician, 2007—. Master: Royal Coll. Physicians Ireland; fellow: Royal Australasian Coll. Physicians. Avocations: sports, golf. Office: Alfred Hosp Commercial Rd Prahan Melbourne Victoria 3004 Australia Business E-Mail: d.keating@alfred.org.au.

KEATING, THOMAS PATRICK, health care administrator, educator; s. Thomas Wilbur and Margaret (Gahllagher) K.; m. Carolyn Elizabeth Kraft, Sept. 4, 1976; children: Jerrod Patrick, Kerri Ann, Zane, Kriste, Marite. BS in Bus., Cleve. State U., 1971; MS in Bus., U. Toledo, 1973. Cert. health care exec., prof. human resources, 2011, NC State U., Raleigh, 1981; lic. in long-term care adminstrn. SC, 1985. Asst. dir. facilities U. Kans. Med. Ctr., Kansas City, 1977-80; dir. mgmt. svcs. Charleston (S.C.) County Park and Recreation Commn., 1980-84; adminstr. Children's Health Sys., Med. U. of S.C., Charleston, 1984-2001, instr., 1987-2001, preceptor adminstrv. residency, master health svcs. adminstrn., 1990-93; asst. supt. Bibb County Schs., 2001—03, tchr. recruiter, 2003—08; with Womack Army Cmty. Hosp., 1974—76, 5th Combat Support Hosp. MUST, 1976—77, 325th Gen. Hosp., 1978—80, 3271st US Army Hosp., 1980—82, US Army Command & Gen. Staff Coll., 1985—91, Acad. Health Scis., USA, 1991—94. Adj. instr. Cen. Mich. U., Mt. Pleasant, 1979—, Rockhurst Coll., Kansas City, 1979-80, Kansas City (Kans.) Cmty. Jr. Coll., 1978-80, Fayetteville (N.C.) Tech. Inst., 1974-75; accredited cons. SBA, Charleston, 1980-91; adj. prof. Webster U., St. Louis, 1982-2000, faculty U. Ala., New Coll., 1974; nursing home cons. Charleston County Mental Retardation Bd., Charleston, 1987-88; vol. Appalachian Tech. Coll., 2003—06. Contbr. articles to profl. jours. Vol. Driftwood Health Care Ctr., Charleston, 1981-83. Capt. US Army, 1973-77, with, 1978-94, lt. col. USAR ret. Recipient Outstanding Young Men of America, Marriott Svc. Excellence Award. Fellow Am. Coll. Health Care Execs., Am. Acad. Med. Adminstrs.; mem. Toastmasters (CTM adminstrv. v.p. 1985-86), Sigma Phi Epsilon (com. chmn. 1970-71), Alpha Kappa Psi (com. chmn. 1972-73). Roman Catholic. Avocations: writing, exercise, gardening, history. Home: 1223 Shadowood Dr Spartanburg SC 29301

KEBEDE, KEBRET THEODORE, orthopedic surgeon, professor; s. Kebede Bahta and Wudie Gebre Medhin; m. Ethiopia N. Asmerom, Apr. 24, 1995; children: David Alexander Alula Kebret, Mara Ruth Kebret. MD, Aristotle U., Greece, 1985. Cert. orthopedic surgeon Gen. Med. Coun., London, UK, 1992. Dir. Coll. So. Nev., 2004—05, instr.; prof. Nev. State Coll., Henderson, 2005—. Orthop. surgeon U. Glasgow, 1995—96. Contbr. scientific papers. Physician Inernat. Spartathlon Com., Athens, Greece, 1995; med. mission Christian Med. Dental Soc., 2007; sec. Nev. State Coll. Faculty Senate, 2006—07; vice chair Nev. State Coll, 2007—08. Lt. col. Airborne M.C. Ethiopian Army, 1988. Recipient Gold medal, H.I.M. Haile Sellasie I Ethiopia, 1974, King Solomon Silver Trophy, 1974, Silver Medal, 1974, Gold Trophy, Harar Acad., 1973, Sword of honor, Mil. Med. Doctors Sch.-Commdg. Gen., 1985, AST Top Program Dir. award; nominee Regents award. Mem.: Assn. Surgeons Gt. Britain & Ireland, Gen. Med. Coun., Internat. Soc. Laser Surgery, Am. Assn. Anatomists, Human Anatomy Physiology Soc., World Med. Assn., Internat. Acad. Orthop. Medicine. Non-Partisan. Christian Ch. Achievements include research in cemented vs uncemented arthroplasties, total joint replacement-training residents. Avocations: hiking, racquetball, horseback riding, reading. Office: Nev State Coll 1125 Nev State Dr Henderson NV 89002 Office Phone: 702-992-2614. Home Fax: 702-361-8870. Personal E-mail: drkebede@doctors.net.uk. Business E-Mail: kebret.kebede@nsc.nevada.edu.

KECELI OZCAN, SEMA ASKIN, medical educator; b. Kütahya, Oct. 25, 1966; MD, Marmara U., 1991; PhD, U. London, 1997. Assoc. prof. Kocaeli U. Med. Faculty Dept. Microbiology, 2000—. Mem.: European Clin. Microbiology and Infectious Diseases, Turkish Med. Microbiology Assn. Office: Kocaeli University Med Faculty Dept Microbiology Kocaeli 41380 Turkey Office Fax: 00902623037001. E-mail: keceliozcan@yahoo.com.

KECHIJIAN, PAUL, retired dermatologist, educator; b. Providence, Mar. 17, 1940; s. Harry Maderos and Annette (Rhia) Paré; m. Janice Ann Kechijian, July 31, 1976; children: Douglas Paul, Lisa Ann. AB in Psychology, Brown U., 1961, ScM in Biology, 1964; MD, Albany Med. Coll., 1968. Lic. Nat. Bd. Med. Examiners, N.Y. State Med. Lic.; diplomate Am. Bd. Dermatology, diplomate Dermatopathology Am. Bds. of Dermatology and Pathology. Med. intern, med. resident Barnes Hosp., St. Louis, 1968-69, 69-70; dermatology resident Mass. Gen. Hosp., Boston, 1970, U. Miami (Fla.) Sch. of Medicine, 1973-75; dermatopathology fellow NYU Med. Ctr., NYC, 1975-76; instr. clin. dermatology NYU Sch. of Medicine, NYC, 1975-78, clin. asst. prof. dermatology, 1978-84, clin. assoc. prof., 1984—2002; asst. attending physician to assoc. attending physician Bellevue Hosp., 1976—2002, NYU Med. Ctr., 1976—2002; asst. attending dermatologist to sr. asst. North Shore U. Hosp., 1978—2002, hon. mem., 2002—. Chief inpatient dermatology svc. Bellevue Hosp., 1976—86; cons. Holy Martyrs Armenian Day Sch., 1976—; hon. surgeon in dermatology N.Y.C. Police Dept., 1981—2011; chief nail sect. NYU Med. Ctr., 1983—2002; presenter and lectr. in field. Contbg. editor: Jour. Dermatologic Surgery and Oncology, 1983-85; contbr. reports and articles to profl. jours. and chpt. to books. Fellow ACP, Am. Acad. Dermatology (com. on evaluation 1980-84, coun. on govtl. liaison key contact program 1986—96), Am. Soc. Dermatopathology; mem. AMA, N.Y. Acad. Scis., Dermatology Found., Soc. for Investigative Dermatology, Nassau County Med. Soc., L.I. Dermatol. Soc., others. Personal E-mail: pkech1@verizon.net.

KECK, PAUL E., JR., psychiatrist; b. Pitts., July 22, 1957; s. Paul Edgar and Shirley (Painter) K.; m. Susan Lynn McElroy; children: Timothy Daniel, Jason Samuel. AB, Dartmouth Coll., 1979; MD, Mt. Sinai Sch. Medicine, 1983. Intern internal medicine Beth Israel Med. Ctr., NYC, 1983-84; psychiat. resident McLean Hosp., Belmont, Mass., 1984-87, asst. psychiatrist, 1987-89; instr. in psychiatry Harvard Med. Sch., Boston, 1987-89, asst. prof. of psychiatry, 1989-91; assoc. prof. U. Cin. Coll. Medicine, 1991—2006, Lindner prof., 2006—, vice-chmn. rsch., 1997—2006, co-dir. biol. psyc. program, 1991—; dir. GCRC, Cin. VA Med. Ctr., 2004—06; pres., CEO, Lindner Ctr. of Hope, Mason, Ohio, 2006—. Asst. dir. Sleep Research Lab., McLean Hosp., Belmont, 1989-90. Contbr. 350 articles to profl. publs. Research grantee Nat. Inst. Arthritis Metabolism, 1982, Mass. Charitable Soc.; fellowship Tucker Found., 1983, Scottish Rite Schizophrenia Program, 1987, Stanley Found., 1994—, NIDA, 1995—, NIMH, 1994—, Am. Diabetes Assn. Fellow Soc. Biol. Psychiatry (disting.); mem. AAAS, Am. Psychiat. Assn., Collegium Internat. Psychopharmacologicum, MY Acad. Sci., Am. Coll. Physician Execs., Internat. Copernicus Scientists. Office: 1 Cin Coll Medicine Dept Psychiatry 231 Albert Sabin Way ML 559 Cincinnati OH 45267-0559 E-mail: paul.keck@uc.edu.

KEDES, LAURENCE HERBERT, biochemistry professor, physician, researcher; b. Hartford, Conn., July 19, 1937; s. Sammuel Ely and Rosalyn (Epstein) K.; m. Shirley Beck, June 15, 1958; children: Dean Hamilton, Maureen Jennifer, Todd Russell. Student, Wesleyan U., 1955-58; BS with distinction, Stanford U., 1961, MD, 1962; BS (hon.), Wesleyan U., Middletown, CT, 2009. Intern Presbyn. U. Hosp., Pitts., 1962-63, asst. resident, 1963-64; rsch. assoc. lab. biochemistry Nat. Cancer Inst. Peterson, 1964-66; sr. asst. med. resident Peter Bent Brigham Hosp., Boston, 1966-67; surgeon USPHS, 1964-66; postdoctoral fellow dept. biology MIT, 1967-68; jr. assoc. in medicine and hematology assoc. Peter Bent Brigham Hosp., Boston, 1967-69; rsch. trainee in embryology Marine Biol. Lab., Woods Hole, Mass., 1969; instr. biology MIT, Boston, 1969-70; asst., assoc. then prof. medicine Stanford U., 1970-89, dir. admissions med. sch., 1978-81; William M. Keck prof. biochemistry and medicine U. So. Calif. Keck Sch. Medicine, LA, 1989—2009, dir. Inst. Genetic Medicine, 1989—2008, chair biochemistry, 1989—2002; William M. Keck prof. emeritus biochemistry and medicine U. So. Calif. Keck Sch. Medicine, 1989—2002; vis. prof. biological chemistry, Geffen School of Medicine at UCLA, 2009—. Staff physician VA, 1970-92; vis. scientist Lab. Molecular Embryology, Naples, Italy, 1969-70, Dept. Animal Genetics, U. Edinburgh, 1970, Imperial Cancer Rsch. Fund, London, 1976-77; instr. embryology Marine Biol. Lab., Woods Hole, 1976; investigator Howard Hughes Med. Inst., 1974-82; founder, dir. IntelliCorp., Mountain View, Calif., 1980-90, chmn., 1982-86. Mem. editorial bd. Jour. Biol. Chemistry, 1982-88, Molecular and Cellular Biology, 1982-89, Jour. Applied Molecular Biology, 1982-85, Oxford Surveys on Eukaryotic Genes, 1983-94, Trends in Genetics, 1984-88; assoc. editor Jour. Molecular Evolution, 1982-90; cons. editor Circulation Rsch., 1994-99. Mem. fellowship award com. Am. Cancer Soc., 1978-81; co-principle investigator BIONET, 1984-89; mem. rsch. com. Am. Heart Assn., 1987; mem. sci. adv. bd. Muscular Dystrophy Assn., 1988-93, chair, Massry Prize Selection Com, 1999- Fellow Med. Found. Boston, 1967-69, John Simon Guggenheim Found. fellow, 1976-77; Leukemia Soc. Am. scholar, 1969-74, 1994 Mem. Western Soc. for Clin. Rsch., Am. Soc. Clin. Investigation, Assn. Am. Psysicians, Am. Soc. Microbiology, Am. Soc. Biochemistry and Molecular Biology, Internat. Soc. Devel. Biology, Alpha Omega Alpha. Office: 2234 Chislehurst Dr Los Angeles CA 90027 Office Phone: 323-442-1144. Business E-Mail: kedes@usc.edu.

KEE, KEHKOOI, medical educator; b. Sitiawan, Malaysia, May 5, 1973; PhD, Weill Cornell Med. Coll., 2003. Prof. Tsinghua U., 2010— Office: Rm B106 Med Sci Bldg Beijing 100084 China Business E-Mail: kkee@tsinghua.edu.cn.

KEEFER, LARRY KAY, medical researcher; b. Akron, Ohio, Oct. 28, 1939; s. Wesley Orville and Harriet Jane (Earhart) K.; m. Julie Ann Klestadt, June 24, 1962; children: Steven Howard, Simona Nicole. AB in Chemistry cum laude, Oberlin Coll., 1961; PhD in Organic Chemistry, U. NH, 1965. Asst. prof. oncology Chgo. Med. Sch., 1965-68, asst. prof. biochemistry U. Nebr. Med. Sch., Omaha, 1968-71, NIH spl. postdoctoral fellow Nat. Cancer Inst., NIH, Bethesda, 1971-72, sr. staff fellow, 1972-74, head analytical chemistry sect., 1974-83, chief Chemistry Sect. Frederick, Md., 1983—, chief Lab. of Comparative Carcinogenesis, Ctr. Cancer Rsch., 1997—. Editl. adv. bd. Nitric Oxide Biology and Chemistry, 1997—. Mem. AAAS, Am. Chem. Soc., Am. Assn. Cancer Rsch. Achievements include discovery of and patents on compositions incorporating the nitric oxide-releasing diazeniumdiolate functional group, compositions useful for studying the physiological and pathophysiological effects of nitric oxide's critical bioregulatory actions; research the unique chemical properties of these compositions for a variety of possible clinical advances. Office. Nat Cancer Inst at Frederick Lab Comparative Carcinogenesis PO Box B Bldg 538 Rm 205F Frederick MD 21702-1201 Office Phone: 301-846-1467. Office Fax: 301-846-5946. E-mail: keefer@ncifcrf.gov. *

KEEFFE, EMMET BRITTON, medical educator; b. San Francisco, Apr. 12, 1942; s. Emmet Britton and Corinne M. (Walsh) K.; m. Melenie M. Laskey, June 18, 1966; children: Emmet III, Brian, Meghan. BS, U. San Francisco, 1964, secondary teaching credential, 1965; MD, Creighton U., 1969. Intern Oreg. Health Sci. U., Portland, 1969-70, resident, 1970-73, fellow gastroenterology, 1973-74, asst. prof. medicine, 1979-83, assoc. prof. medicine, 1983-89, prof. med., 1989-92; fellow gastroenterology U. Calif., San Francisco, 1977-79, clin. prof. medicine, 1992—95; chief divsn. gastroenterology, hepatology Calif. Pacific Med. Ctr., San Francisco, 1992—95, med. dir. liver transplant program, 1992—95; prof. medicine, chief of hepatology, co-dir. liver transplant program Stanford Univ. Med. Ctr., 1995—2008; prof. medicine emeritus Stanford U. Sch. of Medicine, 2008—; v.p., chief med. officer Romark Labs., Tampa, Fla., 2008—11; prin. med. fellow Vertex Pharms., Cambridge, Mass., 2011—, Vertex Pharm., Cambridge, Mass. Author: Flexible Sigmoidoscopy, 1985, Handbook of Liver Disease, 1998, 2004, 2011, Atlas of Gastrointestinal Endoscopy, 1998; editor: Liver Update, 1991—94; mem. editl. bd. Hepatology, 1993—2006, 2000—07; mem. editl. bd.: Am. Jour. Gastroenterology, 2002—06, Alimentary Pharmcology Therapeutics, 2003—08, Liver Transplantation, 2006—09, Gastroenterology, 2008—, Therapy, 2008—; assoc. editor Liver Transplantation and Surgery, 1995—2000, Digestive Health and Nutrition, 1999—2004, Reviews in Gastroenterological Disorders, 2000—07, sec. editor Current Opinion in Organ Transplantation, 2000—07; exec. editor: GastroHep.com, 2000—; editor-in-chief Current Hepatitis B Reports, 2007—08, Digestive Diseases and Sciences, 2008—, Gastroenterology and Heptology, 2007—, World Jour. Gastroentology, 2009—, World Jour. Hepatology, 2009—11; contbr. chapters to books, articles to profl. jours. Lt. comdr. USN, 1974-77. Master: ACP; fellow: RCP (Ireland), Am. Gastroent. Assn., Am. Soc. Gastrointestinal Endoscopy (sec. 1991—94, pres. elect 1994—95, pres. 1995—96), Am. Coll. Gastroenterology; mem.: RCP(London), AMA, Am. Gastroent. Assn. Rsch. Found. (vice chair, individual & physician giving 2004—), Asian Pacific Assn. Study of Liver, Am. Bd. Internal Medicine (chair subspecialty bd. gastroenterology 2007), Internat. Liver Cancer Assn., Am. Digestive Health Found., Am. Clin. and Climatology Assn., European Assn. Study of Liver, Western Gut Club (pres. 1991), Internat. Assn. for Study of Liver, Internat. Liver Transplantation Soc., Am. Fedn. Clin. Rsch., Am. Soc. Transplantation, Am. Assn. Study Liver Diseases, Am. Gastroenterologic Assn. (v.p. 2002—03, pres. 2004—05), Am. Liver Found. (bd. dirs. 1991—95, bd. dirs., North Calif. chpt. 2008—). Home: 22 Weatherly Dr Mill Valley CA 94941-3272 Office: 2320 Marinship Way Ste 250 Sausalito CA 94965 Office Phone: 650-498-5691. Business E-Mail: ekeeffe@stanford.edu.

KEEGAN, ANDREW, gastroenterologist; b. Sydnev, 1955; BSc in Medicine, U. Sydney, 1978, MBBS, 1980, PhD, 1994. Cons. gastroenterologist Nepean Hosp., 1989—, dep. dir. gastroenterology and hepatology, 2006—11, vice chmn., med. staff, 2009—11. Adj. assoc. prof. Sydney Med. Sch., U. Sydney, 2009—11. Mem. mgmt. com. U. Football Club; mem. fellowship selection panel Winston Churchill Meml. Trust; state chmn. pres.'s med. liaison coun. MDA Nat. Fellow: Am. Gastroenterology Assn., Australian Med. Assoc. (mem. state coun. 1999—2011, pres. 2006—08, Pres.'s award), Royal Australasian Coll. Physicians; mem.: Internat. Soc. Biomed. Rsch. on Alcoholism, Gastroenterology Soc. Australia. Office: 1A Barber Ave Kingswood NSW 2747 Australia Office Phone: 61 247225550. Office Fax: 61 247225551. Personal E-mail: adkeegan@pnc.com.au.

KEEGAN, CHRIS A., surgical technologist; Cert. of Surg. Tech., Evansville (Ind.)-Vanderburgh Sch. of Health Occupations, 1974; BA in History, BS in Health Svcs., U. So. Ind., 1992, MS in Edn., 1996. Cert. surg. technologist. Surg. technologist St. Mary's Med. Ctr., Evansville, 1974—77; asst. to physician Tri State Otolaryngology, Evansville, 1977—91; surg. technologist St. Mary's Med. Ctr., 1991—92; prof. Vincennes (Ind.) U., 1991—; surg. technologist Meml. Hosp., Jasper, Ind., 2002—. Presenter in field. Co-author (textbook): Pharmacology for the Surgical Technologist, 1999, 2d edit., 2006; reviewer (textbook) Miller and Keane's Encyclopedia and Dictionary of Medical, Nursing, and Allied Health, 6th edit., 1997; contbr. articles to profl. jours. Recipient Excellence award, Nat. Inst. for Staff and Orgn. Devel., 1996, Award of Excellence in Vocat. and Tech. Edn., State of Ind., 1999, J. Warren Perry Disting. Author award, Jour. Allied Health, 2000. Fellow: Nat. Assn. Surg. Technologists (chair instr.'s com. 1993—99, chair accreditation review com. 1999—2003, nat. bd. surg. tech. & surg. asst. 2003—09, Instr.'s Scholarship award 1995, Pres.'s award 2000); mem.: Assn. Surg. Technologists (bd. dirs. 2009—), Pinnical Honor Soc., Golden Key Honor Soc. (pres. 1991—92), Phi Alpha Theta. Office: Vincennes Univ 1002 N First St Vincennes IN 47591 Office Phone: 812-888-5893.

KEEHAN, SISTER CAROL ANN, healthcare association administrator; BSN magna cum laude, St. Joseph's Coll., Emmitsburg, Md.; MS in Bus., U. SC, Columbia, 1980; LLD (hon.), Niagara U., NY; D (hon.), St. John's U., Queens, NY; DS (hon.), Cath. U. America, Washington; D in Pub. Svc. (hon.), Coll. Holy Cross, Worcester, Mass.; D in Humane Letters (hon.), DePaul U., Chgo., Marymount U., Arlington. RN. Various leadership positions Sacred Heart Children's Hosp. & Regional Perinatal Intensive Care Ctr., Pensacola, Fla., Sacred Heart Hosp., Cumberland, Md.; v.p. nursing, ambulatory care, and edn. and tng. Providence Hosp., pres., CEO, 1989—2005, Cath. Health Assn. of US, Washington, 2005—. Bd. dirs. Cath. Relief Services, Balt., Holy Family Hosp. of Bethlehem Found., Washington; mem. health, labor & domestic policy coms. US Conf. Cath. Bishops, Washington; mem. fin. com. Archdiocese of Washington; bd. chair Ascension Health's Sacred Heart Health System, Pensacola, Fla.; rep. Internat. Fedn. of Cath. Health Care Associations (AISAC) Pontifical Coun. for Pastoral Health Care; past chairperson Cath. Health Assn. US. Past chair Fla. State Human Rights Advocacy Commn., Ascension Health Sacred Heart Health Sys., Pensacola; bd. dirs. Univ. St. Thomas, St. Paul, St. John's Univ.; past. bd. dirs. Cath. Healthcare Ptnrs., Cin., St. Agnes Hosp., Balt., Mercy Health Sys., Miami, Fla., Cath. Healthcare Audit Network, Clayton, Mo., Support Our Aging Religious (SOAR!), Silver Spring, Md., DC Hosp. Assn., Care First/Blue Cross Md., Nat. Capital Area, Owings Mills, Md. Decorated Medal of Honor, Monsignor George C. Higgins, Pro Ecclesia et Pontifice (Cross for Church & Pontiff), Pope Benedict XVI; recipient Trustee award, Am. Hosp. Assn., 1999, Disting. Alumna award, U. SC Sch. Bus., 2000, Algernon Sydney Sullivan award, 2009, George C. Higgins Labor Advocacy award, Archdiocese of Washington, 2008, Vision award, Cath. Charities USA, 2009, Cardinal Joseph Bernardin award, Cath. Common Ground Initiative, 2009, American Cardinals' Encouragement award, Elizabeth Ann Seton award, SOAR!; named one of The 100 Most Powerful People in Healthcare, Modern Healthcare mag., 2006—09, The 100 Most Influential People in the World, TIME mag., 2010, Top 25 Women in Healthcare, Modern Health mag., 2011. Mem.: Daughters of Charity of St. Vincent dePaul. Office: Catholic Health Association US 1875 Eye St NW Washington DC 20006 Office Phone: 202-296-3993. Office Fax: 202-296-3997. Business E-Mail: ckeehan@chausa.org. *

KEEN, LINDA J., former government agency administrator; BSc in Chemistry with honors, U. Alta., MSc in Agr. Scis. Cert. agrologist. Dir. gen. strategic planning and coord. Agr. and Agri-Food Can.; asst. dep. min. Natural Resources Can., Human Resources Devel. Can.; commr. Can. Nuclear Safety Commn., 2000, pres., CEO Ottawa, Ont., 2001—08. Pres. Convention on Nuclear Safety. Mem. adv. com. Govt. Can. Workplace Charitable Campaign. Recipient 2008 Women in Nuclear Global award. Mem.: Internat. Nuclear Regulators Assn. (pres. 2003), Women In Sci. and Engring. Office: Can Nuclear Safety Commn 280 Slater St PO Box 1046 Stn B Ottawa ON K1P 5S9 Canada Office Phone: 613-992-8828.

KEENAN, MARY ANN, orthopedic surgeon, researcher; b. Phila., Aug. 14, 1950; d. William Joseph and Irene Agnes (Obara) K. AB, U. Pa., 1971; MD, Med. Coll. Pa., 1976. Diplomate Am. Bd. Med. Examiners, Am. Bd. Orthopedic Surgery. Orthop. resident Albert Einstein Med. Ctr., Phila., 1976-81; fellow rehab. Rancho Los Amigos Hosp., Downey, Calif., 1981-82, rsch. dir. Head Trauma Service, 1982-87, chief, 1987-90; chmn. dept. orthop. surgery Albert Einstein Med. Ctr., Phila., 1990-97, dir. neuro-orthop. program, 1997—2002; chief neuro-orthop. program U. Pa., Phila., 2002—, prof. orthop. surgery, 2002—, vice chair grad. med. edn., dept. orthop. surgery, 2007—. Orthop. surgeon, chmn. rehab. team Kaiser Found. Hosp., Bellflower, Calif., 1982-87, regional rehab. cons., 1987-90; asst. prof. orthops. U. So. Calif. Med. Sch., L.A., 1982-88, assoc. prof., 1988-90; prof. orthop. surgery Temple U., Phila., 1990-2000. Contbr. articles in field to profl. jours. Recipient Annual Radiology prize Albert Einstein Med. Ctr., 1977, 78, 79, First Prize in rsch. competition, 1980, Commonwealth Bd. award Med. Coll. Pa., 1994, 1st Ann. Healthcare Breakthrough award Ladies Home Jour., 2002, Jacquelin Perry Rsch. award, 2002, 04-07, 2010, Vernon Nickle Rsch. award, 2009. Mem. Am. Orthop. Assn., Am. Acad. Orthop. Surgeons, Ruth Jackson Orthop. Soc. (bd. dirs., pres. 199-91), Orthop. Rehab. Assn. (pres. 1996-97, 2003-2004), Am. Soc. Surgery of the Hand, Alumnae Assn. Med. Coll. Pa. Democrat. Office: U Pa Dept Orthop Surgery 2 Silverstein 3400 Spruce St Philadelphia PA 19104 Office Phone: 215-349-8695.

KEENAN, RETHA ELLEN VORNHOLT, retired nursing educator; b. Solon, Iowa, Aug. 15, 1934; d. Charles Elias and Helen Maurine (Konicek) Vornholt; m. David James Iverson, June 17, 1956; children: Scott, Craig; m. Roy Vincent Keenan, Jan. 5, 1980. BSN, U. Iowa, 1955; MSN, Calif. State U., Long Beach, 1978. Cert. nurse practitioner adult and mental health. Pub. health nurse City of Long Beach, 1970-73, 94-96, coord. continuing edn., 1999—2000; ret., 2000. Pub. health nurse Hosp. Home Care, Torrance, Calif., 1973-75; patient care coord. Hillhaven, LA, 1975-76; mental health cons. InterCity Home Health, LA, 1978-79; instr. CC Dist., LA, 1979-87; instr. nursing El Camino Coll., Torrance, 1981-86; instr. nursing Chapman Coll., Orange, Calif., 1982, Mt. St. Mary's Coll., 1986-87; cons. in field. Contbg. author: American Journal of Nursing Question and Answer Book for Nursing Boards Review, 1984, Nursing Care Planning Guides for Psychiatric and Mental Health Care, 1987-88, Nursing Care Planning Guides for Children, 1987, Nursing Care Planning Guides for Adults, 1988, Nursing Care Planning Guides for Critically Ill Adults, 1988. Mem. Assistance Leauge of Temecula Valley, Calif.; bd. dir. Inland Valley Symphony, 2008-10. NIMH grantee, 1977-78. Mem. Sigma Theta Tau, Phi Kappa Phi, Delta Zeta, Coachella Valley Symphony Guild. Lutheran. Avocations: travel, writing, reading. Home: 38126 Sunny Days Dr Palm Desert CA 92211

KEENAN, ROBERT J., thoracic surgeon, educator; MD, U. Alta. Diplomate Am. Bd. Thoracic Surgery. Intern St. Michael's Hosp.; resident Univ. Toronto; fellow Royal Coll. of Surgeons of Can.; faculty cardiovascular and thoracic surgery Drexel Univ.; thoracic surgeon McGinnis Thoracic and Cardiovasc. Surg. Assocs.; system chief divsn. of thoracic surgery The West Penn Alleghany Health System; dir. Ctr. for Thoracic Surgery Allegheny Gen. Hosp., hosp. affiliations include, Forbes Regional Hosp., West Penn Allegheny Cancer Inst., McGinnis Cardiovascular Inst., Alle-Kiski Med. Ctr. Office: Allegheny Cancer Center 320 East North Ave Room 363 Pittsburgh PA 15212

KEENE, JACK DONALD, molecular genetics and microbiology educator; b. Jacksonville, Fla., June 21, 1947; s. Jack Donald and Stella Collene (Ellis) Keene; m. Judy May Keene, Sept. 6, 1969; children: Mike, Lisa E. Dugan. AB, U. Calif., Riverside, 1969; PhD, U. Wash., 1974. Staff fellow NINDS/NIH, Bethesda, Md., 1974-78; asst. prof. microbiology and immunology Duke U. Med. Ctr., Durham, NC, 1979-84, assoc. prof., 1984—88, prof., 1988—92, chmn., 1992—2002, James B. Duke disting. prof., 1997—, founder Duke Ctr. RNA Biology, 1999—. Exptl. virology study sect. NIH, 1984—88, mem. molecular biology study sect., 1991—95, chmn., 1993—95; mem. nat. sel. and adv. bd. PEW Scholars in the Biomed Scis., 1991—96; co-chmn. Diversity Biotech. Consortium, Santa Fe, 1994—; dir. basic sci. rsch. Duke U. Comprehensive Cancer Ctr., 1995—2003; with program in genetics and genomics and molecular and cellular biology Duke U.; dir. combinatorial scis. ctr. Duke U. Med. Ctr., 1994—2000; biotech. cons. LipoGen, Inc., BioWhittaker, Inc., Med. and Biol. Labs., Inc., Nagoya, Japan; co-founder SARCO, Inc., Combinatorial Sci. Systems, Inc., ChemCodes, LLC; founder Ribonomics, Inc., Research Triangle Park, NC; bd. dirs. Alpha Vax, Inc.; chmn. bd. sci. counselors NIEHS, NIH; mem. forum on drug disc., devel. & translation Inst. Med. Nat. Acad. Sci. Assoc. editor Virology, 1983-2007, RNA Biology, 2005-; mem. editl. bd. Jour. of Virology, 1985-95, Molecular and Cellular Biology, 1991—2008, Alliance Cellular Signaling; editor Microbiology and Molecular Biology Revs., 1992-2000, editor-in-chief, 2000-05; editor Molecular Diversity, 1995-2000, Jour. Biol. Chemistry, 2003—2000, primary reviewer Jour. Immunology, 1996—. Mem. fellowship com. Arthritis Found., 1990-92, mem. rsch. com., 1990-92. Recipient Faculty Rsch. award Am. Cancer Soc., 1981-86, Devil's Bag award Arthritis Found., 1985-91; Nanaline Duke Faculty Scholar, 1981-84, PEW Scholar in the Biomed. Scis., 1986-90. Fellow Am. Acad. Microbiology; mem. Am. Soc. Virology, Am. Soc. Biochemistry and Molecular Biology, Am. Soc. Microbiology (mem. pub. bd. 2000-05), Ribonucleic Acid Soc., The Henry Kunkel Soc., Ny Acad. Scis. Office: Duke Univ Med Ctr Box 3020 Mol Gen and Microbiol Dept Research Dr/414 Jones Bldg Durham NC 27710 Office Phone: 919-684-5138.

KEENEY, VIRGINIA T., retired child psychiatrist; b. Albany, NY, Mar. 23, 1920; d. Leon Lyle and Mabel Alice Tripp; m. Arthur Hail Keeney, 1942 (dec.); children: Steven Harris, Lee Douglas, Martha Heyburn; m. George Harrison Houston, 2003 (dec.). BS, Coll. of William and Mary, Williamsburg, Va., 1942; MD, U. Louisville, 1954. Dir./creator ethics and humanities program U. Louisville Sch. Medicine, 1974—2004; assoc. prof. dept. cmty. and family medicine U. Louisville, 1974—2004, asst. prof. dept. psychiatry, 1984—2004; ret., 2004. Bd. dirs. Buckhorn Presbyn. Child Welfare Agency. Co-editor (with Arthur Keeney): (book) Dyslexia, 1966. Mem. adv. bd. Salvation Army, Louisville; program dir. Sabin Oral Polio Campaign, 1961—63; elder Presbyterian Ch.; chmn. bd. YWCA, Louisville, 1963—65, Ky. bd. med. lic., 1992—2002; life trustee Am. Printing House for Blind, Louisville, 1981—; life bd. dir. Louisville Orch., 2003; chmn. bd. ARC, Louisville, 1994—96, life bd. dir., 1999; bd. dir. Louisville Hospice, 2000—06. Recipient Clara Barton award, ARC, 1980, 1996; named Citizen Laureate of Louisville, Younger Women's Club, 1964, Woman of Distinction, Ctr. for Women and Families, 1992, Alumna fellow, U. Louisville, 2007. Mem.: Jefferson County Med. Soc. Found. (trustee 2004—10), Ky. Physicians Health Found. (trustee 1985—), River Valley Club, Alpha Omega Alpha. Presbyterian. Avocations: reading, walking, swimming, gardening.

KEEP, MARCUS FLOYD, neurosurgeon; b. NYC, Mar. 15, 1959; s. Charles Russell, Jr. Keep and Nancy Garland Stotz; m. Jenny Karlsson, Nov. 25, 2005; 1 child, Hannah Freyja. AB in Religion, Dartmouth Coll., Hanover, NH, 1980; BS in Chemistry, U. SC, 1981; MD, Med. U. SC, 1988; postgrad., Shanxi U., Taiyuan, China, 1981—82, St. George's U., 1984—85. Surgery intern Med. U. S.C., Charleston, 1988—89; neurosurgery resident Montreal Neurol. Inst., McGill U., Que., Canada, 1989—94; rsch. fellow Restorative Neurology Unit, Lund U., Sweden, 1994—96; pres. Restorative Neurosurgery Found., Honolulu, 1996—; CEO, founder Maas BioLab, LLC, Honolulu, 1997—; asst. prof. dept. neurosurgery U. N.Mex., Albuquerque, 2002—07; med. dir. Swedish Gamma Knife Ctr., Swedish Med. Ctr., Englewood, Colo., 2007—09; co founder www.KeepDNA.net, 2008; med. staff Pinnacle Health Neurol. Surgery Harrisburg Hosp., 2009—; clin. asst. prof. dept. neurosurgery Penn. State Hershey Med. Ctr., 2010—. Rsch. fellow INSERM-Neuromorphology Lab.-Salpetriere Hosp., Paris, 1989—90; asst. prof. dept. surgery John A. Burns Sch. Medicine, U. Hawaii, Honolulu, 1997—2002; rschr. Ctr. for Study of Neurol. Disease, Honolulu,

1997—98, Lab. Matrix Pathology, Honolulu, 1999—2002; asst. prof. dept. anatomy John A. Burns Sch. Medicine, U. Hawaii, Honolulu, 2000—02; mem. sci. adv. bd., bd. dirs. NeuroVive Pharma, Lund, 2007—. Contbr. chapters to books, scientific papers to profl. jours. V.p. Nova Arts Found., Honolulu, 1997—2002; mem. instnl. rev. bd. St. Francis Med. Ctr., Honolulu, 1999—2001; mem. sci. adv. com. Clin. Rsch. Ctr., Honolulu, 2000—01; union rep. Montreal Neurol. Inst., Montreal, Que., Canada, Assn. Residents of McGill, Montreal, 1992—94. Grantee Rsch. grantee, Ingeborg V.F. McKee Fund, 2001, Bradley & Victoria Geist Found., 1998, 1999, 2000, Omina-Freundeshilfe Found., 1994, Rsch. Ctrs. for Minority Instns, NIH, 2001—; fellow, Phadhar Hosp., India, 1988, Burn Unit, Cali, Colombia, Ptnrs. of the Ams., 1987. Fellow: ACS, Soc. Montreal Neurol. Inst. (pres. 1993—94), Royal Coll. Surgeons Can.-Neurosurgery; mem.: Soc. Stereotactic and Functional Neurosurgery, Congress Neurol. Surgeons, Cell Transplant Soc., Hawaii Assn. Neurol. Surgeons (treas. 1997—2000, v.p. 2000—02), Soc. for Neurosci., Am. Soc. for Neural Therapy and Repair, Am. Epilepsy Soc., Am. Assn. Neurol. Surgeons., Internat. Brain Rsch. Orgn., NY Soc. Mayflower Descs., Mass. Soc. Mayflower Descs., Outrigger Canoe Club. Achievements include patents in field. Home: 725 Indiana Ave Lemoyne PA 17043-1566 Office Phone: 505-843-4230.

KEET, LIZELLE, pediatrician; b. Kimberley, South Africa, Sept. 2, 1970; MBChB, U. Free State, 1994, MD in Pediats., 2003. Pediatrician Dept. Pediats., 2003—. Cons. paediatrician in HIV Free State Dept. Health, 2007—11. Office: University Free State Dept Pediatrics Bloemfontein Free State 9301 South Africa Office Fax: 0514443230. Business E-Mail: keetl.md@ufs.ac.za.

KEETON, J. E., retired psychiatrist; b. Brilliant, Ala., Oct. 8, 1925; s. James Willie and Mary Etta (Dodd) K.; m. Mary Ann Trantham, May 31, 1953 (dec. Dec. 1989); children: Jonathan Eric(dec.), David Wright, Adam Blake. BS, Birmingham So. U., 1951; MD, U. Ala., 1955. Intern U. Chgo. Clinics, 1955-56; resident psychiatry Inst. Living, Hartford, Conn., 1956-59; dir. day hosp. Vets. Hosp., Washington, 1960-61, asst. chief psychiatry, 1961-64; pvt. practice psychiatry Bethesda, Md., 1964-78; staff psychiatrist Vets. Med. Ctr., Tuscaloosa, Ala., 1978-97; ret., 1997; clin. asst. prof. dept. psychiatry, 2009—; asst. prof., dept. psychology U. Ala. Psychiatry Clinic, 2010—. Dir. clozapine rsch. Vets. Hosp., Tuscaloosa, 1991-97. Pharmacist mate USN, 1944-46. Mem. Am. Psychiat. Assn. (life; assoc. mem.). Home: Capstone Village 601 5th Ave E Apt 223 Tuscaloosa AL 35407

KEETON, JAMES E., dean, surgeon, educator; BA, U. Miss., 1961, MD, 1965. Cert. American Bd. Urology. Residency in gen. surgery and urology U. Miss. Med. Ctr., Jackson, prof. surgery and pediat., various adminstrv. appointments including interim vice chancellor, chief of staff to the vice chancellor and assoc. vice chancellor clin. affairs, vice chancellor health affairs, dean sch. medicine, 2010—; residency in pediatric urology London; pvt. practice Miss., 1970—. Lt. col. med. corps USN. Fellow: American Acad. Pediat. Office: University Miss Med Ctr Sch Medicine LRC Rm U-016 2500 North State St Jackson MS 39216 Office Phone: 601-984-1010. Office Fax: 601-984-1013. Business E-Mail: jkeeton@umc.edu. *

KEFALIDES, NICHOLAS ALEXANDER, physician, educator; b. Alexandroupolis, Greece, Jan. 17, 1927; came to U.S., 1947, naturalized; s. Athanasios and Alexandra (Aematidou) K.; m. Eugenia Georgia Kutsunis, Nov. 24, 1949; children: Alexandra Jane (dec.), Patricia Ann, Paul Thomas. BA, Augustana Coll., Rock Island, Ill., 1951; BS, U. Ill., Chgo., 1953, MS in Biochemisry, 1956, MD, 1956, PhD in Biochemistry, 1965; MS (hon.), U. Pa., 1971; doctorate (hon.), U. Reims, France, 1987. Resident in internal medicine U. Ill. Coll. Medicine, Chgo., 1960-62, NIH fellow in infectious disease, 1962-64, asst. prof. medicine, 1964-65, U. Chgo., 1965-69, assoc. prof. medicine, 1969-70; assoc. prof. medicine and biochemistry U. Pa., Phila., 1970-74, prof. medicine, 1974—96, prof. medicine emeritus, 1996—, prof. biochemistry and biophysics, 1975—; assoc. dean rsch. U. Pa. Sch. Medicine, 1994-95; pres. Assn. Sr. and Emeritus, Sch. Medicine, U. Penn., 2010—. Vis. prof. Oxford (England) U., 1977—78, 1984—85; mem., chmn. pathobiochemistry study sect. NIH, 1982—86, dir. project on burns, Peru, 1957—60; dir. Connective Tissue Rsch. Inst., Phila., 1977—2002; chmn. Instn. Rev. Bd. U. Pa., 1995—98, exec. chmn., 1998—2003; initiator, chair Gordon Rsch. Confs. on Basement Membranes, 1982; sci. mentor biotech. cos. Sci. Ctr., Phila., 2002—; chair Penn. Assoc. Sr. & Emeritus Faculty Program Com., 2008—11; pres. sr. emeritus faculty Assn. U. Pa. Sch. Med., 2010—. Author: (with J. P. Borel) Basement Membranes: Cell and Molecular Biology, 2005, Echoes from the CobbleStones-A Memoir, 2009(translated to greek); creator lecture series Lunch for Hungry Minds, Phila., 1998—; contbr. chpts. to books, articles to profl. jours. Lt. comdr., surgeon US Public Health Svc., 1957—60. Recipient Borden Rsch. Found. award, 1956, award for pioneering rsch. on connective tissue Collagen Gordon Confs. and Collagen Corp., 1997; Guggenheim fellow, 1977. Fellow AAAS; mem. Am. Assn. Pathologists, Am. Soc. Clin. Investigation, Am. Soc. Biochemistry and Molecular Biology, Am. Soc. Cell Biology. Achievements include discovery of Collagen type IV in basement membranes and its role in suppressing tumor cell growth and angiogenesis. Office: U Pa Univ City Sci Ctr 3711 Market St Rm 467 Philadelphia PA 19104-5502

KEFELI, VALENTIN ILICH, biologist, botanist, educator, researcher; b. Moscow, July 12, 1937; s. Ilia Josef Kefeli and Alisa Michailovna Kefeli-Tongur; m. Galina Michailovna Mzen, Jan. 9, 1932; 1 child, Maria Valentinovna. Student, Agrl. Acad., Moscow, 1954-59; cand. of sci., Inst. Plant Physiology, Moscow, 1965, DSc, 1971. Asst. Inst. Phytopathology, Moscow region, 1959-61; sci. jr. Inst. Plant Physiology, Moscow, 1961-69, sci. sr., 1969-88, head lab., prof. biology, 1986—; dir. Inst. of Soil Sci. and Photosynthesis, Moscow region, 1988—. From vis. prof. to assoc. prof. biology Slippery Rock U., Pa., 1995-98; advisor wetland project & master programs Coll. Health & Human Svcs., 1998-2000; adv. Slippery Rock Watershed Coalition, 2000—, Carnegie Mellon U. Living Lab., Pitts., 2005—; prof. Robert Morris U., Pitts., 2010-. Author: Natural Growth Inhibitors, 1978, 2003, Mechanism of Land-Scape Rehabilitation & Sustainability, 2011; editor: Development of Acetabularia, 1979. V.p. Presidium of Pushchino Biol. Ctr., Moscow region, 1989. Recipient prize Russian Chek Acad., Moscow, 1979. Mem. N.Y. Acad. Sci.; Internat. Inst. of Crimean Karaites (founder). Home: 329 N Main St Slippery Rock PA 16057-1019 Personal E-mail: vkafeli@embarqmail.com.

KEGLER, SCOTT R., statistician; b. St. Paul, Minn., 1956; BS, U. Minn., 1979; PhD, Okla. State U., 1999. Math. statistician Ctrs. Disease Control and Prevention, 2001—. Mem.: Math. Assn. America, Am. Statis. Assn. Office: 4770 Buford Hwy Atlanta GA 30341 Business E-Mail: skegler@cdc.gov.

KEHINDE, ELIJAH OLADUNNI, urological surgery educator, researcher; b. Ogbomoso, Nigeria, Nov. 13, 1953; s. Solomon Atanda and Deborah Mohun (Onifade) K.; m. Funmilola Ajibona, Aug., 1998; children: Yemisi, Olaitan, Mojoyinoluwa, Omolayo. MBBS, U. Ibadan, 1979; diploma urology, U. London, 1987; MD, U Leicester, Eng., 1998. House officer, sr. registrar U. Coll. Hosp., Ibadan, 1979-80, 84-86; registrar U. Tchg. Hosp., Ile-Ife, Nigeria, 1981-83; registar Inst. of Urology, London, 1987-88; rsch. fellow U. Leicester, U.K., 1991-94; asst. prof. Sultan Qaboos U., Muscat, Oman, 1994-98, Kuwait U., 1998—2003, assoc. prof., 2003—08, prof., 2008—. Cons. urol. surgeon Sultan Qaboos U. Hosp., Muscat, 1994-98; cons. urol. surgeon Mobarak U. Hosp., Kuwait, 1998—; referee Brit. Jour. Urology, 1996-2000, Kuwait Med. Jour., 2001—, Med. Principles and Practice, 2003—, Jour. Urology, 2005—, African Jour. Urology, 2005—. Author (with others) Cancer Surveys 23, Preventing Prostate Cancer, 1995; Clinical Presentation of Jaundice in Europe, 1995. contbr. articles to profl. jours. Recipient Disting. Rschr. award in basic applied scis. Kuwait U., 2006; grantee U. Leicester, 1991-94, Bayer U.K. Ltd., 1993-94, Kuwait Univ. 2001—. Fellow Royal Coll. Surgeons Eng., Med. Coll. Surgeons Nigeria; mem. AAAS, Brit. Assn. Urol. Surgeons, Am. Urol. Assn. Baptist. Avocations: travel, tennis. Home: Villa 19 St 14 Area 10 Jabriya Kuwait Home Phone: 965 2531 9597, 965 2531 9030; Office Phone: 965 2531 9475. Personal E-mail: ekehinde@hotmail.com.

KEHL, FRANZ, anesthesiologist, educator; b. Offenbach, Hessen, Germany, Aug. 4, 1963; married. Cert. prof. U. Würzburg, Germany, 2008. Asst. med. dir. U. Würzburg, 1998—2004; predoc. rsch., dept. neuophysiology U. Frankfurt, Hessen, 1987—89; attending Mcpl. Hosp., Hanau, Germany, 1998—98; rsch. fellow, dept. anesthesiology Med. Coll. Wis., Milwaukee, 2000—02; critical fellow Bayerische Julius Maximilians U., Wurzburg, 1998—2000, asst. prof., 1998—2000, assoc. prof., 2002—04, chief anesthesiologist, 2004—08, vice chair, 2004—08; prof. anesthesiology and intensive care medicine chmn. Städt. Klinikum Karlsruhe, Germany, 2008. Office: Städtisches Klinikum Karlsruhe gGmbH Moltkestraße 90 Karlsruhe Baden-Württemberg 76133 Germany Office Fax: 49-721/9741609. Business E-Mail: franz.kehl@klinikum-karlsruhe.com.

KEHOE, PETER HERBERT, optometrist; b. Galesburg, Ill., July 30, 1959; s. Herbert Peter and June Carolyn (Melick) K.; m. Melissa Sue Thomas, June 19, 1982; children: Vincent, Alexandra, Kathryn. Grad., Ind. U., 1977-79; BS, OD, Ill. Coll. Optometry, 1984. Private practice Kehoe Eye Care, P.C. (formerly Kehoe Optical), Galesburg, Ill., 1984—. Fellow Am. Acad. Optometry; mem. Am. Optometric Assn. (bd. trustees 1999—, pres. 2008-09, Ill. Optometric Assn. (former pres., legis. com., Optometrist of Yr., 2001), West Ctrl. Ill. Optometric Soc. (former pres.), Optometric Extension Program (assoc.), Galesburg Area C. of C. (bd. dirs. 1986), Lions. Avocations: flying, golf, racquetball, entrepreneur. Office: Kehoe Eye Care Ste 35 4-L Plaza Galesburg IL 61401 also: Am Optometric Assn 243 N Lindbergh Blvd Saint Louis MO 63141 E-mail: info@kehoeeyecare.com. *

KEHRT, BETTIE F., retired medical transcriptionist; b. Phila., Aug. 20, 1948; d. Reed and Bettie Francis (MacKnight) Knox; m. Randy Mark Kehrt, Mar. 22, 1986; m. Fred Kaplan (div.). At in Paleontology, SD Sch. Mines and Tech., Rapid City, 1992—94. Sec., audit student U. Pa. Hosp., Phila., 1970—82; transcription sec. Salick Health Care, Phila., 1990—98; med. transcriptionist Temple U. Hosp., Phila., 1982—2000, Bapt. Hosp. East, Louisville, 2001—04, Norton Healthcare, Louisville, 2004—10. Docent Acad. Nat. Scis., Phila., 1982—2000; vol. editor, writer Mesozoic Times, 1987—93. Mem.: Soc. Vertebrate Paleontology. Libertarian. Avocations: paleontology, reading. Home: 7415 Crawfordshire Ln Louisville KY 40220-2811

KE-HUNG, CHIEN, ophthalmologist; b. Taichung, Taiwan, May 30, 1979; MD, Nat. Def. Med. Ctr., 2004. Ophthalmologist Tri-Svc. Gen. Hosp., 2006—. Mem.: Ophthal. Soc. Taiwan. Avocation: travel. Office: 325 Sect 2 Cheng-Gong Rd Nei Taipei 886 Taiwan

KEIICHI, MATSUMOTO, nuclear scientist; b. Izushi-gun, Japan, Sept. 1, 1976; s. Matsumoto Amakazu and Matsumoto Hiroe; m. Mihoko Keiichi, Sept. 22, 2001; 1 child, Suzu. Degree in Med. Tech., Kyoto U., Japan, 1998. Cert. radiol. technologist Ministry Health, Japan. Nuclear medicine technologist Kyoto (Japan) U. Hosp., 1998—2001; sr. nuclear medicine technologist Inst. Biomedical Rsch. and Innovation, Kobe, Japan, 2001—. Recipient award, Brain Imaging Coun., 2001. Mem.: Japanese Soc. Radiol. Tech. (instr. 2003, rschr. 2003, Rookie Tech. award 2002), Japanese Soc. Nuclear Medicine Tech. (editor 2003). Avocations: driving, movies, job. Office: Inst Biomed Rsch and Innovation 2-2 Minatojima-Minamimachi Chuo-ku Kobe 650 0047 Japan

KEIJI, KURODA, research scientist; b. Tokyo, May 27, 1976; MD, Juntendo U., 2001, PhD, 2006. Physician Dept. Ob-Gyn. Juntendo U. Hosp., 2001—03, 2005—10, asst. prof., 2005—10, med. specialist, 2006—10, med. specialist, gynecologic and obstetrics endoscopy, 2010; physician Sato Hosp., 2003—04; vis. rschr., dept. physiology Tokyo Women's Med. U., 2004—05; vis. rschr. Inst. Reproductive and Devel. Biology Imperial Coll. London Hammersmith Campus, 2010—. Rsch. fellowship, Uehara Meml. Found., Inter-Inst. Rsch. grant, Naito Found. Mem.: Japan Soc. Endoscopic Surgery, Japan Soc. Fertilization and Implantation, Japan Soc. Gynecologic and Obstetrics Endoscopy and Minimally Invasive Therapy, Japan Soc. Fertility and Sterility, Japan Soc. Ob-Gyn. Avocations: rugby, football. Home: 2-14-5 Misuji Tokyo Taito-ku 111-0055 Japan Home Fax: 81-0-3-5820-2338. Business E-Mail: arthur@juntendo.ac.jp.

KEILL, STUART LANGDON, psychiatrist; b. Binghamton, NY, Oct. 5, 1927; s. Kenneth and Dorothy B. (Langdon) K.; m. Joanne Veness, Sept. 2, 1950; children: Elinor Anne Moran, Patricia J., Brian S., Victoria M. Keill Lo Russo. BA, Princeton U., 1947; MA, Cornell U., 1948; MD, Temple U., 1952. Intern Highland Hosp., Rochester, NY; resident in psychiatry N.Y. State Psychiat. Inst., Presbyn. Hosp., Columbia U., NYC, 1955-58; dir. edn., dir. West Side Community Mental Health Ctr., NYC, 1958-71, Roosevelt Hosp., NYC, 1958-71; regional dir. N.Y. State Dept. Mental Health, 1971-75; prof. clin. psychiatry SUNY, Stony Brook, 1975-80; chmn. dept. psychiatry Nassau County Med. Ctr., East Meadow, NY, 1975-80; clin. prof. psychiatry SUNY, Buffalo, 1980-86, emeritus prof. psychiatry, 1993—; chief psychiat. service VA Med. Ctr., Buffalo, 1981-86; prof. of psychiatry Sch. of Medicine U. Md., 1986-94, vice chmn. dept. psychiatry, 1986-93, prof. sch. social work, 1993-94, acting chmn., 1991-92; clin. prof. psychiatry Sch. Medicine NYU, 1994—; counselor Advocates Coalition for Psychiat. Patients, 1980-86; med. dir. Inst. for Psychiatry and Human Behavior, 1986-93. Mem. adv. com. mental health laws Md. Atty. Gen. Office, 1987-93; hon. rsch. fellow Dept. Psychol. Medicine U. Glasgow, 1994. Author: (with others) Textbook on Administrative Psychiatry, 1992; also 52 articles; mem. editl. bd. Social Work and Health Care, 1975—, Social Work in Mental Health Care, 2000—, Hosp. and Community Psychiatry; assoc. editor Gen. Hosp. Psychiatry Jour., 1981-94. Chmn. Nassau coun. Health Systems Agy., 1977-80; mem. adv. com. Dr. Glory's Children's Theatre, N.Y.C., 1980—; mental health laws adv. com. State's Atty. Gen., 1987; warden Christ Ch., Oyster Bay, 2003-07. Lt. USN, 1953—55. Recipient Julius T. Marcus award dept. psychiatry SUNY, Stony Brook, 1980, Jour. Social Work in Health Care editl. award, 1985, Disting. Svc. award Bishop Diocese LI, 2011; hon. sr. fellow U. Glasgow, Dept. Psychol. Medicine, Scotland, 1994. Fellow Am. Coll. Psychiatrists, Am. Psychiat. Assn. (Distinction in Adminstrn. award 1990); mem. MEDIPP Psychiatry Coun. (dist. chmn. 1981-86), Am. Assn. Psychiat. Adminstrs. (pres. 1981-82), Am. Hosp. Assn. (chmn. psychiat. svcs. sect. 1985), Am. Assn. Gen. Hosp. Psychiatrists (pres. 1985-87), N.Y. Soc. Clin. Psychiatry (pres. 1974-75, chmn. pub. psychiatry com.), Md. Psychiat. Soc.

KEIM, MICHAEL RAY, dentist; b. Sabetha, Kans., June 8, 1951; s. Milton Leroy and Dorothy Juanita (Stover) K.; m. Christine Anne Lorenzen, Nov. 20, 1971; children: Michael Scott, Dawn Marie, Erik Alan. Student, U. Utah, Salt Lake City, 1969-72; DDS, Creighton U., Omaha, 1976. Pvt. practice, Casper, Wyo., 1976—. Mem. vertical math. com. Natrona County Sch. Dist., 1997-2000; mem. Coll. Nat. Finals Rodeo Com., 2002—; adv. com. mem. State of Wyo. Equality Care, 2007-, mem. State Wyo. Cleft Palate Team, 2009-. Mem. organizing bd. dirs. Ctrl. Wyo. Soccer Assn., 1976-77; mem. Casper Mountain Ski Patrol, Nat. Ski Patrol Sys., 1980-2000, 2005—, Big Horn Ski Patrol, 2001-05, avalanche and ski mountaineering advisor No. Divsn. Region III, 1992-96, outdoor emergency care instr. trainer, 1996-99, 1st asst. patrol dir., 1996-98, patrol dir., 1998-99; bd. dirs., dep. commr. for fast pitch Wyo. Amateur Softball Assn., 1980-84; bd. dirs. Ctrl. Wyo. Softball Assn., 1980-84; head coach Big Horn Mountain Ski Team, 2002-05; pres. Wyo. Spl. Smiles Found., 1995-96; mem. organizing com. Prevent Abuse & Neglect thru Dental Awareness Coalition, Wyo., 1996; mem. adv. com. Natrona County Headstart, 1985—; mem. City of Casper Leisure Svc. Adv. Com., 2002—10, vice chair, 2007—10. Recipient Purple Merit Star for Saving a Life, 1992, Hixon award, 2002, Lusche Fellow award, 2008. Master: Acad. Gen. Dentistry; mem.: ADA, Internat. Congress Oral Implantologists, Internat. Coll. Dentistry, Wyo. Donated Dental Svcs. (organizing bd. dirs. 1994, pres. 1995—96, Outstanding Vol. Dentist 2007), Wyo. Dental Hist. Assn. (bd. dirs. 1989—95), Ctrl. Wyo. Dental Assn. (sec.-treas. 1981—82, pres. 1982—83, sec.-treas. 2002—03, pres. 2003—04), Wyo. Dental Polit. Action Com. (sec.-treas. 1985—97), Wyo. Dental Assn. (chmn. conv. 1987—, bd. dirs. 1992—97, chmn. conv. 1993, v.p. 1993—94, ADA alt. del. 1994—95, pres.-elect 1994—95, pres. 1995—96, editor 1997—, chmn. conv. 1999), Wyo. Acad. Gen. Dentistry (sec.-treas. 1980—82, pres. 1982—87, del. 2007—), Pierre Fauchard Acad., Fedn. Dentaire Internat., Am. Acad. Cosmetic Dentistry, Safari Club Internat. (treas. ctrl Wyo. chpt.), Creighton Club (pres. 1982—84), Kiwanis (bd. dirs. 1986—96, v.p. Casper club 1988—89, pres.-elect 1989—90, internat. del. 1989—91, pres. 1990—91, chmn. internat. rels. com. 1992—99, Rocky Mountain dist. lt. gov.-elect divsn. 1 1997—98, lt. gov. divsn. 1 1998—99, it. Gov. divsn. 1 2008—, Hixon award 2002, Lusche fellow 2009). Methodist. Avocations: hunting, skiing, sports, woodworking, photography. Office: 1749 S Boxelder St Casper WY 82604-3538 Home: 3524 Aspen Ln Casper WY 82604-4571 Office Phone: 307-234-6358. Personal E-mail: mogul_mike@msn.com.

KEINÄNEN, MATTI TAPIO, psychiatrist, psychotherapist, educator; b. Kuopio, Finland, Jan. 1, 1953; s. Veikko and Selma Keinänen; m. Kristiina Virtanen; children: Miia, Mika, Matias. MD, Turku U., Finland, 1977. Psychiatrist Student Health Svc., Turku, 1986—; tng. psychotherapist, sr. lectr. psychiatry Turku U., 2002—. Sr. lectr. clin. psychology Jyväskylä U., Finland, 2000—. Author: Psychosemiosis as a Key to Body-Mind Continuum, 2006, The Psychodynamic Psychotherapy of Young Adults, 2007; contbr. articles to profl. jours. Cons. Turku Ch. Adminstrn., 1997—. Office: Student Health Svc Kirkkotie 13 FIN- 20540 Turku Finland Office Phone: 358467101045. Business E-Mail: matti.keinanen@pp.fimnet.fi, matti.keinanen@yths.fi.

KEISER, PAUL HAROLD, retired hospital administrator; b. Dalton, Ohio, June 1, 1927; s. Austin R. and Elrena E. (Tschantz) K.; m. Nancy F. Homan, May 27, 1950; children— James William, Martha Ann Lee, Elizabeth Louise Green, Patricia Elrena Bell. BS, Mt. Union Coll., 1948; MS in Hosp. Adminstrn., Northwestern U., 1952. Adminstr. Community Hosp. Evanston, Ill., 1952-54, Burlington Hosp., Iowa, 1954-67; pres. York Hosp., Pa., 1967-88, ret. Pa., 1988. Lectr., seminar leader Northwestern U., Chgo., 1952-54, U. Iowa Hosp., Iowa City, 1955-59; lectr. George Washington U., 1969-86. Contbr. articles to profl. jours. Bd. dirs. United Way, York, Pa., 1970-78, York Habitat for Humanity, 1992-98, 99-2005, York County Parks Charitable Trust Bd., 1989-2007, vice chmn., 1990-2007; bd. dirs. York County Farm and Natural Land Trust, 1992-98, mem. adv. bd., 1998—2006; dir. adv. bd. Pa. State U., York, 1979—2005; sec. North Codorus Twp. Plan Commn., 1994-96; mem. North Codorus Twp. Bd. Suprs., 1995—2005, vice chmn., 1997-99, chmn. 2000-02, S.E. (York County) Regional Police Bd., chmn. 2002-05; mem. gov. bd. Byrnes Health Edn. Ctr., 1995—2008. Fellow Am. Coll. Hosp. Adminstrn. (life, regent 1964-67); mem. Iowa Interprofl. Assn. (pres. 1963-64), Iowa Hosp. Assn. (pres. 1961-62), Am. Hosp. Assn. (del. 1975-86), Hosp. Assn. Pa. (chmn. bd. dirs. 1983, bd. dirs. svcs. corp. 1986-89), Northwestern U. Hosp. Adminstrn. Alumni Assn. (pres. 1957-58), Rotary (bd. dirs. 1979-82), Sigma Alpha Epsilon. Republican. Presbyterian. Avocations: tennis, woodworking. Home: Apt J 404 950 Willow Valley Lakes Dr Willow Street PA 17584-9663 Personal E-mail: paul.keiser@gmail.com.

KEITH, JEANETTE N., medical educator; BA, Ind. State U., 1983; MD, Ind. U., 1989. Asst. prof. medicine U. Chgo., 1998—2006; assoc. prof. medicine and nutrition U. Ala., Birmingham, 2007—10; assoc.

prof. medicine U. Buffalo, SUNY, 2010—. Mem.: Am. Soc. Gastrointestinal Endoscopy, Am. Soc. Parenteral and Enteral Nutrition (Rhoads Rsch. Found. award), Am. Gastroent. Assn. Office: Buffalo General Hosp 100 High St Buffalo NY 14203 Office Fax: 716-859-3352. Business E-Mail: jkeith2@buffalo.edu.

KEJUN, ZHANG, physician; b. Qingdao, Nov. 11, 1966; D, Shandong U., 2006. Physician Qingdao U., 2003—. Office: 59 Haier Rd Qingdao Shandong 266003 China Business E-Mail: wlsdermyy@163.com.

KELBER, OLAF, pharmacologist, researcher; b. Freiburg, Germany, June 2, 1961; s. Wolfgang J. and Erna A. Kelber; life ptnr. Violetta F. Vollrath. Diploma in biology, Johannes-Gutenberg U., Mainz, Germany, 1989, PhD in Biology, 1991; M of Pharm. Medicine, U. Witten-Herdecke, 2003. Rsch. scientist Inst. Zoology Johannes-Gutenberg U., Mainz, Germany, 1989—91; rsch. scientist dept. pharmacology and toxicology Steigerwald Arzneimittelwerk GmbH, Darmstadt, Germany, 1992—95, head lab. dept. pharmacology and toxicology, 1995—2001, head sci. project mgmt. dept. sci., 2001—, head, med. sci. and clin. rsch., 2007—. Contbr. articles to profl. jours. Mem.: Soc. Phytotherapy (bd. mem.), ICH (EWG mem.), German Soc. Pharm. Medicine, Koop. Phyto., German Soc. Psychiatry, Soc. Medicinal Plant Rsch. (bd. mem.), German Soc. Exptl. and Clin. Pharmacology and Toxicology, German Soc. Atherosclerosis Rsch., European Soc. Neurogastroenterology and Motility, German Pharm. Soc. Office: Steigerwald Arzneimittelwerk GmbH Havelstr 5 Darmstadt 64295 Germany Personal E-mail: o_kelber@kelber.org. Business E-Mail: kelber@steigerwald.de.

KELEMEN, LINDA ELIZABETH, genetic epidemiologist; d. Steve and Barbara Kelemen. BSc, U. BC, Vancouver, Can., 1985—91; MSc, U. Guelph, Can., 1994—95, McMaster U., Hamilton, Can., 1997—2000; ScD, Harvard U., Boston, Mass., 1999—2003. Registered Dietician Commn. US Dietetic Registration, 1993. Diabetes educator Hotel Dieu Hosp., St. Catharines, Ont., Canada, 1992—94; dietician St. Catharines Gen. Hosp., 1993—94; rsch. nutritionist Population Health Rsch. Inst., McMaster U., Hamilton, Ont., Canada, 1996—2002; rsch. assoc. Mayo Clinic Coll. Medicine, Rochester, Minn., 2003—. Nutrition cons. Versar Inc., Springfield, Va., 2000—00. Contbr. articles. Health promotion planning com. Heart and Stroke Found. Ont., Hamilton, 1996—97; mentor Big Sister Assn. Greater Boston, 2001—01. Recipient Doctoral Traineeship award, Heart and Stroke Found. Can., 1999, 2000, 2001; grantee, Heart and Stroke Found. Ont., 2000-2001, Can. Insts. Health Rsch., 2002-2003, 2008—, Rsch. grant, Nat. Cancer Inst., 2006—08; fellow Mayo Clinic Genetic Epidemiology Fellowship, 2003-2006; scholar Percy Walter Perris Scholarship, U. BC, 1987, Entrance Scholarship, 1987, Scholarship, Harvard U., 1999, Harvard U. Assocs. Can. Scholarship, 2000, 2001; Peter D.C. Thomas scholarship, 1999—2000. Mem.: Am. Assn. Cancer Rsch., Soc. Epidemiologic Rsch., Am. Soc. Preventive Oncology. Achievements include development of cultural food frequency questionnaires and nutrient databases for South Asian and Chinese in North America; discovery of genetic risk factors for ovarian cancer and breast cancer. Business E-Mail: lkelemen@post.harvard.edu.

KELEPOURIS, ELLIE, nephrologist, educator; MD, U. Athens. Diplomate Am. Bd. Internal Medicine, Am. Bd. Internal Medicine-nephrology. Hosp. affiliations include Hahnemann Univ. Hosp., Magee Rehab. Hosp.; fellow Am. Heart Assoc.; prof. nephrology Dexel Univ.; chief divsn. nephrology Drexel Univ. Coll. of Medicine. Recipient Lindback award for Disting. Tchg., 2004, Outstanding Leading award, Nat. Kidney Found., Disting. Svc. award, Outstanding Physician award; named Top Doctor, Phila. Mag., 2009, 2011, Best Doctors in America, 2010. Office: Drexel Nephrology 219 N Broad St 9th Fl Philadelphia PA 19107 Office Phone: 215-762-2688. Office Fax: 215-762-2689.

KELLEHER, ROSEMARY CLARE, social worker, researcher; b. Melbourne, June 11, 1949; BA in English Lit. & Anthropology, Monash U., 1970, MSW, 1992; diploma in Social Studies, Melbourne U., 1973. Cert. in bereavement counseling methods Australian Ctr. Grief Edn., 2000. Sr. social worker St. Vincent's Aged Mental Health Svc., 1996—2005; hon. fellow Academic Unit Psychiatry Old Age, U. Melbourne, 1996—. Mem.: Nat. Assn. Loss and Grief, Internat. Psychogeriatric Assn., Australian Assn. Social Workers. Avocations: gardening, reading. Home: 3 Sunnyside Ave Camberwell Victoria 3124 Australia Business E-Mail: roseck@bigpond.net.au.

KELLER, EGON HEINRICH JOSEF, surgeon; b. Remagen, Rheinland, Germany, May 2, 1950; s. Anton Josef and Elsbeth Maria (Louen) K.; m. Angela Anna Pauline Kratzig, May 20, 1978; children: Andrea, Michael, Martin. DrMed, U. Bonn, 1971; MD, Joh.Gutenberg-U. Mainz, 1979. Resident Borromäerinnen-Hosp., Trier, Germany, 1977-78; sr. house oficer dept. surgery Vincenz-Hosp., Mainz, Germany, 1978-80; acad. asst. dept. surgery U. Mainz, 1980-87; asst. med. dir. dept. surgery Gen. Hosp. Heidberg, Hamburg, Germany, 1987-93; sr. surg. dept. vascular surgery Gen. Hosp. Harburg, Hamburg, 1994-95; asst. med. dir. Asklepios Klinik Nord Heidberg, Hamburg, 1993, 1996—. Co-author: Therapie des Magenkarzinoms, 1984, Therapie Gastroenterologischer Erkrankungen, 1986; contbr. articles to profl. jours. With Med. Corps, 1970, 71. Mem. European Soc. Surg. Oncology. Roman Catholic. Avocations: church music, mountain climbing, skiing. Office: Asklepios Klin ik Nord Campus Heidberg Tangstedter Landstr 400 D-22417 Hamburg Germany Business E-Mail: egon@keller-norderstedt.de.

KELLER, NATASHA MATRINA LEONIDOW, nursing administrator; b. Nyack, NY, June 12, 1958; d. Paul and Matrina (Butich) L.; children: Alexandra, Mary, John. AAS, Rockland C.C., 1979; BS in Nursing cum laude, SUNY Coll. Technology, Utica, 1982; MS in Nursing magna cum laude, Syracuse U., 1985. RN, N.Y.; cert. nurse adminstr. Staff nurse Englewood Hosp., N.J., 1979-80; chare nurse Mary Imogene Bassett Hosp., Cooperstown, N.Y., 1980-82, nursing svc. coord., 1983-86, asst. dir. sys. devel., 1986-87; assoc. nursing practice coord. Strong Meml. Hosp.-U. Rochester, N.Y., 1987-88; asst. dir. nursing Bayfront Med. Ctr., St. Petersburg, Fla., 1988—, adminstr. on duty, 1998. Translator: Excellence in Russian Language, 1976 (Otrada award). Served as 1st lt. USAFR, 1990-91, Persian Gulf War, Saudi Arabia. Mem. Fla. Orgn. Nurse Execs., Tampa Bay Orgn. Nurse Execs., Sigma Theta Tau. Office: Bayfront Med Ctr 701 6th St S Saint Petersburg FL 33701-4814 Office Phone: 727-893-6162, 727-893-6078. Business E-Mail: natasha.keller@bayfront.org.

KELLER, RANDAL JOSEPH, toxicology educator; b. Salem, Ind., Nov. 22, 1957; s. Frank Joseph and Virginia Francis (Barrett) K.; m. Pamela Marie Stroman, Sept. 17, 1994. BA, Eisenhower Coll., Seneca Falls, NY, 1979; MS, Utah State U., 1984, PhD, 1988. Cert. indsl. hygienist; cert. safety profl.; diplomate Am. Bd. Toxicology. Postdoctoral fellow Nat. Ctr. Toxicology Rsch., Jefferson, Ark., 1988-90; instr. U. Ark. for Med. Scis., Little Rock, 1990-91, coord. occupl. and environ. health program, 1991-96; assoc. prof. dept. occupl. safety and health Murray (Ky.) State U., 1996—. Peer reviewer Ctr. for Indoor Air Rsch., 1995—. Contbr. articles to profl. jours. Rsch. grantee U.S. EPA, Washington, 1993-96, NIOSH, Morgantown, W.Va., 1993-95. Fellow Am. Acad. Indsl. Hygiene; mem. Am. Indsl. Hygiene Assn. (pres. elect. Ark. sect. 1993-94, pres. 1994-95), Am. Conf. Govt. Indsl. Hygienists, Am. Soc. Safety Engrs., Am. Soc. Toxicology (1st pl. award metals splty. sect. 1986). Republican. Avocations: running, reading. Office: Murray State U Dept Occupl Safety and Health 157 Industry and Tech Ctr Murray KY 42071-3347 Home: 1305 Olive Blvd Murray KY 42071 Office Phone: 270-809-6655. Business E-Mail: randal.keller@murraystate.edu.

KELLER, ROBERTA LYNN, physician, researcher; d. William and Shirley Streifer; m. Bruce Adam Keller, May 18, 2000. MD, U. Calif., San Francisco, 1993. Cert. in neonatal-perinatal medicine Am. Bd. Pediat., 2003. Asst. prof. clin. pediat. U. Calif., San Francisco, 2005—. *

KELLER, STEVEN M., cardiothoracic surgeon; MD, Albany Med. Coll., 1977. Diplomate Am. Bd. Thoracic Surgery, registered NY, 1978. Intern LI Jewish Med. Ctr., 1978; fellow in surgical oncology NIH, 1983, Nat. Cancer Inst., 1983; resident in gen. surgery Mt. Sinai Med. Ctr., 1985; resident in cardiothoracic surgery Meml. Sloan-Kettering Cancer Ctr., 1987; hosp. affiliations include Beth Israel Med. Ctr., Flushing Hosp. Med. Ctr., Jacobi Med. Ctr., Our Lady of Mercy Med. Ctr.; cardiothoracic surgeon Montefiore Med. Ctr., NY. Named one of Top Doctors, NY Mag., 2010. Fellow: ACS; mem.: Soc. of Surgical Oncology, Soc. of Thoracic Surgeons. Office: Montefiore Medical Center 1575 Blondell Ave Bronx NY 10461 Office Phone: 718-405-8378. Office Fax: 718-405-8253.

KELLERMAN, JONATHAN SETH, writer, pediatric psychologist, educator; b. NYC, Aug. 9, 1949; s. David Kellerman and Sylvia Fiacre; m. Faye Marilyn Marder, July 23, 1972; children: Jesse, Rachel, Ilana; 1 child, Aliza. BA in Psychology, UCLA, 1972; MA in Psychology, U. So. Calif., 1973, PhD in Clin. Psychology, 1974. Lic. psychologist Calif. Psychology intern Children's Hosp. LA, 1973-74, founding dir. psychol. prog., 1977—81, postdoc. fellow, 1974-75, U. So. Calif. Keck Sch. Medicine, LA, 1974-75, staff psychologist, 1975-78, asst. clin. prof. pediat., 1978—79, clin. assoc. prof. pediat., 1979-98, clin. prof. pediat. & psychology, 1998—. Author: (non-fiction) Psychological Aspects of Childhood Cancer, 1980, Helping the Fearful Child, 1981, Savage Spawn: Reflections on Violent Children, 1999, With Strings Attached: The Art and Beauty of Vintage Guitars, 2008, (fiction) When the Bough Breaks, 1985 (Edgar Allan Poe award for Best First Novel, 1986), Blood Test, 1986, Over the Edge, 1987, The Butcher's Theater, 1988, Silent Partner, 1989, Time Bomb, 1990, Private Eyes, 1991, Devil's Waltz, 1992, Bad Love, 1993, Daddy, Daddy Can You Touch the Sky?, 1994, Self-Defense, 1994, Jonathan Kellerman's ABC of Weird Creatures, 1995, The Web, 1995, The Clinic, 1996, Survival of the Fittest, 1997, Billy Straight, 1998, Savage Spawn, 1999, Monster, 2000, Dr. Death, 2000, Flesh And Blood, 2001, The Murder Book, 2002, A Cold Heart, 2003, The Conspiracy Club, 2003, Therapy, 2004, Twisted, 2004, Double Homicide, 2005, Gone, 2006, Obession, 2007, Capital Crimes, 2007, Compulsion, 2008, Bones, 2008, True Detectives, 2009, Evidence, 2009, Deception, 2010, Mystery, 2011; co-author (with Thomas H. Cook and Otto Penzler): The Best American Crime Reporting, 2008 (#1 Publishers Weekly bestseller). Recipient Samuel Goldwyn Creative Writing award, UCLA, 1972, Anthony Boucher award, 1986, Disting. Alumnus award, UCLA dept. psychology, 1997. Mem.: Mystery Writers America, American Psychol. Assn. (Media award 1994, Presdl. award 1998). Jewish. Avocations: painting, art and book collecting, guitar. Office: c/o Karpfinger Agcy 357 W 20th St New York NY 10011 E-mail: submit@jonathankellerman.com. *

KELLEY, FRANCES A., occupational therapist, consultant; b. Cheyenne, Wyo., July 26, 1925; BSin Occupl. Therapy, U. So. Calif., 1949; Occupl. Cert. in Supervision, Los Angeles Valley Coll., 1985. Asst. chief occupl. therapy, therapist San Fernando VA Hosp., Calif., 1948-53, rehab. medicine svc. coord., chief occupl. therapy, clin. edn. supr. Calif., 1963-71; dir., bd. dirs. IDEAS Assocs., Inc., 1989-93; chief. occupl. therapy, coord. GM&S occupl. therapy VA Med. Ctr., Sepulveda, Calif., 1971-89, cons., vol. Dept. Occupl. Therapy, 1989—. HHon. clin. faculty dept. occupl. therapy U. Soc. Calif., 1992-95, 95—; presenter in field. Contbr. articles to profl. jours., video. Mem. Am. Occupl. Therapy Found., Calif. Found. Occupl. Therapy. Recipient Lifetime Achievement award Occupl. Therapy Assn. Calif., 1990, Cert. Appreciation Govt. Affairs Commn., 1995. Mem. Am. Occupl. Therapy Assn. (Cert. Recognition commn. on edn. 1994), Am. Occupl. Therapy Polit. Action Com., Occupl. Therapy Assn. (Calif. We. area chpt.), World Fedn. Occupl. Therapy, Nat. Assn. Ret. Fed. Employees, V.A. Retirees, Disabled Am. Vets. Aux., Arleta C. of C., San Fernando Valley Japanese Am. Cultural Ctr., Gold Star Wives Am., Nat. History Assn. San Luis Obispo Coast, Inc., Tau Alpha Epsilon. Home: 9427 Obeck Ave Arleta CA 91331-5521 Home Phone: 805-528-3520; Office Phone: 818-899-8029. Personal E-mail: fkelley725@aol.com.

KELLEY, JOSEPH LEO, III, obstetrician, gynecologic oncologist; MD, St. Louis U. Sch. of Medicine, Mo. Intern Magee Womens Hosp. of Univ. of Pitts. Med. Ctr. (UPMC), 1986, resident, 1989, Univ. of Tex. MD Anderson Cancer Ctr., Houston, 1988, fellow, 1991; hosp. affiliations include Magee-Womens Hosp. of UPMC, UPMC Mercy, UPMC Passavant, UPMC Presbyn., UPMC Shadyside. Fellow: ACS, Am. Congress of Obstetricians and Gynecologists; mem.: Soc. of Gynecologic Oncologists. Office: Magee Gynecologic Cancer Program 300 Halket St Ste 1750 Pittsburgh PA 15213 Office Phone: 412-641-5411.

KELLEY, LISA L., medical association administrator; b. New Bedford, Mass., Mar. 31, 1953; Baccalaureate in Nursing Sci., U. Mass., Fitchburg Campus, 1975; MBA, Fla. Inst. Tech., 1984. Chief oper., chief nursing officer Fawcett Meml. Hosp., 1999—2001; chief oper. officer Kindred Hosp. Ctrl. Tampa, 2002—05; adminstr. Adult & Children's Surgery Ctr., SW Fla., 2006—. Mem.: Fla. Soc. Ambulatory Surg. Ctrs., ASC Assn. Avocation: photography. Office: 5238 Mason Corbin Ct Ste 101 Fort Myers FL 33907 Office Fax: 239-936-9707. E-mail: lkelley@acscswf.com.

KELLEY, PATRICIA HAGELIN, geology educator; b. Cleve., Dec. 8, 1953; d. Daniel Warn and Virginia Louise (Morgan) Hagelin; m. Jonathan Robert Kelley, June 18, 1977; children: Timothy Daniel, Katherine Louise. BA, Coll. of Wooster, 1975; AM, Harvard U., 1977, PhD, 1979. Instr. New Eng. Coll., Henniker, NH, 1979; asst. prof. U. Miss., University, 1979-85, assoc. prof., 1985-89, acting assoc. vice chancellor acad. affairs, 1988, prof., 1989-92, assoc. dean, 1989-90; program dir. NSF, Washington, 1990-92; prof., chmn. dept. geology U. N.D., Grand Forks, 1992-97; prof. U. NC, Wilmington, 1997—, chmn. dept. earth scis., 1997—2003. Editor several books; contbr. articles to profl. jours. Deacon Bethel Presbyn. Ch., Olive Branch, Miss., 1985-90. Rsch. grantee NSF, 1986-89, 90-99, 2000-03, 2008-; NSF fellow, 1976-79. Fellow AAAS, Geol. Soc. Am., Paleontol. Soc. (coun. 1984-85, 95-96, 98-2004, chair S.E. sect. 1984-85, chair N.C. sect. 1995-96, pres.-elect 1998-2000, pres. 2000-02, past pres. 2002-04); mem. Assn. Women Geosci. (Outstanding Educator award 2003), Paleontol. Rsch. Inst. (trustee 2003-, pres. bd. trustees 2004-06), Soc. Econ. Paleontologists and Mineralogists, Nat. Assn. Geosci. Tchrs. (disting. spkr. 2006-09), Sigma Xi, Phi Beta Kappa. Presbyterian. Avocations: writing, music, travel. Office: Dept Geography and Geology Univ NC Wilmington NC 28403-5944 Office Phone: 910-962-7406. Business E-Mail: kelleyp@uncw.edu.

KELLEY, PATRICK W., health science association administrator, preventive medicine physician; MD, U. Va.; DrPhD, Johns Hopkins Sch. of Hygiene and Public Health. Dir. Global Emerging Infections System US Dept. of Defense, Silver Spring, Md., 1990—2002; dir. Preventive Medicine Walter Reed Army Inst. of Research, Silver Spring, Md., 1990—2002; dir., Global Health Bd. Inst. of Medicine-Nat. Academies, Washington, 2003—, dir., African Sci. Acad. Develop. Bd., 2005—. Invited spkr. in field. Fellow: Am. Coll. Preventative Medicine. Office: Inst Medicine 500 5th St NW Washington DC 20001 Office Phone: 202-334-2650. E-mail: africa@nas.edu.

KELLEY, ROBERT OTIS, academic administrator, anatomist; b. Santa Monica, Calif., Apr. 30, 1944; s. David Otis and Onetia May (Nettles) Kelley; m. Marcia Jean Bell; children: Jennifer Leigh, Karin Michelle, Matthew Philip, Sarah Ann. BS, Abilene Christian U., 1965; MA, U. Calif., Berkeley, 1966, PhD, 1969. Asst. prof. U. N.Mex. Sch. Medicine, Albuquerque, 1969-74, assoc. prof., 1974-79, prof., 1979, chmn. dept. anatomy, 1981-97; assoc. vice chancellor rsch., exec. dean grad. coll. U. Ill., Chgo., 1997-99; dean Coll. Health Scis., U. Wyo., Laramie, 1999—2008; pres. U. ND, Grand Forks, 2008—. Vis. scientist Okazaki (Japan) Nat. Labs., 1984-85; mem. study sect. NIH, Bethesda, Md., 1982-86, U.S. Med. Licensing Exam. Step 1, 1995—; anatomy com. Nat. Bd. Mex. Examiners, Phila., 1992—. Author: Basic Histology, 1989; editor Cell and Tissue Rsch., 1970—, Anat. Record, 1970-97; contbr. articles to profl. jours. Patroller Nat. Ski Patrol, 1970—. Recipient Rsch. Career Devel. award NIH, 1972-77, Kaiser award U. Calif., Irvine, 1976; Internat. Exch. Scholar NSF; NIH grantee, 1970—, Svc. award, 1999, Ladman award, Am. Assn. Anatomists, 2002. Mem. Fedn. Am. Socs. for Exptl. Biology (pub. affairs exec. com. 1993—), Am. Soc. Cell Biology, Soc. for Devel. Biology, Electron Microscopy Soc. Am. (bd. dirs. 1987—), Am. Assn. Anatomists (exec. com. 1988—), Assn. Am. Med. Colls. (exec. coun. 1995—, chair assembly 1997-99), Nat. Caucus of Basic Biomed. Sci. Chairs, Nat. Bd. Med. Examiners. Democrat. Avocations: sailing, skiing, scuba diving, backpacking. Home: 1 Yale Dr Grand Forks ND 58203 Office Phone: 701-777-2121. Office Fax: 701-777-3866. E-mail: rkelley@mail.und.edu.

KELLEY, WILLIAM NIMMONS, physician, educator, science administrator, dean; b. Atlanta, June 23, 1939; s. Oscar Lee and Willa Nimmons (Allen) Kelley, m. Lois Faville, Aug. 1, 1959; children: Margaret Paige, Virginia Lynn, Lori Ann, William Mark. MD, Emory U., 1963; MA (hon.), U. Pa., 1989. Diplomate Am. Bd. Internal Medicine (chmn. 1985-1986). Intern in medicine Parkland Meml. Hosp., Dallas, 1963—64, resident, 1964—65; sr. resident medicine Mass. Gen. Hosp., Boston, 1967—68; clin. assoc., sect. on human biochem. genetics NIH, 1965—67; tchg. fellow medicine Harvard U. Med. Sch., 1967—68; asst. prof. to prof. medicine, asst. prof. to assoc. prof. biochemistry, chief divsn. rheumatic and genetic diseases Duke University School Medicine, 1968—75; Macy faculty scholar Oxford U., 1974—75; prof., chmn. dept. internal medicine, prof. dept. biol. chemistry U. Mich. Med. Sch., Ann Arbor, 1975—89; Robert G. Dunlop prof. medicine, biochemistry and biophysics University of Pennsylvania, Phila., 1989—2000, dean Sch. Medicine, 1989—2000; CEO U. Pa. Med. Ctr. and Health Sys., Phila., 1989—2000; prof., 2000—. Human gene therapy subcom. NIH, 1986—92, recombinant DNA com., 1988—92, dirs. adv. com., 1992—95; bd. dirs. Merck & Co., Beckman Coulter, Inc., GenVec, Inc. Author: (with J.B. Wyngaarden): Gout and Hyperuricemia, 1976; author: (with I.M. Weiner) Uric Acid, 1979; author: (with Harris, Ruddy and Sledge) Textbook of Rheumatology, 1981, 5th edit., 1997, now Kelley's Textbook of Rheumatology, 8th edit., 2009, Arthritis Surgery, 1994; author: (with M. Osterweiss and E.R. Rubin) Emerging Policies for Bio-Medical Research (Health Policy Annual III), 1993; editor-in-chief: Textbook of Internal Medicine, 1989, Textbook of Internal Medicine, 3rd edit., 1997; editor-in-chief now Kelley's Textbook of Internal Medicine, 4th edit., 2000; editor-in-chief: Essentials of Internal Medicine, 1994; contbr. articles to profl. jours. Trustee Emory U., 1992—, Emory U., Woodruff Health Scis. Ctr. Recipient C.V. Mosby award, 1963, John D. Lane award, USPHS, 1969, Rsch. Career Devel. award, 1972—75, Geigy Internat. prize rheumatology, 1969, Heinz Karger Meml. Found. prize, 1973, Disting. Med. Achievement award, Emory U., 1985, John Phillips Meml. award and medal, ACP, 1990, Nat. Med. Rsch. award, Nat. Health Coun., 1993, Robert H. Williams award, Assn. Profs. of Medicine, 1995, David E. Rogers award, Assn. Am. Med. Coll., 1999, Emory medal, 2000; scholar, Mead Johnson, 1967, Josiah Macy Found., 1974—75; Clin. scholar, Am. Rheumatism Assn., 1969—72. Master: ACP, Am. Coll. Rheumatology; fellow: AAAS, Am. Philos. Soc., Am. Acad. Arts and Scis.; mem.: Assn. Profs. Medicine (sec.-treas. 1987—89), Am. Soc. Internal Medicine, Am. Soc. Human Genetics, Ctrl. Rheumatism Soc. (pres. 1978—79), Australian Rheumatism Assn. (hon.), Royal Coll. Physicians Ireland (hon.), Am. Coll. Rheumatology (editl. bd. 1972—77, pres. 1986—87, Gold Medal award 1997), Assn. Am. Physicians (Kober medal 2005), Am. Fedn. Med. Rsch. (pres. 1979—81), Am. Soc. Biochemistry and Molecular Biology (editl. bd. 1976—81), Am. Soc. Clin. Investigation (editl. bd. 1974—79, pres. 1983—84, editl. bd. 2007—, pres.

2007—), Inst. Medicine of NAS (chmn. sect. 4 1988—90, chmn. membership com. 1990—94, coun. mem., exec. com. 1996—2001), Ctrl. Soc. for Clin. Rsch. (pres. 1986—87), Alpha Omega Alpha, Sigma Xi. Office: BRB II/III 421 Curie Blvd Ste 1403 Philadelphia PA 19104 Home: 10750 Savannah Dr Vero Beach FL 32963 Personal E-mail: kelleywn@hotmail.com.

KELLMAN, ROBERT M., otolaryngologist, educator; b. Bklyn., Mar. 11, 1952; AB, Cornell U., 1973; MD, SUNY, Upstate Med. Ctr., 1977. Prof., chair otolaryngology and communication sci. SUNY, Upstate Med. U., 1994—. Recipient Anderson award, Am. Bd. Facial Plastic and Reconstructive Surgery. Fellow: ACS, Am. Acad. Otolaryngology - Head and Neck Surgery, Am. Acad. Facial Plastic and Reconstructive Surgery. Avocations: piano, writing. Office: 750 East Adams St Syracuse NY 13210 Office Fax: 315-464-7298. Business E-Mail: kellmanr@upstate.edu.

KELLOGG, HUSTON GLENN, pediatrician, medical educator; b. LA, Apr. 6, 1924; s. William Pitt and Thelma Bernice Kellogg; m. Eleanor Katherine Duncan, June 16, 1990; 1 child, Brian McBride Hodge; m. Dorothy Zulick Kellogg (dec.); children: Jacob William, Paul Huston, Michael Sherman. BS, Yale U., New Haven, 1945; MD, Washington U., St. Louis, 1947. Diplomate Am. Bd. Pediat. Intern St. Luke's Hosp., St. Louis, 1947—48; resident pediat. St. Joseph's Infirmary, Lousiville, Ky., 1948—49, St. Louis U., 1949—50; pvt. practice pediat. San Diego, 1952—62, La Mesa, 1962—95; chief pediat. and infectious disease San Diego County Hosp., 1957—61; faculty U. Calif. San Diego, 1969—. Med. dir. Home of Guiding Hands, Lakside, Calif., 1967—79. Contbr. articles pub. to profl. jour., scientific papers. Bd., chair Grossmont Hosp. Found., La Mesa, 1996—2002; bd. dirs. Home of Guiding Hands, San Diego Regional Ctr. for Devel. Disabilities, 2000—06. Capt. M.C. USNR, 1943—84. Mem.: Acad. Pediat. Poets Rodeo, Marine Corps Tankers Assn., Navy League, Found. for Devel. Disabilities (bd. dirs. 2011—), Grossmont Hosp. Found. (chmn.), San Diego County Med. Soc. Found. Ret. Physicians Soc. (chair 2006—09, bd. dirs. 2006—09), Assn. Mil. Surgeons U.S., Naval Res. Assn., Res. Officers Assn. (nat. surgeon 1976, Civilion Pediat. Residency award), Rotary, Shriners. Republican. Presbyterian. Achievements include the first started civilian Pediatricresldency in the county. Avocations: travel, real estate. Home: 3404 Cromwell Pl San Diego CA 92116-1927 Personal E-mail: hgkell@aol.com.

KELLY, ARTHUR PAUL, physician; b. Asheville, NC, Nov. 23, 1938; s. Joseph Paul and Amanda Lee (Walker) Kelly; m. Beverly Gayle Baker, June 25, 1966; children: Traci Allyce, Kara Gisele. BA, Brown U., 1960; MD, Howard U., 1965. Intern Harper Hosp., Detroit, 1965-66; resident in dermatology Henry Ford Hosp., Detroit, 1968-71; instr. in dermatology Brown U., Providence, 1971-73; asst. prof. internal medicine Charles Drew U. Medicine & Sci., Los Angeles, 1973—77; prof. Charles R. Drew U. Medicine and Sci., LA, 1983; chief div. dermatology King.-Drew Med. Ctr., LA, 1976—2006, interim chmn. dept. internal medicine, 1985-86, vice chmn., 1987-91, chmn., 1992-95; assoc. prof. medicine U. So. Calif., LA, 1977-80; prof. UCLA, 1995—. Contbr. articles to profl jours, chapters to books; editor-in-chief: Jour. Nat. Med. Assn., 1997—2004. Served to capt US Army, 1966—68, Vietnam. Recipient Act-So award, NAACP, 1983. Fellow: Am Acad Dermatology; mem.: Am Dermatology Asn (vpres 1997—98, pres 1998—99), Asn Profs Dermatology (pres-elect 1996—98, pres 1998—2000), Nat Med Asn (chmn sect dermatology 1978—80, Oustanding Minority Dermatology Fellow 1972), Metropolitan LA Dermatology Soc (vpres 1986—87, pres 1987—88). Democrat. Avocations: travel, tennis. Office: King/Harbor Med Ctr 12021 S Wilmington Ave Los Angeles CA 90059-3019 Office Phone: 310-668-4571. Business E-Mail: apkelly@cdrewu.edu. E-mail: apaulkelly@cdrewu.edu.

KELLY, DANIEL JOHN, physician; b. Binghamton, NY, June 23, 1940; s. William James and Mary Elizabeth (Schmitt) K.; m. Lois Ann Lanshe, Aug. 21, 1965; children: Britton James, Jeffrey Daniel, Reid William, Piper Ann. AB in History, Yale U., 1962; MD, Jefferson Med. Coll., 1966. Diplomate in Pathology, Nuclear Medicine, Dermatopathology. Intern Naval Hosp., Boston, 1966-67, resident Oakland, Calif., 1966-71, asst. chief lab. Great Lakes, Ill., 1971-73, chief lab. svcs., 1973-75; co-dir. lab. Highland Park (Ill.) Hosp., 1975-97, dir. lab., 1980-89, 96-97; co-dir. lab. Lake Forest (Ill.) Hosp., 1975-97, dir. lab., 1989-91; with Dean, Hoffman & Clark Pathologists S.C., Lake Forest, 1975-97, Associated Lab. Physician Svcs., Wauwatosa, Wis., 1997-99; chief of staff elect Highland Park (Ill.) Hosp., 1992-94, chief of staff, 1994-96, also bd. dirs.; with Consolidated Pathology Cons., S.C., Lake Bluff, Ill., 1999—2007. Med. exec. com. Highland Park Hosp., 1992-97, Lake Forest Hosp., 1989-91. Bd. dirs. Lake Forest Hist. Preservation Found., 1979-88; mem. bldg. rev. bd. City Govt., Lake Forest, 1989-93; mem. clin. lab. and blood bank adv. bd. Ill. Dept. Pub. Health, 1990-95; mem. Am. Pathology Found. Comdr. USNR, 1966-75. Fellow Coll. Am. Pathology, Am. Soc. Clin. Pathology, Internat. Acad. Pathologists; mem. AMA, Ill. Soc. Pathologists, Am. Soc. Dermatopathology, Internat. Soc. Dermatopathology, Assn. Military Surgeons Roman Catholic. Avocations: reading, art, music, fishing. Home: 499 E Illinois Rd Lake Forest IL 60045-2364 Office: 499 E Illinus Rd Lake Forest IL 60045-2364 Office Fax: 847-234-8032. Personal E-mail: djkellymd@yahoo.com.

KELLY, DANIEL P., cardiologist, molecular biologist; b. Oct. 6, 1955; m. Therese J. Michelau; 3 children. BS in Biology, U. Ill., 1978, MD, 1982. Diplomate Am. Bd. Internal Medicine, Am. Bd. Cardiovasc. Disease. Intern in medicine Barnes Hosp., St. Louis, 1982—83, asst. resident in medicine, 1983—85; chief med. resident John Cochran VA Hosp., Washington U. Svc., 1984—85; rsch. postdoctoral fellow cardiovascular divsn. and dept. biol. chemistry Washington U. Sch. of Medicine, St. Louis, 1985—87, fellow in clin. cardiology, 1987—89, instr. of medicine cardiovascular divsn., 1989—90, asst. prof. medicine cardiovascular divsn., 1990—95, asst. prof. molecular biology and pharmacology, 1993—95, co-dir. Ctr. Adults with Congenital Heart Disease, 1993—, assoc. prof. medicine and molecular biology & pharmacology, 1995—, dir. Ctr. for Cardiovascular Rsch., 1996—, prof. medicine and molecular biology & pharmacology, 1999—, prof. pediatrics, 2000—, co-dir., Cardiovascular Div., Dept. Medicine. Lectr. rsch. and clin. fellowship program Washington U. Sch. Medicine, 1989, lectr. pharmacology and pathophysiology, 94; attending physician medicine and cardiology svcs. Barnes and Jewish Hosps., St. Louis, 1989. Contbr. chapters to books, articles to profl. jours. Recipient Lucille P. Markey Scholar award, Markey Found., 1989, Basal O'Connor Scholar award, March of Dimes, 1991, Rsch. Tng. grantee, NHLBI, 1994—, 1996—. Fellow: Am. Coll. Cardiology; mem.: AAAS, Am. Soc. for Clin. Investigation, Internat. Soc. Adult Congenital Heart Disease, Internat. Soc. Heart Rsch., Am. Heart Assn. (basic sci. coun., Established Investigator award 1995), Am. Fedn. Clin. Rsch., Alpha Omega Alpha, Phi Beta Kappa. Office: Washington U Sch of Medicine Clinical Sciences Rsch Bldg North Addition Rm 810 Saint Louis MO 63110-1010 Office Phone: 314-362-8908, 314-362-8912. Office Fax: 314-362-0186. E-mail: dkelly@burnham.org.

KELLY, DOROTHY HELEN, pediatrician, educator; b. Fitchburg, Mass., July 29, 1944; BS in Nursing magna cum laude, Fitchburg State Co., 1966; BS with distinction, Wayne State U., 1968, MD with distinction, 1972. Diplomate Am. Bd. Pediatrics, Pediatric Pulmonology. Intern Children's Svc. Mass. Gen. Hosp., Boston, 1972-73, resident in pediatrics, 1973-75, fellow in pediatrics pulmonary medicine, 1976-79, co-dir. pediat. pulmonary lab., 1976—83, assoc. dir. pediatric pulmonary unit, 1983—95; teaching fellow Harvard Med. Sch., Boston, 1973-75, clin. fellow, 1972-75, instr. in pediatrics, 1975-81, asst. prof. pediatrics, 1981-89, assoc. prof. pediatrics, 1989-95, U. Tex., Galveston, 1995-97, Houston, 1995—; assoc. dir. S.W. SIDS Rsch. Inst. Meml. Herman S.W. Hosp., Houston, 1995—. Cons. Bur. Community Health Svcs., NEW, 1979-80, FDA, 1986, 88-92, ECRI, 1987-88, also others; chmn. apnea adv. com. Nat. Sudden Infant Death Syndrome Found., 1979-81; mem. com. anesthesiology and respiratory devices panel Ctr. for Devices and Radiol. Health, FDA, 1990-94; chmn. physicians' com. Nat. Assn. Apnea Profls., 1990-91, also others; reviewer numerous jours. in field. Contbr. numerous articles to profl. jours. Recipient Woman of Vision award Nat. Soc. for Prevention of Blindness, Mass. Affiliate, 1981, First Disting. Alumni award Fitchburg State Coll., 1984, grants in field. Mem. Am. Med. Woman's Assn., Am. Acad. Pediatrics (task force on prolonged apnea 1978), Am. Thoracic Soc., Internat. Pediatric Soc., Assn. for Psychophysiol. Study Sleep, Soc. for Pediatric Rsch., Tex. Thoracic Soc., Tex. Med. Assn., Tex. Pediatric Soc., Am. Autonomic Soc., Am. Assn. SIDS Prevention Physicians (bd. dirs., pres.), NH Pediatric Soc, Am. SIDS Inst. (bd. mem.). Office: Western Mass Pediatrics Holyoke MA 01040 Office Phone: 603-484-2803. E-mail: dhkelly@aap.net. *

KELLY, JOHN DAVID, IV, orthopaedic surgeon, educator; MD, U. Cincinnati. Lic. Pa., 1985, diplomate Am. Bd. Orthopaedic Surgery, 1992. Fellow Temple Univ. Hosp., 1990; intern Pa. Univ. Hosp., 1985, resident, 1989, assoc. prof. clin. orthop. surgery, dir. undergraduate orthop. edn., surgeon. Named one of the Top Doctors, Phila. Mag., 2010—11. Mem.: Irish Am. Orthop. Assn., Am. Orthop. Assn., Am. Acad. Orthop. Soc., Eastern Orthop. Assn., Am. Orthop. Soc. Sports Medicine, Arthroscopy Assn. N.Am., Phila. Orthop. Sports Soc., Phila. Orthop. Soc., Pa. Orthop. Soc. Office: Pennsylvania University Hospital Orthopaedic Surgery PA Medicine Radnor 250 King Prussia Rd Radnor PA 19087 Office Phone: 800-789-7366.

KELLY, KATHLEEN, medical researcher; PhD, U. Calif., Irvine. Postdoctoral tng. Harvard Med. Sch.; ind. investigator Nat. Cancer Inst., NIH, 1984—, head signal transduction sect., chief Cell and Cancer Biology Br., Ctr. Cancer Rsch. Office: Nat Cancer Inst Bldg 37 Rm 1068 37 Convent Dr Bethesda MD 20892 Office Phone: 301-435-4651. Office Fax: 301-435-4655. E-mail: kkelly@helix.nih.gov. *

KELLY, LUCIE STIRM YOUNG, retired nursing educator; b. Stuttgart, Germany, May 2, 1925; came to U.S., 1929; d. Hugo Karl and Emilie Rosa (Engel) Stirm; m. J. Austin Young, Aug. 30, 1946 (div. Feb. 1971); m. Thomas Martin Kelly, 1972 (dec. Aug. 2003); 1 child by previous marriage, Gay Aleta (Mrs. Donald Meyer). BS, U. Pitts., 1947, MLitt, 1957, PhD, 1965; D in Nursing Edn. (hon.), U. RI, 1977; LHD (hon.), Georgetown U., 1983; DSc (hon.), Widener U., 1984; D of Pub. Svc. (hon.), Am. U., 1985; DSc (hon.), U. Mass., 1989; DHL (hon.), SUNY, 1996. Instr. nursing McKeesport (Pa.) Hosp., 1953-57, asst. adminstr. nursing, 1966-69; asst. prof. nursing U. Pitts., 1957-64, asst. dean, 1965; prof., chmn. nursing dept. Calif. State U., LA, 1969-72; co-project dir. curriculum rsch. Nat. League for Nursing, 1973-74; project dir. patient edn., office consumer health edn., also adj. assoc. prof. cmty. medicine Coll. Medicine and Dentistry N.J.-Rutgers Med. Sch., 1974-75; prof. pub. health and nursing Sch. Pub. Health and Sch. Nursing Columbia U., NYC, 1975-90, prof. emeritus Sch Pub. Health, Sch. Nursing, 1990—, assoc. dean acad. affairs Sch. Pub. Health, 1988-90, hon. prof. nursing edn. Tchrs. Coll., 1977-93, acting head divsn. health adminstrn. Sch. Pub. Health, 1980-81, 86-88; on leave as exec. dir. Mid-Atlantic Regional Nursing Assn., 1981-82. Cons. U. Nev., Las Vegas, 1970-72, Ball State U., Ind., 1971, Long Beach (Calif.) Naval Hosp., 1971-72, Travis AFB, Calif., 1972, Brentwood VA Hosp., LA, 1971-72, Ctrl. Nursing Office VA, Washington, 1971-94, NJ Dept. Higher Edn., 1974-78, John Wiley Pub., 1974-76, Sch. Nursing and Sch. Pub. Health Am. U. Beirut accreditation visit, 1978; spl. med. adv. group VA Dept. Medicine and Surgery, Washington, 1980-84; cons. nursing com. AMA, 1971-74, Citizen's Com. for Children, NYC; v.p. Pa. Health Coun., 1968-69; adv. com. physicians assts. Calif. Bd. Med. Examiners, adv. com. Cancer Soc. LA, 1970-72, com. nursing VA, Washington, 1971-74, chair 1975-90, regional med. programs, Pa., 1967-69, Calif. 1970-72; spl. adv. com. on med. licensure and profl. conduct N.Y. State Assembly, 1977-79, nat. adv. com. Encore (nat. YWCA post-mastectomy group rehab. project), 1977-83; assoc. mem. NY Acad. Medicine, 1988-90; ethics com. Palisades Med. Ctr., 1993-05, bd. govs., 1995-05, mem. profl. and quality rev. com., 1995-05, chair, 1998-05, exec. com., 1998-99; 2d vice chair N.Y. Presbyn. Healthcare Sys., Palisades Med. Ctr., 1999-03, 1st vice chair 2003-05; lectr., cons., guest Beijing Med. Coll., China, 1982, Aga Khan U., Pakistan, 1990; bd. visitors U. Pitts. Sch. Nursing, 1986-93; editl. adv. bd. Am. Jour. Pub. Health, 1992, chair, 1993-97; chair adv. com. grad. program in pub. health U. Medicine and Dentistry NJ, 1995-00; vol. cert. mediator for Hudson County mcpl. cts., 2004-05; lectr. in field Author: (textbooks) Dimensions of Profl. Nursing, 8th edit., 1999, The Nursing Experience: Trends, Challenges, Transitions, 4th edit., 2002; contbg. editor: Jour. Nursing Adminstrn., 1975—82; columnist: jour. Nursing Outlook, editor-in-chief, 1982—91; mem. bd. advisors (jour.) Nurses Almanac, 1978, Nurse Manager's Handbook, 1979, Nursing Administration Handbook, 1992; editor (editl. bd.): (jour.) Am. Health, 1981—91; mem. editl. bd. Nursing and Health Care, 1991—95, Internat. Nursing Index, 1997—2001. Bd. dirs. ARC, LA, 1971-72; bd. dirs. Vis. Nurse Svc. N.Y., 1980-01, mem. exec. com., chmn. human resources, 1989-01; bd. dirs. Concern for Dying, 1983-89; bd. trustees Calif. State Coll. LA Found., 1971-72, U. Pitts., 1984-90, mem. exec. com. 1988-90; chair bd. visitors U. Pitts. Sch. Pub. Health, 1988-90; bd. visitors U. Miami Sch. Nursing, 1986-05; mem. health svcs. com. Children's Aid Soc., N.Y., 1978-84; v.p. Am. Nurses Found., 1980-82; mem. nat. adv. coun. on nurse tng. HRA, 1981-85; mem. nurses leadership coun. Chlorine Chemistry Coun., 1999-03; hon. bd. dirs. NOVA Found., 1998—, Health Professions Panel, Am. Legacy Found., 2000—. Named Outstanding Alumna U. Pitts. Sch. Nursing, 1966, Pa. Nurse of Yr., 1967, Roll of Honor N.J. State Nurses Assn., 1990; named to Tchrs. Coll. Columbia U. Nursing Edn. Alumni Hall of Fame, 1999; recipient Disting. Alumna award U. Pitts. Sch. Edn., 1981, Shaw medal Boston Coll., 1985, Bicentennial Medallion of Distinction, U. Pitts., 1987, R. Louise McManus Medallion for Disting. Svc. to Nursing, Tchrs. Coll. Columbia U., 1987, Dean's Disting. Svc. award Columbia Sch. Pub. Health, 1995, Second Century award in health care, Columbia U. Sch. Nursing, 1996; fellow HEW, 1965. Fellow Am. Acad. Nursing (named Living Legend 2001); mem. ANA (dir. 1978-82, Hon. Recognition award 1992), APHA (Ruth Freeman Pub. Health Nursing award 1993), Pa. Nurses Assn. (pres. 1966-69), Nat. League Nursing (bd. govs. 1991-95), Nurses Ednl. Funds Bd., U. Pitts. Sch. Nursing Alumni (pres. 1959), Vis. Nurse Assn. Ctrl. Jersey (bd. dirs. 1999-2001, mem. bd. trustees), Am. Hosp. Assn. (com. chmn. 1967-68), Assn. Grad. Faculty Cmty. Health/Pub. Health Nursing (v.p. 1980-81), Sigma Theta Tau (sr. editor Image 1978-81, pres.-elect 1981-83, pres. 1983-85, nat. campaign chair Ctr. for Nursing Scholarship 1987-89, chair devel. com. 1989-95, spl. advisor 1995-97, planned giving task force 1998-2001, Mentor award 1985, 93, 97, Spirit of Philanthropy award 1997), Pi Lambda Theta, Alpha Tau Delta (Cert. of Merit 1968). Achievements include collection of papers in Mugar Library, Boston U. Personal E-mail: storm25@wcbr.us.

KELLY, MICHAEL A., orthopedist, surgeon; Attended, U. NC, Georgetown U., 1979. Diplomate Am. Bd. Orthopaedic Surgery, 1987, Am. Bd. Orthopaedic Surgery, 1997. Resident surgery St. Vincent's Hosp., 1980—81; resident orthopaedic surgery Columbia-Presbyn. Hosp., 1981—84; fellow knee surgery Hosp. for Spl. Surgery, 1984—85; with Lenox Hill Hosp.; dir. Insall Scott Kelly Inst.; head team physician NJ Nets; chmn. dept. of orthopaedic surgery Hackensack Univ. Med. Ctr. Co-editor: Surgery of the Knee 2nd Edition. Mem.: Am. Knee Soc. (pres.), Am. Orthopaedic Assn., Am. Orthopaedic Soc. of Sports Medicine. Office: Hackensack University Medical Center Ste 303 360 Essex St Hackensack NJ 07601 Office Phone: 201-336-8867. Office Fax: 201-336-8873.

KELLY, PATRICK JOSEPH, neurosurgeon, educator; b. Lackawanna, NY, Sept. 19, 1941; s. Joseph P. and Mary D. (Conner) K.; m. Carol Huey; children: Patrick D., Michael, Caitlin. BS, U. Mich., 1962; MD, SUNY, Buffalo, 1966. Cert. Am. Bd. Neurol. Surgery 1978. Intern U.S. Naval Hosp., Phila., 1966-67; resident neurosurgery Northwestern U., Chgo., 1970-72; resident neurosurgery med. branch U. Tex., Galveston, 1972—74; from asst. prof. to assoc. prof. U. Tex. Med. Sch., Galveston, 1974—79; assoc. prof. SUNY, Buffalo, 1979-84; prof., cons. Mayo Med. Sch./Mayo Clinic, Rochester, Minn., 1984-93; Joseph P. Ransohoff prof., chmn. neurosurg. dept. NYU Sch. Medicine, 1993—2008. Cons., adv. bd. mem. Jet Propulsion Lab NASA, Pasadena, Calif., 1994—. Author: Tumor Stereotaxis, 1991; co-editor: Computers in Stereotactic Neurosurgery, 1992; mem. editl. bd. Neurosurgery, 1991—, Surg. Neurology, 1990—, Jour. Stereotactic and Functional Neurosurgery, 1986—; contbr. chpts. in books and articles to profl. jours.; profiled Am.'s Top Drs. and Top Drs.: New York Metro Area 2000-2002 of Castle Connolly Guide. Trustee Boys and Girls Club of Am. Lt. comdr. MC USN, 1968—70. Recipient Scoville award World Fedn. Neurol. Surgery, 1997; named Citizen of Yr. Buffalo Evening News, 1982, Best Doctors in Am. Good Housekeeping, 1993, Town & Country, 1992, Am. Health, 1996, Top 100, Irish Am. mag., 1996, 99, Best Drs. N.Y., New York Mag., 1999, 2000-05, Woodward/White, Inc., 1998, 2000, 01, 02, Obrador medal Spanish Neurol. Soc., 1996, Sir Peter Freyer medal, Irish Surgical Soc., 2001, Invitee d'Honneur French Neurosurg. Soc., 2000, Olivacrona medal Karolinska Inst., Stockholm, 2002, Schneider Lectr. Am. Assn. Neurolog. Surgeons, 1996, 2002; named to Boys and Girls Clubs Am. Hall of Fame, 2001. Fellow ACS; mem. Am. Soc. Stereotactic Neurosurgery (past pres., bd. dirs.), Am. Assn. Neurol. Surgeons (Van Wagenen fellow 1977, com. chmn.), Acad. Neurol. Surgery, Soc. Neurol. Surgeons (com.), Soc. Neurochurgic de Lange Francaise., Brain Tumor Found. (founder 1997), World Soc. Stereotactic and Functional Neurosurgery (v.p., bd. dirs.), NY Yacht Club, Metropolitan Club (NY). Roman Catholic. Achievements include development of a computer-assisted image guiding stereotactic neurosurgery for brain tumors. Avocations: sailing, watercolor painting. Office: NYU Med Ctr 530 1st Ave New York NY 10016-6402 Home Phone: 212-751-7751; Office Phone: 212-263-8002. Office Fax: 212-263-8031. Business E-Mail: kellyp01@med.nyu.edu.

KELLY, ROBERT E., hospital administrator, anesthesiologist; b. Phila. MD, U. Cin. Coll. Medicine, 1981. Intern Christ Hosp., Cin.; resident NY Hosp. Cornell U. Medical Ctr., 1982—84, fellow, 1984—85; clinical instr. Cornell U. Medical Ctr., 1985—87, asst. prof., 1987—93, assoc. prof., 1993—99, prof., 1999—; mgmt. positions NY-Presbyn. Hosp. (formerly NY Hosp.), 1995—97; sr. v.p., COO, chief medical officer NY-Presbyn. Hosp., NYC, 1999—2007, group sr. v.p., 2007—11, pres., 2011—. Office: NY-Presbyterian Hospital 161 Fort Washington Ave HIP 14-1456 New York NY 10032 Office Phone: 212-305-0090. Office Fax: 212-305-6740. *

KELLY, THOMAS JESSE, JR., molecular biologist, researcher; b. Birmingham, Ala., Nov. 21, 1941; s. Thomas Jesse and Agnes (Allen) K.; m. Mary Lucinda Schwartz, June 25, 1969; children: Mark Thomas, Andrew Samuel. BA with honors, Johns Hopkins U., 1962, PhD in Biophysics, 1968, MD, 1969. Served with USPHS, 1970-72. Postdoctoral fellow Harvard Med. Sch., Boston, 1968, Johns Hopkins U. Sch. Medicine, Balt., 1969-70; staff assoc. Nat. Inst. Health, Bethesda, Md., 1970-72; asst. prof. microbiology Johns Hopkins U. Sch. Medicine, Balt., 1972-75, assoc. prof., 1976-79, Boury Prof. molecular biology and genetics, 1980—2002, dir. dept., 1982—2002; dir. Sloan-Kettering Inst., NYC, 2002—. Chmn. study sect. virology NIH, 1988-90; served on many nat. adv. boards; mem. adv. com. to dir., NIH, scientific mgmt. review bd. Mem. editorial bd. Jour. Biol. Chemistry, 1982-94, Jour. Virology, 1980-90, Virus Rsch., 1983-93, Oncogene Rsch., 1989-94, Seminars in Virology, 1989-95, Am. Soc. Biochem. Molecular Biology, 1989-94. Awards assembly Gen. Motors Cancer Prize; bd. dirs. Passano Found. Recipient Career Devel. award NIH, 1972-77, Alfred P. Sloane, Jr. award, GM Cancer Rsch. Found., 2004; co-recipient Louisa Gross Horwitz prize, Columbia U., 2010. Fellow Am. Acad. Arts and Sci.; mem. NAS, Am. Soc. Biological

Chemists, Am. Soc. Microbiology, Am. Soc. Virology, Am. Philosophical Soc., Phi Beta Kappa, Alpha Omega Alpha, Inst. Medicine. Office: Sloan-Kettering Institute 1275 York Ave New York NY 10021 Office Phone: 212-639-8614. Office Fax: 646-422-2189. Business E-Mail: tkelly@mskcc.org.

KELMAN, MARYBETH, retired health care consultant, health policy analyst; AS in Nursing, Rutgers U., 1964; BA, Douglas Coll., 1977; MA, Rutgers U., 1988. Program dir. health promotion N.J. Hosp. Assn., Princeton, NJ, 1983-87; policy analyst N.J. Dept. Human Svcs., Trenton, NJ, 1988-89; exec. dir. Eye Screening Coord. Coun. N.J., Inc., Monmouth Junction, NJ, 1989-91; health care cons. N.J. Divsn. Pensions and Benefits, Trenton, 1992—2004; ret., 2004. Trustee Forums Inst. for Pub. Policy, Princeton, 1998—2008, chmn., 1998—2005. Home: 1500 Sawyer Ave Manasquan NJ 08736 Personal E-mail: marybeth.kelman@gmail.com.

KELSEN, DAVID PAUL, medical oncologist; MD, MCP Hahnemann U., 1972. Diplomate Am. Bd. Internal Medicine, Am. Bd. Internal Medicine-med. oncology, registered NY, 1976. Intern Temple Univ. Hosp., 1973, resident, 1976; fellow Meml. Sloan-Kettering Cancer Ctr., NY, 1977, chief gastrointestinal oncology svc. Office: Memorial Sloan-Kettering Cancer Center 1275 York Ave New York NY 10065 Office Phone: 212-639-8470.

KELTY, PAUL DAVID, obstetrician, educator; b. Louisville, Oct. 2, 1947; s. William Theadore and Mary Frances (Hinton) Kelty. BEE, U. Louisville, 1970, MD, 1978; MS, Ohio State U., 1971. Tech. staff Bell Labs., Whippany, NJ, 1970—72; design engr. GE, Louisville, 1972—74; intern St. Mary's Med. Ctr., Evansville, Ind., 1978—79, resident in ob-gyn., 1979—82; pvt. practice Corydon, Ind., 1982—. Clin. instr. dept. ob-gyn U. Louisville Sch. Medicine, 1987—. Mem.: AMA, N.Y. Acad. Scis., Am. Inst. Ultrasound Medicine, Am. Soc. Reproductive Medicine, Sigma Xi, Omicron Delta Kappa, Gamma Beta Phi, Eta Kappa Nu, Sigma Pi Sigma, Sigma Tau, Tau Beta Pi, Phi Kappa Phi. Roman Catholic. Home and Office: 2000 Edsel Ln NW Corydon IN 47112 Office Phone: 812-738-8206. Business E-Mail: paul.keltymd@insightbb.com.

KELTZ, MARTIN D., gynecologist, educator; MD, NYU, 1989. Diplomate Am. Bd. Ob-Gyn, 1996, Am. Bd. Ob-Gyn-reproductive endocrinology, 1998. Resident ob-gyn. NYU/Bellevue Hosp., NYC, 1990—93; fellow reproductive endocrinology Yale Univ. Sch. of Medicine, New Haven, 1993—95; dir. Continuum Reproductive Ctr., NYC, dir. reproductive endocrinology and infertility ob-gyn. dept. St. Luke's-Roosevelt Hosp. Ctr., NYC, 1995—; assoc. clin. prof. ob-gyn. Columbia Univ. Coll. of Physician and Surgeons, NYC, 1995—. Office: 425 West 59th St Ste 5A New York NY 10019 Office Phone: 212-523-7751. Office Fax: 212-523-7575.

KEMENY, M. MARGARET, oncologist, surgeon, hospital administrator, educator; b. Elizabeth, NJ, May 7, 1946; d. George Kemeny and Ellen Sagi. BS, Harvard U., 1968; MD, Columbia U., 1972. Dir. cancer ctr. Queens Cancer Ctr., NYC, 2001—; prof. surgery Mt. Sinai Sch. Medicine, 2005—; divsn. chief surg. oncology SUNY Stony Brook. Mem. editl. bd. Am. Jour. Surgery, Annals of Surgery Oncology; chair, women in surgery com. ACS. Fellow: ACS (bd. govs., vice chair bd. govs.); mem.: Harvard Alumni Assn. (bd. dirs. 2010—), Assn. Women Surgeons (pres.). Home: 36 Perry St New York NY 10014 Office: Queens Cancer Ctr at Queens Hosp 82-68 164th St Jamaica NY 11432 Business E-Mail: kemenym@nychhc.org.

KEMMER, TERESA MARIE, dietician; b. Parkston, SD, Aug. 22, 1961; PhD, U. Wash., Seattle, 2001. Asst. prof. SD State U., 2007—. Dietitian, ret. lt. col. U.S. Army, 1986—2007; adj. prof. Uniformed Svcs. U. Health Scis., 2007—. Recipient Disting. Rschr. award, SD State U. Coll. Edn. and Human Scis., Col. Mary Lipscomb Hamrick Rsch. award, Army Med. Specialist Corps.; grant, Agr. and Food Rsch. Initiative,USDA, Henry M. Jackson Found. Advancement Mil. Medicine. Mem.: SD Dietetic Assn., Soc. Nutrition Edn., Am. Dietetic Assn., Am. Soc. Nutrition. Avocations: golf, cooking, reading. Office: PO Box 2275A Wagner Hall 445 Brookings SD 57007 Business E-Mail: teresa.kemmer@sdstate.edu.

KEMP, STEPHEN FRANK, pediatric endocrinologist, educator, composer; b. Newport, Oreg., Mar. 21, 1947; s. Frank Shirley and Charla Mae (Wait) Kemp. BA, U. Oreg., 1969; PhD in Biochemistry, U. Chgo., 1974, MD, 1976. Diplomate Am. Bd. Pediat. Intern Stanford U., 1976-77, resident in pediat., 1977-78, fellow in pediat. endocrinology, 1978-80; asst. prof. pediat., chief pediat. endocrinology U. South Ala., Mobile, 1980-84; asst. prof. pediat. U. Ark. for Med. Sci., 1984-86, asst. prof. biochemistry, 1985-95, assoc. prof. pediat., 1986-95, chief pediat. endocrinology, 1987—2001, prof. pediat., 1995—. Composer (various choir, organ and orchestral works); contbr. V.p. Ala. affiliate Am. Diabetes Assn., 1982—84, pres., 1986—88, chmn. youth com. Ark. affiliate, mem. camp com.; bd. dirs. Human Growth Found., v.p., 1999—2000, pres., 2000—06; chief editor Endrocrinology in e-Medicine Pediat., 2007—. Recipient Postdoctoral Nat. Rsch. Svc. award, NIH, 1978—80. Fellow: Am. Coll. Endocrinology; mem.: Ark. Med. Soc., Med. Assn. State Ala., So. Pediat. Soc., Endocrine Soc., Am. Fedn. Clin. Rsch., Am. Pediat. Soc. Democrat. Episcopalian. Home: 8 Victoria Cir Maumelle AR 72113-6423 Office: Univ Ark Med Sci Dept Pediat 1 Children's Way Little Rock AR 72202-3591 Office Phone: 501-364-1430. Business E-Mail: kempstephenf@uams.edu.

KEMPEN, PAUL MARTIN, anesthesiologist; b. Grand Rapids, Mich., Sept. 19, 1954; s. Vernon Dominick Kempen and Lorraine Victoria (Yonaish) Curte; m. Inge Kempen; children: Martin Markus, Anna-Lena Bettina, Thomas Maximillian. BS in Biology, U. Mich., 1976; MD, Albert-Ludwig-U., Freiburg, Germany, 1981, PhD, 1989. Diplomate Am. Bd. Anesthesiology; lic. physician Mich., Pa., Ohio, Va., Ind., N.C., Ill., La., Okla. Resident in cariology Benedikt Kreutz REHA Ctr., Bad Kroezingen, Germany, 1982; resident in surgery St. Elizabeth Hosp., Rodalben, Germany, 1982; resident in anesthesia/critical care Kreiskrankenhaus, Bad Saeckingen, Germany, 1982-84; intern in pediat. and internal medicine S.W. Mich. Area Health Edn. Ctr., Kalamazoo, 1984-85; resident in anesthesia U. Mich., Ann Arbor, 1985-87; asst. prof. U. Pitts. Sch. Medicine, 1987-90; staff anesthesiologist Magee Womans Hosp., Pitts., 1987-90; rsch. assoc. Internat. Resuscitation Rsch. Inst., Pitts., 1987-90; chief of anesthesia Bixby Med. Ctr., Adrian, Mich., 1990-91, Riverside Hosp., Toledo, 1992-94; assoc. prof., dir. obstetric anesthesia La. State U. Med. Ctr., Shreveport, 1994-96; staff anesthesiologist Comanche County Meml. Hosp., Lawton, Okla., 1996—. Presenter in field, and contbr. articles to profl. jours., including Critical Care Medicine, Anesthesiology, Jour. AMA, Pediat., others. Mem. AMA, Am. Soc. Anesthesiology, Am. Soc. Regional Anesthesia, Internat. Anesthesia Rsch. Soc., La. State Med. Soc., La. State Soc. Anesthesiologists. Achievements include patented intravenous workstation as a medical organizing device. Home: 3401 W Gore Blvd Lawton OK 73505-6332

KEMPER, CHRISTINA, small business owner, respiratory therapist, elementary school educator; b. St. Louis, Feb. 16, 1952; d. Edward James and Norma Helen (Renner) K.; m. Don Eichholz, Dec. 23, 1972 (div. Apr. 1994); children: Cherie L., Derek V. BS in Edn., U. Mo., St. Louis, 1976, MA in Polit. Sci., 1980; AAS in Respiratory Therapy, Maryville U., 1983. Registered respiratory therapist. Intensive and critical care specialist various hosps., St. Louis, 1974—. Tchr. Parish Sch. Religion, St. Joseph's Ch., Manchester, Mo.; leader Girl Scouts Am., St. Louis. Mem. NOW (treas.), Am. Assn. for Respiratory Care, Nat. Bd. for Respiratory Care, Kappa Delta Pi. Avocations: reading, interior decorating, jewelry designing. Home: 12930 Twin Meadow Ct Creve Coeur MO 63146-1803 Personal E-mail: gemqueen@sbcglobal.net.

KEMPER, LORI, dean; Dir. med. edn. American Osteopath. Assn. Internship and Tempe St. Luke's Hosp. Family Practice Residency; assoc. dean postdoctoral edn. Midwestern University Ariz. Coll. Osteopath. Medicine, Glendale, dean, 2007—. Office: Midwestern University Ariz Coll Osteopath Medicine 19555 N 59th Ave Glendale AZ 85308 Office Phone: 623-572-3300. Office Fax: 623-572-3226. Business E-Mail: lorik@midwestern.edu. *

KEN, CHUIAN-FU, biology professor; b. Taiwan, Aug. 9, 1966; PhD, Nat. Def. Med. Ctr., 2002. Asst. prof. Inst. Biotech., Nat. Changhua U. Edn., 2004—07, assoc. prof., 2007—. Avocations: travel, badminton. Office: 1 Jin-De Rd Changhua 500 Taiwan Business E-Mail: kencf@cc.ncue.edu.tw.

KENAGY, CHERI LYNN, nurse; b. Houston, Nov. 12, 1958; d. Kenneth Leigh and Mary Louise Kenagy; m. William J. Balan, July 30, 1982 (dec. Jan. 15, 1991). Student, San Jacinto Coll., 1980. Lic. vocat. nurse, cert. pediat. advanced life support. Hosp. staff relief Ace Med. Staffing, Houston, 1998—, AHA, Houston, 1998—. Conservative. Presbyterian. Avocations: travel, scuba diving. Home: Box 5885 Pasadena TX 77508-5885 Personal E-mail: txauburn2002@yahoo.com.

KENDALL, JOHN WALKER, JR., internist, researcher, dean; b. Bellingham, Wash., Mar. 19, 1929; s. John Walker and Mathilda (Hansen) K.; m. Elizabeth Helen Meece, Mar. 19, 1954; children: John, Katherine, Victoria. BA, Yale Coll., 1952; MD, U. Wash., 1956. Intern, resident in internal medicine Vanderbilt U. Hosp., Nashville, 1956-59, fellow in endocrinology, 1959-60, U. Oreg. Med. Sch., Portland, 1960-62; asst. prof. medicine Oreg. Health Scis. U., Portland, 1962-66, assoc. prof. medicine, 1966-71, prof. medicine, 1971—, head divsn. metabolism, 1971-80; dean Oreg. Health Scis. U. Sch. Medicine, Portland, 1983—92; assoc. chief staff-rsch. VA Med. Ctr., Portland, 1971-83, dep. chief of staff, 1993, VA disting. physician, 1993-96, acad. affiliates officer, 1997—2010, grad. med. edn. adv. com., 2001—04. Cons. Med. Rsch. Found. Oreg., Portland, 1975-83; sec. Oreg. Found. Med. Excellence, Portland, 1984-89, pres., 1989-91; grad. med. edn. adv. com. Dept. Vets. Affairs, 2001—05; commn. mem. VA Cares, 2003-04; mem. VA Blue Ribbon Com. on Grad. Med. Edn., 2006-10. Lt. comdr. M.C., USN, 1962-64, pres.-elect Oreg. Health Sci., U. Sch. Med. Alumni. Assn., 2010, pres., 2011-. Recipient Outstanding Physician award Found. Med. Excellence, 1995, Outstanding Alumnus award, Oreg. Health Sci. U., 2009. Mem. AMA (governing coun. med. sch. sect. 1989-93, chair 1991-92, alt. del. 1992-93, Oreg. del. 1994-98, rep. Coun. Grad. Med. Edn. 1993-94), Assn. Am. Physicians, Am. Soc. Clin. Investigation, Am. Fedn. Clin. Rsch., We. Soc. Clin. Rsch. (councillor 1972-75), Endocrine Soc., Multnomah County Med. Soc. (treas. 1989, pres. 1991), Med. Rsch. Found. (Mentor award 1992), Royal Soc. Medicine (endocrinology sect. coun. 1999—2004). Presbyterian. Home: 3131 SW Evergreen Ln Portland OR 97205-5816 Office: Oreg Health Scis U Sch Medicine L-607 3181 SW Sam Jackson Park Rd Portland OR 97239

KENDALL, LEIGH WAKEFIELD, surgeon, retired hospital administrator; b. Brattleboro, Vt., Mar. 8, 1937; s. Irwin Samuel and Laura Eliza (Walbridge) Kendall; m. Grace Eleanor Fullarton, July 1, 1961; children: William Leigh, Bradley Edward. AB, U. Pa., Phila., 1959; D of Medicine, U. Vt., 1963; MS, U. Ill., Chgo., 1965. Diplomate Nat. Bd. Med. Examiners, Am. Bd. Surgery, cert. ACLS. Intern then resident surgery U. Ill. Hosp., Chgo., 1963-69; rsch. fellow Am. Cancer Soc., Chgo., 1964-65, clin. fellow, 1968-69; staff surgeon USN Hosp., Great Lakes, Ill., 1969; surgeon USN Hosp. Ships, Vietnam, 1969-70; pvt. practice Lancaster, Pa., 1971-93; med. dir. Alliance Health Plan, Lancaster, 1995—2005, St. Joseph Hosp., Lancaster, 2000—01, Lancaster Regional Med. Ctr., 2000—07; assoc. med. dir. St. Joseph Regional Health Network, Lancaster and Reading, 1999—2000. Instr. surgery U. Ill. Hosp., Chgo., 1968—69; active staff St. Joseph Hosp., Lancaster, 1971—93, sect. chief gen. surgery, 1981—88, chmn. dept. surgery, 1989—93; mem. courtesy staff Lancaster Gen. Hosp., 1971—93; cons. surgery Franklin & Marshall Coll., Lancaster, Pa., Masonic Homes, Elizabethtown, Pa.; staff physician Millersville U., 1993—2004; staff physician cardiac rehab. Lancaster Gen. Hosp. Health Campus, 1995—98. Lt. comdr. M.C. USNR, 1959—71, Vietnam. Decorated 1st Class Mil. Honor medal Republic of Vietnam. Fellow: ACS; mem.: AMA, Am. Coll. Physicians Execs., Royal Soc. Medicine (Eng.), Pa. Med. Soc., Internat. Soc. Surgeons, Warren H. Cole Soc. (pres. 1994—95), Intrepids Club, Sigma Nu. Republican. Episcopalian. Avocations: photography, travel. Home: 1832 Apostle Way Lancaster PA 17603-2300

KENDALL, PHILIP C., psychologist, educator; b. Merrick, NY; BS, Old Dominion U.; PhD in Clinical Psychology, Va. Commonwealth U. Prof. & dir. clinical training U. Minn.; prof. psychology Temple U.; dir. Child & Adolescent Anxiety Disorders Clinic. Named Top Therapist, Philadelphia Mag. Fellow: Ctr. Advanced Study in Behavioral Sciences; mem.: Assn. Advancement Behavior Therapy (former pres.), Soc. Clinical Child & Adolescent Psychology (former pres.), Soc. Clinical Psychology (Disting Contbr. to Sci. of Clinical Psychology), Anxiety Disorders Assn. America (Rsch. Recognition award). Office: Temple University Department of Psychology Weiss Hall 1701 N 13th St Philadelphia PA 19122-6085 Office Phone: 215-204-1558. E-mail: pkendall@temple.edu.

KENDIG, LYNNE E., physician; b. Phila., Dec. 6, 1949; d. Carl M. and Marion (Conkle) Shetzley; 1 child, Megan Alpert; m. Robert Kendig, 2003. BS in Edn., U. Pa., 1971; MS in Computer Edn., Lesley Coll., 1985; MD with honors, U. Colo., 1994. Tchr. elem. edn. Tredyffrin-East town Sch. Dist., Berwyn, Pa., 1976—81, Cherry Creek Sch. Dist., Englewood, Colo., 1982—87; intern, residency St. Joseph's Hosp., Denver, 1994—97; family practice physician Exempla Healthcare Orchard Family Practice, Englewood, 1997—2000; pvt. practice family physician Oasis Family Medicine, Denver, 2000—. IBM edn. cons., Englewood, 1986-87; resident physician St. Joseph Hosp. Family Practice, Denver, 1994-97; mem. admissions com. U. Colo. Med. Sch., Denver, 1993-94. Vol. student physician Stout Street Homeless Clinic, Denver, 1990-94; physician lectr., educator Tar Wars, Denver, 1995-96; mem. Denver Pub. Libr. Friends Found., 1996—; mem. Med. Mission Team, Guatemala, 2005, 07. Mem. AMA, Am. Acad. Family Physicians, Colo. Med. Soc., Alpha Omega Alpha. Avocations: hiking, travel, gardening, fly fishing. Home: 635 Bellaire St Denver CO 80220-4934

KENDLER, KENNETH SEEDMAN, psychiatrist, medical educator; b. NYC, July 12, 1950; BA in Biology and Religion, U. Calif., Santa Cruz, 1972; MD, Stanford U. Sch. Medicine, Calif., 1977; DSc (hon.), U. Birmingham, Eng., 1999. Diplomate Am. Bd. Psychiatry & Neurology. Intern, resident psychiatry Yale U., New Haven, 1977-78; asst. prof. dept. psychiatry Mt. Sinai Sch. Medicine, NYC, 1980-83; assoc. prof. depts. psychiatry and human & molecular genetics Va. Commonwealth U., Richmond, 1983—87, prof. depts. psychiatry and human genetics, 1987—, Rachel Brown Banks disting. prof. psychiatry, 1991—, dir. Va. Inst. Psychiat. & Behavioral Genetics, 1996—. Biol. scientist tng. program fellow Yale U. Sch. Medicine, 1978—80; rsch. assoc. Bronx VA Med.l Ctr., NYC, 1981—83; Thomas William Salmon lectr. NY Acad. Medicine, 2001; Fritz Redlich fellow Ctr. Advanced Study in Behavioral Scis., Stanford, Calif., 2003—04. Mem. editl. bd. Archives Gen. Psychiatry, Bipolar Disorders, Current Psychiatry Reports, Neuropsychiat. Genetics, Schizophrenia Rsch., Social Psychiatry & Psychiat. Epidemiology, Brit. Jour. Psychiatry, mem. internat. adv. panel Indian Jourl. Psychiatry; contbr. articles to profl. jours., chapters to books. Recipient Lieber prize for outstanding rsch. in schizophrenia, Nat. Alliance Rsch. Schizophrenia & Depression, 1995, Stanley R. Dean award, Am. Coll. Psychiatrists, 1998, Kurt Schneider Sci. award, 1998, Edward Strecker award for outstanding contbn. to psychiat. care and treatment, 2000, Edward J. Sachar award for outstanding contbn. to psychiat. rsch., 2001, Rema Lapouse award, Am. Pub. Health Assn., 2002, Erik Stromgren medal, Stromgren Found., Denmark, 2003. Fellow: Am. Psychiat. Assn.; mem.: AAAS, Behavior Genetics Assn., Genetic Epidemiology Soc., Am. Soc. Human Genetics. Office: Va Commonwealth U Dept Psychiatry PO Box 980126 Richmond VA 23298-0126 Office Phone: 804-828-8590. Office Fax: 804-828-1471. Business E-Mail: kendler@hsc.vcu.edu. *

KENDO, KIYOSAWA, retired gastroenterologist; b. Matsumoto, Nagano, Japan, Feb. 25, 1943; MD, Shinshu U., 1967. Prof. Shinshu U., 1995—2007; dir. Nagano Winter Olympic Clinic, 1998, Shinshu U. Hosp., 1999—2003, Nagano Red Cross Hosp., 2007—11. Vis. scientist NIH, 1982—84. Contbr. articles to profl. jours. Mem.: Am. Assn. Study Liver Diseases. Avocation: photography. Home: 270-10 Souza Matsumoto Nagano 3900305 Japan

KENDRICK, BEVERLY ANN, medical/surgical nurse, small business owner; b. Rupert, Idaho, July 17, 1949; d. Robert Alfred and Erna (Plocher) Dockter; m. Sidney Cannon, Aug. 22, 1967 (div.); 1 child, Lisa Ann; m. Budd Leroy Kendrick, Dec. 26, 1978; children: Cassandra Rachelle, Angela Priscilla. Assoc. of Sci., Boise State U., 1989, BS, 1993; grad. bus. program, Idaho Small Bus. Devel. Ctr., Boise, 1997. RN, Idaho; cert. staff devel. continuing edn. nurse; cert. med.-surg. nurse. Coord. infant stimulation program Adult and Child Devel. Ctr., Boise, 1974-78; parent educator St. Alphonsus Regional Med. Ctr., Boise, 1996-97, nurse educator, 1996-97, risk mgr., 1998—2002, hospice nurse, 2002—03; investigator Idaho Bd. of Medicine, 2003—. Owner Angel Essence, Boise, 1995—2005. Author: Infant Stimulation Procedure Manual, 1978. Facilitator Women's Network of Entrepreneurial Tng., 1996-97; bd. dirs. Women's Entrepreneurial Mentoring Sys., v.p., 1996-97, pres., 1998-99; co-founder Small Bus. Adminstrn. Women's Bus. Ctr., 1999. RN scholar St. Alphonsus Regional Med. Ctr., 1988; named Women in Bus. Adv. of Yr. Idaho SBA, 1998; receipent Idaho Women Making History awar, 2005. Mem. Angel Collectors' Club Am. Avocations: travel, reading, collecting angel collectibles, angel art, gourmet cooking. Office Phone: 208-327-7000 ext 236.

KENDRICK, BUDD LEROY, psychologist; b. Pocatello, Idaho, Apr. 19, 1944; s. Oscar Fredrick Kendrick and Miriam Stuart (Thorn) Stewart; m. Sue Lorraine Allen, Nov. 11, 1966; children: Aaron Matthew and Edgar Seth; m. Beverly Ann Dockter, Dec. 26, 1978; children: Cassandra Rachelle, Angela Priscilla. BA, Idaho State U., Pocatello, 1967, MEd, 1969, EdD, 1974. Lic. psychologist, lic. clin. profl. counselor Mont., Idaho; cert. health svc. provider in psychology, nat. cert. counselor; cert. clin. mental health counselor; nat. bd. cert. fellow hypnotherapist; cert. profl. qualification in psychology; interjurisdictional practice cert., Assn. State & Provincial Psychology Bds.; critical incident stress mgmt. provider, Red Cross disaster mental health svc. provider; cert. supr. Idaho Profl. Counselors and Marriage and Family Therapists. Tchr. psychology Pocatello H.S., 1967-69; dir. counseling svcs. Midwestern Coll., Denison, Iowa, 1969-70; rehab. counselor Idaho Divsn. of Vocat. Rehab., Pocatello, 1970-73; counselor (doctoral internship) Counseling Ctr., Idaho State U., Pocatello, 1973-74; rehab. counselor Idaho Divsn. of Vocat. Rehab., Pocatello, 1974-75; chief of psychology Mental Health and Devel. Disabilities Program, Boise, Idaho, 1975—; pvt. practice psychology Boise, 1977—. Vice-chmn. Idaho State Counselor Licensing Bd., 1982-84, chmn. 1984-85, sec. 1985-86; sec., treas. Nat. Bd. Cert. Counselors Inc., Alexandria, Va., 1986-93; mem. licensure com. Idaho Pers. and Guidance Assn., 1975-78, chmn. 1977-78, rep. Am. Pers. and Guidance Assn. Licensure Network, 1977-78; allied clin. staff Intermountain Hosp., Boise, 1983-93, Northwest Passages Adolescent Hosp., Boise, 1986-93, Saint Alphonsus Regional Med. Ctr., Boise, 1986-93; designated examiner and dispositioner involuntary commitments, conservatorships and guardianships State of Idaho, 1981—; cons. Idaho Pers. Commn., 1982—; grad. sch. lectr. Idaho State U., 1975; grad. sch. faculty affiliate, Coll. of Idaho, Caldwell, 1981-86; presenter concerning counselor credentialing issues, 1981-86; treas. Idaho Mental Health Assn., 1980-81; mem. Idaho Psychology, Social Work reclassification task force, 1990-91; mem. Idaho

Assn. Counseling and Devel. Legis. Task Force for Third Party Benefits for Lic. Profl. Counselors, 1990; editl. bd. mem. The Profl. Counselor: Rsch. & Practice Jour. Editor: Directory of the Idaho Psychol. Assn., 1983; author numerous articles on hypnosis, counseling and profl. credentialing. Mem. adv. bd. Trio (Upward Bound, Talent Search, Head Start), Idaho State U., 1975-76; mem. Human Rights Com., Idaho State Sch. and Hosp., 1977; mem. adv. com. Nat. Bd. Cert. Counselors and WHO Internat. Global Counseling Survey, Surrey, Eng., 2005. Recipient Disting. Svc. award Idaho Pers. & Guidance Assn., 1978, Profl. Achievement award Idaho State U., 1987, Spl. Recognition award Idaho Assn. for Counseling and Devel., 1989, Lawrence Schumacher Meml. Employee of Yr. award State of Idaho, 1995, Disting. Grad. award Idaho State U., 2001, Friend of Rsch. and Assessment for Counseling, Inc. Fellow Am. Coll. Advanced Practice Psychologists (founding mem. Idaho chpt.), Idaho Psychol. Assn. (sec. 1982-84); mem. SCV, Idaho Mental Health Counselors Assn. (charter), Idaho Counseling Assn. (leadership coun. 1977-78), ACA (pub. policy and legis. com., mem.-at-large 1992-94, chair nat. licensure subcom. 1992-94), Am. Mental Health Counselors Assn., APA (divsn. 17 counseling psychology, divsn. 30 psychol. hypnosis), Chi Sigma Iota, Idaho Hist. Soc. (cert. Idaho pioneer desc.), Stuart-Mosby Hist. Soc., Kappa Delta Pi, Honor Soc. Edn., Ancora Impara Hon. Soc. (co-founder, v.p.). Avocations: sword collecting, genealogy, history, collecting autographed celebrity photographs. Personal E-mail: psy108@cableone.net.

KENICHIRO, TANAKA, surgeon; b. Japan, Apr. 13, 1969; MD, Tokyo Med. and Dental U., 1994. Med. dir. endocrine surgery dept. surgery Shizuoka Saiseikai Gen. Hosp., 2008—. Med. staff divsn. surg. oncology, dept. surgery Nagoya U. Grad. Sch. Medicine, 2005—07; med. staff divsn. breast surgery Cancer Inst. Hosp., 2007—08, med. staff divsn. head and neck surgery, 2008. Mem.: Japan Thyroid Assn., Japanese Soc. Thyroid Surgery, Japan Surg. Soc., Japan Assn. Endocrine Surgeons, Japanese Breast Cancer Soc. Avocations: guitar, mountain climbing, aquariums. Office: Suruga-ku Ojika 1-1-1 Shizuoka 422-8527 Japan Office Fax: 81-45-285-5179. Business E-Mail: k154768@siz.saiseikai.or.jp.

KENIGSBERG, AARON E., medical director; Grad., Stanford U.; MD, NYU. Diplomate Am. Bd. Internal Medicine, Am. Bd. Internal Medicine-cardiovasc. disease, Am. Bd. Internal Medicine-interventional cardiology. Intern internal medicine Jackson Meml. Hosp./Univ. Miami, resident internal medicine; fellow cardiology New England Deaconess/Harvard Univ.; cath. lab. dir. Holy Cross Hosp.; chief cardilogy sect. Washington Adventist Hosp.; med. staff Md. Heart. Fellow: Am. Coll. of Cardiologists. Office: Washington Adventist Hospital 306 10313 Georgia Ave Silver Spring MD 20902 Office Phone: 301-681-9095. Office Fax: 301-681-8156.

KENISTON, KENNETH, psychologist, educator; b. Chgo., Jan. 6, 1930; s. Hayward and Roberta (Cannell) K.; m. Ellen Uviller, June 20, 1960 (div. Aug. 1975); children: Ann Rogers, Sarah Hayward; m. Suzanne Berger, Jan. 10, 1976; 1 child, Daniel Eben. BA, Harvard Coll., Cambridge, Mass., 1951; DPhil, Oxford U., 1956; LLD (hon.), U. Notre Dame, Ind., 1971; DSc (hon.), Colgate U., Hamilton, NY, 1972. From rsch. asst. to rsch. assoc. dept. social rels. Harvard U., Cambridge, Mass., 1955-62; from asst. prof. to assoc. prof. psych. Yale Med. Sch., New Haven, 1962-68, prof. psych., 1968-75; Andrew W. Mellon prof. human devel. Mass. Inst. Tech., Cambridge, 1975—, prof. emeritus, 2006—. Lectr. on clin. psychology Harvard U., 1958-62, resident fellow, asst. sr. tutor Eliot House, 1953-59; assoc. dir., acting dir., then dir. Behavior Scis. Study Ctr., Yale Med. Sch., 1965-72; fellow Davenport Coll., Yale U., 1962-75; chmn., exec. dir. Carnegie Coun. on Children, New Haven, 1972-78; dir. program in sci., tech. and soc. Mass. Inst. Tech., 1987-92, dir. grad. studies, 1993-96, dir. projects, 1996—; dir. MIT India Program, 1998-06; mem. Carnegie Commn. on Higher Edn., 1968-73, bd. dirs. Overseers Harvard Coll., 1969-75, MacArthur Prize Fellows selection com., 1979-85; com. on selection Guggenheim Found., 1992-94; vis. scholar Ecole de Mines, Paris, 1980-81; vis. prof. U. Paris Sorbonne, 1986-87, Centro de Estudios Avanzados de Ciencias Sociales, Madrid, 1990, Nat. Inst. Advanced Studies, Indian Inst. Sci., Bangalore, 1999-2000, 01-02, Adv. Bd., Microsoft Rsch. India, 2007-. Author: The Uncommitted, 1966, Young Radicals, 1968, All Our Children, 1977, (with D. Guston) The Fragile Contract, 1994, Earth, Air, Fire, Water, 1999, (with J. Ker Conway and L. Marx) Earth, Air, Fire, Water: Humanistic Studies of the Environment, 2000, (with Deepak Kumar) IT Experience in India: Bridging the Digital Divide, 2004, (with Rohit Raj Mathur and R.K. Bagga) The State, IT, and Development, 2005; contbr. articles to profl. jours., chpts. to books. Rhodes scholar Balliol Coll., Oxford U., 1951-53; jr. fellow Harvard U., 1953-56; Guggenheim fellow, 1980-81. Fellow AAAS; mem. Coun. Fgn. Rels., Phi Beta Kappa, Sigma Xi, India Internat. Ctr. (origin mem. 2004-). Office: Mass Inst Tech E51-296A 77 Massachusetts Ave Cambridge MA 02139 Business E-Mail: kken@mit.edu. *

KENJO, MASAMUTSU, speech pathology/audiology services professional, researcher; b. Iwakuni, Yamaguchi, Japan, June 19, 1967; s. Toshio and Hiroko Nishimoto Kenjo. BE, Tokyo Gakugei U., Koganei, 1991; MEd, Kanazawa U., Ishikawa, Japan, 1993. Lic. speech-lang.-hearing therapist Ministry Health, Labor and Welfare, 1999; cert. elem. sch. tchr. Tokyo Bd. Edn., 1991, kindergarten educator Ishikawa Bd. Edn., 1991, tchr. sch. deaf Ishikawa Bd. Edn., 1991, social rschr. 2007. Tchr. U. Tsukuba, Kirigaoka Sch. for the Physically Challenged, Itabashi, Tokyo, 1993—94, Misato Spl. Sch. Mentally Retarded, Japan, 1994—95; rsch. asst. Kyoei Gakuen Jr. Coll., Kasukabe, Japan, 1995—99; asst. prof. Fukuoka U. Edn., Munakata, Fukuoka, Japan, 1999—2001, assoc. prof., 2001—07, prof., 2007—, chief spl. edn. ctr., 2009—, chief officer Students Disability, 2011—. Part-time lectr. Saitama U., 1998—2002, Yokohama Nat. U., 2008—; lectr. Kasuya Town Resource Rm., 1999—2008, Japan Stuttering Assn. Fukuoka Genyukai, 2000—; part-time lectr. Fukuoka Internat. Coll. Health and Welfare, 2002—06; lectr., adviser Fukuoka City Resource Rm., 2003—06; cons. Fukutsu City Resource Rm., Japan, 2005—06; vis. prof. U. Ill., Urbana, 2003—04; part-time lectr. Aso Rehab. Coll., Fukuoka, 2004—07; lectr. Fukuoka City Bd. Edn., 2005—07, Yamaguchi Prefecture Bd. Edn., 2006—, Fukuoka Prefectural Edn. Ctr., 2007—10, Fukuoka Prefecture Bd. Edn., 2007—10, edn. adv., 2009—; adj. lectr. Yanagawa Rehab. Sch., 2010—; lectr. Kitakyushu City Bd. Edn., 2009—. Co-author: (book) Stuttering: A Clinical Casebook, 2004; co-translator (book) Communication and Communication Disorders: A Clinical Introduction, 2005. Recipient Rsch. Encouragement prize, Japanese Speech Lang. Hearing Assn., 2001; grantee, Ministry Edn., Culture, Sports, Sci. and Tech., 1996—97, 1998—2002, 2002—. Mem.: Japanese Assn. Speech Lang. Hearing Therapists, Japan Stuttering Assn. Buddhist. Avocations: museums, sumo wrestling. Office: Fukuoka Univ Edn 1-1 Akamabunkyomachi Munakata Fukuoka 8114192 Japan Office Phone: 81-940-35-1653. Office Fax: 81-940-35-1718. Business E-Mail: mkenjo@fukuoka-edu.ac.jp.

KENKEL, JEFFREY MILLER, plastic surgeon, educator; b. Washington, July 15, 1963; s. John Bonaventure and Grace Marie Kenkel; m. Suzanne Marie Kenkel, May 9, 1992; children: Matthew Miller, Ashley Marie. BS, Boston coll., 1985; MD, Georgetown U., 1989. Diplomate Am. Bd. Plastic Surgery. Resident gen. surgery Georgetown U. Sch. Med., Washington, 1989—94; resident plastic surgery U. Tex. Southwestern Med. Ctr., Dallas, 1994—96, faculty mem., 1996—2000, assoc. prof. to prof., vice chmn. Dept. Plastic Surgery, 2000—, dir. Clin. Ctr. Cosmetic Laser Treatment, Rod J. Rohrich, MD Disting. Professorship wound healing and plastic surgery; dir. Clin. Ctr. Cosmetic Laser Treatment, chief plastic surgery VA Med. Ctr., Dallas. Attending staff mem. Baylor U. Med. Ctr., Children's Med. Ctr., Dallas, Parkland Meml. Hosp., St. Paul U. Med. Ctr., Zale Lipshy Univ. Hosp.; plastic surgeon, team physician Dallas Stars, 1996—. Co-author: Ultrasound-Assisted Liposuction; editor: Body Contouring After Massive Weight Loss; contbr. articles to med. jours. Named one of Best Doctors in Dallas, D Mag., 2005, Best Doctors in America, 2006; grantee Am. Soc. Aesthetic Surg. Rsch. Found., 1997, Plastic Surgery Ednl. Found., 1998, 1999. Fellow: ACS; mem.: AMA, Aesthetic Surgery Edn. and Rsch. Found. (treas.), Am. Soc. Laser Medicine and Surgery, Dallas Soc. Plastic Surgeons (past pres.), Tex. Soc. Plastic Surgeons, Am. Soc. Plastic and Reconstructive Surgeons, Am. Soc. Aesthetic Plastic Surgery (bd. mem.). Avocations: golf, ice hockey, rollerblading, music. Office: U Tex Southwestern Med Ctr Outpatient Bldg 1801 Inwood Rd, 5th Fl Dallas TX 75390-9132 Office Phone: 214-645-2353, 214-645-3112. Office Fax: 214-645-2354. E-mail: jeffrey.kenkel@utsouthwestern.edu.

KENNA, GEORGE ANTHONY, pharmacist, researcher; s. Merrill Carlton and Esther Ann Kenna; m. Nancy Constantino Kenna, May 17, 1981; 1 child, John. BS in Pharmacy, U. RI, 1975, MA in Psychology, 2001, PhD in Psychology, 2003. Registered pharmacist Va. Pharmacist Potomac Hosp., Woodbridge, Va., 1977—80, Liggett Rexall, Middletown, RI, 1980—81, Douglas Drug, RI, 1981—96; grad. asst. U. R.I., 1997, rsch. asst., 1999; pharmacist Walmart Pharmacy, North Kingstown, RI, 1998—2001; clin. pharmacist Kent County Hosp., Warwick, RI, 1999—2007, Westery Hosp., RI, 2007—. Tchg. asst. stats. U. RI, Kingston, 2001—02, asst. adj. prof., 2006—; rsch. fellow dept. biomedicine Brown U., Providence, 2003—04; postdoctoral fellow Ctr. for Alcohol and Addiction Studies, Providence, 2004—07; cons. Brown U., Providence, 2003—04, asst. prof. psychiatry and human behavior, 2007—. Contbr. articles to profl. jours., chapters to books. Recipient Young Investigator award, Rsch. Soc. Alcoholism, 2004, Rsch. Award grant, Ctr. for Alcohol and Addiction Studies, 2004. Mem.: APA, Coll. Psychiat. and Neurol. Pharmacists, Rsch. Soc. Am., Am. Pharm. Assn. Episcopalian. Avocations: skiing, bicycling, golf, writing. Home: 59 Bedford Ln North Kingstown RI 02852 Office: Brown U Box G-BH Providence RI 02908

KENNEDY, CHARLES, retired neuroscientist, retired medical educator; b. Buffalo, Aug. 27, 1920; m. Eulsum Kennedy, Aug. 27, 1968; 3 children from previous marriage. BA in Chemistry cum laude, Princeton U., 1942; MD, U. Rochester, 1945. Diplomate Am. Bd. Pediats., Am. Bd. Psychiatry and Neurology, lic. N.Y., Pa., DC, Maine, Md. Intern pathology New Haven Hosp., 1945—46; instr. pathology Sch. Medicine Yale U., New Haven, 1945-46; fellow in child psychiatry Children's Hosp., Buffalo, 1948-49, resident pediatrician, 1949-51; fellow in physiology Grad. Sch. Medicine U. Pa., Phila., 1951-53, assoc. pediats. Sch. Medicine, 1952-55, assoc. in neurology, 1955-58, asst. prof. neurology in pediats., 1958-61, assoc. prof., 1961-67; chief divsn. neurology, dir. child neurology Children's Hosp., Phila., 1959-67; prof. pediats., neurology Sch. Medicine Georgetown U., Washington, 1971-90, prof. emeritus, 1990—. Vis. fellow in neurology Neurol. Inst. Columbia Presbyn. Med. Ctr., 1957—58; mem. Lab. Clin. Sci. Nat. Inst. Mental Health, 1967—68, Lab. Cerebral Metabolism, 1968—95; lectr. U.S. Naval Hosp., Phila., 1962—68; mem. adv. com. dyslexia State of Tex., 1965; guest lectr. Nat. Naval Med. Ctr. Uniformed Svcs. U. Health Scis., 1977—87. Mem. editl. bd. Pediat. Rsch., 1978—84, Brain Rsch., 1980—96, Jour. Cerebral Blood Flow and Metabolism, 1981—88. Lt. (j.g.) USNR, 1946—48. Fellow, Life Ins. Med. Rsch. Fund, 1951—53. Fellow: Coll. Physicians Phila.; mem.: Profs. Child Neurology, Child Neurology Soc., Soc. Neuroscience, Assn. Rsch. Nervous and Mental Disease, Phila. Neurol. Soc. (v.p. 1967), Phila. Pediat. Soc. (pres. 1964), Internat. Soc. Cerebral Blood Flow and Metabolism, Internat. Soc. Neurochemistry, Nat. Bd. Med. Examiners (mem. pediat. com. 1960—64), Am. Soc. Neurochemistry, Am. Acad. Neurology (chmn. sect. child neurology 1964—66), Am. Neurol. Assn., Am. Acad. Pediats., Am. Pediat. Soc.

KENNEDY, DAVID WILLIAM, otolaryngologist, medical administrator, educator; b. York, Eng., June 27, 1948; s. Michael Leo and Winifred Pearl (Shepherd) K.; m. Edna Mae Schirmer, Apr. 20, 1978; children: Garrett David, Kirin Suzanne. Student in Pre-Med. Program, Ampleforth Coll., York, 1962-66; MD, Royal Coll. Surgeons, Ireland, 1972. Diplomate Am. Bd. Otolaryngology, Am. Bd. Head and Neck Surgery; lic. physician Pa., Md. Intern St. Laurence's Hosp., Dublin, 1972-73; asst. resident in surgery Johns Hopkins U., Balt., 1973-74, asst. resident in otolaryngology, 1974-77, mem. staff, 1977-91, chief resident in otolaryngology, asst. prof. otolaryngology, 1977-78, asst. prof., 1978-86, assoc. prof. otolaryngology-head and neck surgery, 1986-91, assoc. prof. neurosurgery, 1987-91; mem. staff Loch Raven VA Hosp., Balt., 1980-87, cons. physician, 1987-91; mem. staff Sinai Hosp. Balt., 1981-88; chmn. U. Pa. Med. Ctr., Phila., 1991—2003; mem. staff VA Hosp., Phila., 1991—; vice dean profl. svcs. U. Pa. Sch. Medicine, 2002—08; sr. v.p. U. Pa. Health Sys., 2002—08; med. dir. Patient Facilitated Svcs. & Interventional Program, 2006—. Dir. Penn Internat. Rhinology Course, Phila., 1991—; spkr. in field; lectr. in field. Contbg. author: Rhinitis, 2d edit., 1991, Diseases of the Nose, Throat, Ear, Head and Neck, 1991, Otolaryngology, 3d edit., 1991, Surgery for Skull Base Tumors, 1991, Sinus Disease: Guide to First Line Management, 1994, Diseases of the Sinuses: Diagnosis and Management, 2000, Living with Chronic Sinusitis, 2004, Rhinosinusitis: A Guide to Management and Treatment, 2008, others; mem. editl. bd. Ear, Nose and Throat Jour., 1983—, Am. Jour. Rhinology, 1986—, Laryngoscope, 1988—, Auris Nasus Larynx, 1996—, ACTA Oto-Rhino-Laryngologica Belgica, 1995—; editor-in-chief Am. Jour. Rhinology, 1988-10, Current Opinion in Otolaryngology and Head and Neck Surgery, 1992—, Jour. Otolaryngology, 1993—, Rginology and Allergy, 2010-; editor Auris Nasus Larynx, 1996—, ACTA Oto-Rhino-Larynngologica Belgica, 1995—; contbr. numerous articles to profl. jours. Recipient Leonard Abrahamson Meml. Gold medal, 1971, Lyons Meml. medal, 1971, gold medal Coombe Lying-In Hosp., 1971, Reuben-Harvey prize, 1972, Coun.'s prize and gold medal, 1972, Sr. William Wilde medal, 1995, Predl. Citation Am. Acad. Otolarynogology - Head and Neck Surgery, 2002; rsch. grantee Schering Corp., 1981, HHS, 1983-88, Norwich-Eaton Corp., 1984-86, Minn. Mining and Mfg. Co., 1984, Healthtek, 1990-91. Fellow Am. Acad. Otolaryngology-Head and Neck Surgery (mem. hearing subcom. 1985-91, mem. rhinology-paranasal sinus com. 1986-93, 97—, mem. CPT com. 1992-97, legis. alt. bd. govs. 1991—, mem. adv. coun. on continuing edn. with TV subcom. 1994, instr. endoscopic sinus surgery 1985, mem. internat. otolaryngology com. 2000, bd. dirs., coord. govtl. rels. 2004-, pres. elect 2007, pres. 2008-09, chair otolaryngology workplace com. 2009-), Royal Coll. Surgeons (anatomy demonstrator/lectr. 1972-73, vis. prof. 1980-81, Royal Coll. Surgeons (Ireland); fellow ACS (com. on emerging surg. tech. and edn. 1999), AMA (hon.), NAS-Inst. Medicine, Am. Rhinologic Soc. (bd. dirs. 1988-96, v.p. 1989-90, pres. 1992-93, cons. to bd. dirs. 1987-88), Internat. Rhinologic Soc. (bd. dirs. 1995—, pres. elect 2005-07, pres. 2007-09), Phila. Laryngol. Soc., Soc. Univ. Otolaryngologists (mem. nominating com. 1985-86), Nat. Acad. Scis., Inst. of Medicine, Pa. Acad. Otolaryngology, John Morgan Soc., Johns Hopkins Med. and Surg. Assn., Danish Otolaryngology Soc. (hon.), Johns Hopkins Soc. Scholars Achievements include introduction of endoscopic sinus surgery to U.S.; development of extended applications of endoscopic surgical techniques; clinical development of surgical localizers. Office: Univ Pa Med Ctr 5 Ravdin 3400 Spruce St Philadelphia PA 19104-4206 Office Phone: 215-662-6971. Business E-Mail: kennedyd@uphs.upenn.edu.

KENNEDY, FRANK, endocrinologist; b. Ossining, NY, Mar. 7, 1954; MD, Boston U., 1981. Cons., endocrinology, diabetes & nutrition Mayo Clinic, 1988—. Mem.: Am. Assn. Clin. Endocrinologists, Endocrine Soc., Am. Diabetes Assn., Am. Coll. Physicians. Home: PO Box 7036 Rochester MN 55903 Home Fax: 507-284-5745. Business E-Mail: kennedy.frank@mayo.edu.

KENNEDY, GARRY, geriatrician, psychiatrist, educator; MD, U. Tex., 1975. Diplomate Am. Bd. Psychiatry and Neurology, 1980, Am. Bd. Psychiatry and Neurology-geriatric psychiatry, 2000, Am. Bd. Psychiatry and Neurology-psychosomatic medicine, 2005. Resident psychiatry Va Hosp. Univ. Tex., 1976—79; fellow geriatric psychiatry Montefiore Med. Ctr., 1979—81, fellow psychosomatic medicine, 1981—83, dir. divsn. of geriatric psychiatry; prof. dept. of psychiatry and behavioral sciences Albert Einstein Coll. of Medicine. Office: Montefiore Medical Center 111 E 210th St Bronx NY 10467-2401 Office Phone: 718-920-4321, 718-920-4236. E-mail: gkennedy@montefiore.org.

KENNEDY, GARY J., psychiatrist, educator; b. Dallas, Nov. 1, 1948; m. Jenny McCord, Sept. 1, 1969. BA, U. Tex., 1970, MD, 1975. Diplomate Am. Bd. Psychiatry, cert. in geriatric psychiatry. Intern psychiatry Bexar Conty Hosp./U. Tex., San Antonio, 1975—76; resident geriatric psychiatry Va. Hosp., San Antonio, 1976—79; instr. psychiatry Albert Einstein Coll. Medicine, Bronx, NY, 1979-84, rsch. fellow, 1982-84, assoc. prof. psychiatry, 1989-95, prof. psychiatry & behavioral scis., 1996—. Fellow psychiatry & psychobiology Montefiore Med. Ctr., Bronx, 1979—84, dir. divsn. geriatric psychiatry, 1986—; supr. unit psycgeriatrics Bronx Pyschiat. Ctr., 1987—2002. Contbr. articles to profl. jours. Recipient New Investigator Rsch. award, HIH Nat. Heart, Lung & Blood Inst, 1984, Cmty. Svc. award, Bronx Geriatric Mental Health Com., 1990, Extraordinary Psychiatrist award, Nat. Alliance Mentally Ill, 2003; grantee Nat. Inst. Aging rsch. grant, 1986—90; WHO Travel Study fellow, 1983. Fellow: NY Acad. Meidcine; mem.: APHA, Geriatric Mental Health Found., Am. Geriatrics Soc., Gerontol. Soc. America, Am. Assn. Geriatric Psychiatry, Am. Psychiat. Assn. Office: Montefiore Med Ctr 111 E 210th St Bronx NY 10467-2401 Office Phone: 718-920-4236. Business E-Mail: gkennedy@montefiore.org.

KENNEDY, LINDA MANN, neuroscience educator, researcher; b. Malden, Mass., July 29, 1939; d. Alfred William Mann and Etta May (Maglue) Stenquist; m. Richard Dearman Kennedy, Apr. 15, 1961; children: Pamela Lea, Ruth Alexander. Diploma in nursing, New England Deaconess Hosp., 1959; AB, Simmons Coll., 1975; PhD, Harvard U., 1980. RN, Mass. Staff nurse Lahey Clinic, Boston, 1959-61, various hosps., Mass., Ga., 1962-72; tchg. asst. Simmons Coll., Boston, 1972-75; vis. rsch. fellow Cornell U., Ithaca, NY, 1978-81; rsch. assoc. Worcester (Mass.) Found. Exptl. Biology, 1980-83; rsch. asst. prof. Clark U., Worcester, 1983-84, asst. prof., 1984-91, assoc. prof., 1991—2010, rsch. prof., 2010—; assoc. prof U. Mass. Med. Sch., 1995—2000. Co-founder, co-dir., dir. interdisciplinary neurosci. program Clark U., Worcester, 1984—97, chair instnl. rev. bd. for human rsch., 1997—2000, Worcester, 2002—; vis. scientist Weizmann Inst. Sci., Rehovot, Israel, 1991—92; mem. adv. panel various programs NSF, Washington, 1993—, vis. program dir. Sensory Sys. program, 2000—02; mem. study sections various programs NIH, 1988—. Mem. editl. com. Univ. Press New England, 1989-91; contbr. articles to profl. jour. Mem. conservation com. Town of Framingham, Mass., 1973-74. Recipient Grad. fellowship for women Danforth Found., 1975-79, Rsch. Svc. award NIH, 1980-83, multiple Rsch. grants NSF, NIH, 1978—. Mem. New Eng. Psychol. Assn. (hon.), Assn. Chemoreception Sci. (exec. bd. councilor 1986-88), Soc. for Neurosci., Soc. for Values in Higher Edn., European Chemoreception Orgn., Internat. Brain Rsch. Orgn. Unitarian Universalist. Avocations: swimming, classical and jazz concerts, travel, reading mysteries, opera. Office: Clark Univ Dept Biology Worcester MA 01610 Home: 1120 8th Ave 1801 Seattle WA 98101 Office Phone: 508-579-4877.

KENNEDY, TIMOTHY C., critical care specialist; MD, Columbia U., 1971. Diplomate Am. Bd. Internal Medicine, 1974, Am. Bd. Internal Medicine- pulmonary disease, 1976, Am. Bd. Internal Medicine- critical care medicine, 1997. Resident in internal medicine Presbyn- St. Luke's Med. Ctr., Denver, 1972—74; fellow in pulmonary disease Univ. Ariz. Hosps., Tucson, 1974—76; clin. prof. Univ.

Colo.; hosp. affiliation include Exempla St. Joseph Hosp., Presbyn.-St. Luke's Med. Ctr. Office: Presbyterian- Saint Luke's Medical Center 1721 E 19th Ave No 366 Denver CO 80218 Office Phone: 303-863-0300. Office Fax: 303-863-7014.

KENNETH, ZEITZER, radiation oncologist educator; Grad., Thomas Jefferson U., Phila., 1988. Diplomate Am. Bd. Radiology-radiation oncology. Intern Albert Einstein Med. Ctr., Phila., 1989; resident Thom. Jefferson Univ. Hosp., Phila., 1992, fellow, 1993; tchg. appointment Temple Univ. Sch. of Medicine. Office: Albert Einstein Healthcare Newtwork Department Radiation Oncology 5501 Old York Rd Levy Gr Philadelphia PA 19141 Office Phone: 215-456-6280. Office Fax: 215-457-0270.

KENNETT, KEITH FRANKLIN, psychologist, educator; b. Adelaide, Australia, July 18, 1935; s. Ernest Franklin and Olive Myrtle (Bowes) K.; m. Barbara Eileen Henderson, 1957; children: Elizabeth (dec.), Paul, James; m. Gail Louise Hanson, Jan. 4, 1992. Diploma in tchg., Adelaide Tchr.'s Coll., 1955; diploma in edn., U. Adelaide, 1965, BA in English and History, 1967, Assoc. in Polit. Sci., 1968, MEd, 1976; MA in Psychology, U. Saskatchewan, 1969, PhD in Psychology, 1972. Registered psychologist, New South Wales. Prin., owner Oxford Coaching Coll., Adelaide, 1962—68; pvt. practice vocat. guidance Canada, 1970—77; pvt. practice clin. and neuropsychology New South Wales, Australia, 1977—; tchr., prin. So. Australia Edn. Dept., 1955—; head dept. psychology Salisbury Tchr. Coll., So. Australia, 1970; asst. prof. psychology St. Francis Xavier U. and U. Coll. Cape Breton, Canada, 1970—72, assoc. prof. psychology, 1973—77; dean edn. and prof. U. We. Sydney, Nepean, 1977—91; prof. psychology US Sports Acad., 1984—; pres. and mng. dir. Excelsior Coll. Pty. Ltd., Sydney, 1998—2002. Co-creator Cape Breton Playventure Way; exec. dir. Jeffries Industries Ltd., 1993—94; past dep. chmn., internat. coord. Kampala Heart and Gen. Hosp., Uganda, 1996; mng. dir. Power Positive Action, Australian Internat. Edn., Australian Sports Acad., Australian Internat. Quality Health Svcs.; non-exec. chmn. Australian Wine & Living, 1997—2002; chmn., mng. dir. various cos.; assessor, counselor work adjustment tng. programs Province of NS, Canada; vocat. assessor Dept. Manpower Govt. Can.; prin. asst., lectr. U. Sarkatchewm, 1968—69; expert witness psychology and edn. Supreme Ct.; cons., lectr., presenter, spkr. in field; mng. dir. Life Beinlt Edn. P/L, 1996—; pres. Power Positive Action P/L, 2009—. Author: Cash In Your Career: Making the Move, 1999, Cash In Your Career: Setting-Getting Goals, 1999, The Power of Positive Action: Action Intelligence, 2011; co-author: Eng. Lang. Comm. Skills: Basic Phonics, 1997; contbr. chpts. to books, articles to profl. jour. Active various sr. bd., Can. Can. doct. fellow. Fellow: Am. Coll. Forensic Examiners (clin. neuropsychologist, clin. forensic psychologist, internat. cons. edn. psychology, Diploma in Psychology 1996), Am. Assn. Integrative Medicine (Diploma Coll. Pain Mgmt. 2002), Chartered Secs. of Australia; mem.: APA, Internat. Coll. Leadership in Sports (interim pres. 2000—), Nat. Assn. Autism, Autism Soc. NSW (pres. 1985), Assn. Psychologists N.S. (Can., past pres.), Internat. Coun. Psychologists (past exec. dir.), Internat. Coun. Tchg. Effectiveness (chmn. 2001—06), Australian Psychol. Soc. Home: 157 Old Northern Rd 2154 Castle Hill NSW Australia Home Phone: 612-9639-0220.

KENNEY, JOHN PATRICK, dentist; s. John Edward and Nellie Kenney; 1 child, David J. BS Mktg., Christian Bros. Coll., 1960, DDS, Loyola U., Maywood, Ill., 1977; MS Oral Biology, Loyola U., Chgo., 1979. Diplomate Am. Bd. Forensic Odontology, 1986-, Am. Bd. Pediat. Dentistry, 2010. Supr. passenger svcs. Am. Airlines, Chgo., 1969—72; pvt. practice in pediat. dentistry Park Ridge, Ill., 1980—, asst. prof. pediat. dentistry Northwestern U., Chgo., 1993—97, clin. assoc. prof. pediat. dentistry, 1997—2000; assoc. prof. clin. surgery Northwstern U. Med. Sch., 2000—10. Forensic odontologist Cook County Med. Examiner, Chgo., 1984-97, chief, 1991-97; forensic odontologist Kane County Coroner, Geneva, Ill., 1984-97; cons. forensic odontologist Am. Airlines, Chgo., 1979, Midwest Express Airlines, Milw., 1985, Am. Eagle Airlines, Ind., 1995, United Express Airlines, Quincy, Ill., 1996, Comair Airlines, Mich., 1997, U.S. Army Ctrl. ID Lab., Honolulu, 1997—2003, Amtrak, Ill., 1999, NYCME, 2001; mem. Nat. Disaster Med. Sys. D-Mort team USPHS, forensic oversight com., 2001—09; dir. Identification Svcs. Dupage County Ill. Coroners Office, 1997-, Joint POW-MIA Acctg. Command Ctrl. Identification Lab. Hickam AFB, Hawaii, 2003-. Mem. editl. bd. Jour. Forensic Scis., 1997—, Jour. Forensic Identification, 2004—; contbr. articles to profl. jours Dep. coroner DuPage County, 2001— Fellow Am. Acad. Pediat. Dentistry, Am. Coll. Dentists, Am. Acad. Forensic Scis., Pierre Fauchard Soc., Royal Soc. Medicine; mem. ADA, Internat. Orgn. Forensic Odonto-stomatology (v.p. 1984-87), Internat. Assn. for Identification (cert. sr. crime scene analyst 1991—), Am. Acad. Pediat. Dentists, Am. Bd. Forensic Odontology (bd. dirs. 1990-96, 2000-03, treas. 1991-93, v.p. 1994, pres. 1995-96, sec. 2003-04, v.p. 2004-05, pres. 2006-07), Ill. State Dental Soc., Ill. Soc. Pediat. Dentists (bd. dirs. 1987-90), Chgo. Dental Soc.,Park Ridge Ill. Kiwanis, Kiwanis (pres. 1983-84, Disting. Pres. 1984), Forensics Sci. Found. (trustee 2006—, sec. 2010-). Office: 101 S Washington Ave Park Ridge IL 60068-4200 *

KENNING, JAMES A., neurosurgeon; MD, Thomas Jefferson U., 1974. Lic. Pa., 1980, diplomate Am. Bd. Neurol. Surgery, 1983. Intern in gen. surgery Dartmouth-Hithcock Med. Ctr., 1975, resident in neurology, 1980; fellow in gen. surgey Univ. Pitts. Med. Ctr., 1981; affiliate staff Albert Einstein Med. Ctr.; hosp. affiliations include Phoenixville Hosp., Paoli Hosp., Pa., 1988—, Bryn Mawr Hosp., 1988—, Bryn Mawr Rehabilitation Hosp., 1992—, Lankenau Med. Ctr., 1993—; chief neurosurgery dept.; system divsn. chief. Named one of Top Doctors, Phila. Mag., 2002, 2007, 2010. Fellow: Am. Coll. of Surgeons; mem.: Physician Adv. Group, Main Line Health Operating Rm. Com., Montgomery County Med. Soc., Phila. Neurol. Soc., Pa. Med. Soc., Phila. Med. Soc., Pa. Neurol. Soc., AMA, Congress of Neurol. Surgeons, Am. Heart. Assn., Am. Assn. of Neurol. Surgeons. Mailing: Bryn Mawr Hospital 130 S Bryn Mawr Ave Bryn Mawr PA 19010 Office Phone: 866-225-5654.

KENNY, CHARLES, counselor; BA in Psychology, Seton Hall U., 1989, MA in Counseling, 1991; MA in Psychology, New Sch. for Social Reseach, 1997. Lic. profl. counselor N.J., 1999. Adjunctive therapist/mental health worker St. Mary's Hosp., Hoboken, 1991—96; coord. counseling svcs., therapist PSI Family Svcs., Edison, NJ, 1997—2001; family support divsn. dir. Multicultural Cmty. Svcs., Edison, 2001—. Named Big East Academic All-Star, Big East Conf. Mem.: ACA, Am. Mental Health Counselors Assn., N.J. Mental Health Counselors Assn., N.J. Counseling Assn., Kappa Delta Pi, Psi Chi. Office: Multicultural Cmty Services Ste 108 1 Ethel Rd Edison NJ 08817

KENNY, ROBERT WADE, sociology, ethics and rhetoric educator; arrived in U.S., 1989; PhD in Rhetoric, U. Pitts., 1994, MA in Sociology, 1995. Prof. U. Dayton, Pa., 1996—2005, Mt. St. Vincent U., Nova Scotia, Canada, 2005—. Contbr. articles to profl. jours.; author: The Attic, 1985. Personal E-mail: doctorwadekenny@hotmail.com, wade.kenny@msvu.ca.

KENOKI, OHUCHIDA, surgeon, educator; b. Fukuoka, Japan, Sept. 30, 1971; MD, Kyusyu U., 1997, PhD, 2005. Asst. prof. Kyusyu U., 2007—. Recipient Young Scientists prize, Ministry of Edn., Culture, Sports, Sci. and Tech. Office: 3-1-1 Maedashi Fukuoka Kyuhsu 812-8582 Japan Office Fax: 81-92-642-5457. Business E-Mail: kenoki@surg1.med.kyushu-u.ac.jp.

KENT, BARTIS MILTON, retired physician; b. Terrell, Tex., June 23, 1925; s. Bartis William and Annie (Smalley) K.; m. Ann L. Kiel, July 6, 1954; children: Susan Ruth, Martha Lucille, Bartis Michael. Student, So. Meth. U., 1942-44; MD, Baylor U., 1948. Diplomate Am. Bd. Internal Medicine. Intern Jefferson Davis Hosp., Houston, 1948-49; resident pathology Mass. Meml. Hosps., Boston, 1951; resident in internal medicine Baylor U., 1953-56; indsl. physician Humble Oil Co., Houston, 1949-51; instr. dept. medicine U. Iowa, 1956-58; staff physician Iowa City VA Hosp., 1956-58; practice medicine specializing in internal medicine Muskogee, Okla., 1958—2002. Cons. Muskogee VA Hosp.; clin. asst. prof. medicine U. Okla. Sch. Medicine, 1975-98. Chmn. Muskogee County chpt. Am. Nat. Red Cross, 1963-65. With USAF, 1951—53. Decorated Air medal. Fellow A.C.P.; mem. Indsl. Med. Assn., Soc. Nuclear Medicine, Am. Fedn. Clin. Research, Am. Heart Assn., Aerospace Medicine Assn., Am., Okla. socs. internal medicine, Muskogee C. of C. Methodist. Mason (Shriner). Avocations: fishing, gardening. Home: 800 N 45th St Muskogee OK 74401-1505

KENT, GEORGIA L., obstetrician, gynecologist, healthcare executive, educator; b. NYC, May 30, 1950; d. Harry J. and Eva R. K. BS in Biology with honors, U. Pitts., 1971; MD, U. Pa., 1975; MBA, George Washington U., 1991. Diplomate Am. Bd. Obstetricians-Gynecologists; MD, Colo., Calif., N.Y., N.J., Pa. Sr. instr. ob-gyn. Hahnemann U., Phila., 1979-82; obstetrician-gynecologist Kaiser Group Health Assn., Washington, 1982-90; med. dir. Pacificare, Fountain Valley, Calif., 1991-93, Denver, 1993-94; v.p. med. svcs. The Prudential Ins. Co. of Am., Prudential Healthcare, Roseland, N.J., 1994-96; potter, healthcare cons. self employed, West Orange, N.J., 1997-99, Pitts., 1999—; coll. chair undergrad. bus. and mgmt. degree programs U. Phoenix-Pitts. Campus, 2000—03; pvt. practice, 2006—. Guest lectr. U. Calif. Riverside, 1992-93, Denver U., 1993-94; adj. faculty Duquesne U., 1999—; dept. chair undergrad. bus. & mgmt. U. Phoenix, Pitts., 2000-03, Cmty. Coll. Alleghery County, 2001—; pvt. practice Georgia L. Kent, MD FACOG PC, 2006—. Contbg. author, featured in: (book) Women in Medicine and Management: A Mentoring Guide, 1995; exhibited in group shows at N.J. Ctr. for Visual Arts Mem. Show, 1997, 98, Sweetwater Art Ctr., 1999, North Hills Art Ctr., 2000 (hon. mention). Mem. AAUW, Am. Coll. Obstetricians and Gynecologists, Phi Beta Kappa, Beta Gamma Sigma. Avocations: greyhound rescue/adoption, potter, gardening, walking.

KENT, JOAN L., obstetrician, gynecologist; Attended, Weill Cornell Med. Coll. Diplomate Am. Bd. Ob Gyn. Intern NY Presbyn. Hosp. - Weill Cornell Med. Ctr., resident, 1985—88, affiliation ob-gyn. Office: NewYork-Presbyterian Hospital - Weill Cornell Medical Center 235 E 67th St 204 New York NY 10021 Office Phone: 212-772-2900.

KENY, RAMCHANDRA VISHNU, pharmacist, educator; b. Panaji, Goa, India, Aug. 30, 1954; BS in Pharmacy, Bombay U., 1976, PharmM, 1983. Mfg. chemist injectable Roussel Pharm. India Ltd., 1976—78, head dept. pharmaceutics, prof. Goa Coll. Pharmacy, 1978—. Contbr. to profl. publs. Recipient Best Tchr. Shikshak Bhushan award, Shikshak Vikas Parishad, Goa, India, 2008. Mem.: Assn. Pharm. Tchrs. India, Controlled Release Soc. (Indian chpt.), Indian Pharm. Assn. Avocations: theater, sports, movies. Office: Goa Coll Pharmacy 18th June Rd Panaji Goa 403001 India Office Fax: 91-832-2226882. E-mail: rvkenys@rediffmail.com.

KENYON, GARY MICHAEL, gerontologist, educator; b. Montreal, Que., Can., June 12, 1949; s. Raymond George and Frances Evelyn (Duhault) K. B in Commerce cum laude, Loyola U., Montreal, 1970; BA, Concordia U., Montreal, 1977, MA, 1981; PhD, U. B.C., 1985. Postdoctoral fellow Andrew Norman Inst. U. So. Calif., LA, 1985-86; postdoctoral fellow Swedish Inst. Linkoping U., Sweden, 1986-87; prof., chmn. dept. gerontology St. Thomas U., Fredericton, N.B., Canada, 1987—. Adj. prof. McGill U. Ctr. for Studies in Aging, Montreal; hon. rsch. assoc. U. N.B., 1996—. Author: Emergent Theories of Aging, 1988, Metaphors of Aging, 1991, Aging and Biography, 1996, Restorying Our Lives, 1997, Ordinary Wisdom, 2001, Narrative Gerontology, 2001, Storying Later Life, 2011; editor: jour. Gnosis, 1979—81; rev. editor: Can. Jour. on Aging, 1989—90; contbr. articles to profl. jours. Social Scis. and Humanities fellow, Can. Govt., 1983—85. Mem. Gerontology Soc. Am., Can. Assn. Gerontology. Avocations: skiing, cooking, wine, Tai Chi instructor, language study. Office: St Thomas U Dept Gerontology Fredericton NB Canada E3B 5G3 Home: 43 Queen St Saint Andrews NB E5B 1C3 Canada Office Phone: 506-452-0527. E-mail: kenyon@stu.ca.

KEOGH, BRUCE EDWARD, cardiothoracic surgeon; b. Harare, Zimbabwe, Nov. 24, 1954; s. Cecil Alexander and Marjorie Beatrice Keogh; m. Ann Katherine Westmore, Sept. 22, 1979; children: Robert Alexander, Christopher Andrew, William Edward, Michael Edward. BSc, MB, ChB, U. London, 1980, MD, 1989; MD (hon.), U. Birmingham, 2009, U. Sheffield, 2009; DSc, U. Toledo, 2009, U. Coventry, 2010. Specialist register Gen. Med. Coun., 2002. Sr. lectr. cardiac surgery, cons. Royal Postgraduate Med. Sch., Hammersmith Hosp., London, 1991—95; cons. cardiothoracic surgeon, assoc. med. dir. U. Hosp. Birmingham, England, 1995—2004; dir. surgery The Heart Hosp., London, 2004—07; med. dir. Dept. Health Nat. Health Svc., 2007—. Nat. task force coronary heart disease Dept. Health, London, 2000—06; chair clin. strategy group Healthcare Commn., London, 2000—06, commr., Commn. Health Improvement, London, 2002—04, chair nat. svc. frameworks programme bd., 2002—04; standing med. adv. com. Nat. Health Svc., London, 2002—05; prof. cardiac surgery U. Coll. London, 2004—; vis. prof. U. Tokyo, U. Colo., Chinese U. Hong Kong. Author: Normal Surface Anatomy and Imaging; editor: The Evidence Base for Cardiothoracic Surgery; contbr. articles to profl. jours. Recipient knight comdr. Order Brit. Empire. Fellow: ACS (hon.), European Assn. Cardio-Thoracic Surgery (sec. gen. 2004—07), European Soc. Cardiology, Royal Coll. Surgeons Eng., Royal Coll. Surgeons Edinburgh (cert. in cardiothoracic surgery, King James IV prof. 2005), Royal Coll. Physicians London, Royal Coll. Gen. Practitioners (hon.); mem.: Lunar Soc., Royal Soc. Medicine (pres. cardiothoracic sect. 2005—07), Soc. Cardiothoracic Surgeons Gt. Britain and Ireland (pres. 2006—08, Ronald Edwards medal 1991), Soc. Thoracic Surgeons USA (bd. dirs. 2005—). Office: Dept Health Richmond House 79 Whitehall SW1A 2NS London England Business E-Mail: bruce.keogh@dh.gsi.gov.uk.

KEON YEOP, KIM, medical educator; b. Daegu, Jan. 2, 1970; D, Kyungpook Nat. U., 2003. Chief Dept. Occupl. Medicine, DongGang Hosp., 1999—2000; flight surgeon Republic of Korea Air Force, 2000—03; asst. prof. Coll. Medicine Dept. Preventive Medicine, Konyang U., 2003—07, assoc. prof. Sch. Medicine, 2009—; asst. prof. Dept. Preventive Medicine, Coll. Medicine, Chungnam Nat. U., 2007—09. Bd. dir. Acad. Critical Health Policy, 2007—, Korean Assn. Agrl. Medicine & Cmty. Health, 2010—; cons. Korea Healthy Cities Partnership, 2009—, Adv. Com. Health Impact Assessment, 2009—; vis. scholar Dept. Social and Behavioral Health, Sch. Rural Pub. Health, Health Sci. Ctr., Tex. A&M U., 2011—. Recipient award, Nat. Health Ins. Corp., Geumsan County, Muju County. Mem.: Internat. Union Health Promotion and Edn., Korean Soc. Occupation & Environ. Medicine, Korean Soc. Health Edn. and Promotion, Korean Soc. Preventive Medicine. Avocations: movies, badminton, ping pong/table tennis. Office: #101 Dongin 2-ga Jung-gu Daegu 700-422 Republic of Korea Office Fax: 82-53-425-2447. Business E-Mail: pmkky@knu.ac.kr.

KEOWN, LAURISTON LIVINGSTON, JR., consulting psychologist; b. Balt., Feb. 24, 1942; s. Lauriston Livingston and Gladys May (Dykes) K.; m. Patje Alexandra Susemihl, Aug. 7, 1962 (div. 1977); children: Christina, Cassandra, Lauriston, Clayton; m. Nancy Ann Hastie, Mar. 18, 1978 (div. 1990); m. Denise Elaine Parsons, (1993). BA cum laude, U. Balt., 1965; MS, U. Alta., 1970, PhD, 1977. Registered psychologist, Alta.; Can. Register Health Svc. Providers in Psychology. Lectr. Nippissing Coll., Laurentian U., North Bay, Ont., Can., 1968-69; chief sys. analyst Dept. Youth, Edmonton, Alta., Can., 1969-71, rsch. dir., 1971-72; dir. planning and rsch. Dept. Culture, Youth and Recreation, Alta., 1972-74; dir. planning and devel. Dept. Recreation, Pks. and Wildlife, Edmonton, Alta., 1974-75; asst. dir. Transp. Safety Alta. Transp. Dept., 1975-87; dir. Motor Transp. Planning and Bus. Analysis Alta. Transp. and Utilities, 1987-93; sr. psychologist Wainwright Cmty. Mental Health Svcs. Project, Alberta Hosp., Ponoka, 1993-95; regional mental health mgr. East Ctrl. Health Region, 1995-99; psychologist The Family Ctr., 1999—2005, Insight Psychol. Inc., 2002—, Couples First Counselling, 2009—; dir. Donaldson Park Cmty. League, 2005—. Cons. R. Dehaas Assocs., Edmonton, 1979-80, Draherin Group, Edmonton, 1980-82, Denlaur Assocs., 1988-. Author: (with others) Evaluation of Traffic Safety Programs, 1980, Strategic Management of The Motor Transport Industry, 1989, The Obsessive Compulsive Organization, 1993; contbr. more than 200 articles to profl. jours. Mem. Alta. Planning Bd., 1974-82; bd. dirs. Alta. Royal Can. Mounted Police Hist. Celebrations Commn., 1974-75; exec. bd. Traffic Records Commn., Nat. Safety Coun., 1978-93; Minister's Adv. Com. on Traffic Safety, 1992-93.; mem. mental health adv. com. Capital Health Region, 2006-08. Indsl. psychology scholar Lamond Dewhurst & Assocs., U. Alta., 1966. Fellow Am. Traffic Safety Info. Profls., Can. Fedn. Clin. Hypnosis (Alta. Soc.); mem. Eye Movement Desentization and Reprogramming Internat. Assn. Can., Alta. Psychologists Assn. Home: 26-51331 RR 224 Sherwood Park AB Canada T8C 1H3 Office: Insight Psychol Inc Ste 203 9148-23 Ave Edmonton AB T6N 1N9 Canada

KERAMIDAS, DIMITRIS CONSTANTINE, pediatric surgeon, consultant; b. Athens, Attica, Greece, May 28, 1935; arrived in U.S., 1973; s. Constantine Keramidas and Alice Nanopoulos; m. Dimitria Anagnostou, June 14, 1973; 1 child. MD, Athens U. Med. Sch., 1960, PhD (hon.), 1967. Assoc. Pediat. Surgery Aglaia Kyriakou Children's Hosp., Athens, 1970—85; chief surgeon Aghia Sophia Children's Hosp., Athens, 1985—2002; cons. pediat. surgeon Mitera Maternity and Pediat. Hosp., Athens, 2003—. Prof. Pediat. Surgery U. Patras, Greece, 1998—2000; vis. pediat. surgeon Medecins du Monde, Cyprus, 1998. Assoc. editor European Jour. Pediat. Surgery, 1991—; contbr. articles to profl. jours. 1st lt. Greek Med. Corps, 1961—62. Fellow Pediat. Surgery, U. So. Calif., 1973—74. Mem.: Mediterranean Assn. Pediat. Surgeons (pres. 2000—02), Hellenic Surg. Soc. (pres. 2003—04, jour. editor-in-chief 2003—), Greek Assn. Pediat. Surgeons (pres. 1991—92). Achievements include research in pediatric surgery. Avocations: swimming, chess, history, physics. Office: Mitera Maternity & Pediat Hosp 6 Erythrou Stavrou St 15123 Amaroussion Greece Personal E-mail: dimit940@otenet.gr.

KERBER, RICHARD E., cardiologist; b. NYC, May 10, 1939; s. Max and Pauline Kerber; m. Linda K. Kaufman; children: Ross, Justin. AB in Anthropology, Columbia U., 1960; MD, NYU, 1964. Diplomate Am. Bd. Internal Medicine, Am. Bd. Cardiology. Med. intern/resident Bellevue Hosp., NYC, 1964—66; med. resident Stanford (Calif.) U. Hosp., 1968—69, cardiology fellow, 1969—71; asst. prof. internal medicine U. Iowa, Iowa City, 1971—74, assoc. prof. internal medicine, 1974—78, prof. medicine, 1978—. Editor: Echocardiography in Coronary Artery Disease, 1988. Capt. US Army, 1966—68. Grantee RO1 grant, NHLBI, 1995—2008. Fellow: Am. Coll. Cardiology, Am. Heart Assn., Am. Heart Assn. (chmn. coun. on cardiopulmonary and critical care 1997—99, 1997—99, award of Meritorious Achievement 1996, Scientific Coun. Dist. Achievement award 2001), Am. Coll. Cardiology (gov. for Iowa 1976—79, 1976—79); mem.: Assn. Am. Physicians, Assn. Univ. Cardiologists, Am. Soc. for Clin. Investigation, Am. Soc. Echocardiology (sec. 1978—80, treas. 1993—95, v.p. 1995—97, pres. 1997—99, sec. 1978—80, treas. 1993—95, v.p. 1995—97, pres. 1997—99). Office: U Iowa Dept Medicine 200 Hawkins Dr Iowa City IA 52242-1009

KERDEL, FRANCISCO ARMANDO, dermatologist; b. NYC, Apr. 28, 1954; MD, St. Thomas Hosp. Med. Sch., London U., 1979. Cert. in dermatology Harvard Med. Sch., 1983. Physician, pres. Fla. Academic Dermatology Ctrs., 2004—. Dir. dermatology inpatients U. Miami Hosp., 1990—. Recipient Intendis Mentoring award, Am. Osteo. Coll. Dermatology, Reconocimiento al merito, Asociacion Colombiana de Dermatologia; named Practitioner of Yr., Fla. Soc.

Dermatology. Master: Found. Internat. Dermatology Edn., Internat. Soc. Dermatology; mem.: Noah Worcestor Dermatol. Soc., Academia Nacional Medicina (Caracas Venezuela) (corr.), Soc. Investigative Dermatology, Am. Acad. Dermatology. Avocations: fishing, cooking. Office: 1400 NW 12 Ave Ste 4 Miami FL 33136 Office Fax: 305-325-0919. Business E-Mail: dr.kerdel@fadcenter.com.

KERDELHUÉ, BERNARD L., medical educator, medical researcher; s. Joseph Marie and Andrée Kerdelhué; m. Marie-Christine Hélene Lacouture de Bronno Bronska, June 26, 1962; children: Jean-Christophe André, Valérie Marie, Elodie. DSc, Faculty of Sci., Paris, 1967. Asst. rschr. CNRS, Paris, 1967—72, chargé of rsch., 1972—76, dir. rsch., 1976—. Assoc. prof. cell biology Baylor Coll., Houston, 1979—80; assoc. prof. ob-gyn. U. Calif., San Francisco, 1980—82; adj. rsch. prof. ob-gyn. Ea. Va. Med. Sch., Norfolk, 1991—; mem. sci. coun. CNRS, 1997—2003; chmn. sci. coun. Found. Jérome Lejeune, Paris, 1997—; mem. Pontifical Acad. for Life, Vatican City, 1998—. Contbr. articles to numerous profl. jours. Sgt. Air Force, 1961—62, France. Recipient Medal of bronze, Nat. Ctr. Sci. Rsch., 1972. Office: Faculté de Médecine 45 Rue des Saints Pères Paris 75270 Cedex06 France Office Fax: 33 1 42864070. Business E-Mail: bernard.kerdelhue@biomedicale.univ-paris5.fr.

KEREIAKES, DEAN JAMES, cardiologist; b. Louisville, Jan. 8, 1953; s. James G. and Helen (Christy) K.; m. Anne Sugar, June 20, 1981; children: Jennifer, David, Andrew, Nicholas. BS, U. Cin., 1974, MD, 1978. Diplomate Am. Bd. Internal Medicine, Am. Bd. Cardiology. Intern, resident U. Calif., San Francisco, 1978-80; sr. resident Mass. Gen. Hosp., Boston, 1980-81; chief med. resident H.C. Moffitt Hosp., San Francisco, 1981-82; adult cardiology fellow U. Calif., San Francisco, 1982-84; coronary angioplasty fellow San Francisco Heart Inst., 1984, Sequoia Hosp., Redwood City, Calif., 1984; med. dir. The Christ Hosp. Heart & Vascular Ctr., Cin., 2005—; CEO, dir. rsch. Ohio Heart Health Ctr., 2000—05. Med. dir. Carl & Edythe Lindner Ctr. Rsch. & Edn., Cin., 1995—; prof. clin. medicine Ohio State U., 1995—; mem. ACC/AHA task force com on angioplasty and unstable angina guidelines AHA/ACC, 1987-2002. Mem. editl. bd. Circulation, sect. editor, Jour. Invasive Cardiology, mem. editl. bd. Am. Heart Jour., Am. Jour. Cardiology, Jour. Am. Coll. Cardiology. Fellow Am. Coll. Cardiology; mem. AMA, Am. Heart Assn., Alpha Omega Alpha, Phi Beta Kappa. Republican. Avocation: wine collecting. Office: The Ohio Heart and Vascular Ctr 2123 Auburn Ave Ste 136 Cincinnati OH 45219-2906 Office Phone: 513-585-1777. E-mail: lindner@fuse.net.

KEREN-KENDE, GERSHON, epidemiologist; b. Prague, Czech Republic, Apr. 20, 1947; MD, Tel Aviv U., 1975, MSc in Pediat. Cert. in infectious disease Edmonton, Alta., 1984. Head, infectious diseases unit Hillel Yaffe Hosp., Hedera, 2008—. Avocation: photography. Home: Shosan Yamin 15 Kfar Ganim Petah Tikva 49772 Israel Home Fax: 97239094216. Personal E-mail: dr-keren@zahav.net.il.

KERIK, NORA ESTELA, nuclear medicine physician, researcher; b. Buenos Aires, Aug. 10, 1958; d. David Kerik and Paulina Rotenberg; m. Samuel Gorodzinsky, Jan. 19, 1986; children: Alan Gorodzinsky, Dan Gorodzinsky. MD, La Salle U., Mexico city, 1982. Intern Hosp. Espanol, Mexico, 1981—82; resident in nuc. medicine McGill U., Montreal, Canada, 1982—84; attending Hosp. Humana Pedregal, Mexico city, Mexico, 1984—86; chief dept. nuc. medicine Nat. Neurol. and Neurosurg. Inst., Mexico, city, 1985—89; dir. positron emission tomography-cyclotron facility Nat. U., Mexico City, 2000—03. Tng. in operation of CTI RDS-II Cyclotron and FDG Regional Nuc. Pharm., Birmingham, 2001. Contbr. articles. Positron Emission Tomography fellow, UCLA, 1999. Mem.: Com. Tecnico Cientifico de la Unidad Positron Emission Tomography-Cyclotron (assoc.), Com. Acad. Radiologìa Imàgen (assoc.), Soc. Mexican Nuc. Medicine (assoc.), Soc. Nuc. Medicine (assoc.), Internat. Atomic Energy Agy. (assoc.). Jewish. Achievements include development of The First Positron Emission Tomography-Cyclotron Facility In Mexico. Avocation: bicycling. Personal E-mail: drkerik@hotmail.com.

KERKHOFF, THOMAS R., psychology professor; b. Cin., Apr. 12, 1948; BS, Xavier U., 1970; degree in Clin. Psychology, Va. Commonweatlh U., 1976. Clin. prof. U. Fla., 1999—. Rehab. psychologist Shands Rehab. Hosp., 1999—. Fellow: APA Divsn. 22. Avocations: music, motorcycling. Home: 4923 NW 69th Pl Gainesville FL 32653-1195 Home Fax: 352-265-5420. Personal E-mail: t.kerkhoff@cox.net.

KERLIKOWSKE, KARLA, research scientist; BS in Med. Tech. magna cum laude, Mich. State U., East Lansing, 1978; MS in Nutrition, U. Calif., Berkeley, 1984; MD, U. Calif., San Francisco, 1988. Intern, medicine U. Calif., 1988—89, resident, primary care medicine, 1989—91, clin. instr., asst. physician, dept. medicine, 1991—93, asst. prof. in residence, dept. medicine, 1994—, asst. prof. in residence, dept. epidemiology & biostatistics, 1994—, assoc. prof. in residence, dept. medicine, 2000—, assoc. prof. in residence, dept. epidemiology & biostatistics, 2000—, prof. in residence, dept. epidemiology & biostatistics, 2006; fellow, gen. internal medicine Veterans Affairs Med. Ctr., San Francisco, 1991—93, assoc. dir., women's clinic, 1993—99, dir., women's clinic, 1999—. Mem. U. Calif. Comprehensive Cancer Ctr., San Francisco; prin. investigator Nat. Cancer Inst.-funded San Francisco Mammography Registry, Outcomes Core; co-investigator NIH-funded, U. Calif. San Francisco Breast Cancer SPORE. Contbr. articles to profl. publications. Recipient Tower Guard award for Scholastic Achievement, 1975, Am. Cancer Soc. award for Primary Care Physicians, 1994—96. Mem.: Alpha Omega Alpha. Office: Veterans Affairs Medical Center VAMC 111A1 San Francisco CA 94143 Office Fax: 415-379-5573. E-mail: karla.kerlikowske@ucsf.edu.

KERLIN, PAUL, gastroenterologist; b. Brisbane, Australia, Jan. 24, 1947; s. Arthur William and Catherine Mary (Mahon) K.; m. Rosemary Heath, Jan. 17, 1976; children: Douglas, Beata, Victoria, Amelia. MB, BS with honors, U. Queensland, Australia, 1972, BA, 1973; FRACP, Royal Australian Coll. Phys., Australia, 1979; MD, U. Queensland, Australia, 1983. Resident Royal Brisbane Hosp., Australia, 1973; resident, registrar Royal Canberra Hosp., Australia, 1974-75; registrar The Queen Elizabeth Hosp., Adelaide, Australia, 1976-77; rsch. fellow U. So. Calif., LA, 1978-79, Mayo Clinic, Rochester, Minn., 1979-81; dir. dept. gastroenterology Princess Alexandra Hosp., Brisbane, 1981-90; clin. prof. U. Queensland, Brisbane, 1991—; cons. gastroenterologist & hepatologist Wesley Hosp., Brisbane, 1991—. Contbr. 100 articles to profl. jours. Recipient Fulbright Postdoctoral fellowship, 1978-81, Mayo Rsch. fellowship, 1979-81, Rappaport Clinician-Investigator award, 1980. Fellow Royal Australasian Coll. Physicians, Am. Coll. Gastroenterology, Am. Gastroenterol. Assn.; mem. Gastroenterology Soc. Australia (coun. 1987—), Australian Med. Assn., Australian Inst. Co. Dirs. Roman Catholic. Office: Wesley Hosp Level 4 Sandford Jackson Bldg 30 Chasely St Auchenflower QLD 4066 Australia Business E-Mail: paul.kerlin@wesley.com.au.

KERMAN, JULES, psychiatrist, educator; b. Bklyn., Jan. 9, 1944; BA, Columbia U., 1964; MD, Albert Einstein Coll. Medicine, 1972, PhD, 1977. Diplomate Am. Bd. Psychiatry and Neurology. Intern Einstein/Bronx Mcpl. Hosp., 1972-73, resident in psychiatry, 1973-76; fellow in psychiatry Payne Whitney, NY Hosp., 1976—77; practice specializing in psychiatry and psychoanalysis NYC, 1976—; post grad. Columbia U. Psychoanalytic Ctr., NYC, 1984—89, assoc. clin. prof., tng. and supervising analyst, chmn. tng. and supervising com., mem. exec. com. Mem. Am. Psychoanalytic Assn., Assn. Psychoanalytic Medicine (pres. 2009-11). Office: 239 Central Park W New York NY 10024-6038 *

KERN, DONALD MICHAEL, internist; b. Belleville, Ill., Nov. 21, 1951; s. Donald Milton and Dolores Olivia (Rust) K. BS in Biology, Tulane U., 1973; MD magna cum laude, U. Brussels, 1983. ECFMG cert.; lic. Calif. Intern in surgery Berkshire Med. Ctr., Pittsfield, Mass., 1983-84; intern in psychiatry Tufts New England Med. Ctr., Boston, 1984-85; resident in internal medicine Kaiser Found. Hosp., San Francisco, 1985-87; with assoc. staff internal medicine Kaiser Permanente Med. Group, Inc., San Francisco, 1987-89; assoc. investigator AIDS Clin. Trial Unit Kaiser Permanente Med. Ctr., Stanford U., Nat. Inst. Allergy & Infectious Disease, San Francisco, 1988-90; mem. staff internal medicine Kaiser Permanente Med. Group, South San Francisco, 1989-96; mem. staff Desert Med. Group, Palm Springs, Calif., 1996—, assoc. med. dir., 2002—. Democrat. Roman Catholic. Avocations: theater, ballet, travel, antiques. Office: Desert Medical Group 275 N El Cielo Rd Palm Springs CA 92262

KERN, JOSIPA, medical educator, researcher; d. Fridrik and Vjekoslava Kern; m. Silvije Vuletic, Oct. 14, 2004. Mathematician, Zagreb U., 1972, MSc in Math. Stats., 1981, PhD in Biology, 1990. Asst. prof. U. Med. Sch., Zagreb, Croatia, 1991—96, assoc. prof., 1996—2002, prof. med. informatics, 2002—. Master: Croatian Soc. for Med. Informatics (corr.); mem.: Acad. of Med. Sci. in Croatia, Internat. Assn. of Med. Informatics (corr.), European Fedn. for Med. Informatics (corr.). Office: Andrija Stampar Sch of Pub Health Rockefellerova 4 Zagreb 10000 Croatia

KERN, SCOTT E., pathologist; b. Benton, Ill., Sept. 5, 1959; s. Teddy Roosevelt and Audra Blondell (Mings) K.; m. Mary Jo Steel, Nov. 1, 1991; 1 child, Lisa. BS in Biomed. Scis., U. Mich., 1981, MD, 1983. Diplomate Am. Bd. Pathology. Resident, dept. pathology U. Mich., Ann Arbor, 1983-87; fellow, gastrointestinal pathology Johns Hopkins U., Balt., 1987—88, postdoctoral fellow, oncology, 1988—90, instr. pathology and oncology, 1990-91, asst. prof. oncology and pathology, 1991—97, assoc. prof., oncology and pathology, 1997—2002, prof. oncology and pathology, 2002—, preceptor human genetics program, 1992—. Contbr. articles to profl. jours. Recipient Upjohn award Am. Assn. Cancer Rsch., 1989, Clinician Scientist award, John Hopkins Hosp., 1991-92, McDonnell Found. Scholar award, 1993. Achievements include discovery of prognostic value of genetic changes in colorectal cancer, p53 protein binding of specific DNA sequences, mutant p53 protein inhibition of transcriptional function of wild-type p53. Office: Sidney Kimmel Comprehensive Cancer Ctr at Johns Hopkins Harry & Jeanette Weinberg Bldg Ste 1100 401 North Broadway Baltimore MD 21231

KERNAHAN, CHARLES, medical association administrator; Group mng. dir. Allied Healthcare Ltd., UK; v.p. mktg. EMEA ConvaTec (divsn. Bristol Myers Squibb), UK; CEO Kidney Rsch. UK, Peterborough. Bd. dir. Medicines & Healthcare Products Regulatory Agy. Office: Kidney Rsch UK Kings Chamber Priestgate PE1 1FG Peterborough England *

KERNER, JOHN ALAN, pediatrician, educator; b. San Francisco, Nov. 16, 1947; BA, Stanford U., 1969; MD, U. Calif., San Francisco, 1973. Prof. pediat. Stanford U. Med. Ctr., 1979—. Med. dir., children's home pharmacy Lucile Packard Children's Hosp., 1994. Recipient Joseph W. St. Geme, Jr. Edn. award, Western Soc. Pediatric Rsch. Fellow: AAP; mem.: ASPEN, NASPGHAN. Avocation: writing. Office: 750 Welch Rd Ste 116 Palo Alto CA 94304 Office Fax: 650-498-5608. Business E-Mail: jkerner@stanfordmed.org.

KERNS, GERTRUDE YVONNE, psychologist; b. Flint, Mich., July 25, 1931; d. Lloyd D. and Mildred C. (Ter Achter) B. BA, Olivet Coll., 1953; MA, Wayne State U., 1958; PhD, U. Mich., 1979. Sch. psychologist Roseville (Mich.) Pub. Schs., 1958—68, Grosse Pointe (Mich.) Pub. Schs., 1968—86; pvt. practice psychology Grosse Pointe, 1980—; instr. psychology Macomb C.C., 1959—69. Author: A Second Heartbeat, 1979. Mem.: Lakeshore Psychol. Assn. (pres. 1988—89), Mich. Psychol. Assn., Am. Psychol. Assn., Psi Chi. Home: 28820 Grant St Saint Clair Shores MI 48081-3207 Office: 131 Kercheval Ave Ste 140 Grosse Pointe Farms MI 48236-3630

KEROS, PREDRAG ANTE, physician, neurosurgeon; b. Zagreb, Croatia, Sept. 17, 1933; d. Ante Silvestar Keros and Vilka; m. Jadranka D. Stom, Dec. 24, 1967; 1 child, Tomislav. Degree, U. Zagreb, 1958, PhD, 1963, MS in experimental biology, 1970. Asst. U. Zagreb, 1960—65, asst. prof., 1965—70, assoc. prof., 1970—75, prof., 1975—98, prof. emeritus, 2001—; sr. rsch. counselor Ministry of Sci., Rep. Croatia, 1978—; head dept. anatomy and physiol. Sch. Health Studies, 1999—. Head polyclinic, dept. neurosurgery U. Clinical Hosp., Zagreb, 1976—2004; vice provost Rectorship of U. Zagreb, 1986—88; sr. fellow Croatian Acad. Med. Scis., 1988—. Editor in chief Jour. Libri Oncologici, 1974—92; editor: Jour. Arta Facultatis Medicae Zagrebiernsis, 1976—91, publs., author 349 scientific and profl. articles, 38 profl. med. books, editor 15 profl. and ednl. books. Mem. advisory scientific council Ministry of Sci., Zagreb, 1991—92; sec. exec. com. Croatian League for Fight Against Cancer, Zagreb, 1970—73; pres. Croatian Soc. Ergonomics, Zagreb, 1987—89; pres. com. for ecology Pub. Council of Zagreb, 1986—90. Recipient Decoration for merit with silver star, Decrete of Pres. of SFRY J.B. Tito, 1975, Sci. award, Mcpl. Authorities of Zagreb, 1989, State award for promotion of sci., Croatian State Assembly, 2001, J.J. Strossmayer award, Croatian Acad. Sci. Art, 2007, award, City of Zagreb, 2009. Mem.: World and European Assn. Neurosurgical Soc., Croatian Neurosurgical Assn., Croatian Med. Assn. Croatian Folk Party. Roman Catholic. Office: Univ Zagreb Sch Medicine Salata 11 Zagreb 10000 Croatia Home: Amruseva St 15 10-000 Zagreb Croatia

KERR, ALLEN STEWART, retired psychologist; b. Evanston, Ill., Nov. 13, 1928; s. Charles Allen and Mildred (Latham) Kerr; m. Charlyn Floyd, July 19, 1952; children: Betsy Kerr Hedding, Chet, Peggy Kerr Ihinger, Cindy Kerr Levesque. BA, Brown U., 1950; D of Psychology, Forest Inst. Profl. Psychology, 1988. Salesman Sleepeck Printing Co., Bellwood, Ill., 1953—68, v.p. sales, 1968—83; staff psychologist The Bradley Ctr., Columbus, Ga., 1988—94; sr. psychologist The Pastoral Inst., Columbus, Ga., 1994—99; ret., 1999. Lt. j.g. USN, 1950—53. Recipient Bell Ringer award, Mental Health Assn., Columbus, Ga., 1995. Mem.: APA, Rotary (Muscogee charter mem., pres. 1997—98), Minne Tonka Rotary Club. Methodist. Avocations: golf, photography, writing, travel. Home: 10451 Greenbrier Rd Apt 201 Minnetonka MN 55305 Business E-Mail: askchar@earthlink.net.

KERR, DAVID JAMES, oncologist; b. Glasgow, Scotland, June 14, 1956; arrived in England; s. Robert and Sarah P. (Hogg) K.; m. Anne M. Young, July 11, 1980; children: Stewart, Sarah, Fiona. BS with 1st class honors, U. Glasgow, 1977, MBChB, 1980, MS in Clin. Pharmacology, 1986, MD, 1987, PhD, 1989, DSc, 1997; MA, U. Oxford, 2002. House officer Glasgow Royal Infirmary, 1980-81; sr. house officer Western Infirmary, Glasgow, 1981-83; lectr. in endocrinology U. Glasgow, 1983-84, lectr. in med. oncology, 1984-89, sr. lectr., 1989-92; prof. clin. oncology U. Birmingham, England, 1992—2001; Rhodes prof. cancer therapeutics and clin. pharmacology, dir. Nat. Cancer Rsch. Network U. Oxford, England, 2001—. Co-author numerous books; contbr. articles to profl. jours. Named Comdr. of Brit. Empire, 2002; grantee, Cancer Rsch. Campaign, 1992, Med. Rsch. Coun., 1994, Regional Health Authority, 1995. Fellow: Royal Coll. Physicians (London), Royal Coll. Physicians (Glasgow), Acad. Med. Scis.; mem.: European Soc. Med. Oncology (pres. 2007). Mem. Labour Party and Reform Club. Avocations: flying, soccer. Office: U Oxford Radcliffe Infirmary Dept Clin Pharmacology Oxford England also: Sidra Medical & Research Ctr Qatar Foundation PO Box 26999 Doha Qatar Office Phone: 441865617020. Office Fax: 441865617022. Personal E-mail: david.kerr@clinpharm.ox.ac.uk.

KERR, DOUGLAS ANTHONY, neurologist, researcher; b. Aug. 12, 1966; BA in Biology (magna cum laude), Princeton U., 1988; PhD in Biochemistry and Molecular Biology, Coll. Grad. Studies, Thomas Jefferson U., Phila., 1995; MD summa cum laude, Thomas Jefferson U., Jefferson Med. Coll., 1995. Am. Bd. Psychiatry & Neurology, 2000. Resident, dept. internal medicine The Graduate Hosp., Phila., 1995—96; resident, dept. neurology John Hopkins Hosp., Balt., 1996—98, chief resident, dept. neurology, 1998—99; assoc. prof., neurology John Hopkins Sch. Medicine, Balt., 1999—; asst. prof., dept. molecular microbiology and immunology John Hopkins Sch. Pub. Health, Balt., 1999—; dir. John Hopkins Transverse Myelitis Ctr., 1999—. Platform presentation, Neural Stem Cells in Motor Neuron Disease Soc. for Neuroscience, 2000; invited spkr. in field; bd. dir. Ctr. for Amyotrophic Lateral Sclerosis Rsch., John Hopkins U.; affiliated faculty, Barker Firm, Osler Med. Tng. Program John Hopkins Hosp.; mem. Data Safety Monitoring bd. NIH sponsored hematopoietic stem cell transplantation trials network; dir. John Hopkins Project RESTORE; invited testimony, State Senate and House of Representatives for the MD Stem Cell Act 2005, Annapolis, Md. Contbr. articles to profl. jours.; peer reviewer Annals Neurology, Human Molecular Genetics, Jour. Neurovirology, Jour. Immunology, Exptl. Neurology, Jour. Clin. Investigation, Jour. Neurological Sciences, Jour. Neurology, Neurosurgery & Psychiatry, Jour. Rheumatology, Neurology, Spinal Cord, Jour. Cerebral Blood Flow & Metabolism. Recipient Howard Hughes Med. Inst. award for Clinician Scientist, 1999, Mentored Scientist award, NIH, 1999, Rsch. Develop. award, Muscular Dystrophy Assn., 1999—2001, Rsch. Grant, Parkinson's Disease Found., 1999—2000, Clinician Scientist award, John Hopkins Hosp., 1999, Agarni Found. award for best Scientific Talk, 2nd Internat. Congress in Neuroscience, Terni, Italy, 2000; named Hero for Hope for work on spinal cord regeneration, Keck Ctr. for Collaborative Neuroscience (The Spinal Cord Injury Project), 2004. Mem.: Transverse Myelitis Assn. (bd. dir.), Soc. for Neuroscience, Internat. Assn. for Neurovirology, Am. Soc. Microbiology, Am. Acad. Neurology, Alpha Omega Alpha. Office: Johns Hopkins Transverse Myelitis Ctr 600 N Wolfe St Baltimore MD 21287 Office Phone: 410-502-7099. Office Fax: 410-502-6736. E-mail: dker@jhml.edu.

KERR, JOHN FOXTON ROSS, pathologist, educator; b. Sydney, NSW, Australia, Jan. 24, 1934; s. John Ross and Mary Maud Kerr; m. Mary Margaret Field, Nov. 25, 1994. BS, U. Queensland, Brisbane, Australia, 1955, MB, BChir, 1957, DSc, 1998; PhD, U. London, 1964. Intern Royal Brisbane Hosp., 1958—59, pathology registrar, 1960—61; sr. lectr. pathology U. Queensland, Brisbane, 1965—72, reader in pathology, 1973—74, prof. pathology, 1974—95, prof. emeritus, 1996—. Adj. sr. prin. rsch. fellow Queensland Inst. Med. Rsch., Brisbane, 1988—95. Contbr. articles to profl. jours. Recipient Paul Ehrlich prize, Paul Ehrlich Found., Frankfurt am Main, Germany, 2000, Charles IV prize, Charles U., Prague, 2002; fellow, Australian Acad. Sci., 1998. Achievements include description of process of cell death by apoptosis and definition of its main biological and medical implications. Avocation: collecting and studying butterflies and moths. Home: 29 Hipwood Rd Hamilton Brisbane QLD 4007 Australia

KERR, KIM M., medical educator; b. Pa., Dec. 2, 1960; BS, U. Rochester, 1982; MD, Temple U., 1986. Clin. prof. medicine U. Calif. San Diego, 1995—. Office: 9300 Campus Point Dr M/C 7381 La Jolla CA 92037 Business E-Mail: kmkerr@ucsd.edu.

KERR, KIRKLYN M., academic administrator, veterinarian, pathologist; b. Green Bank, W.Va., May 1, 1936; married, 1957; 3 children. BS, U. W.Va., 1961, MS, 1966; DVM, Ohio State U., 1961; PhD in Vet. Pathology, Tex. A&M U., 1970. Diplomate Am. Coll. Vet. Pathology. Vet. practitioner North Side Vet. Clinic, Carlisle, Pa., 1961-62; rsch. assoc. vet. microbiology & pathology W.Va. U., Morgantown, 1962-65; form instr. to assoc. prof. vet. pathology Tex. A&M U. Coll. Vet. Medicine, 1965-72; assoc. prof. vet. pathobiology, dir. divsn. applied pathology Ohio State U. Coll. Vet. Medicine, 1972-78, dir. Ohio Agrl. Rsch. & Devel. Ctr., prof. poultry sci., 1987-91, prof. vet. preventive medicine, mem. faculty dept. preventive medicine, 1991-93; asst. dean rsch. and advanced studies, head vet. sci. La. State U. Sch. Vet. Medicine, La. State U. Agrl. Ctr., 1978-87; dean, dir. Coll. Agr. and Natural Resources U. Conn., Storrs

Mansfield, 1993—2008, prof. vet. pathology, 2008—. Mem. AVMA, Am. Assn. Avian Pathologists, Am. Coll. Vet. Pathologists, Farm Bur., Conn. Vet. Medicine Assn. Achievements include research in veterinary pathology, mycoplasmatacea, cancer research in animals. Office: Univ Conn Coll Agriculture & Natural Rsch 61 N Eagleville Rd Unit 3089 Storrs Mansfield CT 06269-4066 Office Phone: 860-486-2918. Business E-Mail: kirklyn.kerr@uconn.edu.

KERR, NANCY KAROLYN, pastor, mental health services professional; b. July 10, 1934; d. Owen W. and Iris Irene (Israel) K.; m. Richard Clayton Williams, June 28, 1953 (div.); children: Richard Charles, Donna Louise. Student, Boston U., 1953; AA, U. Bridgeport, 1966; BA, Hofstra U., 1967; postgrad. in clin. psychology, Adelphi U. Inst. Advanced Psychol. Studies, 1968-73; MDiv, Associated Mennonite Bibl. Sems., 1986. Ordained pastor Mennonite Ch., 1987; apptd. pastor Kamloops Presbyn. Ch., Can., 1992. Pastoral counselor Nat. Coun. Chs., Jackson, Miss., 1964; dir. teen program Waterbury (Conn.) YWCA, 1966-67; intern in psychology N.Y. Med. Coll., 1971-72, rsch. cons., 1972-73; coord. home svcs., psychologist City and County of Denver, 1972-75; cons. Mennonite Mental Health Svcs., Denver, 1975-78; asst. prof. psychology Messiah Coll., 1978-79; mental health cons., 1979-81; called to ministry Mennonite Ch., 1981; pastor Cin. Mennonite Fellowship, 1981-83, mem. Gen. Conf. Peace and Justice Reference Coun., 1983-85; instr. Associated Mennonite Bibl. Sems., 1985; tchg. elder Assembly Mennonite Ch., 1985-86; pastor Pulaski Mennonite Ch., 1986-89; exec. dir., pastoral counselor Bethesda Counseling Svcs., Prince George B.C., 1989-99; pvt. practice, 1999—. Spl. ch. curriculum Nat. Coun. Chs., 1981; mem. Cen. Dist. Conf. Peace and Justice Com., 1981-89; mem. exec. bd. People for Peace, 1981-83. Sec. Ft. George Housing Soc., 2002—09; clin. supr. St. Stevens. Sem., Edmonton, Canada; cons. Phoenix House, 2010—; active Prince George Ministerial Assn., chmn. edn. and airport chapel coms., 1990—92; elder St. Giles Presbyn. Ch., 1996—2000; mem. St. Andrews Worship Com.; bd. dirs. Tri-County Counselling Clinic, Memphis, Mo., 1980—81, Boulder ARC, 1977—78, PLURA, B.C. Synod, 1995—98, Prince George Neighbor Link, 1995—99, Davis County Mins. Assn., v.p., 1988—89; mem. Waterbury Planned Parenthood Bd., 1964—67, MW Children's Home Bd., 1974—75, Mennonite Disabilities Respite Care Bd., 1981—86, Prince George Children's Svcs. com., 1992—94; adv. com. Prince George Planning Coun., 1997—98; mem. housing Prince George adv. bd. Mennonite Cen. Com., 1998—99; mem. UCC Ministerial Com., 2007; with Phoenix House Counselor, 2010, Counsel Srs. Cons., 2010—; intern spr. Yorkville U., Fredericton, Canada; bd. mem. Crisis Ctr. PG, 2010—. Mem. APA (assoc.), Can. Psychol. Assn., Soc. Psychologists for Study of Social Issues, Christian Assn. Psychol. Studies, Soc. Bibl. Lit. & Exegesis (sec. Ft. Geol. bd., 2004-09). Office: Nancy Kerr Counselling Svc 302-2DW 1R7AI Prince George BC Canada V2L1G6

KERSCHNER, JOSEPH E., dean, educator, otolaryngologist; MD, Med. Coll. Wis. Cert. American Bd. Otolaryngology. Residency U. South Fla., Tampa, 1996; fellowship in pediat. otolaryngology Children's Hosp. Wis., Milw., 1996—98, physician; CEO Children's Specialty Group, Wis.; faculty mem. Med. Coll. Wis., 1998—, sr. assoc. dean clin. affairs - Children's Specialty Group, interim chmn., prof. dept. otolaryngology and comm. sciences, interim dean and exec. v.p., 2011—. Mem. sci. rev. panels NIH Nat. Inst. on Deafness and Other Communication Disorders. Named one of Best Doctors in America, 2004—. Fellow: American Acad. Otolaryngology; mem.: American Acad. Pediat., American Coll. Surgeons. Office: Med Coll Wisconsin Office of Dean 8701 Watertown Plank Rd Milwaukee WI 53226 *

KERSHAW, MAVIS MAISIE, psychologist; b. Doncaster, Yorkshire, Eng., June 24, 1944; d. Arthur and Ethel Annie White; m. Terence Kershaw, Sept. 7, 1963; children: Sean Terence, Simon, Julian Nathan. BA, Swinburne U., Melbourne, Australia, 1996; BA with honours, Deakin U., Melbourne, Australia, 1997, PhD, 2005. Contbr. articles to profl. jour. publs. Mem.: Psychologist Registration Bd. Victoria, Assn. Psychiatry, Psychology & Law (Australia & New Zealand), Australian Psychol. Soc. Achievements include research in financial competence assessment inventory. Office: Matek Pty Ltd 21 Carronvale Rd Mooroolbark Victoria 3138 Australia Office Phone: 03 9727 1521. Personal E-mail: maviskershaw@optusnet.com.au. Business E-Mail: matek1@optusnet.com.au.

KESER, IBRAHIM, geneticist, researcher; b. Malatya, Turkey, Nov. 1, 1964; s. Vahap and Zahre Keser; m. Ilkay Kayacan, Aug. 17, 2002. PhD, Akdeniz U., Antalya, Turkey, 1994, DSc, 2002. From rsch. asst. to asst. prof. Akdeniz U., 1988—2000, asst. prof., 2000—. Contbr. articles to profl. jours. (Poster Presentation award, 2001). With med. corp. Turkish Army, 1993. Fellow, TUBTAK, 1994—96. Mem.: European Cytogenetic Assn. (assoc.). Peace Party. Avocations: travel, running, swimming, climbing, driving. Home: 189SokNo 26 Kat 2/7 Antalya TR 07050 Turkey Office Fax: 00902422274482.

KESHAVJEE, SHAF, thoracic surgeon, educator; b. Feb. 22, 1961; MD, U. Toronto Med. Sch., Ontario, Can., 1985, MS, 1990. Intern, resident gen. surgery U. Toronto Hospitals, 1985—91, cardiothoracic residency, 1991—93; fellow thoracic surgery Toronto Gen. Hosp., 1991—93; asst. prof. surgery U. Toronto, 1994—99, assoc. prof. surgery, 1999—2002, prof. surgery, 2002—, prof., chair divsn. thoracic surgery, 2004—. Dir. thoracic surgery rsch. Toronto Hosp. Rsch. Inst., 1994—, dir. lung transplant program, 1997—. Contbr. articles to profl. jours. Fellow: ACS, Royal Coll. Surgery Can. Achievements include development of a technique whereby donor lung tissue is modified so that it is less susceptible to injury upon transplantation; a lung preservation solution to preserve donor lungs en route to transplant. Office: Toronto Gen Hosp 9th Fl Rm 9N946 200 Elizabeth St Toronto ON M5G 2C4 Canada Office Phone: 14163404010. Office Fax: 14163404556. E-mail: shaf.keshavjee@uhn.on.ca. *

KESKIN, SIDDIK, medical educator; b. Ardanuc, Jan. 19, 1973; MS, Ankara U., 1998, PhD, 2002. Faculty medicine Yuzuncu Yil U., Van, 2004, adj. prof., 2008. Office: Yuzuncu Yil University Faculty Medicine Van 65200 Turkey

KESLER, JAMES L., ophthalmologist; b. Vincennes, Ind., July 8, 1949; s. Richard Kesler and Bonnie L. (Perrott) Treece; m. Jana L. Blake, Aug. 29, 1970; children: Jason, Jessica. BS Biochemistry with distinction, U. Ill., 1971; MD, Washington U., 1975. Diplomate Am. Bd. Ophthalmology, Nat. Bd. Med. Examiners. Resident U. Va., Charlottesville, 1975-76, Barnes Hosp./Washington U., St. Louis, 1976-79; ophthalmologist Coastal Carolina Eye Clinic, Wilmington, N.C., 1979—. Cons. in ophthalmology Duke U., 1998—. James scholar U. Ill., 1967-71. Fellow ACS (bd. dirs. N.C. chpt. 1997-2002, alt.gov. 2004—2008, govs.2008-), Am. Acad. Ophthalmology (councillor 1996-2000); mem. AMA, N.C. Med. Soc. (cmty. com. 2005-, nominating com., 2005-07), N.C. Soc. Ophthalmology (pres. 1988), New Hanover-Pender County Med. Soc. (pres. 1991), Excellence in Primary Eye Care (founding mem.), Nat. Parliamentarian Soc., Cmty. Eyecare (bd. dirs. 1999-2003), Phi Beta Kappa, Alpha Omega Alpha, Bronze Tablet Avocations: biking, tennis, baseball, basketball, reading. Office: Coastal Carolina Eye Clinic 1120 Med Ctr Dr Wilmington NC 28401

KESSELRING, ULRICH KILIAN, plastic surgeon; b. Bern, Switzerland, June 13, 1940; s. Oscar Ulrich and Gertrud Kesselring; m. Felicitas Tschappeler-Kesselring, Sept. 29, 1969; children: Sandra, Francis. Med. diploma, U. Zurich, Switzerland, 1967; MD, Univ. Hosp. Zurich, 1967. Cert. bd. in gen. surgery Swiss Med. Assn., bd. in plastic surgery Swiss Med. Assn. Resident, chief resident dept. surgery Univ. Hosp. Basel, Switzerland, 1968—73; trainee Pvt. Plastic Surgery Unit, Lausanne, Switzerland, 1973—75; cofounder, sr. ptnr. Ctr. de Chirurgie Plastique, Lausanne, 1977—. Prof. postgrad. edn. in aesthetic plastic surgery Internat. Soc. Aesthetic Plastic Surgery, 1999—. Author or coauthor: handbooks and articles on plastic surgery. Achievements include originator of liposuction. Office: Ctr de Chirurgie Plastique 4 Av Marc-Dufour 1007 Lausanne Switzerland Home Phone: +41-21-695 2010; Office Phone: +41 21 3112376.

KESSINGER, MARGARET ANNE, medical educator; b. Beckley, W.Va., June 4, 1941; d. Clisby Theodore and Margaret Anne (Ellison) K.; m. Loyd Ernst Wegner, Nov. 27, 1971. MA, W.Va. U., 1963, MD, 1967. Diplomate Am. Bd. Internal Medicine and Med. Oncology. Internal medicine house officer U. Nebr. Med. Ctr., Omaha, 1967-70, fellow med. oncology, 1970-72, asst. prof. internal medicine, 1972-77, assoc. prof., 1977-90, prof., 1990—, assoc. chief oncology hematology sect., 1988-91, chief oncology hematology sect., 1991-99, assoc. dir. clin. rsch., Eppley Cancer Ctr., 1999—2008. Contbr. articles to profl. publs. Fellow ACP, Am. Assn. Cancer Edn.; mem. Am. Soc. Clin. Oncology, Am. Assn. Cancer Rsch., Internat. Soc. Exptl. Hematology, Am. Soc. Hematology, Sigma Xi, Alpha Omega Alpha. Republican. Methodist. Avocations: aviation, gardening, canning, skiing. Office: U Nebr Med Ctr 987680 Nebraska Med Ctr Omaha NE 68198-0001

KESSLER, DAVID AARON, medical educator, writer, former federal agency administrator; b. NYC, May 31, 1951; m. Paulette Kessler; children: Elise, Benjamin. BA, Amherst Coll., 1973; JD, U. Chgo., 1978; MD, Harvard U., 1979. Cert. Advanced Profl. Cert. NYU Grad. Sch. Bus. Adminstrn., 1986. Intern pediat. Johns Hopkins Hosp., Balt., 1979—80, resident pediat., 1980—82; spl. asst. to pres. Montefiore Med. Ctr., NYC, 1982—84; med. dir. Albert Einstein Coll. Medicine affiliate hosp., NYC, 1984—90; instr. food & drug law Columbia Law Sch., NYC, 1986—90; commr. of the FDA, US Dept. Health & Human Svcs., Rockville, Md., 1990—97; prof. pediat., internal medicine & pub. health, dean Yale U. Med. Sch., New Haven, 1997—2003; prof. pediat., dean, vice chancellor med. affairs U. Calif. San Francisco Sch. Medicine, 2003—07, prof. pediat., epidemiology & biostatistics, 2007—. Cons. US Senate Labor & Human Resources Com., 1981—84; bd. dirs. Doctors of the World, Columbia U. Nat. Ctr. Addiction& Substance Abuse; mem. White House Commn. Presdl. Scholars. Author: A Question of Intent: A Great American Battle with a Deadly Industry, 2001, The End of Overeating: Taking Control of the Insatiable American Appetite, 2009 (Books for a Better Life award, Nat. Multiple Sclerosis Soc., 2010); contbr. articles to profl. jours. Chmn. bd. dirs. Elizabeth Glaser Pediatric AIDS Found.; bd. dirs. Henry J. Kaiser Family Found. Recipient Medal of Honor, Am. Cancer Soc., 1996, Pub. Welfare Medal, NAS, 2001, Pub. Health Hero award, U. Calif. Berkeley Sch. Pub. Health, 2008, Nat. Pub. Affairs Spl. Recognition award, Am. Heart Assn., Sheldon W. Andelson Pub. Policy Achievement award, Am. Fedn. AIDS Rsch., Pub. Svc. award, Am. Acad. Pediat., Franklin Delano Roosevelt Leadership award, March of Dimes. Fellow: Am. Acad. Arts & Scis.; mem.: Inst. Medicine. Office: U Calif, San Francisco Med Sci 224 Box 0110 513 Parnassus Ave San Francisco CA 94143-0110 Office Phone: 415-476-2342. Office Fax: 415-476-0689. E-mail: kesslerd@medsch.ucsf.edu. *

KESSLER, IRVING ISAR, epidemiologist, consultant; AB in Math., NYU, 1952; MA in Endocrinology, Harvard U., 1955, PhD in Epidemiology, 1969; MD, Stanford U., 1960; MPH, Columbia U., 1962. Diplomate Nat. Bd. Med. Examiners, Am. Bd. Preventive Medicine; lic. physician Md. Prof. epidemiology Johns Hopkins U., 1972-84; chmn. dept. epidemiology and preventive medicine U. Md. Sch. Medicine, Balt., 1978-88; prof. oncology U. Md. Sch. Medicine Cancer Ctr., Balt., 1984—; prof. medicine U. Md. Sch. Medicine, Balt., 1985—, prof. dermatology, 1995—. Prof. dept. epidemiology & preventive medicine U. Md. Sch. Medicine, 1988-2001; emeritus, 2002-, exec. com. U. Md. Med. Sys., 1984-88; bd. dirs. Md. Med. Rsch. Inst.; v.p. for health scis., bd. dirs. ECRI, Plymouth Meeting, Pa., 1992-93; sci. adv. bd. Ctr. for Indoor Air Rsch., 1988-2001; mem. hazardous and toxic substances study commn., State of Md., 1983-84; cons. and lectr. in field. Bd. dirs. Israel Cancer Rsch. Found.; chmn. advisory panel on toxic shock syndrome AMA, 1984-85. Capt. USPHS res. Recipient Faculty Rsch. award Am. Cancer Soc. Fellow Am. Pub. Health Assn., Am. Coll. Preventive Medicine; mem. AAAS, Am. Epidemiol. Soc., Am. Assn. for Cancer Rsch., Am. Coll. Occupl. Medicine, N.Y. Acad. Sci., Md. Gerontological Assn. (founder, bd. dirs., chmn., program com., pres. 1984-85, Gerontology Recognition award 1989), D.A. Boyes Soc. Gynaecologic Oncology (hon.), Phi Beta Kappa, Soc. Sigma Xi. Office: University Md Med Sys Howard Hall 142 C 660 W Redwood St HH 142 C Baltimore MD 21201-1596 Office Phone: 410-706-7866. Business E-Mail: ikessler@epi.umaryland.edu.

KESSLER, WILLIAM EUGENE, retired healthcare executive; b. St. Louis, Dec. 15, 1944; s. Joseph John and Margaret Mary (Burns) K.; m. Patricia Christine Wilson, Nov. 9, 1968; children: Christina, William, John, Timothy, Jennifer, Catherine, Joseph, Daniel. BS in Commerce, St. Louis U., 1966, MHA, 1968; MTS, Quincy U., 2006. Various positions St. John's Hosp., St. Louis, 1963-67; adminstrv. resident St. Mary's Hosp., Grand Rapids, Mich., 1967-68; pres. St. Anthony's Health Ctr., Alton, Ill., 1971—2007. Chmn., prof. and tech. adv. com. Joint Commn. on Accreditation Healthcare Orgn., 1990-94; speaker profl. and community settings, 1972—; preceptor St. Louis U., 1980-2006, U. Mo., Columbia, 1991; bd. dir. Hosp. Assn. Met. St. Louis, 1975-85. Contbr. articles to profl. jour., 1972—. Admissions advisor US Mil. Acad., 1973-83; treas., bd. dir. Cath. Childrens' Home Alton, 1981-89; v.p. diocesan bd. edn. Diocese of Springfield, Ill., 1981-82, pres. 1982-84, mem. bd. edn. 1986-92; mem. diocesan fin. coun., 1987—; ordained permanent deacon Cath. Ch., 2007; Deacon, St. Ambrose Parish, 2008-; chmn. ARC, Alton, 1983-85; bd. dir. Am. Cancer Soc., Alton, 1984-90; pres. St. Louis Metropolitan Hosp. Coun., 1996. Served to capt. US Army, 1968-71. Decorated Army Commendation medal; recipient Alton Jaycees Disting. Svc. award, Alumni Merit award St. Louis U., 1994; named Knight of the Equestrian Order of the Holy Sepulchre, 1997; recipient Pro Ecclesia et Pontifice Cross Pope John Paul II, 2002, Mercy H.S., Alumni Merit award, 2002. Fellow: Am. Coll. Healthcare Execs. (regent's adv. coun. 1987—93, nominating com. 1991—94, regent 2002, chair ethics com., Regent's award, Sr. Healthcare Exec. of the Yr. award 1993); mem.: Diocese of Springfield, Order of Deacons, Coun. Regents, Southwestern Ill. Indsl. Assn. (exec. com. 1983—88, bd. dirs. 1989—, chmn. 1997), St. Louis U. Hosp. Administrn. Alumni Assn. (pres. 1978), Cath. Health Assn. U.S.A. (bd. dirs. 1987—, exec. com. 1989—92, chmn.-elect 1990—, chair 1991), Ill. Hosp. Assn. (exec. com. 1981—86, chmn. 1984—85), Am. Hosp. Assn. (Ho. of Dels. 1984—88), Stadium (St. Louis), Rotary (pres. Alton chpt. 1981-82, Paul Harris fellow 1985), Rotary (pres. Alton chpt. 1981—82, Paul Harris fellow 1979, 1985). Avocations: photography, sports. Office: Saint Ambrose Parish 820 W Homer Adams Parkway Godfrey IL 62035 Home: 401 Timber Ridge Dr Grafton IL 62037

KETCHERSID, WAYNE LESTER, JR., medical technologist; b. Seattle, Oct. 16, 1946; s. Wayne Lester and Hazel May (Greene) K.; m. Wilette LaVerne Mautz, Oct. 6, 1972; 1 son, William Les. BS in Biology, Pacific Luth. U., 1976, BS in Med. Tech., 1978; MS in Adminstrn., Ctrl. Mich. U., 1990; postgrad., Kennedy Western U., 1996—. Cert. med. technologist; cert. clin. lab. dir. Nat. Cert. Agy. for Med. Lab. Pers. Staff technologist Tacoma Gen. Hosp., 1978-79, chemistry supr., 1979-81, head chemistry, 1981-83, Multicare Med. Ctr., 1984-86, mgr., 1986-93, clin. lab. scientist, 1993—2011; ret. Contbr. articles to profl. jours. Mem. Nat. Rep. Com. With U.S. Army, 1966-68. William E. Slaughter Found. scholar, 1975-76. Mem. Am. Soc. Clin. Lab. Sci. (cert., chmn. region IX adminstrn. 1984-94, nat. del. 1984—, vice chmn. govt. affairs com. 1991-92, chmn. 1992-93, vice chair 1993-94, bd. trustees polit. action com. 1991-97, treas. 1994-97, nat. licensure coord. 1996—, sec./treas. bd. dirs. 1996-2001, jud. com. 2001-04, nominee Mem. of Yr. 1992, Bd. Dirs. award 1994, Mendelson award 1994, Pres. award 1996), Wash. State Soc. Clin. Lab. Sci. (chmn. biochemistry sect. 1983-86, dist. pres. 1986-99, co-chair ann. meeting 1996, cert. merit 1983, 84, 86, 88, pres. 1988-89, 89-90, mem. of yr. 1990, chmn. govt. affairs com. 1991-92, chmn. 1992—, Pres.'s award 1996, 97), Am. Soc. Clin. Pathologists (med. technologist), N.w. Med. Lab. Symposium (chmn. 1986-88, 90, 92), Alpha Mu Tau. Lutheran. Office: 2906 S 274th Pl Federal Way WA 98001-1803 Personal E-mail: wayketch@aol.com.

KETEFIAN, SHAKÉ, nursing educator; d. Krikor and Zaghganoush (Soghomonian) K. BSN, Am. U. Beirut, 1963; MEd, Columbia U., 1968, EdD, 1972. From asst. prof. nursing to prof. NYU Sch. Edn., Health, Nursing and Arts Professions, NYC, 1972-84; dir. continuing edn. in nursing NYU, NYC, with U. Mich., 1984—, prof., assoc. dean for grad. studies, dir. doctoral and postdoctoral studies U. Mich. Sch. Nursing, Ann Arbor, 1984—91, dir. internat. affairs, 1996—, acting dean, 1991-92. Contbr. articles to profl. jours. Fellow AAUW, Am. Acad. Nursing (governing coun.); mem. ANA, Midwest Nursing Rsch. Soc. (chair sci. integrity task force 1994-96, 2001-03), NC Nurses Assn., Internat. Network Doctoral Edn. in Nursing (founding pres.), Sigma Theta Tau Internat. Office: U Mich Sch Nursing 400 N Ingalls Ann Arbor MI 48109 Office Phone: 734-763-6669. Business E-Mail: ketefian@umich.edu.

KETHEESAN, NATKUNAM, biomedical researcher, educator; s. Rajaratnam and Anna Natkunam; m. Prasani Dilruksi Jayamaha, Nov. 11, 1989; children: Sarangan, Sanjeevan. MD, Vinnitsa State Med. U., Ukraine, 1987; MSc, U. Leeds, England, 1989, PhD, 1995. Resident Ministry Health, Colombo, 1989—91; grad. scholar U. Leeds, Leeds, 1991—94, rsch. fellow, 1994—95; rsch. officer U. Western Australia, Australia, 1995—97; rsch. fellow U. Queensland, Australia, 1997—2000; lectr. James Cook U., Townsville, Queensland, 2000—02, sr. lectr., 2003—05, prof., 2006—. Rsch. leader Australian Inst. Tropical Medicine, James Cook U., Townsville, 2004—; sr. rsch. fellow Townsville Hosp., 2000. Contbr. articles to profl. jours. Fellow, Australasian Coll. Tropical Medicine, 1999; Postgraduate scholar, U. Leeds, 1991, Postdoctoral fellow, U. Queensland, 1997. Mem.: Australian Soc. Med. Rsch., Australasian Soc. Immunology, Brit. Soc. Immunology. Achievements include research in involvement of lymphocytes in the development of immunity to tropical infections. Office: James Cook U University Dr 4811 Townsville QLD Australia Office Fax: 61 7 4779 1528. Business E-Mail: n.ketheesan@jcu.edu.au.

KETTE, FULVIO, emergency physician; 2 children. MD, U. Trieste, 1981, splty. degree in anesthesia and intensive care therapy, 1984; splty. degree in hygiene and preventive medicine, U. Udine, 2002. Physician dept. anesthesia and ICU U. Trieste, 1981—82, asst. physician, 1982—91, attending physician, 1991—97; rsch. fellow dept. medicine U. Health Scis., North Chicago, Ill., 1988—90; attending physician dept. anesthesia and ICU U. Udine, 1997—99; attending physician emergency dept. Udine Hosp., 2000—01; head emergency dept. San Vito al Tagliamento (Italy) Hosp., 2001—. Mem. exec. com. European Resuscitation Coun., Antwerp, Belgium, 1994—98; founding mem. Italian Resuscitation Coun., Milan, 1994, mem. exec. com., Bologna, 1997—99, head ALS subcom., 2000—01; instr. more than 60 courses on trauma and cardiac emergency procedures. Contbr. articles to profl. jours. Office: Emergency Dept Via Savorgnano 2 33078 San Vito al Tagliamento Italy Office Fax: 0434-841606. E-mail: fulvio.kette@ass6.sanita.fvg.it.

KETTELKAMP, DONALD BENJAMIN, retired orthopedist; b. Anamosa, Iowa, Jan. 21, 1930; s. Enoch George and Elsie (Norden) K.; m. Alice June Mencke, Dec. 30, 1954; children: Karen June, Lisa Marie, Suzanne D., Jonathan B.; m. Clemencia Oliveros Brandon, Apr. 28, 1989. BA, Cornell U., Mt. Vernon, Iowa, 1952; MD, U. Iowa, 1955, MS, 1960. Diplomate Am. Bd. Orthop. Surgery. Intern Thomas D. Dee Meml. Hosp., Ogden, Utah, 1955—56; resident orthopedic surgery U. Iowa, Iowa City, 1958—61; practice medicine specializing in orthopaedic surgery Anchorage, 1961—64; asst. prof. Albany (N.Y.) Med. Coll., 1964—66, assoc. prof., 1966—68, U. Iowa, Iowa City, 1968—71, prof., 1971; prof., chmn. dept. orthopaedic surgery U. Ark., Little Rock, 1971—74, Ind. U., Indpls., 1974—84; assoc. dean Tex. Tech. U., El Paso, 1984—87; exec. dir. Am. Bd. Orthop. Surgery, Chgo., 1986—94. Trustee: Jour. Bone and Joint Surgery, 1991—96. With USPHS, 1956—58. Mem.: ACS, Knee Soc., Assn. Orthopaedic Chairmen (pres. 1981), Am. Orthopaedic Assn. (pres. 1989—90), Am. Soc. Surgery of Hand, Am. Acad. Orthopaedic Surgeons.

KETTLES, ALYSON MCGREGOR, mental health nurse, educator; b. Perth, Perthshire, Scotland, June 1, 1956; d. Kettles Alan and Margaret Anderson McGregor; m. Clinton Mark Williams, Aug. 20, 1999; 1 child, Mhairi McGregor Williams. BSc in Nursing, Abertay U., Dundee, 1984; MSc in Health Psychology, City U., London, 1992; PhD in Nursing, U. Aberdeen, 2005; diploma in Criminology, 2008. Registered mental nurse, Nursing and Midwifery Coun., 1984, Gen nurse, Nursing & Midwifery Coun., 1984, nurse teacher, NMCU. Surrey, 1989, cert. tchr. & asst.clin. practice, English Nat. Bd., 1987. Staff nurse Brookwood Hosp., Woking, Surrey, England, 1984—85, sister, charge nurse, 1985—86; cmty. psychiat. nurse West Surrey NE Hampshire Health Authority, Farnboroug, Surrey, 1986—88; nurse tchr. South West Surrey Health Authority, Guildford, Surrey, 1988—89; lectr. dept. mental health nursing & psychology Frances Harrison Coll. Nursing U. Surrey, Guildford, 1989—94; chair Forensic Nurses R & D Group, London, 2005—; asst. prof. Coll. Nursing, Jesenice, Slovenia; r & d officer NHS Campaign, 1994—2011; devel. officer NHS Campion, 2011; vis. scholar & sr. lectr. U. Alexander, 2000—11. Mem., rcn mental health field practice adv. panel Royal Coll. Nursing, London, 2000—04; mem., nat. bd. r & d com. Nat. Bd. Nursing, Midwifery & Health Vis., Edinburgh, 1997—2005. Contbr. scientific papers. Contbr. Scottish Soc., Scotland, 1974—2009. Fellow Fellowship, Royal Soc. of Medicine, 2007 onwards, The Higher Edn. Acad., 2007 onwards. Fellow: Royal Soc. Medicine; mem.: register experts NHS Edn., Networ Psychiat. Nursing Rsch. (life; regional rep. 1996—2009), Scottish Mental Health Nursing Forum. Office: CSHAD West Gask University Aberdeen Longharen Peterhead Aberdeenshire Cornhill Hosp Cornhill Rd Aberdeen Aberdeenshire AB25 9ZH Scotland Office Phone: 0 1224 557677. Office Fax: 0 1224 557855. Business E-mail: alyson.kettles@nhs.net, a.kettles@abdn.ac.uk.

KETTLING, VIRGINIA, retired health facility administrator; b. Toldeo, Aug. 9, 1932; d. Charles Albert and Elizabeth (Knapp) Reuthe; m. George Kettling, June 16, 1962; children: Elys, Kandys, Gynevra, Geoff. BSN, Capital U., 1955; MA, Ohio State U., 1962. Cert. nursing admin. advanced. Asst. dir. nursing Christ Hosp., Cin., 1962—65; asst. prof., dir. baccalaureate program U. Cin., 1965-71; asst. v.p., nursing dir. Bethesda Hosp. Sch. Nursing, Cin., 1971-77; clin. asst. prof. U. Wis., Milw., 1981-88; chief nurse exec. Mt. Sinai Med. Ctr., Milw., 1977-88; v.p. patient care United Samaritans Med. Ctr., Danville, Ill., 1988-97; cert. parish nurse Bethel Luth. Ch., Danville, 1997—2002; parish nurse Christ the King Luth. Ch., 2003—, Advent Luth. Ch. and St. John Luth. Ch., 2004—09. Cons. assoc. degree program D.A.C.C., 1998—; interim .pres. Lakeview Coll. Nursing, Danville, 1999—2000, planning devel. fiscal officer, 2000. Named nominee, Wisc. Nurse Exec. Yr. Mem.: Midwest Alliance Nursing, Am. Coll. Healthcare Execs., Am. Hosp. Pub. (reviewer books), Ill. Orgn. Nurse Execs., Am. Orgn. Nurse Execs., Exec. Club Danville. Home: 333 W Walters St Apt 3J Port Washington WI 53074-1456 Personal E-mail: vkettling@att.net.

KETTUNEN, JUKKA SAKARI, orthopedist, surgeon, researcher; b. Säyneinen, Finland, Feb. 16, 1961; s. Lauri Sakari and Kaisa Lyydia Kettunen; m. Sanna Elina Rautiainen, Oct. 10, 1988; children: Henna, Emmi. Degree in Medicine, Kuopio U., Finland, 1987, MD, 1999. Orthop. surgeon Kuopio U. Hosp., 1996—2001, asst. chief surgery, 2001—; asst. surgeon Mikkeli Ctrl. Hosp., 1988—92; fellow surgery Kuopio U. Hosp., 1992—94, fellow orthop., 1994—96. Mem.: Finnish Orthop. Assn., Dirty Dozen Golfers. Avocations: golf, hunting, cross country skiing, reading. Office: Kuopio Univ Hosp 70211 Kuopio Finland

KEUCHEL, MARTIN, gastroenterologist, nephrologist; b. Frankfurt/Main, Germany, Apr. 25, 1958; m. Karin Schmöcker; children: Lena, Ellen. MD, Philipps U., Marburg/Lahn, Germany, 1987. Lic. Hessen County Exam. Office Health Care Profls., cert. in internal medicine Hamburg Physicians Chamber, in nephrology Hamburg Physicians Chamber, in gastroenterology Hamburg Physicians Chamber. Intern Fulda Mcpl. Hosp., Germany, 1985—86; resident Univ. Hosp., Marburg/Lahn, 1985—86; asst. physician dept. nephrology and Transplant Ctr. Philipps U., Marburg/Lahn, 1986—90; asst. physician dept. clin. Bernhard-Nocht Inst. Tropical Medicine, Hamburg, Germany, 1990—93; cons. dept. gastroenterology Asklepios Klinik Altona, Hamburg, 1993—2010; asst. physician Clinic Nephrology, Hamburg, 1995—97; head dept. internal medicine Bethesda Krankenhans Bergedorf, Hamburg, 2010—. Co-editor: Atlas of Video Capsule Endoscopy, 2006. Mem.: German Soc. Endoscopy and Imaging Techniques, Am. Soc. for Gastrointestinal Endoscopy, Hamburg Med. Assn., German Soc. Infectiology, German Soc. Nephrology, German Soc. Digestive and Metabolic Diseases. Office: Glindersweg 80 Hamburg 21029 Germany

KEUM, DONGYOON, thoracic surgeon; b. Daegu, Republic of Korea, June 1, 1963; s. Hansoon Kwon; m. Hyekyeong Chung, Jan. 22, 1989; children: Kayeon, Inkook. PhD, Keimyung U., Daegu, 2002. Diplomate Korean Soc. Thoracic and Cardiovasc. Surgery Bd., 1996. Asst. prof. Eulji Hosp., Daejun, Republic of Korea, 1997—2002; assoc. prof. Dongsan Med. Ctr., Keimyung U., Daegu, 2003—. Rsch. fellow Mass. Gen. Hosp., Boston, 2006—07. Author: (book) General Surgery: Principles and International Practice, 2nd edit.; contbr. articles to profl. jours. Asst. Gyungsan Vol. Ctr., 2008. Recipient award, Min. Health and Welfare, 1990. Mem.: Korean Soc. Thoracic and Cardiovasc. Surgery. Achievements include research in lung transplantation in animal lab. Home: 201-206 Garden-Heights Apt HwangKum-Don Daegu 706-794 Republic of Korea Office: Dongsan Med Ctr Dongsan-Dong Jung-Gu 194 700-712 Daegu Daegu Republic of Korea Office Fax: 82-53-250-7307. Business E-Mail: kdy@dsmc.or.kr.

KEUM-IL, JANG, science educator; b. Seoul, Republic of Korea, Sept. 21, 1971; PhD, Chungbuk Nat. U., 2002. Assoc. prof. Chungbuk Nat. U., 2009—. Office: 52 Naesudong-ro Heungdeok-gu Cheongju Chungbuk 361-763 Republic of Korea Office Fax: 82-43-271-4412. Personal E-mail: jangki@hanmail.net.

KEVELIGHAN, EUAN, obstetrician, gynecologist; b. Dublin, Jan. 30, 1963; s. Herbert Kevelighan and Elizabeth Corbett Mcpheator. MB ChB BAO, U. Coll. Dublin, 1981—87; diploma in Med. Edn., Dundee U., 2007. Cons. in obgyn Swansea NHS Trust, Singleton Hosp., Swansea, Wales, 2000—; sr. clin. tutor Med. Sch. Swansea, Swansea, Wales, 2001—; dir. All Wales OB-GYN Tng. Programme, 2006—, Royal Coll. Regional Advisors South Wales, 2011—. Recipient scholarships for med. edn., RCOG, London, 1998—99. Fellow: Royal Coll. Obstetricians and Gynaecologists. Avocations: travel, lecturing. Office: Consultant O&G Singleton Hospital Sketty Lane Swansea SA2 8QA Wales Fax: 01792-285060. Personal E-mail: euankevelighan@hotmail.com.

KEY, JAMES EVERETT, ophthalmologist; b. Freeport, Tex., July 19, 1944; s. James Everett and Margaret Ann (Parker) K.; m. Betty Wilson, Dec. 22, 1967; children: Peter Wilson and Courtney Brooke (twins). BA, U. Tex., 1966; MD, Baylor U., 1970. Diplomate Am. Bd. Ophthalmology. Mem. staff Coll. Medicine Baylor U., Houston, 1976-89, clin. assoc. prof. ophthalmology, 1989-93, clin. prof. ophthalmology, 1994—. Chief ophthalmology St. Luke's Episcopal Hosp., Houston, 1987—. Contbr. articles to jours., chpts. to books, editor medical textbooks. Trustee U. of South, Shawnee, Tenn., 1991—96, 1998—2000; mem. exec. bd. Episc. Diocese Tex.; bd. mem. Tex. Map Soc. Lt. med. officer USN, 1971—73. Recipient Honor award Am. Acad. of Ophthalmology, 1990; named Outstanding Alumnus, Baylor Coll. Medicine, 2006. Fellow Am. Acad. Ophthalmology (Hon. award); mem. AMA, Contact Lens Assn. Ophthalmologists (past pres.), Harris County Med. Assn., Tex. Ophthal. Assn. (past bd. dirs.), Houston Ophthal. Soc. (past pres.), Phi Beta Kappa. Episcopalian. Avocation: map collecting. Office: Methodist Eye Assoc 6560 Fannin 450 Houston TX 77030 Home Phone: 713-529-9025; Office Phone: 713-441-8843. Office Fax: 713-793-1636.

KEY, RICHARD DUANE, pathologist; b. Jacksonville, Fla., Sept. 1956; s. Herbert Calvin and Mary Elaine Key; m. Laurie Beth Gribas, Oct. 3, 1981; children: Trevor Scott, Amelia Catherine. AA, Northeast Miss. Jr. Coll., 1976; BA, Miss. Coll., 1978; MD, U. Miss., 1982. Diplomate Am. Bd. of Pathology. Intern Eugene Talmadge Meml. Hosp., Augusta, Ga., 1982—83; resident in pathology Med. Coll. Ga., Augusta, 1983—86; med. dir. lab. Flowers Hosp., Dothan, Ala., 2002—. Mem.: AMA, CAP, Ala. Assn. Pathologists, Am. Soc. Clin. Pathology. Home: 102 Fair Oak Dr Dothan AL 36303 Office: Flowers Hosp 4370 W Main St Dothan AL 36305 Business E-Mail: rkey@flowershospital.com. E-mail: ratl_key@juno.com.

KEYDAR, IAFA, virology educator; b. Yassy, Romania, July 6, 1923; arrived in Israel, 1941; d. Zeev and Sara (Rosenzweig) Pomerliano; m. Abraham Tiberius Keydar Klein, July 9, 1942 (dec. 1982); 1 child, Yael. Degree in nursing, Nurses Tng. Coll., Tel Aviv, 1950; BSc in Zoology, Tel Aviv U., 1956, MSc in Microbiology, 1958; PhD, Hebrew U., 1967. Nurse Kibbutz Maagan, Israel, 1950-53; rsch. assoc. Inst. for Cancer Rsch., Columbia U., NYC, 1969-71; sr. lectr. microbiology Tel Aviv U., 1971-74, assoc. prof., 1974-82, prof., 1982—, prof. emeritus, 1993—. Chair dept. microbiology, Tel Aviv U., 1974-76, dean faculty of life scis., 1984-89; dir. Moise and Frida Eskenasy Inst. for Cancer Rsch., 1990-92; vis. prof. Inst. for Cancer Rsch., Columbia U., N.Y.C., 1976-78. Mem. editl. bd. Jour. of Women's Cancer, 2000. Mem. N.Y. Acad. Sci, Internat. Assn. Breast Cancer Rsch. (pres. 1989), Israel Cell Biology Assn., Israel Microbiology Assn. Office: Tel Aviv U Dept Cell Rsch and Immunology 69978 Tel Aviv Israel

KEYMLING, MICHAEL, gastroenterologist, researcher; married. Privatdozent Dr. Med. Habil, Justus Liebig Universität, Giessen, Germany. Head dept. gastroenterology Klinikum Meiningen GmbH, Meiningen, Germany, 1995—. Contbr. articles to profl. jours. Achievements include development of the percutaneous gastrostomy tube; research in quality control in gastrointestinal endoscopy, malnutrition, jejunal tub feeding, and intestinal stenting. Home: Ueberm Dorf 4 Bad Hersfeld 36251 Germany Office: Medizinische Klinik Klinikum Meiningen Bergstrasse 3 Meiningen 98617 Germany Office Fax: +40369390181028. E-mail: med2.keymling@klinikum-meiningen.de.

KHABBAZ, RIMA, public health service officer; BS, Am. U. Beirut, 1975, MD, 1979. Cert. in internal medicine. Internal medicine tng. Am. U. Beirut Med. Ctr., Lebanon, 1978—80; fellowship in infectious diseases U. Md.; resident internal medicine Union Meml. Hosp., Balt.; epidemic intelligence officer Centers for Disease Control, 1980; dep. dir. Divsn. Viral and Rickettsial Diseases Nat. Ctr. Infectious Diseases, Centers for Disease Control, assoc. dir. epidemiologic sci., acting dep. dir., dir., 2005—08; dir., Nat. Ctr. Preparedness, Detection and Control Infectious Diseases Centers for Disease Control and Prevention, dep. dir., dir. Office Infectious Diseases. Blood product adv. com. US Food & Drug Adminstrn., 1995—99. Contbr. chapters to books, articles to profl jours. Fellow: Infectious Disease Soc. Am. (scientific program com. 1999—2002); mem.: Am. Soc. of Tropical Medicine and Hygiene, Am. Bd. for Microbiology, Am. Epidemiologic Soc. Office: Nat Ctr Infectious Diseases CDC Bldg 1 Rm 6013 1600 Clifton Rd NE Atlanta GA 30333 Business E-Mail: rima.khabbaz@cdc.hhs.gov. *

KHADJOOI, KAYVAN, physician, university lecturer; b. Tehran, Iran, 1971; s. Ali and Afsar Khadjooi. MD with honors, Tehran Azad U. Sch. Medicine, Iran, 1998. Cert. in med. edn. U. Dundee, 2009. Sr. house officer, dept. medicine Modarres Gen. Hosp., Saveh, Iran, 2000—02, Conquest Hosp., St. Leonards, East Sussex, England, 2002—03, Good Hope Hosp., Birmingham, West Midlands, England, 2003—06, rsch. fellow, dept. cardiology, 2006—07; hon. lectr. U. Birmingham, Divsn. Med. Scis., 2006—07; specialist registrar, acute medicine East Yorkshire Hosps. NHS Trust, England, 2007—; hon. lectr. Hull York Med. Sch., Yorkshire, 2007—. Head, Med. Students Assn. Tehran Azad U. Sch. Medicine, 1994—98; coord. investigator inter-heart study U. Tehran, Sch. Medicine, 2000—02; trainee drs., rep. Brit. Med. Assoc., 2007—. Contbr. articles to profl. jours. Mem. Soc. Support Children Suffering from Cancer, Tehran, 1992—2002.

Mem.: RCP (London), Am. Heart Assn., Brit. Med. Assn., Soc. Acute Medicine. Achievements include research in cardiac resynchronization therapy; dyssynchrony in heart failure. Business E-mail: kayvan@nhs.net.

KHAIRY, GAMAL AHMED, surgeon, educator; b. Dongula, Sudan, July 15, 1956; s. Ahmed Khairy and Zubaida Ali Edrees; m. Salwa Araheem, Sept. 15, 1992; children: Abdulrahman, Amro, Abeer. MS, Khartoum U., 1990. Sr. registrar Dept. Surgery Kkuh, Riyadh, Saudi Arabia, 1990—2000; spl. registrar The Royal Liverpool (Eng.) U. Hosp., 2000, fellow in breast surgery, 2001; head Dept. Surgery King Fahad Hosp., Albaha, Saudi Arabia, 2001—02; asst. prof. dept. surgery King Saud U. Coll. Medicine and King Khalid U. Hosp., Riyadh, 2002—, cons. gen. surgeon dept. surgery, 2002—. Contbr. articles to profl. jours. Fellow: Royal Coll. Surgeons Edinburgh; mem.: Endoscopic and Laparaoscopic Surgeons Asia, Soc. Saudi Gastroenterology Assn. Avocations: swimming, volleyball.

KHALED, SHERIF AHMED, orthopedist; b. Giza, Egypt, June 16, 1973; s. Ahmed Radwan Khaled and Mahassen Aly Hassan; m. Yasmin Rady Saad; children: Yehia Sherif, Youssef Sherif, Ahmed Sherif. MBBCh in Medicine, Cairo U. Sch. Medicine, 1995; MSc in Orthop., Cairo U., 1999, PhD in Orthop., 2003. Asst. lectr. orthop. Cairo U. Dept Orthop., 2000—04, lectr. orthop., 2004—09, asst. prof. orthop., 2009—. Mem. Egyptian Orthop. Assn., Cairo, 1999—; alumni mem. AO Assn., Switzerland, 2003—, internat. mid. east faculty, 2009—; nat. faculty, instr. advanced AO Assn. Egyptian Chpt., Cairo, 2004—; internat. affiliate mem. SICOT Assn., Canada, 2010—. Contbr. to profl. publs. (Internat. Publ. award, 2009). Shoulder Resident Inst. De La Main Paris fellow, Ministry External Affairs France, 2004—05. Office: 32 Falaky street-Awkaf Building Cairo 11211 Egypt Office Fax: 202-27956339; Home Fax: 202-27956339. Personal E-mail: sherifakhaled@yahoo.com.

KHALIFA, MAHA, pharmacist, educator; b. Cairo, Oct. 14, 1970; PhD in Pharmacy, 1992. Assoc. prof., pharm. chemistry Al-Azhar U., 1994—; asst. prof., pharmacy, 2003. Reviewers Letters Drug Discovery and Design, 2008. Mem.: Syn. Pharmacy. Home: Sheraton El Matar Misr el Taemer 5th Cairo Misr el-Gedida 11754 Egypt Personal E-mail: maha_khalifa@hotmail.com.

KHALIL, ABDALLA SALEM, oncologist; b. Nazareth, Aug. 6, 1962; D, Timishoara U., 1989; degree, Haifa U., 2003. Pediatric hemato-oncologist Meyer-Children's Hosp. Haifa, 2000—, sr. pediatric hemato-oncologist, 2000. Sr. pediatric physician Ziev Hosp. Zefat, 1995—2000. Office: Turan 199 Nazareth 16950 Israel Office Fax: 972-4-854-2007. Business E-Mail: k_abdalla@ambam.health.gov.il.

KHALIL, MOHAMMED WESAM ABDELRAHMAN, thoracic surgeon; b. Cairo, June 8, 1969; s. Abdelrahman Amin Khalil and Nadia Abbas Morsi; m. Marwa Kamel Hussein, July 19, 2002; children: Malak, Yusuf, Mariam. MBBS, U. Nigeria, Enugu, 1992. Registrar U. Nigeria Tchg. Hosp., 1995—2001; cons. surgeon, gen., thoracic Aminu Kano Tchg. Hosp., Kano, Nigeria, 2002—03; specialist registrar thoracic surgery Trent Deanery Hosps., Glenfield, England, Nottingham, England, Sheffield, England, 2006—08; trust grade surgeon Castle Hill Hosp., Cottingham, England, 2008—. Fellow: RCS (Ireland), RCS (Edinburgh), RCS (Glasgow), West African Coll. Surgeons. Muslim. Avocations: history, archaeology. Office: Castle Hill Hosp Castle Road HU16 5JQ Cottingham England Personal E-mail: wesam@doctor.com.

KHALKHALI, IRAJ, radiologist, educator; b. Tehran, Iran, Apr. 4, 1948; MD, Tehran Faculty Med., 1973. Prof. radiol. scis. David Geffen Sch. Medicine -UCLA, 1989—. Dir., breast diagnostic Ctr. Harbor-UCLA Med. Ctr., 1989. Recipient Excellence award, Du Pont Pharmaceuticals; numerous grants, NCI. Fellow: Am. Coll. Nuc. Physicians, Am. Coll. Radiology. Avocations: swimming, hiking, reading. Office: 21840 S Normandie Ste # 506 Torrance CA 90502 Office Fax: 310-222-5173. Business E-Mail: nephrad@aol.com.

KHAMANARONG, KIMAPORN, anatomist, educator; b. Udorn Thanee, Thailand, Apr. 12, 1954; MD in Anatomy, Khon Kaen U., Thailand; MS in Anatomy, Mahidol U., 1996; degree in Family Medicine, Med. Coun. Thailand, 2002. Assoc. prof. Khon Kaen U., 1999—. Office: Khon Kaen University Mitraparp Rd Khon Kaen 40002 Thailand E-mail: kimapor@yahoo.com.

KHAN, ABDUL JAMIL, surgeon, dean, dentist; Founding prin. Frontier Med. Coll.; former prin., head of medicine dept., bd. dirs. Bolan Coll., Quetta, Pakistan; founding prin., head of medicine dept., bd. dirs. Ayub Med. Coll., Abbottabad, Pakistan; v.p. EMRO (Eastern Mediellerranean, Region) Regional Com.; bd. dirs. Sheikh Zayed Hosp., Jinnah Postgrad. Med. Centre, Karachi, Pakistan; dir. gen. of health Govt. of Pakistan, fed. min., adv. com. of health, mem. and health system monitoring com.; dean faculty of health sciences Bahria Univ, Islamabad, Pakistan. Leader Pakistan delegation World Health Assembly of UN. Recipient SITARA-E-IMTIAZ. Mem.: Pakistan Red Crescent Soc. (bd. dirs.), Nat. Inst. of Cardiovascular Diseases (bd. dirs.), Nat. Inst. of Health (bd. dirs.), Pakistan Med. & Dental Coun. (pres.). Office: Frontier Medical College Mansehra Rd Abbottabad Pakistan Office Phone: 920992383568/380190. Office Fax: 0992381028. *

KHAN, AHSAN YAQOOB, psychiatrist, educator; b. Karachi, Sindh, Pakistan, Feb. 3, 1963; s. Mohammed Yaqoob Khan and Raisa Begum; m. Naila Aziz, Aug. 4, 1996; children: Maaz Ahsan, Faraz Ahsan. MD, U. Kans. Sch. Medicine, Wichita, 2000. Diplomate in psychiatry Am. Bd. Psychiatry and Neurology, 2002. Resident psychiatrist U. Kans. Sch. Medicine, 1996—2000, assoc. prof., 2000—. Med. dir. Via Christi Psychiat. Clinic, Wichita, 2000—. Contbr. scientific papers presentation to conf. (George Winokar Rsch. award, 2006, 1st Pl., 2000), chapters to books, articles to profl. jours. Cons. psychiatrist Nat. Alliance Mental Illness, Wichita, 2000—08. Recipient Excellence Psychopharmacology Rsch. award, Psychiat. Rsch. Inst., 2000, Cmty. Svc. Recognition award, Nat. Alliance Mental Illness, 2001, 2004, Irma Bland Excellence Tchg. award, Am. Psychiat. Assn., 2005; named Tchr. of Yr., U. Kans. Sch. Medicine, Dept. Psychiatry, 2004, 2007. Fellow: Am. Psychiat. Assn.; mem.: AMA, Assn. Physicians Pakistani Descent N.Am., Kans. Psychiat. Soc. Office Phone: 316-858-0050. Business E-Mail: akhan@kumc.edu. E-mail: ayk63@hotmail.com.

KHAN, ALI S., federal agency administrator; b. Bklyn., June 14, 1963; MD, Downstate Med. Ctr., NY, 1987; MPH, Emory U., Ga., 2000. Diplomate Nat. Bd. Med. Examiners. Joint residency in internal medicine and pediatrics U. Mich., Ann Arbor; joined as an epidemic intelligence svc. officer Ctrs. Disease Control and Prevention and the US Health Svc. Commd. Corps, 1991; dep. dir. nat. ctr. emerging zoonotic infectious diseases Ctrs. Disease Control and Prevention, 2006—10, asst. surgeon gen., dir. office pub. health preparedness and response, 2010—. Cons. NASA, Ministries of Health, WHO; adj. prof. Emory U., 2005—11. Decorated Meritorious Svc. medal US Pub. Health Svc., Commendation medal, Outstanding Svc. medal; recipient Outstanding Unit Citation award, Sec.'s award. Fellow: ACS, Am. Acad. Physicians; mem.: Delta Omega, Alpha Omega Alpha. Office: 1600 Clifton Rd MS D44 Atlanta GA 30329 Business E-Mail: ask0@cdc.gov. *

KHAN, GULFARAZ, pathologist, educator; b. Kashmir, Pakistan, Feb. 7, 1965; BSc, U. London, 1988, PhD, 1993; MS, London Sch. Hygiene and Tropical Medicine, 1989. Sr. scientist St. Bartholomew's Hosp. Med. Coll., London, Glasgow U. Med. Sch.; lectr. pathology Anglia Ruskin U., Cambridge, England, 2002—04; sr. lectr. cellular pathology Kingston U., Kingston upon Thames, Surrey, England, 2004—08; assoc. prof., viral pathology United Arab Emirates U., 2008—. Author: Du'a: The Essence of Worship; mem. editl. bd.: Pakistan Jour. Pathology, 2005—, Pakistan Jour. Med. Scis.; contbr. articles to profl. jours. Rsch. Fellow, Tufts U., Sch. Medicine, Boston. Fellow: Royal Inst. Pub. Health, Royal Soc. Medicine; mem.: Internat. Soc. Infectious Diseases, Asian Pacific Orgn. Cancer Prevention & Control, Path. Soc. Gt. Brit. and Ireland. Office: Dept Microbiology and Immunology United Arab Emirates University Al Ain Abu Dhabi 17666 United Arab Emirates

KHAN, INAYAT, pharmacologist; b. Peshawar, Pakistan, Mar. 2, 1929; arrived in Switzerland, 1970; s. Shahzad K.; m. Shamim, Mar. 2, 1960; children: Haleem, Ayub, Afshan, Seema. MB, BS, King Edward Med. Coll., Lahore, Pakistan, 1952; PhD, Edinburgh U., Scotland, UK, 1959. Tchr. in pharmacology, Pakistan, 1959-69; dir. NIH, Islamabad, 1969-70; sr. med. officer WHO, 1970-90; cons. in field, 1990—. Chief med. officer psychoactive drugs WHO, Geneva, 1976-90; hon. prof. Ayub Med. Coll., Abbottabad, Pakistan; Beijing Med. U. China, U. Buenos Aires, Argentina. Author: (book) Guidelines for the Control of Narcotic & Psychotropic Substances, 1984, Rational Use of Psychoactive Drugs in Pakistan, 1990, Use and Misuse of Psychoactive Drugs Who Report of a seminar in Beijing, 1983, The Use of the Psychoactive Drugs, 1981, Clandestinely Produced Analogues & Precursors, 1987, Les Medicaments Psychoactifs Pour Une Meilleure Prescription and numerous others, 1990. Fellow Royal Coll. Psychiatrists London. Achievements include research in drug abuse control in WHO. Home and Office: Meyrin 1217 0 Geneva Switzerland E-mail: ina@optimasa.com.

KHAN, JAFFER, surgeon; MB, BS. Initial plastic surg. tng. Cork Univ. Hosp., St. Bartholomew's, Royal London Hosps.; fellow in cosmetic surgery leading Harley st. practice London; former cons. plastic surgeon England; dir. and head cons. Aesthetics Internat.; cons. plastic and reconstructive surgeon Med. Internat. Specialist Centre, United Arab Emirates. Contbr. various sci. publs. and several internat. presentations. Achievements include as the 1st Surgeon in the Region to pass the Specialty Fellowship examination of the Joint Royal Colleges in Plastic Surgery; pioneer of Facial Resurfacing, having introduced the first Erbium YAG laser to Riyadh, Saudi Arabia in 1997 and to Dubai in 1998. Office: Medical International Specialist Centre Al Wasl Rd Jumeirah PO Box 71753 Dubai United Arab Emirates Office Phone: 97143499100. Office Fax: 97143443577. *

KHAN, KHALEQUE NEWAZ, physician; b. Dhaka, Bangladesh, Dec. 25, 1958; s. Ali Newaz and Anwara (Begum) K.; m. Motoko Miyamoto, Nov. 17, 1996. MD, Dhaka U. Med. Sch., Mymensingh, Bangladesh, 1982; PhD, Nagasaki U. Sch. Medicine, Japan, 1993. Med. officer Govt. Rural Hosp., Dhaka, Bangladesh, 1982-86; clin. assoc. U. Hosp., Mymensingh, Bangladesh, 1986-87; lectr. U. Rsch. Inst., Dhaka, Bangladesh, 1987-88; guest rsch. fellow Nagasaki U. Hosp., Japan, 1993-99, asst. prof., 1999—. Cons. in field. Inventor in field. Organizer blood donation, organ donation Rotary, Lions, Bangladesh, 1982-88; organizer diarrheal disese in control program Pub. Health Ctrs., Bangladesh, 1982-88. Monbusho fellow, Govt. Japan, 1988. Mem. Asian Pacific Assn. for Study of Liver, Assn. Hepatology Japan, Soc. Gastroenterology Japan, Am. Fedn. Cancer Rsch., Japan Soc. Ob-Gyn., Internat. Friendship Soc. Japan, Am. Soc. Reproductive Immunology, European Soc. Endocrinology, World Endometriosis Soc., Japanese Soc. Endometriosis, Soc. Fertility and Sterility. Avocations: reading, music, travel, tennis, swimming. Home: 21-3 Chitose machi #303 Nagasaki 852-8135 Japan Office: Nagasaki U Sch Medicine 1-7-1 Sakamoto Nagasaki 852-8501 Japan Personal E-mail: nemokhan76@hotmail.com. Business E-Mail: nemokhan@nagasaki-u.ac.jp.

KHAN, MOHAMMED YOUSUF, physician, consultant; arrived in U.S., 1960; s. M.K. and H.K. Durrani; m. Yasmin Yousef Jan, Oct. 31, 1971; children: Irfan, Zeshan. MBBS, Punjab U., Pakistan, 1958; PhD, U. Minn., Mpls., 1969. Diplomate Am. Bd. Internal Medicine, Am. Bd. Infectious Diseases. Resident internal medicine U. Minn., 1962-66, fellow infectious disease, 1966-69; cons. Pakistan Internat. Airlines, Karachi, Pakistan, 1970-72; head infectious diseases Hennepin County Med. Ctr., Mpls., 1972-83; co-dir. Sexually Transmitted Diseases Clinic, 1972-83; asst. prof. Dept. Med., U. Minn., 1972-83; head infectious diseases King Fahad Hosp., Riyadh, Saudi Arabia, 1983-98, King Khalid Hosp., Jeddah, Saudi Arabia, 1998-2000; chief infectious disease Maricopa Med. Ctr., Phoenix, 2000—06; assoc. prof. medicine Mayo Med. Sch., Rochester, Minn., 2001—. Keynote speaker Riyadh Med. Forum, Suadi Arabia, 1992. Contbr. articles to jours., chpts. to books. Recipient Physician Recognition award AMA, 1996. Fellow ACP, Infectious Disease Soc. Am., Royal Coll. Physicians. Avocations: fishing, hiking, reading, coin collecting/numismatics. Office: Maricopa Med Ctr Dept Medicine 2601 E Roosevelt Phoenix AZ 85008 Personal E-mail: md1khanyou@yahoo.com.

KHAN, MOHAMMED ZAHIRUL ISLAM, pharmaceutical executive, pharmacist; b. Comilla, Bangladesh, Apr. 16, 1956; arrived in Australia, 1989; s. Md Abdur Razzaque and Zilhazz (Begum) Khan; m. Nasrin Sultana Jolly, May 29, 1986; children: Zahida (Jenny) Sultana, Shohan Mohammed. MSc in Pharmacy, Pyatigorsk Inst. Pharmacy, USSR, 1982; PhD in Pharmaceutics, U. Queensland, Brisbane, Australia, 1993. Pharmacist-in-charge Ministry of Health, Lusaka, Zambia, 1982—83; pharmacist mgr. Nat. Drug Co., Lusaka, 1983-87, prodn. pharmacist, 1987-89; tutorial asst. U. Queensland, Brisbane, 1989-91, tutorial fellow, 1991-92; rsch. fellow level B Monash U., Melbourne, 1992—94; devel. pharmacist Sigma Pharms. Pty Ltd., Melbourne, 1994—97; project mgr. drugs devel. PLIVA d.d, Zagreb, Croatia, 1997—99, head solid dosage forms labs, 1997—99, dir. pharm. tech., 1999—2001, corp. dir. pharm. tech., 2001—02, dir. pharm. devel., 2002—03; sr. dir. project competitive advantage PLIVA d.d., Zagreb, Croatia, 2004—; sr. dir. pharm. devel. PLIVA Rsch. Inst. Ltd., Zagreb, Croatia, 2003—04, sr. dir. strategic devel., 2004—; chief sci. officer PLIVA Krakow S.A., Poland, 2004—05. Mgmt. bd. mem. PLIVA R&D Polska Ltd., Krakow, 2004—05; chmn. bd. PLIVA Rsch. Pvt. Ltd., Goa, India, 2004—; sr. dir. Strategic Devel., 2004—05, sr. global dir., 2005—. Contbr. articles to profl. jour., chapters to books. Recipient Bibliography appeared in the Who's Who in the European Rsch. & Devel., 3rd Edit., K. G. Saur, Munchen, 2003, Bibliography appeared in the Who's Who in the World - 1996, 13th Edit., Marquis Who's Who, New Providence, 1995; scholar The U. of Queensland Postgraduate Rsch. Scholarship, The U. of Queensland, 1990-1992, Scholarship for Undergraduate and Grad. Studies Leading to Master Degree, Coun. for Mut. Economy (COMECON), 1976-1982, Excellence in Studies, Pyatigorsk Inst. of Pharmacy, Russia, 1977—82, Talent Scholarship, Bangladesh Agrl. U., Mymensing, Bangladesh, 1976, Merit Scholarship, Bd. of Intermediate and Secondary Edn., Comilla, Bangladesh, 1972-1978. Mem.: Controlled Release Soc., Am. Assn. Pharm. Scientists, Pharm. Soc. Japan, Pharm. Soc. Australia (MPS). Muslim. Achievements include 2 PCT patent applications on Novel Drug Delivery Systems. Avocations: gardening, world politics, fishing. Office: PLIVA Rsch and Devel Ltd Prilaz Baruna Filipovica 29 10 000 Zagreb Croatia Home Phone: +385-1-377-6873; Office Phone: +385-1-372-2546. Office Fax: +385-1-372-2108. Business E-Mail: zahir.khan@pliva.com.

KHAN, MOHIUDDIN MOHAMMAD TAIMUR, engineering educator, researcher; b. Khulna, Bangladesh, Dec. 8, 1972; PhD, U. Tokyo, 2002. Adj. prof., rsch. faculty U. Tokyo, 2002—11, U. N.Mex, N.Mex., 2010—, Mont. U. Reviewer in fields. Contbr. articles to profl. jours. Japan Soc. Promotion Sci. Fellowship, Japan Ministry Edn., Monbusho scholarship, Merit scholarship, Bangladesh Ministry Edn. Mem.: ASCE, Environ. Engrs. and Sci. Profs., WateReuse Assn., ASM, IEB, NAMS, IWA. Avocations: travel, movies, hiking. Home: 945 Buena Vista Dr SE Apt H 203 Albuquerque NM 87106 Office Phone: 505 277 1018. Personal E mail: t2000aimur@yahoo.com.

KHAN, MUSHFIQUDDIN, neuropharmacologist, researcher; s. Noor Mohammad Khan and Aqila Begum; m. Salma Ansar, June 15, 1966 (dec.); children: Tooba, Talha, Hamza. BSc with honors, Aligarh Muslim U., India, 1976, MSc, 1978, MPhil, 1980. Postdoctoral rschr. Ehime U., Matsuyama, Shikoku, Japan, 1984—86; rsch. scientist-pool officer Aligarh Muslim U., Uttar Pradesh, India, 1986—88; lectr. Shibli Nat. Postgraduate Coll., Azamgarh, Uttar Pradesh, India, 1988—90; postdoctoral rschr. Med. U. SC, Charleston, 1994—98, asst. prof., 2002—. Scientist Modern Foam Industries, Janupur, 1990—94; sr. scientist Ariz. Inst. for Biomedical Rsch., Scottsdale, 1999—2001, grant reviewer NIH, Washington. Mem. AMU Rsch. Student's Assn., Aligarh, 1980—82. Recipient Mitchell I. Rubin rsch. award, Children's Hosp., MUSC; grantee, NINDS, NIH, Bethesda, MD, 2000—05; Monbusho fellow, Govt. of Japan, jr. rsch. fellow, CSIR, Govt. of India, sr. rsch. fellow. Mem.: AAAS, Indian Soc. for Mass Spectrometry, Am. Soc. for Neurochemistry, Am. Assn. for Biochemistry and Molecular Biology. Avocations: travel, classical music, humor, handball. Home: 3529 Ashwycke St Mount Pleasant SC 29466 Office: Med Univ SC 173 Ashley Ave 508 CRI Charleston SC 29425 Business E-Mail: khanm@musc.edu.

KHAN, NADEEM KAMAL MUSTAFA, health facility administrator, accountant; b. Karachi, Sind, Pakistan, July 22, 1952; s. Mohammad Mustafa and Suraiya Mustafa Khan; m. Imrana Afridi, Dec. 16, 1983; children: Usman, Anam, Erum, Kiran. BA, U. Peshawar, Pakistan, 1971; BSc in Econs. with honors, U. London, 1974. Chartered acct., 1977; cert. quality mgr. Am. Soc. Quality, lead auditor, ISO, 1997. Trainee acct. to investigation sr. Price Waterhouse and Co., London, 1974-79; sr. Hays Allan, London, 1979-80; asst. fin. mgr. Aga Khan Univ. Hosp., Karachi, Pakistan, 1981-82, fin. mgr., 1982-87, dir. fin. and info. systems, 1987-89, dir. profl. svcs., 1989—97, COO, 1997—2000, dir. gen., CEO, 2001—. Fellow Inst. Chartered Accts. Eng., Wales and Pakistan. Muslim. Avocations: speaking on skills development, travel, economics and mgmt. lit. Office: Aga Khan U Hosp Stadium Rd PO Box 3500 Karachi 74800 Pakistan Home: 25/II/I Kh-e-Momin DHAV Karachi Pakistan 75500 Business E-Mail: nadeem.khan@aku.edu.

KHAN, NAJM US-SAQIB, plastic surgeon, consultant; b. Karachi, Pakistan, Nov. 28, 1958; s. Abdul Wahab Khan and Shaheeda Bano; m. Samina Najm Siddiqui, Jan. 13, 1990; children: Areeb, Sobia, Hiba. MB, BChir, Dow Med. Coll., 1983. Diplomate Bd. Cert. Royal Coll. of Physicians and Surgeons of Glasgow, 1989. Cons. and head of plastic surgery units Al-Qassimi and Kuwait Hospitals, United Arab Emirates, 1995—; cons. plastic surgeon King Khalid Hosp., Hail, Saudi Arabia, 1994—95; registrar plastic surgery Odstock Hosp., Salisbury, 1990—94; sr. ho. officer plastic surgery Middlesbrough Gen. Hosp., Middlesbrough, 1989—90; sr. ho. officer gen. surgery North Tees gen. Hosp., Stockton-on-Tees, 1987—88, Burnley Gen. Hosp., Burnley, 1986—87. Moderator adv. bd. Al-Qassimi Hosp., United Arab Emirates, 2000—. Author: (scientific paper on laser treatment) Laser in Medical Science; contbr. scientific papers. Merit scholarship, Secondary bd. Karachi, 1975, President's Scholarship Scheme, 1977. Mem.: Plastic Surgery Soc. Emirates Med. Assn. (v.p. 1996—2003), Pan Arab Assn. of Plastic Surgeons (assoc.), Internat. Confederation for Plastic, Reconstructive and Aesthetic Surgeons (assoc.), Internat. Soc. of Aesthetic Plastic Surgeons (assoc.), Brit. Assn. of Plastic Surgeons (assoc.). Avocations: travel, current affairs, history, photography, movies.

KHAN, SHAHNAWAZ, pharmacist, director; b. Nawabshah, Sind, Pakistan, May 22, 1955; arrived in U.S., 1974; s. Abdul Q. Khan and Mehmooda Begum; m. Ghazala Jabeen, June 10, 1988; children: Sidra, Sarah, Shahzaib, Malik. BS in Pharmacy, U. Karachi, Pakistan, 1979. Cert. surg. fitter Phila. Coll., 1989, registered pharmacist NY, NJ, cert. orthotist NY, NJ, lab. technician NY, NJ. Supr. pharmacist Tri-Star Pharmacy, NYC, 1982—84, Empire State Drugs, Bronx, NY, 1984—86; clin. pharmacist Harlem Hosp. Ctr., NYC, 1986—93, clin. coord., 1993—99, dir. pharmacy dept., 2000—. Mem. Franklin Dem. Club, NYC, 2003. Recipient Jim Wright Vulnerable Populations award, 2003. Mem.: Am. Hosp. Pharmacy Assn., Am. Coll. Clin. Pharmacy, Am. Diabetes Assn., Am. Pharmacist Assn., Pakistani Am. Pharm. Assn. (sec.). Democrat. Achievements include development of Once Daily Dosing of Gentamicin: Implementation of Pharmacy on Infectious Diseases; Antibiotic Control Program: Switch from IV to PO dosage of antibiotic and H2 antogonist; Usage of Neuromuscular Blocking Agent. Avocation: reading, driving. Office: Harlem Hosp Ctr 506 Lenox Ave New York NY 10037 Office Phone: 212-939-1761. E-mail: khan2512@aol.com.

KHANDAY, FIRDOUS AHMAD, biology professor; b. Kashmir, India, Sept. 4, 1973; PhD, Jammu & Kashmir Sainik Sch., 1991; PhD in Biotech., 2002. Asst. prof. U. Kashmir, 2005—. Recipient Innovative Young Biotechnologists award, Dept. Biotech. Govt. of India. Office: Hazratbal Srinagar Jammu and Kashmir 190006 India Business E-Mail: khanadayf@kashmiruniversity.net.

KHANDEKAR, JANARDAN DINKAR, oncologist, educator; b. Indore, India, Feb. 1, 1944; came to U.S., 1971; s. Dinker and Sulaochan (Dawlae) K.; m. Amita Oomen, Aug. 28, 1971; children: Manoj, Melin. MD, MBBS, U. Indore, 1969; sabbatical, Northwestern U., Baylor U., 1992. Diplomate Am. Bd. Internal Medicine, Am. Bd. Med. Oncology. Intern M.Y. Hosp., Indore, 1967-70; resident in medicine Allegheny Gen. Hosp., Pitts., 1972-73; head divsn. med. oncology Evanston (Ill.) Hosp., 1975-98, from asst. attending physician to assoc. attending physician, 1975-79, sr. attending physician, 1979—; fellow Med. Rsch. Coun., Montréal, Que., Canada, 1970-71, Tufts U., Boston, 1973-75; asst. prof. medicine Northwestern U., Chgo., 1975-80, assoc. prof., 1980-86, prof. medicine, 1986—, Kellogg/Scanlon chair in oncology, 1991-98; dir. cancer control Northwestern U. Cancer Ctr., Chgo., 1991—; assoc. dir. Kellogg Cancer Care Ctr. Evanston Hosp., 1979-87, dir., 1987—; Louise Coon chmn. dept. medicine Evanston Northwestern Healthcare, 1998—. Active NIH Ad Hoc Com. on Nat. Prostate Cancer Program, NIH Team for Audit Clin. Trials at Yale U., Roswell Park Meml. Inst., Mayo Clinic, etc.; chmn. rsch. com. and adv. com. Searle Clin. Pharmacology Unit; sr. investigator Eastern Coop. Oncology Group, 1976-83, Community Clin. Oncology Program, 1983—; lectr. in field. Author (with others): (novels) Radiation-Associated Thyroid Carcinoma, 1977, Adjuvant Therapy of Cancer, 1977; editor: (Archives) of Internal Medicine, 2004; contbr. articles. Recipient cert. of merit Nat. Cancer Inst. Humanitarian award Cancer Wellness Ctr., 2003; grantee Ill. Cancer Coun., 1983 98, Duke U., 1983 90, Nat. Cancer Inst., 1983—, Women's Health Inst., 1993, Evanston Hosp., 1993—, NIH, 1988-91, 93—. Fellow ACP (laureate); mem. AAAS, Am. Soc. Clin. Oncology, Am. Fedn. Clin. Rsch., Am. Assn. Cancer Rsch., Inst. Medicine (Chgo.). Office: Evanston Hosp 2650 Ridge Ave Evanston IL 60201-1781

KHANDELWAL, CHIRANJIVA, gastroenterologist, oncologist; b. India, Oct. 8, 1952; s. Sitaram and Manbhari K.; m. Poonam Jalan, May 19, 1977; children: Manish, Piyush. BSc, Patna U., 1971, MBBS, 1977, MS in Surgery. Sr. rsch. fellow ICMR, India, 1979-82; pool officer CSIR, India, 1989-92; prof. gastrointestinal surgery, head of dept. Indira Ghandi Inst. Med. Scis., Patna, India, 1995—2002; head surg. oncology Mahaver Cancer Sansthan. Cons. Indian Cancer Soc., Bihar, 1987. Fellow Cleve. Clinic. Fellow RCS (Eng.), Internat. Coll. Surgeons, Internat. Union Against Cancer; mem. Indian Acd. Med. Specialists, Indian Soc. Gastroenterology, Rotary Internat. (dist. gov.). Home: 6 Nehru Nagar Patna 800013 India Home Phone: 91-612-2270731. Personal E-mail: drkhandelwal@hotmail.com. E-mail: khandelwal3250@gmail.com.

KHANDHERIA, BIJOY K., cardiologist; b. India, May 11, 1956; MS, U. Baroda, Vadodara, Gujarat, India; MD, 1979. Cert. Internal Medicine, 1997. Resident in internal medicine Shree Sayaji Gen. Hosp., India, St. Agnes Med. Ctr., Hahnemann U., Phila.; fellow in cardiovascular diseases Mayo Grad. Sch. Medicine, Rochester, Minn.; mem. divsn. cardiovasc. diseases Mayo Clinic, Scottsdale, Ariz., chair cardiovasc. diseases, prof. medicine, 2003—. Office: Mayo Clinic 13400 E Shea Blvd Scottsdale AZ 85259 E-mail: khandheria@mayo.edu.

KHANDJI, ALEXANDER G., neuroradiologist, educator; Grad., SUNY, 1980. Diplomate Am. Bd. Radiology, Am. Bd. Radiology-neuroradiology. Intern Hershey Med. Ctr., resident in surgery, 1981—82; resident in diagnostic radiology Columbia Presbyn. Med. Ctr., 1982—85, fellow neuroradiology, 1985—87, clin. prof. of radiology, vice chair for clinical affairs, assoc. dir. of radiology svc. Office: New York Presbyterian/ Columbia University Medical Center 622 West 168th St New York NY 10032 Office Phone: 212-305-2500.

KHANDPUR, SUJAY, dermatologist, consultant; b. Pondicherry, India, June 4, 1971; s. Subhash Chander and Jayanti Khandpur; m. Shaifali Manocha Khandpur; 1 child, Saanchi. MBBS, Delhi U., 1990, MD, 1998. Intern Maulana Azad Med. Coll., New Delhi, 1994, jr. resident, 1995—98, sr. resident, 1998—2001, sr. rsch. assoc., 2001; asst. prof. All India Inst. Med. Scis., New Delhi, 2001—. Author: Lecture Series in Geriatrics, 2000, Practical Guidelines in the Management of Psoriasis, 2002, Clinical Geriatrics - Disorders of Skin, 2003; contbr. articles to profl. jours. Mem., trainer Nat. Leprosy Eradication Program, New Delhi, 1995—, Nat. AIDS Control Program, New Delhi, 1995—, Coordination Com. on Leprosy Control, New Delhi, 1998—. Mem.: Assn. Cutaneous Surgeons of India, Indian Assn. for Study of Sexually Transmitted Diseases & AIDS, Indian Assn. Dermatologists, Venereologists, Leprologists (Certificate of Hon. 1996—97, Young Dermatologist Continued Med. Edn. Trophy 1998—99), Nat. Acad. Med. Scis. Office: Dept Dermatology and Venereology All India Inst Med Scis New Delhi 110029 India Home: 59 Sfs Hauz Khas Apts 110 016 New Delhi India

KHANNA, ATUL, plastic surgeon, consultant; b. Hyderabad, India, Nov. 21, 1960; s. Harish Chand and Santosh Khanna; m. Sunanda Shahi, Nov. 25, 1988; children: Akshay, Anant. MBBS, Osmania U., Hyderabad, India, 1983; MBA, Open U., Milton Keynes, Eng., 1994. Diplomate European Bd. Plastic and Reconstructive Surgery. Sr. registrar in plastic surgery Radcliffe Infirmary, Oxford, Eng., 1996; fellow in hand surgery Derbyshire NHS Trust, Derby, Eng., 1996; locum cons. City Hosp. NHS Trust, Birmingham, Eng., 1996-97; specialist registrar in plastic surgery Nottingham (Eng.) City Hosp. NHS Trust, 1998; cons. Selly Oak Hosp., Birmingham, 1998-99, Sandwell Healthcare NHS Trust, Birmingham, 1999—. Hon. sec.

West Midlands Surg. Adv. Com. in Plastic Surgery; surg. coll. tutor Sandwell Gen. Hosp. Contbr. articles to profl. jours. Nat. Merit scholar, 1974, State Merit scholar, 1976. Fellow Royal Coll. Surgeons Glasgow, Internat. Coll. Surgeons; mem. Brit. Assn. Plastic Surgeons, Brit. Assn. Aesthetic Plastic Surgeons (coun. mem.), Brit. Burn Assn., Brit. Med. Assn. (chmn. Birmingham divsn. 2003-04), Soc. Expert Witnesses, Overseas Drs. Assn. (jr. drs. rep., sec.). Hindu. Avocations: swimming, cricket, walking, bicycling. Office: Sandwell Healthcare Lyndon West Bromwich B71 4HJ England Office Phone: 0121 607 3455. Office Fax: 0121-607-2498. Business E-Mail: atulkhanna@doctors.org.uk.

KHANNA, GEETIKA, medical educator; b. Amritsar, Punjab, India, July 5, 1973; MBBS, All India Inst. Med. Scis., 1997; MD, U. Iowa Hosps. and Clins., 2002. Assoc. prof. Mallinckrodt Inst. Radiology, 2008—. Office: 510 S Kingshighway Campus Box 8131 Mal St Louis MO 63110 Office Phone: 314-454-6229. E-mail: khannag@mir.wustl.edu.

KHANNA, SUNALI, dental educator; b. Bhopal, Madhya Pradesh, India, Nov. 30, 1978; d. Sundeep and Rita Khanna. BDS in Dental Surgery, Coll. Dental Scis., Davangere, Karnataka, India, 2001; MDS in Dental Surgery, U. Bombay, Nair Hosp. Dental Coll., 2005; Postgrad. diploma in Hosp. & Health Mgmt., Symbiosis Inst. Health Scis., Pune, Maharashtra, 2008; Postgrad. diploma in Medicolegal Sys., Symbiosis U., Pune, 2009. Cert. in computer info. Maharashtra Govt., 2007; diplomate Govt. of India, 2005, cert. in clin. rsch. U. Pune, 2010; Nat. Bd. Examinations, 2006. Asst. prof. Nair Hosp. Dental Coll., Mumbai, 2005—; faculty Maharastra U. Health Sci. Guest spkr., Maldives, 2006, Iran, 07, Japan, 07, France, 08, China, 2008—10; peer review bd. mem. Internat. Jours. Contbr. chapters to books, articles to profl. jours. Mem.: Nat. Bd. Examinations, Indian Acad. Oral Medicine & Radiology (exec. com. mem. 2006—08, hon. treas.), Indian Dental Assn., Indian Soc. Dental Rsch., Nat. Acad. Med. Scis., Internat. Assn. Dentomaxillofacial Radiology (Japan) (life; adv. bd. mem., 18th Internat. Congress 2011). Office: Nair Hosp Dental Coll Dr ALNair Rd Mumbai Ctrl Mumbai Maharashtra 400008 India Home Phone: 91-9821459013. Personal E-mail: sunali3011@yahoo.com, sunailkhanna@gmail.com.

KHANNA, YASH KUMAR, family practice physician, pediatrician; b. Lahore, India, Dec. 28, 1941; came to U.S., 1970; s. Sohan Lal and Savitri (Mehra) K.; m. Christine Anne Warren, Sept. 22, 1972; children: Rajan Yash, Nisha, Dev Yash. MBBS, King George Michael Coll., Lucknow, India, 1964. Diplomate Am. Bd. Pediat., Am. Bd. Forensic Examiners, Child Health Royal Coll. Physicians and Surgeons, London. Sr. house officer Monsall Hosp., Booth Hall Children's Hosp., Manchester, England, 1966-68, Joyce Green Hosp., Dastford, England, 1969-70; house officer, emergency physician St. Mary's Hosp., Orange, NJ, 1971-87, resident in pediat., 1971-73; pvt. practice physician Orange, NJ, 1973—; med. dir. Quick Med.-West Essex Med. Group, Caldwell, NJ, 1983—, pres.-elect, 1997-2000, pres. med. staff, 2001—06. Asst. surgeon Ctrl. Health Svcs., New Delhi, 1965-66; house physician and surgeon Irwin Hosp., New Delhi, 1964-65; mem. med. staff Hosp. Ctrs. at Orange, N.J., 1973—2004, pres. med. staff, 1986-87, 2001-04; bd. govts. Cathedral Healthcare Sys. N.J., 2001-04. Mem. adv. com. to the handicapped Twp. of Livingston, N.J.; trustee Hosp. Ctr. at Orange, 1986-96; bd. govs. Cath. Healthcare, 2001-04. Recipient Med. Outreach award Grace Reformed Bapt. Ch., Newark, 1997, Hind Ratann award NRI Soc. India, 2002. Mem. Am. Assn. Physicians from India, N.J. Med. Soc., Orange Mountain Med. Soc., Indian Physicians Assn. N.J. (v.p. 2002-03, pres. 2004—), Asian Music Acad. (founder, pres. 1999—). Democrat. Hindu. Avocations: music, antiques. Home: 112 Shrewsbury Dr Livingston NJ 07039-3404 Office: Family Medicine/Pediat 310 Central Ave East Orange NJ 07018 also: Quick Med-West Essex Med Group 825 Bloomfield Ave Verona NJ 07044 Office Phone: 973-678-2900. Personal E-mail: yashk@aol.com.

KHARAT, AMIT TULSHIRAM, radiologist, hospital administrator; s. Kharat Dagdu and Draupada Kharat Tulshiram; m. Reeta Tulshiram Newnani, Feb. 17, 2004. MB, BChir, BJ Med. Coll., Pune, 1997; diploma in med. radio diagnosis, Pune U., 2002; postgrad. diploma in hosp. adminstrn., Indira Gandhi Nat. U., India, 2004. Diplomate Nat. Bd. Radiology, India, 2004. Intern Ruby Hall Clinic, Pune, India, 1998—99, Primary Health Ctr., Bhigwan, India, 1998—99, med. officer Chickhaldhara Amravati, India, 1999—2000; resident in radiodiagnosis Rural Med. Coll., Loni, Ahmednagar, India, 2000—02; radiologist Dr. D. Y. Patil Hosp. and Rsch. Ctr., Pimpri, India, 2002—, Yeshwantrao Chavan Mcpl. Corp. Hosp., Pune, 2002—. Med. officer in charge Dist. Health Orgn. Amravati, Chickhaldhara, India, 1999—2000; cons. in field. Contbr. articles to profl. jours. (Best paper award, 2004, 05). Mem.: Nat. Acad. Med. Scis., Indian Radiology Soc. (life). Achievements include research in musculoskeletal ultrasound. Home: New Alandi Road Shantinagar Yerawada Maharashtra Pune 411006 India Office: Dr D Y Patil Hospital & Research Centre Sant Tukaram Nagar Pimpri 411018 India Personal E-mail: kharatamit@yahoo.co.in.

KHARBANDA, KUSUM K., biologist, educator; d. Duni Chand and Vidya Wati Kharbanda. MSc, U. Delhi, India, 1981, PhD, 1988. Postdoctoral rsch. assoc. All India Inst. Med. Scis., New Delhi, 1988—92; rsch. assoc. U. Nebr. Med. Ctr., Omaha, 1992—96, rschr., 1996—99, asst. prof., 1999—2009, assoc. prof., 2009—; rsch. biologist Dept. Veterans Affairs Med. Ctr., Omaha, 1999—. Project mgr. Jr. League, Lincoln, Nebr., 1992—96; bd. dirs. Nebr. Polio Survivors Assn., Omaha, 1997—. Recipient Internal Medicine Basic Sci. Rsch. award, U. Nebr. Med. Ctr., Dept. Internal Medicine, 2005; Jr. Rsch. fellow, Coun. Sci. and Indsl. Rsch., 1982—84, Sr. Rsch. fellow, 1984—87. Mem.: Sigma Xi, Rsch. Soc. on Alcoholism, Am. Assn. Study Liver Disease. Achievements include research in prognostic prediction of human brain tumors based on cell culture characteristics; the effect of alcohol consumption on liver lysosomes; acetaldehyde-malondialdehyde-protein adducts on the pro-fibrogenic and pro-inflammatory properties of hepatic stellate cells; betaine administration on alcohol-induced alterations in methionine metabolism. Office Phone: 402-995-3752. Business E-Mail: kkharbanda@unmc.edu.

KHARCHENKO, VASYL, physicist; b. Sumy, Ukraine, Apr. 25, 1984; PhD, NAS Ukraine, 2009. Sr. staff scientist Inst. Applied Physics, 2010. Office: 58 Petropavlovskaya Sumy 40030 Ukraine Business E-Mail: vasiliy@imag.kiev.ua.

KHARE, DEVENDRA KUMAR, surgeon; b. Jhansi, Uttar Pradesh, India, Oct. 20, 1967; s. Mukta Prasad and Siya Khare. MBBS, GSVM Med. Coll., Kanpur, 1991; MS, KG Med. Coll., Lucknow, 1995. Sr. resident gen. surgery King George's Med. Coll., Lucknow, 1996; sr. resident surg. gastroenterology Sanjay Gandhi Postgrad. Inst. Med. Scis., Lucknow, 1997—2000; asst. prof. gen. surgery Himalayan Inst. Med. Scis., Dehradun, Uttaranchal, India, 2001—04, Sri Ram Murti Smarak Inst. Med. Scis., Bareilly, Uttar Pradesh, India, 2004—05, Adesh Inst. Med. Scis. and Rsch., Bathinda, Punjab, India, 2005—06; practicing surgeon Various Hosps., Jhansi, 2006—. Author: (book) Debates in Gastrointestinal Surgery; contbr. articles to profl. jours. Recipient Internat. Health Profl. of Yr. award, IBC Cambridge Eng., 2010. Mem.: Assn. Minimal Access Surgeons India, Assn. Surgeons India. New Alliance. Home: Village- Londi PO Baghera Jhansi Uttar Pradesh India Office: Omkar Bhawan Kargava Ji Rd 284 128 Jhansi India Personal E-mail: dkk67@yahoo.co.in.

KHARIA, ANKIT ANAND, healthcare educator; b. Mandla, Madhya Pradesh, India, Dec. 12, 1981; PharmB, RMES's Coll. Pharmacy, 2004; PharmM, HKES'S Coll. Pharmacy, 2007; attended, Uttarakhand Tech. U. Asst. prof. Oriental Coll. Pharmacy, 2008—. Recipient Gold medal, HKES's Coll. Pharmacy. Home: A-48 Siddharth Lake City Anand Nagar Bhopal Madhya Pradesh 462021 India Personal E-mail: ankitanandkharia@yahoo.co.in.

KHATAMEE, MASOOD AHMAD, obstetrician, gynecologist; b. Mashhad, Iran, Feb. 12, 1936; s. Ahmad and Cobra (Tadbir Kashani) K.; married, Mar. 11, 1966; children: Pira, Neda, Yalda. MD, Shiraz U., Iran, 1961. Diplomate Am. Bd. Ob-Gyn. Intern Nemazee Hosp., 1960-61; resident in ob-gyn. Bellevue Hosp. Ctr., NYC, 1962-66, fellow in infertility, 1966-67; exec. dir. Fertility Rsch. Found., NYC; mem. staff Lenox Hill Hosp., NYC, Beth Israel-North Divsn., NYC, NYU Med. Ctr., NYC. Clin. prof. NYU Sch. Medicine; pres. Iranian Am. Med. Assn., 1998-2000; founder Soc. Prevention Human Infertility; founder, pres. Shiraz U. Sch. Medicine Alumni Assn. USA, Inc., 1988-89, mem., bd. dirs., past pres. Co-author: The Fertility Sourcebook, Doctor Are You Listening?; contbr. articles to sci. jours. Pres. Iranian Am. Rep. Party, N.Y.C., 1994—. Recipient Ronald Regan Gold medal, Nat. Republican Congressional Com., 2004—05, Citation award, Royan Inst. Molecular Biology, Iranian Congress Med. Scis.; named Physician of Yr., White House, 2003; named one of America's Top Obstetricians, Consumer Rsch. Coun.; nominee Top Ten Iranian Am. Physicians; fellow, WHO. Fellow ACOG; mem. Am. Fertility Soc., Fertility Rsch. Found., Physicians Adv. Bd., Nat. Republican Com., Russian Am. Med. Assn. (hon.), America's Registry Outstanding Profls., Canadian Soc. Iranian Engrs. & Archs. (Citation award). Home: 23 Church St Alpine NJ 07620 Office: Fertility Rsch Found NYU Sch Medicine 877 Park Ave New York NY 10075-0341 Office Phone: 212-288-3737. Office Fax: 212-744-6536. Personal E-mail: frfbaby@msn.com.

KHATER, HANEM FATHY, medical educator, researcher; d. Fathy Khater and Fawzia Ahmed El- Sherbini; m. Saeed Mohamed Abdel-Bary, Dec. 20, 2005; children: Galal El-Deen Abou-Ella, Nour El-Deen Abou-Ella. PhD (hon.), Faculty Vet. Medicine, Zagazig U., Benha bransh, Egypt, 2003. Tchg. asst., parasitology Faculty Vet. Medicine, Qalyubia, 1993—95, sr. tchg. asst., 1995—2004, asst. prof. parasitology, 2004—08, assoc. prof. parasitology, 2008—; journalist, pub. awarness Al- Watan Newspaper, Shuwikh, Kuwait, Kuwait, 2006—. Contbr. articles to profl. jours. (Sci. reward, 2004). Office: Faculty Veterinary Medicine Benha Un Moshtohor-Toukh Benha Qalyubia Governorate 13736 Egypt Mailing: Gulf Newspaper distribution and printables Co P.O. Box 42057 70651 Shuwaikh Kuwait Office Fax: 002- 2013- 2463074. Personal E-mail: hafkahter@yahoo.com.

KHATIB, RUSTOM ATFAT, gynecologist, endocrinologist, researcher, consultant; b. Beirut, Sept. 3, 1962; s. Atfat Rustom and Samia Ibrahim (Jannoun) K.; m. Mona Adnan Tabbara, Feb. 11, 1993; children: Samia Karla, Ryan Atfat. BS with honors, Am. U. Beirut, 1984, MD, 1988; MBA, Hamilton U., Wyo., 1995, PhD in Bus. Adminstrn., 2001; postgrad diploma in econs., U. London, 2000, MSc in Fin. Mgmt., 2006. Resident in ob-gyn. Am. U. Beirut, 1992-94; fellow in reproductive endocrinology Mich. State U., Saginaw, 1994, clin. instr., 1992-94; clin. cons. Rizk Hosp., Beirut, 1994—2005. Clin. cons., dir. fertility unit European Heart Ctr., Saida, 1994—96; chmn. ob-gyn. United Med. Group, Beirut, 1996—2007, dir. fertility unit, 1997—2007; sci. cons. Beirut Fertility Ctr., 1994—99; dir. fertility svc. Jubeily Hosp., Saida, 1996—99; cons. fertility unit Kasab Hosp., Saida, 2000—; dir., sr. cons. IVF Systems, Beirut, 2007—; prof. and cons. Janeen Fertility Ctr., Manama, Bahrain, 2006—; mem. acad. coun. London Diplomatic Acad. Contbr. articles to profl. jours. including Gynecologic Oncology, Fertility and Sterility, European Jour. Obstets., Clin. Consultation in Ob-Gyn. Founding cabinet mem. World Peace and Diplomacy Forum, Cambridge; sec. gen. United Cultural Conv., Raleigh, NC, 2000—. Recipient Physician's Recognition award AMA, 1994, Ob-Gyn. Rsch. award Saginaw Coop. Hosps., 1994. Fellow Am. Coll. Surgeons; mem. Am. Soc. for Reproductive Medicine, NY Acad. Scis., European Soc. for Human Reproduction and Embryology, Am. Soc. for Reproductive Medicine, Greenpeace. Office: IVF Systems Almabani Bldg Abdul Aziz Str Box Beirut 14 5354 Lebanon Office Phone: 9611741900. Office Fax: 9611749695. Business E-Mail: drrustomkhatib@iuf_systems.com.

KHATOD, MONTI, surgeon; b. Ajmer, India, Mar. 25, 1970; BA, UC Berkeley, 1992; MD, UC San Diego, 1996. Surgeon Southern Calif. Permanente Med. Group, 2003—. Fellow: Am. Acad. Orthop. Surgeons. Avocations: skiing, surfing. Office: Dept Orthopedics Surgery 1011 Baldwin Park CA 91706 Business E-Mail: monti.x.khatod@kp.org.

KHATTAB, ABDUL-ZAHER MOSELHY, pathologist, educator; b. Minyet-Al-Qamh, Nov. 15, 1959; MBBCh with honors, Faculty Medicine, 1984; MD, Layola U., Chgo., 1997; PhD in Pathology, Zagazig U., Egypt. Prof., surg. and molecular pathology, 2008—. Recipient, Egyptian Syndicate. Mem.: World Soc. Pathology Arab Divsn., Egyptian Soc. Pathology. Home: 7-Ghashaam St Zagazig Sharkiya 3424 Egypt Personal E-mail: abdulzaherkhattab@yahoo.com.

KHATTAB, AHMED D., professor of medicine, physician, educator; b. Ninawa, North Iraq, Iraq, Nov. 23, 1956; s. Dhia S. Khattab and Alyia D. Younis; m. Ibtisam S. Al-Samarraie, Feb. 11, 1983; 1 child, Ali A. MBChB, Royal Coll. Medicine, Baghdad, Iraq, 1980; PhD, U. Reading, 1992; C.Biol, M.I.Biol, Inst. Biology, London, 1989; FRSPH, Royal Soc. of Pub. Health, London, UK, 2009; FRIPHH, Royal Inst. of Pub. Health & Hygiene, London, UK, 1995; MIHE, Inst. Health Edn., London, 1994. Rsch. scientist Inst. Health & Cmty. Studies, Bournemouth, Dorset, 1992—94; sr. lectr. Bournemouth U., 1996—2004, reader, med. rsch., 2004—07, head, biomed. & clin. rsch., 2004—; vis. prof. Anglo-European Coll., Chiropractic, Bournemouth, 2007—. Physician gen., medicine & medicine elderly & stroke Royal Bournemouth Hosp., 1996—2002; vis. sr. lectr. U. Reading, Berkshire, 1991—2000; cons. advisor Dept. Health, London, 2004—07; advisor Fgn. & Commonwealth Office, London, 2006—; cons. Ctr. Postgrad. Med. Rsch. & Edn., Bournemouth, Dorset, 2007—. Contbr. articles to profl. jours. Supporting & advising rsch. matters Stroke assn., London, 2005—08; with Fgn. & Commonwealth Office, London, 2006—09; promoting & appointing prof. Anglo-European Coll. Chiropractic, Bournemouth, 2006—09, advising tng. & edn., 2006—09; with Ctr Postgrad Med. Rsch. & Edn., 2007—09, Royal Coll. Nursing & Bournemouth U., 1997—2008; coord. Bournemouth U., 2000—09. Fellow: FRIPHH, FRSPH; mem.: Institue Health Edn., Inst. Biology (Chartered Biologist 1989), Gen. Med. Coun. Avocations: reading, history. Office: Bournemouth Univ 17 Christchurch Road BH1 3LH Bournemouth England Office Phone: 00441202967281. Office Fax: 00441202967398. Personal E-mail: aliawd@hotmail.com. Business E-Mail: akhattab@bournemouth.ac.uk.

KHAVARI, KHALIL AKHTAR, psychology professor; b. Tehran, Iran, Nov. 10, 1932; s. Ardeshir Akhtar and Rouhanghiz Khalili K.; m. Sue Williston, June 6, 1959; children: Paul, Katherine. BS, Bradley U., 1960, MS, 1963; PhD, Ind. U., 1967. Asst., assoc. then prof. psychology U. Wis., Milw., 1967-95, founder, dir. Midwest Inst. on Drug Use, 1974-77, co-founder, coord. peace studies program, 1987-89. Referee, cons. in field. Author: Creating a Successful Family, 1989, Together Forever: A Practical Guide to Successful Marriage, 1993, Introduction to the Baha'i Faith, 1997, Spiritual Intelligence, 2000. Mem. aux. bd. Baha'i Faith, Milw., 1981-86, founding mem. Baha'i Internat. Health Assn., Ft. Lauderdale, Fla., 1984-90; life mem. Tlinget Indian Tribe, Alaska. Avocations: reading, travel, tennis, hiking, gardening.

KHEDER, EMAM MOHAMED, orthopedist, surgeon, consultant; b. Shobra Al Khima, Egypt, Feb. 19, 1956; arrived in Saudi Arabia, 1992; s. Mohamed Abdul Razek Kheder and Aziza Ahmed Sharawi; m. Nevien Nagi Faried, Aug. 15, 1985; children: Hadeer Emam, Areej Emam. MB CHB, Ain Shams U., Cairo, 1980, MSc in Orthopedics, 1987. Intern Ain Shams U. Hosp., Cairo, 1981—82; orthop. resident Internat. Locomotor and Neuroscience Inst., Giza, Egypt, 1983—87, orthop. registrar, 1987—90, Al Amal Polyclinic, Yanbu, Saudi Arabia, 1990—92, Riyadh (Saudi Arabia) Mil. Hosp., 1992—98, sr. orthop. registrar, 1998—2002, sr. orthop. spinal registrar, 2002—04; cons. orthop. King Fahd Mil. Med. Complex, Dhahran, Saudi Arabia, 2004—. Tutor Riyadh (Saudi Arabia) Mil. Hosp., 1997—2001. Named Orthop. Resident Friend, Saudi Bd. Orthop. Program, 1998; fellow, Internat. Coll. Surgeons, 2000, ACS, 2002. Fellow: Royal Coll. Surgeons Glasgow, Royal Coll. Physicians and Surgeons Glasgow; mem.: Egyptian Orthop. Assn. (life). Muslim. Achievements include research in intercondylar notch giew - its value in ACL reconstruction. Avocations: travel, swimming, reading. Home: Kornish Al Nile North Cairo Maadi Egypt Office Fax: 0096614736615. Personal E-mail: emamk@hotmail.com.

KHO, EUSEBIO, surgeon; b. Philippines, Dec. 16, 1933; came to U.S., 1964; s. Joaquin and Francisca (Chua) K.; m. Grace Casas Lim, May 24, 1964; children: Michelle Mae, April Tiffany, Bradley Jude, Jaclyn Ashley, Matthew Ryan. AA, Silliman U., The Philippines, 1955; MD, State U. Philippines, 1960. Diplomate Am. Bd. Surgery. Rotating intern Philippine Gen. Hosp., U. Philippines, 1959-60; resident gen. practice Silliman U. Med. Ctr., 1960-63; virology rschr. Van Howelling Lab. Silliman U., 1963-64; intern in surgery Francis Scott Key Med. Ctr., 1964-65, resident in gen. surgery, 1965-67; fellow in surgery Johns Hopkins, 1965-67; rsch. assoc. pediat. surgery U. Chgo. Hosps., 1967-68; resident in gen. surgery then chief resident U. Tex. Hosp., San Antonio, 1968-70; hosp. surgeon St. Anthony Hosp., Louisville, 1970-72; practice medicine specializing in surgery Scottsburg, Ind., 1972—. Chmn. dept. surgery Scott County Meml. Hosp., 1973—; cons. surgeon Washington County Meml. Hosp., Salem, Ind., Clark County Meml. Hosp., Jeffersonville, Ind., 1973—; courtesy surgeon Suburban Hosp., Louisville, 1973—; gen. surgeon 5010 U.S. Army Hosp., Louisville, 1980—. Bd. dirs. Make-A-Wish Found., Ind., 1992—. Col. M.C., USAR, 1980—, Operation Desert Storm, 1990-91. Named to Chgo. Filipino Am. Hall of Fame, 1998; recipient Outstanding Svc. Overseas award U. Philippines Med. Alumni Soc., 2002. Fellow: ACS, Am. Coll. Emergency Physicians, Am. Soc. Abdominal Surgeons; mem.: APHA, AMA (Physician's Recognition award 1969, 1972), Phillipine Med. Assn. of Ky. (Disting. Svc. award 2000), Am. Heart Assn., Am. Soc. Law and Medicine, Am. Cancer Soc., Am. Soc. Parenteral and Enteral Nutrition, Soc. Laparoscopic Surgeons, N.Y. Acad. Scis., Surgeons in Am. (life), Assn. Philippine Practicing Physicians in Am. (life), Assn. Mil. Surgeons U.S. (life), Res. Officers Assn. U.S. (life), Soc. Philippine Surgeons in Am. (life), Bradley Aust. Surg. Soc., Mark Ravitch Surg. Assn., Ind. Philippines Med. Assn., Ky. Med. Assn., Soc. of The Philippines, Ind. State Med. Assn., Am. Coll. Internat. Physicians (founding, trustee 1974—), U. Chgo. Med. Alumni Assn., Philippine Heritage Endowment Found., Philippine Ednl. and Cultural Endeavor (life), Silliman U. Alumni Assn. (life), U. Philippines Med. Alumni Soc. Am. (life), Assn. U.S. Army (life), Silliman Alumni Internat., Johns Hopkins Med. Alumni Assn., Optimists, Masons, Hon. Order Ky. Cols. Presbyterian. Home: 14 Carla Ln Scottsburg IN 47170-9707 Office: 137 E Mcclain Ave Scottsburg IN 47170-1846 Office Phone: 812-752-5659.

KHOJASTEH, ALI, medical oncologist, hematologist; b. Shiraz, Pars, Persia, Nov. 10, 1947; arrived in U.S., 1974; s. Mostafa and Pari Jan (Azimi) K.; children: Artemis, Amitis. Degree, Pahlavi U., Shiraz, 1968, MD, 1974. Vice dean Sch. Medicine Shiraz U., 1980-82, chmn. med. dept. Sch. Medicine, 1982-83; chief med. oncology Ellis Fischel Cancer Ctr., Columbia, Mo., 1983-87, chmn. med. dept., 1987-90, chief of staff, 1988-89; med. dir. St. Mary Cancer Ctr., Jefferson City, Mo., 1993—; pres. Columbia Comprehensive Cancer Care Clinic and Rsch. Inst., 1990—. Assoc. prof. U. Mo., Columbia, 1989—; prin. investigator Ellis Fischel CCOP, Columbia, 1988-90; chmn. Mo. Acad. Sci. Oncology, 1988-89, Mo. Cancer Pain Initiative, 1991-96; investigator Nat. Cancer Inst., US, 1990—, Nat. Cancer Inst., Canada,

2002—; liaison Am. Coll. Surgeons, 1992—, Top Physicians Consumers Rsch. Coun. America, 2003—, Best Drs. in Am., 2003-04, Top Oncologist Consumer Rsch. Coun. America, 2008-10; reviewer Clin. Drug Investigations Jour., Current Cancer Drug Targets Jour. Contbr. articles to New Eng. Jour. Medicine, Cancer, Am. Jour. Medicine, Am. Jour. Hematology, Jour. Clin. Oncol. Cancer Bull., Jour. Pain Sys. Mgmt., Can. Jour. Medicine, Jour. Expert Opinion UK Blood; author: (with others) Pulmonary Medicine, Cancer and Heart, Chemotherapy Resource Book, Small Intestinal Disease. Named one of Top Oncologist, Consumers Rsch. Coun. America, 2008—11, AstraZeneca Lab., 2011; grantee, Purdue Fredrick Co., Conn., 1994—, Adria Lab., Columbus, 1988—, Glaxo Rsch. Lab., Research Triangle Park, N.C., 1988—91, Ciba-Geigy Co., 1990—91, Merrill Dow Co., 1991—95, Viventia Biotech. Lab., 1995, Pfizer, 1995—, Matrix Pharm., 1996, Ross Lab., 1996, Aronex Pharm., 1997, Merck Rsch. Lab., 1997, Ligand Lab., 1997, Maxim-Pharm., 1998, Nat. Cancer Inst. (Can.), 1998, Glaxo-Wellcome, 1998, Bayer Lab., 1999, Amgen, 1999, Arugon Lab., 1999, Pharmacia & Upjohn Lab., 2000, Hoffman-Roche Lab., 2000, Sanofi-Synthelabo Lab. (France), 2000, PI of prospective study of hemalologic and neoplastic disorders, UN Project, 2001, UN, 2001, Pro-Neuron Lab., 2002, Johnson and Johnson Lab, 2003, Aventis Lab., 2003, Bristol Meyers Squib Lab., 2003, Biovest Lab., 2004, Viventia Biotec, 2005, Endo Pharms., 2005, Nuvelo Rsch. Lab., 2006, Genentech, 2006, Vical Lab., 2007, Otsuka Pharm. Devel., 2007, others, Kosan Bioscis., 2007, Insys Therapeutics, 2008, Tragara Pharm., 2008, Biogen, 2008, Translational Rsch. Lab., 2009. Fellow ACP, Royal Soc. Medicine (Eng.); mem. Am. Soc. Clin. Oncology, Am. Soc. Internat. Medicine, Smithsonian Soc., N.Y. Acad. Sci., Mo. Acad. Scis. (chmn. oncology sect. 1988-89), So. Med. Assn., Am. Soc. Hematology, Am. Jour. Medicine (reviewer). Zoroastrian. Home: 2801 Greenbriar Dr Columbia MO 65203-3663 Office: Columbia Comprehensive Cancer Care Clinic 500 Keene St Ste 202 Columbia MO 65201-8104 Office Phone: 573-893-6404, 573-442-6800. Personal E-mail: drk5c@socket.net.

KHOL, CHAREL L., psychologist; b. Cleve., Apr. 2, 1943; divorced; children: Adrienne Marie, Matthew Philip. BS in Edn., Ohio State U., 1965; MS in Edn., Ohio U., 1969; PhD, Kent State U., 1982. Lic. psychologist, Ohio. Psychologist Kevin Coleman Ctr., Ravenna, Ohio, 1983-87; pvt. practice Ravenna and Kent, 1984—2008; psychologist Child Guidance Ctr., Akron, Ohio, 1987 2006. Cons., expert witness. Named Jennings Scholar for Tchr. Excellence, Jennings Trust, 1967. Mem.: APA, OSU Varsity O. Avocations: reading, quilting, collecting.

KHOMUTOVA, ELENA YURIEVNA, radiologist; b. Omsk, Russia, Dec. 22, 1968; MD, Omsk State Med. U., 1983. Radiologist Omsk Regional Hosp., 1993, Omsk State Med. U., 2000—. Named Best Dr. of Yr., Siberian Govt., 2005. Mem.: ECR, ESGAR. Avocations: travel, music. Office: Berezovaya 3 Omsk 644111 Russia Office Phone: 79136281547. Office Fax: 73812359364. Business E-Mail: elenahomutova@rambler.ru.

KHONSARI, ROMAN HOSSEIN, maxillofacial surgeon; b. Teheran, Iran, Jan. 19, 1979; MSc, École Normale Supérieure, Paris, 2002; MD, U. Paris VI, 2004; PhD, King's Coll. London, 2011. Surgeon Ctr. Hosp. U. Nantes, 2004; rsch. fellow King's Coll. London, 2009—11. Avocations: piano, history, literature. Home: 12 rue Laromiguière Paris 75005 France Business E-Mail: roman.khonsari@kcl.ac.uk.

KHOOBEHI, KAMRAN, plastic surgeon; married. MD, St. Louis U., 1986—90. Diplomate Am. Bd. Surgery, 1999, Am. Bd. Plastic Surgery, 2000. Gen. surgery La. State Univ. Health Sci. Ctr., New Orleans, 1990—95, clin. prof. surgery; plastic surgeon Solo Practitioner, Metairie, La., 1997—; hosp. affiliations include Tulane-Lakeside Hosp., East Jefferson Gen. Hosp., Univ. Med. Ctr., Lakeview Regional Med. Ctr., Ochsner Baptist Med. Ctr. Recipient Tchg. Excellence in Aesthetic Surgery, 2005. Fellow. Am. Coll. of Surgeons; mem.: Am. Soc. of Reconstructive Microsurgery, La. Soc. of Plastic Surgeons, Am. Soc. for Aesthetic Plastic Surgery, Am. Soc. of Plastic Surgery. Avocations: deep sea fishing, swimming, spending time with his children. Office: Kamran Khoobehi, M.D. 3901 Veterans Blvd Metairie LA 70002 Office Phone: 504-273-7267.

KHOPKAR, UDAY SHARADCHANDRA, dermatologist, consultant; b. Pune, Maharashtra, India, Aug. 25, 1962; s. Sharadchandra Rajaram and Sulochana Sharadchandra Khopkar; m. Sunita Shriram Nagavkar, Aug. 15, 2001. MBBS, Topiwala Nat. Med. Coll., Mumbai, India, 1984, diploma in venereology and dermatology, 1985, MD in Dermatology, 1988. Diplomate Nat. Bd. of Examinations, New Delhi, India, 1989. Lectr. dermatology T. N. Med. Coll. and B.Y.L. Nair Charitable Hosp., Mumbai, Maharashtra, India, 1988—93, sr. lectr. dermatology, 1993—94, assoc. prof. dermatology, 1994—2000, prof. dermatology, 2000—02; prof., head dept. dermatology Seth GS Med. Coll. and KEM Hosp., 2002—. Cons. dermatologist Dr. Ctr. Kemps Corner, Mumbai, 2005—. Chief editor (journal) Indian Journal of Dermatology, Venereology and Leprology; author: (book) Handbook of Skin and Sexually Transmitted Infections, editions 1 to 5, Synopsis of HIV Infection and AIDS in India; contbr. chapters to books. Adviser Social Justice, Mumbai, 1999. Recipient AC Parikh award, IADVL Maharashtra State Br., 1985; fellow, NYU Med. Ctr., NY, 1992, Inst. Dermatopathology, Jefferson Med. Coll., Pa., 1995; scholar, Nat. Merit Scholarship Bd., 1977—83, U. Mumbai, 1979—87, World Congress Dermatology, 1992, Rotary Internat., 1994. Mem.: Cosmetology Soc. India (life), Pemphigus and Pulse Therapy Found. (life), Dermatopathology Soc. India (life), Dermatopathology Soc. Mumbai (life; sec. 1996), Indian Assn. Dermatologists, Venereologists and Leprologists (life; sec. Maharashtra state br. 1993—2000, Best Br. award 1993, 1998, 1999). Achievements include first to Initiate Dermatopathology Referral Service first time in India at a public hospital - 1997; Indigenously developed and popularized ultraviolet therapy chambers in public hospitals of Mumbai; Initiate Day Care Centre and Pulse Therapy for Pemphigus in Mumbai. Avocations: travel, trekking, stamp collecting/philately, history. Home: 2/7 Government Colony Haji Ali Mumbai 400 034 India Office: KEM Hosp & Seth GS Med Coll Acharya Donde Marg Parel Mumbai 400012 India Office Fax: 91-22-24143435. Personal E-mail: drkhopkar@gmail.com. Business E-Mail: ukhopkar@rediffmail.com.

KHORANA, ALOK ANAND, oncologist, medical researcher; arrived in US, 1996; s. Anand Bhushan and Suman Anand Khorana; m. Melissa Marie Khorana; children: Ethan Alok, Matthew, Michael, Benjamin. MBBS, Maharaja Sayajirao U., Baroda, Gujarat, India, 1995; MD, SUNY, Buffalo, NY, 1999. Diplomate Am. Bd. Internal Medicine, 1999, in med. oncology Am. Bd. Internal Medicine, 2002. Fellow in hematology and oncology U. Rochester, Rochester, NY, 1999—2002, sr. instr. James P. Wilmot Cancer Ctr., 2002—04, asst. prof. medicine James P. Wilmot Cancer Ctr., 2004—08, assoc. prof. medicine, 2008—, vice chief divsn. hematology oncology, 2009—. Mem. oncology expert com. U.S. Pharmacopoeia, 2005—; mem. sci. program com. ASCO, 2005—07; mem. rsch. implementation workgroup comprehensive cancer control plan N.Y. State, Albany, NY; mem. gastrointestinal cancers com. S.W. Oncology Group, 2003—. Contbr. (TV series) Second Opinion, Sta. PBS-TV, 2005; contbg. author: Narrative Matters, 2006, assoc. editor: Cancer Investigation; editor: Cancer Associated Thrombosis: New Findings in Translational Science, Prevention & Treatment, 2007; contbr. chapters to books, articles to profl. jours. Med. adv. coun. Gilda's Club, Rochester, 2005—06. Recipient Dr. H. P. Shastry Academic Excellence Gold medal, South Gujarat U., 1991, Academic Excellence in Pharmacology Gold medal, Maharaja Sayajirao U., 1993, Creative Excellence Faculty award, U. Rochester, Med. Humanities Divsn., 2001—02; grantee, Cancer Action, Gilda's Club, Rochester, 2001, Dr. Robert Cooper Trust, 2003, Nat. Cancer Inst., 2006—; James P. Wilmot Cancer Rsch. fellow, U. Rochester, 2001—04, V Found. fellow, 2006. Fellow: ACP; mem.: Internat. Soc. Thrombosis and Haemostasis (co-chair, sci. subcom. hemostasis & malignancy 2009—), Am. Soc. Clin. Oncology (mem. venous thromboembolism guidelines panel 2006—). Hindu. Achievements include research in elucidating risk factors related to cancer-associated thrombosis. Office: University of Rochester 601 Elmwood Ave Box 704 Rochester NY 14467

KHORANA, HAR GOBIND, chemist, educator; b. Raipur, India, Jan. 9, 1922; arrived in US, 1960, naturalized, 1966; s. Shri Ganpat Rai Khorana and Shrimati Krishna (Devi) Knorana; m. Esther Elizabeth Sibler, 1952; children: Julia Elizabeth, Emilie Anne; 1 child, Dave Roy. BS, Punjab U., 1943, MS, 1945; PhD, Liverpool U., Eng., 1948; DSc (hon.), U. Chgo., 1967, Simon Fraser U., Vancouver, Can., 1969, U. Liverpool, Eng., 1971, U. Punjab, India, 1971, U. Miami, 1994; degree (hon.), U. Bergen, Norway, 1996; others (hon.). Head organic chemistry group BC Rsch. Coun., Vancouver, 1952—60; vis. prof. Rockefeller Inst., NYC, 1958—; prof., co-dir. Inst. Enzyme Rsch., U. Wis., Madison, 1960—70, prof. dept. biochemistry, 1962—70, Conrad A. Elvehjem prof. life scis., 1964—70; Alfred P. Sloan prof. biology and chemistry MIT, Cambridge, 1970—92, Alfred P. Sloan prof. emeritus, sr. lectr., dept. Biology, 1992—. Vis. prof. Stanford U., 1964; mem. adv. bd. Biopolymers; rschr. chem. methods for synthesis of nuccleotides, coenzymes and nucleic acids, elucidation on the genetic code, lab. synthesis of genes, biol. membrane and light-transducing pigments. Author: Some Recent Developments in the Chemistry of Phosphate Esters of Biological Interests, 1961; editl. bd. Jour. Am. Chem. Soc., 1963—, contbr. numerous articles to profl. jours. Recipient Merck award, Chem. Inst. Can., 1958, Gold medal, Profl. Inst. Pub. Svc. Can., 1960, Dannie-Heinneman Preiz, Göttingen, Germany, 1967, Remsen award, Johns Hopkins U., 1968, Am. Chem. Soc. award for creative work in synthetic organic chemistry, 1968, Louisa Gross Horwitz prize, 1968, Lasker Found. award for basic med. rsch., 1968, Nobel prize in medicine, 1968, elected to Deutsche Akademie der Naturforscher Leopoldina, HalleSaale, Germany, 1968; fellow Overseas, Churchill Coll., Cambridge, Eng., 1967. Fellow: AAAS, Am. Acad. Arts and Scis., Chem. Inst. Can.; mem.: NAS, others, Japanese Biochem. Soc. (fgn. hon.), Royal Soc. Edinburgh, Pharm. Soc. Japan (hon.), Royal Soc. (London), Pontifical Acad. Scis. (Rome), Indian Acad. Scis. (fgn. mem.), Am. Philos. Soc. Office: 68-680A Dept Biol MIT 77 Massachusetts Ave Cambridge MA 02139-4307 *

KHORRAM-MANESH, AMIR, surgeon, regional medical advisor; b. Tehran, Iran, July 7, 1958; s. Mohammad and Fakhrosadat (Hosseini) Khorram Manesh; m. Marina Sussane Khorram Manesh, Mar. 20, 1961; children: Yasmin, Nicki. MD, Gothenburg U., Sweden, 1988, PhD in Endocrine Surgery, 2004. Cert. specialist I gen. surgery Swedish Nat. Bd. Health and Welfare, 1994, Gen. Med. Coun., UK, 1995, instr. ATLS Swedish Surg. Assn., 2005. Chief cons. trauma and emergency surgery Sahlgrenska U. Hosp., Gothenburg, 2001—05, co-chair dept. urology, 2009—10; chmn. dept. gen. and orthop. surgery Kungälvs Hosp., Sweden, 2005—09; co-med. dir. Perhosp. and Disaster Medicine Ctr., Gothenburg, 2007—. Co-dir. studies in surgery Gothenburg U., 2000—01; dir. studies for non-Swedish physicians Sahlgrenska Acad., Gothenburg, 2000—02, dir. study in surgery for fgn. students, 2001—03; chmn. Swedish-Iranian Med. Assn., Gothenburg, 2002—04, 2007—09. Author: articles in profl. jours. Grantee, Swedish Med. Assn., Gothenburg Med. Assn., 1999, 2004, 2005, 2006, Assn. Gabnelssons Fund, 2008—10. Mem.: World Assn. Disaster & Emergency Medicine, Assar Gabriblssons, European Soc. Trauma & Emergency Surgery, Swedish Soc. Disaster Medicine, Brit. Med. Assn., Soc. Peritoneal Cavity, Swedish Trauma Assn., Swedish Surg. Assn., Swedish Med. Assn. Office: Prehosp Disaster Medicine Ctr Regionnens HUS Gothenburg 40544 Sweden Business E-Mail: amir.khorram-manesh@surgery.gu.se. E-mail: amir.khorram-manesh@vgregion.se.

KHORSHID, FATEN ABDULRAHMAN, medical educator; b. Riyadh, Saudi Arabia, Apr. 20, 1960; d. Abdulrahman Fuad and Saleha Hassan (Akbar) Khorshid; m. Aboulmaali Abdullatif Abdullah, Nov. 28, 1977; children: Ahmed Aboulmaali Abdullatif, Anas Aboulmaali Abdullatif, Asmaa Aboulmaali Abdullatif. BA, King Abdulaziz U., Jeddah, 1983; MA, King Adulaziz U., Jeddah, 1989; PhD in Cell Engring., Glasgow U., 2001. Lectr. faculty medicine King Abdulaziz U., Jeddah, 1990—2002, asst. prof. faculty medicine, 2002—. Head tissue culture unit King Fahd Med. Rsch. Ctr., Jeddah, 2003—; head female rsch. group of world supreme Coun. for Commn. on Sci. Signs of Quran and Sunnah, Muslim World League, Jeddah, 2004—; mem. female group World Assembly of Muslim Youth, Jeddah, Saudi Arabia, 2004—; mem. Gulf Fedn. for Cancer Control, Doha, Qatar, 2005—; presenter in field. Author: Laboratory Manual of Biology, Part I, 2004, Laboratory Manual of Biology, Part II, 2005. Muslim. Achievements include invention of anticancer agent; research in tech. for studying keloid. Home: AlSamer Jeddah 80215 Saudi Arabia Office: King Abdulaziz Univ PO Box 80215 King Abdulaziz University St Jeddah 21589 Saudi Arabia Office Fax: + 966-2-695-2076; Home Fax: + 966-2-695-2076. Personal E-mail: fatenkhorshid@yahoo.com. Business E-Mail: fkhorshid@kaau.edu.sa.

KHOSA, ROBIN, oncologist; b. Bathinda, Punjab, India, Jan. 25, 1980; MD, MGM Med. Coll., 2008. Sr. resident radiation oncology Batra Hosp. And Med. Rsch. Ctr., 2008—11; jr. cons. radiation oncology Action Cancer Hosp., 2011—. Mem.: Aroi (India) (Dr G.C. Pant Young Drs. award 2009). Office: Fc-34 A-4 Paschim Vihar New Delhi 110063 India Personal E-mail: drrobin25@gmail.com.

KHOSHBIN, ESPEED, surgeon; s. Ehsanollah and Zohreh Khoshbin; m. Tracy White. MBChB, Aberdeen U. Lic. physician Gen. Med. Coun., England. Specialist registrar U. Leicester, England. Pres. doctors mess Glenfield Hosp., Leicester. Contbr. articles to profl. jours. Mem.: Med. Protection Soc., Soc. Cardiothoracic Surgeons Gt. Britain and Ireland, Brit. Med. Assn., Royal Coll. Surgeons. Achievements include research in adult and paediatric cardiopulmonary surgery, transplantation and extracorporeal life support. Avocations: skiing, swimming, travel, cooking, movies. Office: University of Leicester Leicester Royal Infirmary Leicester LE2 7LX England Personal E-mail: khoshbinuk@yahoo.co.uk. Business E-Mail: ek68@le.ac.uk.

KHOSLA, POOJA, epidemiologist, consultant; b. Ludhiana, Dec. 23, 1973; MD, CMC, Ludhiana, 2001. Cons. Sir Ganga Ram Hosp., 2005. Lectr. CMC, 2001—03. Fellowship, Maluana Azad Med. Coll., 2007. Avocations: reading, movies. Home: 748 Gurdev Nagar Ludhiana Punjab 141001 India Home Fax: 919818288194. Personal E-mail: poojakhosla@hotmail.com.

KHOSLA, VED MITTER, oral and maxillofacial surgeon, educator; b. Nairobi, Kenya, Jan. 13, 1926; s. Jagdish Rai and Tara V. K.; m. Santosh Ved Chabra, Oct. 11, 1952; children: Ashok M., Siddarth M. Student, U. Cambridge, 1945; L.D.S., Edinburgh Dental Hosp. and Sch., 1950, Coll. Dental Surgeons, Sask., Can., 1962. Prof. emeritus, dir. postdoctoral studies in oral surgery Sch. Dentistry U. Calif., San Francisco, 1968—; chief oral surgery San Francisco Gen. Hosp. Lectr. oral surgery U. of Pacific, VA Hosp.; vis. cons. Fresno County Hosp. Dental Clinic.; Mem. planning com., exec. med. com. San Francisco Gen. Hosp. Contbr. articles to profl. jours. Examiner in photography and gardening Boy Scouts Am., 1971-73, Guatemala Clinic, 1972. Granted personal coat of arms by H.M. Queen Elizabeth II, 1959 Fellow Royal Coll. Surgeons (Edinburgh), Internat. Assn. Oral Surgeons, Internat. Coll. Applied Nutrition, Internat. Coll. Dentists, Royal Soc. Health, AAAS, Am. Coll. Dentists, mem. Brit. Assn. Oral Surgeons, Am. Soc. Oral Surgeons, Am. Dental Soc. Anesthesiology, Am. Acad. Dental Radiology, Omicron Kappa Upsilon. Clubs: Masons. Office Phone: 650-348-7587.

KHOSROSHAHI, AREZOU, rheumatologist; b. Tehran, Iran, Sept. 1, 1976; MD, Tehran Med. Sch., 2001. Rheumatology assoc. Mass. Gen. Hosp., 2010—. Attending physician Carney Hosp., 2007—08. Arthritis Found. grant. Fellow: ACR. Home: 26 Westwood St Newton MA 02465 Business E-Mail: akhosroshahi@partners.org.

KHOUQEER, FAREED AHMED, cardiac surgeon, executive management consultant; s. Ahmed Mohammadali Khouqeer and Aisha Medammad Magadmi; m. Nahla Mohammadali Hammad, Mar. 21, 1974; children: Ahmad Fareed, Noor Fareed, Abdallah Fareed, Abraheem Fareed, Mohammadali Fareed. MD, King Saud U., Riyadh, 1979; MBA, U. Tenn., 2001. Diplomate Am. Bd. Surgery, 1989. Cardiac surgery cons. King Faisal Specialist Hosp. and Rsch. Ctr., Riyadh, Saudi Arabia, 1989—, exec. dir. med. and rsch. Jeddah, Saudi Arabia, 2000—. Dept. chmn., cvd King Faisal Specialist Hosp. and Rsch. Ctr., Jeddah, Saudi Arabia, 2000—01, dept. chmn. critical care, 2000—01. Dir.: (executive management) Executive Director; author: (medical) Doudenal Varix, Thoracoabdominal Aneurysm, Brain Protection In Heart Surgery, (research) Cytokines Change Due To Cardiopulmonary Bypass. Fellow: Am. Coll. Chest Physicians, Am. Coll. Critical Care Medicine, Am. Coll. Surgeons, ACS; mem.: M E DeBakey Surg. Soc. Muslim. Achievements include invention of Khouqeer Shunt, Pulmonary Hypertension. Avocations: travel, humanitarian missions. Office: Kfsh&Rc Zahrawi St Cr Riyadh 11211 Saudi Arabia Home: P0 Box 75538 11588 Riyadh 11588 Saudi Arabia Office Fax: +966-1- 442-6125. E-mail: khouqeer@hotmail.com.

KHOURI, GEORGE GEORGE, ophthalmologist; b. Beirut, May 24, 1957; came to U.S., 1976; BA summa cum laude, Rollins Coll., 1978; MD, Am. U. of Beirut, 1983. Diplomate Am. Bd. Ophthalmology. Intern in internal medicine Am. U. Hosp. and Med. Ctr., Beirut, 1982-83; rsch. fellow in ocular pharmacology and physiology Wilmer Inst., Johns Hopkins Hosp., Balt., 1983-84; resident in ophthalmology U. Chgo. Hosps. and Clinics, 1984-87; clin. fellow Retina Assocs. & Schepens Eye Rsch. Inst. Mass. Eye and Ear Infirmary/Harvard Med. Sch., Boston, 1987-88; asst. prof. Tufts U. Sch. Medicine, Boston, 1988-92; staff ophthalmologist Dept. Vets. Affairs Med. Ctr., Boston, 1988-92, Malden (Mass.) Hosp., 1992-93, Melrose (Mass.)-Wakefield Hosp., 1992-93; pvt. practice West Palm Beach, Fla., 1994—. Presenter in field. Contbr. articles to profl. publs. Vol. eye surgeon Aravind Eye Hosp., India, 1993, Lumbini (Nepal) Eye Hosp., 1993, Nepal Eye Hosp., Kathmandu, 1993, Lighthouse for Christ Eye Ctr., Mombasa, Kenya, 1993. Eye rsch. grantee Mass. Lions, 1992-93, VA, 1990-92. Fellow Am. Acad. Ophthalmology; mem. Am. Soc. Cataract and Refractive Surgery. Avocations: swimming, travel, horseback riding. Office: Palm Beach Eye Ctr Ste 8100 1411 N Flagler Dr West Palm Beach FL 33401-3411 Office Phone: 561-366-8300. Business E-Mail: info@palmbeacheye.com.

KHOURY, GHASSAN WADIE, orthopedic surgeon, consultant; b. Ramallah, Palestine, Aug. 16, 1953; s. Wadie Odeh Khoury and Najla AbdulNoor Awwad; m. Rania Salim Khalilieh, July 9, 1994; children: Wadie Ghassan, Tamara Ghassan, Leen Ghassan. BSc, Am. U. Beirut, 1975; MD, Am. U. Med. Sch., 1982. Cert. in orthopedic surgery U. Bermingham, 1986. Fellow in upper extremity and microsurgery U. Toronto, 1988; chief of staff Consulting Clinics, Riyadh, Saudi Arabia, 1992—2001; chmn. dept. surgery Kingdom Hosp., Consulting Clinics, Riyadh, 2002—. Chmn. Pvt. Orthop. Club, Riyadh, 1989—. Editor: (journal) Arabian Orthopedic News. Chmn. Am. U. Alumni, Riyadh, 1994—98. Fellow: ACS (life). Office: Kingdom Hosp Makkah Rd Box 61022 Riyadh 11565 Saudi Arabia Office Fax: +96614616334. Personal E-mail: gwkhoury@gmail.com.

KHOURY, KHALIL BUTRUS, supervisor nurse; b. Haifa, Israel, Aug. 12, 1971; s. Butrus Khalil and Angel Khalil Khoury; m. Shahraban Marwan Khoury. MSc, Sch. Pharmacy, Hebrew U., Jerusalem, 2003. Cert. BSN — nursing sch. Hadassah hosp., Hebrew U., 1996. R. nurse Hadassah Hosp., Jerusalem, 1996—99, clin. supr., 1997—2001, nurse mgr. asst. internal medicine A, 1999—2007, supervisor nurse, coord. procedures and profl. instrns., 2007—. Contbr. articles to profl. jours. Recipient Excellence Nursing, Hadassah Hosp., 2000, Best nursing staff, 2007, first Pl. best dept. hospitalized patients, Israeli servey, 2003, Hadassah Excellent Worker, 2003. Mem.: Israeli Assn. Internal Medicine. Home: fassouta village 25170 PO Box 183 Israel Office: Hadassah Hosp PO Box 12000 Jerusalem 91120 972 Israel Home Phone: 972-2-5815814, 972 0507874482; Office Phone: 972 2 6777075. Office Fax: 972 2 6777394; Home Fax: 972-2-5815814. Personal E-mail: khourykl@netvision.net.il. Business E-Mail: khoury_khalil@hotmail.com, khoury@hadassah.org.il.

KHOYNEZHAD, ALI, surgeon, educator; b. Mashad, Khorasan, Iran, Feb. 11, 1970; arrived in U.S., 1998; s. Reza Khoynezhad and Zhaleh Yousefein; m. Ziba Jalali, Mar. 31, 1998. MD, U. Cologne Coll. Medicine, 1996, PhD, 1998. Diplomate Am. Bd. Surgery, 2004, Am. Bd. Thoracic Surgery, 2006. Instr., prosector anatomy U. Cologne Coll. Medicine, Koeln, Germany, 1992—93; instr. surgery Humboldt-University, Berlin, 1996—98, North Shore U.-L.I. Jewish Med. Ctr., New Hyde Park, 2002—03, adminstrv. chief resident gen. surgery, 2002—03; instr. surgery Montefiore Med. Ctr. Affiliated Hosp., Bronx, 2004—05, adminstrv. chief resident cardiothoracic surgery, 2004—05; staff surgeon vascular and endovascular surgery Harbor-UCLA Med. Ctr., 2005—10; asst. prof. Cardiovasc. and Thoracic Surgery divsn. U. Nebr. Med. Ctr., Omaha, 2006—10, Creighton U. Med. Ctr., 2006—10; assoc. prof. surgery Cedars-Sinai Med. Ctr., dir. aortic surgery, 2010—. Exec. com. mem. Oper. Rm. Quality Assurance Com., New Hyde Park, NY, 2001—02, Grad. Med. Edn. Com., New Hyde Park, 2002—03, Credentials Com., Bronx, 2004—05, Thoracic Surgery Resident Assn., NYC, 2004—; rschr. in field. Recipient First Prize, Murry Friedman Competition, Coll. Surgeons, 2002; E. Ferdinand Sauerbruch Grant in Aid, E. Ferdinand Sauerbruch Competition, 1996-1998. Mem.: ACS (licentiate), Am. Coll. Cardiology (licentiate), Am. Coll. Chest Physicians (licentiate Poster of Distinction award 2002), Iranian AMA (licentiate), So. Med. Assn. (licentiate), Internat. Soc. Heart and Lung Transplantation (licentiate), Cardiothoracic Surgery Network (licentiate), Soc. Thoracic Surgeons (licentiate), German Soc. Thoracic & Cardiovasc. Surgery (licentiate). Avocations: photography, travel. Home: 3405 Pacific Ave Manhattan Beach CA 90266 Office: Cedars-Sinai Med Ctr 8700 Beverly Blvd NT 6215 Los Angeles CA 90048 Office Phone: 310-423-3851. Personal E-mail: akhoy@lycos.com. Business E-Mail: akhoy@cshs.org.

KHRAISAT, AHMAD, internal medicine, adult cardiovascular medicine; b. Al-Salt, Balqa', Jordan, Feb. 13, 1972; s. Sameh Khraisat and Alia Jaser; m. Eshraq Al-jaghbeer, July 4, 2001; children: Aya, Raya, Bilal. MD, U. Jordan Sch. Medicine, Amman, 1996. Cert. in Medicine Am. Bd. Internal Medicine, 2003. Chief med. resident Chgo. Med. Sch., 2002—03, asst. clin. prof. medicine, 2003—08, cardiology fellow, 2006—; attending physician Home Physicians, Chgo., 2003—, cons., 2003—; internat. cardiologist St. Luke's Med. Ctr., Milw., 2010—. Dir. Mt. Sinai Hosp. Med. Ctr., Chgo., 2003—06. Author: (new model for morning reports) Morning Report e-mails; clinical educator, internal medicine resident Internal Medicine Resident, internship in medicine Internal Medicine Intern, medical student (medical student). Recipient Alpha Omega Alpha award, AOA Honor Med. Soc., 2003, Max Harry Weil Disting. Clin. Educator award, 2003, Honor Degree award, 1996; named one of Outstanding Intern, 2000, Outstanding Graduating Med. Resident award, 2002. Mem.: ACP. Achievements include research in attenuating ischemia reperfusion injury on cardiac myocytes using Ranolazine; ischemia reperfusion injury, the blood brain barrier. Office: Rosalind Franklin Univ Medicine 3333 Green Bay Rd North Chicago IL 60064 Office Fax: 773-257-6726. Business E-Mail: ahmad.khraisat@rosalindfranklin.edu.

KHUBCHANDANI, INDRU TEKCHAND, colon and rectal surgeon; b. Karachi, India; s. Tekchand and Sarsati Khubchandani; m. Lynne Adderley, July 11, 1965; children: Joya, Mona, Sonya. MD, Grant Med. Coll., Bombay, India, 1956; postgrad., Royal Coll. of Surgeons, Eng., 1960; MS, Temple U., 1964; D (hon.), U. Santacruz, Bolivia. Diplomate Am. Bd. Colon and Rectal Surgeons. Fellowship. in gen. surg. New Eng. Hosp., Boston, 1961-62; res. Temple Univ. Med. Sch., Phila., 1962-64; chief divsn. colon and rectal surg. Healtheast Teaching Hosps., Allentown, PA, 1979-93; prog. dir. colon and rectal residency bd. dirs., 1983-93; prof. surgery Pa. State U., Hershey, 1995—, Hanneman U., Phila.; assoc. U. Pa. Bd. dirs. Healtheast, 1983—90, Slate Belt Med. Ctr.; hon. prof. U. Guadalajara, 2004. Editor: Indian Jour. Coloproctology, Surgical Treatment of Hemorrhoids, 2008, Khubchan Dani Endowed Chair in Colon & Rectal Surgery, Penn. State U., 2007; mem. editl bd. Jour ColoProctology, 1980, Phila. Jour. Diseases of Colon and Rectum, 1980-96, Revista Brasileira de ColoProctologia, Italian Jour. of ColoProctology, 1997—, referee Brit. Jour. of Surgery. Pres. Harry E. Bacon Found., 1985; fund raiser Rep. Party. Recipient medal of honor, Assn. Latin Am. de Coloproctologia, Tchr. of Yr. award, Lehigh Valley Hosp., 2000, 2001, 2002, 2003, Tcrh. of Yr. award, 2004, 2006—07. Fellow Royal Coll. Surgs. (Edinburgh); mem. Am. Soc. Colon and Rectal Surgs. (chmn. sci. and comml. exhibits 1979-94, Best Paper awds. 1970, 81, Rowell awd. 1985), Am. Gastroenterological Soc., Cuban Soc. Coloproctology (hon.), Assn. Surgeons India (hon.), Assn. Colon and Rectal Surgeons India (pres. 1990), Royal Soc. Med., N.E. Soc. Colon and Rectal Surgeons (pres. 1988), Pa. Soc. Colon and Rectal Surgeons (pres. 1978), Internat. Soc. of Univ. Colon and Rectal Surgeons (dir. gen. 1980-), Chilean Soc. Coloproctology (hon.), Venezuelan Soc. Colon and Rectal Surgeons (hon.), Sociedad Gallegade De Patologia Digestiva, La Coruna, Spain (hon.), Yugoslovia Soc. Coloproctology, Brazilian Soc. Colon and Rectal Surgeons (hon.), Assn. of Colon and Rectal Surgeons of India (hon.), Italian Soc. Coloproctology (hon.), Union League (Phila.), Internat. Coll. Surgeons (hon.), Hindu Club, Lehigh Country Club, Contemporary Club, Pa. Soc. Club, Rotary, Masons. Office: 1275 S Cedar Crest Blvd Allentown PA 18103-6207 Office Phone: 610-433-7571. Personal E-mail: indruk@aol.com.

KHULPATEEA, NEEKIANUND, gynecologic oncologist, educator; MD, Israel, 1972. Diplomate Am. Bd. Ob-Gyn., 1981. Resident ogb-gyn. Meth Hosp., Brooklyn, 1973—76; asst. dir. ob-gyn. Kings County Hosp.; assoc. clin. prof. Mt. Sinai Sch. Med.; pvt. practice Winthrop Univ. Hosp., Mid Island Hosp.; fellow gynecologic oncology SUNY Downstate, 1976—78, ass.t clin. prof. ob-gyn.; chief gynecology and oncology Coney Island Hosp., attending gynecologic oncology, assoc. dir. ob-gyn.; staff physician Maimonides Med. Ctr., dir. gynecology, 1994, dir. gynecologic oncology, 1994. Office: Maimonides Medical Center 4802 Tenth Ave Brooklyn NY 11213 Office Phone: 718-283-6000.

KHUNTIA, ANJANA (ANNIE KHUNTIA), pediatrician, educator; MD, Wayne State U., Detroit. Diplomate Am. Bd. Pediatrics, Am. Bd. Allergy and Immunology. Intern U. Chgo. Med. Ctr.; fellowship U. Mich., Ann Arbor; clin. assoc. prof. pediat. U. Chgo. Corner Children's Hosp., 2000—. Contbr. articles to profl. jours. Mem.: Am. Coll. Allergy & Immunology, Am. Acad. Pediat., Am. Acad. Allergy & Immunology. Achievements include research in allergic rhinitis, asthma and quality of life issues for children with asthma. Office: U Chgo Med Ctr 5841 S Maryland Ave MC 0730 Chicago IL 60637 Office Phone: 773-834-8109. Office Fax: 773-363-8075.

KHURAIJAM, GOURASHYAM SINGH, physician; b. Imphal Manipur, India, Mar. 1, 1941; arrived in U.K., 1977; s. Maipak Singh and Pati Devi Khuraijam; m. Nongthombam Mema Devi; children: Monica Devi, Jessica Devi. BSc with honors, D.M. Coll., Manipur, India, 1961; MB BS, M. Azad Med. Coll., Delhi, 1966; MD, Delhi U., 1973. Asst. prof. medicine Northeastern Regional Inst. Med. Sci., Manipur, 1974—77; cons. physician in respiratory, geriatric and gen. medicine Noble's Isle of Hosp., Douglas, Isle of Man, 1984—. Mem. Disability Appeal Tribunal, Isle of Man, 1995—. Author: General Science and Hygiene, 1969, Yaipha-Yumbal, 1969; contbr. articles to profl. jours. Recipient "C" Merit Award in Medicine, Isle of Man Health Svcs., 1990. Fellow: Royal Coll. Physicians of Edinburgh, Royal Coll. Physicians of London (adv. com. 2005), Royal Coll. Physicians Glasgow; mem.: Smoke Buster (chief patron 2000—), Burma Star Assn. (v.p. 2000—03, pres. 2004—), Isle of Man Med. Soc. (pres. 2000—01). Avocations: golf, badminton, gardening, hockey. Home: 12 Cronk Drean Douglas IM2 6AY Isle of Man Office: Noble's Hospital Dept General Medicine Douglas IM4 4RJ Isle of Man

KHURANA, RITU, rheumatologist; d. M. and M. Maira; m. Vikas Khurana; 1 child, Vriti. MD, ACGME, 2004. CCD ISCD, 2005; cert. in rheumatology ACGME, 2006. Chief rheumatology Crozer Keystone Health Sys., Upland, Pa., 2008—. Personal E-mail: ritu.khurana@gmail.com.

KHURANA HERSHEY, GURJIT, pediatrician, pulmonologist, educator; BS, U. Iowa, 1985; MD, PhD, Washington U. Sch. Medicine, 1992. Resident St. Louis Children's Hosp., 1992—95, fellow, 1995—97; dir. divsn. asthma rsch. Cinn. Children's Hosp. Med. Ctr.; assoc. dir. physician scientist training program U. Cin. Coll. Medicine, prof. pediatrics. Editorial bd. Jour. Allergy & Clinical Immunology. Mem.: Am. Acad. Allergy, Asthma & Immunology (exec. coun., Spl. Recognition award 2007), Am. Pediatric Soc. Office: 3333 Burnet Ave Cincinnati OH 45229-3039 Office Phone: 513-636-7054. Office Fax: 513-636-1657. E-mail: gurjit.hershey@cchmc.org.

KHUSH, GURDEV SINGH, geneticist; b. Rurkee, Punjab, India, Aug. 22, 1935; arrived in Philippines, 1967; s. Kartar Singh and Pritam Kaur (Dosanjh) Kooner; m. Harwant Kaur Grewal, Dec. 31, 1961; children: Ranjiv, Manjeev, Sonia, Kiran. BS in Agr., Punjab U., India, 1955; PhD, U. Calif., Davis, 1960; DSc (hon.), Punjab Agr. U., 1987, Tamil Nrdu Agr. U., 1995, CS Azad U. Agr. & Tech., 1995, G.B. Pant U. Agr. and Tech., 1996, De Montfort U., 1998, Assam Agrl. U., 2000, U. Cambridge, 2000; ND, U. Agr. and Tech., 2003. Rsch. asst. U. Calif., Davis, 1957-60, asst. geneticist, 1960-67; plant breeder Internat. Rice Rsch. Inst., Manila, 1967-72, plant breeder, head dept. plant breeding, 1972-85, prin. plant breeder, head dept. plant breeding, 1986—2002. Cons. rice breeding programs Burma, Bangladesh, China, India, Indonesia, Iraq, Egypt, Sri Lanka, Bhutan, Cambodia, Vietnam, Korea, Australia, Laos. Author: Cytogenetics of Aneuploids, 1973, Host Plant Resistance to Insects, 1995; editor: Rice Genetics Newsletter; contbr. articles to books and profl. jours. Recipient Borlaug award Coromandal Fertilizeers Ltd., Delhi, India, 1977, Japan prize Sci. and Tech. Found., Tokyo, 1987, Internat. Agronomy award Am. Soc. Agronomy, 1989, World Food prize World Food Prize Found., Des Moines, Iowa, 1996, Rank Prize, Rank Prize Found., London, 1998, Wolf prize Agrl., Wolf Found., Israel, 2000. Fellow Rice Genetics Coop. (elected, sec. 1985—); mem. Genetic Soc. Am., Am. Soc. Agronomy (fellows award 1987), Indian Soc. Genetics and Plant Breeding (fellows award 1988), Royal Soc. London, Crop Sci. Soc. Philippines (fellows award 1986), Indian Nat. Sci. Acad., U.S. NAS (fgn. assoc.), Third World Acad. Scis. Avocations: reading, jogging. Home: 39399 Blackhawk Davis CA 95616 Business E-Mail: gurdev@khush.org.

KIANG, NELSON YUAN-SHENG, medical educator; b. Wuxi, China, July 6, 1929; came to US, 1934; naturalized, 1961; m. 1957, 1976. PhB, U. Chgo., 1947, PhD in biopsychology, 1955; MD (hon.), U. Geneva, 1981; MS (hon.), Harvard U., 1984. Rsch. asst. Eaton-Peabody Lab. Mass. Eye and Ear Infirmary, Boston, 1957-62, dir., 1962—96; staff mem. rsch. lab. electronics MIT, Boston, 1955—96, Eaton-Peabody prof. dept. brain and cognitive scis., 1986—96, Eaton-Peabody prof. health scis. and tech., 1993—96; neurophysiologist, neurology svc. Mass. Gen. Hosp., Boston, 1977—96; prof. physiology, dept. otology and laryngology Harvard Med. Sch., Boston, 1984—96; emeritus on all appts., 1996—. Mem. communicative scis. study sect. NIH, 1968-72, behavior and neuroscis. study sect. NIH, 1985-89; mem. Com. Hearing Bioacoustics and Biomechanics NAS/NRC, Collegium Otorhinology-Laryngology Amiticiam Sacrum, Deafness Rsch. Found, Internat. Brain Rsch. Orgn.; hon. prof. Zhejiang U., Hangzhou, China, 1997, Peking Union Med. Coll., Beijing, 2001, Sun Yat-sen Med. U., Guangzhou, China, 2001; adv. prof. Fudan U., Shanghai, China, 1997; hon. advisor Chinese Med. Assn. Recipient Beltone award, 1968. Mem. AAAS, Soc. Neurosci., Am. Physiol. Soc., Acoustical Soc. Am., Am. Otology Soc., N.Y. Acad. Sci., Am. Acad. Arts and Scis., Assn. for Rsch. in Otolaryngology, Am. Vet. Med. Frontiers (trustee 2011-), Eastern Psychol. Assn., History of Sci. Soc., Philosophy of Sci. Assn., Royal Soc. Medicine, Psychonomic Soc., Union Internat. Univs. (advisor), Triglav Cir., Sigma Xi. Rsch. in physiology of auditory and other sensory systems; relation of brain to behavior. Office: Eaton Peabody Lab MA Eye & Ear Infirmary 243 Charles St Boston MA 02114 Business E-Mail: bnk@epl.meei.harvard.edu.

KIAT-AMNUAY, SUDARAT, prosthodontist, educator; arrived in U.S., 1996; d. Sompong and Suwanna Kiat-amnuay; m. Kwai Wa Cheng, Feb. 14, 2004; children: Natalie Kiat-amnuay Cheng, Teresa Kiat-amnuay Cheng, Emika Kiat-amnuay Cheng. BS, Rajsima Wittayalai U., Thailand, 1988; DDS with 2d Class Hons., Khon Kaen U., Thailand, 1994; MS in Prosthodontics, U. Louisville, 1999. Cert. in maxillofacial prosthetics and dental oncology U. Tex. M. D. Anderson Cancer Ctr., 2000, diplomate Am. Bd. Prosthodontics, Am. Bd. Clin. Anaplastology. Instr. faculty dentistry Khon Kaen U., Thailand, 1994—2000; adj. asst. prof. Sch. Dentistry U. Louisville, 1999—; vis. investigator Houston Biomaterials Rsch. Ctr., 2000—02; assoc. prof., clinic dir. postgrad general dentistry AEGO residency program U. Tex. Dental Br., Houston, 2001—; assoc. prof. M.D. Anderson Cancer Ctr., U. Tex., 2004—. Contbr. articles to profl. jours., chapters to books. Recipient 1st, 3d Pl. winner, poster presentation rsch. competition, Am. Acad. Maxillofacial Prosthetics, Internat. Congress of Maxillofacial Prosthetics, 1999—2001, Kosair Charities award, Kosair Children Hosp., 1997—99; grantee, Khon Kaen U., 1993, U. Louisville, 1998—2002, U. Tex. M. D. Anderson Cancer Ctr., 1999, v.p. rsch., U. Louisville, 2002, Nat. Inst. Dental and Craniofacial Rsch., NIH, 2003—08, U. Tex. Health Sci. Ctr., Houston, 2004—05; scholar, U. Louisville, 1998; grant, HSRA, 2010—. Fellow: Am. Acad. Maxillofacial Prosthetics (mem. materials and devices com. 2002, mem. rsch. com. 2003, 1st pl. poster presentation rsch. 1999, 2001), Internat. Congress Oral Implantologists, Am. Coll. Prosthodontists (diplomate); mem.: Am. Anaplastology Assn., Minority Faculty Assn., Assn. Women Faculty, Acad. Laser Dentistry, Internat. Assn. Dental Rsch., Am. Coll. Oral Implantology, Am. Assn. Dental Rsch., Phi Delta, Sigma Xi. Office: Univ Tex Dental Br 6516 M D Anderson Blvd Suite # 493 Houston TX 77030 Office Phone: 713-500-4194. Business E-Mail: sudarat.kiat-amnuay@uth.tmc.edu.

KIBA, TAKAYOSHI, internist, researcher; b. Tokyo, Mar. 31, 1964; MD, Yokohama City U., Japan, 1989, PhD, 1993. Resident internal medicine Hosp. Yokohama City U., 1989—93, clin. instr. third dept. internal medicine, 1996—99, staff third dept. internal medicine, 2001—04; sr. resident internal medicine Nat. Cancer Ctr. Hosp., Tokyo, 1993—96; vis. fellow molecular biology sect. Craniofacial and Devel. Biology and Regeneration Br. Nat. Inst. Dental and Craniofacial Rsch., NIH, Bethesda, Md., 1999—2001; lectr. Kyoto U. Grad. Sch. Medicine and Outpatient Oncology Unit, 2004—05; asst. dir. R&D and Bus. Integration Kyoto U. Hosp., 2004—07; assoc. prof. dept. med. oncology Kanazawa Med. U., 2005—07; prin. investigator mem. supr. team Found. for Biomed. and Innovation Translational Rsch. Informatics Ctr., 2007—11; chief, divsn. modern med. tech. Inst. Clin. Rsch., Nat. Hosp. Orgn. Kure Med. Ctr. & Chugoku Cancer Ctr., 2011—. Recipient Scholar award, Japanese Soc. Hepatology, 1994, Found. Scholar award, Yokohama City U., 1995, Young Clinicians award, World Congress Gastroenterology in Vienna, 1998. Office: Divsn Modem Med Tech Inst Clin Rsch Nat Hosp Orgn Kure Med Ctr & Chugoku Cancer Ctr 3-1 Aoyama cho Kure Hiroshima 737 0023 Japan Office Phone: 81 823-22-3111. Office Fax: 81-823-21-0478. Personal E-mail: takkiba@hotmail.com.

KIBLER, WILLIAM BENJAMIN, orthopedist, surgeon; b. Kingsport, Tenn., Sept. 29, 1946; s. Jacob B. and Della M. Kibler; m. Elizabeth Fay Mugler, June 20, 1970; children: B. Chase, David. BA, Vanderbilt U., 1968, MD, 1972. Cert. Am. Bd. Orthopedic Surgery, 1978. Intern, surgery Parkland Hosp., Dallas, 1972—73; resident, orthop. surgery Vanderbilt U., Nashville, 1973—77; staff physician Lexington Clinic, Ky., 1977—, head sect. orthop surgery, 1998—2007, med. dir. Sports Medicine Ctr., 1984—; med. dir. Shoulder Ctr. Ky., 2006—; bd. dirs. Vanderdict Med. Alumni Assn., 2010—. Bd. dirs. Am. Coll. of Sports medicine, Indpls., 1990—96; pres. Soc. Tennis Medicine and Sci., NYC, 1990—99; lectr. various national and internat. orthop. soc. Author: The Athletic Preparticipation Exam, 1990, Functional Rehabilitation of Sports Injuries, 1998; contbr. articles various profl. jours. Recipient Citation award, Am. Coll. of Sports Medicine, 1998, Plagenhof Sci. award, Profl. Tennis Registry, 1998, Hughston award, Am. Physical Therapy Assn., 2008, Edn. Merit award, Internat. Tennis Hall of Fame, 2010; named Best Dr. America Inc., 2004—. Fellow: Am. Acad. Orthop. Surgeons; mem.: Womens Tennis Assn. (cons.), US Tennis Assn. Sports Sci. Com., Arthoscopy Assn. America, Internat. Soc. Arthroscopy, Knee Surgery and Orthopedic Sports Medicine, Am. Orthopedic Assn., Am. Coll. Sports Medicine, Am. Shoulder and Elbow Surgeons, Am. Orthop. Soc. for Sports Medicine. Methodist. Avocations: sports, travel, hiking, bible study. Home: 240 Mkt St Lexington KY 40507 Office: Lexington Clinic 1221 S Broadway Lexington KY 40504 Office Phone: 859-258-8575. Office Fax: 859-258-8562. Personal E-mail: wkibler@aol.com. Business E-Mail: bkibl@lexclin.com. *

KIBRICK, ANNE, retired nursing educator, dean; b. Palmer, Mass., June 1, 1919; d. Martin and Christine (Grigas) Karlon; m. Sidney Kibrick, June 16, 1949; children: Joan, John. RN, Worcester Hahnemann Hosp., Mass., 1941; BS, Boston U., 1945; MA, Columbia Tchrs. Coll., 1948; EdD, Harvard U., Cambridge, Mass., 1958; LHD (hon.), St. Joseph's Coll., Windham, Maine, 1973. Asst. edn. dir. Cushing VA Hosp., Framingham, Mass., 1948—49; asst. prof. nursing Simmons Coll., Boston, 1949—55; dir. grad. div. Boston U. Sch. Nursing, 1958—63, dean, 1963—68, prof., 1968—70; chmn. dept. nursing Boston Coll. Grad. Sch. Arts and Sci., 1970—74; founding chmn. Sch. Nursing Boston State Coll., 1974—82; founding dean Sch. Nursing U. Mass., Boston, 1974—88, prof., 1988—93, prof. emeritus, 1993—. Mem. adv. coun. Coll. Nursing and Health Scis. U. Mass., Boston, 2004—. Mem. editl. bd. Mass. Jour. Cmty. Health. Mem. Brookline Town Meeting, 1995—2000; mem. nat. adv. bd. Hadassah Nurses Coun., 1996—2006; bd. dirs. Brookline Mental Health Assn., Met. chpt. ARC, Children's Ctr. Brookline and Greater Boston, Inc., 1984—89, Boston Health Care for Homeless, 1988—90, Landy-Kaplan Nurses Coun., 1992—, treas., 1994—96. Named to, Nursing Edn. Alumni Assn. Tchr.'s Coll., Columbia U. Hall of Fame, 1999. Fellow: Am. Acad. Nursing; mem.: Mass. Assn. RNs (charter mem., Living Legend award 2006), Inst. of Medicine of NAS, Mass. Blueprint 2000, Mass. Orgn. Elder Ams. (bd. dirs. 1988—2000), Mass. Med. Soc. (postgrad. med. inst. 1983—96, bd. dirs. 1983—96, exec. com. 1989—96), Nat. Acads. of Practice, Mass. Nurses Found. (v.p. 1983—86), AIDS Internat. Info. Found. (founding mem. 1985), Mass. Nurses Assn. (dir. 1982—86, charter inductee Hall of Fame 2000), Nat. Mass. League Nursing (pres. 1971—73), ANA, Pi Lambda Theta, Sigma Theta Tau. Home: # 312 130 Seminary Ave Auburndale MA 02466 E-mail: akibrick@lasell.edu.

KIDD, JAMES MARION, III, allergist, immunologist, educator; b. Baton Rouge, Dec. 15, 1950; s. James Marion, Jr. and Germaine Elizabeth (Hunt) Kidd; children: Mackenzie Elizabeth, Katherine Anne. MD, La. State U., 1976. Diplomate Am. Bd. Allergy and Immunology, lic. physician La., Fla., Wis. Resident physician La. State U. Sch. Medicine, New Orleans, 1977—79; rsch. fellow Med. Coll. Wis., Milw., 1980-82; pvt. practice in allergy and immunology Allergy, Asthma, and Immunology Clinic, Baton Rouge, 1982—; clin. asst., prof. medicine La. Sch. Medicine, New Orleans, 1982—; clin. asst., prof. community medicine and pub. health Tulane U. Sch. Medicine, New Orleans, 1992—2003. Dir. Baton Rouge Pollen Counting Sta., Nat. Allergy Bur. Paul Harris fellow, Rotary. Fellow: ACP, Baton Rouge Allergy Soc. (pres. 1990—95), La. Allergy Soc. (pres. 1989—90, exec. sec.-treas. 1992—96), Royal Soc. Medicine (U.K.), Am. Acad. Allergy and Immunology. Office: 8017 Picardy Ave Baton Rouge LA 70809-3538 Fax: 225-768-7642. E-mail: drjmkidd3@aol.com.

KIDD, MICHAEL RICHARD, physician, educator; b. Melbourne, Victoria, Australia, Nov. 11, 1959; s. Richard Edward and Jill Dulcie (East) K. MB BS, U. Melbourne, 1983; diploma in cmty. child health, Flinders U., Adelaide, Australia, 1989; MD, Monash U., Melbourne, 1995. Sr. lectr. Monash U., 1990-95; prof. gen. practice U. Sydney, 1996—2007, head dept. gen. practice, 1999—2005; exec. dean Faculty Health Scis., Flinders U., 2009—. Fellow Royal Australian Coll. Gen. Practitioners, (pres. 2002-06); mem. World Orgn. Family Drs. (pres.-elect, 2010-), Australasian Soc. for HIV Medicine (treas. 1997-99), Australian Med. Assn., Australian Gen. Practice Computing Group (chair 1998-2002), Order of Australia. Office: Flinders Univ GPO Box 2100 Adelaide SA5001 Australia Business E-Mail: michael.kidd@flinders.edu.au.

KIECOLT-GLASER, JANICE KAY, psychologist; b. Oklahoma City, Okla., June 30, 1951; d. Edward Harold and Vergie Mae (Lively) Kiecolt; m. Ronald Glaser, Jan. 18, 1980. BA in Psychology with honors, U. Okla., 1972; PhD in Clin. Psychology, U. Miami, 1976. Lic. psychologist, Ohio. Clin. psychology intern Baylor U. Coll. Medicine, Houston, 1974-75; postdoctoral fellow in adult clin. psychology U. Rochester, N.Y., 1976-78; asst. prof. psychiatry Ohio State U. Coll. Medicine, Columbus, 1978-84, assoc. prof. psychiatry and psychology, 1984-89, prof. psychiatry and psychology, 1989—, dir. divsn. health psychology, 1994—, active various coms. Mem. AIDS study sect. NIMH, 1988-91. Editl. bd. Brain, Behavior and Immunity jour., 1986—, Health Psychology jour., 1989—, Brit. Jour. Health Psychology, 1996—, Jour. Behavioral Medicine, 1994—, Psychosomatic Medicine, 1990—, Jour. Cons. and Clin. Psychology, 1992—, Jour. Gerontology, 1992—; reviewer Jour. Personality and Social Psychology, Psychiatry Rsch. jour.; author: Detecting Lies, 1997, Unconscious Truths, 1998, Handbook of Human Stress and Immunity, 1994; contbr. articles to profl. jours., chpts. to books. NIMH grantee, 1985—, recipient Merit award NIMH, 1993, Ohio State Disting. scholar, 1994, Devel. Health Psychology award, Divsn. Health Psychology and Adult Devel. and Aging, Norman Cousins award, Psychoneuroimmunology Rsch. Soc., 1998. Fellow Am. Psychol. Assn. (Outstanding Contbns. award 1988), Acad. Behavioral Medicine Rsch.; mem. Phi Beta Kappa, Inst. Medicine. Avocations: jogging, fiction writing. Office: Ohio State U Coll Medicine Dept Psychiatry 1670 Upham Dr Columbus OH 43210

KIEFFER, BRIGITTE, neuroscientist, PhD in chemistry and biochemistry, U. Strasbourg, postdoctoral fellow, Friedrich Miescher Inst. Prof. dept. neurobiology Inst. Genetics, Molecular and Celluar Biology, U. Strasbourg, France. Recipient Richard Lounsbery award, NAS (USA), 2004. Achievements include expert in molecular neurobiology of opioid-controlled behavior. Office: Inst de Genetique et de Biologie Moleculaire et Cellulaire Univ Strasbourg BP 10142 67404 Illkirch France Business E-Mail: briki@igbmc.u-strasbg.fr

KIENSTRA, KATHLEEN O., radiation therapist professor, program director; d. Johannes Daniel and Anneliese Elisabeth Oelke; m. Mark Joseph Kienstra, Aug. 17, 1985; children: Stefanie Kathleen, Therese Elizabeth, Christopher Mark. MA in Tcgh., Webster U., St. Louis, 2000. Cert. in radiologic tech. Am. Registry Radiologic Tech., 1980, in radiation therapy Am. Registry Radiologic Tech., 1981. Radiation therapy program dir. Barnes Jewish Hosp. Nursing & Allied Health, St. Louis, 1990—2007, St. Louis U., 2007—. Bd. dir. Lindbergh Sch. Dist., St. Louis, 2008—. Mem.: Chgo. Area Radiation Therapists, Mo. Soc. Radiologic Technologists, Assn. Educators Imaging & Radiologic Scis., Am. Soc. Radiologic Technologists, Lambda Nu Honor Soc. (sec. 2005—08). Office: Saint Louis Univ 3437 Caroline St Saint Louis MO 63104 Personal E-mail: kkienstra@gmail.com. Business E-Mail: kkienst1@slu.edu.

KIENY, MARIE-PAULE, international organization administrator; b. France; PhD, U. Montpelier, 1980, diploma in economics; diploma, U. Strasbourg, 1995. Asst. sci. dir. Transgene S.A., France, 1981—88; dir. rsch., head of hepatitis C virus molecular virology group INSERM Inst. Virology, France, 1999—2000; joined spl. program for rsch. & tng. in tropical diseases WHO, Geneva, 2001, dir. initiative for vaccine rsch., 2001—10, asst. dir.-gen. innovation, info. evidence and rsch., 2010—. Contbr. articles to profl. jours. Decorated Prix de l'Innovation Rhône-Poulenc, Prix Génération 2000-Impact Médecin, Chevalier de l'Ordre Nat. du Mérite, au titre du Ministère de la Recherche. Office: WHO avenue Appia 20 1211 Geneva Switzerland *

KIER, ANN B., pathology educator; b. Littlefield, Tex., June 26, 1949; d. Robert Merlin and Martha (Bond) Yarbrough; m. Friedhelm Schroeder, Dec. 9, 1978; 1 child, Hilary. BA, U. Tex., 1971; BS, Tex. A&M U., 1973, DVM, 1974; PhD, U. Mo., 1979. Diplomate, Am. Coll. Lab. Animal Medicine. NIH fellow U. Mo., Columbia, 1976-79, asst. prof., 1979-84, assoc. prof., 1984-87; assoc. prof. dept. pathology U. Cin. Med. Sch., 1987-91, prof., dir. divsn. comparative pathology, dept. pathology, 1991-93; prof., head dept. pathobiology Tex. A&M U., College Station, 1994—2005. Cons. NIH, Washington, 1983—, Comparative Pathology, Frann Sci., Cin., 1987—. Contbr. articles to profl. jours. NIH grantee, 1980—. Mem. AAAS, Am. Assn. Pathologists. Avocations: scuba diving, reading. Home: Tex A & M University PO Box 500 Wellborn TX 77881-0500 Office: Tex A&M Univ Dept Pathobiology College Station TX 77843-0001 Office Phone: 979-862-1509. Business E-Mail: akier@cvm.tamu.edu.

KIERAN, MARK W., pediatric oncologist; PhD, U. Alberta, Canada, 1983; MD, U. Calgary, 1986. Resident Montreal Children's Hosp., 1989—92; fellow Boston Children's Hosp., 1991—95, instr. pediatrics; asst. prof. dept. pediatrics Harvard Med. Sch., 2008; dir. pediatric med. neuro-oncology Dana-Farbar Cancer Inst. Office: Dana-Farber Cancer Institute 44 Binney St SW Rm 331 Boston MA 02115 Office Phone: 617-632-4907. Office Fax: 617-632-4897. Business E-Mail: mark_kieran@dfci.harvard.edu.

KIESMANN, MICHELE, neurologist; b. Paris, Apr. 15, 1955; D, U. Strasbourg, Alsace, France, 1986. Sr. registrars Faculty Medicine Strasbourg, 1986; neurologist Pole Geriat., 1988; physician U. Hosp. Strasbourg, 1990—. Courses in charge U. Strasbourg, 1990. Mem.: Movement Disorders Soc., Soc. Française Gériatrie et Gérontologie, Soc. Française Neurology. Avocations: skiing, painting. Office: 83 rue Himmerich Strasbourg Alsace 67091 France Business E-Mail: michele.kiesmann@chru-strasbourg.fr.

KIKAWADA, MASAYUKI, respiratory medicine physician; b. Nakano-ku, Japan, Nov. 29, 1963; s. Takashi and Mutsuko Kikawada; m. Naoko Yoshida, June 12, 1994; children: Shoko, Tomoyuki, Mako. MD, Tokyo Med. U., 1993, PhD in Immunology, 1999. Lic. physician Japanese Ministry of Health and Welfare. Resident in internal medicine Tokyo Med. U., Shinjuku-ku, Japan, 1993—95, fellow in respiratory medicine, 1995—98, fellow in geriat. medicine, 1998—2000, attending physician in geriat. medicine, 2000—04, instr. geriat. medicine, 2004—. Indsl. physician CSK Corp., Shibuya-ku, Japan, 2000—04; asst. prof. Clin.-Welfare Coll., Nerima-ku, Japan, 2003—, Ryogoku Rehab. Coll., Sumida-ku, Japan, 2003—. Contbr. articles to profl. jours. Fellow: ACP, Japanese Respiratory Soc., Japan Soc. Respiratory Endoscopy, Japanese Soc. Internal Medicine, Japan Geriat. Soc.; mem.: Japanese Assn. Infectious Disease, Japan Lung Cancer Soc., Asian Pacific Soc. Respirology. Avocations: golf, swimming. Office: Tokyo Med U 6-7-1 Nishishinjuku Shinjuku 160-0023 Japan Office Fax: 81-3-33422305. Business E-Mail: kikawada@tokyo-med.ac.jp.

KIKUCHI, MOTOO, physician; b. Mishima City, Shizuoka, Japan, July 12, 1961; s. Itsuo Kikuchi, Tazuko Kikuchi; m. Rika Murakami, Aug. 10, 1997; children: Gen, Yuka. MD, Nagoya U., Japan, 1990. Diplomate in internal medicine Japan. Resident Nagoya City U. Hosp., Aichi, 1991—92; physician Shizuoka Saiseikai Gen. Hosp., Shizuoka City, Shizuoka, Japan, 1993. Contbr. articles to profl. jours. Office: Fujita Health Univ Nanakuri Sanatorium 424-1 Otori Tsu 514-1295 Japan Home Phone: +81-52-806-3046; Office Phone: 81-59-252-1555. Office Fax: 81-59-252-1383. Business E-Mail: mtkikuchi-u@umin.ac.jp.

KIKUCHI, SHINICHI, orthopedist; b. Fukushima, Dec. 15, 1946; MD, Fukushima Med. U., 1971, PhD, 1983. Prof. & chmn., orthopaedic dept. Fukushima Med. U., 1990—2007, pres., 2007—. Pres. Internat. Soc. Study Lumbar Spine, 2005—06, Japanese Soc. Spine Surgery & Related Rsch., 2006. Recipient award, Volvo, ISSLS. Avocations: antiques, travel. Office: Fukushima Med University 1 Hikarigaoka Fukushima 960-1295 Japan Home Phone: 03-6450-1093; Office Phone: 81-24-547-1000. Office Fax: 81-24-547-1010. Business E-Mail: sinichk@db3.so-net.ne.jp.

KIKUCHI, SHIRO, oncologist, surgeon, educator; b. Kawasaki, Japan, Mar. 25, 1957; s. Junichiro and Miyako Kikuchi; m. Rie Furuhashi, Aug. 6, 1988; children: Yuichiro, Maria. MD, Kitasato U., Japan, 1981. Resident Kitasato U. Hosp., Sagamihara, Japan, 1981—83, Nat. Cancer Ctr., Tsukiji, Japan, 1983—86; fellow Kitasato U., 1986—87; fellow dept. surgery Moabit Hosp., Berlin, 1988—90; chief surgery Izu-shimoda Hosp., Shimoda, Japan, 1991—94; asst. prof. Kitasato U., 1995—; vice dir. Kitasato U. East Hosp., 2006—, assoc. prof., 2007—, dir., 2009—, prof. surgery, 2010—. Contbr. articles to profl. jours. Grantee, Cancer Rsch. Soc. Berlin, 1989, Japan Ministry of Edn., 1997. Mem.: Internat. Soc. Surg. Found., Internat. Assn. Surgeons & Gastroenterologists, Japan Soc. Surgery. Roman Catholic. Avocations: fishing, travel. Office: Kitasato University East Hospital 2-1-1 Asamizodai Minami Sagamihara Kanagawa 252-0380 Japan Office Phone: 81-427-48-9111. Fax: 427-45-5582.

KILEY, THOMAS, rehabilitation counselor; b. Mpls., Aug. 28, 1937; s. Gerald Sidney and Veronica (Roberts) K.; m. Jane Virginia Butler, Aug. 25, 1989; children: Martin, Truman, Tami, Brian. BA in English, UCLA, 1959; MS in Rehab. Counseling, San Francisco State U., 1989. Cert. rehab counselor. Former rsch. profl., businessman various S.E. Asian cos., U.S. Army; sr. social worker Episcopal Sanctuary, San Francisco, 1986-88; dir. social svcs. Hamilton Family Ctr., San Francisco, 1988-89; rehab. specialist Intracorp, Honolulu, 1989-91; pres. Heritage Counseling Svc., Honolulu, 1991—. Pres. Hunter Employment Svcs., Yuma, Ariz., 1995—, Algo Enterprises, Yuma, 1998—; pres. Hunter Leasing Svc., Yuma, 2006—, Heritage Am., Phoenix, 2011-. Mem. Am. Counseling Assn., Internat. Assn. Rehab. Profls., Am. Rehab. Counselors Assn. (profl.), Nat. Rehab. Assn., Rotary, Phi Delta Kappa. Office: Heritage Counselling Svcs PO Box 5945 Yuma AZ 85366-5945

KILINC, MEHMET OKYAY, medical educator; b. Turkey, Apr. 23, 1970; PhD, Bosphorus U., 2002. Rsch. asst. prof. U. Buffalo, 2006—. DOD grant, Dept. Def., Postdoc. fellowship, James Graham Brown Cancer Ctr. Mem.: Internat. Soc. Biol. Therapy Cancer (mem., Early Career Scientists Com. 2011), Am. Assn. Cancer Rsch., Witebsky Ctr. (assoc.). Home: 216 Robert Dr North Tonawanda NY 14120 E-mail: mokilinc@buffalo.edu.

KILLEBREW, ELLEN JANE (MRS. EDWARD S. GRAVES), cardiologist, educator; b. Tiffin, Ohio, Oct. 8, 1937; d. Joseph Arthur and Stephanie (Berion) K.; m. Edward S. Graves, Sept. 12, 1970. BS in Biology, Bucknell U., Lewisburg, Pa., 1959; MD, NJ Coll. Medicine, 1965. Diplomate in cardiovasc. disease Am. Bd. Internal Medicine. Intern U. Colo., 1965-66, resident, 1966-68; cardiology fellow Pacific Med. Ctr., San Francisco, 1968-70; dir. coronary care Permanente Med. Group, Richmond, Calif., 1970-83; asst. prof. U. Calif. Med. Ctr., San Francisco, 1970-83, assoc. prof., 1983-93; clin. prof. medicine U. Calif., San Francisco, 1992—, mem. admissions panel, 1998—. Admissions panel joint med. program U. Calif. San Francisco/U. Calif. Berkeley, 1998—; expert med. reviewer Calif. Med. Br., 1999, Bd. of Med. Examiners Calif., 1999—. Contbr. chapters to books. Contbr. Resolution Firm Calif. State Assmebly, 2005. Recipient Physician's Recognition award continuing med. edn., Lowell Beal award Permante Med. Group/House Staff Assn., 1992, Commendation State Assembly of Calif. for Contbr to Women and Heart Disease, 2005; Robert C. Kirkwood Meml. scholar in cardiology, 1970. Fellow ACP, Am. Coll. Cardiology; mem. Fedn. Clin. Rsch., Am. Heart Assn. (rsch. chmn. Contra Costa chpt. 1975—, v.p. 1980, pres. chpt. 1981-82, chmn. CPR com. Alameda chpt. 1984, pres. Oakland Piedmont br. 1995—, bd. dirs. western affiliate). Home: 30 Redding Ct Belvedere Tiburon CA 94920-1318 Office: 280 W Macarthur Blvd Oakland CA 94611-5642 also: 901 Nevin Ave Richmond CA 94801-3143 Business E-Mail: ellen.killebrew@kp.org.

KILLINGSWORTH, CLEVE L., JR., retired insurance company executive, board member; b. Chgo., May 5, 1952; BS in Mgmt., Mass. Inst. Tech., 1974; MPH, Yale U., 1976. Sr. mgmt. positions with Blue Cross Blue Shield, Rochester, NY, 1986—94, Kaiser Found. Health Plan, 1994—97, Hosp. of the Univ. of Pa., American Hosp. Assn., Group Health Coop. of Puget Sound; sr. v.p. ins. and managed care Henry Ford Health Sys., 1998—2003, sr. v.p., 2003—04; pres., CEO Health Alliance Plan, 1998—2004; pres., COO Blue Cross Blue Shield Mass., 2004—05, pres., CEO, 2005—10, chmn., 2008—10. Bd. dirs. RGS Energy Group, 1998—, Rochester Gas and Electric, 1999—, The Travelers Co., Inc., 2007—, Nat. Ctr. for Healthcare Leadership, Nat. Inst. for Health Care Mgmt.; dir. Reynolds and Reynolds Co., 1997—2006; trustee Blue Cross Blue Shield of Mass. Found., 2007—10, MITRE Corp., 2008—; lectr. Sch. Medicine and Dentistry Univ. of Rochester Med. Ctr., NY; adj. prof. health svcs. adminstrn., Wharton Sch. of Bus. Univ. of Pa.; faculty mem. Harvard Sch. Pub. Health. Trustee The Mus. of Fine Arts Boston Univ.; bd. overseer Tchr. Ins. and Annuity Assn. of America (TIAA) and Coll. Retirement Equities Fund (CREF), 2007—; founding mem. Exec. Leadership Coun., Washington; trustee Northwood U., 1999—2006, Greater Boston C. of C., 2005—10, Jobs for Mass., 2005—10, Babson Coll., 2006—08, Initiative for a New Economy, 2008—10; bd. mem. Boys and Girls Clubs Boston, Mass. Bus. Roundtable, The United Way Mass. Bay; bd. mem. Carroll Sch. Mgmt. Boston Coll.; bd. fellow Harvard Med. Sch.; bd. dirs. League of Black Women. *

KILMAN, JAMES WILLIAM, surgeon, educator; b. Terre Haute, Ind., Jan. 22, 1931; s. Arthur and Irene (Piker) K.; m. Priscilla Margaret Jackson, June 20, 1968; children: James William, Julia Anne, Jennifer Irene. BS, Ind. State U., 1956; MD, Ind. U., 1960. Intern Ind. U. Med. Ctr., Indpls., 1960-61, resident surgery, 1961-66, asst. prof., 1966-69, assoc. prof., 1969-73; prof. surgery Ohio State U. Coll. Medicine, 1973-91, prof. surgery emeritus, 1991—; chmn. dept. thoracic surgery Children's Hosp., 1975-91; attending surgeon Univ. Hosp., Columbus, Ohio; attending staff Children's Hosp., Columbus, pres. staff, 1978; attending staff Grant Hosp., Riverside Hosp. Cons. surgeon VA Hosp., Dayton; pres. Columbus Acad. Medicine, 1977. Contbr. articles to profl. jours. Trustee Central Ohio Heart Assn., Acad. Medicine Edn. Found., Children's Hosp., 1978—. Served with USNR, 1951-55. USPHS Cardiovascular fellow, 1963-64; recipient Alumni Achievement award, Ind. State U., 1989. Fellow ACS, Am. Coll. Cardiology, Am. Acad. Pediats., Coll. Chest Physicians; mem. Columbus Surg. Soc. (hon., pres. 1974), Columbus Acad. Medicine (coun. 1971-73), Am. Surg. Assn., Soc. Univ. Surgeons, Am. Assn. Thoracic Surgery, Cen. Surg. Assn., Western Surg. Assn., Soc. Vascular Surgery, Internat. Cardiovasc. Soc., Internat. Soc. Surgeons, Chest Club, Cardiovasc. Surgery Club, City Club, Palm Aire Country Club, Faculty Club, Capital Club, Columbus Athletic Club, Pickaway County Country Club, Am. Boxer Club (bd. dirs. 2000-03, pres. 2001-03, AKC del. 2002-05), Pinnacle Club (Grove City, Ohio), Sigma Xi, Alpha Omega Alpha. Achievements include research in infant cardiopulmonary bypass and surgery for congenital heart lesions. Home: 4231 Jackson Pike Grove City OH 43123 Personal E-mail: leoline@aol.com.

KILMER, SUZANNE L., dermatologist, educator; MD, U. Calif., Davis, 1987. Diplomate Am. Bd. Dermatology, 2009. Resident dermatology Univ. Calif. Davis Med. Ctr., Sacramento, 1988—91; asst. clin. prof. dermatology Univ. Calif. Davis, Sacramento, fellow laser surgery Mass. Gen. Hosp., Boston, 1991—92, founding dir. Laser and Skin Surgery Ctr. of Northern Calif.; hosp. affiliation include Mercy Gen. Hosp. Author numerous articles and chapters on cutaneous laser surgery; reviewer (jour.) Laser in Surgery and Medicine, Archives of Dermatology, Dermatologic Surgery and Jour. of Cutaneous Laser Surgery. Recipient Ellet Drake lectureship award. Mem.: Am. Acad. of Dermatology, Am. Soc. for Dermatologic Surgery (bd. dirs.), Am. Soc. for Laser Medicine and Surgery (pres. 2002—03, bd. dirs., laser certification task force, laser safety dir., v.p.). Office: The Laser & Skin Surgery Center 3835 J St Sacramento CA 95816-5520 Office Phone: 916-456-0400.

KILPATRICK, SARAH J., obstetrician, gynecologist, educator; PhD in Biopsychology, U. Chgo.; MD, Tulane U. Sch. Medicine. Cert. obstetrics & gynecology, maternal fetal medicine. Resident & fellow U. Calif., San Francisco; divsn. dir. maternal fetal medicine U. Ill. Med. Ctr.; prof. & head dept. ob-gyn. U. Ill. Chgo. Coll. Medicine, vice dean. Assoc. editor Am. Jour. Obstetrics & Gynecology. Mem.: Am. Coll. Obstetrics & Gynecology (chmn. obstetric practice com.), Am. Bd. Obstetrics & Gynecology (MFM bd. mem.), Soc. Maternal Fetal Medicine (pres. elect). Office: 820 S Wood St M/C 808 Chicago IL 60612 Office Phone: 312-996-7006. Office Fax: 312-996-4238.

KIM, BOK RYANG, biochemist, educator; b. Jeonju, Republic Of Korea, Apr. 19, 1957; s. Byungchan and Hyungrye Kim; m. Kyungmi Cho, Mar. 10, 2008; children: Juyoung, Sohyeon. PhD, Korea Advanced Inst. Sci. and Tech., Seoul, 1990. Instr. Wonkwang U., Iksan, Cheonbuk, Republic of Korea, 1986—90, asst. prof., 1990—94, assoc. prof., 1994—99, prof., 1998—. Rsch. assoc. Vanderbilt U., Nashville, Rutgers U., Piscataway, NJ, 2001—03; gen. sec. Korean Soc. Free Radical, Iksan, 2005—07. Home: Lucky-Wooa 2-1304 Wooadong Jeonju Cheonbuk 561-771 Republic of Korea Office: Wonkwang Univ Dept Biochemistry 344-2 Shinyongdong 570-749 Iksan Jeollabuk-do Republic of Korea Office Fax: 82-63-841-1616. Personal E-mail: blue0310410@hotmail.com. Business E-Mail: bokim@wonkwang.ac.kr.

KIM, BONG-HYUN, ophthalmologist; b. Seoul, Republic of Korea, May 17, 1967; s. Kyung-Gu Kim and Min-Ja Heo; m. Young-Ah Oh, Apr. 3, 1993; children: Won-Jun, Won-Jae. BA, MD, Chung-Ang U., Seoul, 1991, PhD, 2003. Lic. Ministry Health Welfare, Republic of Korea, 1991, Korean Bd. Ophthal. Ministry Health Welfare, 1996. Internship Chung-Ang U. Hosp., Seoul, 1991—92, residency, 1992—96; dir. ophthal. St. Columban's Hosp., Mokpo, Republic of Korea, 1996—99; pres. HenAm Kim Eye Ctr., Haenam, Republic of Korea, 1999—2007; fellow Mass. Eye Ear Infirmary Harvard Med.

Sch., Boston, 2004—05; pres. Seer & Ptnr. Eye Inst., Seoul, 2007—. Contbr. articles to profl. jours. Mem.: European Soc. Cataract Refractive Surgery (assoc.), Korean Soc. Cataract Refractive Surgery (assoc.), Korean Med. Assn. (assoc.), Am. Soc. Cataract Refractive Surgery (assoc.), Am. Acad. Ophthal. (assoc.). Achievements include patents pending in field. Avocations: exercise, films. Office: Henam Kim Eye Ctr 1103-4 Hae-Ri Haenam Eup Haenam Jeon-Nam Republic of Korea Office Fax: 82-2-511-0571. Business E-Mail: nunsusul@yahoo.co.kr.

KIM, BYUNG GON, medical educator; b. Seoul, Republic of Korea, Dec. 27, 1968; s. Chang K. and Hee J. (Choi) Kim; m. Hyang Woon Lee, July 12, 1997; 1 child, Hyun Woo. MD, Seoul Nat. U., 1993; PhD, Georgetown U., Washington, 2005. Diplomate Korean Bd. Neurology, lic. physician Korea. Resident in adult neurology Seoul Nat. U. Hosp., 1994—98; sci. rev. adminstr. Heath Sci. Tech. Planning and Evaluation Bd., Seoul, 1998—2001; asst. prof. Brain Disease Rsch. Ctr., Ajou U. Sch. Medicine, Suwon, Kyunggi, Republic of Korea, 2005—. Med. care provider Rafael Clinic for Fgn. Workers, Seoul, Republic of Korea, 1998—2000. Capt., 1998, Korean Army. Scholar, Georgetown U. Grad. Sch. Art and Sciences, 2001. Mem.: Soc. for Neurosci. Achievements include research in regeneration and plasticity in spinal cord injury. Office: Ajou Univ Sch Medicine San 5 Wonchon-Dong Yeongtong-Gu Kyunggi Province Suwon 443-721 Republic of Korea Office Fax: 82-31-216-6381. Business E-Mail: kimbg@ajou.ac.kr.

KIM, BYUNG GUK, otolaryngologist, educator; b. Seoul, Republic of Korea, July 13, 1966; PhD, Cath. U. Korea, 1991. Dir., dept. otorhinolaryngology-HNS St. Paul's Hosp., 2007—11; assoc. prof. Cath. U. Korea, 2007—. Fellow: Korean Rhinology Soc.; mem.: Internat. Rhinology Soc., Korean Otolaryngology Soc. Office: 620-56 Jeonnong-dong Dongdaemun-gu Seoul 130-709 Republic of Korea Business E-Mail: coolkim@chol.ac.com.

KIM, BYUNG-OCK, dentist, educator; b. Gwangju, Aug. 1, 1959; married; 2 children. PhD in Dentistry, Sch. Dentristry Kyunghee U., Seoul, Republic of Korea, 1993. Lic. dentist Ministry Health Welfare, Republic of Korea, 1984. Dentist Chosun U. Dental Hosp., Gwangju, Republic of Korea, 1984, resident, 1985—87, instr., 1990—93, chmn. dept. periodontics, 1984—2007, dir. clin. dept., 1998—2007; prof. Chosun U. Coll. Dentistry, 2006—07, dean, 2007—. Contbr. articles to profl. jours. Capt. Korean Army, 1987—90. Recipient New Rschr. award, Korean Acad. Periodontology, 1993. Mem.: Internat. Assn. Dental Rsch., Am. Acad. Periodontology. Baha'I. Achievements include invention of guided bone regeneration technique, ultrasound in periodontology, oxygen free radicals. Avocations: golf, movies, writing. Home: 102-504 Hankok Adeitum Gwangu Sotaedong Dong-gu 501-828 Republic of Korea Office: Chosun Univ Sch Dentistry Seosukdong 421 501-825 Donggu Gwangju Gwangju Republic of Korea Home Fax: 82622244664. Personal E-mail: bobkim@chosun.ac.kr.

KIM, CHANG-JU, medical educator, researcher; b. Daegu, Republic of Korea, Mar. 16, 1958; s. Young-Ju Lim; m. Chang-Ju Kim, Oct. 20, 1985; children: You-Jung, Sang-Hoon. MD, Kyung Hee U., Coll. Medicine, Seoul, Republic of Korea, PhD, 1990. Cert. prof. Kyung Hee U, Coll. Medicine, 2004. Rschr. coll. medicine Kyung Hee U., 1984—, assoc. prof. coll. medicine, 1999—2004, prof., 2004—. Contbr. articles to jour. Maj. Air Force Korean Army, 1991—94, Suwon. Achievements include research in. Office: Dept Physiology Coll Medicine Kyung Hee Univ Hoegi-dong Dongdaemungu Seoul 130-701 Republic of Korea Office Phone: 82-2-961-0407. Office Fax: 82-2-964-2195. Business E-Mail: changju@khu.ac.kr.

KIM, CHANG-SIK, ophthalmologist, educator; b. Daejon, Republic of Korea, Nov. 27, 1961; s. Eun-duk Lee Kim; m. Haeran Lee Kim, Oct. 1, 1986; children: Hyung-jun, Si-yun. MD, Chungnam Nat. U., Daejon, 1986. MD Korean Ministry Health and Welfare, 1986. Instr. Chungnam Nat. U. Coll. Medicine, Daejon, 1996—98, asst. prof., 1998—2002, assoc. prof., 2002—. Clin. fellow dept. ophthalmology Yamanashi U. Hosp., Kofu, Japan, 1997—97; rsch. fellow glaucoma svc. dept. ophthalmology U. Iowa Hosps. and Clinics, Iowa City, 1999—2000. Contbr. articles to profl. jours. Shaffer Internat. Rsch. fellow, Glaucoma Rsch. Found., 1999—2000. Mem.: Assn. for Rsch. in Vision and Ophthalmology, Korean Glaucoma Soc., Korean Ophthal. Soc. (mem. editl. bd. 2002—), Korean Med. Soc. Achievements include patents for an intraocular lens for cataract operation; a fluid drainage device for treating glaucoma. Office: Ophthalmology Chungnam Univ Hosp Daesa-Dong Jung-Ku 640 301-721 Daejeon Daejeon Republic of Korea Office Fax: 82-42-255-3745. Business E-Mail: kcs61@cnu.ac.kr.

KIM, CHAN-HYUNG, psychiatrist, educator; b. Seoul, Republic Of Korea, Mar. 10, 1961; m. Ji-Yong Jeon; 1 child, Jae-Won. MD, Yonsei U., Seoul, 1986. Cert. psychiatrist Korean Health Ministry, Seoul, 1990. Prof. Yonsei U. Coll. Medicine, 2003. Contbr. scientific papers. Recipient Best Prof. award, 2005. Office: Severance Mental Hosp 696-6 Tanbul-dong Gyeonggi-si Gyeonggi-do 464-100 Republic of Korea Office Fax: 82-31-764-8662. E-mail: spr88@yuhs.ac.

KIM, CHANWOONG, emergency physician; b. Kwangju, Jan. 13, 1972; MD, Chungang U., 1996. Assoc. prof. Chungang U., Med. Coll., 2005; gen. sec. Korean Soc. Health Communication, 2009—11, Korean Soc. Simulation Healthcare, 2009—. Faculty mem. Advanced Cardiac Life Support Korean Assn. Cardiopulmonary Resuscitation, 2011—; chief editor Jour. Korean Soc. Simulation Healthcare, 2011—. Mem.: Korean Soc. Traumatology, Korean Soc. Critical Care Medicine, Korean Soc. Emergency Medicine. Home: 224-1 Heukseok-Dong Dongjak-Gu Seoul 156-755 Republic of Korea Business E-Mail: whenever@cau.ac.kr.

KIM, CHARLES WESLEY, microbiology educator; b. Nashville, Mar. 20, 1926; s. Herbert Hyungsik and Kyung Sook Kim; m. Soo Johung, June 9, 1956; 1 child, Charles W. Jr. BA, U. Calif., Berkeley, 1949; MS in Pub. Health, U. NC, 1952, PhD in Parasitology and Microbiology, 1956. Instr., asst. prof. NY Med. Coll., NYC, 1956-59, 59-64; assoc. scientist, scientist Brookhaven Nat. Lab., Upton, NY, 1965-68, 68-70; assoc. dean basic health sci. SUNY, Stony Brook, 1972-74, assoc. vice provost, 1974-83, assoc. prof., 1970-87, prof. microbiology and medicine, 1987—, prof. emeritus, 1996—. Author: Microbiology Review, 1962, 11th edit., 1995; editor: Trichinellosis, 1974, 4th edit., 1985; editl. bd. Exptl. Parasitology, 1984—; reviewer Am. Jour. Tropical Medicine and Hygiene, 1990-93. Moderator N.E. Synod Presbyn. Ch., 1997—98; bd. dirs. Mountain Retreat Assn., 2000—03; mem. gen. assembly coun. Presbyn. Ch. (USA), 2000—04, mem. exec. com. gen. assembly coun., 2003—04, chair worldwide ministries com., 2003—04; bd. govs. Friends of Sunwood, Stony Brook, 1973—85, Suffolk Symphonnic Soc., Suffolk County, NY, 1975—77; mem. devel. com. Mus. Stony Brook, 1983—85; bd. govs. L.I. Coun. Chs., 1999—2003; mem. gov. bd. Three Village Hist. Soc., 2000—01; trustee Med. Benevolence Found., 2005—08. Tropical medicine fellow La. State U. Sch. Medicine, 1958, USPHS fellow Argonne Nat. Lab., U. Chgo., 1964-65, Royal Soc. Tropical Medicine and Hygiene fellow, London, 1975. Mem. Internat. Commn. Trichinellosis (pres. 1988-93), Am. Soc. Parasitologists (chmn. nominating com. 1987), Am. Soc. Tropical Medicine and Hygiene, NY Soc. Tropical Medicine (pres. 1985-86), Sigma Xi (chpt. pres. 1993-94), Delta Omega.

KIM, CHONG SOON, nuclear medicine physician, researcher; b. Seoul, Republic of Korea, Feb. 23, 1953; s. Yung Gon Kim and Wha Soon Jin; m. Eun Hee Han, May 1, 1981; children: Jung Soo, Ye Sul. MD, Seoul Nat. U., 1977, MS, 1980, PhD, 1987. Diplomate Korean Bd. Nuc. Medicine, Korean Bd. Internal Medicine. Intern Hanil Hosp., Seoul, Republic of Korea, 1977—78, resident in internal medicine, 1978—82, chief, dept. nuc. medicine & internal medicine, 1989—2007; chief dept. nuc. medicine Nat. Med. Ctr., Seoul, 1985—89; vis. scholar MD Anderson Cancer Ctr., Tex., 1988—89, Kyoto U. Hosp., Japan, 1994, Rsch. Ctr. Julich, Germany, 1994; dir., Korea Electric Power Corp. Radiation Health Rsch. Inst., Seoul, 1999—2001, dir., Korea Hydro & Nuc. Power, 2001—07; pres. Korea Inst. Radiol. and Med. Scis., Seoul, 2007—. Invited prof. Seoul Nat. U., 1998—; adj. prof. Cath. U., Seoul, 2005—, Korean U. Sci. & Tech., Seoul, 2007—; pres. Korea Inst. Radiol. and Med. Scis., Seoul, 2007—. Contbr. articles to profl. jours. Med. svc. for homeless Seoul City Sta., 2003—04; med. svc. for country side Around Power Plant, 2004—05. Capt., 1982—85, Korean mil. Recipient Disting. Svc. award, Ministry Sci. and Tech., 2001, Korea Hydro & Nuc. Power Co., 2002. Mem.: Korea Nuclear Internat. Coop. Found. (trustee 2007—), Korean Thyroid Soc. (chmn. bd. trustees 2008), Korean Assn. Radiation Rsch., Asia Assn. Radiation Rsch. (cong. com. chair 2005—, v.p. 2006—, coun. mem., sec. gen.), Asian Oceania Assn. Radiation Protection (sec. gen. 2006), Korean Assn. Radiation Protection (v.p. 2006), Korean Soc. Internal Medicine, Korea Nuc. Soc. (coun. mem. 2005), Korean Assn. Radiation Biosciences, Korea Radioisotope Assn. (trustee 2004—), Korean Soc. Nuc. Medicine (Disting. Svc. award 1997), World Fedn. Nuc. Medicine and Biology (sec. gen. 9th World Congress), Internat. Assn. Radiopathology (trustee 2006—). Achievements include patents in field. Avocations: badminton, movies, travel, mountain climbing. Home: Bldg #33-1304 Hyandar Apt Ogum-dong Songpa Gu Seoul 138-130 Republic of Korea Office Phone: 82-2-970-2000. Business E-Mail: kjsoon@kirams.re.kr.

KIM, CHONG-RAK, engineering educator, professional society administrator; b. Seoul, Republic of Korea, Oct. 31, 1954; s. Kyo-young and Chong-suk (Choi) Kim; m. Hee-ok Ha, Apr. 22, 1987; children: Ji-young, Ji-eun. PhD, Seoul Nat. U., 1991. Chmn. U. Coun. Inje U., Kimhae, Republic of Korea, 1987—89, dean rsch. affairs, 1993—95; dean Coll. Biomed. Sci. and Engring., Kimhae, 1999—2001; dir. biomed. engring. devel. project Ministry Edn., Kimhae, 1999—2001; pres. Korean Soc. Biomed. Lab. Scis., Seoul, 2004—. Vis. scientist in cardiology U. Conn. Health Ctr., Farmington, Conn., 1992—93; vis. scientist in cell biology Duke U. Med. Ctr., Durham, NC, 2002—03; ad hoc reviewer Korea Sci. and Engring. Found., Daejeon, Republic of Korea, 2004—, Korea Health Industry Devel. Inst., Seoul, 2004—; com. mem. Korea Bio-IT Foundry Ctr., Busan, Republic of Korea, 2004—, 27th World Congress Biomed. Lab. Sci., Seoul, 2006. Chmn. Cath. Lay Apostolate Coun. Korea, Busan, 2004—; mem. adv. bd. Gyeongnam Provincial Police Agy., Changwon, Republic of Korea, 2000—. Named Prof. of Excellence, Inje U., 2003. Mem.: Korean Soc. Molecular and Cell Biology, Korean Soc. Biochemistry and Molecular Biology, Korean Assn. Biol. Scis. Avocation: travel. Office: Inje U Obang-Dong 607 621-749 Kimhae Gyeongsangnam-do Republic of Korea Office Fax: +82-55-334-3426. Business E-Mail: bioxgeny@inje.ac.kr.

KIM, CHONG-SUNG, anesthesiologist, director; b. Jinhae, Republic of Korea, Oct. 7, 1952; s. In-Kyu and Jin-Kie Kim; m. Sung-Youb Choi, Feb. 2, 1977; children: Jungsun, Junghyun. MD, Seoul Nat. U., 1977, MS, 1986, PhD, 1989. Cert. bd. anesthesiology Ministry Health & Social Affairs, 1984. Prof. Seoul Nat. U., Coll. Medicine, Republic of Korea, 1999—; chmn. dept. anesthesiology Seoul Nat. U., Republic of Korea, 2004—07; dir. children's hosp. Seoul Nat. U. Hosp., Republic of Korea, 2007—10. Editl. bd. Korean Soc. Anesthesiologists, Seoul, Republic of Korea, 2000—02, pres., 2006—08, Korean Soc. Pediatric Anesthesia, Seoul, Republic of Korea, 2000—06. Editor (co-editor): (textbook) Pediatric Respiratory Care; contbr. chapters to books. Capt. US Army, 1977—80. Recipient Academic awards, Korean Soc. Anesthesiologists, 1994. Mem.: Nat. Acad. Medicine Korea. Home: Gangdong-ku Seoungnae-dong 447-18 Seoul 134-885 Republic of Korea Office: Seoul Nat Univ Children's Hosp 101 Daehang-no Jongno-gu Seoul 110-744 Republic of Korea Office Fax: 82-2-745-5587; Home Fax: 82-2-474-8112. Business E-Mail: kimcs@snu.ac.kr.

KIM, CHUN-BAE, medical educator; b. Seoul, Republic of Korea, Mar. 24, 1962; MD, Chung-Ang U., Republic of Korea, 1987; PhD, Yonsei U., Republic of Korea, 1996. Resident Dept. Preventive Medicine & Pub. Health, Coll. Medicine, Yonsei U., 1988—91, rsch. instr., 1994—96; instr. Dept. Preventive Medicine, Wonju Coll. Medicine, Yonsei U., 1996—97, asst. prof., 1997—2002, assoc. prof., 2002—07, prof., 2007—, chief dir. prof., 2008—. Intern Cheonggu Gen. Hosp., 1987—88; army surgeon Korean Army, 1991—94; vis. prof. Clin. Outcomes Rsch. Ctr., Sch. Pub. Health, U. Minn., 2003—05; mem. Vaccine Internat. Congress. Recipient Merit award, First China-Japan-Korea Joint Symposium Med. Informatics, 1999, Excellent Achievements Prof. Commendation award, Pres. Yonsei U., 2000, Dean Wonju Coll. Medicine, Yonsei U., 2010, Excellent Achievements Rsch. Investigator award, Korea Health Industry Devel. Inst., 2001. Mem.: Acad. Health, Korea Soc. Health Policy and Adminstrn., Korean Soc. Preventive Medicine, Korean Med. Assn. Avocations: hiking, movies, travel. Office: 162 Ilsan-Dong Wonju Kangwon 220-701 Republic of Korea Office Fax: 82-33-747-0409. Business E-Mail: kimcb@yonsei.ac.kr.

KIM, DAE-HYUN, medical educator; b. Busan, Republic of Korea, July 19, 1969; B, Dong-A U., 1995; PhD, Chungnam Nat. U., 2006. Stroke fellowship Samsung Med. Ctr., 2003—04; clin. asst. prof. Ulsan U. Hosp., 2004—05; asst. prof. Chungnam Nat. U. Coll. Medicine, 2005—09, Dong-A Coll. Medicine, 2009—. Mem.: World Stroke Congress. Office: 1 3-Ga Dongdaesin-dong Seo-gu Busan 602-715 Republic of Korea Personal E-mail: kdh6542@hanmail.net.

KIM, DAMIAN BYUNGSUK, psychiatrist, consultant, counselor, writer; b. Seoul, Korea, Mar. 15, 1934; arrived in U.S., 1964; s. Bong-Ju Kim and Sang-Im Park; children: Steven Namgi, Jeanhee, Andrew Wonki. MD, Seoul Nat. Univ., Seoul, Korea, 1959. Diplomate psychiatry Am. Bd. Psychiatry, cert. psychoanalyst Am. Inst. for Psychoanalysis. Chief alcoholism treatment program Coney Island Hosp., Bklyn., 1978—82, dir. psychiatic outpatient divsn., 1982—, assoc. chmn., 1986—. Asst. clin. prof. SUNY Med. Sch., Bklyn., 1979—; faculty Am. Inst. for Psychoanalysis, NYC, 1982—97. Author: I Still Want to Live (in Korea), 2000, The Road to American Dreams, 2002; editor: (anthology of poems) Mother & Dove. Pres. Soc. for Korean Studies at Stony Brook, NY, 1994; founder, pres. Inst. for Korean Am. Culture, 1996—; chmn. bd. dirs. Assn. for Trad. Korean Performing Arts, NY, 1986—96. Capt. medicine Korean Air Force, 1959—64, Korea. Named Outstanding Korean -Am., Whomki Kim Found., 1993, Assn. of Korea, 1994. Fellow: Am. Acad. of Psychoanlyas; mem.: Am. Soc. of Clin. Hypnosis, Am. Psychiatry Assn. (life). Buddhist. Avocations: golf, yoga, meditation, writing. Office Phone: 718-460-5190.

KIM, DO KYUNG, science educator; b. Gwangju, Republic of Korea, Mar. 6, 1967; s. Sung Hwan Kim and Jung Sook Choi; m. Kyung Jin Park, Apr. 20, 1968; children: Hyung Chul, Chae Won. BS, Chosun U., Gwangju City, Republic of Korea, 1989, MS, 1990—92, PhD, 1996. Post doctoral rschr. Toho U., Tokyo, 1997—97, Wonkwang U., Iksan City, Republic of Korea, 1998, Kyorin U., Tokyo, 1999—2002; instr. Chosun U., Gwangju, Republic of Korea, 2002—03, asst. prof., 2004—. Recipient Young Investigator award, Asian Soc. Toxicology, 2000, Japanese Soc. Molecular Nephrology, 2001. Office: Chosun Univ 375 Seosuk-dong Dong-gu Gwangju 501-759 Republic of Korea Home: 101-1506 Woosung Apt Moonheung-Dong 500-110 Gwangju Republic of Korea E-mail: kdk@chosun.ac.kr.

KIM, DOHERN, surgeon, educator; b. Donghae City, Oct. 3, 1970; MS, Hallym U., 2004. Asst. prof. dept. surgery Burn Ctr., Hangang Sacred Heart Hosp., 2005. Mem.: Korean Surg. Soc., Korean Burn Soc. Avocation: golf. Office: 94-200 Youngdeungpo-dong Seoul Youngdeungpo 150-719 Republic of Korea Business E-Mail: dohern@hallym.ac.kr.

KIM, DONG CHUNG, biochemistry professor; b. Jeju, Republic of Korea, Dec. 4, 1967; PhD, Seoul Nat. U., 2003. Asst. prof. Suncheon First Coll., 2000—07; vis. rschr. U. Cambridge, 2006—07; rsch. assoc. prof. Sungkyunkwan U., 2007—09; asst. prof. Chungwoon U., 2009—. Subcom. chmn. Korean Soc. Ginseng, 2007—; editl. bd. Korean Soc. Biotechnology and Bioengineering, 2011—. Recipient award, Chungwoon U., Small and Medium Bus. Adminstrn. Mem.: Korean Soc. Applied Biol. Chemistry, Korean Soc. Ginseng. Avocation: travel. Office: San 29 Namjang-ri Hongseong Chungnam 350-701 Republic of Korea Office Fax: 82-41-634-8740.

KIM, DONG IK, surgeon, educator; b. Jeju, Korea, Dec. 12, 1959; s. Ki Su and Seo Bae Kim; m. Sung Hee Park, Mar. 20, 1988; children: Mu-Kun, Mu-Jun. BSc, Hanyang U., Seoul, 1980, MD, 1984, MS, 1988, PhD, 1996. Diplomate Nat. Bd. Medicine of Korea, Korean Bd. Surgery. Rotating intern Hanyang Univ. Hosp., Seoul, 1984-85, asst. resident, 1988-91, chief resident, 1991-92; fellow Osaka (Japan) Univ. Hosp., 1992-94; staff surgeon Samsung Med. Ctr., Seoul, 1994—; prof. surgery Sungkyunkwan U., Seoul, 1995—; dir. divsn. vascular surgery Samsung Med. Ctr., 1999—. Mem. bd. Korean Soc. Vascular Surgery; editor-in-chief Internat. Jour. Stem Cells, 2008, v.p., Asian Venous Forum. Author: Diabetic Foot, 2006, Vascular Sugery, 2006, Phlebology, 2007, Carotid Artery Disease, 2011; editor: Internat. Jour. Angiology, Jour. Lymphology & Oncology, Annals Vascular Diseases, Jour. Korean Med. Sci. Nat. del. Korean Soc. Phlebology; Capt. Korean Army, 1985-88. Recipient Investigators award Samsung Med. Ctr., 1997, Korean Surg. Soc., 1997, Investigator award Korean Soc. for Vasc. Surgery, 2000, 02, IUA, 2001. Fellow: ACS, Internat. Coll. Angiology; mem.: Internat. Union of Angiology, European Soc. for Vascular Surgery. Avocation: golf. Office: Samsung Med Ctr/Vasc Surg 50 Irwon-Dong Kangnam-ku 135-710 Seoul Republic of Korea Business E-Mail: dikim@smc.samsung.co.kr.

KIM, DONG WOO, research scientist; b. Pusan, Republic of Korea, Feb. 25, 1969; PhD, Pukyong Nat. U., 1999. Rsch. chief Natural F&P, 2002—. Avocations: skiing, golf. Office: Munjeong-Dong 99-5 Natural B/D Seoul Songpa-Gu 138-200 Republic of Korea Office Fax: 82-2-400-4419. Business E-Mail: drkimdw@daum.net.

KIM, DONG-HYUN, pharmacist, educator; b. Cheju, Republic of Korea, Nov. 17, 1956; m. Joo Han Han. PhD, Toyama Med. and Pharm. U., Japan, 1987. Cert. in pharmacy Republic of Korea, 1979, academic diploma Korean Soc. Ginseng, 2003. Dean Kyung U., Coll. Pharmacy, Seoul, Republic of Korea, 2003—05; v.p. Korean Soc. Ginseng, Seoul, 2006—. Contbr. scientific papers to profl. jours. With edn., rsch. KFDA, Seoul, 1995—2008. Recipient Excellent Rsch. award, Pharm. Soc. Korea, 1998. Fellow: Korean Soc. Sci. and Tech. Office: Kyung Hee University Hoegi Dongdaemun-gu Seoul 130-701 Republic of Korea Office Fax: 82-2-957-5030. Business E-Mail: dhkim@khu.ac.kr.

KIM, DONG-JUN, orthopedist, educator; b. Busan, Republic of Korea, Sept. 20, 1959; MD, Yonsei U., 1985, PhD, 1998. Prof. Ewha Womans U. Hosp., 1993—. Mem.: Korean Orthop. Assn., Korean Soc. Spine Surgery (exec. sec. 2008—, Hyangsan award, Medtronic Travelling fellowship), North Am. Spine Soc. Avocations: mountain climbing, skiing. Office: 911-1 Mok Dong Yangcheon Ku Seoul 158-710 Republic of Korea Business E-Mail: djkim@ewha.ac.kr.

KIM, DOO-KWUN, medical educator; b. Hadong, Gyeongnam, Republic of Korea, Dec. 11, 1961; MD, Inje U. Coll. Medicine, 1987; PhD, Dong-A U. Coll. Medicine, 1999. Chmn., dept. pediat. Dongguk U. Hosp., 2006—07; prof. Dongguk U. Coll. Medicine, 2005—. Bd. mem. Korean Pediatric Neurology Assn., 2009—11. Project grant, Dongguk U. Med. Inst. Mem.: Asian and Oceanian Congress Child Neurology, Korean Epilepsy Soc., Korean Pediat. Assn., Korean

Pediatric Neurology Assn., Korean Med. Assn. Avocations: rock climbing, golf, swimming. Office: 1090-1 Sukjang-Dong Dept of Peidatrics Gyeongju Gyeongbuk 780-350 Republic of Korea Office Fax: 82-770-8378. Business E-Mail: pedepi@medimail.co.kr.

KIM, DUCKSOO, radiologist, inventor, educator; b. Seoul, Korea, Aug. 16, 1948; came to U.S., 1977; s. Changkun and Sunchom (Cho) K.; m. Eunjoo Lee, May 22, 1978; children: LeeAnn, SueAnn, Andrew. BS, Cath. U., Seoul, 1969, MD, 1973; postgrad., Stanford U., Calif., 1981-83. Diplomate Am. Bd. Radiology; lic. physician, Mass., N.Y., Calif. Intern St. Mary's Hosp., Seoul, 1976-77, McKeesport Hosp., Pa., 1977-78; resident in diagnostic radiology Beth Israel Hosp., Newark, 1978-81; NIH fellow in cardiovascular and interventional radiology Stanford U. Med. Ctr., Calif., 1981-83; instr. radiology Harvard Med. Sch., Boston, 1983-86, asst. prof. radiology, 1986-92, assoc. prof. radiology, 1992-98; dir. divsn. cardiovascular and interventl. radiology Beth Israel Hosp., Boston, 1983-96; co-dir. divsn. cardiovascular and interventional radiology Beth Israel Deaconess Med. Ctr., Boston, 1996-98; prof. radiology and surgery U. Mass. Med. Sch., Worcester, 1999—2006; prof. radiology Boston U. Med. Sch., 2006—; dir. divsn. cardiovascular and interventional radiology U. Mass. Med. Ctr., Worcester, 1999—2006, Boston U. Med. Ctr., 2006—. Vis. prof. radiology U. Zurich, 1987, Nat. Rsch. Ctr. of Surgery, Ministry of Health, Russia, 1992; lectr. in field; rschr. in field. Author: Peripheral Vascular Imaging and Intervention, 1992; reviewer Catheterization and Cardiovascular Diagnosis, 1992-94, Hepatology, 1993; contbr. articles to profl. jours., chpts. in books. Sec. Korean Cath. Community, Boston, 1988-89, v.p., 1989-91, pres., 1991-92. Capt. Korean Army, 1973-76. Cath. U. Med. Coll. scholar, 1969-73; NIH grantee, 1981-83. Fellow Am. Coll. Angiology, Internat. Coll. Angiology, Am. Heart Assn., Soc. of Cardiovascular and Interventional Radiology; mem. AMA, Radiol. Soc. N.Am., Am. Coll. Radiology, New Eng. Soc. for Cardiovascular and Interventional Radiology (pres. 1992-93), New Eng. Korean Med. Soc., Norfolk Dist. Med. Soc., Mass. Med. Soc., Soc. of Magnetic Resonance in Medicine, Soc. of Magnetic Resonance Imaging, New Eng. Alumni Assn. of Cath. U. Med. Coll. (pres. 1991-92). Roman Catholic. Avocations: tennis, golf. Home: 9 Cedar Hill Rd Dover MA 02030-1631 Office: Boston Med Ctr 88 East Newton St Boston MA 02118 Home Phone: 508-395-3110. Personal E-mail: dicksookim@comcast.net.

KIM, EDWARD WILLIAM, ophthalmic surgeon; b. Seoul, Korea, Nov. 25, 1949; came to U.S., 1957; s. Shoon Kul and Pok Chu (Kim) K.; m. Carole Sachi Takemoto, July 24, 1976; children: Brian, Ashley. BA, Occidental Coll., Los Angeles, 1971; postgrad., Calif. Inst. Tech., 1971; MD, U. Calif., San Francisco, 1975; MPH, U. Calif., Berkeley, 1975. Diplomate Nat. Bd. Med. Examiners, Am. Bd. Ophthalmology. Resident in ophthalmology Harvard U.-Mass. Eye and Ear Infirmary, Boston, 1977-79; clin. fellow in ophthalmology Harvard U., 1977-79, clin. fellow in retina, 1980; practice medicine in ophthalmic surgery Laguna Hills, San Clemente, Calif., 1980— . Vol. ophthalmologist Eye Care Inc., Ecole St. Vincent's, Haiti, 1980, Liga, Mex., 1989, Tonga, 1997; chief staff, South Coast Med. Ctr., 1988-89; assoc. clin. prof. dept. ophthalmology, U. Calif., Irvine. Founding mem. Orange County Ctr. for Performing Arts, Calif., 1982, dir. at large, 1991; pres. Laguna Beach Summer Music Festival, Calif., 1984. Reinhart scholar U. Calif. San Francisco, 1972-73; R. Taussig scholar, 1974-75. Fellow ACS, Am. Acad. Ophthalmology, Internat. Coll. Surgeons; mem. Calif. Med. Assn., Keratorefractive Soc., Orange County Med. Assn., Mensa, Expts. in Art and Tech. Office: Harvard Eye Assocs 24401 Calle De La Louisa Ste 300 Laguna Hills CA 92653

KIM, EE-HWA, medical association administrator, educator; s. Su-Hae Kim and Myung-Soon Kang; m. Yang-On Kim; children: Na-Yeon, Su-Yeon. PhD, Kyung-Hee U., Seoul, 1998. Diplomate oriental medicine Kyung-Hee Hosp., 1998. Prof. Semyung U., Jecheon, Chungbuk, Republic of Korea, 1998—; dir. Clin. Trial Ctr. Semyung U. Hosp., Jecheon, 2006—, Clin. Trial Ctr. Bio-Industry, Jecheon, 2007— . Author: (textbook) Acupuncture, A Practical Exercise of Acupuncture. Dir. Bio-Cluster, Jecheon, 2005. Fellow: Soc. Meridian & Acupoint; mem.: Soc. Acupunture. Office: Semyung Univ Shinwol-Dong 579 390-711 Jecheon Chungcheonbuk-do Republic of Korea Office Phone: 82-43-653-6300. Office Fax: 82-43-652-1348.

KIM, EUGENE, orthopedist; b. Aug. 9, 1966; PhD, Yonsei U., 1991. Invited prof. Osaka U. Sch. Medicine, 2011—; assoc. prof. Sungkyunkwan U., Sch. Medicine, 2006—. Recipient award, Japan Orthop. Assn., 2005. Mem.: Korean Orthop. Assn. (mem. specialist bd. orthop. 1998). Avocation: photography. Office: Kangbuk Samsung Hosp 108 Pyongdong Seoul 110-746 Republic of Korea Business E-Mail: eugene0809@skku.edu.

KIM, EUN-CHEOL, oral pathologist, educator; b. Jeonbuk, Republic of Korea, Jan. 6, 1964; s. Hyun-Ju Kook; m. JI-Youn Kim, Jan. 27, 2004; children: Jong-Jin, Hae-Won. Bachelor magna cum laude, Wonkwang U., Iksan, Republic of Korea, 1988, Master, 1990, PhD, 1996. Cert. dentist Ministry Health and Welfare. Prof. Dental Coll. Wonkwang U., Iksan, 1996—, dir. dept. predental course, 2002—04, vice dean Dental Coll., 2005—, head dept dentistry, grad. sch., 2006; vis. assoc. NIH, Rockville, Md., 1999—2001; program mgr. Korea Rsch. Found., Seoul, 2006—08. Editor: Jour. Korean Oral Maxillofacial Pathology, 1997—; contbr. articles to profl. jours. Dental svc. Jeonbuk Blind Sch., Iksan, 2002. Mem.: Korean Assn. Oral Biologists, Korean Assn. Oral and Maxillofacial Pathologists (fin. dir. 2005—), Internat. Assn. Oral and Maxiiofacial Pathologists, Internat. Assn. Dental Rsch. Home: Busongdong Regencivill Apt 503-606 Iksan City Jeonbuk Republic of Korea Office: Kyung Hee University Dept Maxillofacial Tissue Regeneration Heogi-dong 1, Dongdaemoon-gu Seoul 130-701 Republic of Korea Office Phone: 82-2-961-0746. Office Fax: 82-2- 960-1457. Business E-Mail: eckim@khu.ac.kr.

KIM, GI EUN, engineering educator; b. Seoul, Sungbukgu, Republic of Korea, Mar. 30, 1958; Dr.-Ing., Tech. U. Berlin, 1984. Prof. engring. Seokyeong U., 1998. Master: KOFWST, Austrian Coun.; mem.: Korea Women Engineer's Soc. Avocations: skiing, dance, golf, boating. Office: Jungnung 16-1 Seoul Sungbukgu 136-704 Republic of Korea Office Fax: 8229190345. Business E-Mail: gkeun@skuniv.ac.kr.

KIM, GON SUP, science educator, researcher; s. Eun Hee Kim. DVM, Seoul, 1984; PhD, Seoul Nat. U., 1998. Prof. Gyeong Nat. U., Chinju, Gyeongnam, Republic of Korea, 1992—. Dir. Korea Nat. Animal Rsch. Resource Ctr., Chinju, 2006—08, Korea Nat. Animal Bio Resource Bank. Mem.: Internat. Rotary Club (pres. 2000—08). Office: Gyeongsang Nat Univ Gazwadong 660-701 Chinju Gyeongsangnam-do Republic of Korea Home Phone: 55-748-9654; Office Phone: 011-834-5823, 55-751-5823. Office Fax: 055-751-5803. Business E-Mail: gonskim@gnu.ac.kr.

KIM, GWANG-CHUL, architecture educator; b. Republic of Korea, Oct. 22, 1968; BS, Seoul Nat. U., 1991, PhD, 1999. Asst. prof. Chonbuk Nat. U., 2002—07, assoc. prof., dept. housing environ. design, 2008—. Recipient award, Korean Furniture Soc. Fellow: Korean Soc. Wood Sci. & Tech. (academic award). Avocation: guitar. Office: 664-14 1Ga Duckjin-dong Jeonju Chonbuk 561-756 Republic of Korea Office Fax: 82-63-270-3649. Business E-Mail: gckim@jbnu.ac.kr.

KIM, HACK SEANG, retired pharmacologist, educator; b. Okchon, Chungbuk, Republic of Korea, Mar. 28, 1936; m. Hae-Ja Park; 1 child, Seung Hwan. BSc in Pharmacy, Chungbuk Nat. U., Cheongju, Korea, 1960; MSc in Pharmacology, Sydney U., 1974; PhD in Pharmacy, WonKwang U., Iri, Korea, 1975. Asst. prof. pharmacy Chungbuk Nat. U., Cheongju, 1963—2001, prof. emeritus, pharmacologist, 2001—. Dean coll. pharmacy Chungbuk Nat. U., Cheongju, 1983—85, dean grad. sch., Cheongju, 1998—2000; adv. mem. FDA, Seoul, 1995—97. Cons. Korea Sci. and Tech. Consulting Corps, Seoul, 1996. Fellow, Colombo Plan, 1972—73; Fulbright Found. scholar, U. Ill., 1980. Mem.: Korean Acad. Sci. and Tech. (Presidental Acad. award 1988). Achievements include patents for antinarcotic drugs with ginseng. Home: Su-Dong # 339 361-112 Cheongju Chungbuk Republic of Korea Office Fax: 82-877-3902.

KIM, HAK YANG, gastroenterologist, educator; b. Seoul, June 6, 1956; s. Soon Kyung Kim and Won Yim Cho; m. You Jeon Lee, June 12, 1987; children: Min Kee, Pyung Kee. MD, Kyung Hee U., 1982, PhD, 1996. Intern, resident Kyung Hee U., Seoul, 1982-86; lectr., asst. prof. Hallym U., Seoul, 1988-97; assoc. prof., 1997—2002, prof., 2002—, head dept. internal medicine, 2001—11, chief gastroenterology divsn., 2005—09; dir. Digestive Disease Ctr., Health Promotion Ctr., 2011—. Rsch. fellow Baylor Coll. Medicine, Houston, 1992-93. Editor The Korean Jour. of Helicobacter Research and Practice, 2002-2004, contbr. articles to profl. jours. Mem. Korean Soc. Internal Medicine, Korean Soc. Gastroenterology, Korean Soc. Gastrointestinal Endoscopy. Avocations: sports, travel. Office: Kangdong Sacred Heart Hosp Seoul 134-010 Republic of Korea Office Phone: 82 2 2224 2113. Business E-Mail: bacter@hallym.or.kr.

KIM, HAN SU, surgeon, educator; b. Seoul, Republic of Korea, Jan. 13, 1973; s. Jong Gun Kim and Yon Sook Paik; m. Hyun Jung Choi, July 6, 2002; children: Yejune, Yena. MD, Yonsei U., Coll. Medicine, Seoul, 1997, PhD, 2007. Diplomate Dept. Health, Republic of Korea, 1997. Head & neck surgery fellow Yonsei U. Severance Hosp., 2002—03; asst. prof. Ewha Womans U. Sch. Med., Seoul, 2004—08, assoc. prof., 2009. Achievements include research in tissue engineering and laryngology. Office: Ewha Womans Univ Sch Medicine Yangcheon-Gu Mok 6 Dong 911-1 Seoul 158-710 Republic of Korea Office Phone: 82-2-2650-2686. Office Fax: 82-2-2653-5135. Business E-Mail: sevent@ewha.ac.kr.

KIM, HAN-SEONG, medical educator; b. Seoul, Republic Of Korea, Mar. 18, 1966; s. Bong-gil Kim and Yun-Hee Cho; m. Hi-Soo Rhee; children: Grace, Joy, Daniel. MD, Coll. Medicine, Korea U., Seoul, 1991; PhD, Coll. Medicine, Seoul Nat. U., Seoul, 1999. Cert. Bd. Pathology, Ministry of Health and Welfare, 2000. Clin. instr. Ilsan Paik Hosp., Goyang, Republic of Korea, 2000—01; instr. Coll. Medicine, Inje U., Gim Hae, Republic of Korea, 2001—03, asst. prof., 2003—07, assoc. prof., 2007—. Mem. Korean Soc. Gastroent., Seoul, 2000—; clin. cons. Internat. BioServe, Seoul, 2002—04; councilor Korean Soc. Pathologist, Seoul, 2003—08, dir. Diagnostic Electron Microscopy Study Group, 2004—07; cons. US Care Edn. Sch., Goyang, 2008—; toxicologic pathologist Korean Soc. Toxicologic Pathology, Seoul. Pub. health practitioner Ministry of Health and Welfare, Yun-Chun gun; dir. Ilsan Paik Hosp. Ch., Goyang, 2002—08. Recipient Rsch. award, Ilsan Paik Hosp., 2007, Good Rsch. award, Inje U., 2004. Office: Inje Univ Ilsan Paik Hosp Daehwadong 2240 Ilsan Seu Gu 411-702 Goyang Gyeonggi Republic of Korea Office Fax: 82-32-910-7139. Business E-Mail: hskim@paik.ac.kr.

KIM, HEE-JE, immunologist, internist, biologist; s. Sam-Cheol Kim and Bok-Soon Jeong; m. Kyung Kim, Jan. 9, 1993; children: Dong-Hyun, Se-Hoon. MD, Cath. Med. U., Korea, 1989; PhD in Med. Sci., Cath. Med. Coll. of Korea, 1999. Diplomate Korean Soc. Internal Medicine, 1994, lic. in Hematology and Oncology Korean Bd. Internal Medicine, 1999. Fellow in oncology Johns Hopkins U., Balt., 1999—2001; resident St. Mary's Hosp. Cath. Med. Coll., Seoul, Republic of Korea, 1990—94, mem. tng. program internal medicine St. Mary's Hosp., 1990—94; fellow hematology Cath. Stem Cell Transplantation Ctr. Cath. Coll. Medicine, 1997—98; instr. internal medicine Cath. U. Korea Coll. Medicine, Seoul, 1998—2001, asst. prof. internal medicine, 2002—06, assoc. prof. internal medicine, 2006—. Mem. editl. bd.: Pharmacogenomics, 2003—; contbr. articles to profl. jours. Capt. Korean Army, 1994—97. Recipient Outstanding Poster award, Congress Asia-Pacific BMT Group, 1998; grantee, Internat. Soc. Exptl. Hematology, 2001, Ministry Health and Welfare Korea, Nat. Cancer Ctr. Korea, 2003, Ministry Health and Welfare Korea, 2005; fellow, Johns Hopkins U. Sch. Medicine, Balt., 1999—2001. Mem.: Korean Assn. Medicine, Korean Soc. Immunology, Korean Soc. Hematopoietic Stem Cell Transplantation, Korean Soc. Hematology, European Hematology Assn., Korean Soc. Internal Medicine (diplomat 1994), Internat. Soc. Exptl. Hematology (corr.), Am. Soc. Hematology (corr.), Korean Cancer Assn. (life). Roman Catholic. Achievements include research in The role of anti-apoptotic molecule 'FLIP' and apoptotic 'Fas Ligand' in the normal and malignant Stem Cells; The role of KIR and NK alloreactivity in haploidentical hematopoietic stem cell transplantation; The clinical implications of mixed lymphocyte immune reaction with leukemic cells; Transduction of donor HSCs with FasL using Lentiviral vector; development of A novel haploidentical HSCT in AML, Korea; Treatment of elderly AML with newly designed combination chemotherapy regimens; Triple alkylating chemotherapy in patients with high-risk acute leukemia; design of novel mutations in the FLT3 gene in adult patients with refractory AML. Avocations: travel, music. Office: St Mary's Hospital CHSCTC 62 Youido-dong Youngdungpo-ku Seoul 150-713 Republic of Korea Office Fax: 82-2-780-3132. Business E-Mail: cumckim@catholic.ac.kr.

KIM, HEE-YOUNG, otolaryngologist; b. Busan, Republic of Korea, July 7, 1963; s. Moon-Sung Kim and Myung-Ja Kim; m. Min-Soo Chung, Nov. 5, 1994; children: So-Yoon, Ji-Yoon. Master Pathology, Chung-Ang U., Seoul, Republic Of Korea, 1997, MD, 1990, D in Pathology, 1999. Intern Chung-Gu Sung-Shim Hosp., Seoul, 1993—94, resident dept. of otolaryngology, 1994—98; attending dept. otorhinolaryngology-head and neck surgery Chung-Ang U. Hosp., Seoul, 1999—2000; attending otolaryngologist An-Yang Hosp., Anyang, Republic of Korea, 2000; co-dir. Koh Ear, Nose and Throat Clinic, Seoul, 2001; dir. Shinil Ear, Nose and Throat Clinic, Seoul, Republic of Korea, 2002—. Consulting physician NHN Corp., Seongnam, Republic of Korea, 2004—08; guest mem. reporter Korean Med. Doctor's News, Seoul, 2006—09; mem. adv. com. Korean Med. Assn., 2010—; guidepoint global advisors Coleman Rsch. Group's Exec. Forum. Author: (column) Korean Medical Doctor's News; contbr. articles to profl. jours. Recipient President's Active Lifestyle Award, 2010, President's Champions, Bronze Award, 2010. Mem.: Hearing Loss Assn. America, Advisory Com. Korean Med. Assn., Korean Audiological Soc., Korean Otologic Soc., Am. Acad. Otolaryngology-Head and Neck Surgery (internat. regular), Korean Soc. Otorhinolaryngologic Clinician, Am. Acad. Otolaryngology-Head and Neck Surgery Found., Seoul Gwanakgu Med. Assn. (licentiate; dir. offcl. info. 2006—09, dir. med. affairs 2009—, Letter of Commendation 2006), Korean Med. Assn. (licentiate), Korean Soc. Otorhinolaryngology-Head and Neck Surgery (assoc.), Postgraduate Assn. Harvard Med. Sch. Dept. Continuing Edn. (life), Chung-Ang Otolaryngology Club, Seoul St Mary Otolaryngology Club, Goryeo Guro Otolaryngology Club, Seonam Otolaryngology Club, Samsung Otolaryngology Club. Avocations: violin, golf

KIM, HONG JIN, oncologist, educator; b. Seoul, Republic of Korea, Oct. 2, 1966; BA, Dartmouth Coll., 1988; MD, U. Va., 1992. Assoc. prof. UNC Sch. Medicine, 2001—. Clin. dir., tissue procurement facility Lineberger Comprehensive Cancer Ctr., 2005; fellowship dir., surg. oncology UNC, 2008, chief, sect. pancreas and hepatobiliary surgery, 10. James Wood Faculty grant, UNC, Med. Alumni Endowment grant, Acad. Educators fellow. Mem.: Surg. Biology Club, Assn. Academic Surgery, Soc. U. Surgeons, Soc. Surg. Oncology, Alpha Omega Alpha. Avocation: scuba diving. Office: Dept Surgery & Surg Oncology Chapel Hill NC 27599 Office Fax: 919-966-8806. Business E-Mail: kimhj@med.unc.edu.

KIM, HOWARD LYNN, neurologist; b. La Mirada, Calif., June 17, 1964; BS, U. Calif. Irvine, 1986; MD, Northwestern U. Sch. Medicine, 1990. Assoc. clin. prof. Irvine Sch. Medicine U. Calif., 2002—11, dir. Irvine Med. Ctr. Neurodiagnostic Lab. & Intraoperative Monitoring, 2002—10, clin. dir. Irvine Comprehensive Epilepsy Program, 2004—10; intraoperative neurophysiologist Biotronic NeuroNetwork, 2011—. Mem.: Am. Acad. Neurology, Am. Soc. Neurophysiol. Monitoring, Am. Clin. Neurophysiology Soc. Office Phone: 734 213 3020. Personal E-mail: hkspearo@gmail.com.

KIM, HUI TAEK, orthopedist, surgeon, educator, researcher; b. Chilgok, Kyungbuk, Republic Of Korea, Nov. 25, 1958; s. Bong Gi Kim and Pil Eun Chang; m. Mi Kyung Jang; children: Hui Kyung, Ji Soo. MD, Pusan Nat. U., Republic of Korea, 1983, Master, 1994. Lic. med. doctor Ministry Health and Sci., 1983, diplomate Korean Bd. Orthopaedics, 1988. Intern Pusan Nat. U. Hosp., 1983—84, resident, 1984—88; clin. fellow Seoul Nat. U. Children's Hosp., 1993; clin. rsch. fellow U. Calif. Children's Hosp., San Diego, 1994—95, Tex. Scottish Rite Hosp. Children, Dallas, 1998, 2002. Lectr. Pusan Nat. U. Coll. Medicine, 1992—94, asst. prof., 1994—98, assoc. prof., 1998—2003, prof., 2003—. Contbr. articles to profl. jours. Capt. Korean Air Force M.C., 1988—91, Pusan. Recipient award, Coll. Medicine Pusan Nat. U., 1998. Mem.: N. Am. Pediat. Orthop. Soc., Asia Pacific Orthop. Assn., Internat. Orthop. Trauma Surgery Soc., Korean Assn. for Study and Application of Ilizarov Method, Korean Fracture Soc., Korean Pediat. Orthop. Soc. (award 2000, fellow 2005), Korean Orthop. Assn. (award 1996, 2004, 2005). Home: 11-1001 Lucky APT 707 Oncheon-2dong Pusan 607-753 Republic of Korea Office: Pusan Nat Univ Hosp Dept Orthop Surgery 1-10 Ami-dong Seo-gu Pusan 602-739 Republic of Korea Office Phone: 82-51-240-7248. Office Fax: 82-51-247-8395. Business E-Mail: kimht@pusan.ac.kr.

KIM, HWAN MOOK, biologist, researcher; s. Ku Hong and Young Hee Kim; m. Sung Eun Kim, Jan. 14, 1984; children: Jun Ho, Bo Min. BS in Pharm. Scis., Seoul Nat. U., Korea, 1982; PhD, Korea Advaced Inst. Sci. and Tech., Taejon, 1987. Cert. pharmacist Republic of Korea, 82. Sr. rsch. scientist Korea Rsch. Inst. Biosci. and Biotech., Taejon, Republic of Korea, 1987—97, dir., bio-evaluation ctr., 1990—, prin. rsch. scientist, 1997—; joint prof. Korea Advanced Inst. Sci. and Tech., 1998—. Govt. rep. Environ. Program UN, 1992—2001; com. mem. Nat. Ctrl. Com. of Pharm. Affairs, Korea (South), 1997—2001; mem. adv. com. rsch. evaluation Korea Food and Drug Adminstrn., 2000—00; mem. adv. com. Ministry of Fgn. Affairs and Trade, 2000—02. Deacon DaeDuk Ch., Korea (South), 1990—2003. Pvt. Korean Army, 1987—90. Recipient IR52 JangYoungSil award, Ministry of Sci. & Tech., 1999. Mem.: The Korean Soc. of Toxicology, Korea Pharm. Assn., Asian Soc. of Toxicology (assoc. Poster Awards 1997). Achievements include patents pending for a new fungal strain; various treatments of diabetes mellitus. Office: Kribb 685-1 Yangcheong Ochang Cheongwon Chungcheongbuk-do 363-883 Republic of Korea Office Fax: 82-43-240-6529. Business E-Mail: hwanmook@kribb.re.kr.

KIM, HYE RYOUN, medical educator; b. Seoul, Republic of Korea, Apr. 24, 1966; PhD, Chung-Ang U. Coll. Medicine, 1999. Assoc. prof. Chung-Ang U. Coll. Medicine, 2009—11. Korea Rsch. Found. grant, Korean Govt. Mem.: Korean Soc. Lab. Medicine. Office: 224 1 Heukseok-Dong Dongjak Seoul 156 755 Republic of Korea Office Fax: 82-2-6298-8630. Business E-Mail: hyekim@cau.ac.kr.

KIM, HYOUNJU, nutritionist, educator; b. Cheju, Republic of Korea, Jan. 8, 1969; Degree in Nutrition, Cheju U., 1991; PhD, Tohoku U., 1997. Lectr. Josai U., 2002—. Office: Keyakidai 1-1 Sakado Saitama 350-0295 Japan Business E-Mail: hyounju@josai.ac.jp.

KIM, HYUN SEOK, plastic surgeon; Grad., Seoul Nat. U. Med. Coll. Bd. cert. tng. plastic surgery dept. Seoul Nat. Univ. Hosp., Seoul Nat. Univ. Bundang Hosp.; dir. Dream Plastic Surgery Clinic. Mem.: Internat. Confederation Plastic reconstructive and Aesthetic Surgery,

Korean Cleft-Palate-Craniofacial Assn., Korean Microsurgical Soc., Korean Soc. Reconstructive Hand Surgery, Korean Med. Assn., Korean Soc. Aesthetic Plastic Surgery, Korean Soc. Plastic and Reconstructive Surgeons. Office: Dream Plastic Surgery Clinic Apkujung Subway Sta Seoul Republic of Korea Office Phone: 8225461616. Office Fax: 8225461614. *

KIM, HYUN SOO, gastroenterologist, educator; b. Chungju, June 16, 1966; MD, Yonsei U., Seoul, Republic of Korea, PhD, 2001. Assoc. prof. Divsn. Gastroenterology, Dept. Internal Medicine, Yonsei U. Wonju Coll. Medicine, 2005—10, prof., 2010—; vis. assoc. prof. M. D. Anderson Cancer Ctr., Epigenetics Rsch. Ctr., Dr. Jean-Pierre Issa Lab., 2006—08. Chair, sci. com. Korean Assn. Study Intestinal Disease, 2011. Mem.: Am. Assn. Cancer Rsch., Korean Gastric Cancer Assn., Korean Soc. Gastrointestinal Motility (Dr. Paul Janssen award), Korean Soc. Gastrointestinal Endoscopy (head, lower GI part sci. com. 2009—, Weolbong award), Korean Soc. Gastroenterology. Avocation: swimming, golf. Office: 162 Ilsan-Dong Wonju Kangwon 220-701 Republic of Korea Office Fax: 82-33-741-1228. Business E-Mail: hyskim@yonsei.ac.kr.

KIM, HYUNG-JEE, urologist, educator; b. Seoul, Republic of Korea, May 15, 1961; s. Yoon-Cheon Kim and Kyung-Soon Hwang; m. Young-Rahn Lee, Jan. 29, 1988; children: Min-Jung, Min-Jee. DSc, Korea U., Seoul, 1990. Lic. Korean Med. Assn., 1987. Assoc. prof. coll. medicine Dankook U., Cheonan, Republic of Korea, 2002—; mgr. pub. rels. team Dankook U. Hosp., Cheonan, Republic of Korea, 2005—. Chair of publications Korean Continence Soc., Seoul, 2005—. Contbr. articles to profl. jours. Recipient Pharmacia and Upjohn award, Korean Andrological Soc., 1998. Mem.: Korean Continence Soc. (chmn. pub. rels. 2005—, award 2001). Avocations: golf, sightseeing. Office: Dept Urology Dankook Univ Hosp Anseodong 29 Cheonan 330-715 Republic of Korea Business E-Mail: killtumor@dankook.ac.kr, killtumar@yahoo.co.kr.

KIM, HYUNG-JOO, urologist, researcher; m. Shin-Ah Kim. PhD student, Korea Advanced Inst. Sci. and Tech., Seoul, 2006—. Diplomate Korean Bd. Urology, 1996. Dir. Dept. Urology, Hallym U. Hosp., Seoul, 2007—. Contbr. articles to med. jours. Office Fax: (82) 2-2632- 5383. Business E-Mail: urokhj@naver.com.

KIM, HYUNGSIN, research scientist; b. Seoul, Republic of Korea, Feb. 6, 1978; PhD, Northwestern U., 2003; PhD student, Ga. Inst. Tech. E-learning specialist DuPont Asia Pacific, 2003—04; rschr. Korea U., 2004—06, Ga. Inst. Tech., 2006—, Northwestern U. Anne Robinson Clough Conf. Grant. Mem.: IEEE Computing and Soc., Assn. Computing Machinery (women com. mem.). Avocations: movies, swimming. Home: 860 Peachtree St Unit 1816 Atlanta GA 30308

KIM, HYUN-JEONG, pain clinician, researcher; b. Seoul, Republic of Korea, Sept. 2, 1967; d. Myung-Ok Kim and Yeo-Sook Park; m. Tae-Gyoon Yoon, Nov. 5, 1995; 1 child, Yeo-Sang Yoon. MD, Seoul Nat. U., 1992, MPH, 1998; PhD, Korea U., 2001. Cert. Anesthetic Specialist. Intern Seoul Nat. U. Hosp., 1992—93, resident, 1993—97, fellow, 1997—99, instr., 1999—2003, asst. prof., 2003—. Gen. sec. Korean Dental Soc. of Anesthesiology, Seoul, 2001. Contbr. articles to prof. jours. Grantee Gen. Rsch. Fund, Seoul Nat. U., 2000, 2002, Korea Health 21 Rsch. Devel., Ministry Health Welfare, 2002. Mem.: Internat. Assoc. Study Pain, Japanese Dental Soc. Anesthesiology, Korean Pain Soc. Achievements include invention of Neurolytics with Botulinum Toxin Type A 2001. Avocations: swimming, yoga. Office: Dept Dental Anesthesiology Seoul Nat U Coll Dentistry 28 Yongondong Chongno-gu 110-768 Seoul Republic of Korea

KIM, IN HO, gastroenterologist, educator; b. Daegu, Republic of Korea, Apr. 11, 1952; MD, Kyungpook Nat. U., 1976; PhD, Chonbuk Nat. U., 1991. Prof. Keimyung U. Sch. Medicine, 1984—, prof., chmn. dept. surgery, 2007—10; dir. Keimyung U. Inst. Med. Sci., 2007—09, Keimyung U. Dongsan Cancer Ctr., 2008. Bd. dirs. Korean Gastric Cancer Assn., 2000—, Korean Soc. Parenteral Nutrition & Enteral Nutrition, 2000—08; pres. Korean Soc. Surg. Metabolism & Nutrition, 2010—; v.p. Korean Soc. Gastroenterology, 2010—; pres. Daegu Surg. Soc., 2010—. Recipient Best Article award, Korean Assn. Internal medicine; named Best Prof., Keimyung U. Dongsan Med. Ctr. Mem.: Korean Cancer Assn., Korean Soc. Surg. Metabolism & Nutrition, Internat. Gastric Cancer Assn., Korean Gastric Cancer Assn., Korean Med. Assn. Avocation: golf. Office: Keimyung University 56 Dalsungro Choong-Ku Daegu 700-712 Republic of Korea Office Fax: 82-53-250-7322. Business E-Mail: kih309@dsmc.or.kr.

KIM, INKYEOM, pharmacologist, researcher; b. Yecheon, Kyungpook, Republic Of Korea, Oct. 14, 1961; s. SeungRyong Kim; m. YoungSun Seok, Mar. 10, 1991; children: JaeYoung, JiEun, Jennifer JaeHee, JaeEun. MD, Kyungpook Nat. U., Daegu, 1986; PhD, Kyungpook Nat. U., 1992. Visting scientist Boston Biomed. Rsch. Inst., 1997—99; fellow Harvard Med. Sch., Boston, 2001—03; prof. Kyungpook Nat. U., 2006—, chmn., 2005—. Translator: Principles of Pharmacology. Vol. Parents Chaperone Corps., Daegu, 2007—08. Capt. US Army, 1992—95, Daegu. Recipient Appreciation award, New Eng. Biol. Soc., 1999, Eulgi Med. Coll., 2000; grantee, Ministry Edn., 2007, Ministry Sci. and Tech., 2008. Fellow: Korean Soc. Pharmacology (sec. 2009—). Office: Kyungpook Nat Univ 101 Dongin-2-Ga Daegu 700422 Republic of Korea Office Fax: 82-53-426-7345. Business E-Mail: inkim@knu.ac.kr.

KIM, JAE CHAN, ophthalmologist, educator; b. Chungju, Republic of Korea, Oct. 9, 1952; s. Sa Dal Kim and Nam Soon Jo; m. Tae Sook Kwon, Nov. 30, 1979; children: Sung Hee, Min Hee, Jung Hee. MD, Coll. of Medicine, Chung-Ang U., Seoul, Korea. Med. Diploma Ministry of Health and Soc., 1977, Ophthal. Dr. Korean Ophthal. Soc., 1982. Rsch. fellow, dept. ophthalmology Chung-Ang U. Yongsan Hosp., Seoul, 1985—86, asst. prof., dept. ophthalmology, 1986—90; associated prof. Dept. of Ophthalmology, Chung-Ang U. Yongsan Hosp., Seoul, Republic of Korea, 1990—95; exch. prof. Rochester U., 1991—92, Bascom-Palmer Inst., Miami U., 1991—92; prof., dir., dept. ophthalmology Chung-Ang U. Yongsan Hosp., 1995—, chmn., clin. rsch. ctr., 1995—. Advisor Korean Occupl. Safety and Health Agy., Seoul, 1995—. Contbr. numerous articles in profl. jours.; editor: (book) Atlas of Ophthal., Cornea, Cataract, Ophthalmology; contbr. articles to profl. jours. (Top Con Acad. award, 2010). Master: Korean Contact Lens Soc.; mem.: NY Assn. Sci., Assn. for Rsch. in Vision and Ophthalmology, Am. Assn. Ophthalmology, Asia Pacific Acad. of Ophthalmology, Korean External Eye Disease Soc., Korean Basic Ophthalmology and Visual Rsch. Club, Korean Ophthal. Soc. Buddhist. Achievements include first in the world clinical application of amniotic membrane; patents for wound healing promotive agent or cell therapeutic agent containing mesenchymal stem cells and/or substance P. Avocation: golf. Home: Family Apt 216 1003 Moon Jung Dong Song Pa Ku Seoul 138 793 Republic of Korea Office: Dept of Ophthalmology Chung Ang University Med Ctr 224 1 Heuk Seok Dong Dongjak gu Seoul 156 755 Republic of Korea Office Phone: 82-2-6299 1689. Office Fax: 82-2-795-6295. Personal E-mail: jck50ey@kornet.net.

KIM, JAE GYU, gastroenterologist, educator; b. Jinju, Republic of Korea, May 5, 1962; s. Joon Il Kim and Jae Hee Cho; m. Sang Hee Choi, Nov. 10, 1996; children: Kwang Mo, Joon Mo. PhD, Coll. Medicine, Seoul Nat. U., Seoul, MD, 1999. Diplomate Ministry Health Welfare, 1987, cert. Bd. Internal Medicine, Ministry Health Welfare, 1995. Prof. Coll. Medicine, Chung-Ang U., Seoul, Republic of Korea, 1996—; mem. bd. meeting Korean Assn. Internal Medicine, Seoul, 2007—10, chmn. academic com., treas., 2010—, Seoul Internat. Digestive Symposium, 2007—09; vice sec. gen. Korean Soc. Gastroenterology, Seoul, 2007—09; mem. scientfic com. Korean Gastric Cancer Assn., Seoul, 2007—09, dir. ethics com., 2011—; sec. gen. Korean Coll. Helicobacter and Upper Gastrointestinal Rsch., Seoul, 2008—10; editl. bd. Jour. Gastroenterology And Hepatology, Australia, 2009—; dir. planning com., organizing com. World Congress Internat. Medicine, 2011—. First lt. Korean Army, 1988—91, Seoul. Recipient Young Clinician award, APDW, 2000, Academic award, Korean Assn. Internal Medicine, 2004. Mem.: Internat. Gastric Cancer Congress (Seoul), Am. Gastroent. Assn. Office: Chung-Ang University Hosp 224-1 Heukseok-dong Dongjak-gu Seoul 156-755 Republic of Korea Office Phone: 82-2-6299-3147. Office Fax: 82-2-749-9150. Business E-Mail: jgkimd@cau.ac.kr.

KIM, JAE KYU, radiologist, educator; b. Na ju, Chonnam, Republic of Korea, Jan. 8, 1955; s. Ki Dong Kim and Il Soon Nah; m. Sung Hee Lee; children: Do Yeon, Hee Jong, Tae Heung. MD, Chonbuk Nat. U., Sch. Medicine, Jeon Ju, Republic of Korea, 1980, PhD, 1988. Chmn., dept. radiology Chonnam Nat. U. Hosp., Gwangju, 2005—; vice-dean Chonnam Nat. U. Med. Sch., 2006—08. Editor Korean Radiology Soc., Seoul, Republic of Korea, 2000—. Mem.: Radiol. Soc. N.Am. Office: Chonnam Nat Univ Dept Radiology Hackdong 8 501-757 Gwangju Republic of Korea Office Fax: 82-62-226-4380. Business E-Mail: kjkrad@chonnam.ac.kr.

KIM, JAE MIN, rehabilitation physician, professor; s. Yong Hwan Kim and Jin Suk Park; m. Hyo Jung Yu, Sept. 24, 2005; children: Beom-Gu, Beom-Seo. MD, Med. Coll. Cath. U. Korea, Seoul, Republic of Korea, 2001, M, 2005; PhD, Cath. U., Seoul, 2010. Cert. Korean Bd. Rehabilitation Medicine, 2006. Mem., med. info. Korean Acad. Med. Scis., Seoul, 2003—04; mgr. Korean Assn. Pain Medicine, Seoul, 2006—. Contbr. articles to profl. jours. Mem.: Korean Acad. Neuromusculoskeletal Sonography, Korean Soc. Ultrasound Medicine, Korean Soc. Brain-Neurorehabilitation, Korean Stroke Soc., Korean Soc. Sports Medicine, Korean Assn. Rehab. Medicine, Korean Assn. EMG Electrodiagnostic Medicine (Best Scientist award 2008). Office: Incheon St Marys Hosp Bupyeong 6-Dong Bupyeong-Gu 665 403-720 Incheon Incheon Republic of Korea Office Fax: 82-32-280 5040. Personal E-mail: destrudo@catholic.ac.kr.

KIM, JAEHWANG, coloproctologist, surgeon, medical educator, researcher; b. Gumi, Republic of Korea, Nov. 26, 1957; s. Heeyoung Kim and Imdo Lee; m. Hae-Sook Kim, Oct. 3, 1985; children: Sujin, Ikhyoun, Suahn. MD, Med. coll. of Kyungbook Nat. U., 1978—82; PhD, Yeungnam U., 1986—91. MD Korea, 1982, Bd. Surgery Korea, 1990. Instr. surgery Med. Coll. Yeungnam U., Daegu, Republic of Korea, 1991—93, prof. sugery, 2002—. Capt. Army surgeon, 1983—86, Korea. Recipient Med. Design Excellence award BMS, NY, 2004, Korean Med. Sci. award new intraoperative colonic irrigation and intraoperative colonoscopy technique, Seoul, 2005. Mem.: Korean Assn. Coloproctology, ASCRS. Achievements include invention of Bowel management sys; intraoperative colonic irrigator; patents for Fecal diverting device; invention of rotatble laparoscopic monitor. Avocations: painting, travel, tennis. Home: Yeungnam Apt JIsandong Suseonggu Daegu Republic of Korea Office: Yeungnam Univ Med Ctr 317-1 Daemyung-Dong Nam-Gu 705-717 Daegu Daegu Republic of Korea Office Fax: 053 624 1213. Personal E-mail: jhkimgs@yumail.ac.kr. Business E-Mail: jhkimgs@ynu.ac.kr.

KIM, JANG YOUNG, physician, educator; b. Busan, July 13, 1968; MD, Wonju Coll. Medicine, Yonsei U., 1994; PhD, Yonsei Coll. Medicine, 2007. Assoc. prof. Wonju Coll. Medicine, Yonsei U., 2008—; physician Wonju Christain Hosp., 2002—11. Sub primary investigator Arirang studies Korean Genome Rural Cohort, 2005—11; assoc. editor Jour. Cardiovasc. Ultrasound, 2006—11. Cmty. Cohort grant, Total Budet Cohort Team. Fellow: Korean Soc. Circulation. Avocation: golf. Office: Yonsei University Wonju Coll Medicine 162 Ilasn-Dong Wonju Gangwon 220-701 Republic of Korea Office Fax: 82-33-741-1219. Business E-Mail: kimjy@yonsei.ac.kr.

KIM, JANG-RAK, preventive medicine physician; b. Yeongduk, Gyeongbuk, Republic of Korea, Mar. 9, 1959; s. Tae-Hyun Kim and Soon-Ki Shin; m. Hye-Song Ryu, Apr. 17, 1988; children: Ka-Young, Keun-Mok. Dr. in Pub. Health, Kyungpook Nat. U., 1992. MD Ministry of Health and Welfare, 1983. Prof. dept. preventive medicine sch. medicine Gyeongsang Nat. U., Jinju, Republic of Korea, 1991—. Capt. Army, 1983—86. Mem.: Korean Soc. for Preventive Medicine. Home: Shinan-Dong Pyeonggeo-Hyundai A 103-501 Gyeongnam Jinju 660-290 Republic of Korea Office: Gyeongsang Sch Medicine Chilam-Dong 92 660-751 Jinju Gyeongsangnam-do Republic of Korea Office Fax: 82-55-772-8099. Business E-Mail: jrkim@gnu.ac.kr.

KIM, JEONG KYU, otolaryngologist, educator; b. Daegu, Republic Of Korea, Aug. 25, 1970; s. Soon Tae Kim and Kyung Ja Jeong; m. So Hyun Sung, Aug. 23, 1998; children: Sang Jin, Tae Eun. BSc, Kyungpook Nat. U., Daegu, 1995, MSc, 1998, PhD, 2007. Cert. med. dr. Ministry Health and Welfare, 1995, otolaryngologist 2000. Intern and resident Kyungpook Nat. U. Hosp., Republic of Korea, 1995—2000, fellow, 2003—04; instr. Cath. U. Daegu, 2004—06, asst. prof., 2006—. Contbr. scientific papers to profl. jours. Naval officer, 2000—03. Home: 101-2306 Muhak Apt Jisan-dong Suseong-gu Daegu 706-787 Republic of Korea Office: Cath U Daegu 3056-6 Daemyung4-Dong Nam-Gu 705-718 Daegu Daegu Republic of Korea Office Phone: 82-53-650-4071. Office Fax: 82-53-650-4525. Personal E-mail: doctorjkkim@hotmail.com.

KIM, JEONG-HO, pathologist, educator; b. Seoul, Republic of Korea, Sept. 10, 1958; s. Chun Soo Kim and Yn Sung Shin; m. Euna Choi; children: Sungseek, Jesun. MD, Yonsei U. Coll. Medicine, Seoul, 1983; MS, Yonsei U. Grad. Sch., 1986, PhD, 1995. Lic. physician Ministry of Health, Republic of Korea, 1983, cert. clin. pathologist 1987. Prof. Yonsei U. Coll. Medicine, 2004—; editor-in-chief Korean Soc. Lab. Medicine, Seoul, 2006—; dir. Gangnam Med. Rsch. Ctr., Seoul, 2007—. Editor Korean Jour. Lab. Medicine. Trustee So-mang Cmty. Disabled, Gongju-si, Chungcheongnam-do, 2002—08. Mem.: Am. Assn. Clin. Chemistry. Office: Gangnam Severance Hosp Yonsei Univ 712 Eonjuro Gangnamgu Seoul 135-720 Republic of Korea Office Fax: 82-2-2019-4822. Personal E-mail: jeong_ho_kim@hotmail.com. Business E-Mail: jeongho@yuhs.ac.

KIM, JEONG-TAE, plastic surgeon, educator; s. Young-Soek Kim and Dong-Suk Jo; m. You-Kyeong Choi, Feb. 7, 1970; 1 child, Se-Jin. PhD in Medicine, Han Yang U., 1987, MD, 1987. Cert. plastic surgeon Korea. Assoc. prof. Dong-A U., Sch. Medicine, Busan, Republic of Korea, 1996—2002, Hanyang U., Seoul, Republic of Korea, 2002—; cons. St. Andrews Ctr., Chelmsford, England, 2005—06. Vis. asst. prof. Kawasaki Med. Sch., 1998; cons. St. Andrews Ctr., Chelmsford, England, 2005—06. Contbr. articles to profl. jours. Capt. Korean Army, 1992—95, Kangwha, Community Public Health Doctor. Mem.: Korean Soc. Surgery of Hand (mem. congress and sci. com. 2000—06, bd. dirs. 2000—06), Korean Burn Soc., Korean Cleft Palate-Craniofacial Assn., Korean Microsurg. Soc. (bd. dirs. 2001—), Korean-Japan Soc. Plastic and Reconstructive Surgeons, Internat. Confedn. for Plastic, Reconstructive and Aesthetic Surgery, Internat. Soc. Aesthetic Surgery, Korean Soc. for Head and Neck Oncology, Korean Soc. Reconstructive Hand Surgery (bd. dirs. 1999—), Korean Soc. Aesthetic Plastic Surgery, Korean Soc. Plastic and Reconstructive Surgeons (bd. examiners 2000—, internat. affairs com. 2000—). Roman Catholic. Avocation: travel. Office: Hanyang Univ Med Sch Dept Plastic & Reconstructive Surg 17 Haengdang-Dong Seongdong-Gu 133 792 Seoul Republic of Korea Office Fax: +82-2-2293-8560. Business E-Mail: jtkim@hanyang.ac.kr.

KIM, JIM YONG, academic administrator, preventive medicine physician; b. South Korea, Dec. 8, 1959; m. Younsook Lim; 2 children. BA, Brown U., 1982; MD, Harvard U., 1991, PhD in anthropology, 1993. Assoc. prof. med. Harvard U., co- dir. Program in Infectious Disease and Soc. Change, 1996; founding mem. Working Group. on DOTS-Plus WHO, Geneva, 1999, dir. HIV/AIDS dept., 2004—06; attending physician Dept. of Internal Med. Brigham & Women's Hosp., Boston, chief Divsn. Global Health Equity; chief. Div. of Soc. Med. & Health Inequalities Harvard Med. Sch., chair Dept. Global Health and Social Medicine, prof. social medicine; Francois-Xavier Bagnoud prof. health & human rights Harvard Sch. Pub. Health, 2006—09, dir. Francois-Xavier Bagnoud Ctr. for Health & Human Rights (FXB), 2006—09; pres. Dartmouth Coll., Hanover, NH, 2009—. Co-founder, exec. dir. Partners in Health, 1987—. Author: (book) Dying for Growth: Global Inequality and the Health of the Poor; contbr. book. Named a MacArthur fellow, John D. & Catherine T. MacArthur Found., 2003; named one of The 100 Most Influential People in the World, TIME mag., 2006. Mem.: Inst. Medicine. Office: Dartmouth Collage Office of President Parkhurst, Room 207 Hanover NH 03755 Office Phone: 603-646-2223. E-mail: Jim.Y.Kim@Dartmouth.edu. *

KIM, JIN SU, medical researcher; b. Busan, June 1, 1973; PhD, Seoul Nat. U., 2009. Rsch. assoc. Nuc. Medicine, Seoul Nat. U., 2001—07; sr. rschr. Korean Inst. Radiol. and Med. Scis., 2007—; prof. U. Sci. and Tech., 2008. Advisor Korea Basic Sci. Inst., 2007, PET Instrumentation Team, Korea PET Com., 2008—. Recipient Travel award, IEEE Med. Imaging Conf., Young Investigator award, Tng. Rsch. Career award, Seoul Nat. U. Mem.: Korean Soc. Med. Physics, Korean Soc. Nuc. Medicine (Sai Han award), Korean Soc. Mech. Engring., Inst. Physics and Engring. Medicine, Soc. Nuc. Medicine (Travel award). Office: 75 Nowon Gil Gongneung dong Nowongu Seoul 100380 Republic of Korea Business E-Mail: kjs@kirams.re.kr.

KIM, JIN WANG, plastic surgeon, educator; b. Seoul, Jan. 12, 1962; s. Ki-Soo Kim and Kyu-Kyung Choi; m. Joung-Ok Lee, June 20, 1987; children: Hyum Ji, Hyun Woo. MB, Yonsei U., Seoul, Korea, 1986, MD, 1991, PhD, 2001; MBA, Seoul Nat. U., 2007. Intern, resident Yonsei U. Severance Hosp., 1986—91; supt. Best Well Hosp., Seoul, Republic of Korea, 1991—2003; sec. gen. Asian Pacific Assn. for Lasers in Medicine and Surgery, Seoul, Republic of Korea, 1996—2000; pres. Internat. Soc. for Lasers in Medicine and Surgery & Asian Pacific Assn. for Lasers in Medicine and Surgery, Seoul, Republic of Korea, 2000—, Fedn. Lasers in Medicine and Surgery and World Plastic Surgery; prof. Dan Kook U., Chun-Ahn, Republic of Korea, 2001—; clin. prof. Yonsei U., Seoul, 2002—; prof. In Ha U., Inchoon, Republic of Korea, 2003—04, Hallym U. Hosp., Seoul, Republic of Korea, 2004—. Faculty ISAPS, OSAPS, Tokyo, 1996—; pres. ISELS, Seoul, 2000—; dep. gen., hon. adv. bd. IPRAS, Berlin, 2003—; gen. sec., amb. gen. United Cultural, UNESCO Convention, 2007—; supt. Bestwell Inst., 2008; surgeon world Best Blepharoplasty Lipoplasty, 2009; pres. exec. dir. Korean Soc. Aesthetic Medicine & Surgery, Korean Acad. Aesthetic Med. Sci., 2010; founder KBLS KAIA, 2011. Author, editor: Art and Science of Laser Surgery, 2000; author: Innovation of Plastic Surgery, 2007, IPRAS, 2009. Recipient award, Am. Soc. Aesthetic Surgery, 1999, 2000, Best Lecture award, Firenze-Italy 17th ISLMS, Achievement award, ASAPS, 1998, Best Speech award, ISLSM Tokyo, 2009. Fellow: Am. Soc. for Lasers in Medicine and Surgery; mem.: Korean Acad. Aesthetic Surgery & Medicine (chief exec. dir. 2010—11), Korean Acad. Laser Application (pres. 2011), Acad. Aesthetic Medicine & Surgery (exec. chief dir. 2010—), Korean Soc. of Aesthetic Med. & Surgery (pres, exec. dir. 2010, pres. KOFSTISLSM 2010, pres. KALA 2011), Internat. Conf. for Plastic Reconstructive Aesthetic Surgery (hon. advisory bd. 2007—, pres. ISAPS offcl. course 2011), Internat. Soc. Lasers in Surgey & Med. (pres. 2010—13), ISALMS (pres. 2008), Global Med. (pres., CEO, MBA 2007—), World Acad. Letters (vice chancellor 2006—), IBC (hon. dir. gen. 2006—, nominee Einstein's Genuine & Davinci award, IBC 2009), ABI (order of Am. amb. 2006—), Asia Pacific Aesthetic Plastic Surgery (pres. 2008—11), Korean Soc. Hand Surgery (v.p. 2006), Korean Soc. Plastic and Reconstructive Surgery (treas. 2006), Korean Soc. for Laser in Medicine and Surgery (treas., bd. dir. 2006), Internat. Plastic, Reconstructive and Aesthetic Surgery (mem. adv. bd. & faculty), Oriental Aesthetic Plastic Surgery Soc., Internat. Soc. Photodynamic Therapy (hon.; bd. dir. 2006—). Achievements include first to introduce laser bone surgery in 1998 and lasers in medicine & surgery in Korea; laser bone surgery and lasers in medicine and surgery in korea; patents for first introduce minimal invasive endoscopic bone contouring saw and tools; first introducer laser led Lipolysis, epithelial stem cell and lipo precursor fat stell cell therapy in plastic surgery. Avocations: golf, soccer, tennis, swimming, fishing. Home: Hyundai Apt 87 Dong 202 Ho Seoul 135-100 Republic of Korea Office: Best Well Hosp Kang Nam Gu Sin Sa Dong 638-5 Seoul Republic of Korea Office Phone: 82-2-511-3713. Office Fax: 822 517 3713. Personal E-mail: khg000@unitel.co.kr. Business E-Mail: jinwang@naver.com.

KIM, JIN-SUNG, neurosurgeon, consultant; b. Seoul, Republic of Korea, July 4, 1971; BA, Cath. U. Coll. Medicine, Seoul, 1991, MD, 1997, MS, 2009, PhD student, 2010—. Neurosurgery med. specialist, minimally invasive spinal surgery. Intern St. Vincent Hosp., Suwon, Republic of Korea, 2000—01; clin. fellow, with dept. thoracic spine disease, neurosurg. resident Wooridul Spine Hosp., neurosurgeon, dept. neurosurgery, cons. spine surgeon, 2008—. Author: (book) Neurosurgery Board Review in Korea, 2006, (books) 2nd edit., 2007; contbr. articles to numerous profl. jours. Named Outstanding Fellow, Wooridul Spine Hosp., 2006—07, Outstanding Dr., 2009. Mem.: Congress of Neurol. Surgeons, Internat. Soc. Minimal Intervention in Spine Surgery, N.Am. Assn. Laser Therapy, Spine Arthroplasty Soc., Korean Neurosurg. Soc., Korean Spinal Neurosurgery Soc., Korean Spine Arthroplasty Soc. Avocation: languages. Office: Wooridul Spine Hosp Dept Neurosurgery 47-4 Chungdam-dong Gangnam-gu Seoul 135-100 Republic of Korea Office Phone: 82-2-513-8151. Office Fax: 82-2-513-8146. Business E-Mail: mddavidk@dreamwiz.com.

KIM, JONG BAE, medical educator; b. Seoul, Republic of Korea, Feb. 18, 1957; s. Young-Deok Kim and Soon-Keum Hur; 1 child, Kayoung. PhD, Seoul Nat. U., 1985. Cert. DVM Ministry Agr., 1981. Asst. prof. Geong-Sang Nat. U., Chinju, Republic of Korea, 1986—89; visting prof. Wash. State U., Pullman, 2003—04; prof. Yonsei U., Wonju, Kangwon, Republic of Korea, 1989—. Contbr. articles to sci. jours. Mem.: Korean Soc. Biomedical Lab. Scis. Office: Yonsei Univ Dept Biomedical Lab Sci Maeji Heung-Up 234 220-701 Wonju Gangwon-do Republic of Korea Office Phone: 82-33-760-2423. Office Fax: 82-33-760-2561. Business E-Mail: kimjb70@yonsei.ac.kr.

KIM, JONG-MIN, dermatologist, educator; b. Seoul, Republic of Korea, Feb. 15, 1949; m. Youn Yung Heuy, Feb. 6, 1977; children: Yoon Chung, Yoon Gang. BS, MD, Seoul Nat. U., Korea, 1974, PhD, 1986. Cert. dermatologist Ministry Health and Welfare, 1978. Intern Seoul Nat. U Hosp., 1974—75, resident, 1975—79; prof. med. sch. Hallym U., Seoul, 1983—2001; pvt. practice Seoul, 1991—. Vis. clinician Mayo Clinic, Rochester, Minn., 1990—91; cons. Editor: Textbook of Dermatology, 2001; contbr. articles to profl. jours. Maj. Korean Army, 1979—82. Recipient Dong-A Sci. award, Dong-A Pharm Co., 1986. Mem.: Korean Dermatology Assn., Am. Acad. Dermatology, Korean Dermatology Assn. (bd. dirs. 1993—2001), Am. Acad. Dermatology, Dermatologic Assn. (pres. alumni 2006). Avocations: tennis, mountain climbing, billiards. Home: 1661-4 Shin Rim 8 Dong Kwanak-Ku Seoul 151 903 Republic of Korea Office: Kim Jong Min Skin Clinic 676-103 Manan-Ku Anyang 4 Dong 430-013 Anyang Gyeonggi-do Republic of Korea Personal E-mail: yungheny@hotmail.com.

KIM, JONG-RYOUL, oral surgeon; b. Pusan, Republic of Korea, May 18, 1955; s. Hae Ok Kim and Yeonee Hur; m. Hyunhee Park Kim, Dec. 8; children: Soojung, Seung Taek, Yookyung. DDS, Seoul Nat. U., 1979, MSD, 1982, PhD, 1987. Lic. oral/maxillofacial surgeon, maxillofacial plastic surgeon. Resident Seoul Nat. Univ. Hosp., 1979—82; head dept. Maryknoll Hosp., Pusan, 1985—86; lectr. Pusan Nat. U., 1986—89, from asst. prof. to assoc. prof., 1989—98, prof., 1998—. Vis. scholar U. N.C., Chapel Hill, 1994—95. Author: (book) Textbook of Oral/Maxillofacial Surgery, 1998, Oral Cancer, 2002. Capt. Korean Army, 1982—85. Recipient Editor's award, Am. Speech Lang. Assn., 1997. Fellow: Rotary; mem.: Korean Assn. Maxillofacial Plastic Surgeons (sec.-gen. 2001—). Avocations: golf, skiing. Home: Lotte Apt 8-604 Woo-Dong Haeundae Pusan Republic of Korea Office: Pusan Nat U Dental Sch 1-10 Ami-Dong Pusan Republic of Korea Office Fax: 82 51 244 8334. E-mail: jorkim@pusan.ac.kr.

KIM, JOON YONG, urologist; b. Seoul, Republic of Korea, Apr. 23, 1971; s. Hyun Cheol Kim and Kyung Hwa Heo; m. Hyun Seung Seo, May 24, 1972; 1 child, Byung Moo. MD, PhD, The Cath. U., Seoul, 2003. Diplomate Korean Bd. Urology Ministry of Health and Welfare, 2001. Clin. dir. Manomedi Clinics for Urology and Andrology, Seoul, 2003—; clin. prof. Ewha Woman's Coll. Medicine, Seoul, 2004—, Soonchunhyang Coll. Medicine, Seoul, 2005—. Author: The Lifestyle Counselor's Guide for Weight Control, Handbook of Obesity Treatment. Master: Internat. Profl. Assn. Andrology and Sexology (assoc.); mem.: Dr.'s Assn. Obesity Rsch. (pres. 2001—05), European Urology Assn. (assoc.), Am. Soc. Andrology (assoc.), Am. Urology Assn. (assoc.). Avocations: travel, reading. Office: Manomedi Clinics for Urology and Sexology 142-2 Jung-il B/D Nonhyun-dong Kangnam-gu Seoul 135-822 Republic of Korea Office Fax: 82-2-3446-8215; Home Fax: 82-2-3446-8215. Personal E-mail: kjy2344@naver.com.

KIM, JOONG-GAHNG, otolaryngologist, educator; b. Daegu, Republic of Korea, July 13, 1940; s. Sam-Won Kim and Boo-Suk Choi; m. Dong-Hee Suh, Nov. 12, 1969; children: Hyong-Yong, Sun-Young, Ki-Yong. BS, Korea U. Coll. Medicine, Seoul, 1966; MS, Kyung Pook Nat. U., Daegu, 1975, PhD, 1979. Registered Ministry Health and Welfare, Republic of Korea, 1966, Bd. Otolaryngology Ministry Health and Welfare, Republic of Korea, 1972. Chief dept. otolaryngology Combined-Army Hosp., Daegu, 1973—75, Dongsan Presbyn. Hosp., Daegu, 1976—80; prof. dept. otolaryngology Keimyung U. Sch. Medicine, Daegu, 1981—2005; prof. emeritus Daegu, 2005—; chief and chmn. dept. otolarynology Keimyung U. Sch. Medicine, Daegu, 1981—93, dir. med. libr., 1995—96; dir. Deafness Rsch. Ctr., Dongsan Med. Ctr. Keimyung U., Daegu, 1986—2005; pres. Gawon Hearing Ctr. for Children, Daegu, 2001—. Adv. bd. Daegu Med. Assn., 1983—89; vis. prof. dept. otolaryngology-head and neck surgery U. Iowa Coll. Medicine, 1985—86. Author: (book) Textbook of Otolaryngology, 1987; contbr. over 100 articles to profl. jours. Head lay believer Samduck Cath. Ch., Daegu, 2003—05; adv. bd. steering com. Daegu City Welfare Ctr. for the Deaf and Speech Disorders, 2002—05, advisor to hearing and speech, edn., 2006—; med. missionary Missionary Welfare Ctr., Dongsan Med. Ctr. Keimyung U., Daegu, 2004—05; vol. med. svcs. for the hearing impairment and deaf of children Dongsan Med. Ctr. Keimyung U., Daegu, 1978—98; advisor to prof. New Voice Daegu, Internat. Assn. Laryngectomy (Am. Cancer Soc.), 1976—88. Maj. Army Forces, 1972—75, Republic of Korea. Recipient Nat. Medal for Ednl. Svcs., Ministry Adminstrn., Pres. Republic of Korea, 2005, Certification Appreciation, Internat. Assn. Laryngectomy (Am. Cancer Soc.), 1981, 1986. Mem.: Korean Fedn. Cath. Med. Assns. (vice pres. 2004—), Korean Med. Assn., Korean Soc. Otolaryngology (pres. 1999—2000, Disting. Svc. award 1999, 2000, Social Svcs. award 2004), Internat. Microsurgical Soc., Hearing Internat., Internat. Soc. Logopedics and Phoniatrics, Am. Acad. Otolaryngology- Head and Neck Surgery (corr.). Roman Catholic. Achievements include research in epidermiology of Otitis Media with Effusion; Newborn Hearing Screening Program; Oxygen Free Radicals in Otitis Media in Effusion; School Screening of Otitis Media over 10 years. Avocations: travel, poetry, calligraphy, music. Office: Gawon Joseph Ear Nose and Throat Clinic 76-1 Soo Dong Joong Gu Daegu 700-220 Republic of Korea Home: #201-1803 Hyperion Apt Sinchun-dong Daegu Dong 701-780 Republic of Korea Office Fax: 82-53-257-2275; Home Fax: 82-0505-424-4758. Personal E-mail: hear713@gmail.com.

KIM, JUNG H., medical researcher, educator; b. Pusan; m. Sung H. Kim; 1 child, Jeannette S. MD, Pusan Nat. U., Korea, 1964; MA (hon.), Yale U., New Haven, 2003. Diplomate in anatomical pathology Am. Bd. Pathology, 1976, in clinical pathology Am. Bd. Pathology, 1976, in neuropathology Am. Bd. Pathology, 1983. Attending physician Yale-New Haven Hosp., 1981—; assoc. prof. pathology Yale U. Sch. Medicine, New Haven, 1996—2002, dir., neuropathology program, 1996—2007, prof. pathology, 2002—07, sr. rsch. scientist, 2007—, prof. emeritus, 2007—. Cons. Pathology Hosp. St. Raphael, New Haven, 1993—2007. Contbr. articles to profl. sci. jours. Bd. mem. Alzheimer's Assn. South Ctrl. CT Chpt., New Haven, 1984—91; vice chmn. Saturday Korean Lang. Sch., Orange, Conn., 2004, bd. dirs., 2004. Recipient Andrew W. Mellon Found. award, 1980—83, Alzheimers Recognition award, Alzheimers Assn. South Ctrl. Connecticut Chpt., 1995, Dr. Averill A. Liebow award Excellence in Tchg., 2001. Fellow: Am. Assn. Neuropathologists. Achievements include research in chronological ultrastructural and microscopic alterations in brains of experimental Creutzfeldt-Jakob disease, neuronal and glial density in human epilepsy, and glial role in epileptogenesis; mechanism of neuronal loss via excitoxicity in Alzheimer's disease; neuropathological evaluation of the brain subjected to experimental explosive blasts. Office: Yale Univ Sch of Medicine 310 Cedar St New Haven CT 06520-8023 Office Phone: 203-785-5486. Business E-Mail: jung.kim@yale.edu.

KIM, JUNG HOON, radiologist, educator; b. Seoul, Republic of Korea, Apr. 3, 1968; s. Woo Young Kim and Soon Ja Lee; m. Hyo Won Eun. MD, PhD, Cath. U., Seoul. Cert. by Korean bd. diagnostic radiology Korea Med. Assn., 2000, Iowa Bd. Medicine, 2000. Asst. prof. Soonchunhyang U. Hosp., Dept. Radiology, Seoul, 2001—08; vis. assoc. prof. radiology Iowa U. Hosp., 2008—. Mem.: European Soc. GastroIntestinal and Abdominal Radiology (France). Home: 1509 Mckinley Place Iowa City IA 52246 Office: Radiology Univ Iowa Hosp 200 Hawkins Dr 3897 JPP Iowa City IA 52242-1077 Office Phone: 319-356-7222. Office Fax: 319-356-2220. Personal E-mail: jhkim2008@gmail.com.

KIM, JUNG JU, pharmacologist, researcher; b. Boryeong, Chungnam, Republic of Korea, Jan. 3, 1963; s. Gyocheon Kim and Huichoon Choi; m. Mikyung Kong, Apr. 29, 1989; children: Jiyoon, Boyoon, Dukyoon. BS in Pharmacy, Seoul Nat. U., Republic Of Korea, 1986, PharmM, 1988; PhD in Phramacy, Purdue U., West Lafayette, Ind., 1999. Cert. pharmacist Ministry Health and Welfare, 1986. Chief scientist Amorepacific R&D Ctr., Yongin-si, Republic of Korea, 1999—2005, dir., 2005—07; chief sci. officer Daewoong Pharm., Republic of Korea, 2008—. Author: Glucose-sensitive Hydrogel Membranes; contbr. articles to profl. jours. Mem.: Controlled Release Soc., Pharm. Soc. Korea (sec. gen. affairs 2007—), Korean Soc. Pharm. Sci. and Tech. (indsl. sec. 2004—, mem. editl. bd. 2002—, Rsch. Excellence award 2003), Korean Pharm. Assn., Am. Assn. Pharm. Scientists. Achievements include patents for transdermal preparations containing non-steroidal anti-inflammatory drugs; novel transdermal preparation and its producing method; sustained-releasing injectable formulation for the treatment or prevention of bone-related diseases comprising bisphosphonate-containing polymeric microparticles; multi-stage oral drug controlled-release system; Film-forming agent for drug delivery and preparation for percutaneous administration containing the same; transdermal ketorolac formulation for increasing transdermal absorption of ketorolac; biodegradable polymeric matrix containing hydrophilic or salt-form drug; film-forming composition for transdermal delivery of active ingredients and percutaneous administration formulation containing the same; medicinal adhesive for percutaneous administration. Avocations: golf, tennis. Home: Gaepowoosung Apt 9-203 Daechi-1-dong Gangnam-gu 135-828 Seoul Republic of Korea Office: Daewoong Life Sci Res Ins 501-2 Samgye Pogok Cheoin Yongin Gyeonggi-do 449-814 Republic of Korea Office Phone: 82-31-271-8310. Office Fax: 82-31-322-7152. Personal E-mail: jjkim355@hanmail.net. Business E-Mail: jjkim@daewoong.co.kr.

KIM, JUNG MOGG, healthcare educator; b. Seoul, Republic of Korea, Aug. 10, 1959; s. Changhee Kim and Insook Hyun; m. Kyoung-Ho Kim; 1 child, Hanseung. MD, Hanyang U., Seoul, 1985, PhD in Microbiology and Immunology, 1990. Lic. MD Ministry of Health Republic of Korea, 1985. Rsch. scientist U. Calif., San Diego, 1986—88; prof. Hanyang U. Coll. Medicine, Seoul, 1988—. Com. mem. Ministry Edn., Seoul, 2004—05. Mem. editl. bd.: Jour. Bacteriology and Virology, 2001—. Com. mem. Ministry Edn., Seoul, 2004—05. Capt. Mil. Med. Republic of Korea Army, 1991—94. Recipient Best paper award, Korean Soc. Internal Medicine, 1995, Sci. award, 1997, Best Prof. award, Hanyang U., 2002, Sci. award, Japanese Soc. Helicobacter Rsch., 2002, Best paper award, Korea-Japan Joint Meeting for Helicobacter, 2002, Sci. award, 2004, Poster award, 2005, China-Korea-Japan Joint Meeting for Helicobacter, 2008. Fellow: Korean Soc. Helicobacter and Upper Gastrointestinal Rsch., Korean Soc. Microbiology; mem.: Internat. Soc. Mucosal Immunology, Korean Soc. Gastroenterology (mem. editl. bd. 1999—). Achievements include research in host-parasite relationships, especially bacterial toxin-related immune responses. Avocations: running, mountain climbing, walking. Home: Olympic Apt 315-802 Songpa-gu Seoul Republic of Korea Office: Hanyang Univ Coll Medicine 17 Haengdang-dong Sungdong-gu Seoul 133-791 Republic of Korea Office Phone: 82-2-2282-0645, 82-2-2220-0645. Business E-Mail: jungmogg@hanyang.ac.kr, jungmogg@hanmail.net.

KIM, JUNG WHEE, psychiatrist, educator; b. Gimcheon, Gyeonsangbuk-do, Republic of Korea, May 4, 1940; s. Pal Man and Pil Sun (Song) Kim; m. Myung Ja Son; children: Sungwon, Sung Min. MD, Kyungpook Nat. U., Daegu, Republic of Korea, 1964. Cert. med. specialist Ministry Health & Welfare, 1974. Intern First Army Hosp., Daegu, 1964—65; med. officer Korea Army, 1964—69; resident, dept. neuropsychiatry Kyungbook Nat. U., 1970—74, lectr., dept. neuropsychiatry, 1985—90; dir. Korea Neuropsychiatric Clinic, Daegu, 1974—; neuropsychiatrist Deagu Juvenile Detention & Classification, Ministry of Justice, Daegu, 1979—2000. Lectr. Legal Rsch. & Tng. Inst., Ministry of Justice, Daegu, 1980—2000; pres. Daegu & Kyungbook Sects., Korean Neuropsychiatric Assn., 1984—85; dir., bd. dirs. Daegu Sect., Life Line, 1985—2002; pres. Nam-Gu Med. Assn., Daegu, 1991—92; mem., adv. com. med. affairs Daegu Dist. Pub. Prosecutor's Office, 1991—94; lectr., Daegu Edn. Tng. Inst. Daegu Met. Office Edn., 1993—96, com. mem. spl. edn., 1995—; com. mem. mental hygiene Daegu Met. City Hall, 1997—2000. Author: (book) A Preliminary Study for the Development of a Predictive Scale for Delinquency, 1976, A Study of Personality Characteristics and Traits in Delinquents, 1979, A Study on the Psychiatric Dynamics of Juvenile Delinquents Among Korean, 1984, A Study of the Influences of Symptom Checklist-90-revision on the Delinquents, 1996, The Effects of Meditation on a Measure of Eco-Identity in Delinquent Adolescents, 1997. Capt. Korean Army, 1964—69. Recipient Prime Min.'s Citation award, 2000. Roman Catholic. Avocations: meditation, reading, yoga.

KIM, JUNGHOON, neurosurgeon; b. Incheon, Republic of Korea, Dec. 30, 1973; MD, Inha U., 1998, PhD in Neurosci. and Biophysics, 2003. Fellow surgeon, brain and spine surgery Neurosurg. Dept. Severance U. Hosp., 1999—2003; neurosurgeon Dept. Neurosurgery Himchan Hosp., 2003—07; chief, neurosurg. dept. Brain and Spine Ctr. Tntn-Hosp., 2007—. Outpatient assoc. prof., spine surgery Dept. Neurosurgery Severance U. Hosp., 1999—2011; med. cons. Assn. Korean Profl. Volleyball Players, 2006—11; med. cons., spine and sports injury Korean Med. Assn. Group, 2007—11. Recipient Appreciation plaque, Welfare Dept. Seoul City Office. Mem.: Korean Assn. Minimal Invasive Spine Surgery (Outstanding Achievement award), Asia-pacific Assn. Spine Surgery, Korean Assn. Spine Surgery, Korean Med. Assn., Korean Assn. Neurosurgery. Avocations: antiques, music, motorcycling. Office: Tntn Hosp 1126-34 Guro 3-Dong Guro Seoul 152-880 Republic of Korea Office Fax: 822-851-9400. Personal E-mail: ns733@hanmail.net. Business E-Mail: tntnhospital@hotmail.com.

KIM, JUNGIN, dietician, educator; b. Busan, Republic Of Korea, Feb. 4, 1959; d. Namkyung and Duckja Kim; m. Cheolhwa Noh, July 17, 1982; children: Soonhyun Noh, Soonwook Noh. BA, Seoul Nat. U., Republic Of Korea, 1981; MS, Mass. Inst. Tech., Cambridge, 1984; PhD, U. Calif., Berkely, 1988. Registered dietician Ministry Health and Welfare, 1981; cert. mid. and high sch. tchr. Ministry Edn. Sci. and Tech., 1981. Vis. scholar U. Calif., 1996—97; lectr. Inje U., Gimhae, Gyungnam, Republic of Korea, 1989—91, asst. prof., 1991—97, assoc. prof., 1997—2004, prof., 2004—. Editor J. Cmty. Nutrition Korea, Seoul, 2002—07; exec. Korean Nutrition Soc., Seoul, 2004—06; editor J. Food Sci. and Biotech., Seoul, 2005—; panel mem. Health Promotion Program Expert Adv. Com., Busan, Republic of Korea, 2005—; exec. Korean Soc. Cmty. Nutrition, Seoul, 2008—. Contbr. articles to profl. jours. Recipient Pub. Heath Promotion award, Gimhae, 2004, Pharmbio award, Korean Endourological Soc., 2006, award, Min. Edn. Sci. and Tech., 2007. Mem.: Korean Nutrition Soc. (Outstanding Poster Presentation award 2004, 2005), Korean Soc. Cmty. Nutrition. Avocations: travel, music, recorder, hiking, reading. Office: Inje Univ Obang-Dong 607 621-749 Gimhae Gyeongsangnam-do Republic of Korea Office Phone: 82-55-320-3236. Office Fax: 82-55-321-0691. Personal E-mail: moojoo@hanafos.com. Business E-Mail: fdsnkiji@inje.ac.kr.

KIM, JUN-MO, medical educator; b. Seoul, Aug. 3, 1969; B, Soonchunhyang U., 1994, PhD, 2005. Assoc. prof. dept. urology Soonchunhyang U., Bucheon Hosp., 2008—. Mem. Korean med. guideline com. Korean Acad. Med. Scis., 2010—. Gra, Nat. Rsch. Found. Korea. Mem.: Korean Assn. Urogenital Tract Infection and Inflammation (exec. dir. state affair 2010—), Korean Soc. Pediatric Urology (exec. dir. info. com. 2011—), Korean Children's Continence and Enuresis Soc. (sec. gen. 2010—), Korean Urol. Assn. (mem. informational com. 2011—). Avocation: tennis. Office: 1174 Jung-dong Wonmi-gu Bucheon Gyeonggi 420-767 Republic of Korea Office Fax: 82-32-621-5016. Business E-Mail: urojun@schmc.ac.kr.

KIM, JUN-SANG, medical educator; b. Yesan, Republic Of Korea, Dec. 25, 1965; s. Chang-Hyeon Kim and Young-Sook Lim; m. Eun-Kyeong Jo, Dec. 10, 1992; children: Ha-Young, Ju-Young. BS in Medicine, Chungnam, Daejeon, 1990, MS in Medicine, 1997; PhD in Medicine, Chungnam Nat. U., Daejeon, 1999. Cert. radiation oncology Ministry Health and Welfare, 1999. Rsch. fellow Cancer Rsch. UK Laboratories, Dept. Cancer Medicine, Imperial Coll., London, 2003—04; asst. prof. medicine Chungnam Nat. U., 2004—; chief radiation oncology dept. Chungnam Nat. U. Hosp., 2005—. Contbr. articles to profl. jours. Mem.: Korean Soc. Therapeutic Radiology & Oncology (licentiate Excellent Paper Exhbn. award 2005, 2006), Am. Soc. Therapeutic and Radiation Oncology (licentiate). Office: Chungnam Nat U Hosp Daesa-dong Jung-gu Daejeon 301-721 Republic of Korea Office Fax: 82-42-280-7899. Business E-Mail: k423j@cnu.ac.kr.

KIM, KE CHUNG, entomology, systematics, and biodiversity educator, researcher; b. Seoul, Mar. 7, 1934; came to US, 1957, naturalized, 1973; s. Yong Shik Kim and Yong Im Cho, m. Young Hee Kim, Apr. 11, 1964; children: Stuart, Sally. BS, Seoul Nat. U., Korea, 1956; MA, U. Mont., 1959; PhD, U. Minn., 1964. Rsch. assoc. U. Minn., St. Paul, 1964-68; asst. prof. entomology Pa. State U., Univ. Pk., 1968—72, assoc. prof., 1972-79, prof., 1979—2008, prof. emeritus, 2008—, dir. emeritus, Ctr. BioDiversity Rsch., 1988—2008. Fulbright lectr., rschr., Korea, 1975-76; vis. prof. Seoul Nat. U., 1993-94; Gast prof. Heidelberg U., 1976; chmn. Internat. Adv Coun. for Biosystematic Svcs. in Entomology, 1985-92; pres. Pa. Biol. Survey, 1996-97. Author, editor: Coevolution of Parasitic Arthropods and Mammals, 1985, Sucking Lice of North America, 1986, Black Flies, 1987, Evolution of Insect Pests, 1993, Biodiversity and Landscapes: A Paradox of Humanity, 1994, Biodiversity Korea 2000: A Strategy to Save, Study and Sustainably Use Korea's Biotic Resources, 1994, Biodiversity, Our Living World: Your LIfe Depends On It!, 2001. Mem. coun. Trinity Luth. Ch., State College, Pa., 1983-86; bd. dirs. Temporary Housing, Inc., State College, 1988-93. Fulbright sr. scholar, 1993—94. Mem. AAAS, Entomol. Soc. Am. (chmn. Sect. A 1985-86), Entomol. Soc. Pa., Soc. Systematic Biologists, Soc. Conservation Biology, Assn. Systematics Collections (chmn. coun. on applied systematics and society 1985-87), Korea Acad. Sci. and Tech. (life), Sigma Xi (chpt. pres. 1992-95), DMZ Forum Inc.(chair 1997-). Avocations: photography, nature conservation, walking, music. Office Phone: 814-863-2863. Business E-Mail: kck@psu.edu.

KIM, KEE-DEOG, dentist, educator; b. Daejeon, Republic of Korea, Jan. 27, 1962; s. Young-Kuk Kim and Soo-Ok Lee; m. Hyang-Yi Kim; 1 child, Min-Kyung. DDS, Yonsei U., Seoul, Republic of Korea, 1988, PhD, 1997. Prof. Yonsei Univ. Coll. Dentistry, Seoul, 1996—; chmn. dept. advanced gen. dentistry, Dental Hosp. Yonsei U., Seoul, 2006—, dir. Continuing Edn. Ctr., 2008—. Author: (articles) Dental & medical informatics (PACS & EMR), various image processing & three-dimensional image application in oral & maxillofacial diagnostic science, and forensic & anthropologic radiology in association with human identification; contbr. articles to profl. jours. Recipient Best Prof. award, Yonsei U., 2004. Mem.: Korean Acad. Geriat. Dentistry (sec. gen. 2009—10). Achievements include development of Picture Archiving and Communications System (PACS) in Yonsei University College of Dentistry Dental Hospital, the first real Dental Full PACS implementation. Office: Yonsei University Coll Dentistry 250 Seongsanno Seodaemun-gu Seoul 120-752 Republic of Korea Home: 101-1304 Hongjewon Hyundai Apt Hongje-dong Seodaemun-gu Seoul 120 788 Republic of Korea Office Fax: 82-2-2227-8906. Business E-Mail: kdkim@yuhs.ac.

KIM, KI HUN, surgeon; b. Seoul, Republic of Korea, June 20, 1966; s. Myung Hwan and Yun Hee Kim. BS, Med. Coll., Korea U., Seoul, MD, 1992; MS, Grad. Sch., Korea U., Seoul, 1999, PhD, 2003. Diplomate Korean Surg. Soc., 1998. Instr. Surgery, Inje U., Seoul Paik Hosp., Seoul, 2000—01, Surgery, Ulsan U., Asan Med. Ctr., Seoul, 2001—04, asst. prof., 2004—08, assoc. prof., 2008—. Vis. prof. Kobe U., Republic of Korea, 2006. Recipient Best Video Presentation award, APDW Com., 2005. Mem.: Korean Med. Assn., Internat. Liver Transplantation Soc., Internat. Assn. Surgeons and Gastroenterologists, Internat. HPB Assn., Korean Soc. Transplantation, Korean Assn. HBP Surgery, Korean Surg. Soc. Avocations: motorcycling, travel. Office: Surgery Asan Med Ctr 388-1 Pungnap-dong Songpa-gur Seoul 138-736 Republic of Korea Office Phone: 82-2-3010-3495. Office Fax: 82-2-474-9027. Business E-Mail: khkim620@amc.seoul.kr.

KIM, KI WOONG, medical educator; s. Sung Yong Kim and Bog Ja Song; m. Sae Youn Kim; children: Taehyung, Taejoo. PhD, Seoul Nat. U. Grad. Sch., Republic of Korea, 1999. Diplomate MD Ministry Health Welfare, Republic of Korea, 1989, in psychiatry 1994. Intern. Seoul Nat. U. Hosp., 1989—90; resident Dept. Neuropsychiatry, Seoul Nat. U. Hosp., 1990—94, clin. fellowship, 1997—99; med. dir. Kyunggi Provincial Hosp. Elderly, Yongin, Republic of Korea, 2000—02; assoc. prof. Dept. Neuropsychiatry, Sungkyunkwan U. Coll. Medicine, Seoul, 2001—02, Seoul Nat. U. Coll. Medicine, 2003—. Chmn. Gyeonggi chpt. Korean Assn. Dementia, Seongnam, Republic of Korea, 2004—, Korean Consortium Health and Aging Rsch., Seongnam, 2005—; mng. editor Psychiatry Investigation, Seoul, 2010; v.p. Korean Coll. Geriatric Psychoneuropharmacology, Seoul, 2003—05, bd. dir., 2006—; sec. gen. Korean Soc. Cognitive Sci., Seoul, 2008—. Singer: (chorus) Medichior Annual Performances; author: (book) Dementia, Telling a Hope, CERAD-K Assessment Packet, Occupational Therapy for Dementia Patients, The Health of the Elderly and Clinical Laboratory Tests, Dementia Care Assessment Packet. Capt. Army, 1994—97, Pocheon, Gyeonggido, Korea. Recipient Disting. Svc. award, Seoul Nat. U. Bundang Hosp., 2004; named Joongang Best Articles of Yr., Korean Neuropsychiatric Assn., 2007—08. Mem.: Korean Assn. Dementia (bd. dir. 2002—08), Gyeonngi Assn. Dementia (chmn. 2004—08), Editl. Com. Korean Neuropsychiatric Assn., Am. Assn. Geriatric Psychiatry, Korean Dementia Registry Ctr., Planning Com. Korean Neuropsychiatric Assn., Korean Dementia Nurse Edn. Com., Korean Soc. Biol. Psychiatry, Korean Soc. Psychopathology and Psychiat. Classification, Korean Neuropsychiatric Assn. Achievements include patents for safe indwelling foley catheter. Office: Seoul Nat Univ Bundang Hosp Gumidong Bundanggu 300 462-707 Seongnam Gyeonggi-do Republic of Korea Office Phone: 82-31-787-7432. Office Fax: 82-31-787-4058; Home Fax: 82-2-557-5498. Business E-Mail: kwkimmd@snu.ac.kr.

KIM, KIMBERLY, medical educator; b. Ych, Feb. 1, 1965; PhD, UWM, 1997. Postdoc U. Calif. San Francisco; assoc. prof. CSUEB, 2001—. Mem.: STTI (Hall of Fame Nu Xi at Large chpt.). Avocation: reading. Office: 25800 Carlos Bee Blvd Hayward CA 94542 Office Fax: 510-885-2156. Business E-Mail: kimberly.kim@csueastbay.edu.

KIM, KWANG SEOG, plastic and reconstructive surgeon, professor; b. Gwangju, Republic of Korea, Apr. 5, 1963; s. Hee Choong Kim and Bok Kyoung Ju; m. Ji Young Park, Apr. 17, 1998; children: Min Seo, Jinwoo. BS in Med. Sci., Grad. Sch., Chonnam Nat. U., Republic of Korea, 1988; MS in Med. Sci., Grad. Sch., Chonnam Nat. U., 1994, PhD, 1997; PhD in Pub. Health, Nat. Pub. Health Care Ctr., Republic of Korea, 1991. Cert. med. practice 1988, specialy bd. plastic and reconstructive surgery 1997, subspecialty bd. in surgery of the hand 2005; Korean Subspeciality Bd. Surgery Hand, 2010. Intern Chonnam Nat. U. Hosp., Gwangiu, Republic of Korea, 1991—92, resident, 1993—97; lectr. Chonnam Nat. U. Hosp., Grad. Sch., 1997—99; fellowship Chonnam Nat. U. Hosp., 1999—2000, clin. prof., 2000—04; asst. prof. Chonnam Nat. U. Hosp., Grad. Sch., 2004—08; assoc. prof. Dept. Plastic & Reconstructive Surgery Chonnam Nat. U. Hosp., Grad. Med. Sch., Republic of Korea, 2008—. Dir. Chonnam Nat. U. Hosp., Hand Surgery Ctr., 2000—02, Chonnam Nat. U. Hosp., Microsurgery Ctr., 2003—, Chonnam Nat. U. Hosp., Burn Ctr., 2004—; pub. health rschr. Nat. Pub. Health Care Ctr., Chonnam, Republic of Korea, 1988—91. Contbr. articles various profl. jours., chapters to books. Pub. health br. Nat. Pub. Health Care Ctr., Chonnam, Republic of Korea, 1988—91. Lt., med. officer Korean Army, 1988, Korea. Rsch. grant, Chonnam Nat. U. Hosp., 1999—2011, Chonnam Nat. U., 1999—2011. Mem.: Korean Soc. Microsurgery (dir. ex officio 2008—, mem. publ. & editl. Svc. Com. 2008—), Korean Soc. Surgery Hand (dir. ex officio 2008—, mem. publ. & editl. svc. com. 2009—, chmn. fin. com. 2010—11), Korean Plastic Surgery Rsch. Coun. (dir. 2007—), World Soc. Reconstructive Microsurgery, Korean Cleft Palate-Craniofacial Assn. (exec. dir. 2001—03, treas. 2003—05, award 1997), Korean Soc. for Surgery of the Hand (award 1997), Korean Soc. Aesthetic Plastic Surgery (chmn. internal affairs com. 2010—, award 1997), Korean Soc. Plastic and Reconstructive Surgeons (mem. sci. programs com. bd. exem. com. 2008—, award 1997), Internat. Conf. for Plastic, Reconstructive and Aesthetic Surgery (award 1997). Avocations: swimming, climbing, golf, Asian checkers. Office: Chonnam Nat University Med Sch Dept Plastic and Reconstructive Surgery 42 Jebong ro Dong-gu Gwangju 501-757 Republic of Korea Office Phone: 82-62-220-6363 Ext. 6352. Office Fax: 82-62-227-1639. Business E-Mail: pskim@chonnam.ac.kr.

KIM, KYEONG SEOP, biomedical engineer; b. Inchon, Republic of Korea, Dec. 7, 1957; s. Byeong Geol Kim and Un Soon Huh; m. Young Mi Choi, Mar. 10, 1960; children: Jane Young, Simon Young. PhD, U. of Ala., Huntsville, 1994; MS, Yonsei U., Seoul, Korea, 1981; BS, Yonsei U., 1979. Professor, Konkuk U., 2001. Prin. rschr. Samsung Advanced Inst. of Tech., Kihung, 1995—2001; prof. Konkuk U., Chungju, 2001—. Achievements include patents for biometric apparatus and method using bio-signals; biometric identification apparatus and method using bio-signals and artificial neural networks. Home: YeonSoo Dong 418 Bunji Youwon Apt2-907 Chungju Si Republic of Korea Office: Konkuk University Sch Biomed Engineering Dan Wall Dong 322 380-701 Chungju Si Chungcheongbuk-do Republic of Korea Office Fax: +82-43-851-0620; Home Fax: +82-43-851-0620. Personal E-mail: kyeong@kku.ac.kr.

KIM, KYU-HONG, neurosurgeon, department chairman; b. Republic of Korea, Mar. 20, 1964; BS, Busan Nat. U., 1983; MD, Dong-A U., 1997. Cert. neurosurg. specialist. Chmn., neurosurg. dept. Samsung Changwon Hosp., 2005—. Office: Samsung Changwon Hosp 50 Hapsung-dong Masan Hoewon-gu Changwon Gyeongsangnam 630-723 Republic of Korea Office Fax: 82-55-290-6245. Business E-Mail: unikkh@unitel.co.kr.

KIM, KYUNG HWAN, pharmacologist, educator; b. Hayang, Kyungbuk, Korea, July 16, 1946; s. Seok Do and Gwee Jo (Lee) K.; m. Won Sook Kang, Feb. 8, 1974; children: Aejoo, Daeyun. MD, Yonsei U., Seoul, Korea, 1970, M.M.Sc., 1973, PhD, 1977. Teaching and rsch. asst. Yonsei U. Coll. Medicine, Seoul, 1970-74, instr., 1977-80, asst. and assoc. prof., 1980-87, chmn. dept. pharmacology, 1987-96, prof. pharmacology, 1988—, head dept. clin. pharmacology, 1996-2000, dean, 2004—06; chief rsch. div. Aeromed. Rsch. Ctr., Seoul, 1974-77; rsch. assoc. U. Newcastle Upon-Tyne Med. Sch., 1978-79. Vis. instr. Brown U., Providence, 1979-80; vis. prof. U. Manchester, U.K., 1988-89; head Yonsei Med. Tech. Evaluation Ctr., 1997-99; dir. basic med. sci. Korean Acad. Med. Sci., 1997-2000; dir. Brain Korea 21 project med. sci. Yonsei U., 1999—2006. Editor: Lecture on Pharmacology, 1984, 5th edit. 2003; editor Korean Jour. Pharmacology, 1985-96, Asian Pacific Jour. Pharmacology, 1991-2000. Maj. M.C., Korean Air Force, 1974-77. Recipient Scientific award Korean Soc. Gastroenterology, 1995. Mem. Korean Soc. Pharmacology (v.p. 1991-93, pres. 1993-94, Sci. award 1997), Korean Med. Assn. (Scientific award, 1997), Internat. Union Pharmacology (nat. del. 1993—2004), Korean Med. Assn., Korean Acad. Sci. and Tech., Korean Soc. Clin. Pharmacology and Therapeutics (pres. 2003-05), Nat. Acad. Medicine Korea. Avocations: music record collecting, mountain climbing, golf. Office: Yonsei Univ Coll of Med Dept Pharmacology Seoul 120-752 Republic of Korea Home Phone: 82-(0)31-904-8988; Office Phone: 82-(0)2-2228-1732. Business E-Mail: hwan444@yuhs.ac.

KIM, KYUNGMOK, electronics engineer, researcher; b. Republic of Korea, June 19, 1977; PhD, Oxford U., Eng., 2006. Chief rsch. engr. LG Electronics, Republic of Korea, 2006—07; commd. rsch. scientist Korea Inst. Sci. and Tech., 2007—08; rsch. engr. Ecole Nat. Supérieure des Mines, 2009—11. Office: Ecole Nationale Supérieure des Mines 15 Saint-Etienne 42023 France Personal E-mail: kyungmok@yahoo.co.kr. Business E-Mail: kkim@emse.fr.

KIM, MI KYUNG, research scientist, educator; b. Seoul, Republic Of Korea, Aug. 8, 1964; d. Sun Sik Kim and Eun Seop Yoon. BS in Food & Nutrition, Yonsei U., Seoul, 1986, MS in Nutritional Biochemistry, 1989, PhD in Nutritional Epidemiology, 1996. Cert. Ministry of Health & Welfare, Korea, 1986. Postdoc. tng. Cath. U. Korea, Seoul, 1998—99, rsch. prof., 2000—04, educator, Grad. Sch. Occupl. Health, 2000—. Postdoc. tng. Asan Med. Ctr., Seoul, 1996—97; with Ajou U. Hosp., 1997—98; educator Kangnung U., 1996—99, Dongduck U., 1997—, Changwon U., 1999—99, Kongju U., 1999—99; vis. scientist Nat. Cancer Ctr. Rsch. Inst. East, Japan, 2001—03, Nat. Inst. Health & Nutrition, Tokyo, 2003—04. Contbr. scientific papers. Office: Nat Cancer Ctr Ilsan-Gu 411-769 Gyeonggi-do Gyeonggi-do Republic of Korea Office Fax: 82.31.920.2006. Business E-Mail: alrud@ncc.re.kr.

KIM, MICHAEL CHONG, medical educator, director; b. Aug. 3, 1958; BA in English Lit., Georgetown U. Sch. Medicine, 1990, MD, 1994. Diplomate Am. Bd. Internat. Medicine. Asst. prof., med. dir. Mt. Sinai Med. Ctr., 1994—. Office: Mount Sinai Medical Ctr One Gustave L. Levy Pl New York NY 10029 Office Phone: 212-241-6422. Business E-Mail: michael.kim@mountsinai.org.

KIM, MIHYUNG, pharmacist; b. Republic of Korea, Nov. 18, 1968; PhD, Ewha Woman's U., 2002. Bd. dir. Anterogen Co., Ltd., 2008, mng. dir., 2008—. Office: 405 Namsung-Plz 345-30 Gasan-dong Seoul 153-802 Republic of Korea Business E-Mail: mhyungk@anterogen.com.

KIM, MIN YOUNG, nursing educator, researcher; b. Seoul, Republic of Korea, Jan. 17, 1974; PhD, Seoul Nat. U., 2008. RN nurse practitioner, advanced oncology Seoul Nat. U. Hosp., 1996—2005; rschr. Jeju Regional Cancer Ctr., 2009—11; prof. Jeju Nat. U., 2011—, ednl. rschr., 2011—. Mem.: Korean Soc. Hospice and Palliative Care, Korean Oncology Nursing Soc., Korean Acad. Nursing Adminstrn., Oncology Nursing Soc., Korean Soc. Nursing Sci. Avocations: piano, singing, cooking. Office: Coll Nursing Jeju Nat University Jejudaehakno 102 Jeju 690-756 Republic of Korea Personal E-mail: musemy2@jejunu.ac.kr.

KIM, MOO HYUN, internist, educator; b. Hadong-Gun, Kyungsangnam-Do, Korea, Apr. 20, 1960; s. Sang Bong and Sang Nam Kim; m. Ann Mi Kyung, Jan. 23, 1988; children: So Yeon, Sung Woo. PhD, Pusan Nat. U., 1993. Lic. physician Korea, 1984, diplomate Korean Bd. of Internal Medicine, Korean Bd. of Cardiology. Intern Pusan Nat. U. Hosp., Busan, Republic of Korea, 1984—85, resident, 1985—88, 1991—92; instr. Dong-A Med. Coll., Busan, Republic of Korea, 1992—94, asst. prof., 1994—98, assoc. prof., 1998—2003, prof., 2003—. Dir. cardiology Dong-A U. Hosp., Busan, 2001—. Contbr. articles to profl. jours., chapters to books. Capt. Korean Army, 1988—91, Daegu. Grantee, Korean Sci. Rsch. Found. grantee, 2001. Fellow: Soc. of Cardiac Catheterization and Cardiac Intervention (life; bethesda, md 1978—2003), Am. Coll. of Cardiology (life; bethesda 1977—2003). Home: #102-1402 Woosung Bora Soo Young-Gu Pusan 613-816 Republic of Korea Office: Dong-A Univ Hosp Dept Cardiology 3-1 Dongdaeshin-Dong Pusan 602-715 Republic of Korea Office Fax: 82-51-242-1449. Personal E-mail: kmh60@chollian.net. E-mail: kmh60@damc.or.kr.

KIM, MOON YOUNG, gynecologist; b. Seoul, Republic of Korea, Apr. 10, 1963; MD, Ewha Women's U., 1988; PhD, Kyung Hee U., 2004. Divsn. dir. maternal fetal medicine Cheil Gen. Hosp., Sch. Medicine, Kwan Dong U., 2006—09, prof. dept. ob-gyn., 2006—. Editor-in-chief Korean Soc. Perinatology, 2009—, Korean Soc. Ultrasound in Ob-gyn., 2006—07, chmn. pub. rels., 2010—. Fellow: Korean Soc. Ob-gyn.; mem.: Internat. Soc. Ultrasound in Ob-gyn. Office: 1-19 Muk Jung Dong Jung Ku Seoul 100-380 Republic of Korea Office Fax: 82-2-2000-7793. E-mail: mykimdr@yahoo.co.kr.

KIM, MYOUNG S., researcher; b. Pusan, Republic of Korea, Nov. 25, 1969; PhD, Pusan Nat. U., 2000. Instr. Johns Hopkins U. Sch. Medicine, 2007—. Mem.: Am. Assn. Cancer Rsch. Office: 1550 Orleans St Baltimore MD 21231 Business E-Mail: mkim51@jhmi.edu.

KIM, MYUNG-GOOD, plastic surgeon; Hon. dr., Uzbekistan; md palstic surgery dept. Seoul Nat. Univ. Hosp.; resident plastic surgery divsn. Seoul Paik Hosp.; surgeon Real Cosmetic Clinic. Prof. coll. medicine Seoul Nat. Univ.; prof. plastic surgery dept. Seoul Nat. Univ. Borame Hosp., Seoul Nat. Univ. Bundang Hosp. Office: Real Cosmetic Clinic Asio B/D 580 Shinsa-Dong Gangnam-Gu Seoul 135892 Republic of Korea Office Phone: 8225121616. Office Fax: 8225111313. *

KIM, NAM KEUN, research scientist, medical educator; b. Buankun, South Korea, June 24, 1960; s. Yeun Seop Kim and Jung Ja Hur; m. Keum Duk Kang, Nov. 13, 1988; children: Eo Jin, Nu Ri. PhD, Seoul Nat. U., 1985—90. Lectr. Seoul Nat. U., Republic of Korea, 1989—90; post-doc Oak Ridge Nat. Lab., Tenn., 1991—92, U. Tex. Med. Br., Galveston, 1992—93; rsch. fellow Ajou U., Suwon, Kyonggi-do, Republic of Korea, 1993—94; rsch. scientist CHA Gen. Hosp., Seoul, Republic of Korea, 1995—2000; asst. prof. Pochon CHA U., Kyonggi-do, Republic of Korea, 2000—, lab dir. Seongnam, Kyonggi-do, Republic of Korea, 2001—. Fellow: Korean Jour. Genetics. Achievements include patents pending for MTHFR 677TT genotype for prediction and prevention of an ischemic stroke. Home: #420-1104 Seohyun-dong Bundang-ku Kyonggi-do Seongnam 463-777 Republic of Korea Office: Pochon CHA Univ Yatap-Dong Bundang-Ku 351 462-712 Seongnam Gyeonggi-do Republic of Korea Office Fax: +82-31-780-5766. Personal E-mail: namkkim@naver.com. Business E-Mail: nkkim@cha.ac.kr.

KIM, OKSOO, nursing educator; d. Byungguu and Guiran Kim; m. Namson Hong, Feb. 16, 1986; children: Sungki Hong, Kahon Hong. BSN, MSN, Ewha Womans U.; PhD, U. Nebr., Omaha, 1996. RN Bd. Nursing Lic., Nebr., 1992. Staff nurse Ewha Womans U. Hosp., Seoul, 1980—83, prof., 1997—. Prof. Mokpo Cath. U., 1984—91. Com. mem. Seoul Women Com., 2005—07, Upper Rm. Evangelist Assn., Seoul, 1999—2007. Mem.: Seoul Nurses Assn. (life), Korean Nurses Assn. (life), Korean Acad. Adult Nursing (life), Korean Soc. Nursing Sci. (life), Sigma Theta Tau Internat. (life). Methodist. Office: Ewha Womans U 11-1 Daehyun-dong Seodaemoon-gu Seoul 120-750 Republic of Korea Office Fax: 02-3277-2850. Business E-Mail: ohong@ewha.ac.kr.

KIM, PETER SUNGBAI, pharmaceutical research and development company executive, educator; b. Atlanta, Apr. 27, 1958; s. Mi Heh (Ryu) K.; m. Kathryn H. Spitzer; children: Michael, Jeremy, Alexander. AB magna cum laude with distinction, Cornell U., 1979; PhD, Stanford U., 1985; DSc (hon.), Pohang U. Sci. and Tech., 2011. Whitehead fellow Whitehead Inst., Cambridge, 1985—88, assoc. mem., 1988—92, mem., 1992—2001; asst. prof. biology MIT, Cambridge, 1988—92, assoc. prof., 1992—95, prof. biology, 1995—2001; asst investigator Howard Hughes Medical Institute, Cambridge, 1990—93, assoc. investigator, 1993—97, investigator, 1997—2001; exec. v.p. R&D Merck Research Laboratories, West Point, Pa., 2001—02, pres., 2003—; exec. v.p. Merck & Co., Inc., 2008—. Bd. dirs. Fox Chase Cancer Ctr., 2003—09, Whitehead Inst. Biomed. Rsch., 2005—; mem. coun. Inst. Medicine NAS, 2006—; mem. oversight com., divsn. earth and life studies The Nat. Acads., 2006—08, Coun. Global HIV Vaccine Enterprise, 2009—; bd. trustees Alfred P. Sloan Found., 2009—. Recipient Excellence in Chemistry award ICI Pharms., 1989, Walter J. Johnson prize Jour. Molecular Biology, 1989, Nat. Acad. Sci. Molecular Biology award, 1993, Eli Lilly Biol. Chemistry award Am. Chem. Soc., 1994, DuPont Merck Young Investigator award Protein Soc., 1994, Ho-Am prize for basic sci. Samsung Found., 1998, Hans Neurath award The Protein Soc., 1999, Harvey lectr., The Harvey Soc., 2002. Fellow AAAS, Biophys. Soc., Am. Acad. Microbiology, Am. Acad. Arts & Scis.; mem. NAS, Inst. Medicine (coun. mem.). Office: Merck Rsch Labs UG4CD-01 351 N Sumneytown Pike North Wales PA 19454

KIM, S. PETER, psychiatrist, educator, health facility administrator, researcher; b. Seoul, Oct. 8, 1939; s. Chong Soon Kim and Soon Bok Lim; m. Oksuk Mary Lee, Mar. 30, 1963; children: John, Katherine. CPM, Seoul Nat. U., 1957; MD, Seoul Nat. U. Coll. of Medicine, 1963; PhD, Toho U. Grad. Sch., Japan, 1984; MBA, U. Hawaii Sch. Bus. Adminstrn., 2002. Asst. prof. psychiatry N.Y. U. Sch. of Medicine, NYC, 1976—82, assoc. prof. psychiatry, 1982—88; prof. psychiatry and pediat. U. Ga. Med. Sch., Augusta, 1988—94; prof. psychiatry Sungkyoon Kwan Sch. of Medicine, Seoul, Republic of Korea, 1994—97, U. Hawaii Sch. of Medicine, Honolulu, 1997—. Program dir. child and adolescent psychiatry N.Y. U. and Bellevue Med. Ctrs., NYC, 1979—88, dir. divsn. child and adolsecent psychiatry; program dir. child and adolescent psychiatry U. Ga. Med. Coll. of Ga., Augusta, 1988—94; dept. chmn. psychiatry Sungkyoon Kwan U. Sch. of Medicine, Seoul, Republic of Korea, 1994—97; dir. Samsung-

Johns Hopkins Internat. Clinics, Seoul, 1994—97; program dir. child and adolescent forensic psychiatry U. Hawaii Sch. of Medicine, 1999—2006. Pres. Hawaii Psychiatric Med. Assn., Korean Am. Med. Assn. of Hawaii, Honolulu, 1999—2001. Fellow: Pacific Rim Coll. Psychiatrists, Am. Orthopsychiatric Assn., Am. Coll. Psychiatrists, Am. Acad. Child and Adolescent Psychiatry, Am. Psychiatric Assn.; mem.: Hibiscus Lions Club (pres. 2002—03). Office: Dept Psychiatry 4th Fl U Hawaii Sch Medicine 1356 Lusitania St Honolulu HI 96813 Business E-Mail: kimp@dop.hawaii.edu.

KIM, SAE-CHUL, urologist, educator; b. Taegu, Korea, June 2, 1946; m. Jung-Hwa Lee, June 23, 1973; children: Sun-Young, Ye-Young, Hee-Young, Hee-Tae. B Medicine, Kyung-Pook U., Taegu, 1971, M Medicine, 1974, PhD in Medicine, 1980. Diplomate Bd. Urology. Intern Kyung-Pook Nat. U. Hosp., Taegu, Republic of Korea, 1971-72, resident, 1972-76; asst. prof. Chung-Ang U. Med. Sch., Seoul, 1980-85, assoc. prof., 1985-90, prof., chmn. dept. urology, 1990—; supt. gen. Chung-Ang U. Yongsan Hosp., 1996—97; dir. gen. Chung-Ang U. Med. Ctr., Seoul, 2005—08; v.p. Chung-Ang U., 2007—08; pres. Kwandong U., Myongji Hosp., 2011—. Author: Andrology, 1989, Sociology of Sex, 1990, Urology, 1991, Diagnosis and Treatment of Impotence, 1994, The Prostatic Disease, 1996; contbr. articles to profl. jours. Maj. Korea Mil., 1976-79. Recipient Excellence in Medicine award Seoul Med. Sco., 1986, Excellence in Sci. Rsch. award Chung-Ang U., Seoul, 1988, 2000; named Hon. Alumnus Kyung-Pook Nat. U., 1998. Mem.: Korean Soc. Quality Assurance in Healthcare (pres. 2010—), N.Y. Acad. Scis., Internat. Soc. Andrology, Am. Soc. Andrology, Am. Fertility Soc., Asia-Pacific Soc. Sex Med. (sec.-gen. 1989—91, pres. 2004—05, excellence of urology award 1989), Korean Soc. Fertility (v.p. 1988—90, pres. 1998—2000), Korean Andrologic Assn. (v.p. 1990—94, pres. 1994—97), Korean Acad. Sci. and Tech., Korean Urologic Assn. (pres. 2005—06, excellence of urology award 1975, 1991, 1993, 1999), Am. Urol. Assn. (corr.; sec. gen. 3rd Asian Congress of urology 1996). Avocations: swimming, playing violin, photography. Office: Chung-Ang Univ Hosp Dept Urol Heukseok-Dong Dongjak-Gu Seoul 156-861 Republic of Korea

KIM, SA-JIN, obstetrician, educator; b. Jochiwon, Korea, Dec. 15, 1958; s. Byuk-Soo Kim and Jung-Ja Jun; m. Eun-Kyung Kwon, Jan. 20, 1987; children: Kyu-Lim, Sung-Min. PhD, Cath. U., Seoul, 1996. Physician Cath. U., Kangnam Gu, Republic of Korea, 1977—, prof., 2005—. Chief ob-gyn. Cath. U. Holy Family Hosp., Pucheon, Republic of Korea, 2003—; mem. ob-gyn. med. bd. Cath. U., Seoul, 1987—91; auditor Korean Perinatology, 2010. Author: Ultrasound of Fetal Anomalies. Recipient DSM. Mem.: Korean Soc. Ob Gyn. (licentiate; gen. sec. 2001—03, fin. chmn. 2003—05, info. comm. com., v.p. 2011—). Home: Yangcheon Gu Bok-Dong Hyperion 101-2102 Seoul 158-724 Republic of Korea Office: Cath U Holy Hosp Pucheon City Wonmigu Sosa Dong Gyeonggi 420-717 Republic of Korea Office Fax: 82-32-340-7069. Personal E-mail: ksajin@yahoo.co.kr. E-mail: ksajin@catholic.ac.kr.

KIM, SANG GYUN, physician, educator; b. Seoul, Republic of Korea, Jan. 19, 1971; MD, Seoul Nat. U., PhD, 1996. Asst. prof. Seoul Nat. U. Coll. Medicine, 2005—. Office: Daehangno 101 Jongno-gu Seoul 110-799 Republic of Korea Business E-Mail: harley1333@hanmail.net.

KIM, SANG-HA, retired ophthalmology educator; b. Taegu, Korea, May 30, 1933; s. Chang-Woo and Bock-Dong (Park) K.; m. Kui-Duk Suk; children: Eoen-A, Han-Chul, Jin-Chul, Eoen-Joeng. MD, Kyungpook U., Taegu, 1958; DOMS, Vienna U., 1965; MD, Ruprecht-Karl U., Heidelberg, Germany, 1968. Scientific asst. dept. ophthalmology U. Eye Clinic, Vienna and Heidelberg, 1962-68; chief dept. ophthalmology Mary Knol Hosp., Pusan, Korea, 1972-76; prof., chmn. dept. ophthalmology Kyung Pook U. Hosp., Taegu, 1976-98, prof. emeritus, 1998; med. dir., advisor The Most Holy Trinity Hosp., 1999—2004. Supt., med. dir. Kyungpook U. Hosp., Taegu, 1987-89; pres. Korean Retina Soc., Seoul, 1989-92, Cath. Physician Guild, Taegu, 1992-96; internat. cons. Highlight of Ophthalmology, 1990—. Capt. Korean Air Force, 1958-61. Mem. Internat. Soc. Eye Rsch., Internat. Soc. Clin. Electrophysiology, Korean Ophthal. Soc. (pres. 1995-96). Home: 165-22 Boem-Oe-Dong Susong-ku Taegu 706-012 Republic of Korea

KIM, SANGTAEK, engineering educator; b. Republic of Korea, Feb. 1, 1975; PhD, U. Colo., Boulder, 2008. Assoc. specialist U. Calif., San Francisco, 2008—. Mem.: AAPM. Avocations: tennis, skiing, basketball. Office: 185 Berry St Ste 350 San Francisco CA 94107 Personal E-mail: taktek@gmail.com.

KIM, SARA S., pharmacist; b. Seoul, Republic of Korea, June 27, 1973; BS in Pharm., St. John's U., 1996, PharmD, 2004. Clin. oncology pharmacist Mt. Sinai Med. Ctr., 2006—. Home: 457 W 57th St 612 New York NY 10019 Personal E-mail: sarasound@aol.com.

KIM, SEOK-KWUN, medical educator, director; b. Ha-Dong, Kyung-nam, Republic of Korea, Apr. 9, 1952; m. Jae-Hee Ryu. MD, Busan Nat. U., PhD, 1977. Prof. Dong-A U. Hosp., Busan, Republic of Korea, 1990—; dean Dong-A U. Sch. Medicine, 2004—07. Pres. Korean Cleft Palate-Craniofacial Assn., Seoul, 2003—05. Recipient Paper award, Korean Sci. & Tech., 2006. Mem.: Nat. Acad. Medicine Korea (life). Achievements include research in plastic surgery. Office: Dong-A Univ Hosp 3Ga-1 Dongdaesin-Dong Seo-Gu Pusan 602-715 Republic of Korea Home Phone: 82-51-204-1949; Office Phone: 82-51-240-2807, 82-51-240-5411. Office Fax: 82-51-248-1527. Business E-Mail: sgkim1@dau.ac.kr.

KIM, SEONG DEOK, plastic surgeon; Grad., Seoul Nat. U. Med. Coll. Bd. cert. tng. palstic surgery dept. samsung med. ctr. Samsung Seoul Hosp.; adv. dr. plastic surgery dept. Samsung Med. Ctr.; chmn. plastic surgery dept. Kangnam Gen. Hosp.; dir. Dream Plastic Surgery Clinic. Mem.: Internat. Confederation Plastic reconstructive and Aesthetic Surgery, Korean Cleft-Palate-Craniofacial Assn., Korean Microsurgical Soc., Korean Soc. Reconstructive Hand Surgery, Korean Med. Assn., Korean Soc. Aesthetic Plastic Surgery, Korean Soc. Plastic and Reconstructive Surgeons. Office: Dream Plastic Surgery Clinic Apkujung Subway Sta Seoul Republic of Korea Office Phone: 8225461616. Office Fax: 8225461614. *

KIM, SEONG HWAN, internist; b. Seoul, Republic of Korea, Apr. 6, 1970; s. Pyeong Sam Kim and Byeong Sook Lee; m. Juri Park; 1 child, Naryoung. MD, Korea U., Seoul, 1995, MSc, 2003, PhD, 2008. Cert. internal medicine Korean Assn. Internal Medicine, 2004. Internship Korea U. Med. Ctr., Seoul, 1995—96, residency, 1999—2003; clin. instr. Korea U. Anam Hosp. Cardiovasc. Ctr., Seoul, 2003—04; clin. prof. Hallym U. Sacred Heart Hosp., Anyang-si, Republic of Korea, 2005—06; asst. prof. Hallym U. Hangang Sacred Heart Hosp., Seoul, 2006—07, Korea U. Ansan Hosp., 2007—. Lt. Army, 1996—99, Kangwon-do, Republic of Korea. Mem.: Korean Soc. Sleep Medicine, Korean Soc. Hypertension, Korean Soc. Echocardiography, Korean Soc. Internal Medicine, Korean Soc. Circulation (life). Office: Korea Univ Ansan Hosp Gojan 1-dong Danwon-gu Ansan-si Kyeonggi-do 425-707 Republic of Korea Office Phone: 82-31-412-5546. Office Fax: 82-31-412-5604. E-mail: cardioguy@korea.ac.kr.

KIM, SEONG-KYU, medical educator; b. Pohang, Republic of Korea, July 14, 1968; s. Deuk-Ho Kim and Chun-Ja Lee; m. Hee-Jin Choi; children: Na-yeon, Na-yun, Yeong-Jae. PhD, Hanyang U., Seoul, Republic of Korea, 2005. Cert. physician Ministry for Health, Welfare, and Family Affairs, 1997. Asst. prof. Dankook U., Cheonan, Republic of Korea, 2005—07, Cath. U. Daegu, Republic of Korea, 2007—. Editl. bd. mem. Korean Rheumatism Assn., Seoul, 2007—. Mem.: Korean Assn. Internal Medicine (Seoul) (Best Paper award 2005), Asia Pacific League Assn. Rheumatology (Yokohama) (Young Investigator award 2008). Office: Cath Univ Daegu 3056-6 Daemyung 4-Dong Namgu 705-718 Daegu Daegu Republic of Korea Office Fax: 82-53-6298248. Business E-Mail: kimsk714@cu.ac.kr.

KIM, SEONG-MAN, medical educator; b. Busan, Republic Of Korea, Nov. 25, 1968; s. Chun-Ja Choi; m. Young-Hi You, Feb. 10, 1996; children: Su-Bin, Geon-Woo. PhD, Kosin Med. Sch., Republic Of Korea, 2008. Cert. Internal Medicine Bd., Seoul, 2003. Cardiology fellow Kosin Gospel Hosp. Med. Sch., AmNam dong, Busan, 2001—03; asst. prof. Busan Paik Hosp. Inje U., GaeGeum Dong, Busan, 2003—. Grant, Inje Med. Sch., 2004. Achievements include patents for diagnostic and guiding coronary catheter. Office: Inje Univ GaeKeum Dong Busan 614-735 Republic of Korea Home: Yongho Dong Lg Metrocity 223-1804 608-091 Busan Busan Republic of Korea Personal E-mail: kimseongman@gmail.com.

KIM, SEON-TAE, otolaryngologist, director; b. Republic of Korea, July 1, 1963; MD, Korea U., 1988, PhD, 1999. Resident, dept. otolaryngology Korea U. Guro Hosp., 1989—92; with Gil Med. Ctr., 1995—99; prof. Gachon Med. Sch., 1999; postdoc. fellow U. Calif., San Francisco, 2002—04; dir., dept. otolaryngology Gachon U. Gil Med. Ctr., 2009—. Dir., academic affairs Gachon U. Medicine and Sci. Sch. Medicine, 2008—; bd. mem. Korean Rhinologic Soc., 2009—11. Mem.: Internat. Rhinologic Soc., Korean Allergy & Immunology Soc., Korean Acad. Otolaryngology, Head & Neck (Seogdang Academic award). Avocations: golf, travel. Office: Gil Hosp Gachon Med Sch Guwoldong 1198 Namdong-Gu Inchon 405-760 Republic of Korea Office Fax: 82-32-467-9044. Personal E-mail: rhinokim2002@hanmail.net.

KIM, SEUNG TAIK, oncologist, educator; b. Jinhae, Republic of Korea, Aug. 31, 1953; MD, Seoul Nat. U., 1978, PhD, 1988. Prof. Chungbuk Nat. U., 2000—. Dean Chungbuk Nat. U. Sch. of Medicine, 1999—2001; dir. Chungbuk Nat. U. Hosp., 2003—06; pres. Chungbuk Nat. U., 2010. Recipient Presdl. award, Republic of Korea. Mem.: Korean Soc. Clin. Oncology, Korean Soc. Hematology, Korean Soc. Internal Medicine. Avocation: mountain climbing. Office: 410 Seongbongro Heungduk-gu Cheongju Chungbuk 361-763 Republic of Korea Office Fax: 82-43-273-3252. E-mail: stkim@chungbuk.ac.kr.

KIM, SEUNG-HO, surgeon; b. Daegu, Republic of Korea, July 12, 1961; s. Chun-Ok Byun; m. Myung-Nan Kim, Sept. 28, 1986. MD, Kyungpook Nat. U., 1986. Medical diplomate Korean Med. Assn., 1986. Assoc. prof. Sungkyunkwan U., Seoul, Republic of Korea, 2002—05; dir. Madi Hosp., Seoul, 2005—. Recipient Jema Sports Medicine award, Korean Soc. for Sports Medicine, 2004. Office: Madi Hosp 192-5 Nonhyeon-dong Gangnam-gu Seoul 135-010 Republic of Korea Office Fax: 82-2-2056-8010. E-mail: shk@madi.or.kr.

KIM, SHIN-KON, surgeon, educator, hospital administrator; b. Hwasun, Chonnam, Republic of Korea, May 16, 1944; s. Yong-Il and Shin-Bang (Lee) K.; m. Chung-Woo Kim, Dec. 6, 1969; children: Yu-Jin, Jong-Seon, Jong-Jin. Diploma, Chonnam U., Kwangju, Korea, 1968, MS, 1982; PhD, Jeonbuk U., Chonju, Korea, 1985. Dir. emergency dept. Chonnam U. Hosp., Kwangju, 1983-85, dir. med. edn., 1988-90, chmn. dept. surgery, 1993-96, gen. dir., 1996-99; prof. surgery Chonnam U. Med. Sch., 1988—2009, assoc. dean acad. affairs, 1990-92. Editor textbooks: Nephrology, 1990, Emergency Medicine, 1991, A Guide to the Medical Fellowship in USA, 1997, Surgery of the Stomach and Intestine, 2000, Principles of Surgery, 2006. 1st lt. Korean Air Force, 1968-71. Fellow Internat. Coll. Surgeons; mem. Aerospace Med. Assn., Collegium Internat. Chirurgiae Digestivae, Korean Surg. Soc. (bd. dirs. 1994-98, pres. 2007-), Korean Hosp. Assn. (bd. dirs. 1996-99), Korean Soc. Vascular Surgery (pres. 2005-06), Korean Soc. Transplantation (pres. 2006-07), Kwangju City Med. Assn. (v.p. 1994-96), Chonnam Nat. U. Alumni Assn. (v.p. 1996-02). Roman Catholic. Avocations: golf, stamp collecting/philately. Office: Sangmoo Gen Hosp Dept Surgery 1240 Chipyeongdong Gwangju 502-270 Republic of Korea Home: Lausantium Pk # 1209 Chipyeongdong 502-827 Gwangju Seogu Republic of Korea Office Phone: 82-62-600-7126. Personal E-mail: sgkkim@hanmail.net. Business E-Mail: sgkim@chonnam.ac.kr.

KIM, SHIN-YOON, surgeon, medical educator; b. Daegu, Republic of Korea, Sept. 14, 1957; s. Jang-Soo and Kui-Jo Kim; m. Byung-Heun Choi, Feb. 9, 1985; children: Hye-Ihn, hye-Weon, Hye-Ryng. BS, Kyungpook Nat. U., Daegu, 1983, MA, 1986; PhD, Yeungham U., Gyungsam, 1996; MD, Korean Med. Assn., 1983. Asst. prof. Kyungpook Nat. U., Daegu, 1993—97, assoc. prof., 1997—2002, prof., 2002—. Clin. rsch. fellow U. Pitts. Med. Ctr., 1996—98. Office: Kyungpook Nat U Dept Orthop Surgery Sch Medicine Sam-Duck 2 Ga 50 700-721 Jung-gu Daegu Daegu Republic of Korea Home Phone: 8253 475 9739; Office Phone: 8253 420 5635. Business E-Mail: syukim@knu.ac.kr.

KIM, SI-OH, anesthesiologist, medical educator; b. Daegu, Republic of Korea, Mar. 13, 1960; s. Chan-Soo Kim and Jeong-Ok Lim; m. Sue-Yeo Choi, Dec. 31, 1963; children: Jae-Yeol, Ji-Min, Ki-Hwan. Doctorate, Kyungpook Nat. U., Daegu, Korea, 1996. Cert. anesthesiologist South Korea, 1989. Assoc. prof. Kyungpook Nat. U., Daegu, Republic of Korea, 2002—. Capt. Korean Army Hosp., 1989—92. Mem.: Soc. Cardiovascular-thoracic Anesthesia, Am. Soc. Anesthesiologist (assoc.). Office: Kyungpook Nat University Hosp Dept Anesthesiology Samdok-2ga Choong-Gu # 50 Daegu 700-721 Republic of Korea Office Fax: +82-53-426-2760. E-mail: sokim@knu.ac.kr.

KIM, SOBIN, engineering educator; b. Seoul, Republic of Korea, Jan. 20, 1971; BS, Seoul Nat. U., 1993; PhD, Columbia U., 2001. Asst. prof. Rutgers U., 2004—. Office: 599 Taylor Rd Piscataway NJ 08854 Business E-Mail: sobinkim@rci.rutgers.edu.

KIM, SOK WON, physicist, educator; b. Busan, Republic of Korea, Aug. 2, 1959; s. Dohee and Myungyun Kim; m. In Sook Song; children: Youngmin, Hyunwoo. PhD, Korea Advanced Inst. Sci. & Tech., Daejon, 1987. Cert. HS tchr. Seoul Edn. Agy., 1982. Sr. rschr. Korea Rsch. Inst. Sci. & Standards, Daejon, 1978—93; vis. prof. Purdue U., West Lafayette, Ind., 1990—91; prof. U. Ulsan, Republic of Korea, 1993—; vis. scholar Tex. A&M U., Coll. Stn., Tex., 2000—01. Head Busan-Ulsan Medium and Small Industry Agy., 2005. Contbr. articles to profl. jours. Head Bus. Incubator Assn., 2006—08. Recipient 1st NETZSCH award, 2005, KPS award, 2008. Office Phone: 82-52-259-2388. Office Fax: 82-52-259-1693. Personal E-mail: high-5k@hanmail.net. Business E-Mail: sokkim@ulsan.ac.kr.

KIM, SOO-JIN, medical educator; b. Incheon, Republic of Korea, Apr. 29, 1967; MD, Korea U., PhD, 1992. Prof. Konkuk U. Med. Ctr., 2011—. Mem.: Korean Pediatric Heart Assn. Office: 4-12 Hwayang-dong Gwangin-gu Seoul 143-729 Republic of Korea Office Phone: 82-2-2030-7678. Personal E-mail: ksoojn@yahoo.co.kr.

KIM, SOON OK, microbiologist, science educator, researcher; b. Dae-gu, Republic Of Korea, Dec. 17, 1960; d. Jong-Hoi Kim and Jung-Hee Park; m. Sung Seo, Jan. 8, 1984; children: Young-Kyung Seo, Hae-Kyung Seo. BS, Kyungpook Nat U., Dae Gu, 1982; MS, Kyungpook Nat. U., Dae Gu, 1984, PhD, 1990. Postdoctoral rschr. Kobe U., Japan, 1992—93; lectr. Chung Ju U., Chung Ju, Republic of Korea, 1994; rsch. prof. Myungji U., Young-In, Republic of Korea, 1995—99; R&D dir. Chem.-Tech. Rsch. Inc., Suwon, Republic of Korea, 2000—; dir. product devel. union Korea Pharm Co., Ltd, 2010—. Mem.: Korea Soc. Microbiology and Biotech. Roman Catholic. Home: LG Village 208-301 Mang-Po Young-Tong Suwon Gyeonggi-do 443-769 Republic of Korea Office: Product Devel Union Korea Pharm Co Ltd 389-1 Wonwae B/D 3F Pungnap-2 dong Songpa-gu Seoul 138-878 Republic of Korea Office Phone: 822 489 3611.

KIM, SOO-SHIN, plastic surgeon; Started Soo-Shin Scholarship, Yanbian, 2002; chief plastic surgery dept. Korea Univ. Guro Hosp., Inje Univ. Paik Hosp., Seoul Nat. Univ. Hosp., advisor palstic surgery dept.; founder Real Cosmetic Clinic, 1991, surgeon. Med. sch. prof. Seoul Univ., Korea Univ.; adjunct prof. Korea Univ. Coll. Surgeons, Inje Univ. Coll. Surgeons; exch. prof. med. ctr. NYU. Achievements include world renowned in the field of finger reattachment surgery; 1st in the world to develop jawline and cheekbone reduction techniques; 1st cosmetic surgeon to develop and apply the use of endoscopes in facelifts. Office: Real Cosmetic Clinic Asio B/D 580 Shinsa-Dong Gangnam-Gu Seoul 135892 Republic of Korea Office Phone: 8225121616. Office Fax: 8225111313. *

KIM, SOUNG MIN, surgeon, educator; b. Republic of Korea, Apr. 25, 1969; PhD, Seoul Nat. U., 2003. Assoc. prof. Kangnung Nat. U., 2001—08, Seoul Nat. U., 2009—. Achievements include research in oral and maxillofacial reconstruction, dental implant, congenital facial defect reconstruction. Office: 62-1 Changgyeonggung-no Jongnogu Seoul 110-768 Republic of Korea Office Fax: 82-2-766-4948. Business E-Mail: smin5@snu.ac.kr.

KIM, STEPHEN S., surgeon, educator; BA, U. Va., Charlottesville, 1990, MD, 1994. Nat. Bd. Med. Examiners, 1995, lic. Wash., 2001, Calif., 2003, Va., 2008, diplomate Am. Bd. Surgery, 2002, 2009, pediat. surgery 2004. Res. surgery U. Chgo., 1994—2001; rsch. fellow surgery Harvard U. Boston Children's Hosp., 1996—98; fellow pediat. surgery U. Wash. Sch. Medicine, Seattle, 2001—03, asst. prof. surgery, 2004—08; asst. prof. pediat. surgery Stanford U. Sch. Medicine, Calif., 2003—04; faculty Inst. Stem Cell Regenerative Medicine, Seattle, 2005—08; prin. investigator Seattle Children's Hosp. Rsch. Inst., 2006—08; assoc. prof. surgery Va. Commonwealth U. Sch. Med., 2008—. Adj. asst. prof. bioengring. elec. engring. U. Wash., Seattle, 2005—08. Named America's Top Surgeons, Consumers Rsch. Coun. America, 2009, 2010; grantee, Children's Hosp. Basic Sci. Steering Com., 2006. Fellow: ACS, Am. Acad. Pediat., Seattle Surg. Soc. (clin. rsch. award 2002); mem.: Med. Soc. Va., North Pacific Surg. Assn., Pacific Assn. Pediat. Surgeons, Soc. Am. Gastrointestinal Endoscopic Surgeons, Internat. Pediat. Endosurgery Group, Am. Pediat. Surg. Assn., Tissue Engring. Regenerative Medicine Soc. Internat., Assn. Academic Surgery (student rsch. award 1994), Henry N. Harkins Surg. Soc., Korean AMA (basic sci. rsch. award 1997), King County Med. Assn., Wash. State Med. Assn. Office: Pediatric Surgical Group 3301 Woodburn Rd #205 Annandale VA 22003 Office Phone: 703-560-2236. Office Fax: 703-876-4960. Business E-Mail: skim@psgkids.com.

KIM, SU-GWAN, dental educator, oral surgeon, medical researcher; b. HaeNam, Republic of Korea, Aug. 23, 1964; s. Wan Sik and Jeong-Im Kim; m. Sun-Mi Kim, Dec. 24, 1995; children: Yu-Jeong, Yu-Min. DDS, Chosun U., GwangJu, Republic of Korea, 1989, MSD, 1992, PhD, 1998. Prof. Chosun U., 2002; chmn. Dept. Oral and Maxillofacial Surgery, Chosun U. Hosp., GwangJu, 1999. Dir. Korean Assn. Maxillofacial Plastic and Reconstructive Surgeons, 1990, Korean Assn. Oral and Maxillofacial Surgeons, 1990, Korean Acad. Laser Dentistry, 2001. Contbr. articles to profl. jours. including Oral and Maxillofacial Surgery, Internat. Jour. Oral and Maxillofacial Surgery. Capt. Korean Army. Recipient Pres. Award (scholarship for Rsch.)- 5 times, Chosun Univ./GwangJu, Republic of Korea, 1999—2003, Pres. Award (scholarship for Rsch.), Minister of Health and Welfare/ Seoul, Republic of Korea, 2002, Sci. Rsch. Award, Asia Pacific Congress Craniofacial Distraction Osteogenesis/Male, Republic of Maldives, 2004. Fellow: Internat. Assoc. of Oral and Maxillofacial Surgeons; mem.: Acad. of Osseointegration, Acad. of Laser Dentistry. Achievements include patents for dental screw, 2001; anchorage plate for teeth, 2002; notable findings: development of bone substitute using particulate dentin, 2000-2012. Office: Chosun U Hosp Dept Oral Maxillofacial Surgery Seo Suk-Dong Dong-Gu 421 501-825 Gwangju Republic of Korea Business E-Mail: sgckim@chosun.ac.kr.

KIM, SUN I., biomedical engineer, educator; b. Seoul, Korea, Dec. 2, 1952; s. Kyungduck Kim and Yeoupboon Lee; m. Youngock Kwon, Oct. 8, 1977; children: Heounjoo, Heounmo. Bachelor, Seoul Nat. U., 1976, MS, 1978; PhD, Drexel U., Phila., 1987. Chief engr. Seoul Nat. U. Hosp., 1979—82; rsch. fellow Drexel U., Phila., 1982—87; rsch. assoc. Mayo Clinic, Rochester, NY, 1987—88; prof. Hanyang U., Seoul, Republic of Korea, 1988—. Pres. 2006 World Congress on Med. Physics and Biomedical Engring., Seoul, Korea (South), 2000—; com. mem. DICOM, Seoul, Korea (South), 1998—; sec. gen. The 4th Asia-Pacific Med. Info., Seoul, 2003—. Contbr. articles to profl. jours. Pvt. Korean Army, 1978—79, Korea. Recipient KOREA Web awards, Korea Times, 2002, The Award of Best Rschr., Hanyang U., 2002, The Best Internat. Rsch. award, 2003. Fellow: The Korean Soc. of Human Brain Mapping, Internat. Fedn. for Med. and Biol. Engring.; mem.: IEEE, Korean Soc. Biomed. Engring. (Award of Biomed. Engring. 1995), Korean Fedn. Sci. and Tech. Socs. (Award of Sci. Tech. Best Rsch. 2001), The Radiol. Soc. of N.Am. Achievements include patents pending for visual displaying device for virtual reality with a built-in biofeedback sensor; system and method of correlating virtual reality with biofeedback for enhancing attention; system and method of providing service for enhancing attention on internet. Avocations: golf, skiing. Home: 36-802 Hanshin 3rdAPT Banpodong Seochoku Seoul 137-040 Republic of Korea Office: Hanyang Univ Dept Biomed Engring 17 Haengdang-dong Sungdong-ku Seoul 133-791 Republic of Korea Office Fax: 02-2296-5943. Business E-Mail: sunkim@hanyang.ac.kr.

KIM, SUNG HUN, orthopedist; b. Pusan, Republic of Korea, May 6, 1970; MD, Yonsei U., 1997, MD, 2002. V.p., chief shoulder & upper extremity dept. Yonsei Sarang Hosp., 2008—11; dir. Yonsei Kyunwoo Shoulder Hosp., 2011—. Home: 172-1704 Jamsil Els Apt Jamsil 2-dong Seoul 138-910 Republic of Korea Business E-Mail: orthoksh@gmail.com.

KIM, SUNG SOO, medical educator, researcher; s. Young Hoon Kim and Geuk Choon Kim (Bang); m. Hyun Sook Song, Aug. 2, 1959; children: Ara, Ayeon. MD, Kyung Hee U., Seoul, 1982; PhD, SUNY, Buffalo, NY, 1992. Diplomate Korean Ministry Pub. Health and Social Affairs, 1982. Prof. Kyung Hee Med. Sch., Seoul, Republic of Korea, 1998—. Chmn. Kyung Hee Med. Sch., 1994—. Contbr. articles to profl. jours. Capt., 1983—86, Korean Army. Mem.: Korean Soc. Med. Biochemistry and Molecular Biology (com. mem. 1998—2001). Office: Kyung Hee Med Sch Dept Molec Biology 1 Hoegi-dong Dongdaemoon gu Seoul 130 701 Republic of Korea Office Fax: 82-2-959-8168. Personal E-mail: sgskim@hotmail.com. E-mail: sgskim@khu.ac.kr.

KIM, SUNG-GON, psychiatrist, educator; b. Pusan, Republic of Korea, Jan. 8, 1961; s. Tae-Jin Kim and Heong-Ja Shin; m. Jin-Ryeong Park, Apr. 26, 1986; children: Yeon-Sue, Ji-Sue. MD, Pusan Nat. U., 1985, MSc, 1991, PhD, 1999. Lic. Korean Bd. Psychiatry. Chmn. dept. psychiatry Bongsaeng Meml. Hosp., Pusan, Republic of Korea, 1992—93; vis. scholar U. Pa., Phila., 1993—94, vis. prof., 1999—2000; clin. instr. Pusan Nat. U., 1994—97, asst. prof., 1997—2001, assoc. prof., 2001—05, prof., 2006—. Dir. sci. com. Korean Acad. Addiction Psychiatry, Seoul, 2002—04; sec. spl. affairs Korean Coll. Neuropsychopharmacology, 2007—. Contbr. articles to profl. jours.; transl. author: book The BRENDA Approach, 2002, mem. editl. bd.: Korean Acad. Addiction Psychiatry, 1996—, Korean Neuropsychiat. Assn., 2001—, Korean Soc. Biol. Psychiatry, 2002—, Psychiat. Investigation, 2004—. Dir. pub. com. Korean Acad. Addiction Psychiatry, Seoul, 2006—08, dir. Internat Affairs, 2008—; com. mem. Judgement Com. for Drug-Related Criminals, Seoul, 2001—03, Judgement Com. Mental Health, Pusan, 2003—04, Mgmt. Ctr. for Health Promotion in Metrocity, Pusan, Republic of Korea; chmn. Pusan Alcohol Counseling Ctr., 2002—. 1st lt. Korean Army, 1985. Recipient Poster award, Korean Neuropsychiat. Assn., 2002, 2004, 2005. Mem.: Korean Soc. Depressive and Bipolar Disorder (sec. spl. affairs 2007—), Internat. Soc. Biomed. Rsch. on Alcoholism, Korean Soc. Biol. Therapies in Psychiatry (sec. internat. affairs 2006—), Am. Psychiat. Assn. (internat. mem. 1998—99), Rsch. Soc. Alcoholism. Avocations: golf, Korean chess. Office: Pusan Nat Univ Sci Medicine Beomeo-rI Mulgeum-eup Yangsan-si Gyeongnam 626 770 Republic of Korea Office Phone: 82 51 240 7304. Office Fax: 82 51 242 5364. E-mail: sungkim@pusan.ac.kr.

KIM, SUNG-JAE, medical educator; b. Daegu, Kyungbook, Republic of Korea, Nov. 18, 1949; s. Kim Yong-Chul and Kwon Moon-Kyo; m. Lee Kyung-Soon, Nov. 28, 1975; children: Soo-Min, Jhung-Suk. MD, Yonsei U., 1975, PhD, 1989. Prof. Yonsei U., Seoul, 1983—; fellow Harvard U. Med. Coll., Boston, 1988—90; dir. arthroscopy and joint rsch. inst. Yonsei U., 2005—, prof., chmn., dept. orthops., 2007—10; hon. pres. Asia Arthroscopy Congress, 2010—. Vis. physician Orthopaedic Arthritic Hosp., Toronto, 1988; rsch. fellow Harvard U., Boston, 1988-90; vis. prof. U. Calif., Irvine, 1990.; guest prof. Peking U. Health Sci. Ctr., China, 2010-12. Mem. editl. bd.: Arthroscopy Jour., 2001—06, Jour. Orthopedic Sci., 2003. Sci. bd. mem. Soc. Internat. Orthopedic Surgery & Traumatology, 2000—04. Recipient Med. Sci. award Seoul Med. Assn., 1996. Fellow Am. Coll. Surgeons; mem. Korean Orthopaedic Assn. (gen. sec. 1987, Malae scholar 1996), Korean Knee Soc. (counselor 1990—), Korean Soc. Sports Medicine (bd. dirs. 1994—), Korean Arthroscopy Assn. (gen. sec. 1994—), Korean Shoulder and Elbow Assn. (counselor 1994—), Asia Athroscopy Congress (hon. pres. 2010-). Avocations: hiking, skiing. Office: Yonsei University Coll Medicine 134 Shinchon-dong Seodaemun-gu Seoul 120-752 Republic of Korea Office Phone: 82-2-2228-5679. Office Fax: 8223631139. Business E-Mail: sungjaekim@yuhs.ac, severanscopy@yuhs.ac.

KIM, SUNGJOO, transplant surgeon; b. Kwangju, Republic of Korea, Feb. 13, 1960; s. Sangho Kim and Booja Park; m. Myunghee Kim, June 27, 1985; children: YouJin, Youmin. MD in Med. Sci., Cath. U., 1986, MS in Med. Sci., 1990; PhD in Med. Sci., Tokyo U., 2000. Lic. Korea, 1986. Fellow Sch. Medicine Sungkyunkwan U., Soowon, Republic of Korea, 1995—96, asst. prof. dept. surgery, 1996—2001, assoc. prof., 2001—07, prof., 2007—; clin. fellow U. Minn., 1997, U. Wisc., 1998; fellow U. Emory, 2000—02. Contbr. articles to profl. jours. Mem.: Internat. Cell Therapy Soc., Internat. Transplantation Soc., Korean Soc. Immunology, Korean Soc. Transplantation, Korean Soc. Sugery. Office: Samsung Med Ctr #50 ilwon Dong Kangnam Ku Seoul 135-710 Republic of Korea Home Phone: 82-2-575-1935; Office Phone: 82-2-3410-3476. Office Fax: 82-2-3410-0040. Business E-Mail: kmhyj111@skku.edu.

KIM, SUN-HAE, retired medical/surgical nurse, writer, nurse midwife, physical therapist; b. Jinju, Republic of Korea, July 16, 1941; arrived in U.S., 1971; d. Sampil Kim and Bok-Sun Lee. BA in Eng. Lit., Youngnam U., 1966. Chief nurse Swedish Saved Children Fedn., Pusan, Republic of Korea, 1966—70; staff nurse Cook County Hosp., Chgo., 1971—72, Harper Hosp., Detroit, 1972—73, Queens Hosp. Ctr., Jamaica, NY, 1973—90, Elmhurst Hosp., NY, 1990—97, ret., 1997. Author: Among Hibiscus and Roses, 2004. Army nurse South Korean Army, 1960—66. Avocations: reading, walking. Home: 152-18 Union Turnpike Apt 12F Flushing NY 11367 Office Phone: 718-969-7135. Personal E-mail: kimsunhae@webtv.net.

KIM, SUNHYO, nutritionist, educator; b. Kongju, Republic of Korea, Aug. 16, 1958; d. Kipyung Kim and Jungae Won; m. Byungchul Ryu; children: Whayeon Ryu, Hoyun Ryu. BA, Kongju Nat. Tchr.'s Coll., 1981; MS, Ewha Woman's U., Seoul, Republic of Korea, 1983; PhD, Chung Ang U., Seoul, 1990. Cert. tchr. Republic of Korea. Prof. Kongju Nat. U., 1990—, counseling dir., 1993—95, 2003—05, chmn. dept. home econs. edn., 1999—2001, chmn. dept. foodsvc mgmt nutrition, 2005—07; vis. scholar U. Otago, Dunedin, New Zealand, 1994, U. Calif., Davis, 1996—97, 1998, postgrad. rschr., 2002—04. Cons. in field; supr. exhbns. on nutrition edn. Dir.: Korean Jour. Human Ecology. Mem.: Asian Soc. Home Econs. (editor), Korean Soc. Cmty. Nutrition (editor), Korean Nutrition Soc. (dir.), Korean Assn. Women's Studies. Avocations: nature watching, walking, cooking, travel. Home: Daewoo Apt 104-1303 Kyo-Dong 314-090 Kongju Chungcheongnam-do Republic of Korea Office Phone: 82-41-850-8307. Business E-Mail: shkim@kongju.ac.kr.

KIM, TACK JOONG, biology professor; b. Seoul, Republic of Korea, May 28, 1974; PhD, Hokkaido U., 2005. Prof. Yonsei U., 2008—. Office: 1 Yonseidae-gil Wonju Gangwon-do 220-710 Republic of Korea Office Phone: 82-33-760-2242. Office Fax: 82-33-760-2183. Business E-Mail: ktj@yonsei.ac.kr.

KIM, TAE HYEON, medical educator; b. Jeonju, Republic Of Korea, May 9, 1965; s. Si joong Kim and Yang lee Lee; m. Gyeong Soon Choi; children: Jeong yeon, Do yoon. MD, Ministry of Health and Welfare, 1991; PhD, Jeonbuk Nat. U., Republic Of Korea, 2003. Cert. Bd. Korean Assn. Gastrointestinal Endoscopy, 2001, Bd. Korean Assn. Internal Medicine, 1996, Bd. Korean Assn. Gastroent., 2001. Fellow, gastroent. dept. Wonkwang U. Hosp., Iksan, Republic of Korea, 1999—2001, dir. Health Promotion Ctr., 2007—; instr. medicine Wonkwang U., Sch. Medicine, 2001—03, asst. prof., 2003—07, assoc. prof., 2007—; exch. prof. dept. gastroent. U. Wash., Seattle, 2005—07. Contbr. articles to profl. jours. Mem.: Am. Soc. Gastrointestinal Endoscopy. Achievements include research in new method to treat biliary stone; treatment of acute pancreatitis; assessment of severity of chronic hepatitis B. Home: Hyo Ja-3 seogok Daelim apt 104-1001 Jeonju Jeonlabukdo Republic of Korea Office: Wonkwang Univ Hosp Sinyong Dong 344-2 570-711 Iksan Jeollabuk-do Republic of Korea Office Fax: 82-63-855-2025. Business E-Mail: kth@wonkwang.ac.kr.

KIM, TAE-HEUNG, dermatologist, researcher; b. Daegu, Republic of Korea, Mar. 17, 1959; s. Soong-Jong and Hee-Han (Lee) Kim; m. Eun-Mee Gil, Apr. 26, 1986; children: Na-Hyun, Keun-Woo. Diploma in Medicine, Seoul Nat. U., 1984, MSc, 1991, PhD, 1995. Registered Korean Bd. Dermatology Ministry Health & Welfare, 1991, lic. Korean Med. Assn. Intern Seoul Nat. U. Hosp.; residency Dept. Dermatology Seoul Nat. U. Hosp.; prof., chmn. dermatology Gyeongsang Nat. U. Coll. Medicine, Jinju, Kyungnam, Republic of Korea, 1991—2003; pres. White-Line Skin Group, Kyungnam, Republic of Korea, 2003. Dir. White-Line Skin Rsch. Ctr., Changwon, 2004—. Contbr. articles to profl. jours. Mem.: Korean Dermatol. Assn. (licentiate), Korean Soc. Photomedicine (corr.), Am. Soc. Photobiology (assoc.). Home: Daedong Apt 121-702 Changwon 641 777 Republic of Korea Office: White-Line Skin Clinic Fl 5 26 W Madimi Rd Seongsan-ku Changwon Gyeongsangnam-do 642-832 Republic of Korea Office Fax: 82-55-274-0054. Personal E-mail: derkim@hanmail.net. Business E-Mail: derkim@paran.com.

KIM, TAE-HOON, medical educator; b. Seoul, Republic of Korea, June 29, 1961; s. Sang-Kyo and Dae-Sook Kim; m. Jung-Hye Chae; 1 child, Suk. PhD, Kyung Hee U., Seoul, 1995. Cert. prof. Dankook U., Chungnam, 2007. Assoc. prof. Dankook U., Cheonan, Chungnam, Republic of Korea, 2001—07, chmn., dept. radiology, 2003—04, prof., 2007—. Dir.: (society interventional radiology). 1st lt. med. affairs, navy, 1997—2000, Korea, south. Office: Dankook Univ San 29 Anseodong Cheonan Chungnam 330-714 Republic of Korea Office Fax: 82-41-550-7163. Business E-Mail: radiology@dankook.ac.kr.

KIM, V. NARRY, biological scientist, science educator; BA in Microbiology, Seoul Nat. U., 1992, MS in Microbiology, 1994; PhD in Biochemistry, Oxford U., 1998. Postdoc. fellow Howard Hughes Med. Inst., U. Pa., 1998—2001; rsch. asst. prof. Seoul Nat. U., 2001—04, asst. prof., 2004—08, assoc. prof., 2008—. Coun. mem. Presdl. Acv. Coun. Sci. & Tech., Korea. Recipient Macrogen Young Investigator award, Korean Soc. Molecular & Cell Biology, 2004, Macrogen Women Scientist award, 2006, Rsch. award, Seoul Nat. U., 2006, Sci. Citation Laureate award, Thomson Corp., 2007, Young Scientist award, Korean Ministry Sci. & Engring., 2007, L'Oréal-UNESCO Women in Sci. award, 2008, Nat. Honor Scientist award, South Korean Ministry Edn., Sci. & Tech., 2010; named Women Scientist of Yr., Korean Ministry Sci. & Engring., 2007. Office: Bldg 504 Rm 522 School Biological Sciences Seoul National University Seoul 151-742 Republic of Korea Office Phone: 82 2 880 9120. Office Fax: 82 2 887 0244. Business E-Mail: narrykim@snu.ac.kr. *

KIM, WAN JONG, biologist, educator; b. Gujwamyun, Jeju, Republic of Korea, Sept. 18, 1956; m. Jae Hwa Lee. PhD, Yonsei U., Seoul, Republic of Korea, 1988. Prof., dept. biology Soochunhyang U., Asan City, Choongnam, Republic of Korea, 1994—. Dean student affairs, Office Student Affairs, Asan City, 2007—08, chief dept. life sci. Achievements include research in study of cell ultrastructure using electron microscopy; effects of some cytokines on wound healing have been reported. Home: Sungjeongdong Cheonan City Choongnam 330-935 Republic of Korea Office: Soonchunhyang University Dept Biology Shinchangmyun 336-745 Asan Chungcheongnam-do Republic of Korea Home Phone: 820415728942; Office Phone: 82-041-530-1251. Business E-Mail: wjkim56@sch.ac.kr.

KIM, WEON-YOO, orthopedist; b. Seongju, Gyungsanguk-do, Republic of Korea, Aug. 2, 1955; s. Young-Gyuk Kim and Gyu-Soon Park; m. Gweon-Hee Weon, Sept. 21, 1956. MD, PhD, Cath. U., Seoul, 1992. Surgeon Korea, 1981. Head dept. orthop. surgery., prof. Daegeon St.Mary's Hosp., Cath. U., Daejeon, Republic of Korea, 2000—. Editor: J. Korean Hip Soc., 2004. Mem.: Orthop. Trauma Assn. Achievements include research in effect of pin location on stability of pelvic external fixation. Office: Saint Mary's Hosp Daehung-Dong Jung-Gu 301-723 Daejeon Daejeon Republic of Korea Office Fax: 82-42-221-0429. E-mail: weonkim@hotmail.com.

KIM, YANG SOO, infectious diseases physician, educator; b. Seoul, Republic of Korea, Nov. 30, 1960; m. Young Ju Cho; 1 child, Jung Hwan. MD, Ministry Health, Welfare & Family, 1986; PhD, Seoul Nat. U. Sch. Medicine, 1996. Cert. in internal medicine Ministry Health, Welfare & Family, 1990, in infectious diseases Korean Soc. Internal Medicine, 1997. Prof. U. Ulsan Coll. Medicine, Seoul, 1995—; dir. Dept. Hosp. Infection Control, Asan Med. Ctr., Seoul, 2000—, Dept. Infectious Diseases, Asan Med. Ctr., Seoul, 2002—. Dir. Ctr. Antimicrobial Resistance & Microbial Genetics, U. Ulsan, Seoul, 2000—. Author: (journals) Best Scientific Article. Capt. US Army. Recipient award, Ministry Health, Welfare and Family, 1992, Acad. award, Korean Soc. Infectious Diseases, 2005. Home: 104-901 Samsung Apt Oksu-dong Sondong-gu Seoul 133-758 Republic of Korea Office: Univ Ulsan Asan Med Ctr 388-1 Pungnap-2dong Songpa-gu Seoul 138-736 Republic of Korea Office Fax: 82-2-3010-6970; Home Fax: 82-2-2282-4225. Business E-Mail: yskim@amc.seoul.kr.

KIM, YANG WOOK, medical educator; b. Pusan, Republic of Korea, July 2, 1963; MD, Inje U., PhD, 1987. Prof. Inje Med. Sch. Haeundae Paik Hosp., 2009—. Cons. Novartis, 2009. Mem.: ISPD, Internat. Soc. Nephrology, Am. Soc. Nephrology. Avocations: travel, golf, movies. Office: 1435 Jwa-dong Haeundae-goo Pusan 612-862 Republic of Korea Business E-Mail: kyw8625@chol.com.

KIM, YEON-DEOK, ophthalmologist; b. Seoul, Republic of Korea, Apr. 25, 1976; MD, Cath. U. Korea, Med. Coll., 2002, MS in Med. Sci., 2008, PhD student, 2009—. Intern Cath. Med. Ctr., 2002—03, resident in ophthalmology, 2003—07; fellow in glaucoma Seoul Nat. U. Hosp., 2007—08; staff physician HanGil Eye Hosp., 2008—. Adj. asst. prof. Cath. U. Korea, Med. Coll., 2010. Mem.: Assn. Rsch. in Vision and Ophthalmology, Korean Med. Assn., Korea Glaucoma Soc., Korean Ophthal. Soc. Avocations: music, weightlifting. Office: #543-36 Bupyeong-dong Bupyeong-gu Incheon 403-010 Republic of Korea Home Phone: 82 2 6249 4110. Office Fax: 82-32-503-0801. Personal E-mail: oijee@hanmail.net.

KIM, YEONG HOON, medical educator, director; b. Seoul, Republic Of Korea, Feb. 15, 1962; d. Min Chae and Soon Ja Kim; m. Jong Jin Kim, June 4, 1988; children: In Jee, In Suh, In Hoo. Student, Kyung Hee U., Seoul, 1980—86, MSc, 1989, PhD, 1993. Cert. MD Ministry Health and Wellfare, 1986. Chief, nephrology divsn. Busan Paik Hosp. InJe Med. Sch., Republic of Korea, 1990—, lectr., 1990—94, asst. prof., 1995—98, assoc. prof., 2001—05, prof., 2006—, dir., paik organ transplantation ctr., 2008—, chief, dept. internal medicine, 2008—; rsch. fellow U. Mich., Ann Arbor, 1998—2000. Contbr. scientific papers. Mem.: Korean Soc. Transplantation (gen. dir. 2008—), Am. Soc. Nephrology, Korean Soc. Nephrology (dir. pub. comm. 2006—, dialysis specialist 1999), Korean Assn. Internal Medicine. Home: 206-302 LGmetrocity Yonghodong Namgu Busan Republic of Korea Office: Busan Paik Hosp Inje Med Coll 633-165 Gaegeumdong Jingu 614-735 Busan Busan Republic of Korea Office Fax: 82-51-891-1837. Business E-Mail: yeonghnl@inje.ac.kr.

KIM, YEONG-DAE, medical educator, director; b. Pusan, Republic of Korea, Oct. 24, 1965; s. Jun-Tae Kim and Bok-Ryae Park; m. Ji-Young Kim; 1 child, Bu-Gyeom. MD, Ministry Health & Welfare, Republic of Korea, 1990, Pusan Nat. U., 2002. Intern, resident Pusan Nat. U. Hosp., 1990—95, postdoc. fellow, 1998—2000, dir., trauma team, 2007—, dir., hospice & palliative care, 2007—10; physician, thoracic surgery Nat. Masan Tubrculosis Hosp., Republic of Korea, 1996—98; asst. prof. Pusan Nat. U., 2000—08, assoc. prof., 2008—. Dir., Cancer Control Inst. Pusan Cancer Ctr., 2008—09. Com. mem., civil affair Busan Dist. Ct., Pusan, 2006—. Capt. Republic of Korea Army. Mem.: Korean Assn. Traumatology, Internat. Assn. Study Lung Cancer, Korean Soc. Critical Care Medicine, Korean Soc. Hospice & Palliative Cars, Korean Assn. Study Lung Cancer, Korean Soc. Thoracic & Cardiovasc. Surgery. Office: Pusan Nat Univ Hosp 305 Gu-duck Ro Se Gu Pusan 632-739 Republic of Korea Office Fax: 82-51-243-9389. Business E-Mail: domini@pnu.edu.

KIM, YEONSIL, oncologist, educator; b. Seoul, Feb. 1, 1965; MD, Cath. U. Korea, 1989, PhD, 2000. Assoc. prof. Cath. U. Korea, 2004—10, prof., 2010—. Master: Korean Soc. Radiation Biosci.; mem.: Korean Assn. Study Lung Cancer, Korean Soc. Head & Neck Oncology, Korean Cancer Assn. (GSK award), Korean Soc. Therapeutic Radiology and Oncology (Excellent Poster award). Avocations: travel, mountain climbing. Office: #505 Banpo-dong Seoul Seocho-gu 137-041 Republic of Korea Business E-Mail: yeonkim7@catholic.ac.kr.

KIM, YONG JIN, medical educator; b. Chungbuk, Republic of Korea, Apr. 10, 1971; PhD, Soonchunhyang U., 2007. Assoc. prof. Soonchunhyang U. Hosp., 2010—. Office: Yongsan Gu Hannam Dong 657 Seoul 140-743 Republic of Korea Business E-Mail: yjkim@hosp.sch.ac.kr.

KIM, YONG JUN, medical educator; b. Wonju-si, Republic of Korea, Sept. 7, 1949; PhD, Seoul Nat. U., 1988. Tchg. asst. Seoul Nat. U., 1979—81; vet. officer Ministry of Agr. and Forestry, 1982—89; lectr. Sin Ku U., 1987, Yonsei U., 1987—89; prof. Chonbuk Nat. U., 1989—, dir., tchg. vet. hosp., 1992—96, dean, Coll. Vet. Medicine, 2005—07. Pres. Korean Assn. Edn. for Vet. Clinics, 2007—09, Korean Assn. Profs. of Vet. Obstetrics and Theriogenology, 2007—11, Korean Soc. Vet. Clinics, 2009—11. Grant, Min. of Agr. and Forestry, scholarship, Ministry Agr. of France, Govtl. Rsch. fellowship, Japan Soc. for Promotion Sci., DFG, Germany. Mem.: Accreditation Bd. for Vet. Edn. Korea, Korea Com. Nat. Exam. for Veterinarians, Korean Fedn. Sci. and Tech. Socs. Avocations: music, tennis, mountain climbing. Office: Coll Vet Medicine Chonbuk Nat University Deokjindong 1-Ga 664-14 Jeonju-si Jeonrabuk-do 561-756 Republic of Korea Office Fax: 82-63-270-3780. Business E-Mail: yjk@jbnu.ac.kr.

KIM, YONG-GWON, engineering educator; b. Jeju, Republic of Korea, Jan. 25, 1971; PhD, Korea U., 2008. Lectr. Konyang U., 2009—. Mem.: Korea Academia-Indsl. Cooperation Soc., Inst. Electronics Engrs. Korea. Avocations: fishing, golf. Office: Rm 314 Myoung Gok Med Sci Bldg Daejeon 302-718 Republic of Korea Office Fax: 82-42-600-6459. Business E-Mail: ygkim@konyang.ac.kr.

KIM, YONG-IN LUKE, surgeon, educator; s. Heung-Dong and Mimal Agnes Kim; m. Mi-Kyung Agnes Choi, July 2, 1988; children: In-Wha Gabriella, June Raphael, Young Michael. MD, Kyung Hee U., Seoul, Korea, 1982; PhD in Med. Sci., Cath. U. Leuven, Belgium, 2000. Lic. physician Ministry Health, Korea, 1976, cert. med. dr. Edn. Com. for Foreign Med. Grads., 1983, lic. physician Ministry Health, Belgium, 1986, cert. specialist in cardiothoracic surgey Belgian Assn. Cardiothoracic Surgery, 1992, in thoracic and cardiovascular surgery Ministry Health, Korea, 1997, lic. physician Pa., 1997, cert. critical care medicine specialist 2009. Surg. resident in gen. and cardiothoracic surgery Cath. U. Leuven, 1986—92, clin. fellow in cardiac surgery, 1992—95; asst. prof. Kyung Hee U., Seoul, Republic of Korea, 1995—97, Pocheon Joongmoon Med. Sch., Pocheon, Kyonggi-province, Republic of Korea, 1997—98; assoc. staff in cardiovasc. and thoracic surgery St. Francis Med. Ctr., Pitts., 1998—2001; attending staff in cardiothoracic surgery Nat. Med. Ctr., Seoul, 2001—02; assoc. prof. in cardiothoracic surgery Inje U., Seoul Paik Hosp., 2002—. Assoc. cardiac surgeon European Homograft Bank, Brussel, 1994—95; consulting mem. Gerson Lehman Group, NYC, 2005—; rsch. boad advisors Am. Biog. Inst., Raleigh, NC, 2006—; cons. Soc. Industry Leaders, Std., Poor's Vista Rsch., NYC, 2007—. Author: (book) Clinical Cardiology, 1998, (poetry books) Collecting Memories, 2001, The Best Poems and Poets of 2002, 2002, Theater of the Mind, 2003; contbr. articles to profl. jours. Mem. Malguyou Med. Svc. Team, Seoul, 1978—2003; chmn. Yonggok, Kimpo City, Republic of Korea, 2003—09; chmn. bd. dir. MGU. Recipient Excellent Article award, Kyung Hee U. Med. Sch. Alumni, 1995, Editor's Choice award, Internat. Libr. Poetry, 2001. Mem.: Soc. Heart Valve Repair (gen. sec.), Korean Soc. Critical Care Medicine, Royal Belgian Soc. Surgery, Belgian Assn. Cardiothoracic Surgery, European Soc. Cardiovasc. Surgery, Internat. Soc. Heart and Lung Transplantation, European Assn. Cardiopthoracic surgery, Internat. Soc. Minimally Invasive Cardiac Surgery, Korean Med. Assn., Korean Soc. Thoracic and Cardiovasc. Surgery, Soc. Thoracic Surgeons, Internat. Soc. Poets (Silver Merit award 2002). Roman Catholic. Achievements include development of no-transfusion double valve replacement using retrograde autologous priming; minimally invasive simultaneous correction of congenital heart diseases with pectus excavatum; unilateral videoscopic assisted thoracoscopic ablation of atrial fibrillation. Avocations: travel, golf, music. Office: Inje Univ Seoul Paik Hosp 85 2d Str Jeo-dong Joong-gu Seoul 100-032 Republic of Korea Office Fax: 82-2-2270-0038. Personal E-mail: yongin@hotmail.com.

KIM, YONG-SHIN, anesthesiologist; b. Kongju, Chung-num, Republic of Korea, May 10, 1965; d. On-Sik Kim and Myoung-Ho Kang; m. Won-Kyoung Park Kim; children: Hong-Shik, Jae-Shik. MD, Ewha Women U. Korea, Republic of Korea, 1989; MSc, Cath. U. Med. Coll., 2000; PhD, ChungNam U. Med. Coll., 2005. Clin. fellow Cath. U., St. Vincent Hosp., Suwon, Republic of Korea, 1997—98, instr., 1998—2001, asst. prof., 2001—05, assoc. prof., 2005—, prof., 2010—. Achievements include research in anesthesia & body temperature. Office: St Vincent Hosp 93 Gi-Dong Paldal-Gu Suwon Gyounggi-Do 442-723 Republic of Korea Office Fax: 82-31-258-4212. Business E-Mail: aneskim@catholic.ac.kr.

KIM, YONG-UNG, pharmacist, educator; b. Dongdaemun-gu, Seoul, Republic of Korea, June 6, 1967; s. Geuksu and Sinja Kim; 1 child, Ujung. BS in Pharmacy, Seoul Nat. U., 1990, MS in Pharmacy, 1992, PhD in Pharmacy, 2000. Cert. pharmacist Ministry Health, Welfare and Family Affairs, Republic of Korea, 1990, oriental medicine dispenser Ministry Health, Welfare and Family Affairs, Republic of Korea, 1996. Postdoc. fellow Seoul Nat. U., Gwanak-gu, 2000—05; lectr. Coll. Nursing, Nat. Med. Ctr., Jung-gu, Seoul, 2002—03, Korea Nat. Police U., Yongin-si, Gyeonggi-do, 2003, Korea Nat. Open U., Jongno-gu, Seoul, 2004; korea sci. and engring. found. rsch. fellow Seoul Nat. U., Gwanak-gu, 2004—05; lectr. Sookmyung Women's U., Yongsan-gu, Seoul, Republic Of Korea, 2005—05; rschr. Chung-Ang U., Dongjak-gu, Seoul, 2005—06; committeeman Korea Inst. Sci. and Tech. Info., Yuseong-gu, Daejeon, Republic of Korea, 2008—; prof. Daegu Haany U., Gyeongsan-si, Gyeongsangbuk-do, Republic of Korea, 2008—. Pvt., 2nd class Med. Br., 1992—99, Seoul. Postdoc. fellowship, Japan Soc. Promotion Sci., 2005. Mem.: Japanese Soc. Pharmacognosy, Med. and Pharm. Soc. WAKAN-YAKU, Pharm. Soc. Korea, Korean Soc. Microbiology and Biotech., Japan Wood Rsch. Soc., Japan Soc. Biosci., Biotech. and Agrochemistry, Pharm. Soc. Japan, Korean Soc. Applied Biol. Chemistry. Achievements include patents pending for reductase inhibitors & phenazine methosulfate for curing benign prostatic hypertrophy; patents for menaquinone 7 for curing benign prostatic hypertrophy & reductase inhibitors, abietic acid from resina pini of pinus spp. Office: Daegu Haany University 290 Yugok-dong Gyeongsan-si Gyeongsangbuk-do r712-715 Republic of Korea Office Fax: 82-53-819-1272. Business E-Mail: ykim@dhu.ac.kr.

KIM, YONG-WOOK, gynecologist, educator; b. Jeonju, Republic of Korea, Nov. 5, 1963; MD, Cath. U. Korea, 1988, PhD, 2000. Rsch. fellow, divsn. gynecologic oncology Dept. Gynecology and Obstetrics Johns Hopkins Hosp., 2003—05; dir., dept. ob-gyn. Incheon St. Mary's Hosp., 2009—, dir., Laparoscopic Surgery Ctr., 2009—; prof., dept. ob-gyn. Cath. U. Korea, 2010—. Recipient Korea Global Med. Supply award, iMBC, DongA.com ISPLUS, 2010. Mem.: Am. Assn. Gynecologic Laparoscopists, Korean Soc. Gynecologic Oncology and Colposcopy, Korean Soc. Gynecologic Endoscopy and Minimal Invasive Surgery, Korean Soc. Ob-Gyn. Office: 665 Bupyeong 6-dong Bupyeong-gu Incheon 403-720 Republic of Korea Business E-Mail: ywk@catholic.ac.kr.

KIM, YOON BERM, immunologist, educator; b. Pyongnam, Republic of Korea, Apr. 25, 1929; arrived in U.S., 1959, naturalized, 1975; s. Sang Sun and Yang Rang (Lee) K.; m. Soon Cha Kim, Feb. 23, 1959; children: John, Jean, Paul. MD, Seoul Nat. U., 1958; PhD, U. Minn., 1965. Intern Univ. Hosp. Seoul Nat. U., 1958-59; asst. prof. microbiology U. Minn., Mpls., 1965-70, assoc. prof., 1970-73; mem., head lab. ontogeny of immune sys. Sloan Kettering Inst. Cancer Rsch., Rye, NY, 1973-83; prof. immunology Cornell U. Grad. Sch. Med. Scis., NYC, 1973-83, chmn. immunology unit, 1980-82; prof. microbiology, immunology & medicine Rosalind Franklin U. Medicine and Sci., Chgo. Med. Sch., 1983—2006, prof. emeritus microbiology, immunology & medicine, 2006—, chmn. dept. microbiology and immunology, 1983—2004, acting dean Sch. Grad. and Postdoctoral Studies, 1994-95. Mem. Lobund adv. bd. U. Notre Dame, 1977-88. Contbr. numerous articles on immunology to profl. jours. Recipient Rsch. Career Devel. award USPHS, 1968-73, Morris Parker Meritorius Rsch. award U. Health Scis., Chgo. Med. Sch., 1984, Ham Choon Disinction in Med. Rsch. Grand prize Seoul Nat. U. Coll. Medicine Alumni Assn., 2003, Disting. Alumni award Seoul Nat. U., 2004. Fellow Am. Acad. Microbiology; mem. AAAS, Korean Acad. Sci. and Tech., Assn. Gnotobiotics (pres.), Internat. Assn. for Gnotobiology (founding), Am. Assn. Immunologists, Am. Soc. Microbiology, Am. Assn. Pathologists, Korean-Am. Med. Assn., NY Acad. Scis., Soc. for Leucocyte Biology, Internat. Soc. Devel. Comparative Immunology, Harvey Soc., Internat. Soc. Interferon and Cytokine Rsch., Korean Acad. Sci. and Tech., Chgo. Assn. Immunologists (pres.), Assn. Med. Sch. Microbiology and Immunology Chairs, Internat. Endotoxin Soc. (charter), Soc. Natural Immunity (charter), Sigma Xi, Alpha Omega Alpha. Achievements include discovery of the unique germfree dolostrum-deprived immunologically "virgin" piglet model used to investigate ontogenic development and regulation of the immune system including T/B lymphocytes, natural killer/killer cells, and macrophages; research on ontogeny and regulation of immune system, immunochemistry and biology of bacterial toxins, host-parasite relationships, gnotobiology and immunotherapy of cancer. Home: 313 Weatherford Ct Lake Bluff IL 60044-1905 Office: Rosalind Franklin U Medicine and Sci Chgo Med Sch 3333 Green Bay Rd North Chicago IL 60064-3037 Home Phone: 847-295-5286; Office Phone: 847-578-8847. Business E-Mail: yoon.kim@rosalindfranklin.edu.

KIM, YOON-WON, physician, educator; b. Korea, Oct. 21, 1955; MD, Seoul Nat. U., 1981, PhD, 1987. Prof. Hallym U., 1986—. CEO ImmuneMed, Inc., 2000—11. Recipient Excellent Paper award, Asia-Pacific Forum on Andrology, Dongsin Smith Keine award, Korean Med. Assn. Mem.: Bio Electro Magnetic Soc., Am. Soc. Microbiology. Achievements include research in anti-viral substance secreted from body; manufacturing of diagnostic kit for acute febrile illness. Office: Hallym University 1 Hallymdaehak-gil Chuncheon Gangwon 200-702 Republic of Korea Office Fax: 82-33-241-1664. Business E-Mail: ywkim@hallym.ac.kr.

KIM, YOUN H., dermatologist, educator, oncologist, educator; MD, Stanford U., 1984. Diplomate Am. Bd. Dermatology, 1989. Intern Kaiser Permanente San Francisco Med. Ctr., 1985; resident dermatology Met. Hosp., NYC, 1986—89; prof., oncology, dermatology Med Ctr. Line Stanford Sch. of Medicine; hosp. affiliation include Stanford Hosp. and Clinics. Office: Medical Dermatology 450 Broadway St Pavilion B 4th Fl MC 533 Redwood City CA 94063 Mailing: Cutaneous Oncology 875 Blake Wilbur Dr Clinic A Stanford CA 94305 Office Phone: 650-723-6316, 650-723-6316. Office Fax: 650-721-3476.

KIM, YOUNG CHEOL, agricultural studies educator; b. Goheung, Sept. 09; PhD, Utah State U., 1999. Prof. Chonnam Nat. U., 2000—. Dir. Inst. Environmetally-Friendly Agr., 2011. Mem.: Am. Phytopath. Soc. Avocation: fishing. Office: Inst Environmentally-Friendly Agr Gwangju 500-757 Republic of Korea E-mail: yckimyc2@hanmail.net.

KIM, YOUNG DAE, pediatrician, educator; b. Seoul, Sept. 25, 1966; MD, Hanyanng U., Seoul, 1994, PhD, 2009. Resident, pediat. Hanyang U. Hosp., 1998—2002, pediat. fellowship, 2002—04; lectr. Inje U., Seoul Paik Hosp., 2004—07. Cons. Kaya Constrn. Co., 2002—08, Kaya Energy Co., 2005—08; pres. Alumni Assn., 2004—06. Recipient Best Med. Resident award, Hanyang U. Hosp., 1998; named Best Dr. of Yr., 1999. Mem.: Korean Soc. Pediat. Hematology-Oncology, Korean Pediat. Soc., Korean Cancer Assn., Korean Soc. Hematology, Korean Coll. Pediat. Clin. Immunology. Office: Dept Pediat Inje University 85 Seoul 100-032 Republic of Korea Office Fax: 82-2-2270-0264. Business E-Mail: kmsc29@hanmail.net.

KIM, YOUNG DON, medical educator; b. Pusan, Republic of Korea, Mar. 9, 1966; B, Pusan Nat. U., 1991, M, 1995. Asst. prof. Ulsan U. Coll. Medicine, Republic of Korea, 2002—06; rsch. fellow Hosp. Sick Children Rsch. Inst., Toronto, Canada, 2006—07; pediatrician Hanmaeum Hosp., Jeju, Republic of Korea, 2007—08; clin. asst. prof. Pusan Nat. U. Hosp., Republic of Korea, 2008—10; assoc. prof. Jeju Nat. U. Sch. Medicine, 2010—. Dir., regional ctr. neontal ICU Jeju Nat. U. Hosp., 2010; editl. bd. mem. Jour. Korean Soc. Neonatology, 2010, Korean Jour. Perinatology, 2011. Mem.: Korean Soc. Perinatology, Korean Soc. Neonatology, Korean Pediatric Soc. Avocation: photography. Office: 1753-3 Ara-1dong Jeju 690-716 Republic of Korea Personal E-mail: cardion@hanmail.net.

KIM, YOUNG GON, molecular medicine biologist, researcher; b. Iksan, Republic of Korea, Sept. 27, 1947; s. Jinyeo Shin and Yangyong Kim; m. Seongja Song; 1 child, Sah Rok. PhD, U. N.Mex., 1990. Cert. tchr. 1975, Radiation Safety specialist 1995. Head dept. biology Chosun U., Kwangju, Republic of Korea, 1997—99; chief Chosun Life Sci. Inst., Kwangju, Chollanamdo, Republic of Korea, 2000—. Adv. com. Biotechnology Ctr., Kwangju, 2001; visiting scholar NC State U., Raleigh, 1995—96. Author: Free Radicals in Medicine, 1997 (Best author from Korea Civilization & Tourism Resource, 1997), Biology of Aging, 2000, Gene Therapy, 2001, Antioxidants, 2005 (Best author, Nat. Acad. Sci.), Aging Clinic, 2007. Com. Living of Earth, Seoul, Republic of Korea, 2001. Sgt. med. affairs Army of Republic of Korea, 1970—73. Fellow: Chollabukdo Ednl. Orgn. (Ist Prize from mid. graduation in Chollabukdo Ist prize(1964)); mem.: AAAS (membership membership in science(1997)), Korean Soc. Molecular Biology, Internat. Soc. Free Radical Rsch., Korean Soc. of Gerontology (hon.), Subis (Current awareness in Biomedicine 2001). Presbyn. Avocation: citizenship. Office: Natural Sci Chosun U Seosukdong Dongku 375 501-759 Gwangju Republic of Korea Home Phone: 82-62-652-0834; Office Phone: 82-62-230-6656. Home Fax: 82-62-234-4326. Business E-Mail: ygnkim@mail.chosun.ac.kr.

KIM, YOUNG HO, microbiologist, educator; b. Kimhae, Kyungnam, South Korea, Feb. 16, 1958; s. Seuk Chool and Bok Jeum Kim; m. Do Youn Jun, June 5, 1959; children: Mhin Jine, Yae Jine. BS, Kyungpook Nat. U., Taegu, South Korea, 1980; MS, Kyungpook Nat. U., Teagu, South Korea, 1982; PhD, Kyungpook Nat. U., Taegu, South Korea, 1985. Instr. Taegu Health Coll., 1981—82; tchg. asst. Kyungpook Nat. U., Taegu, 1982—83, rsch. asst., 1984—86; instr. Coll. of Natural Sci., Kyungpook Nat. U., Taegu, 1986—88, asst. prof., 1988—94, assoc. prof., 1994—99, prof., 1999—; chmn. dept. microbiology Coll. Natural Sci., Kyungpook Nat. U., 1995—97, chmn. Sch. Life Sci., 1996—97. Vis. fellow Gerontology Rsch. Ctr., Nat. Inst. Aging, NIH, Balt., 1989—92, assoc., 1999—2000. Contbr. articles to profl. jours. Recipient Best Promotion of Rsch. award, Korean Soc. Indsl. Microbiology, 1987, Best Rsch. Paper award, Korean Soc. Microbiological Biotechnology, 2003. Avocation: tennis. Office: Kyungpook Natl Univ Dept Microbiol Sangkyuk-Dong Buk-Ku 1370 702-701 Daegu Daegu Republic of Korea Office Fax: 82-53-955-5522. Business E-Mail: ykim@knu.ac.kr.

KIM, YOUNG HOON, surgeon, educator; b. Jinhae, Republic of Korea, Dec. 7, 1953; s. Hong Ju Kim and Jung Im Jo; m. Shin Jae Kang, Oct. 10, 1987; children: Jee Yun, Seung Hyun. MD, Cath. U. Med. Coll., Seoul, PhD, 1979. Cert. surgeon Gen. Surgery Bd., Korea, 1985. Dir. prof., dept. surgery Dong-A U., Busan, Republic of Korea, 1990—. Dir. Korea HBP Assn., Busan, 2004—08. Capt. 25 army divsn., 1979—81, Korea. Master: Busan HBP & Transplant Assn. Home: 101-2505 Adels Apt U-1dong Haeundaegu Busan 612-875 Republic of Korea Office: Dong-A Univ Hosp 3-1 Dongdaesindong Seogu 602-715 Busan Busan Republic of Korea Home Phone: 82-51-621-5281; Office Phone: 82-51-240-2981. Office Fax: 82-51-247-9316. Business E-Mail: yhkim1@dau.ac.kr.

KIM, YOUNG JIN, dermatology registrar; b. Incheon, Republic of Korea, Dec. 1, 1977; s. Kwang Ho and Soon Boon Kim; m. Seung Hee Jin, May 18, 2007. B in Med. Sci., U. Sydney, 1998, M in Medicine, 2006; MB BChir with honours, U. NSW, Sydney. Lic. Korean Med. Bd., Seoul, Republic of Korea, 2004. Gen. practice registrar Queen St. Clinic, Grafton, NSW, 2007; dermatology registrar Queensland Inst. Dermatology, Greenslopes, Australia, 2008—, Mater Misericordiae Hosp., South Brisbane, 2009—, Royal Brisbane and Women's Hosp., Houston, 2010, Princess Alexandra Hosp., Woolloongabba, 2011—; assoc. lectr. Sch. Medicine, U. Queensland, 2009—11. Dermatology rsch. fellow Royal Prince Alfred Hosp., Sydney, 2005—06. Leader Youth Charismatic Prayer Group, Sydney, 2002—07, Korea Cath. Youth Charismatic Prayer Group. Fellowship, Australasian Coll. Dermatology, 2011. Personal E-mail: kimabel@hanmail.net.

KIM, YOUNG JOON, plastic surgeon; Grad., Seoul Nat. U. Med. Coll.; postgrad., Seoul Nat. U. Bd. cert. tng. plastic surgery dept. Seoul Nat. Univ. Hosp.; chief dir. Dream Aesthetic Medicine rsch. Ctr.; surgeon Dream Plastic Surgery Clinic. Fellow: Am. Soc. Laser Medicine and Surgery; mem.: Internat. Confederation Plastic reconstructive and Aesthetic Surgery, Korean Cleft-Palate-Craniofacial Assn., Korean Microsurgical Soc., Korean Soc. Reconstructive Hand Surgery, Korean Med. Assn., Korean Soc. Aesthetic Plastic Surgery, Korean Soc. Plastic and Reconstructive Surgeons. Office: Dream Plastic Surgery Clinic Apkujung Subway Sta Seoul Republic of Korea Office Phone: 8225461616. Office Fax: 8225461614. *

KIM, YOUNG JU, medical educator; b. Seoul, Republic of Korea, Oct. 31, 1963; d. Am San Kim and Soon Myung Ahn, Dong Soon Shin (Stepmother); m. Myung Geol Pang, Oct. 4, 1991; children: Won Ki Pang, Jun Ki Pang. MD, Ewha Womans U., Shinchon, Seoul, Republic of Korea, 1988; MS, Ewha Womans U. Coll. Medicine, Shinchon, Seoul, Republic of Korea, 1992, PhD, 1997. Lic. in medicine Republic of Korea, 1988, cert. Specialist Republic of Korea, 1993. Internship Ewha Womans U. Hosp., Republic of Korea, 1988—89, residency, 1989—92, fellow, 1993—94; instr. Ewha Womans U., Republic of Korea, 1994, asst. prof., 1997—2002, assoc. prof., 2002—07, prof., 2007—. MPH Yonsei U., Seoul, Republic of Korea, 2001—03. Recipient award, Korean Meternal Fetal Medicine, 2004, Fering award, Korena Metrnal Fetal Medicine, 2008, award, Korean Women Med. Assn., 2008; named Best Dr., Ewha Womans U., 2006. Mem.: Korean Soc. Ob-Gyn. (award 2006). Home: 120-902 Mok-Dong Apt Yangcheon-ku Seoul 158-710 Republic of Korea Office: Ewha Womans Univ MokDong Hosp 911-1 MokDong Yangcheon-ku Seoul 158-710 Republic of Korea Office Fax: 82-2-2647-9860. Business E-Mail: kkyj@ewha.ac.kr.

KIM, YOUNG JUN, dean; b. Seoul, Republic of Korea, Sept. 3, 1970; s. Dong Hoon Kim and Sun Ho Song; m. Hee Joo Kim; 1 child, Seo Yoon. PhD, Cornell U., Ithaca, NY, 2001. Postdoc. rsch. assoc. Boyce Thompson Inst., Ithaca, 2001—02, Cornell U., 2002—04; dept. dean Korea U., Jochiwon, Chungnam, Republic of Korea, 2006—. Editor Korean Soc. Food Sci. Tech., Seoul, 2005—07; adj. rsch. dir. Nat. Inst. Animal Sci., Pyong Chang, Kangwon, Republic of Korea, 2008—; editl. bd. mem. Korean Soc. Poultry Sci., Cheonan, Chungnam, 2008. Office: Korea Univ Seochang-Dong 208 339-700 Jochiwon Chungcheongnam-do Republic of Korea Office Fax: 82-41-865-0220. Business E-Mail: yk46@korea.ac.kr.

KIM, YOUNG OK, nephrologist; b. Buyeo, Chungnam, Republic of Korea, June 1, 1962; s. Bok Hyun Kim and Il Hee Song; m. In Suk Kwon, Feb. 1, 1963; children: In Soo, Jung In. MD, Cath. U. Korea, Seoul, 1988. Nephrologist Cath. U. Korea, 2005—. Home: Kunyoung Apt 310-904 JungKye 1-Dong Seoul 139-221 Republic of Korea Office: Cath U Korea 65-1 Kumoh-Dong 480-130 Uijongbu-City Gyeonggi-do Republic of Korea Office Fax: 82-31-847-2719. Personal E-mail: cmckyo@yahoo.co.kr. Business E-Mail: cmckyo@catholic.ac.kr.

KIM, YOUNG OK, healthcare educator; b. Seoul, Republic of Korea, Dec. 2, 1950; MPH, Yonsei U., 1975; PhD, U. London, 1981. Prof., dept. food and nutrition Dongduk Women's U., 1992—2011; dean Coll. Natural Sci., Dongduk Women's U., 2010; dir. Sungbuk Children's Food Svc. Mgmt. Ctr., 2011; pres. Korean Soc. Cmty. Nutrition, 2010—. Rschr., dept. human nutrion Food and Nutrition Policy and Planning Unit, London Sch. Hygine and Tropical Medicine, U. London, 1977—81; vis. asst. prof. U. Colo. Health Sci. Ctr., 1988—90; cons. IBRD, 1990—90. Named Best Rschr. of Yr., Dongduk Women's U.; grant, Das Diakonische Werk Der Ekd, Germany. Mem.: Korean Nutrition Soc., Korean Soc. Epidemiology, Japanese Soc. Nutrition and Dietetics, Nutrition Soc., Soc. Nutrition Edn. Avocations: running, skateboarding, mountain climbing. Office: #23-1 Wolgok-dong Sungbuk-gu Seoul 136-714 Republic of Korea Office Fax: 82-2-940-4193. Business E-Mail: yok@dongduk.ac.kr.

KIM, YOUNG RAN, pharmacist, educator; b. Republic of Korea, July 7, 1966; BS in Pharmacy, Chonnam U., 1990, PhD in Pharmacy, 1997. Rsch. prof. Chonnam U., 2003—05; prof. Dongshin U.,

2006—. Office: Dongshin University Gunjaero Naju Jeonnam 520-714 Republic of Korea Business E-Mail: kimyr@dsu.ac.kr.

KIM, YOUNG SUN, gastroenterologist, educator; b. Seoul, Republic of Korea, Mar. 4, 1970; PhD, Ewha Womans U., 1994. Asst. prof. Seoul Nat. U. Hosp., Healthcare Sys. Gangnam Ctr., 2003—. Mem.: Korean Soc. Gastrointestinal Endoscopy (Best Rsch. award), Korean Assn. Study of Intestinal Disease, Korean Soc. Gastroenterology. Avocation: classical music. Office: Seoul Nat University GFC 39th Fl Seoul 135-987 Republic of Korea Personal E-mail: pandayoung@yahoo.co.kr.

KIM, YOUNG-CHUL, medical researcher, educator; b. Gwangju, Republic of Korea, Sept. 23, 1962; s. Myung-Won Kim and Woo-Soon Shim; m. Min-Sun Kang, Mar. 28, 1987; children: SoYeon, TaeHee. M.D., Chonnam Nat. U., Gwangju, Korea, 1981—87; PhD, Chonnam U. Grad. Sch., Gwangju, Korea, 1988—95. Medical Doctor Ministry of Health and Wellfare, 1987, Board of Internal Medicine Ministry of Health and Wellfare, Korea, 1991, Subspecialty in Pulmonology and Critical Care Medicine Korean Acad. of Internal Medicine, 1998, cert. Ednl. Commn. for Fgn. Med. Grads. Rsch. assoc. Duke U. Med. Sch., Durham, NC, 1997—99; prof. Chonnam Nat. U. Med. Sch., Gwangju, Republic of Korea, 1995—2008. Trustees Korean Assn. for the Study of Lung Cancer, Seoul, 2000—. Author: (research publication) Prognostic significance of molecular genetic aberrations on chromosome segment 11p15.5 in non-small-cell lung cancer., Apoptosis and bcl-2 expression as predictors of survival in radiation-treated non-small cell lung cancer, Different cutoff values of cyfra 21-1 for cavitary and noncavitary lung cancers, SSA/RO52gene and expressed sequence tags in an 85 kb region of chromosome segment 11p15.5., The interactive effect of ras, her2, p53 and bcl-2 expression in predicting the survival of non-small cell lung cancer, other numerous research papers. Capt. Army, Korean, 1991—92, South Korea. Mem.: Korean Acad. of Tb and Respiratory Medicine, Internat. Assn. of Study of Lung Cancer (life), Am. Thoracic Soc. (life), Korean Assn. of Internal Medicine (life), Korean Med. Assn. (life). Office: Chonnam Nat Univ Hwasun Hosp Ilsim-Ri Hwasun-Eup 160 519-809 Hwasung Jeollanam-do Republic of Korea Business E-Mail: kyc0923@chonnam.ac.kr.

KIM, YOUNG-HOO, medical educator, surgeon; b. Seoul, Republic of Korea, May 29, 1944; s. Jin-Taek Kim and Mee-Kyung Lee; m. Hee-Ja Kim, Dec. 25, 1996; children: Una, Ian. MD, Yonsei U. Coll. Medicine, 1969. Diplomate Korean Bd. Orthopaedic Surgery. Intern, resident Yonsei U. Med. Ctr., Seoul, 1969—74; resident Toronto Western Hosp., 1974—75, U. Chgo. Hosps., 1976—79; clin. instr. U. So. Calif., LA, 1980—82; asst., assoc. prof. Yonsei U. Coll. Medicine, Seoul, 1983—89; assoc. prof. Tex. Tech. U. Hosp., Lubbock, 1989—91; prof. Pochon Joongmun U., Seoul, 1996—98; pres. HaeMin Gen. Hosp., 2000—; dir. Joint Replacement Ctr. of Korea Ewha Women's U., Dong Dae Mun Hosp., Seoul, 2000—, prof., 2003—. Spkr. and presenter in field. Contbr. articles to profl. jours. Fellow, Mass. Gen. Hosp., Boston, 1979—80, Birgham and Women's Hosp., Boston, 1982—83. Mem.: Korean Orthopaedic Assn., Asian Pacific Orthopaedic Assn. (chmn. knee sect.), Tex. Orthopaedic Assn., Am. Assn. Hip and Knee Surgeons, Soc. Internat. Chirugie Orthopedique et Traumatologie, Orthopaedic Rsch. Soc., Am. Acad. Orthopedic Surgery. Office: Ewha Women's U Dong Dae Mun Hosp 70 Chongro 6Ga Chong Ro=Gu Seoul C110-1267 Republic of Korea Office Phone: 822-760-5000. Fax: 822 457-2632. E-mail: younghookim@netsgo.com.

KIM, YOUNG-JOON, neurosurgeon, educator; b. Seoul, Republic Of Korea, July 28, 1955; m. Min-Sook Park, Mar. 15, 1957; children: Yun-Ji, Hyo-Geun, Chang-Geun, Jae-Geun. PhD, Hanyang U., Seoul, 1988. Lic. Neurosurgeon Korea, 1988. Prof., chmn. dept. neurosurgery Dankook U. Coll. Medicine, Cheonan, Choongnam, Republic of Korea, 1993—. Publ. com. chair Korean Neurol. Soc., 2009—. Mem.: Korean Soc. Neurosurgery (bd. dirs. 1998—), Korean Soc. Intravascular Neurosurgery (pres. 2002—04). Achievements include research in endovascular aneurysm coiling with stent & endovascular care of acute stroke. Office: Dankook Univ Coll Med Dept Neurosurgery Anseo-Dong Cheonan 29 330-714 Choongnam Chungcheongnam-do Republic of Korea Office Phone: 82-11-397-8999. Office Fax: 82-41-552-6870. Business E-Mail: kimyj@dku.edu, kimyj@dankook.ac.kr.

KIM, YOUNGJUN, chemistry professor; b. Buan, Republic of Korea, Mar. 28, 1967; PhD, U. Ill., Chgo., 2004. Postdoc. rschr. U. Calif., San Diego, 2004—08; asst. prof. Konkuk U., 2008—. Mem.: KSMS, KSBE, KSMCB, KSBMB, Korean Chem. Soc. Avocation: hiking. Office: Konkuk University Damwoldong 322 Chungju Chungbuk 380-701 Republic of Korea Office Fax: 82-43-840-3929. Business E-Mail: ykim@kku.ac.kr.

KIM, YOUNG-WAN, biotechnologist, educator; b. Seoul, Republic of Korea, Oct. 26, 1969; PhD, Seoul Nat. U., 2002. Postdoc. fellow U. BC, 2003—06; assoc. prof. Korea U., 2007—. Fellowship, Michael Smith Found. Health Rsch., Can., 2006, Rsch. grant, Ministry of Edn., Sci. and Tech., Republic of Korea, 2011—. Office: Seochang-Ri 208 Korea University Jochiwon Chungchengnam 339-700 Republic of Korea Business E-Mail: ywankim@korea.ac.kr.

KIM, YOUNGWOO, physician; b. Seoul, Republic of Korea, Apr. 30, 1964; MSc, Seoul Nat. U., 1992, PhD, 1998. Head physician, gastric cancer Nat. Cancer Ctr., 2006—. Prin. scientist Gastric Cancer Br. Divsn. Common Cancers Rsch. Inst. Nat. Cancer Ctr., 2006—11. Recipient Young Investigator award, Dept. Orthop. Surgery Seoul Nat. U. Hosp., Meritorious award, Ministry of Knowledge Economy, Republic of Korea; Rsch. fellow, Korean Cancer Assn. Mem.: Nat. Cancer Control Program (steering com.), Japanese Gastric Cancer Assn., Soc. Laparoscopic Surgeon, Soc. Am. Gastrointestinal Endoscopic Surgeons, Internat. Gastric Cancer Assn., Gastric Cancer Br. Cancer Prevention and Early Detection Com. Avocations: golf, travel, reading. Office: Jungbalsanro 323 Ilsandonggu Goyangsi Gyeonggi-Do 410-769 Republic of Korea Office Fax: 82319202799. Business E-Mail: gskim@ncc.re.kr.

KIM, YU JUNG, medical educator; b. Seoul, Republic of Korea, Oct. 5, 1975; MD, Seoul Nat. U., 2001, MSc, 2005. Asst. prof. Seoul Nat. U. Bundang Hosp., 2007—. Recipient Young Investigator award, Asian Pacific Cancer Conf. Mem.: Am. Soc. Clin. Oncology. Office: Seoul Nat University Bundang Hospital 1 Seongnam Gyeonggi-do 463-707 Republic of Korea Office Fax: 82-31-787-4051. Personal E-mail: cong1005@gmail.com.

KIM, YUN-HEE, medical educator; b. Iksan, Jeonbuk, Republic of Korea, Dec. 25, 1957; d. Hyoung-Il Kim and Ok-Nyou Choi; children: Bareun Choi, Joeun Choi. MD, Yonsei U., Seoul, 1982, PhD, 1996. Lic. doc. Ministry of Health and Social Welfare, Korea, 1982, cert. rehab. medicine Korea, 1986, electrodiagnsis US, 1996. Attending staff, chief dept. rehab. medicine Presbyn. Med. Ctr., Chonju, 1986—92; asst. prof. & chief dept. rehab. medicine Chonbuk Nat. U. Med. Sch. & Hosp., Chonju, Republic of Korea, 1992—98; assoc. prof., chief dept. rehab. medicine Chonbuk Nat. U. Medial Sch. & Hosp., Chonju, Republic of Korea, 1998—2002, Coll. of Medicine, Pochon Cha U., Bundang Cha Gen. Hosp., Sungnam, Republic of Korea, 2002—03; prof., chair dept. phys. medicine & rehab. Sungkyunkwan U. Sch. Medicine, Samsung Med. Ctr., Seoul, 2003—. Supr. North-Wanju Cmty. Rehab. Project, Republic of Korea, 1988—92; vis. scholar cognitive neurology and alzheimer's disease ctr. Northwestern U. Med. Sch., Chgo., 1996—98. Contbr. scientific papers to profl. jours. Grantee, Korean Ministry of Health and Social Welfare, 2000—02, 2006—07, Korean Sci. & Engring. Found., 2000—03, 2006—07, Korean Rsch. Found., 2001—02, Ministry of Health & Social Welfare, 2001—03, Ministry of Sci. & Tech., Korea, 2006—, 21st century Frontier Rsch. grant, 2003—06. Mem.: Korean Stroke Soc., Korean Soc. Neurorehab. (dir. bd. 2006—), Orgn. Human Brain Mapping, Am. Congress Phys. Medicine and Rehab., Am. Acad. Electrodiagnostic Medicine, Am. Soc. Neurorehab., Am. Assn. Phys. Medicine and Rehab., Soc. Neurosci., Korean Soc. Rehab. Medicine, Korean Soc. Neurosci. Achievements include research in the large-scale neural network for spatial attention displays multifunctional overlap but differential asymmetry; facilitative effect of high frequency subthreshold repetitive transcranial magnetic stimulation on complex sequential motor learning in humans; plastic changes of motor network after constraint-induced movement therapy; ipsilateral motor pathway confirmed by diffusion tensor tractography in a patient with schizencephaly; virtual reality induced cortical reorganization in a child with hemiparetic cerebral palsy; cortical reorganization associated with motor recovery in hemiparetic stroke patient; reorganization of cortical language areas in patients with aphasia; computer-assisted cognitive rehabilitation program for patients with brain injury; restoration of corticospinal tract compressed by hematoma; diffusion tensor tractography study; virtual reality-induced Cortical reorganization and associated locomotor recovery in chronic stroke; experimenter-blind randomized study; rTMS-induced corticomotor excitability and associated motor skill acquistion in chronic stroke; facilitating visuospatial attention for the contralateral hemifield by repetitive TMS on the posterior parietal cortex; effects of single-dose methyphenidate on cognitive performance in patients with traumatic brain injury; double-blind placebo-controlled study; longitudinal FMRI study for locomotor recovery in patients with stroke; dissociable modulating effect of repetitive TMS on sensory and pain perception, plasticity of attentional after brain injuri and cognitive training; plasticity of attentional network after brain injuri and cognitive training; effects of hippotherapy on gait parameters in children with bilateral spastic cerebral palsy; longitudinal changes of resting state functional connectivity during motor recovery after stroke; effects of robot assisted gait training on cardiopulmonary fitness in subacute stroke patients. Office: Samsung Med Ctr Dept Phys Med & Rehab 50 Ilwon-dong Kangnam-gu Seoul 135-710 Republic of Korea Office Fax: 82-2-3410-0052. Personal E-mail: yunkim1225@empal.com. Business E-Mail: yunkim@skku.edu.

KIM, YUN-SOOK, physician, educator; b. Dangjin-gun, Chungnam, May 1, 1972; PhD, Soonchunhyang U., 2008. Asst. prof. Soonchunhyang U. Cheonan Hosp. Ob-gyn., 2009—. Office: 23-20 Bongmyeong-Dong Cheonan Choongcheongnam 330-821 Republic of Korea Office Fax: 82-41-571-7887. Business E-Mail: drsook@schmc.ac.kr.

KIM, ZAEZEUNG, allergist, immunologist, educator; b. Hamhung, Korea, Feb. 21, 1929; came to U.S., 1967; s. Suh and Suyeo (Hahn) K.; m. Youngju Kim, June 2, 1961; children: Keungsuk, Maria. Student, Hamhung Med. Coll., Korea, 1946-50; MD, Seoul U., Korea, 1960; PhD in Immunology, U. Cologne, Fed. Republic of Germany, 1968. Diplomate Am. Bd. Allergy and Immunology. Intern Seoul Nat. U. Hosp., 1960-61, resident in medicine, 1961-63, Heidelberg U. Hosp., Fed. Republic of Germany, 1963-64; research fellow Max-Planck Inst., Cologne, 1965-67; fellow in hematology U. Tex., Houston, 1967-68; resident in allergy and immunology Temple U. Hosp., Phila., 1968-69; fellow in medicine Ohio State U., Columbus, 1969-71; instr. medicine Med. Coll. Wis., Milw., 1972-75, asst. prof., 1975-78, assoc. clin. prof., 1978—; practice medicine specializing in allergy and immunology Racine, Wis. Hon. staff Milw. (Wis.) County Med. Complex, 1993. Contbr. articles to profl. jours. Fellow Am. Acad. Allergy and Immunology, Am. Coll. Allergists; mem. AMA. Home: 461 W Sunnyview Dr Apt 13 Oak Creek WI 53154-3893

KIMBALL, ALEXA BOER, dermatologist; b. Boston, Oct. 21, 1968; d. F. Peter and Ellen Boer; m. Ranch Cannon Kimball. AB cum laude, Princeton U., NJ, 1990; MD cum laude, Yale U., New Haven, 1994; MPH, Johns Hopkins U., Balt., 2000. Bd. cert. Am. Bd. Dermatology; lic. Calif., Mass., Md. Intern, clin. fellow, internal medicine Beth Israel Hosp., Boston, 1994—95; chief resident, dermatology Stanford U. Med. Ctr., 1995—98, dir. clin. trials, dermatology, asst. prof., 2000—04; assoc. dermatologist Mass. Gen. and Brigham and Womens Hosps., 2004—, dir. Clin. Unit Rsch. Trials in Skin (CURTIS), chair, Clin. Investigation Com. BWH, mem. Women in Acad. Medicine Com., staff dermatologist, Dana Farber Cancer Inst.; asst. prof. Harvard Med. Sch., 2005—07, assoc. prof., 2007—; vice chair dermatology Mass. Gen. Hosp., 2008—. Intern, polit.-military and sci. sec. US Embassy, Paris, 1989; mem. scientific adv. bd. Magen Biosciences, Inc., 2007. Assoc. editor Jour. Am. Acad. Dermatology, 2004—; contbr. chapters to books, scientific papers to profl. publs. Recipient Women's Dermatol. Soc. Mentorship grant, Stanford U. Med. Ctr., 1997, Disting. Cmty. Svc. award, Yale U. Sch. Medicine. Fellow: NIH (dermatology br. 1998—2000); mem.: AMA (del. 2000—02), Soc. Investigative Dermatology (bd. dirs. 2008), San Francisco Dermatol. Soc. (mem. exec. com. 2001—04), Am. Assn. Med. Colls. (mem. adv. panel 1997—99), Am. Acad. Dermatology (chair 2006—), Nat. Psoriasis Found. (med. bd. 2004—), Phi Beta Kappa, Delta Omega Alpha. Avocations: travel, tennis, skiing, languages.

KIMBALL, HARRY RAYMOND, medical association administrator, educator; b. LA; MD, U. Wash., 1962. Intern King County Hosp., Seattle, 1962—63; resident in internal medicine U. Wash. Hosps., Seattle, 1963—64, 1967—68; fellow infectious diseases NIH Hosps., Bethesda, Md., 1964—67; pres. Am. Bd. Internal Medicine, Phila., 1991—2004; prof. medicine, sr. advisor to dean Sch. Medicine U. Wash., Seattle, 2004—. Office: Uw School Of Medicine 815 Mercer St # 4c Seattle WA 98109-4714 Office Phone: 206-221-4743. Office Fax: 206-221-2999. Business E-Mail: hkimball@u.washington.edu.

KIMBALL, MOLLY, dietician, nutritionist; BS in Dietetics, magna cum laude, La. State U. Agrl. & Mech. Coll., 1998, BS in Food. Sci. and Tech., magna cum laude, 1999. Registered dietician, cert. specialist in sports dietetics. Dietetic internship Touro Infirmary Hosp., New Orleans, 1999; sports & lifestyle nutritionist, mgr. nutrition program Elmwood Fitness Ctr., Ochsner Health Found., New Orleans. Nutrition columnist The Times-Picayune, New Orleans; host weekly segment 'Get Fit with Molly' ABC 26's Good Morning New Orleans. Regular appearances as nutritional expert NY Times, Vogue, Newsweek, Shape, Fitness, Runner's World, Cosmopolitan, ABCNews-.com, WebMD, CNN.com. Mem.: Am. Dietetic Assn. Office: Elmwood Fitness Ctr 1200 S Clearview Pkwy Ste 1200 New Orleans LA 70123 Office Phone: 504-842-9572. Business E-Mail: molly@mollykimball.com.

KIMBERLY, ROBERT PARKER, medical educator; b. New Haven, July 29, 1946; s. John Taylor and Beatrice Eileen (Branch) K.; m. Susan Johnson Alesbury, June 17, 1972; children: Christopher, Taylor, Sarah, Michael, Thomas. AB, Princeton U., 1968; MA, New Coll., Oxford, Eng., 1970; MD, Harvard U., 1973. Diplomate Am. Bd. Internal Medicine. Intern Hosp. of U. Pa., Phila., 1973—74, resident in medicine, 1974—75; fellow in rheumatology Applied Rsch. Br., NIAMDDK, NIH, Bethesda, Md., 1975-77, Hosp. Spl. Surgery-Cornell Med. Ctr., NYC, 1977-79; asst. prof. medicine Cornell U. Med. Coll., NYC, 1979-84, assoc. prof. medicine, 1984-91, prof. medicine, 1991—96; dir. biomedical component and program dir. Cornell Arthritis Ctr., 1988—96; prof. immunology Cornell Grad. Sch. Med. Sciences, 1991—96; Howard L. Holley Prof. Medicine U. Ala. Sch. Medicine, Birmingham, 1996—; program dir. and sr. scientist U. Ala. Arthritis Ctr., 1996—; prof. microbiology and sr. scientist U. Ala. Comprehensive Cancer Ctr., 1996—, sr. assoc. dean rsch., 2007—. Andrew Mellon Found. tchr., scientist, 1980; sci. adv. bd. Alliance for Lupus Rsch.; trustee Arthritis Found. Contbr. numerous articles to profl. jours. Lt. comdr. USPHS, 1975-77. Rhodes Trust scholar, 1968. Fellow ACP, Am. Coll. Rheumatology (pres. N.E. chpt. 1990-91); mem. NY Rheumatism Assn. (pres. NYC chpt. 1992-93), Am. Assn. Immunologists, Am. Soc. Clin. Investigation. Office: Univ Ala Dept Rheumatology Immunology 1530 3rd Ave S Shelby 172D Birmingham AL 35294 Office Phone: 205-934-5306.

KIMBER-TROJNAR, ZANETA, physician; b. Ciechanów, Poland, Sept. 21, 1976; MD, Med. U. Lublin, 2001, PhD, 2003. Resident U. Med. Sch. Tchg. Hosp. No 4, Lublin, 2005—10, jr. asst., 2010—11, sr. asst. Ind. Pub. U., 2011—. Recipient Sci. Congress Young Scientist award, Polish Pediat. Soc., Warsaw, 2000, Polish Soc. Pediat. Pathology; fellowship, Weill Cornell Med. Coll. Mem.: Polish Soc. Perinatal Medicine, Polish Gynaecol. Soc. Office: Jaczewskiego 8 Lublin 20-950 Poland Business E-Mail: zkimber@poczta.onet.pl.

KIMBRELL, DEBORAH ANN, geneticist, educator; b. San Angelo, Tex., July 22, 1950; d. Billy Lee and Dorothy (Babish) K.; m. S. Ingemar C. Olsson, June 15, 1991. BA in Biology and Psychology with honors, Mills Coll., 1972; PhD in Genetics, U. Calif., Berkeley, 1985. Rsch. tech. dept. respiration physiology Max Planck Inst. Exptl. Medicine, Göttingen, Germany, 1973-74; NIH predoctoral trainee dept. genetics U. Calif., Berkeley, 1979-85; Am. Cancer Soc. post-doctoral fellow dept. genetics U. Cambridge, England, 1985-88; Swedish MRC vis. scientist fellow dept. microbiology U. Stockholm, 1988-90; asst. prof. dept. biology and Inst. Molecular Biology, U. Houston, 1991—97; sr. faculty fellow dept. biochemistry and cell biology Rice U., Houston, 1997—99; assoc. rsch. geneticist molecular and cellular biology U. Calif., Davis, 1999—. Ad hoc grant reviewer various books and profl. jours., 1990—, NIH, Wash., DC, 2002—; founder immunity workshops Annual Drosophila Rsch. Conf., 1995—; contbr. Sci. Am. On-line, Ask the Experts, 1996. Contbr. articles to profl. jours. Mem. US Coast Guard Aux., Calif., 2001—. Pres. Rsch. and Scholarship Fund grantee U. Houston, Rsch. grantees Am. Cancer Soc., 1992-99, NIH, 1999-03, Cancer Rsch. Coordinating Com. U. Calif., 2001, 04, NASA, 2004-, NASA Flight Investigator Rsch. grantee, 2005-. Mem.: Am. Soc. Gravitational and Space Biology, Genetics Soc. Am.

KIME, RYOTARO, exercise physiologist, researcher; b. Kitakyusyu-shi, Fukuoka, Japan, Nov. 30, 1972; s. Noriyoshi and Kyoko Kime. BS, Tokyo Gakugei U., 1995; MPE, Nat. Inst. Fitness and Sports, Kagoshima, Japan, 1997; PhD in Medicine, Tokyo Med. U., 2003. Rsch. fellow Tokyo Med. U., Shinjuku, 2001, asst. prof., 2003—; vis. scholar U. Pa., Phila., 2001—03. Lectr. Tokyo Denki U., Inzai-shi, Chiba, Japan, 2004—, Tokyo Internat. U., Kawagoe-shi, Saitama, Japan, 2004—05, Tokyo Denki U., Inzai-shi, Chiba, Japan, 1998—2001. Contbr. articles to profl. jours. Recipient Best Rsch. award, Japan Soc. for Med. and Biol. Engring., 2004; grantee, Ministry of Edn., Sci., Sports and Culture Japan, 2005; scholar, The Japan Scholarship Found., 1995—97, 1997—2001. Mem.: Japan Soc. Exercise and Sport Physiology, Japan Soc. Phys. Edn., Health and Sport Sci., Japanese Soc. Phys. Fitness and Sports Sci., Am. Coll. Sports Medicine, European Coll. Sport Sci. (Young Investigators award 1999). Avocations: baseball, hiking, karaoke. Home: B-302 4-4-10 Syakujii-dai Nerima-ku Tokyo 177-0045 Japan Office: Dept Sports Medicine for Health Promotion Tokyo Med Univ 6-1-1 Shinjuku Shinjuku 160-8402 Japan Office Fax: +81-3-3226-5277. E-mail: kime@tokyo-med.ac.jp.

KIM-FARLEY, ROBERT JAMES, epidemiologist, educator; b. Troy, NY, Jan. 24, 1948; s. Robert James and Glennie Jean Farley; m. Han Ju Kim-Farley, Sept. 18, 1976; 1 child, Jean. BSEE, U. Calif., Santa Barbara, 1970; MPH, UCLA, 1975; MD, U. Calif., San Francisco, 1980. Cert. preventive medicine and pub. health. Med. epidemiologist Ctrs. Disease Control and Prevention, Atlanta, 1981—2004; dir. communicable disease control and prevention Los Angeles County Dept. Pub. Health, LA, 2004—. Regional advisor WHO, New Delhi, 1984—88, dir. expanded programme on immunization, Geneva, 1989—93, rep., Jakarta, Indonesia, 1994—99, New Delhi, 1999—2002; prof. UCLA, 2003—. Recipient Surgeon Gen.'s Exemplary Svc. medal, USPHS, 1993. Mem.: APHA. Avocation: swimming. Business E-Mail: rkimfarley@ph.ucla.edu.

KIMMEY, JAMES RICHARD, JR., foundation administrator; b. Boscobel, Wis., Jan. 26, 1935; s. James Richard and Frances Dale (Parnell) Kimmey; m. Sarah Webster Eastman, June 21, 1958; children: Elisabeth Webster, James Richard III. BS, U. Wis., 1957, MS, 1959, MD, 1961; MPH, U. Calif., Berkeley, 1967. Diplomate Am. Bd. Preventive Medicine. Intern Univ. Hosps., Cleve., 1961-62; med. resident Univ. Hosp., Madison, 1962-63; served from surgeon to med. dir. USPHS, 1963-68, chief kidney disease br., 1964-66, regional health dir. NY, 1967-68; exec. dir. Cmty. Health Inc., NYC, 1968-70, Am. Pub. Health Assn., 1970-73; sec. Health Policy Coun. Wis., 1973-75; pres. James R. Kimmey Assos., Inc., 1975-85; dir. Midwest Ctr. Health Planning, 1976-79; exec. dir. Inst. Health Planning, 1979-87; prof. pub. health, dir. Ctr. for Health Svcs. Edn. Rsch. St. Louis U. Med. Ctr., 1987-91; dean sch. pub. health St. Louis U., 1991-93, v.p. health scis., 1993-98, exec. v.p., 1998-2000, emeritus prof. cmty. health, 2001—; dir. Inst. Urban Health Policy, 2000-2001; pres. Mo. Found. for Health, 2001—. Adj. prof. NYU, NYC, 1968—70; lectr. Johns Hopkins, 1971—73; clin. instr. U. Wis., 1974—87; pres. Inst. Health Planning, 1979—86; chair Task Force Accreditation Health Professions, 1997—99, St. Louis ConnectCare, 1998—2001; dir. Ctr. Engring. Tech., 1998—2001; vice chair St. Louis Access Health, 1999—2001. Editor: (book) The Nation's Health, 1972—73; mng. editor: Am. Jour. Pub. Health, 1970—73, mem. editl. adv. bd.: Health Cost Mgmt., 1983—87; contbr. articles to profl. jours. Pres. World Fedn. Pub. Health Assns., 1972—73; mem. sci. adv. bd. Gorgas Inst., 1970—73; bd. dirs. Internat. Union Health Edn., 1970—73. Decorated USPHS Commendation medal. Fellow: APHA (governing coun. 1978—81, chmn. cmty. health planning sect. 1979—80, governing coun. 1983—87, 1989—92), Am. Coll. Preventive Medicine, mem.: Grant Makers Health (dir. 2006—11, chair 2009—11), Gateway Ctr. for Giving (bd. dirs. 2002—09, vice chair 2007—08, chair 2008—09), Prospective Payment Assessment Commn. (commr. 1991—97), Mo. Pub. Health Assn. (Mo. Communicator of the Yr. award 1994), Am. Coll. Health Adminstrs., Am. Health Planning Assn. (dir. 1974—75, 1977—78, corp. sec. 1977—78, pres. 1980—81, Richard H. Schlesinger award 1978, James R. Kimmey award 1994), Alpha Sigma Nu, Delta Omega, Alpha Omega Alpha, Phi Eta Sigma. Democrat. Episcopalian. Office: Ste 400 1000 St Louis Union Sta Saint Louis MO 63103 Home: 1805 Park Ave #2D Saint Louis MO 63104 Home Phone: 314-621-3424; Office Phone: 314-345-5500. Business E-Mail: jkimmey@mffh.org.

KIMURA, AKATSUKI, biology professor; b. Moscow, Dec. 2, 1974; PhD, U. Tokyo, 2002. Assoc. prof. Nat. Inst. Genetics, 2006—. Office: Yata 1111 Mishima Shizuoka 411-8540 Japan E-mail: akkimura@lab.nig.ac.jp.

KIMURA, AKIHIKO, pediatrician, educator; b. Japan, Oct. 23, 1952; MD, Kurume U. Sch. Medicine, Fukuoka, Japan, PhD, 1979. Asst. prof. dept. pediat & child health Kurume U. Hosp., 2000—11. Office: Kurume University Sch Medicine Dept Pediat and Child Health 67 Asahi-mchi Kurume Fukuoka 830-0011 Japan Business E-Mail: hirof@med.kurume-u.ac.jp.

KIMURA, DOREEN, psychology professor, researcher; b. Winnipeg, Man., Can. 1 child, Charlotte Vanderwolf. BA, McGill U., Montreal, Que., Can., 1956, MA, 1957, PhD, 1961; LLD (hon.), Simon Fraser U., 1993, Queen's U., 1999. Lectr. Sir George Williams U. (now Concordia U.), Montreal, 1960-61; rsch. assoc. otol. rsch. lab. UCLA Med. Ctr., 1962-63; rsch. assoc. Coll. Medicine, McMaster U., Hamilton, Ont., 1964-67; assoc. prof. psychology U. Western Ont., London, 1967-74, prof. psychology, 1974-98, coord. clin. neuropsychology program, 1983-97. Supr. clin. neuropsychology Univ. Hosp., London, 1975-83; vis. prof. psychology Simon Fraser U., 1998—. Author: Neuromotor Mechanisms in Human Communication, 1993, Sex and Cognition, 1999, French, Japanese, Swedish, Spanish, Portuguese, and Polish edits.; co-author: Women, Men and the Sciences, 2009, (with Jerre Levy) The Sci. on Women & Sci., C.H. Sommers, 2009, AEI; contbr. numerous articles to profl. jours., chapters to books. Recipient Outstanding Sci. Achievement award Can. Assn. Women in Sci., 1986, John Dewan award Ont. Mental Health Found., 1992, Kistler prize for lifetime achievement in human rsch. Found. for the Future, 2006; fellow Montreal Neurol. Inst., 1960-61, Geigy fellow Kantonsspital, Zürich, Switzerland, 1963-64, D.O. Hebb Disting. Contbn. award, Can. Soc. Brain, Behav. & Cogn. Sciences, 2005. Fellow Royal Soc. Can., Can. Psychol. Assn. (Disting. Contbns. to Sci. award 1985); mem. Soc. Acad. Freedom and Scholarship (founding pres. 1992-93, 98-2000). Office: # 624 3338 Wesbrook Mall Vancouver BC V6S 0A6 Canada Business E-Mail: dkimura@sfu.ca.

KIMURA, GENKI, virologist, educator; b. Shimonoseki, Yamaguchi Ken, Japan, Jan. 3, 1937; s. Noboru and Chika Kimura; m. Yoshiko Kunigoshi, Apr. 8, 1963; children: Koki, Yuki. MD, Kyushu U., Fukuoka, Japan, 1961, PhD, 1966. Intern St. Luke's Internat. Hosp., Tokyo, 1961—62; asst. prof. Kyushu U. Sch. Medicine, Fukuoka, 1966—67, prof. tumor virology, 1977—82; prof. virology Med. Inst. Bioregulation, Kyushu U., Fukuoka, 1982—2000; non-resident lectr. Kyushu U., Fukuoka, 2002—04, prof. emeritus, 2000—; assoc. prof. Tottori U. Sch. Medicine, Yonago, Japan, 1967—74, prof. virology, 1974—77; prof. Daiichi Pharm. Coll., Fukuoka, Japan, 2004—07, dean, 2004—07. Head baseball coach Kyushu U., Japan, 1977—90; vis. scientist Salk Inst. for Biol. Studies, San Diego, 1968—70; cons. Chlorella Industry Co., Chikugo, Japan, 2000—01; vis. lectr. U. Air Fukuoka, 2002—04. Contbr. over 164 articles to profl. jours. Recipient Asahi Sci. Promotion award, Asahi Shimbun, Tokyo, 1973; fellow, Am. Cancer Soc., Geneva, 1968. Fellow: Assn. Union Internat. Contre le Cancer Fellows (life); mem.: Japanese Soc. for Virology (councillor 1982—2010), Japanese Cancer Assn. (life). Home: 4-2-15 Torikai Jonan-Ku Fukuoka 814-0103 Japan Home Phone: 81928436583.

KIMURA, HIROSHI, physician, educator; b. Tokyo, Sept. 12, 1951; MD, Kanazawa U., 1978; PhD, Chiba U., 1985. Asst. prof. Chiba U. Sch. Medicine, 1992—97, assoc. prof., 1997—2001; prof. Nara Med. U. Sch. Medicine, 2001—. Fellow: Am. Coll. Chest Physicians; mem.: Asian Pacific Soc. Respirology (Fukuchi award 2010), European Respiratory Soc., Am. Thoracic Soc. Avocations: travel, classical music, photography. Office: 840 Shijo-cho Kashihara Nara 634-8522 Japan Office Fax: 81-744-290907.

KIMURA, MASASHI, biologist, educator; b. Tohma Chou, Hokkaido, Japan, Jan. 26, 1966; s. Kazuo and Yuriko Kimura. PhD in Sci., Tsukuba U., Japan, 1993. Asst. prof. Gifu U. Sch. Medicine, Japan, 1993—. Office Phone: 81 58 230 6208. Office Fax: 0582306209. Business E-Mail: yo@gifu-u.ac.jp.

KIMURA, MASATO, nursing educator; b. Sapporo, Hokkaido, Japan, Apr. 21, 1948; MD, Tokyo U., PhD, 1974. Prof. Sch. Nursing U. Shizuoka, 1997—. Fellow: Japanese Soc. Nephrology (coun.). Avocations: fishing, cooking, reading. Office: University Shizuoka Sch Nursing Shizuoka Suruga-ku 422-8526 Japan Office Fax: 81(0)54-264-5461. E-mail: kimuram@u-shizuoka-ken.ac.jp.

KIMURA, TAKANORI, health facility administrator, physician; b. Yawatahama, Ehime, Japan, Dec. 27, 1930; s. Masao and Shizuko (Koizumi) K.; m. Tomoko Inoh, Oct. 24, 1961; children: Takashi, Yoshiye, Hiromi. MD, Kyushu U., 1955. Resident contagious diseases Cook County Hosp., Chgo., 1958—59; resident tuberculosis Sea View Hosp., SI, NY, 1959—60; resident gen. practice Louise Obici Meml. Hosp., Suffolk, Va., 1964—66; chief examiner Ministry Health and Welfare, Tokyo, 1962—63; dep. dir. Nakamura-shimin Hosp., Japan, 1972—73; chief family practice, dir. Benda Hosp., Pineland Center, Maine, 1976—77; dir. radiology NTT Matsayama Hosp., Japan, 1978—82; dep. dir. Iyo Hosp., Japan, 1982—83, Matsuyama Bethel Hosp., Japan, 1983—86; dir. Tojima Clinic, Uwajima, Japan, 1987—. Co-author: Handbook of Everyday Practice, 1987; author: (mag.) The Den-den jidai, 1979; contbr. articles to profl. jours. Recipient Disting. Svc. cert. Japan Primary Care Assn., 1987, Disting. Svc. cert. Nat. Health Ins. Groups, 1993, 2007, Disting. Med. Svcs. Ehime Prefecture, Japan, 2006 Fellow Am. Acad. Family Physicians; mem. Japan Med. Assn. (cert. specialist in occupational health 1991). Buddhist. Avocations: writing, reading, photography, art. Office: Tojima Clinic 2014 Tojima Uwajima Japan Office Phone: 0895 640210. Business E-Mail: tojima-cl@city.uwajima.lg.jp.

KIMURA, TETSU, anesthesiologist, educator; b. Tokyo, Oct. 30, 1963; s. Hiroshi and Sachiko Kimura; m. Kaori Inoe; children: Sho, Chika. MD, U. Tsukuba, Ibaraki, Japan, 1989. Cert. Japanese Soc. Anesthesiologists, 1995, Japan Soc. Pain Clinicians, 2008. Resident U. Tsukuba, Ibaraki, 1989—95; rsch. fellow Johns Hopkins U., Baltimore, Md., 1997—99; instr. Akita U. Sch. Medicine, Japan, 1999—2008, asst. prof., 2008—. Mem.: Sakura Yu Club (Japan) (advisor 2005). Avocations: skiing, driving. Office: Akita Univ Sch Medicine Hondo 1-1-1 Akita 010-8543 Japan Office Phone: 81-18-884-6175. Office Fax: 81-18-884-6448. Business E-Mail: kimtetsu@doc.med.akita-u.ac.jp.

KIMURA, TOKIHISA, endocrinologist; b. Isawa, Yamanashi, Japan, June 1, 1940; s. Jishu and Chie Kimura; m. Ishimori Katsuko, Apr. 11, 1969; children: Kyoko, Osamu, Takako. MD, Tohoku U., Sendai, Miyagi, Japan, 1966, PhD, 1974. Diplomate internal medicine, endocrinology. Intern Mizusawa Mcpl. Hosp., Japan, 1969—70; rsch. fellow dept. medicine Tohoku U. Sch. Medicine, Sendai, 1970-71, instr. dept. physiology, 1971-72, instr. dept. medicine, 1973-78, asst. prof. dept. medicine, 1981-92, assoc. prof., 1993-97, 1998—2005; clin. prof. endocrinology, nephrology and hypertension Tohoku U., Sendai, 2000—; adminstr., pres. Furukawa City Hosp., 1998—2006; asst. prof. dept. physiology U. Tenn., Memphis, 1979-80; supt. Hosp. Adminstrn. Bur., Miyagi Prefecture, 2007—. Chief doctor dept. internal medicine Tohoku U., Sendai, 1992-94. Author: Annuals New York Academy Science, 1993; editorial bd. Advances in Neuroimmunology, 1991—; contbr. articles to profl. jours. Recipient Golden prize for established researcher Tohoku U., Sendai, 1991; rsch. grantee Ministry of Edn. Japan, Tokyo, 1989, 92. Mem. Am. Physiol. Soc., Am. Endocrine Soc., Japan Endocrine Soc., Japan Med. Soc., Japan Neuroendocrine Soc., N.Y. Acad. Sci., Am. Heart Assn. Avocations: jogging, reading, music. Home: Aobaku Higashi-Katsuyama 3-33-8 Sendai 980 Japan Office. Hosp Adminstrn Bur Miyagi Prefecture Govt 3-8-1 Honcho Aobaku Sandai Miyagi 980-8570 Japan

KIMURA, YOSHINOBU, microbiologist, educator; b. Gifu, Japan, May 25, 1940; s. Katsuji and Harue (Urasaki) K.; m. Makiko Araya, Apr. 10, 1966; 1 child, Kota. MD, Nagoya U. Med. Sch., Japan, 1965, PhD in Medicine, 1973. Postgrad. fellow dept. microbiology Germfree Life Rsch. Inst. Nagoya U. Sch. Medicine, 1966-70, rsch. assoc. dept. microbiology Germfree Life Inst., 1970-79, lectr. dept. microbiology Germfree Life Inst., 1979-80, assoc. prof. dept. microbiology Germfree Life Rsch. Inst., 1980-81; prof. dept. microbiology Fukui U. Sch. Medicine, Japan, 1981—2006; prof. dept. med. tech. Gifu U. Med. Sci., Japan, 2006—10; dir. Fukui Ajisai Long Term Care Health Facility, 2011—. Rsch. fellow Karolinska Inst. Sch. Medicine, Stockholm, 1975-77; vis. scientist U. Calif., San Francisco, 1988. Author: (textbook) Medical Microbiology, 1987; editor, author: (textbook) Modern Medical Microbiology, 1984. Mem. Japanese Soc. for Infectious Diseases (hon.). Avocations: violin, cello, yachting. Home: Komegawaki-4 2-38 Mikuni-cho Fukui 913-0057 Japan Office: Fukui Ajisai Long Term Care Health Facility Fukui 918 8041 Japan Office Phone: 81 776 33 5911. Office Fax: 81 776 33 6691. Business E-Mail: kimura@mx4.fctv.ne.jp.

KIMURA, YUKIKO, pediatric rheumatologist, educator; b. Kobe, Japan, May 25, 1955; MD, Albert Einstein Coll. Medicine, NY, 1982. Diplomate Am. Bd. Pediat., cert. Am. Bd. Pediat. Rheumatology. Intern pediat. Babies & Children's Hosp., Columbia Presbyn., 1982—83, resident pediat. rheumatology, 1983—85, fellowship pediat. rheumatology, 1987—90; chief pediat. rheumatology Children's Hosp., Hackensack U. Med. Ctr., NJ, 1991—. Vis. prof. pediat. rheumatology Am. Coll. Rheumatology, 2007; assoc. prof. pediat. U. Medicine & Dentistry NJ, Newark. Editor: (med. textbook) Arthritis in Children and Adolescents, 2006; contbr. articles to profl. jours. Recipient Clinician Scholar Educator award, Am. Coll. Rheumatology, 2007; named one of NY's Best Dr.'s, Castle Connolly Med. Ltd. Fellow: Am. Coll. Rheumatology, Am. Acad. Pediat.; mem.: Pediat. Rheumatology Collaborative Study Group, Childhood Arthritis and Rheumatology Rsch. Alliance (chair, juvenile arthritis). Office: Hackensack Univ Med Ctr 30 Prospect Ave Hackensack NJ 07601 Office Fax: 201-996-9815. Business E-Mail: ykimura@humed.com.

KIMYAI-ASADI, ARASH, surgeon; s. Taghi Kimyai-Asadi and Fatemeh Milani; m. Ming Hewy Jih, May 24, 2003; children: Leila, Zane. BA, Johns Hopkins U., Balt., 1995, MD, 1999. Diplomate Am. Bd. Dermatology. Mohs surgeon DermSurgery Assocs., Houston, 2004—. Contbr. Fellow: Am. Coll. Mohs Surgery; mem.: Am. Acad. Dermatology, Am. Soc. for Dermatologic Surgery, Phi Beta Kappa. Office: DermSurgery Assocs 7515 Main Ste 290 Houston TX 77030 Home: 6615 Belmont St Houston TX 77005 Office Fax: 713-791-9927. Personal E-mail: akimyai@yahoo.com. *

KINCANNON, ELIZABETH ANNE, neonatologist, hospital administrator; b. LA, Feb. 24, 1954; d. William Thomas and Inez (Stout) K.; m. Patrick Clebert Payne, Nov. 30, 1985; 1 child, MacKenzie Payne. BS with distinction, Stanford U., 1975; MD, Harvard U., 1979. Diplomate Am. Bd. Pediatrics. Resident U. Colo. Health Scis. Ctr., Denver, 1979-82; neonatologist So. Calif. Permanente Med. Group, San Deigo, 1986-93, Colo. Permanente Med. Group, Denver, 1985—86, 1994—, assoc. medical dir. network, strategy and bus. devel. Chmn. dept. pediatrics St. Joseph Hosp., Denver, 1995—; physician reviewer utilization mgmt. Colo. Permanente MEd. group, 1994—. Advisor Women Creating NewLives, San Diego, 1992-93. Neonatology fellow The Children's Hosp., Denver, 1983-84. Fellow Am. Acad. Pediatrics; mem. Phi Beta Kappa. Avocations: tennis, skiing, science fiction, entertaining. Office: Colo Permanente Med Group 2045 Franklin St Denver CO 80205-5437

KINDBERG, SHIRLEY JANE, pediatrician; b. Newark, Feb. 4, 1936; d. John Bertil and Mabel Jacoba (deJonge) Kindberg; m. Charles Dale Coln, May 12, 1962; children: Sara Goldstein, Eric Coln, Lois Thompson, Ruth Skipper, Mary Mielenz. BS, Wheaton Coll., 1957; MD, Baylor U., 1961. Intern Tex. Children's Hosp., Houston, 1961-62; resident Children's Med. Ctr., Dallas, 1962-63; fellow in pediat. pulmonary disease U. Tex. S.W. Med. Sch., Dallas, 1963-64, fellow in pediat. infectious disease, 1965-67; pvt. practice gen. pediat. Dallas, 1969-81; pvt. practice newborns, 1981—2004. Active Park Cities Presbyn. Ch.; mem. Dallas Symphony Assn. Republican. Avocations: cooking, travel, music, exercise. Personal E-mail: colnoma@sbcglobal.net. *

KINDBLOM, JON, oncologist; b. Gothenburg, Sweden, Apr. 16, 1969; MD, Gothenburg U., 1997, PhD, 2003. Cons., clin. oncology Sahlgrenska U. Hosp., 2003—. Sec. Swedish Soc. Urooncology, 2008. Mem.: Swedish Soc. Oncology. Office: Sahlgrenska University Dept Oncology Gothenburg 41345 Sweden Personal E-mail: jon.kindblom@gu.se.

KINDLER, JEFFREY BRUCE, retired pharmaceutical executive; b. Upper Montclair, NJ, May 13, 1955; m. Sharon Sullivan; children: Joshua, Samantha. BA summa cum laude, Tufts U., 1977; JD magna cum laude, Harvard Law Sch., 1980. Bar: DC 1980. Law clk. to Hon. David L. Bazelon US Ct. Appeals (DC Cir.), Washington, 1980—81; law clk. to Justice William J. Brennan, Jr. US Supreme Ct., Washington, 1981—82; assoc. then ptnr. Williams & Connolly, LLP, Washington, 1982—90; sr. counsel litig. & legal policy General Electric Co., Fairfield, Conn., 1990—94, v.p., sr. counsel litig. and legal policy, 1994—96; sr. v.p., gen. counsel McDonald's Corp., Oak Brook, Ill., 1996—97, exec. v.p. corp. rels., gen. counsel, 1997—2001, chmn. CEO Boston Market Corp., 2000—01, pres. Partner Brands, 2001—02; sr. v.p., gen. counsel Pfizer, Inc., NYC, 2002—04, vice chmn., gen. counsel, chief compliance officer, 2004—06, CEO, 2006—07, chmn., CEO, 2007—10. Bd. dirs. Pfizer Inc., 2006-10, Fed. Reserve Bank NY, 2009-2011; chmn. Pharm. Rsch. & Manufacturers of America (PhRMA), 2010; mem. President's Mgmt. Advisory Bd. (PMAB), 2010- Editor: Harvard Law Rev. Bd. mem. Brennan Ctr. for Justice, Corporate ProBono.Org, Inst. for Legal Reform U.S. Chamber of Commerce, Legal Aid Soc., Tufts U., Manhattan Theatre Club, NY Philharmonic, Partnership for NYC, Ronald McDonald House Charities, Bus. Council for NY State, Transparency Internat., United Way NYC. Recipient Stephen E. Banner award, UJA Fedn., Lawyers divsn., 2002, Stand Tall with NY award, Greater NY Chapter of the Am. Corp. Counsel Assn., 2002, Pro Bono Publico award, ABA, 2003, Northeast Region Employer of Choice award, Minority Corp. Counsel Assn., 2004, Exemplar award, The Nat. Legal Aid & Defender Assn., 2005, Expeditioner's award, NYC Outward Bound, 2005, Pro Bono Publico, The Legal Aid Soc., 2005, Pub. Svc. Corp. award, 2005, Exemplar award, Nat. Legal Aid & Defender Assn., 2005, Expeditioner's award, NYC Outward Bound, 2005, Laurie D. Zelon award, Pro Bono Inst. Georgetown Univ., 2006. Mem.: Assn. Gen. Counsels. *

KINDRED, LYNN HERBERT, cardiologist; b. Emporia, Kans., July 6, 1937; MD, U. Kans., 1963. Diplomate Am. Bd. Internal Medicine, Am. Bd. Cardiology. Intern U. Kans., Kansas City, 1963-64, resident, 1964-66, fellow in cardiology, 1966-67; mem. staff St. Luke's Hosp., Kansas City; clin. prof. U. Mo. Med. Sch., Kansas City; ptnr. group practice Mid Am. Cardiology, Kansas City, Mo. Named a Kans. City Super Doctor, Kans. City mag., 2007. Fellow ACP, Am. Coll. Cardiology, Am. Coll. Chest Physicians; mem. CCC. Office: Mid Am Cardiology 4321 Washington St Kansas City MO 64111-5905 also: 3901 Rainbow Blvd Mail Stop 4023 Kansas City KS 66160 Office Phone: 913-588-1227.

KING, DAVID PAUL, health services executive, lawyer; b. Washington, June 20, 1956; s. Ivan Robert and Alice King. AB, Princeton U., 1977; JD, U. Pa., 1982. Bar: Ga. 1984. Law clk. to Hon. Alvin B. Rubin, US Ct. Appeals (5th cir.), Baton Rouge, 1982-83; assoc. Rogers & Hardin, Atlanta, 1983-85, Covington & Burling, LLP, Washington, 1985-87, Hogan & Hartson, L.L.P., Balt., 1990-92, ptnr., 1992—2001; asst. US atty. Dept. Justice, Balt., 1987-90; sr. v.p., gen. counsel, chief compliance officer Lab. Corp. Am. Holdings, 2001—04, exec. v.p. strategic planning and corp. devel., 2004—05, exec. v.p., COO, 2005—06, pres., CEO, 2007—09; chmn., pres., CEO Laboratory Corp. of America Holdings, 2009—. Adj. prof. U. Md. Law Sch., Balt. Mem. ABA, Md. Bar Assn., DC Bar Assn., Ga. Bar Assn. Office: Lab Corp Am Holdings 358 S Main St Burlington NC 27215 *

KING, EARL D., pulmonologist; MD, Pa. State U., 1986. Diplomate Am. Bd. Internal Medicine, Am. Bd. Internal Medicine-critical care medicine, cert. pulmonology, lic. Pa. Intern Temple Univ. Hosp., Phila., 1987, resident, 1989, Johns Hopkins Univ., Balt., 1993; dir. pulmonary function lab. and respiratory care unit Fox Chase Cancer Ctr., Phila. Office: Fox Chase Cancer Center 333 cottman ave Philadelphia PA 19111-2497 Office Phone: 215-728-6900.

KING, HUESTON CLARK, retired otolaryngologist, educator; b. Bklyn., Feb. 3, 1929; s. William Clark and Alice Packard (Hueston) K.; m. Wilma Marguerite Grove, June 13, 1953; children: Brian G., Melinda K. AB in Biology, Princeton U., 1950; MD, Columbia U., 1954. Diplomate Am. Bd. Otolaryngology; lic. physician, Fla., NC; cert. Nat. Bd. Med. Examiners. Intern Jackson Meml. Hosp., U. Miami (Fla.) Sch. Medicine, 1954-55; resident in otolaryngology Walter Reed Army Med. Ctr., Washington, 1956-58; staff Coral Gables (Fla.) Hosp., 1962-82, Bapt. Hosp., 1962-82, Mercy Hosp.,

1962-82, South Miami Hosp., Fla., 1962-82, Cedars of Lebanon Hosp., 1962-82, Jackson Meml. Hosp., 1962-82; with Venice (Fla.) Hosp., 1983-94. From clin. faculty to assoc. prof. dept. otolaryngology U. Miami Med. Sch., 1962-82; clin. prof. dept. otolaryngology U. Tex. Southwestern Med. Ctr., Dallas, 1998-2006, U. Fla.; lectr. in field. Author: (textbook) An Otolaryngologist's Guide to Allergy, 1991; sr. author: (textbook) A Practical Guide to Management of Nasal and Sinus Disorders, 1993, Allergy in ENT Practice: A Basic Guide, 1998, 2d edit. 2004; editor: Otolaryngologic Allergy, 1981; editor Allergy Digest, food allergy sect. Current Sci., allergy sect. Current Opinion, 1999-01; contbr. chpts. to books, articles to profl. jours. Bd. dirs. Woodmere at Jacaranda, Venice, 1997—99; committeeman Venice Found., 1995—97. Fellow ACS (emeritus), Am. Acad. Facial Plastic and Reconstructive Surgery (emeritus), Am. Acad. Otolaryngic Allergy (past pres. 1979-80, dir. med. edn. 1983-88), Am. Coll. Allergy, Asthma and Immunology; mem. Fla. Med. Assn., Sarasota Couty Med. Assn., Venice Yacht Club. Personal E-mail: huestoncking@verizon.net.

KING, LLOYD ELIJAH, dermatologist, educator; b. Mayfield, Ky., Sept. 10, 1939; MD, U. Tenn., Memphis, 1967, PhD, 1969. Asst. mem. biochemistry St. Jude Children's Rsch. Hosp., 1975—77; asst. prof. medicine in dermatology U. Tenn. Health Scis. Ctr., Memphis, 1976—77; chief, dermatology svc. Va. Med. Ctr., Nashville, 1977—88; assoc. prof. medicine in dermatology Vanderbilt U., 1977—82, chmn., founder dermatology program, 1979—2002, prof. medicine in dermatology, 1982—. Rsch. Assoc. grant, Advanced Splty. Tng. Program, Vets. Adminstrn., 1972—77, Clin. Investigator fellowship, 1978—81, Rsch. grant, NIH R01 Grants Epidermal Growth Factor, 1979—96, Veterans Adminstrn. Merit Rev. grants, 1981—96. Fellow: ACP, Am. Acad. Dermatology; mem.: Am. Dermatol. Assn., Assn. Profs. Dermatology, Soc. Investigative Dermatology (bd. dirs., v.p.). Avocation: travel. Office: Vanderbilt Dermatology 100 Oaks 406 Thompson Ln Ste 26300 Nashville TN 37204 Office Phone: 615-322-6485. Office Fax: 615-343-2591, 415-967-9030. Business E-Mail: lloyd.e.king@vanderbilt.edu.

KING, MARJORIE LOUISE, cardiologist; b. 1953; MD, Pa. State U., 1979. Diplomate Am. Bd. Internal Medicine. Intern NYU-Manhattan VA Hosp., 1979-80, resident in internal medicine, 1980-82, fellow in cardiology, 1982-84; staff Helen Hayes Hosp., West Haverstraw, NY, 1984—, dir. cardiac svcs. Mem. AMA; Am. Assn. Cardiovascular and Pulmonary Rehab. (pres. 2005-06) Office: Helen Hayes Hosp Rte 9W West Haverstraw NY 10993

KING, MARY-CLAIRE, geneticist, educator; b. Evanston, Ill., Feb. 27, 1946; m. 1973; 1 child, Emily King Colwell. BA in Math. (cum laude), Carleton Coll., Northfield, Minn., 1966; PhD in Genetics, U. Calif., Berkeley, 1973; PhD (hon.), Carleton Coll., Bard Coll., Smith Coll., Dartmouth Coll. Postdoctoral tng. U. Calif.-San Francisco; prof. genetics & epidemiology U. Calif. Berkeley, 1976—95; American Cancer Soc. rsch. prof. genome sciences & medicine U. Wash., Seattle, 1995—. Mem. bd. sci. counselors Nat. Cancer Inst., Meml. Sloan-Kettering Cancer Ctr., mem. NRC com. to advise Dept. Def. on the Breast Cancer Rsch. Program., NIH Genome Study Sect.; served on Nat. Commn. on Breast Cancer of the President's Cancer Panel; mem. adv. bd., NIH Office of Rsch. on Women's Health, Coun. of the NIH Fogarty Ctr., Nat. Action Plan for Breast Cancer, NIH Breast Cancer Program Review Group; affiliate mem. Fred Hutchinson Cancer Rsch. Ctr., Seattle; cons. Com. for Investigation of Disappearance of Persons, Govt. Argentina, Buenos Aires, 1984; carried out DNA Identifications for the UN War Crimes Tribunial; mem. UN Forensic Anthropology Team; mem. adv. bd. Robert Wood Johnson Found. Minority Med. Faculty Develop. program Contbr. articles to profl. jours. Recipient Clowes award, Basic Rsch., American Assn. Cancer Rsch., Jill Rose award, American Breast Cancer Found., Brinker award, Susan G. Komen Breast Cancer Found., 1999, Genetics prize, Peter Gruber Found., 2004, Weizmann Women & Sci. award, American Com. for Weizmann Inst. Sci., 2006; co-recipient Pearl Meister Greengard prize, Rockefeller U., 2010; named Woman of Yr., Glamour Mag. Fellow AAAS, Inst. Medicine, Acad. Arts & Sciences; mem. American Soc. Human Genetics, Soc. Epidemiologic Research, NAS, Phi Beta Kappa, Sigma Xi. Achievements include identifying the close similarity of the human and chimpanzee genomes; discovery of a gene (BRCA1) that predisposes to breast cancer; introduced direct sequencing of PCR-amplified segments of mitochondrial DNA for identifying people or their remains by comparing their DNA to that of relatives. Office: Dept Medicine and Genome Sciences Health Sciences RM K-160 U Washington Sch Medicine Box 357720 Health Sciences Room K-160 Seattle WA 98195-7720 Office Phone: 206-616-4294. Office Fax: 206-616-4295. E-mail: mcking@u.washington.edu.

KING, MICHAEL JAMES, podiatric surgeon; b. Sandusky, Ohio, Oct. 17, 1957; s. James Everett and Nola Jean (potts) K.; m. Laura Ann Novak, June 4, 1983; children: Lindsay, Christopher. BS, Baldwin-Wallace Coll., 1979; D of Podiatric Medicine, Ohio Coll. Podiatric Medicine, 1983. Diplomate Am. Bd. Podiatric Surgery, Am. Bd. Pediatric Surgery. Surg. resident Toledo Riverside Hosp., 1983-85; podiatric surgeon pvt. practice Howell, N.J., 1985-87; podiatric surgeon Foot Care Assocs., Inc., Fall River, Mass., 1987—. Trustee Fund for Podiatric Med. Edn., 1994—. Author: (book chpts.) Infectious Diseases of the Lower Extremity, 1990. Fellow Am. Coll. Foot Surgeons (1st Pl. for papers written 1985), Mass. Podiatric Med. Soc. (1st v.p. 1992-94, pres. 1995-97, trustee Fund for Podiatric Med. Edn.); mem. American Podiatric Med. Assn. (pres. 2011-). Avocations: flying, baseball, golf. Office: 222 Milliken Blvd Fall River MA 02721-1623 *

KING, ORDIE HERBERT, JR., oral pathologist; b. Memphis, Aug. 11, 1933; s. Ordie Herbert and Hazel (Eaton) King; m. Violette Papagianis, Mar. 21, 1974; children: Catherine Ann, Alexander Carlos;children from previous marriage: Anna LaVelle, Ordie Herbert III. BS, Memphis State U., 1957; DDS, U. Tenn., 1959, PhD, 1965. Diplomate Am. Bd. Oral and Maxillofacial Pathology. USPHS postdoctoral fellow U. Tenn., 1960-62, rsch. assoc. dept. pathology, 1963-65, asst. prof. pathology, 1965, resident oral pathology City of Memphis Hosps., 1962-63; asst. prof. pathology Northwestern U., 1966; assoc. prof. oral pathology St. Louis U., 1967-69, prof., 1969-70, chmn. dept., 1967-70, chmn. dept. dentistry univ. hosps., 1967-70; acting chmn., vis. assoc. prof. oral pathology Washington U., St. Louis, 1969-70, clin. prof. pathology Sch. Dental Medicine, 1979-80; prof. oral pathology, assoc. prof. pathology W.Va. U., Morgantown, 1970-74, prof. pathology, 1974, dir. Cytopathology Lab., Med. Ctr., 1971-74; prof. pathology Sch. Dental Medicine So. Ill. U., Alton, 1974-97, chmn. dept. diagnostic specialties Sch. Dental Medicine, 1979-92. Dir. So. Ill. Pathology Lab., Ltd., Godfrey, 1977—; dental cons. to chief med. examiner State of Tenn., 1963—65; mem. exec. com. St. Louis U. Hosps., 1967—70; mem. med. staff W. Tenn. Cancer Clinic, 1962—65, W.Va. U. Hosp., 1970—74; mem. med./dental staff dept. pathology Alton Meml. Hosp., 1986—; cons. VA Hosp., Clarksville, W.Va., 1973—74; dental cons. St. Louis County Med. Examiner, 1968—70; cons. cancer control program Nat. Ctr. Chronic Disease Control, USPHS, 1967—70; mem. Mo. Bd. Dental Splty. Examiners, 1982—84. Fellow: Am. Acad. Oral Pathology; mem.: ADA, Am. Cancer Soc. (bd. dirs. W.Va. divsn. 1972—74), Am. Soc. Cytopathology, Ill. Walking Horse Assn. (bd. dirs. 2000—08, v.p. 2009), Spotted Saddle Horse Assn. Ill. (v.p. 2001, pres. 2002—04, v.p. 2005—07, pres. 2009—10), Tenn. Walking Horse Breeders and Exhibitors Assn., Spotted Saddle Horse Breeders and Exhibitors Assn., Omicron Kappa Upsilon, Phi Rho Sigma, Kappa Alpha Order, Delta Sigma Delta. Home: 6111 Vollmer Ln Godfrey IL 62035-1062 Office: So Ill Path Lab Ltd Godfrey IL 62035

KING, ROBERT CHARLES, biologist, educator; b. NYC, June 3, 1928; s. Charles James and Amanda (McCutchen) King. BS, Yale U., 1948, PhD, 1952. Scientist biology dept. Brookhaven Nat. Lab., 1951-55; mem. faculty Northwestern U., 1956—, prof. biology, 1964-99, prof. emeritus, 2000—. Chmn. 8th Brookhaven Symposium in Biology, 1955; vis. investigator, fellow Rockefeller U., 1959; NSF sr. postdoctoral fellow U. Edinburgh, Scotland, 1958, Commonwealth Sci. and Indsl. Research Orgn. Div. Entomology, Canberra, Australia, 1963, Sericultural Expt. Sta., Tokyo, Japan, 1970 Author: Genetics, 2d edit., 1965, A Dictionary of Genetics, 8th edit., 2011, (with W.D. Stansfield and P.K. Mulligan) Ovarian Development in Drosophila melanogaster, 1970, also numerous papers; editor: Handbook of Genetics Series, 5 vols., (with H. Akai) Insect Ultrastructure, 2 vols., 1982. Fellow AAAS; mem. Am. Soc. Zoologists, Histochem. Soc., Am. Soc. Cell Biology (treas. 1972-75), Electron Microscopy Soc. Am., Genetics Soc. Am., Am. Soc. Naturalists, Soc. Devel. Biology, Entomol. Soc. Am., Genetics Soc. Can., Genetics Soc. Korea, Sigma Xi (pres. Northwestern U. chpt. 1966-67) Home: 2890 Fredric Ct Northbrook IL 60062-7504

KING, SHELDON SELIG, health facility administrator, educator; b. NYC, Aug. 28, 1931; s. Benjamin and Jeanne (Fritz) King; m. Ruth Arden Zeller, June 26, 1955 (div. 1987); children: Tracy Elizabeth, Meredith Ellen, Adam Bradley; m. Xenia Tonesk, 1988. AB, NYU, 1952; MS, Yale U., 1957. Adminstrv. intern Montefiore Hosp., NYC, 1952, 1955; adminstrv. asst. Mt. Sinai Hosp., NYC, 1957—60, asst. dir., 1960—66, dir. planning, 1966—68; exec. dir. Albert Einstein Coll. Medicine-Bronx Mcpl. Hosp. Ctr., Bronx, NY, 1968—72; asst. prof. Albert Einstein Coll. Medicine, NYC, 1968—72; dir. hosps. and clinics Univ. Hosp., assoc. clin. prof. U. Calif., San Diego, 1972—81; acting head div. health care scis., dept. cmty. medicine U. Calif. Sch. Medicine, 1978—81; assoc. v.p. Stanford U., Calif., 1981—85, clin. assoc. prof. cmty., family and preventive medicine; exec. v.p. Stanford U. Hosp., 1981—85, pres., 1986—89, Cedars-Sinai Med. Ctr., LA, 1989—94, CEO, 1989—94; exec. v.p. Salick Health Care, Inc., LA, 1994—99, pres. ea. region, 1996—98; interim dir. UCLA Med. Ctr., 1995; interim COO INFOHEALTH Mgmt. Corp., 1999—2000, bd. dirs., 2000—; prin. Creative Intellectual Commerce, 2001—. Mem. adminstrv. bd. Coun. of Tchg. Hosps., 1981—86, chmn. adminstrv. bd., 1985; preceptor George Washington U., Ithaca Coll., Yale U., U. Mo., CUNY; chmn. health care com. San Diego County Immigration Coun., 1974—77; adv. coun. Calif. Health Facilities Commn., 1977—82; chmn. ad hoc bd. advisors Am. Bd. Internal Medicine, 1985—91; mem. exec. com. St. Joseph Health Sys., 1990—94; acting chmn. Am. Health Properties, 1996—; nat. adv. com. Robert Wood Johnson Exec. Nurse Fellows Program, 1998—2010; trustee Carondelet Found., Carondelet Health Sys., Tucson, 2003—, chmn., 2009—10; mem. health care adv. coun. TLContact Inc., 2003—08; mem. adv. coun. Precyse Solutions, Inc., 2004—08; mem. exec. adv. coun. The Beryl Cos., 2006—10, Crime Victims Compensation Bd., Pima County, 2010—; adv. bd. mem. Rise Health Inc., 2009—. Mem. editl. adv. bd. (book) Who's Who in Health Care, 1977, mem. editl. bd. Jour. Med. Edn., 1979—84. Adv. bd. Rise Health Corp., 2009—, Reid Pk. Zoological Soc.; bd. mem. Pima County Crime Victim Compensation, 2010—; bd. dirs. hosp. coun. San Diego and Imperial Counties, 1974—77, treas., 1976, pres., 1977; bd. dirs. United Way San Diego, 1975—80, Vol. Hosps. Am., 1990—94; mem. Accreditation Coun. for Grad. Med. Edn., 1987—90, Prospective Payment Assessment Commn., 1987—90; bd. dirs. Hosp. Fund, 1987—2000, Tucson Zool. Soc., Reid Park Zoo, 2006—. With US Army, 1952—55. Fellow: APHA, Am. Hosp. Assn. (governing coun. Met. sect. 1983—86, coun. on fin. 1987, ho. of dels. 1987—89), Am. Coll. Health Care Execs.; mem.: Ariz. Arts, Sci. and Tech. Acad. (founder), Inst. of Medicine, Am. Podiatric Med. Assn. (project coun. 2000 1985—86), Calif. Hosp. Assn. (trustee 1978—81). Personal E-mail: xenshel@comcast.net.

KING, SPENCER BIDWELL, III, cardiologist, educator, medical educator; b. Asheville, SC, May 12, 1937; s. Spencer B. and Caroline Paul King; m. Judith Gail Hayes; children: Spencer B., Susan Gail. AB, Mercer U., Macon, Ga., 1959; MD, Med. Coll. Ga., Augusta, 1963. Diplomate in internal medicine, cardiovasc. disease and interventional cardiology Am. Bd. Internal Medicine. Intern, internal medicine Walter Reed Army Med. Ctr., Washington, 1963—64; capt. M.C., U.S. Army, Honolulu and Vietnam, 1964—66; med. resident, cardiology Emory U. Sch. Medicine, Atlanta, 1966—68, cardiology fellow, 1968—70, dir., cardiac catheterization labs., 1972—90, dir. interventional cardiology, 1985—2000, prof. medicine; cardiologist St. Luke's Hosp. / U. Colo., Denver, 1970—72; dir. Andreas Cardiovasc. Ctr., Atlanta, 1986—2000; Fuqua chair interventional cardiology Fuqua Heart Ctr., Piedmont Hosp., Atlanta, 2000—08; exec. dir., academic affairs St. Joseph's Heart Vascular Inst., 2008—, pres., 2008—. Bd. dirs. Surgivision, Inc., Columbia, Md.; chair interventional cardiology bd. Am. Bd. Internal Medicine, 1997—. Co-author: (book) Coronary Angiography and Angioplasty, Atlas of Interventional Cardiology, Hurst's the Heart; author and co-author of other books., editor-in-chief JACC: Cardiovasc. Interventions, mem. editl. boards for several publications, editl. cons. The New England Journal of Medicine; contbr. several articles to profl. jours. Trustee Mercer U., Macon, Ga., 1982—2002, 2007—; bd. of visitors Mercer U. Sch. Medicine, Macon, Ga., 1982—84. Capt. US Army, 1963—66. Decorated Bronze Star; recipient Disting. Alumnus award, Med. Coll. Ga., 1992, RO1 Rsch. award, NHLBI, 1987-1997. Fellow: Am. Coll. Physicians, European Soc. Cardiology (Ethica Award 2000), Soc. Cardiac Angioplasty and Interventions (pres. 1990—91, First Founders Lecture 1990), Am. Coll. Cardiology (pres. 1998—99, Master). Achievements include development of multipurpose coronary arterography and invetion of beta radiation catheter endovascular brachytherapy. Avocation: golf. Office: St Joseph Hosp Heart and Vascular Inst 5665 Peachtree Dunwoody Rd NE Atlanta GA 30342 Office Fax: 404-851-7339. Business E-Mail: sbking@sjha.org.

KING, STEPHANIE ANGELA, gynecologic oncologist, educator; BS summa cum laude, U. Pa. Sch. of Medicine, MD. Diplomate Am. Bd. Ob-Gyn. Intern Hosp. of the Univ. Pa., resident ob-gyn, 1984—88, fellow ob-gyn, 1988—90; hosp. affiliation includes: Hahnemann Univ. Hosp.; assoc. prof. Drexel Univ. Coll. of Medicine. Recipient Angela Carlino award for Excellence in Ovarian Cancer Rsch./Care., 2008, Cert. of Appreciation for Tchg., Dept. of Ob-Gyn., Jefferson Med. Coll.; named one of Best Doctors for Women, Phila. Mag., 2000, 2002—06. Mem.: AMA, Soc. of Laparoendoscopic Surgeons, Soc. of Gynecologic Oncologist, Phila. County Med. Soc., Phila. Obstet. Soc., Am. Coll. of Ob-Gyn. Office: Fox Chase Cancer Center 333 Cottman Ave Philadelphia PA 19111-2497 Office Phone: 215-728-6900.

KING, TALMADGE E., physician; b. Feb. 24, 1948; BA, Gustavus Adolphus Coll., 1970; MD, Harvard U., 1974. Vice chair dept. medicine U. Colo., Denver, 1992-97; exec. v.p. Nat. Jewish Med. and Rsch. Ctr., Denver, 1992-95; vice chmn. medicine U. Calif., San Francisco, 1997—2007, chair medicine, 2006—; chief med. svc. San Francisco Gen. Hosp., 1997—2007. Editor: Interstitial Lung Disease, 2000; co-editor: Medical Management of Vulnerable and Underserved Patients, 2006. Trustee Gustavus Adolphus Coll., St. Peter, Minn., 1993—2002. Mem.: Inst. Medicine, Am. Bd. Internal Medicine (bd. dir. 2006—), Am. Thoracic Soc. (pres. 1997—98). Office: Univ Calif 505 Parnassus Ave M-994 San Francisco CA 94143 Office Phone: 415-476-0909. Business E-Mail: tking@medicine.ucsf.edu, tkina@medicine.ucsf.edu.

KING, THOMAS, physiologist, educator; b. Shanghai, June 1, 1934; came to U.S., 1965; s. Tsung Ming and Yen Vee (Sung) K.; m. Amy Penn, July 15, 1959; children: Susan, Caroline. MB, Ch.B., U. Edinburgh, 1959, MD, 1963. Asst. prof. medicine Cornell U. Med. Ctr., NYC, 1970—73, assoc. prof. medicine, 1973—, acting chief divsn. pulmonary and critical care medicine, 1982—85, acting chief divsn. pulmonary and ciritical care medicine, 1991—93, assoc. prof. physiology and biophysics NYC, 1975—. Vis. prof. U. Hong Kong, 1981, U. Guadalajara, Mexico, 1985, U. Taiwan, 1989, 97. Recipient Pulmonary Acad. award Nat. Heart & Lung Inst., 1972-77. Fellow Royal Coll. Physicians London, Am. Coll. Chest Physicians; mem. N.Y. Trudeau Soc. (pres. 1978-79), Chinese-Am. Med. Soc. (pres. 1984-85), Am. Thoracic Soc., Med. Rsch. Soc. U.K., Am. Fedn. Clin. Rsch., Am. Physiology Soc. Office: Cornell U Med Ctr 520 E 70th St Starr # 505 New York NY 10021-9800 Office Phone: 212-746-2250.

KING, TURI EMMA, geneticist; d. Alan John and Daphne King; married. BA with honor, U. Cambridge, 1996; MSc, U. Leicester, Eng., 1997, PhD, 2007. Postdoc. rsch. assoc. dept. genetics U. Leicester, 2007—11; project mgr. rsch. fellow Impact Diasporas Making Britain, 2011—. Collaborator People Brit. Isles Project, Oxford, 2008—; mem. Roots Brit. Project, Leicester, 2009—; mem. steering group Genes Gallgoidil Rsch. Group, Nottingham. Sch. gov., Leicester, 2008—. Recipient Doc. Inaugural Lectr. award, U. Leicester, 2008, award, Sch. Biol. Scis., 2008. Mem.: Genetics Soc. Office: University Leicester University Road LE1 7RH Leicester England

KING, WILLIAM DOUGLAS, physician; b. Inglewood, Calif., Feb. 18, 1964; MD, U. Ill., Urbana, 1996; JD, U. Ill., Urbana-Champaign, 1995. CEO W King Health Care Group, 2010—. Chief resident Cambridge Hosp., 1999—2000; pres. Charles R. Drew Med. Soc., 2010—. Contbr. articles to profl. publs. Fellow UCLA Robert Wood Johnson Clin. fellowship, Robert Wood Johnson Found.; MATP Postdoc. fellowship, Adult AIDS Clin. Trial Group. Mem.: Am. Coll. Legal Medicine, Am. Acad. HIV Medicine, Charles R. Drew Med. Soc. Avocations: sports, reading. Office: 3756 Santa Rosalia Dr Ste 506 Los Angeles CA 90008 Personal E-mail: drwdking@gmail.com.

KINGDON, HENRY SHANNON, retired internist, biochemist, science administrator; b. Puunene, Maui, Hawaii, July 2, 1934; s. Robert Wells and Anna Catherine (McCune) K.; m. Mary Lee Colman, June 22, 1957 (dec. Aug. 28, 1983); children: Holly, Catherine, Henry Colman; m. Jodi Kremiller, Jan. 26, 1985 AB in Chemistry, Oberlin Coll., 1956; MD, Western Res. U., 1963, PhD in Biochemistry, 1963; postgrad., U. Wash., 1962-63. Intern Univ. Hosp., Seattle, 1963-64; resident U. Wash. Affiliated Hosps., Seattle, 1964-65; practice medicine specializing in internal medicine Chgo., 1967-72, Chapel Hill, N.C., 1973-81; asst. prof. medicine and biochemistry U. Chgo., 1967-71, asso. prof., 1971-73, acting chmn. dept. medicine, summer 1971, dir. med. internship program, 1971-72; prof. medicine and biochemistry U. N.C., Chapel Hill, 1973-81; med. dir. Hyland Therapeutics div. Travenol Labs., Glendale, Calif., 1981-84; v.p., med. dir. Hyland div. Baxter Healthcare Corp., Glendale, Calif., 1984-90, v.p., gen. mgr., 1990-91; v.p. sci. affairs, chief med. officer Blood Therapy Group Baxter Healthcare Corp., Deerfield, Ill., 1991-93; v.p., med. dir. Gene Therapy Unit Baxter Biotech., Deerfield, 1993-95; v.p. tech. affairs Baxter Biotech., Deerfield, 1996-99; ret., 1999. Contbr. articles on mechanisms of blood coagulation, primary structure of proteins, and on regulation of anabolic nitrogen metabolism to profl. jours. Served with USPHS, 1965-67. Guggenheim Meml. Found. fellow, 1972-73; NIH grantee, 1957-59, 69-81 Mem. Am. Soc. Biol. Chemists, Am. Soc. Hematology, Internat. Soc. Thrombosis and Haemostasis, Central Soc. Clin. Research, So. Soc. Clin. Research, Phi Beta Kappa, Sigma Xi. Achievements include methods developed regarding eliminating AIDS and hepatitis infectivity from blood products; patentee in field. E-mail: hskingdon@aol.com. *

KINGSBURY, ELLEN ANN DAGON, anesthesiologist, general practitioner; b. Balt., Feb. 3, 1936; d. Emmett Paul and Annie (Sollers) Dagon; m. Lyle Jordan Millan IV, Dec. 21, 1963; children: Lyle Jordan V, Elizabeth Lyle, Ann Sheridan Worthington.; m. T. Marshall Duer, Jr., Aug. 23, 1985; m. Milton D. Kingsbury, Oct. 13, 2006. AB, George Washington U., 1959; MD, U. Md., 1964; postgrad., Johns Hopkins U., 1965—68. Intern Union Meml. Hosp., Balt., 1964—65; resident in anesthesiology Johns Hopkins Hosp., Balt., 1965—68, fellow in surgery, 1965—68; practice medicine specializing in anesthesiology Balt., 1968—; faculty Ch. Home and Hosp., Balt., 1969—; attending staff Union Meml. Hosp., Ch. Home and Hosp., Franklin Sq. Hosp., Children's Hosp., James Lawrence Kernan Hosp., Balt., 1982—94; co-chief anesthesiology James Kernan Hosp., 1983—94, med. dir. out-patient surgery dept., 1987—94; med. dir. Northern Neck Free Health Clinic, 2009. Affiliate cons. emergency room Ch. Home and Hosp., Balt., 1969—, med. audit and utilizaions com., 1970-72, mem. emergency and ambulatory care com., 1973-74, chief emergency dept., 1973-74; cons. anesthesiologist Md. State Penitentiary, 1971; fellow in critical care medicine Md. Inst. Emergency Medicine, 1975-76; infection control com. U. Md. Hosp., 1975—; instr. anesthesiology U. Md. Sch. Medicine, 1975—; staff anesthesiologist Mercy Hosp., 1978—, audit com., 1979-80, 82; asst. prof. anesthegiology U. Md. Med. Sch., 1989-94; med. exec. com. Kernan Hosp., 1990-94, v.p. 1990, chief of staff, 1992—; active Tappahannock Family Practice, 1994-96, Rappahannock Gen. Hosp. Family Practice, 1996—, Rappahannock Gen. Hosp., 1996—, ethics com., 1997—; med. examiner No. Neck of Va., 1996—; active Commonwealth of Va. Med. Bd. Mem. AMA, Am. Coll. Emergency Physicians, Am. Acad. Gen. Practitioners, Met. Emergency Dept. Heads Am., Md. Soc. Anesthesiologists, Balt. County Med. Soc., Mid. Peninsula Med. Soc., No. Neck Med. Soc., Med. Soc. Va., Med. and Choir Faculty Med., Chirurg. Soc., Internat. Congress Anaesthesiologists, Internat. Anesthesia Rsch. Soc. Anglican. Home: 244 Oak Hill Rd Lancaster VA 22503 Office Phone: 804-435-0575.

KINGSLEY, JOHN RAYMOND, surgeon; b. Kansas City, Mo., Oct. 27, 1941; s. James Gordon Kingsley and Blanche Sybil Payne Peak; children: Jennifer Nicole, John Randolph, Sarah Ashley. AA, Pensacola Jr. Coll., Fla.; BS, U. Fla., 1964, MD, 1970. Diplomate in surgery and gen. vascular surgery Am. Bd. Surgery, American Coll. Phlebology. Intern U.S. Naval Hosp., Bethesda, Md., 1970-71, resident in gen. surgery, 1971-75; attending surgeon Naval Med. Ctr., Pensacola, 1975-78, Mid-Columbia Med. Ctr., The Dalles, Oreg., 1978-92, Klickitat Valley Hosp., Goldendale, Wash., 1978-92, Russell Hosp., Alexander City, Ala., 1992-97, Carraway Meth. Med. Ctr., Birmingham, Ala., 1997—, Brookwood Med. Ctr., Birmingham, Ala., 2001—; chmn. dept. surgery Norwood Clinic, 2000—02, Carraway Meth. Med. Ctr., 2000—. Chmn. bd. Vein Assoc. Am., 2005—. Contbr. articles to profl. jours. Recipient Svc. Appreciation award DAV, 1977, Sheard-Sanford award for clin. pathology, 1970, Roger Schnell award for clin. neuorlogy, 1970, others; recognized as one of top surgeons in U.S., Consumers' Rsch. Coun. Am. Fellow ACS, S.E. Surg. Congress, So. Assn. for Vascular Surgery; mem. AMA, Am. Soc. Outpatient Surgeons (pres. 1992-95), Ala. Vascular Soc. (exec. bd. 2001—), Pacific N.W. Vascular Soc. (exec. coun. 1989-92), Am. Coll. Phlebology, Am. Med. Tennis Assn., Beta Beta Beta, Phi Theta Kappa. Avocations: tennis, horses, writing. Office: Ala Vascular & Vein Ctr Ste 210 700 Montgomery Hwy Birmingham AL 35216-1869 Office Phone: 205-823-0151. Personal E-mail: johnkingsley@mindspring.com. Business E-Mail: johnkingsleymd@alabamavascular.com.

KINGSMORE, STEPHEN FRANCIS, physician, research scientist; b. Motherwell, Scotland, Sept. 3, 1960; came to U.S., 1988; s. Brian and Rona K. (Ritson) K.; m. Fiona J. McQuaid, Nov. 7, 1987; children: Daniel R., Rebekah F.P., Francesca S. BSc in Med. Microbiology, Queen's U., Belfast, Ireland, 1982; MB, ChB, BAO, Queen's U., Belfast, No. Ireland, 1985. Diplomate Am. Bd. Internal Medicine. Intern Craigavon Hosp., Portadown, No. Ireland, 1985-86; resident Queen's U., Belfast, 1986-88; fellow Duke U., Durham, NC, 1988-89, intern, 1989-90, resident, 1990-91, fellow, 1991-93, assoc. in medicine, 1993-94; asst. prof. U. Fla., Gainesville, 1994-97; COO Molecular Staging Inc., New Haven; v.p. rsch. CuraGen Corp., New Haven, 1997—2004; pres., CEO Nat. Ctr. for Genome Resources, Santa Fe, 2004—. Contbr. articles to profl. jours. Recipient Sr. Scholar awrd Am. Coll. Rheumatology, 1994, Arthritis Investigator award Arthritis Found., 1995, Jr. Faculty Rsch. award Am. Cancer Soc., 1996. Mem. Am. Fedn. Clin. Rsch. (Trainee Investigator award 1994, Jr. Faculty award 1996), Internat. Mammalian Genome Soc. Office: Pres Nat Ctr for Genome Resources 2935 Rodeo Pk Dr East Santa Fe NM 87505 Home Phone: 505-820-7852; Office Phone: 505-995-4466. Business E-Mail: sfk@ncgr.org.

KINGTON, RAYNARD STUART, academic administrator, former federal agency administrator; b. Balt., Md., July 7, 1960; BS with distinction, U. Mich., MD, 1982; MBA, U. Pa., PhD in Health Policy and Economics. Cert. Internal Medicine, Pub. Health and Preventive Medicine. Resident internal medicine Michael Reese Med. Ctr., Chgo.; Robert Wood Johnson Clin. Scholar U. Pa.; sr. scientist RAND Corp.; co-dir. Drew/RAND Ctr. Health & Aging; dir. divsn. health examination stats. Nat. Ctr. Health Stats., Ctrs. Disease Control & Prevention; assoc. dir. behavioral & social sciences rsch. NIH, Bethesda, Md., 2000—03, dep. dir., 2003—10, acting dir., 2008—09, Nat. Inst. Alcohol Abuse & Alcoholism, Bethesda, Md., 2002; pres. Grinnell Coll., Iowa, 2010—. Grantee Fontaine Fellowship, U. Pa. Wharton Sch. Fellow: NAS. Office: Grinnell College Office of President 1121 Park St Grinnell IA 50112-1690 Office Phone: 641-269-3000. *

KINLOCH-DE LOES, SABINE IRENE, epidemiologist, educator; b. Geneva, Feb. 4, 1954; MBBS, Geneva U., 1979, MD, 1995. Rsch. fellow Geneva U. Hosp. Dept. Infectious Diseases, 1991—96, sho, registrar, 1988—91; sho Geneva U. Hosp. Dept. Internal Medicine, 1981—83; dr. Hong Kong Red Cross, 1979—81; clin. lectr. U. Coll. London Dept. Infection and Immunity, 1996—. Contbr. articles to profl. med. jours. Mem.: Children HIV Assn., Brit. HIV Assn., HYPNET. Avocations: music, gardening, theater. Home: 29 Walpole St London SW34QS England Home Fax: 44(0)2077307993. Personal E-mail: sabine@kinloch.u-net.com.

KINMONTH, ANN-LOUISE, physician, medical educator, researcher; b. London, Jan. 8, 1951; d. Maurice Henry and Gwendoline Stella (Phillipps) K. MB BChir, Cambridge U., Eng., 1975, MD, 1984; MSc, London U., 1989. Prin. in gen. practice Aldermoor Health Ctr., Southampton, Eng., 1983-96; sr. lectr. in primary med. care Southampton U., 1985, reader in primary med. care, 1981-82, prof. primary med. care, 1992-96, convenor health care devel. group, 1992; found. prof. gen. practice U. Cambridge, 1997—; assoc. dir. Primary Care, 2005—07. Med. officer Oxfam, N.W. Somalia, 1981; cons. Latvian Med. Acad., 1993; mem. rsch. bd. MRC Health Svcs., London, 1994, 97, Wellcome, 1998; dir. internat. seminar on gen. practice Brit. Coun., Eng., 1995. Editor: Evidence Base for Diabetes Care, 2002; contbr. articles to profl. publs. Recipient Exhibitioner award Cambridge & St. Thomas' Hosp., 1975; grantee MRC, Wellcome Trust, Nat. R&D Funds, 1993. Fellow Royal Coll. Gen. Practitioners (James Mackenzie prize 1991), Royal Coll. Physicians, Acad. Med. Sci. (mem. coun. 1998), Zool. Soc. London; mem. Inst. Medicine (fgn. assoc.), Brit. Diabetic Assn., Soc. Acad. Primary Care, UK Soc. Behavioral Medicine, CBE Brit. Empire (comdr. 2002), Nat. Inst. Health Rsch. (cons. 2006-), Nat. Sch. Primary Care Rsch. Office: Cambridge U IPH Forvie Site University Forvie Site Robinson Way CB2 0SR Cambridge England Office Phone: 01223 330329.

KINNEY, BRIAN MALTBIE, plastic surgeon; b. Baton Rouge, Apr. 28, 1954; s. Kenneth Lee and Louise Estelle (Walker) Kinney; BS in Mech. and Biomedical Engring., MIT, 1976, MS in Mech. and Biomedical Engring., 1980; MD, Tulane U. Sch. Medicine, New Orleans, 1982. Diplomate Am. Bd. Plastic Surgery, Nat. Bd. Med. Examiners, registered US Dept. Justice Drug Enforcement Adminstrn. Intern, resident gen. surgery UCLA Med. Ctr., 1982—87, plastic & reconstructive surgery fellowship, 1987—89; pvt. practice Century City, Calif., 1989—. Clin. asst. prof. plastic surgery U. So. Calif. Keck Sch. Medicine. Clin. editor Aesthetic Surgery Jour.; contbr. articles to profl. jours. Past. pres. Plastic Surgery Ednl. Found. US; chmn. bd. dirs. Nat. Endowment Plastic Surgery; bd. dirs. Internat. Confederation Plastic, Reconstructive & Aesthetic Surgery. Recipient Disting. Svc. award, Plastic Surgery Ednl. Found. US. Fellow: ACS; mem.: Am. Soc. Aesthetic Plastic Surgery (bd. dirs. 2002—08), Am. Soc. Plastic Surgery (bd. dirs. 1983—2010), Am. Soc. Mech. Engring., Am. Inst. Physics, Am. Soc. Plastic & Surgeons. Office: Century City Med Plz 2080 Century Park E Ste 1110 Los Angeles CA 90067-2014 Office Phone: 310-277-5112.

KINNIBURGH, ALAN JAMES, not-for-profit administrator, molecular biologist; b. Elmhurst, Ill., Oct. 3, 1951; s. Theodore and Elizabeth (Pitcairn) K. BS, U. Ill., 1973; PhD, U. Chgo., 1977. Rsch. assoc. U. Wis., Madison, 1977-82; asst. prof. Roswell Park Cancer Inst., Buffalo, 1982-87, assoc. prof., 1987-91, prof., 1992—2000; sr. v.p. rsch. adminstrn. Leukemia & Lymphoma Soc., White Plains, NY, 2000—05; CEO Nat. Hemophilia Found., NYC, 2005—07; pres. AJK Consulting, Bethesda, Md., 2007—10; exec. dir. Nat. Strength and Conditioning Assn., Colorado Springs, 2010—. Mem. adv. bd. Assn. for Rsch./Childhood Cancer, Buffalo, 1990—; mem. hematology rev. bd. VA, Washington, 1990-93. Recipient Louis Pasteur award U. Ill., 1973. Mem. AAAS, Am. Assn. Microbiology, Am. Assn. Cancer Rsch., N.Y. Acad. Sci. Achievements include discovery of introns in mRNA precursors, B-thalassemia is an RNA processing disorder; discovery that DNA triplexes increase transcription of proto-oncogenes. Office: NSCA 1885 Bob Johnson Dr Colorado Springs CO 80906 Office Phone: 719-632-6722. Office Fax: 719-632-6367. *

KINNULA, VUOKKO LIISA, medical educator; b. Kauhajoki, Finland, July 29, 1947; PhD in Biochemistry, U. Oulu, 1974, MD, 1987. Vis. prof. Duke U., 1989—91; prof., chief dept. pulm med Oulu U. Hosp., 1995—2003; pulmonary fellow Helsinki U. Hosp., 1987—89, physician, asst. prof., 1992—94, prof. pulmonary medicine, 2003—. Pres. Finnish Respiratory Soc., 1999—2002, Finnish Med. Soc. Duodecim, 2008—10. Recipient Maud Kuistila award, Prize Supervising Young Scientists, 2011. Mem.: Finnish Med. Soc., Finnish Med. Assn., Free Radical Soc., Am. Thoracic Soc. Office: Haartmaninkatu 4 Helsinki 00029 Finland Business E-Mail: vuokko.kinnulu@helsinki.fi.

KINO, MASAYA, hospital administrator, physician; b. Osaka, Japan, Jan. 19, 1947; s. Takeshi and Chiyoko K.; m. Sumiko Chiba, Nov. 5, 1978; children: Mayumi, Keiichiro. MD, Osaka Med. Coll., Takatsuki, Japan, 1971. Resident Osaka Med. Coll. Hosp, Japan, 1971-73; tchg. fellow cardiology Tufts U. Med. Sch., Boston, 1973-74; intern Faulkner-Lemuel Shattuck Hosp., Boston, 1974-75; resident New Eng. Deaconess Hosp., Boston, 1975-76; cardiology fellow Beth Israel Hosp., Boston, Boston, 1976—77; physician Osaka Med. Coll. Hosp., Japan, 1977-86; pres. Hokusetsu Gen. Hosp., Takatsuki, Japan, 1986—; clin. prof. medicine Osaka Med. Coll., 2002—; dir. cardiology Osaka Med. Coll. Hosp., Japan, 1981—84. V.p. Japanese Edn. Clin. Cardiology Soc., 1986—2004, pres., 2005—; councillor Fellow's Assn. of Japanese Soc. Internal Medicine, 1997—, v.p., 2000—04, pres., 2004—07. Fellow: ACP, Japanese Soc. Internal Medicine, Japanese Circulation Soc., Am. Coll. Cardiology, Am. Heart Assn. (internat.). Avocations: guitar, golf, watching movies. Office: Hokusetsu Gen Hosp 6-24 Kitayanagawa-cho Takatsuki Osaka 569-8585 Japan

KINOSHITA, AKITOSHI, oncologist, pulmonologist; b. Nagasaki, Japan, Aug. 5, 1959; s. Hisaaki and Jitsuko Kinoshita; children: Yuko, Mayumi, Takaaki. MD, Nagasaki U., 1984, PhD, 1993. Staff, 2d dept. internal medicine Nagasaki U. Sch. Medicine, 1984-86, 88-92; chief dept. pulmonology Hokusho Ctrl. Hosp., Nagasaki, 1986-88, Nagasaki Mcpl. Citizens' Hosp., 1992-96, NHO Nagasaki Med. Ctr., Omura, Japan, 1996—2011; v.p. Nagasaki Prefecture Shimabava Hosp., 2011—. Reviewer Am. Cancer Soc. Mem. Japanese Soc. Med. Oncology, Japanese Soc. Palliative Medicine, Internat. Assn. for Study of Lung Cancer, Japanese Cancer Assn., Asian Pacific Soc. Respirology, Japanese Respiratory Soc., Japan Soc. Clin. Oncology, Japanese Soc. Internal Medicine, Japan Soc. Bronchology, Japan Lung Cancer Soc. Home: 748-11-807 Nishihonmachi Omura 856-0837 Japan Office: Nagasaki Prefecture Shimabara Hosp Shimo Kawaziri Machi 7895 Shimabara 8550861 Japan

KINOSHITA, TAKAHIRO, oncologist; b. Kanazawa, Japan, Apr. 24, 1969; MD, Kanazawa U., 1994, PhD, 1999. Guest surgeon Eberhard Karls U. Tuebingen, Germany, 2001—03; lectr. Toho U. Sakura Med. Ctr. Hosp., Japan, 2004—10; head surgeon dept. surg. oncology Nat. Cancer Ctr. Hosp. East, Japan, 2010—. Office: 6-5-1 Kashiwanoha Kashiwa Chiba 277-8577 Japan Office Fax: 81-4-7131-9960. Personal E-mail: kino_tuebingen@yahoo.co.jp.

KINRA, PRATEEK, pathologist; b. India, Oct. 2, 1972; MBBS, Armed Forces Med. Coll., Pune, 1995, MD in Pathology, 2003. Wing comdr. Indian Air Force, 2010—. Assoc. prof. Armed Forces Med. Coll., 2010—11. Decorated Chief of Air Staff Commendation medal Indian Air Force, Comdr.-in-Chief Commendation medal; recipient Lt. Col. Jagdish Rai Meml. medal, Indian Armed forces, 2003, Maj. Gen. Subramaniam award, Armed Forces Med. Coll. Mem.: Indian Assn. Pathologist. Office: Armed Forces Med Coll Wanowrie Dept Pathology Pune Maharashtra 411040 India Office Fax: 02026363301. Personal E-mail: pkinra_in@yahoo.com.

KINSMAN, SARA B., pediatrician, adolescent medicine; MD, U. Pa., Phila., 1990. Diplomate Am. Bd. Pediatrics-adolescent medicine, 2005, Am. Bd. Pediatrics, 2008. Resident pediat. Children's Hosp. Phila., 1990—93, fellow adolescent medicine, 1993—95, attending physician Pa., 1996—. Office: Children's Hospital of Philadelphia 3550 Market St Fl 4 Philadelphia PA 19104 Office Phone: 215-590-3537.

KINTSCH, WALTER, retired psychology professor; b. Temesvar, Romania, May 30, 1932; arrived in US, 1955; s. Christof and Irene (Hollerbach) Kintsch; m. Eileen Hoover, June 27, 1959; children: Anja, Julia. PhD, U. Kans., 1960. Prof. U. Colo., Boulder, 1968—2004; ret., 2004. Editor: Pyschol Rev, 1989—94; author: books. Office: U Colo Dept Psychology Institute Cognitive Scis Boulder CO 80309-0344 Office Phone: 303-492-8663. Business E-Mail: walter.kintsch@colorado.edu.

KINTSCHER, ULRICH, pharmacologist, research scientist; b. Wuppertal, Nordrhein Westfalen, Germany, Oct. 23, 1967; s. Walter and Eva Kintscher; m. Frederike Kintscher-Schmidt, Aug. 14, 1998; children: Cedrik, Oona. MD, U. Hamburg, Hamburg, 1995. Clin. resident in cardiology German Heart Inst., Berlin, 1996—99; rsch. fellow in endocrinology U. Calif., LA, 1999—2001; rsch. scientist, group leader Charité-U. Medicine Berlin, Ctr. Cardiovasc. Rsch., Inst. Pharmacology, Berlin, 2002—. Contbr. articles to profl. jours. Recipient New Investigator award, North Am. Vascular Biology Orgn., 2001; Gonda Goldschmied Diabetes fellow, U. Calif., L.A. Fellow: Am. Heart Assn. (New Investigator award for European Fellows 2003); mem.: German Soc. Pharmacology, German Hypertension Soc. (Rsch. award for Hypertension and Obesity 2004), North Am. Vascular Biology Orgn., German Soc. Cardiology, European Soc. Cardiology. Achievements include research in pleiotropic action of angiotensin receptor blockers; PPARalpha inhibits TGF-beta-induced beta5 integrin transcription in vascular smooth muscle cells by interacting with Smad4; angiotensin type 1 receptor blockers induce PPARgamma activity; molecular characterization of new selective PPARgamma modulators with angiotensin receptor blocking activity. Office: Charité-Univ Medicine Berlin Hessische Str 3-4 Berlin 10115 Germany Office Fax: +4930450525901. E-mail: ulrich.kintscher@charite.de.

KINUGASA, YUSUKE, colon and rectal surgeon; b. Tokyo, June 23, 1973; M.D., Ph.D., Tokyo Med. and Dental U., 1998. Chief, colon and rectal surgery Shizuoka Cancer Ctr. Hosp., 2006. Office: 1007 Shimonagakubo Nagaizumicho Suntogun Shizuoka 411-8777 Japan Business E-Mail: y.kinugasa@scchr.jp.

KINYA, OKAMOTO, medical researcher; b. Japan, Sept. 20, 1969; MD, Tottori U., 1996. Rsch. assoc. Tottori U., 2008—. Office: Nishi-cho 36-1 Yonago Tottori 683-0854 Japan Office Fax: 81 859 386529. Business E-Mail: okamotka@grape.med.tottori-u.ac.jp.

KINZIE, JEANNIE JONES, retired radiation oncologist, retired nuclear medicine physician; b. Great Falls, Mont., Mar. 14, 1940; d. James Wayne and Lillian Alice (Young) Jones; m. Joseph Lee Kinzie, Mar. 26, 1965 (div. Sept. 1982); 1 child, Daniel Joseph. Student, Oreg. State U., 1960; BS, Mont. State U., 1961; MD, Washington U., 1965; MBA, U. Phoenix, 1997. Diplomate Am. Bd. Radiology; diplomate Am. Bd. Nuclear Medicine; cert. master gardener Colo. State U., 1997. Intern. in surgery U. N.C., Chapel Hill, 1965-66; resident in therapeutic radiology Washington U., St. Louis, 1968-71, instr. in radiology, 1971-73; asst. prof. in radiology Med. Coll. of Wis., Milw., 1973-75, U. Chgo., 1975-78, assoc. prof. in radiology, 1978-80; assoc. prof. of radiation oncology Wayne State U., Detroit, 1980-85; prof. radiology U. Colo., Denver, 1985-95; dir. radiation oncology U. Hosp., Denver, 1985-91; fellow in nuclear medicine U. Colo., 1996-98, asst. clin. prof. nuclear medicine, 1998—2005; staff radiologist Denver Vets. Hosp., Denver, 2003—08. Cons. Denver Vets. Hosp., 1985-98, Denver Gen. Hosp., 1985-95, Rose Med. Ctr., 1986-95, FDA Ctr. for Devices and Radiologic Health, 1986-2003; mem. sci. adv. bd. Cancer League Colo., 1985-88; examiner Am. Bd. Radiology, 1985-88; adv. physician Colo. Med. Found., 1988-98; chmn. faculty promotion com. U. Colo. Health Scis. Ctr., 1988-89. Assoc. editor Internat. Jour. Radiation Oncology Biology and Physics, 1985-95; contbr. articles to profl. jours.; chpts. to books. Mem. Faith Bible Chapel Ch. NIH grantee, 1973-75. Fellow: Am. Coll. Radiology; mem.: AMA, Am. Cancer Soc. (bd. dirs. Denver unit 1986—87), Am. Soc. Therapeutic Radiologists, Rocky Mountain Oncology Soc. (bd. dirs. 1989—93, pres. 1991—93), Colo. Radiol. Soc., Denver Med. Soc., Colo. Med. Soc. (del./alt. del. ho. of dels. 1989—2006), Am. Coll. Nuclear Physicians. Republican. Avocations: gardening, rug latching, mountain climbing, tai chi, painting, poetry, hiking. Personal E-mail: jeannie.kinzie@att.net.

KIPROFF, PAUL M., radiologist, educator; MD, Jefferson Med. Coll. Diplomate Am. Bd. Radiology, cert. vascular and interventional radiology. Fellow Presbyn. Univ. Hosp.; assoc. prof. radiologic sci. Drexel Univ.; practice Allegheny Radiology Assocs.; resident Allegheny Gen. Hosp., system chmn. dept. diagnostic radiology, dir. divsn. of vascular and interventional radiology. Named one of Top Doctors, Pitts. mag., 2011. Office: Allegheny General Hospital 320 E N Ave Pittsburgh PA 15212 Office Phone: 412-359-3131. Office Fax: 412-359-4108.

KIRBY, RUSSELL STEPHEN, epidemiologist, geographer, researcher; b. New Haven, June 8, 1954; s. Frank Eugene and Emily (Baruch) K.; m. Elizabeth Margaret Ivens, July 9, 1977; children: Rachel Anne, Amelia Jeanne, Jocelyn Eileen. BA, U. Wis., 1974, MS, 1977, PhD, 1981, MS, 1991. Lectr. U. Wis., Madison, 1980, 82-83; rsch. analyst 3 Wis. Ctr. for Health Stats., Madison, 1981-83, rsch. analyst 5, 1983-85, rsch. analyst 6 maternal and child health statistician, 1985-88; sr. rsch. analyst maternal and child health Ark. Ctr. Health Statistics, Little Rock, 1988-91; instr. dept. pediat. U. Ark. Med. Scis., Little Rock, 1989-93, asst. prof., 1993-96; assoc. prof. dept. ob.-gyn. Milw. Clin. Campus U. Wis. Med. Sch., 1996-01, prof., 2001—02; prof., vice chair dept. maternal and child health, sch. pub. health dept. of pediat. and ob-gyn U. Ala. at Birmingham, 2002—08; Marrell chair. prof., dept. cmty. family health, dept. pediat., psychiatry and ob-gyn. dept. child and family studies U. South Fla., Tampa, 2008—. Vis. asst. prof. Beloit Coll., 1987—88; adj. asst. prof. U. Ark., Little Rock, 1988—95; adj. assoc. prof. Coll. Bus. and Mgmt. Cardinal Stritch U., 2000—02; sci. dir. Ark. Reproductive Health Monitoring Sys., 1991—94, dir., 1994—96, cons., 1996—98. Book rev. editor Jour. Perinatology, 1992-99; mem. bd. editors Jour. Childs

Health, 2003-04, Birth, 2003—, Pediatric and Perinatal Epidemiology, 2003-, Public Health Reports, 2009-, Annals Epidemiology, 2009-, Am. Jour. Perinatology, 2005, Spatial and Spatio-Temporal Epidemiology, 2009-, Disability and Health Jour., 2010-; contbr. articles to profl. jours. Recipient Callon-Leonard award Wis. Assn. for Perinatal Care, 1994, Byron L. Hawks award Ark. Perinatal Assn., 1995, Fraternalist of Yr. award Ct. Razorback Ind. Order Foresters, 1996, Pres.'s award Nat. Birth Defects Prevention Network, 2005; named Vol. of Yr. SE chpt. Wis. March of Dimes Birth Defects Found., 1998, Outstanding Advocate for Maternal and Child Health Wis. Maternal and Child Health Coalition, 1999, Outstanding Faculty Pub. Health Svc. award, UAB Sch. Pub. Health, 2007, Nat. Maternal and Child Health Epidemiology award for Excellence in Teaching, 2007, Godfrey P. Oakley Jr. award, Nat. Birth Defects Prevention Network, 2007, Outstanding Faculty rsch. award, USF, 2009. Fellow Am. Coll. Epidemiology; mem. APHA, Assn. Am. Geographers (life), Agrl. History Soc. (life), So. Hist. Soc. (life), Wis. Assn. for Perinatal Care (bd. dirs. 1996-2002, pres.-elect 1998-99, pres. 1999-2000, past pres. 2000-01, Pres. award, 2003), Perinatal Found. (bd. dirs. 1996-2002, 09-, treas. 2000-02), Ark. Perinatal Assn. (pres. 1991-92), Soc. for Epidemiologic Rsch., Nat. Perinatal Assn. (bd. dirs. 1990-92, 95-98, ann. conf. chair 1999), Nat Birth Defects Prevention Network (pres. 1999, past pres. 2000, exec. com. 1997—2008, pres. award, 2005), Soc. for Pediatric and Perinatal Epidemiologic Rsch. (exec. com. 2000-04, pres. 2009-10, past pres. 2010-11), Teratology Soc., Ala. chpt. Mar. of Dimes (bd. dirs. 2002—08, chpt. chair 2005—06), Assn. Tchrs. Maternal and Child Health (treas. 2005-06, pres. 2008-10, past pres. 2010-). Avocations: writing, computers. Office: USF Coll Pub Health 13201 Bruce B Downs Blvd MDC 56 Tampa FL 33612 Home: 15906 Layton Ct Tampa FL 33647 Office Phone: 813-396-2347. Business E-Mail: rkirby@health.usf.edu.

KIRCH, DARRELL GENE, medical association administrator, former dean; b. Denver, May 3, 1949; m. Deborah M. Kirch; children: Samantha M., Madeline A. BA in Philos., U. Colo., 1973, MD magna cum laude, 1977. Diplomate Am. Bd. Psychiatry & Neurology. Resident psychiatry U. Colo. Health Scis. Ctr., Denver, 1977—82; med. staff fellow adult psychiatry br. NIMH, Washington, 1982—84, sr. staff fellow neuropsychiatry br., 1984—87, med. dir. Neuropsychiatric Rsch. Hosp., 1987—89, dep. sci. dir. Bethesda, Md., 1992—93; prof. dept. psychiatry, prof. Sch. Grad. Studies Med. Coll. Ga., Augusta, 1994—2000, dean Sch. Medicine, 1994—2000, dean Sch. Grad. Studies, 1995—99, sr. v.p. clin. activities, 1998—2000; prof. dept. psychiatry, sr. v.p. health affairs Pa. State U., Hershey, 2000—06, dean Coll. Medicine, 2000—06; CEO Milton S. Hershey Med. Ctr., 2000—06; pres., CEO Assn. Am. Med. Colls., Washington, 2006—. Examiner Am. Bd. Psychiatry & Neurology, Deerfield, Ill., 1985—. Assoc. editor: Schizophrenia Bull., 1989—95, Psychopharmacology Bull., 1990—98. Capt. USPHS, 1986—94. Decorated Commendation medal. Mem.: AMA, Inst. Medicine, Assn. Am. Med. Coll. (chair med. schs. sect. 1998—99, mem. coun. deans adminstrv. bd. 2000—05, chair 2003), Soc. Exec. Leadership in Acad. Medicine, Am. Psychiat. Assn. Office: Assn Am Med Colls 2450 N St NW Washington DC 20037-1126 Office Phone: 202-828-0460. E-mail: aamcpresident@aamc.org.*

KIRI, VICTOR A., epidemiologist; arrived in UK, 1983; s. Dokubo A. and Tarikoro D. Kiri; m. Furo Kiri, Dec. 12, 1980; children: Victor A. Kiri Jnr, Janet T. BSc, U. Nigeria, 1979; MSc, U. Sussex, 1984; PhD, U. Bradford, 1988. Chartered statistician Royal Statis. Soc. U.K., 1998, chartered scientist UK Sci. Coun., 2010. Lectr. Liverpool John Moore's U., 1988—90, London Sch. Hygiene and Tropical Medicine, 1998—99; rsch. fellow U. Surrey, 1990—98; mgr. epidemiology GlaxoSmithKline, London, 1999—2007; dir. epidemiology PAREXEL Internat., London, 2007—; chartered scientist Science Coun. UK, 2010. Cons. Nat. Heart Rsch. Fund, Leeds, England, 1988—91; cons. Nat. Ctr. Health Outcomes Devel. London (England) Sch. Hygiene and Tropical Medicine, 1999—; adj. prof. U. Limerick, Ireland, 2007—. Contbr. articles to profl. jours. Recipient Best Grad. award, U. Nigeria, 1979, Excellence in Sci. award, GlaxoSmithKline R&D, 2005. Fellow: Royal Statis. Soc. (fellowship 1989). Bahai. Avocation: chess. Home: 39 Juniper Close Surrey Guildford GU1 1NX England Office: PAREXEL Internat The Quays 101-105 Oxford Road UB8 1LZ London England Office Fax: 44 18956277. Business E-Mail: victor.kiri@parexel.com.

KIRIIKE, NOBUO, psychiatrist, educator; b. Osaka, Japan, June 4, 1946; s. Masanobu and Harue (Hiraoka) K.; m. Hiroko Watanabe, Apr. 26, 1976; children: Yoshiko, Yusuke, Yasuko, Atsuko. MD, Med. Sch. Osaka City U., 1971, postgrad., 1971-73, PhD, 1981. Residency Osaka City U. Med. Sch. Hosp., 1973-75; asst. Osaka City U. Med. Sch., 1975-77, 80-82, lectr., 1982-92, assoc. prof., 1992-99, prof., chmn., 1999—; with Kitano Hosp., Osaka, 1977-78; rsch. fellow dept. pharmacol. rsch. Nebraska State U., 1979-80. Mem. psychiat. rev. bd. Osaka City Govt., 1993—. Contbr. articles to profl. jours. Fellow Japanese Soc. Psychiat. Diagnosis, Japanese Soc. Biol. Psychiatry; mem. Japanese Soc. Psychiat. Neurology, Internat. Soc. Neurochemistry, N.Y. Acad. Sci. Avocations: music, golf. Home: Sumiyoshi-ku 1-10-19 Tezukayamanishi Osaka 558-0052 Japan Office: Osaka City U Grad Sch Medicine 1-4-3 Asahi-cho Abeno-ku Osaka 545-8585 Japan Office Phone: 06 6645 3821.

KIRINCIC, MARIE, orthopedist; MD, Palacky Univ., Czech Republic. Cert. Bd. Physical Medicine and Rehab. Examiners, Pain Medicine. Clin. rsch. instr., Northwestern Univ. Feinberg Sch. Medicine; staff physician Rehab. Inst. Chgo., Hinsdale Hosp., Good Samaritan Hosp., Silver Cross Hosp.; physician Hinsdale Orthopaedic Assoc., S.C., 2003—. Intern, residency Loyola Univ., Maywood, Ill.; fell., pain mgmt. Rehab. Inst., Chgo. Mem.: Am. Assn. Electrodiagnostic Medicine, Psychiatric Assn. Spine, Sports, Occupational Rehab, Midwest Pain Soc., Ill. Soc. Physical Medicine and Rehab., Am. Pain Soc., Am. Acad. Physical Medicine and Rehab. Office: Hinsdale Orthopaedic Assoc 550 W Ogden Ave Hinsdale IL 60521

KIRKLAND, REBECCA TRENT, endocrinologist; b. Durham, NC, Dec. 27, 1942; d. Josiah Charles Trent and Mary Duke (Biddle) Trent-Semans; m. John Lindsey Kirkland III, June 24, 1965. BA, Duke U., 1964, MD, 1968. Intern Baylor Coll. Medicine, 1968-69, resident in pediatrics, 1969-70, fellow in pediatric endocrinology, 1971-73, asst. prof. dept. pediatrics, 1975-81, assoc. prof., 1981-88, prof., 1988—, sr. assoc. dean med. edn. London, 2000; registrar Guy's Hosp., Hosp. for Sick Children, London, 1970; with U. Pa. Sch. Medicine, 1973-74, fellow, 1974-75. Asst. physician divsn. endocrinology Children's Hosp. Phila., 1973-75; mem. staff Tex. Children's Hosp., 1975—, Harris County Hosp. Dist., 1975—; head ambulatory svcs. Tex. Children's Hosp., 1984—, dir. jr. league outpatient dept., 1984—. Contbr. articles and revs. to profl. jours. Active Leadership Tex., Leadership Houston; pres. Greater Houston Women's Found., 1994—96; bd. dirs. AVANCE, Inc., 1992, YWCA, 1992; trustee Mus. Med. Sci., 1984—88; pres. Josiah C. Trent Meml. Found., Inc., 1983—, v.p., 1977—83; bd. dirs. Am. Leadership Forum, 1991, mem. selection com., 1989, 1990, sec. bd. dirs. Houston/Gulf Coast chpg., 1989, 1990, pres.-elect, 1991, pres., 1991—93; bd. dirs. Mus. Health and Med. Scis., 2001—. NIH fellow, 1971-73; recipient Alumnae award Baldwin Sch., 1983, Disting. Alumni award Durham Acad., 1984, Goodheart Humanitarian award B'nai B'rith, 1986, Disting. Svc. award Duke U. Med. Alumni Assn., 1992, Recognition award Ctr. for Interaction: Man, Sci. and Culture, 1993, One Voice for Children award Tex. Network for Medically Fragile and Chronically-Ill Children, 1993; named one of five Outstanding Women of Yr. Channel 13, Houston, 1984, Woman on the move Houston Post, 1989. Fellow Am. Acad. Pediatrics; mem. Endocrine Soc., Am. Fedn. For Clin. Rsch., So. Soc. for Pediatric Rsch., Lawson-Wilkins Pediatric Endocrine Soc., Houston Pediatric Soc., Tex. Pediatric Soc., Tex. Med. Assn., Soc. for Pediatric Rsch., Pediatric Endocrinology Soc. Tex., Ambulatory Pediatric Assn., Am. Pediatric Soc., Am. Acad. Pediatrics (pediatric endocrine sect.) 1990), Tex. Diabetes and Endocrine Assn. Business E-Mail: rebeccak@bcm.tmc.edu.

KIRKPATRICK, CHARLES HARVEY, immunologist, researcher; b. Topeka, Nov. 5, 1931; s. Hazen Leon and Clarice Opal (Privott) K.; m. Janice Faye Fosha, July 11, 1959; children: Heather, Michael, Brian. BA, U. Kans., 1954; MD, U. Kans., Kansas City, 1958. Diplomate Am. Bd. Internal Medicine, Am. Bd. Allergy and Immunology. Asst. prof. U. Kans., Kansas City, 1965—67, assoc. prof., 1968; sr. investigator Nat. Inst. Allergy and Infectious Diseases, NIH, Bethesda, Md., 1968-79; dir. allergy and clin. immunology Nat. Jewish Ctr., Denver, 1979-93; prof. U. Colo., Denver, 1979—; dir. rsch. Innovative Therapeutics, Inc., 1993-96; pres. Cytokine Sci., Inc., Denver, 1996-99. Active NIH study sects., Bethesda. Editor: 4 books; contbr. numerous articles to profl. jours. NIH research grantee, 1981-86. Fellow ACP, Am. Acad. Allergy and Immunology, Molecular Med. Soc.; mem. Am. Soc. Clin. Investigation, Am. Assn. Immunologists. Episcopalian. Office Phone: 303-724-7197.

KIRKPATRICK, SHARON MINTON, nursing educator, academic administrator; b. Independence, Mo., Aug. 31, 1943; d. Charles Russell and Minnetta (Brotherton) Minton; m. John P. Kirkpatrick; children: John Brent, Kraig Russell. Grad. in nursing, Ind. Sanitarium and Hosp., Independence, 1965; AA, Graceland Coll., Lamoni, Iowa, 1965; BSN, Calif. State U., Sacramento, 1976; M in Nursing, U. Kans., 1981, PhD in Nursing, 1988. RN, Mo., Iowa. Office coordinator Family Practice Physicians, Cupertino, Calif., 1965-67; head nurse Truman Med. Ctr. East, Kansas City, Mo., 1977-79; teaching asst. U. Kans. Med. Ctr., Kansas City, 1980; asst. prof. nursing Graceland Coll., 1980-86, chmn. div. nursing, 1986-94, prof., dean Independence Campus, 1990-94, v.p., dean. nursing, 1994—2002, v.p. instl. advancement, 2002—05, v.p. independence campus, 2005—. Dir. cmty. health projects Haiti, Dominican Republic, Jamaica, Zambia, Malawi, Nepal, India, Congo. Contbr. articles to profl. jours. Trustee Independence Sanitarium and Hosp., 1977-86, Independence Regional Health Ctr., 2000—, Med. Ctr. of Ind., 2003—; mem. corp. body Truman Neurol. Ctr., Kansas City, 1979-86. Mem. ANA (coun. on cultural diversity), Mo. Nurses Assn. (bd. dirs., pres. 1991-93), Profl. Nurses Assn. (pres. 1982-84), Collegiate Nurse Educators Greater Kansas City (pres. 1991-92), Jr. Women's Club Cupertino (past pres.), Sigma Theta Tau. Mem. Reorganized Lds Ch. Avocations: travel, cultural studies, backpacking, boating, reading. Home: 5665 NE Northgate Xing Lees Summit MO 64064-1240 Office: Graceland Univ Lamoni IA 50140 Office Phone: 816-833-0524. Business E-Mail: kirkpat@graceland.edu.

KIRKPATRICK, WILLIAM NIALL ALEXANDER, plastic surgeon, consultant; s. William Arthur and Marlise Meta Erna Kirkpatrick; m. Anahita Houshangi Kermani, May 15, 1993; children: Guy, Sean, Louis. BDS, Guy's Hosp. Dental Sch., London, 1984; MBBS, Guy's Hosp. Med. Sch., London, 1990; MD, U. London, 1996. Cons. plastic surgeon Chelsea & Westminster Hosp., London, 2003—; cons. craniofacial and plastic surgeon, lead clinician craniofacial unit Chelsea and Westminster Hosp., London; cons. plastic surgeon Royal Marsden Hosp., London, 2003—. Fellow: Royal Coll. Surgeons. Office: The Consulting Ste 82 Portland Pl W1B 1NS London England Office Phone: 442079276512. Fax: 442079276511. Business E-Mail: niallkirkpatrick@theconsultingsuite.co.uk.

KIRKSEY, AVANELLE, nutrition educator; b. Mulberry, Ark., Mar. 23, 1926; BS, U. Ark., Fayetteville, 1947; MS, U. Tenn., Knoxville, 1950; PhD, Pa. State U., University Park, 1961; postdoctoral, U. Calif., Davis, 1976; DSc honoris causa, Purdue U., Ind., 1997. Assoc. prof. Ark. Polytechnic U., Russellville, 1950—55; rsch. asst. Pa. State U., University Park, 1956—58, fellow Gen. Foods, 1958—60; assoc. prof. Purdue U., West Lafayette, Ind., 1961—69, prof. nutrition, 1970—85, disting. prof., 1985—96, disting. prof. emeritus, 1997. Prin. investigator nutrition project in rural Egypt; coord. nutrition program Indonesian Univs., 1987—91. Contbr. articles to profl. jours. Recipient endowment, Kirksey Annual Lecture Series, Purdue U., 1997, Borden award, Am. Home Econs. Assn., 1980; named Meredith Disting. Prof. Nutrition, Purdue U.; named to Nutrition Hall of Fame, 2007. Fellow Am. Inst. Nutrition (Lederle award 1994); mem. N.Y. Acad. Scis., Phi Kappa Phi, Sigma Xi. Office: Purdue U Dept Food Nutrition West Lafayette IN 47907 Office Phone: 479-452-2340. Personal E-mail: akirksey01@cox.net.

KIRKWOOD, JOHN MUNN, medical educator; b. NYC, Mar. 5, 1948; BA, Oberlin Coll., 1969; MD, Yale U., 1973. Prof. medicine, dermatology, and translational sci. U. Pitts. Sch. Medicine, 1985—. Cons. JMK Consulting LLC, 1995. Mem.: ECOG, ISBT, AACR, ASCO. Avocations: bicycling, music, sports. Home: 282 Shephard Rd Gibsonia PA 15044 Business E-Mail: kirkwood@pitt.edu.

KIRKWOOD, MELISSA L., surgeon, educator; b. Winter Pk., Fla., Dec. 15, 1977; BS, U. Fla., 2000; MD, Yale U., 2004. Gen. surgery resident U. Chgo. Med. Ctr., 2004—09; vascular surgery fellow U. Pa. Med. Ctr., 2009—; asst. prof., surgery U. Tex. Southwestern Med. Ctr., 2011—. Vascular surgery grand rounds, presenter U. Pa. Med. Ctr., 2009—10; plenary session spkr. Soc. Vascular Surgery Ann. Meeting, Boston, 2010; spkr. Eastern Vascular Soc. Ann. Meeting, NYC, 2010; rsch. spkr. Del. Valley Vascular Soc. Meeting, 2011. Recipient Dean's award, Yale U. Sch. Medicine, Commencement Spkr. award, Outstanding Rsch. award, U. Fla. Microbiology. Mem.: Resident Recruitment Com., Surg. Edn. Com., Alpha Omega Alpha Honor Med. Soc. Avocations: running, travel, swimming. Home: 1900 McKinney Ave Apt 1106 Dallas TX 75201 Office: 5959 Harry Hines Blvd Ste 620 Dallas TX 75390 Office Phone: 214-645-0538. Business E-Mail: melissa.kirkwood@utsouthwestern.edu.

KIRLAND, MATT, III, surgeon; MD, Thomas Jefferson Med. Coll. Diplomate Am. Bd. Surgery. Intern Pa. Hosp., resident, 1988—, clin. asst. prof. surgery. Named one of Top Docs, Phila. Mag., 2002, 2010—11. Mem.: Phila. County Med. Soc., AMA, Am. Soc. Gen. Surgeons, Am.Soc. Abdominal Surgeons, Intenat. Coll. Surgeons, ACS, Soc. Laparoendoscopic surgeons. Office: Pennsylvania Hospital 700 Spruce St Ste 305 Philadelphia PA 19104 Office Phone: 215-829-3697. Office Fax: 215-829-8431.

KIRSCH, NANCY ROSENTHAL, physical therapist, educator; m. Sheldon J. Kirsch, Apr. 8, 1973; children: Rebekah Sara, Hannah Rachel, Shira Arielle, Jessica Leah, Saul Jay, Avra Miriam. BS, Temple U., Phila., 1971; MA, Montclair State U., 1977; PhD, UMDNJ, Newark, 2003; DPT in Phys. Therapy, MGH, Boston, 2005. Health care mgmt. cert. Seton Hall U., 2000. Prof. UMDNJ, phys. therapist program dir. Bd. phys. therapy examiners Divsn. Consumer Affairs-NJ, Newark, 1990—. Contbr. columns in newspapers. Pres. White Meadow Temple, Rockaway, NJ, 1992—94. Recipient Health Profl. of Yr. award, Nat. Multiple Sclerosis Soc.-NJ chpt., 2001, Master Educator Guild, UMDNJ, 2006, Lucy Blair Svc. award, Am. Phys. Therapy Assn., 2006, Pres. award, Fedn. State Bds. PT, 2008, Fedn. State Bd. Phys. Therapy, 2008; named Adopt a Doc, APTA Sect. Edn., 2002; Rsch. grant, Fedn. State Bds. PT, 2007. Mem.: Fedn. State Bds. Phys. Therapy, Fedn. State Bds. (Svc. award 2003), Am. Phys. Therapy Assn. (pres. 1979—81, Outstanding Svc. award 1982). Office Phone: 973-972-2371. Office Fax: 973-972-3717. Business E-Mail: kirschna@umdnj.edu.

KIRSCH, SCOTT DOUGLAS, family practice physician, director; b. Bronx, NY, Nov. 4, 1946; s. Max Milton Kirsch and Linda Paley Sokoloff; m. Bonnie E. Becker; children: Geoffrey Z., Laura G. BA, Queens Coll., 1967; MD, SUNY, Buffalo, 1971. Diplomate Am. Bd. Family Practice. Asst. dir. family practice residency program South Nassau Cmtys. Hosp., Oceanside, NY, 1980—82, dir., 1982—99, dir. dept. family practice, 1989—99, emeritus mem. dept. family practice, 2001—; assoc. dir. family practice residency program Southside Hosp., Bayshore, 1999—2006, Presbyn. Intercmty. Hosp., Whittier, Calif., 2006—10; faculty FP Residency Program Southside Hosp., Bay Shore, NY, 2010—. Donor Project SMILE TRAIN. Recipient award for dedication to Hispanic Cmty., Nat. Hispanic Med. Assn., 2002, legis. resolution for disting. svc., N.Y. State Senate, 1999, NY State Acad. Family Physicians, Family Practice Educator of Yr., 2005. Mem.: N.Y. State Acad. Family Physicians (pres. 2001—02, Family Practice Educator of Yr. 2005), Am. Acad. Family Physicians (del. to nat. conv. 1999—2006, mem. commn. on continuing med. edn. 2002—06, chair adv. bd. home study program 2004—06). Avocations: history, travel, baseball. Office: Southside Hosp 301 E Main St Bay Shore NY 11706 Personal E-mail: scottkirsch@roadrunner.com.

KIRSCHENBAUM, IRA H., orthopedist; b. June 30, 1957; BS magna cum laude, Brown U., 1979; MD, Albert Einstein Coll. Medicine, 1984. Intern, gen. surgery Montefiore Med. Ctr., Bronx, NY, 1984—85, resident, orthop. surgery, 1986—90; fellow, joint replacement surgery Pa. Hosp. Rothman Inst., 1990—91; attending White Plains Hosp. Ctr., NY, 1991; chief reconstructive surgery Kaiser Permanente; founding exec. dir. orthopaedics Medscape; orthopedist Westchester Orthopaedic Inst. White Plains Hosp. Ctr. Recipient Vohs Quality award, Kaiser Permanente, 1994. Mem.: Am. Bd. Orthopaedic Surgery, Bd. Arthritis Found., Am. Acad. Orthopaedic Surgeons, Orthopaedic Rsch. Soc., Am. Assn. Hip & Knee Surgeons. Office: 244 Westchester Ave Ste 205 White Plains NY 10604 Office Phone: 914-328-5111. Office Fax: 914-328-5211.

KIRSCHNER, BARBARA STARRELS, gastroenterologist; b. Phila., Mar. 23, 1941; m. Robert H. Kirschner (dec.). MD, Women's Med. Coll. Pa., 1967. Diplomate Am. Bd. Pediatrics; cert. in pediatric gastroenterology and nutrition. Intern U. Chgo., 1967-68, resident, 1968-70; mem. staff U. Chgo. Children's Hosp., 1977-83, asst. prof. pediatrics, 1984-88, prof. pediatrics and medicine, 1988—. Contbr. articles to profl. jours. Pediatric Gastroenterology fellow U. Chgo., 1975-77; recipient Davidson award in Pediatric gastroenterology Acad. Pediatrics, 1993, Joseph Brenneman award Chgo. Pediat. Soc., 2001. Mem. Am. Gastroenterologic Assn., N.Am. Soc. Pediatric Gastroenterology, Soc. Pediatric Rsch., Alpha Omega Alpha. Office: U Chgo Med Ctr 5839 S Maryland Ave # MC 4065 Chicago IL 60637-5417 Home Phone: 773-288-2299; Office Phone: 773-702-6418.

KIRSCHNER, MARC WALLACE, biochemist, cell biologist; b. Chgo., Feb. 28, 1945; BA, Northwestern U., 1966; PhD in Biochemistry, U. Calif., Berkeley, 1971. Postdoctoral rsch. U. Calif., Berkeley, U. Oxford; asst. prof. Princeton U., 1972-77, prof. biochemistry, 1977-78; prof., chmn. dept. biochemistry and biophysics U. Calif., San Francisco, 1978—93; prof., chmn. dept. cell biology Harvard U., Boston, 1993—. Adv. com. to dir. NIH. Co-author (with John C. Gerhart): Cells, Embryos, and Evolution, 1997, The Plausibility of Life: Resolving Darwin's Dilemma, 2005; contbr. articles to profl. jours. Recipient Rsch. Career Devel. award NIH, 1975-80; NSF fellow U Calif., 1971-72, Gairdner Found. Internat. award, 2001, William C. Rose award, Am. Soc. for Biochemistry and Molecular Biology, 2001. Mem. NAS (Richard Lounsberg award 1991), Am. Soc. Biol. Chemists, Am. Soc. Cell Biology (former pres.), Am. Acad. Arts and Sci., Royal Soc. London (fgn. mem.), Academia Europaea (fgn. mem.). Achievements include research in mechanism of microtubule assembly, regulation of mitosis and cell division in amphibian eggs, biophysical studies of macromolecules, embryonic induction. Office: Harvard Medical Sch Dept Systems Biology 200 Longwood Ave Boston MA 02115 Office Phone: 617-432-2250. Office Fax: 617-432-0420. Business E-Mail: marc@hms.harvard.edu. *

KIRSHENBAUM, RICHARD IRVING, retired public health physician; b. Bklyn., Aug. 19, 1933; s. Joseph and Anne (Hantman) K.; m. Jean Shicher, Aug. 17, 1957; children: Miriam, Susan, Rachel. AB, Temple U., 1955; DO, Phila. Coll. Osteo. Medicine, 1959; MPH, Columbia U., 1971. Diplomate Am. Bd. Preventive Medicine. Resident intern Met. Hosp., Phila., 1959-60; pvt. practice medicine Bklyn.,

1960-70; resident in pub. health N.Y.C. Dept. Health, 1970-73, pub. health physician, 1973-81, regional health dir. for Queens County, 1977-80, chief epidemiologist for Manhattan Borough, 1980-81; pub. health physician N.Y. State Dept. Health, NYC, 1981-98; retired, 1998. Contbr. articles to profl. jours. Lt. col. med. corps. NY Nat. Guard, 1981—91, lt. col. med. corps. USAR, 1991—93. Recipient Physician's Recognition award AMA 1973, 76, 79, 82, 85, 88, 90, 93, 96, 98. Home: 313 Whitman Dr Brooklyn NY 11234-6935 Home Phone: 718-241-6007. Personal E-mail: bd67124@optonline.net.

KIRTLEY, GEORGE E., cosmetic dentist, educator; Team dentist NBA Ind. Pacers; pvt. practice. Nat. lectr. Dentistry Today and Contemporary Esthetics; product rsch. cons. Dental Product companies; tchr. aesthetic advantage programs NYU, NYC, instr. aesthetic advantage programs, West Palm Beach Atlantic Coast Rsch. Ctr., Univ. Ky. Author: (articles) Dentistry Today and Contemporary Esthetics. Named one of America's Top Ten Cosmetic Dentist, More Mag., 2001; named to GenR8Next Dental Hall of Fame, 1999. Mem.: Acad. Gen. Dentistry, ADA, Brit. Acad. of Cosmetic Dentistry, Am. Acad. of Cosmetic Dentistry. Office: 7465 E 82nd St Indianapolis IN 46256 Office Phone: 317-841-1111.

KISCHER, CLAYTON WARD, human embryologist, educator; b. Des Moines, Mar. 2, 1930; s. Frank August and Bessie Erma (Sawtell) K.; m.Linda Sese Espejo, Nov. 7. 1964; children: Cynthia Ann, Eric Armine, Frank Henry. BS in Biology, U. Omaha, 1953; MS, Iowa State U., 1960, PhD, 1962. Asst. prof. biology Ill. State U., 1962-63; rsch. assoc. Argonne (Ill.) Nat. Lab., 1963; asst. prof. zoology Iowa State U., 1963-64; NIH postdoctoral fellow in biochemistry M.D. Anderson Hosp, Houston, 1964-66; chief sect. electron microscopy S.W. Found. Rsch. and Edn., San Antonio, 1966-67; assoc. prof. anatomy U. Tex. Med. Br., Galveston, 1967-77, U. Ariz. Coll. Medicine, Tucson, 1977—95, prof. emeritus, 1995—. Dir. Scanning electron microscopy lab. Shrine Burns Inst., Galveston, 1969-73, cons. Am. Life League, Stafford, Va., other right to life groups; chmn. Am. Bioethics Adv. Commn.; lectr. in biomed. ethics Pima C.C., 2002-05. Co-author: The Human Development Hoax: Time to Tell the Truth; author sci. and pub. policy; contbr. articles to profl. jours. Cubmaster pack 107 Island Dist., Galveston, 1974-76; bd. dirs. YMCA. With USN, 1947-49. NIH Rsch. grantee, 1968-89; Morrison Trust grantee, 1975-76. Mem. SAR, Galveston Rsch. Soc. (pres. 1971-72), Am. Soc. Cell Biology, Electron Microscopy Soc. Am., Am. Assn. Anatomists, Tex. Soc. Electron Microscopy (hon.) (editor newsletter 1969-73, pres. 1975-76), Ariz. Soc. Electron Microscopy (pres. 1980-81), Gamma Pi Sigma. Home: 6249 N Camino Miraval Tucson AZ 85718-3024 Personal E-mail: wardkischer@yahoo.com.

KISELEVA, IRINA V., virologist; b. Leningrad, Russia, Dec. 6, 1951; MS, Leningrad State U., 1974; PhD, Inst. Exptl. Medicine, St. Petersburg, Russia, ScD, 2001. Sr. rsch. scientist Inst. Exptl. Medicine, 1993—2001, leading specialist, 2001—09, sect. chief, 2009—. Cons. Merck, 2002—03, Nobilon, Netherlands, 2005—08, GPO, Thailand, 2009. Office: 12 Acad Pavlov St Saint Petersburg 197376 Russia

KISH DOTO, JULIA, healthcare educator; BS, U. Del., Newark, 1993; MS, Pa. State U., State Coll. Pa., 1995; PhD, U. Md., Coll. Pk., 2003. Health communication specialist RTI Internat., Rockville, Md., 1995—. Evaluation specialist CDC, NCI, and FDA. Recipient Pub. Health Edn. and Health Promotion Early Career award, APHA, 2009, President's award, RTI Internat., 2009. Office: RTI Internat 6110 Exec Blvd Ste 902 Rockville MD 20852 Business E-Mail: jkdoto@rti.org.

KISHIDA, YUTAKA, physician, researcher; b. Kyoto City, Japan, Feb. 19, 1949; s. Hideo and Shinako (Suma) K.; m. Taeko Kageishi, Apr. 29, 1978; children: Masashi, Yuki, Maki. MD, Nara Prefectural Med. Coll., Kashihara, Japan, 1974; PhD, Osaka U., 1982. Diplomate Japanese Bds. Internal Medicine, Gastroenterology, Hepatology, Oriental Medicine, Gastroenterol. Endoscopy, Occpl. Environ. Medicine. Rsch. trainee Osaka U. Med. Sch., 1974-77; med. staff Osaka U.Med. Sch., 1976-82; med. staff internal medicine Osaka Prefectural Hosp., 1974-76, chief med. staff internal medicine, 1982-83; head med. staff in internal medicine Shin-Senri Hosp., Suita, Japan, 1983-85; subhead of internal medicine Osaka Rousai Hosp., Sakai, Japan, 1985-92, acting head of gastroenterology, 1992—94; head gastroent. endoscopy Osaka Kousei Nennkin Hosp., 1992-94; med. dir. Japan Tobacco Inc./Ctr. Preventive Medicine, Osaka, 1994—2009; vice-head dept. internal medicine Ikeda Kaisei Hosp., Osaka, Japan, 2009—10; dir. dept. internal medicine gastroenterology hepatology Osaka Kaisel Hosp., 2010—. Dir. Uemachidai Liver Conf. Group, Osaka, 1993—; lectr. Senri Nursing Sch., Suita, 1983-85, Osaka Rousai Hosp. Nursing Sch., 1985-92; assoc. staff in internal medicine Osaka Kousei Nennkin Hosp., 1994-2003, assoc. staff in gastroenterology, 2008-; cons. Unitika Co. Ltd. Med. Inst., 1983—; assoc. staff gastroenterology Osaka Prefectural Gen. Med. Ctr., 2003-08, assoc. staff. in Gastroentrology Osaka Kaiser Hosp., 2008-. Contbr. articles to profl. jours. Mem. AAAS (internat. mem.), Am. Gastroenterol. Assn. (internat. mem.), Japan Soc. Internal Medicine, Japan Soc. Gastroenterology, Japan Soc. Hepatology, Japan Soc. Gastroenterol. Endoscopy, Japan Soc. Biochemistry, Japan Soc. Ultrasonics in Medicine, Japanese Cancer Assn., Japan Soc. Occupational Health, NY Acad. Scis., Am. Assn. Advancing Sci. (internat. mem.), Am. Gastroenterol. Assn. (internat.), Asian Pasific Assn. For Study Of Liver (internat. mem.) Buddhist. Avocations: skiing, mountain climbing, walking, art, reading. Home: 66 Uguisu Dai Nagaokakyo Kyoto 617 0815 Japan Office: Osaka Kaisei Hosp 1-6-10 Miyahara Yodogawa Osaka 532 0003 Japan Office Phone: 81-6-6393-6234. Business E-Mail: y-kishida@muse.ocn.ne.jp.

KISHIMOTO, TADAMITSU, medical educator; b. Tondabayashi, Osaka, Japan, May 7, 1939; s. Tadanobu and Yasuko Kishimoto; m. Chizuko Tamura, Nov. 4, 1967. MD, Osaka U. Med. Sch., Japan, 1964, PhD in Medicine, 1969. Rsch. fellow Johns Hopkins U. Sch. Medicine, Balt., 1970—73, asst. prof., 1973—74; asst. prof., dept. medicine Osaka U. Med. Sch., 1974—79, prof. pathology and medicine, 1979-83, prof. immunology, 1983-91, prof., chmn. medicine, 1991-98, emeritus prof., dean, 1995-97, pres., 1997—2003; prof. Inst. for Molecular and Cellular Biology, Osaka, 1983—91. Vis. prof. Lab Immune Regulation Grad. Sch. Frontier Biosciences, Osaka U. 2003-; mem. Coun. for Sci. and Tech. Policy at the Cabinet Office, adj prof. Memorial Sloan Kettering Cancer Ctr., Inst. for Virus Rsch., Kyoto U.; chair 7th Internat. Congress on AIDS in Asia and the Pacific, 2005; lectr. in field. Contbr. several articles to peer-reviewed jours.; mem. of several editl. bds. Decorated The Order of Culture, 1998; recipient Osaka Sci. prize, 1983, Asahi prize, 1988, Person of Cultural Merit award, 1990, Imperial prize Japan Acad., 1992, Sandoz prize for immunology, 1992, Robert Koch Gold medal 2003, Erwin Von Balz Prize, Takeda Prize, Asahi Prize; co-recipient Crafoord prize in Polyarthritis, Royal Swedish Acad. Sciences, 2009, Japan prize, 2011. Mem. NAS (fgn. assoc.), Japan Acad., Japan Soc. for Immunology (pres. 1991-92, coun.), Japanese Soc. Allegology (coun.), Internat. Soc. for Immunopharmacology (pres. 1991-94), Internat. Cytokine Soc. (pres. 1994-95), Am. Assn. Immunologists (hon.), Am. Soc. Hematology (hon.), Internat. Myeloma Found. (mem. Scientific Adv. Bd.). Achievements include discovery in interleukin 6; pioneering work with collegues to isolate interleukins, determine their properties and explore their role in the onset of inflammatory disease. Office: Immunology Frontier Rsch Ctr Osaka University 3-1 Yamada Oka Suita City Osaka 565 0871 Japan Office Phone: 81-6-6879-4431, 81 6 6879 4956. Office Fax: 81-6-6879-4437. Business E-Mail: kishimoto@ifec.osaka-u.ac.jp. E-mail: kishimot@imed3.med.osaka-u.ac.jp.

KISHINO, TOMONORI, internist, researcher; b. Musashino, Tokyo, Japan, Dec. 1, 1964; MD, Yamanashi Med. Coll., 1991; PhD, Kyorin U., 1999. Lic. Dr. Japan, 1991. Resident in gastroenterology and hepatology, dept. internal medicine Kyorin U. Sch. Medicine, Tokyo, 1991—93, staff physician, instr. in gastroenterology and hepatology, dept. internal medicine, 1997—2001, instr. ultrasonography medicine, gastroenterology and hepatology, dept. lab. medicine, 2001—04, asst. prof. ultrasonography medicine, lab. medicine, gastroenterology and hepatology, dept. lab. medicine, 2004—; resident, dept. internal medicine Cardiovasc. Inst. Hosp., Tokyo, 1993—94; staff radiologist, dept. radiology Tokyo Met. Geriatric Hosp., 1994—97. Investigator Tokyo Met. Inst. Gerontology, 1995—97. Contbr. scientific papers, articles to profl. jours. Fellow: Japanese Soc. Gastroenterology, Japanese Soc. Internal Medicine; mem.: Japan Soc. Lab. Medicine. Achievements include research in lipids. Office: Dept Lab Medicine Kyorin Univ 6-20-2 Shinkawa Mitaka Tokyo 181-8611 Japan Office Fax: +81 422 79 3471. Business E-Mail: kishino@kyorin-u.ac.jp.

KISHORE, BELLAMKONDA KRISHNA, biomedical researcher, educator; b. Visakhapatnam, India, Aug. 2, 1953; arrived in U.S., 1993; s. Dharma Rao and Kamala Devi Bellamkonda; m. Ratnavathi Rolla, Feb. 24, 1989; children: Satya, Dharma. MBBS, Sri Venkateswara U., Tirupathi, India, 1975; MD, Banaras Hindu U., Varanasi, India, 1980; PhD in Biomedical Scis., Cath. U. Louvain, Brussels, 1990; MBA, U. Utah, 2009. Prof. medicine, physiology Ctr. Aging, U. Utah Health Scis. Ctr., Salt Lake City; prin. investigator VA Salt Lake City Health Care Sys., Salt Lake City. Mem. editl. bd. Am. Jour. Physiology, Open Urology and Nephrology Jour.; expert reviewer med. jours. Recipient Citation award, European Biog. Directory. Fellow: Am. Soc. Nephrology, Inst. Biology (chartered biologist 1988); mem.: Faculty 1000 Biology (renal fluid & electrolyte physiology mem. 2008—), Nat. Kidney Found., Internat. Soc. Nephrology, Soc. Nephrology, Am. Heart Assn. (coun. kidney in cardiovasc. diseases 2008—), Am. Physiol. Soc., Smithsonian Inst. (assoc.). Hindu. Achievements include patents for therapies; innovative therapies for erythropoietin-responsive anemia and water balance disorders. Avocations: photography, writing, art, travel, philosophy. Office: U Utah Health Scis Ctr 50 N Medical Dr Rm 4R312 Salt Lake City UT 84132 Business E-Mail: BK.Kishore@hsc.utah.edu.

KISIS, JANIS, dermatologist, consultant; b. Riga, Latvia, Dec. 23, 1956; s. Janis Roberts Kisis and Irena Kise; m. Ligija Kise, Sept. 10, 1976; children: Janis, Martinsh. BA, Riga Med. Inst., 1975, MBA, 1981. Nursing asst. P. Stradina Clin. Hosp., Riga, 1972—74, asst. med. advisor outpatient dept. skin and sexual diseases, 1981—82, venerologist, head outpatient dept., 1986—88, v.p. advisors, 1988—97, surgeon, 1997—. Lectr. Med. H.S. on Dermatology, Riga, 1982—86, Riga Med. Inst., 1988—; assoc. prof. Riga Stradina U. (formerly Latvian Med. Acad.), 2002. Author: Syphilis Mortality in Latvia, 1999, Epidemiology of Syphilis, 2000, Tuberculosis Eruptical, 2000. Asst. com. European Acad. Dermatology and Venerology, Latvia, 1997; bd. dirs. Acad. Dermatology and Venerology, Baltic Dermatology Assn., Latvian Dermatology Assn. Lt. Latvian armed forces. Recipient named honored lectr., Latvia Sci. Soc., 1982—92; grantee, EADV, 1993—94. Mem.: Lativa Assn. Dermatology (pres. 1999), Eruopean Dermatol. Acad., Basketball Club (bd. dirs. 1995). Lutheran. Avocations: fishing, sports, literature, art, travel. Home and Office: Kr Baroma 40-6 1011 Riga Latvia E-mail: kisis@namatevs.lv.

KISLAL, FATIH MEHMET, pediatrician, researcher; b. Turkey; m. Gülgün Kislal. Degree in Pediats., Hacettepe U., Ankara, 2003. Faculty, medicine Hacettepe U., 1985—93; cons. malpractice com. Ministry of Health, Ankara, 2007—. Author: Pediatrics International, Clinical Pediatrics. Mem.: WHO (translator com.), Nat. Pediat. Assn. Personal E-mail: fatihkislal@gmail.com.

KISO, YOSHINOBU, research scientist; b. Hanno, Saitama, Japan, Oct. 17, 1953; PhD, Tohoku U., 1983. Chief planning officer Suntory Ltd. Inst. Health Care Sci., 2002—09; exec. gen. mgr., chief planning officer Inst. Health Care Sci., Suntory Wellness Ltd., 2009—, sr. specialist, 2011—. Mem.: Japanese Soc. Nutrition and Food Sci., Japan Soc. Biosci., Biotech., and Agrochemistry. Avocation: hiking. Office: 1-1-1 Wakayamadai Shimamoto-cho Mishima Osaka 618-8503 Japan Office Fax: 81-75-962-1690. Business E-Mail: yoshinobu_kiso@suntory.co.jp.

KISS, ISTVAN, geneticist, biologist, researcher; b. Pápa, Hungary, May 29, 1943; s. Istvan and Vilma Kiss; m. Enikõ Kuthy; children: Enikõ, Istvan, Gergely. PhD, U. Szeged, Hungary, 1966. Sci. investigator Biol. Rsch. Ctr., Szeged, 1981—98, sci. advisor, 1999—curr. Contbr. articles to profl. jours. Scholar Internat. Rsch., Howard Hughes Med. Inst., 1995. Mem.: AAAS. Office: Biol Rsch Ctr PO Box 521 H-6701 Szeged Hungary Office Phone: (36)(62)599 686. Business E-Mail: kiss43@brc.hu.

KISSLER, HERBERT, physician, researcher; b. Butzbach, Hesse, Germany, July 14, 1946; s. Wilhelm and Herta Kissler; m. Gabriele Hager, Dec. 22, 1972; children: Simone, Daniel-Benjamin, Julia. MD, U. Freiburg im Breisgau, Germany, 1974. Lic. Regierungspräsidium, Stuttgart, Baden-Würtemberg. Med. practitioner U. Giessen, Germany, 1975—76; asst. physician, intern Bundeswehrkrankenhaus, Giessen, 1977—78; gen. practitioner Butzbach, Germany, 1980—. Assoc. mem. Soc. for Exptl. Biology and Medicine, NY, 2001. Contbr. articles to profl. jours. Achievements include a comparison of the old map of malaria with the geographic distribution of Multiple Sclerosis led to a reevaluation of the former idea of a malarial cause of MS. Avocations: philosophy of science, history of medical thought. Home: Holzheimerstrasse 57 35510 Butzbach Germany Home Phone: 06033-64997. E-mail: herbert_kissler@gmx.de.

KISZKA, SONIA ANN, nurse practitioner, educator; b. NYC, Apr. 4, 1938; d. Hermann William and Gertrude (Hohensteiner) Schumann; m. David F. Madden, Feb. 16, 1957 (div. Oct. 1975); children: David F., Michael P., Daniel J., Lisa M.; m. Lawrence F. Kiszka, Nov. 27, 1975; stepchildren: Lawrence V., Patricia, Valerie. AAS in Nursing cum laude, Maria Coll., Albany, NY, 1973; BS cum laude, Skidmore Coll., 1991; MEd, St. Michael's Coll., Colchester, Vt., 1995. Nat. cert. nurse practitioner in adult medicine, physician asst. Intensive/critical care nurse, dept. medicine Ellis Hosp., Schenectady, NY, 1979-80, nurse practitioner dept. medicine, 1980-82, dir employee/student health svcs., 1982-85; asst. dir. health svc., health educator Skidmore Coll., Saratoga Springs, NY, 1985-89, dir. Health and Wellness Ctr., 1997—2000; dir. health svcs., health educator St. Michael's Coll., 1989-97, GlaxoSmithkline Pharmaceuticals Vaccine Divsn., Phila., 2000—04; P.N. program coord., asst. prof. nursing Maria Coll., Albany, NY, 2004—07. Cons., spkr. in field. Contbr. articles to profl. jours. Bd. dirs. N.Y. State Coalition Nurse Practitioners, 1985-90, 98—, pres. Saratoga/Warren/Washington chpt., 1998—2004; bd. dirs. New England Coll. Health Assn., 1994-97; active Vt. State HIV/AIDS Task Force. Recipient award for HIV/AIDS edn., Vt. Dept. Health/Dept. Edn., 1995. Mem. Vt. State Nurses Assn. (bd. dirs. 1990-93), Am. Coll. Health Assn. (Vt. rep., chair task force on campus violence, rep./spkr. internat. conf. on sexual assault on campus), New Eng. Coll. Health Assn. (bd. dirs. 1994-97), Vt. Nurse Practitioners Assn. (v.p. 1991-92), Nat. Commn. Certification Physician Assts., NY State Coll. Health Assn. (chair Capital Region 1999-2000), NY State Coalition Nurse Practitioners, NY State Physician Asst. Assn. Roman Catholic. Avocations: needlecrafts, swimming, travel. Home Phone: 518-580-1982. Fax: 518-580-2339.

KITA, ETSUKO, health facility administrator; b. Hyogo, Japan, Aug. 18, 1939; MD, Nara Med. U., 1965, PhD, 1976. Chief project officer health and nutrition UNICEF Afghan Programme Office, 1988—90; dir. expert svc. Internat. Med. Ctr. Japan, 1992—97; chief field support EHA WHO, 1997—99, prof. Japanese Red Cross Kyushu Internat. Coll. Nursing, 2001—04, pres., 2005—. Mem. dean's com. Johns Hopkins U. Sch. Pub. Health, 1999—; vis. prof. Grad. Sch. Waseda U., 1999—2006; advisor JBIC and JICA, 2000—09; mem. tech. evaluation reference group Global Fund, 2003—05. Recipient Gt. award, Avon, Yomiuri Med. Svc. award, Yomiuri Newspaper, Sen Kayoko Internat. award, Internat. Soroptimist Japan; nominee Women Courage award, US Embassy Tokyo. Mem.: NY Acad. Sci., Carnegie Coun., Japanese Assn. Internat. Health. Avocation: reading. Office: 1 Asty Munakata Fukuoka 811-4157 Japan Office Fax: 81 940 35 7021. Business E-Mail: et-kita@jrckicn.ac.jp.

KITA, TOSHIHIRO, medical researcher; b. Saito, Miyazaki, Japan, Aug. 30, 1960; MD, Miyazaki Med. Coll., 1985, PhD, 1991. Postdoctoral fellow Monsanto Corp. Rsch., St. Louis, 1992—95; asst. U. Miyazaki, Japan, 1998—. Contbr. articles to profl. jours. Fellow: Japanese Soc. Hypertension. Achievements include discovery of human uroguanylin. Office: Univ Miyazaki 5200 Kihara Kiyotake Miyazaki 889 1692 Japan Office Fax: 81-985-85-6596. Business E-Mail: t-kita@po.sphere.ne.jp.

KITADAI, HUMBERTO KEN, cardiologist; b. Sao Paulo, Brazil, July 25, 1958; MD, CCMB PUC-SP, 1981; PhD, UNIFESP, 2002. Assoc. prof. orthop and traum. dept. UNISA-Med. Sch., 1985—2001. Mem.: Nucleo de Estudos em Ortopedia e Traumatologia, IMA (Keio), Soc. Brasileira de Ortopedia e Traumatologia. Home: Av Manoel Reis Araujo 953 São Paulo 04664-000 Brazil Personal E-mail: hkitadai@uol.com.br.

KITAGAKI, HIROSHI, microbiologist, researcher; s. Tadahisa and Yoko Kitagaki, Tsuyoshi (Stepfather) and Etsuko Morikami (Stepmother); m. Naomi Morikami; children: Ryota, Kazuma, Yuto. B in Agrl., U. Tokyo, 1993, M in Agrl., 1995, PhD, 2004. Protein rschr. U. Tokyo, 1993—95; brewing analyst Osaka Regional Taxation Bur., Japan, 1996—2000; brewing microbiologist Nat. Rsch. Inst. Brewing, Higashihiroshima, Japan, 2001—; sphingolipid rschr. Med. U. SC, Charleston, 2005—06; brewing microbiologist Nat. Rsch. Inst. Brewing, Higashihiroshima City, 2006—. Author: (textbook) Complex Microbial Flora During Brewing, 2004, The Mechanism of Ethanol-induced Death of Yeast and Its Potential Application for Formentation Industry, 2008; contbr. scientific papers in field. Recipient Young Investigator award, Japanese Soc. Brewing, 1999, Soc. Biotech. Japan, Found. Agrl. Scis. Japan, 2008, Most Impressive Presentation award, Japan Soc. Biosci., Biotech., 2007, Young Scientists prize, Mister Edn., Culture, Sports, Sci. and Tech. Mem.: Nat. Rsch. Inst. Brewing (corr.). Achievements include discovery of role, existence and dynamics of yeast mitochondria during alcohol fermentation; the mechanism of production of antioxidant activity of sake during sake brewing; a novel glycosylphosphatidyglinositol-anchored protein involved in cell wall biosynthesis of saccharomyces cerevisiae; the dynamics of cell wall protein dependent on the culture conditions in saccharomyces cerevisiae; patents for a new method of treating active carbon before applying to foods and drinks; research in elucidated the activation mechanism of calpain protease family, one of which is responsible for muscle dystrophy; elucidated the biosynthesis pathway of sphingolipid in mitochondria; development of mitochondria-targeted breeding system of brewerg geasts. Office: Natl Saga U Faculty Agriculture Honjo-cho 1 Saga City Saga 840-8502 Japan Office Fax: 81 952288709. Business E-Mail: ktgkhrs@cc.saga-u.ac.jp.

KITAGAWA, MASANOBU, medical educator; b. Yokohama, Sept. 28, 1956; MD, Tokyo Med. and Dental U., 1981, PhD, 1985. Prof. Tokyo Med. and Dental U., 2005—. Mem.: Japanese Cancer Assn., Japanese Soc. Pathology (Rsch. Encouragement award). Office: 1-5-45 Yushima Bunkyo Tokyo 113-8519 Japan Office Fax: 03-5803-0123. Business E-Mail: masa.pth2@tmd.ac.jp.

KITAGAWA, TORU, surgeon, researcher; b. Takatsuki, Osaka, Japan, Nov. 26, 1960; s. Akira and Miyoko Kitagawa. MD, PhD, Osaka U., 1989. Cert. Japan Surg. Soc., 2004. Surgeon Kure Nat. Hosp., Hiroshima, Japan, 1990—96; vis. rsch. instr. U. Pitts., 1996—99; assoc. prof. Osaka U., Suita, 1999—. Contbr. articles to profl. jours. Grantee, Japan Soc. for Promotion of Sci., 2000, 2003,

2005. Mem.: Japan Soc. Clin. Oncology (coun. mem. 2001—). Achievements include research in anti-cancer drug sensitivity test; cancer gene therapy. Avocation: tennis. Office: Osaka Univ 2-2-E1 Yamadaoka Osaka Suita 565-0871 Japan

KITAHARA, SHIZUO, allergist; b. Tokyo, Nov. 20, 1922; s. Buntaro and Tamiko K.; m. Yoko Kitahara, April 19, 1931; 1 child, Taeko. MD, Tokyo U., 1945. Intern and resident Tokyo U. Hosp., 1946-56; chief allergist Doai Meml. Hosp., Tokyo, 1956-69; CEO Allergy Clinic, Tokyo, 1969—. Author: Treatment of Bronchial Asthma, 1985, Cure for Asthmatic Patients, 1994, Treatment for Bronchial Asthma, Atopic Dermatitis, Up-date, 2000, Bronchial Asthma & Allergy, 2000, Cure Bronchial Asthma, 2007. Fellow Japan Allergy Soc.; mem. Am. Coll. Allergists, Am. Acad. Allergists, NY Acad. Sci. Avocation: music. Home: 32-20 Minami-Ogikubo 4 Suginami-ku Tokyo 167 Japan Office: Allergy Clinic 11-18 Kita-Otsuka 1 Tokyo 170 Japan Office Phone: 81339404769. Business E-Mail: tkshiz@blue.b-city.net.

KITAMI, MASAHIRO, radiologist, researcher; b. Kitakata-City, Fukushima-Prefecture, Japan, Dec. 15, 1973; m. Maki Kitami, Mar. 4, 2001; children: Yuma, Miyu. M in Med. Sci., Tohoku U., Sendai, Miyagi, Japan, 1998, PhD in Med. Sci., 2004. Radiological specialist Japan Radiol. Soc., 2006. Radiologist Ishinomaki Red-Cross Hosp., Ishinomaki-City, Japan, 1998—2000, sub-chief radiologist, 2007—09; dr., dept. diagnostic radiology Tohoku U. Hosp., Sendai-City, Japan, 2001—04; radiologist Takeda-General Hosp., Aizu-Wakamatsu-City, Japan, 2005—07; chief radiologist Miyogi Children's Hosp., Sendai City, Japan, 2010—. Contbr. articles to profl. jours. Recipient Cyber-Poster award, Japan Radiol. Soc., 2005, Platinum Medal award, 2006, Itai award, 2006. Mem.: Japan Colleage Radiology. Avocations: tanka, travel. Home: 3-5-29 Kashiwagi Aobaku Sendai Miyagi 981-0933 Japan Office Fax: 81 22 717 7316. Business E-Mail: mshkitami@rad.med.tohoku.ac.jp.

KITAMURA, HIRONORI, anatomist, educator; b. Fukuyama, Japan, Dec. 18, 1920; s. Yukichi and Masa (Mitsunari) K.; m. Mitsuko Yasuda, Dec. 25, 1948; children: Akihide, Emi. DDS, Tokyo Med. Dental U., 1942, D in Med. Sci., 1960; BA in Psychology, Nippon Mgmt. U., 1972; PhD, Union U., 1984. Pvt. practice, Fukuyama, Japan, 1946-55; asst. prof. Tokyo Med. and Dental U., 1956-61; rsch. assoc. dental sch. U. Wash., Seattle, 1961-63; rsch. assoc. cleft palate rsch. ctr. U. Pitts., 1963-65; prof. anatomy Kanagawa Dental Coll., Yokosuka, Japan, 1965-88, prof. emeritus, 1988—. Oral anatomy educator Sch. Dental Hygienists, Hiratsuka, Japan, 1987-97. Author: Atlas of Developmental Anatomy of Face, 1966, Embryology of Mouth and Related Structures, 1989; author, editor: Color Atlas of Human Oral Histology, 1992, Oral Embryology and Pathohistology, 1998, Dental Malformations and Pathohistology, 1998, Human Soul and Body: One Spirti with Four-souls, 1999. Mem. Japanese Assn. Anatomists (councillor 1956—), Japanese Assn. Oral Biologists (councillor 1965—). Home: Minami-ku Nagata Higashi 3-8-5 #406 Yokohama 232-0072 Japan

KITAMURA, MITSUTAKA, physician, educator; b. Matsuyama, Apr. 1, 1946; M, Kyoto U., 1970, D, 1978. Prof., physician U. Hyogo, 2005—. Home: 665-7 Minamikume-cho Matsuyama Ehime 790-0924 Japan Home Fax: 089-907-0468. Personal E-mail: kitamuralabo@energy.ocn.ne.jp.

KITAMURA, NAOTO, physician, educator; b. Japan, Apr. 11, 1971; MD, Keio U. Sch. Medicine, PhD, 1996. Asst. prof. Keio U., Sch. Medicine, 2004. Recipient Young Investigator's award, EASL. Avocations: skiing, golf. Home: 217 E 96th St Apt #23B New York NY 10128 Business E-Mail: yib03642@nifty.com.

KITAMURA, TOSHINORI, psychiatrist; b. Yokohama, Kanagawa, Japan, Oct. 16, 1947; s. Masanori and Kikuko (Matsumoto) K.; m. Fusako Oami, Mar. 17, 1973. MD, Keio Gijuku U., Tokyo, 1972. Psychiatrist Inst. Psychiatry, Tokyo, 1973-76; hon. rsch. fellow U. Birmingham, England, 1976-80; clin. instr. Keio Gijuku U., Tokyo, 1980-83, lectr., 1983; chief sect. mental health for elderly NIMH, Ichikawa, Japan, 1983-91, dir. dept. sociocultural environ. rsch., 1991-2000; prof., head dept. clin. behavioural scis. Kumamoto (Japan) U. Sch. Medicine, 2000—10, Kitamura Inst. Mental Health Tokyo, 2010—; disting. vis. prof. Wash. U. Sch. Medicine, 2011. Vis. lectr. Keio Gijuku U., 1986—; head Group for Rsch. Assessment in Psychiatry, Tokyo, 1981—; mem. com. Med. Selection Japanese Astronauts, 1987-88, 95-96, com. Psychiat. Diagnostic Criteria Japan, 1987-89, com. Guideline for Psychiat. Treatment, 1987-88. Editor-in-chief Archives of Psychiat. Diagnostics and Clin. Evaluation, Tokyo, 1989-91; editor Brit. Jour. Psychiatry, 1994-97, Internat. Jour. Behavioral Medicine, 1994-97, Internat. Jour. Offender Therapy Comparative Criminology, 1998—, Arch. Women's Mental Health, 1998—2010; contbr. articles to profl. jours. including Brit. Jour. Psychiatry, Psychol. Medicine, Jour. Affective Disorder, others. Fellow: Japanese Assn. Psychiatry and Neurology (coun. 1991—94), Brit. Coun. Japan Assn., Royal Coll. Psychiatrists. Home: 305 Akasaka 8-12-4 Minato Tokyo 107 0052 Japan Office: Kitamura Inst Mental Health 101 Akasaka 8-5-13 Minato Tokyo 107 0052 Japan Office Phone: 81-3-6804-5662. Business E-Mail: kitamura@institute-if.mental.health.jp.

KITAZONO, MASAKI, physician; b. Kagoshima, Sept. 21, 1965; MD, PhD, 1989. Physician dept. digestive surgery Kagoshima U., 1989—, asst. prof., 2004—11. Home: Arata 1-32-6 Kagoshima 890-0054 Japan Personal E-mail: curan55@gmail.com.

KITOH, HIDEAKI, physician, researcher; b. Ube, Yamaguchi, Japan, Mar. 6, 1974; s. Masaaki and Yoshiko Kitoh; m. Tomoko Hatabe, Aug. 19, 2002; 1 child, Chisato. PhD, Yamaguchi U., 1999. Physician Yamaguchi U. Sch. Medicine, Ube, Japan, 1999—2000, 2001—05, Ube Central Hosp., 2000—01, 2005—. Mem.: Japanese Cancer Assn. (assoc.), Japanese Soc. Internal Medicine (assoc.), Japan Gastroent. Endoscopy Soc. (assoc.), Japanese Soc. Gastroenterology (assoc.). Achievements include research in genetic alterations of pancreatic cancers using cells obtained by endoscopic ultrasonography guided by fine needle aspiration before surgery. Avocations: Karate, guitar. Home: Nishikiwa 2504-2 Ube Yamaguchi 755 0151 Japan Office: Ube Central Hosp Nishikiwa 750 Ube Yamaguchi 755-0151 Japan Personal E-mail: kitoh916@c-able.ne.jp.

KITRIDOU, RODANTHI C., medical educator; b. Almyros, Greece, Oct. 6, 1938; d. Constantin D. Kitridis and Eudoxia C. Kitridou. MD, U. Athens, Greece, 1962. Diplomate internal med & rheumatology Am. Bd. Internal Med., 1972. Assoc. prof. medicine U. Southern Calif. Sch. Medicine, LA, 1975—89, prof. medicine, 1989—2005, prof. emerita medicine, 2005—. Contbr. articles to profl. jours., chapters to books. With CARES, 2006. Col. Am. Med., 1985—2000, LA. Master: Am. Coll. Rheumatology (regional pres., com. 1996—97); fellow: ACP. Greek Orthodox. E-mail: kitridou@usc.edu.

KITSOS, CONSTANTINE NICHOLAS, plastic surgeon; b. Athens, Greece, Aug. 10, 1938; came to U.S., 1946; s. Nicholas E. and Bessie N. Kitsos; children: Katie, Kristina, Nicholas, Kevin. BA, U. Wash., 1960, MD, 1964. Diplomate Am. Bd. Surgery, Am. Bd. Plastic Surgery. Intern U. Miami, 1964-65, gen. surg. resident; resident in plastic surgery Loyola U.; pvt. practice Miami, Fla., 1973—; chief staff Highland Park Gen. Hosp., Miami, Fla., North Shore Med. Ctr., Miami, 2000—03; staff North Shore Med. Ctr. & Drs. Hosp. Capt. M.C., U.S. Army, 1965-67. Mem. Am. Soc. Plastic Surgeons. Greek Orthodox. Office: 9000 NE 2d Ave Miami FL 33138

KITTISUPAMONGKOL, WEEKITT, physician; b. Bangkok, Sept. 25, 1983; s. Wirat Kittisupamongkol and Sae Chua Tuangtip. MD, Chulalongkorn U., Bangkok, 2007. Gen. practitioner Surin Hosp., Aumpur Muang, Surin, Thailand, 2007—08, Hua Chiew Hosp., Pomprap, 2008—. Assoc. editor Jour. Med. Case Report, 2008—; academic editor in chief World Jour. Gastroenterology, 2010—. Contbr. articles to profl. med. jours. (BMJ Endgame Competition Winner, 2008). Office: Hua Chiew Hosp 665 Bumrungmuang Rd Bangkok Pomprap 10100 Thailand Home: Yaowaraj Rd Talad Kao 251 10100 Bangkok Sumpantawong, Bangkok Thailand Personal E-mail: weekitti@gmail.com.

KITTLE, CHARLES FREDERICK, surgeon; b. Athens, Ohio, Oct. 24, 1921; s. Frederick F. and Ida (Falls) K.; m. Jeane Mignon Groenier, 1945 (div. 1973); children: Candace Mignon, Bradley Dean, Leslie Jeane, Brian David; m. Ann Catherine Bates, 1981. AB with honors, Ohio U., Athens, 1942, LLD, 1967; MD with honors, U. Chgo., 1945; MS in Surgery, U. Kans., 1950. Diplomate Am. Bd. Surgery, Am. Bd. Thoracic Surgery (mem. bd. 1967-75, chmn. 1973-75). Intern U. Chgo. Clinics, 1945-46; resident gen. and thoracic surgery U. Kans. Med. Center, 1948-52; spl. tng. radio-isotopes for med. use Oak Ridge Inst. Nuclear Studies, 1950, cons. med. div., 1950-55; mem. faculty U. Kans. Sch. Medicine, 1950-66; assoc. prof. surgery, lectr. history medicine, 1959-66; cons. thoracic surgery VA Hosp., Wadsworth, Kans., 1954-57, cons. gen. surgery, 1957-60; attending gen. surgery VA Hosp. Kansas City, Mo., 1954-66, Wichita, Kans., 1955-62; prof. surgery, head sect. thoracic and cardiovascular surgery U. Chgo. Clinics, 1966-72; prof. surgery, dir. thoracic surgery sect. Rush Med. Coll. and Presbyn.-St. Luke's Hosp., 1973-92, prof. emeritus, 1992—; dir. Rush Cancer Ctr., 1978-86; mem. staff McNeal Hosp., Berwyn, Ill., 1986-92. Cons. Mcpl. TB Sanatorium, Chgo., 1968-74, Hines VA Hosp., Maywood, Ill., 1973-92; spl. rsch. cardiovascular surgery, control of blood flow. Life trustee Chgo. Served as lt. (j.g.) USNR, 1946-48. Recipient Konneker award Ohio U., 2004; clin. fellow Am. Cancer Soc., 1950-52; Markle scholar med. scis., 1952-58. Mem. AAAS, ACS (bd. dirs. Kans. 1965-68), Am. Assn. History Medicine, Am. Assn. Thoracic Surgery, Am. Coll. Cardiology (bd. dirs. Kans. 1963-66), Chgo. Surg. Soc. (pres. 1972-73), Am. Heart Assn. (chmn. program com. cardiovasc. surgery 1965-88, exec. com. cardiovasc. surgery coun. 1962-74, chmn. coun. 1972-74), Am. Physiol. Assn., Cen. Surg. Soc., Chgo. Med. Soc., Am. Surg. Assn., Internat. Cardiovasc. Soc. (sec. 1965-71), Internat. Soc. Surgery, Soc. Med. Hist. (pres. Chgo. 1983-85), N.J. Thoracic Surgery Soc., Ill. Thoracic Surgery Soc. (pres. 1983-84), Soc. Clin. Surgery, Soc. Surg. Oncology, Soc. Vascular Surgery, Soc. U. Surgeons (pres. 1966-67), Soc. Thoracic Surgery, U. Village Assn. (bd. dirs. 1986-89, pres. 1989), Arthur Conan Doyle Soc., Caxton Club (pres. 1999-2001), Chgo. Literary Club, Hounds of Baskerville, Baker Street Irregulars, Grolier Club, Phi Beta Kappa, Sigma Xi, Alpha Omega Alpha, Newberry Libr. (life; trustee, 2001-). Home: 811 S Lytle St Apt 510 Chicago IL 60607-4152 Office Phone: 312-243-4310. E-mail: kittle856@mindspring.com.

KITZ, RICHARD JOHN, anesthesiologist, educator; b. Oshkosh, Wis., Mar. 25, 1929; s. Edward G. and Lona M (Schneider) Kitz; m. Jeanne Hogan, Feb. 27, 1954; 1 child, Anne Marie. BS, Marquette U., Milw., 1951, MD, 1954, DSc (hon.), 2000; MA (hon.), Harvard U. Med. Sch., Cambridge, Mass., 1969. Diplomate Am. Bd. Anesthesiology (dir.). From intern in surgery to assoc. prof. Columbia U., 1954—66, assoc. prof., 1966—69; prof. rsch. and tchg. in anesthesia Harvard U.-MIT, co-dir. divsn. health scis. tech., 1985—91; anaesthetist-in-chief Mass. Gen. Hosp., Boston, 1969—94; from prof. to prof. Med. Sch. Harvard U., 1969—2004, prof. emeritus, 2004—. Prin. investigator Harvard Anaesthesia Rsch. and Rsch. Tng. Ctr., 1969—93. Editor: This is No Humbug! Reminiscences of the Department of Anesthesia at the Massachusetts General Hospital, 2002; editor: (with E.M. Papper) Uptake and Distribution of Anesthetic Agents, 1963; editor: (with M.B. Laver) Sci. Basis of Anesthesia; editor-in-chief Jour. Clin. Anesthesia, 1987—95; contbr. articles to profl. jours. With M.C. USN, 1955—57. Fellow: Coll. Anesthesiologists; mem.: Royal Coll. Surgeons Ireland (hon. mem. faculty anesthetists), Mass. Soc. Anesthesiologists, Am. Soc. Anesthesiologists, Royal Coll. Anesthetists Eng. (hon.), Japan Soc. Anesthesiologists (hon.), German Soc. Anesthesiologists and Intensive Care (hon.), Australian Soc. Anesthetists (hon.), Assn. Univ. Anesthetists, Inst. Medicine, NAS. Roman Catholic. Office: Mass Gen Hosp Dept Anesthesia Boston MA 02114 Home: 10 Longwood Dr Apt 419 Westwood MA 02090-1144 Business E-Mail: richard_kitz@hms.harvard.edu.

KITZES, JUDITH, medical educator; b. Mpls., Nov. 12, 1945; MD, Drexel U., 1974; MPH, Harvard Sch. Pub. Health, 1980. Chief med. officer USPHS Indian Health Svc., 1980—; assoc. prof. internal medicine, palliative care U. N.Mex. Sch. Medicine, 2001—. Decorated Disting. Svc. medals USPHS. Mem.: Am. Assn. Hospice and Palliative Medicine. Avocations: walking, reading. Office: MSC11 6020 1 University New Mex Albuquerque NM 87108 Business E-Mail: jkitzes@salud.unm.edu.

KITZHABER, JOHN ALBERT, Governor of Oregon, emergency physician; b. Colfax, Wash., Mar. 5, 1947; s. Albert Raymond and Annabel Reed (Wetzel) K.; m. Sharon Lacroix (div. 2003); 1 child, Logan. BA, Dartmouth Coll., 1969; MD, U. Oreg., 1973. Intern Gen. Rose Meml. Hosp., Denver, 1976-77; Emergency physician Mercy Hosp., Roseburg, Oreg., 1974-75; mem. from 45th Dist. Oreg. House of Reps., 1979-81; mem. from 23rd Dist. Oreg. State Senate, 1981—93, pres., 1985—93; gov. State of Oregon, 1995—2003, 2011—; pres. Estes Park Inst., Englewood, Colo., 2003—; endowed chair Found. for Med. Excellence, Portland, Oreg., 2003—; pres. Kitzhaber Ctr. Lewis & Clark Coll., Portland, Oreg., 2004—. Assoc. prof. Oreg. Health Sci. U., 1989-1995; MD chmn. health policy Found. Med. Excellence, 2003-. Pres. Estes Park Inst., Colo., 2003—; founder Archimedes Movement, Oreg., 2006. Recipient Neuberger award, Oreg. Environ. Coun., 1987, Dr. Nathan Davis award, AMA, 1992. Mem. Am. Coll. Emergency Physicians, Inst. Medicine, Douglas County Med. Soc., Physicians for Social Responsibility, Am. Council Young Polit. Leaders, Oreg. Trout. Democrat. Office: Found Med Excellence Ste 800 1 SW Columbia St Portland OR 97258 also: Office of Governor 160 State Capitol 900 Court St Salem OR 97301-4047 E-mail: kitz@wecandobetter.org. *

KITZKE, EUGENE DAVID, research and development company executive; b. Milw., Sept. 2, 1923; s. Leo R. and Regina R. (Tomczyk) Kitzke; m. Lorraine Grace Shummon, Sept. 2, 1946; children: Mary Victoria, Paul Simon, Patrice Lynn, Jerome Peter. BS, Marquette U., 1945, MS, 1947; diploma in basic clin. sci., Med. Coll. Wis., 2002. Instr. microbiology St. Mary's Sch. Nursing, Grand Rapids, Mich., 1946-47; assoc. prof. Aquinas Coll., 1947-51; lab researcher S.C. Johnson & Son, Inc., Racine, Wis., 1951-57, research mgr., 1957-76, v.p. corp. R&D, 1976-81; pres. Oak Crete Block Corp., South Milwaukee, Wis., 1980—; developer Wind Crest Subdiv., Wind Lake, Wis., 1993. Adj. prof. dept. environ. medicine Med. Coll. Wis., Milw., 1973—81; owner Danel Enterprise, South Milwaukee; judge Marquette U. Sci. Fair; bd. dirs. Songcards, inc. Author: (book) For the Next Generation, 1986; contbr. articles to tech. jours., fiction and poetry to mags.:, author pubs. in field. Mem. pres.' coun. Alverno Coll., 1979—87. Recipient H. F. Johnson Cmty. Svc. award, 1996; Disting. scholar, Marquette U., 1995. Mem.: AAAS, Hist. Sci. Soc., Palm Soc. (exec. bd., past pres.), Sigma Xi, Sigma Tau Delta, Phi Sigma. Roman Catholic. Achievements include patents in field. Home: 616 Aspen St South Milwaukee WI 53172-1702 Office: PO Box 413 South Milwaukee WI 53172-0413 also: 7101 S Pennsylvania Ave Oak Creek WI 53154-2439

KIVANC, MERIH, biology professor; b. Aksehir, Konya, Jan. 28, 1954; D, Atatürk U., 1983. Prof. Anadolu U., 1995—. Chpt. pres., dept. biology Anadolu U., 1995—98, 2002—05. Avocations: painting, travel. Office: Anadolu University Faculty Sci Eskisehir Tepe Basi 26470 Turkey Business E-Mail: mkivanc@anadolu.edu.tr.

KIVELA, SIRKKA-LIISA, medical educator; b. Temmes, Finland, Jan. 14, 1947; MD, Oulu U., 1971; PhD, Tampere U., 1983. Family Dr. Posio Health Ctr., Finland, 1971-72, chief med. officer, 1972-80; sr. lectr. Tampere U., Finland, 1980-88; prof. family medicine Oulu U., 1988-2000, Turku U., 2000—11; adj. prof. geriat. pharmacotherapy Helsinki U. Avocations: sports, poetry. Home: Perustie 13A9 00330 Helsinki Finland Office: Helsinki University Dept Social Pharmacy PO Box 56 Helsinki 00014 Finland Office Phone: 358-2-3338424. Fax: 358-2-3338439. Business E-Mail: sirkiv@utu.fi.

KIVIAHO-TIIPPANA, ARJA HELENA, podiatrist; b. Saari, Finland, Feb. 5, 1955; MSN, Kuopio U., 1990. Cert. podiatrist Mikkeli U. Applied Scis., 2000. Lectr. Savonlinna Health Care Instn., 1991—96; sr. lectr. nursing and podiatry Mikkeli U. Applied Scis., 1996—. Pres. Podiatry Assn., Finland, 2011. Grant, Finnish Cultural Found. Mem.: Finnish Nursing Assn., Trade Union Edn. in Finland. Avocations: dance, languages, music. Home: Hauenleuka 14 Savonlinna 57210 Finland Personal E-mail: arja.tiippana@mamk.fi.

KIVIKOSKI, ASKO ILMARI, retired obstetrician, gynecologist; b. Helsinki, Finland, Aug. 3, 1932; came to U.S., 1984; MD, U. Turku, Finland, 1958, DSc, 1967. Diplomate Am. Bd. Ob-gyn. Intern U. Turku, 1962, resident in ob/gyn., 1962-65, asst. prof., 1966-76; resident in surgery City Hosp., Turku, 1965-66; researcher Washington U., St. Louis, 1971-72; fellow in perinatology Mt. Sinai Hosp., NYC, 1978-79; head dept. ob/gyn. Ctrl. hosp., Lahti, Finland, 1976-84; staff Barnes Hosp., St. Louis, 1984-87, 97—; chief gynecol. svcs. St. Louis Regional Med. Ctr., 1987-97; Connect Care, 1998-2001; asst. prof. Washington U., St. Louis, 1984-92, assoc. prof., 1992-2001, assoc. prof. emeritus, 2001—. Author articles on anatomy, obstetrics, perinatology and ultrasound.

KIWERSKI, JERZY EDWARD, spinal surgeon; b. Warsaw, June 24, 1937; s. Antoni and Halina (Jaworska) K.; m. Dorota Szymczak, Jan. 9, 1963; children: Małgorzata, Katarzyna, Magdalena, Bartosz. MBChB, Med. Acad., Szczecin, Poland, 1963; MD, Med. Acad., Warsaw, 1971, habilitation, 1975. Specialist in med. rehab. I, 1967, II, 1969; specialist in orthopaedics and traumatology I, 1971, II, 1974. Asst., anatomical dept. Med. Acad., Szczecin, 1956-62, asst., path. anatomy dept. Warsaw, 1962-64, asst., rehab. clinic, 1965-71, asst. prof., rehab. clinic, 1971-76, assoc. prof., rehab. clinic, 1976-84, prof., 1984. Head spinal dept. rehab. ctr., Konstancin, Poland, 1973-98; head rehab. clinic Warsaw Med. Acad., 1982-2007; cons. rehab., Warsaw, 1982-2002, Country Cons. Rehab, 2002-08; dir. rehab. ctr., Konstancin, 1991-98; pres. High Sch. Rehab., 2007—. Author: 16 books includes Rehabilitation, 1992, Cervical Spinal Injury, 1993 (also editor), Diseases and Injuries of the Spine, 2d edit., 2001, Biomechanics and Rehabilitation Engineeering, 2004, Medical Rehabilitation, 2005, Polish Rehabilitation, 2009; contbr. more than 600 articles to nat. and internat. med. jours.; author more than 440 congress presentations. Mem.: Polish Soc. Med. Bioengring. (v.p. 2010), Polish Soc. Biomed. Engring. (v.p. 2010), Social Health Found. (pres. 1999), Polish Sci. Acad. (com. biocybernetics and biomed. engring. 1953—, com. rehab. and social adaptation 1990—, v.p. com. rehab. 1996—2000, pres. 1999—2007), Polish Soc. Biomechs. (v.p. 1993—94, 1996—2000), Polish Rehab. Soc. (pres. 1992—95, 1995—98, hon. mem. 2002), European Spine Soc., Paraplegia Soc., NY Acad. Scis. Roman Catholic. Achievements include patents for system of supporting grasping movements, and hybrid device for the control of hand functions. Home: Chyliczki Orchidei 4 05-500 Piaseczno Poland Office: Rehabilitation Ctr Wierzejewskiego 12 05-511 Konstancin Poland Personal E-mail: kiwerski_jerzy@poczta.onet.pl. Business E-Mail: kiwerski@stocer.pl.

KIYOHISA, KAMIMURA, radiologist; married. MD, PhD, Kagoshima U., 1998. Med. staff Kagoshima U. Med. and Dental Hosp., 1998—2000, Kagoshima Prefectural Oshima Hosp., 2000—02, Nanpuh Hosp., Kagoshima, 2002—04, Fujimoto Hayasuzu Hosp., Miyakonojo, Miyazaki, Japan, 2004—08. Contbr. articles to profl. jours. (Japanese Jour. Clin. Radiology award, 2006). Mem.: Japanese Coll. Radiology. Office: Fujimoto Hayasuzu Hosp 17-1 Hayasuzu-cho Miyakonojo Miyazaki 885-0055 Japan

KIYOKAWA, YASUSHI, veterinarian, researcher; b. Tokyo, 1977; PhD, DVM, U. Tokyo, Bunkyo-ku. Asst. prof. U. Tokyo, 2010—. Office: Lab Vet Etho Univ Tokyo 1-1-1 Yayoi Bunkyo-ku Tokyo 113-8657 Japan Office Fax: 81-3-5841-8190. Business E-Mail: kiyokawa-ns@umin.ac.jp.

KIYONO, HIROSHI, immunologist, educator; b. Nagano, Japan, Mar. 17, 1953; s. Seiichi and Masako Kiyono; m. Momoyo Miwa; 1 child, Erika. DDS, Nihon U., Matsudo, Japan, 1977; PhD, U. Ala., Birmingham, 1983. Clin. & rsch. asst. prof. U. Ala., Birmingham, 1984—87, assoc. prof., 1988—90, prof., 1991—2003, co-dir. Immunobiology Vaccine Ctr., 1992—96, adj. prof., 2004—; prof., chmn. Osaka U., Japan, 1994—2003; prof. U. Tokyo, 2003—, chmn. dept. microbiology & immunology, 2005—07, assoc. dean Inst. Med. Sci., 2007—. Vis. sr. scientist Max-Planck Inst. Biology, Germany, 1986—87; mem. study sect. Nat. Inst. Dental Rsch., NIH, 1992—97; adj. clin. prof. Ariz. State U., 2007—. Editor: Mucosal Immunology, 1994, Mucosal Vaccines, 1996, Essential of Mucosal Immunology, 1996, The Mucosal Immune System: Gut is a Commanding Tower for the Host Immune System, 2001. Mem. ADA Nat. Bd. Test Construction Com., 1988—93. Recipient New Investigator award, NIH, 1984—87, Rsch. Career Devel. award, 1988—93, Hideyo Noguchi Meml. award, Japan Soc. Promotion of Sci., 2007. Mem.: Japanese Soc. Vaccinology (bd. dirs. 2003—, Takahashi prize 2007), Japanese Soc. Immunology (bd. dirs. 2005—), Soc. Mucosal Immunology (bd. dirs. 2003—, pres. 2005—07). Office: U Tokyo Inst Med Sci 4-6-1 Shirokanedai Minato-ku Tokyo 108-8639 Japan Office Fax: +81-3-5449-5411. Business E-Mail: kiyono@ims.u-tokyo.ac.jp. *

KIYOTA, HEIDE PAULINE, psychologist; b. Bamberg, Germany, July 6, 1942; came to U.S., 1970; d. Fritz and Marcella (Schropfer) S.; m. Ronald Masaki Kiyota, Dec. 26, 1982; children: Heather E., Catherine M., Michelle H. BS, U. Md., 1975, MA, 1979; PhD, U. Hawaii, 1986. Lic. psychologist, Hawaii; accelerated hypnotherapy cert. The Wellness Inst., 1996. Counselor-trainee Regional Inst. for Children & Adolescents, Balt., 1976-77; supr.-counselor Multiple Offender Alcoholism Program, Balt., 1977-80; therapist-intern VA, Honolulu, 1983-84; clin. psychologist Kalihi-Palama Counseling Svcs., Honolulu, 1987-89; pvt. practice psychologist Honolulu, 1988—. Presenter in field. Contbr. articles to profl. jours. Mem. Am. Psychol. Assn., Hawaii Psychol. Assn., Phi Kappa Phi. Home: 1812 Nahenahe Pl Wahiawa HI 96786-2627 Office: 319 A Cane St Wahiawa HI 96786-1844 Office Phone: 808-621-1820.

KIYOTAKA, KABATA, agricultural studies educator; b. Fukuoka, Japan, Mar. 7, 1951; MS, Simane U., 1975; PhD, Kyushu U., 1980. Prof., faculty agr. Tokai U., 1991 . Office: Minamiaso Aso Kuma moto 869-1404 Japan Office Fax: 0967-67-3960. Business E-Mail: kkabata@agri.u-tokai.ac.jp.

KIYOTAKA, KAWAUCHI, medical educator, researcher; b. Takashima, Shiga, Japan, Jan. 14; MD, kyorin U., Tokyo, 1981. Lic. practical mediciner Nat. Bd. Japan, 1981. Postdoc. fellow Toronto U., Ontario, Canada, 1991—94; assoc. prof. Tokyo Women's Med. U., 2000—. Office: Tokyo Women's Med Univ Med Ctr East 2-1-10 Nishiogu Arakawa-ku Tokyo 116-8567 Japan Office Phone: 81-03-3810-1111.

KIZER, KENNETH WAYNE, physician, executive, educator; b. Decatur, Ind., May 28, 1951; s. Homer Martin Kizer and Ellen Hope Howland; m. Suzanne A. Stoddard, Aug. 26, 1972; children: Kelli Christina, Kimberly Casey. BS with honors, Stanford U., 1972; MD with honors, MPH in Epidemiology, UCLA, 1976; DSc (hon.), NY State U., 2006, Med. U. SC, 2008. Rotating internship Naval Regional Med. Ctr., Portsmouth, Va., 1977; undersea medicine fellowship Naval Undersea Med. Inst., Groton, Conn., 1977; resident in diagnostic radiology U. Calif, San Francisco, 1980-81, resident in occupl. medicine, 1982-83; firefighter; emergency physician; dir. Emergency Med. Svcs. Authority State of Calif., 1983-84; chief dep. dir. and chief of pub. health Calif. Dept. Health Svcs., Sacramento, 1984-85, dir., 1985-91; prof., chmn. dept. cmty. and internat. health U. Calif., Davis, 1991-94; undersec. for health US Dept. Vets. Affairs, Washington, 1994-99; dir. Health Sys. Internat., Inc., 1994-97; pres., CEO Nat. Quality Forum, Washington, 1999—2005; chmn. Medsphere Sys. Corp., Aliso Viego, Calif., 2002—, pres., 2005—07, CEO, 2005—07, cons., 2007—10; dir. Inst. Population Health Improvement, UC Davis Health Sys., 2010—11; disting. prof. U. Calif. Davis Sch. Medicine, Betty Irene More Sch. Nursing. Contbr. numerous articles to profl. jours., chpts. to books. Chair Radiation Emergency Screening Team, 1988-91, Hazardous Waste Appeal Bd., 1990; co-chair Calif. AIDS Leadership Com.; mem. Diving Control Bd. U. Calif., 1980-91, Gov.'s Emergency Ops. Exec. Coun., 1984-91, Governing Bd. Calif YMCA Model Legislature Program, 1986-90, Chem. Emergency Planning and Response Commn., 1988-90; chair S.W. Low Level Radioactive Waste Compact Commn., 1990-91, tobacco edn. oversight com. State Calif., 1990-91, bd. dirs. Calif. Wellness Found., 1992-2003, Matthews Found., 1991-94, Ctr. for AIDS Rsch., Edn. and Svcs., 1992-94, Infection Control Coun., 1991-94; mem. adv. bd. Preventive Sports Medicine Inst., 1991-94. Lt. USN, 1976-80. Recipient Humanitarian Svc. medal Dept. of Def., 1979, Spl. Recognition award No. Calif. Emergency Med. Care Coun., 1984, Golden State Med. Assn., 1986, Calif. Div. Am. Lung Assn., 1988, Calif. Health Fedn., 1988, cert. of Recognition Calif. Asian Pacific Health Coalition, 1989, Spl. Achievement award Calif. Emergency Physician Med. Group, 1989, Jean Spencer Felton award for Excellence in Sci. Writing, 1989, spl. awards from March of Dimes, Am. Cancer Soc., Calif. State Senate, Calif. Conf. Local Health Officers, others, 1991—, Healthcare Heroes award Calif. State Assembly, 1996, Cert. of Recognition award, 1996, Dr. Nathan Davis award AMA, 1998, Literacy Achievement award Am. Coll. Physician Execs., 1998, Founders award Wilderness Med. Soc., 1998, Justin Kimball Innovator's award Am. Hosp. Assn., 1998, Lifetime Achievement award Assn. Health Systems Pharmacists, 2002, Founders award Am. Coll. Med. Quality, 2004, Gustov O. Lienhard award, Inst. Medicine/Nat. Acad. Scis., 2004, Ernest S. Codman award Joint Commn. Accreditation Healthcare Orgs., 2005, Special Recognition award Am. Legion, 2007, Award for Excellence Am. Pub. Health Assn., 2008; named Toll fellow Coun. State Govts., 1987, Torch award, 2009, Beverlee A. Meyers award Calif. Dept. Pub. Health, 2011.Named Leaders of Today, 2010, UCLA Health Scis. Alumni Assoc. Fellow Am. Coll. Physician Execs. (disting.), Am. Coll. Preventive Medicine, Am. Coll. Emergency Physicians, Am. Coll. Occupl. Environ. Medicine, Am. Acad. Clin. Toxicology, Royal Soc. Health, Royal Soc. Medicine, Am. Coll. Med. Toxicology, Am. Acad. Med. Adminstrs., Explorers Club; mem. APHA, Internat. Soc. Toxicology, Inst. Medicine NAS, Wilderness Med. Soc., Undersea and Hyperbaric Med. Soc., Nat. Soc. YMCA Youth Govs., Nat. Assn. Underwater Instrs. (Outstanding Contribution to Diving award 1984), Inst. Medicine, Nat. Acad. Sci., Delta Tau Delta (Beta Rho chpt. Hall of Fame 1987), Alpha Omega Alpha, Delta Omega, Nat. Acad. Pub. Adminstrns. Independent. Avocations: scuba diving, hiking and backpacking, photography, racquet sports, book collecting. Office Phone: 916-734-4754.

KIZILDAG, SEFA, research scientist, educator; b. Izmir, Turkey, Dec. 4, 1973; PhD in Med. Biology, 2004. Rsch. scientist, med. faculty Dokuz Eylul U., 1995—. Office: Dokuz Eylul University Med Faculty Izmir Inciralti 35340 Turkey Business E-Mail: sefa.kiildag@deu.edu.tr.

KIZILISIK, AYDIN TARIK, surgeon, researcher; b. Istanbul, Turkey, July 20, 1959; s. Karani Ozer Akra and Gulen Kizilisik, Suat Kizilisik (Stepfather); m. Semiha Reha Duldur, Nov. 19, 1984; 1 child, Basak. MD, Ankara U. Med. Sch., 1984; M in Exptl. Surgery, U. Alta., Edmonton, Alta, Can., 1994; MBA in Healthcare Adminstrn., Ind. Wesleyan U., 2010. Intern Ankara U. Hosps., 1983—84; resident in surgery Gulhane Mil. Med. Acad. and Hosps., Ankara, 1986—91; sr. med. examiner, med. advisor to the gov. Tosya, Kastamonu, Turkey, 1984—86; fellow in liver transplantation U. Alta. Hosps., Edmonton, 1991—93; cons. liver transplant and hepatobiliary surgeon King Fahad N.G. Hosp., Riyadh, Saudi Arabia, 1994—98; fellow in multiorgan transplantation U. Tenn. Hosps., Memphis, 1999—2001, transplant surgeon, 2001—02; asst. prof. surgery Vanderbilt U. Med. Ctr., Nashville, 2002—06; attending transplant surgeon VA Med. Ctr., Nashville, 2002—06, St. Thomas Hosp., Nashville, 2002—06; dir. kidney transplant program Luth. Hosp. of Ind., Fort Wayne, 2007—. Instr. ACLS program King Fahad N.G. Hosp., Riyadh, 1994—98, instr. advanced trauma life support program, 1994—98; presenter in field. Contbr. articles more than 100 to profl. jours. Named to 2007 Guide to Am.'s Top Surgeons, Consumers' Rsch. Coun. Am.; Helen Boone scholar, Nora's Life Gift Found., 1999. Fellow: ACS, Internat. Coll. Surgeons, Am. Soc. Transplant Surgeons, Internat. Soc. Surgery, Transplantation Soc., Am. Soc. Transplantation (Trainee Travel award 2000); mem.: Internat. Pancreas & Islet Transplant Assn., H. William Scott Jr. Surg. Soc., European Soc. Organ Transplantation, Internat. Liver Transplantation Soc., Mid. Ea. Soc. Organ Transplantation, Turkish Nat. Soc. Surgery, NY Acad. Scis., Turkish Med. Assn. Achievements include research in graft versus host disease after small bowel transplantation; analysis of donor criteria and its implications on the outcome of liver transplants; development of microsurgery training for transplantation research purposes; research in impact of long term chronic immunosuppressive therapy on health and quality of life after orthotopic liver transplantation; quality of life after solid organ transplants; development of pancreas transplantation with portal-enteric drainage; administrative development and cultural change in organizational development of transplant centers. Business E-Mail: tkizilisik@ioheart.com.

KJOS, NILS PETTER, nutritionist, researcher; b. Drammen, Norway, Aug. 3, 1959; s. Arne and Solveig Kjos. PhD, Agrl. U. of Norway, 1985—89. Lectr. Buskerud Agrl. Coll., 1984; rschr. Agrl. U. Norway, 1985—2001, prof., 2002—. Chmn. Nedre Eiker Agrl. Union, 2001. 2d lt. Norwegian Home Def., 1993—2005. Avocations: farm work, entomology. Office: Norwegian U Life Scis Dept Animal Aquacultural Scis Postboks 5003 Nlh 1432 Aas Norway Business E-Mail: nils.kjos@umb.no.

KLAASSEN, PAUL J., personal care industry executive; m. Terry Klaassen. Founder, chmn., CEO Sunrise Sr. Living, 1981—2008; non-exec. chmn. Sunrise Senior Living, Inc., 2008—. Founding chmn., dir Assisted Living Fed. Am.; bd. trustees Hudson Inst., Inst. Am. Values, Ethics Public Policy Ctr., Trinity Forum; adv. com. Dept. Healthcare Policy Harvard Univ. Med. Sch.; bd. dirs. Netherland-Am. Found., Nat. Investment Ctr., US C. of C. Office: Sunrise Sr Living 7900 Westpark Dr Ste T900 Mc Lean VA 22102-4217 Office Phone: 703-273-7500. Office Fax: 703-744-1601. *

KLAEWKLA, JEERANUN, nutritionist, educator; b. Thailand, May 15, 1962; DSc, Mahidol U., 2000. Assoc. lectr., dept. nutrition, faculty pub. health Mahidol U., 2000—. Adj. prof. Tokai U., 2006. Office: Rachvithi Rajthevee Rd Bangkok 10400 Thailand Office Fax: 662 6409839. Business E-Mail: phjsw@mahidol.ac.th.

KLAKEG, CLAYTON HAROLD, retired cardiologist; b. Big Woods, Minn., Mar. 31, 1920; s. Knute O. and Agnes (Folvik) Klakeg; children: Julie Ann, Robert Clayton, Richard Scott. Student, Concordia Coll., Moorhead, Minn., 1940; BS, ND State U., 1942; BS in Medicine, ND U., 1943; MD, Temple U., 1945; MS in Medicine and Physiology, U. Minn., Mayo Found., 1954. Diplomate Am. Bd. Internal Medicine. Intern Med. Ctr., Jersey City, 1945—46; mem. staff Va. Hosp., Fargo, ND, 1948—51; postdoc. fellow medicine and cardiology Mayo Found., Rochester, Minn., 1951—55; internist, cardiologist Sansum Med. Clinic Inc., Santa Barbara, Calif., 1955—2008; mem. staff Cottage Hosp., St. Francis Hosp. Contbr. articles to profl. jours. Bd. dirs. Sansum Med. Rsch. Found., pres., 1990. Capt. M.C. USAF, 1946—48. Fellow: ACP, Am. Heart Assn. (mem. coun. clin. cardiology), Am. Coll. Chest Physicians, Am. Coll. Cardiology; mem.: Santa Barbara Soc. Internal Medicine (pres. 1963), Mayo Clinic Alumni Assn., Santa Barbara County Med. Assn., LA Acad. Medicine, Calif. Med. Assn., Santa Barbara County Heart Assn. (pres. 1959—60, Disting. Svc. award 1958, Disting. Achievement award 1971), Calif. Heart Assn. (pres. 1971—72, Meritorious Svc. award 1968, Disting. Svc. award 1972, Disting. Achievement award 1975), Channel City Club, Phi Beta Pi, Sigma Xi. Republican. Lutheran. Home: 5956 Trudi Dr Santa Barbara CA 93117-2175

KLAMERUS, KAREN JEAN, pharmacist, researcher; b. Chgo., Aug. 10, 1957; d. Robert Edward and Jane Mary (Nawoj) Klamerus. BS in Pharmacy, U. Ill., 1980; PharmD, U. Ky., 1981. Registered pharmacist Ky., Ill., Pa. Staff pharmacist Haggin Meml. Hosp., Harrodsburg, Ky., 1980-81, Regional Med. Ctr., Madisonville, Ky., 1982, critical care liasion, 1982; clin. pharmacist resident U. Nebr., Omaha, 1983; clin. pharmacist cardiothoracic surgery U. Ill., Chgo., 1983-88, clin asst. prof. dept. pharmacy practice, 1983-86, asst. prof., 1986-88, departmental affiliate dept. pharmaceutics, 1986-88; sr. pharmacokineticist Wyeth-Ayerst Rsch., Phila., 1988-91, asst. dir. clin. pharmacology, 1991-95, assoc. dir. clin. pharmacology, 1995-97; dir. med. rsch. Roche Global Devel., Palo Alto, Calif., 1997—2001; dir. clin. rsch. Vical, Inc., San Diego, 2002; dir. clin. pharmacology Pfizer, Inc., 2002—04, sr. dir., clin. pharmacology, 2004—. Fellow: Am. Coll. Clin. Pharmacology (indsl. rels. com. 1995); mem.: Mid-Atlantic Coll. Clin. Pharmacology (sec. 1991, pres. 1992—94), Am. Soc. Clin. Pharmacology and Therapeutics (edn. com. mem. 2007—10). Avocations: softball, scuba diving, gardening, sewing. Office: Pfizer-La Jolla 10646 Science Center Dr CB10 San Diego CA 92121 Personal E-mail: kjklamerus@yahoo.com.

KLAPHOLZ, ARI, pulmonologist, educator; MD, NY Med. Coll., Valhalla, 1984. Diplomate Am. Bd. Internal Medicine, 1987, Am. Bd. Internal Medicine-pulmonary disease, 1990, Am. Bd. Internal Medicine-critical care medicine, 1991. Fellow in critical care medicine Mt. Sinai Hosp., NY, 1989—90; asst. prof. medicine Mt. Sinai Sch. Medicine; resident in internal medicine Beth Israel Med. Ctr., NY, 1985—87, fellow in pulmonary medicine, 1987—89, pulmonologist Milton & Caroll Petrie divsn. Office: Beth Israel Medical Center 275 7th Ave 3rd Fl New York NY 10001 Office Phone: 646-778-3475. Office Fax: 646-778-3485.

KLAPHOLZ, HENRY, obstetrician, gynecologist, educator; b. NYC, Oct. 13, 1941; s. Jakob and Frida (Nussbaum) Klapholz; m. Madelyn Hyman, June 6, 1971; children: Meredith, Judith, Lauren, Jacob. BEE, CCNY, NYC, 1963; MEE, NYU, NYC, 1964; MD, Albert Einstein U., NYC, 1971. Diplomate Am. Bd. Ob-Gyn. Intern Montefiore Hosp., NY, 1971—72; resident Beth Israel Hosp., Boston, 1972—76, vice chmn. ob-gyn., 1989—2001; assoc. prof. Harvard Med. Sch., Boston, 1989—; assoc. prof. HST divsn. MIT, Cambridge, Mass., 1998—; clin. prof. Tufts U. Sch. Medicine, Boston, 2001—; chmn. ob-gyn. Metrowest Med. Ctr., Framingham, Mass., 2001—. Host, prodr. (cable TV program) Dr.'s on Call, 2001—. Maj. US Army, 1976—78. Recipient S. Robert Stone Tchr. award, Harvard Med. Sch., 1985, Tchg. award, Tufts U., 2002, 2003, 2004, Irving London Tchg. award, MIT, 2008; named one of Best of Boston, Boston Mag., 1993. Fellow: ACOG, Boston Obstet. Soc. Jewish. Avocations: photography, videography, TV production, piano, computers. Home: 25 Rockport Rd Weston MA 02493 Office: MetroWest Med Ctr 115 Lincoln St Framingham MA 01701 Office Phone: 508-383-8727. Personal E-mail: henry@klapholz.org. *

KLARES, SCOTT, pulmonologist; MD, NY Med. Coll., Valhalla, 1992. Diplomate Am. Bd. Internal Medicine, Am. Bd. Internal Medicine-critical care medicine, Am. Bd. Internal Medicine-pulmonary disease. Intern in internal medicine New Eng. Deaconess Hosp., Boston, resident in internal medicine, 1993—95; fellow in pulmonary disease & critical care medicine Boston Med. Ctr., Mass., 1995—98; pulmonologist Northern Westchester Hosp. Office: Northern Westchester Hospital 90 S Bedford Rd Mount Kisco NY 10549 Office Phone: 914-241-1050.

KLASE, DANIEL, physician, consultant; Sr. house officer U. Schleswig-Holstein, Luebeck, Germany, 2001—07, cons. and specialist neurosurgical pain therapy, 2005—, cons. neurosurgery, 2008—09, resident, neurosurgeon & specialist neurosurg. pain therapy, 2009—. Contbr. articles to profl. jours. Mem.: German Soc. Neurosurgery, German Soc. Neuromodulation. Avocations: football, interior decorating. Office: Med Practice Neurorothenbaum Rothenbaumchaussee 38 Hamburg 20148 Germany Home: Rittersporweg 8a Luebeck 23566 Germany Office Phone: 49 40 41469173. Office Fax: 49 40 41469174. Business E-Mail: klase@neurorothenbaum.de.

KLASKO, STEPHEN KENT, dean, obstetrician, gynecologist, b. Phila., Dec. 23, 1953, MD, Hahnemann U., Phila.; MBA, U. Pa. Diplomate Am. Bd. Ob-Gyn. Resident in ob-gyn. Allentown Hosp., Pa.; chmn. residency program, dir. ob-gyn. Lehigh Valley Hosp., Allentown, Pa.; prof. clin. ob-gyn., assoc. chmn. dept. ob-gyn. Pa. State U.; dean Coll. Medicine Drexel U., Phila., prof. ob-gyn., dean grad. med. edn.; CEO, medicine, nursing and public health U. South Fla., Tampa, 2009—, dean Coll. Medicine, 2004—. Pres. bd. dirs. Lehigh Valley Physician's Group; dir. Trexlertown Women's Health Mall. Fellow Am. Coll. Ob-Gyn., Am. Fertility Soc.; mem. Am. Assn. Gynecol. Laparoscopists, Am. Inst. Ultrasound in Medicine, Gynecol. Laparoscopy Soc. Office: Office of Dean College Medicine Univ South Fla 12901 Bruce B Downs Blvd Tampa FL 33612 *

KLASS, PERRI ELIZABETH, pediatrician, writer; b. Tunapuna, Trinidad, Apr. 29, 1958; d. Morton and Sheila Solomon K.; children: Benjamin Orlando Klass, Josephine Charlotte Paulina Wolff, Anatol Elvis Klass AB, Harvard U., 1979; postgrad., U. Calif., Berkeley, 1979-81; MD, Harvard U., 1986. Diplomate Am. Bd. Med. Examiners. Researcher Inst. Parasitology, Rome, 1981-82; instr. expository writing Harvard U., Cambridge, Mass., 1982-83; resident in pediatrics Children's Hosp., Boston, 1986-89, staff pediatrician, 1989-90; rsch. fellow Boston City Hosp., 1990; prof. journalism pediatrics NYU; med. dir. Reach Out and Read Nat. Ctr.; asst. prof. pedait. Boston U. Sch. Medicine. Author: (novels) Recombinations, 1985, Other Women's Children, 1990, The Mystery of Breathing, 2004, (short stories) I Am Having an Adventure, 1986, Love and Modern Medicine, 2000, Two Sweaters For My Father, 2003, (essay collection) A Not Entirely Benign Procedure: Four Years as a Medical Student, 1987, Baby Doctor: A Pediatrician's Training, 1992; co-author (with Eileen Costello): Quirky Kids: Understanding and Helping Your Child Who Doesn't Fit In, 2003; co-author: (with Sheila Solomon Klass) Every Mother Is A Daughter, 2006; author: The Mercy Rule, 2008, Treatment Kind & Fair: Letters to a Young Doctor, 2007. Recipient O. Henry award Doubleday, 1983, 84, 91, 92, 95, Women's Nat. Book Assn. award, 2006., award Am. Acad. Pediat. Edn. award, 2007 Fellow Am. Acad. Pediatrics mem. PEN., Acad. Pedait. Assn., Barbara Dyne Soc., Betry Tacy Soc. Avocations: knitting, travel, spicy foods. Office Phone: 212-998-7992.

KLATSKY, ARTHUR LOUIS, cardiologist, epidemiologist; b. NYC, Oct. 24, 1929; s. Martin Max and Rose M. (Hurwitz) Klatsky; m. Eileen Selma Rohrberg, June 21, 1953; children: Jennifer Ann, Benjamin Paul. BA, Yale U., 1950; MD, Harvard U., 1954. Diplomate Am. Bd. Internal Medicine, Am. Bd. Cardiovascular Disease. Intern in medicine Boston City Hosp., 1954-56; resident in internal medicine and cardiology Boston VA Hosp., 1958-60; trainee in cardiology U. Calif., San Francisco, 1960-61; clin. instr. in medicine U. Calif. Med.

Ctr., San Francisco, 1961-68, asst. clin. prof. medicine, 1968-80; staff physician internal medicine and cardiology Kaiser Found. Hosp., Oakland, Calif., 1961-80, sub-chief dept. medicine, 1973, chief divsn. cardiology, 1978-94; assoc. divsn. rsch. Kaiser Permanente Med. Care Program, Oakland, 1975—; sr. cons. in Cardiology, 1995—. Mem. med. adv. coun. Wine Inst., San Francisco, 1978—. Contbr. articles to profl. jours., chpts. to books. Mem. profl. edn. com. Alameda County Heart Assn., 1969—. With Med. Corps, 1956-58. Recipient rsch. award, Med. Friends of Wine, 1984, 1st Thomas Turner award for Excellence in Alcohol Rsch., Alcoholic Beverage Med. Rsch. Found., 1992, Morris Collen Lifetime Rsch. Achievement award, 2004; fellow Am. Heart Assn. Coun. on Epidemiology, 1975—. Fellow ACP, Am. Coll. Cardiology; mem. Am. Wine Alliance for Rsch. and Edn. (bd. dirs. 1989—), Disting. Practioner in Medicine, Nat. Acad. of Practice (Disting. Practitioner award 1995), Alcoholic Beverage (bd. trustee 2008-), Medical Rsch. Found. Avocations: long distance running, music, gardening, travel. Office: Kaiser Found Hosp 280 W Macarthur Blvd Oakland CA 94611-5642 Office Phone: 510-752-6538. Business E-Mail: arthur.klatsky@kp.org.

KLATTE, TOBIAS, urologist; b. Schonebeck, Germany, May 5, 1980; s. Detlef and Sabine Klatte; m. Michela de Martino; children: Bianca, Emma. MD, U. Magdeburg, Germany, 2005, PhD, 2007; MS, Open Mgmt. Sch., Cologne, Germany. Cert. German Bd. Drs. Sachsen-Anhalt, Germany, 2005. Fellow UCLA, 2006—07; resident physician Med. U. Vienna, 2008—. Contbr. scientific papers (Clin. Sci. award, German Soc. Immunotherapy, 2002). Mem.: European Assn. Urology (1st Poster prize 2008), German Urol. Assn., Am. Urol. Assn. (1st Poster prize 2007). Office: Medical Univ Vienna Urology Wahringer Gurtel 18-20 Vienna 1090 Austria Office Fax: 43-1-404002332. Personal E-mail: tobias.klatte@gmx.de. Business E-Mail: tobias.klatte@meduniwien.ac.at.

KLEBANOFF, SEYMOUR JOSEPH, medical educator; b. Toronto, Ont., Can., Feb. 3, 1927; s. Eli Samuel and Ann Klebanoff; m. Evelyn Norma Silver, June 3, 1951; children: Carolyn, Mark. MD, U. Toronto, 1951; PhD in Biochemistry, U. London, 1954. Intern Toronto Gen. Hosp., 1951—52; postdoctoral fellow dept. path. chemistry U. Toronto, 1954—57; postdoctoral fellow Rockefeller U., NYC, 1957—59, asst. prof., 1959—62; assoc. prof. medicine U. Washington, Seattle, 1962—68, prof., 1968—2000, prof. emeritus, 2000—. Mem. adv. coun. Nat. Inst. Allergy and Infectious Diseases, NIH, 1987—90. Author: The Neutrophil, 1978; contbr. over 200 articles to profl. jours. Recipient Merit award, NIH, 1988, Mayo Soley award, Western Soc. for Clin. Investigation, 1991, Bristol-Myers Squibb award for Disting. Achievement in Infectious Disease Rsch., 1995, Disting. Rsch. Biomed. Sci. award, Assn. Am. Med. Coll., 2007. Fellow: AAAS; mem.: NAS, Am. Acad. Arts and Scis., Inst. of Medicine, Soc. for Leukocyte Biology (Marie T. Bonazinga rsch. award 1985), Endocrine Soc., Infectious Diseases Soc. Am. (Bristol award 1993), Assn. Am. Physicians, Am. Soc. Biol. Chemists, Am. Soc. Clin. Investigation. Home: 509 Mcgilvra Blvd E Seattle WA 98112-5047 Office: U Wash Dept Medicine Div Al & Infectious Disease PO Box 357185 Seattle WA 98195-7185 Office Phone: 206-685-1876. Business E-Mail: seym@u.washington.edu.

KLEIN, ARNOLD WILLIAM, dermatologist; b. Mt. Clemens, Mich., Feb. 27, 1945; s. David Klein; m. Malvina Kraemer. BA, U. Pa., 1967, MD, 1971. Intern Cedars-Sinai Med. Ctr., LA, 1971—72; resident in dermatology Hosp. U. Pa., Phila., 1972—73, UCLA, 1973—75; pvt. practice Beverly Hills, Calif., 1975—. Prof. dermatology/medicine U. Calif. Ctr. Health Scis.; mem. med. staff Cedars-Sinai Med. Ctr.; asst. clin. prof. dermatology Stanford U., 1982—89; from asst. clin. prof. to prof. dermatology/medicine UCLA, trustee David Geffen Sch. Medicine, 2003—; mem. adv. bd. Botox, Allergan Inc.; retained cons., investigator Elan Pharms.; cons., investigator Inamed Aesthetics, Q-Med, Medicis, Skin-Medica, Ortho-Neutrogena; presenter seminars in field. Assoc. editor: Jour. Dermatologic Surgery and Oncology, reviewer: Jour. Sexually Transmitted Diseases, Jour. Am. Acad. Dermatology; mem. editl. bd. Men's Fitness mag., Shape mag., Archives Dermatology; contbr. articles to profl. jours. Mem. CAlif. State Adv. Com. Malpractice, 1983—89; med. adv. bd. Skin Cancer Found., Lupus Found. Am.; founder R. Tarlow/Dr. Arnold Klein Fund Breast Cancer Treatment. Mem.: AFTRA, AMA, Am. found. AIDS Rsch. (founder, bd. dirs.), Soc. Cosmetic Chemists, Am. Venereal Disease Assn., Jennifer Jones Simon Found. (trustee), Hereditary Disease Found. (bd. dirs.), Discovery Fund Eye Rsch. (bd. dirs.), Lupus Found., Internat. Psoriasis Rsch. Inst., Scleroderma Found., Dermatology Found., Am. Acad. Dermatology, Met. Dermatology Soc., Am. Coll. Chemosurgery, LA Med. Assn., Assn. Sci. Advisors, Am. Assn. Cosmetic Surgeons, Internat. Soc. Dermatologic Surgery, Am. Soc. Dermatologic Surgery, Calif. Med. Assn., Children's Mus. LA (founder), Dance Gallery LA (founder), LA Mus. Contemporary Art (founder), Friars Club, Delphos, Phi Beta Kappa, Sigma Tau Sigma. Office: 435 N Roxbury Dr Ste 204 Beverly Hills CA 90210-5004 Office Phone: 310-275-5136. Personal E-mail: awkleinmd1@aol.com.

KLEIN, DONALD FRANKLIN, psychiatrist, research scientist, educator; b. NYC, Sept. 4, 1928; s. Jesse and Rose K.; m. Rachel Gittelman, Dec. 29, 1968; children: Beth, Geri, Hilary, Michelle, Erika. BA magna cum laude, Colby Coll., Waterville, Maine, 1947; MD, SUNY, Bklyn., 1952, DSc, 1998. Rotating intern USPHS Hosp., SI, NY, 1952-53; resident in psychiatry Creedmoor State Hosp., 1953-54, 56-58; dir. rsch. and evaluation, dept. psychiatry L.I. Jewish-Hillside Med. Center, 1972-76; prof. psychiatry SUNY Med. Sch., Stony Brook, 1972-76; dir. rsch. and therapeutics NY State Psychiat. Inst., NYC, 1976—2007; attending psychiatrist NY Presbyn. Hosp., NYC, 1977—; prof. psychiatry Columbia U. Coll. Physicians and Surgeons, NYC, 1978—2007, prof. emeritus, 2007—; rsch. prof. NYU Child Study Ctr., NYC, 2007—; rsch. psychiatrist Nathan S. Kline Inst., Orangeburg, NY, 2008—. Chmn. clin. psychopharmacology study sect. NIMH, 1973-75; sr. sci. advisor Alcohol Drug Abuse Mental Health Adminstrn., 1989-91; cons. Nat. Inst. Drug Abuse, 1990-99, Nat. Inst. Alcoholism and Alcohol Abuse, 1996-99. Co-author: Diagnosis and Drug Treatment of Psychiatric Disorders: Adults and Children, 2d edit., 1980, Mind, Mood and Medicine, 1981, Understanding Depression, 1993; co-editor: Critical Issues in Psychiatric Diagnosis, 1978, Anxiety: New Research and Changing Concepts, 1981; contbr. articles to med. jours. Sr. asst. surgeon USPHS, 1954-56. Recipient A.E. Bennett Neuropsychiat. Rsch. award, 1964, Nat. Assn. Pvt. Psychiat. Hosp. Rsch. award, 1965, 1971, Samuel W. Hamilton award, APPA, 1980, William R. McAlpin award, NAMH, 1988, Found.'s Fund prize, Am. Psychiat. Assn., 1988, Gold medal, Soc. Biol. Psychiatry, 1990, Heinz Lehmann Rsch. award, N.Y. State Office of Mental Health, 1991, Thomas W. Salmon medal, N.Y. Acad. Medicine, 1993, Lifetime Achievement award, Soc. Biol. Psychiatry, 1996, Exemplary Psychiatrist award, Nat. Alliance for the Mentally Ill, 1997, Castillo del Pino prize, 1999, Disting. Svc. in Psychiatry award, Am. Coll. Psychiatrists, 2004, Ist Highly Cited Rschr. award. Fellow Psychiat. Rsch. Soc.(pres. 1980), Am. Psychopathol. Assn. (past pres., Hamilton award 1980), Am. Coll. Neuropsychopharmacology (life, past pres. 1981, Paul Hoch award 1991), Royal Coll. Psychiatrists (founding); mem. Am. Soc. Clin. Psychopharmacology (pres. 1992-96, v.p. 1997-2005), Phi Beta Kappa. Home: 1016 5th Ave Apt 14D New York NY 10028-0132 Office: NY State Psychiat Inst 1051 Riverside Dr New York NY 10032-1013 Address: 171 E 84 St Ste 16D New York NY 10028 Office Phone: 212-543-6249, 212-628-2841. Personal E-mail: donaldk737@aol.com.

KLEIN, ERIC ALAN, surgical oncologist, urologist; b. Bristol, Pa., Dec. 25, 1955; s. Milton and Sylvia Klein; m. Susan Kerins, Dec. 27, 1980; 1 child, Mira Lamson. B, Johns Hopkins U., Balt., 1977; MD, U. Pitts. Sch. Medicine, 1981. Diplomate Am. Bd. Urology, Nat. Bd. Med. Examiners. Intern Cleve. Clinic Found., 1981-82, resident in urology, 1982-86; fellow in urology Meml. Sloan Kettering Cancer Ctr., NYC, 1986-89; head sect. urol. oncology Cleve. Clinic Glickman Urol. & Kidney Inst., 1989—; prof. surgery Cleve. Clinic Lerner Coll. Medicine, 2004—. Editor: Renal Cell Carcinoma: Immunotherapy, 1993, Biology of Renal Cell Carcinoma, 1995, Management of Prostate Cancer, 1999, 2d edit., 2004; assoc. editor Seminars in Urologic Oncology, 1994—, mem. editl. bd. The Prostate Jour., 1997—, Molecular Urology, 1997—; contbr. articles to profl. jours. Trustee-at-large Am. Cancer Soc., Ohio, 1996. Recipient George & Grace Crile Traveling Fellow award, Cleve. Clinic Found., 1986, Internat. Traveling Fellow award, 1986, Nightingale Physician Collaboration award, 2000, Norman K. Probstein award for meritorious contbn. to oncology, Wash. U. Sch. Medicine, 2001; named Tchr. of Yr., Glickman Urol. & Kidney Inst., 2005—06, Best Practices Tchr., Cleve. Clinic Lerner Coll. Medicine, 2007; named a Top Doc, Cleve. Mag., 1998—2008. Fellow: ACS; mem.: Am. Assn Genitourinary Surgeons, Soc. Urol. Oncology (exec. com. 1998—), Am. Urol. Assn. (exam. com. 1988—, Internat. Acad. Exch. award 1994). Avocations: photography, 20th century history. Office: Cleve Clinic Dept Urology 9500 Euclid Ave Cleveland OH 44195-0001 Office Phone: 216-444-5591. Business E-Mail: Kleine@ccf.org.

KLEIN, FRIEDER, retired surgeon; b. Erlangen, Germany, Nov. 7, 1945; s. Kurt and Anneliese Klein; m. Martina Jrrgang, Mar. 24, 1979; children: Alexandra, Markus. Med. exam, Tech. U., Munich, 1972; PhD, U. Munich, 1973. Cert. GJ-tract surgeon, gen. surgeon. Med. intern City Hosp., Traunstein, Germany, 1972—74, resident, 1975—77, Kantonsspital, St. Gallen, Switzerland, 1974, Hosp. Wien-Lainz, Wien, Austria, 1974, Queen's Hosp., London, 1975, Hosp. Thorax Klinik, Heidelberg, Germany, 1977—79; head dept. surgery Klinikum, Traunstein, 1991—2004. Guest physician Meml. Sloan Kettering Cancer Ctr., NYC, 1976, Stanford, UCLA, U. Utah, 1990, various orgns., Japan, 1990; lectr. in field. Author: (books) Interne Qualitaetssicheruug, 1999; contbr. articles to profl. jours. Cons. Bayer Aerztekammer, Bavaria, Germany, 1991—. Oberstabsarzt Gebirgsjaeger, 1964—65, Germany. Mem.: several German surg. socs. Home: Axdorfer Feld 164 Traunstein D-83278 Germany Office: Klinikum Surg Dept Cuno-Niggl-Str 3 Traunstein D-83278 Germany Office Phone: 49-861-15834. Personal E-mail: klein.frieder@t-online.de. Business E-Mail: frieder.klein@gmx.de.

KLEIN, GORDON LESLIE, pediatrician, educator; b. NYC, Aug. 26, 1946; s. Hyman David and Ruth Harriet (Katz) K.; m. Joann Pamela Schulz, July 1, 1973; children: Andrew Howard (dec.), Adrienne Lindsay. BA, Columbia U., 1967; postgrad., Cambridge U., 1970-71; MD, Albert Einstein Coll. Medicine, 1971; MPH, UCLA, 1980. Cert. Am. Bd. Pediat., 1976, in pediat. gastroenterology and nutrition Am. Bd. Pediat., 1990. Intern, resident in pediat. Stanford U. Med. Ctr., Calif., 1971-74, Internat. Ctr. Med. Rsch. and Tng., Colombia, 1973; postdoctoral fellow pediat. nutrition Johns Hopkins U. Med. Sch., Balt., 1976-78, Nutrition Rsch. Inst., Lima, Peru; postdoctoral fellow in pediat. gastroenterology UCLA, 1978-80, adj. asst. prof. pediat., 1980-82; asst. prof. pediat. Tulane U. Med. Sch., New Orleans, 1982-84; pediat. gastroenterologist City of Hope Med. Ctr., Duarte, Calif., 1984-86; assoc. prof. pediat. and preventative medicine U. Tex. Med. Br., Galveston, 1986-95, prof. pediat., 1995—2009, clin. prof. orthop. surgery, 2010—, mem., med. staff, Shriners Burns Hosp.; prof. pediat., dir. pediat. nutrition U. Ky., Coll. Medicine & Ky. Pediat. Rsch. Inst., Lexington, 2009—10. Mem. com. revision US Pharmacopeia, Rockville, Md., 1990-2000, chmn. gastroenterology adv. panel, 1990-2005, exec. com. rev., 1995-2000; cons. on malnutrition Nicaraguan Ministry Health, 1992, FDA, NICHD aluminum toxicity in infants, 1996; mem. spl. rev. panel osteoporosis NIH, 1997; spl. govt. cons., FDA, 1998-2006, evaluator NICHD Best Pharm. Children Act, 2010, Best Pharm. Children Act, Hematology Working Group, 2011; vis. prof. Okayama U., Kyushu U., Japan, 1996, Baylor Coll. Medicine, Houston, 1999, U. Sheffield, Eng., 2000, Sanjay Gandhi Postgrad. Inst. Med. Scis., Lucknow, India, 2009, Cin. Children's Hosp., U. Cin., 2009, U. Pitts., 2010, Hosp. U. d'Etat Haiti, Port-au-Prince, 2010; invited lectr. Hosp. Necker, Paris, 1991, Columbia U., 1997, Harvard U., 1994, 99, 2009, U. Melbourne, U. Sydney, Australia 1995, Japan, 1996, 2003, China, 1997, 99, 2002, 2009, Asian Pacific Osteoporosis Conf. & Internat. Soc. Clin. Densitometry, Beijing, 2009, Cambridge U., 2004, 06, Am. Soc. Bone and Mineral Rsch., 2004, Pediat. Acad. Soc., 2005, NIH, 2005, Oxford U., 2005, 09, US Army Inst. Surg. Rsch., 2006, 2008, Johns Hopkins U., 2000, 2006, 4th Internat. Conf. on Children's Bone Health, 2007, sci. adv. com., 2007, All India Inst. Med. Scis., New Delhi, 2009, 7th Asia Pacific Bur. Congress, New Delhi, 2009, Sanjay Gandhi Postgrad. Inst. Med. Scis., King George V Med. Coll., Lucknow, 2009, Internat. Soc. Clin. Densitometry, Beijing, 2009, Asia Pacific Osteoporosis Conf., 2009, Red Cross Hosp., U. Cape Town, South Africa, 2010; mem. sci. adv. com. Internat. Osteoporosis Conf., Shanghai, 2002; organizing com. pharmacology and pediat. bone workshop NIH and Am. Soc. for Bone and Mineral Rsch., 2005-, sr. editor proceedings, 2007; combined expert adv. panel Internat. Conf. Children's Bone Health and Internat. Soc. Clin. Densitometry, 2007. Editor: Metabolic Bone Disease in Total Parenteral Nutrition, 1985; co-editor: Current Opinion in Pharmacology: Endocrine and Metabolic Diseases, 2005; mem. internat. adv. bd. Jour. of Bone and Mineral Metabolism, 2005-, mem. editl. bd. Jour. Burns and Wounds, 2006-08, Jour. Bone and Mineral Rsch., 2008-; contbr. articles to profl. jours. Lt. comdr. USN, 1974—76. Named Clin. Assoc. Physician NIH, 1980-82; recipient Nat. Rsch. Svc. award, 1979-80, Travel award Internat. Conf. Calcium Regulating Hormones, Melbourne, 1995; nominee Howard Hughes Investigatorship in Translational Rsch., 2001; Nutrition Program fellow Project HOPE Nicaragua, 1992, Commdg. Gen. Medallion of Exellence, US Army, 4th Inf. Divsn., San Antonio, Tex, 2006. Fellow Am. Acad. Pediat., Am. Gastroent. Assn.; mem. N.Am. Pediat. Bone and Mineral Working Group (founder, sec.-treas. 1984-85), Soc. for Pediat. Rsch., Am. Soc. Bone and Mineral Rsch. (lectr. 2004), Am. Soc. Nutrition, Am. Gastroent. Assn., Am. Pediat. Soc., Princeton Club NY, English Speaking Union (mem. exec. bd. Houston br., 2011-). Achievements include development of the Pediatric Bone Disease Initiative with the American Society for Bone and Mineral Research and the NIH; FDA rule governing aluminum contamination of intravenous solutions used for nutrition of hospitialized patients; characterization of the toxic damage of aluminum to bones and liver; characterization of bone loss following burn injury including abnormalities in vitamin D, calcium, parathyroid hormone and treatment for the bone loss; collaborative studies with US Army Institute for surgical research on the effects of combat injury on calcium and bone metabolism. Avocations: travel, reading, horseback riding, music. Personal E-mail: gordonklein@ymail.com.

KLEIN, HARVEY, medical educator; b. NYC, Aug. 29, 1937; s. Emanuel and Rose (Sanderman) K.; m. Phyllis Levine, Sept. 22, 1963; children: Laura, Daniel. SB, U. Chgo., 1959; MD, Harvard U., 1963. Diplomate Am. Bd. Internal Medicine. Intern N.Y.-Cornell, NYC, 1963-64, asst. resident, 1964-65, sr. resident, 1967-68, chief resident, 1968-69, fellow in medicine, 1969-70; asst. prof. medicine Cornell U. Med. Coll., NYC, 1970-75, assoc. prof., 1975-88, William S. Paley prof. clin. medicine, 1992—. Capt. USAF, 1965-67. Office: Weill Cornell Med Coll 1305 York Ave New York NY 10021-4870 Office Phone: 646-962-4101.

KLEIN, JEFFREY HOWARD, oncologist, internist; b. Cleve., Jan. 24, 1943; s. Joseph Bart and Tillie Alice Klein; m. Nancy Klein, June 5, 1971; 1 child, Bart Edward. Student, Brown U., 1961-64; BS in Medicine, Northwestern U., 1966, MD, 1968. Diplomate Am. Bd. Internal Medicine, Am. Bd. Med. Oncology, Am. Bd. Hospice & Palliative Medicine. Intern Cleve. Met. Gen. Hosp., 1968-69, resident, 1969-70, Rush-Presbyn. St. Luke's Med. Ctr., Chgo., 1970-71, Am. Cancer Soc. clin. fellow, 1971-72; pvt. practice internist, oncologist Lombard Med. Group, Thousand Oaks, Calif., 1974-2000; chief of medicine Los Robles Regional Med. Ctr., Thousand Oaks, 1976-77, chief of staff, 1979-81; med. dir. hospice Vitas Healthcare Corp., LA, 2000—. Trustee Columbia/Los Robles Med. Ctr., Thousand Oaks, 1995-98. Maj. USAF, 1972-74. Mem. Am. Soc. Clin. Oncology, So. Calif. Acad. Clin. Oncology (charter), Am. Acad. of Hospice and Palliative Medicine, Phi Beta Kappa, Pi Kappa Epsilon, Alpha Omega Alpha. Avocations: philosophy, tennis, skiing, music. Office Phone: 800-757-4242. E-mail: jeffrey.klein@vitas.com.

KLEIN, MICHAEL ELIHU, physician; b. NYC, Apr. 6, 1946; s. Leo and Edith (Rigrod) K.; m. Elizabeth Angela McGehee, Oct. 8, 1988; children: Michael, Debra, Daniel. BA, Wesleyan U., Middletown, Conn., 1967; MD, MPH, Yale U., 1972. Diplomate Am. Bd. Internal Medicine. Asst. dir. hematology U. Md., Balt., 1979-83; sr. investigator U. Md. Cancer Ctr., Balt., 1979-83; cons. in hematology, oncology Pinnacle Health Sys., Harrisburg, 1983—2007, Cowley Assocs., Camp Hill, Pa., 1983—87, Holy Spirit Hosp., Camp Hill, 1983—2007, Ctrl. Pa. Hematology & Oncology, Lemoyne, 1997—2007, Thomas Jefferson U., Phila., 2007—, hospitalist Oncology Sold Tumor Svc., 2007—, assoc. prof. oncology, 2008—, dir. Solid Tumor Inpatient Svc., 2010—. Chmn. blood usage com. Holy Spirit Hosp., Camp Hill, Pa., 1998—2000, Camp Hill, 2003—06; chief hematology Pinnacle Health Sys., 2002—07, chmn. blood utilization com., 1988—2007; assoc. clin. prof. U. Pa., Hershey, 2004—07; asst. clin. prof. Pa. Coll. Osteopathic Medicine, Phila., 2004—07. Author: Political Dynamics National Health Insurance in New York, 1972; contbr. articles to profl. jours., chpts. to books. Founder, bd. dirs. Number Nine, New Haven, 1971. Comdr. lt. USPHS, 1974-77. Recipient Best Tchr. award, Jefferson U., 2008—09. Fellow Internat. Acad. Clin. and Applied Thrombosis/Hemostasis; mem. AMA, Am. Soc. Clin. Research, Am. Soc. Clin. Oncology, Am. Soc. Hematology, Am. Legion, Balt. Blood Club (pres. 1979-83). Avocations: stamp collecting/philately, baseball, reading. Office: Jefferson University Hosp Curtis Bldg 1215 Walnut St Ste 1008 Philadelphia PA 19107 Office Phone: 215-955-9317. Personal E-mail: orioledh@aol.com. Business E-Mail: michael.klein@jefferson.edu.

KLEIN, NEIL CHARLES, physician; b. NYC, Jan. 6, 1935; s. Martin and Jeannette F. (Pazow) K.; divorced; children: Lisa, Susie, David; m. Phyllis Klein, Nov. 26, 1989. AB, Columbia U., 1956; MD, Cornell U., 1960. Diplomate Am. Bd. Internal Medicine, Am. Bd. Gastroenterology, Nat. Bd. Med. Examiners. Intern N.Y. Hosp., 1960—61, resident, 1964—67; fellow in medicine Cornell Med. Coll., 1965—67, clin. instr. in medicine, 1967—70, asst. clin. prof. medicine, 1970—77; assoc. clin. prof. medicine N.Y. Med. Coll., 1977—84, clin. prof. medicine NYC, 1984—98, Columbia U., NYC, 1998—; asst. clin. attending physician N.Y. Hosp., 1970—77, St. Joseph's Hosp., Stamford, Conn., 1967—72; from asst. to assoc. attending physician Stamford Hosp., 1967—, assoc. chief medicine, 1972—75, chief divsn. gastroenterology, 1978—84. Bd. dirs. Conn. Med. Ins. Co., 1988-2002, fin. com., 1988-2002, sec., 1990-2002; bd. dirs. Stamford Health Network, 1987-93, chmn. fin. com., 1994-2001; mem. sci. adv. coun. Fairfield-Westchester Ileitis-Colitis Found., 1982—; mem. Commn. of Aging, Stamford, 1971-82. Fellow ACP, Am. Coll. Gastroenterology, Royal Soc. Tropical Medicine and Hygiene; mem. Fairfield County Med. Assn. (trustee 1980-87, chmn. bd. trustees 1984-85, pres. 1985-86), Conn. State Med. Assn., Am. Soc. Gastrointestinal Endoscopy, Am. Gastrointestinal Assn., Cornell Med. Coll. Alumni Assn. (pres. 1976-78, sr. advisor 1978—), Stamford Med. Soc. (pres. 1990-91). Office: Shoreline Med Group 1450 Washington Blvd Stamford CT 06902-2451 Office Phone: 203-327-9321. Business E-Mail: neilklein@shorelinemedicallp.com.

KLEIN, NORMAN IRA, allergist, immunologist; MD, SUNY, Brooklyn, 1976. Diplomate Am. Bd. Pediatrics, Am. Bd. Allergy and Immunology, registered NY, 1977. Intern Brookdale Hosp. Med. Ctr., NY, resident in pediat., 1979; fellow in allergy and immunology Albert Einstein Med. Ctr., 1980; hosp. affiliations include Bklyn. Hosp. Ctr. (Downtown Campus), Bklyn. Hosp. Ctr. (Caledonian Campus); dir. allergies and immunology divsn. Brookdale Hosp. Med.

Ctr. Named one of Top Doctors, NY Mag., 2010. Office: Brookdale Hospital Medical Center 1648 E 14th St Brooklyn NY 11229 Office Phone: 718-627-0183. Office Fax: 718-627-1019.

KLEIN, VICTOR, obstetrician-gynecologist, educator; MD, State U. of NY. Downstate. Diplomate Am. Bd. Ob-Gyn, Am. Bd. Med. Genetics-clin. genetics, cert. maternal and fetal medicine. Resident internal medicine Kings County Hosp. Ctr., Bklyn., 1980—81; resident, obstetrics and gynecology Johns Hopkins Hosp., Balt., 1981—85; fellow clin. genetics Univ. of Texas Southwestern Med. Ctr., Dallas, 1985—87, fellow maternal and fetal medicine, 1985—87; practices ob-gyn. Great Neck Obstetrics, NY. Assoc. clin. prof. obstetrics and gynecology NYU Sch. of Med. Office: Great Neck Obstetrics 900 Northern Blvd Ste 220 Great Neck NY 11021 Office Phone: 516-466-0778. Office Fax: 516-466-0825.

KLEINAU, SANDRA, medical researcher, educator; b. Uppsala, Sweden, Feb. 2, 1961; BSc, Uppsala U., 1989, PhD, 1993. Prof. Uppsala U., 2008—. Recipient award, Göran Gustafsson's Found., Royal Swedish Acad. Scis. Anna-Greta & Holger Crafoord Found., Viking prize, Scandinavian Jour. Immunology. Mem.: Swedish Soc. Immunology, Scandinavian Soc. Immunology, Am. Assn. Immunologists. Office: Husargatan 3 Box 596 Uppsala SE-75124 Sweden Business E-Mail: sandra.kleinau@icm.uu.se.

KLEINDORFER, DAWN OLSON, neurologist, educator; b. Dec. 8, 1970; BS in Biology with high honors, Ind. U.; MD, Washington Univ. Sch. Medicine, 1997. Med. residency, dept. neurology U. Mich., 1998—2001; fellowship, cerebrovascular disease divsn., dept. neurology U. Cinn., Coll. Medicine, 2001—02; chief resident, dept. neurology U. Mich., 2000—01; asst. prof., neurology U. Cinn. Selected participant Early Career Women in Academic Medicine Profl. Develop. Seminar, 2004. Contbr. articles to profl. jours. Recipient Top Enrollment award, PROFESS study, Platinum Level, Outstanding Resident Rsch. award, Mich. Neurological Assn., Am. Heart Assn. Health Initiatives Vol. award, 2004; Nat. Stroke Assn. Rsch. Fellowship award, 2002. Mem.: AMA, Am. Stroke Assn., Phi Beta Kappa. Recipient of the Hazel K. Goddess Scholar grant for stroke research in women, 2004-2006. In a two-year study running concurrently in Atlanta and Cincinnati, African American beauticians will be educated about the signs of a stroke, and they will then educate their clientele during their appointments. Office: Univ Neurology Inc 222 Piedmont Ave # 3200 Cincinnati OH 45219-4217 Office Phone: 513-475-8730, 513-558-5328. Office Fax: 513-475-8033. Business E-Mail: dawn.kleindorfer@uc.edu.

KLEINMAN, RONALD ELLIS, pediatrician; b. Buffalo, June 16, 1946; BS in Biology, Trinity Coll., Hartford, Conn., 1968; MD, NY Med. Coll., 1972; MS, Harvard U. Med. Sch., Boston, 1998. Diplomate Am. Bd. Pediats. with subspecialties in pediat. gastroenterology and nutrition. Resident pediat. Montefiore Hosp. Med. Ctr., Albert Einstein Coll. Medicine, Bronx, NY, 1972—75, chief resident pediat., 1975—76; fellow human devel. biology, dept. microbiology and immunology Albert Einstein Coll. Medicine, 1976—77; clin. rsch. fellow, pediat. gastrointestinal and nutrition unit Mass. Gen. Hosp., Boston, 1977—80; rsch. fellow, pediat. Harvard U. Med. Sch., 1977—80, instr. pediat., 1980—82, asst. prof. pediat., 1982—88; chief pediat. gastroenterology and nutrition Mass. Gen. Hosp., 1986—, attending pediatrician, 1987—. Assoc. prof. pediat. Harvard U. Med. Sch., 1988—98, prof. pediat., 1988—, mem. nutrition adv. com., 1995—; mem. WHO Treatment Effects Monitoring Com., 1995—98; chief, pediat. cons. USDA Evaluation of Sch. Breakfast Prog. Pilot Project, 2000—02; mem. Steering Com. Nat. Cholesterol Edn. Prog., 1993—; sci. adv. bd. mem. Inst. Nutrition, Lima, Peru, 2002—; acting physician-in-chief, chair dept. pediat. Mass. Gen. Hosp., 2006—. Sr. assoc. editor (med. publ.) Journal of Pediatric Gastroenterology and Nutrition, 1989—2002; contbr. articles to profl. jours. Named a Best Dr., Boston Mag., 2007. Mem.: Nutrition Curriculum Devel. Com. (chair 1995—98), Am. Cancer Soc. (adv. grp. on diet and nutrition 1991—94), Am. Acad. Pediat. (chmn. com. on nutrition 1989—93), FDA Food Adv. Panel, Internat. Soc. Behavioral Nutrition and Physical Activity (pres. 2003—04). Office: Mass Gen Hosp 55 Fruit St YAW 6 Boston MA 02114 E-mail: rkleinman@partners.org.

KLEINSCHNITZ, CHRISTOPH, neurologist; b. Wuerzburg, Germany, Oct. 8, 1973; s. Michael and Erika Kleinschnitz; life ptnr. Konstanze Barthel. Attending, Friedrich Koenig Gymnasium, Wuerzburg, 1993—; Degree, U. Wuerzburg, 2001. Resident, dept. neurology U. Wuerzburg, 2001—, cons., dept. neurology, 2008. Contbg. editor. Office: Univ Wuerzburg Josef-Schneider St 11 Wuerzburg 97080 Germany Office Fax: 4993120123488.

KLEJNOT, GETHA JEAN, school nurse practitioner, music educator; b. Stroudsburg, Pa., July 28, 1950; d. Robert Roger and Betty Wilson Snyder; m. Gerald Francis Klejnot, Sr., Feb. 14, 1986 (div. Apr. 2, 1998); 1 child, Andrew Robert. AA in nursing, C.C. Balt., 1976; MusB, Peabody Conservatory, 1980. RN Md., 1976, CPR, Am. Heart Assn., 1976; wound care cert. Nat. Alliance Wound Care. Oncology and bone marrow transplant nurse Johns Hopkins Hosp., Balt., 1976—80; head nurse Balt. City Hospitals, 1980—84; home health nurse Bay Area Home Health, Annapolis, 1984—85; icu-ccu nurse SRT Med Staff, Balt.; pvt. piano tchr. for large studio Annapolis, 1987—; sch. health nurse Anne Arundel County Health Dept, 1995—; with wound team U. Splty. Hosp, Balt. Tchg. asst. pre-sch. music theory Eastman Sch. Music, U. Rochester, NY, 1968—70. Mem.: Nat. Guild Piano Tchrs. Achievements include Piano study with Maria Luisa Faini, Julio Esteban, Alexander Paskanov; Harpsichord study with Shirley Matthews; Piano pedagogy with Tinka Knopf; Master classes with Eugene List and Ignor Kipnis. Avocation: kayaking. Home: 1217 Plateau Pl Annapolis MD 21401 Office: Univ Splty Hosp 601 S Charles St Baltimore MD 21230 Personal E-mail: gesny@comcast.net.

KLEMENS, JONATHAN MARK, pharmacy educator, speaker, writer; b. Tarentum, Pa., July 3, 1948; s. Stanley Daniel Klemens and Winona Katherine Klemens (Wilcox); m. Linda Ellen Bailich, Sept. 9, 1972; children: Lauren Morelli, Aaron. BS in Pharmacy, Duquesne U., 1976, BS in Biol. Rsch., 1970; postgrad., U. Ark., 1998—2000; MS in Leadership and Bus. Ethics, Duquesne U., Pitts., 2007. Registered pharmacist. Dir., pharmacy Highlands Hosp., Connellsville, Pa., 2000—02, Dept. Vets. Affairs Med. Ctr., Butler, Pa., 2002—08, Jefferson Regional Med. Ctr., Pitts., 2008—11; clin. pharmacist CVS Caremark, Pitts., 2011; spkr. Integrative Medicine Antigoarian. Instr. in pharmacy practice CC Allegheny County, 1979; instr. in sterile products U. Pitts., 1976—81. Author: Mountains and Rivers: Complementing your Healthcare with Alternative Medicine, 2003, Quick Guide to Common Herb Side Effects and Interactions, 2005, (hist. fiction) Mississippi Mud, numerous other works. Korean martial arts instr. (black belt) Taekwon-Do. Recipient Black Belt, Taekwon-Do. Fellow: Soc. Antiquaries Scotland; mem.: Am. Coll. Healthcare Execs., Pa. Soc. Health-Sys. Pharmacists. Avocations: Scottish history, writing, history. Home: 3298 Cramlington Dr Gibsonia PA 15044 Personal E-mail: jkwriter@live.com.

KLEMENT, ANDREAS, physician, researcher; b. Bielefeld, Germany, Dec. 27, 1966; s. Rudolf Richard and Hella Magarethe Bleschkowski; m. Julia Maria Klement, Sept. 6, 2002; children: Jonas Köpsel, Charlotte Maria, Isabel Luise, Johannes Valentin. MD, Charite Med. Sch., Berlin, 1996. Cert. surgeon Bd. Physicians Berlin, 2001, gen. practitioner Bd. Physicians Saxony, 2004. Rsch. assoc. Inst. Gen. Practice U. Leipzig, Germany, 2004—05, U. Halle-Wittenberg, 2006—09, head sect. gen. practice, 2010—. Prin. gen. practice Practice Jacobi & Klement, Dresden, Germany, 2005—. Mem.: German Coll. Gen. Practice. Office: Sect Gen Practice Magdeburger St 8 Halle Saale 06112 Germany Office Fax: 0049-345-557-5340. Business E-Mail: andreas.klement@medizin.uni-halle.de.

KLENK, ROSEMARY ELLEN, pediatrician, educator; b. Pitts., June 16, 1948; d. Joseph Albert and Frieda (Roppolo) Meisner; m. Kenneth Klenk, June 26, 1977; children: Kara, Jacob, Caitlin, David, Colin, Kevin. BA in History, U. Rochester, 1970; BSN, Columbia U., 1972; MD, Cornell U., 1980. Diplomate Nat. Bd. Med. Examiners, Am. Bd. Pediat.; RN. Intern pediatrics Babies Hosp., Columbia Presbyn. Med. Ctr., NYC, 1980—81, resident, 1981—83; ptnr. pvt. practice New England Pediat., Stamford, Conn., 1983—; assoc. chief pediatrics Stamford Hosp. Part-time instr. Coll. Physicians & Surgeons Columbia U., 1983—. Contbr. articles to profl. jours. Bd. advisors Arts for Healing. Named one of Top Drs., Conn. Mag., 2010, NY Metro Area, 2010. Fellow Am. Acad. Pediat.; mem. Conn. State Med. Soc., Fairfield County Med. Soc. Office: New England Pediatrics 183 Cherry St New Canaan CT 06840-5409 also: 166 W Broad St Ste 103 Stamford CT 06902-3661 Office Phone: 203-323-1770, 203-972-5232. Office Fax: 203-348-1510, 203-972-5234. Business E-Mail: reklenk@nepeds.com.

KLEPPER, ELIZABETH LEE, retired physiologist; b. Memphis, Mar. 8, 1936; d. George Madden and Margaret Elizabeth (Lee) K. BA, Vanderbilt U., 1958; MA, Duke U., 1963, PhD, 1966. Rsch. scientist Commonwealth Sci. and Indsl. Rsch. Orgn., Griffith, Australia, 1966-68, Battelle Northwest Lab., Richland, Wash., 1972-76; asst. prof. Auburn U., Ala., 1968-72; plant physiologist USDA Agrl. Rsch. Svc., Pendleton, Oreg., 1976-85, rsch. leader, 1985-96; ret., 1996. Assoc. editor Crop Sci., 1977-80, 88-90, tech. editor, 1990-92, editor, 1992-95; mem. editl. bd. Plant Physiology, 1977-92, Irrigation Sci., 1987-92; mem. editl. adv. bd. Field Crops Rsch., 1983-91; contbr. articles to profl. jours., chpts. to books. Mem. Umatilla Basin Watershed Coun., 2005—, Umatilla County Critical Groundwater Taskforce, 2005—09. Marshall scholar Brit. Govt., 1958-59; NSF fellow, 1964-66; Recipient First Citizen award, Pendleton, 2005, White Rose award, March of Dimes, Portland, 2005. Fellow: AAAS, Am. Soc. Agronomy (monograph com. 1983—90, bd. dirs. 1995—98), Soil Sci. Soc. Am. (fellows com. 1986—88), Crop Sci. Soc. Am. (fellows com. 1989—91, pres.-elect 1995—96, pres. 1996—97, Monsanto Disting. Career award 2004, Presdl. award 2006); mem.: Agronomic Sci. Found. (bd. dirs. 1993—99, 2011—), Sigma Xi. Home: 1454 SW 45th Pendleton OR 97801 Home Phone: 541-276-8416. E-mail: klepper.betty@gmail.com.

KLEPPINGER, ERIKA L., pharmacist, educator; b. Allentown, Pa., Sept. 11, 1977; PharmD, U. Scis. Phila., 2001. Bd. cert. pharmacotherapy specialist; cert. diabetes educator. Assoc. clin. prof. Auburn U. Harrison Sch. Pharmacy, 2003—. Pharmacy practice resident Temple U. Hosp., 2001—02; ambulatory care pharmacy resident Phila. Coll. Pharmacy, 2002—03. Recipient Preceptor of Excellence, Auburn U. Harrison Sch. Pharmacy, 2005—06, 2009—10, Outstanding Faculty, 2010. Mem.: Nat. Lipid Assn., Am. Coll. Clin. Pharmacy, Am. Pharmacists Assn., Am. Diabetes Assn., Am. Assn. Colls. Pharmacy. Office: Auburn University Dept Pharmacy 2131 Walker Bldg Auburn AL 36849 Office Fax: 334-844-4410. Business E-Mail: kleppel@auburn.edu.

KLEWER, JÖRG, physician; b. Velbert, Germany, Feb. 24, 1971; s. Heinz and Anneliese K. MD, PhD, Bochum Med. Sch., Germany, 1997; DrPH, Dresden Sch. Pub. Health, 2003. Jr. house officer Bethesda Hosp., Wuppertal, Germany, 1997-98, 98-99, Oshakati Regional Hosp., Namibia, 1998; rsch. fellow Dresden Med. Sch., Germany, 1999-2000; vice regional health dir. Chemnitz Govt., Germany, 2000—03; cons. Fed. Ins. Authority, 2003—04; prof. U. Applied Sci., Zwickau, Germany, 2004—. Advisor Fed. Ministry Work and Social Affairs, 2004—, Saxonian State Ministry Social Affairs, 2009—10. Mem. editl. bd.: HIV & AIDS Review, 2003—, Heilberufe Sci., 2008—; contbr. articles to profl. jours. Lance corp. Air Force, 1990-91. Fellow Royal Soc. Pub. Health; mem. APHA, German Soc. Social Medicine and Prevention. Office Phone: 49 375 536 3405.

KLEZL, ZDENEK, orthopedic & spinal surgeon, educator; b. Prague, Oct. 20, 1956; s. Zdenek Klezl and Helena (Lomicka) Klezlova; m. Radka Kostnerova; children: Zdenek, Katerina. MD, Charles U., 1983, PhD, 1996. Diplomate Bd. Orthopedics and Bd. Traumatology. Resident in gen. surgery NNF-Praha, 1984-85; resident in orthopedics Ortho-univ. Hosp., Praha, 1985-88, head sub-dept. ICU Prague, 1988-91; fellow dept. orthopedics U. Louisville, Ky., 1991-92; head subdept. ortho sta. Univ. Hosp., Prague, 1992-95; dep. head Ortho-trauma dept. Ctrl. Mil. Hosp., Prague, 1995—2005; head postgrad. tng. program Mil. Med. Acad., Hradec Kralove, Czech Republic, 1997—2005; head pvt. orth clinic Prague, 1994—2003; assoc. prof., 2005—; cons. orthop. & spinal surgeon Royal Hosp. Derby & Nuffield Health Derby. Contbr. articles to profl. jours., chpts. to books. Mem. SICOT, Czech Spine Soc., Czech Soc. for Orthopedics and Taumatology, Czech Med. Chamber, German Soc. for Orthopedics and Traumatology, World Ortho Soc., Mil. Surg. Soc. Roman Catholic. Avocations: tennis, sailing, windsurfing, travel. Home: Nad Kralovskou Oborou 41 170-00 Prague 7 Czech Republic also: 86 Muirfield Dr Mickleover Derby DE3 9YF England Office Phone: 44 77 246 305 71. E-mail: zklezl@aospine.org.

KLIEFOTH, A. BERNHARD, III, neurosurgeon; b. San Antonio, Nov. 1942; S. Arthur Bernhard, Jr. and Pauline (Gray) K.; m. Ingrid R. Kunde, Apr. 22, 1968; children: Karena, Tanya. AB in Chemistry, Princeton U., 1965; MD, U. Tex. Med. Br., Galveston, 1970. Diplomate Am. Bd. Neurol. Surgery, 1980. Intern Naval Hosp., Oakland, Calif., 1970-71, resident gen. surgery San Diego, 1972-73; neurosurg. tchr. Washington U., St. Louis, 1973-78, chief resident, 1976—77, instr. in neurosurg., 1976—78, rsch. fellow dept. radiation scis., 1977-78; commd. ensign USN, 1969, advanced through grades to comdr., 1977; staff neurosurgeon Naval Regional Med. Ctr., Oakland, 1978-81; capt. USNR, 1985; practice medicine specializing in neurosurgery Knoxville, Tenn., 1981—; mem. staff U. Tenn. Hosp., St. Mary's Hosp.; chmn. dept. surgery, 1989-90; clin. assoc. prof. surgery U. Tenn.; chmn. IRB St Marys, 1984—2008, sec. med. staff, 1990. Bd, dirs. Tenn. Donor Svcs., Cole Neurosci. Found., Knoxville Donor Svcs., Epilepsy Found. Ea. Tenn., vis. prof. Bethesda Naval Hosp./Nat. Naval Med. Ctr. Pres., treas/ Princeton Alumni Assn. Knoxville and Ea. Tenn.; mem. exec. com. West Hills Assn.; treas. Westborough Assn. Commd. ensign USN, 1969, med. officer, radiation safety officer USS Bainbridge DLG (N)-25 USN, 1971—81, with USNR, 1981—96, med. officer in charge reserve unit drs. & nurses PRIMUS. Recipient Disting. Southern Neurosurgeon award, So. Neurosurgery Soc., 2003—. Fellow ACS, Stroke Coun. Am. Heart Assn.; mem. AMA, Am. Assn. Neurol. Surgeons, Am. Soc. Stereotactic and Functional Neurosurgery, Tenn. Neurosurg. Soc., World Soc. Stereotactic and Functional Neurosurgery, Congress Neurol. Surgeons, So. Neurosurg. Soc., So. Med. Assn., Tenn. Med. Assn., Knoxville Acad. Medicine, San Francisco Neurol. Soc., Soc. Med. Cons. to Armed Forces, Assn. Mil. Surgeons U.S., Soc. Neurosci. Avocations: photography, coin collecting/numismatics, stamp collecting/philately, computers, travel, scuba diving. Office: 6901 Office Park Cir Knoxville TN Address: PO Box 51648 Knoxville TN 37950-1648 Office Phone: 865-524-9400.

KLIMEK, JOSEPH JOHN, physician, educator; b. Wilkes-Barre, Pa., Sept. 14, 1946; s. Joseph John and Frances Carol (Pavloski) K.; m. Jane Marie Stout, June 26, 1971 (div.); 1 child, Adam. AB cum laude, Princeton U., 1968; MD, Pa. State U., 1972. Diplomate Am. Bd. Internal Medicine, Am. Bd. Infectious Diseases. Intern, resident in internal medicine Hartford U., Conn., then fellow in infectious disease, 1972—76, chief epidemiology, 1976—87, dir. subsplty. medicine, 1985—87, assoc. dir. medicine, 1987—90, assoc. dir. dept. medicine and chmn. AIDS program, 1987—90, dir. dept. medicine, 1990—2005, v.p. for med. affairs, 2006—, v.p. physician rels., 2010—, chmn. AIDS task force, 1985—90, assoc. chmn. dept. medicine, 1995—; asst. prof. medicine U. Conn., Farmington, 1977—84, assoc. prof., 1984—90, prof., 1990—; assoc. chmn. dept. medicine U. Conn. Sch. Medicine, 1995—. Conn. mem. numerous faculties pharm. industry. Sr. assoc. editor Am. Jour. Infection Control, 1980-95; med. editor Asepsis, The Infection Control Forum; also mem. numerous editl. bds. in field; contbr. articles to med. jours. Recipient Disting. Alumnus award, 1970, ABC award, 1986. Fellow ACP, Infectious Disease Soc. Am.; mem. APHA, AAAS, Am. Profls. in Infection Control, Am. Soc. Microbiology, Am. Fedn. Clin. Rsch., Soc. Hosp. Epidemiologists Am., Am. Venereal Disease Assn., Am. Med. Writers Assn. Achievements include integrated internal medicine residency of Hartford Hospital with University of Connecticut School of Medicine; developed hospital community linkage network for AIDS care in Greater Hartford; introduced primary care medicine practice model to all ambulatory services; expanded care to indigent with two bilingual satellite practices; developed hospital cardiac services product line; developed hospital-wide Program in Integrative Medicine; initiated formal hospitalist program for care of inpatients; facilitated hospital-wide program in palliative medicine; initiated a formal approach to patient safety and quality with a new vice president position; initiated a 24 hours transfer center; initiated physician relations council for an advanced care organisation. Home: 31 Main St Farmington CT 06032-2229 Office: Hartford Hosp 80 Seymour St Hartford CT 06115-2701 Office Phone: 860-545-1444. Business E-Mail: jklimek@harthosp.org.

KLIN, BARUCH, surgeon, educator; b. Curitiba, Parana, Brazil, Mar. 2, 1954; MD, Faculdade Evangelica de Medicina do Parana, 1977; degree in Gen. Surgery, Hadassah Ein-Kerem Med. Ctr., Jerusalem, 1990, degree in Pediat. Surgery, 1996. Resident gen. surgery Hadassah Ein-Kerem Med. Ctr., 1981—87; resident pediat. surgery Assaf Harofeh Med. Ctr., 1987—94. Sr. lectr. surgery Sackler Sch. Medicine, Tel-Aviv U., 2004. Recipient Hon. award, Beterem Orgn. Children's Security, Safe Kids Israeli Chpt., Excellence Tchg. award, Sackler Med. Sch., Tel-Aviv U., Henrieta Szold Nursing Sch., Affiliated to Hadassah Nursing Sch., Jerusalem. Mem.: Israeli Soc. Gen. Surgery, Israeli Soc. Pediat. Surgery. Avocations: piano, sports, classical music. Home: Yasmin St 88/1 Mevasseret Ziyyon 90805 Israel Home Fax: 972-2-5709005. Personal E-mail: klin2@netvision.net.il.

KLINE, FRANK MENEFEE, psychiatrist; b. Cumberland, Md., May 14, 1928; s. Frank Huber and Margaret (Menefee) K.; m. Shirley Steinmetz, June 27, 1953; children: Frank F., Margaret L. BS, U. Md., 1950, MD, 1952; PhD, So. Calif. Psychoanalytic Inst., 1977. Diplomate Am. Bd. Psychiatry and Neurology (examiner 1970—). Intern Cin. Gen. Hosp., 1952-53; resident Brentwood VA Med. Ctr., West L.A., 1955-58; regional chief West Ctrl. Mental Svc., L.A. County Dept. Mental Health, LA, 1967—68; assoc. dir. adult psychiatry out-patient dept. L.A. County, U. So. Calif. Med. Ctr., 1968—77, acting dir. adult psychiat. dept., 1977, attending physician, 2008—, LAC-USC-MC, 2009—; attending staff Harbor-UCLA-MC, 2009—; chief psychiatry VA Med. Ctr., Long Beach, Calif., 1977-91. Clin. prof., vice-chair U. Calif., Irvine, 1978—91, prof. emeritus, 1995—, U. So. Calif.; clin. prof. Drew King, 1992—2004; reviewer Hosp. Cmty. Psychiatry, 1978—, Am. Jour. Psychiatry, 1978—, Readings, 1995—2002; cons. Los Angeles County Dept. Mental Health, 1992—2008; attending staff LAC-USC-MC, 2008—11, Harbor-UCLA-Med. Ctr., 2009—. Editor: A Handbook of Group Psychotherapy, 1983. 1st lt. M.C., U.S. Army, 1953-55. E-mail: frank.kline1@cox.net.

KLINE, HOWARD JAY, cardiologist, educator; b. White Plains, NY, Nov. 5, 1932; s. Raymond Kline and Rose Plane; divorced; children: Michael, Ethan; m. Ellen Sawamura, June 13, 1987; 1 child, Christopher. BS, Dickinson Coll., 1954; MD, N.Y. Med. Coll., 1958. Intern San Francisco Gen. Hosp., 1958—59; resident Mt. Sinai Hosp., NYC, 1959—61; sr. resident U. Calif. Med. Ctr., San Francisco, 1961—62; cardiology fellow Mt. Sinai Hosp., NYC, 1962—64; dir. cardiology tng. program St. Mary's Hosp., San Francisco, 1970—90, Calif. Pacific Med. Ctr., San Francisco, 1992—. Clin. prof. medicine and cardiology U. Calif. Med. Ctr., San Francisco, 1984—; vis. prof. Nihon U., Tokyo, 1986; dir. cardiology Valley Forge Gen. Hosp; Lt. col. U.S. Med. Corps, 1967-69. Cardiology editor Hosp. Practice, Cardiology, 1992—; contbr. articles to profl. jours. Recipient Spinal Recognition award, U. Calif. San Francisco Sch. Medicine. Fellow ACP, Am. Heart Assn., Am. Coll. Cardiology, Am. Coll. Chest Physicians; mem. Golden Gate Tennis Club, U. San Francisco Masters Swim Team. Avocations: painting, reading, running, skiing, tennis, swimming. Office: 1 Sharder St Ste 600 San Francisco CA 94117 Office Phone: 415-379-9500. Personal E-mail: hklinemd@gmail.com.

KLINE, SUSAN ANDERSON, internist, dean, educator; b. Dallas, June 4, 1937; d. Kenneth Kirby and Frances Annette (Demorest) Anderson; m. Edward Mahon Kline, Dec. 26, 1964 (dec. July 1990). BA, Ohio U., 1959; MD, Northwestern U., 1963. Diplomate Am. Bd. Internal Medicine, Nat. Bd. Med. Examiners (bd. dirs. 1977-81). Asst. physician NY Hosp., 1967—68, physician-to-outpatients, 1968—69, electrocardiographer, 1968—70, asst. attending physician, 1969—76, physician-in-charge cardiopulmonary lab., 1970—71, dir. adult cardiac catheterizaion lab., 1970—71, dir. adult cardiac catheterization lab., 1971—79, assoc. attending physician, 1976—85, emeritus attending physician, 1985—, emeritus dir. adult cardiac catheterization lab., 1985—; assoc. dean student affairs Cornell U. Med. Coll., NYC, 1974—78; assoc. dean admissions and student affairs Cornell Med. Sch., Ithaca, NY, 1978—80; mgr. occupl. med. programs GE Co., 1980—84; sr. assoc. dean student affairs NY Med. Coll., Valhalla, 1984—94, interim dean, v.p. med. affairs, 1994—96, exec. vice dean acad. affairs, vice provost univ. student affairs, 1996—. Mem. test com. Ednl. Commn. on Fgn. Med. Grads., Phila., 1985—92; mem. U.S. Med. Licensing Exam test accommodations com. Nat. Bd. Med. Examiners, Phila., 1992—97; chmn. unmatched student com. Nat. Residency Matching Program, 1998—2000, mem. exec. com., 2003—, chair second match com., 2003—05, pres.-elect, 2004—05, pres., 2005—06, chair nominating com., 2005—06, bd. dirs.; mem. Liaison Com. Med. Edn., 1998—2004, chair ad hoc subcom. rev. accreditation stds., 2000—01, exec. com., 2002—04, policy com., 2003—04; chmn. adv. com. Electronic Residency Application Svc., 1996—2001. Bd. visitors Coll. Arts, Ohio U., Athens, 1981—91; bd. dirs. Burke Rehab. Hosp., White Plains, 1997—2006. Recipient Leaders of the Future award, Nat. Coun. Women, N.Y.C., 1978, Cert. of Appreciation, Ohio U., 1978. Fellow: ACP, Am. Soc. Internal Medicine, Am. Coll. Cardiology; mem.: Phi Kappa Phi, Am. Assn. Med. Colls. (chmn. 1989—93, mem. sr. mgmt. adv. com. 2001—05, chmn. N.E. group on student affairs), N.Y. Cardiologists Soc., Am. Heart Assn. (fellow coun. on clin. cardiology), Cruising Club Am., Alpha Omega Alpha, Phi Beta Kappa. Avocation: sailing. Home: 561 Pequot Ave Southport CT 06490-1366 Office: NY Med Coll Sunshine Cottage Valhalla NY 10595 Personal E-mail: sakline@attglobal.net. Business E-Mail: kline@nymc.edu.

KLINGE, BJORN CHRISTER, periodontics educator; b. Alingsas, Sweden, Jan. 12, 1950; s. Björn Wiking and Anna-Lisa (Augustsson) K.; m. Kerstin Maria Tengwall, 1984; children: Anna, Magnus. DDS, Lund U., 1977, PhD, 1984. Asst. prof. Lund U. Oral Health Sci., Malmo, Sweden, 1977-84, assoc. prof., 1984-94; prof., chmn., dean Karolinska Inst., Stockholm, 1994—, dean faculty of odontology, 1996—. Mem. AAAS, Scandinavian Soc. of Periodontology. Home: Koltrastvägen 4 S-17839 Ekero Sweden Office: Karolinska Inst Perio Dept PO Box 4064 S-14104 Huddinge Sweden Office Phone: 46852480000. Business E-Mail: bjorn.klinge@ki.se.

KLINGEL, CHRISTINE, pharmacist, director; b. St. Louis, Dec. 14, 1976; PharmD, U. Iowa, 2002. Pharmacy dir. Columbia Valley Cmty. Health, 2010—. Mem.: Bd. Pharm. Specialties, Am. Pharmacists Assn., Am. Coll. Clin. Pharmacists. Home: 2710 Gracie Ln East Wenatchee WA 98802 Personal E-mail: cklingel@cvch.org.

KLINMAN, JUDITH POLLOCK, biochemist, educator; b. Phila., Apr. 17, 1941; d. Edward and Sylvia Pollock; m. Norman R. Klinman, July 3, 1963 (div. 1978); children: Andrew, Douglas. BA, U. Pa., 1962, PhD, 1966, degree (hon.), 2006; PhD (hon.), U. Uppsala, Sweden, 2000. Postdoctoral fellow Weizmann Inst. Sci., Rehovoth, Israel, 1966—67; postdoctoral assoc. Inst. Cancer Rsch., Phila., 1968—70, rsch. assoc., 1970—72, asst. mem., 1972—77, assoc. mem., 1977—78; asst. prof. biophysics U. Pa., Phila., 1974—78; assoc. prof. chemistry U. Calif., Berkeley, 1978—82, prof., 1982—, Miller prof., 1992, 2003—04, prof. molecular and cell biology, 1993—, chair chem. dept., 2000—03, Joel Hildebrand chair, 2002—03, chancellor's prof., 2009—. Mem. ad hoc biochemistry and phys. biochemistry study sects. NIH, 1977—84, phys. biochemistry study sect., 1984—88. Mem. editl. bd.: Jour. Biol. Chemistry, 1979—84, Biofactors, 1991—98, European Jour. Biochemistry, 1991—95, Biochemistry, 1993—, Ann. Rev. Biochemistry, 1996—2000, Accts. Chem. Res., 1995—98, Current Opinion in Chemical Biology, 1997—, Chemical Record, 2000—, Advances in Physical Organic Chemistry, 2003—; contbr. articles to profl. jours. Fellow, NSF, 1964, NIH, 1964—66, Guggenheim, 1988—89. Fellow: ACS, AAAS; mem.: NAS, Royal Soc. Chemistry, Am. Philos. Soc., Am. Soc. Biochemistry and Molecular Biology (membership com. 1984—86, pub. affairs com. 1987—94, program com. 1995, pres.-elect 1997, pres. 1998, past pres. 1999, Merck award 2007), Am. Acad. Arts and Scis., Am. Chmn. Soc. (exec. coun. biol. divsn. 1982—85, chmn. nominating com. 1987—88, program chair 1991—92, Repligen award 1994, Remsen award 2005), Sigma Xi. Office: U Calif Dept Chemistry Berkeley CA 94720-0001 Office Phone: 510-642-2668.

KLIPPEL, JOHN H., medical association administrator, physician; BA in Chemistry and Math., magna cum laude, Bowling Green State U., Ohio; MD, U. Cin. Coll. Medicine. Diplomate Am. Bd. Internal Medicine, cert. in rheumatology. Resident internal medicine Yale-New Haven Hosp.; rheumatology fellow NIH, U. Calif., San Diego; clin. dir. Nat. Inst. Arthritis & Musculoskeletal & Skin Diseases, NIH; med. dir. Arthritis Found., Atlanta, 1999—2003, pres., CEO, 2003—. Contbr. articles to profl. jours. Recipient Burroughs-Wellcome Vis. Prof. award, Royal Soc. Medicine, London, Surgeon Gen.'s Exemplary Svc. award, Borden Rsch. award. Fellow: ACP, Am. Coll. Rheumatology; mem.: Omicron Delta Kappa, Phi Eta Sigma, Alpha Omega Alpha. Office: Arthritis Found PO Box 7669 Atlanta GA 30357-0669 Office Phone: 404-965-7671. Business E-Mail: jklippel@arthritis.org. *

KLITZNER, THOMAS S., pediatric cardiologist; b. LA, Sept. 4, 1948; AB in Physics, Harvard U., Cambridge, Mass.; MS in Mech. Engring., Mass. Inst. Tech., Cambridge; MD, U. Pa. Sch. Med., 1977, PhD, 1979. Diplomate Am. Bd. Pediat., Am. Bd. Pediat. Cardiology. Intern pediat. UCLA Sch. Med., 1978—79, resident pediat., 1979—80, fellow pediat. cardiology, 1980—84, prof., chief divsn. pediat. cardiology. Vice-chair academic affairs, dept. pediat UCLA Med. Sch., dir. med. home. project; dir. Calif. children's svcs. prog. Mattel Children's Hosp., LA. Healthy Tomorrows Partnership for Children Grant, Fed. Health Resources Svcs. Adminstrn. Mem.: Joint Coun. Congenital Heart Disease, Am. Heart Assn. (past pres.), Am. Acad. Pediat. (exec. com. cardiology, cardiac surgery, Excellence in Pediat. Rsch. award). Office: David Geffen Sch Med UCLA Div Pediat Cardiology 10833 Le Conte Ave Los Angeles CA 90095 Office Phone: 310-825-7148. Office Fax: 310-825-9524. Business E-Mail: tklitzner@mednet.ucla.edu.

KLOEHN, RALPH ANTHONY, plastic surgeon; b. Milw., Dec. 18, 1932; s. Ralph Charles and Virginia Mary (Kosak) K.; m. Mary Theresa Landers, Nov. 4, 1961; Children: Colleen, Gregory, Kristine, Patricia, Timothy, Philip, Michelle. BS, Marquette U., 1954, MD, 1958. Diplomate Am. Bd. Plastic Surgery. Rotating intern Charity Hosp. La., New Orleans, 1958-59; gen. surgery resident Marquette U. Hosps., Milw., 1961-65; resident in plastic and maxillofacial surgery U. Tex. Med. Br., Galveston, 1965-68; fellowship in plastic and reconstructive surgery African Med. Rsch. Found., Nairobi, Kenya, 1968-69; pvt. practice medicine specializing in plastic surgery Milw., 1969—; med. dir. Lake County Medi-Spa, Pewaukee, Wis., 2003—09; ind. contractor Wis. Vein Ctr. & MediSpa, Pewaukee, 2009—. Former med. cons. McGhan Med. Corp., Santa Barbara, Calif., Mentor/Sonique Surg. Sys., Santa Barbara. Contbr. articles to profl. jours. Lt. USNR, 1959-61. Fellow ACS, Internat. Coll. Surgeons; mem. AMA, Am. Soc. Aesthetic Plastic Surgery, Am. Soc. Plastic Surgery, Am. Soc. Maxillofacial Surgeons, Can. Soc. Aesthetic for (Cosmetic) Plastic Surgery. Republican. Roman Catholic. Avocations: photography, sports fishing, oil and watercolor painting.

KLOOR, MATTHIAS JOHANNES, research scientist; b. Landau, Rhineland-Palatinate, Germany, Sept. 24, 1972; s. Werner Kloor and Gisela Beck. MD, Med. Sch., Heidelberg, 2000. Resident U. Heidelberg, Dept. of Surgery, Baden-Wuerttemberg, Germany, 2000—02; postdoctoral fellow U. Heidelberg, Inst. Pathology, Germany, 2002—. Spkr. in field. Contbr. articles to profl. jours. Achievements include research in Colorectal cancer, hereditary tumors, microsatellite instability, tumor immunology; development of Novel Marker System For Microsatellite Instability Analysis. Avocation: classical music. Office: U Heidelberg Im Neuenheimer Feld 220/221 Heidelberg D-69120 Germany Office Fax: 49 (6221) 565981. Personal E-mail: m.kloor@gmx.de. E-mail: matthias.kloor@med.uni-heidelberg.de.

KLORIN, GEULA, medical researcher; b. Israel, Dec. 17, 1959; DSc, Israel Inst. Tech., 1992. Rsch. scientist NIH, NCI, CCR, 2003—06; head cytology rsch. lab. Rambam Human Health Care Campus, 1994—2003, sr. rsch. assoc., 2007—. Office: PO Box 9602 Haifa 31096 Israel Office Fax: 972-4-8541784. Business E-Mail: g_klorin@rambam.health.gov.il.

KLOSS, LINDA L., healthcare management consultant; B in Health Info. Mgmt., Coll. St. Scholastica, Minn., 1968; M in Orgn. Devel. Registered health info. adminstr. American Health Info. Mgmt. Assn.; cert. assn. exec. American Soc. Assn. Executives. Former sr. mgr. MediQual Systems, Inc., Mass., InterQual, Inc., Chgo.; exec. v.p., CEO Am. Health Info. Mgmt. Assn., Chgo., 1995—2010; pres. Kloss Strategic Advisors, 2010—. Bd. dirs. Am. Health Info. Mgmt. Assn., 1980—86, pres. bd. dirs., 1985; bd. dir. Nat. Alliance for Health Info. Tech., 2004—. Recipient Sr. Alice Lamb award for achievement, Coll. St. Scholastica, 1984; named one of Top Women in Healthcare, Modern Healthcare, 2002—07. Fellow: American Health Info. Mgmt. Assn. Office: Kloss Strategic Advisors 240 E Randolph St Chicago IL 60601-7950 Office Phone: 312-624-9750. Business E-Mail: linda@kloss-strategicadvisors.com. *

KLOTH, DAVID S., pain medicine physician; MD, NYU, 1987. Diplomate Am. Bd. Anesthesiology-pain medicine, Am. Bd. Anesthesiology, Am. Acad. Pain Mgmt. Resident anesthesiology Hosp. of the Univ. of Pa., 1988—91; med. dir. Anesthesia Pain Ctr. Danbury Hosp., co-dir. Acute Pain Mgmt. Svc.; founder Conn. Pain Care, med. dir. Mem.: Soc. of Interventional Pain Mgmt. Surgery Centers (dir.), Am. Interventional Pain Physicians, Internat. Spinal Injection Soc., New England Pain Assoc., Am. Acad. of Pain Medicine, Am. Pain Soc., Am. Soc. of Interventional Pain Physicians (former pres., ethics com.), Conn. Pain Soc. (exec. dir.). Office: Connecticut Pain Care 109 Newton Rd Danbury CT 06810 Office Phone: 203-792-7246. Office Fax: 203-792-9636.

KLOTMAN, PAUL, academic administrator, physician; BS, U. Mich., 1972; MD, Ind. U., 1976. Tng. in medicine and nephrology, faculty mem., assoc. prof. medicine Duke U. Med. Ctr., 1976—83; chief molecular medicine sect. NIH Lab. Devel. Biology, 1988—98; chief NIDR/NIH Viral Pathogenesis Lab., 1993—94; Irene and Dr. Arthur M. Fishberg prof. medicine, chief nephrology divsn. Mt. Sinai Sch. Medicine, 1994—2001, chmn. Samuel Bronfman dept. medicine, 2001—10; pres., CEO Baylor Coll. Medicine, 2010—. Chmn. study sections NIH, Am. Heart Assn., Nat. Kidney Found, VA Rsch. Svc.; bd. mem. on various sci. adv. boards to biotech., pharm. and healthcare companies. Contbr. more than 200 publs. Mem.: Assn. Am. Physicians, Am. Soc. Clin. Investigation. Office: Baylor College Medicine One Baylor Plz Houston TX 77030 Office Phone: 713-798-4951. *

KLOUCHE, SHAHNAZ, medical researcher; b. Algeria, Oct. 1, 1967; MD, Medecine U., 1990. Clin. rsch. physician La Croix St.-Simon Hosp., 2007—10; clin. rsch. coord. Ambroise Paré Hosp., 2010—. Home: 85 Bd Pasteur Paris 75015 France Personal E-mail: klouche_shahnaz@yahoo.fr.

KLUMPP, SUSANNE, biochemist, educator, pharmacist; PhD, U. of Tübingen, 1982, Habilitation, 1989. Prof. Westf. Wilhelms-Univ., Münster, Germany, 2002—, Marburg U., Germany, 1995—2002; vis. assoc. prof. CalTech, Pasadena, Calif., 1994—95; heisenberg scholar CalTech / KFA (Germany), Pasadena, Calif., 1992—95; asst. prof. U. of Tübingen, Germany, 1985—91, rsch. fellow. Coun. mem. for rsch. support & funding com. Westf. Wilhelms-Univ., Münster, Germany, 2003—; dep. to ombudsman U. of Marburg, Germany, 1999—2002, dean of pharmacy, Germany, 1998—2000; student advisor U. of Tübingen, Germany, 1985—92. Editor: (book) Methods in Enzymology vol. 366: Protein Phosphatases; discoverer (patent) Histidine Protein Phosphatase. Grantee, Deutsche Forschungsgemeinschaft (DFG), 1989-2003; fellow, Heisenberg, 1992-1995. Mem.: GBM, ISN. Office: Inst für Pharm & Med Chemie der WWU Hittorfstr 58-62 Muenster 48149 Germany

KLUMPP, THOMAS RUSSELL, bone marrow transplant physician, educator; b. Santa Monica, Calif., Oct. 18, 1956; s. Allan Russell and Susan Wing Klumpp; m. Maria Gumas; children: John Allan, David Thomas. Degree magna cum laude, Williams Coll., 1978; MD, U. Pa., Phila., 1982. Cert. SAS Inst., Inc.; in oncology Am. Bd. Internal Medicine, 1989, in hematology Am. Bd. Internal Medicine, 1990, diplomate Am. Bd. Internal Medicine, 1985. Asst. prof. medicine Temple U. Sch. Medicine, 1990—96, assoc. prof. medicine, 1996—2006, prof. medicine, 2006—. Chief info. officer Temple U. BMT Program, 1990—. Contbr. scientific papers to numerous profl. jours. Parishioner Ch. Holy Apostles, Wynnewood, Pa., 1990—. Named Humanistic Physician of Yr., Dartmouth Med. Ctr., 1985. Mem.: AMA, ACP, Am. Soc. Clin. Oncology, Am. Soc. Hematology, Am. Soc. Blood and Marrow Transplantation, Phi Beta Kappa, Alpha Omega Alpha. Achievements include development of cancer research information systems. Office: Temple Univ BMT Program 7604 Central Ave Philadelphia PA 19111-2442 *

KLUN, BORIS, retired neurosurgeon; b. Ljubljana, Slovenia, July 6, 1925; s. Jakob and Marija (Hafner) Klun; m. Hermina Dreo, May 30, 1959 (dec. 1991); children: Nina, Barbara; m. Tatjana Lesjak, 2003. MD, Med. Faculty Ljubljana, 1952, PhD, 1971. Intern U. Med. Ctr., Ljubljana, 1953-54, resident in neurosurgery, 1954-59, U. Chgo., 1959-60; asst. prof. U. Med. Ctr., Ljubljana, 1972-77, prof., 1977-99; ret. U. Chgo., 1999. Head dept. neurosurgery Univ. Med. Ctr., 1975-87, dir. surg. depts. and svcs., 1977-82, sr. sci. advisor, 1987-92; officer Slovenian Med. Chamber. Author: Brain Injuries, 1997; editor: Slovenian Medical Dictionary; contbr. articles to profl. jours. Mem. Am. Assn. Neurol. Surgery, European Assn. Neurol. Surgery (officer tng. com. 1980-87), Academia Euro-Asiana Neurochirurgica, Hungarian Neurosurgeon Soc. (hon.), Slovenian Soc. Humanistic Scholars (pres.). Roman Catholic. Avocations: classical music, chess, photography, mountain climbing, skiing. Home: Goce Delceva 72 1000 Ljubljana Slovenia

KLUTZOW, FRIEDRICH WILHELM, neuropathologist; b. Bandoeng, Dutch East Indies, Aug. 6, 1923; arrived in US, 1953; s. Rudolph F.W. and Pauline (Van Thiel) K.; m. Apr. 2, 1954; children: Judith A., Michael J.; m. Merlene Hutto Byars, Dec. 10, 1999. MD, U. Utrecht, Netherlands, 1951. Diplomate Am. Bd. Neuropathology and Anatomic Pathology., 1972. Chief of staff Cmty. Meml. Hosp., Oconto Falls, Wis., 1965-68; pathology resident U. Wis., Madison, 1968-71, Armed Forces Inst. Pathology, Washington, 1971—72; neuropathologist VA Hosp., Mpls., 1972-75, dir. pathology dept. Brockton, Mass., 1975-83, Wichita, Kans., 1983-87, chief of staff Bath, N.Y., 1987-90, neuropathologist Bay Pines, Fla., 1991—2011. Clin. assoc. prof. pathology U. Rochester (N.Y.) Sch. Medicine, U. South Fla., Tampa; cons. in neuropathology Minn. Bd. Med. Practice, 1998—2011, Internat. Biographical Ctr., 2007; invited spkr. Oxford U., England, 1997, Lisbon, Portugal, 99, U. Cambridge, England, 2001. Prin. author: Neuropathology Manual: The Practical Approach, 1996; contbr. articles to profl. jours. Col. USAR, 1979-85. Recipient Paul Harris fellowship, Rotary Internat., Bath, NY, 1990, Outstanding Career award, Dept. Vet. Affairs, Washington, 1990; named to Hall Fame, Am. Biog. Inst., 2002. Fellow: Coll. Am. Pathologists; mem.: Internat. Soc. Neuropathology, Am. Assn. Neuropathologists. Republican. Achievements include research in persistent vegetative state; practical approach to lesions in neuropathology; the therapeutic potential of food, which can virtually cure any illness, including many cancers. Home: PO Box 3387 West Columbia SC 29171-3387 Office Phone: 727-398-9309. Home Fax: 803-794-4869. Personal E-mail: needle1@msn.com.

KNABLE, MICHAEL, psychiatrist, medical researcher; BS, DO, Ohio U. Clin. instr. dept. psychiatry George Wash. U. Med. Ctr.; dep. med. dir. Nat. Inst. Mental Health, 1992—98; med. dir. Stanley Med. Rsch. Inst., 1998—2003, exec. dir., 2003—08; pres. Bethesda Behavioral Scis., 2008—. Bd. dir. Ahead with Autism Found., Psychiatric Genomics, Inc., DarPharma, Inc. Co-author (with E. Fuller Torrey): Surviving Manic Depression, 2001. Office: Bethesda Behavioral Sciences 43 Montgomery Ave Bethesda MD 20814-4412 Office Phone: 301-652-6260. *

KNAPP, ALBERT BRUCE, gastroenterologist; b. NYC, Aug. 9, 1955; s. Russell Sage and Bettina K. BA, Columbia U., 1975, MD, 1979. Intern, resident Albert Einstein Med. Ctr., NYC, 1979-82; fellow in gastroenterology Brigham & Women's Hosp. and Harvard Med. Sch., Boston, 1982-85; attending physician Lenox Hill Hosp., NYC, 1985—, NYU Hosp. Ctr., NYC, 1991—; asst. clin. prof. medicine NYU Med. Ctr., NYC, 1990—2004, assoc. clin. prof. medicine, 2005—08, clin. prof. medicine, 2008—. Author major textbook in field, 1982; contbr. numerous articles to profl. jours. Fellow: NIH rsch. grantee, 1982. Fellow ACP (jour. reviewer Annals of Internal Medicine 1985—); mem. Am. Gastroenterol. Assn. (jour. reviewer Gastroenterology 1985—), Am. Assn. Gastrointestinal Endoscopy, Am. Assn. for Study of Liver Disease (Rsch. award 1984), Coun. on Fgn. Rels. Office: 760 Park Ave New York NY 10021-4152 Business E-Mail: office@knappmd1.com.

KNAPP, CYNTHIA L. CORLETT, microbiologist, director; b. Cleve., Aug. 11, 1954; d. Donald F. and Betsy L. Corlett; m. K. Brad Knapp, July 29, 1978; 1 child, Kelly Danielle. BS, Ashland U., Ohio, 1976; MS, Cleve. State U., 1984. Head spl. projects R&D Cleve. (Ohio) Clinic, 1975—96; dir. lab. svcs. TREK Diagnostic Sys., Cleve., 1996—. Adv. Clin. Labs. Stds. Inst., Wayne, Pa., 1997—2000; presenter in field. Contbr. chapters to books, over 100 articles to profl. jours. Mem.: Am. Soc. Clin. Pathology, Am. Soc. Microbiology. Avocations: sailing, hiking. Office: Thermo Fisher Scientific 982 Keynote Cir Cleveland OH 44131 Office Phone: 216-351-8735. Business E-Mail: cknapp@trekds.com.

KNAPP, DAVID ALLAN, pharmaceutical educator, researcher, former dean; b. Cleve., Feb. 25, 1938; s. Frederick Allan and Ethel R. (Ogden) Knapp; m. Deanne Evander, June 2, 1962; 1 child, Wendy Kay Knapp Steagall. BS, Purdue U., West Lafayette, Ind., 1960, MS, 1962, PhD, 1965. Asst. prof. Ohio State U. Coll. Pharmacy, Columbus, 1964-67, assoc. prof., 1967-71; assoc. prof. to prof. pharm. health svcs. rsch. U. Md. Sch. Pharmacy, Balt., 1971—, assoc. dean grad. edn. & rsch., 1981-83, chmn. dept. pharm. practice & adminstrn. sci., 1987-91, dir. Ctr. on Drugs and Pub. Policy, 1987-96, acting dean Sch. Pharmacy, 1989-91, dean, 1991—2007. Vis. scholar U. Mich. Sch. Pub. Health, 1970—71, Agy. Healthcare Rsch. & Quality, HHS, 2001—02; intramural rschr. Nat. Ctr. Health Svc. Rsch. HHS, Hyattsville, Md., 1978. Author: Pharmacy Drugs and Medical Care (5 edits.), 1972—92; contbr. articles to profl. jours. Fellow: APHA, AAAS, Am. Soc. Hosp. Pharmacists, Am. Pharms. Assn., Am. Assn. Colleges of Pharmacy (scholar in residence 1986—87, bd. dirs. 1986—89, 1993—96, pres. 1994—95, Volwiler Rsch. Gold medal 1986), Am. Found. Pharm. Edn. (bd. dirs. 1994—96, exec. com. 1995—96), Am. Assn. Pharm. Scientists; mem.: Rho Chi, Sigma Xi. Unitarian Universalist. Office: U Md Sch Pharmacy 20 North Pine St Baltimore MD 21201-3480 Business E-Mail: dknapp@rx.umaryland.edu.

KNAPP, HOWARD RAYMOND, internist, clinical pharmacologist; b. Red Bank, NJ, Oct. 5, 1949; s. Howard Raymond and Jane Marie (Ray) K.; m. Brenda Louise Carr, 1984; 1 child, Matthew. AB in Biology, Washington U., St. Louis, 1971; MD, Vanderbilt U., 1977, PhD in Pharmacology, 1984. Diplomate Am. Bd. Internal Medicine, cert. clin. densitometrist. Asst. prof. medicine and pharmacology Vanderbilt U., Nashville, 1984-89, assoc. prof., 1990; assoc. prof. internal medicine and pharmacology U. Iowa, Iowa City, 1990-97, prof. internal medicine and pharmacology, 1997-2000, assoc. dir. NIH Clin. Rsch. Ctr., 1997-2000; exec. dir. Billings Clin. Res. Divsn., Mont., 2000—05, v.p. rsch. Mont., 2006—. Mem. NIH Nutrition Study Sect., Bethesda, Md., 1994—96; cons. pharm. firms, grant orgns. and govtl. entities; mem. applied pharmacol. task force Nat. Bd. Med. Examiners, 1997—2000; mem. expert panel on cardiovasc. and renal drugs U.S. Pharmacopeia, 2000—05. Editor-in-chief Lipids, 1995-2006; contbr. numerous articles to profl. jours., chpts. to books. Grantee NIH, Am. Heart Assn., others. Fellow ACP, Am. Heart Assn. (vascular biol. rsch. rev. com. 1993-95, arteriosclerosis coun.); mem. Ctrl. Soc. for Clin. Rsch. (chair clin. pharmacol. sect. 1992-95), Am. Soc. for Clin. Pharmacology and Therapeutics, Am. Oil chemists Soc. (gov. bd., 2002-04, v.p., 2005-06, pres., 2006-07), Am/ Diabetes Assn., NY Adad. Sci., Am. Chem. Soc. Achievements include first demonstration that calcium ionophores stimulate eicosanoid synthesis; first evidence that N-3 fatty acids reduce platelet activation and blood pressure in patients; first demonstration of the effects of 5-lipoxygenase inhibition in humans. Office: Billings Clinic Rsch Ctr 1045 N 30th St Billings MT 59101-0733 Office Phone: 406-255-8475. Business E-Mail: hknapp@billingsclinic.org.

KNAPP, MILDRED FLORENCE, retired social worker; b. Detroit, Apr. 15, 1932; d. Edwin Frederick and Florence Josephine (Antaya) K. BBA, U. Mich., 1954, MA in Cmty. and Adult Edn., 1964, MSW, 1967. Social work master's lic. Dist. dir. Girl Scouts Met. Detroit, 1954-63; planning asst. Coun. Social Agys. Flint and Genessee Counties, 1965; sch. social worker Detroit Pub. Schs., 1967-98, ret., 1998. Field instr. Alumnae bd. govs. U. Mich., 1972-75, scholarship chair, 1969-70 76-80, chair spl. com. women's athletics, 1972-75, class agt. fund raising Sch. Bus. Adminstrn., 1978-79; active Founders Soc. Detroit Inst. Art, 1969—, Friends Children's Mus. Detroit, 1978— Women's Assn., Detroit Symphony Orch., 1982-89, Mich. Humane Soc., 1991—; vol. Coun. Detroit Symphony Orch., 1990—; trustee, fin. chmn. Children's Mus.; charter mem. World War II Meml. Recipient Appreciation cert.; grantee, HEW, 1966; fellow, Mott Found., 1964. Mem. NASW, Acad. Cert. Social Workers, Nat. Cmty. Edn. Assn. (charter), Sch. Social Work Assn. Am. (charter), Outdoor Edn. and Camping Coun. (charter), Mich. Sch. Social Workers Assn. (pres. 1980-81), Detroit Sch. Social Workers Assn. (past pres.), Detroit Assn. U. Mich. Women (pres. 1980-82), Detroit Fedn. Tchrs., Madame Alexander Doll Club, WWII Meml. (charter mem.). Methodist. Home: 702 Lakepointe St Grosse Pointe Park MI 48230-1706

KNAPP, RICHARD DAVID, psychiatrist, educator; BS in Biology, Fairleigh Dickinson U., NJ, 1967; DO, Phila. Coll. Osteo. Medicine, 1971. Lic. Fla., 1978, diplomate Am. Bd. Psychiatry and Neurology-psychiatry, 1985, Am. Bd. Psychiatry and Neurology-addiction psychiatry, 1993. Intern Tri-County Hosp., 1972; resident psychiatry Belmont Behavioral Health (formerly Phila. Psychiat. Ctr.), Phila., 1972—75; pvt. practice gen. medicine Miami, Fla., 1979—82; clin. dir. adolescent substance abuse program Humana Hosp. South Broward, Hallandale, Fla., 1982—86; pvt. practice gen., geriatric and addictions psychiatry Miami, Fla., 1982—86; asst. assoc. clin. prof. Coll. Osteo. Medicine Nova Southeastern Univ., Miami, Fla., 1983—94; pvt. practice gen., geriatric and addictions psychiatry Hollywood, Fla., 1986—2001; prin. investigator Fla. Clin. Rsch. Ctr. LLC, 2001—; hosp. affiliations includes Meml. Regional Hosp. Office: Memorial Regional Hospital 3501 Johnson St Hollywood FL 33021 Office Phone: 954-961-1500.

KNAPP, RICHARD MAITLAND, association executive; b. Hartford, Conn., July 23, 1941; s. Maitl K.; m. Elizabeth Burgoyne, Apr. 1969; children: Heather, Peter. BA, Marietta Coll., 1963; MA, U. Iowa, 1965, PhD in Hosp. and Health Adminstrn., 1968. Trainee USPHS, 1964-65; project dir. Tchg. Hosp. Info. Ctr., Coun. of Tchg. Hosps., Assn. Am. Med. Colls., Washington, 1968-69; dir. divsn. tchg. hosps. Assn. Am. Med. Colls., Washington, 1969-73, dir. dept. tchg. hosps., 1973-87, sr. v.p., 1987-93, exec. v.p., 1994—; mem. adv. com. ambulatory dental svcs. program Robert Wood Johnson Hosp., 1978-83. Bd. dirs. Nat. Assn. Biomed. Rsch., chmn. exec. com. 1993-95; chmn. exec. com. Ad Hoc Group for Med. Rsch., 1992—. Contbr. articles to profl. jours.; mem. editl. bd. Inquiry, 1983-88. Bd. dirs. Hosp. Fund, Inc., 1984-2000; adv. com. The Commonwealth Fund Exec. Nurse Devel. Program, 1984-93; trustee Inova Health Sys. Bd., 1986-2005, chmn., 1999-2003; trustee Inova Health Care Svcs. Bd., 1982-98, chmn. 1993-98; mem. oper. bd. Fairfax Hosp., 1987-92, sec. bd., 1987-89, chmn. bd., 1990-92; mem. vestry St. Anne's Episc. Ch., Reston, Va., 1979-83. Mem.: Va. Hosp. and Health Care Assn. (bd. dirs. 2001—03), Inst. Medicine of NAS, Am. Hosp. Assn., W.Va. Thoroughbred Breeders Assn., Throughbred Owners and Breeders Assn., Hidden Creek Country Club, Cosmos Club, Delta Upsilon. Office: Assn Am Med Colls 2450 N St NW Washington DC 20037-1167 Office Phone: 202-828-0410. Business E-Mail: rmknapp@aamc.org.

KNAPP, ROBERT CHARLES, retired obstetrics and gynecology educator; b. NYC, Jan. 19, 1927; s. Jack and Hilda (Knapp); m. Miriam Hermanos, Nov., 1955; children: Louise, Jennifer, Michael. AB, Columbia U., 1949; MD, SUNY Downstate Med. Center, Bklyn., 1953; MA, Harvard U., 1982; DSc (hon.), SUNY, Bklyn., 2003. Diplomate Am. Bd. Ob-Gyn. Intern Kings County Hosp., Bklyn., 1953-54, resident, 1954-58; instr. ob-gyn SUNY, Bklyn., 1958-62, Am. Cancer Soc. fellow, 1962-63, asst. prof. ob-gyn, 1962-63; asst. prof. Cornell U., 1963-69, assoc. prof., 1969-70, vis. scholar ob-gyn. Weill Med. Coll., 1998—; chmn. dept. ob-gyn. Nassau County Med. Center, East Meadow, NY, 1967-70; assoc. prof. ob-gyn. Harvard Med. Sch., Boston, 1970-75, William H. Baker prof. gynecology, 1975-93, William H. Baker prof. emeritus, 1993—; assoc. chief of staff Boston Hosp. for Women, 1975—80; dir. gynecology surgery and oncology Brigham and Women's Hosp., Boston, 1980-89. Dir. gynecology Sidney Farber Cancer Inst., 1975-89; vis. scholar Weill Med. Coll., Cornell U., 2000-. Served with U.S. Army, 1944-46. Fellow ACOG, ACS; mem. AAAS, Am. Soc. Clin. Oncology, Am. Fedn. Clin. Rsch., Obstet. Soc. Boston, Am. Radium Soc., Boston Surg. Soc. Soc. Gynecologic Oncology, Am. Assn. for Cancer Rsch., Soc. Surg. Oncologists, Internat. Soc. Gynecologic Oncologists. Home: 20 Sutton Pl S New York NY 10022-4165 Office Phone: 212-829-1209. Business E-Mail: robert_knapp_ma82@post.howard.edu.

KNATTERUD, MARY E., editor, educator, writer; b. Pipestone, Minn., Mar. 21, 1954; BA, Concordia Coll., 1974; MA, U. Minn., 1979, PhD, 1997. Editor/writer U. Minn. Pub. Ctr., Mpls., 1981—86; user documentation tng. specialist Higher Edn. Assistance Found., St. Paul, 1986—87; assoc. prof./sr. rsch. assoc. U. Minn., Dept. Surgery, Mpls., 1987—2008; assoc. prof. U. Ariz., Tucson, 2008—. Author: First Do No Harm: Empathy and the Writing of Medical Journal Articles, 2002. Fellow: Am. Med. Writers Assn. (pres. north ctrl. chpt. 1992—93, Pres.'s award 2002, Golden Apple Tchg. award 2010); mem.: Coun. Sci. Editors, 4Cs, Nat. Coun. Tchrs. English. Democrat. Lutheran.

KNAUB, MARK A., orthopedist, director; b. York, Pa., Feb. 3, 1971; MD, U. Pitts. Sch. Medicine, 1993. Dir., orthopaedic spine svc. Penn State Hershey Med. Ctr., 2006—. Asst. prof., dept. orthopaedic surgery Penn State U. Coll. Medicine, 2004—; assoc. dir. Penn State Hershey Spine Ctr., 2008—. Fellow: Am. Acad. Orthopaedic Surgery; mem.: North Am. Spine Soc. Avocations: winemaking, golf. Office: 30 Hope Dr Bldg A Hershey PA 17033 Business E-Mail: mknaub@psu.edu.

KNECHT, RICHARD ARDEN, family practitioner; b. Grand Rapids, Mar. 7, 1929; s. Fredrick William and Eva Rae (Blakley) K.; m. Joan Matson, Dec. 26, 1951 (div. 1975); children: Richard Arden, Karrie Jo, Jeffrey Paul; m. Patricia Irene Gilmore, Aug. 14, 1976; 1 child, Kimberly Kahler. BS, U. Mich., 1951, MD, 1955. Diplomate Am. Bd. Family Practice, Am. Bd. Geriatric Medicine; cert. med. dir. Intern St. Mary Hosp., Grand Rapids, Mich., 1955-56; pvt. practice, Fife Lake, Mich., 1956—. Fellow Am. Acad. Family Physicians, Am. Geriatric Soc., Royal Soc. Medicine; mem. Mich. Med. Soc. (com. on aging 1988—), Mich. Acad. Family Practice (chmn. com. on aging 1986-88, pub.'s award 1988), Mich. Med. Dirs. Assn. (pres. 1996-97). Avocations: archaeology, motorcycling, geology, hunting, fishing. Home: 8851 W River Beach Ln Garden City ID 83714-1812 Personal E-mail: r.knecht@charter.net.

KNESEL, ERNEST ARTHUR, JR., health facility administrator, chemicals executive; b. New Orleans, Dec. 11, 1945; s. Ernest Arthur and Catherine Charlotte (Maier) K.; m. Lavina Lynn Menge, June 2, 1968; children: Eric Ernest, Tami Lynn, Bradley William. Student, Armstrong Coll., 1963—64; BS, Fairleigh Dickinson U., 1968, MS, 1970. Cert. clin. chemist. Technologist Am. Biol. Control Lab., Tenefly, NJ, 1966—68; sr. technologist Englewood Hosp., NJ, 1968—69; founder, v.p. Biomed. Reference Labs., Inc., Burlington, NC, 1969—82; sr. v.p. Roche Biomed. Labs., Inc., Burlington, 1982—95; pres., founder Roche Image Analysis Sys., Inc., Elon College, NC, 1989—96; exec. v.p., founder Autocyte, Inc., Elon College, 1996—99; v.p., founder TriPath Imaging, 1999—2000; cons. True North Group, 2000—01; founder, pres. Select Diagnostics Inc., 2001—11; co-founder, pres. Synermed Select Ptnrs., Inc., 2003—10. Founder, mgr. CellSolutions LLC, 2007—, Select Labs. SC, 2007—; chmn., pres. Select Labs. Ptnrs., Inc., 2010—. Inventor serum filter/dispenser vial, automated aliquoting system, cyto-rich automated cytology preparation system and simultaneous machine and human interactive cytology evaluation system, Cell Solution 120 high capacity thin-layer cytology preparation system, Cell Solution 30 and BestCyte Imaging System. Mem. Am. Assn. Clin. Chemistry, Am. Soc. Clin. Pathologists (assoc.). Roman Catholic. Avocation: magic. Office: Select Lab Ptnrs Inc 1100 Revolution Mill Dr # 1 Greensboro NC 27405

KNIBEL, MARCOS FREITAS, health facility administrator, intensive care physician; b. Petrópolis, Brazil, Apr. 17, 1953; s. Moacyr and Hercilia Knibel; m. Marcia Paranhos Knibel, Feb. 18, 1978; children: Marcela, Frederico, Felipe. MD, Faculdade de Medicina de Teresópolis, Brazil, 1976. With intensive care unit Hosp. Marcilio Dias, Brazil, 1982—85, INCA, Brazil, 1989—; head intensive care unit Santa Casa, Brazil, 1991—, Cardio Trauma Ipanema, Brazil, 1999—, Hosp. São Lucas, Brazil, 2001—. Author: Medicina Intensiva, 2003. Mem.: Associação Medicina Intensiva Brasileira. Home: Rua Capuri 1484 22610-310 Rio de Janeiro RJ Brazil

KNIEWALD, JASNA, toxicologist, educator, scientist; b. Zagreb, Croatia, June 24, 1938; d. Radivoj and Jelena (Operman) Novak; m. Zlatko Kniewald, July 14, 1962; children: Ines, Hrvoje. BSc, Tech. U. Zagreb, 1962, PhD, 1965. Rsch. assoc. Inst. Physical Chem., Zagreb, Croatia, 1962-75; sr. rsch. assoc. Technol. Faculty U. Zagreb, 1976-86; from rsch. advisor to prof., head toxicology lab. Faculty Food Sci. & Biotech. U. Zagreb, 1987—. Co-author: Food and Development, 1987, Technology and Development, 1989, Food Technology and Biotechnology, 1990; author: (textbooks) Methods in Scientific Work, 1993, Toxicology-Practice, 1997; co-editor: Current Studies in Biotechnology: Vol. 1, Biomedicine, 2000, Vol. 2, Environment, 2001, Vol. 3, Food, 2003; contbr. articles to profl. jours. Mem. European Soc. Toxicology, European Sci. Found., Croatian Acad. Engring., NY Acad. Scis. Avocations: skiing, swimming. Home: Rakovčeva 6 10000 Zagrab Croatia Office: U Zagreb Pierotti Str 6 10000 Zagreb Croatia Office Phone: 3851 4605288. E-mail: jasna.kniewald@pbf.hr.

KNIGHT, ANN, rheumatologist; b. Stockholm, Jan. 25, 1957; MD, Karolinska Inst., 1982; PhD, Uppsala U., 2007. Physician Akademiska sjukhuset, 2000—. Office: Akademiska sjukhuse Dept Rheumatology Uppsala 751 85 Sweden Business E-Mail: ann.knight@medsci.uu.se.

KNIGHT, DELVIN R., JR., cardiologist, researcher; b. Houston, Aug. 15, 1952; BS in Biol. Sci., Tex. A&M U., 1975; PhD in Med. Physiology and Biophysics, U. Okla., Health Scis. Ctr., 1982. Postdoc. fellow in medicine Harvard Med. Sch., 1982—86, instr. in cardiovasc. medicine, 1986—89; rsch. fellow Pfizer, Inc., 1989—. Sect. editor Current Opinion in Investigational Drugs, 1999—2010; editl. bd. mem. Am. Jour. Physiology, 2007—11. Postdoc. fellowship, NIH. Fellow: Am. Heart Assn. (mem., Coun. Basic Cardiovasc. Sci., chmn., comm. com., heritage affiliate 1995—97, named Outstanding Vol., Conn. affiliate, Grant-in-Aid); mem.: NY Acad. Scis., Am. Physiol. Soc. Office: MS 8220-2266 Eastern Point Rd Groton CT 06340 Business E-Mail: delvin.r.knight@pfizer.com.

KNIGHT, EDWARD HOWDEN, retired hospital administrator; b. Vancouver, BC, Can., Apr. 13, 1933; s. Edward Allen and Helen Blackley (Howden) K.; m. Glenda Carol Wiggins, Mar. 6, 1964; children: Carolyn, Patricia, Brett. B of Commerce, diploma in hosp. adminstrn., U. B.C., 1956. Adminstrv. asst. Vancouver Gen. Hosp., 1956-57; adminstr. Prince Rupert Gen. Hosp., 1957-61, Red Deer Gen. Hosp., 1961-72, Dr. Richard Parsons Aux. Hosp., 1963-72, Valley Pk. Manor Nursing Home, 1969-72; dep. exec. dir. Calgary Gen. Hosp., Calgary, Alberta, Canada, 1972-74, exec. dir., 1974-83, pres., 1983-88, E.H. Knight & Assoc. Inc., Calgary, Alberta, Canada, 1988-92. Lectr. Red Deer Coll., 1968-72; adj. asst. prof. faculty medicine U. Calgary, 1978-91; trustee Alta. Blue Cross Plan, 1963-68; mem. Fed. Task Force on Cost of Health Svc. in Can., 1969. Recipient Queen's Silver Jubilee medal, 1977. Fellow Can. Coll. Health Svc. Execs. (dir. 1972-74, founding charter mem.), Am. Coll. Healthcare Execs. (regent for Alta. 1973-76, 79-82); mem. Can. Hosp. Assn. (dir. 1981-83), Alta. Hosp. Assn. (dir. 1977-84, pres. 1983), Assn. Can. Tchg. Hosp. (pres. 1986-87), Rotary (asst. dist. gov. 2005-08), Rancho Bernardo (pres. 2003-04), Kinsmen Club (pres. 1971-72), Phi Delta Theta. Home: 820 Windridge Cir San Marcos CA 92078-7917 E-mail: ehknight@roadrunner.com.

KNIGHT, EDWARD R., judge, psychologist, law educator; b. Milw., Oct. 5, 1917; s. Harry and Lillian (Bachman) K.; m. Judith A. Weidberg, July 6, 1941; 1 child, Barbara Jane. AB, U. Wis., 1940, JD, 1941; AM, NYU, 1942, PhD, 1943. Bar: Wis. 1941, N.J. 1976; diplomate Am. Bd. Profl. Psychology. Master Oxford Acad., Pleasantville, NJ, 1941, psychologist, 1942, head psychologist, 1943, asst. headmaster, 1945-47, headmaster, 1947-73, emeritus, 1973—. U.S. magistrate judge, 1976—; judge Mcpl. Ct., Margate City, N.J., 1976-81; ptnr. Fox, Rothschild, Atlantic City, N.J., 1976—; dir. First Fidelity Bank, 1950-90. Pres. bd. govs. Atlantic City Med. Ctr., 1973-87, chmn. emeritus, 1987—; chmn. Master Planning Bd., Egg Harbor Twp., N.J., 1961-73; chmn. Atlantic County (N.J.) Charter Study Commn., 1973-74. Author: Self-Discipline and Academic Failure; mem. editl. bd. Parental Delinquency; contbr. articles on edn. and psychology to profl. jours. Capt., USAAF, 1943-45; personnel com., personnel div. ATSC, Wright Field. Named Trustee of Century, Atlantic City Med. Ctr., 1998. Fellow APA (sch. psychologists div.); mem. Ea. N.J. psychol. assns., Nat. Assn. Ind. Schs., N.J. Assn. Sch. Psychologists, Interam. Soc. Psychology, Boarding Sch. Headmasters Assn. Mid. States (pres. 1966-67), Wis. Alumni Assn., U. Wis. Mem. Union (life), Atlanticare Health Sys. (vice-chmn. bd.), Phi Delta Kappa, Kappa Delta Pi. Office: US Dist Ct 1301 Atlantic Ave Fl 3 Atlantic City NJ 08401-7207 Home: 5 Baycrest Ct Margate City NJ 08402-1601

KNIGHT, JACK VERNON, medicine and microbiology educator; b. Osceola, Mo., Sept. 6, 1917; m. Elizabeth Gordon; 4 children. AB, William Jewell Coll., 1939, DSc (hon.), 1982; MD, Harvard U., 1943. Diplomate Am. Bd. Internal Medicine. Intern Mass. Meml. Hosp., Boston, 1943; resident Cornell U.-N.Y. Hosp. Med. Ctr., NYC, 1946-47, from asst. in medicine to asst. prof., 1948-54; assoc. prof. medicine Vanderbilt U. Sch. Medicine, Nashville, 1954-59; clin. dir. Nat. Inst. Allergy and Infectious Diseases, NIH, Bethesda, Md., 1959-66; prof., chmn. dept. microbiology and immunology Baylor Coll. Medicine, Houston, 1966-88, prof. infectious disease sect. dept. medicine, 1966—, prof. biotech., dir. Ctr. for Biotech., 1989-94, prof., acting chmn. dept. molecular physiology-biophysics, 1994-99, prof. molecular physiology and biophysics, 1994—, Kyle and Josephine Morrow disting. prof., 1984. Sr. attending physician Meth. Hosp., Houston, 1966—; attending physician Ben Taub Gen Hosp., Houston, 1966—; physician, cons. VA Hosp., Houston; bd. dirs. Viratek, Inc., Costa Mesa, Calif., 1980-94; mem. med. scis. rev. panel to NASA, Am. Inst. Biol. Scis., 1976-80; profl. cons. U.S. Army Med. Rsch. Inst. Infectious Diseases, 1962-81. Patentee on small particle aerosol generator for treatment respiratory disease including lungs; patentee for small particle aerosol liposome and liposome-drug combinations for med. use. Bd. dirs. Contemporary Arts Mus., Houston, 1977-82, Gorgas Meml. Inst. Tropical and Preventive Medicine, Washington, 1977-91. With M.C., USN, 1944-46, ETO. Recipient Guy R. Odum, Jr. award M.D. Anderson Hosp. and Tumor Inst., 1986; Disting. Svc. Prof. award Baylor Coll. Medicine, 1986, Disting. Faculty award, 1987. Mem. ACP, Am. Clin. and Climatol. Assn., Am. Fedn. for Clin. Rsch., Am. Soc. for Clin. Investigation, Am. Soc. for Microbiology, Am. Soc. for Virology, Assn. Am. Physicians, Assn. Med. Sch. Microbiology Chairmen (pres. 1981), Infectious Diseases Soc. Am. (emeritus), Internat. Assn. Aerobiology, Internat. Leprosy Assn., Soc. for Exptl. Biology and Medicine, Tex. Med. Assn., Harris County Med. Soc., Sigma Xi, Alpha Omega Alpha. Business E-Mail: jvknight@houston.rr.com.

KNIGHT, LESTER B., healthcare company executive; b. NYC, May 15, 1958; BS of Indsl. Engring., Cornell U., 1980; MBA, Cornell Johnson Sch. Mgmt., 1981. Various positions Baxter International, Inc., 1981-90, corp. v.p., 1990-92, exec. v.p., 1992-96; chmn., CEO, Allegiance Corp., 1996-99; vice chmn. Cardinal Health, Inc., 1999; founder, mng. ptnr. Roundtable Healthcare Partners, 2001—; non-exec. chmn. AON Corp. (AON Brokerage Group), 2008—. Bd. dirs. Baxter Internat. Inc., 1995—96, Cardinal Health Inc., 1999, Aon Corp., 1999—, Health Industry Mfrs. Assn., Evanston Hosp. Corp., Jr. Achievement of Chgo., The Baxter Allegiance Found., Evanston Northwestern Healthcare. Trustee Northwestern U.; mem. Lincoln Found. for Bus. Excellence. Mem.: Bus. Roundtable (Mid-Am.

com.)., Chgo. Coun. on Fgn. Rels., Econ. Club Chgo., Chgo. Commonwealth Club, Chgo. Club, Comml. Club Chgo. Office: Roundtable Healthcare Partners 272 E Deerpath Rd Ste 350 Lake Forest IL 60045

KNIGHT, PATRICIA MARIE, biomedical engineer, consultant; BS in Engring. Sci., Ariz. State U., MSChemE; PhD in Biomed. Engring., U. Utah. Teaching and rsch. asst. Ariz. State U., Tempe; product devel. engr. Am. Med. Optics, Irvine, Calif., mgr. materials rsch.; rsch. asst. U. Utah, Salt Lake City; dir. materials rsch. Allergan Surg. Products, Irvine, dir. rsch., v.p. rsch., devel. and engring., 1991—2002; v.p. rsch., devel. Advanced Med. Optics, Santa Ana, Calif., 2002—03; cons. biomed. product rsch. and devel. Laguna Niguel, Calif., 2003—. Contbr. articles to profl. jours. E-mail: pkbiomed@cox.net.

KNIGHTS, EDWIN MUNROE, pathologist; b. Providence, Dec. 25, 1924; s. Edwin Munroe and Viola Ruth (Koreb) K.; m. Ruth Lindsay Currie, Sept. 23, 1961; children: Edwin B., Jessie B., Ross D., David J. (dec. 1979). AB, Brown U., 1948; MD, Cornell U., 1948. Intern Bellevue Hosp., NYC, 1948-49; resident in pathology R.I. Hosp., Providence, 1949-50, Henry Ford Hosp, Detroit, 1952-54; assoc. pathologist Harper Hosp., Detroit, 1954; dir. labs. Hurley Hosp., Flint, Mich., 1957-62, Providence Hosp., Southfield, Mich., 1963-75; dir. Northland Oakland Med. Labs., Southfield, Mich., 1964-75, Bio Sci. Labs., Detroit, 1975-85, Smith Kline Bio-Sci. Labs., Detroit, 1985-89; dir. labs. Kern Hosp., Warren, Mich., 1977-81; pres. Coll. Terr. Inc., Flint, Mich., 1968—2003; dir. Performance Assurance Profls., Bloomfield Hills, Mich., 1988-94; pres. Life Sci. Inc., Flint, 1971-72, Vet. Med. Labs., 1973-75; clin. prof. pathology Mich. State U., 1974-75; rep. Comprehensive Health Planning Coun. S.E. Mich., 1973-85, trustee, 1986-87; mem. lab. peer rev. com. Mich. Dept. Social Svcs., 1979-84; med. dir. Smith Kline Beecham Labs., Detroit, 1990-92, Nat. Health Labs., Flint, 1992-94. Pres. Life Sci. Inc., Grantham, 1996-98; pathologist Project Hope, Indonesia and Vietnam, 1961, Peru, 1962, Ecuador, 1964; bd. dirs. GeneSaver DNA Preservation Svcs., 1996—. Author: Ultramicro Methods for Clinical Laboratories, 1957, 2d edit., 1962; editor: Minicomputers in the Clinical Laboratory, 1970, Lifelines, 1971-75, For Want of an "A" Confusion Reigns. The Day Nature Goofed, 2004, Harvesting Health from your Family Tree, 2007; contbg. editor Jour. Foot Surgery, 1983-89; contbr. articles to profl. jours. and mags. Emeritus mem. adv. coun. New Eng. Hist. Geneal. Soc., trustee, 2001—07; mem. long range planning com. Eastman Cmty. Assn., 1997-2003; bd. overseers USS Constn. Mus., 2005—; bd. dirs. Thomas Jefferson Heritage Soc., 2005—, Am. Theater, 1943-45, Lt. MC USNR, 1950-52, 50-52, ETO, Korean War, squadron med. officer, cominron 8, USPHS grantee, 1957-66. Fellow ACP, Coll. Am. Pathologists, Am. Soc. Clin. Pathology (Mich. councillor 1966-68); mem. AMA, Am. Coll. Med. Genetics (affil. doctoral mem. 2005-06), Oakland County Med. Soc. (pres. 1974), Mich. Soc. Pathologists (pres. 1970, del. Mich. State Med. Soc. 1986-93), Internat. Acad. Pathology, Mich. State Med. Soc., Assn. Clin. Scientists, Gen. Soc. Mayflower Descs., Roger Williams Family Assn., Wardroom Club (Boston), Phi Chi Achievements include patents in field. Home and Office: 10 Allds St Apt 112 Nashua NH 03060

KNOBLOCH, FERDINAND J., psychiatrist, educator; b. Prague, Czech Republic, Aug. 15, 1916; emigrated to Can., 1970; s. Ferdin and Marie (Verunac) K.; m. Susana Hartman (dec. 1944 victim of Holocaust); m. Jirina Sorkovska, Sept. 5, 1947; children: Katerina, Gohana. Maturity degree, Realgymnasium, Prague, 1935; student, Charles U. Med. Sch., Prague, 1935—46; psychoanalytic tng., Charles U. Med. Sch., 1945-53, 1945—53. Successively lectr., asst. prof., assoc. prof. psychiatry Charles U., Prague, 1946-70; mem. faculty U. B.C., Vancouver, Canada, 1970—, prof. psychiatry, 1971-83, prof. emeritus, 1983—; clin. dir. Day House Univ. Hosp., 1972-90. Vis. prof. U. Havana, 1963, U. Ill., Chgo., 1968-69, Columbia U., 1969-70, Albert Einstein Med. Coll., 1970; pres. European seminar mental health and family WHO, 1961, 3d Internat. Congress Psychodrama, 1968; co-chmn. Internat. Symposium Non-Verbal Aspects and Techniques of Psychotherapy, 1974; hon. dir. psychodrama Moreno Inst., NYC, 1974. Author: (with Jirina Knobloch) Forensic Psychiatry, 1967 (award Czechoslovak Med. Soc. 1968), Psychotherapy, 1968, Neurosis and You, 1962, 63, 68, Integrated Psychotherapy, 1979 (transl. into German 1983, Japanese 1984, Czech 1993, 1999, Chinese, 1995), Integrated Psychotherapy in Action, 1999; contbr. articles on psychotherapy integration, psychology of music and evolutionary psychology to profl. jours. Polit. prisoner of Gestapo, 1943-45. Recipient award, Min. Foreign Affairs, 2004. Fellow Am. Psychiat. Assn. (disting. life), Czechoslovak Soc. Advancement Psychoanalysis and Integration of Psychotherapy (pres. 1968-72), Am. Acad. Psychoanalysis, Polish Psychiat. Assn. (corr.), Can. Psychiat. Assn., Am. Group Psychotherapy Assn., Can. Soc. for Integrated Psychotherapy and Psychoanalysis (pres. 1972—), World Psychiat. Assn. (co-chmn. sect. psychotherapy 1983-93, chmn. 1993-96).

KNOEBEL, SUZANNE BUCKNER, cardiologist, educator; b. Ft. Wayne, Ind., Dec. 13, 1926; d. Doster and Marie (Lewis) Buckner. AB, Goucher Coll., 1948; MD, Ind. U.-Indpls., 1960. Diplomate: Am. Bd. Internal Medicine. Asst. prof. medicine Ind. U., Indpls., 1966-69, assoc. prof., 1969-72, prof., 1972-77, Krannert prof., 1977—. Asst. dean rsch. Ind. U., Indpls., 1975-85; assoc. dir. Krannert Inst. Cardiology, Indpls., 1974-90; asst. chief cardiology sect. Richard L. Roudebush VA Med. Ctr., Indpls., 1982-90; editor-in-chief ACC Current Jour. Rev., 1992-2000. Fellow Am. Coll. Cardiology (v.p. 1980-81, pres. 1982-83); mem. Am. Fedn. Clin. Research, Assn. Univ. Cardiologists Office: Krannert Inst 1701 N Senate Ave Indianapolis IN 46202 Home Phone: 317-841-9233; Office Phone: 317-962-0061. Business E-Mail: sknoebel@iupui.edu.

KNOLL, ANDREW HERBERT, biology professor; b. West Reading, Pa., Apr. 23, 1951; s. Robert Samuel and Anna Augusta (Meyer) K.; m. Marsha Craig, June 22, 1974; children: Kirsten C., Robert A. BA with highest honors, Lehigh U., 1973; MA, Harvard U., 1974, PhD, 1977; PhD (hon.), Uppsala U., Sweden, 1996; DSc (hon.), Lehigh U., 1998. Asst. prof. geology Oberlin Coll., Ohio, 1977-82; assoc. prof. Harvard U., Cambridge, Mass., 1982-85, prof. biology, 1985-2000, curator bot. mus., 1985—, prof. earth and planetary sci., 1985—, chmn. dept. organismic and evolutionary biology, 1992-98, 2004—05, Fisher prof. natural history, 2000—, assoc. dean faculty Arts and Scis., 2000—03. Mem. com. on planetary biology U.S. Space Sci. Bd., 1982-88, NRC Bd. on Earth Scis., 1987-88, 92-95, space studies bd., 1989-90, 97-2000; Crosby vis. lectr. MIT, 1999; mem. sci. team NASA MER 2003 Mars Mission. Assoc. editor Paleobiology, 1980-92, Precambrian Rsch., 1985—, Trends in Ecology and Evolution, 1987-92, Rev. of Palaeobotany and Palynology, 1987—, Am. Jour. Sci., 1990—, Geology, 1992-98, Palaios, 1996-2002, Palaeography Palacoclimatology Palaeocology, 1997—, Internat. Jour. Plant Scis., 1998—; contbr. articles to profl. publs. Bd. dirs. U.S. Nat. Mus. Nat. Hist., 1993-97. Recipient Walcott medal, Nat. Acad. Scis., 1987, Chang prize in paleontology, Am. Mus. Natural History, 2001, Moore medal, Soc. Sedimentary Geology, 2005, Bownocker medal, Ohio State U., 2005, medal, Paleontological Soc., 2005, Wollaston medal, Geol. Soc. London, 2007; named one of Time/CNN America's Best Scientists, 2002; fellow, Geol. Soc. Am., Linnean Soc., London, Am. Acad. Arts and Scis., 1987, Guggenheim, 1987; Vis. fellow, Gonville and Caius Coll., Cambridge, Eng., 1991—92. Fellow AAAS, European Union Geoscis. (hon.); mem. NAS, Bot. Soc. Am., Am. Philos. Soc., Paleontol. Soc. (Schuchert award 1987, medal, 2005), Am. Acad. Microbiology, Phi Beta Kappa (book award in sci. 2003), Sigma Xi. Avocations: travel, reading, cooking, choral music. Office: Harvard Univ Botanical Museum 26 Oxford St Cambridge MA 02138-2902 E-mail: aknoll@oeb.harvard.edu.

KNOLL, JÓZSEF, pharmacology researcher; b. Kassa, Hungary, May 30, 1925; s. Jakab and Blanka (Deutscher) K.; m. Éva Teleki, Jan. 26, 1950 (dec. Oct. 1981); 1 child, Julia; m. Berta Knoll, Oct. 24, 1984. MD, Semmelweis U. of Medicine, Budapest, Hungary, 1951. Teaching asst. Dept. of Pharmacology Semmelweis U. of Medicine, Budapest, Hungary, 1949-51, asst. prof., 1951-58, dozent, 1958-62, acting head, 1962, prof. pharmacology, 1963—, chmn. Dept. of Pharmacology, 1963-92; prof. emeritus, 2004. Author: Theory of Active Reflexes, 1969, Handbook of Pharmacology, 1st edit., 1965, Handbook of Pharmacology, 8th edit., 1995, The Brain and Its Self. A Neurochemical Concept of the Innate and Acquired Drives, 2005; contbr. articles to profl. sci. jours. V.p. Semmelweis U. of Medicine, Budapest, 1964-70, Hungarian Acad. Scis. Class of Medicine, 1967-76; councillor Internat. Union of Pharmacology, 1982-84, 1st v.p., 1984-87. Recipient Nat. prize State of Hungary, 1985, Disting. Svc. award European Pharmacol. Soc., 1999, Excellence award in anti-aging medicine, 2001, Szechenyi prize State of Hungary, 2003; named Hon. doctor Med. Acad., Magdeburg, Germany, 1984, Bologna (Italy) U., 1989, Hon. fellow Royal Soc. of Medicine London, 1990. Mem. Hungarian Pharmacol. Soc. (gen. sec. 1962-67, pres. 1967-83, life hon. pres. 1983—), Hungarian Acad. Scis. (chmn. com. of pharmacology 1962—, corr. mem. 1970, full mem., 1979), Leopoldina Acad. Natural Scis., Polish Acad. Art and Scis. (fgn. mem. 1995). Achievements include patents for 53 patents in field. Avocation: fine arts. Home: Jászai Mari tér 4/b 1137 Budapest Hungary Office: Semmelweis U Faculty Gen Medicine Dept Pharmacol Pharmacother Nagyvarad ter 4 1089 Budapest Hungary Office Phone: 36 1 210 4405. E-mail: jozsefknoll@hotmail.com.

KNOPF, PAUL MARK, immunologist; b. Trenton, NJ, Apr. 4, 1936; s. David and Beatrice Knopf; m. Carol Lois Harrison, June 29, 1958; children: Jeffrey William, Steven Harrison, Rachel Analiese. BSc, MIT, 1958, PhD, 1962. Postdoctoral fellow MRC Lab. Molecular Biology, Cambridge, Eng., 1962-64; spl. research assoc. Salk Inst., La Jolla, Calif., 1964-72; prof. med. sci. Brown U., Providence, 1972—2003, Charles A. and Helen B. Stuart prof. med. sci., 1992—2003, chmn. sect. molecular, cellular and devel. biology, 1990-94, chmn. dept. molecular microbiology and immunology, 1994-97, Stuart prof. emeritus med. sci., 2003—. Program dir. ACS Inst. Rsch. Grant, 1976—85; mem. study sect. on parasitic disease NIH, 1985—87; mem. sci. rev. com. Progeria Rsch. Found., 2002—; cons. EpiVax, Inc., 2003—, Ctr. for Internat. Health Rsch., 2005—. Recipient Career Devel. award NIH, 1966-72; named Tchr. of Yr. in Life Scis., Brown U., 1998; grantee NIH, 1966-76, 84-88, 91-99, Rockefeller Found., 1972-80, Edna McConnell Clark Found., 1976-85, WHO, 1979-94, MS Soc., 1989-90; Fulbright-Hays sr. fellow, 1978-79, Fogarty sr. internat. fellow, 1986-87. Mem. AAAS, Am. Assn. Immunologists, Am. Soc. Tropical Medicine and Hygiene, Soc. Neurosci., Am. Soc. Microbiology, New Eng. Assn. Parasitology. Office: Brown U Divsn Biology and Medicine PO Box G-B6 Providence RI 02912-9107 Office Phone: 401-863-1607. Business E-Mail: Paul_Knopf@Brown.edu.

KNOPMAN, DAVID S., neurologist; b. Phila., Oct. 6, 1950; AB, Dartmouth Coll., 1972; MD, U. Minn., 1975. Diplomate Am. Bd. Psychiatry and Neurology. Intern Hennepin County Med. Ctr., 1975-76; resident U. Minn., 1976-79, asst. prof. neurology Mpls., 1980-86, assoc. prof. neurology, 1986-98, prof., 1998—2000; cons. dept. neurology Mayo Clinic, Rochester, Minn., 2000—; prof. Mayo Clinic Coll. Medicine, Rochester, 2000—. Office: Mayo Clinic Dept Neurology Rochester MN 55905 Office Phone: 507-284-2511.

KNORR, UWE, orthopaedic surgeon; b. Marbach, Germany, Mar. 13, 1960; s. Hans and Irmtraud Knorr; m. Bettina-Ulrike Hettler, May 27, 1988; children: Stefanie Isabel, Tobias Sebastian. Grad., U. Ulm, 1986. Med. asst. Klinik Albstadt, Germany, 1987—89, Klinik Bethesda, Stuttgart, 1989—90, Krankenhaus Bietigheim, 1990—92, Argental Clinic, Isny, 1992—96, Orthopadische Klinik Kassel, 1996—99; orthopaedic surgeon pvt. practice, Muehlacker, 1999—2006. V.p., instr. MWE chirotherapy Dr. Karl-Sell-Aerzteseminar, Neutrauchburg, Germany, 1994—, mem. exec. bd., 1997—, v.p. MWE chirotherapy; del. Assn. Scientific Med. Socs. Germany, 2005—. Avocations: basketball, saxophone, gardening, skiing. Home: Uhlandstrasse 26 74321 Bietigheim-Bissingen Germany Office: Bahnh of strasse 43 75417 Muehlacker Germany Office Phone: 00497041 811011. Personal E-mail: knorr.uwe@web.de.

KNOSPE, WILLIAM HERBERT, medical educator; b. Oak Park, Ill., May 26, 1929; s. Herbert Henry and Dora Isabel (Spruce) K.; m. Adris M. Nelson, June 19, 1954. BA, U. Ill., Chgo. and Urbana, 1951; BS, U. Ill., 1952; MD, U. Ill., Chgo., 1954; MS in Radiation Biology, U. Rochester, 1962. Diplomate Am. Bd. Internal Medicine and Subspecialty Bd. on Hematology. Rotating intern Upstate Med. Ctr. Hosps-SUNY-Syracuse, 1954-55; resident in medicine Ill. Central Hosp., Chgo., 1955-56, VA Research Hosp-Northwestern U. Med. Sch., Chgo., 1956-58; investigator radiation biology Walter Reed Army Inst. Research, Washington, 1962-64, investigator hematology, asst. chief dept. hematology, 1964-66; attending physician med. service Walter Reed Gen. Hosp., Washington, 1963-64, fellow in hematology, 1964-65; asst. chief hematology service, chief hematology clinic Walter Reed Army Inst. of Rsch., Washington, 1964-66; asst. attending staff physician Presbyn. St. Luke's Hosp., Chgo., 1967-68, asst. dir. hematology radiohematology lab., 1967-74, assoc. attending staff physician, 1968-74, sr. attending staff physician, 1974—; asst. prof. medicine U. Ill.-Chgo., 1967-69, assoc. prof., 1969-72; assoc. prof. medicine Rush Med. Coll., Chgo., 1971-74, prof. medicine, 1974—; dir. sect. hematology Rush-Presbyn.-St. Luke's Med. Ctr., Chgo., 1974-93; Elodia Kehm prof. hematology Rush-Med. Coll., Chgo., 1986-94, prof. emeritus, 1994—; prof. medicine U. N.Mex., Albuquerque, 1994—2002, emeritus, 2002—. Speaker at profl. confs. U.S. and abroad; vis. prof. medicine dept. hematology U. Basel, Switzerland, 1980-81, Cancer Ctr., U. N.Mex., 1992-93. Contbr. numerous articles to profl. publs. Trustee Ill. chpt. Leukemia Soc. Am., 1977-88, v.p., 1979-80; trustee Bishop Anderson House (Rush-Presbyn.-St. Luke's Med. Ctr.), 1980-94. Served to capt. M.C., USAR, 1958-61, to lt. col., U.S. Army, 1961-66. Fellow ACP; mem. Am. Fedn. Clin. Research, AMA, Am. Soc. Hematology, Am. Soc. Clin. Oncology, Central Soc. Clin. Research, Chgo. Med. Soc., Inst. Medicine Chgo., Internat. Soc. Exptl. Hematology, Radiation Research Soc., Southeastern Cancer Study Group, Polycythemia Vera Study Group, Eastern Coop. Oncology Group, Ill. State Med. Soc., Assn. Hematology-Oncology Program Dirs., Sigma Xi, Chgo. Literary Club. Office: 310 Big Horn Ridge Dr NE Albuquerque NM 87122-1455

KNOTHE, ULF R., orthopedist; b. Hamburg, Germany, Feb. 3, 1963; MD, U. Bern, Switzerland, 1992, DSc in Medicine, 2000. Clin. scholar dept. orthop. surgery Cleve. Clinic, 2001—02, staff surgeon, 2002—. Rsch. fellow orthop. rsch. lab Dept. Orthop. Surgery, Mt. Sinai Sch. Medicine, NY, 2000, clin. fellow musculoskeletal oncology, 2000—01. Recipient award, Wallace H. Coulter Found. Mem.: AMA, Ohio State Med. Assn. Avocations: sailing, skiing. Office: 9500 Euclid Ave A41 Cleveland OH 44195 Office Fax: 216-444-9198. Business E-Mail: knotheu@ccf.org.

KNOWLES, MICHAEL RAY, medical educator, researcher; m. Marilyn Goodman; children: Joshua, Rachel. AB, U. NC, Chapel Hill, 1967, MD, 1971. Diplomate Am. Bd. Internal Medicine, 1974, Pulmonary Disease Subspecialty Bd. Medicine, 1980. Chief internal medicine USAF Malcolm Grow Med. Ctr., Andrews AFB, DC, 1975—78; instr. dept. medicine U. NC, Chapel Hill, 1980—82, asst. prof. medicine, 1982—87, assoc. prof. medicine, 1987—94, prof. medicine, 1994—. Prin. investigator Nat. Consortium to Study Genetic Disorders of the Lung, 2003—. Author: (textbook) Cystic Fibrosis in Adults; contbr. articles to profl. med. jours. Maj. USAF, 1975—78, Andrews AFB. Recipient Jefferson Pilot award, U. NC, Chapel Hill, 1983—87; named one of Best Doctors Am., 1992—2010; Rsch. Sabbatical, Cambridge, Eng., 1988—89. Mem.: Alpha Omega Alpha. Office: UNC Chapel Hill 7019 Thurston Bowles Bldg CB7248 Chapel Hill NC 27599-7248 Business E-Mail: knowles@med.unc.edu. *

KNOX, GEOFFREY M., psychotherapist, business owner; b. Manchester, Eng., July 14, 1971; s. Vic and Eunice Knox; m. Chelsea Knox; children: Liam children: Hannah. MB ChB, Victoria U., Manchester, England, 1994; Dip. Hlt Mgt, 2001. Registered Royal Coll. Anaesthetists, 2002. With Univ. Hosp., South Manchester, 1994—98, NW Anesthesiology Program, 1998—2005, The Walton Ctr. for Neurology, 2001—02; mng. and clin. dir. Pain Solutions, Accrington, England, 2005—. Fellow: RCA. Achievements include patents pending for test for each individual's genetic abililty to respond to analgesics; design of new model of care for pain patients; development of new system of care for pain patients; first to set up and run an independent NHS specialist pain service. Office: Pain Solutions 7-11 Abbey St Accrington Lancashire BBS 1EN England Office Phone: 08450569595. Business E-Mail: painsolutions@consultant.com.

KNOX, MICHAEL DENNIS, medical educator, charitable foundation administrator; b. Wyandotte, Mich., May 9, 1946; s. Harold L. and Mary (Latta) K.; children: John M.P., James R.S. BA, Ea. Mich. U., 1968; MSW, U. Mich., 1971, MA Psychology, 1973, PhD Psychology, 1974. Lic. clin. psychologist, Fla., Va. Dir. Applied Sci., Inc., Ann Arbor, Mich., 1974—76; clin. dir. Cmty. Mental Health Ctr., Inc., Huntington, W.Va., 1976—78; clin. instr. Marshall U. Sch. Medicine, Huntington, 1977—78; dir. We. Tidewater Mental Health Ctr., Suffolk, Va., 1978—86; dir. Ctr. for HIV Edn. and Rsch. U. South Fla., Tampa, 1988—2011. Adj. prof. psychology Marshall U., 1977-78; asst. prof. Ea. Va. Med. Sch., Norfolk, 1979-86; chmn., bd. dirs. Applied Sci. Corp., Tampa, 1985-1999; assoc. prof., chmn. dept. cmty. mental health U. South Fla., 1986-91, disting. prof., 1991-2001, disting. prof. psychology, 1991-, disting. prof. medicine dept. internal medicine Coll. Medicine, U. South Fla., 1994—, exec. com. faculty senate, 1992-99, pres. faculty senate, 1995-97, disting. prof. gerontology, 2002-05, disting. prof. cmty. and family health Coll. Pub. Health, 1997-2004, disting. prof. global health coll. pub. health, 2004—; disting. prof. dept. mental health law and policy Louis de la Parte Fla. Mental Health Inst., 2001—, disting. prof. aging studies, 2005—11; chmn. adv. coun. faculty senates Fla. State U. Sys., 1996-98; cons. USPHS, Bethesda, Md., 1990-96, NIMH, Rockville, Md., 1990-98; tech. advisor state and local govts.; dir. Fla./Caribbean AIDS Edn. and Tng. Ctr., 1999-2011; vis. scholar dept. psychiatry Oxford (Eng.) U., 1999; lectr. in field. Author books including: Last Wishes: A Handbook to Guide Your Survivors, 1995, HIV and Community Mental Healthcare, 1998; editor: US Peace Registry, 2006-; contbr. more than 150 articles on AIDS, peace studies and psychology; invited reviewer 5 acad. jours., internat. spkr. 1982—. Adv. Joint Commn. on Accreditation of Hosps., Chgo., 1982-84; co-chair Am. Found. for AIDS Rsch. Nat. HIV/AIDS Update Conf., 2004; mem. steering com. S.E. Region STD/HIV Prevention Tng. Ctr., 2004—11; chmn., CEO, US Peace Meml. Found., Inc., 2005—; mem. cmty. adv. bd. U. Miami Develop. Ctr. AIDS Rsch., 2007-. Recipient Disting. Svc. award Nat. Coun. Cmty. Mental Health Ctrs., 1984, Resolution of Appreciation, 1993, Millennium Appreciation award, Tampa General Hosp. Infectious Disease Ctr., 2000, Million Dollar Rschr. Award, gold mem., USF, 2005-2006, Marsella prize for Psychology of Peace and Social Justice, 2007; grantee Emory U., 1988-91, NIMH, 1991-93, U. Miami, 1991-99, U. Calif. 2001, HHS, 1999-, Fla. Dept. Health 2001-. Fellow APA, Assn. Psychol. Sci.; mem. Internat. AIDS Soc., U. Mich. Alumni Assn., Nat. Assn. AIDS Edn. and Tng. Centers, U.S. Power Squadron (bd, dirs. 1983-84), Sigma Xi. Achievements include research in HIV/AIDS risk factors for the seriously mentally ill, HIV/AIDS risk reduction, peace research, AIDS prevention, knowledge and attitudes regarding AIDS among treatment providers. Avocations: boating, bicycling, walking. Office: University South Fla MHC 2606 13301 Bruce B Downs Blvd Tampa FL 33612-3807 Business E-Mail: knox@usf.edu.

KNUDSON, ALFRED GEORGE, JR., medical geneticist; b. LA, Aug. 9, 1922; s. Alfred George and Mary Gladys (Galvin) Knudson; m. Anna T. Meadows, June 20, 1977; children from previous marriage: Linda, Nancy, Dorene. BS, Calif. Inst. Tech., 1944, PhD, 1956; MD, Columbia U., 1947; DSc (hon.), Thomas Jefferson U., 1992; MD (hon.), U. Oslo, 2000. Chmn. dept. pediat. City of Hope Med. Ctr., Duarte, Calif., 1956—62, chmn. dept. biology, 1962—66; assoc. dean Health Sci. Ctr., SUNY, Stony Brook, 1966—69; dean Grad. Sch. Biomed. Scis., U. Tex. Health Sci. Ctr., Houston, 1970—76; dir. Inst. Cancer Rsch., Fox Chase Cancer Ctr., Phila., 1976—83, sr. mem., 1976—, disting. sci., 1992—, pres., 1980—82. Mem. Assembly Life Scis. NRC, 1975—81. Author: Genetics and Disease, 1965; contbr. articles to profl. jours. Recipient Charles S. Mott prize, GM Cancer Rsch. Found., 1988, medal of honor, Am. Cancer Soc., 1989, Charles Rodolphe Brupbacher Found. prize, 1995, Gairdner Found. Internat. award, 1997, Lasker-DeBakey Clin. Med. Rsch. award, Lasker Found., 1998, John Scott award, City of Phila., 1999, Lila Gruber Meml. Cancer Rsch. award, Am. Acad. Dermatology, 2000, Kyoto prize, 2004, Bristol-Myers-Squibb Cancer award, 2005. Fellow: AAAS; mem.: NAS, Am. Soc. Pediatric Hematology/Oncology (Disting. Career award 1999), Am. Assn. Cancer Rsch. (Lifetime Achievement award 2005), Am. Pediat. Soc., Assn. Am. Physicians, Am. Soc. Human Genetics (pres. 1978, Allan award 1991), Internat. Soc. Pediatric Oncology, Am. Acad. Arts and Scis., Am. Philos. Soc. Achievements include research in genetics of human cancer. Office: Fox Chase Ctr 333 Cottman Ave Philadelphia PA 19111 Business E-Mail: ag_knudson@fccc.edu. *

KNUDSON, DUANE VICTOR, kinesiology educator, researcher; b. West Allis, Wis., Oct. 1, 1961; s. Henry T. and Rosa Ellen (Shondel) K.; m. Lois Mary Reinders, Aug. 5, 1983; children: Joshua Thomas, Amanda Kay. BS, U. Wis., Oshkosh, 1983; MS, Baylor U., 1984; PhD, U. Wis., Madison, 1988. Grad. asst. U. Wis., Madison, 1985-88, Baylor U., Waco, Tex., 1983-84, lectr. and asst. prof., 1984—97; prof., assoc. dean Calif. State U., Coll. Commn. and Edn., Chico, 1997—2009; prof. chair Health & Human Performance Tex. State U., 2009—. Contbr. articles on biomechanics rsch. and sports medicine to scholarly and profl. jours.; author three books; reviewer Phys. Therapy, Jour. Biomechanics. Rsch. grantee Victor Sports, Inc., 1986, Apple Computer, 1987, 88, U.S. Tennis Assn., 1987, 89, 92, 94, 96, 98, 2000, 01, 02. Mem. AAHPER and Dance, Am. Soc. Biomechanics, Internat. Soc. Biomechanics in Sports; fellow Am. Coll. of Sports Medicine, Internat. Soc. Biomech. Sports, USTA (sport sci. tech. com.). Office: Tex State University Health & Human Performance San Marcos TX 78666 Office Phone: 512-245-2561. Business E-Mail: dknudson@txstate.edu.

KNUTSEN, ALAN PAUL, pediatrician, immunologist, allergist; b. Mpls., July 21, 1948; m. Kim A.; children: Laura Joelle, Brian A., Benjamin C., Elizabeth G., Katherine M., Amy S., Summer A. BA in Biology, U. Calif., 1971, MD, St. Louis U., 1975. Resident pediatrics St. Louis U. Med. Ctr., 1975-78, fellow allergy Duke U. Med. Ctr., Durham, NC, 1978-80;, 1980-93; dir. dept. allergy and immunology St. Louis U. Med. Ctr., 1985—; prof. St. Louis U., 1993—, 1993—. Mem. infectious disease com., 1980—; dir. pediatric immunology lab, 1983—; dir. pediatric allergy/immunology trng. program. Contbr. articles to profl. jours. Mem. Am. Acad. Allergy/Immunology, Clin. Immunology Soc., Phi Beta Kappa, Alpha Omega Alpha. Democrat. Lutheran. Office: St Louis U Pediatric Rsch Inst 1465 S Grand Blvd Saint Louis MO 63104-1003 Home: 44 S Gore Ave Saint Louis MO 63119-2910 Home Phone: 314-961-3179; Office Phone: 314-268-4014. Business E-Mail: knutsenm@slu.edu.

KO, JIH-YANG, orthopedist, educator; s. Jih-Lu Ko and Jen-Jen Yang; m. Lih-Ching Hsiu; children: Yng-Ruu, Shu-Ruey. MD, Taipei Med. U., Taiwan, 1980. Cert. prof. Chang Gung U. Coll. Medicine. Chief, dept. orthop. surgery Chang Gung Meml. Hosp., Kaohsiung Med. Ctr., Kaohsiung Hsien, Taiwan, 2002—, program dir., 2002—10. Reviewer Jour. Shoulder and Elobw Surgery, Jour. Formosa Med. Assn., Jour. Orthop. Rsch., Chang Gung Med. Jour.; reviewer study proposals Nat. Sci. Coun. Taiwan; bd. com. mem. Taiwan Ankle Foot Soc., Taiwan, 2005—07, Taiwan Arthroscope and Knee Soc., 2004—, Taiwan Orthop. Rsch. Soc., 2008—, Taiwan Insall Soc.; pres. Taiwan Pediat. Orthop. Soc., 2006—08, Taiwan Shoulder and Elbow Soc., 2006—07. Contbr. articles to profl. jours. Numerous rsch. grants, fellowship, Jikei U., Japan, 1983—84, U. Calif., San Diego Sch. Medicine, 1993, Mayo Clinic Dept. Orthop., Rochester, 1993. Achievements include research in knocking-down dickkopf-1 alleviates estrogen deficiency induction of bone loss; modulation of dickkopf-1 attenuates glucocorticoid induction of osteoblast apoptosis, adipocyte differentiation and bone mass loss; inflammation induction of dickkopf-1 mediates chondrocyte apoptosis in osteoarthritis joint; dickkopf-1 promotes hyperglycemia-induced accumulation of mesangial matrix and renal dysfunction; increased dickkopf-1 expression accelerates bone cell apoptosis in femoral head osteonecrosis. Avocation: music. Office: Chang Gung Meml Hosp 123 Ta Pei Rd Niao Sung Hsiang Kaohsiung Hsien 83305 Taiwan Office Fax: 886-7-7354309. Business E-Mail: kojy@adm.cgmh.org.tw.

KO, KWAI FU, neurologist, researcher; b. Hong Kong, Oct. 31, 1953; s. Yau Shau Ko and Sai Kwan Lee; m. Sanny Chiu, June 14, 1987; children: Dora, Ka Young. MBBS, U. Hong Kong, 1978; MHA, U. NSW, Australia, 1999; PhD in Health Sci., U. S.Australia, 2004. Lic. dr. in neurology Med. Coun. Hong Kong, 1979. Dir. electrodiagnostic medicine Hosp. Authority, Kowloon, 1995—;.cons. Hosp. Authority Hong Kong, Kowloon, 1995—; program dir. Neurology Splty. Bd., Hong Kong, 1996—2007, Advance Medicine Splty. Bd., Kowloon, 2007. Contbr. articles to profl. jours. Program dir. Hong Kong Acad. Medicine, Kowloon, 1995—2007. Named Hon. Prof., U. Hong Kong, 1989, Chinese U. Hong Kong, 1995, Hon. Cons., Wong Tai Sin Hosp., 1995. Fellow: Hong Kong Acad. Medicine, Royal Coll. Physicians, Hong Kong Acad. Medicine (hon.; advance medicine splty. bd. 2007). Achievements include research in a comprehensive stroke unit to Chinese stroke patients. Home: Block 5 19 D City Garden Electric Rd North Point Hong Kong Office: Kwong Wah Hosp 25 Waterloo Rd Kowloon Hong Kong Home Phone: 852-25711466; Office Phone: 852-35175038. Office Fax: 852 35175259. Business E-Mail: kokwaifu@yahoo.com.hk.

KO, SANG-HUN, orthopedist, educator; b. Seoul, Republic of Korea, Aug. 1, 1962; s. Hwa-Young and Young-Hee (Lee) Ko; m. HyunJoo Lee, Mar. 16, 1997; children: Young Kyeong, Seo-Young. Prof. Ulsan U., Ulsan, Republic of Korea. Fellow Kyunghee U., Seoul, SamSung Med. Ctr., Seoul, Yonsei U. Servance Hosp., Seoul. Contbr. articles to profl. jours. (Award for Outstanding Rsch., 2006). Dir. Korean Orthop. Assn., Busan Ulsan, Republic Of Korea, 2006—08. 2d lt. South Korean Mil., 1987—90. Fellow, UCLA Med. Ctr., U. So. Calif., Columbia U. Mem.: Korean Shoulder Elbow Soc. (com. mem., Award for Textbook Compilation 2008), Korean Orthop. Assn. (com.mem.). Achievements include first to Arthroscopic single-row supraspinatus tendon repair with a modified mattress locking stitch: a prospective randomized controlled comparison with a simple stitch; research in 13. Instability after total knee arthrosplasy; first to Meniscus stabilizing function of the meniscofemoral ligament: experimental study of pig knee joints; research in 15. Early loosening of femoral component after primary total knee arthroplasty; first to Arthroscopic management of septic arthritis of the shoulder joint; Manual of Arthroscopic Surgery; research in 18. The evaluation for the usefulness of arthroscpic miniopen repair which related with large and massive sized full thickness rotator cuff tear and clinical results; first to 19. Idiopathic scoliosis in the eleven years old —prevalence study-; research in 20. Pancreatic cancer presenting as dermatomyositis; 21. Clinical and Functional Result after Internal Fixation of Floating Shoulder; Disability Evaluation — Orthopedic field — 1st Edition; research in 2. All Arthroscopic Repairs with Massive Cuff Stitch in Medium-sized Full Thickness Rotator Cuff Tears; 23. Thoracic myolopathy due to thoracolumbar kyphosis and spinal stenosis in achondroplasia; 24. All arthroscopic repairs with biceps incorporation in large, massive sized full thickness rotator cuff tears; 25. Early results of primary high flex total knee arthroplasty; first to 26. MRI of acute septic arthritis of the shoulder joint; correlation with arthroscopic findings; research in 27. Arthroscopic reconstruction in mega-frequency of recurrent anterior shoulder dislocations; 28. Histological assessment of degeneration of anterior curciate ligament in arthritis knee; 29. Degeneration of the cruciate ligaments in osteoarthritis knee; 30. The use of bio suture anchor in the arthroscopic repair of medium sized full thickness rotator cuff tear in sports injury; 31. Paraspinal abscess communicated with epidural abscess after extra articular facet joint injection; 32. Internal fixation with plate and bone graft of mid shaft clavicle nonunion; 3. Early Results of Mini-incision vs Conventional Total Knee Arthroplasties; 33. Comparison of arthroscopic versus mini open repair in medium and large sized full thickness rotator cuff tear — short term preliminary results; 34. Arthroscopic capsular release in refractory adhesive capsulitis of the shoulder; 35. Anterior Cruciate Ligament Reconstruction Using Tibialis Tendon Allograft —A Short Term Follow-Up Result -; first to 36. Arthroscopic Decompression and Shaving of Popliteal Cyst Using Posteromedial Portal — Technical Note-; research in 37. Arthroscopic Reduction and Pull-out Suture Fixation for the Intercondylar Eminenece Fracture of the Tibia; 38. Treatment of Femoral Intertrochanteric Fracture with Proximal Femoral Nail. 17-1:1-6, J of Korean Fracture Society; first to Popliteal cystoscopic excisional debridement and removal of capsular fold of valvular mechanism of large recurrent popliteal cyst; research in 40. Spur like lesion on the lateral tibial condyle — a sign of chronic ACL tear -; 41. Discoid Meniscal Cyst — Report of 3 Cases-; 42. Arthroscopic Repair of Full Thickness Rotator Cuff Tear; 4. Total Knee Arthroplasty with NexGen® System - 3-8 Year Follow-up Results -; 43. The Use of Hook Plate on the Management of Unstable Neer II Lateral End Fracture of The Clavicle; 44. Treatment of a High Pressure Injection Hand Injury; 45. Patterns of Meniscus Injury with Acute Anterior Curciate Ligament Tears; 46. Arthroscopic Assisted Reduction and Internal Fixation of Patella Fractures. J of Korean Society of Fractures; 47. Arthroscopic Excisional Debridement of Cyst-like lesion in juxta-articular Knee Joint; first to Arthroscopic Treatment of Septic Arthritis of the Hip; research in 49. Modified Tension Band Wiring using Cortical Screw for Displaced Medial Malleolar Fractures; 50. Allogeneous Bone Interference Screw and Achilles Allograft used in ACL Reconstruction; 51. Minimal incision Wolter Plate Fixation in Displaced Lateral End Fracture of the Clavicle and the Acromioclavicular Dislocation; 52. Arthroscopic Shaving Cystectomy of Popliteal Cyst; 5. Arthroscopic repair of Type II SLAP lesion with bioabsorbable knotless suture anchor: surgical technique and clinical results; 53. Comparison between Screw Fixation and Modified Tension Band Wiring for Medial Malleolar Fracture; 54. Comparative Analysis of Interlocking IM Nailing and LC-DCP fixation in the Treatment of Distal Tibial Fracture; 55. Anterior Cruciate Ligament Reconstruction using Human Bone Screw in Sports Injury; first to 56. Treating Septic Hip with Hip Arthroscopy; research in 57. Effects of X ray irradiation on survival and development of Metagonumus yokogawai in rats; 58. Bone spur and Over Weight in Painful Heel Syndrome and Tenderness; 59. Treatment Using Arthroscopic Reduction and Fixation in Tibial Intercondylar Eminence Frature; 60. Hemiarthroplasty for Treatment of Proximal Humerus Fracture; 61. Limited Open Reduction and Internal Fixation of the Tibial Pilon Fractures; 62. Analysis of Prognostic Factors in Surgical Treatment for Lumbar Disc Herniation; Shoulder & Elbow Surgery; research in 63. Surgical Repair of Achilles Tendon Ruptures - modified lindholm method-; 64. Remodelling of Angular Deformity in Split Russel Traction for Femoral Shaft Fractures in Children(According to Site & Direction & Acceptable Angulation); 65. Traumatic Fracture - Dislocation of the Hip; 66. Comparison of Hemiarthroplasty and Compression Hip Screw on Elderly Unstable Intertrochnateric Fractures; 67. Complications of Interlocking Intramedullary Nailing for Humeral Shaft Fracture; 68. A Oprerative Treatment of the Tibial Pilon Fractures -For minimize soft tissue injury-; 69. Treatment of Lateral Humeral Condyle Fractures in Children Using Closed Reduction and Percutaneous Pinning; 70. Normal Variation and Incidence of Coincided Alignment on Lisfranc Joint on Normal Foot Radiography; 71. The Treatment of Supracondylar Fracture of The Humereus in Children; 72. Attritional Rupture of the Flexor Tendons after Malunion of Distal Radial Fracture; 10. ACL reconstruction using transtibial femoral tunnel at 10 or 2 o'clock position — technical note-; 76. The Treatment of the Proximal Humeral Fracture using Bifurcate Blade Plate in Adult; 77. Treatment of Fracture-Dislocation of Tarsometatarsal Joint; 78. Transcatheter arterial embolization of Aneurysmal Bone Cyst in Pubic Bone; 79. The operative treatment of supracondylar fractures of the humeurs in children -closed reduction and percutaneous pinning or open reduction and internal fixation; 11. One stage revision anterior cruciate ligament reconstruction using achilles tendon allograft; 12. Use of massive cuff stitch in arthroscopic repair of rotator cuff tears. Avocations: running, tennis, skiing, hiking. Home: 30 East St Winchester MA 01890 Office: U Ulsan 290-3 Jeon Ha-Dong Dong-Gu 682-714 Ulsan Republic of Korea Office Phone: 1-617-696-0785, 82-52-250-8114. Personal E-mail: shkoshko@hanmail.net, sanghunko@yahoo.com, shkoshko@uuh.ulsan.kr, shkoo@mail.ulsan.ac.kr.

KO, TAESUNG, physical therapy educator; b. Seoul, Republic of Korea, May 22, 1969; MS, Young In U., 2001; PhD, Sahmyook U., 2008. Prof. Daewon U. Coll., 2006—. Asst. prof., dept. phys. therapy, 2006—11. Office: 316 Daehak Rd Jecheon Chungbuk 390-702 Republic of Korea Office Fax: 82-43-649-3690. E-mail: intkts@korea.com.

KO, YOUNG-GUK, medical educator; b. Jeju, Republic of Korea, May 1, 1966; MD, Bonn U., Germany, 1992. Instr. Severance Cardiovasc. Hosp. Yonsei U., 2003, asst. prof., 2005, assoc. prof., 2008—. Office: 250 Seongsanno Seodaemu-gu Seoul 120-752 Republic of Korea Business E-Mail: ygko@yuhs.ac.

KOAY, LOK BENG, gastroenterologist, consultant; b. Penang, Malaysia, Aug. 2, 1952; s. Theam Soo Koay and Buan Huah Teoh; m. Yi Chen Lin, Feb. 6, 1991; children: Mai Ke, Mi Chi. MD, Taipei Med. U., Taiwan, 1981. Resident Taipei Med. U. Hosp., 1981—84, cons. physician, 1985—87; cons. physician and gastroenterologist Chi-Mei Med. Ctr., Tainan, Taiwan, 1987—, chief cons. nutritional support unit, 1990—2001. Mem.: Chinese Taipei Soc. Ultrasound Medicine (hon.), Digestive Endoscopy Soc. Taiwan (hon.), Gastroent. Soc. Taiwan (hon.). Avocations: sports, music, travel. Office: Chi Mei Found Hosp Dept Medicine 901 Chung Hwa Rd Tainan Taiwan Office Fax: 886-6-2828928. E-mail: lbkoay@mail.chimei.org.tw.

KOBAK, ALFRED JULIAN, JR., obstetrician, gynecologist; b. Chgo., Feb. 10, 1935; s. Alfred J and Rose B (Baron) Kobak; m. Sue B Stein, May 3, 1959; children: William, Steven, Jane, Deborah. BS, U. Ill., Chgo., 1957, MD, 1959. Diplomate Am Bd Ob-Gyn. Intern Michael Reese Hosp., Chgo., 1959-60; resident Cook County Hosp., 1960-62, 64-65; practice medicine specializing in ob-gyn. Valparaiso, Ind., 1965—; physician in charge Kobak Ctr. Women's Health, Valparaiso, 2007—. Mem. med. staff Porter Hosp., Valparaiso, 1965—, chmn. dept. Ob/Gyn., pres. med. staff, 1981—82; clin. assoc. prof. ob-gyn. Ind. U. Sch. Medicine; with Ob-Gyn. Assocs., 1970—2006. Contbr. articles to profl jours. Bd. dirs. NW Ind. Jewish Fedn., 1970—84, Porter County Bd. Health, 1991—, pres., 1997. Capt USAF, 1962—64. Fellow: ACS, Am. Coll. Ob-Gyn., Internat. Coll. Surgeons; mem.: AMA, Chgo. Gynecol. Soc. (v.p. 1998—99), Porter County Med Soc (pres. 1979, 1986), Ctrl. Assn. Obstetricians and Gynecologists, Ind. Med. Assn., Am. Soc. Reproductive Medicine. Office: 1101 Glendale Blvd Ste 108 Valparaiso IN 46383-3724 Office Phone: 219-531-7500. Business E-Mail: drk@kobakcenter.com.

KOBARI, MASAHIRO, neurologist; b. Tokyo, Oct. 12, 1952; s. Matahiko and Yasuko (Tokunaga) K.; m. Junko Kitahara, June 24, 1984; children: Kazutoshi, Yusuke, Asuka. MD, Keio U., 1977. Diplomate Japanese Bd. Neurology and Internal Medicine. Instr. dept. neurology Keio Univ. Sch. Medicine, Tokyo, 1984; head dept. neurology Mihara Meml. Hosp., Isesaki, 1985-87; chief neurology clinic Keio Univ. Hosp., 1990-96; chief dept. neurology Tachikawa Hosp., 1996—2006, Shizuoka Red Cross Hosp., Japan, 2006—, dep. dir., 2008—. Mem. Japanese Soc. Neurology (coun.), Japanese Soc. Stroke (coun.), Japanese Soc. Cerebral Blood Flow and Metabolism (coun.)., Internat. Soc. Cerebral Blood Flow and Metabolism, Internat. Stroke Soc. Home: 2-23-14 Minamiogikubo Suginami-ku Tokyo 167-0052 Japan Office: Shizuoka Red Cross Hosp Dept Neurology 8-2 Otemachi Aoi-ku Shizuoka 420-0853 Japan

KOBASHIGAWA, JON AKIRA, internist, cardiologist, researcher, educator; b. Honolulu, Sept. 25, 1954; s. Eikichi and Alice K. BS, Stanford U., 1976; MD, Mt. Sinai Sch. Medicine, 1980. Diplomate Am. Bd. Internal Medicine, Am. Bd. Cardiology. Intern, resident, cardiology fellow UCLA Med. Ctr., 1980-86, from clin. instr. medicine to clin. prof. UCLA, 1986-99, clin. prof. medicine, 1999—, med. dir. heart transplant program, 1994—, chief divsn. clin. faculty medicine, 1998—. Contbr. articles to profl. jours. Upjohn clin. scholar, 1980; grantee in field. Mem. AAAS, Am. Coll. Cardiology (past chmn. heart failure and transplant com.), Internat. Soc. Heart Lung Transplantation (bd. dirs., program chair 1999—, pres. 2004), Am. Soc. Transplantation, Am. Heart Assn. (chair 1998—), Alpha Omega Alpha. Office: Univ Cardiovasc Med Group 100 UCLA Med Plz Ste 630 Los Angeles CA 90095-0001 Office Fax: 310-794-1211. Business E-Mail: jonk@mednet.ucla.edu.

KOBAYASHI, HIROSHI, microbiologist, educator; b. Ohmachi-shi, Nagano-ken, Japan, June 23, 1946; m. Toshiko Shinkai, Nov. 24, 1974; children: Chiharu, Reiji. BA, U. Tokyo, 1969, MA, 1971, PhD, 1974. Rsch. fellow U. Tokyo, 1974-75; postdoctral fellow U. Colo., Denver, 1976-77; assoc. prof. Chiba U., Japan, 1978-95, prof., 1996—. Vis. rschr. U. Mich., Ann Arbor, 1985-86. Co-author: Sugar Transport and Metabolism in Gram-Positive Bacteria, 1987; contbr. to profl. jours. Recipient Young Scientist award Pharm. Soc. of Japan, 1990. Mem. Am. Soc. Microbiology, Japanese Biochem. Soc., Pharm. Soc. Japan. Home: 982-2 Naniwa-cho Hanamigawa-ku Chiba 262-0024 Japan Office: Grad Sch Pharm Scis Chiba U 1-8-1 Inohana Chuo-ku Chiba 260-8675 Japan Home Phone: 81-43-275-7915. Business E-Mail: hiroshi@p.chiba-u.ac.jp.

KOBAYASHI, HIROSHI, ophthalmologist; b. Nagano, Japan, Apr. 25, 1955; MD, Kyoto U., 1981; PhD, Kyoto U. Grad. Sch., 1991. Dir. dept. ophthalmology Kanmon Med. Ctr., 2009—. Office: Kanmon Med Ctr 1-1 Chofu-satou Shimonoseki Yamaguchi Pref 752-8510 Japan Office Fax: 81-83-241-1319. Business E-Mail: kobi@earth.ocn.ne.jp.

KOBAYASHI, HIROYUKI, medical educator; b. Yoshikawa, Saitama-ken, Japan, July 1, 1960; s. Tsugio and Kazuko Kobayashi; m. Akiko Sugimoto. MD, Juntendo U., Tokyo, 1987; PhD, Juntendo U., Tokyo Japan, 1992. Cert. pediat. surgery Japan, 2002. Resident in gen. surgery Juntendo U. Hosp., Bunkyo-ku, Tokyo, 1987—89; asst. prof. pediat. surgery Juntendo U., Bunkyo-ku, Tokyo, 1995—2002, assoc. prof. pediat. surgery, 2002—. Contbr. articles to profl. jours. Pediat. Surgery fellow, Juntendo U., 1990—91, Sr. Rsch. fellow, Our Lady's Hosp. Sick Children, 1992—94. Fellow: Japanese Soc. Pediat. Surgery (assoc.); mem.: Brit. Assn. Pediat. Surgery (assoc.), Japanese Soc. Surgery (assoc.). Achievements include research in biliary atresia; Hirschsprung's disease; intestinal neuronal dysplasia. Office: Dept Pediatric Surgery Juntendo Univ 2-1-1 Tokyo Bunkyo 113-8421 Japan Office Fax: +81-3-5802-2033. Business E-Mail: koba@med.juntendo.ac.jp.

KOBAYASHI, KUNIHIKO, medical educator; b. Takasaki, Gunma, Japan, Feb. 4, 1958; s. Tokuro and Noriko Kobayashi; m. Reiko Takei. Grad., Nippon Med. Sch., Tokyo, 1983; PhD, Tokyo, 1991. Prof.

Saitama Med. U., Hidaka, Japan, 2007—. Editor in chief Japanese Soc. Palliative Med., Osaka, Japan, 2008—. Dir. North East Japan Study Group, Tokyo, 2005—08. Mem.: ASCO. Achievements include patents for biochemical modulation in intestine. Office: Saitama Med Univ 1397-1 Yamane Hidaka Saitama 350-1298 Japan Office Fax: 81-42-984-4667. Business E-Mail: kobakuni@saitama-med.ac.jp.

KOBAYASHI, MARK ROBERT, plastic surgeon, educator; b. Feb. 25, 1957; MD, Tulane U., 1984. Cert. Am. Bd. Plastic Surgeons. Intern surgery UCLA, resident plastic surgery, fellowship microsurgery; assoc. clin. prof. surgery Aesthetic and Plastic Surgery Inst., U. Calif. Irvine; plastic surgeon U. Calif. Irvine Med. Ctr. Office: UCI Manchester Pavilion 200 South Manchester Ave, Ste 650 Orange CA 92868 Office Phone: 714-456-3077.

KOBAYASHI, NAMI, nursing educator, researcher; b. Japan, Sept. 29, 1969; PhD, U. Tokyo, 1998. Prof. Kitasato U., 2009—11. Chair person Family Sys. Care Japan, 2008—11. Recipient Outstanding Rsch. award, Japan Jour. Nursing Studies. Mem.: Internat. Family Nursing Assn. Achievements include research in systems of family relation and illness based on brain science. Office: #2-1-1 Kitasato Minami Sagamihara Kanagawa 252-0329 Japan Business E-Mail: namikoba@nrs.kitasato-u.ac.jp.

KOBAYASHI, NOZOMU, endoscopist; b. Japan, Nov. 9, 1972; MD, Mie U., 1997. Chief, dept. diagnostic imaging Tochigi Cancer Ctr., 2005—. Office: 4-9-13 Yonan Utsunomiya Tochigi 320-0834 Japan Personal E-mail: nokobaya2@tcc.pref.tochigi.lg.jp.

KOBAYASHI, SHUZO, physician, hospital administrator; b. Osaka, Japan, June 13, 1955; m. Tokako Kobayahsi, Mar. 9, 1987; children: Alisa Kobayahsi, Miki Calorine Kobayahsi. MD, Hamatsu U., Japan, 1980, PhD, 1986. Vis. asst. prof. U. Tex. Health Sci. Ctr., San Antonio, 1988—90; dir. medicine NTT Izu Teishia Hosp., Shizuoka, Japan, 1992—97; asst. prof. medicine Nat. Def. Med. Sch., Tokorozawa, Japan, 1997—99; v.p. Shonan Kamakura (Japan) Gen. Hosp., 1999—. Author: (book) Hemodialysis Treatment, 2002. Recipient Spl. award, Sankyo Life Sci., 1988. Avocations: classical music, clarinet. Office: Shonan Kamakura Gen Hosp 1202-1 Yamazaki Kamakura 247-8533 Japan Office Fax: 81-467-45-0190. Business E-Mail: shuzo@shonankamakura.on.jp.

KOBAYASHI, TOSHIYUKI, psychiatrist, educator; s. Tomiji and Mitsu Kobayashi; m. Kazumi Ide, June 1, 1991; children: Akane, Yume. MD, Jichi Med. Sch., Shimotsuke, Tochigi, Japan, 1987, PhD, 2000. Resident Jichi Med. Sch., 1987—89; physician Asama Gen. Hosp., Saku, Nagano, 1989—92; rsch. fellow Shinshu U., Matsumoto, Nagano, 1992—93; chief psychiatrist Anan Hosp., Nagano, 1993—97; rsch. fellow Jichi Med. U., Shimotsuke, 1997—2001, lectr., 2001—10, assoc. prof., 2010—. Contbr. articles to profl. jours. (Japanese Assn. Pathography award, 2005, 2009). Mem.: Japanese Soc. Schizophrenia Rsch. (coun. 2007), Tochigi Psychiat. Assn. (editor 1999), Japanese Assn. Pathography (editor 2002, dir. 2003). Avocation: viola. Office: Jichi Med Univ 3311-1 Yakushiji Shimotsuke Tochigi 329-0498 Japan Office Fax: 81-285-44-6198. Business E-Mail: kabakun@jichi.ac.jp.

KOBBELTVEDT, THERESE, psychology professor; PhD in Psychology, U. of Bergen, Norway. Rsch. fellow Norwegian Naval Acad./U. of Bergen, Bergen, Norway, 2000—03; assoc. prof., gen. psychology U. Bergen, Norway, 2006—; assoc. prof. Mgmt. Norwegian Sch. Economics, 2009—. Personal E-mail: kobba@online.no.

KOBER, GISBERT HERBERT, cardiologist, clinician; b. Ziegenhals, Germany, Aug. 30, 1939; s. Kurt B. and Hildegard E. (Mucha) K.; m. Ingeborg Geier, Apr. 5, 1965; children: Andreas, Henning, Philipp. Med. student, J.W. Goethe U., Frankfurt, Germany, 1959-62, U. Vienna, Austria, 1962-63, U. Marburg, Germany, 1963-64; MD, J.W. Goethe U., 1965, specialist in internal medicine, 1973, specialist in cardiology, 1974, habilitation, 1974. Med. asst. Univ. Hosp., Giessen, 1965-67; rsch. fellow in medicine Berlin U. Physiology, 1967-68; trainee in internal medicine Univ. Hosp., Frankfurt, 1968-73, trainee in cardiology, 1973-74, prof. internal medicine and cardiology, 1977-91; chief Clinic Nordrhein, Bad Nauheim, Germany, 1991—2001; with Cardiology Ctr. Bethanien, Frankfurt, 2001—. Author: Die Koronare Herzerkrankung, 1976, Koronarangiographie, 1980; editor, author: Nitrate und Nitrattoleranz in der Behandlung der KHK, 1983, Nitrates IV, 1983. Recipient Kurt Adam award Soc. Med. Edn., Berlin, 1981, Nitrolingual award Pohl-Boscamp, Hohenlockstedt, 1981, Arthur Weber award, 1991. Fellow Am. Heart Assn., European Soc. Cardiology; mem. German Cardiology Assn. (chief working group cardiomyopathy 1982-86, chief working group coronary interventions 1986-90), Rotary. Avocations: biking, hiking, tennis, classical music. Office: Cardiology Ctr Bethanien Am Prueffing 23 60389 Frankfurt Germany Office Phone: 069-945028-0. E-mail: g.kober@ccb.de.

KOBER, THILO, health researcher; b. Mannheim, Germany, Sept. 21, 1948; s. Freimut Kober and Lydia Sandri; m. Anne Margaret McNaughton, Sept. 25, 1965; children: Rebekah, Benjamin. M in Nursing Adminstrn., U. NSW, 1987; PhD, U. Cologne, 2005. Exec. officer Cochrane Hematological Malignancies Group, Cologne, 1999—2006; asst. dir. Australian Govt. Dept. Health and Ageing, Canberra, 2006—08. Project and liaison officer Australian Cancer Soc., Sydney, 1992—97. Avocations: cooking, motorcycling, horseback riding. Office: Smiling Press Internat 3 Ulm St 2614 Canberra ACT Australia Office Phone: 61 2 6255 2838. Office Fax: 61 2 6255 2838. Personal E-mail: tk_smilingpress@bigpond.com.

KÖBLER, SUSANNE, audiologist; b. Augsburg, Germany, Dec. 3, 1968; MSc, Erlangen U., Germany, 1994; PhD, Karolinska Inst., Sweden, 2007. Audiological scientist Uppsala U. Hosp., 2007—. Home: Blåhakevägen 4 Uppsala Uppland 75652 Sweden Personal E-mail: susanne.kobler@bredband.net.

KOC, YENER, hematology and oncology educator; b. Konya, Turkey, Dec. 17, 1962; s. Hilmi Koc; m. Ebru Koc, Oct. 23, 2004; children: Fulya, Funda. MD, Hacettepe U. Sch. Medicine, 1985. Lic. physician Turkey. Mem. faculty dept. rsch. Evans meml. Boston U. Med. Ctr., 1992—95; assoc. prof. Hacettepe U. Inst. Oncology, Ankara, Turkey, 1999—2005; prof., dir. hematology/oncology Yeditepe U. Hosp., Istanbul, Turkey, 2005—. Insp. European Bone Marrow Transplant Registry, Barcelona, 2004—. Recipient Sci. Achievement award, Spl. Fellowship Program Prof. Dr. Kanti Rai, 1997; named Fellow of the Yr., Boston U. Med. Ctr., 1995. Mem.: Am. Soc. Hematology, Am. Soc. of Bone Marrow Transplantation. Achievements include research in clinical stem cell transplantation. Office: Yeditepe Univ Hosp Kozyatagi 34752 Istanbul Istanbul Turkey Personal E-mail: yener@mac.com.

KOCABAY, GONENC, physician; b. Ankara, June 2, 1978; MD, Istanbul U., Turkey, 2001. Cardiologist Kartal Kosuyolu Heart Rsch. and Edn. Hosp., Istanbul, 2007—10; diabetologist Istanbul U., Istanbul Med. Sch., 2006—07, specialist, internal medicine, 2001—06. Recipient award, Turkish Sci. and Tech. Found., Eastern Anatolia Region, 1994, 2006, Soc. Turkish Cardiology Bd., 2008, European Soc. Cardiology, 2010. Mem.: Turkish Soc. Internal Medicine, Turkish Soc. Cardiology. Home: Hurriyet Mah Uzmanlar Cad Reyhan Sok Yakacik-Kartal-Istanbul 34800 Turkey Personal E-mail: gonenckocabay@yahoo.com.

KOCAKUSAK, AHMET, surgeon; b. Antalya, Turkey, Nov. 9, 1967; s. Oktay and Sidika Kocakusak; m. Canan Kabaca, May 15, 1999; children: Ege, Ece Lara. MD (hon.), Marmara U., Istanbul, Turkey, 1994; philos. degree in Anatomy, Istanbul U., 1998; PhD in Gen. Surgery, Haseki Tchg. and Rsch. Hosp., Istanbul, 2002, PhD in Diagnostic and Therapeutic Endoscopy, 2006. Diplomate in gen. surgery Ministry of Health, in anatomy, in diagnostic and theraputic endoscopy, in med. faculty. Technician Cagdas Roentgen Lab., Istanbul, 1985—86; translator German and English Barit Mine, Istanbul, 1990—92; govt. physician Ministry of Health Ercis Child and Woman Health Assn., Van, Turkey, 1994—95; resident in anatomy Istanbul U. Med. Faculty, 1995—98; resident in gen. surgery Haseki Tchg. and Rsch. Hosp., 1998—2002, gen. surgeon; anatomy tchr. Fatih Pvt. HS for Nurses, Istanbul, 2000—01. Head invoice commn. Haseki Tchg. and Rsch. Hosp. Editor: Haseki Med. Bull., 2005—; referee: Med. Principles and Practice, 2003—, Indian Jour. Med. Scis., 2003—, Med. Prins. Practice; contbr. articles to profl. jours. Lt. Turkish Rep. Land Forces, 2002—04. Mem.: Turkish Trauma Assn. (assoc.), Istanbul Surg. Soc. (assoc.), Turkish Surg. Soc. (assoc.), Istanbul Med. Chamber (assoc.), Assn. Grads. Marmara U. Med. Faculty, Assn. Grads. German Pvt. Sch., SCUBA Deep Sea Diving Assn., Windsurfing Assn. Socialist. Muslim. Avocations: languages, archaeology, mythology, rafting, windsurfing. Home: Medine Apt Semsettin Gunaltay Cad 197/23 Erenkoy Istanbul 34738 Turkey Office: Haseki HastanesiHaseki Tchg Hosp Millet Cad Aksaray Istanbul Turkey Personal E-mail: ahmetkocakusak@yahoo.com.

KOCH, CHRISTIAN ALBERT, endocrinologist, educator; b. Nuremberg, Germany, Feb. 3, 1965; arrived in US, 2006; MD, Friedrich-Alexander-U., 1991; PhD, U. Leipzig, 2003. Diplomate Am. Bd. Internal Medicine, 1999, lic. Saxonian Physician Chamber, 2002, diplomate German Bd. Internal Medicine, 2002. Capt. and physician Germany Army, Leipzig, Germany, 1993—94; intern, resident internal medicine Ohio State U., Columbus, Ohio, 1994—97; clin. fellow NIH, Bethesda, Md., 1998—2001, attending physician, 2000—02; attending physician, assoc. prof. medicine U. Leipzig, Germany, 2002—06; prof. U. Miss., Jackson, Miss., 2006—, dir., 2006—. Recipient, Am. Assn. Clin. Endocrinologist, 2001. Fellow: ACP, Am. Coll. Endocrinologists. Office: Univ Miss 2500 N State Street Jackson MS 39216 Business E-Mail: ckoch@medicine.umsmed.edu.

KOCH, MICHAEL GERHARD, epidemiologist; b. Prenzlau, Germany, Aug. 21, 1941; s. Gerhard Walter and Hildegard Helene (Hirschberg) K.; m. Lisbeth Andersson, June 7, 2000; children: Ivar Nathan, Jessica Feyl, Viveca Miriam, Angelica Dalia. MD, U. Kiel, 1966. Physician various hosps., Sweden, 1967-71; state physician Karlsborg, Sweden, 1972-80; head health dist., 1981-90; regimental physician, 1991—2006. Epidemiologist, Bavaria, 1988-89, Switzerland, Sweden, Germany, 1989-2007. Recipient Bejerot award Swedish Carnegie Inst., 1989. Avocations: animal rights/health, protection of nature, prevention of drug abuse, gender science, emerging diseases. Home: Bjurvall Satra SE 54694 Undenas Sweden Personal E-mail: mgkoch@gmail.com.

KOCH, MICHAEL OSCAR, urologist; married. MD, Dartmouth Med. Sch., Hanover, NH, 1981. Diplomate Am. Bd. Urology, 1987. Chmn. urology Ind. U. Sch. Medicine, Indpls., 1998—2008. Home: 2173 Caledonian Ct Greenwood IN 46143 Business E-Mail: miokoch@iupui.edu.

KOCH, RICHARD, retired pediatrician, educator; b. ND, Nov. 24, 1921; s. Valentine and Barbara (Fischer) K.; m. Kathryn Jean Holt, Oct. 2, 1943; children: Jill, Thomas, Christine, Martin, Leslie. BA, U. Calif., Berkeley, 1958; MD, U. Rochester, 1951. Mem. staff Children's Hosp., LA, 1952—75, 1977—2003, dir. child devel. divsn., 1955-75; dep. dir. Calif. Dept. Health, 1975-76; prof. pediat. U. So. Calif., 1955—75, 1977—2003; dir. Phenylketonuria Collaborative Study, 1966-82; med. dir. Spastic Children's Found., LA, 1980-85. Mem. Project Hope, Trujillo, Peru, 1970; dir. Regional Ctr. for Developmentally Disabled at Children's Hosp., L.A., 1966-75; mem. rsch. adv. bd. Nat. Assn. Retarded Citizens, 1974-76; mem. Gov.'s Coun. on Devel. Disabilities, 1981-83; bd. dirs. Down's Syndrome Congress, 1974-76; prin. investigator Maternal Phenylketonuria Project Nat. Inst. Child Health and Human Devel., Washington, 1985-2003; mem. forensic assessment team South Ctrl. Regional Ctr. for Developmental Disabilities, 1999—. Author: (with James Dobson) The Mentally Retarded Child and his Family, 1971, (with Kathryn J. Koch) Understanding the Mentally Retarded Child, 1974, (with Felix de la Cruz) Downs Syndrome, 1975; contbr. articles to profl. jours. Recipient Albert L. Anderson award for outstanding health care profl., 1997, Homer Smith Rsch. award, 1998; Carrie D. Jones scholar, U. Calif., Berkeley, 1941. Mem. Am. Assn. on Mental Deficiency (pres. 1968-69), Am. Acad. Pediat., Soc. for Study Inborn Errors Metabolism, Soc. Inborn Metabolic Disorders, Sierra Club (treas. Mineral King task force 1972). Achievements include research in mental retardation, phenylketonuria and maternal PKU phenyl Ketonaria, Kuvan Therapy. Home: 2125 Ames St Los Angeles CA 90027-2902 Home Phone: 323-664-6902. Personal E-mail: drpku@sbcglobal.net.

KOCHAN, PIOTR, medical educator, researcher; MD, Jagiellonian U. Med. Coll., Cracow, Malopolskie, Poland, 2002. Registered Chamber of Physicians, 2003. Intern Rydygier Voivodship Hosp., Cracow, 2002—03; academic tchr., rschr. Jagiellonian U. Med. Coll., 2004—. Internat. conf. coord. EUPROBIO, 2005, 08; amb. Ctrl. & Eastern Europe, 2011—. Translator (editor): (med. book) Polish Edit., Sanford Guide for Antimicrobial Therapy. Grantee, Polish Min. Sci. and Higher Edn., 2008; Project grants, European Union, 2004—07. Mem.: Am. Soc. Microbiology (amb. ctrl. & eastern Europe), Polish Soc. Probiotics and Prebiotics (Cracow) (bd. dirs. 2007—), Polish Soc. Clin. Microbiology, Polish Soc. Hosp. Infections, Polish Soc. Microbiologists, European Soc. Clin. Microb & Infect Disesses Profl. Affairs Subcom. Office: Jagiellonian Univ Med Coll Ul. Czysta 18 31-121 Cracow Poland Office Fax: 4812 423 39 24. Business E-Mail: pkochan@cm-uj.krakow.pl.

KOCHANEK, PATRICK MICHAEL, pediatrician, educator; b. Detroit, July 1, 1954; s. Julius E. and Stella A. (Mrowiec) K.; m. Denise Marie Kochanek; children: Ashley, Stanton, Jillian. BS, U. Mich., 1976; MD, U. Chgo., 1980. Intern, then resident U. Calif., San Diego, 1980-83; fellow pediatric critical care medicine Children's Hosp. Nat. Med. Ctr., Washington, 1983-86; guest scientist Naval Med. Rsch. Inst., Bethesda, Md., 1983-86; from asst. prof. to prof. U. Pitts., 1986—2002, prof., 2002—, dir. Safar Ctr. for Resuscitation Rsch., 1994—; dir. pediatric critical care medicine rsch. Children's Hosp. Pitts., 1992—2009. Editor in chief Pediatric Critical Care Medicine, 2000—. Recipient Investigator award Soc. Critical Care Medicine, 1994—95, Disting. Investigator award Am. Coll. Critical Care Medicine, 2007, Disting. Career award Critical Care Sect. Am. Acad. Pediat., 2008. Office: Safar Ctr Resuscitation Rsch 3434 5th Ave Pittsburgh PA 15260 Home Phone: 412-561-5987; Office Phone: 412-383-1900. Business E-Mail: kochanekpm@ccm.upmc.edu.

KOCHER, MININDER SINGH, pediatric orthopaedic surgeon, epidemiologist; b. Rochester, NY, Dec. 23, 1966; s. Haribhajan Singh and Ranjit Kaur Kocher; m. Michele Mary Dupre, June 4, 1994; children: Sophia Dupre, Isabelle Dupre, Calvin Dupre, Ava Dupre, Henry Dupre. AB, Dartmouth Coll., 1989; MD, Duke U., 1993; MPH, Harvard U., 2000. Bd. cert. Am. Bd. Orthopaedic Surgeons, 2002, cert. Am. Bd. Orthopaedic Surgeons Sports Medicine, 2009. Intern Beth Israel Hosp./Harvard Med. Sch., 1993—94; resident Harvard Combined Orthop. Surgery Residency program, 1994—98; fellow pediat. orthop. surgery Boston Children's Hosp., 1998—99; fellow sports medicine Steadman Hawkin's Clinic, 1999—2000; pediatric orthop. surgeon Children's Hosp. Boston, 2000—; asst. prof. orthop. surgery Harvard Med. Sch., Boston, 2000—06, assoc. prof. orthop. surgery, 2006—; cons. Steadman Hawkins Sports Medicine Found., Vail, Colo., 2000—. Dir. Children's Hosp. Orthop. Inst. for Clin. Effectiveness, Boston, 2000—; assoc. dir. divsn. sports medicine Children's Hosp., Boston, 2005—. Sci. adv. com. Steadman Hawkins Sports Medicine Found., Vail, Colo., 2000; med. adv. com. Leading-MD.com, LA, 2001. Recipient Wilburt Davidson award, Duke U. Sch. Medicine, 1993, Harris Yett award, Harvard Combined Orthop. Program, 1994, Von Meyer award, Children's Hosp. Boston, 1998, Zimmer award, Am. Orthop. Assn., 1999, Richard Kilfoyle award, New Eng. Orthop. Soc., 1999, Clin. Rsch. prize, Arthroscopy Assn. N.Am., 2000, 2001, Vernon Thompson award, Western Orthop. Assn., 2000, Kappa Delta award, Otherpedic Rsch. and Edn. Found., 2005; Nat. Honor Soc. scholar, LG Balfour, 1985—89, Nat. Merit Scholarship, 1985—89, Rufus Choate scholar, Dartmouth Coll., 1988—99. Fellow: Am. Acad. Orthop. Surgeons (Kappa Delta Clin. Rsch. award 2005); mem.: Am. Orthop. Soc. for Sports Medicine, Anterior Cruciate Ligament Study Group, Pediat. Orthop. Soc. N.Am. (clin. effectiveness com. 2002—, bd. dirs. 2005, Angela Kuo award 2004), Phi Beta Kappa. Office: Childrens Hosp Boston 300 Longwood Ave Boston MA 02115 Business E-Mail: mininder.kocher@childrens.harvard.edu.

KOCIĆ, IVAN BOGOLJUB, pharmacologist, researcher; b. Leskovac, Serbia, Apr. 1, 1962; arrived in Poland, 1990; s. Bogoljub and Smilja (Nikolić) K.; m. Beata Katarzyna Groth, June 4, 1988; children: Milan, Adam, Eliza. MD, Med. Faculty, Nish, Yugoslavia, 1986; PhD, Med. U., Gdańsk, Poland, 1995; habil, Med. U., 2005. Rschr. Pharm. Factory Zdravlje, Leskovac, 1986-90; asst. Dept. Pharmacology, Gdańsk, 1990-95, adj., 1995—, prof., 2010. Rsch. fellow dept. cardiovasc. disease Tokyo Med. and Dental U., 1999-2001; assoc. prof. pharmacology, 2005-, head dept. pharmacology Med. U. Gdansk, 2007-. Contbr. to profl. jours. Japanese Soc. Promotion Sci. fellow, Tokyo, 1998. Mem. Polish Pharm. Soc., Gdańsk Soc. Scis., European Soc. Cardiology. Avocations: chess, playing guitar, soccer. Home: Podlaska Str 5/3 81-325 Gdynia Poland Office: Dept Pharmacology Ul. Debowa 23 80-204 Gdansk Poland Business E-Mail: ikocic@amg.gda.pl, ikocic@gumed.edu.pl.

KOCIJAN LOVKO, SANDRA, psychiatrist, educator; b. Zagreb, Croatia, June 6, 1974; MD, U. Medicine, Zagreb, 1998, MS, 2008. Head, outpatient dept. psychiatry Gen. Hosp. Zabok, 2000—. Mem.: Croatian Soc. Quality Improvement in Health Care, Croatian Psychiat. Assn. Home Fax: 3851 3740168. Personal E-mail: sandra.kocijan@zg.t-com.hr.

KODA-KIMBLE, MARY ANNE, pharmacologist, educator, dean; PharmD, U. Calif., San Francisco, 1969. Lic. pharmacist Calif., 1969, cert. diabetes educator. Faculty U. Calif. San Francisco Sch. Pharmacy, 1970—, dean, 1998—, also prof. clin. pharmacy, Thomas J. Long Endowed chair in chain pharmacy practice. Mem. nonprescription drugs adv. com. FDA; mem. Calif. State Bd. Pharmacy. Coeditor: Applied Therapeutics for Clinical Pharmacists, 1975, Basic Clinical Pharmacokinetics, 1980, Applied Therapeutics: Clinical Use of Drugs, 1988, Basic Clinical Pharmacokinetics, 1988, Handbook of Applied Therapeutics, 3d edit., 1996; contbr. numerous articles to profl. jours., chpts. to books.; mem. editl. bd. Internat. Jour. Clin. Pharmacology, 1979—82, Drug Interactions Newsletter and Update, 1981, Diabetes Forecast, 1986—89. Recipient Alumnus of Yr., UCSF Sch. Pharmacy Alumni Assn., 1993; named Pharmacist of Yr., Calif. Soc. Hosp. Pharmacists, 1991; named to Calif. Pharmacists Hall of Fame, 1997. Mem.: Nat. Acad. Practice in Pharmacy (founding mem.), Am. Coun. Pharm. Edn., Am. Coll. Clin. Pharmacy (bd. dirs., Paul F. Parker Medal 2007), Calif. Soc. Health-System Pharmacists (bd. dirs., Pharmacist of Yr.), Am. Pharm. Assn. (task force on edn.), Am. Assn. Colleges of Pharmacy (pres.), Inst. Medicine. Office: UCSF Sch Pharmacy C 156 Box 0622 521 Parnassus Ave San Francisco CA 94143-0622 Office Phone: 415-476-8010. Office Fax: 415-476-6632. Business E-Mail: kodakimblem@pharmacy.ucsf.edu.

KOECH, KENNEDY JERRY, oral surgeon; b. Sotik, Kenya, Mar. 4, 1966; BDS, U. Nairobi, 1992, MDS, 2005. Maxillofacial surgeon Kenyatta Nat. Hosp., 2005—. Surg. vol. Operation Smile, 2003—11; lectr. U. Nairobi, 2005—; cons. surgeon Smile Train, 2010—. Fellow: AO, Eastern Africa Assn. Oral & Maxillofacial Surgeons, Internat. Assn. Oral & Maxillofacial Surgeons. Avocations: exercise, golf. Office: Argwings Kodhek Nairobi 00202 Kenya E-mail: kennedykoech@yahoo.co.uk.

KOEHL, JOERG, microbiologist, researcher, medical educator; b. Gladbeck, North Rhein/Westfalia, Germany, Oct. 1, 1960; s. Paul and Rita Koehl; m. Gabriele Karwath, 1991; children: Vera, Anja. MD, U. Mainz, Germany, 1988. Cert. physician Nat. Office for Social, Youth and Family, 1988, specialist in med. microbiology Lower Saxony, 1994. Asst. prof. Med. Sch. Hannover, Germany, 1995—99, assoc. prof., 1999—2002; prof. pediat. Cin. Children's Hosp., 2002—. Contbr. over 90 articles to profl. jours. Grantee molecular regulation of immune complex disease, NIH, 2004—, complement in allergic asthma: role of C3a and C5a, 2004—. Achievements include patents for muteins of the C5a anaphylatoxin, nucleic acid molecules encoding such muteins, and pharmaceutical uses of muteins of the C5a anaphylatoxin; patents pending for organ transplantation solutions and methods for transplanting organs. Home: 6965 Crystal Springs Rd Cincinnati OH 45227-4437 E-mail: joerg.koehl@chmcc.org.

KOENEN, KARESTAN, psychologist, educator; BA in Economics, Wellesley Coll., 1990; MA in Developmental Psychology, Columbia U., 1996; PhD in Clinical Psychology, Boston U., 1999. Lic. clinical psychologist. Fellow in psychiatric epidemiology Columbia U.; adj. asst. prof. psychiatry Boston U. Sch. Medicine; asst. prof. society, human devel. & health Harvard Sch. Pub. Health. Office: Harvard School of Public Health Kresge Bldg 677 Huntington Ave 7th Fl Boston MA 02115 E-mail: kkoenen@hsph.harvard.edu.

KOEPKE, JOHN ARTHUR, hematologist, clinical pathologist; b. Milw., Mar. 25, 1929; s. Elmer Paul and Meta Clara (Jennrich) K.; m. Evelyn Mae Lovekamp, June 18, 1955; children: Mary Evelyn, John Frederick, Mark David, James Robert. BA, Valparaiso U., 1951; MD, U. Wis., 1956; MS, Marquette U., 1964. Intern, resident in clin. pathology and internal medicine Milw. Hosp., 1956-60; mem. faculty U. Ky. Coll. Medicine, 1961-71, assoc. prof., 1965-71; dir. clin. pathology, prof. pathology U. Iowa, Iowa City, 1972-79, vice chmn. dept., 1972-79; prof. pathology, assoc. prof. internal medicine Coll. Medicine, Duke U., Durham, NC, 1979-94; dir.clin. transfusion svc. hematology lab. Duke U. Med. Ctr., 1979-88, prof. emeritus, 1994—. Vis. scientist Karolinska Inst., Stockholm, 1967-68, Royal Postgrad. Med. Sch., London, 1978. Author 7 books in field; editor 6 books; bd. editors Am. Jour. Clin. Pathology, 1976—, Clin. and Lab. Hematology, 1978-94, Blood Cells, 1985-98; assoc. editor Cytometry, 1993-1998, Comms. in Clin. Cytometry, 1994-99, Lab. Hematology, 1994—; contbr. over 250 articles to profl. jours., 25 chpts. to books. Recipient Pres.'s award Valparaiso U., 1951, also Disting. Alumnus award, 1980. Fellow Am. Soc. Clin. Pathology, Coll. Am. Pathologists; mem. AMA, Internat. Coun. for Standards in Hematology (secretariat 1978—, v.p. 1990-92, pres. 1992-94). Lutheran. Home: 3142 Gracefield Rd Apt MG 521 Silver Spring MD 20904-5858 Personal E-mail: nckoepke@mindspring.com.

KOEPSELL, HERMANN, biomedical scientist; b. Lüneburg, Germany, Feb. 22, 1944; s. Eberhard and Elisabeth (Aberle) K.; m. Iliane Sacher, Aug. 1, 1969 (div. Apr. 1986); children: Kilian, Bettina, Philip; m. Kornelia Stendal, Sept. 30, 1988. MD, U. Münster, Germany, 1971. Rsch. asst. Anatomical Inst., Münster, 1972-74; rsch. assoc. Max-Planck Inst. Biophysics, Frankfurt, 1975-78, leader rsch. group, 1978-92; prof. anatomy and cell biology, chmn. dept. U. Würzburg, Germany, 1993—. Mem. editl. bd.: Molecular Pharmacology. Rsch. grantee Deutsche Forschungsgemeinschaft, 1979—, German-Israeli Found., 1987-90. Mem. Anatomy Assn., Assn. Biochemistry & Molecular Biology, Assn. for Nephrology, Am. Soc. Pharmacology & Exptl. Therapeutic, German Acad. Scis. Leopoldina. Achievements include research on detection of inactive state of the Na-K-ATPase in plasma membrane; detection and cloning of membrane-associated protein that regulates plasma membrane transporters; detection/cloning of polyspecific cation transporter that participates in renal and hepatic drug excretion and was the first member of a new transporter family; identification of high and low affinity binding sites in polyspecific organic cation transporter; detection of a glucose ligated channel. Office: U Würzburg Inst für Anatomie und Zellbiologie Koellikerstraße 6 97070 Würzburg Germany Home Phone: 49-931-4043296; Office Phone: 49-931-3182700. E-mail: Hermann@Koepsell.de.

KOGA, ITARU, physician; b. Saga, Japan, Nov. 14, 1965; s. Shintaro and Kazue Koga; m. Mariko Nakada, June 1, 2001. MB, Saga Med. Sch., Japan, 1990; PhD, Uppsala U., Sweden, 2003. Registered anesthetic doctor Japanese Govt., 1993, specialist anesthesiologist Japanese Soc. Anesthesiologist, 2007. Mgr., dept. anesthesiology Mejiro Hosp., Tokyo, 1999—. Grant, Laerdal Found. for Acute Medicine, 1996, 1997. Achievements include research in validated sophisticated monitoring application of splanchnic perfusion. Personal E-mail: i_koga@hotmail.com, i_koga@auone.jp. Business E-Mail: itaru.koga@surgsci.uu.se.

KOGA, KOMATSU, gastroenterologist, director; b. Sendai City, Japan, May 12, 1964; MD, Yamagata U. Sch. Medicine, 1991; PhD, Tohoku U. Grad. Sch., 1997. Med. staff Miyagi Social Ins. Hosp., 1997—99, Akita U. Sch. Medicine, 1999—2001, asst. prof., 2003—05, adj. asst. prof., 2009—11; rsch. fellow Vanderbilt U. Med. Ctr., 2001—03; dir. gastroenterology Honjo Daiichi Hosp., 2005—. Vice chmn., bd. trustees, CEO Med. Corp. SEIRAN-KAI, 2010—11. Rsch. fellowship, Uehara Meml. Found., Maeda Toyokichi Meml. Gastroent. Found. Fellow: Japan Gastroent. Endoscopy Soc., Japanese Gastroent. Assn., Japanese Soc. Helicobacter Rsch., Japanese Soc. Gastroenterology, Japanese Soc. Internal Medicine. Office: 110 Iwabuchishita Yurihonjo Akita 015-8567 Japan Office Fax: 81-184-22-0120. Business E-Mail: komami@live.jp.

KOGA, MSAFUMI, physician; b. Saga, Japan, Mar. 6, 1951; MD, Osaka U. Sch., 1975, PhD, 1989. Dir. health care ctr. Kinki Ctrl. Hosp., 2000—. Assoc. prof. Osaka U. Sch., 1994—95. Avocation: Go. Office: 3-1 Kuruma-zuka Itami Hyogo 664-8533 Japan Office Fax: 81-72-779-1567. Business E-Mail: koga_m@kich.itami.hyogo.jp.

KOGA, YASUHIRO, medical researcher, microbiologist; b. Sasebo, Nagasaki, Japan, Nov. 4, 1952; s. Takehiko and Atsuko Koga; m. Yasuhiro Koga, Dec. 1, 2000. MD, Kyushu U., Fukuoka, Japan, 1978. Lic. physician Health And Welfare Ministry, Japan, 1978. Prof. Tokai U. Sch. Medicine, Isehara, Kanagawa, Japan; pres. Japanese Soc. Probiotics Sci., Isehara, 1998—. Contbr. scientific papers. Achievements include discovery of daily intake of a probiotic lactobacillus strain as food decrease the risk of gastric cancer of the human infected with Helicobacter pylori. Home: Shimokasuya 2254-10 Isehara Kanagawa 259-1143 Japan Office: Tokai Univ Sch Medicine Shimokasuya 143 Isehara Kanagawa 259-1193 Japan Office Fax: 81-463-94-2976; Home Fax: 81-463-95-6369. Business E-Mail: yasuhiro@is.icc.u-tokai.ac.jp.

KOGAN, INNA, psychiatrist, educator; b. Kharkov, USSR, Sept. 5, 1940; came to U.S., 1979; d. Alexander and Fanya (Ioffe) Epelbaum; 1 child, James B. MD, Med. Sch., Perm, USSR, 1957-59, Med. Sch., Riga, Latvia, 1964. Tng. in ophthalmology Med. Sch., Riga, 1964-65; staff ophthalmologist Outpatient Clinic, Riga, 1964-78; physician asst. to William S. Harris, M.D., Dallas, 1980-83; flexible intern U. Tex. Southwestern Med. Sch., Dallas, 1984-85, resident in ophthalmology, 1985-86, resident in psychiatry, 1987-90, clin. instr. psychiatry dept., 1990-95, clin. assoc. prof., 1995—, clin. prof. dept. psychiatry, 2008—; mem. staff Terrell (Tex.) State Hosp., Dallas, 1990-92; pvt. practice Dallas, 1992—. Head statis. divsn. Ministry Pub. Health Latvia, Riga, 1975-78; med. dir. Psychiatric Svcs. Meth. Med. Ctr., Dallas, 1993-94. Contbr. articles to med. jours., including Contact and Intraocular Lens Med. Jour., Am. Intraocular Implant Soc. Jours. Recipient Cert. Excellence, Nancy A.A. Roeske, 2000, Cert. Appreciation, U. Tex. S.W. Med. Sch., 2002, 2004, 2005, Arthur M. Griffin award, 1997—98, Jewish Family Svc. Appreciation award, 1995, Terrell State Hosp. Appreciation award, 1987—92, Nat. Leadership award, Nat. Rep. Congl. Com.; named Am. Top Psychiatrists, Consumer's Rsch. Coun. America, 2007. Mem. Am. Psychiat. Assn., North Tex. Soc. Psychiat. Physicians, Tex. Soc. Psychiat. Physicians, Dallas Area Women Psychiatrists (chmn.). Republican. Avocations: music, art, travel, reading. Office: Ste 504 13101 Preston Rd Dallas TX 75240-5231 Office Phone: 469-791-9000.

KOGAN, RICHARD J., former pharmaceutical company executive; b. NYC, June 6, 1941; s. Benjamin and Ida K.; m. Susan Linda Scher, Aug. 29, 1965. BA, CCNY, 1963; MBA, NYU, 1968. V.p. planning and adminstrn. pharm. divsn. Ciba-Geigy Ltd., Summit, NJ, 1975-76, pres. Can. pharm. ops., 1976—79, pres. U.S. pharm. divsn., 1979—82; exec. v.p. pharm. ops. Schering-Plough Corp., Kenilworth, NJ, 1982—86, pres., COO, 1986—96, pres., CEO, 1996—2003, chmn. bd. dirs., 1998—2002. Bd. dirs. Colgate-Palmolive Co., The Bank of NY Co., Inc.; trustee St. Barnabas Corp. and Med. Ctr. Trustee NYU, bd. overseers Stern Sch. Bus. Mem.: Coun. Fgn. Rels. Office Phone: 973-379-6560. Personal E-mail: rjk@rjkogan.com.

KOGER, MICHAEL PIGOTT, SR., physician, writer; b. Balt., Jan. 20, 1953; s. Linwood Jr. and Margaret (Pigott) K.; children: Michael Pigott Koger Jr. Student, Morgan State U., 1970, Fisk U., 1971-73, MIT, 1973-74; MD, Meharry Med. Coll., 1979; BA Journalism, Ga. State U., 2001, BA in Spanish, 2002; MA in Health Sci., U. Ala., 2003, postgrad., 2002—06. Internal med. resident Franklin Sq. Hosp., Balt., 1979—82; attending physician Provident Hosp., Balt., 1982-85, VA Hosp., Marion, Ill., 1986-88, Central State Hosp., Milledgeville, Ga., 1988—92, Northwest Ga. Regional Hosp., Rome, 1992—96, Complete Wellness Med. Ctr., Atlanta, 1997; news dir. Sta. WRAS, Ga. State U., Atlanta, 2000—03; with Applied Rsch. Ltr., Ga. State U., 1999—2002; announcer WVUA FM Tuscaloosa New Rock 90.7 FM, 2002—03. Chmn. dept. quality assurance and utilization review Hancock Meml. Hosp., Sparta, Ga., 1985-86; mem. sci. adv. bd. Nutrition Superstore.com, 1999-2001. Columnist Sparta Ishmaelite, 1985-86, Signal (Ga. State U.), 2000. Vol. com. Olympic Games, Atlanta, 1996, Hands on Atlanta, 1996-97, Atlanta Cmty. Food Bank, 1996-97, organizing com. Atlanta Paralympic, 1996, Am. Heart Assn., Marietta, Ga., 1996. Mem. AMA, Soc. Profl. Journalists, Journalism History Soc. Home: 2024 Dinford St Apt 311 Laramie WY 82072-5386 Business E-Mail: mkoger@alum.mit.edu.

KOGSTAD, RAGNFRID ELINE, science educator; b. Oslo, July 15, 1953; Degree in Sociology, U. Bergen, 1984, PhD, 2011. Assoc. prof. Hedmark U. Coll., 2006—. Assoc. prof. Gjövik U. Coll., 2010—; fellow Rsch. Network, Human Rights and Mental Health Care. Recipient Best Publ. award, Hedmark U. Coll., 2010. Avocation: music. Home: Östregate 102 C Hamar Hedmark 2317 Norway Personal E-mail: ragnfrid.kogstad@hihm.no.

KOH, ANDREW YOUNG, pediatrician, director; b. Manhattan, Kans., Sept. 4, 1966; AB, Harvard Coll., 1988; BA in English, Oxford U., 1990; MD, Harvard Med. Sch., 1996. Chief resident Children's Hosp. Boston, 1999—2000; instr., pediat. Harvard Med. Sch., 2004—09; asst. prof. pediat. and microbiology U. Tex. Southwestern Med. Ctr., 2009, dir. pediat. hematopoietic stem cell transplantation, 2009—. Mem.: Soc. Pediat. Rsch., Am. Soc. Hematology, Am. Soc. Blood and Marrow Transplantation, Pediat. Bone Marrow Consortium, Am. Soc. Microbiology. Avocation: music. Office: University Tex Southwestern Med Ctr 5323 Harry Hines Bl Dallas TX 75390-9063 Office Fax: 214-648-3122. Business E-Mail: andrew.koh@utsouthwestern.edu.

KOH, BO KYUNG, dermatologist; d. Kwang Sam Koh and Jeong Seon Park; m. Sang Hak Yoon, Jan. 23, 2000; children: Sung Yeon Yoon, Hee Yeon Yoon. MD, 1997; PhD, Cath. U., Seoul, 2003. Cert. MD Korean Med. Assn., 1997, dermatologist Korean dermatol. Assn., 2003. Instr. Catolic U., St. Mary's Hosp., Uijongbu, Kyunggido, Republic of Korea, 2003—04; codir. CNP Skin & Laser Clinic, Seoul, 2004—10, Seoul Vets. Hosp., 2011—. Contbr. scientific papers to profl. jours. (Hyundai Pharmacy Acad. award). Mem.: Korean Dermatolo. Assn., Korean Med. Assn. Office: Seoul Veterans Hosp Dept Dermatology Dunchon 2-dong Gangdong-gu Seoul 134-791 Republic of Korea Office Phone: 82-2-2225-1388. Office Fax: 82-2-471-5514. Business E-Mail: kohbo@catholic.ac.kr.

KOH, BONG KYUNG, science educator; b. Daegu, Republic of Korea, July 16, 1961; PhD, Kans. State U., 1993. Prof. Keimyung U., 1995—. Adj. prof. Food Sci. and Human Nutrition, Mich. State U., 2005—06. Mem.: Korean Soc. Food Sci. and Tech. Avocations: running, painting. Office: 1000 Sindang Dong Dalsuh Gu Daegu 704-701 Republic of Korea Business E-Mail: kohfood@kmu.ac.kr.

KOH, BYUNGHEE, medical educator; b. Jeonju, Jeonbook, Republic of Korea, Oct. 7, 1953; BS, Kyunghee U., 1979, PhD, 1986. Dir. Dept. Sasang Constl. Medicine, Kyunghee U. Med. Ctr., 1993—2009; pres. Korea Inst. Oriental Medicine, 2000—03; prof. Kyunghee U., 1988—; dir. Internat. Studies Oriental Medicine, Kyunghee U., 2004—09. Exec. sec. Inst. Oriental Med. Kyung-Hee U., 1994—97. Recipient Best Paper award, Assn. Korean Oriental Medicine, Silver prize, Kowhang Found., Bronze prize, Gold prizes, Inst. Oriental Medicine, Kyung-Hee U.; Constl. Cohorts grant, KCDC, Ministry of Health, Korea. Master: Soc. Sasang Constl. Medicine (bd. mem. 1996—2011, pres. 1994—96); fellow: Soc. Info. Oriental Medicine (pres. 1992—94), Korean Soc. Oriental Medicine Music Therapy (pres. 2008—10); mem.: Korean Assn. Traditional Oncology, Soc. Acupuncture. Avocations: archery, music, travel. Office: Oriental Medicine Hosp 1 Hoegidong Dongdaemun-gu Seoul 130-702 Republic of Korea Office Fax: 82-2-958-9234. Business E-Mail: kohbh@khu.ac.kr.

KOH, DEAN C., colon and rectal surgeon; b. Singapore, Dec. 9, 1970; MBBS, Nat. U. Singapore, 1994; degree in Gen. Surgery, 2003. Cons. surgeon Tan Tock Seng Hosp. Singapore, 2003—06; cons. colorectal surgeon Nat. U. Health Sys., Singapore, 2006—10, sr. cons. colorectal surgeon, 2010—. Asst. prof., surgery Yong Loo Lin Sch. Medicine, Nat. U. Singapore, 2006—. Recipient Health Manpower Devel. Programme award, Ministry of Health, Singapore, Nat. Excellent Svc. award, SPRING Singapore, Svc. Champion award, Nat. Healthcare Group Singapore. Fellow: Royal Coll. Physicians and Surgeons Glasgow, Royal Coll. Surgeons Edinburgh, Acad. Medicine Singapore; mem.: Soc. Endoscopic and Laparoscopic Surgeons Asia, Am. Soc. Colon and Rectal Surgeons. Home: 19 Greenwood Ln Singapore 286947 Singapore Personal E-mail: dean_koh@nuhs.edu.sg.

KOH, HOWARD KYONGJU, federal agency administrator, former academic administrator; b. Cambridge, Mass., Mar. 15, 1952; s. Kwang Lim and Hesung (Chun) Koh; m. Claudia Anne Arrigg; children: Steven, Daniel, Katherine. BA, Yale Coll., 1973; MD, Yale U. Sch. Medicine, 1977; MPH, Boston U., 1995; Degree (hon.), Merrimack Coll. Diplomate American Bd. Dermatology, American Bd. Internal Medicine, cert. in hematology & med. oncology. Med. intern Boston City Hosp., 1977—78, resident internal medicine, 1978—82, resident dermatology, 1981—82; resident hematologic oncology Mass. Gen. Hosp., Boston, 1982—85; prof. dermatology, medicine & pub. health Boston U.; dir. cancer prevention & control Boston U. Med. Ctr.; commr. pub. health State of Mass., 1997—2003; dir. divsn. pub. health practice, assoc. dean Harvard Sch. Pub. Health, Boston, 2003—09, Harvey V. Fineberg prof. practice of pub. health, 2005—09; asst. sec. for health US Dept. Health & Human Services, Washington, 2009—. Chmn. Mass. Coalition Healthy Future, 1995—97; Presdl. appointee Nat. Cancer Adv. Bd., 2000—02. Mem. editl. Jour. Clin. Oncology, Jour. Disaster Medicine & Pub. Health Preparedness; contbr. numerous articles to profl. jours. Bd. dirs. American Cancer Soc., 1986—97, American Soc. Law, Medicine & Ethics, Harvard U. Advanced Leadership Initiative, Partnership HealthCare Excellence, Blue Cross Blue Shield Mass. Found. Recipient Disting. Svc. award, American Cancer Soc., Drs. Jack E. White/LaSalle D. Leffall Cancer Prevention award, American Assn. Cancer Rsch./Intercultural Cancer Coun., Disting. Alumni award, Boston U. Sch. Pub. Health; named one of The Most Influential Persons in the Fight Against Tobacco, New Eng. divsn. American Cancer Soc., K100-The 100 Leading Korean Americans in the First Century of Korean Immigration to US. Fellow: ACP; mem.: Inst. Medicine. Office: US Dept Health & Human Services 200 Independence Ave SW Washington DC 20201 Office Phone: 202-690-7694. E-mail: ASH@hhs.gov. *

KOH, HWEE-LING, pharmacist, educator, book author, consultant; BSc in Pharmacy with honors, Nat. U. Singapore, 1990, MSc in Pharmacy, 1992; PhD, Cambridge U., Eng., 1996. Registered pharmacist, Singapore. Pre registration pharmacist Singapore Genl. Hosp., 1990-91; rsch. asst. Nat. U. Singapore, 1991, assoc. prof., 2007—; pharmacist Guardian Pharmacy, Singapore, 1992, asst. prof., 1996—2006. Mem. food adv. com. Ministry of Environment, Singapore, 1998; cons. Ctr. Drug Adminstrn., Health Scis. Authority, 2003-; tech. assessor, expert Singapore Accreditation Coun. Singapore Lab. Accreditation Scheme 2003-, cons. Ctr. for Drug Evaluation, Ctr. for Pharmaceutical Adminstrn, Health Scis. Authority, 2003-05; mem. com. Nat. Traditional Chinese Medicine Taskforce, 2000-02; grant reviewer Rsch Grants Coun. of Hong Kong, 2004-08, Wellcome Trust Translation awards, 2004-, Nat. Med. Rsch. Coun., 2008-. Reviewer Jour. Chromatography A, Trends In Pharmacological Scis., Jour. of Pharm. Biomedical Analysis, Jour. Alternative and Complementary Medicine, Health Policy; contbr. articles to profl. jours. Recipient Prime Min.'s Book prize Min. Edn., 1983; EDB-Glaxo scholar Econ. Devel. Bd. Singapore, 1992-96, Herchel Smith Endowment Fund scholar, 1992-96; Outstanding Mentor award, Sci. Mentorship Program, Ministry Edn., 2004, Gen. Edn. Module Incentive Scheme award Nat. U. Singapore, 2004-05.Singapore Accreditation Coun. Assessor Bronze award, 2008. Fellow Japan Soc. for the Promotion of Sci.; mem. Am. Assn. Pharm. Scientists, Pharm. Soc. Singapore (Book prize 1986), Internat. Soc. for Magnetic Resonance in Medicine, Pharm. Scis. Group, Royal Pharm. Soc. Gt. Britain. Office: Nat U Singapore Dept Pharmacy/Fac Sci 18 Science Dr 4 117543 Singapore Singapore Office Phone: 65-65167962. E-mail: phakohhl@nus.edu.sg.

KOH, KYUNG BONG, psychiatry educator; b. Seoul, Republic of Korea, Nov. 10, 1947; s. Joon Sam Koh and Shin Bock Huh; m. Sung Sook Cho, Sept. 25, 1982; children: Jin Young, Jin Woo. MB, Yon Sei U., Seoul, 1974, MS, 1978, PhD, 1988. Diplomate in Psychiatry. Intern, then resident Severance Hosp., Seoul, 1974-79; research fellow Yonsei U. Severance Hosp., Seoul, 1982-83; instr., chief dept. psychiatry Yongdong Severance Hosp., Seoul, 1983-85, asst. prof., dir. consultation and liaison dept. psychiatry, 1985—, dir. research, 1986-87, assoc. prof., 1990—96, prof., 1996—. Mem. adv. editl. bd. Biopsychosocial Medicine, 2006—; chmn. organising com. 13th Asian Coll. Psychosomatic Medicine, 2008, 21st World Congress Psychosomatic Medicine, 2011. Editor: Korean Jour. Psychosomatic Medicine, 1992—94. Served as maj. Korean armed forces, 1979-82. Mem.: European Conf. on Psychosomatic Rsch. (internat. adv. com. 2004—06), Internat. Coll. Psychosomatic Medicine (internat. sci. adv. com. 2001—06), Korean Psychosomatic Soc. (pres. 2000—02), Am. Psychosomatic Soc., Korean Neuropsychiat. Assn. Avocations: tennis, golf. Office: Yonsei U Severance Hosp Dept Psychiatry 50 Yonsei Yo Seoul 120-752 Republic of Korea Office Phone: 82-2-2228-1624. Business E-Mail: kbkoh@yuhs.ac.kr.

KOH, SEONG-HO, medical educator; b. Seoul, Mar. 14, 1971; MD, Hanyang U., PhD, 2007. Asst. prof. Hanyang U. Coll. Medicine, 2007—. Recipient award for Best Rsch. Presentation, Korean Assn. for Neurodegenerative Disorders. Mem.: Korean Neurol. Assn.

(Young Investigator award). Office: 249-1 Gyomun-dong Gyeonggi Guri-city 471-701 Republic of Korea Office Phone: +82-31-560-2267. Office Fax: +82-31-560-2267. Business E-Mail: ksh213@hanyang.ac.kr.

KOH, YOUNG YOUP, cardiologist, educator; b. Gwangju, Republic of Korea, Aug. 1, 1964; s. Woon Seok Koh and Ok Hyun Cho; m. Jeong Joo Woo, May 23, 1992; 1 child, Byoung Wook. MD, Chosun U., Gwangju, 1989, PhD, 2001. Cert. in Korean nat. bd. exam. Ministry Health and Social Affairs, Republic of Korea, 1989, Korean bd. internal medicine cert. Korean Assn. Internal Medicine, cert. in Korean bd. cardiology. Cardiology fellow Sejong Gen. Hosp., Bucheon, Gyeonggi Province, Republic of Korea; dir. divsn. cardiology Sun Gen. Hosp., Daejeon, Republic of Korea, dir. Cardiac Catheterization Lab.; asst. prof. Chosun U. Coll. Medicine, 2001—06, assoc. prof., 2006—11, prof., 2011—; tchg. staff and rschr. Harvard U. Beth Israel Deaconess Med. Ctr., Boston, 2007—08. Mem. splty. Health Care and Evaluation Com. Health Ins. and Assessment Svc., Republic of Korea. Contbr. articles to profl. jours. Capt., med. officer Korean Army, 1994—97. Mem.: Korean Soc. Interventional Cardiology, Korean Soc. Echocardiography, Korean Soc. Hypertension, Korean Soc. Cardiology, Korean Assn. Internal Medicine, Korean Med. Assn. Home: Acroriver 752-36 Banghae-Dong Seocho-Gu Seoul 137-826 Republic of Korea Office: Chosun Univ Hosp Seosuk-Dong Dong-Gu 588 501-717 Gwangju Republic of Korea Office Fax: 82-62-234-9653.

KOH, YOUNG-DO, orthopedist, educator; b. Seoul, Republic of Korea, Apr. 13, 1962; s. Jungsuk Koh and Yeon Kim; m. Hyunsoo An, Nov. 10, 2002; children: Byungchul, Seungyeon. PhD, Seoul Nat. U., South Korea, 1998. Cert. in MD Divsn. Welfare, 1987, clin. orthop. bd. Korean Med. Assn., 1992. Asst. prof. Chungbuk Nat. U., Chungbuk, Republic of Korea, 1992—96; vis. fellowship U. Utah, Saltlake City, 1995, Med. Coll. Wis., Milw., 1996. Mem. Korean Soc. of Spine Surgery, Seoul, 1994—, Korean Orthop. Assn., Seoul, Republic Of Korea, 1992—, Korean Fracture Soc., Seoul, Republic Of Korea, 1994—, NASS, 1999—. Mem.: NASS, Korean Fracture Soc., Korean Soc. Spine Surgery, Korean Orthop. Assn. Office: Ewha Womans' Univ Sch Medicine 911-1 Mok-dong Yangcheon-ku Seoul 158-710 Republic of Korea Home: #106-602 Seocho-Raemian Apt Seachodong Seocho-ku Seoul 137-070 Republic of Korea Office Phone: 82-10-8875-5608. Office Fax: 02-2644-0128. Business E-Mail: ydkoh@ewha.ac.kr.

KOH, YOUNGIL I., allergist, medical educator; s. Kwang-Sik Koh and Duk-Youp Lim; m. Kyoung-Myoung Seo, Jan. 23, 1994; children: Eun-Jung, Ka-Hyun, Seung-Woo. B in Medicine, Chonnam Nat. U. Med. Sch., Republic of Korea, 1985—91, M in Medicine, 1992—94, MD, 1994—97. Lic. Ministry Health and Social Affairs, Republic of Korea, 1991, Allergy specialist Korean Assn. Internal Medicine, Republic of Korea, 1998. Intern Chonnam U. Hosp., Gwangju, 1991—92, resident, 1992—96, fellowship, 1996—97, 2000—01, clin. instr., 2001—03; asst. prof. Chonnam Nat. U. Med. Sch., Gwangju, 2003—. Capt. med. officer, 1997—2000, South Korea. Recipient Seo-Bong Med. Prize, Chonnam Nat. U. Med. Sch., 2003.

KOH, YOUNG-SANG, medical educator; s. Tae-Min Koh and Sun-Saeng Yang; m. Hwa-Jin Oh; children: Eun-Ji, Min-Hyuk, Youn-Hyuk. BS magna cum laude, Coll. Natural Scis. Seoul Nat. U., 1989; MS, Seoul Nat. U. Grad. Sch., 1991, PhD, 1996. Rschr. Rsch. Ctr. Molecular Microbiology Seoul Nat. U., 1993—94; postdoctoral fellow Harvard Med. Sch. and Mass. Gen. Hosp., Boston, 1996—97, Baylor Coll. Medicine, Houston, 1997—98; full-time lectr. Coll. Medicine Cheju Nat. U., Jeju, Republic of Korea, 1998—2000, asst. prof., 2000—04, assoc. prof., 2004—; prof. Jeju Nat. U. Sch. Medicine, 2009—. Rschr. Microbial Genome Ctr. Skin Infection Coll. Medicine Seoul Nat. U., 2001—05; chmn. dept. microbiology Coll. Medicine Cheju Nat. U., Jeju, 2001—06; com. sci. promotion Cheju Nat. U., 2002—04, steering com. Rsch. Instrument Ctr., 2003—05, com. rsch. and tng., com. med. curriculum, 2003—05, evaluation com. accreditation med. edn., 2004; asst. dean basic medicine Coll. Medicine Cheju Nat. U., 2003—05; adv. bd. Jeju Hi-Tech Industry Devel. Inst., 2003—04; vis. assoc. prof. Dana Farber Cancer Inst., Harvard Med. Sch., Boston, 2006—08. Author: Medical Microbiology, 3rd edit., 2004, 4th edit., 2005, 6th edit., 2009; contbr. articles to profl. jours. Recipient Excellent Dissertation award, Seoul Nat. U., 1996. Fellow: Microbiological Soc. Korea, Korean Soc. Microbiology. Achievements include research in Orientia tsutsugamushi Genome Project. Avocations: swimming, reading. Office: Jeju Nat University Sch Medicine 102 Jejudaehakno Jeju 690-756 Republic of Korea Office Fax: 82 64 702 2687. Business E-Mail: yskoh7@jejunu.ac.kr.

KOHAN, DARIUS, otolaryngologist, educator; b. Mar. 8, 1959; MD, NYU, 1984. Diplomate Am. Bd. Otolaryngology, 1990. Resident in surgery Beth Israel Med. Ctr., 1984—86; resident in otolaryngology NYU Med. Ctr., 1986—90, fellow in otology, 1990—91; assoc. prof. dept. of otolaryngology Sch. of Medicine NYU; assoc. adj. surgeon NY Eye and Ear Infirmary. Office: New York Eye and Ear Infirmary 310 E 14th St New York NY 10003 Office Phone: 212-979-4000.

KOHAN, RAUL E., healthcare company executive; Grad., Gen. San Martin Mil. Acad., Argentina; MBA in Economics, U. Buenos Aires, 1975. Contr., budget and econ. analysis dir. Pfizer, Inc., Argentina, treas., L.Am. region; fin. dir. through gen. mgr., pres. Schering-Plough Venezuela, 1984—86; v.p., fin. ops. Schering-Plough Internat., 1990—93; ops. dir., L.Am., Far East regions Schering-Plough Corp., 1986—88, pres., global animal health, 2003—, group head, global splty. ops., 2003—07, dep. head, animal health, sr. v.p., corp. excellence and adminstrv. svcs., 2007—08, sr. v.p., 2007—09, pres., Intervet/Schering-Plough Animal Health, 2008—09; exec. v.p., pres. animal health Merck & Co., Inc., 2009—. Office: Merck & Co Inc One Merck Dr Whitehouse Station NJ 08889-0100 Office Phone: 908-423-1000. Office Fax: 908-735-1253. Business E-Mail: Raul.Kohan@spcorp.com. *

KÖHLER, HUGO FONTAN, physician; b. Recife, Brazil, Feb. 8, 1975; MD, UNICAMP, 1998. Physician UNICAMP, 2005—. Office: Rua Santana 142 Sala 42/43 São Roque São Paulo 18130-555 Brazil Office Fax: 11-4784-4413. E-mail: hkohler75@uol.com.br.

KOHLER, PETER OGDEN, academic administrator, internist, educator; b. Bklyn., July 18, 1938; s. Dayton McCue and Jean Stewart (Ogden) K.; m. Judy Lynn Baker, Dec. 26, 1959; children: Brooke Culp, Stephen Edwin, Todd Randolph, Adam Stewart. BA, U. Va., 1959; MD, Duke U., 1963; PhD in Pub. Svc. (hon.), U. Portland, 2003; PhD (hon.), Oreg. Health Sci. U., 2006. Diplomate Am. Bd. Internal Medicine and Endocrinology. Intern Duke U. Hosp., Durham, NC, 1963-64, fellow, 1964-65; clin. assoc. Nat Cancer Inst., Nat Inst. Child Health and Human Devel., NIH, Bethesda, Md., 1965-67, sr. investigator, 1968-73, head endocrinology service, 1972-73; resident in medicine Georgetown U. Hosp., Washington, 1969-70; prof. medicine and cell biology, chief endocrinology divsn. Baylor Coll. Medicine, Houston, 1973-77; prof., chmn. dept. medicine University of Arkansas, 1977-86, interim dean, 1985-86; chmn. Hosp. Med. Bd., 1980-82, chmn. council dept. chmn., 1979-80; prof., dean Sch. Medicine, U. Tex., San Antonio, 1986-88; pres. Oreg. Health & Sci. U., Portland, 1988—2006, pres. emeritus, 2006; vice chancellor NW U. Ark. for Med. Scis., 2007—. Cons. endocrinology merit rev. bd. VA, 1985—86; mem. bd. sci. counselors NICHD, 1987—92, chair, 1990—92; chair task force on health care delivery AAHC, 1991—92, Inst. Medicine, 1994—; bd. dirs. Stancorp Fin. Group, 1990—2011; bd. dirs., Portland br. Fed. Res. Bank San Francisco, 2002—06; chair IOM Task Force on Improving Quality of Long-Term Care, 2004; mem. adv. bd. Loaves and Fishes, 1989—99; mem. Gov.'s adv. com. Commn. on Tech. Edn., 1989—92; chair Oreg. Health Coun., 1993—95; various positions Am. Bd. Internal Medicine, 1987—93, NIH; mem. numerous bd. dirs. and adv. bds. Editor: Current Opinion in Endocrinology and Diabetes, 1994-97, Diagnosis and Treatment of Pituitary Tumors, (with G. T. Ross), 1973, Clinical Endocrinology, 1986; assoc. editor: Internal Medicine, 1983, 87, 90, 94, 98; contbr. articles to profl. jours. Mem. campaign cabinet United Way, 1999—2004. With USPHS, 1965-68. NIH grantee, 1973—; Howard Hughes Med. Investigator, 1976-77; recipient NIH Quality awrds, 1969, 71, Disting. Alumnus award Duke Med. Sch., 1992, MRF Mentor award, Med. Rsch. Found., 1994, Humanitarian award Am. Lung Assn., 1996, Jewish Nat. Fund Tree of Life award, 1998, Internat. Citizens award Oreg. Consular Corps., 1999, Human Rels. award Am. Jewish Com., 2002, Leadership award Coun. for Advancement and Support of Edn., 2004; named Honored Citizen, Archl. Found. Oreg., 2002; named one of Twenty Leaders of Change, The Bus. Jour., 2004, Nat. Multiple Sclerosis Soc. Hope award, 2005, Oregon Health Forum Lifetime Leadership award, 2007 Master ACP; mem. AMA (William Beaumont award 1988), Inst. Medicine, Am. Soc. Clin. Investigation, Am. Fedn. Clin. Rsch. (nat. coun. 1977-78, pres. so. sect. 1976), So. Soc. Clin. Investigation (coun. 1979-82, pres. 1983, Founder's medal 1987), Am. Soc. Cell Biology, Assn. Acad. Health Ctrs. (chmn. 1998-99, bd. dirs.), Assn. Am. Physicians, Am. Diabetes Assn., Endocrine Soc. (coun. 1990-93), Raven Soc., Phi Beta Kappa, Sigma Xi, Alpha Omega Alpha, Omicron Delta Kappa, Phi Eta Sigma. Methodist. Office: UAMS NW 1125 N College Ave Fayetteville AR 72703 Office Phone: 479-713-8000. Business E-Mail: pkohler@uams.edu.

KOHLI, GURMANDER SINGH, plastic surgeon; b. Quetta, India, Oct. 27, 1945; s. Asa Singh Kohli and Jaswant Kaur Sethi; m. Maninder Kaur Dutta, Apr. 13, 1974; children: Sanjivan, Moneet, Manpreet, Harjivan, Sukhjivan. MBChB, U. Glasgow, 1973. Diplomate Am. Bd. Plastic Surgery, 1984, lic. Mass., Calif., England, Lithuania. Resident Boston Med. Ctr., 1975—79, 1979—81; plastic surgeon pvt. practice, Boston, 1981—2004; chief plastic surgery Boston Regional Med. Ctr., Stoneman, 1989—99, Whidden Meml. Hosp., Everett, 1992—2001; asst. clin. prof. surgery Tufts U. Sch. Medicine, Boston, 2002—; asst. clin. prof. plastic surgery U. Calif., San Diego, 2004—; plastic surgeon pvt. practice, Irvine, Calif., 2004—; assoc. prof. dept. plastic surgery Loma Linda U. Sch. Medicine, 2006—. Fellow, Plastic Surgery Ednl. Found., 2002—, Nat. Endowment Plastic Surgery, 2002—. Fellow: Am. Coll. Surgeons; mem.: Am. Soc. Plastic Surgeons. Sikh. Home: 15 Photinia Irvine CA 92620-2218 Office Phone: 888-882-4119, 949-954-8382. Office Fax: 888-834-8776, 949-272-0430. Business E-Mail: gsk@kohli.com.

KOHLS, NIKOLA BORIS, psychologist; Diploma in Psychology, U. Freiburg, Germany, 1998, PhD, 2004. Sr. rsch. fellow U. Northampton, England, 2005—08. Office: Generation Rsch Program Prof-Max-Lange 83646 Bad Tölz Germany Office Fax: 0049-8041-79929-11. Business E-Mail: kohls@grp.hwz.uni-muenchen.de.

KOHN, JEAN GATEWOOD, retired health facility administrator, pediatrician; b. Chgo., July 8, 1926; d. Gatewood and Esther Lydia (Harper) Gatewood; m. Martin M. Kohn, Feb. 10, 1951; children: Helen, Joel, Michael, David. BS, U. Chgo., 1948, MD, 1950; MPH, U. Calif., Berkeley, 1973. Diplomate Am. Bd. Pediatrics. Physician Permanente Med. Group, San Leandro, Calif., 1953-60; pediatric cons. Calif. Children Svcs., 1961-72; lectr. maternal and child health U. Calif., 1973-91; med. advisor rehab. engring. ctr. Packard Children's Hosp. at Stanford, Calif., 1976-97, med. dir. child prosthetic clinic Calif., 1977-97, ret. Calif., 1997, pediatrician Mary L. Johnson Infant Devel. Unit, 2000—. Asst. neurologic diagnostic ctr. U. Calif., San Francisco, 1960-72; pediatric cons. Project HOPE, Nicaragua, 1966, Peru, 1962; pediatric cons. sch. pub. health U. Hawaii, Okinawa, 1975. Contbr. chpts. to books and articles to profl. jours. Mem. adv. panel State of Calif. Dept. Spl. Edn., Calif. Children Svcs.; bd. dirs. Mental Health Assn., United Cerebral Palsy Assn., Head Start, San Mateo County, 1993—. Recipient Lyda M. Smiley award Calif. Sch. Nurses Orgn., 1987. Fellow Am. Acad. Pediats., Am. Acad. Cerebral Palsy and Devel. Medicine; mem. Project HOPE Alumni Assn. (pres. 1988-92). Office Phone: 650-725-8995.

KOHN, MARY LOUISE BEATRICE, nurse; b. Yellow Springs, Ohio, Jan. 13, 1920; d. Theophilus John and Mary Katherine (Schmitkons) Gaehr; m. Howard D. Kohn, 1944; children: Marcia R., Marcia K. Epstein. AB, Coll. Wooster, 1940; M in Nursing, Case Western Res. U., 1943. Nurse, 1943-44, Atlantic City Hosp., 1944, Thomas M. England Gen. Hosp., U.S. Army, Atlantic City, 1945-46, Peter Bent Brigham Hosp., Boston, 1947, Univ. Hosps., Cleve., 1946-48; mem. faculty Frances Payne Bolton Sch. Nursing Case Western Res. U., Cleve., 1948-52; vol. nurse Blood Svc. ARC, 1952-55; office nurse Cleve., 1955—94; freelance writer. Author: Berry and Kohn's Operating Room Technique, 1951, 11th edit., 2007; asst. editor: Cleve. Physician Acad. Medicine, 1966-71. Bd. dirs. Aux. Acad. Medicine Cleve., 1970-72, officer, 1976; active Cleve. Health Mus. Aux., Am. Cancer Soc. vol.; women's com. Cleve. Orch., 1970, Sta. WVIZ-TV. Mem.: ANA, Assn. Prevention of Cruelty to Animals, Assn. Oper. Rm. Nurses, Assn. Oper. Rm. Nurses of Greater Cleve. (charter, plaque 2004), Greater Cleve. Nurses Assn., Nat. Wildlife Fedn., Cleve. Zool. Soc., Coun. World Affairs, Friends of Cleve. Ballet, Alumni Assn. Wooster Coll., Frances P. Bolton Sch. Nursing Alumni Assn. (pres. 1974—75, bd. dirs. 1997—2000), Western Res. Hist. Soc., Am. Heart Assn., Cleve. Playhouse, Internat. Fund for Animal Welfare, Cleve. Animal Protective League, U.S. Humane Soc., Smithsonian Instn., Cleve. Children's Mus., Alzheimer's Assn., Sierra Club, Antique Automobile Assn. Am., Women's City Club (Jewel award 1992), Cleve. Racquet Club (social com. 1999—2000), Sigma Theta Tau Internat.

KOHN, MELVIN A., state agency administrator, public health service officer; BA in Russian and European Studies, Yale U., New Haven, 1981; pre-med, Columbia U., NYC; MD, Harvard U., Mass., 1990; MPH, Tulane U. Sch. Pub. Health and Tropical Medicine. Cert. in pediat., in preventive medicine. Intern and resident in pediat. Children's Hosp., Boston; officer, epidemic intelligence svc. Ctrs. Disease Control and Prevention, Atlanta; asst. prof. pediat. Tulane U. Sch. Medicine, New Orleans; med. dir. La. Office Pub. Health, New Orleans; dep. state epidemiologist Oreg. Dept. Human Services, Portland, 1999—2000, state epidemiologist, 2000—08, adminstr., office disease prevention and epidemiology, asst. dir., state pub. health divsn., 2008—, state health officer, 2008—. Contbr. articles to profl. jours. Office: Oreg Dept Human Services Pub Health Divsn 800 NE Oregon St Portland OR 97232 Office Phone: 971-673-1222. Office Fax: 971-673-1299.

KOHN, ROGER ALAN, surgeon; b. Chgo., May 1, 1946; s. Arthur Jerome and Sylvia Lee (Karlen) K.; m. Barbara Helene, Mar. 30, 1974; children: Bradley, Allison. BA, U. Ill., Urbana, 1967; MD, Northwestern U., Evanston, Ill., 1971. Diplomate Am. Bd. Ophthalmology. Internship UCLA, 1971-72; residency Northwestern U., Chgo., 1972-75; fellowship U. Ala., Birmingham, 1975, Harvard Med. Sch., Boston, 1975-76; chmn. dept. ophthalmology Kern Med. Ctr., Bakersfield, Calif., 1978-87; asst. prof. UCLA Med. Sch., 1978-82, assoc. prof., 1982-86, prof., 1986—. Vice chmn. dept. ophthalmology Santa Barbara Cottage Hosp., Calif., 2004—05, chmn. dept. ophthalmology, 2006—, dir. Author: Textbook of Ophthalmic Plastic and Reconstructive Surgery, 1988; contbr. numerous articles to profl. jours.; author chpts. in 16 additional textbooks; patentee in field. Bd. dirs. Santa Barbara Symphony, Calif., 1990—. Capt. USAR, 1971-77. Name applied to med. syndrome Kohn-Romano Syndrome. Mem. Am. Soc. Ophthalmic Plastic and Reconstructive Surgery (cert.), Am. Acad. Ophthalmology (Honor award 1995), Santa Barbara Ophthalmologic Soc. (pres. 1998), Pacific Coast Ophthal. Soc. (bd. dirs. 1986—, 1st v.p. 1990). Jewish. Avocations: guitar, tennis. Office: 525 E Micheltorena St Ste 201 Santa Barbara CA 93103-4212

KOHRMAN, ARTHUR FISHER, pediatrics educator; b. Cleve., Dec. 19, 1934; s. Benjamin Myron and Leah (Fisher) K.; m. Claire Hoffenberg, Nov. 10, 1955; children: Deborah, Benjamin, Ellen, Rachel. BA, BS, U. Chgo., 1955; MD, Western Res. U., 1959. Diplomate Am. Bd. Pediatrics. Lic. Ill., Ind. Intern Cleve. Met. Gen. Hosp., 1959-60; resident in pediatrics Case Western Res. U., Cleve., 1960—62; post doctoral fellow Stanford U., Palo Alto, Calif., 1965-68; from asst. prof. to prof. Mich. State U., East Lansing, 1968—81, assoc. chmn. dept. human devel., 1968—78, assoc. dean Coll. Human Medicine, 1977—81; prof., assoc. chmn. dept. pediatrics U. Chgo., 1981-96; pres. La Rabida Children's Hosp. and Research Ctr., Chgo., 1981-96; prof. pediatrics, assoc. chmn. Northwestern U. Sch. Medicine and Children's Meml. Hosp., Chgo., 1997—2002; prof. preventive medicine Sch. Medicine, Northwestern U., Chgo., 2000—02, prof. emeritus pediatrics and preventive medicine, 2003—. Congl. fellow Office Tech. Assessment, U.S. Congress, 1980-81; pres. Children's Hospice Internat., 1983-86; chmn. instl. rev. bd. U. Chgo., 1986-96. Contbr. numerous scholarly articles to profl. jours. Served to capt. USAF, 1962-65. Recipient Outstanding Service award Am. Diabetes Assn. Mich. chpt., 1977. Fellow Am. Acad. Pediatrics (chmn. com. on bioethics 1990-94); mem. Am. Pediatric Soc., Ambulatory Pediatric Assn., Soc. Pediatric Rsch., Lawson Wilkins Pediatric Endocrine Soc., Alpha Omega Alpha.

KOHRMAN, MICHAEL H., pediatrician, educator, neurologist; MD, Rush Med. Coll., Chgo. Cert. Pediat., Psychiatry & Neurology, with a spl. competency in child neurology, Sleep Medicine, Clin. Neurophysiology. Intern U. Chgo. Hospitals, resident, fellow; fellow, clin. neurophysiology U. Ill.; practicing since, 1981—; assoc. prof. pediat. and neurology U. Chgo. Med. Ctr., mem. pediat. epilepsy ctr. team, dir., pediat. clin. neurophysiology lab. Mem.: Tuberous Sclerosis Alliance, Epilepsy Found. America, Child Neurology Soc., Am. Sleep Disorders Assn., Am. Epilepsy Soc., Am. Electroencephalographic Soc., Am. Acad. Neurology. Office: Center for Advanced Medicine 5758 S Maryland Ave Chicago IL 60637 Address: U Chgo Corner Children's Hosp 5721 S Maryland Ave Chicago IL 60637 Mailing: U Chgo Hospitals 5841 S Maryland Ave MC3055 Chicago IL 60637 Office Phone: 773-702-6487. Office Fax: 773-702-4786. Business E-Mail: mkohrman@peds.bsd.uchicago.edu.

KOHUT, ROBERT IRWIN, otolaryngologist, educator; b. Chgo., Nov. 29, 1932; s. Emil and Ruth Irene Kohut; m. Joanne Kay Hughes, Dec. 26, 1953 (dec. Oct. 1982); children: James, Paul, Robert, John; m. Frances Irene Speas, June 6, 1983 (div. 1999). BA, Wittenburg Coll., 1956; MD, U. Chgo., 1960. Diplomate Am. Bd. Otolaryngology (bd. dirs. 1979). Intern U. Chgo., 1961—62, resident in otolaryngology, 1962—65, NIH fellow, 1965—66, instr. in otolaryngology, 1965—66; asst. prof. U. Fla., Gainesville, 1966—68, assoc. prof., 1968-71, assoc. prof., acting chmn., 1971—72; prof., chief otolaryngology U. Calif., Irvine, 1972—79; prof., chmn. otolaryngology Wake Forest U. Sch. Medicine, Winston-Salem, NC, 1979—99, emeritus prof., chair, 1999—. Mem. study sect. Nat. Insts. Neurol. and Communicative Disorders and Stroke/NIH, Bethesda, Md., 1981—86; cons. NASA, 1982—84; mem. adv. bd. Nat. Inst. Deafness and Other Comm. Disorders, 1991—94; exec. v.p. med. affairs, med. dir. Deafness Rsch. Found., 1999—2001. Contbr. numerous chpts. to books and articles to profl. jours.; editor otology divsn. Head and Neck Surgery-Otolaryngology; mem. editorial bd. Am. Jour. Otology, 1992-2000, Am. Jour. Otolaryngology, 1982-2000, Archives of Otolaryngology, 1980-2000, Laryngoscope, 1976-2000. With USAF, 1950-53. Recipient Norvel Pierce award Chgo. Laryngological Soc., 1965, Basic Rsch. award Acad. Ophthalmology and Otolaryngology, 1968. Fellow ACS, mem. AMA (rep. residency review com. otolaryngology 1975-80), Soc. Univ. Otolaryngologists (pres. 1978-79), Barany Soc., Am. Laryngological, Rhinological and Otological Soc. (exec. coun. 1987-90, Edmund Fowler award 1974, Guest of Honor, So. sect. 1996), Am. Broncho-Esophagological Ass., Am. Neurotology Assn., Otosclerosis Study Group, Am. Otological Soc. (sec.-treas. 1987-92, pres.-elect 1992-93, pres. 1993-94), Assn. Acad. Depts. Otolaryngology, Pacific Coast Oto-Ophthalmol. Soc., Forsyth County

Med. Soc., N.C. Med. Soc., N.C. Soc. Otolaryngology Head and Neck Surgery (v.p. 1985, pres. 1986-87), Assn. for Rsch. in Otolaryngology, Am. Acad. Otolaryngology-Head and Neck Surgery, Am. Soc. Head and Neck Surgery, Internat. Fedn. Oto-Rhino-Laryngological Soc. (chmn. emeritus standing com. edn. 2004), others. Avocations: fishing, hunting, sailing. Office: Wake Forest U Sch Medicine Dept Otolaryngology Medical Center Blvd Winston Salem NC 27157-0001 Personal E-mail: rikohut@att.net.

KOICHIRO, KANEKO, physician; b. Fukuoka, Japan, Feb. 10, 1970; s. Keiko Kaneko; m. Mika Satoi, Sept. 16, 2000; children: Mayu Kaneko, Koki Kaneko. PhD, Kyushu U., Fukuoka, 2004. Cert. radiologist Japan Radiol. Soc., 2003, nuc. physician Japanese Soc. Nuc. Medicine, 2006. Adviser Kyushu U. Hosp., 2005—. Home and Office: Kyushu Univ Dept Radiology Maidashi 3-1-1 Higashi-ku Fukuoka 812-8582 Japan Office Phone: 81-92-642-5695. Office Fax: 81-92-642-5708.

KOIZUMI, TOMOMI, medical educator; b. NYC, Oct. 18, 1965; MD, Yamaguchi U. Sch. Medicine, Japan, 1993; PhD, Chiba U. Grad. Sch. Medicine, Japan, 2002. Facc Am. Coll. of Cardiology, 2007. Postdoc. fellow Stanford U., Calif., 2003—06; asst. prof. medicine, cardiology Saitama Med. U. Internat. Med. Ctr., Hidaka, Japan, 2006—. Contbr. chapters to books. Stanford-St. Jude Med. scholarship Program, St. Jude Med. Japan Co., Ltd., 2003. Fellow: Am. Coll. Cardiology. Office: Saitama Med Univ 1397-1 Yamane Hidaka Saitama 350-1298 Japan Office Fax: 81-42-984-4741. Business E-Mail: tomomikzm@yahoo.com.

KOJI, HIGUCHI, physician; b. Tokyo, Oct. 13, 1974; MD, Tokyo Med. and Dental U., PhD, 2000. Physician Musashino Red Cross Hosp., 2001—06, Tokyo Med. and Dental U., 2006—; rsch. assoc. CARMA Ctr., U. Utah, 2011—. Mem.: Japanese Heart Rhythm Soc. (St. Jude Med., Fukuda Denshi fellowship), Japanese Circulation Soc., Heart Rhythm Soc. Avocations: basketball, snowboarding, music. Office: 30 N 1900 E CARMA Ctr Salt Lake City UT 84132 E-mail: gucchon.cvm@gmail.com.

KOJIMA, HIROSHI, medical educator; b. Fukuoka, Japan, Aug. 9, 1952; PhD in Medical Scis., Kyoto U., 1986. Prof. Tamagawa U., 2005—. Adv. bds. mem. Knowledge Engring. and Discovery Rsch. Inst., Auckland U. Tech., 2008—. Mem.: Soc. Neurosci. Avocation: painting. Office: Coll Engineering Tamagawa University 6-1-1 Tamagawagakuen Machida Tokyo 194-8610 Japan Office Fax: 81-42-739-8434. Business E-Mail: hkojima@lab.tamagawa.ac.jp.

KOJIMA, SATOKO, urologist, educator; b. Kanagawa, Japan, June 8, 1969; MD, Tsukuba U., 1994; PhD, Chiba U., 2001. Assoc. prof. Teikyo U. Chiba Med. Ctr., 2007—. Finalist Oral Communication award, Internat. Fedn. Fertility Socs., 2001. Mem.: Am. Assn. Cancer Rsch., Japanese Urol. Assn., Am. Urology Assn. Office: 3426-3 Anesaki Ichihara Chiba 299-0111 Japan Office Fax: 81-436-61-4773. Business E-Mail: jason@pa2.so-net.ne.jp.

KOJIMA, SHINSUKE, medical researcher; s. Akio and Takeko Kojima; m. Akiko Hara Kojima, Mar. 23, 2004; children: Kanako, Richie, Lily. MD, Kyoto U. Sch. Medicine, PhD, 1999. Resident Kyoto U. Hosp., 1999—2001, Kyoto City Hosp., 2001—02; fellow Div. Clin. Trial Design & Mgmt., Translational Rsch. Ctr., Kyoto U. Hosp., 2002—06; clin. trial supr. Translational Rsch. Informatics Ctr., Found. for Biomed. Rsch. and Innovation, Kobe, 2006 . Contbr. articles to profl. jour. Grant, Japan Health Scis. Found., 2004—06. Office: Translational Rsch Informatics Ctr 1-5-4 Minatojima-minamimachi Chuo-ku Kobe Hyogo 650-0047 Japan Office Phone: 81 78 303 9093. Office Fax: 81 78 303 9094. Business E-Mail: shinkx@tri-kobe.org.

KOK, TIAN YUE, nuclear medicine physician; b. Singapore, Mar. 1, 1976; MBBS, Nat. U. Singapore, 2002. Nuc. medicine physician Singapore Gen. Hosp., 2007—. External lectr. Nanyang Poly., Sch. Health Scis., 2007. Recipient award, Singapore Health Svcs. Fellow: Royal Coll. Radiologists (Eng.); mem.: Radiologic Soc. N.Am. Avocations: classical music, films, golf, tennis. Office: Outram Rd Singapore 169608 Singapore Business E-Mail: kok.tian.yue@sgh.com.sg.

KOKESH, JOHN, otolaryngologist; b. Seattle, Jan. 12, 1962; MD, U. Wash., 1988. Chief, otolaryngology Alaska Native Med. Ctr., 1994—. Sr. clin. advisor Alaska Fed. Health Care Access Network, 2000. Fellow: Am. Telemedicicine Assn.; mem.: Am. Acad. Otolaryngology, Head and Neck Surgery. Office: Dept Otolaryngology Head and Neck Surgery Alaska Native Med Ctr 4315 Diplomacy Dr Anchorage AK 99508 Business E-Mail: jkokesh@anthc.org.

KOKOTAILO, PATRICIA K., pediatrician, educator; MD, Northwestern U., Feinberg, 1982. Diplomate Am. Bd. Pediatrics, 1987, cert. Am. Bd. Pediatrics-adolescent medicine, 2009. Intern Johns Hopkins Hosp., Baltimore, resident pediat., 1983—85, fellow adolescent medicine, 1987—89; hosp. affiliation includes Am. Family Children's Hosp., Meriter Hosp.; prof. pediat. Univ. Wis.; pediatrician Univ. of Wis. Hosp. and Clinics. Office: University of Wisconsin Ste 200 2800 University Ave Madison WI 53705 Office Phone: 608-263-6421. Office Fax: 608-263-0423.

KOKUBO, YUJI, dentist, educator; b. Japan, Mar. 13, 1962; DDS, Tsurumi U., 1986, PhD, 1990. Clin. prof. Shimane U., 2008; guest rschr. Malmo U., 1999—2000; asst. prof. Tsurumi U., 2003—. Councilor Japan Prosthodontic Soc., 2006, Japanese Assn. Oral Implantology, 2009. Recipient ITI World Symposium award, Stramann. Mem.: Internat. Assn. Dental Rsch., European Assn. Osseointegration, Asian Acad. Prosthodontics (award), Internat. Coll. Prosthodontics. Office: Tsurumi University 2-1-3 Tsurmi Tsurumi Yokohama Kanagawa 230-8501 Japan Business E-Mail: kokubo-y@tsurumi-u.ac.jp.

KOKUDO, NORIHIRO, surgeon, educator; b. Kagawa, Japan, June 5, 1956; MD, U. Tokyo, 1981, PhD, 1988. Staff surgeon Cancer Inst. Hosp., Tokyo, 1995—2001, sr. staff surgeon, 2001—01; assoc. prof. U. Tokyo, Dept. HPB Surgery, 2001—07, prof., chmn., 2007—. Mem.: Internat. Assn. Surgeons, Gastroenterologists & Oncologists, Internat. Soc. Surgery, Soc. Surg. Oncology, Internat. Hepato-Pancreato-Biliary Assn. Office: 7-3-1 Hongo Bunkyo-ku Tokyo 113-8655 Japan Office Fax: 81-3-5684-3989. Business E-Mail: kokudo-2su@h.u-tokyo.ac.jp.

KOLANSKY, HAROLD, physician, psychiatrist, psychoanalyst, psychotherapist; b. Carbondale, Pa., Aug. 15, 1924; s. Abe and Miriam (Raker) K.; m. Elsa Harwitz, June 8, 1948; children: Jeffrey, Betta, Daniel. Student, U. Scranton, 1942-44; MD cum laude, Georgetown U., 1948. Rotating intern Walter Reed Army Hosp., Washington, 1948-49; resident Coatesville (Pa.) VA Hosp. and Deans' Com. Program, Phila., 1949-52; practice medicine specializing in psychiatry and psychoanalysis Phila., 1952—, Elkins Park, Pa., 1959—; clin. assoc. prof. psychiatry U. Pa. Sch. Medicine, 1972-77, clin. prof., 1977, 91—, mem. steering com. Psychoanalytic Cluster, 1991—, chair steerimg com. Psychoanalytic Cluster, 1997-99; prof. psychiatry and human behavior Jefferson Med. Coll., Thomas Jefferson U., Phila., 1977-91, dir. sect. child and adolescent psychoanalysis, 1980-90, dir. sect. psychoanalysis, 1982-90; mem. faculty child and adolescent psychiatry Children's Hosp. Phila., 1991—, mem. grad. edn. commn., dept. child psychiatry, 2010—. Mem. psychiatry staff Albert Einstein Med. Ctr., 1952-69, 82—, sr. attending, 1983—, dir. divsn. child psychiatry, 1955-69, acting chmn. dept. psychiatry, 1968-69, dir. child psychiatry fellowship, 1960-69, dir. ctr. for psychoanalysis, 1991—, mem. exec. com., ednl. com. and curriculum com., 1991—; mem. faculty Inst. Phila. Assn. Psychoanalysis, 1960—, chmn. administrv. bd., 1966-69, dir. divsn. childrn and adolescent psychoanalysis, 1975-84, tng. and supervisory analyst, 1976—, chmn. tng. analyst com., 1982-83, 93-94, 95-96, chmn. curriculum com., 1982-88, dir. consultation and evaluation divsn., 1988-89, mem. ednl. com., 1989-94, mem. ednl. com., vice chmn., 1997, mem. ednl. com., 1997-2000, chmn. edn. com., 2000-2001, vice-chmn., 1997-2001, chmn. faculty com., 1997—, chmn., liaison com. med. edn., 1994—, chair ednl. com., 2000-01; mem. staff psychiatry Phila. Psychiat. Ctr., 1952 81; pres. Regional Coun. Child Psychiatry, Pa., S.E. N.J., Del., 1967-68, 72-73, chmn. exec. com., 1970-73; chmn. med. bd. Ea. State Sch. and Hosp., Trevose, Pa., 1966-69; asst. prof. psychiatry Hahnemann Med. Coll. and Hosp., Phila., 1952-60; mem. Pa. Task Force on Mental Health Children, 1971-74; vis. prof. psychiatry U. P.R. Sch. Medicine, 1982—; mem. steering com. psychoanalytic cluster U. Pa. Sch. Med., 1991—, chmn., 1997-99. Contbg. author to numerous texts on psychoanalysis and psychiatry including: A Handbook of Child Psychoanalysis, 1968, Behavior Pathology of Childhood and Adolescence, 1973, Controversy in Psychiatry, 1978, Prognosis, 1981; contbr. numerous articles on child and adult psychiatry and psychoanalysis to profl. jours. Capt. M.C., U.S. Army, 1950-51, Korea, coord. child psychiat.analysis Childrens Hosp. Phila., 2006, mem. grad. med. edn. com. Dept. Adj. Property Childrens Hosp. Phila, 2010 Recipient 1st prize biochemistry Georgetown U., 1945, Robert Waelder award for Teaching Excellence in Psychiatry Thomas Jefferson Med. Coll., 1987, Dedication to Edn. award, 1990, award for tchg. excellence dept. psychiatry Albert Einstein Med. Ctr., 1993, award for tchg. excellence, 1996, 2000, 02, 04, Outstanding Tchr. award Children's Hosp. of Phila. 2003, 07-08, Elizabeth Weller award, 2009; 1st pl. U.S. in Surgery Nat. Bd. Med. Examiners, 1948. Fellow: Phila. Coll. Physicians, Am. Acad. Child Psychiatry (chmn. com. continuing med. edn. 1974—82, councillor, citation for developing continuing med. edn. program 1976), Am. Psychiat. Assn.; mem.: AMA, Phila. County Med. Soc., Pa. Med. Soc., Am. Psychoanalytic Assn. (exec. counselor 1969—73, 1977—82, fellow bd. profl. standards 1983—89, 1992—98, mem. com. on child and adolescent analysis 1981—90, 1999—, acting fellow bd. on profl. standards 1989, mem. univ. and med. edn. com. 1995—2000, budget and fin. com. 1996—98, all exec. counselor 1999—2001, Edith Sabshin Teaching award 2000), Internat. Psychoanalytic Assn., Phila. Psychiatric Soc. (Psychiat. Educator award 2002), Assn. Child Psychoanalysis, Phila. Assn. Psychoanalysis (bd. dirs. 1984—86, pres. 1984—86, Gersld Pearson prize award 1960).

KOLAROV, VLADIMIR PANAYOTOV, cardiac surgeon; b. Sofia, Bulgaria, Oct. 18, 1953; s. Panayot Stanchev and Maria Inanova Kolarov; m. Diana Marinova Kolarova; children: Plamen, Victor. MD, Med. Acad. Sofia, 1979. Cert. gen. surgery, cardiac surgery. Surgeon Regional Hosp., Kubrat, Razgrad, Bulgaria, 1979—81; cardiac surgeon Nat. Heart Hosp., Sofia, Bulgaria, 1981—2001. Mem.: Internat. Soc. Minimally Invasive Cardiac Surgery. Home: 9 Dobri Voinikov str Sofia 1164 Bulgaria Office: Nat Heart Hosp 65 Miko Papo str Sofia 1309 Bulgaria Office Phone: 359 2 8833 49. Personal E-mail: kolarov@mail.orbitel.bg.

KOLASINSKI, SHARON LEE, rheumatologist, educator; BA in Biology, U. Pa., 1978; MD, NYU, 1985. Diplomate Am. Bd. Internal Medicine-internal medicine, rheumatology, lic. to practice Pa., 1986. Intern, resident Temple Univ. Hosp.; fellow Hosp. Univ. Pa., NYU; physician lead for rheumatology Perelman Ctr. for Advanced Medicine, Penn Medicine, Radnor; assoc. prof. clin. medicine, interim divsn. chief, chief clin. svcs. U. Pa. Sch. Medicine. Dir. Rheumatology Fellowship Program; chair Rheumatology Electronic Med. Record Governance Com. Co-author: (publs.) Relationships between biochemical markers of bone and cartilage degradation with radiological progression in patients with knee osteoarthritis receiving risedronate: the Knee Osteoarthritis Structural Arthritis randomized clinical, 2008, Connective Tissue Disorders: To Flap or Not to Flap, 2009, Hepatic artery aneurysm: An unusual case of biliary obstruction, Yoga for the Management of Knee Osteoarthritis, 2010, Fish oil in rheumatic diseases, 2011, and numerous others; author: Dietary Supplements in Rheumatologic Disorders, 2010, Complementary and Alternative Medicine in Rheumatology, 2011. Named Top Doc, Phila. Mag., 2011. Fellow: ACP, Am. Coll. Rheumatology. Office: Hospital of the University of Pennsylvania Division of Rheumatology 8 Penn Tower 34th St Civic Center Blvd Philadelphia PA 19104-4283 Office Phone: 215-662-2789. Office Fax: 215-662-4500. E-mail: sharonk@mail.med.upenn.edu.

KOLATA, GINA, journalist, writer; b. Balt., Feb. 25, 1948; d. Arthur and Ruth Lillian (Aaronson) Bari; m. William George Kolata; children: Therese Bari, Stefan Matthew. BS in Microbiology, U. Md., 1969, MA in Applied Math., 1973. Copy editor Sci. Mag., Washington, 1973-74, writer, 1974-87; columnist Jour. Investigative Dermatology, 1985—87; sci. & medicine reporter The New York Times, 1987—. Author/co-author (nonfiction) The Baby Doctors: Probing the Limits of Fetal Medicine, 1990, Sex in America: A Definitive Survey, 1994, Clone: The Road to Dolly and the Path Ahead, 1998, FLU: The Story of the Great Influenza Pandemic of 1918 and the Search for the Virus That Caused It, 1999 (NJ Coun. Humanities Book award), Ultimate Fitness: The Quest for Truth About Exercise and Health, 2003, Rethinking Thin: The New Science of Weight Loss -- and the Myths and Realities of Dieting, 2007. Recipient Sound Sci. in Journalism award, Advancement of Sound Sci. Coalition, 1995, Front Page award, News Women's Club NY, 1999, Statis. Reporting Excellence award, American Statis. Assn., 2004. Avocations: bicycling, running. Office: NY Times 620 8th Ave New York NY 10018 E-mail: kolata@nytimes.com. *

KOLB, DAVID ALLEN, psychologist, educator; b. Moline, Ill., Dec. 12, 1939; s. John August and Ethel May (Petherbridge) K.; m. Alice Yoko; 1 son, Jonathan Demian. AB cum laude, Knox Coll., 1961; PhD, Harvard U., 1967; ScD (h.c.), U. N.H., 1984; PhD (h.c.), Internat. Mgmt. Ctr., Buckingham, 1988; LittD (h.c.), Franklin U., 1994; DHL (h.c.), SUNY, 1996. Asst. prof. organizational psychology MIT, Cambridge, 1965-70, assoc. prof., 1970-75; prof. organizational behavior and mgmt. Case Western Res. U., Cleve., 1976—, deWindt Prof. Leadership and Enterprise Devel. Weatherhead Sch. Mgmt., 1992-97, chmn. dept., 1984-90. Vis. prof. mgmt. London Grad. Sch. Bus., 1971; dir. Devel. Research Assos., 1966-80; mgmt. cons., U.S., Australia, N.Z., Indonesia, Singapore, Malaysia, Thailand, Japan. Author: Experiential Learning: Experience as the source of learning and development, 1984, Kolb Learning Style Inventory 3.1, 2005; co-author: Organizational Behavior: An Experiential Approach, 8th edit, 2007, Organizational Behavior: A Book of Readings, 8th edit, 2007, Changing Human Behavior: Principles of Planned Intervention, 1974, Innovation in Professional Education: Steps on Journey from Teaching to Learning, 1995, Conversational Learning: An Experiential Approach to Knowledge Creation, 2002. Woodrow Wilson fellow, 1962; named Ednl. Pioneer of the Yr. Nat. Soc. Exptl. Edn., 2008 Mem. Internat. Assn. Applied Social Scientists (charter), Soc. Intercultural Edn., Tng. and Rsch. (charter), Coun.l Advancement of Experiential Learning (Research Excellence award 1984, Morris T. Keaton Adult and Experiential Learning award 1991, Case Weatherhead Rsch. Recognition award 2002-03 Office: Case Western Res U Dept of Orgn Behavior Cleveland OH 44106 Office Phone: 216-368-2050. E-mail: dak5@msn.com.

KOLBE, THOMAS, agricultural studies educator; b. Bielefeld, Germany, Mar. 28, 1966; Degree in Agrl. Engring., U. Goettingen, 1995, Dr. sc. agr., 1998. Asst. prof. Biomodels Austria, 2006—. Mem.: ISTT, GV-SOLAS. Avocation: reading. Office: Veterinaerplatz 1 Vienna 1210 Austria Office Fax: 00431250772890. Business E-Mail: tkolbe@gmx.at.

KOLCH, WALTER, cell biologist, medical researcher; MD, U. Vienna, 1985; habilitation, Ludwig-Maximillians U., Munich, 1996. Group leader Beatson Inst. for Cancer Rsch., Glasgow, Scotland, 1998; prof. molecular cell biology U. Glasgow, Scotland, 2000, founder, dir. Sir Henry Wellcome Functional Genomics Facility, 2001—04; dir. Sys. Biology Ireland, a Centre for Sci., Engring. & Tech. (CSET) Conway Inst. of Biomolecular and Biomedical Rsch., U. Coll. Dublin, Ireland, 2009—10, dir., 2010—. Office: UCD Conway Institute University College Dublin, Belfield 4 Dublin Iceland Office Phone: (+353 1) 716 6700. Office Fax: (+353 1) 716 0701. E-mail: walter.kolch@ucd.ie. †

KOLDEN, GREGORY G., psychology professor; B, St. Olaf. Coll., Minn.; PhD in Clin. Psychiatry, Northwestrn U., 1988. Prof. psychology, psychiatry U. Wis. Med. Sch., Madison, dir. clin. psychology, dir. depression rsch. program; rsch. scientist HealthEmotions Rsch. Inst. Bd. dirs. Camp Randall Rowing Club. Office: Univ Wis Psychiatric Inst & Clinics Box 9601 6001 Research Park Blvd Madison WI 53719 Office Phone: 608-263-6082. Office Fax: 608-362-0265. E-mail: ggkolden@facstaff.wisc.edu.

KOLEGA, JOHN, medical educator; b. Manchester, Conn., Feb. 23, 1957; BS, MIT, 1978; PhD, Yale U., 1984. Postdoc. fellow NIH, 1984—85, NYU Med. Ctr., 1985—89; spl. rsch. faculty Carnegie Mellon U., 1989—93; assoc. prof. SUNY, Buffalo, 1993—. Editl. bd. mem. Open Enzyme Inhibition Jour., 2009—, ISRN Vascular Medicine, 2011—. Recipient Didaskalos award, Buffalo Campus Ministries, 2011; grant, NSF, Am. Heart Assn. Mem.: AAAS, Am. Soc. Cell Biology. Office: Dept Pathology & Anatomical Scis Buffalo NY 14214 Business E-Mail: kolega@buffalo.edu.

KOLETTIS, PETER, medical educator; b. South Bend, Ind., Sept. 22, 1964; BS, U. Notre Dame, 1987; MD, U. Chgo. Pritzker Sch. Medicine, 1991. Asst. prof. surgery U. Ala., Birmingham, 1998—2003, assoc. prof., 2003—08, prof. surgery, 2008—. Named one of Best Drs. in Am. Mem.: Soc. Reproductive Surgeons, Am. Soc. Reproductive Medicine, Soc. Male Reproduction and Urology, Soc. Study Male Reproduction, Am. Urol. Assn. Avocations: music, sports. Office: University Ala Divsn Urology 1530 Third Ave South FOT 1105 Birmingham AL 35294-3411 Office Fax: 205-934-4933. Business E-Mail: peter.kolettis@ccc.uab.edu.

KOLF-CLAUW, MARTINE, toxicology educator, researcher; b. Lille, Nord, France, Nov. 28, 1957; René Kleber and Denise Marie (Lequart) Clauw; m. Philippe Reně Kolf; children: Nicolas, Vincent, Mathilde. DVM, Maisons-Alfort, France, 1983; postgrad. studies, Agregation French Vet. Schs., 1988; Diploma in Histopathology, U. Paris VI, 1996; PhD in Toxicology, U. Paris VII, 1997. Asst. tchr. Vet. Sch., Alfort, France, 1982-86, prof. toxicology, 1998—; rschr. Rhone-Poulenc, Vitry, France, 1986-87. Cons. French Pesticides Commn., 1989-97; bd. dirs. Animal Poison Ctr., Alfort, France, 1992-97. Contbr. articles to Teratology. 1984— Mem. Urbanism Commn., Couilly, France, 1995-97. Recipient Bronze medal for DVM thesis, U. Paris XII, 1984, Cover Figure, Teratology (Jour.) 1996, 97. Mem. ETS, SFT. Avocations: sailing, swimming, dance, reading, travel. Office: ENVA Toxicology Dept 7 Ave Gen de Gaulle 94704 Maisons-Alfort Cedex France

KOLINSKA, JIRINA, biochemist, researcher; d. Karel Kolinsky and Jirina Kolinska. MS in Biochemistry, Charles U., Prague, 1956; PhD, Inst. Microbiology, Czech Acad Sci., Prague, 1962. Board Certified Diplomate Prague, 1962. Rsch. assoc., dept. biochemistry, Chgo. Med. Sch., 1962—63; rsch. asst., dept. cell membrane transport, inst. microbiology Czech Acad Sci., Prague, Czech Republic, 1964—65. Rsch. asst. prof. Inst. Biochemistry, U. Zurich, 1966—67; editl. bd. mem. Internat. Jour. Interferon, Cytokine and Mediator Rsch., 2008. Contbr. articles to jours. publs. Grant, Ministry Edn., 1991—2008. Mem.: Czech Soc. Probiotics Application, Czech Soc. Biochemistry Molecular Biology. Avocation: gymnastics. Home: Starolazenska 286/17 Prague 159 00 Czech Republic Office: Inst Physiology Acad Sci CZ Videnska 1083 Prague 142 20 Czech Republic Office Phone: 420 241 062 557. Office Fax: 420 244 472 269. Business E-Mail: kolinska@biomed.cas.cz.

KOLINSKY, MICHAEL ALLEN, emergency physician; b. Phila., Dec. 23, 1947; BA, U. Wis., 1970; MD, Rush U., 1979. Diplomate Am. Bd. Emergency Medicine. Staff physician emergency dept. River Parishes Hosp., LaPlace, La., 1982-85, Rutland Regional Med. Ctr., Vt., 2005—; co-med. dir. emergency dept. Meadowcrest Hosp., Gretna, La., 1985-92; co-med. dir. City of New Orleans Emergency Med. Svcs., 1987—2004; med. dir. emergency dept. Tulane U. Med. Ctr., New Orleans, 1992—2008, staff physician, 2008—; staff physician emergency dept. Bapt. Hosp., New Orleans, 2009—. Office: Ochsner Bapt Hosp Emergency Dept 2700 Napoleon Ave New Orleans LA 70115 E-mail: kolinsky@tulane.edu.

KOLKER, ADAM ROSS, plastic surgeon, educator; s. Paul and Susan Kolker; m. Lauren Pia Silverman, Jan. 27, 2001. BS in Bio Arts, Union Coll., NY, 1988; MD cum laude, Albany Med. Coll., 1990. Diplomate Am. Bd. Plastic Surgery, Am. Bd. Surgery, Nat. Bd. Med. Examiners. Clin. asst. prof. surgery Mt. Sinai Sch. Medicine, assoc. clin. prof. Attending plastic surgeon Lenox Hill Hosp., Manhattan Eye, Ear and Throat Hosp., The Mt. Sinai Hosp. Fellow, Harvard Med. Sch., U. Melbourne, Australia. Fellow: ACS; mem.: Am. Soc. Aesthetic Plastic Surgeons, Am. Soc. Plastic Surgeons. Office: 710 Park Ave New York NY 10021 Business E-Mail: drkolker@kolkermd.com.

KOLLAR, EDWARD JAMES, retired biology educator; b. Forest City, Pa., Mar. 3, 1934; s. I. J. and Mary (Zaverl) K.; m. Catherine Ann Tobin, Feb. 23, 1963; children: Michelle, Elizabeth, Rachael, Brian, Rebecca. BS, U. Scranton, 1955; MS, Syracuse U., 1959, PhD, 1963. Instr., zoology, rsch. assoc. U. Chgo., 1963-66, asst. prof., biology, rsch. assoc., zoology, 1966-67, asst. prof., anatomy, biology, 1967-69, asst. prof., anatomy, 1969-71; assoc. prof., oral biology U. Conn. Health Ctr., 1971-76, prof., oral biology, 1976-97, prof. emeritus, 1998—, acting head, dept. oral biology, 1985-86, 96-98, oral biology grad. program dir., 1983-88, assoc. dean acad. affairs, 1988-98, program dir., dentist sci. award program, 1990-97. Vis. prof. Guy's Hosp. Med. Sch., London, 1978, Inst. Molecular Biology, Salzburg, Austria, prof., 1971-90; presenter in field. Editor-in-chief Archives of Oral Biology, 1978-97; mem. editl. bd. Saudi Dental Jour., Epithelial Cell Biology. Numerous exec. positions various ednl. coms. Grantee NIH; recipient Quantrell award, U. Chgo., 1968, Issac Schour Meml. Basic Sci. award, 1981, City of Paris medal, 1986. Mem. Am. Soc. Zoologists, Internat. Soc. Devel. Biologists, Cranofacial Group Internat. Assn. (pres. 1983), Internat. Soc. Differentiation, Devel. Biology, Tissue Culture Assn., Bone Tooth Soc., Sigma Xi (treas. Chgo. chpt. 1969, sec. 1970). Democrat. Roman Catholic. Business E-Mail: kollar@nso.uchc.edu.

KOLLEF, MARIN HRISTOS, physician, educator; b. Greenwich, Conn., Feb. 24, 1958; MD, U. Rochester, 1983. Prof. medicine Wash. U., 1983—. Office: 660 S Euclid Ave Saint Louis MO 63110 Office Fax: 314-454-5571. Business E-Mail: mkollef@dom.wustl.edu.

KOLLER, LOREN D., veterinary medicine educator; b. Pomeroy, Wash., June 16, 1940; s. Edwin C. and Doris K. (Shelton) K.; m. Kathleen Noel Ringness, Sept. 7, 1963; children: Susan E., Michael D., Christopher L. DVM, Wash. State U., 1965; MS, U. Wis., 1969, PhD, 1971. Head diagnostic and comparative pathology Nat. Inst. Environ. Health Scis., Research Triangle Park, NC, 1971-72; rsch. assoc. dept. vet. medicine Oreg. State U., Corvallis, 1972-76, assoc. prof., 1976-78, prof., 1995—2001, dean Coll. Vet. Medicine, 1985-95; assoc. prof. dept. vet. medicine, asst. dean U. Idaho, Moscow, 1978-81, assoc. prof., assoc. dean, 1981-82, prof., assoc. dean, 1982-85; owner Loren Koller & Assocs., LLC, 2001—. Rsch. asst. dept. vet. sci. U. Wis., Madison, 1968-71; assoc. veterinarian Blue Cross Vet. Clinic, Corvallis, 1965-66; mem. Nat. Adv. Com. to Establish Acute Exposure Guidelines for Hazardous Substances Commn.; chair expert consultation panel provisional adv. levels Nat. Homeland Security Rsch. Ctr. Office Rsch. and Devel. US EPA. Contbr. articles to profl. jours., chpts. to books. Served to capt. M.C., U.S. Army, 1966-68. Grantee NIH, USDA, Dow Chem. Co., EPA, WHO, FDA, Merck Sharp & Dohme, Warner-Lambert, Pew Found. Fellow Acad. Toxicol. Sci.; mem. AVMA, NAS (mem. com. toxicology and Inst. of Medicine). Personal E-mail: kollerl@g.com.

KOLLER, SILVIA, physician; b. Graz, Austria, Apr. 4, 1977; MD, Karl-Franzens-U. Graz, 2001. Physician Med. U. Graz, 2002—. Office: Auenbruggerplatz 8 Graz Styria 8036 Austria Business E-Mail: kollers@gmx.at.

KOLLEROV, VYACHESLAV VLADIMIROVICH, research scientist; b. Vladikavkaz, Russia, Oct. 10, 1982; PhD, Pushchino State U., 2009. Staff rschr. Inst. Biochemistry and Physiology of Microorganisms, Russian Acad. Scis., Pushchino, Moscow Region, 2004—. Home: cvartal D 20 Pushchino Moscow Region 142290 Russia Personal E-mail: svkollerov@rambler.ru.

KOLODNER, RICHARD DAVID, biochemist, educator, director; b. Morristown, NJ, Apr. 3, 1951; s. Ignace Izack and Ethel (Zelnick) Kolodner; m. Karin Ann Gregory, Aug. 6, 1983 (div. May 1991); m. Jean Y.J. Wang, Dec. 2, 2004. BS, U. Calif., Irvine, 1971, PhD, 1975; MS (hon.), Harvard U., 1988. Rsch. fellow Harvard U. Med. Sch., Boston, 1975-78; from asst. prof. to prof. biochemistry Dana Farber Cancer Inst. and Harvard U. Med. Sch., Boston, 1978—97; chmn. divsn. cellular molecular biology Dana-Farber Cancer Inst., 1991-94, head x-ray crystallography lab., 1991-97, chmn. divsn. of human cancer genetics, 1995-97; prof. medicine, mem. Cancer Ctr. U. Calif. Med. Sch., San Diego, 1997—; mem. Ludwig Inst. Cancer Rsch., San Diego, 1997—, assoc. dir., 2004—05, exec. dir. lab. sci. and tech., 2006—10, head acad. affairs, 2010—. Editor: PLASMID Jour., 1986—95; assoc. editor: Cancer Rsch. Jour., 1995—2000, Cell jour., 1996—; mem. editl. bd. Molecular Cellular Biology Jour., 1999—2001, Jour. Biol. Chemistry, 2000—05, DNA Repair Jour., 2003—; contbr. articles to sci. jours. Recipient Jr. Faculty Rsch. award, Am. Cancer Soc., 1981, Faculty Rsch. award, 1984, Merit award, NIH, 1993, Charles S. Mott prize, GM Cancer Rsch. Found., 1996; grantee, NIH, 1978—; rsch. grantee, Am. Cancer Soc., 1980—82. Fellow: Am. Acad. Arts Scis., Am. Acad. Microbiology; mem.: NAS, Am. Assn. Cancer Rsch. (Kirk Landon award 2007), Genetic Soc. Am., Am. Soc. Microbiology, Am. Soc. Biochemistry and Molecular Biology. Home: 13468 Kibbings Rd San Diego CA 92130-1231 Office: Ludwig Inst for Cancer Rsch 9500 Gilman Dr CMME 3058 La Jolla CA 92093-0669 Home Phone: 858-259-9027. Business E-Mail: rkolodner@ucsd.edu.

KOLODNER, ROBERT MARK, retired federal official; b. Baltimore, Md., Sept. 20, 1948; BS, Harvard Coll., 1970; MD, Yale U. Sch. Medicine, 1974. Cert. Psychiatry. Clin. fellowship, medicine Harvard Univ. Sch. Medicine, 1975; psychiatric residency Washington Univ. Sch. Medicine, 1975—78; chair, mental health spl. interest user group Veterans Health Adminstrn., US Dept. Veterans Affairs, 1983—89, acting co-chair, clin. record spl. interest user group, 1989—91, chair, clin. applications requirements group, 1991—93, dir., med. info. resources mgmt. office, 1993—96, assoc. chief info. officer for enterprise strategy (formerly bus. enterprise solutions and tech.), Office of Info., 1996—2005, chief health information officer (CHIO), 2005—06; interim nat. health info. tech. coord. US Dept. Health & Human Services, Washington, 2006—07, nat. health info. tech. coord., 2007—09. Lectr. on med. informatics throughout the US. Mem. of several editl. boards; contbr. articles to several med. jours., chapters to books. Achievements include involvement with the development and oversight of VistA, Veterans Affairs electronic health records system and My HealtheVet, Veterans Affairs personal health records for veterans; establishment of the Federal Health Information Exchange (FHIE) program. E-mail: Rob@RobKolodner.com.

KOLODNY, EDWIN HILLEL, neurologist, geneticist, director; b. Boston, Mar. 15, 1936; s. Myer Zeman and Naomi Lillian (Zalkind) K.; m. Roselyn Leinwand, May 31, 1958; children: Nancy, Leonard Benjamin, Robin, Noah Jacob. AB in Econs. cum laude, Harvard Coll., 1957; MD with honors, NYU, 1962. Diplomate Am. Bd. Psychiatry and Neurology, Am. Bd. Med. Genetics. Intern, resident in internal medicine Bellevue Hosp., NYC, 1962-64; resident in neurology Mass. Gen. Hosp., Boston, 1964-67; spl. fellow lab. neurochemistry Nat. Inst. Neurol. Diseases, Bethesda, Md., 1967-70; asst. prof. neurology Harvard Med. Sch., Boston, 1970-76, assoc. prof., 1976-85, prof., 1985-91; Bernard and Charlotte Marden prof. dept. neurology NYU Med. Ctr., NYC, 1991—, chmn. dept. neurology, 1991—2010. Vice-chmn. exec. com. Med. Bd. Tisch Hosp., NY, 1993-97, chmn., 1997-99; vis. prof. Weizmann Inst. Sci., Rehovot, Israel, 1988, 90; assoc. dir. Eunice Kennedy Shriver Ctr., Mental Retardation, Inc., Waltham, Mass., 1976-83, acting dir., 1983-84, dir., 1984-90; assoc. neurologist Mass. Gen. Hosp., Boston, 1976-87, neurologist, 1988-91; chmn. com. Rsch. Ctrs. Forward Planning Mental Retardation, Nat. Inst. Child Health and Human Devel., 1983-84; cons. pres.'s com. Mental Retardation, 1982; adv. genetic svcs. Dept. Pub. Health Mass., 1977-80; mem. Mass. Nat. Inst. Health Centennial Com., 1987-88, profl. adv. bd. Internat. Rett Syndrome Assn., 1986-94, sci. adv. bd. United Leukodystrophy Found., 1986-94, sci. med. adv. com. Canavan Found., 1994—; mem. expert com. Gaucher Initiative Project Hope, 2000—, chmn. 2006-2010; mem. steering com. Global Orgn. for Lysosomal Diseases, 2002—06. Mem. editl. bd. Annals of Neurology, 1984-89; contbr. articles to profl. jours. Mem. sci. adv. bd. Nat. Tay Sachs and Allied Diseases Assn., 1970—; mem. med. adv. bd. Dysautonomia Found., 2001—; v.p., trustee Temple Emanuel, Newton, Mass., 1983—89; trustee Hebrew Coll., Brookline, Mass. Recipient Solomon A. Berson Med. Alumni Achievement award clin. sci. NYU Sch. Medicine, 1993, Above and Beyond award Nat. Tay Sachs and Allied Diseases Assn., 2003, Disting. Svc. award ROFEH Internat., 2004, Art of Listening award Genetic Alliance, 2006., Bernard Sachs. Med. award Clin.Practice, Nat. Tay-Sachs and Allied Disease Assn.,2007 Fellow Am. Coll. Med. Genetics, Am. Acad. Neurology (S. Wier Mitchell award 1970); mem. Am. Assn. Neuropathology (Moore award 1975), Am. Neurol. Assn., Am. Soc. Human Genetics, Am. Soc. Neurochemistry, Child Neurology Soc., Harvard Varsity Club (Cambridge), Assn. for Rsch. in Nervous and Mental Diseases (bd. dirs. 1993-2010), Alpha Omega Alpha. Avocations: judaica, photography. Home: 110 Bleecker St Apt 24D New York NY 10012-2106 Office: NYU Med Ctr 550 1st Ave New York NY 10016-6402 Home Phone: 212-677-9500; Office Phone: 212-263-6549. Personal E-mail: ekolc@yahoo.com. Business E-Mail: edwin.kolodny@nyumc.org.

KOLODNY, STANLEY CHARLES, oral surgeon, retired military officer; b. NYC, Feb. 22, 1923; s. Aaron and Lea (Stern) K.; m. Mary Kathryn Leigh, Feb. 22, 1947; children: Kathleen Susan, Carter Leigh, Stanley Charles. BA, U. Tex., 1944; D.D.S., Baylor U., 1947; MS, U. Ill., 1961. Diplomate: Am. Bd. Oral and Maxillofacial Surgery. Commd. 1st lt. USAF, 1951, advanced through grades to maj. gen., 1981; cons. in oral surgery Surgeon Gen. U.S. Air Force, 1966; chmn. dept. oral surgery Wilford Hall USAF Med. Center, San Antonio, 1969-75, dir. dental services, 1975-77; asst. surgeon gen. for dental services Bolling AFB, Washington, 1979-82. Clin. prof. dept. surgery U. Tex. Dental Br., Houston, 1969-77; clin. asso. prof. dept. surgery U. Tex. Med. Sch., San Antonio, 1969-77 Contbr. chpt. to book, articles to profl. jours. Bd. dirs. Am. Cancer Soc., 1970-77. Decorated D.S.M., Legion of Merit with oak leaf cluster, Air Force Commendation medal; recipient cert. of achievement for outstanding oral surgery USAF. Fellow Am. Coll. Dentists, Am. Assn. Oral and Maxillofacial Surgeons; mem. ADA, Soc. Air Force Clin. Surgeons. Home: USAF 6401 Red Bud Dr Flower Mound TX 75022-5859

KOLTS, IVO, medical educator; b. Tallinn, Estonia, Feb. 7, 1957; Dr. med., Tartu U., 1981; MD, Kiel U., Germany, 1993. Assoc. prof. Tartu U., 1996—. Office: Ravila 19 Tartu 5411 Estonia Business E-Mail: ivo.kolts@ut.ee.

KOMARNICKY, LYDIA, radiation oncologist educator; Grad., U. Pa.; MD, Drexel U. Diplomate Am. Bd. Radiology-radiation oncology. Med. advisor Nat. Women's Health Resource Ctr.; bd. dirs. Breast Health Inst.; prof., chair radiation oncology dept. Drexel Univ. Coll. of Medicine; dir. Drexel Univ. Coll. of Medicine Cancer Program; assoc. prof. radiation oncology Thomas Jefferson Univ. Hosp., dir. hosp. residency program; clin. svc. chief Hahnemann Univ. Hosp. Author numerous articles on cancer in peer review jours.; co-author (with Dr. Anne L. Rosenberg): (book) What to Do If You Get Breast Cancer. Spokesperson Linda Creed Breast Cancer Found. Recipient Best Doctors, 2009—12; named one of Top Docs, Phila. Mag. Office: Hahnemann University Hospital Broad and Vine Streets Philadelphia PA 19102 Mailing: Graduate Hospital Tuttleman Center Lower Level 1840 S St Philadelphia PA 19146 Office Phone: 215-762-8409, 215-762-8409. Office Fax: 215-762-3053, 215-893-7362.

KOMATA, TADASHI, neurosurgeon, researcher; b. Niigata, Japan, June 25, 1963; s. Hideo and Michi Komata; m. Masami Eto, Mar. 28, 1993; children: Tatsuki, Mayu. MB, MD, Niigata U., Japan, 1988, PhD, 1997. Cert. in neurosurgery Japan Neurosurg. Soc. Vis. scientist dept. immunology Queensland Inst. Med. Rsch., Brisbane, Australia, 1998—99; rsch. fellow dept. neurosurgery Cleve. Clinic Found., 1999—2000; rsch. coord. dept. neurosurgery Mt. Sinai Sch. Medicine, NYC, 2000—01; part-time instr. dept. neurosurgery, Brain Rsch. Inst. Niigata U., 2001—. Recipient Sammy's award, 3rd pl., 2004; fellow, Sumitomo Life Social Welfare Services Found., 1999. Mem.: Japan Neurosurg. Soc. (licentiate). Achievements include research in gene therapy and molecular target therapy on malignant brain tumor. Avocations: surfing, snowboarding, juggling, igo, dijeridoo. Office: Brain Rsch Inst Niigata Univ 1-757 Asahimachi-dori Niigata 951-8585 Japan Office Fax: 81-25-227-0819; Home Fax: 81-250-21-3357. E-mail: tadashi@bri.niigata-u.ac.jp, tdskmt5@yahoo.co.jp.

KOMATSU, KOGA, gastroenterologist, director; b. Sendai, Japan, May 12, 1964; MD, Yamagata U., 1991; PhD, Tohoku U. Grad. Sch., 1997. Med. staff Miyagi Social Ins. Hosp., 1997—99, Akita U. Sch. Medicine, 1999—2001, asst. prof., 2003—05, adj. asst. prof., 2009; rsch. fellow Vanderbilt U. Med. Ctr., 2001—03; dir. gastroenterology Honjo Daiichi Hosp., 2005—. Vice chmn. bd. trustees, CEO Med. Corp. SEIRAN-KAI, 2010. Rsch. fellowship, Uehara Meml. Found., Maeda Toyokichi Meml. Gastroent. Found. Fellow: Japanese Gastroent. Assn., Japanese Soc. Helicobacter Rsch., Japanese Soc. Gastroenterology, Japan Gastroent. Endoscopy Soc., Japanese Soc. Internal Medicine. Office: 110 Iwabuchishita Yurihonjo Akita 015-8567 Japan Office Fax: 81-184-22-0120. Business E-Mail: koga-k@qb3.so-net.ne.jp.

KOMATSU, SEI, cardiologist; b. Kochi, Japan, July 10, 1969; MD, Kyushu U., Fukuoka, Japan, 1995; PhD, Tsukuba U., Ibaraki, Japan, 2001. Clin. fellow Osaka Police Hosp., Japan, 1995—97; rschr. RIKEN, Genome Sci. Lab, Tsukuba, Japan, 1997—2001; mid-carrier cardiologist Cardiovasc. Divsn., Osaka Police Hosp., 2001—. Achievements include research in Establishing Plaque Map in silico CT Analysis. Office: Osaka Police Hosp 10 31 Kitayama cho Tennoji ku Osaka 543 8502 Japan Office Fax: 81 6 6775 2845. Personal E-mail: donai@muc.biglobe.ne.jp.

KOMECHAK, MARILYN GILBERT, retired psychologist, writer; b. Wabash, Ind., Aug. 28, 1936; d. Russell and Evelyn Georgianna (Snyder) Gilbert; m. George J. Komechak, Aug. 23, 1958; children: Kimberly Ann, Gilbert Matthew. BS, Purdue U., Ind., 1958, Tex. Christian U., Ft. Worth, 1966, MEd, 1968; PhD, North Tex. State U., 1975. Grad. asst. Tex. Christian U., 1967—68; counselor clin. staff Child Study Ctr., Ft. Worth, 1968—74; assoc. dir. Behavioral Ctr. Cmty. Svc., North Tex. State U., Denton, 1974—77; pvt. practice psychology Ft. Worth, 1977—96. Adj. prof. Tex. Christian U., U. Tex., Arlington; dir. Jon Pierce, Inc.; mem. Sanger-Harris Adv. Bd. Dallas, Ft. Worth, 1983; mem. chancellor's alumni adv. com. U. North Tex., 1987, bd. dirs., dance theater arts dept., 1989—96; cons. to schs. mgmt.; presenter in field; coord. Centennal Celebration, Ft. Worth, Tex Poetry Soc., 2010. Author: Getting Yourself Together, 1982, 2nd edit., 2002, The Prairie Tree, 1987, Morals and Manners for the Millennium, 2002 (Finalist Judy and A.C. Greene Lit. Pub. Festival Anthology), Paisano Pete: Snake-Killer Bird, 2003 (named Best Juvenile Book, Okla. Writers Fedn., 2004), Aries Lit. Jour., Tex. Wesleyan U., 2005; contbr. poetry to lit. jours., short stories to various publs., articles counseling and psychology to profl. jours., poetry to anthologies; co-author: Pronto Pete Screenplay (Okla. Writers Fedn. award, 2007); author: Flash Fiction story, 2009, Tex. Poetry Calendar Poems, 2002—03, 2008—09; presenter Ekphrastic Poetry with Abstract Paintings, 2009—; contbr. poetry to anthology. Co-coord. Pen Women's Artist's Gallery Night, Ft. Worth, 2011. Recipient Outstanding Alumnus award, La Fontaine HS, Ind., 2004; named one of Notable Women of Tex., 1984—85. Mem.: DAR, Nat. League Am. Pen Women, Ft. Worth Writers, Inc., Ft. Worth Poetry Soc. (Mem.'s Contest award 1999, 2002, 2006), Tex. State Poetry Soc., Ft. Worth Women's Club (judge, lit. divsn. 2005—), Psi Chi, Delta Gamma. Episcopalian.

KOMEMUSHI, ATSUSHI, radiologist; b. Osaka, Japan, Nov. 2, 1972; s. Sadao and Kazuko Komemushi. MD, Kansai Med. U., 1997, PhD, 2002. Cert. radiologist Japan Radiol. Soc., 2002, interventional radiologist The Japanese Soc. Interventional Radiology, 2004. Resident dept. radiology Kansai Med. U., Moriguchi, Japan, 1997—98, med. staff dept. radiology, 1999—2002, instr. staff dept. radiology, 2002—; resident dept. radiology Rinku Gen. Med. Ctr., Izumisano, Japan, 1998—99. Office: Kansai Medical U Dept Radiology 2- 3-1 Shinmachi Hirakata Osaka 573 1191 Japan Home: 2-2-3-414 Zengenji Miyakojima Osaka 534-0015 Japan Office Phone: 81-6-6992-1001. Office Fax: 81-6-6993-3865.

KOMESU, MARILENA CHINALI, dentist, educator; b. Lins, Brazil, June 2, 1958; d. Seigui and Izabel Chinali Komesu. Degree in Dental Surgery, Lins Sch. Dentistry, Brazil, 1978; specialist in Endodontics, Bauru Sch. Dentistry, Brazil, 1983; MS in Dentistry, Ribeirao Preto Sch. Dentistry, Brazil, 1985, PhD, 1991. Prof. oral pathology Barretos Ednl. Found., Brazil, 1986—87, Araras Assn. Superior Sch., Brazil, 1987; asst. prof. prosthesis Fed. U. Uberlandia, Brazil, 1987—89; assoc. prof. U. São Paulo-Ribeirao Preto, Ribeirao Preto, Brazil, 1989—. Contbr. articles to profl. jours. Recipient Hon. citation, Dental Congress, 1998, 1999, 2001. Mem.: Assn. paulista de Cir. Dentist, Brazillan Soc. Stomatology, Internat. Assn. Dental Rsch. Office: FORP Univ São Paulo Via do Café s/n 14040904 Ribeirão Preto Brazil Office Phone: 55 16 3602 3985. Business E-Mail: mckomesu@usp.br.

KOMISAR, ARNOLD, otolaryngologist, educator; b. NYC, Nov. 27, 1947; s. Samuel and Sonia (Schwartz) K.; m. Marcella Massa Komisar, children: Alexandra Danielle, Jonathan Reed. BS, Bradley U., Peoria, Ill., 1968; DDS, NYU, 1972, MS in Health Care Mgmt., 2004; MD, Hahnemann Med. Coll., Phila., 1975. Diplomate Am. Bd. Otolaryngology, Nat. Bd. Med. Examiners, Nat. Bd. Dental Examiners. Resident in surgery Beth Israel Med. Ctr., NYC, 1975-76; resident in otolaryngology Mt. Sinai Med. Sch., NYC, 1976-79; asst. prof. otolaryngology Albert Einstein Coll. Medicine, NYC, 1979-85, assoc. prof., 1985-86, assoc. clin. prof., 1986-90; assoc. dir. head and neck surgery Albert Einstein Affiliated Hosps., NYC, 1982-86; attending otolaryngologist Montefiore Hosp. and Med. Ctr., NYC, 1979-90, Bronx Mcpl. Hosp. Ctr., NYC, 1979-90, North Ctrl. Bronx Hosp., NYC, 1979-90, N.Y. Hosp.-Cornell U. Med. Ctr., NYC, 1997—; clin. assoc. prof. otolaryngology Cornell U. Med. Coll., NYC, 1994—98, clin. prof., 1998—2000; attending otolaryngologist N.Y. Hosp.-Cornell U. Med. Ctr., NYC, 1997—2000; clin. prof. otolaryngology NYU, 2000—. Otolaryngologist Lenox Hill Hosp., NYC, 1986—, asst to dir. resident edn. dept. otolaryngology, 1986—, adj. otolaryngologist, 1987—, attending otolaryngologist, 1989—, assoc. dir. otolaryngology, 1990—, vice-chmn., 2003-2005, acting chmn., 2006-07; cons. otolaryngology NY Eye and Ear Infirmary, NYC, 1986-89; courtesy staff surgery-otolaryngology Drs. Hosp., NYC, 1986-90; attending staff Manhattan Eye Ear and Throat Hosp., 1995—; attending otolaryngologist NY Hosp. Cornell U. Med. Ctr., 1997-2000; presenter in field. Contbr. articles to profl. jours., chpts. in books. Recipient Centurion award Bradley U., 1997, Resident Tchg. award, Manhattan Eye Ear Throat Hosp., 1999, Stanley M. Blaugrund Tchg. award NYU, 2003, 07 Fellow ACS, Am. Soc. Head and Neck Surgery, Am. Acad. Otolaryngology/Head and Neck Surgery (Honor award 1998, Disting. Svc. award 2009), Triological Soc. (Mosher award 1989), Am. Bronchoesophalogical Soc., NY Acad. Medicine, Am. Laryngol. Assn.; mem. AMA, Am. Acad. Anti-Aging Medicine, Med. Soc. NY, NY Laryngol. Soc., NY County Med. Soc., Am. Thyroid Assn., Am. Coll. Physician Executives Avocations: reading, travel. Office: 1421 Third Ave 4th Fl New York NY 10028 Office Phone: 212-861-8888. Personal E-mail: axk2@aol.com.

KOMIYA, NORIHIRO, physician, cardiologist, electrophysiologist; s. Komiya Kenji and Komiya Hiroko; m. Komiya Rie; children: Yuki, Ryohei. MD, Nagasaki U., Japan, 1999; PhD, Nagasaki U., 2004. Rschr. Nagasaki U. Hosp., 2004—07, associated prof., 2007—08. Contbr. articles to profl. jours. Office: Nagasaki Univ Hosp 1 7 1 Sakamoto Nagasaki 8528501 Japan Office Phone: 81-95-819-7288. Office Fax: 81 95 819 7290. Business E-Mail: nkomi@net.nagasaki-u.ac.jp.

KOMORI, AKIRA, orthodontist, educator; b. Kurume, Fukuoka, Japan, Nov. 3, 1962; s. Saizou and Junko Komori; m. Tomoko Komori; children: Mao, Daisuke. PhD, Nagasaki U. Sch. Dentistry, 1992. Diplomate Japanese Orthodontic Soc. 1996. Orthodontist Koyata Dental Office, Urawa, Saitama, Japan, 1992—93; rsch. fellow Nippon Dental U., Chiyoda-ku, Tokyo, Japan, 1993—99, sr. asst. prof., 1999—2007, assoc. prof., 2007—09. Vis. prof. U. Ferrara, Sch. Dentistry, Postgrad. Sch. Orthodontics. Editor (jour.): Odontology, 2001; contbr. articles to profl. jours. Mem.: RCS (Edinburgh), European Orthodontic Soc. (london, eng. 2002), Internat. Assn. for Dental Rsch. (alexandria, va. 2002), Am. Assn. Orthodontists (st. louis, mo. 2002). Citizens. Office: Nippon Dental Univ Fujimi 2-3-16 Chiyoda-ku Tokyo 102-8158 Japan Home: 2-9-12 Komaba Meguro Ku Tokyo 153-0041 Japan Office Phone: 81-3-3261-5511. Office Fax: 81-3-3261-3924. Business E-Mail: komo@msi.biglobe.ne.jp, como@tky.ndu.ac.jp.

KOMORNY, KENNETH MICHAEL, pharmacist; b. Toledo, May 16, 1970; s. Robert Edgar and Veronica Komorny; m. Lynn Marie Pyles, Mar. 19, 1994; children: Hannah Noel, Grace Nicole. BS in Pharmacy, U. Toledo, 1993; PharmD, U. Cin., 1995. Registered pharmacist Ohio State Bd. of Pharmacy, 1993, cert. pharmacotherapy specialist Bd. of Pharm. Specialties, 1999. Cert. specialist of poison info. Cin. Drug and Poison Info. Ctr., 1993—97; clin. pharmacist St. Luke Hosp. - East, Ft. Thomas, Ky., 1995—97; clin. lead pharmacist Summa Health Sys., Akron, Ohio, 1997—99, ednl., investigational, and clin. coord., 1999—2008, mgr., 2008—09; sys. dir. pharmacy Cubicin Outcomes Registry, 2009—, investigator. Presenter in field. Contbr. articles to profl. jours. Pres. Jerusalem Evangel. Luth. Ch., 2007. Mem.: Am. Soc. Health-Sys. Pharmacists, Ohio Coll. Clin. Pharmacy (assoc.), Am. Coll. Clin. Pharmacy (assoc.). Lutheran. Achievements include investigator of Summa Health Sys. Cubicin Outcomes Registry and Experience for the treatment of serious gram positive infections; research in the clinical and economic impact of Methicillin reserve with the National Nosocomial Resistance Surveillance Group; the effect of formulary conversion from ceftazidime to cefepime on the in-vitro sensitivities of pseudomonas aeruginosa, enterobacter cloacae, and klebsiella pneumoniae to selected antibiotics. Avocations: fishing, hunting, soccer. Home: 8760 Guilford Rd Seville OH 44273 Office. Summa Health Sys 525 E Market St Akron OH 44309-2090 Personal E-mail: komorny@hughes.net. Business E-Mail: komornyk@summahealth.org.

KON, ELIZAVETA, orthopaedic surgeon, researcher; b. Moscow, Aug. 2, 1969; d. Alexander Kon; m. Alessandro Franco, Sept. 25, 2004. Degree in Medicine and Surgery, U. Bologna, Italy, 1994. Cert. specialist in orthopaedics and traumatology U. Bologna, 1999. Orthopaedic surgeon Rizzoli Orthopaedic Inst., Sport Orthpaedic and Traumatology Dept., Bologna, 2000; rschr. Biomechanics Lab., Rizzoli Inst., Bologna, 2000—; asst. prof. Motor Scis. U. Bologna, 2003—; mem. Gen. Bd. ICRS; dir. Nano-Biotech. Lab; chair fellowship, scholarships & grants ICRS. Mem. sci. bd. Kolana Surgery. Mem.: Club Internat. Cartilage Repair Soc., Young Scientist Orthopaedic Surgeon (pres.), European Soc. Sports Traumatology Knee Surgery and Arthroscopy (assoc.), Internat. Soc. Arthroscopy Knee Surgery and Orthopaedic and Sports Medicine (assoc.), European Tissue Engring. Soc. (assoc.), Italian Soc. Knee, Arthroscopy, Sport, Cartilage and Orthopaedic Technologies (assoc.; cartilage rsch. bd., pres.), European Soc. Sports Traumatology Knee Surgery and Arthroscopy (assoc.), Internat. Cartilage Repair Soc. (assoc.), European Orthopaedic Rsch. Soc. (assoc.). Office: Rizzoli Orthopaedic Inst Biomechanics Lab 10 Via di Barbiano 1 40136 Bologna BO Italy Office Fax: +39 051583789. Business E-Mail: e.kon@biomec.ior.it.

KONDO, NORIHIRO, cardiovascular surgeon; MD, Hirosaki U. Sch. Medicine, 1999. Trainee Hirosaki U. Sch. Medicine, Aomori, Japan, 1999—2000; surgeon Hirosaki Mcpl. Hosp., 2000—00, Aomori Rosai Hosp., Hachinohe, 2000—02; rschr. Hirosaki U. Surgery 1, Hirosaki, 2002—05; cardiovasc. surgeon Aomori Mcpl. Hosp., 2005—. Office: Aomori Mcpl Hosp Dept Cardiovasc Surgery 1-14-20 Katta Aomori 030-0821 Japan Business E-Mail: kondo18@r66.7-dj.com.

KONDO, RYOICHI, thoracic surgeon; b. Japan, Apr. 3, 1968; MD, Shinshu U., PhD, 1997. Chief gen. thoracic surgery Nat. Hosp. Orgn. Matsumoto Med. Ctr., 2009—. Mem.: Am. Thoracic Soc. Office: 811 Kotobuki-Toyooka Matsumoto Nagano 3990021 Japan Office Fax: 81-263-86-3190. Business E-Mail: kryoichi@shinshu-u.ac.jp.

KONDO, TAKAYUKI, neurologist, researcher; b. Shizuoka, Shizuoka, Japan, Dec. 20, 1960; s. Toshiyuki and Toyoko Kondo; m. Akiko Sasahara, Feb. 8, 1967; 1 child, Ikumi. MD, Kyoto U., 1987. Cert. Neurologist Societas Neurologica Japonica, 1992. Postdoctoral fellow Neuroimmunology Br., NIH, Nat. Multiple Sclerosis Soc., Bethesda, Md., 1997—99; sect. chief Cellular Immunology Sect., Dept. of Immunology, Nat. Inst. of Neuroscience, Nat. Ctr. of Neurology and Psychiatry, Kodaira, Tokyo, Japan, 1999—2001; head Dept. of Neurology, Fukui Redcross Hosp., Fukui, Fukui, Japan, 2001—04, Dept. of Clin. Rsch., Nagasaki Med. Ctr. of Neurology, Higashisonogi, Nagasaki, Japan, 2004—. Home: 16-13 Huis Ten Bosch Nagasaki Sasebo 859-3243 Japan Office: Nagasaki Med Ctr of Neurology 2005-1 Shimogumi Kawatana Nagasaki Higashisinogi 859-3615 Japan Office Fax: 81-956-82-3710; Home Fax: 81-956-58-6789. Personal E-mail: takakon78@hotmail.com. E-mail: tkondo@mist.ocn.ne.jp.

KONDO, YOSHIAKI, pediatrician, educator, nephrologist, researcher; b. Ise, Mie, Japan, Nov. 4, 1956; MD, Tohoku U. Sch. Medicine, 1981; PhD, Tohoku U. Grad. Sch. Medicine, 1990. Prof. Tohoku U. Grad. Sch. Medicine, 2002—10, vis. prof., 2011, Nihon U. Sch. Medicine, 2008—10, prof., 2011—. Adj. lectr. Iwate Med. U., 2009. Recipient IPA award, Info.-Tech. Promotion Agy., Japan, Oshima award, Japanese Soc. Nephrology, Arakawa award, Dept. Pediat., Tohoku U. Sch. Medicine. Mem.: Am. Med. Informatics Assn., Internat. Soc. Nephrology, Japanese Soc. Pediat. Nephrology, Japanese Soc. Nephrology, Japanese Pediat. Soc. Avocations: piano, travel. Office: 30-1 Oyaguchi-Kamicho Itabashi Tokyo 173-8610 Japan Office Fax: 3-5964-7036. Personal E-mail: ykondox@gmail.com.

KONDOH, YASUHIRO, physician; b. Nagoya, Aichi, Japan, May 1, 1959; s. Yozo and Yanako Kondoh; m. Akiko Sugiura; 1 child, Ryo. Degree, Nagoya U. Grad. Sch. Medcine, 1985; PhD, Nagoya U., 1994. Lic. Health and Welfare Ministry, 1985. Resident Tosei Gen. Hosp., Seto, Aichi, 1985—89, dir., dept. respirarory medicine and allergy, 1993—; fellow Nagoya U. Grad. Sch. Medicine, 1989—92. Contbr. rsch. articles to profl. jours. Recipient Incentive award, Japanese Soc. Internal Medicine, 1993. Achievements include research in acute exacerbation of idiopathic pulmonary fibrosis in English for the first time. Avocation: reading. Office: Tosei Gen Hosp 160 Nishioiwake-Cho Seto Aichi 489-8642 Japan Office Phone: 81-561-82-5101. Office Fax: 81-561-82-9139. Business E-Mail: kondoh@tosei.or.jp.

KONDRATYEV, ANATOLY NICOLAEVICH, anesthesiologist; b. Leningrad, Russia, June 4, 1950; s. Nicolay Vasilievich Kondratyev and Ludmila Konstantinovna Kondratyeva; m. Irina Grygorievna Babikova, May 7, 1974; children: Ekaterina Anatolievna Kondratyeva, Sergey Anatolievich. MD, Pediatrical Med. Acad., Leningrad, 1973. Chef dept. anesthesiology Kalinigrad State Hosp., Russia, 1974—81; chef intensive care and anesthesiology dept. Polenov Neurosurg. Inst., St. Petersburg, 1986. Mem. adv. bd. Postgrad. Med. Acad., St. Petersburg, 2003. Author: (book) Intracranial Meningioma, Anesthesiology and Intensive Care Injury of Nerve System Surgical Endocrinology; contbr. articles to profl. jours. Mem.: Mem. European Soc. Anesthesiology (assoc.), Assn. North-West Anesthesiologists (assoc.; pres.). Achievements include discovery of Intensive Care and Prognosis in Vegetative State Patients; Usage of Alpha-2 Agonists in Neuroanesthesia. Home: Belgradskaya 22 - 2 - 58 Saint Petersburg 192212 Russia Office: Polenov Neurosurgical Inst ul. Mayakovskogo 12 191014 Saint Petersburg Sankt-Pyetyerburg Russia Office Fax: 78122738759. Personal E-mail: eak2003@mail.ru.

KONDZIOLKA, DOUGLAS, neurosurgeon; b. Montreal, Que., Can., Sept. 12, 1961; came to U.S., 1989; MD, U. Toronto, 1985; MSc, U. Pitts., 1991. Prof. neurol. surgery U. Pitts., 1992—. Recipient Lars Leksell award World Fedn. of Neurosurg. Socs., 197, Stephen Mahaley award Am. Assn. Neurol. Surgeons/Congress Neurol. Surgeons, 1997, 99. Mem. Am. Assn. Neurol. Surgeons, Congress Neurol. Surgeons., Am. Soc. Stereotactic & Functional Neurosurgery (pres. 2001-03), Internat. Stereotactic Radiosurgery (pres. 2003-05), Congress Neurol. Surgeons (pres. 2006-07). Office: U Pitts Med Coll 200 Lothrop St Ste B-400 Pittsburgh PA 15213-2546 Business E-Mail: kondziolkads@upmc.edu. *

KONE, BRUCE C., medical educator, nephrologist, scientist, former dean; b. Frankfurt, Germany, Jan. 29, 1958; s. Kenneth M. and Dorothy Kone; m. Daisy Linda Waller, June 10, 1992; children: Natalie Audrey, Justine Dorothy, Lindsey Jane. AB, Princeton U., NJ, 1979; MD, U. Fla., Gainesville, 1983. Internal Medicine Am. Bd. Internal Medicine, 1984, Nephrology Am. Bd. Internal Medicine, 1994; cert. nephrology Am. Bd. Internal Medicine, 2004. Resident Johns Hopkins Hosp., Baltimore, Md., 1983—86; renal fellow Brigham and Women's Hosp., Boston, 1986—88; instr. medicine Johns Hopkins U. Sch. Medicine, Baltimore, Md., 1989—91; asst. prof. medicine U. Fla. Coll. Medicine, Gainesville, 1991—95, dean, 2007—08, Folke H. Peterson/deans disting. professorship, prof. medicine and biochem. & molecular biology, 2007—09; assoc. prof. medicine U. Tex. Med. Sch., Houston, 1995—99, prof. medicine, 2000—07, dir., divsn. renal diseases and hypertension, 2000—07, vice chair, dept. internal medicine, 2000—04, James T. and Nancy B. Willerson chair, 2001—07, chmn. internal medicine, 2004—07, vis. prof. medicine, 2009—10, prof. medicine, 2010—; chief, sect. nephrology U. Tex. M.D. Anderson Cancer Ctr., Houston, 2000—07; pres. chmn. Fla. Proton Therapy Inst., Inc., 2008; dir. Shands Healthcare Bd., 2007—08, U. Tex. Physicians Bd., 2005—07, vice chair, 2006—07; dir. Meml. Hermann Hosp. Sys. Physicians Tex. Bd., 2007, Med. Svc., R. & D. Plan Bd., U. Tex. Health Sci. Ctr. Houston, 2002—05. Gov. Tobacco Edn. & Use Prevention Adv. Coun., Fla. Dept. Health, 2007—08. Named Best Dr. in America, 2005—; grantee Clin. Investigator award, NIH, RO1 Individual Rsch. awards, All-Am., US Masters Swimming, 2010; fellow Nat. Rsch. Svc. award, NIH. Fellow: Am. Soc. Nephrology, AAAS, Am. Coll. Clin. Pharmacology, ACP, Am. Heart Assn. (Established Investigator award); mem.: So. Soc. Clin. Investigation (councilor 2003—07, pres. 2007—08, adv. coun. 2009—), Alpha Omega Alpha Honor Med. Soc. Avocation: swimming. Office: Univ Tex-Houston Divsn Renal Diseases MSB 5 124 6431 Fannin St Houston TX 77030 Home: 1104 Berthea Houston TX 77006

KONERMANN, MARTIN, physician, researcher; b. Münster, Nordrhein-Westfalen, Germany, Jan. 21, 1956; s. Clemens Heinrich and Ursula (Springer) K.; m. Gabriele Angelika Lange, Aug. 24, 1978; 1 child, Philipp. Med. diploma, Westfälische Wilhelms U., Münster, Germany, 1980, MD, 1983. Med. asst. Marienhospital, Marl, Germany, 1982, Franz-Hosp., Dülmen, Germany, 1983-84, Herz-Jesu-Krankenhaus, Münster, Germany, 1984-87, Ruhruniversität, Bochum, Germany, 1987-92, med. superior, 1993-96; med. dir. Marienkrankenhaus, Kassel, Germany, 1996—. Asst. med. educator Ruhruniversität, Bochum, 1989-92, med. tchr., 1993—; clin. dir. Marienkrankenhaus Kassel, Germany, 1996, hosp. dir., 1999—. Author (editor): Sleep Related Breathing Disorders of Children and Adults, 1994; author: Sleep Related Disorders, 1997; editor (in-chief): (journal) Somno Jour., 2000—; contbr. articles to profl. jours. Capt. Bundeswehr, 1981-82, Germany. Recipient Indsl. award Bristol-Myers Squibb, 1993, Boehringer Mannheim, Germany, 1994. Mem. Lions Club Internat., Marburger Bund, Deutsche Gesellschaft für Schlafforschung und Schlafmedizin, Bund Deutscher Internisten. Roman Catholic. Avocations: art exhibitions, skiing, running, fishing, sponsoring art. Home: Vor der Prinzenquelle 22 34130 Kassel Hessen Germany Office: Marienkrankenhaus Marburger Str 85 34127 Kassel Hessen Germany Office Fax: 561-80734200. E-mail: m.konermann@mariankrankenhaus-kassel.de.

KONES, RICHARD, cardiologist, medical services company executive; s. Joseph Irwin and Ruth (Winkler) K. BSChemE, NYU, 1960, MD, 1964; DSc in Physiology, Somerset U., Eng., 1988, PhD in Exercise Physiology and Nutrition, 1990. Diplomate Am. Bd. Internal Medicine, Nat. Bd. Med. Examiners. Intern Kings County Hosp., Bklyn., 1964-65; resident in surgery Bronx Mcpl. Hosp., NYC, 1965-66; resident in medicine Lenox Hill Hosp., NYC, 1966-68; fellow cardiology VA Hosp., New Orleans, 1969—71; physician in charge CCU Arthur Logan Hosp., 1968—69; USPHS-NIH fellow in cardiology, chief resident Sch. Medicine, Tulane U., New Orleans, 1969-71; asst. prof. cardiology N.Y. Med. Coll., NYC, 1971, chief CCU, 1971-75; cons. and chief CCU CCU Midtown Hosp.-NYU, Cmty. Hosp., NYC, 1971—79; chief exec. officer Community Med. Offices, Inc., Houston and NYC, 1974—; asst. physician, dir., ECG conf. coord. Cornell Med. Ctr. Park City Hosp., Bridgeport, Conn., 1975-78, st. cardiologist Cabrini Med. Ct.-NYU, NYC, 1978—88; physician and cons. in cardiology SW Meml. Hosp., 1979-81, Alief Gen. Hosp., Houston, 1979—81; lectr. medicine U. Tex., 1979; faculty Inst. Spirituality & Health Tex. Med Ctr., 2009—; editor Medpedia Project, Cardiovasc. Disease, 2009—; editor-in-chief Rsch. Reports Clin. Cardiology, Dove Med. Pres, 2010—. Asst. prof. to assoc. prof. medicine NY Med.Coll., 1971—; vis. rsch. cardiologist, Tulane U. Sch. Medicine, New Orleans, 1969-1992; med. dir., chief Nutrition, Sports, Health Clinic, Houston,1989—; lectr. medicine & cardiology U. Tex. Health Sci. Ctr., Houston Med. Ctr.; CCU Nursing CME lect., Spring Branch Hosp., Houston, 2007-9; Med. Dir., Cardiometabolic Rsch. Inst. & Found., Houston, 2006--. Author, editor books on biochemistry, physiology, cardiology, nutrition, metabolism, nutrition and sports medicine; contbr. rsch. papers to profl. pubs. Sponsorer US Olympic Com., 2008; advocacy, "You're the Cure" program Am. Heart Assn., 2009, spkr's bur., 2020 CV Mortality Goals-Life's Simple 7, 2011—. Recipient Faculty Excellent Recognition award, Academic Congress Internat. China, 2011, Outstanding Contribution Clin. Rsch. Key Investigator, NY Med. Coll. & Sandoz, 1994, Physicians Recognition awards, AMA, 1993, Best Doctors in America Plaque, Best Doctors in America, 1981, Advances in Molecular Cardiology Plaque, Sec. Health, Hosp. Juarez, 1980, Appreciation Biol. Edn. award, Am. Inst. Biol. Scis., 1978, Investigator award, Dobutamine study excellence, NY Med Coll, 1976, Appreciation Outstanding Voluntary Svc. award, Hosp. & Cmty. Svc. Plaque, Arthur Logan Hosp. Harlem, NY, 1969, Faculty Excellence Recognition award, Academic Congress Internat. China, 2011, award, Internat. Conf. Pharmaceuticals, 2011, Colegio de Medicina Interna Mex., 2011, Editl. award, Medpedia, 2010. Fellow European Soc. Cardiology, Royal Soc. Medicine, Royal Soc. Health, NY Cardiological Soc., Am. Coll. Pharmacology, Am. Geriatric Soc., Am. Coll. Angiology, Internat. Coll. Angiology, Am. Soc. Angiology, Am. Coll. Nutrition, Internat. Coll. Nutrition, Internat. Soc. Noninvasive Monitoring Electrocardiography; mem. Am. Heart Assn., Am. Soc. Clin. Pharmacology Exptl. Therapeutics, Am. Soc. Clin. Pharmacology Therapeutics, World Heart Fedn., European Atherosclerosis Soc., Am. Physiol. Soc., Am. Soc. Cardiovasc. and Pulmonary Rehab., Physiological Soc. (London); Nutrition Soc. (London), French Soc. Cardiology (Paris), NY Acad. Scis., Coun. Clin. Cardiology, Am. Soc. Preventive Cardiology, Heart Rhythm Soc., European Heart Rhythm Soc., Am. Coll. Sports Medicine, Soc. Gen. Internal Medicine, Am. Soc. Nutrition, Heart Failure Soc America, Am. Soc. Hypertension, European Soc. Cardiac Prevention and Rehab, Am. Assn. Clin. Chemistry, Am. Chem. Soc., European Soc. Clin. Nutrition and Metabolism, Am. Med. Athletic Assn., Inflammation Rsch. Assn., Nutritional Rsch. Coun., Am. Fedn. Clin. Rsch., Am. Dietetic Assn., Am. Soc. Internal Medicine, Am. Thoracic Soc., Am. Diabetes Assn., Am. Pub. Health Assn., So. Med. Assn., Brit. Soc. Nutritional Medicine. Avocations: tennis, electronics, music.

KONG, BYEONG SEON, surgeon; b. Busan, Republic of Korea, Apr. 19, 1968; s. Hoo Sik and Jeong Hae; m. Kyoung Ah Kim; children: Joon Kyu, Seo Yeon. Diploma in Medicine, Busan Nat. U. Med. Coll., 1993; M, Grad. Sch. Dong-A U., Busan, 2001, PhD, 2004. Cert. med. dr. Korean Med. Assn., 1994, in orthop. surgery 1998, in hand surgery 2005. Physician, hand and microsurgery dept. Seil Hosp., Busan, 1999—2001; chief, hand and microsurgery dept. Choonhae Hosp., Busan, 2001—06, Good Moonwha Hosp., Busan, 2006—07; dir., planning divsn. Westbusan Hosp., Busan, 2009—, hand and microsurgery physician, 2009—. Guest physician Wurzburg U., Germany, 1999; rsch. fellow, hand and upper extremity svc. Mass. Gen. Hosp., 2008. Contbr. nemurous articles & sci. papers to profl. jours. Recipient Academic prize, Busan-Ulsan-Kyeongnam Orthopaedic Soc., 2004. Mem.: Korean Foot & Ankle Soc., Korean Soc. Surgery Hand, Korean Microsurg. Soc. (Academic prize 2005), Korean Orthop. Assn. Avocation: movies. Home: Lucky Apt 5-501 Oncheon 2 Dong Dongraegu Busan 607-753 Republic of Korea Office: Busan Microorthop Clinic 85-14 Guseo 1 Dong Geumjung Gu 609-854 Busan Busan Republic of Korea Office Phone: 82-51-329-3000, 82-51-514-1400. Office Fax: 82-51-329-3100, 82-51-514-0400. Personal E-mail: gongja2000@yahoo.co.kr.

KONG, KAM FU JAMES, orthopedist, surgeon; MBBS, U. Hong Kong, 1991; diploma in sports and exercise medicine, U. Bath, England, 2004, MSc, 2006; postgrad., Manchester Met. U., 2006; MD. Diplomate Am. Bd. Ind. Med. Examiners, 2005, cert. pers. trainer Nat. Acad. Sports Medicine, 1997, in orthop. & traumatology. Intern Queen Mary Hosp., Hong Kong, 1991—92, med. officer surg. unit, 1994—95, med. officer orthop. unit, 1995—97, 1999—2000, Grantham Hosp., Hong Kong, 1992—94, Duchess Kent Children's Hosp., Hong Kong, 1998—99; traveling fellow shoulder surgery U. Zurich, Switzerland, 2001; traveling fellow knee surgery Dr. Dejour, Lyon, France, 2001, U. Pitts., 2001; traveling fellow shoulder surgery San Antonio Orthop. Group, 2001, So. Calif. Orthop. Inst., LA, 2001; hon. clin. asst. prof. dept. orthop. surgery U. Hong Kong, 2002—; pvt.

practice Hong Kong, 2003—. Hon. orthop. cons. Shanghai Comml. Bank Ltd., 2004; lectr., presenter in field. Contbr. articles to profl. jours. Hon. med. adv. Hong Kong Indsl. Assn., 2005—. Recipient Yearly Math's prize, UK, 1985, Meml. Math's prize, 1986; Elective Travel grant, Wong Chi Ming Med., Hong Kong, 1991, Scholarship, 1991. Fellow: HKAM, HKCOS, RCS, Hong Kong Acad. Medicine, Coll. Orthop. Surgeons Hong Kong, Coll. Surgeons Edinburgh, Coll. Surgeons Hong Kong. Office: Melbourne Plaza 33 Queen's Rd. Hong Kong Hong Kong Island Hong Kong Office Phone: 3527 3535, 2523-6880.

KONGSAP, PIPAT, ophthalmologist, educator; s. Manus and Wannee Kongsap; m. Nuanrat Patpitak, Nov. 12, 1994; children: Thanwarat, Prima. MD, Chulalongkorn U., Bangkok, 1991. Diplomate in ophthalmology Chulalongkorn U., 1997. Dir. hosp. Kaosaming Hosp., Trat, 1992—95; ophthalmologist Prapokklao Hosp, Meung, Chanthaburi, Thailand, 2005—, asst. prof., 2005—, assoc. prof., 2009—. Assoc. prof. Chulalongkorn U., 1998—, asst. prof., 2009—. Contbr. articles to profl. jours. Recipient Prevention Blindness award, Asia-Pacific Ophthalmology, 2006; nominee Honors Sci. Deliberation, Internat. Soc. Manual Small Incision Cataract Surgeons, 2007. Mem.: Am. Acad. Ophthalmology. Achievements include first to surgical technique for manual small incision cataract surgery named The kongsap technique; development of prechop manual phacofragmentation, nylon loop manual phacofragmentation. Office: Dept Ophthalmolo Prapokklao Hosp Leubneun Rd Meung Chanthaburi 22000 Thailand Office Phone: 663 9323905. Office Fax: 663-9324861. Business E-Mail: pkongsap@yahoo.com.

KONIARI, IOANNA CHRISTOS, cardiologist researcher; b. Athens, Greece, Apr. 21, 1982; MD, Sch. Medicine, U. Patras, Greece, 2006, PhD, 2011. Rsch. fellow, cardiothoracic surgery dept. U. Patras, 2006—. Resident in pathology, 2010—11. Contbr. articles to profl. jours. Mem.: Hellenic Med. Assn. Avocations: writing, travel, art. Home: Andrea Miaouli 15 Arachovitica Patras Achaia 26504 Greece Personal E-mail: iokoniari@yahoo.gr.

KÖNIG, PETER, pediatrician, educator; b. Cluj, Romania, Feb. 14, 1938; came to U.S., 1976; s. Rudolf and Irina (Grünwald) K.; m. Lea Schiffer, Sept. 30, 1965; 1 child, Orly. Graduate, Timisoara Med. Sch., Romania, 1959; MD, Hebrew U., Jerusalem, 1966; PhD, U. London, 1974. Resident Hadassah Hosp., Jerusalem, 1969—70, Bikur Cholim Hosp., Jerusalem, 1970-71, staff, 1974-76; fellow in pulmonary diseases Brompton Hosp., London, 1971-74; asst. prof. child health U. Mo., Columbia, 1976-80, assoc. prof. child health, 1980-84, prof. in child health, 1984—. Fellow Am. Acad. Allergy; mem. Am. Thoracic Soc., Acad. Allergy, Soc. Pediatric Research, Chilean Asthma Found., Sigma Xi. Home: 1310 Vintage Dr Columbia MO 65203-4878 Office: U Mo Child Health 1 Hospital Dr Columbia MO 65212-5276 Office Phone: 573-882-6978. Business E-Mail: KonigP@health.missouri.edu.

KONO, ATSUSHI, medical educator; b. Hiroshima, Japan, Apr. 3, 1976; MD, Kobe U. Sch. Medicine, 2002, PhD, 2010. Resident Kobe U. Hosp., 2002—03, Hyogo Brain and Heart Ctr., 2003—06; sr. resident Nat. Cardiovasc. Ctr., 2008—10; asst. prof. Kobe U. Hosp., 2010—. Recipient Cert. Merit, Radiol. Soc. N.Am. Mem.: Japan Soc. Magnetic Resonance Medicine, Japanese Soc. Nuc. Medicine, Japan Radiol. Soc., European Soc. Radiology, Soc. Cardiovasc. Magnetic Resonance. Avocations: skiing, movies. Office: 7-5-2 Kusunoki-cho Chuo-ku Kobe Hyogo 650-0017 Japan Office Fax: 81-78-382-6129. Business E-Mail: akono@med.kobe-u.ac.jp.

KONOPINSKI, VIRGIL JAMES, retired safety engineer; b. Toledo, July 11, 1935; BSChemE, U. Toledo, 1956; MSChemE, Pratt Inst., 1960; MBA, Bowling Green State U., 1971. Registered profl. engr., Ind., Ohio, Calif., cert. safety profl., indsl.hygienist retired. Assoc. engr. Owens Ill., Toledo, 1956, 60; real estate developer Grand Rapids, Ohio, 1961; chem. engr. USPHS, Cin., 1961-64; sr. environ. engr. Vistron Corp., Lima, Ohio, 1964-67; environ. specialist, asst. to dir. environ. control Owens Corning Fiberglas, Toledo, 1967-72; gen. mgr. Midwest Environ. Mgmt., Maumee, Ohio, 1972-73; staff specialist, indl. hygienist Williams Bros. Waste Control, Tulsa, 1973-75; dir. divsn. indsl. hygiene and radiol. health Ind. State Bd. Health, Indpls., 1975-87; exec. v.p. ACT Ind., Indpls., 1987-89; sr. cons. Occusafe, Chgo., 1990-91; regional safety engr., human resources analyst/safety U.S. Postal Svc., Bloomingdale, Ill., 1991—2003; cons. in field, 2003—. Bd. dirs. IOSHA Indsl. Hygiene, 1975—83; cons. indoor air, occupl. health aND safety, Zionsville, 1987—91; cons. indoor air, safety, Cary, 1991—2003, Maumee, Ohio, 2003—. Contbr. articles to profl. jours. With USNR, 1956—59. Mem.: Am. Indsl. Hygene Assn., Am. Soc. Safety Engrs., Mil. Officers Assn. Republican. Roman Catholic. Home and Office: 7206 Longwater Dr Maumee OH 43537 Office Phone: 419-878-3158.

KONOROVA, IRINA L'VOVNA, pathologist; b. Moscow, Nov. 27, 1960; DSc in Pathophysiology, 2010. With rsch. ctr. neurology Russian Acad. Med. Scis., 1988—. Cons. Sci. Jour. 'Pathophysiology & Exptl. Therapy', 2005—. Mem.: Vinogradov's Soc. Rheology, Russian Soc. Microcirculation & Regional Haemodynamics. Office: Volokolamskae shosse 80 Moscow 125367 Russia Office Fax: 7-495-4902210. E-mail: konorova.irina@yandex.ru.

KONRAD, ANDREAS, neurologist and psychiatrist, researcher; b. Darmstadt, Germany, Apr. 24, 1969; s. Adolf and Heidi Konrad; m. Verena Doell; children: Sophie Margarete, Amelie Louise. MD, Rheinische Friedrich-Wilhelms-U., Bonn, Germany, 1997. Cert. in health economics BWL Acad., Germany, 2005. Asst. Clinic Neurology, Ludwigshafen, Germany, 1997—2001; asst., dept. psychiatry Johannes Gutenberg-U., Mainz, Germany, 2001—06, sr. physician asst. dept. psychiatry, 2007—, cons., 2007—. Lt. Logistics German Army, 1988—90, Hardheim. Mem.: DGPPN, OHBM, Soc. Neurosci. Achievements include imaging genetics findings in schizophrenia, structural and functional disconnectivity in adult ADHD, and structural and functional cerebral correlates of working memory. Avocations: bicycling, skiing, history. Office: Johannes Gutenberg-Univ Untere Zahlbacher Strasse 8 Mainz 55131 Germany Office Phone: 49-6131-172158. Office Fax: 49-6131-173459. Personal E-mail: andreas_konrad@gmx.de. Business E-Mail: konrad@psychiatrie.klinik.uni-mainz.de.

KONSTANTINIDIS, KONSTANTINOS M., surgeon, educator; b. Rhodes, Greece, Oct. 28, 1956; s. Michael Konstantinidis and Sofia Pazartzis; m. Marilena Vlachou, Feb. 23, 1993; children: Sofia, Michael. MD, Aristotelian U., Thessaloniki, Greece, 1980; PhD, Dimokritio U. Thrace, Alexandroupoli, Greece, 1995. Cert. Am. Bd. Surgery, European Bd. Surgery. Intern Riverside Meth. Hosp., Columbus, 1982—83, intern in gen. surgery, 1983—84, resident in gen. surgery, 1984—87, chief resident in gen. surgery, 1987—88; tutor surgery Ohio State U. Sch. Medicine, Columbus, 1988—89, asst. clin. prof., 1989—92; dir. gen. and laparoscopic surgery Athens Med. Ctr., Greece, 1992—. Pres. sci. soc. Athens Med. Ctr., 2000—; lectr. in field. Fellow: ACS; mem.: Internat. Fedn. for Surgery of Obesity, Soc. Am. Gastrinal and Endoscopic Surgeons. Achievements include first to apply robotic and laparoscopic surgery in Greece. Avocations: tennis, soccer, scuba diving, swimming, folklore dancing. Office: 354 Kifisias Ave 15233 Athens Greece Office Phone: +30-210-6107165. E-mail: k.konstantinidis@laplaser.gr.

KONSTANTINOU, GEORGE N., consultant in allergy and clinical immunology; b. Thessaloniki, Greece, May 8, 1975; s. Nestoras G. Konstantinou and Spiridoula G. Tsekoura-Konstantinou; m. Evangelia N. Georgiou. MD, Aristotle U. Thessaloniki, 1999; MSc in Biostats., Nat. and Kapodistrian U. Athens, Greece, 2006; PhD, Aristotle U., 2009. Dir. allergy and clin. immunology dept. 417 NIMTS Army Hosp., Athens, 2008—09, 424 Gen. Mil. Tng. Hosp. Office: Dept Allergy& Clinical Immunology Siru 21 544 53 Thessaloniki Greece Personal E-mail: gnkonstantinou@gmail.com.

KONTOS, GEORGE JOHN, JR., surgeon; b. Chgo., May 26, 1958; s. George John and Sherry Knox Kontos; m. Sherry Knox Reed, Aug. 24, 1991; children: Alexis Reed, Nicholas John. BA, Northwestern U., 1979; MD, Loyola U., Maywood, Ill., 1982. Diplomate Am. Bd. Thoracic Surgery, 1992, Am. Bd. Surgery, 1988. Resident, gen. surgery Mayo Clinic, Rochester, Minn., 1982—88; resident, cardiac surgery U. Ala., Birmingham, 1988—91; cardiovasc. and thoracic surgeon Midwest Cardiovasc. Ctr., Sioux Falls, SD, 1992—94, Ctrl. Ala. Thoracic and Cardiovasc. Surgery, Montgomery, 1994—2002; surgeon U. Tenn., Memphis, 2002—03; thoracic, cardiovasc. surgeon Helena Surgery Assoc., Ark., 2004—07; thoracic surgeon Genesis Health Group Surg. Assocs., Silvis, Ill., 2007—. Guest reviewer Jour. Applied Physiology, Houston, 1991—92, Transplantation, Boston, 1991—97, Am. Jour. Cardiology, Dallas, 2001, 2002, 2004. Mem. Am. Hellenic Philanthropic Orgn., Montgomery, Ala., 1994—2002. Grantee, Am. Heart Assn., 1992. Fellow: Am. Coll. Chest Physicians, Am. Coll. Cardiology, Southeastern Surg. Congress, Am. Coll. Surgeons; mem.: Johns Hopkins Med. and Surg. Assn., Priestly Soc., Mayo Clinic, N.Y. Acad. Scis., Soc. Thoracic Surgeons. Greek Orthodox. Avocations: fountain pen collector, water sports, sailing. Home: 3392 Valleywynds Dr Bettendorf IA 52722 Office: Genesis Health Group 855 Illini Dr Silvis IL 61282 Office Phone: 309-281-2120.

KONTSEVAYA, ANNA V., cardiologist; b. Russia, Apr. 16, 1979; Degree in Medicine, Ivanovo State Med. Acad., 2002, PhD, 2005. Med. tchr. Ivanovo State Med. Acad., 2005—06; leading rschr. Nat. Rsch. Ctr. Preventive Medicine, 2006—. Administr. Soc. Cardiology Russian Fedn., 2007—10, head young cardiologist working group, 2010; head preventive project Sberbank Russia, 2011. Decorated Purple Heart; recipient Young Scientists award, Soc. Vardilogy Russian Fedn. Mem.: European Soc. Cardiology. Avocation: exercise. Home: Moldagulovoy 28 2 kv 110 Moscow 111538 Russia

KOO, BON-KWON, medical educator; b. Daegu, Republic Of Korea, Dec. 14, 1967; s. Ja-Young Koo and Tae-Go Lee; m. Hyo-Jin Lee, July 15, 1996; children: Keon-Woo, Min-Jeung. PhD, Yonsei U., Seoul, Korea. Asst. prof. Seoul Nat. U., 2004—; postdoc. fellow Stanford U., Calif., 2007—. Contbr. articles to profl. jours. Recipient Best Manuscript award, Korean Soc. Circulation, 2002, Best Challenging Case award, TCT-AP, 2006, Best Abstract award, 2005. Achievements include research in physiologic evaluation of coronary side branches. Office: Seoul National Univ Hosp Yeongon-dong Jongno-gu Seoul 110-744 Republic of Korea Office Phone: 82-2-2072-2062. Business E-Mail: bkkoo@snu.ac.kr.

KOO, DEOG-BON, research scientist; b. Daegu, Republic of Korea, Oct. 18, 1967; s. Ja-Woon Koo and Ok-Yi Shin; m. Soon-Yeon Choi, Apr. 16, 1994; children: Hyun-Mo, Jeong-Ha, Jeong-Young. PhD, Kon-Kuk U., Seoul, 1998. Sr. rsch. scientist KRIBB, Daejoen, Republic of Korea, 2003—05, prin. rsch. scientist, 2006—08; prof. dept. biotech. coll. engring. Daegu U., Jillyang, Gyeongsan, Republic of Korea. Achievements include research in Proteomics; Life Sciences; Fertil Steril; JBC; Hum Reprod; Mol Reprod Dev; Anim Reprod Sci; BBRC; Theriogenology; Biomed Microdevices; Biol Reprod; Embo J; J Biol Chem; FEBS Letters; Nat Genet; Transgenic Research; Anim Reprod Sci; Small Ruminant; Dev Dyn; biochem biophys res commun; patents for beta-casein gene targeting vector using homologous recombination; an improved method for production of porcine clone embryos via somatic cell nuclear transfer. Home: 109-1503 Hanwool Shinsung-dong Yuseong Daejeon 305-707 Republic of Korea Office: Daegu Univ Coll Engring Dept Biotech Jillyang Gyeongsan 712-714 Gyeongbuk Gyeongsangbuk-do Republic of Korea Home Phone: 82-42-382-5528; Office Phone: 82538506557. Office Fax: 82-42-860-4608, 82 53 850 6559. Personal E-mail: dbkoo86@hanmail.net. Business E-Mail: dbkoo@kribb.re.kr, dbkoo@daegu.ac.kr.

KOO, HYUN YOUNG, nursing educator; b. Republic of Korea, Dec. 30, 1970; PhD, Cath. U. Korea, 1999. Nurse St. Marys Hosp., 1994—97; tchg. asst. Inha U., 1997—99; lectr. Cath. U. Daegu, 2001—02, asst. prof., 2003—06, assoc. prof., 2007—11. Basic Sci. Rsch. grant, Nat. Rsch. Found. Korea, 2007—08, 2010, 2011. Mem.: Korean Academic Soc. Nursing Edn., Korean Acad. Child Health Nursing, Korean Soc. Nursing Sci. Avocations: art, music, mountain climbing, travel. Office: 3056-6 Daemyung 4 Dong Namgu Daegu 705-718 Republic of Korea Business E-Mail: hykoo@cu.ac.kr.

KOO, JA-WON, medical educator, department chairman; b. Daegu, Kyungsangbuk-do, Republic of Korea, Sept. 27, 1966; s. Min Hae Koo and Joo Hee Kim; m. Hyejin Kwon, Sept. 3, 1993; children: Bonjae, Yoonji. MD, Seoul Nat. U., Republic of Korea, 1991, MS, 1998, PhD, 2004. Cert. Ministry of Health and Social Welfare, Republic of Korea, 1991, Korean Bd. Otolaryngology, Ministry of Health and Social Welfare, 1999. Fellow Seoul Nat. U. Hosp., 1999—2001; rsch. assoc. U. Pitts. Med. Ctr., 2001—02; asst. prof. Seoul Nat. U. Bundang Hosp., Seongnam, Kyunggi-do, 2003—08, chmn., dept. otolaryngology, 2008—; asst. prof. Seoul Nat. U. Coll. Medicine, 2004—08, assoc. prof., 2008—. Sci. com. bd. mem. Korean Soc. Otolaryngology, 2005—07; gen. sec. Korean Balance Soc., Seoul, 2007—; edn. com. bd. mem. Korean Otology Soc., Seoul, 2007—; judge Judging Com. Indsl. Ins., Ministry of Labor, Seoul, 2008—; assoc. editor Korean Jour. Audiology. Recipient Sci. Presentation Hon. award, Korean Balance Soc., 2007; named Excellent Investigator of Yr., 2007—08; Internat. Travel grant, Am. Acad. Otolaryngology-Head and Neck Surgery, 2002. Mem.: Korean Otology Soc., Korean Audiology Soc., Korean Balance Soc., Korean Soc. Otorhinolarynogology-Head and Neck Surgery, Barany Soc., Politzer Soc., Am. Acad. Otolaryngology-Head and Neck Surgery Found. (Alexandria, Va.), Assn. Rsch. Otolaryngology, (Mt. Royal, NJ). Achievements include research in neurotology, vestibular disorder. Office: Seoul Nat Univ Bundang Hosp Bundang-Gu Gumi-Dong 300 463-707 Seongnam Kyunggi-do Republic of Korea Office Fax: 82-31-787-4057. Business E-Mail: jwkoo99@snu.ac.kr, jawonkoo@snubh.org.

KOO, JOHN YING MING, psychiatrist, dermatologist; b. Tokyo, Jan. 9, 1955; arrived in U.S., 1967; s. Kwang Ming Koo and Amy Tsai Ma; m. Nancy Chiang, July 7, 1978; children: Kathie, Jennifer, Jocelyn, Jonathan, Karina. BA in Biochemistry, U. Calif., Berkeley, 1977; MD, Harvard U., 1981. Cert. psychiatry and dermatology. Intern UCLA Ctr. Health Scis., 1981—82; resident in psychiatry UCLA Neuropsychiatric Inst., 1982—85; resident in dermatology U. Calif.-San Francisco Med. Ctr., 1985—88; dir. Psoriasis and Skin Treatment Ctr., U. Calif., San Francisco, 1988—; prof. and vice chmn. dept. dermatology, prof. U. Calif., San Francisco, 1989—. Med. adv. bd. Nat. Psioriasis Found., Portland, Oreg., 1995; cons. in field. Mem. editl. bd.: Jour. Am. Acad. Dermatology, 1994; editor: Dermatology and Psychosomatics, 1999. Scholar Harvard Nat. scholar, Harvard Med. Sch., Boston, 1981. Mem.: Am. Psychiat. Assn., Am. Acad. Dermatology, Assn. for Psychocutaneous Medicine N.Am. (founder). Avocations: philosophy, military history. Office: U Calif San Francisco Psoriasis and Skin Treatment Ctr 515 Spruce St San Francisco CA 94118 Office Fax: 415-502-4126.

KOOI-MOW, SIM, chemistry professor; b. Perak, Malaysia, Dec. 6, 1970; BS in Chemistry, U. Malaya, 1995, PhD, 2001. Sr. lectr. Tunku Abdul Rahman Coll., 2001—04; asst. prof. U. Tunku Abdul Rahman, 2004—09, assoc. prof., dept. head, 2010—. Recipient 42nd IUPAC Young Chemist award, Royal Soc. Chemistry; Sci. and Tech. Rsch. grant, Malaysia Toray Sci. Found., Sci. Fund grant, Ministry of Sci. Tech. and Innovation Malaysia. Mem.: Malaysian Inst. Chemistry. Office: Universiti Tunku Abdul Rahman Faculty Sci Bandar Barat Kampar Perak 31900 Malaysia Office Fax: 6054661676. Business E-Mail: simkm@utar.edu.my.

KOOK, JOONG-KI, biochemist, educator, dentist; b. Gwang-ju, Republic of Korea, June 11, 1967; s. Hong-Sub Kook and Hae-Sim Park; m. Mi-Hyang Jung, Mar. 20, 1993; children: Seo-Hyun, Seo-Lin. BA, Coll. of Dentistry, Chosun U., Gwang-ju, Republic of Korea, 1992; MSc, Seoul Nat. U., 1995, PhD, 1997. Instr. Coll. of Dentistry, Chosun U., Gwang-ju, Republic of Korea, 2000—02, asst. prof., 2003—. Contbr. articles to profl. jours. Grantee, Korean Sci. and Engring. Found., 2001—02, Korea Rsch. Found., 2001, 2002, Korean Sci. and Engring. Found., 2003. Office: Coll Dentistry Chosun Univ Seo-Suk Dong Dong-Gu 375 501-759 Gwangju Republic of Korea Office Fax: 82-62-224-3706. Business E-Mail: jkkook@chosun.ac.kr.

KOOK, YOON-AH, orthodontist, educator; b. Iksan, Republic of Korea, May 16, 1960; s. Chang-ryong Kook and Chung-hee Shin; m. Seon-wha Jin, Jan. 20, 1990; children: Jin-hyeok, Do-hyun. BA in Dentistry, Wonkwang U., 1985; MS in Orthodontics, Wonkwang U., Iksan, 1988, U. So. Calif., LA, 2000; PhD, Chonbuk Nat. U., Chonju, 1995. Dental Lic. Calif., 2000, lic. Orthodontics U.S., 2000, Dental Lic. Seoul, 1985. Capt., mil. dentist South Korean Army, South Korea, Republic of Korea, 1988—91; assoc. prof. Wonkwang U., Iksan, Chonbuk, Republic of Korea, 1992—2000; assoc. prof., chmn. Grad. Sch. of Clin. Dental Sci., Cath. U. of Korea, Seoul, Republic of Korea, 2002—. Author: Textbook in Orthodontics, 1998, OrthodTADs: The Clinical Guide and Atlas, 2007. Grantee, Dept. of Edn., Govt. of South Korea, 1996. Mem.: Korean Dental Assn. (dir. 2006—), Korean Assn. Orthodontics (fin. dir. 2008—). Achievements include patents for Korean type orthodontic archwire (patent pending). Office: Kangnam St Mary's Hosp Dentistry #505 Banpo-Dong Seocho-gu Seoul 137-701 Republic of Korea Office Fax: 82-2-537-2374. E-mail: kook190036@yahoo.com.

KOOP, C. EVERETT (CHARLES EVERETT KOOP), former Surgeon General of the United States, educator; b. Bklyn., Oct. 14, 1916; s. John Everett and Helen (Apel) K.; m. Elizabeth Flanagan, Sept. 19, 1938; children: Allen van Benschoten, Norman Apel, David Charles Everett, Elizabeth. AB, Dartmouth Coll., 1937, DSc (hon.), 1989; MD, Cornell U., 1941; DSc in Medicine, U. Pa., 1947, DSc (hon.), 1990; LLD (hon.), Ea. Bapt. Coll., 1960, Phila. Coll. Osteo. Medicine, 1979, LaSalle Coll., 1983, Colby-Sawyer Coll., 1988, Princeton U., 1989, Hahnemann U., 1989, U. Miami, 1991, U. Cin., 1991; MD (hon.), U. Liverpool, Eng., 1968; LHD (hon.), Wheaton Coll., 1973, Phila. Theol. Sem., 1980, Chgo. Med. Sch., 1988, Brown U., 1990; DSc (hon.), Gwynedd Mercy Coll., 1978, Washington and Jefferson Coll., 1979, Marquette U., 1983, Ea. Mich. U., 1985, N.Y. Med. Coll., 1985, Ball State U., 1987, Kirksville Coll. Osteo. Med., 1988, Albany Med. Coll., 1988, Colby Coll., 1988, Yeshiva U., 1988, Phila. Coll. Pharmacy and Sci., 1988, Baylor Coll. Medicine, 1988, U. Mass., Boston, 1989, Brandeis U., 1990, Northwestern U., 1990, U. New England, 1991; D. Pub. Svc. (hon.), George Washington U., 1991; DPH, Cedar Crest Coll., 1995; D in Humanities, So. Utah U., 1997, LLD, Med. Coll. Pa., 1997. Diplomate Am. Bd. Surgery, Nat. Bd. Med. Examiners. Intern Pa. Hosp., Phila., 1941-42; fellow in surgery U. Pa. Hosp., Phila., 1942-47; fellow in pediat. surgery Children's Hosp., Boston, 1946; surgeon-in-chief Children's Hosp. of Phila., 1948-81; with U. Pa. Sch. Medicine, 1942-85, prof., 1959-85; former dep. asst. sec. for health HHS; surg. gen. of U.S. US Dept. Health & Human Services, 1981-89; former dir. internat. health USPHS, from 1982; chair Safe Kids Nat. Campaign, Washington; dir. Elizabeth De Camp McInery prof. surgery C. Everett Koop Inst. Dartmouth-Hitchkock Med. Ctr., Hanover, NH, 1993—. Cons. USN, 1964—81; sr. scholar C. Everett Koop Inst. at Dartmouth; dir. Ready to Learn Program Carnegie Found., 1993—95; McEnerny prof. surgery Dartmouth Med. Sch. Author: Visible and Palpable Lesions in Children, The Right to Live, The Right to Die, 1976, The Right to Live, The Right to Die, rev. edit., 1980, Smoking: The New Book of Knowledge, 1989; author: (with E. Koop)) Sometimes Mountains Move, 1979; author: (with F. A. Schaeffer)) Whatever Happened to the Human Race?, 1979; author: Koop: The Memoirs of America's

Family Doctor, 1991; author: (with T. Johnson)) Let's Talk, 1992; editor: surgery sect. Jour. Clin. Pediatrics, 1961—64; mem. editl. bd.: Zeitschrift fur Kinderchirugie and Grenzgebiete, 1964—81, editor-in-chief: Jour. Pediatric Surgery, 1965—77, editl. cons.: Japanese Jour. Pediatric Surgery and Medicine, 1970—81, chmn. editorial bd.: PHS Reports, 1982—89, mem. editorial adv. bd.: Tobacco Control: An Internat. Jour.; contbr. publs. in surg. physiology, biomed. ethics, physiology of surg. neonate, tech. advances in pediatric surgery. Bd. dirs., pres. Nat. Health Mus. Inc.; bd. dirs., chmn. sci. adv. com. Biopure; chmn. Patient Med. Edn., 1993—96, Patient Med. Record, Inc., 1997—; Bd. dirs. Med. Assistance Programs, Inc., Brunswick, Ga., Friends Nat. Libr. of Medicine. Decorated chevalier Legion of Honor France, Order Duarte, Sanchez and Mella Dominican Republic, Chevalier French Legion of Honor; recipient medal, City of Marseille, Presbyn. Man of Yr. award, Presbyn. Social Union Phila., 1975, Super Achiever of Yr. award, Phila. chpt. Juvenile Diabetes Found., 1975, Man of Yr. award, Jewish Community Chaplaincy Svc. Phila., 1975, Copernicus medal, Polish Surg. Soc., 1977, Gold medal, Children's Hosp. Phila., 1981, Sec. of Health of Commonwealth of Pa. award, 1981, Thomas Linacre award, Nat. Fedn. Cath. Physicians Guild, 1981, Key to City of St. Louis, 1985, Award of Distinction, Alumni Assn. Cornell U. Med. Coll., 1988, Humanitarian Svc. award, City of Boston, 1989, Harry S. Truman award, City of Independence, Mo., 1990, Daniel Webster award, Dartmouth Coll., 1990, John Wiley Jones Disting. Lectr. award, Rochester Inst. Tech., 1990, NAS Public Welfare medal, 1990, Tyler prize, U. So. Calif., 1991, Albert Schweitzer prize, Johns Hopkins U., 1991, Person of Yr. award, Nat. Hosp. Orgn., 1991, C. Everett Koop Hon. Lectr. medal named in his honor, Anchor & Caduceus Soc., 1991, C. Everett Koop Health Adv. award named in his honor, Am. Soc. for Health Care Mktg. and Pub. Rels., Gustav O. Lienhard award, Inst. Medicine, 1992, Presdl. medal of Freedom, 1995, Heinz Found. award, 1995, Medal of Honor, Am. Cancer Soc., 2000, Presdl. Medal of Freedom; named Hon. Citizen, City of Balt., 1985; scholar Disting. scholar to Carnegie Found. for advancement of teaching. Fellow: ACS, Am. Acad. Pediatrics (William E. Ladd Gold medal), Royal Coll. Physicians and Surgeons of Glasgow (hon.), Royal Coll. Surgeons Eng. (hon.); mem.: AMA, Societé Suisse De Chirurgie Infantile, Deutschen Gesselschaft für Kinderchirugi, Societé Française de Chirurgie Infantile, Assn. Mil. Surgeons U.S. (pres. 1982, 1987, Founders medal), Internat. Soc. Surgery, Brit. Assn. Pediatric Surgeons (Dennis Browne Gold medal), Soc. U. Surgeons, Royal Soc. Medicine, Am. Surg. Assn., Sigma Xi. Office: Dartmouth Coll Dartmouth-Hitchcock Ctr C Everett Koop Inst Hanover NH 03755 *

KOPEC, SCOTT EUGENE, medical educator; b. Passaic, NJ, May 29, 1963; MD, Rush Med. Coll., 1989. Asst. prof. medicine U. Mass.-Meml. Med. Ctr., 1990—. Office: 55 Lake Ave N Worcester MA 01655 Business E-Mail: kopecs@ummhc.org.

KOPECEK, JINDRICH (HENRY KOPECEK), chemist, pharmaceutical scientist, professor; b. Strakonice, Czech Republic, Jan. 27, 1940; s. Jan and Herta Zita (Krombholz) Kopecek; m. Marie Porcari, Aug. 11, 1962 (div. 1984); m. Pavla Hrusková, Apr. 27, 1985. MS in Macromolecular Chemistry, Inst. Chem. Tech., Prague, Czechoslovakia, 1961; PhD in Macromolecular Chemistry, Czechoslovak Acad. Scis., Prague, 1965, DSc in Chemistry, 1990. Rsch. sci. officer Inst. Macromolecular Chemistry, Czechoslovak Acad. Scis., 1965-67, 68-72, head lab. med. polymers, 1972-80, head lab. biodegradable polymers, 1980 88; vis. prof. U. Utah, Salt Lake City, 1986—88, co-dir. Ctr. Controlled Chem. Delivery, 1986—, prof. bioengineering, pharmaceutics & pharm. chemistry, 1989—2002, chair dept. pharmaceutics & pharm. chemistry, 1999—2004, disting. prof. bioengineering, pharmaceutics & pharm. chemistry, 2002—. Mem. com. on new polymers Ministry Health, Czechoslovakia, 1976—86; vis. prof. U. Paris-Nord, 1983, 2000, Acad. Scis. Czech Republic, 1995, 2005, Tokyo Women's Med. U., 1999; chair NIH Biomaterials & Biointerfaces Study Sect., 2003—06, Gordon Rsch. Conf. Drug Carriers in Medicine & Biology, Big Sky, Mont., 2004; Busse lectr. U. Wis., 2006; Disting. H. Morawetz lectr. Bklyn. Poly. U., 2006; hon. prof. Sichuan U., China, 2007; CIMA lectr. U. Minn., 2009. Mem. editl. bd. Biomaterials, 1980—, Critical Reviews in Therapeutic Drug Carrier Systems, 1981—, Jour. Controlled Release, 1984—, Jour. Biomaterials Sci.: Polymer Edit., 1987—, Drug Delivery, 1991—, European Jour. Pharmaceutics & Biopharmaceutics, 1992—, Bioconjugate Chemistry, 1993—, Advanced Drug Delivery Reviews, 2001—, Jour. Drug Delivery Sci. & Tech., 2002—, European Jour. Pharm. Scis., 2002—, Current Drug Delivery, 2004—, Biomacromolecules, 2007—, Macromolecular Biosci., 2009—, Molecular Pharmaceutics, 2010—; contbr. numerous articles to profl. jours. Recipient Disting. Rsch. award, U. Utah, 1993, Clemson award for basic rsch., Soc. Biomaterials/Clemson U., 1995, Millennial Pharm. Scientist award, World Congress Pharm. Scis., 2000, Paul Dawson Biotechnology award, American Assn. Colleges of Pharmacy, 2001, J. Heyrovsky Hon. Medal for Merit in Chem. Scis., Acad. Scis. Czech Republic, 2003, Disting. Internat. Scientist award, Japanese Biomaterials Soc., 2006, Lifetime Achievement award, Jour. Drug Targeting, 2011; fellow Biomaterials Sci. & Engring., Internat. Union Societies of Biomaterials Sci. & Engring., 1999. Fellow: American Inst. Med. & Biol. Engring., American Assn. Pharm. Scientists, Controlled Release Soc. (bd. govs. 1988—91, v.p. 1993—94, pres. 1995—96, Founders award 1999); mem.: AAAS, NAE, American Assn. Cancer Rsch., Czech Learned Soc. (hon.), Biomaterials Soc., American Chem. Soc. Achievements include research in the design, synthesis and characterization of biorecognizable biomedical polymers; patents in field. Office: U Utah Dept Pharm and Pharm Chemistry 20 S 2030 E BPRB Rm 205 Salt Lake City UT 84112-5820 E-mail: jindrich.kopecek@utah.edu. *

KOPECKY, STEPHEN LOUIS, cardiologist; b. San Antonio, May 23, 1954; MD, U. Tex., Houston, 1981. Staff Heart Group San Antonio, 1987—89; cons. dept. internal medicine, divsn. cardiovasc. diseases Mayo Clinic, 1992—. Mem. Acad. Pharm. Physician Investigators, 2002—, academic membership com., 2003—. Recipient Edward C. Rosenow Endowed Professorship Internal Medicine Residency award, Mayo Clinic. Fellow: AMA, ACP, Am. Coll. Cardiology; mem.: Am. Soc. Preventive Cardiology (publs. com. mem. 2010—, bd. mem. 2008—10, sec., treas. 2010—), Am. Bd. Internal Medicine. Office: Mayo Clinic 200 First St SW Rochester MN 55905 Office Fax: 507-266-0228. Business E-Mail: kopecky.stephen@mayo.edu.

KOPELMAN, MICHAEL D., nueropsychiatrist; b. London, Feb. 8, 1950; s. Harry and Joan Margaret Kopelman; m. Sophie J. Thomson, Dec. 23, 1985; 2 children. BA in Psychology and Economics, U. Keele, Eng., 1972; MBBS, U. London, 1978, PhD, 1988. Rschr. to lectr. Inst. Psychiat., London, 1988; sr. lectr. & cons. Charing Cross Med. Sch., London, 1988—89; sr. lectr. to reader neuropsychiat. UMDS Guys & St. Thomas Med. Schs., London, 1989—97; prof. neuropsychiat. Kings Coll., London, 1998—. Co-author: (book) Lishman Organic Psychiatry, 2009; co-editor: Handbook of Memory Disorders, 2002, Forensic Neuropsychology in Practice, 2009; contbr. articles to profl. jour. Recipient Denis Hill prize, Maudsley Hosp., London, 1983. Fellow: Acad. Med. Scis., Royal Coll. Psychiatrists (Rsch. medal 1985), British Psychol. Soc.; mem.: British Acad. Forensic Scis. (pres. 2011—), Internat. Neuropsychiat. Assn. (pres. 2011—), British Neuropsychol. Soc. (pres. 2004—06), Internat. Neuropsychol. Soc. (bd. govs. 1999—2002), Soc. Expert Witnesses, Exptl. Psychology Soc., Memory Disorders Rsch. Soc. Achievements include research in retrograde and anterograde amnesia. Office: Neuropsychiatry and Memory Disorders Clinic South Wing Saint Thomas Hosp London SEI7EH England Office Phone: 442071885396. Office Fax: 442076330061. Business E-Mail: michael.kopelman@kcl.ac.uk.

KOPELMAN, RIMA G., rheumatologist, educator; Studied, Columbia U., NYC, 1977. Diplomate Am. Bd. Internal Medicine, Am. Bd. Internal Medicine-rheumatology. Intern Columbia Presbyn. Med. Ctr., resident internal medicine, 1978—81, fellow rheumatology, 1981—83; asst. prof. medicine-rheumatology Columbia Univ.; with Valley Hosp. Office: Valley Hospital 301 Godwin Ave Midland Park NJ 07432-1544 Office Phone: 201-444-4526.

KOPELOFF, IRIS HOPE, dermatologist; d. Arnold and Marcia Kopeloff; m. Michael Rahmin; children: Samantha, Austin, Gabrielle. BA summa cum laude, Wellesley Coll., Mass., 1985; MD, Mt. Sinai Sch. Medicine, NYC, 1989. With Dermatology Ctr. Ridgewood, NJ. Fellow: Am. Acad. Dermatology; mem.: Phi Beta Kappa. Office: Dermatology Ctr Ridgewood LLC One Sears Dr Paramus NJ 07652 Office Phone: 201-265-2994.

KOPENHAVER, PATRICIA ELLSWORTH, podiatrist; Student, Columbia U., 1950-53; BA, George Washington U., 1954; MA, Columbia U., 1956; Dr. Podiatric Medicine, N.Y. Coll. Podiatric Medicine, 1963, postgrad., 1980; LLD (hon.), Barry U., 1998; MD (hon.), Internat. U. Health Scis. Sch. Medicine, 2001; MD (hon.), Internat. Univ. of the Hlth. Sci., 2001. Diplomate Nat. Bd. Podiatry Examiners. Pvt. practice podiatry, Greenwich, Conn., 1964—, staff podiatrist Havenhealth Care Ctr., Greenwich, 2003—. Mem. staff Laurelton Convalescent Hosp., Greenwich; trustee N.Y. Coll. Podiatric Medicine, 1998. Bd. dirs. Monmouth Opera Guild, 1965; trustee Monmouth Opera Festival, 1966, v.p., 1964; mem. Greenwich Arts Coun.; program chmn. Greenwich Women's Rep. Club, 1983-84, 4th dist. rep., 1984-85, 87—; trustee N.Y. Coll. Podiatric Medicine, 1998—. Recipient Hosp. Fund award for med. research translations ARC, Alumni award of distinction N.Y. Coll. Podiatric Medicine, 1997; scholarship named in her honor N.Y. Coll. Podiatric Medicine, 1997. Mem. AAUW (v.p. 1991, pres. Greenwich br. 1992-94, bd. dirs. 1996), NOW, Conn. Podiatric Med. Assn., Hist. Soc., Asian Soc., Fairfield Podiatry Assn., Am. Assn. Women Podiatrists (founding charter pres. 1969-78), Acad. Podiatry, Am. Podiatry Coun., UN Assn. U.S.A., Acad. Podiatric Medicine (chmn. nominating com. 1981, 1st v.p. 1983-84, chmn. fundraising 1984-85, chmn. women's issues 1985, chmn. cmty. edn. 1989), NY Coll. Podiatry Med. (bd. amb.), Am. Acad. Sports Medicine, Am. Acad. Podiatric Sports Medicine (assoc. 1989), George Washington U. Alumni Assn., Columbia Alumni Assn., Fairfield County Alumni Assn. Columbia U., Coast Soc. Founders Barry U. (treas. 1998), Nat. Fedn. Rep. Women, Bruce Mus., Nature Conservancy, Federated Garden Clubs Conn., St. Mary Ladies Guild, Greenwich Gardeners, Womans' Club (ways and means com. 1989, pres.), English Speaking Union, Soroptimists Internat. Am. (pres. Greenwich br. 1990—, bd. dirs. 1997-98), Inc. (vice chmn. program com. 1985—, regional med. scholarship chmn. 1987, med. scholarship chmn. N.E. region 1988, program dir. 1988—, pres. Greenwich br. 1990-92), Toastmasters, Travel Club (program com. 1984—), Soroptimist (bd. dirs. 1997, 2000—), Greenwich Woman's Club (chair gardeners judges 2001—), Pi Epsilon Chi. Home: 2 Sutton Pl S New York NY 10022-3070 Office: 119 E Putnam Ave # 2 Cos Cob CT 06807-2604

KOPERSKI, NANCI CAROL, legal nurse consultant, women's health nurse; b. Omaha, Sept. 14, 1962; d. William S. Jr. and Ethel A. (Friday) Koperski; divorced. Student, Marquette U.; BSN cum laude, Creighton U., 1984; MBA, MHSA, Ariz. State U. RN, Ariz.; cert. women's health nurse. Staff nurse Phoenix Meml. Hosp., Phoenix Gen. Hosp., Community Hosp., Phoenix, Phoenix Indian Med. Ctr.; clin. care coord. Ahwatukee Foothills Samaritan Health Ctr., 1992—2001; staff nurse Alegent Health, Omaha, 2001—04; legal nurse cons. Omaha, 2004—. Mem. Assn. Women's Health, Obstet. and Neonatal Nurses, Ariz. Nurses Assn., Sigma Theta Tau. Personal E-mail: nancikinaz@aol.com.

KOPF, GEORGE MICHAEL, retired ophthalmologist; b. Chilton, Wis., Oct. 20, 1935; s. George and Mary (Schmid) K.; m. Sandra Mary Nolte, Dec. 29, 1962; children: Karen, Jennifer, Nancy. BS, U. Wis., 1958, MD, 1961. Diplomate Am. Bd. Ophthalmology. Intern Luther Hosp., Eau Claire, Wis., 1961-62; resident Milw. County Hosp., 1962-63, Detroit Gen. Hosp., 1965-68; ophthalmologist pvt. practice, Zanesville, Ohio, 1968—; ret., 1999. Mem. med. staff Bethesda Hosp., Zanesville; mem. med. staff Good Samaritan Med. Ctr., Zanesville, pres., 1978, sec. bd. dirs., 1986-96. Capt. USAF, 1963-65. Fellow ACS, Am. Acad. Ophthalmology; mem. Ohio Ophthalmology Soc. (pres. 1976-77), Muskigum County Acad. Medicine (pres. 1983), Ohio State Med. Assn., Rotary. Republican. Roman Catholic. Avocations: tennis, swimming, hiking, reading, travel. Home: 22030 Longleaf Tr Bonita Springs FL 34135 Personal E-mail: kopfgs@comcast.net.

KOPKA, ANDREAS F. J., anesthesiologist; b. Iburg, Niedersachsen, Germany, June 26, 1963; s. Werner B. and Irmgard B. (Gerbracht) Kopka; m. Sigrun Becker, Aug. 21, 1992; children: Moritz, Max. Grad., Free U. Berlin, 1991, MD, 1992. Cert. in emergency medicine and in anesthesiology. Cons. anaesthetist South Glasgow U. Hosps., Glasgow, Scotland, 2005—; rsch. fellow Western Infirmary, Glasgow, Scotland, 2004. Specialist registrar in anaesthesia North Glasgow U. Hosps., 1999—2004; sr. house officer in anaesthesia Falkirk (Scotland) and Dist. Royal Infirmary, 1998—99; asst. physician in anesthesiology, intensive care, pain therapy and emergency medicine Klinikum Schaumburg, Stadthagen, 1993—98; house officer in surgery Cumberland Royal Infirmary, 1993; ho. officer in medicine Thanet and Dist. Gen. Hosp., Kent, England, 1992—93; house officer Westmorland Gen. Hosp., Kendal, England, 1991—92; rsch. fellow Inst. of Pathology, Berlin, 1988—91; anat. demonstrator Free U. of Berlin, 1987—89; presenter in field. Contbr. articles, abstracts and revs. to sci. jours. Fellow: Royal Coll. Anaesthetists London; mem.: Med. and Dental Def. Union of Scotland, European Soc. Anaesthesiologists, Scottish Soc. Anaesthetists, Glasgow and West of Scotland Soc. Anaesthetists, Clober Golf Club. Achievements include research in simple, yet effective cricoid pressure biofeedback trainer. Personal E-mail: a.kopka@doctors.org.uk.

KOPKE, RICK D., otolaryngologist; b. Boise, Idaho, Jan. 6, 1955; BS, U. Wash., 1977, MD, 1981. Cert. Neurotology Bd., 2004. Staff neurotologist, dir.-basic sci. rsch., co-dir. dept. def. spatial orientation ctr., dept. otolaryngology Naval Med. Ctr., 1996—2004; COO Hough Ear Inst., 2004—05; staff physician VA Med. Ctr., Okla. City, 2004—06, Otologic Med. Clinic Inc., 2004—; CEO Hough Ear Inst., 2005—. Asst. prof. surgery Uniformed Svcs. U. Health Scis., 1998—2004; cons. NASA Neurology IPT Hearing and Balance, 1999—2004; adj. faculty, rsch. mem. Okla. Med. Rsch. Found., 2004—; clin. prof., dept. otorhinolaryngology U. Okla. Health Scis. Ctr., 2004—; adj. clin. prof. surgery Okla. State U. Ctr. Health Scis., 2009—; with leading rsch. team Inner Ear Biology, 2011—. Contbr. to profl. publs. Decorated Legion Merit award US Army, Meritorious Svc. medal, Army Commendation medal, Navy-Marine Commendation medal US Navy; recipient Edmond Prince Fowler award, Triological Soc.; Tng. fellowship, Albert Einstein Coll. Medicine, Neurotology & Neurobiology, 1994—96. Avocations: fly fishing, hiking, skiing. Office: 3400 NW 56th St Oklahoma City OK 73112 Office Phone: 405-917-1270. Business E-Mail: rkopke@houghear.org.

KOPLAN, JEFFREY POWELL, academic administrator, epidemiologist; b. Boston, Jan. 3, 1945; s. Samuel R. and Kate G. K.; m. Carol R. Bassuk, May 18, 1969; children: Adam, Kate BA, Yale Coll., 1966; postgrad., Tufts U., 1966-68; MD, Mount Sinai Sch. Medicine, NYC, 1970; M.P.H., Harvard U., 1978. Diplomate Am. Bd. Internal Medicine, Am. Bd. Preventive Medicine. Intern, resident Montefiore Hosp. and Med. Ctr., Bronx, NY, 1970-72; epidemic intelligence service officer Centers for Disease Control & Prevention, US Dept. Health & Human Services, Atlanta, 1972-74; resident Stanford U. Hosp, Calif., 1974-75; med. epidemiologist Calif. State Dept. Health, Berkeley, 1975, Caribbean Epidemiology Ctr., Port of Spain, 1975-77; med. officer Office of Program Planning Centers for Disease Control & Prevention, US Dept. Health & Human Services, Atlanta, 1978-82, asst. dir. pub. health practice, 1982-88; dir. Nat. Ctr. Chronic Disease Prevention and Health Promotion, Atlanta, 1989-94; asst. surgeon gen. US Dept. Health & Human Services, Rockville, 1989-94, dir. Centers for Disease Control & Prevention Atlanta, 1998—2002; exec. v.p., dir. Prudential Ctr. for Health Care Rsch., Atlanta, 1994-95, pres., 1995-98; v.p. for acad. health affairs, global health Emory U., Atlanta, 2002—08, dir. Emory Global Health Inst., 2002—. Contbr. articles to profl. jours. With USPHS, 1970-94. Recipient Order of Bifurcated Needle WHO, 1979; Saul Horowitz award Mt. Sinai Sch. Medicine, 1983; Commendation medal USPHS, 1984 Fellow ACP, Am. Coll. Epidemiology; mem. Assn. Tchrs. Preventive Medicine, Am. Pub. Health Assn., Soc. Med. Decision Making, Inst. Med. Office: Emory Global Health Inst Emory Univ MS 1599 001 1AH 1599 Clifton Rd NE Ste 6101 Atlanta GA 30322-4250

KÖPP, WERNER, internist, psychoanalyst, physician; b. Bad Kissingen, Germany, Nov. 19, 1949; s. Hans Dieter Köpp and Erika Sporer. Diplomate Free U., Berlin, 1975. Head eating disorders dept. Free U. Berlin, 1994—2002; psychoanalyst pvt. practice Berlin, 2002—. Assoc. prof. U. Hop. Charite, Berlin. Author: Inpatient Psychotherapy (Christina Barz Rsch. award, 2000). Recipient Christina Barz Rsch. prize, German Soc. Sci. Founds., 2000. Mem.: German Psychoanalytic Soc. Achievements include research in inpatient psychotherapy of eating disorders; role of leptin in eating disorders; training problems in psychotherapy education. Office: Maassenstr Berlin 10777 Germany

KOPPEL, AUDREY FEILER, electrologist, educator; b. NYC, Sept. 25, 1944; d. Jules Eugene and Lee (Gibel) Feiler; m. Mark Alyn Koppel, May 28, 1967; children: Jason, Seth. BA, Bklyn. Coll., 1972; diploma in electrolysis, Hoffman Inst., 1975; post grad., Kree Inst., 1980, George Washington U., 1984, Essex C. C., 1984. Cert. corrective cosmetics paramedical tng. program Dermablend Corp. for Corrective Cosmetics, in paramedical skin care Dermablend Corp. for Corrective Cosmetics, in advanced aesthetics paramedical skin care and camouflage application, lic. esthetician cosmetologist, realtor N.J., electrolysis N.J., 2005, nat. bd. cert. electrolysis 1985. Electrologist, Bklyn., 1976, Glemby Internat., NYC, 1976—78, Island Electrolysis, Manhasset, NY, 1982—84; registrar, supr. instr. Kree Inst., NYC, 1978—82; pres. North Shore Electrolysis, Manhasset, 1982—84; dir., electrologist Bklyn. Studio, 1982—; pres. Ray Internat., 1986—. Editor, author: pamphlet Glossary for Electrolysis, 1985; contbr. articles to profl. jours. Active Boy Scouts Am., 1977—84; chmn. hosp. and med. coms. Share, 1993—94; gov. Corzine Electrolojist Adv. Bd., 2008, 2010—11; v.p. Electrolysis Adv. Com. Gov. Christy, NJ. Mem.: Aesthetics Internat. Assn., Soc. Clin. and Med. Electrologists, Internat. Guild of Electrologists (Merit award 1978), N.Y. Electrolysis Assn. (corr. sec. 1983—85, pres. 1985—90, bd. trustee 1990—94, advisor 1990—94), Nat. Esthetic Rehab. Assn., Am. Electrology Assn. (v.p. 1984—, continuing edn. coord. 1985, chmn. pub. rels. com. 1989—, v.p. govs. adv. com. 2009—), U.S. Power Squadron (flag lt.), Bklyn. Yacht Club (v.p. ladies aux. 1989—90, pres. 1990—94). Democrat. Jewish. Avocations: boating, swimming, music. Office: Bklyn Studio of Electrolysis 2380 Ocean Ave Brooklyn NY 11229 Mailing: 83 Peasley Dr Marlboro NJ 07746 Office: Sunset Commons Ste 204 3200 Sunset Ave Ocean NJ 07712 Office Phone: 732-996-3586. Personal E-mail: audrey@koppel.net, ridhair@koppel.net.

KOPPLE, JOEL D., medical educator, researcher; s. Louis A. and Evelyn I. Kopple; m. Madelynn G. Kopple; children: David, Michael, Deborah, Joshua. MD, Northwestern U., 1958, U. Ill., 1962; Doctorate (hon.), P.J. Sfarik U., Kosice, Slovak Republic, 1995, U. Szeged, Hungary, 2002, U. Auvergne, Clermont-Ferrand, France, 2010. Diplomate Am. Bd. Internal Medicine, 1969, subspecialty of nephrology

Am. Bd. Internal Medicine, 1974, clin. nutrition Am. Bd. Nutrition, 1980, cert. specialist in clin. hypertension Am. Soc. Hypertension, 2011. Asst. prof. medicine, 1969—73; asst. prof. medicine, pub. health, 1973—76; assoc. prof. UCLA Sch. Medicine and Pub. Health, 1976—78; prof. medicine and pub. health UCLA Sch. Medicine, Torrance, Calif., 1978—; med. investigator VA Wadsworth Med. Ctr., LA, 1976—81; chief divsn. nephrology and hypertension Harbor-UCLA Med. Ctr., Torrance, 1982—2007. Co-editor: (book) Nutritional Management of Renal Disease; contbr. articles 470 profl. sci. jours. Pres. Nat. Kidney Found., 1998—2000, Coun. Am. Kidney Socs., 1998—99, Am. Soc. for Parenteral and Enteral Nutrition, 1990—91, Internat. Soc. for Renal Nutrition and Metabolism, 1991—94, Internat. Fedn. Kidney Foundations, 2000—03; mem. Am. Bd. Nutrition, 1984—90. Recipient David M. Hume Meml. award, Nat. Kidney Found., 1983, Ann. Joel D. Kopple award, 2001—, Internat. Fedn. Kidney Found., 2010—, E.V. McCollum award, Louis Pasteur medal and award, U. Strasbourg, France, 1988, Thomas Addis medal, Interna. Soc. Renal Nutrition & Metabolism, 1996, Robert H. Herman award, Am. Soc. Clin. Nutrition, 1996, 2004, Malpighi medal, U. Messina, Italy, 2000, Sandor Koranyi award, Hungarian Soc. Nephrology, 2005, Belding H. Scribner award, Am. Soc. Nephrology, 2006, Lifetime Achievement award, Ann. Dialysis Conf., 2007. Office: Harbor-UCLA Medical Center 1000 W Carson St Box 406 Torrance CA 90509 Office Phone: 310-222-3891. Office Fax: 310-782-1837. Business E-Mail: jkopple@labiomed.org.

KOPROWSKI, HILARY, microbiologist, educator; b. Warsaw; s. Pawel and Sonia (Berland) Koprowski; m. Irena Grasberg; children: Claude Eugene, Christopher Dorian. BA, Nikolaj Rej Gymnasium of Luth. Congregation, Warsaw; MD, U. Warsaw; grad., Warsaw Conservatory Music and Santa Cecilia Acad., Rome; DSc (hon.), Ludwig-Maximilian U., Munich, Widener Coll.; D in Medicine and Surgery, U. Helsinki, Finland; MD (hon.), U. Uppsala, Sweden; LittD (hon.), Thomas Jefferson U.; DMS (hon.), U. Lublin, Poland, Univ. Coll. Dublin, U. Poznan, Poland, U. Warsaw Acad. Medicine, La Salle U. Rsch. asst. dept. exptl. and gen. pathology U. Warsaw, 1936—39; staff Yellow Fever Rsch. Svc., Rio de Janeiro, 1940—44; staff rsch. divsn. Am. Cyanamid Co., 1944—46; asst. dir. viral and rickettsial rsch. Lederle Lab., Pearl River, NY, 1946—57; dir. Wistar Inst., Phila., 1957—91, prof., 1957—93, prof. laureate, 1993—; Wistar Inst. prof. of rsch. medicine U. Pa., 1957—; prof. microbiology and immunology Thomas Jefferson U., Phila., 1992—, vice chmn. dept. cancer biology, 2008—; dir. Ctr. Neurovirology, Biotech. Found. Labs., 1992—. Cons. WHO, 1950—; mem. microbiology study sect. NIH, 1956—60; mem. PAHO; mem. adv. com. Nat. Multiple Sclerosis Soc., 1970—78; mem. immunobiology adv. com. NIH, USPHS, 1975—76; mem. bd. sci. counselors divsn. cancer etiology Nat. Cancer Inst., 1982—86, chmn., 1987—90; mem. biol. response modifiers program deicision network com. NIH, 1985—87. Co-editor: Methods in Virology, Viruses and Immunity, Current Topics in Microbiology and Immunology, 1965—. Hon. trustee Kosciuszko Found., 1993—. Decorated commandeur Order du Mérite pour la Rsch. et l'Invention, chevalier Order Royal De Lion Belgium, officer Order of the Polish Republic, comdr. Order of The Lion of Finland, chevalier Legion d'honneur (France), Greater Order of Merit Poland; recipient Alvarenga prize, Coll. Physicians Phila., 1959, Alfred Jurzykowski Found. Polish Millenium prize, 1966, Felix Wankel Tierschutz prize, 1979, Phila. Cancer Rsch. award, Phila. Cancer Club, 1989, San Marino award, 1989, Nicolaus Copernicus medal, Polish Acad. Scis., 1989, The Phila. award, 1990, John Scott award, 1990, Andrzeja Drawicza award, Pres. of Poland, 2005, Lifetime Achievement award, Monte Jade Sci. and Tech. Assn. Mid-Atlantic, Alexander von Humboldt Sr. U.S. Scientist award, Inglis House Disability Awareness award, 1997, Gt. Order of Merit & Star award, Pres. of Poland, 1998, Grand Cross Order of Polonia Restituta, 2007, Mid-Atlantic Lifetime Achievement award, Monte Jade Sci. & Tech. Assn., 2001, Order of Smile, Poland, 2002, Pioneer in NeuroVirology award, Soc. NeuroVirology, 2004, Albert B. Sabin Gold medal, 2007, Strittmatter Outstanding Leadership award, Phila. County Med. Soc., 2008; named hon. trustee, Kosciuszko Found., 1993; scholar Fulbright scholar, Max Planck Inst. für Verhaltensphysiologie, Seewiesen, Fed. Republic Germany, 1971. Fellow: AAAS, Phila. Coll. Physicians, N.Y. Acad. Medicine; mem.: NAS, N.Y. Acad. Scis. (pres. 1959, trustee 1960—72), Finnish Acad. Arts and Scis., Russian Acad. Med. Scis., Polish Acad. Scis., Yugoslavian Acad. Scis., Nat. Acad. Arts and Scis., Order of the Smile. Achievements include development of first oral polio vaccine which ultimately led to elimination in 1992 of polio from the Americas; new rabies vaccine for humans, reducing the number of injections and of oral vaccine in bait for immunization of wildlife; research in mechanism of damage of cells in brain in neurotropic virus infection; development of first monoclonal antibody for treatment and cure of colorectal cancer. Office: Thomas Jefferson Univ Dept Cancer Biology JAH-M85 1020 Locust St Philadelphia PA 19107 Home Phone: 610-649-1327; Office Phone: 215-503-4761. Business E-Mail: hilary.koprowski@jefferson.edu.

KOPTAGEL-ILAL, GÜNSEL, psychiatrist, educator; b. Istanbul, Turkey, Oct. 1, 1933; d. Baha and Hikmet Koptagel; m. Gürkan Ilal, Nov. 27, 1973. BA, Robert Coll., Istanbul, Turkey, 1953; MD, Istanbul U., 1959. Lic. psychiatrist Istanbul U. and Free U. Berlin, 1964. Asst. doctor U. Istanbul Psychiatry Clinic, 1959—60, Neuropsychiatry Clinic Free U. Berlin, 1960—64; psychoanalysis training Berlin Psychoanalytic Inst., 1960—64, specialist, 1964—68; asst. prof. U. Istanbul Psychiatry Clinic, 1968—72, docent, 1972; prof. psychiatry Istanbul U. Cerrahpasa Med. Faculty, 1972, head psychosomatic and psychotherapy divsn., 1974—2000, dir. dept. psychiatry, 1982—83. Guest prof. psychosomatic dept. Giessen U., Germany, 1985—87; guest prof. Kassel U., Germany, 1987—88. Contbr. over 274 articles to profl. jours. Del. Turkey human rights divsn. com. prevention torture Coun. Europe, Strasbourg, France, 2002—06. Recipient Fgn. Publ. award, Turkish Soc. Psychiat. Health, 1984, Rsch. Work award, Istanbul U., 1999, 2000, 2000. Mem.: German Coll. Psychosomatic Medicine, Turkish Acad. Medicine, Turkish Soc. History Medicine, German Psychoanalytic Soc., Internat. Coll. Psychosomatic Medicine (v.p. 1979—2000), Turkish Neuro-Psychiatry Assn. (v.p. 1975—83), Turkish Psychosomatic and Psychotherapie Soc. (pres. 1978—2009), Internat. Soc. Psychopathology of Expression and Art-Therapy (vice chmn. 1970—2000). Avocations: music, literature, painting, sports. Home: Ebekizi SokNo:14 D:9 Ebekizi Apt Sisli Istanbul 34363 Turkey Home Fax: +90-212-225 64 29. Personal E-mail: gkoptagel@superonline.com.

KORETZKY, GARY ALAN, rheumatologist, educator; b. Orange, NJ, May 5, 1956; MD, U. Pa., 1984, PhD in immunology. Cert. Internal Medicine, 1987, Pediatric Rheumatology, 1992. Resident in medicine U. Calif., San Francisco, 1984—87, fellow in rheumatology, 1987; prof. U. Iowa, 1991—99, Kelting prof. rheumatology; dir. signal transduction and investigator Abramson Family Cancer Rsch. Inst., U. Pa., Phila., 1999—; prof. pathology and lab. medicine U. Pa., Phila., 1999—2004, Leonard Jarett prof. pathology and lab. medicine, 2004—, chief rheumatology divsn., 2005—, vice chair rsch. and chief sci. officer, dept. medicine, 2008—. Exec. com. U. Pa. Cancer Ctr., Phila.; editor in chief Immunological Reviews. Fellow: AAAS; mem.: Am. Assn. Physicians, Inst. Medicine, Am. Soc. Clin. Investigation (pres. 2000—01). Office: 3400 Civic Ctr Blvd Ste 300 S Philadelphia PA 19104 E-mail: koretzky@mail.med.upenn.edu.

KORFALI, ENDER, neurosurgeon, educator; b. Ankara, Turkey, Oct. 30, 1945; MD, Hacettepe U., 1969. Chmn. Uludag U., 1976, prof., physician, 1978—. Mem.: CNS, AANS. Avocation: skiing. Office: Uludag University GORUKLE Campus Bursa 16059 Turkey Office Fax: 902244429263. Business E-Mail: ekorfali@uludag.edu.tr.

KORHONEN, PÄIVI ELINA, physician; b. Harjavalta, Oct. 3, 1965; MD, U. Tampere, 1991; PhD, U. Turku, 2009. Specialist internal medicine Ctrl. Satakunta Health Fedn. Municipalities, 2004—. Clin. advisor U. Turku, 2010. Fellow: Internat. Coll. Angiology. Avocations: literature, sports. Home: Jokikatu 3 Harjavalta Satakunta 29200 Finland Personal E-mail: paivi.e.korhonen@fimnet.fi.

KORIS, MARK JOSEPH, surgeon; b. Elizabeth, NJ, Aug. 19, 1953; MD, Case Western Res. U., 1982. Upper extremity surgeon, orthop. surgeon, 1988—2007. Recipient Ewald prize, Elbow Soc. Mem.: MMS, ABOS, Am. Assn. Orthop. Surgeons. Achievements include development of cemented total elbow removal hardware. Avocations: snowboarding, skiing, fishing. Home: 11 Heath Hill St Brookline MA 02445 Personal E-mail: mkoris@partners.org.

KORISTKOVA, BLANKA, pharmacist; b. Ostrava, Czech Republic, Aug. 9, 1972; PharmD, Charles U. Prague, Czech Republic, 1995; PhD, Palacky U., Olomouc, Czech Republic, 2001. Pharmacist Hosp. Pharmacy, U. Hosp., Czech Republic, 1995—96; jr. lectr. Med. Faculty, U. Ostrava, Czech Republic, 2011; clin. pharmacist Dept. Clin. Phramacology, U. Hosp., Ostrava, Czech Republic, 1995—. Master: Drug Utilization Rsch. Group Czech Republic; mem.: Czech Soc. Clin. Pharmacology, Czech Soc. Exptl. & Clin. Pharmacology & Toxicology. Office: Dept Clin Pharmacol University Hosp Trida 17 listopadu 1790 Ostrava Poruba 70852 Czech Republic Business E-Mail: blanka.koristkova@seznam.cz.

KORMOS, ROBERT L., surgeon; BA in Psychology, U. We. Ont., Can.; MD, U. We. Ont., 1976. Resident neurosurgery, gen. surgery and cardiovasc. surgery Toronto Gen. Hosp., Canada, clin. fellow cardiovasc. surgery; fellow Univ. of Pitts. Med. Sch.; dir. artificial heart program Univ. Pitts. Med.Ctr., co-dir. heart transplantation; hosp. afilliations include Magee-Womens Hosp. of UPMC, Children's Hosp. of Pitts. of UPMC, UPMC Passavant, UPMC Presbyterian; med. dir. Vital Engring., Alberta, Canada. Co-author: (publs.) Successful cidofovir treatment in an adult heart transplant recipient with severe adenovirus pneumonia, 2008, Long-term outcome of lung and heart-lung transplantation for idiopathic pulmonary arterial hypertension, 2008, Prolonged use of right ventricular assist device for refractory graft failure following orthotopic heart transplantation, 2009. Recipient President's award, Internat. Soc. for Heart and Lung Transplantation, 1987; named one of America's Top Doctors, Castle Connolly Med., Ltd., 2001. Mem.: Internat. Soc. for Heart and Lung Transplantation (pres. 1999—2000), Soc. for Thoracic Surgeons Workforce on End-Stage Cardiopulmonary Disease (chair), Am. Soc. for Thoracic Surgeons (bd. dirs.). Office: University of Pittsburgh Medical Center Department of Cardiothoracic Surgery Ste 5B 200 Lothrop St Pittsburgh PA 15213 Office Phone: 412-648-6200.

KORN, DAVID, pathologist, educator; b. Providence, Mar. 5, 1933; s. Solomon and Claire (Liebman) Korn; m. Phoebe Richter, June 9, 1955 (div. Dec. 1993); 1 adopted child, Joanna M. Fiduccia children: Stephen James, Daniel Clair, Michael Philip; m. Carol Scheman, Dec. 24, 1997. BA, Harvard U., 1954, MD, 1959. Intern Mass. Gen. Hosp., Boston, 1959—60, resident in Pathology, 1960—61; rsch. assoc. NIH, 1961—63, asst. pathologist, 1963—68; mem. staff Lab. Biochem. Pharmacology; prof. pathology Sch. Medicine, Stanford (Calif.) U., 1968—97, chmn. dept. pathology Sch. Medicine, 1968—84; physician-in-chief pathology Stanford Hosp., 1968—84, dean Sch. Medicine, 1984—85, v.p., dean, 1986—95; cons. pathology Palo Alto VA Hosp., 1968—84; sr. v.p. biomed. and health scis. rsch. Assn. Am. Med. Colls., 1997—. Sr. surgeon USPHS, 1961—66; cell biology study sect. NIH, 1973—77, chmn., 1976—77; bd. sci. counselors, divsn. cancer biology and diagnosis Nat. Cancer Inst., 1977—82, chmn., 1980—82; chair Nat. Cancer Adv. Bd., 1984—91; disting. scholar-in-residence Assn. Am. Med. Colls., 1995—97; sr. fellow sci. and health policy Assn. Acad. Health Ctrs., 1995—97. Mem. editl. bd. Human Pathology, 1969—74, assoc. editor, 1974—88, mem. editl. bd. Jour. Biol. Chemistry, 1973—79. Founding mem., chmn. bd. Calif. Transplant Donor Network, 1987—95. Recipient Disting. Young Scientist award, Md. Acad. Sci., 1967. Fellow: AAAS, Am. Soc. Clin. Pathology (hon.); mem.: Inst. Medicine, Assn. Pathology Chmn. (Disting. Svc. award 1999), Fedn. Am. Soc. Exptl. Biology (bd. dirs., exec. com.), Am. Soc. Investigative Pathology (Gold-headed Cane award 2003), Am. Soc. Biochemistry and Molecular Biology. Office: AAMC 2450 N St NW Washington DC 20037-1167 Home: 151 Beacon St Apt 4 Boston MA 02116-1406 Business E-Mail: dkom@aamc.org.

KORNBERG, ROGER DAVID, biochemist, structural biologist; b. St. Louis, Apr. 24, 1947; s. Arthur and Sylvy Ruth (Levy) Kornberg; m. Yahli Deborah Lorch, Sept. 18, 1984; children: Guy, Maya, Gil. BS in Chemistry, Harvard U., Cambridge, Mass., 1967; PhD in Chemistry, Stanford U., Calif., 1972. Postdoc. fellow MRC Lab. Molecular Biology, Cambridge, England, 1972—73, jr. fellow, 1973—74, mem. sci. staff, 1974-75; asst. prof. biol. chemistry Harvard Med. Sch., 1976-77; prof. structural biology Stanford U. Sch. Medicine, 1978—, chmn. dept., 1984-92, Winzer prof. structural biology. Co-chmn. Skolkovo Sci. and Technical Coun., 2010—. Contbr. articles to profl. jours. Recipient Eli Lilly award, 1981, Passano award, 1982, Ciba-Drew award, 1990, Harvey prize, Technion-Israel Inst. Tech., 1997, Gairdner Found. Internat. award, 2000, Hoppe-Seyler award, Soc. Biochemistry & Molecular Biology, Germany, 2001, Welch Found. award in chemistry, 2001, Merck award, Am. Soc. Biochemistry & Molecular Biology, 2002, Pasarow award in cancer rsch., 2003, Massry prize, 2003, GM Cancer Rsch. award, 2005, Dickson prize, U. Pitts., 2006, Nobel prize in chemistry, 2006, Louisa Gross Horwitz prize, Columbia U., 2006. Mem.: NAS, European Molecular Biology Orgn. (fgn. assoc.), Am. Acad. Arts & Scis., Japanese Biochem. Soc. (hon.). Office: Stanford U Dept Structural Biology Fairchild Bldg 1st Fl 299 Campus Dr Stanford CA 94305-5126 E-mail: kornberg@stanford.edu. *

KORNBLUTH, IRA DAVID, medical association administrator; b. Arlington, Va., Sept. 24, 1971; MA in Med. Scis., Boston U., 1994; MD, Jefferson Med. Coll., 1999. Med. dir. Smart Pain Mgmt., 2008—. Mem.: ABPMR. Office: 826 Washington Rd Ste 112 Westminster MD 21157 Office Fax: 866-605-3654. Personal E-mail: drira@hotmail.com.

KORNER, ANTHONY JAMES, psychiatrist; b. London, Apr. 25, 1955; MBBS with honors, U. Sydney, 1978, MS in Psychotherapy, 1999. Psychiatrist, sr. staff psychiatrist Sydney West Area Health Svc., 1995—2011; lectr. U. Sydney, Westmead, 1995—2004, sr. clin. lectr., 2005—11, acting dir., Westmead Psychotherapy Program, 2010—. Chmn., organizing com. 6th World Congress for Psychotherapy, World Coun. Psychotherapy, 2003—11; mem. Borderline Personality Guideline Devel. Com. Nat. Health and Med. Rsch. Coun., 2011—. Recipient Inaugural Ann. Writer's award, Jour. Psychotherapy in Australia, 2006. Fellow: Royal Australian and New Zealand Coll. Psychiatry; mem.: Australian and New Zealand Assn. Psychotherapy, NSW RANZCP Sect. Psychotherapy Com., World Coun. Psychotherapy (exec. bd. mem.). Avocations: music, piano, flute, theater, acting. Office: Mental Health Scis Ctr PO Box 7118 Locked Parramatta Sydney NSW 2124 Australia Office Fax: 02 98403572. Business E-Mail: anthony_komer@wsahs.nsw.gov.au.

KORNETSKY, CONAN, pharmacology professor; b. Portland, Maine, Feb. 9, 1926; BA, U. Maine, Orono, 1948; grad., U. Ky., 1952, PhD. Rsch. psychologist USPHS Hosp., Rsch. Dept., Lexington, Ky., 1948—52; rsch. scientist Nat. Inst. Methal Health, 1952—59; prof. psychiatry & pharmacology Boston U. Sch. Medicine, 1959—. Recipient Disting. Alumnus award, Dept. Psychology, U. Ky., 1997—98, Bernard Lown Alumni Humanitarian award, U. Maine Alumni Assn., 2011. Fellow: APA, AAAS, Am. Coll. Neuropharmacolgy; mem.: Coll. Problems Drug Dependence (Nathan Eddy Meml. Award, Mentoring award), Am. Am. Soc. Pharmacology and Exptl. Therapeutics. Avocations: skiing, bicycling, tennis. Office: 80 E Concord St R-620 Boston MA 02118 Office Fax: 617-638-5254. Business E-Mail: ckornets@bu.edu.

KORNGUTH, STEVEN EDWARD, biologist; b. NYC, Dec. 1, 1935; s. Eugene Irving and Helen (Pardes) K.; m. Margaret Livens, Aug. 29, 1958; children: Ingrid Laura Taylor, David Gregory. BA, Columbia Coll., 1957; PhD, U. Wis., 1961. Rschr. Psychiat. Inst. Columbia U., NYC, 1961-62; from asst. prof. to prof. neurology and physiol. chmn. U. Wis., Madison, 1963-98; dir. neurol. scis. NSF, Washington, 1981-83; dir. Biol. Scis. Inst. Advanced Tech., prof. pharmacy U. Tex., Austin, 1985—. Mem. Army Sci. Bd. Editor: Prof. Scholar, 1991; contbr. over 110 articles to profl. jours.; patentee in field. Avocations: piano, bicycling, reading. Business E-Mail: steve_kornguth@iat.utexas.edu.

KORNSTEIN, ANDREW, plastic surgeon; Grad. in Biochemical Genetics magna cum laude, U. Pa., 1982; MD, Cornell U. Diplomate Am. Bd. Plastic Surgery. Resident gen. surgery and plastic surgery Lukes- Roosevelt Hosp. Ctr., fellow aesthetic plastic surgery, attending physician divsn. of plastic and reconstructive surgery; assoc. adj. surgeon dept. of gen. plastic surgery NY Eye and Ear Infirmary. Recipient George S. Meister award, 1986, Golden Cannula award. Fellow: NIH; mem.: Am. Soc. for Aesthetic Plastic Surgery, Technique-Lipoplasty Soc. of North Am., Phi Beta Kappa. Office: 1050 Fifth Ave New York NY 10028 Office Phone: 212-987-1300.

KOROLIJA, DRAGAN, surgeon; b. Zadar, Croatia, Feb. 26, 1964; m. Snjezana Tadic-Korolija, June 25, 1988. MD, Med. Sch., Zagreb, Croatia, 1988, PhD, 2001. Cert. in gen. surgery Ministry of Health, Zagreb, 1995. Cons. surgeon Gen. Hosp. Zabok, Croatia, 1997—2001, Clin. Hosp. Ctr. Zagreb, Croatia, 2001—. Dir. laparoscopic ventral hernia repair postgraduate course Med. Sch. Zagreb, 2005—06. Pres. city dist. Zagreb City Coun., 2005—06. Mem.: European Assn. Endoscopic Surgery. Avocations: swimming, tennis. Home: Bleiweisova 24 Zagreb 10 000 Croatia Office: Clin Hosp Ctr Zagreb Kispaticeva 12 Zagreb Croatia Home Fax: 00385 21 533031. Personal E-mail: dragan.korolija-mominic@zg.t-com.hr.

KOROLKIEWICZ, KONSTANTY ZBIGNIEW, retired pharmacologist; b. Wilno, Poland, Nov. 15, 1927; s. Konstanty and Aleksandra (Wertynska) Korolkiewicz; m. Izabella Maria Majorkiewicz, Oct. 9, 1966; 1 child, Roman Pawel. MD, Med. U., Gdansk, Poland, 1952, PhD, 1961. Diplomate internal diseases, clin. pharmacology. Asst. dept. pharmacology Med. U., Gdansk, 1957-58, lectr. pharmacology, 1958-68, asst. prof. dept. pharmacology, 1968-77, prof. dept. pharmacology, 1977—98, prorector sci. and rsch., 1980—83; ret., 1998. Sci. cons. Pharm. Works, Starogar-Gdanski, 1961—2002. Contbr. articles to profl. jours. Maj. Med. Army Hosp., 1952—57. Decorated Disting. Cross Polonia Restituta; recipient award, Ministry Health and Social Affairs, 1994. Mem.: Sci. Soc. Gdansk, Polish Physiol. Soc., Polish Pharmacological Soc. Avocation: yachting. Office Phone: 48 58 349 1815. Personal E-mail: kokor@amg.gda.pl. Business E-Mail: kokor@umed.edu.pl.

KORONES, SHELDON BERNARR, retired pediatrician, educator; b. NYC, Apr. 26, 1924; s. Samuel Aaron and Estelle (Goldstein) K.; m. Judith Ann Kest, June 15, 1952; children: David N., Susan Gifford. BS, U. Tenn., 1944; MD, U. Tenn., Memphis, 1947. Diplomate Am. Bd. Pediatrics, Am. Bd. Neonatal/Perinatal Medicine. Intern Boston City Hosp., 1948-49; asst. resident pediat. Babies Hosp., NYC, 1950-51, 53-54; asst. in pathology Children's Med. Ctr., Boston, 1949-50; asst. clin. prof. pediat. U. Tenn., 1961-68, assoc. prof. newborn svcs. dept. pediats., 1968-72, prof. pediats., dir. newborn svcs., 1972-89, prof. ob-gyn., 1982-89, alumni disting. svc. prof. pediat. ob-gyn., 1989—2009. Project dir., prin. investigator collaborative perinatal project NIH, Bethesda, 1960-75; dir. newborn ctr. Regional Med. Ctr. Memphis, 1968-2004; perinatal adv. com. State Tenn., 1974—, chmn. subcom. standards regionalization perinatal care, 1975—, subcom. liaison, legis. funding and cmty. edn., 1979—, subcom. perinatal transp., 1979-86, gov.'s task force prevention mental retardation, 1980-83, gov.'s task force healthy children, 1983-86, subcom. follow-up, 1983-86, subcom. evaluation, 1983-86, subcom. med. home., 1983-86, task force child devel. standards dept. human svcs., 1984-86; med. svc. adv. com. March of Dimes, 1974-78, edn. adv. com., 1979-1987, exec. com. west Tenn. chpt., 1986-92; bd. examiner oral exams maternal and fetal medicine Am. Bd. Ob-Gyn., Chgo., 1975; study panel bur. med. devices diagnostic products FDA, 1976-93; prin. investigator Nat. Heart, Lung, Blood Inst., Bethesda, Md., 1976-83, Coop. Multictr. Network Neonatal Intensive Care Rsch., Bethesda, 1986-2001; profl. edn. rsch. com. Am. Lung Assn. Tenn., 1977-81; pres.-elect med. staff Regional Med. Ctr. Memphis, 1982-83, pres. 1983-84; adv. bd. Office Drug Policy, Memphis, 1991; subcom. ob-gyn. newborn svcs. TLC Family Care Healthplan, Memphis, 1994—; mem. perinatal com. devel. clin. practice guidelines TennCare, First Mental Health, Inc., 1996; spkr., cons. in field. Author: High Risk Newborn Infants: The Basis for Intensive Nursing Care, 1972, 4th edit., 1986, Spanish translation, 1979, Russian translation, 1981; co-author: Neonatal Decision Making, 1993; author, co-author: (chpts.) Synopsis of Pediatrics, 1963, 6th edit., 1984, Resuscitation of the Newborn, 3d edit., 1973, Iatrogenic Problems in Neonatal Intensive Care, 1976, Current Diagnosis, 1977, Standards and Recommendations for Hospital Care of Newborn Infants, 6th edit., 1977, Current Therapy in Obstetrics and Gynecology, 1980, 83, Assisted Ventilation of the Newborn, 1981, The Use of Computers in Perinatal Medicine, 1982, Parent-Baby Attachment in Premature Infants, 1983, Infant Stress under Intensive Care, 1985, Gynecology and Obstetrics, Vol. 2, 1985, Teratogen Update: Environmentally Induced Birth Defect Risks, 1986, Assisted Ventilation of the Neonate, 1988, 4th edit., 2003, Comprehensive Pediatrics, 1990; author: (introduction) Planning and Design for Perinatal and Pediatric Facilities, 1977; editor Ross Labs., Columbus, Ohio, 1975-82, Perinatal Press, U. Tenn., Memphis, 1976-78, Brentwood Pub. Corp., L.A., 1977-88, Am. Baby Hosp. Network Adv. Bd., 1984—, Jour. Perinatology-Neonatology, 1988—, Am. Baby Mag., 1992—; reviewer C.V. Mosby Co., 1976-77, 81, 83, J.B. Lippincott Co., 1979, Williams and Wilkins Co., 1981, Polymorph films, 1985, Pediats., 1974—, New Eng. Jour. Medicine, 1975—, Am. Jour. Ob-gyn., 1979, 92, 97, Jour. Pediats., 1997, Pediat. Nephrology, 1997-2004, Pediat. Infectious Disease Jour. 1997-2000, 2003-04, Arch. Pediat. and Adolescent Medicine, 1999, Jour. Perinatology, 2001-04, Acta Paediatrica, 2003; contbr. over 300 articles to profl. publs. Bd. dirs. Memphis Orch. Soc., 1961-70. With USPHS, 1951-53. Named Citizen of Yr. Newspaper Guild Memphis, 1974, Who's Who in Medicine, Memphis Mag., 1984-88, Top Doctors, 1996; recipient Myrtle Wreath award Hadassah, 1976, Contribn. to Perinatal Medicine commendation Commr. Pub. Health Tenn., 1978, Cmty. Svc. award Nat. Conf. Christians and Jews, 1982, City Coun. Memphis, 1982, L.M. Graves Meml. Health award Mid-South Med. Ctr. Coun., Inc., 1984, Cert. Appreciation, Gov. Lamar Alexander, 1986, Key to City Memphis, Mayor Richard Hackett, 1988, Alumni Svc. award U. Tenn. Nat. Alumni Assn., 1989, Themis award March of Dimes, 1991, Meritorious Svc. commendation State Tenn. Ho. of Reps., 1992, Person of Vision award Alliance for Blind Visually Impaired, 1994, Meritorious Svc. award Tenn. Hosp. Assn., 1995; Sheldon B. Korones Chair Neonatology U. Tenn. Coll. Medicine named in his honor, 1989, Sheldon B. Korones Newborn Ctr. named in his honor, 2004; grantee NIH, 1960-75, 1971-75, 1985-2001, Merck, Sharpe and Dohme, 1970-73, Tenn. Dept. Health, 1970—, Memphis Regional Med. Program, 1972-75, Tenn. Dept. Human Svcs., 1972—96, March of Dimes, 1973-80, Nat. Heart, Lung, Blood Inst., 1976-83, Nat. Inst. Child Health Human Devel., 1986-91, 91-96, 96—, Tenn. Dept. Children's Svcs., 1996-2001. Fellow Am. Coll. Ob-Gyn. (assoc.); mem. So. Soc. Pediat. Rsch., Am. Acad. Pediats. (com. fetus and newborn 1969-75, liaison com. perinatal health Am. Coll. Ob-Gyn. 1965-74, rep. to joint com. newborn hearing Am. Speech Hearing Assn., Am. Acad. Ophthalmology Otolaryngology 1969-75, task force on circumcision 1973-74), Tenn. chpt. Pediatrician of Yr. 1994), Tenn. Pediat. Soc., Memphis Pediat. Soc., Am. Pediat. Soc., Tenn. Perinatal Assn. (bd. dirs. 1983—), Russian Perinatologists Assn. (hon. pres. 1996), Nat. Assn. Perinatal Social Workers (hon. 1980), Sigma Xi, Alpha Omega Alpha. Office: U Tenn 853 Jefferson Ave Rm 201 Memphis TN 38103-2807 Home Phone: 901-682-3692. Business E-Mail: skorones@utmem.edu, skorones@uthsc.edu.

KOROSHETZ, WALTER J., neurologist, educator; b. Bklyn. Grad, Georgetown U.; MD, U. Chgo. Prof. neurology Harvard Med. Sch., 1990—; vice chmn. neurology svc. Mass. Gen. Hosp., dir. stroke & neurointensive care svcs.; dep. dir. Nat. Inst. Neurological Disorders & Stroke, 2007—. Office: NIH/NINDS MSC 2540 31 Center Dr Bldg 31 Rm 8A52 Bethesda MD 20892-2540 E-mail: koroshetzw@ninds.nih.gov.

KORPELA, RIITTA ANNELI, nutritionist, professor; d. Kauko and Carita Korpela. MS in Nutrition Sci., U. Helsinki, 1980; PhD, U. Kuopio, 1995. Registered clin. and public health nutritionist Nat. Bd. Health, 1983, cert. docent 2003, clin. nutritionist Authorized Nat. Boards Medicolegal Affairs, 1995; lic. in nutrition sci. and microbiology U. Helsinki, 1994, cert. in med. nutrition physiology 2008. Mgr., nutrition and health Valio Ltd, R&D, Helsinki, Finland, 1990—2004, v.p., rschr., 2004—10; sci. sec. Found. Nutrition Rsch., Helsinki, 1994—2008; prof. med. nutrition physiology U. Helsinki, Inst. Biomedicine, 2008—; chmn. Strategic Ctr. Health & Wellbeing, 2009—10. Mem. Assn. Clin. and Pub. Health Nutritionists, 1978—, mem. bd., 1981—86, Socs. Biochemica, Biophysica et Microbiologica Fenniae, 1981—, Finnish Soc. Food Rsch., 1984—85, Finnish Soc. Nutrition Sci., 1988—94, pres., 2008—; mem. pr com. Finnish Dietetic Assn., 1982—85; pres. Assn. Clin. and Pub. Health Nutritionists, 1985—86, Nordic Dietetic Assn., 1987—89; mem. Internat. Soc. Study Fatty Acids and Lipids, 1991—, Finnish Pharmacological Soc., 1995—, Finnish Hypertension Soc., 1995—2004, European Acad. Nutritional Sci., 1996—; finnish rep. standing com. nutrition Internat. Dairy Fedn., 1995, mem. nat. com., 2006—, chmn. nat. com., 2008—; pres. Finnish Soc. Nutrition Rsch., 2008—; mem. functional foods task force Internat. Life Sci. Inst., 1999—2008; mem. external adv. bd. European Union, 1999—2002; mem. nutrition sci. bd. & world jour. gastroenterology European Dairy Fedn., 2005—08; editor Intl. Jour. Probiotics & Prebiotics, 2006—, World Jours. Gastroenterology and Functional Food Forum U. Turku; mem. sci. adv. bd. U. Oulu, Lab. Biotechnology, Finland, 2007—, Joint Programming Initiative A Health Diet Healthy Life. Contbr. articles to profl. jours., chapters to books. Office: University Helsinki Inst Biomedicine PO Box 63 Helsingin Yliopisto Helsinki FIN-00014 Finland Office Phone: 358 9 191 25354. Office Fax: 358 9 191 25364. Business E-Mail: riitta.korpela@helsinki.fi.

KORTH, RUTH-MARIA, research physician; b. Kiel, Germany, Mar. 7, 1950; d. Kurt and Hildegard (Galle) Kramer; m. Harald Korth, Aug. 3, 1968; 1 child, Anja. Master's degree, Ludwig-Maximilians U., Munich, 1979; MD in Gen. Medicine, Bavarian State Med. Bd., Munich, 1984. Staff Inst. for Prevention of Heart and Circulation Diseases U. Munich, 1989; rsch. staff Paris INSERM U., 1990—97; rschr. gen. medicine FIDA, 1990—, MECUM, Ludwig Maximilains U., 2004—. Contbr. rsch. articles to profl. jours. Poste verte INSERM, 1988, hon. vis. rsch. fellow Royal North Shore Hosp., Sydney, 1991. Mem. AAAS, German Soc. Gen. Med., DFG (rsch. fellow), German Rsch. Soc. (rsch. fellow 1980-83, 84), The Planetary Soc., European Atherosclerosis Soc., N.Am. Vascular Biology Orgn. Roman Catholic. Avocations: sports, music, modern art. Office: Practice Rsch Forschung Allgemeinmedizin FIDAR Fidabus FidadermR Palestrinastr 7a D-80639 Munich Germany E-mail: ruth-maria.korth@i-dial.de.

KORU, OZGUR, medical educator; b. Istanbul, Jan. 1, 1970; MD, Gulhane Mil. Med. Acad., 1994, PhD, 2003. Chief med. parasitology lab., dept. microbiology, divsn. med. parasitology Gulhane Mil. Med. Acad., 2009, asst. prof., dept. microbiology, 2009—. Mem.: Turkish Soc. Med. Microbiology, Turkish Soc. Parasitology, Am. Soc. Tropical Medicine and Hygiene. Avocations: fishing, water sports. Office: Gulhane Military Medical Acad Dept Microbiology Ankara Etlik 06018 Turkey Office Fax: 903123043402. Business E-Mail: okoru@gata.edu.tr.

KORYTKOWSKI, MARY T., endocrinologist; Attended, U. NC, Chapel Hill, NC. Diplomate Am. Bd. Internal Medicine-endocrinology, diabetes and metabolism, Am. Bd. Internal Medicine. Resident John Hopkins Bayview Med. Ctr., Balt., fellow; with ctr. for diabetes and endocrinology Univ. of Pitts. Med. Ctr. Office: University of Pittsburgh Medical Center Center for Diabetes and Endocrinology 3601 Fifth AveSte 3B Pittsburgh PA 15213 Office Phone: 412-586-9700.

KOS, ARTHUR OCTAVIO A., medical educator; b. Rio de Janeiro, June 27, 1932; s. Jose Arthur C. and Eunice D'Avila Kos; m. Maria Altina Ripper, Feb. 12, 1961; children: Jose, Maria Altina, Mariado Carmo, Maria Isabel, Arthur, M. Luisa, Maria. MD, Fed. U. Rio de Janeiro, 1957. Fellow Fac. Medicine Bordeaux, France, 1960, Harvard Med. Sch., Boston, 1964—65; asst. prof. Escola de Medice Cirurgia, Rio de Janeiro, 1958—76, Nat. Faculty Medicine, Rio de Janeiro, 1976—81, assoc. prof., 1981—85, prof., 1985—2002, prof. emeritus, 2005—. Recipient Bordeaux Citizen award, Maire of Bordeaux, France, 1984. Mem.: Am. Acad. Otolaryngology. Avocations: music, literature, wine, sports. Office: R Visconde de Piraja 351 22410-003 Rio de Janeiro Brazil Home, Rua Garcia D'Avila 25 - Apt 602 22421-010 Rio de Janeiro RJ Brazil Office Phone: 55-21-2523-4949. Personal E-mail: ao@kos.med.br.

KOSAKA, MASAAKI, plastic surgeon, educator; b. Japan, Dec. 6, 1958; MD, Kinki U., 1984; PhD, kinki U., 1990. Dir., plastic surgery Fukuoka Sanno Hosp., 2009. Prof. Internat. U. Healt and Welfare, 2009. Mem.: Japanese Soc. Plastic and Reconstructive Surgery. Office: Momochihama 3-6-45 sawara-ku Fukuoka 814-0001 Japan Office Phone: +81-92-832-1100. Office Fax: +81-92-832-1102. E-mail: kosaka@kouhoukai.or.jp.

KOSAR, MUBERRA, pharmacist, educator; b. Eskisehir, Turkey, Mar. 17, 1969; PhD, Anadolu U., 1999. Asst. to assoc. prof. Anadolu U. Faculty Pharmacy, 1990—2008; prof., rschr. Erciyes U. Faculty Pharmacy, 2008—, dean faculty pharmacy, 2009. Mem.: PSE. Avocation: music. Office: Erciyes University Faculty Pharmacy Kayseri 38039 Turkey Business E-Mail: mkosar@erciyes.edu.tr.

KOSCHEYEV, VICTOR S., emergency physician, researcher; s. Semon M. Koscheyev and Polina I. Pavlova; m. Margarita A. Volostnikova, Mar. 24, 1962; 1 child, Inna Linder. MD, PhD, Inst. of Biophysics, Moscow, DSc, 1979. Mem. Med. Acad. of Sci. (Russia), 1986. Head dept. human protection Inst. of Biophysics, Moscow, 1975—89; dir. Ctr. for Disaster Medicine, Moscow, 1989—92; dept. head Ministry Health, Moscow, 1991—92; prof. and fellow Radiobiology Rsch. Inst., Bethesda, 1993—94; lab. head health and human performance in extreme environments U. of Minn., Mpls., 1995—. Cons. 3M, Mpls., 1987—92. Contbr. articles to profl. pubs. Chmn. Nat. Commn. Sci. Degree Certification, Moscow, 1988—92. Recipient Nat. prize, U.S.S.R., 1979, Nat. medal, 1987, 1988; grantee, NASA, 1995—98, 3M Corp., 1998, NASA, 1999—2002, 2003—05, U. Minn., 2002—04. Mem.: Aerospace Med. Assn., World Assn. for Disaster and Emergency Medicine (assoc.; bd. dirs.). Office: U Minn 1901 University Ave SE Minneapolis MN 55455 Business E-Mail: kosch002@umn.edu.

KOSECOFF, JACQUELINE BARBARA, health care company executive; b. L.A., June 15, 1949; d. Herman Plaut and Betty (Bass) Hamburger; m. Robert Henry Brook, Jan. 17, 1982; children: Rachel Brook, Davida Brook. BA in Applied Mathematics, UCLA, 1970; MS in Applied Mathematics, Brown U., 1971; PhD in Applied Mathematics, UCLA, 1973. Prof. medicine & pub. health UCLA, 1975—2006; pres., co-CEO Value Health Sciences, Santa Monica, Calif., 1988—98; v.p. Value Health, Inc., Avon, Conn.; pres., founder Protocare, Inc., 1998—2002; exec. v.p., Pharmaceutical Services PacifiCare Health Sys., Inc., Cypress, Calif., 2002—05; CEO Prescription Solutions UnitedHealth Group Co., 2005—. Bd. dirs. Steris, 2002—, Sealed Air Corp., 2005—, CareFusion Corp., 2009—. Author: An Evaluation Primer, 1978, How to Evaluate Education Programs, 1980, Evaluation Basics, 1982, How to Conduct Surveys, 1985; contbr. numerous articles to profl. publs. Bd. dirs. City of Hope, 1999—. Regents scholar UCLA, 1967-71; NSF fellow, 1971-72. Mem. Am. Pub. Health Assn., Assn. for Health Services Research. Democrat. Jewish. Office: UnitedHealth Group Co PO Box 1459 Minneapolis MN 55440

KOSHIBA, MASAHIRO, immunologist, researcher, physician; s. Takuma and Ayako Koshiba; m. Naoko Suehiro, Nov. 1, 1987; children: Yuya, Kyoko. PhD, Kyoto U., Japan, 1993, MD, 1984. Vis. fellow NIH, Bethesda, Md., 1993—98; asst. prof. Kobe U., Japan, 1998—2004, assoc. prof., 2004—06; prof. Hyogo Coll. Medicine, 2006—. Mem.: Japanese Soc. Internal Medicine, Japanese Soc. Gastroenterology, Japanese Soc. for Immunology, Japan Rheumatism Assn., Am. Assn. Immunologists. Office: Dept Clin Lab Medicine 1-1 Mukogawa-cho Nishinamiya 663-8501 Japan

KOSKENTAUSTA, TERHI, psychiatrist; b. Helsinki, Finland, Dec. 17, 1959; d. Topi and Outi Urponen; m. Kimmo Koskentausta, Sept. 27, 1986; children: Elina, Lauri, Sakari, Juho. MD, U. Turku, Finland, 1985; PhD in Child Psychiatry, U. Helsinki, 2007. Cert. specialist in psychiatry U. Tampere, 2004, intellectual disabilities specialist Finnish Med. Assn., 2008. Sr. physician Spl. Care Dist. Pirkanmaa, Ylojarvi, Finland, 1985—86; health care physician Health Ctr. Ylojarvi, 1986; sr. physician Spl. Care Dist. Pirkanmaa, 1987—88; health ctr. physician Health Ctr. Mouhijarvi, 1988—90; specialist Mental Health Clinic Mantta, 1990—92; sr. physician Paajarvi Joint Mcpl. Authority, Lammi, Finland, 1999—2001; specialist Ctrl. Hosp. Paijat-Hame, 2001—04, Paajarvi Joint Mcpl. Authority, Lammi, Finland, 2004—07, chief physician, 2008—, Eteva Joint Mcpl. Authority, 2009—10; dep. chief physician Helsinki U. Ctrl. Hosp., 2011—. Achievements include research in psychiatric disturbances in persons with intellectual disability. Business E-Mail: terhi.koskentausta@eteva.fi.

KOSKI, TYLER, neurosurgeon, educator; b. Escanaba, Mich., Nov. 23, 1973; MD, Mich. State U. Coll. Human Medicine, 2000. Asst. prof. Northwestern U. Feinberg Sch. Medicine, 2006—. Bd. dirs. One Spine Soc., 2009—; adv. bd. Spine CME.org, 2010—. Mem.: Am. Assn. Neurol. Surgeons, Congress Neurol. Surgeons, Scoliosis Rsch. Soc. Office: 676 N St Clair Ste 2210 Chicago IL 60611 Business E-Mail: tyler.koski@nmff.org.

KOSLOW, STEPHEN HUGH, health science association administrator, pharmacologist, neuroscientist; s. Julius and Lillian Koslow; m. Diane Heisler, Aug. 18, 1962; children: Karin, James. BS, Columbia U., 1962; PhD, U. Chgo., 1967. Internat. postdoctoral fellow Swedish Med. Rsch. Coun., Karolinski Inst., 1968-69; pharmacologist, chief neurobiology unit St. Elizabeth's Hosp., Washington, 1970-77; chief biol. rsch. sect. Clin. Rsch. br. NIMH, Rockville, Md., 1975-81, chief Neurosci. Rsch. br., 1981—85, chief Basic Scis. Neurosci. Rsch., 1985—88, dep. dir. divsn. Basic Brain and Behavioral Scis., 1989—90; dir. divsn. Basic and Clin. Neurosci. Rsch. NIMH-NIH, Rockville, 1990—99; assoc. dir., dir. office neuroinformatics NIMH, Rockville, 1999—2004; dir. external rels. Allen Inst. Brain Sci., Seattle, 2005, Biomedical Consulting, 2006—; rsch. dir. Am. Found. Suicide Presentation, 2009—10; cons. U. Miami Med. Sch., 2011—. Project dir. NIHM-CRB Collaborative Program on Psychobiology of Depression-Biol. Study, 1975-85; mem. adv. bd. Tourette Syndrome Assn., Bayside, NY, 1984; chair fed. coordinating com. on the Human Brain Project, 1991—; chair neuroinformatics subgroup of Office Econ. Coop. & Devel., Megasci. Forum, Biol. Working Group, 1996-99; co-chair US/EC com. on neuroinformatics, 1998—, chair global sci. forum neuroinformatics working group, 2000-02; editl. bd. mem. Translational Psychiatry, 2011—. Mem. editl. bd. Neuropsychopharmacology, 1987-92, Critical Revs. in Neurobiol., 1991-2001, Human Brain Mapping, 1993-2004, Psychopharm. Bull., 1989-99, Neuroimage, series editor Progress in Neuroinformatics Rsch., 1996-2001, Neuroimage, 1995-2001, CNS Drug Revs., 1995-99, Biomednet, 1999-2003; editor: Databasing the Brain From Data to Knowledge, 2005, Integrative Neuroscience and Personalized Medicine, 2010; assoc. editor Jour. Integrative Neurosci. Recipient NIMH Quality Increase award, 1977-78, Health Adminstr.'s award for Meritorious Achievement, 1986, Pub. Health Svc. Spl. Recognition award, 1992, Alumni Achievement award U. Chgo. Club of Washington, 1995, two Dir.'s awards NIH, 1996, Pres. award Internat. Neural Network Soc., 2001; Swedish Med. Rsch. Coun. internat. postdoctoral fellow, 1968-69, Spl. NATO fellow, 1969. Fellow AAAS, Am. Coll. Neuropsychopharmacology, Am. Coll. Med. Informatics; mem. Am. Soc. for Neurochemistry, Am. Soc. Pharmacology and Exptl. Therapeutics, Collegium Internat. Neuro Psychopharmacologium, Soc. for Neurosci., Soc. Biol. Psychiatry. Home and Office: 8642 Falcon Green Dr West Palm Beach FL 33412 Personal E-mail: stevekoslow@gmail.com.

KOSMA, MARIA, physical education educator; d. Loukas and Angeliki Kosma; m. Marc V.J. Parijs, Apr. 8, 2004. BS, Nat. and Kapodistrian U., Greece, 1997; MS with hons., U. Jyväskylä, Finland, 1999; PhD, Oreg. State U., Corvallis, 2003. Rsch. asst. Nat. and Kapodistrian U., Athens, 1995—98, Oreg. State U., 2000—03; assoc. prof. La. State U., Baton Rouge, 2003—. Rschr. in field; fellow Rsch. Consortium, 2008. Contbr. articles to profl. jours. Mem.: NASPSPA, AAHPERD (Rsch. Consortium Grad. Student Rsch. award 2003, Mabel Lee award 2007), Internat. Fedn. Adapted Phys. Activity. Office: La State U 112 HP Long Fieldhouse Kinesiology Baton Rouge LA 70803 Office Phone: 225-578-8016. Business E-Mail: mkosma@lsu.edu.

KOSMADAKIS, NIKOLAOS MYRON, surgeon; b. Bergisch Gladbach, Germany, Mar. 11, 1966; s. Pelagia Kosmadaki; m. Panagiota Basilis Moschogianni; children: Basilis Nikolaos, Myron Nikolaos. MD in Surgery, U. La Sapienza, 1994. Cert. in gen. surgery Med. Bd. The Prefecture Of Athens, 2003. Rural gen. practitioner Gen. Hosp. Zante, Zakynthos, Greece, 1995—97; resident gen. surgery Ippokratio U. Hosp., Athens, Greece, 1997—2003; sr. specialist registrar gen. surgery Gen. Hosp. Zakynthos, 2003—. Instr. in field. Fellow: Hellenic Trauma Soc. (corr.; rep. 2004—); mem.: European Assn. Endoscopic Surgery (assoc.). Office: General Hospital Of Zakynthos 3 Perivola Street Zakynthos 29100 Greece Office Fax: 2695024143. Business E-Mail: nkosma@otenet.gr.

KOSMAS, CHRISTOS, oncologist; b. Athens, Greece, May 17, 1961; MD, Athens U., 1985; PhD, London U., 1993. Clin. rsch. fellow Hammersmith Hosp. Royal Postgrad. Med. Sch., 1988—92; rsch. scientist, physician, med. oncology Laikon Gen. Hosp. Athens U. Sch. Medicine, 1992—96; attending, med. oncology Helena-Venizelou Hosp., 1996—2001; cons. med. oncologist Metaxa Cancer Hosp., 2001—. Contbr. more than 150 articles to profl. publs. Scholar, State Scholarships Found. Greece. Mem.: European Soc. Med. Oncology, Am. Soc. Clin. Oncology. Avocations: basketball, music. Home: 21 Apolloniou Athens Attiki 16341 Greece Home Fax: 30210-9962917. Personal E-mail: ckosm1@ath.forthnet.gr.

KOSNETT, MICHAEL J., medical toxicologist; b. Newark, Mar. 11, 1957; s. Irwin and Sylvia Kosnett; m. Jan Kosnett. BS magna cum laude, Yale U., New Haven, 1979; MD, U. Calif., San Francisco, 1983; MPH, U. Calif., Berkeley, 1988. Diplomate Am. Bd. Internal Medicine, 1986, Am. Bd. Med. Toxicology, 1990, Am. Bd. Preventive

Medicine, 1991. Asst. prof. medicine U. Calif., San Francisco, 1991—95; assoc. clin. prof. medicine U. Colo. Health Sciences Ctr., Denver, 1999—; lead review panel EPA Sci. Adv, Bd., 2010—, Nat. Inst. Occupl. Bd. Sci. Counselors, 2011—; bd. sci. counselor Nat. Inst. Occpl. Safety & Health, 2010—. Mem. toxicology com. Nat. Rsch. Coun., Washington, 1999—2001; pres. Am. Coll. Med. Toxicology, Schaumburg, Ill., 2002—04; cons. WHO, Geneva, 2002—04; childhood head poisoning prevention CDC Adv. Com., 2007—. Mem. lead review panel EPA Sci. Advisory Bd., 2010—; mem. bd. sci. counselors Nat. Inst. Occupl. Safety and Health, 2011—. Recipient Asst. Administrator's Spl. Svc. award, Agy. for Toxic Substances and Disease Registry, 2003; grantee Spl. Emphasis Rsch. Career award, Nat. Inst. for Occupl. Safety and Health, 1991. Fellow: Am. Coll. Med. Toxicology (pres. 2002—04, Outstanding Svc. award 2008). Achievements include clinical research and publication regarding heavy metal intoxication. Office: 1630 Welton St Ste 300 Denver CO 80202 Office Phone: 303-571-5778. Business E-Mail: michael.kosnett@ucdenver.edu.

KOSOFSKY, BARRY E., pediatric neurologist; BA in Biophysics, MA in Biophysics, Johns Hopkins U.; MD, Johns Hopkins U. Sch. Medicine, PhD in Neuroscience. Cert. neurology. Resident Boston Children's Hosp.; asst. resident & chief resident Mass. Gen. Hosp., fellow, assoc. neurologist & dir. child neurology; instr. neurology Harvard Med. Sch.; prof. pediatrics Weill Cornell Med. Ctr., chief divsn. pediatric neurology, prof. pediatrics in radiology. Mem.: Child Neurology Soc. (chmn. scientific selection program com.). Office: Weill Cornell Medical College Helmsley Tower 3rd Fl 505 E 70th St New York NY 10021 Office Phone: 212-746-3321. Office Fax: 212-746-8137.

KOSS, LEOPOLD G., pathologist, educator; b. Gdansk, Poland, Oct. 2, 1920; arrived in U.S., 1947, naturalized, 1952; s. Abram and Rose (Merenholc) Kon; m. Lydia Palla (dec. 2008); children: Michael S., Andrew C., Richard P. MD, U. Berne, Switzerland, 1946; Doctorate (hon.), Pomeranian Med. Acad., Poland, 2002, U. Bern, Switzerland, 2007. Intern Lincoln Hosp., NYC, 1947-48; tng. pathology St. Gallen, Switzerland, 1946-47, Kings County Hosp., Bklyn., 1949-52; instr. pathology LI U. Coll. Medicine, NY, 1949-52; mem. staff Meml. Hosp. Cancer and Allied Diseases, NYC, 1952-70, attending pathologist, 1961-70, chief cytology svc., 1961-70; pathologist-in-chief Sinai Hosp. Balt., 1970-73; prof., chmn. dept. pathology Montefiore Hosp., Med. Ctr. Albert Einstein Coll. Medicine, Bronx, NY, 1973-92, prof., chair emeritus, 1993—; hon. alumnus US SUNY Downstate Med. Ctr., 2010; disting. univ. prof. emeritus, US Alumnus SUNY Downstate Med. Ctr., 2011—. Hon. prof. pathology Severance Med. Coll., Seoul, Korea, 1956; assoc. mem. Sloan-Kettering Inst. Cancer Research, NYC, 1957-70; assoc. prof. pathology Sloan-Kettering div. Postgrad. Sch. Med. Sci., Cornell U., 1957-70; prof. pathology Jefferson Med. Coll., Phila., 1970-73; clin. prof. pathology U. Md. Med. Sch., 1971-73; vis. pathologist James Ewing Hosp., NYC, 1952-60; former cons. pathologist NY State Dept. Health, Hosp. Spl. Surgery, NYC; cons. pathologist Walter Reed Army Med. Ctr., Nassau County Med. Ctr.; Frost lectr., Balt., 1999. Author: Diagnostic Cytology and Its Histopathologic Bases, 5th rev. edit. 2006, Tumors of the Urinary Bladder, 1975, Supplement, 1984, Aspiration Biopsy: Cytologic Interpretation and Histologic Bases, 2d rev. edit. 1992, Introduction to Gynecologic Cytology, 1999; editor: Advances in Clinical Cytology, Vol. I, 1981, Vol. II, 1984, Papillomaviruses and Human Diseases, 1987, Errors and Pitfalls in Diagnostic Cytology, 1997; contbr. more than 390 articles to profl. jour. and 40 chpts. to books also monographs. Served to maj. M.C., AUS, 1955-57. Recipient Wien award Papanicolaou Cancer Inst., 1963, Alfred P. Sloan award cancer rsch., 1964, Fred Stewart award, 1984, Vandenberge-Hill award, 1984, Meritorious medal U. Brussels, 1987, Jurzykowski award, 1991, Disting. Pathologist award US and Can. Acad. Pathology, 2001, Disting. Pathologist award Assn. Pathology Chairs, 2002. Fellow: AAAS, Internat. Acad. Cytology (Goldblatt award 1962, Kazumasa Masubuchi Life-Time Achievement award in clin. cytology 1995), Coll. Am. Pathologists, Am. Soc. Clin. Pathology, Royal Coll. Pathologists (hon. Found. lectr. 1997), Royal Coll. Pathologists (hon.); mem.: AMA, Am. Soc. for Colposcopy and Cervical Pathology (Disting. Svc. award 1996), Internat. Soc. of Urol. Pathology (F.K. Mostofi Disting. Svc. award 1995), German Acad. Sci. (Leopoldina), Peruvian Soc. Ob-Gyn., Polish Soc. Pathology, Japanese Soc. Pathology, Argentinian Soc. Cytology, Mex. Soc. Cytology, Brit. Soc. Clin. Cytology (hon.), Royal Acad. Medicine Spain (corr.), Korean Med. Assn., NY State Soc. Pathology (Lansky-Ratner award 1989), NY Pathology Soc. (pres. 1985—87, Middleton-Goldsmith lectr. 1992), Internat. Acad. Pathology (Maude Abbott lectr. 1989), Am. Soc. Cytology (pres. 1962, Papanicolaou award 1966), James Ewing Soc., Am. Soc. Exptl. Pathology (Gold Cane award 1993), Order of Merit Republic of Poland (officer, medal 2004). Office Phone: 718-920-5185. Business E-Mail: lkoss@montefiore.org.

KOSTADINOV, STEFAN, pathologist, educator; b. Kazanlak, Bulgaria, Feb. 10, 1965; s. Georgi Georgiev and Margarita Georgieva; m. Mira Kostadinov; children: Gloria, Nellia, Vivien. MD, Trakia U., Stara Zagora, Bulgaria, 1991. Diplomate Bulgaria, 1991, cert. Am. Bd. Pathology, 2008, Ednl. Comision Fgn. Med. Grads. Staff perinatal pathologist Women and Infants Hosp., Providence, 2004; asst. prof. pathology Alpert Med. Sch. Brown U., Providence, 2004—. Staff perinatal pathologist Women and Infants Hosp. RI, 2004—. Recipient Recognition Exemplary Tchg. award, Brown U. Med. Sch. Mem.: Coll. Am. Pathologists.

KOSTECKI, JACEK, physician; b. Mikołów, Jan. 24, 1969; MD, PhD, Med. U. Silesia, 1993; MBI, Warsaw Sch. Economics, 2001. Physician Med. U. Silesia, 2005. Mem.: Polish Soc. Vascular Surgeons, Polish Phlebological Soc., Polish Soc. Surgeons. Avocations: sports, travel, camping. Office: Edukacji 102 Tychy Slask 43-100 Poland Office Fax: 48323254245. Business E-Mail: kosteckj@op.pl.

KOSTEN, THERESE A., neuroscientist, psychologist, researcher; d. Emmett and Ruth Kinney; m. Thomas Kosten, Aug. 12, 1978; children: Molly, Neal. BA in Psychobiology, SUNY, Purchase, 1978; PhD in Psychology, Yale U., 1986. Tchg. fellow Yale U., 1982—85, lectr., 1986—87; vis. asst. prof. Wheaton Coll., 1986—87; assoc. rsch. scientist Yale U. Sch. Medicine, New Haven, 1987—92, rsch. scientist, 1992—95, asst. prof., 1995—2003, assoc. prof., 2003—06, rsch. scientist, 2003—06; assoc. prof., dept. pschiatry Baylor Coll. Med., Houston, 2006—. Invited spkr. in field. Contbr. articles to profl. jours.; mem. editl. bd. Jour. Substance Abuse Treatment, 1991, Ad hoc reviewer for numerous jours. Grantee, Donaghue Med. Rsch. Found., 2000—03; Yale U. Fellowship, 1980—84, Com. for the Problems of Drug Dependence Travel Fellowship, 1989, BIRCWH Scholar, Yale IWHR Scholar Program on Women and Drug Abuse, 2001—06. Mem.: Coll. on the Problems of Drug Dependence, Soc. for Neurosciences, Sigma Xi. Office: Baylor Coll Medicine Research Service Line 151 MEDVAMC 2002 Holcombe Blvd Houston TX 77030 Office Fax: 713-794-7240. Business E-Mail: tkosten@bcm.edu. E-mail: therese.kosten@yale.edu.

KOSTEN, THOMAS RICHARD, psychiatrist, educator; b. Bklyn., Feb. 16, 1951; s. Richard Kosten; m. Therese Kosten, Aug. 12, 1978; children: Molly, Neal. BS, Rensselaer Polytechnic Inst., Troy, NY, 1973; MD, Cornell U. Med. Coll., NYC, 1977; MA, Yale U. Sch. Medicine, New Haven, Conn., 1995. Diplomate Am. Bd. Psychiatry and Neurology, 1984, Am. Bd. Psychiatry and Neurology, Addiction Psychiatry. Intern Greenwich Hosp., Conn., 1977—78; resident Yale U. Sch. Medicine, New Haven, 1978—81, asst. to assoc. prof., psychiatry, 1983—94, assoc. dir. to dir., substance abuse treatment unit, 1984—92, dir., divsn. substance abuse, 1992—96, prof. psychiatry, 2000—06; prof. Yale Grad. Sch., 2000—06; chief of psychiatry VA Conn. Healthcare Sys., West Haven, Conn., 1996—2000, dep. chief psychiatry, 2000—; prof. psychiatry and neuroscience Baylor Coll. Medicine, Houston, 2006—. Courtesy faculty appointments Yale-New Haven Hosp., Conn., Conn. Mental Health Ctr., New Haven; rsch. dir. VA Nat. Substance Use Disorders Quality Enhancement Rsch. Initiative; congl. fellow US House Representatives, House Subcommittee on Human Resources, Washington, 1998—99; vis. rsch. prof., dept. medicine U. Minn., 1987; vis. prof., med. divsn. US Army European Command, Heidelberg, Germany, 1988; vis. prof., dept. toxicology Med. Sch. Hosp. de la Sta. Creu i Sant Pau, Barcelona, 1989, Barcelona, 90, Barcelona, 94; vis. prof., dept. medicine and psychiatry, Addiction Rsch. Found. U. Toronto, Canada, 1991; vis. prof. Beijing Med. U. & Chinese Nat. Inst. on Drug Dependence, 1991; disting. prof. Universidad Complutense de Madrid, Facultad de Medicina, Madrid, 1993; vis. prof., dept. psychiatry U. Athens, Greece, 1995, Greece, 98; disting. vis. prof. North Shore U. Hosp., Einstein Med. Sch., NY, 1998; mem. of several nat. advisory and review groups; lectr. in field; presenter in field. Dep. editor to sr. dep. editor Am. Jour. on Addictions, dep. editor to editor-in chief Am. Jour. Drug and Alcohol Abuse, co-editor for Substance Abuse, Guilford Press, cons. editor Clin. Advances in the Treatment of Psychiatric Disorders, mem. editl. bd. Am. Jour. Psychiatry, Drug and Alcohol Dependence, Jour. Nervous and Mental Disease, Jour. Studies on Alcohol, Brain Pharmacology, Neuropharmacology, Sci. & Practice Perspectives; contbr. chapters to books, articles to profl. jours. Congl. fellow, u.s. ho. of rep. Ho. Subcommittee on Human Resources (Christopher Shays, Chair), Washington, 1998—99. Recipient Rsch. Scientist Develop. award, Nat. Inst. on Drug Abuse, 1987—96, Joseph Cochin award for Rsch. in Substance Abuse, Com. on Problems of Drug Dependence, Chartered Com. NAS, 1990, Nyswander award for Contributions to Rsch. in Oplate Dependence, Am. Methadone Treatment Assn., 2000, Sr. Scientist award, Nat. Inst. on Drug Abuse, 2000—; named one of New York Mag. Best Doctor, 2001—05; named to America's Top Doctors, 1st, 2nd, 3rd, 4th, 5th, 6th, 7th, 8th & 9th editions, Top Doctors, New York Metro Area, 5th, 6th, 7th, 8th & 9th editions, Castle Connolly Med. Ltd., 2001—05; NSF Fellow in Biophysics, Rensselaer Polytechnic Inst., 1972, Travel Fellowship, Com. on Problems of Drug Dependence, 1985. Fellow: Coll. on Problems of Drug Dependence (pres.-elect 2005, bd. dir., program chair, credentials com.), Am. Coll. Neuropsychopharmacology (program chair, human rsch. com., Joel Elkes Internat. award for Outstanding Contributions to Psychopharmacology 1993), Collegium Internationale Neuro-Psychopharmacologicum, Am. Acad. Addiction Psychiatry (pres. 1998—2000, founding mem., bd. dir.), Am. Psychiatric Assn. (vice chair, coun. on addictions); mem.: Inst. of Medicine. Achievements include being the founder of the divison of substance abuse at Baylor and Yale U; neroimaging research includes detecting and treating cocaine induced cerebral perfusion defects, and using functional MRI to predict pharmacotherapy outcome; medication contributions include a cocaine vaccine, immunotherapy for hallucinogens, buprenorphine for opioid dependence, disulfiram for cocaine dependence, vasodilators for cocaine induced cerbral perfusion defects, & combining medications with contingency management for opioid & cocaine dependence. Avocations: tennis, ice skating. Office: Baylor College Medicine Research 151 Bldg 110 Rm 229 Michael E DeBailey VA Med Ctr 2002 Holcombe Blvd Houston TX 77030 also: One Baylor Plaza BCM 350 Houston TX 77030 Office Fax: 713-794-7240. Business E-Mail: kosten@bcm.edu.

KOSTER, JOHN FREDERICK, insurance executive; b. Ancon, Canal Zone, Sept. 6, 1950; s. Frederick Eugene and Margaretta (Lillystrand) K.; m. Laura Plikerd, June 11, 1971; children: Kimberly, Erik, Krista. BS in Biology, N.Mex. Tech. U., 1972; MD, U. N.Mex., 1976. Diplomate American Bd. Internal Medicine. Intern Providence Hosp., Portland, Oreg., 1976; resident internal medicine U. N.Mex., Albuquerque, 1977; assoc. Internal and Family Medicine Assocs., Albuquerque, 1979-88; pvt. practice, 1980—88; med. dir. Blue Cross and Blue Shield N.Mex., Albuquerque, 1988-90; sr. v.p. healthcare Rocky Mountain Healthcare Corp., Denver, 1990—91; v.p. Presbyn. Healthcare Svcs., Albuquerque, 1992—93; v.p targeted mem. svcs. VHA Inc., Irving, Tex., 1993—97, sr. v.p. targeted mem. svcs., dir., chmn., 2008—11; dir. First Choice Health Network Inc.; v.p. clin. physician svcs. Sisters of Providence Health System, 1997; exec. v.p., COO Providence; dir. system ops. Providence Health System, Seattle, 1997—2002, acting pres., CEO, 2003, pres., CEO, 2003—06, Providence Health and Svcs., 2006—. Cons. Govs. Health Policy Adv. Com., N.Mex., 1990-91; advisor to physcians and mgmt. staff in various healthcare orgs. Mem. AMA (Physicians Recognition award 1985—), American Coll. of Physician Execs. Office: Providence Health and Services 4800 37th Ave SW Seattle WA 98126-2793 Office Phone: 206-937-4600. Office Fax: 206-923-4001. E-mail: John.Koster@providence.org. *

KOSTERICH, JOE MAX, physician; b. Perth, Australia, Jan. 24, 1961; MBBS, U. Western Australia, 1985. Chmn. gen. practice coun. Australian Med. Assn., 1996—99; med. dir. Endeavour Healthcare, 2001—04, Onsite Health Solutions, 2004—08; pvt. practice, 1988—. Clin. lectr. U. Western Australia, 2007. Avocations: movies, winemaking, travel. Office: PO Box 453 Floreat West Australia 6015 Australia Office Fax: 61892850898. Business E-Mail: joe@drjoe.net.au.

KOSTICK, ALEXANDRA, ophthalmologist; BSc, MD, U. Man., Winnipeg, Can., 1990. Surg. intern St. Boniface Hosp./U. Man., Winnipeg, 1990-91; rsch. fellow in ocular pathology Storm Eye Inst./Med. U. SC, Charleston, 1991-92; resident in ophthalmology U. Sask., Saskatoon, Can., 1992-95; fellow corneal diseases U. Mo., Columbia, 1995-96; practice ophthalmology specializing in cornea and external diseases, Ormond Beach, Palm Coast, Fla., 1996—. Contbr. articles to profl. jours. Fellow ACS, Am. Acad. Ophthalmology; mem. Am. Soc. Cataract and Refractive Surgeons, European Soc. Cataract and Refractive Surgeons, Royal Coll. Physicians and Surgeons Can., Castroviejo Corneal Soc., Paton Eye Bank Soc., Can. Ophthalmology Soc., Royal Acad. Dancing (London). Office Phone: 386-446-9590.

KOSTIS, JOHN BASIL, cardiologist; b. Yannina, Greece, June 14, 1936; came to US, 1964; s. Basil John and Vasiliki Ilia (Masouras) K.; m. Barbara Charleston, June, 1969; children: William Jason, Steven Lawrence. MD, U. Salonica, Greece, 1960; student, USAF Sch. Aerospace Medicine, 1963. Diplomate Am. Bd. Internal Medicine, subspecialty cardiovascular disease, specialty clin. hypertension, Am. Bd. Clin. Lipidology. Resident internal medicine Evangelismos Hosp., 404 Gen. Hosp., Athens and Larissa, Greece, 1963-64; intern Bklyn.-Cumberland Med. Ctr., 1964-65, med. resident, 1965-67; fellow cardiology Phila. Gen. Hosp., 1967-69; instr. physiology and aviation medicine Sch. Aviation Medicine, Athens, 1969-70; assoc. clin. medicine, asst. prof. medicine U. Pa., Phila., 1971-72; assoc. prof. Coll. Medicine and Dentistry NJ-Rutgers Med. Sch., New Brunswick, 1972-76; chief cardiology Robert Wood Johnson U. Hosp., New Brunswick, 1980—97. Adj. prof. biomed. engring. Rutgers U. Coll. Engring., Piscataway, NJ, 1975—, Grad. Sch. Biomed. Engring., 1976—; prof. medicine U. Medicine and Dentistry NJ-Robert Wood Johnson Med. Sch., New Brunswick, 1976—, chief div. cardiovascular disease, 1982-84, chief div. cardiovascular disease and hypertension, 1984-97, prof. pharmacology, 1986—, John G. Detwiler prof. cardiology, 1987—, chmn. dept. medicine, 1990—; cons. pharm. industry. Co-editor: Essentials of Cardiovascular Diagnosis, 1984, Beta Blockers in the Treatment of Cardiovascular Disease, 1984, The Pharmacological Treatment of Cardiovascular Diseases, 1986, Angiotensin Converting Enzyme Inhibitors, 1987, The Prevention of Sudden Cardiac Death, 1990; assoc. editor Cardiology, mem. editl. bd. Am. Jour. Cardiology, Clin. Therapeutics, Cardiovasc. Drug Revs., others, co-inventor device noninvasive diagnostic system for coronary artery disease. Grantee pharm. industry, Nat. Heart Lung and Blood Inst., NIH, Nat. Inst. Aging. Fellow ACP, Am. Heart Assn. (disting. leadership in rsch. award 1986), mem. Am. Coll. Cardiology, Assn. U. Cardiologists, Am. Soc. Hypertension, Internat. Soc. Hypertension, Assn. Profs. of Medicine. Office: U Med and Dentistry NJ Robt Wood Johnson Med Sch PO Box 19 New Brunswick NJ 08903-0019 Office Phone: 732-235-7685. Business E-Mail: kostis@umdnj.edu.

KOSTMAN, JAY R., infectious disease physician, educator; MD, Yale U. Diplomate Am. Bd. Internal Medicine, Am. Bd. Internal Medicine-infectious disease. Resident Temple Univ. Hosp., fellow; clin. assoc. prof medicine infectious diseases divsn. medicine dept. U. Pa.; head infectious diseases divsn. Presbyterian Med. Ctr. Named one of Top Docs, Phila. Mag., 2005, 2006, 2007, 2008, 2009, 2010, 2011, Best Doctors in America, 2003—04, 2005—06, 2007—08, 2009—10. Mem.: ACP, Am. Soc. for Microbiology, Infectious Diseases Soc. of America. Office: Penn Presbyterian Medical Center 2nd Fl 3910 Powelton Ave Philadelphia PA 19104 Office Phone: 800-789-7366.

KOSZEGI, TAMÁS, physician, educator; b. Pécs, Hungary, Jan. 5, 1955; MD, U. Pécs, PhD, 1979. Assoc. prof. complementary medicine U. Pécs, Inst. Lab. Medicine, 2001—. Dir. bd. trustees Melius Found., 2001. Széchenyi István scholarship, Ministry of Edn., Hungary. Mem.: Hungarian Soc. Biophysics, Hungarian Soc. Chem. Pathology. Avocations: photography, gardening. Office: Ifjúság Pécs Baranya H-7624 Hungary Office Fax: 36 72 536 121. Business E-Mail: koszegit@freemail.hu.

KOSZEWSKI, BOHDAN JULIUS, retired internist, medical educator; b. Warsaw, Dec. 17, 1918; Came to U.S., 1952; s. Mikolaj and Helen (Lubienski) K.; children Mikolaj, Joseph, Wanda Marie, Andrzej Bohdan. MD, U. Zurich, Switzerland, 1946; MS, Creighton U., 1956. Resident in pathology U. Zurich, 1944-46, resident in internal medicine, 1946-50, assoc. in medicine, 1950-52; intern St. Mary's Hosp., Hoboken, NJ, 1953; practice medicine specializing in internal medicine Omaha, 1956-90. Mem. staff St. Joseph's Hosp., Mercy and Meth. Hosps.; instr. internal medicine Creighton U., 1956-57, asst. prof., 1957-65, assoc. prof. internal medicine, 1965-90; cons. hematology Omaha VA Hosp., 1957-90. Author: Prognosis in Diabetic Coma, 1952; contbr. numerous articles to profl. jours. Served with Polish Army, 1940-45. Fellow ACP, Am. Coll. Angiology; mem. AAAS, Am. Fedn. Clin. Research, Internat. Soc. Hematology, Polish-Am. Congress Nebr. (pres. 1960-68, 82-92). Home: 1400 Broadmoor Ave Lincoln NE 68506

KOTANI, HIDEHITO, biologist, biomedical researcher; b. Ochanomizu, Japan, Dec. 27, 1967; s. Chikae Kotani; m. Suwako Ito, Dec. 12, 1993; 1 child, Hidetaka Frederick. PhD, Thomas Jefferson U., 1993. Head of genomics Banyu Tsukuba Rsch. Inst., Japan, 1998—2005; head of oncology and genomics Banyu Tsukubsa Rsch. Inst., 2005—; rsch. fellow Whitehead Inst. for Biomedical Rsch., MIT, Cambridge, Mass., 1995—98, Pfizer Ctrl. Rsch., Groton, Conn., 1993—95. Author: (journals) Roles of RNA in Pairing Event (Avis award, 1993). Fellow Pfizer Post-Doctoral Rsch. awards, Pfizer Inc., 1993. Mem.: Japanese Assn. of Molecular Biology, Japanese Assn. of Molecular Cancer Theraputics, The Japanese Cancer Assn. Achievements include discovery of use of RNA in gene therapy, anti-histamine for treatment of obesity, novel gene for obesity; patents for prediction of anticancer therapy outcome; research in application of DNA arrays in drug discivery. Home: 1 Sengen Tsukuba 3050047 Japan Office: MSD K K 1-13-12 Kudan-kita Chiyoda Tokyo 102-8667 Japan Business E-Mail: hidehito_kotani@merck.com.

KOTAPKA, MARK J., neurosurgeon; MD, U. Md., 1985. Diplomate Am. Bd. Neurol. Surgery, Am. Bd. Surgery. Intern in gen. surgery Hosp. Univ. Pa., 1986, resident in neurology, 1991; fellow in otolaryngology Univ. Pitts. Med. Ctr., 1992; fellow in pediatric neurology Children's Hosp. Phila., 1992; hosp. affiliation includes Albert Einstein Med. Ctr., Pa. Named one of Top Doctors, Phila. Mag., 2010. Office: Albert Einstein Medical Center Klein Bldg Ste 400 5401 Old York Rd Philadelphia PA 19141 Office Phone: 215-456-6127. Office Fax: 215-456-7223.

KOTAS, ROBERT VINCENT, pediatrician, educator; b. Buffalo, Nov. 26, 1938; s. Vincent John and Regina K.; m. Ilona Rae Fielding, Mar. 2, 1968; children: Nicole, Timothy, Robert, Rebecca. BS, Canisius Coll., 1959; MD, U. Buffalo, 1963. Diplomate: Am. Acad. Pediatrics. Research assoc. McGill U., 1969-70; intern Buffalo Children's Hosp., 1963-64; resident in pediatrics Johns Hopkins Hosp., Balt., 1964-66; asst. prof. pediatrics U. Okla. Med. Sch., 1970-72, dir. newborn services, 1970-72; dir., div. devel. physiology; career investigator W.K. Warren Med. Research Center, Tulsa, 1972-76, sci. dir., 1976-80; dir. William and Natalie Warren Med. Inst., Tulsa, 1980-83; chief pediatrician Ella Austin Health Ctr., San Antonio, 1989-95, med. dir., 1993-95; lab. dir., 1993-95; pediatrician UTHSC-SA Primary Care Cmty. Pediat., San Antonio, 1995-98, Minor Emergency Ctr., San Antonio, 1998-99; assoc. Fernando A. Guerra, MD, San Antonio, 1998-99, Lonestar Pediats., Kaufman, Tex., 1999—2002; lead staff physician Cmty. Outreach Clinic/Bluitt-Flowers, Dallas, 2003; pvt. practice, 2006—. Clin. prof. pediats. U. Okla. Med. Sch., Tulsa, 1977-99; clin. instr. pediats. U. Tex. Southwestern Med. Ctr., Dallas, 2002; assoc. prof. pediats. U. Tex. Health Sci. Ctr., San Antonio, 1983-98, dir. rsch. devel., 1993-94, also med. dir.; guest scientist Nat. Inst. Child Health and Human Devel., Bethesda, Md., 1975-77, also cons.; cons. Am. Lung Assn., others; cons. pediatrician San Antonio Ind. Sch. Dist. Contbr. articles to profl. jours. and books. Served as capt. USAF, 1966-68. Recipient continuing edn. awards AMA; Best M.D. Written Book award Am. Med. Writers Assn., 1980; Mosby scholar, 1963; grantee NIH, 1969-70, 75-79, 84-88; grantee USPHS, 1968-69, 91-95; others. Mem. Johns Hopkins Med. and Surg. Assn., So. Soc. Pediatric Rsch., Soc. Pediatric Rsch., Am. Physiol. Soc., Soc. Gynecol. Investigation, Tex. Med. Assn., Raufman County Med. Soc. Home: 604 Courageous Dr Rockwall TX 75032-5768

KOTB, REHAB MOHAMED SALAH, pedodontist; b. Egypt, Sept. 10, 1979; BS in Dental Medicine & Surgery with honors, Faculty Dentistry, Alexandria, 2001, MS in Pediat. Dentistry, 2008. Intern Ras El-Teen Hosp., Shark el Madina Hosp., 2001—02, Faculty Dentistry, Alexandria U., resident pedodontist, 2004—07, registeral pedodontist, 2007—09; dentist Ministry Health, 2002—04; pedodontist Alexandria Dental Rsch. Ctr., 2009—. Contbr. articles to profl. jours. Recipient First prize, Internat. Conf. Egyptian Soc. Pediat. Dentistry. Muslim. Home: 264 Abdelsalam Aref Street Alsaraya Alexandria 264 Egypt Home Phone: 03-3584384, 0127376322. Personal E-mail: hrl79@hotmail.com.

KOTHBAUER, KARL F., neurosurgeon, researcher; b. St. Polten, Austria, Apr. 9, 1962, arrived in U.S., 1996, permanent resident, 1997; m. Ingrid J. Kothbauer-Margreiter, June 19, 1993. MD, U. Vienna, Austria, 1980—88. Cert. Austrian Med. Chamber, 1996. Neurosurgeon Neurochirurgische Klinik, Inselspital, Bern, Switzerland, 1995—99; neurophysiologist, Inst. Neurology and Neurosurgery Beth Israel Med. Ctr., Singer Divsn., NYC, 1996—98, fellow in pediat. neurosurgery, 1998—99, pediat. neurosurgeon, Inst. Neurology and Neurosurgery, 1999—; asst. prof. neurosurgery Albert Einstein Coll. Medicine, NYC, 2000—. Mem.: AAAS, Austrian Soc. for Neurol. Surgery, European Neurol. Soc., New York Acad. of Scis., Congress of Neurol. Surgeons. Avocations: sailing, running, travel. Home Phone: 201-761-0279; Office Phone: 212-870-9600. Office Fax: 212-870-9810. Business E-Mail: kkothbau@bethisraelny.org.

KOTHERA, LYNNE MAXINE, psychologist; b. Cleve., Dec. 18, 1938; d. Leonard Frank and Lillian (Shackleton) K.; m. Richard Litwin, Oct. 24, 1965 (dec.). BA with hons., Denison U., Granville, Ohio, 1960, MA, NYU, 1983; PhD, L.I. U., Bklyn., 1989; postgrad. psychotherapy/psychoanalysis, NYU, 2003. Dancer Martha Graham Dance Co., NYC, 1961-62, Carmen DeLavallade Dance Co., NYC, 1965-68, Glen Tetley Dance Co., NYC, 1965-69; prin. dancer John Butler's, NYC, 1971; artist-in-residence Boston High Schs. - Title III, 1969-71, Hobart-Smith Coll./Denison U., 1973; auditor N.Y. State Council of the Arts, NYC, 1974-78; predoctoral fellow clin. psychology Yale-New Haven Hosp., 1987-88; postdoctoral fellow neuropsychology Inst. of Living, Hartford, Conn., 1989-91; with dept. rehab. medicine Mt. Sinai Med. Ctr., NYC, 1991—2006, co-dir. tng. inpatient, 1995—2006; adj. asst. prof. Hunter Coll., NYC, 1998-99. Mem.: APA. Democrat. Avocations: the arts, ballroom dancing. Home: PO Box 1138 Bridgehampton NY 11932

KOTLER, ROBERT, cosmetic surgeon; b. Chgo., Ill., Sept. 16, 1942; Attended, U. Wisconsin, 1960—63; BS in Medicine, Northwestern U., Chgo., 1964; MD, Northwestern U. Med. Sch., 1967; completed specialty tng., Northwestern U. and U. Ill., 1973, and several others. Lic. Calif., Ill., Va., diplomate Nat. Bd. Med. Examiners, Am. Bd. Otolaryngology/Head and Neck Surgery, 1973, Am. Bd. Cosmetic Surgery, 1980. Student rsch. fellow, dept. medicine Northwestern U. Med. Sch., 1966, tchr. asst., dept. anatomy, 1966; lab. rsch., rsch. lab. VA Adminstrn. Hosp., Chgo., 1966; intern Kaiser Found. Hosp., San Francisco, 1967—68; resident, gen. surgery Cook County Hosp., Chgo., 1968—69; resident, head and neck surgery Northwestern U., Chgo., 1969—70, U. Ill., Chgo., 1971—73; fellowship, cosmetic and reconstructive surgery of the face, head and neck Am. Acad. of Facial Plastic and Reconstructive Surgery; clin. instr., divsn. head & neck surgery, dept. surgery UCLA Med. Sch.; cons., attending surgeon VA Med. Ctr., LA; private practice Beverly Hills, Calif., 1977—; founder Cosmetic Surgery Specialists Group, Beverly Hills. Chief, head and neck dept. DeWitt Army Hosp., Fort Belvoir, Va.; cons., residency program instr. Walter Reed Army Med. Ctr., Washington; founder, pres. Am. Nasal and Facial Surgery Inst., Inc.; commr., reg. cons. Med. Bd. Calif., Dept. Consumer Affairs; cons. City of LA, County of LA; spkr. in field. Author: Chemical Rejuvenation of the Race, Secrets of a Beverly Hills Cosmetic Surgeon, 2002, The Consumer's Guidebook to Cosmetic Facial Surgery, The Expert's Guide to Safe, Successful Surgery, The Essential Cosmetic Surgery Companion, Don't Consult A Cosmetic Surgeon Without This Book!, 2005; contbr. to several med. publs. and presentations, to several med. and lay books; guest appearances Dr. 90210, Access Hollywood, EXTRA, Oprah, Deborah Noville Tonight, Entertainment Tonight. Maj. med. corps. US Army, 1973—75. Mem.: Am. Soc. Outpatient Surgeons (fmr. head and neck sect. chmn.), AMA, Calif. Med. Assn., LA County Med. Assn., Am. Acad. Cosmetic Surgery, Pan-Pacific Surgical Soc., Calif. Soc. Specialty Plastic Surgeons, Canadian Soc. Facial Plastic Surgery, Am. Soc. Outpatient Surgeons, European Soc. Facial Surgery, Am. Soc. for Laser Medicine & Surgery, Internat. Coll. Surgeons, Am. College Surgeons, Am. Soc. for Dermatologic Surgery, Internat. Soc. Cosmetic Surgeons, Karl Meyer Surgical Soc., Am. Acad. Ophthalmology and Otolaryngology, Soc. Mil. Head and Neck Surgeons, Assn. Mil. Surgeons, Am. Acad. Facial Plastic Surgery and Reconstructive Surgery. Office: 436 N Bedford Dr Ste 201 Beverly Hills CA 90210 Office Phone: 310-278-8721. Office Fax: 310-278-0114.

KOTOVSKAYA, YULIA V, cardiologist; b. Kiev, USSR, Mar. 5, 1968; d. Larissa I Bondareva and Victor N Bondarev; 1 child, Natalia V. MD, Russian Peoples' Friendship U., 1992. Cardiologist Russian Peoples' Friendship U., 1992. Asst. prof. Russian Peoples' Friendship U., Moscow, 2003—05, prof., 2005—. Recipient G. Arabidze Diploma of Honors, Russian Soc. of Arterial Hypertension, 1999, Diploma of Honor, Armenian Acad. of Sci., 2001. Mem.: Russian Soc. of Cardiology. Office: Russian Peoples Friendship Univ Vavilova str 61 Hosp N 64 Moscow 117292 Russia Office Fax: +7 495 134 83 06. Business E-Mail: kotovskaya@bk.ru.

KOTSALOU, IRINI, medical researcher; d. Evaggelia Kotsalou. MD, U. Athens, PhD, 2004, Capodistrian U., Athens, 2008. Resident nuc. medicine Nimts Hosp., Athens, 2005—. Contbr. articles to profl. jours. Mem. youth office archbishop, Athens. Mem.: Hellenic Med. Soc., Hellenic Assn. Nuc. Medicine, European Assn. Nuc. Medicine.

KOTSANOS, NIKOLAOS I., dental educator; b. Thessaloniki, Greece, Jan. 9, 1954; DDS, Aristotle U., Greece, 1977; PhD, Bristol U., 1982. Prof. Aristotle U., 1984—. Avocations: basketball, tennis, sailing. Office: Kyriakidi 19 Thessaloniki Macedonia 54636 Greece Business E-Mail: kotsanos@dent.auth.gr.

KOTSEV, STRAHIL NINOV, anesthesiologist, consultant; 2 children. MBBS, MD, Coll. Medicine, Pleven, Bulgaria, 1981—87. Diplomate European Acad. Anaesthesiology, Med. Bd. Sofia. Cons. in anesthesia and critical care AWH, Dubai, United Arab Emirates, 2005—. Contbr. articles to profl. jours. Fellow: European Acad. Anesthesiology; mem.: European Soc. Anesthesiologists (assoc.). Achievements include being the first Bulgarian doctor to be a diplomate of the European Academy of Anaesthesiology; authoring the first publication about retrograde intubation below the first tracheal ring. Avocations: swimming, jogging, travel, martial arts. Home: 1 'King Boris I'str 'Zdravets' Cherven Briag Bulgaria E-mail: strahilkotsev@hotmail.com.

KOTTAMASU, MOHAN RAO (K.V.R. MOHAN RAO), physician, health facility administrator; b. Gudivada, India, Jan. 13, 1947; arrived in U.S., 1973; s. Janardana Rao and Kantharatnamma (Maddi) Kottamasu; m. Sarada Devi Vusirikala, Dec. 20, 1992; children: Pallavi, Aamani. MBBS, Gulbarga Med. Coll., 1972. Diplomate Am. Bd. Internal Medicine, 1977, in pulmonary disease Am. Bd. Internal Medicine, 1980. House surgeon Govt. Gen. Hosp., Gulbarga, India, 1971-72; intern St. Vincent's Med. Ctr. Richmond, SI, NY, 1973-74, resident, 1974-76, chief resident, 1976-77; pulmonary diseases fellow Lahey Clinic and Deaconess Hosp., Boston, 1977-79; clin. fellow Harvard Med. Sch., Boston, 1978-79; assoc. Valley Pulmonary and Med. Assocs., Springfield, Mass., 1979-81, ptnr., v.p., 1981—, pres., 2008. Adj. asst. prof. clin. pharmacy Mass. Coll. Pharmacy and Allied Health Scis., 1984—; pres. med. staff Mercy Hosp., Springfield, 1989—91. Pres. house staff St. Vincent's Med. Ctr., 1976; founding pres. Indian Assn. Greater Springfield, 1985—86. Fellow: ACP, Am. Coll. Chest Physicians; mem.: AMA, Hampden Dist. Med. Soc. (pres.-elect 1999, pres. 2000—01, Cmty. Clinician of the Yr. 2001), Mass. Med. Soc., Am. Thoracic Soc. Hindu. Avocations: chess, gardening. Home: 112 Twin Hills Dr Longmeadow MA 01106-2952 Office: Valley Pulmonary Med Assocs 222 Carew St Springfield MA 01104-4103 Office Phone: 413-739-5661.

KOTTURESHA, HALLADARASTHAPURAMATH VRUSHABHENDRA SWAMY, neonatologist, pediatrician, consultant; b. Shikaripura, India, Feb. 9, 1955; s. H. Vrusharhendra Swamy and Kamalamma; m. Suvarna Kotturesha, Feb. 22, 1992; children: Animisha, Aniketha. DCH, Jawaharlal Nehru Med. Coll., Belgaum, Karnataka, India, 1986, MBBS, 1989. Sr. ho. officer Bapuji Hosp., Davanagere, India; neonatology trainee Kasturba Med. Coll., Manipal, India, 1993—95, B.J. Wadia Hosp., Mumbai, India, 1995—99, P.V.S. Meml. Hosp., Cochin, India, 1999; consulting obstetrician and gynecologist Kotturesha Hosp., Shimoga, India. Dist. coord., dir. Kotturesha Edn. Soc., Shikaripura, India. Mem.: Pediat. Cardiac Soc. of India, Indian Med. Assn., Nat. Neonatology Forum, Indian Acad. Pediat. (life; sec. Malnad br. 2002—04, Appreciation award 2003). Office: Kotturesha Hosp Kamala Nivasa Achutha Rao Layout 1st Cross Near Jail Cir Shimoga 577 201 India Home Phone: 08182-227541; Office Phone: 08182-221432. Personal E-mail: drhvkotturesha@yahoo.co.in.

KOU, VICTORIA, medical educator; BA in Econs., Northwestern U., Evanston, Ill., 1988; MD, George Wash. U., 1997. Rsch. assoc. Prudential, Newark, 1989—91; resident Mt. Sinai Hosp., NYC, 2002—05; asst. prof. UMDNJ Med. Sch., Newark, 2005—11; EMS med. dir. U. Hosp. UMDNJ, 2009—11, Hackersack U. Med. Ctr., 2011—. Comdr. USN, 1997—. Scholar, US Navy, 1993. Mem.: Am. Coll. Emergency Physicians. Office: UMDNJ Dept Emergency Medicine 30 Bergen St ADMC 11 Rm 1110 Newark NJ 07101 also: Mackersack University Med Ctr Emergency Trauma Dept 30 Passport Ave Hackensack NJ 07601 Office Phone: 201-996-5726. Personal E-mail: vwkou@aol.com. Business E-Mail: vkou@humed.com. E-mail: kouvw@umdnj.edu.

KOUAKAM TAKOUGANG, CLAUDE, cardiologist, researcher; b. Dschang, Cameroon, May 27, 1962; s. Thomas Bertin Takougang and Bernadette Kenko; m. Ide Marlise Tchougouoc Djomo, May 30, 1992; children: Laetitia Kenko, Maelis Tchuendem, Cédric Thomas. MD, Lille U. of Medicine, 1990; degree in Emergency Medicine, Lille U., 1992, diploma of Cardiology, 1990—94. Asst. cardiologist Lille U. Hosp., France, 1991—95, sr. cardiologist, 1995—. Sr. clin. rschr. Lille U. of Medecine, 1998—; cons. Guidant CRM, Rueil Malmaison, 1999—. Contbr. articles to profl. jours. Mem. Africans' French Rep. Coun., Lille, 2000—03. Mem.: European Heart Rhythm Assn., European Soc. Cardiology, French Soc. Cardiology (assoc.; working group on arrhythmia). Achievements include research in improvement of medical practice. Home: Chemin des Bois Blancs Wavrin 59136 France Office: Cardiology Hosp CHRU Blvd du Pr J Leclercq Lille 59037 France Office Fax: 33 3 20 44 68 98. Personal E-mail: ckouakam@wanadoo.fr. E-mail: c-kouakam@chru-lille.fr.

KOUBASSOV, ROMAN VICTOROVICH, physiologist, researcher; b. Archangelsk, Russia, Jan. 20, 1973; s. Lyubov Gennadyevna Koubassova and Victor Ivanovich Koubassov; m. Elena Dmitrievna Koubassova, Jan. 10, 2004. Grad., No. State Med. U., Archangelsk, 1993—99, MD, 2005. Lic. pediatrician No. State Med. U., 2006. Pediatrician Archangelsk Regional Children's Hosp., Russia, 1999—2000; from asst. to rsch. fellow lab. endocrinology Inst. Environ. Physiology, Archangelsk, 2000—. With Archangelsk Regional Children Hosp., 2006. Contbr. articles to profl. jours. (JTEMB, Human Physiology). Rsch. grants, Archangelsk Gov. Adminstrn., 2003, 2004, 2006, Rsch. grant, Russian Acad. Scis., 2004. Mem.: Russian Soc. Physiologists (assoc.). Office: Inst Enviorn Physiology Lomonosov Av 249 163061 Archangelsk Russia Office Phone: 78182200927. Office Fax: 78182652992. Personal E-mail: romanas2001@mail.ru. Business E-Mail: rvk@atnet.ru.

KOUCHOUKOS, NICHOLAS THOMAS, surgeon; b. Grand Rapids, Mich., Dec. 26, 1936; s. Thomas Paul and Antoinette (Karver) K.; m. Judith Buell, Aug. 24, 1966; children: Nicholas Thomas, Robert Buell, Thomas Paul. Student (James B. Angell scholar), U. Mich., 1954—57; MD cum laude, Washington U., St. Louis, 1961. Diplomate Am. Bd. Thoracic Surgery. Intern Barnes Hosp., Washington U. Med. Ctr., St. Louis, 1961-62, asst. resident in surgery, 1962-65, chief adminstrv. resident, 1965-66; asst. in surgery Sch. Medicine Washington U., St. Louis, 1961-65, instr. surgery, 1965-67, John M. Shoenberg prof. cardiovascular surgery, 1984-96, vice chmn. dept. surgery, 1991-96; sr. clin. trainee in surgery USPHS, 1966-67, surgery study sect. Bethesda, Md., 1977-80; rsch. fellow surgery Sch. Medicine, U. Ala., Birmingham, 1967-68, instr. surgery, 1967-69, advanced trainee thoracic and cardiovascular surgery, 1968-70, asst. prof. surgery, 1969-71, assoc. prof., 1971-74, prof., vice-dir. div. thoracic and cardiovascular surgery, 1974-81, John W. Kirklin prof. cardiovascular surgery, 1981, clin. prof., 1981-84; cardiovascular surgeon in-chief Jewish Hosp. of St. Louis, 1984-96, surgeon in chief, 1988-96; thoracic and cardiovascular surgeon Mo. Bapt. Med. Ctr., St. Loius, 1996—. Ad hoc cons. Specialized Centers in Rsch. Arteriosclerosis, Nat. Heart and Lung Inst., Bethesda, 1971-72, mem. ad hoc rev. com. for collaborative studies on coronary artery surgery, 1973-75, surgery A study sect., 1976-77; mem. merit rev. bd. in cardiovascular studies VA, Washington, 1976-78; mem. cardiovascular rsch. study com. Am. Heart Assn. 1977-79. Editl. bd. Jour. Cardiac Rehab., 1979-84, Current Topics in Cardiology, 1977-92, Circulation, 1978-81, 86-88, Cardiology Update, 1979-92, Annals Thoracic Surgery, 1980-89, Cardiosat, 1984-92; assoc. editor Jour. Thoracic and Cardiovascular Surgery, 1994-98. Fellow: ACS, Am. Coll. Cardiology (asst. treas. 1997—99, sec. 1999—2000, finalist Young Investigators award 1962); mem.: AAUP, AMA, Am. Bd. Thoracic Surgery (bd. dirs. 1989—96), Internat. Cardiovascular Soc., Soc. Vascular Surgery, Soc. Univ. Surgeons, So. Surg. Assn., So. Thoracic Surg. Assn., St. Louis Thoracic Surg. Soc. (pres. 1993—95), Soc. Thoracic Surgeons (treas. 1992—97, v.p. 1998, pres. 1999—2000, historian 2007—), John Kirklin Soc., St. Louis Met. Med. Soc., Internat. Surg. Soc., Assn. Acad. Surgery, Assn. Clin. Cardiac Surgeons, Am. Surg. Assn., Am. Assn. Thoracic Surgery, Alpha Omega Alpha, Phi Beta Kappa. Home: 25 Picardy Ln Saint Louis MO 63124-1606 Office: Mo Bapt Med Ctr 3009 N Ballas Rd Ste 360C Saint Louis MO 63131-2308 Office Phone: 314-996-5287.

KOUCHOUKOS, PHILIP LAWRENCE, emergency physician; b. Joliet, Ill., Feb. 1, 1946; MD, U. Ill., 1971; MS, U. Chgo., 2002. Emergency physician Emergency Med. Specialists, 2001—. Avocations: gardening, music, computers. Home: 130 Old Barrington Rd North Barrington IL 60010-1927 Personal E-mail: freebison@sbcglobal.net.

KOUDRIAVTSEVA, TATIANA, neurologist; b. Moscow, Sept. 7, 1960; MD, U. Rome La Sapienza, 1989. Philos. physician U. Rome La Sapienza, 1993—98, neurologist, 1993, Hosp. Belcolle Viterbo, 1998—2000, Hosp. S. Giovanni Addolorata Rome, 2000—07, dir., multiple sclerosis regional ctr., 2003—07, Inst. Regina Elena - IFO - Rome, 2009—, neurologist, 2007—. Mem.: AISM, SIN. Avocations: classical music, travel. Office: Via Elio Chianesi 53 Rome Lazio 00144 Italy Business E-Mail: koudriavtseva@ifo.it.

KOUFAKIS, DIMITRIS, ophthalmologist, medical retina specialist; b. Athens, Attiki, Greece, Aug. 31, 1972; s. Ioannis Koufakis and Agathoniki Chalvatzoglou; m. Theodora Tetsiou, Sept. 11, 2004; 1 child, Ioannis. PhD, U. Thessaly Med. Sch., Greece, 2006. Resident Gen. Hosp. Larissa, Greece, G. Papanikolaou Gen. Hosp., Thessaloniki, Greece; pvt. health care provider. Fellow, U. Hosp. Larissa, Moorfields Eye Hosp., London. Fellow: European Bd. Ophthalmology; mem.: Internat. Tear Film and Ocular Surface Soc., European Assn. Vision and Eye Rsch., Assn. Rsch. Vision and Ophthalmology, European Vitreo Retinal Soc. Greek Orthodox. Avocations: volleyball, motorcycling, water-skiing. Home: 20 Gyzi Str Larissa 41447 Greece Office: 9 Panagoulis Str Larissa 41223 Greece Office Phone: 0030 2410 23947. Personal E-mail: dimkouf@hotmail.com.

KOUIMTSIDIS, CHRISTOS, psychiatrist, educator; b. Kavala, Greece, Oct. 5, 1966; arrived in Eng., 1994; s. Dimitris Kouimtsidis and Niki Papadaniel; m. Anastasia06041994 Revi; 1 child, Dimitris. MBBS, Aristotle U., Thessaloniki, Greece, 1990; MSc, U. London, 1996. Lectr. substance misuse St. George's Hosp. Med. Sch., London, 1999—2001, cons., sr. lectr., 2003—; specialist registrar SW London & St. George's, London, 2001—02. Cons. Hertfordshire Ptnr. Trust, Hepts, England, 2003. Contbr. articles to profl. jours. Mem.: Royal Coll. Psychiatrists. Avocation: writing. Home: 10 Westways 43 Hamilton Rd London W5 2EE England Office: St George's Hosp Med Sch Cranmer Terr London SW17 0RE England Personal E-mail: drckouimtsidis@hotmail.com.

KOUL, DEEPAK, cardiologist, researcher; s. Moti Lal and Pyari Koul. MD with honors, Govt. Med. Coll., Srinagar, Kashmir, India, 1995, M.P. Shah Med. Coll., Jamnagar, India, 1999. Diplomate Am. Bd. Internal Medicine, 2005, Am. Bd. Geriat. Medicine, 2006. Tutor, rsch. assoc. M.P. Shah Med. Coll. and Irwin Group Hosps., Jamnagar, Gujurat, India, 1999—2001; resident in internal medicine Wayne State U./Detroit Med. Ctr., 2002—05, fellow geriat. medicine, 2005—06; fellow in cardiology St. John Hosp. and Med. Ctr., Detroit, 2006—. Com. mem. nat. sch. health screening program Irwin Hosp./Govt of India, Jamnagar, 1995—97. Contbr. articles to profl. jours. Vol. WHO Pulse Polio Immunization, Jamnagar, 1997—2000; vol. bus drivers health screen Detroit Med. Ctr., 2002—04. Recipient L.B.Mahajan prize, Saurashtra U., 1996, Cert. of Distinction, 1996, award, Glaxosmithkline Diagnostic Challenge, 2004. Fellow: Am. Coll. Cardiology (assoc.; 2006 - current); mem.: AMA (assoc.), ACP (assoc.), Mich. Assn. Physicians of Indian Origin (assoc.), Mich. State

Med. Soc. (assoc.). Hindu. Achievements include patents for erythropoietin in cardiovascular diseases; research in outcomes after renal angioplasty and stent placement in hypertensive African Americans with critical renal artery stenosis; prevalence of metabolic syndrome in coronary microangiopathy and left ventricular remodeling after acute myocardial infarection on transthoracic echocardiography; reviews on current concepts in diastolic heart failure, transient apical ballooning and atrial flutter. Avocations: swimming, mountain biking, white-water rafting, hiking, travel. Office: St John Hosp and Med Ctr Cardiac Cath Lab 2nd Fl VEP 22101 Moross Rd Ste 126 Detroit MI 48236 Office Phone: 313-343-4612. Personal E-mail: deekoul@yahoo.com.

KOULOURIS, NIKOLAOS G., pulmonologist, educator; s. George and Maria Koulouris; m. Marilena Melea, Feb. 7, 1999; 1 child, George. Ptychion Iatrikis, Athens U. Med. Sch., Greece, 1980, MD, 1985; diploma in Thoracic Medicine, U. London, 1982, PhD, 1989. Cert. Tb & pulmonary medicine specialist Greek Ministry Health Wellfare, 1985. Rsch. fellow U. Athens Med. Microbiology Dept., 1980—81, sr. house officer, 1981—82; rsch. fellow U. London-Royal Brompton Hosp., 1982—84, U. London Royal Brompton & King's Coll. Hops., 1986—89; med. registrar Air-Force Internal. Medicine Dept., Athens, 1984—86; med. sr. registrar Athens U. Respiratory Medicine Dept., 1989—92, lectr. respiratory medicine, 1993—98, asst. prof. respiratory medicine, 1998—2004, assoc. prof., 2004—; postdoc. rsch. fellow McGill U. Meakins Christie Labs., Montreal, Quebec, Canada, 1992—93. Mem. formulary com. Greek Nat. Drug Adminstrn., Athens, 2000—02. Contbr. articles to profl. jours. Lt. capt. Greece Air Force, 1984—86. Med. fellowship, NATO, 1986—87, Excellence Med. fellowship, Can. Med. Ctr., 1992—93. Mem.: Brit. Thoracic Soc., Am. Thoracic Soc., European Respiratory Soc. Office: Nat Univ Athens 152 Mesogeion Ave Athens Attica GR-11527 Greece Office Fax: 30 210 776 3454. Business E-Mail: koulnik@med.uoa.gr.

KOUNO, AKIHISA, forensic pathologist, health facility administrator; b. Tennoji, Osaka, Japan, Nov. 10, 1961; s. Takao and Eiko Kouno; m. Mika Akamatsu, Mar. 3, 1995; 1 child, Reika. MD, Fujita - Gakuen Health U., Toyoake, Aichi, Japan, 1987; PhD, Osaka U., 2000. Cert. anesthesiologist, supreme forensic pathologist. Resident Osaka University Hospital, Osaka, Osaka, Japan, 1988—89, Minoo Munincipal's Hospital, Minoo, Osaka, Japan, 1989—90; regular anesthesiologist Tondabayashi Hosp., 1990—92; rsch. fellow Westfalische Wilhelms U., Münster, 1995—96; chief anesthesiologist Kouno Clinic, Sakai, Japan, 1992—95, exec. dir., 1996—2005, dir., 2005—. Med. examiner Osaka Med. Examiner's Office, 1989—; asst. prof. Shiga U. Med. Sci., 2004—; guest prof. Fujita-Gakuen Health U., 2010. Author: (book) Child Suffering in the World, 2000; editor: (jour.) Child Abuse in Japan, Perinatal Care 19(13), 2000; author: (book) A Handbook of Sudden Infant Death Syndrome, 1999, Child Abuse, A Global View, 2001; co-author (with Kizuaton-Shinjitsu): Novels of Child Abuse and Neglect, 2008; contbr. articles and reports to profl. publs., chpts. to books; mem. editl. bd. Forensic Sci., Medicine and Pathology, 2005—. Mem. Prefectural adv. com. on child abuse and neglect Osaka and Hyogo Prefectures, 2002—. Mem.: Medico-Legal Soc., Japan Med. Assn. Achievements include research in differential diagnosis of sudden infant death cases; diagnostic approach to child abuse and neglect. Avocations: piano, cooking, swimming, skiing, travel. Home: 2-2-6 Wakamatsu-dai Osaka Sakai 590-0116 Japan Office: Kouno Clinic 2 - 2 - 6 Wakamatsu - dai Osaka Sakai 590 - 0116 Japan Home Phone: 81-72-293-1501; Office Phone: 81-72-291-0232. Office Fax: 81-72-293-3121; Home Fax: 81-72-293-3121.

KOURI, GUSTAVO PEDRO, virologist; b. Havana, Cuba, Jan. 11, 1936; s. Pedro and Mercedes (Flores) K.; m. Lidia Cardella (div. 1979); children: Lilliam, Vivian, Gustavo; m. Maria G. Guzman, Nov. 25, 1980; 1 child, Pedro. MD, Havana U., 1962; PhD, Nat. Ctr. Sci. Rsch., Havana, 1973; ScD, Charles U., Prague, Czechoslovakia, 1990. Chief virology dept. Nat. Ctr. for Sci. Rsch., Havana, 1965-70, dep. dir., 1965-70; vice-dean med. faculty Havana U., 1970-73, vice rector, 1973-76; nat. dir. for sci. Ministry of Higher Edn., Havana, 1976-78; dir. gen. Tropical Medicine Inst. "Pedro Kouri", Havana, 1979—; dir. WHO Collaborating Ctr. for Biol. Vector Control, Havana, 1990—. Temp. advisor Pan Am. and WHO to present; lectr. in field; cons. in field. Contbr. numerous articles to profl. jours. Grantee TDR, 1979, 81, 82, 83, 84, 85, 86, IDRC, 1983, 86, 2003, French Govt., 1989; recipient Carlos Finlay Nat. Order and medal Cuban State Coun., 1990, Silver medal Charles U., 1988, Cesar Uribe medal NIH, Colombia, 1991, Hero of the Republic of Cuba, 1996. Fellow Third World Acad. Scis.; mem. AAAS, N.Y. Acad. Sci., Cuban Acad. Sci. (mem. de merito, v.p. 1996), Real Academia de Medicina y Cirujia de Galicia, Royal Soc. Tropical Medicine Hygiene, Latin Am. Fedn. Tropical Medicine (pres. 1993-97), Cuban Soc. Microbiology and Parasitology (pres. 1980), Latin Am. Fedn. Parasitology (pres. 1995-97), Latin Am. Soc. Microbiology (pres. 2000—02), Coun. Internat. Soc. Infectious Diseases. Achievements include research on Dengue Hemorrhagic Fever. Office: Inst Medicina Tropical Autopista Novia del Mediod Havana Cuba E-mail: gkouri@ipk.sld.cu.

KOURI, JUAN BAUTISTA, government agency administrator; b. Havana, Cuba, May 2, 1941; arrived in Mexico, 1994; s. Pedro Kouri and Mercedes Flores; 1 child, Maythe. MD, Havana U., Cuba, 1966. Dir. nat. ctr. sci. rsch. Ministry Higher Edn., Havana, 1976—84; vice min. sci. and tech. Pub. Health Ministry, Havana, 1985—90; cons. prof. Ameijeras Hosp., Havana, 1990—94; with Nat. Inst. for Orthop., Havana, 1990—94; prof., head dept. exptl. pathology Soc. Electronic Microscopy, Mexico City, 1994—, pres. Cuban Interamerican Com., 2004—. Temp. cons. Pan-Am. Health Orgn., Havana. Mem.: Internat. Com. of Electron Microscopy Socs. of Am. (gen. sec. 1985—2002). Office: Cinvestav-Ipn Ave Ipn # 2508 07360 Mexico City Mexico Home Phone: 52-55-52771530; Office Phone: 52-55-50613343. Office Fax: 52-55-57479890. Business E-Mail: bkouri@enigma.red.cinvestav.mx.

KOURI, TIMO T, associate chief physician, consultant; b. Kemi, Finland, 1953; s. Vilho Olavi Kouri and Salme Marjatta Kouri s Torvinen; m. Ulla K Pylvas, June 25, 1983; children: Marjaana, Panu, Sampo. MD, PhD, Turku U., Med. Faculty, Finland, 1985. Specialist in clin. chemistry Turku U., Finland, 1989. Rsch. asst. Turku U., Dept. Med. Biochemistry, Finland, 1978—86; postdoc. fellow Dept. Basic and Clin. Rsch., Scripps Clinic, La Jolla, Calif., 1987—88; resident clin. chemistry Turku U. Hosp., Dept. Clin. Chemistry, 1988—90; specialist physician, clin. chemistry Tampere U., Finland, 1990—2001, docent clin. chemistry, 1995; assoc. chief physician, lab. Oulu U. Hosp., Finland, 2001—; adminstrv. competence Oulu U., Finland, 2002. Cons. urinalysis Labquality, Helsinki, Finland, 1990—; chmn., european urinalysis group European Confederation Lab. Medicine, Germany, 1996—2000. Author: European Urinalysis Guidelines. Fellow, European Bd. Med. Biocpathology, UEMS, 2004. Mem.: Finnish Soc. Med. Specialists Clin. Chemistry (chmn. 2007—, Finnish Clin. Chemist Ann. award 2002), Am. Assn. Clin. Chemistry. Achievements include research in reference procedure for urine particle counting. Avocation: music. Office: Oulu Univ Hosp Lab Adminstrn PL 50 90029 Oulu Finland

KOURIDES, IONE ANNE, endocrinologist, researcher, educator; b. NYC, Sept. 1, 1942; d. Peter T. and Anne E. (Spetseris) K.; m. Charles G. Zaroulis, Nov. 30, 1974; children: Anna Larisa, Andrew, Christina, Peter. BA, Wellesley Coll., 1963; MD, Harvard U., 1967. Diplomate Am. Bd. Internal Medicine, Am. Bd. Endocrinology and Metabolism. Intern Jewish Hosp., Washington U., St. Louis, 1967-68; resident Montefiore, Albert Einstein Med. Sch., Bronx, NY, 1968-69; fellow Beth Israel, Harvard U., Boston, 1970-72; assoc. prof. medicine Cornell U. Med. Coll., NYC, 1981—; sr. med. dir., worldwide team leader endocrine care Pfizer Inc., NYC, 2004—09; med. cons. Biotech Pharms. Industry, 2009—; sr. med. dir. Diabatis Fized Inc, NYC, 1990—2004. Mem. editl. bd. Endocrinology, Jour. Clin. Endocrinol Metabolism, also others; contbr. over 100 articles to sci. jours., chpts. to books. Mem. nat. campaign Harvard Med. Sch., Boston, 1986-92; nat. bd. dirs. Philoptochos Soc. Greek Orthodox Archdiocese. Grantee NIH, 1979-84. Fellow ACP; mem. Am. Soc. Clin. Investigation, Am. Assn. Physicians, Am. Thyroid Assn. (coms.), Endocrine Soc. (coms.). Achievements include discovery of alpha-secreting pituitary tumors; measurement of amniotic fluid thyroid stimulating hormone that can be used to diagnose hypthyroidism in utero; development of insulin secretagogue Glucotrol XL. Office: 1070 Park Ave New York NY 10128-1000 Business E-Mail: ionc.kourides@gmail.com.

KOURILSKY, OLIVIER, nephrologist; b. Boulogne-Billancourt, France, Apr. 1, 1945; s. Raoul and Simone (Develay) K.; 1 child, Gregory. Diploma in Immunology, Pasteur Inst., Paris, 1970, MD, 1973, Habilitation to Direct Rsch., 1993. Intern, Paris, 1969-72; asst. chief clinic Tenon Hosp., Paris, 1973-82; head dept. nephrology Centre Hosp Sud Francilien, Evry, France, 1982—2010; assoc. prof. Coll. Medicine Hopitaux, Paris, 1993; ret. Mem. sci. commn. #5, INSERM, Paris, 1979-82; expert Clin. Rsch. Commn., Paris, 1999-2006; mem. coun. faculty medicine U. Paris XI, 2000-07. Author: Nephrology, Urology for Nurses, 1995, 4 Thrillers (Littré prize 2010); co-author: Management of the Critically Ill Patient, 1983, Nephrology, 1997 (Nat. Acad. Medicine prize 1998); contbr. articles to profl. jours. Decorated chevalier de la Légion d'Honneur; grantee INSERM-CIBA Found., London, 1973, Paris Hosps. Med. Soc., 1974-78. Mem. Internat. Soc. Nephrology, Internat. Soc. Hypertension, Am. Soc. Nephrology, French Soc. Nephrology (coun. 1991-97, 2005-11). Avocations: music, piano, Judo, cinema, literature. Home: 34 Rue Serpente 75006 Paris France

KOUTLIANOS, NIKOLAOS, exercise physiologist, educator; b. Thessaloniki, Greece, June 17, 1974; s. Aggelos Koutlianos and Aggeliki Siozou; m. Anna Petridou, Sept. 10, 2005. BPE, Aristotle U., 1996, PhD in Human Performance and Health, 2001. Rschr. Aristotle U. Thessaloniki, 1995—2005, lectr., 2005. Seaman Greek Navy, 2001—03. Scholar, Rsch. Com. Aristotle U. Thessaloniki. Mem.: European Assn. Rehabilitation in Chronic Kidney Disease, European Assn. Cardiovascular Prevention of Rehabilitation, European Coll. Sport Sci., Fedn. Intern. Du Medicine Sportive. Achievements include research in sports medicine. Home: Grigoriou E 10 Thessaloniki Triandria 55337 Greece Office Fax: 00302310992183; Home Fax: 00302310992183. Business E-Mail: koutlixy@phed.xuth.gr.

KOUTSIARIS, ARISTOTLE, biomedical engineer, applied science professor; b. Larissa, Greece, Nov. 16, 1970; s. George Koutsiaris and Olga Koutsiari. Diploma in Engring., Aristotle U. Thessaloniki, Greece, 1993; MSc in Biomed. Engring., U. Dundee, Scotland, 1994; PhD in Biomed. Engring., U. Patras, Athens, Greece, 2000. Rschr. U. Athens, 2001—04. Contbr. articles to profl. jours. Grantee, Nat. Scholarship Found., Athens, 1996—99. Mem.: Internat. Soc. Clin. Hemorheology, European Soc. Microcirculation, Inst. Physics Engring. in Medice, Inst. Elec. Engrs. Achievements include first implementation of particle image velocimetry without laser and fluroscence at cylindrical glass micro tubes; quantification of the human eye microcirculatory hemodynamics in relation to vessel diameter; velocity profile equation for blood flow in-vivo.

KOVACHEV, LJUBOMIR STEFANOV, surgery educator; b. Dimitrovgrad, Haskovo, Bulgaria, Nov. 26, 1942; s. Stefan Lazarov and Stefanka Yankova (Lambeva) K.; m. Anelia Ljubomirova Panteleeva, Feb. 7, 1981; 1 child, Stefan Ljubomirov. MD, Higher Inst. Medicine, Sofia, Bulgaria, 1972; PhD, Higher Med. Inst., Pleven, Bulgaria, 1985. Registrar in surgery City Hosp., Dulovo, Bulgaria, 1972-75, Dist. Hosp., Pernik, Bulgaria, 1975; asst. prof. surgery Higher Med. Inst., Pleven, Bulgaria, 1976-85, assoc. prof., 1986—2005, prof., 2005—, head dept., 1987—, dean, 1987-93. Contbr. articles to med. jours., including Internat. Surgery, Surgery Today-Japan Jour. Surgery, Lancet, Zentralblat für Chirurgie, Surg. Radiol. Anatomy, Brit. Jour. Surgery, European Jour. Surgery, Hernia. Mem.: Eurosurgery. Orthodox. Achievements include research in treatment of groin hernia, pancreatic and biliary diseases and other areas of gastrointestinal surgery. Avocations: sports, history, geography. Home: Entr D Apt 2 George Kochev St 39 5800 Pleven Bulgaria Office: Higher Med Inst Kl Ohridsky St 1 5800 Pleven Bulgaria Home Phone: 359.64.804053; Office Phone: 359 64 886 152. Business E-Mail: lskovachev@abv.bg.

KOVACHY, EDWARD MIKLOS, JR., psychiatrist, consultant; b. Cleve., Dec. 3, 1946; s. Edward Miklos and Evelyn Amelia (Palenscar) K.; m. Susan Eileen Light, June 21, 1981; children: Timothy Light, Benjamin Light. BA, Harvard U., 1968, JD, MBA, Harvard U., 1972; MD, Case Western Reserve U., 1977. Diplomate Nat. Bd. Med. Examiners. Resident in psychiatry Stanford U. Med. Ctr., Stanford, Calif., 1977-81; pvt. practice psychiatry, mediation, exec. coaching Menlo Park, Calif., 1981—. Presenter ann. meeting Am. Psychol. Assn., 1998, Calif. Assn. Marriage and Family Therapists, 1999. Co-prodr. Jolson and Company, Century Ctr. for the Performing Arts, N.Y.C., 2002; columnist The Peninsula Times Tribune, 1983-85. Trustee Mid-Peninsula H.S., Palo Alto, Calif., 1990-2001, mem. bd. advisors, 2001—; mem. gift com. Harvard Coll. Class of 1968, 25th reunion chmn. participation, San Francisco, 1993, 30th reunion chmn. participation, West Coast, 1998, nat. co-chmn. participation and assocs. giving, 1999—, nat. co-chmn. participation, 35th reunion, 2003, nat. co-chmn. participation, 40th reunion, 2008. Recipient Albert H. Gordon award Harvard U., 2000, 05, 07, Joseph R. Hamlen award Harvard U., 2003, 08; named to Hall of Fame, Shaker Heights Alumni Assn., 2003 Mem. Am. Psychiat. Assn. (life, presenter annual meetings 1984, 98), Physicians for Social Responsibility, Assn. Family and Conciliation Cts., No. Calif. Psychiat. Soc., Harvard Alumni Assn. (dir. 2006—09). Presbyterian. Avocations: personal activism, musical comedy, athletics. Office: 1187 University Dr Menlo Park CA 94025-4423 Office Phone: 650-329-0600. Personal E-mail: edkovachy@aol.com.

KOVACS, DONALD J., physician; b. Cleve., Dec. 31, 1949; BA, Coll. Wooster, 1971; MD, U. Cin., 1976. Ptnr. Yellow Breeches Family Practice, 1979—. Dir., med. edn. Carlisle Regional Med. Ctr., 1994—. Mem.: Pa. Med. Soc. Avocations: photography, bicycling. Office: 1358 Lutztown Rd Boiling Springs PA 17007 Office Fax: 717-258-0311. Business E-Mail: quakerdoc07@aol.com.

KOVACS, ILLES, ophthalmologist; b. Pecs, Hungary, Dec. 20, 1974; MD, Med. U. Pecs, 1999, PhD, 2005. Asst., dept. ophthalmology Semmelweis U., 2001. Mem. steering com. Hungarian Assn. Rsch. Vision and Ophthalmology, 2008. Tchrs. Travel grant, Italian Ministry of Fgn. Affairs, European Bd. Ophthalmology, grant, Austrian ARVO, Marie-Curie fellowship. Mem.: ESCRS, AVRO. Office: 39 Maria Str Pest Budapest 1085 Hungary Personal E-mail: kovacsilles@yahoo.com.

KOVACS, JOZSEF, physician, philosopher, psychotherapist, bioethicist; b. Budapest, Hungary, June 14, 1955; s. Jozsef Kovacs and Klara Gilde; m. Katalin Fehervari, July 1, 1982; children: David, Kristof, Adam. MD, Semmelweis U. Medicine, Budapest, 1979; degree in Philosophy, Eotvos Lorand U., Budapest, 1983. Cert. in cmty. medicine Hungary, 1985, in psychotherapy Hungary, 2002. Jr. mem. Dept. Cmty. Medicine, Inst. Postgraduate Med. Studies, Budapest, Hungary, 1979—82; asst. prof. med. ethics Semmelweis U. Medicine, Inst. Social Scis., Unit Med. Ethics, Budapest, 1982—90, asst. lectr., 1990—93, asst. lectr. bioethics, 1993—97; assoc. prof. dept. bioethics Semmelweis U., Inst. Behavioural Scis., 1997—, prof. bioethics, 2010—. Expert mem. bioethics adv. com. Hungarian Parliament, Budapest, 1991—94; mem. rsch. staff Tchg. and Rsch. Network, Bioethics of European Coun., 1993—95; mem. rsch. project on fertility, infertility and human embryo European Commn., 1994—95; mem. sci. and rsch. ethics com. Health Care Sci. Coun. Hungary, Budapest, 1995—; cons. in field. Author: The Fundamentals of Modern Medical Ethics. An Introduction to Bioethics, 1997, 2d edit., 1999, 2006, (in Hungarian) Bioethical Questions on Psychiatry and Psychotherapy, 2007; contbr. articles to profl. jours. Szechenyi Professorial Fellowship. Mem.: Hungarian Assn. Philosophy, Hungarian Assn. Bioethics, Hungarian Psychiat. Assn., Internat. Assn. Bioethics, European Soc. Philosophy of Medicine and Health Care. Achievements include research in patient's rights in Hungary. Avocations: literature, music, walking. Office: Semmelweis Univ Budapest Nagyvarad ter 4 Budapest 1089 Hungary Office Fax: (36-1)-210-2955.

KOVALCHUK, VITALY VLADIMIROVICH, neurologist, educator; b. Vilnius, Lithuania, Oct. 14, 1967; Degree, Pavlov's St. Petersburg Med. U., 1993. Resident Pavlov's St. Petersburg Med. U., Dept. Neurology, 1993—95, rschr., 1995—97; neurologist Clinic 89, 1997—98; head dept. neurology rehab. Hosp. 38, 1998—; assoc. prof. med. faculty, dept. therapy St. Petersburg U., 2008—10. Chmn. St. Petersburg's Soc. Rehab., 2008; adj. prof. Assn. Neurologists Russian's NW Region, 2009. Contbr. articles to profl. publs. Recipient Best People of Pushkin Region, Govt. of Pushkin Region, St. Petersburg, Honored Deed, Minister of Healthcare and Social Devel. of Russian Fedn., 2011; named Best Rschr. of Yr., Acad. Med. Scis. Russia, Best Doctor of Russian Fedn., 2011. Master: Coordination Coun. Elaboratoin Med. Stads. in Rehab., St. Petersburg's Com. Reorganization Stroke Rehab. svc.; mem.: Coordination Coun. Elaboratoin Med. Stads. in Neurology, St. Petersburg's Com. Reorganization Stroke svc., St. Petersburg's Assn. Neurologists. Home: Leningradskaya St 85/12 155 Pushkin Saint Petersburg 196605 Russia Home Fax: 7(812)4666226. Personal E-mail: vikoval67@mail.ru.

KOVALEVA, NATALIA VITALIYEVNA, geneticist, consultant; b. St. Petersburg, Russia, July 30, 1952; d. Vitaliy A. Kovalev and Zoya I. Kovaleva; m. Eugeniy V. Kouvalchouk, May 4, 1985. MS in Animal Genetics, St. Petersburg State U., Russia, 1976; PhD, Rsch. Inst. Animal Genetics and Breeding, St. Petersburg, 1984. Sr. lab. asst. Inst. Exptl. Medicine, St. Petersburg, 1977—84, rschr., 1984—89, sr. rschr., 1989—97, Inst. Ob-gyn., St. Petersburg, 1997—2000; postdoctoral fellow Baylor Coll. Medicine, Houston, 2001—02; cons. St. Petersburg (Russia) Ctr. Med. Genetics, 2003—; assoc. prof. St. Petersburg Med. Acad. Postgrad. Studies, 2006—. Expert North-West Ecol. Union, St. Petersburg. Mem.: St. Petersburg (Russia) Soc. Med. Genetics (chmn. 2004—), European Soc. Human Genetics. Avocation: gardening. Office: St Petersburg Ctr Med Genetics ul. Tobol'skaya 5 194044 Saint Petersburg Sankt-Pyetyerburg Russia Personal E-mail: kovaleva@robotek.ru. E-mail: kovaleva@admiral.ru.

KOVARIK, JOHN MARK, pharmacologist; b. St. Paul, Feb. 11, 1958; BA in Chemistry summa cum laude, Macalester Coll., 1980; BS in Pharmacy, U. Minn., 1985, PharmD, 1985; PhD, Royal U. Utrecht, The Netherlands, 1990. Lic. pharmacist, Minn. Clin. instr. pharmacy U. Minn., Mpls., 1985-87; clin. rsch. investigator Univ. Hosp. Utrecht, 1987-90; postdoc. rsch. asst. pharmacology Sandoz Pharma Ltd., Basle, Switzerland, 1991; pharmacokineticist Novartis Pharma, Inc., Basle, Switzerland, 1992—. Author: Applications of Pharmacokinetics Principles in Drug Development, 2004; contbr. articles to profl. jours. Am. Soc. Hosp. Pharmacists fellow Hennepin County Med. Ctr., Mpls., 1985-87. Fellow Am. Coll. Clin. Pharmacology, Phi Beta Kappa. Office: Novartis Pharma Clin Pharmacol WSJ 210 427 4002 Basel Switzerland Business E-Mail: john.kovarik@novartis.com.

KOVE, MIRIAM, psychotherapist; b. Chotin, Romania, Feb. 17, 1941; came to U.S., Sept. 12, 1962; d. Avrum and Riva (Nussenbaum) Wolkove; m. Marc L. Kouffman, Aug. 16, 1964 (div. Oct. 24, 1989); children: Avra, Paulette. BA in English Lit., Sir George Williams U., 1962; MA in Early Childhood, Hunter Coll., 1975; Cert. in Psychoanalytic Psychotherapy, New Hope Guild, NYC, 1979; MSW, Adelphi U., 1983. Tchr. various pub. schs., Montreal, Can., 1957-58; actress

NYC, 1962—; tchr. early childhood Emanuel Nursery Sch., NYC, 1964-74; adj. lectr. early childhood Cmty. Coll., Bklyn., 1974-75; psychotherapist, clinician New Hope Guild Ctr., NYC, 1979-81; intake dir., clinician Insts. of Religion and Health, NYC, 1983-84; pschotherapist NYC, 1984—; faculty, supr. New Hope Guild Ctr., NYC, 1990—; dir. day care on-site therapy program C.I.S. Counseling Ctr., NYC, 1992-94. Author: (book) Myths and Madness, 2007. Mem. People for the Am. Way, Warsaw Gathering of Holocaust Survivors. Recipient Hebrew prize Sir George Williams U., 1962; recommended for English prize Concordia U. Fellow Nat. Orgn. Social Work, Soc. for Clin. Social Work Psychotherapists (edn. com.); mem. New Hope Grad. Soc. (steering com.), Am. Bd. Examiners in Clin. Social Work. Jewish. Home and Office: 320 E 25th St Apt 8ee New York NY 10010-3100 Office Phone: 212-689-1442. Personal E-mail: miriamkove@hotmail.com.

KOWALCEK, INGRID, biomedical researcher; Diploma in Psychology, Philipps U., Marburg, Germany, 1985; MD, U. Marburg, Germany, 1992; habilitation, U. Schleswig Holstein, Lübeck, Germany, 2002. Prof., clin. practice in prenatal medicine, reproductive medicine, dept. gynecology & obstetrics Med. U. Schleswig Holstein, 2006—. Author: Psychomatic in Reproductive Medicine, Psychosomatic Aspects in Prenatal Medicine. Achievements include research in gender specific psychosomatic aspects in reproductive medicine and in prenatal medicine anxiety by pregnant women with prior miscarriage before and after prenatal diagnosis, body mind medicine psychology, nutrition, yoga, phytotherapic; culturspecific aspect of illness e.g. menopause; preferred mode of delivery, pregnancy and delivery after assisted conception, Psychological aspects reducing multiple pregnancy after ART, Parets of Multiple Births after ART Phythotherapy. Office: Fertility Ctr Lübeck Inst Women Brahmstr 10 23556 Lübeck Germany E-mail: kowalcek@t-online.de.

KOWALCZYK, MACIEJ STANISLAW, obstetrician, gynecologist, sexologist; b. Krakow, Poland, June 8, 1956; s. Bogumil Wieslaw and Teresa Maria (Matowska) K.; m. Tamara Halina Kolany, Jan. 20, 2005; 1 child, Maciej Stanislaw Jr. MD, Med. Acad., Krakow, 1984; postgrad., Polish Acad. Sci., Krakow, 1984, Inst. Gyn.-Ob, 1988-91, Instn. Sexology and Pathology Interhuman Bonds, Warsaw, 1990-93. Intern Narutowicz Hosp., Krakow, 1984-85; gen. practice medicine ambulatory Krakow-Srodmiescie, 1984-85; gen. practice ambulatory medicine First Aid Svc., 1985-87; asst. obstetrician and gynecologist Szpital Polozniczy, Krakow, 1986—2004; obstetrician and gynecologist Maternity Amb. for Sch. Tchrs., Krakow, 1987-92. Tchr. Cathedral Normal Anatomy, Med. Acad., Krakow, 1984-86; prof. Med. Coll. for Midwives, 1991; mem. commn. in Social Ins. Instn., Krakow, 1986-88; mem. govtl. commn. med. examiners, 2000-2004. Contbr. articles to profl. jours. Recipient Organon Poster award, Yokohama, Japan, 1995. Mem. AAAS, Polish Gynecol. Soc., Polish Andrological Soc. (initiator), Polish Sexological Soc., Polish Radiol. Soc. (ultrasound sect.), Am. Soc. Colposcopy and Cervical Pathology, N.Y. Acad. Sci., Internat. Soc. Ultrasound in Ob-Gyn., Am. Inst. Ultrasound in Medicine, Polish Sonographic Soc., European Soc. Contraception, European Menopause and Andropause Soc., European Soc. Human Reprodn. and Embryology, Internat. Fedn. Profls. and Assns. in Favor of Abortion and Contraception, European Tourist Club, Planetary Soc., Galician Sch. Health Assn. (treas. 2000-04). Roman Catholic. Avocations: coin collecting/numismatics, diving, photography. Office: Gabinet Lekarski Polozniczo-Ginekologiczny i Seksuologiczno-Andrologiczny ul Krowoderska 5/7 Cracow 31-141 Poland Office Phone: 48501333512. Personal E-mail: maciej.s.kowalczyk@neostrada.pl. Business E-Mail: glpgisa@mp.pl.

KOWALCZYKOWSKI, STEPHEN CHARLES, biochemist, biophysicist, microbiologist, cellular and molecular biologist, educator; b. Dec. 18, 1950; BS in Chemistry, Rensselaer Poly. Inst., Troy, NY, 1972; PhD in Chemistry, Georgetown U., Washington, 1976. Am. Cancer Soc. postdoctoral fellow molecular biology U. Oreg., Eugene, 1976—81; asst. prof. molecular biology Northwestern U. Med. Sch., Chgo., 1981—87, assoc. prof., 1987—91; prof. microbiology and molecular and cellular biology U. Calif., Davis, 1991—, chmn. sect. microbiology, 1992—99, dir. Ctr. Genetics and Devel., 2000—06, disting. prof. microbiology and molecular and cellular biology, 2005—. Contbr. articles to sci. jours.; mem. editl. bd.: Jour. Biol. Chemistry, 2003—, mem. editl. adv. bd.: Am. Chem. Soc. Chem. Biology, 2006—, assoc. editor: Genes to Cells. Recipient MERIT award, NIH, 2000—. Fellow: AAAS, Am. Acad. Arts & Scis., Am. Acad. Microbiology; mem.: NAS, Biophysical Soc., Am. Soc. Microbiology, Am. Chem. Soc. (biol. chemistry divsn.), Am. Soc. Biochemistry and Molecular Biology. Achievements include patents in field. Office: U Calif Davis Microbiology Sect Briggs Hall Rm 310 1 Shields Ave Davis CA 95616-8665 Office Phone: 530-752-5938, 530-752-5939. E-mail: sckowalczykowski@ucdavis.edu.

KOWALENKO, TERRY, emergency physician program director; b. Dearborn, Mich., June 27, 1962; MD, U. Chgo., 1987. Dir. continuing profl. devel. U. Mich., 2011, program dir., 2001—. Fellow: Am. Coll. Emergency Physicians. Office: UMHS Medical Ctr 1500 E Ann Arbor MI 48109 Office Fax: 734-763-9298. Business E-Mail: terryk@med.umich.edu.

KOWALEWSKI, RADOSLAW ANDRZEJ, surgeon; b. Wegorzewo, Poland, Sept. 18, 1971; s. Wladyslaw Kowalewski and Irena Kowalewska; married, 2009. MD, Med. U., Poland, 1996. Cert. in gen. surgery Ctr. Exams. in Medicine, 2005, in vascular surgery Ctr. Exams. in Medicine, 2009. Asst., dept. vascular surgery and transplantology Med. U. Bialystok, Poland, 1996—. Contbr. articles to profl. jours. Scholar, Karolinska U., Stockholm, 1998. Mem.: Polish Soc. for Vascular Surgery (life), Assn. of Polish Surgeons (life), European Soc. for Vascular Surgery (life). Achievements include research in haemostatic properties of synthetic vascular grafts; vessel wall extracellular matrix composition. Avocations: skiing, music, bicycling, travel. Office: Dept Vascular Surgery M Curie-Sklodowskiej 24A Bialystok 15-276 Poland Home: Ul. Adama Mickiewicza 46B/26 15-232 Bialystok Poland Office Phone: 48857468276. Personal E-mail: korado@2com.pl.

KOWALSKI, THOMAS E., gastroenterologist, educator, physician; BS, Cornell U., 1980; MD, SUNY, Buffalo, 1988. Diplomate Am. Bd. Internal Medicine, Am. Bd. Internal Medicine-gastroenterology. Resident internal medicine Johns Hopkins Hosp., 1991; fellow gastroenterology Univ. Pa., 1993, fellow advanced endoscopy, 1994; assoc. prof. Medicine Thomas Jefferson Univ., physician; dir. gastrointestinal endoscopy dept. Thomas Jefferson Univ. Hosp., hosp. affiliation includes Meth. Hosp. divsn. Co-author: Accuracy of Magnetic Resonance Cholangiography As Compared To Endoscopic Retrograde Cholangiography In The Evaluation of Patients With Biliary Obstruction, 1994, A Simple Method of Retrieving Migrated Esophageal Stents, 1997, EUS Guided Fine Needle Aspiration of the Liver. Indications, Yield, and Safety from an International Survey of 167 Cases, 2000, EUS Guided Fine Needle Aspiratin of the Liver. International Survey of Preparation, Procedureal and Monitoring Techniques, 2000, Peripancreatic Neoplasms: Diagnosis and Staging By MR and Endoscopic Ultrasonography (EUS), 2001, various publs. Named one of the Top Doctors, Phila. Mag., 2010. Office: Thomas Jefferson University Ste 480 132 S 10th St Philadelphia PA 19107 Office Phone: 215-955-8900. Office Fax: 215-503-2527.

KOWARSKI, ALLEN AVINOAM, endocrinologist, educator; b. Tel Aviv, Dec. 30, 1927; s. Hanoch and Sima (Tkazh) K.; m. Hanna Rose Zas, Mar. 24, 1950; children: David, Ruth. Student, Hebrew U., Jerusalem, 1946—47, MD, 1955; student, U. Lausanne Med. Sch., Switzerland, 1949—52. Acad. physician Hebrew U., 1955-62; instr., fellow Johns Hopkins U., Balt., 1962-68, asst. prof., 1968-72, assoc. prof., 1972-81; prof. U. Md., Balt., 1981—; pres. Kay Labs., Inc., 1974—. Patentee in field; contbr. over 170 articles to profl. jours. Grantee NIH, 1979-97, McNeil Pharm., 1984-86, DuPont Critical Care, 1985-90, Genentech Found. for Growth & Devel., 1994-95, Lilly Rsch. Lab. 1996-98. Mem. Am. Pediat. Soc., Soc. Pediat. Rsch., Lawson-Wilkins Pediat. Endocrine Soc., The Endocrine Soc., Am. Fedn. Clin. Rsch., Am. Diabetes Assn. (Diabetes Rsch. award 1983, Charles H. Best medal for disting. svc. 1994). Achievements include invention of nonthromogenic blood withdrawal sys., nonthrombogenic glucose monitor; discovery of DAWN phenomenon in diabetes and bioinactive growth hormone syndrome (Kowarski syndrome); integrated concentration of growth hormone method for diagnosis of growth hormone deficiency. Office: Kay Labs Inc 5801 Nicholson Ln Unit 1135 Rockville MD 20852-5734 *

KOWLESSAR, MURIEL, retired pediatric educator; b. Bklyn., Jan. 2, 1926; d. John Henry and Arene (Driver) Chevious; m. O. Dhodanand Kowlessar, Dec. 27, 1952; 1 child, Indrani. AB, Barnard Coll., 1947; MD, Columbia U., 1951. Diplomate Am. Bd. Pediatrics. Instr. Downstate Med. Ctr., Bklyn., 1958-64, asst. prof., 1965-66; asst. prof. clin. pediatrics Temple U., Phila., 1967-70; assoc. prof. Med. Coll. Pa., Phila., 1971-83, dir. pediatric group svcs., 1975-90, acting chmn. pediatrics dept., 1981-83, vice chair pediatrics dept., 1982-91, prof., 1983-91, prof. emeritus, 1991—; mentor Big Brother Big Sister Program, 2011—; vol. reviewer Dept. Children & Families State Mass., 2009—. Contbr. articles to med. jours. Mem. Pa. Gov.'s Task Force on Spl. Supplemental Food Program for Women, Infants and Children, Harrisburg, 1981-83, Phila. Bd. Health, 1982-86; vol. Phila. Com. for Homeless, 1991-92, Gateway Literacy Program, YMCA, Germantown Bridge, Pa., 1992-93. Fellow Am. Acad. Pediatrics (emeritus); Cosmopolitan Club Phila., Phi Beta Kappa. Democrat. Avocations: ballroom dancing, opera, travel.

KOYAMA, HIDENORI, medical researcher; b. Kato-gun, Hyogo-Pref, Japan, Sept. 13, 1962, s. Tadashi and Asako Koyama, m. Yuko Fuchiwaki. MD, PhD, Osaka City U., Japan, 1987. Lic. physician Govt. Japan, 1987. Postdoctral fellow U. of Wash., Seattle, 1994—97; rsch. assoc. Osaka City U. Sch. Medicine, 1998—2002, lectr., 2002—. Recipient Young Investigator award, Am. Soc. Bone and Mineral Rsch., 1993, Japanese Cardiovasc. Endocrinology Metabolism, 1997, Mayor's award, Osaka City, 2005; grantee, Ministry Edn., 1999—, Japan Heart Found./Pfizer Pharms., 1997, Ono Med. Rsch. Found., 1997, scholar, Ministry Edn., 1994—95. Achievements include research in pathophysiology of atherosclerosis. Office: Osaka City U Grad Sch Medicine 1-4-3 Asahi-machi Abeno-ku Osaka 545-8585 Japan Office Fax: +81-6-6645-3808. Business E-Mail: hidekoyama@med.osaka-cu.ac.jp.

KOYAMA, KATSUSHI, medical association administrator; b. Nagoya, Japan, Jan. 14, 1962; MD, Nagoya City U., PhD, 1987. Dir., dept. nephrology Kariya Toyota Gen. Hosp., 2002—, dir., Med. Edn. Ctr., 2010. Clin. prof. Grad. Sch. Med. Scis. Nagoya City U., 2005. Mem.: Eurorean Renal Assn. Avocations: mountain climbing, skiing. Office: 5-15 Sumiyoshi-cho Kariya Aichi 448-8505 Japan Office Fax: 81-566-22-2493. Personal E-mail: nephkidedta@do9.enjoy.ne.jp.

KOYAMA, NOBUYUKI, medical educator; b. Tokyo, Apr. 28, 1966; MD, Shinshu U., 1992; PhD, Tokyo Med. and Dental U., 2001. Asst. prof. Saitama Med. U., 2006—. Rsch. grant, Japanese Soc. Promotion Sci., Daiwa Securities Health Found. Master: Japanese Med. Assn., Japanese Bd. Cancer Therapy, Japanese Resiratory Soc., Japanese Soc. Internal Medicine; mem.: Am. Soc. Clin. Oncology. Avocation: skiing. Office: 1397-1 Yamane Hidaka-shi Saitama 350-1298 Japan Business E-Mail: nkoyama@saitama-med.ac.jp.

KOZAK, MILAN, cardiologist, medical educator; b. Brno, Czech Republic, Mar. 5, 1967; s. Slavka and Miloslav Kozak; m. Martina Kocab, Sept. 9, 1989; children: Kristian, Magdalena. MD, MD, Masaryk U., Brno, Czech Republic, 1991, PhD, 2000. Diplomate in Internal Medicine Ministry of Health, Czech Republic, 1994, in Cardiology Ministry of Health, 1999, Cardiostimulation - surgical part Assn. of Czech Physicians, 1999, Cardiostimulation - cardiological p. Assn. of Czech Physicians, 1999, Electrophysiology Soc. of Czech Physicians, 1999. Physician anesthesiology dept. anesthesiology Univ. Hosp., Brno, Czech Republic, 1993—94, head std. internal ward dept. medicine and cardiology, 1997—2000, head group for electrophysiology and icd dept. medicine and cardiology, 1998—, head coronary unit dept. medicine and cardiology, 2000—; asst. prof. med. faculty Masaryk U., Brno, Czech Republic, 1997—. Author: (presentations, articles- in extenso) Treatment of malignant arrhythmias with ICDs (Young rschr., 1997), (competition of young cardiologists) Analysis of indications for ICD implantation (Young cardiologist, 1999); contbr. articles to profl. jours. Mem. group for arrhythmias and pacing Czech Soc. Cardiology, Prague, 1997—2001; mem. acad. senate faculty medicine Masaryk U., Brno, Czech Republic, 2000—02. Grantee, Vasovagal Syncope, 1997 - 1998. Mem.: Group for Arrhytmias and Pacing (life), Czech Soc. Cardiology (life). Avocations: cyckling, jogging, climbing. Home: Lipova 1A Brno 602 00 Czech Republic Office: Univ Hosp Dept Cardiology Jihlavská 20 Brno 639 00 Czech Republic Office Fax: +420547192611. E-mail: kozak.milan@post.cz.

KOZIAN, RALF, medical researcher; b. Magdedurg, Saxonia- Anhalt, Germany, Jan. 20, 1963; s. Herbert and Eleonore Kozian. Diplomate U. Magdeburg, 1989. Physician U. Jena, Germany, 1990—95, Stadtroda, Germany, 2006. Home: Ernst- Löbe Str 11 Stadtroda Thuringia D- 07646 Germany Office: Asklepiosklinik Bahnhofstr 1a Stadtroda Thuringia D-07646 Germany Personal E-mail: nimz01@web.de.

KOZIARA, MICHAEL, accountant, insurance company executive; BA, Ctrl. Mich. U., Mt. Pleasant; M in acctg., Ea. Mich. U., Ypsilanti. CPA. Healthcare audit mgr. Coopers & Lybrand, Detroit; dir. fin. adminstrn. Allegiance LLC; dir. managed care svc. Mercy Health Svc., 1997—2000; CFO Care Choices (Now Priority Health), 2000—07; v.p. network strategy Priority Health, COO, 2011—. Office: Priority Health 1231 E Beltline NE Grand Rapids MI 49525-4501 *

KOZIN, SCOTT H., orthopedist; b. Pa., Sept. 23, 1960; MD, Hannemann U. Sch. Medicine, 1986. Orthrop. surgeon Shriners Hosps. Children, 1990—. Office: 3551 N Broad St Philadelphia PA 19140 Business E-Mail: skozin@shrinenet.org.

KOZLOFF, LLOYD M., dean, microbiologist, educator; b. Chgo., Oct. 15, 1923; s. Joseph and Rose (Hollobow) K.; m. Judith Bonnie Friedman, June 16, 1947; children: James, Daniel, Joseph, Sarah BS, U. Chgo., 1943, PhD, 1948. Asst., then assoc. prof. biochemistry U. Chgo., 1949-61, prof., 1961-64; prof. microbiology U. Colo., Denver, 1964-80, chmn. dept. microbiology, 1966-76, assoc. dean, prof., 1976-80; dean, prof. U. Calif., San Francisco, 1981-91, prof., dean emeritus, 1991—. Career investigator USPHS, U. Chgo., 1962 Founding editor Jour. Virology, 1966-76; contbr. articles to profl. jours., chpts. to books. Chmn. bd. dirs. Proctor Fund., 1981-91; v.p. San Francisco Alliance for Mental Illness, 1993-96; pres. emeritus U. Calif. San Francisco Faculty Assn., 1996-2000. With USN, 1944-46. Commonwealth Fund fellow, 1953, Lederle Found. fellow, 1954; recipient Disting. Svc. award U. Chgo., 2004. Fellow AAAS, Am. Acad. Microbiol. (hon.); mem. Am. Soc. Biol. Chemistry, Am. Soc. Microbiology (head virology sect. 1974-76), Am. Chem. Soc., N.Y. Acad. Sci. Home: 43000 Lyndon Ln Fort Bragg CA 95437 Office: U Calif Grad Divsn San Francisco CA 94114-2732

KOZLOV, ALEXANDER A., health facility administrator, researcher; b. Ivanovo region, Russia, Aug. 20, 1966; s. Alexander P. Kozlov and Marija M. Kozlova; m. Olga A. Nesterova, July 18, 1993. Therapeutist, Russian State Med. U., Moscow, 1993; Highest qualification category Psychiatry and Narcology (hon.), Ctrl. Attestation Bd., Moscow, 2002; PhD in Med. Scis. (hon.), Rsch. Inst. Narcology, Moscow, 1999. Cert. narcology and psychiatry State Narcology Rsch. Ctr., Ministry Health Russian, 1997, Psychotherapy Russian Med. Post-graduate Acad., 2003, Psychiatry Sechenov Moscow Med. Acad., 2005, Health svcs. adminstrn. Russian Med. Post-graduate Acad., 2006. Attending MD State Narcology Rsch. Ctr., Ministry Health and Med. industry Russian, Moscow, 1993—95; sr. scientist rschr. Nat. Sci. Ctr. Narcology Ministry Health Russian Fedn., Moscow, 1998—2003; head dept. Psychiat. Clinic Fed. Bur. Med. and Social Expertise Ministry, Moscow, 2003—04; psychotherapy expert Clin. Sanatorium 'Barviha'Russian Pres. Adminstrn., Moscow, 2004—05; Psychologist Russian Pres. Acad. State Svcs., Moscow, 2009—; head sect. Fed. Drug Control Svc. Russian Fedn., Moscow, 2005—. Bd. mem. Europad (European Opiate Addiction Treatment Assn.), Pisa, Italy, 2003—. Author: (textbook) Medical and Social Consequences of Drug Addiction Narcology, V. I, Chapter 17.; co-author (book) Addictions. Medical and Social Consequences. Treatment., Medical, Psychological, Psychophysiological Support of Operational Officers of Law-Enforcement Organizations., (textbook) Pharmacotherapy of Drug Addictions., Particularities of Formation of Clinical Picture and Clinical Course of Drug Addiction Women., Therapeutic Approaches to HIV-infected Drug Users. Heroin Addiction: current developments.; contbr. scientific papers to numerous profl. jours. Mem.: Soc. Russian Psychiatrists, Assn. European Psychiatrists. Office Fax: +74956214655; Home Fax: +74956355044. Personal E-mail: aakozlov@inbox.ru.

KOZLOW, BEVERLY KAY, retired physical therapist, psychologist, realtor; b. Detroit, Aug. 10, 1931; d. Samuel and Genevieve Ione (Griffin) K.; m. Roy Carl Gleaves, Apr. 16, 1959 (div. 1975). BS, Eastern Mich. U., 1953; MS, UCLA, 1959; PhD, Sierra U., 1987. Registered physical therapist. Phys. therapist Walter Reed Army Med. Ctr., Washington, 1953-55, Crippled Children's Soc., Rockville, Md., 1955-56, San Bernardino (Calif.) County Hosp., 1957-59; coord. pre phys. therapy program UCLA, 1959-67; home health phys. therapist Vis. Nurses Assn. L.A., 1967-68; from staff to dir. phys. therapy L.A. County Med. Dept., 1968-73; dir. in-patient/out-patient acute and rehab. svcs. Valley Med. Ctr., Van Nuys, Calif., 1973-81; contract phys. therapist LA, 1981-89; home health phys. therapist Vis. Nurses Assn., Stuart, Fla., 1992-96; CPS Great River Property, Guerneville, Calif., 1997—2002; ret., 2002. Adj. faculty U.S. Army Command and Gen. Staff Coll., Ft. Leavenworth, Kans., 1986-92. Ret. col. U.S. Army. Mem. Am. Physical Therapy Assn. (life), Ret. Officers Assn. Democrat. Jewish. Avocations: reading, travel, gardening. Home: 14317 Datetree Dr Elizabeth Lake CA 93532-1433 Personal E-mail: bevkoz@roadrunner.com.

KOZUCH, PETER, medical oncologist, educator; MD, Hahnemann U., Pa., 1994. Diplomate Am. Bd. Internal Medicine, 1997, Am. Bd. Internal Medicine-hematology, Am. Bd. Internal Medicine-med. oncology, 2000, lic. Mass., 1997, registered NY, 2000. Intern Boston Med. Ctr., 1995, resident in internal medicine, 1997; fellow in med. oncology MD Anderson cancer ctr. Tex. Univ., Houston, 1997—2000; assoc. prof. clin. medicine Albert Einstein coll. medicine Yeshiva Univ., NY; med. oncologist Milton & Caroll Petrie divsn. Beth Israel Med. Ctr.; hosp. affiliations include St. Lukes Hosp., St. Lukes Roosevelt Hosp. Named one of Top Doctors-NY Metro Area, Castle Connolly, 2009. Office: Beth Israel Medical Center 10 Union Sq E Ste 4C New York NY 10003 Office Phone: 212-844-8070. Office Fax: 212-844-2027.

KRABILL, ROBERT ELMER, osteopathic physician; b. Wayland, Iowa, June 4, 1934; s. Robert H. and Amanda (Wyse) K.; m. Ellen Savage, Sept. 1, 1963; children: Keith Andrew, Angela Kay, Valerie Ann, Kelly Dawn. BS, Iowa Wesleyan Coll., 1961; DO, Kirkville Coll. Osteo. Medicine, 1966. Diplomate Am. Bd. Family Practice. Intern Cuyahoga Falls Gen. Hosp., Ohio, 1966—67, mem. staff, 1967—; gen. practice osteo. medicine Uniontown, Ohio, 1967—.

Sec., treas. gen. practice dept. Cuyahoga Falls Gen. Hosp., 1985-86. Named one of Outstanding Young Men of Am., U.S. Jaycees, 1969. Mem. Am. Osteo. Assn., Ohio Osteo. Assn., Am. Coll. Gen. Practitioners Osteo. Medicine and Surgery. Mennonite. Home: 3733 N Vista St NW Uniontown OH 44685-8496 Office: PO Box 399 Uniontown OH 44685-0399

KRACH, DALE JAMES, science educator, athletic trainer; b. Phila., Jan. 12, 1947; s. James and Laura Abel Krach; m. Donna Rae Davis, Aug. 1, 1970; children: Joshua Dale, Nathan Jarrett, Amy Meredith. AB in Psychology, W.Va. U., 1970; MS in Environ. Sci., Drexel U., 1977; Postgrad. in sports medicine, Pa. State U., 1984; Cert. sci. tchr., U. West Ga., 1999, Cert. in ednl. leadership, 2002. Cert. athletic trainer Nat. Athletic Trainers Assn., master athletic adminstr. Nat. Interscholastic Administrators Assn., EMT Pa. Field supervising environ. protection specialist Bucks County Dept. of Health, Doylestown, Pa., 1971—77; health edn. instr., emergency care program asst. Pa. State U., State College, 1977—84; athletic trauma and rehab. specialist PAPP Clinic, Newnan, Ga., 1984—92; sci. tchr., head athletic trainer Northgate H.S., Newnan, 1996—. Sports medicine cons. U.S. Women's Olympic Weightlifting, Marietta, Ga., 1990—95; sports medicine staff 11th Pan Am. Games, Indpls., 1987; asst. chief athletic trainer, EMT Centennial Olympic Games, Atlanta, 1996. Mem. med. staff Boy Scouts of Am. Nat. Jamboree, Fort A.P. Hill, Va., 1989—2001; athletic trainer, mem. med. staff Ga. State Games, Augusta, 1990—2000, Atlanta; 2d v.p. Lambda Omicron chpt. Alpha Phi Omega, Morgantown, W.Va., 1969—70. Recipient Silver Beaver award, Boy Scouts Am., 1995; named Eagle Scout, 1963, Region Athletic Dir. of Yr., 2002—03. Mem.: AAHPERD (corr.), Ga. Athletic Trainers Assn. (corr.), Nat. Interscholastic Athletic Adminstrs. Assn. (corr.), Nat. Athletic Trainers Assn. (corr.), Nat. Assn. Secondary Sch. Prins. (assoc.), Kappa Delta Pi, Eta Sigma Gamma. Avocations: camping, outdoor sports, military memorabilia, reading, travel. Home: 145 Marsha Way Sharpsburg GA 30277-3377 Office: Northgate HS 3220 Fischer Rd Newnan GA 30265 Office Fax: 770-463-4982. Personal E-mail: dkrach@charter.net. E-mail: dale.krach@cowetaschools.org.

KRAEMER, HELENA ANTOINETTE CHMURA, psychiatry educator; Degree, Stanford U., 1963. With Stanford U., 1964—, prof. biostats. in psychiatry, Dept. Psychiatry and Behavioral Scis., 1991—, mem. Comprehensive Cancer Ctr. Mem. editorial bd. Jour. Child & Adolescent Psychopharmacology. Co-author: How Many Subjects?: Statistical Power Analysis in Rsch., 1987, Evaluating Medical Tests: Objective & Quantitative Guidelines, 1992, To Your Health: How to Understand What Research Tells Us About Risk, 2005. Recipient Harvard award in psychiat. epidemiology and biostats., 2001. Mem.: Inst. Medicine. Office: Stanford U Dept Psychiatry and Behavioral Scis 300 Pasteur Dr Stanford CA 94305 also: Stanford Comprehensive Cancer Ctr 875 Blake Wilbur Dr Stanford CA 94305

KRAEMER, JORGE LUIZ, medical educator; b. Porto Alegre, May 20, 1953; MD, UFRGS, 1977; MSc, UNIFESP, PhD, 1992. Prof. livre-docente UFCSPA, 2006—. Chief ICU, 1992. Mem.: Brasilian Soc. Neurosurgery (Prêmio Eliseu Paglioli). Office: Rua Padre Chagas 415/702 Porto Alegre RS 90570-080 Brazil Business E-Mail: jkraemer@doctor.com.

KRAFT, GEORGE HOWARD, physician, educator; b. Columbus, Ohio, Sept. 27, 1936; s. Glen Homer and Helen Winner (Howard) K.; children: Jonathan Ashbrook, Susannah Mary. AB, Harvard U., 1958; MD, Ohio State U., 1963, MS, 1967. Diplomate Am. Bd. Phys. Medicine and Rehab. (subspecialty in spinal cord injury medicine), Am. Bd. Electrodiagnostic Medicine. Intern U. Calif. Hosp., San Francisco, 1963—64, resident in phys. medicine and rehab., 1964—65, Ohio State U., Columbus, 1965—67; assoc. U. Pa. Med. Sch., Phila., 1968—69; asst. prof. U. Wash., Seattle, 1969—72, assoc. prof., 1972—76, prof., 1976—, Alvord prof. MS rsch., 2005—; chief of staff U. Wash. Med. Ctr., Seattle, 1993—95. Dir. electrodiagnostic medicine U. Wash. Hosp., 1987—, dir. Multiple Sclerosis Ctr., 1982—; co-dir. Muscular Dystrophy Clinic, 1974—; bd. dirs. Am. Bd. Electrodiagnostic Medicine, 1993-2000, chmn., 1996-2000 Co-author: Chronic Disease and Disability, 1994, Living with Multiple Sclerosis: A Wellness Approach, 2000, The M.S. Workbook, 2006; cons. editor: Phys. Medicine and Rehab. Clinics, 1990—, EEG and Clin. Neurophysiology, 1992-96; assoc. editor Jour. Neurol. Rehab. and Neurol. Repair, 1988-2000, Muscle and Nerve, 1998-2000; contbr. articles to profl. jours. Sci. peer rev. com. C Nat. Multiple Sclerosis Soc., N.Y.C., 1990-96, chmn., 1993-96, med. adv. bd., 1991—; bd. sponsors Wash. Physicians for Social Responsibility, Seattle, 1986—; nat. adv. bd. NCMRR (NIH), 2009-. Rsch. grantee Rehab. Svcs. Adminstrn., 1976-81, Nat. Inst. Handicapped Rsch., 1984-88, Nat. Multiple Sclerosis Soc., 1990-92, 94-95, 2005—Nat. Inst. Disability and REhab. Rsch., 1998—. Fellow Am. Acad. Phys. Medicine and Rehab. (pres. 1984-85, Zeiter award 1991, Krusen award 2002); mem. Am. Assn. Electrodiagnostic Medicine (pres. 1982-83. Lifetime Achievement award 2004), Assn. Acad. Physiatrists (pres. 1980-81), Am. Acad. Clin. Neurophysiology (pres. 1995-97), Am. Acad. Neurology, Internat. Rehab. Medicine Assn., Alpha Omega Alpha. Episcopalian. Office: Dept Rehab Med U Wash PO Box 956490 Seattle WA 98195 Home Phone: 206-467-0206.

KRAFT, SUMNER CHARLES, physician, educator; b. Lynn, Mass., Aug. 21, 1928; s. Ansel and Bella (Rome) K.; m. Patricia F. Pink, June 23, 1963; children: Gary Andrew, Jennifer Rose, Steven Russell. BS, Tufts U., Medford, Mass., 1948; AM, Boston U., 1949; MD, U. Chgo., 1955. Diplomate Am. Bd. Internal Medicine, Am. Bd. Gastroenterology; cert. med. rev. officer, 2009-. Intern Boston City Hosp., 1955-56; asst. resident in medicine U. Chgo. Hosp., 1956-57, jr. asst. resident, 1957-58, resident, 1958-59, fellow in gastroenterology, 1958-60, instr. medicine, 1959-61, USPHS spl. fellow, 1961-66; rsch. fellow immunology Scripps Clinic & Rsch. Found., 1964—66; asst. prof. medicine U. Chgo., 1961—68, assoc. prof. medicine, 1968—73; USPHS rsch. career devel. fellow Nat. Inst. Allergy and Infectious Diseases, 1967-72; prof. medicine, 1974—; prof. com. on immunology, 1974-93; emeritus staff mem. U. Chgo. Med. Ctr.; locum tenens ind. contr. in primary care and gastroenterology, 1996—. Ad hoc cons. food allergy and gastrointestinal immunology; faculty lectr. Nat. Ctr. Advanced Med. Edn., Chgo., 1969-96; vis. prof. medicine, then affil. prof. medicine Uniformed Svcs. U. Health Scis., Bethesda, Md., 1979-87. Chmn. editl. bd. Jour. Medicine on the Midway, 1981-96 contbr. articles to med. jours. Merit badge counselor Calumet coun. Boy Scouts Am., former scoutmaster, troop com. chmn., 1966-81; judge Chgo. Non-Pub. Sch. Sci. Exposition, 1981-82. Col. USAR, 1957-96. Recipient William Beaumont award for clin. rsch., 1977, U.S. Army Order of Mil. Med. Merit, 1994, Disting. Mem. Regiment award U.S. Army Med. Dept. Regiment, 1997, Legion Merit award, US Army, 1998. Fellow ACP, Am. Gastroent. Assn. (editl. bd. 1976-81); mem. AAAS, Am. Assn. Immunologists, Am. Fedn. Clin. Rsch., Am. Bd. Internal Medicine (mem. subspecialty examining bd. gastroenterology 1978-83), Army Reserve Assn., Am. Soc. Gastrointestinal Endoscopy, Assn. Mil. Surgeons U.S., Ctrl. Soc. Clin. Rsch., Chgo. Assn. Immunologists, Chgo. Soc. Gastroenterology (organizing com. 1967-68, exec. com. 1968-71, pres. 1969-70), Chgo. Soc. Gastrointestinal Endoscopy, Chgo. Soc. Internal Medicine, Gastroenterology Rsch. Group, Inst. Medicine Chgo., Sr. Army Reserve Comdrs. Assn. (life), Midwest Gut Club (steering com. 1969-72), N.Y. Acad. Scis., Res. Officers Assn. (life), Soc. Exptl. Biology and Medicine, U.S. Army War Coll. Alumni Assn.(life), Nat. Eagle Scout Assn. (life), Sigma Xi, Alpha Epsilon Pi (life). Avocations: skiing, travel. Office: U Chgo Hosp Mail Code 4076 5841 S Maryland Ave Chicago IL 60637-1463 Personal E-mail: sckraft1@hotmail.com.

KRAGH-MÜLLER, GRETHE KRARUP, psychologist, educator; d. Martin and Valborg Jespersen; m. Claus Michael Kragh-Müller, Aug. 10, 1974; children: Thomas Krarup, Tanja Maria, Ajaja Martine, Sune Alexander. Degree in psychology, U. Copenhagen, 1973. Cert. clin. psychologist Danish Ministry Edn., 1986, supr. child psychology Danish Psychol. Soc., 2000, specialist in child psychology Danish Psychol. Soc., 2000. Cons. psychologist Boerneringen, 1978—; rschr., various rsch. programs Danish U. Sch. Edn., Aarhus U., Copenhagen NV, 1996—, assoc. prof., 1999—, DPU Flarhus U., 2002. Editor, asking questions about children Monthly Mag. Parents, Egmont Mags., Copenhagen, 1998—; cons., tv programs devel. of children Danish Nat. TV, Channel 1, Copenhagen, 2000—; writer Daily Newspaper Info., Copenhagen, 2007—. Contbr. articles to profl. jours. Psychol. cons. mem., dealing with placing children outside home. Region Copenhagen, 1996; mem. Rsch. Unit Gender Equality Diversity & Subjectification, Copenhagen, 2003. Grant, BUPL, Denmark, 2006. Achievements include research in gracelity in early childhood education. Office: Danish University Edn Ark University Tuborgvej 164 2400 Copenhagen Denmark Office Phone: 45 88889000.

KRALJ, MLADEN, cosmetic dentist; BA in Biology, Ind. U.; DDS, Tufts U., Boston. Cert. Invisalign 1, Invisalign advanced 2, Invisalign Premier Provider 2006, 2007, 2008. Clin. instr. Heartland Inst., Effingham, Ill. Specialized advanced aesthetic and restorative tng. Pacific Aesthetic Continuum, San Francisco. Mem.: Art. Ist. Chgo., Museum Contemporary Art, ADA, Ill. State Dental Assn., Chgo. Dental Soc., Acad. Laser Dentistry, World Congress Minimally Invasive Dentistry, Internat. Assn. Comprehensive Esthetics, Acad. Comprehensive Esthetics, Am. Acad. Cosmetic Dentistry. Office: Ora Dental Studio 712 N Dearborn Penthouse Chicago IL 60654 Office Phone: 312-867-8766.

KRAMAN, DAVID J., urologist; Grad., U. Pa., MD, 1987. Diplomate Am. Bd. Urology, lic. Pa. Resident gen. surgery Sch. Medicine Univ. Pa., fellow urology dept. Sch. Medicine; urologist Aria Health. Named Top Dr., Phila. Mag., 2011, Recognized Dr., HealthGrades. Fellow: ACP; mem.: AMA. Office: Aria Health Calvanese Bldg Ste 2D 2137 Welsh Rd Philadelphia PA 19115 Office Phone: 215-698-7333.

KRAMER, BARNETT SHELDON, oncologist, retired federal agency administrator; b. Balt., July 29, 1948; s. Mervin and Muriel Hannah (Woolf) Kramer; m. Ruth Solomon, June 25, 1972; 1 child, Jeremy. MD, U. Md. Med. Sch., 1973; MPH, Johns Hopkins U. Sch. Hygiene & Pub. Health, Balt., 1991. Diplomate Am. Bd. Internal Medicine, Am. Bd. Med. Oncology. Intern Washington U., St. Louis, 1973-74, med. resident, 1974-75; fellow Nat. Cancer Inst. (NCI) NIH, Bethesda, Md., 1975-78, sr. investigator, 1986-90, assoc. dir. NCI, 1990-96, dep. dir. divsn. cancer prevention & control, 1996-97, dep. dir. divsn. cancer prevention, 1997-2000, dir. office med. applications rsch., Office Disease Prevention (ODP), 2000—10, assoc. dir. disease prevention, ODP, 2001—10; asst. prof. U. Fla., Gainesville, 1978-83, assoc. prof., 1983-86. Assoc. editor Jour. of Nat. Cancer Inst., 1988—94, editor-in-chief, 1994—; clin. prof. medicine Uniformed Svcs. U. of Health Scis., Bethesda, 1990—. Co-editor (with P. Greenwald and D. Weed): Cancer Prevention and Control, 1995; co-editor: (with J. Gohagan and P. Prorok) Cancer Screening Theory and Practices, 1999; co-editor: (with C. Allegra) Understanding Clinical Trials, 2000; mem. editl. bd. Physicians Data Query; contbr. articles to profl. jours., chapters to books. Fellow: ACP; mem.: Delta Omega, Am. Soc. Clin. Oncology, Alpha Omega Alpha. Avocation: fountain pen collecting. Office: Nat Cancer Inst 6116 Executive Blvd Rockville MD 20852 Office Phone: 301-594-9050. Business E-Mail: barry.kramer@nih.gov. *

KRAMER, BARRY ALAN, psychiatrist, educator; b. Phila., Sept. 9, 1948; s. Morris and Harriet (Greenberg) K.; m. Paulie Hoffman, June 9, 1974; children: Daniel Mark, Steven Philip. BA in Chemistry, NYU, Bronx, 1970; MD, Hahnemann Med. Coll., Phila., 1974. Resident in psychiatry Montefiore Hosp and Med. Ctr., Bronx, N.Y., 1974-77; practice medicine specializing in psychigary, NYC, 1977-82; staff psychiatrist L.I. Jewish-Hillside Med. Ctr., Glen Oaks, N.Y., 1977-82; asst. prof. SUNY, Stony Brook, 1978-82; practice medicine specializing in psychiatry, LA, 1982—; asst. prof. psychiatry U. So. Calif., 1982-89, assoc. prof. clin. psychiatry, 1989-94, prof. clin. psychiatry, 1994-98; ward chief L.A. County/U. So. Calif. Med. Ctr., 1982-98. Med. dir. ECT, Cedars Sinai Med. Ctr., 1998—; cons. Little Neck Nursing Home (N.Y.), 1979-82, L.I. Nursing Home, 1980-82; dir. ECT U. So. Calif. Sch. Medicine, 1990; adj. asst. prof. U. So. Calif., Sch. Pharmacy, 2004—. Reviewer Am. Jour. Psychiatry, Hosp. and Cmty. Psychiatry; mem. editl. bd. Convulsive Therapy; contbr. articles to profl. juors., papers to sci. meetings. Grantee NIMH, 1979-80, UCLA/U. So. Calif. Long-Term Gerontology Ctr., 1985-86, NARSAD, 2001—; named one of Am.'s Top Doctors, Castle Connolly Med. Ltd., 2001-11, Am.'s Top Psychiatrists, Consumers Rsch. Coun. Am., 2007, Southern Calif. Super Drs., LA Mag., 2010-11. Fellow Am. Psychiat. Assn., Assn. Convulsive Therapy (editl. bd.); mem. AMA, Soc. Biol. Psychiatry, Calif. Med. Assn., L.A. Med. Assn., Am. Assn. Geriatric Psychiatry, Gerontol. Soc. Am., So. Calif. Psychiat. Soc. (chair ETC com.). Jewish. Office: Cedars Sinai Med Ctr Thalians 306-C 8730 Alden Dr Los Angeles CA 90048 also: PO Box 5792 Beverly Hills CA 90209-5792 Office Phone: 310-423-4014. Personal E-mail: barryakramer@yahoo.com. Business E-Mail: krameb@cshs.org.

KRAMER, KIM, oncologist; b. Bronx, NY, Mar. 25, 1964; MD, SUNY Syracuse, 1989. Assoc. mem. Meml. Sloan-Kettering Cancer Ctr., 1993—. Office: 1275 York Ave Box 429 New York NY 10065 Office Fax: 212-717-3239. Business E-Mail: kramerk@mskcc.org.

KRAMER, MICHAEL STUART, pediatric epidemiologist; b. NYC, July 8, 1948; arrived in Can., 1978; s. George and Beatrice (Jacobs) K.; m. Claire Yael Sasportas, June 14, 1981; children: Eric, Elise, Philippe. BA, U. Chgo., 1969; MD, Yale U., 1973. Diplomate Am. Bd. Pediatrics, Am. Coll. Epidemiology. Intern in pediat. Yale New Haven (Conn.) Hosp., 1973-74, resident in pediat., 1974-76; fellow clin. epidemiology Yale U., 1976-78; asst. prof. faculty medicine McGill U., Montreal, Que., Canada, 1978-82, assoc. prof., 1982-87, prof., 1987—. Com. mem. U.S. Inst. Medicine/NAS, Washington, 1986—; vis. scientist Nat. Perinatal Epidemiology Unit, Oxford, England, 1991—92; cons. WHO, Geneva, 1984—, Nat. Health R&D Program Can., 1992—97; Nat. Health Scientist, 1992—97; disting. scientist Can. Inst. Health Rsch., 1997—2002, sr. investigator, 2002—07, sci. dir. Inst. Human Devel. and Child and Youth Health, 2003—. Author: Clinical Epidemiology and Biostatistics, 1988, Nutrition During Pregnancy, 1990, Adverse Events Associated With Childhood Vaccines, 1994, Improving Birth Outcomes, 2003, Reducing Birth Defects, 2003. Violinist:New Haven Symphony, 1969-73, I Medici di McGill, Montreal, 1990-94. Nat. Health Rsch. scholar, 1982-88; recipient Prix d'excellence Insvc. Clubs Coun. Que., Montreal, 1987, Chercheur Boursier Sr. FRSQ, Que., 1988-91, Rsch. award Ambulatory Pediatric Assn., 1993, Sanofi Pasteur award for pediat. rsch. Can. Pediat. Soc., 2006, Greg Alexander award, 2007, Prix Léo Parisan award ACFAS, 2008, Earl W. Crampton award, 2009, Pediatr. Chairs Can Paediatr. Acad. Leadership, Clinical Investigator Award, 2010, Royal Soc. Can., 2011. Fellow: Royal Soc. Can.; mem.: Soc. Pediat. and Perinatal Epidemiol. Rsch. (pres. 1997—98, Mentoring award 2009), Soc. Epidemiol. Rsch. (John Cassel Meml. lectr. 2004), Soc. Pediat. Rsch. (coun. 1986—89). Avocations: skiing, hiking, tennis, squash, violin. Office: McGill U 2300 Tupper St Montreal PQ Canada H3H 1P3 Business E-Mail: Michael.Kramer@mcgill.ca.

KRAMER, PETER DAVID, psychiatrist, educator; m. Rachel M. Schwartz, June 29, 1980; children: Sarah Elizabeth, Jacob Aaron, Matthew Charles. AB, Harvard Coll., 1970; postgrad., Univ. Coll., London, 1970-72; MD, Harvard Med. Sch., 1976. Diplomate in psychiatry and in adolescent psychiatry Am. Bd. Psychiatry and Neurology. Resident in internal medicine U. Wis. Hospitals, Madison, 1976-77; resident in psychiatry Yale U., New Haven, 1977-80; acting dir. divsn. sci. Alcohol, Drug Abuse, Mental Health Adminstrn., Rockville, Md., 1980-82; outpatient dir. R.I. Hosp., Providence, 1982-84; asst. prof. dept. psychiatry Brown U., Providence, 1982-91, assoc. prof., 1991-95, prof., 1995—; asst. prof. psychiatry George Washington U., 1981-82; med. adv. bd. mem. Foch Tech. House, 2009—. Author: Moments of Engagement, 1989, Listening to Prozac, 1993, Should You Leave?, 1997, Spectacular Happiness, 2001, Against Depression, 2005, Freud: Inventor of the Modern Mind, 2006; mem. editl. bd. Psychiat. Times, 1985—, The Psychodynamic Letter, 1990-92, Am. Jour. Psychotherapy, 1996—; contbr. articles to profl. jours.; host syndicated pub. radio show The Infinite Mind, 2005-06. Mem. Am. Psychiat. Assn. (pvt. practice com. 1988-94, chmn. 1992-94), R.I. Med. Soc., R.I. Psychiat. Soc. (pres. 1990-91). Office: 196 Waterman St Providence RI 02906-2212

KRAMER, RICHARD JAY, gastroenterologist, educator; b. Morristown, NJ, Mar. 31, 1947; s. Bernard and Estelle (Mishkin) K.; m. Leslie Fay Davis, June 28, 1970; children: Bryan Jeffrey, Erik Seth Davis. Student, UCLA, 1965-68; MD, U. Calif., Irvine, 1972. Diplomate Am. Bd. Internat. Med., Am. Bd. Gastroenterology. Intern Los Angeles County Harbor Gen. Hosp., Torrance, Calif., 1972-73; resident Santa Clara Valley Med. Ctr., San Jose, Calif., 1973-76; fellow gastroent. Stanford (Calif.) U. Hosp., 1976-78; pvt. practice San Jose, 1978—2003; tchr. gastroenterology Santa Clara Valley Med. Ctr., San Jose, 2003—. Clin. assoc. prof. of medicine Stanford (Calif.) U., 1984—; chmn. med. dept. Good Samaritan Hosp., San Jose, 1988-90. Pres. Jewish Family Service Bd., San Jose, 1974. Recipient Regents scholarship U. Calif., 1965, 68, Mosby Book award, Mosby Books, Inc., Irvine, Calif., 1972. Fellow Am. Gastroent. Assn.; mem. Am. Coll. Physicians, Calif. Med. Soc., Santa Clara County Med. Soc., No. Calif. Soc. Clin. Gastroenterologists, Internat. Brotherhood Magicians, Mystic 13 (pres. 1986-87, San Jose), Masons, Alpha Omega Alpha. Jewish. Avocations: magic, travel.

KRAML, JIRI, medical educator; b. Prague, Czech Republic, Apr. 23, 1930; s. Jan Kraml and Ruzena Vlckova Kramlova; m. Marie Pavlova, July 21, 1956; children: Pavel, Jana Krenkova. MD, Charles U., Prague, 1955; PhD, Charles U., 1965; DSc, Czech Acad. Sci., Prague, 1989. Physician med. dept. Dist. Hosp., Chomutov, Czech Republic, 1955—59; rsch. assoc. chemistry dept. Ind. U., 1965—66; prof. biochemistry, Charles U. First Faculty Medicine, 1959—, vice-dean, 1990—93, head dept. med. biochemistry, 1990—98, cons., 2009—. Editor: (textbook) Harper's Biochemistry - Czech Translation; contbr. scientific papers. Recipient Presidium award, Czechoslovak Med. Soc., 1966, Golden Commemorative Medal, Charles U., 2010. Fellow: Czech Med. Acad. (coun. mem. 2006); mem.: Czech Soc. Biochemistry & Molecular Biology (hon.). Home: Hrusicka 2511/4 Prague 141 00 Czech Republic Office: Charles Univ First Faculty Med Katerinska 32 121 08 Prague Czech Republic Home Phone: 420 272772964; Office Phone: 420 224964267. Office Fax: 420 224964280; Home Fax: 420 272772964. Business E-Mail: kraml@cesnet.cz.

KRANIAS, EVANGELIA G., medical educator; b. Thessaloniki, May 24, 1947; PhD, Northwestern U., 1974. Prof. U. Cin., 1978—. Office: 231 Albert Sabin Way Cincinnati OH 45243 Office Fax: 513-558-2269. Business E-Mail: litsa.kranias@uc.edu.

KRASIL'NIKOV, MIKHAIL, medical educator; b. Moscow, Apr. 10, 1954; MD, Second Moscow Med. Inst., 1977; PhD, Russian Cancer Rsch. Ctr., 1982. Prof. Russian Cancer Rsch. Ctr., 2002—. Grant, Russian Found. Fundamental Rsch. Office: Kashirskoye Shosse Moscow 115478 Russia Business E-Mail: krasilnikovm@main.crc.umos.ru.

KRASNOFF, ERIC, health products executive; s. Abraham Krasnoff; m. Robin Krasnoff; 2 children. BA in Anthropology, Columbia Univ. Various exec. positions, including v.p., sr. v.p., group v.p., exec. v.p., pres., COO Pall Corp., East Hills, NY, 1975—94, chmn, CEO, 1994—2006, chmn., pres., CEO, 2006—. Chmn. bd. Nat. Blood

Found., 2001—; Presdl. adv. bd. Nat. Ctr. for Disability Svcs.; vice chmn. Am. Bus. Conf.; bd. dir. Nassau Healthcare Corp., 2004—. Bd. trustees Long Island Univ., 1992—. Office: Pall Corp 25 Harbor Park Dr Port Washington NY 11050-4605 Office Phone: 516-484-5400.

KRAU, ARY, plastic surgeon; MD, NYU. Diplomate Am. Bd. Plastic Surgery. Resident gen surgery Jackson Meml. Hosp.; resident plastic surgery King's County Hosp.; fellow plastic surgery Miami Heart Inst. Fellow: Am. Coll. of Surgeons; mem.: Greater Miami Soc. of Plastic and Reconstructive Surgeons, Am. Soc. of Plastic Surgeons. Office: 1143 Kane Concourse Bay Harbour Islands Miami FL 33154 Office Phone: 305-861-6881.

KRAU, EDGAR, psychologist, educator, research scientist; b. Stanislau, Poland, Apr. 9, 1929; arrived in Israel, 1977; s. Adolf and Ella (Lam) K.; m. Mary Epure, Dec. 27, 1958; 1 child, Nicole. MA, U. Cluj, Romania, 1951, PhD, 1964. Lic. psychologist Israel. Chief rsch. fellow Inst. Pedagogical Scis., Cluj, Romania, 1961-63; with U. Cluj, Romania, 1963-77; head psychology dept. Acad. Romanian Republic, Cluj, 1968-77; prof. U. Haifa, Israel, 1977-81, Tel-Aviv U., Israel, 1981-97, prof. emeritus, 1997—; prof. Thames Valley U., Haifa, Israel, 1997—. Mem. Internat. Test Commn., 1971-73; chmn. Internat. Colloquium on Human Resources Devel., Jerusalem, 1984; mem. sci. com. XXI Internat. Congress of Applied Psychology, 1986; editor-in-chief (jour. of labor studies) Man and Work, 1987—, hon. dir. gen. Internat Biographical Ctr. Cambridge, 2008. Author: The Contradictory Immigrant Problem, 1991, Social and Economic Management in the Competitive Society, 1998, (with P. Goguelin) Projet Professionnel - Projet de Vie, 1992, (with A. Globerson) Organizations and Management: Towards the Future, 1993, The Realization of Life Aspirations Through Vocational Careers, 1997, A Meta-Psychological Perspective on the Individual Course of Life, 2003, Toward Globalization with a Human Face, 2009; co-author: Treatise on Industrial Psychology, 1967 (Romanian Acad. Vasile Conta award 1972); co-author, editor: Self-realization, Success and Adjustment, 1989; author Jour. Vocational Behavior, 1981-89 (hon. mention award 1986). Recipient diploma of high ctr. for logic and comparative scis. award, Bologna, Italy, 1972, Homagial Biography-Bibliography, Revue Européenne de Psychologie Appliquée, 1993, World Order Sci.-Edn.-Culture, 2002, Am. Order of Excellence, 2003, Legion of Honor United Cultural Conv., 2005, Order of Am. Ambs., 2006. Mem. APA (affiliate), Israeli Psychol. Assn. (instr. 1979—), NY Acad. Scis., London Diplomatic Acad. (mem. acad. coun. 2002), World Acad. Letters (Einsteinian chair sci. 2004), Internat. Order of Merit. Home: 2 Hess St 33398 Haifa Israel E-mail: edgark@inter.net.il.

KRAUS, CHADD KENNETH, physician; b. St. Marys, Pa., Apr. 15, 1978; MPH, Johns Hopkins Bloomberg Sch. Pub. Health, 2005; DO, Phila. Coll. Osteo. Medicine, 2010. Clin. rschr. Johns Hopkins Dept. Emergency Medicine, 2002—07, course coord., head tchg. asst. Johns Hopkins Bloomberg Sch. Pub. Health, 2006—08, emergency medicine resident Lehigh Valley Health Network, 2010—; v.p. bd. dirs. Alpha Sigma Nu, 2006—09, admission com.; mem. Phila. Coll. Osteo Medicine, 2008—10, V.p., bd. dirs. Alpha Sigma Nu, 2006—09. Mem.: Emergency Medicine Residents Assn. (med. student editor 2008—10), Am. Acad. Emergency Medicine, Am. Osteo. Assn., Soc. Academic Emergency Medicine, Am. Coll. Emergency Physicians. Home: PO Box 275 Mechanicsville PA 18934 Personal E-mail: chaddkraus@hotmail.com.

KRAUS, GUENTHER JOSEPH, radiologist; b. Klagenfurt, Austria, Feb. 8, 1967; m. Verena Leitner, 1 child, Fabian. MD, Vienna Med. U., Austria, 1994; MSc, Donau U. Krems, 2008. Cert. gen. practicioner AMA, 1999, bd. cert. radiologist AMA, 2005. Internship Ikh-Klagenfurt, 1996—2000, Deutsch Ordens Spital-Friesach, 2000—03, U. Graz, Harvard U., 2003—05; pvt. practice radiologist Vienna, 2002—; sr. radiologist Klinikum, Amstetten, 2005—06, Diagnostikzentrum Urania, Vienna, 2006—. Mem.: Oesterreichische Radiologische Gesellschaft, Radiol. Soc. N.Am. Office: Diagnostikzentrum Urania DZU Laurenzerberg 2 1010 Vienna Austria Office Phone: 0043-1-200200 51. Personal E-mail: krausgj@hotmail.com.

KRAUS, HELEN, plastic surgeon; MD, Northwestern U. Med. Sch.; grad., U. Notre Dame. Diplomate Am. Bd. of Plastic Surgery, lic. Wis., Fla. Internship gen. surgery Northwestern Meml. Hosp., Chgo., resident plastic surgery; fellow pediatric plastic sugery Children's Meml. Hosp., Chgo.; chief plastic surgery Resurrection Med. Ctr., chief surgery; attending plastic surgeon Osceola Regional Med. Ctr., St. Cloud Med. Ctr., Fla. Hosp. Named Top Doc, Connolly Castle. Mem.: Phi Beta Kappa Soc., Am. Soc. of Plastic Surgeons. Office: St. Cloud Regional Medical Center 2906 17th St Saint Cloud FL 34769 Office Phone: 407-892-2135. Office Fax: 407-892-4835.

KRAUSE, CHARLES JOSEPH, otolaryngologist; b. Des Moines, Apr. 21, 1937; s. William H. and Ruby I. (Hitz) Krause; m. Barbara Ann Steelman, June 14, 1962; children: Sharon, John, Ann. BA, State U. Iowa, 1959, MD, 1962. Diplomate Am. Bd. Otolaryngology. Intern Phila. Gen. Hosp., 1962—63; resident in surgery U. Iowa, 1965—66, resident in otolaryngology, 1966—69; fellow dept. plastic surgery Marien Hosp., Stuttgart, Germany, 1970; asst. prof. otolaryngology U. Iowa, 1969—72, asso. prof., 1972—75, vice chmn. dept. otolaryngology, 1973—77, prof., 1975—77; prof., chmn. dept. otolaryngology U. Mich. Med. Sch., Ann Arbor, 1977—92; pres. Am. Bd. Otolaryngology, Houston. Prof. dept. otolaryngology U. Mich., 1977—2000, emeritus prof., 2000—, asst. dean for clin. affairs, 1986—89, sr. assoc. dean med. sch., 1992—96, chief clin. affairs, 1992—95, sr. assoc. hosp. dir., 1995—96; chief clin. affairs U. Mich. Hosps., Ann Arbor, 1986—89; bd. dirs. Am. Bd. Otolaryngology, 1984—2002, pres., 1998—2000. Author: book in field; contbr. chapters to books, articles to profl. jours. Capt. USAF, 1963—65. Fellow: Am. Soc. Head and Neck Surgery (coun. 1980—83, chmn. rsch. com. 1980—83, pres. 1987—88); mem.: Am. Bd. Otolaryngology (bd. dirs. 1984—, exam. com. chair 1993—, pres.-elect 1996—98, pres. 1998—2000), Centurions of Deafness Rsch. Found., Am. Laryngol. Assn., Am. Laryngol., Rhinol. and Otol. Soc., Am. Cancer Soc. (med. adv. com. Washtenaw County unit), Walter P. Work Soc. (pres. 1987), Soc. United Otolaryngologists, Am. Acad. Depts. Otolaryngology, Mich. Otolaryngol. Soc., Mich. State Med. Soc., Washtenaw County Med. Soc. (exec. com. 1979—82), Assn. Rsch. in Otolaryngology, Am. Asssn. Cosmetic Surgeons, Assn. Head and Neck Oncologists, ACS (adv. coun. otolaryngology 1979—83), Am. Acad. Facial Plastic and Reconstructive Surgery (regional v.p. 1977—80, chmn. rsch. com. 1977—80, pres. 1981—82), Am. Acad. Otolaryngology Head and Neck Surgery (bd. dirs. 1987—93, sec.-treas. 1987—93, pres.-elect 1995, pres. 1996), AMA. Republican. Presbyterian. Home and Office: 880 Sea Dune Ln Marco Island FL 34145-1840 E-mail: cjkrause1@aol.com.

KRAUSE, HELEN FOX, retired otolaryngologist; b. Boston, Mar. 20, 1932; d. Nathan and Frances Lena (Rich) Fox; children: Merrick Eli, Beth Riva Harper, Kim Debra Codd. BS, U. Maine, 1954; MD, Tuft U., 1958. Diplomate Am. Bd. Otolaryngology. Intern Health Ctr. Hosps. Pitts., 1958-59; resident Eye & Ear Hosp., Children's Hosp., VA Hosp., 1959-62; pvt. practice Pitts., 1962—2003; ret., 2003. Mem. otolaryngology adv. bd. U.S. Pharmacopea, 1991-96, 00—, chmn., 1995-00; prof. U. Pitts. Sch. Medicine; vis. prof. Pan Hellenic Otorhinolaryngology Soc., Crete, Greece, 1993, Panama, Argentina, 1998, China, Hong Kong, 1999, Thailand, China, Taiwan, 2000, Pan Am. Otolaryn. Soc., 2000; pres., dir. 1st World Congress of Otorhinolaryngologic Allergy, Endoscopy and Laser Surgery, Athens, 1998, 01; bd. dirs. Bayer Pharm. Women's Health Initiative; vis. prof. Thailand, Singapore; lectr. 2nd World Congress Otolaryngology, Allergy and Immunology, 2001; chairperson Nat. Hadassah Physicians Coun. Author, editor: Otolaryngic Allergy and Immunology, 1989; lectr., vis. prof. Singapore, Bangkok, Hong Kong (multiple tng. programs 1990); contbr. chpts. to books and articles to profl. jours. Pres. North Hills Jewish Cmty. Ctr., Pitts., 1973-74; cons. North Allegheny Sch. Bd., Pitts., 1977; lectr. North Allegheny Sr. High Sch., Wexford, 1979-84; chmn. Desert Storm Project, North Hills Bus. and Profl. Women, 1991. Recipient Disting. Svc. award, Pa. Acad. Otolaryngology, 1993, Hon. Achievement award, Am. Acad. Otolaryngology Head and Neck Surgery, 1993, Bd. Govs. Chair award, 2000, Bd. Govs. award, Practioner of Excellence, 2003, Presdl. citation, 2004, Bd. Govs. Volunteerism award, 2004, Bd. Govs. Vounteerism award, 2005, Recognition award, Panhellenic Soc. ORL-HNS, 2001, Lifetime Achievement award, Am. Acad. Otolaryngic Allergy, 2002; scholar Jackson Meml. Labs., Bar Harbor, Maine, 1954. Fellow ACS, Am. Acad. Otolaryngology Head and Neck Surgery (bd. govs. 1982-89, 90—, Practitioner Excellence award 2003, Presdl. citation 2004, Volunteerism award 2004, 05, 06), Am. Acad. Otolaryngologic Allergy (pres. 2984-85, Lifetime Achievement award 2002, Svc. award 1990, cert. appreciation 1991, Pres.'s award 1997, Spl. Achievement award 1997), Am. Acad. Facial Plastic and Rsch. Surgery; mem. Pa. Acad. Otolaryngology (pres. 1989-90), Internat. Soc. Otorhinolaryngic Allergy and Immunology (pres. 1995-98), Pitts. Otological Soc. (pres. 1983-85), Phi Beta Kappa, Phi Kappa Phi. Office: 1301 Aviara Pl Gibsonia PA 15044-8042 Personal E-mail: hfk@zoominternet.net.

KRAUSE, JOHN L., retired optometrist; b. Portland, Oreg., Oct. 26, 1917; m. Nancy D., Sept. 30, 1942; children: Diana L., Karen L., Ronald L. Student, Northwestern U., 1935—37; OD, Ill. Coll. Optometry, 1947. Pres. class practice optometry, Niles, Ill., 1978—87; ret., 1987. USAF Med. Service liaison officer, Northwestern U. Med. Sch., Chgo., 1964-91. Author: Sight Check Your Child, 1961, Holiday Fax, 1991, 3d edit., 2006, Win-Win, Inc., 1994; contbr. articles to nat. mags.; patentee card holder, 1967. Bd. overseers S.E. Univ. Coll. Optometry, North Miami Beach, Fla., 1993, liaison to optometry Nat. Alliance Mental Health, 1993; pres. ins. coun. City Tamarac, Fla., 1993—2009, chmn., 2002-09, ombudsman State of Fla., Broward County, 1996-2000. Served with U.S. Army, 1941-45, to lt. col. USAF, ret., 1970. Decorated Bronze Star with cluster, Combat Medic badge; recipient hon. award, Armed Forces Optometric Soc., 2002; named Alumnus of the Yr., Ill. Coll. Optometry, 2007; named to Sr. Hall of Fame, Broward County Fla., 2000. Mem. Am. Optometric Assn., Ill. Optometric Assn., Fla. Optometric Assn. Armed Forces Optometric Soc. (Honor award 2002), Air Force Assn., Fla. Pub. Health Assn. (chmn.-elect vision sect. 1992), Fla. Ret. Optometrists Assn. (pres. 1993-95, editor 1995—2007, Alumnus of Yr. Ill Coll. Optometry, 2007), Kappa Phi Delta, Phi Theta Upsilon, Phi Mu Delta. Achievements include patents for eyedrop transport apparatus, 2002, 2004. Avocations: golf, stamp collecting/philately. Home: 7270 Fairfax Dr Tamarac FL 33321-4305 Personal E-mail: dockrause@comcast.net.

KRAUSE, PETER CARL, physician, educator; b. Washington, Nov. 5, 1966; AB, Harvard U., 1990; MD, Stanford U., 1996. Asst. prof. La. State U. Health Sci. Ctr., 2002—. Office: La State University Orthopaedic Clinic 200 W Esplana Kenner LA 70065 Office Fax: 504-412-1701. Business E-Mail: pckrause@mac.com.

KRAUSE, RICHARD MICHAEL, medical scientist, government official, educator, researcher; b. Marietta, Ohio, Jan. 4, 1925; s. Ellis L. and Jennie Mae (Waterman) Krause. BA, Marietta Coll., 1947, DSc (hon.), 1978; MD, Case Western Res. U., 1952; DSc (hon.), U. Rochester, 1979, Med. Coll. Ohio, Toledo, 1981, Hahnemann Med. Coll. and Hosp., 1982; LLD (hon.), Thomas Jefferson U., 1982. Rsch. fellow dept. preventive medicine Case Western Res. U., 1950—51; intern Ward Med. Svc., Barnes Hosp., St. Louis, 1952—53, asst. resident, 1953—54; asst. physician to hosp. Rockefeller Inst., 1954—57, asst. prof., assoc. physician to hosp., 1957—61; prof. epidemiology Sch. Medicine, Washington U., St. Louis, 1962—66, assoc. prof. medicine, 1962—65, prof. medicine, 1965—66; assoc. prof., physician to hosp. Rockefeller U., 1966—68, prof., sr. physician, 1968—75; dir. Rockefeller U. (Animal Rsch. Ctr.), 1974—75, Nat. Inst. Allergy and Infectious Diseases, NIH, HEW, Bethesda, Md., 1975—84; USPHS surgeon, 1975—77; asst. surgeon gen., 1977—84; dean Emory U. Sch. Medicine, Atlanta, 1984—89, Robert W. Woodruff prof. medicine, 1984—89; mem. program com. Inst. Medicine, 1986—87; sr. sci. adv. Fogarty Internat. Ctr. NIH, Bethesda, 1989—; sr. investigator NIAID NIH, Bethesda, 2000—. Bd. dirs. Mo.-St. Louis Heart Assn., 1962—66, mem. rsch. com., 1963—66; mem. exec. com. coun. on rheumatic fever and congenital heart disease Am. Heart Assn., 1963—66, chmn. coun. rsch. study com., 1963—66, mem. assn. rsch. com., 1963—66, mem. policy com., 1966—70; mem. commn. streptococcal and staphylococcal diseases U.S. Armed Forces Epidemiol. Bd., 1963—72, dep. dir., 1968—72; bd. dirs. N.Y. Heart Assn., 1967—73, chmn. adv. coun. on rsch., 1969—71, mem. dirs. coun., 1973—75; cons. WHO, 1967—, mem. coccal expert com., 1967—; mem. steering com. Biomed. Sci. Scientific Working Group, WHO, 1978; mem. infectious disease adv. com. Nat. Inst. Allergy and Infectious Disease, NIH, 1970—74; bd. dirs. Royal Soc. Medicine Found., Inc., 1971—77, treas., 1973—75; bd. dirs. Allergy and Asthma Found. Am., 1976—77, Lupus Found. Am., 1977—79. Assoc. editor: Jour. Immunology, 1963—71, sect. editor: Viral and Microbial Immunology, 1974—75; editor: Jour. Exptl. Medicine, 1973—75; adv. editor:, 1976—84, mem. editl. bd.: Bacteriological Revs., 1969—73, Infection and Immunity, 1970—78, Immunochemistry, 1973—80, Clin. Immunology and Immunopathology, 1976—78; contbr. articles to profl. jours. With US Army, 1944—46. Decorated Gumhuria medal Egypt; recipient DSM, HEW, 1979, C. William O'Neal Disting. Am. Svc. award, Robert Koch Medal in Gold, Berlin, 1985, Sr. U.S. Scientist award, Alexander Von Humboldt Found., Fed. Republic Germany, 1986. Mem.: AAAS, Am. Epidemiol. Soc., Practitioner's Soc. NY, Royal Soc. Medicine, Infectious Diseases Soc. Am., Am. Coll. Allergists, Harvey Soc., Am. Soc. Microbiology, Am. Assn. Immunologists, Am. Soc. Clin. Investigation, Am. Soc. Biol. Chemists, Am. Acad. Allergy, Assn. Am. Physicians, Inst. Medicine, U.S. Nat. Acad. Scis., Cosmos, Century Assn. Achievements include research in pathogenesis and epidemiology of streptococcal diseases; immunochem. studies on streptococcal antigens; immunogenetics; recognition of rabbit antibodies with molecular uniformity, genetics of immune response. Home: 4000 Cathedral Ave NW Apt 413B Washington DC 20016-5268 Office: NIAID NIH Rm 202 16 Center Dr Bldg 16 Bethesda MD 20892-0001 E-mail: richard_krause@nih.gov.

KRAUSER, ROBERT STANLEY, healthcare executive; b. NYC, Aug. 24, 1937; s. Benjamin and Eva (Ferester) K.; m. Mary Kay Edwards, June 12, 1977 (dec. May 1999); children: Robert Edwards, Kathryn Edwards. BA, U. Vt., 1958; MS, Columbia U. Grad. Sch. Bus., 1959. Rschr., portfolio analyst Merrill, Lynch, Pierce et al, NYC, 1961-63; dir. spl. situations rschr. Orvis Bros., NYC, 1964-66; dir. rsch. Amott, Baker, NYC, 1966-69; v.p. rsch. counsel Bruns, Nordemann & Rea, NYC, 1970-75; v.p. rsch. assoc. Rosenkrantz, Ehrenkrantz, NYC, 1976-77; investment banker Herzfeld & Stern, Stamford, Conn., 1978-82; chmn., pres. Viral Response Sys., Inc., Greenwich, Conn., 1983—. Patentee in field. With USAR, 1959. Recipient Cert. of Recognition Eli Whitney Mus., 1987. Mem. Nat. Assn. Chain Drug Stores, Am. Mensa (Philanthropic award 1987), Inventors Assn. Conn. (Inventor of Yr. 1988), U.S. Tennis Assn. (ranked 1995), The Wimbledon Soc., Landmark Club, East Hampton Tennis Club (mixed doubles champ 1972), Armonk Tennis Club, Grand Slam Tennis Club (singles champ 1977, 78), San Diego Tennis and Racquet Club, Balboa Tennis CLub. Avocations: tennis, skiing, swimming, travel, medical reading. Home and Office: 444 Taconic Rd Greenwich CT 06831-2850

KRAUSPE, RUEDIGER, orthopedist, surgeon, educator; b. Luenen, Nordrhein-Westfalen, Germany, Sept. 20, 1953; s. Rudolf Karl Reinhold and Rosemarie Krauspe; m. Irene Claudia Goerttler, June 4, 1982; children: Jan Christian, Elena Maria, Jonas David, Philipp Jonathan. Approbation, U. Kiel, Germany, 1980; PhD, U. Wuerzburg, 1993. Cert. orthop. surgeon Aerztekammer Baden-Wuerttemberg, 1987, specialist in orthop. surgery Aerztekammer Bayern, 1996. Staff surgeon U. Wuerzburg, 1987—96, prof., 1996—99; specialist, orthop. surgeon Aerztekammer Bayern, Stuttgart, Germany, 1995; full prof., head orthop. dept. U. Duesseldorf, Germany, 1999—. Contbr. chapters to books, articles to profl. jours. Master: Vereinigung fuer Kinderorthopaedie (pres. 2000); fellow: European Fedn. Nat. Assns. Orthopaedics and Traumatology (sci. advisor 2000—01), Deutsche Gesellschaft fuer Orthopaedie und Orthopaedische Chirurgie; mem.: Deutscher Sportaerzteverband, Deutscher Hochschullehrerverband, Edn. Bd. of the AO-Spine Internat., Arbeitsgemeinschaft fuer Osteosynthesefragen, AO-Deutschland, European Soc. Foot and Ankle Surgeons, European Pediatric Orthopaedic Soc. (bd. mem. 2004). Office: Universitaetsklinikum Duesseldorf Moorenstraße 5 40225 Duesseldorf Germany Office Fax: +49-(0)211 8116281. E-mail: krauspe@med.uni-duesseldorf.de.

KRAUSS, HENRY FREDERICK, JR., optometrist; b. Sewickley, Pa., Apr. 10, 1952; s. Henry Frederick and Mirella Anna (Guerrieri) K.; m. Sally Winston Miller, July5, 1975; children: Molly Anne, Henry Neil, Malinda Paige, Michael Winston. BS, Centre Coll., Ky., 1976; OD, U. Houston, 1980. Optometrist, owner Eye Care Assocs., Richardson, Tex., 1980—. V.p. ProComp Systems Inc., Albuquerque, 1983-86; ptnr. K-W Distbrs., Dallas, 1983-86, Summit Seminars, Richardson, 1985—; owner, operator Profl. Enhancement Strategies, 1997—; pres. Simplified Web Solutions, 2004-. Bd. dirs. Found. for Edn. and Rsch. in Vision, 1988-89, S.W. Vision Svc. Plan, 1982-84. Fellow Am. Acad. Optometry; mem. Am. Optometric Assn., Tex. Optometric Assn. (Young Optometrist of Yr. award 1985), North Tex. Optometric Assn. (pres. 1983-84), Am. Pub. Health Assn. (vision care sect.). Republican. Mem. Lds Ch. Avocations: photography, horsemanship, sailing, scuba diving. Office: Eye Care Assocs 660 W Campbell Rd Richardson TX 75080-3301 Home Phone: 972-235-4314; Office Phone: 972-231-9595. E-mail: drkrauss@ecarichardson.com, hkrauss@ecatexas.net.

KRAUSS, HERBERT HARRIS, psychologist; b. Phila., June 13, 1940; s. Leon and Ethel Sarah (Cohen) K.; m. Beatrice Joy Osgood, Aug. 26, 1965; children: Michael Conal, Daniel Avram. BS, Pa. State U., 1961, MS, 1962; PhD, Northwestern U., 1966. Lic. psychologist, N.Y. Intern in med. psychology U. Oreg. Med. Sch., 1962-63; asst. prof. psychiatry, psychology U. Kans. Med. Sch., Kansas City, Kans., 1966-67; asst. prof. psychiatry, psychology, chief psychologist in child psychiatry Ohio State U. Coll. Medicine, Columbus, 1967-69; assoc. prof. psychology U. Ga., Athens, 1969-71; prof. psychology Hunter Coll., CUNY, NYC, 1971-2001, chmn. dept. psychology, 1992-99; dir. rehab. rsch. and outcomes mgmt. Internat. Ctr. for the Disabled, NYC, 1984—2002; prof., chmn. dept. psychology Pace U., NYC, 2001—10, prof. emeritus, 2010; with Family Ctr., Goshen, NY, 2010—; prof. emeritus Hunter Coll., CUNY, 2001. Cons. Managed Health Network, N.Y.C., 1979-90, PhD Program, NYU, rehab. counselling, 1991—; adj. assoc. prof. psychiatry Cornell Med. Sch., N.Y.C., 1978—; assoc. attending psychologist Payne Whitney Clinic, N.Y. Hosp., 1978—; ptnr. Health Resources Mgmt. Co-author: Living with Anxiety and Depression, 1974; co-editor: Between Survival and Suicide, 1976, A Provider's Guide to Psychiatric Services in the General Hospital, 1986, The Aging Workforce: A Guide for University Administrators, 1992, Violence in the Schools: Cross-National and Cross-Cultural Perpsectives, 2005, Violence and Exploitation against women and girls, Vol. 1087 N.Y. CAcad. Scis.; co-editor Internat. Jour. Group Tensions, 1995-2000, assoc. editor, 2000—; cons. editor Jour. Individual Psychology, 1996—. Cons. Irvington, N.Y. Drug Coun., 1983; coach football and wrestling Irvington Sunnysiders, 1978-83, soccer Am. Youth Soccer Orgn., Houston, 1976-78. Named Outstanding Teacher Psychology, N.Y. Psychol. Assn., 1972. Fellow APA(Gen. Psychology Divsn. & Clin. Psychology Divsn. 12); mem. N.Y. Acad. Scis., Ea. Psychol. Assn., Internat. Orgn. for Study of Group Tensions (v.p., co-pres. 1999—), Am. Coun. on Germany, Am. Evaluation Assn., Cornell Club, Sigma Xi. Home: 520 Grand Ave

Newburgh NY 12550-1929 Office: Family Ctr 305 Main St Goshen NY 10924 Home Phone: 845-565-7063; Office Phone: 845-294-4240. Business E-Mail: hharriskrauss@gmail.com.

KRAUSS, WILLIAM, neurosurgeon; b. Ill., Oct. 17, 1961; AB, Harvard Coll., 1983; MD, Columbia U., 1987. Cons. neurol. surgery Mayo Clinic, 1993. Office: Mayo Clinic Dept Neurological Surgery Rochester MN 55905 Business E-Mail: krauss.william@mayo.edu.

KRAUT, JEFFREY ALAN, nephrologist, educator; b. Jersey City, Dec. 28, 1946; BA, Bucknell U., 1968; MD, NY Med. Coll., 1972. Chief dialysis unit, prof. medicine Veterans Adminstrn. Greater LA Healthcare Sys., UCLA Sch. Medicine, 1978—. Mem.: Western Soc. Clin. Investigation, Am. Soc. Nephrology. Achievements include research in diagnosis and treatment of acid-base disorders with special emphasis on elucidating the mechanisms of cellular dysfunction and injury and developing new methods of treatment. Avocation: reading. Office: 11301 Wilshire Blvd Los Angeles CA 90073 Office Fax: 310-268-4996. Business E-Mail: jkraut@ucla.edu.

KRAUT, RICHARD A., dentist; DDS, NYU. Diplomate Am. Bd. Oral & Maxillofacial Surgeons, Am. Bd. Oral Medicine, Internat. Congress of Oral Implantologists. Intern Ford Ord US Army Hosp., Calif.; resident Fitzsimons Army Garrison Fitzsimons Gen. Hosp., Colo.; resident Fort Sam Brooke Army Med. Ctr., Houston, chief oral and maxillofacial surgery svc., chief dentistry dept., dir. oral and maxillofacial surgery residency program; fellow Am. Dental Soc. of Anesthesiology; chief dentistry dept. Tripler Army Med. Ctr., Honolulu, dir. oral and maxillofacial surgery residency program; prof. dentistry dept. Montefiore Med. Ctr., Bronx, NY, dir. oral and maxillofacial surgery residency program, chmn. dentistry dept. Lectr., Russia, South Africa, Japan, India; and throughout Europe. Co-author: (publs.) Dental implants in geriatric patients: a retrospective study of 47 cases, 2007, Prosthodontic management of sulcoplasty and sialodochoplasty with a conforming surgical stent, 2008, Bisphosphonate use and health history questionnaire, 2008, Outcomes of placing dental implants in patients taking oral bisphosphonates: a review of 115 cases, 2008, Malignant ameloblastoma: a case report of a recent onset of neck swelling in a patient with a previously treated ameloblastoma, 2009, Root and pulp response after intentional injury from miniscrew placement, 2009, Cementum, pulp, periodontal ligament, and bone response after direct injury with orthodontic anchorage screws: a histomorphologic study in an animal model, 2009, Outcomes of placing short dental implants in the posterior mandible: a retrospective study of 124 cases, 2009, Use of tilted implants in treatment of the atrophic posterior mandible: a preliminary report of a novel approach, 2010. Recipient Drummond-Jackson prize, 1985. Fellow: Am. and Internat. Coll. of Dentists. Office: Montefiore Medical Center 3332 Rochambeau Ave Bronx NY 10467 Office Phone: 888-700-6623. Office Fax: 718-515-5419.

KRAVITZ, JOSEPH, cosmetic dentist; m. Renee Kravitz; 4 children. MS in Oral Biology, U. Md., DDS. Cert. prosthodontics U. Md. Fellow implant dentistry NYU, prof., implant dentistry; prof., aesthetic dentistry Univ. Md.; rschr. PEARL Network; with Wash. DC Dental Implants. Adj. clin. faculty mem. periodontics and prosthodontics Nat. Naval Med. Ctr. Office: Washington DC Dental Implants 11247 Lockwood Dr Silver Spring MD 20901

KRAVTSOV, GENNADI, biophysicist, researcher; b. Bogoduchov, Ukraine, Apr. 17, 1950; s. Michael and Polina (Evsukova) K.; m. Alla Bogdanchikova, May 30, 1983; 1 child, Grigory. BSc, Moscow State U., 1972, PhD, 1977. Jr. rschr. Pub. Health Ctr., Russia, 1976-80, sr. rschr., 1981-89; group chief Cardiol. Ctr., Russia, 1990-93; rsch. officer U. Hong Kong, 1993—. Contbr. articles to profl. jours. Mem. AAAS, European Soc. Hypertension, N.Y. Acad. Scis. Avocations: music, reading, tennis, travel. Office: Univ Hong Kong Dept Physiology 4 F Laboratory Blk 21 Sassoon Rd Hong Kong China Home Phone: 852 28724735. Business E-Mail: gmkravts@hku.hk.

KRAWETZ, STEPHEN ANDREW, molecular medicine and genetics scientist, educator; b. Ft. Frances, Ont., Can., Sept. 17, 1955; s. Stephen and Michaelene (Medynski) K.; m. Lorraine Ruth St. John, Aug. 19, 1977; children: Rhochelle Tairaesa, Alexandra Renée. BSc, U. Toronto, Ont., 1977, PhD, 1983. Tchr. Scarborough Bd. Edn., Ont., 1976-77; Alberta Heritage Found. Med. Rsch. postdoc. fellow U. Calgary, Alta., Canada, 1983-89; asst. prof. rsch. ctr. for molecular biology Wayne State U., Detroit, 1989, asst. prof. molecular biology and genetics, 1989-92, asst. prof. obstetrics and gynecology and molecular biology and genetics, 1992-94, assoc. prof. ob/gyn. and molecular medicine and genetics, 1994-2000, prof. ob-gyn. and molecular medicine and genetics Inst. Sci. Computing, 2000, Charlotte B. Failing prof. ob-gyn. and molecular medicine and genetics, 2001—, dir. Bioinformatics Node Mich. Life Scis. Corridor, 2001—06, dir. Ctr. of Excellence for Combating the Paternal Impact of Toxicol. Waste on the Next Generation, dir. translational reproductive sys., 2004—07; assoc. dir. C.S. Mott Ctr. Human Growth & Devel., 2010—. Biotech. cons., Calgary, 1985-89, Grosse Pointe Woods, Mich., 1989—; co-founder Genetic Imaging, Inc., 1988. Mem. editl. bd. Ag Biotech News and Info., Cellular and Molecular Biology Letters, Gene Therapy and Molecular Biology, EIC SBiRM Systems Biology in Reproductive Medicine; contbr. numerous articles to scholarly jours. Recipient B.C. Childrens Hosp. Rsch. award, Vancouver, 1984, Computer Applications in Molecular Biology award IntelliGenetics Inc., Mountain View, Calif., 1988, others, Bd. of Govs. award Wayne State U., 2004; named Outstanding Basic Scientist, C.S. Mott Ctr., 1999; Alta. Heritage Found. Med. Rsch. fellow, 1985-88. Mem. AAAS, Am. Soc. Human Genetics, Soc. for the Study of Reprodn. Achievements include development of a computer-based imaging system for biological data, of the basis of biological sequence alignment algorithm; first definition of sequence interpretation errors in the GenBank database; first to define a genic domain in human sperm; research in gene therapy targeted to the amelioration of human disease; showed that selective potentiation of our genome mediates cell-phenotype; sperm also deliver RNA at fertilization.

KRAYBILL, WILLIAM GRESS, JR., surgical oncologist, educator; b. Omaha, Feb. 15, 1943; s. William Gress Sr. and Betty (Dunsmore) K.; m. Judith Adams, Feb. 18, 1974; children: Anna, Lindsay, Jacob. BS, Earlham Coll., Richmond, Ind., 1965; MD, U. Cin., 1969. Intern Santa Clara Valley Med. Ctr., San Jose, Calif., 1969-70, U. Oreg. Health Scis. Ctr., Portland, 1972-76, surg. oncology fellow, 1974—75, chief resident, 1976—77, surg. oncology fellow in rsch. tumor immunology, 1977-78; surg. oncology fellow Meml. Sloan-Kettering Cancer Ctr., NYC, 1978-80; assoc. dir. surgery Ellis Fischel State Cancer Ctr., Columbia, Mo., 1980-85, acting dir. surgery, 1980-85, vice chief of staff, 1982-84, med. dir. of surg. ICU, 1982-88, med. cons. to rehab. svc., 1982-88, chmn. residency rev. com., 1983-84, chmn. surg. ICU com., 1983-88, dir. surgery, 1985-88, chmn. cancer registry com., 1986-88, sec. med. staff, 1987-88, cons. staff mem., 2009—; surgery prof. Ohio State U. James Cancer Hosp. Courtesy staff Columbia Regional Hosp., St. Louis, 1988-95; assoc. staff mem. Jewish Hosp., St. Louis, 1988-95; cons. staff mem. Children's Hosp., St. Louis, 1988—; attending staff mem. St. Louis Regional Med. Ctr., 1988-95; assoc. sci. in surgery Cancer Rsch. Ctr., Columbia, 1980-88; asst. prof. Dept. of Surgery U. Mo. Health Scis. Ctr., Columbia, 1980-86; prin. investigator Nat. Surg. Adjuvant Breast Project, Columbia, 1980-88; participant Cancer and Leukemia Group B, 1986-88; assoc. clin. prof. of surgery Washington U. Sch. of Medicine, St. Louis, 1987-88, asst. prof. of surgery, 1988—; mem. steering com. U. Mo., Columbia, 1999-, Carlos Perez-Mesa lectr. humanities, 1999-, assoc. prof. surg., SUNY, 1995-02, prof., 2002-06, Clin. dir., Sarcoma Melanoma Svc., 1995-2000, Roswell Pk. Cancer Inst., 1995-2006, prof. surg. UMKC, med. dir., St. Lukes Hosp., 2007-09, James Cancer Hosp. Ohio State U., 2009-. Mem. editl. bd. Jour. Surg. Oncology, Current Treatment Options in Oncology, Jour. Clin. Oncology, 2001-04; ad hoc reviewer: Cancer, Cancer Rsch., Oncology; contbr. more than 100 articles to profl. jours.; contbr. chpts. to books. Host Eagle Scout Career Day, 1999-2001. Capt. USAF, 1970-72, Vietnam. Recipient Disting. award, Oreg. Health Sci. Ctr. Surg. Alumni; named one of Best Drs. in Am., 2003—04, 2005—10; grantee, Roswell Park Alliance Found., 1997—2000, Schering Corp., 1999—2004, Empire State, 2001—03. Fellow ACS (chmn. Field Liason Program Mo. Commn. on Cancer 1985-91, rep. of Fellowship of Commn. on Cancer 1987—, mem. Cancer Liason Com. Commn. on Cancer 1989-91—, mem. Patient Care and Rsch. Com. Commn. on Cancer 1987-90, mem. Task Force on Staging 1989—, mem. PCF subcom. 1989—, vice chmn. commn. on cancer 1993-94, mem. edn. com. 1995-97, nominating com. 1997-99, NIH Sarcoma Program rev. planning com. 2003-04); mem. AAAS, Am. Joint Com. on Cancer, Am. Assn. Cancer Edn., Am. Assn. Cancer Rsch., Am. Soc. of Clin. Oncology (program com. 1995), Ctrl. Surg. Assn., Mo. State Med. Assn., Mo. State Surg. Soc., St. Louis Metro. Med. Soc., St. Louis Surg. Soc., Soc. of Am. Gastrointestinal Endoscopic Surgeons, Soc. of Critical Care Medicine, Soc. of Head and Neck Surgeery, Soc. Pelvic Surgeons, Soc. of Surg. Oncology (issues com. 1994-96, tng. com. 1996-98, tng. program program dirs. subcom. 2003-, membership com. 2003-), N.Am. Hyperthermia Soc., N.Y. Acad. of Sci., Am. Cancer Soc. (rsch. fellow 1975-78, 1978-80, Jr. Faculty Clin. fellow 1977-78), Buffalo Surg. Soc., Am. Surg. Assn. Home: Ohio State University 410 W 10th Ave N924 Doan Hall Columbus OH 43210 Office Phone: 614-293-7742. Office Fax: 614-293-3465. Business E-Mail: william.kraybill@osumc.edu.

KREBS, WILLIAM HOYT, industrial hygienist, health science association administrator; b. Detroit, Apr. 6, 1938; s. William Thomas and Mary Louise (Hoyt) K.; m. Susan Kathryn Bartholomew, Aug. 8, 1964 (div. July 1976); children: Elizabeth Louise, William Thomas II; m. Jane Germer Meikle, June 18, 1983 (dec. May 2004); stepchildren: David Andrew, Sarah Elizabeth. BS, U. Mich., 1960, MPH (IH), 1963, MS, 1965, PhD, 1970. Rsch. asst. U. Mich., Ann Arbor, 1962-63; indsl. hygienist Lumbermens Mut. Casualty Co., Chgo., 1963-64, GM Corp., Detroit, 1970-77, mgr. toxic materials control activity, 1977-81, dir. toxic materials control activity, 1981-90, dir. indsl. hygiene activity, 1990-93; v.p. Indsl. Health Scis., Inc., Grosse Pointe Park, Mich., 1993—94, pres., 2004—. Mem. asbestos adv. com. Mich. Occupational Health Standards Commn., Lansing, 1984—. Contbr. articles to profl. jours. Mem. Grosse Pointe Meml. Ch., Grosse Pointe Farms, 1954; mem. health and safety com. Detroit Area coun. Boy Scouts Am., 1980; mem. environment and energy com. Detroit Regional Chamber. Fellow Am. Indsl. Hygiene Assn. (hon. mem.; bd. dirs. 1976-79, v.p. 1986-87, pres. 1988-89); mem. AAAS, APHA, Mich. Indsl. Hygiene Soc. (pres. 1980-81), Brit. Occupational Hygiene Soc., Internat. Occupational Hygiene Assn. (v.p. 1990-91, pres. 1992-93), Internat. Commn. on Occpl. Health, Soc. Automotive Engrs. Presbyterian. Home: 1014 Bishop Rd Grosse Pointe Park MI 48230-1421 Office: Indsl Health Scis Inc 1014 Bishop Rd Grosse Pointe Park MI 48230-1421 Office Phone: 313-885-8225.

KREEK, MARY JEANNE, physician; b. Washington; d. Louis Francis and Esperance (Agee) K; m. Robert A. Schaefer, Jan. 24, 1970; children: Robert A., Esperance Anne BA, Wellesley Coll., 1958; MD, Columbia U., Coll. Physicians and Surgeons, 1962; PharmD (hon.), Uppsala U., Sweden, 2000; Doctoris Honoris Causa (hon.), Tel Aviv U., 2007; D (hon.), U. Bologna, 2010. Med. rschr. NIH, Bethesda, Md., 1957—62; intern, resident Cornell N.Y. Hosp. Med. Ctr., NYC, 1962—65, fellow, 1965—67; instr. medicine Cornell Med. Coll., 1966—67; clinician specializing in internal medicine, endocrinology, gastroenterology, hepatology, pharmacology, neurosci., molecular genetics NYC, 1966—. Mem. staff N.Y.-Presbyn. Hosp.-Weill Sch. Medicine of Cornell U., 1968—77, clin. asst. prof., asst. attending physician, now assoc. attending physician, adj. assoc. prof.; vis. scientist, Rockefeller Inst. Med. Rsch. Rockefeller U., 1964—67, asst. prof., 1967—72, sr. rsch. assoc., physician, 1972—83, assoc. prof., physician, 1983—94, prof., sr. physician, head of lab., 1994—; head Ind. Lab. on Biology of Addictive Disease, 1975—94, head of lab., 1994—; sr. physician Rockefeller U. Hosp., 1994—; adj. prof. Beijing Med. U., 1996—2000, Peking U., 2000—, Karolinska Inst., 2001; mem. gen. medicine study sect. NIH, 1973—77; co-chmn. John E. Fogarty (NIH) Internat. Conf. Hepatotoxicity Due to Drugs and Chems., 1977, charter mem. peer rev. oversight group, 1996—2000; vis. prof. Pahlavi U., Shiraz, Iran, 1977; spl. adv. Nat. Inst. Drug Abuse, 1976—86, mem. nat. adv. coun., 1991—95, mem. molecular genetics consortium, 1999—; prin. investigator Rsch. Ctr. Biol. Basis Addictive Diseases, 1987—; mem. gastroenterology adv. com. FDA, 1975—79, 1992—96, NIH Gen. Clin.; mem. gen. rsch. ctr. study sect. NIH, 1979—83, chmn., 1982—83; mem. exec. com. Coll. Problems Drug Dependence, 1982—87, 1989—94, chmn. exec. com., 1985—87, chair sci. program com., 1991—96; fellow CPDD, 1992—; dir. NIH-Nat. Inst. Drug Abuse Rsch. Ctr., 1987—. Recipient Borden Rsch. award, 1962, Career Scientist award Health Rsch. Coun. City NY, 1974-75, Dole/Nyswander award, 1984, Rsch. Scientist award NIH Gen. Clin. sect., 1978—, Mentor of Mentors award Am. Soc. Addiction Medicine, 1995, Assn. for Med. Edn. and Rsch. in Substance Abuse-Betty Ford award for outstanding rsch., 1996, R. Brinkley Smithers Disting. Scholar award Am. Soc. Addiction Medicine, 1999, Nathan B. Eddy award, Lifetime Rsch. award Coll. on Problems of Drug Dependence, 1999, Gold Medal Lifetime Excellence award Columbia U. Coll. Physicians and Surgeons Alumni Assn., 2004, Marian Fischman award, Coll. Ptnrs., 2005, Founders award, Intenat. Narcotic Rsch. Conf., 2005 Fellow: ACP (life), Am. Coll. Psychiatry, Harvey Soc., NY Acad. Scis., Am. Fedn. for Clin. Rsch., Assn. Am. Physicians (life), Am. Coll. Neuropsychopharmacology (mem. coun. 2004—); mem.: Soc. on Neuroscis., Rsch. Soc. on Alcoholism, Coun. Fgn. Rels. (life), Internat. Narcotic Rsch. Conf. (exec. com. 1993—97, pres.-elect 2001—03, pres. 2003—06, past pres. 2006—), Internat. Assn. Study Liver, Am. Assn. Study Liver Diseases, Endocrine Soc., N.Y. Gastroent. Assn. (pres. 1987), Am. Gastroent. Assn., Shakespeare Soc. of Wellesley, Phi Beta Kappa, Sigma Xi. Office: Rockefeller U New York NY 10021

KREGER, DAVID LAWRENCE, gastroenterologist; b. Portsmouth, Va., Feb. 8, 1946; s. H. Sol and Ruth S. (Silverman) K.; m. Ruth H., Mar. 31, 1974; children: Seth Adam, Senta Lauren. BA, Duke U., 1968; MD, Med. Coll. Va. Intern Med. Coll. Va. Hosp., Richmond, 1972-73, resident, 1973-75; gastroenterologist Gastroen. Assocs. Tidewater, Norfolk, Va., 1978—. Gastroenterology fellow, Duke U. Med. Ctr., Durham, N.C., 1975—77. Office: Gastroen Assocs Tidewater 160 Kingsley Ln Ste 200 Norfolk VA 23505-4600 Home Phone: 757-440-0705; Office Phone: 757-889-6800.

KREGER, MARY, medical researcher; b. Phoenix, Ariz., Nov. 21, 1949; PhD, MPH, U. Calif., Berkeley, 1987. Policy analyst, office pres. U. Calif., 1995—2001, sr. rschr. San Francisco, 2001—. Mem. Environ. Evaluators Adv. Com., 2010, Regional Asthma Mgmt. Adv. Com., 2001. Burden Asthma Schs. grant, Calif. Endowment, Cmty. Case Mgmt. grant, Health and Edn. grant, Hewlett Found., Evaluation Health Inequities Policy and Sys. grant, Ctrs. Disease Control and Prevention. Mem.: APHA. Avocation: photography. Office: University Calif San Francisco CA 94118 Office Fax: 415-476-0705. Business E-Mail: mary.kreger@ucsf.edu.

KREIBORG, SVEN, dental educator, researcher; b. Copenhagen, Nov. 1, 1944; s. Svend and Ebba Kreiborg; children: Jesper, Birgitte. DDS, Sch. Dentistry, Copenhagen, 1968, PhD, 1975, cert. orthodontist, 1974, D of Odontology, 1981. Cert. dentistry, orthodontics. Pvt. practice H. Scheil, DDS, Copenhagen, 1968—70; rsch. assoc. U. Ill., Chgo., 1970—71; asst. prof. Sch. Dentistry, Copenhagen, 1975—78, assoc. prof., 1978—85, prof., head dept., 1985—; prof. Copenhagen U. Hosp., 1999—. Recipient Rsch. award, Ingeborg and Leo Dannin's Fund, 1987, Sheldon Friel Meml. Lecture award, 2009. Office: U Copenhagen Norre Allé 20 Copenhagen DK-2200 Denmark Home: Lundely 13 Hellerup DK-2900 Denmark Home Phone: +45 3927 0028; Office Phone: +45 3532 6750. Office Fax: +45 3532 6760. Business E-Mail: skrei@sund.ku.dk.

KREIDER, CLEMENT HORST, JR., neurosurgeon; b. Annville, Pa., Oct. 14, 1932; s. Clement Horst and Eleanor Lucille (Etter) K.; m. Yvonne Maria Vignone, Mar. 6, 1983; children: Clement H. III, John William H., George E. Etter (dec. Jan. 2001); stepchildren: Michael A. Ketcham (dec. July 1997), David C. Ketcham. Student, Yale U., 1949-51, 53-54; BS, Bethany Coll., W.Va., 1957; MD, Temple U., 1963. Lic. physician, Pa., N.J. Intern Pa. Hosp., Phila., 1963-64; resident in gen. surgery Temple U. Hosp, Phila., 1964-65, resident in neurosurgery, 1965-69; pvt. practice neurosurgery Harrisburg, Pa., 1969-72, Ocean, N.J., 1972-99; chief sect. neurosurgery Jersey Shore Med. Ctr., Neptune, N.J., 1972-96, attending neurosurgeon, 1996-99, emeritus, 2000—. Sr. attending Monmouth Med. Ctr., Long Branch, N.J., 1972-99, emeritus attending, 2000—; full attending Riverview Med. Ctr., Red Bank, N.J., 1972-99, emeritus, 2000; cons. emeritus CentraState Med. Ctr., Freehold, N.J.; courtesy staff emeritus Med. Ctr. of Ocean County, Point Pleasant, N.J., Kimball Med. Ctr., Lakewood, N.J., Bayshore Cmty. Hosp., Holmdel, N.J.; clin. instr. surgery Hershey (Pa.) Med. Ctr., 1970-72, Hahnemann Med. Ctr., Phila., 1970-72. Contbr. articles to profl. jours.; mem. com. on pub. N.J. Medicine, Lawrenceville, 1985-99. With U.S. Army, 1951-53. Fellow Stroke Coun., Am. Heart Assn.; mem. Congress of Neurol. Surgeons, Am. Assn. Neurol. Surgeons Joint Sect. on Cerebrovasc. Surgery, Med. Soc. N.J., N.J. Neurosurg. Soc., Monmouth County Med. Soc., Acad. Medicine of N.J. Avocation: cooking. Office Phone: 732-280-7374.

KREISBERG, ROBERT A., physician, researcher, former dean; Student, U. Ala., U. South Ala.; MD, Northwestern U., 1958. Vice chair dept. medicine U. Ala., Birmingham, prof.; interim dean U. South Ala. Coll. Med., Mobile, 2000, dean, 2001—06, v.p. med. affairs; program dir. Bapt. Health Sys., Ala., 2006—. Fellow Am. Coll. Physicians (gov. Ala., regent, chair scientific program subcom., ednl. policy com., gen. chair, Disting. Tchr. award 1994); mem. Am. Fedn. Clin. Rsch. (pres. 1974-75). Office: Bapt Health Sys 840 Montclair Rd Birmingham AL 35213 Office Phone: 205-592-5135. *

KREISEL, DANIEL, thoracic surgeon, educator; b. Dorohoi, Romania, Nov. 24, 1969; MD, Mt. Sinai Sch. Medicine, 1995; PhD, U. Pa., 2002. Asst. prof. surgery, pathology & immunology Wash. U., St. Louis, 2006—10, assoc. prof. surgery, pathology & immunology with tenure, 2010—. Editl. bd. mem. Transplantation Procs., 2010; assoc. editor Jour. Immunology, 2011. Recipient Jonathan Rhoads Rsch. award, U. Pa., Arthur Aufses prize, Mt. Sinai Sch. Medicine, Vanguard prize, Am. Soc. Transplant Surgeons; grant, NIH. Fellow: ACS; mem.: Am. Soc. Transplant Surgeons, Am. Soc. Transplantation, Soc. Thoracic Surgeons, Am. Assn. Thoracic Surgeons. Office: 660 S Euclid Ave Queeny Tower Saint Louis MO 63110 Business E-Mail: kreiseld@wudosis.wustl.edu.

KREITER, CLARENCE DENNIS, medical educator; b. Iowa, 1953; PhD, U. Iowa, 1990. Prof. U. Iowa, 1990—. Office: University Iowa Coll Medicine Iowa City IA 52242 Business E-Mail: clarence-kreiter@uiowa.edu.

KREITZER, JOEL M., pain medicine physician, anesthesiologist, educator; MD, Albert Einstein Coll. Medicine, 1985. Diplomate Am. Bd. Anesthesiology, Am. Bd. Anesthesiology-pain medicine. Resident internal medicine Montefiore Med. Ctr.; resident anesthesiology Mt. Sinai Hosp., NY, 1986—89, fellow pain medicine, 1988—89; assoc. clin. prof. in anesthesiology Mt. Sinai Med. Ctr. Named one of Best Doctors, NY Mag., 2009. Office: Upper East Side Pain Medicine, PC 1540 York Ave New York NY 10028 Office Phone: 212-288-2180. Office Fax: 212-288-2305.

KREITZER, PAULA MICHELLE, pediatric endocrinologist; MD, U. NC, Chapel Hill, 1982. Diplomate Am. Bd. Pediatrics, cert. pediatric endocrinology. Intern LI Jewish Med. Ctr., NY, pediatric endocrinology; resident pediat. Schneider Children's Hosp., NY, fellow; pediatric endocrinology Steven & Alexandra Cohen Children's Med. Ctr. Office: Steven and Alexandra Cohen Children's Medical Center 400 Lakeville Rd Ste 180 New Hyde Park NY 11040

KRELL-MORRIS, CHERI LEE, psychologist; b. Toledo, Mar. 23, 1949; d. Leonard Charles and Doris Leone (Sharples) Krell; children: Marci Lynn, Cari Ann. BEd, U. Toledo, 1975; MS, U. Nev., 1979; postgrad., Immaculata U., 2003. Cert. sch. psychologist, lic. psychologist Pa. Health edn. cons. Ohio Dept. Health, Divsn. Alcoholism, Columbus, 1975—77; dir. social svcs. Cherry Hill Med. Ctr., NJ, 1979—80; mgr. StayWell Control Data Corp., Norristown, Pa., 1980—82, edn. & lifestyle change cons., 1982; counselor New Life Youth & Family Svcs., 1985—2003; sch. psychologist Spring-Ford Sch. Dist., 2003—; pvt. practice Innovative Counseling Assocs., 2001—. Dir. Ohio's Ann. Teenage Inst. Alcohol & Other Drugs, Columbus, 1975—77; faculty Midwest Inst. Alcohol Studies, Notre Dame, Ind., Kalamazoo, 1977. Served with USAF, 1968—72. Mem.: Nat. Assn. Sch. Psychologists, Pa. Psychol. Assn., Eta Sigma Gamma. Mem. United Ch. Of Christ. Home: 212 Salford Station Rd Perkiomenville PA 18074-9740 Office: Spring-Ford High Sch S Lewis Rd Royersford PA 19468-2499 Office Phone: 610-326-2728, 610-705-6032. Business E-Mail: cmorr@spring-ford.org.

KREMIN, DANIEL PAUL, clinical forensic psychologist; b. Bklyn., Sept. 26, 1946; s. Harry and Ruth Kremin; m. Diane Joyce Siesel, Mar. 18, 1972; children: Sean, Todd. BA, Fairleigh Dickinson U., 1967, MA, 1974; MS, Yeshiva U., 1976, SpC., 1977, PhD, 1978. Diplomate Am. Bd. Forensic Medicine, Am. Bd. Forensic Examiners, Am. Bd. Adminstrv. Psychology, Am. Bd. Psychol. Specialties, cert. in clin. and forensic psychology Profl. Acad. Custody Evaluators, registered custody evalator Am. Coll. Forensic Exmainers; cert. bd. cert. sch. and emergency crisis response, bd. cert. homeland security. Sr. psychologist Columbia Presbyn. Hosp., 1975-76; mem. com. on handicapped N.Y. Bd. Edn., 1977-81, psychologist, 1977-78, clin. coord., 1978-79, coord. learning disabilities identification program, 1979, asst. to regional coord., 1979-80, chmn., 1980-81; dir. spl. svcs. Teaneck (N.J.) Pub. Schs., 1981-89; dir. spl. edn. and pupil pers. svcs. Hicksville (N.Y.) Pub. Schs., 1989-92, asst. supt., 1992-2000; pvt. practice clin. and forensic psychology, specializing in custody evaluations, 1992—. Fellow clin. psychology Rousso Ctr., Albert Einstein Coll. Medicine. Tchg. fellow Fairleigh Dickinson U., 1974. Fellow Am. Coll. Forensic Examiners, Am. Acad. Experts in Traumatic Stress, Nat. Ctr. Crisis Mgmt.; mem. APA, Soc. Pediat. Psychology, Nat. Honor Soc. Psychology, NY State Psychol. Assn. (pres. divsn. forensic psychology), Am. Coll. Forensic Psychology, Nat. Register of Health svc. Providers in Psychology, Police Surgeon Fraternal Order of Police. Avocation: skiing. Home Phone: 576-567-1313; Office Phone: 516-333-4066. Personal E-mail: doctorKrem@aol.com.

KRENGLI, MARCO, oncologist, radiologist, educator; b. Novara, Italy, Apr. 15, 1957; s. Alessandro Krengli and Maria Quazzone; m. Patrizia Vietti, Sept. 24, 1988. MD, Turin U., Italy, 1982; postgrad. in oncology, Pavia U., Italy, 1985; postgrad. in radiotherapy, Modena (Italy) U., 1989; postgrad. in radiology, U. Turin, 1992. Med. asst. Hosp. Maggiore, Novara, 1985-95; asst. prof. radiotherapy U. Turin Faculty of Medicine, 1996-98; assoc. prof. radiotherapy U. East Piedmont Faculty of Medicine, Novara, 1998—2006, full prof. radiotherapy, 2006—. Rsch. fellow Harvard U. Med. Sch., Boston, 1995-96; cons. European Inst. Oncology, Milan, 1997-98; dir. dept. radiotherapy, Hosp. Maggiore, Novara, 1998 ; dir. sch. radiology, U. East Piedmont, 1999-2003, dir. rsch. radiotherapy, 2004—, Med. Sch. U. East Predmont, 2007-;sci. bd.CNAO Found. Novara. Contbr. chpt. to book, articles to profl. jours., including Brit. Jour. Cancer, European Jour. Cancer, Internat. Jour. Radiation Oncology, Biology and Physics, Oncology. Mem. coun. Italian League Against Cancer, Novara, 1999 (Massimo Lupo award 1992); bd. dirs., U. East Piedmont, Vercelli, Italy, 2000 05. Capt., Med. Corps, 1983-84, Vercelli. Mem. Am. Soc. Therapeutic Radiation Oncology, European Soc. Therapeutic Radiation Oncology, Italian Assn. Radiation Oncology-Piedmont (mem. coun. 1999-2001, 05—), Lions. Achievements include: radiochemotherapy in head and neck cancer, multimodal images for treatment plans in radiotherapy,intraoperative radiotherapy, proton therapy in skull base tumors. Office: U Piemonte Orientale Via Solaroli I-28100 Novara Italy Business E-Mail: krengli@med.unipmu.it.

KRESGE, BRUCE ANDERSON, retired physician; b. Detroit, Dec. 20, 1931; s. Stanley Sebastian and Dorothy Eloise (McVittie) Kresge; m. Peggy Ann Sale, June 14, 1952; children: Deborah Kresge McDowell, Katherine Kresge Lutey, Susan Kresge Drewes, Cynthia Kresge Furlong, Stephen. BA, Albion Coll., 1953; MD, Wayne State U., 1956. Intern Detroit Receiving Hosp., 1956-57; resident U. Mich. Hosp., 1959-60; pvt. practice Rochester, Mich., 1960-90; mem. staff St. Joseph Mercy Hosp., Pontiac, Mich., Pontiac Gen. Hosp., 1960-67, Crittenton Hosp., Rochester, 1967—. Pres. Rochester br. YMCA, 1975—77; trustee Kresge Found., 1967—2003, Crittenton Hosp., 1993—99; hon. trustee Albion Coll., 1999—. With M.C. US Army, 1957—59. Mem.: AMA. Republican. Methodist. Home: 1071 N Lake Angelus Rd Lake Angelus MI 48326-1026

KRESH, J. YASHA, cardiovascular researcher, educator; b. Russia, July 13, 1948; came to U.S., 1967; m. Myrna Blickman. BSEE, N.J. Inst. Tech., 1971; MSBME, Rutgers U., 1973, PhD, 1976. Rsch. assoc. Beth Israel Med. Ctr., Newark, 1976-79; dir. rsch. Jefferson Med. Coll., Phila., 1979-86; prof. medicine, dir. cardiovascular biophysics and computing Cardiovascular Rsch. Ctr., Phila., 1986—; prof., dir. rsch. cardiothoracic surgery Drexel U. Coll. Medicine, Phila., 1986—. Prof. biomed. and mech. engring. Drexel U., 1984—. Author: Complex Systems Science in Biomedicine, 2006; author more than 200 publs. in physiol. cardiology and bioengring. jours.; patentee in field. Fellow Am. Coll. Cardiology, Biomed. Engring. Soc., Am. Heart Assn., Am. Inst. Med. and Biol. Engring.; mem. IEEE, AAAS, NY Acad. Sci., Am. Soc. Artificial Internal Organs, Sigma Xi, Tau Beta Pi, Eta Kappa Nu. Avocations: computers, porschephile, biocomplexity. Office: Drexel U Coll Medicine MS # 111 245 N 15th St Philadelphia PA 19102-1192 Office Phone: 215-762-1703. Business E-Mail: jkresh@drexelmed.edu.

KRESPI, YOSEF P., otolaryngologist, educator; MD, Israel, 1973. Diplomate Am. Bd. Otolaryngology, 1981. Resident in surgery Mt. Sinai Hosp., 1974—76, resident in otolaryngology, 1976—80; fellow in surgery Northwestern Meml. Hosp., Chgo., 1980—81, assoc. prof. dept. of otolaryngology, 1984—85; prof. divsn. of otolaryngology SUNY, 1985, chmn. divsn. of otolaryngology, 1985; cons. Cook County Hosp.; staff physician Lakeside Veteran's Adminstrn. Med. Ctr., 1980—85; chief otolaryngology Kings County Hosp. Ctr., 1985—89; cons. Brookdale Hosp. Med. Ctr., 1985—90; chief otolaryngology State Univ. Hosp., 1985—89; prof. clin. otolaryngology Columbia Univ., 1990—; chmn. dept. of otolaryngology St. Luke's Roosevelt Hosp. Ctr., 1990—2011, chmn. dept. of dentistry, 2000—, chmn. dept. of oral and maxillofacial surgery, 2000—; dir. Ctr. for Sleep Disorders NY Head and Neck Inst.; assoc. dir. head and neck svc. line Lenox Hill Hosp. Recipient Resident Essay Contest award, Am. Bronchoesophacological Assn., 1979, House Staff Excellence award, Attending Staff/Bella Trachtenberg Assn., 1980. Office: Lenox Hill Hospital 425 W 59th Fl 10 New York NY 10019-1128 Office Phone: 212-262-2929.

KRESS, DOUGLAS W., pediatric dermatologist; MD, Jefferson Med. Coll., 1988. Diplomate Am. Bd. Dermatology, Am. Bd. Dermatology-pediatric dermatology. Intern Univ. of Pitts., 1992, resident, 1993; fellow Children Hosp. of Pitts., 1995; chief divsn. pediatric dermatology Children's Hosp. of Pitts. of UPMC; clin. assoc. prof. Univ. of Pitts. Mem.: Pitts. Acad. of Dermatology, Pa. Acad. of Dermatology, Soc. for Pediatric Dermatology, Am. Acad. of Dermatology. Office: Childrens Hospital of Pittsburgh of UPMC Division of Pediatric Dermatology 11279 Perry Hwy Ste 108 Wexford PA 15090 Office Phone: 724-933-9190. Office Fax: 724-933-9194.

KREUTZBERG, GEORG W., neuroscientist; b. Ahrweiler, Germany, Sept. 2, 1932; s. Josef H.A. and Hanni (Niessen) K.; m. Karin Franken; children: Achim, Jan. MD, U. Freiburg, Germany, 1961; Docent in Neuropathology, U. Tech., Munich, 1971; D (hon.), Med. U. Szeged, Hungary, 1991. Intern U. Hosp., Freiburg, 1957-58, Bonn, Germany, 1959; postdoctoral fellow Neuropathology Inst., Bonn, 1960; rsch. assoc. Max Planck Inst., Munich, 1961-64, sect. chief, 1968-77, mem., head dept. neuromorphology, 1977-2000, chmn. bd. dirs. for psychiatry, 1985-95; prof. emeritus, ret. dir. Max Planck Inst. of Neurobiology, 1995—. Rsch. fellow dept. psychology MIT, Cambridge, 1964—65; guest scientist Rockefeller U., NYC, 1967; prof. Med. Sch. U. Tech., Munich, 1977—; mem. Otto Loewi Ctr. Hebrew U., Jerusalem, 1986—; chmn. ad-hoc com. on history of neurosci. Internat. Brain Rsch. Orgn., 2001—; vis. prof. & Peter Lampert Meml. lectr. U. Calif., San Diego, 2006. Author/editor 15 books in neurosci.; mem. editl. bd. 15 internat. jours. in neurosci.; contbr. numerous articles to profl. jours. Recipient Rudolf F. Weiss prize, German Soc. Phy Pharmacology, 1987, K.J. Zuelch prize, 1991, GSF prize, 1992, Fed. German Disting. Svc. medal, 2007. Mem. Internat. Soc. Neuropathology (hon; v.p. 1986-90, pres. 94-97), German Cell Biology Soc. (pres. 1981-85), Internat. Brain Rsch. Orgn. (councillor 1976-84), German Neurosci. Soc. (pres. 1999-2000), Sci. in Dialogue (PUSH prize with Helmut Kettenmann 1999), Internat. Soc. for History of the Neuroscis. (pres. 2006-08). Office: Max Planck Inst Neurobiology Am Klopferspitz 18 82152 Planegg Martinsried Germany Office Phone: 49-89-8578-3650. Business E-Mail: gwk@neuro.mpg.de.

KREUZ, PETER CORNELIUS, orthopedist, researcher, surgeon; b. Munich, Mar. 5, 1973; s. Dietrich Giselbert and Edda Annamaria Kreuz. Diploma in Italian (hon.), Inst. Michelangelo, Florence, Italy, 1990; degree (hon.), Bad Zwischenahn Mil. Hosp., Germany, 1993; MD, Tech. U., Munich, 1999; MD magna cum laude (hon.), Ludwig Maximillian U., Munich, 2001. Cert. radiation protection GSF Rsch. Ctr., Neuherberg, Germany. Mem. clin. staff Kantonsspital Sanct Gallen, Switzerland, 1998—99, Harborview Med. Ctr., Seattle, 1999, Tech. U. Hosp., 1999; intern LMU U. Hosp., Munich, 1999—2001; resident Albert Ludwig U. Hosp., Freiburg, Germany, 2001—, orthopaedic surgeon, 2006. Organizer congress the diabetic foot syndrome Munich Soc. Diabetes, 2000; coord., cons. clin. cartilage rsch. Valley Tissue Engring. Ctr., Freiburg, 2002—; cons., instr. in workshops for autologous chondrocyte transplantation Co. Ormed, Freiburg, 2002—; reviewer Jour. Osteoarthritis and Cartilage, 2005—. Lance cpl. German armed forces, 1992—93. Recipient Poster prize, Internat. Cartilage Repair Soc., 2004, Internat. Soc. for Orthopaedics, Traumatology and Sports Medicine, 2005, 2006; winner ARCUS TERRA triathlon, German Assn. Sports Medicine, 2003, travel grantee, Sci. Soc. Freiburg, Toronto, 2002, San Diego, 2006, rsch. grantee, Arbeitsgemeinschaft fur Osteosynthesefragen, Switzerland, 2005. Mem.: Tölzer Boys Choir (life). Roman Catholic. Achievements include first to biomechanical behaviour of different PFN designs in the treatment of unstable pertrochanteric fractures; development of operating and biomechanical guide for the implantation of the PFN in unstable pertrochanteric fractures; guidelines in the treatment of diabetic neuropathic osteoarthropathy-the Charcot foot; guidelines in the surgical therapy of early and late infections of total knee endoprosthesis; guidelines in the surgical treatment of spondylitis; new matrix containing growth factors to induce differentiation of mesenchymal stem cells into hyaline like cartilage; new matrices to improve the results after microfracture in the knee; new surgical approach to posterior osteochondral defects of the talus: the tibial wedge osteotomy; Development of a new classification system of periosteal hypertrophy after autologous chondrocyte transplantation of full thickness chondral defects of the knee; research in long term durability of different ACT (autologous chondrocyte transplantation) techniques; degeneration of the repair tissue after microfracture of full thickness chondral defects of the knee; long term durability of different surgical techniques in the treatment of osteochondral talar lesions; The Napoleon sign: a clinical test for the differentiation between total and partial subscapularis tendon tears; prognostic factors in the treatment of subscapularis tendon tears. Avocations: piano, violin, jogging, swimming, bicycling, windsurfing, singing.

KREUZBERG, BORIS, radiologist; b. Pilsen, Czech Republic, May 29, 1950; s. Boris Kreuzberg and Eva Kreuzbergova; m. Jaroslava Koleckova, Sept. 28, 1996; children: Eva Brozova, Adam, Katerina Kostakova, Karina Divisova. MD, Charles U., Pilsen, PhD, 1974. Cert. radiologist Postgrad. Edn. Inst., Prague, Czech Republic, 1982. Asst. prof. Med. Faculty, Charles U., 1968—74; physician Faculty Hosp., Pilsen, 1974—90; head dept. radiology Faculty Hosp. and Med. Faculty, Pilsen, 1992—. Dean faculty Med. Faculty Charles U., Pilsen, 1997—2003. Mem. regional min. environ. affairs Coun. Pilsen Region, 2004—08; chmn. exec. bd. St.Lazar s Hospice, Pilsen, 1998—2006. Recipient Silver and Golden medal, Chancellor Charles U., 2000, 2003. People'S Party. Roman Catholic. Avocations: history, philosophy, literature. Home: Kralovicka 5 Pilsen 320 00 Czech Republic Office: Faculty Hosp Alej Svobody 80 304 60 Pilsen Czech Republic Office Fax: 420377103438. Personal E-mail: karuna@volny.cz. Business E-Mail: kreuzberg@fnplzen.cz.

KREVANS, JULIUS RICHARD, academic administrator, internist; b. NYC, May 1, 1924; s. Sol and Anita Krevans; m. Patricia N. Abrams, May 28, 1950; children: Nita, Julius R., Rachel, Sarah, Nora Kate. BS Arts and Scis, N.Y. U., 1943, MD, 1946. Diplomate: Am. Bd. Internal Med. Intern, then resident Johns Hopkins Med. Sch. Hosp., mem. faculty, until 1970, dean acad. affairs, 1969—70; physician in chief Balt. City Hosp., 1963—69; prof. medicine U. Calif., San Francisco, 1970—, dean Sch. Medicine, 1971—82, chancellor, 1982—93, chancellor emeritus, 1993—. Contbr. articles on hematology, internal med. profl. jours. With USMC, 1948—50, AUS. Mem. ACP, Assn. Am. Physicians. Address: 32 Birch Bay Dr Bar Harbor ME 04609 Personal E-mail: krevansmaine@roadrunner.net.

KRIEGEL, DAVID A., dermatologist; MD, Boston U. Diplomate Am. Bd. Dermatology. Resident internal medicine Mount Auburn Hosp.; resident dermatology dept. Boston City Hosp.; dir. dermatologic and mohs surgery divsn. Mount Sinai Med. Ctr., assoc. clin. prof. dermatology; founder Procedural Dermatology; fellow MOHS-Micro Surgery, SUNY. Named one of Best Doctors, New York Mag., 2009; named to New York Magazine, The New York Times Best Doctors edit., America's Best Cancer Doctors Guide by Castle Connolly. Office: Manhattan Center for Dermatology Ste 825 250 W 57th St New York NY 10107 Office Phone: 212-489-6669. Office Fax: 212-489-1685.

KRIEGEL, ROBIN, medical association administrator; BA, Hofstra U., 1971. Exec. dir. Am. Soc. Parenteral & Enteral Nutrition, Silver Spring, Md., 2000, Am. Assn. Med. Soc. Execs., 1988—2000. Fellow: Am. Soc. Assn. Execs.; mem.: Greater Washington Soc. Assn. Execs., Assn. Forum Assn. Execs., N.Y. Soc. Assn. Execs. Office: Am Soc Parenteral Enteral Nutrition 8630 Fenton St Ste 412 Silver Spring MD 20910-3803 *

KRIEGER, JAMES, public health service officer, physician; b. Nov. 24, 1956; BA, Harvard U., 1978; MD, U. Calif., San Francisco, 1984. Chief, assessment, policy devel. & evaluation Pub. Health - Seattle & King County, 1989—2007, chief, chronic disease & injury prevention, 2007—. Clin. prof. medicine & health svcs. U. Wash.; panel mem. NHLBI Nat. Asthma Edn. & Prevention Program Guidelines Implementation Expert Panel, 2006—08, Inst. Medicine Com. Childhood Obesity Prevention Actions Local Governments, 2008—09, Inst. Medicine Roundtable Health Disparities, 2007—09; mem. Nat. Ctr. Healthy Housing Sci. Adv. Coun., 2008—11. Recipient Ann. award, Wash. State Pub. Health Assn., Innovation Prevention award, Sec. US HHS, Children's Environ. Health Excellence award, US EPA. Mem.: ACP, APHA, Phi Beta Kappa. Avocations: skiing, hiking, photography. Office: 401 5th Ave Ste 900 Seattle WA 98104

KRIEGER, KARL HEMINGWAY, cardiothoracic surgeon; b. Boulder, Colo., June 10, 1948; s. Frederick Wilhelm and Nancy Adele (Hemingway) K. BA, Amherst Coll., 1970; MD, Johns Hopkins U., 1975. Diplomate Am. Bd. Surgery, Am. Bd. Thoracic Surgery; lic. physician, Md., N.Y. Intern, thoracic surgery Johns Hopkins Hosp., 1974-75, resident cardiothoracic surgery, 1975-76, NYU-Bellevue Med. Ctr., 1976—79, chief resident, 1978-79, fellow thoracic and cardiovascular surgery, 1979-81; asst. attending surgeon NYU Hosp., 1981-85, Bellevue Hosp., 1981-85, Manhattan VA Hosp., 1981-85, N.Y. Hosp., 1983-89, assoc. attending surgeon, 1989, attending surgeon, 1994. Teaching asst. NYU Sch. Medicine, 1976-78; clin. instr. NYU Sch. Medicine, 1976-81, instr. surgery, 1981-84, asst. prof., 1984-85; asst. prof. surgery Cornell U. Med. Coll., 1985-89, assoc. prof., 1989; dir. cardiothoracic tng. program Cornell U. Med. Ctr., 1985, dir. cardiothoracic rsch. lab., 1985; dir. surg. rsch. NYU Hosp., 1982-85, dir. cardiovascular rsch., 1985; Philip Geier prof. cardiothoracic surgery, vice-chmn. cardiothoracic surgery, attending surgeon N.Y. Presbyn. Hosp. Weill Cornell Med. Ctr. Contbr. articles to profl. jours. Recipient Peter Brunett Howe award, Stanley V. and Charles B. Travis award. Fellow ACS; mem. Internat. Soc. Heart Transplantation, Am. Coll. Chest Physicians, Soc. Thoracic Surgery, Royal Soc. Medicine, N.Y. Soc. Thoracic Surgery (chmn. nominating com. 1988-91), Am. Heart Assn., Am. Assn. Thoracic Surgeons, Am. Coll. Cardiology, Heart Valve Soc. America. Office: NY Hosp-Cornell Med Ctr Cardiothoracic Surg Dept 525 E 68th St # 2106 New York NY 10021-4885 Office Phone: 212-746-5152. Office Fax: 212-746-8388. E-mail: khkriege@med.cornell.edu.

KRIEGLSTEIN, JOSEF, pharmacology professor; b. Pechgruen, Germany, Mar. 10, 1938; m. Marlene; children: Kerstin, Heike, Roland. PhD, U. Erlangen-Nuernberg, Germany, 1965; MD, U. Erlangen-Nuernberg, 1967; habil. in Pharmacology and Toxicology, U. Mainz, Germany, 1970. Lectr. U. Mainz, 1970-72, assoc. prof., 1972-73, sci. councillor, prof., 1973-74; prof. pharmacology and toxicology U. Marburg, Germany, 1974—2006, mng. dir. Inst. Pharmacology and Toxicology, 1975—2006, dean faculty Pharmacy, 1976—77, 1986—87, 1997—98; guest prof. U. Muenster, Germany, 2006—08, sr. prof., 2009—. Named Internat. Hon. Citizen City of New Orleans, 1999; recipient Order of Merit, Fed. Rep. Germany, 2004 Office: Inst Pharmacology & Toxicol Ketzerbach 63 35037 Marburg Hessen Germany Office Phone: 4964212825833. Business E-Mail: krieglst@uni-muenster.de.

KRIEGSTEIN, ARNOLD, neurologist, educator; BA cum laude, Yale U., 1971; MS in physiology, NYU, 1974, MD, PhD in physiology, 1977. Lic. Calif., 1978, Mass., 1979, Conn., 1991, NY, 1993. Intern in medicine Harbor Gen. Hosp., Torrance, Calif., 1977—78; resident in neurology Boston, 1978—81; instr. physiology NYU, 1973—77; asst. prof. neurology Stanford U., 1981—88, assoc. prof. neurology, 1988—91; cons. prof. neurology Palo Alto Veterans Hosp., 1981—91; clin. assoc. prof. neurology Yale U., 1991—93; assoc. prof. neurology Columbia U., 1993—99, assoc. prof. pathology, 1993—99, prof. neurology and pathology, 1999—2004, investigator Lieber Ctr. Schizophrenia, 2000—04, John and Elisabeth Harris prof. neurology, 2001—04, sci. dir. Neural Stem Cell Ctr., 2003—04; prof. neurology U. Calif., San Francisco, 2004—, dir. Inst. Regeneration Medicine, 2004—. Recipient Javits Neuroscience Investigator award, NIH, 1999—2006; scholar Mellon Found., 1982—84. Mem.: AMA, AAAS, Inst. Medicine, Internat. Soc. Stem Cell Rsch., Am. Neurological Assn., Epilepsy Found. of Southern NY, New Haven County Med. Soc., Royal Soc. Medicine, Nat. Headache Found., Am. Epilepsy

Soc., Soc. Neuroscience, Am. Acad. Neurology. Office: U Calif San Francisco HSW-1201F Box #0525 San Francisco CA 94143-0525 Office Phone: 415-476-0766. Office Fax: 415-514-2346. E-mail: kriegsteina@stemcell.ucsf.edu.

KRINGLEN, EINAR, psychiatrist, scientist, educator; b. Norway, June 6, 1931; m. Gerd Winge Knutsen. MD, U. Bergen, 1958. Intern Vestfold Sentralsykehus, Tonsberg; resident dept. psychiatry Dikemark Hosp., U. Oslo, 1960-64; research fellow Norwegian Research Council for the Scis. and Humanities, 1965-67; assoc. prof. psychiatry U. Bergen, Norway, 1967-69, prof. clinical psychology, 1969-71; prof. behavioral sci. in medicine U. Oslo, 1976-83, prof. psychiatry and physician in chief Dept. Psychiatry, 1984—. Research fellow Nat. Inst. Mental Health, Bethesda, Md., 1965-66, Ctr. Advanced Study in Behavioral Scis., Stanford, Calif., 1974-75. Author several books. Mem.: Norwegian Acad. Sci. and Letters. Achievements include pioneering work in psychiatric twin research, epidemiological studies and history of psychiatry. Home: Jornstadv 7 1394 Nesbru Norway Office: Dept Psychiatry U Oslo Vinderen Oslo 3 Norway Home Phone: 47-66845850; Office Phone: 47-22029963. Business E-Mail: einar.kringlen@medisin.uio.no.

KRISHNAMURTHI, VENKATESH, surgeon; b. Cleve., May 24, 1967; MD, Case Western Res. U. Sch. Medicine, 1993. Staff surgeon Cleve. Clinic, 1993—. Office: Cleveland Clinic Cleveland OH 44195 Business E-Mail: krishnv@ccf.org.

KRISHNAMURTHY, GERBAIL THIMMEGOWDA, retired nuclear physician; b. Gerbail, N.R. Pura, Chickmagalore, Karnataka, India, Aug. 3, 1937; s. Thimmegowda and Manjamma K.; m. Shakuntala Naik, Dec. 26, 1969; children— Anil Raj, Kalpana. M.B., BS, U. Mysore, India, 1964; MS, UCLA, 1971. Staff physician in nuclear medicine Wadsworth VA Hosp., Los Angeles, 1971-77; asst. prof. medicine UCLA, 1972—77, asso. prof., 1977; chief nuclear medicine VA Hosp., Portland, Oreg., 1977—92; prof. radiology, pathology and medicine Oreg. Health Scis. U., Portland, 1977-93, dir. nuclear medicine residency program, 1977—93; staff physician VA Med. Ctr., Portland, 1992-93, Tucson, 1993-97, Tuality Cmty. Hosp., Hillsboro, Oreg., 1997—. Vis. prof. U. Rio de Janeiro, Brazil, 1976, U. Hawaii program, Okinawa, Japan, 1985. Contbr. articles to profl. jours.; co-author: Nuclear Hepatology, Hepatobiliary Diseases, 2nd edit., 2009. Recipient Rajyostava award, Karnataka State Govt., India. Fellow ACP; mem. Am. Coll. Nuclear Physicians, Soc. Nuclear Medicine, Indian Soc. Nuclear Medicine, Indo-Am. Soc. Nuclear Medicine (pres. 1985-86, Sarabai Meml. award India 1986), Indo-Am. Med. Assn. (founding pres. 2003-05), UCLA Club Oreg. (pres. 1992-93). Hindu. Achievements include development of hepatoliliary software for analysis of liner and gallbladder function. Home: 7570 SW Westgate Way Portland OR 97225-1231 Office Phone: 503-681-1745. Personal E-mail: gtkrishna@aol.com.

KRISHNAMURTHY, JAYASHREE, pathologist, educator; b. India, Mar. 24, 1962; MBBS, Mysore U., 1985, MD, 1995. Prof. J. S. S. U., 1997—. Grant, Dept Sci. and Tech. Avocations: drawing, painting, reading. Home: NS Rd Mysore Karnataka 570004 India Personal E-mail: dr.jayashree_k@yahoo.co.in.

KRISHNAMURTHY, VENKATESAN, biochemist, director; b. Chennai, Tamil Nadu, India, Mar. 22, 1952; BSc, Loyola Coll., Chennai, 1972; MSc in Med. Biochemistry, JIPMER, Puducherry, 1975. Rsch. officer NJILOMD (ICMR), 1983—89, sr. rsch. officer, 1989—94, asst. dir., 1994—99, head biochemistry divsn. and lab. divsn., 1996, dep. dir., 1999—2006; scientist f, dep. dir. Nat. JALMA Inst. Leprosy & Other Mycobacterial Diseases (ICMR), 2006—. Guest tchg. faculty in fields, 1998. Recipient Dr. CGS Iyer award, Indian Coun. Med. Rsch. Mem.: Indian Pharmacological Soc. Avocation: reading. Home: 39 JALMA Campus Miyazaki Marg Taj Gan Agra Uttar Pradesh 282001 India Home Fax: 91-562-2331755. Personal E-mail: venkatesan_52@rediffmail.com.

KRISHNAN, ANAND, medical educator; b. Rajgangpur, Orissa, India, June 10, 1964; s. Krishnan Subraminan and Seetha Krishnan; m. Prema Easwar, Nov. 13, 1993; children: Kritika Anand, Keertana Anand. MBBS, Delhi U., 1986; MD, AIIMS, 1990. Asst. prof. Ctr. Cmty. Medicine, All India Inst. Med. Scis., New Delhi, 1994—2003, assoc. prof., 2003—. Short term profl. (NCD surveillance) WHO (SEARO), New Delhi, 2002—03. Contbr. articles to profl. jours. Recipient BC Shrivastava award, Indian Coun. Med. Rsch., 2000; fellowship, Indian Assn. Preventive and Social Medicine, 2007, Indian Pub. Health Assn., 2006. Office: All India Inst Medical Scis Ansari Nagar New Delhi 110029 India Office Fax: 91-129-2211227. Personal E-mail: dranandkrishnan@rediffmail.com. E-mail: anand.drk@gmail.com.

KRISHNAN, KRISHNASWAMY RANGA RAMA R., psychiatry educator; b. Madras, Tamilnadu, India, Apr. 22, 1956; came to U.S., 1981; s. N. Krishnaswamy and Sulochana Krishnaswamy Reddy; m. Sripriya Chitamoor, May 21, 1987; children: Vaishnavi, Prahlad. PUC, Loyola Coll., Madras, India, 1973; MBBS, U. Madras, 1978. Chief resident Duke Med. Ctr., Durham, 1981—83, asst. prof., 1984—89, assoc. prof., 1990—95, prof., 1995—, chmn. psychiatry, 1998—. Vice dean Duke Grad. Med. Sch.- Nat. U., Singapore, 2006—. Mem.: Inst. Medicine. Office: Duke U Med Ctr Box 3950 Durham NC 27710-0001 Office Phone: 919-684-5616. Business E-Mail: krish001@mc.duke.edu.

KRISHNASAMY, PRASANNA V., physician; b. India, Apr. 2, 1980; MD, Dr. MGR Med. U., 2003; MPH, Portland State U., 2006. Internal medicine faculty physician Legacy Health, 2009—. Recipient Dr. Tony Andrews Meml. award, Legacy Health, Dr. Stephen Jones award, Found. Med. Excellence. Mem.: ACP. Avocations: bicycling, motorcycling, hiking. Office: 2800 N Vancouver Ave Ste 230 Portland OR 97227 Office Fax: 503-413-4898. Business E-Mail: pkrishna@lhs.org.

KRISHNASASTRY, KAMBHAMPATY V., surgeon, educator; b. Guntur, India, June 21, 1949; MBBS, Guntur Med. Coll., 1973. Dir. vascular surgery NYHQ, 1996—2004; chief vascular endovascular surgery NSLIJ Health Sys., 2004—. Clin. assoc. prof. surgery Weill Cornell Med. Sch., 1998—2008; assoc. prof. surgery Hofstra Med. Sch., 2009—. Recipient Krishnasastry award, NSLIJ Dept. Surgery; named one of Best Tchr., Residents Surgery. Mem.: NY Surg. Soc., Assn. Program Dirs. Vascular Surgery, Ea. Vascular surgery, Soc. of Clin. Vascular Surgery, Soc. vascular Surgery. Avocations: tennis, jogging, reading. Home: 63 Knolls Dr N Manhasset Hills NY 11040 Home Fax: 516-233-3605. Business E-Mail: kkrishna@nshs.edu.

KRISTENSEN, CYNTHIA, nephrologist; b. Ames, Iowa, Feb. 11, 1949; BA, Antioch Coll., 1971; MD, U. Minn., 1977. Physician Denver Nephrologists, 1991—. Office: 10099 Ridgegate Pky #310 Lone Tree CO 80124 Business E-Mail: ckristensen@denverneph.net.

KRISTROM, BERIT OHMAN, pediatrician; b. Umea, Sweden, Aug. 2, 1949; MD, Umea U., 1974, PhD, 1999. Cons. Umea U., 1990, asst. prof. dept. pediat., 2005—. Mem.: European Soc. Pediat. Endocrinology. Office: Umea University Dept Pediat Umea SE-90185 Sweden Office Fax: 46-90-123728. Business E-Mail: berit.kristrom@pediatri.umu.se.

KRITCHEVSKY, STEPHEN BENNETT, epidemiologist, educator; b. Phila., July 15, 1960; s. David and Evelyn S. Kritchevsky; m. Nannette C. Gover, Feb. 2, 1982; children: Alexander, Samuel, Caleb. BA, U. Chgo., 1982; MSPH in epidemiology, U. NC Sch. Pub. Health, 1986, PhD in epidemiology, 1989. Asst. prof. U. Tenn., Memphis, 1989—95, assoc. prof., 1995—2001, prof. preventive medicine, 2001—03; prof. dept. internal medicine, sect. on gerontology and geriatric medicine Wake Forest U. Med. Sch., Winston-Salem, 2003—, acting dir., J. Paul Sticht Ctr. on Aging and Rehabilitation, 2003—06, dir., J. Paul Sticht Ctr. on Aging and Rehabilitation, 2006—; dir., & Claude D. Pepper Older Americans Independence Ctr. Wake Forest U. Baptist, 2006—. Reviewer for a variety of medical journals, including New England Journal of Medicine, Annals of Internal Medicine, Journal of the American Medical Association and American and European Journals of Epidemiology. Mem. Soc. for Epidemiologic Rsch., Soc. Healthcare Epidemiology, Am. Coll. Epidemiology, Gerontol. Soc. Am., Am. Soc. for Nutritional Scis. Office: Wake Forest Univ J Paul Sticht Ctr on Aging Medical Center Blvd Winston Salem NC 27157 Office Phone: 336-713-8548. Business E-Mail: skritche@wfubmc.edu.

KRITEK, PATRICIA ANNE, critical care specialist; MD, U. Conn., 1998. Diplomate Am. Bd. Internal Medicine, 2001, Am. Bd. Internal Medicine- pulmonary disease, 2004, Am. Bd. Internal Medicine- critical care medicine, 2005. Resident in internal medicine Brigham and Women's Hosp., Boston, 1999—2001, fellow in pulmonary, 2001—03, hosp. affiliation includes. Office: Brigham and Women's Hospital 75 Francis St Boston MA 02115-6110 Office Phone: 617-732-6770.

KRIZ, FRANK KENNETH, JR., surgeon; s. Frank Kenneth and Virginia Mary Kriz; m. Jeanette Elizabeth Kriz; 5 children. BS, U. Md., College Park, 1954; MD, U. Md., Balt., 1958. Diplomate Am. Bd. Orthop. Surgery. Clin. asst. prof. U. S. Fla., Tampa, 1971—. Lt. col. US Army, 1958—69. Fellow: ACS, Am. Acad. Orthop. Surgeons; mem.: N.Am. Spine Soc. Office: 800 Dr M L King Jr Blvd Ste 1 Tampa FL 33603

KRIZAN, KELLY JOE, physician, leather craftsman; b. Winner, SD, Jan. 16, 1951; s. Miles Woodrow and Sadie Mae (DeSmet) Kelly; m. Susan Barker Krizan, Aug. 21, 1971 (div. Aug. 1983); children: Nicholas Miles, Jennifer Rebecca; m. Cynthia Lydia Obras, Aug. 6, 1983. BS, SD State U., 1973; BS medicine, U. SD, 1976; MD, Tufts U., 1978. Diplomate Am. Bd. Family Practice, commd. Am. Bd. Radiology. Intern USAF Med. Ctr., Scott AFB, Ill., 1978—79, resident Ill., 1979—81; staff physician USAF Hosp., Hill AFB, Utah, 1981—83, chief emergency svcs., chief family practice Utah, 1983—84, USAF Hosp., Ircirlik AB, Turkey, 1983—84; chmn. dept. family practice USAF Hosp., Hill AFB, 1985—86; resident radiology U. Wash., 1986—90, clin. asst. prof., 1990—; chmn. dept. radiology 13th AF Med. Ctr., Clark AB, Philippines, 1990—91, St. Mary's Health Care Ctr., Pierre, SD, 1993—2005, chief staff, 1997, Walla Walla (Wash.) Gen. Hosp., 2006—09; pres. bd. dirs. Oahe Inc., 2001—05; med. dir. North Spokane Advanced Imaging, W.Va., 2009—10; south sound radiologist Providence St. Peters Hosp., Olympia, Wash., 2010—; staff physician Providence St Peters Hosp., Olympia, Wash., 2010. Bd. dirs. St. Mary's Found., Pierre, SD, Walla Walla Gen. Hosp. Leather goods, (various awards). Bd. dir. Pierre Players, Short Grass Art Coun. First active duty capt. USAF, 1978—92, lt. col. USAF, 1984. Recipient Winner Regional Healthcare Ctr., St. Mary's Found., 1993—94, 2009; named one of Am. Top Radiologists, Rsch. Coun. Am., Am.'s Top Physicians. Fellow: Am. Acad. Family Physicians; mem.: Radiol. Soc. N. Am., Am. Roentgen Ray Soc., Am. Coll. Radiology (rural econ. com. mem. 2003—), Phi Kappa Phi. Roman Catholic. Office Phone: 509-527-8000 ext. 1320. Business E-Mail: kellykrizan@mac.com.

KRNJEVIC, KRESIMIR IVAN, neurophysiologist; b. Zagreb, Croatia, Yugoslavia, Sept. 7, 1927; arrived in Canada, 1964; s. Juraj Krnjevic and Nada K. (Hirsl) Krnjevic Marullaz; m. Jeanne W. Bowyer, Sept. 27, 1954; children— Peter Juraj, Nicholas John M.B.Ch.B., Edinburg U., Scotland, 1949; BSc with honors, Edinburgh U., Scotland, 1951, PhD, 1953. Joseph Morley Drake prof. physiology, chmn. dept. McGill U., Montreal, Canada, 1978—2001, dir. dept. anaesthesia research Canada, 1965—2000, prof. physiology emeritus, 2001—. Contbr. articles to profl. jours.; editor Can. Jour. Physiology and Pharmacology, 1972-78 Bd. govs. Montreal Children's Hosp. Rsch. Inst., 1982-88. Named to Order of Can., 1987; recipient Sarrazin award Can. Physiol. Soc., 1984, Gairdner Found Internat. award, 1984, Wilder Penfield prize, 1997, Spiridion Brusina prize, 2001; Beit Meml. fellow U. Edinburgh, 1952-54 Fellow Royal Soc. Canada; mem. Can. Physiol. Soc. (pres. 1979-80), Internat. Union of Physiol. Socs. (council mem. 1983—93, chmn. admissions commn.) Avocations: swimming, reading, music. Office: McGill Univ Dept Physiology #1228 3655 Drummond St Montreal PQ Canada H3G 1Y6 Office Phone: 514-398-6001. E-mail: kresimir.krnjevic@mcgill.ca.

KROBATH, KRISTA ANN, pharmacist; b. Pottsville, Pa., July 8, 1962; d. James Joseph and Gaye Diane (Anderson) E.; m. Gilbert Krobath; 1 child, Kelleigh Ann. BS in Pharmacy, Temple U., 1985. Registered pharmacist. Pharmacist People's Drug, Harrisburg, Pa., 1985-86; pharmacist, mgr. Amcare Health Svcs., Harrisburg, 1986-96; pharmacist Pharmerica, Harrisburg, 1996-99, Express Scripts, Harrisburg, 1999—. Mem.: Capital Area Pharm. Assn., Pa. Pharm. Assn.

KROBOTH, PATRICIA DOWLEY, dean, pharmacy educator; BS in Pharmacy, SUNY, Buffalo; MS, PhD, U. Pitts. Sch. Pharmacy. Lic. pharmacist NY, Pa. Asst. prof. U. Pitts., 1980—87, assoc. prof., 1987—95, prof., 1995—, dir. clin. pharm. scientist prog., 1984—96, dir. Pharmacodynamic Rsch. Ctr., 1985—2002, chair dept. pharmacy & therapeutics, 1988—96, chair dept. pharm. scis., 1996—2002, assoc. dean faculty & academic planning, 2001—02, interim dean Sch. Pharmacy, 2002—04, dean, 2004—. Co-editor: Pharmacokinetics and Pharmacodynamics: Research Design and Analysis, 1986, Pharmacodynamic Research: Current Problems, Potential Solutions, 1988; contbr. articles to profl. jours., chapters to books. Fellow: Am. Assn. Pharm. Scientists, Am. Coll. Clin. Pharmacy; mem.: Soc. Biol. Psychiatry, Soc. Neurosci., Am. Soc. Clin. Pharmacology & Therapeutics, Am. Assn. Colleges of Pharmacy, Pa. Soc. Hosp. Pharmacists, Western Pa. Soc. Hosp. Pharmacists, Am. Soc. Health-System Pharmacists, Acad. Gen. Practice, Allegheny County Pharmacists Assn., Pa. Pharmacists Assn., Am. Pharmacists Assn., Acad. Pharm. Scis., Am. Pharm. Assn., Phi Lambda Sigma, Rho Chi. Office: U Pitts Sch Pharmacy Ste 1100 Salk Hall 3501 Terrace St Pittsburgh PA 15261 Office Phone: 412-624-2400.

KROCK, CURTIS JOSSELYN, pulmonologist; b. Fort Smith, Ark., Oct. 11, 1935; s. Frederick Henry and Hazel Armiger (Josselyn) Krock; m. Ruth Leone Johnson, Apr. 27, 1968; children: Eric Gregory, Lynn Alyson; m. Susan de la Fuente, July 15, 2006. BA, Stanford U., 1957; MD, Johns Hopkins U. Sch. Medicine, 1961. Diplomate Am. Bd. Internal Medicine, Am. Bd. Pulmonary Medicine. Intern Barnes Hosp., St. Louis, 1961-62, resident in internal medicine, 1963-65; resident in pathology Johns Hopkins U. Sch. Medicine, Balt., 1962-63; pulmonary fellow Duke U., Durham, NC, 1965-66; pvt. practice Holt-Krock Clinic, Ft. Smith, Ark., 1968-72, Carle Clinic, Urbana, Ill., 1972-2001, also bd. dirs., 1978-80, chief medicine dept., 1996-99; clin. asst. prof. U. Ill., Urbana, 1976-99, clin. assoc. prof., 2000—; interim chief of medicine UICOM-UC, 2005—07; chief of medicine Carle Found. Hosp., 2003—08. Capt. US Army, 1966—68. Fellow: ACP; mem.: Sierra Club, Sigma Xi. Avocations: violin, reading. Office: Carle Clin Edn Ctr Forum Bldg 611 W Park Urbana IL 61801-2530 Home: 2310 Blanche Ln Champaign IL 61822 Office Phone: 217-383-4617. Personal E-mail: ckrock1935@aol.com. Business E-Mail: curtis.krock@carle.com.

KROFT, STEVEN HOWARD, pathologist, director, medical educator; b. San Antonio, June 2, 1965; s. Arthur Ellis and Roslyn Ann Kroft; children: Maxwell Alexander, Charles William, Henry Oliver. BS, MIT, 1986; MD, U. Ill., 1991. Diplomate in anatomic and clinical pathology Am. Bd. Pathology, 1996, in hematology Am. Bd. Pathology. Resident anat. & clin. pathology McGaw Med. Ctr. Northwestern U., Chgo., 1991—96; fellow hematopathology U. Mich. Med. Sch., Ann Arbor, 1996—97; asst. prof. pathology U. Tex. Southwestern Med. Sch., Dallas, 1997—2002, assoc. prof. pathology, 2002—05, Med. Coll. Wis., 2005—07, prof. pathology, 2007—; dir. hematopathology Froedtert Hosp. & Med. Coll. Wis., Milw., 2005—, vice chair edn. and academic affairs, 2010—. Med. dir. hematology lab. Parkland Meml. Hosp., Dallas, 1997—2003; med. dir., clin. flow cytometry Veripath Labs. U. Tex. Southwestern Med. Ctr., Dallas, 2003—05; dir. hematopathology fellowship Med. Coll. Wis., 2005—11, assoc. dir. pathology residency, 2008—09, dir. pathology residency, 2009—; assoc. editor Clin. Cytometry, 2002—07, Lab. Medicine, 2004—07; mem. editl. bd. Am. Jour. Clin. Pathology, 2002—, Internat. J. Lab. Hematology, 2007—, Clin. Cytometry, 2007—, Annals of Diagnostic Pathology, 2009—. Editor: (textbook) Color Atlas of Hemoglobin Disorders; contbr. chapters to books, articles to various peer-reviewed profl. jours. Recipient Pathology Resident Tchg. award, U. Tex. Southwestern, 1999, Outstanding Tchr. award, U Tex. Southwestern, 1999, Pathology Resident Tchg. award, U. Tex. Southwestern, 2000; named one of Best Doctors in Am., 2003—. Fellow: Am. Soc. Clin. Pathology (bd. dirs. 2006—, chair commn. assessment 2007—09, chair commn. continuing profl. devel. 2009—11, v.p. 2011—), Coll. Am. Pathologists (mem. hematology & clin. microscopy resource com. 1998—2005, chair hematology & clin. microscopy resource com. 2006); mem.: Wis. Soc. Pathologists (bd. dirs. 2009—), Coun. Med. Splty. Soc. (fin. com. 2008—10), Internat. Soc. Lab. Hematology, Soc. Hematopathology, US & Can. Acad. Pathology, Am. Soc. Hematology, Clin. Cytometry Soc. Office: MCW Dept Pathology 8701 Watertown Plank Rd Milwaukee WI 53226 Business E-Mail: skroft@mcw.edu.

KROHN, KENNETH ALBERT, radiologist, educator; b. Stevens Point, Wis., June 19, 1945; s. Albert William and Erma Belle (Cornwell) K.; 1 child, Galen. BA in Chemistry, Andrews U., 1966; PhD in Chemistry, U. Calif., 1971. Acting assoc. prof. U. Wash., Seattle, 1981-84, assoc. prof. radiology, 1984-86, prof. radiology and radiation oncology, 1986—, adj. prof. chemistry, 1986—. Guest scientist Donner Lab. Lawrence Berkeley (Calif.) Lab., 1980-81; radiochemist, VA Med. Ctr., Seattle, 1982—; affiliate investigator Fred Hutchinson Cancer Rsch. Ctr., 1997—. Contbr. articles to profl. jours.; patentee in field. Recipient Aebersold award, 1996; fellow, NDEA. Fellow AAAS; mem. Am. Assn. for Cancer Rsch., Am. Soc. Clin. Oncology, Am. Chem. Soc., Radiation Rsch. Soc., Soc. Nuclear Medicine, Acad. Coun., Sigma Xi. Home: 550 NE Lakeridge Dr Belfair WA 98528-8720 Office: U Washington Imaging Rsch Lab Box 356004 Seattle WA 98195-6004 Office Phone: 206-598-6245. Business E-Mail: kkrohn@u.washington.edu.

KROL, GEORGE, neuroradiologist, educator; b. Kielkow, Poland, June 11, 1944; arrived in US, 1970; MD, Krakow Med. Acad., Poland, 1968. Diplomate Am. Bd. Radiology, Am. Bd. Radiology-neuroradiology. Resident Brooklyn-Cumberland Med. Ctr.; fellow SUNY Downstate Med. Ctr.; dir. neuroradiology Meml. Sloan-Kettering Cancer Ctr., 1988—; clin. mem. Sloan-Kettering Inst., 1993—; prof. radiology Cornell Univ. Med. Ctr., NYC, 1994—. Author: MR table surveyor, various publs. Mem.: Am. Soc. Neuroradiology (organizing com. mem.). Libertarian. Roman Catholic. Avocations: Polish, English, German. Office: Memorial Solan-Kettering Cancer Center 1275 York Ave New York NY 10065 Office Phone: 212-639-7273.

KROLICK, MERRILL A., cardiologist; b. NYC, Oct. 14, 1959; s. Stanley David and Barbara Krolick; m. Dana Konopka, Oct. 19, 1989; children: Matthew, Alex. BS, Rensselaer Poly. Inst., 1981; DO, Coll. Osteo. Medicine, NY, 1985. Bd. cert. Internal Medicine, Cardiology, Interventional Cardiology. Cardiologist Prince William Cardiology, Manassas, Va., 1992—94, The Heart and Vascular Inst. of Fla., Largo, Fla., 1994—. Contbr. articles to med. jours. Pres. Am. Heart Assn. Pinellas County, Largo, 1996. Republican. Office: Heart & Vascular

Inst of Fla 1345 W Bay Dr Largo FL 33770 Home: 10316 Longwood Dr Seminole FL 33777-1311 Home Phone: 727-546-0952; Office Phone: 727-489-5400. Personal E-mail: mkrolick@tampabay.rr.com.

KRONENBERG, RICHARD SAMUEL, physician, administrator; b. Chgo., Aug. 7, 1938; s. Frank Paul and Ruth Ida (Zaretzsky) K.; m. Carole Marie Hurd, Oct. 11, 1963; children: Karen, Marilyn, Brenda. BA, Northwestern U., 1960, MD, 1963; MBA, LaTourneau U., Longview, Tex., 1998. Cert. internal medicine & pulmonary disease 1972. Intern Parkland Meml. Hosp., Mpls., 1967-68, resident in internal medicine, 1968; rsch. fellow Cardiovascular Rsch. Inst. U. Calif., San Franciso, 1968-70; asst. prof. medicine U. Minn., 1970-74, assoc. prof., 1974-79, prof., dir. pulmonary div., 1979-84; prof. U. Tex. Health Sci. Ctr., Houston, 1984—2002; prof. medicine, exec. v.p. for clin. affairs U. Tex. Health Ctr., Tyler, 1984—2002; sr. v.p. Mother Frances Health Sys., 2002—. Reviewer subsplty. programs in internal medicine Accreditation Coun. Grad. Med. Edn., Chgo., 1985—. Mem. editorial rev. bd. The Asbestos Monitor, Nat. Asbestos Coun. Jour., 1990-93; contbr. chpts. to books. Capt. USAF, 1965-67. Recipient Rsch. Career Devel. award NIH, 1973-78. Fellow ACP, Am. Coll. Chest Physicians; mem. Nat. Asbestos Coun. (bd. dirs. 1990-93), Asbestos Disease Assn. (pres. 1990-93), Ctrl. Soc. Clin. Rsch. Avocation: bicycling. Home: 5615 Cedar Hill Cir Tyler TX 75703-3912 Business E-Mail: kronen.r@tmfhs.org. E-mail: kronenr@tmfhs.org. *

KROTENBERG, ROBERT, physician, educator, medical facility director; b. Newark, Mar. 24, 1947; s. Joseph and Sylvia Krotenberg; m. Barbara Krotenberg, June 27, 1981; 1 child, Alyson. BSc, Ohio State U., 1968; MD, U. Rome, 1977. Diplomate Am. Bd. Phys. Medicine and Rehab., Am. Acad. Pain Mgmt. Intern Hackensack (N.J.) Med. Ctr., 1978—79; resident in rehab. medicine VA Med. Ctr., East Orange, NJ, 1976—80, U. Medicine and Dentistry N.J., Newark, 1983—84, chief resident in rehab. medicine, 1984; pvt. practice Bellleville, NJ, 1980—83, Miami, Fla., 1980—83; assoc. attending Clara Maass Hosp., Belleville, NJ, 1980—85, South Miami (Fla.) Hosp., 1981—82, Bapt. Hosp., Miami, 1981—82, Univ. Hosp., Newark, 1985—87; staff physiatrist Kessler Inst. Rehab., East Orange, 1985—87, assoc. med. dir., 1987—93, med. dir., 1994—, sr. med. officer, 1997—. Acting med. dir. Welkind Rehab. Hosp., Chester, NJ, 1990; cons. Univ. Hosp. U. Medicine and Dentistry N.J., Newark, 1987—, clin. instr., 1985—88, asst. prof., 1998—. Co-author: (book) Advances in Clinical Rehabilitation, Vol. 3, 1991; contbr. articles to profl. jours. Mem.: AMA, Essex County Med. Soc., Med. Soc. N.J., Fla. Med. Assn., N.J. Soc. Phys. Medicine and Rehab. (treas. 1986—88, v.p. 1988, pres. 1988—90), Am. Congress Rehab. Medicine, Am. Pain Soc., Assn. Academic Physiatrists, Am. Coll. Physician Execs. Business E-Mail: rkrotenberg@kessler-rehab.com.

KROTHAPALLI, SRINIVASA BABU, neurologist; b. Tenali, July 7, 1958; PhD, Christian Med. Coll., 1990. Head neurophysiology lab. Christian Med. Coll., 1989—2011, rsch. scientist, 1999—. Grant, DST-CTI. Mem.: Soc. Neuroscis. Achievements include research in intra-operative monitoring of neurosurgical and orthopedic cases; development of instruments to assess hand function and also to study the role of amygdala in the generation and propagation of epilepsy. Avocation: photography. Office: Christian Med Coll Dept Neurological Scis Vellore Tamilnadu 632004 India Business E-Mail: srinivas@cmcvellore.ac.in.

KROWKA, MICHAEL JOSEPH, physician; b. Evanston, Ill., Sept. 15, 1946; m. Christine McGraw. MD, U. Nev., Reno, 1980. Cert. ABIM Pulmonary Medicine, 1985. Prof. medicine Mayo Clinic, Rochester, Minn., 1986—. Staff sgt. USAF, 1969—73. Office: Mayo Clinic 200 1st St SW Rochester MN 55905 Office Phone: 507-284-5398. Office Fax: 507-266-4372. Business E-Mail: krowka@mayo.edu. *

KRŠIAK, MILOSLAV, pharmacologist, educator; b. Bratislava, Slovakia, May 7, 1939; arrived in Czech Republic, 1947; s. Mikuláš and Ludmila (Baxantová) K.; m. Miloslava Slavíčková, June 25, 1963; children: Helena, Jan. MD, Charles U., Prague, Czechoslovakia, 1962, PhD, 1966, DSc, 1982. Asst. dept. pharmacology, faculty paediatrics Charles U., Prague, 1962-63; postdoctoral fellow dept. pharmacology U. Coll., London, 1967-69; rsch. scientist Inst. Pharmacology/Czechoslovak Acad. Sci., Prague, 1969-93; head pharmacology dept. Charles U., Prague, 1991—, prof., 1993—. Chmn. adverse drug reactions com. Ministry Health, Prague, 1988-96, presidium of rsch. coun. of ministry, 1994-98; chmn. com. for pharmacology Grant Agy. Ministry Health, Prague, 1994-99. Contbr. articles to profl. jours. Riker fellow Internat. Union Pharmacology, 1967; recipient J.E. Purkynje medal Czech Med. Soc., 1983, Zdenek Klein Hon. award, 2008. Mem. European Behavioral Pharmacological Soc. (com. mem. 1986-92), Internat. Soc. for Rsch. on Aggression (coun. mem. 1991-98), Internat. Brain Rsch. Orgn., Czech Pharmacological Soc. (hon. mem., chmn. 1998-2002), Czech Med. Acad-.(vice chmn. 2011-), Soc. for Neuroscience, Internat. Assn. Study of Pain, Czech Med. Soc. (hon.). Avocations: human ethology, philosophy. Office: Charles Univ Dept Pharmacology 3rd Med Faculty 100 00 Prague Czech Republic Office Phone: +420267102487. Business E-Mail: miloslav.krsiak@lf3.cuni.cz.

KRUEGER, ANDREAS, orthopaedic surgeon; b. Kulmbach, Germany, July 7, 1973; s. Manfred and Runheid Krueger. MD, U. Bern, 2007. Resident U. Hosp., Inselspital Orthop. Dept., Bern, Switzerland, 2002—06, attending mem., 2008—; resident U. Hosp., Balgrist Orthop. Dept., Zurich, Switzerland, 2006—07. Reviewer Jour. Orthop. Surgery and Rsch., London, 2008—; officer Bone Bank U. Bern, 2008—; with exam com. U. Bern, 2008—. Contbr. sci. articles. Dist. physician Bavarian Red Cross, Bayreuth, Germany, 2002—08. Recipient Best Poster, SGO, 2006, EFORT, 2007. Mem.: ATLS. Achievements include invention of aluminium mold for intraoperative production of cement spacer during total knee revision surgery. Avocations: horseback riding, skiing, mountain climbing. Office: Inselspital Freiburgstrasse Bern 3000 Switzerland Personal E-mail: drmedkrueger@gmail.com. Business E-Mail: andreas.krueger@insel.ch.

KRUEGER, GERALD G., dermatologist, educator; BA, Union Coll., 1962; MD, Loma Linda U., 1996. Diplomate Am. Bd. Dermatology, 1973. Resident dermatology Univ. Colo. Med. Ctr., Denver, 1969—72; prof. dermatology dept. Univ. of UT Health Care, Benning Presidential Endowed chair. Co-author: (jour.) Association between IL13 Polymorphisms and Psoriatic Arthritis is modified by smoking. J Invest Dermatol, 2009, Plaque thickness and morphology in psoriasis vulgaris associated with therapeutic response. Br J Dermatol, 2009, Psoriatic arthritis is a strong predictor of sleep interference in patients with psoriasis. J Am Acad Dermatol, 2009, Further genetic evidence for three psoriasis-risk genes: ADAM33, CDKAL1, and PTPN22. J Invest Dermatol, 2009, and numerous others. Office: University of UT Health Care Department of Dermatology 30 N 1900 E 4A330 School of Medicine Salt Lake City UT 84132 Office Phone: 801-581-6465.

KRUEGER, GERALD PETER, psychologist; b. Evanston, Ill., Apr. 3, 1944; s. Albert August and Pauline Mary (Didier) K.; m. Jessica Ann Prendergast, Aug. 26, 1967; children: Michael G., Deborah L., Kevin A. BA in Psychology, U. Dayton, 1966; MA in Exptl. and Engring. Psychology, Johns Hopkins U., 1975, PhD in Exptl. Psychology, 1977; grad., U.S. Army Command and Gen. Staff Coll., 1980, U.S. Army War Coll., 1988. Cert. profl. ergonomist Bd. Certification Profl. Ergonomics. Rschr. engring. psychology Bunker-Ramo Corp., Wright-Patterson AFB, Ohio, 1966—69; human factors rsch. psychologist U.S. Army Human Engring. Lab., Aberdeen, Md., 1969—71; R & D coord. Def. Advanced Rsch. Projects Agy., Saigon, Vietnam, 1971—72; mil. police ops. officer U.S. Army, Ft. Meade, Md., 1972, aviation psychologist Aeromed. Rsch. Lab. Ft. Rucker, Ala., 1976—80; R & D programs staff officer U.S. Army Med. R & D Command, Ft. Detrick, Md., 1980—84; dep. chief dept. behavioral biology Walter Reed Army Inst. Rsch., Washington, 1984—88; dir. biomed. applications rsch. divsn. U.S. Army Aeromed. Rsch. Lab., Ft. Rucker, 1988—90; comdr., sci. tech. dir. U.S. Army Rsch. Inst. Environ. Medicine, Natick, Mass., 1990—94; ret. col. U.S. Army, 1994; v.p. ergonomics R & D svcs. Biomechanics Corp. Am., Melville, NY, 1994—95; prin. rsch. scientist, ergonomist Star Mountain, Inc., Alexandria, Va., 1995—98; pres. Krueger Ergonomics Cons., Inc., 1998—; prin. scientist, ergonomist Wexford Group Internat., Vienna, Va., 2000—06. Tchr. U.S. Armed Forces Inst., Saigon, 1971, Johns Hopkins U., 1974-75, U. So. Calif., 1977-80; adj. asst. prof. med.-clin. psychology Uniformed Svcs. U. Health Scis., Bethesda, Md., 1997—; mem. sci. coun. to UTEK Corp., Plant City, Fla., 1999-2010; bd. dirs. Commonwealth Biotechs., Inc., Richmond, Va., 2004-07; mem. sci. adv. coun. Innovaro, Inc., Tampa, Fla., 2010-. Book review editor Ergonomics in Design Mag., 1995—; assoc. editor Mil. Psychology, 1991-2003, mem. editl. bd., 2003—; guest editor jours. in field; contbr. articles to profl. jours. Recipient Richard M. Griffith Meml. award So. Soc. Philosophy and Psychology, 1978, Order of Mil. Med. merit for career contbns. Army Med. Dept., 1992, numerous mil. awards, medals and skill proficiency badges, including Legion of Merit, 1994, Bronze Star U.S. Army, 1972, Meritorious Svc. medals with 2 oak leaf clusters. Fellow APA (pres. divsn. mil. psychology 1995-96, pres. divsn. engring. psychologists 2001-02), Human Factors and Ergonomics Soc. (pres. Potomac chpt. 2003); mem. Assn. US Army, Nat. Def. Indsl. Assn., Inst. Ergonomics and Human Factors, Fedn. Assns. in Behavioral and Brain Scis. (mem. bd. dirs. 2007-10), Aerospace Med. Assn., Aerospace Human Factors Assn., Soc. for Human Performance in Extreme Environments, Army War Coll. Alumni Assn., VFW, Am. Legion. Roman Catholic. Office: Krueger Ergonomics Consultants 4105 Komes Ct Alexandria VA 22306-1252 Office Phone: 703-850-6397. E-mail: jerrykrueg@aol.com.

KRUG, ARNO, retired surgeon; b. Schneidemühl, Germany, Feb. 16, 1935; s. Willy and Berta Krug; m. Christine Hartwig, Nov. 5, 1955; children: Ulrike, Torsten, Christian, Hannes. MD, U. Med. Sch., Marburg, Germany, 1959; PhD, U. Med. Sch., Kiel, Germany, 1972. Rsch. fellow German Rsch. Soc., Marburg, 1962—67; surgeon Univ. Hosp., Kiel, 1968—78; chief surgeon City Hosp., Hof, Germany, 1978—98. Prof. Tchg. Hosp., Hof, 1962—98. Contbr. articles to profl. jours. Mem.: Bavarian Surg. Soc., German Surg. Soc. Avocations: sports, chess, languages, sailing. Home: Theodor Fontane Str 20 D-95032 Hof Saale Germany Fax: 09281794863. E-mail: arnokrug@yahoo.de.

KRUGER, FREDERIK CORNELIS, gastroenterologist; b. Pretoria, July 27, 1969; MBChB, Stellenbosch U., MMED, 2003, PhD, 2008. Cons. Stellenbosch U., 2001—06, gastroenterologist Durbanville Mediclinic, 2006—. Reviewer European Jour. Hepatology, Liver Internat. and SAMJ; examiner Colls. Medicine South Africa. Recipient Best Presentation award, SAGES, Rsch. award, Med. Rsch. Coun.; grant, Harry and Doris Crossley Found., Stellenbosch U. Mem.: Coll. Medicine SA, SAGES, AGA. Avocations: skiing, music, art. Office: Ste 106 Durbanville Mediclinic Well Cape Town Western Cape 7550 South Africa Business E-Mail: ckruger@gastrosa.com.

KRÜGER, REJKO, neurologist, educator; b. Recklinghausen, Germany, Dec. 7, 1969; m. Maren Runte, July 8, 2004; children: Yannis, Fenya. Cert. neurologist Bd. Ärztekammer Baden-Württemberg, 2005. Residency and postdoc. rsch. fellow Neurology and Molecular Human Genetics, Ruhr-U., Bochum, Germany, 1996—2001, Ctr. Neurology and Hertie-Inst. Clin. Brain Rsch., Tübingen, Germany, 2001—04, assoc. prof., 2005—; dir. Lab. Functional Neurogenomics Ctr. Neurology & Hertie-Inst. Clin. Brain Rsch., 2005—. Contbr. chapters to books (Rsch. award, German Parkinson's disease Assn., 2001). Mem.: German Soc. Neurology, Movement Disorders Soc., Soc. Neurosci. Achievements include discovery of second known mutation worldwide in Parkinson's disease gene alpha-synuclein; novel gene for Parkinson's disease; patents for mutations in the Omi/HtrA2 gene in Parkinson's disease; research in genetic risk factors for Parkinson's disease. Office: Ctr Neurology and Hertie-Inst Hoppe-Seyler Str 3 Tübingen 72076 Germany Office Phone: 49-7071-2982340. Office Fax: 49-7071-295260. Business E-Mail: rejko.krueger@uni-tuebingen.de.

KRUGMAN, RICHARD DAVID, pediatrician, academic administrator, educator; b. NYC, Nov. 28, 1942; s. Saul and Sylvia (Stern) K.; m. Mary Elizabeth Kerber, July 9, 1966; children: Scott, Joshua, Todd, Jordan. AB, Princeton U., 1963; MD, NYU, 1968. Resident U. Colo. Sch. Medicine, Denver, 1968-71; staff assoc. Nat. Inst. Health, Bethesda, Md., 1971-73; asst. prof. U. Colo. Sch. Medicine, 1973-78, assoc. prof., 1978-87, prof. pediatrics, 1988—, dean, 1992—, vice chancellor health affairs, 2007—. Author: The Battered Child, 5th edit., 1997; editor: (jour.) Child Abuse/Neglect, 1986-2001. Chmn. U.S. Adv. Bd. Child Abuse and Neglect, Washington, 1989-91; dir. Kempe Nat. Ctr. for Prevention and Treatment of Child Abuse and Neglect, Denver, 1981-92; trustee Princeton U., 2001-2005. Recipient C. Henry Kempe award Nat. Conf. on Child Abuse, 1989, St. Geme award U. Colo. Sch. Medicine, 1992, 98; Paul Harris fellow Rotary Internat., Sydney, Australia, 1992. Mem. Internat. Soc. Prevention of Child Abuse and Neglect (pres. 1992-94), Am. Acad. Pediatrics (Ray Helfer award 1995, Brandt Steele award 1996), Am. Pediatric Soc., Inst. Medicine. Office: U Colo Sch Medicine 13001 E 17th Pl Aurora CO 80045 Office Phone: 303-724-0882. Business E-Mail: richard.krugman@ucdenver.edu. *

KRUKEMEYER, MANFRED GEORGE, medical researcher; Student, U. Keil, U. Bonn, 1982—89; MD, U. Vienna, Austria, 1990, U. Vienna, Kiel, Germany, 1990, U. Vienna, Bonn, Germany, 1990. Bd. cert. surgeon Germany, bd. cert. emergency physician Germany, bd. cert. nutritionist Germany. Resident, surgery Med. Sch., Linz, Austria, 1991, Duesseldorf, Germany, 1992—93, Med. Sch., Charité, Berlin, 1993—94; pres. Berit Hosp., St. Gallen, Switzerland, 1993—; mng. dir. Paracelsus Hosp. Corp., Osnabrueck, Germany, 1994—2000; lectr., rschr. surg. rsch. U. Muenster, Med. Sch., Germany, 2001—. Contbr. more than 50 publs. profl. jours. Mem.: German Med. Assn. Westfalen-Lippe, German Surg. Assn. Office: Dept Radio-Oncology Paracelsus Hosp Sedanstr 109 D-49076 Osnabruck Germany

KRUMBOLTZ, JOHN DWIGHT, psychologist, educator; b. Cedar Rapids, Iowa, Oct. 21, 1928; s. Dwight John and Margaret (Jones) K.; m. Helen Brandhorst, Aug. 22, 1954 (div. Aug. 1986); children: Ann, Jennifer; m. Betty Lee Foster, Nov. 8, 1987. BA, Coe Coll., Cedar Rapids, 1950; MA, Columbia Tchrs. Coll., 1951; PhD, U. Minn., 1955; PhD (hon.), Pacific Grad. Sch. Psychology, 1991. Counselor, tchr. W. Waterloo (Iowa) H.S., 1951-53; from teaching asst. to instr. U. Minn., 1953-55; from asst. prof. ednl. psychology to assoc. prof. Mich. State U., 1957-61; faculty Stanford U. Sch. Edn., 1961-66, prof. edn. and psychology, 1966—. Vis. sr. research psychologist Ednl. Testing Service, 1972-73; fellow Ctr. for Advanced Study in Behavioral Scis., 1975-76, Advanced Study Ctr., Nat. Ctr. for Research in Vocat. Edn., Ohio State U., 1980-81; vis. colleague dept. psychology Inst. Psychiatry, U. London, 1983-84 Author: (with others) Learning to Study, 1960; (with Helen B. Krumboltz) Changing Children's Behavior, 1972; editor: Learning and the Educational Process, 1965, Revolution in Counseling, 1966; (with Carl E. Thoresen) Behavioral Counseling: Cases and Techniques, 1969, Counseling Methods, 1976; (with Anita M. Mitchell and G. Brian Jones) Social Learning and Career Decision Making, 1979; (with Daniel A. Hamel) Assessing Career Development, 1982; contbr. articles to profl. jours. With USAF, 1955-57. Recipient Eminent Career award Nat. Career Devel. Assn., 1994, Living Legend award Am. Counseling Assn., 2004, Outstanding Achievement award, U. Minn., 2006; Guggenheim fellow, 1967-68. Mem. APA (pres. div. counseling psychology 1974-75, award for disting. profl. contbns. to knowledge 2002), Am. Ednl. Rsch. Assn. (v.p. div. E. 1966-68), Am. Pers. and Guidance Assn. (Outstanding Rsch. award 1959, 66, 68, Disting. Profl. Svcs. award 1974, Leona Tyler award 1990).

KRUMHOLZ, HARLAN MARC, cardiologist, internist, educator; b. St. Louis, Mo., Mar. 21, 1958; BS, Yale Coll., 1980; MD, Harvard Med. Sch., 1985; MSc, Harvard Sch. Pub. Health, 1992. Cert. Internal Medicine, Cardiovascular Disease. Intern & resident, internal medicine U. Calif., San Francisco, 1985—88; chief resident Moffitt Hosp.; fellow, cardiology Beth Israel Hosp., Boston; hosp. affiliation Yale New Haven Hosp., New Haven; asst. prof. medicine (cardiology) and epidemiology and pub. health Yale Sch. Medicine, 1992—97, assoc. prof. medicine (cardiology) and epidemiology and pub. health, 1997—2002, full prof. medicine (cardiology) and epidemiology and pub. health, 2002—05, Harold H. Hines, jr. prof. medicine and epidemiology and pub. health (cardiology), 2005—; founder, dir. Yale-New Haven Hosp. Ctr. for Outcomes Rsch. and Evaluation, 1992—; co-dir. Robert Wood Johnson Clin. Scholars Program, 1996—. Chair steering com. Am. Heart Assn. Ann. Scientific Forum on Quality of Care and Outcomes Rsch. in Cardiovascular Disease & Stroke; co-clinical coord. Nat. Project for Myocardial Infarction, Centers for Medicare & Medicaid Services; chair, cardiovascular conditions clin. adv. panel Joint Commn. on Accreditation of Healthcare Organizations; chair, writing com. to develop performance measures on acute myocardial infarction Am. Coll. Cardiology/Am. Heart Assn.; cardiovascular expert panel of the performance measurement coordinating coun. AMA, Joint Commn. on the Accreditation of Healthcare Organizations, Nat. Com. for Quality Assurance; chair, technical expert panel for pub. reporting Centers for Medicare & Medicaid Svcs.; chair, quality care and outcomes rsch. expert panel Am. Heart Assn.; mem. nat. scientific adv. coun. Am. Fedn. for Aging Rsch.; chair, Nat. Peer Review Com. for Outcomes Rsch. Am. Heart Assn.; mem. exec. coun. Heart Failure Soc. Am.; mem. writing com. to revise the 1999 guidelines for mgmt. of patients with acute myocardial infarction Am. Coll. Cardiology/Am. Heart Assn.; chair, Working Group on Outcomes Rsch. in Cardiovascular Disease Nat. Heart, Lung and Blood Inst. Contbr. articles to profl. jours.; assoc. editor Circulation, editor Journal Watch Cardiology, serves on several editl. bds.; author: The Expert Guide to Beating Heart Disease, 2005. Paul Beeson Faculty Scholar, 1996—99. Mem.: Inst. Medicine, Assn. Am. Physicians, Am. Soc. for Clin. Investigation. Office: Sect Cardiovascular Medicine Yale U Sch Medicine I-Wing Ste 456 333 Cedar St PO Box 208017 I New Haven CT 06510 Office Phone: 203-785-4114. Business E-Mail: harlan.krumholz@yale.edu.

KRUMHOLZ, OTTO WERNER, anesthesiologist, educator; b. Giessen, Hessen, Germany, Apr. 27, 1956; s. Max Otto and Johanna Waltraud Krumholz; m. Petra Gabriela Brûck, June 16, 1988; children: Maximilian, Konstantin, Sophie, Leonard. MD, U. Giessen, 1983. Sci. collaborator U. Giessen, 1983-92, lectr., 1992—; head dept. Bethlehem Hosp., Stolberg, Germany, 1996—; lectr. U. Aachen, Germany, 1996—; assoc. prof. U. Giessen, 2004. Contbr. articles to profl. jours. Capt. German Med. Corps, 1982. Lutheran. Avocations: photography, model-making, shooting, historical research. Office: Bethlehem Krankenhaus Steinfeldstrasse 5 52222 Stolberg Germany E-mail: wkrumholz@gmx.de.

KRUMLAUF, ROBERT EUGENE, neuroscientist, educator, medical researcher; BSChemE, Vanderbilt U., Nashville, 1970; PhD in Devel. Biology, Ohio State U., 1979. Chief chem. engr. Capital City Products Inc., Columbus, Ohio, 1970—75; fellow dept. biochemistry Ohio State U., 1975—79; postdoc. fellow Dr A. Balmain Beatson Inst. Cancer Rsch., Glasgow, Scotland, 1979—82, Dr S. Tilghman Inst. Cancer Rsch., Phila., 1982—85; group leader to adj. group leader Nat. Inst. Med. Rsch., London, 1985—2000; adj. group leader NIMR, 2000; sci. dir. Stowers Inst. Med. Rsch., Kansas City, Mo., 2000—. Prof. oral biology U. Mo. Sch. Dentistry, Kansas City, 2000—; prof. dept. anatomy & cell biology U. Kans. Med. Sch., Kansas City, 2001—. Editor: Devel. Biology, 1995—; mem. editl. bd.: New

Biologist, 1989—92, Mechanisms of Devel., 1990—, Nucleic Acids Rsch., 1992—, Current Biology, 1993—2000, Portland Press, 1994—2000, Devel., 1994—, Molecular and Cellular Neurobiology, 1995—, Human Molecular Genetics, 1996—98, Genes and Function, 1997—98, InScight, 1998—. Fellow: Acad. Med. Scis.; mem.: Am. Acad. Arts & Scis., Soc. Pathology and Teratology, Acad. Med. Scis. UK, The Genetical Soc., Am. Soc. Microbiology, Am. Assn. Anatomists, Soc. Devel. Biology, Brit. Soc. Devel. Biology, European Molecular Biology Orgn., European Devel. Biology Orgn. (sec. 1997—2001). Office: Stowers Institute for Medical Research 1000 E 50th St Kansas City MO 64110 Home Phone: 913-831-7680; Office Phone: 816-926-4051. Business E-Mail: rek@stowers.org. *

KRUPATKIN, ALEXANDER ILYICH, clinical physiologist researcher, neurologist; b. Moscow, Feb. 17, 1961; s. Ilya Lvovich and Eva Naumovna (Roytberg) K. MD, Med. Inst., Tver, Russia, 1983, Dr.-Neurologist, 1984; Cons. in Psychotherapy, Med. Inst., Moscow, Russia, 1987; PhD, Ctrl. Inst. Traumatology, Moscow, Russia, 1989; DMSc, Ctrl. Inst. Traumatology, Moscow, 1999. Physician Regional Hosp., Tver, Russia, 1983-84; jr. rschr. Ctrl. Inst. Traumatology & Orthopaedics, Moscow, 1984-90, rschr., 1990-91, sr. rschr., 1991—2000, leading rschr., 2000—. Prof. pathophysiology Ctrl. Inst. Traumatology, Moscow, 2006—. Author: Polarographic Method in Traumatology & Orthopedics, 1986, Clinical Neuroangiophysiology of the Limbs, 2003, Laser Doppler Flowmetry, 2005; contbr. articles to profl. jours. Mem. N.Y. Acad. Scis., Russian Assn. Functional Diagnosis. Avocations: stamp collecting/philately, exercise. Home: Voljsky bulvar kvartal 95 korpus 3 kvartira 4 109125 Moscow Russia Office: Ctrl Inst Traumatology & Orthopaedics Ul Priorova 10 127299 Moscow Russia Office Phone: 8-495-450-37-01. Personal E-mail: arch2003@mail.ru.

KRUPNICK, ALEXANDER SASHA, thoracic surgeon; b. Kiev, Russia, June 30, 1969; MD, U. Mich., 1996. Thoracic surgeon Wash. U. St. Louis, 2004—. Cons. Galaxo-Smith-Klein, 2010. Fellow: ACS; mem.: AOA, Southern Thoracic Soc., Soc. Thoracic Surgeons, Am. Assn. Immunologists. Office: Box 8234 660 South Euclid Saint Louis MO 63110 Business E-Mail: krupnicka@wudosis.wustl.edu.

KRUPNICK, JANICE LEE, psychologist, psychotherapist, educator; b. Newark, Mar. 7, 1950; d. Jacob and Betty (Katz) K.; m. Richard Michael Suzman, July 21, 1976; children: Daniel, Jessica. AB, Oberlin Coll., 1972; MSW, U. Mich., 1974; MA, U. Calif., Berkeley, 1985, PhD, 1988. Lic. psychologist, Md., D.C. Social worker Long Beach (Calif.) Neuropsychol. Inst., 1974-75; fellow Mt. Zion Hosp./Med. Ctr., San Francisco, 1975-77; program analyst NIMH, Rockville, Md., 1980-81; asst. clin. prof. U. Calif., San Francisco, 1977-83; cons. NAS, Washington, 1983-84; asst. clin. prof. Georgetown U., Washington, 1984-90; asst. rsch. prof. George Washington U., Washington, 1988-91; assoc. clin. prof. Georgetown U., Washington, 1990-94, clin. prof., 1994—, rsch. prof., 2000—. Cons. NIMH, Bethesda, Md., 1990-91, Am. Psychiat. Assn., 1990-91; tchr. dynamic psychotherapy seminar for advanced psychiat. residents Georgetown U., lectr. interpersonal psychotherapy course. Co-author: Personality Styles and Brief Psychotherapy, 1984; contbr. articles to psychiat. and psychol. jours. Participant rallies for women's rights, Washington, 1986—. Clin. fellow NIMH, 1975-77, rsch. fellow NIMH, 1986-88. Mem. Am. Psychol. Assn., Soc. for Clin. Social Work, Soc. for Psychotherapy Rsch. Jewish. Avocations: reading, movies, travel, swimming. Home: 4100 Oliver St Chevy Chase MD 20815-7120 Office: 5480 Wisconsin Ave Ste 220 Chevy Chase MD 20815-3503 Office Phone: 301-654-2142. Business E-Mail: krupnicj@georgetown.edu.

KRUSTRUP, PETER, physical education educator; b. Copenhagen, June 16, 1970; s. Jørgen Jens Jacobsen and Inge Krustrup; m. Birgitte Rejkjaer Krustrup; children: Sarah, Andrea. PhD, U. Copenhagen, Denmark, 2004. Assoc. prof. Dept. Exercise and Sport Scis., Copenhagen, 2005—; vicehead, dept. exercise and sport scis. U. Copenhagen, 2007—10; leader Soccer Health Project; prof. sport & health sci. U. Exeter, 2011—. Contbr. articles to profl. jours. (Young Investigator award, 1997, U. Publicity award, 2007). Bd. mem. sports clubs Danish Sports Fedn. Recipient Sports Organizer award, Unibank, 1995, Mens Health award, 2010. Office: Univ Copenhagen Universitetsparken 13 2100 Copenhagen Denmark Office Fax: 45 35321600. Business E-Mail: pkrustrup@ifi.ku.dk.

KRYGSMAN, ANNADIE, physiologist, researcher; b. Johannesburg, Apr. 10, 1971; PhD, Utrecht U., Netherlands, 2004. Sr. scientist South African Med. Rsch. Coun., 2004—09; lab. mgr. Stellenbosch U., 2009—. Mem.: Physiology Soc. South Africa. Office: Stellenbosch University Dept Physiological Scis Stellenbosch Western Cape 7505 South Africa Business E-Mail: akrygsman@sun.ac.za.

KRYSINSKI, ZDZISLAW JAN, dental surgeon, educator; b. Poznan, Poland, Jan. 8, 1934; s. Mieczyslaw and Maria (Vidal) K.; m. Romana Teresa Krysztoforska, June 26, 1958; children: Ida, Karolina BDS, Poznan U. Med. Sch., 1957, DDS, 1963, DSc, 1975. Diplomate prosthetic dentistry. Instr., asst. prof. Poznan U. Med. Sch., 1958—76, assoc. prof., 1976—84, prof., chmn., 1984—2004, emeritus prof., 2005—11. Rsch. fellow I.P. Pavlov Med. Inst., Leningrad, USSR, 1971, U. Turku, Finland, 1976; vis. prof. U. Ife, Nigeria, 1984-86, Wroclaw (Poland) U. Sch. Medicine, 1998—2004; part-time prof. Pomeranian Sch. Medicine, Szczecin, Poland, 1989-94; cons. Polish Rys. Health Svc., 1974-98, 2d State Clin. Hosp., Poznan, 1984-2003; hon. cons. Unife Tchg. Hosps. Complex, Ife, 1984-86; regional cons. prosthodontist Ministry Health and Social Care, Poland, 1997— Contbr. articles to profl. jours Capt. Polish Army Health Svc., 1963-65 Recipient Order Polonia Restituta, Pres. Republic Poland Mem.: AAAS, NY Acad. Scis., European Prosthodontic Assn., Pierre Fauchard Acad., Polish Stomatological Soc. (hon.; Poznan br. pres. 1988—97, exec. com. 1988—, v.p. 1997—2008, Bene Meritus award 1994). Avocations: bibliophilism, touring. Office: Inst Stomatology ul Bukowska 70 PL 60 812 Poznan Poland Home: ul J H Dabrowskiego 43 m 8 60-842 Poznan Poland Office Phone: 4861 8547122.

KRYSTAL, GEOFFREY WOLFE, physician, educator; b. Bklyn., Apr. 3, 1952; PhD, SUNY at Stony Brook, 1979; MD, U. Miami, 1982. Prof. medicine Va. Commonwealth U., 1988—. Chief hematology-oncology sect. McGuire DVA Med. Ctr., 2002. Office: McGuire DVA Med Ctr 111K 1201 Broad Rock Blvd Richmond VA 23249 Office Fax: 804-675-5447. Business E-Mail: gkrystal@vcu.edu.

KRYSTAL, JOHN HARRISON, psychiatrist, educator; b. Detroit, Feb. 27, 1958; s. Henry and Esther (Reichstein) Krystal; m. Bonnie Becker; children: Samuel Ethan, Hannah Lauren. BA, U. Chgo., 1980; MD, Yale U., New Haven, 1984. Intern Hosp. St. Raphael, New Haven; resident in psychiatry Yale U. Sch. Medicine, 1984-88, asst. prof., 1989-93, assoc. prof., 1993-96, Albert E. Kent prof. psychiatry, 2000—03, Robert L. McNeil Jr. prof., 2003—, chair dept. psychiatry. Co-founder, dir. Alcoholism Rsch. Ctr., Yale-VA Med. Ctr., West Haven, 1991—2011; mem. bd. sci. counsellors Nat. Inst. Mental Health, 2001—07, chair, 2004—07; chief psychiatry Yale-New Haven Hosp.; dir. clin. neurosci. divsn. Nat. Ctr. Post-Traumatic Stress Disorder, West Haven; med. dir. Schizophrenia Biol. Rsch. Ctr., US Dept. Vets. Affairs; dir. Nat. Inst. Alcohol Abuse & Alcoholism (NIAAA) Ctr. Translational Neurosci. of Alcoholism. Mng. editor Psychopharmacology, 1999—2006; editor: Biol. Psychiatry, 2006—; contbr. articles to profl. jours., chapters to books. Recipient Han Jönas Weitbrecht Sci. award, Germany, 2003, Anna-Monika prize in depression rsch., 2009, Jack Mendelson award for clin. rsch., Nat. Inst. Alcohol Abuse & Alcoholism, 2010; Burroughs Wellcome fellowship, 1986—88. Fellow: American Coll. Neuropsychopharmacology (coun. mem. 2006—, pres. elect 2011, Joel Elkes Internat. award 2001, George N. Thompson award 2011), American Psychiat. Assn. (Penwait award 1988, Kempf award 2005); mem.: Nat. Readers Scis., American Coll. Psychiatrists (Stanley Dean award 2010), Soc. Biol. Psychiatry (ex-officio bd. dirs.), Rsch. Soc. Alcoholism (bd. dirs. 2005—), Inst. Medicine, Internat. Soc. Traumatic Stress Studies (Chaim Danielli award 1989), Soc. Neurosci., Soc. Nuc. Medicine, Phi Beta Kappa. Office: Yale U Dept Psychiatry 00 George St Ste 901 New Haven CT 06511 E-mail: john.krystal@yale.edu.

KRZEWICKI, JERZY HIERONIM, surgeon; b. Gorlice, Poland, Oct. 14, 1946; s. Julian Krzewicki and Barbara Fahrensperk-Stormke; m. Katarzyna Litwiniszyn, June 13, 1970; children: Lukasz, Karolina Romera Krzewicka. MD, PhD, Med. Acad. Kraków, 1976. Registered specialist in surgery Cert. of Postgrad. Med. Edn., Warsaw, 1978. Lectr. Med. Acad. Kraków, Poland, 1974—91; head Dept. Surgery Provincial Hosp., Kielce, Poland, 1991—2005. Dir. Surg. Found., Kielce, Poland; lectr. Swietokrzyska Acad., Kielce, Poland, 2003—. Contbr. articles to profl. jours. Primate coun. Polish Cath. Ch., Warsaw, 1981—83. Mem.: Polish Surg. Soc. (life; pres. 2003—09, hon. mem.). Office: Provincial Hospital Grunwaldzka 45 Kielce 25-736 Poland Home: Ul. Artura Grottgera 16 25-441 Kielce Poland Personal E-mail: j.krzewicki@wp.pl.

KU, CHIH-HUNG, medical educator; b. Nan-Tou County, Taiwan, Nov. 12, 1960; s. Tsai-Tsan Ku and Su-Jiao Ku-Liu; m. Ching-Fang Anna Tsao; children: Lin-Kai Ken, Lin-Chieh Joe. BS, Nat. Def. Med. Ctr., 1983; DSc, Harvard U., 1999. Asst. prof. Sch. Pub. Health Nat. Def. Med. Ctr., Taipei, Taiwan, 1999—2004, assoc. prof. Sch. Pub. Health, 2005—. Grant reviewer Environ. Protection Adminstrn., Taipei, Taiwan, 2000—05, Vet. Affairs Commn., Taipei, 2001—02; mem. master degree com. Sch. Nursing Nat. Yang-Ming U., Taipei, 2000—01; cons. in field. Reviewer Jour. Med. Sci.; contbr. articles to profl. jours. Col. Taiwanese Army, 2006. Decorated Order Loyalty and Diligence Office of Pres., Scholarship medal Ministry Nat. Def., Army Achievement medal, Silver hon.; recipient Outstanding Tchr., Nat. Def. Med. Ctr., 2004; named, 2003, Nat. Def. U., 2004; fellow, Ministry Nat. Def., 1994—99, 2004—05. Mem.: Internat. Soc. Environ. Epidemiology, Chinese Soc. Environ. Health (life), Harvard Club Republic of China (life). Buddhist. Avocations: swimming, hiking, badminton, camping, bicycling. Office: Nat Def Med Ctr P Box 90048-509 Nei-Hu Dist Taipei 114 Taiwan Office Fax: 886-2-8792-9059. Personal E-mail: chihhung.ku@gmail.com.

KU, PO-WEN, physical activity and health educator; b. Taiwan, Apr. 28, 1971; PhD, U. Bristol, 2005, Nat. Yang-Ming U., 2010. Sect. chief Sports Affairs Coun., Exec. Yuan, 1998—2006; asst. prof. Nat. Changhua U. Edn., 2006—09, assoc. prof., 2009—; exec. dir. Human Rights Edn. Found., 2009—. Adj. assoc. prof. Nat. Yang-Ming U., 2011. Recipient Young Investigator award, Internat. Soc. Aging and Phys. Activity, Rsch. Excellence award, Nat. Changhua U. Edn. Mem.: Internat. Assn. Applied Psychology. Office: 1 Jin-De Rd Changhua City 500 Taiwan Office Phone: 886 (4)7232105 ext. 1991. Business E-Mail: powen.ku@gmail.com.

KU, SEUNG-YUP, medical educator, physician; b. Seoul, Republic of Korea, Feb. 10, 1967; s. Pyong Sahm Ku and Yj Kim; m. Jy Hong, Nov. 17, 1969; children: J.H., J.B. MD, Seoul Nat. U., 1991, PhD, 2001. Cert. physician Ob-Gyn. Bd., Korean Soc. of Obstetrics and Gynecology, 1996, Am. Bd. Anti-Aging Medicine, 2003. Asst. prof. Coll. Medicine, Seoul Nat. U., 2002—; practitioner N.Am. Menopause Soc., 2003—. Co-author: (textbook) Anti-Aging Medicine, 2003; exec. editor Anti-Aging Med. Rsch. Jour., 2004—; contbr. articles to profl. jours. Mem.: Korean Soc. Menopause (mem. sci. com. 2004—), Korean Soc. Contraception (mem. sci. com. 2003—), Korean Acad. Anti-Aging Medicine (dir. internat. affairs 2002—), Am. Acad. Anti-Aging Medicine (mem. adv. bd. scientific com. 2002—), Korean Soc. Assisted Reproduction (mem. com. info. and comm. 2003—), Korean Soc. Fertility and Sterility (exec. sec. 2000—02, mem. publ. com. 2002—). Office: Seoul Nat U Dept Ob-Gyn 28 Yonkeun-dong Chongno-gu Seoul 110-744 Republic of Korea Office Fax: 82-2-762-3599. Business E-Mail: jyhsyk@snu.ac.kr.

KU, WAI-HUNG, pediatrician; b. Hong Kong, June 19, 1973; MBChB, Chinese U. Hong Kong, 1997. Med. officer, specialist Hosp. Authority, 1998. Fellow: Hong Kong Coll. Paediatricians. Office: Tseung Kwan O Hosp Hong Kong 852 Hong Kong Business E-Mail: kuwh2002@yahoo.com.hk.

KUAN, YEH CHUNN, medical educator; b. Klang, Malaysia, Nov. 7, 1976; MBBS, U. Malaya, 2001. Physician Hosp. Tengku Ampuan Afzan, 2007—08; asst. prof. Internat. Islamic U. Malaysia, 2008—. Master: Royal Coll. Physicians Edinburgh; mem.: Med. Protection Soc., Malaysian Thoracic Soc. Home: 37 Lorong Bukit Ubi 22 Taman Sekilau Me Kuantan Pahang 25200 Malaysia Home Fax: 095171897. Personal E-mail: kychunn@yahoo.com.

KUBANKOVA, HELENA, physician; b. Kadan, Czech Republic, Nov. 8, 1957; MD, Charles U., Plzen, Czech Republic, 1983. Physician, dept. transfusion medicine Hosp. Ceske Budejovice, 1983—84, physician, dept. internal medicine, 1984—86, physician, dept. transfusion medicine, dept. hematology, 1986—91, dep. head physician, dept. transfusion medicine, 1991—. Working group making nat. guidelines immunohaematological prenatal & perinatal testing Czech Soc. Transfusion Medicine, 2008—10. Mem.: Czech Med. Assn. J.E.Purkyne (Czech Soc. Transfusion Medicine & Czech Soc. Haematology), Internat. Soc. Blood Transfusion. Avocations: computers, singing, hiking. Home: J Bendy 28 Ceske Budejovice Region South Bohemia 370 05 Czech Republic Personal E-mail: h.banzetova@worldonline.cz.

KUBICKA-TRZASKA, AGNIESZKA, ophthalmologist, educator; b. Opole, Poland, Sept. 3, 1967; MD, Nicolas Copernicus Med. Acad., Cracow, 1992, PhD. Sr. lectr., dept. ophthalmology Med. Coll. Jagiellonian U., Cracow, 1992. Master: Malopolski Sect. Age-Related Macular Degeneration Soc.; mem.: Polish Soc. Ophthalmologists. Avocations: skiing, horseback riding, swimming. Home: Lea Str 244/7 Cracow Malopolska 31-133 Poland Personal E-mail: akubicka@onet.pl.

KUBIK, CAROLYN J., reproductive endocrinologist; MD, George Wash. Univ. Sch. of Medicine, Wash., DC. Diplomate Am. Bd. Ob-Gyn, cert. reproductive endocrinology and infertility. Resident ob-gyn., fellow reproductive endocrinology and infertility Magee-Womens Hosp.; adminstrv. chief resident ob-gyn. residency program Magee-Womens Hosp. of Univ. of Pitts. Med. Ctr., 1981—82, med. dir. assisted reproductive tech. program, 1986—91; maj., staff ob-gyn. USAF Hosp., Dover, Del.; clin. assoc. prof. Univ. Pitts. Sch. of Medicine; med. dir. Reproductive Health Specialists. Mem. Pitts. Academic and Rsch. Cmty. Named one of Top Docs, Pitts. Mag. Mem.: ACOG, Allegheny County Med. Soc., Am. Soc. Reproductive Medicine. Office: Magee-Womens Hospital of UPMC 300 Halket St Pittsburgh PA 15213 Office Phone: 412-641-1000.

KUBISTA, KATHARINA E., ophthalmologist; b. Vienna, Apr. 3, 1977; d. Josef and Inge Schmid; m. Bernd Kubista. D, Med. U. Vienna, 2001. Resident Dept. Oncology, Med. U. Vienna, 2001—02, AUVA Trauma Hosp. Meidling, Vienna, 2002—02; internship, dept. neurosurgery Rudolf Found. Clinic, Vienna, 2003—04, resident, dept. ophthalmology, 2004—08; tutor Med. U. Vienna, Vienna, 2006—10; rsch. fellow Dept. Ophthalmology, Mayo Clinic, Rochester, Minn., 2008—09. Rschr. Ludwig Boltzmann Inst., Vienna, 2002—. Recipient Sci. award, Mayor Vienna, 2006; grant, Max Kade Found., 2008, Travel grant, Felix-Mandel-Found., 2006, Brain-Power Group, 2008. Roman Catholic. Achievements include research in ophthalmology, specialized on age-related macular degeneration. Avocations: travel, bicycling, scuba diving, swimming, hiking. Office: Privatklinik Doebling Heiligen Staedter Str 46 48 Vienna 1190 Austria Personal E-mail: katharina.kubista@proeyes.at. Business E-Mail: kubista@proeyes.at.

KUBO, KEITARO, research scientist; b. Tokyo, Oct. 18, 1969; s. Seiichi and Fusako Kubo; m. Nagako Hateruma, Jan. 5, 1969. BA in Edn., U. Saitama, 1992; PhD, U. Tokyo, 2000. Rsch. assoc. U. Tokyo, 2000—. Mem. Sport and Med. Com. Saitama, Japan, 2000—; mgr. Sci. Congress for Sports and Exercise Tng., Tokyo, 2000—, Japan Soc. Phys. Edn., Tokyo, 2001—, Union Phys. Edn. U., Tokyo, 2001—; presenter in field. Grantee, Ministry Edn., Sci., Sports and Culture, 2001—, Meiji Found. for Health Sci., 2001, Takeda Sci. Found., 2002, Naito Sci. Found., 2002, Mizuno Sci. Found., 2002, Descente Found. for the Promotion Sports Sci., 2003. Mem.: Japan Soc. Biomechanics, Japan Soc. Phys. Edn., Am. Coll. Sports Medicine. Avocations: weightlifting, jogging, Judo. Home: Sekiguchi 3-9-6-203 Bunkyo-ku Tokyo 112-0014 Japan Office: Life Scis Sports Scis Komaba 3-8-1 Meguro-ku Tokyo 153-8902 Japan Office Fax: +81-3-5454-4317; Home Fax: +81-3-3941-2970. E-mail: kubo@idaten.c.u-tokyo.ac.jp.

KUBOHARA, YUZURU, biology professor; b. Matsumoto, Japan, Oct. 31, 1958; PhD, Kyoto U., 1991. Assoc. prof. Gunma U. Inst. Molecular and Cellular Regulation, 1999—. Office: 3-39-15 Showamachi Maebashi Gunma 371-8512 Japan Business E-Mail: kubohara@showa.gunma-u.ac.jp.

KUBOTA, HIROSHI, cardiac surgeon; b. Kofu, Yamanashi, Japan, Nov. 9, 1961; s. Teruo and Tokiko Kubota; m. Yumiko Iwaki, June 21, 1992; children: Mayuko, Yugo. MD, Tsukuba U., Ibaraki, 1986. Diplomate 1995, cert. specialist of surgery 1990, specialist of cardiac surgery 1994. Intern Tokyo U., 1986—87, resident, 1990—94, instr., 1994—96, 1998—2001, assoc. prof., 2001—02; resident Tokyo Met. Police Hosp., 1987—90; spl. intern Clermont-Ferrand Univ., Auvergne, France, 1996—98; assoc. prof. Kyorin U., 2002—. Contbr. articles to profl. jours. Grantee Sci. Rsch. grantee, Japanese Min. of Edn., 1999, 2000, 2001—, grantee for arrhythmia treatment, Japanese Heart Found. and Pfizer, 2000. Office: U Kyorin Dept Cardiovascular Surgery 6-20-2 Shinkawa Mitaka Tokyo 181-8611 Japan Home Phone: 81-3-3483-1047; Office Phone: 81-422-47-5511, 81-422-47-7587. Home Fax: 81-3-3483-1247. Business E-Mail: kub@kyorin-u.ac.jp.

KUBOTA, KEISUKE, oncologist, surgeon; b. Taraki Kuma, Kumamoto, Japan, Apr. 18, 1966; MD, U. Tokyo, 1985, PhD, 1991. Cert. Japan Surg. Soc., 1995, Japanese Soc. Gastroent. Surgery, 1998, Japan Gastroent. Endoscopy Soc., 2000, Japan Soc. Gastroenterology, 2005. Resident Nat. Cancer Ctr. Hosp., Chuo-ku, Tokyo, 1995—98; asst. prof. Tokyo U. Hosp., Bunkyo-ku, Tokyo, 1998—2005; lectr. Internat. U. Health and Welfare Mita Hosp., Minato-ku, Tokyo, 2005—. Contbr. scientific papers, articles to profl. jours. Named Most Excellent Lectr., Forum of Gastrointestinal Disease, 2004; grantee, Ministry of Edn., Culture, Sports, Sci. and Tech., 2001—. Master: Tokyo UGI Soc.; mem.: Japanese Soc. Abdominal Emergency Medicine, Japan Soc. Clin. Oncology, Japan Esophageal Soc., Japanese Gastric Cancer Assn., Japanese Soc. Gastroenterology, Japan Gastroent. Endoscopy Soc., Japanese Soc. Gastroent. Surgery, Japan Surg. Soc. Office: IUHW Mita Hosp Mita 1-4-3 Minato-ku Tokyo 108-8329 Japan Office Fax: +81-3-3454-0067. E-mail: kubota@iuhw.ac.jp.

KUBOTA, KIYOSHI, physician; b. Tokyo, Dec. 1, 1952; s. Sakae and Chie (Masuda) Kubota; m. Noriko Yamada, July 26, 1991; 1 child, Junko. MD, Hokkaido U., Sapporo, Japan, 1978. Lic. physician, Japan. Resident Hokkaido U., Sapporo, 1978—83; rsch. fellow Clin. Rsch. Inst. Nat. Med. Ctr., Tokyo, 1983—84; rotating intern Nat. Med. Ctr., Tokyo, 1984—86; rsch. assoc. Clin. Rsch. Inst. Nat. Med. Ctr., Tokyo, 1986—89; rsch. fellow U. Calif., San Francisco, 1989—91; vis. colleague Drug Safety Rsch. Unit, Southampton, England, 1991—94, hon. rsch. fellow, 1994—96, hon. sr. rsch. fellow, 2001—; assoc. prof. phamacoepidemiology U. Tokyo, 1996—2008, prof. pharmacoepidemiology, 2008—. Chmn. bd. trustees Drug Safety

Rsch. Unit Japan, 2001—. Contbr. articles to profl. jours. Grantee Yasuda Meml. Scholarship, Tokyo, 1989, The British Coun. Tokyo, 1991. Office: U Tokyo Dept Pharmacoepidem 7-3-1 Hongo Bunkyo-ku Tokyo 113-8655 Japan Office Phone: 81-3815-5411 Ext. 35821, 81338155411. Office Fax: 81-3-5802-3323. Business E-Mail: kubotape-tky@umin.ac.jp.

KUBOTA, SATOSHI, dentist, researcher; PhD, Kyoto U., 1990. Diplomate dental Ministry Health and Welfare, Japan, 1990. Adj. rsch. asst. prof. Thomas Jefferson U., Phila., 1999—; assoc. prof. Okayama U., Japan, 2004—. Author: (scientific book) International Review of Cytology (award). Recipient Jr. Investigator award, Thomas Jefferson U., 1996; Rsch. grant, Japan Soc. Promotion Sci., 1999—. Master: Japanese Soc. Cartilage Metabolism. Achievements include patents for preventing human immunodeficiency virus infection. Office: Okayama Univ 2-5-1 Shikata-cho kita-ku Okayama 700-8525 Japan Office Fax: 81 86 235 6649. Business E-Mail: kubota1@md.okayama-u.ac.jp.

KUBOTA, TAKEHIKO, periodontist, educator; b. Niigata, Japan, Oct. 24, 1967; DDS, Niigata U., 1992, PhD, 1996. Assoc. prof. Dept. Periodontology, Niigata Med. and Dental Hosp., 2005—. Office: 2-5274 Gakko-cho St Chuo Ward Niigata 951-8102 Japan Office Fax: 81252280808. Business E-Mail: kubota@dent.niigata-u.ac.jp.

KUCEROVA, HELENA, psychiatrist; b. Olomouc, Czechoslovakia, Apr. 18, 1949; d. Jan and Marta (Svejnarova) Kucera. MD, Coll. Medicine, Olomouc, Czech Republic, 1974; diploma in Psychiatry level I, Prague, 1979, diploma in Psychiatry level II, 1983. Diplomate of Medicine, Psychiatry. Asst. lectr. Coll. Medicine, Hradec Kralove, Czech Republic, 1974-76; med. registrar Mental Tchg. Hosp., Hradec Kralove, 1976-83; jr. cons. Mental Hosp., Brno, 1983-86, Sternberk, 1986-90; outpatient psychiatrist cons. pvt. practice, Hranice na Morave, 1991—. Contbr. articles to profl. jours. Author: Dementia in Casuistics Grada, 2006, Schizophrenia in Casuistics Granda, 2010. Recipient Lifetime Achievement award, IBC, 2002, Honorary DG, 2006. Mem.: Czech Psychia.c Soc., Czech Med. Chamber, N.Y. Acad. Scis. Avocations: music, painting, architecture, photography. Office: MUDr Kucerova Helena Svatoplukova 10 753 01 Hranice Czech Republic Office Phone: 0420-581-601-602. Office Fax: 0420-581-601-602. Business E-Mail: hlnkucerova@seznam.cz.

KUCHAN, ANTHONY MARK, psychologist, educator; b. Canton, Ill., Apr. 21, 1930; s. Anthony Mark Sr. and Loraine Vesta (Walker) K.; m. Martha Katherine VeDepo, May 9, 1953; children: Mark, Cathryn, Christine, Susanne, Jeanne. BA, St. Ambrose Coll., 1952; MA, Bradley U., 1955; PhD, Purdue U., 1964. Lic. psychologist, Wis. Jr. engr. Caterpillar Tractor Inc., Peoria, Ill., 1952-54, psychometrist Bradley U. Guidance Ctr., 1954-55; tchg. asst. psychol. clinic Purdue U., West Lafayette, Ind., 1955-57; intern in psychology Galesburg State Rsch. Hosp., Ill., 1957-58, psychologist adolescent unit Ill., 1958-60; instr. psychology Marquette U., Milw., 1960-64, asst. prof. psychology, 1964-97, assoc. dean grad. sch., 1967—72, chair dept. psychology, 1977—87. Cons. St. Charles Youth and Family Svcs., Milw., 1964—, cons. psychologist House of The Good Shepherd/Cedarcrest Girl's Residence, 1965-72; founding mem., clin. prof. Wis. Sch. Profl. Psychology, 1978—; psychol. cons. Wis. Province, Soc. Jesus, 1979—. Pres. parish coun. St. Catherine Parish, Milw., 1971-73, 90-91, lector and communion distributor, 1968—; chair Milw. Archbishop's Spl. Commn., 2002; mem. Archdiocesan Rev. Bd., 2003—. Recipient All Univ. Pere Marquette Tchg. award, 1994, Lifetime Achievement award, Milw. Area Psychol. Assn., 2011, Fellow Wis. Psychol. Assn. (ethics com. chair 1976-89, ombudsman/profl.issues com. 1989—, Disting. Profl. Svc. award 1984); mem. APA, AAUP (chpt. pres. 1975-76), Nat. Register Health Svc. Providers in Psychology, Wis. Psychol. Assn., Milw. Area Psychol. Assn.(lifetime Achievement award 2011), Brown Deer Tennis Team (capt. 4.0 state league 1990-2006), Danihy Alumni Club, Alpha Sigma Nu-Nat. Jesuit Hon. Soc. (chpt. pres. 1996-2003, Lifetime Svc. award 2009). Roman Cath. Avocations: tennis, fishing, gardening, piano. Home: 5760 W Green Brook Dr Brown Deer WI 53223-2333 Office: Marquette Univ Dept Psychology PO Box 1881 Milwaukee WI 53233-1881 Office Phone: 414-288-7219. Personal E-mail: tonykuchan@aol.com.

KUCHARCZUK, JOHN CHARLES, thoracic surgeon; MD, U. Pa., 1992. Diplomate Am. Bd. Thoracic Surgery, Am. Bd. Surgery, lic. Pa., 1994. Intern gen. surgery Pa. Hosp., 1993, resident gen. surgery, 1999, resident cardiothoracic surgery, 2001, hosp. affiliations includes, interim chief divsn. of thoracic surgery, edn1. coord. thoracic surgery; assoc. prof. surgery Univ. Pa. Named one of Best Doctors in America, 2007—08, 2009—10, Top Physicians, Suburban Life Mag., 2010, Top Doctors, Phila. Mag., 2010—. Fellow: ACS; mem.: Soc. of Thoracic Surgeons, Sigma Xi Sci. Rsch. Study, Pa. Assn. for Thoracic Surgery. Office: Pennsylvania Hospital Garfield Duncan Bldg Ste 305 700 Spruce St Philadelphia PA 19106 Office Phone: 800-789-7366.

KUCHEKAR, BHANUDAS SHANKARRAO, pharmaceutical chemistry educator, researcher; b. Pusegaon, Maharashtra, India, Apr. 8, 1955; s. Shankarrao Krishnaji Kuchekar and Narmada Shankarrao Kuchekar; m. Sanjivani Bhanudas Kuchekar, Mar. 20, 1983; Ashwin, Shantanu. B in Pharmacy, Govt. Coll. of Pharmacy, 1978; LLB, New Law Coll., 1983; M in Pharmacy, Poona Coll. Pharmacy, 1988; FIC (hon.), Indian Inst. of Chemists, 1994. Chartered chemist Indian Inst. of Chemists. Asst. lectr. Poona Coll. of Pharmacy, Pune, India, 1978-79, lectr., 1979-91; asst. prof., head dept. pharm. chemistry Govt. Coll. of Pharmacy, Karad, India, 1991—. Assoc. cons. Mitcon Ltd., Pune, 1984-90; advisor student chpt. ISTE, Karad, India, 1993-97; chmn. bd. studies pharmacy Marathwada U., 1997-99; faculty of pharmacy Maharashtra U. of Health Scis., Nashik, 1999—; mem. bd. studies Pharmacy Shivaji U., Kolhapur, 1994—. Author: Pharmaceutical Jurisprudence, 1993, Concise Inorganic Pharmaceutical Chemistry, 1985; contbr. articles to profl. jours. including Indian Drugs, 1994, Eastern Pharmacist. Mem. Ahilyadevimandal, Pune, 1990—. Fellow Instn. of Chemists India; mem. Indian Pharm. Assn. (life), Gazetted Officer's Club (life), Assn. of Pharm. Tchrs. of India (life) Indian Soc. for Clin. Pharmacology and Therapeutics (life), Indian Soc. for Tech. Edn. (life). Achievements include research on dissolution technology in pharmaceutical science; development of methods for drug analysis. Home: Atharva A-2 OM Colony Vidyanagar Karad 415 124 Maharashtra India Office: Govt Coll Pharm Vidyanagar Dist Satara 415 124 Maharashtra India Fax: 91-02164-271196. E-mail: bskuchekar2000@yahoo.com.

KUCHER, TARAS, surgeon; b. St. Petersburg, Russia, Sept. 17, 1971; MD, Pavlov State U., 1995; degree in Vascular Surgery, Beth Israel Hosp., Newark, 2005. Ptnr. So. Conn. Vascular Ctr., 2005—. Recipient 1st, Internat. Congress Soc. Endovascular Specialists. Mem.: Soc. Vascular Surgeons. Avocations: tennis, hiking. Office: 999 Silver Ln Ste 2B Trumbull CT 06611 Personal E-mail: taraskucher@yahoo.com.

KUCHERLAPATI, RAJU, geneticist, educator; m. Melanie Haas; 1 child, David H. MS (hon.), Harvard U., Cambridge, Mass.; PhD, U. Ill., Urbana, 1972. Chmn. Albert Einstein Coll. Medicine, Bronx, NY, 1989—2001; Paul C. Cabot prof. genetics Harvard Med. Sch., Boston, 2001—; sci. dir. Harvard Partners Ctr. for Genetics and Genomics Brigham and Women's Hosp., Boston. Mem. bd. dirs. Millennium Pharm., Cambridge, 1993—2008. Fellow: AAAS; mem.: Inst. Medicine, NAS. Office: Harvard Med Sch 77 Ave Louis Pasteur Boston MA 02115 E-mail: rkucherlapati@partners.org.

KUCHNER, EUGENE FREDERICK, neurosurgeon, neuroscientist, educator; b. NYC, 1945; s. Morton H. and Edna Estelle Kuchner; m. Joan Ruth Freedman, Sept. 2, 1968; children: Marc Jason, Eric Benjamin. AB, Johns Hopkins U., 1967; MD, U. Chgo., 1971. Diplomate Am. Bd. Neurol. Surgery, Am. Bd. Med. Examiners. Resident in surgery Yale U. Sch. Medicine, New Haven, 1971—72; postdoc. fellow Yale U., New Haven, 1972; resident in neurosurgery Montreal Neurol. Inst., McGill U., Que., Canada, 1972—76, spine fellow, 1976; neurosurgeon SUNY Downstate Sch. Medicine, Bklyn., 1976—79, SUNY Sch. Medicine, Stony Brook, 1979—97, assoc. prof., 1983—, acting chief neurosurgery, 1979—81; cons. neurosurgeon North Shore U. Hosp./NYU Sch. Medicine, 1997—99. Mem. staff North Shore U. Hosp.-Cornell Med. Ctr., 1977—97, cons. surgeon, 1992—97; mem. neurosurgery attending staff Univ. Hosp., Stony Brook, 1979—97, Nassau County Med. Ctr., 1977—2000, St. John's Episcopal Hosp., 1976—99, Mt. Sinai-NYU Health Sys., 1997—; clin. assoc. prof. neurosurgery Cornell U. Med. Coll., NY, 1990—97. Contbr. articles to profl. publs.; specialist in microsurgery, magnetic resonance imaging, spinal trauma, pituitary surgery. Recipient K.G. McKenzie Meml. award, Royal Coll. Physicians and Surgeons Can., 1976, Open Scholarship award, Johns Hopkins U., yearly, 1963—66, Scholarship award, U. Chgo., yearly, 1967—70; fellow, NSF, Blackman-Hoffman Found., 1969—70; NSF chemistry fellow, MIT, 1968, USPHS fellowship, Divsn. Epidemiology Columbia U. Sch. Pub. Health, N.Y.C., 1969. Fellow ACS; mem. AMA, Am. Assn. Neurol. Surgeons, Congress Neurol. Surgeons, NY Acad. Scis., LI Neurosci. Acad., Suffolk Acad. Medicine, Montreal Neurol. Ins. Fellows Soc., NY State Neurosurg. Soc., NY State Med. Soc., NY State Soc. Surgeons, Am. Coll. Med. Quality, Healthcare Info. and Mgmt. Sys. Soc., Am. Epilepsy Soc., Am. Soc. Law Medicine and Ethics, Nat. Alumni Schs. Com. Johns Hopkins U., Yale Surg. Soc., Yale Club NYC, Princeton Club NY, John Hopkins Club, Sigma Xi. Office: Stony Brook Med Ctr PO Box 771 Stony Brook NY 11790-0721

KUDO, TOSHIFUMI, surgeon, researcher; b. Ajisu, Yamaguchi, Japan, Jan. 25, 1968; s. Takao and Kimiko Kudo; m. Sonoe Mitake, July 10, 1994; children: Yukari, Asuka. MD, PhD, Tokyo Med. and Dental U., 1993. Diplomate Japan Surgical Bd., lic. physician Japan. Attending surgeon Tokyo Med. and Dental U. Hosp., 2002—03, 2006—; endovascular rsch. fellow UCLA Gonda Vascular Ctr., 2003—06. Contbr. scientific papers to profl. jours. Recipient World Coll. Vascular Diseases prize, Internat. Congress of the Asian Vascular Soc., 2002. Mem.: Internat. Soc. Vascular Surgery (instl. rep. 2006—), Internat. Soc. Endovascular Specialists. Achievements include development of surgical devices. Business E-Mail: t-kudo.srg1@tmd.ac.jp.

KUDSK, KENNETH ALLAN, surgeon; b. Chgo., May 27, 1949; s. Kenneth and Hildegard Amanda (Toepel) K.; married. BA, U. Wis., 1971; MD, U. Ill., Chgo., 1975. Diplomate Am. Bd. Surgery, Am. Bd. Surg. Critical Care. Intern Ohio State U., Columbus, 1975-76, resident in surgery, 1977-79, 81-83; fellow in trauma San Francisco Gen. Hosp., 1979-81. Co. dir. trauma svcs. Ohio State U., 1983-87, dir. nutrition support svcs., 1984-87, asst. prof. surgery, 1983-87; staff Regional Med. Ctr., Memphis; assoc. prof. surgery U. Tenn., 1987-93, dir. surg. rsch., 1988-2001, assoc. prof. anesthesiology, 1989-2001, prof. surgery 1993-2001, prof. emergency medicine, 1994-2001; dir. nutrition support svcs. William F. Bowld Hosp., Memphis, 1995-2001; dir. surg. intensive care Regional Med. Ctr., Memphis, 1991-2001, nutrition support svcs.; prof. surgery U. Wis., Madison, 2001—. Contbr. over 300 articles to profl. jours., chpts. to books. Fellow ACS; mem. Am. Surg. Assn., Am. Assn. for Surgery of Trauma, Am. Soc. for Parenteral and Enteral Nutrition, Assn. for Acad. Surgery, Shock Soc., Surg. Infection Soc., S.E. Surg. Congress, Soc. Internat. de Chirurgie, Ea. Assn. for the Surgery of Trauma, Soc. of Mucosal Immunology, Soc. Critical Care Medicine, Soc. for Surgery of Alimentary Tract, Soc. Univ. Surgeons, So. Surg. Assn. Lutheran. Home: 125 N Hamilton St 1404 Madison WI 53703 Office Phone: 608-262-6246. E-mail: kudsk@surgery.wisc.edu.

KUEHL, W. MICHAEL, medical researcher; MD, Harvard U. Resident in internal medicine Case Western Res. U.; postdoctoral fellow NIH, Albert Einstein Coll. Medicine; from asst. prof. to prof. U. Va. Med. Sch., 1974—82; sr. investigator Nat. Cancer Inst., NIH, 1982, sr. investigator Genetics Br., head molecular pathogenesis of myeloma sect., Ctr. Cancer Rsch. Office: Genetics Br Ctr Cancer Rsch NNMC Bldg 8 Rm 5101 8901 Wisconsin Ave Bethesda MD 20889-5105 Office Phone: 301-435-5421. Office Fax: 301-496-0047. E-mail: wmk@helix.nih.gov. *

KUEHNER, MARVIN ERNEST, surgeon; b. Pflugerville, Tex., Oct. 12, 1934; s. Ernest Frank and Blanche Annie (Kilian) K.; m. Hope Stephanie Maki, Mar. 31, 1990; children: Mark, Jon, Daryl, Kathryn, Michael, David, Steven, Karolyn, Daniel. BS in Pharmacy, U. Tex., 1957; MD, Washington U., 1961. Diplomate Am. Bd. Surgery. Resident surgery Jewish Hosp., St. Louis, 1961-66; staff surgeon Interstate Med. Ctr., Red Wing, Minn., 1969-74, Marshfield Clinic, Wis., 1974—, chmn. salary com, 1983—93, mem. salary com., 1994—2008, dir. med. divsn., 2008—. Contbr. articles to profl. jours., 1994-2008 With AUS, 1966-69. Fellow ACS; mem. AMA, Soc. Vascular Surgery, Midwestern Vascular Surgery Soc., Midwest Surgical Assn Lutheran. Avocations: electronics, running, skiing, wood working. Office Phone: 715-389-3210. Business E-Mail: kuehner.marvin@marshfieldclinic.org.

KUES, IRVIN WILLIAM, financial planner; b. Balt., Apr. 23, 1936; s. Harry Irvin and Theresa Frances (Seliga) K.; m. Mary Carolyn Gaff, Oct. 24, 1959; Pamela, Janet, Lynne, Leslie. BS in Engring. Sci., Johns Hopkins U., 1957, M in Bus. Sci., 1959. Cert. data processer. Rsch. analyst Am. Newspaper Rsch. Inst., Chgo., 1957-59; mgmt. analyst Western Elec. Co., Balt., 1959-61; asst. supt. E.D.P. Bethlehem (Pa.) Steel Co., 1961-66; v.p. data processing Comml. Credit Corp., Balt., 1966-74; CFO Johns Hopkins Hosp., Balt., 1974-86, Johns Hopkins Health System, Balt., 1986-94; chmn. provider reimbursement rev. bd. U.S. Dept. HHS, Balt., 1994—. Bd. dirs. Francis Scott Key Hosp., Balt., Med. Svcs. Corp., Balt., Dome Corp., Balt., Med. Ctr. Ins. Co., Bermuda; mem. fin. coun. Md. Hosp. Assn., Towson; chmn. Health Svcs. Cost Rev. Commn., 2003—. Co-author: Yearbook of Healthcare Mgmt., 1991—. Advisor Villa Julie Coll., Stevenson, Md., 1991. Fellow Healthcare Fin. Mgmt. Assn.; mem. Healthcare Rate Coun., Ctr. Club. Avocations: tennis, golf, reading. Home: 17929 SE 85th Causton Ct The Villages FL 32162 Office Phone: 410-321-0109. Business E-Mail: kues1@msn.com. E-mail: ikues@verizon.net.

KUGLER, LANCE, ophthalmologist; b. Omaha, May 2, 1975; BA, DePauw U., 1997; MD, Case Western Res. U., 2001. Cataract and refractive surgeon First Eye Assocs. PC, 2005—09; cornea, refractive surgery fellow Wang Vision Inst., 2009—10; lasik and cataract surgeon Cornea Assocs. PC, 2010—. Dir. refractive surgery U. Nebr. Med. Ctr., 2010. Fellow: Am. Acad. Ophthalmology, Am. Bd. Ophthalmology; mem.: Cornea Soc., Internat. Soc. Refractive Surgery, Am. Soc. Cataract and Refractive Surgeons (Best Paper award). Avocations: skiing, golf, photography. Office: 13923 Gold Cir Omaha NE 68144 Business E-Mail: lkugler@me.com.

KUGUOGLU, SEMA, nursing educator; permanent resident, USA; d. Emin and Ummeti Yazici; m. Irfan Kuguoglu, Dec. 13, 1997; children: Ismail Hakki, Okan Eren. BS in Gen. Nursing, Istanbul U. Florence Nightingale Coll. Nursing, 1986; MS in Pediatric Nursing, Istanbul U. Health Sci. Inst., Dept. Pediat. Nursing, 1989; PhD in Nursing, Istanbul U. Health Sci. Inst., 1995. Rsch. asst. Marmara U. Vocat. Coll. Health Svcs. Nursing Dept., Istanbul, 1986—89, lectr., 1990—93; founder, mgr. Marmara U. Hosp. Nursing Svcs. Mgmt., 1988—90; lectr. Marmara U. Dept. Pediat. Nursing, 1993—96, asst. prof., 1996—98, assoc. prof., 1998—2006, prof., 2006—; emeritus prof. Marmara U., Health Sci. Faculty, Divsn. Nursing. Cons. Istanbul City Health Dept., 2007—. Contbr. articles. Fellow: European Soc. Paediat. & Neonatal Intensive Care; mem.: Pediat. Nursing Assn., Sigma Theta Tau Internat. Honor Nursing. Muslim. Avocation: travel. Home: 450 95th St B4 Brooklyn NY 11209 Personal E-mail: skuguoglu@gmail.com.

KUHL, DAVID EDMUND, nuclear medicine physician, educator; b. St. Louis, Oct. 27, 1929; s. Robert Joseph and Caroline Bertha (Waldermeyer) Kuhl; m. Eleanor Dell Kasales, Aug. 7, 1954; 1 child, David Nicholas. AB, Temple U., Phila., 1951; MD, U. Pa., 1955; LHD (hon.), Loyola U. Chgo., 1992. Diplomate Am. Bd. Radiology, Am. Bd. Nuc. Medicine (a founder; life trustee 1977-). Intern, then resident in radiology Sch. Medicine and Hosp. U. Pa., 1955—56, 1958—63, mem. faculty, 1963—76, chief div. nuc. medicine, 1963—76, prof. radiology, 1970—76, vice chmn. dept., 1975—76; prof. bioengring. Moore Sch. Elec. Engring. U. Pa., 1974—76; prof. radiol. scis. UCLA Sch. Medicine and Hosp., 1976—86, chief div. nuc. medicine, 1976—84, vice-chmn. dept., 1977—86; prof. internal medicine and radiology U. Mich. Sch. Medicine, Ann Arbor, 1986—2000, chief divsn. nuc. medicine, dir. Positron Emission Tomography Ctr., 1986—2002, prof. radiology, 2000—11, prof. emeritus. Disting. faculty lectr. in biomed. rsch. U. Mich. Med. Sch., 1992, Henry Russel lectr., 98; mem. adv. com. Dept. Energy, NIH, Internat. Commn. on Radiation Units and Measures, Max Planck Soc. Mem. editl. bd.: various jours.; contbr. articles to med. jours. Served as officer M.C. USNR, 1956—58. Recipient Rsch. Career Devel. award, USPHS, 1961—71, Ernst Jung prize for medicine, Jung Found., Hamburg, 1981, Emil H. Grubbe gold medal, Chgo. Med. Soc., 1983, Berman Found. award peaceful uses atomic energy, 1985, Steven C. Beering award for advancement med. sci., Ind. U., 1987, Disting. Grad. award, U. Pa. Sch. Medicine, 1988, William C. Menninger Meml. award, ACP, 1989, Javits Neurosci. Investigator award, NIH, 1989, Charles F. Kettering prize, GM Cancer Rsch. Found., 2001, Japan prize, Japan Prize Found., 2009, Gold medal, Am. Roentgen Ray Soc., 2010, John Scott award, City Trusts Phila., 2011. Fellow: Am. Inst. for Med. and Biol. Engring., Am. Coll. Nuc. Medicine, Am. Coll. Radiology; mem.: Inst. Medicine Nat. Acad. Scis., Am. Neurol. Assn. (Foster Elting Bennett Meml. lectr. 1981), Soc. Nuc. Medicine (ann. lectr. 1991, Nuc. Pioneer citation 1976, Disting. Scientist award 1981, Herman L. Blumgart, M.D. Pioneer award 1979, George Charles de Hevesy Nuc. Medicine Pioneer award 1995, Benedict Cassen prize for rsch. 1996), Radiol. Soc. N.Am. (ann. orator 1982, Outstanding Rschr. award 1996), Assn. Univ. Radiologists, Assn. Am. Physicians, Alpha Omega Alpha. Office: U Mich Hosp Divsn Nuc Medicine 1500 E Medical Center Dr Ann Arbor MI 48109-0028 Business E-Mail: dkuhl@umich.edu.

KUHL, PATRICIA K., science educator; b. Mitchell, SD, Nov. 5, 1946; d. Joseph John and Susan Mary (Schaeffer) K.; m. Andrew N. Meltzoff, Sept. 28, 1985; 1 child, Katherine. BA, St. Cloud State U., Minn., 1967; MA, U. Minn., 1971, PhD, 1973. Postdoctoral research assoc. Cen. Inst. for Deaf, St. Louis, 1973-76; from rsch. assoc. to prof. U. Wash., Seattle, 1976—82, prof., 1982—, William P. and Ruth Gerberding prof., 1997—, dept. chair, 1994—, dir. Inst. Learning and Brain Scis., 2003—. Gov. bd. Am. Inst. Physics, 1994-96; trustee Neurosci. Rsch. Found., 1994—; bd. dirs. Wash. Tech. Ctr., U. Wash., 1994-96; invited presenter White House Conf. on Early Learning and the Brain, 1997, Early Childhood Cognitive Devel., 2001. Editor Jour. Neurosci., 1989-96. Recipient Women in Research citation Kennedy Council, 1978, Virginia Merrill Bloedel Scholar award, 1992-94. Fellow AAAS, Am. Psychol. Soc., Acoustical Soc. Am. (assoc. editor Jour. 1988-92, chair medals and awards, 1992-94, v.p. 1997, Silver medal 1997, pres. 1999—); mem. NAS, Am. Acad. Arts and Scis. Office: Inst Learning and Brain Sci Dept Speech & Hearing Sciences 357988 Seattle WA 98105-6247 Office Phone: 206-685-1921. Business E-Mail: pkkuhl@u.washington.edu.

KUHLER, DEBORAH GAIL, grief therapist, former state legislator; BA, Dakota Wesleyan U., 1974; MA, U. N.D., 1977. Cert. profl. counselor, lic. prof. coun. SD Bd. of Coun. Examiners, 1992, cert. in Thanatology Assoc. for Death Edn. and Counceling, 2003. Outpatient therapist Ctr. for Human Devel., Grand Forks, ND, 1975-77; mental health counselor Community Counseling Services, Huron, SD, 1978-88, 91-93; owner, dir. bereavement svcs. Kuhler Funeral Home, Huron, 1978—; adj. prof. Huron U., 1979—83, 1990—2002; mem. from dist. 23 S.D. Ho. Reps., Pierre, 1987-90; mem. House Judiciary com., chair House Health and Welfare Com., Pierre, 1990. Active First United Meth. Ch. Named Young Alumnus of Yr., Dakota Wesleyan U., 1989, Woman of Yr. Bus. and Profl. Women, 1989. Mem. ACA, PEO, Am. Mental Health Counselors Assn., Assn. for Death Edn. and Counseling. Methodist. Avocations: reading, sewing, piano, quilting. Office Phone: 605-352-4234.

KUHLMAN, JEFFREY, chief White House physician, military officer; B, So. Adventist U., Collegedale, Tenn., 1983; MD, Loma Linda U. Med. Ctr., Calif., 1987. Internship and residency Loma Linda U. Med. Ctr.; fellowship John Hopkins Hosp., Balt.; Navy physician through the grades to capt. US Navy, deployments to Calif., Hawaii and London, Eng.; sr. flight surgeon Marine Helicopter Squadron One; White House physician White House Mil. Office, Washington, 2001—09, physician to the Pres. of US, dir. of White House Med. Unit, chief White House physician, 2009—. Office: White House Med Unit c/o White House Mil Office 1600 Pennsylvania Ave NW Washington DC 20500 *

KUHLMANN, MARTIN K., nephrologist, diabetologist, researcher; b. Göttingen, Germany, Nov. 11, 1959; s. Horst Werner and Charlotte Kuhlmann. MD, Med. Sch., U. Freiburg, Germany, 1986. Cert. internist State of Saarland, Homburg, Germany, 1985, nephrologist 1998, diabetologist State of Berlin, 2007. Asst. prof. medicine and nephrology U. Saarland, 2000—03, 2005—06; vis. prof. medicine Albert Einstein Coll. Medicine, NYC, 2003—05; clin. rsch. lab. dir. Renal Rsch. Inst., NYC, 2003—05; dir. divsn. nephrology Vivantes Klinikum im Friedrichshain, Berlin, 2006—. Mem.: Am. Soc. Nephrology. Achievements include development of EFFICACY software and a phosphate education program fro dialysis patients. Office: Vivantes Klinikum im Friedrichshain Landsberger Allee 49 Berlin 10249 Germany Office Phone: 49-30-13023-1322. Office Fax: 49-30-130232046. Business E-Mail: martin.kuhlmann@vivantes.de.

KUHN, ANNEGRET, dermatologist, researcher, educator; d. Heinz-Wolfgang and Ursula Kuhn; MD, U. Munich, 1994. Lic. dermatologist U. Duesseldorf, 2001. Resident dept. dermatology, U. Duesseldorf, Germany, 1994—99; lise-meitner-scholar Inst. Cell Biology, Ctr. for Molecular Biology Inflammation, U. Muenster, Germany, 1999—2002; sr. staff fellow dept. dermatology, U. Duesseldorf, 2002, asst. prof., 2003; Heisenberg assoc. prof. Max-Planck-Inst. Molecular Biomedicine, Muenster, Germany, 2004—05, German Cancer Rsch. Ctr., Heidelberg, Germany, 2005—08; prof. dept. dermatology U. Duesseldorf, Germany, 2007—08; prof. Dept. Dermatology U. Muenster, Germany, 2008—. Lise-Meitner scholarship, Ministerium für Wissenschaft und Forschung, NRW, 1999—2002, Heisenberg scholarship, German Rsch. Found., 2004—08. Office: Dept Dermatology Von-Esmarch-Strasse 58 Muenster D-48149 Germany Business E-Mail: kuhnan@uni-muenster.de.

KUHN, KLAUS A., medical educator, writer; m. Birgitta M Kuhn; children: Alexander M., Sebastian B., Christopher B. Diploma in Informatics, U.Stuttgart, Germany, 1977; Diploma in Math., U. Stuttgart, Germany, 1977; MD, U. Freiburg, Germany, 1984. Physician, scientist U. Heidelberg, Germany, 1983—84; lectr. U. Ulm, Germany, 1993, physician, scientist, 1985—96; prof. med. informatics Philipps U., Marburg, Germany, 1996—2004, Tech. U., Munich, 2004—. Mem. editl. bd.: Methods of Info. in Medicine, 2002—; mem. editl. bd. Internat. Jour. Med. Info., 2003—; editor: MEDINFO Proceedings, 2007; contbr. articles to profl. jours. and books. Fellow: Am. Coll. Med. Inform.; mem.: German Assn. Comp. Sci. (co-chair, sect. life sci. 2007—), German Assn. Med. Inform (pres. 2007—09, v.p. 2009—11). Business E-Mail: klaus.kuhn@tum.de.

KUHN, MARK D., gynecologist, obstetrician; married; 3 children. Grad., U. Pa.; MD, U. Medicine and Dentistry of NJ-Sch. Health Related Prof, 1985. Diplomate Am. Bd. Ob-Gyn. With Ctr. for Women's Health, 1995—; staff mem. St. Mary Med. Ctr., Langhorne, Pa., Lower Bucks Hosp., Bristol. Named one of Top Doctors, Phila. mag., 2006, 2007, 2008. Avocations: skiing, hiking, bicycling, camping. Office: Lower Bucks Hospital 501 Bath Rd Bristol PA 19007 Office Phone: 215-785-9200.

KÜHNE, GERT-EBERHARD, psychiatrist, educator; b. Breslau, Germany, July 25, 1936; s. Paul and Margarete (Nawroth) K.; m. Rosemarie Heid, June 4, 1975; 1 child, Katharina. MD, Martin Luther U., Halle-Wittenberg, Germany, 1960, PD, 1969, DMS, 1972. Assoc. prof. Martin Luther U., 1970-73; prof., dir. psychiat. clinic Med. Acad., Magdeburg, Germany, 1974-83, Hans Berger Clinic, Friedrich Schiller U., Jena, Germany, 1983-92; prof., head divsn. substance abuse Psychosomatic Clinic, Bad Blankenburg, 1993-97, prof., sen. psychiat. Bad Soden Ts, Germany, 1998—99, Orb Sp, Germany, 2000—01, Bad Wildungen, Germany, 2002—06. Pres.-elect Curatorium Psychiat. Danube Symposia, Linz, Austria, 1980-82; cons. WHO-Expert Adv. Panel of Mental Health, Geneva, 1981-97, joint project on diagnosis and classification alcohol, drug abuse, mental health adminstrn. WHO investigator group composit internat. diagnostic interview, Geneva, 1981-97; dir. State Project Rsch. Group Psychoneurol. Disorders, Magdeburg, 1981-83; mem. Curatorium Rudolf Steiner Acad., Weimar-Taubach, Germany, 1999—2004. Author: (with J.U. Grünes and G. Koselowski) The Structured Psychopathological Evaluation System, 1983 (State Rsch. award 1984); editor: (with H. Klepel and J. Molcan) Neurobiological Aspects in Psychiatry, 1984, (with R.J. Vovin) Psychopharmacotherapeutic Bases in Rehabilitation of Mental Disorders, 1989, (with H.D. Brenner and G. Huber) Cognitive Therapy in Schizophrenics, 1990. Recipient Karl Bonhoeffer medal Assn. Psychiatry and Neurology of Germany, 1986, Albert Schweitzer medal Austrian Assn. Albert Schweitzer, 1991. Mem. Psychiat. Assn. Purkyne (corr.), Internat. Brain Rsch. Orgn., German Assn. Psychiatry, Psychotherapy and Nerve Sci., St. Andrew Vol. Corps (hon.), Souvereign Order St. John Jerusalem (Knight of Honor 1992—). Evangelical Lutheran. Home: Hausbergstrasse 1 07749 Jena Germany E-mail: gert.e.kuhne@web.de.

KUIKEN, TODD ALAN, medical researcher, rehabilitation services professional, educator; b. Champaign, Ill., Mar. 28, 1960; m. Lisa Bierman. BS in Biomedical Engring., Duke U., 1983; PhD in Biomedical Engring., Northwestern U., 1989, MD Northwestern U. Med. Sch., Chgo., 1990. Diplomate Am. Bd. Of Phys. Medicine And Rehab. Intern, physical medicine and rehab. Evanston Hosp., Ill.,

1991; resident, physical medicine and rehab. Rehab. Inst. Chgo./Northwestern U. Med. Sch., 1992—95, Frankel Rsch. fellow Ill., 1992; dir. of amputee svcs. Rehab. Inst. Chgo., 1999—, vice chief staff Ill., 2000—01, chief of staff, 2001—03, dir. neural engring. ctr. for artificial limbs, 2004—; asst. prof., phys. medicine and rehab. Northwestern U. Feinberg Sch. Medicine, Chgo., 1997—2004, assoc. prof., dept. physical medicine and rehab., 2004—, assoc. dean, 2003—; assoc. dean of academic affairs Rehab. Inst. Chgo., Feinberg Sch. Medicine, 2002—; asst. prof., dept. biomedical engring. Northwestern U., 2005—. Bd. dirs. Rehab. Inst. Of Chgo., 2001—03. Recipient Sarah Bakin Rsch. award, 1995, Scholl Recognition award for rehab. rsch., 1995, Da Vinci award for Innovated Engring., Nat. Multiple Sclerosis Soc., 2005, Grand award winner for Best Tech. of 2005, Popular Sci. Mag., 2005; named one of Breakthrough Doctors, Chgo. Mag., 2003, Best Doctors in Chgo., 2004, Top Doctors in Chgo., Chgo. Hosp. News, 2004;, NIH grantee, 2003—. Mem.: Internat. Soc. Prosthetics and Orthotics (Best paper, runner-up IX World Congress, Internat. Soc. for Prosthetics and Orthotics, Amsterdam, Netherlands 1998), IEEE, Assn. Academic Physiatrists, Am. Acad. Physical Medicine and Rehab. (chmn. prosthetics & orthotics, wheelchairs & human biomechanics group 1997—99), Am. Acad. of Orthotists and Prosthetists. Achievements include patents for stand up wheelchair. Home: 1220 Forest Ave Oak Park IL 60302 Office: Rehab Inst Chicago 345 E Superior Rm 1309 Chicago IL 60611 also: Northwestern Univ Feinberg Sch Medicine RIC 1309 303 East Chicago Ave Chicago IL 60611-3008 Office Fax: 312-238-1166. E-mail: tkuiken@rehabchicago.org, tkuiken@northwestern.edu.

KUIPER, MICHAEL ALEXANDER, neurologist, researcher; b. Amsterdam, Oct. 1, 1960; s. Tiny Kuiper-Mook and George Kuiper; m. Clasien Van Der Houwen; children: Boris Cornelis, Lucie Andrea. MD, Free U. Amsterdam, 1990, PhD, 2001. Cert. neurologist Netherlands Soc. Neurology, 1999, intensivist Netherlands Soc. Intensive Care medicine, 2001. Med. dir. Med. Ctr. Leeuwarden, Netherlands, 2002—05, dir., rsch., 2005—. Mem., sci. coun. Netherlands Resuscitation Coun., Bilthoven, Netherlands, 2007—. Editor: (book) Die Another Day, Reducing ICU Mortality, jour. Initiator, sec. Hermes Ciritical Care Group, Amsterdam, 2005. Fellow: Am. Coll. Chest Physicians, Soc. Critical Care Medicine; mem.: Neurocritical Care Soc., Netherlands Soc. Neurology, Netherlands Soc. Intensive Care Medicine (chair 2005—), European Soc. Intensive Care Medicine. Achievements include research in measurement of nitrate and nitrite in cerebrospinal fluid. Avocations: music, travel, bicycling. Office: Med Ctr Leeuwarden Henri Dunantweg 2 Leeuwarden 8934 AD Netherlands Office Phone: 3158 2866737. Office Fax: 31 2866715.

KUIRY, SURESH CHANDRA, materials engineer, researcher; arrived in U.S., 2001; s. Kailash Chandra and Chanchala Kuiry; m. Pritikana Prasad, June 27, 1997; 1 child, Shounak. BEngring in Metall. Engring., Regional Engring. Coll., Durgapur, 1986; MTech in Metall. and Materials Engring., Indian Inst. Tech., Kharagpur, India, 1991, PhD in Metall. and Materials Engring., 1996. Metall. engr. Tata Motors, Jamshedpur, Bihar, India, 1986—89; asst. mgr. R&D Asea Brown Boveri Ltd., Vododara, Gujarat, India, 1996—96; mgr. R&D Mukand Ltd., Mumbai, Maharashtra, India, 1996—2001; rsch. assoc. U. Ctrl. Fla., Orlando, 2001—04; sr. rsch. scientist Ctr. for Tribology, Inc., Campbell, Calif., 2004—. Contbr. articles to profl. jours. Recipient Nat. Young Metallurgist award, Ministry Steel and Mines, Govt. India, 1998, U. Gold medal, U. Burdwan, India, 1986; Nat. Merit scholar, Govt. West Bengal, India, 1979. Mem.: Electrochem. Soc., Am. Ceramic Soc., Materials Rsch. Soc., Indian Inst. Metals (life; hon. sec. 1998—2000). Achievements include research in development of nanomaterials for biological applications such as anti-aging, aleviation of free radical cell damage, treatment age-related problems in humans. Mailing: 1395 Saratoga Ave Apt 18 San Jose CA 95129

KUITUNEN, MARKKU TAPIO, biologist, consultant, environmental science educator; b. Tyrväntö, Häme, Finland, Nov. 22, 1953; s. Paul Bernhard and Signe Irene (Taube) K.; m. Pirjo Irmeli Soini, Dec. 10, 1983 (div. 2005); children: Juho-Pekka, Selja Elina, Milja Maaria. MSc, U. Jyväskylä, Finland, 1982, PhD, 1989. Rschr. Ministry Agr. and Forestry, Helsinki, Finland, 1980-82; asst. prof. U. Jyväskylä, 1982-88, assoc. prof., 1988, prof., 1989—. Vis. prof. U. Minn., Duluth, 1996, 2005, Murdoch U. Perth, Western Australia, 2006; cons. City of Helsinki, 1992, 97; rschr. Internat. Inst. Cultural Edn., Budapest, Hungary, 1982-85.Ghana, 2005. Contbr. articles to profl. jours.; editor-in-chief Soc. Finnish Biologists Periodical Sci. Jour., 1982-85. Grantee Acad. of Finland, 1994, 96, 98, 2003, 05. Mem. Brit. Ecol. Soc., Soc. for Conservation Biology, Internat. Assn. Landscape Ecology, Int Assn. Impact Assessment Lutheran. Avocations: photography, birds on stamps, gardening. Office: U Jyväskylä PO Box 35 FIN40351 Jyväskylä Finland Business E-Mail: markku.kuitune@jyu.fi.

KUJI, ICHIEI, radiologist, educator; b. Tokyo, Apr. 14, 1964; MD, Kanazawa U., 1990, PhD, 1994. Assoc. prof., vice-dir. Saitama Internat. Med. Ctr., Saitama Med. U., 2004—. Assoc. editor Japanese Soc. Nuc. Medicine, 2009—, councilor, 2011—. Mem.: Lepidopterist Soc., Japanese Coll. Radiology, Soc. Nuc. Medicine, Japanese Soc. Radiology. Avocations: tennis, butterfly collecting. Office: 1397-1 Yamane Hidaka Saitama 350-1298 Japan Office Fax: 81-42-984-4146. Business E-Mail: kuji@saitama-med.ac.jp.

KUKIATTRAKOON, BOONLERT, dental educator; b. Hat Yai, Thailand, July 16, 1970; DDS (hon.), Prince Songkla U., Hat Yai, Songkhla, 1994; MS in Prosthodontics, Chulalongkorn U., Bangkok, 2000; LLB, Sukhothai Thammathirat Open U., Bangkok, 2001. Assoc. prof. Prince Songkla U., 2009—. Dep. head Dept. Adminstrn., 2009—. Sgt. 1st class Reserve Comdr. Unit. Recipient Knight Commander 2nd Class Noble Order Crown, Thailand. Mem.: Thai Dental Coun., Thai Dental Assn. Buddhist. Achievements include research in dental ceramic and tooth surface loss to improve human being. Avocations: football, chess, puzzles. Office: Kanchanavanich Rd 15 Songkhla 90112 Hat Yai Thailand Office Phone: 66-74-287703. Office Fax: 66-74-429877. Personal E-mail: boonlert.k@psu.ac.th.

KUKLENYIK, ZSUZSANNA, chemist, researcher; b. Nyiregyhaza, Hungary, May 15, 1963; d. Ferenc and Zsuzsanna Ferencne Mosolygo; m. Peter Kuklenyik, May 21, 1988; children: Andrea Ester, Elizabeth Clara, Daniel Ernest. MS in Chem. Engring., Tech. U. Budapest, 1987; PhD in Chemistry, Emory U., 1996. Rsch. assoc. Emory U., Atlanta, 1996—98; sr. rsch. scientist Centers for Disease Control and Prevention, Atlanta, 2001—. Mem. Cross Roads Cmty.

Ch., Lawrenceville, Ga., 2001—05. Avocation: tennis. Office: Centers for Disease Control and Prev 4770 Buford Highway MS: F-17 Atlanta GA 30341 Office Fax: 770-488-4609. Business E-Mail: zkuklenyik@cdc.gov.

KUKLINA, ELENA V., epidemiologist; d. Victor Kuklin and Nina Kuklina; m. Andrew Liashenko, 1994; children: Varvara Liashenko, Tamara Liashenko. MD, Urals State Med. Acad., Ekaterinburg, 1993; PhD, Emory U., Atlanta, 2004. Epidemiologist Ctrs. Disease Control and Prevention, Atlanta. Reviewer Jour. AMA, European Jour. Ob-Gyn., Med. Monitor, Jour. Stroke, Jour. Pediat., Jour. Nutrition, BJOG: Internat. Jour. Ob-Gyn., Jour. Clin. Epidemiology, Current Women's Health Reviews, Maternal and Child Health Jour., Jour. Women's Health. Contbr. articles to numerous profl. jours. Office: Ctrs Disease Control and Prevention 4770 Buford Hwy NE Mailstop K-47 Atlanta GA 30341 Office Phone: 770-488-6529. Business E-Mail: ekuklina@cdc.gov.

KUKURA, VLASTIMIR, gynecologist; b. Sibenik, Mar. 8, 1953; MD, Sch. Medicine, U. Zagreb, 1976. Assoc. prof. dept. ob-gyn. Sch. Medicine, U. Zagreb, 1997; chmn. dept. ob-gyn. Merkur U. Hosp., 2008. Master: Croatian Soc. Gynecol. Oncology; mem.: European Soc. Gynecol. Oncology. Office: Ivana Zajca 19 Zagreb 10000 Croatia Office Phone: 385 1 2431 391. Office Fax: 385 1 2431 391. Business E-Mail: vlastimir.kukura@zg.t-com.hr.

KULA, KATHERINE SUE, dentist; b. Dayton, Ohio, Oct. 5, 1945; d. James Adam and Adelaide Charlotte (Thaler) Miller; m. Theodore John Kula Jr., Aug. 2, 1969; children: Stacy Charlotte, Theodore John III. BS, U. Dayton, 1966, MS, 1972; DMD, U. Ky., 1977; MS, cert. in pediat. dentistry, U. Iowa, 1979. Cert. in orthodontics U. Md., 1992, diplomate Am. Bd. Orthodontics, 2005. Sci. tchr. Lexington Cath. HS, Ky., 1969-71, chmn. sci. dept., 1971-73; resident U. Iowa Dental Sch., Iowa City, 1977-79; asst. prof. U. Md. Dental Sch., Balt., 1979-84, assoc. prof., 1984-92; assoc. prof. dept. orthodontics and pediatric dentistry U. NC Dental Sch., Chapel Hill, 1992-97, adj. prof., 1998; chair dept. orthodontics & dentofacial orthopedics U. Mo., Kans. City, 1998—2007; chair dept. orthodontics & oral facial genetics Ind. U., Sch. Dentistry, Indpls., 2008—; Jarabak Endowed prof., 2009—. Mem. staff U. N.C. Hosp., Chapel Hill, 1992-97, dental faculty practice, 1992—97; mem. staff St. Luke's Hosp., Kansas City, Mo., 2003—07, Staff Craniofacial Team, Riley Hosp., Indpls.; outside grant reviewer NIH-NIDR, Washington, 1993—97; manuscript reviewer Pediatric Dentistry Jour., Chgo., Angle Orthodontist, Am. Jour. Ortho Dentofac Orthoped, World Jour. Orthop. Contbr. articles to profl. jour. and chpts. to books. Bd. dir. Bridges-Leadership for Women, Chapel Hill, 1995-96, Virginia Brown Found., Kansas City, 2002-07. Grantee NIH-Nat. Insts. Dental Rsch., 1994, 2009, Am. Assn. Dental Schs., 1997. Fellow Am. Coll. Dentists, Am. Acad. Pediatric Dentists (1st pl. table clinic ednl. rsch. 1994, Rsch. award 1980); mem. Md. Soc. Dentistry for Children (pres., sec.-treas. 1979-92), Am. Assn. Dental Rsch. (sec.-treas. Balt. sect. 1979-92, Am. Dental Edn. Assn. (sec., chair, councilor orthodontics sect. 1993-2001, mem.-at-large coun. of sects. 2001-02, sec. 2002, chair 2004, 1st pl. Rsch. award 2000, 1st pl. World Wide Web Instrnl. Materials 2002), Am. Assn. Orthodontists (rep. to Am. Assn. Dental Edn. Assn.), Internat. Assn. Dental Rsch., Coll. Diplomates, Am. Bd. Orthodontics. Avocation: gardening. Home: 7604 Peaking Fox Ln Indianapolis IN 46237

KULAKSIZOGLU, ISIN BARAL, psychiatrist, educator; b. Eskisehir, Turkey, Feb. 7, 1966; d. Huseyin and Semra Baral; m. Haluk Kulaksizoglu, Mar. 15, 1997; 1 child, Efe. Lic. specialist in psychiatriy Turkish Ministry Health, 1996. Assoc. prof. psychiatry Med. Sch. Istanbul (Turkey) U., 1999—2003; head Dept. Geriatric Psychiatry Med. Sch. Istanbul (Turkey) U., 2003—, prof. Med. Sch., 2003—; chmn. Dept. Psychiatry MedIstanbul Clinic, Istanbul, 2004—. Mem. adv. bd. Istanbul (Turkey) Met. Mcpl. Geriatric Support Project; co-dir. adv. bd. Alzheimer's Paltform, Istanbul, 2003—. Mem.: Turkish Alzheimer's Soc. (v.p. 2004—), Internatioal Psychogeritaric Assn., Am. Psychiat. Assn. Achievements include research in alzheimer's disease and geriatric depression. Office: Istanbul Univesity Medical Schoool Capa Istanbul 34310 Turkey Business E-Mail: isinbaral@yahoo.com.

KULICK, ROY G., orthopedist, surgeon, educator; MD, Cornell U., 1973. Diplomate Am. Bd. of Orthopedic Surgery, Am. Bd. of Orthopedic Surgery-hand surgery. Resident surgery St. Lukes-Roosevelt Hosp., 1974—75; resident orthopaedic surgery Columbia-Presbyn. Hosp., 1975—78; fellow hand surgery Hosp. for Spl. Surgery, 1978—79; assoc. prof. orthopaedic surgery Albert Einstein Coll. of Med.; with Montefiore Med. Ctr. Office: Montefiore Medical Center The Tower at Montefiore Medical Pk Fl 2 1695 Eastchester Rd Bronx NY 10461 Office Phone: 718-920-2060.

KULIKOWSKI, CASIMIR ALEXANDER, computer scientist, engineer, educator; b. Hertford, Herts, Eng., May 4, 1944; arrived in U.S., 1961; s. Victor A. and Isabel S. (Tuckett) Kulikowski; m. Christine A. Wilk, May 31, 1969; children: Michael Edward, Victoria Anne. BE with honors, Yale U., New Haven, Conn., 1965, MS, 1966; PhD, U. Hawaii, Manoa, 1970. From asst. prof. to assoc. prof. Rutgers U., New Brunswick, NJ, 1970—77, prof., 1977—97, chmn. dept. computer sci., 1984—90, dir. Lab. Computer Sci. Rsch., 1985—96, bd. govs. prof., 1997—. Mem. bd. sci. counselors Nat. Libr. Medicine, Bethesda, Md., 1984—87; mem. biomed. libr. rev. com. NIH, 1994—99, chair, 1997—99; co-chair sci. program com. World Congress on Med. Informatics, 2004. Author: A Practical Guide to Designing Expert Systems, 1984, Computer Systems that Learn, 1992; editor: Artificial Intelligence Expert Systems and Languages in Modeling & Simulation, 1988; co-editor: Yearbook of Medical Informatics, 2001—; assoc. editor: Artificial Intelligence in Medicine Jour., 2001—; mem. editl. bd. Jour. Am. Med. Informatics Assn., 1993—98, Methods Info. in Medicine, 1999—, Iterations: An Interdisciplinary Jour. Software History, 2001—05. Pres. Highland Park Residents Assn., NJ, 1983—88. Fellow: IEEE, AAAS, Am. Inst. Med. and Biol. Engring., Am. Coll. Med. Informatics, Am. Assn. Artificial Intelligence; mem.: Internat. Med. Informatics Assn. (v.p. 2007—), NAS Inst. Medicine. Office: Rutgers U Dept Computer Sci Hill Ctr Busch Campus New Brunswick NJ 08903 Office Phone: 732-445-2006.

KULIKOWSKI, JANUS JOSEPH, visual neuroscientist, educator; b. Warsaw, May 28, 1935; s. Jozef Kulikowski and Janina v. Karvat. MSc in Engring., Warsaw Tech. U., Poland, 1956; PhD in Tech.,

Polish Acad. Sci., Warsaw, 1962; PhD in Physiology, Nencki Inst. Exptl. Biology, Poland, 1970. Tchg. asst. Tech. U. Poznan, Poland, 1953—55; sci. officer, lectr. Polish Acad. Scis., Warsaw, 1956—70; Wellcome Rsch. fellow Physiol. Lab., Cambridge, England, 1970—71; lectr. gen. physiology U. Manchester, England, 1971—73; reader, dir. visual scis. dept. ophthalmic optics U. Manchester Inst. Sci. and Tech., 1974—89, prof. visual neurosci., optometry and neurosci., 1989—. Contbr. over 200 articles to profl. jours. Mem.: Royal Soc. Medicine, Brit. Neurosci. Assn., European Brain and Behaviour Soc., Fedn. European Neurosci. Socs., Assn. Rsch. in Vision and Ophthalmology, Soc. Neurosci. USA (fgn.), Physiol. Soc. UK and Ireland, Internat. Color Vision Soc. (hon.). Achievements include finding that visual images are analyzed by fundamental filters at detection thresholds: spatial, temporal and chromatic. Avocations: visual arts, hill walking. Office: Univ Manchester Faculty Life Scis Moffat Bldg PO Box 88 Manchester M60 1QD England Office Phone: 44 161 3063882. Office Fax: 44 161 3063887.

KULKARNI, KANCHAN, physician, director; b. India, Jan. 5, 1975; MD, Topiwala Nat. Med. Coll., 1999. Dir. Nuc. Endocrinology, 2004—. Asst. prof. Georgetown U., 2009. Mem.: Soc. Nuc. Medicine. Avocations: cooking, sports. Office: Washington Hosp Ctr 110 Irving St Washington DC 20010 Office Fax: 202-877-6601. E-mail: kpk002@yahoo.com.

KULLEN, SHIRLEY ROBINOWITZ, psychiatric epidemiologist, consultant; b. Balt., Sept. 6, 1922; d. Joseph and Rose (Collins) Robinowitz; m. Joseph Stephen Reff, Sept. 14, 1941 (div. 1958); children: Richard Brian, Robert Alan; m. Sidney Irving Margolis, Oct. 28, 1973 (dec. Dec. 1988); m. Sol Kullen, Jan. 10, 1993 (dec. May 21, 2008). BS, Am. U., 1959, MBA, 1961, PhD, 1972. Statistician NIMH, Bethesda, Md., 1964-72, health scientist adminstrn., 1972-93; cons. psychiatric epidemiologist, Chevy Chase, Md., 1993—. Adj. prof. Am. U. Washington, 1961, 69, 70, 74, 87, seminar developer, 1987; lectr. Howard U., Washington, 1963-67. Bd. dirs. Jewish Cmty. Ctr. Greater Washington, Rockville, Md., 1979—90, Hebrew Home Washington, Rockville, 1980—85, Fed. Credit Union, Rockville, 1987—93; exec. v.p. S-K Family Partnership, 1996—2005. Recipient Helen Palmer Kettler Soc. award, Am. U., 2004. Mem. APHA (adv. bd. mental health sect. 1990-93), AAUW, Cosmos Club. Avocations: golf, music, writing. Office: 5610 Wisconsin Ave Chevy Chase MD 20815 Office Phone: 301-652-3655. Personal E-mail: sugar906@aol.com.

KULSHRESTHA, RITU, medical educator; b. Mumbai, Sept. 22, 1971; MBBS, DNB, KEM Hosp. and G.S. Med. Coll., Mumbai, MS, 1994. Asst. prof. Vallabhbhai Patel Chest Inst., 2007—. Founder sec. Pulmonary Pathology Soc. India, 2008. Geraldine Zeiler fellowship, Mayo Clinic, Scottsdale, Ariz. Mem.: Nat. Acad. Med. Scis. Avocation: photography. Office: Vallabhbhai Patel Chest Inst University Delhi 110007 India Personal E-mail: ritukumar71@yahoo.com.

KULWICHIT, WANLA, medical educator, researcher; s. Yen Lieh Cheng and Kanchana Kulwichit. MD (hon.), Chulalongkorn U., Bangkok, Thailand, 1987; degree in infectious diseases, U. N.C., 2000. Diplomate Thai Bd. Internal Medicine, Thai Bd. Infectious Diseases, cert. Ednl. Commn. Fgn. Med. Grad., 1990; Goethe Institut, 1987. Resident in internal medicine Prince of Songkla U., Thailand, 1987—90, chief resident in internal medicine, 1990; clin. fellow in infectious diseases Chulalongkorn U., Bangkok, 1991—92; clin. and rsch. fellow Lineberger Comprehensive Cancer Ctr., U. N.C., Sch. Medicine, Chapel Hill, 1992—97, rsch. assoc., 1998—2000; clin. and rsch. instr. infectious diseases Chulalongkorn U., Bangkok, 2000—03, asst. prof. medicine, 2003—. Dep. editor Jour. Infectious Diseases and Antimicrobial Agents; contbr. articles to profl. jours. Recipient First Runner-up English As a Fgn. Lang., MAC Acad. Ctr., Bangkok, Thailand, 1979; grantee Rsch. scholar Dengue Rsch., Thailand Rsch. Fund, 2006—; Rsch. scholar Sci. Medicine, King Ananda Mahidol's Found., 2002—04, Rsch. scholar Dengue Rsch., Thailand Rsch. Fund, 2003—05. Mem.: Med. Assn. Thailand (life), Thai Med. Coun. (life), Royal Coll. Physicians Thailand (life), Infectious Disease Assn. Thailand (life). Achievements include first to dengue virus detection methods in urine and oral fluids; dengue virus detection methods in blood and urine dried on filter papers and detection of persistent dengue virus in humans. Office: Dept Medicine Faculty Medicine Chulalongkorn Univ Bangkok 10330 Thailand E-mail: wkulwich@gmail.com.

KUMAGAI, MASAHIRO, oral surgeon; b. Sendai, Miyagi, Japan, Feb. 25, 1959; s. Sachio and Yoko Kumagai; m. Sumi Yoshida, Feb. 4, 1990. BS, Tohoku U. Sch. Dentistry, Sendai, Japan, 1985, PhD, 1993. Cert. dr. of Dental Surgery Ministry Health and Welfare, Japan, 1985. Resident Tohoku U., Dept. Oral and Maxillofacial Surgery II, Dental Hosp., Miyagi, 1985—91; staff Tohoku Kosai Hosp., Dept. Dentistry, 1991—95; chief surgeon Tohoku Kosai Hosp., Dept. Oral and Maxillofacial Surgery, 1995—. Clin. prof. Tohoku U., Grad. Sch. Dentistry, 2006—. Mem.: Japanese Soc. Oral and Maxillofacial Surgeons (specialist 1994—). Office: Tohoku Kosai Hosp 2-3-11 Kokubuncho Aoba-ku Sendai Miyagi 980-0830 Japan Office Phone: 81-22-227-2211. Office Fax: 81-22-227-2228. Business E-Mail: kumar@mug.biglobe.ne.jp.

KUMAGAI, TAKASHI, physician, researcher; s. Yukio and Reiko Kumagai; m. Hiroko Anzai, June 21, 1997; 1 child, Tomoya. BS, Tokyo U., 1984; MD, Tokyo Med. and Dental U., 1990, PhD, 1999. Board certificated member Japanese Soc. Internal Medicine, 1995, Japanese Soc. Hematology, 2000, board certificated instructor 2005, 2004. Resident in internal medicine Tokyo Med. and Dental U., 1990—91, resident in hematology, 1993—94, clin. assoc. prof., 2007—, clin. prof., 2011—; resident in hematology Tokyo Met. Komagome Hosp., 1994—95; resident in internal medicine Ohme Mcpl. Gen. Hosp., 1991—93, dep dir. dept. hematology, 2004—07, dir. dept. hematology, 2007—; staff physician in hematology Tokyo Teishin Hosp., 1999—2001; rsch. fellow, dept. hematology, oncology Cedars-Sinai Med. Ctr., UCLA Sch. Medicine, 2001—04. Instr. Tokyo Met. Ohme Nursing Sch., Japan, 2008—. Contbr. articles to profl. jours. Recipient Tanaka Michiko award for Cancer Rsch., Tokyo Med. and Dental U., 1999. Fellow: Japanese Soc. Hematology (bd. cert. instr.), Japanese Soc. Internal Medicine (bd. cert. instr.); mem.: Am. Assn. Cancer Rsch., Japanese Soc. Clin. Hematology, Am. Soc. Hematology. Achievements include research in anti-tumor activity of the vitamin D analog, paricalcitol; molecularly targeted therapy in cancers; Methylation analysis of the tumor suppressor genes in cancers; discovery of anti-apoptotic effect of the proto-oncogene Bcl-6 in myogenesis. Home: 3-13-7 Morooka-cho Rm 201 Ohme Tokyo 198-0031 Japan Office: Ohme Municipal General Hospital 4-16-5 Higashi-Ohme Ohme Tokyo 198-0042 Japan Office Fax: 81-428-24-5126; Home Fax: 81-428-23-8450. Personal E-mail: kumamed1_2001@yahoo.co.jp.

KUMAR, ANAND, medical educator; b. Allahabad, Uttar Pradesh, India, Dec. 16, 1952; s. Kamla Devi Agrawal; m. Shashi Khattri, May 12, 1979; children: Anshu Gupta, Ashish Agrawal. MBBS, Banaras Hindu U., Uttar Pradesh, MS, 1978. Reader dept. gen. surgery, Inst. Med. Scis. Banaras Hindu U., 1990—96, prof. dept. gen. surgery, Inst. Med. Scis., 1997—, med. supt., SS Hosp., 1998—2002, 2009—. Contbr. scientific papers. Named Outstanding Tchr. of State, 1996; fellow, Indo Netherland, U. Grants Commn., 1998. Fellow: Nat. Acad. Med. Scis. (editl. mem. 2007—08). Achievements include research in breast cancer. Home: B-143 Brij Enclave Sunderpur Varanasi Uttar Pradesh 221005 India Office: Banaras Hindu Univ Varanasi Uttar Pradesh 221005 India Office Phone: 91-542-2369033. Office Fax: 91-542-2369569. Personal E-mail: profanandkumar52@gmail.com.

KUMAR, ASHUTOSH, cardiologist; b. India, June 24, 1977; MBBS, Sri Krishna Med. Coll. Muzaffarpur, 2000; MD, Inst. Med. Sics., Banaras Hindu U., 2006. Chief interventional cardiologist Gsl Med. Coll., Rajahmundry, 2009—. Fellow: Am. Coll. Cardiology; mem.: Indian Acad. Geriat., Cardiol. Soc. India. Avocation: music. Home: House 75 DBV Raju Villas Diwanchervu Rajahmundry Andhra Pradesh 533296 India Personal E-mail: ashutoshvani@yahoo.co.in.

KUMAR, ASHWANI, biotechnologist, educator; b. India, June 10, 1979; PhD, Kurukshetra U. NDRI, Karnal, 2007. Asst. prof. JMIT, 2008—. Office: Dept Biotechnology JMIT Radaur Yamunanagar Haryana 135133 India Personal E-mail: ashwanindri@rediffmail.com.

KUMAR, KANAGARAJ GANESH, biologist, educator; b. Trichy, Tamil Nadu, India, Oct. 4, 1951; s. A. Kanagaraj and Thirupura Sundari; m. Kalyani G. Kalyani J., Feb. 26, 1978; children: Sundari G., Shyam G. MS, St. Joseph's Coll., Madras U., Trichy, India, 1973; PhD, Mysore U., India, 1978. Assoc. prof. Case Western Res. U., Cleve., 1978—2006; prof. Dept. Med., U. Chgo., 2007—. Study sect. mem. NIH, RIBT, DC, 2005—. Contbr. articles to profl. jours. Grantee, Am. Thoracic Soc., 1987—89; Rsch. grant, Am. Lung Assn., 1991—92, grant, NIH, 1992—93, Rsch. grant, NIH; Heart, Lung and Blood Rsch. Inst., 1995—2001, NIH, Heart, Lung and Blood Rsch. Inst., 2001—06, NIH, Heart Lung & Blood Rsch. Inst., 2008—. Mem.: Am. Physiol. Soc., Am. Assn. Biochemistry and Molecular Biology. Liberal. Hindu. Avocations: tennis, meditation, travel. Office Fax: 773-834-5252. Business E-Mail: gkumar@medicine.bsd.uchicago.edu.

KUMAR, PRIYANKA SETHI, orthodontist, educator; b. New Delhi, Oct. 1, 1980; BDS, Kle's Inst. Dental Scis., Belgaum, Karnataka, India, 2001, MDS, 2008. Asst. prof. Santosh Dental Coll. & Hosp., Ghaziabad, Uttar Pradesh, India, 2008—. Cons. Delhi Heart & Lung Inst., New Delhi, 2009. Recipient Dr Shivaratna Csavadi's award, Indian Orthodontic Soc., Dr J G Kannappan's award. Mem.: Indian Orthodontic Soc. Avocations: reading, writing. Home: C - 110 Sector 61 Noida Uttar Pradesh 201301 India Personal E-mail: priyankakumar@rediffmail.com.

KUMAR, S. SADISH, professor, pharmaceutical chemist; b. Chennai, India, Apr. 30, 1972; s. Shanmugam and Banumathy, m. Arutchelvi, Jan. 26, 2001; 1 child, Smisha PharmM, Tamil Nadu Dr. M.G.R. Med. U., 1996; PhD, Gautam Buddh Tech. U., 2010; MBA, Alagappa U., 2010. Asst. prof. Vel's Coll. Pharmacy, 1996—2003; lectr., reader Dr. K.N. Modi Inst. Pharm. Edn. & Rsch., 2003—05; reader, prof. I.T.S. Paramed. Coll., 2005—11, academic adv. bd. mem., 2007—11, selection bd. mem., 2008—11. Bd. studies mem. Gautam Buddh Tech. U., 2008—11; reviewer Taylor & Francis Pub. Academic Jours.; advisor editl. bd. IJPFR, academic adv. bd. mem., selection bd. mem.; Org. Sec & Sci. Comm Mem. AICTE Spon Nat. Sem. UP, India. Recipient Rsch. Project of Yr. award-II, IPC Trust, 2010. Fellow: Indian Chem. Soc.; mem.: Royal Soc. Chemistry, Tamil Nadu Pharmacy Coun., Assn. Pharm. Tchrs. India. Hindu. Achievements include res. papers pubd. 15 intl. jour, 2 nat jour. 6 intl. conf pres. 10 Nat conf. papers; guided 23 pharm M proj. Avocations: guitar, drawing, cricket. Office: ITS Paramedical Coll Delhi Meerut Rd Murad Nagar Ghaziabad UP India Personal E-mail: jesisjes@yahoo.co.in.

KUMAR, SANJAY, research scientist; b. India, Sept. 27, 1975; MTech, IT BHU, Varanasi, India, 2005; PhD, IIT, Guwahati, Assam, India, 2011. Postdoc. rschr. U. Windsor, 2010—. Asst. mgr., process Kothari Fermentation & Biochem Pvt Ltd, India, 1999—2003; biochem. engr. Winsome Breweries Pvt Ltd, 1999; sr. rsch. fellow project IIT, 2010. Mem.: All India Biotech Assn. Avocations: badminton, cooking, travel. Office: Dept Civil & Environ Engineering UoW Windsor Ont N9B 3P4 Canada Business E-Mail: sanjay27@uwindsor.ca.

KUMAR, SUDERSHAN, veterinarian, educator; b. Jammu, India, Feb. 9, 1954; BVSc & AH, Govind Ballabh Pant U. Agrl. and Tech., Pantnagar, 1978; PhD, Sher-e-Kashmir U. Agrl. Scis. & Tech., Jammu, 2010. Asst. project officer Rajasthan State Dairy Devel. Corp., 1978—; vet. asst. surgeon, cons. J&K State Govt., Animal Husbandry Dept., 1979—2001; asst. prof., jr. scientist Sher-e-Kashmir U. Agrl. Scis. & Tech., 2001—05, assoc. prof., sr. scientist, 2005—. Recipient Color award, Punjab Agrl. U.; Jr. fellowship, Indian Coun. Agrl. Rsch. Mem.: Indian Soc. Animal Prodn., Indian Soc. Advancement Canine Practice, Indian Soc. Study Animal Reprodn. Avocations: ping pong/table tennis, reading, theater. Home: 123/124 Jantpur Housing Colony Jammu Jammu & Kashmir 180007 India Home Fax: 911923250639. Personal E-mail: drsudarshandogra@yahoo.com.

KUMAR, SUNIL, physician; b. Kathadih, Jharkhand, India, Nov. 30, 1977; s. Tulsi Modi and Mandodari Devi; m. Ritu Kumari. MBBS, Pune U., India, 2002; MD, Postgrad. Inst. Med. Edn. And Rsch., Chandigarh, 2005. Cert. in biostats. and epidemiology Postgrad. Inst. Med. Edn. and Rsch., 2004, ECFMG, Phila., 2006. Chief resident Postgrad. Inst. Med. Edn. and Rsch., 2005, housestaff internal medicine, St. Luke's Roosevelt Hosp., Columbia U., NYC, 2007—; postdoc. rschr. Cin. Children's Hosp., U. Cin., 2006—07. Contbr. numerous articles to med. jours. Team leader, pulse polio immunization Directorate Family Welfare, Pune, 2001. Recipient award, B. J. Med. Coll., Pune U., 1997, 2nd Best Rsch. Poster, Rsch. Com., St. Luke's Roosevelt Hosp., 2008; named Runner Up, Dept. Pediat., B. J. Med. Coll., Pune U., 2000; Travel grant, Cin. Rsch. Trustee Found., 2007. Mem.: AMA, Am. Coll. Physician, Maharashtra State Med. Coun., Med. Coun. India, Assn. Am. Physicians Indian Origin, Am. Heart Assn. Achievements include research in strong association of promoter tagging variant of Apolipoprotein E (APOE) with obstructive sleep apnea; obese adolescents who also have obstructive sleep apnea usually have higher soft tissue volume around neck, especially retropalatal area; robotic cardiac resynchronization therapy (CRT) is superior to Endo CRT in promoting reverse remodeling and decreasing the combined endpoint of heart failure hospitalization and mortality. Personal E-mail: drsunil06@gmail.com. Business E-Mail: skumar@chpnet.org.

KUMAR, SUNIL, physician; b. Godda, Jharkhand, May 10, 1970; MBBS, RIMS, Ranchi, 1995, MD, PGDGM, 2000. Physician JNMC, DMIMSU, Sawangi, 2000—, assoc. prof., 2004. Home: Af-10 Doctor'S Quarter Hosp Campus Wardha Maharastra 442005 India Personal E-mail: drsunilkr_med@rediffmail.com.

KUMAR, SUNIL, pharmacist, educator; b. Haryana, India, May 21, 1978; PharmB, Guru Jambheshwar U. Sci. & Technolgy, Hisar, Haryana, India, 2000; PharmM, Poona Coll. Pharmacy, Pune, Maharashtra, India, 2003. Lectr. Kurukshetra U., Haryana, 2004—06, asst. prof., 2006—. Contbr. articles to profl. jours. Recipient Young Tchrs. award, All Indian Coun. Tech. Edn., New Delhi; Merit scholarship, Govt. Haryana, grant, All Indian Coun. Tech. Edn., New Delhi. Mem.: Assn. Pharm. Profls., Assn. Pharm. Tchrs. India, Indian Pharm. Assn., Indian Pharm. Grad. Assn., Soc. Pharmacists & Technocrats. Avocations: cricket, singing, dance. Office: Inst Pharm Scis Kurukshetra Haryana 136119 India Personal E-mail: sunilmadhuban@yahoo.com.

KUMAR, VIKAS, neuropharmacologist, researcher; b. Palwal, Faridabad, Haryana, India, Feb. 16, 1973; s. Ajit Kumar and Savitri Arya; m. Pooja Arya, Mar. 7, 2008. PharmD, Dayananda Sagar Inst. Pharmacy, Bangalore, 1990; B in pharmacy, Gulbarga U., 1995, PharmM, 1997; PhD, Banaras Hindu U., Varanasi, India, 2000; postdoc in Neuropharmacology, ex. Tech. Sch. Pharmacy, Amarillo, Tex., 2006. Registered pharmacist State Pharmacy Coun., 1991. Lectr. Hindu Coll. Pharmacy, Sonepat, Haryana, India, 1997—98; sr. rsch. fellow Banaras Hindu U., Varanasi, India, 1998—2000, assoc. prof. pharmacology, dept. pharmaceutics, Inst. Tech., 2006—; scientist to sr. scientist Indian Herbs Rsch. & Supply Co. Ltd, Saharanpur, India, 2001—03; rsch. assoc. Lupin Rsch. Pk., Pune, Maharashtra, India, 2003—04, Tex. Tech Sch. Pharmacy, Amarillo, 2004—06. Cons. Indo Phytochem Pharms., Sirmour, India, 2004—05. Recipient Semi Khatib Gold medal, Luqman Coll. Pharmacy, 1996, Servier Young Investigators' award, Inst. Rsch. Internat. Servier, France, 1999; named Internat. Scientist of Yr., 2007, Leading Scientist of World, 2008; Sr. Rsch. fellow, Indian Coun. Med. Rsch., Govt. of India, New Delhi, 1999, Post Doctoral fellow, So. Ill. U., 2002. Mem.: Internat. Brain Rsch. Orgn., Acad. Pharm. Scientists Gt. Britain, Am. Assn. Pharm. Scientists, Assn. Pharm. Tchrs. India (life), Soc. for Phytomedica (life), Indian Soc. Biomedical Scientists (life), Indian Sci. Congress Assn. (life), Indian Soc. Chemists & Biologists (life), Indian Pharmacy Graduates' Assn. (life), Assn. Physiologists and Pharmacologists India (life), Indian Acad. Neurosciences (life), Indian Pharm. Assn. (life), Soc. Young Scientists (life), Indian Pharmacological Soc. (life). Achievements include Established the neuropsychopharmacology laboratory at R&D centre of Indian Herbs Ltd., Saharanpur. Business E-Mail: vikas.phe@itbhu.ac.in.

KUMAR, VINOD, ophthalmologist, educator; b. Muktsar, Punjab, India, Feb. 23, 1980; MBBS, Maulana Azad Med. Coll., New Delhi, 2001; MS in Ophthalmology. Registrar sr. resident Guru Nanak Eye Ctr., Maulana Azad Med. Coll., 2006—09; fixed term specialty tng. appointee Wrexham Maelor Hosp., Wrexham, Wales, 2009—10; asst. prof. U. Coll. Med. Scis. & GTB Hosp., 2010—. Contbr. scientific papers to profl. jours. Fellow: Royal Coll. Physians and Surgeons (Glasgow); mem.: Nat. Acad. Med. Scis., Am. Acad. Ophthalmology, Vitreo Retinal Soc. India, Delhi Ophthalmic Soc., All India Ophthalmic Soc. Avocations: badminton, mountain climbing, music. Home: 57 Sadar Apt Mayur Vihar Phase 1 Ext New Delhi 110091 India Personal E-mail: drvinod_agg@yahoo.com.

KUMATE RODRIGUEZ, JESUS, physician; b. Mazatlan, Sinaloa, Mex., Nov. 11, 1924; s. Efren Kumate and Josefina Rodriguez; m. Bertha Guerra Rovelo, Mar. 2, 1957. BSc, Escuela Preparatoria, Mazatlan, Mex., 1940; MD, Med. Militar, Mexico City, 1946; PhD, Escuela Nal. Cienc. Biol., Mexico City, 1963; DSc (hon.), U. de Nuevo Leon, Monterrey, Mex., 1990, U. de Sinaloa, Mex., 1995. Diplomate Bd. Infectious Diseases. Asst. prof. Escuela Med. Militar, Mexico City, 1949-54; physician Hosp. Infantil, Mexico City, 1953-80; assoc. prof. Facultad de Medicina, Mexico City, 1960-70, prof., 1970-80; lectr. Polytechnic Inst., Mexico City, 1974-80; investigator Instituto Mexicano Seguro Social, Mexico City, 1981—. Dir. Hosp. Infantil, 1979-80; coord. Nat. Insts. Health, Mexico City, 1983-84; undersec. Health Svcs., Mexico City, 1985-88, sec., 1988-94. Author: Manual de Infectologia. Maj. Mex. Army, 1940-54. Recipient Legion of Honor, Govt. of France, 1978-88, Disting. Svcs. award Def. Sec. Mex., 1988, Oswaldo Robles award Govt. Guatemala, 1993, Sacred Treasure Band, Japan, 1997, Order of Merit, Italy, 1998. Roman Catholic.

KUME, AKITO, physician; b. Nagoya, Japan, Dec. 23, 1957; MD, Nagoya U., 1982, PhD, 1992. Head KUME Clinic, 2004—. Clin. rsch. physician Eli Lilly Japan, 1999—2004. Mem.: Japanese Soc. Neurology. Office: 1-8 Marune Mizuho Nagoya Aichi 467-0054 Japan Office Fax: 81-52-831-9980. Business E-Mail: kumeiin@nifty.com.

KUME, KEIICHIRO, medical educator; b. Yokohama, Japan, July 10, 1962; PhD, U. Occupl. and Environ. Health, Sch. Medic, Japan, 1994. Assoc. prof. third dept. internal medicine U. Occupl. and Environ. Health, Japan Sch. Medicine, 2005—. Office: 1-1 Iseigaoka Yahatanishi-ku Kitakyushu Fukuoka 8078555 Japan Office Fax: 81-93-692-0107. Business E-Mail: k-kume@med.uoeh-u.ac.jp.

KUMM, DIETMAR ALFRED, orthopedist, consultant, surgeon; b. Munich, Jan. 20, 1959; s. Alfred Wilhelm and Hedy (Diekaemper) Kumm; children: Lars, Leslie, Linda. Student, Friedrich-Wilhelms U., Bonn, Germany, 1978—84; MD, U. Bonn., 1984, PhD, 1985. Intern Basle U., Switzerland, 1984, resident in internal medicine, 1984—85; asst. surgeon EV KRHS, Bad Godesberg, 1984—89; asst. prof. U. Cologne, Cologne, Germany, 1989—94, asst. CI, 1994—96; ltd.

oberazt U. Witten-Herdecke, Witten, 1996—2003; chefarzt, dept. dir., head dept. Bethesda KRHS, Duisburg, Germany, 2003—. Cons. in field. Contbr. articles to profl. jours. With German Air Force, 1977—78. Recipient Am. Medal of Honor, 2005. Fellow: IBA (life); mem.: Am. Acad. Orthop. Surgery, NY Acad. Sci., German Assn. Sports Medicine, German Assn. Orthop. and Orthop. Surgery. Achievements include invention of fixation of artificial joints, sliding screw for fixation of SCFE; patents in field. Avocation: sailing. Office: Orthopaedic Clinic Bethesda KRHS Heer Str 219 Duisburg D-47053 Germany Business E-Mail: d.kumm@bethesda.de.

KUMRA, SANJIV, psychiatrist, educator; b. Toronto, Ont., Can., Sept. 30, 1967; s. Surender and Asha Kumra; m. Neerja Suri-Kumra, Mar. 18, 1969; children: Amit, Rohit. MD, U. Toronto, 1990. Diplomate Am. Bd. Psychiatry, cert. in Child/Adolescent Psychiatry, Neurology. Intern dept. internal medicine Toronto Gen. Hosp., 1990—91; resident adult psychiatry Harvard Med. Sch., Boston, 1991—93, child/adolescent fellowship, 1993—95; sr. staff fellow NIH, Bethesda, Md., 1995—98; asst. prof. psychiatry U. Toronto, 1998—2000, Albert Einstein Coll. Medicine, Bronx, NY, 2000—; asst. prof. dept. psychiatry, dir. child & adolescent psychiatry U. Minn., Mpls., 2006—. Rsch. psychiatrist Zucker Hillside Hosp., Glen Oaks, NY. Contbr. articles to profl. jours. Recipient Career Devel. award, NIH, 1990, Young Investigator award, Nat. Assn. Rsch. on Schizophrenia & Depression, 2002. Fellow: Royal Coll. Physicians & Surgeons; mem.: Am. Acad. Child & Adolescent Psychiatry. Achievements include research in childhood-onset schizophrenia. Office: U Minn Dept Psychiatry 2312 S 6th St Minneapolis MN 55454 also: LI Jewish 7559 263rd St Glen Oaks NY 11021 Office Phone: 612-273-9778.

KUNAVARAPU, CHANDRA, cardiologist; married. Cert. in adult cardiovacular disease Am. Bd. Internal Medicine, 2006, in adult cardiology, in nuc. cardiology, in echocardiography, in angiography. Med. dir., heart failure & transplant Tex. Transplant Physicians Group, 2006—. Fellow: Am. Coll. Cardiology; mem.: Heart Failure Soc. America, Internat. Soc. Heart & Lung Transplantation. Achievements include development of heart failure and transplant program. Office Phone: 210-575-8485.

KUNDU, SUMAN, research scientist, educator; b. Habra, West Bengal, India, Jan. 26, 1971; PhD, Banaras Hindu U., India, 2000. Postdoc. Iowa State U., 2000—04; proteins interactions rsch. assoc. Pioneer Hi Bred-Dupont, 2004—06; asst. prof. Banaras Hindu U., 2006; assoc. prof. U. Delhi South Campus, 2006—. Chief editor Jour. Proteins and Proteomics, 2010—. Contbr. articles to numerous rsch. jours. & publs. Fellow, Indo-US Sci. and Tech. Forum, Travel grant, Dept. Sci. and Tech., Govt of India. Achievements include patents in field. Home: F-1 NII-Near JNU E Gate Aruna Asaf Delhi New Delhi 110067 India Office Phone: 91-11-24117460. Business E-Mail: suman.kundu@south.du.ac.in.

KUNE, GABRIEL ANDREW, surgeon, educator, oncologist, consultant; b. Kosice, Slovak Republic, Dec. 21, 1933; arrived in Australia, 1948; s. Andrew and Ann (Skriba) Kun; m. Susan Bannerman, Apr. 8, 1967 (div. May 1992); 1 child, Randall Joshua. MB, BS, U. Melbourne, Australia, 1957, MD, 1988. Surg. intern and registrar Royal Melbourne Hosp., 1958-61, staff surgeon, 1967-77, cons. surgeon, 1977—; sr. surg. registrar St. Mary's Hosp., Guy's Hosp., London, 1963-64; first asst. in surgery Lahey Clinic, Boston, 1965; prof. surgery U. Melbourne, 1977-88, emeritus prof. surgery, 1989—. Author: The Current Practice of Biliary Surgery, 1972, The Practice of Biliary Surgery, 1980, Chirurgia Della Via Biliari, 1981, Biliary Surgery (in Japanese), 1986, The Psyche and Cancer, 1992, Causes and Control of Colorectal Cancer, a Model for Cancer Prevention, 1996, Nothing is Impossible, The John Saunders Story, 1999, Reducing the Odds: A Manual for the Prevention of Cancer, 1999, Cancer Prevention in the Third Millenium, 2001, Home Health Guide to a Cancer-Free Family, 2003, Home Health Guide to a Cancer Free Family Chinese Edit., 2005, Home Health Guide to a Cancer Free Family Indian Edit., 2006; contbr. chpts. to books and numerous articles to profl. jours. Fellow ACS, Royal Australasian Coll. Surgeons, Royal Coll. Surgeons Eng. (Arris & Gale lectr. 1970, Hunterian prof. 1976), Royal Soc. Medicine; mem. Australian Med. Assn., Internat. Soc. for Nutrition and Cancer (exec. coun.), Royal South Yarra Tennis Club, Kooyong Lawn Tennis Club, Thredbo Alpine Club. Avocations: music, tennis, skiing, travel, discovering the causes of cancer. Home: 41 Power St Toorak VIC 3142 Australia Office: 41 Power St Toorak Vicrtoria 3142 Australia Business E-Mail: gkune@unimelb.edu.au.

KUNES, PAVEL, surgeon; b. Turnov, Czech Republic, June 29, 1955; d. Pavel Kuneš and Božena Hartmanová; life ptnr. Kvetuše Soucková, Dec. 10, 1977; children: Mariana Kunešová, Diana Kunešová. MD, Charles U. Prague, Med. Sch. Hradec Králové, Czech Republic, 1981. Head critical care unit Dept. Cardiac Surgery, Hradec Králové, 1989—2002, attending physician, 2003—. Rsch. fellow Charles U. Prague, 2005—. Contbr. articles to med. jour. Achievements include research in behavior of Pentraxin 3 and mainly inter leukin 33 in cardiac surgery patients. Avocation: writing. Home: Hodesovice 121 Byst 53322 Czech Republic Home Phone: 420 718 138 628; Office Phone: 420 495 388 362. Business E-Mail: kunes.pavel@fnhk.cz.

KUNG, DAVID S., plastic surgeon; married; 2 children. BA with honors, Columbia Coll., 1984; DDS with distinction, Columbia U. Coll. Dental Medicine, 1989; MD, Harvard Med. Sch., 1992. Diplomate Am. Bd. Oral and Maxillofacial Surgery, Am. Bd. Plastic Surgery. Intern in surgery Mass. Gen. Hosp., Boston, 1989, resident in surgery, 1992-95; resident in plastic surgery U. N.C., 1996-98, fellow in craniofacial surgery, 1998; clin. instr. divsn. plastic surgery Georgetown U. Med. Ctr., Washington, 1998—; bd. dirs. Ecladent, NC, 2009—; pres. Kung Plastic Surgery PA, 2004—; attending division of plastic surgery Nat. Children's Med. Ctr., Washington, 1998—; adj. faculty Coll. Pharmacy and Health Sci. Butler U., Indpls., 2009—. Clin. preceptor Harvard Med. Sch., 1995; reviewer, publ. rev. com. Harvard Med. Sch. Office of Med. Edn., 1990—92, exec. com., 1990—92. Editor-in-chief: Columbia U. Office Profl. Edn., 1985—86. Pres. Honor and Rsch. Soc., Columbia U., 1985—88. Recipient Nat. Rsch. Svc. award NIH, 1986, award of achievement Am. Assn. Oral and Maxillofacial Surgery, 1989; named one of Am.'s Top Surgeons, 2006; Top Drs. award, News Channel 8, 2006, Patients' Choice award, 2010-11; nominated as Internat. Health Profl. of yr., 2004. Fellow: ACS; mem.: World Assn. Plastic Surgeons Chinese Descent, Md. Soc. Plastic Surgeons, Am. Soc. Aesthetic Plastic Surgery, Am. Soc. Plastic Surgeons, Chinese Am. Med. Soc. (bd. dirs. 2000—), Am. Soc. Maxillofacial Surgeons, Chinese Med. and Health Assn. (bd. dirs. 1998—), Nat. Capital Soc. Plastic Surgeons (mem. exec. bd. 1999—2000), Omicron Kappa Upsilon. Office: Ste 635 5454 Wisconsin Ave Chevy Chase MD 20815-6910 Office Phone: 301-986-8878. Office Fax: 301-986-8879. E-mail: dk@kungmd.com.

KUNG, PATRICK CHUNG-SHU, biotechnologist; b. Nanjing, China, July 10, 1947; came to U.S., 1969; s. Tao and Yuing (Li) K.; m. Yie Lu; children: Julia, Calvin, Charles Shen. BS, Fu Jen U., Taiwan, 1968; PhD, U. Calif., Berkeley, 1974. Rsch. fellow MIT, Cambridge, 1974-77; sr. rsch. fellow Ortho Pharm. Co., J & J, Raritan, NJ, 1978—81; v.p. rsch. Centocor Inc., Malvern, Pa., 1982-83; co-founder, exec. v.p., vice chmn. T Cell Sci., Inc./Avant Immunotherapies, Inc., Cambridge, 1984—98; bd. dirs. PhytoCeutica, Inc., New Haven. Exec. bd. Coll. Letters and Scis. U. Calif., Berkeley, 1989-91; bd. dirs. PhytoCeutica, Inc., pres., CEO, 1999-2003; bd. dirs. Briglow, Ltd., 2007. Contbr. articles to profl. jours. Trustee Park Sch., Brookline, Mass., 1992-95. Recipient Philip Hoffman award Johnson & Johnson Co., 1979, Achievement award Chinese Inst. Engrs., 1988, Discoverers award U.S. Pharm. Mfrs. Rsch. Assn., 1991, Thomas Alva Edison award N.J. Rsch. Coun., 1991. Mem. Soc. Chinese Bioscientists in Am. (pres. bio/pharm. scis. divsn. 1994, 95).

KUNG-WOO, NAM, medical researcher, educator; b. Republic of Korea, Oct. 17, 1966; PhD, Seoul Nat. U., Republic of Korea, 2004. Rsch. scientist NPRI, Seoul Nat. U., 1995—2004; postdoc. rschr. BWH, Harvard Med. Sch., 2005—06; with Jung San Biotech. Co., 2007—09; rsch. instr. Dept. Neurosci., 2010—. GRI grant, GSBC. Mem.: Korean Soc. Toxicology, Korean Soc. Applied Pharmacology, Pharm. Soc. Korea. Avocations: hiking, fishing, mountain climbing. Office: 126-1 5-Ga Anam-Dong Seongbuk-Gu Seoul 136-705 Republic of Korea Office Fax: 82-2-953-6095. Business E-Mail: kwnam1@korea.ac.kr.

KUNITOMO, ADACHI, medicinal chemist; b. Fukuoka, Japan, Mar. 9, 1959; BS in Pharm. Scis., U. Tokyo, 1981, PhD, 1986. Mgr. Mitsubishi Tanabe Pharma Corp., 1986—. Postdoc. fellow U. Oxford, England, 1987—89; vis. lectr. faculty pharm. scis. Toho U., Japan, 2010—11. Mem.: Soc. Synthetic Organic Chemistry (Japan), Pharm. Soc. Japan. Avocations: reading, tennis, japanese chess. Office: 1000 Kamoshida-cho Aoba-ku Yokohama Kanagawa 227-0033 Japan Business E-Mail: adachi.kunitomo@mc.mt-pharma.co.jp.

KUNKLER, ARNOLD WILLIAM, retired surgeon, educator; b. St. Anthony, Ind., Nov. 18, 1921; s. Edward J. and Selma (Hasenour) K.; m. Muriel Burns, 1954; m. Barbara McElroy, 2004; children: Lisa, Arnold William, Carolyn, Christine, Phillip, Kevin. AB, Ind. U., 1943, MD, 1949. Diplomate Am. Bd. Surgery. Intern Ind. U. Med. Ctr., Indpls., 1949-50, asst. resident in surgery, fellow vascular surg. research, 1950-54, resident in surgery, 1954-55, faculty, 1955—76, clin. prof. surgery, 1976-94, emeritus clin. prof. surgery, 1995—. Individual practice medicine specializing in gen. surgery, Terre Haute, Ind., 1955-94; dir. med. edn. Terre Haute Regional Hosp., 1970-79; staff Terre Haute Center Med. Edn.; chief of staff Terre Haute Regional Hosp., 1989-90. Contbr. articles to profl. jours. Pres. Terre Haute Med. Edn. Found., 1972-73, 78-81, bd. dirs., 1967-86; pres. cmty. adv. coun. Terre Haute Center Med. Edn., 1976-80; treas. Wabash Valley Cmty. Blood Program, 1974-78; trustee Terre Haute Regional Hosp., 1978-84, chmn. bd., 1981-84, Vigo County Bd. Health, 1990-97. With U.S. Army, 1943-46, ETO. Fellow ACS (pres. Ind. chpt. 1980-81); mem. Ind. State Med. Assn. (com. med. edn. 1986-92), Vigo County Med. Soc., Pam. Am. Med. Assn., Pan Pacific Surg. Assn., Midwest Surg. Assn., Aesculapian Soc. Wabash Valley, Pres.'s Cir. Ind. U., Dean's Coun. Ind. U. Sch. Medicine, Rotary Club of Terre Haute, Sagamore of the Wabash, Columbia Club, Highland Country Club, Commons Club (Bonita Springs, Fla.). Democrat. Roman Catholic.

KUNNUMMAL, MUHAMMED, dermatologist, educator, consultant; b. Kozhikode, Kerala, India, June 1, 1957; s. Pavirootty and Sainaba Kunnummal; m. Sabeena Kunnummal, Jan. 20, 1985; children: Hasanul Banna, Lamya. BSc, U. Calicut, Kerala, India, 1979, DVD, 1989; MBBS, Med. Coll. Calicut, Kerala, India, 1984. Diplomate Nat. Bd. Exams, India, 1998. Asst. surgeon Pub. Health Svcs., Kerala, 1991—94; lectr. Med. Coll. Calicut, Kerala, 1994—98, sr. lectr., 1998—2002, asst. prof., 2002—08, assoc. prof., 2008—, additional prof., 2010—. Pvt. practice, Calicut, 1992—; cons. Alhind Cosmetology Clinic, Calicut, 2005—; bd. dirs. Floreat Internat. Sch., Kondotty; founding mem. Crescent Ednl. and Cultural Trust Kalaranthiri, Kerala; trustee 2 schs. Contbr. articles to profl. jours. Fellow: Am. Acad. Dermatology; mem.: Indian Assn. Dermatologists, Venereologists and Leprologists (hon. sec. 2009—11, Best Br. award 2011), Internat. Hyperhidrosis Soc., CosmetologySoc. India, Lymphology Soc. India, Acad. Med. Specialists, Nat. Acad. Med. Scis., Indian Assn. Leprologists, Indian Med. Assn. (sec. 2003—04, award for article writing 1995), Muslim Svc. Soc. Muslim. Avocations: gardening, reading. Home: Koroth School Rd Badagara Kozhikode Kerala 673101 India Office: Med Coll Dept Dermatology Kozhikode 673008 India Office Phone: 0495-3253564. Business E-Mail: drmuhammedk@rediffmail.com.

KUNOS, GEORGE, pharmacologist; b. Budapest, Hungary, May 14, 1942; came to U.S., 1987; s. Istvan and Gabriella (Kalman) K.; m. Ildiko Vermes, June 11, 1967; children: Anne-Marie, Doreen. MD, Budapest Med. U., 1966; PhD, McGill U., Montreal, Can., 1973. Asst. prof. dept. pharmacology McGill U., 1974-79, assoc. prof., 1979-83, prof. dept. pharmacology and dept. of medicine, 1984-88; lab. chief Nat. Inst. Alcoholism, Bethesda, Md., 1987-92; prof., chmn. dept. pharmacology Va. Commonwealth U., Richmond, 1992—2000; scientific dir. Nat. Inst. Alcohol Abuse and Alocholism, Nat. Inst. Health, 2000—. Mem. pharmacology task force Nat. Bd. Med. Examiners, 1996-99. Editor monographs in field; contbr. over 200 sci. articles to profl. jours. Recipient Monat-Fraser Associateship award McGill U., 1981-87. Mechoulam award Internat. Cannabinoid RSch. Soc., 2005, dir. award NIH, 2008. Fellow Am. Heart Assn. (coun. on high blood pressure; mem. Am. Soc. Pharmacol. Exptl. Therapy, Am. Soc. Biochem. Molecular Biology, Soc. for Neurosci., Hungarian Acad. Scis. Achievements include identification of role of endogenous opioid peptides of the brain in regulation of blood pressure and in antihypertensive drug action, unique mechanisms in regulation of hormone receptors role of endogenous cannabinoids in cardiovascular, appetite and metabolic regulation. Office: Nat Inst Alcohol Abuse & Alcoholism Nat Inst Health PO Box 9413 Bethesda MD 20892-9413 Office Phone: 301-443-2069.

KUNSCHNER, LARA J., neurologist, educator; MD, U. Pitts. Diplomate Am. Bd. Neurology. Intern St. Joseph Mercy Hosp., St. Charles, Mo.; resident Uni. Mich. Hosps., Ann Arbor, Minn.; fellow Anderson Cancer Hosp., Houston; practice Allegheny Neurological Assocs.; soc. prof. neurology Drexel Univ.; co- dir. neuro-oncology Allegheny Gen. Hiosp. Named one of Top Doctors, Pitts. mag., 2011. Office: Allegheny General Hospital 320 E N Ave Pittsburgh PA 15212 Office Phone: 412-359-3131. Office Fax: 412-359-4108.

KUNTZ, CHARLES, IV, neurosurgeon; b. Oct. 21, 1964; married; 2 children. BA in Chemistry magna cum laude, Holy Cross Coll., 1987; MD in Infectious Disease, Case Western Res. U., 1991. Intern, resident, fellow U. Washington Affiliated Hosps., Seattle, 1991-2000; assoc. prof., vice chmn., dir. spine and peripheral nerve surgery dept. neurosurgery Mayfield Clinic and Spine Inst., U. Cin., 2000—. Contbr. articles to profl. jours. Mem. AMA, Am. Assn. Neurol. Surgeons, Congress Neurol. Surgeons, N.Am. Spine Soc., Phi Beta Kappa, Alpha Omega Alpha. Office: Ste 3100 222 Piedmont Ave Cincinnati OH 45219 Office Phone: 513-475-8667. Office Fax: 513-475-8033. Personal E-mail: charleskuntz@yahoo.com.

KUNTZ, EDWARD LAWRENCE, healthcare executive; b. Phila., Feb. 22, 1945; s. Samuel J. and Mary S. (Shulman) K.; m. Caroline L. Lessner, Aug. 3, 1969; m. Stuart M., David M., Beth. BA, Temple U., 1966, JD, 1969, ML, 1978. Pvt. practice, Phila., 1970-78; asst. gen. counsel ARA Svcs., Phila., 1978-79, sector counsel, 1979-84, assoc. gen. counsel, 1984-85; exec. v.p. ARA Living Ctrs., Houston, 1985-92; chmn., CEO Living Ctrs. Am., Houston, 1992-97, Vencor Inc. (now Kindred Healthcare), Louisville, 1999—2003; pres. Kindred Healthcare, Louisville, 1999—2002; chmn. of bd. Kindred Healthcare, Inc., Louisville, 2004—. Dir. Alzheimer's Assn., Houston, 1993—; advisor Woodway Fin. Group, Houston, 1994—; mem. com. Am. Health Care Assn., Washington, 1986—. Co-chmn. fundraising campaign United Way, Med. Ctr., Houston, 1993; bd. dirs. Alley Theater, 1994-97, mem. facilities com., 1994; bd. trustees, adminstrv. and pers. com. Enamu-El, 1996-97. Mem. Thyroid Soc. of Houston (bd. dirs., vice chmn. 1995—), Am. Health Care Assn. (chmn. multifacility steering com., bd. dirs., exec. com., long term financing task force 1997, former mem. numerous coms.), Alzheimer's Assn. (bd. dirs. 1992-97), Thyroid Soc. (vice chmn. bd. dirs., chmn. fund devel. 1996, chmn. bd. 1997), Anti-Defamation League (bd. dirs. 1996-97). Home: 8807 Stable Crest Blvd Houston TX 77024-7035 Office: Kindred Healthcare 680 S Fourth St Louisville KY 40202 *

KUNTZMAN, RONALD, research and development company executive; b. Bklyn., Sept. 17, 1933; s. Herman and Fanny Kuntzman; m. Bernice Russman, May 29, 1955; children: Fred, Gary. BS, Bklyn. Coll., 1955; MS, George Washington U., 1957, PhD in Biochemistry, 1962. Biochemist lab. chem. pharmacology Nat. Heart Inst., NIH, Bethesda, Md., 1955-62; sr. biochemist Wellcome Research Labs.-Burroughs Wellcome & Co. U.S.A. Inc., Tuckahoe, NY, 1962-66, dep. head biochem. pharmacology dept., 1967-70; assoc. dir. dept. biochemistry and drug metabolism Hoffmann-La Roche Inc., Nutley, NJ, 1970-71, assoc. dir. biol. research, 1972-73, dir. therapeutics research, 1973-79, asst. v.p., 1974-81, dir. pharm. R & D, 1980-81, v.p. pharm. R&D, 1981-84, v.p. R&D, 1984-92; adj. prof. dept. chem. biology and pharmacognosy Rutgers U. Coll. Pharmacy, Piscataway, NJ, 1990—2010; adj. mem. Roche Inst. Molecular Biology, Nutley, NJ, 1992-96. Adv. coun. Nat. Orgn. for Rare Disorders, 1987-91; adj. prof. Rutgers U., 1990—. Mem. editl. bd. Biochem. Pharmacology, 1966-68, Neuropharmacology, 1970-78, Xenobiotica, 1970-84, Archives of Biochemistry and Biophysics, 1971-78, Life Scis., 1973-78; contbr. articles to profl. jours. Mem. AAAS, Am. Soc. Pharmacology and Exptl. Therapeutics (editorial bd. jour. 1968-75, nominating com. 1972, chmn. divsn. nominating com. 1977, chmn. divsn. drug metabolism 1978-81, sec.-treas. 1981-83, coun. 1981-83, chmn. long-range planning com. 1987-92, exec. com. divsn. drug metabolism 1973-76, John Jacob Abel award 1969), Am. Soc. Biol. Chemists, Am. Coll. Neuropsychopharmacology, Soc. Toxicology, George Washington U. Alumni Assn. (Dist. Alumni Achievement award 1988), Roche Inst. Molecular Biology (adj. 1992-96), Sigma Xi. Achievements include research on steroids and other normal body constituents which are metabolized by drug metabolizing enzymes; discovered P448, the hemoprotein inducible by hydrocarbon; demonstrated that DOPA-5HTP decarboxylase are the same enzyme. Address: 16 Reunion Rd Rye Brook NY 10573-1085 E-mail: ronkfun@aol.com.

KUNZ, ALEXANDRA CAVITT, physician, anthropologist, researcher; b. Waukegan, Ill., Aug. 3, 1944; d. Hamilton Cavitt and Evelyn Lucille (Becker) Goding; m. Louis William Kunz, Jan. 27, 1968 (div. July 1981); children: Jacob Alexander (dec.), Carmen Rachel. BS with Distinction, U. Nebr., 1966; MD, Ea. Va. Med. Sch., 1991; CPH, Harvard U., 1992, post-grad. Evolutionary Anthropology, 1995—2000. Registered dental hygienist. Mem US Pub. Health Team, Hawaii, 1966; periodontal hygienist Nebr., Hawaii, Calif. Ariz., Mass., Va., 1966—91; med. rschr. Harvard U., Boston, 1992—. Rschr. Wampumpeag, Inc. Mem.: AMA (mem. com. on alcohol and health), AAAS, Hydrocephalus Assn., Found. Internat. Edn. Neurosurgery, Mass. Med. Soc., Am. Assn. Neurol. Surgeons Rsch. Found., Physicians Social Responsibility, Physicians Human Rights. Avocations: ice skating, cross country skiing, piano. Business E-Mail: ARKunz@post.harvard.edu.

KUO, DAVID DA-WEI, dentist, educator; b. Taipei, Taiwan, Mar. 1, 1975; Master of Dental Sci., Boston U., 2005; DDS, Chung Shan Med. Sch. Cert. dental specialities Chung Shan Med. Sch., adv. grad. studies periodontology Boston U., 2005. Clin. instr. Landmark Dental Hosp., Taipei, 2005—06, Nat. Def. Med. Ctr., Taipei; clin. asst. prof., periodontology U. Hong Kong, 2008—. Home: 5f-2 No3 Sec3 Hsin-I Rd Taiwan Taipei 106 Taiwan Office Phone: 852-2859-0521. Personal E-mail: drdavidkuo@yahoo.com.tw.

KUO, IRENE C., ophthalmologist, educator; MD, U. Calif., San Francisco, 1994. Assoc. prof., med. dir. Wilmer Eye Inst., White Marsh, 2000—. Recipient Sci. award, Eye Bank Assn. America; Heed fellowship, Heed-Knapp Orgn. Fellow: Am. Acad. Ophthalmology; mem.: Am. Soc. Cataract and Refractive Surgery, Am. Bd. Ophthalmology. Office: Wilmer Eye Inst 4924 Campbell Blvd Baltimore MD 21236 Business E-Mail: ickuo@jhmi.edu.

KUO, YAO-LUNG, physician, educator; b. Tainan, Taiwan, July 10, 1972; MD, U. Heidelberg, 2001. Vis. staff, asst. prof. Nat. Cheng Kung U., 2006—. Office: 138 Sheng-Li Rd Tainan 704 Taiwan

KUO, YUNG-CHIH, biomaterials scientist, chemical physicist, bioengineer, chemical engineer; b. Taiwan, Republic of China, Mar. 1, 1966; s. Wen-Yu Kuo and Ching Cheng. PhD, Nat. Taiwan U., 1996. Contbr. articles to profl. jours. Mem. AAAS, N.Y. Acad. Scis., Phi-Pau-Phi., Asian Fedn. of Biotechnology, American Nano Soc., Asia-Pacific Chem., Biol. and Environ. Engring. Soc. Presbyterian. Avocations: music composition, photography, literature. Home: 6-19 Min-Tsu Rd Ma-Tou Tainan 72103 Taiwan Office: Nat Chung Cheng U Dept Chem Engring Chiayi 62102 Taiwan Business E-Mail: chmyck@ccu.edu.tw.

KUPEK, EMIL JAKOB, epidemiologist, psychologist; b. Zadar, Dalmatia, Croatia, Oct. 16, 1959; s. Jakob Adam and Karmela Simica K.; m. Beatriz de Freitas Monteiro, June 12, 1993 (div. Aug. 1998); 1 child, Daniela. BSc, U. Belgrade, 1984, MSc, 1991; PhD in Pub. Health Medicine, U. London, 1997. Clin. Psychologist Dept. Psychology, Univ. Belgrade, 1984. Rsch. asst. Inst. Psychology, U. Belgrade, 1985-87; rsch. fellow Inst. Criminology and Sociology, Belgrade, 1987-88; asst. prof. dept. psychology U. Belgrade, 1988-91; rsch. assoc. Imperial Coll. Sch. Medicine, St. Mary's Hosp. Med. Sch., London, 1993-95; prof. epidemiology dept. pub. health U. Fed. Santa Catarina, Florianopolis, Brazil, 1998—. Vis. prof. CNPq, 1997-98. Contbr. articles to profl. jours. including Archives of Sexual Behavior, Social Science and Medicine, Brazilian Jour. of Infectious Diseases, Transfusion Medicine, Jour. of Viral Hepatitis. Prevention of HIV transmission and support for the HIV infected FAÇA, Florianopolis, Santa Catarina, Brazil, 1997—2003. Grantee European Sci. Found., 1991. Fellow Soc. for Social Medicine; mem. AAAS. Achievements include research on estimation of number of sexual partners and its relationship with sexual attitudes, epidemiology of infectious diseases in Brazil and Great Britain. Office: Health Campus U Dept Pub Trindade-Florianopolis 88040-900 Santa Catarina Brazil E-mail: kupek@ccs.ufsc.br.

KUPERMAN, ROMAN GREGORY, toxicologist, ecologist; b. Moscow, May 20, 1957; arrived in USA, 1986; s. Gregory I. Kuperman and Olga R. Blau; m. Frances L. Pergericht, Feb. 24, 1982; 1 child, Natalie Jill. BSc in Biology and Chemistry, Moscow State Pedagogical U., 1980; PhD, Ohio State U., 1993. Program mgr., sr. scientist Geo-centers, Inc., Aberdeen Proving Ground, Md., 1999—2002; rsch. biol. scientist Edgewood Chem. Biol. Ctr., Aberdeen Proving Ground, Md., 2002—. Leader key tech. area Tech. Coop. Program, 2003—10; chmn. contaminated soils adv. group Soc. Environ. Toxicology and Chemistry, Pensacola, Fla., 2002—04; liaison rep. to NAS, U.S. nat. com. for soil sci. Soil Ecology Soc., 2005—. Grantee, Strategic Environ. Rsch. and Devel. Program, 2000—04. Mem.: Soc. Environment Toxicology and Chemistry, Sigma Xi Soc. Office: Edgewood Chem Biol Ctr RDCB DRT E E5641 5183 Blackhawk Rd Aberdeen Proving Ground MD 21010-5424 Office Fax: 410-612-5399. Business E-Mail: roman.g.kupermanciv@mail.mil.

KUPERSMITH, MARK, ophthalmologist, neurologist; Attended, Northwestern U. Med. Sch., Chgo., Ill., 1974. Diplomate Am. Bd. of Ophthalmology, 1981, Am. Bd. of Psychiatry and Neurology-neurology, 1981. Resident opthalmology NY Univ. Med. Ctr., 1976—77, resident neurology, 1978—80; prof. neurology and ophthalmology Albert Einstein Sch. of Medicine; dir. neuro-ophthalmology St. Luke's-Roosevelt, NY Eye and Ear Infirmary, Inst. of Neurology and Neurosurgery. Named one of Best Doctors, NY Mag., 2008, Top Doctors, Castle Cannolly, 2009. Office: St Lukes Roosevelt Hospital Center 1000 10th Ave New York NY 10019 Office Phone: 212-523-4000.

KUPFER, DAVID J., psychiatry professor; b. NYC, Feb. 14, 1941; s. Alex and Muriel (Greenfield) Kupferstein; m. Barbara Stern Burstin, June 1963 (div. Mar. 1975); m. Ellen Frank, June 1975; children: Andrea, Jeffrey, Deborah, Nancy, Erica, Tonia. BA magna cum laude, Yale U., 1961, MD, 1965. Diplomate Am. Bd. Psychiatry and Neurology. Med. intern Montefiore Hosp. Ctr., NYC, 1965—66; clin. fellow in psychiatry Yale U. Sch. Medicine, New Haven, 1966—67; postdoctoral fellow, chief resident in psychiatry Dana Psychiat. Clinic, Yale-New Haven Hosp., 1969—70; asst. prof. Yale U. Sch. Medicine, New Haven, 1970—73; assoc. prof. psychiatry U. Pitts., 1973—75, prof., 1975—, chmn. dept., 1983—; dir. rsch. Western Psychiat. Inst. and Clinic Western Psychiat. Inst. and Clinic, Pitts., 1973—, Thomas Detre prof., chmn. dept. psychiatry, 1994—. Office: U Pitts Western Psychiat Inst & Clinic 3811 Ohara St Pittsburgh PA 15213-2593

KUPFERBERG, BRADLEY J., medical practice administrator; b. Chgo., Sept. 8, 1952; s. Cyril William and Lois Kupferberg; m. Cathy A. Collins, June 19, 1977; children: Shaun F., Kimberly H. BS in Fin., U. Ill., 1974; MBA in Fin., Roosevelt U., 1977. Cert. Am. Coll. Med. Profl. Execs. Hosp. adminstr. U. Chgo. Hosp., 1974-76; fin. officer Northwestern U. Dental Sch., Chgo., 1976-81; CFO Scholl Coll. Podiatry, Chgo., 1982-88; assoc. v.p. fin. Med. Coll. wis., Milw., 1988-90; exec. dir. Children's Surg. Found., Chgo., 1991-2000, CMH Faculty Practice Plan, Inc., Chgo., 1999—. Cons. Kuperberg & Assoc., Schaumburg, Ill., 1981, 90; adv. bd. Stage Left, Chgo.; pres. Assembly of Surg. Practices, 1997-98, Ill. Med. Group Mgmt. Assn., 2006-07. Mem. Med. Group Mgmt. Assn. (cert.). Avocations: sports, weightlifting. Office: 540 W RUHL RD Palatine IL 60074-1041 E-mail: bkupferberg@childrensmemorial.org.

KUPFERWASSER, LEON IRI, cardiologist, researcher; s. Israel and Gerda Kupferwasser; m. Deborah Kahler; children: Hannah E., Noah I. MD, Johannes Gutenberg U., Mainz, Germany, 1991. Cert. in adult echocardiography NBE, 2002, diplomate in internal medicine ABIM, 2003, cardiology 2006, interventional cardiology 2007, cert. in nuclear cardiology CBNC, 2005. Resident medicine, fellowship cardiology Johannes Gutenberg U., Mainz, Germany, 1991—97, rschr., resident med. care, 2001—03; rschr. Harbor UCLA Med. Ctr., Torrance, Calif., 1997—2003; staff physician Cedars Sinai Med. Ctr., LA, 2003—, mem. staff, interventional fellowship, 2006—07. Ptnr. Heart Group, Van Nuys, Calif., 2007—. Contbr. rsch. articles to profl. sci. jours. Recipient Solomon Scholars Rsch. award, 2002, Poster Price, ACP Chpt. Calif., 2002, Nat. Winner Poster Prize, 2003, Aspirin award, Internat. Young Rschrs., 2003; named Fellow of Yr., 2004, Outstanding fellow, 2005, H.J.C. Swan, 2006; Rsch. grant, German Rsch. Found., 1997—99, fellow, European Soc. Cardiology, 2001, Am. Coll. Cardiology, 2006—07. Mem.: ACP, Am. Heat Assn., Am. Soc. Echocardiography, Am. Soc. Nuc. Cardiology. Achievements include discovery of aspirin exhibits anti staphylococcal effects. Office: 10515 Tennessee Ave Van Nuys CA 91406 Office Phone: 818-904-6782. Office Fax: 818-904-5896.

KUPPERMANN, NATHAN, emergency medicine physician, educator; b. Urbana, Ill., July 16, 1958; married. BS, Stanford U., Palo Alto, Calif., 1981; MD, U. Calif. San Francisco Sch. Medicine, 1985; MPH, Harvard U. Sch. Pub. Health, Boston, 1993. Diplomate American Bd. Pediat., cert. in pediatric emergency medicine. Intern, resident pediat. Harbor-UCLA Med. Ctr., Torrance, Calif., 1985—90; fellow in pediatric emergency medicine Children's Hosp. Boston, 1990—93; assoc. prof. U. Calif. Davis Sch. Medicine, 1995—2005, prof. emergency medicine and pediat., 2005—, Bo Tomas Brofeldt endowed chair dept. emergency medicine. Founding chair Pediatric Emergency Care Applied Rsch. Network (PECARN), 2001—08. Contbr. articles to profl. jours. Recipient Dean's award for excellence in rsch. & clin. mentoring, U. Calif. Davis Sch. Medicine, 2003, Outstanding Contbn. to Faculty Devel. & Diversity award, 2007, Miller-Sarkin Mentoring award, Academic Pediatric Assn., 2009, Nat. Heroes award, US Dept. Health & Human Services, 2010. Mem.: American Acad. Pediat., Inst. Medicine, Western Soc. Pediatric Rsch., Soc. Academic Emergency Medicine (Excellence in Rsch. award 2010), American Pediatric Soc., American Coll. Emergency Physicians, Ambulatory Pediatric Assn. Achievements include research in infectious disease emergencies in children including bacteremia, bronchiolitis, meningococcemia and ketoacidosis. Office: UC Davis Health Sys 2315 Stockton Blvd Sacramento CA 95817 Business E-Mail: nkuppermann@ucdavis.edu. *

KUPTNIRATSAIKUL, VILAI, physician, educator; b. Bangkok, Aug. 12, 1959; MD, Mahidol U., 1985; MS in Health Devel., Chulalongkorn U., 2004. Assoc. prof. Mahidol U., 1991—. Office: Prannok Bangkok 10700 Thailand Office Fax: (662)-411-4813. Business E-Mail: sivkp@mahidol.ac.th.

KURACHI, AKEMI, psychologist, educator; b. Kyoto, Aug. 29, 1951; d. Shogo and Emiko Kurachi. BA, Doshisha U., Kyoto, Japan, 1974; MEd, U. Ill., 1978, PhD, 1982. Postdoctoral fellow Stanford U., Palo Alto, Calif., 1982—83; rsch. coord. Inst. Child Behavior and Development U. Ill., Urbana, 1983—84; asst. prof., then assoc. prof. Ritsumeikan U., Kyoto, 1986—93; assoc. prof. Hiroshima U., Japan, 1993—2000, prof., 2001—, chair dept. Grad. Sch. Edn., 2006—08; vis. prof. Tohoku U., Sendai, Japan, 1992—94; vis. scholar Columbia U., NYC, 2008—09. Bd. dirs. Jour. Support Network, Hiroshima, 1994—, transcultural mental health care advisor, 2002—; councilor Hiroshima Internat. Ctr., 2006—. Author: Dialogue: A Path Leading Beyond Cultural Diversity, 1992, Change From Within: A New Development for Transcultural Communication, 1998, Education across Diverse Cultures and Related Fields, 2006, Assessment & Japanese Education, 2010; contbr. articles to profl. jours. Recipient Letitia Walsh fellowship, U. Ill., 1981—82, Univ. fellowship, 1981—82. Mem.: Am. Ednl. Rsch. Assn., Intercultural Edn. Soc. (bd. dirs. 1996—2007, 2009—), Japanese Soc. Transcultural Psychiatry (bd. dirs. 2000—), Phi Delta Kappa, Phi Kappa Phi. Office: Hiroshima U Grad Sch Edn 1-1-1 Kagamiyama Higashi Hiroshima 7398524 Japan Business E-Mail: akemi@hiroshima-u.ac.jp.

KURAMOTO, TAKESHI, gynecologist, director; b. Yanai, Yamaguchi, Japan, Apr. 29, 1952; MD, Kurume U., 1979; PhD, Yamaguchi U., 1985. Asst. dir. Dept. Ob-Gyn. Yamaguchi Grand Med. Ctr., 1985—88, dir., 1988—95, Kuramoto Women's Clinic, 1995—. Med. specialist Fukuoka Prefecture Med. Assn., 2006; part time lectr. Kyushu U., 2007—09, Yamaguchi U., 2010. Mem.: Fukuoka Prefecture Med. Assn., Japan Soc. Reproductive Medicine (advising dr. 2006), Japan Soc. Ob-Gyn. (media specialist 1987), ASRM, ESHRE. Office: 1-1-19 Hakataeki-higashi Hakata-ku Fukuoka 8120013 Japan Business E-Mail: kwc@kuramoto.or.jp.

KURATA, YOSHIAKI, orthopedist; b. Tokyo, Feb. 24, 1970; MD, Tokyo Med. & Dental U., 1996. Surgeon, dept. traumatology and critical care medicine Sapporo Med. U. Hosp., 1996—99, surgeon, dept. orthop. surgery, 1999—2008; surgeon, trauma ctr. Sapporo Tokushukai Hosp., 2008—, Sapporo Higashi Tokushukai Hosp., 2011—. Mem.: Japanese Soc. Surgery Hand, Japanese Soc. Fracture Repair, Japanese Assn. Surgery Trauma, Japanese Assn. Acute Medicine, Japanese Orthop. Assn. Office: Sapporo Higashi Tokushukai Hospital Kita 33 Higashi 14 Higashi-ku Sapporo Hokkaido 065-0033 Japan Business E-Mail: ykurata@h5.dion.ne.jp.

KURBEGOV, AMETHYST CAMILLE, pediatrician, gastroenterologist, educator; b. Austin, Tex., July 8, 1970; BA, Rice U., 1991; MD, Baylor Coll. Medicine, 1997. Resident U. Colo. Sch. Medicine, 1997—2000, chief resident, pediatrician, 2000—01, asst. prof., pediat., 2007—; pediat. GE fellow Baylor Coll. Medicine, Tex. Children's Hosp., 2001—04; asst. prof., pediat. U. Miami Sch. Medicine, 2004—07. Mem.: Am. Assn. Study Liver Diseases, Nat. Soc. Pediat. Gastroenterology, Hepatology, and Nutrition, Crohn's and Colitis Found. America (med. adv. bd. mem., Rocky Mountain Br. 2008—). Avocations: writing, travel, hiking. Office: 2121 E La Salle Ste 201 Colorado Springs CO 80909 Office Fax: 719-365-1524. Business E-Mail: amethyst.kurbegov@childrenscolorado.org.

KUREKCI, EMIN, pediatrician, hematologist, educator; b. Ceyhan, Turkey, Aug. 15, 1962; s. Mehmet and Elmas Kurekci; m. Sema Teke, Mar. 19, 1971; 1 child, Ipek. Diploma, Gulhane Mil. Med. Acad., Ankara, 1986. Diplomate Ministery of Health. Fellow faculty medicine Ankara U., Turkey, 1998—2000; assoc. prof. pediat. hematology, chief dept. pediat. hematology Gulhane Mil. Med. Acad., 2000—. Dir. dept. pediat. hematology Gulhane Mil. Med. Acad., Ankara, 2000—. Avocation: travel. Office: Gülhane Military Med Acad Etlik Ankara 06018 Turkey Office Fax: +90 312 304 4381. Business E-Mail: ekurekci@gata.edu.tr.

KURIAN, PIUS, nephrologist, educator; b. Arpookara, India, May 9, 1959; s. Pylo and Mariamma Kurian; m. Sally Kurian, May 11, 1986; children: Michelle Maria, Matthew Paul, Catherine Tresa. BSc, Kuriakose (India) Elias Coll., 1979; MB, BChir, Kottayam (India) Med. Coll., India, 1986. Diplomate Am. Bd. Internal Medicine, Am. Bd. Nephrology, Am. Bd. Forensic Examiners; specialist clin. hypertension, Am. Soc. Hypertension. Resident in internal medicine Nassau County Med. Ctr., East Meadow, NY, 1988-91, fellow in nephrology, 1991-94; attending physician in nephrology Mercy Med. Ctr. and Cmty. Hosp., Springfield, Ohio, 1994—. Asst. prof. dept. medicine Wright State U., Dayton, Ohio, 1998; chief divsn. internal medicine Mercy Med. Ctr., Springfield, Ohio, 1999, chmn., dir. dept. medicine Mercy Med. Ctr., Springfield, Ohio, 2000; med. dir. Cmty. Physicians Dialysis, Springfield, 2000—, DaVita Midwest Dialysis Springfield, Urbana, Fairborn, Ohio; chmn. ethics com. Cmty. Hosp., Springfield; mem. governing bd. Cmty. Mercy Health Ptnrs. Health Sys., Springfield, 2006. Fellow ACP, Am. Soc. Nephrology, Am. Soc. Hypertension (specialist in clin. hypertension); mem. AAAS, AMA, Am. Coll. Physicians Execs., Internat. Soc. Nephrology, Renal Physicians Assn., Am. Soc. Nephrology, NY Acad. Scis., Clark County Med. Soc. (pres. 2004). Roman Catholic. Office: 247 S Burnett Rd Springfield OH 45505-2639 Home Phone: 937-390-3144; Office Phone: 937-322-7364. Personal E-mail: piuskurian@doctor.com.

KURIBAYASHI, TOSHIRO, physician; b. Kurume, Japan, Feb. 16, 1945; s. Tetsuji and Yaeko (Noda) K.; m. Chizuko Takakura, Apr. 10, 1976; children: Yuko, Yoshiko BS, Kyoto U., 1967; MD, Kyoto Prefectural U. Medicine, 1976, PhD, 1987. Cert. in cardiology. Asst. prof. Kyoto Prefectural U. Medicine, 1986—90, assoc. prof., 1990—94, guest prof., 1994—; physician Red Cross Hosp., Kyoto, 1994—96; dir. Kuribayashi Clinic, Fukuoka, Japan, 1996—. Guest rschr. NIH, Bethesda, Md., 1991-92 Co-author: Developmental Mechanism of Heart Disease, 1995; contbr. articles to Am. Jour. Physiology, Pediat. Rsch., Am. Jour. Cardiology, others Japanese Govt. grantee, 1986, 90, 93 Mem. Japanese Circulation Soc., Japanese Soc. Internal Medicine Avocations: horticulture, bicycling. Home and Office: Ozasa 5-5-18 Chuo-Ku Fukuoka 810-0033 Japan Home Phone: 092-525-3202; Office Phone: 092-525-3200. Personal E-mail: kuriba@basil.ocn.ne.jp.

KURIC, LUTVO, medical researcher; b. Sarajevo, SA, Bosnia-Herzegovina, Aug. 22, 1941; m. Semka Herceg, Jan. 29, 1970; children: Adem, Eldin. Cert. sr. expert collaborant Sarajevo BiH, 1986. Economical Faculty, Rijeka, Croatia, 1973—77; dir. economical and fin. dept. Municipality, Novi Travnik, SBK, Bosnia-Herzegovina, 1990—97; dir. Fed. Office Stats., Dept. SBK Canton, Travnik, 1998—2006, Fed. Office Stats., Dept. Sci. Rsch., Sarajevo, 2004—05. Cons. Inst. Genetics, Sarajevo, 2007—08. Contbr. articles to jours. Pres. Charity Merhamet, Novi Travnik, SBK, 1997—2004. Recipient Internat. Hippocrates award, Outstanding Med. Achievement Cert., 2011, Gold medal, 2011; named Internat. Health Profl. of Yr., 2010. Achievements include patents pending for New methodologies for enchantment of the researching phenomenas in medicine and genetics. Home: Kalinska 7/7 SBK 72290 Novi Travnik Bosnia-Herzegovina Office Phone: 00387 62 208279. Personal E-mail: lutvokuric@yahoo.com.

KURIEN, SANTHA T., psychiatrist; b. Perumpavoor, Kerala, India, June 15, 1945; came to US, 1973; d. Varghese and Mary (Thomas) Koshy; m. Thomas K. Kurien; children: Susan, Miriam. MD, Calicut Med. Coll., Kerala, India, 1970. Diplomate Am. Bd. Psychiatry Neurology; cert. geriatric psychiatry; cert. addiction psychiatry, clin. psychopharmacology, Consumers Rsch. Coun. America, 2007, Peers Conn. Mag., 2008, 2009. Sr. house surgeoncy Vellore Med. Coll., Madras, 1970-71; gen. med. practice St. Thomas Memorial Hosp., Vadasscrikara, Kerala, India, 1971-72; psychiat. residency Fairfield Hills Hosp., Newtown, Conn., 1973-76, staff psychiatrist, 1976-77, Danbury Hosp., Conn., 1977-82; psychiatrist pvt. practice, Danbury, 1982—. Consulting psychiatrist Pope John Paul Ctr., Danbury, Conn., 1991 2000. Named one of Americas Top Psychiatrists, Coun. America, 2007, Conn. Top Drs., Conn. Mag., 2008—10. Mem. Am. Psychiat. Assn., Am. Assn. Geriatric Psychiatry, New Haven County Med. Assn., Danbury Med. Soc., Assn. Kerala Med. Grads., Am. Soc. Clin. Psychopharmacology (cert.). Office: 27 Hospital Ave Ste 304 Danbury CT 06810-5954 Office Phone: 203-743-3833. Business E-Mail: santha.t.kurien@snet.net.

KURIHARA, ATSUSHI, research scientist, drug metabolism; b. Yokohama, Japan, Sept. 27, 1962; s. Takeshi and Yoshie Kurihara; m. Naomi Kawauchi; children: Misa, Kei. M, U. Tokyo, 1987, PhD, 1996. Dir. Sankyo Co. Ltd., Tokyo, 1987—2007, Daiichi Sankyo Co. Ltd., Tokyo, 2007—. Vis. scientist UCLA Sch. Medicine, 1997—99. Contbr. articles to profl. jours. Mem.: JSDDS, JSSX. Achievements include discovery and development of antiplatelet drug prasugrel and antihypertensive drug olmesartan. Avocations: walking, swimming. Home: Tsuzuki Yokohama Japan Office: Daiichi Sankyo Co Ltd 1-2-58 Hiromachi Shinagawa-ku Tokyo 140 8710 Japan

KURIHARA, HIDEO, surgeon, educator; b. Maebashi, Gunma, Japan, Aug. 11, 1928; s. Eiichi and Tama Kurihara; m. Kouko Fukushi; children: Kasumi Nakaya, Hideko. MD, PhD, Tohoku U., Sendai, Japan, 1960. Diplomate Ministry Health, 1955. Vice dir. Noguchi Hosp., Beppu, Ohita, Japan, 1960—65; chief head, neck surgery Iwate Inst. Ctrl. Hosp., Morioka, Japan, 1965—81; dir. Kurihara Thyroid Clinic, Morioka, 1981—, Kurihara Thyroid Lab., 1981—. Prof. emiritus Jilin U. Med. Sch., Changchun, China, 1993—, Harbin Med. U., Amur, China, 1994—. Contbr. articles to sci. publs. Commr. Tohoku Thyroid Soc., Tohoku, Japan, 1987—2008, advisor Tohoku, 1987—2008. Mem.: Japan Endocrine Surg. Assn., Japan Surg. Assn., Japan Thyroid Surgery Assn., Japan Thyroid Assn., Japan Endocrine Assn. Achievements include research in original surgical technique and method for thyroid disease. Office: Kurihara Thyroid Clinic 1-16-4 Honchodori Morioka Iwate 020-0015 Japan Office Phone: 81-19-654-7123, 81-19-654-7040. Office Fax: 81-19-654-7113. Business E-Mail: kclinic@rnac.ne.jp.

KURIHARA, SHINTARO, medical educator; b. Japan, Jan. 30, 1970; BS, Nagasaki U., 2000. Asst. prof., infection control and edn. ctr. Nagasaki U. Hosp., 2006—. Grants, Japan Soc. Promotion Sci. Avocation: reading. Office: Sakamoto1-7-1 Nagasaki 8500036 Japan Office Fax: 81-958197766. Business E-Mail: kurihiro@nagasaki-u.ac.jp.

KURIHASHI, KATSUAKI, ophthalmologist, dacryologist; b. Muroran, Hokkaido, Japan, Dec. 23, 1944; s. Yoshio and Yone Kurihashi; m. Fumiko Ota, Apr. 11, 1971; children: Miyako, Daisuke. MD, Sapporo Med. Coll., Japan, 1971. Dir. Kurihashi Eye Clinic, Hamamatsu, Japan, 1980—; temp. lectr. Hamamatsu U. Sch. Medicine, 1989—. Author: Dacryology, 1998; patentee apparatus for intubation of lacrimal drainage pathway, Nunchaku-style silicone tubing; contbr. articles to profl. jours., ency.; mem. editl. bd. European Soc. Dacriology, 1992—. Mem.: Japanese Soc. Ophthalmic Surgeons (exec. com. 2002). Avocations: photography, films, walking. Office: Kurihashi Eye Clinic 1366-1 Hatsuoi-cho Hamamatsu 433-8112 Japan E-mail: k-eyemed@poem.ocn.ne.jp.

KURIYAMA, GENSHIN, physician, researcher; b. Tokyo, Jan. 24, 1969; s. Teiko Kuriyama; children: Minami, Gentaro. MD, Jikei U., 1996, PhD, 2004. Cert. Japanese Soc. Internal Medicine, 2005. Physician Jikei U. Sch. Medicine, Tokyo, 1997—2000, Utsunomiya Nat. Hosp., Tochigi-ken, Japan, 2004—. Grantee, Japan Smoking Rsch. Found., 2001—03. Avocations: fishing, skiing, swimming, travel. Office: Utsunomiya National Hosp 2160 Shimo okamoto Kawachi machi Kawachi gun Tochigi 329 1193 Japan Ken Office Fax: 028-673-6148; Home Fax: 03-3699-1430. Personal E-mail: kuri_gen0101@yahoo.co.jp.

KURIYAMA, SHINICHI, epidemiologist, educator; b. Osaka, Japan, Oct. 5, 1962; s. Rokuichi and Hatsue Kuriyama; m. Yuka Goto, May 5, 1987; children: Koichi, Tatsuya, Tomoya. BS, Tohoku U., 1987, PhD, 2004; MD, Osaka City U., 1993. Med. diploma Japan, 1993. Physician Osaka City U. Hosp., 1993; med. dir. Daido Mutual Life Ins. Co., 1993—2003; asst. prof. dept. pub. health and forensic medicine Tohoku U. Grad. Sch. Medicine, Sendai, Japan, 2003—05, assoc. prof., 2005—. Recipient Young Investigator award, Japan Epidemiol. Assn., 2005, Gold prize, Tohoku U. Sch. Medicine, 2008. Achievements include discovery of effects of green tea in humans. Avocations: reading, travel, swimming. Home: 2-39-7 Kunimigaoka Aoba-ku Sendai Miyagi 989-3201 Japan Office: Tohoku Univ Grad Sch of Medicine 2-1 Seiryo-machi Aoba-ku Sendai Miyagi 980-8575 Japan Office Fax: +81-22-717-8125. Business E-Mail: s-kuri@mail.tains.tokoku.ac.jp.

KURK, MITCHELL, physician; b. NYC, Aug. 25, 1931; s. Benjamin and Frieda (Steinbaum) K.; m. Marcia Carol Leon (dec. 1981); children: Hope, Nancy, Cindy. BS, MS, Columbia U., 1954; OD, Mass. Coll. Optometry, 1955; DO, Phila. Coll. Osteopathic, 1960; MD, U. Calif., 1962. Diplomate Am. Bd. Family Practice. Pvt. practice, NYC, 1962—. Attending physician Peninsula Hosp. Ctr. Author: Prescription for a Long Life, 1997. Fellow Internat. Coll. Applied Nutrition, Am. Acad. Family Physicians; mem. AMA, Internat. Acad. Preventive Medicine, Am. Holistic Med. Assn., N.Y. State Med. Soc., Nassau County Med. Soc., Nassau Acad. Medicine. Republican. Office Phone: 516-239-5540.

KURKUS, JAN OLGIERD, nephrologist; b. Warsaw, Jan. 7, 1939; arrived in Sweden, 1982; s. Marian Stanislaw and Romana Irena Kurkus; m. Jadwiga Maria Wojtulewicz, Jan. 7, 1967; 1 child, Jan Michal. MD, Warsaw Med. Sch., 1962, PhD, 1972. Cert. splty. bd. internal medicine Warsaw, 1973, Stockholm, 1985, splty. bd. nephrology Stockholm, Ednl. Coun. for Fgn. Med. Grads. Examination, 1974, Fgn. Med. Grad. Examination in Med. Scis., 1987. Postgrad. intern and resident Warsaw Med. Sch. Hosp., 1962—64, mem. tchg. staff, 1964—75, 1976—80; spl. fellow medicine Meml. Sloan Kettering Cancer Ctr., NYC, 1975—76; resident dept. hematology and nephrology Uppsala (Sweden) U., 1984—85; resident dept. nephrology U. Lund, Sweden, 1985—89; cons., sr. cons. dept. nephrology U. Hosp. Lund, 1989—, assoc. prof., 1998—. Cons. Polish Red Cross, Warsaw, 1970—74; cons. internal medicine U. Benghazi, Libya, 1980—82; vis. investigator Meml. Sloan Kettering Cancer Ctr., NYC, 1982; investigator Internat. Nutritional Rsch. Inst., Stockholm, 1983; head dialysis dept. U. Lund, 1991—2004; med. dir. dialysis dept. Gambro Healthcare Sweden, Lund, Sweden, 2004—05. Contbr. chapters to books, articles to profl. jours. Recipient reward, Polish Students Assn., 1962, Bronze medal, Polish Red Cross, Warsaw, 1974, reward, Polish Acad. Sci., Warsaw, 1979, Warsaw Med. Sch., 1979. Mem.: Polish Med. Assn. in Sweden (exec. com. 1992—2006), Swedish Soc. Transplantation, Swedish Soc. Nephrology, Swedish Med. Assn. Avocations: sailing, skiing, photography. Home: Knut Wicksells Vg 17 224 66 Lund Sweden

KURLAND, GEOFFREY, pediatric pulmonologist, educator; MD, Stanford U., 1973. Diplomate Am. Bd. Pediatrics, Am. Bd. Pediatrics-pediatric pulmonology, Am. Bd. Allergy and Immunology. Resident Stanford U., Stanford, Calif., 1976; fellow Children's Hosp., 1978; hosp. affiliations include/s Children's Hosp. of Pitts. of UPMC, UPMC Children's Surgery Ctrs.; prof. pediatrics Univ. of Pitts. Recipient Outstanding Achievement in Patient Care award, 2003, Faculty Recognition award, Univ. of Pitts.; named one of Top 25 Physicians, Children's Hosp. of Pitts. Office: Childrens Hospital of Pittsburgh of UPMC Division of Pediatric Pulmonology 4401 Penn Ave Fl 3 Pittsburgh PA 15224 Office Phone: 412-692-5630. Office Fax: 412-695-6645.

KURLANSKY, PAUL ALAN, cardiovascular and thoracic surgeon; b. Hartford, Conn., Oct. 14, 1952; s. Philip and Roslyn (Solomon) K.; m. Helaine Schneuder, June 13, 1976; children: Aaron, Dylan. AB, Harvard U., 1975; MD, Tufts U., Boston, 1980. Diplomate Am. Bd. Surgery, Am. Bd. Thoracic Surgery. Intern Columbia U., NYC, 1980-81, residency, 1981-85, post doctoral rsch., 1985, cardiothoracic surgical residency, 1986-87; pvt. practice Miami, 1988—97; assoc. med. dir. Allied Health Group, 1998—99; dir. rsch. Miami Heart Rsch. Inst., 1999—. Presenter in field; contbr. articles to profl. jours. Recipient Disting. Recognition award, Spl. Recognition award, 1990, Honoree chmn, 1991, Outstanding Svc. in Profl. Edn., 1992, Am. Heart Assn.; named Honoree Physician award Bikkur Cholim, 1996. Fellow Am. Coll. Surgeons, Am. Coll. Chest Physicians, Am. Coll. Cardiology; mem. Soc. Thoracic Surgeons, Internat. Soc. Heart Transplantation, NY Acad. Sciences, Fla. Soc. Thoracic and Cardiovascular Surgeons, Dade County Med. Assn. Office: Miami Heart Rsch Inst 4770 Biscayne Blvd 5th Fl Miami FL 33137 Office Phone: 305-674-3154. Office Fax: 305-674-3009. E-mail: doctorwu18@aol.com.

KURLINSKI, JOHN PARKER, physician; b. Buchanon, W.Va., Jan. 17, 1948; s. John Peter and Jean (Holloway) K.; m. Claire Sawyer, June 12, 1971; children: Joshua John, Ryan Edward, Seth Parker. AB cum laude, Williams Coll., 1970; MD, Johns Hopkins Sch. Medicine, 1974. Intern, then resident Johns Hopkins Hosp., Balt., 1974-77; fellowship neonatal/perinatal medicine U. Calif., San Diego, 1977-79; chief resident pediatrician Johns Hopkins Hosp., 1979-80; pediatrician, co-dir. neonatology S.W. Regional Neonatal Ctr. at Sunrise Hosp. and Med. Ctr., Las Vegas, 1980-93; vice chief pediat. Sunrise Children's Hosp., Las Vegas, 1983-90, vice chief of staff, 1989-90, chief of staff, 1990-95, dir. NICU, 1994—2002; clin. assoc. prof. pediatrics U. Nev. Sch. Medicine, Reno, 1994—2007. Bd. dirs. S.W. Regional Neonatal Ctr. Edn. Found.; chmn. bd. dirs. Sunrise Children's Hosp. Found.; mem. Med.-Legal Screening Panel, Nev., 1986—; many hosp. coms., 1980—. Bd. dirs. So Nev. chpt. March of Dimes, Las. Vegas, 1984—. Mem. AMA, Am. Acad. Pediatrics (v.p. Nev. chpt. 1987-90, pres. 1990-93, coun. mem. dist. VIII sect. on perinatal pediatrics), Clark County Med. Soc., Las Vegas Pediatric Soc. (founding), Phi Beta Kappa. Avocations: rugby, skiing, hiking, camping. Home: 3322 Beam Dr Las Vegas NV 89139-5902 Office: Sunrise Childrens Hosp 3186 S Maryland Pky Las Vegas NV 89109-2317 Office Phone: 702-361-5167. Personal E-mail: kurli@cox.net.

KURMIS, ANDREW PAUL, medical educator, consultant, researcher; b. Adelaide, Australia, Feb. 3, 1978; s. Peter and Patricia Anne Kurmis. BAppSc in Med. Radiations, U. So. Australia, 1997, B in Med. Radiations with honors, 1998; PhD in Orthopaedics, Flinders U., 2003, postgrad., 2005—. Cert. IV ambulance studies So. Australia Ambulance Svc., 2001; II small bus. mgmt. Flinders U. / YAA, 2002. Rsch. officer Inst. Med. Vet. Sci., Adelaide, Australia, 2003—04; orthop. rsch. fellow Flinders U., Bedford Park, Australia, 2004—05; orthop. rsch. cons. Repatriation Gen. Hosp., Daw Park, Australia, 2005—. Rsch. cons. So. Australian Ambulance Svc., Adelaide, 2003—; bd. mem. Sch. Medicine, Flinders U., Bedford Park, 2004. Mem. editl. bd.: journal Radiography, Soc. and Coll. Radiographers, London, 2004—; contbr. articles in field. Recipient Richard T. Southwood Orthop. prize, Flinders Med. Ctr., 2005. Mem.: AMA, Australian and New Zealand Bone and Mineral Soc., Flinders Ctr. Epidemiology and Biostatistics, Australian and New Zealand Orthop. Rsch. Soc., Australian Inst. Radiography (Rsch. award 2003), Australian Coll. Ambulance Profls. (assoc.), Internat. Soc. Radiographers and Radiol. Technologists (assoc.). Achievements include patents pending for IVD hydration state semi-quantitative ranking model.

KURNICK, NATHANIEL BERTRAND, retired oncologist, hematologist; b. Bklyn., Nov. 8, 1917; s. Jacob and Celia (Levine) K.; m. Dorothy Manheimer, Oct. 4, 1940 (dec. Dec. 1985); children: John E., Katherine(dec.), James T.; m. Sally Ann Kreeger, June 23, 1989; children: Helen Seigel, Miriam Seigel-Stern, Lynn Seigel-Boettner, Glenn Steiner, Bruce Steiner. BA, Harvard U., 1936, MD, 1940. Diplomate Am. Bd. Internal Medicine, Am. Bd. Med. Oncology, Am. Bd. Hematology, Am. Bd. Med. Examiners. Intern Mt. Sinai Hosp., NYC, 1941-42, chief resident internal medicine, 1946; asst. prof. medicine Tulane U. Med. Sch., New Orleans, 1949-54; chief hematology svc. VA Hosp., Long Beach, Calif., 1954-59, cons., 1959—; assoc. clin. prof. medicine U. Calif., LA, 1954-64, clin. prof. medicine Irvine, 1964-99; pvt. practice Long Beach, 1959-83; dir. Bixby Hematology-Oncology Lab. Long Beach Cmty. Med. Ctr., 1982—99. Chmn. cancer activities, 1968—90; chmn. dept. medicine, 1966—68; chmn. dept. med. oncology and hematology, 1982—87; pres. Long Beach Soc. Internal Medicine, 1971; chmn. Franklin Bank of Calif., Orange, Calif., 1988—2004. Contbr. over 150 articles to jours. in field. Trustee Garden Grove, Calif. Unified HS Dist., 1960-64. Capt. U.S. Army Med. Corps., 1942—46, Pacific Ocean area. Am. Cancer Soc./NRC fellow, 1946-47, Rockefeller Inst., 1946-47, Nobel Inst., 1947-49; NIH/Am. Cancer Soc. grantee, 1949-1972; Henry Hunter Workman rsch. fellow Harvard Med. Sch./Mass. Gen. Hosp., 1940-41. Fellow ACP; mem. Intern. Soc. Exptl. Hematology, Am. Soc. Hematology, Western Soc. Clin. Rsch., Cen. Soc. Clin. Rsch., Sigma Xi (fellow 1951). Democrat. Jewish. Avocations: sailing, skiing, travel.

KURODA, HAJIME, pathologist, researcher; b. Tokyo, Tokyo, Japan, June 11, 1968; s. Setsuo and Hisayo Kuroda; m. Mina Kawasaki, June 2, 2000. PhD, Tokyo U., 1998. Diplomate Japanese Soc. of Pathology, 1999. Asst. Saitama Med. Ctr., Kawagoe, Saitama, Japan, 1998—.

KURODA, SHINJI, dental educator; b. Tokyo, Mar. 11, 1970; DDS, Tokyo Med. and Dental U., 1995, PhD, 1999. Postdoc. rsch. fellow Rush U. Med. Ctr., 2001—03; tchg. asst. Tokyo Med. and Dental U., 1998—99, clin. staff, 1999—2000, asst. prof., 2000—. Mem.: Japanese Soc. Inflammation and Regeneration, Internat. Congress Oral Implantologists, Internat. Assn. Dental Rsch., Orthop. Rsch. Soc., Am. Soc. Bone and Mineral Rsch. Office: 1-5-45 Yushima Bunkyo-ku Tokyo 113-8549 Japan Office Fax: 81-3-5803-4656. Business E-Mail: skuroda.mfc@tmd.ac.jp.

KUROI, KATSUMASA, physician; m. Kuroi Sayamoto; children: Kuroi Miki, Kuroi Shoko, Kuroi Ryo. PhD, Hiroshima U., Japan, 1987. Cert. Health, Labour and Welfare Ministry, 1984. Dir. Tokyo Met. Komagome Hosp., Bunkyo-ku, 2007—. Office: Tokyo Met Komagome Hosp 3-18-22 Honkomagome Bunkyo-ku Tokyo 113-8677 Japan Home: 1-11-9-404 Honkomagome Bunkyo-ku Tokyo 113 0021 Japan Office Phone: 81-3-3823-2101. Office Fax: 81-3-3824-1552. Business E-Mail: kurochan@dd.iij4u.or.jp.

KUROIWA, TOSHIHIKO, neurosurgeon, educator; b. Okayama, Japan, Jan. 12, 1954; MD, Osaka Med. Coll., Takatsuki, Japan, PhD, 1985. Cert. neurosurgeon Japan Neurosurgical Soc., 1985. Prof. Osaka Med. Coll., 2000—, chmn., 2000—. Mem.: World Fedn. Neurosurgical Soc. Office: Osaka Med Coll 2-7 Daigakumachi Takatsuki Osaka 569-8686 Japan Office Phone: 81-72-683-1221. Business E-Mail: neu040@poh.osaka-med.ac.jp.

KUROKI, HIROSHI, orthopedic surgeon; b. Miyazaki, Japan, Mar. 7, 1966; MD, Miyazaki Med. Coll., 1990. Resident Miyazaki Med. Coll., 1991—92, physician, 1994—97, instr., 1997—2005; physician Miyazaki Kohnan Hosp., 1991—92, Miyazaki Nat. Sanatorium, 1992—93; resident in anesthesia Kanto Teishin Hosp., Tokyo, 1993—94; asst. prof. faculty medicine U. Miyazaki, 2005—. Avocations: reading, golf. Office: U Miyazaki Faculty Medicine 5200 Kihara Kiyotake Miyazaki 889-1692 Japan Home: 2-6-25 Segashira Miyazaki 8800867 Japan Office Phone: 81-985-85-0986. Business E-Mail: hiroshik@med.miyazaki-u.ac.jp.

KURPAD, UMESH A., insurance company executive; b. Burla, Orissa, India, Dec. 23, 1957; came to U.S., 1979; s. Anantharam Shamanna and Indira (Rao) K.; m. Debra Ann Webb, Aug. 6, 1983. BS in Civil Engring., Delhi Coll. of Engring., India, 1979; MBA, U. Florida, 1981. Systems analyst Fireman's Fund Ins. Companies, San Rafael, Calif., 1982-83, sr. systems analyst, 1983-84, sr. fin. analyst Novato, Calif., 1984-86; fin. planner Kaiser Health Plan, Kaiser Permanente, Oakland, Calif., 1986—; v.p. health care bus. develop. for Asia/Pacific unit of CIGNA Intenat. CIGNA Corp., asst. v.p. provider and internat. strategy, asst. v.p. and controller of managed care ops.; CFO Munich Reinsurance America; sr. v.p., CFO Tufts Health Plan, 2008—. Grad. assistantshipU. Fla., 1980-81. Avocation: tennis. Office: Tufts Health Plan 705 Mt Auburn St Watertown MA 02472 *

KURTZ, MYERS RICHARD, retired hospital administrator; b. Schaefferstown, Pa., June 18, 1924; m. Linda Bewan, Dec. 26, 1988; 1 child, Ronald Hayden; 1 stepchild, Erin B. Brown. BS, U. Md., 1958; MBA, Ind. U., 1963. Served as enlisted man U.S. Army, 1942-51, commd. 2d lt., 1951; advanced through grades to lt. col. Med. Svc. Corps, 1965; mem. staff Army Surgeon Gen., Washington, 1963-67; ret., 1967; affiliation adminstr. NYU Med. Ctr., NYC, 1967-69; exec. dir. Ephrata Community Hosp., Pa., 1969-76; supt. Longview State Hosp., Cin., 1976-79; asst. dir. Ohio Dept. Mental Health and Mental Retardation, Columbus, 1979-81, dir., 1981-82; sr. v.p. Cleve. Met. Gen. Hosp., 1982-83; supt., CEO Ctrl. State Hosp., Milledgeville, Ga., 1983-93; adminstr., CEO G. Pierce Wood Meml. Hosp., Arcadia, Fla., 1995-98, ret., 1998. Adj. asst. prof. dept. psychiatry U. Cin., 1977-83. V.p., bd. dirs. Coordinated Home Care Agy., Inc., Lancaster County; pres. Lancaster County Hosp. Coun.; bd. dirs. Pa. Hosp. Assn., Baldwin County United Way, 1986-91, Baldwin County Salvation Army; mem. adv. bd. Youth Devel. Ctr., 1984-91. Decorated Legion of Merit, Army Commendation medal with oak leaf cluster, Soldiers medal. Fellow Royal Soc. Health; mem. Am. Coll. Hosp. Adminstrs. (life fellow), Am. Acad. Med. Adminstrs., Am. Hosp. Assn., Milledgeville-Baldwin County C. of C. (bd. dirs. 1984-87, exec. com. 1986—, treas. 1987—), Nassau County Vol. Ctr. (bd. dirs. 1998-, pres. 2002-03), Sigma Iota Epsilon, Rotary Internat. Home: 95485 Captains Way Fernandina Beach FL 32034-4346 Personal E-mail: LmKurtz@bellsouth.net.

KURTZ, ROBERT C., gastroenterologist, educator; MD, Jefferson Coll., 1986. Diplomate Am. Bd. Internal Medicine, Am. Bd. Internal Medicine-gastroenterology. Resident internal medicine Meml. Sloan-Kettering Cancer Ctr., NYC, 1969—71, fellow gastroenterology, 1971—73, former pres. med. staff; prof. medicine Weill Med. Coll., NYC, chief gastroenterology and nutrition svc., co-dir. hepatobilliary disease mgmt. team. Office: Memorial Sloan-Kettering Cancer Center Gastroenterology and Nutrition Service 1275 York Ave New York NY 10065 Office Phone: 212-639-7620.

KURTZBERG, JOANNE, pediatrician, educator; b. NYC, Nov. 18, 1950; d. Lawrence Kurtzberg; m. Henry S. Friedman; children: Joshua, Sara. BA, Sarah Lawrence Coll., 1972; MD, N.Y. Med. Coll., 1976. Intern in pediats. Dartmouth Med. Ctr., Hanover, NH, 1976—77; resident in pediats. Upstate Med. Ctr., Syracuse, NY, 1977—79, clin. rsch. fellow in pediat. hematology/oncology, 1979—80; mem. faculty Duke Comprehensive Cancer Ctr., Durham, NC, 1983—; sr. rsch. fellow in pediat. hematology/oncology Duke U. Med. Ctr., Durham, NC, 1980—86, asst. prof., assoc. prof. pediat., 1983—88, prof. pediat., 1993—, dir. pediatric bone marrow lab., 1989—, dir. pediat. blood and marrow transplant program, 1989—2004, mem. grad. faculty Grad. Sch. pathology dept., 1993—, assoc. prof. pathology, 1991—2003, prof. pathology, 2003—, dir. Carolinas cord blood bank, 1996—, chief divsn. pediatric blood and marrow transplant, 2004—. Recipient R. Wayne Rundles award for excellence in cancer rsch., 1993, Basil O'Connor Starter Scholar Rsch. award, 1985-87. Fellow Leukemia Soc. Am. (spl. fellow, scholar 1986-89); mem. Internat. Soc. for Hematotherapy and Graft Engring., Am. Soc. for Blood & Marros & Transplantation, Am. Soc. Pediat. Hematology/Oncology, Am. Soc. Hematology, Soc. for Pediat. Rsch., Pediat. Oncology Group, Alpha Omega Alpha. Home: 1808 Faison Rd Durham NC 27705-2439 Office: Duke U Med Ctr PO Box 3350 Durham NC 27702-3350 Home Phone: 919-383-6157; Office Phone: 919-668-1119. *

KURTZKE, JOHN FRANCIS, SR., neurologist, epidemiologist; b. Bklyn., Sept. 14, 1926; s. John Ambrose and Teresa Rose (Knipper) K.; m. Margaret Mary Nevin, June 30, 1950; children: John Francis Jr., Catherine Kurtzke Brown, Elizabeth Kurtzke Siebert, Patricia Margaret(dec.), Joan Kurtzke Brennan, Robert, James, Christine Kurtzke Hughes. BS summa cum laude, St. John's U., NY, 1948; MD, Cornell U., Ithaca, NY, 1952; MD (hon.), U. Ferrara, Italy, 2000; med. diploma (hon.), U. degli Studi di Ferrara, Italy, 2008. Diplomate in neurology Am. Bd. Psychiatry and Neurology, 1958 (asst. examiner, then examiner and sr. examiner in neurology 1964-96, cert. appreciation 1969, 90). Intern Kings County Hosp., Bklyn., 1952—53; resident in neurology VA Hosp., Bronx, NY, 1953-56, chief neurology svc. Coatesville, Pa., 1956—63, Washington, 1963—95; chief neuroepidemiology sect. VA Med. Ctr., Washington, 1995—2002, cons. in neurology, 1995—, cons. in neuroepidemiology, 2002—; cons. in neurology VA Multiple Sclerosis Ctr. Excellence East, Balt., 2004—. Mem. faculty Jefferson Med. Coll., Phila., 1958-63, asst. prof. clin. neurology, 1963; mem. faculty Georgetown Med. Sch., Washington, 1963—, prof. neurology, 1968-2000, prof. emeritus, 2000—, vice chmn. dept. neurology, 1976-95, prof. cmty. and family medicine, 1968-95; Disting. prof. neurology Uniformed Svcs., U. Health Scis., Bethesda, 1992—, USN med. student liaison officer, 1979-85; vis. prof. neurology and neuroepidemiology Temple U. Sch. Medicine, 1984-89; cons. neurology Nat. Naval Med. Ctr., Bethesda, 1966-2000, Surgeon Gen. Navy, 1970-97; mem. med. adv. bd. Nat. Multiple Sclerosis Soc., 1966-94, hon. mem., 1995—, mem. working group on design of clin. studies in multiple sclerosis, 1976-84, mem. exec. com., 1981-83, mem. task force on epidemiology, 2006—; mem. med. adv. bd. Internat. Fedn. Multiple Sclerosis Socs., 1972—, hon. mem., 1998—; mem. com. multiple sclerosis World Fedn. Neurology, 1967—, com. neuroepidemiology, 1977—; chmn. epidemiology sect. NIH Epilepsy Adv. Com., 1973-76; med. rsch. program specialist for neurology and neurobiology VA Rsch. Svc., 1977-80; chmn. work group epidemiology HEW Commn. Control of Huntington's Disease, 1976-78; mem. naval exam. bd. Naval Med. Command, 1980-83; mem. Residency Rev. Com. Neurology, 1983-88, vice chmn., 1985-86, chmn., 1987-88; chmn. US Naval Res. Med. Flag Coun., 1985-86; mem. instnl. rev. bd. Nat. Inst. Neurol. Diseases and Stroke, 1989-98; established investigator Nat. Multiple Sclerosis Soc., 1987—; mem. spl. panel Inst. Medicine, 1990; mem. oversight com. War-Related Illness and Injury Ctr., VAMC, Washington, 2002—; mem. oversight com. MS Ctrs. of Excellence, VA, 2003—; mem. Am. Com. Treatment and Rsch. in Multiple Sclerosis, L.Am. Com. on Treatment and Rsch. in Multiple Sclerosis, Consortium of Multiple Sclerosis Ctrs. Author, co-author: Epidemiology of Multiple Sclerosis, 1968, Epidemiology of Cerebrovascular Disease, 1969, Epidemiology of Neurologic and Sense Organ Disorders, 1973, Neuroepidemiology, 1998, Psychiatry/Neurology, 1998, Practice Questions. Book One, 1998, Psychiatry/Neurology, 1998, Book Two, 1998, Encyclopedia of the

Neurological Disorders (Neuroepidemiology), 2003; mem. editl. bd. Neuroepidemiology, 1980—, Neurology, 1984-92, Stroke, 1986-2000, Jour. Clin. Epidemiology, 1988-2005, Jour. Neurol. Sci., 1990-96, Acta Neurologica Scandinavica, 1990-97; contbr. 550 articles to profl. jours., chpts. to books. Served with USN, 1944—46, rear adm. M.C. USNR, 1946—86, rear adm. USN ret., 1986—. Decorated Legion of Merit (2), Navy Commendation medal, Armed Forces Res. medal with gold hourglass, others; recipient cert. of merit, Surgeon Gen. Navy, 1969, Gold Bicennial medal, Georgetown U., 1982, Sec.'s Disting. Career award, Dept. Vets. Affairs, 1998, Dystel award for MS Rsch., NMSS, AAN, 1997, Charcot award, Internat. Fedn. MS Socs., 1999, Lifetime Achievement award, Consortium of MS Ctr., 2003, others, Kurtzke Clinician Scientist fellowship, AANF & CMSC, 2009. Fellow: ACP (life), AAAS (life), Pan Am. Med. Assn. (coun. neurology sect.), Am. Coll. Preventive Medicine, Am. Coll. Epidemiology, Am. Acad. Neurology (chmn. sect. on neuro-epidemiology 1971—75, chmn. com. nat. needs in neurology 1981—85, subcom. nat. needs in neurology 1985—86, mem. work force task force 1997, John Jay Dystel prize for mulitple sclerosis rsch. 1997), NY Acad. Sci., Am. Heart Assn. (stroke coun. 1991—2000); mem.: AMA, AAUP, Consortium Multiple Sclerosis Ctrs. (Lifetime Achievement award 2003), Lat. Am. Com. Treatment and Rsch. in Multiple Sclerosis, Am. Com. Treatment and Rsch. in Multiple Sclerosis, Soc. Med. Cons. to Armed Forces (com. on res. affairs 1980—83, com. on manpower 1984—98, com. on med. edn. 2001—09), Sr. Stroke Soc., Res. Officers Assn. (life), Naval Inst. (life), Fleet Res. Assn. (life), Naval Officers Assn. Am. (life), Am. Neurol. Assn. (hon.; chmn. bylaws ad hoc com. 1990—91), Danish Neurol. Soc. (hon.), French Soc. Neurology (hon.; fgn.), Assn. Nicolò Copernico (hon.), German Soc. Neurology (hon.), Assn. Mil. Surgeons (life), Naval Res. Assn. (life), Naval Order US (life), Internat. Stroke Soc., Am. Soc. Microbiology, Am. Epilepsy Soc., Assn. Rsch. in Nervous and Metal Disease, Internat. Epidemiol. Assn., Am. Epidemiol. Soc., So. Med. Assn., Navy League (life). Home: 7509 Salem Rd Falls Church VA 22043-3240 Office Phone: 703-560-6016. Office Fax: 703-560-6490. Business E-Mail: kurtzke2@aol.com.

KURTZMAN, JAMES TODD, medical educator; b. Santa Monica, Calif., Apr. 25, 1962; BA, Stanford U., 1984; MD, U. Calif., San Diego, 1988. Assoc. prof. maternal-fetal medicine U. Calif., Irvine Med. Ctr., Loma Linda U. Med. Ctr., 1999—. Ob-gyn. dept. chmn. Saddleback Meml. Med. Ctr., 1999. Recipient Nat. award, Assn. Profs. Ob-Gyn. Fellow: Am. Coll. Obstetricians and Gynecologists; mem.: Am. Inst. Ultrasound Medicine, Soc. Maternal-Fetal Medicine (Nat. award 1998—99, 2003, 2009), Phi Beta Kappa. Avocations: running, walking, piano. Home: 11234 Anderson St Ste 3400 Loma Linda CA 92354 Business E-Mail: jtk@stanfordalumni.org.

KURUKULASURIYA, LILAMANI ROMAYNE GOONETILLEKE, medical educator; b. Colombo, Sri Lanka, Dec. 1, 1963; MBBS, Faculty Medicine, 1991. Assoc. prof. U. Mo. Columbia, 2000—. Fellow: Am. Assn. Clin. Endocrinologists. Avocation: travel. Office: D109 Diabetes And Endocrinology Ctr Columbia MO 65212 Office Fax: 573-884-4609. Business E-Mail: kurukulasuriyar@health.missouri.edu.

KURY, BERNARD EDWARD, lawyer; b. Sunbury, Pa., Sept. 11, 1938. AB, Princeton U., 1960; LLB, U. Pa., 1963. Bar: NY 1964. Assoc. Dewey, Ballantine, Bushby, Palmer & Wood, NYC, 1963-71, ptnr., 1971—2004; v.p., gen. counsel Guidant Corp., Indpls., 2004—06. Contbg. editor Ency. of Venture Capital; bd. trustees Keck Grad. Inst. (KGI), 2006—. Editor: Pa. Law Sch. Review. Mem.: NY State Bar Assn., Assn. of the Bar of the City of NY, ABA. Mailing: Keck Grad Inst 535 Watson Dr Claremont CA 91711

KURZIK-DUMKE, URSULA BARBARA, science administrator, educator; b. Silesia, Poland, Sept. 21, 1952; arrived in Germany, 1976; m. Andres Dumke; 1 child, Martin Dumke. Grad in Bioscis., U. Silesia, Katowice, Poland, 1976, MS in Biology; Dr.rer.nat, U. Leipzig, Germany, 1981. Rsch. asst. dept. chemistry of biologically active substances U. Leipzig, Germany, 1981—83; head lab. Inst. Environ. Hygiene, Leipzig, Germany, 1984; head cell culture lab. Inst. Pathobiochemistry, Faculty Medicine, U. Leipzig, Germany, 1985—89; lectr., head Comparative Tumor Biology Group, Biology Faculty, Inst. Genetics, Johannes Gutenberg U., Mainz, 1989—2004; prof., faculty medicine, inst. med. microbiology & hygine Johannes Gutenberg U., 2005—; mem. Commn. Protection Animals, Ministry Edn. & Sci., 2005. Guest prof. Faculty Biology, U. Silesia, 2001—. Contbr. articles to profl. jours. Named to Great Woman, 21St Century Hall Fame, ABI, 2008. Mem.: New Yorker Acad. Scis., German Genetics Soc., German Soc. Cell Biology, Am. Assn. Cancer Rsch., European Assn. Cancer Rsch., German Cancer Rsch. Soc. Avocations: music, piano, literature, art, travel. Office: University Med Ctr Johannes Gutenberg University Verfugungsgebaude Forchung & Entwicklung Obere Zahlbacher Str 63 Mainz D 55131 Germany Office Phone: 0049-6131-17 9221, 0049-6131-17 9337. Business E-Mail: Kurzik@uni-mainz.de.

KURZMAN, MICHEAL A., dermatologist; MD, NY Med. Coll.; attended, Yeshiva U. Diplomate Nat. Bd. of Med. Examiners, Am. Bd. Internal Medicine. Postgrad. tng. Maimonides Med. Ctr., internal medicine intership, residency; dermatology residency NY Med. Coll., clin. asst. prof. dermatology dept.; co-dir. dermatology divsn. Staten Island Univ. Hosp. Fellow: The Am. Acad. of Dermatology. Office: Staten Island Office 401 Bloomingdale Rd Staten Island NY 10309 Mailing: Bayside Office 7308 Springfield Blvd Oakland Gardens NY 11364 Office Phone: 718-317-0941. Office Fax: 718-464-0109.

KUSAKA, SHUNJI, physician; b. Tokushima, Japan, Sept. 11, 1961; s. Toshio and Tsuneko K.; m. Kanae Yamada; children: Takuya, Hiroki. MD, Osaka U., Japan, 1986, PhD, 1998. Resident Osaka U. Med. Sch., Japan, 1986-87; faculty Tane Meml. Eye Hosp., Osaka, 1991-92; asst. prof. Ehime U. Sch. Medicine, Japan, 1992-97, Osaka U. Med. Sch., 1997—. Author: A Guidebook for Ophthalmic Assistant, 1996; contbr. articles to profl. jours. Clin. fellow Nat. Osaka Hosp., 1987-91, rsch. fellow U. Mich., Ann Arbor, 1994-97. Mem. Am. Acad. Ophthalmology, Soc. Neurosci., Assn. Rsch. & Ophthalmology and Visual Sci. Office: Osaka U Med Sch 2-2 Yamada-oka Osaka 565-0871 Japan

KUSH, MICHELLE L., physician, educator; b. Ill., Oct. 25, 1971; MD, Loyola U. Stritch Sch. Medicine, 1998. Asst. prof. U. Md., 2002—. Med. dir. Perinatal Outreach. Fellow: SMFM, ACOG. Office: 22 S Greene St N6W104F Baltimore MD 21202 Office Phone: 410-328-3613. E-mail: michellekush@yahoo.com.

KUSHEL, YURY, neurosurgeon; b. Minsk, Belorussia, June 21, 1970; s. Vadim and Marianna Kushel. MD, PhD, Sechenov's Moscow Med. Acad., 1994. Bd. cert. neurosurgeon Russian Acad. Postgrad. Med. Edn., 2000. Neurosurgical resident Burdenko Neurosurg. Inst., Moscow, 1994—99, staff neurosurgeon, assoc. prof., 1999—. Recipient Braakman Diploma of Excellence, European Assn. Nneurosurg. Soc. Tng. Com., 2000, Peter The Gt. Sci. medal, Russian Acad. Natural Sci., 2005. Mem.: Am. Assn. Neurol. Surgeons (corr.). Office: Burdenko Neurosurgical Inst ul. Tvyerskaya-Yamskaya 4-Ya # 524 125047 Moscow Moskva Russia Personal E-mail: kuszel@mail.ru. Business E-Mail: kuszel@nsi.ru.

KUSHIBIKI, TOSHIHIRO, medical educator, researcher; b. Osaka, Japan, Sept. 4, 1975; MSc in Pharm. Sci., Osaka U. Pharm. Scis.; PhD in Polymer Chemistry, Kyoto U., 2005. Lic. pharmacist 1998. Asst. prof., biomed. engring. Osaka U., 2006—, assoc. prof., biomed. engring., 2006—11. Rschr. Japan Sci. Tech., Precursory Rsch. Embryonic Sci. Tech., Tokyo, 2006—10; vis. rschr. Mass. Gen. Hosp., 2008—; vis. assoc. prof. Havard Med. Sch., 2008—10. Contbr. scientific papers to profl. publs. Recipient prize, Japanese Soc. Laser Surgery and Medicine, 2006, Lazer Soc. Japan, 2007, Young Sci. prize, Ministry Edn., Culture, Sports, Sci. and Tech. Japan, 2008. Office: Osaka Univ 2-1 Yamadaoka Suita Osaka 565-0871 Japan

KUSHIKATA, TETSUYA, anesthesiologist, educator; b. Ichikawa City, Chiba, Japan, May 31, 1963; s. Kazuo and Miyo Kushikata; m. Yasuko Shimomura, Mar. 29, 1965. MD, U. Hirosaki Sch. Medicine, Japan, 1989; PhD, U. Hirosaki, 2002. Bd. cert. Japanese Soc. Anesthesiologist, 1995, cert. med. practitioner conducting advanced clin. tng. Ministry Health and Welfare, 1999. Instr. dept. anesthesiology U. Hirosaki Sch. Medicine, 1993, 1999—, lectr. dept. anesthesiology, 2007; rsch. assoc. dept. physiology U. Tenn., Memphis, 1996; rsch. assoc. dept. vet. medicine Wash. State U., Pullman, 1997—98. Recipient award, Japanese Soc. Intravenous Anesthesia, 2005, 2008—10, 2011—;, Ministry Edn., Sci. & Culture, 2001—02, 2003, grant, Ministry Edn., Sci. & Culture JPN, 2001—02, 2003, 2005, 2008—10, 2011—. Mem.: Am. Chem. Soc., Internat. Brian Rsch. Orgn., Soc. Neurosci., USA, Japanese Neurosci. Soc., Japanese Assn. Acute Medicine, Japanese Soc. Intensive Care Medicine, Japanese Soc. Anesthesiologists (bd. mem. 1995). Office: Univ Hirosaki Sch Medicine Zaifu 5 Hirosaki 0368562 Japan Aomori Office Phone: 81172395113, 81172335111. Office Fax: 81172395112. Business E-Mail: masuika@cc.hirosaki-u.ac.jp, tetsuyak@cc.hivosaki-u.ac.jp.

KUSHLAN, SAMUEL DANIEL, internist, educator, hospital administrator; b. New Britain, Conn., Feb. 17, 1912; s. H. David and Bessie M. K.; m. Ethel Ross, June 24, 1934; children: Nancy Kushlan Wanger, David Ross. BS, Yale U., 1932, MD, 1935. Diplomate: Am. Bd. Internal Medicine with subsplty in gastroenterology. Intern New Haven Hosp., 1935-36, asst. resident, 1937; vol. research fellow Mass. Gen. Hosp., 1938; assoc. physician-in-chief Yale-New Haven Hosp., 1967-82, cons. to chief staff, 1982—; clin. prof. medicine Yale U., 1967—. Contbr. numerous articles to profl. jours. Mem. bequest and endowment program Yale Med. Sch. Alumni Fund, 1977—; cons. to office of alumni affairs Yale Med. Sch., 1990—. Named Physician of Yr. Conn. Digestive Disease Soc., 1975, recipient Yale medal, 2007. Mem. AMA, Am. Gastroenterol. Assn., Am. Soc. Gastrointestinal Endoscopy, Conn. State Med. Soc., New Haven Med. Assn., Conn. Regional Soc. for Gastrointestinal Endoscopy, World Med. Assn., Assn. Yale Alumni in Medicine (pres. 1957-59), Yale Alumni Fund (bd. dirs. 1986-91), ACP (Lifetime Achievement award Conn. chpt. 2003), Sigma Xi, Alpha Omega Alpha. Office: Suite 1063 CB Yale-New Haven Hosp New Haven CT 06504 Office Phone: 203-688-2604.

KUSHNER, BRIAN HARRIS, oncologist; b. NYC, July 8, 1951; s. William Isidore and Sheila Elaine (Kasselbranar) Kushner; m. Phyllis Debra Levinberg, Feb. 22, 1986; children: Sarah Lynn, Carolyn Joy. AB, Harvard U., 1972; MD, Johns Hopkins U., 1976. Diplomate Am. Bd. Pediatrics, Am. Bd. Pediatric Hematology-Oncology. Pediatric intern and resident Babies Hosp. of Columbia-Presbyn. Med. Ctr., NYC, 1976-78; pediatric sr. resident N.Y. Hosp., NYC, 1978-79; clin. fellow in pediatric hematology-oncology Children's Hosp., Boston, 1979-80; staff pediatrician Boston City Med. Clinics, North End Cmty. Health Ctr., 1980-81; coord. in-patient svc., dir. ICU dept. pediatrics Lincoln Hosp., N.Y. Med. Coll., Bronx, 1982-83; clin. rsch. fellow in pediatric hematology-oncology Meml. Sloan-Kettering Cancer Ctr., NYC, 1983-86, chief fellow dept. pediat., 1985-86, spl. fellow dept. pediat., 1986-87, clin. asst. pediatrician, 1987-92; asst. attending pediatrician dept. pediat. N.Y. Hosp., NYC, 1988—; asst. attending pediatrician Meml. Sloan-Kettering Cancer Ctr., NYC, 1992—99, assoc. attending pediatrician, 1999—2003, attending pediatrician, 2003—. Staff physician Internat. Rescue Com., Khao-I-Dang Refugee Camp, Thailand, 1981, Oxfam Relief, Khlam, Lebanon, 1983; instr. pediat. Cornell U. Med. Coll., NYC, 1987—, asst. prof. pediat., 1993—. Contbr. articles to profl. jours. Recipient Clin. Scholars Nat. Rsch. Svc. award, 1988—90, Career Devel. award, Am. Cancer Soc., 1990—93; Am. Cancer Soc. grantee, 1993—95. Mem.: Am. Soc. Pediatric Hematology-Oncology, Am. Soc. Hematology, Am. Soc. Clin. Oncology, Am. Assn. Cancer Rsch., Am. Acad. Pediat. Office: Meml Sloan Kettering Cancer Ctr 1275 York Ave # 299 New York NY 10021-6094 Office Phone: 212-639-6793.

KUSHNER, JACK, physician executive; b. Montgomery, Ala., Dec. 5, 1939; s. Louis Harry and Rose (Feldman) K.; m. Annetta Esther Horwitz, June 21, 1964; children: Reyna, Eve. Student, U. Sheffield, 1959—60; BA in History, Tulane, 1960; MD, U. Ala., 1964; MGA in Fin., U. Md., Coll. Pk., 1990. Diplomate Am. Bd. Neurosurgery, 1976, cert. in Neurosurgery. Intern George Washington U. Hosp., Washington, 1964; resident in surgery U. Mich., Ann Arbor, 1965-66; resident in neurosurgery Bowman Gray Sch. Medicine Wake Forest U., Winston-Salem, NC, 1968-72; instr. neurosurgery Johns Hopkins U., 1972—79; pvt. practice neurosurgery Annapolis, Md., 1972-95; clin. asst. prof. neurosurgery George Washington U., 1976—80; founder Transcriptions Internat., 1990; pres., CEO, Futuristic Instruments, Annapolis, 1995-98; chmn., bd. dirs. Telehealth, 1999. Bd. mgrs. Anne Arundel Med. Ctr., Annapolis, Md., 1978-80; mem. Mil. Leadership Coun., U. Md., 2003—; bd. dirs. E-Global Telehealth, 1999—; chmn., CEO Am. Opportunity Portal, Annapolis, 2003-09; lectr. UMUC-Graduate Sch. Bus. Author: Preparing To Tack: When Physicians Change Careers, 1995, Coping Successfully with Changing Winds and Tides: A Neurosurgeon's Compass 2009-, When Universities are Destroyed, 2010, Courageous Judicial Decisions in Alabama, 2011; contbr. articles to profl. jours. With U.S Army, 1966-68, combat surgeon, Vietnam Capt. 91st Evacuation Hosp. US Army, 1966—68, Tuy Hoa, Vietnam. Decorated Bronze Star; recipient Most Disting. Alumnus award U. Md., 2001, laureate Marie Curie award for contbns. to neurosurgery and emerging med. tech. Oxford U., 2006, Lifetime Achievement award World Forum, Washington, 2007, 1st place Bronze Divsn., World Ball Rm. Dancing, Las Vegas, Nev., 2008; named Amb. of Knowledge, U. Cambridge, 2010; named to Hall of Fame Oxford U., Eng., 2008. Fellow ACS (emerging tech. and edn. com.), Internat. Coll. Surgeons; mem. Am. Assoc. Neurol. Surgeons, Congress of Neurol. Surgeons, So. Neurosurg. Soc., Pan Pacific Neurosurg. Soc., Tulane U. Alumni Assn. (bd. dirs., dir.-at-large), Tulane Med. Sch., Strategic Global Initiative, Tulane Assoc. (bd. dir.), US Naval Acad. Golf Assn.(sr. men's tournament dir.), Sheffield in Am., 1902 Soc.(founding mem.) Republican. Jewish. Avocations: golf, yacht racing, ballroom dancing. Home: Ferry Farms 2030 Homewood Rd Annapolis MD 21409-5970 Personal E-mail: jkaoportal@comcast.net.

KUSHNER, MICHAEL JAMES, neurologist, consultant, educator; b. Hackensack, NJ, July 18, 1951; s. Samuel and Ruth Ellen (Paul) K.; m. Sarah Joan Warden, Aug. 14, 1976; children: Hunter Paul, Paul Macrae (dec.). BA in Physics, Yale U., 1973; MD, NYU, 1977. Diplomate Am. Bd. Psychiatry, Am. Bd. Neurology, Am. Bd. Med. Examiners; cert. Am. Bd. Electrodiagnostic Medicine, Am. Bd. Pain Medicine. Intern Parkland Meml. Hosp., U. Tex., Dallas, 1977-78; resident in neurology Neurol. Inst., Columbia-Presbyn. Med. Ctr., NYC, 1978-81; rsch. assoc. U. Pa., Phila., 1981-83, asst. prof. neurology, 1983-90; attending physician Hosp. of U. Pa., Phila., 1983-90; with Wilson (N.C.) Neurology Ctr., 1992—; clin. asst. prof. East. Carolina U. Sch. Medicine, 1997—. Dir. SPECT facility Hosp. of U. Pa., 1986-90, asst. dir. neurovascular lab., 1987-90; mem. sensory disorders and lang. study sect. NIH, Bethesda, Md., 1988-90; staff neurologist Wilson (N.C.) Orthop. Surgery Neurology Ctr.; legal medicine cons.; neurology physician advisor N.C. Blue Cross/Blue Shield; asst. prof. East Carolina U. Sch. Medicine; dir. Wilson Regional MRI Ctr. Contbr. numerous articles to profl. jours. Interviewer alumni schs. com. Yale U., Phila., 1984—. Fellow Am. Acad. Neurology, Am. Heart Assn. (stroke coun.); mem. AMA, Internat. Soc. for Blood Flow and Metabolism, N.C. Neurol. Soc. (pres. 1995-97), Yale of N.Y.C., Yale of Cen. N.C., Yale of N.C. Republican. Episcopalian. Avocations: oenology, travel, exercise, art. Home: 1110 Salem St NW Wilson NC 27893-2137 Office: Wilson Neurology Ctr PO Box 3148 Wilson NC 27895-3148 Office Phone. 252-243-9629.

KUSHNIR, IGAL, physician; b. Petachtikva, Israel, Nov. 11, 1945; m. [illegible], Aug. 3, 1969; children: Tali Bar David, Alon, Dafna Weiss, Sharon. MD (hon.), Tel Aviv U., grad. cum laude. Cert. pediat. specialist Israel, 1973. Founder, CEO MTRE, Or-Akiva, Israel, 1996—2000, Deep Breeze, Or-Akiva, 2001—08; physician Israel, 1972—. Philanthropic activities, Israel. Achievements include invention of human thermo-regulation device; VRI vibration response imaging. Home: Shekdim St 11 Pardess Hanna 37011 Israel Home Phone: 972 544 204 583. Personal E-mail: igalkush@gamil.com, dr@igalkushnir.com.

KUSS, BRYONE JEAN, hematologist; b. Adelaide, Australia, Apr. 30, 1961; MBBS, Sch. Medicine, Adelaide U., 1985, PhD in Molecular Haematology, 1997. Head unit SA Pathology, Flinders Med. Ctr., 2011—. Head molecular medicine Sch. Medicine Flinders U., 2009, assoc. dean Flinders Clin. and Molecular Medicine, 11. Recipient Albert Baikic medal, HSANZ; Howard Florey fellow, Royal Soc., Postdoc. Rsch. fellowship, NHMRC, Leukaemia Rsch. fellowship, Peter Nelson Found. Fellow: Royal Coll. Pathologists Australasia, Royal Australian Coll. Physicians; mem.: Australasian Leukaemia Lymphoma Group, Haematology Soc. Australia and New Zealand, Am. Soc. Haematology. Avocations: dance, music. Office: Dept Haematology & Genetic Pathology Bedford Park 5042 Australia Office Fax: 618 82045706. Business E-Mail: bryone.kuss@flinders.edu.au.

KUSSMAN, MICHAEL JAMES, retired federal agency administrator; b. Troy, NY, May 22, 1944; MD, Boston U., 1968; MS, Salve Regina U., 1994; grad., Army War Coll.; grad. (hon.), Command Gen. Staff Coll. Cert. internal medicine. Joined US Army, 1970, advanced through ranks to brig. gen., 1996; med. resident Joslin Clinic, Boston, 1972—74; pvt. practice Pittsfield, Mass., 1974—79; chief internal medicine Tripler Army Med. Ctr., Honolulu, 1979—84; chief, Dept. Medicine Brooke Army Med. Ctr., San Antonio, 1984—88, dep. comdr. clin. svcs.; chief cons. in internal medicine Army Surgeon Gen., 1988; gov. Army Region, ACP, 1988; comdr. Martin Army Comty. Hosp., Ft. Benning, Ga., 1993—95, Walter Reed Health Care Sys., Washington, Europe Regional Med. Command; command surgeon US Army Europe; TRICARE lead agt. for Europe; prin. dep. under sec. for health US Dept. Veterans Affairs, Washington, 2005—06, acting under sec. for health, 2006—07, under sec. for health, 2007—09. Mem. faculty Uniformed Svcs. U. Health Sciences. Decorated DSM, Legion of Merit with three oak leaf clusters, Defense Meritorious Svc. medal, Order of Military Medical Merit; recipient Laureate award, ACP/Am. Soc. Internal Medicine. Master: ACP.

KUTLUBAY, ZEKAYI, dermatologist; b. Malatya, Turkey, Apr. 10, 1970; Specialist Istanbul U. Cerrahpasa Med. Faculty, 1994. Dermatology specialist Cerrahpasa Med. Faculty, 2000. Mem.: Turkish Soc. Dermatlogists, Dermatoloji Akademisi Dernegi, Kozmetik Dermatoloji Akademisi Dernegi. Office: Istanbul Universitesi Cerrahpasa Tip Fakültesi Istanbul 34000 Turkey Personal E-mail: zekayikutlubay@hotmail.com.

KUTSCHERA, ULRICH, biologist, researcher; b. Freiburg, Germany, Feb. 2, 1955; s. Alfred and Esther Kutschera; m. Renate Bernot, Sept. 2, 1983; children: Verena, Jens, Lena. BS in Biology and Chemistry, U. Freiburg, 1980, MS in Zoology, 1981, PhD in Plant Physiology, 1985. Rsch. fellow Carnegie Inst. Stanford U., 1985—87, vis. prof., Carnegie Inst., 2007—; rsch. assoc. Mich. State U., East Lansing, 1987—88; lectr. U. Bonn, Germany, 1988—93; prof. U. Kassel, Germany, 1993—, dean dept. biology, 1998—99. Mem., fellow Alexander-von-Humbold Found., 1985—. Author: Grundpraktikum zur Pflanzenphysiologie, 1998, Evolutionsbiologie, 2001, 3d edit., 2008, Prinzipien der Pflanzenphysiologie,2nd edit., 2002, Streitpunkt Evolution, 2004, Kreationismus in Deutschland, 2007, Tatsache Evolution, 2009; contbr. articles to 200 sci. publs. Recipient Goedecke-Forschungspreis, 1986. Mem.: Assn. German Biologists (v.p. 2005—), European Soc. Evolutionary Biology, Fedn. European Societies Plant Physiology. Achievements include discovery of several leech species and growth promoting symbiotic bacteria; epidermal growth control theory of stem elongation; synade model of macroevolution. Office: U Kassel Biology Dept Heinrich-Plett-Str. 40 34132 Kassel Germany Office Fax: 0049-561-804-4009. E-mail: kut@uni-kassel.de.

KUTTER, DOLPHE, chemist, educator; b. Trier, Germany, July 28, 1932; s. Joseph and Rosalie (Sedlmayr) Kutter; m. Delphine Guggenbichler, June 6, 1972; children: Pierre-Joseph, Jean. MS in Chemistry, U.Lausanne, 1954; DSc, U. Lausanne, 1957; MD (hon.), Charite U., Berlin, 1990. Dir. lab. Labs. Reunis, Junglinster, Luxembourg, 1959—2004. Prof. U. Lausanne, Switzerland, 1968—88, Centre U., Luxembourg, 1988—98; vis. prof. Charles U., Prague, Czech Republic, 1996—2000. Contbr. over 200 articles to profl. jours. Cpl. Health Svc. Luxembourg Army, 1958. Office: Labs Reunis POB 11 Junglinster 6101 Luxembourg Home: 48 Kiem 5337 Moutfort Luxembourg

KUTTLER, JUDITH ESTHER, retired psychotherapist; b. Paterson, NJ, Feb. 26, 1938; d. Theodor Herzl and Roslyn Unterman; children: Hillel Moshe, David Eli, Nadine Eve. BA, Marymount Manhattan Coll., NYC, 1974; MSW, Hunter Coll. Sch. Social Work, NYC, 1978, post-masters cert. in adv. clin. social work in family therapy, 1982. RN Beth Israel Hosp. (now known as Beth Israel Med. Ctr.), NYC, 1960. Psychotherapist Creedmoor Psychiatric Ctr., Queens, NY, 1972—84, social worker, Manhattan Children's Psychiatric Ctr., Ward's Island, NY, 1986—88, Creedmoor Psychiatric Ctr., Queens, 1988—94; self-employed psychotherapist Adv. Ctr. for Psychotherapy, Jamaica Estates, 1994—2002. Com. mem. Penn South Housing Complex, NYC. Jewish. Avocations: reading, hiking, poetry, travel, writing. Home: 365 W 25th St Apt 20H New York NY 10001-5825

KUTTY, PREETA, epidemiologist; b. Kuwait, Apr. 2, 1971; MPH, Boston U., 2005; MD, Kasturba Med. Coll., 1998. Med. epidemiologist Ctrs. Disease Control & Prevention, 2005—. Named one of Shea Trainee of Yr., Soc. Healthcare Epidemiology America, 2006. Avocations: swimming, painting. Home: 1326 Briarhill Ln NE Atlanta GA 30324 Personal E-mail: preeta.kutty@gmail.com.

KUTZ, JOSEPH EDWARD, hand surgeon, educator; b. Standish, Mich., June 11, 1928; s. Joseph M. and Hazel (Stock) K.; m. Mary Jane Templeton, June 15, 1957; children: Anthony, Karen, Bradley. BS, U. Detroit, 1953, MS, 1955; MD, U. Mich., 1958. Diplomate Am. Bd. Surgery. Rotating intern Springfield (Ohio) City Hosp., 1958-59; resident in gen. surgery U. Louisville Med. Sch., 1959-63; fellow in surgery of hand U. Louisville, 1963-64, asst. clin. prof. surgery, 1968-74, assoc. clin. prof., 1974-88, clin. prof. surgery, 1988. Chmn. divsn. hand surgery U. Louisville Med. Sch., 2004. Contbr. numerous articles to profl. jours. With AUS, 1946—48. Mem. ACS, Am. Soc. Surgery of Hand, Caribbean Soc. Surgery of Hand, Am. Med. Assn., Ky. Med. Assn., Greater Lousiville Med. Soc. (pres. 1988-89), Louisville Surg. Soc., Pan-Pacific Surg. Soc., Southeastern Surg. Congress., Am. Soc. Plastic Surgeons, Internat. Soc. Reconstructive Microsurgery (founder, treas. 1983-91), World Soc. for Reconstructive Microsurgery (founding mem.), Am. Soc. for Reconstructive Microsurgery (pres. 1986-87), Sunderland Soc. (charter), SC Orthop. Assn. (hon.), Group for Advancement Microsurgery. Office: 225 Abraham Flexner Way Louisville KY 40202-1846 Office Phone: 502-561-4263.

KUTZSCHE, STEFAN, physician; b. Frankfurt, Germany, Apr. 15, 1954; MD, U. Hamburg, 1983; PhD, U. Oslo, 2002, M in Health Adminstrn., 2006; M in Health Profl. Edn., U. Maastricht, 2011. Sr. cons., dept. anaesthesiology Oslo U. Hosp., 1991—2000; rsch. fellow U. Oslo, 1994—98; sr. cons. Oslo U. Hosp. Women and Child Clinic, 2000—; chief physician Norwegian Air Ambulance Found., 2009—10. Mem., leader Com. Licencing Matters and Fgn. Med. Drs. Faculty Medicine U. Oslo, 1998—2008; chief editor Jour. Norwegian Assn. Pediatricians, 2009; bd. mem. Norwegian Assn. Pediatricians, 2009. Decorated Emergency Svc. medal Russian Border Directorate. Mem.: Norwegian Med. Assn., Assn. Med. Edn. Europe. Office: Kirkeveien 166 Oslo 0407 Norway

KUUSISTO, JOHANNA MARIA, cardiologist, scientist; b. Vaasa, Finland, Apr. 27, 1959; d. Isak and Saara Johanna (Pennanen) K.; m. Markku Heikki Sakari Laakso, May 11, 1996; 1 child, Annamaria Aleksandra. Licent of medicine, U. Kuopio, Finland, 1984, MD, 1996, docent of internal medicine, 1996. Asst. physician dept. medicine Kuopio U. Hosp., 1985-90, sr. physician dept. medicine, 1991-97, lectr. in medicine, 1996-98, cardiologist, 1998—, acting chief physician cardiology unit, 2005—07, acting prof. cardiology, 2007—10, acting chief physician dept. medicine, 2010—, acting prof. medicine, 2010—. Vis. scientist dept. medicine/divsn. cardiology U. Wash., Seattle, 1993-94. Contbr. articles to profl. jours. Mem. European Cardiac Soc., Am. Heart Assn., Finnish Cardiac Soc. Avocations: literature, architecture, music, sports, riding. Office: Kuopio U Hosp Cardiology Unit Dept Medicine PO 1777 70211 Kuopio Finland Office Phone: 358 17 173949. Business E-Mail: johanna.kuusisto@kuh.fi.

KUWABARA, CLEUZA CATSUE TAKEDA, nursing administrator; b. Londrina, Dec. 23, 1958; Degree, U. Estadual de Londrina, 1980; PhD in Nursing, USP Ribeirão Preto, 2009. Advisor material resources U. Estadual de Londrina - U. Hosp., 1998—2004, hosp. risk mgr., 2002—10, don, 2006—10, dir. Lab. Medicines, 2011—. Pvt. practice, 2010. Recipient Best Sci. Paper award, Congress Nursing and Tech., 2000. Home: Ave Voluntários da Pátria 241 Londrina Paraná 86061120 Brazil Personal E-mail: cleuzak@yahoo.com.br.

KUWAHARA, TOSHIYA, dentist, prosthodontist; b. Osaka, Japan, Mar. 1, 1960; s. Setsushi and Akiko (Kawamura) K.; m. Shigeyo Kojima, Apr. 30, 1993; children: Lisa, Riku. DDS, Osaka U., 1984, PhD, 1989. Cert. oro-facial pain Japanese Soc. Temporomandibular Joint. Jr. instr. Osaka U. Dental Sch., 1989-91, sr. instr., 1991-96; postdoctoral fellow in maxillofacial surgery SUNY, Buffalo, 1993-95. Vis. rsch. prof. SUNY, Buffalo, 1993-95. Mem. Internat. Coll. Prosthodontists, Am. Soc. Temporomandibular Joint Surgeons, Am. Acad. Fixed Prosthodontics. Avocation: scuba diving. Home: 1-103-6 Bessho Hachioji Tokyo 192-0363 Japan Office: Kuwahara Dental Clinic 1001-3 Takahata Hino Tokyo 191-0031 Japan

KUWAJIMA, SHIROU, physician; b. Taipei, Taiwan, Feb. 28, 1943; s. Yosio and Tomie Kuwajima; m. Noriko Okada, May 14, 1976; children: Yumiko, Masako. BA, Nat. Kyoto U., Japan, 1965; MD, Osaka City U., Japan, 1970, PhD, 1975; postgrad., Nat. Osaka U., 1975—76. Staff 3rd dept. internal medicine Osaka City U. Med. Sch., Japan, 1977—85, staff, lectr. dept. lab medicine, 1985—91; vice-dir. Yaenosato Hosp. Med. Corp., Higashi-Osaka City, Osaka Prefecture, Japan, 1991—96; from vice-dir. to dir. Haruki Hosp., Med. Corp., Kishiwada City, Osaka Prefecture, Japan, 1996—99; dir. Toho Hosp., Med. Corp., Osaka City, Osaka Prefecture, Japan, 1999—2002, Honankai Hosp. Med. Corp., Toyonaka City, Japan, 2002—03; physician Toho-Kasiba Hosp. Med. Corp., Nara Prefecture, 2003—04; dir. Toho Hosp., Osaka City, 2004—; also chmn. bd. dirs.; physician Toho Hosp. Med. Corp. Osaka City, 2011—. Chmn. bd. dirs. Toho Hosp. Group, Japan, 2004—; bd. dirs. Toho Hosp. Med. Corp., Osaka City, physician, 2011. Contbr. scientific papers to profl. med. jours. and publ. Mem.: Japan Med. Assn., NY Acad. of Sci. Buddhist. Avocation: Go.

KUWASAKO, KENJI, internist; b. Miyazaki, Japan, Oct. 23, 1965; s. Toshio and Akiko Kuwasako; m. Ayuko Miyaji, Dec. 24, 2005. MD, Miyazaki Med. Coll., Kiyatake, Japan, 1991, PhD, 1998. Intern Miyazaki Med. Coll., 1991—93, physician, 1999—, Junwakai Meml. Hosp., Miyazaki, Japan, 1993—94. Vis. rschr. Shionogi and Co. Ltd., Settsu, Osaka, Japan, 1998—99; asst. prof. Miyazaki Med. Coll., U. Miyazaki, 2004—; spkr. in field. Mem. editl. bd.: Internat. Jour. Pharmacology, 2005. Recipient Young Investigator's award, Japanese Soc. Hypertension, 2003, Japanese Soc. Cardiovasc. Endocrinology and Metabolism, 2003; grantee, Uehara Meml. Found., 2003, Novartis Pharma, 2004, Japanese Soc. Hypertension and Vascular Metabolism, 1998. Mem.: Japanese Soc. Cardiovascular Endocrinology and Metabolism, Japanese Soc. Hypertension, Am. Soc. Biochemistry and Molecular Biology. Avocations: reading, driving, music, movies, painting. Home: 87-2 Yanagimaru-cho Miyazaki 880-0844 Japan Office: Miyazaki Med Coll U Miyazaki Dept Internal Medicine 5200 Kihara Miyazaki 889-1692 Japan Office Phone: +81 985-85-0872. Fax: +81 985-85-6596. Business E-Mail: kuwasako@fc.miyazaki-med.ac.jp.

KUWAYAMA, S. PAUL, physician, immunologist, allergist; b. Sapporo, Hokkaido, Japan, Nov. 8, 1932; s. Satoru and Chiyoko (Nishikawa) K.; m. Barbara Ann Dresback, June 29, 1974; children: David, Steven, Jason. BS, Hokkaido U., Sapporo, 1955, MD, 1959. Diplomate Am. Bd. Pediatrics, 1965, Am. Bd. Allergy & Immunology, 1972, Am. Bd. Pediatric Allergy, 1970; lic. Nat. Bd. Med. Examiners of Japan, 1960, Wis. State Bd. Med. Examiners, 1968, Ariz. State Bd. Med. Examiners, 1987, N.Mex. State Bd. Med. Examiners, 1987, Tenn. State Bd. Med. Examiners, 1992. Intern U.S. Naval Hosp., Yokosuka, 1959-60, St. Mary's Hosp., Milw., 1960-61; jr. resident in pediatrics Temple U. Sch. of Medicine, Phila., 1961-62; chief pediat. resident W.Va. U. Sch. of Medicine, Morgantown, 1962-63; postdoctoral fellow in immunology, jr. fellow in pediatric allergy The Children's Mercy Hosp.-U. Kans. Sch. of Medicine, Kansas City, 1964-65; staff pediatrician Atomic Bomb Casualty Commn. in Hiroshima, U.S. Nat. Acad. of Scis.-U.S. Atomic Energy Commn., 1966-67; sr. pediatric allergist, dept. immunobiology U. Kans. Sch. of Medicine, 1967-68. Asst. clin. prof. pediatric allergy and immunology Med. Coll. Wis., Milw., 1970—. Contbg. author texts and forward to books. Fulbright scholar, 1960-63. Fellow Am. Acad. Pediat. (sect. on allergy and immunology), Am. Coll. Allergy, Asthma and Immunology, Am. Assn. Cert. Allergists, Am. Acad. Allergy, Asthma and Immunology, Am. Assn. Clin. Immunology and Allergy; mem. AMA, Fulbright Scholarship Grantee Alumni Assn., Milw. Pediatric Soc.

KUWERT, PHILIPP, psychiatrist, trauma researcher; b. Essen, Germany, July 1, 1969; s. Ernst Karl and Erika Kuwert; m. Anne Bluttner, Oct. 30, 1998; children: Leander, Helene, Simon, Malte. Dr. med., U. Marburg, 1997. Cert. physician U. Marburg, 1997. Assistenzarzt U. Greifswald, Germany, 2002—05, oberarzt, 2006—. Office: Univ Greifswald Rostocker Chaussee 70 Stralsund 18437 Germany Business E-Mail: kuwert@uni-greifswald.de.

KUZMIN, VLADIMIR SEMENOVICH, chemist, educator; b. Smolensk, Russia, June 23, 1946; ChD, IGICh RAS, 1991. Leading rsch. scientist State Rsch. Inst. Organic Chemistry and Tech., 1994—2008; leading expert Sci. Ctr. Expertize Med. Goods, 2011—. Prof. I.M.Sechenov Moscow Med. Acad., 2009. Avocations: photography, travel. Home: Martenovskaja ul 30 29 Moscow 111394 Russia Personal E-mail: vsk46@yandex.ru.

KUZNETSOV, VADIM A., medical educator, director; b. Novosibirsk, Russia, Oct. 18, 1956; MD, Novosibirsk State Med. U., 1980. Dir., prof., cardiology Tyumen Cardiology Ctr., 1991—. Contbr. articles to profl. publs. Named one of Honored Scientist, Govt. of Russian Fedn. Master: Soc. Cardiology of Russian Fedn. (chmn., Tyumen br., bd. mem.); fellow: Internat. Soc. Cardiovasc. Ultrasound (Russian Chpt.), European Soc. Cardiology; mem.: European Assn. Echocardiography. Achievements include patents in field. Avocations: singing, poetry. Office: 111 Melnikaite St Tyumen 625026 Russia Office Fax: 7-3452-205349. Business E-Mail: kuznets@cardio.tmn.ru.

KUZNETSOVA, TATJANA JURIEVNA, cardiologist; b. Petrozavodsk, Russia, Apr. 22, 1964; MD, PetrSU, 1987, PhD. Cardiologist Vishnevski's Surgery Inst., Moscow. Chair, faculty therapy dept. Petrozavodsk State U., 2007—. Mem.: Assn. Heart Failure Specialists, Russian Cardiologists Assn. Home: Karl Marks 22 21 Petrozavodsk Karelia 185035 Russia Home Fax: 8-814-2-78-15-50. Personal E-mail: eme@karelia.ru.

KUŹNICKI, LESZEK, cell biologist; Chmn. Com. for Futures Studies/Poland 2000 Plus. Mem. Polish Acad. Scis. (pres. 1993-98), Internat. Commn. Protozoology. Office: Polish Acad Scis Nencki Ins Ul. Ludwika Pasteura 3 02-093 Warsaw Poland Office Phone: (4822) 822-42-78. Business E-Mail: kuznicki@nencki.gov.pl.

KVARSTEIN, BERNT, urological surgeon; b. Lierne, Norway, Aug. 21, 1930; s. Gunnvald and Gudrun (Berge) K.; m. Anne-Kari Hegna, June 23, 1955 (dec. June 1986); children: Helene, Gunnvald, Bernt Kristian. MD, U. Oslo, 1959, PhD, 1971. Intern Lillehammer Fylkessykehus and Sel and Heidal dists., 1960-61; sci. asst. Inst. Path. Anatomy U. Oslo, 1962-63, rsch. fellow Inst. Thrombosis Rsch., 1965-69; resident and registrar dept. ob/gyn. Univ. Hosp., Oslo, 1964, 69-70, registrar dept. surgery, 1970-73, sr. registrar divsn. urology, 1975-78; registrar, sr. registrar dept. surgery Drammen Hosp., Norway, 1973-75; specialist in gen. surgery, 1976; in urology, 1978; surgeon-in-chief Home for Congl. Sisters, Oslo, 1978-79; asst. surgeon-in-chief dept. surgery Akershus Ctrl. Hosp., U. Oslo, 1979-82, head sect. urology, 1982-89; urologist-in-chief dept. urology Ulleval Hosp., U. Oslo, 1988-89; head sect. urology Akerstrüs Cen. Hosp., 1989—; cons. urologist, 2000—. Contbr. articles on endocrinology, cardiovascular surgery and urology to profl. jours. Recipient C.R. Bard award, 1982, Astra Meditec award, 1991. Mem. Norwegian Med. Assn., Norwegian Surg. Assn., Norwegian Assn. Patients with Urol. Diseases (initiator found., hon. mem., chmn. 2001—), Nordic Surg. Assn., Norwegian Assn. Urology (hon., pres. 1986-89), Nordic Urol. Assn., Société Internationale d'Urologie, Internat. Continence Soc., European Assn. Urology, N.Y. Acad. Scis. Address: Lijordveien 25 1359 Eiksmarka Norway Home Phone: +47 6714 6033. E-mail: kvarste@online.no.

KVETINA, JAROSLAV, pharmacologist; b. Racineves, Czech Republic, May 19, 1930; s. Jaroslav and Marie (Aimova) K.; m. Helena Mala, Apr. 15, 1960 (div. 1973); 1 child Libnarova Marketa; m. Miluse Simkova, Feb. 7, 1975; children: Petr, Jan. RND, Masaryk U., 1953; PhD in Medicine, Charles U., Prague, 1964, DSc, 1975; D (hon.), U. Brno, 2000. Lectr. Med. Faculty, Hradec Kralove, Czech Republic, 1955—69; prof. Faculty Pharmacy, Hradec Kralove, Czech Republic, 1969—90; dir. Inst. Exptl. Biopharmaceutics, Hradec Kralove, Czech Republic, 1990—2007; prof. Vet. U., Brno, 1991—; scientist Inst. Exptl. Biopharmacentist, 2007—. Head dept. pharm. Med. Faculty Charles U., 1968-71, Faculty Pharmacy, dean, 1969-90. Contbr. articles to profl. jours. Hon. emeritus prof. Charles U. Mem. Czech Med. Acad. (v.p., 2005), Czech Acad. Sci. (v.p 1980), Czech Med. Assn. (hon.), French Pharm. Assn. (hon.), Slovak Pharm. Assn. (hon.). Home: M Horakove 268 500 06 Hradec Králové Czech Republic Office: Inst Exptl Biopharmaceutics Heyrovskeho 1207 500 03 Hradec Králové Czech Republic Business E-Mail: kvetina@ueb.cas.cz.

KVETON, JOHN F., otolaryngologist, educator; MD, St. Louis U., 1978. Diplomate Am. Bd. Otolaryngology, Am. Bd. Otolaryngology-neurotology. Resident in otolaryngology Yale- New Haven Hosp., Conn., 1979—82; fellow in neurotology The Otology Group, Nashville, 1982—83; clin. prof. otolaryngology Yale Univ.; otolaryngologist St. Raphael Hosp., Yale- New Haven Hosp. Mem.: Cmty. Med. Group. Office: Yale- New Haven Hospital 20 York St. New Haven CT 06510 Office Phone: 203-688-6937. Office Fax: 203-688-4242.

KVICEROVA, JANA, parasitologist; b. Mestec Kralove, June 6, 1980; DVM, U. Vet. and Pharm. Scis., 2005. Rsch. scientist, Inst. Parasitology, Acad. Scis. Czech Republic, 2005—. Medicus vets. Pvt. Vet. Clinic, 2005—. Office: Branisovska 31 Ceske Budejovice 370 05 Czech Republic Business E-Mail: janaq@centrum.cz.

KWAAN, JACK HAU MING, retired physician; b. Hong Kong, Apr. 1928; came to U.S., 1953; s. Y.K. and Rose W. Kwaan; m. Min K. Ho, Feb. 11, 1973; children: Mary, Peter, Rebecca, Nicholas. MD, U. Hong Kong, 1952. Diplomate in diagnostic radiology, radiotheraphy, nuc. medicine, Am. Bd. Radiology, Am. Bd. Surgery, Am. Bd. Thoracic Surgery. Resident in radiology Roswell Park Meml. Inst., 1955-56; chief resident Peter Bent Brigham Hosp., 1956-57; rsch. fellow in radiology Harvard Med. Sch., Boston, 1956-57; sr. cancer rsch. radiol. therapist Roswell Park Meml. Inst., Buffalo, 1958-59; asst. prof. radiology U. Ky., Lexington, 1963-65; resident in surgery U. Calif., Irvine, 1965-68; rsch. fellow oncologic surgery M.D. Anderson Hosp., Houston, 1968-69; resident in thoracic U. Calif., Irvine, 1969-71, chief resident thoracic surgery, 1970, asst. prof. surgery, 1972-73; chief vascular surgery sect., co-dir. vascular surgery tng. program U. Calif. Irvine/Long Beach VA Med. Ctr., 1974-87; prof. surgery U. Calif., Irvine, 1983-87; sr. resident in thoracic surgery U. So. Calif./L.A. County Med. Ctr., 1971; staff thoracic cardiovasc. surgeon Long Beach VA Hosp., 1972-73; asst. chief dept. surgery Valley Med. Ctr., Fresno, Calif., 1973-74; prof. surgery U. Okla., Tulsa, 1987-93; ret., 1993. Chief dept. surgery Valley Med. Ctr., Fresno, Calif., 1973-74; chief vascular surgery sect. Long Beach VA Med. Ctr., 1974-87; surgical cons. Kaiser Permanente Hosp., resident pathology U. Tex. Galveston, 1957-58, register surgery, Colchestar Gr. Hosps. Eng., 1959-62. Contbr. articles to profl. jours. Fellow Am. Coll. Surgeons; mem. Brit. Med. Assn., Gen. Med. Coun. London (registrant), Assn. Mil. Surgeons of U.S. (life), Assn. VA Surgeons, Internat. Cardiovascular Soc. Home: PO Box 50183 Long Beach CA 90815-6183

KWABI-ADDO, BERNARD, medical educator; b. Aug. 2, 1967; PhD, U. London, 1997. Assoc. prof. Howard U., 2007—. Recipient Idea Devel. award, Dept. Def. Mem.: Am. Assn. Cancer Rsch. (Minority Instn. award). Avocations: music, theater, swimming, travel. Office: Howard University Cancer Ctr #511 20 Washington DC 20060 Office Fax: 202-667-1686. Business E-Mail: bkwabi-addo@howard.edu.

KWACK, KYUBUM, medical educator; b. Seoul, Republic of Korea, May 22, 1960; PhD, U. Iowa, 1995. Postdoc. fellow Harvard Med. Sch., 1995—98; rsch. prof. Ulsan U., 1999—2001; proteomics & transcriptomics sect. chief Korea Nat. Inst. Health, 2001—04; prof. CHA U., 2004—. Jr. scientist Cheil Sugar Co., 1984—89. Decorated Order of Ministry of Health and Welfare. Mem.: Am. Soc. Hematology. Office: 222 Yatap-dong Bundang-gu CHA Rsch I Seongnam Gyeonggi-do 463-836 Republic of Korea Office Fax: 82-31-725-8350. Business E-Mail: kbkwack@cha.ac.kr.

KWAK, JAE HYOCK, chemist; b. Seoul, Republic of Korea, Apr. 6, 1970; PhD, Rugers U., 2003. Rsch. assoc. Monell Chem. Senses Ctr., 2003—. Mem.: Assn. Chemoreception Scis. Office: 3500 Market St Philadelphia PA 19104 Business E-Mail: jkwak@monell.org.

KWAK, JAE-YONG, medical educator; s. Im Hwan Kwak and Chun Ja Lee; m. Hyeon Sook Kim; children: Jie Hoon, Jeong Hoon. MD, Chonbuk Nat. U. Med. Sch., Jeonju, Jeonbuk, Republic of Korea; PhD, Chonbuk Nat. U. Grad. Sch., 1996. Cert. Korean Assn. Internal Medicine, 1996, lic. Korean Med. Assn., Seoul. Instr. Chonbuk Nat. U. Med. Sch., 1996—98, asst. prof., 1998—2002, assoc. prof., 2002—07, dir., divsn. hematology & oncology, 2006—, prof., 2007—; rsch. assoc. U. Utah, Salt Lake City, 2004—06. Leader, bone marrow transplantation program Chonbuk Nat. U. Hosp., Jeonju, 1999—; mem., lymphoma working party Korean Soc. Hematology,

2006—, mem., multiple myeloma working party, 2006—, mem., KSH CML working party, 2006—, ad hoc mem., KSH AML/MDS study sec., 2008—, ad hoc mem., KSH all study sect., 2008—, mem., KSH AA working party, 2008—; editl. bd., korean jour. internal medicine Korean Assn. Internal Medicine, 2008—. Contbr. articles to profl. jours. Mem.: Korean Assn. Internal Medicine, Korean Med. Assn., Korean Soc. Blood & Marrow Transplantation, Korean Cancer Assn., Am. Soc. Hematology, Internat. Soc. Exptl. Hematology, Am. Soc. Clin. Oncology. Avocations: photography, travel. Office: Chonbuk Nat Univ Med Sch 634-18 Keumam-Dong 561-712 Jeonju Jeonbuk Republic of Korea Office Fax: 82-63-254-1609. Business E-Mail: jykwak@chonbuk.ac.kr.

KWAK, JIN YOUNG, radiologist, educator; b. Daegu, Republic Of Korea, Dec. 24, 1969; m. Ho Jung Kim; children: Young Eun Kim, Young Kwan Kim. D, Chungnam Nat. U., Daejeon, 2006. Diplomate in radiologic border Ministry Health and Social Affairs, Republic of Korea, 2001. Asst. prof. Gangnam CHA Gen. Hosp., Seoul, Republic of Korea, 2002—06; clin. asst. prof. Severance Hosp., Seoul, 2006—08, asst. prof., 2008—, assoc. prof., 2010—. Editl. bd. mem. Jour. Korean Soc. Med. Ultrasound, Seoul, 2004—, Korean Jour. Radiology, Seoul, 2005—, Jour. Korean Acad. Med. Sci., Seoul, 2007—. Author: (book) State of the Art. Thyroid Sonography, Thyroid gland: Imaging diagnosis and intervention, Breast Diagnostic Imaging, Textbook of diagnostic radiology; contbr. articles to profl. jours. Recipient Bronze award, Korean Soc. Ultrasound Medicine, 2007; Grant, Korean govt., 2008, Yonsei U. Coll. Medicine, 2008, Yonsei U., 2008. Mem.: Korean Thyroid Soc., Korean Soc. Med. Ultrasound, Korean Radiol. Soc. (ins. bd. mem. 2003—07, Gold award 2007), Korean Med. Assn., Asia and Oceania Thyroid Assn. Avocations: swimming, travel. Office: Yonsei University Coll Medicine 250 Seongsanno Seodaemun-gu Seoul 120-752 Republic of Korea Office Fax: 82-2-393-3035. Business E-Mail: docjin@yuhs.ac.

KWAK, JONG-YOUNG, biochemist, medical educator; b. Busan, Republic of Korea, Oct. 5, 1961; s. Hyun-Bo Kwak and Bok-Dal Kim; m. Mi-Sook Choi, Aug. 25, 1990; children: Eun-Bee, Seung-Ha. BS, Pusan Nat. U., 1987, MS, 1989, PhD, 1991. Lic. doctor Korean Med. Assn., 1987, ECFMG, 1994. Postdoctoral staff Emory U. Med. Sch., Atlanta, 1994—96; asst. prof. Keon-Yang U. Med. Coll., Non-San, Chung-Nam, Republic of Korea, 1996—97; assoc. prof. Dong-A U. Coll. Medicine, Pusan, Republic of Korea, 1997—, chmn. Dept. Biochemistry, 1999—; dir. Inst. Med. Sch. Dong-A U., Pusan, 2001—02. Dir. Med. Rsch. Ctr. for Cancer Molecular Therapy, Pusan, 2002—, vis. prof. Emory U. Med. Sch., Atlanta, 1997, Kobe U. Med. Sch., Japan, 1998. Author: Recent Research Developments in Biophysical Chemistry, 2002; contbr. articles to profl. jours. Capt. Korean Ctrl. Med. Mil. Rsch. Ctr., 1991—94. Recipient Travel awards, Fujisawa Pharm. Co., 1998, Grand-Prix prize, Internat. Soc. Impotence Rsch., 1998; grantee Med. Rsch. and Engring. Ctr., Korean Ministry Sci. and Tech., 2002, scholar, Fujisawa Pharm. Co., 1990. Mem.: AAAS, Korean Soc. for Med. Biochemistry and Molecular Biology (corr.), N.Y. Acad. Sci. (assoc.), Soc. for Leukocyte Biology (assoc.). Achievements include research in Apoptotic signaling of Phagocytic Cells. Home: 106-409 WooSung Apt Pusan 617-020 Republic of Korea Office: Dong A Univ Coll Medicine 3Ga-1 Dongdaeshin-dong Pusan 602-714 Republic of Korea Office Fax: 82-51-241-6940. Business E-Mail: jykwak@dau.ac.kr.

KWAK, LARRY W. (LAWRENCE WONSHIN KWAK), oncologist, researcher, medical researcher; b. Rochester, NY, Mar. 19, 1959; BS in Med. Sci., Northwestern U., 1979, MD, 1982, PhD in Tumor Cell Biology, 1984. Cert. Internal Medicine, 1987, Med. Oncology, 1989. Internship internal medicine Stanford U. Med. Ctr., Calif., 1984—85, resident internal medicine Calif., 1985—87, fellowship med. oncology Calif., 1987—91; mem. Biological Response Modifiers Program Nat. Cancer Inst., 1992; head vaccine biology sect. NIH, 1996; assoc. dir. Ctr. Cancer Immunology Rsch. U. Tex. M. D. Anderson Cancer Ctr., Houston, 2004—, prof., chmn. Dept. Lymphoma/Myeloma, Divsn. Cancer Medicine, Justin disting. endowed chair in leukemia rsch. Spkr. in field. Contbr. articles to med. jours. Recipient Asian and Pacific Islander-Am. Orgn. Outstanding Sci. Achievement Award, NIH, 2000, NCI Tech. Transfer Award, Ctr. for Cancer Rsch., 2003; named one of The 100 Most Influential People in the World, TIME mag., 2010. Mem.: European Acad. Scis., Am. Assn. Immunology, Am. Soc. Clin. Investigation, Am. Soc. Clin. Oncology (Young Investigator Award 1989), Am. Soc. Hematology. Office: University of Texas MD Anderson Cancer Center 1515 Holcombe Blvd, Unit 0429 Houston TX 77030 *

KWAK-KIM, JOANNE YOUNG HEE, medical association administrator; b. Honolulu, Feb. 10, 1960; MD, Yonsei U. Coll. Medicine, MPH, 1984, Med. Coll. Wis., 2008. Dir., reproductive medicine Chgo. Med. Sch. at Rosalind Franklin U. Medicine and Sci., 2003—. Pres. Am. Soc. Reproductive Immunology, 2006—08; exec. coun. Internat. Soc. Immunology Reproduction, 2010—. Recipient J. Christian Herr award, Am. Soc. Reproductive Immunology, Outstanding Svc. award, Lawrence R. Medoff award, Rosalind Franklin U. Medicine and Sci. Mem.: Am. Soc. Reproductive Medicine, Internat. Soc. Reproduction Immunology, Am. Soc. Reproductive Immunology. Avocation: piano. Office: 830 West End Ct Ste #400 Vernon Hills IL 60061 Office Fax: 847-247-6951.

KWAN, BENJAMIN CHING KEE, ophthalmologist; b. Hong Kong, July 12, 1940; came to U.S., 1959. s. Shun Ming and Lurk Ming (Lai) K.; m. Catherine Ning, Aug. 29, 1964; children: Susan San, David Daiwai. MD, Wash. U., St. Louis, 1967. Diplomate Am. Bd. Ophthalmology. Ptnr. So. Calif. Permanente Med. Ctr., Harbor City, 1976—2003, chief of svc. ophthalmology, 1976-88; clin. prof. dept. ophthalmology UCLA, 1995—. Chmn. winter blossom ball Chinese Am. Debutante's Guild, 1993; bd. dirs. Asian Am. Sr. Citizens Svc. Ctr., 1993-. Capt. U.S. Army, 1969-71. Recipient Svc. award Asian Am. Sr. Citizens Svc. Ctr., 1993, Proclamation award Calif. Sec. of State, 1993, Svc. award East L.A. Chinese Everspring Sr. Assn., 1994. Fellow Am. Acad. Ophthalmology; mem. Chinese Am. Ophthal. Soc. (pres. elect 1997-99, pres. 1999-00, Svc. award 1994, 2006), Chinese Physician's Soc. So. Calif. (bd. dirs., pres. 1983, Svc. award 1983, 89), Orgn. Chinese Ams. (pres. L.A. chpt. 1986-87). Roman Catholic. Avocations: ballroom dancing, singing, skiing. Home: 6327 Tarragon Rd Rancho Palos Verdes CA 90275-5834 Personal E-mail: benckwan@hotmail.com.

KWAN, JUN, cardiologist; b. Seoul, Republic Of Korea, May 11, 1960; s. Do-won Kwan and Hyun-ja Gwak; m. Seung-Mi Jung, Aug. 20, 2005; m. Jung-won Shin, Jan. 10, 1991 (div.); children: Sang-don, Jung-ah, Hee-Jae. MD, Yonsei Med. Coll., Seoul, PhD, 1986. Cert. cardiologist Korean Assn. Internal Medicine, 1995. Prof. Inha U. Hosp., Incheon, Republic of Korea, 2004, dir. cardiology dept., 2005—. Dir. rsch. com. Korean Soc. Echocardiography, Seoul, 2005—07, dir. internat. com., 2007—. Contbr. articles to profl. med. jours. Mem.: Asian Pacific Congress Cardiology, Korean Soc. Intervention, Korean Soc. Circulation, Am. Soc. Echocardiography, Korean Soc. Cardiology, Korean Soc. Hypertension, Korean Soc. Echocardiography. Home: Sangji RitzVil Seocho-dong Seocho-gu Seoul Republic of Korea Office: Inha Univ Hosp 3-Ga Jung-Gu Sinheung-Dong 400-711 Incheon Incheon Republic of Korea Office Fax: 8232-882-6578. Personal E-mail: kuonmd@inha.ac.kr. Business E-Mail: kuonmd@inha.as.kr.

KWANG, JIMMY, lab administrator, educator; b. China, Aug. 24, 1949; PhD, U. Calif., Davis, 1987. Prof., sr. prin. investigator Temasek Life Scis. Lab., Nat. U. Singapore, 1999—. Office: Nat University Singapore 1 Research Link Singapore 117604 Singapore Business E-Mail: kwang@tll.org.sg.

KWAST-RABBEN, OLGA, physiologist; d. Galina and Aleksey Furman; m. Terje Rabben, Oct. 1, 1988; children: Svetlana Furman, Jörgen Rabben. MS, State U., Moscow, 1971; PhD, U. Warsaw, 1985. Jr. asst. State U., 1971—74; sr. asst. Dist. Hosp., Warsaw, 1976—79; asst. prof. Child Health Ctr., Warsaw, 1981—88; neurophysiologist U. Hosp., Umeå, 1987—. Congress grant, Internat. Fedn. Clin. Physiology, 1983, 1985, 1987, 1990, 1995, Rsch. grant, Danish Ministry Edn., 1985, Clin. Neurosci. Umea U., 1993—94, 2000, 2003, 2006—07. Achievements include research in clinical neurophysiology. Office: Unit Clin Neurophysiology Univ Nothern Sweden Umeå 90 185 Sweden E-mail: olga.kwast.rabben@vll.se.

KWETKAUSKIE, JOHN A., medical technologist; b. Elizabeth, NJ, June 25, 1947; s. Albert and Genevieve Kwetkauskie; m. Patricia Manning, May 13, 1972; children: Brian R., Lara A. BS in Life Scis., N.Y. Inst. Tech., 1970. Registered med. technologist. Med. technologist Geisinger Wyoming Valley Med. Ctr., Wilkes-Barre, Pa., 1974-96, Med. Transport, Inc., Hazleton, Pa., 1988—97, Columbia Diagnostics, Inc., Canton, Mass., 1997-99, Greiner Bio-one N.Am., Monroe, NC, 1999—. EMT, edu. coord., designated officer Med. Transport, Inc., Hazleton, Pa., 1988-97; EMT, instr. Pa. Dept. Health, Harrisburg, 1990—; adj. faculty Luzerne County C. C., 1994—; cons. Ea. Safety Health, Inc., Nanticoke, Pa. Author: (instrn. manual) Prevention of Infectious Diseases - for EMS Providers, 1996. With U.S. Army, 1970-74, 90-91. Mem. Am. Med. Technologists, Nat. Assn. EMS Educators, Am. Socl Clin. Lab. Scis., Clin. Lab. Mgmt. Assn. Avocations: camping, boating, outdoor activities, golf. Office: Greiner Bio One 4238 Capital Dr Monroe NC 28110 Office Phone: 704 [illegible] 1617.

KWIK, CHRISTINE IRENE, physician, retired military officer, foreign service officer; b. Lvov, Poland, Sept. 12, 1939; d. Karol Stanislaus and Leonarda Fryderica (Senluk) Kostek; widowed; children: Christine and Catherine. Grad. summa cum laude, Med. Acad. Cracow, Poland, 1956-62; grad. primary flight medicine, Brooks AFB, Tex., 1985; completed chief of profl. staff, Sheppard AFB, Tex., 1988. Diplomate Am. Bd. Emergency Medicine, Am. Bd. Internal Medicine, Poland, cert. Edn. Coun. Fgn. Med. Grad.; re-cert. Extended Allergy Care Provider. Intern. Med. Acad., Cracow, Poland, 1962-63; residency internal medicine II Clinic Internal Diseases, Cracow, Poland, 1963-66, staff II Clinic of Internal Diseases, Cracow, Poland, 1966-69; gen. med. officer Gen. Hosp., Sokoto, Nigeria, 1969-72; intern. Frankford Hosp., Phila., 1972-73; house physician Holy Redeemer Hosp., Meadowbrook, Pa., 1973-74; emergency room physician John F. Kennedy Hosp., Phila., 1974-76, Emergency Rm. dir., 1976-78; commd. capt. USAF Med. Corp, 1978, advanced through grades to colonel, 1993; primary care physician USAF Clinic Emergency Rm., Ramstein, Germany, 1978-81; officer in charge Emergency Rm. and Gen. Practice Clinic, Peterson Field, Colo., 1981-84; primary care physician Malcolm Grow Med. Ctr., Andrews AFB, Md., 1984-88; chief clinic svc. 63d Med. Group/SGH, Norton AFB, Calif., 1988-93; staff physician 60h Med. Group, Travis AFB, Calif., 1993-96, Occupl. and Environ. Health and Safety Svc., Ft. George Meade, Md., 1996-99; ret. col. USAF, 1999; regional med. officer Dept. of State, 1999—2005. Asst. tchr., sr. asst. tchr. Inst. Descriptive Anatomy, Cracow, Poland 1963-69; emergency physician on call First Aid Sta., Cracow, Poland 1966-69. Vol. Phila. Med. Res. Corps., Med. Res. Corps. Fellow: Am. Coll. Emergency Physicians; mem.: AMA, World Med. Assn. Avocations: photography, travel, gourmet cooking. Personal E-mail: kwikci@yahoo.com.

KWITEROVICH, PETER OSCAR, JR., medical science educator, researcher, physician; b. Danville, Pa., June 24, 1940; s. Peter O. Sr. and Mary E. (Marks) K.; previous marriage Kathleen Ann Justin, Aug. 14, 1965; children: Kris Ann, Peter III, Karen Ann.;m. Martha Walker, June 5, 1999, children: Adam, Shelton AB, Holy Cross Coll., Worcester, Mass., 1962; B in Med. Sci., Dartmouth Coll., 1964; MD, Johns Hopkins U., 1966. Intern Boston Children's Meml. Hosp., 1966-67; staff assoc. NIH, Bethesda, Md., 1967-70; resident Johns Hopkins Hosp., Balt., 1970-72; from asst. prof. to assoc. prof. in med. sci. Johns Hopkins U., Balt., 1972-84, prof. in med. sci., 1984—. Dir. Specialized Ctr. Rsch. Arteriosclerosis, 1991—96; bd. dirs. lipid clinic Johns Hopkins Hosp., 1971—; chmn. steering com. prin. investigation Nat. Dietary Investigation Study in Children, 1987-1997. Author: Beyond Cholesterol, 1989 (Blakeslee award 1991, Helen B. Taussig award 1992, Sanctal Crucis award, 2007); contbr. articles to profl. jours; editor: Johns Hopkins textbook of Dyshipidemia, 2009. Platt rep., Roland Park Civic League, Balt., 1986-88, v.p., 1988-89, pres., 1989-91. Surgeon USPHS, 1967-70. Fellow Coun. Arteriosclerosis; mem. Soc. Pediatrics Rsch., Am. Soc. Clin. Investigation. Republican. Roman Catholic. Avocations: boating, running, fishing, wildlife, reading. Office: Johns Hopkins Lipid Rsch Unit 200 N Wolfe St Suite 3096 Baltimore MD 21287

KWOK, SAMUEL PO YIN, surgeon; MBBS, U. Hong Kong, 1983. Cons. surgery Prince of Wales Hosp., Hong Kong, 1994—95; chief of svc. and cons. surgeon United Christian Hosp., Hong Kong, 1995—2002, dir. minimally invasive surgery devel. ctr., 2000—02; dir. minimally invasive and endoscopic surgery ctr. Hong Kong Sanatorium and Hosp., Hong Kong, 2002—. Hon. cons. surgery United Christian Hosp., Hong Kong, 2003—; hon. clin. assoc. prof. Chinese U. Hong Kong, 1997—. Mem. editl. bd. (jour.) Asian Surg. Jour., 2002, Techniques in Coloproctology, 2003. Named one of Ten Outstanding Young Person's, Hong Kong Jr. Chamber, 1998. Fellow: Hong Kong Acad. Medicine, Coll. Surgeons Hong Kong, Royal Coll. Surgeons Edinburgh, Royal Australasian Coll. Surgeons; mem.: Endoscopic and Laparoscopic Surgeons Asia (sec.-gen. 1999—), Hong Kong Soc. Minimal Access Surgery (past. pres. 1997—2000), Hong Kong Soc. Coloproctology (pres. 1997—). Office: Hong Kong Sanatorium and Hosp 2 Village Rd Happy Valley Hong Kong Hong Kong Fax: 852 2892 7511. E-mail: samuelkwok@hksh.com.

KWON, CHUL SOO, psychiatrist; b. Seoul, Korea, Sept. 10, 1948; m. Sung Hee Chung, Apr. 6, 1974; 1 child, Soon Jeong (Susan). MD, Seoul Nat. U., 1974. Diplomate in psychiatry and in psychosomatic medicine and geriatric psychiatry Am. Bd. Psychiatry and Neurology and Psychosomatic Medicine. Intern Washington Hosp. Ctr., 1975—76, resident in gen. surgery, 1976—77; resident in psychiatry Johns Hopkins Hosp., Balt., 1977—80; fellow in behavioral sci. Johns Hopkins U., Balt., 1977—80, asst. in psychiatry, 1980—86; dir. partial hospitalization program North Charles Genl. Hosp., Balt., 1981—88; med. dir. partial hospitalization program Homewood Hosp. Ctr., Balt., 1988—91; med. dir. psychiat. partial hospitalization program Union Meml. Hosp., Balt., 1991—; physician St. Joseph Med. Ctr., Towson, Md., 1991—, Church Hosp., Balt., 1991—99, Md. Gen. Hosp. (U. Md. Med. System), Balt., 1991—98, 2000—, Taylor Manor, Ellicott City, Md., 1987—98; mgmt. mem. EHP Group Practice, 1993—; physician JL Kernan Hosp., Balt., 1995—2000, Sheppard-Enoch Pratt Hosp., 1998—2001. Instr. psychiatry Johns Hopkins U., 1986—96; physician, sub-investigator Ctr. Behavioral Health, 1999—2004; psychiat. cons. U. Splty. Hosp. (U. Md. Med. System), 2001—09; psychiatrist-in-charge, cons. Harbor Hosp. (Medstar Health Sys.), Balt., 2001—07; physician Good Samaritan Hosp. (Medstar Health SYs), Balt., 2008—. Mem.: APA, AMA, Internat. Neuropsychiat. Assn., Korean Am. Med. Assn., Internat. Psychogeriatric Assn., Am. Soc. Clin. Psychopharmacology (cert.), Md. Psychiat. Soc., Johns Hopkins Med. and Surg. Assn., Am. Neuropsychiat. Assn. Home: 2908 Chainita Ct Ellicott City MD 21042-7625 Office: 711 W 40th St Ste 406 Baltimore MD 21211 Office Phone: 410-235-2880. Fax: 410-313-9641. Business E-Mail: cskwon@jhu.edu.

KWON, E. HYOCK, science academy executive, preventive medicine physician; b. Seoul, Korea, July 13, 1923; Grad., Seoul Nat. U. Coll. Medicine, Korea, 1947, Seoul Nat. U. Grad. Sch., 1951; MPH, U. Minn., 1956, PhD, Seoul Nat. U., 1960. Asst. prof., assoc. prof., prof. Seoul Nat. U., Republic of Korea, 1956-80, dean Coll. Medicine, 1970-76, dean Sch. Pub. Health, 1976-78; gen. dir. Seoul Nat. U. Hosp., 1979-80; pres. Seoul Nat. U., 1980-83; min. Ministry Edn., Republic of Korea, 1983-85; pres. Korea Nat. U. Edn., 1985-88; min. Ministry Health and Social Affairs, Republic of Korea, 1988; chmn. Korea Green Cross Corp., 1989—91; pres. Korean Fedn. Sci. and Tech. Edn., 1990—91; min. Ministry of Environment, Republic of Korea, 1991-92; chmn. bd. trustees Sungkyunkwan U., Republic of Korea, 1996—2007. Vis. prof. U. Calif., Sch. Pub. Health, Berkeley, 1969. Pres. World Zero Tuberculosis Movement. Fellow: World Acad. Art and Sci.; mem.: Nat. Acad. Scis. Korea (pres. 1992—96, chmn. Wookang Health Forum). Home: 31-4 Sungbuk-Dong Sungbuk-Gu Seoul 136-822 Republic of Korea Office: 136-46 Korea Christian Bldg Ste 303 Yeonji-dong Chongro-gu Seoul Republic of Korea Business E-Mail: zerotb@zerotb.net.

KWON, HEEJIN, radiologist, educator; b. Pusan, Republic of Korea, May 12, 1977; MB, Dong-A U., 2002, M, 2005. Intern Dept. Radiology, Dong-A U. Hosp., 2002—03, resident, 2003—07, fellow, 2007, instr., 2008—09, asst. prof., 2010—. Mem.: Korean Soc. Ultrasound Medicine, Korean Soc. Abdominal Radiology, Korean Soc. Radiology. Office: Dong-A University Dept Radiology Dongd Pusan Kyungnam 602-714 Republic of Korea

KWON, HOWER, child and adolescent psychiatrist, educator; BS in Biology, MIT, 1985—89; MD, NYU, 1989—93. Diplomate Am. Bd. Psychiatry and Neurology, 1999, Am. Bd. Psychiatry and Neurology, 2009, Am. Bd. Psychiatry and Neurology-child and adolescent psychiatry, 1999, Am. Bd. Psychiatry and Neurology-child and adolescent psychiatry, 2009. Resident gen. psychiatry UCLA Neuropsychiatric Inst., 1993—96, chief resident geriatric psychiatry, 1996—97, fellow child and adolescent psychiatry, 1997—99; NIMH T32 postdoc. rsch. fellow pediatric neuroimaging Standford Univ., 1999—2001; attending psychiatrist Stanford Pervasive Devel. Disorders Clinic, 1999—2004; attending psychiatrist Harman Multidisciplinary Neurology clinic Lucile Packard Children's Hospital at Stanford, 1994—2004; sr. rsch. scientist Stanford Psychiatry Neuroimaging Lab., 2001—03; dir. outpatient psychiatry clinics Stanford Divsn. Child and Adolescent Psychiatry; attending Psychiatrist inpatient psychiatric unit and consultation svc. Children's Hosp. and Regional Med. Ctr., Seattle, 2004—05; attending psychiatrist Univ. Wash. Autism Ctr., 2004—09; asst. prof. Univ. Wash. Sch. Medicine, 2004—05, asst. clin. prof., 2006—08, assoc. clin. prof.; consulting psychiatrist Renton Acad., Newcastle, Wash., Fircrest Sch., Shoreline, Wash.; attending psychiatrist Seattle Children's Autism Ctr.; pvt. practice child and adolescent psychiatrist Bellevue Child Behavior Ctr. Office: Bellvue Child Behavior Center 365 118th Ave SE Ste 118 Bellevue WA 98005 Office Phone: 425-454-2911. Office Fax: 425-454-2966.

KWON, IK HYUN, internist; b. Korea, Aug. 22, 1937; S. Soo Myong and Jin Joo (Rhim) K.; m. Sook Ja Kwon, 1986; children: Esther, James. MD, Seoul Nat. U., 1962; PhD, Rutgers U., 1974. Intern Martland Med. Ctr., Newark, 1966-67; resident in internal medicine Bklyn.-Cumberland Med. Ctr., 1967; pvt. practice specializing in internal medicine South Plainfield, N.J., 1976—. Mem. staff John F. Kennedy Med. Ctr., Edison, N.J., Muhlenberg Regional Med. Ctr., Plainfield, N.J. Served with Korean Army, 1963-66. Fellow: ACP. Home and Office: 1526 New Durham Rd South Plainfield NJ 07080-2317 Office Phone: 732-287-2273. E-mail: lhkwon@pol.net.

KWON, JAEHWAN, otolaryngologist; 2 children. MD, PhD, Busan Nat. U., 2006. Cert. MD Korea Med. Assn., 1995. Chmn., ENT dept. Maryknoll Med. Ctr., Busan, 2003—; clin. rsch. fellow, dept. facial plastic reconstructive surgery & dept. otolaryngology Stanford U., 2007—08. Home: Lucky Apt 15-601 Onchun 2dong Dongraegu Busan 607-759 Republic of Korea Office: Maryknoll Med Ctr Daechungdong 4-12 Jung-Gu 600-730 Busan Busan Republic of

Korea Office Phone: 82-51-461-2205, 82-51-461-2441, 82-51-17-553-0364. Office Fax: 82-51-461-0297. Personal E-mail: entkwon@gmail.com, entkwon@hanmail.com.

KWON, JEE-HYUN, physician; b. Incheon, Republic of Korea, Apr. 4, 1973; MD, Inha U., 1997, PhD, 2004. Physician Ulsan U. Hosp., 2006. Office: 290-3 Jeon-ha dong Dong-gu Ulsan 682-714 Republic of Korea Personal E-mail: jhkwon-or@hanmail.net.

KWON, JEONG-YI, physiatrist, educator; b. Seoul, May 26, 1968; MD, Seoul Nat. U., Coll. Medicine, 1993, PhD, 2007. Asst. prof. Cath. U. Korea, St. Vincent's Hosp., 2005—08; assoc. prof. Sungkyunkwan U. Sch. Medicine, Samsung Med. Ctr., 2008—. Sec. Korean Soc. Pediatric Rehab. & Devel. Medicine, 2006—. Mem.: Internat. Soc. Phys. & Rehab. Medicine, Korean Acad. Rehab. Medicine. Office: 50 Ilwon-dong Gangnam-gu Seoul 135-710 Republic of Korea Business E-Mail: jeongyi.kwon@samsung.com.

KWON, KUNG ROCK, dentist, educator; b. Daegu, Republic of Korea, July 29, 1961; PhD, Kyung Hee U., 1995, MBA, 2010. Prof., chmn. dept. prosthodontics Sch. Dentistry, Kyung Hee U., 2007—. Sec. Korean Acad. Prosthodontics, 2009—11; v.p. Korean Acad. Sports Dentistry, 2009—11, Korean Acad. Esthetic Dentistry, 2009—11, ICOI Korea, 2009—11, Korean Acad. Geriatric Dentistry, 2011—. Fellow: Internat. Team Implantology. Avocations: golf, reading, painting. Office: KyungHee University Hoegi-dong Dongdaemun-gu Seoul 130-701 Republic of Korea Office Fax: 82-2-958-9349.

KWON, OH JUNG, surgeon; m. In Hee Park, Jan. 5, 1958; 1 child, Huyk Ju. MD, Hanyang U., Seoul, 1982, MA, 1986, PhD, 1992. Diplomate Korean Board of Surgery. Intern Hanyang U. Hosp., Seoul, 1982—83, resident, 1983—87; prof. Hanyang U. Med. Coll., Seoul, Republic of Korea, 1994—. Capatin Korean mil., 1987—90. Mem.: Transplantation Soc. Roman Catholic. Avocations: climbing, travel. Office: Hanyang Univ Med Coll Haengdangdong 17 Seoungdongku Seoul 133-792 Republic of Korea Office Fax: 82-2-2281-0224. Personal E-mail: ojkwon@hanyang.ac.kr.

KWON, SOON CHAN, neurosurgeon; b. Busan, Republic Of Korea, Nov. 17, 1970; s. Kwon Im Ho and Park Song Hee; m. Kim Hye Kyoung; 1 child, Kwon Min Jae. MD, KyoungHee U., Seoul, Republic Of Korea, 2006. Cert. dr. Ministry Health and Welfare, Republic Of Korea, 1994. Instr. U. Inje Coll. Medicine, Seoul, 2004—05; asst. prof. Ulsan U. Hosp., Coll. Medicine, Republic of Korea, 2005—. Contbr. articles to sci. jours. Capt. Capital Army Forced Hosp., 1999—2002, Seoul. Mem.: Korea Neurosurgery Soc. Office: Ulsan Univ Hosp 290-3 Jeonha-Dong Dong-Gu 682-714 Ulsan Republic of Korea Office Fax: 82-52-250-7138. E-mail: sckwon21@hanmail.net.

KWON, SUNKUK, medical educator; b. Republic of Korea, Jan. 12, 1977; PhD, Tex. A&M U., 2006. Asst. prof. U. Tex. Health Sci. Ctr., Houston, 2009—. Office: 1825 Pressler St IMM UTHSC-H Houston TX 77030 Business E-Mail: sunkuk.kwon@uth.tmc.edu.

KWON, YONG-SOON, medical educator; b. Seoul, Republic of Korea, Feb. 20, 1973; MD, Ulsan U., PhD, 2009. Asst. prof., divsn. gynecologic oncology, dept. ob-gyn. Cheil Gen. Hosp., 2008—10; clin. fellowship, divsn. gynecologic oncology, dept. ob-gyn. Asan Med. Ctr., 2006—07; asst. prof., divsn. gynecologic oncology, dept. ob-gyn. Coll. Medicine, Ulsan U. Hosp., 2011—. Office: Dong-Gu Jeonha-Dong 290-3 Ulsan 682-714 Republic of Korea

KWONG MING, FOCK, gastroenterologist; b. Singapore, June 12, 1949; MBBS, Nat. U. Singapore, 1973, M in Internal Medicine, 1978. Sr. cons., dept. gastroenterology Changi Gen. Hosp., 1990—, clin. prof., 2001. Chmn. Singhealth Clin. Governance Coun., 2008; chief risk officer Singapore Health Svcs., 2009. Recipient Pub. Adminstrn. Silver medal, Govt. of Singapore, Svc. medal, Changi Gen. Hosp. Master: Acad. Medicine, Singapore; mem.: Asian Pacific Assn. Gastroenterology, Asian-pacific Soc. Digestive Endoscopy, Singapore Med. Assn., Internat. Gastro-surg. Club. Office: 2 Simei St 3 Singapore 529889 Singapore Office Phone: 65 6850-3987.

KYLE, ROBERT ARTHUR, medical educator, hematologist; b. Bottineau, ND, Mar. 17, 1928; s. Arthur Nichol and Mabel Caroline (Crandall) K.; m. Charlene Mae Showalter, Sept. 11, 1954; children: John, Mary, Barbara, Jean. AA, N.D Sch. Forestry, 1946; BS, U. N.D., 1948; MD, Northwestern U., 1952; MS, U. Minn., 1958. Diplomate Am. Bd. Internal Medicine; subsplty. Hematology. Fellow Mayo Grad. Sch., Rochester, Minn., 1953-59; clin. asst. Tufts U. Sch. Medicine, Boston, 1960-61; cons. internal medicine Mayo Clinic, Rochester, 1961—; prof. medicine and lab. medicine Mayo Med. Sch., Rochester, 1975—. Pres. med. subjects unit Am. Topical Assn., Johnstown, Pa., 1976-81; chmn. standards, ethics and peer rev. orgn. Cancer & Acute Leukemia Group B, Scarsdale, NY, 1978-82; Waldenström lectr., Stockholm, 1988, chmn. Myeloma Com. Eastern Coop. Oncology Group, 1984-1996. Author: The Monoclonal Gammopathies, 1976, Medicine and Stamps, vols. 1 and 2, 1980, vol. 3, 2004; author, editor: Neoplastic Disease of the Blood, 4th edit., 2003, Myeloma: Biology and Management, 1995, 3rd edit. 2004 Chmn. bd. trustees First Presbyn. Ch., Rochester, Minn., 1967; chmn. Rochester Med. Ctr. Ministry, 1979-86; chmn. adv. bd. Internat. Waldenstrom's Macroglobulinemia Found. Capt. USAF, 1955-57. Named Disting. Topicl Philatelest, Am. Topical Soc., 1982; Recipient Waldenström award Internat. Workshop for Myeloma, Italy, 1991, Henry S. Plummer Distinguished Internist award Mayo Clin., 1995, Mayo Distinguished Clinician award 1996, Sioux award U. N.D., 1998, Robert A. Kyle Lifetime Achievement award IMF, 2003, Mayo Clinic Disting. Alumni award, 2005; Bruce Wiseman lectr. Ohio State U., 1991, Kauffman Meml. lectr. Meml. Sloan Kettering Med. Ctr., N.Y.C., 1997; Clement Finch prof. U. Wash., 1993, Joseph Michaeli award for Myeloma, 2006, David A. Karnofsky award and Lectr., ASCO, 2007, Wallace Coulter award Am. Soc. Hematology, 2008 Master ACP; mem. Royal Coll. Pathologists (hon.), N.Y. Acad. Scis., Am. Soc. Hematology, Internat. Soc. Hematology (sec.-gen. Inter-Am. divsn. 1990-96), Am. Assn. Cancer Rsch., Internat. Myeloma Found. (chmn. sci. adv. bd. 1995-), Internat. Soc. Amyloidosis (pres. 2001-06), Phi Beta Kappa, Internat. Waldenstroms Macroglobulinemia Found. (chmn. sci. adv. com 1998-), Internat. Myeloma Soc.,(pres. 2007-.) Republican. Avocation: stamp collecting/philately. Office: Mayo Clinic 200 1st St SW Rochester MN 55905-0002 also: 6-26 Stabile Rochester MN 55905-0001 Home Phone: 507-285-9138; Office Phone: 507-284-3039. Business E-Mail: kyle.robert@mayo.edu.

KYNCL, JOHN JAROSLAV, pharmacologist; b. Prague, Czechoslovakia, Aug. 16, 1936; arrived in US, 1971; s. Jan Petr and Marie (Mikesova) K.; m. Mila Marie Tomaides, Mar. 4, 1961; children: Marketa Kyncl Leisure, John Anthony. PhD, Komensky U., Bratislava, 1963; ScC, Czech. Acad. Sci., 1967. Pharmacologist Rsch. Inst. for Biochemistry & Pharmacy, Prague, 1963—68; A. von. Humboldt fellow U. Heidelberg, Germany, 1968—71; rsch. fellow Cleveland Clinic Found., 1971—72; E. Volwiler rsch. fellow Abbott Labs., North Chicago, Ill., 1972—. Contbr. over 100 articles to profl. jours. Fellow Coun. for High Blood Pressure Rsch. Am. Heart Assn., Am. Soc. Exptl. Biology; mem. Am. Hypertension Soc., Am. Endocrine Soc., Internat. Hypertension Soc. (Paris). Achievements include invention of terazosin (Hytrin) and terlipressin (Glypressin); patents in field. Home: 800 Green Bay Rd Lake Bluff IL 60044-1829 Personal E-mail: kynclj@comcast.net.

KYRGIDIS, ATHANASSIOS APOSTOLOS, oral & maxillofacial surgeon, medical researcher; b. Thessaloniki, Greece, Sept. 10, 1975; s. Apostolos Athanassios and Elizabeth Savvas Kyrgidis; m. Georgia Konstantinos Galimani, Dec. 30, 2006; 1 child, Anastasia. BS in Optometry & Optics, Tech. Sch. Highest Edn., Athens, 1997; Degree in Medicine, Aristotle U. Thessaloniki, Greece, 2002; MSc in Med. Rsch. Methodology, 2008—08; Degree in Dentistry, Aristotle U., Thessaloniki, 2009. Cert. optician Greek Ministry Health & Welfare, 1997, diplomate Greek Ministry Health & Welfare, 2002. Asst. mgr. Nitrofarm Sa, Thessaloniki, Greece, 1994—97; gen. mgr. Vis Vitalis Fitness Ctr., Ampelokipi, Thessaloniki, Greece, 2002—04; sr. ho. officer surgery Kavala Gen. Dist. Hosp., Greece, 2005—06; splty. registrar, oral & maxillofacial surgery Theagenio Cancer Hosp., Thessaloniki, 2007, G. Papanikolaou Gen. Hosp., Thessaloniki, 2007—. Mem., instl. rev. bd. Sch. Medicine, Aristotle U., Thessaloniki, 2007—. Contbr. articles to prof. med. jours. Soldier - medic Greek Spl. Forces, Unorthodox Warfare, 2003—04, Rentina, Volvi, Thessaloniki. Master: Postgraduate student assn.; mem.: Greek Soc. Oral & Maxillofacial Surgeons, Med. Assn.Thessaloniki, Greek Soc. Cancer Rsch. Office: Aristotle Univ Thessaloniki Egnatia St Thessaloniki GR 541 24 Greece Home: Papazoli Yeorg. 3 546 30 Thessaloniki Greece Home Phone: 302310546701; Office Phone: 306947566727. Personal E-mail: akyrgidi@gmail.com.

KYRIAKIDIS, ALEXANDR VLADIMIR, surgeon; b. Essentouki, Kaukaz, Russia, Oct. 20, 1966; s. Vladimir Semion Kyriakidis and Valentina Charlampii Kyriakidou; m. Nadia Gkiourii Antoniskis, May 22, 1968; children: Vladimir Alexandr, Sergey Alexandr. Diploma, 1st State Med. U. I.P. Pavlov, St. Petersburg, 1989; D, Med. U. I.P.Pavlov St.Petresbourgh Russia, St. Petersburg, 1996. Resident Surgery Clinic I.P. Pavlov, St. Petersburg, 1989—91, cons. endoscopy unit, 1991—92; gen. physician Med. Unit Andros, Greece, 1993—94; resident Sismanogleion Gen. Hosp. Surgery Clinic, Athens, 1995—2000; cons. ICU Sismanogleion Gen. Hosp., 2000—01, Gen. Hosp. Amfissa Surgery Clinic, 2001—. Contbr. articles to profl. jours. Recipient 3d award, Hellenic Surg. Soc., 1997, 2d award, 1998, 3d award, 2000. Mem.: Hellenic Soc. Digestive Surgery (assoc.), Hellenic Surg. Soc. (assoc.), Russian Soc. Endoscopic Surgery (assoc.). Home: Frouriou 95 Amfissa 33100 Greece Office: Gen Hosp Of Amfissa Oikismos Drosohoriou Amfissa 33100 Greece Office Fax: 65022086; Home Fax: 65022086. Personal E-mail: alkidi@hotmail.com. E-mail: gamfiss@otenet.gr.

KYRIAZIS, ARTHUR JOHN (ATHANASIOS IOANNIS KYRIAZIS), lawyer, molecularbiologist, patent attorney; b. Thessaloniki, Greece, Nov. 2, 1958; came to U.S., 1960; s. George A. and Elpis (Halkedis) K.; m. Maria M. Zissimos, Aug. 31, 1986; children: Cassandra Hope, Michael John, George Athanasios II. AB, Harvard U., 1981; postgrad., Pepperdine U., 1982—83; JD cum laude, Temple U., 1985; MSCE in Biotechnology, U. Pa. Engring., Submatriculated Wherton Sch. Bus., 2008. Bar: USPTO, 2003, US Supreme Ct. 1994. Vol. Med. Coll. Hahneman U., Pa., 1974—76, lab. rsch. technician mouse mammers tumor virus project Coll. Medicine, 1977—78; assoc. Cardillo & Corbett, NYC, 1983; law clk. to Hon. Norma J. Shapiro U.S. Dist. Ct. (ea. dist.) Pa., 1984; law clk. to Arnold R Silversteih Esq., 1984—85; law clk. to Hon. James Gardner Colins Commonwealth Ct. Pa., Phila., Harrisburg, 1985—86; assoc. Rawle & Henderson, Phila. and Marlton, NJ, 1987—88, Lesser & Kaplin and predecessor firm, Phila., Blue Bell, Pa. and Marlton, 1988—89; prin. Kyriazis & Assocs., Springfield, 1989—92; intellectual property coord. ESI, 2000—03, Reactred, Inc., 1993—. Arbitrator Phila. Ct. Common Pleas, 1988—, Delaware County Ct. Common Pleas, 1993—; pro bono counsel Am. Assn. Univ. Students, 1989—; solicitor to Register of Wills, Montgomery County, Pa., 2000; law clk. Registrar Wills Del. County, 2002; rsch. assoc. clin. trials emergency medicine project Judd Hollander U. Pa. Hosp., 1999—2000; tutor chemistry U. Pa., 1994—2000. Pa. co-coord. Dukakis for Pres., 1987-88; del. Nat. Fin. Com., Dem. Conv., Atlanta, 1988; mem. Hellenic Am. for Dukakis, Pa., 1987-88; founder Am. Assn. Univ. Students, Cambridge, Mass. and Phila., 1978-79; pres. Hercules-Spartan Phila. chpt. 26 Am. Hellenic Progressive Edn. Assn., 1990-91; alumni assn. bd. trustees Haverford Sch., 1997-06. Mem. ATLA, ABA (young lawyers divsn., litig. and bus. law sect., bus., real estate sects.), Am. Hellenic Lawyers Assn. (founder, treas. 1992-94), Phila. Bar Assn. (exec. com. young lawyers sect. 1988-90, fin. sec. exec. com. 1990, sec. exec. com. 1989, co-chmn. law related edn. com. 1988—, bar edn. found. com. 1988—, mem. Bill Rights 200 coms., fed. cts. 200 com., chmn. debate com. and mock trial 1987—, debate dir. fed. cts. 200 nat. high sch. debate tournament 1990—), Pa. Bar Assn. (litig., young lawyers jud. adminstrn.), Pa. Trial Lawyers Assn., Am. Arbitration Assn. (comml. arbitrator 1988—), Pa. Bar Assn., State Bar Calif. (litig., intellectual property, entertainment), Am. Assn. Univ. Students (legal counsel 1989—), Coll. Admissions Inst. Am. (adv. bd. 1992—), Hellenic Univ. Club (bd. trustees 1996-98), Harvard Club, Penn Club, Maxwell Football Club, Nat. Press Club, Harvard-Radcliffe Club (schs. com., chmn. Del. county schs. com.), Penn Faculty Club. Republican. Greek Orthodox. Office: 336 Bay Ave Unit 503 Ocean City NJ Business E-Mail: akbiotech@comcast.net.

KYRIAZIS, VASSILIOS, biomedical engineer, educator; b. Ioannina, Epirus, Greece, May 10, 1969; s. Christoforos Kyriazis and Despina Manou Kyriazis; m. Xanthi Toutounzoglou, Sept. 13, 2003. BSEE, Nat. Tech. U. Athens, Greece, 1993; PhD in Biomedical Engring., U. Ioannina, 2000. Vis. asst. prof. Tech. Ednl. Inst. Epirus, Arta, Greece, 2000—03; rsch. asst. prof. U. Ioannina, 2003—. Cons. elec. engr., Ioannina, 2002—. Contbr. articles to profl. jours. Mem.: IEEE, Greek Chamber Engrs., Internat. Soc. Biomechanics. Avocations: stamp collecting/philately, coin collecting/numismatics. Office: U Ioannina Dept Materials 45110 Ioannina Greece Home: Ariva 15 453 32 Ioannina Greece Personal E-mail: vkyriazi@cc.uoi.gr.

KYSOR, DANIEL FRANCIS, psychologist; b. Corry, Pa., Aug. 3, 1956; s. Darrell Francis and Louise Mary (Col) K.; m. Kate Galbraith Morrison, Sept. 7, 1991; children: Kenneth Jon Kron, Samuel Morrison, Charles Col. BS, Edinboro U., 1980; MS in Ednl. Psychology, Edinboro U., Pa., 1988; MEd in Secondary Sch. Adminstrn., Edinboro U., 1994; postgrad., Miss. State U., 1991—. Cert. elem. edn., guidance, elem. and secondary adminstr., sch. psychologist; lic. psychologist, Pa., in theol. seminary Lay Pasta, pitts., 2011. Tchr. Calhoun County Schs., Grantsville, W.Va., 1982; counselor, tchr. Bradford Children's Home, Pa., 1983; residential program counselor Assn. for Retarded Citizens, Meadville, 1984—86; resident hall dir. Edinboro U., 1984—86, counselor Edinboro Summer Acad. for the Gifted, 1985—96; guidance counselor Cranberry Sch. Dist., Seneca, 1986; dropout prevention counselor Erie Sch. Dist., 1988; sch. psychologist Seneca Highlands Intermediate Unit #9, Coudersport, 1989—. Pvt. practice Addis & Assocs., Bradford, Pa., 1994-97; CEO, dir. psychol. svc. Port Psychol. Svcs., Inc., 1996-2007; psychologist, Beacon Light Behavioral Health Sys., 2007-09; CEO, divsn. psychol. svcs. Port Psychol. Svcs., 2009-. Pa. Rural Leadership Program scholar Pa. State U., 1989; Rsch. grantee St. Bonaventure U., N.Y.; recipient citations Pa. House of Reps., 1991, 93, 95. Mem. ACA (life), NASP, Am. Sch. Counselor Assn., Nat. Fedn. Interscholastic Ofcls. Assns., Pa. Interscholastic Athletic Assn., Pa. Sch. Bds. Assn., Ea. Wrestling League, Ea. Ind. Officials Wrestling Assn., Nat. Wrestling Officials Assn., Clowns of Am. Internat., Inc./POCO Clowns. Democrat. Presbyterian. Avocations: wrestling officiating, reading, bicycling. Home: 109 Chestnut St Port Allegany PA 16743-1248 Office: Seneca Highlands IU #9 306 N Main St Coudersport PA 16915-1626 E-mail: kysor@zitomedia.net.

KYUNG, SEUNG HYUN, dental educator; b. Seoul, Republic of Korea, June 30, 1961; PhD, Yonsei U., 1996. Assoc. prof. Sunggyunkwan U., 2004—. Chair, dept. ortholdontics Samsung Med. Ctr., 2003—05. Recipient Excellent Presentation award, IKM. Mem.: Am. Assn. Orthodontists. Avocation: golf. Office: Samsung Bule Dental Clinic Dong-ha B/D Seoul 135-280 Republic of Korea Personal E-mail: shkyung@gmail.com.

LA, PEIQING, engineering educator; b. Linxia, China, Dec. 24, 1971; PhD, CAS, 2002. Prof. Lanzhou U. Tech., 2005—. Office: Langongping Rd 287 Lanzhou Gansu 730050 China Business E-Mail: pqla@lut.cn.

L.A. SATHISH, physics professor; b. Mandya, Karnataka, India, May 20, 1973; s. L. Appajaiah and Swarna; m. B. M. Meenakshi L.A., May 29, 2002; 1 child, Dhruthi M. Sathish. MSc, U. Mysore, India, 1996, PhD, 2004. Head dept. physics, lectr. Nat. First Grade Coll. Hennur Cross, Bangalore, 1996—97; lectr. physics Sharada Vilas Coll. Mysore, 1997—99; with Oxford Sr. Secondary Sch., Bangalore, 1997; jr. rsch. fellow dept. physics U. Mysore, 1998—2000; lectr. physics. JSSATE, Noida, 2000—03; asst. prof. physics sr. lectr. SIR M VIT, Bangalore, Karnataka, India, 2003—06; asst. prof., postgrad. dept. physics Govt. Sci. Coll., Bangalore, India, 2006—, coord., 2010—; register JSSATE, asst. supt. Exec. com. mem. Nuclear Track Soc. India, 2009—11; mem. Nat. Organizing Com. MS U., Baroda, 2011. Contbr. articles to profl. jours. Jr. Rsch. fellowship, Bd. Rsch. Nuc. Sci., Bhabha Atomic Rsch. Ctr., Govt. India, Mumbai, grants, Am. Assn. Radon Scientists and Technologists, U. Grants Commn., New Delhi, 2007, Dept. Sci. and Tech. Travel grants, 2010, Travel grant, Conf. Secretariat, Internat. Orgn. Med. Physics and Mid. East Fedn. Med. Physics, Iran, 2011. Mem.: Indian Assn. Aerosol Sci. and Tech., Nuc. Track Soc. India (exec. com. mem.), Indian Aerosol Sci. & Tech. Assn. (life), Indian Soc. Radiation Physics (life). Hindu. Achievements include executing UGC sponsored major research projects and guiding students for their PhD. Avocation: writing. Office: Govt Sci Coll Postgrad Dept Physics Nrupathunga Rd Bangalore Karnataka 560001 India Home: 3009/4 Mahavi II Main II Stage 17 Cross Banashankari Bangalore 560 070 India Office Fax: 918022212924. E-mail: lasgayit@yahoo.com.

LAAKSI, ILKKA TUOMAS, physician, educator; b. Kotka, Finland, Oct. 4, 1968; s. Seppo and Riitta Laaksi; m. Leena Eeva Maria Tuohimaa-Laaksi, July 30, 1994; children: Iida Anna Maria, Akseli Tapio Tuomas, Lotta Eeva Maija. MD, U. Turku, Finland, 1998. Physician Health Ctr., Hämeenlinna, Finland, 1998—, Mänttä, Finland, 1999—2002, Virrat, Finland, 2001—, Valkeakoski, Finland, 2004—. Lectr. U. Tampere, 1999—. Author: (book) Vitamin D Deficiency Increases Risk of Prostate Cancer, 2004. 2d lt. Häme tank br., 1988—89. Grantee, Finnish Cultural Found., 2001, Pirkanmaa Hosp. Dist. Competitive Rsch. Funding, 2002, 2004, 2005. Mem.: Finnish Med. Assn., Finnish Endocrinology Assn. Achievements include research in antiproliferative action of vitamin D; 25-hydroxyvitamin D3 as an active hormone in human primary prostatic stromal cells; vitamin D fortification as public health policy; the association between serum 25(OH)D concentrations and bone stress fractures in Finnish young men; an association of serum concentrations of vitamin D with acute respiratory tract infections in young Finnish men; vitamin D supplementation for the prevention of acute respiratory tract infections; a randomized double-blinded trial in young Finnish men. Office: Tampere U Medisiinarinkatu 3 Tampere 33014 Finland Business E-Mail: ilkka.laaksi@uta.fi.

LAAKSO, LIISA, physiotherapist, educator; d. Toivo Armas and Elsi Elina Laakso. BPhty, U. Queensland, Brisbane, Australia, 1981, PhD, 1994; grad. cert. in health mgmt., Queensland U. Tech., Brisbane, 1999. Acting asst. dir. Royal Brisbane Hosp., 1994—95; sr. physiotherapist, clin. lectr. Royal Brisbane Hosp. /U. Queensland, 1996—99, sr. physiotherapist, conjoint lectr., 1999—2002; sr. lectr. Griffith U. Sch. Physiotherapy and Exercise Sci., Gold Coast, Queensland, 2002—. Scholar, Sir Robert Menzies Meml. Found., 1991—92; Palliative Care Nat. Incentive Scheme grantee, Commonwealth Dept. Human Svcs. and Health, 1995—96. Fellow: Australian Med. Laser Assn. (v.p. 2005); mem.: Menzies Meml. Scholars Assn., Australian Physiotherapy Assn. (nat. rsch. and quality practice com. 1995—2005, mem., convenor various coms.), Australian Physiotherapy Assn.

LABAYEN, IDOIA, nutritionist, educator; b. Pamplona, Spain, May 18, 1968; Degree in Biology, U. Navarra, 1991; degree in Nutrition, U. Granada, 1993. Rsch. scientist U. Navarra, 2000—02; asst. prof. U. Basque Country, 2002—. Office: Paseo de la Universidad 7 Vitoria Alava 01006 Spain Business E-Mail: idoia.labayen@ehu.es.

LABBÉ, DANIEL SEBASTIEN, plastic surgeon; b. St. Germain en Laye, France, Nov. 23, 1951; s. Jacques and Nadine (Bertrand) L.; m. Monique Germaine Krief, Feb. 5, 1979; children: Raphaël, Sarah, Chine. Internat., Sch. of St. Germain en Laye, 1968; Baccalaureat, Sch. of Germainenlaye, 1970; MD, Paris Medical Sch., 1983. Asst. medical doctor Univ. Caen HOsp., 1985-87, first asst. plastic and reconstructive surgery, 1987—. Contbr. numerous articles to profl. jours in field of Facial Palsy. Recipient Silver medal Paris Medical Sch., 1983. Mem. French Soc. Plastic Reconstructive Surgery (First prize 1996), French Assn. Maxillo Facial Surgery. French Soc. Otorhinolaryngology and Cervico Surgery. Avocations: art, music, skiing, jogging. Home: 9 Rue Pemagnie 14000 Caen France Office: 4 Place Fontette 14000 Caen France

LABBIE, ANDREW SCOTT, pediatric urologist, surgeon; b. Miami, Fla. MD, Northwestern U., Ill., 1982. Diplomate Am. Bd. Urology, lic. Fla. Intern U. Tex., Dallas, 1982—83, resident, 1983—88; fellowship Tex. Children's Hosp., Baylor U., Houston, 1988—89; staff urologist, chief dept. surgery Miami Children's Hosp., 1990—. Clin. assoc. prof. urology U. Miami Sch. Med.; bd. dirs. Miami Children's Hosp. Contbr. articles to profl. jours. Mem.: Am. Acad. Pediat. Office: Children's Hosp 3200 SW 60th Ct Ste 105 Miami FL 33155 Office Phone: 305-669-6448. Office Fax: 305-663-8464.

LABUSCHAGNE, MATHYS JACOBUS, ophthalmologist; b. Sannieshof, South Africa, June 9, 1963; MBChB, U. Free State, 1987, MMed in Ophthalmology, 2006. Pvt. practice, 1990—2002; med. specialist U. Free State, 2007—. Recipient Prestige award, U. Free State. Mem.: South African Med. Assn., Internat. Soc. Simulation Healthcare, Ophthal. Soc. South Africa. Avocations: classical music, gardening. Office: Nat Hosp White Block First fl Bloemfontein Free State 9300 South Africa Office Fax: 27514302225. Business E-Mail: mathyslab@mweb.co.za.

LABUTTI, RONALD STEPHAN, orthopedist; b. Tacoma, Oct. 12, 1965; s. Ronald Justin and Judith Ann LaButti; m. Robin Michelle Ford, Sept. 2, 2001. BA in Psychology, Providence Coll., RI, 1987; DO, U. New England Coll. Osteopathic Medicine, Biddeford, Maine, 1994. Cert. Am. Osteo. Bd. of Orthop. Surgery. Intern, clin. instr., dept. internal medicine RI Hosp./Brown U., Providence, 1994—95; orthop. surgery resident Okla. State U. Coll. Osteo. Medicine, Tulsa, 1995—99, assoc. clin. prof., orthop. surgery, 2002—, asst. program dir. orthop. surgery residency program, 2003—; pediatric orthop. surgery rotation Shriners Hosp. for Children, Spokane, Wash., 1997—98; hip and knee reconstruction rotation U. Utah Med. Ctr., 1998; orthop. sports medicine rotation Detroit Med. Ctr./Hutzel Hosp., 1998; hand surgery rotation Detroit Med. Ctr./Harper Hosp., 1998; dept. orthop. surgery, lower extremity and joint reconstruction fellow Buffalo Gen. Hosp./SUNY, Buffalo, 1999—2000; pvt. practice Central States Orthop. Specialists, Inc, Tulsa, 2000—. Clin. instr. Okla. State U. Coll. Osteo. Medicine Western U. Health Scis., 1995—99; team physician Tulsa Pub. Schools, Tulsa, Okla., 1995—99, Internat. Profl. Rodeo Assn. Longhorn Rodeo, Tulsa, Okla., 1995—99, Cleve. Pub. Schools, Cleve., 1995—99, Tulsa Roughnecks Soccer Team, 1999; mem. orthop. peer review com. (rotating mem.) St. Francis Hosp., 2001—; mem. surgical morbidity and mortality com. Tulsa Regional Med. Ctr., 2000—; presenter in field; bd. trustees Okla. State Med. Assoc., 2009—11; bd. dirs. Arthritis Found. Eastern Okla. Chpt. South Ctrl. Region, 2011—. Contbr. articles various profl. jours. Physician for student history and phys. exams for athletic participation Cleve. Pub. Sch., Cleve., Okla., Holland Hall Sch., Tulsa, Okla., Jenks Pub. Schools, Jenks, Okla.; bd. trustees Okla. State Med. Assn., 2009—10; bd. examiner Am. Ostheoparthic Bd.; lifetime mem. Osteo. Founders Found., Tulsa, 2003—04, chmn., Winterset Ball" Stepping Out 2004" Charity Ball, 2004; benefactor LaButti Scholarship for Academic Excellence, Okla. State U. Coll. Osteo. Medicine, 2001—; premier sponsor Tulsa Running Club, 2003—04. Named one of Am.'s Top Physicians, Consumers' Rsch. Coun. Am., 2004—05, Leading Physicians of World, Internat. Assn. Orthop. Surgeons. Fellow: Am. Osteo. Acad. Orthop.; mem.: Tulsa Osteo. Med. Soc., Tulsa Orthop. Soc., Tulsa Orthop. Network, Tulsa County Med. Soc., Okla. Osteo. Assn., Am. Acad. Orthop. Surgeons, Am. Osteo. Acad. Orthop. Surgery (mem. newsletter com. 2003—), Am. Osteo. Assn. (Psi Sigma Alpha 1994), Psi Sigma Alpha. Achievements include being the first orthopedic surgeon in Tulsa to offer and perform ceramic-on-ceramic total hip replacement; the first orthopedic surgeon in Oklahoma to perform computer assisted total knee replacement. Avocations: fishing, hunting, playing the guitar. Office: Ctrl States Orthop Specialists Inc William Med Bldg 6585 S Yale Ste 200 Tulsa OK 74136 Home: 1203 E 19th St Tulsa OK 74120 Home Phone: 918-592-7080; Office Phone: 918-481-2767. Office Fax: 918-481-7611. Personal E-mail: ronlabutti@cox.net.

LACHANCE, PAUL ALBERT, food science educator, clergyman; b. St. Johnsbury, Vt., June 5, 1933; s. Raymond John and Lucienne (Landry) Lachance; m. Therese Cecile Cote; children: Michael P, Peter A, M-Andre, Susan A. BS, St. Michael's Coll., 1955; postgrad., U. Vt., 1955-57; PhD, U. Ottawa, 1960; cert. in pastoral counseling, N.Y. Theol. Sem., 1981; DSc (hon.), St. Michael's Coll., 1982. Diplomate Am. Assn. Integrative Medicine, 2005; ordained deacon Roman Cath. Ch., 1977. Assigned to St. Paul's Ch., Princeton, NJ; aerospace biologist Aeromed. Research Labs., Wright-Patterson AFB, Ohio, 1960-63; lectr. dept. biology U. Dayton, Ohio, 1963; flight food and nutrition coordinator NASA Manned Spacecraft Center, Houston, 1963-67; assoc. prof. dept. food sci. Rutgers U., New Brunswick, NJ, 1967-72, dir. Sch. Feeding effectiveness research project, 1969-72, prof., 1972—2004, prof. emeritus, 2005—, faculty rep. to bd. trustees, 1988-90, dir. grad. program food sci., 1988-91, chmn. food sci. dept., 1991-97, chmn. univ. senate, 1990-93, faculty rep. to bd. govs., 1990-94, dir. The Nutraceuticals Inst., 1989—2007. Trustee religious ministry com. Princeton Health Care Sys., 1968—, on-call chaplain, 1968—; mem nutrition adv comt Whitehall-Robins/Centrum Consumer div, 1989—2000; mem sci adv bd Roche chem div Hoffmann La Roche Co, 1976—88; mem nutrition policy comt Beatrice Food Co, 1979—86; mem. Am. Coll. Nutration, Cert. Bd. Nutritional Scis.; bd. dirs. J. R. Short Milling Co., 1990—2008; cons. Nutritional Aspects Food Processing, Nutraceuticals. Mem. editl. adv. bd.: Nutrition Reports Internat., 1963—83, Sch. Food Svc. Rsch. Rev., 1977—82, Profl. Nutritionist, 1977—80, mem. editl. adv bd.: Jour. Med. Consultation, 1985—2002, Jour. Medicinal Foods, 1998—, Food and Chem. Toxicology, 2000—07, Jour. Nutraceuticals Functional & Health Foods, 2000—05; contbr. articles to profl. jours. Served to capt USAF, 1960—63. Recipient Endel Karmas award for excellence in tchg. food sci., 1988, Lifetime Achievement award, NSF Internat. Food, Safety and Security Summit, Washington, 2008; named to Academic Hall of Fame, St. Michael's Coll., 2002. Fellow: Am. Assn. Integrative Medicine, Am. Soc. Nutritional Sci., Am. Coll. Nutrition, Inst. Food Technologists (William Cruess award for excellence in tchg. 1991, Babcock-Hart award 2001); mem.: APHA, AAAS, Soc. Free Radical Biology and Medicine, Nat. Assn. Cath. Chaplains, Soc. Nutrition Edn., Am. Dietetic Assn., N.Y. Acad. Sci., Am. Soc. Clin. Nutrition, N.Y. Inst. Food Technologists (chmn 1977—78), Am. Assn. Cereal Chemists, Sigma Xi, Delta Epsilon Sigma. Home: 34 Taylor Rd Princeton NJ 08540-9521 Office: Rutgers U Food Sci 65 Dudley Rd New Brunswick NJ 08901-8520 Personal E-mail: drpal@aol.com.

LĀCIS, ARIS, health facility administrator, cardiac surgeon; b. Jelgava, Latvia, Aug. 1, 1936; s. Teodor and Zelma (Gedrovics) L.; m. Aija Ozolina, Sept. 8, 1958; children: Aigars, Andis. MD, Riga Med. Inst., Latvia, 1961. Resident gen. surgery Jelgava (Latvia) Gen. Hosp., 1961-62; resident thoracic surgery P. Stradina Clin. Hosp., Riga, Latvia, 1962-64; surgeon The Latvian Ctr. Pulmonary Surgery, Riga, 1964-69; asst. prof., chief surgeon Clinic Gen. and Cardiovascular Surgery, Riga Med. Inst., Riga, 1969-94; prof., head Latvian State Cardiology Ctr. Children, Riga, 1994—2006; head Clinic for Children's Cardiology, Latvian Med. Acad., Riga. Spl. editl. cons. Latvian Med. Acad., Riga, 1990—; dep. dirs. gen. JBC, 1997—; head Clinic Children's Cardiology & Cardiovasc. Surgery, U. Hosp. Children, Riga Stredius U. Contbr. articles to med. jours., chpts. to books; author 3 monographs; editl. bd. Latvian Pediat., Latvian Surgeon. Recipient Bronze medal in Sci., Soviet Union Ctrl. Exhibn. for Scientific Achievement, 1977, Commemorative medal Man of the Yr., Am. Biographical Inst., 1995, Meml. award, 2008; named Officier of the Three Star Order, 2001. Mem. The World Med. Assn. (assoc.), European Soc. Cardiology, Riga Hansa Rotary Club (pres. 1998-99), Internat. Soc. Cardiovascular Surgery, Assn. for European Paediatric Cardiology (nat. del.), World Soc. Cardiovasc. Surgeons, Latvian Soc. Cardiovasc. Surgery (pres.). Lutheran. Avocation: swimming. Home: Raunas str 45/3-108 1084 Riga Latvia Office: University Hosp Children Riga Vienibas gatve 45 Riga LV 1004 Latvia Home Phone: 371-7565227; Office Phone: 26446113. Business E-Mail: aris.lacis@apollo.lv.

LACIS, JANIS, medical educator; b. Riga, Latvia, Aug. 1, 1935; MD, Riga Stradins U., 1961. Assoc. prof. Riga Stradins U., 1976—. Fellow: European Soc. Cardiology. Avocations: fishing, travel, gardening. Office: Pilsonu 13 Riga LV 1002 Latvia Business E-Mail: janis.lacis@stradini.lv.

LACKMAN, RICHARD D., orthopaedic surgeon, educator; MD, U. Pa., Phila., 1977. Lic. Pa., 1978, diplomate Am. Bd. Orthopaedic Surgery, 1985. Fellow orthop. oncology Mayo Clinic, Minn., 1983; intern gen. surgery Pa. Univ. Hosp., 1978, resident orthop. surgery, 1982, prof. orthop. srugery, dir., assoc. dir. patient family svcs., surgeon. Recipient Best Dr., Best Doctors in America, 2008, 2010; named one of the Top Doctors, Phila. Mag., 2006—11, America's Top Doctors, 2007—08, 2010. Office: Pennsylvania University Hospital Garfield Duncan Bldg Ste 2C 301 S 8th St Philadelphia PA 19106 Office Phone: 800-789-7366.

LACKNER, JAMES ROBERT, aerospace medicine educator; b. Virginia, Minn., Nov. 11, 1940; s. William and Lillian Mae (Galbraith) L.; m. Ann Martin Graybiel, Aug. 26, 1970. BSc, MIT, 1966, PhD, 1970. Asst. prof. psychology Brandeis U., Waltham, Mass., 1970-74, assoc. prof. psychology, 1974-79, Riklis prof. physiology dept. psychology, 1977—, chmn. dept. psychology, 1975-83, provost, dean faculty, 1986-89, dir. Ashton Graybiel Spatial Orientation Lab., 1982—. Research assoc. dept. psychology and clin. research ctr. MIT, Cambridge, 1970-80; sci. adv. bd. Space Biomed. Research Inst., Houston, 1982—, Aphasia Research Ctr. Boston U. Sch. Med., 1977-82, Eunice Kennedy Shriver Ctr. Harvard U. Med. Sch., Cambridge, 1980-90; sci. adv. panel astronaut longitudinal health program Johnson Space Ctr., NASA, 1983, exec. sec. space adaptation syndrome steering com., 1982-84, pre-adaption trainer working group, 1986—, artificial gravity working group, 1987—; fabricant com. life scis. experiments for a space sta., 1982; space scis. bd. sensory motor panel NAS, 1984-86; com. on hearing, bioacoustics and biomechanics NRC, 1985-89, com. on vision, 1987-92, com. on space, biology and medicine, 1991-99, mem. com. virtual reality rsch. and devel., 1992-95. Mem. editorial bd. Presence, 1992—, Jour. Vestibular Rsch., 1991-2001, Jour. Neurophysiology, 1995—, Exptl. Brain Rsch., 1997—, Jour. Exptl. Psychology, 2001—; contbr. more than 250 articles to sci. jours. Mem. Am. Soc. for Gravitational and Space Biology, Aerospace Med. Assn. (Arnold B. Tuttle award), Soc. for Neurosci., Psychonomics Soc., Internat. Brain Research Orgn., Barany Soc. (hon.), Internat. Acad. Astronautics (hon.). Achievements include research in human sensory-motor coordination and spatial orientation. Home: Boyce Farm Rd Lincoln MA 01773-4813 Office: Brandeis U Ashton Graybiel Lab 415 South St Waltham MA 02453-2728

LACOMB-WILLIAMS, LINDA LOU, community health nurse; b. Galion, Ohio, Oct. 1, 1948; d. Horace Allen and Roberta May (Black) Braden; m. Robert Earl LaComb, Feb. 1, 1970 (div. Aug. 1984); children: Robin Marie, Patrick Alan; m. Robert Allen Williams, Aug. 30. 1991; children Erin, Megan. BSN, Capital U., 1970; MPH, U. South Fla., 2002. RN, Fla., Ohio; cert. health edn. specialist. Staff nurse St. Anne's Hosp., Columbus, Ohio, 1970; pub. health nurse Hillsborough County Health Dept., Tampa, Fla., 1970-80, cmty. health nurse supr., 1980-87, RN supr., Joyce Ely Health Ctr., 2003—06, nursing program specialist, 2006—10; sr. cmty. health nurse Polk County Dept. Health, Lakeland, Fla., 1987-88, sr. cmty. health nurse supr., 1999—2003; sr. RN supr. Children's Med. Svcs., Tampa, 1988-91, Lakeland, 1991-99. Adj. faculty U. Tampa, Fla., Springfield Coll., Tampa, 2008. 1st lt. flight nurse res. USAF, 1971-75. Recipient Boss of Yr. award, Strawberry chpt. Am. Bus. Women's Assn., 1985. Mem.: ARC, ANA, Fla. Assn. Pub. Health Nurses, Fla. Pub. Health Assn., Hillsborough County Med. Res. Corp., Bay Care Faith Cmty. Nurse, Fla. Nurses Assn. (grievance rep. state employees profl. bargaining unit 1976, pres. 1984—87, 1st v.p. 1989—91, dist. 2d v.p. 1998, Undine Sams award 1987, Nurse of Yr. award Dist. Four 1987, Excellence award 2004), Eta Sigma Gamma, Sigma Theta Tau, Phi Kappa Phi. Republican. Presbyterian. Avocations: walking, nurses' rights, writing. Home: PO Box 1491 Valrico FL 33595-1491 Office: Hillsborough County Health Dept PO Box 5135 Tampa FL 33675-5135 Personal E-mail: lacombwilliams@aol.com.

LACOSTE, ALAN DANIEL, physician, educator, medical company executive; b. New Orleans, Aug. 25, 1943; s. Charles and Viola Lacoste; 1 child, Natasha. BA, Loyola U., New Orleans, 1971; MD, La. State U., New Orleans, 1975. Cert. Am. Bd. in Opthalmology. CEO The Eye Clinic, Lake Charles, La., 1979—; clin. prof. opthalmology La. State U. Sch. Medicine, 1997—. Physician, surgeon Benevolent Missions Internat., Africa, 1986—, 1986—, Belieze, El Salvador, Bolivia, Fiji. Office: The Eye Clinic 1717 Oak Park Blvd Ste 100 Lake Charles LA 70601 Office Phone: 337-478-3810. Office Fax: 337-478-6360.

LACOUR, DELESE, physician; b. Ohio, Feb. 25, 1972; MD, U. Cin., 1994. Physician Johns Hopkins Hosp., 2008—. Fellow: ACOG; mem.: NASPAG. Home: 1429 BAttery Ave Baltimore MD 21230 Business E-Mail: dlacour1@jhmi.edu.

LADAS, SPIROS D. (SPYRIDON LADAS), gastroenterologist, educator; b. Lixouri, Kefallonia, Greece, Mar. 20, 1946; s. Dimitrios S. and Asimina Ladas; m. Eleni Malamou, Apr. 28, 1974; 1 child, Dimitris S. Degree, Nat. U. Athens, Greece, 1970; PhD in Medicine, Med. Sch., Athens U., Greece, 1977. Cert. specialist in internal medicine Greek Ministry Hygiene, 1976, specialist in gastroenterology Greek Ministry Hygiene, 1979. Lectr. internal medicine Med. Sch., Athens U., 1978—87, reader internal medicine, 1988—95, assoc. prof. internal medicine, gastroenterology, 1996—2003, prof. medicine, gastroenterology, 2004—. Chmn. Dept. Internal Medicine-Propaedeutic, Laiko U. Gen. Hosp. Athens, 2007—. Editor: (book) Medical Ethics. Focus on Gastroenterology and Digestive Endoscopy, 2002; contbr. chapters to books, articles to profl. jours. publs. Mem. governing coun. Hellenic Found. Gastroenterology Nutrition, Athens, 2000—08. Mem.: United European Gastroenterology Fedn. (pub. affairs com. 2006—), European Soc. Gastrointestinal Endoscopy (v.p. 2007—08). Office: Laiko Univ Gen Hosp Athens 17 Ag Thoma Athens 11527 Greece Business E-Mail: sdladas@otent.gr.

LADD, VIRGINIA, medical association administrator; Pres., exec. dir. Lupus Found. America; founder Chronic Illness Awareness Coalition; founder, pres., exec. dir. Am. Autoimmune Related Diseases Assn., E. Detroit, Mich. Past bd. mem. Nat. Heath Coun.; mem. bd. contbrs. Inst. Voluntary Orgns. USA; mem. bd. dirs. UN NGO Health Com.; mem. various committees NIH; mem. expert panel on autoimmune diseases Agency Toxic Substances and Diseases Registry; founder, facilitator Nat. Coalition Autoimmune Patient Groups. Recipient Jefferson award, Am. Inst. Pub. Svc., 1995. Office: Am Autoimmune Related Diseases Assn Inc 22100 Gratiot Ave Eastpointe MI 48021 also: Ste 1100 750 17th St NW Washington DC 20006 Office Phone: 586-776-3900. *

LADEIRA, MARCELO SADY PLÁCIDO, geneticist; b. Rio de Janeiro, June 30, 1969; Degree in Biology, UNICOR, 1990; degree in Genetics, U. Estadual Paulista, 1990. Prof., nutrigenomics postgrad. pathology program botucatu med. sch. U. Estadual Paulista, 2005; CEO, sci. cons. Multigene - Edn., Rsch., Consult and Svcs. Human, Molecular and Toxicological Genetics, 2008—. Avocation: yoga. Office: José Barbosa 1780 Fazenda Lageado Botucatu São Paulo 1860609 Brazil Office Fax: 55(14) 3811-7110. Business E-Mail: mladeira@fmb.unesp.br.

LADENHEIM, JULES CALVIN, neurosurgeon; b. Union Hill, NJ, Apr. 21, 1923; s. Solomon and Miriam (Preminger) L.; m. Janet Bloom (dec.), Feb. 15, 1959; children: Eric, Fred (dec.), Karen. AB, Harvard U., 1944; MD, NY Med. Coll., 1947. Diplomate Am. Bd. Surgery, Am. Bd. Neurologic Surgery. Intern Queens Gen. Hosp., NYC, 1947-48; resident gen. surgery NY Med. Coll., 1948-50, Pitts. Med. Ctr., 1952-53, Mt. Sinai, Cleve., 1953-54; resident neurosurgery Serafimer Hosp., Stockholm, 1954-56, Med. Coll. Va., Richmond, 1956-57; resident in neurosurgery Neurology Inst. NY, 1957-58; resident neurosurgery Mary Hitchcock, Hanover, NH, 1958-60; pvt. practice Hackensack, NJ, 1960—. Staff neurosurgeon Hackensack U. Hosp., 1960—, Holy Name Hosp., Teaneck, NJ, 1960—, Meadowland Hosp., Secaucus, NJ, 1987—, St. Mary Hosp., Hoboken, 1987—. Co-author: Arteriovenous Aneurysm, 1956; author: Intraventric Meningiomas, 1961, Leonard Bertapaglia, 1991, Firearms and Ballistics, 1996, Alien Horseman, 2003, Custer's Thorn, 2007, The Jarrett-Palmer Express of 1876, 2008, Abe Lincoln Afloat, 2009, Grant Keeper, 2011. Lt. USNR, 1950—52. Decorated Navy and Marine Corps medal. Mem. Am. Assn. Neurologic Surgeons, Congress of Neurosurgery, Nordiska Neurokirugiska Forening, Abraham Lincoln Soc. (pres. 1993-94), USS Columbus Vets. Assn., Harvard Club NY. Office: 664 River Rd Teaneck NJ 07666-1642 E-mail: julescalvin@aol.com.

LADENSON, PAUL, endocrinologist; MD, Harvard U., 1975. Prof. medicine Johns Hopkins Med. Instn., Balt., dir. divsn. endocrinology and metabolism, 1989—; dir. Johns Hopkins Thyroid Tumor Ctr., Balt, 1991—. Office: Johns Hopkins Univ 1830 E Monument St Ste 333 Baltimore MD 21287 Office Fax: 410-955-8172.

LADENSTEIN, RUTH LYDIA, pediatrician; b. Vienna, Dec. 25, 1956; MD, Med. U. Vienna, PhD, 1998; MBA in Internat. Health Care Mgmt., U. Salzburg, 2006. Cert. sr. project mgr. Internat. Project Mgmt. Assn. Sr. paediatric haemotologist, oncologist St. Anna Children's Hosp. and Rsch. Inst., 1982—; assoc. prof. Med. U. Vienna, 1998. Chair Austrian Group Paeditric Haemato-Oncology, 2005—11; bd. pres. SIOPEN Assn., 2007—11; pres. SIOP Europe European Soc. Paediatric Oncology, 2009—. Recipient Paediatric Haemato-Oncology Sci. award, Dachverband der Österreichischen Kinder-Krebs-Hilfe-Orgn., 1998, European Rsch. award, 7th Framework Programme EU Health, 2010, Woman award, Woman Mag., 2010. Avocations: ballroom dancing, sailing, hiking, jogging, tai chi. Office: Zimmermannplatz 10 Vienna 1090 Austria Office Phone: 43-1-404-70-4750. Office Fax: 43-1-404-70-7430. Business E-Mail: ruth.ladenstein@ccri.at.

LADER, MALCOLM HAROLD, pharmaceutical consultant; b. Liverpool, England, Feb. 27, 1936; s. Abe and Minnie (Sholl) L.; m. Susan Ruth Packer, Apr. 16, 1961; children: Deborah, Vicki, Charlotte. BSc, U. Liverpool, 1956, MB, ChB, 1959, MD, 1964; PhD, U. London, 1963, DSc, 1978; LLB, Coll. Law, 2006. Rsch. staff MRC, England, 1966—2001. Cons. Maudsley Hosp., 1970—2001; prof. clin. psychopharmacology U. London, 1978—2001, emeritus prof., 2001—; advisor WHO, 1995—2002; trustee Psychiatry Rsch. Trust. Author: Biological Treatments in Psychiatry, 1996, Tranquillisers and Antidepressants, 2008; contbr. articles to profl. jours. Decorated Order of Brit. Empire. Fellow: Acad. Med. Scis., Royal Soc. Psychiatrists, Soc. for Study of Addiction (hon.), Am. Coll. Psychiatry (hon.), Brit. Assn. Psychopharmacology (hon.). Avocations: antiques, paintings. Home: 16 Kelsey Park Mansion 78 Wickham Rd BR3 6QH Beckenham England Office Phone: 44-207-848-0372. Personal E-mail: malcolm.lader@kcl.ac.uk.

LADRON DE GUEVARA PUERTO, ABELARDO, health facility administrator, obstetrician, gynecologist; b. Mexico City, Jan. 27, 1966; s. Abelardo Ladron de Guevara Herrera and Herlinda Puerto Pavon; 1 child, Abelardo Ladron de Guevara Apodaca. MD, U. Nacional Autónoma de México FES Iztacala, Tlalnepantla, Estado de Mexico, 1991. Consejo Mexicano de Ginecología y Obstetricia Nat., 1995. Physician gynecology and obstetric staff Instituto Mexicano del Seguro Social Hosp. Gen. de Zona # 98, Coacalco, Estado de Mexico, 1995—2004, Instituto Mexicano del Seguro Social Hosp. Gen. Regional # 72, Tlalnepantla, 2004—. Chmn. reproductive healt jurisdictional Instituto de Salud del Estado de Mex., Tlalnepantla, 2004—. Fellow: ACOG (licentiate), La Asociacion Mexicana de Ginecologia y Obstetrica (licentiate). Roman Catholic. Office: Inst Health of Mexico State Profirio Diaz / Guerrero 54000 Tlalnepantla Mexico Home: Circuito Circunvalacion Oriente # 33A 53100 Ciudad Satelite Mexico

[The remaining body text continues in multiple columns with numerous biographical entries including LADWIG HAROLD ALLEN, LAERUM OLE DIDRIK, LAFARGA JUAN BAUTISTA, LAFAYE CLAUDINE YVONNE LOUISE, LAFFEY JOHN G, LAFLEUR KENNETH CHARLES, LAFRANCE WILLIAM CURT PHILLIP JR, LAGANGA LINDA ROSE, LAGERBERG DAGMAR ANNA-GRETA, LAGOS NESTOR WILSON, LAGRANGE JEAN-LEON, LAGUNOFF DAVID, LAHDENKARI ANNE-TIINA, LAHIFF MARILYN J, LAHITA ROBERT GEORGE, LAHOUD GEORGE YOUSSEF GEORGE.]

N.E. Yorkshire Trust, North Yorkshire, England, 1994—2007; assoc. prof. anaesthesia U. Leeds Sch. Medicine, 2007—. Presenter in field. Recipient Physician's Recognition award, AMA, 1994—97. Fellow: Royal Coll. Anaesthetists, Mass. Med. Soc., Royal Coll. Surgeons Ireland (fellow faculty anaesthetists); mem.: AAAS, Assn. Dental Anaesthetists, Assn. Anaesthetists Gt. Britain and Ireland (licentiate). Conservative. Roman Catholic. Achievements include advanced clinical research in combined conscious sedation for patients requiring ambulatory diagnostic or surgical procedures and for pain relief in labour; pioneer a new sevoflurane inhalation conscious sedation for children having dental treatment. Avocations: painting, photography, classic music, travel, fine cuisine. Home: 33 Carlton Manor Deepdale Ave YO11 2UF Scarborough YO11 2UF England Home Fax: 44 (0)1723 385160. Personal E-mail: drlahoud@aol.com.

LAHOWCHIC, NICHOLAS JOHN, consulting company executive; b. NYC, Apr. 11, 1947; s. Nicholas and Mary Ellen (Dunn) La H.; m. Diane Forrest; children: Tara Anne, Nicole Marie. Student, Marquette U., Milw., 1964—66; BS in Acctg., Fairleigh Dickinson U., Teaneck, NJ, 1970; MBA, Pace U., NYC, 1980; DSc, Logistic Healthcare Strategy Bd., 2011. Acct. Okonite Cable Corp., Passaic, NJ, 1966-68; cost analyst Philips Broadcast Equip. Corp., Paramus, NJ, 1968-69; from corp. acct. to mgr. Thomas J. Lipton, Inc., Englewood Cliffs, NJ, 1969—77, mgr. ops. planning, 1977—79; gen. mgr. McGraw Hill Book Co., NYC, 1979-81; dir. inventory mgmt. Nabisco Brands, Inc., Parsippany, NJ, 1981-84, 1984-85, dir. logistics planning, systems and adminstrn., 1985-87; dir. logistics Colgate-Palmolive, Inc., NYC, 1987-89, dir. customer svc. and logistics, 1989-91; v.p. corp. logistics Becton Dickinson & Co., Franklin Lakes, NJ, 1991-95; pres. Becton Dickinson Supply Chain Svcs., Franklin Lakes, NJ, 1995-97; pres., CEO Ltd. Logistics Svcs., Columbus, 1997—; exec. v.p. Ltd. Brands, Inc., 2004—07; pres. Diannic LLC, Port St. Lucie, Fla., 2007—. Bd. dirs. Express Scripts, Inc.; bd. advisory dir. Whirlpool Co.; cons. in field. Mem. editl. adv. bd. Supply Chain Mgmt. Rev., Med. Product Sales mag; contbr. articles to bus. publs. Trustee United Way, Greater Columbus, Ohio, 1999-2005, Columbus C. of C., 2003-06, Columbus Jazz Group, 2006-07, Compete Columbus, 2006-07. Recipient Harry Salzburg medallion award, 1997, Thinkurt Movers award, 2010. Mem. Nat. Assn. Accts., Am. Mgmt. Assn., Am. Prodn. and Inventory Control Soc. (dir. 1979-80), Nat. Coun. Phys. Distbn. Mgmt. (v.p. 1982-83), Health Industry Distbn. Assn. (bd. dirs. 1997-2001), Health Industry Mfrs. Assn., Health Industry Bar Code Coun., Grocery Mfrs. Assn. (chmn. distbn. ops. steering com.), Coun. Logistics Mgmt., Internat. Materials Mgmt. Soc. Pace U., Columbus C. of C. (bd. dirs. 2001-2005). Office: PO Box 9618 Port Saint Lucie FL 34985 Office Phone: 614-561-7100. Business E-Mail: nlahowchic@diannicllcltd.com.

LAHÓZ MOYA, GABRIEL BUENO, physical therapist, educator; b. Sao Paulo, Brazil, Sept. 13, 1982; Degree in Phys. Therapy, USP, 2004 M 2009. Physiotherapist USP, 2005—; phys. therapy cons. Sanitas Corpus, 2009—. Bd. dirs. Sanitas Corpus, 2009—. Avocation: guitar. Home: Rua Embaixador Raul Garcia 24 Bosque d São Paulo 04127-010 Brazil Personal E-mail: gabriel.moya@sanitascorpus.com.br.

LAI, CHOON HIN, surgeon; b. Singapore, Aug. 3, 1955; MBBS, Nat. U. Singapore, 1979. Adult reconstruction fellow Mayo Clinic, Rochester, Minn., 1989—90; instr. Mayo Med. Sch., 1989—90; cons. adult reconstruction & orthopaedic surgeon Tan Tock Seng Hosp., Singapore, 1990—97, sr. cons. adult reconstruction & orthopaedic surgeon, 1997—. Founding pres. ASEAN Arthroplasty Assn., 2007—08, bd. mem., 2008—11; pres. Singpore Orthopaedic Assn., 2007—08. Recipient Howard Eddy medal, Royal Australasian Coll. Surgeons; Merit scholarship, Pub. Svc. Commn., Singapore. Fellow: Royal Coll. Surgeons, Edinburgh; mem.: ASEAN Arthroplasty Assn., Singapore Orthopaedic Assn. Home: 5 Stone Ave Singapore 588227 Singapore Personal E-mail: chpclai@gmail.com.

LAI, ERIC PONG SHING, family physician, educator; b. Kowloon, Hong Kong, May 20, 1946; arrived in Can., 1968; s. Man Hoi and Lai Ming (Chiu) L.; m. Mimi Maria Mak Lai, Sept. 11, 1972; children: Gordon, Jennifer. BSc, Acadia U., Wolfville, Nova Scotia, 1971; MB, B CH, LRCS, LLMRCP, U. Ireland, Dublin, 1977; DFM, Chinese U. Hong Kong, 1989. Med. diplomate, Ireland, UK, Hong Kong. Rsch. fellow Med. Sch. McGill U., Montreal, Can., 1971; resident in medicine Chesterton Hosp. Cambridge (Eng.) U., 1977; resident New Addenbrooke Hosp., Cambridge, 1978; resident in gynecology Princess Margaret Hosp., Kowloon, Hong Kong, 1979-81; pvt. practice family physician Hong Kong, 1981—2001; dir. G-Way Health Ctr., Richmond, B.C., Canada; med. dir, 1998—2008. Bd. dirs. First Med. Mgmt. Ltd., Calgary, Alta., Can., 1989; found. dir. Chinese Recreation Assn., Calgary; lectr. Hong Kong U., 1986-92, Chinese U. Hong Kong, 1986-92; facilitator Hong Kong Coll. Gen. Practitioners, 1986-92; internat. dir. World Orgn. Health Promotion, 1993-2002; cons. G-Way Holdings Internat. Inc., 1993-2009; internat. med. dir. G-Way Health Centre, Can., 1993-2009. Mem. Hong Kong Dem. Found., 1990-92, Hong Kong Bd. Edn. Coll. Gen. Practitioners, 1986-92, chmn., 1991-92, com. chmn. refresher course, 1991-92; vice chmn. found. Kidney Ctr. Precious Blood Hosp., 1991; adviser S.E. Asia Rsch. Inst., 1992; mem. Pub. Edn. Com., 1993-95; med. cons. World Orgn. Health Promotion, Can., 1993-2002. Named Henry Burton De Wolfe scholar to McGill U., 1971. Mem. Internat. Lions Club (v.p. Mt. Cameron chpt. 1986-90, pres. 1990-91, zone chmn. Internat. Club 1991-92, Melvin Jones fellow 1991-2002), KSJ, OSJ (Australia). Democrat. Avocations: reading, meditation, poetry, walking, boxing. Office: G-Way Health Ctr 3700 No 3 Rd Richmond BC V6X 3X2 Canada

LAI, JUI-YANG, engineering educator; b. Taiwan, Aug. 14, 1975; BS in Chem. Engring., Nat. Ctrl. U., 1997; PhD in Chem. Engring., Nat. Tsing Hua U., 2006. Postdoc. rsch. fellow Nat. Tsing Hua U., 2006—07; asst. rsch. fellow Chang Gung U., 2007, asst. prof., 2007—10, assoc. prof., 2010—. Recipient Triangle Rsch. Collaboration award, 3rd Asian Internat. Symposium Biomaterials & Drug Delivery Sys. Mem.: Tissue Engring. & Regenerative Medicine Internat. Soc., Soc. Biomaterials, Polymer Soc., Taipei, Biomed. Engring. Soc. ROC, Assn. Rsch. Vision & Ophthalmology. Avocations: reading, writing, travel. Office: 259 Wen-Hwa 1st Rd Kwei-Shan Taoyuan 33302 Taiwan Business E-Mail: jylai@mail.cgu.edu.tw.

LAI, LESLIE, pathologist, consultant, lecturer; b. Malacca, Malaysia, Sept. 26, 1959; s. Philip and Irene (Toh) L. MBBS, Guy's Hosp., London, 1983; MSc, Charing Cross and Westminster Hosps., 1987; MD, London U., 1990. Cons., sr. lectr. in clin. biochemistry Freeman Hosp., Newcastle upon Tyne, Eng., 1990-96; prof. clin. biochemistry and metabolic medicine U. Putra Malaysia, Selangor, 1997—2001, dep. dean Med. Sch., 1997—2001; dean Postgrad. Med. Sch. Internat. Med. U., 2001—04; cons. endocrinologist Gleneagles Intan Med. Ctr., 2004—09, dir. pathology, 2009—; cons. endocrinologist Prince Ct. Med. Ctr., 2007—; cons. endocrinologist, clin. dir. pathology Sunway Med. Ctr., 2004—09. Chmn. organizing com. WASPaLM 2007 Congress, Kuala Lumpur, Malaysia. Editor Malaysian Jour. Clin. Biochemistry, 1998-2000; mem. editl. bd. Clin. Biochemist Revs., Pathology, 1998—, Malaysian Jour. Pathology, 1998-, assoc. editor, 2008-, clin. biochemistry assoc. editor, 2008-, Clin. Chemistry and Lab. Mgmt., 2008, Indian Jour. Clin. Biochemistry, 2007-; contbr. articles to profl. jours. Chmn. Tyneside Cancer Trust, Eng., 1994-96. Named Outstanding Young Malaysian for Acad. Leadership and Accomplishment, 1999. Fellow Royal Coll. Pathologists, Royal Coll. Physicians; mem. Internat. Fedn. Clin. Chemistry (exec. com. edn. and mgmt. divsn. 2004-, vice-chmn. 2008-, chmn, vis. lectr. prog. 2008-), Soc. Endocrinology, Assn. Clin. Biochemists, Malaysian Assn. Clin. Biochemists, Acad. Medicine Malaysia, Asian-Pacific Fedn. Clin. Biochemistry (v.p. 2004—10, pres. 2010-, travelling lectr. 2007-08), Coll. of Pathologists (mem. coun.2002-08, chmn. lab. quality assurance scheme, 1998-). Avocations: classical music, playing piano, travel. Office: Gleneagles Intan Med Ctr 282 & 286 Jalan Ampang 50450 Kualalumpur Malaysia Office Phone: 603-42510433.

LAI, MARIA ELIANA, internist, educator; b. Desulo, Nuoro, July 16, 1948; Degree in Medicine, Med. Sch. Cagliari, Sardinia, Italy, 1973; degree in Internal Medicine, Postgrad. Sch. Internal Medicine Cagliari, 1984. Rsch. fellow Inst. Infectious Diseases U. Cagliari, 1973—80, rschr. Inst. Internal Medicine, 1980—2000, assoc. prof. internal medicine, 2000—, dir. Adult Thalassemic Ctr., 2000—11, dir. Liver Diseases Ctr., 2006—11. Mem.: Italian Soc. Internal Medicine, Italian Soc. Study Thalassemia & Other Hemoglobinopathies. Avocations: exercise, swimming, tennis. Home: Viale Armando Diaz 182 Cagliari Sardinia 09125 Italy Home Fax: 39 070 6095511. Business E-Mail: laie@pacs.unica.it.

LAI, TIMOTHY Y. Y., ophthalmologist, educator; MD, Chinese U. Hong Kong; MS in Med. Scis., U. Hong Kong; MB, BChir, U. Sydney. Assoc. prof. dept. ophthalmology & visual scis. Chinese U. Hong Kong, 2007—. Recipient Nakajima award, Asia-Pacific Acad. Ophthalmology, 2008; named one of Ten Outstanding Young Persons, Jr. Chamber Internat. Hong Kong, 2008. Fellow: RCS (Edinburgh), Coll. Ophthalmologists Hong Kong, Hong Kong Acad. Medicine. Achievements include research in diagnosis and treatment of retinal diseases, uveitis and visual electrophysiology. Office: Chinese Univ Hong Kong Hong Kong Eye Hospital 147K Argyle St Kowloon Hong Kong Business E-Mail: tyylai@cuhk.edu.hk.

LAI, TZE LEUNG, mathematician, educator; b. Hong Kong, China, June 28, 1945; s. Chi Yau Lai and Wai Chun Cheng; m. Letitia Chow, June 23, 1975; children: Peter, David. PhD, Columiba U., 1971. Prof. stats., health rsch & policy dir. fin. math., co-dir. biostats Cancer Ctr. Ctr. Innovative Study Design Stanford U., Calif., 1987—; prof. math. stats. Columbia U., New York, 1977—87. Adv. bd. mem. Academia Sinica, Taipei, Taiwan, 1991—. Author books and jour. articles. Recipient Guggenheim Fellowship, Guggenheim Found., 1983—84. Fellow: Am. Statis. Assn. (COPSS Award 1983). Office: Stanford Univ Sequoia Hall Serra Mall Stanford CA 94305-4065 Office Phone: 650-723-2622. Business E-Mail: lait@stanford.edu.

LAI-BO, SAN PAUL, surgeon; Grad., Chinese U., Hong Kong. Cluster coord. surg. svc. new territories east cluster (NTEC) Hosp. Authority; surg. tng. gen. surgery Hong Kong, Edinburgh; joined Chinese Univ., Hong Kong, 1990, asst. dean gen. affairs faculty medicine, chmn. surgery dept.; hon. chief svc. and cons. surgeon Prince Wales Hosp. Office: Prince Wales Hospital 30-32 Ngan Shing St Sha Tin New Territories Hong Kong Office Phone: 85226451222.
*

LAIER JOHNSEN, HELLE BIRGIT, occupational health physician; b. Kjellerup, Denmark, Aug. 31, 1958; d. Karl Aage and Gudrun Laier; m. Sigbjoern Johnsen, Aug. 8, 1987; children: Emma Kristine, Jens Aage, Ida Marie. MD, U. Copenhagen, 1987; PhD, U. Oslo, 2009. Rsch. fellow Faculty Divsn. Akershus U. Hosp., U. Oslo, Loerenskog, Norway, 2003—08; chief occupl. health dept. HMS East, Occupl. Health Dept., Furnes, Norway, 1988—2010, Frisk HMS, 2010—; occupl. health physicain Nat. Inst. Occupl. Health, 2009—. Mem.: Norwegian Med. Assn., Am. Quarter Horse Assn. Home: Vesleenga Bjoergevegen 29 Brumunddal N-2380 Norway Office: Frisk HMS Storgate 133 2390 Moelv Norway Personal E-mail: helle.laier@dadlnet.dk. Business E-Mail: helle@oppfrisk.no.

LAIHINEN, ARTO OLAVI, neurologist; b. Rauman mlk, Finland, Feb. 23, 1952; arrived in Germany, 1998, permanent resident, 1998; m. Ulrike Halsband, Apr. 8, 1990. MD, U. Turku, Finland, 1977, PhD, 1983. Lectr. neurology U. Turku, 1989; med. dir. Rehamed Neuro GmbH, Stuttgart, Germany, 2005—. Rsch. fellowship, UBC, Vancouver, Can., 1984. Achievements include research in parkinson's disease, dopaminergic brain mechanisms, positron emission tomography, cognitive neuroscience. Clinical areas: neurology, rehabilitation, traffic medicine. Avocation: literature. Home: Grundackerstrasse 14 Emmendingen DE-79312 Germany Home Phone: 49-173-378 72 75. Business E-Mail: arto.laihinen@gmx.de.

LAINO, LUIGI, dermatologist; b. Rome, Apr. 4, 1974; Degree in Medicine and Surgery, U. Rome La Sapienza, 2000, degree in Dermatology and Venereology, 2004. Exec. physician Dermatol. Inst. San Gallicano Rsch. and Care, 2009—. Prof. HS Allergology and Immunology, U. Rome La Sapienza, 2004—05; cons. High Law Ct. Rome, 2006; mem., directive coun. Order Med. Drs. Rome, Italy, 2008; reviewer European Jour. Dermatology, 2009, Archives Dermatology, 2010. Fellow: Internat. Found. Med. Thermography, Italian Fedn. Sports Dermatology, Dermatol. Acad. Rome; mem.: Italian Hosp. Dermatologists Assn., Internat. Soc. Dermoscopy. Avocations: chess, guitar. Office: Via Elio Chianesi 53 Rome Lazio 00144 Italy Office Fax: 390652662889. Business E-Mail: laino@ifo.it.

LAINSON, RALPH, parasitologist, researcher; b. Upper Beeding, Sussex, Eng., Feb. 21, 1927; s. Charles Harry and Anne (Denyer) L.; m. Ann Patricia Russell, 1956 (div. 1976); children: Karen Susan, Amanda Jane, Stephen Paul; m. Zéa Constante Lins, Apr. 12, 1989. BSc, London U., 1951, PhD, 1955, DSc, 1964; D (hon.), U. Fed. Pará, Brazil, 1982. Lectr. London Sch. Hygiene and Tropical Medicine, 1955-59, rsch. worker, 1962-65; officer-in-charge Dermal Leishmaniasis Unit, Cayo Dist., Belize, 1959-62; dir. The Wellcome Tropical Unit, Belém, Brazil, 1965-92; rsch. worker, cons. leishmaniasis and the Coccidia Inst. Evandro Chagas Fundação Nat. de Saude, Belém, 1992—. Contbr. over 350 articles to profl. jours. Mem. steering com. WHO, Geneva, 1977-83. Named to Order of Brit. Empire, 1996; recipient Chalmers medal and Manson medal Royal Soc. Tropical Medicine and Hygiene, 1971, 83. Fellow Royal Soc. of London; mem. 3d World Acad. Scis. (assoc.), London Sch. Hygiene and Tropical Medicine (hon.), Royal Soc. Tropical Medicine and Hygiene, Brit. Soc. Parasitology (hon.), Soc. Protozoologists (hon.), Am. Soc. Tropical Medicine & Hygiene (hon.). Anglican. Avocations: philately, music, lepidoptera, fishing. Office: Inst Evandro Chagas Avenida Almirante Barroso 492 66093-020 Belém PA Brazil Business E-Mail: ralphlainson@iec.pa.gov.br.

LAISHRAM, RANBIR SINGH, pediatrician, educator; s. Ador Singh Late Laishram and Ibechaobi Devi Laishram; m. Sakila Devi Kshetrimayum, Feb. 14, 1979; children: Romila Devi, Veerjit Singh, Sheronica. MBBS, Patna Med. Coll., India, 1976, MD in Pediatrics, 1981. Registrar pediat. Regional Inst. Med. Scis., Imphal, 1983—93, asst. prof. pediat., 1993—2000, faculty mem., med. edn. unit, 1999—2003, assoc. prof. pediat., 2002—06, prof., head pediat., 2006—, editl. bd. mem., Jour. Med. Soc. Mem. Bd. Studies Med. Scis., Manipur U., Imphal, 1994—; mem. various com. HIV, AIDS Manipur State AIDS Control Soc., Imphal, 1997—; state and nat. trainer on HIV, AIDS, Indian Acad. Pediat., UNICEF, WHO Nat. AIDS Control Orgn., Manipur, 1997—, mem., rev. com. implementation art, New Delhi, 2004, mem., expert com. pediat. ARV formulations treatment for HIV, AIDS, 04, mem., Ist Nat. Consultative Meeting Pediatric HIV, AIDS Bd. India, Indian Acad. Pediat., UNICEF, Ptnr. WHO, Clinton Found., 06, mem., 06; insp. Med. Coun. India, New Delhi, 2007; pediatric cons. Anteretroviral Therapy Ctr, Regional Inst. Med. Scis., Imphal, 2004—; mem. task force meet pediat. HIV, AIDS Indian Coun. Med. Rsch., New Delhi, 2007; ctrl. coordinating team mem. Clin. Epidemiol. Network India, New Delhi, 2006—; editor Sci. Bull., Indian Acad. Pediat., Manipur. Contbr. articles to profl. jours., columns in newspapers. Hony pediat. cons. Manipur Network Positive People, Imphal, 2006—08. Recipient Internat. Med. Excellence award, India Internat. Friendship Soc., 2002, Marvel award, All Manipur Antidrug Assn., 2007; fellow Home and Cmty. Care HIV, AIDS Thailand, WHO, 2003. Fellow: Indian Acad. Pediat. (Manipur Br.) (hony. sec. 1992—96, editor 2000—02, fellow 2005, Cert. of Appreciation 1994—); mem.: Indian Acad. Pediat. (Neurology, Nephrology and Infectious Disease chpt.), Breast Feeding Promotion Network India, Indian Med. Assn., East Zone Indian Acad. Pediat. Coordinating Com. (sci. com. mem. 2000—06, v.p. 2007—08, 2008—, East Zone Purbanchal Pioneer award 2003), Rotary Club (Imphal) (Cert. of Appreciation 1994—), Core Group Trainers HIV, AIDS (Manipur). Achievements include research in project on survey of blood pressure height and weight of school children in Manipur; rapid assessment of newborn care situation and needs in national rural health mission, priority states of india under PATH/INCLEN, detection and treatment outcome of congenital hypothyroidism among term newborns. Office: Regional Inst Med Scis Lamphelpat Imphal Manipur 795004 India Home: Kwakeithel Moirangpurel Leikai 795 001 Imphal India Office Fax: 91-385-2414625. Personal E-mail: drranbirlai@yahoo.co.in.

LAITURI, TONY, engineering executive; b. Mich., Jan. 12, 1966; BSME, Mich. Tech U., 1986, MSME, 1988. Tech. specialist Ford Motor Co., 1989—. Recipient Ralph H. Isbrandt Automotive Safety award, SAE Internat., US Govt. Spl. award, DOT/NHTSA. Mem.: SAE. Avocation: tennis. Office: Research and Innovation Ctr MD 2115 Dearborn MI 48121 Business E-Mail: tlaituri@ford.com.

LAKE, CAROL LEE, anesthesiologist, physician, educator; b. Altoona, Pa., July 14, 1944; d. Samuel Lindsay and Edna Winifred (McMahan) L. BS, Juniata Coll., 1966; MD, Med. Coll. Pa., 1970; MBA, U. Calif., Irvine, 1997; MPH, U. Mich., 2000. Intern Mercy Hosp., Pitts., 1970-71, resident in anesthesiology, 1971-73; staff anesthesiologist Pitts. Anesthesia Assocs., 1973-75; asst. prof. anesthesiology U. Va., Charlottesville, 1975-80, assoc. prof., 1980-89, prof. anesthesiology, 1989-94; prof. anesthesiology, chair U. Calif., Davis, 1994-95, prof. clin. anesthesiology, 1996; chief of staff Roudebush VA Med. Ctr., 1997-99; asst. dean, prof. anesthesia Ind. U., Indpls., 1997-99; prof. anesthesiology, chair U. Louisville, 1999—2004, assoc. dean for continuing med. edn., 1999—2004, asst. v.p. for health affairs/continuing edn., 2002—04; CEO Verefi Techs., Inc., Elizabethtown, Pa., 2005—08; ret., 2009. Sr. assoc. examiner Am. Bd. Anesthesiology, 1981—2005. Author: Cardiovascular Anesthesia, 1985; editor: Pediatric Cardiac Anesthesia, 1988, 4th edit., 2004; Clinical Monitoring, 1990, 2d edit., 2000; editor Seminars in Cardiothoracic and Vascular Anesthesia, 1999—06; co-editor: Blood: Hemostasis, Transfusion and Alternatives in the Perioperative Period, 1995; editor Advances in Anesthesia, 1993-2008. Mem. Assn. Cardiac Anesthesiologists (pres. 1987-88), Soc. Cardiovascular Anesthesiologists (bd. dirs. 1988-92), Alpha Omega Alpha. Presbyterian. Avocations: music, entomology, gardening. Home Phone: 717-583-0842. E-mail: carol.lake@verefi.com.

LAKE, WESLEY WAYNE, JR., internist, allergist, medical educator; b. New Orleans, Oct. 11, 1937; s. Wesley Wayne and Mary McGehee (Snowden) L.; m. Abby F. Arnold, Aug. 1959 (div. 1974); children: Courtenay B., Corinne A., Jane S.; m. Melissa Bowman, Mar. 1999. AB in Chemistry, Princeton U., 1959; MD, Tulane U., 1963. Diplomate Am. Bd. Internal Medicine, Am. Bd. Allergy and Immunology. Intern Charity Hosp. of La., New Orleans, 1963-64, resident internal medicine, 1966-69; NIH fellow allergy and immunology La. State U. Med. Ctr., 1969-70; instr. dept. medicine Tulane U., New Orleans, 1967-69; fellow dept. medicine La. State U., New Orleans, 1969-70, instr. dept. medicine, 1970-73, asst. clin. prof. medicine, 1973-77; chief allergy clinic La. State U. Svc. Charity Hosp. La., New Orleans, 1970-77; assoc. clin. prof. medicine Tulane U., 1978—93. Temp. staff positions various hosps., 1963-70, including Baton Rouge Gen. Hosp., Our Lady of the Lake Hosp., Glenwood Hosp., St. Francis Hosp., Monroe, La., Lallie Kemp Charity Hosp., Independence, La., Huey P. Long Hosp., Pineville, La.; gen. med. officer outpatient clinic Hunter AFB, Savannah, Ga., 1964-65, gen. med. officer internal medicine svc., 1965-66; cons. physician Seventh Ward Gen. Hosp., Hammond, La., 1971-77, Slidell (La.) Meml.

Hosp., 1971-89, St. Tammany Parish Hosp., Covington, La., 1977-85; cons. physician East Jefferson Hosp., Metairie, La., 1971-77, staff physician, 1990—; asst. vis. physician Charity Hosp. New Orleans, 1970-75, staff physician, 1975-77, vis. phys. Tulane divsn., 1979-93; assoc. physician So. Bapt. Hosp., New Orleans, 1970-75, chmn. dept. medicine, chmn. internal medicine com., 1982-84, chmn. pharmacy and therapeutics, 1980-82, mem. investigative rev. com., 1984-85, mem. internal medicine quality assurance com., 1989-94; staff physician Kenner (La.) Regional Med. Ctr. (formerly St. Jude Med. Ctr.), 1985-99, chmn. quality assurance com., 1987-89; staff physician Drs. Hosp. of Jefferson, 1988—2005; mem. pharmacy and therapeutics com. and continuing med. edn. com. East Jefferson Gen. Hosp., 1997—. Author: (with others) Infiltrative Hypersensitivity Chest Diseases, 1975; contbr. articles to profl. jours. including Jour. Immunology, Internat. Archives Allergy and Applied Immunology, Jour. Allergy and Clin. Immunology; also chpts. in books concerning chest diseases. Fellow ACP, Am. Coll. Allergy, Sigma Xi; mem. New Orleans Acad. Internal Medicine, Musser-Burch Soc., S.E. Allergy Soc., La. Allergy Soc. (sec. 1975-76, v.p. 1976-77, pres. 1977-78). Republican. Episcopalian. Home: 4636 Perrier St New Orleans LA 70115-3920 E-mail: lakejrmd@aol.com.

LAKEY, DAVID L., state agency administrator; BS in Chemistry, Rose-Hulman Inst. Tech., Terre Haute, Ind.; MD, Ind. U. Sch. Medicine. Resident in internal medicine & pediat. medicine Vanderbilt U. Med. Ctr., Nashville, fellow in adult and pediat. infectious disease; faculty mem., assoc. prof. medicine U. Tex. Health Ctr., Tyler, 1998—2007, chief, divsn. clin. infectious disease, med. dir., Ctr. Pulmonary and Infectious Disease Control; assoc. dir., infectious disease and biosecurity U. Tex. Ctr. Biosecurity and Pub. Health Preparedness; commr. Tex. Dept. State Health Services, Austin, 2007—. Office: Tex Dept State Health Services PO Box 149347 Austin TX 78714-9347 Office Phone: 512-458-7375. Office Fax: 512-458-7477.

LAKHANI, PARAS, radiologist, educator; b. Skokie, Ill., Apr. 18, 1977; BA, U. Calif. Berkeley, 1999; MD, U. Pa., 2005. Radiologist Hosp. U. Pa., 2006—, Thomas Jefferson U., 2011—, asst. prof., 2011. Contbr. articles to numerous sci. profl. publs. Mem.: Soc. Imaging Informatics Medicine (Rsch. grant), Am. Imaging Informatics Assn., Am. Roentgen Ray Soc. (Rsch. award), Radiol. Soc. N.Am. (Trainee Rsch. prize), Am. Coll. Radiology, Phi Beta Kappa. Avocations: computers, basketball, exercise. Home: 113 N Bread St Apt 10e Philadelphia PA 19106 Personal E-mail: paras42@yahoo.com.

LAKIN, JAMES DENNIS, allergist, immunologist, director; b. Harvey, Ill., Oct. 4, 1945; s. Ora Austin and Annie Pitranella (Johnson) L.; m. Sally A. Stuteville, July 22, 1972 (dec. July 27, 2002); children: Tracey A., Margaret K., Matthew A., Christian J., Anne E.; m. Debra J. Franz, May 29, 2004. PhD, Northwestern U., 1968, MD, 1969; MBA in Med. Group Mgmt., U. St. Thomas, 1996. Diplomate Am. Bd. Internal Medicine, Am. Bd. Allergy and Immunology; cert. comml. pilot FAA, cert. flight instr., sr. aviation med. examiner. Dir. allergy rsch. Naval Med. Rsch. Inst., Bethesda, Md., 1974-76; clin. prof. U. Okla., Oklahoma City, 1976-89; dir. lab., chmn. allergy and immunology dept. Oxboro Clinics, Bloomington, Minn., 1989—2001; dir. Fairview Allergy and Asthma Svcs., Bloomington, 1995-2001; mng. ptnr. Minn. Allergy and Asthma Consultants, LLP, 2001—. Bd. dirs. Okla. Med. Rsch. Found., Oklahoma City, 1980-89; regional cons. Diver Alert Network, Duke U., Chapel Hill, N.C., 1987—; cert. diving med. officer NOAA, 1988. Co-author: Allergic Diseases, 1971, 3d edit., 1986; contbr. articles, revs. to profl. publs. Councilperson Our Lord's Luth. Ch., Oklahoma City, 1978-88, Faith Luth. Ch., Lakeville, Minn., 1990-91. Lt. comdr. USN, 1970—76, Vietnam, ret. Fellow ACP, Am. Acad. Allergy and Immunology, Am. Coll. Allergy and Immunology,Am. Coll. Chest Physicians, Am. Coll. Med. Practice Execs. (E.B. Stevens Article of Yr. award 1998); mem. Am. Assn. Immunologists, Med. Group Mgmt. Assn. (bd. dirs. 2002-06, E.B. Stevens Article of Yr. award, 1998), Am. Coll. Physician Execs. Achievements include research in characterization of the immunoglobulin system of the rhesus monkey, alterations in allergic reactivity during immunosuppression. Office: James Lakin 675 E Nicollet Blvd Ste 250 Burnsville MN 55337-6768 Office Phone: 952-223-3040. Business E-Mail: jdlakin@minnesotaallergy.com.

LAKSHMANADOSS, UMASHANKAR, medical association administrator; b. India, Nov. 18, 1975; MD, Unity Health Sys., 2010. With CIMS divsn. JH Bayview; house staff Unity Health Sys., 2007—10; dir., inpatient med. consult svc. Johns Hopkins U., 2010—. Recipient Humanist award, Unity Hosp. Sys., Outstanding Intern award; Cardiology fellow, Guthrie Clinic Robert Packer Hosp. Mem.: Am. Coll. Physician, Soc. Hosp. Medicine, Am. Coll. Cardiology, Am. Heart Assn. Office: 5200 Eastern Ave MFL West 6th Fl Baltimore MD 21224 Office Fax: 410-550-2972. Personal E-mail: drlumashankar@gmail.com.

LAKSHMANAN, PALANIAPPAN, surgeon, registrar; b. Madras, India, June 16, 1975; s. Lakshmanan Palaniappan and Unnamalai Lakshmanan; m. Jayanthi Palaniappan, Dec. 13, 2000; children: Unnamalai Palaniappan, Lakshmanan Palaniappan. MB, BS, Tamil-Nadu Dr. MGR Med. U., India, 1998; MS in Orthops., Madras Med. Coll., India, 2001. Intern Coimbatore Med. Coll. and Govt. Gen. Hosp., India, 1997—98; resident in trauma and orthop. surgery Madras Med. Coll. and Govt. Gen. Hosp., 1998—2001; fellow in spinal surgery U. Hosp. Wales, Cardiff, 2001; specialist registrar - trauma & orthopaedics No. Deanery, Newcastle-Upon-Tyne, Equatorial Guinea, 2005—. Specialist registrar. Contbr. articles pub. to profl. jour. Recipient Pres. Award, Scouts and Guides, Republic of India Govt., 1992, Gov. Award, Scouts & Guides, TamilNadu Govt, 1990, Gold Medal in Surgery, Indian Med. Assn., 1996, Best Outgoing student in Med. Sch., India Med. Assn., 1996, Gold Medal in Ist MBBS, Coimbatore Med. Coll., 1992, Highest Proficiency in Pathology, 1995, Highest Proficiency in Biochemistry, 1993. Fellow: Royal Coll. Surgeons Ireland (assoc.). Achievements include research in New hypothesis on the mechanism of odontoid fractures in the elderly, finding a relationship between upper cervical spine osteoarthritis and Type II odontoid fractures; New technique for patellar tendon bone grafting in patients undergoing Total knee arthroplasty with previous patellectomy; 26 Internat. and Nat. presentations in Trauma and Orthopaedics in the yr. 2004, and 23 Internat. presentations in the yr. 2005. Office: Wansbeck Gen Hosp Woodhorn Ln Ashington NE63 9JJ England Home: 36 Greenhills NE12 5BB Newcastle upon Tyne England Home Fax: +44 (0)1670 521212. Personal E-mail: lakunns@gmail.com.

LAL, PURSHOTAM, cardiologist; MD; AB, USA. Cert. Am. Specialty Bd.; ACC. Sr. interventional cadiologist Apollo Hosps., 1991; attending cardiologist Cornell Med. Ctr., 1994; sr. interventional cardiologist & co-ordinator dept. of cardiology Indraprastha Apollo Hosps., New Delhi, 1996; chmn. interventional cardiology Metro Heart Inst., 1997—, dir. interventional cardiology, 1997—. Mem. Ctrl. Coun. of Health & Family Welfare; mem. expert com. for medical devices Ministry of Health & Welfare; demonstrator dept. of anatomy Govt. Med. Coll., 1976; asst. clinical prof. Mich. Univ., 1983; registrar dept. of cardiology Am. Heart Assn., vis. cons., England, Am. Med. Assn., Germany. Orator Dr. V.V. Shah Oration, Annual Conf. of Cardiological Soc. of India, 1992, Dr. B.L. Tanjea Meml. Guest Lecture and Oration, 47th Annual awards, Delhi Med. Assn., 2004, Dr. William Ganz Oration, World Congress on Clin. and Preventive Cardiology, 2009, Bharat Ratna Dr. A.P.J. Abdul Kalam oration, World Congress on Clin. and Preventive Cardiology, 2010. Recipient 2nd Jawaharlal Lal Nehru Internat. Excellence award, UK, 1990, Mother India award, Honorable Spkr. Lok Sabha, 1992, Padma Shri award, 1993, Lifetime Achievement award, Delhi Med. Assn., 2002, Padma Bushan, 2003, Dr. B C Roy Nat. award for innovations in Interventional Cardiology, 2004, Indira Gandhi Excellence award, Nat. Med. Forum, New Delhi, 2006, Distinguished Achievement award of Highest Order, Nat. Forum of Indian Med. Assn., 2006—07, Padma Vibhushan, 2009, Lifetime Achievement award, World Congress of Cardiology, 2010; named Best Interventional Cardiologist of the Year, State of Tamil Nadu, 1991. Fellow: Royal Coll. of Physicians (Canada), Indian Coll. of Cardiology, Am. Coll. of Cardiology, Am. Coll. of Medicine; mem.: Delhi Med. Coun., German Soc. of Cardiovasc. Rsch., British Cardiovasc. Interventional Soc., Soc. of Cardiac Angiography and Interventions (USA). Office: Metro Heart Institute Sector-16 A New Delhi India *

LALEZARI, PARVIZ, retired medical educator; b. Iran, Aug. 17, 1931; MD, Tehran U., 1954. Prof., medicine and pathology Montefiore Med. Ctr. Albert Einstein Coll. Medicine, 1957—2011. Dir., blood bank Montefiore Med. Ctr., 1961—71; pres., CEO Bergen Cmty. Regional Blood Ctr., 1986—2001. Recipient Henry Moses Rsch. award, Montefiore Med. Ctr.; Rsch. grant, NIH. Mem.: Am. Soc. Hematology, Am. Soc. Clin. Investigation. Avocation: gardening. Office: Montefiore Med Ctr 111 E 210 Bronx NY 10467 Office Fax: 718-653-3284. Personal E-mail: lalezari2@aol.com.

LALIC, HRVOJE, medical educator; b. Rijeka, Croatia, Mar. 12, 1960; s. Mladen Lalic and Nada Turato; 1 child, Vedrana. MD, U. Rijeka, 1983, PhD, 1998. Prof., dept. occupl. and sport medicine Jeneteal U., Croatia, 2002—; chief dept. occupational health U. Rijeka, 2003—. Contbr. scientific papers to profl. pubs. Mem.: Croatian Med. Assn. Avocation: hunting. Office: Ho Health Rijeka Dept Occupational Medicine Ive Marinkovica 11 Rijeka 51000 Croatia Home: Franje Brentinija 5 51-000 Rijeka Croatia Home Phone: 00385-51-371-094; Office Phone: 00385-51-322-359. Business E-Mail: hlalic@inet.hr.

LALITHA, PALLE, radiologist, educator; b. Hyderabad, Andhra Pradesh, India, Sept. 22, 1976; MBBS, Jawaharlal Inst. Postgrad. Med. Edn. & Rsch., 2000; MD, Osmania Med. Coll., DNB, 2004. Sr. resident Nizams Inst. Med. Scis., 2005—06; cons. radiologist, asst. prof. Focus Diagnostics, Shadan Inst. Med. Scis., 2006—, cons., 2006—11. Recipient Dr. Sashi Goel Gold medal, USCON XIX, 2010. Mem.: EOSR, AMS, ESR, RSNA, ICRI, IJRI. Avocations: reading, travel. Office: Focus Diagnostics Dwarakapuri Colony Hyderabad Andhra Pradesh 500082 India Personal E-mail: lalithamanohar@rediffmail.com.

LALLY, JOANNE ELIZABETH, research scientist; b. Stockton on Tees, Eng., Feb. 27, 1969; d. James and Patricia Ling; m. Sean Lally; children: Patrick James, Roisin Lally, Ciaran Noel. BA with honors, U. Liverpool, Eng., 1990; MPH, Inst. Health and Soc., Newcastle U., Eng., 2000. Rsch. fellow Newcastle U., 2003—. Tng. fellowship, Med. Rsch. Coun., 2003. Office: Newcastle Univ Inst Health and Soc NE2 4HH Newcastle upon Tyne England Business E-Mail: j.e.lally@ncl.ac.uk.

LALLY, MARGARET S., dermatologist; MD, U. Pitts., 1985. Diplomate Am. Bd. Dermatology. Resident Univ. Pitts. Med. Sch.; hosp. affiliations include Univ. Pitts. Med. Ctr. St. Margaret, Allegheny Gen. Hosp. Avocation: French. Office: 1382 Old Freeport Rd Pittsburgh PA 15238 Office Phone: 412-967-1192.

LALWANI, ANIL KUMAR, otolaryngologist; b. Sept. 17, 1960; MD, U. Mich., 1985. Diplomate Am. Bd. Otolaryngology. Intern Duke U., Durham, NC, 1985—86, resident in gen. & thoracic surgery, 1986—87; resident in otolaryngology & head & neck surgery U. Calif., San Francisco, 1987-91, fellow in otolaryngology skull base surgery, 1987—91; sr. staff fellow NIH, Bethesda, Md., 1992—94; staff U. Calif., San Francisco, 1994—2003; Mendik Found. prof. otolaryngology NYU Sch. Medicine, chmn. otolaryngology, 2003—09, prof. physiology, neurosci. and pediat. Surgeon NYU Cochlear Implant Ctr. Mem.: ACS, Am. Acad. Otolaryngology and Head and Neck Surgery. Mailing: NYU Sch Medicine 540 1st Ave Skirball 7Q New York NY 10016 Office Phone: 212-263-6344. Business E-Mail: anil.lalwani@nyumc.org.

LAMARQUE GARNIER, VERONIQUE, health facility administrator, director; d. Michel and Nicole Hauser; children: Edouard Lamarque, Charlotte Lamarque. MS in Human Biology, Besançon U., 1986, MD, 1988; Postgrad. in Exptl. and Clin. Pharmacology, St. Antoine U., Paris, 1987. Cert. in statis. methodology Kremlin Bicetre U., Paris, 1986. Investigator phase 1 clin. studies and med. advisor for regional pharmacovigilance ctr. Hosp. Pharmacology Dept., Besançon, 1986—90; global head drug safety Beaufour Ipsen Group, Paris, 1990—92; head pharmacovigilance and med. info. SANDOZ, Paris, 1992—96, head med. affairs, 1996—97; head pharmacovigilance and pharmacoepidemiology NOVARTIS, Paris, 1997—2003; european sr. dir. vigilance and med. surveillance BAXTER, Paris, 2003—05; sr. dir. health evaluation, safety and risk mgmt. PFIZER, Paris, 2005—. Mem.: Assn. Pharmacovigilance Rsch., ARME-P, French Soc. Pharmacology & Therapeutics, Assn. French Speaking Epidemiologists, Internat. Soc. Pharmacovigilance. Office: Pfizer 23 25 avenue du Docteur Lannelongue 75668 Paris France Office Phone: 33 1 58 07 41 10. Office Fax: 33 1 58 07 42 43. Business E-Mail: veronique.lamarque@pfizer.com.

LAMB, IRENE HENDRICKS, medical researcher; b. Ky., May 9, 1940; d. Daily P. and Bertha (Hendricks) Lamb. Diploma in nursing, Ky. Bapt. Hosp.; student, Berea Coll., Ky., Calif. State U. L.A. RN, Ky. Charge nurse, head nurse acute medicine, med. ICU, surgical ICU, emergency room various med. ctrs., 1963—67; staff nurse rsch. CCU U. So. Calif./L.A. County Med. Ctr., 1968, nurse mgr. clin. rsch. ctr., 1969—74; sr. rsch. nurse cardiology Stanford U. Sch. Medicine, Calif., 1974—85, rsch. coord. pvt. clin., 1988; dir. clin. rsch. San Diego Cardiac Ctr., 1989—92; sr. cmty. health nurse Madison County Health Dept., Berea, Ky., 1993—97, sr. clin. rsch. mgr. stroke program, U. Ky. Coll. Medicine, Lexington, 1997—2002. Contbr. articles to profl. jours., chapters to books. Bd. dirs. Ky. Stroke Assn., 1998—2000. Mem.: Am. Heart Assn. Home: 107 Lorraine Ct Berea KY 40403-1317 Business E-Mail: ireneh.lamb@ky.gov.

LAMB, MICHAEL E., psychology professor, researcher; b. Lusaka, Zambia, Oct. 22, 1953; came to U.S., 1973, Eng., 2004; s. Francis B. and Michelle M. (de Lestang) L.; m. Kathleen J. Sternberg (dec.); children: Damon G., Aya Lewkowicz, Darryn N., Jeanette M., Philip D.; m. Hilary S. Clark; stepchildren: Amy Jaffa, Kate Jaffa, Lily Jaffa. BA, U. Natal, Durban, Republic of South Africa, 1972; MA, Johns Hopkins U., 1974; MS, MPhil, Yale U., 1975, PhD, 1976; PhD honoris causa, U. Göteborg, Sweden, 1995; DCL honoris causa, U. East Anglia, 2006. Asst. prof. psychology U. Wis., Madison, 1976-78; asst. prof. U. Mich., Ann Arbor, 1978-80; prof. psychology, psychiatry, pediatrics U. Utah, Salt Lake City, 1980-87; sr. scientist and sect. chief NIH, Bethesda, Md., 1987—2004; prof. psychology in the social scis. U. Cambridge, England, 2004—, head, dept. social devel. psychology, 2005—10, head faculty social & polit. sci., 2007—08. Vis. prof. U. Haifa, Israel, 1980, Hokkaido U., Sapporo, Japan, 1985, U. Osnabruck, Germany, 1989, Martin Luther U., Halle, Germany, 1997; mem. UK Econ. Social Rsch. Coun., 2006-11; chair Internat. Advisory Com., 2007-2010; mem. Higher Edn. Funding Coun. Rsch. Excellence Framework Sub-Panel on Psychology, Psychiatry & Neurosci., 2011-; fellow Sidney Sussex Coll., 2008-. Editor: The Role of the Father in Child Development, 1976, rev. edit., 1981, 97, 2004, 10, Social and Personality Development, 1978, Social Interaction Analysis, 1978, Advances in Developmental Psychology vol. I, 1981, vol. 2, 1982, vol. 3, 1984, vol. 4, 1986, Infant Social Cognition, 1981, Sibling Relationships, 1982, Nontraditional Families, 1982, Adolescent Fatherhood, 1986, The Father's Role: Applied Perspectives, 1986, The Father's Role: Cross-Cultural Perspectives, 1987, Developmental Science: An Advanced Textbook, 1982, rev. edits., 1988, 92, 99, 2005, 11, Infant Development: Perspectives from German Speaking Countries, 1991, Child Care in Context: Cross-Cultural Perspectives, 1992, Adolescent Problem Behaviors, 1994, Parenting and Child Development in Nontraditional Families, 1999, Conceptualizing and Measuring Father Involvement, 2004, Hunter-gatherer childhoods, 2005, Child Sexual Abuse: Disclosure, Delay and Denial, 2007, Children's Testimony, 2011, others; co-author: Development in Infancy, 1982, rev. edits., 1987, 92, 2002, Socialization and Personality Development, 1982, Infant-Mother Attachment, 1985, Child Psychology Today, 1986, Investigative Interviews of Children, 1998, Tell Me What Happened: Structered Investigative Interviews of Child Victims and Witnesses, 2008. Recipient Young Psychologist award Am. Psychol. Assn., 1976, Boyd McCandless award Am. Psychol. Assn., 1978, Superior Rsch. award U. Utah, 1985, Disting. Rsch. award U. Utah, 1986, Salt Lake County Childrens Justice award, 2011. Fellow Assn. Psychol. Sci. (James McKeen Cattell award for lifetime contbn. to applied psychology 2003); mem. Soc. Rsch. in Child Devel., Brit. Psychol. Assn., Am. Psychol. Assn. Office: Faculty Human Social & Political Scis University Cambridge Divsn Social & Devel Psychology Free Sch Ln Cambridge CB2 3RQ England Personal E-mail: mel37@cam.ac.uk.

LAMB, SHAWN D., medical association administrator; BS in Bus Comm., George Mason U., Fairfax, Va., 1989. Dep. dir. Soc. Toxicology, 1991—93, exec. dir., 1993—; founder, pres., CEO Assn. Innovation and Mgmt., Inc., 1999—. Mem.: American Soc. Assn. Executives. Office: Assn Innovation Mgmt Inc 1821 Michael Faraday Dr Ste 300 Reston VA 20190 Office Phone: 703-438-3103. Office Fax: 703-438-3113. *

LAMBERT, GEORGE H., physician, director; MD, U. Ill., 1972. Diplomate in pediats. and neonatal-perinatal medicine Am. Bd. Pediatrics. Intern Johns Hopkins Hosp., Balt., 1972—73, resident in pediats., 1973—74; rsch. assoc. molecular teratology NIH, Bethesda, 1974—76; fellow in neonatal medicine and pharmacology Children's Hosp. Phila., 1976—77; physician dept. pediats. Robert Wood Johnson Med. Sch., New Brunswick, NJ, 1987—; dir. divsn. pediat. pharmacology and toxicology EPA/NIH; dir. NIH Ctr. Childhood Neurotoxicology and Exposure Assessment Rutgers U., 2001—, Robert Wood Johnson Med. Sch., 2001—; with Harvard Bus. Sch., 2011. Assoc. prof. pediatrics Robert Wood Johnson U. Hosp., New Brunswick, NJ, 1984—. Contbr. articles to profl. pubis. Achievements include patents in field. Business E-Mail: glambert@umdnj.edu.

LAMBERT, VICKIE ANN, retired dean, nursing consultant; b. Hastings, Nebr., Oct. 28, 1943; d. Victor E. and Edna M. (Hein) Wagner; m. Clinton E. Lambert, Jr., June 30, 1974; 1 child, Alexandra. Diploma, Mary Lanning Sch. Nursing, 1964; BSN, U. Iowa, 1966; MSN, Case Western Res. U., 1973; DNSc, U. Calif., San Francisco, 1981. RN, Ga., Va. Staff and head nurse U. Iowa Hosp., Iowa City, 1966—68; instr. Sch. Nursing U. Iowa, 1968—70; instr. Robert Packer Sch. Nursing, Sayre, Pa., 1970—71; instr. dept. nursing St. John's Coll., Cleve., 1973—74; asst. prof. Sch. Nursing U. Pa., Phila., 1974—78; assoc. prof., acting chair dept. nursing adminstrn. Med. Coll. Ga., Augusta, 1982-84, coord. doctoral program nursing, 1984-85, George Mason U., Fairfax, Va., 1986-88; assoc. dean Case Western Res. U., Cleve., 1989-90; dean Sch. Nursing Med. Coll. Ga., Augusta, 1990-2001, emeritus dean Sch. Nursing, 2001—; prof. Yamaguchi U., Japan, 2001—03, Wuhan U., China, 2003—08, Prince Songkla U., Thailand, 2007—10, Mahidol U., 2011—. Internat. vis. prof. Lambert and Lambert Nursing Cons., Springfield, Va., 2001—. Contbr. articles to profl. jours., chapters to books. Fellow Am. Acad. Nursing; mem. ANA, Sigma Theta Tau Methodist. Avocation: travel. Home: Apt 520 7418 Spring Village Dr Springfield VA 22150

LAMBERT, WILLIAM DAVID, biology professor; b. Cin., Nov. 11, 1963; BA in Biology, U. Chgo., 1986; PhD in Zoology, U. Fla., 1994. Asst. prof. biology St. Peter's Coll., 1995—98; biology instr. La. Sch. Math, Sci. and Arts, 1998—2011, Oxbridge Acad. Palm Beaches, 2011—. Adj. prof. Northwestern State U., 2002—08. Mem.: AAAS, Soc. Vertebrate Paleontology. Avocations: writing, astronomy, fly fishing. Office: Oxbridge Acad Palm Beaches 3 West Palm Beach FL 33409 E-mail: w.david.lambert@gmail.com.

LAMBERTON, JACQUELYN EDMUNDS, retired psychotherapist; b. Dover, NH, July 15, 1924; d. Guy Ordway and Marjorie Gladys (Cheney) Edmunds; m. Bruce Alexander Lamberton, July 5, 1947 (dec. Mar. 9, 1988); children: Karen(dec.), Christopher J., Andrew B, Valerie A.; m. George Louis Frigie, Dec. 17, 1994. BS, Simmons Coll., Boston, 1947; Grad., Gestalt Inst., Cleve., 1991. Lic. ind. chem. dependency counselor. Therapist United Meth. Ch. Orgn., Berea, Ohio, 1980—85; therapist outpatient family program Glenbeigh Hosp., Cleve., 1985—87; dir. assessment, svcs. Glenbeigh Outpatient Family Program, 1987—89, dir., 1989—92; therapist chem. dependency Taylor, Dean, Masci, Inc., Broadview Heights, Ohio, 1992—95; addictions therapist Mosaics Integrated Health, Independence, Ohio, 1995—99; pvt. practice therapy Independence, Ohio, 1999—2006, Pepper Pike, 2003—06; ret., 2006. Instr. 4-week pub. edn. intervention program Glenbeigh of Rock Creek, Ohio, 2000. Author: Intervention - Why?...Why Not?... Alcohol is a Drug, and Drugs Kill...That's Why, 2004—05. Citizen advocate for C.D. prevention Ohio Citizen Advocates, Columbus, 2001—05; vestry woman St. Thomas Episcopal Ch., Berea, Ohio, 1997—2003; co-chair commn. on alcoholism Episcopal Diocese of Cleve., 1990—91. Mem.: Nat. Assn. Alcohol and Drug Abuse Counselors. Episcopalian. Avocations: music, pianist.

LAMBERTSEN, KATE LYKKE, medical educator; b. Harbooere, Denmark, Oct. 8, 1971; MSc, U. Southern Denmark, 1999, PhD, 2004. Rsch. asst. prof. U. Southern Denmark, 2004—09, assoc. prof., 2009—. Bd. mem. Danish Soc. Neurosci., 2007—11; vis. rsch. asst. prof. Miami Project to Cure Paralysis, 2008—09. Lundbeck Found. grant, Novo Nordic Found. grant. Mem.: Women Neurotrauma Rsch., Nat. Neurotrauma Soc., Soc. Neurosci., FENS, Danish Soc. Neurosci. Office: JB Winsloewsvej 21 St Odense C Fyn 5000 Denmark Business E-Mail: klambertsen@health.sdu.dk.

LAMBREW, JEANNE MARIE, federal official, healthcare educator; b. 1967; BA, Amherst Coll., 1989; MA in Health Policy, PhD in Health Policy, U. N.C. Sch. Pub. Health. Asst. prof. Georgetown U.; assoc. prof. George Washington Sch. Pub. Health & Human Svcs.; assoc. dir. Office Mgmt. & Budget, Exec. Office of the Pres., 1997—2001; sr. health analyst Nat. Econ. Coun., 1997—2001; assoc. prof. pub. affairs U. Tex. Lyndon Johnson Sch. Pub. Affairs, 2007—09; dir. Office Health Reform US Dept. Health & Human Services, Washington, 2009—11; dep. asst. to Pres. for health policy The White House, Washington, 2011—; sr. fellow Ctr. for American Progress, 2003—09. Co-author (with Tom Daschle): Critical: What We Can Do About the Healthcare Crisis, 2008. Office: The White House 1600 Pennsylvania Ave NW Washington DC 20500 *

LAMBROPOULOU, MARIA CHISTOS, medical educator, researcher; d. Christos Dionysios Lambropoulos and Aggelika Andreas Lambropoulou; m. George Triantaphyllos Alexiadis, Dec. 1, 1995; children: Triantos George Alexiadis, Christina-Aggelika George Alexiadi. MD, Democritus U. Thrace, Med. Sch., Alexandroupolis, Evros, Greece, 1995, PhD, 2005. Lectr. histology-embryology Democritus U. Thrace, Med. Sch., 2006—. Contbr. scientific papers to profl. publs. Vol. Actionaid, Ratanakiri, Cambodia, 2007—. Achievements include research in experimental medicine. Office: Democritus Univ Thrace Dragana 681 00 Alexandroupolis Greece Business E Mail: mlambro@med.duth.gr.

LAMBROS, VAL (VASILIOS S. LAMBROS II), plastic surgeon; b. Washington, 1948; MD, Rush Med. Coll., 1974. Diplomate Am. Bd. Plastic Surgery. Intern Rush Presbyn. St. Luke's Med. Ctr., Chgo., 1974—75, resident plastic surgery, 1980—82; associated with Calif. Emergency Physicians, 1975—76; resident surgery UCLA Ctr. for Health Scis., 1976—78; fellowship, asst. dir. microsurgical rsch. UCLA Harbor Microsurgical Lab., 1978—79; fellow burn surgery U. Calif. Irvine (UCI) Burn Unit, 1979; fellow hand surgery U. Miami, 1980; cosmetic surgical fellowship with Bruce F. Connell, MD, Santa Ana, Calif., 1982; dir. Burn Unit and Hand and Reconstructive Surgery King Faisal Hosp., Saudi Arabia, 1982—83; plastic surgeon Western Med. Ctr., Santa Ana, Calif.; pvt. practice Newport Beach, Calif., 1984—. Clin. instr. U. Calif., Irvine; spkr. in field. Contbr. articles to med. jours. Mem.: Orange County Soc. Plastic Surgeons, Orange County Med. Assn., Lipoplasty Soc. N.Am., Calif. Soc. Plastic Surgery, Am. Soc. Plastic Surgery, Am. Soc. Aesthetic Plastic Surgery. Office: 360 San Miguel, Ste 406 Newport Beach CA 92660 Office Phone: 949-759-4733. Office Fax: 949-759-5458. E-mail: LAMBROSONE@aol.com.

LAMKIN, CELIA BELOCORA, physician; b. Dinalupihan, Bataan, Philippines, Mar. 10, 1957; d. Crispiniano and Rufina Paule Belocora; m. Ronald Phillip Lamkin, Feb. 14, 1997; children: Jericho Belocora Santos, John Raymond Belocora Sablan. BS in Biol. Scis., U. Philippines, Manilla, 1978; MD, De La Salle U., Cavite, Philippines, 1984; post grad. in Occupl. Health and Safety, Coll. Pub. Health U. Philippines, Manila, 1989. Cert. physician Profl. Regulation Commn., Philippines, 1986, specialist in assistive tech. Calif. State U., Northridge, 2003. Intern U. Philippines, Philippines Gen. Hosp, Manila, 1984—85; physician Cainta Rural Health Ctr., Cainta Rizal, 1986; cons. and med. examiner Anthony Med. Clinic, Manila, 1987—89; med. examiner Insular Life Ins. Co., Makati City, 1988—90; co. physician M. Greenfield Garment Factory, Paranaque City, 1989—90, Drugmakers Laboratories, Inc., Paranaque City, Philippines, 1989—90; pvt. practice gen. practitioner Ermita, Manila and Cainta Rizal, 1986—93; HIV/ADS specialist and program coord. Pub. Sch. Sys., Saipan, Commonwealth No. Marianas Islands, 1995—96; human svcs. provider Philippine Consulate, Saipan, 1996—97; assistive tech. program coord. Coun. on Devel. Disabilities, 1997—2003; counselor and disability svcs. coord. No. Marianas Coll., 2003—05; ret. health & disability adv., 2005—. Workshop condr. disabilities and assistive tech.; vis. cons. Med. Ctr. Manila, 1988—91; translator U.S. Dist. Ct., 2002—05; spkr. in field. Vol. HIV instr. Am. Red Cross, first aid and CPR instr. Recipient cert. appreciation, No. Marianas Coll., 2005, Gov.'s Coun. Devel. Disabilities, Commonwealth No. Marianas Islands, 1998, 2003, Organizing Com. Internat. Biophilia Rehab. Acad., Philippines, 2004, Ho. Reps. Commonwealth No. Marianas Islands, 2004, Saipan and No. Islands Mcpl. Coun., 2004, Cert. award, Help Hosptalized Vets., Boystown, Am. Diabetes Assn., Feed The Children, 2009. Mem.: WWF, AMA, Paralyzed Vets. America, Assistive Tech. Higher Edn. Network, Devel. Gateway Found., Arthritis Found., Cystic Fibrosis Found., Internat. Biophilia Rehab. Acad. (cert. appreciation 2004), Biophilia Rehab. Acad. Japan, Am. Diabetes Assn., Pacific Disability Forum, U. Philippines Alumni Assn. Roman Catholic. Avocations: piano, organ, cooking. Home: PO Box 7497 Saipan MP 96950-7497 Personal E-mail: clamkinmd@yahoo.com.

LAMOURE, JOEL, pharmacist, educator, scientist; b. Tillsonburg, Ontario, Canada, Sept. 9, 1969; s. Wayne Clarence Lamoure and Shirley Esther Garon; m. Susan Northey, June 5, 1993; children: Lindsay Joelle, Jocelyn Dianne. BSc, U. Toronto, 1987—91. Tchg. assoc. faculty pharmacy U. Toronto, 1997—; mental health pharmacist London Health Scis. Ctr., London, Ontario, 2003—; assoc. prof. dept. psychiatry, medicine U. Western Ont., London, 2006—; asst. dir. CME, 2008—; assoc. scientist Lawson Health Rsch. Inst., 2010; asst. CME dir. UWO, 2008—. Contbr. articles to profl. jours.; co-author: Psychopharmacology in Severe Mental Illnesses. Chair ACCME UWO Medicine, 2009—10. Recipient Tchg. Excellence award, U. Toronto, 2006, Western Ont. U., 2005—10, CME award, 2007, 2010. Fellow: Am. Soc. Cons. Pharmacists; mem.: ACCME (chair Western Ont. U., dept. psychiatry 2009—), Ont. Coll. Pharmacists, Canadian Soc. Cons. Pharmacists. Office: London Health Scis Ctr Dept Psychiatry 375 South St W737 PO Box 5375 Stn B London ON Canada N6A 4G5 Office Phone: 519-685-8500 ext. 75018. Office Fax: 519-667-6811; Home Fax: 519-667-6811. Business E-Mail: joel.lamoure@lhsc.on.ca.

LAMOUREUX, GLORIA KATHLEEN, nurse, consultant, retired military officer; b. Billings, Mont., Nov. 2, 1947; d. Laurits Bungaard and Florence Esther (Nielsen) Nielsen; m. Kenneth Earl Lamoureux, Aug. 31, 1973 (div. Feb. 1979). BS, U. Wyo., 1970; MS, U. Md., 1984. Staff nurse, ob-gyn DePaul Hosp., Cheyenne, Wyo., 1970; enrolled USAF, 1970, advanced through grades to col.; staff nurse ob-gyn dept. 57th Tactical Hosp., Nellis AFB, Nev., 1970-71, USAF Hosp., Clark AB, Republic Philippines, 1971-73; charge nurse ob-gyn dept. USAF Regional Hosp., Sheppard AFB, Tex., 1973-75, staff nurse ob-gyn dept. MacDill AFB, Fla., 1976-79; charge nurse ob-gyn dept. USAF Med. Ctr., Andrews AFB, Md., 1979-80, MCH coord., 1980-82; chief nurse USAF Clinic, Eielson AFB, Alaska, 1984-86, Air Force Systems Command Hosp., Edwards AFB, Calif., 1986-90; comdr. 7275th Air Base Group Clinic, Italy, 1990-92, 42d Med. Group, Loring AFB, Maine, 1992-94; 347th Med. Group, Moody AFB, Ga., 1994-96; chief nursing svcs. divsn. Hdqrs. Air Edn. and Tng. Command, Randolph AFB, Tex., 1996-2000. Ind. cons. Customers First Cons., Universal City, 2000—05, v.p., 2000—05; sr. cons. NCI, San Antonio, 2002—10, PSI, San Antonio, 2010—11, ZCore 808 Solutions Inc., 2011—. Mem. Assn. Women's Health Obstetric and Neonatal Nurses (sec.-treas. armed forces dist. 1986-88, vice-chmn. armed forces dist. 1989-91), Air Force Assn., Bus. and Profl. Women's Assn. (pub. rels. chair Prince George's County chpt. 1981-82), Bulverde Area Rep. Women (sec. 2007, v.p. 2008-, pres. 2009), San Antonio Cons. Soc., Comal County Hist. Commn. Commr., Sigma Theta Tau. Republican. Lutheran. Avocations: reading, needlecrafts, piano, photography. Home: 383 Indigo Run Bulverde TX 78163 Office Phone: 210-365-3015. Business E-Mail: glamoureux@gvtc.com. *

LAMPANARIS, GEORGIOS PANAGIOTIS, urologist; b. Youngstown, Ohio, Jan. 24, 1976; s. Panagiotis Georgios Labanaris and Athanasia Labanari; m. Maria Gkanidou. MD, U. Novi Sad, 2000; degree, Zeisigwaldkliniken Bethanien, 2006, PhD student, 2009—. Diplomate U. Novi Sad, Sch. Medicine, Republic of Serbia, 2000. Country dr. Med. Health Ctr., Servia, Kozani, Greece, 2003—05; urologist-in-tng. Zeisigwaldkliniken Bethanien, Chemnitz, Sachsen, Germany, 2006—11, postdoc. fellow, 2009—. Mem.: German Soc. Residents in Urology, Endourological Soc., European Assn. Urology, Am. Urol. Assn. Greek Orthodox. Avocations: swimming, skiing, travel, basketball, movies. Home: Zeisigwaldstr 79 Chemnitz Sachsen 09130 Germany Office: Zeisigwaldkliniken Bethanien Zeisigwaldstr 101 Chemnitz Sachsen 09130 Germany Home Phone: 00493714047842; Office Phone: 00493714301748. Personal E-mail: georgelabanaris@yahoo.gr.

LAMPERT, RACHEL, cardiologist, educator; BA, Harvard Coll., 1983; MD, Vanderbilt U., 1987. Intern & resident Bellevue-NYU; fellow Yale U. Sch. Medicine, assoc. prof. cardiology & electrophysiology. Office: Yale University School of Medicine Department of Internal Medicine Box 208017 New Haven CT 06520-8017 Office Phone: 203-785-4114. E-mail: rachel.lampert@yale.edu.

LAMPERT, S. HENRY, retired dentist; b. Bklyn., Mar. 10, 1929; s. Joseph and Sadie (Bass) L.; m. Jacqueline Adler, Mar. 27, 1955; children: Karen Ann, Beth Robin, Judith Ellen. BA, U. Ill., 1950; DDS, NYU, 1954. Intern in dentistry Mt. Sinai Hosp., NYC, 1954-55; gen. practice dentistry Essex Junction, Vt., 1957-95; ret., 1995. Dir. Temporo Mandibular Joint Program, Med. Ctr. Hosp. Vt., Burlington, 1970-76, attending staff 1957-92, peer rev. com., 1978-92; mem. staff Fanny Allen Hosp., Winooski, Vt., 1961-89; assoc. prof. Sch. Allied Health Scis., U. Vt., Burlington, 1963-73, clin. instr. Coll. Medicine, 1974-75, clin. instr. dept. oral surgery, 1986-96. Sec., Vt. Bd. Dental Examiners, 1973-76, pres., 1976-77; instr. photography Church St. Ctr. for Cmty. Edn., U. Vt., until 1998; mem. N.E. Regional Bd. Dental Examiners, 1973-84, 96-98, cons. and examiner; CPR instr. Vt. Heart Assn., 1977-2000; photographer Essex (Vt.) Reporter, 1997—02; instr. photography Essex Town Parks and Recreation Dept., 1999—; lectr. in field Contbr. articles to profl. jours., photographs pub. in numerous mags. and jours. Capt. AUS, 1955-57, USAR, 1957-60; col. Vt. State Guard, 2005; photography judge Champlain Valley Exposition, 1991-. Fellow Internat. Coll. Dentists; mem. ADA (standard setting com. of coun. on nat. bd. exams. 1978-81), Champlain Valley Dental Soc. (pres. 1961-62), Acad. Operative Dentistry, Am. Prosthodontic Soc., Vt. Dental Soc., Masons, Rotary, Alpha Omega. Jewish (bd. govs. synagogue 1967-70, 72-73, chmn. bd. edn.). Home: 13 Hopkins St Voorhees NJ 08043 Personal E-mail: jackieejvt@mac.com.

LAMPRECHT, MANFRED, physiologist; b. Graz, Styria, Austria, Sept. 21, 1966; s. Adolf and Ida Lamprecht; m. Sabine Erna Zirngast, May 6, 2006; children: Jan Dukic-Wolfensson, Jennifer Zirngast, Sabrina Surowitz. Project mgmt. Styrian Health Assn., Graz, 2004—08; head Inst. Tng. Scis. and Sport Consulting, Graz, 2007—. Adv. bd. mem. Austrian Nutrition Soc., Vienna, 2005—, European Nutraceutical Assn., Basel, Switzerland, 2008—. Contbr. articles to profl. jours. Grant, Austrian Nutrition Soc., 1997, Fund Healthy grant, Austrian Govt., 2004—08. Mem.: European Nutraceutical Assn. Office: Med Univ Graz Harrachgasse 21/II Graz Styria 8010 Austria Office Fax: 433163809610. Business E-Mail: manfred.lamprecht@meduni-graz.at.

LAMSTER, IRA BARRY, dean, academic administrator; b. NYC, Mar. 6, 1950; s. Nathan and Mollie (Garber) L.; m. Gail Maxine Marcovitz, Aug. 28, 1971; children: Rachel Amy, Stephanie Anne. BA, CUNY, 1971; SM, U. Chgo., 1972; DDS, SUNY, Stony Brook, 1977; M.M.Sc., Harvard U., 1980; grad. splty. training in periodontology and oral medicine, Harvard U. Sch. Dental Medicine. Diplomate Am. Bd. Periodontology, Am. Bd. Oral Medicine. Assoc. prof., dir. rsch. ctr. Coll. Dental Medicine Fairleigh Dickinson U., Hackensack, NJ, 1980-88; dir. divsn. periodontics Columbia U. Sch. Dental and Oral Surgery, NYC, 1988—98, vice dean, 1998—2001, dean, 2001—. Cons. VA, various oral health care companies. Inventor in field; contbr. chpts. to books and articles to profl. jours. Recipient Young Investigator Rsch. award Pub. Health Svc., 1982-85, Individual Rsch. award 1985-89, 2002-08, prin. Investigator Program Project 1991-97. Fellow: Am. Coll. Dentists. Mem.: AAAS, ADA, Am. Acad. Periodontology (editorial bd.), Am. Assn. Dental Rsch., Am. Acad. Oral Medicine, N.Y. Acad. Scis., Northeastern Soc. Periodontists (contbg. editor). Avocations: golf, tennis, reading. Office: Columbia U Coll Dental Medicine Dean's Office Box 20 630 W 168th St New York NY 10032 Office Phone: 212-305-4511. Business E-Mail: ibl1@columbia.edu.

LAN, CHING, physiatrist, educator; b. Taipei, Taiwan, Oct. 18, 1955; s. Chih-Kang Lan and Tseng-I Tso; m. Li-Chu Huang, Mar. 2, 1960; children: Hsin, Chiang. BS, Nat. Taiwan U., Taipei, 1978; MD, Kaohsiung Med. U., 1987. Staff physiatrist Nat. Taiwan U. Hosp., Taipei, 1991—, asst. prof., 2001—. Cons. Dept. of Health, Taipei, 1995—. Contbr. articles to profl. jours. Jr. officer, 1978—80, Chung-Li, Taiwan. Recipient Contbn. award, Internat. Tai Chi Chuan Fedn., Taiwan, 2002. Mem.: Rehab. Medicine Assn., Am. Coll. Sports Medicine (assoc.; indpls.). Achievements include research in health benefits of Chinese Tai Chi Chuan. Office: Nat Taiwan Univ Hosp 7 Chung-Shan South Rd Taipei 100 Taiwan Office Fax: 886-2-23832834; Home Fax: 886-3-5968510. Personal E-mail: chinglan@seed.net.tw. E-mail: clan@ha.mc.ntu.edu.tw.

LAN, YIN, ophthalmologist; b. Guangdong, China, Jan. 1, 1981; M, Gen. Hosp. Pla, 2010. Ophthalmologist, 2003—. Office: Fucheng Rd 51 Beijing 10048 China Personal E-mail: doc_yl@126.com.

LANATA, CLAUDIO FRANCO, epidemiologist, physician; b. Lima, Peru, Feb. 4, 1951; s. Ernesto F. and Juanita M. (de las Casas) L.; m. Ana Isabel Gil, Sept. 07, 2007; children: Fiorella, Cristina Mariana. MD, Peruvian U. Cayetano Heredia, Lima, 1977, MPH, Johns Hopkins U., 1983. Resident in internal medicine St. Vincent's Med. Ctr., Bridgeport, Conn., 1977-80; fellow in infectious diseases U. Md. Sch. Medicine, Balt., 1980-82; fellow in geog. med. Johns Hopkins U. Sch. Medicine, Balt., 1983; rsch. dir. Nutrition Rsch. Inst., Lima, 1985-88, sr. rschr., 1983—, gen. dir., 1987-93. Vis. sr. rsch. fellow London Sch. Hygiene and Tropical Medicine, 1991-92; hon. sr. lectureship, 1996-2002, hon. prof. dept. epidemiology & population scis., 2002-; assoc. dept. internat. health Johns Hopkins U., Baltimore, 1986—; dir. maternal and child tng. program Esan Bus. Sch., Lima, 1996-99; vol. faculty mem., clin. asst. prof. Sch. Medicine, U. Md., 2000-; prof. Sch. Medicine, Peruvian U. Applied Scis., 2007-; assoc. mem. Peruvian Acad. Medicine, 2008-; mem. steering com. and tech. adv. group WHO, 1986—, also numerous consultancies on health projects; mem., chmn. sci. working group Pan Am. Health Orgn., Washington, 1984-87. Contbr. 24 chpts. to books; author 1 book, 15 monographs; contbr. 89 articles to profl. jours. Mem. Internat. Epidemiol. Assn. Avocation: tennis. Office: Nutrition Rsch Inst Ave la Molina 1885 Lima Peru

LANCASTER, CARROLL TOWNES, JR., health services executive; b. Waco, Tex., Mar. 14, 1929; s. Carroll T. and Beatrice L.; m. Catherine Virginia Frommel, May 29, 1954; children: Loren Thomas, Barbara, Beverly, John Tracy. Student, U. Tex., 1948-51, 52-53. Sales coord. Union Tank div. Butler Mfg. Co., Houston, 1954-56, sales rep. New Orleans, 1956-57, br. mgr., 1957-60; asst. to exec. v.p. Maloney-Crawford Mfg. Co., Tulsa, 1960-62; mktg. cons., sr. assoc. Market/Product Facts, Tulsa, 1962-63; market devel. asst. Norriseal Controls divsn. Dover Corp., Houston, 1963-66; area dir. Arthritis Found., Houston, 1966-69, regional dir., 1969-71; exec. dir. United Cerebral Palsy, Tex. Gulf Coast, 1971-74, Leukemia Soc. Am., Gulf Coast, 1974-76, Lancaster & Assocs., 1976—. Christian edn. tchr., 1970, supr. 1971, asst. youth football coach, Bellaire, 1967-68, 70-71; mem. Houston-Galveston Area Health Commn. Study Group, 1972-76, co-chmn. 1976; dir. essayist Tex. Low Vision Coun., 1976-79, sec.-treas., 1978-81, pres. 1981-85; pres. Bellaire Civic Action Club, 1987-88, del. Houston Interfaith Sponsoring Com., 1979-81; bd. dirs. Coun. Chs. Greater Houston, 1966-68, v.p. 1968. Active USN, 1946—48, active USNR, 1951—52. Recipient award for securing free blood for indigent Harris County Hosp. Dist., 1968. Mem. Am. Mktg. Assn., Huguenot Soc., Military Order of Stars and Bars, San Marcos Acad., Ex-Students Assn. (pres. 1982-84), SAR, Delta Sigma Phi. Episcopalian (vestryman 1975-78).

LANCASTER, KATHY, insurance company executive; BS, Loyola Marymount U. Various positions at Prudential Ins. Co., 1981—98, v.p., healthcare delivery, 1995—98; with Kaiser Permanente, Oakland, Calif., 1999—, acting CFO, 2005, sr. v.p. strategic planning, sr. v.p., CFO, 2005—. Office: Kaiser Permanente 1 Kaiser Plz Oakland CA 94612 Office Phone: 510-271-5800. Office Fax: 510-267-7524. *

LANCE, PETER, medical educator; b. London, May 11, 1947; BA, U. Cambridge, MA, 1968, MB, BChir, U. Cambridge; MD, SUNY, 1972. Chief gastroenterology, staff physician U. Buffalo and Roswell Pk. Cancer Inst., 1987—2001; prof. medicine and molecular & cellular biology U. Ariz. Ariz. Cancer Ctr., 2001—, chief cancer prevention, control officer, 2007. Fellow: RCP (London). Office: Ariz Cancer Ctr 1515 N Campbell Ave Tucson AZ 85724 Business E-Mail: plance@azcc.arizona.edu.

LANDAU, BARBARA, neuroscientist; BA in Sociology, U. Pa., Phila., 1970, PhD in Psychology, 1982; EdM in Ednl. Psychology,

Rutgers U., NJ, 1977. Asst. to assoc. prof. psychology Columbia U., NYC, 1983—91; assoc. to full prof. psychology U. Calif., Irvine, 1990—96; assoc. prof. psychology & linguistics U. Del., Newark, 1995—97, prof. psychology & linguistics, dir. cognitive sci. program, 1997—2000; Dick and Lydia Todd prof. cognitive sci. Johns Hopkins U., Balt., 2001—, acting chair, dept. cognitive sci., 2003. Mem. adv. bd. Early Literacy in the Blind, Am. Printing House the Blind, 1989; mem. program com. Cognitive Sci. Soc., 2000, 05. Mem. editl. bd.: Cognition, 1985—, Spatial Cognition and Computation, 1998—, Lang. Learning and Devel., 2002—; co-author (with L.R. Gleitman): Language and Experience: Evidence from the Blind Child, 1985; co-author: (with J. Sabini, J. Jonides, E. Newport) Perception, Cognition, and Language: Essays in Honor of Henry and Lila Gleitman, 2000; co-editor (L.R. Gleitman): Acquisition of the Lexicon, 1994; contbr. articles to profl. jours., chapters to books. Sloan Post-Doctoral fellow, U. Pa., 1982—83, vis. scientist, 1992—93, vis. instr. psychology, Princeton U., 1983. Fellow: APA (mem. bd. sci. advisors 2006—09, Boyd McCandless Young Scientist award 1990), Am. Psychol. Soc.; mem.: Am. Acad. Arts & Sciences, Psychonomics Soc., Soc. Rsch. in Child Devel. Office: Dept Cognitive Sci Johns Hopkins Univ 241 Krieger Hall Baltimore MD 21218 Office Phone: 410-516-5255. Office Fax: 410-516-8020. Business E-Mail: landau@cogsci.jhu.edu.

LANDAU, LOUIS I., pediatrician; b. Melbourne, Australia, Aug. 11, 1942; s. Jack and Hilda (Pahoff) L.; m. Miriam Erlich, Jan. 19, 1965; children: Jonathan, Peter. MBBS, U. Melbourne, 1965, MD, 1974. FRACP. Resident med. officer Royal Melbourne Hosp., 1966-67, Royal Children's Hosp., Melbourne, 1968-70, rsch. fellow, 1971-72, rsch. fellow, acting dir., dept. thoracic medicine, 1974-76; Uncle Bob's Travel fellow/Med. Rsch. Coun. of Can. McGill U., Montreal, Que., Can., 1973-74; hon. cons., pediatric. thoracic medicine Royal Children's Hosp. and Queen Victoria Med. Ctr., Melbourne, 1977-84; prof. paediatrics U. Western Australia, 1984-95, exec. dean faculty of medicine and dentistry, 1996—2004; chmn. Inst. for Child Health Rsch., Perth, Australia, 1990-94; bd. Women's and Children's Health Authority, 2000—04; prof. pediats. U. Western Australia; chair Postgrad. Med. Coun. Western Australia, 2005—; prin., med. advisor Western Australian Dept. Health, 2006—. Hon. cons., pediatric thoracic medicine, Mercy Maternity Hosp. and Royal Women ' s Hosp., Melbourne, Australia, 1977-84; vis. fellow Health Scis. Ctr., Tucson, Ariz., 1980-81, Hadassah U. Hosp., Jerusalem, 1980-81; prin. rsch. fellow Royal Children's Rsch. Found., 1981-83; tutor in pediatrics, Ormond Coll./Univ. Melbourne, 1975-80, tutor/sr. assoc., 1975-84, part-time lectr. dept. physiology, 1978-84; vis. prof. Health Scis. Ctr., U. London, 1992, U. Capetown, S. Africa, 1993, U. Bristol, U.K.; bd. dirs. Western Australia Inst. for Mus. Rsch.; chair Cystic Fibrosis Assn., Autism Australia, Lung Inst. Western Australia, Coop. Rsch. Ctr. Asthma. Author: Cystic Fibrosis, 1984, Respiratory Illness in Children, 1990, Pediatric Respiratory Medicine, 1999; contbr. 200 articles to profl. jours. Fellow Royal Astralasian Coll. Physicians; mem. Australian Coll. Paediatrics, Thoracic Soc. Australian/New Zealand, European Respiratory Soc., Am. Thoracic Soc. Office: U Western Australia Faculty Medicine/Dentistry Sch Pediats and Child Health Nedlands 6009 Australia Business E-Mail: louis.landau@uwa.edu.au.

LANDAW, STEPHEN ARTHUR, physician, educator; b. Paterson, NJ, June 20, 1936; s. Louis and Ida (Machowsky) L.; children: Jared Lawrence, Nicole Renee. BS, U. Wis., 1955; MD, George Washington U., 1959; PhD, U. Calif., Berkeley, 1969. Cert. internal medicine, hematology, med. oncology, nuc. medicine. Intern Mt. Sinai Hosp., NYC, 1959-60, resident in internal medicine, 1960-61; fellow in hematology Med. Coll. Va., 1962-63; fellow in nuclear medicine Donner Lab., U. Calif., 1963-69, asst. physician, 1970-73; chief isotope lab. Highland-Alameda County Hosp., Oakland, Calif., 1970-73; asso. prof. SUNY, Syracuse, 1973-78, prof., 1978-99; assoc. chief staff research and devel. VA Med. Center, Syracuse, 1973-94; chief, hematology VA Med. Ctr., Syracuse, 1997-99; vis. prof. Rockefeller U., NYC, 1988; vis. physician Rockefeller U. Hosp., NYC, 1988; dep. editor, hematology Uptodate, Inc., Waltham, Mass., 1999—; attending physician hematology-oncology Beth Israel Deaconess Med. Ctr., Boston, 2003—. Pres. Ctrl. NY Rsch. Corp., 1989—94; lectr. medicine Harvard Med. Sch., Boston, 2003—09, assoc. clin. prof. medicine, 2009—. Contbr. in field. Weekend guide Mus. Fine Arts, Boston, 2005—. With US Army, 1961—62. VA grantee, 1973-93; NASA grantee, 1976-82; recipient NASA Kosmos Achievement awards, 1975, 77 Fellow ACP; mem. Am. Soc. Hematology. Jewish. Office: Uptodate Inc 95 Sawyer Rd Waltham MA 02453-3471 Office Phone: 781-392-2021. Personal E-mail: slandaw@uptodate.com.

LANDEFELD, CHALES S., geriatrician, educator; MD, Yale U., 1982. Diplomate Am. Bd. Internal Medicine, 1982. Intern UCSF Med. Ctr., 1980, resident internal medicine, 1980—83; fellow geriatric medicine Brigham-Women's Hosp., 1983—85; prof. medicine UCSF. Office: UCSF Medical Center 500 Parnassus Ave San Francisco CA 94143-0296 Office Phone: 415-476-1000.

LANDEIRA-FERNANDEZ, ANA MARIA, biology professor; b. Rio de Janeiro, May 15, 1965; PhD, Fed. U. Rio de Janeiro, 1999, Stanford U., 2003. Assoc. prof. Inst. Bioquímica Médica, CCS, U. Fed. Rio de Janeiro, 2002—. Fellowship, Pew Charitable Trust. Avocations: swimming, volleyball. Home: Av Erico Verissimo 380 Apt 301 Rio de Janeiro 22621180 Brazil Personal E-mail: landeira@bioqmed.ufrj.br.

LANDER, ERIC STEVEN, geneticist, molecular biologist, mathematician; b. Bklyn., Feb. 3, 1957; BA in Math. with hons., Princeton U., 1978; DPhil in Math., Oxford U., Eng., 1981. Asst. prof. Grad. Sch. Bus., Harvard U., 1981-86, assoc. prof., 1987-90; Whitehead fellow MIT, Cambridge, 1986, vis. scientist, 1984-89, assoc. prof., 1989-93, prof. dept. biology, 1993—, mem. Whitehead Inst. Biomed. Rsch., 1989—, founder, dir. Whitehead Ctr. Genome Rsch., 1990—, founding dir., Broad Inst., 1990—. Med. geneticist Mass. Gen. Hosp., Boston, 1993—; Ralph R. Braund disting. vis. prof. U. Tenn., 1994; mem. US Presdl. Commn. Nat. Medal Sci., 1995—97; mem. genetics working group NIMH, 1997—; Christian A. Herter disting. lectr. NYU, 1993; Gladstone disting lectr. Gladstone Inst., 1994; Herbert Boyer lectr. genetics U. Calif., San Francisco, 1995; co-chair Pres.'s Coun. of Advisors on Sci. and Tech. (PCAST), 2009—. Contbr. articles to profl. jours. Recipient Beckman prize for lab automation, Chiron prize in biotechnology, Woodrow Wilson prize for pub. svc., Princeton U., Dickson prize in cancer, Rhodes prize in cancer, Gairdner Found. Internat. award, 2002, Pub. Understanding of Sci. and Tech. award, AAAS, 2004; co-recipient Albany Med. Ctr. prize in Medicine, 2010; named Millennium Lectr., The White House, 1999, Scientist of Year, Nat. Disease Rsch. Interchange, 2003, R&D Mag., 2003; fellow MacArthur fellow, 1987; scholar Rhodes scholar, 1978. Fellow: AAAS; mem.: NAS (mem. Math. and Molecular Biology Com. 1989—90), Inst. Medicine, Am. Assn. Cancer Rsch., Am. Acad. Forensic Sci., Math. Assn. America, Am. Soc. Human Genetics, Genetics Soc. America, Human Genome Orgn., Inst. Medicine, Am. Acad. Arts and Scis. Achievements include founding the center which is the leading contributor to the Human Genome Project. Address: MIT 77 Massachusetts Ave Cambridge MA 02139-4307 Office: Whitehead Inst/MIT 9 Cambridge Center Cambridge MA 02142-1479 Office Phone: 617-252-1906. Office Fax: 617-258-0903. E-mail: lander@genome.wi.mit.edu. *

LANDER, JOYCE ANN, retired nursing educator, medical/surgical nurse; b. Benton Harbor, Mich., July 27, 1942; d. James E. and Anna Mae Remus LPN, Kalamazoo Practical Nursing, Ctr., 1967; AAS, Kalamazoo Valley C.C., 1981, Grad. Massage Therapy Program, 1995. LPN-RN Bronson Meth. Hosp., Kalamazoo, 1972-82; RN med./surg. unit Borgess Med. Ctr., Kalamazoo, 1982-84; RN pediat. Upjohn Home Health Care, Kalamazoo, 1984-88; supr. nursing lab Kalamazoo Valley Comm. Coll., 1982—2005, ret., 2005; asst. Parish nurse First Presby. Ch., Kalamazoo, 2009—. Therapeutic massage therapist in client homes with Business Kneading Peace Therapeutic Massage, Kalamazoo, 1995—; nursing asst., instr. State of Mich. Observer, 1990-96. Author: What Is A Nurse, 1980. Address: 3300 Woodstone Dr E Apt 108 Kalamazoo MI 49008-2548

LANDER, RUTH A., medical association administrator; b. Fitchburg, Mass., Dec. 13, 1948; d. H. Allison and Violet K. (Erickson) Linné; m. C. Stephen Lander, June 28, 1968; children: Timothy, Mary. BA, Ohio State U., 1978. Cert. med. practice exec. 1994. Dir. fin. Luth. Svc. Assn. New England, Natick, Mass., 1973—76; gen. mgr. Logos, Columbus, Ohio, 1976—87; practice adminstr. Columbus Oncology Assocs., Inc., 1987—. Sec., treas. Adminstrs. Oncology Hematology Assembly, Englewood, Colo., 1994-95, legis. liaison, 1994-95, pres.-elect, 1995-96, pres., 1996-97; spkr. med. group mgmt. issues. Editor Administrs. in Oncology Hematology Assembly News, 1994-95; mem. editl. bd. Oncology Issues Mag., 1998-2000; mem. editl. adv. bd. for coding and reimbursement Oncology & Hematology, 2001; contbr. articles to profl. jours. Mem. task force Cmty. Oncology Alliance, 2004-05. Fellow Med. Group Mgmt. Assn., Am. Coll. Med. Practice Execs. (nat. chair membership devel. com. 1999, nat. bd. dir. 2004-06, exam. com., 2006—); mem. Am. Soc. Clin. Oncology (assoc.), Nat. Oncology Soc. Network, Ctrl.-Ohio Med. Group Mgmt. Assn. (pres. 1993-94, sec. 1992-93, program dir. 1991-92, exec. com. 1990-97), Assn. Cmty. Cancer Ctr. (editl. bd. mag. 1998-2000), Ohio Med. Group Mgmt. Assn. (exec. com. 1994-2001, sec. 1995-96, pres. 1998, rep. to Medicare POE adv. group 2003—, grass roots legis. group 1994—), Ohio Oncology Med. Group Mgmt. Assn. (pres. 1997), Ohio State Med. Assn. (assoc.; group practice task force 2000—), Columbus Med. Assn. (group practice mgrs. task force 2002—), Oncology Practice Mgmt. (mem. editl. adv. bd., 2011-). Republican. Avocations: reading, computers, crafts, knitting, bible study. Office: Columbus Oncology Assocs 810 Jasonway Ave Ste A Columbus OH 43214-2329

LANDERS, CHERI, pediatrician; b. Boone County, Mo., Sept. 23, 1966; MD, U. Mo., Columbia, 1993. Assoc. prof. pediat. U. Ky., 1999—. Pediatric critical care divsn. chief Dept. Pediat., U. Ky., 2005—08; med. dir. Ky. Children's Hosp. PICU, 2005—08; dir. quality and safety Ky. Children's Hosp., 2008—, med. dir. pediatric sedation, 2006—11. Recipient Jacqueline Noonan Role Model award, U. Ky. Pediatric Residents; named to Best Doctors in Am., 2007, 2009, 2011. Fellow: Am. Assn. Pediat., Soc. Critical Care Medicine; mem.: Ky. Pediatric Soc., Soc. for Pediatric Sedation. Avocations: chocolatier, church choir. Office: 800 Rose St Room MN480 Lexington KY 40536 Office Phone: 859-323-1496. Business E-Mail: cdland2@uky.edu.

LANDIS, DONNA MARIE, nursing administrator, women's health nurse; b. Lebanon, Pa., Sept. 5, 1944; d. James O.A. and Helen Joan (Fritz) Muench; m. David J. Landis, Feb. 4, 1967 (div. Jan. 1985); children: Danielle M. Landis Barry, David J., Derek J.; m. John C. Broderick, May 8, 1990 (div. Jan. 1995). RN Md., 1993, cert. DXA technologist. Clin. dir., clin. rsch. coord. Osteoporosis Assessment Ctr., Wheaton, Md., 1985-95; pvt. practice as cons. in osteoporosis, bone densitometry & bone health Donna M. Landis, LLC, 2004—. Mem. nurses adv. bd. NPS Pharms., 2005—06; cons. applied physics lab. Johns Hopkins U., 2007. Mem. task force on osteoporosis State of Md., 1996—2006. Named one of Md.'s Top 100 Women in Bus., 2002. Mem.: Nat. Osteoporosis Risk Assessment Project (specialist practice and lead technologist trainer 1997—98), Allied Health Profls./Arthritis Found. (pub. policy contact), Nat. Osteoporosis Found. (pub. policy contact), Internat. Soc. Clin. Densitometry (steering com. 1993—94, contbg. editor SCAN newsletter 1994—2002, cert. com. technologists and physicians 1995—2000, sci. adv. com. 1996—2009, trustee 1999—2002, technologist edn. subcom. 2000—03, facility accreditation coun. 2004—09), St. Joseph's Hosp. Alumni Assn., Balt. Bone Club, Washington Met. Bone Club (steering com. 1996, bd. dirs. 1999—2001, sec. 1999—2001, bd. dirs. 2007—11), Kiwanis Internat. (bd. dirs. Prince Georges County 1997—2002, pres. Prince Georges County 2000—01, Satellite Club Capital Dist. lt. gov. 2003—04, Prince Georges County Club advisor to U. Md. CKI 2005—11, Capital Dist. Key Leader site coord. 2008—09, Club advisor to K-Kids club 2008—09, charter mem., bd. dirs. Prince Georges County 2008—11, Brownie Brownfield award 2005). Office Phone: 301-512-3648. Personal E-mail: donna.m.landis@gmail.com.

LANDIS, STORY CLELAND, federal agency administrator, neurobiologist; m. Dennis Landis; 1 child, Michael. BA in Biology, Wellesley Coll., Mass., 1967; MA, Harvard U., 1970, PhD, 1973. Faculty dept. neurobiology Harvard Med. Sch.; assoc. prof. pharmacology, dir. Ctr. Neuroscis. Case Western Res. U. Sch. Medicine, Cleve., 1985—95, chair dept. neuroscis., 1990—95; sci. dir. Nat. Inst. Neurol. Disorders & Stroke (NINDS), NIH, Bethesda, Md., 1995—2003, dir. NINDS, 2003—. Chair NIH Stem Cell Task Force, 2007—. Contbr. articles to profl. jours. Named one of The 100 Most Powerful Women in DC, Washingtonian mag., 2009. Fellow: AAAS, Am. Neurol. Assn., Am. Acad. Arts & Scis.; mem.: Soc. Neurosci. (pres.-elect 2002). Achievements include research in the study of the developmental interactions required for the formation of functional synapses. Office: NINDS Bldg 31 Rm 8A52 31 Ctr Dr MSC 2540 Bethesda MD 20892 Office Phone: 301-496-9746. Office Fax: 301-496-0296. E-mail: story.landis@nih.gov. *

LANDO, JEROME BURTON, macromolecular science educator; b. Bklyn., May 23, 1932; s. Irving and Ruth (Schwartz) L.; m. Geula Ahroni, Dec. 2, 1962; children: Jeffrey, Daniel, Avital. AB, Cornell U., 1953; PhD, Poly. Inst. Bklyn., 1963. Chemist Camille Dreyfus Lab., Research Triangle Inst., Durham, NC, 1963-65; asst. prof. macromolecular sci. Case Western Res. U., Cleve., 1965—68, assoc. prof., 1968—74, prof., 1974—2005, prof. emeritus, 2005—; pres., CEO Edison Polymer Inovation Corp., 2000—. Dept. chmn. Case Western Res. U., Cleve., 1978—85; Erna and Jakob Michael vis. prof. Weizmann Inst. Sci., Rehovot, Israel, 1987; Lady Davis vis. prof. Technion, Haifa, Israel, 1992—93. Author: (with S. Maron) Fundamentals of Physical Chemistry, 1974; mem. editl. adv. bd. Polymers for Advanced Techs. Served to lt. U.S. Army, 1953-55. Named Alexander Von Humboldt Sr. Am. Scientist U. Mainz, Germany, 1974, disting. alumnus Poly. U., 1990. Fellow Am. Phys. Soc.; mem. Am. Chem. Soc., Am. Crystallographic Assn., Soc. Plastics Engrs. (rsch. award 1994, edn. award 1999), Sigma Xi. Jewish. Home: 21925 Byron Rd Cleveland OH 44122-2942 Office: Case Western Res U Dept Macromolecular Sci Kent Hale Smith Bldg 321 Cleveland OH 44106 Office Phone: 216-368-6366. Business E-Mail: jbl2@case.edu.

LANDOLPH, JOSEPH RICHARD, molecular biologist, educator; b. Phila., Pa., Nov. 09; BS in Chemistry, Drexel U., Phila., 1971; PhD in Chemistry, U. Calif., Berkeley, 1976. Grad. student, rsch. asst., tchg. asst., dept. chemistry U. Calif., Berkeley, 1971—76; postdoc. fellow Keck Sch. Medicine, U. Southern Calif., 1977—80, asst. prof. pathology, 1980—82, asst. prof. microbiology and pathology, 1982—87, assoc. prof. molecular microbiology and immunology, pathology, and molecular pharmacology and toxicology, 1987—. 2nd lt. US Army, 1971, ROTC. Recipient Superior Cadet award, US Army ROTC, Drexel U., Phila., 1971, Cleland Excellence Tchg. award, Dept. Pathology, U. Southern Calif., 1985. Mem.: Forensive Expert Witness Assn., LA chpt., Am. Soc. Cell Biology, Am. Assn. Cancer Rsch., Soc. Toxicology. Avocations: skiing, martial arts, football, baseball, basketball. Office: Cancer Rsch Lab Rm #218 1 Los Angeles CA 90033 Office Fax: 323-224-7679. Business E-Mail: landolph@usc.edu.

LANDONI, GIOVANNI, anesthesiologist, researcher; b. Milan, Nov. 27, 1971; s. Gabriele and Gianna (Veronese) Landoni; m. Elena Pinna, Aug. 19, 2002; children: Giulia, Mattia. MD, Milan U., 1996, specialist in anesthesiology and intensive care, 2000. Registered surgeon 1997. Anesthesiologist, gen. practitioner St. Mary's Hosp. Lagor, Gulu, Uganda, 1998—2000; sr. anesthesiologist San Raffaele Hosp., Milan, 2000—; mem. Italian Food and Drug Adminstrn. (CTJ-AIFA), 2009—; asst. prof. Vita-Salute U., Milan, 2003—; exec. bd. Italian Assn. Cardiothoracic Anesthesiologists, Milan, 2006—11. Head rsch. Anesthesia and Intensive Care Dept., Milan, 2002—; basic life support trainee Vita-Salute U., 2005—; mem. editl. bd. Jour. Cardiothoracic and Vascular Anesthesia & HSR Proceedings, 2005—; reviewer Critical Care Medicine Circulation Annals Internal Medicine, 2009. Project mgr. Indian Inst. Mother and Child, Kolkota, India, 1993, 1998, 2002, 2006, 2008; vol. UNICEF, Italy, 1994—96; project coord. Internat. Fedn. Med. Student's Assn., Amsterdam, 1995—97. Recipient Hon. Mention award, Global Youth Action, 2001; finalist Third Pl., Internat. Championship Math., Lombardia, Italy, 1995. Mem.: Project for People Onlus (pres. 2003—04, project mgr. 2000—), Societa-Italiana Anestesia, Analgesia Rianimazione and Terapia Intensiva, European Assn. Cardiothoracic Anesthesiologists. Achievements include patents in field. Office: Istituto Scientifico San Raffaele Via Olgettina 60 20132 Milan MI Italy Office Phone: 39 02 2643 6154. Office Fax: 39 02 2643 6154. Business E-Mail: landoni.giovanni@hsr.it.

LANDRETH, BARBARA HORAN, pediatrician, educator; b. Havana, Cuba, Nov. 29, 1952; BS, NYU, 1975, MD, 1987. Cert. Pediat., 1992. Intern pediat. NY-Presbyn. Hosp./ Weill Cornell Med. Ctr., NYC, 1987—88, resident pediat., 1988—90, resident, 1990—91, asst. attending pediatrician; clin. instr. pediat. Weill Cornell Med. Coll. Office: 115 E 67th St, Ste 1C New York NY 10021 Office Phone: 212-772-7596. Office Fax: 212-327-4966.

LANDRIGAN, PHILIP JOHN, epidemiologist; b. Boston, June 14, 1942; s. John Joseph and Frances Joan (Conlin) Landrigan; m. Mary Florence Magee, Aug. 27, 1966; children: Mary Frances, Christopher Paul, Elizabeth Marie. AB, Boston Coll., 1963; MD, Harvard U., 1967; MS, DIH, London Sch. Hygiene and Tropical Medicine, 1977. Diplomate Am. Bd. Pediat., Am. Bd. Preventive Medicine, Am. Bd. Occupl. Medicine, Am. Coll. Epidemiology. Intern Cleve. Met. Gen. Hosp., 1967—68; resident in pediatrics Children's Hosp. Med. Ctr., Boston, 1968—70; fellow in pediatrics Harvard U. Med. Sch., Boston, 1969—70; clin. instr. pediatrics Emory U. Sch. Medicine, Atlanta, 1970—71; epidemic intelligence service officer Ctrs. for Disease Control, Atlanta, 1970—73, dir. research and devel. smallpox erradication program, 1973—74, chief environ. hazards activity, 1974—79; dir. div. Surveillance, Hazard Evaluations and Field Studies Nat. Inst. for Occupational Safety and Health, Cin., 1979—85; prof. community medicine and pediatrics Mt. Sinai Sch. Medicine, NYC, 1985—, dir. div. environ. and occupational medicine, 1985—90, prof., chmn. dept. community and preventative medicine, 1990—. Mem. bd. on toxicology and environ. health hazards NAS, Washington, vice chmn., 1981—86, chmn. com. on pesticides in the diets of infants and children, 1988—93; sr. advisor to adminstr. on children's health and environment U.S. EPA, Washington, 1997—98; clin. prof. environ. health Sch. Pub. Health U. Wash., Seattle, 1983—. Contbr. numerous articles to prlfl. jours.; cons. editor: Archives of Environ. Health, 1982—, Am. Jour. Indsl. Medicine, 1979—, editor-in-chief: Environ. Rsch., 1987—. Recipient Vol. award, Dept. HEW, 1973, Pub. Health Svc. Career Devel. award, 1975, group citation as mem. of Ctr. for Disease Control beryllium rev. panel, 1978, Meritorious Svc. medal, USPHS, 1985. Fellow: Royal Soc. Medicine; mem.: AAAS, APHA, Soc. for Epidemiologic Rsch., Am. Epidemiol. Soc., Inst. of Medicine Internat. Commn. on Occupl. Health. Home: 915 Stuart Ave Mamaroneck NY 10543-4124 Office: Mt Sinai Sch Medicine Dept Community Medicine 1 Gustave L Levy Pl # 1057 New York NY 10029-6500 E-mail: phil.landrigan@nasa.gov.

LANDRÓN, ANA, school psychologist; d. Sidney Kruset and Carlina Figueroa; m. Jose R. Landron, June 29, 1974; children: Rafael A. Landron, Miguel O. Landron. BS in Psychology, Queens Coll. CUNY,

1969; MS in Sch. Psychology, St. John's U., 1995, postgrad., 1999—, PsyD, 2009. Cert. in sch. psychology U. State NY, 1996, lic. bilingual sch. psychologist NYC Dept. Edn., 1996, primary and advanced practicum in rational emotive behavior therapy Albert Ellis Inst. Family counselor Children's Aid Soc., Sloane Head Start, NYC; sch. psychologist NYC Dept Edn., Forest Hills; bilingual sch. psychologist Oyster Bay-East Norwich Sch. Dist., NY, 1995—. Mem. Sen. Marcellino's Mental Health Adv. Com., Nassau County, NY, 2001; bd. advisor Centro Cultural Hispano de Oyster Bay-East Norwich y Vecinidades; mem. majority task force on children's health and safety NY State Senate. Recipient cert. acad. excellence, St. John's U., 1995, Woman of Distinction, Humanitarian award, Town of Oyster Bay, 2001. Mem.: APA, Soc. for Study of Peace, Conflict, and Violence, Soc. for Psychol. Study of Ethnic Minority Issues, Nat. Assn. Sch. Psychologists. Avocations: reading, hiking, gardening. Office: Roosevelt Elem Sch 150 W Main St Oyster Bay NY 11771

LANDRY, DONALD WILLIAM, physician, educator, scientist; b. Jersey City, May 19, 1954; s. Donald O. and Gloria A. Landry; m. Maureen O'Reilly, Sept. 3, 1978; children: Christopher D., Michael J. BS in Chemistry summa cum laude, Lafayette Coll., 1975; PhD in Organic Chemistry, Harvard U., 1979; MD, Columbia U. Coll. Physicians & Surgeons, 1983. Diplomate Nat. Bd. Med. Examiners, Am. Bd. Internal Medicine, Am. Bd. Nephrology; Lic. NY. Intern, resident in medicine Mass. Gen. Hosp., Boston, dir. divsn. exptl. therapeutics, 1998—, dir. divsn. nephrology, 2003—08; prof. medicine with tenure, chair dept. medicine Columbia U. Physicians and Surgeons, NYC, 2008—. Contbr. chapters to books; mem. editl. bd. Regenerative Medicine, 2005. Recipient Presdl. Citizen's medal, 2009. Mem. Am. Soc. Clin. Investigation, Am. Assn. Physicians, Alpha Omega Alpha, Phi Beta Kappa. Roman Catholic. Achievements include patents in field of ten. Avocation: running. Home: 29 Claremont Ave #2-S New York NY 10027-6802 Office: Columbia U Coll Physicians & Surgeons Rm 10-445 630 W 168th St New York NY 10032 Office Phone: 212-305-5838. Business E-Mail: dwl1@columbia.edu. *

LANDRY, MARK EDWARD, podiatrist, researcher; b. Washington, May 24, 1950; s. John Edward and Daphne (Fay) L.; m. Mary Ann Kotey, Sept. 7, 1974; children: John Ryan, Christopher John, Jessica Marie. D in Podiatry, Ohio Coll. Podiatric Medicine, 1975; MS in Edn., U. Kans., Lawrence, 1982. Diplomate Am. Bd. Podiatric Surgery, Am. Bd. Podiatric Orthopedics and Primary Podiatric Medicine; cert. NAUI, 2000, RADI scuba diver, 2004. Gen. practice podiatry, Kansas City, Mo., 1977—, Overland Park, Kans., 1980—; clin. asst. prof. U. Health Scis., Kansas City, 1985-98; clin. assoc. prof. Coll. Podiatric Medicine and Surgery U. Osteo. Medicine and Health Scis., Des Moines, 1985-92; clin. instr. Sch. Medicine U. Mo., Kansas City, 1987-95. Founder, bd. dirs. Kansas City Podiatric Residency Program, Kansas City, 1982-91; adv. bd. Rockport Shoe Co., 1988-89; chmn. podiatry dept. Park Lane Med. Ctr., Kansas City, Mo., 1995-97; dir. continuing edn. Kans. Podiatric Med. Assn., 1997—, sec.-treas., 2010-. Contbr. articles to profl. jours. Cons. Mid-Am. Track and Field Assn., Lenexa, Kans., 1978-88; com. chmn. Boy Scouts Am., Overland Park, Kans., 1986; coach Johnson County Soccer League, 1987-90; head coach 6th and 7th grade girls' Cath. Youth Orgn. Basketball, 1995-96, 97; sponsor 8 & 11 Baseball League, 1987-90. 1st lt. USAF, 1975-77. Recipient Pres.'s award Ohio Sch. Podiatric Medicine, 1975; USAF scholar Armed Forces Health Professions, 1973-75. Fellow Am. Coll. Foot and Ankle Surgeons, Acad. Podiatric Sports Medicine; mem. Kans. Podiatric Med Assn. (bd. dirs. 1997—, continuing edn. dir. 1997-, Sec. treas. 2010-), Brit. Podiatry Assn. (hon.), Am. Bd. Primary Podiatric Medicine (founding dir., bd. examiner 1994-2000), Holy Cross Social Club (pres. 1983-84), Prairie Life Club, Leukemia Assn. of Am. (team in tng. 1997-2000, 2005, team capt. 1999, K.C. corp. challenge participant 1997-99), K.C. (4th degree 1995—, chancellor 1998, 99), KC Ski Club (trip capt. 1999), Fifty States Marathon Club, 50 State Marathon Group, D.C. Marathon Group, Johnson County CC (mem. brown and gold adv. bd., 2011-). Republican. Roman Catholic. Avocations: triathlon, skiing. Office: 10550 Quivira Rd Ste 260 Overland Park KS 66215-2375 Office Phone: 913-438-9898.

LANDSBERG, LEWIS, endocrinologist, medical researcher, former dean; b. NYC, Nov. 23, 1938; AB, Williams Coll., 1960; MD, Yale U., 1964. Intern Yale-New Haven Hosp., 1964—65, resident in internal medicine, 1965—66, 1968—69; fellow in endocrinology NIH, 1966—68; from instr. to asst. prof. medicine Sch. Medicine Yale U., 1969-72; from asst. prof. to assoc. prof. Harvard Med. Sch., 1972-77, from assoc. prof. to prof., 1977-86; Irving S. Cutter prof., chmn. dept. medicine Northwestern U. Feinberg Sch. Medicine, Chgo., 1990—2000, dir. Ctr. Endocrinology, Metabolism & Nutrition, 1990-93, dean, v.p. for medical affairs, 1999—2007, Irving S. Cutter prof. medicine emeritus, dean emeritus, 2007—. Assoc. physician Yale-New Haven Hosp., 1969-71, attending physician, 1971-72, Beth Israel Hosp., 1974-79, physician, 1979-88, sr. physician, 1988-90; attending physician West Haven VA Hosp., 1970-72; assisting physician Boston City Hosp., 1972-73, assoc. vis. physician, 1973-74; physician-in-chief dept. medicine Northwestern Meml. Hosp., 1990—. Fellow ACP, AAAS; mem. Am. Fedn. Clin. Rsch., Endocrine Soc., N.Y. Acad. Scis., AHA, Am. Soc. Pharmacology and Exptl. Therapeutics, Am. Physiology Soc., Am. Soc. Clin. Investigators, Am. Clin. and Climatological Assn., Assn. Am. Physicians. Achievements include rsch. in catecholamines and the sympathoadrendal system, nutrition and the sympathetic nervous system, obesity and hypertension. Office: Northwestern Univ Med Sch Morton 4-656 310 East Superior St Chicago IL 60611-2958

LANDZBERG, JOEL SERGE, cardiologist; b. NYC, Dec. 20, 1958; s. Sol and Marilyn Joy (Aboff) L.; m. Barbara Eugenie Ross, May 1, 1983; children: Rebecca, Elizabeth, David, Jessica. BA summa cum laude, Columbia Coll., 1979; MD, Columbia U., 1983. Resident medicine Vanderbilt U., Nashville, 1983-86, chief resident medicine, 1987-88; rsch. fellow cardiology U. Calif. San Francisco, Cardiovascular Rsch. Inst., 1986-87; cardiology fellow Brigham & Woman's Hosp., Boston, 1988-90; instr. medicine Harvard U., Boston, 1990-91; pvt. practice cardiology Westwood, N.J., 1991—. Fellow Am. Coll. Cardiology; mem. AMA, Clin. Assoc. Prof. of Medicine, Phi Beta Kappa. Office: Westwood Cardiology 333 Old Hook Rd Ste 200 Westwood NJ 07675-3267

LANE, DOROTHY SPIEGEL, preventive medicine physician; b. Bklyn., Feb. 17, 1940; d. Milton Barton and Rosalie (Jacobson) Spiegel; m. Bernard Paul Lane, Aug. 5, 1962; children: Erika, Andrew, Matthew. BA, Vassar Coll., 1961; MD, Columbia U., 1965, MPH, 1968. Diplomate Am. Bd. Preventive Medicine, Am. Bd. Family Practice. Resident in preventive medicine NYC Dept. Health Dist., 1966-68, project dir. children and youth project Title V, HHS Rockaway, 1968-69; med. cons. Maternal and Child Health Svc. HHS, Rockville, Md., 1970-71; asst. prof. preventive medicine Sch. Medicine SUNY, Stony Brook, 1971-76, assoc. prof., 1976-92, prof., 1992—2002, Disting. Svc. prof., 2002—, assoc. dean, 1986—; chair dept. cmty. medicine, dir. med. edn. Brookhaven Meml. Hosp. Med. Ctr., Patchogue, NY, 1972-86. Contbr. articles to profl. jours. Exec. com. LI divsn. Am. Cancer Soc., 1975—96, pres. LI divsn., 1982, mem. nat. assembly, 1996—2001, nat. bd. dir., 1994—96; corp. mem. Nassau Suffolk Health Sys. Agy, 1977—97; bd. dir. Cmty. Health Plan Suffolk, Hauppauge, NY, 1986—91. Grantee, HHS-USPHS, 1977—2002, 2004—, Nat. Cancer Inst., 1987—2008, Nat. Heart, Lung and Blood Inst., 1994—, Ctrs. for Disease Control, 2005—. Fellow: APHA, Am. Bd. Preventive Medicine (trustee 1991—2000, chair 1998—2000), NY Acad. Medicine, Am. Acad. Family Physicians, Am. Coll. Preventive Medicine (regent 1988—96, sec.-treas. 1994—96, pres.-elect 1998—2001, pres. 2001—03, immediate past pres. 2003—05, past pres. 2005—07), Assn. Tchrs. Preventive Medicine (pres. 1996—98); mem.: Accrediation Coun. Grad. Med. Edn. (bd. dirs. 2009—), Accreditation Coun. for Continuing Med. Edn. (bd. dirs. 2002—06, exec. commn. 2005—06). Office: SUNY at Stony Brook Sch Medicine Health Scis Ctr L2 Rm 142 Stony Brook NY 11794-8222 Home Phone: 631-751-9471; Office Phone: 631-444-2094. Business E-Mail: dorothy.lane@stonybrook.edu.

LANE, H. CLIFFORD, internist; b. Detroit, June 15, 1950; s. Henry Talbot Lane, Jr. and Clara Elizabeth Lane; m. Linda Susan Scott, May 16, 1998; children: Rebecca Triantis, Chelsea Edwards, Emily Judith, Claire Elizabeth. BS, U. Mich., Ann Arbor, 1972; MD, U. Mich., 1976. Diplomate Am. Bd. Internal Medicine with subspecialties in diagnostic and clin. lab. immunology and infectious diseases. Resident in internal medicine U. Mich., Ann Arbor, 1976—79; clin. assoc. NIAID/NIH, Bethesda, Md., 1979—82, sr. investigator lab. immunoregulation, 1982—, clin. dir., 1991—. Contbr. over 260 articles to profl. jours. With USPHS. Recipient DSM, USPHS; named to Knight of the Order of Mali Nat. Fellow: Infectious Diseases Soc. Am.; mem.: ACP, Internat. Assn. Physicians AIDS Care, Inst. Scientific Info., Inst. Medicine Nat. Acad. Scis., Assn. Am. Physicians. Achievements include invention of co-inventor use of IL-2 in HIV infection. Office: National Institutes of Health Bldg 10/Rm 4-1479 Bethesda MD 20892 Office Phone: 301-496-7196. *

LANE, RICHARD ALLAN, preventive medicine physician, educator; b. Camp LeJuene, NC, Feb. 5, 1956; s. Howard Allan and Elizabeth Jane (Fischer) L.; m. Cynthia Diane Gastineau, Jan. 7, 1978; children: Tiffany Marie, Laurel Christina. BS, U. Md., 1978, MD, 1982; MPH in Tropical Medicine, Tulane U., 1986. Diplomate Am. Bd. Preventive Medicine. Intern Md. Gen. Hosp., Balt., 1982-83; squadron flight surgeon, 363rd Tactical Fighter Wing USAF, Shaw AFB, 1983-85, resident in aerospace medicine Brooks AFB, 1986-87, advanced through grades to maj., 1983-87; chief aeromed. svcs. Warner Robins Air Logistics Ctr., Robins AFB, 1987-89; staff physician, microbiology instr. Liberty U., Lynchburg, Va., 1989-91, assoc. prof. health scis., 1991—; dir. Liberty U. Health Svcs. Ctr. Med. Group, 2011—; pvt. med. practitioner Light Med., 1991—2009. Cons., spkr. Liberty Godparent Home, Lynchburg, 1989—2000; mem. residency adv. bd. Meharry Med. Coll., Nashville, Tenn., 1987-89; adj. faculty health sci. Internat. Health Honduras project James Madison U., Harrisonburg, Va., 1993-2000; adj. clin. prof. nurse practitioner program Old Dominion U., 1997-2000, James Madison U., 2009-11; sentinel provider U.S. Influenza Surveillance Network, 2004—; mem. AstaZeneca Spkrs. Bur., 2006—09. Contbr. articles to profl. jours. Bd. dirs. Network for Women in Crisis, Lynchburg, 1990-91; exec. bd. Lynchburg chpt. ARC, 1991-93; founder Emmanuel Bapt. Ch., chpt. AWANA, Warner Robins, Ga., 1987-89; trainer Youth at the Crossraods Internat. AIDS Prevention Program, 1996—; bd. dirs. Freedom 4/24, 2009-; med. cons. World Help. Fellow Am. Coll. Preventive Medicine; mem. APHA, Gideons Internat. (camp treas. 1988-89), ACSM. Republican. Evangelical. Business E-Mail: rlane@liberty.edu.

LANE, WENDY EVRARD, health facility administrator; b. Milw., Apr. 27, 1951; d. John Raymond and Connie Fae (van Ert) Evrard; m. Frederick Carpenter Lane, June 9, 1973; children: Jesse, Eliza BA, Wellesley Coll., 1973; MBA, Harvard Bus. Sch., 1977. Assoc., Investment Banking Goldman Sachs & Co., NYC, 1977—80; assoc. cons. Temple, Barker & Sloan, Lexington, Mass., 1980; prin. Donaldson, Lufkin & Jenrette, v.p. NYC, 1980—83, sr. v.p., 1983—86, mng. dir., 1986—92; chmn. Lane Holdings, Inc., 1992—. Bd. dirs. Willis Group Holdings Ltd., UPM-Kymmene Corp., Lab. Corp. of America Holdings, 1996—. Trustee US Ski & Snowboard Team Found. Durant scholar, 1973. Mem. Doubles, The Greenwich Field Club, The Greenwich Skating Club, Bus. Leadership Coun., Phi Beta Kappa. Republican. Roman Catholic. Avocations: athletics, involvement with children's education and gifted children. Office: Laboratory Corp of America Holdings Bd Directors 531 S Spring St Burlington NC 27215 Office Phone: 336-436-5274. Office Fax: 336-436-1569. E-mail: lanew@labcorp.com. *

LANE, WILLA JOAN MANES, retired psychologist; b. Okla. City, May 25, 1930; d. Marvin Talmadge and Ethel May (Southern) Manes; m. Lynn Roland Lane (div.); 1 child, Lee Nathan. BA, U. Ariz., Tucson, 1951; MA, Ariz. State U., Tempe, 1967; PhD, Walden U., Mpls., 1981. Lic. tchr. Ariz., 1951, cert. counselor Ariz., 1967, lic. sch. psychologist Ariz., 1971, cert. counselor Tex., 1989, lic. psychologist Tex., 1995. Tchr. Williams AFB, Chandler, Ariz., 1951—53; dancer Hormel Girls Caravan, Hormel Foods, Austin, Minn., 1953—54; tchr. Madison Sch. Dist., Phoenix, 1961—71; counselor, psychologist Creighton Sch. Dist., Phoenix, 1971—88; counselor Joshua Ind. Sch. Dist., Tex., 1990—97, Roswell Ind. Sch. Dist., N.Mex., 1998—2003; mem. counselor Ariz. Elem. Sch., Ariz. Sch. Psychologist. Sunday sch. adult class tchr. 1st United Meth. Ch., Glen Rose, Tex., 2006. Mem.: NEA, Am. Psychol. Assn., Am. Sch. Counselor Assn., Nat. Assn. Sch. Psychologists, Ariz. Sch. Psychologists, Ariz. Elem. Sch. Counselors. Republican. Avocations: reading, theater, meditation, travel, self-help workshops. Home: 408 Grace St Glen Rose TX 76043-4835

LANG, ELVIRA VALENTINA, radiologist, educator, medical products executive; b. West Germany, Oct. 7, 1953; married. MD magna cum laude, U. Heidelberg, Germany, 1978. Diplomate Am. Bd. Radiology, qualified interventional radiology. Intern in radiology, surgery, medicine U. Heidelberg, 1977-78, resident in radiology, 1978-83, jr. faculty radiologist, 1983-84; intern, fellowship in angiography U. Calif., San Diego, 1985-86, resident in radiology, 1986-88; fellowship in interventional and vascular radiology Mallinckrodt Inst. of Radiology, St. Louis, 1988-89; asst. prof. of radiology Stanford U. Sch. of Medicine, 1989-94; assoc. prof. radiology U. Iowa Coll. of Medicine, Iowa City, 1994—98, dir. of interventional radiology, 1994—98; chief vascular interventional radiology Beth Israel Deaconess Medical Ctr., Boston, 1998—2006; assoc. prof. radiology Harvard Medical Sch., 1999—; v.p., chief medical officer Omnisonics Medical Technologies Inc., 2006—. Chief of vascular and interventional radiology VA med. Ctr., Palo Alto, 1989-94, head of radiology rsch. lab., 1989-94. Reviewer Am. Jour. Roentgenology, Jour. Vascular and Interventional Radiology, Investigative Radiology, Acad. Radiology. Rsch. grantee Dept. of Vets. Affairs HSR&D Field Program, 1994—, grantee Nat. Inst. Mental Health/Office for Alternative Medicine, 1996; recipient numerous rsch. grants. Mem. Am. Roentgen Ray Soc., Radiol. Soc. N.Am., Assn. Univ. Radiologists, Soc. Cardiovasc. and Interventional Radiology (mem. rsch. com. 1992—), Am. Assn. Women Radiologists, Western Angiographic and Interventional Soc., Am. Coll. Radiology, Soc. Minimally Invasive Therapy, Internat. Soc. Exptl. Clin. Hypnosis. Office Phone: 978-657-9980. Office Fax: 978-657-9982.

LANG, GUNTER, JR., orthodontist; b. Erlangen, Bavaria, Germany, Sept. 30, 1969; s. Günter Lang, Sr. and Alida Lang. DDS, U. Tuebingen, Germany, 1997. Asst. dentist Dr. H. Putze, Stuttgart, Germany, 1998—99; asst. for postgraduation in orthodontics Dr. G. Lang Sr., Leonberg, Germany, 2000—01; sci. asst. dept. orthodontics U. Hosp., Tuebingen, 2002—04; pvt. practice, 2004—. Lectr. in field. Contbr. articles to profl. jours. Fellow: Landsmannschaft Schottland; mem.: German Orthodontic Soc. Avocations: skiing, golf, travel. Office: Brennerstr 1 71229 Leonberg Germany Home: Finkenweg 28 70839 Gerlingen Germany Office Phone: 0049-7152-35657-0. Office Fax: 0049-7152-35657-27; Home Fax: 0049-7156-4379823. E-mail: drs.g.lang@t-online.de.

LANG, JESSICA LANG, psychologist; b. Speyer, Rheinland-Pfalz, Germany, Oct. 17, 1978; d. Gerardo Ippolito and Graziella Kunz; m. Jonas W.B. Lang, July 29, 2006; children: Julian S.C., Sophia D.A. Diploma in Psychology, U. Mannheim, Germany, 2004, Dr. rer. soc., 2006. Cert. psychol. trainer Deutsche Psychologen Akademie, Germany, 2006, stress coping trainer 2006. Rsch. psychologist Inst. Occupl. Medicine, RWTH Aachen U., NRW, Germany, 2008—. Reviewer Internat. Archives Occupl. and Environ. Health, 2008, Applied Psychology: An Internat. Review. Contbr. articles to sci. jours. Rsch. contractor US Army Med. Rsch. Unit Europe, 2003—08, Heidelberg, Germany. Recipient Scheffel prize, Literarische Gesellschaft/Scheffelbund Karlsruhe, 1998; scholar Student Rsch. Participation Program, Oak Ridge Inst. Sci. Edn., 2005—06. Mem.: APA, German Soc. Occupl. Environ. Medicine, Soc. Indsl. and Orgnl. Psychology (Bowling Green) (reviewer 2006), German Psychol. Soc. Avocations: travel, music. Office: RWTH Aachen Univ Hosp Pauwelsstrasse 30 Aachen NRW 52074 Germany

LANG, SAMUEL, thoracic surgeon, educator; MD, U. Ala., 1978. Diplomate Am. Bd. Thoracic Surgery. Resident surgery UCLA Med. Ctr., Los Angeles, 1978—82, fellow cardiothoracic surgery, 1983—85; resident thoracic surgery NYU Med. Ctr., NYC, 1982—83; fellow pediatric cardiac surgery Hosp. for Sick Children, London, 1985—86; dir. cardiothoracic surgery NY Hosp. Queens, 1996—99, chmn. cardiothoracic surgery dept., 2009; sect. chief cardiothoracic surgery St. Vincent Cath. Med. Ctr.; lectr. Weill med. coll. Cornell Univ.; lectr. sch. medicine NYU; lectr. UCLA. Vis. prof. of surgery, China, 1988, Bolivia, 89. Mem.: Am. Heart Assn., Am. Coll. of Surgeons, Soc. of Thoracic Surgeons. Office: New York Hospital Queens 56-45 Main St Flushing NY 11355 Office Phone: 718-670-2000.

LANG, SHELDON, pathologist; b. NY, Jan. 31, 1932; s. Emil and Anna Lang; m. Marie Christabel Hoyos; children: Melissa Ellen, Maximilian Edward. BA, NYU, 1953; MD, SUNY, Bklyn., 1957. Lic. doctor NJ, 1958, Calif., 1958, Nev., 1988. Pvt. practice pathogist, Henderson, Nev., 1964—. Dir. lab. Beth Israel Hosp., Passaic, NJ, 1975—89. Author: A FLAWED VISION: A History of Battlecruisers. Lt. med. corps. USN, 1959—61. Fellow: Coll. Am. Pathologists. Independent. Avocations: history, painting. Home: 1981 Moyer Dr Henderson NV 89074 Home Fax: 702-837-8732. Personal E-mail: sheldonlang@cox.net.

LANGE, ANDRZEJ HENRYK, haematologist and transplantologist; b. Cracow, May 7, 1942; MD, Med. Sch., Wroclaw, 1971; Prof. of Medicine, Nominated by the Pres. of the Polish Republic. Leverhulme fellow Middlesex Hosp. Med. Sch., London, 1973—74; prof., head K. Dluski Hosp., Divsn. Immunotherapy, 1980—2002, Lower Silesian Ctr. Cellular Transplantation with Nat. Bone Marrow Donor Registry, 2002; prof., head dept. clin. immunology L. Hirszfeld Inst. Immunology and Exptl. Therapy, Polish Acad. Scis., 1980—; vis. scientist Inst. Exptl. Biology and Medicine, Borstel, Germany, 1982—93. Mem. standardization commn. WHO, IUIS, ILAR, 1980—85; founder, med. dir. Nat. Polish Marrow Donor Registry, 1992; internat. sci. coord. stemnet project European Commn., 2000—04; founder, pres. Polish Soc. Immunogenetics, 2001—08; nat. Polish cons. clin. immunology Polish Ministry Health, 2006; fellow Ramazzini Coll., Italy. Recipient medal, Polish Soc. Transplantation, Polish Soc. Immunogenetics, Best Poster award, European Bone Marrow Transplantation Group, Interlaken, 1987, European Fedn. Immunogenetics, 2004, 2009. Mem.: Polish Soc. Hematology, Polish Soc. Immunology, Polish Union Transplantation Medicine, Am. Soc. Hematology (medal). Avocation: horseback riding. Office: Grabiszynska 105 Wroclaw Dolnoslaskie 53-439 Poland Office Fax: 48713621512. Business E-Mail: andrzej-lange@wp.pl, lange@dctk.wrac.pl.

LANGE, BEVERLY J., pediatric oncologist; b. 1945; MD, Temple U. Sch. Med., Pa., 1971. Diplomate Am. Bd. Pediat., cert. Pediat. Hematology, Oncology. Intern Phila. Gen. Hosp., resident; fellowship Children's Hosp. Phila., med. dir. divsn. oncology. Assoc. chair clin. rsch. Children's Oncology Grp. Contbr. articles to profl. jours. Achievements include research in genetic variations among individuals influence response to cancer treatment and the severity of the side effects to treatment. Office: Children's Hosp Phila 4th Fl Wood Bldg 3615 Civic Ctr Blvd Philadelphia PA 19104 Office Phone: 215-530-2253. Business E-Mail: lange@email.chop.edu.

LANGE, JOS HUBERTUS MARIA, medical researcher, chemist; b. St. Hubert, Noord Brabant, Netherlands, Mar. 29, 1959; s. Koos Lange and Marie van der Poel; m. Jannet Hinderkien Siccama, Sept. 23, 1993. BA, Cath. U., Nijmegen, Netherlands, 1980, MS, 1984, PhD, 1989. Sr. scientist drug discovery Abbott Healthcare Products, Weesp, Netherlands, 1988—; prin. scientist Solvay Pharms., 2005—. Lectr. sci. symposia; reviewer Drug Discovery Today, Current Opinion Drug Discovery and Devel. and Chem. Record. Mem. editl. bd.: Recent Patents CNS Drug Discovery, Open Structural Biology Reviews and Recent Patents on Biotechnology., Current Chem. Biology, Open Structural Biology Jour. & Pharmaceuticals, Global Jour. Organic Chemistry, Jour. Pharmacology & Pharmacy; contbr. scientific papers to profl. jours. (over 45 peer reviewed papers and three invited reviews). Mem.: Royal Netherlands Chem. Soc. (assoc.). Achievements include invention of orally active cannabinoid receptor antagonists and agonists highly cited from different chemical classes; co-inventor of ibipinabant; research in cannabinoid drug discovery; 34 patents in field and 46 peer-reviewed sci. publs. Office: Abbott Healthcare Products BV C J van Houtenlaan 36 1381 CP Weesp Netherlands Office Phone: 0031 0 294479731.

LANGER, ALOIS, biomedical engineer; b. Pitts. BSEE, MIT, 1967; PhDEE, Carnegie Mellon U., 1973. Project engr., chief engr. Medrad/Intec, 1973—91; founder, past pres. Cardiac Telecom Corp., Pitts., 1991—. Named to National Inventors Hall of Fame, 2002. Achievements include invention of Telemetry @ Home; design of of automatic implantable cardioverter defibrillator. Personal E-mail: a.a.la@gmx.net.

LANGER, ELLEN JANE, psychologist, educator, writer, artist; b. NYC, Mar. 25, 1947; d. Norman and Sylvia (Tobias) L. BA, NYU, 1970; PhD, Yale U., 1974. Cert. clin. psychologist. Asst. prof. psychology The Grad. Ctr. CUNY, 1974-77; assoc. prof. psychology Harvard U., Cambridge, Mass., 1977-81, prof., 1981—. Cons. NAS, 1979-81, NASA; mem. div. on aging Harvard U. Med. Sch., 1979—, mem. psychiat. epidemiology steering com., 1982-90; chair social psychology program Harvard U., 1982-94, chair Faculty Arts and Scis. Com. of Women, 1984-88. Author: Personal Politics, 1973, Psychology of Control, 1983, Mindfulness, 1989, The Power of Mindful Learning, 1997, On Becoming an Artist: Reinventing Yourself Through Mindful Creativity, 2005; editor: (with Charles Alexander) Higher Stages of Human Development, 1990, (with Roger Schank) Beliefs, Reasoning and Decision-Making, 1994, Counterclockwise Mindful Health and the Power of Possibility, 2009; contbr. articles to profl. and scholarly jours.; exhibits at Julie Hellery Gallery, Provincetown, Mass., J&W Gallery, New Hope, Pa. Guggenheim fellow; grantee NIMH, NSF, Soc. for Psychol. Study of Social Issues, Milton Fund, Sloan Found., 1982; recipient Disting. Contbn. of Basic to Applied Psychology award APS, 1995. Fellow Computers and Soc. Inst., Am. Psychol. Assn. (Disting. Contributions to Psychology in Public Interest award 1988, Disting. Contributions of Basic Sci. to Applied Psychology 1995); mem. Soc. Exptl. Social Psychology, Phi Beta Kappa, Sigma Xi. Democrat. Jewish. Avocations: tennis, horseback riding. Office: Harvard U Dept Psychology 33 Kirkland St Cambridge MA 02138-2044 Business E-Mail: langer@wjh.harvard.edu.

LANGER, GLENN ARTHUR, cellular physiologist, educator; b. Nyack, NY, May 5, 1928; s. Adolph Arthur and Marie Catherine (Doscher) L.; m. Beverly Joyce Brawley, June 5, 1954 (dec. Nov. 1976); 1 child, Andrea; m. Marianne Phister, Oct. 12, 1977. BA, Colgate U., 1950; MD, Columbia U., NYC, 1954. Diplomate Am. Bd. Internal Medicine. Asst. prof. medicine Columbia U. Coll. Physicians and Surgeons, NYC, 1963-66; assoc. prof. medicine and physiology UCLA Sch. Medicine, 1966-69, prof., 1969-97, Castera prof. cardiology, 1978-97, assoc. dean rsch., 1986-91, dir. cardiovascular rsch. lab., 1987-97, emeritus prof., 1997—. Griffith vis. prof. Am. Heart Assn., L.A., 1979; cons. Acad. Press, N.Y.C., 1989-97; founder, dir. Partnership Scholars Program, 1996—. Author: Understanding Disease, 1999; editor: The Mammalian Myocardium, 1974, 2d edit., 1997, Calcium and the Heart, 1990; mem. editl. bd. Circulation Rsch., 1971-76, Am. Jour. Physiology, 1971-76, Jour. Molecular Cell Cardiology, 1974-97; contbr. more than 200 articles to profl. jours. Co-pres., dir., founder Partnership Scholars Program for disadvantaged youth, 1996—. Capt. U.S. Army, 1955-57. Recipient Disting. Achievement award Am. Heart Assn. Sci. Coun., 1982, Heart of Gold award, 1984, Cybulski medal Polish Physiol. Soc., Krakow, 1990, Pasarow Found. award for Cardiovascular Sci., 1993, Outstanding Acad. Title citation Choice mag., 2001, Spl. award LA County, 2006, Humanitarian award Colgate U., 2010; Macy scholar Josiah Macy Found., 1979-80. Fellow AAAS, Am. Coll. Cardiology, Internat. Soc. for Heart Rsch.; mem. Am. Soc. Clin. Investigation, Am. Assn. Physicians. Achievements include research on control of cardiac contraction. Personal E-mail: glang@mcn.org.

LANGER, JUDITH ANN, psychologist; b. NYC; BA, CUNY, 1962, MSEd, 1965; PhD; Hofstra U., Hempstead, NY, 1978; PhD (hon.), U. Uppsala, Sweden, 2005. Asst. prof. LI U., 1973-78; asst. prof. dept. ednl. psychology NYU, 1978-80; sr. rschr. lang. behavior rsch. lab. U. Calif., Berkeley, 1980-84; assoc. prof. sch. of edn. Stanford U., 1984-87; prof. SUNY, Albany, 1987—, disting. prof., 2001—. Dir. Albany Inst. for Rsch. in Edn., Nat. Rsch. Ctr. on English Learning & Achievement; co-dir. Nat. Rsch. Ctr. Lit. Tchg. and Learning; trustee Rsch. Found.; task force mem. Nat. Commn. on Edn. Stds. and Testing; adv. com. New Stds. in Edn. Project, Literacy Unit, LRDC and Nat. Ctr. on Edn. and the Economy; adv. bd. Nat. Coun. of Chief State Sch. Officers, Nat. Objective in Reading, Nat. Assessment of Ednl. Progress, Reading and Writing Assessments, 1980—; cons. Calif. Assessment Program, NC English Lang. Arts Standards, Calif. State Dept. Edn., Ctr. for Lang. Edn. and Rsch., Ctr. for the Study of Writing, Rev. of Rsch. on Reading and Writing Relationships, Mich. State Edn. Dept. Author: Reader Meets Author/Bridging the Gap, 1982, Understanding Reading and Writing Research, 1985, Children Reading and Writing: Structures and Strategies, 1986, Language, Literacy, and Culture, 1987, Issues of Society and Schooling, How Writing Shapes Thinking: Studies of Teaching and Learning, 1987, Literature Instruction: A Focus on Student Response, 1992, Literature Instruction: Practice & Policy, 1994, Envisioning Literature, 1995, 2nd edit., 2010, Effective Literacy Instruction: Building Successful Reading and Writing Programs, 2002, Getting To Excellent: How to Create Better Schools, 2004, Envisioning Knowledge: Gaining Literacy in the Academic Disciplines, 2010; contbr. articles to profl. jours.; editor: Research in the Teaching of English, 1984-92; editl. bd. English Internat., Discourse Processes, Jour. of Reading Behavior, Newsletter, Lab. of Comparative Human Cognition, Jour. of Reading and Writing, Internat. Jour. of Reading and Writing; reviewer in field. Recipient numerous grants, Presdl. award for lifetime achievement, Hofstra U., 1992, Chancellor's award for Exemplary Contbns. to Rsch., 2001, Albert J. Harris award, 2003; fellow, Rockefeller Found., Internat. Reading Hall of Fame; Benton fellow, U. Chgo., 1997. Fellow Am. Psychol. Assn., Am. Ednl. rsch. Assn., Nat. Conf. on Rsch. in English; mem. MLA, Am. Ednl. Rsch. Assn., Am. Psychol. Soc., Conf. on Coll. Composition and Comm., Internat. Reading Assn., Nat. Reading Conf., Nat. Coun. of Tchrs. of English. Office: Univ at Albany 1400 Washington Ave Albany NY 12222-0100 *

LANGER, ROBERT SAMUEL, JR., chemical and biomedical engineering educator; b. Albany, NY, Aug. 29, 1948; s. Robert Samuel and Mary (Swartz) Langer; m. Laura Feigenbaum, July 31, 1988; children: Michael David, Susan Katherine, Samuel Alexander. BSChemE, Cornell U., NYC, 1970; DSChemE, MIT, 1974; PhD (hon.), ETH, Switzerland, 1996, Technion U., Israel, 1997, Cath. U. Louvain, Brussels, 1999, Hebrew U., 2002, U. Liverpool, 2003, U. Uppsala, 2005, Pa. State U., 2005, U. Nottingham, 2005, Albany Med. Coll., 2006, Northwestern U., 2006, Yale U., 2007. Chmn. math. and sci. dept. The Group Sch., Cambridge, Mass., 1972—74; rsch. asst. MIT, 1972—74, asst. prof. nutritional biochemistry, 1977—81, assoc. prof. biochemical engring., 1981-85, prof. biochemical engring., 1985—88, Kenneth J. Germeshausen prof. chemical & biochemical engring., 1988—2005, David H. Koch Inst. prof., 2005—. Rsch. assoc. Children's Hosp. Med. Ctr., Boston, 1974—; endowed lectr. U. PR, 1983, Case Western Res. U., 1986, U. Mich., 1987, 98, U. Wash., 1988, U. Kans., 1989, U. Calif., San Francisco, 1991, U. Wis., 1991, Ga. Inst. Tech., 1991, Ohio State U., 1991, U. Pitts., 1992, Purdue U., 1992, U. Del., 1993, Pa. State U., 1993, Beth Israel Hosp., 1994, Cornell U., 1994, Calif. Inst. Tech., 1995, Ill. Inst. Tech., 1995, Ohio State Med. Sch., 1995, U. Calif., 1996, U. Tenn., 1996, U. NC, 1997, 97, U. Pa., 1998, Wash. U., 1998, U. Tex., San Antonio, 1998, U. Calif., Berkeley, 1999, U. Notre Dame, 1999, U. Liverpool, 2000, Brown U., 2001, Stanford U., 2001, Cornell U., 2001, U. Pa., 2002, U. Louisville, 2002; mem. FDA Sci. Bd., 1995—2002, chmn., 1999—2002; sr. lectr. Harvard U., 1999—; bd. dirs. Boston Life Scis. Co-author: Group School Chemistry Curriculum, 1972, Laboratory in Applied Biology, 1978, Analaytical Practices in Biochemistry, 1979, Temporal Control of Drug Delivery, 1991; co-editor: Medical Applications on Control Release, 1984, Biodegradable Polymers in Drug Delivery, 1990, Angiogenesis, 1992; contbr. articles to profl. jours. Recipient John W. Hyatt Svc. to Mankind award, Soc. Plastics Engineers, 1995, Gairdner Found. Internat. award, 1996, Wiley medal, FDA, 1997, Killian award, 1997, Lemelson-MIT prize, 1998, Dickson prize for Sci., U. Pitts., 2002, Heinz award for Tech., Economy & Employment, 2003, John Fritz award, Am. Assn. Engring. Societies, 2003, Harvey prize, Technion-Israel Inst. Tech., 2003, General Motors Kettering prize for cancer rsch., 2004, Dan David prize in Materials Sci., Tel Aviv U., 2005, Albany Med. Ctr. prize in Medicine and Biomedical Rsch., 2005, 2006 Nat. Medal of Sci., Max Planck Rsch. award, 2008, Prince of Asturias award for Technical and Scientific Rsch., 2008, Millennium Tech. prize, Finland, 2008; named one of 25 Most Important Individuals in Biotechnology, Forbes Mag., 1999, BioWorld Daily, 1990, 15 Innovators World Wide who will Reinvent our Future, Forbes Mag., 2002, The 100 Most Influential People, TIME mag., 2001, America's Best in Science or Medicine, CNN, 2001, 20 Most Important People in Biotechnology, Discovery mag., 2002; named to Nat. Inventors Hall of Fame, 2006. Fellow: World Tech. Network (Health & Medicine award 2005), Am. Inst. Med. & Biol. Engineers (founding fellow), Am. Assn. Pharm. Scis. (Disting. Pharm Sci. award 1993), Soc. Biomaterials (Clemson award 1990); mem.: NAE (Charles Stark Draper prize 2002, Founders award 2010), AIChE (Food, Pharm. & Bioengring. award 1986, Profl. Progress award 1990, Charles M. Stine Materials Sci. & Engring. award 1991, William Walker award 1996), NAS, Controlled Release Soc. (bd. governers 1981—85, chmn. regulatory affairs com. 1985—89, pres. 1991—92, Founders award 1989, Millerial Pharm. award 2000, Glaxo Wellcome award 2000, Nagai Innovation award 2002), Am. Soc. Artificial Internal Organs (mem. program com. 1984—87), Biomed. Engring. Soc. (bd. dirs. 1991—94), Internat. Soc. Artificial Internal Organs (Organon-Teknika award 1991), Am. Chem. Soc. (Creative Polymer award 1989, Phillips Applied Polymer Sci. award 1992, Polymer Chemistry award 1999, Materials award 2007), Am. Acad. Arts & Scis., Inst. Medicine. Achievements include pioneering research of many new technologies, including transdermal delivery systems which allow the administration of drugs or extraction of analytes from the body through the skin without needles or other invasive methods. Avocations: magic, jogging. Office: MIT Dept Chemical Engring Bldg E25-519 77 Massachusetts Ave Cambridge MA 02139 Office Phone: 617-253-3107, 617-253-3123. Business E-Mail: rlanger@mit.edu. *

LANGLAND, OLAF ELMER, retired dental educator; b. Madrid, Iowa, May 30, 1925; s. Raymond F. and Minnie Margaret (Kinsey) L.; m. Carolyn Anderson, Oct. 1955 (div. 1973); children: Sara Mindell, Beth Langland (dec. Feb. 2002); m. Ruth Klabunde, July 1, 1975 (dec. Jan. 1985); children: Julie Van Delden, Gary Kablunde; m. Gwen E. Stokes, Apr. 25, 1991; children: Renee' Schatz, Richard Stokes, Deborah Stark-Fato, Kimra Lynn Stokes (dec.), D. Scott Stokes. DDS, U. Iowa, 1951, MS, 1961. Prof., head dept. oral diagnosis U. Iowa Sch. Dentistry, Iowa City, 1963-68; prof., head dept. oral diagnosis, medicine and radiology La. State U. Med. Ctr. and Dental Sch., New Orleans, 1968-74; prof., head div. oral and maxillofacial radiology U. Tex. Health Sci. Ctr., San Antonio, 1975-99, prof. emeritus, 1999—. Rotator U.S. Hope Ship, Maceio, Brazil, 1973. Author: Textbook of Dental Radiology, 1984, Radiology for Dental Assistants and Dental Hygienists, 1987, Principles and Practice of Panoramic Radiology, 1989, Diagnostic Imaging of the Jaws, 1994, Principles of Dental Imaging, 1997, 2nd edit. 2001. With inf. AUS, 1943-45, ETO. Decorated Purple Heart, Combat Infantry badge with star, Bronze Star; recipient Outstanding Tchr. award U. Tex. Health Sci. Ctr., 1992. Fellow Am. Coll. Dentists, Internat. Assn. of Dental Maxillofacial Radiology (hon.); mem. Am. Acad. Oral and Maxillofacial Radiology (diplomate, pres. 1984-85), Am. Acad. Dental Schs. (pres. sect. oral radiology 1974-75), Orgn. Tchrs. Diagnosis (pres. 1975-76), Masons, Shriners, Mil. Order of Purple Heart, Am. Legion. Home: 2027 Lemonberry Ln Carlsbad CA 92009 Personal E-mail: glangland@msn.com, olangland@msn.com.

LANGLEY, GEORGE ROSS, retired medical educator; b. Sydney, NS, Can., Oct. 6, 1931; s. John Goerge Elmer and Freda Catherine (Ross) L.; m. Jean Marie Ballantyne, June 22, 1957; children: Joanne Marie, Mark Ross, Richard Graham. BA, Mt. Allison U., 1952; MD, Dalhousie U., 1957. Intern Victoria Gen. Hosp., Halifax, N.S., 1957, resident, 1958, Toronto Gen. Hosp., 1960, U. Melbourne, Australia, 1961, U. Rochester, NY, 1962; John and Mary Markle scholar in acad. medicine Dalhousie U., Halifax, 1963-68, from lectr. to prof. medicine, 1963-69, prof., chmn. dept. medicine, 1974-82; chief of service medicine Camp Hill Hosp., Halifax, 1969-74; head dept. medicine Victoria Gen. Hosp., 1974-82; prof. medicine Dalhousie U., Queen Elizabeth II Health. Sci. Ctr., 1982—2002; exec. dir. Strategic Hlth. Svcs. Dept. Hlth. Provinces, Nova Scotia, Canada, 1998-2000, prof. emeritus, 2002—, Dalhousie U., 2002—. Chmn. clin. investigation grants com. Med. Rsch. Coun., 1976-78; chmn. clin. and epidemiol. research adv. com., bd. dirs. Nat. Cancer Inst. Can., 1978 86 Contbr. articles to profl. jours. Recipient Queen's Silver Jubilee medal, 1977, Laureate, Am. Coll. Physicians, 1996, Queen's Golden Jubilee medal, 2002, Dalhousie Med. Alumnus of Yr., 2003, Svc. award, Med. Soc. NS, 2007; grantee John and Mary Markle scholar, 1963—68. Master ACP (bd. govs. 1973-78, laureate Atlantic region 1996, Mastership 2007); fellow Internat. Soc. Hematology, Royal Coll. Physicians and Surgeons Can.(v.p., coun., Wightman vis. prof. 1990, Drs. Nova Scotia Disting. Svc. award 2007), Royal Coll. Physicians (Edinburgh); mem. Can. Hematology Soc. (pres. 1976-78), Can. Soc. Clin. Investigation, Am. Soc. Hematology, Can. Soc. Oncology, Alpha Omega Alpha. Mem. United Ch. Can. Home and Office: 6025 Oakland Rd Halifax NS Canada B3H 1N9 Office Phone: 902-429-5045. Business E-Mail: ross.langley@dal.ca.

LANGLEY, RICKY LEE, occupational medicine physician; b. Fountain, NC, Aug. 31, 1957; s. Ernest Lee and Janie Ruth (Fulford) L.; m. Sandra Jane Ward, June 7, 1980; children: Patrick, Nicholas, Megan. BS magna cum laude, NC State U., Raleigh, 1979; MD, Bowman Grey Sch. Medicine, 1983; MPH, U. NC, 1988. Diplomate Am. Bd. Internal Medicine, Am. Bd. Preventive Medicine. Intern East Carolina Sch. Medicine, Greenville, NC, 1983-84, resident, 1984-86; asst. prof. dept. preventive medicine and health policy East Carolina U., Greenville, 1989-91, adj. asst. prof. dept. family medicine, 1989-91, adj. asst. prof. dept. environ. health, 1989-98, asst. prof. dept. internal medicine, 1991; fellow Sch. Medicine Duke U., Durham, NC, 1986-88, asst. cons. prof. in occupl. medicine, 1989-90, asst. clin. prof. dept. cmty. and family medicine, 1991-96; pvt. practice occupl. medicine Health and Hygiene, Inc., Greensboro, NC, 1988-89; med. dir. Mebane (NC) Med. Ctr., 1996-98, Kernodle Clinic, Inc., 1998; pub. health physician Occupl. and Environ. Epidemiology, Dept. Health & Human Svc., Raleigh, NC, 1998—. Adj. asst. prof. dept. biol. and agrl. engring. NC State U., 1996—99; cons. in field; mem. planning com. on agrl. safety NC State Fair, 1991; mem. task force Agri-Bus. for Gov.'s Commn. on Reduction of Infant Morality, 1992; mem. NC State Task Force on Blood-Borne Pathogens NC Occupl. Health and Safety Adminstrn., 1991—92; presenter in field.; mem. Nat. Pork Procedures Coun. Task Force on Worker Health and Safety, 1995; occupl. medicine residency program evaluator for NIOSH, 1992—96, mem. spl. emphasis panel, 1996—; mem. agrl. safety and health coun. NC Dept. Labor, 1996; mem. NC Pesticide Bd., 1998—, chair, NC, 2007—; occupl. medicine residency adv. com. Duke U., 1998—; mem. bd. collaborators NC Inst. Health and Safety in Agr., Forestry & Fisheries, 2001—. Author: Sex and Gender Differences in Health and Disease, 2003; editor: Safety and Health in Agriculture, Forestry and Fisheries, 1997, (textbook) Animal Handlers; guest editor NC Med. Jour., 1992-93, 95, mem. editl. bd., 1999—; mem. editl. bd. Jour. Agromedicine, 2004-09; co-editor Environmental Health Secrets, 2001; reviewer, contbr. articles to profl. jours. Vol. Greenville Cmty. Shelter, 1990, Health Hotline, WITN, 1990, 91, State Employee Wellness Day 1989, Adopt-A-Hwy. Project, 1989; Dr. of the Day, NC State Legislature, 1991; doctor on call blood drive ARC, Greensboro, 1989; vol. Freemont Peoples Clinic, 1993, Open Door Clinic, Burlington, 2006-11; pub. affairs officer, mem. USCG Aux., 1996-99, flotilla 18-11, 1995-98; hunting safety educator, NC, 1996-2005; mem. Alamance County (NC) Bd. Adjustment, 1997-99. Lloyd T. Weeks scholar, 1978, Benjamin Elloit Ibie and Benjamin Elliot Ibie Jr. Meml. scholar, 1976. Fellow ACP, Am. Coll. Occupl. and Environ. Medicine (del. 1995-98), Am. Coll. Preventive Medicine, Acad. Wildarness Medicine, 2009; mem. AMA, NC Med. Soc. (environ. health subcom. 1991-2001, vice chair 1999-2000, chair 2000-01), Am. Occupl. Med. Assn. (med. ctr. occupl. health com. 1990-97), Carolinas Occupl. Med. Assn. (sec.-treas. 1991-92, pres-elect 1992-93, pres. 1993-94, del. 1995-98), NC Archeol. Soc. (exec. bd. 1998-2000), Tarheel Archaeology Soc. (edn. chair 1996-2000), Found. for Advanced Lithics Studies (sec.-treas. 2000—), Alamance County Astronomy Club (founding mem.), Sigma Xi, Phi Kappa Phi, Phi Eta Sigma, Gamma Sigma Delta, Alpha Epsilon Delta. Avocations: astronomy, archaeology. Home: 1506 Miles Chapel Rd Mebane NC 27302-9008 Office: Mebane Med Clinic Mebane NC 27302 Office Phone: 919-707-5920, 919-707-5913, 919-707-5900. Personal E-mail: rick.langley@ncmail.net. Business E-Mail: rick.langley@dhhs.nc.gov.

LANGONE, KENNETH G., investment company executive; b. Roslyn Heights, NY, Sept. 16, 1935; m. Elaine Langone; 3 children. BA, Bucknell U., 1957; MBA, NYU. Exec. v.p. R.W. Pressprich & Co.; founder, chmn. Vantis Capital Mgmt. LLC; founder, chmn., CEO Invemed Associates, LLC, 1974—, bd. dirs., 1999; former bd. dirs. Home Depot Inc., 1978; co-founder Home Depot, Inc., 1978—; chmn., interim pres. & CEO Geeknet, Inc., 2010—. Bd. dirs. TRICON Global Restaurants, AutoFinance, Inc., US Satellite Broadcasting of Minn.; former mem. NY Stock Exch.; bd. dirs. Unifi, Inc., 1969—, InterWorld Corp., 1996—2001, DBT Online, Inc., 1996—, Yum Brands, Inc., 1997—, GE, 1999—, Choicepoint, Inc., 2000—. Vice-chmn. bd. overseers Stern Sch. Bus.; chmn. bd. trustees NYU Med. Sch.; trustee, chmn. nominating com., chmn. endowment com., mem. exec. com. Bucknell U.; contbr., adv., transformation team Mayor Rudolph Giuliani, 1993; chmn. NY State Sen. Bob Dole, presdl. election, 1996; trustee, chmn. nominating com., chmn. endowment com., mem. exec. com. NY Philharm., Children's Oncology Soc. (Ronald McDonald House), Robin Hood Found.; trustee, mem. exec. com. NYU; bd. dirs., vice-chmn. bd. develop. Damon Runyon-Walter Winchell Found.; trustee Ctr. for Strategic & Internat. Studies (CSIS). Named one of 400 Richest Ams., Forbes mag., 2006. Office: Invemed Associates LLC 375 Park Ave Ste 2205 New York NY 10152-2201 Office Phone: 212-421-2500. Office Fax: 212-421-2523. Business E-Mail: kenneth.langone@nyu.edu.

LANGOWSKI, JÖRG, biophysicist; b. Husum, Germany, Aug. 14, 1955; s. Horst and Isolde Langowski; m. Katalin Tóth; children: Judith, Eva. PhD, U. Hannover, Hannover, Germany, 1982. Scientist U. Hannover, Hannover, Germany, 1980—83; post-doc Dept. of Chemistry, U. of Wash., Seattle, 1983—84; group leader European Molecular Biology Lab., Grenoble, France, 1985—94; head of divsn. and prof. German Cancer Rsch. Ctr., Heidelberg, Germany, 1994—. Heisenberg Fellowship, German NSF (DFG), 1984-1986. Office: German Cancer Rsch Ctr Im Neuenheimer Feld 580 Heidelberg 69120 Germany Office Fax: +49-6221-423391. E-mail: jl@dkfz.de.

LANGRIDGE, ROBERT, biophysicist, educator, computational biologist; b. Essex, Eng., Oct. 26, 1933; came to U.S., 1957; naturalized, 1987. s. Charles and Winifred (Lister) L.; m. Ruth Gottlieb, June 26, 1960; children: Elizabeth, Catherine, Suzanne. BSc in Physics (1st class honours), U. London, Eng., 1954, PhD in Crystallography, 1957. Vis. research fellow biophysics Yale, 1957-59; research assoc. biophysics M.I.T., 1959-61; research assoc. pathology Children's Cancer Research Found., Boston; research assoc. biophysics, lectr. biophysics, also tutor biochem. scis. Harvard, 1961-66; research assoc. Project MAC, Lab. for Computer Sci., M.I.T., 1964-66; prof. biophysics and info. scis. U. Chgo., 1966-68; prof. chemistry and biochem. scis. Princeton, 1968-76; prof. pharm. chemistry, biochemistry and biophysics, dir. Computer Graphics Lab. U. Calif., San Francisco, 1976-94, prof. emeritus, 1994—, mem. adv. com. resource for biocomputing visualization and informatics, 1998—2004. Vis. prof. computer sci. Stanford U., 1983-84; vis. prof. biochem., biophys. Oreg. State U., 1995-97; mem. computer and biomath. rsch. study sect. NIH, USPHS, 1968-72, chmn., 1975-77, mem. nat. adv. rsch. resources coun., 1992-96, mem. adv. com. to dir., 1993 95, mem. biomed. informatics expert panel, 2004—; mem. vis. com. biology dept. Brookhaven Nat. Lab., 1977-80, mem. adv. com. neutron diffraction, biology dept., 1980-83; mem. sci. and ednl. adv. com. Lawrence Berkeley Labs., 1988-92; chair U. Calif. Berkeley/U. Calif. San Francisco Grad. Group in Bioengrng., 1991-93; mem. computer sci. and telecomm. bd. NRC, NAS, 1988-91. Guggenheim fellow, 1983-84, named one of 35 Who Made a Difference, Smithsonian Mag., 2005. Fellow AAAS; mem. NAS, Inst. of Medicine.

LANGSNER, ALAN MICHAEL, pediatric cardiologist; b. NYC, Dec. 21, 1948; s. Herman and Celeste (Prince) L.; m. Hilary Schmidt, Dec. 19, 1971. BA in Psychology, Fairleigh Dickinson U., 1970; MD, U. Autonomia Guadalajara, Jalisco, Mex., 1977; postgrad., NYU, 1977-78. Cert. Am. Bd. Pediat. and Pediat. Cardiology. Resident in pediatrics N.Y. Med. Coll./Met. Hosp. Ctr., NYC, 1978-79, resident in pediatrics-primary care tng. program, 1979-80, chief resident in pediatrics primary care tng. program, 1980-81; pvt. practice pediatric cardiology NYC, 1983—; attending pediatrics, sr. cons. pediatric cardiology St. Barnabas Med. Ctr., Livingston, NJ, 1983—; assoc. cons. pediat. cardiology St. Vincent's Med. Ctr., SI, NY, 1983—2009; cons. pediat. cardiology St. Clare's Med. Ctr., Denvillen, NJ, 1996—2010; cons. pediatric cardiology Somerset Med. Ctr., Somerville, NJ, 1999—; chief dept. pediatric cardiology Children's Hosp. of N.J. at Newark Beth Israel Hosp., 1999—2004. Cons. pediatric cardiology, asst. prof. pediat. NYU Sch. Medicine,1983—, SI U. Hosp., 1985-2003; perinatal rev. com., med. bd. St. Barnabas Med. Ctr.; presenter in field Contbr. articles to profl. jours. Fellow: Am. Acad. Pediatrics, Am. Coll. Cardiology (councilor NJ chpt. 2006—, exec. coun. NJ chpt. 2004—); mem.: Essex County Med. Soc. Office: 405 Northfield Ave West Orange NJ 07052-3023 Office Phone: 973-736-9997. Personal E-mail: alangsner@gmail.com. Business E-Mail: alan.langsner@nyumc.org.

LANGSTON, EDWARD LEE, physician, pharmacist; b. Logansport, Ind., Sept. 28, 1944; m. Linda Langston; 2 children. BS in pharmacy, Purdue U. Sch. Pharmacy; MD, Ind. U. Sch. Medicine. Bd. cert. in family practice. Resident in family practice St. Mary's Grad. Med. Ctr., Evansville, Ill.; chair Commn. on Legis.; dir. family practice program, assoc. prof. Tex. Med. Ctr., 1993—96; v.p. med. affairs and med. edn. Trinity Regional Health Sys., Rock Island, Ill., 1996—2000; pvt. practice family physician Lafayette, Ind., 2000—. Affiliate asst. prof. Purdue U., Sch. Pharmacy, West Lafayette, Ind.; mem. adv. com. State Medicaid Prescription Drug; coord., sec. Lafayette Med. Edn. Found., 2001—; vol. faculty Cmty. Hosp. Family Practice Residency Program, dir., 1988—92; mem. bd. trustees US Pharmacopoeia, 1995—2000; bd. dir. Accreditation Coun. on Grad. Med. Edn., 1998—2003; bd. commr. Joint Commn. on Accreditation of Healthcare Orgn., 2005—. Mem.: AMA (house del. 1987—, mem., coun. on med. edn. 1997—2003, bd. trustees 2003—11, chair-elect bd. trustees 2006—07, chmn. bd. trustees 2007—08, mem., chair, specialty and svc. soc.), Ind. State Med. Assn., Am. Acad. Family Physicians (bd. dir. 1991—93, v.p. 1994, chair delegation 1999—2002), Ind. Acad. Family Physicians (pres. 1982—83), Alpha Omega Alpha. Avocations: jogging, reading, furniture refinishing. Office: 2323 Ferry St Ste 101 Lafayette IN 47904 Office Phone: 765-448-4511. *

LANHAM, RICHARD J., oncologist, educator; b. St. Louis, June 7, 1935; s. Richard Horatio and Helen Edwards Lanham; children: Richard Edwards, Richard Renault, Winifred Brook. BA, CCNY, 1966; MD, Albert Einstein Coll. Medicine, 1972. Cert. internal medicine Am. Bd. Internal Medicine, hematology Am. Bd. Internal Medicine, med. oncology Am. Bd. Internal Medicine, med. rev. officer Am. Soc. Med. Rev. Officers. Med. internship Johns Hopkins Hosp., 1972—73; med. resident Montefiore Hosp. and Med. Ctr., Albert Einstein Coll. Medicine, NYC, 1973—74, hematology resident, 1973—74; hematology fellow Cabrini Health Care Ctr., NYU Sch. Medicine, NYC, 1975—76; med. oncology fellow Bronx Mcpl. Hosp. Ctr., Albert Einstein Coll. Medicine, NYC, 1982—83; clin. instr. medicine Albert Einstein Coll. Medicine, NYC, 1978—83, asst. clin. prof. medicine, 1978—88, Wright State U. Coll. Medicine, Dayton, Ohio, 1985—88, Sch. Medicine and Biomed. Scis. of SUNY, Buffalo, 1990—96; pvt. practice NY and Ohio; prof., religion St. Matthews Cathedral Coll., 2010—; ordained Diaconate in the Ind. Anglican Ch. Can. Synod 1934, 2011. Presenter and lectr. in field. Contbr. articles to profl. jours. and chpts. to books. Deacon Anglican Ch. Mem.: Pure Knowledge, Inc. (founder, pres. 2007), Am. Assn. for Chronic Fatigue Syndrome (mem. clin. affairs com.), Johns Hopkins Alumni Assn., Albert Einstein Coll. Medicine Alumni Assn., Nat. Assn. Scholars, Math. Assn. Am., Assn. Literary Scholars and Critics, Am. Coll. Occupl. and Environ. Medicine, Am. Soc. Med. Rev. Officers, Hist. Soc. Avocations: rollerblading, wilderness hiking, camping, canoeing, sailing, collecting Inuit artifacts and carvings. Personal E-mail: richardjlanham@gmail.com. Business E-Mail: pureknowledge.net@gmail.com.

LANIGAN, SEAN WILLIAM, dermatologist, consultant; b. Newport, Wales, Feb. 17, 1955; s. William Patrick and Winifred (Pugh) Lanigan; m. Clare Hilary Carr, Oct. 20, 1990; children: Stuart James, Eleanor Clare. MB, BChir, U. Wales, Cardiff, 1978, MD, 1992; diploma in child health, Royal Coll. Physicians, London, 1981. House physician Royal Alexandra Hosp., 1978-79; house surgeon Cardiff Tchg. Hosp., 1979; sr. house physician Nevill Hall Hosp., Abergavenny, 1979-80; rotating registrar Glan Clwyd Hosp., Bodelwyddan, 1980-83; registrar in dermatology U. Coll. Hosp., London, 1983-86; lectr., hon. sr. registrar U. Leeds, Eng., 1986-89; cons. dermatologist Bridgend Princess of Wales Hosp., 1989—2001; med. dir. Lasercare Clinics, Harrogate, England, 2001—. Hon. clin. tchr. U. Wales Coll. Medicine, Cardiff, 1989—2001; adv. bd. Disfigurement Guidance Ctr., Fife, Scotland, 1992—; cons. dermatologist City Hosp. NHS Trust, Birmingham, 2001—; expert adviser Med. Devices Agy. and Nat. Inst. Clin. Excellence, 2000—; regional rep. Brit. Skin Found. Author: Lasers in Dermatology, 2001; editor-in-chief: Lasers in Med. Sci., 2001—06; contbr. articles to profl. jours. Rsch. fellow Psoriasis Rsch. Inst., Stanford, Calif., 1988-89, Travel fellow British Dermatol. Surgery Soc., 1988; recipient Silver medal Assn. Brit. Insurers Med. Cmty. awards, 1991, Nat. Clin. Excellence Bronze award, 2004. Fellow Royal Coll. Physicians, Am. Soc. for Laser Medicine and Surgery (internat. affairs com. 2000—, chmn. 2004); mem. Brit. Assn. Dermatologists, Brit. Med. Laser Assn. (exec. com. 1997—), European Soc. for Lasers and Aesthetic Surgeons, European Acad. Dermatovenereology, European Soc. for Laser Dermatology. Avocations: modern jazz, welsh rugby. Office: Skin Ltd 34 Harborne Rd Edgbaston Birmingham B153AA England Office Phone: 121 5678204. Business E-Mail: sean.lanigan@sknclinics.co.uk.

LANKINEN, KARI SAKARI, physician, researcher; b. Helsinki, Dec. 10, 1958; s. Pentti Tapani and Kerttu Kaarina (Angeria) L. MD, U. Oulu, Finland, 1984, PhD, 2003; diploma in tropical medicine and hygiene, U. Liverpool, Eng., 1990; diploma in pub. health, Nordic Sch. Pub. Health, Gothenburg, Sweden, 1996. Clin. rsch. physician Orion Corp., Helsinki, 1987-89, med. advisor, 1994-95, unit, project mgr., 1995-96; gen. practice Suomussalmi Health Ctr., Finland, 1990-91, 2004—05; rsch. physician Nat. Pub. Health Inst., Helsinki, 1991-93, sr. scientist, 1996 99; project dir. evaluation of immunization programs European Union, PSR Cons. Ltd., 1998—2000; mng. dir. PSR Cons. Ltd., Helsinki, 1992-2000; project dir. European Rsch. Programme for Improved Vaccine Safety Surveillance, Helsinki, 2001 03; project mgr. pub. markets Schering Oy, 2005—06; assoc. chief physician Kuhmo Health Ctr., Finland, 2007; physician Kuusamo Health Ctr., 2008; chief physician Mediverkko Ltd., 2009; sr. med. officer Finnish Medicines Agy., 2010—. Freelance cons. in internat. pub. health and pharm. medicine, 2004—; mem. nat. adv. com. vaccination Nat. Inst. Health & Welfare, 2010—. Editor: Health and Disease in Developing Countries, 1994, Production and Quality Control of Tetanus Vaccine, 1994. With Finnish Navy, 1977-78. Mem.: Royal Coll. Physicians (U.K.), Faculty Pharm. Medicine. E-mail: kari.lankinen@welho.com.

LANSEN, THOMAS, neurosurgeon, educator; BA, Marquette U.; MD, Med. Coll. Wis., 1973. Diplomate Am. Bd. Neurol. Surgery, Am. Coll. of Surgeons. Intern NYU Med. Ctr.; resident Lenox Hill Hosp., 1974—75; resident and chief resident neurol. surgery coll. of medicine Univ. Fla., 1975—80; with White Plains Hosp. Med. Ctr., White Plains, St. Vincent's Hosp., Our Lady of Mercy Med. Ctr., Bronx, Sound Shore Med. Ctr., New Rochelle; asst. clin. prof. neurosurgery Yale Univ.; assoc. clin. prof. dept. of neurosurgery NY Med. Coll., Valhalla; chief sect. of neurosurgery Lawrence Hosp., Bronxville, Northern Westchester Hosp., Mt. Kisco, co-dir. gamma knife. Mem. Westchester County AIDS Coun., NY State Neurosurgical Soc.; mem. credentials conv. Com Med. Soc. State of NY, mem. house of del.; mem. Med. Soc. of the State of NY; bd. dir. Westchester County Med. Soc.; key contract mem. Med. Soc. State of NY; chmn. pub. rels. com. Westchester County Med. Soc.; med. bd. mem. Westchester Med. Ctr., Valhalla, Lawrence Hosp., Bronxville, Westchester Hosp., Mt. Kisco. Fellow: Am. Heart Assn., ACS; mem.: AMA, Alt.Del. to the Am. Med. Assn. Office: Northern Westchester Hospital Ste 310 244 Westchester Ave West Harrison NY 10604 Office Phone: 914-948-6688.

LANSMAN, STEVEN L., thoracic surgeon, educator; PhD in Biophysics, SUNY, Brooklyn, 1977, MD, 1977; trained in Cardiac Surgery, SUNY; trained in Cardiac Transplantation, Stanford U. Diplomate Nat. Bd. Med. Examiners, Am. Bd. Surgery, Am. Bd. Thoracic Surgery. Resident surgery Montefiore Med. Ctr., Bronx, NY, 1977—82; fellow thoracic surgery Univ. Hosp., Brooklyn, 1982—84; interim chief cardiothoracic surgery SUNY, Brooklyn; with The Brooklyn VA Hosp., Kings County Hosp.; staff Mt. Sinai Hosp., NYC, 1985, interim chmn. dept. of cardiothoracic surgery, 2002; prof. surgery NY Med. Coll.; chief of cardiothoracic surgery Westchester Med. Ctr., NY. Co-author: (publs.) Extended Aortic Arch Anastomosis For Repair Of Coarctation In Infancy, 1986, Urgent Operations for Acute Transverse Aortic Arch Dissection, 1989, History of Cardiac Transplantation, 1989, The History of Heart and Heart-Lung Transplantation, 1989, Intraluminal Graft Repair of Ascending Arch, Descending and Thoracoabdominal Aortic Segments For Dissection and Aneurysmal Disease: Long Term Follow-up, 1991, and numerous others. Mem.: The Am. Assn. for Thoracic Surgery, NY Surg. Soc., NY Soc. for Thoracic Surgery, Assn. of Academic Surgeons, Internat. Soc. for Heart/Lung Transplantation, Soc. of Thoracic Surgeons, ACS. Office: Westchester Medical Center 100 Woods Rd Valhalla NY 10595 Office Phone: 914-493-7000.

LANTHALER, MONIKA LANTHALER, plastic surgeon; b. Hall, Tyrol, June 12, 1975; MD, Innsbruck Med. U., 2000. Registered asst. prof. Innsbruck Med. U., 2011. Intern gen. practitioner Hosp. Hall/Tyorl, 2000 03; cons., asst. prof. dept. visceral-thoracic and transplantation surgery U. Hosp. Innsbruck, 2004—11, resident dept. plastic, reconstructive and aesthetic surgery, 2011—. Mem.: Austrian Soc. Gen. Surgery. Avocations: bicycling, swimming, sports, reading. Home: Planoetzenhofstrasse 19 B12 Innsbruck Tyrol 6020 Austria Personal E-mail: m.lanthaler@mac.com.

LANTZY, ALAN, neonatal-perinatal pediatrician; MD, U. Pitts., 1976. Cert. Pa., 1977, diplomate Am. Bd. Pediatrics-neonatal-perinatal medicine, Am. Bd. Pediatrics. Intern Children's Hosp. of Pitts., resident, 1979; fellow Univ. of Pitts. Med. Ctr. Magee Womens Hosp., 1990; hosp. affiliation include Allegheny Gen. Hosp.; asst. prof. pediat. Temple Univ.; chmn. dept. of pediat. The Western Pa. Hosp. Named one of the Top Doctors, Pitts. mag. Office: The Western Pennsylvania Hospital Department of Pediatrics W3 4800 Friendship Ave Pittsburgh PA 15224 Office Phone: 412-578-5858. Office Fax: 412-578-1529.

LANZA, ROBERT PAUL, medical scientist; b. Boston, Feb. 11, 1956; s. Samuel and Barbara (Corbett) L. BA, U. Pa., 1978, MD, 1983. Sr. scientist Biohybrid Techs., Shrewsbury, Mass., 1990-93, dir. transplantation biology, 1993-98; clin. assoc. prof. surgery Tufts U., 1994-95; sr. dir. tissue engrng. and transplant medicine Advanced Cell Tech., Inc., Worcester, Mass., 1999-2000; med. dir., v.p. rsch. and sci. devel. Advanced Cell Tech. Group Inc., Worcester, Mass., 1999, chief scientific officer. Rschr. Lab. of Richard Hynes, 1975, Gerald Edelman, 1976, Jonas Salk, 1978, B.F. Skinner, 1979-81, Christiaan Barnard, 1981-84; assoc. surgery Harvard Med. Sch., 1991-93; adj. prof. Inst. Regenerative Medicine, Wake Forest U. Sch. Medicine, 2004-. Author: Xeno, 2000; editor: Heart Transplantation, 1984, Medical Science and the Advancement of World Health, 1985, Procurement of Pancreatic Islets I, 1994, Immunomodulation of Pancreatic Islets II, 1994, Immunoisolation of Pancreatic Islets III, 1994, One World: The Health & Survival of the Human Species in the 21st Century, 1996, Tissue Engineering/Cellular Medicine Series, 1995—, Yearbook of Cell and Tissue Transplantation, 1996—, Principles of Tissue Engineering, 1997, 3rd edit., 2007, Encapsulated Cell Technology and Therapeutics, 1999, Methods of Tissue Engineering, 2001, Principles of Cloning, 2002, Handbook of Embryonic Stem Cells, 2004, Handbook of Adult and Fetal Stem Cells, 2004, Essentials of Stem Cell Biology, 2005, 2nd edit., 2009, Methods in Enzymology: Embryonic Stem Cells, 2006, Methods in Enzymology: Adult Stem Cells, 2006, Principles of Regenerative Medicine, 2007, 08, Biocentrism, 2009; contbr. articles to profl. and lit. jours.; featured in the following media CNN, TIME, Newsweek, People, NY Times, Wall Street Journal, Washington Post, among others. Active Conservation Commn., Town of Clinton, 1998—, open space com., 1996-98; founder, dir. South Meadow Pond and Wildlife Assn., 1998—; bd. dirs. Clinton Greenway Conservation Trust, 2001-07. Prof. Howe Buck scholar, 1974-75, Benjamin Franklin scholar, 1975-78, Univ. scholar, 1976-83, Fulbright scholar, 1978-79; Hon. Christiaan Barnard fellow, 1981-84, Mary K. Iacocca Transplantation fellow, 1988-90; recipient Rave award in Medicine, WIRED, 2005, 2006 All Star award for Biotechnology. Achievements include cloned first endangered species; first to reverse aging using nuclear transfer; was part of team that cloned first human embryo for medical purposes; first to demonstrate "proof-of-principle" for therapeutic cloning; patents in field. Home: South Meadow Pond Island 35 S Meadow Rd Clinton MA 01510-4327 Office: Advanced Cell Tech 33 Locke Dr Marlborough MA 01752 Office Phone: 508-756-1212 ext. 315. Fax: 508-756-4468. Business E-Mail: rlanza@advancedcell.com.

LANZAFAME, RAYMOND JOSEPH, surgeon, researcher; b. Rochester, NY, Sept. 30, 1952; s. Ray J. and Mary Vera (DeMeis) L.; m. Patricia Marie Volkmar, Apr. 26, 1980; children: Mark Raymond, Karen Elizabeth. BS with honors and distinction, Cornell U., Ithaca, NY, 1974; MD, George Washington U., DC, 1978; MBA, U. Rochester, NYC, 1999. Diplomate Nat. Bd. Med. Examiners, Am. Bd. Surgery. Clin. asst. prof. U. Rochester, NY, 1983-87, asst. prof., 1987-97, assoc. prof., 1997—2003. Laser task force N.Y. State Dept. of Health, 1990; dir. laser tng., chmn. laser usage com., Rochester Gen. Hosp. 1983-2005, dir. surg. laser rsch. lab., 1988—, dir. Laser Ctr., 1984-2005; cons. gen. and plastic surgery devices panel CDRH FDA, 2003—; bd. dir. Rochester Gen. Hosp. Found., 1990—2009; v.p. med. affairs Lakeside Meml. Hosp., 2004-06. Sr. editor Jour. Clin. Laser Medicine and Surgery, 1987-93, co-editor-in-chief, 1993-96, editor-in-chief, 1996 2004, referee, 1987 ; mem. editl. bd. Laser Medicine and Surgery News and Advances, 1988-90, Jour. Laparoendoscopic Surgery, 1991—, Surgery Alert, 1991-94, Lasers Surg. Medicine, 1995—, Jour. Soc. Laparoendoscopic Surgery, 1996-02, asst. editor, 2003—, Laser Med. Sci., 1997—; referee Jour. Investigative Surgery, 1997—; cons. editor Biomed. Optics, 1992—; asst. editor Gen. Surgery, 2002—; editor-in-chief Photomedicine and Laser Surgery, 2004—. Grantee Am. Cancer Soc. Fellow: ACS (councillor upstate N.Y. chpt. 1992—97, young surgeon rep. 1992—, sec.-treas. 1997—98, pres. 1999—2000, coun. 2000—); mem.: Biomed. Gateway LLC (ptnr. 2010—), N.Am. Assn. Laser Therapy (pres. 2005—08, pres. emeritus 2008), Soc. Laparoendoscopic Surgeons (bd. dir. 2000—, sec.-treas. 2004—05, v.p. 2005, pres. 2005—06, dir. CME 2007—), Soc. Univ. Surgeons, Biomed. Optics. Soc., Soc. Photo-Optical Instrumentation Engrs., Ctrl. Surg. Assn., Soc. Surgery Alimentary Tract, Internat. Soc. Surgery, Internat. Soc. for Lasers in Surgery and Medicine, Acad. Surg. Rsch., Assn. for Acad. Surgery, Am. Soc. for Laser Medicine and Surgery (Ellet Drake Lectureship 1999, Pres. Citations 2000, Mark award 2001, Pres. Citations 2006, 2008, 2011), Rochester Surg. Soc., Monroe County Med. Soc., Med. Soc. State N.Y., Am. Soc. Laser Surgery and Medicine (bd. dir. 1992—, pres. 1995—96, dir. CME 1999—), Laser Inst. Am. (sr.). Office: 757 Titus Ave Rochester NY 14617-3930 Office Phone: 585-266-2150. Business E-Mail: raymond.lanzafame@gmail.com.

LANZKRON, SOPHIE, hematologist, educator; b. Houston, Apr. 23, 1965; MD, Albert Einstein Coll. Medicine, 1991; MHS, Johns Hopkins Bloomberg Sch. Pub. Health, 2009. Asst. prof. to assoc. prof., medicine & oncology Johns Hopkins Sch. Medicine, 2000—. Mem.: Am. Soc. Hematology, Alpha Omega Alpha. Office: 1830 E Monument St Ste 7300 Baltimore MD 21205 Office Fax: 410-614-8601. Business E-Mail: slanzkr@jhmi.edu.

LAORWONG, KONGKIAT, surgeon; Diploma, Thai bd. Family Medicine, 2006; med. degree, Prince of Songkla U., Thailand. Cert. Internat. Soc. Gen. surg. residency Pramongkutklao Army Hosp., Bangkok, 2002; fellowship tng. Internat. Soc. Hair Restoration Surgery (ISHRS), 2007; trained with dr. Damjerng Pathomvanich; surgeon Phuket Aesthetic Ctr., Thailand. Guest lectr. hair transplantation at plastic and reconstructive surgery and ear nose and throat dept. Chulalongkorn Hosp., Bangkok. Contbr. scientific papers Eyebrow Transplantation in Asians Dermatologic Surgery, Volume 35, Issue 3, Pages496 - 504, 2009, Eyebrow transplantation using donor hair from sideburns pages54-55 International Society of Hair Restoration Surgery Hair Transplant Forum Internat., 2009. Mem.: Internat.

Soc. of Hair Restoration Surgery (ISHRS). Office: Phuket Aesthetic Center Bangkok Hospital Phuket 2/1 Hongyok Utis Rd Muang Dist Phuket 83000 Thailand Office Phone: 6676254425. Office Fax: 6676254430. *

LAPIERRE, PAUL, medical association executive; Degree in Social Sci., Coll. Ahuntsic, Montreal, Que., Can., 1981; degree in Polit. Sci., Douglas Coll., New Westminster, BC, 1986. Exec. dir. Kali Shiva AIDS Svc., Winnipeg, 1997—2001, Can. AIDS Soc., Ottawa, 2002—06; v.p. pub. affairs & cancer control Can. Cancer Soc., Toronto, 2006—. Bd. mem. Manitoba AIDS Co-operative. Office: Can Cancer Soc Nat Office 200-10 Alcorn Ave Toronto ON M4V 3B1 Canada Office Phone: 613-230-3580 ext. 118. Office Fax: 613-563-4998. Business E-Mail: Paull@cdnaids.ca.

LAPIN, BORIS ARKADIEVICH, pathologist; b. Kharkov, USSR, Aug. 10, 1921; s. Arkady Julievich and Faina (Borisovna) Lapin; m. Ester Illinichna Kurdina, June 10, 1944 (dec. Jan. 1969); children: Elena B. Lapina, Arkady B.; m. Lelita Andreevna Yakovleva, Dec. 20, 1969. MD, Moscow 2d Med. Inst., 1949; PhD, Acad. of Med. Scis., Moscow, 1952, Dr.M.Sci., 1960. Pathologist 13th Clin. Hosp., Moscow, 1950-52; rsch. scientist Med.-Biol. Sta., Acad. of Med. Sci., Sukhumi, USSR, 1952-53; rsch. dir. Inst. Exptl. Pathology and Therapy Acad. of Med. Sci., Sukhumi, USSR, 1953-57, dir., 1958-92, Inst. of Med. Primatol. Russian Acad. of Med. Sci., Sochi-Adler, Russia, 1992—. Head dept. pathology Inst. Exptl. Pathology and Therapy Acad. of Med. Sci., 1953—57; adviser to presidium Acad. Med. Sci., 1992—; chair prof. Dept. Exptl. Pathology Abkhasian State U., 1980—92. Author: Monkey Diseases as a Model of Human Diseases, 1959; co-author: Comparative Pathology in Monkeys, 1963; co-author: (with L. Yakoleva) Vergleichende Patologie der Affen, 1964, Pathology of Simian Primates, 1972; co-author: Nonhuman Primates and Medical Research, 1974, Hemoblastoses in Primates, 1979, Guidance in Medical Primatology, 1987; mem. bd. Jour. Med. Primatology, 1972—96, Exptl. Pathology, 1968—90; contbr. articles to profl. jours. Dep. Supreme Soviet of Abkhazia, 1967—71, 1975, 1983, Supreme Soviet of Georgia, Tbilisi, 1975—80, 1980—85, 1985—90; chmn. primate commn. Acad. Med. Sci., 1969—. Lt. Russian Airforce, 1941—44. Decorated Order of Peter Great 1st degree, Order of Golden Eagle; recipient Medal of Astronaut Gagarin, 1981, Korolev medal, 1981, V. Timakov prize in virology, 1984, prize of Russian Govt., Russia, 1997, also 10 orders, 20 medals, State prize of RF, Russia, 2002, R. Virchov's medal, 2003, A. Nebolsin's medal, 2004, N. Pirogov's award, 2005, Marie Curie award, 2006; named Honored Citizen of Sochi, Russia, 1997. Mem.: AAAS, Gerontol. Soc. Russian Acad. Scis. (elected v.p. 2005), Russian Med. Soc., Nat. Geographic Soc., Internat. Primatological Soc., Internat. Assn. Comparative Leukemia and Related Diseases (v.p. 1977—79, pres. 1979—81), Hungarian Soc. Microbiology, Russian Soc. Pathologists, Internat. Acad. Astronautics, Internat. Acad. Sci. (Russian sect.), N.Y. Acad. Sci., Russian Acad. Natural Sci., Russian Acad. Med. Sci., German Nat Acad of Scis, Am. Soc. Primatology. Avocations: collecting minerals, collecting rosary. Home and Office: Russian Acad Med Sci Inst Med Primatology 354376 Sochi Veseloye 1 Russia Office Phone: 7(8622)416-239. Personal E-mail: blapin@yandex.ru.

LAPLANTE, MITCHELL P., sociologist, educator; b. Worcester, Mass., Jan. 25, 1955; PhD, Stanford U., 1985. Prof. U. Calif., 1985—. Mem. editl. bd. Disability and Health Jour., 2007—11, Jour. Gerontology: Social Scis., 2009—11. Recipient Career Commendation award, Nat. Assn. Rehab. Rsch. and Tng. Ctrs. Mem.: APHA, Gerontol. Soc. America. Avocation: glass blowing. Office: University Calif 3333 California St San Francisco CA 94118 Business E-Mail: mitch.laplante@ucsf.edu.

LAPOOK, JONATHAN, gastroenterologist, medical correspondent; b. Mineola, NY; married; 2 children. B in Biology, cum laude, Yale U., New Haven, 1975; MD, Columbia U., NYC, 1980. Cert. in internal medicine, in gastroenterology. Residency in internal medicine NY-Presbyn. Hosp. Columbia U. Med. Ctr., NYC, fellowship in gastroenterology; asst. physician NY-Presbyn. Hosp., 1985—86, asst. attending physician, 1986—2001, assoc. attending physician, 2001—; instr. in clin. medicine Columbia U., 1985—86, asst. prof. clin. medicine, 1986—2001; med. corr. CBS Evening News, NYC, 2006—. Contbr. articles to profl. jours. Office: Columbia Eastside 16 E 60th St Ste 322 New York NY 10022 also: CBS News 524 W 57th St New York NY 10019 Office Phone: 212-326-8405. Office Fax: 212-326-8495. *

LAPORTE, STEVEN M., cardiologist; b. 1947; Attended, Temple U. Diplomate Am. Bd. Internal Medicine, 1976, Am. Bd. Internal Medicine-cardiovasc. disease, 1983. Intern Med. Coll. Hosp. of Pa., resident, fellow; intern The Med. Coll. of Pa., resident, fellow; joined Paoli Hosp., 1978, chief of cardiology medicine dept.; hosp. affiliations include Bryn Mawr Hosp., 1988—, Lankenau Med. Ctr., 1996—. Recipient Top Doctors, Phila. Mag., 2011. Mem.: Am. Coll. of Cardiology. Office: Paoli Hospital MOB III Ste 234 255 W Lancaster Ave Paoli PA 19301 Office Phone: 866-225-5654.

LAPPAS, JOHN, radiologist, educator; b. Lafayette, Ind., Sept. 5, 1950; AB, Ind. U., 1972, MD, 1976. Prof. Ind. U. Sch. Medicine, 1980—. Fellow: Am. Coll. Radiology; mem.: Soc. Abdominal Imaging, Soc. Gastrointestinal Radiologists, Am. Roentgen Ray Soc., Radiol. Soc. N.Am. Office: 550 N University Blvd Indianapolis IN 46202 Business E-Mail: jlappas@iupui.edu.

LAPPIN, MICHAEL BRUCE, ophthalmologist, surgeon, medical educator; b. Poplar Bluff, Mo., Dec. 11, 1941; s. Morris and Nettie Lappin; m. Cyli Teitelbaum, Apr. 20, 1968; children: Lauri, Steven, Sarah. BS, U. Fla., Gainesville, 1963; MD, U. Tenn., Memphis, 1967. Diplomate Am. Bd. Ophthalmology. Med.-surg. intern LA County and U. So. Calif. Med. Ctr., LA, 1967—68; resident in orthopedic surgery LA County Harbor, UCLA Med. Ctr., Torrance, Calif., 1968—69; resident in ophthalmology Baylor Coll. Medicine, Houston, 1971—74; assoc. clin. prof. ophthalmology U. Calif. Coll. Medicine, Irvine, 1977—; chmn. dept. ophthalmology Western Med. Ctr., Santa Ana, Calif., 1981, 1987—88. Commr. oral exams. med. licensure Calif. Bd. Med. Quality Assurance, 1976—90. Ophthal. assoc. Rsch. to Prevent Blindness, LA, 1975—; qualified med. evaluator State of Calif. Maj. Med. Corps USAF, 1969—71. Fellow: ACS, Am. Acad. Ophthalmology; mem.: AMA, Orange County Med. Assn., Calif. Med. Assn., Am. Soc. Cataract and Refractive Surgery, Orange County Soc. Ophthalmology (pres. 1979—80), Alpha Omega Alpha. Avocations: classical and contemporary music, literature, racket sports. Office: 801 N Tustin Ave # 700 Santa Ana CA 92705 Office Phone: 714-541-4185.

LAQUAGLIA, MICHAEL PATRICK, pediatric surgeon, neuroblastoma researcher; b. Newark, Aug. 6, 1950; s. Michael and Dorothy Theresa (Livsey) LaQ.; m. Joanne Drako, June 26, 1982; children: Michael Joseph, Catherine Elizabeth. BS, N.J. Inst., 1972, MD, 1976. Diplomate Am. Bd. Surgery; Cert. Spl. Competence Pediatric Surgery. From intern to chief resident in gen. surgery Mass. Gen. Hosp., Boston, 1976-83, clin. fellow in transplantation, 1980-81, clin. fellow in vascular surgery, 1984; hon. sr. registrar in surgery Broadgreen Regional Chest Ctr., Liverpool, Eng., U.K., 1982; assoc. chief resident in pediatric surgery Children's Hosp. Med. Ctr., Boston, 1985-86, chief resident in pediatric surgery, 1986-87; assoc. surgeon and mem., assoc. attending pediatrician Meml. Sloan-Kettering Cancer Ctr., NYC, 1987—, chief pediatric surgery, 1994—, Burchenal chair pediat.; assoc. attending Cornell U. Med. Ctr., NYC, 1989—, assoc. prof. surgery Med. Sch., 1989—. Fellow: Am. Surg. Assn.; mem.: AAAS, Soc. Surg. Oncology, Am. Pediatric Surg. Assn., Am. Assn. Cancer Rsch. Office: Meml Sloan Kettering Cancer Ctr Box 325 1275 York Ave New York NY 10065-6094 Office Phone: 212-639-7002.

LARA, JERRY MENDOZA, radiographer; b. San Fernando, Pampanga, Philippines, Feb. 25, 1957; s. Godofredo and Lydia Mendoza Lara; m. Mary Jean Morales, Mar. 15, 2003. A.Radiologic Tech., Emilio Aguinaldo Coll., Manila, Philippines, 1981. Cert. radiologic technologist Philippines. Nuclear medicine radiographer Lung Ctr. of the Philippines, Quezon City, 1984—88, St. Luke's Med. Ctr., Quezon City, 1988—90, King Aboulaziz U. Hosp., Jeddah, Saudi Arabia, 1990—91, King Khalid Nat. Guard Hosp., Jeddah, 1991—94; prin. radiographer Nat. Univ. Hosp., Singapore, 1994—. Mem.: Soc. of Nuclear Medicine. Avocations: softball, music, fishing. Office: Nat Univ Hosp Pte Ltd 5 Lower Kent Ridge Rd Singapore 119074 Singapore Home: Blk 409 Clementi Avenue 1 # 1406 120409 Singapore Singapore E-mail: jm_lara2000@yahoo.com.

LARACH, FERNANDO C., rheumatologist, researcher; b. San Pedro Sula, Cortes, Honduras, July 27, 1955; s. Jose Cruz and Emily Larach; m. Carole J. Aschi, Nov. 5, 1988; children: Joseph, Helaine, Caroline. MD, Nat. Autonomous U. Honduras, Tegucigalpa, 1981; MBA, Fla. Met. U., 2002, U. South Fla., 2003. Diplomate Am. Bd. Quality Assurance and Utilization Rev. 1993, Am. Acad. Pain Mgmt. 1991. Resident in internal medicine Wright State U., Dayton, Ohio, 1982—85; fellow in rheumatology Loyola U. of Chgo., Maywood, Ill., 1985—87; pres. A-Bay Area Med. Clinic, P.A., St. Petersburg, Fla., 1987—. Med. dir. Humana Ctr. #529, Pasadena, Fla., 1988—93. Contbr. articles to profl. jours.; editl. review bd. Jour. Managed Care Medicine (JMCM). Vol. Fla. Med. Assn./Pinellas County Med. Soc., 1996. Recipient Physician's Recognition award, 1985—, 2006, 2009. Fellow: Am. Inst. for Healthcare Quality, Interam. Coll. Physicians and Surgeons, Am. Coll. Rheumatology (contact to legis. affairs 1991—94); mem.: AMA, Southern Med. Assn., Am. Coll. Physician Execs. (life), Am. Profl. Practice Assn. (life), Am. Coll. Managed Care Medicine, Nat. Assn. Managed Care Physicians, Am. Coll. Med. Quality. Roman Catholic. Avocations: reading, music. Mailing: 202 Hancock Ct Safety Harbor FL 34695 Office: A Bay Area Med Clinic 202 Hancock Ct Safety Harbor FL 34695 Office Phone: 727-327-0879. Office Fax: 727-724-9720. Personal E-mail: f_c_larach@msn.com.

LARAGH, JOHN HENRY, physician, scientist, educator; b. Yonkers, NY, Nov. 18, 1924; s. Harry Joseph and Grace Catherine (Coyne) L.; m. Adonia Kennedy, Apr. 28, 1949; children: John Coyne, Peter Christian, Robert Sealey; m. Jean E. Sealey, Sept. 22, 1974. MD, Cornell U., 1948. Intern Presbyn. Hosp., NYC, 1948-49, asst. resident, 1949-50; cardiology trainee Nat. Heart Inst., 1950-51; rsch. fellow N.Y. Heart Assn., 1951-52; asst. physician Presbyn. Hosp., 1950-55, asst. attending, 1954-61, assoc. attending, 1961-69, attending physician, 1969-75, pres. elect med. bd., 1972-74; faculty Coll. Physicians and Surgeons Columbia U., 1950-75, prof. clin. medicine, 1967-75, spokesman exec. com. faculty coun., 1971-73; vice-chmn. bd. trustees for profl. and sci. affairs Presbyn. Hosp., 1974-75; dir. Hypertension Ctr., chief nephrology divsn. Columbia-Presbyn. Med. Ctr., 1975—76; Master prof. medicine, dir. Hypertension and Cardiovascular Ctr., N.Y. Hosp.-Cornell Med. Ctr., 1975—96, chief cardiology divsn., 1975—96. Cons. USPHS, 1964-. Editor-in-chief Am. Jour. Hypertension, 1988-2005, Cardiovascular Reviews and Reports, 1980—; Editor: Hypertension Manual, 1974, Topics in Hypertension, 1980, Frontiers in Hypertension Rsch., 1981; editor Hypertension: Pathophysiology, Diagnosis, and Management, 1990, 1995; editorial bd.: Am. Jour. Medicine, Am. Jour. Cardiology, Kidney Internat., Jour. Clin. Endocrinology and Metabolism, Hypertension, Jour. Hypertension, Circulation, Am. Heart Jour., Procs. of Soc. Exptl. Biology and Medicine. Mem. policy adv. bd. hypertension detection and follow-up program Nat. Heart and Lung Inst., 1971, bd. sci. counselor, 1974-79; chmn. U.S.A.-USSR Joint Program in Hypertension, 1977-93. With U.S. Army, 1943-46. Recipient AHA Stouffer prize Med. Rsch., 1969, J.K. Lattimer award Am. Urol. Assn., 1989, Robert Tigerstedt award Am. Soc. Hypertension, 1990, John P. Peters award Am. Soc. Nephrology, 1990, Lifetime Achievement in Medicine award NY Acad. Medicine, 1993, Disting. Alumnus award Cornell U. Med. Coll., 1993, Bristol Myers Squibb award for disting. achievement cardiovalcular rsch., 1996, Disting. Achievement award Coun. High Blood Pressure Rsch., Am. Heart Assn., 1999, Stevo Julius awrd for edn. in hypertension Internat. Soc. Hypertension, 2002, Lewis and Jack Rudin NY prize medicine and health, 2005; subject of Time Mag. cover story, 1975; Most Frequently Cited Scientist: Top Ten Advances in Cardiopulmonary Medicine, 1946-75. Fellow Am. Coll. Cardiology; mem. ACP (Master), Am. Heart Assn. (chmn. med. adv. bd. coun. high blood pressure rsch. 1968-72), Am. Soc. Clin. Investigation, Assn. Am. Physicians, Assn. Univ. Cardiologists, Endocrine Soc., Am. Soc. Nephrology, Am. Soc. Hypertension (founding pres. 1986-88), Internat. Soc. Hypertension (pres. 1986-88), Harvey Soc., Kappa Sigma, Nu Sigma Nu, Alpha Omega Alpha, Country Club of Fla., Shinnecock Hills Golf Club (Southampton, N.Y.). Achievements include discovery of the renin-angiotensin-aldosterone hormonal control system and the revelation of its causal role in malignant, and in most essential hypertension. Office: NYP Hosp-Weill Cornell Med Coll 525 E 68th St Mailbox 266 New York NY 10065-4805 Home: 5 Sandpiper Dr Village Of Golf FL 33436 Home Phone: 561-369-1851; Office Phone: 212-746-2206. Business E-Mail: jhl2001@med.cornell.edu.

LARAYA-CUASAY, LOURDES REDUBLO, pediatrician, pulmonologist, educator; b. Baguio, Philippines, Dec. 8, 1941; came to U.S., 1966; d. Jose Marquez and Lolita (Redublo) Laraya; m. Ramon Serrano Cuasay, Aug. 7, 1965; children: Raymond Peter, Catherine Anne, Margaret Rose, Joseph Paul. AA, U. Santo Tomas, Manila, Philippines, 1958, MD cum laude, 1963. Diplomate Am. Bd. Pediatrics. Resident in pediatrics U. Santo Tomas Hosp., 1963-65, Children's Hosp. Louisville, 1966-67, Charity Hosp. New Orleans-Tulane U., 1967-68; fellow child growth and devel. Children's Hosp. Phila., 1968-69; fellow pediatric pulmonary and cystic fibrosis programs St. Christopher's Hosp. for Children, Phila., 1969-71, rsch. assoc., 1971-72; clin. instr. Tulane U., New Orleans, 1967-68; asst. prof. pediatrics Temple Health Scis. Ctr., Phila., 1972-77; assoc. prof. pediatrics Thomas Jefferson Med. Sch., Phila., 1977-79, U. Medicine & Dentistry N. J., Robert Wood Johnson Med. Sch., New Brunswick, 1980-85, prof. clin. pediatrics, 1985-98, prof. pediat., 1998—2005; med. dir. pediat. asthma ctr. K. Hovnanian Children's Hosp., Jersey Shore U. Med. Ctr., Neptune, NJ, 2006—07; pediat. pulmonologist Cardon Children's Med. Ctr., 2008—. Dir. pediatric pulmonary divsn. and cystic fibrosis ctr. U. Medicine and Dentistry, Robert Wood Johnson Med. Sch., New Brunswick, 1981-2004 Co-editor: Interstitial Lung Diseases in Children, 1988. Recipient Pediatric Rsch. award Mead Johnson Pharm. Co., Manila, 1965. Fellow Am. Coll. Chest Physicians (steering com., chmn. cardiopulmonary diseases in children 1976—), Airways Network, Am. Acad. Pediatrics (tobacco free generation rep. 1986-92); mem. Am. Ambulatory Pediatric Soc., Am. Thoracic Soc., Am. Sleep Disorder Assn., N.J. Thoracic Soc. (chmn. pediatric pulmonary com. 1986-91, governing coun. mem. 1981-94), European Respiratory Soc. Avocation: piano. Home: 45 E Ninth Pl 39 Mesa AZ 85201-4336 Office: Desert Med Pavilion Ste 403 1432 S Dobson Rd Mesa AZ 85202 Business E-Mail: lourdas.laraya@banarhealth.com. *

LAREDO, JAMES, surgeon, educator; b. Chgo., June 11, 1965; s. Josue C. and Cristina M. Laredo; m. Tatiana N. Korobkova, Jan. 17, 1994; children: Jonathan Alexander, Alexander Nikolai. BS in Pharmacy, U. Md., Balt., 1988, PhD in Physiology, 1995, MD, 1996. Lic. Mass. Bd. Registration Medicine, 1999, in medicine Ill. Dept. Profl. Regulation, 2002, DC Health Profl. Licensing Adminstrn., 2004, Va. Dept. Health Professions, 2004, Md. Bd. Physicians, 2006, US Med. Licensing Exam., 1997, diplomate Am. Bd. Surgery, 2003, in vascular surgery 2006, registered vascular technologist Am. Registry Diagnostic Med. Sonographers, 2005, physician in vascular interpretation 2007. Hosp. pharmacist NW Hosp. Ctr., Randallstown, Md., 1988—96; resident gen. surgery Beth Israel Deaconess Med. Ctr., Boston, 1996—2001, chief resident gen. surgery, 2001—02; clin. fellow surgery Harvard Med. Sch., Boston, 1996—2002; fellow vascular surgery Loyola U. Med. Ctr., Maywood, Ill., 2002—04; physician Alexian Bros. Med. Ctr., Ill., 2002—04; cardiothoracic surgery physician Good Samaritan Hosp., Downers Grove, Ill., 2002—04; asst. prof. surgery Georgetown U. Med. Ctr., Washington, 2004—10; surgeon Wash. DC Veterans Affairs Hosp., 2006—; assoc. prof. surgery George Wash. U. Med. Ctr., 2011—. Reviewer Jour. Vascular Surgery, Washington, 2004—. Recipient Travel award, Dupont Merck Pharm. Co., 1994, Merck Young Investigator award, Am. Heart Assn., 1996, Gen. Surgery Resident Tchg. award, Harvard Med. Sch. Beth Israel Deaconess Med. Ctr., 2001—02, William J. Von Liebig Found. award, 2004, William J. Von Liebig Vascular Academic award, Peripheral Vascular Surg. Soc., 2006; Clin. Electives Program Clerkship, Nat. Cancer Inst., 1995, Cardiothoracic Surgery Clerkship, Cambridge U. Sch. Clin. Medicine, 1996. Mem.: AMA, ACS, Am. Venous Forum, Am. Coll. Phlebology, Peripheral Vascular Surg. Soc., Soc. Vascular Surgery. Office: George Wash University Med Faculty Associates 1800 Town Ctr Dr Ste 218 Reston VA 20190 Personal E-mail: jameslaredomd@yahoo.com.

LA REGINA, MICAELA, physician; b. Polla, Salerno, May 10, 1973; Medicine, U. Cattolica del Sacro Cuore, Rome, 1997, degree in Internal Medicine, 2003. Med. dir. dept. internal medicine ASL 5, Liguria, 2004—. Mem sci. com. 5th Internat. Conf. Autoinflammatory Diseases. Recipient Young rschr. award, U. Cattolica Sacro Cuore. Mem.: Federazione Associazioni Dirigenti Ospedalieri Internisti (nat. coord., Young Internist award, Ligurian sect.). Avocations: writing, reading, theater, travel. Home: Viale Italia 211 La Spezia Liguria 19124 Italy Business E-Mail: micaela.laregina@rm.unicatt.it.

LARET, MARK R., hospital administrator; BS in Polit. sci., UCLA; M in Polit. sci., U. So. Calif. Asst. dir. UCLA Med. Ctr., 1985, assoc. dir. marketing and planning, 1990, dep. dir., 1994; CEO UCLA Med. Group, 1994, Univ. Calif. Irvine Med. Ctr., Orange, Calif., 1995—2000, exec. dir., 1995; CEO University California San Francisco (UCSF) Medical Center, 2000—, University California San Francisco (UCSF) Children's Hospital, 2000—. Exec. com. bd. Univ. Healthcare Consortium; bd. dir. CaloPTIMA, 1997, AAMC Coun of Teaching Hosp. and Health Systems (COTH), 2003—04. Named Orange County Manager of Year, Soc. for Advancement of Mgmt., 1999. Office: Med Ctr Adminstrn Univ Calif San Francisco Box 0296 500 Parnassus Ave MU 509E San Francisco CA 94143-0296 Office Phone: 415-353-2733. Office Fax: 415-353-2765. Business E-Mail: mark.laret@ussfmedctr.org. *

LARHS, ANTHONY EMIL, nuclear medicine physician; arrived in U.S., 1998; m. Andreea M. Larhs, Aug. 15, 1998. MD, U. Toronto, Can., 1993, BS, 1989. Diplomate Am. Bd. Radiology, Am. Bd. Nuc. Medicine, cert. Bd. Nuc. Cardiology, Am. Bd. Scis. in Nuc. Medicine. Internship U. Toronto, 1993—94, residency radiology, 1994—98; nuc. medicine W. Pa., Phila., 1998—2000; dir. nuc. medicine and clin. P.E.T. TRA Med. Imaging, Tacoma, 2000. Acct. Northwest P.E.T. Philips, 2002—; advisor Coun. for Zevalin; advisor, biomed. tech. Nat. Coun. Healthcare Advisors. Participant 1st Nuc. Medicine Delegation People to People Amb. Program Internat., 2001—. Mem.: Australia and New Zealand Assn. Nuc. Medicine, European Assn. Nuc. Medicine, Soc. Nuc. Medicine. Avocations: travel, symphony, collecting art, skiing, tennis. Office: TRA Med Imaging 3402 S 48th St Tacoma WA 98405 Home: 20501 10th Pl SW Normandy Park WA 98166-4107 Home Phone: 206-878-1980; Office Phone: 253-383-1099. Business E-Mail: alarhs@tramedicalimaging.com.

LARI, ABDUL-REDA, plastic surgeon; Grad., Ireland, 1982; postgrad., Scotland; MA in Art of Aesthetic Surgery. Cons. plastic surgeon Lari Clinic, Kuwait. Author various articles about plastic and aesthetic surgery procedures. Mem.: West of Asia Soc. of Aesthetic Surgery (WASAPS) (pres.), Internat. Soc. of Aesthetic Plastic Surgery (ISAPS) (nat. sec. Kuwait 2000—08), Internat. Confederation for

Plastic, Reconstructive and Aesthetic Surgery (IPRAS) (nat. del. Kuwait 1992—2004, exec. com. mem. 2003—07), Kuwait Med. Assn. Jour. (editl. bd. mem. 1995—99), Pan Arab Assn. of Burns and Plastic Surgery (pres. 2001—03), Gulf Cooperation Coun.-Assn. of Plastic Surgeons (pres. 2002—04), Gulf Assn. of Plastic Surgeons (founder mem. and gen. sec. 1994—2004), Kuwait Soc. of Plastic Surgeon (founder and pres. 1994—2003), Plastic Surgery Dept. (chmn. 1993—2003). Achievements include first to work in the field of Body Contouring, Obesity and Liposuction. Office: Royal Hayat Hospital Lari Clinic 4th Ring Rd 90805 Hawalli Kuwait Office Phone: 9652617770. Office Fax: 9652619900. *

LARIA OCHAITA, CARLOS, ophthalmologist; b. Guadalajara, Spain, Mar. 11, 1966; s. Jose Florentino Laria Asenjo and Maria Nieves Ochaita Tello; m. Maria Elena Perez Lago. D, Alicante U., Spain, 1989. Cert. ophthalmologist Hosp. Clinico U. De Santiago De Compostela. Spain, 1993. Ophthalmologist Hosp. Comarcal, Monforte De Lemos., Spain, 1993—99; med. subdir. Clin Ica Oftalmologica, Badajoz, Spain, 1999—2001. Pediat. ophthalmologist Vissum Inst. Oftalmologico De Alicante, 2001—. Author: (book) "Terapéutica combinada no esteroidea de la inflama—ción ocular., "El Oftalmólogo responde a los padres. Manual de consulta oftalmológica"., "El Oftalmólogo responde. Manual de la visión adulta", "El Oftalmólogo responde. Manual de la tercera edad".; contbr. articles to profl. jours., chapters to books. Med. coord. Jorge Alio Found. Blindness Prevention, Alicante, 2001—08. Mem.: Consejo Latinoamericano de Estrabismos., Internat. Strabismological Assn., European Strabismological Assn., Sociedad Española de Ergoftalmología., Sociedad de Oftalmología Pediátrica Latinoamericana, European Paediatric Ophthal. Soc., Sociedad Española de Estrabología., Sociedad Gallega de Oftalmología., Sociedad Española de Oftalmología. Office: VISSUM Inst Oftalmolgico Alicante Avda Denia s/n 3016 Alicante Spain Office Fax: 34 965260530. Personal E-mail: laria1@telefonica.net.

LARICCIA, PATRICK J., internist, acupuncturist, medical researcher; BA in Psychology, Youngstown State U., Ohio, 1969; MA in Psychology, Temple U., Phila., 1971; MD, U. Ghent, Belgium, 1978; MS in Clin. Epidemiology, U. Pa., Sch. Medicine, 2007. Cert. in internal medicine 1981, lic. Conn., Ky., Ohio, Pa., in acupuncture. Instr. psychology Camden County CC, Blackwood, NJ, 1971—72; intern internal medicine Akron City Hosp., Ohio, 1978—79, resident internal medicine, 1979—81; asst. dept. medicine Presby. Med. Ctr. Phila., 1983—, med. dir. incontinence treatment ctr., 1986—93; med. dir. Milton H. Erickson Inst. Phila., 1986—; clin. assoc. dept. rehab. medicine U. Pa. Sch. Medicine, 1993—, adj. scholar epidemiology, 2009—. Bd. dirs. Acupuncture Soc. Pa., 1986—97, pres., 1988—91, v.p., 1991—94. Contbr. chapters to books, articles to med. jours. Fellow: Nat. Acad. Acupuncture and Oriental Medicine (mem. editl. com. 1993—2000), Internat. Coll. Acupuncture and Electro-Therapeutics, Am. Coll. Acupuncture; mem.: ACP, AMA (reviewer 1999—), Soc. Behavioral Medicine, Phila. County and Pa. Med. Socs., NY Soc. Acupuncture Physicians and Dentists (bd. dirs. 1990—, v.p. 1995—97, pres. 1997—99), Nat. Alliance Acupuncture and Oriental Medicine, Am. Soc. Acupuncture, Am. Psychosomatic Soc., Am. Coll. Advancement in Medicine, Am. Acad. Med. Acupuncture, Am. Assn. Acupuncture and Oriental Medicine, Acupuncture Soc. Pa. Office: Pa Presby Med Ctr 51 North 39th St Philadelphia PA 19104 Office Phone: 215-662-8988. Personal E-mail: plariccia@aol.com.

LARIKKA, MARTTI JOHANNES, nuclear medicine physician, researcher; b. Helsinki, Finland, July 27, 1957; s. Pekka Johannes Hamalainen and Marja-Riitta (Haukka) Larikka, Yrjo Larikka (Stepfather); m. Marjatta Ritva Elvi Puustinen, June 23, 1985; children: Jari Johannes, Sara Maria. MD, U. Kuopio, 1983; PhD, U. Oulu, 2004. Resident U. Hosp. Kuopio, 1987—90; chief physician lab. Lansi-Pohja Ctrl. Hosp., Kemi, Finland, 1991—, med. dir., 2004—05. Cons. clin. physiology and nuc. medicine U. Kuopio, 1990; rschr. U. Oulu, 1996—. Contbr. articles to profl. jours. First lt. Air Force, 1976—77, Finland. Mem.: European Assn. Nuc. Medicine. Avocation: pilot, flight instructor. Office: Lansi-Pohja Ctrl Hosp Lab Kauppakatu 25 94100 Kemi Finland Office Phone: 358 16 243641. Office Fax: 358 16 243657. Business E-Mail: martti.larikka@lpshp.fi.

LARIONOV, VLADIMIR L., medical researcher; PhD Inst. Exptl. Medicine, USSR Acad. Med. Sciences, Leningrad, 1977; DSc Inst. Cytology, Russian Acad. Sciences, 1983. Postdoctoral fellow Leningrad State U., Enhelhardt Inst. Molecular Biology, Moscow; staff scientist Inst. Cytology, Russian Acad. Sciences, chief Lab. Genetics, 1984—91; vis. scientist Lab. Molecular Genetics Nat. Inst. Environ. Health Sciences, NIH, 1991, leader Gene Isolation Unit, 1997; sr. investigator Lab. Biosystems and Cancer Ctr. Rsch. Rsch., Nat. Cancer Inst., NIH, 2000—06, chief genome structure and function sect., Lab. Biosystems and Cancer, 2000—, sr. investigator Lab. Molecular Pharmacology, 2006—. Office: Lab Biosystems and Cancer Ctr Cancer Rsch 37 Convent Dr Bldg 37 Rm 5032A Bethesda MD 20892 Office Phone: 301-496-7941. Office Fax: 301-480-2772. E-mail: larionov@mail.nih.gov. *

LARIVIERE, WILLIAM R., medical educator; b. Montreal, Mar. 23, 1971; PhD, McGill U., 2000. Asst. prof. anesthesiology U. Pitts. Sch. Medicine, 2003—. Editl. bd. mem. Open Jour. Pain, 2010. Postdoc. fellowship, Natural Scis. and Engring. Rsch. Coun. Can., Fonds pour la Formation de Chercheurs et l'Aide a la Recherche, Que., Can., grant, NIH/NIDA, NIH/NCCR. Mem.: Internat. Mammalian Genome Soc., Am. Pain Soc. (mem. adv. bd. Genetics and Pain SIG 2006, co chair 2008—10), Internat. Assn. Study Pain (sec. Genetics and Pain SIG 2010—, grant). Avocations: hockey, skiing, motorcycling. Office: W1356 BST 200 Lothrop St Pittsburgh PA 15213 Office Fax: 412-648-9587. Business E-Mail: lariwr@upmc.edu.

LARKAM, BEVERLEY MCCOSHAM, clinical social worker, marriage and family therapist; b. Vancouver, Can., Mar. 3, 1928; arrived in U.S., 1951; d. William Howard and Marjorie Isobel (Jerome) McCosham; children: Elizabeth, Charles, Daphne, Peter, John. A Royal Conservatory of Mus., U. Toronto, Toronto, 1948; BA, U. B.C., Can., 1949; BSW, U. B.C., 1950, MSW, 1951. Bd. cert. diplomate in clin. social work; LCSW; lic. marriage and family therapist, Tex., diplomate Internat. Conf. Advanced Profl. Practice of Clin. Social Work. Psychiat. social worker Brackenridge Hosp., 1952-54; chmn. dept. sr. high. sch. Univ. Presbyn. Ch., Austin, Tex., 1952-55, mem. Christian edn. com., 1961-67, bd. dirs. developing and organizing nursery sch., 1967-70; social worker Counseling-Psychol. Svcs. Ctr., U. Tex., 1971-72; psychiat. social worker, chief supr. Adult, Children's Mental Health Human-Devel. Ctr.-South, Austin, Tex., 1972-79; pvt. practice marriage and family therapy, sex therapy and individual and group psychotherapy Austin, Tex., 1975—, Georgetown, Tex., 1979—. Field supr. Sch. Social Work U. Tex.; cons. in field. Mem. cmty. orgn. to establish classes for mentally retarded children, 1966-68, City of Austin Commn. for Women, 1978—, chmn., 1982-84, emeritus, 1985—2009; organizer Austin Assn. for Marriage and Family Therapy, 1980-82, bd. dirs. Tex. Assn. for Marriage and Family Therapy, 1980-82; vol. usher Austin Symphony Orch. Soc., 1974-; mem. Heritage Soc. Austin, Georgetown Heritage Soc., Women's Symphony League of Austin, Austin Art Mus., Williamson County Hist. Mus.; mem. Dean Sch. Social Work, profl. linkage com., 1993—; vol. family therapist Child Inc./Headstart Ranch Weekends, 1995-96. Mem. NASW, Am. Assn. Marriage and Family Therapy (approved supr., com. on racial, ethnic and cultural diversity 1992-95, Honored Svc. Austin chpt., 1998), Am. Group Psychotherapy Assn. (cert. group psychotherapist), Southwestern Group Psychotherapy Soc. (sr. faculty), Austin Group Psychotherapy Soc., Am. Assn. Sexuality Educators, Counselors and Therapists (cert. diplomate sex therapy), Acad. Cert. Social Workers, Register Clin. Social Workers, cert. Eye Movement Desenitization Reprocessing, Tex. Soc. for Clin. Social Work (bd. dirs. 1990—, pres. 1997-99, chmn. Austin study groups 2006—), Clin. Social Work Fedn. (fin. chmn. 1998-2000), Austin Commn. Women (honored Austin city coun. 30yr svc.), PEO Sisterhood (50 Yr. Golden Mem. award 2009), Austin Woman's Forum (pres. 1994-95, 2002-03). Presbyterian (elder, session of Univ. Presbyterian Ch. 1997—). Home and Office: 2102 Raleigh Ave Austin TX 78703-2128 also: 207 E 9th St Georgetown TX 78626-5908 Office Phone: 512-476-4182. Personal E-mail: blarkam@earthlink.net.

LARKIN, GREGORY NEIL, public health service officer, state official; b. Feb. 9, 1949; MD, Ind. U., 1974. Diplomate Am. Bd. Family Medicine. Practiced family medicine, Greencastle, Ind., 1975—86; pres. City Park, Greencastle, Ind.; chmn. Ops. Life, Greencastle, Ind.; coroner Putnam County, 1976—80; mem. Healthy Ind. Task Force; chmn. Indpls. Med. Soc., Ind. Blood Ctr.; dir. corp. health services Eli Lilly & Co.; chief med. officer Ind. Health Info. Exch.; commr. Ind. Dept. Health, Indpls., 2010 . Pres. Ind. affiliate Am. Heart Assn.; pres-elect Ind. Acad. of Family Practice. Fellow: Am. Coll. of Occupl. and Environ. Medicine, Am. Acad. of Family Practice. Office: Indiana State Department of Health 2 North Meridian St Indianapolis IN 46204 Office Phone: 317-233-1325. *

LAROCHE, ROGER RENAN, psychiatrist; b. St. Paul, July 12, 1960; s. Gerard Auguste and Carolyn Mae (Seese) L.; m. Elizabeth Ann Tollerud, June 25, 1988; children: Austin, Hope, Cordon, Nathan. BA, Bethel Coll., St. Paul, 1982; MD, U. Minn., 1987. Diplomate Nat. Bd. Med. Examiners, Am. Bd. Psychiatry and Neurology, Am. Soc. Addiction Medicine, Am. Bd. Addiction Medicine, Geriatric Psychiatry, Addiction Psychiatry. Med. intern Hennepin County Med. Ctr., Mpls., 1987-88; resident dept. psychiatry Mayo Clinic Grad. Sch. Medicine, Rochester, Minn., 1988-91, fellowship addiction medicine dept. psychiatry, 1991-92; med. dir. dept. psychiatry Bradford (Pa.) Regional Med. Ctr., 1992—; med. dir. Cattaraugus County Coun. on Alcoholism and Substance Abuse, 1995 , Maple Manor Residential Rehab. Treatment Ctr., 2002—. Psychiat. cons. Beacon Light Behavioral Health Sys. for Children and Adolescents, 1998—; forensic psychiatrist cons. McKean County Fed. Corrections Inst., 1993-98; rotating med. student educator Mayo Med. Sch., 1987-92; contract forensic psychiatrist U.S. Bur. Prisons, Fed. Med. Ctr., Rochester, 1990-91, prin. investigator for carbamazepipe in smoking cessation Mayo Clinic, Rochester, 1991-92, psychiat. rsch. com. cons., 1991-92; pvt. and cons. psychiatrist, Bradford, Pa., 1992—; staff sec.-treas. Bradford Regional Med. Ctr., 1995—96, pres. med. staff, 1997-98, chmn. credentials com., 2001—04; chmn. Bradford Nursing Pavillion's Utilization Rev. Com., 1999-, vice chair bd. Twin Tiers Pregnancy Care Ctr., 2002-04; chmn. bd. Twin Tiers Pregnancy Care Ctr., 2005—; med. dir. Maple Manor Rehab. Ctr., 2002—; sr. high sunday tchr., 2005-. Contbr. articles to profl. jours. County del. Rep. Party Conv., Rochester, 1990. Recipient Medtronic Corp.'s Med. Fellow scholarship of excellence in leadership and acads., 1983, Acad. Writing Excellence award Mayo Clinic, 1991; Mayo Clinic Grad. Sch. Medicine grantee, 1991-92. Mem. AMA (resident physician sect. nat. del. 1990, 91), Am. Psychiat. Assn., Am. Soc. Addiction Medicine, Minn. Med. Assn. (del. ho. of dels. 1990, 91, resident physician sect. state governing officer 1990, 91), Pa. Med. Assn., Pa. Psychiat. Soc., Pa. Soc. Addiction Medicine, McKean County Med. Soc. Avocations: violist, vocal soloist, painting, weight training, distance biking. Home: 80 Stone Ave Bradford PA 16701-1050 Office Phone: 814-362-2287.

LAROCHELLE, PATRICIA ANNE, technologist; b. Bath, Maine, Apr. 21, 1952; d. Oliver George and Minnie V. (Dinsmore) Wass; m. Marc Joseph Larochelle, Feb. 23, 1974; children: Meghan Joy, Robert Oliver. BA in Med. Tech., U. Maine, 1976. Med. technologist chemistry Maine Med. Ctr., Portland, 1976—80, asst. chemistry supr., 1980—83; supr. Park Ave. lab. Oncology, Hematology Assocs., Portland, 1983—85; med. technologist Diamed/Diaexport, Windham, Maine, 1987—90, Westbrook (Maine) Cmty. Hosp., 1990—99; sr. med. technologist Mercy Westbrook Lab., Mercy Hosp., 1999—2010; microbiologist Mercy Hosp. Lab., 2010—. Sec. Maine chpt. Am. Soc. Med. Technologists, 1981—83, del. Maine to nat. convs., 1981—82; fund-raiser, mem. Windham Youth Football, 1999—2003; videographer Windham H.S. Football, 2000—; bd. dirs. Little Sebago Lake Assn., Maine, 1996—97. Mem.: Clin. Lab. Mgrs. Assn., Am. Soc. Clin. Pathologists (registrant). Avocations: gardening, kayaking, shopping, walking. Office: Mercy Lab 144 State St Portland ME 04101 Home Phone: 207 892 2478. Business E-Mail: larochellep@mercyme.com.

LA ROSA, CORINNA, medical educator; b. Civitavecchia, Italy, Mar. 5, 1965; PhD, U. Pisa, 1993. Assoc. rsch. prof. City Of Hope, 2008—. Office: 1500 E Duarte Rd Duarte CA 91010 Business E-Mail: clarosa@coh.org.

LA ROSA, FRANCISCO GUILLERMO, pathologist, researcher, educator; b. Lima, Peru, Jan. 17, 1949; came to U.S., 1981; s. Anibal and Carmen (de la Pascua) La R.; m. Clara Ann Dufficy, May 21, 1989; children: David, Anamaria, Joseph, MarieCarmen. MD, U. Nacional Federico Villarreal, Lima, 1975. cert. (AP/CP), 1995. Instr. U. Nacional Federico Villarreal, Lima, 1973-79, asst. prof., 1979-81; resident in clin. pathology U. de San Marcos, Lima, 1977-79; postdoctoral fellow in immunology U. Colo., Denver, 1981-85, instr., 1985-87, asst. prof., 1987—92, resident in pathology, 1992-95, fellow in lung pathology, 1995-96; lab. dir. Miners Colfax Med. Ctr., Raton, N.Mex., 1996—2000; clin. asst. prof. dept path., immunology U. Colo. Health Sci. Ctr., Denver, 1996—2002, asst. prof. prostate cancer rsch. lab, dept. pathology, 2001—09, assoc. prof., 2009—, fellow in prostate cancer Prostate Cancer Rsch. Labs., 2002—04. Pathologist Sterling Regional Med. Ctr., 1996-00, Longmont United Hosp., Colo., 2002-03; pres. Pathology Cons., PC, 1995—, Telepathology Cons., PC, 1996—; cons. Ortho Pharm., Lima, 1979-81, Reaads Med. Products, Inc., Denver, 1991; bd. dirs. comm. Christian Life Movement, Denver, 2005-; chair pathology informatics com. U. Colo. Health Sci. Ctr., Dept. Pathology, 2006-09, vice chmn. Am. Telemedicine Assn. L.Am. & Caribbean Chpt., 2007-09, vice-sect. Assn. Ibero Americana de Telesalud & Telemedicina, 2011- Contbr. chpts. to books, revs. and articles to 57 profl. jours. Krock Found. fellow, 1985-86, Juvenile Diabetes Found. fellow, 1985-86; NIH grantee, 1988-91; recipient award Diabetes Rsch. and Edn. Found., 1987-88, Butcher award, 2006-2007; hon. prof. U. Nat. Federico Villareal, 2003. Mem. Coll. Am. Pathologists, Transplantation Soc., Soc. Española Immunologia, Am. Assn. Immunologists, Am. Soc. Clin. Pathologists, Am. Telemedicine Assn., Peruvian Soc. Clin. Pathology, Peruvian Soc. Immunology and Allergy, Colo Med. Soc. Roman Catholic. Avocations: photography, videotaping, web page design, telepathology. Office: U Colo Denver Anschutz Prostate Cancer Rsch Lab Stop 8104 PO Box 6511 Aurora CO 80045-0508 Office Phone: 303-724-3782. Business E-Mail: francisco.larosa@ucdenver.edu. E-mail: flarosa@telepathology.com.

LARSEN, GARY LOY, physician, researcher; b. Wahoo, Nebr., Jan. 10, 1945; s. Allan Edward and Dorothy Mae (Hengen) L.; m. Letitia Leah Hoyt, Dec. 22, 1967; children: Kari Lyn, Amy Marie. BS, U. Nebr., 1967; MD, Columbia U., 1971. Diplomate Am. Bd. Pediat., Am. Bd. Pediatric Pulmonology (chmn. 1990-92). Pediatric pulmonologist Nat. Jewish Med. and Rsch. Ctr., Denver, 1978—2010, head divsn. pediatric pulmonary medicine, 1989—2010; mem. faculty U. Colo. Sch. Medicine, Denver, 1978—2010, dir. sect. pediatric pulmonary medicine, 1987—2003, prof. pediat., 1990—; head dept. respiratory medicine The Children's Hosp., Denver, 2002—03. Editl. councillor Pediat. Pulmonology; editl. adv. bd. Child Mag., 2006—07. Assoc. editor: Jour. Allergy and Clin. Immunology; contbr. articles to prof. jours. Mem. sci. adv. panel Nat. Urban Air Toxics Rsch. Ctr., 1998-2005. Maj. M.C., U.S. Army, 1974-76. Grantee Med. Rsch., NIH, 1981—2007. Mem. Am. Thoracic Soc. (chmn. pediatric assembly 1987-88), Soc. Pediatric Rsch., N.Y. Acad. Scis., Chilean Respiratory Soc. (hon.), Western Soc. Pediat. Rsch., Phi Beta Kappa, Alpha Omega Alpha. Lutheran. Office: Nat Jewish Med & Rsch Ctr 1400 Jackson St Denver CO 80206-2761

LARSEN, JORGEN NEDERGAARD, medical researcher; b. Hørsholm, May 7, 1957; MSc, U. Copenhagen, 1985, PhD, 1991. Rsch. scientist U. Copenhagen, 1985—91, ALK-Abello, 1991—2000, sci. communication mgr., 2000—05; sr. sci. affairs mgr. ALK, 2005—. Mem.: Am. Acad. Allergy, Asthma and Immunology, European Acad. Allergology and Clin. Immunology, Collegium Internat. Allergologicum, Danish Soc. Allergology, Danish Soc. Biochemistry and Molecular Biology. Office: Boge Alle 3 Hørsholm Nordsjaelland 2970 Denmark Business E Mail: jnldk@alk abello.com.

LARSEN, RALPH S(TANLEY), retired pharmaceutical executive; b. Bklyn., Nov. 19, 1938; s. Andrew and Gurine (Henningsen) L.; m. Dorothy M. Zeitfuss, Aug. 19, 1961; children: Karen, Kristen, Garret. BBA, Hofstra U., 1962. Mfg. trainee, then supr. prodn. and dir. mfg. Johnson & Johnson, New Brunswick, NJ, 1962—77, v.p. ops., v.p. mktg. McNeil Consumer Products Co. div. Johnson & Johnson, Ft. Washington, Pa., 1977—81; pres. Becton Dickenson Consumer Products, Paramus, NJ, 1981—83; pres. Chicopee divsn. Johnson & Johnson, New Brunswick, NJ, 1983—85, co. group chmn., 1985—86, vice chmn., exec. com., bd. dirs., 1986—89, chmn. bd., pres., CEO, 1989—2002, bd. dirs., mem. exec. com. Bd. dirs. General Electric Co., 2002—. Trustee Robert Wood Johnson Found. Independent. Avocations: skiing, boating, art. Office: 100 Albany St Ste 200 New Brunswick NJ 08901

LARSEN, RANDY JOHN, psychology professor, department chairman; b. Lake City, Iowa, Aug. 27, 1954; s. Floyd William and Mary Ellen (Stewart) L. MA, Duquesne U., 1979; PhD, U. Ill., 1984. Asst. prof. Purdue U., West Lafayette, Ind., 1984-89, U. Mich., Ann Arbor, 1989-92, assoc. prof., 1992-97, prof., 1997-98; William R. Stuckenberg prof. human values Washington U., St. Louis, 1998—, chmn. dept. psychology. Mem. NIH Study Sect. on Emotion and Personality, 1992-95. Mem. editl. bd. Jour. Personality and Social Psychology, 1985-91, Jour. Personality, 1990—, Jour. Rsch. in Personality, 1990—; author: (chpt.) A Process Approach to Personality, 1990; assoc. editor Jour Personality and Social Psychology, 1998—; contbr. articles to profl. jours. David Ross grantee Purdue U., 1987-89, NIH, 1987-90, 87-93. Mem. AAAS, Am. Psychol. Assn. (Disting. Sci. Achievement award 1991), Am. Psychol. Soc., Soc. for Psychophysiol. Rsch. Achievements include research in affect intensity as a personality dimension, occurence, duration and emotional impact of illness, personality and susceptibility to emotion states. Office: Wash Univ Dept Psychology Psychology Bldg 206 One Brookings Dr Saint Louis MO 63130 Office Phone: 314-935-8560. Business E-Mail: rlarsen@wustl.edu.

LARSEN, STEVEN B., federal agency administrator; BA, Gettysburg Coll., Pa.; MA in Pub. Policy, Rutgers U.; JD, Rutgers Camden Sch. Law. Ptnr. Saul Ewing, LLP; ins. commr. State of Md., 1997—2003; exec. v.p. health plan ops., Md. CEO Amerigroup Corp., 2004—07, sr. v.p. state & govt. rels., 2008—10; dep. dir. oversight, Office Consumer Info. & Ins. Oversight, US Dept. Health & Human Services, Washington, 2010—11, dep. adminstr., dir. Ctr. Consumer Info. & Ins. Oversight (CCIIO), 2011—. Chmn. Md. Pub. Svc. Commn., 2007. Recipient Disting. Pub. Svc. award, Md. Hosp. Assn., 2003. Mailing: Centers for Medicare & Medicaid Services 7500 Security Blvd Windsor Mill MD 21244 Office Phone: 757-490-6900. Office Fax: 757-222-2330. Business E-Mail: slarsen@amerigroupcorp.com. *

LARSON, DALE GEORGE, psychology professor; b. Joliet, Ill., Jan. 28, 1949; BA, U. Chgo., 1971; PhD, U. Calif. Berkeley, 1977. Prof. Santa Clara U., 1982—. Sr. editor Finding Our Way: Living With Dying in America, 2000—01. Recipient Kara Pioneer award, Palo Alto, Calif.; scholar, Fulbright Orgn. Fellow: APA (Counseling and Health Psychology Divsns.); mem.: Internat. Work Group Death,

Dying, and Bereavement. Avocations: backpacking, basketball. Office: Santa Clara University Dept Counseling Psychology Santa Clara CA 95053-0201 Office Fax: 408-554-2392. Business E-Mail: dlarson@scu.edu.

LARSON, DANIEL E., retired foundation administrator; Regional dir. Fellowship Christian Athletes, 1977—88; nat. mgmt. cons. Nat. Multiple Sclerosis Soc., 1988—93; pres., CEO Polycystic Kidney Disease Found., 1993—2011, sr. advisor, CEO-emeritus, 2011—. Office: Polycystic Kidney Disease Found 9221 Ward Pky Ste 400 Kansas City MO 64114-3367 Office Phone: 816-268-8455. *

LARSON, DAVID LEE, surgeon; b. Kansas City, Mo., Dec. 9, 1943; s. Leonard Nathaniel and Mary Elizabeth (Stuck) L.; m. Sherrill Ankli, Apr. 16, 1977; children: Jeffrey David, Dawn Elizabeth, Bradley Jesse. BS, Bowling Green State U., 1965; MD, La. State U., 1969. Diplomate Am. Bd. Plastic Surgery (bd. dirs. 1996—, sec.-treas. 1998—). Intern Charity Hosp. of La., New Orleans, 1969-70; resident otolaryngology Baylor Coll. Medicine, Houston, 1972-76; plastic surgery resident Ind. U., Indpls., 1976-78; surgeon M.D. Anderson Cancer Ctr., Houston, 1978-85; prof., chmn. dept. plastic and reconstructive surgery Med. Coll Wis., Milw., 1986—, George S. Korkos prof. plastic surgery, 2007. Alano J. Ballantyne prof. in head and neck surgery M.D. Anderson Cancer Ctr., Houston, 1985; sec.-treas. Am. Bd. Plastic Surgery, 1996-2002. Editor: Cancer in the Neck, 1987, Essentials of Head and Neck Oncology, 1998. Capt. USNR, 1991—. Mem. Am. Assn. Plastic Surgeons, Nat. Inst. Healthcare Rsch. (chmn. bd. dirs. 1995-2000), Plastic Surgery Ednl. Found. (pres. 2001—02). Avocations: reading, exercise. Home: 13510 Braemar Dr Elm Grove WI 53122-2509 Office: Med Coll Wis 8700 Watertown Plank Rd Milwaukee WI 53226-3522 E-mail: dlarson@mcw.edu.

LARSON, ERIC B., medical educator, director, internist; BA in History (with great distinction), Stanford Univ., Stanford, Calif, 1969; MD, Harvard Med. Sch., 1973; MPH, U. Wash. Sch. Pub. Health, Seattle, Wash., 1977. Cert. Nat. Bd. Med. Examiners (Parts I, II, III), 1974, diplomate Am. Bd. Internal Medicine, 1977, lic. Wash., 1975. Assoc. diener, dept. pathology Children's Hosp., Boston, 1969—71; intern, medicine Beth Israel Hosp., Harvard Med. Sch., Boston, 1973—74, asst. resident, medicine, 1974—75; internist, outpatient dept. Harborview Med. Ctr., Seattle, 1975—77; rsch. assoc. Va. Mason Hosp./Rsch. Found., Seattle, 1975—77; chief resident, medicine U. Hosp., Seattle, 1977—78, attending physician, 1977—; Robert Wood Johnson Clin. scholar, sr. fellow, dept. medicine U. Wash., Seattle, 1975—77, assoc. dean clin. affairs; med dir. U. Wash. Med. Ctr., 1989—2002; sr. investigator, dir., Group Health Coop. Ctr. for Health Studies, Seattle, 2002—06, exec. dir., Group Health Coop., 2006—. Instructor, medicine Harvard Med. Sch., Boston, 1973—75; acting instructor, medicine U. Wash. Sch. Medicine, Seattle, 1977—78, assoc. dean for clin. affairs, 1989—2002; asst. prof., medicine U. Wash., Seattle, 1978—82, assoc. prof., medicine, 1982—88, prof. medicine, 1988—; adj. asst. prof., cmty. medicine Sch. Pub. Health, Seattle, 1979—82; adj. assoc. prof., health services & cmty. medicine U. Wash. Sch. Pub. Health, Seattle, 1982—88, adj. prof., health services & cmty. medicine, 1988—; sect. head, gen. internal medicine U. Hosp., Seattle, 1988—89; sr. investigator and dir. Ctr. for Health Studies, Group Health Coop., 2002; commr. Joint Commn. for Accreditation Health Care Orgns., 1999—. Contbr. articles to profl. jours.; assoc. editor: Jour. of Gen. Internal Medicine, 1989—94, editl. bd.: Annals of Internal Medicine, 1992—95, Health Services Rsch., 1994—, Am. Jour. Medicine, 1997—, Primary Care Case Reviews, 1988—, editl. adv. bd.: Rsch. and Practice, 1998—. Nat. reviewer, abstract selection Soc. of Gen. Internal Medicine (SGIM), 1984, co-chmn., NW regional mtg., 1983, chmn., NW regional mtg., 1986, regional rep., 1986—87, coun., 1986—89, pres., 1994—95; commr. Joint Commn. on Accreditation of Healthcare Orgns., 2003; nat. reviewer Am. Fedn. for Clin. Rsch.-Clin. Epidemiology-Health Care Rsch., 1983—88, western regional reviewer, 1985, chmn., abstract selection, 1990 Nat. Mtg., 1989—90; DHHS Adv. Panel on Alzheimer's Disease Office of Tech. Assessment, 1987—89, chmn., 1993—98. Henry J. Kaiser Family Found. Faculty Scholar in Gen. Internal Medicine, 1981. Fellow: ACP (regent 1998—2006, chmn. publications comm. 2000—03, chair-elect, bd. regents 2003, chair, bd. regents 2004, master 2006, George Morris Piersol Tchg. and Rsch. Scholar 1978, Laureate award, Wash. Chpt. 2006); mem.: AMA, Inst. Medicine, ACP Jour. Club (editl. adv. bd. 1990—), Wash. State Medical Soc., King County Med. Soc. (editl. adv. bd. 1987—90), Am. Fedn. for Med. Rsch. (clin. epidemiology-Health Care Rsch., Nat. reviewer 1983—88, clin. epidemiology-Health Care Rsch., Western Regional Reviewer 1985, chmn., abstract selection 1990 Nat. Mtg. 1989—90), Seattle Acad. of Medicine, Soc. Gen. Internal Medicine (co-chmn., northwest regional mtg. 1983, nat. reviewer, abstract selection 1984, chmn., Northwest Regional Mtg. 1986, regional rep. 1986—87, councilor 1986—89, pres. 1994—95, Robert J. Glaser award 2004), Am. Clin. and Climatological Assn., Am. Soc. Clin. Investigation, Am. Geriatrics Soc. (editl. bd. 1988—91, Service award 1992), Assn. Am. Physicians, Phi Beta Kappa. Office: Ctr for Health Studies Ste 1600 1730 Minor Ave Seattle WA 98101-1448 Office Phone: 206-287-2988. Business E-Mail: larson.e@ghc.org. E-mail: ebl@u.washington.edu.

LARSON, KYLE SCOTT, marketing executive; b. Wichita, Kans., Feb. 20, 1987; BA in Mktg., Wichita State U., 2011; M in Healthcare Leadership, Friends U. Bus. mgr. Ctr. Women's Health, 2009—. Mem.: Nat. Acad. Sports Medicine. Avocations: exercise, football, guitar. Office: 1855 N Webb Rd Wichita KS 67206 Office Fax: 316-634-0050. E-mail: klarson@cwhwichita.com.

LARSON, RICHARD ALLEN, physician, educator; b. SD, Feb. 20, 1951; MD, Stanford Sch. Medicine, 1977. Prof. medicine U. Chgo., 1983—. Office: University Chgo Med Ctr 2115 5841 S Maryland Ave Chicago IL 60637 Business E-Mail: rlarson@medicine.bsd.uchicago.edu.

LARSON, ROLAND ELMER, health facility administrator; b. Chgo., Jan. 21, 1939; s. Elmer Gustav and Anna (Alphida) L.; children: Eric R., Jennifer L., Melissa K. BA, Augustana Coll., 1961; MHA, U. Iowa, 1963; postgrad., Harvard U., 1978. Adminstrv. asst. U. Vt. Med. Ctr., Burlington, 1962-64; assoc. adminstr. Roger Williams Hosp., Providence, 1964-73; v.p. adminstrn. Norwalk (Conn.) Hosp., 1973-81; pres., chief exec. officer Nashoba Community Hosp., Ayer, Mass., 1981-88; v.p. Charles River Assn., Boston, 1988-90; cons. Charles River Assocs., Boston, 1990-93; ind. healthcare cons. Harvard, Mass., 1990—. Chmn. Harvard (Mass.) Coalition Against Drugs and Alcohol, Opportunities, Inc., Providence, 1966-68, Greater Norwalk Community Coun., 1980; bd. dirs. Nat. Arthritis Found., N.Y.C., 1967-71, Am. Cancer Soc., Stamford, Conn., 1978-81; bd. mem., Timberbrook Assn., Belmont, Mass. Fellow Am. Coll. Healthcare Execs.; mem. Cen. Mass. Hosp. Coun. (chmn. 1987-88), Rotary. Avocations: sailing, bicycling, golf, squash, woodworking. Home and Office: Larson & Assocs PO Box 602 Boylston MA 01505-0602

LARSON, SIGNE S., pediatrician; MD, SUNY, Stony Brook, 1978. Diplomate Am. Bd. Pediatrics, Am. Bd. Pediatrics-pediatric endocrinology. Resident in family medicine Vancouver Gen. Hosp., Canada, 1978—84; resident in pediat. St. Luke's Med. Ctr., NY, 1979—82; fellow in pediatric endocrinology Mt. Sinai Hosp., 1982—84; pediatrician Mt. Sinai Med. Ctr. Office: Mount Sinai Medical Center 1245 Pk Ave New York NY 10128 Office Phone: 212-427-0540. Office Fax: 212-534-1086.

LARSON, VICKI LORD, academic administrator, communication disorders educator; b. Prentice, Wis., Sept. 21, 1944; d. Edward A. and Stella Mae Lord; m. James Roy Larson, Sept. 3, 1966. BSEd, U. Wis., Madison, 1966, MS, 1968, PhD, 1974. Speech-lang. pathologist Coop. Ednl. Svc. Agy. 2, Minoqua, Wis., 1967—69; instr. U. Wis., Whitewater, 1969—71, rsch. asst. Madison, 1971—73, asst. prof. Eau Claire, 1973-77, assoc. prof., 1977—81, prof. communication disorders, 1981—91, dept. chair, 1978—83, asst. dean grad. studies and univ. rsch., 1984—89, assoc. dean grad. studies and univ. rsch., 1989—91, interim chancellor, 2005—06, prof. comm. Oshkosh, 1991—2000, dean Grad. Sch. Rsch., 1991—94, provost, vice chancellor acad. affairs, 1994—2000. Acquistions editor Thinking Publs., Eau Claire, 2001—04, acquistions mgr., 2004—06. Author: Adolescents: Communication Development and Disorder, 1983, Communication Assessment and Intervention Strategies for Adolescents, 1987; contbr. Handbook of Speech-Language Pathology and Audiology, 1988, Language Disorders in Older Students, 1995, Working Out With Listening, 2002, Communication Solutions for Older Students, 2003, S-MAPs curriculum-based assessment, 2004, Aspergers Syndrome: Strategies for Solving the Social Puzzle, 2005; contbr.: Working Out With Writing, 2005. Fellow: Am. Speech, Lang., Hearing Assn. (councilor); mem.: Wis. Speech, Lang., Hearing Assn. (pres. 1976, honors 1991, pres. found. 2000—04, v.p. 2005—07, treas. 2005—07), Golden Key, Phi Kappa Phi, Omicron Delta Kappa. Avocations: traveling, quilting, reading. E-mail: larsonvl@uwec.edu.

LARSON BONCK, MAUREEN INEZ, rehabilitation consultant; b. Madison, Minn., Mar. 10, 1955; d. Alvin John and Leona B. (Bornhorst) Larson; m. Michael Bonck, Jan. 8. BFA in Psychology & Fine Arts cum laude, U. Minn., 1977; MA in Counseling & Guidance, U. N.D., 1978. Cert. vocational rehab. counselor, disability mgmt. specialist. Employment counselor II, coordinator spl. programs Employment Security div. State of Wyo., Rawlins, 1978-80; employment interviewer Employment Security divsn. State of Wash., Tacoma, 1980; lead counselor Comprehensive Rehab. Counseling, Tacoma, 1980-81; dir. counseling Cascade Rehab. Counseling, Tacoma, 1981-87, dist. mgr., 1987-90; regional mgr. Rainier Case Mgmt., Tacoma; owner Maureen Larson and Assocs., Gig Harbor, Wash., 1992—2005, Maureen Larson Consulting, Tacoma, 2005—; chair Facilities Commn., St. Vincent Paul Parish, Fed. Way, Wash., 2010—; pres. Northshore Homeowners, 2010—; bd. dirs. Assn. Tacoma, 2006—. State capt. legis. div. Provisions Project, Am. Pers. and Guidance Assn., 1980. Advocate Grand Forks (N.D.) Rape Crisis Ctr., 1977-78; mem. Pierce County YMCA; bd. dir. Boys and Girls Clubs of Tacoma, 1991-98, chair sustaining drive, 1991-98, sec.-treas., 1992-93, pres., 1994, auction com. and spl. events com.; founding bd. dir., bd. devel. chair, events chair, co-chmn. Literacy Plus!, 1999-2001; chairperson adv. bd. Gig Harbor br. Tacoma C.C., 2002—. State of Minn. scholar, 1973-77; recipient Alice Tweed Tuohy award U. Minn., 1977, Nat. Disting. Svcs. Registry award Libr. of Congress, 1987; named bd. mem. vol. of Yr. Boys and Girls Clubs of Tacoma, 1992. Mem.: Nat. Rehab. Adminstrs. Assn. (bd. dir. 1993), Nat. Rehab. Counseling Assn. (bd. dir. 1993, State of Wash. Counselor of Year 1991, Pacific Region Counselor of Year 1992), Nat. Rehab. Assn. (bd. dir. Olympic chpt. 1988—97, pres. 1990—91, chmn. state conf. planning com. 1993, 1996, 1990), Nat. Fedn. Bus. & Profl. Women (rec. sec. 1978—80, runner-up Young Careerists' Program 1980), Washington Self-Insured Assn., Rotary Gig Harbor Midday Club (charter mem., dir. vocat. svcs. 2002—08), Pi Gamma Mu. Avocations: sailing, aerobics, ballet, art. Office: M Larson Consulting 4325 Country Club Dr NE Tacoma WA 98422-4612 Office Phone: 253-943-5272. Office Fax: 253-943-5279. Business E-Mail: maureen@mlarsonconsulting.com.

LARSSON, MARIE, biology professor; b. Sweden, Aug. 27, 1966; PhD, Linköping U., Sweden, 1997. Prof. Linköping U., 2005. Office: Linköping University Molecular Virology Lab 1 plan 13 Linköping 58185 Sweden Business E-Mail: marie.larsson@liu.se.

LARSSON, P.G., obstetrician, gynecologist, consultant; b. Malmö, Sweden, Mar. 17, 1953; MD, U. Uppsala, 1980; PhD, U. Linköping, 1991. Cons. Dept. Ob-Gyn., 1987—. Prof. U. Skövde, 2008. Mem.: SFOG. Avocations: skiing, skateboarding. Office: Dept Obstetrics and Gynecology Kärns Skövde SE-541 85 Sweden Business E-Mail: p-g.larsson@vgregion.se.

LARWOOD, LAURIE, psychologist, artist; b. NY, Nov. 23, 1941; PhD, Tulane U., 1974. Pres. Davis Instruments Corp., San Leandro, Calif., 1966—71; cons., 1969—; asst. prof. orgnl. behavior SUNY, Binghamton, 1974—76; assoc. prof., chair dept. psychology Claremont (Calif.) McKenna Coll., 1976—83, assoc. prof. bus. adminstrn., 1976—83, Claremont Grad. Sch., 1976—85; prof., head dept. mgmt. U. Ill., Chgo., 1983—87; dean sch. bus. SUNY, Albany, 1987—90; dean Coll. Bus. Adminstrn. U. Nev., Reno, 1990—92, prof., 1990—2003, prof. emerita, 2003—; dir. Inst. Strategic Bus. Issues, 1992—2003; mng. ptnr. Quail Lane Studios, Tucson, 2003—. Western regional adv. coun. SBA, 1976-81; dir. Mgmt. Team; pres. Mystic Games, Inc.; mng. ptnr. Quail Lane Studios, 2003-. Author: (with M.M. Wood) Women in Management, 1977, Organizational Behavior and Management, 1984, Women's Career Development, 1987, Strategies-Successes-Senior Executives Speak Out, 1988, Women's Careers, 1988, Managing Technological Development, 1988, Impact Analysis, 1999; mem. editl. bd. Sex Roles, 1979-2003, Consultation, 1986-91, Jour. Orgnl. Behavior, 1987-2003, Jour. Vocat. Behavior, 1999-, Group and Orgn. Mgmt., 1982-84, editor, 1986-91; founding editor Women and Work, 1983, Jour. Mgmt. Case Studies, 1983-87; artist: artistic digital photography; contbr. articles to profl. jours. Mem.: Nat. Assn. Photoshop Profls., So. Ariz. Arts Guild. Libertarian. Office: Quail Ln Studios 10225 N Quail Ln Tucson AZ 85742 Mailing: Box 89789 Tucson AZ 85752 Personal E-mail: larwood@earthlink.net.

LASALA, JOHN M., cardiologist, medical educator; b. Stamford, Conn., Aug. 11, 1953; s. Alfred Lasala and Teresa Maria Del Monaco Lasala; m. Carolyn Francis Watkins, July 29, 1960; children: Stephanie, Erica, Olivia. BA in Chemistry with honors, Drew U., 1975; PhD in Anatomy and Neurobiology, St. Louis U., 1979; MD, U. Conn., 1983. Cert. cardiovascular and interventional cardiology Am. Bd. Internal Medicine. Postdoctoral fellow anatomy and neurobiology Washington U. Sch. Medicine, St. Louis, 1979; intern and resident dept. internal medicine Washington U. Sch. Medicine/Barnes-Jewish Hosp., St. Louis, 1983—86; asst. prof. medicine Washington U. Sch. Medicine, St. Louis, 1992—97; assoc. prof. medicine Washington U. Sch. Medicine/Barnes-Jewish Hosp., St. Louis, 1997—, dir. interventional cardiology, 1995—, dir. cardiac catherization lab., 1996—; fellow cardiology Yale U. Sch. Medicine, New Haven, 1986—89, interventional fellow cardiology, 1989—90; pvt. practice St. Louis, 1990—91. Spkr. in field. Editor: Video Jour. Cardiology, 1993—95; mem. editl. bd.:, Coronary Artery Disease, Circulation, Catheterization & Cardiovasc. Diagnosis, Am. Jour. Cardiology, Am. Heart Jour., Jour. Thoracic Surgery, Jour. Hypertension; contbr. articles to profl. jours. Recipient Outstanding Cardiology Alumnus award, Yale U. Sch. Medicine, 2000; named a Best Doctor in America, St. Louis mag., 2007; Med. Student Rsch. grantee, March of Dimes, 1980, Am. Heart Assn. Rsch. fellow, 1988. Fellow: Soc. for Cardiac Angiography and Intervention; mem.: Am. Heart Assn., Am. Coll. Cardiology. Office: Washington Univ Sch Medicine 660 S Euclid Ave 14100 Queeny Tower Saint Louis MO 63110 also: One Barnes-Jewish Hospital Plz Saint Louis MO 63110 Home Phone: 314-362-3729. Fax: 314-747-1417. E-mail: jlasala@im.wustl.edu.

LAŠAS, LIUDVIKAS, biotechnologist; b. Kaunas, Lithuania, June 4, 1933; s. Vladas and Janina (Mackevičaite) L.; m. Danute Terese Mockute, Aug. 14, 1965; children: Lina, Tomas. Diploma in Biotechnology, Kaunas Technol. U., 1956, PhD, 1962; DS, St. Peterburg Technol. Inst., Russia, 1989. From asst. to assoc. prof. Kaunas Technol. U., 1959—78; prof. Kaunas U. Medicine, 1993; chief lab. Inst. Endocrinology br. Kaunas Med. Acad. former USSR, 1978—90; dir. Inst. Endocrinology Kaunas U. Medicine, 1990—2004, head rsch. lab., 1990—, chmn. coun. Inst. Endocrinology, 1993—; dir. Endocrinology Ctr. Lithuania, Kaunas, 1994—. Dir. rsch. lab. Plant Endocrinic Preparations, Kaunas, 1971-86; prof. Med. Univ., Kaunas, 1993—; mem. senate, bd. dirs. Med. Univ., Kaunas, 1991—2004. Author: Human Growth Hormone, 1982, Obesity and its Treatment, 1998, Human Growth Hormone, Its Deficit and Treatment, 2003, Sources and Development of Endocrinology of Lithuania, Who is Who, 2006, Inst. Endocrinology, 2007, Turner Syndrome, 2008, Diagnosis, Monitoring and treatment of Turner Syndrome, 2009; contbr. over 300 articles to profl. jours. Named Inventor of USSR, 1986; recipient Laureate of Vladas Lašas (Nominal Premium medicine) Acad. Scis. Lithuania, 2001. Mem. Internat. Growth Hormone Rsch. Soc., Internat. Soc. Endocrinologists, Internat. Osteoporosis Fedn. (bd. dirs.). Achievements include 30 patents and inventions. Avocations: reading, nature. Office: Inst Endocrinology Kaunas U Medicine Eiveniu 2 LT-50009 Kaunas 7 Lithuania Home: Aukstaiciu G. 37 44158 Kaunas Lithuania Home Phone: 370 37 200848; Office Phone: 370 37 797888. Business E-Mail: liudvikas.lasas@med.kmu.lt.

LASBLEIZ, JEREMY, radiologist, researcher; b. Granville, France, July 23, 1972; s. Alain and Veronique Lasbleiz; m. Murielle Cantin, Sept. 6, 2003; children: Simon, Capucine. MD, U. Rennes, France, 2005. With U. Caen, France, 1990—98, U. Rennes, 1998—2005. Contbr. articles to profl. jours. Home: 24 Rue Des Courtines Montgermont 35760 France Personal E-mail: jeremy.lasbleiz@laposte.net.

LASHER, LARA ELAINE, epidemiologist, researcher; d. Lawrence and Natalia Lasher. BS in Microbiology with honors, U. Calif., Santa Barbara, 1995; MPH in Epidemiology, UCLA, 2003. Instr. yoga and fitness Kabala Resort, Hawaii Athletic Club, Honolulu Club, 1989—; rsch. writer Hawaii State Dept. Health, Honolulu, 2002—06, epidemiologist, 2004—06, influenza surveillance coord., 2005—06. Tchg. asst. med. microbiology U. Hawaii, Honolulu, 2000—01; rsch. asst. lung cancer study UCLA, LA, 2001—03. Contbr. articles to profl. jours. Pres. Golden Key Nat. Honor Soc., Santa Barbara, 1994—95. Mem.: Golden Key Nat. Honor Soc. (life; pres. 1994—95, Grad. award 1995). Avocations: mountain hiking, ocean swimming, marathon running, yoga, skydiving.

LASHLEY, FELISSA ROSE, dean, nursing educator, researcher; b. NYC, Apr. 6, 1941; d. Jack and Ruth (Dorbin) Lashley; divorced; children: Peter, Heather, Neal. BS, Adelphi Coll., 1961; MA, NYU, 1965; PhD, Ill. State U., 1973. Cert. Am. Bd. Med. Genetics., Am. Coll. Med. Genetics. Dean Coll. Nursing, Rutgers U., Newark, 2002—. Author: Clinical Genetics in Nursing Practice, 1998 (book of yr. award); editor: The Person with AIDS: Nursing Perspectives, 1987 (Book of Yr. award), Tuberculosis: A Sourcebook for Nursing Practice and Women, Children and HIV/AIDS (Book of Yr. award, 1993), Emerging Infectious Diseases: Trends and Issues, 2002, The Person with HIV/AIDS: Nursing Perspectives, 2000. Mem.: AAAS, ANA (coun. nurse researchers), Am. Coll. Med. Genetics, Ill. Nurses Assn., Midwest Nursing Rsch. Soc., Nat. League Nursing, Am. Acad. Nursing, Am. Soc. Human Genetics. Office Phone: 973-353-5293 ext. 647. Business E-Mail: flashley@rutgers.edu.

LASHOF, JOYCE COHEN, public health service officer, educator; b. Phila. d. Harry and Rose (Brodsky) Cohen; m. Richard K. Lashof, June 11, 1950; children: Judith, Carol, Dan. AB, Duke U., 1946; MD, Women's Med. Coll., 1950; DSc (hon.), Med. Coll. Pa., 1983. Dir. Ill. State Dept. Pub. Health, 1973—77; dep. asst. sec. for health programs and population affairs Dept. Health, Edn., and Welfare, Washington, 1977—78; sr. scholar in residence IOM, Washington, 1978; asst. dir. office of tech. assessment U.S. Congress, Washington, 1978—81; dean sch. pub. health U. Calif., Berkeley, 1981—91; prof. pub. health U. Calif. Sch. Pub. Health, Berkeley, 1981—94, prof. emeritus, 1994—. Co-chair Commn. on Am. after Roe vs. Wade, 1991—92; mem. Sec.'s Coun. Health Promotion and Disease Prevention, 1988—91; chair Pres.'s Adv. Com. on Gulf War Vets. Illnesses, 1995—97. Mem. editl. bd.: Wellness Letter, 1984—, Ann. Rev. of Pub. Health, 1987—90. Recipient Alumni Achievement award, Med.

Coll. Pa., 1975, Sedgewick Meml. medal, APHA, 1995. Avocation: hiking. Office: U Calif Sch Pub Health 140 Earl Warren Hl Berkeley CA 94720-7360 Home: 2431 Mariner Square Dr Apt 105 Alameda CA 94501-1679 Office Phone: 510-642-2493. Business E-Mail: jlashof@berkeley.edu.

LASK, GARY P., dermatologist, educator; MD, Universidad Autonoma de Guadalajara, 1977; grad., U. So. Calif. Diplomate Am. Bd. Dermatology, 1983. Resident dermatology Martin Luther King Jr Hosp., LA, 1980—83, intern, fellow dermatology; clin. prof. Ronald Reagan UCLA Med. Ctr., dir. dermatologic surgery service, dir. Dermatology Laser Ctr., dir. mohs' micrographic skin cancer surgery unit. Office: Ste 530 16260 Ventura Blvd Encino CA 91436 Office Phone: 818-788-4022.

LASKAR, MOHAMMED SHAWKATUZZAMAN, medical educator; b. Gopalgonj, Bangladesh, June 1, 1967; MD, Tashkent State Med. Inst., Uzbekistan, 1993; PhD, Yamaguchi U. Sch. Medicine, Japan, 2000. Prof. cmty. medicine, vice prin., with governing body MH Samorita Med. Coll. & Hosp., 2011—. Postdoc. Rsch. fellowship, Japan Soc. Promotion Sci. Mem.: Japanese U. Alumni Assn. Bangladesh. Avocations: movies, music, reading. Office: 13/A Panthapath Dhaka 1215 Bangladesh E-mail: laskarms@gmail.com.

LASKE, DOUGLAS W., neurosurgeon, educator; MD, Columbia U., 1985. Lic. Pa., 1995, diplomate Am. Bd. Neurol. Surgery, 1996, lic. NJ, 2010. Intern in gen. surgery Va. Commonwealth Univ. Med. Ctr., 1986, resident in neurosurgery, 1991; fellow in neurology NIH Clin. Ctr.; asst. prof. neurosurgery Temple Univ. Health Sciences Ctr., Pa.; hosp. affiliations include Fox Chase Cancer Ctr., Temple Univ. Hosp. Mem.: Fox Chase Temple: Neuro-Oncology Program (dir.). Office: Temple University Hospital 3401 N Broad St Philadelphia PA 19140 Office Phone: 215-707-7200.

LASKEY, RICHARD ANTHONY, biomedical device executive; b. NYC, Oct. 24; s. Charles Lewis and Gertrude Ann (Stolzenhaler) L.; m. Frances M. Pollack; children: Victoria Ann, Deborah Lea. BS in Chemistry, MS in Organic Chemistry; PhD in Organic Chemistry, Sussex U., Eng.; JD, U. Chgo.; MD (hon.), Med. Coll. S.A., fellow psychiatry, 1976; postgrad. in ob-gyn., U. Pa., 1989-99; CME, Yale John Hopkins Harvard Med. Sch. Diplomate Am. Bd. Examiners in Psychotherapy. With Hydron Labs., North Brunswick, NJ; v.p. biomed. rsch. Datascope Corp., Paramus, NJ; pres., CEO Millbrook Labs., Inc., Rochelle Park, 1982-2000. Cons. in field; inventor, patentee. Recipient Doctor's award Chgo. Med. Coll., 1975; fellow Am. Acad. Behavioral Sci., 1976. Fellow Am. Inst. Chemists; mem. NRA, AAAS, Md. Med. Soc., Idaho Med. Soc., Nat. Med. Soc., Internat. Coll. Physicians and Surgeons, Am. Inst. Chemist, Am. Psychotherapy Assn., Nat. Psychol. Assn., Assn. Advancement Med. Instrumentation, Soc. Rsch. Adminstrs. Biomed., Am. Soc. Reproductive Medicine, 1997, Harvard Med. Sch. Post Grad. Assn. E-mail: [illegible]

LASKIN, DANIEL M., oral and maxillofacial surgeon, educator; b. Ellenville, NY, Sept. 3, 1924; s. Nathan and Flora (Kaplan) L.; m. Eve Pauline Mohel, Aug. 25, 1945; children: Jeffrey, Gary, Marla. Student, NYU, 1941—42; BS, Ind. U., 1947; MS, U. Ill., 1951; DSc (hon.), Ind. U., 2001. Diplomate Am. Bd. Oral and Maxillofacial Surgery, Am. Dental Bd. Anesthesiology. Faculty U. Ill., Chgo., 1949-84, prof. dept. oral and maxillofacial surgery, 1960-84, head dept., 1973-84, clin. prof. surgery, 1961-84, dir. temporomandibular joint and facial pain research center, 1963-84; prof., chmn. dept. oral and maxillofacial surgery Med. Coll. Va., Richmond, 1984—2002, chmn. emeritus, 2003, dir. temporomandibular joint and facial pain rsch. ctr., 1984—2002; affiliate clin. prof., dept. psychology Va. Commonwealth U.; head dept. dentistry MCV Hosp., Richmond, 1986—2002; former attending oral surgeon Edgewater, Swedish Covenant, Ill. Masonic, Skokie Valley Cmty. hosps., Chgo.; former chmn. dept. oral surgery Cook County Hosp., Chgo. Cons. oral surgery to Surgeon Gen. Navy, 1977-83; dental products panel FDA, 1988-92, cons., 1993-95; Francis J. Reichmann Lectr., 1971, Cordwainer lectr., London, 1980, Donald B. Osborn Meml. lectr., 1999. Author: Oral and Maxillofacial Surgery, Vol. I, 1980, Vol. II, 1985; contbr. articles to profl. jours.; editor-in-chief: Jour. Oral and Maxillofacial Surgery, 1972-2002; mem. editl. bd. Internat. Jour. Oral and Maxillofacial Surgery, 1978-88, Topics in Pain Mgmt., Densat, Internat. Jour. Oral and Maxillofacial Implants, Quintessence Internat., Revista Latino America Cirugia Traumatologia Maxilofacial, Va. Dental Jour., Jour. Dental Rsch.; mem. internat. editl. bd. Headache Quar.; mem. editl. bd. Greek Jour. Oral and Maxillofacial Surgery, Electronic Jour. Dentistry; assoc. editor Odontology; mem. internat. adv. bd. Asian Jour. Oral and Maxillofacial Surgery; OMFS editor Jewish Med. Jour. Nat. hon. chmn. peer campaign A.A.O.M.S. Edn. and Rsch. Found., 1990; bd. dirs. Internat. Assn. Oral and Maxillofacial Surgeons Found.; chmn. Nat. Acad. Dentistry, 1997-99; pres.-elect Nat. Acad. of Practice, 1999, pres., 2002—04. Recipient Disting. Alumni Svc. award, Ind. U., 1975, William J. Gies editl. award 1st prize, 1978—79, 1984, 1987, 1989, 1992, 1996, 2001, Simon P. Hullihen Meml. award, 1976, Arnold K. Maislen Meml. award, 1977, Thomas P. Hinman medallion, 1980, W. Harry Archer Achievement award for rsch., 1981, Heidbrink award, 1983, Disting. Alumnus award, Ind. U. Sch. Dentistry, 1984, U. Ill. Coll. Dentistry, 2003, Rene Lefort medal, 1985, Semmelweis medallion, Semmelweis Med. U., 1985, Golden Scroll award, Internat. Coll. Dentists, 1986, Internat. award, Friends Sch. Dental Med., U. Conn. Health Ctr., Donald B. Osbon award, 1991, Achievement medal, Alpha Omega, 1992, Norton M. Ross Excellence in Clin. Rsch. award, 1993, Va. Commonwealth U. Faculty award of excellence, 1994, named Zendium Lectr., 1989, Edward C. Hinds Lectr., 1990, Disting. Practitioner Nat. Acads. Practice, 1992, Hon. Diplomate Am. Soc. Osseointegration, 1992, Silver Scroll award, Internat. Coll. Dentists, 2004, Distinction medal, U. Seville, 2005, Alumni Achievement award, U. Ill., 2006; named Laskin Lectureship, U. Ill. Coll. Dentistry, 2009; fellow in dental surgery, Glasgow Royal Coll. Physicians and Surgeons (hon.), Royal Coll. Surgeons Eng. Fellow: AAAS, Am. Acad. Implant Prosthodontists (academia), Internat. Coll. Dentists (Spl. Editl. citation 1999, Silver Scroll award 2004), Am. Coll. Dentists (Lifetime Achievement award 2007), Acad. Internat. Dental Studies (hon.), Internat. Assn. Oral and Maxillofacial Surgeons (hon.; exec. com. 1980—95, pres. 1983—86, sec. gen. 1989—95, exec. dir. 1995—99, gen. chmn. 14th Internat. Conf. on Oral and Maxillofacial Surg. 1999, found. cons.); mem.: ADA (adv. com. advanced edn. in oral surgery 1968—75, cons. Coun. on Dental Edn. 1968—82, mem. Commn. on Accreditation 1975—76), Colo. Soc. Oral & Maxillofacial Surgeons (Lifetime Achievement award 2009), Internat. Jour. Dentistry (editl. bd. mem.), Hungarian Assn. Oral and Maxillofacial Surgeons, Odontographic Soc., William F. Harrigan Soc., Nat. Chronic Pain Outreach Assn. (adv. bd.), Am. Dental Bd. Anesthesiology (pres. 1983—92), Japanese Soc. for Temporomandibular Joint (hon.), Am. Soc. Laser in Dentistry (hon.), Internat. Study Group for Advancement of TMJ Arthroscopy (hon.), Can. Assn. Oral and Maxillofacial Surgeons (hon.), Japanese Soc. Oral and Maxillofacial Surgeons (hon.), Scandinavian Assn. Oral and Maxillofacial Surgeons (hon.), Turkish Assn. Oral and Maxillofacial Surgeons (hon.), Phillipine Coll Oral & Maxillofacial Surgeons (hon.), Edward H. Angle Soc. Orthodontists (hon.), Brazilian Coll. Oral and Maxillofacial Surgery and Traumatology (hon.), Chilean Soc. Oral and Maxillofacial Surgery (hon.), Hellenic Assn. Oral Surgery (hon.), Sadi Fontaine Acad. (hon.), Internat. Congress Oral Implantologists (hon.), Soc. Maxillofacial and Oral Surgeons South Africa (hon.), Royal Soc. Medicine, Am. Assn. Dental Editors, Am. Soc. Exptl. Pathology, Am. Dental Soc. Anesthesiology (pres. 1976—78), Internat. Assn. Dental Rsch., Am. Assn. Oral and Maxillofacial Surgeons (editor Forum 1965—96, pres. 1976—77, editor AAOMS Today 1996—, Disting. Svc. award 1972, rsch. recognition award 1978, William J. Gies award 1979, dedication 73d ann. meeting and sci. sessions 1991), Ill. Splty. Bd. Oral Surgery, Sigma Xi, Omicron Kappa Upsilon. Rsch. and publs. on connective tissue physiology and pathology, particularly cartilage and bone metabolism, craniofacial growth, oral maxillofacial surgery, and pathology of temporomandibular joint. Office: Va Commonwealth U Dept Oral/Maxillofac Surg PO Box 980566 Richmond VA 23298-0566 Office Phone: 804-828-3547. Business E-Mail: dmlaskin@vcu.edu.

LASKIN, KEITH J., gastroenterologist; BA in Biology magna cum laude, Harvard U., 1979; MD, NYU. Diplomate Am. Bd. Internal Medicine, Am. Bd. Internal Medicine-gastroenterology. Resident internal medicine Temple Univ. Hosp., fellow gastroenterology; on-staff Paoli Hosp., 1989—, med. dir. Celiac Ctr., attending physician; physician Main Line Endoscopy Ctr. Contbr. articles on inflammatory bowel disease and on the use of laser treatment for esophageal cancer. Mem. Celiac Disease Found, Crohn's and Colitis Found. of Am. Recipient Sol Sherry award for Clin. Rsch., Komarov prize for Clin. Rsch. Mem.: ACP, Am. Coll. of Gastroenterology, Am. Soc. of Gastrointestinal Endoscopy, Celiac Sprue Assn., Am. Gastroent. Assn., Alpha Omega Alpha. Office: Main Line Gastroenterology Associates 2nd Fl 325 W Central Ave Malvern PA 19355 Office Phone: 610-644-6755. Fax: 610-647-2063.

LASKO, ALLEN HOWARD, pharmacist; b. Chgo., Oct. 27, 1941; s. Sidney P. and Sara (Hoffman) L.; m. Janice Marilynn Chess, Dec. 24, 1968 (div. Aug. 1993); children: Stephanie Paige, Michael Benjamin. BS, U. Ill., 1964. Staff pharmacist Michael Reese Hosp. and Med. Ctr., Chgo., 1964-68; clin. pharmacist City of Hope Med Ctr., Duarte, Calif., 1968-73; chief pharmacist Monrovia (Calif.) Cmty. Hosp, 1973-74, Santa Fe Meml. Hosp., L.A., 1974-77; pvt. investor, 1977-93; clin. pharmacist Foothill Presbyn. Hosp., Glendora, Calif., 1993—. Author: Diabetes Study Guide, 1972, A Clinical Approach to Lipid Abnormalities Study Guide, 1973, Jet Injection Tested As an Aid in Physiologic Delivery of Insulin, 1973. Mem. Magic Castle. Recipient Roche-Hosp. Pharmacy rsch. award, 1972-73; James scholar U. Ill. Mem. Mensa (life), Rho Pi Phi. Jewish. Home: 376 Hill St Monrovia CA 91016-2340 Office: Foothill Presbyn Hosp 250 S Grand Ave Glendora CA 91741-4218 E-mail: allenlasko@aoi.com.

LASKY, RICHARD DONALD, psychoanalyst, educator; b. NYC, Jan. 22, 1943; s. Sidney Lasky and Alice Presser; m. Judith Faye Sherman. PhD in Psychology, NYU, 1970, postdoctoral cert., 1974. Lic. psychologist, N.Y.; diplomate Am. Bd. Profl. Psychology. Jr. rsch. scientist Rsch. Found. State N.Y., Downstate Med. Ctr., SUNY, Bklyn., 1964-68; asst. prof. L.I. Univ., Greenvale, N.Y., 1969-74; clin. assoc., supr. psychologist doctoral program psychology CUNY, NYC, 1975—; assoc. dean tng. Inst. Psychoanalytic Tng. and Rsch., NYC, 1985—2000; clin. prof. psychology postdoctoral program NYU, 1990—. Author: Multiple Personality and the Related Dissociative Disorders, 1984, Dynamics of Development and the Therapeutic Process, 1993; editor: Symbolization and Desymbolization: Essays in Honor of Norbert Freedman, 2002. Rsch. fellow VA, 1968, NIMH fellow, 1969-71. Fellow Acad. of Psychoanalysis; mem. APA, Internat. Psycho-Analytical Assn., Am. Psychoanalytic Assn., Nat. Register of Health Care Providers in Psychology. Office Phone: 212-595-0442. E-mail: richardlasky@nyc.rr.com.

LASLETT, LAWRENCE J., physician, educator; b. Boston, Apr. 17, 1942; BS, Iowa State U., Ames, 1964; MD, U. Iowa, Iowa City, 1969. Diplomate in internal medicine, cardiology and interventional cardiology Am. Bd. Internal Medicine. Intern Hennepin County Gen. Hosp., Mpls., 1969-70; resident in internal medicine U. Calif., Davis, 1973-76, fellow in cardiology, 1976-78, asst. prof. clin. medicine, 1978-85, assoc. prof. clin medicine, 1985-96, dir. fellowship tng. in cardiology, 1994—2002, prof. clin. medicine, 1996—2004, prof. emeritus, 2005—; dir. cardiac catheterization lab. U. Calif. Davis Med. Ctr., Sacramento, 1984-94. Contbr. articles to med. jours. Mem. tech. adv. com. on free-standing catheterization labs. Calif. Dept. Health Svcs., Sacramento, 1990-94. Served to lt. comdr. USPHS, 1969-71. Fellow Am. Coll. Cardiology (past chair Calif. chpt. and nat. govt. rels. coms., No. Calif. gov. 2003-06). Office: U Calif Davis Divsn Cardiology 4860 Y St Ste 2800 Sacramento CA 95817-2307 Office Phone: 916-734-3764. Business E-Mail: ljlaslett@ucdavis.edu.

LASMEZAS, CORINNE IDA, neuroscientist, researcher; b. Paris, Jan. 2, 1968; Degree, Toulouse Vet. Sch., France, 1990; MS in Aeronautic and Space Medicine, Toulouse U. Medicine, 1990; DVM, Toulouse U., 1993; MS in Neuroscience, Pierre & Marie Curie U., Paris, 1991, PhD in Neuroscience, 1995; degree in Neurolinguistic Program, 2004. Asst. prof. Coll. Indsl. Physics & Chemistry, Paris, 1996; prin. investigator Atomic Energy Commn., Fontenay-aux-Roses, France, 1997—2002, dir. prion pathogenesis lab., 2002—05; prof. Scripps Rsch. Inst., Jupiter, Fla., 2005—. Mem. Spongiform Encephalopathy Adv. Com., London, 2003—09; advisor Dept. Environment, Food and Rural Affairs, London, 2003—; coun. mem. Gerson Lehrman Group, NYC, 2004—; expert prion diseases WHO, US Govtl. Agys. and European Agy.; reviewer Nat. Inst. Health. Contbr. articles to profl. publs.; reviewer (profl. jours. articles). Achievements include patents in field. Avocations: singing, cello, swimming, skiing, dance, Aikido. Office: Scripps Rsch Inst 130 Scripps Way #3C1 Jupiter FL 33458 Office Fax: 561-228-3098. Business E-Mail: lasmezas@scripps.edu.

LASS, JONATHAN HERSCHEL, ophthalmologist; b. Orange, NJ, July 14, 1949; s. David and Stella Lass; m. Leah Lass, Aug. 23, 1970; children: Michael, Jessica. BA magna cum laude, Boston U., 1972, MD cum laude, 1973. Diplomate Am. Bd. Ophthalmology, 1987. Rotating intern Mount Auburn Hosp., Cambridge, Mass., 1973-74; resident in ophthalmology Boston U. Med. Ctr., 1974-77; clin. fellow in ophthalmology Harvard Med. Sch. Mass. Eye/Ear, Boston, 1977-79; asst. prof. ophthalmology Case Western Res. U., Cleve., 1979-87, assoc. prof. ophthalmology, 1987-93, Charles I Thomas prof. ophthalmology, 1993—, chmn. dept. ophthalmology, 1994—; dir. dept. ophthalmology U. Hosps. of Cleve., 1994—; dir. Case Western Reserve U. Visual Scis. Rsch. Ctr., Cleve., 1996—. Active staff U. Hosp. of Cleve., 1979—, St. Vincent Charity Hosp., 2001—, UHHS Richmond Heights Hosp., 2001—; chmn. adv. com. Ophthalmic Technician Program, Lakeland Cmty. Coll., 1990—. Author: Corneal Surgery, 1986, Advances in Ocular Immunology, 1994; contbr. articles to profl. jours.; reviewer Investigative Ophthalmology and Vis. Sci., 1983—. Named Top Opthalmologist, Northern Ohio Live Mag., 2001; named one of Best Doctors in Cleve., Cleve. Mag., 2002-04. Am. Acad. Opthamology (honor award, 1987, sr. honor award, 2004), Assn. for Rsch. in Vision and Opthalmology, Cleve. Opthal. Soc., Contact Lens Assn. Opthalmologists, Cornea Soc., Eye Bank Assn. America, Northern Ohio Med. Assn., Ocular Microbiology and Immunology Group, Ohio Opthal. Soc., Phi Beta Kappa, Alpha Omega Alpha. Avocation: cleveland chamber music society. Home: 33176 Woodleigh Rd Pepper Pike OH 44124-5262 Office: U Hosps Case Med Ctr 11100 Euclid Ave Cleveland OH 44106-1736

LASSER, GAIL MARIA, psychologist, educator; b. Saddle River, NJ, Feb. 29, 1960; d. Dominick A. and Genevieve M. Sanzo; children: Michael, Jason, Jonathan. BA, Seton Hall U., 1971; postgrad., Seton HaLL u., 1975—77; tchg. cert., William Paterson Coll., 1973; MA, Montclair State Coll., 1975. Cert. staff clin. psychologist N.J., 1977; lic. real estate agt. N.J., 1977, notary pub. Pub. rel. rep. European Health Spa, 1970—71; med. asst. Sci. Prevention and Rehab. Assn., 1973; grad. tchg. and rsch. asst. Montclair State Coll., 1973—74; clin. asst. Dr. Brower, 1974; instr. psychology Essex County Coll., 1976—77; clin. psychologist intern Cmty. Mental Health Ctr., Mt. Carmel Guild, Newark, 1976—77; lectr. St. Michaels Med. Ctr.-N.J. Coll. Medicine, 1977—80; instr. psychology Bergen Cmty. Coll., Paramus, NJ, 1977—. Asst. to ct. adminstr. Bergen County Cts., 1977—78; cons. telecom., 1994. Vol. Am. Heart Assn. Mem.: Am. Soc. Phy. Rsch., Am. Psychol. Assn., Psi Chi, Pi Lambda Theta. Home: 7 Westwind Ct Saddle River NJ 07458-3211

LASSO DEL CASTILLO, JAIME LEONEL, obstetrician, gynecologist, director; b. Panama, Panama, Feb. 10, 1961; s. Jaime Leonel Lasso and Silvia Rene Del Castillo; m. Astrid Liliana Jaramillo, Dec. 6, 2001; m. Maria Elena Diaz, Apr. 20, 1982 (div. Oct. 20, 1995); children: Valeria Lasso, Michelle Marie Lasso, Andres Felipe Lasso, Jaime Leonel Lasso. MD with honors, U. Panama, Panama City, 1985, grad. in ob-gyn., 1991. Reproductive biology fellow U. Pa. Med. Ctr., Phila., 1992—94; med. dir. Clinic Reproduction, Panama, 1994—; co-dir. Panama Fertility Group, 2000—02. Sr. rschr. Ctr. for Rsch. in Human Reproduction WHO, Panama, 1994—96; ad honorem prof. U. Panama Sch. Medicine, 1994—; assoc. cons. physician Colombian Ctr. of Fertility and Sterility, Bogota, Colombia, 2003—; cons. editor Medica Mag., Panama, 2005—. Contbr. articles to profl. jours., chapters to books. Active Marine Live, Panama. Scholar, Rockefeller Found., 1992; Rsch. grant, 1994—96. Mem.: ACOG, Panama Soc. Ob-Gyn., Am. Soc. Reproductive Medicine, Nat. Assn. Forestation, Diablo Spinning Club, Panamenian Fishing and Yachts Club. Independent. Roman Catholic. Achievements include research in sperm antioxidants enzymes. Avocations: fishing, snorkeling, horses and cows farms, teak plantation for reforestation. Home: Altos Del Golf Panama 0832-2596 WTC Panama Office: Paitilla Med Ctr Marbella 53 ST 832 Panama Provincia de PanamÉf Panama Office Fax: 507 2062439. Personal E-mail: lassodelc@cableonda.net.

LASSWELL, MARCIA LEE, psychologist, educator; b. Oklahoma City, July 13, 1927; d. Lee and Stella (Blackard) Eck; m. Thomas Lasswell, May 29, 1950 (div. July 1990); children: Marcia Jane, Thomas Ely, Julia Lee. BA, U. Calif., Berkeley, 1949; MA, U. So. Calif., 1952; postgrad., U. Calif., Riverside, U. So. Calif., U. N.C. Individual practice psychotherapy, marriage/family therapy, Claremont, Calif.; asst. prof. Pepperdine Coll., LA, 1959—60; asst. prof. psychology behavioral sci. dept. Calif. State U., Pomona, 1960—64, assoc. prof., 1965—69, prof., 1970—, chmn. dept., 1964—69, emeritus, 2005—; assoc. clin. dir. Human Rels. Ctr. U. So. Calif., 1975—98. Vis. assoc. prof. Scripps Coll., 1968-69, U. So. Calif., 1969-70, Occidental Coll., 1971-72; lectr. various Calif. univs.; mem. staff spl. project alcoholics and narcotics offenders Calif. Prison System, 1970-73; mem. Calif. Accreditation Com. Secondary Schs. and Colls., 1965—1990; mem. commn. accreditation for marriage and family tng. US Dept. Edn., 1981-87. Author: College Teaching of General Psychology, 1967, Love, Marriage and Family, 1973, No-Fault Marriage, 1976, Styles of Loving, 1980, Marriage and Family, 1982, rev. edit., 1987, 91, Equal Time, 1983. Recipient Outstanding Tchrs. award Calif. State U., 1971, Outstanding Contbn. to Marriage and Family Therapy, 1991, Disting. Clin. Mem. award Calif. Assn. Marriage and Family Therapists, 1995, award Outstanding Marriage and Family Therapy Orgn., 1999; named Outstanding Woman of Yr. LA City Club, 2010. Fellow Am. Assn. Marital and Family Therapy (bd. dirs. 1970-72, 87-91, pres. elect 1993-95, pres. 1995-97, past pres. 1997-98); mem. AAAS, Nat. Coun. Family Rels. (exec. com. 1978-80), Am. Acad. Family Therapy, So. Calif. Assn. Marital and Family Therapy (pres. 1972-73), Groves Family Conf. Acad., Groves Family Conf. (sec. 2001-2004), Alpha Kappa Delta, Phi Delta Gamma, Pi Gamma Mu. Home: 800 W 1st St Apt 2908 Los Angeles CA 90012-2444 Office: 250 W First St # 352 Claremont CA 91711 Office Phone: 909-624-4641. Personal E-mail: mlass@aol.com.

LASTER, LEONARD, internist, gastroenterologist, academic administrator, educator, writer, researcher; b. NYC, Aug. 24, 1928; s. Isaac and Mary (Ehrenreich) L.; m. Ruth Ann Leventhal, Dec. 16, 1956; children: Judith Eve, Susan Beth, Stephen Jay. AB, Harvard U., Cambridge, Mass., 1949, MD, 1950. Diplomate Nat. Bd. Med. Examiners, Am. Bd. Internal Medicine (gastroenterology). From intern to resident medicine Mass. Gen. Hosp., Boston, 1950—53; vis. investigator Pub. Health Rsch. Inst., NYC, 1953—54; commd. lt. USPHS, 1954, advanced through grades to asst. surgeon gen. (rear adm.), 1971, ret., 1973; exec. dir. Assembly Life Scis., also divsn. med. scis. NAS-NRC, 1973—74; v.p. acad. and clin. affairs Med. Ctr., also dean Coll. Medicine, prof. medicine SUNY Downstate Med. Ctr.,

Bklyn., 1974—78; pres., prof. medicine Oreg. Health Scis. U., Portland, 1978—87; chancellor U. Mass. Med. Ctr., Worcester, 1987—90, chancellor emeritus, 1990—, Disting. prof. medicine and health policy, 1990—2002, emeritus, 2002—; adj. scientist Marine Biol. Lab., Woods Hole, Mass., 2002—. Bd. dirs. TEI Biosci., Boston; lab. investigator Marine Biol. Lab., Woods Hole, 1962—69, chmn. organizer symposia on nat. policy and biomed. scis., 1971—72, libr. reader, 1973—76; chmn. steering com. Falmouth Forum, 1994—2002, mem. coun. visitors, 2003—; cons. in field; mem. staff Nat. Inst. Arthritis, Metabolic and Digestive Diseases NIH, Bethesda, Md., 1954—73, chief digestive and hereditary diseases br., 1969—73; from spl. asst. to asst. dir. human resources Pres.'s Office Sci. and Tech., 1969—73; instr. medicine Harvard Med. Sch., Mass. Gen. Hosp., 2007—; mem. Harvard Inst. Learning in Retirement, 2007—. Author: Life After Medical School, 32 Doctors Describe How They Shaped Their Medical Careers, 1996; contbr. articles on gastrointestinal disease, inborn errors of metabolism, devel. biology to profl. jours.; contbr. op-ed column and other pieces to Washington Post, essays to Hosp. Practice and MD Mag. columnist Cape Cod Times, 2002-07. Columnist falmouth Enterprise, 2008-, Active Found. Advanced Edn. Scis., Bethesda, 1965-69, Bedford Stuyvesant Family Health Ctr., Bklyn., 1975-78, Med. Rsch. Found., Oreg., 1979-87, Oreg. Symphony, 1979-85, Oreg. Contemporary Theatre, 1981-83; pres. Burning Tree Elem. Sch. PTA, Bethesda, 1972-73; bd. dirs. Internat. Artists Series, Worcester, 1988-91, Mass. Biotech. Ctrs. for Excellence, Boston, 1988-96, Mass. Biotech. Rsch. Inst., Worcester, 1988-90, Worcester Bus. Devel. Corp., 1988-91; co-chmn. United Way Ctrl. Mass., COMEC Campaign, 1989; mem. exec. com. Worcester Econ. Club, 1988-91; mem. citizen gov. bd. Worcester Fights Back, 1990-95; chmn. corp. liaison com. Marine Biol. Lab., 1991-92; mem. Worcester Com. Fgn. Rels. (affiliated with Coun. Fgn. Rels.), 1992-96. Fellow gastro-enterology, Mass. Meml. Hosp., 1958—59. Fellow ACP; mem. Am. Fedn. Clin. Rsch., Am. Gastroenterol. Assn., Am. Soc. Biol. Chemists, Am. Soc. Clin. Investigation (emeritus), Marine Biol. Lab. Corp., Portland C. of C. (dir. 1980-84), Mass. Med. Soc., Harvard Inst. for Learning in Retirement (apptd. mem. 2007-), Cosmos Club, Harvard Club NYC, Harvard Club, Harvard Faculty Club, Phi Beta Kappa, Alpha Omega Alpha. Home and Office: 8 Lawrence Farm Rd Woods Hole MA 02543-1416 Personal E-mail: lencolumn@aol.com.

LASTER, RICHARD, biotechnologist, consultant; b. Vienna, Nov. 10, 1923; arrived in U.S., 1940, naturalized, 1944; s. Alan and Caroline (Harband) L.; m. Liselotte (Schneider), Oct. 17, 1948; children: Susan Laster Rubenstein, Thomas. Student, U. Wash., 1941-42; BChE cum laude, Poly. Inst. Bklyn., 1943; postgrad., Stevens Inst. Tech., 1945-47. With Gen. Foods Corp., 1944-82, corp. R & D Hoboken, NJ, 1944-58, ops. mgr. Franklin Baker divsn., 1958-64, ops. mgr. Atlantic gelatin divsn. Woburn, Mass., 1958-64, mgr. R & D Jell-O divsn. White Plains, NY, 1967-68, exec. v.p. Maxwell House divsn., 1968-69, pres. Maxwell House divsn., 1969-71, corp. v.p., 1971-73, exec. v.p., 1974-82, also dir. R & D and food-away-from-home, 1975-82. Bd. dirs., DNA Plant Tech. Corp., 1982-94, chmn., 1988-94, CEO, 1982-92, pres., 1982-91; mgmt. cons., 1994—; bd. dirs., Rice Tec; bd. dirs., vice chmn. Well Gen, Inc. Contbg. articles to profl. pub.; patentee in field. Mem. Sch. Bd., Chappaqua, NY, 1971—74, pres., 1973—74; chmn., bd. dirs., 1st v.p. United Way of Westchester, 1978; chmn. adv. com. Poly. Inst. Westchester, 1977; trustee Poly. Inst. N.Y., 1978—; mem. coll. coun. SUNY Purchase, Purchase Coll. Found., 1986—2007; mem. corp. N.Y. Bot. Garden; mem. subcom. export adminstrn. Pres.'s Export Coun., 1995; chmn. Westchester Edn. Coalition, 1992—2001, Holocaust & Human Rights Edn. Ctr., 1994—, Am. Soc. Plant Physiologists Edn. Found., 1995—2000; mem. New Castle Town Bd., 1996—2001; dir. Weizmann Inst., 2007—. Recipient Disting. Alumnus award, 1996, Disting. Svc. award,NCCJ, Poly Inst. N.Y. fellow. Mem. AAAS, AIChE (Food and Bioengring. award 1972), N.Y. Acad. Sci., Am. Chem. Soc., Am. Inst. Chemists, Tau Beta Pi, Phi Lambda Upsilon. Home: 23 Round Hill Rd Chappaqua NY 10514-1622 Office: 103 S Bedford Rd Mount Kisco NY 10549-3440 Home Phone: 914-238-8892; Office Phone: 914-241-4959. E-mail: rilaster@aol.com.

LASYS, JOAN, medical/surgical nurse, educator; b. Siauliai, Lithuania, Sept. 1, 1924; arrived in Can., 1948; came to U.S., 1960; d. Joseph-Apolinarius and Elena (Šlapokaite) Barceviõius; m. Bill Lasys, July 31, 1949. RN degree, Lithuanian Red Cross Sch. Nursing, 1945; student, Ariz. State U., Tempe, 1981—86, Ea. Ariz. Coll., Thatcher, 1981—86. RN, Can., Nebr.; cert. nursing tchr., Ariz.; C.C., occupl. tchg. cert. Ariz. Staff RN St. Mary's Hosp., Montreal, Canada, 1949—51, Montreal Gen. Hosp., 1951—53, 1959—60; pvt. duty Nurses Registry, Montreal, 1953—56; Can. civil svc. RN R.H.O. Ctr. Dept. Vets. Affairs, Ottawa, 1956—57, Queen Mary Vets. Hosp., Montreal, 1957-58; staff RN St. Joseph's Hosp., Omaha, 1968—69, Meryvale Hosp., Phoenix, 1969—71, Valley View Hosp., Youngtown, Ariz., 1971—72, Boswell Hosp., Sun City, Ariz., 1972—76; RN Kivel Care Ctr., Phoenix, 1986—93, 2000—02. Past v.p. and officer Pine-Strawberry Health Svcs., Ariz.; columnist/reporter Payson Roundup, Ariz. Pub. (mag.) Small Town U.S.A.; prodr. audio tapes: Time Management, Nursing Communications; author numerous poems Mem. Payson Regional Med. Ctr. Aux.; mem Rep. Presdl. Task Force. Recipient Bronze Poet of Merit medal, Poetry Conv. and Symposium Intl. Soc. Poets, 2005, Silver bowl Outstanding Achievement in Poetry, 2005, Crystal tower, 2006, Poetry Gold Medal of Excellence, Famous Poets, 2007; named Poet of Yr., Nat. Soc. Poetry, 2007. Mem.: AAUW, Libr. Congress, Nat. Mus. Women in the Arts, Payson Libr., County Attys. and Sheriffs Assn. (hon.), Kivel Geriatric Ctr. Aux. (life), Arbor Day Found., Nature Conservancy, Cooking Club of Am. (charter). Republican. Roman Catholic. Avocations: cooking, poetry, public speaking, arts and crafts. Home: 4029 E Pershing Ave Phoenix AZ 85032-6721

LÁSZLÓ, CZAKÓ, physician; b. Szeged, Hungary, Jan. 5, 1966; s. Czakó László and Csomor Piroska; m. Stájer Anette, Apr. 21, 2002; children: Bálint, Ákos Géza. Health economist, U. Szeged, 1999, med. diploma, 2000. Cert. specialist internal medicine Nat. Qualifying Bd., 1995, specialist endoscopy, gastroenterology, hepatology Nat. Qualifying Bd., 1998, specialist Diabetes Mellitus Nat. Qualifying Bd., 2006. Rsch. assoc. U. Szeged, 1990—95, asst. prof., 1995—2002, assoc. prof., 2002—. Recipient Medicom Glaxo award, Hungarian Soc., 1995, Young Investigator's award, Internat. Assn., 1998, award, World Gastroenterology Orgn., 1998, Bólyai János award, Hungarian Acad. Scis., 2004, Markusovszky Lajos díj, Orvosi Hetilap, 2006. Mem.: European Pancreatic Club (assoc.), Hungarian Soc. Gastroenterology (assoc. Most Valuable Gastroenterol. Publ. of Yr. 1999, 2000, 2005, Magyar Imre 2001). Office: University of Szeged Korányi fasor 8-10 H-6720 Szeged Hungary Business E-Mail: czal@in1st.szote.u-szeged.hu.

LÁSZLÓ, ZOLTÁN, cardiologist; b. Budapest, Sept. 5, 1955; s. Lajos and Gyöngyi (Tóth) L.; m. Judit Schilling, July 28, 1979; children: Bálint, Márton, Kristóf. MD, Semmelweis U., Budapest, 1980, PhD, 2002. Cert. in cardiology and internal medicine. Rschr. Semmelweis U. Med. Sch., Budapest, 1976-79, resident, 1980-84, asst. prof. cardiology, 1985-92, cons. in cardiology, 1992-98; head dept. cardiology Weiss Manfred Hosp., Budapest, 1998—2001; head dept. internal medicine St. Borbala Hosp., Tatabanya, Hungary, 2001—03; head dept. cardiology St. Margit Hosp., Budapest, 2003—10, St. Janos Hosp., 2011—. Contbr. articles to profl. jours. Named European Cardiologist, European Soc. Cardiology, 2000. Mem.: Hungarian Soc. Cardiology, Hungarian Soc. for Internal Medicine, Am. Soc. for Integrative Physiology. Achievements include research in gravitational physiology. Avocation: mountain biking. Home: Tutaj Utca 6/A 1133 Budapest Hungary Office: Saint Janos Hosp Cardiology Dept Dios arok 1-3 Budapest H-1125 Hungary Home Phone: 36 1 7866645; Office Phone: 36-1-4584546. E-mail: laszlo.zoltan.dr@chello.hu.

LATANÉ, BIBB, social psychologist; b. NYC, July 19, 1937; s. Henry Allen and Felicité Gillman (Bibb) L.; children: Julia Gillman, Claire Augusta, Henry Arbiter. BA, Yale U., 1958; PhD, U. Minn., 1963. Mem. faculty dept. social psychology Columbia U., NYC, 1962-68; prof. psychology, dir. behavioral scis. lab. Ohio State U., Columbus, 1968-82; prof. psychology, dir. Inst. Research Social Sci. U.N.C.-Chapel Hill, 1982-90. Pres. Social Sci. Confs., Inc., 1990—; founder Nags Head Confs., Sea Frolic Conf. Ctr., Ctr. Human Sci., sr. fellow, 2000—. Contbr. articles to profl. jours. Guggenheim fellow, 1974-75; James McKeen Cattell fellow, 1981-82; NSF, Office of Naval Research grantee. Mem. APA (coun. rep. 1971-75), Soc. Personality and Social Psychology (pres. 1976-79, Campbell award 1986), Midwestern Psychol. Assn. (pres. 1981-84), Acad. Mgmt., AAAS (Socio-Psychol. prize 1968, 80), Soc. Exptl. Soc. Psychology (Disting. Scientist award 1998), Am. Sociol. Assn., Animal Behavior Soc. E-mail: latane@humanscience.org.

LATELLA, GIOVANNI, gastroenterologist, educator; b. San Bartolomeo in Galdo, Benevento, Italy, Mar. 22, 1957; MD, U. Rome, La Sapienza, 1982, degree in Gastroenterology & Gastrointestinal Endoscopy, 1986. Prof. gastroenterology U. L'Aquila, Italy, 1995—. Home: Via Pusiano 9 Rome 00199 Italy Home Fax: 39.06 86275506. Business E-Mail: giolatel@in.it.

LATHAM, PATRICIA S., physician; b. Annapolis, Md., Aug. 22, 1946; BS, Simmons Coll., 1968; MD, U. So. Calif., 1972. Intern Yale-New Haven Hosp., 1972-73, resident, 1973-75, fellow in hepatology, 1975-78; resident in anatomic pathology U. Toronto (Can.) Hosp., 1978-80; asst. prof. pathology and medicine U. Md., 1981-88, Nat. Cancer Inst., 1988-90, George Washington U., 1990-92, assoc. prof. pathology and medicine, 1992—2011, prof. pathology and medicine, 2011—. Office: George Wash U 2300 I St NW Washington DC 20037-2336 Office Phone: 202-994-3391. *

LATHI, ELLEN S., neurologist; b. Phila., Pa., May 18, 1952; MD, SUNY Syracuse Health Sci. Ctr., 1976. Intern, neurology SUNY Upstate Med. Ctr., Syracuse, 1976—77; resident Tufts U., New Eng. Med. Ctr., 1977—80; dir. Multiple Sclerosis Ctr. Caritas St. Elizabeth's Med. Ctr., Boston, staff neurologist; asst. prof. neurology Tufts U. Mem.: Central New England Chpt. Nat. MS Soc. (clinical adv. com., Physician Health Care Profl. Vol. award 2006), Am. Acad. Neurology. Office: Caritas Neurology Group 736 Cambridge St CCP 8 Brighton MA 02135 Office Phone: 617-789-2375. Office Fax: 617-789-5117.

LATIES, VICTOR GREGORY, psychologist, educator; b. Racine, Wis., Feb. 2, 1926; s. Simon Gregory and Rima (Kapnik) L.; m. Martha Ann Fisher, July 29, 1956; children: Nancy, Andrew, Claire. AB, Tufts U., 1949; PhD, U. Rochester, NYC, 1954. Ford Found. teaching intern Brown U., 1954-55; instr., asst. prof. dept. pharmacology Johns Hopkins U. Sch. Medicine, 1955-65; assoc. prof. U. Rochester Sch. Medicine and Dentistry, 1965-71, prof., 1971—, dir. toxicology tng. program, 1978-91, 95-96. Mem. preclinical psychopharmacology research rev. com. NIMH, 1967-71; mem. bd. on toxicology and environ. health hazards Nat. Acad. Sci.-NRC, 1977-80, mem. toxicology info. program com., 1981-85; mem. sci. rev. com. for health research EPA, 1981-89. Editor: Jour. Exptl. Analysis of Behavior, 1972-76, exec. editor, 1966-72, 76—; editor: (with B. Weiss) Behavioral Toxicology, 1975, Behavioral Pharmacology, 1976; mem. editorial bd.: Jour. Pharmacology and Exptl. Therapeutics, 1965-71, Psychopharmacology, 1968-78, 81-89, The Behavior Analyst, 1980-82, Experimental and Clinical Psychopharmacology, 1993-99; contbr. articles to profl. jours. Served with USN, 1944-46. Fellow Am. Psychol. Assn. (pres. div. psychopharmacology 1968-69, div. exptl. analysis of behavior 1979-82, bd. sci. affairs 1983-85), Behavioral Pharmacology Soc. (pres. 1966-68), Am. Soc. Pharmacology and Exptl. Therapeutics, Assn. for Behavior Analysis, Soc. Toxicology, Soc. for Exptl. Analysis of Behavior (sec.-treas. 1966—). Home: 55 Dale Rd E Rochester NY 14625-2137 Office: U Rochester Medical Ctr Dept Environ Medicine Box EHSC Rochester NY 14642

LATNER, SELMA, retired psychoanalyst; b. Bronx, Aug. 11, 1920; d. Isidore and Jennie (Reisman) Levy; m. Harold Latner, Mar. 23, 1959 (dec. 1972); children: Gail, Karen, Irwin. BBA, CCNY, 1942; MSW, U. Pitts., 1945; PsyD Psychoanalysis, Heed U., 1984. LCSW, lic. marriage and family therapist NJ, cert., lic. psychoanalyst, specialist eating disorders. Caseworker Clin. Social Worker, NJ, Jewish Family Svcs., NYC, 1949—53, Cmty. Svc. Soc., Queens, 1953—65; sr. caseworker Jewish Family Svcs., Hackensack, NJ, 1965—68; sr. family and marriage therapist Bergen County Family Counseling Svc., Hackensack, 1968—83; pvt. practice psychoanalyst Teaneck, NJ, 1981—2002. Recipient Outstanding Profl. Human Svcs. plaque, Am. Acad. Human Svcs., 1974—75. Mem.: NASW (Gold Card), NJ Inst. Tng. Psychoanalysis, Nat. Assn. Advancement Psychoanalysis, NJ Soc. Clin. Social Work, Am. Anorexia Bulimia Assn. (bd. dirs. Teaneck chpt. 1984—88, v.p., founder, dir. Group Therapy Program at Hackensack Med. Ctr. 1984—95, Eating Disorders Outstanding Svcs. award 1991, state award, 2 nat. awards), Nat. Alliance Family Life. Avocations: tennis, music, art, dance. Home: 27 Oakdale Ct North Haledon NJ 07508-2920

LA TORRE, MARCO, colon and rectal surgeon; b. Rome, Oct. 11, 1979; MD, U. Rome, Sapienza, 2004. Physician U. Sapienza, 2004—. Mem.: European Soc. Colon Proctology. Office: Via di Grottarossa Rome 00189 Italy Business E-Mail: netlat@tiscali.it.

LATOUR, ROBERT A., biomedical engineer, educator; b. July 15, 1957; BS, U. Va., 1979; MS, U. Pa., PhD, 1989. McqQeen-Quattlebaum prof. bioengring. Clemson U., 2008—. Recipient Faculty Excellence award, Clemson U. Bd. Trustees, 2010. Fellow: Am. Inst. Med. and Biol. Engring.; mem.: AVS, Am. Chem. Soc., Soc. Biomaterials. Avocations: kayaking, backpacking, canoeing. Office: Clemson University Dept Bioengineering Clemson SC 29634 Office Fax: 864-656-4466. Business E-Mail: latourr@clemson.edu.

LATROFA, FRANCESCO, medical educator, researcher, physician, endocrinologist; b. Bari, Italy, June 12, 1964; s. Vito Latrofa and Serafina Ottolino; m. Maristella Lombardi, July 19, 1997; children: Sara, Ania, Vittorio. Degree with honors, Med. Sch., U. Bari, 1992; PhD in Endocrinology with honors, Sch. Endocrinology and Metabolic Disease, U. Pisa, Italy, 1999. Italian med. lic. U. Bari, 1992. Postdoc. rschr. autoimmune disease unit Cedars-Sinai Rsch. Inst. and Sch. Medicine, U. Calif., LA, 2000—03; asst. prof. dept. endocrinology U. Hosp., Pisa, 2004—. Contbr. articles to profl. publs. Fellowship, U. Bari, 1992, Sch. Endocrinology and Metabolic Disease, Pisa, 1994. Mem.: Endocrine Soc., Italian Thyroid Assn., Italian Soc. Endocrinology. Home: Via Tealdi 13 Pisa 56124 Italy Office: Dept Endocrinology Via Paradisa 2 56124 Pisa PI Italy Office Fax: 39050578772. Business E-Mail: latrofaf@libero.it.

LATTA, GEORGE HAWORTH, III, neonatal/perinatal nurse practitioner; b. Chattanooga, Sept. 4, 1960; s. George Haworth Jr. and Charlotte (Major) L. BS in Physics, Ga. Inst. Tech., 1982; MD, East Tenn. State U., 1986. Cert. in pediat., neonatology. Intern, resident in pediat. Dartmouth (N.H.) U., 1986-88; resident in pediat. Stanford (Calif.) U., 1988-89; fellow in neonatology Vanderbilt U., Nashville, 1989-90, U. Tenn., Memphis, 1990-92; attending neonatologist Rose Med. Ctr., Denver, 1992-94, Forrest Gen. Hosp., Hattiesburg, Miss., 1994-95, Meth. Hosps., Memphis, 1995-99; neontalogist Intermountain Healthcare, Provo, Utah, 2000—05, Children's Hosp. Ctrl. Calif., Madera, 2006—07, Kaweah Delta Hosp., 2007—; med. dir. Kaweah Delta Med. Ctr., 2007—. NIH pulmonary trainee grantee Vanderbilt U., 1989; March of Dimes scholar East Tenn. State U., 1984, Johnny J. Jones scholar, 1981. Fellow: Am. Acad. Pediat.; mem.: Wildnerness Med. Soc., Phi Eta Sigma. Roman Catholic. Avocations: skiing, camping, jazz, aquariums, scuba diving. Personal E-mail: ghlatta3@comcast.net. Business E-Mail: uvglatta@ihc.com.

LAU, CLARA BIK SAN, medical educator; d. Tony Pui Chuen Lau and Angelina Wai Yee Cheung; m. Timothy Chit Ming Tam, Oct. 9, 2004. BPharm, 1993; PhD in Pharmacy, U. London, 1998. Lectr. pharmacy U. Bradford, England, 1997—2000; asst. prof. pharmacy Chinese U. Hong Kong, Shatin, Hong Kong, 2000—08; adj. asst. prof. pharmacy U. So. Calif., LA, 2003—08; asst. dir. Inst. Chinese Medicine, Chinese U. Hong Kong, 2008—. Advisor Chinese Medicine Coun. Hong Kong, Registration Chinese Proprietary Medicines, Hong Kong, 2004—; external examiner Hong Kong Inst. Vocat. Edn., Hong Kong, 2006—. Contbr. articles to profl. jours. Grantee Rsch. grant, Innovation and Tech. Commn., 2002—05, Rsch. Grants Coun., 2005—08. Mem.: Royal Pharm. Soc. Great Britain, Am. Soc. Pharmacognosy. Achievements include research in natural products with potential anti-cancer and anti-diabetic activities. Office: Chinese Univ Hong Kong Inst Chinese Medicine Shatin New Territories Hong Kong Office Phone: 852 26096109. Personal E-mail: claratim@netvigator.com. Business E-Mail: claralau@cuhk.edu.hk.

LAU, H. LORRIN, obstetrician, gynecologist; b. Honolulu, Apr. 21, 1932; s. Henry S. and Helen (Lee) L.; m. Maureen Lau; children: David, Marianne, Mike, Mark, Linda. AB cum laude, Harvard U., 1950-54; MD, Johns Hopkins U., 1954-58, MPH, 1970-71. Asst. prof. Sch. Med. Johns Hopkins U. (Balt.), 1964-82; assoc. prof. U. Hawaii, 1982-84; chief ob-gyn. St. Francis West Hosp., Honolulu, 1990-92, Kuakini Hosp., Honolulu, 1994-95. Fellow AMA; mem. ACOG, Internat. Soc. Biology and Medicine. Inventor pregnancy tests, helped introduce alpha-fetoprotein tests into obstetrics in USA, 1971. Home: 1121 Wilder Ave 1700B Honolulu HI 96822 Office: 1010 S King St Honolulu HI 96814-1701 Office Phone: 808-596-0164. Personal E-mail: drhllau@yahoo.com.

LAUCHE, HERVÉ MICHEL, oncologist; b. Bordeaux, Gironde, France, July 1, 1952; s. Michel Georges and Simone Marie (Rousseau) L.; m. Eliane Marguerite Vollmer, May 26, 1979; children: Anne-Sophie, Olivier. MD, Med. Sch. Strasbourg, France, 1977. Bd. cert. in oncology and radiation oncology; expert in oncology. Intern U. Hosp. Cancer Ctr., Strasbourg, 1975-77, resident, 1978-79, sr. asst., 1981-87; oncology specialist French Cancer Ctr., Strasbourg, 1987; head dept. oncology Clinique Clementville, Montpellier, France, 1988—. Asst. clin. faculty Med. Sch. Strasbourg, 1982-87; clin. rsch. asst. Thermology Lab., U. Strasbourg, 1982-87; pres. Tumors Register of Herault, Montpellier, 1992-99. Editor-in-chief Bull. French Soc. Pvt. Oncology, 1989-2002. With French Mil., 1979-80. Mem.: French Soc. Pvt. Oncology (gen. sec. 1989—), French Soc. Cancer, European Orgn. Rsch. Treatment of Cancer, European Soc. Therapeutic Radiation Oncology, European Soc. Med. Oncology, Am. Soc. Therapeutic Radiology and Oncology, Am. Soc. Clin. Oncology. Roman Catholic. Avocations: tennis, skiing, bridge. Office: Clinique Clementville 25 Rue de Clementville 34070 Montpellier France Office Phone: 33 04 67 92 61 55. E-mail: lauche@oncoclem.org.

LAUDE, AUGUSTINUS, ophthalmologist; b. Jakarta, Indonesia, Aug. 2, 1973; MBChB, U. Edinburgh, 1996; MSc, U. Manchester, 2000. Cons. Nat. Healthcare Group Eye Inst., Tan Tock Seng Hosp., Singapore, 2010—. Recipient award, Hereford Med. Soc., Eng., Courage Star and medal award, Courage Fund, Singapore, Nat. Excellent Svc. award, SPRING Singapore. Fellow: Acad. Medicine (Singapore), Royal Coll. Surgeons Edinburgh. Office: Tan Tock Seng Hosp11 Jalan Tan To Singapore 308433 Singapore Business E-Mail: laude_augustinus@ttsh.com.sg.

LAUDERDALE, DIANE S., epidemiologist, educator; BA in Religion, Harvard U., 1977; MA in Divinity, U. Chgo., 1979, MA in Libr. Sci., 1981; PhD in Epidemiology, U. Ill. Chgo. Sch. Pub. Health, 1996. Assoc. prof. health studies U. Chgo. Med. Ctr.; program dir.

Dept. Health Studies MS for Clinical Profl. Recipient Investigator award, Robert Wood Johnson Found. Office: 5841 S Maryland Ave MC 2007 Rm W254 Chicago IL 60637 Office Phone: 773-834-0913. Office Fax: 773-702-1979.

LAUENER, ROGER P., pediatrician, allergist; MD, Zurich U. Med. Sch. Cert. pediatrician and allergologist Switzerland bd. Physician-in-chief Children's Allergy & Asthma Hosp., Hochgebirgsklinik Davos, Switzerland, 2008—. Home: Switzerland Office: Children's Allergy & Asthma Hosp Hochgebirgsklinik Davos-Wolfgang 7265 Switzerland

LAUERMAN, WILLIAM, medical educator; b. NYC, Dec. 27, 1954; s. Sidney and Veronica Lauerman; m. Cynthia Tull, Sept. 24, 1983; children: Katie, Kevin. BA in Natural History, Johns Hopkins U., Balt., 1978; MD, Georgetown U., DC, 1982. Lic. orthopaedic surgeon Am. Bd. Orthopaedic Surgeons, 1990. Intern surgery Georgetown U. Med. Ctr., 1982—83, resident orthop. surgery, 1983—87; fellow spine surgery U. Minn., 1987—88; maj., orthop. surgeon USAF Med. Ctr., 1988—92; asst. prof. U. Pitts. Med. Ctr., 1992—95; assoc. prof. Georgetown U. Med. Ctr., DC, 1995—2000, prof. orthopaedic surgery, 2000—. Maj. USAF, 1988—92, Lackland AFB, Tex. Fellow: Am. Acad. Orthopaedic Surgeons (chair subcom. on spine evaluation 2004—07), Scoliosis Rsch. Soc. Avocations: skiing, golf, travel. Office: Georgetown Univ Hosp 3800 Reservoir Rd NW Washington DC 22066

LAUFER, IRA JEROME, physician; b. NYC, Mar. 29, 1928; s. Irving and Evelyn (Weisman) L.; m. Barbara Alfandari, July 10, 1955; children: Tina, David. BA, NYU, 1948; MD, NYU Sch. Medicine, 1953. Diplomate Am. Bd. Internal Medicine. Instr. clin. medicine NYU Sch. Medicine, NYC, 1959-69, asst. prof. clin. medicine, 1969-83, clin. assoc. prof. medicine, 1983—; dir. diabetes svc. Cabrini Med. Ctr., NYC, 1966-89; dir. medicine N.Y. Eye and Ear Infirmary, NYC, 1978-91; med. dir. Diabetes Treatment Ctr., NYC, 1985-92; physician-in-charge Diabetes Treatment Program, NYC, 1992—; with diabetes treatment program Cabrini Med. Ctr., NYC, 1992—2008; assoc. attending physician NYU Med. Ctr., 1983—. Lectr. and cons. in field. Co-author: Diabetes Explained, 1976. Capt. USAF, 1955-57, Korea. Recipient Svc. award Am. Diabetes Assn., 1990. Fellow Am. Coll. Clin. Pharmacology, Am. Coll. Endocrinology; mem. ACP. Avocations: tennis, sailing. Office Phone: 212-475-2535.

LAUFER, NATHAN, cardiologist; b. Montreal, Quebec, Can., Mar. 12, 1953; came to US, 1981, Naturalised; s. Jack and Pearl (Brachfeld) Laufer; m. Judy Franceska Egett, Sept. 2, 1986; 1 child, Andrew. DCS, McGill U., Montreal, Quebec, 1972, MD, 1977. Diplomate Nat. Bd. Med. Examiners, Am. Bd. Internal Medicine; cert. Profl. Corp. Physicians Que., Am. Bd. Internal Medicine, Caridiology & Interventional Cardiology. Intern, resident U. Toronto, Can., 1977-81; fellow cardiology U. Mich., Ann Arbor, 1981-83, faculty dept. cardiology, 1983-84; cardiologist Affiliated Cardiologists, Phoenix, 1984-2001, mng. cardiologist, 1996-2001; med. dir. Heart & Vascular Ctr. Ariz., 2001—; chief cardiovascular svcs. Banner Estrella Med. Ctr., 2004—07. Dir. coronary care Good Samaritan Hosp., Phoenix, 1986—92, dir. interventional cardiology, 1987—; vis. prof. Chigasaki Tokushi-kai Med. Ctr., Kanagawa-ken, Japan, 1988, Leningrad Postgrad. Med. Inst., St. Petersburg, Russia, 1991; bd. dirs. Integrated Cardiovascular Group, Maricopa Med. Ctr., 2002—04; pres. Maricopa County Med. Soc., 2011. Contbr. articles to profl. jours. Fellow ACP, Am. Coll. Cardiology, Am. Coll. Chest Physicians, Royal Coll. Physicians and Surgeons Can., mem. AMA, N.Am. Soc. Pacing and Electrophysiology, Soc. Cardiac Angiography and Intervention, Am. Assn. Nuclear Cardiology, Ariz. Med. Assn., Can. Cardiovascular Soc., Maricopa County Med. Assn.(bd. dirs., 2002-, pres, 2011), Cardiovascular Soc. Ariz. (founder, pres.). Avocations: skiing, tennis, music, films, computers. Office: Heart & Vascular Ctr Ariz 1331 N 7th St Ste 375 Phoenix AZ 85006-2712 Home Phone: 480-443-1722; Office Phone: 602-307-0070.

LAUGHLIN, EDWARD HUMES, surgeon, educator; b. Huntsville, Ala., July 22, 1932; s. James Burnett and Mary Cleophas (Mahoney) Laughlin; children: Page Lewis, Leedy Stockton. BA, U. Va., Charlottesville, 1954; MD, Duke U., 1958. Diplomate Am. Bd. Surgeons. Intern Johns Hopkins Hosp., Balt., 1958—59; resident in surgery U. Va. Hosp., Charlottesville, 1959—64; surgical fellow Lahey Clinic, Boston, 1962; chmn. surg. programs U. Ala. Sch. Primary Med. Care, Huntsville, 1975—79; prof. surgery U. Ala. Sch. Medicine, Huntsville, 1998—. Author: Coming to Terms with Cancer, 2001, Cancer from A to Z, 2008. Lt. col. USAR, 1986—88. Fellow: ACS; mem.: Am. Soc. Clinical Oncologists, Soc. Surgical Oncology. Avocations: fishing, hunting, weight training. Home: 1901 Asbury Rd Huntsville AL 35801

LAUGHLIN, LARRY W., academic administrator, military officer; B, Millikin U., 1967; MD, St. Louis U., 1971; M, U. London, 1979, PhD, 1982. Diplomate Am. Bd. Preventive Medicine, Am. Bd. Internal Medicine, cert. in pub. health, gen. preventive medicine. Past commdg. officer Naval Med. Inst., Bethesda, Md.; with Uniformed Svcs. U. of Health Sciences, Bethesda, Md., 1992—, chmn. dept. preventive medicine and biometrics, 1998—, Sanford chmn. in tropical medicine, dean F. Edward Hebert Sch. Medicine, 2002—. Capt. (ret.) US Army. Office: Uniformed Services Univ Health Sciences 4301 Jones Bridge Rd Bethesda MD 20814 *

LAUGHTON, BARBARA, pediatrician; b. Cape Town, South Africa, May 20, 1962; MBCHB, U. Cape Town, 1986; FCPaed(SA), Coll. Medicine South Africa, 1995. Devel. paediatrician Stellenbosch U., 1999—. Mem. exec. Pediat. Neurology & Devel. Assn. South Africa, 2005. Fellow: Coll. Paediatricians South Africa. Office: Tygerberg Children's Hosp Francie v Tygerberg Western Cape 7505 South Africa E-mail: blaughton@mweb.co.za.

LAUMANN, ANNE ELIZABETH, dermatologist; b. Beaconsfield, Bucks, Eng., Jan. 31, 1946; came to U.S. 1976; d. Richard M. and Suzanne Marie (Weissman) Solomon; m. Edward Otto Laumann, June 21, 1980; chil dren: Christopher Richard, Timothy Otto. MB, ChB, Birmingham Med. Sch., Eng., 1968. Diplomate Am. Bd. Dermatology, 2009. Resident in dermatology U. Chgo., 1977-79; asst. prof. dermatology U. Ill., Chgo., 1980-85; clin. asst. prof. U. Chgo., 1987-90; clin. practice dermatology Group Practice South Side Chgo., 1979—99, Michael Reese Hosp. Health Plan Humana HMO, 1986—97, Advocate Health Care, 1997—99; clin. asst. prof. dermatology U. Ill., Chgo., 1990—99; divsn. dir. dermatology Michael Reese Hosp., Chgo., 1995—99, vice chmn. IRB, 1998—99; assoc. prof. dermatology Northwestern U. Chgo., program dir. medine dermatology residency program, asst. to assoc. prof., 2005—; dir. gen. dermatology Feinberg Sch. Medicine, Northwestern U., Chgo., 2010—; asst. prof. clin. med. Sect. Dermatology, U. Chgo., 2000—05, physician, practice dir. Mem. various coms. Michael Reese Hosp., Humana HMO. Fellow Am. Acad. Dermatology, Inst. Medicine of Chgo.; mem. Royal Coll. Physicians, Brit. Assn. Dermatology, Am. Women's Dermatology Assn., Chgo. Dermatology Soc. (v.p. 1997-98), Ill. Dermatology Soc. (pres., 2001-02), Am. Soc. Psychocutaneous Medicine, Med. Dermatology Soc. (bd. mem., 2010-), Am. Dermatoepidemiology Network, Assn. Prof. of Dermatology. Episcopalian. Avocations: hiking, cooking. Office: Northwestern University 676 N St Clair#1600 Chicago IL 60611 Home: 21 East Huron #2705 Chicago IL 60611 Office Phone: 312-695-8106. Business E-Mail: a-laumann@northwestern.edu. *

LAUPU, WENDY KAY, medical/surgical nurse; b. Christchurch, Canterbury, New Zealand, Oct. 6, 1965; arrived in Australia, 1990; d. Peter Dillon Shallard and Jean Dorothy van Asch; m. Gelly Ulec Laupu, Feb. 17, 2002; children: Max Stossel, Gordon Maneb. BNSc, PhD student, James Cook U. RN 2010. Enrolled nurse Cairns Base Hosp., Queensland, Australia, 1994—2009. Trainer, examiner, com. mem. Australian Sports Medicine Fedn., Melbourne and Cairns, 1992—99. Contbr. scientific papers to profl. jours. Recipient Queensland Nursing Coun. scholarship, Queensland Nursing Coun., 2006, Nursing Excellence award, 2008. Achievements include development of first cleaning solution to remove residual protein/prions from reusable laryngeal mask airways and anesthetic equipment; research in examining protein cross contamination on reusable laryngeal mask airways. Personal E-mail: wendylaupu@optusnet.com.au.

LAURELL, ASA CRISTINA, retired physician, educator; b. Uppsala, Sweden, Dec. 20, 1943; MD, U. Lund, Sweden, 1971; PhD in Sociology, U. Naocial Autónoma de Mex., 1987; D with honoris causa, U. Buenos Aires. Prof. U. Lund, 1972—2000; sec. health Mex. City Govt., 2000—06; pvt practice, 2007—11. Mem.: Assn. L.Am. Medicina Social. Avocations: literature, travel. Home: Callejon Chilpa 23-9 Mexico City 04000 Mexico Personal E-mail: laurell9998@gmail.com.

LAURELL, GÖRAN FRANS EMANUEL, otolaryngologist, researcher; b. Stockholm, Jan. 19, 1954; s. Ingemar Frans Emanuel Laurell and Kerstin Maria Elisabet Ström; m. Birgitta Tyrn Ester Wahlman, Apr. 3, 1993; children: Maria, Gustaf. MD, Karolinska Inst., Stockholm, 1983, PhD, 1991. Assoc. prof. Karolinska Inst., 1996—; cons. dept. otolaryngology Karolinska Hosp., 1997—; prof. Dept. Clin. Scis., Umea U., 2006—. Office: Umea Univ Hosp Dept ENT 90185 Umeå Sweden Office Phone: +468 51774728. E-mail: goran.laurell@karolinska.se.

LAURENCE, JEFFREY CONRAD, immunologist, educator; b. NYC, Oct. 21, 1952; s. Harry and Stephanie (Maderic) L.; children: Auden, Galen, Luca. BA summa cum laude, Columbia U., 1972; MD, U. Chgo., 1976. Diplomate Am. Bd. Internal Medicine. Rsch. assoc. Inst. for Cancer Rsch., Osaka, Japan, 1974-75; intern, resident, then hematology fellow N.Y.C. Hosp.-Cornell, 1976-82; assoc. physician The Rockefeller U., NYC, 1980-84; asst. prof. Cornell U. Med. Coll., NYC, 1982-87, assoc. prof., 1988-2000, prof., 2001—; dir. Lab. AIDS Rsch. Cornell Med. Coll., NYC, 1986—; attending physician N.Y. Presbyn. Hosp., NYC, 2001—. Sr. dir. Immune Tech, Inc., N.Y.C., 1986-95; sr. scientist Am. Found. AIDS Rsch., N.Y.C. and Beverly Hills, Calif., 1986—. Author: (play) Many Happy Returns, 1982; editor-in-chief The AIDS Reader, 1991-2008; editor AIDS Targeted Info. Newsletter, 1987-92; assoc. editor AIDS Rsch. and Human Retroviruses, AIDS, 1987-95; editor-in-chief AIDS Patient Care and STDs, 1996—, Translational Rsch., 2006—; cons. editor Infections in Medicine, 1987—; patentee in field Recipient Clinician-Scientist award Am. Heart Assn., 1980-85; William S. Paley Found. fellow, 1982-84; Henry Luce Found. scholar, 1974, Rhodes scholar-elect, 1973. Mem. NIH (mem. study sect.), AMA, Fedn. Am. Soc. Exptl. Biology-Medicine, Am. Soc. Microbiology, Am. Soc. Clin. Investigation, Phi Beta Kappa. Presbyterian. Avocations: sports, art, book collecting. Home: 86 Brookside Dr Greenwich CT 06831-5345 Office: NY Presbyn Hosp-Cornell Med Ctr Dept Medicine Lab AIDS Rsch 310 E 67th St New York NY 10065 Business E-Mail: jlaurenc@med.cornell.edu.

LAURENCIN, CATO THOMAS, orthopaedic surgeon, professor, former dean; b. Phila., Jan. 15, 1959; s. Cyril Alexander and Helen Isabella (Moorehead) Laurencin. BSChemE, Princeton U., NJ, 1980; MD magna cum laude, Harvard Med. Sch., Boston, 1987; PhD in Biochemical Engring., MIT, 1987. Diplomate American Bd. Orthop. Surgery. Surg. house officer Pa. Hosp., Phila., 1987—88; resident orthop. surgery Beth Israel Hosp./Harvard Med. Sch., 1988—93; fellow sports medicine & shoulder surgery Cornell U. Med. Ctr., NYC, 1993—94; rsch. prof. chem. engring. Drexel U., Phila., 1994—98, rsch. prof. materials engring., 1994—2003, Helen I. Moorehead prof. chemical engring., dir. Ctr. Advanced Biomaterials & Tissue Engring., 1998—2003, vice chmn. dept. orthop. surgery, 2002—03; assoc. prof. orthop. surgery MCP Hahnemann U. Sch. Medicine (merged with Drexel U. Coll. Medicine), Phila., 1994—98, clin. assoc. prof. orthop. surgery, 1998—2001, clin. prof., 2001—02, dir. shoulder surgery, Hahnemann Hosp., 2000—03; Lillian T. Pratt disting. prof. & chair dept. orthop. surgery U. Va., Charlottesville, Va., 2003—08, also Univ. prof., prof. biomedical & chem. engring, orthop. surgeon-in-chief U. Va. Health Sys.; v.p. heath affairs, dean Sch. Medicine U. Conn., 2008—11, Van Dusen endowed chair academic medicine, disting. prof. orthop. surgery, 2008—, prin. investigator, CEO Conn. Inst. Clin. & Translational Sci., 2011—, dir. Inst. Regenerative Engring. Mem. NIH Nat. Adv. Coun. Arthritis, Musculoskeletal & Skin Diseases, 2002; mem. nat. sci. adv. bd. FDA, 2003—; mem. NSF Engring. Adv. Com., 2007—. Recipient Disting. Alumni award, Princeton U., 1998, William Grimes award, AICE, 2002, Nicolas Andry award, American Assn. Bone & Joint Surgeons, 2006, Robert A. Bland award, U. Va. Coll. Engring., 2007, Presdl. award for excellence, White House Office Sci. & Tech. Policy, 2009; named one of America's Leading Doctors, Black Enterprise mag., 2001, Top 50 Innovators, Sci. American Mag., 2008, 100 Chem. Engineers of the Modern Era, AICE, 2009. Fellow: ACS, Biomed. Engring. Soc., American Inst. Med. & Biol. Engring. (Pierre Galletti Award 2009), Third World Acad. Scis., American Acad. Orthop. Surgeons; mem.: NAE (Presdl. Excellence award), American Soc. Engring. Educators, American Orthop. Assn., Nat. Med. Assn. (spkr. of house 2003—05), Inst. Medicine. Office: U Conn Health Ctr 263 Farmington Ave Farmington CT 06030-3800 Office Phone: 860-679-2594. E-mail: LAURENCIN@UCHC.EDU. *

LAURENT, PHILIPPE EMILE, medical association administrator, researcher; b. Oullins, France, Nov. 16, 1949; MD, Med. U. Lyon, 1977. Physician clin. immunology Montgelas Gen. Hosp., 1980—2011; rsch. lab dir. Pasteur Inst., 1977—87; rsch. sci. dir. Lafon - Cephalon, 1987—97; v.p. Becton Dickinson, 1997—. Recipient Clin. Trial award, Becton Dickinson. Office: Aristide Berges Le Pont De Claix Isere 30800 France Business E-Mail: philippe_laurent@europe.bd.com.

LAUTER, M. DAVID, physician; b. Wilmington, Del., Jan. 7, 1951; s. Aaron Mordecai and Anne Marguerite (Scondin) L.; m. Diane Ruel, Oct. 11, 1980; children: Michael, Sara. B in Engring. Scis., Johns Hopkins U., 1973, MA in Organic Chemistry, 1974; MD, Jefferson Med. Coll., 1978. Diplomate Am. Bd. Family Physicians. Resident family practice Ctrl. Maine Med. Ctr., Lewiston, 1978-81; clin. dir. USPHS Indian Hosp., Red Lake, Minn., 1981-84; pvt. practice as family doctor York, Maine, 1984—, Portmouth, NH, 2004—. With Pub. Health Svc., 1981-84. Office: 200 Griffin Rd Ste 11 Portsmouth NH 03801-7145 Office Phone: 603-433-7500. E-mail: mdavidlautermd@aol.com.

LAUTERBACH, EDWARD CHARLES, psychiatric educator; b. Chgo., Mar. 21, 1955; s. Edward G. and Virginia C. (Pochelski) L. AB cum laude, Augustana Coll., Rock Island, Ill., 1977; MD, Wake Forest U., 1982. Lic. psychiatrist, Mo., Pa., N.J., N.C. Ga.; diplomate Nat. Bd. Med. Examiners, Am. Bd. Psychiatry and Neurology with qualifications in geriat. psychiatry. Intern Washington U. Sch. Medicine/Barnes Hosp., St. Louis, 1982-83, resident in psychiatry, 1983-86, clin. asst., 1982-86; instr. neurology movement disorder fellow U. Medicine and Dentistry of N.J., New Brunswick, 1986-87; asst. prof. Mercer U. Sch. Medicine, Macon, Ga., 1988-92, chief div. adult and geriatric psychiatry, dept. psychiatry and behavioral scis., 1988-98, coord. grand rounds dept. psychiatry and behavioral scis., 1989-98, assoc. prof., 1992-96, prof., 1996—, prof. internal medicine/neurology, 1996—, prof. radiology, 1996—, prof. emeritus, psychiatry and neurology, 2009; pvt. practice Charlotte, NC, 1987-88. Chair free comm. IVth World Congress Biol. Psychiatry, Phila., 1985; mem. neurology staff Lyons VA Hosp., 1986; med. staff privileges in neurology Mercy Hosp., Charlotte, 1987, cons., 1987; privileges in psychiatry Med. Ctr. Ctrl. Ga., 1994—, Coliseum Psychiat. Hosp., 1994—, dir. med. staff continuing edn., 1994-96, Middle Ga. Hosp., 1997-2002; med. dir. geropsychiatry program The Sr. Ctr., Middle Ga. Hosp., 1997-2002; founding dir., dir. emeritus Mercer U. Ctr. Translation Studies in Alzheimer's, Parkinson's, and Other Neurogenerative Diseases, 2008-. Guest editor Psychiatric Annals, 2002; editor: Psychiatric Management in Neurological Disease, 2000, Psychiatric Management in Neurological Disease, Spanish and Italian edits., 2002; editl. reviewer Neuropsychiatry, Neuropsychology and Behavioral Neurology, Biological Psychiatry, Movement Disorders, assoc. editor Jour. Neuropsychiatry and Clin. Neuroscis., 1999—; contbr. articles to profl. jours. Recipient Med. Dir. of Yr. award S.E. region, Horizon Mental Health Mgmt., Inc., 1999—2001; scholar Rock Sleyster scholar, Wake Forest U., 1981. Fellow: Am. Psychiat. Assn. (course dir. 1990—92, 1994—95, symposium chmn. 1995—97, co-dir. 1998—2001, symposium chmn. 2001, Disting.), Am. Neuropsychiat. Assn. (rsch. com. 1992—, vice-chair 1998—99, chmn. 1999—2008); mem.: Charlotte Psychiat. Soc., Movement Disorder Soc., Med. Assn. Ga., Mecklenburg County Med. Soc., N.C. Psychiat. Assn., Bibb County Med. Soc., Ga. Psychiat. Physicians Assn. (state com. on contg. med. edn.), Am. Acad. Neurology, AMA. Home: 331-48 College St Macon GA 31201

LAUTERSTEIN, JOSEPH, cardiologist; b. Vienna, Dec. 1, 1934; came to US, 1940, naturalized, 1945; s. Bernard and Hajnalka (Stern) L.; m. Erika Stein, Jan. 24, 1964 (dec. Aug. 13, 1990); children: Deborah Ann Ehret, Brenda Rose Horton; m. Elisabeth Spiegl Lazaroff, Nov. 27, 1994. BA, Syracuse U., 1955; MD, U. Vienna, 1964. Lic. physician, NY. Intern, then resident in internal medicine The Bklyn. Cumberland Med. Ctr., 1964-66, 68-69, fellow in cardiology, 1969-70; attending physician, cons. internal medicine and cardiology Hamilton Ave. Hosp., Monticello, NY, 1970-78, Catskill Regional Med. Ctr., Harris, NY, 1970—2005, chief cardiology, 1971—2005, chief of staff, 1981—82; mem. courtesy staff dept. internal medicine and cardiology The Bklyn. Hosp. Ctr., 1971-95; clin. asst. dept. internal medicine and cardiology St. Vincent's Hosp. and Med. Ctr. N.Y., 1974-80, asst. attending physician, 1981-86, assoc. attending physician, 1987-94, attending physician, 1995—2005; with Sullivan Internal Medicine Group, P.C., Monticello, 1970—2005; ret., 2005. Dir. ICU Catskill Regional Med. Ctr., Harris, 1971—79, dir. CCU, 1978—2005, dir. spl. diagnostics, 1984—2005, pres. med. bd., 1981—82; mem. pacemaker task force Empire State Med. Sci. and Ednl. Found., 1985—89; med. dir. Sullivan County EMT-D Program, 1989—2005; police surgeon Village of Monticello, 1972—, Sullivan County, 1972—2005; med. advisor Monticello Vol. Ambulance Corps, 1970—80, 1989—2004; mem. Sullivan County Emergency Svcs. Coun., 1990, 91; instr. outdoor emergency care, 1991—. Co-contbr. articles to Jour. Cardiovascular Surgery, Annals of Thoracic Surgery, Angiology, Chest. Trustee Catskill Regional Med. Ctr., 1981-82, Catskill Regional Med. Ctr. Found., 1990-2004, 2007—, v.p., 2009-, hon. trustee, 2004—07; mem. Nat. Ski Patrol, 1979—, med. advisor So. NY region, 1989-94, 97—, med. advisor So. Catskill sect., 1994-97; patroller Holiday Mountain Ski Patrol, 1979—; bd. dir. Hospice of Orange and Sullivan Counties, 2005-, mem. fin. exec. com., 2006-, mem. profl. adv. com., 2007—. Capt. med. corps USAF, 1966—68. Named Citizen of Yr., SYDA Found. Sullivan County, 1991. Fellow Am. Coll. Cardiology (emeritus; NY state chpt. councilor 1991—, com. mem. 1990—), Am. Coll. Chest Physicians (assoc.), Am. Coll. Angiology, Internat. Coll. Angiology, NY Cardiol. Soc. (exec. bd. dirs. 1982—, mem. various coms.), NY Acad. Medicine; mem. AMA, Am. Geriatrics Soc., ACP/Am. Soc. Internal Medicine, Soc. for Critical Care Medicine, NY Acad. Scis., N.Am. Soc. for Pacing and Electrophysiology, Med. Soc. State of NY (cardiology del. to interspecialty com., cardiology del. to ho. of dels.), others. Avocations: stamp collecting/philately, classical music, skiing. Home Phone: 845-794-1737. Personal E-mail: joe_lauterstein@yahoo.com.

LAVE, JUDITH RICE, economics professor; b. Campbellton, May 18, 1939; d. J.H. Melville and G.A. Pauline (Lister) Rice; m. Lester Bernard Lave, June 21, 1965; children: Tamara Rice, Jonathan

Melville. BA in Econs., Queen's U., Kingston, Ont., Can., 1957-61; MA in Econs., Harvard U., 1964, PhD, 1967; LLD, Queen's U., 1994. Lectr., asst. prof. econ. Carnegie Mellon U., Pitts., 1966-73, assoc. prof., 1973-78; dir. econ. analysis Office of Sec., Dep. of Asst. Sec. Planning and Evaluation, Washington, 1978-79; dir. office of rsch. Health Care Fin. Adminstrn., Washington, 1980-82; prof. health econ. U. Pitts., 1982—, co-dir. Ctr. for Rsch. on Health Care, 1996—2010, chair dept. health policy and mgmt., 2003—10. Cons. Nat. Study Internal Medicine Manpower, Chgo., 1976, Wash. State Hosp. Assn., 1984, Horty, Springer & Mattern, Pitts., 1984, Hogan and Hartson, Washington, 1989, Ont. Hosp. Assn., Conn. Hosp. Assn., 1991; cons. various agys. U.S. HHS (formerly U.S. HEW), 1971-89; mem. adv. panel Robert Wood Johnson Found., Princeton, N.J., 1983-84, 96—, Leonard Davis Inst., Phila., 1984, U.S. Congress, 1977, 82, 83—; com. mem. Inst. Medicine Coms., Washington, 1975-, Project 2000 Commn. on Future of Podiatry, Washington, 1985-86. Editl. bd. Wiley Series in Health Svcs., 1989-90, Health Svcs. Rsch., 1970-74, Inquiry, 1979-82, AUPHA Press, 1986, Jour. of Health Policy Politics and Law, Health Affairs, 1998—; co-author: Hospital Construction Act - An Evaluation of the Hill Burton Program, 1948-73, 74, Health Status, Medical Care Utilization and Outcome: A Bibliography of Empirical Studies (4 vols.) 1989, Providing Hospital Services, 1989; contbr. numerous articles to profl. jours. Mem. Prospective Payment Assessment Commn., 1993—97, Medicare Payment Adv. Commn., 1997—2000; mem. planning com. ARC, Pitts., 1986—; mem. rev. com. United Way, Pitts., 1988—90, Bd. Health Svcs., Inst. Medicine; bd. dirs. Craig House, Pitts., 1976—77, Presbyn. Sr. Care, Pitts., 1999—, Jewish Health Care Found., 2002—07. Woodrow Wilson fellow, 1961—62. Disting. fellow Acad. Health (pres. 1977-88, bd. dirs. 1983-93); mem. Found. for Health Svcs. Rsch. (pres. 1988-89, bd. dirs. 1983—), Am. Pub. Health Soc., Am. Econ. Soc. (com. mem.), Inst. Medicine (bd. health svcs. 2000-10), Nat. Acad. Social Ins., Robert Wood Johnson Found. (com. on econ. impact of health sys. change 1996—). Democrat. Home: 1008 Devonshire Rd Pittsburgh PA 15213-2914 Office: U Pitts A620 Pub Health Pittsburgh PA 15213 Office Phone: 412-624-0898. Business E-Mail: lave@pitt.edu.

LAVEN, DAVID LAWRENCE, nuclear and radiologic pharmacist, consultant; b. Detroit, Jan. 31, 1953; s. Harold Sanford and Ada Rae (Blumenthal) Laven; m. Maxine Frances Miller, May 14, 1977 (div.); children: Ryan Stuart, Cameron Alexander; m. Lois Marion Vitagliano, Oct. 8, 2004. BA in History and Biology, Albion Coll., 1975; BS in Pharmacy, U. N.Mex., 1981. Cert. disting. rep. 2011. Rsch. technologist, biodistbn. specialist U. N.Mex. Coll. Pharmacy, Albuquerque, 1978-81; asst. mgr. Syncor, Inc. (formerly Pharmatopes), Miami, Fla., 1981-84; instr. nuc. pharmacy U. Miami, 1982-85; pres., owner Gammascan Cons., Longwood, Fla., 1982—; staff pharmacist Hollywood (Fla.) Med. Ctr., 1983-84; asst. mgr. Nuclear Pharmacy, Inc., Sunrise, Fla., 1984-85; dir. nuc. pharmacy program VA Med. Ctr., Bay Pines, 1985-96; exec. dir. Ala. Pharmacy Assn., 1996-98; poison control splst./mgr. PET Cyclotron/Pharmacy Kans. U. Med. Ctr., Kansas City, Kans., 1998-2001; lead PET nuc. pharmacist Eastern Isotopes/IBA, 2001—02; pharmacist Eckerds Corp., 2002—03, Priority Healthcare Corp., 2003—04, Am. Pharm. Svcs./Omnicare, 2004—05, Kindred Pharmacy Svcs., Orlando, Fla., 2005—06; drug insp. Bur. Statewide Pharm. Svcs., Fla. Dept. Health, Orlando, 2005—. Mem. adv. panel in radiopharms. U.S. Pharmacopeial Conv., Inc., Rockville, Md., 1985—96; cons. nuc. pharmacy Nat. Assn. Bds. Pharmacy, Chgo., 1987—2000; adj. asst. clin. prof. U. Fla. Coll. Pharmacy, Gainesville, 1986—98, Nova-Southeastern U. Coll. Pharmacy, North Miami Beach, Fla., 1990—98, Mercer U. Coll. Pharmacy, 1995—98, U. Kans. Coll. Pharmacy, 2000—01; edn. cons. Nuclear Tech. Rev. Series Rev., Inc., 1988—; mem. splty coun. on nuclear pharmacy Bd. Pharm. Specialities, 1988—91; mem. Ala. Coun. Assn. Execs., 1996—98, Nat. Coun. State Pharmacy Execs., 1996—98, Govs. Task Force Prevention Tobacco Use in Ala., 1997—98; chair Smoking Cessation Workgroup. Co-author: Pharmacologic Alterations in the Biorouting/Performance of Select Radiopharmaceuticals Used in Cardiac Imaging, 1990, Pharmacologic Alterations with Biorouting/Performance of Radiopharmaceuticals Used in Nuclear Medicine Abscess, Liver/Spleen, and Tumor/Inflammation Imaging Procedures, 1992, Pharmacologic Alterations in the Biorouting of Radiopharmaceuticals Used in Nuclear Medicine Adrenal, Cerebral, Hepatobiliary, Pulmonary, and Renal Scintigraphic Studies, 1993, International Handbook of Drug-Radiopharmaceutical Interactions and Incompatibilities, 1994; Pharmacologic Alterations in the Biorouting/Performance of Radiopharmaceuticals Used in Cistmography, Ferrokinetic Studies, Gastrointestinal Imaging, Schillings Testing, Thrombus Localization, Thyroid Uptake/Imaging, and Other Nuclear Medicine Procedures, 1994, A Pharmacist's Guide to Pharmaceuticals Used in Medical Imaging, 2001; editor Ala. Pharmacy Jour., 1996-98, APA Newsletter, 1996-98, Pratique Extrordinaire Newsletter, 1997-98, editor, co-pub. Clini-Scan Monthly, 1982-84; co-guest editor Jour. Pharmacy Practice, Radiologic Pharmacy I, 1989, II, 1989, III, 1994, IV, 2001, mem. editl. bd., 1991—; guest editor Fla. Jour. Hosp. Pharmacy, 1990, cons. editor, 1986-96; guest author In-Svc. Rev. in Nuclear Medicine, 1990—, Poison Control - Part I, 2000, Part II, 2000, Jour. Pharmacy Practice, Radiologic Pharmacy IV, Parts I and II, 2001, Drug Diversion and Counterfeiting, Parts I and II, 2006; mem. editl. bd. New Perspectives in Cancer Diagnosis and Management, 1992-99, Annals of Pharmacotherapy, 2003—, our. Pharmacy Practice, 1991—; nat. field editor ASHP Signal Newsletter, 1985-87; contbr. chpt. to book. Mem. Henry Morgan chpt. B'nai B'rith, Southfield, Mich., 1975-77; sec. Ala. Pharmacy Assn. Rsch. and Edn. Found., 1996-98; trustee Fla. Pharmacy Assn. Found., 2002-04. Fellow: Acad. Pharmacy Practice and Mgmt. (nuc. pharmacy sec. ednl. affairs com. 1983—2009, regulatory affairs com. 1984—2004, del. 1986—2002, edn. cons. 1987—2001, profl. and sci. affairs com. 1988—2004, Practitioner Merit award 1990, Presentation award 1990—91, Poster award 1990—91, Presentation award 1994, Poster award 1994, Disting. Achievement award in Nuc. Pharmacy 2003), Am. Soc. Health-Sys. Pharmacists (edn. program assoc. 1988—95, practice adv. panel 1992—93, chmn. specialized practice group on radiologic pharmacy 1993—95, continuing edn. 1995—98); mem.: Oakstone Med. Pubs. (coord. editor in-svc. revs. nuc. medicine tech. 2004—), Ctrl. Fla. Pharmacy Assn. (sec. 2002—06, treas. 2007—09, newsletter editor 2009—, Pharmacist of Yr. 2004), Ala. Pharmacy Assn. (exec. dir. 1996—98), Polk County Pharmacy Assn., Hillsborough County Pharmacy Assn. (sec. 1991—92, exec. com. 1991—96, pres.-elect 1993—94, pres. 1994—95, newsletter editor 1994—96, pres. 1995—96, Pharmacist of Yr. award 1994, Pres. award 1994—96), Pasco-Hernando Pharmacy Assn. (treas. 1990—93, exec. com. 1990—94, Pharmacist of Yr. award 1995), Pinellas Pharmacists Soc. (exec. com. 1989—97, pres.-elect 1991—92, pres. 1992—93, newsletter editor 1992—96, Pharmacist of Yr. award 1992, Pres' award 1993, FPA Unit Assn. Recognition award 1993, PPS Merit award 1994, Practice Merit award 1994, FPA Unit Assn. Recognition award 1995, Lifetime Merit award 1996), Soc. Nuclear Medicine (S.E. chpt., govt. affairs com. 1985—86, program com. 1988—89, edn. cons. 1989—, Brewster Bill task force 1995, NRC com. 1995—97, chair pharmacy liaison com. 1995—2000), Internat. Pharm. Fedn. (edn. cons. Pharmacy World Congress 1992—93, editor procs. spl. session Pharmacy World Congress 1993, vice chmn. nuc. pharmacy subsect. 1994—95, chmn. nuc. pharm. group 1994—97, edn. con. Pharmacy World Congress 1995—96, chair SIG on radiologic pharmacy bd. of pharm. scis. 1997—2002, edn. con. Pharmacy World Congress 1999, 2001—02, editor Radioimmunopharm.: Current and Future Considerations, Sci. Poster award Sect. Hosp. Pharmacists 1992), Fla. Nuclear Medicine Technologists (exec. coun. 1992—97, editor Procs. 22nd ann. meeting 1993, 24th ann. meeting 1995, 25th ann. meeting 1996), Fla. Soc. Hosp. Pharmacists, Acad. Pharmacy Practice (chmn. nuc. pharmacy sect. 1987—89, chmn. 1988—90, chmn. nuc. pharmacy sect. 1991—93, chmn. 1993—95, 2001—02, Poster Presentation 1st Pl. award 1995), Fla. Pharmacy Assn. (chmn. nuc. pharmacy sect. 1987—89, edn. cons. 1987—96, chmn. acad. pharmacy practice 1988—90, del. 1988—96, budget and fin. com., chmn. ednl. affairs coun., pres. com. 1989—90, task force on mission of pharmacy in Fla. 1989—92, conv. planning com. 1989—93, Region XII rep., exec. com. 1989—96, chmn. nuc. pharmacy sect. 1991—93, chmn. orgnl. affairs coun. 1992—93, chmn. acad. pharmacy practice 1993—95, editor numerous procs. for nuc. pharmacy lectr. series 1993—96, pres. com., budget and fin. com. 1994—95, conv. planning com., task force on mission of pharmacy in Fla. 1995, chmn. nuc. pharmacy sect. 2001—02, trustee 2002—04, exec. com., Region V rep. 2002—06, edn. cons. 2004—, chmn. orgnl. affairs coun. 2005—07, mem. orgnl. affairs coun. 2009—, Acad. Pharmacy Practice Merit award 1992, Number 1 Club 1990, Disting. Young Pharmacist award 1990, Acad. Pharmacy Practice Practitioner Merit award 1992, Sidney Simkowitz Pharmacy Involvement award 1992, Disting. Svc. award 1993, Unit Assn. Newsletter awards 1994—96, Acad. Pharmacy Practitioner Merit award 2008), Am. Soc. Pharmacy Law, Ala. Coun. Assn. Execs., Nat. Coun. State Pharmacy Assn. Execs., Am. Assn. Colls. Pharmacy (taskforce on residency programs and support 1990—91, task force on assessment of exptl. function 1994—95), Ad Hoc Com. Practice Environ. and Quality of Worklife, Am. Pharmacists Assn. (nuc. pharmacy sect., ednl. affairs com. 1983—2008, regulatory affairs com. 1984—2004, chmn.-elect, edn. adv. com. 1988—89, profl. and sci. affairs com. 1988—2004, chmn. sect. on specialized pharm. svcs. 1989—90, chmn.-elect 1992—93, edn. adv. com. 1992—94, chmn. sect. on nuc. pharmacy 1993—94, at-large sect. officer, edn. adv. com. 2000—02, chmn.-elect nuc. pharmacy 2002—03, policy com. Acad. Pharmacy Practice and Mgmt. 2002—04, chmn. nuc. pharmacy sect., chmn. 2003—04), Beta Beta Beta, Phi Alpha Theta, Psi Chi, Kappa Psi. Avocations: art collecting, sports, camping, travel, writing. Office: 455 Twisting Pine Cir Longwood FL 32779 Personal E-mail: dlavenrx@earthlink.net.

LAVENSTEIN, BENNETT, neurologist, educator; b. Balt., Nov. 21, 1945; BS, George Washington U., 1966; MD, U. Md., 1970. With Georgetown U. Sch. Medicine, 1980—; prof. neurology and pediat. Children's Nat. Med. Ctr., 1998—. Fellow: Am. Acad. Neurology; mem.: Am. Soc. Exptl. Neurotherapeutics, Child Neurology Soc., Movement Disorders Soc., Profs. Child Neurology. Avocations: tennis, sailing, art. Office: 111 Michigan Ave Washington DC 20010 Business E-Mail: blavenst@cnmc.org.

LAVERY, HILARY ANNE, dermatologist; d. John and Anne Patton; m. James Tees Lavery, Dec. 20, 1972; children: Alice, John, Michael, Paul, Caroline. MB, BChir, BAO, Queens U., Belfast, 1975, MD, 1980. Ho. officer Aras Hosp., Newtownards, 1975—76; sr. ho. officer dermatology Royal Victoria Hosp., Belfast, 1976—77, registrar dermatology, 1977—78, sr. registrar gentiourinary medicine, 1979—82; cons. physician Royal Victoria Hosp. and Ulster Ind. Clinic, 1982—86; registrar dermatology Belfast City Hosp., 1978—79; cons. physician genitourinary medicine and vulva skin disease Ulster Ind. Clinic, Belfast, 1982. Sr. tutor in medicine dept. medicine Queens U., Belfast, 1979—82; vis. physician dept. dermatology Mayo Clinic, Rochester, Minn., 1981; lectr. in field. Contbr. chapters to books, articles to profl. jours. McGrath Clin. scholar in og-byn., 1975. Mem.: Royal Soc. Medicine, Royal Coll. Physicians Edinburgh, Royal Coll. Physicians and Surgeons Glasgow. Avocations: golf, tennis, chess, reading, table tennis. Office: Ulster Ind Clinic 245 Stranmillis Rd Belfast BT9 5JH Northern Ireland Home: 74 Craigdarragh Road BT19 1UB Bangor Northern Ireland Office Phone: 01144 2891853148. E-mail: jameshillav@yahoo.co.uk.

LAVERY, ROBERT MICHAEL, internist, cardiologist; b. Pitts., Feb. 7, 1951; BS magna cum laude, Univ. Notre Dame, 1972; MD, Johns Hopkins U., 1976. Diplomate Am. Bd. Internal Medicine, Am. Bd. Cardiology. Intern Boston U. Hosp., 1976-77, resident in internal medicine, 1977-78; fellow in cardiology Boston U. Med. Ctr., 1978-80; pvt. practice Cardiology Assoc. of Manchester, NH, 1980—86, NH Cardiology Cons., Manchester, NH, 1986—, chief of cardiology, 2002—; clin. asst. prof. Boston U. Sch. Medicine, 2003—. Mem. staff Elliot Hosp., Manchester, Cath. Med. Ctr., Manchester. Named one of Top Cardiologists in NH, NH Mag., 2000, 2001, 2006, 2008. Fellow Am. Coll. Cardiology (coun. on clin. cardiology, NH affiliate pres. 1987-88, bd. dir. 1981-2000, gov. NH 2000-03, tri-state No. New Eng. chpt. pres. 2001-02); mem. Hillsborough County Med. Soc. Office: NH Cardiology Cons Ste 100 1 Elliot Way Manchester NH 03103-3547

LAVEZZI, ANNA MARIA, pathologist, educator; d. Francesco Lavezzi and Adele Fabris; m. Angelo Ghirardelli, May 15, 1972; 1 child, Marco Ghirardelli. DSc in Biol. Sci., U. Milam, 1968; MD in Med. and Surgery, U. Milan, 1989. Assoc. prof. pathology U. Milan, 1996—, chmn., 2001—04; mem. sci. com. Rsch. Ctr. Lino Rossi, 2004—. Ofcl. tchr. Technicians Sch. Pathol. Anatomy. Contbr. articles to profl. jours. Mem. work group Regional Ctr. Network, 2005—. Achievements include research in neuropathology and cardiovascular pathology. Office: Lino Rossi Dept Surg Reconstructive and Diagnostic Univ Milan Milan Italy Office Phone: 39-02-50320821. Office Fax: 39-02-50320823. Business E-Mail: anna.lavezzi@unimi.it.

LAVIE, CARL J., cardiologist, researcher; MD, LSU Sch. Medicine. Intern & resident Ochsner Med. Ctr., dir. cardiac rehabilitation & prevention, dir. exercise lab.; fellow in cardiovascular training Mayo Clinic Found. Grad. Sch. Medicine; assoc. editor for population medicine Ochsner Journal. Fellow: Am. Coll. Cardiology. Office: 1514 Jefferson Hwy New Orleans LA 70121 Office Phone: 504-842-5874.

LAVILLA, FRANCISCO JAVIER, nephrologist; b. Barcelona, Nov. 27, 1966; MD, U. Navarra, 1990. Nephrologist Clinica U. de Navarra, 1990—. Office: Pio XII 36 Pamplona Navarra 31180 Spain E-mail: jlavilla@unav.es.

LAVIN, PABLO, gynecologist, educator; b. Santiago, Chile, Apr. 21, 1947; MD, Medicine U. Chile, 1973; MPH, Pub. Health Johns Hopkins-North Carolina, PhD, 1987. Chmn. ob-gyn. clinica svc. Hosp. Barros Luco, 2002—10; prof. chmn. ob-gyn. dept. Facultad de Medicina U. Chile Campus Sur, 1985—. Bd. dir. Soc. Chilena de Climaterio y Menopausi, 2008—, Soc. Chilena de Endocrinología Ginecológica, 2008—, Soc. Chilena de Medicina Reproductiva, 2010—. Mem.: European Soc. Contraception, Am. Reproductive Medicine Soc., European Menopause and Andropause Soc., N.Am. Menopause Soc., Internat. Menopause Soc. Avocations: sports, travel, reading. Office: Gran Avenida 3204 San Miguel Santiago 8900085 Chile Office Fax: 56-2-555-3331. Business E-Mail: plavin@med.uchile.cl.

LAVIN, PHILIP TODD, medical executive; b. Rochester, NY, Nov. 21, 1946; s. Albert A. and Mary (Rapkin) Lavin; m. Mary Ellen Saunders, Aug. 23, 1970; children: Andrew, Abby. AB, U. Rochester, 1968; PhD, Brown U., Providence, 1972. Rsch. asst. prof. Brown U., Providence, 1972-74, SUNY Buffalo, Amherst, 1974-77; asst. prof. Sch. Pub. Health Harvard U., Harvard Med. Sch., Boston, 1977-83, assoc. prof. surgery, 1983—2005. Trainee NSF, 1968—72; pres., founder Averion Internat. (formerly Boston Biostatistics, Inc.), Southborough, Mass., 1983—; exec. dir., founder Boston Biostat Rsch. Found., Framingham, Mass., 1988—; cons. FDA, 1983—86, spl. govt. employee, 1992—; co-chmn. clin. trial com. Mass. Biotech. Coun., 2003—09. Fellow: Am. Statis. Assn., RAPS; mem.: Biometric Soc., Mass. Biotech Coun., N.Am. Spine Soc., Soc. Clin. Trials. Achievements include founding an international contract research organization and not for profit research foundation; supporting 63 FDA approvals for drugs, devices and biologics; conducting research in biomarkers, oncology, obesity, cardiology, transplantation, orthopedics, pain control and periodontology; authoring or co-authoring over 150 professional publications and winning awards from professional societies for key publications in fertility and periodontology. Home: 3 Cahill Park Dr Framingham MA 01702-6105 Office: Aptiv Solutions 225 Turnpike Rd Southborough MA 01772 Business E-Mail: philip.lavin@aptivsolutions.com.

LAVIOLETTE, PAUL A., investment company executive; b. 1957; BA, Fairfield U.; MBA, Boston Coll. With Kendall Co. (Hosp. Products Divsn.); v.p., USCI Divsn. C.R. Bard, Inc., 1990—91, v.p., gen. mgr., USCI Angioplasty Divsn., 1991—93, pres., USCI Angioplasty Divsn., 1993, pres., USCI Divsn., 1993; pres. Boston Sci. Internat., Natick, Mass., 1994—95, 1998; sr. v.p., group pres., interventional cardiology, peripheral interventions, vascular surgery, electrophysiology & neurovascular bus. Boston Scientific Corp., Natick, Mass., sr. v.p., group pres., nonvascular bus., 1995—98, sr. v.p., group pres., Scimed, EP Technologies & Target Divsn., 2000, pres., Scimed, 2001, COO, 2004—08, adv., 2008; venture ptnr. SV Life Sciences Advisers, LLC. Bd. dirs. Advanced Med. Tech. Assn., New Eng. Heath Care Inst. Office: SV Life Sciences Advisers LLC 60 State St Ste 3650 Boston MA 02109-1925 Office Phone: 617-367-8100. Office Fax: 617-367-1590. Business E-Mail: Paul.LaViolette@svlsa.com.

LAVIZZO-MOUREY, RISA JUANITA, medical foundation administrator; b. Seattle, Sept. 25, 1954; d. Philip V. and Blanche (Sellers) Lavizzo; m. Robert J. Lavizzo, July 21, 1975; children: Rel, Max. Student, U. Wash.; B, SUNY, Stony Brook, 1975; MD, Harvard Med. Sch., 1979; MBA, U. Pa. Wharton Sch., 1986. Med. resident Brigham & Women's Hosp., Boston, 1979—82; clin. instr. Temple U. Med. Sch., Phila., 1982; asst. prof. medicine U. Pa. Sch. Medicine, Phila., 1986—92, assoc. prof., 1992—97, Sylvan Eismann prof. medicine, 1997—2001, dir. Inst. Aging, chief divsn. geriatric medicine, 1984—92, 1994—2001; assoc. chief of staff geriatrics & extended care Phila. Vets. Adminstrn. Med. Ctr.; dep. adminstr. Agy. Healthcare Policy & Rsch. HHS, Washington, 1992—94; dir. Health Care Group, sr. v.p. Robert Wood Johnson Found., Princeton, NJ, 2001—03, pres., CEO, 2003—, bd. trustees. Mem. Pres.'s Commn. Consumer Rights & Quality in Healthcare Industry, 1997—98; past mem. White House Task Force Health Care Reform; bd. dirs. Genworth Fin. Inc., 2007—. Contbr. articles to profl. jours. Named one of 25 Visionary Doctors, Modern Physician mag., 2003, 100 Most Powerful Women, Forbes mag., 2008, 2009; Robert Wood Johnson Clin. Scholar, U. Pa., 1984. Master: ACP; fellow: Am. Soc. Internal Medicine, Am. Geriatric Soc.; mem.: NAS, Nat. Med. Assn., Assn. Academic Minority Physicians, Am. Soc. Internal Medicine, Inst. Medicine. Office: Robert Wood Johnson Found PO Box 2316 College Rd E & Rte 1 Princeton NJ 08543-2316 Office Phone: 877-843-7953. *

LAVOIE, LIONEL A., physician, health science association administrator; b. St. Brieux, Sask., Can., Aug. 24, 1937; s. Athanase T. and Ella Marie (Mevel) L.; m. Mary Tina Luchenski, Oct. 12, 1964; children: Robert, Michelle, Nicole, Andrea. BA, Ottawa U., Ont., Can., 1958, MD, 1964. Intern, then resident Univ. Hosp., Sask.; clin. prof. family medicine U. Sask., 1978—; chief of staff Melfort Union Hosp., Sask., 1985-90. Commr. Med. Care Ins. Commn., 1984-88. Chmn. Melfort Dist. Minor Sports, 1978-80, Melfort Pks. and Recreation, 1983-86, Sask. Summer Games 1988, 1986-88. Recipient Ramstead award, Jaycees of Province Sask., 1975, Dedication award, Sask. Parks, Recreation and Culture, 1988, Cmty. Recreation award, Melford C. of C., 1989, Commemorative medal, 125th Anniversary Can. Confedn., 1993, Recognition award, Coll. Medicine, U. Sask., 1999, award of merit, Faculty of Medicine U. Ottawa Alumni Assn., 2001, Rural Long Service award, Soc. Rural Physicians Can., 2002, Queen's Jubilee medal Can., 2002, Award of Merit, Can. Paraplegic Assn., 2005, Sask. Centennial medal, 2005. Fellow Coll. Family Physicians (Can., cert.),; mem. Can. Med. Assn. (sr., bd. dirs. 1978-83, pres. elect 1989-90, pres. 1990-91, life), Sask. Med. Assn. (bd. dirs. 1971-76, v.p. 1974, pres. 1975, life), Can. Acad. Sports Medicine, Am. Geriatric Soc., Coll. Family Physicians Can. (sec. Sask. province 1967-70), Sask. Acad. Sports Medicine (pres. 1986-88, Cert. of Merit 2004), Coun. Med. Assn. (chmn. 1985-89), Sask. Paraplegic Assn. (bd. dirs. 1978—), Can. Cancer Soc. (adv. com. Sask. div. 1986—),

Nat. Aerospace Med. Assn., KC (grand knight 1980-81), Rotary (pres. Melfort club 1987-88). Avocations: golf, curling, horticulture. Home: 402 Stovel E Melfort SK Canada S0E 1A0 Office: Can Med Assn 1867 Alta Vista Dr Ottawa ON Canada K1G 0G8 Personal E-mail: lionelmarylavoie@hotmail.com.

LAVRANOS, GIAGKOS, medical researcher; b. Piraeus, Attica, Greece, Dec. 15, 1983; s. Micky and Maro Lavranos. MD (hon.), Athens U. Med. Sch., Attica, 2007. Rschr. Athens U., 2003—. Rsch. coord. CEREPRI, Athens, 2007—08. Contbr. scientific papers. Olympic games vol. IOC, Athens, 2004. Grant, Propondis Found. Liechtenstein, 2007—, Athens U., 2005—07. Master: RCP; mem.: Hellenic Soc. Andrology. Personal E-mail: giagkos83@gmail.com.

LAVYNE, MICHAEL H., neurosurgeon, educator; Studied, Williams Coll.; MD, Cornell U., 1972. Diplomate Am. Bd. Neurol. Surgery. Resident Mass. Gen. Hosp., Boston, 1974—79; fellow Beth Israel Hosp., Boston; assoc. attending surgeon NY Presbyn. Hosp.; clin. prof. of neurol. surgery Cornell Univ., NYC. Office: Cornell University 110 E 55th St New York NY 10022 Office Phone: 212-486-9100. Office Fax: 212-486-9024.

LAWLESS, MICHAEL RHODES, pediatrics educator; b. Baytown, Tex., Oct. 13, 1942; s. Wallace Ervin and Amy Ruth (Broussard) L.; m. E. Sandra Johnson, Aug. 27, 1967; children: Melanie Lawless York, Stephanie Lawless Setzer. BA in Zoology, U. Tex., 1964, MD, 1968. Diplomate Am. Bd. Pediat. Intern City Memphis Hosp., 1968-69; resident in pediat. U. Tex. Med. Br., Galveston, 1969-71; instr. U. Rochester (N.Y.) Sch. Medicine, 1971-72; staff pediatrician Portsmouth (Va.) Naval Hosp., 1972-74; asst. prof. pediat. Wake Forest U. Sch. Medicine, Winston-Salem, NC, 1974-80, assoc. prof. pediat., 1980-2001, prof. pediat., 2001—08, dep. assoc. dean student affairs, 1988-96, chief gen. pediat. and adolescent medicine, 1997—2005. Lt. comdr. USNR, 1972-74. Fellow U. Rochester, 1971-72. Fellow Am. Acad. Pediat. (legis. liaison 1980—); mem. Am. Profl. Soc. on Abuse of Children, N.C. Pediatric Soc. (child adv. 1974—), Coun. Med. Student Edn. in Pediat. (pres. 1998-00), Academic Pediatric Assn., Am. Bd. Pediat. (bd. dirs. 2003—08). Avocation: outdoor activities.

LAWLEY, THOMAS JOSEPH, dean, medical educator; b. Buffalo, 1947; m. Christine Lawley, 1969; children: Thomas Jr., John, Megan. Grad., Canisius Coll., 1968; MD, SUNY Sch. Medicine, Buffalo, 1972. Intern SUNY Sch. Medicine, Buffalo, 1973—74; resident Yale U. Affiliated Hosps., 1974—75; sr. investigator dermatology br. Nat. Cancer Inst. NIH; prof. and chair. dept. dermatology Emory U. Sch. Medicine, Atlanta, 1988—96, William Patterson Timmie Prof. Dermatology, 1993—, exec. assoc. dean, 1995—96, dean, 1996—; vice chair Emory U. Sys. Health Care, Atlanta, 1996—; core dir. Emory Skin Disease Rsch. Ctr., Atlanta. Pres. Emory Med. Care Found., Emory Children's Ctr.; adminstrv. coun. Assn. Am. Med. Colls. Mem.: Am. Profs. Dermatology, Soc. Investigative Dermatology, Am. Acad. Dermatology (Marion Sulzberger Award 1995), Assn. Am. Physicians, Am. Soc. Clin. Investigators. Office: Emory U Sch Medicine Woodruff Health Scis Ctr Adminstrv Bldg 1440 Clifton Rd NE Atlanta GA 30322-1053 *

LAWRENCE, ALBERT EDWARD, III, counselor; b. Brockton, Mass., Sept. 26, 1980; BA, Franklin Pierce Coll., 2002; MEd, Bridgewater State Coll., 2007. Clin. intern Mclean Hosp., 2006, Arbour Fuller Hosp., 2006, clin. intern, clinician Mass. Soc. Prevention of Cruelty to Children, 2006—08; secure treatment clinician Dept. Youth Svcs., 2008—11; lic. mental health counselor Dr. Karen Ruskin and Assocs., 2011—. Mental health counseling adv. bd. mem. dept counselor edn. Bridgewater State Coll., 2005—06; rsch. assoc. psychiatry Harvard Med. Sch., Mclean Hosp., 2006. Decorated Outstanding Heroism Am. Legion. Mem.: Am. Mental Health Counselors Assn., Chi Sigma Iota (hon.). Avocations: swimming, reading, hiking. Office: 36 S Main St Ste B Sharon MA 02067 Office Fax: 1-781-784-3112. E-mail: albertlawrenceiii@gmail.com.

LAWRENCE, DAVID M., retired health facility administrator; b. 1940; BA, Amherst Coll., Mass., 1962, DSc (hon.) (hon.), 1994; MD, U. Ky., 1966; MPH, U. Wash., 1973; LittD (hon.) (hon.), Colgate U., 1995. Cert. gen. preventive medicine. Intern in internal medicine, pediat.; health officer, dir. Multnomah County, Oreg.; v.p., area med. dir. N.W. Permanente Kaiser Found. Health Plan and Hosps., Portland, Maine, 1981—85, v.p., reg. mgr. Colo., 1985—88, sr. v.p., reg. mgr. NC, 1988—89, vice chmn. bd. dirs. Oakland, Calif., 1990—91, CEO, 1992—2002. Bd. dirs. Pacific Gas and Elec. Co., Hewlett Packard, Healthcare Forum, Bay Area Coun., Calif. Coll. Arts and Crafts, Colby Coll.; trustee Rockefeller Found.; bd. dirs. Agilent Technologies Inc., Dynavax Technologies Corp., Raffles Med. Group, Inc., McKesson Corp., 2004—. Named Outstanding Alumnus of the Sch. Pub. Health and Cmty. Medicine, U. Wash., 1980, Outstanding Alumnus of the Coll. Medicine, U. Ky., 1995. Mem.: APHA, Inst. of Medicine of NAS (bd. dirs.), The Conf. Bd. (bd. dirs.), Calif. Bus. Roundtable, Western Consortium for Pub. Health, Group Health Assn. Am., Calif. Assn. Hosps. and Health Sys., Am. Coll. Preventive Medicine, Am. Hosp. Assn., Alpha Omega Alpha. Office: McKesson Corp One Post St San Francisco CA 94104 Office Phone: 415-983-8300. Office Fax: 415-983-8464. Business E-Mail: david.lawrence@mckesson.com. *

LAWRENCE, JANICE ELAINE, psychiatric and mental health nurse; b. Brockton, Mass., Jan. 7, 1954; d. George Freemont and Marjorie Elsie Glidden; m. James George Lawrence, Sept. 11, 1971; children: Jennifer Lynn, Jillian Lee, James George, Justin James. AS, Massasoit CC, Brockton, Mass., 1983. RN Mass. Nursing asst. Hallmark nursing Home, East Bridgewater, Mass., 1979—83, evening nursing supr. Blue Hills Nursing Care Ctr., Staughton, Mass., 1983—84; evening charge nurse psychiat. unit, emergency dept. psychiat. evaluator Brockton (Mass.) Hosp., 1984—; pres. Cyborg Equipment Corp. Inc. Author numerous poems. Active Girl Scouts Am., East Bridgewater, 1978—84, Boy Scouts Am., Bridgewater, 1992—. Baptist. Avocations: writing, horseback riding, music, gardening, dogs. Home: 298 High St Bridgewater MA 02324 Office: Brockton Hosp 680 Centre St Brockton MA 02302 Personal E-mail: jl02324@aol.com.

LAWRENCE, JANICE FLETCHER, psychologist; d. Charlie J. and Garnet Roberts Fletcher; 1 child, Vicci Leigh. AB, Marshall U., 1955, MA, 1957, MA, 1979; EdD, Va. Polytechnic Inst. & State U., 1979. Lic. sch. psychologist W.Va. Dept. Edn., 1978, Nat. Sch. Psychology, 1989, sch. psychologist, ind. practioner W.Va. Bd. Psychologists, 1995. Psychologist Kanawha County Schs., Charleston, W.Va., 1967—74; coord. psychologists W.Va. State Dept., Charleston, 1974—89; sch. psychologist Kanawha County Schs., Charleston, 1984—89; adj. clin. prof. psychology Marshall U., South Charleston, W.Va., 1978—2001; pvt. practice Cmty. Behavioral Svcs., Inc., Dunbar, W.Va., 1990—2008; cons. Sch. Sys., 2008—. Trustee Nat. Sci. Bd., Charleston, 1974—84. Gifted Edn. grant, W.Va. Dept. Edn., 1978—83, Handicapped Children grant, 1981—84. Mem.: Nat. Assn. Sch. Psychologists. Avocations: gardening, reading.

LAWRENCE, NAOMI, dermatologist, educator; BA, Tulane U., 1983, MD, 1987. Diplomate Am. Bd. Dermatology, Am. Bd. Dermatology-dermatopathology. Intern Tulane Med. Ctr. Hosp. & Clinic, resident; fellow Univ. Tex. Southwestern Med. Ctr.; mohs micrographic surgery and cutaneous oncology fellowship under Willis Cottel Dallas; instr. dermatology residents Cooper Univ. Hosp., head divsn. dermatology sect. of procedural dermatology, assoc. prof. medicine; instr. med. students UMDNJ-Robert Wood Johnson Med. Sch. Mem.: Am. Acad. of Cosmetic Surgery, Am. Coll. of Mohs Micrographic Surgery, Am. Acad. of Dermatology, Am. Soc. of Dermatologic Surgery. Office: Cooper University Hospital Ste 10103 10000 Sagemore Dv Marlton NJ 08053 Office Phone: 856-596-3040. Office Fax: 856-596-5651.

LAWRENCE, ROBERT SWAN, physician, educator; b. Phila., Feb. 6, 1938; s. Thomas George and Catherine (Swan) Lawrence; m. Cynthia Starr Cole, July 1, 1960; children: Job Scott, Matthew Swan, Hannah Starr, Jin Sook, Sang Bo. AB magna cum laude, Harvard U., Cambridge, Mass., 1960, MD, 1964. Intern, resident in internal medicine Mass. Gen. Hosp., 1964—66; surgeon USPHS, 1966—69; resident in internal medicine Mass. Gen. Hosp., 1969—70; asst. prof., then assoc. prof. medicine, chief divsn. cmty. medicine Med. Sch. U. NC, 1970—74; dir. divsn. primary care Harvard U. Med. Sch., 1974—91, assoc. prof. medicine, 1980—81, Charles S. Davidson assoc. prof. medicine, 1981—91; prof. medicine Johns Hopkins Sch. Medicine, Balt., 1996—; prof. environ. health sci., health policy, internat. health Johns Hopkins Bloomberg Sch. Pub. Health, Balt., 1995—, Edyth Schoenrich prof. preventive medicine, 2000—06, Ctr. Livable Future prof., 2008—. Chmn. dept. medicine Cambridge Hosp., Mass., 1980—91; adj. prof. NYU Sch. of Medicine, 1992—95; assoc. dean profl. edn. Johns Hopkins Bloomberg Sch. Pub. Health, 1995—2006; mem. com. human rights NAS, 1986—97; chmn. bd. health promotion and disease prevention IOM, 1981—86, chmn. com. health and human rights, 1990—94; chmn. U.S. Preventive Svc. Task Force HHS, 1984—89, active mem., 1990—96; fellow Ctr. Advanced Study in Behavioral Scis., 1988—89; dir. health scis. Rockefeller Found., 1991—95; found. dir. Ctr. Livable Future, John Hopkins Bloomberg Sch. Pub. Health, 1996—; mem. global health advisory com. Open Soc. Inst., 2005—; bd. trustees Albert Schweitzer Fellowships, 2003—. Editor Am. Jour. Preventive Medicine, 1990—92; contbr. articles to profl. jours., chapters to books. Bd. trustees Columbia U. Tchrs. Coll., 1992—98; bd. dir. Physicians for Human Rights, 1986—91, 1997—2003, 2007—, pres., 1999—2003, 2007—, chair, bd. dirs., 2007—. Epidemic intelligence svc. CDC, 1966—69, commissioned officer USPHS. Recipient Maimonides prize, 1964, John Atkinson Ferrell prize, 1997, Albert Schweitzer Humanitarian prize, 2002, Zubrow award, Pa. Hosp., 2008, Sedgwick Meml. medal, APHA, 2009. Master: ACP; fellow: Am. Coll. Preventive Medicine (Spl. Recognition award 1988); mem.: APHA, Soc. Tchrs. Preventive Medicine (Spl. Recognition award 1993), Soc. Gen. Internal Medicine (pres. 1978—79, Leadership award 1997), Inst. Medicine NAS, Phi Beta Kappa, Delta Omega. Home: Highfield House 1112 4000 N Charles St Baltimore MD 21218-1760 Office Phone: 410-614-4590. Business E-Mail: rlawrenc@jhsph.edu.

LAWRENCE, RODERICK JOHN, social sciences educator; b. Adelaide, Australia, Aug. 30, 1949; s. Keith and Babette Naomi (Radford) L.; m. Clarisse Christine Gonet, Sept. 30, 1977; children: Xavier Gerard, Adrien Keith, Kevin John. BS with first class hons., Adelaide U., Australia, 1972; MS, Cambridge U., Eng., 1977; PhD, Ecole Poly., Lausanne, Switzerland, 1983. Architect Edwards, Madigan and Torzillo, Sydney, Australia, 1972-74, S. Australian Housing Trust, Adelaide, 1973-76; rsch. scholar St. John's Coll., Cambridge U., Eng., 1975-77; asst. prof. Ecole Poly. Fed., Lausanne, Switzerland, 1978-84; cons. Econ. Commn. Europe, Geneva, 1984—; master tchr. and rschr. U. Geneva, 1984-99, prof. Faculty of Social and Econ. Scis., 1999—. Vis. prof. U. Que., Montreal, 1987; vis. fellow Flinders U., Adelaide, 1985; mem. editl. bd. Arch. and Behavior, 1980, Open House Internat., 1986, Netherlands Jour., Housing and the Built Environment, 2002-, Archtl. Sci. Rev., 2006-; mem sci. adv. bd. on health and environ., WHO, 1994—, mem. European task force on housing and health, 2001--; cons. Urban Affairs divsn., Environment Directorate, OECD, Paris, 1992—; speaker, guest lectr. various European and Australian univs. Author: Le Seuil Franchi..., 1986, Housing, Dwellings, and Homes, 1987, Better Understanding Our Cities: The Role of Urban Indicators, 1997; editor: Sustaining Human Settlement: A Challenge or the New Millennium, 2000, Socially Sustainable Cities: Principles and Practice, 2000; guest editor: jours. Nat. Sci Found. Switzerland fellow, 1984. Mem. Internat. Assn. Study of People and their Phys. Surroundings (bd. dirs. 1986—, exec. bd. 1994-2002, treas. 1994-2002), Environ. Design Rsch. Assn., People and Phys. Environ. Rsch. Soc., Open House Internat. Assn., N.Y. Acad. Sci. Avocations: photography, bushwalking, skiing. Office: U Geneva/Inst Environ Scis Human Ecology Group route de Drize 7 1227 Carouge Switzerland

LAWRENCE, RUTH ANDERSON, pediatrician; b. NYC; d. Stephen Hayes and Loretta (Harvey) A.; m. Robert Marshall Lawrence, July 4, 1950; children: Robert Michael, Barbara Asselin, Timothy Lee, Kathleen Ann, David McDonald, Mary Khalil, Joan Margaret, John Charles, Stephen Harvey. BS in Biology summa cum laude, Antioch Coll., 1945; MD, U. Rochester, 1949; DD (hon.), St. Bernard's Sch. Theology, 2009. Diplomate Am. Bd. Pediatrics 1960. Internship and residency in pediatrics Yale New Haven (Conn.) Hosp., 1949-50; asst. resident in Medicine Yale New Haven (Conn.) Community Hosp., 1950-51; postdoctoral fellow Yale New Haven Hosp., 1951, chief resident newborn svc., 1951; cons. in medicine U.S. Army, Ft. Dix, N.J., 1952; from clin. instr. to sr. instr. in pediatrics U. Rochester, N.Y., 1952-64, assoc. resident N.Y., 1957-58, asst. prof. N.Y., 1964-70, assoc. prof. N.Y., 1970-85, prof. pediatrics, ob.-gyn. N.Y., 1985—. Rsch. pediatrician Monroe County Health Dept., Rochester, 1952-58; dir. Finger Lakes Regional Poison Control Ctr., 1958—2010; chief nursery svc. Strong Meml. Hosp., Rochester, 1960-73, chief dept. pediatrics, The Highland Hosp., Rochester, 1960-91; adj. prof. Sch. Pub. Health, SUNY, Albany, 1996-99, editor-in-chief Breast Feeding Medicine, 2005-; rsch. in field. Author: Breastfeeding: A Guide for the Medical Profession, 6th edit., 2005, 7th edi, 2010; editor: various periodicals; contbr. numerous articles to profl. publs. Mem. Safety Coun. Rochester and Monroe County, also past pres.; bd. dirs., past pres. Life Line. Recipient Gold Medal award U. Rochester Alumni Assn., 1979, William Keeler award Rochester Safety Coun., 1982, Civic Contribution citation Rochester Safety Coun., 1984, Career Achievement award Girl Scouts U.S. of Genesee Valley, 1987, Rochester Diocesan award for women, St. Bernard's Inst., 1989, Albert David Kaiser medal, 1991, Chamber Civic Health Care award, 1996, Humanism in Medicine award Am. Assn. Med. Colls., 1999, Edward Mott Moore award, Monroe County Med. Soc., 2001, Nat. Best Physician award, 2002-03, Lifetime Achievement award Healthy Children, 2003, 1st Annual Leading Lady award Leading Lady Cos., Beachwood, Ohio, 2003, Dr. of Divinity St. Bernard's Inst. Tech., 2008, Martha Mae Eliot award Am. Pub. Health Assn., 2009, Disting. Alumnae award U. Rochester Sch. Medicine, 2010, numerous svc. awards; named Woman of Yr. Girl Scouts U.S. of Monroe County, 1968; hon. fellow Am. Sch. Health Assn., 1960, rsch. fellow Jackson Meml. Rsch. Labs., 1945. Fellow Am. Pediatric Soc., Am. Acad. Clin. Toxicology (past trustee, Lifetime Achievement award 2002); mem. Internat. Soc. for Rsch. in Human Milk and Lactation (exec. com. 1995-98), Human Milk Banking Assn. N.Am. (adv. bd. 1980-2005), NAS (subcom. on nutrition during lactation), Acad. Breastfeeding Medicine (founding bd. dirs. 1994—, pres. 1997-98), Alpha Omega Alpha. Roman Catholic. Office: U Rochester Sch Medicine 601 Elmwood Ave Box 777 Rochester NY 14642 Office Phone: 585-275-4354. Business E-Mail: ruth_lawrence@urmc.rochester.edu.

LAWRENCE, SANFORD HULL, physician, immunochemist, author; b. Kokomo, Ind., July 10, 1919; s. Walter Scott and Florence Elizabeth (Hull) L. AB, Ind. U., 1941, MD, 1944. Fellow in biochemistry George Washington U., 1941; intern Rochester (N.Y.) Gen. Hosp., 1944-45; resident Halloran Hosp., Staten Island, NY, 1946-49; chief med. svce. Ft. Ord Regl. Hosp., 1945-46; dir. biochemistry rsch. lab. San Fernando (Calif.) VA Hosp.; asst. prof. UCLA, 1950—. Cons. internal medicine and cardiology U.S. Govt., Los Angeles County; lectr. Faculte de Medicine, Paris, various colls. Eng., France, Belgium, Sweden, USSR, India, Japan; chief med. svc. Ft. Ord Regional Hosp.; chmn. Titus, Inc., 1982—. Author: Zymogram in Clinical Medicine, 1965, Gyert, 2000, Whitley Heights, 2002; contbr. articles to sci. jours.; author: Threshold of Valhalla, Another Way to Fly, My Last Satyr, and other short stories; traveling editor: Relax Mag. Mem. Whitley Heights Civic Assn., 1952—; pres. Halloran Hosp. Employees Assn., 1947-48. Served to maj. U.S. Army, 1945-46. Recipient Rsch. award TB and Health Assn., 1955-58, Los Angeles County Heart Assn., 1957-59, Pres. award, Queen's Blue Book award, Am. Men of Sci. award; named one of 2000 Men of Achievement, Leaders of Am. Sci., Ky. Col., named Hon. Mayor of West Point, Ky. Mem. AAAS, AMA, N.Y. Acad. Scis., Am. Fedn. Clin. Research, Am. Assn. Clin. Investigation, Am. Assn. Clin. Pathology, Am. Assn. Clin. Chemistry, Los Angeles County Med. Assn. Republican. Methodist. Avocations: bridge, comml. pilot, piano, organist. Home: Whitley Heights 2014 Whitley Ave Los Angeles CA 90068-3235 also: 160 rue St Martin 75003 Paris France

LAWRENCE, THEODORE, retired physician; b. Phila., Feb. 13, 1921; MD, U. Pa., 1950. Diplomate Am. Bd. Internal Medicine, Am. Bd. Cardiovascular Disease. Intern Bryn Mawr Hosp., 1950-51, resident, 1951-52, Long Beach VA Hosp., 1952-53, Phila. VA Hosp., 1953-54, staff physician, 1965-80, Haverford State Hosp., Pa., 1980-97, ret. Pa., 1997. Fellow ACP. Home: 808 Galer Dr Newtown Square PA 19073-3503 *

LAWRENCE, THEODORE S., oncologist, educator; MD, Cornell Med. Coll., 1980; PhD, Rockefeller U., 1979. Cert. Internal Medicine, 1983, Med. Oncology, 1985, Radiation Oncology, 1987. Resident Stanford U. Med. Sch., 1983, Nat. Cancer Inst., 1987; faculty U. Mich., Ann Arbor, 1987—; Isadore Lampe prof. and chair radiation oncology U. Mich. Med. Sch., Ann Arbor; prof. environ. health U. Mich. Sch. Pub. Health, Ann Arbor. Chair, bd. sci. councilors Nat. Cancer Inst. Mem.: Inst. Medicine, Am. Soc. Therapeutic Radiology and Oncology, Am. Soc. Clin. Oncology. Office: U Hosp 1500 E Med Ctr Dr Rm B2C490 Ann Arbor MI 48109-0010 Office Phone: 734-647-9955. Office Fax: 734-763-7371.

LAWRENCE, WALTER, JR., surgeon, educator; b. Chgo., May 31, 1925; s. Walter and Violette May (Matthews) L.; m. Susan Grayson Shryock, June 20, 1947; children: Walter Thomas, Elizabeth, William Amos, Edward Gene. Student, Dartmouth Coll., 1943-44; PhB, U. Chgo., 1944, SB, 1945, MD with honors, 1948. Diplomate Am. Bd. Surgery (examiner 1974-78, sr. mem. 1978—). Intern Johns Hopkins, 1948-49, asst. resident, 1949-51; fellow Meml. Sloan-Kettering Cancer Ctr., 1951-52, 54-56, rsch. fellow, 1956, asst. mem., asst. attending surgeon, 1957-60, assoc. mem., assoc. attending surgeon, 1960-66; practice medicine specializing in surgery NYC, 1956-66, Richmond, Va., 1966—. Instr. surgery Cornell U., 1957-58, asst. profl. clin. surgery, 1958-63, clin. assoc. prof., 1963-66; vis. investigator Queen Victoria Hosp., East Grinstead, Eng., 1964-65; prof. surgery Med. Coll. Va., Richmond, 1966-90, prof. emeritus, 1990--, chmn. divsn. surg. oncology, 1966-90, exec. vice chmn. dept. surgery, 1966-73, acting chmn., 1973-74, Am. Cancer Soc. prof. clin. oncology, 1972-77; dir. Massey Cancer Ctr., 1974-88, dir. emeritus, 1988—; chmn. surgery test com. Nat. Bd. Med. Examiners, 1973-77; med. dir.-at-large Va. divsn. Am. Cancer Soc., 1967—, med. v.p. Am. Cancer Soc., 1975-77, pres., 1977-79, nat. del., 1972-76, mem. nat. coun. for rsch. and clin. investigation, 1974-78, mem. profl. edn. com., 1982-96, bd. dir., 1985-98, vice chmn., chmn. M&S com., 1986-88, chmn. M&S exec. com., 1989-90, pres. elect, 1990-91, nat. pres., 1991-92, past office dir., 1993-99, hon. life mem., 1999—; bd. sci. counsellors Nat. Cancer Inst., 1978-82, chmn. surg. oncology rsch. devel. com.; mem. Nat. Cancer Adv. Bd., 1988-94; governing coun. Internat. Union Against Cancer, 1994-2002. Author: (with J.J. Terz) Cancer Management, 1977, (with J.J. Terz, J.P. Neifeld) Manual of Soft Tissue Surgery, 1983; mem. editl. bd. Va. Med., 1977-93, Jour. Surg. Oncology, 1978—, assoc. editor, 1991—, dep. editor, 2005-09; editl. bd. Jour. Cancer Edn., 1986; asst. editor Cancer, 1962-65, assoc. editor, 1991-2000, mem. editl. bd., 2000-06; contbr. articles to med. jour. Served with USNR, 1942-46, with US Army, 1952-54. Recipient Cancer Rsch. award Alfred P. Sloan Found., 1964; J. Shelton Horsley award Am. Cancer Soc., 1973; Disting. Svc. award U. Chgo., 1976; Va. Commonwealth U. Univ. Award for Excellence, 1988, Disting.

Faculty award Med. Coll. Va. Alumni Assn., 1988, Va. Cultural Laureate award, 1992, OBICI award, 1992, Dean's award for Disting. Svc., 1992; named to Humera Soc. (hon.), 1992, Beckstrand Cancer Found. Cancer Fighter of Yr., 1999, Presdl. medallion Va. Commonwealth U., 2000, Lifetime Sci. Achievement award Sci. Mus. Va., 2002; Disting. Svc. Award of Richmond Acad. Medicine, 2003, Robert Irby award, MCV Found., 2009, St. George Nat. award Am. Cancer Soc., 2010. Fellow ACS, Am. Cancer Soc.(commn. on cancer 1973-85, chmn. 1979-81, St. George Nat. award 2010), NY Acad. Sci., Royal Soc. Medicine, Soc. Black Acad. Surgeons (hon.), mem. AAAS, AMA, Am. Assn. Cancer Edn., Am. Assn. Cancer Rsch., Am. Gastroenterol. Assn. (coun. on cancer 1972-76), Am. Surg. Assn., Halsted Soc. (pres. 1975), James Ewing Soc., Soc. Head and Neck Surgeons, Am. Soc. Clin. Oncology, Am. Radium Soc. (exec. coun. 1985-87), Soc. Surgery Alimentary Tract (founder), Soc. Surg. Oncology (exec. com. 1976-77, v.p. 1977-78, pres. 1979-80, chmn. exec. coun. 1980-81, Heritage honoree 2002), Soc. Univ. Surgeons, Surg. Biol. Club III (founding mem.), Transplantation Soc., Collegium Internat. Chirurgiae Digestive, Southeastern Surg. Congress, Pan Am. Med. Assn., Sociètè Internationale de Chirurgie, Va. Surg. Soc. (v.p. 1973-74), Richmond Surg. Soc. (pres. 1986-87), Richmond Acad. Medicine (trustee 1986-87, 1st v.p. 1988, Disting. Svc. award 2003), So. Surg. Assn. (1st v.p. 1999-2000, hon. fellow, 2004), Argentine Surg. Assn. (hon.), Sigma Xi, Alpha Omega Alpha. Home: 6501 Three Chopt Rd Richmond VA 23226-3118 Office: Med Coll Va Hosps 1200 E Broad St PO Box 980011 Richmond VA 23298-0011 Business E-Mail: wlawrence@mcvh-vcu.edu.

LAWRENCE, WALTER THOMAS, plastic surgeon; b. Balt., Md., Sept. 5, 1950; s. Walter Jr. and Susan (Shryock) L.; m. Marsha Blake, May 30, 1987. BS, Yale U., 1972; MPH, Harvard U., 1976; MD, U. Va., 1976. Diplomate Am. Bd. Plastic Surgery. Intern and resident in gen. surgery U. NC, Chapel Hill, 1976-78; resident gen. surgery Med. Coll. Va., Richmond, 1978-81; resident plastic surgery U. Chgo., 1981-83; expert NIH, Bethesda, Md., 1983-85; asst. prof. U. NC, Chapel Hill, 1985-92, assoc. prof., div. chmn., 1992-95; prof., divsn. chmn. U. Mass. Med. Ctr., 1995-99, U. Kans. Med. Ctr., Kans. City, 1999—2009, U. Iowa Hosps. & Clinics, 2010—. Treas. Plastic Surgery Rsch. Coun., 1991—94, Plastic Surgery Ednl. Found., 2005—06; mem. Residency Rev. Com. for Plastic Surgery, 2000—06; pres. Assn. Academic Chmn. in Plastic Surgery, 2006—07. Contbr. articles to profl. jours. Fellow ACS; mem. Am. Assn. Plastic Surgeons(bd. trustees. 2006-09), Am. Soc. Plastic Surgeons (bd. dirs. 2007-09), Assn. Academic Chmn. Plastic Surgery, Plastic Surgery Rsch. Coun., Humera Soc., Womack Soc., Wound Healing Soc. Avocations: skiing, sailing, tennis, bicycling. Office: University Iowa Hosps & Clinics Divsn Plastic Surgery 200 Hawkins Dr 1541 JCP Iowa City IA 52242 Business E-Mail: thomas-lawrence@uiowa.edu.

LAWRIE, GERALD MURRAY, cardiovascular and thoracic surgeon, educator; b. Murwillumbah, N.S.W., Australia, Oct. 15, 1945; came to U.S., 1974; s. Charles Malcolm and Heather (Murray) L.; m. Susan Wagner, Dec. 28, 1978; children: Heather Cristina, Charles Murray, Elizabeth Jane. Attended, Scots Coll.; MB, BS, U. Sydney Med. Sch., Australia, 1969; MD, Baylor Coll. Medicine, 1974. Resident in gen. surgery Prince Henry/Prince of Wales Teaching Hosps., U. NSW, Sydney, 1969-72, sr. registrar in cardiothoracic surgery, 1973-74; resident in gen. surgery Royal Coll. Surgeons Eng., London, Plymouth Gen. Hosp., U.K., 1972; cardiovascular fellow Baylor Coll. Medicine, Houston, 1974-75, assoc. surgeon, dept. surgery, 1975, instr., 1975-76, asst. prof., 1976-78, assoc. prof., 1978-84, prof., 1984—97, clin. prof. surgery, 1997—, dir. thoracic surgery residency program, 1992-94; assoc. surgeon with Dr. DeBakey, 1975; attending surgeon Methodist Hosp., Houston, 1978—, Michael E. DeBakey Prof. Cardiac Surgery, 2008—, med. dir., Heart Valve Inst.; attending surgeon VA Hosp., Houston, 1980—, Ben Taub Hosp., Houston, 1975—; vice chmn. rsch., dept. surgery St. Joseph Hosp./Baylor Coll. Medicine, Houston, 1995-96; group practice Tex. Surgical Associates, 1997—; cardiothoracic surgeon Methodist DeBakey Heart & Vascular Ctr., Houston. Helped set up cardiovascular surgery programs in Saudi Arabia and Indonesia; helped set up a cardiac surgery program, Glasgow, Scotland, 1994; actively involved in the develop. of new surgical tng. facility, Methodist Inst. for Tech., Innovation and Edn. Methodist Hosp., mem. med. audit com., 1975, med. records com., 1981—82, chmn., cardiovascular patient care com., 1982—84, mem. surgical adv. com., 1983—84, mem. operating room com., 1994—95, mem. quality mgmt. com., 1997—, mem. exec. com., 1999—; mem. admissions com. Baylor Coll. Medicine, 1977—79, course curriculum com., cancer etiology, pathophysiology and prevention, 1980—91, mem. student promotions com., 1981—82, mem. curriculum com., adv. com. for pub. affairs, 1986—88, mem. grad. med. edn. com., 1992—93, mem. curriculum com., 1992—93; mem. ops. com. DeBakey Methodist Heart Ctr., 1999—; invited lectr. in field. Author of several published sci. articles and book chpts. Commonwealth Scholarship Holder, 1963-69; recipient James McRae Yeates prize for Clinical Surgery; Decorated Merit Order of Republic of Egypt, 1980; named leading adult heart surgeon in the U.S.A., Good Houskeeping Mag., 1996. Fellow Royal Coll. Surgeons (Edinburgh), Royal Australasian Coll. Surgeons, Royal Coll. Surgeons Can., Am. Coll. Cardiology (Gov.'s award 1983); mem. ACS, AMA, Am. Heart Assn. (pres. Houston chpt. 1985-86, bd. dirs. Tex. chpt. 1986-89, editl. task force, Houston Divsn. 1983-84, chmn. program com., Houston Divsn., 1984-85, Meritorious Svc. award, 1983, Vol. Recognition award, Houston, 1986), Am. Coll. Chest Physicians, South Tex. chpt. ACS, DeBakey Internat. Cardiovascular Soc., Houston Cardiology Soc. (sec./treas. 1980-81, v.p. 1981-82, pres. 1982-83), Harris County Med. Soc., Southwestern Surg. Congress, Tex. Med. Assn., Royal Soc. Medicine (assoc.), Soc. Thoracic Surgeons, Soc. for Vascular Surgery, Internat. Cardiovascular Soc. (N.Am. chpt.), Internat. Soc. for Minimally Invasive Cardiac Surgery, Am. Assn. for Thoracic Surgery, Soc. for Thoracic Surg. Edn., So. Surg. Assn., N.Am. Soc. Pacing and Electrophysiology, Soc. Med. Consultants to the Armed Forces, Houston Electrophysiological Soc. (treas. 1982-83, v.p. 1983-84, pres. 1984-85). Presbyterian. Participated in the surgical care of notable figures such as Shah of Iran, President of Turkey, the King of Belgium, and a number of royal figures; invented a technique called the American Correction; first to use a surgical robot to successfully repair a mitral valve using this advanced technique, 2007; performed heart surgery on Former First Lady Barbara Bush in 2009. Office: 6560 Fannin St Ste 1842 Houston TX 77030 Office Phone: 713-790-2089. Office Fax: 713-794-0576. Business E-Mail: glawrie@TexasSurgical.com.

LAWS, EDWARD RAYMOND, JR., neurosurgeon, educator; s. Edward Raymond and Jessie (Mancini) L.; m. Margaret Patricia Anderson, Sept. 15, 1962; children: Elizabeth, Margaret, Victoria, Eleanor. MD, Johns Hopkins U., Balt., 1963. Diplomate Am. Bd. Neurol. Surgery (bd. dirs. 1989—). Intern & resident Johns Hopkins Hosp., 1963—71, asst. prof. neurosurgery, 1971—72; asst. to prof., neurosurgery Mayo Clinic, Mayo Med. Sch., Rochester, Minn., 1972—87; prof. & chair, neurosurgery George Wash. U., Washington, 1987—92; prof. neurosurgery, medicine & pediat. U. Va., Charlottesville, 1992—2007; prof. neurosurgery, neurology & neurol. sci. Stanford U., Calif., 2007—08; prof. neurosurgery Harvard U., Boston, 2008—. Pres. Congress Neurol. Surgeons, 1984-85. Author: Pituitary Adenomas, 1976, Orbital Tumors, 1988, Glioma, 1992; editor: Neurosurgery, 1987-92; contbr. over 250 papers to profl. jours. Bd. dirs. Nat. Found., Balt., 1968-72, Nat. Found. for Brain Rsch., Washington, 1988—. Lt. comdr. USPHS, 1964—66, CDC, Atlanta, Ga. NIH grantee. Mem. Am. Acad. Neurol. Surgery, Am. Assn. Neurol. Surgeons (former pres., bd. dirs. 1988—), Am. Coll. Surgeons (past pres.), Congress Neurological Surgeons (former pres.), Inst. Medicine, Soc. Neurol. Surgeons, So. Neurosurg. Soc., Internat. Soc. Pituitary Surgeons, World Fedn. Neurol. Socs. (former pres.), Sigma Xi, Alpha Omega Alpha. Roman Catholic. Office: Brigham & Women's Hosp 15 Francis St Boston MA 02115

LAWSON, EDWARD EARLE, neonatologist; b. Winston-Salem, NC, Aug. 6, 1946; s. Robert Barrett and Elsie Chatterton (Earle) L.; m. Rebecca Newhall Fitts, June 21, 1969; children: Katherine Tabor, Robert Barrett II. BA magna cum laude, Harvard U., 1968; MD, Northwestern U., 1972. Diplomate Am. Bd. Pediat. and Neonatal/Perinatal Medicine. Intern then resident pediat. Children's Hosp., Boston, 1972-75, fellow neonatology, 1975-78; from asst. prof. pediat. to prof. pediat. U. N.C., Chapel Hill, 1978-99, chief divsn. neonatal medicine, 1987-95, interim chmn. dept. pediat., 1993-95; vice chmn., dept. pediat., 1995-99; prof. pediat., vice chair dept. pediat. Johns Hopkins U., Balt., 1999—; chief divsn. neonatology, dept. pediat. Johns Hopkins U. Hosp., Balt., 1999—. Editor-in-chief Jour. Perinatology, 2001—; assoc. editor Jour. of Pediat., 1985-95; contbr. numerous articles to profl. jours. Recipient Sidney Farber Meml. Rsch. award United Cerbral Palsy, 1982, Rsch. Career Devel. award NIH, 1982-87; E.L. Trudeau fellow, 1978-81, Alexander Von Humboldt fellow, 1985-86; NIH grantee, 1979—2006. Fellow Am. Acad. Pediat.; mem. Am. Lung Assn. (sci. adv. com. 1989-91), Am. Thoracic Soc. (bd. dirs. 1988-90), Am. Pediat. Soc., Perinatal Rsch. Soc. Achievements include research on developmental aspects of respiratory control, particularly physiology and neurobiology. Office: Johns Hopkins Hosp Dept Pediatrics 600 N Wolfe St NH2-133 Baltimore MD 21287-0001 Office Phone: 410-955-5259. Business E-Mail: elawson@jhmi.edu.

LAWSON, GEORGES MAGLOIRE, surgeon, researcher; b. Cotonou, Atlantique, Benin, Dec. 15, 1951; s. Pierre and Marie-Aimée (Agbodjogbe) Lawson; life ptnr. Christine Claudine Goset; children: Patrick Michel I., Clovis Morel T.; children: Jean-Yves Lionel M., Iris Mylene. MD, Nat. U. Benin, Cotonou, 1981; LLB, Nat. U. Benin, Calavi, 1983; BS in Pub. Health Care, Pub. Health Care Sch.WHO, Bamako Mali, 1986; BS in Gen. and Reconstructive Surgery, U. Louvain Med. Sch., Brussels, Belgium, 1990—92; MS in ENT Neck and Head Surgery, Cath. U. Louvain Med. Sch., Brussels, Belgium, 1992. Intern gen. med. Provincial Hosp., Natitingou, Atacora, Benin, 1982—83, resident gen. surgery, 1983—84; asst. specialist U. Hosp. of Louvain, Yvoir, Belgium, 1992—94, resident, 1994—96, asst. sr. registrar, 1997—99, clin. lectr., 1997—2000, assoc. prof., 2000—04, prof., 2004—. Dir. provincial health Nat. Health Ministry, Natitingou, Atacora, Benin, 1984—87. Contbr. articles to profl. jours., chpts. to books, 1991. 2° classe Infantery Benin Army, 1975—76, Ouidah. Grantee Public Health Care, WHO, 1986. Mem.: European Orgn. for Rsch. and Treatment of Cancer, European Laser Assn., Am. Head and Neck Soc., Groupe d'Etude des Tumeurs Tete et Cou (France), Groupe Belge de Contact de pathologie cervicale, Assn. Francaise d'ORL Pediatrique, European Group of Dysphagia and Globus, Soc. Francaise de Carcinologie Cervico-Faciale, European Laryngol. Soc., French Ear Nose and Throat Head and Neck Surgery Soc., Belgian Ear, Nose and Throat, Head and Neck Surgery Soc., Nat. Inst. of Laser Enhanced Sciences, Niles, Cairo, Egypt. (hon.), Club D'Anesthesie Réanimationen ORL. Roman Catholic. Avocations: photography, travel. Home: Rue Du Cato N7 Namur Profondeville 5170 Belgium Office: Univ Hosp Louvain Mont-Godinne Av. Dr. Gaston-Therasse 1 5530 Yvoir B - 5530 Belgium Home Phone: 00 32 81412423; Office Phone: 00 32 81423707. Office Fax: 00 32 81 423703. E-mail: george.lawson@orlo.ucl.ac.be.

LAWSON, IAN JAMES, physician; b. Woodford, Essex, Eng., Mar. 10, 1956; s. William John and Edna Muriel Lawson; m. Anne Coulson, Sept. 18, 1956; children: Kate, Jack. MB, BS, Newcastle Med. Sch., Newastle Upon Tyne, 1979. Diploma Royal Coll. Obstetricians and Gynecologists Royal Coll. Obs and Gyn London, 1982, membership Faculty Occupl. Medicine RCP London, 1991. Trainee The Mt. Group Practice, Doncaster, South Yorkshire, 1980, gen. med. practitioner, 1983—87; regional med. officer Rolls Royce plc, Derby, 1987—98; chief med. officer, occupl. physician Rolls-Royce plc, Derby, 1998—. Med. reference panel Dept. Trade and Industry, London, 1999—; mem. indsl. injuries adv. coun. mem. Dept. Work and Pension, London, 2003—. Contbr. chapters to books. Trustee Addaction, London, 2001—03. Fellow Faculty Occupl. Medicine, RCP London, 1998. Fellow: RCP, Am. Coll. Occupl. and Environ. Medicine; mem.: Soc. Occupl. Medicine (pres. 2004—05). Achievements include expert witness in Hand-arm vibration syndrome. Office: Rolls-Royce plc PO Box 31 Derbyshire Derby DE 24 8BJ England Office Fax: +44(0)1332 244296. Business E-Mail: ian.lawson@rolls-royce.com.

LAWSON, WILLIAM, otolaryngologist, educator; b. NYC, Nov. 23, 1934; s. Alexander and Sophia (Elkind) L.; m. Miriam Patkin, Nov. 7, 1965; 1 child, Vanessa Ann. BA, NYU, 1956, DDS, 1961, MD, 1965. Diplomate Am. Bd. Otolaryngology, Am. Bd. Cosmetic Surgery, Am. Bd. Facial Plastic Surgery. Intern Mt. Sinai Hosp., NYC, 1965-66, rsch. fellow in otolaryngology, 1969-70, resident in otolaryngology, 1970-73; resident in gen. surgery Bronx (N.Y.) VA Hosp., 1966-67, chief otolaryngology, head and neck surgery, 1974—2003, cons., 2003—; prof. Mt. Sinai Sch. Medicine, NYC, 1980—; vice chmn., 1996—. Co-dir. Paranasal Sinus Rsch. Lab.; dir. facial plastic surgery clini Mt. Sinai Hosp., N.Y.C.; cons. Nat. Space Biomed. Rsch. Consortium, cons. in physical anthropology, Am. Mus. Natural History, Eugene Grabscheid rsch. prof. otolaryngology. Author: Paraganglionic Chemoreceptor Systems, 1982, Surgery of the Paranasal Sinuses, 1988, 2nd edit., 1992, External Ear, 1995; contbr. over 280 articles to med. jours., chpts. to books. Capt. Med. Corps. US Army, 1967—69. Fellow ACS, Am. Acad. Facial Plastic and Reconstructive Surgery (svc. awrd), Am. Soc. Head and Neck Surgery, Am. Soc. Maxillofacial Surgeons, Am. Rhinologic Otologic and Laryngologic Soc. (v.p. award, pres. award), Am. Laryngol. Soc., Am. Rhinologic Soc.; mem. Am. Acad. Otolaryngology (svc. award), Am. Bronchoesophagologic Soc. (included in Best Drs., named Top Drs. Am., Best Drs. in N.Y.). Avocations: photography, art history, horology. Office: Mt Sinai Med Ctr Box 1191 1 Gustave L Levy Pl New York NY 10029-6500

LAWSON-NDU, OVUNDA A., emergency physician, surgeon; b. Elelenwo, Nigeria, 1951; s. Lawson Ngbachi and Esther Adanma (Nwogbe) N.; m. Elsie Nnenne Jenewari, Dec. 13, 1977 (div. Jan. 1980); children: Jennifer Mboma, Sandra Njimole; m. Donna Marie Grimes, June 27, 1986; 1 child, Anuugo Michelle. BS in Chemistry with highest honors, U. Wis., 1977; DO, U. Health Sci., 1980. Diplomate Am. Bd. Emergency Medicine. Intern Metro Health Ctr., Erie, Pa., 1981-82; resident in gen. surgery Howard U. Hosp., Washington; mem. staff Lower Bucks Hosp., Bristol, Pa. Mem. hypertension and diabetes screening program Rivers State, Nigeria, 1992—; vice chmn. dept. emergency medicine Temple U. Hosp., Bristol, Pa., 1997—, asst. dir., 1997-2000, assoc. dir., 2000-, adj. clin. asst. prof. medicine Temple U. Health Sys., 1998-2000. Active Nat. Exch. Club, Amnesty Internat. Fellow Am. Coll. Emergency Physicians, Am. Acad. Emergency Medicine. Address: PO Box 640 Medford NJ 08055-0640

LAXMINARAYANA, DAMA, geneticist, researcher, educator; b. Hyderabad, India, Apr. 20, 1953; came to U.S., 1990; s. Kishtaiah and Sathyamma; m. Dara Jayalakshmi; children: Dama Bhargavi, Dama Sriharsha, Dama Vishnupriya. BSc, Osmania U., Hyderabad, 1974, MSc, 1976, PhD, 1982. Jr. sci. asst. dept. genetics Osmania U., 1977-78, lectr. dept. zoology, 1985-90; jr. rsch. fellow Indian Dept. Atomic Energy, 1978-81, postdoctoral fellow, 1982-83, rsch. assoc., 1983-85; postdoctoral fellow dept. medicine Case Western Res. U. Sch. Medicine, Cleve., 1990-91; rsch. assoc. dept. internal medicine Wake Forest U. Sch. Medicine, Winston-Salem, N.C., 1991-94, rsch. instr., 1994-98, rsch. asst. prof., 1998—. Conf. presenter in field; editor-in-chief Clin. Medicine: Pathology, 2007-; editl. bd. mem. Clin. Medicine: Arthritis and Musculoskeletal Disorders, 2007- Contbr. articles to sci. jours., chpts. to books. Mem. AAAS, Am. Assn. Immunologists, Am. Coll. Rheumatology, Environ. Mutagen Soc. India, India Soc. Cell Biology, Soc. Geneticists and Cytologists India, N.Y. Acad. Scis. Home: 444 Lynn Ave Winston Salem NC 27104 Office: Wake Forest U Sch Medicine Dept Internal Medicine Medical Center Blvd Winston Salem NC 27157 Office Phone: 336-716-0616. Personal E-mail: laxmina@triad.rr.com. Business E-Mail: dlaxmina@wfubmc.edu.

LAY, GREGG R., pharmacist; b. Fremont, Nebr., Aug. 1, 1949; s. Albertus Nies and Rachel Constance Lay; m. Pamela Kay Geu, Sept. 23, 1972 (div. May 1996); children: Cody Michael, Rikki Allison; m. Crystal Lynn Sughroue, May 19, 1997; children: Cari Lee Ferguson, Willie Joe Ferguson. BS in pharm., U. Nebr., 1972; PharmD, U. Kans., 2003. Registered pharmacist State of Nebr. Pharmacy intern Baker's Pharmacy, Lincoln, Nebr., 1970, Mary Lanning Meml. Hosp., Hastings, Nebr., 1971—72, registered pharmacist, 1975—2005, Gibson Pharmacy, Norfolk, Nebr., 1972—75. Clin. asst. prof. pharmacy Creighton U. Sch. Pharmacy, Omaha, 1977—79; cert. pharmacy preceptor Creighton U., 1980—2004, U. Nebr. Med. Ctr., Omaha, 1980—2004; adj. asst. prof. pharmacy Creighton U. Sch. Pharmacy, 1980; clin. instr. U. Nebr. Med. Ctr., 1990. Spkr. YMCA Family Asthma Conf., Hastings, 1998; pharmacist vol. Adams County Vital Signs Health Fair; spkr. Mary Lanning Meml. Hosp. Cardiac/Cardiopulmonary Rehab. Mem.: Am. Soc. Health Sys. Pharmacists, Nebr. Soc. Health Sys. Pharmacists, Am. Soc. Parenteral and Enteral Nutrition. Republican. Presbyterian. Achievements include development of 26 original computer programs to assist physicians and pharmacists with pharmacokinetic dosing and complete dosing calculations for Neonatal ICU and Adult Critical Care Total Parenteral Nutrition. Avocations: fishing, hunting, softball, skiing, travel. Home: 611 N Shore Dr Hastings NE 68901 Office Phone: 402-461-5138. Personal E-mail: grlay1@yahoo.com.

LAY-HARN, GAM, medical educator, researcher; b. Malaysia, Dec. 14, 1966; BSc, U. Malaya, 1990; PhD, U. Sains Malaysia, 2001. Assoc. prof. U. Sains Malaysia, 2001—, lectr., rschr., 2001—. Recipient Intelectual Property award, Ministry of Domestic Trade Malaysia. Mem.: Am. Assn. Cancer Rsch. Avocations: reading, gardening. Office: University Sains Malaysia Sch Pharmaceutical Scis Minden Penang 11800 Malaysia Office Fax: 604-6570017.

LAYKE, JOHN C., plastic surgeon, researcher; b. Milw., May 29, 1974; s. John D. and Suzanne J. Lacke. BS, Marquette U., Milw., 1996; DO, Nova Southeastern U. COM, Ft. Lauderdale, Fla., 2002. Cert. in gen. surgery Ill., 2007, ACS, 2008, diplomate AMA, 2002. Resident gen. surgery U. Ill. Met. Group Hosps., Chgo., 2002—07, adminstrv. chief resident, 2006—07; fellow plastic & reconstructive surgery Nassau U. Med. Ctr., East Meadow, NY, 2007—. Contbr. articles to profl. jours. including Esophageal Cancer & Gastric Cancer. Recipient Leadership & Excellence award. Mem.: ACS, AMA, Am. Soc. Plastic Surgeons. Personal E-mail: jlayke@yahoo.com.

LAYMAN, DALE PIERRE, retired medical educator, researcher, writer; b. Niles, Mich., July 3, 1948; s. Pierre Andre and Delphine Lucille (Lenke) L.; m. Kathleen Ann Jackowiak, Aug. 8, 1970; children: Andrew Michael, Alexis Kathryn, Allison Victoria, Amanda Elizabeth. AS in Life Sci., Lake Mich. Coll., Benton Harbor, 1968; BS in Anthropology and Zoology with distinction, U. Mich., Ann Arbor, 1971, MS in Physiology, 1974; EdS in Physiology and Health Sci., Ball State U., Muncie, Ind., 1979; PhD in Health and Safety Studies, U. Ill., Champaign-Urbana, 1986; Grand PhD in Medicine, World Info. Distributed U., Belgium, 2003. Histological technician in neuropathology U. Mich. Med. Sch., Ann Arbor, 1971-72, tchg. fellow human physiology, 1972-74; instr. human anatomy, physiology, and histology Lake Superior State U., Sault Ste. Marie, Mich., 1974-75; prof. med. terminology, human anatomy and physiology Joliet Jr. Coll., Ill., 1975—2007, part time prof., 2008—10; ret., 2007. Author: The Terminology of Anatomy and Physiology, 1983, The Medical Language: A Programmed Body-Systems Approach, 1995, Biology Demystified, 2003, Anatomy Demystified, 2004, Physiology Demystified, 2004, Medical Terminology Demystified, 2005; contbr. articles to profl. jours. Founder Robowatch. Mem. Ill. C.C. Faculty Assn. (campus coord.), London Diplomatic Acad. (mem. acad. coun.), European Acad. Informatization (cavalier-knight, prof.), Internat. Assn. Bus. Leaders (life), Phi Kappa Phi, Kappa Delta Pi. Avocations: running, swimming, reading. Home: 509 Westridge Rd Joliet IL 60431-4883 Business E-Mail: drdlayman@sbcglobal.net. *

LAYNE, JAMES NATHANIEL, retired vertebrate biologist; b. Chgo., May 16, 1926; s. Leslie Joy and Harriet (Hausmann) L.; m. Lois Virginia Linderoth, Aug. 26, 1950; children: Linda Carrie, Kimberly, Jamie Linderoth, Susan Nell, Rachel Pratt. BA, Cornell U., Ithaca, NY, 1950, PhD, 1954. Grad. teaching asst. Cornell U., Ithaca, NY, 1950-54, assoc. prof. zoology, 1963-67; asst. prof. zoology So. Ill. U., Carbondale, 1954-55; asst. prof., then assoc. prof. biology U. Fla., 1955-63; asst. curator, then assoc. curator mammals Fla. State Mus., Gainesville, 1955-63, research assoc., 1963-65; dir. research, then exec. dir. Archbold Biol. Sta.; Archbold curator mammals Am. Mus. Natural History, 1967-85; sr. rsch. biologist Archbold Biol. Sta., 1985-94, sr. rsch. biologist emeritus, 1994—. Rsch. assoc. Fla. State Collection of Arthropods, Am. Mus. Natural History; vis. scientist primate ecology sect. Nat. Inst. Neurol. Diseases and Blindness, summers 1961-62; adj. prof. biology U. South Fla., 1968-89; adj. prof. biol. scis. Fla. Atlantic U., 1980-84; cons. ecology sect. WHO, 1969; mem. Fla. com. Rare and Endangered Plants and Animals; mem. Fla. Panther Recovery team US Dept. Interior; mem. rodent specialist group Species Survival Commn.; mem. reclamation rsch. com. Fla. Ins. Phosphate Rsch.; mem. resource planning and mgmt. com.Kissimee River. Contbr. articles and chpts. to profl. jours. and books. Hon. trustee Fla. Defenders of Environment; bd. dirs. Fla. Audubon Soc.; mem. Fla. Nongame Wildlife Adv. Council, Peace River Basin Bd., Fla. Panther Tech. Adv. Council. Served with USAAF, 1944-46. bd., Inst. of Environ. Studies U. of South Fla. Fellow AAAS; mem. Am. Soc. Zoologists, Am. Soc. Mammalogists (pres. 1970-72, hon. mem. 1993, C. Hart Merriam award 1976), Ecol. Soc. Am., Soc. for Study of Evolution, Am. Soc. Naturalists, Wildlife Soc., Wildlife Disease Assn., Nature Conservancy (trustee Fla. chpt.), Fla. Acad. Scis. (pres. 1984-85, medalist 1995), Orgn. Biol. Field Stas. (pres. 1986-87), Phi Beta Kappa, Sigma Xi, Phi Kappa Phi, Phi Sigma. Home Phone: 863-465-4240. Business E-Mail: jlayne@strato.net.

LAYTON, ROBERT GLENN, radiologist; b. Bklyn., Oct. 14, 1946; s. Irving and Charlotte (Bell) L.; m. Judith Helene Bohrer, May 31, 1969; children: Andrew, Julia. BS, Union Coll., 1968; MD, Boston U., 1972. Diplomate Am. Bd. Radiology. Resident in radiology Boston City Hosp., 1972-75; jr. attending radiologist L.I. Jewish Hosp., Hillside, NY, 1975-76; staff radiologist Cedars Med. Ctr., Miami, Fla., 1978-98, chief of radiology, 1999—2003; assoc. med. dir. MedSolutions Inc., Franklin, Tenn., 2004—. Radiologist Highland Park Gen. Hosp., Miami, 1978-84; clin. asst. prof. U. Miami Sch. Med., 1985-87. Pres. Michael-Ann Russell Jewish Cmty. Ctr., Miami, 1980-82; bd. dirs. Jewish Cmty. Ctrs. South Fla., 1982-86; trustee Temple Sinai of North Dade, North Miami Beach, 1982-01, v.p., 1985-92, pres., 1992-94; nat. bd. dirs. Union Am. Hebrew Congregations, trustee, 1999-2004; dir., Aspen Jewish Congregation, 2007-09, Union Reform Judaism, 2009-; Served to maj. USAF, 1976 78. Mem. AMA, Am. Coll. Radiology, Colo. Radiol. Soc., Begg Soc., Alpha Omega Alpha. Avocations: skiing, golf, art. Office Phone: 615-468-4181. Personal E-mail: rglmd1@yahoo.com.

LAZÂR, CÂLIN CONSTANTIN, plastic surgeon, writer; b. Bucharest, Romania, Dec. 21, 1974; s. Stefan and Olga Lazâr; m. Sophie Deneuve, Aug. 5, 2006. Degree in Biol. and Med. Scis., Rouen U. Medicine, France, 2002; diploma in Head and Neck Surg. Anatomy, Paris V U. Medicine, 2004, diploma in Gen. Surg. Anatomy, 2006; diploma in Microsurgery and Exptl. Surgery, Rouen U. Medicine, France, 2004, MD, 2006, diploma in Plastic, Reconstructive and Aesthetic Surgery, 2008; diploma in Breast Diseases, Paris VII U. Medicine, 2005. Surgeon internship Charles Nicolle U. Hosp., Rouen, 2001—06; clin. chief asst. in plastic, reconstructive and aesthetic surgery Regional Hosps. Aulnay Sous Bois and Pontoise, Paris, 2006—08, plastic, reconstructive and aesthetic surgeon, 2008—; staff cons. physician plastic, reconstructive & aesthetic surgery unit Regional Hosp. Meulan, 2010—. Med. writer Grego-Vernazobres Book Publishers, Paris; translator Tech. Assistance to Commonwealth Ind. States Internat. Project, Paris, 1997; tchr. Nurse Tng. Sch., Rouen, France, 2004—05. Contbr. scientific papers to profl. publs. Treas. Assn. Protection French Med., Paris, 2002—04. Achievements include invention of medical treatment device. Office: Meulan les Mureaux Regional Hosp 1 rue du Ft Meulan 78250 France Office Phone: 33-6-63199061. Personal E-mail: lazarcalin@yahoo.fr.

LAZAR, FLORIN, social sciences educator; b. Bucharest, Sept. 13, 1975; D, U. Bucharest, 2009. Asst. prof. U. Bucharest, 2001—. Office: Schitu Magureanu 9 Bucharest 170000 Romania E-mail: lazarflorinl3@gmail.com.

LÁZÁR, GEORGE, pathophysiologist, researcher; b. Kismarja, Bihar, Hungary, Mar. 12, 1934; s. János and Ágnes (Szilber) L.; m. Elisabeth Husztik, Aug. 15, 1960; children: George, Stephen. MD, Albert Szent-Györgyi Med. U., Szeged, Hungary, 1958, Specialist in Lab. Investigation, 1964; PhD, Hungarian Acad. Scis., Budapest, Hungary, 1970, Dr.Med.Scis., 1975. Asst. Albert Szent-Györgyi Med. U., 1958-68, asst. prof., 1968-73, assoc. prof., 1973-77, prof. Inst. Pathophysiology, 1977—. Vis. prof. U. Pierre and Marie Curie, Paris, 1989-90. Contbr. more than 200 articles to profl. jours. Res. Officer Hungarian Army. Recipient Literary prize Hungarian Writers' Assn., 1952, Acad. prize Hungarian Acad. Scis., 1974, Szeged-1956 Commemorative medallion City of Szeged, 1997, Albert Szent Györgyi prize, 1999, medal for Szeged, 2000; named Accomplished Tchr., Ministry of Edn., Budapest, 1976; fellow U. Montreal, 1971-72, U. Groningen, The Netherlands, 1986, INSERM, Paris, 1976, 82, 84, 87. Mem. European Reticuloendothelial Soc. (v.p. 1982-86, bd. dirs. 1984-86), Hungarian Physiol. Soc. (bd. dirs. 1972-80), Hungarian Soc. Chemotherapy (bd. dirs. 1985—). Avocations: hammer-throwing, literature. Home: Petőfi S St 40/B 6722 Szeged Hungary Office: Albert Szent-Gyorgyi Med U Szeged Inst Pathophys Pf. 427 6700 Szeged Hungary Home Phone: (62) 450 317; Office Phone: (62) 545 112. Business E-Mail: lazar@patph.szote.u-szeged.hu.

LAZAR, HAROLD LEE, cardiothoracic surgeon; AB, Boston U., 1970, MD, 1974. Diplomate Am. Bd. Surgery, Am. Bd. Thoracic Surgery. Resident in gen. surgery U. Mich. Med. Ctr., Ann Arbor, 1974-81; rsch. fellow in cardiac surgery UCLA Med. Ctr., 1977-79; fellow in cardiothoracic surgery Columbia-Presbyn. Med. Ctr., NYC, 1981-83; attending surgeon Univ. Hosp., Boston, 1984—, Boston City Hosp., 1984—, VA Med. Ctr., Boston, 1990—. Asst. dir. thoracic surgery Boston City Hosp., 1990—; chmn. Mass. Consortium Lung Transplantation, Boston, 1992; from asst. prof. to prof. cardiothoracic surgery Med. Sch., Boston (Mass.) U., 1984-98, prof., 1998—. Editor: Current Therapy for Acute Coronary Ischemin, 1993; mem. editl. bd. Jour. Thoracic and Cardiovascular Surgery, 2002-. Fellow ACS, Am. Coll. Cardiology, Mass. Med. Soc.; mem. Am. Coll. Chest Physicians (sec. sect. cardiac surgery 1993—), Am. Assn. Thoracic Surgery, Soc. Thoracic Surgery, Soc. Univ. Surgeons. Office: Boston U Med Ctr 88 E Newton St Boston MA 02118-2308 Office Phone: 617-638-7350. E-mail: harold.lazar@bmc.org.

LAZAR, IRVING, psychologist; b. NYC, Feb. 20, 1926; s. Charles and Sylvia L.; m. Jules M. Marquart, Dec. 24, 1981; children: Kathryn S., James Bradford, Richard Alan. BS, CCNY, 1948; MA, Columbia U., 1950, PhD, 1954. Intern Menninger Clinic, Topeka, 1946—47; instr. clin. psychology U. Rochester, NY, 1948—49; instr. psychology Bard Coll., Amandale-on-Hudson, NY, 1949—50; instr. child devel. U. Ill. Coll. Edn., Urbana, 1950—54; assoc. chief mental health sect. Nev. State; sr. scientist US Pub. Health Svc. Dept., Las Vegas, 1954—91; dir. Peterson-Guedel Family Ctr., Beverly Hills, Calif., 1960—64; exec. dir Neumeyer Found., Beverly Hills, 1963—68; western mgr. Kirschner Assoc., LA, 1968—70; assoc. dir. Appalachian Regional Commn., Washington, 1969—72; prof. dept. human svc. studies Cornell U., 1972—91, prof. emeritus, 1991—; external faculty Santa Fe Inst., 1994—99; rsch. prof. Vanderbilt U., Nashville, 1991—98, resident scholar Kennedy Ctr. Rsch. Human Devel., 1991—. Cons. in field. Contbr. articles to profl. jour. Trustee Coalition for Quality Children's Media, Santa Fe, 1994—. Rsch. Fellow Population Inst., East-West Ctr., Honolulu, 1987. Home: 313 Cana Cir Nashville TN 37205 Home Phone: 615-354-1505. Personal E-mail: i.lazar@comcast.net. Business E-Mail: irving@santafe.edu.

LAZAR, MITCHELL AVERY, physician, educator; b. Frankfort, Germany, Apr. 24, 1956; arrived in US, 1956. s. Marvin Lazar and Fern (Menkis) Gordon; m. Althier Margaret Pino, July 16, 1988; 1 child, Zachary George. SB, MIT, 1976; MD, Stanford U., 1982, PhD, 1987. Cert. Internal Medicine, 1985. Intern Brigham and Women's Hosp., Boston, 1982-83, resident, 1983-85; fellow in endocrinology Mass. Gen. Hosp., Boston, 1985-86; rsch. assoc. Howard Hughes Med. Ctr., Boston, 1986-88; instr. Med. Sch. Harvard U., Boston, 1988-89; asst. prof. medicine U. Pa., Phila., 1989—95, assoc. prof. medicine, 1995—99, chief, divsn. endocrinology, diabetes and metabolism, 1996—, prof. medicine and genetics, 1999—, Sylvan H. Eisman prof. medicine and genetics, 2002—, dir. Inst. Diabetes, Obesity and Metabolism, 2005—. Recipient Outstanding Investigator award, Am. Fedn. Med. Rsch., 1999, Yamanouchi USA Rsch. award, 2002. Fellow Am. Acad. Arts and Sciences; mem. NAS Inst. Medicine, Am. Soc. Clin. Investigation (mem. coun.), Assn. Am. Physicians, Am. Thyroid Assn. (Van Meter prize, 1994), Endocrine Soc. (Richard E. Weitzman prize, 1995, Edwin B. Astwood lecture award, 2006), Am. Fedn. for Clin. Rsch (AFCR Found.-Merck Early Career Devel. award). Achievements include discovery of multiple thyroid hormone receptors including a pituitary specific form. Home: 507 Lafayette Rd Merion Station PA 19066 1009 Office: U Pa Divsn Endocrinology Diabetes & Metaboli 415 Curie Blvd Philadelphia PA 19104-6149 Office Phone: 215-898-0198. Office Fax: 215-898-5408. E-mail: lazar@mail.med.upenn.edu.

LAZAR, RANDE HARRIS, otolaryngologist; b. NYC, Feb. 27, 1951; s. Irving and Dorothy (Tartasky) L.; m. Linda Zishuk, Aug. 11, 1974; 1 child, Lauren K. BA, Bklyn. Coll., 1973; MD, U. Autonoma de Guadalajara, Mexico, 1978; postgrad., N.Y. Med. Coll., 1978-79. Diplomate Am. Bd. Otolaryngology-Head and Neck Surgery; lic. physician, N.Y., Ohio, Tenn. Gen. surgery resident Cornell North Shore Community Hosp., Manhasset, NY, 1979-80, Cleve. Clinic Found., 1980-81, otolaryngology-head and neck surgery resident, 1980-84, chief resident dept. otolaryngology & communicative disorder, 1983-84; physician Otolaryngology Cons. Memphis, 1984—. Fellow pathology head and neck dept. otolaryngologic pathology Armed Forces Inst. Pathology, Washington, 1983; pediatric otolaryngology fellow Le Bonheur Children's Med. Ctr., Memphis, 1984-85, dir. pediatric otolaryngology fellowship tng., 1989—, chief surgery, 1989, chief staff East Surgery Ctr.; chmn. dept. otolaryngology head and neck surgery Meth. Health Systems, 1990-91; courtesy staff Bapt. Meml. Hosp., Bapt. Meml. Hosp.-East, Eastwood Med. Ctr., Meth. Hosp., Germantown, Tenn.; chief dept. otolaryngology Les Passees Rehab. Ctr., 1988—. Contbr. articles to profl. jours. Bd. dirs. Bklyn. Tech. Found. Recipient award of honor Am. Acad. Otolaryngology-Head and Neck Surgery, 1991. Fellow Internat. Coll. Surgeons; mem. AMA, Am. Acad. Otolaryngology-Head and Neck Surgery (Disting. Svc. award 2010), Am. Acad. Facial Plastic and Reconstructive Surgery, Am. Acad. Otolaryngic Allergy, Centurions Deafness Rsch. Found., Am. Auditory Soc., Nat. Hearing Assn., Soc. Ear, Nose Throat Advances in Children, Am. Soc. Laser Medicine and Surgery, So. Med. Assn., N.Y. Acad. Scis., Tenn. Med. Soc., Tenn. Acad. Otolaryngology-Head and Neck Surgery, Memphis and Shelby County Med. Soc., Memphis/Mid South Soc. Pediatrics Office: Otolaryngology Cons Memphis 791 Estate Pl Memphis TN 38120 E-mail: Lazarent@aol.com.

LAZAR, RICHARD BECK, physician, medical administrator; b. NYC, Oct. 9, 1954; s. Harold Paul and Molly (Beck) L.; m. Jessica Elaine Tampas, Feb. 8, 2003; children: Spencer Berman, Winston Harold, Graham Henry Duke, John Peter Lazar. BA in Biology cum laude, Harvard U., Cambridge, Mass., 1976; MD, Northwestern U., Evanston, Ill., 1979. Attending physician Northwestern Meml. Hosp., Chgo., 1984-94, Rehab. Inst. Chgo., 1986-92; exec. v.p., med. dir. Schwab Rehab. Hosp., Chgo.; chair dept. phys. medicine & rehab. Mt. Sinai Hosp., Chgo., 1992-2000; clin. assoc. prof. surgery Pritzker Sch. Medicine, U. Chgo., 1994-98, program dir., chief subsect. phys. medicine & rehab., 1994—2000, clin. prof. surgery Pritzker Sch. Medicine, 1998-2003. Mem. adv. com. patient mgmt. & tech. Nat. MS Soc., N.Y.C., 1992-96; hon. com. Nat. Head Injury Found., Chgo., 1994; profl. adv. com. Nat. Easter Seal Soc., Chgo., 1994. Co-author: Handbook of Neurorehabilitation, 1994, Spinal Injury: Medical Management and Rehabilitation, 1994; editor: Principles of Neurologic Rehabilitation, 1997. Fellow Am. Acad. Neurology, Am. Acad. Phys. Medicine, Assn. Acad. Physiatrists, Am. Congress Rehab. Medicine, Am. Soc. Neurorehab. (pres.-elect 1994-96, pres. 1996-98, Outstanding Svc. & Leadership award 1990-94). Home: 1340 N State Pkwy Chicago IL 60610 Office: Schwab Rehab Hosp & Care Network 1401 S California Blvd Chicago IL 60608-1696 Office Phone: 773-522-2010 ext 5857. Business E-Mail: richard.lazar@qtm.net.

LAZAR, RONALD M., neuropsychologist; BA, NYU, 1971; PhD, Northeastern U., 1977. Chief neuropsychologist Kings County Med. Ctr., 1984—93; asst. prof. neurology, dir. neuropsychology svc. SUNY, Downstate Med. Ctr., Bklyn, 1984—93; prof. clin. neuropsychology Columbia U. Coll. Physicians & Surgeons, 1993—; profl. neuropsychologist NY Presbyn. Hosp., 1994—; dir. Richard & Jenny Levine cerebral localization lab. Neurol. Inst., Columbia U. Med. Ctr., 1994—. Cons. advisor Ctr. Devices & Radiol. Health US FDA, 2002; editor-in-chief Neuropsychology Rev., 2006—08; chartered mem. ANIE Rev. Panel, NIH, 2009—; editl. rev. bd. mem. Stroke, AHA Jour., 2011—. Grant, NIH. Fellow: APA (neuropsychology divsn. mem.), Andrew Mellon Found., Am. Coll. Forensic Medicine, Am. Heart Assn. (nat. co-chair ECC rsch. working group for neurologic outcomes 2009—), Am. Acad. Neurology. Office: Neurological Inst 710 West 168th St New York NY 10032 Business E-Mail: ral22@columbia.edu.

LAZARE, AARON, psychiatrist, educator, former academic administrator; b. Newark, Feb. 14, 1936; s. H. Benjamin and Anne (Storfer) L.; m. Louise Cannon; children: Robert, Jacqueline, David, Sam, Sarah, Hien, Thomas, Naomi. AB, Oberlin Coll., 1957; MD, Case Western Reserve U., 1961. Intern in medicine Bronx Mcpl. Hosp. Ctr., NY, 1961-62; resident in psychiatry Mass. Mental Health Ctr., 1962-65; asst. in psychiatry Mass. Gen. Hosp., Boston, 1967-68; chief day hosp. inpatient unit Yale-New Haven Hosp., 1967-68; assoc. dir. adult outpatient psychiatry Mass. Gen. Hosp., Boston, 1968-70, dir. adult outpatient psychiatry, 1970-75, acting dir. residency tng., 1972, dir. outpatient psychiatry, 1975-82, dep. chief psychiatry, 1976-82, clin. dir. psychiatry, 1978-82; prof. Harvard U., 1982; prof., chmn. dept. psychiatry U. Mass. Med. Sch., Worcester, 1982—90, interim dean, 1989-90, dean, 1990, chancellor, 1991—2007, Celia and Isaac Haidak prof. med. edn., prof. psychiatry, 2007—. Editor: Outpatient Psychiatry, 1979, 1989, 2nd edit.; contbr. articles to profl. jours.; co-author of books in field. Capt. US Army, 1965—67. Named for Disting. Pub. Svc. Commonwealth of Mass., honorable mention U. Mass., 1987, Commonwealth of Mass., U. Mass., Boston, 1988, Brotherhood award NCCJ, 1992, Maimonides award for outstanding commitment as a physician and educator Anti-Defamation League New Eng., 1993, Friend and Leader award Mass. Assn. Mental Health Inc., 2001. Mem. AAAS, AMA, Am. Psychiat. Assn. (Benjamin Rush award 1992), Mass. Psychiat. Soc. Office: U Mass Med Ctr 55 Lake Ave N Worcester MA 01655-0002

LAZARUS, ARNOLD ALLAN, psychologist, educator; b. Johannesburg, Republic of South Africa, Jan. 27, 1932; came to U.S., 1963; s. Benjamin and Rachel Leah (Mosselson) L.; m. Daphne Ann Kessel, June 10, 1956; children: Linda Sue, Clifford Neil. BA with honors, U. Witwatersrand, Johannesburg, 1956, MA, 1957, PhD, 1960. Diplomate: Am. Bd. Profl. Psychology, Am. Bd. Med. Psychotherapists (fellow), Internat. Acad. Behavioral Medicine, Counseling and Psychotherapy. Pvt. practice clin. psychology, Johannesburg, 1959-63, 64-66, vis. asst. prof. dept. psychology Stanford (Calif.) U., 1963 64; prof. psychology Temple U. Med. Sch., Phila., 1967-70; dir. clin. tng. Yale U., New Haven, 1970-72; disting. prof. Rutgers U., New Brunswick, NJ, 1972-98; pres. Ctr. for Multimodal Psychol. Svcs., Princeton, NJ, 1998—2005; exec. dir. Lazarus Inst., Skillman, NJ, 2005—. Mem. adv. bd. Psychologists for Social Responsibility, 1984—; cons. in field. Author: (18 books including) Behavior Therapy and Beyond, 1971, Multimodal Therapy, 1981, rev. edit., 1989, In the Mind's Eye, 1984, Martial Myths, 1985, Mind Power: Getting What You Want Through Mental Training, 1987, The Essential Arnold Lazarus, 1991, A Dialogue with Arnold Lazarus, 1991, Don't Believe It For A Minute!, 1993, Abnormal Psychology, 1995, Brief But Comprehensive Psychotherapy, 1997, The 60 Second Shrink, 1997, I Can If I Want To, 2000, Marital Myths Revisited, 2001, Dual Relationships and Psychotherapy, 2002; editl. bd.: sci. jours.; contbr. articles to profl. jours.; editor: (assoc. editor) Focus on Ethics, 2008. Recipient Disting. Svc. award Am. Bd. Profl. Psychology, Disting. Career Achievement award Am. Bd. Med. Psychotherapists, Outstanding Contbns. to Mental Health award Psychiat. Outpatient Ctrs. of the Americas, 1991, Presdl. award ACA, 2003, NJ Psychol. Assn., 2003. Fellow APA (Disting. Psychologist award divsn. of psychotherapy 1992, 1st Ann. Cummings Psyche award 1996, Disting. Profl. Contbns. award Divsn. Clin. Psychology 1997), Am. Bd. Profl. Psychology (diplomate), Internat. Acad. Eclectic Psychotherapists, Acad. Clin. Psychology, Am. Psychotherapy Assn. (mem. exec. adv. bd. 2001—); mem. Internat. Assn. Marriage and Family Counselors (Disting. Presenter Series award 2000), Am. Acad. Psychotherapy, Assn. for Advancement Psychotherapy, Nat. Acads. Practice in Psychology (distng.), Soc. for Exploration of Psychotherapy Integration, Calif. Psychol. Assn. (Lifetime Achievement award 1999), Assn. Advancement Behavior Therapy (Lifetime Achievement award 1999), Internat. Assn. Marriage and Family Counselors (Disting. Presenter award 2000), Am. Counseling Assn. (presdl. award 2003), N.J. Psychol. Assn. (presdl. award 2003). Home: 56 Herrontown Cir Princeton NJ 08540-2924 Office Phone: 609-240-3612. E-mail: aalaz@aol.com.

LAZARUS, GEORGE M., pediatrician, educator; Attended, Columbia U. Coll. Physician and Surgeons. Diplomate Am. Bd. Pediatrics. Intern Babies & Children's Hosp. Columbia Presbyterian Med. Ctr., NY, resident in pediat., 1972—74; assoc. clin. prof. pediat. Columbia Univ. Coll. Physicians & Surgeons; with NY Presbyn. Hosp. / Weill Cornell; pediatrician NY Presbyn. / Morgan Stanley Children's Hosp. Office: NewYork-Presbyterian 106 E 78th St New York NY 10075 Office Phone: 212-744-0840. Office Fax: 212-535-3730.

LAZARUS, GERALD SYLVAN, dermatologist, educator, dean; b. NYC, Feb. 16, 1939; s. Joseph W. and Marion (Goldstein) Lazarus; m. Sandra Jacob, Sept. 3, 1961 (dec. 1985); children: Mark, Elyse, Lynne, Laura; m. Audrey Fedyszyn Jakubowski, Apr. 7, 1990. BA, Colby Coll., 1959; MD, George Washington U., 1963. Intern, then resident U. Mich., Ann Arbor, 1963—64, resident in medicine, 1964—65; rsch. asso. NIH, Bethesda, Md., 1965—68; resident in dermatology Harvard U., Cambridge, Mass., 1968—70; rsch. fellow Strangeways Labs., Cambridge, England, 1970—72; assoc. prof. medicine, co-dir. dermatology tng. program Albert Einstein Med. Coll., NYC, 1972—75; J. Lamar Callaway prof. Duke U., Durham, NC, 1977—82, chief dermatology, 1975—82; Milton B. Hartzell prof. U. Pa. Sch. Medicine, Phila., 1982—, chmn. dept. dermatology,

1982—93; dean Sch. Medicine U. Calif., Davis, 1993—97; vis. scholar U. Calif., Inst. Health Policy Rsch., San Francisco, 1997—98; prof. dermatology, biol. chemistry U. Calif. Scholar Inst. for Health Policy, 1998—99; dean, prof. emeritus U. Calif. Davis Sch. Medicine, 1999—; prof. dermatology Johns Hopkins Med. Inst., Balt., 2002—; dir. Johns Hopkins Medicine Wound Healing Ctr. Sr. investigator Arthritis Found., 1972—77; mem. study sect. NIH, 1976—80; prof. dermatology U. Calif., San Francisco; faculty Inst. of Health Policy; advisor to univ. pres. and hosp. dir. advisor Ministry of Health; vis. prof. Peking Union Med. Coll., Beijing, 1999—2002; advisor to pres. Peking Union Med. Coll. Hosp.; co-dir. China Med. Be. Mgmt. Program. Author (with L. Goldsmith): Diagnosis of Skin Disease, 1980; author: (with Herman Beerman) Tradition of Excellence: History of Dermatology at Univ. Pa. Sch. of Medicine; assoc. editor Jour. Investigative Dermatology, 1977—82; contbr. numerous articles to profl. jours. Trustees George Washington U., Washington, 2005—. With USPHS, 1965—68. Grantee, NIH; fellow John Simon Guggenheim, U. Geneva, 1986. Fellow: ACP, Am. Soc. Clin. Investigation, Assn. Am. Physicians; mem.: Am. Acad. Dermatology (Sultzberger award 1986), Biochem. Soc., Soc. Investigative Dermatology (pres. 1996—97, dir., Disting. Alumnus award George Washington U. 1996), Am. Dermatol. Assn. (Carl Herzog fellow 1970—72). Republican. Jewish. Office: Johns Hopkins Bayview Med Ctr 4940 Eastern Ave Baltimore MD 21224 Office Phone: 410-550-4724, 410-490-0183. Office Fax: 410-550-1232. Business E-Mail: glazarv1@gmail.com.

LAZARUS, HERBERT, pediatrician, educator; MD, U. Med. & Dentistry, NJ, 1983. Diplomate Am. Bd. Pediat., cert. Pediat. Rheumatology. Intern pediat. NYU Med. Ctr., 1983—84, resident pediat., 1984—86, clin. fellowship pediat. rheumatology, 1986—88, clin. assoc. prof., dept. pediat. Contbr. articles to profl. jours. Named one of NY's Best Dr.'s, Castle Connolly Med. LTD. Office: NYU Med Ctr Dept Pediat 390 W End Ave New York NY 10024 Office Phone: 212-787-1444. Office Fax: 212-799-8620.

LAZARUS, JEREMY A., psychiatrist; b. Chgo. m. Debbie Lazarus; 3 children. B in chemistry, Northwestern U.; MD with honors, U. Ill. Coll. Medicine. Intern Michael Reese Hosp., Chgo.; chief resident and tchg. fellow U. Colo. Health Sci. Ctr. (UCHSC), Denver, clinical prof. psychiatry; pvt. practice psychiatry, Denver, 1972—. Med. dir. Colo. Met. State Coll. Student Health Svc.; vol. assoc. prof. psychiatry U. Miami Sch. Medicine. Author several articles, chpt., books and other med. publ. on issues from ethics to managed care, Entering Private Practice: A Handbook for Psychiatrists, musician, singer. Recipient Presdl. Commendation, Am. Psychiatric Assn., 2003, Assembly Warren Williams award, 2004; fellow, Am. Coll. Psychiatrists; disting. fellow, Am. Psychiatric Assn. Mem.: AMA (vice speaker House of Dels. 2003—07, rep. Ride for World Health 2007, spkr. House of Dels. 2007—11, chair bd. task force on medicare/health sys. reform, mem. bd. audit and orgn. and ops. coms., (found.) Uniting for the Future of Medicine campaign steering com., vice chair, Nat. Adv. Coun. on Violence and Abuse, liaison to the Coun. on Med. Svc., pres.-elect 2011—, nominee for Isaac Hays, M.D. and John Bell, M.D. award for leadership in med. ethics and professionalism 1998), Fla. Med. Assn., Am. Inst. Parliamentarians, Nat. Assn. Parliamentarians, Colo. Med. Soc. (past pres.), Colo. Psychiatric Soc. (pres., Spokesperson Yr. 1995, Outstanding Achievement Award 2008), Arapahoe County Med. Soc. (pres.). Achievements include 13-time Ironman Triathlon finisher; 13-time marathon finisher. Office: Jeremy A Lazarus 7555 E Hampden Ave Ste 301 Denver CO 80231-4834 Office Phone: 303-771-0353. *

LAZARUS, MARK DAVID, orthopaedic surgeon; BA, Johns Hopkins U.; MD, U. Medicine and Dentistry of NJ-Sch. Health Related Prof, Newark, NJ, 1988. Lic. Pa., 1990, NJ, 1995, diplomate Am. Bd. Orthopaedic Surgery. Resident orthop. surgery Pa. Univ. Hosp., 1993, fellow orthop. surgery, 1994; hosp. affiliation include Bucks County Splty. Hosp.; physician Thomas Jefferson Univ. Hosp. Contbr. articles Arthritis of the Glenohumeral Joint, 2001, Acute and Chronic Dislocations of the Shoulder, 2002, Complications of Instability Surgery, 2007, Chronic Anterior Dislocation: Open Reduction and Tendon/Bone Transfers, 2007, Anterior Glenohumeral Instability-Treatment/Reduction Acute Injury, 2007. Named one of the Top Doctors, Phila. Mag., 2010—11. Office: Thomas Jefferson University Hospital 925 Chesnut St 5th Fl Philadelphia PA 19107 Office Phone: 800-321-9999.

LAZENBY, GWENETH BRATTON, gynecologist, educator; b. Rock Hill, SC, Feb. 27, 1978; BS, U. SC, 2000, MD, MSCR, 2004. Asst. prof., reproductive infectious diseases, dept. ob-gyn. Med. U. SC, 2008—, med. dir., Sexual Assault Nurse Examiners, 2011. Bd. dirs. Florence Crittenton Home, 2011. Mem.: Infectious Diseases Soc. Am., Am. Coll. Ob-Gyn., Infectious Diseases Soc. Ob-Gyn. Avocations: yoga, surfing, sports. Office: 96 Jonathan Lucas St Ste 628 Charleston SC 29425 Office Fax: 843-792-0533. Business E-Mail: lazenbgb@musc.edu.

LAZERA, MARCIA DOS SANTOS, medical researcher; b. Rio de Janeiro, Jan. 19, 1950; MD, PhD, Fed. U. Rio de Janeiro, 1974, IOC-FIOCRUZ, 1985. Rschr. human mycoses FIOCRUZ Found. IPEC, 1989—2011, head med. lab., 2006—. Mem.: Soc. Brasileira Micologia. Avocation: piano. Office: IPEC-FIOCRUZ Found Av Brasil 4365 Rio de Janeiro 21040-900 Brazil Office Fax: 55 21 22904532 23659657. Business E-Mail: marcia.lazera@ipec.fiocruz.br.

LAZO, JOHN, JR., physician; b. Passaic, NJ, Nov. 29, 1946; s. John and Mary (Beley) Lazo; m. Donnalynn Margaret Materna, July 22, 1972; children: Jonathan Christopher, Ashley Jude. BS, Fairleigh Dickinson U., 1974; MD, Univ. Autonoma de Guadalajara, Mex., 1978. Diplomate Am. Bd. Emergency Medicine, Am. Bd. Forensic Examiners, Am. Bd. Forensic Medicine. Intern Akron (Ohio) City Hosp., 1980-81, resident in emergency medicine, 1981-83, chief resident in emergency medicine, 1982-83; med. dir. emergency svcs. Parma (Ohio) Cmty. Gen. Hosp., 1986-93, chmn. emergency dept., 1994-95, vice-chmn. emergency dept., 1995-99, chmn. emergency dept., 2000—05. Dir. Paramedic Edn. Program, Parma, 1986—93; med. dir. Emergeny Medicine Physicians - Cuyahoga County, LLC, 2002—03. Sgt. USAF, 1966—70. Fellow: Am. Coll. Emergency Physicians. Republican. Russian Orthodox. Avocations: photography, cooking. Home: 545 Eastwood Dr Hinckley OH 44233-9496 Office: Parma Cmty Gen Hosp 7007 Powers Blvd Parma OH 44129-5437 Office Phone: 440-743-2375. Personal E-mail: doclexus@aol.com. E-mail: jlazo@emp.com.

LAZZARA, RALPH, cardiologist; b. Tampa, Fla., Aug. 14, 1934; s. Bennie Lazzara and Rosalie Spoto; m. Barbara Jolly; children: Ralph, Melissa, Rosalie D'Innella. BS, U. of Chgo., 1955; MD, Tulane Med. Sch., La., 1959. Lic. Am. Bd. of Internal Med, 1967, Cardiovascular Diseases Am. Bd. of Internal Medicine, 1968. Cardiology sect. chief U. of Okla. Health Scis. Ctr., Oklahoma City, 1978—98, prof. of medicine, 1978—; med. dir. Heart Rhythm Inst., Oklahoma City, 1998—. Author: (3 medical textbooks) Cardiology Medical Textbooks; contbr. 64 med. texbook chpts., over 269 peer-rev. jour. articles to med. jours. Lt. col. US Army, 1967—70, Denver, CO. Recipient Disting. Scientist award, Heart Rhythm Soc., 1999, Regent's Prof. of Medicine, U. of Okla. Health Scis. Ctr., 2003, Disting. Alumnus award, Tulane Med. Sch., 2010. Fellow: European Soc. Cardiology, Heart Rhythm Soc. (nat. pres. 1995—96), Am. Coll. of Cardiology; mem.: AHA. Achievements include patents for System For Prevention Of Paroxysmal Supraventricular Tachycardia. Office: University Okla Health Scis Ctr Heart Rhythm Inst 1200 Everett Dr Rm 6E103 Oklahoma City OK 73104

LAZZARI, CARLO GIUSEPPE, medical psychologist, researcher; b. Caracas, Venezuela, May 11, 1957; s. Luigi and Maria (Barillari) L. MD, U. Rome, 1982; MSc in Human Behavior & Devel., Drexel U., 1985; postgrad. diploma in infectious diseases, U. Bologna, Italy, 1993; diploma in psychotherapy, Italian Inst. Thanatology, Bologna, 1995; PhD in Work and Orgnl. Psychology, U. Bologna, 1997, MSc in Labour and Indsl. Rels., 2000; ClinPsyD, Salesian Pontifical U., Rome, 2005. Med. diplomate in psychology. Rsch. asst. Drexel U., Phila., 1984-85, NIH, Bethesda, Md., 1989-90, rsch. fellow Rome, 1992—98; chief clin. psychologist Inst. Infectious Diseases, Bologna, 1987—97. Collaborator Corriere della Sera, Milan, Italy, 1992-99; rsch. fellow Network C-AIDS Hot., Bologna, 1992-98. Author: Psychological Assistance of AIDS Patients, 1992, Sex and AIDS, 1993, A Guide to Doctor-Patient Communication, 1994, Psychosocial Aspects of AIDS and other STDs, 1994, Guide to Communication with the Terminally Ill Patient, 1995, Counselling in Medicine, 1996, Tales from the End of Life, 1996, Coping with Work Conflicts, 1996, How to Cope with Work Harassment, 1997, The Helping Relation, 1998, A Guide to the Helping Relation, 1999, Poetry on Childhood, 1999, Ethical Economy, 2000, Poetry on Life, 2002, Poetry and Psychology, 2002, Psychology and Ethics of Workplace and Organizations, 2004, Psychology and Ethics of Companies and Industrial Relations, 2005, The Helping Relationship, 2006, How the Mind Works, 2007, Spiritual Counseling in Medicine, 2009. Home: Via Raiale 112 65128 Pescara PE Italy Personal E-mail: sianca@micso.net. E-mail: lazzari.carlo@tiscali.it.

LAZZARO, RICHARD, thoracic surgeon, educator; MD, Albany Med. Coll., 1988. Diplomate Am. Bd. Surgery, Am. Bd. Thoracic Surgery. Resident surgery North Shore Univ. Hosp., Manhasset, NY, 1988—94; fellow cardiothoracic surgery SUNY Downstate Med. Ctr., Brooklyn, 1994—97, asst. clin. prof. surgery; fellow thoracic surgery Univ. Pitts. Med. Ctr., 1997—98; dir. of gen. thoracic surgery Maimonides Med. Ctr.; chief of thoracic surgery NY Meth. Hosp. Office: New York Methodist Hospital 506 Sixth St Brooklyn NY 11215 Office Phone: 718-780-3000.

LAZZERINI DENCHI, EROS, research scientist, educator; b. Italy, Sept. 17, 1974; PhD, Open U., Eng., 2004. Asst. prof. Scripps Rsch. Inst., 2009—. Office: 1550 N Torrey Pines Rd San Diego CA 92037 Business E-Mail: edenchi@scripps.edu.

LE, CAROLINE M., dentist; BS, Cornell Univ.; DDS, Univ. Md. Dental Sch. Private practice dentist San Francisco Dental Assoc. Mem.: San Francisco Dental Soc., Calif. Dental Assn., Am. Dental Assn. Office: San Francisco Dental Assoc Ste 2234 450 Sutter St San Francisco CA 94108 Office Phone: 415-692-6874.

LE, JENNIFER, medical educator; b. Vietnam, May 21, 1973; PharmD, U. Calif. San Francisco, 2000. Cert. Bd. Pharm. Scis., 2007. Assoc. prof. clin. pharmacy U. Calif. at San Diego Skaggs Sch. Pharmacy, 2009—. Grant, NIH-NIAID. Office: 9500 Gilman Dr MC0714 La Jolla CA 92093 Business E-Mail: jenle@ucsd.edu.

LE, QUANG ANH, medical educator; b. Saigon, Vietnam, July 21, 1971; BS, UCLA, 1999; PharmD, U. Southern Calif., PhD, 2010. Asst. prof. Western U. Health Scis., 2010—. Office: 309 E Second St Pomona CA 91766 Business E-Mail: quangle@usc.edu.

LEACH, BERTON JOE, medical educator; b. Tuscola, Ill., Mar. 30, 1932; s. William Howard Leach and Frances Margaret De Haven; m. Barbara English, June 5, 1955; children: Laura Anne, Berton Franklin. AB, Washington U., 1957; MA, U. Mo., 1960, PhD, 1963. Assoc. prof. George Washington U., Washington, 1963—66; scientist adminstr. NSF, Washington, 1966—69; chmn., prof. Ctrl. Meth. Coll., Fayette, Mo., 1969—74; exec. sec. NIH, Bethesda, Md., 1974—76; sr. scientist pvt. industry, Rockville, Md., 1976—89; scientist Omni Rsch., Capital Sys. Group, 1976—89; admissions registrar, team leader Shady Grove Adventist Hosp., Rockville, 1988—; adj. prof. neurosci. Georgetown U., Washington, 1989—2003. Vis. scholar Harvard U., Cambridge, Mass., 1969; gen. reader Marine Biol. Lab., Woods Hole, Mass., 1985—87; guest rschr. NIH/Brain Behavior Lab., Poolesville, Md., 1991—92. Author: Structure and Development of Vertebrates, 1973, Vertebrate Biology Courseware, 1979, Human Neuroanatomy, 1999. Program chmn. Rotary Internat., Bethesda, 1975; vol. swimming instr. Rockville Swim Ctr., 2001; pres. Meth. Men's Club, Columbia, Mo., 1960. Decorated Am. Spirit Honor medal U.S. Army; named F. H. Dearing endowed prof., Ctrl. Meth. Coll., Fayette, 1970—74; grantee, NSF, Washington, 1973—74; fellow USPH rsch. fellow, NIH, Bethesda, 1962—63. Mem.: Am. Soc. Mammalogists (life), Sigma Xi. Republican. Methodist. Achievements include first scientist to ovulate polyovular follicles using exogenous hormones. Avocations: gardening, landscaping. Home: 12707 Weiss St Rockville MD 20853 Office: Shady Grove Adventist Hosp Admissions 9901 Medical Center Dr Rockville MD 20850

LEACH, BRIAN, dermatologist; b. Houma, La., Aug. 8, 1967; BS in Biology, Centenary Coll. La., 1989; MD, Tulane U. Sch. Medicine, 1993. Asst. prof. dermatologic surgery & dermatology Med. U. SC, 2009—, mohs micrographic surgeon. Fellow: Am. Coll. Mohs Surgery. Home and Office: Med University SC Dept Dermatology 135 Rutledge Ave Charleston SC 29425 Personal E-mail: leachbc@comcast.net.

LEACH, KENT, engineering educator; b. Ark., July 29, 1974; PhD, U. Okla., 2003. Assoc. prof. UC Davis, 2005—. Mem.: Soc. Biomaterials, Tissue Engring. and Regenerative Medicine Internat. Soc., Biomed. Engring. Soc. Office: Dept Biomed Engring 45 Davis CA 95616 Business E-Mail: jkleach@ucdavis.edu.

LEACH, MATTHEW JOHN, district nurse, educator, naturopath, researcher; BN with honors, U. S.Australia, Adelaide, 1994; PhD in Nursing, U. S.Australia, 2005; Diploma in Applied Sci. Naturopathy, South Australia Coll. Natural and Traditional Medicine, Adelaide, 1998; Diploma in Clin. Nutrition, Internat. Acad. Nutrition, 2008. RN Nurses Bd. South Australia, 1994. RN Adecco NSB, Adelaide, 1996—2000, Royal Dist. Nursing Svc., Adelaide, 2000—; lectr. naturopathy U. South Australia, Adelaide, 2004—; rsch. fellow U. S. Australia, Adelaide, 2008—. Mem. divsn. health scis. human rsch. ethics com. U. South Australia, Adelaide, 2006—08. Reviewer: Jour. Wound Care, 2006; contbr. articles to profl. jours. Mem. course evaluation panel Office Higher Edn., Dept. Edn. and the Arts, Queensland Govt., Brisbane, Australia, 2006—08. Recipient High Achiever award for Graduating Nurses, Royal Coll. Nursing, Australia, 1995, Award for Excellence in Naturopathic Studies, South Australia Coll. Natural and Traditional Medicine, 1999, Australian Postgraduate award, U. South Australia, 2001—04; WJC Willson Undergraduate scholar, 1992—94, Bachelor of Nursing Honors scholar, 2000, Florence Nightingale Edn. and Rsch. grantee, Australian Nurses Fedn., 1995. Mem.: Australian Soc. Med. Rsch., Australian Traditional Medicine Soc. (Simon Schot Edn. grant 2006), Internat. Soc. Complementary Medicine Rsch. Avocations: reading, swimming, travel, research. Office: University South Australia North Terrace 5000 Adelaide SA Australia Business E-Mail: matthew.leach@unisa.edu.au.

LEACH, ROBERT ELLIS, orthopedist, surgeon, educator; b. Sanford, Maine, Nov. 25, 1931; s. Ellis and Estella (Tucker) L.; m. Laurine Seber, Aug. 20, 1955; children: Cathy, Brian, Michael, Craig, Karen, Diane. AB, Princeton U., 1953; MD, Columbia U., 1957. Diplomate Am. Bd. Orthopedic Surgery (treas. 1986-93). Resident orthopedic surgery U. Minn., 1957-62; orthopedic surgeon Lahey Clinic, Boston, 1964-68, chmn. dept., 1968-70; prof., chmn. dept. Boston U. Med. Sch., 1970—. Head physician U.S. Olympic Team, 1984; chmn. sports medicine coun. U.S. Olympic Com., 1984-93; vice chmn. sports medicine coun. U.S. Tennis Assn., 1988-2002. Editor-in-chief Am. J. Sports Med.; editor emeritus Am. Jour. Sports Medicine, 2002; contbr. articles to profl. jours. Served to lt. comdr. USNR, 1962-64. Recipient Rovere Career Tchg. award, 1995, Ernst Jokl Sports Medicine award, 2000; named Sports Medicine Man of Yr., 1988; named to Sports Medicine Hall of Fame, 2003; Am., Brit., Can. Orthop. Travelling fellow, 1971. Mem. Am. Acad. Orthopedic Surgeons, Continental Orthopedic Soc. (sec. 1966), Am. Orthopedic Assn. (pres. 1994), Am. Orthopedic Soc. Sports Medicine (pres. 1983), Longwood Cricket Club. Home: 40 Rockport Rd Weston MA 02493-1428 Office: 230 Calvary St Waltham MA 02453-8366

LEACOCK, RODNEY OWEN, neurologist, educator; b. Cornwall, Ontario, Can., Aug. 18, 1959; arrived in U.S, 1995, permanent resident; s. Raymond Joseph and Rona Violet (Haynes) Leacock; m. Valerie Nell Hicks, June 24, 2000. BS, Concordia U., Montreal, Quebec, Can., 1985; MD, Howard U., Washington, 1992. Diplomate Am. Bd. Psychiatry and Neurology in Neurology, 2001. Intern Howard U., Washington, 1992—93; resident Dalhousie U., Halifax,, Nova Scotia, Canada, 1993—95, Temple U., Phila., 1995—98; fellow Wayne State U., Detroit, 1998—99, Saint Louis U., 1999—2000, instr., 2000—02, asst. prof., 2002—. Mem.: AMA, Soc. Critical Care Medicine, Nat. Med. Assn. (Mound City Med. Forum), Am. Acad. Neurology, Am. Heart Assn. (mem. Am. Stroke Assn.). Avocations: sports, modern jazz, reading. Home: 12 Willow Side Ct Fairview NC 28730-8549

LEADLEY, KATRIN, medical device company executive; MD, Ludwig-Maximilian U., Munich, 1989. Dir. clin. affairs Advanced Stent Technologies; dir. clin. rsch. Pulmonx; global sr. med. dir. clin. sciences Boston Scientific Corp., 2009—11; chief med. officer Jena-Valve Tech. Inc., 2011—. Recipient Clin. Sciences Impact award, Boston Scientific Corp., 2008. Avocations: German, English. Office: JenaValve Technology Incorporated Wilmington Downtown 1000 N West St Suite 1200 Wilmington DE 19801 Office Fax: 302-295-4897, 302-295-4801.

LEAF, ALEXANDER, preventive medicine physician, epidemiologist; b. Yokohama, Japan, Apr. 10, 1920; arrived in U.S., 1922, naturalized, 1936; s. Aaron L. and Dora (Hural) Leaf; m. Barbara Louise Kincaid, Oct. 1943; children: Caroline Joan, Rebecca Louise, Tamara Jean. BS, U. Wash., 1940; MD, U. Mich., 1943; MA, Harvard, 1961. Intern Mass. Gen. Hosp., Boston, 1943—44, mem. staff, 1949—, physician-in-chief, 1966—81; resident Mayo Found., Rochester, Minn., 1944—45; rsch. fellow U. Mich., 1947—49; practice internal medicine Boston, 1949—90; faculty Med. Sch., Harvard, 1949—66, Jackson prof. clin. medicine, 1966—81, Ridley Watts prof. preventive medicine, 1980—90, chmn. dept. preventive medicine and clin. epidemiology, 1980—90, Jackson prof. clin. medicine emeritus, 1990—; Disting. physician VA Medical Ctr. Brockton/W. Roxbury Hosps., Boston, 1992—97. Capt. M.C. US Army, 1945—46. Recipient Outstanding Achievement award, U. Minn., 1964; fellow Vis. fellow, Balliol Coll., Eng., 1971—72, Guggenheim, 1971—72. Master: ACP; fellow: Am. Acad. Arts and Scis.; mem.: NAS, Internat. Soc. Nephrology (A.M. Richards award 1997), Assn. Am. Physicians (Kober medal 1995), Biophys. Soc., Am. Physiol. Soc., Am. Soc. Clin. Investigation (past pres.), Inst. Medicine. Home: 5 Sussex Rd Winchester MA 01890-3846 Office: Mass Gen Hosp Bldg 149 13th St Charlestown MA 02129 Office Phone: 617-726-5908. Business E-Mail: aleaf@partners.org.

LEAKE, DEIRDRE, plastic surgeon; BS in Biochemistry summa cum laude, U. Tenn., 1990—94, MD, 1994—98. Diplomate Am. Bd. Otolaryngology, Am. Bd. of Facial Plastic & Reconstructive Surgery. Internship in gen. surgery Univ. of Rochester Med. Ctr., Rochester, NY, 1998—99, resident in otolaryngology head and neck surgery, 1999—2003; fellow in facial and plastic & reconstructive surgery Univ. Mich., 2003—04; fellow Am. Acad. of Facial Plastic &

Reconstructive Surgery, Am. Acad. of Cosmetic Surgery. Mem.: AMA, Assn. of Women Surgeons, Skin Cancer Found., Fla. Soc. of Otolaryngology, Fla. Soc. of Facial Plastic & Reconstructive Surgery, Fla. Med. Soc., Am. Coll. of Surgeons, Am. Acad. of Otolaryngology. Office: Facial Rejuvenation Center Suite 10 1750 Tree Blvd Saint Augustine FL 32084

LEAL, ERMELINDO C., cell and molecular researcher; b. Coro, Venezuela, Oct. 13, 1979; PhD in Cell Biology, U. Coimbra, 2008. Rsch. asst. Ctr. Ophthalmology and Vision Scis., 2007—08; postdoc. rschr. Ctr. Neuroscis. and Cell Biology, 2009—, Harvard Med. Sch. BIDMC, 2011—. Mem.: EASD, Portuguese Soc. Diabetologia, Portuguese Bioquemistry Soc., Portuguese Soc. Neurosci. Avocations: reading, theater, sports. Office: 21 Colbourne Cresent Brookline MA 02445 Office Phone: +351919504536. Business E-Mail: ecieal@cnc.uc.pt. E-mail: ecleal@gmail.com.

LEANDRO-MERHI, VANIA APARECIDA, nutritionist, educator; b. São Joaquim da Barra, São Paulo, Brazil, Feb. 3, 1963; M, Fed. U. São Paulo, 1997; PhD, State U. Campinas, São Paulo, 2002. Prof., rschr. Pontifical Cath. U. Campinas, 1987—. Editor-in-chief Brazilian Jour. Nutrition, 2010. Home: Ave Carlos Grimaldi 1171 Quadra:D-13 Campinas São Paulo 13091-906 Brazil

LEAR, ERWIN, anesthesiologist, educator; b. Bridgeport, Conn., Jan. 1, 1924; s. Samuel Joseph and Ida (Ruth) L.; m. Arlene Joyce Alexander, Feb. 15, 1953; children: Stephanie, Samuel MD, SUNY, 1952. Diplomate Am. Bd. Anesthesiology, Nat. Bd. Med. Examiners. Intern L.I. Coll. Hosp., Bklyn., 1952-53; asst. resident anesthesiology Jewish Hosp., Bklyn., 1953-54, sr. resident, 1955, asst., 1955-56, adj., 1956-58, assoc. anesthesiologist, 1958-64; attending anesthesiologist Bklyn. VA Hosp., 1958-64, cons., 1977—; assoc. vis. anesthesiologist Kings County Hosp. Ctr., Bklyn., 1957-80, staff anesthesiologist, 1980-81; vis. anesthesiologist Queens Gen. Hosp. Ctr., 1955-67; dir. anesthesiology Queens Hosp. Ctr. Jamaica, 1964-67; chmn. dept. anesthesiology Catholic Med. Ctr., Queens and Bklyn., 1968-80; dir. anesthesiology Beth Israel Med. Ctr., NYC, 1981-98; clin. instr. SUNY Coll. Medicine, Bklyn., 1955-58, from clin. asst. prof. to clin. prof., 1958-80, prof., vice-chmn. clin. anesthesiology, 1980-81; prof. anesthesiology Mt. Sinai Sch. Medicine, 1981-94, Albert Einstein Coll. of Medicine, 1994—. Cons. in field. Author: Chemistry Applied Pharmacology of Tranquilizers; contbr. articles to profl. jours. Served with USNR, 1942-45 Fellow: N.Y. Acad. Medicine (sec. sect. anesthesiology 1985—86, chmn. sect. anesthesiology 1986—87), Am. Coll. Anesthesiologists; mem.: AMA, SUNY Coll. Medicine Alumni Assn. (pres. 1983, trustee alumni fund 1980), N.Y. County Med. Soc., N.Y. State Med. Soc. (chmn. sect. anesthesiology 1966—67, sec. sect. 1977—81), N.Y. State Soc. Anesthesiologists (chmn. pub. rels. 1963—73, assoc. editor Bulletin 1963—77, chmn. com. local arrangements 1968—73, dist. dir. 1972—73, bd. dirs. 1972—94, v.p. 1974—75, pres. 1976, chmn. jud. com. 1977—81, editor Sphere 1978—87, Disting. Svc. award 1996), Am. Soc. Anesthesiologists (ho. of dels. 1973—94, dir. 1981—97, chmn. com. on by-laws 1982—83, editor newsletter 1984—98, chmn. adminstrv. affairs com. 1987—94), Alpha Omega Alpha. Address: 1 Harriman Dr Sands Point NY 11050-1246 E-mail: erwinlear@aol.com.

LEARRETA, JORGE ALFONSO, dentist, educator; b. Buenos Aires, Dec. 11, 1949; s. Pedro Jose Learreta and Nelida Ruiz Perera; life ptnr.; children: Maria de las Mercede, Maria Sol, Jorge Pedro Ivan. DDS, Buenos Aires U., 1971; MS International Coll. Cranio Mandibular Orthopedics, 1996. Diplomate Argentine Orthodontics Soc., 1991, Am. Acad. Craniofacial Pain, 2003, Acad Panameña de Prótesis y Oclusión, 2006. Asst. Orthodontic Chair Legal Dentistry, Buenos Aires, 1972—75, chief practice work, 1976—85; adj. prof., Sci. Health Faculty Argentine Cath. U., Buenos Aires, 1991—93, chmn., Specialist in Orthodontics Career, Sci. Health Faculty, 1994—98; chmn., growth and devel. chair Faculty, La Plata U., Buenos Aires, 1994—96; chmn., Specialist Orthodontics Career Salta Cath. U., Buenos Aires, 2000—, chmn., Specialist Temporomandibular Joint Career, 2000—. Cons. TMJ Air Force, Buenos Aires, 1999—; pres. Sociedad Argentina de Ortodoncia, Buenos Aires, 1986—90. Author: (scientific book) Compendio Sobre Diagnóstico de las Patologias de la ATM, Atlas de imagenes sanas y patologicas de la Articulación Temporomandibular. Fellow: World Federación Orthodontics; mem.: Circulo Argentino Odontología, Asociación Odontológica Argentina, Sociedad Argentina Ortodoncia, Internat. Coll. Dentists, Pierre Fouchard Acad. Roman Catholic. Office: Consultorio Beruti 3208 Buenos Aires 1425 Argentina Office Fax: 5411 4822 3300. Personal E-mail: jorgelearreta@fibertel.com.ar.

LEARY, KIMBERLYN, psychologist; b. New Orleans, July 24, 1960; PhD, U. Mich., 1988; MPA, Harvard Kennedy Sch., 2009. Chief psychologist Cambridge Health Alliance, Harvard Med. Sch., 2004—. With, network faculty Program Negotiation, Harvard Law Sch., 1997—. Pub. Svcs. fellowship, Harvard Kennedy Sch. Mem.: APA (award), Am. Psychoanalytic Assn. (program com. chair 2010, Karl Menninger award, Ticho award). Avocation: photography. Office: 201 Brookline St #1 Cambridge MA 02139 E-mail: kimleary9@gmail.com.

LEATH, MARY ELIZABETH, medical/surgical nurse; b. Cochran, Ga., Aug. 12, 1949; d. Warren Shaw Leath and Hattie Mae (Blackshear) Sterling; divorced; children: Myisha Renee, Shamara Antonea. Diploma, City Hosp., 1972; BS, Johns Hopkins U., Balt., 1988; ADN, Catonsville C.C., 1990; BSN, U. Md., 1993; MS, Johns Hopkins U., Balt., 1995; PhD, Cath. U., 1997. Cert. ACLS, critical care, ICU/trauma specialist, med./surg., phlebotomy and respiratory therapy, PICC lines, IV therapy and maintenance, cardiac care, peripheral intravenous cardiac catheterization. LPN staff MIEMSS, Balt., 1973-80, Ft. Howard (Md.) VA Med. Ctr., 1981-90; staff nurse Ft. Howard (Va.) VA Med. Ctr., 1990-96, Washington Trauma Ctr., 1996—; legal nurse cons., 1998—. Mem. ANA, Black Nurses Assn., Woodmoor Cmty. Health Assn. (instr. 1984—), Pres.'s Coun. on Physical Fitness, D.C. Nursing Assn., Phi Beta Kappa, Alpha Kappa Phi.

LEAVELL, ELIZABETH BOYKIN, retired pediatrician; b. Sumter, SC, 1924; d. William de Saussure and Elizabeth (Hood) Boykin; m. Seth Eugene Latham (dec.); children: Seth Eugene Latham Jr., Margaret Elizabeth Latham Davis, Richard Boykin Latham, William deSaussure Latham; m. Lewis Edward Leavell, Jr., Aug. 16, 1985 (dec.). BS in Biology, Winthrop U., Rock Hill, SC, 1946; MD, Med. U. SC, Charleston, 1950. Diplomate Am. Bd. Pediat., 1956. Rotating intern Roper Hosp., Charleston, 1950—51, resident Pediat., 1951—53, chief resident, 1953—54; pediatrician Civil Svc. Tripler Army Hosp., Honolulu, 1954—55; pediatrician Aiken, SC, 1955—61, Atlanta, 1962—86; ret., 1986. Chief pediat. Holy Family Hosp., Atlanta, 1967, South Fulton Hosp., Atlanta, 1970; clinic pediatrician Crippled Children's Clinic, Atlanta, 1980—85; dir. med. edn. Pediat. St. Joseph Hosp., Atlanta, 1962—68; med. dir. Ctrl. Presbyn. Baby Clinic, Atlanta, 1962—68; pres. Sumter County Hist. Soc., 2007—08. Recipient Mary Mildred Sullivan Outstanding Alumna award, Winthrop U., 1970; tchg. fellow dept. pediat., Med. U. SC, 1953—54. Fellow: Am. Acad. Pediat. (chmn. Fetus and Newborn com. Ga. chpt.). Home: 623 Antlers Dr Sumter SC 29150

LEAVITT, BRUCE JASON, medical educator; b. Albequerque, Dec. 26, 1955; BA, U. Maine, 1976; MD, U. Vt., 1981. Prof., surgery U. Vt. Coll. Medicine, 1988—. Recipient Medicine and Cmty. award, U. Vt. Med. Alumni Assn. Fellow: Am. Coll. Surgeon; mem.: New Eng. Surgery Soc., Soc. Thoracic Surgery, Am. Assn. Thoracic Surgery. Office: Fletcher Allen Health Care 111 Colchest Burlington VT 05403 Office Fax: 802-847-8158. Business E-Mail: bruce.leavitt@vtmednet.org.

LEAVITT, MICHAEL OKERLUND, consulting firm executive, former United States Secretary of Health and Human Services; b. Cedar City, Utah, Feb. 11, 1951; s. Dixie and Anne (Okerlund) Leavitt; m. Jacalyn Smith; children: Michael Smith, Taylor Smith, Anne Marie Smith, Chase Smith, Weston Smith. BA in Economics & Bus., Southern Utah U., 1978. CPCU. Sales rep. Leavitt Group, Cedar City, 1972-74, account exec., 1974-76, mgr. underwriting Salt Lake City, 1976-82, COO, 1982-84, pres., CEO, 1984-92, gov. State of Utah, 1993—2003; adminstr. EPA, Washington, 2003—05; sec. US Dept. Health & Human Services, Washington, 2005—09; co-founder, chmn. Leavitt Partners LLC, Salt Lake City, 2009—. Chmn. Nat. Governors Assn., 1999—2000. Chmn. instl. coun. Southern Utah State U., Cedar City, 1985-89, chmn, Utah St. Bd. Regents, 1989-92, campaign chmn. to Senator Orrin Hatch, 1982, 88, US Sen. Jake Garn, 1980, 86; cons. campaign Gov. Norman Angerter, 1984; mem. staff Reagan-Bush '84. 2d lt. USNG, 1969-77. Named Disting. Alumni Southern Utah State Coll. Sch. Bus., 1986; recipient China Pub. Health award Mem. CPCU. Republican. Mem. Lds Ch. Avocation: golf. Office: Leavitt Partners LLC 299 South Main St Ste 2300 Salt Lake City UT 84111 Office Phone: 801-656-9716. Office Fax: 801-538-1111.

LEBER, GEOFFREY EVANS, plastic surgeon; BA in Biochemistry, U. Ariz., 1988, MD, MCP Hahnemann U., Phila., 1993. Diplomate Am. Bd. Plastic Surgery, Am. Bd. Surgery, lic. Calif., Ariz. Resident gen. surgery Baystate Med. Ctr., Springfield, Mass., 1993—98; resident plastic surgery Med. Coll. of Wis., Milwaukee, Wis., 1998—2000; fellowship Ellenbogen Advanced Aesthetic Plastic Surgery, Beverly Hills, Calif., 2000; hosp. appointments include Banner Desert Med. Ctr., Mesa, Ariz., Scottsdale Healthcare Shea, Scottsdale Healthcare Osborn; with Samaritan Surgicenters of Ariz., Tempe Surg. Ctr. Inc., Paradise Valley Cosmetic surgery Ctr. Office: Ste D-500 5410 N Scottsdale Rd Paradise Valley AZ 85253 Office Phone: 480-945-5522.

LE BIHAN, DENIS, radiologist; b. France, July 30, 1957; m. Christiane Le Bihan; children: Armelle, Carolyn. Higher Studies Degree in Computer Sci., U. Paris, 1977, Extensive Studies Degree in Biomathematics, Data Processing, and Statistics, with major in Math. Models in Medicine, 1978, Higher Studies Degree in Neurophysiology and Ctrl. Nervous System Functional Exploration, 1979, BS in fundamental physics with high distinction, 1983, MA in fundamental physics with high distinction, 1984, extensive studies degree in nuclear and elementary particles physics with distinction, 1985, PhD in physical Sci., 1987, MD with distinction, 1984. French Bd. Cert. in Radiology, 1987. Resident in neurosurgery, nuclear medicine and radiology U. Paris, 1981—87; chief diagnostic radiology rsch. sect., Clin. Ctr. NIH, Bethesda, Md., 1990—94, vis. assoc., diagnostic radiology dept., Clin. Ctr., 1987—90; clinical asst. prof. radiology, dept. radiology, divsn. neuroradiology Georgetown U. Hosp., Washington, 1989—91, clin. assoc. prof. radiology, dept. radiology, divsn. neuroradiology, 1991—96; dir. lab. anatomical and functional neuroimaging, dept. med. rsch. Atomic Energy Commn., Orsay, France, 1999—; dir. Federative Rsch. Inst. Functional Imaging, Paris, 2000—06, Neurospin, Saclay, France, 2007—. Cons. Magnetic Resonance Dept. Thomson-CGR, Buc, France/General Electric Med. Systems, Milwaukee, 1987, Guerbet Group, Aulnay-sous-bois, France, 1992, Yokogawa Med. Systems, 1993—94; hon. lectr. European Congress Radiology, 2002; mem. scientific adv. bd. of Nat. and Internat. Organizations and rsch. funding agencies; dir. Neurospin, project of CEA. Author over 200 articles in fields of MRI, Imaging, neuroscience and radiology; cons. to editor Radiology, assoc. editor Human Brain Mapping, mem. editl. bd. Journal of Magnetic Resonance Imaging, Journal of Computer Assisted Tomography, 1993—95, Magnetic Resonance in Medicine, Internat. Journal of Neuroradiology, Neuroimage and others, referee Stroke, Science, Proceeding of the NAS, Journal Magnetic Resonance, American Journal Roentgenology, Investigative Radiology, NMR in Biomedicine and others; author: Imagerie par Resonance Magnetique: Bases Physiques (first textbook on MRI physics in French), 1984, Magnetic Resonance Imaging of Diffusion and Perfusion: Applications to Functional Imaging (Only textbook on Diffusion MRI, first textbook published on fMRI), 1995. Recipient Michel Katz award, French Soc. Radiology, 1985, Rene Djindjian award, French Soc. Neuroradiology, 1986, Foucault award for Achievements in Applied Physics, French Soc. Physics, 1989, Sylvia Sorkin Greenfield award in Medical Physics, Am. Assn. Physicists in Medicine, 1991, Award of the European Soc. Magnetic Resonance in Medicine and Biology, 1994, Richard Lounsbery award, Nat. Acad. Scis., USA, 2002, Louis D. Found. award, Inst. France, 2003. Fellow: Internat. Soc. Magnetic Resonance in Medicine (Gold medal 2001); mem.: French Acad. Scis. (corr. Kodak award for Scientific Achievement in Imaging Rsch. 1995), Am. Soc. NeuroRadiology (hon.), French Acad. Tech. (hon.). Achievements include patents in field. Avocations: meteorology, golf, classical piano, Japanese sightseeing, language, gardening, cooking. Office: Neurospin Botiment 145 Cea Saclay 91191 Gif-sur-Yvette France Office Phone: 33 0 1 69 08 82 05. Office Fax: 33 0 1 69 08 82 13. Personal E-mail: denis.lebihan@gmail.com.

LEBLANC, STACIE SCHRIEFFER, lawyer, educator; b. La., Aug. 24, 1964; BA in Liberal Arts Curriculum, La. State U., Baton Rouge, 1986; MA in Early Childhood Edn., U. New Orleans, 1989; JD, Loyola U. New Orleans, 1990. Asst. dist. atty., supr. Felony Child Abuse Program, Terrebonne Parish Dist. Atty.'s Office, 1990—99, bd. dirs., 1997—98; dept. head Audrey Hepburn CARE Ctr. Children's Hosp., 2000—; exec. dir. New Orleans Children's Adv. Ctr. Children's Hosp.; dir. legal advocacy Jefferson Parish Dist. Atty.'s Office. Law lectr. in numerous schs. & colls., 1990—; bd. mem. Met. Battered Woman's Bd., 1999, La. Partnership for Children and Families, 2008—10; bd. dirs. Jefferson Parish Children's Advocacy Ctr., 2000; mem. La. Commn. Multidisciplinary Teams, 2000; chair, legis. com. New Orleans Task Force on Child Sexual Abuse, 2004; adv. bd. mem. La. Partnership for Children and Families, 2010—, Abused Kids with Disabilities, 2010. Recipient Recognition award, Met. Battered Woman's Program, 1997, Outstanding Prosecutor award, Victims and Citizens Against Crime, Inc., 1998; MAPS grant, Crime Victim Assistance Funds, 1998—99, VINE grant, Violence Against Women Act Funds, 1998—99. Mem.: Timberline Garden Club (pres. 2003). Office: Audrey Hepburn CARE Ctr Children's Hosp 200 Henry Clay Ave New Orleans LA 70118 Office Fax: 504-896-7295. Business E-Mail: sleblanc@chola.org.

LEBOFF, MERYL SUSAN, physician, medical educator; b. Bklyn., Mar. 14, 1949; married; 2 children. MD, U. Med. and Dentistry of N.J., 1975. Diplomate Am. Bd. Internal Medicine. Fellow in endocrinology Harvard Med. Sch., Boston, 1979-82; intern, resident, chief resident U. So. Calif./Los Angeles County Hosp., LA, 1979-82; assoc. physician Brigham and Women's Hosp., Boston, 1982—; instr. in medicine Harvard Med. Sch., Boston, 1982-84, asst. prof. medicine, 1984-95, assoc. prof. medicine, 1995—, mem. search com. for asst. prof., 1989; dir. skeletal health and osteo. ctr. Brigham and Women's Hosp., Boston, 1987—, dir. housestaff tng. program in endo-hypertension, 1990, dir. skeletal health and osteo. program, 1993—. Councilor Am. Soc. Bone and Mineral Rsch., 2007—. Mem. editl. bd. Jour. Bone and Mineral Rsch., Jour. Clin. Density; contbr. articles to profl. jours. Recipient Boy Frame award Am. Soc. Bone and Mineral Rsch., 2002; grantee NIH, 1983-87, 94-97, 95—, Dept. Def., 1999—; named Harvard Sandoz Scholar in Medicine, 1990-93, The Best Drs. Am., 1996-2009, One of 50 Most Intriguing Women in Boston, 1997, among Best Physicians in Women's Health, Boston Mag., 2001, Best Physician in Endocrinology, Boston Mag., 2002, Best Drs. in America, 2003-09. Mem. AMWA, ACP, AAAS, NOW, Nat. Osteoporosis Found., Inc. (mem. sci. adv. bd.), Paget's Disease Found., Inc., Soc. Tchg. Scholars, Brigham and Women's Hosp. Avocation: classical music. Office: Brigham and Womens Hosp 221 Longwood Ave Boston MA 02115-5804 Office Phone: 617-732-6155.

LEBOVICS, EDWARD, gastroenterologist, director; MD, NYU, 1980. Diplomate Am. Bd. Internal Medicine, Am. Bd. Internal Medicine-gastroenterology. Intern internal medicine Barnes-Jewish Hosp., St. Louis, resident internal medicine, 1981—83; fellow hepatology Mt. Sinai Hosp., NYC, 1983—84; fellow gastroenterology NY Med. Coll., Valhalla, NY, 1984—86, dir. gastroenterology and hepatobiliary diseases dept., prof. medicine, chief gastroenterology and hepatobilliary diseases sect. Westchester Med. Coll., Valhalla; med. staff Greenwich Hosp., Conn. Named one of Best Doctors in NY, NY Mag., 2005. Office: Westchester Medical Center Munger Pavilion Rm 206 100 Woods Rd Valhalla NY 10595 Office Phone: 914-493-7337. Office Fax: 914-594-4317.

LEBOVICS, ROBERT, otolaryngologist; MD, SUNY, 1982. Diplomate Am. Bd. Otolaryngology. Resident in surgery Montefiore Hosp. and Med. Ctr., 1982—83, resident in otolaryngology, 1983—87; chief of the clin. otolaryngology svc. Nat. Insts. of Health, Bethesda, Md.; lectr. Georgetown Univ.; chief of otolaryngology Cabrini Med. Ctr., 1999—2002; with head and neck surgical group St. Luke's Roosevelt Hosp. Ctr., 1997, dir. of the Inflammatory Disorders of the Respiratory Tract Program. Named one of Top Doctors- NY Metro Area, Castle Connolly, 2009. Office: St. Luke's-Roosevelt Hospital Center 425 W 59th St 10 Fl New York NY 10019 Office Phone: 212-262-0056.

LEBOVITZ, PAUL J., gastroenterologist, educator; MD, Yeshiva U. Diplomate Am. Bd. Internal Medicine-gastroenterology. Intern Univ. Pa., resident; fellow Univ. Pitts.; asst. prof. medicine Drexel Univ.; practice Alegheny Gen. Hosp.; dir. divsn. gastroenterology Allegheny Gen. Hosp., dir. gastroparesis ctr. Named one of Top Doctors, Pitts. mag., 2011. Office: Allegheny General Hospital 320 E N Ave Pittsburgh PA 15212 Office Phone: 412-359-3131. Office Fax: 412-359-4108.

LEBRANCHU, YVON, immunologist, educator; b. Dinan, France, May 10, 1947; MD, U. Grenoble, PhD, 1975. Asst. prof. clin. immunology U. Tours, France, 1981—92, head, transplantation and clin. immunology, rsch. unit dendritic cells and GRAFTS, 1985, 2002, prof. clin. immunology, 1992—. Pres. French Assn. U. Profs. Med. Immunology, 2001, French Speaking Soc. Transplantation, 2003—06, Nat. Bd. Appointing the Profs. Med. Immunology, 2010. Office: Blvd Tonnelle Tours Touraine 37044 France Business E-Mail: lebranchu@med.univ-tours.fr.

LEBRETON, OLIVIER, ophthalmologist; b. Libourne, Sept. 2, 1974; MD in Ophthalmology, U. Franche Comté, 2003. Chef, clinique, asst. des hôpitaux CHU Besançon, U. Franche Comté, 2004—06; hosp. pratician CHU Nantes, 2006—. Medaille d'or l'internat fellowship, Hosp. Besançon. Mem.: Soc. Française d'Ophtalmologie. Office: Service Ophtalmologie CHU Nantes 1 p Nantes Pays de la Loire 44093 France Business E-Mail: olivier.lebreton@chu-nantes.fr.

LEBWOHL, MARK GABRIEL, dermatologist, educator; b. Bklyn., Apr. 27, 1952; married, 1978; 2 children. BA summa cum laude, Columbia Coll., 1974; MD, Harvard Med. Sch., 1978. Diplomate Am. Bd. Internal Medicine, Am. Bd. Dermatology. Intern in internal medicine Mt. Sinai Med. Ctr., NYC, 1978-79, resident in internal medicine, 1979-81, resident in dermatology, 1981-82, NIH fellowship, 1982-83, asst. prof. dermatology, 1983-88, assoc. prof. dermatology, 1988-92, prof. dermatology, 1993—, dir. phototherapy unit, 1982—, clin. dir. dept. dermatology, 1983—, vice chmn. dept. dermatology, 1989—. Dir. divsn. clin. dermatology Mt. Sinai Sch. Medicine, NYC, 1989—, chmn. dept. dermatology, 1996—; dir. skin cancer screening clinic Mt. Sinai Hosp., NYC, 1985—93; chmn. PXE symposium Mt. Sinai Med. Ctr., NYC, 1987, chmn. phototherapy symposium, 92; dir. dermatology course N.Y. Coll. Podiatric Medicine, 1989—; med. adv. bd. Nat. Psoriasis Found., 1990—, chmn. med. bd., 2003—; chmn. Psoriasis Symposium, Istanbul, Turkey, 1993, Ankara, Turkey, 93, Adana, Turkey, 93, New Orleans, 93.

Author: Difficult Diagnoses in Dermatology, 1988, Atlas of the Skin and Systemic Disease, 1995, Psoriasis, 1995, Treatment of Skin Disease, 2002, 2d edit., 2006, 3rd edit., 2010, The Skin and Systemic Disease, an Atlas and Text, 2d edit., 2003, Mild to Moderate Psoriasis, 2009, Moderate to Severe Psoriasis, 2009; asst. editor The Mount Sinai Jour. of Medicine, 1989—2000; mem. editl. bd. Nat. Psoriasis Found. Bull., 1990—, Jour. Am. Acad. of Dermatology, 1993—. Fellow ACP, Am. Acad. Dermatology (faculty genodermatoses symposium 1985, skin cancer campaign coord N.Y. State 1985-93, nat. adv. coun. 1986—, faculty itch symposium 1993—, psoriasis symposium 1993—, dir. diagnostic update symposium 1993—); mem. AMA, N.Y. County Med. Soc., Soc. for Investigative Dermatology (chmn. psoriasis symposium 1991), Dermatol. Soc. of Greater N.Y., Manhattan Dermatol. Soc. (pres. 1985-86), Internat. Dermatology Soc., N.Y. State Soc. for Dermatology (pres. 2001-02), N.Y. Dermatol. Soc. (pres. 2003-04), N.Y. Acad. Medicine (chmn. dermatology sect. 1996), Phi Beta Kappa. Office: Mt Sinai Sch Medicine 5 E 98th St New York NY 10029-6501 Office Phone: 212-241-9728.

LECHEVALIER, HUBERT ARTHUR, microbiology educator; b. Tours, Indre et Loire, France, May 12, 1926; came to US, 1948; s. Jean Gaston and Marie Emilie L.; m. Mary Pfeil, Apr. 10, 1950; children: Marc, Paul. L ès Sci., Laval U., 1947, MS, 1948, DSc (hon.), 1983; PhD, Rutgers U., 1951. Asst. prof. Rutgers U., New Brunswick, NJ, 1951-56, assoc. prof., 1956-66, prof. microbiology, 1966-91, assoc. dir. Waksman Inst., 1980-88; prof. emeritus, 1991—. Vis. scientist Acad. of Scis. USSR, Moscow, 1958-59, Pasteur Inst., Paris, 1961-62 Author: (with others) A Guide to the Actinomycetes and Their Antibiotics, 1953, Neomycin--Its Nature and Practical Application, 1958, Antibiotics of Actinomycetes, 1962, Three Centuries of Microbiology, 1965, Hungarian transl., 1971, The Microbes, 1971, The Development of Applied Microbiology at Rutgers, 1982; co-editor: CRC Critical Reviews in Microbiology (1970-78), CRC Handbook of Microbiology (1970-89); contbr. numerous articles to profl. jours.; 4 patents. Trustee Am. Type Culture Collection, Rockville, Md., 1973-79. Recipient Lindback award 1976, Bergey award 1989; inducted into NJ Inventors Hall of Fame, 1990. Mem. Soc. Française de Microbiologie (hon.), Soc. Indsl. Microbiology (emeritus); Charles Thom award 1982, Soc. for Actinomycetes Japan (hon.) Home: 131 Goddard-Nisbet Rd Morrisville VT 05661-8041 Personal E-mail: mheques@comcast.net.

LECHEVALIER, MARY PFEIL, retired microbiologist, educator; b. Cleve., Jan. 27, 1928; d. Alfred Leslie Pfeil and Mary Edith Martin; m. Hubert Arthur Lechevalier, Apr. 7, 1950; children: Marc E.M., Paul R. BA in Physiology-Biochemistry, Mt. Holyoke Coll., 1949; MS in Microbiology, Rutgers U., 1951. Rsch. fellow Rutgers U., New Brunswick, NJ, 1949-51, rsch. assoc. inst. microbiology, 1962-74, from asst. to assoc. rsch. prof., 1974-85, rsch. prof. Waksman inst. microbiology, 1985-91, prof. emerita, 1991—; ind. rschr., 1955-59; microbiologist steroid preparative lab. E.R. Squibb and Sons, New Brunswick, 1960-61; vis. investigator Inst. Biology Czechoslovak Acad. Scis., Svc. de Mycologie Pasteur Inst., Prague, Paris, 1961-62. Cons. in field. Contbr. over 100 chpts. to books and articles to rsch. jours.; mem. adv. com. actinomycetes Bergey's Manual of Determinative Bacteriology, 8th edit.; chair adv. com. muriform actinomycetes Bergey's Manual, 9th edit. Assoc. mem. Bergey's Trust, 1989—92. Recipient Charles Thom award, Soc. Indsl. Microbiology, 1982, Waksman award, Theobald Smith Soc., 1991. Mem. AAAS, US Fedn. Culture Collections (exec. com. 1982-85, J. Roger Porter award nominating com. 1983-84, 87-88, chair 1989-90, J. Roger Porter award 1992), Soc. for Actinomycetes Japan, Sigma Xi (pres. Rutgers U. chpt. 1977-78). Achievements include patents in field. Home: 131 Goddard-Nisbet Rd Morrisville VT 05661-8041

LE CHEVALIER, THIERRY, medical oncologist; b. Lisieux, France, Aug. 12, 1948; s. François and Jacqueline (Deshayes) Le C.; m. Françoise D'Ornellas, Mar. 2, 1973; children: Isabelle, Clemence, Stanislas, Edouard. MD, U. Paris Sud, 1979. Fellow French Health Assistance, Yaounde, Cameroun, 1973-74; head lung unit Inst. Gustave Roussy, Villejuif, France, 1979—2005, asst. medicine, 1981—88, v.p., 2005—06, chief of unit Villejuif, 1988—94, chief of svc., 1994—2000, chmn. clin. trial com., 1998—2005, head dept. medicine, 2000—05; dir. internat. affairs French Nat. Cancer Inst., 2005—06; v.p. GlaxoSmithKline, 2006—09, R & D Oncology Europe, 2006—09; cons. Inst. Gustave Roussy & Ctr. Chirurgical Marie Lannelongue, 2009—; head Inst. Thoracic Oncology, 2010—. Vis. assoc. prof. Georgetown U., Washington, 1983-84; pres. Lung Group of French Cancer Ctr., 1982-2003; chmn. French Intergroup of Thoracic Oncology, 1999-2004. Assoc. editor Annals of Oncology, 1999-2006, Jour. Thoracic Oncology, 2005-06; contbr. over 300 articles to profl. jours. Mem. Am. Soc. Clin. Oncology, European Soc. Med. Oncology, Internat. Assn. for Study of Lung Cancer, French Cancer Soc. Roman Catholic. Office: Dept Medicine Inst Gustave Roussy 94800 Villejuif France Home: 19 avenue Emile Deschanel 75007 Paris France Office Phone: 3314 211 43 24, 33142114592. Business E-Mail: thierry.lechevalier@igr.fr.

LECHLEITER, JOHN C., pharmaceutical executive; b. 1953; BS in Chemistry summa cum laude, Xavier U., Cin., 1975; MS in Organic Chemistry, Harvard U., 1980, PhD, 1980; D in Bus. Adminstrn. (hon.), Marian Coll., Indpls., 2006. Sr. organic chemist process R & D Eli Lilly & Co., 1979—82, head process R & D, 1982—84, dir. pharm. product devel. Lilly Rsch. Ctr. Ltd. Windlesham, England, 1983—86, mgr. rsch. devel. projects Europe Indpls., 1986—88, dir. devel. projects mgmt., pharm. regulatory affairs, 1988, dir. chemistry, mfg. and control, 1989, exec. dir. pharm. product devel., 1991—93, v.p. pharm. prodn. & devel., 1993—94, v.p. regulatory affairs, 1994—96, v.p. devel. & regulatory affairs, 1996—98, sr. v.p. pharm. products, 1998—2001, exec. v.p. pharm. products & corp. devel., 2001—04, exec. v.p. pharm. ops., 2004—05, pres., COO, 2005—08, pres., CEO, 2008—09, chmn., pres., CEO, 2009—. Bd. dirs. Great Lakes Chemical Corp., 1999—2005, Eli Lilly & Co., 2005—, Nike Inc., 2009—, Pharmaceutical Rsch. & Manufacturers America. Vis. com. Harvard Bus. Sch., 2004—; health policy and mgmt. coun. Harvard Sch. Pub. Health, 2004—; bd. trustees Xavier U., Cin.; disting. advisor Children's Mus. Indpls.; Dean's adv. bd. Ind. U. Sch. Med.; bd. dirs. Fairbanks Inst., United Way Ctrl. Ind. Mem.: Am. Chem. Soc. Office: Eli Lilly & Co Lilly Corp Ctr Indianapolis IN 46285 Office Phone: 317-276-2000. *

LECHNER, JON ROBERT, nursing administrator, educator; b. Detroit, Nov. 5, 1957; s. Monroe Stanley and Helen Cecelia (Schneider) L. Cert. in practical nursing, Oakland C.C., Southfield, Mich., 1983; ADN, Mercy Coll. Detroit, 1991, BSN, 1992; MSA, Ctrl. Mich. U., 1998. Cert. EMT; RN, ANCC, Mich. Coord. emergency med. svcs., paramedic William Beaumont Hosp., Royal Oak, Mich., 1979-84, nurse, 1986—92, asst. nursing mgr., 1992-97, nursing mgr., 1997—2001; pastoral assoc. St. Mary's Parish & Sch., Toledo, 1984-86; adj. clin. instr. Oakland C.C., Waterford, Mich., 1993—; program mgr. Vis. Nurse Assn. of Southeast Mich., Oak Park, 2001—. Cert. BLS instr. Am. Heart Assn., Southfield, 1986—. Vol. Project Health-O-Rama, 1992—, Wellness Networks, Inc., 1992—; voting mem. region I State of Mich. HIV Planning & Prevention Commn., Detroit, 1994-2002. Mem. Am. Assembly Men Nursing, Am. Assn. Neurosci. Nurses, Acad. Med. Surg. Nurses (charter), Assn. Nurses AIDS Care, Sigma Theta Tau. Democrat. Roman Catholic. Avocations: reading, hiking, walking, bicycling, theater. Home: 28450 Universal Dr Warren MI 48092-2441 Office: Visiting Nurse Assn of Southeast Michigan 25900 Greenfield Rd Ste 600 Oak Park MI 48237 Office Phone: 248-967-8377. E-mail: jlechner@vna.org.

LECHNER, MATTHIAS ALEXANDER, physician; b. Innsbruck, Tirol, Austria, Oct. 29, 1981; s. Justus Lechner and Silvia Lechner-Steinleitner. MD, U. of Innsbruck, Austria, 2004. Dr. in tng. Hyperbaric Med. Ctr., Sharm-el-Sheikh, Sinai, Egypt, 2004, Castle Hill Hosp., Cottingham, Yorkshire, England, 2005—, Oxford Radcliffe Hosp., Oxford, England, 2006—07; rsch. assoc. and dr. in tng. Med. U. of Innsbruck, 2004—05; physician U. Hosp. Innsbruck, Austria; dr.in tng. Dr. Sardjito Hosp., Indonesia, 2007—08; rsch. fellow U. Coll. London, 2008—; with U. Hosp. Innsbruck, Austria, 2007—08. Grantee Med. Grad. grantee, Ministry of Edn., Sci., and Culture, 2004. Achievements include research in development of non-invasive diagnostic means. Avocations: skiing, diving, surfing, dance, opera. Office: Univ Coll London UCL Cancer Inst London England Personal E-mail: m.lechner@ucl.ac.uk. Business E-Mail: matthias.lechner@doctors.org.uk.

LECK, IAN MAXWELL, epidemiologist; b. Coventry, Eng., Feb. 14, 1931; s. Arthur Simpson and Margaret Mortimer (Jagger) Leck; m. Ann Patricia Sarson, July 25, 1959; children: Susan Margaret, Christopher James, Patricia Mary, Jonathan Peter. MB ChB, U. Birmingham, Eng., 1954, PhD, 1961, DSc, 1983. House officer Walsall Gen. Hosp., England, 1954—55; rsch. fellow U. Birmingham, England, 1957—59, lectr. social medicine, 1959—66; sr. lectr. cmty. medicine Univ. Coll. Hosp. Med. Sch., 1966—71; reader U. Manchester, 1971—78, prof., 1979—91, prof. emeritus, 1991—. Spl. cons. USPHS, 1964—68; assoc. editor Teratology: the Jour. of Abnormal Devel., 1972—80; mem. editl. bd. Jour. of Epidemiology & Cmty. Health, 1978—92, Jour. Med. Screening, 2001—06. Author (with G.J Draper): Childhood Cancer in Britain: Incidence, Survival & Mortality, 1982; editor (with N. Wald): Antenatal & Neonatal Screening, 2000; contbr. chapters to books, articles to profl. jours. Hon. sec. Ch. Together in Oxfordshire, 2000—05; methodist; local preacher, 1955—. Cap. Royal Army Med. Corps., 1955—57. Fellow: Royal Coll. Physicians London (Milroy Lectr. 1993), Faculty Pub. Health; mem.: Soc. Social Medicine (sec. 1993—95). Labour. Meth. Avocations: bicycling, walking. Home: 20 Upper Brook Hill Woodstock Oxfordshire OX 20 IUA England E-mail: iannleck@supanet.com.

LECKBAND, DEBORAH E., biomedical engineer, educator; b. May 30, 1959; BS, Humboldt State U., 1982; PhD, Cornell U., 1988. Prof. U. Ill., 1985—. Fellow: Am. Inst. Med. and BioEngring., Am. Chem. Soc.; mem.: Biomed. Engring. Soc. Achievements include research in surface science pertaining to biomaterial interactions with proteins and cells; investigations include studies of single molecules at surfaces and of protein transmission of mechanical information across cell membranes. Office: 600 S Mathews Ave Urbana IL 61801 Office Fax: 217-333-5052. Business E-Mail: leckband@illinois.edu.

LECKMAN, LINDA C., physician; b. Watonga, Okla., Oct. 2, 1947; d. Kenneth L. and Clara I. (Driever) Cordell; m. Scott L. Leckman, June 12, 1983; children: Matthew S., Eric A. BA, Tex. Christian U., 1969; MD, U. N.Mex., 1977. American Bd. Surgery. Intern, resident Univ. UT Affiliated Hosps., Salt Lake City, 1977-82; gen. surgeon Cottonwood Hosp.; gen. surgeon Alta View Hosp. Intermountain Healthcare, bd. trustees, v.p., 1996—; CEO Intermountain Med. Group, 1996—. Bd. trustees UT Med. Assn., Salt Lake City, 1986—; bd. dirs. Health Insight, Salt Lake City Named one of 25 Women in Healthcare, Modern Healthcare mag., 2011. Fellow ACS; mem. UT Med. Assn. (trustee, disting. svc. award), Assn. Women Surgeons, American Coll. Physician Execs., Alpha Omega Alpha. Office: Intermountain Healthcare 36 S State St 16th Fl Salt Lake City UT 84111 Office Phone: 801-442-3930. *

LECLÈRE, FRANCK MARIE PATRICK, microsurgeon; b. Neuilly sur Seine, France, Mar. 29, 1978; MD, U. Cath. Louvain, Bruxelles, 2004; BA in Economics, Haute Ecole de Commerce, Bruxelles, 2004; MS, U. Paris XI, 2009; PhD student, U. Lille, France, 2009. Plastic surgeon U. Heidelberg, U. Lille, U. Hannover. Contbr. articles to profl. jours. Recipient Whipple award, European Wrist Arthroscopy Soc., Gimbernat award, 2009. Mem.: European Wrist Arthroscopy Soc., Group Advancement Microsurgery. Avocations: piano, languages. Home: 4 rue Larribe Paris 75008 France Personal E-mail: franckleclere@yahoo.fr, franck.leclere@inserm.fr.

LEDEBOER, NATHAN ALLEN, pathologist, director; b. Willmar, Minn., Oct. 6, 1977; BA, Dordt Coll., 2000; PhD, U. Iowa, 2005. Med. dir., microbiology and molecular pathology Med. Coll. Wis., 2007. Office: 9200 West Wisconsin Ave Milwaukee WI 53150 Office Fax: 414-805-7560. Business E-Mail: nledeboe@mcw.edu.

LEDEEN, ROBERT WAGNER, neuroscientist, educator; b. Denver, Aug. 19, 1928; s. Hyman and Olga (Wagner) L.; m. Lydia Rosen Hailparn, July 2, 1982. BS, U. Calif., Berkeley, 1949; PhD, Oreg. State U., 1953. Postdoctoral fellow in chemistry U. Chgo., 1953-54; rsch. assoc. in chemistry Mt. Sinai Hosp., NYC, 1956-59; rsch. fellow Albert Einstein Coll. Medicine, Bronx, NY, 1959, asst. prof., 1963-69, assoc. prof., 1969-75, prof., 1975-91; prof., dir. div. neurochemistry U. Medicine and Dentistry N.J., Newark, 1991—. Contbr. articles to profl. jours.; dep. chief editor Jour. Neurochemistry. Mem. neurol. scis. study sect. NIH; mem. study sect. Nat. Multiple Sclerosis Soc. With US Army, 1954—56. NIH grantee, 1963—; Nat. Multiple Sclerosis Soc. grantee, 1967-74, 97—; recipient Humboldt prize, Javits Neurosci. Investigator award. Mem. Internat. Soc. Neurochemistry, Am. Soc. Neurochemistry, Am. Chem. Soc., Am. Soc. Biol. Chemists, N.Y. Acad. Sci. Jewish. Achievements include discoveries in the biochemistry of brain glycolipids and myelin. Home: 8 Donald Ct Wayne NJ 07470-4608 Office: U Medicine and Dentistry NJ Dept Neuroscis 185 S Orange Ave Newark NJ 07103-2757 Home Phone: 973-696-3091; Office Phone: 973-972-7989. Business E-Mail: ledeenro@umdnj.edu.

LEDERER, DAVID JOSHUA, medical educator; b. LI, NY, Oct. 23, 1971; MD, SUNY Downstate, 1999; MSc, Columbia U., 2007. Herbert Irving asst. prof. medicine Columbia U., 2006—. Rsch. dir. NY Presbyn. Lung Transplant Program, 2008; co-dir. NYP, Columbia Interstitial Lung Disease Program, 2008. Recipient Chancellor's award, SUNY, Harald A. Lyons award. Fellow: Am. Coll. Chest Physicians (Young Investigator award); mem.: Internat. Soc. Heart & Lung Transplantation, Am. Thoracic Soc. Office: 622 W 168th St PH-14 Rm 104 New York NY 10032

LEDERER, JOHN A., wholesale distribution executive; BA in Economics, York U. Pres. Loblaws Supermarkets Ltd.; sr. leadership positions Loblaw Companies Ltd., exec. v.p., merchandising, ops. and profit performance Toronto, Canada, pres., 2001—06, bd. dirs., 2002—06; pres., food distbn., segment George Weston Ltd., 2006; chmn. & CEO Duane Reade Holdings, Inc., NYC, 2008—10, bd. dirs., 2008—10; CEO & pres. US Foodservice, Inc., 2010—, bd. dirs., 2010—. Bd. dirs. Tim Hortons Inc., 2007—. Office: US Foodservice Inc 9399 W Higgins Rd Ste 500 Rosemont IL 60018 Office Phone: 847-720-8000. *

LEDERER, SUSAN HENDLER, speech/language pathologist, educator; d. Arthur Joel and Gloria Spector Hendler; m. Richard Brian Lederer, July 20, 1986; 1 child, Spencer Michael. BS, N.Y. U., 1979, MA, 1981, PhD, 1996. Lic. speech-lang. pathologist N.Y., cert. tchr. of speech and hearing handicapped N.Y. Speech-lang. pathologist, NY, 1981—; adminstr. SteppingStone Day Sch., Kew Garden Hills, NY, 1984—97; assoc. prof. Adelphi U., Garden City, NY, 1997—, chair depart. comm. sci. and disorders, 2005—08. Author: Pre-Read: An Integrated Emergent Literacy Program, 2005, I Can Say That, 2006, I Can Do That, 2008, I Can Play That, 2010, (CD) Storybook Yoga, 2008. Grantee, N.Y. State Devel. Disabilities Planning Coun. and Dept. Social Services, 1993—97. Mem.: L.I. Speech-Lang.-Hearing Assn. (univ. counselor 1997—2000), N.Y. State Speech-Lang.-Hearing Assn., Am. Speech-Lang.-Hearing Assn. (cert.). Avocations: yoga, swimming, walking, travel, reading. Office: Adelphi U Hy Weinberg Ctr Cambridge Ave Garden City NY 11530 Office Phone: 516-877-4770. Business E-Mail: lederer@adelphi.edu.

LEDERMAN, SALLY ANN, nutritionist, researcher; b. NYC, July 8, 1937; d. Joseph Edward and Leanora Rossi; m. Lawrence Lederman, Jan. 26, 1958 (div. Feb. 1991); children: Leandra, Evin. BS in Chemistry, Bklyn. Coll., 1957; MS in Nutrition, Columbia U., 1976, PhD, 1980. Analytical chemist U.S. FDA, NYC, 1957—62; lectr. dept. chemistry Bklyn. Coll., 1962-66, 74; postdoctoral fellow Inst. Human Nutrition Columbia U., NYC, 1980—82, postdoctoral fellow obstetrics and biochemistry, 1983, asst. prof. Sch. Pub. Health, 1983—90, assoc. prof. Sch. Pub. Health, 1990—94, prof. Tchrs. Coll., 1994—97, rschr. Tchrs. Coll., 1997—99; rsch. assoc. divsn. endocrinology, diabetes, nutrition St. Luke's-Roosevelt Hosp. Ctr., NYC, 1998—2003. Spl. lectr. Mailman Sch. Pub. Health, Inst. of Human Nutrition, Columbia U., 2000—. Editor: Controversial Issues in Public Health Nutrition, 1983; contbr. articles to profl. jours. Mem. APHA, AAAS, Am. Nutrition Soc., Am. Women in Sci., N.Y. Acad. Sci. Office: Inst Human Nutrition 630 W 168th St New York NY 10032 Office Phone: 212-305-4808. Business E-Mail: sal1@columbia.edu.

LEDERMAN, STEPHANIE, medical association administrator; BA in English, Emerson Coll., Boston, 1972; EdM, Boston U., 1975. Program mgr. Am. Heart Assn., Phila., 1977—78, Meml. Sloan Kettering Cancer Ctr., 1977—80; dir. health services Am. Red Cross, Greater NY, 1981—85; exec. dir. The Children's Health Fund, Nat. Ctr. Health Edn., 1986—90, Am. Fedn. Aging Rsch., NYC. Fellow: NY Acad. Medicine; mem.: NY Acad. Sciences. Office: Am Fedn Aging Rsch 55 W 39th St 16th Fl New York NY 10018 Office Phone: 212-703-9977. Office Fax: 212-997-0330. *

LEDFORD, DENNIS KEITH, physician; b. Johnson City, Tenn., May 10, 1950; s. Lawrence and Dorothy Ruth (Swatzell) L.; m. Jennifer L. Shelton, June 15, 1974; 3 children. BCE, Ga. Inst. Tech., 1973; MD, U. Tenn., 1976. diplomate Am. Bd. Allergy and Immunology. Med. intern U. Tenn. Hosps., Memphis, 1977, asst. and assoc. resident, 1978-79; chief resident City of Memphis Hosps., 1979-80; fellow in clin. immunology and rheumatology NYU, NYC, 1980-82; fellow in clin. allergy and immunology U. South Fla., Tampa, 1983-85, asst. prof. medicine, 1985-91, assoc. prof. medicine, 1991-99, prof. medicine, 2000—. Instr. dept. medicine U. Tenn. Ctr. Health Scis., Memphis, 1979-80; clin. assoc. internal medicine U. South Fla., 1983-85, dir. tng. program in clin. and lab. immunology, 1992-2004; mem. AIDS adv. com. James A. Haley VA Hosp., 1987-94; mem. infection control com. Univ. Cmty. Hosp., 1987-96; mem. adv. com. Blue Cross/Blue Shield, 1987-94; med. dir. Asthma and Allergy Clinic of Judeo-Christian Clinic, 1988—; chief allergy, immunology sect. Univ. Cmty. Hosp., 1996—; chmn. med. student selection com. U. South Fla., 1994-98, 2002-06; bd. dirs. Am. Bd. Allergy and Immunology, Annals of Allergy, Asthma and Immunology; mem. editl. bd. Annals of Allergy, Asthma and Immunology, 1988-03, Jour. Allery & Immunology, 2003—. Mem. editl. bd.: Jour. Allergy and Clin. Immunology, 2003—07, assoc. editor:, 2007—. Mem. med. adv. coun. Fla. chpt. Nat. Hemophilia Found., 1990-92; mem. AIDS edn. adv. coun. Hillsborough County Sch. Bd., 1992-95. Recipient Outstanding Spkr. award Marion County Med. Assn., 1987, Vol. of Yr. award Vol. Ctr. Hillsborough County, 1994. Fellow Am. Acad. Allergy Asthma & Immunology (bd. dirs. 2004-, chair underserved underrequested task force, pres. 2011-); mem. AMA, ACP, Am. Soc. Internal Medicine, Am. Rheumatism Assn. (Fellowship award 1981), Am. Coll. Allergy and Immunology (mem. ann. meeting postgrad. program com. 1996-98, 2002-03), Am. Acad. Allergy and Immunology (mem. continuing med. edn. com. 1987-90, chmn. 1989-90, mem. AIDS com. 1989-98, chmn. 1998-99, postgrad. edn. planning com. 1992-93, mem. core curriculum com. for clin. and diagnostic lab. immunology tng. programs 1993—, co-chair, bd. rev. course 1996-98, 2005—, co-chmn. clin. lab com. 1999-2001), Fla. Allergy and Immunology Soc. (sec. 1989-90, v.p. 1990-91, pres. 1991-93, bd. dirs. 1993-96). Avocations: gardening, hiking, fishing, music. Office: U South Fla Coll Medicine VA Med Ctr 13000 Bruce B Downs Blvd # 111D Tampa FL 33612-4745 Home Phone: 813-948-1410. Business E-Mail: dledford@hsc.usd.edu. *

LEDGER, WILLIAM JOE, obstetrician, gynecologist, educator; b. Turtle Creek, Pa., 1932; BA, Princeton U., 1954; MD, U. Pa., 1958; MS, Temple U., 1964. Diplomate Am. Bd. Ob-Gyn. Intern Hamot Hosp. Assn., Erie, NY, 1958-59; resident Temple U. Hosp., Phila., 1961-64; attending physician Women's Hosp.-Mich. Med. Ctr., 1964-72; assoc. prof. U. Mich., Ann Arbor; prof. U. So. Calif., LA, 1972-79; Given Found. prof., chmn. ob-gyn. Cornell U. Med. Coll., NYC, 1979—99, chmn. emeritus, 1999—. Served to capt. USMC, 1959-61 Fellow ACS, Am. Coll. Ob-Gyn. Office: NY Presbyn Hosp Weill Med Coll Cornell U 525 E 68th St Ste J-130 New York NY 10021-4870 Home Phone: 609-924-7569. Business E-Mail: wjledger@med.cornell.edu.

LEDLEY, ROBERT STEVEN, biophysicist; b. NYC, June 28, 1928; DDS, NYU, 1948; MA in Theoretical Physics, Columbia U., 1949. Rsch. physicist Columbia U. Radiation Labs., Columbia, 1948—50; instr. physics Columbia U., 1949—50; vis. scientist Nat. Bur. Standards, 1951—52; physicist, 1953—54; ops. rsch. analyst Johns Hopkins U., 1954—56; assoc. prof. elec. engring George Washington U., 1957—60; instr. pediat. Johns Hopkins U., Sch. Medicine, 1960—63; prof. elec. engring. George Washington U., 1968—70; prof. physiology, biophysics & radiology Georgetown U., 1970—; pres., rsch. dir. Nat. Biomed. Rsch. Found., 1960—; pres. Digital Info. Sci. Corp., 1970—75. Contbr. articles to profl. jours. and author of several books; editor-in-chief Pattern Recognition, Elsevier Science, Oxford, Eng., Computers in Biology and Medicine, Computerized Medical Imaging and Graphics, Computer Languages. Recipient Nat. medal of Tech., U.S. Dept. Commerce, 1997, Morris E. Collen, MD award, Am. Coll. of Medical Informatics, 1998, Goldhaber award, Harvard Sch. Dental Medicine, 1998, Cert. of Appreciation, Nat. Inst. Dental Rsch., NIH, 1998, Disting. Alumni NYU, 1999; named to Nat. Inventor Hall of Fame, 1990. Mem.: NIH, IEEE, NAS (mem. Inst. Medicine), Pattern Recognition Soc., N.Y. Acad. Scis., Biophys. Soc., Soc. Math. Biophysics. Achievements include invention of CT Scanner.

LEDOUARIN, NICOLE MARTHE, molecular biologist; b. Aug. 20, 1930; BS, U. Paris, 1954, DSc, 1964. Lectr. Clermont-Ferrand U., 1965—66; prof. Nantes U., 1971—75; dir. Inst. Embryology, 1975—; prof. Coll. France, 1988—2000. Co-recipient Ralph W. Gerard prize in Neuroscience, Soc. for Neuroscience, 2007. Mem.: NAS, Royal Soc. UK, Am. Acad. Scis., Acad. Scis. Paris (permanent sec.). Office: Coll de France 3 rue d'ulm 75005 Paris France E-mail: nicol.ledouarin@wanadoo.fr.

LEDOUX, JEAN-MARIE, veterinarian; b. Roubaix, France, Feb. 5, 1958; s. Gaston Ledoux and Fernande Berte. DVM, Nat. Vet. Sch. Toulouse, France, 1980; degree in Biology, Faculty of Medicine, Lille, France, 1987. Vet. practitioner, Lys-Lez-Lannoy, France, 1985—. Contbr. articles to profl. jours. Recipient Laureate for vet. doctoral thesis, 1980. Home and Office: 17 Rue Jules Guesde 59390 Lys-Lez-Lannoy France Personal E-mail: ledoux.jean-marie@wanadoo.fr.

LEE, AMANDA JOAN, nutritionist, director; b. Melbourne, Australia, Nov. 20, 1956; BSc in Nutrition, Deakin U., 1978; PhD, Sydney U., 1992. Dir., nutrition and phys. activity Queensland Health, 2000—. Chair Dietary Guidelines Working Com. NHMRC, 2008; conjoint assoc. prof. U. Queensland, 2008—10; adj. prof. Queensland U. Tech., 2011. Mem.: Pub. Health Assn. Australia, Dietitan's Assn. Australia. Office: 15 Butterfield St Herston Queensland 4006 Australia Business E-Mail: amanda_lee@health.qld.gov.au.

LEE, ANNEMARIE, physical therapist; b. Box Hill, July 25, 1974; BS in Physiotherapy, U. Melbourne, 1996, PhD, 2009. Lectr. U. Melbourne, 2008—. Physiotherapist Alfred Health, 2004—11. Grant, Physiotherapy Rsch. Found., Monash U. Fellow: Inst. Breathing and Sleep; mem.: Thoracic Soc. Australia and New Zealand, Australian Physiotherapy Assn. Avocations: exercise, theater. Office: 200 Berkeley St Carlton Victoria 3010 Australia Office Fax: 03 8344 4188. Business E-Mail: annemarie.lee@alfred.org.au.

LEE, BANG HUN, dentist, director; b. Seoul, Republic of Korea, June 22, 1971; s. Byungtae Lee and Boomi Park; m. Jinkyung Jun, Aug. 29, 1997; 1 child, Kenneth Yejun. DDS, NYU, 2004. Mng. clin. dir. Aspen Dental, Harrisburg, Pa., 2005—08; pvt. practice Palisades Pk., NJ. Personal E-mail: newyorkdds@hotmail.com.

LEE, BENJAMIN YUEHTUNG, genetic biochemist, nutrition researcher; b. Tianjin, China, July 1, 1930; arrived in U.S., 1986; s. Zhongyao Li and Guizhi Sun; m. Liwei Zhao, Nov. 20, 1985 (div. Oct. 20, 1996); m. Gongfu Bai Lee, Jan. 9, 1998; children: James, John, Hui Lin, Rong Bai. BS, Yenching U. of Am Chs. Union, Beijing, 1952; MD, Peking Union Med. Coll., Beijing, 1957. Intern in internal medicine Beijing Med. Coll. Hosp./Peking Union Med. Coll. Hosp., 1956—57; resident in internal medicine Peking Union Med. Coll. Hosp./Beijing Tiantan Hosp., 1957—58; resident, physician Lake Xingkai State Farm (Concentration Camp) Hosp., Black Dragon River Province, China, 1958—62; physician Beijing Jianguomen Clinic, 1962—85; clin. assoc. prof. Beijing Tropical Medicine Rsch. Inst., 1977—85; rsch. assoc., postdoctoral fellow, instr. pediat. genetics La. State U. Health Scis. Ctr., Shreveport, 1986—. Author: (series) New Nutrition Diseases, 1997; guest editor: Greater Chinese Encyclopedia, 1984—86. Roman Catholic. Achievements include discovery of nutritional diseases; design of nutritional deficiency may be the basic etiology of several surgical diseases. Office: La State U Health Scis Ctr Dept Pediat 1501 Kings Hwy Shreveport LA 71130 Office Phone: 318-675-6339. E-mail: blee1@lsuhsc.edu.

LEE, BEOM-JIN, pharmaceuticals professor, researcher, pharmaceutical executive, dean; b. Jeonbuk, Republic of Korea, Oct. 9, 1962, s. Hong-Won and Yeon-Soon Lee; m. Mina Lee, Sept. 29, 1962; children: Jeong-Eun, Sang-A, Hoon-Young. BS, Seoul Nat. U. Coll. Pharmacy, Republic of Korea, 1984; MS, Seoul Nat. U. Coll. Pharmacy, 1986; PhD, Oreg. State. U., Corvallis, 1993. Lic. pharmacist 1984. Vice dean Coll. Pharmacy, Kangwon Nat. U., Chuncheon, Republic of Korea, 1999—2001, dir. Rsch. Inst., 2001—03, prof., 2003—, dean, 2005—07; CEO Pharm. Tech. Rsch. Inc., 2000—. Adv. bd. mem. Korean FDA, Seoul, 1998—; vis. prof. Sch. Pharmacy, U. London, 1998—99. Author: (book) Development of Drug Products with Advanced Technologies, (textbook) Principles and Technologies of Dosage Forms, Biopharmaceutics and Pharmacokinetics, Dispensing and Pharmaceutical Care, Physical Pharmacy, Thermodynamics. Adv. bd. mem. Korean Food and Drug Adminstrn., 1999—. Recipient Achievement award, Pres. Kangwon Nat. U., 2003—06, Excellent Achievement award, Gov. Sonpa-Gu, 2003, Lee-Sun-kyu award, 2005; vis. scholar, Sch. Pharmacy, U. London, 1998—99. Master: Korean Soc. Pharm. Sci. and Tech. (corr.; chief gen. sec. 1999—2004, internat. coop.-in-chief 2005—, Acad. award 1999), Korean Am. Pharm. Assn. Scientists (corr.; mem. adv. bd. 1999—, pres. 2006—, v.p. 2000—01); mem.: Controlled Release Soc., Am. Assn. Pharm. Scientists, Pharm. Soc. Korea (corr.; gen. sec. 2005—, Acad. award 2000). Roman Catholic. Achievements include patents in field. Avocations: golf, squash, tennis. Office: Kangwon Nat U 192-1 Hyoja-2-Dong 200-701 Chuncheon Gangwon-do Republic of Korea Business E-Mail: bjl@kangwon.ac.kr.

LEE, BUMSUK, occupational therapist, educator; b. Republic of Korea, July 16, 1972; PhD, Gunma U., 2010. Asst. prof. Gunma U., 2007—. Avocation: hiking. Office: 3-39-15 Showa Maebashi Gunma 371-0027 Japan Office Fax: 81-27-220-8999. E-mail: bslee@health.gunma-u.ac.jp.

LEE, BYEONG-KYU, research scientist, educator; s. Jangho Lee and Sookrye Jung; m. Haengah Kim Lee, Oct. 26, 1965; children: Curie, Kangjun. PhD, U. Mass., Lowell, 1995. Rschr. Agy. for Def. Devel., Daejon, Republic of Korea, 1987—93; rsch. assoc. Mass. Toxics Use Reduction Inst., Lowell, 1993—96; vis. scientist Bio-Rad Digilab, Cambridge, Mass., 1996; prof. U. Ulsan, Ulsan, Republic of Korea, 1996—; vis. scientist Harvard U., Cambridge, Mass., 2003—. Assoc. dir. Environ. Rsch. Inst., Ulsan, Republic of Korea, 1996—; dir. Brain Korea 21, 1996—, Environ. Engring. Program, 1996—; outstanding prof. Air Emission, YougJong Ind., 2008—, Sludge Energy Study, Korean Minn. Know & Environ., 2008—, Atopy Study, Minn. Environ., 2009—, AWMA, 2010. Mem. editl. bd.: KOSAE, 1999—; contbr. articles to profl. jours.; author: Global Warming: Engineering Solutions, 2009. Edn. instr. Korean Ministry of Environment, Ulsan, Republic of Korea, 1998—2010; adv. com. Met. City of Ulsan, Republic of Korea, 1997—2010, Met. City of Busan, Republic of Korea, 1999—2003. Recipient, Agy. for Def. Devel., 1992; named Hon. Citizen, City of Tulsa, Okla., Okla., Outstanding Prof., AWMA, 2010; grantee, Commonwealth of Mass., 1994-1995, LG Chem. Co., 1996-1999, Korean Housing Co., 1996-2001, Met. City of Ulsan, 1996-2002, Korean Ministry of Environ., 1997—2008, Korean Sci. Reseach Found., 1997-2003, Korean Ministry of Edn., 1997-1998, Hyundai Constrn. Co., 1998-2002, Internat. Brotherhood of Teamsters, 2000-2005, Hanla, 2001-2002, YoungJong Co., 2001-2002, 2005—10, AlcanDaehan, 2001-2002, Bomyun Co., 2001-2003, Boston Transp. Dept., 2002-2003, Islands Cmty. Med. Services, Inc., 2003, ECO-TSC Co., 2003—05, Il-Shin Constrn., 2005, Ministry Indsl. Resources, 2006—08, Yu Sung Co. Ltd., 2007—, KOENTEC, 2008—, Met. Ulsan, 2009—10, Korean Ministry Knowledge & Economy, 2008—10, Korean Ministry Environ., 2009; scholar, Busan Nat. U., 1981-1987, U. of Mass., 1993-1995. Mem.: Internat. Ozone Assn. (corr.), Korean Soc. Environ. Engrs. (corr.; bd. dirs. 2006—,), Air and Waste Mgmt. Assn. (corr.), Korean Soc. Waste Mgmt. (life), Korean Soc. Environ. Scis. (life; dir.), Korean Soc. Atmospheric Environ. (life; editl. bd., reviewer 2006—10, Outst Rsch. award 2002). Christian. Achievements include patents for Dry and Wet Deposition Collector. Office: U Ulsan Dept Civil and Environ Engring San 29 Moogeo-Dong Nam-Gu 680-749 Ulsan Republic of Korea Office Fax: 82-52-259-2629. Business E-Mail: bklee@ulsan.ac.kr.

LEE, BYUNG MU, education educator; b. Buan, Chunbuk, Republic of Korea, Oct. 30, 1954; arrived in US, 1984; s. Gong Soo and Yoo Soon (Kim) Lee. BS, SungKyunKwan U., Seoul, 1982; MPH, Seoul Nat. U., 1984; MS in Pub. Health, U. SC, 1987; DPH, Columbia U., NYC, 1989; postgrad., Johns Hopkins U., 1989—90. From asst. prof. to assoc. prof. SungKyunKwan U., Suwon, Republic of Korea, 1990—98, prof., 1999—. Adv. bd. Nat. Inst. Toxicol. Rsch., Seoul, 1994—, Korea FDA, Seoul, 1994—, Dept. Human Health and Svcs., Seoul, 2003, Seoul, 05. Mem. editl. bd.: Jour. Toxicology and Environ. Health, Asian Pacific Jour. Cancer Prevention; contbr. articles to profl. jours. Sgt., 1975—78, Korean Army. Recipient Young Scientist award, Brookhaven Symposium, 1989, Yun-Ho Lee award, Internat. Sci. Coun., 2000; scholar, NIH, 1997. Mem.: Asia Soc. Toxicology (v.p.), Korea Environ. Mutagen Soc. (v.p. 2005), Korea Soc. Toxicology (v.p. 2005), Internat. Assn. Environ. Mutagen Soc. (counselor 2005). Avocations: music, mountain climbing, travel. Office: SungKyunKwan Univ Coll Pharmacy Gyeonggi-Do Chonchondong 300 Suwon 440-746 Republic of Korea Office Phone: 82-31-290-7708. Business E-Mail: bmlee@skku.ac.kr, bmlee@skku.edu.

LEE, BYUNG-ILL, orthopedist; s. Ck Lee and Jj Chung; m. Bong-Soo Lee, Mar. 10, 1974; children: Hae-Seoung, Dong-Joo. PhD, Yonsei Grad. Sch., Republic of Korea, 1983. Bd. cert. Korean Orthop. Soc., 1981. Prof. Soonchunhyang U. Hosp., Seoul, Republic of Korea, 1982—2008; dir. Korean Knee Soc., Seoul, 1984—2008. Dir. Korean Shoulder and Elbow soc., Seoul, 1992—2008. Med. svc. Achievements include research in arthroscopic surgery. Home: 113-1 1ka Sungbook-dong Sungbook-gu Seoul 136-821 Republic of Korea

LEE, BYUNGLAN, anatomist, educator; b. Yeonpyungdo, Republic Of Korea, Feb. 17, 1953; d. Manho Lee and Jae Oh; m. Wooho Kim, Dec. 16, 1983; children: Younghoon Kim, Hyesung Kim. MD, Seoul Nat. U. Coll. Medicine, 1978, PhD, 1986; MS, U. Mich., Ann Arbor, 1983. Prof. Seoul Nat. U. Coll. Medicine, Republic of Korea, 1986—. Contbr. scientific papers (Clin. Cancer Rsch. grant, 2003, 2005, 2007). Achievements include research in gastric cancer. Office: Seoul Nat Univ Coll Medicine 28 YonGeon-dong Seoul 110-799 Republic of Korea Office Fax: 82-2-745-9528.

LEE, BYUNG-WAN, medical educator; b. Chungju, Sept. 18, 1969; PhD, Sungkyunkwan U. Sch. Medicine, 2005. Prof. Yonsei U. Coll. Medicine, 2006—. Office: 134 Shinchon-dong Seodaemun-gu Seoul 120-752 Republic of Korea Office Fax: 82-2-393-6884. Business E-Mail: bwanlee@yuhs.ac.

LEE, CAROL M., ophthalmologist, educator; Attended, Yale U.; MD, SUNY Downstate Med. Ctr., 1984. Diplomate Am. Bd. of Ophthalmology. Intern Meml. Sloan-Kettering Cancer Ctr., 1984—85; resident ophthalmology NYU Med. Ctr., 1986—89; fellow Univ. Ill. Hosp. and Clinics, 1985—86, Wash. Univ. Med. Ctr., 1989—91; clin. prof. dept. of ophthalmology NYu Langone Med. Ctr. Contbr. (articles) Quantification of diabetic macular edema, Quantification of macular ischaemia in sickle cell retinopathy, Modified grid laser photocoagulation for diffuse diabetic macular edema. Long-term visual results, Surgical management of subfoveal choroidal neovascularization, Mascular laser Photocoagulation for the Advanced Cases of Diabetic Macular Edema, and numerous other articles. Office: NYU Langone Medical Center and School of Medicine 550 1st Ave New York NY 10016 Office Phone: 212-263-7300.

LEE, CHANG UK, psychiatrist, educator; b. Seoul, Apr. 19, 1961; MD, Cath. U. Korea, 1986, PhD, 1997. Instr. Cath. U. Korea, Kangnam ST. Mary's Hosp., 1993—97, asst. prof., dept. psychiatry, 1997—2001, assoc. prof., 2001—06, prof., dir., 2006—; vis. asst. prof. Harvard Med. Sch., Mass., 1999—2001. Cons. Korea Labor Welfare Corp., 2005—, Nat. Pension Svc., 2007—10, Nat. Health Ins. Corp., 2009—; bd. dirs. Korean Neuropsychiatric Assn., 2009—; v.p. Korean Assn. Geriatric Psychiatry, 2010—. Recipient Commendation award, Nat. Health Ins. Corp., Rsch. award, Janssen Rsch. Found., 21st century award, Internat. Biog. Centre, Cambridge, Eng., 5th Whanin Academic Achievement award, Korean Neuropsychiatric Assn. Fellow: Korean Soc. Psychopharmacology, Korean Soc. Biol. Psychiatry; mem.: Internat. Psychogeriatric Assn., World Fedn. Socs. Biol. Psychiatry, Korean Med. Assn. Avocations: golf, travel. Office: 505 Banpo-dong Seocho-gu Seoul 137-701 Republic of Korea Office Fax: 82-2-536-8744. E-mail: jihan@catholic.ac.kr.

LEE, CHANG-SEOP, medical educator; b. Jeonju, Republic of Korea, May 12, 1970; MD, Chonbuk Nat. U. Med. Sch., Jeonju, Republic of Korea, 1996, MS, 2000, PhD, 2008. Cert. physician 1996, Korean Bd. Internal Medicine, 2001, Korean Bd. Infectious Disease, 2006. Intern Chonbuk Nat. U. Med. Sch., 1996—97, resident, dept. internal medicine, 1997—2001, clin. instr., divsn. infectious diseases, 2005—06, chief, infection control dept., 2005—, chief, divsn. infectious disease, dept. internal medicine, 2005—, lectr., 2006—08, assoc. prof., dept. internal medicine, Divsn. Infectious Disease, Rsch. Inst. Clin. Medicine Jeonju, 2008—; KOKA physician Ministry Fgn. Affairs & Trade Seoul, Republic of Korea, Bangladesh Korea Friendship Hosp. Dhaka, 2001—04; clin. fellow Divsn. Infectious Disease Seoul Nat. U., 2004—05. Recipient Citation award, Ministry Fgn. Affairs & Trade, 2005—09, Citation of Contbn., 2009, Seoul Nat. U. Hosp., 2005, Jeonju City Coun., 2010, Med. Assn. Jeollabukdo, 2010, Outstanding Rsch. award, Chonbuk Nat. U. Hosp., 2011; named Prof. of Yr., Chonbuk Nat. U. Med. Sch., 2008. Mem.: Korean Soc. Clin. Microbiology, Korean Soc. Zoonoses, Korean Soc. Immuncompromised Host, Korean Soc. AIDS, Korean Soc. Infectious Disease, Korean Assn. Internal Medicine, Korean Med. Assn. Office: Chonbuk Nat University Med Sch Divsn Infectious Disease Dept Internal Medicine Rsch Inst Clin Medicine 634-18 Geum-am Deokjin-gu Jeonju Jeonbuk 561-712 Republic of Korea Office Fax: 82-63-254-1609. Business E-Mail: lcsmd@jbnu.ac.kr.

LEE, CHANG-SHING, computer engineer, educator; b. Wan Ton, Taiwan, May 29, 1968; s. Ming-Xing and Xian Lee; m. Mei-Hui Wang, Feb. 28, 1990. B, Chung Yan Christian U., Chung-Li, 1992; M, Nat. Chung Cheng U., Chia-Yi, 1994; PhD, Nat. Cheng Kung U., Tainan, 1998. Asst. prof. dept. info. engring. Kun Shan Inst. Tech., Tainan, 2000—01; chief Computer Ctr. Software Developing Group Chang Jung Christian U., Tainan, 2001—02, asst. prof. Dept. Info. Mgmt., 2001—03, assoc. prof. Dept. Info. Mgmt., 2003—05, chief Dept. Computer Sci. and Info. Engring., 2004—05; assoc. prof. Dept. Computer Sci. and Info. Mgmt. Nat. U. Tainan, 2005—08, prof. dept. computer sci. and info., 2008—. Dir. Computer Ctr. Nat. U. Tainan, 2006—. Author (reviewer): Rsch. Project Nat. Sci. Coun. Taiwan, 2002—05, Fuzzy Sets and Systems, 2001—05, Jour. Info. Sci. and Engring., 2001—05, Internat. Jour. Fuzzy Systems, 2001—05; mem. editl. bd.: Applied Intelligence and Open Cybernetics and Sys. Jour., guest editor in field:; contbr. chapters to books, articles to profl. jours. Recipient Excellence prize, Nat. Ctr. High Performance Computing, 2004, Best Display prize, 2004, Qualification prize, 2004, 1st prize Info. Mgmt. Group, Ministry Edn., 2002, Excellence prize, Info. Mgmt. Project Performance Contest, 2001, 1st prize Internet Group, 2001, 3d prize Info. Tech. Group, 2001, 1st prize Nation wide Organizing Group, Nation-wide Computer Program Design Contest, 2000, 1st prize So. Taiwan Group, 2000. Mem.: Taiwanese Assn. Artificial Intelligence (Master Thesis prize 2005), Taiwan Fuzzy Systems Assn., Computational Intelligence, IEEE (tech. com. World Congress on Computational Intelligence 2008, program. com. 2008). Achievements include invention of Design and Hardware Synthesis of Adaptive Weighted Fuzzy Mean Image Filter; Design and Hardware Synthesis of Adaptive Weighted Fuzzy Mean Image Filter; An approach for documents classification; Automatic ontology construction system and approach. Avocations: travel, jogging, badminton, tennis. Office: Dept Computer Sci Info Engring Nat Univ Tainan Tainan 700 Taiwan Office Phone: 886 6 2606123 ext. 7709. Business E-Mail: leecs@mail.nutn.edu.tw.

LEE, CHAVA CHERTA, psychotherapist, consultant; arrived in Thailand, 1980, arrived in U.S., 1980; s. Khoua Pao Lee and True Thao; m. Chaeng Moua, Dec. 5, 1963; children: Linda, David L., Elvis, Yen, Tumuakong. AA, Fresno City Coll., 1986, ASc, 1987; BS, MS, Nat. U., 1992; postgrad., Family Therapy Tng. Inst., Milw., 1996—98; PhD, U. Devonshire, 2000. Cert. marriage and family therapist Wis. Psychotherapist Aurora Health Care, Milw., 2001—, Chava Counseling Practice, LLC, Milw., 1996—. Cons. Sebatian Family Psychology Practice, Milw. Mem.: Am. Mental Health Counselor Assn., Am. Assn. Marriage and Family Therapy.

LEE, CHOONG WON, hospital administrator; b. Busan, Sept. 20, 1963; m. Hye Jin Lee; 1 child, Suah. MD, PhD, Busan Nat. U., 1989. Cert. in internal medicine Korea Assn. Medicine, 1997. Instr. Yonsei Severance Hosp., Seoul, Republic of Korea, 1997—98; rsch. fellow U. Ala., Birmingham, 1998—2000; dir. Wallace Meml. Bapt. Hosp., Busan, 2000—. Deacon Yale Bapt. ch., Busan, 2000—. Capt. inf., 1989—92, Korea. Home: Namgu Daeyoun 3 Dong Chunggu APT 101-901 Busan 609-728 Republic of Korea Office: Wallace Memorial Baptist Hosp Gumjunggu Namsan-Dong 374-72 609-728 Busan Busan Republic of Korea Business E-Mail: choong@wmbh.co.kr.

LEE, CHOON-KEY, orthopedist; b. Pusan, Republic of Korea, Mar. 30, 1971; s. Ou-Bang Lee and Choon-Ja Kim; m. Min-Jung Chang; 1 child, Tae-Hun. MD, Korean Med. Assn., 1996; B, Pusan Nat. U., 1996, M, 2000, PhD, 2006. Cert. Korean Orthop. Assn., 2001. Intern Pusan Nat. U. Hosp., 1996—97, resident, 1997—2001, fellow knee & sports medicine, 2004—06; fellow shoulder & sports medicine Funabashi Orthop. Hosp., 2008; fellow Tohoku U. Hosp., Sendai, Japan, 2008; orthop. physician Good Samsun Hosp., Pusan, 2006—, Himchan Hosp., Gangbuk, Seoul, 2010—. Cons. orthop. physician Korea Workers Compensation & Welfare Svc., Pusan, 2006—. Armed Forces Hosp., Pusan, 2006—. Contbr. articles to profl. jours. With

Korean Army, 2002—04. Mem.: Korean Sports Medicine Assn. (active mem. 2008—), Korean Knee Soc. (active mem. 2003—), Korean Shoulder & Elbow Soc. (active mem. 2003—), Korean Arthroscopy Soc. (active mem. 2003—), Korean Orthop. Assn. (active mem. 2001—), European Soc. Sports Traumatology Knee Surgery & Arthroscopy (internat. mem. 2010), Arthoscopy Assn. N.Am. (internat. mem. 2008—). Avocations: travel, golf. Office: Himchan Hosp Gangbuk 650-46 Chang-Dong Dobong-Gu 131-040 Seoul Republic of Korea Business E-Mail: choonkeylee@gmail.com.

LEE, CHRISTINE MARIE, nursing consultant; b. Peru, Ill., May 10, 1956; BSN, U. Ill., 1979; MS in Healthcare Adminstrn., Bellevue U., 2005. Nurse mgr. Long-Term Care Facilities, Clinics, Home Health, Staff Nurse, 1976—98, Asbury Meth. Village, 1990—98; project dir. Logistics Applications Inc., 1998—2004; dep. project dir. Wright Solutions Inc., 2005—09, Zimmerman Assocs. Inc., 2009—11; nurse cons. Social & Sci. Sys., 2005—. Mil. nurse capt. US Army Nurse Corps, 1979—86; project mgr. Fed. Contractor, 1998—2011. Decorated Army Achievement medal US Army. Mem.: ANA. Home: 7 Centerway Ct Gaithersburg MD 20879 Personal E-mail: christin_lee.7@comcast.net.

LEE, CHUNG-SOO, education educator; b. Seoul, Republic of Korea, June 1, 1953; m. Eun-Sook Han, Dec. 25, 1985; 1 child, Min-Sung. PhD, Seoul Nat. U., 1986. M.D. Ministry Health & Welfare/South Korea, 1979. Prof. Chung-Ang U., Seoul, 1984—. Councilor Ctrl. Drug Evaluation Coun. Korean Food and Drug Assn., 2002—04; pres. Med. Sci. Inst., Chung-Ang U., 2005—. Contbr. Jour. of Neurochemistry, Biochemical Pharmacology (Sci. award of Chung-Ang U., 2001). Office: Coll Med Chung-Ang Univ Dongjak-Gu Seoul 156-756 Republic of Korea Office Fax: 82-2-815-3856. Business E-Mail: leecs@cau.ac.kr.

LEE, DAE HO, oncologist; b. Seoul, Dec. 26, 1968; s. Hee Sook Jung; m. Rodis Chae Eun Paik, Oct. 30, 2003; 1 child, Joanne Inyoung. MD, PhD, Seoul Nat. U., Republic of Korea, 2007. Diplomate in hematology-oncology Korean Bd. Internal Medicine, 2002. Asst. prof. U. Ulsan Coll. Medicine, Asan Med. Ctr., Seoul, Republic of Korea, 2006—. Achievements include research in clinical and translational in Oncology. Office: Asan Med Ctr 388-1 Pungnap 2 Dong Songpa Gu Seoul 138736 Republic of Korea Office Fax: 82-2-3010-6961. Business E-Mail: leedaeho@amc.seoul.kr.

LEE, DAVID BO, dentist; b. Cambodia, Nov. 21, 1965; s. Chin Lee and Khim Lay; m. Sim Chou, Dec. 28, 1991; children: Brian C., Lily S. BS cum laude, Calif. State Poly. U., 1990; DDS, UCLA, 1999. Elec. engr. Gen. Dynamics, Rancho Cucamonga, Calif., 1990—92; dentist Buena Park, Calif., 1999—. Mem.: ADA (assoc.), Calif. Dental Assn. (assoc.), Tau Beta Pi, Eta Kappa Nu, Golden Key. Office: 942 W Orangethorpe Ave Fullerton CA 92832 Personal E-mail: davidblee@sbcglobal.net.

LEE, DO-HYUNG, ophthalmologist, researcher; b. Seoul, Republic of Korea, Aug. 23, 1967; s. Soo Young Lee and Ei Sook Oh. Bachelor, Chung Ang U., Seoul, 1993, Master, 1996, PhD, 1993, MD, 1999. Chmn. ophthalmology Ilsan Paik Hosp., Koyang, Kyunggyido, Republic of Korea, 1999—. Co-author (with others): Advances in Corneal Rsch., 1997; contbr. chapters to books, articles to profl. jours. Mem.: European Soc. Cataract and Refractive Surgery, Assn. Rsch. in Vision and Ophthalmology, Am. Soc. Cataract and Refractive Surgery. Home: 504-7 Changchun-dong Sudaemun-ku Seoul 120-180 Republic of Korea Office: Ophthalmol Ilsan Paik Hosp Inje Univ 2240 Daewha-dong Ilsan-Ku Kyunggyi-do Koyang-shi 411706 Republic of Korea Home Phone: 82-2-334-9879; Office Phone: 82-31-910-7240. Office Fax: 82319117241; Home Fax: 8223322356. Personal E-mail: dhlee@ilsanpaik.ac.kr, eyedr0823@hotmail.com.

LEE, DOMINIC H., urologist; b. Daegu, Republic of Korea, Dec. 23, 1962; MD, Kyung Hee U., MBA, 1987, PhD, 1996. Chmn., dept. urology Sch. Medicine, Kyung Hee U., Gangdong, 1996—, prof., 2007. Recipient award, Am. Biog. Inst. Mem.: European Assn. Urology, Am. Urol. Assn., Korean Urol. Assn. Office: Kyung-Hee University Hosp Gangdong Dept Urology #149 Sangil-Dong Gangdong-Gu Seoul 134-727 Republic of Korea Office Phone: 82-2-440-6160. Office Fax: 82-2-440-7744. Business E-Mail: hllee61@hanmail.net.

LEE, DONALD HAN, surgeon, orthopedist; b. Huntington, W.Va., Oct. 28, 1955; s. Kwan Ho and Kay Hee Lee; m. Dawn Thomas Thomas, May 13, 1989; children: David Thomas, Dana Elizabeth, Diane Louise, Daniel Thomas, Dustin Thomas. BS, Georgetown U., 1977; MD, W.Va. Sch. Medicine, 1982. Diplomate Nat. Bd. Med. Examiners, 1983, Am. Bd. Orthop. Surgeons, 1991. Intern surgery W. Va. U. Sch. Medicine, 1982—83, George Washington U. Sch. Medicine, 1983—84, resident orthop. surgery, 1984—88; Hand fellowship Columbia Presbyn. Med. Ctr., 1988—89; assoc. prof. orthop. surgery U. Ala., Birmingham, 1989—2005; prof. orthop. surgery Vanderbilt U., Nashville, 2005—, dir. hand fellowship, 2005—. Dir. hand fellowship U. Ala., Birmingham, 1993—2005; dir. hand and upper extremity fellowship Vanderbilt U., Nashville, 2005—; bd. examiner Am. Bd. Orthop. Surgery; joint com. surgery of hand Am. Bd. Orthop. Surgeons; reviewer Jour. Bone and Joint Surgery, Clinical Orthopedics and Related Rsch., Jour. Shoulder and Elbow Surgery. Pres. parish coun., 2000—01. Rsch. grantee, Merck and Co., Biomet, Inc. Mem.: Am. Soc. Reconstructive Microsurgery, Am. Soc. Surgery of Hand, Am. Acad. Orthop. Surgeons, Assn. Bone and Joint Surgeons, Am. Orthop. Assn. Office: Vanderbilt Orthop Inst Med Ctr East South Tower Ste 3200 Nashville TN 37232-8829 E-mail: donald.h.lee@vanderbilt.edu.

LEE, DONG HO, radiologist; b. Seoul, Republic of Korea, Dec. 17, 1954; s. Kyo Woong Lee and Chae Hee Oh; m. Hae Young Jung, Mar. 4, 1984; children: Kyung Eun, Han Myung. MD, Seoul Nat. U., Korea, 1979, PhD, 1990. Diplomate Republic of Korea, 1983. Prof. Kyung Hee U., Seoul, Republic of Korea, 1986—; clin. rschr. NYU, NYC, 1992—93. Mem.: Radiological Soc. N. Am. (corr.), Am. Roentgen Ray Soc. (corr.). Office: Kyung Hee University Hospital 1 Hoegidong Dongdaemun-gu Seoul 130 702 Republic of Korea Office Fax: 011-822-968-0787. Business E-Mail: donghlee@hanafos.com.

LEE, DONG HO, gastroenterologist, educator; b. Seoul, Republic Of Korea, July 9, 1960; s. Je Won Lee and Hong Young Ja; m. Ji Soo Lee, May 26, 1989; children: Won Suk, Yeon Suk. MD, PhD, Seoul Nat. U., 1995. Diplomate Ministry Health, Welfare, 1985, cert. in internal medicine Ministry Health, Welfare, 1989, in gastroenterology Korean Soc. Internal Medicine, 1997, Korean Soc. Gastroent. Endoscopy, 1998. Prof. Divsn. Gastroenterology, Dept. Internal Medicine., Seoul, 1996—; vis. prof., rsch. fellow U. Calif. Divsn. Gastroenterology, Dept. Internal Medicine, San Diego, 1999—2000. Vice sec. gen. Korean Soc. Gastrointestinal Endoscopy, Seoul, 2004—06. Contbr. articles to profl. med. jours. Com. mem. evaluation safety med. equipment Korean Food, Drug Adminstrn., Seoul, 2007—. Capt. Army, 1989—92, Seoul. Recipient award, Med. Communication Mass Media, 2006—07, Rsch. Fund Korean Electronics Tech. Inst., 2006—08. Mem.: Internat. Assn. Surgeons, Korean Soc. Study of Liver, Korean Soc. Gastrointestinal Motility, Korean Soc. Gastrointestinal Endoscopy, Korean Soc. Gastroenterology, Korean Assn. Internal Medicine, Korean Soc. Gastroenterology, Korean Med. Assn., Am. Gastroenterology Assn., Asian Neurogastroenterology Motility Assn. Roman Catholic. Achievements include development of more effective form of gastrointestinal endoscopy room. Avocations: travel, movies, music, history, photography. Office: Seoul Nat Univ Bundang Hosp Gumi-Dong Bundang-Gu 300 469-707 Seongnam-Si Republic of Korea Home: 104 901 Gusung Paragon Apt Mabuk dong Giheung-gu Yongin-si Gyeonggi do 446 511 Republic of Korea Home Phone: 82-31-275-2716; Office Phone: 82-31-787-7019, 82-11-787-7009, 82317877009, 82-10-5243-2414. Office Fax: 82-31-787-4051; Home Fax: 82-31-275-2716. Personal E-mail: dhljohn@yahoo.co.kr. Business E-Mail: dhljohn@snubh.org.

LEE, DONGHO, ophthalmologist; b. Seoul, Republic Of Korea, July 7, 1964; s. Jae Soon Lee and Soo Jung Hong; m. Regina Kim, Aug. 1, 1989; children: Soon Min, Yoanna. MD, Yonsei U., Seoul, 1989; PhD in Ophthalmology, Yonsei U., 1999. Lic. ophthalmologist Nat. Bd. Ophthalmology, 1994. Asst. prof. Ajou U., Suwon, Gyung-gi do, Republic of Korea, 1997—99; dir. ophthalmology Yonsei Eye Ctr., Seoul, 1999—. Contbr. articles to profl. jours. Mem. directing com. Roman Cath. Ch., Seoul, 2003—05. Capt. Korean Army, 1994—97, Pohang. Recipient Best Paper award, ASCRS, 2004; Internat. Rsch. fellow, Duke U. Eye Ctr., 2005—06. Mem.: Internat. Soc. Refractive Surgery (mem. internat. coun. 2005—), Korean Ophthalmology Soc., Am. Soc. Cataract and Refractive Surgery, Am. Acad. Ophthalmology (Korea rep. 2005—), Korean Ophthalmology Assn. Roman Catholic. Achievements include treatment of presbyopia with excimer laser; mitomycin-C in refractive surgery; development of M-LASEK treatment for high myopia. Avocations: golf, photography, travel. Office: Apgujeong Yonsei Eye Ctr Ssang-Bong Bd 3F Sinsadong 638-13 Seoul 135-896 Republic of Korea Office Phone: 82-2-517-8686. Office Fax: 82-2-517-8696. Personal E-mail: donghlee64@hananet.net. Business E-Mail: donghlee64@hanafos.com.

LEE, DONG-JOON, plastic surgeon; b. Pusan, Republic of Korea, Jan. 14, 1960; s. Hyang-Wu and Jung-Hi C. Lee; m. Kaaren McConaughy; children: Brian, David, Kevin. AB, Dartmouth Coll., 1982; MD, U. Vt., 1986. From resident to chief resident SUNY, Bklyn., 1986—91; resident in plastic surgery U. So. Calif., LA, 1991—93; hand, micro fellow U. So. Calif., Boyes Found., LA, 1993—94; plastic surgeon Kaiser West LA, 1994—; assoc. clin. prof. & assoc. program dir. divsn. plastic surgery U. So. Calif., 1994—. Fellow: ACS. Office: Dept Plastic Surgery, SCPMG 6041 Cadillac Ave Los Angeles CA 90034 Office Phone: 323-857-2758. Office Fax: 323-857-3690. Business E-Mail: dong-joon.lee@kp.org.

LEE, EUI JU, medical educator; b. Repubic of Korea, Nov. 13, 1968; PhD, Kyung Hee U., 1998, MBA, 2011. Com. mem. Korean Health Ins. Rev. Agy., 2004—08; editor Soc. Sasang Constl. Medicine, 1998, v.p., 2010; vis. prof. Ctr. Integrative Medicine, U. Md. Sch. Medicine, 2008—09; assoc. prof. Kyunghee U., Seoul, Republic of Korea, 2007. Bd. dirs. Kyung Hee Oriental Medicine Hosp., 2010; coun. mem. Traditional Korean Medicine Soc. Ins. Medicine, 2010. Mem.: Rsch. Ctr. Oriental Medicine, Korean Inst. Oriental Medicine, Kyung Hee Oriental Medicine Hosp. Avocations: sports, swimming, drawing. Office: #1 Hoeki-Dong Dongdaemun-gu Seoul 130-702 Republic of Korea Office Fax: 82 2 958 9274. Business E-Mail: sasangin@khu.ac.kr.

LEE, EUN NAM, critical care nurse, educator; b. Seoul, Republic of Korea, Aug. 25, 1958; d. Seong Soon Lee and Bok Soon Kim; m. Yeon Yook Choe, July 27, 1986; children: Il Sun Choe, Sun Yee Choe. BS, Seoul Nat. U., 1981, MS, 1984, PhD, 1998. Cert. nurse, Korean Nurses Assn., 1981. Nurse Seoul Nat. Hosp., 1981—85; asst. prof. Daedong Nursing Coll., Busan, 1985—98; prof. Dong-A U., Busan, 1998—; chmn. Curriculum Coun. Emergency Nurse Practitioner, Busan, 2008—. Vis. prof. Iowa U., 2001—02; program mgr. Korea Rsch. Found., Seoul, 2006. Author: (book) Emergency Nursing. Pres. pub. svc. young Nightingale Busan Br. Republic Korea Nat. Red Cross, 2009—. Recipient Best Tchr. award, Dong A U., 2004—05, 2010. Fellow: Korean Soc. Muscle & Joint Health (regional pres., Busan 1995—2009, editl. bd. mem., Seoul 2008—, Excellent Rsch. award 2006); mem.: Korean Acad. Soc. Nursing Edn., Korean Acad. Fundamental Nursing, Korean Academic Soc. Rehab. Nursing, Korean Soc. Critical Care Nursing (Seoul) (article reviewer 2008—), Adult Nursing Assn. (Seoul) (article reviewer 2008—), Korean Soc. Nursing Sci. (Seoul) (article reviewer 2008—). Home: Mangmi-dong Suyoung Gu Busan Republic of Korea Office: Dong-A University Dongdaesin Dong 3 Ga-1 Seo Gu 602-714 Busan Busan Republic of Korea Office Fax: 82-51-240-2920. Business E-Mail: enlee@dau.ac.kr.

LEE, EUN SEONG, biomedical engineer; b. Tongyoung, Kyeongsangnam-do, Republic of Korea, July 1, 1975; s. Jeong Tae Lee and Sam Sun Kim; m. Hyeryeon Jo, Oct. 8, 2005; 1 child, Jessica Minhee. B, Sungkyunkwan U., 1998; M, Gwangju Inst. Sci. and Tech., South Korea, 2000, PhD, 2004. Rsch. scholar U. Utah, Salt Lake, 2002—03, fellow, 2006—08; specialist Amore-Pacific Corp. R&D Ctr., Pharm. and Health Rsch. Inst., Yongin, Kyeonggi-do, Republic of Korea, 2004—06; prof. Cath. U. Korea, Bucheon, 2008—. Cons. Korea Invention Promotion Assn., Seoul, 2006; reviewer Internat. jour. of pharmaceutics, 2006—, Jour. Microencapsulation, 2007—. Contbr. articles to profl. jours. Scholar, South Korea, 1998—2004. Achievements include research in protein delivery; design of cancer specific targeting; reversal of multi-drug resistance in cancer; drug-carrier design and biodegradable functional polymer synthesis; patents pending in field. Office: Divsn Biotech Cath Univ Korea 43-1 Yeokgok 2-dong Wonmi-gu Bucheon 420-743 Republic of Korea Personal E-mail: hejulu@hanmail.net. E-mail: eslee@catholic.ar.kr.

LEE, GLENN RICHARD, medical administrator; b. Ogden, Utah, May 18, 1932; s. Glenn Edwin and Thelma (Jensen) L.; m. Pamela Marjorie Ridd, July 18, 1969; children— Jennifer, Cynthia. BS, U. Utah, 1953, MD, 1956. Intern Boston City Hosp.-Harvard U., 1956-57, resident, 1957-58; clin. asso. Nat. Cancer Inst., NIH, 1958-60; postdoctoral fellow U. Utah, 1960-63; instr. U. Utah Coll. Medicine, 1963-64, asst. prof. internal medicine, 1964-68, assoc. prof., 1968-73, prof., 1973-96, assoc. dean for acad. affairs, 1973-76, dean, 1978-83, prof. emeritus, 1996—; chief of staff Salt Lake VA Med. Ctr., 1985-95. Author: (with others) Clinical Hematology, 10th edit, 1998; Contbr. (with others) numerous articles to profl. jours.; editorial bd.: (with others) Am. Jour. Hematology, 1976-79. Served with USPHS, 1958-60. Markle Found. scholar, 1965-70; Nat. Inst. Arthritis, Metabolic and Digestive Disease grantee, 1977-82. Mem. A.C.P., Am. Soc. Hematology, Am. Soc. Clin. Investigation, Western Assn. Physicians, Am. Inst. Nutrition. Mem. Lds Ch. Home and Office: 194 Harvest Run Idaho Falls ID 83404 Personal E-mail: grichardl@cableone.net.

LEE, GREGORY PRICE, neuropsychology educator; b. Orange, NJ, July 3, 1952; s. John Landon and Olga (Squeo) Lee; m. Susan L. Haverstock, Oct. 3, 1988; children Stuart Haverstock Lee, Claudia Elinor Bernheim. BA in Psychology, U. No. Colo., 1975; MA in Clin. Psychology, Lone Mountain Coll., 1975; PhD in Clin. Psychology, Fla. Inst. Tech., 1980. Diplomate Am. Bd. Clin. Neuropsychology, Am. Bd. Profl. Psychology; lic. psychologist, Ga. Predoctoral intern Harlem Valley Psychiat. Ctr., White Plains, NY, 1977—79; instr. dept. psychology Coll. V.I., St. Thomas, 1981—82; rsch. assoc. Tex. Rsch. Inst. Mental Sci., Tex. Med. Ctr., Houston, 1983—84; postdoctoral fellow dept. psychology, sect. neuropsychology U. Houston, Baylor Coll. Medicine, 1983—84; postdoctoral fellow dept. neurology U. Wis. Med. Sch., Milw., 1984—86; dir. neuropsychology svc. neurosurgery and psychiatry Med. Coll. Ga., Augusta, 1986—2002, asst./assoc. prof. dept. neurosurgery, 1986—2001, prof. dept. neurology, 2001—. Dir. adult neuropsychology svc. Med. Coll. Ga.; oral examiner Am. Bd. Clin. Neuropsychology, 1989—2009, bd. dirs., 2004-11; cons. editor Jour. Internat. Neuropsychol. Soc., 1994-97, Archives of Clin. Neuropsychology, 2002—; mem. Med. Student Promotions Com. Med. Coll. Ga., 1989-2001, clin. rsch. I and II, Neurosci., 2001-, Brain & Behavior, others; bd. trustees Am. Bd. Profl. Psychology, 2005—2010. Author: Neuropsychology of Epilepsy and Epilepsy Surgery; co-author: Amobarbital Effects and Lateralized Brain Function: The Wada Test; contbr. numerous articles to profl. jours.; contbr. chpts. to books. Pres. Am. Bd. Profl. Psychology, 2010-; mem. med. adv. com. Alzheimer's Disease and Related Disorders Assn., 1986-97; bd. dirs. Red Devil, Inc., 1985-92. Grantee, Med. Coll. Ga. Found./Smith Kline Glaxo, 2003—07, Med. Coll. of Ga. Rsch. Inst., 2002—07, NIH/NINDS, 2003—10, Berlex Labs., 2002—03. Fellow APA (divsn.40, membership program com. 2000-05, chair awards com., 2000-06), Nat. Acad. Neuropsychology (chair publs. com., mem. investment com. 2001-04, program com. 2000-05); mem. Internat. Neuropsychol. Soc., Am. Acad. Neurology, Am. Epilepsy Soc., Am. Bd. Profl. Psychology (bd. trustees, pres. 2011-), Sigma Xi. Office: Med Coll Ga Dept Neurology (BA-3278) 1120 15th St Augusta GA 30912-3275 Office Phone: 706-721-3851. Business E-Mail: glee@georgiahealth.edu.

LEE, HAE WAN, surgeon, educator; b. Seoul, Republic of Korea, Oct. 19, 1957; s. Kyu Yong Lee and Jung Soo Kim; m. Mi Young Kim; children: Han Joo, Min Ji. MD, Seoul Nat. U. Coll. Medicine, 1983; MS, Seoul Nat. U., 1991, PhD, 1998. Diplomate Korean Bd. Gen. Surgery, 1991. Army physician Korean Army, 1983—86; intern Seoul Nat. U. Hosp., 1986—87; resident in surgery Seoul Nat. U. Hosp., 1987—91, fellow in surgery, 1991—92; postdoctoral rsch. fellow Gastrointestinal Rsch. Lab. Vets. Affairs Med. Ctr. Dept. Medicine U. Calif., San Francisco, 1998—99; assoc. prof. medicine Hallym U., Chunchon, Kangwon-do, Republic of Korea, 1998—2005, prof. Coll. Medicine, 2005—. 1st lt. Korean Army, 1983—86. Mem.: Korean Gastric Cancer Assn., Korean Surg. Soc., Korean Cancer Assn. (life). Avocations: fishing, travel. Office: Hallym U Sacred Heart Hosp Pyungchon-Dong Dongan-Gu 896 431-070 Anyang-si Kyungki-do Republic of Korea Office Fax: 82-31-385-0157. Business E-Mail: leehw@hallym.or.kr.

LEE, HAE-RAN, hospital administrator; Grad., Yonsei U., 1978. Dept. of pediat. chief Kangdong Sacred Heart Hosp., dir. of planning, pres., 2006, v.p. of medicine, 2004; dept. of pediat. chair Hallym Univ. Coll. of Medicine, sr. v.p., 2006—08, pres., 2008—. Office: Hallym University Medical Center 94-195 Yeongdeungpo-dong Yeongdeungpo-gu Seoul Republic of Korea *

LEE, HARRY ANTONIUS, allergist, immunologist; b. Jakarta, Indonesia, June 27, 1954; arrived in US, 1973, naturalized, 1991; s. Djoe Eng and Jan Nio (Tjan) L.; m. Johanna Francisca Setiawan, Nov. 23, 1977; children: Edwin Christopher, Vanessa Theresa. BS in Biology, magna cum laude, Fairmont State Coll., 1977; MD, St. George's U., 1982. Diplomate Am. Bd. Allergy and Immunology, Am. Bd. Pediat., 1988, Am. Bd. Allergy Immunology, 1993. Resident in pediat. Marshall U. Sch. Medicine, Huntington, W.Va., 1983-86; fellow in allergy and immunology U. South Fla./All Children's Hosp., St. Petersburg, 1989-91; chief Air U. Regional Hosp.-Maxwell AFB, Montgomery, Ala., 1991-93; with Bapt. Med. Ctr., Montgomery, 1994—, Jackson Hosp., Montgomery, 1994—. Contbr. articles to profl. jours. Maj. USAF, 1986—93. Decorated USAF Commendation medal; recipient Schering Travel award, Schering-Plough Pharm., 1990. Fellow Am. Acad. Pediats., Am. Acad. Allergy, Asthma, and Immunology, Am. Coll. Allergy, Asthma, and Immunology; mem. Ala. Soc. Allergy & Immunology (treas. 2004-05, v.p. 2005-06, pres. 2006-07), Joint Coun. Allergy, Asthma, and Immunology, Med. Assn. State Ala., Med. Soc. Montgomery County (bd. trustees 2006), Soc. Air Force Physicians, Ala. Soc. Allergy and Immunology (pres. 2007). Republican. Roman Catholic. Avocations: travel, golf, swimming, reading, computers. Office: Allergy Asthma & Immunology Montgomery 1420 Narrow Ln Pky Montgomery AL 36111-2654 Home Phone: 334-244-2928; Office Phone: 334-284-4196. Office Fax: 334-284-4256. Business E-Mail: dochlee@knology.net.

LEE, HEE-JOO, microbiologist, educator, lab administrator, director; b. Seoul, Republic of Korea, Jan. 27, 1954; d. Jong-Man Lee and Ja-Hyang Kim; m. Soon-Moo Soh; children: Jeong-Soo Soh, Yun-Soo Soh. MB, YonSei U., Seoul, 1978, MS in Medicine, 1981, MD, 1984. Specialist in lab. medicine Seoul, 1983. Resident Severance Hosp., Seoul, 1979—83; dir. lab. medicine Incheon Christian Hosp., Republic of Korea, 1983—90; vis. scientist, dept. microbiology & immunology Bonn U., Germany, 1990—91; asst., assoc. prof. Incheon Jr. Nursing Coll., 1983—93, Kyung Hee U., Seoul, 1993—2002, prof., 2002—, dir. lab. medicine, Med. Ctr., 2007—; pres. Korean Soc. Clin. Microbiology, Seoul, 2008—. Home: DoGok Dong 164-6 Poscourt Apt 101-203 Seoul 135-270 Republic of Korea Office: Kyung-Hee Univ Hoe-Gi Dong #1 Seoul 130-702 Republic of Korea Home Phone: 82-10-8944-1725; Office Phone: 82-2-958-8672. Office Fax: 82-2-958-8609. E-mail: leehejo@khmc.or.kr.

LEE, HEUNG BUM, medical educator; s. Gae Wan Lee and Ok Ja Kim; m. Jeong Hee Kim; children: Dong Hoon, Soo Yeon. PhD, Chonbuk Nat. U., Jeon-ju, Republic of Korea, 1999. Cert. Bd. Internal Medicine, 1997, splty. respiratory disease Korean Med. Assn., 1999. Clin. fellow Chonbuk U. Hosp., Jeon-ju, 1997—98, dir., 2007—08; faculty Chonbuk Nat. U., Jeon-ju, 1998—; vis. scientist Mayo Clinic, Rochester, Minn., 2005—07. Presenter in field. Mem.: European Respiratory Soc., Am. Thoracic Soc. Achievements include research in respiratory diseases, bronchial asthma, COPD, intensive care. Office: Chonbuk Nat Univ Keum-am Dong San 2-20 561-712 Jeon-ju Chonbuk Republic of Korea Office Fax: +82-632541609. Business E-Mail: lhbmd@chonbuk.ac.kr.

LEE, HEUNG-MAN, otolaryngologist, educator; s. Gil Moon Lee and Young Ja Park; m. Myoung-Suk Kim; children: Chang Shin, Hyun Shin. MD, Korea U., Seoul, 1984, PhD, 1991. Clin. fellow Korea U. Coll. Medicine, Seoul, 1991—94, prof., 1994—, asst. prof. otorhinolaryngology-head and neck surgery, 1994—97, assoc. prof. otorhinolaryngology-head and neck surgery, 1997—2003, prof. otorhinolaryngology-head and neck surgery, 2003—; chief, dir. dept. otorhinolaryngology-head and neck surgery Korea U., Guro Hosp., Seoul, 2000—06. Vis. rschr. dept. pulmonology Cardiovasc. Rsch. Inst. U Calif., San Francisco, 1997—99; dir. Clin. Trial Ctr. for Med. Devices Korea U., Seoul, 2005—. Mem.: Collegium Oto-Rhino-Laryngologicum Amicitiae Sacrum, Korean Rhinologic Soc., Korean Soc. Otolaryngology (dir. sci. com. 2003—05, Sug Dang Hag Sul Sang award 1994). Achievements include research in allergic rhinitis and sinusitis.

LEE, HOCHANG BENJAMIN, psychiatrist, educator; b. Seoul, Republic of Korea, Sept. 15, 1969; MD, Jefferson Med. Coll., 1997. Assoc. prof. Johns Hopkins U. Sch. Medicine, 2003—. Dir. rsch. devel. Johns Hopkins Bayview Med. Ctr., 2008. Mem.: Acad. Psychosomatic Medicine (Dlin Fischer award). Avocations: classical music, reading. Office: 5300 Alpha Commons Dr 4th Fl Baltimore MD 21224 Business E-Mail: hochang@jhmi.edu.

LEE, HOI YOUNG, medical educator; s. Kim Lee; m. Hye Kyung Chang; 1 child, Yun. PhD, U. Tex., Austin, 1992. Vis. assoc. NIH, Bethesda, Md., 1992—95; instr. Gyeongsang Nat. U. Coll. Medicine, Chinju, Gyeongsangnamdo, Republic of Korea, 1995—97; prof. Konyang U. Coll. Medicine, Nonsan, Chungnam, Republic of Korea, 1998—. Achievements include research in signal transduction of autotaxin. Office: Coll Medicine Konyang Univ 821 Medical Sci Bldg 681 Gasuwon-dong Seo-gu Daejeon 302-918 Republic of Korea Office Fax: 8242-541-4626. Business E-Mail: hoi@konyang.ac.kr.

LEE, HON CHEUNG, physiology educator; b. Hong Kong, May 7, 1950; came to the U.S., 1967; s. Chai Chong and Yee Chin (Ng) L.; m. Miranda Wong, Aug. 1981; 1 child, Cyrus W. BA, U. Calif., Berkeley, 1971, MA, 1973, PhD, 1978; degree (hon.), U. Genoa, Italy, 1997. Postdoc. rsch. U. Calif., Berkeley, 1978—79, Stanford U., Pacific Grove, Calif., 1979—81; asst. prof. U. Minn., Mpls., 1981—86, assoc. prof., 1986—90, prof., 1990—, McKnight Disting. Univ. prof., 1996—; chair, prof., head physiology U. Hong Kong, China, 2006—. Mem. Reproductive Biology Study Sect., NIH, Bethesda, Md., 1993-97; chmn. Reproductive Biology Spl. Emphasis Panel, NIH, Bethesda, 1994; chair prof. and head dept. physiology U. Hong Kong, 2006-. Contbr. articles to profl. jours. Rsch. grantee NIH, Bethesda, 1983—, 94—, NSF, Washington, 1986-89. Mem. AAAS, Am. Soc. Cell Biochemistry and Molecular Biology. Achievements include discovery of Cyclic ADP-ribose and NAADP, messenger molecules for regulating cellular calcium; patents for Cyclic ADP-ribose antagonists and novel caged nucleotides. Office: U Hong Kong Dept Physiology Hong Kong China Office Phone: 612-625-7120. Business E-Mail: leehc@tc.umn.edu, leehc@hku.hk.

LEE, HOO-YEON, medical researcher; b. Republic of Korea, Aug. 8, 1975; MD, Ewha Woman's U. Coll. Medicine, PhD, 2000. Early detection br. Nat. Cancer Ctr., 2008—. Office: 323 Ilsan-ro Ilsandong-gu Goyang-si Gyeonggi-do 410-769 Republic of Korea Business E-Mail: hoo@ncc.re.kr.

LEE, HOYEON, neurosurgeon; b. Seoul, Republic of Korean, Jan. 3, 1965; s. Bongjoon Lee and Eunpok Park; m. Youngmi Cho, Jan. 20, 1990; children: Joonil, Haeun, Joonyoung. PhD, U. Ulsan, Republic of Korea, 2003. Lic. Medical Doctor Min. of Health & Welfare, 1989, cert. Korean Neurosurgl. Soc., 1995. Clin. instr. Asan Med. Ctr., Seoul, 1995—96; dir.neurosurgery Wooridul Spine Hosp., Seoul, 1998—, pres. med. affairs, 2006—08, hon. pres., 2009—. Contbr. articles to profl. jours. Ordinee Good News Ch., Seoul, 2003. Mem.: Am. Assn. Neurological Surgeons, Am. Bd. Minimally Invasive Spinal Surgery, Am. Acad. Minimally Invasive Medicine and Surgery (life). Achievements include patents for calcium phosphate artificial bone; design of endoscopic forceps designs and development of Robin Hood Locker. Avocation: bicycling. Office: Wooridul Spine Hosp 47-4 Chungdam-Dong Gangnam-Gu Seoul 135-100 Republic of Korea Office Phone: 82 2 513 8212. Office Fax: 82-2-513-8146. Personal E-mail: mediple@yahoo.co.kr.

LEE, HYUN KOO, neurosurgeon; b. Chungju, Chconbuk, Republic of Korea, June 23, 1948; s. Rock Shin Lee and Eng Sun Oh; m. Eun Kyung Cho; children: Soo Jin, Sun Yong. PHD, Seoul Nat. U., Republic of Korea, 1988. Cert. neurosurgeon Republic of Korea, 1982. Med. pres. St. Mary's Hosp., Chungju, 1987—; pres. Deajun-Chungchung Neurosurg. Soc., Chungchungdo, Republic of Korea, 2006—07. Pres. Chungchung divsn. Korean Hosp. Assn., Chungju, 2005—06. Mem.: Korean Neurosurg. Soc. Office: Saint Mary's Hosp Jujungdong Sangdanggu 360-568 Chungju Chungbuk Republic of Korea Office Fax: 82-43-212-5001. Business E-Mail: hyunkli@hanmail.net.

LEE, HYUNG SIK, medical educator; b. Gyeongju, Republic of Korea, Mar. 16, 1959; MD, Busan Nat. U., 1984, PhD, 1996. Prof. Dong-A U. Med. Ctr., 1992—, dir., planning & coordination dept., 2009. Mem.: Korean Soc. Therapeutic Radiation Oncology (Best Paper award 2003), European Soc. Therapeutic Radiology & Oncology, Am. Soc. Therapeutic Radiology & Oncology. Avocations: golf, mountain climbing. Office: 1-3 Dongdaisindong Seo Gu Busan 602-715 Republic of Korea Business E-Mail: hyslee@dau.ac.kr.

LEE, IL-OK, anesthesiologist, education educator; b. Seoul, Republic of Korea, Nov. 10, 1958; d. Byoung-Cheol Lee and Soon-Rye Shin; m. Jae-Ryong Lee, May 11, 1991; children: Ji-Hyun, Tae-Sun. Bachelor's degree, Korea U., Seoul, 1984, M in Medicine, 1988, PhD, 1992. Cert. bd. anesthesia and pain medicine Korea Med. Assn., 1989. Assoc. prof. Korea U., Seoul, Republic of Korea, 1998—2002, prof., 2003—. Rsch. fellow Harvard Med. Sch., Boston, 1995—96; vis. prof., rsch. assoc. Dept. Anesthesiology, Pharmacology and Therapeutics Med. Sch. U. BC, Vancouver, Canada, 2006—07. Author: (articles) Corresponding author, (article) Corressponding author; contbr. articles pub. to profl. jour. (Abott academic award, 2000, Korea U. Alumni Award, 2002). Mem. com. Cert. Bd Examination Of Anesthesia; mem. Com. Academic Affairs. Grantee, Korea U. Med. Rsch. Found., 2005, Korea Academic Rsch. Found., 1997, Korea Sci. Found., 1999, Korean Rsch. Found., 2006—07. Mem.: Com. Acad. Affair KSA, Korea Assn. of Pain Rsch., Korea Assn. of Pediatric Anesthesia, Korea Assn. of Neuroanesthesia, Korea Soc. Anesthetic Pharmacology, Korea Assn. of Anesthesiology (assoc.). Roman Catholic. Achievements include research in C-Fos In Spinal Preemption glycine and gaba receptor in neuropathic pain; glycine or GABA receptor. Avocation: travel. Home: Shinjung dong 1279 MokHyundai Apt106-906 Seoul 158-072 Republic of Korea Office: Korea Univ Guro Hosp Guro-dong 80 Guro ku Seoul 152-703 Republic of Korea Office Phone: 82-2-2626-1420, 82-2-2626-3234. Office Fax: 82-2-851-9897. Business E-Mail: iloklee@korea.ac.kr.

LEE, IMSHIK, biotechnologist, educator; b. Hadong, Gyung-Nan, Republic of Korea, Sept. 1963; s. Jong-Whan Lee and Tae-Sim Park; m. Taiyan Lee, May 18, 1997; children: David, Joshua, Grace. BA, Pusan Nat. U., 1986; PhD, U. Bristol, 1993. Rsch. fellow Chinese Acad. Scis., Beijing, 1995—97, Hong Kong U., 1997—98; sr. rschr. Case Western Res. U., Cleve., 1998—2002; vis. prof. Tokyo Med. and Dental U., 2002—03; prof. Nankai U., Tianjin, China, 2003—; adj. prof. Yanbian U. Sci. Tech., Jilin, 1993—. Disciple-making, 1992—2005. Recipient Outstanding Young Rschr. Travel award, World Congress Biomaterials, 2000; named Outstanding Prof., Nankai U., 2003, Spl. Prof., 2005; grantee, Japanese Ministry of Edn., 2003. Achievements include first to identify single molecular kinetics of ligan(fibrinogen) - recetor(alpha2b.beta3) system in-vitro; research in nanohydrogel particles' single molecular kinetics at the liquid-solid interfaces; controlling growth of platinium nanoparticle; molecular designs for targeting duplex DNA; nanobio-interfacial under electromagnetic fields. Business E-Mail: ilee@nankai.edu.cn

LEE, IN HO, medical educator; b. Chungcheongnam-do, Republic of Korea, Dec. 24, 1974; MD, Chungnam Nat. U., 1999, PhD, 2008. Clin asst prof. Chungnam Nat. U. Hosp., 2010—. Mem., European Soc. Radiology, Korean Soc. Neuroradiology and Head & Neck Radiology, Korean Soc. Ultrasound in Medicine, Korean Soc. Radiology. Office: 282 Munhua ro Jung gu Daejeon 301 721 Republic of Korea Office Fax: 82 42 253 0061.

LEE, INAH, psychology professor; b. Seoul, Republic of Korea, Oct. 17, 1970; s. Taeheang Lee and Sukyung Baek; m. Sujeong Lee, children: Serin, Sejune. BA in Psychology, Seoul Nat. U., 1996; PhD, U. Utah, Salt Lake City, 2002. Rsch. fellow U. Tex. Med. Ctr., Houston, 2002—04; rsch. fellow Ctr. for Memory and Brain, Boston U., 2004—05; asst. prof. dept. psychology U. Iowa, Iowa City, 2006—. Contbr. articles to profl. jours. Recipient James W. Prahl Meml. award, U. Utah, 2002; Pickwick Postdoctoral Rsch. fellow, Nat. Sleep Found., 2004—05, Old Gold Summer Rsch. fellow, U. Iowa, 2006, rsch. grantee, NIH, 2007. Office: U Iowa E11 SSH Dept Psychology Iowa City IA 52242 Office Fax: 319-335-0191. Business E-Mail: inah-lee@uiowa.edu.

LEE, INKYU, endocrinologist, educator; s. Mahnjung and Soyeun Lee; m. Eun-Mee Park, May 12, 1984; 1 child, Jinhyung. MD, Kyungpook Nat. U., Taegu, 1982, PhD, 1988. Cert. internal medicine Korean Med. Assn., 1985, nuc. medicine Korean Med. Assn., 1996. Rsch. fellow Joslin Diabetes Ctr., Boston, 1994—95; prof. Keimyung Univ., Med. Sch., Taegu, Republic of Korea, 1998—2003, chief, 1998—. Mem. editl. bd.: Korean Diabetes Jour. (award internal medicine Korean Med. Assn., 2002). Bd. adolescent dept. Cath. Ch., Taegu, 1994—99. Achievements include invention of Dumbbell Type Decoy. Office Fax: 82-53-250-7892; Home Fax: 82-53-250-7434. Business E-Mail: inkyulee@dsmc.or.kr.

LEE, JAE CHEOL, pulmonologist, researcher; b. Mokpo, Republic of Korea, Mar. 19, 1964; s. Tae Hyeong Lee and Young Sook Son; m. Yoo Mi Kim, Feb. 19, 1994; 1 child, Min Keon. MD, Seoul Nat. U., Republic of Korea, PhD, 2002. Diplomate Nat. Bd. Med. Practitioner, Korea Med. Assn., 1989. Chief, chest medicine Korea Cancer Ctr. Hosp., Seoul, 1998—. Mem.: Korean Assn. Internal Medicine, Korean Acad. Tb and Respiratory Diseases, Internat. Assn. Study Lung Cancer. Achievements include research in lung cancer. Home: Kangnam-gu Ilwon-dong Woosung Apt Seoul 135-946 Republic of Korea Office: Korea Cancer Ctr Hosp Nowon-gu Gongneung-dong 215-4 Seoul 139-706 Republic of Korea Business E-Mail: jclee@kcch.re.kr.

LEE, JAE WON, surgeon, educator; b. Kyungnam, Republic of South Korea, Oct. 9, 1957; s. Younghan Lee and Yunsuk Ha; m. Sang Sook Lee, Feb. 28, 1983; children: Eun Young, Jungki, Namhun. MD, Seoul Nat. U., Republic of Korea, 1982, PhD, 1991. Bd. cert. in thoracic surgery Korean Ministry of Health. Chmn. Gil Gen. Hosp., Incheon, Republic of Korea, 1987—93; assoc. prof. ASAN Med. Ctr., Seoul, Republic of Korea, 1993—; clin. fellow Toronto Hosp., Ont., Canada, 1996—97. Dir. ICU ASAN Med. Ctr., Seoul, Republic of Korea, 2001—. Recipient Song Chon award, Husaengshinbo newspaper, 1982, Samil award, Samil Pharm. Co., 1992, Walton Lillehei award for clinical excellence, St Jude Med., Korean Soc. for Thoracic Surgery, 2002. Mem.: Korean Circulation Soc. (life), Korean Soc. for Thoracic Surgery (life; publ. com. 1999—2003). Home: Samsung-green #101-401 Sangil-dong kangdon Seoul Republic of Korea Office: ASAN Med Ctr 388-1 Pungnap Dong Seoul 138-736 Republic of Korea Office Fax: 82-2-30106966; Home Fax: 82-2-30106966. Business E-Mail: jwlee@amc.seoul.kr.

LEE, JAE-CHUL, medical educator; b. Seoul, Republic of Korea, Feb. 26, 1968; PhD, Hallym U., 2000. Tchg. and rsch. asst., dept. anatomy Coll. Medicine Hallym U., 1998—2000; postdoc. fellow Ewha Inst. Neurosci. Ewha Womans U., 2000—04; rsch. asst. prof., dept. nanotech. Ewha Womans U., 2004—07; rsch. asst. prof., dept. neurosci. Coll. Medicine Korea U., 2007; clin. rsch. prof. Clin. Rsch. Inst. Seoul Nat. U., 2007—. Office: 28 Yeongeon-dong Jongno-gu Seoul 110-744 Republic of Korea Personal E-mail: anajclee@hanmail.net.

LEE, JAN LOUISE, nursing educator; b. Grundy Center, Iowa, Oct. 30, 1953; d. Robert L. and B. Lucille (Frey) Thede; m. Henry M. Lee (div.). BSN, U. Iowa, 1975; MN, UCLA, 1980; PhD, U. So. Calif., 1988. Patient care coord. Queen of the Valley Hosp., West Covina, Calif., 1977-78; rsch. clin. nurse specialist Wadsworth VA Med. Ctr., LA, 1980-83; asst. prof. nursing U. So. Calif., LA, 1983-88, UCLA, 1988-95; dir. undergrad. and non-traditional programs U. Mich. Sch. Nursing, Ann Arbor, 1995—2003; prof., assoc. dean U. Tenn. Coll. Nursing, Knoxville, 2003—. Mem. ANCC Commn. on Cert. Contbr. articles to profl. jours. Grantee NIH, U. So. Calif., UCLA, others. Mem. Tenn. Nurses Assn., Sigma Theta Tau (past chpt. pres.). Home: 9746 Dawn Chase Way Knoxville TN 37931 Office: U Tenn Knoxville Coll Nursing 1200 Volunteer Blvd Knoxville TN 37996-4180 Home Phone: 865-531-1921. E-mail: jlee39@utk.edu.

LEE, JEN-JYH, medical association administrator; b. Taipei, Dec. 10, 1952; B, Nat. Taiwan U., 1977. Sect. chief, sect. treatment planning Buddhist Tzu Chi Gen. Hosp., 1982—; pres. Nat. Tuberculosis Assn., Taiwan. Sec. chief TB Lab Sect. Buddhist Tzu Chi Gen. Hosp., 2009—. Office: 707 Sect 3 Chung Yang Rd Hualien Hualien 970 Taiwan Office Phone: 886-3-8561825 ext 2118. Business E-Mail: e0139@tzuchi.com.tw.

LEE, JEONG KEUN, oral, maxillofacial surgeon, director; b. Seoul, Republic of Korea, Apr. 27, 1966; s. Moon Su Jung; m. Anna Yi; 1 child, Nam Kyeong. B Dentistry, Seoul Nat. U., 1990, MS in Dentistry, 1994, PhD, 2001. Diplomate Korean Assn. Maxillofacial Plastic and Reconstructive Surgeons. Vis. faculty mem. U. Ill., Chgo., 2002—03; assoc. prof., chair Ajou U., Suwon, Republic of Korea, 2004—09; head dept. dentistry Ajou U. Hosp., 2004—09, dir. Dentofacial Ctr., 2005—09; dir. Ilwoong Cleft Lip/Palate Med. Svc. Corp., 2006—; tenured prof. Ajou U., 2010—. Dir. Ilwoong Cleft Lip/Palate Svc. Corp., 2006—; comm. chair, bd. of Bone Bank Korean Assn. of Oral and Maxillofacial Surgeons, 2008—; assoc. editor Editorial bd., Surgical Techniques Development; tenured prof. Ajou U., 2010—. Contbr. articles to profl. jours.; editor: (textbook) Maxillofacial Plastic & Reconstructive surgery 2nd edn.; assoc. ed. (ed. bd.) the Surgical Tech. Develop. Grantee, Korean Ministry Commerce, Industry and Energy, 2004—08. Achievements include research in retrospective multicenter cohort study of the clinical performance of 2-stage implants in South Korean populations; inactivation patterns of p16/INK4A in oral squamous cell carcinomas; clinical study on the prognosis after secondary osteoplasty in the cleft alveolus patients; clinical study on current jaw fractures of Koreans; differential diagnosis of class III profile; emergency medicine in oral and maxillofacial area; adenomatoid odontogenic tumor; clinical study of the mandibular canal location in mandibular molar areas using Dentascan, comprehensive treatment of unilateral complete cleft lip and palate; lateral cephalometric study on the soft tissue changes after orthognathic surgery in patients diagnosed as mandibular prognathism; soft tissue change according to skeletal change following BSSRO with advancing genioplasty; complications of orthognathic surgery; prognosis after secondary bone graft using iliac PMCB in the cleft alveolus patients; treatment protocol for cleft lip and/or palate patients; a probable case of oral bisphosphonate-associated osteoradionecsis of the jaw and recovery with parathyroid hormone treatment; outfracture osteotomy on lateral maxillary wall as a modified sinus graft technique; relationship of synovial TNF-alpha & IL-6 to the temporomandibular disorders; angled eccentric osteosynthesis, a new technique for simple mandibular fractures; inventor of oligopeptide for enhancing osseointegration and bone formation; inventor of bone biology for the implant dentistry in atrophic aleveolar ridge: theory and practice in dental implants. Office Fax: 82-31-219-5329. Business E-Mail: arcady@ajou.ac.kr.

LEE, JEONG-HO, nephrologist, medical educator; b. Seosan, Republic of Korea, Nov. 4, 1956; s. Pyeong-Jae Lee and Taek Jie; m. Hyun-Sook Shim, Jan. 19, 1986; children: Jamin, Dong-Kyu. B, Chungam Nat. U., 1979—84; M, Chungnam Nat. U., 1986—88; PhD, Keimyung U., 1995—97. MD Ministry of Health and Welfare, Korea, 1985, Bd. Internal Medicine Ministry Health and Welfare, Korea, 1991, Bd. Nephrology Korean Med. Assn., Seoul, 1996, Specialist Renal Dialysis Korean Soc. Nephrology, Korea, 1998, Human Care and Use of Animals in Rsch. and Tchg. U. Mo., Columbia, 1998. Dir. Kyongju Pub. Health Ctr., 1986—88; instr. Dongguk U. Med. Ctr., 1991—93, asst. prof., 1994—97, assoc. prof., 1998—2002, prof., 2003—, dir. nephrology divsn., 1994—, dir. dept. internal medicine, 2002—; rsch. assoc. U. Mo.-Columbia, 1998—99. Ednl. com. Korean Soc. Nephrology, 2001—02, rsch. com., 2003—, exam. com., 1999—, bd. rev., 1999—; exam. com. Korean Med. Assn., 1994—, bd. rev., 1999—, Jour. Korean Med. Sci., 1999—. Contbr. articles to profl. jours. Dir. Hwangsung Cath. ch., 1999—2003. 1st lt. Pub. Health Dr., 1978—79, Daejeon, Korea. Recipient Project of Elimination of Pulmonary Tb, Ministry of Health and Welfare, Korea, 1987, Best Abstract award, Ann. Dialysis Conf., 2005, Academic prize, Samil Co. MBC Broadcasting Sta., Korea, 2005. Mem.: Korean Med. Assn. (corr.), Korean Soc. of Nephrology (corr.), Internat. Soc. of Peritoneal Dialysis (assoc.), Am. Soc. of Nephrology (assoc.). Peace And Freedom. Roman Catholic. Achievements include research in metabolism of peritoneal membrane. Avocations: golf, fishing. Home: Hyundai APT 101-1304 Hwangsung-dong Gyeongju 780-130 Republic of Korea Office: Dongguk Univ Med Ctr 1090-1 Sukjang-Dong 780-350 Gyeongju Gyeongsangbuk-do Republic of Korea Office Fax: 82-54-770-8565. Personal E-mail: petlee@hanmail.net. Business E-Mail: jhlee@dongguk.ac.kr.

LEE, JHEMON HOM, physician; b. Redwood City, Calif., July 1, 1970; s. Billy Tom and Yuen Han Lee, m. Misa Catherlyn Nguyen BA in Engring. summa cum laude, Harvard U., 1990; MD cum laude, U. Md., 1994. Diplomate Nat. Bd. Med. Examiners. Resident in diagnostic radiology U. Chgo., 1994—98, chief resident, 1997—98; fellow in abdominal imaging Brigham and Women's Hosp./Harvard Med. Sch., Boston, 1998—99; radiologist, ptnr. MemRAD Med. Group, Long Beach, Calif., 1999—2006; vice chair dept. diagnostic imaging Los Alamitos Med. Ctr., 2002—08; ptnr. Los Alamitos Radiology Group, 2006—; med. dir. Diagnostic Sonography Program

Platt Coll., 2010—. Bd. dir. Radiologic Practice Mgmt., Inc., 2004—05; med. dir. Diagnostic Med. Sonography Program, Platt Coll., 2010—. Editor-in-chief UMAB news, 1993; news editor East Wind, 1987-90; contbr. articles to profl. jours. Mem. steering com. United Asian Am. Orgns., Chgo., 1996-98; mem. Leadership Ctr. for Asian Ams., Chgo., 1997-98. Recipient Chgo. Chpt. Recognition award, Nat. Assn. of Asian Am. Profl., 1998, Lifetime Achievement award, 2002; named one of Am. Top Radiologists, Consumers' Rsch. Coun. America, 2002—03, 2009, Am. Top Physicians, Consumers' Rsch. Coun. of Am., 2004—05. Mem. Radiol. Soc. N.Am., Nat. Coun. Asian Pacific Islander Physicians (sec., bd. mem.), Assn. Asian Am. Studies, Harvard Club Southern Calif., Nat. Assn. Asian Am. Profls. (nat. pres., 1998-2000, exec. v.p. 2002-04, bd. advisor, Orange county chpt.), Asian Pacific Am. Med. Students Assn. (pres. adv. bd.), Asian Profl. Exch. (chair Healthcare Spl. Interest Group, dir. profl. devel. 2000-01), Orgn. Chinese Ams. (bd. mem., Orange county chpt., pres. Orange County chpt. 2003-06), Cold Tofu Improv, East West Players Edn. Com. & Actors Conservatory (edn. advisor), Phi Beta Kappa, Alpha Omega Alpha. Avocations: writing, films, computers. Home: 13710 Alderton Ln Cerritos CA 90703 Office Phone: 562-799-3294. Business E-Mail: jhemon@post.harvard.edu.

LEE, JI WOONG, medical educator; b. Daegu, Republic of Korea, June 21, 1977; MS, Kyungpook Nat. U. Sch. Medicine, 2005. Clin. asst. prof. Dept. Ophthalmology, Kyungpook Nat. U. Sch. Medicine, 2008—09; instr. Dept. Ophthalmology, Pusan Nat. U. Sch. Medicine, 2009—11, asst. prof., 2011—. Recipient award, Korean Ophthal. Soc. and Taejoon. Mem.: Korean Ophthal. Soc. Avocation: golf. Office: 1-10 Ami-Dong Seo-Ku Busan 602-739 Republic of Korea Office Fax: 82 51 242 7341. Business E-Mail: alertlee@hanmail.net.

LEE, JOHN Y. K., neurosurgeon, director; BS in Molecular Biophysics and Biochemistry, Yale U., 1994; MD, U. Medicine and Dentistry of NJ, 1998. Diplomate Am. Bd. Neurol. Surgery, 2009, cert. gamma knife stereotactic radiosurgery Univ. Pittsburgh, 2005, cyberknife stereotactic radiosurgery Accuray, 2011. Intern in surgery Univ. Pitts., 1998—99, resident in neurol. surgery, 1999—2005; fellow in stereotactic and functional neurosurgery Cleve. Clinic, 2005—06; asst. prof. neurosurgery Pa. Hosp., med. dir. Penn Gamma Knife Ctr. Co-author (with M. Mata and D.J. Fink): Vector-Mediated Gene Transfer to Express Inhibitory Neurotransmitters in Dorsal Root Ganglion Reduces Pain in a Rodent Model of Lumbar Radiculopathy, 2006; co-author: (with A. Deogaonkar, M. Deogankar, Z. Ebrahim and A. Schubert) Propofol-Induced Dyskinesias controlled with Dexmedetomidine during Deep Brain Stimulation Surgery, 2006; co-author: (with M. Deogaonkar and A. Rezai) Deep Brain Stimulation for Patients with Dystonia, 2006; co-author: (with M. Smith) Role of Stereotactic Radiosurgery in Managing Brain Metastasis, 2007; co-author: (with M. Deogaonkar and A. Rezai) Deep Brain Stimulation of Globus Pallidus Interna for Dystonia, 2007; co-author: various others. Named one of Top Doctors, Phila. Mag., 2011. Mem.: Pa. Hosp. (med. exec. com.). Office: Pennsylvania Hospital Department of Neurosurgery Washington Sq. W Bldg 235 S 8th St Philadelphia PA 19106 Office Phone: 215-829-5189. Office Fax: 215-829-6645. Business E-Mail: leejohn@uphs.upenn.edu.

LEE, JONG HWA, physician, educator; b. Pusan, Republic of Korea, Dec. 24, 1963; s. Mal Hee Park; m. Seon Young Koh, May 5, 1990; children: Seo Jeong, Chae Eun, Seong Yun. BA, Pusan Nat. U., 1988, SM in Diagnostic Radiology, 1991, PhD in Diagnostic Radiology, 2002. Internship Pusan Nat. U. Hosp., 1988—89; residency Dept. Diagnostic Radiology, Pusan Nat. U. Coll. Medicine, 1989—92; dir. Diagnostic Radiology Heaseong Gen. Hosp. Asan Welfare Found., Ulsan, 1992—97; lectr. Dept. Diagnostic Radiology, U. Ulsan Coll. Medicine, 1997—99, asst. prof., 1999—2003, assoc. prof., 2003—. Mem.: Korean Soc. Radiology. Home: Apt 109-1402 1639-1 Nam-gu Ulsan 680-010 Republic of Korea Office: Ulsan Univ Hosp 290-3 Jeonha-Dong Dong-Gu 682-714 Ulsan Republic of Korea Office Fax: 82-52-252-5160; Home Fax: 82-52-252-5160. E-mail: jhlee@uuh.ulsan.kr.

LEE, JONGHO, thoracic surgeon, educator; b. Seoul, Apr. 17, 1967; PhD, Coll. Medicine, Cath. U. Korea, 2006. Assoc. prof. dept. thoracic & cardiovasc. surgery Daejeon St. Mary's Hosp., Coll. Medicine, Cath. U Korea, 2011—. Mem.: Korean Soc. Thoracic and Cardiovasc. Surgery. Avocations: running, baseball. Office: 520-2 Daeheung-Dong Jung-gu Daejeon 301-723 Republic of Korea

LEE, JONG-HO, medical association administrator; b. Kyung-Nam, Republic of Korea, Mar. 18, 1957; DDS, Seoul Nat. U., 1982, PhD, 1991. Dir. Oral Cancer Ctr. Seoul Nat. U., 2005—, Korean Soc. Oral Cancer, 2009—11. Pres. Koean Tempromandibular Joint Corp., 2009—11. Fellow: ITI; mem.: Internat. Assn. Oral Cancer, World Soc. Reconstructive Microsurgery, AOCMF. Office: Dept Oral & Maxillofacial Surgery Chongro-Ku Seoul 110-768 Republic of Korea Office Fax: 82-2-766-4948. Business E-Mail: leejongh@snu.ac.kr.

LEE, JONG-MIN, oncologist, gynecologist, medical researcher; b. Seoul, Republic of Korea, Apr. 13, 1965; s. Moo-Young Lee and Jeong-Bo Sim; m. Myung-Sim Hwang, May 12, 1996; children: Eun-Sol, Eun-Gyul. MD, Korea U., Seoul, 1991, MS, 1999, PhD, 2001. Diplomate Ministry Health & Welfare Korea, 1991. Instr. Gachon Med. Sch. Gil Med. Ctr., Inchon, Republic of Korea, 1997—2001, asst. prof., 2001—05, assoc. prof., 2005—06, Kyunghee U. East-West Neo Med. Ctr., Seoul, 2006—. Mem. Korean Gynecol. Oncology Group, Seoul, 2002—. Mem. editl. bd.: Korean Jour. Gynecologic Oncology, 2004—; contbr. articles to profl. jours. Grantee, Kyunghee U., 2006, 2007, Korea Rsch. Found., 2007; fellow, Korea Cancer Ctr. Hosp., Seoul, 1996—97. Mem.: Korean Soc. Oncology, Korean Soc. Gynecol. Oncology and Colposcopy, Korean Soc. Ob-Gyn., Internat. Gynecol. Cancer Soc. Roman Catholic. Home: 604-303 Ssang-Yong APT 852 Sanghyun-dong Suji-gu Yongin-si 448-523 Republic of Korea Office: East-West Neo Med Ctr Kyunghee U 149 Sangil-dong Gangdong-gu Seoul 134-890 Republic of Korea Office Fax: 82-440-7894. Personal E-mail: kgo02@hanmail.net.

LEE, JOO-EUN, ophthalmologist, educator; b. Republic of Korea, Dec. 14, 1971; MD, Pusan Nat. U., PhD, 1997. Instr. Pusan Nat. U. Hosp., 2002—04; dir. Maryknol Med. Ctr., 2004—08; postdoc. rsch. fellow Mass. Eye and Ear Infirmary, Harvard Med. Sch., 2008—10; asst. prof. Inje U. Haeundae Paik Hosp., 2010—. Recipient Excellence award, Korean Ophthal. Assn.; Young Ophthalmologist fellowship, TaeJun-Santen Com. Mem.: Korean Ophthal. Soc., Korean Soc. Clin. Electrophysiology Vision, Korean Retina Soc., Am. Soc. Retina Specialists, Am. Acad. Ophthalmology. Avocations: skiing, computers. Office: 1435 Jwa-dong Haeundae-gu Busan 612-030 Republic of Korea Business E-Mail: jooeun2@korea.com.

LEE, JOON KYOO, otolaryngologist, educator; b. Seoul, Republic of Korea, July 19, 1973; s. Jeong Rhyeol Lee and Yeon Deok Park; m. Kun Hee Cho, Nov. 3, 2001; children: Ka-Hyeon, Ji-Myoung. B in Medicine, Chonnam Nat. U. Med. Sch., 1998; MD, Chonnam Nat. U. Med. Sch., Republic of Korea, 1998, PhD, 2007. Lic. Korean Med. Assn., Seoul, 1998. Intern Chonnam Nat. U. Hosp., Republic of Korea, 1998—99, resident, dept. otolaryngology-head and neck surgery, 2000—04, specialist in otolaryngology-head and neck surgery, 2004, head and neck surgeon, 2004—, fellow, dept. otolaryngology-head and neck surgery, 2004—05, clin. prof. dept. otolaryngology-head and neck surgery, 2005—06; prof. Chonnam Nat. U. Med. Sch. & Hosp., 2006—. V.p. Dae Han Surg. Clinic, Gwangju, 1999—2000. Mem.: Korean Thyroid Assn., Korean Soc. Logopedics and Phoniatrics, Korean Broncho-esophagological Soc., Korean Soc. Head and Neck Oncology, Korean Soc. Head and Neck Surgery, Korean Soc. Otolaryngology Head and Neck Surgery (life). Presbyterian. Avocations: guitar, basketball, music, drums. Home: 102-1706 Humancia Apt Banglim-dong Nam-gu Gwanhju 503-804 Republic of Korea Office: Chonnam National University Hospital Hak-Dong Dong-Gu 8 501-757 Gwangju Republic of Korea Office Fax: 82-62-228-7743. Personal E-mail: joonkyoo@hanmail.net. Business E-Mail: joonkyoo@chonnam.ac.kr.

LEE, JOON SUP, cardiologist; MD, Duke U., Durham, NC. Diplomate Am. Bd. Internal Medicine-cardiovascular disease, Am. Bd. Internal Medicine, Am. Bd. Internal Medicine-interventional cardiology. Resident Mass. Gen. Hosp., Boston, fellow; with cardiovascular inst. Univ. of Pitts. Med. Ctr. Office: University of Pittsburgh Physicians Cardiovascular Institute 200 Lothrop St Ste 5B Pittsburgh PA 15213 Office Phone: 412-647-6000.

LEE, JOO-YOUNG, research scientist; b. Won-Ju City, Republic of Korea, Dec. 20, 1973; PhD, Seoul Nat. U., 2005. Postdoc. rsch. fellow Kyushu U., 2008—. Office: 4-9-1 Shiobaru Minami-ku Fukuoka Kyushu 815-8540 Japan Business E-Mail: romans54@snu.ac.kr.

LEE, JUNG HIE, psychiatry professor; d. Tae Joo Lee and Joong Sook Hwang; m. Chang Kil Park, Apr. 15, 1989; 1 child, Kyung Chae Park. MD, Seoul Nat. U., 1980, PhD, 1989. Diplomate Korean Bd. Psychiatry and Neurology, 1984, Am. Bd. Sleep Medicine, 1991. Intern Seoul Nat. U. Hosp., Republic of Korea, 1980—81, resident dept. neruopsychiatry, 1981—84; staff psychiatrist dept. neuropsychiatry Incheon Christian Hosp., Republic of Korea, 1985—89; fellowship Stanford Sleep Rsch. Ctr., Calif., 1989—90; asst. prof. dept. psychiatry and neurology Case Western Res. U. Sch. Medicine, Cleve., 1990—93; rsch. prof. Aging and Phys. Culture Rsch. Inst. Seoul Nat. U. Coll. Medicine, 1994—99; asst. to prof. dept. psychiatry Kangwon Nat. U. Coll. Medicine, 2000—; lectr. divsn. sleep medicine Havard Med. Sch., 2010—11. Dir. Ctr. Sleep and Chronobiology Kangwon Nat. U. Hosp., 2003—; dean Kangwon Nat. U. Coll. Medicine, 2005—07; vice chair, mem. organizing com. 9th World Congress Sleep Apnea, Seoul, 2006—09; vis. prof. divsn. sleep medicine Harvard Med. Sch., 2008—09. Grantee Rsch. grant, Govt., 2004. Mem.: Korean Soc. Sleep Rsch. (pres.), Internat. Coll. Geriat. Psychoneuropharmacology (councilor), Korean Coll. Geriat. Psychoneuropharmacology (chair, bd. dirs.), Korean Assn. Dementia (bd. dirs.). Achievements include research in sleep medicine. Office: Kangwon Nat Univ Hosp 17-1 Hyoja-3-Dong 200-947 Chunchon Gangwon-do Republic of Korea Office Phone: 033-258-2005. Office Fax: 82 33 256 3344. Business E-Mail: jhielee@kangwon.ac.kr.

LEE, JUNG-KIL, neurosurgeon; b. Gwangju, Republic of Korea, Dec. 10, 1965; s. Gab-Rye Ban; m. Hye-Kyung Noh, Nov. 21, 1992; children: Ji-Soo, Soo-Min. MD, Chonnam Nat. U., Gwangju, 1989, PhD, 1998. Diplomate Chonnam Nat. U. Intern Chonnam Nat. U. Hosp., Gwangju, Republic of Korea, 1990, resident, 1994, neurosurgeon, spine specialist. Assoc. prof. Chonnam Nat. U. Hosp., 2004—. Editor review bd. Jour. Korean Neurosurgical Society. Med. dir. Fgn. Missionary, Gwangju, 2007—. Capt. Korean Army, 1994—97. Mem.: Korean Neurosurgical Soc. (life). Presbyterian. Achievements include research in animal brain infarction and spinal cord injury. Office: Chonnam Nat Univ Hosp Dept Neurosurgery Jebongno Dong-Gu 671 501-757 Gwangju Republic of Korea Home Phone: 82 62 2347539; Office Phone: 82622206606, 82622206602. Office Fax: 82622249865. Business E-Mail: jkl@chonnam.ac.kr.

LEE, KATHLEEN MARY, health facility administrator, nursing executive; b. Phila., Apr. 12, 1948; d. Daniel Joseph and Mary Ann (Daly) Glackin; m. Gary Douglas MacClay, May 2, 1970 (div. 1980); 1 child, Jeffrey Daniel; m. Glenn Patrick Lee, Feb. 14, 1981. RN diploma, Phila. Gen. Hosp., 1969; BS, St. Joseph Coll., 1985; M Health Svcs. Adminstrn., St. Josephs Coll., 1990; PhD in Health Svcs., Walden U., 1992. RN, Ga., R.I., Pa., Miss.; cert. nursing adminstr. Head nurse, nursery Jeanes Hosp., Phila., 1969-78; adminstrv. supr. Roger Williams Hosp., Providence, 1981-83; head nurse, nursery svcs. King Fahad Hosp., Rivadh, Saudi Arabia, 1983-85; charge nurse psychiatric N.E. Ga. Med. Ctr., Gainesville, 1986-87; v.p. patient svcs. St. Joseph's Hosp., Dahlonega, Ga., 1987-95, Coffee Regional Med. Ctr., Douglas, Ga., 1996-98; assoc. adminstr. Nursing and Profl. Svcs., Ocean Springs, Miss., 1998—2009. Founder, UNITE, Parent Support Group, Phila., 1976; co-founder, Neonatal Soc. San Antonio, 1979. Capt. USAF, 1978-81. Fellow: Am. Coll. Healthcare Execs.; mem.: ANA, Ga. Nurses Assn. (Ga. Nurses Make a Difference award 1991, dist. honoree 1992), Am. Orgn. Nurse Execs., Miss. Nurses Assn. (Dist. Specialty Nurse of Year award 2000), Sigma Theta Tau (Excellence in Nursing Adminstrn. award Zeta Gamma chpt. 2005). Democrat. Roman Catholic. Home: 2527 Venture Cir Gainesville GA 30506 Personal E-mail: kathleen39553@gmail.com.

LEE, KENNETH K. W., surgeon; Attended, U. Chgo., Chgo. Diplomate Am. Bd. Surgery. Resident Univ. of Chgo. Pritzker Sch. of Medicine, fellow; with surg. oncology divsn. Univ. of Pitts. Med. Ctr. Office: University of Pittsburgh Physicians Digestive Disorders Center 200 Lothrop St 3rd Fl Pittsburgh PA 15213 Office Phone: 412-647-0457.

LEE, KENNETH STUART, neurosurgeon, educator; b. Raleigh, NC, July 23, 1955; s. Kenneth Lloyd and Myrtie Lee (Turner) L.; m. Cynthia Jane Anderson, May 23, 1981; children: Robert Alexander, Evan Anderson. BA, Wake Forest U., 1977; MD, East Carolina U., 1981. Diplomate Nat. Bd. Med. Examiners, Am. Bd. Neurol. Surgeons; med. lic. N.C., Ariz. Intern, then resident in neurosurgery Wake Forest U. Med. Ctr., Winston-Salem, N.C., 1981-88; fellow Barrow Neurol. Inst., Phoenix, 1988-89; clin. asst. prof. neurosurgery East Carolina U., Greenville, NC, 1989-93, clin. assoc. prof. neurosurgery, 1994—2001, clin. prof. neurosurgery, 2001—, adj. assoc. prof. health edn., 1997—. Assoc. editor Current Surgery, 1990—; contbr. 30 articles to profl. jours. and 6 chpts. to books. Mem. Ethicon Neurosurgical Adv. Panel, 1989-95. Bucy fellow, 1988. Fellow ACS, Am. Heart Assn. (stroke coun.); mem. AMA, N.C. Med. Soc., Am. Assn. Neurol. Surgeons, Am. Soc. Stereotactic and Functional Neurosurgery, So. Med. Assn., Congress Neurol Surgeons, N.C. Neurosurg. Soc. (sec.-treas. 1991-93, pres. 1994-95), So. Neurosurg. Soc., Leksell Gamma Knife Soc., Alpha Omega Alpha. Republican. Baptist. Achievements include research on the efficacy of certain surgical procedures, particularly carotid endarterectomy, in the prevention of strokes. Home: 792 Lexington Dr Greenville NC 27834 Office: ECU Neurosurg & Spine Ctr 2325 Stantonsburg Rd Greenville NC 27834-7534 Office Phone: 252-752-5156. Business E-Mail: leeke@ecu.edu.

LEE, KEUN YOUNG, obstetrician, gynecologist, educator; b. Seoul, Republic Of Korea, July 27, 1953; s. Sung Min and Bong Ju Lee; m. Sung Ji Nam, Jan. 24, 1981; children: Han No, Kyung No. MD, Chung Ang U., Seoul, 1978, PhD, 1984. Cert. Bd. Ob-gyn., Seoul, 1983. Pres. Kangnam Sacred Heart Hosp., Hallym U., Seoul, 2006—; chair Korean Soc. Maternal & Fetal Medicine, Seoul, 2008—. Chair Dept. Ob-gyn., Seoul, 2006—. Recipient awards, Health Adminstrn., 2003, Adademic prize, Korean Soc. Ultrasound Ob-gyn., 2007. Office Phone: 82-2-829-5357. Business E-Mail: mfmlee@hallym.ac.kr.

LEE, KOONJA, medical researcher, educator; b. Busan, Republic of Korea, Jan. 9, 1958; m. Sung Lee, Dec. 17, 1982; children: Junwhan, Jiwhan. BS in Biochemistry, Yonsei U., Seoul, 1980; MS in Biochemistry, Yonsei U., 1984, PhD in Biochemistry, 1994. Prof. Eulji U., 1991—, prof. ocular ananotomy & contact lens optometry Sungnam, 1991—; prof. anatomy histology Med. Sch., Hanyang U., Seoul, Republic of Korea, 1989—91; vis. scholar Borish Ctr. Ophthalmic Rsch., Indiana U., Bloomington, Ind., 2005—06; key opinion leader Contact Lens, Bauch&Lomb, Rochester, 2006—; hon. prof. Contact Lens, Ciba Vision Korea, Seoul, 2007—08; prof. contact lens Ciba Vision Acad., 2008—; v.p. Korean Soc. Vision Sci., 2006—, editor in chief, 1999—2003, editor & reviewer, 1999—; reviewer Korean Ophthalmic Optics Soc., 2007—; v.p. Internat. Assn. Contact Lens Educators, Sydney, 2008—. Contbr. chapters to books. Recipient Excellence Rsch. Paper award, Bumsuk JanghakJadan, 2000, Korean Optometric Assn., 2000—01, 2003, Korean Ophthalmic Optics Soc., 2008, 2010. Fellow: Internat. Assn. Contact Lens Educators (Sydney); mem.: Korean Ophthalmic Optics Soc. Seoul, Korean Soc. Vision Sci. (Seoul). Achievements include discovery of glaucoma autoantibodies; research in wound healing mechanism in cornea, endothelial change in cornea with diabetes mellitus, corneal changes in orthokeratology, contact lens care and management, ophthalmic anthropometry for dimensions of spectacle framepolyamine mechanismtoxic effects of anticancer drugs and agricultural chemicals. Avocations: walking, gardening, travel. Office: Eulji University Dept Optometry Yangji-Dong Sujeong-Gu 212 461-713 Seongnam Gyeonggi Republic of Korea Office Phone: 82 31 740 7182. Office Fax: 82 31 740 7195. Business E-Mail: kjl@eulji.ac.kr.

LEE, KYO RAK, radiologist, educator; b. Seoul, Republic of Korea, Aug. 3, 1933; arrived in US, 1964, naturalized, 1976; s. Ke Chong and Ok Hi (Um) Lee; m. Ke Sook Oh Lee, July 22, 1964; children: Andrew, John. MD, Seoul Nat. U., 1959. Diplomate Am. Bd. Radiology; cert. in pediat. radiology. Intern Franklin Sq. Hosp., Balt., 1964—65; resident U. Mo. Med. Ctr., Columbia, 1965—68; instr. dept. radiology U. Mo., Columbia, 1968—69, asst. prof., 1969—71; asst. prof. dept. radiology U. Kans., Kans. City, 1971—76, assoc. prof., 1976—81, prof., 1981—. Contbr. articles to med. jours. Served with, 1950—52, Republic of Korea Army. Recipient Richard H. Marshak award, Am. Coll. Gastroenterology, 1975. Fellow: Am. Coll. Radiology; mem.: Soc. Pediat. Radiology, Korean Radiol. Soc. N.Am., Wyandotte County Med. Soc., Greater Kans. City Radiol. Soc., Kans. Radiol. Soc., Assn. U. Radiologists, Am. Roentgen Ray Soc., Radiol. Soc. N.Am. Home: 9800 Glenwood St Shawnee Mission KS 66212-1536 Office: U Kans 39th St and Rainbow Blvd Kansas City KS 66103 Office Phone: 913-588-6832. Business E-Mail: klee@kumc.edu.

LEE, KYONG SIK, surgeon, educator; b. Seoul, Republic of Korea, Jan. 1, 1937; s. Jei Eun Lee and Kum Gang Yang; m. Soin Kim, Apr. 16, 1965; children: Sung Jin, Seung jean. MD, Yonsei U., 1961, MS, 1971, PhD, 1975. Lic. physician Dept. Health, Korea, 1961, diplomate Korean Bd. Surgery, 66. Intern Severance Hosp. Yonsei U., Seoul, Republic of Korea, 1961—62, resident surgery Severance Hosp., 1962—66, prof. surgery Coll. Mediicine, 1969—2002, prof. emeritus, 2002—. Supt. Yonsei U. Hosp., Seoul, 1995—99; prof. surgery Pochan (Korea) Cha U., 2002—; dir. Bundang Cha (Korea) Hosp. Author: Management of Breast Cancer. Maj. Korea AF, 1966—69. Recipient Dedicated Med. Svc. award, Korea Hosp. Assn., 1998; named Best Breast Surgeon in Korea, Moon Hwia TV Broadcasting Co., 1997, Leader Dream Team Breast Cancer Treatment, Dong-A Newspaper Co., 2001. Fellow: ACS; mem.: Asian Breast Cancer Soc., Nat. Acad. Medicine Korea, Korean Cancer Assn., Korean Soc. Coloproctology (mem. adv. bd. 1995—, pres. 1994—95), Korean Surg. Soc. (pres. 2001—02, mem. adv. bd. 2002—), Korean Assn. Against Drug Abuse. Presbyn. Avocation: golf. Office: Bundang Cha General Hosp 351 Yatap dong Bundang gu Sungnam Gyonggi 403 712 Republic of Korea Home: Bangbai Raemlan Evernew Apt 408 137-070 Seoul Seoul Republic of Korea Office Phone: 031 780-5005. Business E-Mail: ksl@chamc.co.kr.

LEE, KYOUNG JIN, medical educator; b. Mokpo, Republic of Korea, Feb. 18, 1970; MD, Yonsei U., 1995; PhD, CHA U., 2009. Asst. prof. Gangnam CHA Hosp., CHA U., 2003—. Avocation: hiking. Office: 650-9 Yeoksam-dong Gangnam-gu Seoul 135-081 Republic of Korea Business E-Mail: jlee3575@hanmail.net.

LEE, KYU SUP, gynecologist; b. Busan, Republic Of Korea, May 1, 1954; m. Jin Sook Kim, June 7, 1980; children: Seo Wao, Jae U. PhD, Pusan Nat. U., Busan, 1987. Lic. Md Korea Med. Assn., 1978. Dir. Med. Rsch. Inst., Busan, 2004—; prof., chmn. Pusan Nat. Univ. Hosp., Busan, 2006—. Home: Centum Park Apt 113-1102 1200 Jaesong-dong Haeundae-gu Busan 612-050 Republic of Korea Office:

Pusan Nat Univ Hosp 1-10 Amidong Seoku Busan 602-730 Republic of Korea Office Fax: 82-51-248-2384; Home Fax: 82-51-248-2384. Business E-Mail: kuslee@pusan.ac.kr.

LEE, KYUNGJONG, medical educator; b. Seoul, Republic of Korea, Feb. 2, 1958; MD, Yonsei U., 1984, PhD, 1993. Prof. Ajou U. Sch. Medicine, 1994—. Cons. Korea Workers Compensation & Welfare Corp., 2005—11; editors bd. mem. Jour. Korean Occupl. and Environ. Medcine, 2008—11. Mem.: Korean Preventive Medicine and Pub. Health, Korean Occupl. and Environ. Medicine. Avocation: reading. Office: 5 Wondhon-dong Youngtong-gu Suwon Kyonggi-do 443-721 Republic of Korea Office Fax: 82-31-2195294. Business E-Mail: leekj@ajou.ac.kr.

LEE, KYUNGSOO, biomedical engineer, researcher; b. Busan, Republic of Korea, Sept. 2, 1973; Ph.D, Seoul Nat. U., 2007. Rsch. dir. AnC Bio, 2007—09; mktg. mgr. FMC Korea, 2009—10; rsch. scientist U. Mich., 2010—. Mem.: ASAIO. Home: 2309 Stone Rd Ann Arbor MI 48105 Personal E-mail: jake0902@gmail.com. Business E-Mail: jake0902@snu.ac.kr.

LEE, KYUNG-YIL, pediatrician, educator; b. Seoul, Republic of Korea, Apr. 19, 1954; s. Jong-Jin Lee and Young-Sook Jang; m. Moon-Sun Lee, Sept. 26, 1980; children: Soo-Ho children: Sung-Ho. MD, Cath. U. Korea, Seoul, 1979, PhD, 1992. Internship and resident Cath. Med. Ctr., Seoul, Seoul, Republic of Korea, 1982—86; asst. prof. Cath. U. Korea Sch. Medicine, Seoul, Republic of Korea, 1989—96, assoc. prof. Seoul, 1997—2001, prof. Seoul, 2001—; postdoctoral vis. rschr. Kyushu U. Inst. Bioregulation, Fukuoka, Japan, 1994—95. Dir., dept. pediat. Cath. U. Korea, Daejeon St. Mary's Hosp., 1993—. Contbr. articles to profl. jours. Capt. Republic of Korea Air Force, 1979—82. Roman Catholic. Avocation: Go. Office: Daejeon St Mary's Hosp Dept Pediatrics Daeheung-Dong 301-723 Daejeon Daejeon Republic of Korea Office Fax: 82-42-221-2925. Personal E-mail: leekyungyil@catholic.ac.kr.

LEE, LEONARD Y., thoracic surgeon, educator; BA, Lehigh U., Bethlehem, Pa.; MD, U. Medicine and Dentistry, 1992. Diplomate Am. Bd. Thoracic Surgery. Resident surgery St. Vincent's Hosp., NYC, 1993—97; fellow thoracic surgery Cornell Med. Ctr., NYC, 1999—2001; dir. cardiac surgery surgery program NY Meth. Hosp., chief divsn. of cardiothoracic surgery; asst. attending physician NY-Presbyn. Med. Ctr., Meml. Sloan Kettering Cancer Ctr., St. Barnabas Hosp.; assoc. clin. prof. cardiothoracic surgery Weill med. coll. Cornell Univ., NYC; dir. advanced aortic and valvular heart surgery Hackensack Univ. Med. Ctr., NJ. Recipient Disting. House Staff Award, Alumni Assn. Dept. of Cardiothoracic Surgery - NY-Presbyn. Hosp. Fellow: ACS, Am. Coll. of Chest Physicians, Am. Coll. of Cardiology. Office: Hackensack University Medical Center 30 Prospect Ave Hackensack NJ 07601 Office Phone: 201-996-2000. Office Fax: 201-343-0609.

LEE, LILLIAN VANESSA, microbiologist; b. NYC, June 1, 1951; d. Wenceslao and Ada (Otero) Cancel; m. Thomas Christopher Lee, June 11, 1972; children: Tovan, John-Peter, Phillip-Michael. BS in Biology, St. Johns U., 1972; MS in Microbiology, Wagner Coll., 1974. Cert. registered microbiologist Nat. Registry Microbiologists, specialist in microbiology Nat. Registry Microbiologists, Am. Soc. Clin. Pathologists. Grad. lab. asst. in microbiology Wagner Coll., SI, NY, 1972—74; clin. microbiology technologist Queens Hosp. Ctr., Jamaica, NY, 1974—81, supr. clin. microbiology, 1981—84; sect. head microbiology Nyack Hosp., NY, 1984—93, acting lab. mgr., 1992—93; mgr. microbiology Beth Israel Med. Ctr., NYC, 1994—97, Cabrini Med. Ctr., NYC, 1997—98, Columbia Presbyn. Med. Ctr., NYC, 1998—2002; chief gen. and enteric microbiology lab., chief microbiology biothreat response lab., chief std molecular test lab., chief microbiology svcs. N.Y.C. Dept. Health and Mental Hygiene, 2002—, chief std molecular test lab., 2005—08, chief parasitology lab., 2008—; quality assurance officer Biothreat Response Lab., 2008—. Mem. Mayor's Task Force on Biol. Warfare, 1997-2003; mem. adv. com. to Asst. Commr. on Bioterrorism and Emerging Pathogens, 2004-. Recipient Disting. Svc. award, Dept. Health Mental Hygiene, NYC, 2007. Mem.: Clin. Lab. Mgmt. Assn. (program com. 1996—97), N.Y.C. Soc. Infectious Diseases, Med. Mycology Soc. N.Y., Am. Acad. Microbiology, Am. Soc. Microbiology (N.Y.C. br. coun. 1992—, chair program com. 1993—96, co-chair program com. 1997—2001, pres. N.Y.C. br. 1999—2001), Am. Soc. Clin. Pathologists. Home: 530 E 23rd St Apt MF New York NY 10010-5046 Office: NYC DOHMH Pub Health Labs 455 First Ave New York NY 10016 Home Phone: 212-529-6585. Personal E-mail: lvlee5@yahoo.com. Business E-Mail: llee2@health.nyc.gov.

LEE, MARIE CATHERINE, medical educator; MD, Northeastern Ohio U. Coll. Medicine, 2001. Resident, gen. surgery Lenox Hill Hosp., 2005, chief resident, gen. surgery, 2006; fellow, surgical breast oncology U. Mich. Cancer Ctr., 2007, rsch. fellow, breast oncology, 2007; asst. mem. H. Lee Moffitt Cancer Ctr. & Rsch. Inst., Fla., 2007; clin. lectr., dept. surgery Mich. Comprehensive Care Ctr., 2007—. Contbr. articles to profl. jours. Office: 3302 Cancer & Geriatrics Center 1500 E Medical Center Dr Ann Arbor MI 48109-0932 Office Phone: 734-936-8771.

LEE, MARK CHONG, surgeon; b. China, Oct. 30, 1975; BS, Yale U., 1997; MD, Albert Einstein Coll. Medicine, 2001. Pediatric orthopaedic surgeon Conn. Children's Med. Ctr., 2008—. Mem.: Pediatric Orthopaedic Soc. N.America. Office: 282 Washington St Hartford CT 06106 Personal E-mail: marklee007@gmail.com.

LEE, MAU-HWA, hospital administrator; MD, Chung-Shan Med. Coll., Taiwan, 1967—72; MSc, Nat. Taiwan U., 1999—2001. Dep. supt. Chung-Hsiao Hosp., Taipei City, Taiwan, 1994—98, head dept. of internal medicine, 1997—98; dep. dir. gen. Bur. of Med. Affairs, Taipei, Taiwan, 1998—2003; supt. dept. health Taichung Hosp., Taiwan, 2003; supt. Keelung Hosp., Taiwan, 2003—09; supt. dept. of health Fong-Yuan Hosp., Taiwan, 2009—. Lectr. Sch. of Nursing King-Kuo Inst. of Technology, 1995—. Contbr. of several papers to Chinese Journal of Gastroenterology. Recipient The Efficient Hosp. of combating SARS award, Exec. Yuan, Taiwan, 2003, The Efficient Supt. of combating SARS award, 2003, Svc. Quality award, 2003, Golden Ax award, 2004. Office: Fong Yuan Hospital Department of Health No 100 An-Kan Rd Fong-Yuan City Taichung County Taiwan E-mail: info@fyh.doh.gov.tw. *

LEE, MENG-SUI, dermatologist; b. Taiwan, July 15, 1977; M, Nat. Taiwan U., 2009. Physician Taipei City Hosp., 2002—. Avocation: reading. Office: 4f 38-1 Tongde Rd Nangang Dist Taipei 115 Taiwan Personal E-mail: leemengsui@hotmail.com.

LEE, MING-TING, biochemistry professor, researcher; b. Chia-I, Taiwan, July 1, 1949; s. Kwei-Jiunn and Yeh-Shia Lee; m. Ping-Ping Hwang, Dec. 5, 1979; children: Amy Yu-Lin, Kevin Po-Hao. BS, Nat. Taiwan U., 1978; PhD, Auburn U., Ala., 1985. Vis. assoc. prof. Sch. Medicine Nat. Taiwan U., Taipei, 1992—93; assoc. prof. Inst. Biol. Chemistry Academia Sinica, Taipei, 1994—. Spkr. in field. Contbr. articles to jour. Sgt. Taiwanese Army, 1970—73. Grantee, NSC, 1995—2005. Mem.: Am. Assn. Cancer Rsch. (corr.). Home and Office: Inst Biol Chemistry Academia Sinica Academia Rd Taipei 115 Taiwan Home Fax: 886-2-27889759. Business E-Mail: mtlee@gate.sinica.edu.tw.

LEE, MINNIE JOYCELYN See ELDERS, JOYCELYN

LEE, MIN-WEI CHRISTINE, physician; b. Taipei, Taiwan, Nov. 18, 1964; BS, U. Calif., Davis, 1987, MPH, 1989; MD, U. Ill., 1993. Owner, CEO East Bay Laser & Skin Care Ctr. Inc., 1999—. Asst. clin. prof. U. Calif., Dept Dermatol. Surgery, San Francisco, 1999—; LA dermatology resident Baylor Coll. Medicine, Houston, 1995—98. Recipient President's award, Am. Soc. Dermatologic Surgery; Mohs Micrographic Surgery, Laser and Cosmetic Surgery fellowship, U. Calif., San Francisco, 1999. Fellow: Am. Soc. Laser Medicine and Surgery, Am. Acad. Cosmetic Surgery, Am. Soc. Dermatologic Surgery, Am. Acad. Dermatology, Am. Coll. Mohs Surgery. Avocations: skiing, piano, writing. Office: 1479 Ygnacio Valley Rd #209 Walnut Creek CA 94598 Office Fax: 925-256-9066. E-mail: eastbaylaser@aol.com.

LEE, MOU-SEOP, medical educator; b. Busan, Republic of Korea, Feb. 5, 1958; s. Young-Sook Lee; m. Eun-Shim Lee, Oct. 5, 1985; children: Min-Seok, Min-Ji. PhD, Seoul Nat. U., Coll. Medicine, Republic of Korea, 1992. Diplomate physician Ministry Health & Welfare, Republic of Korea, 1983, in neurosurg. 1988. Chmn., neurosurg. dept. Namgung Gen. Hosp., Cheongju, Chungbuk, Republic of Korea, 1991—92, Chungbuk Nat. U. Hosp., Cheongju, 2000—03, 2009—, dir., Clin. Med. Rsch. Inst., 2006—07; prof. Chungbuk Nat. U., Coll. Medicine, Cheongju, 1992—. Rev. bd. mem. Korean Soc. Cerebrovascular Surgery, 2005—, exec. com. mem., 1999—, Korean Spinal Neurosurgery Soc., 1999—; chmn., sci. program com. Korean Neurotraumatology Soc., 2004—; rev. bd. mem. Korean Neurosurg. Soc., Seoul, 2005—, editl. bd. mem., 2009—; mem., local rev. & evaluation com. Health Ins. Rev. Agy., Republic of Korea, 2007—. Contbr. articles to profl. jours. (Excellent Article award, 1998). Deacon Sangdang Ch., Cheongju, 2003—. Capt. Armed Forces Med. Command, 1988—90, Seoul. Mem.: Korean Neurotraumatology Soc. (congress pres. 2011—). Office: Chungbuk Nat Univ Hosp Gaeshin-dong Heungduk-gu Cheongju Chungbuk 361-763 Republic of Korea Office Fax: 82-43-273-1614. Business E-Mail: mslee@chungbuk.ac.kr.

LEE, PATRICK Y. H., colon and rectal surgeon, educator; BSChemE with honors, U. Calif., Davis, 1978—83; MD, Northwestern U., Chgo., 1984—88. Diplomate Am. Bd. Surgery, 2004, Am. Bd. Colon and Rectal Surgery, 2007. Resident in gen. surgery Loyola Univ. Med. Ctr., Maywood, Ill., 1988—90, Oregon Health Sciences Univ., Portland, 1990—94, assoc. clin. prof.; resident in colorectal surgery Cleve. Clinic Found., Ohio, 1994—95; clin. preceptor physician asst. program. Pacific Univ.; hosp. affiliations include Colon and Rectal Clinic, Legacy Good Samaritan Hosp. and Health Ctr., Providence Portland Med. Ctr., Oreg. Co-author: Total Pelvic Mesh Repair, A Ten Year Experience., 2001, Effects of Endorectal Ultrasound in the Surgical Management of Rectal Adenomas and Carcinomas, 1999, Parastomal Hernia Repair with Polypropylene Mesh Is it Safe?, 2003, Complete Pelvic Floor Repair in Treating Fecal Incontinence, 2005, Is there a role for concomitant pelvic floor repair in patients with sphincter defects in the treatment of fecal incontinence?, 2005, various others. Mem. Oreg. Crohn's and Colitis Found., 1995. Recipient Sir William Osler award, 1986, Best Resident Clin. Rsch. award, Portland Surgical Soc., 1994, Young Surgeon Travel award, ACS, 1996; named one of Top Doctors, Portland Monthly Mag., 2005—07, Portland's Best Physicians in the Portland Area, 2008, numerous others. Fellow: ACS, Am. Soc. Colon and Rectal Surgeons; mem.: Columbia River Oncology Group, Nat. Cancer Inst., Multnomah Med. Soc., Oreg. Med. Assn., Northwest Soc. Colon and Rectal Surgeons, Portland Surgical Soc., North Pacific Surgeons, Pacific Coast Surgical, Internat. Soc. Colon and Rectal Surgeons. Office: Providence Portland Medical Center 4805 NE Glisan St Portland OR 97213 Office Phone: 503-215-1111.

LEE, PAUL P., ophthalmologist, educator, lawyer; b. Taipei, Taiwan, 1960; BA, U. Mich., 1981, MD, 1986; JD, Columbia U., 1986. Bar: Md. 1987, D.C. 1988. Congl. intern U.S. House Select Commn. on Aging, Washington, 1980; biologist NASA, Cape Canaveral, Fla., 1981; med. intern Beth Israel Hosp., Boston, 1986—87; resident ophthalmology Johns Hopkins Hosp., Balt., 1987—90; fellow glaucoma Mass. Eye & Ear Infirmary, Boston, 1990—91; asst. prof. U. So. Calif., LA, 1991—95, assoc. prof., 1995—97; prof. Duke U., Durham, NC, 1997—, James Pitzer Gills III, MD and Joy Gills prof. ophthalmology, 2003—; sr. advisor, chancellor Duke U. Health Sys., 2009—. Bd. dirs. ARVO Found., Prevent Blindness Am. Mem. editl. bd. Archives Ophthalmology, Evidence-Based Ophthalmology, Chinese Jour. Ophthalmology; contbr. articles to profl. jours. Rsch. fellowship Brookdale Inst. on Aging, 1985; sr. fellow Ctr. Aging Duke U., Ctr. for Clin. Health Policy Rsch. Duke U.; Stone scholar Columbia U. Law Sch., 1985 Mem. AMA, ABA, Am. Acad. Ophthalmology (bd. trustees 2000-04), Chinese-Am. Ophthalmology Soc., Assn. for Rsch. in Vision and Ophthalmology Office Phone: 919-681-2793. Business E-Mail: lee00106@mc.duke.edu.

LEE, PAUL YUE-YAN, surgeon; b. Hong Kong, Aug. 30, 1938; arrived in U.S., 1959; MD, U. Oreg., 1967. Intern Wayne County Gen. Hosp., Eloise, Mich., 1967-68; resident Kern Gen. Hosp., Bakersfield, Calif., 1968-72; with Bellflower Kaiser-Permanente Med. Ctr., Calif., 1972—. Mem.: ACS. Office: Kaiser Permanente Med Ctr 9400 Rosecrans Ave Bellflower CA 90706-2217 Office Phone: 562-461-4622. Personal E-mail: mabalee@aol.com. Business E-Mail: pauly.lee@kp.org. *

LEE, PHIL HYU, neurologist; b. Seogwipo, Republic of Korea, Oct. 1, 1968; s. Cheon Ryun Lee and Chun Ja Han; m. Hyo Young Youm; children: Jee Sun, Jung Wook. MD, Yonsei U., 1994, PhD, 2004. Medical Diplomate Korean Med. Assn., Seoul, 1994, Neurologist Diplomate Korean Neurol. Assn., 1999. Internship Yonsei U. Severance Hosp., Seoul, Republic of Korea, resident; asst. prof. Ajou U. Coll. of Medicine, Suwon, Republic of Korea, 2004—. Contbr. articles to profl. jours. Capt. Army, 1999—2002. Grant, Ministry of Health and Welfare, 2004. Home: Yeongtong 1-Dong Daewoo APT 305-1904 Gyeonggi-Do Suwon 956-2 Republic of Korea Office Fax: 82-31-219-5175. Personal E-mail: phisland@chol.net. E-mail: phlee@ajou.ac kr.

LEE, RAPHAEL CARL, plastic surgeon, biomedical engineer; b. Sumter, SC, Oct. 29, 1949; s. Leonard Powell and Jean Maurice (Langston) L.; m. Kathleen Kelley, Feb. 11, 1983; children: Rachel, Catherine. BS, U. SC, 1971, DSc (hon.), 2000; MS, Drexel U., 1975; MD, Temple U., 1975; ScD, MIT, 1979. Diplomate Am. Bd. Plastic Surgeons, Am. Bd. Surgery. Chief resident gen. surgery U. Chgo. Hosps., 1980-81; chief resident plastic surgery Mass. Gen. Hosp., 1982-83; dir. Elec. Trauma Rsch. Program, 1991—; med. dir. U. Chgo. Burn Unit, 1991-97. Asst. prof. surgery Harvard Med. Sch., 1984—89; VanTassel asst. prof. elec. and bioengring. MIT, 1983—89; asst. prof. bioengring. and surgery Harvard MIT, Divsn. Health Scis. and Tech., 1983—89; Russell prof. surgery, medicine, molecular medicine, anatomy & bioengring. U. Chgo., 1992—, pres. Quadrangle Club; chmn. bd. dirs. Avocet Polymers Techs., Inc., 1996—; exec. com. Biomed. Engring. Inst., Ill. Inst. Tech.; founder, dir. Maroon Biotech., Inc.; founder, chmn. bd. dirs. Electrokinetics Signal Rsch., Inc.; founder, dir. Renacyte BioMolecular Tech., Inc.; Paul Russel prof. Author: Electrical Injury, Multidisciplinary Approach, 1994, Occupational Electrical Injury, 1999; editor: Electrical Trauma, Pathophysiology, 1992; assoc. editor Bioelectromagnetics, 1993—; contbr. more than 200 articles to profl. jours. Recipient Disting. Alumni award Temple Med. Sch., 1995, U. Cardina, 1998, Drexel U., 2009, Searle Scholar award The Searle Found., 1985-88, award for advancing safety and health Am. Electric Power Assn.; named Ams. 100 Brightest Young Scientists Sci. Digest, 1984; MacArthur Prize fellow John D. and Catherine T. MacArthur Found., 1981-86. Fellow ACS (Schering scholar in Surgery 1978), AAAS, Am. Inst. Med. and Biol. Engring.(pres.); mem. IEEE, Am. Burn Assn. (Lindberg award), Am. Phys. Soc., Am. Soc. for Cell Biology, Am. Assn. Plastic Surgeons (James Barrett Brown award 1988), Biophys. Soc., Nat. Med. Assn. (plastic surgery sect. chmn. 1989-91), Soc. for Phys. Regulation in Biology and Medicine (pres. 1995), Soc. Univ. Surgeons, Surg. Biology Club III, Tau Beta Pi, Alpha Omega Alpha, Sigma Xi, Drexel 100 (pres., bd. trustees). Achievements include 12 patents. Office: U Chgo Hosps Pritzker Sch Medicine-Surgery MC6035 5841 S Maryland Ave Chicago IL 60637-1463 Office Phone: 773-702-6302, 312-733-0669. Business E-Mail: r-lee@uchicago.edu, rlee@avocetcorp.com.

LEE, RICHARD VAILLE, internist, educator; b. Islip, NY, May 26, 1937; s. Louis Emerson and Erma Natalie (Little) L.; m. Susan Bradley, June 25, 1961; children: Matthew, Benjamin. BS, Yale U., 1960, MD cum laude, 1964. Diplomate Am. Bd. Internal Medicine, Am. Bd. Family Practice. Intern Grace-New Haven Hosp., 1964-65, asst. resident in internal medicine, 1965-66, 69-70, fellow in inflammatory disease Yale U., New Haven, 1970-71, asst. prof. medicine, 1971-74, assoc. prof. clin. medicine, 1974-76; practice medicine specializing in internal medicine New Haven, 1969-76, Buffalo, 1976—; family practice Poplar, Mont., 1966-68, Chester, Mont., 1968-69; prof. medicine SUNY, Buffalo, 1976—, prof. pediat., 1985—, adj. prof. anthropology, 1989—, prof. obstetrics, 1992—, chief divsn. gen. internal medicine, 1979-82, chief divsn. maternal and adolescent medicine, 1982—, chief divsn. geog. medicine, 1991—; dir. primary care ctr. Yale-New Haven Hosp., 1975-76, dir. med. clinics, 1971-75; chief med. svc. Buffalo VA Hosp., 1976-79, foundary editor, 2008; head dept. medicine Children's Hosp. Buffalo, 1979-96; fellow WHO Collaborating Ctr. for Health in Housing, 1985—, chief med. officer, 1995—. Cons. internal medicine N.Y. Zool. Soc., 1973—; cons. physician Buffalo Zool. Soc., 1980—; aviation med. examiner, 1980—2001; med. dir. Ecology and Environment, Inc., Lancaster, NY; mem. N.Y. State Bd. for Medicine, 1995—2002; mem. com. Nat. Bd. Med. Examiners, 1999—; mem. N.Y. State Office for Profl. Med. Conduct, 2001—10; mem., bd. govs. Shaw Festival, Niagara Lake Ont., Canada, 2010—. Author: Outside Rounds, 2005; editor: When I Was a Boy in China, 2003; sr. editor: Current Obstetric Medicine, 1989—95; corr. editor Jour. Obstetrics and Gynecology, London, 1989—; mem. editl. bd.: Internat. Jour. Environ. Health, 1994—; cons. editor Am. Jour. Medicine, 1976—86, chair editl. bd. Obstetric Medicine, 2008—11; contbr. chapters to books on obstetrics and toxicology, articles to profl. jours. Served with USPHS, 1966-68. Recipient C.G. Barnes award, Internat. Soc. Obs. Medicine, 2006—. Fellow: ACP (sr. editor Med. Care of the Pregnant Patient 2000, contbg. editor Med. Care of the Pregnant Patient, 2d edit. 2008, Laureate award 2002), Royal Soc. Asian Affairs, Royal Geog. Soc., Explorers Club N.Y.C.; mem.: AMA, Am. Coll. Occupl. and Environ. Medicine, Internat. Soc. of Travel Medicine, Soc. Obstetric Medicine (pres. 1991—93, C. G. Barnes award for disting. svc. to obstetric medicine 2006), Infectious Disease Soc. Am., Am. Soc. Tropical Medicine and Hygiene, Gen. Internal Medicine, Am. Fedn. Clin. Rsch. Soc., N.Y. Acad. Sci., Yale China Assn. (trustee 1992—2001, sec. 1995—2001), Nat. Bd. Med. Examiners, Am. Soc. History of Medicine, Royal Soc. Medicine, Great Lakes Interurban Clin. Club, Alpha Omega Alpha. Achievements include editing and reprinting, with introduction and photographs, his grandfather's book When I Was a Boy In China, 2003. Home: 7664 East Quaker Rd Orchard Park NY 14127-2015 Office Phone: 716-684-8060.

LEE, SAI-CHEONG, physician, researcher; b. Hong Kong, China, June 18, 1951; s. Chi-Kong Lee and Kam Chan; m. Chung-Ping Lue; children: Chao-Wei, Chao_Hsuan. MD, Taipei Med. U., Taipei, 1977. Vice-chmn., infection control com. Chang Gung Meml. Hosp., Keelung, Taiwan, 1992—, chief, divsn. infectious diseases, 2002—. Assoc. prof. Chang Gung U., Linkou, 2005—; reviewer Jour. Infectious Diseases Soc. Taiwan. Editor: Infectious Disease Soc. of Taiwan, 1996—; contbr. articles to jours. Rsch. plan reviewer Nat. Sci. Com., Taipei, Taiwan, 2004, Chang Gung Meml. Hosp. Mem.: Am. Soc. Microbiology (assoc.). Achievements include research in invasive candida infections, antifungal susceptibility test, methicilin-resistant S. aureus. Office Fax: 886-24335342. Business E-Mail: lee.sch@msa.hinet.net.

LEE, SANG HEE, microbiologist, educator; b. Youngdong-gun, Chungbuk, Republic of Korea, Sept. 30, 1960; s. Jae Hong Lee and Young Sun You; m. Hye Jeong Song; 1 child, Jaepil David. PhD, Seoul Nat. U., Republic of Korea, 1993. Rsch. assoc. Genetic

Engring. Inst. Seoul (Republic of Korea) Nat. U., 1990—92; postdoctoral rsch. assoc. U. Wis. Madison, 1993—95; assoc. prof. Youngdong U., Youngdong-gun, Chungbuk, Republic of Korea, 1995—2003; prof. Dept. Biol. Sci. Myongji U., Yongin, Republic of Korea, 2003—. Cons. Korean Bus. Newspaper, Seoul, 2000—, Small and Medium Bus. Admintrns., Cheongju, Chungbuk, 2001—; dir.-gen. R&D MB Biotech Inc., 2003—; evaluator Korea Inst. S&T Evaluation and Planning, 2003—, Korean Inst. Indsl. Tech. Evaluation and Planning, 2004—; tech. advisor Lee & Joe Biotech, inc., 2003—, Ovobio Co., Ltd., 2003—; mem. evaluation team Korean broadcasting Sys., 2003—; dep. dir. gen. Internat. Biographical Ctr., England, 2005—. Editor: Microorganisms and Industry, 2003, Korean Jour. Microbiology, 2005—06, Acad. Jours. Inc., 2006—, Recent Patents on Anti-Infective Drug Discovery, 2006—, Jour. Microbiology, 2007—; editor-in-chief: Rsch. Jour. Microbiology, 2006—; reviewer Jour. Applied Microbiology, 2003—. Pvt. Republic of Korea Army, 1981—84. Recipient Min. award, Ministry Edn. and Human Resources Devel., 2003, Best Rsch. award, Youngdong U., 2001, Myongji U., 2006—, Health Industry Devel. Merit award, Korean Ministry Health and Welfare, 2006, Best Edn. award, Ministry Edn. & Human Resources Devel., 2011; named Knight of Justice, Sovereign Order of Knights of Justice, Eng., 2007; fellow, Found. Rsch. Ctr. Molecular Microbiology, Seoul Nat. U., 1990, 1991. Mem.: Am. Soc. Microbiology (full mem. of antimicrobial chemotherapy 2001—). Roman Catholic. Achievements include contributions to design of rapid identification methods for antibiotic resistance genes; discovery of novel antibiotic resistance genes; biochemistry and X-ray crystal structure of extended-spectrum B-lactamase and carbapenemases causing antibiotic resistance; development of novel antibiotics. Avocation: tennis. Office: Myongji Univ Dept Biol Sci San 38-2 Namdong Yongin Gyeonggi 449-728 Republic of Korea Office Fax: 82 31 335 8249. Business E-Mail: sangheelee@mju.ac.kr.

LEE, SANG KOOK, pharmacist, educator; b. Changwon, Republic of Korea, Aug. 24, 1961; s. Seung-Up Lee and Soonja Kang; m. Kyung-mi Cho, Nov. 1, 1992; children: Seung Hoon, Jeong Hoon. BS, Seoul Nat. U., Republic of Korea, 1985, MS, 1987; PhD, U. Ill., Chgo., 1997. Registered pharmacist South Korea. Sr. rschr. Pacific Corp., Seoul, 1987—93; postdoctoral rsch. assoc. U. Ill., Chgo., 1997—99; asst. prof. Ewha Woman's U., Seoul, 1999—. Mem.: Pharm. Soc. Korea, Am. Soc. Pharmacognosy, Am. Assn. Cancer Rsch. Office: Ewha Woman's U Coll Pharmacy 11-1 Daehyun-dong Seoul 120-750 Republic of Korea Office Phone: (02) 3277-3023. Office Fax: (02) 3277-2851. Business E-Mail: sklee@ewha.ac.kr.

LEE, SANG KUN, neurologist, educator; b. Seoul, Republic of Korea, Jan. 6, 1963; s. Hong Soo Lee and Gil Ja Kim; m. Jong Hee Lee, Aug. 25, 1989; children: Kwun Hee, Yoon Ji. MD, Korea U.Coll. Medicine, Seoul, 1987, PhD, 1994. Lic. med. Dr. Seoul Nat. U./Seoul, Korea, 1987, neurologist Seoul Nat. U. Hosp./Seoul, Korea, 1991. Asst. prof. Seoul Nat. U. Coll. of Medicine, Republic of Korea, 1994—2000, assoc. prof., 2000—05, prof., 2005—. Sec. treasurer Korean Neurol. Assn., Seoul, Republic of Korea, 2002—04; sec. gen. Korean Epilepsy Soc.; editor-in-chief Jour. Korean Epilepsy Soc., 2005—07; chair sci. com. Korean Epilepsy Soc., 2007—; consulting editor Epilepsy Rsch., 2011—. Contbr. scientific papers, articles to profl. jours. Achievements include research in epileptology; neuroimaging, epilepsy surgery. Home: 335 Dong-16 Ho Jamwon-dong Seoch-gu Seoul 137-951 Republic of Korea Office: SNUH Dept Neurology #28 Yeungon-dong Chongno-gu Seoul 110-744 Republic of Korea Office Fax: 82-2-2072-1785. E-mail: sangunlee@dreamwiz.com.

LEE, SANG-HO, hospital administrator; MD, Pusan Nat. U., So. Korea; PhD. Founder and pres. Wooridul Spine Hosp, Seoul, Republic of Korea. Author: (poem) The Road Beyond the Fog, 1987, (book) Lumbar Disc, 1998, (text book) Percutaneous Cervical Discectomy with Forceps and Endoscopic Ho: YAG Laser, Lasers in the Musculoskeletal System, 2002. Mem.: Asian Acad. of Minimally Invasive Spinal Surgery (AAMISS) (founding pres.), Internat. Musculoskeletal Laser Soc. (IMLAS) (pres.-elect). Office: Seoul Wooridul Hospital 676 Gwahae-dong Gangseo-gu Seoul 157-822 Republic of Korea E-mail: wipc@wooridul.co.kr. *

LEE, SANG-HUN, medical educator; b. Chuncheon, Kangwon-do, Republic of Korea, Nov. 27, 1969; s. Dong-Su Lee and Gwi-Ye Kim; m. Hee-Jin Lim, May 10, 1997; children: Ui-Jun, Ye-Jun. MD, Kyung-Hee U., Seoul, Korea, 1994; MA, Kyung-Hee U., 2004; PhD, Kyung Hee U., 2006. Lic. Korean Med. Assn., 1994, orthop. surgeon Korean Orthop. Assn., 1999. Asst. prof. Hallym U. Med. Ctr., Youngdungpo-gu, Seoul, 2003—05, Kyung Hee U. Hosp. Gangdong, Kangdong-gu, Seoul, 2006—. Contbr. articles to profl. jours. Capt. pub. health, 1999—2002, Kyunggi-do. Recipient Best Paper award, Korean Orthop. Assn., 2005, Pacific-Asian Soc. Minimally Invasive Spine Surgery, 2005. Mem.: Korean Soc. Spine Surgery (sec. gen. basic rsch. com. 2007—08, Best Paper award 2006), Cervical Spine Rsch. Soc. (corr.), N.Am. Spine Soc. (corr.). Home: 417-1202 Hyundai Apt Seohyun-don Kyunggi-do Seongnam Republic of Korea Office: 149 Sangil-dong Seoul Kangdong-gu 134-727 Republic of Korea Office Phone: 822 440 6152. Office Fax: 822 440 7494. Business E-Mail: shl6@khu.ac.kr.

LEE, SANG-HYUK, psychiatrist, educator; b. Seoul, Republic of Korea, Feb. 7, 1970; s. Myung-Woo Lee; m. Ji-Eun Kim, Sept. 5, 2002; children: Geon-seob, Kang-seob. MD, Yonsei U., Seoul, 1995, PhD, 2007. Clin. fellow Yonsei U., Seoul, 2001—02; asst. prof. Pochon CHA U., Seongnam, Kyounggi, Republic of Korea, 2003—; cons. Nat. Pension Program, Republic of Korea, 2007—, Happy Family Found., Republic of Korea. Bd. mem. gen. com. Korean Acad. Anxiety Disorder, Korean Psychosomatic Soc., Korean Schizophrenia Soc., 2008—. Contbr. articles to profl. jours. Grant, Janssen Korea, 2006, Wyers, 2007. Mem.: Korean Acad. Neuropsychiatry, Korean Psychosomatic Soc., Korean Coll. Neuropsychopharmacology, Korean Schizophrenia Soc., Korean Acad. Anxiety Disorder. Home: 102-1504 Seonkyoung Apartment Yatap Seongnam Kyounggi 101-116 Republic of Korea Office: Psychiatry Bundang CHA Hosp Yatap 351 463-712 Seongnam Kyoung-Gi Republic of Korea Office Phone: 82-31-780-5874. Office Fax: 82-31-780-5862. Personal E-mail: drshlee27@gmail.com. Business E-Mail: drshlee@naver.com.

LEE, SANG-KOON, obstetrician/gynecologist; b. Kwangju, Chollanam-Do, Republic of Korea, Nov. 25, 1929; s. Tae-Sok Lee and Sa-Soon Kim; m. Soo-Nam Yoon, Apr. 24, 1953; 1 child, Chin-Hee. MD, Chonnam U., Kwangju, 1956, MMS, 1962, DMS, 1967; MPH, Johns Hopkins U., 1964. Intern dept. ob-gyn. Chonnam U. Hosp., Kwangju, 1956-57, resident dept. ob-gyn., 1960-63; from instr. to assoc. prof. Med. Sch. Chonnam U., Kwangju, 1964-74; clin. prof. Med. Sch. Jung Ang. U., Seoul, Republic Korea, 1975-80, Med. Sch. Han Yang U., Seoul, 1980—; practice medicine specializing in ob-gyn. Kwangju, 1974—. Contbr. articles to profl. jours. Mem. Internat. Friendship Force, Kwangju, 1985—, UN Assn., Republic Korea, 1997—. Served to capt. Republic KoreaArmy Med. Corps, 1957-60. Mem. Internat. Microsurg. Soc., Royal Asiatic Soc., Korean-Brit. Soc., Planned Parenthood Fedn. Korea, Korean Assn. Vol. Sterilization, Korean Assn. Ob-Gyn. (v.p. 1983-84, pres. 1995-96), Am. Assn. Gyn. Laparoscopists, Am. Fertility Soc., Green Kwangju Club, Rotary Internat. (pres. Kwangju-South chpt. 1977-78, dist. sec. 1985-86, gov. 1994-95). Avocations: walking, jogging, calligraphy, gardening. Home and Office: 38 Daein-dong Dong-ku Kwangju 500 Republic of Korea

LEE, SANG-SOO, medical educator, researcher; b. Daejeon, Republic Of Korea, Sept. 16, 1958; s. Lee and Nam; married; children: Hye-Ree, J-Joon. MD, Korea U., Seoul, 1983, PhD, 1993. Rsch. fellow Mayo Clinic, Rochester, Minn., 1994—96, maj. peripheral nerve; prof. Chungbuk Nat. U., Cheongju-si, Chungbuk, Republic of Korea, 1991—. Mem.: Korean Neurol. Assn. Office: Chungbuk National University Hospital 52 Naesudong-ro Cheongju Chungbuk 361-711 Republic of Korea Office Fax: 82-43-275-7591. Business E-Mail: sslee@chungbuk.ac.kr.

LEE, SANG-YEOL, psychiatrist, educator; b. Jeonju, Jeonbuk, Republic of Korea, Oct. 6, 1962; s. Young-Woo and Mo-Soon Lee; m. Hye-Jin Lee, Oct. 11, 1988; children: Hwa-Yeon, Chan. MD, Wonkwang Med. Sch., Iksan, Cheonbuk, Republic of Korea, 1987; PhD, Jeonbuk Med. Postgrad. Sch., Jeonju, 1991. Lic. psychiatrist. Intern Wonkwang U. Hosp., Iksan, 1987—88, resident, 1988—91; instr. Wonkwang U. Med. Sch., Iksan, 1994—95, asst. prof., 1996—2000, assoc. prof., 2000—. Clin. fellow U. Health Network, Toronto, Ont., Canada, 1998—2000. Author: Functional Dyspepsia, 2000, Irritable Bowel Syndrome, 2003. Recipient Insong award, Korean Psychiat. Assn., Seoul, 1991. Office: Wonkwang Psychiat Hosp 144-23 Dongsan-dong Iksan Cheonbuk Republic of Korea Home: 5th Apt Mottyun-Dong 404-1607 Hyun Dai Iksan Cheonbuk Republic of Korea

LEE, SEI J., geriatrician, researcher; BA in Chemistry, U. Chgo., 1991; MD with honors, U. Ill. Coll. Medicine, 1999. Analytical chemist G.D. Searle & Co., Skokie, Ill., 1993—94; analytical biochemist Calypte Biomed., Berkeley, Calif., 1995; resident internal medicine U. Calif., San Francisco, 1999—2002, fellow geriatrics, 2006—07, asst. prof. medicine, divsn. geriatrics, 2007—; physician Kaiser Permanente, South San Francisco Med.l Ctr., 2002—04; clin. rsch. fellow San Francisco VA Med. Ctr., 2004—06, staff physician, geriatrics & extended care, 2007—. Contbr. articles to profl. jours. Recipient Hartford Geriatrics Health Outcomes Rsch. Scholars award, AGS Found. Health in Aging, 2008. Mem.: Am. Geriatrics Soc., Soc. Hosp. Medicine, Soc. General Internal Medicine. Achievements include research in the prediction of disease outcome among elderly patients and to explore the application of geriatric prognostic information to improve patient care. Office: Univ Calif Box VA 181G 4150 Clement St San Francisco CA 94124 Office Phone: 415-221-4810 ext. 4543. Office Fax: 415-750-6641. E-mail: sei.lee@ucsf.edu, sei.lee@med.va.gov. *

LEE, SEONG-HUN, biotechnologist, researcher; b. Seoul, Republic of Korea, Feb. 3, 1965; s. Dal-Shin Lee and Hong-Ja Do; m. Hyun-Young Kim, Dec. 3, 1994; 1 child, Yoo-Vin. BS in Biology, Konkuk U., Seoul, 1991, MS in Microbiology, 1993; PhD in Molecular Palnt Cell Engring., U. Seoul, 2010. Rschr. Shinpoong Pharm. Co., Ansan, 1994—95, Agr. Tech. Devel. Ctr., Paju, 1998—2002, Nat. Agrl. Products Quality Mgmt. Svc., Seoul, Republic of Korea, 2002—. Rsch. advisor Korea FDA, Seoul, 2004—; spl. cons. Korea Rsch. Inst. Stds. and Sci., Daejeon, 2004—; profl. cons. Korean Agy. Tech. and Stds., Seoul, 2007—, Nat. Inst. Environ. Rsch., Incheon, Republic of Korea, 2007—; spl. advisor Nat. Plant Quarantine Svc., Anyang, 2007—. Contbr. articles to profl. jours. Sgt. Korean Mil., 1987—89. Holiness Ch. Achievements include patents for detection methods for GM maize; detection methods for GM cotton. Avocation: music. Home: 309-901 Dalvit Maeul Hwajeong-Dong Deokyang-Gu Goyang Gyeonggi-Do Republic of Korea 412-271 Office: Nat Agrl Products Quality Mgmt Svc 560 3-Ga Dangsan-Dong Youngdeungpo-Gu Seoul Republic of Korea 150-043 Office Phone: 82-2-2165-6080. Office Fax: 82-2-2165-6005. Personal E-mail: starslee7@hanmail.net. Business E-Mail: starlee65@korea.kr.

LEE, SEONG-RYONG, medical educator; b. Taegu, Republic Of Korea, Jan. 17, 1966; s. Young-Seok Lee and Soo-Jung Song; m. Yeun-Kyung Chu, Dec. 20, 1998; children: Chae-Hyun (Kayla), Yu-Bin, Jun-Hyun. MD, Keimyung U., Taegu, Republic of Korea, 1989; PhD, Korea U., Seoul, 1994. Instr. pharmacology Keimyung U. Sch. Medicine, Taegu, 1997—99, asst. prof. pharmacology, 1999—2003, assoc. prof. pharmacology, 2003—. Planning dir. Brain Rsch. Inst., Keimyung U., 2005—. Contbr. articles to profl. jours. Fellow, Keimyung U. Sch. Medicine, 1992—97; scholar, Mass. Gen. Hosp., Harvard Med. Sch., Dept. Radiology and Neurology, Boston, 2002—04; Joongwae scholar, 2005. Office: Pharmacology Schl of Med Keimyung Univ 194 Dongsan dong Taegu 700-712 Republic of Korea Office Fax: 82-53-250-7016. Business E-Mail: srlee@kmu.ac.kr.

LEE, SEONG-WOOK, molecular biologist, educator; b. Seoul, Republic of Korea, Feb. 8, 1963; s. Eui-Young Lee and Ok-Sook Kim; m. Soonyoung Hwang, July 12, 1989; children: Seok-Joon, Hyun-Ji. BS, Seoul Nat. U., 1985, MS, 1987; PhD, Cornell U., 1995. Rschr. KIST, Seoul, 1988—89; grad. rsch. asst. Meml. Sloan-Kettering Cancer Ctr., NYC, 1989—94; rsch. assoc. Duke U. Med. Ctr., Durham, NC, 1994—97, vis. scholar, 1997—2008; prof. dept. molecular biology Dankook U., Gyeonggi-do, 1997—; co-CEO Genoprot Inc., Seoul, 2000—04; dir. Inst. Nanosensor and Biotech., Republic of Korea, 2004—; adj. rschr. Advanced Insts. Convergence Tech., Gyeonggi-do, 2009—. Author: Gene Therapy for HIV Infection, 1998, Human Gene Therapy, 2003; mem. editl. bd. Biochemistry News, 1998—99, Molecular Biology News, 2000; mem. editl. bd.: Genomics & Informatics, 2004—; editor: JNBT, 2004—, Nucleic Acid Ther, 2011—; contbr. articles to profl. jours.; editl. bd. mem. World Jours. biol. Chemistry, 2010—, pres. Korean Oligonueleotide Therapeutics Soc., 2011—, editl. bd. mem. Oligoneucliotides, 2011—. Lt. Korean Mil., 1987—88. Grantee Rsch. grantee, Korea Rsch. Found., 1997—, Korea Sci. and Engring. Found., 1998—, Ministry of Health and Welfare, 1998—. Mem.: Korea Bioforum, Am. Soc. Gene Therapy. Achievements include noted articles for RNA-based therapeutics and diagnostics; patents for antibody to amino-RNA and its generation method; RNA aptamer against HCV, NFAT, CEA; trans-splicing ribozyme against HCV & cancer and for molecular imaging. Office: Dankook U Dept Mol Biology 126 Jukjeon-dong Suji-gu Yongin Gyeonggi-do 448-701 Republic of Korea Office Phone: 82-31-8005-3195.

LEE, SEUNG HUN, dermatologist, educator; b. Seoul, Jan. 22, 1953; s. Jae Hoon and Eun Gu (Ye) L.; m. Soo Kyung Oh, Dec. 25, 1982; 1 child, Hae Jin. MD, Yonsei U., Seoul, 1977, MS, 1980, PhD, 1985. Intern Yonsei Med. Ctr., Seoul, 1977—78, resident in dermatology, 1978—82; instr. Coll. Medicine Yonsei U., Wonju, Republic of Korea, 1985—87, asst. prof. Coll. Medicine, 1987—88, asst. prof. Wonju Coll. Medicine, 1988—91, assoc. prof., 1991—92, chmn. dept. dermagology Wonju Coll. Medicine, 1991—92, assoc. prof. Coll. Medicine Seoul, 1992—99, prof. Coll. Medicine, 1999—; chmn. dept. dermatology Yonsei U. Coll. Medicine, 2002—07; dir. Skin Biology Rsch. Inst., 2004—07, Human Barrier Rsch. Inst., 2008—; chief dept. dermatology Gangnam Severence Hosp., Seoul, 1992—2001, dir. divsn. edn./rsch., 2001—02, vice gen. dir., 2007—09. Author (in Korean): Common Skin Disease, 1993, Skin Disease, 1994, Skin Tumor Atlas, 1997, Focus in Dermatology, 1999, Skin Aesthetics, 2002, Medical Body Care, 2006, Medical Skin Care, 2009, Skin Barrier, 2010. Bd. dirs. Upper Room Evangelistic Assn., Seoul, 1985-2008. 2d lt. Korean inf., 1982-85. Mem. Korean Dermatol. Assn. (acad. affairs, exec. com. 1995-97, ednl. program 1997-99, bd. dirs. 1999—2008, v.p. 2009-10), Seoul Dermatol. Soc. (sec. gen. 1986-88, sci. affairs 1994-96), Aerospace Med. Assn. Korea (bd. dirs. 1994-2001), Korean Sexually Transmitted Disease Assn. (exec. com. acad. affairs 1993-95, bd. dirs. 2000-2004), Korean Soc. Skin Barrier Rsch. (v.p. 1995-99, pres. 1999-02, hon. pres. 2004—), Korean Soc. for Investigative Dermatology (bd. dirs. 2000-02), Korean Soc. Cosmetic Dermatology (chmn. bd. dirs. 2000-04, pres. 2006—08), Pan Asian Pacific Skin Barrier Rsch. Soc. (pres. 2010-). Office: Yonsei U Coll Medicine Gangnam Severance Hosp 146-92 211 Eonjuro Gangnam Seoul 135-270 Republic of Korea Home Phone: (02) 516-8669. Business E-Mail: ydshderm@yuhs.ac.

LEE, SEUNG-KOOK, plastic surgeon; Grad., Yonsei U. Coll. Medicine. Plastic surgery specialist Inje Univ. Paik Hosp; surgeon Real Cosmetic Clinic. Mem.: Korean Cleft-Palate-Craniofacial Assn., Korean Soc. Aesthetic Plastic Surgery, Korean Soc. Plastic and Reconstructive Surgeons. Office: Real Cosmetic Clinic Asio B/D 580 Shinsa-Dong Gangnam-Gu Seoul 135892 Republic of Korea Office Phone: 8225121616. Office Fax: 8225111313. *

LEE, SEUNG-OK, medical educator; b. Jeonju, Republic of Korea, Aug. 27, 1966; MD, Chonbuk Nat. U., Republic of Korea, 1991, PhD, 2001. Assoc. prof., divsn. gastroenterology, hepatology, dept. internal medicine Chonbuk Nat. U. Med. Sch. & Hosp., 2002—. Office: 634-18 Keumam-Dong Deokjin-Ku Jeonju Jeonbuk 561-180 Republic of Korea Office Fax: 82-63-254-1609. Business E-Mail: solee@chonbuk.ac.kr.

LEE, SHAO-LUN, engineering educator; b. Taiwan, Nov. 8, 1969; PhD, Tamkang U., 2004. Asst. prof. Oriental Inst. Tech., 2004—. Office: 58 Sec 2 Sihchuan Rd Pan-Chiao Dist New Taipei 22061 Taiwan Business E-Mail: sllee@mail.oit.edu.tw.

LEE, SHIN-DA, physical therapy professor, department chair; b. Taichung, Taiwan, Mar. 30, 1970; s. Chin-Shou Lee and Mei-Chin Chen; m. Shu-Ping Lee, Mar. 6, 2004. BS in Phys. Therapy, Kaohsiung Med. U., Taiwan, 1993; MS, SUNY, Buffalo, 1999, PhD, 2001. Lic. phys. therapist Health Adminstrn. Taiwan, 1996. Asst. prof. dept. phys. therapy Chung-Shan Med. U., Taichung, 2001—05; dept. chair, assoc. prof. dept. phys. therapy China Med. U., Taichung, 2005—08; chair, prof. dept. phys. therapy Grad. Inst. Rehabitation Sci. China Med. U.; dean internat. affairs China Med. U., 2011—. Contbr. articles to profl. jours. Recipient Carlton R. Meyers award, SUNY Buffalo, 1999, Travel Grand award, Am. Thoracic Soc., 2000, Top Ten Outstanding Young Person award, Taiwan, 2010. Achievements include research in cardiopulmonary abnormalities in modern diseases such as obesity, diabetes, hypertension, metabolic syndrome and sleep apnea. Home: 13F No369 Sanmin W Rd Taichung 40244 Taiwan Office: China Medical University 91 Hsueh-Shih Rd Taichung 40202 Taiwan Office Fax: 886-422065051; Home Fax: 886-422065051. Personal E-mail: leeshinda@gmail.com. Business E-Mail: shinda@mail.cmu.edu.tw.

LEE, SHIN-SEOK, medical educator; b. Gwangju, Republic of Korea, Apr. 13, 1965; s. Ahn-Seop Lee and Hwan Kook; m. Hyang-Lim Kim, Jan. 14, 1967; children: Soo-Hoon, Soo-Min, Soo-Hyun. MD, PhD, Chonnam Nat. U. Med. Sch., Gwangju, 1998. Medical Diplomate Korean Med. Assn., 1989, Board of Internal Medicine Korean Med. Assn., 1994, Board of Rheumatology Korean Med. Assn., 2000. Clin. instr. Chonnam Nat. U. Hosp., 1997—2002; asst. prof. Chonnam Nat. U. Med. Sch., Gwangju, 2002—08, assoc. prof., 2008—. Vis. prof. Johns Hopkins U., 2005—07. Deacon by election Gwangju First Presbyn. Ch., 2003—. Capt. Korean Army, 1994—97, Seoul. Recipient First Prize, Korean Assn. of Internal Medicine, 2003, Korean Rheumatism Assn., 2003, 2002, Best Mil. Servie, Divisino Comdr., 1997. Mem.: Korean Med. Assn. (licentiate), Korean Assn. Internal Medicine (licentiate), Korean Rheumatism Assn. (licentiate), Am. Coll. Rheumatology (corr.). Catholic. Achievements include research in Rheumatology. Avocation: travel.

LEE, SHUISHIH SAGE, pathologist; b. Soo-chow, Kiang su, China, Jan. 5, 1948; came to U.S., 1972, naturalized, 1979; m. Chung Seng Lee; children: Yvonne Claire, Michael Chung. MD, Nat. Taiwan U., 1972; PhD, U. Rochester, 1976. Resident in pathology Strong Meml. Hosp., Rochester, NY, 1976-78, Northwestern Meml. Hosp., Chgo., 1978-79; dir. cytology and electron microscopy Parkview Meml. Hosp., Ft. Wayne, Ind., 1979—. Clin. prof. Ind. U. Med. Sch. Contbr. articles to profl. jours. Fellow: Am. Soc. Clin. Pathologists, Coll. Am. Pathologists; mem.: AMA, Internat. Assn. Chinese Pathologists (pres. 1999—2001), Ft. Wayne Acad. Physicians and Surgeons (pres. 1990), Ft. Wayne Med. Soc. (pres. 2001—02, chair bd. 2002—), Electron Microscopy Soc. Am., Internat. Acad. Cytology, Internat. Acad. Pathology, Am. Soc. Cytology, Am. Assn. Pathologists, N.Y. Acad.

Scis., Ind. Assn. Pathologists, N.E. Ind. Pathologists Assn. (sec. 1984), Ind. Med. Assn. Home: 5728 The Prophets Pass Fort Wayne IN 46845-9659 Office: Parkview Meml Hosp 2200 Randallia Dr Fort Wayne IN 46805-4699

LEE, SIKYUNG, food scientist, educator; b. Seoul, Republic Of Korea, Aug. 14, 1954; s. JinIl Lee and YoungSoon Park; m. HeaSook Jung, May 28, 1983; children: JungHyun, Seung Ah. PhD, Konkuk U., Seoul, 1991. Cert. in food processing Korea, 1979. Sr. rschr. Doosan Rsch. Ctr., Seoul, South Korea, Republic of Korea, 1983—94; prof. Konkuk U., Seoul, 1994—. Consulting Seoul Functional Food Co., Seoul, Seoul, 2000—07. Coop. pastor Seoul Sekwang Ch., Seoul, 2005—07. Lance cpl. Korean armed forces, 1995—97. Achievements include patents for frozen dough bread preparation using ferment; Chungkookjan preparation method adding Yucca extract; Bacillus subtilis CG-1 and Lactobacillus delbrueckii CG-2 and the preparation of fermented soybean by mixed culture of them. Avocations: swimming, mountain climbing, hiking. Home: Reamian Apt 112-2003SadangDongDonggakku South Korea Seoul 156-301 Republic of Korea Office: Konkuk Un 1 Hwayangdong Kwangginku South Korea Seoul 143-701 Republic of Korea Home Phone: 82 2 3477 2788; Office Phone: 82 2 450 3759. Office Fax: 82 2 456 7183. Business E-Mail: lesikyung@konkuk.ac.kr.

LEE, SIMON, orthopedist; BS in Bio, Univ. Ill., Champaign-Urbana, 1993; MD, Rush Univ. Med. Ctr., 1997. Diplomate Am. Bd. Orthopaedic Surgery, 2005, lic. Physician and Surgeon Ill., No. Carolina. Clin. instr., dept. gen. surgery Rush Med. Ctr., Chgo., 1997—98, Univ. Ill., 1998—2002, Carolinas Med. Ctr., Charlotte, NC, 2002—03; orthopedist Rush Univ. Med. Ctr., asst. prof., dept. gen. surgery, 2003—. Spkr. in field. Contbr. articles to numerous profl. jours. Office: Midwest Orthopaedics Ste 1063 1725 W Harrison St Chicago IL 60612 Office Phone: 312-432-2348. Office Fax: 312-942-1516. Business E-Mail: simon.lee@rushortho.com.

LEE, SIOW MING, professor of medical oncology, consultant; s. Boon Choo Lee and Chin Ho Yeow; m. Monica Liew, Apr. 18, 1978; children: Lennard, Julian. MBBS, Imperial Coll., St Mary Hosp. Med. Sch., London, 1982; PhD, U. Manchester, 1994. CCST Med. Royal Colls., UK, 1997. Cons. med. oncologist U. Coll. Hosp., London, 1997—; hon. sr. lectr. U. Coll. London, prof., 2010—. Clin. scientist Cancer Rsch. UK, London, 1998—; chief investigator Designing and Developing Clin. and Transl. Trials. Steering com. mem. NCRI, London, 2003—08. Recipient McElwain prize, Assn. Cancer Physicians, UK, 1994. Fellow: RCP (London) (accreditation med. oncology JCHMT 1996); mem.: BTOG, London Lung Cancer Group, Am. Assn. Cancer Rsch., ASCO. Achievements include research in lung cancer clinical trials. Office: Univ Coll Hosp 250 Euston Road NW1 2PG London England Office Fax: 44(0)2073809055.

LEE, SOO-KEUN, physician; b. Daejeon, Republic of Korea, Feb. 10, 1968; s. Jonghwa Lee and Younhee Choi; m. Minyun Rho, children: Jungmin, Seoyeon. MD, Seoul Nat. U., Med. Coll., Republic of Korea, 1992; M, Seoul Nat. U., Postgrad. Sch. Medicine, 1997, PhD, 2004. Cert. by bd. dermatology Korean Dermatol. Assn., 1997. Resident Nat. Med. Ctr., Dept. Dermatology, Seoul, 1993—97; staff, med. officer Capital Armed Forces Gen. Hosp., Dept. Dermatology, Seoul, 1998—2000; staff dr. Leejiham Skin Clinic, Seoul, 2000—03; pres. Mein Skin Clinic, Seoul, 2003—. Cons. dr. Seoul Nat. U. Hosp., Dept. Dermatology, 2003—; internat. fellow Am. Acad. Dermatology, Schaumburg, Ill., 2003—; dir. Korean Soc. Aesthetic and Dermatologic Surgery, Seoul, 2006—; ednl. dir. Assn. Korean Dermatologists, Seoul, 2009—. Contbr. articles to profl. jours., chapters to books. Deacon Youngrak Bapt. Ch., Suwon, Republic Of Korea, 2000. Lt. sr. med. officer, 1997, Repulic of Korea. Mem.: Am. Acad. Dermatology (Schaumburg, Ill.), Korean Dermatol. Assn. (Seoul), Korean Med. Assn. (Seoul), Internat. Soc. Cosmetic and Laser Surgeons (Chgo.). Avocations: swimming, tennis. Office: Mein Skin Clinic 1306-1 Seocho-4-dong Seocho-ku Seoul 137-855 Republic of Korea Office Phone: 8210 6375 8697. Business E-Mail: drleesookeun@gmail.com.

LEE, STEVE, orthopedist, surgeon, educator; Attended, Duke U., 1989—93. Diplomate Am. Bd. of Orthopaedic Surgery, Am. Bd. of Orthopaedic Surgery-hand surgery. Intern Yale Univ. Sch. of Medicine, 1993—98, resident, 1993—98; clin. fellow hand surgery NY Univ. Sch. of Medicine, 2002—03, asst. prof. orthopaedic surgery; with NY Univ. Langone Med. Ctr.; assoc. chief NY Univ. Hosp. for Joint Diseases. Co-author: (publs.) A biomechanical study of extensor tendon repair methods: introduction to the running-interlocking horizontal mattress extensor tendon repair technique, 2010, Avulsion injuries of the flexor digitorum profundus tendon, 2011, Comparison of radiographic stress views for scapholunate dynamic instability in a cadaver model, 2011, Perilunate dislocations, 2011, and numerous other publications. Office: New York University Hospital for Joint Diseases 240 E 18th St Rutherford Pl New York NY 10003 Office Phone: 212-598-6697. Office Fax: 212-598-6560.

LEE, SUN, surgeon; b. Korea, June 2, 1920; 6 children. MD, Seoul U., Republic of, 1945, Cook County Grad. Sch. Medicine, Chgo., 1950. Intern Wheeling Gen. Hosp., W.Va., 1951; gen. residency Ohio Valley Gen. Hosp., Wheeling, 1952; gen. surg. residency Pitts., 1955; fellow asst. prof. surgery Univ. Pitts., 1955—64; assoc. immunopathology Scripps Clinic, La Jolla, Calif., 1967; dir. San Diego Microsurg. Inst., San Diego, 2003—; vol. clin. prof. surgery U. Calif. San Diego Med. Sch., 2003—05. Mem.: Transplanation, Internat. Soc. For Experimental Microsurgery (founder), Worlds Microsurgical Soc. (hon.). Achievements include research in rat blood vessel surgery under Professor Bernard Fisher; rat organ transplants except the heart and intestines; consecutive organ transplant, where older vital organs are transplanted into young rats and removed when older and transplanted into a young rat; rats' life span of 24 months; extending rat pancreas to survive to 52 months; endocrine glands implanted into the spleen; the benign turmors at usual rat's life term showing malignant at a prolonged period; recycling human vital organs to fight the organ shortage problem; tech-immunological, pathophysiological investigation using rodents; first to use rodents in organ transplant research to replace domestic animals thus reducing public sentiments and research expenditures. E-mail: msurgical@yahoo.com.

LEE, SUNG-BOK, ophthalmologist, educator; b. Daejeon, Aug. 22, 1971; MD in Medicine, Chungnam Nat. U., 1996, PhD in Ophthalmology, 2007. Lic. physician Korea, 1996, ophthalmologist 2001. Instr. Chungnam Nat. U., 2004—06, asst. prof., 2006—10, assoc. prof., 2010—. Contbr. articles to profl. jours., chapters to books. With Korean Army, 2001—04. Mem.: Korean Soc. Ophthalmic Plastic and Reconstructive Surgery, Korean Ophthalmol. Soc. Office: 640 Daesa-Dong Jung-Gu Daejeon 301-721 Republic of Korea Office Phone: 82-42-280-7604. Business E-Mail: sblee@cnu.ac.kr.

LEE, SUN-HO, neurosurgeon, educator; b. Daegu, Republic Of Korea, Oct. 10, 1972; s. Jae-Kook Lee and Young-Hee Kim; m. Hee Kyung Park; children: Jun-Seung, Joo-Heon. MD, Kyungpook U., Daegu, 1997, PhD, 2007. Lic. physician Ministry Health and Welfare, 1997, cert. specialist neurosurgery 2005. Asst. prof. Kyungpook Nat. U. Hosp., Daegu, 2006—08, Samsung Med. Ctr., Seoul, Republic of Korea, 2008—. Contbr. numerous articles to publs. Mem.: Korean Spinal Neurosurgery Soc., Korean Neurosurg. Soc. Office: Dept Neurosurgery Samsung Med Ctr 50 Ilwon-dong Gangnam-gu Seoul 135-710 Republic of Korea Office Phone: 82-2-3410-2457. Office Fax: 82-2-3410-0048. Personal E-mail: sobotta72@hotmail.com. E-mail: sobotta@dreamwiz.com.

LEE, SUN-MEE, pharmacist, educator; b. Republic Of Korea, Jan. 7, 1959; m. Keun Chang Yi; children: Kyung-Hwan Yi, Woo-Jin Yi. BS, Sungkyunkwan U., Republic of Korea, 1981, MS, 1983, PhD, 1986. Lic. pharmacist Ministry for Health Welfare Family Affairs, S. Korea. Instr. Yonsei U., Sch. of Medicine, Seoul, Republic of Korea, 1987—89; asst. prof. Sungkyunkwan U., Suwon, Republic of Korea, 1992—96, assoc. prof. chmn., 1996—2001, prof., 2001—. Recipient Excellence Paper award, Sungkyunkwan U., 2005; named one of Best Rsch. award, Korean Fedn. Sci. Tech. Soc., 2002. Mem.: Shock Soc., Korean Soc. Applied Pharmacology (Poster award 2003, Acad. award 2008), Korean Physiol. Soc., Pharm. Soc. Korea (Acad. award 2004, Paper award 2005). Home: 5-404 Ginheung APT 1315 Suhcho-dong Seoul Republic of Korea Office: Sungkyunkwan Univ 300 Cheoncheon-dong Changan-gu Suwon Gyeonggi-do 440 746 Republic of Korea Office Fax: 82 31 290 7732. Business E-Mail: sunmee@skku.edu.

LEE, SUSAN, dentist, microbiologist; b. Jellico, Tenn., June 2, 1943; d. Roy Pickerell and Florida Maybell (Weaver) Savage; m. Joseph James Lee, Dec. 30, 1969 (dec. Dec. 1980); 1 child, Susan. BS, Cumberland Coll., 1965; DMD, U. Louisville, 1976. Lic. real estate agt., Ky. Asst. head dept. microbiology Norton Children's Hosp. (formerly Norton Meml. Infirmary, Louisville, 1964-69; head dept. microbiology St. Anthony's Hosp., Louisville, 1969-72; mgr. office, cons. Drs. Med. Plaza, Louisville, 1976-82; dentist Office Richard S. Bonn, DMD, Louisville, 1982-86; hygienist, dentist, cons. Office James Lewis, DMD, Louisville, 1986—. Cons. in field, 1982—. Named Hon. Order Ky. Cols. Mem. Louisville Soc. Physicians and Surgeons (sec., treas.), So. Med. Soc., Fraternal Order Police. Republican. Baptist. Avocations: tennis, gardening, boating, quilting, cooking. Home and Office: 6303 Crest Creek Ct Louisville KY 40241-5801 Personal E-mail: leemissmarco@aol.com.

LEE, TAE KYUNG, psychiatrist; s. Dae Keun Hong; m. Joong Hee Hong, Apr. 24, 1994; children: Jong Won, Jong U. MD, Ministry of Health & Social Affairs, 1991; PhD, Grad. Sch. Hanyang U., Seoul, Republic Of Korea, 2003. Cert. Bd. Psychiatry, Ministry of Health and Welfare, Republic Of Korea, 1996. Chief, army dr. Dept. Psychiatry, Daejeon Armed Forces Hosp., Republic of Korea, 1997—99; dir. Dept. Psychiatry, Hyemin Hosp., Seoul, 1999—2000; staff psychiatrist Karam Neuropsychiat. Clinic, Seoul, 2000—01; sr. dep. dir. Alcohol and Drug Addiction Ctr., Seoul Nat. Hosp., 2001—05; vis. fellow Divsn. Addictions, Cambridge Health Alliance, Harvard Med. Sch., Medford, Mass., 2005—06; dir. Dept. Addiction Psychiatry, Seoul Nat. Hosp., Ministry for Health, Welfare, 2006—09. Standing mem. adv. com. Korea Prevention and Cure Ctr. Gambling Problem, Seoul, 2001—; mgr. Instl. Rev. Bd. Seoul Nat. Hosp., 2004—; standing mem. Supporting Orgn. Prevention and Rehab. Alcoholism, Seoul, 2007—; IRB mem. Nat. Evidence based Healthcare Collaborating Agy., Republic of Korea, 2010—; mem. sub com. for addiction prevention & treatment Nat. Gaming Control Commn., Republic of Korea, 2010—. Contbr. articles to profl. jours. (Best Poster award, Seoul Regional Congress of World Psychiat. Assn., 2007). Recipient Spl. award, Minister of Health, Welfare & Family Affairs, 2008. Office: Seoul Nat Hosp 398 Neung-dong Ro Gwang-Jin Gu Seoul 143-711 Republic of Korea Office Phone: 82-2-2204-0179. Office Fax: 82-2-2204-0394. Personal E-mail: tkleemd@gmail.com. Business E-Mail: atman@korea.kr.

LEE, TAE SUNG, obstetrician, gynecologist, medical educator, dean; b. Sungjugun, Republic of Korea, Jan. 18, 1952; m. Un Mi Park, Mar. 25, 1955; children: Joo Hyun, Chang Hwan. MD, Kyungbook Nat. U., 1970—76; PhD, Cath. U., 1984—87. Chmn.dept. ob-gyn. Sch. Medicine, Cath. U. Daegu, Namgu, 2000—, dean, 2007—, Rsch. Inst. Med. Sci., Namgu, 2002—07. Mem.: Korean Soc. Perinatology (bd. dirs. 2003—), Internat. Gynecologic Cancer Soc., Am. Soc. Colposcopy and Cervical Pathology, Korean Soc. Gynecol. Oncology and Colposcopy, Korean Soc. Ob-Gyn. (bd. dirs. 2000—). Office: Catholic Univ Daegu Daemyung 4 Dong Daegu Namgu 705-034 Republic of Korea Home: 102/803 Jungwha Woobang Palace Sangdong 706-828 Soosunggu Daegu Republic of Korea Office Fax: 82-53-650-4078. E-mail: leets@cu.ac.kr.

LEE, TAT-SUM, physician; b. Kwang See, China, July 19, 1944; came to U.S., 1970; s. Kai-Hung and Lai-See (Wong) L.; m. Hilda Ondruska, Sept. 27, 1975; children: Paula, Monica. MB BS, Taipei Med. Coll., 1970. Diplomate Am. Bd. Emergency Medicine, Am. Bd. Family Practice; cert. quality assurance physician. Sch. physician Pine Valley Ctrl. Sch., South Dayton, N.Y., 1977—, Cassadaga (N.Y.) Ctrl. Sch., 1984—2007; med. dir. in emergency dept. Lake Shore Health Care, Irving, N.Y., 1993—; dir. Lash Stone Ward Ctr., Duesenberg, NY. Med. dir. Cassadaga Job Corps, 1978—; diplomate Am. Assn. Physician Specialists. Rescuer, fire fighter Cherry Creek (N.Y.) Vol. Fire Co., 1977—. Fellow Am. Coll. Emergency Physicians, Am. Acad. Family Physicians Avocations: fishing, skiing, hunting. Office: 618 Center St Cherry Creek NY 14723-9792 Office Phone: 716-363-1515. Office Fax: 716-296-8229.

LEE, THERESA M., psychology professor, department chairman; AB in Biol. Sciences, Ind. U., 1975; PhD, U. Chgo., 1982. Pharmacolgy sr. analyst Inolex Pharm. Co., Park Forest, Ill., 1975—78; post-doctoral fellow, dept. psychology U. Calif., Berkeley, 1982—85, assoc. rsch. psychologist, 1985—88; asst. prof., dept. psychology U. Mich., Ann Arbor, 1988—94, assoc. prof., dept. psychology, 1994—99, prof., neuroscience program, 1999—, rsch. scientist, reproductive sci. program, 1999—, prof., dept. psychology, 1999—, chair, dept. psychology, 2004—. Invited spkr. in field. Mem.: AAAS, Soc. Rsch. on Biol. Rhythms (mem. program com. 2005—06), Am. Soc. Mammalogists, Soc. Neuroscience, Assn. the Study Animal Behavior, Soc. Behavioral Neuroendocrinology (mem. program com. 2004—07), Mich. Soc. Med. Rsch. Office: Univ Mich Dept Psychology 4030 East Hall 525 E University Ave Ann Arbor MI 48109-1109 Office Phone: 313-936-1495. Business E-Mail: terrilee@umich.edu.

LEE, THOMAS HENRY, internist, cardiologist, healthcare executive; b. Schenectady, NY, Dec. 2, 1953; Grad., Harvard Coll., 1975; MD, Cornell U., 1979; MSc, Harvard U., 1987. Bd. cert. internal medicine 1982, bd. cert. cardiovasc. disease. Intern Harvard Med. Sch., Boston, 1980—82; resident Brigham and Women's Hosp., Boston, 1982—84, cardiology fellow, 1984—85, internist, cardiologist; assoc. prof. dept. health policy and mgmt. Harvard Med. Sch., Boston; chief med. officer Partners Healthcare Sys., network pres., 2004—; CEO Partners Cmty. Healthcare, Inc., 2004—. Bd. dirs. Mass. Quality Partnership, Bridges to Excellence; dir. Partners Signature Initiatives. Assoc. editor: The New England Journal of Medicine, editor-in-chief: The Harvard Heart Letter, author numerous scholarly articles. Office: Partners Cmty Health Care Inc Prudential Twr Ste 1150 800 Boylston St Boston MA 02199 also: Brigham Internal Medicine Assoc 75 Francis St Boston MA 02115 E-mail: thlee@bics.bwh.harvard.edu, thlee@partners.org. *

LEE, THOMAS TEHWEN, neurosurgeon; b. Tainan, Taiwan, Dec. 27, 1967; s. Chang Kuei and Shiu-Hoa Shu L.; m. Margaret Yu, Aug. 31, 1993. BA magna cum laude, U. Calif., Berkeley, 1989; MD, UCLA, 1993; MBA, George Washington U., DC, 2007. Diplomate Am. Bd. Neurol. Surgery, Nat. Bd. Med. Examiners. Resident in neurosurgery U. Miami - Jackson Meml. Med. Ctr., 1993-99; attending neurosurgeon Westchester Med. Ctr., NY, 1999—; clin. asst. prof. Mt. Sinai Sch. Medicine, NYC, 2005—; chief sect. neurosurgery St. John's Riverside Hosp., 2001—. Credentials com. Phelps Meml. Hosp., Sleepy Hollow, NY, 2001—; med. bd. St. John's Riverside Hosp., Yonkers, NY, 2003—05, vice chairman bd. dirs., chmn. auditing com., mem. fin. com., 2007—; chair legis. com., bd. dirs., v.p. Westchester County Med. Soc., 2007—, v.p., 2011—; with Am. Coll. Healthcare Executive; mem. com. legis. adv. Med. Soc. State NY, 2010—. Mem. editl. rev. bd. The Spine, 1999—; contbr. articles to profl. jours., chpt. to books in field. Mem. med. response team Championship Auto Racing Team, 1995-99. Recipient Congressional Recognition award, NY State Bd. Profl. Conduct, 2009, award, NY State Bd. Profl. Med. Conduct, 2011—; named one of Best Drs. in NY, Met. Area, Castle Connolly, 2010—; Dean's scholar, UCLA, 1993. Fellow: ACS; mem.: Congress Neurol. Surgeons (med. edn. liaison, mem. com. on edn., mem. sci. program com.), Am. Assn. Neurol. Surgeons, N.Am. Spine Soc., Phi Beta Kappa, Golden Key. Avocations: movie poster collection, swimming, tennis, target shooting. Office Phone: 914-631-9207. Personal E-mail: thomastleemd@aol.com.

LEE, TSUNG-MING, cardiologist, medical researcher, medical educator; b. Tainan, Taiwan, Taiwan, May 28, 1962; MD, Nat. Taiwan U., Taipei, 1989. Board Certified Diplomate Taiwan, 1989. Attending phys. Nat. Taiwan U. Hosp., Taipei, Taipei, Taiwan, 1989—2002; asst. prof. Nat. Taiwan U., Taipei, Taipei, Taiwan, 2000—03. Mem. Fellow: European Soc. Cardiology. Achievements include patents for the use of stains in patients with congestive heart failure. Office: Chi-Mei Med Ctr 901 Chung-Hwa Rd Yang-Kan City Tainan 710 Taiwan Office Fax: +886-6-283-2639. E-mail: tsungm.lee@msa.hinet.net.

LEE, VERNON J., preventive medicine physician; b. Singapore, June 19, 1977; s. Don F.K. Lee and Patricia B.K. Yow; m. Jocelyn L. Goh, June 7, 2003. MB, MBBS, Nat. U. Singapore, 2001; MPH, MBA, Johns Hopkins U., Balt., 2004. Med. officer Singapore Armed Forces, 2002—; pub. health registrar Communicable Disease Ctr., Singapore, 2004—. Vol. Family Svc. Ctr., 1996—97. Maj. US Army, 2002—06, Singapore. Decorated Tsunami relief operation medal Singapore Armed Forces; recipient Book prize, Nat. U. Singapore, 2001; grantee Rsch. grant for HIV study, Nat. Med. Rsch. Coun. Singapore, 2006, Rsch. grant for dengue study, 2006; scholar Local study award, Singapore Armed Forces, 1996. Mem.: Singapore Med. Assn., Delta Omega. Achievements include research in Influenza pandemic planning strategies; Human Immunodeficiency Virus diagnosis and costs; Dengue treatment strategies; Hospital clinical improvement programs. Avocations: golf, tennis, skiing, scuba diving, music. Office: Communicable Disease Ctr 802 Moulmein Rd 308433 Singapore Singapore Business E-Mail: vernonljm@hotmail.com.

LEE, VIRGINIA M.Y., medical educator, health science association administrator; PhD, U. Calif., San Francisco, 1973; MBA, U. Pa., 1984. Prof. dept. pathology and lab. medicine U. Pa. Sch. Medicine, co-dir. neurodegenerative disease rsch., 1992—2002, dir. neurodegenerative disease rsch., 2002—. Mem. grant rev. com. NIH Study Sect., others; mem. med./sci. adv. com. Alzheimer's Assn., S.E. Pa.; mem. coun. Nat. Inst. on Aging. Contbr. papers to profl. jours. Recipient John H. Ware 3d Chair for Alzheimer's Disease Rsch., Stanley N. Cohen Biomed. Rsch. award, 2000. Mem.: Inst. Medicine, Soc. for Neurosci. (elected councilor). Achievements include research in Alzheimer's disease; neuronal cytoskeleton. Office: Ctr for Neurodegenerative Disease Rsch 3d Fl Maloney Bldg 4283 3600 Spruce St Philadelphia PA 19104-4283

LEE, WANG JAE, immunologist, researcher, anatomist, educator; b. Seoul, Rep. of Korea, Apr. 24, 1955; s. Sung Ho Lee; m. Eun Joo Ji, Apr. 27, 1984; 1 child, Hanna. PhD, Seoul Nat. U., 1986—90. Cert. Ministry of Health and Welfare, 1982. Prof., anatomy Seoul Nat. U. Coll. Medicine, Republic of Korea, 1990—, assoc. dean for academic affairs, 2001—02. Capt. Med. Army, 1987—89, Seoul. Methodist. Avocations: golf, travel. Office Fax: 82-2-745-9528. Business E-Mail: kinglee@snu.ac.kr.

LEE, WEI-MING, veterinarian, educator; b. Taipei, Taiwan, June 5, 1962; PhD, Utrecht U., 2004. Lectr., dept. vet. medicine Nat. Chung Hsing U., 1996—2005, assoc. prof., 2005—, dir., Vet. Med. Tchg. Hosp., 2009. Grant, Nat. Chung Hsing U., 2010. Mem.: Taiwan Coll. Vet. Surgeons. Avocation: reading. Office: 250 Kuo Kuang Rd S Dist Taichung 402 Taiwan Business E-Mail: wmlee@dragon.nchu.edu.tw.

LEE, WON HYUK, oral and maxillofacial surgeon; b. Daegu, Republic Of Korea, June 3, 1976; s. Hoon Lee and Kwi Suk Kwon. DDS, Kyoung Buk Nat. U., South Korea, 2002. Chief med. dept. 11th Tactical Fighter Wings Aeromedical Squadron, Republic of Korea Air Force, dir. dental dept. Capt. Air Force, 2006—07, South Korea.

Recipient Gold medal, KAID, 2005; fellowship, Internat. Congress Implantology, 2005—06. Fellow: ICOI (assoc. fellowship); mem.: Korean Assn. Oral and Maxillofacial Surgeons. Home: 102-7-2 Palgong Bosung Apt 1 Daegu 701-771 Republic of Korea Office: Daegu Cath U Hosp Nam-Gu Daemyong 4 Dong Daegu Republic of Korea Office Fax: 82-53-622-7067. Personal E-mail: hyukdent@daum.net. Business E-Mail: hyukdent@hmps.co.kr.

LEE, WON JAY, radiologist; b. Seoul, Korea, Feb. 2, 1938; arrived in U.S., 1965; s. Kang Sei and Choon Ja (Park) L.; m. Moon Jung, Feb. 24, 1968; children: Julie, Lisa, Jennifer. MD, Yonsei U., Seoul, 1962. Diplomate Am. Bd. Radiology, Am. Bd. Nuclear Medicine. Intern Wyckoff Heights Hosp., Bklyn., 1965-66; resident in radiology N.Y. U. Med. Ctr., NYC, 1966-69; fellow, asst. radiologist L.I. Jewish Med. Ctr., New Hyde Park, 1969-71, staff radiologist, 1975-82, chief uroradiology, 1983—2001, hon. staff, 2001—; assoc. radiologist Binghamton Gen. Hosp., 1971-75. Asst. prof. SUNY, Stony Brook, 1975-86, assoc. prof. radiology, 1987-89; prof. radiology Albert Einstein Coll. Medicine, 1989-2002, prof. emeritus radiology, 2002-; clin. prof. diagnostic radiology Yonsei U. Coll. Medicine, Seoul, 1996—; cons. in field. Asst. editor: Jour. Endourology, 1987-96; assoc. editor: Jour. Korean-Am. Med. Assn., 1995-98, editor-in-chief, 1999-2000; contbr. chpts. to books and articles to profl. jours. First lt. Republic of Korea Army M.C., 1962-65. Recipient Sci. Paper award Soc. Uroradiology, 1994, Clin. award Can. Assoc. Radiologists, 1979, Disting. Svc. award Yonsei U. Col. Med. Alumni Assn., 1998. Fellow Am. Coll. Radiology, Soc. Interventional Radiology (emeritus), Soc. Uroradiology (emeritus); mem. AMA, Am. Roentgen Ray Soc. (Merit award 1983), Radiol. Soc. N.Am., Korean-Am. Med. Assn. (chmn. sci. and edn. divsn. 1996), Korean Radiol. Soc. N.Am., Severance Alumni Assn. Am. (pres. 1997). Independent. Presbyn. Avocations: gardening, travel. Office: Lee Radiol Cons 6306 Adirondack Ct Gainesville VA 20155 Office Phone: 703-743-1382. Personal E-mail: wjaylee@yahoo.com.

LEE, WON SUK, neuroscientist, pharmacologist, educator; b. Busan, Republic of Korea, Oct. 12, 1955; s. Jang-Soo Lee and Geum-Ok Kim; m. Bo-Hyun Kim; children: Nam-Kyung, Soon-Wu. MD, Pusan Nat. U., Busan, Republic of Korea, 1980, PhD, 1985. Lic. Ministry Health and Welfare, Republic of Korea, 1980. Prof. dept. pharmacology sch. medicine Pusan Nat. U., Busan, Republic of Korea, 1999—, vice dean sch. medicine, 2003—05. Rsch. fellow Mass. Gen. Hosp., Boston, 1992—94. Lt. Korean Navy, 1985—88. Recipient Choongwae Scholarly award, Korean Soc. Pharmacology, 1999. Mem.: Korean Soc. Pharmacology, Soc. Neurosci., Korean Soc. Brain and Neural Sci. Achievements include research in cerebral ischemia; cerebral blood flow regulation; antimigraine drugs. Home: Prugio Apt 103-1303 93-3 Daeyeon-3-dong Nam-gu 608-744 Busan Republic of Korea Office: Pusan Natl U Sch Med Dept Pharmacology Beomeo-ri Mulgeum-eup Yangsan-si Gyeongsangnam-do Gyeongsangnam-do626870 Republic of Korea Office Phone: 82515108062. Office Fax: 82-51-5108068. Business E-Mail: wonslee@pusan.ac.kr.

LEE, WON-CHANG, veterinarian, educator; b. Seoul, Republic of Korea, July 29, 1935; DVM, Seoul Nat. U., 1958, PhD, 1969. Maj., charge aviation hygiene Aerospace Med. Ctr. Korea Air Force, Republic of Korea, 1958—70, cons., 1970—2010; dean, Grad. Sch. Konkuk U., Seoul, 1998—2000, prof. emeritus, Coll. Vet. Medicine, 1970—. Vis. prof. Dept. Pub. Health, Kobe U. Sch. Medicine, Japan, 1988—89; cons. Korean Air, 1980—2000, Asiana Air, 1980—2010. Recipient Order Svc. Merit award, Academic award, Konkuk U., Korea Pub. Health Assn., Aerospace Med. Assn. Korea. Mem.: Korean Soc. Vet. Pub. Health Assn., Korean Vet. Med. Assn., Korean Pub. Health Assn. Avocation: swimming. Home: Hyundai-Apt 603-704 #610 Guui-dong Seoul 143-760 Republic of Korea

LEE, WONDEOK, medical educator; b. Seoul, Republic of Korea, Oct. 21, 1975; DDS., Seoul Nat. U., 2008. Clin. prof. Seoul Nat. U. Hosp., 2008—. Recipient Mil. Svc. award, Korean Dental Assn. Fellow: Int. Assn. Oral and Maxillofacial Surgury, Korean Assn. Maxillofacial Aesthetic Treatment; mem.: Korean Cleft Lip and Palate Assn., Korean Assn. Plastic and Reconstructive Surgeon, Korean Assn. Oral and Maxillofacial Surgeon. Office: 425 Shindaebang-dong Boramae-Gil Seoul Dongjak-Gu 156-707 Republic of Korea Personal E-mail: lee.wondeok@gmail.com.

LEE, WON-SANG, otolaryngologist; s. Seung Pyo Kim; m. Boo Won Yoon, Nov. 18, 1976; children: Sung Hwan, Jin Hwan. Grad., Yonsei U., 1976, MS in Medicine, 1983; PhD in Otorhinolaryngology, Youngnam U., Daegu, 1997. Diplomate Korean bd. otolaryngology Ministry Health & Welfare, 1983. Intern Yonsei Med. Ctr., 1979—80, resident dept. otorhinolarynology, 1980—83; mem. Korean Otolaryn. Soc., Seoul, 1980—; resident tng. com. dir. Korean Otolaryn. soc., Seoul, 2001—03; chief editor Korean Otolaryngology—Head & Neck Surgery, Seoul, 2000—04; pres. Korean Skull Base Surgery soc., Seoul, 2005—06, Korean Balance soc., Seoul, 2003—05, Korean Otologic soc., Seoul, 2006—08; prof. and chmn. Dept. Otorhinolaryngology, Yonsei U.Med. Ctr., Seoul, 2008—. Vis. scholar dept. otolaryngolog Kyoto U., Japan, 1984; rsch. assoc. divsn. head and neck surgery UCLA Sch. Med., 1987—89; instr. dept. otolaryngology Yonsei U., 1983—87, asst. prof. dept. otolaryngology, 1987—93, assoc. prof. dept. otolaryngology, 1993—98, prof. dept. otolaryngology, 1998—. With Korean Navy, 1976—79. Recipient Gold medal, Young Nam U., 1997, NamHyun Woo award, Yonsei U., 1999. Mem.: Sir Charles Bell Soc. (assoc.), Aeromedical Assn. Korea (assoc.), Korean Soc. for Head and Neck Oncology (assoc.), Korean Audiological Soc. (assoc.), Korean Skull Base Surgery Soc. (assoc.), Korean Balance Soc. (assoc.), Korean Otologic Soc. (assoc.), Barany Soc. (assoc.), Korean Otolaryn. Soc. (assoc.). Avocations: rock climbing, reading. Office: Yonsei U Med Ctr 134 Shinchon-Dong Seodaemun-Gu Seoul 120-752 Republic of Korea Business E-Mail: wsleemd@yuhs.ac.

LEE, WON-SOO, medical educator; MD, Yonsei U., Seoul, Republic Of Korea, 1985, PhD, 1992. Cert. in dermatologist Korean Dermatol. Assn., 1989. Dermatologic residency Yonsei U. Severance Hosp., Seoul, 1985—89; flight surgeon Air Force, Suwon, Kyunggi-Do, Republic of Korea, 1989—92; vis. clin. asst. prof. U. Minn., Mpls., 1996—98; prof. dermatology Yonsei U. Wonju Med. Coll., Wonju, Kangwon-Do, Republic of Korea, 1992—, dir. inst. hair cosmetic medicine, 2003—. Sci. sec. Korean Hair Rsch. Soc., Seoul, 1999—; sec. gen. Korean Soc. Cosmetic Dermatology, Seoul, 2000—. Recipient Young Investigator award, Hair Rsch. Soc., 1995, Best Clin. Poster Award, 1997. Mem.: Korean Soc. Med. Mycology, Korean Soc. Aerospace Medicine, Korean Soc. Med. History, Korean Soc. Investigative Dermatology, Soc. Investigative Dermatology, Am. Acad. Dermatology, Korean Dermatol. Assn., European Hair Rsch. Soc. Office: Yonsei Univ Wonju Med Coll 162 Ilsan-Dong Wonju 220-701 Republic of Korea Office Fax: 82-33-748-2650. Business E-Mail: leewonsoo@yonsei.ac.kr.

LEE, WON-YOUNG, medical educator; b. Seoul, Republic of Korea, Feb. 27, 1967; s. Jong-Beom Lee and Bok-Gang Jeong; m. Hyun-Sook Kim, Dec. 11, 1993; 1 child, Yoo-Gun. MD, Cath. U., Seoul, 1985, PhD, 1991. Cert. Korean Assn. of Internal Medicine, Ednl. Commn. for Fgn. Med. Grads., Korean Soc. Endocrinology. Intern, then resident Kangnam St. Mary's Hosp., Cath. U. Med. Coll., Seoul, 1991—96; instr. St. Mary's Hosp., Cath. U. Med. Coll., Seoul, 1999—2001; asst. prof. Kangbuk Samsung Hosp., Sungkyunkwan U. Sch. of Medicine, Seoul, Republic of Korea, 2001—. Contbr. articles to profl. jours. Recipient Superior Rsch. award, Korean Soc. Bone Metabolism, 2002, Superior Paper award, Korean Soc. Endocrinology, 2001. Mem.: Am. Soc. for Bone and Mineral Rsch., Endocrine Soc., Am. Achievements include research in bone marrow transplantation-related osteoporosis and endocrine complications. Office: Kangbuk Samsung HospSungkyunkwan U Jongro-gu Pyungdong 108 Seoul 110-746 Republic of Korea Office Fax: 82-2-2001-2049. E-mail: drlwy@hanmail.net.

LEE, W.P. ANDREW, plastic surgeon; BA in Physics, Harvard U., 1979; MD, John Hopkins Sch. Medicine, 1983. Cert. Am. Bd. Surgery, Am. Bd. Plastic Surgery; cert. added for Hand and/or Upper Extremity Surgery. Resident gen. surgery John Hopkins Hosp., Md., 1989, chief resident; resident plastic surgery Mass. Gen. Hosp., 1991, chief resident, chief hand surgery svc. dept. surgery, dir. plastic surgery rsch. lab, dir. hand and microvascular fellowship, 1992—2002; fellow microsurgery rsch. John Hopkins U. Sch. Medicine, 1987; fellow clinical Ind. Hand Ctr., 1987; prof. surgery, chief divsn. plastic surgery, dir. hand surgery fellowship U. Pittsburgh Sch. Medicine; with Children's Hosp Hand Surgery, Pa., 2002—. Contbr. several articles to profl. jours. Named one of Pittsburgh's Top Doctors (Hand Surgery), Pittsburgh Mag., 2005—07. Mem.: Plastic Surgery Rsch. Coun., Am. Assn. for Hand Surgery, Am. Soc. Plastic and Reconstructive Surgeons, Am. Soc. for Surgery of the Hand, World Soc. for Reconstructive Microsurgery, Am. Assn. Plastic Surgeons. Achievements include being the led of a team of surgeons to perform double hand transplant at University of Pittsburgh Medical Center in May, 2009. Office: Falk Medical Bldg 3601 Fifth Ave Ste 6B Pittsburgh PA 15213 Address: Children's Hosp Hand Surgery Ctr 45th St and Penn Ave #rd Fl Pittsburgh PA 15201 Office Phone: 412-648-9670, 412-692-8650, 412-692-8622. Office Fax: 412-692-8614. Business E-Mail: andrew.lee@chp.edu.

LEE, YANG DEOK, medical educator; b. Jeonju, Republic of Korea, June 19, 1970; s. Lee Ki Ban and Hwang Giu Uk; m. Kim Hang Na, June 12, 1998; children: Lee Ha Jin, Lee Eun Hyuk. MB, Chonbuk Nat. U., 1996, MS in Medicine, 2000, MD, 2003. Lic. med. doctor Ministry Heath and Welfare, Korea, 1996, specialist internal medicine Ministry Heath and Welfare, Korea, 2002. Intern Chonbuk Nat. U. Hosp., Jeonju, Republic of Korea, 1996—97, resident, 1998—2002; instr. Sch. Medicine Eulji U., Daejeon, Republic of Korea, 2003—05, asst. prof. Sch. Medicne, 2005—10, assoc. prof., 2010—. Mem. staff operation-related area and team on call FIFA World Cup Korea Japan, Seoul, Republic of Korea, 2002; jr. reviewer Med. Sci. Monitor, NYC, 2005—; chmn. Eulji Com. Korea Med. Lic. Exam., Daejeon, Republic of Korea, 2004—05, vice chmn., 2005—; dir. Infection Control Office Eulji U. Hosp., Daejeon, 2005—06. Contbr. articles to profl. jours. Recipient The Best Resident award, Chonbuk Nat. U. Hosp., 2001, Worldcup Appreciation plaque, Ministry Culture and Tourism, 2002, The Best Tchr. award, Eulji U. Sch. Medicine, 2005, Appreciation plaque for tutor, 2007; grantee, 2003, 2005, BumSuk Academic Scholarship Found., 2003, 2006. Mem.: Am. Coll. Chest Physicians, European Acad. Allergology and Clin. Immunology, Am. Thoracic Soc., Europena Respiratory Soc., The Korean Geriat. Soc. (geriatrician 2004), The Korean Acad. Tb and Respiratory Diseases, The Korean Acad. Asthma and Allergy, The Korean Assn. Internal Medicine (subspecialist pulmonology 2004). Avocations: mountain climbing, music, travel. Office: Eulji Univ Hosp Doonsan-Dong Seo-Gu 1306 302-799 Daejeon Daejeon Republic of Korea Home: 205-701 Mokryon Apt Dunsan-dong Daejeon 302 726 Republic of Korea Office Fax: 82-42-259-1111. Personal E-mail: lydmd@hanmail.net. Business E-Mail: lyd@eulji.ac.kr.

LEE, YEU-TSU MARGARET, surgeon, educator; b. Xian, Shensi, China, Mar. 18, 1936; m. Thomas V. Lee, Dec. 29, 1962 (div. 1987); 1 child, Maxwell M. AB in Microbiology, U. S.D., 1957; MD, Harvard U., 1961. Diplomate Am. Bd. Surgery. Assoc. prof. surgery Med. Sch., U. So. Calif., LA, 1973-83; commd. lt. col. U.S. Army Med. Corps, 1983, advanced through grades to col., 1989; chief surg. oncology Tripler Army Med. Ctr., Honolulu, 1983-98; ret. U.S. Army, 1999; assoc. clin. prof. surgery Med. Sch., U. Hawaii, Honolulu, 1984-92, clin. prof. surgery, 1992—. Author: Malignant Lymphoma, 1974; author chpts to books; contbr. articles to profl. jours. Pres. Orgn. Chinese-Am. Women, L.A., 1981, Hawaii chpt., 1988; active U.S.-China Friendship Assn., 1991—. Decorated Nat. Def. Svc. medal, Army Commendation medal, Army Meritorious Svc. medal, Army Humanitarian Svc. medal; recipient Chinese-Am. Engrs. and Scis. Assn., 1987; named Sci. Woman Warrior, Asian-Pacific Womens Network, 1983. Mem. ACS, Soc. Surg. Oncology, Assn. Women Surgeons. Avocations: classical music, movies, hiking, ballroom dancing. Address: PO Box 29726 Honolulu HI 96820 Personal E-mail: ytm_lee@hotmail.com.

LEE, YIH-SHIUNN, orthopedist; m. Chia-Hui Huang; children: Miffy, Angel. MB, Taipei Med. U., Taiwan, 1999. Cert. in orthop. surgery Taiwan, 2005, in gen. surgery Taiwan, 2004. Chief orthop. trauma Lin Shin Hosp., Taichung City, Taiwan, 2007—; orthop. attending staff Taipei City Hosp., 2005—07. Instr. Ctrl. Taiwan U. Sci. and Tech., Taichung City, 2008—. Contbr. articles to profl. jours. Achievements include research in studies related to comparison of surgical methods. Office: Lin Shin Hosp 36 Sect 3 Huizhong Rd Nanton Taichung 408 Taiwan

LEE, YONG CHUL, medical educator; b. Chonju, Republic of Korea, Mar. 14, 1960; B, Chonbuk Nat. U. Med. Sch., Chonju, 1985, MS, 1991; PhD, Chonnam Nat. U. Med. Sch., Kwangju, Korea, 1993. Instr. Chonbuk Nat. U. Med. Sch., Chonju, 1992—94, asst. prof., 1994—, assoc. prof., 1998—. Mem. acad. com. Korean Acad. Asthma and Allergy, Seoul, 2000—. Contbr. articles to profl. jours.; mem. editl. bd.: Korean Acad. TB and Respiratory Disease, 1999. Recipient Best Paper of Yr. award, Korean Acad. Asthma and Allergy, 1996, Korean Fedn. Sci. and Tech. Socs., 2002; named Best Student, Pres. Supreme Ct., 1985. Office: Chonbuk Nat U Dept Internal Medicine/Med Sch 634-18 Keum am Dong 561-712 Chonju Republic of Korea Office Fax: 82-63-254-1609. E-mail: leeyc@moak.chonbuk.ac.kr.

LEE, YONG SANG, endocrinologist, consultant; b. Seoul, Republic Of Korea, Dec. 24, 1971; s. Gu Jong Lee and Hye Ja Choi, Seung Ryul Suh (Stepfather), Gyoung Sook Yang (Stepmother); m. Eun Young Suh; children: Hee Jin, Seong Jae. MS, Yonsei U. Grad. Sch., Seoul, 2008. Cert. medical surgeon Govt. Korea, 2006. Fellow-staff Nat. Cancer Ctr., Goyang-si, Gyeonggi-do, Republic of Korea, 2006—07; intern Severance Hosp., 2001—02, resident dept. surgery, 2002—06, fellow-staff, 2007—08, clin. asst. prof., 2008. Contbr. scientific papers to profl. jours. Capt. US Army. Mem.: The Korean Assn. Endocrine Surgeons. Christian Ch. Achievements include research in genetic expression in poorly differentiated thyroid carcinoma. Avocations: board games, soccer, baseball. Office: Yongdong Severance Hosp 612 Eonjuro Seodaemun-fu Seoul 135-752 Republic of Korea Office Fax: 82-2-3462-5994. Business E-Mail: medilys@yuhs.ac.

LEE, YONG SEOK, medical educator, department chairman; b. Seoul, Republic of Korea, Mar. 23, 1971; MD, Cath. U. Korea, 1997, PhD, 2010. Chmn. dept. ob-gyn. St. Mary's Hosp. Cath. U., 2009—, assoc. prof. Med. Coll. Korea, 2010—. Mem.: Am. Assn. Gynecologic Laparoscopy, Korean Soc. Cancer, Korean Soc. Ob-Gyn., Korean Soc. Gynecologic Oncology. Office: 505 Banpo-dong Seocho-gu Seoul 137-701 Republic of Korea Office Fax: 2-6919-1841. Business E-Mail: gom@catholic.ac.kr.

LEE, YONG SOO, pharmacology professor; b. Sang-ju, Kyungsangbuk-Do, June 14, 1962; s. Ki-Seop Lee and Bok-Yeol Choi; m. Jung-Ae Kim, Apr. 12, 1987; children: Ju-Yeon, Seong-Woo. PhD in Physiology, Loyola U. Chgo., 1993. Lic. pharmacist Korea, 1984. Postdoctoral fellow Loyola U. Med. Ctr., Chgo., 1993—95; prof. Kwandong U., Kangwon-Do, Republic of Korea, 1996—2002, Duksung Women's U., Seoul, 2002—. Post-doc Loyola U. Med. Ctr., Chicago, Ill., 1993—95. Mem. clin. expt. regulation com. Korea FDA, Seoul, 2006—08. Recipient Young Investigator award, Korea Soc. Physiology, 1997, Excellent Sci. Publ. Award, 2007; grantee Regional Scientist grant, Korea Rsch. Found., 1997—2000, Basic Sci. grant, 2001—03, Excellent Rsch. Ctr. grant, 2006—. Mem.: Korea Soc. Applied Pharmacology (assoc.). Adventist. Achievements include patents pending for compound for the treatment of pancreatic cancers. Office: Duksung Women's Univ 419 Ssangmun-Dong Dobong-Gu Seoul 132-714 Republic of Korea Office Fax: 86 2 901 8386. Business E-Mail: yongslee@duksung.ac.kr.

LEE, YONG-SOON, veterinarian, educator; b. Korea, Oct. 16, 1944; DVM, Seoul Agrl. Coll., Republic of Korea, 1972; MS, U. Tokyo, 1975, PhD, 1978. Cert. Korean Bd. Vet. Medicine. Prof. Seoul Nat. U. Coll. Vet. Medicine, 1979—, dean, 1999—2001; commr. Korea Food and Drug Adminstrn., Seoul, 2002—03. Pres. Korea Assn. Lab. Animal Sci., Seoul, 1993—99, Korea Soc. Toxicology, Seoul, 1999—2000, Korean Soc. Vet. Sci., 2003—05. Author: Toxicopathology, 1998, Laboratory Animal Medicine, 2000. Office: Seoul Nat U Coll Vet Medicine Seoul 151-742 Republic of Korea Business E-Mail: leeys@snu.ac.kr.

LEE, YOU MIE, medical educator; b. Muju, Republic Of Korea, Aug. 12, 1961; d. Byung Hee Lee and Seung Bea Yu; m. Chang Rok Kim; children: Jung Hyun Kim, Min Jung Kim. BS, Seoul Nat. U., Coll. Pharmacy, Republic of Korea, 1985, MS, 1986, PhD, 1996. Cert. pharmacist Korean Ministry of Health and Wealfare, 1985. Rsch. fellow Harvard Med. Sch., Children's Hosp., Boston, 2001—03; BK21 prof. Seoul Nat. U., Coll. Medicine, 2003—04. Assoc. prof. Kyungpook Nat. U., Daegu, Republic Of Korea, 2005—. Contbr. articles to med. jours. Mem.: Am. Assn. Cancer Rsch. Home: Jangwon Apt 102-1002 Beomo-dong Daegu 706-739 Republic of Korea Office: Kyungpook Nat Univ Sankyuk-Dong Buk-Gu 1370 702-701 Daegu Daegu Republic of Korea Office Fax: 82-53-943-6925. Business E-Mail: lym@knu.ac.kr.

LEE, YOUNG KEUN, orthopedic surgeon, consultant; b. Gimje, Chonbuk, Republic Of Korea, Mar. 27, 1971; s. Bok Man and Sun Duk Lee; m. Sun A. Jung, Mar. 17, 2002; 1 child, Jung Hun. B, Chonbuk Nat. U., Chonju, Korea, 1996, M, 2000, MD, 2006. Cert. flight surgeon Aeromedical Ctr., ROKAF, 2002, lic. Ministry Health and Welfare, 1996, orthopedic specialist Ministry Health and Welfare, 2001, hand surgery subspecialist Korean Acad. Med. Sci., 2005. Intern Chonbuk Nat. U. Hosp., 1996—97, resident, dept. orthopedic surgery, 1997—2001, clinic lectr., 2004—05; chief aeromedicine 1St Flight Wing, Kwang-ju, Republic of Korea, 2001—04; prof. Eulji U. Med. Sch., Daejon, Republic of Korea, 2005—06; chief, Hand Surgery Ctr. Gangnam Hosp., Daegu, 2007—08; chief Woo and Lee's Inst. for Hand Surgery and Reconstructive Microsurgery Ctr. W Hosp., Daegu, 2008—10; pres. Dason Orthop. Clinic, 2011—. Vis. fellow Prince of Wales Hosp., Shatin, Hong Kong, 2007. Author: (book) Elbow Joint Diseases and Updates of Microsurgery; editl. sec.: Jour. Korean Soc. Microsurgery, 2008; contbr. articles to various profl. jours. Capt. 1st flight wing, 2001—04, Kwangju. Mem.: Korean Soc. Microsurgery, Korean Soc. Surgery of Hand (Excellence award 2010), Korean Orthopedic Assn. Avocations: mountain climbing, trumpet, swimming. Home: 489-1 Sepo-Ri Juksan-Myeon 561-756 Gimje Republic of Korea Office: Dason Orthop Clinic 1572-8 Inhu-Dong Deokjin-gu Jeonju 561-853 Republic of Korea Personal E-mail: trueyklee@yahoo.co.kr.

LEE, YOUNG SEOK, radiologist, educator; b. Daegu, Republic of Korea, Apr. 15, 1952; B, Seoul Nat. U., 1977, PhD, 1989. Dept. dir. Sowha Children's Hosp., 1984—87, Chung-ang Gil Hop., 1987—96; prof. Dankook U. Hosp., 1996—, dir. edn. & rsch., 2001—03, v.p., 2003—04, CEO, 2004—06. Recipient Academic Rsch. award, Korean Soc. Ultrasound Medicine, Outstanding Best Paper award, Korean Fedn. Sci. and Tech. Mem.: Internat. Soc. Pediatric Radiology, Asia-Oceanian Soc. Pediatric Radiology, Korean Soc. Ultrasound Medicine, Korean Soc. Radiology, Radiology Soc. N.Am. Avocations:

board games, mountain climbing. Office: 359 Manghyang-ro Dongnam Cheonan Chungnam 330-715 Republic of Korea Office Phone: 82-41-550-6921. Office Fax: 82-41-552-9674. Business E-Mail: yslee@dkuh.co.kr.

LEE, YOUNG WOO, neurosurgery educator; b. Ulsan City, Republic of Korea, Mar. 9, 1937; s. Jong Kap and Myung Ran (Choi) L.; m. Kyung Ja Kim, Nov. 3, 1969; children: Sang Min, Soon Jeong. MD, Pusan Nat. U., 1962, MSc, 1965, PhD, 1973. Lic. med. practice Ministry Social Welfare, Republic of Korea, 1962, cert. diplomate Korean Bd. Neurosurgery, 1967; lic. radioactive isotope use Korean Atomic Ministry, 1964, marriage counsellor 2004, drug preventive consulting dir. 2004. Intern Pusan Nat. U. Hosp., 1962-63, resident in surgery and neurosurgery, 1963—65, resident in neurosurgery, 1965—67; prof. neurosurgery Pusan Nat. U. Sch. Medicine, Pusan Nat. U. Hosp., 1971—2002, chmn. dept neurosurgery, 1975—2002; rsch. fellow dept. neurology U. Ala., Birmingham Sch. Medicine and Med. Ctr., 1974—75; fellow Dept. Neurosci. LI Coll. Hosp., Bklyn., 1980—81; fellow dept. neurosurgery McGill U., Montreal Neurol. Inst., Canada, 1998—99; prof. emeritus Pusan Nat. U. Hosp., 2002—; hon. supt. Dong-Rae Bong Seng Hosp., 2002—, chmn., 2002—. Co-author: The Great Medical Encyclopedia, 1991; contbr. chapters to books. Maj. Korean Army, 1967—70. Decorated Viet-Nam War medal Pres. Republic of Korea, Merit Viet-Nam Korean Comdr. Viet-Nam War, First Technique Decoration medal Viet-Nam Gov., Civil Decoration medal; recipient award, Pfizer's Med. Co., 1977, Ednl. award, Korean Tchr. Assn., 2001, Pusan Tchr. Assn., 2001, Acad. award, Pusan Med. Assn., 2002, Ockjo award, Korean Gov., 2002, Mil. Merit award, In Heon. Mem.: AAAS, Korean Vet. Soc., Mil. Medalist Assn., World Fedn. Neurosurgeons, Korean Soc. Med. and Biol. Engring., Korean Radioisotope Soc., Korean Soc. Neurobiology and Neurosci., NY Acad. Sci., Am. Assn. Electrodiagnositc Medicine, Korean Med. Assn., Korean Neurosurg. Soc. (v.p. 1988—89, pres. 1987—88). Home: Lucky Apt 19-1205 707 Oncheon 2-dong Tongrae-ku Pusan 607-753 Republic of Korea Office: Busan Nat U Sch Medicine and Pusan Nat U Hosp Dept Neurosurgery 1-10 Ami-dong Busan 602-739 Republic of Korea Office Phone: 82-51-247-0244, 82-51-244-0282.

LEE, YOUNG-HO, hematologist, researcher; b. Busan, Republic of Korea, Feb. 12, 1960; s. Hyun-Keum and Keum-Soo Lee; m. Ki-Roung Kim, Dec. 1, 1985; children: So-Young, Soo-Jin, Joon-Seok. BA, Han-Yang U., Seoul, Republic of Korea, 1984, MA, 1988, PhD, 1992. Diplomate Republic of Korea Pediatric Bd. Intern Busan Baik Hosp. Busan Baik Hosp. Inje U., 1984—85, resident; instr. Coll Medicine Dong-A U., Busan, 1989—92, from asst. prof. to assoc. prof., 1992—2001, prof., 2001—05, dir. dept. edn. & rsch., 2003—, vice dean Coll Medicine, 2004—; prof. Hanyang U. Coll. Medicine, 2005—. Postgraduate rschr. UCLA Sch. Medicine, 1991—92; vis. prof. Baylor Coll. Medicine, Houston, 1996. Mem. editl. bd. Korean Jour. Pediatric Hemato-Oncology, 2003; contbr. articles to profl. jours. Mem. adv. bd. Korean Assn. Childhood Leukemia and Cancer, Seoul, 2000—, Korean Marrow Donor Program, Seoul, 2001—, Korean Ministry of Health and Welfare, Seoul, 2003, Korean FDA, Seoul, 2003; dir. Busan-Kyongnam Cord Blood Bank, 2000—. Grantee, Korean Ministry of Health and Welfare, 2003. Mem.: Internat. Soc. Hematotherapy and Graft Engring., Internat. Soc. Hematology, Am. Soc. Hematology, Korean Soc. Hematopoietic Stem Cell Transplantation (chmn. cord blood com. 2003, grantee 2003), Internat. Cord Blood Soc. (mem. adv. bd. 2002—). Avocation: golf. Home: Shin Gudeok-Woosung Apt #102-1601, Hakjang-Dong, Sasang-Ku Pusan 617-020 Republic of Korea Home Phone: 82-51-322-0383; Office Phone: 82-51-240-2956. Business E-Mail: yhlee1@dau.ac.kr.

LEE, YOUNG-RAN, surgeon; b. Incheon, Republic Of Korea, Apr. 21, 1963; d. Eun-Kap Lee and Won-Sook Yang; m. Yeon-Bum Choi, Dec. 18, 1987; children: Sang-Hoon Choi, Ri-Ye Choi. BMed, Ewha Womans' U., Seoul, 1988; PhD, Juntendo U., Tokyo, 2001. Cert. Ministry Health & Welfare, Republic of Korea, 1988, diplomate family medicine Ministry Health & Welfare, Republic of Korea, 1991, cert. Japanese Soc. Investigative Dermatology, 2000, Internat. Soc. Hair Restoration Surgery, Ill., 2007. Rsch. fellow Dept. Dermatology, Juntendo U., Tokyo, 2003—05; dir. Hair Transplant Ctr., Arumdaunnara Clin., Seoul, 2001—. Contbr. articles, chapters to books. Recipient Bronze Medal, Japanese Soc. Clin. Hair Rsch., 2007, 2nd Pl., Internat. Soc. Hair Restoration Surgery, 2003, Hon. Mention, 2003, Shiseido Rsch. Award, Japanese Soc. Investigative Dermatology, 1997. Mem.: Japanese Soc. Dermatology, Japanese Soc. Aesthetic Surgery (tokyo 2003—09), Japanese Soc. Clin. Hair Rsch. (japan 2007—09), Internat. Soc. Hair Restoration Surgery (ill. 2000—09). Office Phone: 82-2-553-7573. Business E-Mail: arimilee@naver.com.

LEE, YU-JIN, retired military physician; b. Taipei, Taiwan, Feb. 13, 1934; arrived in US, 1966; s. Siong Ai and Sun Lu Chow Lee; m. Marie Louise Willing, Aug. 23, 1969; children: Heather N., Math-Yu E., Jin-Nefer M. MD, Nat. Taiwan U., Taipei, 1961. Lic. physician Del., 1974, Md., 1999. WHO fellow States Serum Inst., Copenhagen, 1961—62; asst. prof. dept. microbiology Nat. Taiwan U., Taipei, 1962—66; rotating intern Toledo Hosp., 1966—67; resident Maryview Hosp., Portsmouth, Va., 1967—68, Wilmington Med. Ctr., Del., 1968—70; pub. health physician II Del. State Bd. Health, Newark, 1970—74; dir. med. svcs. US Naval Hosp., Japan, 1980—82, 1985—89, USN Med. Clinic, Quantico, Va., 1983—85, Naval Hosp., Great Lakes, Ill., 1985—86. Contbr. articles to profl. sci. jours. Capt. USN, 1974—98. Decorated 3 Navy Commendation medals, 2 Nat. Def. Svc. medals, Meritorious Unit Commendation, Overseas Svc. medal, Meritorious Svc. medal; recipient Gold medal for swimming, 2009, Silver medal for swimming. Mem.: AMA. Avocations: swimming, gardening. Home: 902 Song Sparrow Ct Arnold MD 21012

LEE, YUNGLING LEO, medical educator; b. Taiwan, Sept. 30, 1974; MD, Nat. Taiwan U., 1999; PhD, Nat. Cheng Kung U., 2004. Physician Dept. Occupl. and Environ. Medicine, Nat. Cheng Kung U., 2005—09, asst. prof., 2005—09, Inst. Epidemiology and Preventive Medicine, Coll. Pub. Health, Nat. Taiwan U., 2009—; rsch. assoc. Dept. Preventive Medicine, U. Southern Calif., 2006—07. Mem.: Am. Thoracic Soc., Taiwan Pub. Health Assn., Internat. Soc. Environ. Epidemiology (Outstanding Asian Young Environ. Epidemiologist award), Taiwan Environ. and Occupl. Med. Assn. (Outstanding Young Physician award). Office: 17 Xuzhou RD 516R Taipei 100 Taiwan Office Fax: 886-2-23511955.

LEE, YUNHWAN, healthcare educator; married. MD, Yonsei U., 1989, MPH, 1992; DPH, Johns Hopkins U., 1996. Epidemic outbreak investigation officer Korea Ctrs. Disease Control and Prevention, Seoul, 1989—92; postdoctoral rsch. fellow Health Svcs. R&D Ctr. Johns Hopkins U., Balt., 1996—98; asst. rsch. prof. Grad. Sch. Pub. Health Yonsei U., Seoul, 1998—99; asst. prof. Sch. Medicine Ajou U., Suwon, Republic of Korea, 1999—2003, chair dept. pub. policy Sch. Pub. Adminstrn. and Pub. Affairs, 2000—02, internat. affairs officer Med. Ctr., 2003—04, assoc. prof. Sch. Medicine, 2003—, asst. dir. internat. cooperation Office Planning and Coordination Med. Ctr., 2004—06; dir. Inst. Aging, 2008—; vice dean rsch. affairs Ajou U., Sch. Medicine, 2010—; sr. esch. assoc. Josn Hosp. U. Bloomberg Sch. Pub. Health, 2011—. Vis. scientist Tokyo Met. Inst. Gerontology, 2000; mem. adv. panel Planning Bd. of Com. on Nat. Health and Welfare Policy for Older Persons Office for Govt. Policy Coordination, Office of the Prime Min., Seoul, 2001—02; mem. adv. panel Adv. Bd. on Pub. Long-Term Care Sys. for Older People Ministry of Health and Welfare, Seoul, 2003—04, mem. adv. panel Adv. Bd. on Evaluation of Demonstration Projects in Long-Term Care Sys. for Older People, 2005—; vis. scholar Johns Hopkins U., 2006—07; editor-in-chief Jour. Preventive Medicine & Pub. Health, 2009—. Co-founder and co-editor: Communicable Disease Monthly Report for Korea Ctrs. Disease Control and Prevention, 1990—92; contbr. articles to profl. jours. Recipient Spl. Citation, Min. of Health and Social Affairs, Korea, 1991, Grand prize, Alpha chpt. Delta Omega Honor Soc., Bloomberg Sch. Pub. Health, Johns Hopkins U., 1995, Spl. Recognition, Korea Ctrs. Disease Control and Prevention, 2000; fellow, WHO/Pan Am. Health Orgn., 1993—95; Rsch. grantee, Inst. Korean Unification Studies, Yonsei U., 1998—99, Ministry Health and Welfare, Korea, 1999—2002, 2008—09, 2011—, Health Tech. Planning and Evaluation Bd., Ministry of Health and Welfare, Korea, 1998—99, 2002—04, Ajou Inst. Korean Unification and Health Care, 1999—2000, Ministry of Unification, Korea, 2002, Internat. Collaboration on Health Promotion of the Elderly in Asia, Japan Found. for Aging and Health, Japan, 2002—03, Korean Med. Assn., 2005—06, Korean Geriat. Soc., 2008—09, Nat. Rsch. Found., Korea, 2010—. Mem.: APHA (Laurence G. Br. Student Rsch. award gerontol. health sect. 1996), Fed. Gerontol. Korea Socs. (dir.-in-charge acad. bus. 2008—10), Korean Geriat. Soc. (mem. jour. editl. bd. 2008—09), Gerontol. Soc. Am., Korean Gerontol. Soc. (mem. jour. editl. bd. 2001—02, 2006—08, v.p. external affairs 2011—), Korean Soc. Preventive Medicine (life; mem. jour. editl. bd. 2002—04). Office: Ajou University Sch Medicine San 5 Wonchun-dong Youngtong-gu Suwon 443-721 Republic of Korea Office Fax: +82-31-219-5084. Business E-Mail: yhlee@ajou.ac.kr.

LEE, YUNJUNG, nursing educator; b. Republic of Korea, July 27, 1963; PhD, Chungnam Nat. U., 2003. Prof. Woosuk U., 1997—. Office: Woosuk University Samrye-eup Dept Nursing Wanju-gun Jeonbuk 560-701 Republic of Korea Office Phone: 82-63-290-1544. Business E-Mail: yjlee@woosuk.ac.kr.

LEE, YUN-SIL, biomedical researcher; d. Bae; m. Dooil Jeoung, Oct. 13, 2001; 1 child, Seo-Young Jeoung. PhD, Ewha Women's U., Seoul, Republic Of Korea, 1994. Sr. rschr. KIRAMS, Seoul, 1995—2008, divsn. chief, 2004—. Achievements include patents for heptapeptide development for overcoming radio and chemoresistance. Office: KIRAMS 215-4 Gongneung-dong Nowon-ku Seoul 137-240 Republic of Korea Business E-Mail: yslee@kcch.re.kr.

LEEDS, NORMAN E., medical educator, radiologist; b. Jersey City, June 9, 1928; m. Beth G. Leeds, June 12, 1953; children: Frederick G., Patrice G. BA, Yale Coll., 1948; MD, NY Med. Coll., 1953. Diplomate in radiology and in neuroradiology Am. Bd. Radiology. Asst. prof. radiology U So. Calif. Sch. Medicine, LA, 1961—63; asst. prof. U. Pa. Grad. Sch. and Grad. Hosp., Phila., 1962—64, U. Pa. Children's Hosp., 1964—69, Albert Einstein Hosp. Temple U., 1964—69; assoc. prof. Albert Einstein Coll. Medicine, Montefiore Hosp., Bronx, 1969—74, prof., 1974—85, Mt. Sinai Sch. of Medicine, NYC, 1985—90; chair dept. radiology Beth Israel Hosp., NYC; prof., Kennedy chair U. Tex. M.D. Anderson Cancer Ctr., Houston, 1991—2003, clin. prof., 2008—11, Mt. Sinai Sch. Medicine, Mt. Sinai Hosp., 2003—08. With USPHS, 1955—57. Fellow: Am. Heart Assn., Am. Coll. Radiology; mem.: Am. Soc. Neuroradiology (pres. 1973, Gold medal 2003). Home: 5000 Montrose Blvd Apt 8C Houston TX 77006 Business E-Mail: neleeds@mdanderson.org.

LEEPER, MARY ANN, health science association administrator; BS, Drexel U., 1962; MS, Temple U., 1967, PhD, 1971; MBA, Northwestern U., 1978. Biochemist McNeil Labs., 1962—63; radiochemist Wyeth Labs., 1963—65; radiation supr. New England Nuclear Corp., 1966—68; asst. prof. radiopharmaceutical and pharm. chemistry Temple U., 1970—73; tech. mgr. diagnostic Amersham Searle & Co., 1973—74; mgr. radiopharmaceutical rsch. and devel. G.D. Searle & Co., 1974—76, dir. radiopharmaceutical rsch. and devel., 1976—77, exec. asst. to the pres. pharm./consumers product group, 1977—78, dir. bus. devel., 1978—79, dir. mktg., 1979—81, v.p. market devel., 1981—86; v.p., ptnr. Phoenix Health Care, Inc., 1987—; sr. v.p., dir. Wis. Pharmacal, 1987—96; pres., COO Female Health Co. (formerly Wis. Pharmacal), 1996—2006, sr. strategic advisor, 2006—; founder, chair, bd. dirs. Female Health Found., 1997—. Co-founder Bus. Women's Initiative Against HIV/AIDS, 2004; bd. dirs. Neenah Paper, Inc.; adj. prof. Darden Sch. Bus., U. Va. Recipient Woman Entrepreneurship award, Temple U. Sch. Bus., 2003. Home: PO Box 603 Earlysville VA 22936-0603 Home Phone: 312-664-8798; Office Phone: 312-595-9118.

LEES, MARTIN HENRY, retired pediatrician; b. London, May 11, 1929; came to U.S., 1958; s. David William and Lilian Thomson (White) L.; m. Elizabeth McMahon, Sept. 5, 1959; children: Deborah Ann, Jacqueline Mary, Christina Beth. MBBS, London U., 1955, MD, 1962. Diplomate: Am. Bd. Pediatrics, Am. Bd. Pediatric Cardiology, Am. Bd. Fetal/Neonatal Medicine. Intern South Devon Hosp., Plymouth, Eng., 1955-57; resident in pediatrics Hosp. Sick Children, 1957; sr. resident, fellow in pediatric cardiology Boston Children's Hosp., 1958-61; asst. prof. McGill U., Montreal, Que., Can., 1961-62; prof. pediatrics U. Oreg. Health Ctr., Portland, 1963-95. Fellow Royal Coll. Physicians (London); mem. Am. Heart Assn., Am. Pediatric Soc., Soc. Pediatric Rsch. Home: 14 Morningview Ln Lake Oswego OR 97035-8842 Office: Pediatric Cardiology 501 N Graham St Ste 330 Portland OR 97227-2001

LEESON, LEWIS JOSEPH, pharmacist, researcher; b. Paterson, NJ, Apr. 26, 1927; s. Alfred Elias and Rose (Sandow) L.; m. Barbara Rothstein, Dec. 20, 1953; children: Suzanne, Erica, Alex. BS in Pharmacy, Rutgers U., Newark, 1950, MS in Pharm. Chemistry, 1954; PhD in Pharm. Chemistry, U. Mich., Ann Arbor, 1957. Registered pharmacist, N.J., N.Y., Mich. Pharmacist Mack Drug Co., Paterson, N.J., 1950-52, Fried's Drugs, Paterson, 1952-54; lab. asst. Rutgers U. Coll. Pharmacy, Newark, 1952-54, U. Mich., Ann Arbor, 1954-57; rsch. pharmacist, project leader Lederle Labs., Pearl River, NY, 1957—67; dir. product R & D, Union Carbide Co., Greenburgh, N.Y., 1967-69; asst. dir. product R & D, Geigy Pharm., Suffern, N.Y., 1969-71; dir., sr. dir., sr. rsch. fellow Ciba-Geigy Pharm., Summit, N.J., 1971-84; disting. rsch. fellow Ciba-Geigy Corp., Summit, 1984-93, ret., 1993; pres. LJL Assocs. Inc, Pharm. R&D Cons., Montville, N.J., 1993—. Dean Louis W. Busse lectr. U. Wis., 1993; mem. exec. com. USP, 1990—95, mem. expert adv. com., 2000—; mem. exec. com. N.J. DURC, 1984—89; founder, chief sci. officer Cogent Pharm., 1997—. Editor: Dissolution Technology, 1971; contbr. over 40 articles to profl. jours; patentee in field. Recipient Disting. Alumnus award U. Mich., 1990. Fellow Acad. Pharm. Sci., Am. Assn. Pharm. Scientists; mem. Am. Pharm. Assn., Sigma Xi, Rho Chi, Phi Lambda Upsilon. Jewish. Achievements include 14 patents in field. Home and Office: LJL Assocs Inc 134 Ridge Dr Montville NJ 07045-9473 Home Phone: 973-335-2673; Office Phone: 973-265-4637. Personal E-mail: blll@optonline.net.

LEESUNGBOK, RICHARD, dentist, educator; b. Seoul, Republic of Korea, May 13, 1958; DMD, MSD, PhD, Kyung Hee U. Sch. Dentistry, 1984. Head prof., v.p. dental hosp. Kyung Hee U. Sch. Dentistry, 1992—. Recipient Dr. Hiranuma award, 6th Biennial Congress Asian Acad. Prosthodontics, 4 gold medals, Beijing Olympic Game, 2008; grant, European Acad. Osseointegration. Fellow: International Team Implantology (edn. com. mem. 2004—11, edn. del. Korea 2004—11). Office: #149 Sangil-Dong Gangdong-Gu Seoul 134-727 Republic of Korea Office Fax: 82-2-440-7549. E-mail: sbykmw@yahoo.co.kr.

LEFEBER, EDWARD JAMES, JR., internist, educator; b. Galveston, Tex., Jan. 12, 1941; s. Edward James Lefeber and Ellie Hancock Weisiger; m. Faith Linn Gabrielsen, Oct. 18, 1967; 1 child, Karin. BA cum laude, U. South, Sewanee, Tenn., 1962; MD with honors, U. Tex., Galveston, 1966. Cert. internal medicine 1976, 1997, geriatric medicine 1988, 1997. Staff dept. internal medicine William Beaumont Army Hosp., 1971—72; pvt. practice Casa Blanca Med. Grp., Mesa, Ariz., 1972—73; staff physician VAMC, Phoenix, 1973—82, chief gen. internal medicine, dept. medicine, 1982—95; staff physician Temple VAMC, 1995—96, tchg. svc., 1996—98; attending physician Good Samaritan Phoenix VAMC Internal Medicine, 1974—95; acting chief tchg. svc., 1998—99; mem. clin. staff UTHSCSA, 1999—2011. Asst. prof. internal medicine Texas A&M Med. Sch., Tex., 1996—99; credentials com. mem. U. Physicians Grp., 1999—2010, U. Tex. Medicine, San Antonio, 2010—11; staff VTHSCSA, 2011. Vol. State of Tex. Col. USAR, 1966—2001, gen. med. officer US Army, 1967—69, Vietnam, hosp. cmdr. US Army, 403 Combat Support Hosp., active duty US Army, 1970—72, active duty US Army, 1990—91, commdg. officer, major assignment, 1988—92, Phoenix, Saudi Arabia. Decorated Bronze Star Medal US Army, Meritorious Svc. medal; named one of Top Physicians, Consumer Rsch. Coun. America, 2003—11. Fellow: Am. Coll. Physicians; mem.: ACLS, Alpha Omega Alpha. Avocations: hiking, history. Office Phone: 210 450 9100. Office Fax: 210-450-6007. Business E-Mail: lefeber@uthscsa.edu.

LEFEBVRE, PIERRE JEAN, physician, educator; b. Liege, Belgium, Oct. 7, 1931; s. Charles François Lefebvre and Marie Louise Germay; m. Anne Marie Bonhomme, June 2, 1960; children: Philippe Pierre, Catherine, France. MD, U. Liège, Belgium, 1959; D (hon.), Extramadura U., Spain; DSc (hon.), Laval U., Québec, Canada; D (hon.), U. Paris VI, U. Helsinki, Finland, U. Cluj Napoca, Romania, U. Athens, Greece, U. d' Auvergne, Clermont Ferrand, France. Prof. U. Liège, 1967, emeritus prof., 2000—. Pres. Internat. Diabetes Fedn., Brussels, 2003—06; chmn. World Diabetes Found., Copenhagen, 2003—; pres. Global Diabetes Alliance, Seattle, 2008—10; hon. pres. Internat. Acad. Sportology Tokyo, 2011—. Comdt. Belgian Army. Recipient Claude Bernard medal, European Assn. Study Diabetes, 1984, Long Standing Achievement award, Novartis, 2000. Fellow: Royal Coll. Physicians (London). Office: CHU Liege Domaine Univ Du Sart Tilman Liège B 4000 Belgium Home: avenue du Bout du Monde 3 4053 Embourg-Chaudfontaine Belgium Personal E-mail: pierre.lefebvre@ulg.ac.be.

LEFEBVRE, VLADIMIR A., psychologist, researcher; b. St. Petersburg, USSR, Sept. 22, 1936; came to U.S., 1974; s. Alexander Voinov and Olga Lefevr; m. Victorina Dubovskaya, Apr. 26, 1959; 1 child, Andrei; 1 adopted child, Dung Le. MS in Math., Lomonosov State U., Moscow, 1968, PhD in Psychology, 1971; D honoris causa, Internat. Info. Acad., 2000. Engr., lab. technician Rsch. Inst. of Ministry of Def., Moscow, 1961-64; rsch. scientist, head sci. team Automatic Equipment Inst., Moscow, 1965-69; rsch. scientist Cen. Math. Econs. Inst. Acad. of Scis., Moscow, 1969-73; lectr. in psychology Lomonosov State U., 1972-73; researcher dept. psychology U. Calif., LA, 1974-75, lectr. Russian program Humanities Sch. Irvine, 1975-77, researcher Sch. of Social Scis., 1977—. Cons. Scis. Application Internat., Inc., 1981—, RAND Corp., 1985-88. Author: Conflicting Structures, 1967, enlarged edit., 1973, The Structure of Awareness: Toward a Symbolic Language of Human Reflexion, 1977, Algebra of Conscience, 1982, enlarged edit., 2001, The Structure of Human Reflexion: The Reflexional Psychology of Vladimir Lefebvre, 1990, A Psychological Theory of Bipolarity and Reflexivity, 1992, enlarged edit., 2006, The Cosmic Subject, 1997; Lectures on the Reflexive Games Theory, 2010; mem. editl. bd. Jour. Social and Biol. Structures, 1985-89; mem. Editl. bd. Internat. Jour. General Systems 2009-. Sgt. Soviet Army, 1955-58. Recipient gold medal Moldova br. Internat. Info. Acad., 2000, Descartes medal in cognitive studies Ctr. for Advanced Def. Studies, 2006. Mem. AAAS, Am. Psychol. Soc., Soc. for Math. Psychology, Internat. Soc. for Sys. Studies, Russian Acad. Natural Scis. (fgn. mem.), N.Y. Acad. Scis., U. Calif. Univ. Club. Office: U Calif Sch Social Sciences Irvine CA 92697 Personal E-mail: valefebv@uci.edu.

LEFÈVRE, GILBERT YVES, pharmacologist; b. Saint-Lo, Manche, France, Mar. 23, 1962; s. Eugène and Georgette Lefèvre; m. Nadine Noël, Jan. 17, 1960; children: Clément, Marion. PhD, U. Paris VII, 1989. Rschr. French Inst. Health and Med. Rsch., Paris, 1986—89, Clonatec, Paris, 1989—91; mentor Ciba-Geigy Ltd., Paris, 1991—96; sr. expert pharmacokineticist Novartis Pharma Ltd., Basel, Switzerland, 1997—. Recipient award, Fondation de la Vocation Marcel Bleustein-Blanchet, 1986. Avocation: equestrian sports.

Home: 24 rue Principale 68210 Gildwiller France Home Phone: + 33 3 89 25 91 38; Office Phone: + 41 61 324 6114. Office Fax: + 41 61 324 8940. Business E-Mail: gilbert.lefevre@novartis.com.

LEFEVRE, NICOLAS, surgeon; b. Soisy Sous Montmorency, Mar. 12, 1968; MD, BICHAT, 1993. Physician sport surgery, 1993. Mem.: SFA. Office: 36 Blvd Saint Marcel Paris 75005 France Business E-Mail: docteurlefevre@club-internet.fr.

LEFF, ALAN RICHARD, medical educator, researcher; b. May 23, 1945; s. Maurice D. and Grace Ruth (Schwartz) Leff; m. Donna Rae Rosene, Feb. 14, 1975; children: Marni, Karen, Alison. AB cum laude, Oberlin Coll., 1967; MD, U. Rochester, 1971. Diplomate Am. Bd. Internal Medicine, Am. Bd. Pulmonary Disease. Intern U. Mich. Hosp., Ann Arbor, 1971—72, resident, 1974—76; fellow U. Calif., San Francisco, 1976—77, postdoctoral fellow, 1977—79; asst. prof. medicine U. Chgo., 1979—85, assoc. prof. medicine and clin. pharm., 1985—89, prof. medicine, anesthesia, critical care and clin. pharm., 1989—, prof. cell physiology, 1992—, prof. pediats., neurobiology, physiology, 1999—, dir. pulmonary medicine svc., 1984—87, dir. Pulmonary Function Lab., 1979—87, chief sect. pulmonary and critical care medicine, 1987—2000, sr. dir. R&D biol. scis., 2000—02. Dir. NIAID Asthma and Allergic Disease Coop. Rsch. Ctr., Chgo., 1993—97; co-chair asthma sect. NIAID Task Force on Immunology, 1996—98; advisor San Francisco Dept. Pub. Health, 1977—79, Chgo Dept. Health, 1979—89; dir. Ctr. of Excellence in Asthma Glaxo Smith Kline, 2000—. Cons. editor, mem. editl. bd. Jour. Clin. Investigation, mem. editl. bd. Am. Jour. Physiology, Jour. Applied Physiology; editor: Am. Jour. Respiratory Critical Care Medicine, 1994—99, Procs. Am. Thoracic Soc., 2004—; editor, assoc. editor: Am. Rev. Respiratory Diseases, 1989—94, Pulmonary Pharmacology, 1987—92, assoc. editor: European Respiratory Jour., 2006—; contbr. articles to profl. jours. Bd. dirs. Chgo. Lung Assn., 1984—93. With USPHS, 1972—74. Recipient Citation of Merit, Chgo. Lung Assn., 1974, Am. Lung Assn., 1998; named one of Best Drs. in America, 2003—; fellow, Leopold Schepp Found., 1967—69. Fellow: Am. Coll. Chest Physicians; mem.: Am. Assn. Immunologists, Ctrl. Soc. for Clin. Investigation, Am. Thoracic Soc. (Spl. Citation 1999), Assn. Am. Physicians, Am. Physiol. Soc., Am. Soc. Clin. Investigation, Am. Fedn. Clin. Rsch. (councilor 1983—86), Sigma Xi. Avocation: music. Home: 5730 S Kimbark Ave Chicago IL 60637-1615 Office: U Chgo Pritzker Sch Medicine Div Biological Scis MC 6076 5841 S Maryland Ave Chicago IL 60637-1463 Home Phone: 773-955-9555. Business E-Mail: aleff@medicine.bsd.uchicago.edu.

LEFFALL, LASALLE DOHENY, JR., surgeon, educator; b. Tallahassee, Fla., May 22, 1930; s. LaSalle Doheny Sr. and Martha (Jordan) Leffall. BS, Fla. A&M U., 1948; MD, Howard U., Washington, 1952. Diplomate Am. Bd. Surgery. Intern Homer G. Phillips Hosp., St. Louis, 1952-53; asst. resident surgery Freedmen's Hosp., Washington, 1953—54, chief resident, 1956—57; asst. resident surgery DC Gen. Hosp., 1954—55; sr. fellow cancer surgery Meml. Sloan Kettering Cancer Ctr., NYC, 1957—59; faculty Howard University College Medicine, 1962, chmn., dept. surgery, 1970—95, acting dean, 1970, Charles R. Drew prof. surgery, dept. surgery, 1992—. Bd. dirs. Mut. of America Life Ins. Co. Contbr. articles to profl. jours., chapters to books. Chmn., Pres.'s Cancer Panel Nat. Cancer Inst., 2002—. CAPT. US Army, 1960—61. Recipient St. George medal, Am. Cancer Soc., 1977, Minority Health Champion award, Ind. Minority Health Coalition, 2002. Mem.: ACS (pres. 1995—96), AMA, Am. Assn. Cancer Edn., Am. Cancer Soc. (pres. 1978—79), Soc. Surg. Oncology. Avocations: tennis, jazz, foreign languages. Office: Howard University 2400 6th St NW Washington DC 20059 Office Phone: 202-806-6100. Business E-Mail: lleffall@howard.edu. *

LEFFELL, DAVID JOEL, dermatologist, surgeon, writer, photographer, medical school administrator, educator; b. Montreal, Feb. 28, 1956; came to U.S., 1973; s. Allen Bernard and Freda (Deckelbaum) L. BS, Yale U., 1977; MD, McGill U., Montreal, 1981. Diplomate Am. Bd. Dermatology, Am. Bd. Internal Medicine. Resident in internal medicine Meml. Sloan-Kettering Cancer Ctr., NYC, 1981-84; instr. medicine Cornell U. Sch. Medicine, NYC, 1983-84; resident in dermatology Yale U. Sch. Medicine, New Haven, 1984-86; lectr., fellow dermatologic surgery U. Mich., Ann Arbor, 1987-88; chief Mohs micrographic surgery and laser surgery Yale U. Sch. Medicine, New Haven, 1988—, dir. Yale skin cancer detection program, 1988—, med. dir. faculty practice plan, 1996-98, prof. dermatology, plastic surgery and otolaryngology, 1998—2008; David Paige Smith prof. dermatology & surgery, 2008—; assoc. dean clin. affairs Yale U. Sch. Medicine, New Haven, 1999-2000; dir., CEO Yale Med. Group, New Haven, 1999—; sr. assoc. dean clin. affairs Yale U. Sch. Medicine, New Haven, 2001—05, dep. dean clin. affairs, 2005—08. Sci. advisor Nat. Hereditary Hemorrhagic Telangiectasia Found., New Haven, 1991-99; bd. dirs. Am. Coll. Mohs Micrographic Surgery and Cutaneous Oncology. Author: Manual of Skin Surgery, 1996, Total Skin: The Definitive Guide to Whole Skin Care for Life, 2000, Chinese editor, 2007; contbg. editor Jour. Dermatologic Surgery and Oncology, 1992-97; assoc. editor Med. and Surg. Dermatology; mem. editl. bd. Archives of Dermatology, Jour. Aesthetic Dermatology and Cosmetic Surgery, 1999—, Fitzpatrick's Dermatology in Gen. Medicine, 7th edit., 8th edit.; assoc. editor Skin and Aging, 1996-98; editor: Faculty of 1000; inventor laser fluorescence device to measure photoaging; patent: PTC skin cancer gene, 2003. Bd. dirs. Conn. Pub. TV, 2001-04, Artspace, NH, 2007-, Validus, Inc., 2010-, bd. mem., MCIC Bd., 2008-; trustees com. mem. Hopkins Sch., New Haven, 2011-. Recipient Frederic Mohs award Skin Cancer Found., 1988, 91. Mem. Conn. Dermatology Soc. (pres.). Home: 460 St Ronan St New Haven CT 06511-2251 Office: Yale Sch Medicine PO Box 208059 New Haven CT 06520-8059 Office Phone: 203-785-7999. Business E-Mail: david.leffell@yale.edu.

LEFFERT, HYAM LERNER, cell biologist; b. NYC, May 11, 1944; BA, U. Rochester, 1965; MD, Albert Einstein Coll. Medicine, 1971. Prof. UCSD Sch. Medicine, 1980—. Recipient Meml. fellowship, Guggenheim Found. Office: 9500 Gilman Dr La Jolla CA 92093 Business E-Mail: hleffert@ucsd.edu.

LEFFERTS, WILLIAM GEOFFREY, internist, educator; b. Towanda, Pa., Mar. 24, 1943; s. William LeRoy and Beatrice (Smith) L.; m. Susan Lynn Hiles, Oct. 31, 1970. BA, Hamilton Coll., 1965; MD, Hahnemann Med. Coll., 1969. Intern Hahnemann Hosp., 1969-70; resident in internal medicine Cleve. Clinic Hosp., 1970-73, chief med. resident, 1972-73; asst. prof. internal medicine Hahnemann Med. Coll., 1973-77; assoc. prof. Med. Coll. Pa., 1978-82, dir. primary care unit, 1978-82, dir. div. gen. internal medicine, 1979-82; staff physician Cleve. Clinic Found., 1982—. Fellow ACP. Office: 9500 Euclid Ave Cleveland OH 44195-0001

LEFFLER, CAROLE ELIZABETH, retired women's and mental health nurse; b. Sidney, Ohio, Feb. 18, 1942; d. August B. and Delores K. Aselage; children: Veronica, Christopher. ADN, Sinclair C.C., Dayton, Ohio, 1975. Cert. psychiat. nurse supr. Nurse Grandview Hosp, Dayton, 1961—76; substitute sch. nurse Fairborn City Schs., Ohio, 1981—82; dir. nursing Fairborn Nursing Home, 1983; supr. psychiat. nurse Twin Valley Behavioral Health Ctr., 1984—; ret., 2006. Mem. exec. bd. 1199; chmn. disaster mental health com. ARC Ohio. Vol., instr., disaster health nurse ARC, chmn. State of Ohio disaster mental health com.; officer, leader, camp nurse for Girl Scouts, Boy Scouts; Ch. Parish Coun. Recipient Fleur de Lis award Girl and Boy Scouts, Svc. award ARC, Fairborn Mayor's Cert. of Merit for Civic Pride, State of Ohio Govs. award Innovation Ohio, Ohio State Gov.'s award for assistance in N.Y.C. disaster, 2001. Mem. ANA, Ohio Nurses Assn., BPOE and Women of the Moose. Home: 1711 Port Jefferson Rd Sidney OH 45365-1939

LEFING, WILLIAM, dermatologist; BS, Bklyn. Coll., 1958; MD, N.J. Med. Sch., 1962. Bd. cert. dermatology. Intern Beth-El Hosp., Bklyn., 1962—63; resident Skin and Cancer Hosp., Temple U., 1965—68; pvt. practice dermatology Oceanside, NY, 1968—. Lt. USNR, 1963—65. Fellow: Am. Acad. Dermatology; mem.: AMA, NYS Soc. Dermatology Dermatological Surgery, New Marrox Soc. Office: Ste 203 2940 Lower Lincoln Ave Oceanside NY 11572-2915

LEFKOVITS, ALBERT MEYER, dermatologist; b. NYC, June 30, 1937; s. Aaron Melchoir and Muriel (Mark) L.; m. Cheryl Beth Kornberg, Apr. 25, 1971; children, Ari Nathan, Lauren Blair. AB, Cornell U., 1958; MD (Lederle research fellow), NY Medical Coll., 1962. Intern Newark Beth Israel Hosp., 1962—63; resident in dermatology Kings County Hosp. Center, SUNY, Downstate Med. Center, Bklyn., 1963—65; clinical instructor NY Medical Coll., 1966—; chief resident dermatology Mt. Sinai Hosp., NYC, 1965—66, research fellow in dermatology, 1966—67; practice medicine specializing in dermatology NYC, 1966—; clinical asst. Mt. Sinai Hosp., NYC, 1966—70; instr. dermatology Mt. Sinai Sch. Medicine, 1966—70; sr. clinical asst. Mt. Sinai Hosp., 1970—82; sr. clinical instr. Mt. Sinai Sch. Medicine, 1970—82, asst. prof., 1982—, asst. attending physician, 1982—, co-director, Cosmetic Dermatologic NY Surgery Training Program, 2003—, assoc. clinical prof., 2006—. Alumni fund-raising chmn. Horace Mann Sch., 1976-78; treas. Mt. Sinai Alumni, 1988-90, sec., 1991-93, v.p., 1993-95, pres. 1995-97. Served to maj. Army Medical Corps Reserve, 1969—71. Recipient Fredrick Wise Dermatology award N.Y. Acad. Medicine, 1965, Torch of Liberty award Anti-Defamation League, 1987, Maimonides award Keren Or Found. for Handicapped Blind Children, 1994. Mem. med. adv. bd. Skin Cancer Found. Mem. Harvey Soc., Soc. Investigative Dermatology, Dermatology Found., Soc. Tropical Dermatology, Am. Acad. Dermatology (task force on therapeutics and FDA liaison com., comm. coun., physicians practice com.), Am. Acad. Dermatology (comm. coun., physicians practice com.), AMA, Internat. Soc. Human and Animal Mycology, Mycology Soc. Ams., N.Y. Acad. Sci., Am. Physicians Fedn. (trustee, exec. com.), Jewish Chautaugua Soc. (life), Dermatology Soc. Greater N.Y. (pres., chmn. physicians advocacy com.), N.Y. State Med. Soc., Cornell Alumni Assn. N.Y. (bd. govs. 1974-76) Med. Adv. Bd. Skin Cancer Found., 1986—. Jewish (dir. congregation Emanu-El men's club). Clubs: Harmonie, Town, Cornell (N.Y.C.), Friar's, Lawrence Yacht (fleet surgeon 1982-83, sec. 1984, treas. 1985, commodore 1987). Jewish. Office: 1040 Park Ave New York NY 10028-1032

LEFKOWITZ, JOEL M., psychologist, educator; b. NYC, Oct. 17, 1940; s. Frank Morris and Charlotte (Van Dam) L.; m. Merle Ellen Goldner, Sept. 12, 1965 (div. May 1982); children: Jared, Melanie; m. Setha M. Low, June 26, 1994. BBA, CCNY, 1961; MS, Case Western Res. U., Cleve., 1963, PhD, 1965. Lic. psychologist, N.Y.; diplomate Am. Bd. Profl. Psychology. Asst. prof. to prof. psychology Baruch Coll. CUNY, NYC, 1965—2009, emeritus prof., 2009. Ind. cons., N.Y.C., 1965—; nat. bd. mem. Am. Bd. Profl. Psychology, 1995—. Author: Ethics and Values in Industrial-Organizational Psychology, 2003; contbr. articles to profl. jours. Fellow: APA, Assoc. Psychol. Sci., Soc. Indsl. Orgn. Psychology. Avocations: tennis, photography. Office: Baruch Coll Box B8-215 1 Bernard Baruch Way New York NY 10010 E-mail: Joel.Lefkowitz@Baruch.CUNY.edu. *

LEFKOWITZ, LOUIS HIRSCH, obstetrician, gynecologist; b. Bklyn., Oct. 20, 1937; s. Paul Howard and Bertha (Schulman) L.; m. Patricia Smith; 1 child, Andrew Philip. BA, U. N.C., 1959; postgrad., U. Bologna, 1959-62; MD, N.Y. Med. Coll., 1964. Diplomate Am. Bd. Ob-gyn. Intern Beth Israel Med. Ctr., NYC, 1964-65; resident in ob-gyn N.Y. Med. Coll., Flower Fifth Avenue and Met. Hosp. Ctr., NYC, 1965-69; dir. ob-gyn. dept. Good Samaritan Hosp., Suffern, N.Y., 1988-92. Maj. U.S. Army, 1969-71. Fellow ACOG, ACS, Am. Assn. Reproductive Medicine; mem. Am. Assn. Gynecologic Laparoscopy, Rockland County Med. Soc., N.Y. State Med. Soc. Jewish. Office: Tallman Ob-Gyn PC 134 Route 59 Suffern NY 10901-4917 also: 673 Route 17M Monroe NY 10950-3318 Office Phone: 845-535-5333, 845-357-5333. Personal E-mail: mdlou@optonline.net.

LEFKOWITZ, MATTHEW, pain medicine physician; MD, U. Brussels. Diplomate Am. Bd. Anesthesiology, Am. Bd. Anesthesiology-pain medicine. Intern in surgery Lenox Hill Hosp.; resident anesthesiology Mt. Sinai Med. Ctr., 1984—86, fellow in pain mgmt., 1986—87; physician LI Coll. Hosp. Named one of Best Doctors, NY Mag., 2000—10. Mem.: Am. Soc. of Anesthesiologists, Am. Pain Soc. Office: University Hospital of Brooklyn Long Island College Hospital 339 Hicks St Brooklyn NY 11201 Office Phone: 718-780-1000.

LEFKOWITZ, ROBERT JOSEPH, biomedical researcher, educator; b. NYC, Apr. 15, 1943; s. Max and Rose (Levine) Lefkowitz; m. Lynn Tilley, May 26, 1991. BA, Columbia Coll., NYC, 1962; MD, Columbia U. Coll. Physicians and Surgeons, NYC, 1966. Diplomate Am. Bd. Internal Medicine. Assoc. prof. medicine Duke U. Med. Ctr., Durham, NC, 1973—77, prof. medicine, 1977—, James B. Duke prof. medicine, 1982—, prof. biochemistry, 1985—. Investigator Howard Hughes Med. Inst., Durham, 1976—; vis. prof. NYU, 1996. Author: Receptor Binding Studies in Adrenergic Pharmacology, 1978, Receptor Regulation, 1981, Principles of Biochemistry, 1983. Recipient Basic Rsch. prize, 1990, Young Scientist award, Passano Found., 1978, George Thorn award, Howard Hughes Med. Inst., 1979, Oppenheimer award, 1982, Gordon Wilson medal, Am. Clin. and Climatol. Assn., 1982, Lita Annenberg Hazen award, 1983, Outstanding Rsch. award, Internat. Soc. Health Rsch., 1985, H.B. van Dyke award, Coll. Physicians and Surgeons Columbia U., 1986, Steven C. Beering award, Ind. U. Sch. Medicine, 1986, NC award in sci., 1987, Internat. award, Gairdner Found., 1988, Novo Nordsk Biotechnology award, 1990, Biomedical Rsch. award, Assn. Am. Med. Colls., 1990, City of Medecin award, NC, 1991, Alumnus award for disting. achievement in cardiovasc. rsch., Columbia U. Coll. of Physicians and Surgeons, 1992, The Giovani Lorenzini prize for basic biomedical rsch., 1992, Joseph Mather Smith prize, Columbia U. Coll. Physicians and Surgeons, 1993, The Endocrine Soc. Gerald D. Aurbach Lectr. award, Inst. of Medicine NAS, 1995, J. David Gladstone Insts. Disting. Lecture award, 1996, Ciba award, Hypertension Rsch. award, 1996, Glorney-Raisbeck award in cardiology, N.Y. Acad. Medicine, 1997, Novartis/Drew award in biomed. rsch., 2000, F.E. Shideman-Sterling award, U. Minn., 2001, Louis and Artur Lucian award for rsch. in circulatory disease, 2001, Peter Harris Disting. Scientist award, Internat. Soc. for Heart Rsch., 2001, 15th Ann. Pasarow Cardiovasc. Rsch. award, The Robert J. and Claire Pasarow Found., 2002, Bio/Tech. Winter Symposia Feodor Lynen award, Medal of Merit, Internat. Acad. Cardiovasc. Scis., 2003, IPSEN Endocrinology prize, Found. IPSEN, Paris, 2003, Found. Lefoulon-Delalande Grand Prize for Sci. award, Inst. France, 2003, Founding Disting. Scientist award, Am. Heart Assn., 2003, Herbert Tabor Lecture award, Am. Soc. Biol. Chemistry and Molecular Biology, 2004, Shaw prize, Life Sci. and Medicine, Shaw Prize Found., 2007, Nat. Medal Sci., 2007; named Am. Heart Assn. established investigator, 1973—76;, Internat. Acad. Cardiovasc. Scis., 2002. Mem.: NAS (Jessie Stevenson Kovalenko medal 2001), Inst. Medicine, Am. Heart Assn. Basic Rsch. Soc., Am. Acad. Arts and Scis., Am. Fedn. Clin. Rsch. (mem. nat. coun. 1978—83, sec.-treas. 1980—83), Endocrine Soc. (Fred Conrad Koch award 2001), Am. Soc. Pharmacology and Exptl. Therapeutics (John J. Abel award 1978, Goodman and Gilman award 1986), Assn. Am. Physicians (treas. 1989—94, Francis Gilman Blake award 2001), Am. Soc. Clin. Investigation (counselor 1982—85, pres.-elect 1986—87, pres. 1987—88), Am. Soc. Biol. Chemists, Japanese Biochemical Soc. (hon.). Office: Duke U Med Ctr 467 Carl Bldg PO Box 3821 Durham NC 27710 Office Phone: 919-684-2974. Office Fax: 919-684-8875. E-mail: lefko001@receptor-biol.duke.edu.

LEFLER, WADE HAMPTON, JR., ophthalmologist; b. Statesville, NC, Feb. 27, 1937; s. Wade Hampton and Eunice Trudye (Chilcoat) L.; m. Katherine Webb Davis, Apr. 1, 1961; children: Elizabeth Ashley Wilson, Rosemary Kirsten, Ririe. AB, U. N.C., 1959; MD, Bowman Gray Sch. Medicine, 1963. Diplomate Am. Bd. Ophthalmology. Intern N.Y. Hosp./Cornell Med. Ctr., 1963-64; resident in ophthalmology Duke U. Med. Ctr., Durham, N.C., 1966-69; practice medicine specializing in ophthalmology, Hickory, N.C., 1969—; ptnr. Graystone Eye, Ear, Nose and Throat Ctr., Hickory, 1974—; clin. assoc. prof. ophthalmology Duke Med. Ctr., 1969—. Mem. staff Catawba Meml. Hosp., Hickory, Frye Regional Med. Ctr., Hickory, Western Carolina Center, Morganton, N.C., Duke Eye Center, Durham, N.C., Oteen VA Hosp., Asheville, N.C. Trustee Catawba Meml. Hosp., 1990-94. Served to capt. M.C., U.S. Army, 1964-66. Duke U. Med. Ctr. grantee, 1968-70. Mem. AMA, N.C. Med. Soc., Catawba County Med. Soc., Med. Alumni Assn. Bowman Gray Sch. Medicine (pres. 1993, Disting. Svc. award 1995), Lake Hickory Country Club, Phi Beta Kappa, Alpha Omega Alpha. Presbyterian. Home: 1260 6th St NW Hickory NC 28601-2408 Office: PO Box 2588 Hickory NC 28603-2588 E-mail: khlefler@charter.net.

LEFTERIS, DEMETRIOUS, plastic surgeon; m. Pamela Lefteris; 4 children. MD, Vienna U., Austria, 1971; CM in Gen. Surgery, England, 1972. Sr. resident surgeon, England, 1980; intern to Ian Muir Aberdeen Univ. Hosp.; intern Newcastle Univ. Hosp., England, 1986; with Mr. Frederick Nicolle cosmetic surgery England; plastic reconstructive and aesthetic surgeon Timios Stavros Med. Ctr., Larnaca, Cyprus, 1986—. Mem.: The Internat. Fedn. of Sport Medicine, Cyprus Med. Assn., Cyprus Surg. Soc., The Internat. Coll. of Surgeons, Cypriot Soc. of Plastic Surgery, Greek Soc. of Plastic Surgery, European Soc. of Plastic and Reconstructive Surgery, British Assn. of Plastic Surgeons, Internat. Confederation for Plastic Reconstructive and Aesthetic Surgery, Soc. of Aesthetic Plastic Surgery. Achievements include first full time Aesthetic Surgeon in Cyprus. Office: Timios Stavros Medical Center 17 R Santi Rd 6052 Larnaca Cyprus Office Phone: 35799631166. *

LE GAL, GRÉGOIRE, physician, researcher; b. Lesneven, France, May 29, 1973; s. Fanch and Marie-Thérèse Le Gal; m. Caridad Garcia Merchan; children: Inès, Simon. MD, Brest U., France, 2003, PhD, 2007. Clin. and rsch. fellow Geneva U. Hosp., 2003—04; rsch. fellow thrombosis program U. Ottawa, 2007—08; physician Brest U. Hosp., 2004—09; prof. internal medicine Brest U. Sch. Medicine, 2009—. Mem.: Société Nationale Française de Médecine Interne, Internat. Soc. on Thrombosis and Haemostasis. Achievements include research in diagnostic strategies for venous thromboembolism. Office: EA3878 GETBO Brest Univ Hosp Boulevard Tanguy Prigent 29609 Brest France Office Fax: +33298347987. Business E-Mail: gregoire.legal@chu-brest.fr.

LEGATO, MARIANNE, internist, educator; b. NJ, Aug. 17, 1935; MD, NYU, 1962. Bd. cert. internal medicine. Intern Columbia U. Coll. Physicians and Surgeons, NYC, 1962—63, resident internal medicine, 1963—64, Presbyn. Hosp., NYC, 1964—65, fellow cardiology, 1965—68, assoc. attending physician, 1993—; sr. attending physician St. Luke's/Roosevelt Hosp., NYC, 1980—; founder, dir. Partnership for Gender Specific Medicine Columbia U., NYC, 1997—; prof. clin. medicine Columbia U. Coll. Physicians and Surgeons, 1998—; adj. prof. medicine Johns Hopkins U., 2006—. Charter mem. adv. bd. Office Rsch. on Women's Health, NIH. Author: The Female Heart: The Truth About Women and Heart Disease, 1992; author: (with Carol Colman) What Women Need to Know: From Headaches to Heart Disease and Everything in Between, 1997; author: Eve's Rib: The New Science of Gender-Specific Medicine and How It Can Save Your Life, 2002, Why Men Never Remeber and Women Never Forget, 2005; editor: The Principles of Gender Specific Medicine, 2004, 2nd edit., 2010; founder, editor: Gender Medicine, mem. editl. bd.: Cardiovasc. Risk Factors, Prevention Mag. Recipient Howard W. Blakeslee award, Am. Heart Assn., 1992, Leadership in Action award, Women's Action Alliance, 1994, Woman in Sci. award, Am. Med. Women's Assn., 2002, Heart of Gold award, L.I. Heart

Coun., J. Murray Steele award, Sr. Investigator award, Am. Heart Assn., N.Y. Affiliate, Rsch. Career Devel. award, NIH; named Am. Health Hero, Am. Health for Women, 1997, Heroine of Women's Health, Ladies Home Jour., 2000; named one of 300 Am. Women Changing the Face of Medicine, Nat. Libr. Medicine, 2004; named to 1,000 Women for the Nineties, Mirabella Mag., 1994; Martha Lyon Slater fellow. Home and Office: Partnership Gender-Specific Medicine 903 Park Ave, Ste 2A New York NY 10075 Office Phone: 212-737-5663. Business E-Mail: mjl2@columbia.edu.

LEGEAIS, JEAN-MARC J., ophthalmologist; b. Montreuil, France, Aug. 20, 1959; s. Joseph and Jeanine (Guyot) L.; m. Sylvie Massucchetti, May 26, 1984; children: Sophie, Elodie, Thomas. MD, U. Paris, 1984, PhD, 1995. Resident Assistance Public, Paris, 1989; fellow Hotel Dieu Hosp., Paris, 1989; rsch. fellow Bascom Palmer Eye Inst., Miami, 1991; researcher INSERM, Paris, 1993—. Cons. France Chirurgie Instrument, Paris, 1991-96; assoc. prof. Hotel Dieu Hosp., 1993-95, prof., 1997; adj. asst. prof. U. Miami, 1997; prof. Hotel-Dieu Paris Hosp., U. Paris, 1998; dir. lab. Assn.; Claude Bernard, 2001; dir. lab. biotechnologie U. Paris V, 2006. Patentee in field. Mem.: Castroviejo Cornea Soc., Am. Soc. Cataract & Refractive Surgery, Am. Acad. Ophthalmology. Office: Hotel Dieu de Paris Hosp 1 place Jean Paul II Parv Notre Dame 75004 Paris France Office Phone: 33142348364. E-mail: jean-marc.legeais@htd.aphp.fr, jlegeais@wanadoo.fr.

LEGERON, PATRICK R., psychiatrist, consultant; b. Rouen, France, Sept. 8, 1948; s. Bernard Legeron and Renee Cazaux. MD, Nantes U., France, 1977; Psychiatrist, U. Paris V, 1982. Postdoctoral fellow Sch. Medicine, UCLA, Calif., 1979; cons. psychiatrist, tchr. Univ. Hosp. Sainte-Anne, Paris, 1985—; founder, dir. Stimulus, France, 1989—. Author: Stress at Work, 2001; co-author: La Peur des Autres, 1995. Sec. Les Amis des Tuileries, France, 2003—. Recipient E-Europe awards, European Union, 2004; grantee Neuro-Psychiatry grantee, Rank Xerox, 1979. Mem.: French Assn. Cognitive Behavior Therapy (pres. 1989—93, editor-in-chief jour. 1995—). Office: Stimulus 205 rue Saint Honore 75001 Paris France Office Phone: 33142969262. Business E-Mail: patrick.legeron@stimulus-conseil.com.

LEGGAT, PETER ADRIAN, public health physician, university administrator, medical educator; b. Brisbane, Queensland, Australia, Dec. 2, 1961; s. Bruce William and Frances Winifred (Hage) L.; m. Ureporn Kedjarune, Nov. 25, 1993. B in Med. Sci. with distinction, U. Queensland, 1986, MBBChir, 1988; M in Med. Edn., U. Dundee, Scotland, 1992; MPH, U. Otago, New Zealand, 1998; PhD, U. South Australia, 2002; MD, U. Queensland, 2003; MHealth Sci. in Aviation Medicine, U. Otago, New Zealand, 2004; DrPH, James Cook U., Australia, 2005; grad. diploma in Clin. Nutrition, Internat. Acad. Nutrition, 1988; grad. diploma in Edn., Darling Downs Inst. Advanced Edn., 1989; grad. diploma in Tropical Medicine and Hygiene, Mahidol U., Thailand, 1990; grad. diploma in Indsl. Health, U. Otago, New Zealand, 1993; grad. diploma, Corporate Dir. Assn. U. New Eng., 1996; cert. in Addiction Studies, Curtin U., 1992; grad. cert. in Travel Medicine, James Cook U., Australia, 2001, grad. cert. in Astronomy, 2005; grad. cert. in Aeromed. Evacuation, U. Otago, New Zealand, 2002; grad. cert. in Aerospace Medicine, Griffith U., Australia, 2002; grad. cert. in Tertiary Tchg. Edn., James Cook U., 2008; diploma in Mgmt., St. John Ambulance Australia, 2010. Cert. safety exec., safety mgr., safety specialist and safety and security dir. World Safety Orgn.; registered safety profl., Safety Inst. Australia, med. practitioner, specialist in pub. health medicine, Queensland, vocationally registered med. practitioner, Commonwealth Dept. Health; designated aviation med. examiner Commonwealth Civil Aviation Safety Authority; cert. travel health Internat. Soc. Travel Medicine, 2003, med. review officer, Commonwealth Civil Aviation Safety Authority, 2008-, Med. Review Officer Cert. Coun., US, 2008. NHMRC med. undergrad. scholar U. Queensland Med. Sch., 1984-85, clin. tutor/specialist tutor/lectr. dept. social/prev. med., 1985-89; med. officer Dept. Vets. Affairs, Repatriation Gen. Hosp., Greenslopes, Queensland, 1988-89; attached def. officer Australian Embassy, Bangkok, 1990; capt. med. officer Dept. Def., Townsville, 1990-91; officer Commanding Clin. Svcs., Townsville, 1991; sr. lectr. dept. sch. pub. health and tropical medicine James Cook U., Townsville, 1992—98, dep. head, 1997—2000, assoc. prof., 1999—2006, prof., 2007—, mem. 14th coun., 2005—09, mem. 15th coun., 2009—, head, sch. pub. health, tropical medicine and rehab. scis., 2007—10; dep. dir. Anton Breinl Ctr. James Cook U., Townsville, 2005—08, acting pro vice chancellor, 2008—10, acting dir., 2006—07, dep. head, campus head, Sch. Pub. Health, Tropical Medicine & Rehab. Scis., 2011—, dir. rsch. tng., 2011—; adj. prof. Sch. Pub. Health, Queensland U. Tech., Brisbane, 2009—, Queensland U. Tech., 2009—, Southern Cross U., 2011—. Dir. gen. World Safety Orgn., 1997—99, mem. internat. bd. dirs., 1989—99, 2003—10, dir., Collaborating Ctr., 2008—, dep. dir.-gen., 1993—97; cons. Anton Breinl Ctr., James Cook U., 1991, assoc. dean, mem. faculty biomed. and health scis., 1995—97, acad. advisor, 1998—, assoc. dean, faculty affairs, faculty medicine, health and scis., 2007—; vis. med. officer dept. def., Townsville, 1992—; ofcl. accredited rep., liaison officer (World Safety Orgn.) to UN Econ. and Social Commn. for Asia and the Pacific, 1994—2000, 2003—; vis. prof. Prince of Songkla U., Hatyai, Thailand, 1995—, U. Witwatersrand Sch. Pub. Health, Johannesburg, 2000—, Sch. Health, U. Newcastle, 2008—; regional med. officer North Queensland St. John Ambulance, Australia, 2000—08; chair training br. St. John Ambulance, Queensland, 2008—, exec. coun. mem., 2008—, state med. officer, 2008—10, state profl. officer, 2010—; dep. Nat. Dir. Tng., 2011—; short term cons. WHO, 2007; mem. Queensland Injury Prevention Coun., 2008—; mem. Grant Rev. Panel Nat. Health & Med. Rsch. Coun., 2009—10, Queensland Emergency Medicine Rsch. Found., 2009—11, chair grant adv. com., 2011—, chair grant review panel, 2011; with Australian Rsch. Coun. Excellence Rsch., Australia Rsch. Evaluation Com. Pub. & Allied Health, 2010—11, external assessor, 2011—; editor News Share Internat. Soc. Travel Med., 2010. Editor: International Directory of Training in Tropical Medicine, 1994—, The Inaugural Ashdown Oration and Convocation, 1994, Annals of the Australasian College of Tropical Medicine Inc., 1995—2000, Asia-Pacific Safety Directory, 1996—, Primer of Travel Medicine, 1996, 3d revised edit., 2005, Dictionary of Tropical Medicine for Health Professionals, 2001, Tourism in Turbulent Times, 2006, Industrial Health, 2007—; consulting editor Archives of Environmental and Occupational Health, 2008—, dep. editor-in-chief Jour. of Travel Medicine, 2009—; contbr. articles to profl. jours. Hon. sec. Townsville-Thuringowa Local Med. Assn. and voting del. to Queensland br. Australian Med. Assn., 1992—96, pres., 1996—2000, immediate past pres., 2000—04; chmn. Stately Ct. Body Corporate, Townsville, 1993—2005, 2008—09, sec., treas., 2007—; commr. declarations Dept. Justice, Queensland, 1997—98; justice of peace, 1998—; chair Convocation XXI, 2009. Lt. col. Royal Australian Army Med. Corps. Army Reserve, 1999—, aviation med. officer Australian Def. Force, 2006—. Recipient medal, Assn. Mil. Surgeons US, 1991, Australian Def. medal, 2007, Australian Coll. Occupl. Medicine prize, 1984, Merit award, U. Queensland, 1986, Ednl. award, World Safety Orgn., 1992, Fred Katz Meml. medal, Australasian and New Zealand Assn. Med. Edn., WHO, 2001, Concerned Citizen award, World Safety Orgn., 2002, Maj. Gen. John Pearn Surgeon Gen. medal, 2002, James K. Williams award, World Safety Orgn., 2003, Svc. award, Priory of St. John, 2003, Vitae Lampada medal, Queensland Health Australia, 2005, Svc. award, Priory of St. John, 2006, Priory Vote of Thanks, 2006, Ednl. award, World Safety Orgn., 2007, 2008, WSO Achievement award, 2009, Surgeon-Gen. John White medal, Oxford Round Table, Lincoln Coll., 2008, Internat. award, World Safety Org., 2008, 2010, Rsch. & Devel. Achievement award, 2009, Citation award, Queensland Flood & Cyclone, 2011; named World Safety Person of Yr., World Safety Orgn., 1988, Most Outstanding Alumnus, Mahidol U. Tropical Medicine Alumni Assn., 2006, Person of Yr., Thomson Reuters Blake Dawson Inside OHS, 2008, Officer Order St John, 2011; fellow St. Margaret's Coll., U. Otago, 2002; scholar Australian-Am. Fulbright Commn., 2002—03, Internat. Inst. Edn. Am. Mgmt. Assn., 2003; J.G. Hunter rsch. fellow, 1985—86, Faculty Travel Medicine fellowship, Royal Coll. Physicians and Surgeons Glasgow, 2006. Fellow: RCP (pub. health faculty 2011—, Disting. award), Royal Geographical Soc., Australasian Coll. Tropical Medicine, Australian Coll. Educators (World Tchrs. Day Recognition Cert. 2005—06, 2008—10), Royal Soc. Tropical Medicine and Hygiene (Malaysia and Australia centennial lectr. 2007, Centennial Lectr. 2007, 2010), Australasian Faculty Pub. Health Medicine (exe. com. mem., Queensland 2007—), Australian Coll. Rural Remote Medicine, Safety Inst. Australia, Australian Inst. Co. Dirs., Australasian Coll. Tropical Medicine (hon.; hon. sec. 1991—96, pres. 1996—98, councillor, acting hon. sec. 1999—2000, v.p. 2000—01, pres. 2002—04, 4th Anton Breinl Meml. lectr. 2005, pres. 2006—08, past pres. citation 2008, immediate past pres. 2008—09, hon. treas. 2008—, 6th Anton Breinl Meml. lectr. 2009, 2009, chair of convocation XXI 2009, faculty travel medicine, sub faculty expedition medicine, Presdl. medallion 1998, medal 2000, Ednl. award 2002, medal 2004, Bar to Presdl. medallion 2004, Ednl. award 2005, Ednl. Excellence award 2008, Bar to Presdl. medallion 2008, hon. fellow 2011); mem.: Public Health Assoc., Australia (exe. com., Queensland 2008—10), Coll. of Fellows Safety Inst. of Australia, Internat. Soc. Travel Medicine (counselor, exec. bd. 2003—05, dep. editor-in-chief 2009—), South African Soc. Travel Medicine, Colls. Medicine South Africa (assoc.), Coll. Pub. Health Medicine South Africa (assoc.), New Zealand Soc. Travel Medicine (hon. cert. merit 2000), Australian Med. Assn. (60th Ernest Sandford Jackson Meml. lectr. 2008, Distinction medal), Royal Australian Coll. Gen. Practitioners, Golden Key Internat., Phi Beta Delta. Roman Catholic. Avocations: stamp collecting/philately, coin collecting/numismatics, badminton, astronomy. Office: James Cook U Anton Breinl Ctr Ph/Tropical Medicine 4811 Townsville QLD Australia

LEGGE, GORDON E., psychology professor, department chairman, b. Toronto, Can. m. Wendy Legge; 1 child, Alex. B in Physics, Mass. Inst. Tech., Cambridge, 1971; M in Astronomy, Harvard U., Cambridge, Mass., 1972, PhD in Exptl. Psychology, 1976. Postdoctoral rschr. Cambridge U., 1976—77; faculty mem. U. Minn., 1977—, prof. psychology and neuroscience, disting. McKnight univ. prof., chmn. dept. psychology, dir., Minn Lab. Low Vision Rsch. Mem. Nat. Adv. Eye Coun. Author: The Sassaphron Messenger: A Spacetime Adventure, 1995; mem. editl. bd.: Jour. Vision. Office: Univ Wis N218 Elliot Hall 75 E River Rd Minneapolis MN 55455 Office Phone: 612-625-0846. Office Fax: 612-626-2079. Business E-Mail: legge@umn.edu.

LEGGETT, WILLIAM C., biology professor, academic administrator; b. Orangeville, Ont., Can., June 25, 1939; s. Frank William and Edna Irene (Wheeler) L.; m. Claire Holman, May 9, 1964; children: David, John. BA, Waterloo U. Coll., 1962; MSc, U. Waterloo, 1965, DSc, 1992; PhD, McGill U., 1969, DSc, 2001; LLD, Wilfred Laurier U., 1994, Queen's U., 2005; DSc, Laval U., 1996, McMaster U., 2008. From rsch. sci. to rsch. assoc. Essex (Conn.) Marine Lab., 1965-73; asst. prof. McGill U., Montreal, Que., Canada, 1970-72, assoc. prof., 1972-79, prof., 1979—94, chmn. dept. biology, 1981-85, dean of sci., 1986-91, acad. v.p., 1991-94; prin., vice chancellor Queen's U., Kingston, Ont., Canada, 1994—2004, prin. emeritus, prof. emeritus, 2004—; chmn. bd. Huntsman Marine Lab., 1980-89; pres. Quebec Inter univ. Oceanographic Rsch. Group, 1986-91; fellow Sch. Policy Studies Queens U., 2004—; gen. ptnr. Tancho Investment Capital, 2006—; chmn. bd. Can. Found. Innovation, 2007—; chair Trudeau Found. Expert Review Com. Chmn. grant selection com. for population biology Natural Scis. and Engring. Rsch. Coun. Can., 1980-81, chmn. grant selection com. for oceans, 1986-87; exec. com. Coun. Ontario Univs., 1996-2004, vice-chair, 2002-04; mem. com. internationalization Assn. Univ. Colls. Can., 2001-04; bd. dirs. Office for Partnerships for Advanced Skills, 2000-04; chair Ont. Commn. on Interuniv. Athletes, 2002-04; bd. dirs., sec. Conn. River Ecol. Study Found., 2004-. Mem. editl. bd.: Can. Jour. Fisheries and Aquatic Sciences, 1980-85, Le Naturaliste Canadien, 1980-91, Can. Jour. Zoology, 1982-86; contbr. articles in field. Chair svc. learning adv. com. McConnell Found., 2004—. Recipient Fry medal Can. Soc. Zoologists, 1990, Outstanding Biologist award Can. Coun. Biol. Chmn., 1993, John Orr award, 2003, Queen's U., Disting. Svc. award, 2004, Stirling medal, 2004, Isi Highly Cited Rschr. award, 2004—; Paul Harris fellow Rotary Internat., 2004; grantee in field. Fellow Rawson Acad., Royal Soc. Can., Order of Can.; mem. Am. Fisheries Soc. (pres. North-East divsn. 1977-78, Dwight D. Webster award 1989, EO Sette award 1996, Excellence award 1997, Award for Excellence for Fisheries Edn. 1990), Can. Com. for Fishery Rsch., Can. Soc. Zoologists, Am. Soc. Limnology and Oceanography, Am. Soc. Naturalists. Office: Queen's U Dept Biology Kingston ON Canada K7L 3N6 Office Phone: 613-533-6534. Business E-Mail: wleggett@post.queensu.ca.

LEGGIO, MASSIMO, cardiologist; b. Rome, Aug. 7, 1975; s. Francesco Leggio and Matilde Rosa Brancaleon; 1 child, Lucia. BS in Medicine, La Sapienza U., Rome, 1999, BS in Surgery, MS n Cardiology, 2003. Medical Diplomate Italy, 1999. Med. dr. San Filippo Neri Hosp., Cardiovasc. Dept., Rome, 2004—. Reviewer European Heart Jour., 2006—, Europace, 2009—, Internat. Jour. Cardiovasc. Imaging. Contbr. articles to profl. jours. Office: San Filippo Neri Hosp SI Via della Lucchina 41 135 Rome RM Italy Office Fax: 39 0630811972. Business E-Mail: mleggio@libero.it.

LE GRICE, STUART F.J., senior investigator; PhD, U. Manchester, UK, 1976. Postdoctoral tng., Edinburgh, Heidelberg, Germany, Boston; sr. scientist Hoffman La Roche, Basel, Switzerland; assoc. prof. medicine Case We. Res. U., Cleve., 1990—95, dir. Ctr. AIDS Rsch., 1994—99, prof. medicine, biochemistry, and oncology, 1995; joined as chief Resistance Mechanisms Lab. Ctr. Cancer Rsch., Nat. Cancer Inst., NIH, Frederick, Md., 1999, head RT biochemistry sect., chief HIV DRP Retroviral Replication Lab., mem. Sr. Biomed. Rsch. Svc., 2005—, head Ctr. Excellence in HIV/AIDS & Cancer Virology, 2006—. Recipient Outstanding Mentor award, NCI, 2007, Merit award, NIH, 2009. Office: RTBS HIVDRP CCR NCI-Frederick Bldg 535 Rm 312 PO Box B Frederick MD 21702-1201 Office Phone: 301-846-5256. Office Fax: 301-846-6013. E-mail: legrices@mail.nih.gov. *

LEHL, GURVANIT KAUR, dentist, department chairman; b. Patiala, Punjab, India, May 28, 1966; d. Pritam Singh and Birinder Kaur Pannu; m. Sarabmeet Singh Lehl, June 21, 1987; children: Manhit Singh, Dashmeet Singh. M of Dental Surgery, Punjab Govt. Dental Coll. and Hosp., Amritsar, 1991; B of Dental Surgery, Govt. Med. Coll. and Hosp., Patiala, 1987. Faculty Punjab Govt. Dental Coll. and Hosp., 1989—96; prof., head dept. dentistry Govt. Med. Coll. and Hosp., Chandigarh, India, 1997—. Prin. contbr. instrnl. material cert. course dental assts. Tech. Tchrs. Tng. Inst., Chandigarh, 2004; reader Govt. Med. Coll. and Hosp., Chandigarh. Contbg. author (textbook chpt.) Textbook of Pediatric Dentistry, 3d edit., 2006. Named Best Grad., Dental Wing, Govt. Med. Coll., Patiala, 1987. Mem.: Indian Dental Assn. (hon. sec. Chandigarh State br. 2005—07). Sikh. Avocations: photography, painting, music, cooking. Office: Govt Med Coll Hosp Sector 32 Chandigarh India Home: 282 160 011 Chandigarh India

LEHMAN, CONSTANCE DOBBINS, radiologist, researcher; b. Houston; d. William T. and Martha Ann Dobbins; m. Adam K. Lehman; children: Grace, Sam. BA magna cum laude, Duke U., 1983; PhD, MD, Yale U., 1990. Diplomate Nat. Bd. Med. Examiners, 1990, Am. Bd. Radiology, 1995. Intern in surgery U. Wash. Sch. Medicine, Seattle, 1990—91, resident in diagnostic radiology, 1991—95, acting asst. prof. radiology, 1996—97, asst. prof. radiology, 1997—2001, assoc. prof. radiology, 2001—06; sect. chief breast imaging U. Wash., Seattle, 2003—, prof. radiology, 2006—; dir. breast imaging Seattle Cancer Care Alliance, 2000—, dir. radiology, 2007—. Affiliate investigator Pub. Health Sci., 1996—, Group Health Coop., Ctr. Health Studies, Seattle, 2006—; affiliate investigator, pub. health services Fred Hutchinson Cancer Rsch. Ctr., 1997—2003; joint mem. Fred Hutchinson Cancer Rsch. Ctr., Pub. Health Services, 2007—. Fellow: Soc. Breast Imaging; mem.: Nat. Breast Cancer Surveillance Consortium, Wash. State Med. Assn., Wash. State Radiol. Soc., Radiol. Soc. N.Am. (Scientific Merit award 1996), Pacific NW Radiol. Soc., Assn. U. Radiologists, Am. Roentgen Ray Soc., Am. Coll. Radiology, Phi Eta Sigma, Sigma Xi, Phi Beta Kappa. Office: Seattle Cancer Care Alliance PO Box 19023 Seattle WA 98109-1023 Office Fax: 206-288-6556. E-mail: lehman@u.washington.edu.

LEHMAN, THOMAS J. A., pediatric rheumatologist; MD cum laude, Thomas Jefferson U., 1974. Diplomate Am. Bd. Pediatrics, Am. Bd. Pediatrics pediatric rheumatology, lic. Calif., 1975, registered NY 1987. Intern Children's Hosp. of Los Angeles, 1975, resident in pediat., 1975, UC San Francisco Med. Ctr., 1977; fellow pediatric rheumatology Children's Hosp. of Los Angeles, 1979; fellow rheumatology NIH, 1983; pediatric rheumatology faculty Children's Hosp. of Los Angeles; prof. clin. pediat. Weill Cornell Med. Coll.; hosp. affiliations include Blythedale Children's Hosp., Winifred Masterson Burke Rehab. Hosp., NY Presbyn. Hosp.; attending physician Hosp. for Spl. Surgery, NY, sr. scientist, chief pediatric rheumatology, 1987—. Author: (articles) Burden of childhood-onset arthritis, 2010, Should the Food and Drug Administration warning of malignancy in children receiving tumor necrosis factor alpha blockers change the way we treat children with juvenile idiopathic arthritis?, 2010, Neutral lipid storage disease with subclinical myopathy due to a retrotransposal insertion in the PNPLA2 gene, 2010, The importance of visual function in the quality of life of children with uveitis, 2010, Morphea, diabetes mellitus type I, and celiac disease: case report and review of the literature, 2010, various others. Recipient Cassidy award; named one of Best Doctors, NY Mag., 2009—11. Fellow: Western Soc. for Pediatric Rsch., NY Coll. of Medicine, Am. Acad. of Pediat., Am. Coll. of Rheumatology. Office: Hospital for Special Surgery 535 E 70th St New York NY 10021 Office Phone: 212-606-1151. Office Fax: 212-606-1938.

LEHMANN, LISA SOLEYMANI, medical association administrator; b. Phila., Jan. 18, 1965; MD, Johns Hopkins U., PhD, 1993. Dir., ctr. bioethics Brigham and Women's Hosp., Harvard Med. Sch., 2005—. Avocations: music, sailing. Office: 1620 Tremont St Boston MA 02120 Business E-Mail: llehmann1@partners.org.

LEHRHOFF, BERNARD J., urologist, educator; MD, Univ. of Medicine and Dentistry of NJ- NJ Med. Sch., Newark, 1976. Diplomate Am. Bd. Urology. Resident urology Bellevue Hosp., NY, 1978—82, Meml. Sloan Kettering; urologist Consultants in Urology Pa, Westfield, NJ. Asst. clin. prof. Columbia Univ. Coll. of Physicians and Surgeons. Office: Consultants in Urology Pa 275 Orchard St Westfield NJ 07090 Office Phone: 908-654-5100. Office Fax: 908-789-8755.

LEHRMANN, JON A., psychiatrist, educator; b. Milw., Apr. 8, 1964; BS, Carroll Coll., Waukesha, Wis., 1986; MD, Med. Coll. Wis., 1990. Academic psychiatrist Med. Coll. Wis., Va., 1990—; residency tng. dir. Dept Psychiatry and Behavioral Medicine, Med. Coll. Wis., 2004—09, interim chair and assoc. prof., 2010—; mental health divsn. mgr. Milw. VAMC, 2009—. Recipient Disting. Svc. award, Dept. Psychiatry and Behavioral Medicine, Golden Apple Tchg. award, Humanism Medicine award, Med. Coll. Wis. Mem.: Am. Coll. Psychiatry. Office: 8701 Watertown Plank Rd Milwaukee WI 53226 Business E-Mail: jlehrman@mcw.edu.

LEHTONEN, SANNA HELENA, medical researcher; b. Kotka, Finland, Oct. 29, 1967; MSc, U. Jyväskylä, Finland, 1990; PhD, U. Helsinki, Finland, 2004. Rsch. fellow U. Helsinki, 2009—. Office: Haartmaninkatu 3 Helsinki 00290 Finland Business E-Mail: sanna.h.lehtonen@helsinki.fi.

LEI, GUOWEI, physics professor, researcher; b. Nanchang, May 23, 1977; MS, Xiamen U., Fujian, China, 2004. Rschr. Sch. Sci., Jimei U., Xiamen, 2004—11, asst. prof., 2007—. Mem.: IEEE. Avocations: singing, flute, jogging. Office: Jimei University Sch Sci Xiamen Fujian 361021 China Personal E-mail: kuwee.lei@gmail.com.

LEI, YU, medical educator; b. Changchun City, China, June 2, 1972; MD, Capital Med. U., 2008. Assoc. prof., dept. thoracic surgery Beijing Tongren Hosp., 2001—. Recipient Developing Nation awards, Internat. Assn. Study Lung Cancer. Mem.: Chinese Soc. Thoracic and Cardiovasc. Surgery, Internat. Assn. Study Lung Cancer, Internat. Union Against Cancer, Chinese Med. Assn. Office: 1 Dongjiaominxian St Dongcheng Beijing 100730 China Business E-Mail: yulei1118@sohu.com.

LEIBOVICI, VERA, dermatologist; b. Targu-Mures, Romania, June 25, 1953; arrived in Israel, 1980; d. Emeric and Agness (Blau) Lax; m. Marcel Leibovici, Apr. 19, 1975; children: Aviva, Edward. MD, Targu-Mures, 1972; degree in Medicine, U. Targu-Mures, 1978. Resident, dermatology Hadassah U. Hosp., Jerusalem, 1981—86, sr. dermatologist, 1986—2008, lectr., dermatology, 1987—91. Contbr. articles to Jour. Am. Acad. Dermatology, Clin. and Exptl. Dermatology, European Jour. Dermatology. Recipient Excellency award, 1986—2008; grantee, Israeli Ministry Health, 1995—96. Mem. Am. Acad. Dermatology, Internat. Soc. Dermatology (tropical, geog. and ecologic sect.), Internat. Soc. Cosmetic Dermatology. Achievements include research in cutaneous leishmaniasis, widespread tinea corporis and psoriasis. Avocations: music, classic literature.

LEICHTER, DONALD, pediatric cardiologist, educator; MD, Cornell U., Ithaca, NY, 1980. Diplomate Am. Bd. Pediatrics, 1988, cert. Pediatric Cardiology. Pediatric cardiology Overlook Med. Ctr.; intern Children's Hosp. Nat. Med. Ctr., resident pediat. DC, 1981—83; fellow pediatric cardiology Columbia Presbyn. Med. Ctr., NYC, 1983—85; assoc. clin. prof. pediat. Columbia Univ. Coll. Physicians and Surgeons; pediatric cardiology NY-Presbyterian/Morgan Stanley Children's Hosp. Columbia Univ. Med. Ctr. Office: New York-Presbyterian Morgan Stanley Children's Hospital Columbia University Medical Center 630 W 168th St. New York NY 10032 Office Phone: 212-305-2862.

LEICHTLE, CARMEN INA, orthopedist; b. Albstadt, June 16, 1975; Degree, Med. Sch. U. Tuebingen, 2001. Cert. orthopedist and trauma surgeon 2007. Physician BG Trauma Clinic Tuebingen Dept. Trauma and Reconstructive Surgery, 2001—02; physician Dept. Orthop. Surgery U. Hosp. Tuebingen, 2002—, sr. physician, 2008—, leading sr. physician, spine surgery, 2009—. Contbr. numerous articles to profl. publs. Mem.: German Soc. Orthop. and Orthopaedic Surgery, German Spine Soc. Avocations: piano, golf, mountain biking. Office: Hoppe-Seyler-Str. 3 72076 Tuebingen Germany Office Phone: 0049-7071-2986692. Personal E-mail: carmen.leichtle@med.uni-tuebingen.de.

LEIDEN, JEFFREY MARC, venture capitalist, molecular biologist, cardiologist; b. Chgo., Oct. 12, 1955; s. Irving and Rosemary (Rebelsky) Leiden; m. Lisa Leyland, June 23, 1982; children: Benjamin Bradford, Alexander Dow. BA in Biol. Sci. with honors, U. Chgo., 1975, MD with honors, 1979, PhD, 1981. Diplomate Am. Bd. Internal Medicine, Am. Bd. Cardiovascular Diseases, lic. cardiologist Mass., Ill. Chief cardiology, Frederick H. Rawson prof. medicine and pathology U. Chgo.; Elkan R. Blout prof. biological sciences Harvard Sch. Public Health; prof. medicine Harvard Medical Sch.; founder Cardiogene, Inc.; bd. dirs. Abbott, 1999, sr. v.p., chief scientific officer, 2000, exec. v.p. pharmaceuticals, 2000, pres., COO pharmaceutical products group, 2001—06; ptnr. Clarus Ventures, 2006—. Cons. Pfizer, Bristol Meyers-Squibb, Boston Scientific Inc. Bd. dirs. Chgo.'s Mus. Sci. and Industry, Ravinia Festival, Keystone Symposia. Fellow: Am. Acad. Arts and Sciences; mem.: Am. Assn. Physicians, Am. Soc. Clinical Investigation, IOM. Office: Clarus Ventures Llc 101 Main St Cambridge MA 02142-1519

LEIER, CARL VICTOR, internist, cardiologist; b. Bismarck, ND, Oct. 20, 1944; married; 3 children. Grad., Creighton U., MD cum laude, 1969. Diplomate Am. Bd. Internal Medicine, Cardiovascular Medicine, Critical Care Medicine, Geriatric Medicine, Electrocardiography and Advanced Heart Failure & Transplantation Cardiology, Nat. Bd. Med. Examiners; lic. med., Ohio. Intern Ohio State U. Coll. Medicine, Columbus, 1969-70, med. resident (instr.) dept. medicine, 1971-73, chief resident (instr.), 1973-74, fellowship divsn. cardiology, 1974-76; pathology resident dept. pathology St. Vincent Hosp., Worcester, Mass., 1970-71; trainee NIH Tng. Grant, 1974-75; asst. prof. medicine cardiology dept., Ohio State U. Coll. Medicine, Columbus, 1976-80, asst. prof. pharmacology, 1976-80, assoc. prof., 1980-84, faculty mem. grad. sch., 1980—, dir. rsch. divsn. cardiology, 1980-83, James W. Overstreet prof. of medicine, 1983—, prof. of medicine divsn. cardiology, 1984—, prof. pharmacology, dept. pharmacology, 1984—, dir. divsn. cardiology, 1986-98. Mem. rsch. com. ctrl. Ohio chpt. Am. Heart Assn., 1977-84, bd. trustees, 1979-88, exec. rsch. com., 1979-84, vice chmn. rsch. com., 1980-82, chmn. rsch. peer rev. com., 1982-84, v.p., 1984-86, pres. elect, 1986-88; numerous other coms.; cons. AMA on Drugs and Tech., 1985—, FDA Cardiorenal adv. com. 1986-92; mem. chmn. Annual Sci. Sessions of the Am. Coll. of Cardiolog, 1996-97; vis. prof., lectr. and presenter at numerous sci. confs., insts. in U.S. and internationally. Editor: (book) Cardiotonic Drugs, 1986, 2d rev. edit., 1991; co-author: (with H. Boudoulas) CardioRenal Disorders and Diseases, 1986, 2d edit., 1992 (with J. Vincent) Critical Care Medicine: Recent Advances in Cardiovascular Medicine, 1990; contbr. more than 40 chpts. to other medical books and over 200 articles to peer reviewed jours. including: Circulation, Brit. Heart Jour., Jour. Clin. Investigation, Jour. Am. Coll. Cardiology, Am. Jour. Cardiology, Chest, Am. Jour. Medicine, Am. Heart Jour., Annals of Internal Medicine and others; editor in chief Congestive Heart Failure: Index and Revs., 1988-94; mem. editorial bds. of ten medical jours. concerned with heart diseases, the review bds. of others including New Eng. Jour. Medicine, Internat. Jour. Cardiology, Jour. of Lab. and Clin. Medicine. Recipient Upjohn award, 1969, Lange Scholar award, 1969, Golden Apple Student Tchg. award, 1973, 75, Young Investigator award Ctrl. Ohio Heart Chpt., Am. Heart Assn., 1976-78, Rsch. Recognition award, 1978. Fellow Am. Heart Assn., Am. Coll. Cardiology, Am. Coll. Physicians, Coun. on Geriatric Cardiology; mem. AAAS, Am. Fedn. for Clin. Rsch., Ctrl. Soc. for Clin. Rsch., Am. Soc. Clin. Investigation, Assn. Univ. Cardiologists. Office: Ohio State U Med Ctr Divsn Cardiology 473 W 12th Ave Columbus OH 43210-1250 Office Phone: 614-293-8963.

LEIFER, BENNETT, geriatrician; Attended, Brown U., State U. of NY, Syracuse, NY, Mt. Sinai Med. Ctr., NY. Diplomate Am. Bd. of Internal Medicine-geriatric medicine. Resident Hartford Hosp., 1987—89; fellow Mt. Sinai Med. Ctr. Office: The Valley Hospital 223 N Van Dien Ave Ridgewood NJ 07450 Office Fax: 201-447-8000.

LEIFER, JOYCE, pediatrician, educator; b. NYC, May 8, 1954; BA, Brandeis U., 1975; MD, Case Western Res. U., 1980. Physician Forbes Regional Hosp., 1985—2003; clin. assoc. prof. Children's Hosp. Pitts., 2004—. Educator U. Pitts. Sch. Medicine. Fellow: Am. Acad. Pedlat. Office: Childrens Hosp Pitts Pittsburgh PA 15224 Office Fax: 412-692-7038. Business E-Mail: joyce.leifer@chp.edu.

LEIGHTON, KEVIN L., physician; MD, Dalhousie U., Halifax, Can., 1991. Diplomate Am. Bd. Family Practice. Resident Dalhousie Univ., Halifax, Canada, 1993; family medicine physician Butler meml. Hosp. Office: Butler Medical Associates 1022B N main St Butler PA 16001 Office Phone: 724-285-0858.

LEIGHTON, RICHARD FREDERICK, retired dean; BA, Western Md. Coll., 1951; MD, U. Md., 1955; ScD (hon.), Med. Coll. Ohio, Toledo, 2000. Diplomate Am. Bd. Internal Medicine (Specialty Cardiovascular Disease). Intern U. Hosp., Balt., 1955—56; flight surgeon USN, 1956—58; resident Ohio State U. Hosp., 1959—61, resident, cardiology fellow, 1961—64; from asst. prof. to assoc. prof. medicine Coll. Medicine Ohio State U., 1965—74, dir. coronary care unit, 1968—69, dir. cardiac catheterization labs., 1970—74; prof. medicine, chief cardiology Med. Coll. Ohio, 1974—90, acting chmn. dept. medicine, 1988, vice chmn., 1988—90, v.p. acad. affairs, dean Sch. Medicine, 1990—95, sr. v.p. acad. affairs, dean Sch. Medicine, 1995—96, emeritus, ret., 1997; prof. medicine Mercer U. Med. Sch., 1998—; chmn. instnl. rev. bd. Meml. Health U. Med. Ctr., 1998—. Alt. mem. Biomedical Rsch. Alliance NY, IRB, 2007—; med. dir. Ctr. Heart Disease Prevention, St. Joseph's Candler Health Sys., Savannah, Ga., 2007—. Editl. bd. La Lettre du Cardiologue, 1985—; contbr. numerous articles to profl. jours. Fellow ACP, Am. Coll. Cardiology (gov. Ohio chpt. 1985-88), Am. Heart Assn (coun. circulation, epidemiology, clinical cardiology, coun. rep. Ohio 1977-80), Royal Soc. Medicine; mem. Ctrl. Soc. Clin. Rsch., U. Md. Med. Alumni Assn. (Honor award, Gold Key 2005), Societe Francaise Cardiologie (corr.), Alpha Omega Alpha. Office: Meml Health U Med Ctr Dept Internal Med Edn PO Box 23089 Savannah GA 31403-3089 Business E-Mail: leighril@memorialhealth.com. E-mail: rflfsl@bellsouth.net.

LEIKIN-FRENKEL, ALICIA ISABEL, biochemist, educator; b. Argentina, Nov. 10, 1950; Degree in Biochemistry, U. La Plata, Argentina, 1973, PhD in Biochemistry, 1978. Rsch. assoc. U. Chgo., 1980—82; assoc. prof. biochemistry faculty medicinal scis. U. La Plata, 1989—95; rsch. scientist Faculty Medicine, Tel Aviv U. Israel, 1997—2008, assoc. prof. CAMEA, 2008—. Sci. cons. Enzymotec, 2003—04; rsch. cons. GALMED, 2003. Postdoc. fellowship, NIH, Rsch. grant, BARD, Israel- USA, Ministry Health Israel. Mem.: Israeli Assn. Biochemistry and Molecular Biology. Avocations: music, cooking, photography. Office: Haim Lebanon Tel Aviv 69978 Israel Office Fax: 972-3-6407859. Business E-Mail: alicial@post.tau.ac.il.

LEINWEBER, BRUCE KORNBLATT, obstetrician, gynecologist, educator; b. Phila., Sept. 11, 1935; s. Arthur Richter and Florence (Kornblatt) L.; m. Nancy Schwartz, 1960 (dec. 1971); children: Cynthia Beth, Melanie Joy; m. Joan Halperin Glick, 1976; stepchildren: Suzanne Lynn Glick, Jennifer Beth Glick, Adam Brett Glick; 1 child, Dara Hope. BA in Biology, Lafayette Coll., 1955; DDS, Temple U., 1959; MD, Jefferson Med. Coll., 1963. lic. physician, Pa.; diplomate Nat. Bd. Dental Examiners, Nat. Bd. Med. Examiners, Am. Bd. Ob-gyn. Rotating intern, then resident in ob-gyn. Albert Einstein Med. Ctr., Phila., 1963—67, mem. active staff, 1967—2003, affiliate staff, 2003—; mem. active staff Rolling Hill Hosp. divsn. United Hosps. of Phila., Elkins Park, Pa., 1967—91, Frankford Hosp., Phila., 1967—91; pvt. practice ob-gyn. Phila., 1967—78, 1985—92, Bensalem, Pa., 1978—91; clin. asst. prof. ob-gyn. Med. Coll. Pa., Phila., 1976—91; clin. asst. prof. ob-gyn. Sch. Medicine Temple U., Phila., 1976—99; founder Bensalem Premenstrual Syndrome Ctr., 1984; prin. Old York Rd. Ob-Gyn. Assocs., Phila., 1992—95; mem. staff Einstein Women's Health, 1995—2000; clin. asst. prof. ob-gyn. Jefferson Med. Coll., Phila., 2000—; ret., 2000. Panelist Med. Malpractice of southeastern Pa. Contbr. articles to profl. jours. Capt. USAR, 1957-65. Ford scholar, 1951-55. Mem. AAAS, AARP, AMA, Acad. Natural Scis. Phila., Am. Assn. Gynecol. Laparascopists, Am. Assn. Sex Educators, Counselors and Therapists, Am. Coll. Ob-Gyn., Am. Fertility Soc., Fedn. State Med. Bds., Obstet. Soc. Phila., Pa. Med. Soc., Philadelphia County Med. Soc., World Med. Assn., World Affairs Coun. Phila., Zool. Soc. Phila., Assn. Vol. Sterlization, Soc. Laparoendoscopic Surgeons, Am. Soc. Colposcopy and Cervical Pathology, Phi Lambda Kappa. Republican. Jewish. Home: 245 Fairway Dr Warminster PA 18974 Home Phone: 215-885-0377. Personal E-mail: bruclein@comcast.net.

LEIPZIGER, LYLE SETH, plastic surgeon; Grad. with Phi Beta Kappa honors, Johns Hopkins Univ.; MD, cornell U., 1985. Diplomate Am. Bd. Plastic Surgery, registered NY, 1986. Resident in gen. surgery Mt. Sinai Hosp., NY; resident in plastic surgery NY Presbyn. Hosp.-Weill Cornell Med. Ctr., 1990; fellow in craniofacial and microvascular surgery Johns Hopkins Hosp., fellow in plastic surgery, 1991; hosp. affiliation includes Montefiore Med. Ctr.; chief plastic surgery divsn. North Shore Univ. Hosp., LI Jewish Med. Ctr., NY. Author: various publs. Recipient Dean Thomas Meikle prize; named one of America's Top Doctors, Castle Connolly, Best Doctors, NY Mag., 2010. Mem.: Soc. for Anti-Aging Medicine, North Am. Lipoplasty Soc., NY Regional Soc. of Plastic Surgeons, Am. Soc. Plastic Surgeons, Am. Soc. for Aesthetic Plastic Surgery. Office: Long Island Jewish Medical Center 270-05 76th Ave New Hyde Park NY 11040 Office Phone: 516-465-8787. Business E-Mail: lleipzig@nshs.edu.

LEISTEDT, SAMUËL JEAN-JACQUES, medical researcher; b. Baudour, St.-Ghislain, Belgium, June 17, 1977; adopted s. Christian Valentin Leistedt and s. Marie-Christine Monseur; m. Elodie Degroote, Feb. 22, 2003; children: Nora, Vadim, Oliver. MD, U. Liège, 2002. Lic. in psychiatry U. Libre Brussels, 2009. Rsch. fellow, sci. collaborator Erasme Academic Hosp., Brussels, 2005—08; rsch. scholar Harvard Med. Sch., Boston, 2008—. Mem. Mouvement Réformateur, Brussels, 2006—. Grant, FNRS, 2005—, fellowship, Harvard Rsch., 2008—. Office: Erasme Academic Hosp Psychiatric Dept Rt de Lennik 808 Brussels 1070 Belgium Home: 64 Ave Louis Goblet Baudour Hainaut 7331 Belgium Office Fax: 32 2 555 69 55; Home Fax: 32 65 78 73 08. Business E-Mail: samuel.leistedt@me.com, sleisted@bidmc.harvard.edu.

LEITE, CARLOS ALBERTO, physician, educator; b. Rio de Janeiro, Feb. 2, 1939; s. Indayassu and Munira (Raed) L. BSc, Coleg. Ext. Sao Jose, Rio de Janeiro, 1956; MD, U. Brazil, Rio de Janeiro, 1962, PhD, 1972; Prof. honoris causa, U. Iguaçu, Brazil, 1999. Intern Rochester (N.Y.) Gen. Hosp., 1963-64; resident Henry Ford Hosp., Detroit, 1964-65; resident, fellow, researcher Jackson Meml. Hosp. and U. Miami, Fla., 1965-68; ltd. practice Nanticoke Meml. Hosp., Seaford, Del., 1968; prof. medicine U. Fed. de Rio de Janeiro, 1972—; emeritus prof. medicine Faculty Medicine Soc. Ens. Sup. Nova Iguacu, Rio de Janeiro, 1986-99, prof. medicine, 1999—; dir. Hosp. de Nova Iguacu-Posse, Rio de Janeiro, 1991; instr. medicine Fac. Nac. Med., U. Fed. Rio de Janeiro, 1963-72; chief in-patient ward Santa Casa da Misericordia Hosp., Rio de Janeiro, 1968-72, chief out-patient dept., 1968-76, cons. physician surg. unit, 1969—; chercheur visitant temporaire Inst. Pasteur, Paris, 1988; prof. U. Fed. Rio de Janeiro, Brazil, 1993. Prof. medicine Univ. Fed. Fluminense, 1994; expert cons. for EMBRATEL. Med. writer Today's Medicine/Jour. Commerce, 1975—; editor: Metabolic Aspects of 95% Pancreatic Resection, 1971, Medicine, Logique and Reasoning, 1992, Limited Abduction of the Thumb-A New Physical Sign, 1992, Signs and Manoevers in Physical Diagnosis, 1992; editor: Crural Hernias, 1993; contbr. articles to profl. jours. 2d lt. Brazilian Army, 1961-62. Recipient Carlos Chagas medal State of Guanabara, 1972, medal Tiradentes, 1992, Pedro Americo medal, 1993; prize Argentine Meeting of Gastroenterology, 1971. Fellow ACP, Colegio Interamericano de Medicos y Cirurjanos; mem. AMA, Am. Venereal Disease. Brazilian Coll. Surgeons, Clube Monte Libano (counsel mem. 1972—), So. Med. Assn., N.Y. Acad. Scis. Office: Ste 302 595 Rua Visconde de Piraja 22410-003 Rio de Janeiro Brazil Home: Rua Redentor 70 - Apt 101 22421-030 Rio de Janeiro RJ Brazil Office Phone: 55-21-22397847. Personal E-mail: caleite@infolink.com.br.

LEITE, FREDERICO MOTA GONÇALVES, dentist; b. Belo Horizonte, Sept. 17, 1972; Degree in Dentistry, PUC, 1994; TMD, CIODONTO, 2008. Owner Dental Office, 1995—. Mem.: Soc. Brasileira de Cefaléia. Avocation: travel. Home: Rua Francisco Feio 25/302 Gutierrez Belo Horizonte Minas Gerais 30441161 Brazil Personal E-mail: fredericomotagl@yahoo.com.br.

LEITE, GUILHERME KARAM, obstetrician; b. Santos, São Paulo, Brazil, Jan. 1, 1977; Degree in Medicine, U. Severino Sombra, 2005; MD, Santa Casa São Paulo Med. Sch., 2009. Med. resident ob-gyn. Faculdade de Ciencias Medicas da Santa Casa de Misericordia São Paulo, 2009—; specialist ob-gyn. Gynecologic Endoscopy FEBRASGO/AMB. Vol., rschr. Santa Casa São Paulo Med. Sch., 2010. Mem.: Soc. Brasileira Endometriose. Avocations: music, motorcycling. Home: R Raul Pompéia 1061 ap 114 São Paulo 05025-011 Brazil Personal E-mail: guilhermekaram@uol.com.br.

LEITE, RUBENS MARCELO SOUZA, dermatologist; b. Aracaju, Brazil, Oct. 4, 1965; Degree in Medicine, U. Brasilia, 1989, M, 2006. Dermatology prof. U. Catolica de Brasilia, 2004—08; dermatologist clinics chief Camara dos Deputados, 1991—. Dermatology sci. comitee pres. Pediat. Brazilian Soc., 2006—10. Mem.: Internat. Soc. Dermatology, European Acad. Dermatology, Am. Acad. Dermatology, Brazilian Soc. Dermatology. Avocations: philosophy, stamp collecting/philately, languages. Office: SMHN Q 2 N10 Bloco A sala 108 Brasilia 70710980 Brazil Office Fax: 556133277576. Personal E-mail: rubensmsleite@gmail.com.

LEITER, EDWARD HENRY, cell biologist, researcher; b. Columbus, Ga., Apr. 17, 1942; m. Susan Shaw, Sept. 5, 1964. BS, Princeton U., 1964; MS, PhD in Cell Biology, Emory U., 1968. Fellow U. Tex., Austin, 1968-71; asst. prof. in Genetics of Diabetes and Inflammatory Bowel Disease CUNY, Bkyn., 1971-74; assoc. staff scientist Jackson Lab., Bar Harbor, Maine, 1974-75, staff scientist, 1975-90, sr. staff scientist, 1990—. Recipient rsch. award, Juvenile Diabetes Found., 1994. Achievements include research in include research in genetics and immunology of diabetes. Office: Jackson Lab 600 Main St Bar Harbor ME 04609-1500 Office Phone: 207-288-6370.

LEITMAN, I. MICHAEL, health facility administrator; b. Phila., Pa., July 25, 1959; s. Malcolm Bernard and Josephine Yase Leitman; m. Susan Terry Bernstein, June 27, 1995; children: Benjamin Russell, Jonathan Lewis, Amanda Gayle. BA, Boston U., 1981. Diplomate N.Y. Chief surg. critical care, program dir. Lenox Hill Hosp., NYC, 1997—2005; vice chmn., program dir. Beth Israel Med. Ctr., 2005—, chief gen. surgery, assoc. chief med. officer, 2007—. Chief of surg. critical care, physician-in-charge surg. edn. North Shore Univ. Hosp., Manhasset, NY, 1991—97. Contbr. articles to surg. jours. Physician mem. Lenox Hill Health Care Network, NYC, 1999—2005. Grantee, Am. Geriatric Soc., 2002. Office: Beth Israel Med Ctr Ste 2M 10 Union Square E New York NY 10003 Office Fax: 212-844-8440. Business E-Mail: mleitman@chpnet.org.

LEITNER, THOMAS, research scientist; b. Sweden, Jan. 01; PhD, Karolinska Inst., Sweden, 1996. Head HIV & retrovirus sect. Swedish Inst. Infectious Disease Control, 1998—2003, head genomics core facility, 2001—03; staff scientist Los Alamos Nat. Lab., N.Mex., 2003—. Rsch. asst. prof. Med. Rsch. Coun., Sweden, 1998—2002. Numerous grants, NIH. Office: Los Alamos Nat Lab Theoretical Biology & Biophysics Group Los Alamos NM 87545 Business E-Mail: tkl@lanl.gov.

LEITNER, WERNER GEORG, psychologist, educator; b. Küps-Theisenort, Bavaria, Germany, Mar. 21, 1959; s. Josef Anton and Hilde Leitner; 1 child, Doris. Grad. in Edn. sci. and Psychology, U. Bamberg, 1983, PhD, 1995, habilitation, 2009. Sch. psychologist Sch. Psychol. Svc., Kuimbach, Germany, 1988—92; sci. asst. U. Bamberg, Germany, 1992—98; prof. U. Dresden, Germany, 1998—99; scientist U. Bamberg, 1999—2002, U. Giessen, Germany, 2002, U. Leipzig, 1996—2006, U. Köln, 2008—; psychol. psychotherapist Küps, Bavaria, 2002—. Expert for family cts., Germany, 2000—; rschr. Parental Alienation Syndrome, Küps, 1995—. Author: Intervention Guided Single Case Help, 2005, Quality Criteria of Concentration Performance Measures, 1995, 2009, Concentration Performance and Attention Behavior, 2005, International Handbook of Parental Alienation Syndrome. With German Army, 1978—79. Mem.: Internat. Sch. Psychologist Assn. Office: Psychol Psychotherapeutical Practice Kuno Dietrich Siedlung 4u5 96328 Küps Theisenort Bavaria Germany Home: Kuno-Dietrich-Siedlung 5 96328 Küps Theisenort Bavaria Germany Office Phone: 0049 9264 915462, 00491633331230. Office Fax: 0049 9264 915452. Personal E-mail: dr.leitner@web.de.

LEKAS, MARY DESPINA, retired otolaryngologist; b. Worcester, Mass., May 13, 1928; d. Spyridon Peter and Merciny S. (Manoliou) Lekas; m. Harold William Picozzi (dec.). Student, Boston U.; BA, Clark U., 1949, DSc, ScD, Clark U., 1997; MD, Athens U., Greece, 1957; MSc, Brown U., 1986. Diplomate Am. Bd. Otolaryngology. Sci. instr. Hahnemann Hosp. Sch. Nursing; rotating intern Meml. Hosp., Worcester, 1957-58; resident in otolaryngology R.I. Hosp., Providence, 1958-62; resident in otolaryngology and otorhinolaryngology U. Pa. Grad. Sch. Medicine, 1960; surgeon in chief, dept. otolaryngology R.I. Hosp., 1984-96, surgeon-in-chief emerita; pvt. practice Providence, 1962—. Chmn. dept. otolaryngology Brown U., Providnce, 1984, clin. prof. emerita surgery divsn. otolaryngology, head and neck; cons. Cleft Palate Clin. and Craniofacial of R.I. Hosp., 1964—, VA Hosp., Providence, 1967—, St. Joseph Hosp., Providence, 1983—, Miriam Hosp., Providence, 1984—; lectr. profl. orgns.; mem. Project Hope in Columbia, Ceylon/Sri Lanka, SS Hope Hosp. Ship, People-to-People, Inc., Washington, 1968-69. Mem. editl. bd. Am. Jour. Rhinology, 1987—; contbr. articles to profl. jours. Mem. alumni coun. Clark U.; pres. Providence Med. Assn., 1987-88. Recipient Disting. Svc. award, Providence Med. Assn., 1996, Emeriti award, Brown U., 1999, Outstanding Svc. award, Brown Med. Alumni Assn., 1999, Cert. of Recognition, People-to-People, Inc.; named R.I. Woman Physician of Yr., 1992, Endowed Chair in her name, Clark U. Dept. Biology, 1997; Jonas Clark fellow. Fellow ACS, Soc. Univ. Otolaryngologists-Head and Neck Surgeons, Triological Soc. (ea. sect. sec., Presdl. Citation 1993), Am. Acad. Otolaryngology-Head and Neck Surgeons (gov. R.I. chpt. bd. of govs. 1985-), Am. Acad. Facial Plastic and Reconstructive Surgeons, Am. Acad. Broncho-Escophalogy (treas., v.p. 1990); mem. AMA, Assn. Acad. Dept. Otolaryngology-Head and Neck Surgery, Deafness Rsch. Found., Am. Cleft Palate Assn., Am. Med. Women's Assn. (R.I. Woman Physician of Yr. 1992), Am. Broncho-Esophagological Assn. (hon.), New Eng. Otolaryng. Soc. (pres. 1987-88, Cert. of Recognition 1980-81), Centurion Club. Greek Orthodox. Avocations: bicycling, swimming, church choir. Home: 129 Terrace Ave Riverside RI 02915-4726 Home Fax: 401-433-0941.

LEKER LOCKER, CHAIM, surgeon; b. Tel Aviv, Aug. 15, 1963; MD, Ben Gurion U., 1994. Cardiovasc. surgeon Mayo Clinic Rochester, Minn., 2008. Mem. STS, 2010, EACTS, 2010. Mem.. AMA, Mao Alumni, ISMICS. Office: 200 First St SW Rochester MN 55905 Business E-Mail: lekerlocker.chaim@mayo.edu.

LEKSOWSKI, KRZYSZTOF JÓZEF, surgeon, consultant; b. Krakow, Krakowskie, Poland, Mar. 29, 1953; s. Józef Leksowski and Czeslawa Leksowska; m. Teresa Ziarkiewicz, July 27, 1956; children: Anna Leksowska, Lukasz. MD, Mil. Med. Acad., Lodz, Poland, 1989, PhD, 2001. Resident Mil. Med. Acad., Bydgoszcz, 1978—82, assoc. prof., 1982—93, 1993—97; head ward of burns and plastic surgery Mil. Clin. Hosp., Bydgoszcz, 1997—98, head surgical clinic, 1998—. Col. Polish Med. Svc., 1997—. Recipient 1st award for sci. work, Rector Mil. Med. Acad., 1992. Mem.: Polish Assn. Gastroenterology, Polish Soc. Cardiothoracic Surgeons, European Soc. Surgery, Polish-French Soc. Angiology, Assn. Polish Surgeons. Avocation: yachting. Office: Mil Clin Hosp 5 Powstaców Warszawy 85-915 Bydgoszcz Poland Home Phone: 4852 5829779; Office Phone: 4852 3784539. Office Fax: 4852 3211094. Business E-Mail: Klinchir@poczta.onet.pl.

LELAS, SNJEZANA, pharmacologist, researcher, project manager; b. Zagreb, Croatia, Apr. 29, 1971; d. Srdan and Jasmina Lelas. BA, U. Oxford, 1989—92, DPhil, 1993—96. Postdoctoral fellow La. State U. Med. Ctr., New Orleans, 1996—98, Harvard Med. Sch., Southborough, Mass., 1999—2001; sr. rsch. investigator Bristol-Myers Squibb, Wallingford, Conn., 2001—08, prin. scientist, 2008—10, project mgr., 2010—. Contbr. articles to profl. jours. Scholar, U. Oxford, 1991. Mem.: Am. Soc. for Pharmacology and Exptl. Therapeutics, Behavioral Pharmacology Soc., Soc. for Neuroscience. Avocations: travel, writing, sports, theater. Home: 3B Oak Hill Dr Clinton CT 06413 Office: Bristol-Myers Squibb 5 Research Pkwy Wallingford CT 06492 Office Fax: 203-677-7750. Business E-Mail: snjezana.lelas@bms.com.

LEMA, GUILLERMO, anesthesiologist, educator; b. Concepción, Chile, June 19, 1954; MD, U. Chile, 1998. Prof. anesthesiology Pontificia U. Católica Chile, 2006—. Recipient award, Colegio Médico Chile. Avocation: theater. Office: Marcoleta 367 Santiago 833-0024 Chile Business E-Mail: glema@med.puc.cl.

LEMA, MARK JOSEPH, anesthesiologist, educator; b. Buffalo, June 18, 1949; BA in Polit. Sci., Canisius Coll., Buffalo, 1972; MS in Natural Scis., SUNY, Buffalo, 1976, PhD in Physiology, 1978; MD, SUNY, Bklyn., 1982. Diplomate Am. Bd. Anesthesiology, Nat. Bd. Med. Examiners, lic. NY, Mass. Intern SI Hosp., 1982; clin. fellow anesthesiology Brigham & Women's Hosp., Boston, 1983-84; instr. anesthesiology Harvard U. Med. Sch., Boston, 1985-87; asst. prof. anesthesiology SUNY Sch. Medicine & Biomed. Scis., Buffalo, 1987-94, assoc. prof., 1994-99, prof., chair dept. anesthesiology, 1999—, dir. rsch. dept. anesthesia, 1987-92, vice-chmn. acad. affairs, 1992-99. Chmn. dept. anesthesiology, critical care & pain medicine Roswell Park Cancer Inst., Buffalo, 1987—, med. chief cancer pain & palliative care svc., 1988—99; vis. prof. Cornell U., NYC, Dartmouth-Hitchcock Med. Ctr., Lebanon, NH, Cairo U., U. Rochester, NY, SUNY Syracuse, SUNY Bklyn., SUNY Stony Brook, La. State U., Harvard U., Naval Med. Command, Bethesda, Md. Editor: ASA newsletter, 1998—2004; contbr. articles to profl. jours. Recipient Werthamer Fellowship, Perker B. Francis Rsch. Fellowship, Disting. Alumni award, Canisius Coll., Meritorious Svc. award, NY State Dept. Health Office Profl. Med. Conduct, Eliasberg medal for anesthesiology accomplishments, Mt. Sinai Med. Sch. Mem.: NY State Soc. Anesthesiologists (bd. dirs., past pres.), Med. Soc. County Erie, Med. Soc. NY, Internat. Anesthesia Rsch. Soc., Anesthesia Hist. Assn., Am. Soc. Regional Anesthesia (bd. dirs.), Am. Soc. Anesthesiologists (pres.-elect 2005, pres. 2006—08), Internat. Assn. Study of Pain, Am. Pain Soc. Office: Roswell Park Cancer Inst Elm & Carlton St Buffalo NY 14263-0001 Business E-Mail: mark.lema@roswellpark.org.

LEMAISTRE, CHARLES AUBREY, internist, epidemiologist, educator; b. Lockhart, Ala., Feb. 10, 1924; s. John Wesley and Edith (McLeod) LeM.; m. Joyce Trapp, June 3, 1952 (dec. Dec. 2003), Andreae Preyer Behlen, Jan. 29, 2005; children: Charles Frederick, William Sidney, Joyce Anne, Helen Jean; m. Andreae Preyer Behlen, Jan. 29, 2005. BA, U. Ala., 1943, LLD (hon.), 1971; MD, Cornell U., 1947; LLD (hon.), Austin Coll., 1970; DSc (hon.), U. Dallas, 1978, Southwestern U., 1981; D honoris causa, U. Guadalajara, Mex., 1989; D in Humane Letters, Stillman Coll., 2010. Intern to resident in medicine NY Hosp., 1947-49; rsch. fellow infectious diseases Cornell U. Med. Coll., 1949-51, mem. faculty, 1951-54, asst. prof. medicine, 1953-54; mem. faculty Emory U. Sch. Medicine, 1954-59, prof. preventive medicine, chmn. dept., 1957-59; prof. medicine U. Tex. Southwestern Med. Sch., 1959-78, assoc. dean, 1965-66; vice chancellor health affairs U. Tex. Sys., Austin, 1966-68, exec. vice chancellor, 1968-69, dep. chancellor, 1969-70, chancellor, 1971-78, prof. medicine, 1978-96; pres. M.D. Anderson Cancer Ctr. U. Tex., 1978—96, internist, 1978—96, prof. dept. bev. sci.-prevention, 2006—. Cons. epidemiology Communicable Disease Ctr., USPHS, 1953-69; cons. medicine VA, 1954-59; area med. cons. VA (Atlanta area), 1958-59; vis. staff physician Grady Meml. Hosp., Atlanta, 1954-59, Emory U. Hosp., 1954-59; sr. attending staff mem. Parkland Meml. Hosp., Dallas, 1959-66; med. dir. chest divsn. Woodlawn Hosp., Dallas, 1959-65; mem. Surgeon Gen.'s Adv. Com. Smoking and Health, 1963-64, AMA-Edn. Rsch. Found. com. rsch. tobacco and health, 1964-66; chmn. Gov. Tex. Com. Tb Eradication, 1963-64; cons. internal medicine Baylor U. Med. Ctr., Dallas, 1962-66, St. Paul Hosp., Dallas, 1966; cons. divsn. hosp. and med. facilities USPHS, 1966; mem. N.Y.C. Task Force on Tb, 1967; cons. Bur. Physician, HEW, 1967-70; mem. grad. med. edn. nat. adv. com. Health Resources Adminstrn., 1977-80; mem. Tex. Legislature Dept. Health, Edn. and Welfare, 1967, Tex. Legislature Com. on Organ Transplantation, 1968, Carnegie Commn. on Non-Traditional Study, 1971-73; mem. bd. commrs. Nat. Commn. on Accrediting, 1973-76; mem. joint task force on continuing competence in pharmacy Am. Pharm. Assn.-Am. Assn. Coll. in Pharmacy, 1973-74; mem. exec. com. Legis. Task Force on Cancer in Tex., 1984-86; adv. bd. 6th World Conf. on Smoking and Health. Contbr. articles to med. jours.; contbg. author: A Textbook of Medicine, 10 and 11th edits, 1963, Pharmacology in Medicine, 1958, translating author: The Tubercle Bacillus, 1955; mem. editl. bd. Am. Rev. Respiratory Diseases, 1955-58. Mem. President's Commn. White House Fellows, 1971; chmn. subcom. on diversity and pluralism Nat. Coun. on Ednl. Rsch., 1973-75; bd. dirs. Assn. Tex. Colls. and Univs., 1974-75; mem. devel. coun. United Negro Coll. Fund, 1974-78; mem. nat. adv. coun. Inst. for Svcs. to Edn., 1974-78; mem. exec. com. Assn. Am. Univs., 1975-77; mem. Project HOPE com. on Health Policy, 1977; chmn. steering com. Presbyn. Physicians for Fgn. Missions, 1960-62; mem. Ministers Cons. Clinic, Dallas, 1960-62; trustee Austin Coll., 1979-83, Stillman Coll., 1978-84; bd. dirs. Ga. Tb Assn., 1955-59; bd. dirs. Damon Runyon-Walter Winchell Cancer Fund, 1976-83, chmn. exec. com., v.p., 1978, pres., 1979-83; trustee Biol. Humanics Found., Dallas, 1973-82; chmn. health manpower com. Assn. Am. Univs., 1975-78; sec. Coun. So. Univs., Inc., 1976-78, pres., 1977-78; hon. life trustee Menninger Found.; host com. Houston Econ. Summit, 1990. Recipient Cornell Univ. Alumni of Distinction award, 1978, Disting. Alumnus award U. Alabama Sch. Medicine, 1982, Pres.' award Am. Lung Assn., 1987, Gibson D. Lewis award for Excellence in Cancer Control Tex. Cancer Coun., 1988, award of Honor Am. Soc. Hosp. Pharmacists, 1988, Svc. to Mankind award Leukemia Soc. Am. Tex. Gulf Coast chpt., 1991, People of Vision award Tex. Soc. to Prevent Blindness, 1991, Outstanding Tex. Leader award 7th Ann. John Ben Sheppard Pub. Leadership Forum, 1991; Inst. Religion's Caring Spirit Tribute, 1993, AMA Disting. Svc. award, 1995, Ala. Acad. of Honor, 1998, Disting. Svc. award NASA, 1998, Charles A. LeMaiste Clinic Bldg. U. Tex. M.D. Anderson Cancer Ctr., Houston, 1997; named Houstonian of Yr., Houston Sch. for Deaf Children, 1987, Lamar award Assn. Tex. Colls. and Univs., 2000; named to Ala. Healthcare Hall of Fame, 1999. Mem. AMA, (Disting. Svc. award 1995), NASA, NIH (chair joint adv. com. behavioral rsch. 1992), Am. Thoracic Soc. (past v.p.), So. Thoracic Soc. (past pres.), Nat. TB Assn., Tex. Med. Assn., Ga. Med. Assn., Soc. Assn. Oncology (bd. dirs.), Am. Cancer Soc. (Tex. bd. dirs. 1977-89, med. and sci. com. 1974, chmn. study com. on tobacco and cancer 1976, pub. edn. com. 1976-87, chmn., mem. various nat. coms., v.p., pres. 1986, med. dir.-at-large 1977-89, Ted C. Mars award 1998, medal of Honor 1998, Biennial Symposium Founders award 2006), Houston C. of C. (dir. 1979-89), Philos. Soc. Tex. (pres. 1980-81), Greater Houston Partnership (bd. dirs. 1989-96), Alpha Omega Alpha. Presbyterian. Personal E-mail: clemaistre@gmail.com.

LEMAN, ROBERT BURTON, cardiology educator; b. Upper Darby, Pa., Dec. 23, 1947; s. William Walter and Ruth Cordelia Leman; m. Patti Ruth Pennington, June 9, 1973; children: Brian Burton, Heather Michelle. BS, Ursinus Coll., 1969; MD, U. Ark., 1976. Diplomate Am. Bd. Internal Medicine; cert. internal medicine, cardiovascular disease, cardiac electrophysiology; lic. physician, S.C. Intern Med. U. of S.C., Charleston, 1976-77, resident, 1977-79, fellow, 1979-81, instr., 1971-72, dir., 1982—, asst. prof., 1983-89, assoc. prof., 1989-97, prof., 1997—. Dir. pacemaker surveillance Med. U. S.C., Charleston, 1982—2000, dir. adult electrophysiology medicine, 1988—2002; dir. Cath. Lab., Charleston VA, 1986-92;co-dir. electro, 2002—; lectr. in field. Contbr. articles to profl. jours. Active Hibben Meth. Ch.; bd. dirs. Trident Fishing Tournament of Charleston County Park. Grantee Wyeth-Ayerst Labs., 1990, G.D. Searl & Co., 1991, Pfizer, Inc., 1992, 93. Fellow ACP, Am. Coll. Cardiology, Heart Rhythm Soc.; mem. Am. Heart Assn. (fellow coun. in clin. cardiology), N.Am. Soc. Pacing and Electrophysiology, Heart Rhythm Soc., Charleston County Med. Soc., Hobcaw Yacht Club, Alpha Omega Alpha. Avocations: boating, fishing, sailing, gardening. Office: Med Univ SC Divsn Cardiology 25 Courtney Dr Apt 703 MSC 592 Charleston SC 29425-5290 Office Phone: 843-876-4762.

LEMANSKE, ROBERT F., JR., allergist, immunologist; b. Milw., 1948; MD, U. Wis., 1975. Diplomate Am. Bd. Pediats., Am. Bd. Allergy and Immunology. Intern U. Wis. Hosp., Madison, 1975-76, resident in pediats., 1976-78, prof. pediats. medicine, divsn. head pediat. allergy, immunology & rheumatology. Fellow: Am. Acad. Allergy and Immunology, Am. Acad. Pediat. Office: Clin Sci Ctr Rm K4/916 600 Highland Ave Madison WI 53792-0001 Office Phone: 608-265-2206.

LEMANSKI, LARRY FREDRICK, medical educator, academic administrator; b. Madison, Wis., June 5, 1943; s. Fredrick Everett and Marjery Ulila (Hill) L.; m. Sharon Lee Wulf, Aug. 6, 1966; children: Scott Fredrick, Jennifer Lee. BS, U. Wis., Platteville, 1966; MS, Ariz. State U., 1968, PhD, 1971. Asst. prof. U. Calif., San Francisco, 1975-77; assoc. prof. U. Wis., Madison, 1977—79, prof., 1979—83; prof. and chmn. dept. anatomy and cell biology SUNY, Syracuse, 1983—97, cell and molecular biology doctoral tng. program and consortium, 1987—97; rsch. prof. biology Syracuse U., 1988-97; assoc. v.p. for rsch., acting v.p. Tex. A&M. U., College Station, 1997—2001; prof. biomed. sci., biology and chemistry Fla. Atlantic U., 2001—07, v.p. rsch. and grad. studies, pres., CEO of FAU Rsch. Corp.; sr. v.p. Temple U., Phila., 2007—09; provost, v.p. academic affairs Tex. A & M U. Commerce, 2009—. Chmn. spl. study sect. NIH; v.p., IBM bd. gov. LA Grid, dean grad. programs Fla. Atlantic U., 2001—05; mem. bd. dirs. NIH rev. panel Roadmap Rsch. Programs, 2004—05; bd. dirs. Ctr. Human and Machine Cognition, 2004—08; founder divsn. rsch. Fla. Atlantic U.; bd. dirs. Fla. Rsch. Consortium, Fla. Space Rsch. Inst.; mem. Gov.'s Team Fla. in Germany and Switzerland, acad. exchange collaboration India, Mex. and Spain., 2005—; mem. govs. Enterprise Fla. Trade Mission to UK and other ednl. visits for rsch. collaborations, 2006—. Leader Boy Scouts Am., Jamboree nat. staff, 1989, coun. tng. chmn., 1992—94; bd. dirs. Oak Ridge Assn. Univs., 1999—2002, 2004—07, Inst. Human and Machine Cognition, gov.'s appointee, 2004—; bd. dirs. I.B.M Latin Am. Grid, 2005—07, bd. govs., 2005—07; Fla. del. Enterprise Fla. Team Trade Missions to U.K., Germany, Switzerland and Israel, 2005—07; rsch. acad. Trade Missions to China and Japan, 2007; bd. dirs. Fla.-Israeli Inst., 2006—07. Officer USAR, 1965—71. Recipient Pres' award Rsch. SUNY HSC, 1987, Disting. Alumnus award U. Wis., Platteville, 1990, Profl. Excellence award N.Y. State/United Univ. Professions, 1990, 95, SUNY Pres.'s award for affirmative action, 1995, Outstanding Rschr. award SUNY Coll. of Medicine, 1997; NIH fellow, 1968-71, 71-73, Muscular Dystrophy fellow, 1973-75; grantee NIH, 1975—. Mem. AAAS, Am. Heart Assn. (Wis. affiliate rsch. com. 1982-83, mem. nat. review panel 2010-, Louis N. Katz Rsch. prize 1978, Outstanding Rsch. award 1982, Established Investigator award 1976-81, symposium chair Internat. Soc. Heart Rsch. Conf., Brisbane, Australia, 2004, Fla.-Puerto Rican rsch. com. 2004-06, AHA Cardiovascular Devel. Study Sect., 2010-), Electron Microscopy Soc. Am., Tex. Soc. for Biomed. Rsch. (bd. dirs. 1999-2001), Am. Assn. Anatomy, Cell Biology, and Neurobiology (chair nat. coun. 1997—), Am. Assn. Anatomists, Am. Soc. Cell Biology (congrl. liaison com.), Soc. Devel. Biology, Am. Assn. Anatomy Chmn., NY Acad. Scis., Masons (3d degree master), Sigma Xi, Beta Beta Beta, Phi Beta Delta. Avocations: gardening, fishing, boating, camping, music. Home: 2718 McCarley Dr Commerce TX 75428-3828 Office: Tex A & M University Commerce PO Box 3011 Commerce TX 75429-3011 Office Phone: 903-886-5018. Business E-Mail: larry_lemanski@tamu-commerce.edu.

LE MAY, MOIRA KATHLEEN, retired psychology educator; b. NYC, Apr. 12, 1934; d. Bernard Howard and Kathleen (Sullivan) Fitzpatrick; m. Joseph Albert Le May, June 14, 1958; children: Valerie H. (Le May) Teal, Joseph B. BS, Queens Coll., 1956; MS, Pa. State U., 1960, PhD, 1970. Engring. psychologist USN Rsch. Lab., Washington, 1960-62, ITT Fed Labs., Nutley, N.J., 1962-64; instr. psychology Manhattanville Coll., Purchase, N.Y., 1964-68; asst. prof. Skidmore Coll., Saratoga Springs, N.Y., 1968-70; prof. Psychology Montclair State Coll., Upper Montclair, NJ, 1970—98, ret. Cons. in engring. psychol. USAF-WPAFB, Human Resources Lab., Dayton, Ohio, 1978-79, NASA Calif. Tech. Jet Propulsion Lab., Pasadena, 1982-83, USN Air Devel. Ctr. Warminster, Pa., 1986-87, NASA Langley Rsch. Ctr., Hampton, Va., 1989-90, NASA-Ames Rsch. Ctr., Moffett Field, Calif., 1994 Contbr. numerous artticles to profl. jours and papers to sci. meetings. Roman Catholic. Avocations: historical preservation, antiques, architecture. Home: 1023 Hillcrest Rd Ridgewood NJ 07450-1030 Home Phone: 201-447-2471. Personal E-mail: lemayjm@aol.com, moira.lemay@live.com.

LEMBERG, LOUIS, cardiologist, educator; b. Chgo., Dec. 27, 1916; s. Morris and Frances Lemberg; m. Dorothy Feinstein, 1940 (dec. 1969); children: Gerald, Laura Bott, Paula Saltzman; m. Miriam Mayer, Jan. 29, 1971. BS, U. Ill., Chgo., 1938; MD, U. Ill., 1940. Intern Mt. Sinai Hosp., Chgo., 1940-41, resident, 1945-48, asst. prof. med., 1955-58, assoc. prof. med., 1958-70; prof. clin. cardiology U. Miami (Fla.) Sch. Medicine, 1970—, dir. coronary care unit, 1965-75. Chief cardiology Mercy Hosp., 1974-79; chief staff Nat. Children's Cardiac Hosp., 1959-66; cons. cardiology VA Hosp., Miami, 1953-64; dir. cardiology Dade County Hosp., 1953-64, dir. Heart Sta. and Electrocardiography, U. Miami Jackson Meml. Med. Ctr., 1952-75, program dir. Courses in Coronary Care for Practicing Physician, 1970-2003, Courses in Coronary Care for Nurses, 1970-90; Master Approach to Cardiovascular Problems, 1972-82, Cardiology Update for Intensive Care Nurses, Am. Coll. Cardiology, 1978-92, Cardiology Update, 1987-2002. Author: Vectorcardiography, 1969, 2d edit., 1975, Electrophysiology of Pacing and Cardioversion, 1969; editor-in-chief Current Concepts in Cardiovascular Disorders, 1984-86; contbr. to med. publs. Served to maj. AUS, 1941-55, ETO. Recipient U. St. Torres (Philippines) Luis Guerrero hon. lectr. award, 1977, Recognition award U. Miami Sch. Medicine, Lifetime Achievement award Jackson Meml. Med. Ctr. U. Miami, 1997, Key to City of Miami Beach, Fla., Nurses Pioneering Spirit award Am. Assn. Critical Care, 2000, Physicians Recognition awards AMA. Fellow ACP, Am. Coll. Cardiology (editl. bd. jour.); mem. Heart Assn. Greater Miami (pres.), Fla. Heart Assn. (pres.), Am. Heart Assn. (fellow coun. clin. cardiology). Democrat. Jewish. Achievements include pioneer in development Demand Pacemaker, 1964, a chair in cardiology established at the U. Miami Sch. of Medicine entitled The Louis Lemberg Professor of Cardiology, 1990. Home: 720 NE 69th St Apt 18 South Miami FL 33138-5738 Office: U Miami Sch Medicine Divsn Cardiology PO Box 016960 Miami FL 33101 *

LEMBERGER, LOUIS, pharmacologist; b. Monticello, NY, May 8, 1937; s. Max and Ida Lemberger; m. Myrna Sue Diamond, 1959; children: Harriet Felice Schor, Margo Beth. BS magna cum laude, Bklyn. Coll. Pharmacy, LI U., 1960; PhD in Pharmacology, Albert Einstein Coll. Medicine, 1964, MD, 1968; Doctorate (hon.), LI U., 1994. Pharmacy intern VA Regional Office, Newark, summer 1960; postdoctoral fellow Albert Einstein Coll. Medicine, 1964-68; intern in medicine Met. Hosp. Ctr., NY Med. Coll., NYC, 1968-69; rsch. assoc. NIH, Bethesda, Md., 1969-71; clin. pharmacologist Lilly Lab. for Clin. Rsch., Eli Lilly & Co., Indpls., 1971-75, chief clin. pharmacology, 1975-78, dir. clin. pharmacology, 1978-89, clin. rsch. fellow,

1982-93; asst. prof. pharmacology Ind. U., 1972-73, asst. prof. medicine, 1972-73, assoc. prof. pharmacology, 1973-77, assoc. prof. medicine, 1973-77, prof. pharmacology, 1977—, prof. medicine, prof. psychiatry, 1977—, mem. grad. faculty, 1975—; adj. prof. clin. pharmacology Ohio State U., 1975-86; physician Wishard Meml. Hosp., 1976-98. Cons. US Nat. Commn. on Marijuana and Drug Abuse, 1971-73, Can. Commn. Inquiry into Non-Med. Use of Drugs, 1971-73; mem. Pharm. Mfrs. Assn. Commn. on Medicines for Drug Dependence and Abuse, 1990-93, Ind. Optometric Legend Drug Adv. Com., 1991-96; guest lectr. various univs., 1968—; lectr. U. Minn., 1993—; mem. adv. com. Faseb Life Scis. Rsch. Office, 1993-96; commdr. USPHS, 1971-80. Author: (with A. Rubin) Physiologic Disposition of Drugs of Abuse, 1976; contbr. numerous articles on biochemistry and pharmacology to sci. jours.; editorial bd.; Excerpta Medica, 1972-96, Clin. Pharmacology and Therapeutics, 1976-96, Communications in Psychopharmacology, 1975-91, Pharmacology, Internat. Jour. Exptl. and Clin. Pharmacology, 1978-94, Drug and Alcohol Abuse Rsch., 1979-86, Drug Devel. Rsch., 1980-87, Trends in Pharmcol. Scis., 1980-85. Post adviser Crossroads of Am. coun. Boy Scouts Am., 1972-77; comdr. Jewish War Vet. Post 114, 2005—06. Comdr. USPHS, 1969-71. Recipient Disting. Alumnus award, Albert Einstein Coll. Medicine, 1989, LI U., 1990, Pres. award, 1998, Cornerstone award for Outstanding Lifetime Achievement in Health Scis., Am. Drugstore Mus., 2000. Fellow ACP, AAAS, Am. Coll. Neuropsychopharmacology (chmn. credentials com. 1993), Am. Coll. Clin. Pharmacology; mem. Am. Soc. Pharmacology and Exptl. Therapeutics (com. div. clin. pharmacology 1972-78, chmn. com. 1978-83, coun. 1980-83, chmn. long-range planning com. 1984-86, pres. 1987-88, ASPET award in Therapeutics, 1985, Harry Gold award for rsch. and teaching excellence in clin. pharmacology 1993), Am. Soc. Clin. Pharmacology and Therapeutics (chmn. sect. neuropsychopharmacology 1973-80, chmn. fin. com. 1976-83, 89-92, v.p. 1981-82, pres. 1983-84, dir. 1975-81, 84-87, Rawls-Palmer award 1986, Henry Elliot Disting. Svc. award 1992, Oscar B. Hunter award for outstanding achievement in exptl. therapeutics 2003), Am. Soc. Clin. Investigation, Collegium Internat. Neuro-Psychopharmacologicum, Am. Fedn. Clin. Rsch. Ctrl. Soc. Clin. Rsch., Soc. Neuroscis., Jewish War Vets (comdr. Post 114 2005-06), Sigma Xi, Alpha Omega Alpha, Rho Chi. Jewish. Achievements include being first person to administer and study the actions in humans of the antidepressant drug Prozac (fluoxetine), Permax (pergolide) the drug used to treat Parkinson's disease, and the cannabinoid drug Cesamet (nabilone) utilized for the treatment of nausea and vomiting secondary to cancer chemotherapy and Zyprexa (Olanzepine) the drug utilized in schizophrenia and Strattera (atomoxetine) the drug utilized in attention deficit hyperactivity disorder; responsible for directing and spearheading the clinical development of Prozac, Permax and Cesamet through clinical trials, regulatory approval and eventually into the marketplace. Home: 3315 Walnut Creek Dr N Carmel IN 46032-9038 Office: Ind Univ Sch Medicine Dept Pharmacology and Medicine Indianapolis IN 46202

LEMOLE, GERALD MICHAEL, surgeon; b. SI, NY, Dec. 17, 1936; s. Joseph Michael and Mary (Boylan) L.; m. Emily Jane Asplundh, Dec. 8, 1962; children: Lisa Jane, Laura Leigh, Emily Anne, Gerald Michael Samantha Mary, Christopher Robin. BS in Biology, Villanova U., 1958; MD, Temple U., 1962. Diplomate Am. Bd. Surgery, Am. Bd. Thoracic Surgery. Intern S.I. Hosp., 1962-63; resident Temple U., Phila., 1963-67, Baylor Affiliated Hosps., Houston, 1967-69; practice medicine specializing in throacic surgery Phila., 1969—, Browns Mills, NJ, 1972-84; W.L. Samuel CArpenter III disting. chmn. cardiovascular surgery Christiana Care Health Sys., 2006—; assoc. med. dir. Christiana Care Ctr. for Heart and Vascular Health, 2006—. Chief sect. cardiac and thoracic surgery Temple U. Hosp., Phila., 1970-77; prof. surgery Temple U. Health Scis. Ctr., 1975-77; chmn. dept. surgery Deborah Heart and Lung Ctr., Phila., 1972-84; chief sect. cardiovascular surgery Med. Ctr. Del.; vis. prof. cardiac surgery U. Dublin, Ireland, 1974, u. Istanbul, Turkey, 1982, Mil. Med. Coll., Ankara, Turkey, 1985, Beijing Heart Inst., 1991; clin. prof. surgery U. Pa., 1979, Rutgers Med. Sch., Thomas Jefferson U., 1999—; rschr. in field. Contbr. numerous articles on cradiovascular surgery and disease to med. jours. Recipient Disting Alumnus award Villanova U., 1987. Fellow ACS, Coll. Cardiology, Am. Coll. Chest Physicians (cardiovascular com. 1974—); mem. AMA, Am. Assn. Thoracic Surgery, Am. Fedn. Clin. Rsch., Pan Am. Thoracic Soc., Am. Heart Assn. (cardiovascular coun. 1973—, pres. Del. chpt. 1991, chmn. bd. dirs. 1992), Pa. Med. Soc., Pa. Assn. Thoracic Surgery (program chaor 1975—),, Pa. Assn. Thoracic Surgeons, Phila. County Med. Soc., Phila. Acad. Surgery, Phila. Acad. Cardioloby (pres. 1976-79, chmn. exec. com. 1976—), Phila. Coll. Physicians, Internat. Cardiovascular Soc., Assn. Acad. Surgeons, Soc. Casvular Surgery, Denton A. Cooley Cardiovascular Surg. Soc. Home: 404 Tomlinson Rd Huntingdon Valley PA 19006-4818 Office: Med Ctr Del 4745 Ogletown Stanton Rd # 20 Newark DE 19713-2067 Personal E-mail: gmlmd17@aol.com.

LEMOLE, GERALD MICHAEL, JR., neurosurgeon, educator; BS in Biology, Harvard U.; MD, U. Pa., Phila., 1995. Diplomate American Bd. Neurol. Surgery. Intern gen. surgery Maricopa Med. Ctr., Phoenix, 1995—96; fellowship complex spinal surgery & cerebrovascular/skull base surgery Barrow Neurol. Inst., St. Joseph's Hosp. & Med. Ctr., Phoenix, 1996—2000, resident neurol. surgery, 2000—02; head Skull Base Multidisciplinary program U. Ill., Chgo.; co-dir. Chgo. CyberKnife Radiosurgery Ctr.; assoc. prof. surgery, chief divsn. neurosurgery U. Ariz./Univ. Med. Ctr., Tuscon, 2009—. Contbr. articles to profl. jours., chapters to books. Mem.: North American Skull Base Soc., Congress Neurol. Surgeons, American Assn. Neurol. Surgeons. Achievements include gaining national media attention for performing brain surgery on US Rep. Gabrielle Giffords after she was shot in Tucson, removing part of her skull to allow the brain to swell, as well as removing dead brain tissue and skull fragments from her eye. Office: Ariz Health Science Ctr Neurosurgery PO Box 245070 1501 N Campbell Ave Tucson AZ 85724 E-mail: mlemole@surgery.arizona.edu. *

LEMOSY, ELLEN K., medical educator; b. Fla., 1963; BS in Biology, U. Ctrl. Fla., 1984; MD, PhD, Duke U., 1993. Assoc. rsch. scientist Yale U. Sch. Medicine, 2000—01; asst. prof. Georgia Health Scis. U. (formerly Med. Coll. Ga.), 2002—09, assoc. prof., 2009—. Postdoc. fellowship, Am. Heart Assn., Nat. Rsch. Svc. fellow, Nat. Inst. Child Health and Human Devel., fellow, Nat. Inst. Gen. Med. Scis., grant. Mem.: Soc. Glycobiology, Am. Soc. Matrix Biology, Soc. Devel. Biology, Genetics Soc. America, Am. Soc. Cell Biology. Office: Dept Cellular Biology 1120 15th St CB1101 Augusta GA 30912 Business E-Mail: elemosy@mcg.edu.

LENDL, JENNIFER LYNN, psychologist; b. Santa Monica, Calif., July 29, 1951; d. Gerald Lyle and Joyce Lucile (Devine) L. AB in History, Stanford U., 1973, MA in History, 1975; MS in Psychology, San Jose State U., 1982; PhD in Psychology, Internat. Coll., LA, 1984. Lic. psychologist, Calif., History Credential Calif. C.C., 1976, expert in traumatic stress and diplomate Am. Acad. Experts in Traumatic Stress, 1999, cert. therapist and approved cons. in eye movement desensitization and reprocessing, 1999; diplomate, Nat. Inst. Sports, 2003. Head coord. Women's Ctr., San Jose State U., Calif., 1978—79, lectr. dept. sociology, 1978—84; psychol. asst. San Jose, 1982-88; pvt. practice, 1988—; psychologist Family Svc. Ctr., Mare Island Nuclear submarine Base, Vallejo, Calif., 1992. Human rels. specialist Santa Clara County Commn. on Status of Women, San Jose, 1981-82; mgmt. analyst Santa Clara Valley Med. Ctr., San Jose, 1982; tutor in clin. psychology Internat. Coll., 1983-84; affiliate counselor Alum Rock Comm. Ctr., San Jose, 1983-84; fellow Menninger Inst., 1984-86; participant task force on youth suicide NIH, Washington, 1986-87; rsch. asst. Heart Disease Prevention Program Stanford U., Palo Alto, Calif., 1980-81; trainer, facilitator Eye Movement Desensitization and Reprocessing EMDR Inst., WAtsonville, Calif., 1991-; trauma and performance consulting psychologist Amen Clinics for Behavioral Medicine, Newport Beach, Calif., 1996-; sport psychologist Women Involved in Sport Evolution, Ventura, Calif., 1997-, performance & trauma psychologist Amen Clinics, 1995-2001, specially trainer & facilitator EMDR Inst., 1990-, facilitator EMDR Humanitarian Assistance Program, 2003-. Author: EMDR & Performance in the Workplace, 1997. Student mem. Calif. Comn. for Drug Rehab., 1969; asst. to campaign mgr. Campaign for Reelection Mayor Janet Gray Hayes, San Jose, 1978; mem. Santa Clara County Sheriff's Adv. Com. for Women, 1983. Gov.'s scholar State of Calif., 1969, Calif. State scholar, 1969-73, Stanford U. Alumni Assn., 1969-73, Kathryn Uhl Carr scholar Calif. State U. and Coll. Bd. Trustees, 1979-80, scholar NIMH, 1979-81; named Woman of Achievement San Jose Mercury News and Santa Clara County Women's Fund, 1994. Mem. APA (assoc.), Calif. Psychol. Assn. (mem.-at-large divsn. media rels. 1990, sec.-treas. divsn. media rels. 1991-92 mem. pub. info. com., chair pub. interest div. and rep. to bd. dirs.), Santa Clara County Psychol. Assn. (trauma response com. 1989-91, govt. rels. chair 1991-92), Eye Movement Desensitization and Reprocessing Internat. Assn. (founding mem., convention com. 2001-, Francine Shapiro award for outstanding svc. and contbn. 2006), Calif. Assn. Marriage and Family Therapists, Milton H. Erickson Found., Assn. for the Advancement of Applied Sport Psychology, Nat. Inst. Sports (cert. sport psychologist), Stanford U. Alumni Assn. (life), Stanford U. Varsity Block S Assn. (life). Avocations: swimming, theater, home renovation, dowsing. Office: 1142 Mckendrie St San Jose CA 95126-1406 Office Phone: 408-244-6186.

LENFANT, CLAUDE JEAN-MARIE, physician, director; b. Paris, Oct. 12, 1928; arrived in U.S., 1960, naturalized, 1965; s. Robert and Jeanine (Leclerc) Lenfant; children: Philipe, Bernard, Martine Lenfant Wayman, Brigitte Lenfant Martin, Christine. BS, U. Rennes, France, 1948; MD, U. Paris, 1956; DSc (hon.), SUNY, 1988. Asst. prof. physiology U. Lille, France, 1959—60; from clin. instr. to prof. medicine physiology and biophysics U. Wash. Med. Sch., 1961—72; assoc. dir. lung programs Nat. Heart, Lung and Blood Inst. NIH, Bethesda, Md., 1970—72, dir. divsn. lung diseases, 1972—80; dir. Fogarty Internat. Ctr. NIH, 1980—82, assoc. dir. internat. rsch., 1980—82; dir. Nat. Heart, Lung and Blood Inst., 1982—2003, disting. scientist emeritus, 2003—; pres. World Hypertension League, 2000—06; exec. dir. Global Initiative Asthma, and Global Initiative Chronic Obstructive Lung Disease, 2005—. Mem. editl. bd.: Undersea Biomed. Rsch., 1973—75, Respiration Physiology, 1971—78, Am. Jour. Physiology and Jour. Applied Physiology, 1970—76, Am. Rev. Respiratory Disease, 1973—79, Jour. Applied Physiology, 1976—82, Am. Jour. Medicine, 1979—82; editor: Lung Biology in Health and Disease. Elected mem., planning group Global Alliance Against Chronic Respiratory Disease/WHO, 2007—; apptd. mem., Expert Panel Cardiovascular Disease WHO Etpest, 2007—. Recipient Nathan Davis award, AMA, 1998, Gold Heart award, Am. Heart Assn., 2002, European Lung Found. award, 2002. Fellow: Royal Soc. Medicine, Royal Coll. Physicians; mem.: French Nat. Acad. Medicine, USSR Acad. Med. Scis., Inst. Medicine of NAS, Undersea Med. Soc., NY Acad. Scis., Am. Physiol. Soc., French Physiol. Soc., Am. Soc. Clin. Investigation, Assn. Am. Physicians, Alpha Omega Alpha. Home: PO Box 65278 Vancouver WA 98665-0010 Personal E-mail: lenfantc@prodigy.net.

LENG, SHUAI, medical educator; b. China, Dec. 9, 1978; PhD, U. Wis., Madison, 2008. Asst. prof. Mayo Clinic, 2008—. Mem.: SPIE, AAPM, RSNA. Office: 200 1st St SW Rochester MN 55906 Business E-Mail: leng.shuai@mayo.edu.

LENGELE, CHEVALIER BENOÎT G., surgeon, educator; b. Etterbeek, Brussels, Belgium, July 25, 1962; s. Joseph G. Lengelé and Josée J. Dilis; m. Marie-France P. Kempinaire, Mar. 4, 2004; 1 child, Louise-Marie V. Lengelé. MD, U. Catholique de Louvain, Brussels, 1987, PhD, 1997. Resident maxillo-facial surgery Amiens U. Hosp., France, 1990—91; sr. resident plastic surgery St. Luc U. Hosp., Brussels, 1991, clin. chief plastic surgery, 1995; assoc. prof. U. Catholique de Louvain, 1997—2003, prof., head exptl. morphology dept., 2003. Assoc. editor: Surg. Radiol. Anatomy Jour., 2000. Recipient prize, French Soc. Plastic Surgery, Paris, 1999, 2001, European Assn. Plastic Surgeons, Berlin, 2000, Ghent, 2007, Hans Anderl award, 2009. Fellow: European Acad. Facial Plastic Surgery (hon.), Am. Acad. Facial Plastic and Reconstructive Surgery (hon.); mem.: Royal Belgian Acad. Medicine, Royal Coll. Surgeon London (hon.), French Nat. Acad. Surgery (hon.). Achievements include first human face transplantation, in Amiens, France on November, 27th, 2005, ennobled by H.M. King Albert II, 2009. Office: Experimental Morphology Dept UCL Emmanuel Mounierlaan 5251 1200 Brussels Belgium Office Fax: 32-2-764.52.25. E-mail: benoit.lengele@uclouvain.be.

LENGEMANN, FREDERICK WILLIAM, retired physiology educator; b. NYC, Apr. 8, 1925; s. Peter and Dorathea Johanna (Wolter) L.; m. J. Joan Doremus, Dec. 23, 1950; children: Frederick William Jr., David Munson. Student, N.Y. State Sch. Agr., Farmingdale, 1942—43; BS with distinction, Cornell U., 1950, M in Nutrition Sci., 1951; PhD, U. Wis., 1954. Rsch. assoc. U. Tenn.-AEC Agrl. Rsch. Program, Oak Ridge, 1954-55; asst. prof. dept. chemistry U. Tenn. Med. Sch., Memphis, 1955-59; prof. dept. physiology N.Y. State Coll. Vet. Medicine, Cornell U., 1959-88, prof. physiology emeritus, 1988—; biochemist divsn. biology and medicine AEC, 1962-63. Cons. FAO-IAEA, Vienna, Austria, 1966-67, 76-77, Fed. Radiation Coun., 1964-65, NRC, 1970-73, Nat. Com. on Radiation Protection, 1970-73, 79, 82; IAEA expert U. Nacional Agraria, Peru, 1978; lectr., dir. tng. courses. Contbr. articles to profl. jours. Mem. planning bd. Town of Dryden, NY, 1963-68; treas. Rome (Pa.) Presbyn. Ch. Active duty USN, 1943—46, with USNR, 1946—50. Decorated Air medal with 2 stars. Fellow AAAS; mem. Coun. Agrl. Sci. and Tech., Am. Dairy Sci. Assn., Am. Nutrition Soc., Fed. Am. Socs. for Exptl. Biology, Nat., N.Y. State Christmas Tree Growers Assns., Sigma Xi, Phi Kappa Phi. Office: Cornell U NY State Coll Vet Medicine Dept Physiology Ithaca NY 14853 Home: 154 Pleasant St Rome PA 18837

LENGSU, WILLIAM CHIN, emergency physician; b. Kota Kinabalu, Malaysia, Jan. 19, 1969; s. Chin Tain Loi and Koo Nyet Yun. BS, Nat. Taiwan U., Taipei, 1995; MS, Chung Shan U., Taichung, Taiwan, 2002. Dean emergency dept. Da Chien Hosp., Maoli, Taiwan, 1995—. Office: Da Chien Hosp Sin Kuan St No 6 Miaoli 360 Taiwan

LENGY, JACOB ISRAEL, parasitologist, educator; b. Tel Aviv, Mar. 14, 1928; s. Herman Meyer and Shulamith (Leader) L.; m. Sima Hassidoff, Feb. 11, 1958; children: Orith, Amnon, Assaf. BA, Colo. U., 1951; MSc in Biology, Wyo. U., 1957; PhD summa cum laude, Hebrew U., Jerusalem, 1961. Cert. med. technologist. Grad. teaching asst. dept. biology Wyo. U., Laramie, 1955-57; grad. rsch. fellow dept. parasitology Hebrew U., 1958-60; teaching asst. dept. microbiology Tel Aviv U., 1960-61, from instr. to lectr. dept. microbiology, 1961-63, sr. lectr., 1963-66, assoc. prof. Med. Sch., 1966-72, prof. parasitology Med. Sch., 1972-96, prof. emeritus, 1997—, head sect. parasitology Med. Sch., 1972—, chmn. dept. human microbiology Med. Sch., 1981-85, 89-91. Cons. in parasitology Ichilov Mcpl. Hosp., Tel Aviv, 1966—, Zamenhoff Cen. Sick-Fund Lab., Tel Aviv, 1964-91. Author: Guidelines to Parasitology, 1986; contbr. numerous articles to med. jours. Staff sgt. USAF, 1951-53. Grantee Ford Found., 1965, Israel Ministry of Health, 1975, 77, Joint Israel-Egypt Peace Fund, 1988, Zukerman Clin. Parasitology Fund, 1982—. Mem. AAAS, Am. Soc. Parasitologists, N.Y. Acad. Scis., Israel Soc. Parasitology (co-founder, dep. chair 1978-79, chmn. 1980-83), World Fedn. Parasitologists (Israeli rep. 1978-85). Avocations: chess, classical music, tv and radio musical quizzes. Home: 12 Oppenheimer St Tel Aviv Israel Office: Tel Aviv U at Ramat Aviv Sackler Sch Medicine Dept Human Microbiology Tel Aviv Israel

LENHART, CHERYL HAYES, nursing administrator, consultant; b. Pitts., Apr. 18, 1952; d. William Pearse and Virginia Englert Hayes; m. William Terry Lenhart, June 12, 1976; children: Matthew Pearse, Erin Elizabeth. Nursing Diploma, Pitts. Hosp. Sch. Nursing, 1973; BSN, Pa. State U., State College, 1981; M in Human Resource Mgmt., LaRoche Coll., 1998. Staff nurse Allegheny Gen. Hosp., Pitts., 1973—75, nurse mgr., 1975—78, asst. DON, 1978—81, Montefiore Hosp., Pitts., 1981—88, nurse mgr. emergency dept., 1988—91, The Western Pa. Hosp., Pitts., 1991—93, nurse mgr. outpatient ctr. and intravenous therapy, 1991—, nurse mgr. oncology unit, 2000—. Nurse spkr./cons. in field, 2000—. Associate editor: nursing publ. Profl. Paradigms (Merit Award for In Ho. Publications for Hospitals of 500+ Beds, 2005); contbr. articles to profl. jours. Pres. Women's Guild, Pitts., 2002—05. Mem.: Intravenous Nursing Soc., Nat. Oncology Nursing Soc., Oncology Nursing Soc. (pres. 2005—, Greater Pitts. chpt. 2004—05). Achievements include research in relative dose intensity of chemotherapy administration; preventing complications of central venous access devices; use of saline flush only (vs. Heparin) in preventing central line clotting. Office: The Western Pennsylvania Hosp 4800 Friendship Ave Pittsburgh PA 15224 Business E-Mail: clenhart@wpahs.org.

LENKOSKI, LEO DOUGLAS, retired psychiatrist, educator; b. Northampton, Mass., May 13, 1925; s. Leo L. and Mary Agnes (Lee) L.; m. Jeannette Teare, July 12, 1952; children— Jan Ellen, Mark Teare, Lisa Marie, Joanne Lee. AB, Harvard, 1948, spl. student, 1948-49; MD, Western Res. U., 1953; grad., Cleve. Psychoanalytic Inst., 1964. Intern Univ. Hosps., Cleve., 1953-54, resident in psychiatry, 1956-57, dir. psychiatry, 1970-86, chief of staff, 1982-90; dir. profl. services Horizon Ctr. Hosp., 1980; asst. resident in psychiatry Yale U., New Haven, 1954-56; teaching fellow Case Western Res. U., Cleve., 1957-60, from instr. to prof. psychiatry, 1960-93; prof. emeritus, 1993—; assoc. dean Sch. Medicine Case Western Res. U., Cleve., 1982-93, dir. Substance Abuse Ctr., 1990-93. Cons. Cleve. Ctr. on Alcoholism, DePaul Maternity and Infant Home, St. Ann's Hosp., Def. Dept., Cleve. VA Hosp., Psychiat. Edn. br. NIMH; mem. Cuyahoga County Mental Health and Retardation Bd., 1967-73, 94-2002, 2004—09, Health Planning and Devel. Commn., 1967-73, Ohio Mental Health and Retardation Commn., 1976-78; mental health advisor Jewish Family Svcs. Assocs., 2003—. Contbr. articles to profl. jours. Bd. dirs. Hough-Norwood Health Ctr., Hitchcock Ctr., Hopewell Inn, Woodruff Found, 2001-06. 1st lt. USAAF, 1943-46. Decorated D.F.C., Air medal with oak leaf cluster.; Career Tchr. grantee NIMH, 1958-60 Fellow Am. Psychiat. Assn. (life), Am. Coll. Psychiatrists, Am. Coll. Psychoanalysts (pres. 1988-89); mem. AMA, AAAS, Ohio Psychiat. Assn. (pres. 1974—), Am. Psychoanalytic Assn., Assn. Am. Med. Colls., Cleve. Acad. Medicine (bd. dirs. 1987-90), Ohio Med. Assn., Pasteur Club, Am. Assn. Chairmen Depts. Psychiatry (pres. 1978-79), Alpha Omega Alpha. Home Phone: 216-268-3140.

LENNARD-JONES, JOHN EDWARD, retired gastroenterologist; b. Bristol, Eng., Jan. 29, 1927; s. John Edward and Kathleen Mary Lennard-Jones; m. Verna Margaret Down, Feb. 19, 1955; children: David, Peter, Andrew, Timothy. BA, Corpus Christ Coll., Cambridge, Eng., 1947, MA, 1951; MB, BChir, U. Cambridge, 1953, MD, 1965; DSc (hon.), U. Kingston, 1999. Mem. med. rsch. coun. indsl. medicine and burns unit Birmingham Accident Hosp., 1947-48; house surgeon, house physician U. Coll. Hosp., London, 1953-54; sr. house officer Manchester (Eng.) Royal Infirmary, 1954-55; registrar Ctrl. Middlesex Hosp., 1956-58, sr. registrar, 1961-63, mem. med. rsch. coun. gastroenterology rsch. unit, 1963-74; registrar, mem. med. rsch. coun. dept. clin. rsch. U. Coll. Hosp., London, 1958-61, cons. physician, 1965-74; prof. gastroenterology Royal London Hosp., Med. Coll., 1974—87; cons. gastroenterologist St. Mark's Hosp., London, 1965-92; ret., 1992. Chmn. Brit. Assn. for Parenteral and Enteral Nutrition, 1991-95, Sir Halley Stewart Trust, 1997-2007. Joint author: Clinical Gastroenterology, 1968, Inflammatory Bowel Disease, 1992, Constipation, 1994; contbr. articles to profl. jours. Cir. steward Meth. Ch., London, 1986-92. Fellow Royal Coll. Physicians London, Royal Coll. Surgeons London, U. Coll. London, Royal Soc. Medicine London (hon.); mem. Nat. Assn. for Colitis and Crohn's Disease (hon. life pres. 1992—), Brit. Soc. Gastroenterology (hon., hon. sec. 1965-70, pres. 1983, chmn. clin. svcs. com. 1986-90), Digestive Disorders Found. (pres. 1992-2000), Assn. Gastrointestinal Physiologists (pres. 2002-03), Swedish Soc. Gastroenterology (hon.), Swiss Soc. Gastroenterology (hon.) Netherlands Soc. Gastroenterology (hon.), South African Soc. Gastroenterology (hon.), French Soc. Coloproctology (hon.). Methodist/Anglican. Avocations: gardening, ornithology, golf. Home: 1A Cherry Tree Rd Woodbridge IP12 4BL England

LENNON, JEFFREY LYNNE, healthcare educator; m. Chona F. Lennon; 2 children. BA, The King's Coll., NY, 1976; MD, Cetec U. Sch. Medicine, Santo Domingo, Dominican Republic, 1982; MPH, U. Ala., Birmingham, 1986, MSPH, 1991, PhD in Health Edn., Health Promotion, 2001. Cert. health edun. specialist. Postdoc. assoc., dept. epidemiology Yale U. Sch. Medicine, New Haven, 1982—83; heath specialist Ambs. Internat., Dominican Republic, Philippines, 1987—89, Internat. Tech. Assistance Group, Philippines, 1991—98, 2002—06; assoc. prof. Liberty U., Va., 2008—. Reviewer Dengue Bulletin Jour., Health Edn. & Behavior Jour., Simulation & Gaming Jour. Co-author: (book) Things Can Get Better, 2010. Vol. Eagle Scout, 1971. Recipient Mem., Delta Omega-National Pub. Health Honor Soc., Eta Sigma Gamma-National Health Edn. Hon. Mem.: Am. Assn. Health Edn., Eta Sigma Gamma-Nat. Health Edn., Health Honor Soc., Delta Omega-Nat. Pub. Presbyterian. Achievements include development of master of public health program in Silliman University. Office: Liberty University Dept Health Scis 1971 University Blvd Lynchburg VA 24502 Office Phone: 434-592-3759. Personal E-mail: jeffchona2@yahoo.com.

LENOX-SMITH, ALAN, medical researcher, consultant; b. London, Feb. 16, 1958; s. Ian Lenox-Smith; children: Nicholas, Oliver. MRCP Royal Coll. of Physicians, 1987, cert. FFPM 2000. Sr. clin. rsch. physician Lilly Pharms., Basingstoke, England, 2009—. Contbr. numerous article to profl. jours. Fellow: Faculty Pharm. Medicine, Med. Soc. London, mem.: Royal Coll. Physicians, Brit. Assn. Psychopharmacology. Personal E-mail: alan@lenox-smith.co.uk.

LENSKA-MIECIEK, MARTA, neurologist; b. Warsaw, Aug. 12, 1969; MD, Warsaw Med. Acad., 1994; PhD, Med. Ctr. Postgrad. Edn., 2008. Asst. Med. Ctr. Postgrad. Edn., 1997—2009, tchr., 2009—. Mem.: Polish Neurol. Soc. (Best Sci. Work award movement disorders sect. 2006). Avocation: literature. Office: Czerniakowska 231 Warsaw Mazowieckie 00-416 Poland Business E-Mail: martalenska@wp.pl.

LENTZ, EDWARD ALLEN, consultant, retired health administrator; b. Superior, Wis., May 30, 1926; s. Otto Albert and Martha Mary Ann (Gruhl) L.; m. Margaret Ann Denier, May 30, 1952; 1 child, Elizabeth Ann Lentz. BS, U. Cin., 1951; MHA, Wayne State U., Detroit, 1957. Asst. dir. Pub. Health Fedn., Cin., 1954-57; dir. health planning United Cmty. Coun., Columbus, Ohio, 1957-62; asst. dir. Columbus Hosp. Fedn., 1962-65; assoc. exec. dir. Ohio Hosp. Assn., Columbus, 1965-69; exec. dir. Health Planning Assn. of Ohio River Valley, Cin., 1969-70; asst. prof. grad. program in health svcs. adminstrn. Coll. of Medicine, Ohio State U., Columbus, 1970-72, adj. assoc. prof. preventive medicine, 1957—; dep. dir. med. care adminstrn. Ohio Dept. Health, Columbus, 1972-75; pres., CEO Med. Advances Inst., Columbus, 1975-79; v.p. corp. devel. Mt. Carmel Health System, Columbus, 1979-95, cons., 1995-97. Cons. cmty. health planning USPHS; bd. dirs. Scioto Valley Health Sys. Agy. Contbr. articles to profl. jours. Mem., chair Ohio Dept. Jobs and Family Svcs./Ohio Med. Care Adv. Com., Columbus, 1975—2006; bd. dirs., vice chair Netcare Corp., Columbus, 1989-2006. Served with USN, 1944-46; 1st lt. U.S. Army, 1951-53, Korea. Recipient Spl. Citation for hosp. planning and mktg. in Ohio and Delbert L. Pugh Conf., Ohio State U. Coll. Medicine and Ohio Hosp. Assn., 1991. Fellow Am. Pub. Health Assn. (bd. dirs., vice chmn. bd. trustees 1979-83); mem. Ohio Pub. Health Assn. (pres. 1969-70), Am. Assn. Areawide Planning Agencies (pres. 1969-70), Ohio Hosp. Assn. Soc. for Hosp. Planning and Mktg. (pres. 1987-88), Columbus Rotary (com. chair). Presbyterian. Home: 585 Keyes Ln Worthington OH 43085-3503 Home Phone: 614-885-7754. Personal E-mail: lentz43085@gmail.com.

LENZ, CRAIG, academic administrator; married; 3 children. BS in Aerospace Engring., Princeton U.; postgrad., U. Pa.; DOM, Phila. Coll. Osteo. Medicine. Cert. Am. Bd. Emergency Medicine, Am. Bd. Osteo. Family Practitioners. Emergency dept. physician Redington-Fairview Hosp., Maine; clin. clerkship coord., area health edn. program U. New England Coll. Osteo. Medicine; osteo. dir. med. edn. for family practice residency program Ea. Maine Med. Ctr.; dean Coll. Osteo. Medicine of the Pacific Western U. Health Scis., 2000; sr. assoc. dean Coll. Osteopathic Medicine Lincoln Meml. U., Tenn. Fellow: Acad. Osteo. Dirs. and Med. Educators; mem.: Am. Osteo. Assn. Office: College of Osteopathic Medicine Lincoln Meml Univ 6965 Cumberland Gap Pwy Harrogate TN 37752 E-mail: craig.lenz@lumnet.edu.

LENZ, FREDERICK, neurosurgeon; b. Hamilton, Ont., Dec. 7, 1951; arrived in US, 1988, naturalized, 1990; s. Charles and Ruth Lenz; m. Yvonne Istl; children: Richard, David. MD, U. Toronto, 1977, PhD in Sys. Neurosci., 1988. Cert. Am. Bd. Neurol. Surgery, 1993. Asst. prof. neurosurgery Hopkins U., Balt., 1988, prof. neurosurgery, 1998—, clinical assoc. biomed. engring., 2005—; Earl Walker chair nuerosurgery, 2008. Recipient various rsch. operating grants, NIH. Fellow: Royal Coll. Surgeons, Can.; mem.: Soc. Neuroscience, Soc. Neurologic Surgeons (assoc. Grass award). Independent. Episcopalian. Achievements include advances in the understanding of human forebrain mechanisms of sensation, motor control, and plasticity. Avocations: sailing, skiing. Office: Dept Neurosurgery Hopkins Hosp Baltimore MD 21287-7713 Personal E-mail: flenz1@jhmi.edu.

LEO, GARY A., former medical association administrator; BS in Econs. and Psychology, Queens Coll., NY; MS Ednl. Adminstrn., NYU; MS in Social Work Adminstrn. and Planning, Rutgers U., NJ. Exec. dir., nat. v.p., western region Am. Soc. Technion (Israel Inst. Tech.); sr. v.p. devel. Cedars-Sinai Med. Ctr., LA, 2000—04; pres., CEO ALS Assn., Agoura Hills, Calif., 2004—09.

LEON, ARTHUR SOL, research cardiologist, exercise physiologist; b. Bklyn., Apr. 26, 1931; s. Alex and Anne (Schrek) L.; m. Gloria Rakita, Dec. 23, 1956; children: Denise, Harmon, Michelle. BS in Chemistry with high honors, U. Fla., 1952; MS in Biochemistry, U. Wis., 1954, MD, 1957. Intern Henry Ford Hosp., Detroit, 1957-58; fellow in internal medicine Lahey Clinic, Boston, 1958-60; fellow in cardiology Jackson Meml. Hosp.-U. Miami (Fla.) Med. Sch., 1960-61; dir. clin. pharmacology research unit Hoffmann-La Roche Inc.-Newark Beth Israel Med. Ctr., 1969-73; from instr. to assoc. prof. medicine Coll. Medicine and Dentistry N.J., Newark, 1967-73; from assoc. prof. to prof. div. epidemiology U. Minn., Mpls., 1973—, H.L. Taylor prof. exercise sci. and health enhancement, dir. lab. physiol. hygiene and exercise sci., div. kinesiology, Coll. Edn., 1991—, dir. applied physiology and nutrition, 1973-91. Mem. med. eval. team Gemini projects NASA, 1964-67. Editor Procs. of the NIH Consensus Conf. on Phys. Activity and Cardiovasc. Health, 1997; assoc. editor Surgeon Gen.'s Report on Health Benefits of Exercise, 1996; contbr. numerous articles to profl. publs. Trustee Vinland Nat. Sports Health Ctr. for Disabled, 1978—; mem. gov.'s coun. physical fitness sports, 1979-90. Served as officer M.C. U.S. Army, 1961-67, 90-91, col. Res. 1978-92, ret. Recipient Meritorious Svc. medal U.S. Army, 1993, Anderson award AAHPER, 1981, Presdl. award for exercise sci. rsch. Internat. Olympic Com., 1999; Am. Heart Assn. fellow, 1960-61 Fellow Am. Coll. Cardiology, Am. Coll. Chest Physicians, Am. Coll. Clin. Pharmacology, N.Y. Acad. Scis., Am. Coll. Sports Medicine (trustee 1976-78, 82-83, v.p. 1977-79, pres. Northland chpt. 1975-76, Citation award 1995), Am. Assn. Cardiovasc. and Pulmonary Rehab. (trustee 1989-90), Am. Acad. Kinesiology and Phys. Edn.; mem. Am. Physiol. Soc., Am. Soc. Pharmacology and Exptl. Therapeutics, Am. Inst. Nutrition, Am. Heart Assn. (v.p. Hennepin County divsn. 1980-81, pres. 1982-83), Am. Coll. Nutrition, Am. Fedn. Clin. Rsch., Minn. Lung Assn. (trustee 1978-81), Phi Beta Kappa, Phi Kappa Phi. Jewish. Home: 5628 Glen Ave Minnetonka MN 55345-6610 Office: U Minn Sch Kinesiology 202 Cooke Hall Minneapolis MN 55455-0136 Office Phone: 612-624-8271. Business E-Mail: leonx002@umn.edu.

LEON, MARTIN BERT, cardiologist, educator; b. Bklyn., Sept. 5, 1950; MD, Yale Univ., 1975. Cert. Internal Medicine, Cardiovascular Disease. Intern Yale-New Haven Hosp., 1975—76, resident, 1976—78, clin. fellow, cardiology, 1980—82; dir. clin. rsch. Washington Cardiology Ctr., Washington Hosp. Ctr.; clin. prof. medicine Georgetown Univ. Med. Ctr., Washington; founding physician Cardiovascular Rsch. Found., NYC, chmn. emeritus; assoc. dir. Ctr. for Interventional Vascular Therapy; practicing interventional cardiologist NY-Presbyterian Hosp./Columbia Univ. Med. Ctr. Prin. investigator for numerous clin. trials in the field of interventional vascular medicine (STARS, Gamma-1 and SIRIUS trial); dir., founder Transcatheter Cardiovascular; clin. assoc., sr. investigator, dir., catheterization lab., cardiology branch Nat. Heart, Lung, & Blood Inst., NIH, Bethesda, Md.; founder Washington Cardiology Ctr., Cardiology Rsch. Found., Washington. Contbr. articles to profl. jours. Office: Cardiovascular Rsch Found 55 E 59th St and 111 E 59th St New York NY 10022-1122 also: 161 Fort Washington Ave New York NY 10032 Address: 177 Fort Washington Ave New York NY 10032 Office Phone: 212-851-9300, 212-305-7060, 212-305-3640. Office Fax: 212-305-4285, 212-305-7060.

LEON, ROBERT LEONARD, psychiatrist, educator; b. Denver, Jan. 18, 1925; s. Louis and Rae (Brown) L.; m. Willena Lee, Sept. 14, 1947; children: Alexis Kay, Mark Robert, Jeffrey Clayton, Stacy Lee. MD, U. Colo., 1948. Diplomate Am. Bd. Psychiatry and Neurology. Intern U. Mich. Hosp., Ann Arbor, 1948-49; resident in psychiatry U. Colo. Med. Ctr., Denver, 1949-52, child psychiatry fellow, 1951-52, Bur. Mental Hygiene, New Haven, Conn. Dept. Health/Student Health Svc., Yale U., 1952-53; asst. dir., acting dir. child psychiatry Greater Kansas City Mental Health Found., 1953-54; instr. psychiatry U. Kans. Sch. Medicine, Kansas City, 1956-57; asst. prof. psychiatry U. Tex. Health Sci. Ctr. at Dallas, Southwestern Med. Sch., 1957-61, assoc. prof., 1961-65, prof., 1965-67; prof., chmn. dept. psychiatry Sch. Medicine U. Tex. Health Sci. Ctr., San Antonio, 1967-95, interim chmn., 1995-96; Ashbel Smith prof. U. Tex. Health Sci. Ctr., San Antonio, 1990—2003, prof. emeritus, 2003—. Chief psychiatry U. Health Sys., Bexar County, San Antonio, 1967-96; mem. Am. Assn. Chmn. Depts. Psychiatry, 1967-96, pres., 1982-83; cons. psychiatry Audie Murphy Vet.'s Hosp., 1973—; cons. Mental Health Orgn., region IV, HEW, 1957-73; mem. Psychiat. Tng. Rev. NIMH, Rockville, Md., 1970-74; hon. cons. World Health Orgn., Geneva, 1996. Author: Psychiatric Interviewing: A Primer, 1982, 2d edit., 1989; contbr. articles to profl. jours. Sr. surgeon USPHS, 1954-57. Fellow ACP (pres. 1987-88), Am. Psychiat. Assn. (life), Am. Orthopsychiat. Assn. (life), Am. Acad. Child and Adolescent Psychiatry (life), Am. Assn. Social Psychiatry (pres. 1990-92); mem. Benjamin Rush Soc., World Assn. for Social Psychiatry. Avocation: photography. Home: 6866 Stonykirk St San Antonio TX 78240-2743 Office: U Tex Health Sci Ctr 7703 Floyd Curl Dr MS 7792 San Antonio TX 78229-3900 Home Phone: 210-696-3962; Office Phone: 210-567-5408. Business E-Mail: leon@uthscsa.edu.

LEONARD, MARY EILEEN, retired medical technician; b. Charleston, SC, Jan. 9, 1925; d. Edward Andrew and Honora Elizabeth (Price) L. Attended, Barry U., Miami, Fla., 2 yrs.; BS, Coll. of Charleston, 1945; postgrad. in Med. Tech., U. SC, 1947. Med. technologist Med. U. S.C., Charleston, 1946-79, Roper Hosp., Charleston, 1979—2001; ret., 2011. Chmn. adv. com. Trident Tech. Coll., Charleston, 1992-02. Recipient Highest Achievement award, Am. Soc. Clin. Pathology, 2000; named Alumnae of Yr., Coll. Charleston, 2001, Hall of Fame, MUSC Coll. Health Professions, 2008. Mem. Am. Soc. for Clin. Pathology, West Ashley Civitan (bd. dirs. 1998-00). Roman Catholic. Home: 1538 Dunnes Ln Charleston SC 29407-5013

LEONARDI, FABIO, psychologist, psychotherapist; b. Fano, Pesaro e Urbino, Italy, Dec. 26, 1968; Degree in Psychology, U. Padua, 1994; postgrad. in Psychotherapy, Postgrad. Sch. Constructivist-Interactionist Psychotherapy, 2000. Rsch. fellow in psychology I.N-.R.C.A. Italian Nat. Rsch. Ctr. Ageing, 1996—2001; chief rschr. C.S.R.S.S. Studies and Rsch. Ctr. Social Sci., 2000—02; specialist in psychotherapy, clin. psychologist Nat. Health Svc., 2002—. Grad. asst., dept. psychology U. Urbino, 1994—97, U. Padua, 1996—98. Mem.: Psychoterapeutists Register Tuscany (Italy), Psychologists Register Tuscany (Italy). Avocation: writing. Home: Via Fraschetti N23 Livorno 57128 Italy Home Phone: 39 0986 770423; Office Phone: 39 0986223620. Personal E-mail: mifa10@libero.it, leonardifabio@libero.it.

LEON AZOFEIFA, PEDRO, molecular biologist; b. Costa Rica; Grad., Baylor U., U. Oreg. Tchr. to prof. dept. physiology U. Costa Rica Cell and Molecular Biology Rsch. Ctr., San Jose, 1975—, dir.; dir. Ctr. Advanced Technologies Univ. Couns. Pub. Univs., Costa Rica. Contbr. articles to sci. jours. Founding mem., pres. Nat. Parks Found. Recipient George Burch award, Smithsonian Instn., Biology prize, Third World Acad. Scis., 2006; grantee Guggenheim Found. fellowship. Mem.: NAS (fgn. assoc.), Costa Rica Acad. Scis., Orgn. Tropical Studies (pres. exec. com.). Office: U Costa Rica Ciudad Univ Rodrigo Facio Brenes San Pedro de Montes de Oca San Jose Costa Rica E-mail: pleon@conare.ac.cr.

LEONE, AURELIO ANTONIO, physician, researcher; b. Rome, July 21, 1942; s. Oreste and Matilde (Centaro) Leone; m. Elena Archilli, Jan. 10, 1968; children: Oreste Maria, Aldo, Francesco Maria. MD, U. Rome, 1966, cert. in cardiology, 1969; cert. in internal medicine, U. Pise, 1972; cert. in hygiene and preventive medicine, U. Genoa, 1977. Asst. chair pathol. anatomy U. Rome, 1966-69; rschr. in clin. physiology Med. Sch. U. Pise, 1969-73; asst. prof. cardiology City Hosp., La Spezia, 1973-87, chief divsn. medicine Pontremoli, 1987—99, chief med. divsn. Massa, Italy, 1999—2000; dir. med. dept. Hosp. Massa-Cerrara, 2000—02; vis. prof., chmn. angiology dept. cardio-thoracic U. Pise I, 2003—. Editor: Hospital Care, 1981, Drug Addiction, 1984, The Elderly-Medical Aspects, 1985, Sudden Death, 1986, Passive Smoking and Cardiovascular Pathology: Mechanisms and Physiopathological Bases of Damage, 2007, Coronary Circulation in NonSmoking and Smokers, 2008. Fellow: Royal Soc. Health (Eng.); mem.: Italian Soc. Cardiovas. Prevention, Italian Soc. Internal Medicine, World Heart Fedn., Geriat. Cardiology, N.Y. Acad. Scis., Am. Soc. Hypertension, Eques Sancti Gregorii Magni, Lions. Business E Mail: reliol@libero.it.

LEONE, KATHERINE C., legislative staff member; b. Princeton, NJ, 1971; m. Richard C. Leone. BA in Am. Studies, Cornell U., Ithaca, NY; JD, Columbia U., NYC. Atty., antitrust divsn. US Dept. Justice, Washington; sr. policy advisor, Democratic policy com. US Senate, Washington, legis. asst. to Senator Tom Daschle, 2002—03, counsel to Senator Tom Daschle, 2003—04, sr. health counsel to Senator Harry Reid, 2004—. Democrat. Office: 528 Hart Senate Office Bldg Washington DC 20515 Office Phone: 202-224-3542. Office Fax: 202-224-7327.

LEONE, MAURIZIO A., neurologist; b. Torino, Italy, Nov. 3, 1955; Degree in Medicine, U. Torino, 1980, degree in Neurology, 1984. Neurologist Nat. Health Svc., 1987—93, Ospedale Maggiore della Carità, Novara, 1993—2000, head, multiple sclerosis ctr., 2000—. Assoc. editor European Jour. Neurology, European Fedn. Neurol. Scis., 2006, chair, panel substance abuse and neurotoxicology, 06. Mem.: Italian Assn. Neuroepidemiology, NY Acad. Scis., Italian Soc. Neurology. Avocation: antiques. Office: Via Dei Mille 4/A Novara Piedmont 28100 Italy Office Fax: 39 0321 3733298. Business E-Mail: maurizio.leone@maggioreosp.novara.it.

LEONE, NATHALIE, medical researcher; b. Versailles, Yvelines, France, Apr. 9, 1976; d. Claude Leone and Luce Ruelle. MD, Lille II U. Sch. Medicine, France, MPH, 2006. Residency, pub. health and preventive medicine Lille II U. Sch. Medicine, 2002—06; PhD fellow cardio-respiratory epidemiology French nat. Inst. Health & Med. Rsch. Unit 700, Paris, 2006—. Mem.: French Soc. Pub. Health, Assn. Epidemiologists French-Speaking Lang. Office: INSERM U700 Faculté Médecine X Bichat 16 Rue Henri Huchard Paris 75018 France Office Fax: 33 01 57 27 75 51. Personal E-mail: nleone@free.fr. Business E-Mail: nathalie.leone@inserm.fr.

LEONG, ALBIN B., pediatric pulmonologist, allergist, educator; b. Astoria, Oreg., Nov. 8, 1950; BS in Biology, Trinity Coll., Hartford, Conn., 1973; MD, U. Calif., La Jolla, Calif., 1977. Diplomate Nat. Bd. Medical Examiners, 1979, Am. Bd. Pediatrics, 1982, Am. Bd. Allergy & Immunology, 1983. Resident Children's Hosp. of L.A., 1977-79; resident in pediat. U. Calif., San Diego, 1979-80, fellow in pediat. pulmonology, immunology and allergy, 1980-82; pediat. pulmonologist and allergist Sacramento Kaiser Found. Hosp., 1993—. Contbr. articles to profl. jours. Grantee Travel grant, Am. Acad. Alelrgy, 1981, 2004—05, 2006—. Mem.: Calif. Thoracic Soc., Am. Thoracic Soc., Am. Acad. Pediatrics. Office: Kaiser Roseville Med Ctr MOB 2 Pediat Pulmonology 1600 Eureka Rd Roseville CA 95661 Office Phone: 916-474-2250. Office Fax: 916-973-7338. Business E-Mail: albin.leong@kp.org.

LEONG, CHEE-ONN, medical educator; b. Kuala Lumpur, Malaysia, Feb. 18, 1976; BSc in Biomed. Scis., U. Putra Malaysia, 1997; PhD, U. Nottingham, Eng., 2003. Rsch. fellow Harvard Med. Sch., Boston, 2004—08; sr. lectr. Internat. Med. U., Malaysia, 2008—. Recipient MAKNA Cancer Rsch. award, Malaysia; ECOR Rsch. grant, Mass. Gen. Hosp. Mem.: Brit. Assn. Cancer Rsch., European Assn. Cancer Rsch., Am. Assn. Cancer Rsch. Office: Internat Med University 12 Bukit Jalil Kuala Lumpur 57000 Malaysia

LEONOR, CORSINO, physician; b. Dominican Republic, Mar. 1, 1976; MD, PUCMM, 1999; MHS, Duke U., 2009. Physician Duke U., 2006. Office: DUMC Box 3451 Durham NC 27710 Office Fax: 919-668-1559. Business E-Mail: corsi002@mc.duke.edu.

LEOW, MELVIN KHEE SHING, endocrinologist, educator; s. Alvin Yong Keen Leow and Molly Nor Kee Ng; m. Jane Sim Joo Tan, Oct. 1, 1994; children: Veronica May Gwen, Rachel May Wern, Abigail May Shan, Eunice May Jane. MB, BS, Nat. U. Singapore, 1990, MMed in Internal Medicine, 1998; MS in Med. Sci., Am. Internat. U.-Royal Coll. Physicians and Surgeons, 2005, PhD in Med. Rsch., 2007. Cert. insulin pump trainer Minimed, 2002, endocrinologist Specialist Accreditation Bd., Singapore Med. Coun., 2003. Intern in ob-gyn. Kandang Kerbau Women's and Children's Hosp., Singapore, 1990; intern in surgery Singapore Gen. Hosp., 1990—90, resident in emergency medicine, 1993—94, resident in hematology, 1995—96, resident in med. oncology, 1996—97, hematology med. officer (specialist), 1998—99; intern in medicine Toa Payoh Hosp., Singapore, 1990—91, resident in internal medicine, 1994—95; resident in psychiatry Woodbridge Hosp., Singapore, 1991; resident in immunohematology Nat. Blood Ctr., Singapore, 1993; resident in rheumatology Tan Tock Seng Hosp., Singapore, 1994, endocrinology registrar, 1999—2001, assoc. cons. endocrinologist and physician, 2003—04, cons. endocrinologist and physician, 2005—; resident in infectious disease Communicable Disease Ctr., Singapore, 1995; resident in cardiology Nat. Heart Ctr., Singapore, 1996; resident in radiation oncology Nat. Cancer Ctr., Singapore, 1997—98; endocrinology clin. fellow Harvard Med. Sch., Harvard U., Boston, 2001—02. Vis. cons. and med. specialist Mil. Med. Inst., Singapore, 1998—2003; clin. tchr. faculty medicine Nat. U. Singapore, 1999—2004, apptd. examiner for master of nursing degree exams., 2003, clin. lectr. Yung Loo Lin Sch. Medicine, 2004—, faculty mentor for med. students, 2005—; med. rep. for diagnosis-related groups Tan Tock Seng Hosp., Singapore, 2001—04; clin. lectr. Yong Loo Lin Sch. Medicine, Nat. U. Singapore, 2004—; vis. cons. Nat. Neurosci. Inst., 2005—; mem. ethics com. Domain Specific Rsch. Bd.; presenter in field; vis. lectr. Nanyang Poly., Singapore, 2003, Singapore, 05; clin. assoc. prof. Yong Loo Liu Sch. & Medicine Nat. U. Singapore, 2009; acad. cons. Nat. Healthcare group, 2008—; clin. scientist Singapore Inst Clin. Scis. Brener Ctr. Molecular Medicine Agy. Sci. Tech. & Rsch.; dep. chair Domain Specific Review Bd., 2009—; exec. com. mem. Chpt. Endocrinology Coll. Physicians, Singapore, 2009—11; adv. bd. mem. Sing Health Investigation Med., 2009—; assoc. staff Nat. U. Hosp., 2011—; reviewer Singapore Health & Biomed. Congress, 2010—11; v.p. Endocrine Metabolic Soc., 2008—09. Reviewer: Jour. Clinical Endocrinology and Metabolism, Annals Acad. Medicine; contbr. scientific papers. Invited spkr. for med. pub. talks Tan Tock Seng Hosp., Singapore, 1999—2003; vol. in health screening of pub. Med. Soc., Faculty of Medicine, Singapore, 2001; lectr. for continuing med. edn. for gen. practitioners Tan Tock Seng Hosp., Singapore, 1999—2004. Capt. Singpore Armed Forces, 1993—2004. Decorated Excellence award Ministry of Def.; recipient 10-Yr. Long Svc. award, Nat. Healthcare Group, 2002, Courage award for treatment of SARS patients, 2003, Young Investigator award, Nat. Healthcare Group Doctor, 2004, Excellence Svc. award (silver), 2004, Excellence Svc. award (gold), 2005, Health care Svc. award, 2005, Best Reviewer award, 2006—10, Best Tchr. award, 2007, Deans award, 2008, Rschr. scientist Investigator Enabler award, 2008, Investigator Clin. award, 2008; named one of Outstanding Scientists of the 21st Century, 2005, Outstanding Intellectuals of the 21st Century, 2005; fellow Health Manpower Devel. Program, Nat. Healthcare Group, 2001. Fellow: ACP, Coll. Physicians Singapore, Am. Coll. Endocrinologists, Acad. of Medicine, Internat. Soc. of Philos. Enquiry; mem.: Royal Coll. Physicians USA, Am. Assn. of Clin. Endocrinologists, Mass. Med. Soc., The Endocrine Soc., Endocrine and Metabolic Soc. of Singapore (edn. subcom. 2003, sec. 2004—), Singapore Med. Alumni, Singapore Med. Assn., Mensa (Singapore chpt.). Christian. Achievements include research in Mathematical model on dose titration of antithyroid drugs and predicted response of thyroid function tests. Avocations: mathematical modeling, travel, computers, reading, writing. Office: Tan Tock Seng Hosp 11 Jalan Tan Tock Seng Singapore 308433 Singapore Home: 37 Hindhede Walk #01-05 Southaven II 587970 Singapore Singapore Business E-Mail: mleowsj@massmed.org, melvin_leow@ttsh.com.sg.

LEPOR, NORMAN ELLIOTT, cardiologist, director; b. San Diego, Jan. 14, 1958; BS, UCLA, 1978; MD, Johns Hopkins U., 1982. Dir., med. imaging Westside Med. Assocs. LA, 2002—. Clin. prof. UCLA, Geffen Sch. Medicine, 1989—. Fellow: Soc. Coronary Angiography and Interventions, Am. Heart Assn., Am. Coll. Cardiology; mem.: Soc. Cardiac CT, Cedars-Sinai Heart Inst. Achievements include first to coronary CT angiography and green imaging that has revolutionized the diagnostic approach to heart disease. Avocations: travel, skiing. Office: 99 North La Cienega Blvd 203 Beverly Hills CA 90211 E-mail: norman.lepor@gmail.com.

LEPORE, FREDERICK EVERETT, neurologist, educator; b. NYC, Nov. 23, 1949; s. Michael Joseph and Ardean Clough (Everett) L.; m. Adlynn McKeel Gordon, Sept. 9, 1978; children: Adlynn Everett, Meredith Ardean. AB, Princeton U., 1971; MD, U. Rochester, 1975. Diplomate Am. Bd. Psychiatry and Neurology. Intern in internal medicine U. Mich., Ann Arbor, 1975-76; resident in neurology U. Va., Charlottesville, 1976-79; fellow in neuro-ophthalmology Bascom Palmer Eye Inst.-U. Miami, Fla., 1979-80; asst. prof. neurology U. Med. & Dentistry N.J./Rutgers Med. Sch., Piscataway, 1980-86; assoc. prof. neurology U. Med. and Dentistry/Robert Wood Johnson Med. Sch., Piscataway, 1986-94, prof. neurology, 1994—, prof. ophthalmology, 1998—; acting chmn. dept. neurology U. Med. and Dentistry Robert Wood Johnson Med. Sch., Piscataway, 1995—97. Attending physician Robert Wood Johnson Univ. Hosp., New Brunswick, N.J., 1980—; chief neurology svcs., 1994-98; cons. VA Hosp., East Orange, N.J., 1982—. Guest editor (jour.) Seminars in Neurology, 1986; designer Optic Nerve Test Card, 1985. Fellow Am. Acad. Neurology; mem. AAUP (pres. coun. chpts. 2004-06, 2006-10), Am. Neurol. Assn., Assn. for Rsch. in Nervous and Mental Disease, Queen Square Alumnus Assn. Presbyterian. Avocations: photography, hiking. Office: Robert Wood Johnson Med Sch Dept Neurology 125 Paterson St New Brunswick NJ 08901-1928 Home Phone: 609-865-7579; Office Phone: 732-235-7731. Business E-Mail: leporefe@umdnj.edu.

LEPOW, MARTHA LIPSON, pediatric educator, consultant; b. Mar. 28, 1927; d. Harry A. and Anna (Miller) Lipson; m. Irwin H. Lepow, Feb. 7, 1958 (dec. 1984); children: Lauren, David, Daniel. BA, Oberlin Coll., Ohio, 1948, DSc (hon.), 2009; MD, Case Western Res. U., 1952. Intern, resident in pediats. Case Western Res. U., Cleve., 1952—56, fellow, asst. prof. pedit., 1958—67; from assoc. prof. to prof. pediats U. Conn., Farmington, 1967—78; prof. pediats. Albany (NY) Med. Coll., 1978—, dir. Clin. Studies Ctr., 1979—87, vice chmn. pediats, 1981—94, chmn. pediats., 1994—97; attending physician Albany Med. Ctr. Hosp., NY, 1979—, head divsn. pediatric infectious diseases, 1979—, dir. pediatric HIV program, 2006—. Cons. pediat. infectious disease St. Peter's Hosp., 1978—82; spl. fellow USPHS, Oxford, England, 1961—62; bd. dirs. Albany Coll. Pharmacy, 1987—89; mem. study sect. NIH Epidemiology & Disease Control, 1972—76. Contbr. more than 95 articles to profl. jours.; mem. editl. bd.: Pediats., 1976—81. Sec. HEW Task Force on Immunization Practices, 1977—78; mem. Conn. Acad. Sci. and Engring., 1977; mem. adv. com. Inst. Allergy and Infectious Disease, NIH, 1978—82; bd. dirs. Whitney Youhg Health Ctr., Albany, 1985—2004; mem. profl. adv. com. Ctr. for Disabled, Albany; bd. dirs. WYHCR Found., 2005—06. Mem.: Infectious Diseases Soc., Am. Soc. for Microbiology, Am. Pediat. Soc., Am. Soc. Pediat. Rsch., Am. Soc. Immunology (com. on status of women 1982—85), Com. on Vaccines, Inst. Medicine, Capital Dist. Pediat. Soc., Am. Acad. Pediats. (com. infectious diseases 1985—91, assoc. editor report), Alpha Omega Alpha, Sigma Xi. Home: 217 Milner Ave Albany NY 12208 Office: Albany Med Coll MC 88 47 New Scotland Ave Albany NY 12208 Office Phone: 518-262-5332.

LEPPER, MARK ROGER, psychologist, educator; b. Washington, Dec. 5, 1944; s. Mark H. and Joyce M. (Sullivan) L.; m. Jeanne E. Wallace, Dec. 22, 1966; 1 child, Geoffrey William. BA, Stanford U., Calif., 1966; PhD, Yale U., 1970. Asst. prof. psychology Stanford U., 1971-76, assoc. prof., 1976—82, prof., 1982—, chmn., 1990—94, 2000—04, Albert Ray Lang prof. psychology, 2004—. Fellow Ctr. Advanced Study in Behavioral Scis., 1979-80; chmn. mental health behavioral scis. rsch. rev. com. NIMH, 1982-84, mem. basic sociocultural rsch. rev. com., 1980-82. Co-editor: The Hidden Costs of Reward, 1978; cons. editor Jour. Personality and Social Psychology, 1977-85, Child Devel., 1977-86, Social Cognition, 1981-84, Jour. Ednl. Computing Rsch., 1983—, Media Psychology, 1999—; contbr. articles to profl. jours. Recipient Cattell Found. award, 1999; Woodrow Wilson fellow, 1966-67, NSF fellow, 1966-69, Sterling fellow, 1969-70, Mellon fellow, 1975; grantee NSF, 1978-82, 86-88, 2004, NIMH, 1978-86, 88, 2005—, Nat. Inst. Child Health and Human Devel., 1975-88, 90-98, U.S. Office Edn., 1972-73. Fellow APA, AAAS, Am. Psychol. Soc., Soc. Personality and Social Psychology, Soc. Psychol. Study Social Issues, Am. Acad. Arts and Scis., Am. Ednl. Rsch. Assn., Soc. Exptl. Social Psychology,; mem. Soc. Rsch. in Child Devel. Home: 1544 Dana Ave Palo Alto CA 94303-2813 Office: Stanford U Dept Psychology Jordan Hall Bldg 420 Stanford CA 94305-2130

LEPPIK, ILO E., neurologist, educator; b. Tartu, Estonia, Aug. 18, 1942; arrived in U.S., 1950; s. Elmar Emil and Lilly (Hanson) L.; m. Margaret Ann White, June 18, 1967; children: Peter, David, Karina. BS, Haverford Coll., Pa., 1964; MD, U. Pa., 1968. Diplomate Am. Bd. Neurology and Psychiatry, Am. Bd. Clin. Neurophysiology. Rsch. fellow Montreal Neurol. Inst., McGill U., Que., Canada, 1974-76; asst. prof. neurology U. Minn., Mpls., 1976-80, assoc. prof. neurology, 1980-87, prof. neurology, 1987-89, clin. assoc. prof. pharmacy, 1986-89, clin. prof. pharmacy, 1987—2004, prof. pharmacy, 2004—; dir. rsch. MINCEP Epilepsy Care, Mpls., 1990—, clinic practice mem. Adj. prof. neurology U. Minn., 1989—. Author: Contemporary Diagnosis and Management of the Patient with Epilepsy, 1993, 6th edit., 2006, Epilepsy: A Guide to Balancing Your Life, 2006; founding editor Jour. Epilepsy Rsch., 1986—2006; contbr. articles to profl. jours. Bd. dirs. Am. Bd. Clin. Neurophysiology, 1992-94; prin. investigator NIH program epilepsy in elderly, 1997-2008. Maj. USAF, 1969-71. Recipient Lennox Lifetime Achievement award, Am. Epilepsy Soc., 2007. Fellow Am. Acad. Neurology; mem. Am. Epilepsy Soc. (pres. 1992-94, treas. 1983-86; W.G. Lennox award, 2007), Ctrl. Soc. Neurol. Rsch. (pres. 1991-92), Assn. Neurologists of Minn. (pres. 1983-89), Epilepsy Found. Am. (chmn., profl. adv. bd. 1989-91, bd. dirs. 1982-92). Unitarian Universalist. Achievements include development of new drugs for treatment of epilepsy. Avocation: cross country skiing. Office: Coll Pharmacy Rm 461 717 Delaware St Minneapolis MN 55414 Home Phone: 763-546-3328; Office Phone: 612-625-7139. Business E-Mail: leppi001@umn.edu.

LERCHE, EMILE BERNARD, surgeon; b. Neuville St. Remy, France, Aug. 20, 1938; s. Roger Marcel and Mathilde Celina (Boniface) Lerche; m. Brigitte Berthe Habart; children: Eric, Hugues. MD, Faculty of Medicine, Lille, France, 1963. Cert. thoracic and vascular surgery, angiology. Resident in pneumology Faculty of Medicine, Lille, 1965—70, sr. resident in surgery, 1970—72; surgeon Hosp. of Calais, France, 1972—85; visceral, thoracic and vascular surgeon Surg. Clinic of Calais, 1972—. Mem.: Assn. des Chirurgiens Vasculaires Nord-Picardie (pres. 1999—), Syndicat Nat. de Chirurgie Vasculaire (pres. 1992—). Avocations: equitation, chasse a courre.

LERER, RENÉ, health services company executive; b. July 2, 1955; m. Michele Lerer. B in Psychobiology, Oberlin Coll., Ohio; MD, SUNY, Buffalo. Bd. cert. in internal medicine. Sr. v.p. corp. devel. Value Health Scis., 1992—94, sr. v.p. ops., pharmacy and disease mgmt. group, 1995—97; COO Prudential HealthCare, Inc., 1997—99; co-founder, pres. Internet HealthCare Group, 1999—2002; pres., COO Magellan Health Svcs., Inc., Avon, Conn., 2003—08, pres., CEO, 2008—09; chmn., CEO Magellan Health Services, Inc., Avon, Conn., 2009—. Bd. dirs. Digital Ins., Inc., Internet HealthCare Group, RealMed Corp., Magellan Health Svcs. Office: Magellan Health Svcs Inc 55 Nod Rd Avon CT 06001 Office Phone: 860-507-1900. Office Fax: 860-507-1990. *

LERMAN, BRUCE B., cardiac electrophysiologist; MD, Loyola U., 1977. Diplomate Am. Bd. of Internal Medicine, Am. Bd. of Internal Medicine-cardiovasc. disease, Am. Bd. of Internal Medicine-cardiac electrophysiology. Intern internal medicine Northwestern Univ. Meml. Hosp., 1978, resident internal medicine, 1980; fellow Univ. of Mich. Hosp., 1981, Hosp. of the Univ. of Pennsylvania, 1982, John Hopkins Hosp., 1983; dir. cardiac electrophysiology labb. Cornell Univ. Med. Ctr., 1989; chief divsn. of cardiology Weill Med. Coll. of Cornell Univ., 1996; Hilda Altschul master prof. Weill Cornell Med. Coll., 1999, prof. Recipient Established Investigatorship award, Am. Heart Assn., Young Investigators award. Office: New York-Presbyterian 570 East 70Th St Starr Pavilion 4Th Fl New York NY 10021 Office Phone: 212-746-2169. Office Fax: 212-746-6951.

LERMAN, CARYN E., psychology professor; BA in Psychology, Pa. State U., 1981; MA in Psychology, U. So. Calif., 1982, PhD in Clin. Psychology, 1984. Dir. behavioral oncology rsch. Fox Chase Cancer Ctr., Phila.; prof. oncology, psychiatry & pharmacology, assoc. dir. cancer control & population sci. Lombardi Cancer Ctr., Georgetown U. Med. Ctr., Washington, 1993—2001; prof. psychiatry U. Pa. Sch. Medicine, 2001—, prof. Annenberg Pub. Policy Ctr., 2002—, Mary W. Calkins prof. psychiatry, 2003—, dir. Tobacco Use & Rsch. Ctr. Assoc. dir. population scis. Abramson Cancer Ctr., U. Pa., 2001—06, dep. dir. Abramson Cancer Ctr., 2006—10, interim dir., 2010—; mem. adv. coun. Nat. Inst. Drug Abuse; bd. sci. advisors Nat. Cancer Inst. Contbr. articles to profl. jours. Recipient Cullen award for tobacco rsch., American Soc. Preventive Oncology, 2004, Alton Ochsner award relating smoking & health, 2007. Mem.: Soc. Rsch. Nicotine & Tobacco, Inst. Medicine, Soc. Behavioral Medicine (New Investigator award 1989), American Psychol. Assn. (Outstanding Contbn. to Health Psychology award 1995). Office: Univ Pennsylvania 3535 Market St Ste 4100 Philadelphia PA 19104 Office Phone: 215-746-7141. E-mail: clerman@mail.med.upenn.edu. *

LERMAN, MARK JEFFREY, nephrologist, medical administrator; b. Wharton, Tex., Jan. 6, 1947; s. Sol and Lillian Lerman; m. Ray Ann Lerman, June 28, 1970; children: Marci, Marshall. BA, U. Tex., 1969; MD, U. Tex., Galveston, 1973. Diplomate Am. Bd. Internal Medicine. Nephrologist Dallas Nephrology, 1978—; med. dir. Med. City Hosp., Dallas, 1998—. Chmn. com. med. stds. Drs. Hosp., Dallas, 1982. Author: (book chpt.) Pancreas Transplantation, 1999; contbr. articles to med. jours. Fellow ACP; mem. Internat. Soc. Nephrology, Internat. Soc. Heart and Lung Transplantation, Am. Soc. Nephrology, Am. Soc. Transplantation, Tex. Transplant Soc., Phi Beta Kappa, Alpha Omega Alpha. Avocations: computers, golf, travel. Office: Dallas Nephrology Assocs 13154 Coit Rd Dallas TX 75240-5773 Home: 12220 Park Forest Dr Dallas TX 75230-2365 E-mail: mjl972@aol.com.

LERNER, ELLIOT J., neuroradiologist; MD, Brown U., 1985. Diplomate Am. Bd. Radiology, lic. NJ. Intern Mercy Hosp and Med. Ctr., San Diego; resident in diagnostic radiology Hosp. of the Univ. of PA, 1989—91, fellow in neuroradiology, 1989—91; radiologist Radiology Assocs. of Ridgewood, Pa and The Valley Hosp. Mem.: Am. Coll. of Radiology, Soc. of Computer Applications in Radiology, Am. Roentgen Ray Soc., Radiological Soc. of N.Am., Am. Soc. of Neuroradiology. Office: Radiology Associates of Ridgewood, P.A. 20 Franklin Turnpike Waldwick NJ 07463

LERNER, ROBERT GIBBS, internist, hematologist, educator; b. Bklyn., Mar. 30, 1936; s. Morris and Sarah (Kludke) L.; m. Helen Marjorie Halpern, Aug. 31, 1958; children: Rachel Ann, Marcia Lynn, Sharon Ruth. AB, NYU, 1956, MD, 1960. Diplomate Am. Bd. Internal Medicine. Teaching asst. NYU Sch. Medicine, NYC, 1961-62; instr. U. So. Calif. Sch. Medicine, 1965-67; from asst. prof. to prof. medicine N.Y. Med. Coll., NYC, 1967-81, prof. medicine, chief hematology Valhalla, 1981—, acting chmn. dept. medicine, 1996-97; assoc. med. Dir. Westchester Med. Ctr., 1998—2004. Cons. FDA, Rockville, Md., 1972-78, NIH, Bethesda, Md., 1976, 95. Contbr. articles to profl. jours. Served to capt. M.C., U.S. Army, 1963-65. Recipient Research Career Devel. award NIH, 1971. Fellow ACP, Soc. for the Study of Blood (pres. 1995); mem. Island Peer Review Orgn. (bd. dirs. 1995, v.p.), NY State Bd. Medicine (aux. mem. 2004-), Westchester County Med. Soc. (bd. dirs. 2005-, sec. 2011). Home: 11 Dell Dr Eastchester NY 10709-5203 Office: NY Med Coll Grasslands Rd Valhalla NY 10595 Home Phone: 914-337-0936; Office Phone: 914-594-4415, 914-594-4440. Business E-Mail: robert_lerner@nymc.edu.

LERNER, THEODORE RAPHAEL, dentist; b. Bklyn., Sept. 28, 1932; s. Meyer and Tillie (Brimberg) L.; m. Barbara Ellen Bernstein, June 29, 1974; children by previous marriage: Andrea Holly, Evan Andrew. DDS, U. Pa., 1957. Diplomate Am. Bd. Endodontics. Dentist, endodontist pvt. practice, Bklyn., 1957-93, Forest Hills, NY, 1968-93, Boca Raton, Fla., 1992—. Fellow Internat. Coll. Dentists, Am. Coll. Dentists; mem. ADA, 2d Dist. Dental Soc. (pres. 1971), Dental Soc. State of N.Y. (pres. 1983), Fla. Dental Assn. Home: 7040 Lions Head Ln Boca Raton FL 33496-5931 Office: 2499 Glades Rd Ste 204 Boca Raton FL 33431-7201 Personal E-mail: trlray1@bellsouth.net.

LERNER, WAYNE M., hospital administrator; b. Chicago, Ill. BS, U. Ill.; MHA, U. Mich., 1973, DPH, 1988. Adminstrv. positions Rush Presbyterian St. Luke's Med. Ctr., Chicago; pres. Jewish Hosp., St. Louis, 1991—96; developer. exec. v.p. BLC Health System, 1993—96; v.p. Lash Group, Bannockburn, Ill., 1996; pres., CEO Rehab. Inst. Chgo., 1997—2006, Holy Cross Hosp., Chgo., 2006—. Chmn. Am. Hosp. Assn. Com. of Commissioners; mem. exec. com., bd. of commissioners Joint Commn. on Accreditation of Healthcare Orgn. Fellow Am. Coll. of Healthcare Executives. Office: Holy Cross Hosp 2701 W 68th St Chicago IL 60629 Office Phone: 312-908-2720.

LE ROUX, PETER DAVID, neurosurgeon; b. Durban, Republic of South Africa, May 14, 1960; came to US, 1985; s. Petrus Andries Jacobus and Sally Ann Le Roux; m. Eleanor Merle Le Roux, Nov. 6, 1993; children: Peter Donlon, James Patrick, Margot Katherine. MB ChB, U. Cape Town, Republic South Africa, 1983, MD, 1995. Diplomate Am. Bd. Neurological Surgery. Resident in neurosurgery U. Wash., Seattle, 1985-93; fellow neurosci. Ecole Normale Superieure, Paris, 1993-94; asst. prof. neurosurgery NYU, 1994-2000, assoc. prof. neurosurgery, 2001; assoc. prof. dept. neurosurgery U. Pa., Phila., 2001—. Coord. NYU Neurosurgery Residency Program, 1998-2000, acad. coord. dept. neurosurgery, U. Pa., 2001—; mem NIH study sect. Clinical Neurophysiology, Devices and Neuroprosthetics. Editor: Current Management of Cerebral Aneurysms, 1998, 2004—; ad hoc reviewer Jour. of Neurosurgery, Neurosurgery, Jour. of Neurology, Neurosurgery and Psychiatry, Surg. Neurology Jour. Neurosci., Brain Rsch., Critical Care Medicine, Acta Neurochirurchiga, Lancet Neurology, Neurobiology of Disease; contbr. articles to profl. jours. Named Young Neurosurgeon World Fedn. of Neurosurg. Socs., 1993; faculty rsch. fellowship ACS, 1996, Charles Elsberg Neurosurgery fellowship NY Acad. of Medicine, 1993, Whitehead fellowship NYU, 1999; recipient Clin. Investigator Devel. award NIH, 1997. Fellow ACS, Am. Heart Assn. (Stroke fellowship); mem. Am. Assn. of Neurologic Surgeons, Am. Congress of Neurologic Surgeons, Soc. for Neurosci., AANS/CNS (joint sect. on cerebrovascular surgery), Neurotrauma Soc., Neurocritical Care Soc. (bd. dirs.), Leksell Gamma Knife Soc. Office Phone: 215-829-7144. Business E-Mail: lerouxp@uphs.upenn.edu.

LEROY, OLIVIER YVES, physician; b. Sainte Adresse, Apr. 12, 1955; MD, Rouen, 1981. Physician ICU Hosp. Tourcoing, 2005—. Office: 135 Rue Du Président Coty Tourcoing Nord 59200 France Business E-Mail: oleroy@ch-tourcoing.fr.

LERTMANORAT, ZENG, engineering educator; b. Thailand, Nov. 21, 1975; PhD, Case Western Res. U., 2004. Asst. prof. Mahidol U., 2010—. Achievements include first to low-cost implantable nerve stimulator. Office: Mahidol University Faculty Engineering Salaya Nakornpathom 73170 Thailand Business E-Mail: egzlm@mahidol.ac.th.

LERTSAPCHAROEN, PORNTHEP, pediatrician, educator; b. Bangkok, June 3, 1958; MD, Chulalongkorn U., 1982. Assoc. prof. Chulalongkorn U., 2000—. Office: Rama IV Rd Patumwan Bangkok 10330 Thailand E-mail: lpornthep@yahoo.com.

LE SAUX, OLIVIER, medical educator; b. Marseille, France, June 4, 1967; PhD, U. Provence, France, 1997. Asst. prof. John A. Burns Sch. Medicine, 2004—. Office: 651 Ilalo St BSB 222 Honolulu HI 96813 Office Fax: 808-692-1970. Business E-Mail: lesaux@hawaii.edu.

LESAVOY, MALCOLM ALAN, plastic surgeon; b. Allentown, Pa., June 27, 1942; m. Sabine Lesavoy. BA, U. NC, 1964; MD, Chgo. Med. Sch., 1969. Diplomate Am. Bd. Plastic Surgery 1977. Resident gen. surgery U. Chgo., 1969—74; resident plastic and reconstructive surgery U. Miami, 1974—76; chief plastic surgery Harbor-UCLA Med. Ctr., Torrance, 1976—99; plastic surgeon Encino Outpatient Surgery Ctr., Calif., 2000—. Prof. plastic and reconstructive surgery UCLA Sch. Medicine, LA, 1976—99, clin. prof. plastic and reconstructive surgery and hand surgery, 2000—; nat. pres. Millard Plastic Surgery Soc., 1987—89; Frank Hawkins Kenan vis. prof. dept. surgery Duke U., Durham, NC, 2003; Kazanjian vis. prof. divsn. plastic and reconstructive surgery Harvard U., Boston, 2003; Courtemanche vis. prof. U. BC, Vancouver, 2004; vis. prof. Baylor Coll. Med., Houston, 2005. Author: Reconstruction of the Head and Neck, 1981, Hand Surgery Review, 1981, 2d edit., 1985, over 25 book chpts., over 70 articles to profl. jours. in field. Nat. pres. Reconstructive Surgeons Vol. Program, 1990—92. With USAR, 1969—76. Recipient Excellence in Clin. Tchg. award, UCLA Sch. Medicine, 1978, 1992, 1993, 2004; named a Disting. Alumnus, Chgo. Med. Sch., 1983. Mem.: ACS, World Soc. Reconstructive Microsurgery, Plastic Surgery Rsch. Coun., Plastic Surgery Ednl. Found. (bd. dirs. 1984—93, pres. 1991—92), Internat. Coll. Surgeons, Am. Soc. Plastic Surgeons (bd. dirs. 1990—94, chmn. bd. trustees 1995—96), Am. Soc. Maxillofacial Surgeons, Am. Assn. Plastic Surgery (named Clinician of Yr. 2002). Office: 16311 Ventura Blvd Ste 555 Encino CA 91436 Office Phone: 818-986-8270. Office Fax: 818-986-1342. Business E-Mail: mal@dolesavoy.com.

LESCH, OTTO-MICHAEL, medical association administrator; b. Vienna, July 6, 1945; MD, 1983. Prof. head Alcohol Rsch. Group, Med. U., 1976—2010; pres. Austrian Soc. Addicion Medicine, 2004—. Recipient Lautenschläger award, ESBRA. Avocation: tennis. Office: Währingerstrasse 18-20 Vienna A1090 Austria Office Fax: 00431404003472. E-mail: otto.lesch@meduniwien.ac.at.

LESESNE, CARROLL BOUTELL (CAP LESESNE), plastic surgeon; b. Gross Pointe Farms, Mich., Feb. 8, 1955; s. John and Ann L.; m. Elsie Cecilia Nelson, 1994 BA, Princeton U., 1977; MD, Duke U., 1980. Bd. cert., Plastic Surgery, 1987; Diplomate Am. Bd. Plastic Surgery. Resident Stanford U., Palo Alto, 1981—83, NY Hosp., NYC, 1983—85; fellow Sloan Kettering Cancer Hosp., 1985; clin. asst. prof. plastic surgery NYU Med. Ctr. Instr. Cornell Med. Sch. Author: Confessions of a Park Avenue Plastic Surgeon, 2005. Recipient sword of hope Am. Cancer Soc. Office: 620 Park Ave New York NY 10021-6591 also: 101 S Bedford Rd Mount Kisco NY 10549 Office Phone: 212-570-6318. Personal E-mail: clesesesne@aol.com.

LESHINSKY-SILVER, ESTHER, lab administrator; b. Israel, Nov. 21, 1950; PhD, Technion, Israel, 1985. Lab dir. Wolfson Med. Ctr., 1998—. Mem.: UMDF. Office: Halochamim 5 Holon 58100 Israel Office Fax: 972-3-502-8543. Business E-Mail: leshinsky@wolfson.health.gov.il

LESHNER, ALAN IRVIN, science association administrator; b. Lewisburg, Pa., Feb. 11, 1944; s. Saul S. and Martha (Schmidt) Leshner; m. Agnes Farkas, May 18, 1969; children: Sarah, Michael. BS in Psychology, Franklin & Marshall Coll., Lancaster, 1965; MS in Physiol. Psychology, Rutgers U., NJ, 1967, PhD in Physiol. Psychology, 1969. Asst. prof. psychology Bucknell U., Lewisburg, Pa., 1969-73, assoc. prof., 1973-78, prof., 1978-82; dep. exec. dir. Commn. Precollege Edn., Nat. Sci. Bd., 1982 83; dep. dir. divsn. behavioral and neural scis. NSF, Washington, 1983-85, dir. divsn. precollege materials devel. and rsch., 1984-85, exec. officer biol., behavioral and social scis., 1985-87; dep. dir. Nat. Inst. Mental Health (NIMH), NIH, 1988-90, acting dir. NIMH, 1990-92, dir. Nat. Inst. Drug Abuse (NIDA), 1994—2001; CEO AAAS, 2001—. Vis. scientist Postgrad. Med. Sch., Budapest, Hungary, 1974, Wis. Regional Primate Rsch. Ctr., Madison, 1976—77; Fulbright scholar Weizmann Inst. Sci., Rehovoth, Israel, 1977—78; mem. Nat. Sci. Bd., NSF, 2004—. Author: An Introduction to Behavioral Endocrinology, 1978; exec. pub. Sci., 2001—; contbr. articles to profl. jours., chapters to books. Fellow: APA, AAAS, Am. Acad. Arts & Scis., Am. Acad. Pub. Adminstrn., NY Acad. Scis., Am. Psychol. Soc.; mem.: NAS, Inst. Medicine, Internat. Soc. Rsch. Aggression, Phi Beta Kappa. Democrat. Jewish. Office: AAAS 1200 New York Ave NW Washington DC 20005 Office Phone: 202-326-6640. Office Fax: 202-371-9526. E-mail: aleshner@aaas.org.

LESLIE, ALAN M., psychology professor; b. Scotland; Grad., U. Edinburgh, 1974; DPhil, U. Oxford, 1980. Med. rsch. coun. sr. scientist U. London; prof. psychology and cognitive sci. Rutgers U., 1993—, dir. Cognitive Devel. Lab. Fellow: Am. Acad. Arts and Sciences, Assn. Psychological Sci. Office: Cognitive Devel Lab Rutgers U 152 Frelinghuyson Rd Piscataway NJ 08854 Office Phone: 743-445-6152, 732-445-4959. E-mail: aleslie@ruccs.rutgers.edu.

LESLIE, STEVEN W., pharmacologist, educator, former dean; m. Denese Leslie. BS in Pharmacy, Purdue U., West Lafayette, Ind., 1969, MS in Pharmacology/Toxicology, 1972, PhD, 1974. Asst. prof. divsn. pharmacology/toxicology U. Tex. Austin Coll. Pharmacy, 1974—79, assoc. prof., 1979—80, 1982—84, prof., 1984—, assoc. prof. dept. pharmacology, 1980—82, founder, dir. Inst. Neuroscience, 1986—92, Bauerle Centennial prof., 1989—, dean Coll. Pharmacy, 1998—2007, James T. Doluisio chair, 1998—2007, exec. v.p. & provost, 2007—. Assoc. prof. dept. pharmacology U. Ala. Med. Ctr., Birmingham, 1980—82. Office: U Tex Coll Pharmacy 1 Univ Station G1000 Austin TX 78712 Office Phone: 512-471-4363. Office Fax: 512-471-0577. Business E-Mail: sleslie@mail.utexas.edu.

LESSER, ROBERT, rheumatologist, educator; Studied, Ros Franklin U., 1982. Diplomate Am. Bd. Internal Medicine, Am. Bd. Internal Medicine-rheumatology. Resident internal medicine Hahnemann Univ. Hosp., Phila., 1983—85, resident rheumatology, 1986—87; assoc. clin. prof. medicine SUNY Health Sci. Ctr.; rheumatologist dept. of medicine Beth Israel Med. Ctr. Office: Beth Israel Medical Center 4015 Ave U Brooklyn NY 11234-5117 Office Phone: 718-252-5151.

LESSICK, MIRA LEE, nursing educator; d. Jack H. and Shirley E. (Frumkin) Lessick. Diploma in Nursing, Albany Med. Coll., NY, 1969; BSN, Boston U., 1972; MS, U. Colo., 1973; PhD, U. Tex., 1986. Staff nurse Boston City Hosp. and Mass. Gen. Hosp., 1969-72; instr. to asst. prof. nursing, genetics clinician U. Rochester, NY, 1973-79; asst. prof. nursing, practitioner Rush U. Coll. Nursing, Chgo., 1986-91, assoc. prof. nursing, 1992—2001, project dir. genetic health nursing program, 1993—2001; assoc. prof. U. Toledo, 2001—. Human genome rsch. initial rev. group, ethical, legal, and social implications subcom. Nat. Human Genome Rsch. Inst., NIH, 1996-99; peer reviewer Bur. Health Professions, HHS, 2001-02, Nat. Inst. Nursing Rsch., NIH, 2004-09; mem. manuscript rev. panel Nursing Women's Health Jours., 2007-. Mem. editl. bd. Nursing for Women's Health (formerly AWHONN Lifelines), 1999-2007; manuscript rev. panel, Rsch. in Nursing and Health Jour., MEDSURG Nursing, 2005—, Advanced Critical Care Nursing Jour., 2002—; genetics column editor Medsurg Nursing: Jour. Adult Health, 2001-05; contbr. articles to profl. jours.; chpts. to books. Recipient Bd. of Govs. award, Excellence in Pediatric Nursing award Albany Med. Ctr., 1969, Outstanding Nurse Recognition award March of Dimes Birth Defects Found., 1991, Recognition award for Individual Contbn. to Maternal-Child Health Nat. Perinatal Assn., 1993, Founders Award in Edn., Internat. Soc. Nurses in Genetics, 1997, Urologic Nursing Jour. Literary Writers award, 2004, Excellence Tchg. ward U. Toledo, Coll. Nursing, 2011. Mem. Internat. Soc. Nurses in Genetics (chair rsch. com. 1993-2002, co-chair rsch. com. 2003—05, mem. Genetic Nursing Credentialing Commn., 2001-2004, mem. web site editl. bd. 2001-05, mem. rsch. com. 2005-09, hon. mention Genetic Nursing Writer's award 2002), Assn. Women's Health, Obstetric, and Neonatal Nurses (named Manuscript Reviewer of Yr., Nursing for Women's Health Jour., 2009, Excellence in Writing award, 2010), Am. Soc. Human Genetics, Chgo. Nurses Assn. (legis. com. 1990-91), Midwest Nursing Rsch. Soc., Sigma Theta Tau (Luther Christman award for excellence in published writing 1993, Luther Christmas award Excellence Pub. Writing 1998), Phi Kappa Phi. Achievements include development of a genetic health area of concentration within a graduate level nursing program. Office: University Toledo Coll Nursing Health Sci Campus Toledo OH 43606-3390 Home Phone: 419-534-5403.

LESSIN, LAWRENCE STEPHEN, hematologist, oncologist, educator; b. Washington, Oct. 14, 1937; s. Maurice and Anna (Brodsky) L.; m. Judith Ann Lustok, Dec. 23, 1961; children: Jennifer Lynn, Jonathan Lustok, Martine Rose. Student, U. Mich., 1955-58; MD, U. Chgo., 1962. Diplomate Am. Bd. Internal Medicine (assoc. mem. 1976-82). Intern, resident in internal medicine, chief resident, fellow in hematology Hosp. U. Pa., 1962-67; spl. fellow Nat. Heart Inst., Inst. for Cell Pathology, Paris, 1967-68; asst. prof. medicine Duke U., 1968-70; assoc. prof. medicine and pathology George Washington U., 1970-74, prof. medicine and pathology, dir. div. hematology and oncology, 1974—93; dir. George Washington U. Cancer Ctr., Washington, 1991-93; sr. exec. physician Washington Cancer Inst. Washington Hosp. Ctr., 1993—2007, dir., continuing med. edn., 2009—. Vis. physician medicine br. Nat. Cancer Inst., 1971-74; cons. hematology Washington VA Hosp., 1971—; cons. ARC Blood Bank, 1972—, Nat. Naval Med. Ctr., Bethesda, Md., 1974—, NHLBI, 1974, Walter Reed Army Med. Ctr., 1978—; mem. NASA Biomed. Rev. Panel, 1981-88; chmn. div. blood diseases and resources adv. com. Nat. Heart, Blood and Lung Inst., NIH, 1985-86, mem. inst. sci. rev. com., 1997-99; mem. data safety monotoring bd. NHLBI, NIH, 2000—, chmn., program dir. Assn. Hematology Oncology, 1983-87; vol. spl. emphasis panel Comprehensive Sickle Cell SCOR Applications, 1997-99; mem. FDA panel on spongiform encephalopaties, cons. panel on oncology drugs, ODAC; mem. internat. adv. bd. King Hussein Cancer Ctr., Amman, Jordan, 2003—; mem. sci. adv. bd. Capital Tech. Info. Svcs., 2004—; bd. dirs. Internat. Spirit of Life Found., Rockville, Md., 2002—, Ceylinco Health, Colombo, Sri Lanka, 1999—. Editorial reviewer: Annals of Internal Medicine, 1969—, Nouvelle Revue de Hematologie, 1970—, Blood, Jour. Hematology, 1971—, Archives of Internal Medicine, 1972—, Nature, 1973, Jour. Clin. Investigation, 1973—, New Eng. Jour. Medicine; mem. editorial Blood Cells, 1979—, Hematologic Pathology, 1985—; contbr. articles to profl. jours., chpts. to books. Served to capt. M.C. USAR, 1963-69. Named Intern of Year U. Pa. Hosp., 1963; nominee for Golden Apple award, 1975; Nat. Heart Inst. spl. fellow Paris, 1967-68 Master ACP (chair Hematology Med. Knowledge Self-Assessment program 1992-); fellow Internat. Soc. Hematology; mem. Am. Soc. Hematology, Am. Fedn. Clin. Rsch., Am. Soc. Clin. Oncology (pub. info. com. 1999-2003, oncology manpower task force 2003-), Am. Blood Commn., Am. Soc. Internal Medicine, D.C. Med. Soc., Internat. Blood Cells Club, Am. Soc. Clin. Oncology (mem. oncology manpower coms., 2004-07), Cosmos Club (Washington), Annapolis Yacht Club, Sigma Xi, Alpha Omega Alpha. Office: Washington Cancer Inst 110 Irving St NW Washington DC 20010-2976 Office Phone: 202-877-8111. Business E-Mail: lawrence.s.lessin@medstar.net.

LESSIN, STUART R., dermatologist; b. Phila. Grad., Penn State U.; MD, Temple U. Resident tng. dermatology Hosp. of Univ. of Pa.; fellow tng. molecular biology Wistar Inst.; co-dir. cutaneous lymphoma program and pigmented lesion group dermatology dept. Univ. of Pa. Sch. of Medicine; dir. dermatology and melanoma family risk assessment program Fox Chase Cancer Ctr.; dermatologist Bryn Mawr Skin & Cancer. Author 100 med. and sci. publs. Bd. dirs. Dermatology Found., Cutaneous Lymphoma Found. Recipient Physician Scientist award, Nat. Institutes of Health, 1986, Career Devel. award, Dermatology Found., 1990, FIRST award, Nat. Institutes of Health, 1991, Career Devel. award, Dept. of Veterans Affairs, 1991, Mid-Career Devel. award, Nat. Institutes of Health, 1999, Dermatology Program Devel. award, Dermatology Found., 2002; named one of America's Top Doctors, 2003—10, America's Best Doctors for Cancer, 2004—, Top Doctors, Phila., 2004—, Best Doctors in America, 2005—10. Office: Bryn Mawr Skin Cancer Institute Rosemont Business Campus 919 Consetoga Rd Bldg 2 Ste 106 Bryn Mawr PA 19010 Mailing: Bryn Mawr Skin Cancer Institute Main Line Health Center 3855 W Chester Pike Ste 326 Newtown Square PA 19073 Office Phone: 610-525-5028.

LESSING, JEFFREY, urologist; MD, NYU Sch. of Medicine, 1975. Diplomate Am. Bd. Urology. Resident NYU Med. Ctr., NY, 1976—77, Mt. Sinai Hosp., NY, 1977—80; urologist Staten Island Univ. Hosp. North. Office: Todt Hill Urologic Group 78 Todt Hill Road Suite 112 Staten Island NY 10314 Office Phone: 718-448-3880. Office Fax: 718-448-9806.

LESTER, MARK CHARLES, neurosurgeon; b. Pitts., Sept. 23, 1952; AB, Cornell U., 1973; MD, U. Pitts., 1977; MBA, U. Pa., 2002. Diplomate Am. Bd. Neurol. Surgery, cert. physician exec. Intern gen. surgery U. Health Ctr. Hosps., Pitts., 1977—78, resident in neurological surgery, 1978—83; neurosurgeon Allentown, Pa., 1983—2004; chief divsn. neurol. surgery Lehigh Valley Hosp., Allentown, 1992—2001, vice-chmn. opers. dept. surgery, 1999—2004, med. dir. oper. rm., 1999—2004; clin. assoc. prof. Pa. State Coll. Medicine, Hershey, 1995—2004, Mich. State Coll. Human Medicine, Lansing, 2004—09; chief med. officer St. Mary's Mich. Med. Ctr., Saginaw, 2004—09; v.p. chief quality officer Tex. Health Presbyterian Hosp. Dallas, 2009—. Adj. clin. asst. prof. Hahnemann U., Phila., 1988—2004. Fellow: ACS; mem.: Am. Coll. Healthcare Execs., Am. Coll. Physician Execs., Am. Assn. Neurol. Surgeons.

LESTER, RICHARD GARRISON, radiologist, educator; b. NYC, Oct. 24, 1925; s. L. I. and Pauline (Smolan) L.; m. Marion Louise Kurtz, Jan. 17, 1949; children: Elizabeth P., Andrew W. AB, Princeton U., 1946; MD, Columbia U., 1948. Intern N.Y.C. Hosp., 1948-49; asst. resident radiology Stanford Hosp., 1950-51, 53-54; from instr. to asso. prof. radiology U. Minn., 1954-61; prof. radiology, chmn. dept. Med. Coll. Va., 1961-65, Duke Sch. Medicine, 1965-76; prof. radiology U. Tex. Med. Sch., Houston, 1976-84, chmn. dept., 1977-81; interim pres. Meharry Med. Coll., Nashville, 1981-82; dean Eastern Va. Med. Sch., Norfolk, 1984-89, prof. radiology, 1984-93, chmn. dept., 1989-91, prof. emeritus, 1993—; v.p. acad. affairs Med. Coll. of Hampton Roads (formerly Eastern Va. Med. Authority), Norfolk, 1984—89. Trustee Meharry Med. Coll., 1975—. Author: (with others) Congenital Heart Disease, 1965, Exposure of the Pregnant Patient to Diagnostic Radiations, 1985, 2d edit., 1997; also numerous articles. Mem 1st. Bapt. Ch. Oklahoma City, bd. Good Shepherd Minitiries, Okla City, Capt. USAF, 1951-53. Fellow Am. Coll. Radiology, Am. Coll. Chest Physicians; mem. Assn. Univ. Radiologists, Am. Roentgen Ray Soc., Soc. Pediatric Radiology, Radiol. Soc. N.Am. (dir. 1976—, chmn. bd. 1981, pres. 1983). Home and Office: 749 Touchmark Ct Edmond OK 73003-2164 Office Phone: 405 844-6965. Personal E-mail: rglester@aol.com.

LESTER, THOMAS, hematologist, internist, oncologist; Attended, Wash. and Jefferson Coll., 1975; MD, Rutgers U., New Brunswick, NJ, 1979. Diplomate Am. Bd. Internal Medicine, 1982, Am. Bd. Internal Medicine, 1987, Am. Bd. Internal Medicine-hematology, 1984, Am. Bd. Internal Medicine-med. oncology. Intern Mt. Sinai Hosp., NYC, 1980, resident internal medicine, 1980—82, fellow hematology, 1982—84; fellow med. oncology Meml. Sloan - Kettering Cancer Ctr., 1984—86; with Katonah Med. Group; assoc. med. dir. Mt. Kisco Med. Group; chief of med. oncology Northern Westchester Hosp., Mt. Kisco, NY. Office: Northern Westchester Hospital 400 East Main St Mount Kisco NY 10549 Office Phone: 914-666-1200.

LESTIENNE, PATRICK PIERRE, molecular biologist; b. Roubaix, France, Oct. 5, 1950; s. Joseph Pierre and Brigitte Therese (Eeckman) Lestienne; m. Catherine Marie Trouvé, July 7, 1973 (div. Jan. 1991); children: Vincent, Laetitia, Amelie. BTS, ESTBA, Paris, 1972, M in Biochemistry, U. Louis Pasteur, 1974, DEA in Biochemistry, 1975, PhD, 1978, DSc, 1980. Chargé rsch. Poly. Sch., Palaiseau, France, 1980-83, Stanford (Calif.) U., 1983-85, Pasteur Inst., Paris, 1985 86, Angers, France, 1986-88, 1998dir. rsch., 1988, dir. rsch. Bordeaux, France, 1998—. Author: Mitochondrial Diseases, 1999; contbr. articles to profl. jours. Mem.: AAAS, NY Acad. Scis., Soc. French Genetics, European Soc. Human Genetics. Home: 29 Rue Pablo Picasso 33600 Pessac France Office: INSERM U1053 University Bordeaux Victor Segalen Bordeaux 2 146 Rue léo Saignat 33076 Bordeaux France Office Phone: 33557574727. Business E-Mail: patrick.lestienne@inserm.fr.

LETENDRE, DONALD E., dean; BS, Mass. Coll. Pharmacy, Boston, 1976; PharmD, U. Ky. Coll. Pharmacy, Lexington, 1979. Resident dept. pharmacy U. Ky. Albert B. Chandler Med. Ctr., 1976—78, chief resident dept. pharmacy, 1978—79; asst. prof. dept. pharmacy practice U. Kansas Sch. Pharmacy, 1979—82; dir. clin. svcs., asst. dir. accreditation svcs. Am. Soc. Hosp. Pharmacists, 1982—86; dir. accreditation svcs. Am. Soc. Health-System Pharmacists, 1986—2001; prof. pharmacy, dean U. RI Coll. Phalmacy, Kingston, 2001—07; dean U. Iowa Coll. Pharmacy, Iowa City, 2007—. Asst. dir. dept. pharmacy, dir. investigational drug unit U. Kansas Med. Ctr., 1979—82; exec. sec. RI State Crime Lab. Commn., 2001—07. Contbr. articles to profl. jours., chapters to books. Mem. ednl. adv. bd. St. Peter's Elem. Sch., Olney, Md., 1990—91; vol. Habitat for Humanity, 2005—; mem. youth group ministry Christ the King Parish, Lenexa, Kans., 1980—82. Recipient Paul F. Parker Lecture award, U. Ky., 1998, Outstanding Alumni Achievement award, Mass. Coll. Pharmany, 1999; named an Hon. Resident, NY Montefiore Med. Ctr., 1989, U. Wis. Hosp. & Clinics, 1993. Mem.: Am. Pharmacists Assn., Am. Soc. Health-System Pharmacists, Am. Assn. Colleges of Pharmacy, Phi Delta Chi. Office: UI Coll Pharmacy 115 S Grand Ave 118 PHAR Iowa City IA 52242 Office Phone: 319-335-8794. Business E-Mail: donald-letendre@uiowa.edu.

LETH, FRANK VAN, epidemiologist; b. Utrecht, Netherlands, Nov. 17, 1963; s. J Van Leth and G Dreuning; m. Stavros Melachroinos. MD with distinction, U. of Amsterdam, 1989; diploma in Tropical Medicine and Hygiene, Royal Tropical Inst., Amsterdam, 1993; MSc in Epidemiology, London Sch. of Hygiene and Tropical Medicine, 2000; PhD, U. Amsterdam, 2005. Lic. epidemiologist A Dutch Assn. for Epidemiology, 2001, epidemiologist B Dutch Assn. for Epidemiology, 2006. House officer surgery Ysbyty Gwynedd, Bangor, Wales, 1990, Hosp. 'Lichtenberg', Amersfoort, Netherlands, 1991—92; house officer ob-gyn. Hosp. 'Kennemer Gasthuis', Haarlem, Netherlands, 1992—93; med. officer in-charge Misikhu Mission Hosp., Misikhu, Kenya, 1994—98; pub. health officer Dist. Pub. Health Office, Zeist, Netherlands, 1998—99; clin. epidemiologist Internat. Antiviral Therapy Evaluation Ctr., Amsterdam, 2000—05; sr. epidemiologist KNCV Tuberculosis Found., 2005—; epidemiologist Ctr. Poverty Related Communicable Diseases, U. Amsterdam, 2008—. Actor: (theatre) 'De trouwe Johannes' (The Faithful Johannes), 'De toren' (The Tower); asst. designer (theatre cos. 'Travaat', 'De gebroeders Flint', 'Alex d'electrique'); contbr. articles to profl. jours. Mem. mgmt. team Gymnastic Assn., Amsterdam, 2002—; mem., later vice-chair mgmt. team Med. Assn. of Amsterdam Students (MFAS), Amsterdam, 1985—89. Mem.: Internat. Epidemiol. Assn., Dutch Assn. for Epidemiology. Office Phone: 31-70-427-0982. Business E-Mail: vanlethf@kncvtbc.nl.

LETSOS, ARISTEIDIS PETER, orthopedist, surgeon, consultant; b. Athens, Greece, Apr. 1, 1967; s. Peter Sotiris and Mary Aristeidis Letsos; m. Irene Kautrozi, Dec. 25, 1995; 1 child, Peter. Grad., Med. Sch. Athens, 1990, diploma in biochemistry, 2000. Resident in orthop., England, 1990—95; fellow U. Pitts., 1999; cons. orthop.

surgery, traumatology, sports medicine Med. Ctr. Athens, Greece, 2000—. Contbr. chapters to books. Team physician Nat. Volleyball Team, Greece, 2000—. Mem.: Greek Sports Medicine Soc., Greek Orthop. Soc. Office: Karneadhu 4 106 75 Athens Greece

LETSOU, GEORGE VASILIOS, cardiothoracic surgeon; b. Boston, 1958; s. Vasilios George and Helen (Valacellis) L.; m. Jane Elizabeth Carter, June 1, 1985; children: Christopher George, Philip Taylor, John Carter. AB magna cum laude, Harvard U., 1979; MD, Columbia U., 1983. Diplomate Am. Bd. Surgery, Am. Bd. Thoracic Surgery. Resident in gen. surgery Yale-New Haven Hosp., 1983—88, chief resident and instr. surgery, 1987—88, clin. fellow in cardiothoracic surgery, 1988—89, Cystic Fibrosis Found. fellow cardiopulm. transplantation, 1988—89, Winchester scholar in cardiothoracic surg. rsch., 1989—90, resident in cardiothoracic surgery, 1990—91, chief resident in cardiothoracic surgery, 1991—92; attending surgeon Yale U., New Haven, 1992—95, instr. surgery, 1987-88, 91-92, asst. prof. surgery, 1992—95; attending surgeon Yale-New Haven Med. Ctr., 1992—95, Meth. Hosp., Ben Taub Hosp., Houston, 1995—; assoc. prof. surgery Baylor Coll. Medicine, Houston, 1995—99; attending surgeon Meml.-Hermann Hosp., Houston, 1998—, Tex. Heart Inst., 2009—, cardiovasc. surgery staff; assoc. prof. surgery U. Tex., Houston, 1999—2007, prof. surgery, 2007—. Mem. AMA, ACS, Am. Coll. Cardiology, Am. Coll. Chest Physicians, Soc. Thoracic Surgeons, Am. Assn. Thoracic Surgery. Office: Univ Tex-Houston Cardiothoracic Surgery 6410 Fannin St 720 Houston TX 77030-1501 also: 6410 Pannjn #450 Houston TX 77030-1501 Office Phone: 713-500-5323. Office Fax: 713-500-0650. Business E-Mail: George.V.Letsou@uth.tmc.edu.

LETTERIE, GERARD STEVEN, reproductive endocrinologist; b. Phila., Oct. 25, 1950; DO, Phila. Coll. Osteo. Medicine, 1978. Fellow, reproductive endocrinology and infertility NIH, Bethesda, Md., 1984—86; dir. Divsn. Reproductive Endocrinology, Tripler Army Med. Ctr., Honolulu, 1986—91; med. dir. Fertility and Endocrine Ctr., Va. Mason Med. Ctr., Seattle, 1991—2005; practice dir. NW Ctr. Reproductive Scis., Seattle, 2005—11; reproductive endocrinologist Seattle Reproductive Medicine, 2011—. Assoc. prof., Dept. ob-gyn. U. Wash., Seattle, 1991—2011; oral examiner Am. Bd. Ob-Gyn., Dallas, 2002—11. Named one of Top Drs., Seattle Mag., Seattle Met. Mag. Fellow: ACP, Am. Coll. Ob-Gyn.; mem.: Am. Assn. Advancement Sci., Am. Soc. Reproductive Medicine. Avocations: skiing, bicycling, running. Home: 810 W Blaine St Seattle WA 98119 Home Fax: 206-679-2953. Personal E-mail: gerardletterie@integrated.com.

LETTI MULLER, ANA LUCIA, gynecologist; b. Caxias do Sul, Rio Grande do Sul, Brazil, Oct. 12, 1965; MD, U. Fed. do Rio Grande do Sul, 1989, postgrad, 2009. Physician Hosp. De Clínicas De Poro Alegre, 1995—. Office: Palmeira 27/701 Porto Alegre Rio Grande do Sul 90470300 Brazil Business E-Mail: amuller@hcpa.ufrgs.br.

LETTS, ROBERT MERVYN, pediatric orthopaedic surgeon; b. Killarny, Man., Can., June 29, 1940; arrived in United Arab Emirates, 2003; s. Alfred Cyril and Grace Elizabeth Letts; m. Marilyn Janet Frances Jones, May 21, 1964; children: Ian, Eric, Daron. BSc Medicine, U. Man., Winnipeg, 1964, MD honors, 1964; MSc, Queens U., Kingston, Can., 1970. Head orthop. U. Man., Winnipeg, 1976—89; head pediat. surgery Winnipeg Children's Hosp., 1980—89, Childrens Hosp. East Ont., Ottawa, Canada, 1989—2003; head orthop. U. Ottawa, 1994—2000; cons. pediat. orthop. surgery Shaikh Khalifa Med. Ctr., Abu Dhabi, United Arab Emirates, 2003—; pres. Internat. Orthop. Cons. Author: (book) Seating the Disabled, 1991, (textbook) Management of Pediatric Fractures, 2000. Lt. Can. Air Force, 1965—68. Recipient Blount award, Scoliosis Rsch. Soc. N.Am., 1988, Spinal Rsch. Excellence award, Que. Scoliosis Rsch. Soc., 2001, Gov. Gen.'s Bronze medal, Govt. Can., 1958, Emergency Force medal, UN, 1967, Mid. East Def. medal, Govt. Can., 2002, Patient Health Care Excellence award, Authority United Arab Emirates, 2006. Fellow: ACS, Am. Acad. Orthop. Surgeons (internat. com. 1995—2000), Royal Coll. Physicians and Surgeons; mem.: Internat. Orthopaedics Consult. (pres.), Rotary Internat., Can. Orthop. Rsch. Soc. (pres. 1986), Scoliosis Rsch. Soc. (bd. dirs. 1997—2000), Pediat. Orthop. Assn. (pres. 1998), Can. Orthop. Assn. (pres. 1994), Can. Med. Assn. (various coms. 1966—). Avocations: tennis, hockey. Office: #66 261 Botanica Ottawa ON KIY4P9 Canada Personal E-mail: mervandmarvlyn@yahoo.com.

LEUCHTER, ANDREW FRANCIS, psychiatrist, educator; b. Mar. 12, 1954; MD, Baylor Sch. Medicine, 1980. Prof. UCLA, 1986—, dir., Lab. Brain, Behavior, and Pharmacology, 2002. Fellow: Am. Psychiat. Assn. Office: 760 Westwood Pl Rm 37-452 Los Angeles CA 90024 Office Fax: 310-825-7642. Business E-Mail: afl@ucla.edu.

LEUNG, ALEXANDER KWOK-CHU, pediatrician; b. Hong Kong, Oct. 1, 1948; s. Ping and Wai (Tai) Leung; children: Albert, Alex Jr., Amy, Alan, Andrew. MB BS, U. Hong Kong, 1973; DCH, Royal Coll. Physicians London, 1977, Royal Coll. Physicians Ireland, 1979. Intern U. Hong Kong, 1973-74; lectr. in child health U. Queensland, Brisbane, Australia, 1977; resident in pediat. U. Calgary, Alta., Canada, 1974-77, fellow in pediat. endocrinology, 1978-80, clin. asst. prof. pediat., 1980-90, cons. Univ. Med. Info. Svc., 1988—, clin. assoc. prof. pediat., 1990—2010; clin. prof. pediat., 2010—; med. dir. Asian Med. Ctr. in affiliation with U. Calgary Med. Clin., 1994—; cons. pediat. Alta. Children's Hosp., Calgary, 1980—. Hon. advisor Am. Biog. Inst. Rsch., Raleigh, NC, 1987—, Internat. Biog. Ctr., Cambridge, England, 1988—; examiner Med. Coun. Can. Qualifying Examination; mem. editl. bd. Current Pediat. Rev., 2011—, Case Reports Pediat., 2011—, Open Jour. Pediat., 2011—, Physician Info & Edn. Resource, ACP, 2009—. Mem. editl. bd.: Advances in Therapy, 1995—, Can. Clin. Jour. Medicine, 1996—2000, Cons., 2001—, Cons. for Pediatricians, 2002—, Can. Jour. Diagnosis, 2002—; mem. editl. bd. Recent Patents on Inflammation & Drug Discovery, 2008—, The Open Pediat. Med. Jour., 2008—, Recent Patents on Endocrine, Metabolic & Immune Drug Discovery, 2009—, Open Jour. Pediats., 2011—, consulting editor The Contemporary Who's Who; contbr. numerous articles to profl. jours, 324 chpts. to 6 books. Mem. Breastfeeding Com. for Can., 2001—06. Recipient Physician Recognition award, AMA, 1985, 1988, 1990, 1993, 1996, Gold Medal award, Am. Biog. Inst., 1992, Top Pediatrician award, Internat. Assn. Pediatricians. Fellow: Inst. Health Promotion and Edn., Can. Pediat. Soc. (nutrition com. 2000—06), Am. Acad. Pediat. (PREP fellow award 1987, 1990, 1996), Royal Coll. Physicians (London), Royal Coll. Physicians and Surgeons Glasgow, Royal Coll. Physicians Ireland, Royal Coll. Physicians Can., Royal Coll. Pediats. and Child Health, Royal Coll. Physicians Edinburgh, Royal Acad. Medicine, Royal Soc. Health (Eng.); mem.: Royal Soc. South Africa, Royal Soc. New Zealand. Office: # 200 233-16th Ave NW Calgary AB Canada T2M OH5 Office Phone: 403-230-3300. E-mail: aleung@ucalgary.ca.

LEUNG, DEXTER YU-LUNG, ophthalmologist; s. Peter Yuk-woon Leung and Winnie Suk-jing Woo; children: Claudine-Colette, Brendan Cheuk-lok. BS with honors in Medicine, Chinese U. Hong Kong, 1996. Lic. Coll. Ophthalmology Hong Kong, 2004, Royal Coll. Ophthalmology, UK, 2005, Hong Kong Acad. Medicine, 2005. Clin. asst. prof. dept. ophthalmology and visual scis. Chinese U. Hong Kong, 2001—; dep. coord. glaucoma svc. Hong Kong Eye Hosp., 2001—, assoc. cons., 2001—; hon. prof. Shantou U. Med. Coll., 2010—. Mem. standing com. convocation Chinese U. Hong Kong, 2005—. Bd. trustee Shaw Coll., Chinese U. Hongkong, 2009—; counting agt., legis. coun. election spl. adminstrv. region Govt Hong Kong, 2004. Recipient Exemplary Eye Resident award, K. Action Vision, 2003, 2007, Exemplary Eye Specialist award, 2007, Outstanding Sr. Provider award, 2008, award, Asian. Pacific Acad. Ophthalmology, 2009, Best Rsch. award, Action Vision Found., 2009, Outstanding award, Kowloon Ctrl. Cluster Convention, HK Hosp. Authority, 2010, Achievement award, Assian Pacific Acad. Orthop., 2010, Am. Acad. Orthop., 2011; co-recipient Bronze medal, Hong Kong Acad. Medicine, 2005; named Ten Outstanding Young Persons of Yr., Hong Kong, 2010; grantee, South East Asia Glaucoma Interest Group, 2006; fellow, Ho Hung-Chiu Med. Found., 2006. Fellow: Hong Kong Acad. Medicine, Royal Coll. Surgeons Glasgow; mem.: Von Graefe Soc. (exec. dir. and chpt. mem. 2009—), Frontline Doctors' Union (founder, dir. 2002—), Hong Kong Ophthal. Soc. (mem. coun. 2004—, sec. 2009—11, treasurer 2011—), Fedn. Socs. Prevention Blindness (treas. 2005—08), Royal Coll. Surgeons Edinburgh, Assn. Rsch. in Vision Sci., Am. Acad. Ophthalmology (Best Paper award 2007, Internat. Ophthalmologist Edn. award 2009, Achievement award 2011). Achievements include research in defining the role of lens extraction in management of acute angle closure glaucoma; defining silent cerebral infarct as a new risk factor for disease progression in normal tension glaucoma. Office: 8F Dept Ophthalmology Hong Kong Sanatorium Hosp Village Rd Happy Valley Hong Kong Office Phone: 852 27623000. Personal E-mail: dexleung@alumni.cuhk.net. Business E-Mail: dexterleung@hksh.com.

LEUNG, DONALD Y. M., pediatric allergist; b. NYC, Oct. 1, 1949; s. Kwok Choy and Kit (Tsui) Leung; m. Susan Bertarelli, Nov. 10, 1979; children: Allison, Alexander. BA, Johns Hopkin's U., Balt., 1970; PhD, U. Chgo., 1975, MD, 1977. Diplomate Am. Bd. Pediat., Am. Bd. Allergy-Immunology, lic. Mass., Colo. Intern pediat. Children's Hosp. Medical Ctr., Boston, 1977—78, resident pediat., 1978—79, fellow, allergy and immunology, 1979-81; instr. pediat. Harvard Med. Sch., 1981—83, asst. prof. pediat., 1983—87, assoc. prof. pediat., 1987-89; head div. pediat., sr. staff physician Nat. Jewish Ctr. Immunology Respiratory Medicine, Denver, 1989—. Clin. fellow pediat. Harvard Med. Sch., 1977—79; dir. diagnostic allergy, clin. immunology lab. Children's Hosp. Med. Ctr., 1983—87; assoc. clin. dir. immunology prog., dir. allergy prog. Children's Hosp. Medical Ctr., 1987—89; assoc. prof., dept. pediat. U. Colo. Health Sci. Ctr., 1990—91, prof., 1991—, rsch. adv. com., 2006; dir. NIH Gen. Clin. Rsch. Ctr., Denver, 1994. Author: (med. text) Treatment of Atopic Dermatitis, 1991; editorial bd. mem. (to numerous med. jours.); contbr. articles to profl. jours. Recipient Sci. Achievement award, Nat. Jewish med. rsch. Ctr., 2003, Psoriasis Achievement award, Am. Skin Assn., 2004; named to Woodward & White's Best Dr.'s in America, 1992—, Cambridge Outstanding Scientists of the 21st Century, Internat. Biog. Ctr., 2002. Fellow: Am. Coll. Allergy, Asthma, Immunology, Am. Acad. Allergy, Asthma, Immunology; mem.: Am. Soc. Clin. Investigation, European Soc. Pediat. Allergy Clin. Immunology, Soc. Investigative Dermatology, Colo. Allergy Soc., Am. Assoc. Advancement of Sci., New Eng. Soc. of Allergy, Am. Fedn. Clin. Rsch., Am. Assn. Immunologists, Collegium Internat. Allergologicum, Soc. Pediat. Rsch., Eczema Assn. Sci. Edn. (adv. bd. 1988), Am. Acad. Allergy Immunology, Phi Beta Kappa. Achievements include research in treatment of atopic dermatitis and asthma with inmunomodulatory agents; pathogenesis of Kawasaki disease and inmune mechanisms in atopic dermatitis; regulation of the human IgE response; patents for treatment of atopic disorders with gamma-interferon; treatment of steroid resistant diseases. Office: Nat Jewish Med Rsch Ctr Dept Pediat 1400 Jackson St Denver CO 80206-2761 Office Phone: 303-388-4461.

LEUNG, PAK-YIN, hospital administrator; Grad., NSW U., Australia, 1984; MS in Occupl. Medicine, Nat. U. Singapore. Hon. prof. sch. pub. health and primary care Chinese Univ. Hong Kong; contr. ctr. for health Hosp. Authority, dir. quality and safety, 2007, chief exec. With dept. health Govt. Hong Kong, dep. dir. food and environ. hygiene, 2000, dep. dir. health, 02, chmn. expert working group on avian influenza; mem. Med. Coun. Hong Kong; dep. commr. Auxillary Med. Svc., 2007—. Author various publs. including Population Prevalence of Epilepsy in Sydney, Transmission Dynamics of the Etiological Agent of SARS in Hong Kong: Impact of Public Health Interventions, SARS-CoV Antibody Prevalence in All Hong Kong Patient Contacts. Office: Hospital Authority Hospital Authority Bldg 147B Argyle St Kowloon Hong Kong Office Phone: 85228824866. E-mail: pyleung@ha.org.hk. *

LEUNG, PO SING, physiology educator; b. Macao, Jan. 10, 1961; s. Kwok Bun Leung and Kam Luen Fok; m. Wan Chun Hu, July 29, 1988; children: May, Yan. BSc, Nat. Taiwan Normal U., Taipei, 1987; PhD, Queen's U. Belfast, No. Ireland, 1993. Higher Cert. in water pollution control. Insp. Environ. Protection Dept., Hong Kong, 1987-90; postdoctoral fellow Queen's U. Belfast, 1993-94, Japan Sci. and Tech. Agy., 1994-95, Chinese U. Hong Kong, 1995-96; asst. prof. physiology dept. Chinese U., Hong Kong, 1996-98, assoc. prof. dept. physiology, 1998—2003, prof. dept. physiology, 2003—. Mem. editl. bd.: Jour. of Pancreas, Jour. Molecular Endocrinology, Jour. Molecular and Cellular Endocrinology, Pancreas, Internat. Jour. Biochemistry & Cell Biology, Antioxides & Redox Signaling; contbr. articles to sci. jours. including Molecular and Cellular Endocrinology, Jour. Endocrinology, Jour. Membrane Biology, Biochimica et Biophysica Acts, Diabetologia, Diabetes, Gut. Grantee Hong Kong Rsch. Grants Coun., Germany-Hong Kong Joint Rsch. Scheme. Mem. Endocrine Soc., Biochem. Soc., Chinese Physiol. Soc., Internat. Assn. Pancreatology, N.Y. Acad. Scis. Avocations: reading, jogging, ping pong/table tennis. Office: Chinese U Hong Kong Fac Med Sch Biomed Scis Shatin NT Hong Kong Office Phone: (852) 2609 6879. E-mail: psleung@cuhk.edu.hk.

LEUNG, VIVIAN YEE-FONG, radiographer; b. Hong Kong, Jan. 01; PhD, Chinese U. Hong Kong, 2002. Sr. radiographer Prince Wales Hosp., 1988—. Office: Prince Wales Hosp X-ray Dept Shatin New Territories Hong Kong Personal E-mail: leuyf2@ctimail.com.

LEUNG, WALLACE WOON-FONG, engineering educator; b. Hong Kong, Jan. 25, 1954; BSc, Cornell U., 1977; ScD, MIT, 1981. Rsch. engr. Gulf Oil Rsch. & Devel. Co., 1981—84, Schlumberger, 1984—86; dir. process tech. Bird/Baker Hughes, 1986—2004; pres. Advantech, 2004—05; chair prof., innovative products & tech. mech. engring. Hong Kong Poly. U., 2005—. Dir. Rsch. Inst. Innovative Products & Technologies, 2005—11. Recipient Best Engring. award, Baker Hughes. Fellow: Hong Kong Inst. Engrs., Am. Filtration & Separations Soc. (Shoemaker award, Sr. Scientist award). Achievements include research in nanofiber, personal protective equipment against virus, clinical decision support, portable diagnostic, rapid cell culture, osteoarthritis treatment, blind navigation and active stroke rehabilitation; specialize in submicon particulate Filtration Stroke Patient Rehablitation, smart electrical stimulation on osteoarthritis patient. and clinical decision support system. Avocation: swimming. Office: Hong Kong Polytechnique University Rm FG615 Mechanical Engineering Hung Hom Kowloon Hong Kong Business E-Mail: mmwleung@polyu.edu.hk.

LEUNG, YUK MAN, medical educator; PhD, U. Hong Kong, 1996. Postdoc. rsch. assoc. U. Toronto, Canada, 2000—05; assoc. prof. China Med. U., Taichung, Taiwan, 2006—11, prof., 2011—. Contbr. scientific papers. Recipient Rsch. award, China Med. U., 2006—. Mem.: Biophys. Soc. Achievements include research in elucidation of SNARE protein-potassium channel interaction; neuron physiology; drug-channel interaction. Office Phone: 886 4 2205 3366 Ext. 2185.

LEUZZI, ROSEMARIE A., internist, educator; MD, U. Pitts. Diplomate Am. Bd. Internal Medicine. Intern Univ. of Pitts. Med. Ctr., resident; physician Cooper Univ. Hosp.; assoc. prof. medicine dept. Cooper Univ. Named one of the Top Doctor, Phila. Mag., 2011. Office: Cooper University Hospital Bldg 2 Ste 201 900 Centennial Blvd Voorhees NJ 08043 Office Phone: 856-325-6770. Office Fax: 856-673-4300.

LEV, EFRAIM, medical educator; b. Haifa, Israel, Mar. 9, 1958; PhD, Bar Ilan U., 1999. Prof., dept. head U. Haifa, 2008—. Chmn. Israeli Soc. History of Medicine, 2001—03. Fellowship, Koret Found., 2000, Chevening fellow, Brit. Coun., 2001. Mem.: Internat. Soc. History of Medicine (nat. del. 2008). Avocations: running, swimming, hiking. Office: Har Carmel Haifa 31905 Israel Office Fax: 97248240738. Business E-Mail: elev@univ.haifa.ac.il.

LEVAVI-SIVAN, BERTA, agricultural studies educator; b. Israel, Sept. 23, 1958; PhD, Tel-Aviv U., 1983. Prof. Hebrew U., 2007—. Mem.: Soc. Reprodn. Office: Hebrew University Faculty Agriculture Rehovot 76100 Israel Business E-Mail: sivan@agri.huji.ac.il.

LEVCHUCK, SEAN, pediatric cardiologist, educator; MD, St. George U., 1989. Diplomate Am. Bd. Pediatrics, 2008, Am. Bd. Pediatrics-pediatric cardiology. Intern. Winthrop Hosp., resident pediat. Mineola, NY, 1990—92; fellow pediatric cardiology St. Christophers's Hosp. for Children, Phila., 1992—95; dir. pediat. St. Francis Hosp., dir. pediatric cardiology, ptnr. pediatric cardiology LI, attending physician, 1995—2003; clin instr. pediat. State Univ. NY Stoony Brook Sch. Medicine. Co-author: (articles) Am. Jour. Physiology, Pediatric Cardiology and Circulation. Fellow: Am. Acad. Pediat., Am. Coll. Cardiology. Office: St. Francis Hospital The Heaert Center 100 Port Washington Blvd Roslyn NY 11576 Office Phone: 516-365-3340. Office Fax: 516-365-5512.

LEVÉEN, PER, researcher, molecular medicine; b. Lund, Sweden, June 12, 1962; Degree in Pharmacy, Uppsala U., 1986; PhD, Uppsala and Gothenburg U., 1995. Rschr. Lund U., 1997—2009; assoc. prof Lund U, 2008; rschr. Helsinki U., 2010—11; molecular biologist Lab. Medicine Skåne, 2011—. Avocation: music. Office: Sölvegatan 25 Lund Skåne 22362 Sweden Business E-Mail: per.leveen@skane.se.

LEVEEN, ROBERT FREDERICK, radiologist; b. Jersey City, July 24, 1946; s. Harry Henry and Jeanette Lois (Rubricius) LeV.; m. Sandra Sue Hickstein, May 28, 1974; children: Emily, Rob. BA, Grinnell Coll., Iowa, 1968; MD, U. Nebr., Omaha, 1974. Diplomate Am. Bd. Radiology. Intern dept. surgery U. Wash., 1974-75; resident in radiology Coll. Medicine U. Nebr., 1975-78; asst. prof. radiology U. Nebr. Med. Ctr., Omaha, 1978-80; from asst. prof. radiology to assoc. prof. U. Pa., Phila., 1980-90; rsch. assoc. VA Med. Ctr., Phila., 1980-83, clin. investigator, 1985-90; coord. angiography rsch. Dept. Radiology U. Pa., 1985-90; assoc. prof. radiology U. Nebr. Med. Ctr., 1991-99; chief radiology svc. VA Med. Ctr., Omaha, 1991-99; assoc. prof. U. Fla., Gainesville, 1999—. Recipient Career Devel. award, VA, 1985, Innovation Lifetime Achievement award, Intellectual Property Corp. U Nebr., 2007; Stauffer award, Assn. U. Radiologists, 1986. Fellow Am. Coll. Radiology; mem. Soc. Cardiovasc. and Interventional Radiology, Radiologic Soc. N.Am., Assn. U. Radiologists, Nebr. Radiol. Soc. (pres. 1998-99), Fla. Radiol. Soc. Presbyterian. Office: U Fla Coll Medicine Dept Radiology PO Box 100374 Gainesville FL 32610-0374 Personal E-mail: rleveen@cox.net. Business E-Mail: leveer@radiology.ufl.edu.

LÉVEILLARD, THIERRY, research scientist; b. Veules les Roses, Normandie, France, Apr. 26, 1960; s. Bernard and Irene Léveillard; m. Valerie Franc, Oct. 3, 1960; children: Edouard, Louis, Jules. PhD in Molecular and Cellular Biology, U. Rouen, France, 1989. Fellow French Min. Rsch., Rouen, 1986—89; vis. postgrad. rschr. U. Calif., San Diego, 1989—91; rsch. assoc. Salk Inst., San Diego, 1991—92; postdoctoral rschr. CNRS, Strasbourg, Alsace, France, 1992—96, U. Louis Pasteur, Strasbourg, 1997—98; charge de recherche Inserm U592, Paris, 1998—. Cons. Fovea Pharm., Paris, 2005. Recipient award, Found. Fighting Blindness, 2005; fellow, IPSEN Found., 1997. Achievements include patents for Rod derived Cone Viability Factor.

LEVEILLE, GILBERT ANTONIO, food products executive; b. Fall River, Mass., June 3, 1934; s. Isidore and Rose (Caron) L.; divorced; children: Michael, Kathleen, Edward; m. Carol A. Phillips, Aug. 7, 1981. B in Vocat. Agr., U. Mass, 1956; MS, Rutgers U., 1958,

PhD in Nutrition and Biochemistry, 1960; DSc (hon.), Purdue U., West Lafayette, Ind., 2007. Prof. nutritional biochemistry U. Ill., Urbana, 1965-71; chmn. dept. food sci. and human nutrition Mich. State U., East Lansing, 1971-80; dir. nutrition and health sci. Gen. Foods Corp., Tarrytown, NY, 1980-86; v.p. for rsch. and tech. svcs. Nabisco Inc., East Hanover, NJ, 1986-96; pres. Leveille Assocs., Denville, NJ, 1996-99, 2004—; v.p. worldwide, sci. and regulatory affairs McNeil Consumer Healthcare, Fort Washington, Pa., 1999—2001; v.p. tech. food sys. design, dir. food tech. devel. ctr. Cargill, Inc., 2002—04; exec. dir. Wrigley Sci. Inst. William Wrigley Jr. Co., Chgo., 2005—09. Author: The Set Point Diet, 1985 (Nonfiction Bestseller, NY Times); contbr. articles to profl. jours. Served to 1st lt. U.S. Army, 1960-62. Recipient rsch. award Poultry Sci. Assn., 1965, Disting. Faculty award Mich. State U., 1980, Chancellor's Medal, U. Mass., 2000. Mem. AAAS, Am. Chem. Soc., Am. Soc. for Nutrition (pres. 1988-89, Mead Johnson rsch. award 1971, Elvehjem award 2002), Inst. Food Technologists (pres. 1983-84, fellow 1983, Carl Fellers award 1992, Indsl. Scientist award 2004, Nicholas Appert award 2008, Gilbert Leveille Lectureship award 2010). Personal E-mail: leveilleg@optonline.net.

LEVEILLE, SUZANNE G., medical educator; b. Providence, Nov. 27, 1953; BSN, Georgetown U., 1974; PhD, U. Wash., 1995. Epidemiologist, asst. prof. Beth Israel Deaconess Med. Ctr., 2004; prof. U. Mass. Boston, 2009—. Bd. mem. Boston Commn. Persons with Disabilities, 2008. Recipient John A Hartford Geriatric Nursing Rsch. award, Eatern Nursing Rsch. Soc. Mem.: Am. Geriat. Soc., Am. Pain Soc., Gerontol. Soc. Am. Office: 100 Morrissey Blvd Dorchester MA 02125 Business E-Mail: suzanne.leveille@umb.edu.

LEVENSON, ALAN IRA, psychiatrist, physician, educator; b. Boston, July 25, 1935; s. Jacob Maurice and Frances Ethel (Biller) Levenson; m. Myra Beatrice Katzen, June 12, 1960 (div. 1993); children: Jonathan, Nancy; m. Linda Ann Nadell, Jan. 30, 1994 (dec. Aug. 1, 2009). AB, Harvard U., 1957, MD, 1961, MPH, 1965. Diplomate Am. Bd. Psychiatry and Neurology. Intern U. Hosp., Ann Arbor, Mich., 1961-62; resident in psychiatry Mass. Mental Health Ctr., Boston, 1962-65; staff psychiatrist NIMH, Chevy Chase, Md., 1965-66, dir. divsn. mental health svc. programs, 1967-69; prof. psychiatry U. Ariz. Coll. Medicine, Tucson, 1969-2000, prof. emeritus, 2000—, head dept. psychiatry, 1969-89; CEO Palo Verde Mental Health Svcs., Tucson, 1971-91, chief med. officer, med. dir., 1991-93; chmn. bd. dirs., CEO Psychiatrists' Purchasing Group, 1991—; chmn. bd. dirs. Psychiatrists' Risk Retention Group, 1991-2000. Author: (book) The Community Mental Health Center: Strategies and Programs, 1972; contbr. papers and articles to profl. jours. Bd. dirs. Tucson Urban League, 1971—78, Pima Coun. Aging, 1976—83, 2006—, chmn., 2008—. With USPHS, 1965—69. Fellow: The Coll. For Behavioral Health Leadership (v.p. 1980—82, pres. 1982—83), Am. Coll. Psychiatrists (regent 1980—83, v.p. 1983—85, pres.-elect 1985—86, pres. 1986—87), Am. Psychiat. Assn. (treas. 1986—90); mem.: Group Advancement Psychiatry, Harvard Alumni Assn. (bd. dirs. 1988—91). Office: 75 E Calle Resplendor Tucson AZ 85716-4937

LEVENTHAL, BENNETT LEE, psychiatry and pediatrics educator, academic administrator; b. Chgo., July 6, 1949; s. Howard Leonard and Florence Ruth (Albert) L.; children: Matthew G., Andrew G., Julia G. Student, Emory U., Atlanta, 1967—68; BS, La. State U., New Orleans, 1972, MD, 1974. Diplomate Am. Bd. Psychiatry and Neurology in Psychiatry, Am. Bd. Psychiatry and Neurology, Child Psychiatry; lic. physician NC, La., Ill., Va. Undergrad. rsch. assoc. Lab. Prof. William A. Pryor dept. chemistry La. State U., 1968-70; house officer I Charity Hosp. at New Orleans, 1974; resident in psychiatry Duke U. Med. Ctr., Durham, NC, 1974-78, chief fellow divsn. dept. psychiatry, 1976-77, chief resident dept. psychiatry, 1977-78, clin. assoc. dept. psychiatry, 1978-80; staff psychiatrist, head psychiatry dept. Joel T. Boone Clinic, Virginia Beach, Va., 1978-80, staff psychiatrist, faculty mem. dept. psychiatry Naval Regional Med. Ctr., Portsmouth, Va., 1978-80; asst. prof. psychiatry and pediats. U. Chgo., 1978-85, dir. Child Psychiatry Clinic, 1978—2005, dir. Child and Adolescent Psychiatry Fellowship tng. program, 1979-88, Irving B. Harris prof. child and adolescent psychiatry, 1998—, emeritus, 2005—, dir. Sonia Shankman Orthogenic Sch., 2002—05; prof. psychiatry, dir. Ctr. Child Mental Health U. Ill., Chgo., 2005—. Psychiat. cons. Caledonia State Prision/Halifax Mental Health Ctr., Tillery, NC, 1976-77, Fed. Correctional Inst., Butner, NC, 1977-78; cons. Norfolk Cmty. Mental health Ctr., 1978-80; adj. prof. psychology, biopsychology, and devel. psychology U. Chgo., 1990, adj. assoc. prof. dept. psychology and com. on biopsychology, 1987-90; meed. dir. Child Life and Family Edn. program Wyler Children's Hosp. of U. Chgo., 1983-95; dir. child and adolescent programs Chgo. Lakeshore Hosp., 1986-2000; Pfizer vis. prof. dept. psychiatry U. PR, 1992; examiner Am. Bd. Psychiatry and Neurology in Gen. Psychiatry and Child Psychiatry, 1982—; mem. steering com. Harris Ctr. for Devel. Studies, U. Chgo., 1983—; mem. com. on evaluation of GAPS project AMA, 1993-97; treas. Chgo. Consortium for Psychiat. Rsch., 1994; pres. Ill. Coun. Child and Adolescent Psychiatry, 1992-94; vis. scholar Hunter Inst. Mental Health and U. New Castle, NSW, Australia, 1995; mem. Gov.'s Panel on Health Svcs., 1993-94; prof. psychiatry & pediats. U. Chgo., 1990-2005, chmn. dept. psychiatry, 1991-98, Irving B. Harris prof. child & adolescent psychiatry, 1998-2004; presenter in field. Mem. editl. bd. Univ. Chgo. Better Health Letter, 1994-96; cons. editor: Jour. Emo tional and Behavioral Disorders, 1992-96; reviewer: Archives of Gen. Psychiatry, 1983—, Biol. Psychiatry, 1983—, Am. Jour. Psychiatry, 1983—, Jour. AMA, 1983—, Jour. Am. Acad. Child and Adolescent Psychiatry, 1983—, Sci., 1983—; book rev. editor Jour. Neuropsychiatry and Clin. Neuroscis., 1989-92, mem. editl. bd., 1989-92; contbr. articles to profl. jours. Lt. comdr. MC USNR, 1978—80. Recipient Crystal Plate award Little Friends, 1994, Individual Achievement award Autism Soc. Am., 1991, Merit award Duke U. Psychiat. Resident's Assn., 1976, Bick award La. Psychiat. Assn., 1974; Andrew W. Mellon Found. faculty fellow U. Chgo., 1983-84; John Dewey lectr. U. Chgo., 1982. Fellow Am. Acad. Child and Adolescent Psychiatry (Outstanding Mentor 1988, dep. chmn. program com. 1979—, chmn. arrangements com. 1979—, new rsch. subcom. for ann. meeting 1986—, mem. work group on rsch. 1989—), Am. Psychiat. Assn. (Falk fellow, mem. Ittleson Award Bd. 1994-97, mem. Am. Psychiat. Assn./Wisniewski Young Psychiatrists Rsch. Award Panel 1994—), Am. Acad. Pediats., Am. Orthopsychiat. Assn.; mem. AAAS, Am. Coll. Psychiatrists, Brain Rsch. Inst., Ill. Coun. Child and Adolescent Psychiatry, Ill. Psychiat. Soc., Soc. for Rsch. in Child Devel., Soc. of Profs. of Child and Adolescent Psychiatry, Soc. Biol. Psychiatry, Nat. Bd. Med. Examiners, Mental Health Assn. Ill. (profl. adv. bd. 1991—), Sigma Xi. Office: Inst for Juvenile Rsch Dept Psychiatry (M/C 747) U Ill at Chgo 1747 W Roosevelt Rd Rm 155 Chicago IL 60608

LEVENTHAL, CARL M., neurologist, consultant, retired government agency administrator; b. NYC, July 28, 1933; s. Isidor and Anna (Semmel) L.; m. Brigid Penelope Gray, 1962 (dec. 1994); children: George Leon, Sarah Elizabeth Roark, Dinah Susan, James Gray. AB cum laude, Harvard Coll., 1954; MD, U. Rochester, NY, 1959. Diplomate: Am. Bd. Psychiatry and Neurology. Fellow in anatomy U. Rochester, 1956—57; intern, then asst. resident in medicine Johns Hopkins Hosp., 1959-61; asst. resident, then resident in neurology Mass. Gen. Hosp., Boston, 1961-64; commd. officer USPHS, 1963-96, asst. surgeon gen., 1979-83; asso. neuropathologist Nat. Inst. Neurol. Diseases and Blindness, 1964-66; neurologist Nat. Cancer Inst., 1966-68; asst. to dep. dir. sci., 1968-73; acting dep. dir. sci. NIH, 1973-74; dep. dir. bur. drugs FDA, Rockville, Md., 1974-77; dep. dir. Nat. Inst. Arthritis, Diabetes and Digestive and Kidney Diseases, 1977-81; div. dir. Nat. Inst. Neurol. Disorders and Stroke, 1981-96; sr. policy analyst for life scis. Office of Sci. and Tech. Policy, Exec. Office of Pres., 1983; sr. dir. med. affairs INC Rsch., Inc., 2005—. Asst. clin. prof. neurology Georgetown U. Med. Sch., 1966-76 Recipient Commendation medal USPHS, 1970, Meritorious Svc. medal, 1974, 77, 91, Outstanding Svc. medal, 1988, dir's. award NIH, 1992, Disting. Svc. medal, 1997. Fellow Am. Acad. Neurology; mem. Am. Assn. Neuropathologists, Am. Neurol. Assn., Am. Soc. for Exptl. Neurotherapeutics, Alpha Omega Alpha. Home: 10924 Brewer House Rd Rockville MD 20852-3422

LEVENTHAL, JOSEPH ROSS, surgeon; b. NY, Sept. 30, 1963, MD, SUNY Downstate, 1987; PhD, U. Minn., 1996. Assoc. prof. surgery Northwestern U. Feinberg Sch. Medicine, 1998—. Dir. kidney and pancreas transplantation Northwestern Comprehensive Transplant Ctr. Recipient Investigator award, NKF Ill.; Sandoz Transplant fellowship, Am. Coll. Transplant Surgeons. Fellow: ACS; mem.: Am. Soc. Transplantation, Am. Soc. Transplant Surgeons (Pfizer Collaborative Scientist award). Avocations: fishing, swimming, dance. Office: 676 N St Clair Ste 1900 Chicago IL 60611 Business E-Mail: jleventh@nmh.org.

LEVENTHAL, LAWRENCE JAY, rheumatologist, educator; b. NYC, June 5, 1958; s. Samuel and Anne Leventhal; m. Linda Currao, May 15, 1988; 2 children. BA in Biology magna cum laude, Brandeis U., 1980; MD, Hahnemann U., 1984. Resident in internal medicine Albert Einstein Med. Ctr., Phila., 1984-87; fellow in rheumatology U. Pa., Phila., 1987—90, clin. assoc. in medicine, 1989—91, clin. asst. prof. medicine, 1989—97; prof. medicine Drexel U., Phila., 1997—2009; clin. asst. prof. Med. Coll. Pa., Phila., 2007—. Dir. arthritis rsch. edn. Presbyn. Hosp., Phila., 1990—93; assoc. chief rheumatology Grad. Hosp., Phila., 1993—98, chief rheumatology, 1998—, vice chair dept. medicine, 2001—03, chair of medicine, 2003—, assoc. dir., CME Drexel U. Coll. Medicine, 2007. Author: Primer of Rheumatic Disease, 1994; editor: Jour. Clin. Rheumatology; contbr. articles to profl. jours. Named one of Best Drs. in Am., Ctr. for the Study Svcs., 1996—2006. Fellow ACP, Am. Coll. Rheumatology, Phila. Coll. Physicians; mem. AMA (physicians recognition award 1987—), Am. Soc. Internal Medicine, Phila. Rheumatism Soc. (pres. 1996), Arthritis Found. (exec. bd.). Office: 727 Welsh Rd Ste 201 Huntingdon Valley PA 19006 Office Phone: 215-762-2688. Personal E-mail: ljlmd@yahoo.com.

LEVERMORE, MONIQUE A., psychologist, educator; arrived in USA, 1971, naturalized, 1985; d. Oswald and Claudette Levermore; m. Mark Bartolone, Oct. 17, 1998, children: Nino, Kai. BA, U. Miami, Fla., 1988, MS in Edn., 1990; MS, Howard U., Washington, 1993, PhD, 1995. Bd. cert. fellow Am. Bd. Psychol. Specialties, cert. profl. K-6 educator Fla. Clin. fellow Harvard Med. Sch., Cambridge, Mass., 1994—95; resident Psy-Eckerd Youth Devel. Ctr., Okeechobee, Fla., 1995—96; asst. prof. Palm Beach Atlantic U., West Palm Beach, Fla., 1996—97; pvt. practice Levermore Psychol. Svcs., Palmetto Bay, Fla., 1997; asst. prof. Fla. Inst. Tech., Melbourne, 1997—2004; pres. Adolescent Behavioral Inst., Melbourne, 2004—, Miami Tchg. Fellows, 2006—08; assoc. prof., asst. dir. clin. tng. Carlos Albizu U., 2008—; med. staff Baptist Hosp. South Miami Hosp., 2010. Pres. Martique Corp., Levermore Psychol. Svcs. Corp. Contbr. articles to profl. jours. Hon. co-chair physicians adv. bd. Congl. Leadership Award, 2001; chmn. adv. bd. With a Brush of Love, Md., 2002—; mem. Together in Partnership, Brevard County, Fla., 2001—07, Links, Inc., Brevard County, Fla., 2003—08; founder Growing Into Responsible Young Ladies Successfully; bd. dirs. Salvation Army, Melbourne, Fla., 2002—08. Recipient Faculty Mem. of Yr. award, Carlos Albizu U., 2009; named a Woman Distinction-Edn. and Govt., Girls Scouts, Citrus Coun., 2002; grantee, Eckerd Family Found., 1991—2001; Miami Tchg. fellow, 2006—08. Fellow: Am. Coll. Forensic Examiners Internat. (editl. adv. bd. mem.); mem.: APA, Fin. Planning Assn. Democrat. Episcopalian. Avocations: singing, flute, cooking. Office: Carlos Albizu Univ Doctoral Psychology Program 2173 NW 99th St Doral FL 33172 also: Levermore Psychological Services 15715 S Dixie Hwy Ste 404 Miami FL 33157-1812 Office Phone: 305-593-1223 ext. 122, 786-293-0922. Office Fax: 786-293-0923. Business E-Mail: drl@levermore.com.

LEVI, NICK, dentist; DDS in Stomatology, Med. Univ., Sofia, Bulgaria, 1996. Founder Calif. Ctr. Aesthetic Dentistry, 2002. Dentist ABC's Extreme Makeover, 2003, Extreme Makeover radio show, 2003. Author: (Textbook) Orthodontia 2000, 1999. Named one of Medical Profiles, San Francisco Mag., 2005. Mem.: Dental Org. for Conscious Sedation, San Francisco Dental Soc., Calif. Dental Assn., ADA, Da Vinci Group. Office: Aesthetic Dentistry Ste 200 230 California St San Francisco CA 94111 Office Phone: 415-433-4337. Business E-Mail: mydentist@ymail.com.

LEVIEN, DAVID HAROLD, surgeon; b. NYC, Aug. 4, 1948; s. Maurice Berryl and Gloria Anita (Siff) Levien; m. Merril Ann Lirette Levien, Aug. 6, 1977; children: Michael, William, Rachel. BA, Johns Hopkins U., 1970; MD, Georgetown U., 1974. Diplomate Am. Bd. Surgery, Am. Bd. Med. Examiners. Resident Mt. Sinai Hosp., NYC, 1974—76; coordinated surg. resident U. Mass., 1976—79; surg. edn. coord. New Rochelle Hosp., NY, 1980—80; instr. surgery NY Med. Coll., Valhalla, 1980—83, asst. prof. surgery, 1983—90, clin. assoc. prof., 1990—91; cons. surgery Castle Point VA Hosp., 1980—90; clin. assoc. prof. surgery Med. Coll. Pa., Hahnemann U., 1991—; clin. prof. surgery Jefferson Med. Coll., 1996—; dir. surgery Episcopal Hosp.; chmn. surgery St. Vincent's Med. Ctr., Bridgeport, Conn., 2000—03; prof. clin. surgery NY Med. Coll., 2001—03; surgeon Houlton Regional Hosp., Maine, 2003—06; chmn. surgery St. Agnes Hosp., Balt., 2006—; pres. Balt. Acad. Surgery, 2009—. Contbr. articles to profl. jours. Mem. alumni admissions com. Johns Hopkins U., Balt., 1984—90. Mem.: AMA, ACS, Balt. Acad. Surgery, Phila. Acad. Surgery (v.p. 2000), Acad. Surgery Phila. (sec. 1998—99), Pa. Soc. Colon & Rectal Surgery (pres. 1997—98), Assn. Acad. Surgery, Soc. Critical Care Medicine, Am. Soc. Colon & Rectal Surgeons. Office: St Agnes Hosp 900 Caton Ave Box 207 Baltimore MD 21229 Home: 4404 Bedford Pl Baltimore MD 21208 Home Phone: 443-388-9681; Office Phone: 410-368-2745. Personal E-mail: dlevien@stagnes.org.

LEVI-FAICT, THIERRY W., orthopedist, surgeon; b. Paris, Mar. 22, 1957; s. Willy Edmond and Régine Sarah (Alshitz) Levi-Faict; m. Eusheva Cohen Levi-Faict, Oct. 8, 2010; children: Gabriel, Hanna, Alison, David, Sarah. MD, 1988; grad., U. René Descartes Paris V, 1991, U. France Pacifique, Noumea, New Caledonia, 1999, U. Paris V, 2004. Lic. physician Paris, 1988, cert. specialist orthop. surgery Paris, 1991, specialist forensic sciences Paris, 2000. Tchr., surgeon Assistance Publique Hosp., Paris, 1987—91; head surgeon Noumea Hosp., New Caledonia, 1991—99; head surgeon dept. orthop. surgery & forensics U. Hosp., Clermont-Ferrand, France, 1999—2004, prof., head surgeon dept. trauma surgery, 2004—, prof., 2005; expert UNO, 2007. Chief AAHP, 1988—91; health cons. French Nat. Senate, Paris, 1995, 99; dir. social medicine, violences study dept., criminology ward Nat. Health Svcs., Auvergne Country, 1999; law cons. U. Clermont I, Clermont-Ferrand, 1999. Contbr. articles to profl. jours. Comdr. French Army, 1984—2007. Decorated Légion d'Honneur Ortho Nat. Merite, Health Ministry. Mem.: OCF, SFA, CFCOT, ESKSA, SICOT, SOFCOT, Am. Assn. Forensic Sciences (corr.), Lion's Club, Grande Lodge Nat. Française (life; nat. officer, provincial officer, medal Many, such as: OAF medal, national nom). Jewish. Achievements include research in death investigations; non invasive surgery in orthopedic surgery, hip & knee surgery; professional secret and endangered patients law. Avocations: travel, golf, music, painting. Office: CHU de Clermont-Ferrand 58 rue Montalembert Clermont-Ferrand 63000 France Office Fax: 33 473 754 902. Personal E-mail: levifaict@mac.com. Business E-Mail: tfaict@chu-clermontferrand.fr.

LEVI-MONTALCINI, RITA, neurobiologist, researcher; b. Turin, Italy, Apr. 22, 1909; arrived in US, 1947, naturalized, 1956; d. Adamo Levi and Adele Montalcini, Adamo Levi and Adele Montalcini. MD, U. Turin, 1936. Asst. in neurology Inst. Anatomy, Neurology Clinic, Turin Sch. Medicine, 1936—37; rschr. Neurol. Inst. Brussels, 1939; with Allied Health Svc., Italy, 1944—45; resident, assoc. zoologist Washington U., St. Louis, 1947—51, assoc. prof., 1951—58, prof., 1958—77. Dir. neurobiology rsch. program Italian Nat. Rsch. Coun. (CNR), Rome, 1961—69, dir. Inst. Cell Biology, 1969—79; pres. Italian Nat. Commn. United World Colleges, 1993. Author: In Praise of Imperfection: My Life and Work, 1988. Recipient Louisa Gross Horwitz prize, Columbia U., 1983, Albert Lasker Basic Med. Rsch. award, 1986, Nobel prize in physiology/medicine, 1986, Nat. Medal Sci., 1987; named Senator for Life, Italian Parliament, 2001. Mem.: NAS, AAAS, Acad. Arts & Scis. Florence, European Acad. Scis., Arts & Letters, Nat. Acad. Sci. Italy, Belgian Royal Acad. Medicine, Harvey Soc., Nat. Acad. dei Lincei, Pontifical Acad. Scis., Tissue Culture Assn., Am. Assn. Anatomists, Soc. Devel. Biology. Office: European Brain Rsch Inst EBRI Via del Fosso di Fiorano 65 143 Rome RM Italy *

LEVIN, BERNARD, physician; b. Johannesburg, Apr. 1, 1942; came to U.S., 1966, naturalized, 1972; m. Ronelle DuBrow; children: Adam, Katherine. MB, BCh, U. Witwatersrand, 1964. Resident Presbyn. St. Lukes Hosp, Chgo., 1966-68; rsch. fellow U. Chgo., 1968-71, NIH fellow, 1971-72, instr. medicine, 1971-73, asst. prof. medicine, 1973-78, assoc. prof., 1979-84; prof. medicine, chmn. dept. gastro. oncology and digestive U. Tex. Med. Ctr./M.D. Anderson Hosp., Houston, 1984-94, Robert R. Herring prof., 1986-91, Ellen F. Knisely chair, 1991-94, v.p. for cancer prevention, 1994—2007, Betty Marcus chair, 1994—2007, prof. emeritus, 2007—. Mem. large bowel cancer working group Nat. Cancer Inst., 1984-85; cons. spl. study sect. Nat. Cancer Inst., 1976-84, chair nat. adv. com. on colorectal cancer, 1990-2008; chair Nat. Colorectal Cancer Roundtable, 1998-2007; chair World Gastroenterology Orgn. Found., 2006-11; interim dir. Vt. Cancer Ctr., 2008. Mem. editl. bd. Jour. Nat. Cancer Inst.; contbr. articles to profl. jours. Grantee USPHS, 1976-80, Melamid Found. grantee U. Chgo., 1978-83, NCI grantee, 1980-84, 1994; recipient award for sci. excellence in medicine Am. Italian Cancer Found., 2001, Janssen-Cilag Masters in Gastroenterology award Am. Gastroenterological Assn., 2005, Charles A. LeMaistre MD Outstanding Achievement award in cancer M.D. Anderson Cancer Ctr., 2007. Fellow: ACP; mem. AAAS, Am. Assn. Cancer Rsch., Am. Gastroenterol. Assn., Am. Soc. Clin. Oncology (chmn. cancer prevention com. 2002-04, award 2004). Jewish. Office: Apt 33A 2628 Broadway New York NY 10025 Personal E-mail: blevin2628@gmail.com.

LEVIN, FLORA, ophthalmologist, educator; b. Tallinn, Estonia, May 25, 1979; MD, Cornell U., 2004. Asst. prof. Yale U. Sch. Medicine, 2010—. Fellow: Am. Acad. Ophthalmology; mem.: Internat. Thyroid Eye Disease Soc., North Am. Neuro-Ophthalmology Soc. Office: 40 Temple St Ste 3B New Haven CT 06510 Personal E-mail: floralevin@gmail.com.

LEVIN, FRANCES R., psychiatrist, educator; b. Newton, Mass., Nov. 29, 1959; m. Howard Robert Levin; children: Allison Paula, Tamara Stephanie, Charles Jacob. BS magna cum laude, Brown U., 1981; MD, Cornell U., 1985. Diplomate Am. Bd. Psychiatry and Neurology. Kennedy Leavy prof. clin. psychiatry Columbia U.; assoc. attending psychiatry N.Y. Presbyn. Hosp.; resident in psychiatry N.Y. Hosp., Payne Whitney Clinic, NYC, 1985—89, asst. unit chief, 1988—89; rsch. and addiction psychiatry fellow Nat. Inst. on Drug Abuse, U. Md., Balt., 1989—90; asst prof. dept. psychiatry U. Md. Med. Ctr., 1990—92; asst. prof. clin. psychiatry dept. psychiatry Columbia U. Coll. Physicians and Surgeons, 1992—99, assoc. pro. clin. psychiatry dept. psychiatry, 1999—; asst. attending psychiatrist N.Y. Presbyn. Hosp., 1992—99, assc. attending psychiatrist, 1999—. Mem. numerous panels and coms.; presenter in field. Reviewer: numerous profl. jours., mem. editl. bd.: Am. Jour. on Addictions, 2000; contbr. over 100 articles to profl. jours. Recipient Connie Guion scholarship, 1983, AMA-ERF Rock Sleyster Meml. scholarship, 1985; numerous rsch. grants. Fellow: N.Y. Acad. Medicine, Am. Psychiat. Assn.; mem.: AMA, Group for Advancement of Psychiatry,

Coll. on Problems of Drug Dependence, Am. Soc. Addiction Medicine (N.E. region subcom. 1991), Assn. for Med. Edn. and Rsch. in Substance Abuse, Md. Psychiat. Soc. (com. on addiction 1989), Am. Acad. Addiction Psychiatrists (chair area dirs. 2001, bd. dirs. 2001), Sigma Xi, Phi Beta Kappa. Office: NYSPI Columbia Univ 1051 Riverside Unit 66 New York NY 10032 Office Phone: 212-543-5896. Business E-Mail: frl2@columbia.edu.

LEVIN, GRIGORY, orthopedist; b. Gorky, Sept. 6, 1939; MD, Gorky Med. Inst. named after S.M. Kirov, 1962; PhD, Saratov State Med. Acad.; DMS, Ctrl. Inst. Haematology. Head, dept. gravitation surgery and hemodialysis, head, Rsch. Inst. Burn Ctr. Nizhny Novgorod Rsch. Inst. Traumatology and Orthops. Pub. Health Ministry of Russian Fedn., 1984—; prof. HCC. Mem. All-Russia Sci. Bd. Burn Injury, Rsch. Coun. Nizhny Novgorod Rsch. Inst. Traumatology and Orthops.; councillor Nizhny Novgorod Med. Acad. Contbr. articles to numerous profl. publs. Recipient Hon. Sci. Worker award, Govt. Russian Fedn. Master: Nizhny Novgorod Assn. Specialists Hyperbaric Medicine; fellow: All-Russia Assn. Specialists Burn Injury; mem.: All-Russia Assn. Specialists Hyperbaric Medicine. Avocations: reading, computers. Office: Verhne-Volzhskaya Naberezhnaya Nizhny Novgorod Nizhegorodskaya 603155 Russia Office Fax: 7-831-4321758. Business E-Mail: levin@unn.ac.ru.

LEVIN, MARVIN EDGAR, physician; b. Terre Haute, Ind., Aug. 11, 1924; s. Benjamin A. and Bertha Levin; m. Barbara Yvonne Symes; 3 children. BA, Washington U., St. Louis, 1947; MD, Washington U., 1951. Diplomate Am. Bd. Internal Medicine. Intern Barnes Hosp., St. Louis, 1951-52, asst. resident in internal medicine, 1952-53; Nat. Polio Found. fellow in metabolism and endocrinology Sch. Medicine, Washington U., St. Louis, 1953-55; adj. prof. medicine Washington U. Sch. Medicine, St. Louis, 2009—, adj. prof., medicine endocrine, diabetes, metabolism, mem. admissions com. Vis. prof. endocrinology and diabetes People's Republic of China, 1982, Jakarta, Indonesia, Cairo, 92, Taipei, 94, Malvern, England, 96; bd. mem. Soc. Prof. Emeritus, Wash. U. St. Louis. Contbr. Levin and O'Neal's The Diabetic Foot, 7th edit., 2007, The Uncomplicated Guide to Diabetes Complication, 3d edit., 2009; articles to profl. jours., book chpts. Recipient Disting. Alumni award, Washington U., 1989, Arts and Scis. Disting. award, 1998. Fellow Soc. Vascular Medicine and Biology, Am. Coll. Endocrinology; mem. AMA, Am. Diabetes Assn. (nat. bd. dirs. 1984-86, chmn. publ. com. 1986-87, bd. dirs. Mo. chpt. 1987-93, editor in chief Clin. Diabetes 1988-93, co-editor Diabetes Spectrum 1988-93, Outstanding Clinician award 1979, Outstanding Physician Educator award 1991), Am. Dietetic Assn. (hon., Marvin E. Levin, MD Scholarship Program for rsch. in diabetic lower extremity disease named for him), St. Louis Clin. Diabetes Assn. (pres. 1965-66), Am. Thyroid Assn., Endocrine Soc., St. Louis Soc. Internal Medicine, St. Louis Internist Club (pres. 1972), Sigma Xi, Alpha Omega Alpha. Avocations: golf, art. Office: 732 Fairfield Lake Dr Town And Country MO 63017-5928 Office Phone: 314-469-6918. Personal E-mail: blevin0001@aol.com.

LEVIN, PETER J., hospital administrator, public health educator; b. NYC, Apr. 25, 1939; s. Sol and Kate (Gottlieb) L.; m. Judith S. Bolton, June 3, 1967; children: Edward, Gael, Karen. BA, Harvard U., 1961; M.P.H., Yale U., 1965; Sc.D., Johns Hopkins U., 1969. Asso. exec. dir. Bronx (N.Y.) Municipal Hosp. Center, 1970-72; exec. dir. New Haven Health Care, Inc., 1972-74; assoc. commr. Dept. Health, NYC, 1974-77; assoc. v.p. med. affairs, exec. dir. Stanford U. Hosp., 1977-81; asst. clin. prof. dept. epidemiology and pub. health Yale Med. Sch., 1973-75; assoc. clin. prof. dept. community health Albert Einstein Coll. Medicine, 1976-77; clin. assoc. prof. dept. family, community and preventive medicine Stanford U., 1978-81; dean Coll. Pub. Health, prof. health adminstrn. U. Okla., Oklahoma City, 1982-84; dean Coll. Pub. Health U. South Fla., Tampa, 1984-94, prof. pub. health, 1984-97. Vis. scholar Hoover Inst., Stanford U., 1994-95; health policy counsel to Senator Connie Mack U.S. Senate, 1997-2001; dean Sch. Pub. Health, SUNY, Albany, 2001-06 Chmn. Hosp. Cost Containment Bd., State of Fla., 1985-88, Fla. HMO Quality Care Interagy. Task Force, 1987, Hillsborough County Health Care Adv. Bd., 1990-92. Served with U.S. Army, 1961-65, USPHS, 1965-67.

LEVIN, VICTOR A., neurologist, oncologist, educator; b. Milw. MD, U. Wis., 1966. Diplomate Am. Bd. Psychiatry and Neurology. Intern medicine Washington U., St. Louis City Hosp., 1966—67; staff assoc. Lab. Chem. Pharmacology Nat. Cancer Inst., Bethesda, Md., 1967—69; resident neurology Mass. Gen. Hosp., Boston, 1969—72, NINDS spl. fellow dept. neurology, 1971—72; faculty Schs. Medicine and Pharmacy U. Calif., San Francisco, prof. dept. neurosurgery, pharm. chemistry and pharmocology, 1981, chief neuro-oncology svc. Brain Tumor Rsch. Ctr., 1977; prof. dept. neuro-oncology U. Tex. M.D. Anderson Cancer Ctr., Houston, 1988—, chair dept. neuro-oncology, 1988—99, dir. Brain Tumor Ctr., 1993—99. Co-founder Asilomar Conf. for Brain Tumor Rsch. and Therapy, 1975; exec. devel. program Rice U., Houston, 1990—91. Contbr. chapters to books, over 350 articles to profl. jours. Recipient medal med. faculty, Tokyo U., 1982, award in neuro-oncology, Farber Found., 1988, Heath Meml. award for cancer care, 1997. Mem.: Soc. for Neuro-Oncology (founding pres. 1995—97, Gold medal 2003), Nat. Brain Tumor Found., Am. Soc. Clin. Oncology, Am. Brain Tumor Assn., Am. Assn. Neurol. Surgeons (joint sect. on tumors), Am. Assn. for Cancer Rsch., Am. Acad. Neurology. Achievements include research in defining pharmacokinetics of anticancer drugs; development of drug and radiation combination therapies for brain tumors. Office: Victor A Levin MD Neuro Oncology Unit 431 UT MD Anderson Cancer Ctr PO Box 301402 Houston TX 77230-1402 Office Phone: 713-792-8297.

LEVIN, WARREN MAYER, family practice physician; b. Phila., Aug. 20, 1932; s. Israel and Clara Deborah (Cherim) L.; m. Marsha Ann Beinstein, Dec. 24, 1955 (div. 1975); children: Beth Ann, Julie Ruth; m. Frances Susan Teitler, Mar. 20, 1982; 1 child, Erika Alexandra. BS, Ursinus Coll., 1952; MD, Jefferson Med. Coll., 1956. Diplomate Am. Bd. Family Practice, 1973, 80, 87, 94, Am. Bd. Bariatric Medicine, 1973, Am. Bd. Environ. Medicine, 1994, Am. Bd. Chelation Therapy, 1973, Internat. Bd. Advanced Longevity Medicine, 2000, Am. Bd. Clin. Med. Toxicology, 1990; cert. homeopath, 2004. Intern US Naval Hosp., Newport, RI, 1956-57; pvt. practice SI, NY, 1959-74; founder, med. dir. Heights Holistic Health Ctr., Bklyn., 1974-79, World Health Med. Group, NYC, 1979-94; physician Physicians for Complementary Medicine, NYC, 1994-97, Comprehensive Med. Svcs., NYC, 1998—2000, Americas Med. Ctr., Ridgefield, Conn., 1998—2000; founder, med. dir. Integrative Medicine Conn., Wilton, 2001—03, with NYC office, 2001—04; physician Issels Med. Ctr., Phoenix, 2004—05, pvt. practice, Scottsdale, Ariz., 2005—06, Vienna, Va., 2006—. Mem. bd. examiners Internat. Bd. Advanced Longevity Medicine, 1998—2000. Contbr. to books Nutrition in Pregnancy, 1981, to books Challenging Orthodoxy, 1991, to books Alternative Medicine, 1994, to books The Cholesterol Hoax, 1998, to books Whole Body Dentistry, 1999, to books Experts of Lyme Disease, 2008; author: (book) Foreword to Clinical Chemistry Nutrition, 1988. Bd. govs. Internat. Coll. Applied Nutrition, 1974-76; chmn. med. adv. bd. Survive Until a Cure, advisory coun.-Chemical Awareness Rsch. Educ. & Solutions; prin. investigator-A Study on Use of Human Growth Hormone. Lt. M.C., USNR ret. Recipient Disting. Pioneer in Alternative Medicine award Found. for Advancement of Innovative Medicine Fund, 1995, Presdl. Commendation, Am. Coll. for Advancement in Medicine, 1995. Fellow: Am. Acad. Family Pactice, Am. Coll Nutrition, Am. Acad. Environ. Medicine (bd. dirs. 2003); mem.: Nat. Autism Assn. (chmn. biomed. edn. Nova chpt.), Am. Soc. Bariatric Medicine (v.p. 1980—82), Am. Coll. Advancement Medicine (bd. dirs. 1976—80, treas. 1980). Avocations: sailing, swimming. Home: 11743 English Mill Ct Oakton VA 22124 Office Phone: 703-255-0313. Personal E-mail: vadrwmlevin@aol.com. Business E-Mail: info@warrenmlevinmd.org.

LEVINE, ALAN, health facilities company executive; BS in Health Edn. & Cmty. Health, U. Fla., Gainesville, MS in Health Sci., MBA. COO Bayonet Point/Hudson Med. Ctr., Hudson, Fla.; v.p. ops. Columbia Regional Med. Ctrs., Fla.; COO Tallahassee Cmty. Hospitals, Fla.; CEO Doctors' Meml. Hosp., Perry, Fla.; dep. chief of staff, sr. health policy advisor to Gov. Jeb Bush State of Fla., Tallahassee; CEO South Bay Hosp., Sun City Center, Fla., 2000—03; sec. Fla. Agency Health Care Adminstrn., 2004—06; pres., CEO Broward Health, Fla., 2006—08; sec. La. Dept. Health & Hospitals, Baton Rouge, 2008—10; sr. v.p. health devel. ops. & govt. rels. Health Mgmt. Associates, Inc., Naples, Fla., 2010—. Named a Up and Comer in American Healthcare, Modern Healthcare mag., 2005, Heavy Hitter in Health Care, South Fla. Bus. Jour., 2007. Office: Health Management Associates Inc 5811 Pelican Bay Blvd Ste 500 Naples FL 34108 Office Phone: 239-598-3131. *

LEVINE, ARTHUR SAMUEL, pediatric hematologist, dean, educator, oncologist, researcher; b. Cleve., Nov. 1, 1936; s. David Alvin and Sarah Ethel (Rubinstein) L.; m. Ruth Eleanor Rubin, Oct. 14, 1959; children: Amy Elizabeth, Raleigh Hannah, Jennifer Leah. AB, Columbia U., 1958; MD, Chgo. Med. Sch., 1964. Diplomate Am. Bd. Pediatrics, Am. Bd. Pediatric Hematology-Oncology. Intern in pediatrics U. Minn., Mpls., 1964-65, resident in pediatrics, 1965-66, USPHS fellow in hematology and genetics, 1966-67; capt. USPHS, 1967-92, rear adm., asst. surgeon gen., 1992-98; clin. assoc. div. cancer treatment Nat. Cancer Inst., Bethesda, Md., 1967-69, sr. staff fellow, 1969-70, sr. investigator, 1970-73, head sect. infectious disease, pediatric oncology br., 1973-75, chief pediatric oncology br., 1975-82; sci. dir. Nat. Inst. Child Health and Human Devel., Bethesda, 1982-98; sr. vice chancellor for health scis., dean U. Pitts. Sch. Medicine, 1998—, prof. medicine and molecular genetics and biochemistry, 1998—. Clin. prof. medicine and pediatrics Georgetown U., Washington, 1975-98; clin. prof. pediatrics Uniformed Svcs. U. Health Scis., Bethesda, 1983-98; vis. prof. Cold Harbor Spring Lab., N.Y., 1973, Benares Hindu U., India, 1975, U. Minn., 1974, Hebrew U., Israel, 1981, U. Bologna, 1989, Northwestern U., 1992, Moscow State U., 1996; Karon meml. lectr. U. So. Calif., 1983; Seham lectr. U. Minn., 1983; Harris lectr. Va. Commonwealth U., 1995; Markey lectr. Wash. U., 1996; Green lectr. European Molecular Biology Lab. Heidelberg, 1997; Walter Rubin meml. lectr. Drexel U., 2003; John Conley lectr. in med. ethics Am. Acad. Otolaryngology, 2003; vis. dean U. Mich., 2003. Author: Cancer in the Young, 1982; editor-in-chief The New Biologist, 1989-92; contbr. articles to profl. jours. Recipient Disting. Alumnus award Chgo. Med. Sch., 1972, NIH Dir.'s award, 1984, Meritorious Svc. award USPHS, 1987, Disting. Svc. award, 1991, Surgeon Gen.'s Exemplary Svc. award, 1993. Mem. AAAS, Am. Soc. Clin. Investigation, Soc. Pediatric Research, Am. Assn. Cancer Research, Am. Soc. Hematology, Am. Soc. Clin. Oncology, Am. Fedn. Clin. Research, Am. Soc. Microbiology, Am. Soc. Pediatric Hematology/Oncology, Alpha Omega Alpha. Office: U Pittsburgh 3550 Terrace St Pittsburgh PA 15261-0001 Home Phone: 412-687-4007; Office Phone: 412-648-8975. Business E-Mail: alevine@hs.pitt.edu. *

LEVINE, HARVEY DAVIS, retired dentist; b. Bklyn., Dec. 22, 1920; s. William and Minnie Levine; m. Sylvia Shulman, Aug. 17, 1945; children: James Daniel, Matthew Paul, Martin Andrew. BA, Bklyn Coll., 1944; DDS, NYU, NYC, 1945. Pvt. practice, NYC, 1946—87. Sr. clin. asst. dept. dentistry Poly. Hosp., NYC, 1946—52; instr. crown and bridge dept. NYU Coll. Dentistry, NYC, 1946—52. Photographer (exhibitions) NY Scenes, Fla. Maritime Mus. Lt. USNR, 1945—46, lt. USNR, 1952—54. Mem.: ADA, First Dist. Dental Soc., Omicron Kappa Upsilon. Avocations: kayaking, sailing, canoeing, boat building. Home: 3410 Winding Oaks Dr Longboat Key FL 34228-4125

LEVINE, JAMES, biotechnology company executive; BA in Economics, Brandeis U., Waltham, Mass.; MBA in Fin., U. Pa., Phila. With Indsl. Economics, Inc., Cambridge, Mass., Lehman Brothers, Inc., NYC; mng. dir. energy group Goldman Sachs & Co., London, mng. dir. power and utilities group NYC; exec. v.p., CFO Verenium, Corp., San Diego, 2009—11, pres., CEO, 2011—. Office: Verenium Corp 4955 Directors Pl San Diego CA 92121 Office Phone: 858-431-8500. *

LEVINE, JEREMIAH, gastroenterologist, educator; MD, Harvard Coll., 1980. Diplomate Am. Bd. Pediatrics, Am. Bd. Pediatrics-pediatric gastroenterology. Resident in pediat. Albert Einstein Coll. Med. Ctr., Brinx, NY, 1981—83; fellow in pediatric gastroenterology Schneider Children's Hosp., Boston, 1983—85; prof. in pediat. Albert Einstein Coll. Office: Schneider Children's Hospital 26901 76th Ave New Hyde Park NY 11040-1433 Office Phone: 718-470-3000.

LEVINE, JEROME, retired psychiatrist, educator; b. NYC, July 10, 1934; s. Abraham and Sadie (Glowatz) L.; children: Ross W., Lynn R., Andrew R. BA, U. Buffalo, 1954, MD, 1958. Intern, then psychiat. resident E.J. Meyer Meml. Hosp., Buffalo, 1958-61; sr. psychiat. resident St. Elizabeth's Hosp., Washington, 1961-62; staff psychiatrist USPHS Hosp., Lexington, Ky., 1962-64; research psychiatrist, asst. chief psychopharmacology research br. NIMH, 1964-67, chief of br., 1967-81, chief pharmacologic and somatic treatments research br., 1981-84; research prof. psychiatry U. Md. Sch. Medicine, Balt., 1985-94; dep. dir. Nathan Kline Inst. for Psychiat. Rsch., Orangeburg, NY, 1994—2009; rsch. prof. psychiatry NYU, 1994—2009. Instr. psychiatry Johns Hopkins Med. Sch., 1964-72; vis. prof. U. Pisa, Italy, 1977 Author books and papers on psychopharmacology, clin. trial methodology, somatic treatment assessment for psychiat. disorders. Recipient Hofheimer Rsch. prize, Am. Psychiat. Assn., 1970. Mem. Am. Coll. Neuropsychopharmacology. Home: 15 Stony Hollow Chappaqua NY 10514-2014 Personal E-mail: jeromelevine@gmail.com.

LEVINE, JOSEPH, cardiac electrophysiologist; Grad., U. Rochester. Diplomate Am. Bd. of Internal Medicine, Am. Bd. of Internal Medicine-cardiovasc. disease, Am. Bd. of Internal Medicine-cardiac electrophysiology. Intern Yale-New Haven Hosp., resident; fellow Johns Hopkins Hosp.; dir. Arrhythmia and Pacemaker ctr. St. Francis Hosp.; co-dir. clin. electrophysiology lab. John's Hopkins Hosp.; dir. electrophysiology lab. Mercy Med. Ctr.; with Good Samaritan Hosp., Huntington Hosp.; asst. prof. medicine cardiology divsn. Johns Hopkins Univ. Named one of Best Doctors, New York Mag., Best Doctors in America, Castle Connolly. Office: St. Francis Hospital Heart Center 100 Port Washington Blvd Roslyn NY 11576 Office Phone: 516-562-6646. Office Fax: 516-562-6671.

LEVINE, MACY IRVING, physician; b. Johnstown, Pa., May 19, 1920; s. Elliott B. and Ida (Leuin) L.; m. Evelyn B. Levine, June 28, 1948 (dec. July 1996); children: Alan, Amy, Paul, Robert. BS, U. Pitts., 1940, MD, 1943. Diplomate Am. Bd. Internal Medicine, Am. Bd. Internal Medicine and Allergy. Intern U. Pitts. Med. Ctr., 1944; resident in allergy VA Hosp., Aspinwall, Pa., 1947-48, resident in medicine, 1948-49; fellow in medicine Lahey Clinic, Boston, 1950-51; USPHS postdoctoral fellow in medicine Peter Bent Brigham Hosp.-Harvard Med. Sch., Boston, 1951-52; pvt. practice Pitts., 1952—2008. Clin. prof. medicine U. Pitts. Sch. Medicine. Editor: Monograph on Insect Allergy, 4th edit., 2003; editor Bull. of the Allegheny County Med. Soc., 1975-86, Pitt Medicine Med. Alumni Assn., U. Pitts., 1987-99; contbr. more than 70 articles to profl. jours. Bd. dirs. Self Help Group Network, 1989-95, B'nai Israel Congregation, Pitts., 1965-71, Hebrew Free Loan Assn. Pitts., 1980—. Capt. U.S. Army, 1944-46, PTO. Recipient Disting. Svc. award Am. Acad. Allergy and Immunology, 1987, Frederick M. Jacob, M.D. Physician Merit award for Outstanding Svc. Allegheny County Med. Soc., 1988. Fellow Am. Acad. Allergy, Asthma and Immunology (v.p. 1982-83, Outstanding Vol. Clin. Faculty award 1996), Pa. Allergy Assn. (pres. 1970-71, Spl. Recognition award 1989), fellow, ACP; mem. Pitts. Allergy Soc. (pres. 1959-61), U. Pitts. Med. Alumni Assn. (pres. 1976-77), U. Pitts. Alumni Assn. (pres. 1984-85). Avocations: tennis, bridge. Home: 220 N Dithridge St Apt 400 Pittsburgh PA 15213-1421 Home Phone: 412-682-4737.

LEVINE, MARK A., endocrinologist; BA, Brandeis U., 1973; MD, Harvard Med. Sch., 1977. Chief molecular & clinical nutrition section Nat. Inst. Diabetes & Digestive & Kidney Diseases. Office: NIH Bldg 10 Rm 4D52 10 Center Dr Bethesda MD 20892 Office Phone: 301-402-5588. Office Fax: 301-402-6436. E-mail: markl@intra.niddk.nih.gov.

LEVINE, MICHAEL ALAN ALAN, internist, endocrinologist, educator; b. NYC, June 11, 1950; s. Victor Richard and Rita Georgeanna (Ginsberg) L.; m. Barbara Claire Holtz, Apr. 15, 1973; children: Sara, Elizabeth. AB, Rutgers U., 1972; MD, Hahnemann U., 1976. Diplomate Nat. Bd. Med. Examiners, Am. Bd. Internal Medicine, Am. Bd. Endocrinology and Metabolism. Intern in Medicine Johns Hopkins Hosp., Balt., 1976-77, resident in Medicine, 1977-78, sr. resident in Medicine, 1978-79; clin. assoc. NIH, Bethesda, Md., 1979-82, mem. med. staff fellow in Genetics, 1981-82; asst. prof. Medicine Johns Hopkins U., Balt., 1982-86, assoc. prof. Medicine, 1986-92, assoc. prof. Pathology, 1989-92, assoc. prof. Environ. Health, 1991, prof. Medicine and Pathology, 1992—, prof. pediatrics, dir. pediatric endocrinology, 1998—. Founding exec. editor Jour. of Clin. and Translational Sci.; mem. exec. bd. Jour. of Clin. Endocrinology and Metabolism. Reviewer Jour. of Clin. Investigation, New Eng. Jour. of medicine, Endocrinology, Jour. Clin. Endocrinology and Metabolism, Medicine, 1982—; contbr. chpts. to books, 190 articles to profl. jours. Named one of Top Doctors, Phila. Mag., 2010—. Mem. Am. Fedn. Clin. Rsch., Am. Soc. for Bone and Mineral Rsch., The Endocrine Soc., Am. Soc. for Clin. Investigation, Lawson Wilkens Pediatric Endocrine Soc., Assn. of Osteobiology, The Interurban Clin. Club. Jewish. Avocations: film, photography. Home: 2821 Fairmount Blvd Cleveland Heights OH 44118-4019 E-mail: mlevine@jhmi.edu.

LEVINE, RICHARD A., physician; b. Miami Beach, Fla., July 6, 1953; s. Morris Joseph and Sybil R. (Panossian) L.; m. Lidia Foffo; children: Mitchell, Kimberly, David. BS cum laude in zoology, U. Fla., 1975; MD, Universita di Roma, Italy, 1982. Diplomate Am. Bd. Internal Medicine, Am. Bd. Geriatric Medicine; cert. sr. aviation med. examiner FAA. Resident in internal medicine U. Va. Affiliated Hosps., Roanoke-Salem, Va., 1983-86; pvt. practice Boca Raton, Fla., 1987—. Lectr. in field. Dir. med. edn. com. Am. Cancer Soc., Boca Raton, 1990; local coord. 1st pilot program of Put Prevention Into Practice (partnership with ACP and Office of Disease Prevention and Health Promotion, Washington), 1994. Named one of Castle Connolly Best Drs., 2008—11. Fellow ACP; mem. AMA, Fla. Med. Assn., Palm Beach County Med. Soc. (bd. dirs. 1994), Va. Med. Soc. Avocations: marine biology, bicycling, music, travel. Office: 7280 W Palmetto Park Rd Ste 205 Boca Raton FL 33433 Office Phone: 561-368-0191. Business E-Mail: drlevine@priorityconciergemd.com.

LEVINE, ROBERT JOHN, physician, researcher; b. NYC, Dec. 29, 1934; s. Benjamin Bernard and Ruth Florence (Schwartz) L.; m. Jeralea Fooshee Hesse, Nov. 28, 1987; children from previous marriage: John Graham, Elizabeth Braun; stepchildren: Stephen B. Hesse, Katherine F. Hesse. Student, Duke U., 1951—54; MD with distinction, George Washington U., 1958. Diplomate Am. Bd. Internal Medicine. Med. house officer Peter Bent Brigham Hosp., Boston, 1958-59, asst. resident in medicine, 1959-60; clin. assoc. Nat. Heart Inst., Bethesda, Md., 1960-62, investigator, 1963-64; chief med. resident VA Hosp., West Haven, Conn., 1962-63; mem. faculty depts. medicine and pharmacology Yale U., New Haven, 1964-73, chief sect. clin. pharmacology, 1966-74, prof. medicine, lectr. pharmacology, 1973—, co-chair exec. com. interdisciplinary program bioethics, 1999—2005; mem. med. staff Yale-New Haven Med. Ctr., 1964-68, attending physician, 1968—; co-dir. Ctr. Interdisciplinary Rsch. on

AIDS, Law, Policy and Ethics Core, 1997—2000, dir., 1997—; co-dir. Yale U. Interdisciplinary Ctr. Bioethics, 2005—07, sr. fellow, 2008—, chair exec. com., 2011—. Mem. Conn. Adv. Com. on Foods and Drugs, 1967-82, sec. 1969-71, chmn., 1971-73; mem. adv. com. AIDS program U.S. HHS, 1989-95; spl. cons. Nat. Commn. Protection Human Subjects of Biomed. and Behavioral Rsch., 1974-78; bd. dirs. Medicine in the Pub. Interest, Inc., 1976-2002, sec., 1983-2002; mem. ethics subcom. of dir.'s adv. com. Ctrs. Disease Control and Prevention, 1997-2001, 05-08, cons., 2008-; mem. adv. com. Nat. Human Rsch. Protections, 2000-02; dir. Donaghue Initiative in Biomed. and Behavioral Rsch. Ethics, 2003-07. Author: Ethics and Regulation of Clinical Research, 1981, 2nd edit., 1986; co-author: The Belmont Report; editor Clin. Rsch., 1971-76, IRB: Rev. Human Subjects Rsch., 1978-2000, chairperson editl. bd., 2000—; contbr. numerous articles to profl. jours. Mem. Conn. Humanities Coun., 1983-89, chmn. 1988-89, Coun. Internat. Orgn. Med. Scis., co-chmn. steering com. revision internat. ethical guidelines for biomed. rsch. involving human subjects, 1991-93, chmn., 1998-02; chair working group for revision of Declaration of Helsinki, World Med. Assn., 1998-99, Pan Am. Health Orgn.; adv. bd. mem. Internat. Bioethics, 2000-04. Recipient Outstanding Achievement medal, Office Human Rsch. Protection US Dept. Health and Human Svcs., 2004, Lifetime award Excellence in Human Rsch. Protection, Health Improvement Inst., 2004, Lifetime Achievement award Excellence in Rsch. Ethics, Pub. Responsibility in Medicine and Rsch., 2005, Disting. Alumni Scholar award, George Washington U., 2007—08, Spl. Recognition award, Acad. Pharmaceutical Physicians & Investigators; grantee Multiple rsch. grants. Fellow ACP, The Hastings Ctr., AAAS (coun. del. 1987-91); mem. Am. Soc. Clin. Investigation, Am. Soc. Clin. Pharmacology and Therapeutics (bd. dirs. 1981-85), Am. Fedn. Clin. Rsch. (nat. coun. 1967-76, exec. com. 1971-76), Am. Soc. Pharmacology and Exptl. Therapeutics (exec. com. 1974-77), Am. Soc. Law, Medicine and Ethics (bd. dirs. 1986-96, pres. 1989-90, 94-95), Pan Am. Health Orgn. (internat. bioethics adv. bd. 2000-03), Pub. Responsibility in Medicine and Rsch. (bd. dirs. 1984—, v.p. 2007—09), Soc. for Bioethics Consultation (bd. dirs. 1988-94), Sigma Xi, Alpha Omega Alpha. Office: Yale Univ Interdisciplinary Ctr Bioethics PO Box 208293 New Haven CT 06520-8293 Personal E-mail: levinerj@sbcglobal.net.

LEVINE, SELWYN E., pulmonologist; Attended, NYU Sch. Medicine, 1982. Lic. NJ, diplomate Am. Bd. Internal Medicine-pulmonary disease, Am. Bd. Internal Medicine. Resident in internal medicine Bellevue hosp. NYU Med. Ctr., 1983—85; fellow in pulmonary disease Albert Einstein Coll. Medicine, Bronx, 1985—87; hosp. affiliation include Englewood Hosp. and Med. Ctr.; pulmonologist Holy Name Med. Ctr. Office: Holy Name Medical Center 200 Grand Ave Ste 102 Englewood NJ 07631 Office Phone: 201-871-3636. Office Fax: 201-871-2286.

LEVINE, WILLIAM N., sport medicine physician; BA in Human Biology, Stanford U., 1986; MD, Case Western Reserve U. Sch. of Medicine, Cleveland Ohio, 1990. Cert. orthopaedic surgery 1999. Intern Beth Israel Hosp., 1990—91, Harvard Med. Sch., 1990—91; resident Tufts Univ. Med. Sch., 1991—94, New England Med. Ctr., 1991—94, chief resident, 1994—95; fellow shoulder surgery Columbia Shoulder Svc., 1995—96, Columbia-Presbyterian Med. Ctr., 1995—96; fellow sports medicine Univ. of Maryland, 1997—98. Mem.: AMA, Am. Orthopaedic Assn. (AOA), Arthroscopy Assn. of N. America, Am. Shoulder and Elbow Surgeons (ASES), Am. Coll. of Sports Medicine, Am. Orthopaedic Soc. For Sports Medicine, Am. Acad. of Orthopaedic Surgeons (AAOS), The NY Acad. of Medicine, Am. Bd. of Orthopaedic Surgery, Calif. Med. Soc., San Diego Med. Soc. Office: Columbia University Medical Center NewYork-Presbyterian 622 West 168 St PH11-Center New York NY 10032 Office Phone: 212-305-0762, 212-305-4565.

LEVINE, ZACHARY THOMAS, neurosurgeon; b. New Haven, Conn., July 30, 1967; s. Stephen Maxwell Levine, Rhea JC Levine; m. Jennifer Avellino, Aug. 18, 1991; children: Julia, Leah. AB Biology, Dartmouth Coll., 1993. Diplomate Board Medical Examiners 1996, cert. neurological surgery 2004. Resident George Washington U. Med. Ctr., Washington, 1994—99, chief resident, 1999—2000; dir. functional neurosurgery Washington Hosp. Ctr., DC, 2004. Rsch. com. Parkinson's Found., Nat. Capital Area, Fairfax, 2001—. Mem.: Am. Assn. Neurol. Surgeons (assoc.). Achievements include invention of method of cellular transplantation into the brain, 1992. Avocations: sailing, fly fishing, skiing, reading, cooking. Office: Washington Brain & Spine Inst 4927 Auburn Ave Bethesda MD 20814 Home Phone: 301-263-1003; Office Phone: 301-718-9611. Personal E-mail: zlevine@brainsurgery.com. Business E-Mail: info@brainsurgery.com.

LEVINSON, ARNOLD I., dean; b. Balt., Nov. 15, 1944; MD, U. Md., 1969. Chief clin. immunology lab. Walter Reed Army Med. Ctr., 1975—78; prof. medicine and neurology, chief allergy & immunology U. Pa., 1978—2009, assoc. dean rsch. Sch. Medicine, 2009—. Pres. Clin. Immunology Soc., 2002—03; chair Am. Bd. Allergy and Immunology, 1998—99. Recipient Leonard Berwick Tchg. award, U. Pa. Sch. Medicine, Donald Martin Tchg. Svc. award. Fellow: Am. Acad. Allergy, Asthma and Immunology (bd. dirs. 2003—07, Disting. Svc. award); mem.: Am. Soc. Investigation, John Morgan Soc., Alpha Omega Alpha. Avocations: golf, guitar, singing. Home: 115 Pine Tree Rd Radnor PA 19087

LEVINSON, BERNARD, psychiatrist; b. Johannesburg, Gauteng, South Africa, May 5, 1926; m. Sheila Levinson, Jan. 22, 1980. MB, B, Ch., DPM, Witwatersrand U., Johannesburg, 1946—51; diploma in psychol. medicine, South African Med. Coun., 1960. Author: Learning to Love, Waiting on the Edge, (novels) hanging Machine, 2000, Still Mind Strong Heart, 2001. Pvt. South African M.C., 1943—45. Mem.: Med. Art Soc. (founding chmn. 1985—2005). Avocation: sculpting. Personal E-mail: levinson@iburst.co.za.

LEVINSON, DANIEL RONALD, federal agency administrator, lawyer; b. Bklyn., Mar. 24, 1949; s. Gerald Sam and Risha Rose (Waxer) Levinson; m. Luna Frances Lambert, Sept. 13, 1980; children: Luna Claire, Hannah Louise. AB, U. So. Calif., 1971; JD, Georgetown U., 1974; LLM, George Washington U., 1977. Bar: NY 1975, Calif. 1976, DC 1976, US Supreme Ct. 1978; cert. fraud examiner. Law clk. appellate divsn. NY Supreme Ct., Bklyn., 1974-76; assoc. McGuiness & Williams, Washington, 1977-81, ptnr., 1982-83; dep. gen. counsel US Office Pers. Mgmt. (OPM), 1983-85; gen. counsel US Consumer Product Safety Commn., 1985-86; chmn. US Merit Sys. Protection Bd., 1986-93; of counsel Shaw Bransford & O'Rourke, Washington, 1993-94; chief of staff rep. Bob Barr US House of Reps., 1995-98; prin. Law Offices of Daniel R. Levinson, Washington, 1998—2000; insp. gen. GSA, 2001—05; acting insp. gen. US Dept. Health & Human Services, 2004—05, insp. gen., 2005—. Adj. lectr. American U., Washington, 1981—82, Cath. U. American, Washington, 1982; mem. Govt. Accountability and Transparency Bd. Editor-in-chief Jour. Pub. Inquiry, 2002—05; contbr. articles to profl. jours. Bd. dirs. Washington Hebrew Congregation, 1993—96. Mem.: Adminstrv. Conf. US (liaison). Office: US Dept Health and Human Services 200 Independence Ave SW Washington DC 20201 Office Phone: 202-619-3148. Business E-Mail: paffairs@oig.hhs.gov.

LEVINSON, HARRY, psychologist, educator; b. Port Jervis, NY, Jan. 16, 1922; s. David and Gussie (Nudell) L.; m. Roberta Freiman, Jan. 11, 1946 (div. June 1972); children— Marc Richard, Kathy, Anne, Brian Thomas; m. Miriam Lewis, Nov. 23, 1990. BS, Emporia State U., Kans., 1943, MS, 1946; PhD, U. Kans., 1952; DHL (hon.), Mass. Sch. Profl. Psychology, 2004. Coordinator profl. edn. Topeka State Hosp., 1950-53, psychologist, 1954-55; dir. div. indsl. mental health Menninger Found., Topeka, 1955-68; vis. prof. MIT, 1961-62, U. Kans. Bus. Sch., 1967, Texas A&M U., 1976; Thomas Henry Carroll-Ford Found. distinguished vis. prof. Harvard Grad. Sch. Bus., Boston, 1968-72; adj. prof. Coll. Bus. Administrn., Boston U., 1972-74; lectr. Harvard Med. Sch., 1972-85; adj. prof. Pace U., 1972-83; clin. prof. psychology Harvard Med. Sch., 1985-92, emeritus prof., 1992—; head sect. orgnl. mental health Mass. Mental Health Ctr., 1983-92; pres. The Levinson Inst., 1968-91, chmn. bd., 1991—97. Mem. Am. Bd. Profl. Psychology, 1972-80, chmn., 1978-80; Ford Found. prof. Mathur Inst., Jaipur India, 1974; conducted internat. course on social psychiatry Finnish Govt. Inst., 1979. Author: Emotional Health In the World of Work, 1964, Executive Stress, 1970, The Exceptional Executive (McKinsey Found. and Acad. Mgmt. awards), 1968 (James A. Hamilton Hosp. Adminstrs. Book award), Organizational Diagnosis, 1971, The Great Jackass Fallacy, 1973, Psychological Man, 1976, Casebook for Psychological Man; (with S. Rosenthal) CEO: Corporate Leadership in Action (Am. Coll. Health Care Adminstrs. Book award 1986), 1984, Ready, Fire, Aim, 1986, Designing and Managing Your Career, 1989, Career Mastery, 1992, Organizational Assessment, 2002, Psychology of Leadership, 2006, It's Me-Harry, 2008, Consulting Psychology, 2009. Chmn. Kans. adv. com. U.S. Civil Rights Commn., 1962-68; chmn. Topeka Human Relations Commn., 1967-68. Served with F.A. AUS, 1944-46. Recipient Perry Rohrer Cons. Psychology Practice award, 1984, Career award Mass. Psychol. Assn., 1985, Disting. Svc. award Soc. Consulting Psychology, 2004, First award Soc. Psychologists in Mgmt.; Eminent scholar in bus. Fla. Atlantic U., 1995. Fellow APA (award for disting. profl. contbn. to knowledge 1992, Gold medal for life achievement in the application of psychology 2000), Am. Psychol. Found. Address: 4889 Pineview Cir Delray Beach FL 33445-4318 Personal E-mail: hlevinson@bellsouth.net.

LEVINSON, JOSEPH E., retired internist, rheumatologist, educator; b. Cin., Apr. 7, 1920; s. Samuel W. and Rebecca (Lewin) L.; m. Mimi Freiberg, Mar. 21, 1945 (dec. Apr. 1992); children: Steven Henry, Henry Samuel (dec.), Richard Peter (dec.); m. Carol Weihl, Oct. 10, 1993 (dec. Mar. 1999); m. Sophia Ralson, Nov. 10, 2001. Student, Columbia U., NYC, 1937-40; BA, Stanford U., Calif., 1941; MD, U. Cin., 1944. Clin. and rsch. fellow in medicine Harvard U./Mass. Gen. Hosp., Boston, 1950-52; instr. medicine U. Cin., 1953-61, assoc. prof. medicine, 1961-73, prof. medicine and pediatrics, 1973-85, dir. divsn. pediatric rheumatology, 1975-86, Cin. Children's Hosp. Med. Ctr.; assoc. dir. Multipurpose Arthritis Ctr. U. Cin., 1978-82, prof. emeritus medicine and pediatrics, 1985—; med. sec. Cin. Gen. Hosp. & Jewish Hosp., 1944—50. Dir. arthritis tchg. svc. Cin. Gen. Hosp., 1960-64. Contbr. chapters to books, articles to profl. jours. Bd. dirs. Seven Hills Sch., Cin., 1993-2001, Cancer Family Care, Cin., Anthem Found. of Ohio, 1999-2004, Friends of the Spl. Treatment Ctr.; bd. dirs. Planned Parenthood S.W. Ohio Region, 2000— Master Am. Coll. Rheumatology Avocations: tennis, horse and mule wilderness pack trips, travel. Office: Cin Children's Hosp Med Ctr 3333 Burnet Ave Cincinnati OH 45229-3026 Home: Apt 802 2121 Alpine Pl Cincinnati OH 45206-3697

LEVINSON, WENDY S., internist, medical association administrator; b. Toronto; BS, U. Toronto; MD, McMaster U. Faculty Oreg. Health Sci. U., U. Chgo.; prof. U. Toronto, 2001—, Sir John and Lady Eaton Prof., chair, dept. medicine, 2004—; physician in chief Sunnybrook Health Sciences Centre, Toronto. Contbg. editor JAMA. Mem.: Soc. Gen. Internal Medicine (past pres., Robert J. Glaser award 2009), American Bd. Internal Medicine (chair elect 2008—09, chair 2010—11). Office: Dept Medicine Suire Rfe 3-805 190 Elizabeth St Toronto ON M5G 2C4 Canada

LEVITT, JERRY DAVID, medical educator; b. Phila., 1941; s. Abraham and Nettie L.; m. Julie Meranze, 1967; children: Rachel, Daniel, Gabriel. BA, U. Pa., 1962, MD, 1966. Diplomate Am. Bd. Anesthesiology; lic. physician, Pa., Maine. Intern Mt. Sinai Hosp., NYC, 1966—67; resident in anesthesia U. Pa. Hosp., Phila., 1967—69, rsch. fellow, 1971—72; instr. anesthesia U. Pa., Phila., 1972—73, asst. prof. anesthesia, 1973—82; assoc. prof. anesthesiology Med. Coll. Pa. Hahnemann Sch. Medicine, Phila., 1982—2002, Drexel U. Coll. of Medicine, Phila., 2002—. Author: (with others) Basic Pharmacology in Medicine, 1990; contbr. articles to profl. jours. With USPHS, 1969-71. Avocations: photography, sailing, music, motorcycles. Office: Hahnemann Univ Hosp Broad & Vine Sts Philadelphia PA 19102 Office Phone: 215-762-3544.

LEVITT, MARC AARON, pediatrician, director; b. Bklyn., June 6, 1967; MD, Albert Einstein Coll. Medicine, 1993; BA, U. Pa., 1989. Assoc. dir. Cin. Children's Hosp. Colorectal Ctr., 2005—. Office: 3333 Burnet Ave MLC 2023 Cincinnati OH 45229 Office Fax: 513-636-3248. Business E-Mail: tori.hiudt@cchmc.org.

LEVITT, MIRIAM, pediatrician; b. Lampertheim, Germany, June 10, 1946; came to U.S., 1948; d. Eli and Esther (Kingston) L.; m. Harvey Flisser, June 25, 1967; children: Adam, Elizabeth, Eric. AB, NYU, 1967; MD, Yeshiva U., 1971. Diplomate Am. Bd. Pediatrics. Intern Montefiore Med. Ctr., Bronx, N.Y., 1970-71, resident in pediatrics, 1971-73, attending pediatrician, 1975—, mem., exec. med. com., 2007—; instr. pediatrics Albert Einstein Coll. Medicine, NYC, 1973-76, asst. prof. clin., 1976—; med. staff Lawrence Hosp., Bronxville, NY, 1978—, dir. pediatrics, 1988—2003, pres. med. staff, 2002—06, mem. bd. govs., 2002—06; med. dir. Bronxville Sch. Dist., 2003—. Sch. physician Bronxville Bd. Edn., 1983—; mem. faculty coun. faculty of medicine health scis. divsn. Columbia U., 2002—04; police commr. Village Scarsdale, NY, 2010-. Expert office profl. med. conduct N.Y. State Dept. Health, 1996—; trustee Scarsdale Village Bd. Trustees, 2007-; fire commr. Vill. of Scarsdale, NY, 2009-10, mayor, 2011-. Named Hon. Founder, Albert Einstein Coll. Medicine, 1995, hon. founder, 1995—. Fellow Am. Acad. Pediatrics; mem. Westchester County Med. Soc., Albert Einstein Coll. Medicine Alumni Assn. (nat. bd. govs. 1999—2005). Office: 1 Pondfield Rd Bronxville NY 10708-3706

LEVITT, ROBERT E., gastroenterologist; b. Phila., Oct. 22, 1948; s. Martin E. and Miriam G. (Elson) L.; m. Linda Levitt, Mar. 13, 1976; children: Adam, Ashley. BA summa cum laude, Temple U., 1970, MD, 1974. Diplomate Am. Bd. Internal Medicine, Am. Bd. Gastroenterology. Chief hepatology and gastrointestinal rsch. Presbyn. U. of Pa. Med. Ctr., Phila., 1979-88, staff gastroenterologist, 1979—, assoc. dir. Inst. Gastroenterology, 1981-89; chief svc. gastroenterology Bryn Mawr (Pa.) Hosp., 1985—, chief gastrointestinal sect. dept. medicine, 1988—, dir. endoscopy ste., 1988—; asst. prof. medicine U. Pa. Sch. Medicine, 1979—; dir. endoscopy suite Bryn Mawr Hosp., 1988—. Clin. assoc. prof. medicine, Jefferson Med. Coll., Thomas Jefferson U., Phila. Contbr. articles to med. jours., chpts. to med. books; mem. editorial adv. bd. Post-Grad. Medicine. Fellow ACP, Am. Gastroenterol. Assn.; mem. AMA (Physicians Recognition award 1978, others), Am. Coll. Gastroenterology, Am. Soc. for Gastrointestinal Endoscopy, Pa. Soc. Gastroenterology, Med. Club Phila., Phi Eta Sigma, Alpha Omega Alpha. Office: 933 E Haverford Rd Bryn Mawr PA 19010-3819

LEVITT, SEYMOUR HERBERT, radiologist, educator; b. Chgo., July 18, 1928; s. Nathan E. Levitt and Margaret (Chizever) D.; m. Phillis Jeanne Martin, Oct. 31, 1952 (div. Oct. 1981); children: Mary Jeanne, Jennifer Gaye, Scott Hayden; m. Solveig I. Ostberg, Feb. 6, 1983. BA, U. Colo., 1950, MD, 1954, DSc (hon.), 1997. Diplomate Am. Bd. Radiology. Intern Phila. Gen. Hosp., 1954-55; resident in radiology U. Calif. at San Francisco Med. Center, 1957-61; instr. radiation therapy U. Mich., Ann Arbor, 1961-62, U. Rochester, NY, 1962-63; asso. prof. radiology U. Okla., Oklahoma City, 1963-66; prof. radiology, chmn. div. radiotherapy Med. Coll. Va., Richmond, 1966-70; prof., head dept. therapeutic radiology U. Minn., Mpls., 1970—99. Cons. in field. Exec. bd. Am. Joint Com. for End Result Reporting and Cancer Staging; com. radiation oncology studies Nat. Cancer Inst.; trustee Am. Bd. Radiology, 1977-89; chmn. bd. dirs. Radiol. Soc. N.Am, Found. for Rsch. and Edn.; fgn. adj. prof Karolinska Inst., Stockholm, 2002. Bd. dirs., mem. exec. com. Am. Cancer Soc., 1990-95. With M.C., AUS, 1955-57. Recipient Disting. Svc. award U. Colo., 1988, Gold Medal award Gibert Fletcher Soc., 1987, Silver and Gold award Med. Sch., U. Colo., 1992. Fellow: Am. Soc. Therapeutic Radiologists (exec. bd. 1974—78, pres. 1978—79, chmn. bd. [illegible], Gold medal [illegible]), Am. Coll. Radiology (bd. chancellors, Gold medal 1995), Royal Coll Radiology (hon.); mem.: Am. Soc. Clin. Oncology, Soc. Nuclear Medicine, Internat. Soc. Radiation Oncology (pres. 1981—85), Soc. Chmn. Acad. Radiation Oncology Programs (pres. 1974—76), German Soc. Radiation Oncology (hon.), European Cong. Radiology (hon.), German Soc. Radiology (hon.), Am. Roentgen Ray Soc., Am. Cancer Soc. (pres. Minn. divsn. 1979—80, nat. bd., exec. com.), Am. Assn. Cancer Rsch., Radiol. Soc. N.Am. (bd. dirs. 1991—2000, chmn. bd. dirs. 1997—98, pres.-elect 1998, pres. 1999 , Gold medal 2004), Am. Radium Soc. (sec. 1981—83, pres. 1983—84, Janeway medal 1989), Alpha Omega Alpha, Sigma Xi, Phi Beta Kappa. Office Phone: 612-626-6217. Business E-Mail: levit002@umn.edu.

LEVITZKI, ALEXANDER, biochemist, educator; b. Israel; MSc in Chemistry and Bacteriology, summa cum laude, Hebrew U. Weizman Inst. Sci., 1963, PhD in Chemistry, summa cum laude, 1968. Postdoc. fellow U. Calif., Berkeley, 1968—71; sr. scientist Weizmann Inst. Sci., 1970; assoc. prof. Hebrew U., Jerusalem, 1974—76, prof., 1976—, head Silberman Inst. Life Scis., Inst. Advanced Studies, Wolfson Ctr. Applied Structural Biology, Wolfson Family prof. biochemistry. Vis. prof. U. Calif., Berkeley, 1974, U. Oregon, 1974; vis. scientist US Nat. Cancer Inst., 1979—80; vis. scholar Stanford U., Calif., 1993—94; Edward Rotan vis. prof. MD Anderson Cancer Ctr., Houston, 2002—; vis. prof. Miller Inst. Basic Rsch. in Sci., U. Calif., Berkeley, 2007; founder Algen Biopharmaceuticals, 2001, NovoTyr Therapeutics, 2005. Mem. editl. bd.: Anti-Cancer Drug Design, 1995—2002, Molecular Biology Rsch. Comm., 1998, European Jour. Chem. Biology, 2000, Oncology Rsch., 2002, Jour. Biol. Chemistry, 2003, Current Signal Transduction Therapy, 2006; contbr. articles to profl. jours. Recipient Rothschild prize in biology, 1990, Schender prize in pharmacology & drug rsch., 1998, Hamilton-Fairley award, European Soc. Med. Oncology, 2002, Wolf Found. prize in medicine, Israel, 2005, Cancer Rsch. award, Jacqueline Seroussi Meml. Found., 2006, Rsch. award, Prostate Cancer Found., 2006, 2007. Mem.: European Molecular Biology Orgn., Israel Acad. Scis. & Humanities, Am. Soc. Biol. Chemists (hon.). Office: Hebrew Univ Alexander Silberman Inst Life Scis Edmond Safra Campus Givat Rm 91999 Jerusalem Israel Office Phone: 6585404. Office Fax: 6512958. E-mail: levitzki@vms.huji.ac.il. *

LEVY, ALBERT, physician; b. Stanleyville, Congo, Nov. 8, 1948; arrived in US, 1977; s. Moise and Eugenie J. (Menache) Levy; m. Linda Vertannes; children: Antonia G., Eric M. MD, Fed. U. Brazil, Rio de Janeiro, 1973, MS in Medicine, 1976. Diplomate Am. Bd. Family Physicians, Am. Bd. Family Practice, Am. Bd. Geriatric Medicine. Pvt. practice family medicine Manhattan Family Practice, NYC, 1990—; asst. clin. prof. dept. family medicine Albert Einstein Coll. Medicine, Bronx, 1994—; asst. prof. NY Med. Coll., Valhalla, 1994—; asst. prof. medicine Mt. Sinai Sch. Medicine, 1999—. With Beth Israel Med. Ctr., 1986, St. Luke's/Roosevelt Med. Ctr., 1986, Lenox Hill Hosp., 1995, Mt. Sinai Med. Ctr., 1999. Fellow: NY Acad. Medicine, Royal Soc. Medicine (Eng.), Am. Acad. Family Physicians; mem.: AMA, NY County Acad. Family Physicians (v.p. 1992), NY Acad. Scis., Acads. Family Physicians, World Orgn. Nat. Colls., Am. Geriatric Soc. Jewish. Avocations: tennis, opera, travel, golf. Office: Manhattan Family Practice 911 Park Ave New York NY 10021-0337 Office Phone: 212-288-7193. Personal E-mail: alevymd@earthlink.net.

LEVY, ANDREW S., sports medicine physician; BS in Biology, Lehigh U.; MD, Temple U. Sch. of Medicine. Cert. orthopaedic surgeons 1977. Fellow Duke Univ. Med. Ctr., 1994—95; resident

Albert Einstein Med. Ctr., 1990—94; intern Washington Hosp. Ctr., 1994—95. Lectr. Dutch Orthopedic Soc., 1999, ACL 2000, 1999. Co-author: (publications) Chondral Delamination of the Knee in Soccer Players, 1996, Knee Injuries in Women Collegiate Rugby Players, 1997, Graft Selection / Fixation in Revision Anterior Cruciate Ligament Surgery, 1998, Management of a 37-Year-Old Man with Recurrent Knee Pain, 1999, Intra-andInterobserver Reproducibility of the Shoulder Laxity Examination, 1999, and numerous others. Mem.: AMA, NJ Orthopedic Soc., Am. Orthopedic Rugby Football Assn., Internat. Soc. for Cartilage Repair, Piedmont Orthopedic Assn., Am. Acad. of Orthopaedic Surgeons. Office: Saint Barnabas Health Care System 90 Milburn Ave Ste 204 Millburn NJ 07041 Office Phone: 908-598-9199. Office Fax: 908-598-1040.

LEVY, DAVID ALFRED, immunologist, educator; b. Washington, Aug. 27, 1930; s. Stanley A. and Blanche B. (Berman) L.; m. Anne Levy-Badoux; children: Jill, William, Stanley. BS, U. Md., 1952, MD, 1954. Diplomate Am. Bd. Internal Medicine, Am. Bd. Allergy and Immunology. Intern, resident in medicine U. Hosp., Balt., 1954-59; physician VA Hosp., Balt., 1961-62; fellow dept. microbiology Sch. Medicine Johns Hopkins U., 1962-66, asst. prof. radiol. sci. Sch. Hygiene and Pub. Health, 1966-68, assoc. prof., 1968-71, prof. radiol. sci. and epidemiology, 1972-73, prof. biochemistry, 1973-82, with joint appointments in epidemiology and medicine, 1973-82, in pathobiology, 1980-82, prof. immunology and infectious diseases, 1982-86. Mem. FDA Panel on Rev. of Allergenic Extracts, 1975-83; mem. allergy and immunology rev. com. Nat. Inst. Allergy and Infectious Diseases, 1975-77; adj. dir. Centre d'Immunologie et de Biologie, Pierre Fabre, S.A., 1985-90; cons. to pharm. industry, 1990—. Mem. editl. bd. Clin. Immunology and Immunopathology, 1971-76, Revue Francaise d'Allergologie et Immunologie Clinique; contbr. articles to med. jours. and books. Clin. rsch. Centre d'Allergie, Hopital Tenon, Paris, 1991—. With U.S. Army, 1959-61. Fellow: Am. Acad. Allergy and Immunology; mem.: Franco-Am. Allergy Assn., French Soc. Allergology, Am. Assn. Immunologists, Internat. Union Immunol. Socs. (vice chmn. allergen standardization subcom. 1980—83), Sigma Xi. Home and Office: 11 Quai St Michel 75005 Paris France E-mail: dalevy2@wanadoo.fr.

LEVY, JEROME, dermatologist, retired military officer; b. Bklyn., Aug. 17, 1926; s. Alexander and Pauline (Wollkof) L.; m. Leona Elsie Eligator, June 6, 1948; children: Andrew B., Eric J., Peter C., David J. Student, Wesleyan U., 1944—45, postgrad., 1952—54; BA, Yale U., 1947; MD, Albany Med. Coll., 1958. Diplomate Am. Bd. Dermatology. Commd. ensign USN, M.C., 1957, advanced through grades to capt., 1972; intern U.S. Naval Hosp., Newport, RI, 1958—59; resident Phila. (Pa.) Naval Hosp., 1960—62, U. Pa. Grad. Sch. Medicine, Phila., 1962—63, chief dept. dermatology Memphis, 1963—67, Yokosuka, Japan, 1967—70, Long Beach, Calif., 1974—75; head outpatient dermatology clinic San Diego Naval Hosp., 1970—72; sr. med. officer Keflavik, Iceland, 1972—74; ret., 1975; med. dir. dermatology Westwood Pharm. Co., Buffalo, 1975—82; acting chief dermatology dept. Buffalo Gen. Hosp., 1981—82; practice medicine specializing in dermatology Coronado, Calif., 1982—90. Cons. Erie County Health Dept., 1979-82; clin. assoc. prof. SUNY, Buffalo Med. Sch., 1980-82. Contbr. articles to med. jours. and popular mags. Decorated Navy Commendation medal, Joint Svc. Commendation medal; Knight's Cross of the Order of Falcon (Iceland). Fellow ACP, Am. Acad. Dermatology; mem. AMA, So. Med. Assn., Assn. Mil. Surgeons, US Navy League, City Club San Diego, U. Club San Diego, Yale Club San Diego, Alpha Omega Alpha. Democrat. Jewish. Home: 3352 Lucinda St San Diego CA 92106-2932 Personal E-mail: zitzapper@aya.yale.edu.

LEVY, JOSEPH, physician, pediatric gastroenterologist; b. Ciudad Bolivar, Venezuela, Nov. 17, 1946; arrived in US, 1973; s. Abraham Alberto and Clemen (Abadi) Levy; m. Valery Braunstein, Aug. 24, 1968; children: Nomi, Berti. MD, Hebrew U. Hadassah Med. Sch., Israel, 1971. Diplomate Am. Bd. Nutrition, Am. Bd. Pediatrics, Am. Bd. Pediatric Gastroenterology. Resident pediat. Beth Israel Med. Ctr., NYC, 1975-77; hematology rsch. fellow Columbia U. Coll. Physicians and Surgeons, NYC, 1973-75, gastroenterology, nutrition fellow, 1977-79, asst. prof. pediat., 1980-87, assoc. prof. pediat., 1987-90, prof. clin. pediatrics, 1998—; chief divsn. pediat. gastroenterology and nutrition NY Hosp., Cornell Med. Ctr., NYC, 1990-96, pediat. faculty rep., gen. faculty coun., 1996; dir. children's digestive health ctr. NY Presbyn. Children's Hosp., NYC, 1996—. Prof. clin. pediat. Columbia U. Coll. Physicians and Surgeons, 1994—97; dir. pediat. clin. G.I. svc. Columbia Presbyn. Babies & Children's Hosp. NY. Author: (med. text) Practical Approach to Pediatric Gastroenterology, 1988; co-author: Pediatric Gastrointestinal Medical Problems, 1993; reviewer (med. publ.) Journal of Pediatric GI and Nutrition, Journal of Neonatology; contbr. articles to profl. jours. Named an Attending Physician of the Yr., Columbia Presbyn. Babies & Children's Hosp. NY. Fellow: Am. Acad. Pediat.; mem.: Pediat. Gastroenterology Collaborative Rsch. Grp., Am. Assn. Study of Liver Disease, N. Am. Soc. Pediat. Gastroenterology, Hepatology, & Nutrition (chmn. pub. edn. com.), Am. Gastroenterological Assn. Office: Columbia U Med Ctr 630 W 158th St New York NY 10032 Office Phone: 212-305-5693. Office Fax: 212-305-7124. Business E-Mail: JL588@columbia.edu.

LEVY, KENNETH JAY, psychology professor, academic administrator; b. Dallas, Sept. 18, 1946; s. Reuben and Ruth (Okon) L.; children: Ryan S., Scott D. BA, U. Tex., 1968, MA, 1969; PhD, Purdue, 1972. Asst. prof. psychology SUNY, Buffalo, 1972-75, assoc. prof., 1976-78, prof., 1979—, chmn. dept. psychology, 1976-78, dean social scis., 1978-82, various adminstrv. positions, 1985—, assoc. provost, 1987—92, sr. vice provost, 1992—. Contbr. numerous articles to profl. jours.; editorial cons. Psychometrika. Home: 39 Shire Dr S East Amherst NY 14051-1816 Office: SUNY at Buffalo 353 Park Hall Buffalo NY 14260 Office Phone: 716-645-3650 ext. 353.

LEVY, KENNETH ST. CLAIR, barrister, criminologist, psychologist, accountant; b. Brisbane, Australia, Dec. 23, 1949; s. Francis and Grace (Ferguson) Levy; m. Veronica Mary Forster, Jan. 7, 1978; children: Clare, Gregory. BA, U. Queensland, Australia, 1978, B in Commerce, 1980, PhD, 1994; LLB, Queensland U. Tech., 1986. Barrister at Law High Ct. Australia, Supreme Ct. Queensland; registered tax agt., Queensland. Numerous mgmt. and organizatioal positions, 1974—89; dep. dir. gen. Dept. Justice, 1989—2000, dir. gen., 2000—03, cons. psychologist and barrister, 2004—, sr. mem. adminstrv. appeals tribunal, 2004—, dir. acctg. profl. ethical stds. bd., 2006—09; clin. prof. Bond U. Law Faculty, 2007—. Mem. bd. mgmt. Australian Inst. Criminology, 1991—2003, mem. criminology rsch. coun., 1991—2003; prof. law Bond U., 2007—; chair Mgmt. Resource Solutions, 2007—08. Founding mem. Rental Bond Authority, 1989—90; pres. Alternative Dispute Resolution Coun., 1994—2000. Lt. col. Australian Army Res. Fulbright scholar, 1995; recipient Outstanding Law Alumni award Queensland U. Tech., 2002, Res. Force decoration, 1990, Centenary medal, Australia, 2003, Nat. Svc. medal, 2004, Australian Def. medal, 2006. Fellow: CPA Australia (v.p. prof. devel. 1996—97, dep. chair 1997, dep. pres. 1998, dep. chmn. disciplinary com. Queensland divsn. 1998—99, pres. 1999, chmn. Queensland divisional coun. 1999—2000, chair disciplinary com. Queensland divsn. 2000—01, nat. v.p. corp.gov. 2002, nat. dep. pres. 2003, nat. pres. 2004), Inst. Chartered Accts. Australia; mem.: APA, Coll. Forensic Psychology, Bar Assn. Queensland, Australian Psychol. Soc., United Svcs. Club. Avocations: music, reading, travel. Office Phone: 61 418780028. Personal E-mail: ken.levy@bigpond.net.au.

LEVY, LEONARD ALVIN, podiatric medicine educator, college president; b. NYC, Aug. 19, 1935; s. David and Jessie (Frankel) L.; m. Eleanore Auerbach, Dec. 18, 1960; children: Andrew Lincoln, Sarilyn Joan. BA, NYU, 1956; MPH, Columbia U., 1967; D Podiatric Medicine, N.Y. Coll. Podiatric Medicine, 1961. Diplomate Am. Bd. Podiatric Pub. Health, Am. Bd. Primary Podiatric Medicine. Dean, v.p. Calif. Coll. Podiatric Medicine, San Francisco, 1967-74; dean, prof. SUNY Health Sci. Ctr., Stony Brook, 1974-76; cons. to pres. U. Tex. Health Sci. Ctr., Houston, 1976-81; prof. podiat. medicine, dean Coll. Podiat. Medicine/Surgery U. Osteo. Medicine and Health Scis., Des Moines, 1981—, v.p. planning and rsch., 1996—. Cons. USPHS, Rockville, Md., 1967; mem. sec.'s med. adv. group VA, Washington, 1990-94; mem. dean's com., Yale U. Sch. of Medicine, VA Med. Ctr., West Haven, 1993—. Author, editor: (monograph) Clinics in Podiatry/Systemic Diseases, 1985, Principles and Practice of Podiatric Medicine, 1990; contbr. to Podiatric Med. Assisting, 1992—, also over 70 articles to podiatric med. jours. Bd. dirs. Iowa Jewish Sr. Life Ctr., Des Moines, 1983-89, Elsie Mason/Liguitti Towers Sr. Housing, Des Moines, 1988-90, Des Moines Birthing Place-Woman Care, 1990-92. USPHS grantee, 1984—. Fellow APHA, Am. Coll. Podopediatrics (pres. 1987-88); mem. Am. Podiatric Med. Assn. (fellow 1966), Am. Acad. Dermatology (affiliate), Am. Assn. Colls. Podiatric Medicine (chmn. bd. dirs. 1989-90), Gerontol. Soc. Am., Iowa Podiatric Med. Assn. Avocations: travel, oriental cooking.

LEVY, NELSON LOUIS, immunologist, educator, surgeon; b. Somerville, NJ, June 19, 1941; s. Myron L. and Sylvia (Cohen) L.; m. Joanne Barnett, Dec. 21, 1963 (div. 1972); children: Scott, Erik, Jonathan; m. Louisa Douglas Stiles, Dec. 21, 1974; children: Michael, Andrew, David. BA/BS summa cum laude, Yale U., 1963; MD, Columbia U., 1967; PhD, Duke U., 1972. Diplomate Am. Bd. Allergy and Immunology. Intern U. Colo. Med. Ctr., Denver, 1967-68; resident Duke U. Med. Ctr., Durham, NC, 1970-73; rsch. assoc. NIH, Bethesda, Md., 1968-70; asst. prof. immunology Duke U. Med. Ctr., Durham, 1972-75, assoc. prof. immunology and neurology, 1975-80, prof., 1980-81; dir. biol. rsch. Abbott Labs., Abbott Park, Ill., 1981, v.p. rsch., 1981-84; pres. Fujisawa Pharm., Deerfield, Ill., 1992-93; CEO Ill. Tech. Devel. Corp., 1993-95, The Core Techs Corp., Lake Forest, Ill., 1984—92, chmn. bd. dirs., CEO, 1995—. Chmn. bd. dirs. Horizon Quest Inc., Laguna Hills, Calif., 1996—97, ColesCraft Corp., 1997—, IMM UVA Corp., New Orleans, 1997—, ChemBridge Pharms., Inc., 2006—09, Navene Pharm. Co., Lausanne, Switzerland, Chgo., 2009—; bd. dirs. ChemBridge Corp., San Diego, Targeted Genetics Corp., Seattle, Biona PTY Ltd., Laguna Beach, Cary Pharm. Co., Bethesda, Md., ChemBridge Rsch. Labs., LLC, San Diego, zuChem, Inc., Chgo.; chmn. sci. adv. bd. Neoprobe Corp., First Horizon Pharms., Inc.; mem. sci. adv. bd. Ligand Pharms. Inc.; cons. Alcide Corp., 1991—, Ameritech, 1993—, US Dept. Treasury, FTC, 1999—; others. Contbr. chapters to books, articles to profl. jours. Mem. Gov.'s Task Force on Econ. Devel., 1993-98; mem. corp. adv. bd. Family Svc. of South Lake County, 1991—; commr. Lake County, Ill., 1998-, bd. trustees, Writers Theatre, 2009-. Surgeon USPHS, 1968-70. Grantee Am. Cancer Soc., 1970-75, NIH, 1971-81, Nat. Multiple Sclerosis Soc., 1974-81, Ill. Dept. Commerce and Cmty. Affairs, 1993—. Mem. Am. Assn. Immunologists, Am. Assn. Cancer Rsch., Licensing Execs. Soc., Rotary, Phi Beta Kappa, Sigma Xi, Alpha Omega Alpha, Phi Gamma Delta. Avocations: triathlons, biking, rhythm 'n blues. Home: 245 Butler Dr Lake Forest IL 60045-3009 Office Phone: 847-295-3720.

LEVY, NORMAN B., psychiatrist, educator; b. NYC, 1931; s. Barnett Theodore and Lena (Gulnick) L.; m. Lya Weiss (dec.); children: Karen, Susan, Joanne; m. Carol Lois Spiegel, 1 son, Robert Barnett; m. Belle Louise Prieman. BA cum laude, NYU, 1952; MD, SUNY. Diplomate Am. Bd. Psychiatry and Neurology (examiner). Intern Maimonides Med. Center, Bklyn.; resident physician in medicine U. Pitts.-Presbyn. Hosp.; resident in psychiatry Kings County Hosp. Center, Bklyn.; instr. psychiatry SUNY Downstate Med. Ctr. Coll. Medicine, Bklyn., asst. prof., assoc. prof.; prof. State U. N.Y. Downstate Med. Center Coll. Medicine, 1980-95; presiding officer faculty SUNY Downstate Med. Ctr. Coll. Medicine, assoc. dir. med-psychiat. liaison service, 1965-80; prof. psychiatry, medicine, surgery and coordinator psychiat. liaison services NY Med. Coll., 1980-95; clin. prof. psychiatry, adj. prof. of medicine Health Science Ctr. SUNY, Bklyn., 1996—2007; dir. psychiatry Kingsboro Psychiat. Ctr., Bklyn., 2000—06; prof. psychiatry U. So. Calif., 2007—09, prof. clin. psychiatry, 2007—09; dir. psychiatry Southern Calif. Mental Health Assn., 2009—. Dir. liaison svcs. psychiatry divsn. Westchester County Med. Ctr., 1980-95, mem. exec. com. med. staff, 1981-85, 89-92, NY Med. Coll., 1980-95; clin. prof. psychiatry, adj. prof. medicine health sci. ctr. SUNY, Bklyn., 1996—2006; dir., consultation-liaison and emergency psychiatry Coney Island Hosp., Bklyn., 1996-2000; vis. prof. psychiatry and medicine So. Ill. U. Sch. Medicine; vis. prof. psychiatry John A. Burns Sch. Medicine, U. Hawaii, 1981; coord. 1st Internat. Conf. Psychol. Factors in Hemodialysis and Transplantation, 1978, 2nd-13th Internat. Confs. on Psychonephrology; cons. NIMH; chief med. svcs. USAF Hosp., Ashiya, Japan; clin. prof. psychiatry, adj. prof. medicine SUNY Health Sci. Ctr., Bklyn., 1996. Author: (with others), editor: Living or Dying: Adaptation to Hemodialysis, 1974, Psychonephrology I: Psychological Factors in Hemodialysis and Transplantation, 1981, Men in Transition: Theory and Therapy, 1982, Psychonephrology II: Psychological Problems in Kidney Failure and their Treatment, 1983; contbr. articles to jours., chpts. to textbooks in field.; assoc. editor: Gen. Hosp. Psychiatry, 1978-82, sect. editor, 1982-2005; sect. editor: Internat. Jour. Psychiatry in Medicine, 1977-78; mem. editl. bd., book rev. editor Jour. Dialysis and Transplantation, 1979-97, Facta Universitatis, 1997—; mem. editl. bd. Resident and Staff Physician, 1981-91, Internat. Jour. Artificial Internal. Organs, 1983-93, Geriatric Nephrology and Urology, 1990—, Kidney: A Current Survey of World Literature, 1990—, Dialysis and Transplantation, 1979—. Served to capt. M.C. USAF. Recipient William A. Console Master Tchr. award, SUNY, Bklyn., 1991. Fellow ACP, Am. Coll. Psychiatrists, Am. Psychiat. Assn. (pres. Kings County dist. br. 1981-82), Acad. Psychosomatic Medicine (Thomas P. Hackett award 1993); mem. AAAS, Am. Psychosomatic Soc. (coun. 1994-97), NY Acad. Scis., Psychonephrology Found. (pres. 1978—), Internat. Soc. Nephrology, Am. Soc. Nephrology, Soc. Liaison Psychiatry (bd. dirs. 1979-80, sec. 1980-81, pres.-elect 1991-92, pres. 1992-94, bd. dirs. 1995-98, award 1998), Serbian Acad. Medicine, Phi Beta Kappa, Sigma Xi. Office Phone: 646-331-6280. Personal E-mail: nephropsyc@aol.com.

LEVY, PIERRE-YVES, microbiologist, health facility administrator; b. Marseille, France, Mar. 8, 1962; s. Gabriel and Jacqueline (Rispy) L.; m. Anne Sibourg, July 24, 1993; children: Julien, Alice. DEA in Cellular Biology, U. Scis., Marseille, 1987; MD, U. Medicine, Marseille, 1989, DESC in Infectious Diseases, 1990. Fellow Univ. Hosp., Marseille, 1985-89; dir. Lab. Casamance, Aubagne, France, 1989—. Assoc. prof. microbiology Univ. Hosp., Marseille, 2001—. Contbr. articles to profl. jours. Mem. Am. Soc. Microbiology. Jewish. Avocations: tennis, piano. Office: LABM La Casamance 33 Bd des Farigoules 13400 Aubagne France

LEVY, RICHARD M., medical products executive; BA, Dartmouth Coll.; PhD nuclear chem., Univ. Calif., Berkeley. Sales & mktg. positions Varian Associates, sr. v.p., 1989—92, exec. v.p., 1992—99; CEO Varian Med. Systems, Palo Alto, Calif., 1999—2006; chmn. Varian Medical Systems, Inc., Palo Alto, Calif., 2002—. Trustee Palo Alto Med. Found.; bd. dir. Pharmacyclics Inc., Calif. Health Inst.; past. chmn. Am. Electronics Assn.; past bd. mem. Diagnostic Imaging & Therapy Sys. div., Nat. Elect. Mfr. Assn. Office: Varian Medical Systems 3100 Hansen Way Palo Alto CA 94304-1129 *

LEVY, RONALD, medical educator, researcher; b. Carmel, Calif. BS, Harvard U., 1963; MD, Stanford U., 1968. Cert. Internal Medicine, 1973, Med. Oncology, 1979, lic. Commonwealth Mass., 1970, State Calif. Med. License, 1975. Intern, internal medicine Mass. Gen. Hosp., Boston, 1968-69, residency, internal medicine, 1969-70; clin. assoc., immunology branch Nat. Cancer Inst., 1970—72; Helen Hay Whitney Found. fellow in dept. chem. immunology Weizmann Inst. Sci., Rehovot, Israel, 1973-75; fellow, dept. medicine, divsn. oncology Stanford U. Sch. Medicine, 1972—73, mem. faculty Calif., 1975—, asst. prof. medicine, divsn. oncology Calif., 1975—81, assoc. prof. dept. medicine-oncology Calif., 1981—87, prof. medicine, divsn. oncology Calif., 1987—, Robert K. Summy and Helen K. Summy prof. Calif., 1987—; Frank and Else Schilling Am. Cancer Soc. Clin. Rsch. prof., 1987—; chief divsn. oncology Stanford U. Sch. Medicine, Calif., 1993—. Investigator Howard Hughes Med. Inst., 1977—82; chmn., bd. scientific counselors, divsn. cancer treatment NIH, 1989—93; mem. scientific advisory bd. Fred Hutchinson Cancer Rsch. Ctr., 1994—, Coley Pharm. Group, 2001, XTL Therapeutics, Rehovoth, Israel, Therion Inc., Cambridge, Mass., Xeyte Therapeutics, Seattle, Agensys, Santa Monica, Calif., Pointilliste, Mountain View, Calif., Cell Genesis, Foster City, Calif., Five Prime, South San Francisco, Calif.; Woodward vis. prof. Meml. Sloan Kettering Cancer Ctr., NY, 1994; Morton Mason lecture U. Tex. Southwestern, 1995; vis. prof. U. Minn. Cancer Ctr., 1996, U. Nebr. Cancer Ctr., 1999; lectr. in field. Contbr. articles to profl. jours.; Author, co-author of several books and publs. Mem. Dorothy P. Landon Am. Assn. for Cancer Rsch. Translational Cancer Rsch. com., 2001; bd. dir. Damon Runyon Cancer Rsch. Fund, 2002—; mem., Conflict of Interest Com. Stanford U. Sch. Medicine, 2001—; mem. Am. Assn. Med. Sch. Task Force on Fin. Conflicts of Interest in Clin. Rsch., 2001, GM Cancer Rsch. Found. Awards Assembly, 1992—96, 2001—. Recipient Armand Hammer award for Cancer Rsch., 1982, Ciba-Geigy/Drew award in Biomedical Rsch., 1983, Dr. Josef Steiner prize for Cancer Rsch., 1989, Karnofsky award, Am. Soc. Clin. Oncology, 1999, Charles F. Kettering award, GM Cancer Rsch. Found., 1999, Centeon award, 6th Internat. Conf. on Bispecific Antibodies, 1999, C. Chester Stock award, Meml. Sloan-Kettering Cancer Ctr., 2000, Medal of Honor, Am. Cancer Soc., 2000, Key to the Cure award, Cure for Lymphoma Found., 2000, Evelyn Hoffman Meml. award, Lymphoma Rsch. Found. Am., 2001, Jeffrey A. Gottlieb Meml. award, M.D. Anderson Cancer Ctr, 2003, Discovery Health Channel Med. Honors, 2004. Mem. ACP, Inst. Medicine, Am. Soc. Clin. Oncology, Am. Cancer Soc. (chmn. immunology study sect., 1988-92, mem., rsch. coun., 2003-), Am. Soc. Clin. Investigation, Assn. Am. Physicians, Am. Assn. for Cancer Rsch. (chmn., Joseph H. Burchinal award com., 2002, Joseph H. Burchenal Clin. Cancer Rsch. award, 1997), Am. Assn. Immunology (program com. and block chmn. for tumor immunology, 1992-96), Am. Fed. for Clin. Rsch., Am. Soc. Hematology, Western Soc. Medicine, Acad. of Cancer Immunology. Achievements include first to the development of idiotype-based therapeutic vaccines for the treatment of non-Hodgkin's B-cell lymphoma. Office: Levy Lab Divsn Oncology 269 Campus Dr CCSR 1126 Stanford CA 94305-5151 Address: Stanford Sch Medicine 300 Pasteur Dr M207 Stanford CA 94305 Office Phone: 650-725-6452. Office Fax: 650-725-1420. E-mail: levy@stanford.edu.

LEVY, SHELDON GRANT, psychologist, educator; s. Jacob Sydney and Freda Kershnerm Levy; m. Mary Lois Uphoffm Levy, Aug. 21, 1960. AB in Chemistry, Coll. Wooster, Ohio, 1957; MA in Psychology, U. Mich., Ann Arbor, 1959, MA in Pure Math., 1962, PhD in Math. Psychology, 1962. Lectr., psychology, rsch. assoc., Ctr. rsch. conflict resolution U. Mich., 1963—64, asst. prof., dept. psychology, 1965—68, psychologist-in-residence, journalism dept., 1968; vis. assoc. prof., psychology Lemberg Ctr. Study Violence, Brandeis U., Waltham, Mass., 1968—69, Rice U., Houston U., 1970; assoc. prof., psychology. sr. rsch. assocs. Ctr. Urban Studies Wayne State U., Detroit, 1970—73, prof., psychology, 1975—. Cons. Spl. Ops. Rsch. Office, Am. U., 1965; cons. to mayor Detroit's Com. Human Resource Devel., 1968; pres. Peace Sci. Soc., 1992; co founder Asian Network Peace Scientist, 2008. Contbr. articles to profl. publs. Amb. ACLU Mich., 2008—; co-dir., polit. violence Nat. Commn. Causes Prevention Violence, Washington, 1968—69; del., alternate nat. del. Am. Civil Librs. Union. Fellow: APA (chmn., divsn. 9 acad. Freedom com. 1973—81, chmn., divsn. 8 com. on grad. tng. 1976—81), Soc. Exptl. Social Psychology, Soc. Study Social Issues; mem.: AAUP, Peace Sci. Soc., Am. Hist. Assn., Am. Polit. Sci. Assn.,

Am. Sociol. Assn. Home: 2951 Renfrew St Ann Arbor MI 48105 Office: Wayne State University Dept Psychology 5057 Woodward Bldg Detroit MI 48202 Business E-Mail: shelly@umich.edu. E-mail: aa4389@wayne.edu.

LEW, HO MIN, ophthalmologist, educator; b. Seoul, Republic of Korea, Feb. 10, 1947; BS in Medicine, Cath. U., Seoul, 1972; MS in Medicine, Yonsei U., Seoul, 1982. Asst. prof. Dept. Ophthalmology, Yonsei U. Wonju Coll. Medicine, Republic of Korea, 1983—87, assoc. prof., 1987—93, prof., 1993—94; chmn., gen. mgr. Dept. Ophthalmology, Ajou U. Medicine, Suwon, Republic of Korea, 1994—2009, prof., retina svc., 2009—. Mem.: Am. Acad.Ophthalmology, Korean Ophthalmology Soc. (bd. dirs. 2006—08), Korean Retina Soc. Avocations: golf, skiing, fishing. Office: San 5 Woncheon-dong Yeungtong-gu Suwon Kyunggi 443-721 Republic of Korea Office Fax: 82-31-219-5259. Business E-Mail: hmlew@ajou.ac.kr.

LEWANDOWSKI, WENDY ANN, psychiatric nurse practitioner, educator; b. Cleve., Mar. 14, 1955; PhD, Case Western Res. U., 2002. Assoc. prof. nursing, dir. grad. psychiatric mental health nursing program Kent State U. Coll. Nursing, 2002—. Psychiatric mental health clin. nurse specialist Summit County Vis. Nurse Assn., 1987—2002, Cleve. Clinic Found., 2004—. Mem.: ANA, Midwest Nursing Rsch. Soc., Am. Psychiatric Nurses Assn., Sigma Theta Tau Internat. Office: Kent State University 113 Henderson Hall Kent OH 44242 Business E-Mail: wlewando@kent.edu.

LEWENT, JUDY CAROL, retired pharmaceutical executive; b. Jan. 13, 1949; BS in Econs., Goucher Coll., 1970; MSc in Mgmt., MIT, 1972; LHD (hon.), Goucher Coll., 1998; DEng (hon.), Stevens Inst. Tch., 2000; DSc (hon.), NJ Inst. Tech., 2004. With corp. fin. dept. E. F. Hutton & Co., Inc., 1972—74; asst. v.p. for strategic planning Bankers Trust Co., 1974—75; mgr. corp. devel. planning Norton Simon, 1975—76; divsn. contr. Pfizer, Inc., 1976—80; dir. acquisitions and capital analysis Merck & Co., Inc. (formerly Schering-Plough Corp.), Whitehouse Station, NJ, 1980—83, asst. contr., 1983—85, exec. dir. fin. evaluation and analysis, 1985—87, v.p., treas., 1987—90, v.p. fin., CFO, 1990—92, sr. v.p., CFO, 1992—2001, exec. v.p., CFO, 2001—02, exec. v.p., CFO, pres., human health Asia, 2003—05, exec. v.p., CFO, 2005—07; ret., 2007. Bd. dirs. Motorola Solutions Inc., 1995—, Dell Inc., 2001—11, Thermo Fisher Scientific Inc., 2008—, Glaxo Smith Kline, 2011—, Nat. Bur. Econ. Rsch.; life mem. MIT Corp. Trustee Rockefeller Family Trust. Named one of 10 Most Powerful Women in NJ Bus., Star Ledger, 2006. Mem.: Am. Acad. Arts and Scis. *

LEWICKY, ANDREW O., ophthalmologist, consultant, surgeon; came to U.S., 1949; s. Witold George and Irene Anna (Antonowych) L.; m. Daria Marie Kaminsky, Sept. 7, 1968; children: Christina, Mark, Justin. Student, Oberlin Coll., 1963—66; BS, Northwestern U., Chgo., 1967, MD, 1970. Diplomate Am. bd. Ophthalmology. Intern Rush Presbyn. St. Lukes, Chgo., 1970-71, resident in ophthalmology 1971-74; instr. ophthalmology Rush U., Chgo., 1974-77, asst. prof. ophthalmology, 1977—. Founding ptnr. Chgo. Eye Inst., 1979—; co-dir. Ill. Masonic Eye Ctr., Chgo. Co-author: Refractive Surgery: A Text of Radial Keratotomy, 1985, Refractive Corneal Surgery, 1986; mem. editl. bd. Jour. Refractive Surgery; contbr. articles to profl. jours.; inventor chamber maintainer system, lens hook, cystotome, cannula. Adv. bd. to commr. health City of Chgo., 1979-83. Lt. comdr. USN, 1974-76. Fellow ACS, Am. Acad. Ophthalmology; mem. Chgo. Ophthal. Soc. (bd. dirs., eye bank com. 1980—, exec. com. 1983-87), Chgo. Yacht Club. Avocations: sailing, skiing, golf. Office: Chgo Eye Inst 3982 N Milwaukee Ave Chicago IL 60641-2703 Office Phone: 773-282-2000.

LEWIN, JOHN, radiologist; b. Mass., June 2, 1961; MSEE, U. Rochester, 1985; MD, Harvard Med. Sch., 1990. Sect. chief breast imaging Diversified Radiology Colo. PC, 2004—; med. dir. Rose Brent Ctr., 2009—. Fellow: Soc. Breast Imaging; mem.: Radiol. Soc. N.Am., Am. Coll. Radiology. Office: 4700 Hale Pkwy Ste 450 Denver CO 80220 Business E-Mail: jlewin@divrad.com.

LEWIN, JOHN CALVERT, medical association administrator; b. Camden, NJ, Jan. 8, 1946; s. John Edward and Ruth Beatrice (Calvert) L; m. Sandra Patricia Smith, June 17, 1972; children: Jennifer, John, Josanna. BA, U. Calif., Irvine, 1967; MD, U. So. Calif., 1971. Physician, svc. unit dir. US Pub. Health Svc. (USPHS), Kayenta, Ariz., 1972-75; exec. dir., founder the Navaho div. Health Improvement Svcs., Window Rock, Ariz., 1976-79; physician, med. dir. Kula Hosp., Hawaii, 1979-86; dir. health State of Hawaii, 1987—94; exec. v.p., CEO Calif. Med. Assn., 1995—2006; CEO Am. Coll. Cardiology, Washington, 2006—. Office: Am Coll Cardiology Heart House 2400 N St NW Washington DC 20037 Office Phone: 202-375-6180. *

LEWIN, NEAL, internist, educator; MD, SUNY Downstate Med. Ctr., 1970—74. Diplomate Am. Bd. Internal Medicine, 1977, Am. Bd. Emergency Medicine, 2002. Intern internal medicine NYU Langone Med. Ctr., 1974—75, residency tng. internal medicine, 1975—77, prof. dept. of emergency medicine. Co-author: AntimigraineAgent, 2006, Initial Evaluation of the Patient: Vital Signs and Toxic Syndromes, 2006, Principles of Managing The Poisoned or Overdosed Patient, 2006, Cardioactive Steroids, 2006, Artropods, 2006, various publs. Office: New York University Langone Medical Center 550 First Ave New York NY 10016 also: 120 E 36 St 1B New York NY 10016 Office Phone: 212-263-7300.

LEWINSTEIN, ISRAEL, dentist; b. Israel, Oct. 24, 1950; DMD, Hebrew U., 1979, PhD, 1986. Coord. dept. oral rehab. Sch. Dental Medicine, Tel-Aviv U., 1994—. Pres. Israeli Assn. Oral Rehab., 2003—04. Mem.: IADR. Avocations: tennis, history. Home: 5 Hashalom St Mevasseret-Zion 90805 Israel Personal E-mail: lewins@post.tau.ac.il.

LEWIS, ALAN JAMES, pharmaceutical executive, pharmacologist; b. Newport Gwent, UK; BSc, Southampton U., Hampshire, 1967; PhD in Pharmacology, U. Wales, Cardiff, 1970. Postdoctoral fellow biomedical sci. U. Guelph, Ont., Can., 1970-72; rsch. assoc. lung rsch. ctr. Yale U., 1972-73; sr. pharmacologist Organon Labs., Ltd., Lanarkshire, Scotland, 1973-79; rsch. mgr. immunoinflammation Am. home products Wyeth-Ayerst Rsch., Princeton, NJ, 1979-82, assoc. dir. exptl. therapeutics, 1982-85, dir., 1985-87, asst. v.p., 1987-89, v.p. rsch., 1989-93; pres. Signal Pharms. Inc., San Diego, 1994-96, pres., CEO, 1996-2000; pres. signal rsch. divsn. Celgene Corp., 2000—06; pres., CEO, dir. Novocell, Inc., 2006—08; pres., CEO Juvenile Diabetes Rsch. Found. Internat., NYC, 2009—10; chmn. Ambit Biosciences Corp., San Diego, 2009—10, exec. chmn., 2010, pres., CEO, 2010—. Editor allergy sect. Agents & Actions & Internat. Archives Pharmacodynamics Therapy; reviewer Jour. Pharmacology Exptl. Therapy, Biochemical Pharmacology, Can. Jour. Physiol. Pharmacology, European Jour. Pharmacology, Jour. Pharm. Sci. Mem. Am. Soc. Pharmacological and Exptl. Therapeutics, Am. Rheumatism Assn., Mid-Atlantic Pharmacology Soc. (v.p. 1991-93, pres. 1993-94), Pulmonary Rsch. Assn., Inflammation Rsch. Assn. (pres. 1986-88), Pharm. Mfrs. Assn., Internat. Assn. Inflammation Socs. (pres. 1990-95), Bio Bd. Achievements include research in mechanisms and treatment of inflammatory diseases including arthritis and asthma cardiovascular diseases, metabolic disorders, central nervous system diseases, osteoporosis and viral diseases. Office: Ambit Biosciences Corp 4215 Sorrento Valley Blvd San Diego CA 92121 Office Phone: 858-334-2100. Office Fax: 858-334-2192. *

LEWIS, ALVIN EDWARD, pathology educator; b. NYC, Nov. 21, 1916; s. Herman and Libbie (Levy) L.; m. Oct. 23, 1943, (widowed 1974); children: Joan, Elizabeth; m. July, 1, 1976. BA, U. Calif., LA, 1938; MA, Stanford U., 1939, MD, 1944. Chief, pathology sect, atomic energy project UCLA, 1949-53; dir. clin. labs. Mount Zion Hosp., San Francisco, 1953-66; pathology prof. Mich. State U., East Lansing, 1966-72; pathology prof., chmn. U. S. Ala., Mobile, 1972-74; pathology prof. U. Calif., Davis, 1974-87, prof. emeritus, 1987—. Rev. com. mem. Nat. Libr. Medicine, Bethesda, Md., 1972-75, med. quality rev. com. Dist. 3, Sonoma, Calif., 1989-94. Author: Biostatistics, 1966, 1984 (2d ed.), Principles of Hematology, 1970. Lt. (j.g.) USNR, 1945-46. Fellow: Coll. Am. Pathologists; mem.: Am. Physiol. Soc. Republican. Jewish. Avocations: sailing, photography, music (recorder ensemble). Home: 7726 Beaudelaire Cir Galveston TX 77551-1625

LEWIS, ANISHA, medical association administrator; m. Demetrius Lewis; children: Darrien, Nicole. BA in Comm., Howard U., Washington, 1993; MS in Orgnl. Mgmt., Trinity U., San Antonio, 2003. Cert. assn. exec. American Soc. Assn. Executives. Dir. membership services and programs, dep. exec. dir. Nat. Soc. Black Engineers, 1994—2005; founder Exec. Mgmt. Solutions; dep. exec. dir. Nat. Alliance Black Sch. Educators, 2008—09; exec. dir. Assn. Black Psychologists, 2009—. Bd. dirs. Educators Serving the Cmty (EDUSERC). Office: Assn Black Psychologists 7119 Allentown Rd Ste 203 Fort Washington MD 20744 Office Phone: 202-722-0808. Office Fax: 202-722-5941. *

LEWIS, CARLA SUSAN, psychology educator; b. Bklyn. d. Harry Aaron and Mildred Lewis. BA summa cum laude, Fordham U., 1979; MA in Psychology, CUNY, 1984, MPhil, 1986, PhD in Psychology, 1988. Asst. rsch. scientist N.Y. State Psychiat. Inst., NYC, 1987-88; rsch. scientist Columbia Sch. Pub. Health, NYC, 1988-90; adj. asst. prof. MA in program in forensic psychology John Jay Coll. Criminal Justice, NYC, 1990, mem. faculty psychology rsch. lab. Princeton U., NJ, 1992-93, adj. asst. prof. psychology Fordham U., NYC, 1995-95, dep. exec. dir. planning, evaulation and QI Project Hospitality, SI, NY, 2005—09; sr. dir. Children's Health Fund, NYC, 2010—. Rsch. scientist, cons. Columbia Sch. Pub. Health, N.Y.C., 1993-94; rsch. cons. dept. environ. medicine NYU Med. Ctr., 1994, Nat. Devel. and Rsch. Inst., Insts. for Therapeutic Cmty. Rsch., N.Y.C., 1995; sr. rsch. analyst Beth Israel Medical Ctr., 2000-02; presenter in field; chief evaluator Urban Resource Inst., 2002-05, Domestic Violence Shelters U. R.I.; Mt. Sinai Pub. Advocate, 2002; presenter in field. Contbr. articles to profl. jours., Reviewer Violence Against Women. Mem. task force against domestic violence City NY; mem. HIV prevention planning group NYC Dept. Health, chairperson intervention behavioral sci. com. Recipient Disting. Rsch. award Psi Chi Nat. Honor Soc., 1991. Home: 9 E 97th St 3B New York NY 10029 Office: Children's Health Fund 215 W 125th St New York NY 10027 Office Phone: 212-535-9400 Ext. 219. Business E-Mail: clewis@chfund.org.

LEWIS, DAVID ALAN, neuroscientist, psychiatrist, educator; b. Columbus, Ohio, Aug. 9, 1952; MD, Ohio State U., 1979. Cert. Internal Medicine, 1984, Psychiatry, 1988. Resident in internal medicine U. Iowa, resident in psychiatry; endowed prof. translational neuroscience U. Pitts. Med. Ctr., dir. translational neuroscience prog., dir. Conte Ctr. for the Neuroscience of Mental Disorders. Mem.: Inst. Medicine. Office: U Pitts W1653 BST 3811 O'Hara St Pittsburgh PA 15213 Office Phone: 412-624-3934. Office Fax: 412-624-9910. E-mail: lewisda@upmc.edu.

LEWIS, DAVID CARLETON, medical educator, academic administrator; b. Hartford, Conn., May 19, 1935; s. Theodore and Lillian (Levin) L.; m. Eleanor Grace Levinson, Aug. 23, 1959; children: Deborah, Steven. AB magna cum laude, Brown U., 1957; MD, Harvard U., 1961. Intern Beth Israel Hosp., Boston, 1961-62, jr. resident, 1962-63, chief med. resident, 1966-67, dir. emergency unit and med. outpatient dept., 1969-71; sr. resident U. Hosps. Cleve., 1963-64, Parkland Meml. Hosp., Dallas, 1964-66; fellow U. Tex. Southwestern Med. Hosp., Dallas, 1964-66; Sloan Found. fellow Harvard Med. Sch., Boston, 1971-72; med. dir. Washingtonian Ctr. for Addictions, Boston, 1972-77; dir. div. alcohol and substance abuse Roger Williams Gen. Hosp., Providence, 1976-82; dir. program in alcoholism and drug abuse Brown U., Providence, 1976-82, prof. medicine and community health, 1982—, Donald G. Millar prof. alcohol and addiction studies, 1987—, chmn. dept. community health, 1981-86, dir. Ctr. Alcohol and Addiction Studies, 1982-2000. Nat. adv. coun. Nat. Alcohol Inst., Rockville, Md., 1981-85, cons. to dir., 1985-93; sci. adv. bd. Children of Alcoholics Found., 1985-95; cons. WHO, 1986-2000, cocaine global adv. com., 1992-95; chair Physician Consortium on Substance Abuse Edn., 1989—99; mem. Carnegie Substance Abuse Adv. com., 1989-92; scholar-in-residence Nat. Inst. Med., 1991-92; adv. panel to U.S. Pharmacopoeia, 1995—99; mem. Drug Strategies Nat. Adv. Panel, 1994—2000, dir. WHO Collaborating Ctr. at Brown U., 1995-2000; nat. adv. com. Robert Wood Johnson Found. Fighting Back program, 1996—2002; bd. dirs. Nat. Coun. Alchoholism and Drug Dependence, 1995-, dep. chair 2002-04, chair, 2004-08; bd. dirs. Drug Policy Alliance. Author: The Drug Experience: Data for Decision Making, 1970; editor: Providing Care for Children of Alcoholics, 1986; editor Brown U. Digest of Addiction Theory and Application, 1986—2001; exec. editor Substance Abuse jour., 1984—; contbr. numerous articles to profl. jours. Med. dir. Beacon Hill Free Clinic, Boston, 1968—71; chmn. Mayor's Coun. on Drug Abuse, Boston, 1972—80; project dir. Physician Leadership on Nat. Drug Policy, 1997—2004; bd. dirs. Physicians and Lawyers for Nat. Drug Policy, 2004—. Grantee Nat. Alcohol and Drug Insts., 1986—, Robert Wood Johnson Found., 1996—, John D. and Catherine T. MacArthur Found., 1997—99, Open Study Inst., 1997—99; Edward John Noble fellow Harvard U. Med. Sch., 1957-91; receipient Assn. Med. Edn. and Rsch. in Substance Abuse award for Excellence in Medical Edn., 1986, Norman E Zinberg Meml. Lectr. award Harvard Med. Sch., 1996, AMA award, 1997, Excellence in Med. Edn. AMA-ERF, 1997, Silvery Key award, 2008. Fellow: ACP; mem.: NAS, Assn. for Edn. and Rsch. in Substance Abuse (bd. dirs. 1985—), Brown Med. Alumni Assn. (pres. 1974—76), Assn. Med. Edn. and Rsch. in Substance Abuse (pres. 1983—88, Excellence in Medicine award 1986), Inst. Medicine Study on Treatment Alcohol Problems, Am. Acad. on Physician and Patient (bd. dirs. 1998—2001), Am. Soc. Addiction Medicine (bd. dirs. 1995—2005, sec. 2003—05, John P. McGovern award 2004), Sigma Xi, Phi Beta Kappa. Avocations: choral singing, sailing, photography. Office: Brown Univ Ctr Alcohol & Addiction Studies Box G-S121-4 Providence RI 02912 Office Phone: 401-863-6639. E-mail: David_Lewis@brown.edu.

LEWIS, EDWIN REYNOLDS, biomedical engineering educator, academic administrator; b. LA, July 14, 1934; s. Edwin McMurtry and Sally Newman (Reynolds) L.; m. Elizabeth Louise McLean, June 11, 1960; children: Edwin McLean, Sarah Elizabeth. AB in Biol. Sci., Stanford U., 1956, MSEE, 1957, Engr., 1959, PhD in Elec. Engring., 1962. With research staff Librascope div. Gen. Precision Inc., Glendale, Calif., 1961-67; mem. faculty dept. elec. engring. and computer sci. U. Calif., Berkeley, 1967—, dir. bioengring. tng. program, 1969-77, prof. elec. engring. and computer sci., 1971-94, prof. grad. sch., 1994-99, prof. emeritus, 1999—, assoc. dean grad. div., 1977-82, assoc. dean interdisciplinary studies coll. engring., 1988-96. Chair joint program bioengring. U. Calif., Berkeley and San Francisco, 1988-91. Author: Network Models in Population Biology, 1977, (with others) Neural Modeling, 1977, The Vertebrate Inner Ear, 1985, Introduction to Bioengineering, 1996; contbr. articles to profl. jours. Grantee NSF, NASA, 1984, 87, Office Naval Rsch., 1990-93, NIH, 1975-2001; Neurosci. Rsch. Program fellow, 1966, 69; recipient Disting. Tchg. citation U. Calif., 1972, Berkeley citation, 1997; Jacob Javits Neurosci. investigator NIH, 1984-91. Fellow IEEE, Acoustical Soc. Am.; mem. AAAS, Assn. Rsch. in Otolaryngology, Soc. Neurosci., Toastmasters (area lt. gov. 1966-67), Sigma Xi. Office: U Calif Dept Elec Engring & Computer Scis Berkeley CA 94720-1770 Business E-Mail: lewis@eecs.berkeley.edu.

LEWIS, EVAN LARSON, urologist; b. Birmingham, Ala., Nov. 28, 1920; s. Robert Ash Lewis and Freeda Larson; m. Bernardine Buck Lewis, Feb. 26, 1944; children: Sharon, Griffith. BA, Howard Coll., Birmingham, Ala., 1942; MD, Johns Hopkins, Balt., 1945. Intern Johns Hopkins Hosp., Balt., 1946, resident urology Walter Reed Med. Ctr., Washington, 1948—52; chief of surgery 21st EVAC Hosp., Pusan, Republic of Korea, 1953; chief of urology Tokyo Gen. Hosp., 1953—56, Letterman Gen. Hosp., San Francisco, 1956—60, Madigan Gen. Hosp., Tacoma; dep. surgeon 8th Army, Seoul; chief of urology Fitsimmons Gen. Hosp., Denver, 1964—69, Walter Reed Gen. Hosp, Washington, 1969—70, occpl. health Rocky Mountain Arsenal, Denver, 1980—85. Contbr. articles to profl. jours. Col. US Army, 1943—73. Fellow: ACS; mem.: AMA, Am. Urological Assn. Achievements include invention of Lewis Stone forcep. Home: 4043 S Newport Denver CO 80237 Personal E-mail: elewis4449@aol.com.

LEWIS, FRANK RUSSELL, JR., surgeon; b. Willards, Md., Feb. 23, 1941; m. Janet Christensen, 1996. AB in Physics, Princeton U., 1961; MD, U. Md., 1965; postgrad. in med. physics, U. Calif., Berkeley, 1970. Surg. dir. M/SICU San Francisco Gen. Hosp., 1973-80, dir. emergency dept., 1980-83, chief of staff, 1983-85, asst. chief of surgery, 1981-86, chief of surgery, 1986-92; prof. surgery Case We. Res. U., Cleve., 1994—2002; chmn. dept. surgery Henry Ford Hosp., Detroit, 1992—2002; exec. dir. Am. Bd. Surgery, 2001—. Fellow: ACS (gov. 1988—93, 1st v.p. 1995—96); mem.: So. Surg. Assn., Shock Soc. (coun. 1978—, pres.), We. Surg. Soc., Ctrl. Surg. Soc., Am. Assn. for Surgery of Trauma (pres. 1999—2002), Am. Surg. Assn. Office: Am Bd Surgery 1617 JFK Blvd Ste 860 Philadelphia PA 19130 Office Phone: 215-568-4000. Business E-Mail: flewis@absurgery.org. *

LEWIS, GENE EVANS, retired medical equipment company executive; b. Terrell, Tex., May 17, 1928; s. John Evans and Helen Elizabeth (Patterson) L.; m. Sonya Dolishny, Jan. 21, 1950; children: Robert, Melissa. BSEE, Tex. A&M U., 1949. Sales, mktg. and engring. mgr. GE, Schenectady, Dallas, Pittsfield, Holyoke, Lynn, 1950-68, gen. mgr. various bus. Milw., 1970-77; group product mgr. Picker X-Ray, Cleve., 1968-70; pres. sci. instruments div. Am. Optical Corp., Southbridge, Mass., 1977-78, pres. internat. div., 1978-79, pres., 1979—84, Baker Instruments Corp., Allentown, Pa., 1985—88; bd. mem. Novecon Technologies, 1994—99. CEO Sterling Semicondr., Inc., 1996-2001. With Signal Corps U.S. Army, 1949. Mem.: Sea Pines Country Clubc, Calibogue Club. Home: 25 Spartina Cres Hilton Head Island SC 29928-2925 Personal E-mail: gelsl@aol.com.

LEWIS, GLADYS SHERMAN, university professor; b. Wynnewood, Okla., Mar. 20, 1933; d. Andrew and Minnie Elva (Halsey) Sherman; m. Wilbur Curtis Lewis, Jan. 28, 1955; children: Karen, David, Leanne, Cristen. AB, Tex. Christian U., 1956; postgrad., Southwestern Bapt. Theol. Sem., 1959-60, Escuela de Idiomas, San Jose, Costa Rica, 1960-61; MA in Creative Writing, Ctrl. State U., Okla., 1985; PhD in English, Okla. State U., 1992. Mem. nursing staff various facilities, Okla., 1953-57; instr. nursing med. missionary Bapt. Mission and Hosp., Paraguay, 1961-70; vice chmn. edn. commn. Paraguay Bapt. Conv., 1962-65; sec. bd. trustees Bapt. Hosp., Paraguay, 1962-65, 1962-65; chmn. personnel com., handbook & policy book officer Bapt. Mission in Paraguay, 1967-70; trustee Southwestern Bapt. Theol. Sem., 1974-84, chmn. student affairs com., 1976-78, vice chmn. bd., 1978-80; ptnr. Las Amigas Tours, 1978-80, writer, conf. leader, campus lectr., 1959—; owner, publisher Greystone Press, LLC, 1998—2008. Adj. prof. English Ctr. State U., Okla. (now U. Ctrl. Okla.),1990-91, faculty mem., asst. prof., English U. Ctrl. Okla., 1991-95, assoc. prof., 1995-2000, prof., 2000—; exec. editor New Plains Rev., 2000-08. Author: On Earth As It Is, 1983, Two Dreams and a Promise, 1984, Message, Messenger and Response, 1994, Loaves and Hyacinths, 1999, Keeping Women in Their Place, 2004, Reading Cooper, Teaching Cooper, 2006, Valley of the Shadow, 2006; editor: The Jewish Roots of Christian Monotheism, 1999, Sooner Physician's Heartbeat, 1979—82; also religious instrnl. texts in English and Spanish, 1960—75; contbr. articles to So. Bapt. and secular periodicals, chpt. to book. Active Dem. com., Evang. Women's Caucus, 1979-80; leader Girl Scouts U.S.A., 1965-75; Okla. co-chmn. Nat. Religious Com. for Equal Rights Amendment, 1977-

79; tour host Meier Internat. Study League, 1978-81. Recipient Lifetime Achievement award, 2007—08, Vanderford Disting. Tchr. award, 2009. Mem. AAUP (UCO Disting. Tchg. Mentor award, 2009, Faculty Mem. of Yr., 2009), Internat. and Am. Coll. Surgeons Women's Auxs., Okla. State, Okla. County Med Auxs., Am. Nurse Assn. Home: 2708 Portofino Pl Edmond OK 73034 Office Phone: 405-974-5607. Business E-Mail: glewis@ucok.edu.

LEWIS, GUY M., cosmetic dentist; Grad., Baylor Coll. of Dentistry. Cosmetic dentist Houston Rocket, Rocket Powerdancers, Houston Astros, Houston Aeros; adjunct prof. Baylor Coll. of Dentistry. Co-founder Am. Acad. of Cosmetic Dentistry. Named Super Dentist, TexasMonthly Mag., Top Doc, H Texas Mag.; nominee Best Dentists in America. Fellow: Internat. Acad. for Dental Facial Esthetics; mem.: ADA, Texas Dental Assn., Am. Acad. of Cosmetic Dentistry. Office: Texas Center for Cosmetic and Implant Dentistry 4800 W Panther Creek Dr Suite 200 Spring TX 77381 Office Phone: 281-367-6465. Office Fax: 281-367-5516.

LEWIS, HAYLEY, psychologist; b. Kent, Eng., Jan. 19, 1974; BA in Social Scis. with honors, U. Leicester, 1995; MSc in Orgnl. Behaviour, City U., 2003. Lectr. City U.; orgnl. psychologist BBC, 1999—2004, people devel. mgr., 2004—05; orgnl. devel. mgr. Croydon Coun. London Borough, 2005—08, head, strategy and innovation, 2009, head, customer strategy and devel., 2009—. Recipient Transformational HR award, Pub. Sector People Mgrs. Assn.; named Practitioner of Yr., Divsn. Occupl. Psychology Brit. Psychol. Soc., 2009. Office: 5th Fl Taberner House Pk Ln Croydon Surrey CR9 3JS England Personal E-mail: hajlewis@googlemail.com.

LEWIS, JERRY M., psychiatrist, educator; b. Utica, NY, Aug. 18, 1924; s. Jerry M. and Margaret (Miller) L.; m. Patsy Ruth Price, Sept. 24, 1949; children: Jerry M., Cynthia Lewis-Reynolds, Nancy Minns, Tom. MD, Southwestern Med. Sch., Dallas, 1951. Diplomate Am. Bd. Psychiatry and Neurology. Staff psychiatrist Timberlawn Psychiat. Hosp., Dallas, 1957-63, chief women's svc., 1963-66, chief adolescent svcs., 1966-70, dir. profl. edn., 1970-79, psychiatrist-in-chief, 1979-88, dir. rsch., 1988-93. Dir. rsch. and tng. Timberlawn Psychiat. Rsch. Found., Dallas, 1967-88, sr. rsch. psychiatrist, 1988—; clin. prof. psychiatry, family practice and cmty. medicine Southwestern Med. Sch.; cons. in psychiatry Baylor U. Med. Ctr., Dallas. Author: No Single Thread, 1976, How's Your Family, 1978, To Be a Therapist, 1979, The Long Struggle, 1983, Swimming Upstream: Teaching Psychotherapy in a Biological Era, 1991, The Monkey-Rope, 1995, Marriage as a Search for Healing: Theory, Assessment & Therapy, 1997, (with John Gossett, Ph.D.) Disarming the Past: How an Intimate Relationship Can Heal Old Wounds, 1999, Reflections on the Good Life: A Psychotherapist Writes to His Grandchildren, 2005, Famous Marriages: What They Can Teach Us, 2006. Served with USN, 1943-45. Fellow Am. Coll. Psychiatrists (pres. 1985), Am. Psychiat. Assn., So. Psychiat. Assn. (pres. 1979); mem. Group for Advancement of Psychiatry (pres. 1987), Benjamin Rush Soc. (pres. 1994-95), AMA, Tex. Med. Assn. Office: PO Box 270789 Dallas TX 75227-0789 Office Phone: 214-275-4001.

LEWIS, JONATHAN JOSEPH, surgical oncologist, molecular biologist, educator, entrepreneur; b. Johannesburg, May 23, 1958; s. Myer Philip and Maisie (Bagg) Lewis; m. Nanci Lynn Vicedomini, May 20, 1990. MB BCH, Witwatersrand U., Johannesburg, 1982; PhD, Yale U., 1990. Registrar in surgery Witwatersrand U. Sch. Medicine, Johannesburg, 1982-87; postdoctoral assoc. Yale U. Sch. Medicine, New Haven, 1987-90, chief resident, surgery, 1990-92; fellow dept. surgery Meml. Sloan-Kettering Cancer Ctr., NYC, 1992-94, attending surgeon, 1994—, asst. mem., 1994-99, assoc. mem., 1999—2001, mem., 2001—; chmn., CEO, pres. Ziopharm, NYC, 2004—; chmn., joint com. Ziopharm-Intrexon. Asst. prof. surgery Cornell U. Med. Coll., 1994—99, assoc. prof., 1999—2001, prof., 2001—; chief med. officer Antigenics Inc., NYC, 2000—03. Contbr. articles to profl. jours. Bd. mem. Poppa NYPD, Hope Funds Cancer Chmn. Sci. Adv. Coun.; adv. bd. mem. Combat Working Initiative Program. Recipient Abelheim medal, Med. Coun., 1982, Trubshaw medal, Coll. Surgeons, Johannesburg, 1984, OHSE award, Yale U., 1989, Outstanding Tchr. award, Meml. Sloan-Kettering Cancer Ctr., 1997, Hope award, Sarcoma Found., 2009, Vision award, 2009, Brown award, KACR, 2010; Winston fellow, Sloan-Kettering Inst., 1994—95. Fellow: ACS, Royal Soc. Medicine, Royal Coll. Surgeons; mem.: Am. Soc. Hematol., Yale Biotechnology Soc. (bd. mem.), Sweet Rexies LLC. (chmn.), N.Y. Acad. Scis., Soc. Surg. Oncology, Assn. Acad. Surgeons, Am. Soc. Clin. Oncology (Young Investigator award 1994), Am. Assn. Cancer Rsch., Am. Soc. Cell Biology. Jewish. Achievements include research in oncogenes; growth factors; signal transduction; immunotherapy; gene therapy, cancer drug development. Office: ZIOPHARM Oncology Inc 1180 Avenue of the Americas 19th Flr New York NY 10036 also: Parris Bldg Navy Yard Boston MA 02129 also: Seneca Meadows Parkway Germantown MD 20876

LEWIS, MICHAEL JUSTIN, state official, medical educator; s. Jacob Louis Seyfried and Rebecca June Cantley; m. Mino R. Rafee, Dec. 20, 2001; children: Beth Renee Minear, Tana Michelle Uhl. MS in Chem. Engring., Va. Poly. Inst. and State U., Blacksburg, Va., 1966, PhD in Chem. Engring., 1968; MD, W.Va. U., Morgantown, 1974. Cert. Am. Acad. Family Physicians, 1979. Prof. and chmn. family medicine W. Va. U., Sch. Medicine, Morgantown, 1985—92, chmn., bd. dir., 1987—92; assoc v.p. health scis., clin. campus dean sch. medicine W. Va. U., 1992—2001; vice chancellor W.Va. Higher Edn. Policy Commn., Morgantown, 2001—02; vice chancellor, divsn. health scis. East Carolina U., Greenville, 2002—06, exec. asst. chancellor, 2006—08, prof. family medicine, 2008—11; sec. W.Va. Dept. Health & Human Resources, Charleston, 2011—. Contbr. articles to profl. jours. Invited consult king of Nepal Cons. Group Creating New Med. Sch., Kathmandu, 1995; legislative com. C. of C., Greenville, 2007—08; vol. physician uninsured W.Va. Health Right, Charleston, 2008; dir. Wedgewood Summit Retirement Cmty., Charleston, W.Va., 1994—2001. Recipient Disting. award, Gov. W.Va., 2002. Fellow: American Acad. Family Physicians (fellowship 1985). Independent. Avocations: travel, hiking, history. Office: West Virginia Dept Health & Human Resources One Davis Sq Ste 100 E Charleston WV 25301 Office Phone: 304-558-0684. Office Fax: 304-558-1130. E-mail: DHHRsecretary@wv.gov. *

LEWIS, MICHAEL ROBERT, medical researcher, educator; b. Madison, Wis., Sept. 29, 1962; s. Robert Glenn and Sue Ann Lewis; m. Varyanna Chryzhtjanok Ruthengael, Sept. 28, 1991. PhD, City of Hope Grad. Sch. of Biol. Scis., Duarte, Calif., 1994—97. NIH post doc. fellow Wash. U., St. Louis, 1997—2000; asst. prof. U. of Mo. Columbia, 2000—. Study sect. reviewer NIH, Bethesda, Md., 2002—; ad hoc reviewer Bioconjugate Chemistry Internat. Jour. Pharmaceutics, Jour. Nuclear Medicine; mem. bd. dirs. Radiopharmaceutical Scis. Coun. Grantee, Dept. Health and Human Svcs. Nat. Cancer Inst., 2003—, Dept. of Def., 2001—, 2002—, Dept. of Vet. Affairs, 2005—. Mem.: AAAS, Soc. of Radiopharmaceutical Chemistry and Biology, Soc. of Nuc. Medicine (bd. dirs.), Am. Chem. Soc., Alpha Chi Sigma. Office: U MO Columbia 379 E Campus Dr Columbia MO 65211 Business E-Mail: lewismic@missouri.edu.

LEWIS, MITCHELL S., retired hematologist, consultant; b. Kimberley, South Africa, Apr. 3, 1924; s. Coleman James Lewis and Fanny Zweiback; m. Ethel Norma Nochumowitz, Oct. 23, 1959; 1 child, Raymond. BSc, MD, U. Cape Town, South Africa, 1949; diploma in clin. pathology, London U., 1953. Sr. lectr. Royal Postgrad. Med. Sch., London, 1962—67, reader in hematology, 1967—89; emeritus reader in hematology U. London, 1989—2009. Dir. WHO Collaborating Centre Hematology Tech., London, 1989—; founder, dir. UK Nation Extenal Quality Assesment Scheme. Author: Dacie & Lewis Practical Hematology, 10th edit., 2006; emeritus editor 11th edit., 2011; contbr. 350 sci. & clin. papers to profl. publs. Chmn. Internat. Coun. Standardization in Hematology, 1982—96, chmn. emeritus, 2006—. Rsch. fellow hematology, Imperial Coll. London, 2002—. Fellow: Inst. Biomed. Sci., Royal Coll. Pathologists, Internat. Soc. Hematology (counsellor at large 1990—2007); mem.: WHO (mem. adv. panel on health lab. svcs. 1995—2005), Brit. Soc. Hematology (hon.; past pres.). Achievements include development of WHO haemoglobin colour scale. Avocations: music, travel. Office: Hammersmith Hosp DuCane Rd London W12 ONN England Home: 6 Salisbury House Somerset Rd SW19 5HY London England Personal E-mail: smlenl@blueyonder.co.uk. Business E-Mail: sm.lewis@imperial.ac.uk.

LEWIS, PAUL LE ROY, pathology educator; b. Tamaqua, Pa., Aug. 30, 1925; s. Harry Earl and Rose Estella (Brobst) L.; m. Betty Jane Bixby, June 2, 1953; 1 child, Robert Harry. AB magna cum laude, Syracuse U., 1950; MD, SUNY, Syracuse, 1953. Diplomate Am. Bd. Pathology. Intern Temple U. Hosp., Phila., 1953-54; resident in pathology Hosp. of U. Pa., Phila., 1954-58, asst. instr., 1957-58; instr. pathology Thomas Jefferson U. Coll. Medicine, Phila., 1958-62, asst. prof., 1962-65, assoc. prof., 1965-75, prof., 1975-93, hon. prof., 1993—; pathologist Thomas Jefferson U. Hosp., 1958-91; attending pathologist Meth. Hosp., Phila., 1975-93, dir. clin. labs., chmn. dept. pathology, 1975-92, consulting pathologist, 1993—; pathologist pvt. practice Phila., 1993—. Pres. Penndel Labs. Inc., Ardmore, Pa., 1974-85; cons. VA Hosp., Coatesville, Pa., 1976-85; mem. med. adv. com. ARC Blood Bank, Phila., 1978—2006. Contbg. author: Atlas of Gastrointestinal Cytology, 1983; contbr. articles to med. jours. 2d lt. USAAF, 1943-46. Fellow Am. Soc. Clin. Pathologists, Coll. Am. Pathologists; mem. AMA, Pa. Med. Soc., Philadelphia County Med. Soc., Internat. Acad. Pathology, Am. Soc. Cytology, Masons, Phi Beta Kappa, Alpha Omega Alpha, Nu Sigma Nu. Republican. Methodist. Avocations: photography, hiking. Home and Office: 521 Baird Rd Merion Station PA 19066-1301

LEWIS, RANDOLPH VANCE, molecular biologist, researcher; b. Powell, Wyo., Apr. 8, 1950; s. William (Jack) Fredrick and Evelyn Jean (Vonburg) L.; m. Lorrie Dale Emery, May 27, 1972; children: Brian, Daryl (dec.), Karren. BS in Chemistry, Calif. Inst. Tech., 1972; MS in Chemistry, U. Calif., San Diego, 1974; PhD in Chemistry, U. Calif., 1978. Postdoctoral fellow Roche Inst. Molecular Biology, Nutley, N.J., 1978-80; asst. prof. molecular biology U. Wyo., Laramie, 1980-84, assoc. prof., 1984-89, head dept., 1986-91, prof., 1989—2011; USTAR prof. Utah State U., 2011—; dir. NSF EPSCOR Program, 1990—2010. Cons. NIH, Bethesda, Md., 1985—91, Hoffman-LaRoche, Nutley, NJ, 1990—93, DuPont, Wilmington, Del., 1990—94, Protein Polymer Techs., San Diego, 1988—94, Nexia, 1999—; pres. Wyobigen, Laramie, Wyo., 1994—2011; bd. dirs. Wyo. Bus. Devel. Ctr. Author chpts. to books; contbr. articles to profl. jours. Mem. Jr. Livestock Sale Com., Laramie, 1991-98; pres. Albany County 4-H Coun., Laramie, 1994-98. Sloan Found. fellow, 1985; recipient Research Career Devel. award NIH, 1985, Jr. Faculty award Am. Cancer Soc., 1985, Burlington-North Faculty award U. Wyo., 1986, UW Outstanding Faculty, 2007. Mem. Am. Chem. Soc., Am. Soc. Biochemists and Molecular Biologists, N.Y. Acad. Scis., Protein Soc. Republican. Baptist. Achievements include discovery of opioid peptide precursor; sequencing of all 6 different spider silk protein genes; five product licenses; 7 patents. Home: 3832 5250 E Nibley UT 84321 Office: 204 G 650 E Grand Ave North Logan UT 84341 Office Phone: 435-797-9291. Business E-Mail: silk@uwyo.edu, randv.lewis@usu.edu.

LEWIS, RICHARD ALAN, neurologist, educator; s. Bernard and Miriam Lewis; m. Lynn Souchal Kuttnauer, Oct. 25, 1997; m. Christine Marie Guarino, Dec. 27, 1974 (div. Feb. 22, 1995); children: Rachel Devorah, Benjamin David. BS, Union Coll., Schenectady, NY, 1970. Diplomate Am. Bd. Medicine, 1974. Asst. prof. neurology U. Pa., Phila., 1978—80, U. Conn., Farmington, 1980—83; clin. asst. prof. neurology Ea. Va. Med. Sch., Norfolk, Va., 1983—93; assoc. prof. and assoc. chair neurolgoy Wayne State U. Sch. Medicine, Detroit, 1993—98, prof. and assoc. chmn. neurology, 1998—. Bd. mem. ALS, Southfield, Mich., 1994—2008; med. adv. bd. Guillain Barre Sydrome, CIDP Found. Internat., Phila., 2000—08, Myasthenia Gravis Found., Chgo., 2000—08. Fellow: Am. Acad. Neurolgy. Avocation: violin. Office: Wayne State Univ Sch Medicine UHC 8D 4201 Saint Antoine Detroit MI 48201 Office Fax: 313-745-4216. Business E-Mail: ralewis@med.wayne.edu.

LEWIS, ROBERT DAVID, ophthalmologist, educator; b. Thomasville, Ga., Aug. 27, 1948; s. Ralph N. and E. Margaret (Klaus) Lewis; m. Cathleen Ann Polster Lewis, May 26, 1996. BS, St. Louis Coll. Pharmacy, 1971; MD, St. Louis U., 1975. Diplomate Am. Bd. Ophthalmology, registered pharmacist. Intern Cardinal Glennon Hosp. Children, St. Louis, 1975—76, dir. pediat. ophthalmology, 1980—82, 1985, St. Louis U., 1980—82, 1985, resident, 1976—79, asst. prof., 1980—88, assoc. prof., 1988—97, clin. prof. ophthalmology, 1998; pres. St. Louis Ophthal. Soc., 1991—92; adv. bd. Delta Gamma Found. Visually Handicapped Children. Recipient Tchg. award, St. Louis U., 1982. Fellow: ACS; mem.: AMA, St. Louis Opthalmological Soc, Am. Intraocular Implant Soc., Internat. Assn. Ocular Surgeons, Contact Lens Assn. Ophthalmology, Am. Acad. Ophthalmology, St. Louis Med. Soc. (pres. 1991—92), Mo. Med. Assn., Am. Bd. Club. (pres. 1991—92). Office: 12700 Southfork Rd Ste 205 Saint Louis MO 63128-3201 Office Phone: 314-842-0582.

LEWIS, ROBERT EDWIN, JR., pathology and immunology educator, researcher; b. Meridian, Miss., Mar. 11, 1947; s. Robert Edwin and Cecille (Ryan) Lewis. BA in Biology and Chemistry, U. Miss., 1969, MS in Microbiology, 1973, PhD in Pathology, 1976; specialty tng., Barnes Hosp., U. Miami Med. Ctr., U. Tenn. Ctr. for Health Scis., City of Memphis Hosps., St. Jude Children's Research Hosp. Instr. pathology, anesthesiology U. Miss. Med. Ctr., Jackson, 1976-77, asst. prof. pathology, 1977-84, asst. prof. anesthesiology, 1977-85, asst. dir. clin. immnuopathology lab., 1978-81, assoc. dir. tissue typing lab., 1980-84, dir. paternity testing lab., 1981—, assoc. dir. clin. immunopathology lab., 1981-84, asst. prof. nurse anesthesiology, 1981-85, assoc. prof. pathology, 1984-91, prof., 1991—, dir. clin. immunology, tissue typing lab., 1984—, mem. grad. council, 1981—, prof., 1991—. Co-author: Illus. Dictionary of Immunology, 1995, 2003, 3rd edit., 2009, Atlas of Immunology, 1999, 2d edit., 2004, 3rd edit., 2010; co-author: (with J.M. Cruse) Immunology Guidebook, 2004, Historical Atlas of Immunology, 2005; editor (with J.M. Cruse): Concepts in Immunopathology, Vols. 1-8, 1985—91; editor: The Yr. in Immunology-1984-85, 1985, The Yr. in Immunology-1986-8, 1987, The Yr. in Immunology-1988, 1989, The Yr. in Immunology-1989-90, 1990, Progress in Exptl. Tumor Rsch. Vol. 32, 1987, Contributions to Microbiology and Immunology, Vol. 8, 1986, Vol. 9, 1987, Vol. 10, 1989, Vol. 11, 1989, The Yr. in Immunopathology, 1987, Complement Profiles, Vol. 1, 1992, Historical Atlas of Immunology, 2004; sr. editor Immunologic Research, 1981, Pathology and Immunopathology Rsch., 1982—90, Pathobiology, 1990—98, Pathology, 1990—98, Transgenics, 1993, Exptl. and Molecular Pathology, 1999, series editor Concepts in Immunopathology, The Yr. in Immunology, Contributions to Microbiology and Immunology, vol. editor Progress in Exptl. Tumor Rsch, immunology editor Dorland's Illus. Med. Dictionary, 26th and 27th edits., dep. editor-in-chief Pathobiology, 1990—98; contbr. chpts. to books. Am. Cancer Soc. grantee, NIH grantee, Wilson Found. grantee, 1990-2002. Fellow Royal Soc. Health, Royal Soc. Medicine; mem. AAAS, Am. Assn. Pathologists, Am. Assn. Immunologists, Clin. Immunology Soc., Can. Soc. Immunology, Reticuloendothelial Soc., Am. Soc. Microbiology, Am. Soc. Histocompatibility and Immunogenetics (chmn. publs. com. 2000-03, bd. dirs. 2004—), Exptl. Biology and Medicine, N.Y. Acad. Scis., Miss. Acad. Scis., Sigma Xi. Office: U Miss Med Ctr Pathology Dept Dept Pathology 2500 N State St Jackson MS 39216-4500 Home Phone: 601-856-5045; Office Phone: 601-984-1562. Business E-Mail: rlewis@pathology.umsmed.edu.

LEWIS, SANDRA COMBS, research psychologist, writer; b. Troup County, Ga., Oct. 8, 1939; d. Robert Milton and Imogene (Richardson) Combs; children: Virginia Susan Lewis, Charles James III. AB, Wesleyan Coll., 1961; MEd, Mercer U., 1972, Ga. State U., 1976; PhD, U. Ga., 1980. Personnel asst. Sears Roebuck & Co., Atlanta, 1961—62; rsch. asst. bd. regents U. Sys. Ga., 1962—63; asst. psychol. svcs. Bibb County Bd. Edn., Macon, 1972—73; instr. Macon Jr. Coll., 1973, 1982, Wesleyan Coll., 1973—75, 1981; psychometrist Middle Ga. Psychoednl. Ctr., 1975—76; instr. Mercer U., 1980—82. Presenter at profl. confs. Co-author: Christian Love and Problems of Living, 1992, God and Positive Christianity, 1998, Psychology for Life, 2000, A Revolutionary View of Education and Teaching for the Third Millennium, 2002; assoc. editor Truth Seekers Newsletter, 1998-2006, editor, 2007—. Pres. Macon Wesleyan Alumnae Club, 1973-74; bd. dirs. Family Counseling Ctr., Macon, 1975-76; ruling elder, clk. of session Northminster Presbyn. Ch., Macon, 1988-90, 94-96, vice moderator Presbyn. Women, 1989-90, 2002, 08, moderator Presbyn. Women, 1990-91, 2003; trustee Northminster Presbyn. Ch., 2011-; v.p. Fore(In)Sight Found., 1991-2006; pres. Fore(In)Sight Found., 2006—. Mem.: DAR (treas. Mary Hammond Wash. Chpt. 2008—), APA (life), Mid. Ga. Psychol. Assn., Ga. Psychol. Assn. (life). Avocations: gardening, photography. Home and Office: 4976 Oxford Rd Macon GA 31210-3059 Office Phone: 478-474-3869. Business E-Mail: foreignsight@excite.com.

LEWIS, SHARON, federal agency administrator; BFA, Washington U., St. Louis. Pub. policy positions Oreg. Devel. Disabilities Coalition; pub. policy dir. The Arc of Multnomah-Clackamas, Portland, Oreg.; founder DisabilityCompass.org; program mgr. Oreg. Partners in Policymaking; Kennedy pub. policy fellow US Senate Subcom. Children & Families, Washington; sr. disability policy advisor US House Com. Edn. & Labor, 2007—10; commr. Adminstrn. Devel. Disabilities, US Dept. Health & Human Services, 2010—. Fed. mem. Interagency Autism Coordinating Com., HHS, 2010—. Recipient Gold Star award, Assn. Univ. Centers Disabilities, 2008, Disting. Leadership in Nat. Disability Policy award, American Assn. Intellectual & Devel. Disabilities, 2010, Chairman's award, Consortium Citizens with Disabilities. Office: Administration for Children and Families 370 L Enfant Promenade Washington DC 20447 Office Phone: 202-690-6590. *

LEWIS, SHIRLEY JEANE, retired therapist, educator; b. Phoenix, Aug. 23; d. Herman and Leavy (Hutchinson) Smith; m. Edgar Anthony Lewis (div.); children: Edgar Anthony (dec.), Roshaun, Lucy Ann, Jonathan. AA, Phoenix C.C., 1957; BA, Ariz. State U., 1960; MS, San Diego State U., 1975, MA, 1985, Azusa Pacific U., 1982; PhD, U. So. Calif., 1983. Cert. tchr. Calif. Recreation leader Phoenix Parks and Recreation Dept., 1957-62; columnist Ariz. Tribune, Phoenix, 1958-59; tchr. phys. edn. San Diego Unified Schs., 1962—; adult educator San Diego C.C., 1973—94; counselor San Diego County Schs., 1979—97; assoc. prin. Oceanside (Calif.) Unified Sch. Dist., 1997—98; head counselor Gomper Secondary Sch. San Diego (Calif.) Unified Schs., 1998—2003, ret. Gomper Secondary Sch., 2003. Instr. psychology, health, Black studies, 1977—, counselor, 1981—; cmty. counselor S.E. Counseling and Cons. Svcs. and Narcotics Prevention and Edn. Sys., Inc., San Diego, 1973-77; counselor educator, counselor edn. dept. San Diego State U., 1974-77; marriage, family, child counselor Counseling and Cons. Ctr., San Diego, 1977—; inservice educator San Diego Unified and San Diego County Sch. Dists., 1973-77; Fulbright Exch. counselor, London, 1994-96; instr. San Diego (Calif.) C.C., 1977-94, counselor, 1981-94; lectr. in field. Contbr. articles to profl. jours. Girl Scout phys. fitness cons., Phoenix, 1960-62; vol. cmty. tutor for high sch. students, San Diego, 1963; sponsor Tennis Club for Youth, San Diego, 1964-65; troop leader Girl Scouts U.S., Lemon Grove, Calif., 1972-74; vol. counselor USN Alcohol Rehab. Ctr., San Diego, 1978; mem. sch. coun.'s adv. bd. San Diego State U. Named Woman of Yr., Phoenix, 1957, One of

Outstanding Women of San Diego, 1980; recipient Phys. Fitness Sch. award and Demonstration Sch. award Pres.'s Coun. on Phys. Fitness, Taft Jr. H.S., 1975, Excel award Corp. Excellence Edn., 1989; Delta Sigma Theta scholar, 1957-60; Alan Korrick scholar, 1956. Mem. NEA, Calif. Tchrs. Assn., San Diego Tchrs. Assn., Assn. Marriage and Family Counselors, Am. Personnel and Guidance Assn., Calif. Assn. Health, Phys. Edn. and Recreation (v.p. health), Am. Alliance of Health, Phys. Edn. and Recreation, Assn. Black Psychologists (corr. sec. 1993), Assn. African-Am. Educators, Delta Sigma Theta (Delta of Yr. 1987). Democrat. Baptist. Home: 1226 Armacost Rd San Diego CA 92114-3307

LEWIS, SIMON JOHN GEOFFREY, neurologist, researcher; b. Apr. 14, 1970; MBBCh, U. Wales, 1995, degree in Neuroscience, 2003. Physician, dir., parkinson's disease rsch. clin., Brain & Mind Rsch. Inst. U. Sydney, 2009—. Grant, NHMRC, Project grant, Michael J. Fox Found., ARC. Fellow: Royal Australasian Coll. Physicians; mem.: RCP. Avocation: field hockey. Office: Brain & Mind Rsch Inst Sydney NSW 2050 Australia Office Fax: 61 2 95157565. Business E-Mail: simonl@med.usyd.edu.au.

LEWIS, THOMAS JOHN, III, hospital administrator; b. Pitts., Mar. 26, 1952; s. Thomas John and Nancy (Hoser) L.; m. Kathleen Dalrymple, Sept. 4, 1983; children: Benjamin Stephen, Jeffrey Thomas. BA in Biology, Bucknell U., 1974; MHA, Duke U., 1976. Adminstrv. resident Thomas Jefferson U. Hosp., Phila., 1976-77, acting dir. quality assurance and MR, 1977-79, mgr. care program, 1979-82, asst. exec. dir., 1982-85, dir., 1984-85, assoc. exec. dir., 1985-89, exec. dir., chief oper. officer, 1989-90, sr. v.p., chief exec. officer, pres., CEO Thomas Jefferson Univ. Hospital, Phila. Mem. adminstrv. bd. Coun. Teaching Hosps. and Health Systems. Bd. dirs. Phila. Health Acad., Welcon of Delaware Valley, Phila. Mem. Am. Coll. Health Care Execs. (nominee), Delaware Valley Hosp. Coun., Hosp. Assn. Pa. Office: Thomas Jefferson U Hosp Walnut 11th St Philadelphia PA 19107

LEWIS, VERNA MAE, physiatrist; b. Texarkana, Tex., May 31, 1951; d. John Davis and Gladys Vern (Brown) L.; m. Samuel Dubois Robinson, Feb. 20, 1988. BS in Biology, U. Houston, 1972, MS in Microbial and Plant Biochemistry, 1974; MD, Baylor Coll. of Medicine, 1984. Diplomate Am. Bd. Phys. Medicine and Rehab. Rsch. asst. U. Houston, 1973; sr. rsch. asst. Baylor Coll. of Medicine/VA Hosp., Tex. Med. Ctr., Houston, 1975-80; resident in phys. medicine and rehab. Mayo Grad. Sch. of Medicine, Rochester, Minn., 1984-88; chairperson, med. dir. dept. phys. medicine and rehab. Lewis-Gale Hosp., Salem, Va., 1988—. Student asst. dept. edn. U. Houston, 1972-79; guest lectr. annual meeting Am. Coll. Rheumatology, 1990; med. dir., chairperson, Lewis-Gale Regional Rehab. Ctr., Salem.; mem. instl. rev. bd. Lewis-Gale Clinic. Contbr. articles to profl. jours. Active exec. com., utilization rev. com. Lewis-Gale Hosp., 1990—, trustee, 1991—; bd. dirs. Tomorrow's Teacher's Program, Roanoke, Va., 1991, ARC, Roanoke, 1991, Girl Scouts Am., Roanoke, 1993; active Va. Med. Polit. Action Com., Richmond, Va., 1993, Roanoke Continentals. Microbiology Teaching fellow U. Houston, 1973, Immunology Teaching fellow, 1974, Gen. Biology Teaching fellow, 1974, Teaching and Rsch. fellow, 1973-74; Rsch. grantee Mayo Found., 1986-88. Fellow Am. Acad. phys. Medicine and Rehab. (Am. Cong. Rehab. Medicine); mem. AMA, Nat. Med. Assn., Am. Med. Women's Assn., Va. Soc. Phys. Medicine and Rehab., Assn. Acad. Physiatrists, Roanoke Acad. Medicine. Baptist. Avocations: interior decorating, reading, playing the piano, biking. Office: Lewis Gale Hosp 1900 Electric Rd Salem VA 24153-7494 *

LEWIS-WAMBI, JOAN, medical educator; b. Georgetown, Guyana, Nov. 23, 1973; BS, Rutgers U., 1996, PhD, 2002. Asst. prof. Fox Chase Cancer Ctr., 2005—. Recipient Career Devel. award, NCI, NIH, Young Investigator award. Mem.: Am. Assn. Cancer Rsch. Avocations: travel, reading, exercise. Office: 333 Cottman Ave Philadelphia PA 19111 Business E-Mail: joan.lewis@fccc.edu.

LEWITTES, DON JORDAN, psychologist; b. Bklyn., Jan. 21, 1950; s. Morton H. and Laura C. L.; 1 child, Jason D. BA, NYU, 1971; PhD, SUNY, Albany, 1976. Diplomate Am. Bd. Med. Psychotherapists, Am. Bd. Forensic Examiners, Am. Bd. Forensic Medicine, Am. Bd. Psychol. Specialities. Instr. dept. psychiatry Albany Med. Coll., 1976-78; clin. affiliate, prof. of psychology St. John's U., 1983-85; sr. psychologist Schenectady Shared Svcs., Ellis Hosp., 1976-77; dir. adminstrv. and clin. inpatient svcs. South Richmond-South Beach Psychiat. Ctr., SI, NY, 1977-81; chief psychologist South Nassau Cmty. Hosp., Oceanside, NY, 1982-87; cons. Nassau Coalition on Child Abuse and Neglect, Hempstead, NY, 1989-98. Psychol. cons. Gracie Sq. Hosp., N.Y.C., 1989-91; expert cons. N.Y.C. Office Legal Affairs/ACS, 1991—, Kings County and Bronx County Dist. Atty's. Office, 1994—, expert forensic witness US Dept. Defence, USAF, US USN, USMC.; adjunct faculty Grad. Sch. Social Svc. Fordham U., 1995-96; intern dept. psychiatry Rutgers Med. Sch., Piscataway, N.J., 1974-75. Contbr. articles to profl. jours. Mem. Am. Psychol. Soc., Am. Profl. Soc. on the Abuse of Children. Office: Ste 150 30 Hempstead Ave Rockville Centre NY 11570-4033 Home Phone: 212-879-4277; Office Phone: 516-763-1631. Personal E-mail: djlewittesphd@gmail.com.

LEWKOWIEZ, LAURENT, cardiac electrophysiologist, educator; MD, U. SC, 1992. Diplomate Am. Bd. Internal Medicine-cardiovasc. disease, 2000, Am. Bd. Internal Medicine-clin. cardiac electrophysiology. Resident internal medicine Univ. of Colo., 1993—96, fellow nuclear cardiology, 1997—98, asst. prof. medicine. Office: Franklin Medical Offices 2045 Franklin St Denver CO 80205 Office Phone: 303-338-4545, 303-436-8908.

LEWY, ROBERT MAX, physician; b. NYC, Oct. 18, 1945; s. Martin and Ellen (Newmark) L.; m. Barbara, Oct. 4, 1987; children: Jennifer, Sarah. AB, U. Rochester, 1967; MD, U. Medicine and Dentistry N.J., Newark, 1971; MPH, Columbia U., 1977. Diplomate Nat. Bd. Med. Examiners, Am. Bd. Family Practice. Intern Dartmouth Affiliated Hosps., Hanover, NH, 1971-72; resident Maine-Dartmouth Family Practice Program, Augusta, 1974-75; clin. scholar Columbia U., NYC, 1975-77; dir. employee health svcs. Presbyn. Hosp., Columbia-Presbyn. Med. Ctr., NYC, 1977-88, dir. office physician affairs, 1988-91, sr. v.p. med. affairs, 1991-98; assoc. prof. medicine Columbia U., NYC, 1991—2010, sr. assoc. dean health affairs, dir. ctr. med. edn., 1998—2010. Author: Preventive Primary Medicine, 1981, Employees at Risk, 1991; contbr. articles to profl. jours. With USPHS, 1972-74. Fellow Am. Occupational Med. Assn. (sec. chmn. 1984-88), Am. Coll. Preventive Medicine; mem. Am. Pub. Health Assn., N.Y. Occupational Med. Assn. (bd. dirs. 1985—2000). Home: 864 Bradley Pky Blauvelt NY 10913-1127 Office: Columbia U Box 100 630 W 168th St New York NY 10032-3795 E-mail: rl10@columbia.edu.

LEY, RONALD, psychologist, educator; b. Buffalo, Oct. 19, 1929; s. August Andreas and Marie (Jerge) L.; m. Carmen De Brito, Jan. 16, 1965; 1 child, Jessica Elizabeth. BA, U. Buffalo, 1951; PhD, Syracuse U., 1963. Rsch. dir. Madison Area Project, Syracuse, 1962—63; asst. prof. psychology No. Ill. U., DeKalb, 1963—64; asst. prof. grad. faculty New Sch. U., NYC, 1964—66; prof. psychology and stats. SUNY Albany, 1966—99, rsch. prof., 1999—. Cons. Nat. Inst. for Occupational Safety and Health; vis. prof. psychology U. P.R., 1969, cardiac dept., Charing Cross Hosp., London, 1988. Author: A Whisper of Espionage, 1990, Rumores de Espionaje: Wolfgang Köhler y los Monos en Tenerife, 1995; co-editor: Behavioral and Psychological Approaches to Breathing Disorders, 1994; mem. editl. bd. Jour. Behavior Therapy and Exptl. Psychiatry, 1983—, Applied Psychophysiology and Biofeedback, 1997—, Behavior Modification, Jour. Anxiety Disorders, guest editor Biofeedback and Self-Regulation, 1994; guest editor: Behavior Modification, 2001; guest editor Behavior Modification, 2003; contbr. articles to profl. jours. and encys. Bd. dirs. Father's Assn. of the Albany Acad. for Girls, 1981-84. Rsch. fellow SUNY, 1967-68, 70, 74, 76, 78, 91, Rsch. grantee, 1967-72, 74-76, 78, 87-88, 91-92, 96-97, Nat. Inst. Occupl. Safety and Health grantee, 1982-83, 87-88, others. Fellow Am. Psychol. Soc., Behavior Therapy and Rsch. Soc., Assn. for Psychol. Sci.; mem. APA, Anxiety Disorders Assn. Am., Am. Statis. Assn., Assn. Advancement Behavior Therapy, Assn. Applied Psychophysiology and Biofeedback (chmn. sect. applied respiratory psychophysiology 1998-99), Authors Guild, Authors League Am., Ea. Psychol. Assn., Internat. Soc. Advancement Respiratory Psychophysiology (co-founder, pres. 1994-96), Psychol. Assn. Northeastern N.Y. (sec. 1967-68, pres. 1983-84, Disting. Psychologist award 1996), Soc. Psychophysiol. Rsch., Psychonomic Soc., Sigma Xi. Home: 22 Marion Ave Albany NY 12203-1823 Office Phone: 518-442-5055.

LEY, TIMOTHY JAMES, hematologist, molecular biologist; b. Buffalo Ctr., Iowa, June 17, 1953; s. William Dean and Clara Ruth (Odland) L.; m. Patricia Ann Hohn, Aug. 21, 1986; children: Amelia, James, Anna. BA, Drake U., 1974; MD, Washington U., St. Louis, 1978. Diplomate Am. Bd. Internal Medicine and Hematology. Resident in medicine Mass. Gen. Hosp., Boston, 1978-80; fellow in hematology NIH, Bethesda, Md., 1980-83, sr. investigator, 1984-86; fellow in hematology and oncology Washington U. Med. Sch., St. Louis, 1983-84, asst. prof. medicine and genetics, 1986-90, assoc. prof. medicine, 1990-93, prof. medicine and genetics, 1993—. Assoc. dir. basic rsch. Siteman Cancer Ctr., 1999—2008; assoc. dir. cancer genomics Genome Ctr. Wash. U., 2008—. Mem. Gasconade County R2 Sch. Bd., Mo., 2000—09. With USPHS, 1980—86. Fellow AAAS; mem. Inst. of Medicine, NAS, Am. Soc. Hematology, Am. Soc. Biochemistry and Molecular Biology, Am. Soc. for Clin. Investigation (pres. 1997-98), Am. Assn. Physicians (coun. 2007—), Phi Beta Kappa, Alpha Omega Alpha. Democrat. Mem. United Ch. Christ. Achievements include rsch. in practical feasibility of manipulating fetal hemoglobin production in patients with hemoglobinopathies; development of mouse models of human leukemias, genomic studies of acute myeloid leukemia, and determination of roles of proteases in immune effector cell functions. Office: Washington U Med Sch Box 8007 660 S Euclid Ave Saint Louis MO 63110-1010 Home Phone: 573-437-5497; Office Phone: 314-362-8831. Business E-Mail: timley@wustl.edu.

LEYKIN, YIGAL, anesthesiologist, educator; b. Lwow, Ukraine, July 20, 1949; s. Zecharia and Bussia Leykin; m. Cristina Maraffi, Feb. 11, 1962; children: Davide, Michele, Sara, Chiara. MD, U. Bologna, Italy, 1978; MSc, Tel Aviv U., 1985. Specialist tng. Tel Aviv U. Sourasky Med. ctr., 1979—86; sr. anesthesiologist Maggiore Hosp., Bologna, Italy, 1987—95; head toxicology dept. S. Raffaele U., Milan, 1995—96; head anesthesia and intensive care dept. S. Maria Degli Angeli Hosp., Pordenone, Italy, 1998—; prof. Sch. of Specialization in Anesthesia and Intensive Care, U. Udine, Italy, 1998—, U. Trieste, Italy, 1999—. Rschr. Tel Aviv U., 1984—86. Mem. Rotary, Pordenone, Italy, Italy, 1997—2003. Capt. Israeli Med. Corps, 1968—86. Mem.: Soc. Italiana di Anestesia Rianimazione e Terapia del dolore (assoc.). Home: Turati 5 Italy Pordenone 33170 Italy Office: S Maria Degli Angeli Hospital Via Montereale 24 33170 Pordenone PN Italy Office Fax: 0434 399180. E-mail: yigal.leykin@aopn.fvg.it.

LI, BUHONG, physics professor; b. China, Aug. 19, 1973; PhD, Zhejiang U., 2003. Prof. Fujian Normal U., 2007—. Mem.: SPIE. Office: Shangshan Rd 8 Cangshan Dist Fuzhou Fujian 350007 China Business E-Mail: bhli@fjnu.edu.cn.

LI, CHANGGANG, pediatrician, educator; b. Anshan, Liaoning, China, Apr. 6, 1957; D, Hunan Med. Coll., 1982. Head dept. heamato-oncology Shenzhen Children's Hosp., 1998—. Prof., dir. Zhunyi Med. Coll., 2010. Mem.: SIOP, Pediat. Heamatology Guangdong (China), Assn. Prevention And Treatment Pediat. Cancer, Assn. Prevention and Treatment Thalassemia. Avocations: golf, swimming. Office: Shenzhen Children's Hosp Yitian Rd 7019 Shenzhen Guangdong 518026 China Office Fax: 86 755 83939083.

LI, CHAOYING, biomedical researcher, researcher; b. Jingshan, Hubei, China, July 20, 1958; came to U.S., 1990; s. Yi Li and Yulan Liu; m. Chuli Yi, June 10, 1985; 1 child, Shu. MD, Tongji Med. U., Wuhan, Hubei, China, 1983, MS in Neurobiology, 1989. Asst. Tongji Med. U., Wuhan, 1983-89, lectr., 1989-90; vis. fellow NIH, Rockville, Md., 1990-94, intramural rsch. training award fellow, 1994-95, sr. staff fellow, 1995-98; prin. scientist AstraZeneca R&D, Boston, 1998-2000, AstraZeneca CNS Discovery, Wilmington, Del., 2000—09; dir. Wuhan Inst. Neurosci. & Drug Rsch., Jianghan U., China, 2009—. Author: Alcohol, Cell Membranes and Signal Transsolution, 1993; contbr. articles to profl. jours. Mem. Soc. Neurosci. Achievements include first to demonstrate that alcohols affect the function of a neuronal membrane receptor by a direct interaction with the receptor protein, zinc potentiates excitatory action of ATP, copper enhances the function of P2X purinoceptors, protons potentiate ATP-gated ion channel responses to ATP and zinc, magnesium inhibits the function of P2X purinoceptors by decreasing the affinity of the receptor for ATP, inhibitory action of low micromolar concentrations of zinc on P2X purinoceptors, and differential modulation by copper and zinc of P2X receptor function, distinct ATP-activated currents in different types of neurons dissociated from adult rat DRG, ethanol-induced inhibition of a neuronal P2X receptor by an allosteric mechanism, ethanol inhibition of P2X receptors in mammalian central neurons, novel mechanism of inhibition by PPADS of P2X receptors in neurons, histidine mutation of the rat P2X4 receptor alters agonist, antagonist sensitivities, and the mechanism by which ethanol inhibits rat P2X4 receptors, inhibition of GABAA receptor function by tacrine dimers, the impairment of long-term potentiation by fimbria-fornix lesions at the schafter collateral-CAI synapse in the rat in vivos, GABAA receptors alkylene tether-length dependent inhibition of GABAA receptors by tacrine dimers; and inhibition of NMDA receptor-mediated responses by bis (7)-tacrine in rat brain neurons. Home: 11801 Rockville Pike # 514 Rockville MD 20852 Office: Wuhan Inst Neurosci & Drug Rsch Jianghan Univ Wuhan 430056 China Home Phone: 301-738-1990; Office Phone: 86-27-84225807. Personal E-mail: chaoying_li2003@yahoo.com. Business E-Mail: licwhindr@gmail.com.

LI, CHRISTOPHER L., epidemiologist, educator; BS in Biol. Sciences, Stanford U., 1995; MD, U. Calif., San Francisco, 2000; MPH in Epidemiology, U. Wash., 2000, PhD in Epidemiology, 2002. Assoc. mem., pub. health sciences divsn., epidemiology program Fred Hutchinson Cancer Rsch. Ctr., 2006—; rsch. assoc. prof., epidemiology U. Wash., Sch. Pub. Health and Cmty. Medicine, 2006—. Contbr. several articles to profl. jours. Mem.: Am. Assn. for Cancer Rsch. Achievements include research interests that lie principally in the field of breast cancer and understanding factors related to its etiology and outcomes using a multidisciplinary approach; actively investigating the relationships between various hormonal exposures and risks of different types of breast cancer based on their morphology and expression of different tumor markers.

LI, CHUNYU, dean; b. China, Feb. 7, 1957; MD, Yanbian U., China, 1986; PhD, Yonsei U., Republic of Korea, 1999. Dean Sch. Nursing Yanbian U., 2005—. Vice dean Jilin Nurses Assn., 1988. Recipient Outstanding Tchr. award, Govt. of Jilin Province. Mem.: Com. Nat. Nursing Edn. Office: 977 Gongyuan Rd Yanji Jilin 133002 China Office Phone: 0086-433-2436101. Office Fax: 0433-2436100. Business E-Mail: chyli@ybu.edu.cn.

LI, DUO, nutritionist, food scientist, researcher; b. Gansu, China, Mar. 2, 1958; s. Zhijun and Xianglan (Wei) Li; m. Zhen Guo, Oct. 3, 1958; 1 child, Yidan. MB, Lanzhou Med. Inst., Lanzhou, China, 1982; MS, U. Tasmania, Hobart, Australia, 1995; PhD, Royal Melbourne Inst. Tech., Australia, 1998. Rsch. fellow Deakin U., Melbourne, 1998—99; sr. rsch. fellow Royal Melbourne Inst. Tech. U., 2000—01; prof. Hangzhou U. Commerce, China, 2002—03; prof. dept. food sci. and nutrition Zhejiang (China) U., 2004—; dir. Asia Pacific Clin. Nutrition Soc. Ctr. Nutrition Food Safety, 2005—. Editor: Asia Pacific Jour. Clin. Nutrition, 2005—08; co-editor, 2009—; pres. Asia Pacific Clin. Nutrition Soc., 2011—, Asian Vegetarian Union, 2011—. Mem.: Asia Pacific Clin. Nutrition Soc. (dir. Ctr. Nutrition and Food Safety 2005—), China Inst. Food Scis. Tech., Nutrition Soc. China, Am. Oil Chemists Soc., Internat. Union Nutritional Scis., Nutrition Soc. Australia. Office: Zhejiang University 866 Yu Hang Tang Rd Hangzhou 310058 China Home Phone: 86-138-1948-4621; Office Phone: 86-571-8697-1024. Office Fax: 86-57-8697-1024. Business E-Mail: duoli@zju.edu.cn.

LI, EN-CHANG, editor, director; b. Shaanxi, Mar. 15, 1955; MS, Xi'an Jiaotong U., 1985. Dir. Editl. Dept. Jour. Chinese Med. Ethics, 2003—. Invitatory rschr. Applied Ethics Ctr., Chinese Acad. Social Scis., 2006. Mem.: Shaanxi Cultural Study Inst. Office: 76 Yanta W Rd Xi'an Shaanxi 710061 China Business E-Mail: wenhai188@163.com.

LI, HECHENG, surgeon, educator; b. Anhui, China, Oct. 7, 1972; PhD, Shanghai Med. Sch. Fudan U., MD, 2000. Assoc. prof., attending surgeon Shanghai Cancer Hosp., 2005—. Mem.: Am. Assn. Cancer Rsch., Am. Soc. Clin. Oncology. Home: 270 Dong'an Shanghai Shanghai 200032 China Personal E-mail: lihecheng2000@yahoo.com.

LI, HUILIN, biophysicist, educator; b. Changzhou, Jiangsu, China, Nov. 12, 1965; BS, Wuhan U., 1987; PhD, U. Sci. and Tech. Beijing, 1994. Prof. Stony Brook U., 2008—. Rsch. scientist Brookhaven Nat. Lab., 2002. Office: 50 Bell Ave Upton NY 11973 Office Fax: 631-344-3407. Business E-Mail: hli@bnl.gov.

LI, JAMES TUNG CHIEH, physician; b. NYC, Dec. 7, 1953; s. George and Sylvia (Young) L.; m. Susan Rector, June 30, 1955; 1 child, Daniel. BA, Princeton U., 1974; MD, PhD, Duke U., 1981. Resident in medicine Duke U., Durham, N.C., 1981-84; fellow in allergy Mayo Clinic, Rochester, Minn., 1984-85, sr. assoc. cons., 1985-87, cons. allergic diseases, internal medicine, 1987—, chair division Allergic Diseases, Dept. of Internal Medicine; prof. medicine Mayo Clinic Coll. Medicine. Mem. AMA, Am. Coll. Physicians, Am. Acad. Allergy and Immunology (Pres.'s Grant-in Aid award 1985), American Bd. Allergy and Immunology (chair, 2009). Office: Mayo Clinic 200 1st St SW Rochester MN 55905-0002

LI, JIAN YI, pathologist; b. Shandong, China, Aug. 3, 1969; MD, Huabei Med. Coll. Coal Industry, 1991; PhD, Chinese U. Hong Kong, 1998. Rsch. asst. prof. dept. medicine UCLA, 2001—04; resident dept. pathology U. Okla. Health Sci. Ctr., 2004—06; neuropathology fellow Meth. Hosp./MD Anderson Cancer Ctr. Neuropathology Fellowship Program, 2006—08; chief divsn. neuropathology Dept. Pathology and Lab Medicine, North Shore U. Hosp. and LI Jewish Med. Ctr., 2008—10, asst. prof., co-dir. neuropathology, dir. neuropathology Brain Tumor Inst., 2010—. Postgrad. fellowship, Hong Kong U. Assn., 1995—98. Fellow: Am. Bd. Pathology, Anatomic Pathology Neuropathology Bd. Cert., Coll. Am. Pathology; mem.: Am. Assn. Neuropathologists, US & Can. Acad. Pathology. Avocations: reading, hiking, basketball. Office: 6 Ohio Dr Ste 202 Lake Success NY 11042 Office Fax: 516-224-8586.

LI, JIE, research scientist; b. China, Feb. 22, 1972; PhD, Nankai U., 2004. Rsch. instr. U. Cin., 2007—. Mem.: Soc. Neurosci. Office: 231 Albert Sabin Way Cincinnati OH 45267 Business E-Mail: jie.li@uc.edu.

LI, JIH-HENG, alcohol and drug abuse services professional; b. Chia-Yi, Taiwan, Sept. 15, 1954; s. Swei-Mu Li and Su-Lien Li-Liu; m. Ling-Ling Li-Cheng, Dec. 31, 1983; children: Guan-Shen (Grace), Guan-Jay (James). PhD, NY U., New York, New York, 1985—89; BS in Pharmacy, Kaohsiung Med. Coll., Kaohsiung, 1973—77; M.S., Chinese Culture U., Taipei, 1977—79. Pharmacist Exam. Yuan/Taiwan, 1978. Asst. to dir. gen. Nat. Laboratories of Food and Drugs, Taipei, Taiwan, 1981—85, sr. specialist in microbiology, 1985—90; post-doctoral fellow Dept. of Radiation Oncology, U. of Pa., Philadelphia, Pa., 1989—90; chief scientist Nat. Laboratories of Food and Drugs, Taipei, Taiwan, 1990—91; dep. dir. gen. Nat. Narcotics Bur., Taipei, Taiwan, 1991—94, dir. gen., 1994—99, Nat. Bur. of Controlled Drugs, Taipei, Taiwan, 1999—2005; specialist gen. Dept. Health, Taipei, Taiwan, 2005—08, dir. office Avian Influenza control, 2005—08; prof. risk mgmt., dir. office rsch. and devel. Kainan U., Taoyuan, Taiwan, 2008—09; dean Sch. Health Care Mgmt., 2008—09, Coll. Pharmacy, Kaohsiung Med. U., 2009—. Chmn. Rev. Com. on Lab. Certificaton for Urine Drug Testing, Taipei, Taiwan; dept. rep. Rev. Com. for Drug Scheduling, Ministry of Justice, Taipei, Taiwan, 2004—05; vice chmn. Drug Edn. Rsch. Coun., Ministry of Edn., Taipei, 1995—2003. Editor: Drug Abuse 2002, Substance Abuse 2003, Jour. Food and Drug Analysis, 2004; contbr. articles to profl. jours. Cons. Inst. Forensic Medicine, 2000-; mem. Com. Consultation for Athletes' Forbidden Drugs, 2002—. Second lt. Pharm. Supply, 1979—81, Taidong, Taiwan. Recipient Disting. Alumnus, Kaohsiung Med. U., 2003. Mem. Environ. Mutagen Soc., Pharm. Soc. of Taiwan. Achievements include development of licensing and management system for controlled drugs in Taiwan; discovery of mechanism of arsenic inhibition on DNA repair; research in genetic toxicology of cocaine and methamphtamine; drug abuse epidemiology. Avocations: travel, reading. Office: Coll Pharmacy Kaohsiung Med Univ 100 Shih-Chuan 1st Rd Kaohsiung 807-8 Taiwan Office Phone: (07)3121101 ext. 2651. Business E-Mail: jhlitox@kmu.edu.tw.

LI, LIEBER PO-HUNG, otolaryngologist, educator; b. Kaoshiung, Taiwan, June 29, 1967; MD, Nat. Yang-Ming U., 1993, PhD, 2006. Asst. prof. Sch. Medicine, Nat. Yang-Ming U., 2006; prin. investigator Integrated Brain Rsch. Lab., Taipei Veterans Gen. Hosp., 2006; standing staff dept. otolaryngology Cheng Hsin Gen. Hosp., 2008—. Asst. prof. Sch. of Medicine, Nat. Yang-Ming U., 2006; prin. investigator Integrated Brain Rsch. Lab., Taipei Veterans Gen. Hosp., 2006. Performer (singer): 50th Ann. Meml. Concert. Recipient Spl. Tchg. award, Cheng Hsin Gen. Hosp., Taipei, Taiwan, 2010; Travel grant, Internat. Brain Rsch. Orgn., Paris, 2004—05, Young Investigator Travel fellowship, Internat. Fedn. Clin. Neurophysiology, 8th Internat. Evoked Potentials Symposium, Fukuoka, Japan, 2004—10, Young Participant fellowship, Internat. Fedn. Clin. Neurophysiology, Asian and Oceanian Symposium Clin. Neurophysiology, Chiang Mai, Thailand. Mem.: Chinese Med. Assn., Taiwan Soc. Sleep Medicine, Taiwan Otolaryn. Soc. (Excellent award). Avocations: writing, running, singing. Office: 45 Cheng Hsin St Pai-Tou Taipei 112 Taiwan Office Phone: (886)-2-28209589. Office Fax: (886)-2-28263645. Business E-Mail: lieber.li@msa.hinet.net.

LI, LINDA (LINDA JIAN-YUH LI), plastic surgeon; b. Morgantown, WV, Sept. 26, 1969; m. Bill Fulcher; 1 child. BA/MD (six yr. program) cum laude, Boston U., 1993. Cert. Am. Bd. Plastic Surgery, 2002. Intern, plastic surgery U. Southern Calif., LA, 1993—94, resident, surgery, 1994—98; fellow Cornell Med. Ctr., NYC, 1998—2000; attending physician Hosp. Good Samaritan, LA, 2000; pvt. practice Beverly Hills, Calif., 2000—. Featured on Dr. 90210, 2005—. Fellow: Am. Coll. Surgeons; mem.: Calif. Soc. Plastic Surgeons, Am. Soc. Plastic Surgery, Soc. Grad. Surgeons of LA County/U. So. Calif. Med. Ctr. Avocations: exercise, yoga. Office: 433 N Camden Dr Ste 1190 Beverly Hills CA 90210 Office Phone: 310-273-6252. Office Fax: 310-273-6050. Business E-Mail: admins@lindalimd.com.

LI, MING-HUI, counselor educator; s. Wei-Chen Li and Ming Hsu-Li; married. EdD, Tex. Tech U., Lubbock, 2004. Cert. counselor 1994, psychologist 1999; lic. mental health counselor NY, 2006. Assoc. prof. St. John's U., NYC, 2004—; lic. profl. counselor Pa., 2002. Vol. Tzu-chi Acad. NY, New York City, NY, 2006—. Recipient Staff Counselor award, Overseas Chinese Inst. Tech., 1999, award, 1999, Faculty Recognitiion award, St. Johns U., 2008, Acad. Advisor award, Overseas Chinese Inst. Tech., 1999; Summer Rsch. grant, St. John's U., 2006. Mem.: North Am. Assn. Masters in Psychology, Am. Counseling Assn., Am. Ednl. Rsch. Assn., Phi Kappa Phi, Chi Sigma Iota. Office: St Johns University 8000 Utopia Pky Queens NY 11439 Home: 66 19 242 St # 17 A Douglaston NY 11362 Office Phone: 718-990-2756. Personal E-mail: lim@stjohns.edu. Business E-Mail: mikeli7@hotmail.com.

LI, MINQI, medical educator; b. China, Nov. 6, 1970; B, Liaoning Med. U., 1995; PhD, Niigata U., 2004. Asst. prof. Hokkaido U., 2009—. Fgn. Rsch. grant, Japan Soc. Promotion Sci. Mem.: Japanese Soc. Bone Morphometry, Japan Soc. Bone and Mineral Rsch., Internat. Assn. Dental Rsch., European Calcified Tissue Soc., Am. Soc. Bone and Mineral Rsch. Office: Kita 13 Nishi 7 Kita-ku Sapporo Hokkaido 060-8586 Japan Personal E-mail: li_min_qi@hotmail.com.

LI, NINGHUA, epidemiologist, educator; b. People's Republic of China, Jan. 14, 1954; MD, Pub. Health, Beijing Med. Coll., Beijing, 1977; MS in Epidemiology, Microbiology and Immunology, Chinese Acad. Preventive Med. Scis., Beijing, 1987. Lectr. Dept. Epidemiology, Beijing Faculty Pub. Health, Beijing Med. Coll., 1977—84; asst. prof. Dept. Epidemiology, Beijing Inst. Geriat., Beijing Hosp., Ministry of People's Republic of China, 1988—95, assoc. prof., 1995—2001, prof., 2001—. Cons., adj. prof., expert, profl. technique qualification judge Beijing Pers. Bur., 2003—, cons., adj. prof., judge medicine and instrument, 2007; cons., adj. prof. Second Judge Com. Award Sci. and Tech. Chinese Assn. Medicine, 2007—10, First Judge Com. Award Sci. and Tech. Chinese Assn. Preventive Medicine, 2007—, Bur. Supervise and Adminstrn. Drugs and Foods People's Republic of China, 2011—. Contbr. articles to sci. profl. jours. Recipient award, Ministry Sci. and Tech. China, Ministry Health, People's Republic of China. Mem.: Coun. Geriat. Assn. China Health Care and Sci. and Tech. Soc., Chinese Traditional Med. Com., China Internat. Exch. and Promotion Assn. Med. and Health Care, Chinese Practical Medicine and Pharmacology (expert editor). Avocations: sports, music. Office: 1 Dahualu Dongdan Dong Cheng Dist Beijing 100730 China Office Fax: 86-10-65123935.

LI, QINGDI QUENTIN, physician, research scientist, medical educator; b. Guilin, Guangxi, China, Apr. 18, 1956; m. Li Ding; 1 child, Jueli Maggie. MA, MD, Guangxi Med. U., 1987; MS, PhD, U. Md., 2000. Microbiologist, immunologist Guangxi Med. U., Nanning, China, 1983—87; dermatologist Sun Yat-sen Univ. Sch. Medicine, Guangzhou, Guangdong, China, 1987—91; postdoctoral fellow Nat. Cancer Inst., Bethesda, Md., 1996—98; rsch. scientist Balt. VA Med. Ctr., 1998—2000; asst. prof. Sch. Medicine and Health Sci. Ctr. W.Va. U., Morgantown, 2000—06, rsch. coord. MBR Cancer Ctr., 2000—06; rsch. scientist Nat. Cancer Inst., NIH, Bethesda, Md., 2006—08, NIAID, NIH, Bethesda, 2008—. Vis. prof. Wuhan U., China, 2002—, Guangxi Med. U., Nanning, China, 2002—, SE U., Nanjing, China, 2003—, Tongji Med. Coll., Ctrl. China Univ. Sci. and Tech., Wuhan, 2004—, Nanjing Med. U., China, 2006—, Beihai Inst. Endocrine and Metabolic Diseases, China, 2010—. Recipient Intramural Rsch. Award, Nat. Cancer Inst., 1996-1998, Nat. Svc. Award, NIH, 1998-2000. Mem.: AAAS, Chinese Soc. Microbiology, Am. Soc. Microbiology, NY Acad. Sci., Am. Assn. Cancer Rsch., Chinese Med. Assn. Office: NIAID NIH Bethesda MD 20892-1888 Home Phone: 301-208-1945. Personal E-mail: quentinli2004@yahoo.com. Business E-Mail: liquenti@mail.nih.gov, quentin.li@nih.gov.

LI, SARAH SHIU WAI, nursing educator, researcher; arrived in Eng., 1967; d. Sung Yue Tsun and Sau Ngaan Soong; m. David Iu Shun Li, Sept. 9, 1972; children: Louisa San San, Anthony Chun Kit. BA, Open U., Milton Keynes, Eng., 1991; EdB with honors, U. Sussex, Eng., 1993; MA in Sociology, U. London, 1995, PhD in Sociology, 2002. Cert. tchr., English Nat. Bd., 1992, RN for the Mentally Subnormal, UK Ctrl. Coun. for Nursing, Midwifery and Health Visi, 1970, for the Mentally Ill, UK Ctrl. Coun. for Nursing, Midwifery and Health Visi, 1972, Nat. Vocat. Qualification Assessor and Internal Verifier, Inst. Health and Care Devel. Health and Care Ltd., Edexcel, 2002; cert. piano (grade 7) and cello (grade 5) English Associated Bd. Music, 1990. Staff nurse The Manor Hosp., Epsom, Surrey, England, 1971—72, ward sister, 1973—89; nurse tchr. Carshalton (Eng.) Sch. Nursing, 1989—92; lectr. Croydon (Eng.) Coll. Nursing, 1993—95; sr. lectr. Kingston U. and St. George's, Kingston Upon Thames, Surrey, England, 1995—; sr. lectr./rschr. Kingston U. and St. George's, U. London, Kingston Upon Thames, Surrey, 2004—. Curriculum planner for higher edn. Kingston U. and St. George's, U. London, Kingston Upon Thames, 1994—, ednl. auditor, Kingston UponThames, 1995—; MSc course co-ordinator and module leader St. George's, U. London, Tooting, England, 2004—; PhD adviser, supr. Greenwich U., Greenwich, 2004—; first aide provider British Red Cross and St. John's Ambulance; course devel. chair, social sci. curriculum devel. U. Singapore; presenter in field. Jour. article reviewer: Social Sci. and Medicine, Elsevier Publs., 2005—, Qualitative Health Rsch., Sage Publs.; contbr. articles to profl. jours. Interpreter for sick persons in hospitals and gp practices Epsom Chinese Meth. Ch., 2004—05. Mem.: Nursing and Midwifery Coun. (licentiate). D-Liberal. Methodist. Achievements include research in how psychosocial can be delivered in palliative care settings for the dying; discovery of the practices of symbiotic niceness in palliative care settings between dying patients, palliative care nurses and doctors, the therapeutic doctor-patient-nurse relationship. Office: Kingston Univ and St George s Univ Kingston Hill Kingston Upon Thames Surrey KT2 7LB England Office Fax: 0208 547 8744. Business E-Mail: sli@hscs.sgul.ac.uk.

LI, SHAOWU, neurologist; b. Wuhan, Hubei, China, Aug. 16, 1967; MD, Capital Med. U., 2010. Chief Beijing Neurosurg. Inst., 1991—. Office: 6# Tiantan Xili Beijing Dongcheng 100050 China Business E-Mail: lys5@sina.com.

LI, TIEN-SHUN, obstetrician, gynecologist, educator; b. Kaohsiung, Taiwan, Nov. 13, 1932; arrived in U.S., 1968; MD, Nat. Taiwan U., 1960. Diplomate Am. Bd. Ob-Gyn. From intern to resident ob-gyn. Nat. Taiwan U. Hosp., Taipei, 1961—64; resident ob-gyn. St. Barnabas Med. Ctr., Livingston, NJ, 1971—73; clin. asst. prof. U. Medicine and Dentistry N.J., 1978—; pvt. practice Ft. Lee, NJ, 1978—. Attending staff Meadowlands Hosp. Med. Ctr., Secaucus, NJ, 1985—. Fellow: ACOG. Office: 2231 Lemoine Ave Fort Lee NJ 07024-6115 Office Phone: 201-944-1008.

LI, TING-KAI, medical educator, researcher, former federal agency administrator; b. Nanjing, China, 1934; BA in Chemistry and Biology, Northwestern U., Ill.; MD, Harvard U., 1959; DSc (hon.), Northeastern Ohio Universities Coll. Medicine, 1998, Ind. U., 2003, Purdue U., 2003, U. So. Calif., 2010. Chief resident Peter Bent Brigham Hosp., Boston, 1965; dep. dir. biochemistry divsn. Walter Reed Army Inst. Rsch.; faculty, John B. Hickam prof. medicine & biochemistry Ind. U. Sch. Medicine, Indpls., 1971—2002, assoc. dean rsch., 1986—2000, dir. Ind. Alcohol Rsch. Ctr., 2000—02, also Disting. Prof. Medicine; dir. Nat. Inst. Alcohol Abuse & Alcoholism (NIAAA) NIH, Bethesda, 2002—08, ret., 2008; prof. Dept. Psychiatry and Behavioral Scis. Duke U. Sch. Medicine. Contbr. scientific papers numerous articles to profl. jours., chapters to books. Recipient R. Brinkley Smithers Disting. Sci. award, James B. Isaacson award for rsch. in chemical dependency diseases, Jellinek award. Fellow: UK Soc. Study of Addiction (hon.); mem.: NAS Inst. Medicine. Office: Duke University School of Medicine Box 3862 Med Ctr Durham NC 27710 also: Duke-NUS Graduate Medical School 8 College Rd 169857 Singapore Singapore Office Phone: +1 919684 2880, 919-684-2880. Office Fax: +1 919681 8400. E-mail: tk.li@duke.edu.

LI, WEIQUN, research scientist; b. Jinjiang City, China, Dec. 1, 1961; s. Yun Li and Fenglang Wang; m. Youmei Wu; 1 child, Yao. BSc, Nanjing Med. U., China, 1983, MSc, 1986; MD, Free U. Berlin, 1992. Rsch. asst. Nanjing Med. U., 1986—88; vis. fellow Nat. Cancer Inst., Bethesda, Md., 1992—95, vis. assoc., 1995—99; asst. prof. dept. pediat. Georgetown U., Washington, 1999—2000, asst. prof. dept. oncology, 2000—03; rsch. scientist NIH, Bethesda, 2003—. Regular reviewer for cancer rsch.; ad hoc reviewer for numerous jours. in field; spkr., presenter at internat. meetings in field. Contbr. articles to profl. publs. Recipient Young Investigator award, Leukemia Rsch. Found., 2000, V Young Investigator award, Found. for Cancer Rsch., NC, 2001, Sr. Investigator award, Multiple Myeloma Rsch. Found., Conn., 2003; grantee, Concern Found., Calif., 2000, Leukemia Rsch. Found., 2000—01, V Found. for Cancer Rsch., 2001—03. Mem.: Am. Assn. Cancer Rsch. Achievements include research in cellular and genetic mechanisms governing cell proliferation; terminal differentiation and malignant transformation, particularly in hematopoietic malignancies. Avocations: fishing, ping pong/table tennis, travel. Office: Nat Inst Dental and Craniofacial Rsch NIH Bldg 30 Rm 211 30 Convent Dr Bethesda MD 20892 Home Phone: 301-309-0282; Office Phone: 301-402-7435. Personal E-mail: weiqunli03@yahoo.com.

LI, WEIYE, ophthalmologist, educator, biochemist; b. Zhejiang, China, Oct. 10, 1946; arrived in U.S., 1990; s. Zhao-ji and Qin (Yue) Li; m. Xinru Liu, Apr. 12, 1986; 1 child, Yafeng. MD, Peking Second Med. Coll., China, 1970; postgrad., Acad. Med. Scis., China, 1978—80; PhD, U. Pa., 1984. Intern Chao Young Hosp., Peking, 1970—71, resident ophthalmology, 1971—78; rsch. fellow dept. ophthalmology and biochem. grad. sch. Sch. Medicine U. Pa., Phila., 1981—84, postdoctor, asst. prof. dept. ophthalmology Scheie Eye Inst. Sch. Medicine, 1984—85; asst. prof., attending physician ophthalmology Peking Union Med. Coll. Hosp., 1985—86, assoc. prof. ophthalmology, 1986—88, prof. ophthalmology, 1988—, chmn. dept. ophthalmology, 1989—99; prof., dir. rsch. dept. ophthalmology Hahnemann U., Phila., 1990—, attending physician, retinal specialist, Hahnemann U. Hosp., 2003—. Recipient Rsch. award, Internat. Juvenile Diabetes Found., 1984—86, 1st Class Sci. and Tech. Advances prize, Chinese Ministry Pub. Health, 1988; grantee, NIH, 1981—82, 1986—2000, Fight for Sight Inc., 1982—83, Am. Diabetes Assn., 1990—2001; fellow, Internat. Juvenile Diabetes Found., 1982—84. Mem.: Assn. Chinese Ophthalmology Soc., Assn. Rsch. in Vision and Ophthalmology. Avocations: ping pong/table tennis, bicycling, music. Office: Drexel Univ Dept Ophthalmology Coll Medicine 219 N Broad St 3rd Fl Philadelphia PA 19107 Office Phone: 610-892-1708, 215-762-3937. Business E-Mail: weiye.li@drexelmed.edu.

LI, WEI-ZHONG, medical educator; b. Qingdao, Shandong, Aug. 15, 1962; MD, Sch. Dentistry, 1983. Prof. Southern Med. U., Nanfang Hosp., 1999—. Office: Nanfang Hosp Dept Stomatology Guangzhou Guangdong 510515 China

LI, XIAONAN, medical researcher; d. Zhenwen and Zizheng Li; m. Yijiang Chen, Feb. 7, 1987; 1 child, Shuowei Chen. BS, Nanjing Med. Coll., 1984, MS, 1991, MD; PhD, Nanjing Med. U., 2004. Cert. chief physician Health Bur. Jiangsu, China, 2005, prof. Edn. Bur. Jiangsu, 2007. With Göteborg U., Sweden, 1995—96; vis. rschr. Umea U., Sweden, 2001—08. Editor: (book) The People 's Medical Publishing House; contbr. scientific papers and articles to profl. jours. Childhood nutritionist Nutrition Assn., Jiangsu, 2000—08; with Pediat. Med. Assn., Jiangsu, 2006—, Children Health Care Assn., Jiangsu, 2008. Qing-Lan Projects grant, Edn. Bur. Jiangsu Province, 2007, Rsch. grant, Pers. Minstry Jiangsu Province, 2007. Mem.: Nanjing Children Hosp. Achievements include research in epidemic investigation of accident and prevention during 0-14 years of children, obesity related genes expression and regualtion. Office: Nanjing Med Univ Han Zhong Rd 140 Nanjing Jiangsu 210029 China Business E-Mail: xnli@njmu.edu.cn.

LI, YAN, research scientist; b. China, Apr. 20, 1976; D, Dalian U. Tech., Liaoning, China, 2006. Rschr. Dalian U. Tech., 2006. Office: Dalian University Technology 2 Linggong Rd Dalian Liaoning 116023 China Business E-Mail: yanli@dlut.edu.cn.

LI, YANLIN, medical educator; b. Yunnan, China, June 29, 1969; PhD, West China U. Med. Scis., 2000. Prof. First Affiliated Hosp. Kunming Med. Coll., Yunnan, 2000—. Recipient Eighth Tchg. award, Fok Yin Tong Edn. Found., 3rd award, Govt. of Yunnan, 2nd award, Yunnan Edn. Com. Med. Sci. and Tech., Third Youth Sci. and Tech. award, Govt. Kunming, 3rd Excellent Scientist award. Mem.: China Med. Assn. Avocations: sports, music, reading. Home: 209 Xichang Rd Kunming Yunnan 650032 China Personal E-mail: yanlinli1969@yahoo.com.cn.

LI, YANYAN, geriatrician; b. Shandong, China, Nov. 14, 1977; PhD, Nanjing Med. U., 2005. Physician, dept. geriat. First Affiliated Hosp. Nanjing Med. U., 2005—. Office: 300 Guangzhou Rd Nanjing Jiangsu 210029 China Personal E-mail: lyynjmu123@126.com.

LI, ZIZHONG, research scientist; b. Jinyuan, China, June 25, 1965; s. Changhai Li and Minsu Teng; m. Youwen Xu; 1 child, Qing. BSc, Lanzhou U., China, 1986, MSc, 1989; PhD, Auburn U., 1997. Rsch. fellow Nat. Lab. Applied Organic Chemistry, Lanzhou U., 1989—93; grad. rsch. asst. Auburn U., 1993—97; rsch. assoc. NIH Isotope Resources Los Alamos (N.Mex.) Nat. Lab., 1997—99; sr. rsch. assoc. med. dept. Brookhaven Nat. Lab., Upton, NY, 1999—2001, asst. scientist Imaging Sci. Group, 2001—03, assoc. scientist, 2003—; prin. scientist. Contbr. articles to profl. jours.; patentee in field. Mem.: AAAS, Am. Chem. Soc., Phi Lambda Upsilon. Home: 14 Circle Dr Shoreham NY 11786 E-mail: zizhong.li@roche.com.

LIAKAKOS, THEODORE D., oesophageal and gastric surgeon; b. Athens, Attiki, Greece, May 16, 1953; m. Christina Samara, Jan. 15, 1983; 1 child, Dimitrios T. Degree, U. Athens Med. Sch., 1978. Cert. gen. surgeon Bd. Ministry of health, 1986. Assoc. prof. surgery U. Athens Med. Sch., 2003—. Office Phone: 302105326419. Business E-Mail: theodlia@otenet.gr.

LIANG, FENG, research scientist; b. China, July 10, 1977; PhD, Wuhan U., 2003. Asst. prof. Wuhan U., 2004—06; rsch. scientist Biodesign Inst., Ariz. State U., 2006—. Guest editor Mini-Reviews Medicinal Chemistry, 2010, Current Drug Delivery, 2011; editor in chief Internat. Jour. Pharmaceuticals Analysis, 2010; assoc. editor Internat. Rsch. Jour. Plant Scis., 2010; editl. bd. referees Archive Organic Chemistry, 2010. Recipient 1st Class award, Hubei Natural Sci., China. Mem.: Am. Chem. Soc., Sigma Xi. Avocations: hiking, music, soccer. Office: Biodeign Inst SMB 5601 Tempe AZ 85287 Personal E-mail: chemoliangf@yahoo.com.cn.

LIANG, JEROME ZHENGRONG, radiology educator; b. Chongging, China, June 23, 1958; arrived in U.S., 1981; BS, Lanzhou U., China, 1982; PhD, CUNY, 1987. Rsch. instr. Albert Einstein Coll. Medicine, Bronx, NY, 1986—87; rsch. assoc. Duke U. Med. Ctr., Durham, NC, 1987—89, asst. med. rsch. prof., 1990—92; asst. prof. SUNY, Stony Brook, 1992—97, assoc. prof., 1997—2000, prof., 2000—, co-dir. biomed. engring., 1996—. Mem. adv. bd. MDOL, Inc., 1999—; bd. dirs., v.p. R&D, founder Viatronix, Inc., 2000—. Contbr. articles to profl. jours.; mem. editl. bd.: IEEE Transactions on Med. Imaging, 1999—. Recipient NIH awards, 1990—, AHA award, 1996—2001, N.Y. State Biotech. award, 1996—98, E-Z-EM award, 1997—98; grantee, Soc. Thoracic Radiology, 1994—95, ADAC Rsch. Lab., 1994—95. Achievements include development of Bayesian image processing, quantitative emission computed tomography, tissue segmentation from magnetic resonance images, virtual endoscopy, virtual realities in radiology. Avocations: swimming, exercise, tennis.

Office: SUNY Stony Brook Dept Radiology 4th Fl Rm 120 Stony Brook NY 11794-8460 Office Phone: 631-444-7837. Business E-Mail: jerome.liang@sunysb.gov, jzl@mil.sunysb.edu.

LIANG, SHENG-FU, engineering educator; b. Taiwan, Aug. 20, 1971; PhD, Nat. Chiao Tung U., Taiwan, 2000. Postdoc. rschr. Nat. Chiao Tung U., 2001—05, asst. prof., 2005—06, Nat. Cheng Kung U., 2006—10, assoc. prof., 2010—. Mem.: IEEE. Avocations: swimming, art. Office: 1 University Rd Tainan 701 Taiwan Business E-Mail: sfliang@mail.ncku.edu.tw.

LIANG, SHU-MEI YANG, biomedical researcher, educator; d. Tsai and Ying-Jin Lin Yang; m. Chi-Ming Liang, July 6, 1974; 1 child, Tai-Fu Evan. BS, Nat. Taiwan U., 1971; PhD, U. Ark. Med. Scis., 1978. Staff fellow FDA Ctr. Biologics Evaluation and Rsch., Rockville, Md., 1980—83, rsch. chemist, 1986—92; scientist Biogen S.A., Geneva, 1983—85; sr. scientist, dir. N.Am. Vaccine Inc., Beltsville, Md., 1992—97; rsch. fellow Academia Sinica Agrl. Biotechnology Rsch. Ctr., Taipei, Taiwan, 1997—. Mgr. Amvax Inc., Beltsville, Md., 1992—93; prof. Inst. Biotech., Nat. Chen-Kung U., Tainan, Taiwan, 2002—; joint appointment fellow genomic rsch. ctr. Academia Sinica, Taipei, 2005—, acting dir. office pub. affairs, 2006—, dep. dir. agrl. biotech. rsch. ctr., 2006—. Editor: Bio/Pharma Quar., 1994—96; ad hoc reviewer: Jour. Immunology, European Jour. Biochemistry, Jour. Agrl. Food Chemistry, Virus Rsch., others; contbr. articles to profl. jours. Pres. NIH Chinese Assn., Rockville, Md., 1987—88. Recipient Merit award, FDA, 1989, Appreciation award, Chinese Agrl. Chem. Soc., 1998; grantee, Nat. Sci. Coun., Taiwan, 1998—, Academia Sinica, Taiwan, 2001—. Mem.: Am. Soc. Cell Biology, Chinese Biochem. Soc., Protein Soc., Am. Soc. Biochemistry and Molecular Biology. Achievements include development of Method for the high level expression, purification and refolding of the outer membrane group B porin proteins from Neisseria meningitides; Modified immunogenic pneumolysin compositions as vaccines; research in the hybridoma cell line producing monoclonal antibodies against Foot-And-Mouth disease virus and the application of the monoclonal antibody; patents in field. Office: Agrl Biotechnology Rsch Ctr Academia Sinica Number 128 Academia Road Sect 2 Nankang Taipei 11529 Taiwan Business E-Mail: smyang@gate.sinica.edu.tw.

LIANG, YU-CHIH, biomedical researcher, educator; b. Taiwan, Sept. 10, 1966; s. Ting-Jang Liang and Jia-Hao Chang; m. Grace Lee, Jan. 2, 1996; children: Ben-Yu, Ben-Sheng. PhD, Nat. Taiwan U., Taipei, 1998. Cert. med. tchr. Taipei Med. U., Taiwan, 2000. Postdoctoral rschr. Nat. Taiwan U., Taipei, 1999—2000. Recipient Citation Classic award, ISI, 2001. Home: 9F No 5 Ln 84 Sec 7 Hsin-Hai Rd Taipei 116 Taiwan Office: Taipei Med Univ No 250 Wu-Hsing St Taipei 110 Taiwan Office Fax: 886-2-27393447. Business E-Mail: ycliang@tmu.edu.tw.

LIANG-CHENG, CHEN, physician; b. Taipei, Mar. 7, 1965; MD, Nat. Def. Med. Sch., 1991; MS, Inst. Biology & Anatomy Nat. Def. Med. Ctr., 1995. Chief Dept. PM&R Tri-Svc. Gen. Hosp., 2010—. Recipient Outstanding Mil. Med. Staff award, Ministry of Nat. Def. Home: Dept PM & R 325 Sect 2 Cheng-Kung Rd Taipei 114 Taiwan Home Fax: 886-2-87927162. Personal E-mail: clctsgh@yahoo.com.tw.

LIAO, CHIEN-CHUNG, gastroenterologist, endoscopist, consultant; b. Taipei, Taiwan, Aug. 9, 1969; s. Shan-Hsiung Liao and Chiu-Hsia Liao-Kao; m. Tan-Chih Hsu, July 10, 1994; children: Chieh-Yu, Chen-Yu. MD, China Med. Coll., Taichung, Taiwan, 1995. Cert. internist Dept. Health Execs. Yuan, Taiwan, 1998, gastroenterologist Gastroent. Soc. Taiwan, 2000, gastrointestinal endoscopist Digestive Endoscopy Soc. Taiwan, 2001. Intern Chang Gung Meml. Hosp., Lin-Kou, Taiwan, 1994—95; resident dept. internal medicine Cathay Gen. Hosp., Taipei, 1995—98, fellow dept. gastroenterology and hepatology, 1998—2000, gastroenterologist dept. gastroenterology, 2000—; lectr. China Med. U., Taichung, Taiwan, 2003—, Fu Jen Cath. U., Taipei, 2005—07. Cons. dept. gastroenterology Cathay Gen. Hosp., 2000—; vis. clinician Mayo Clinic, Rochester, Minn., 2001—02, Nat. Cancer Ctr., Tokyo, 2007; supt. Liao Clinic, 2007—; rschr. in field. Recipient Young Scientist award, XVth Internat. Workshop Gastrointestinal Pathology and Helicobacter Pylori, 2002. Mem.: Am. Soc. Gastrointestinal Endoscopy (mem. internat. com. 2003—07), Digestive Endoscopy Soc. Taiwan, Soc. Ultrasound in Medicine, Gastroent. Soc. Taiwan. Office: Liao Clinic 23 Xida Rd Hsinchu 30061 Taiwan Home: 23 Zhiping Rd Hsinchu 30067 Taiwan Office Phone: 886-3-5612297. Personal E-mail: cghliaocc@hotmail.com.

LIAO, KENNETH, information technology executive; BS in Computer Sci., Zhongshan U.; M in Math., U. Houston; MEE, Rice U., Houston. Managed tech. teams Digital Transparencies, IBM Corp., Bay Networks; dir., engring., Security Tech. Group Cisco Sys., Inc.; v.p., chief tech. officer eLong, Inc., 2007—. Office: eLong Inc Jiuxianqiao Zhonglu Block B Xing Ke Plz 10 Beijing 100016 China Office Phone: 105-860-2288. Office Fax: 106-431-5872.

LIAO, TA-HSIU, biochemistry educator; b. Taipei, Taiwan, Feb. 22, 1942; s. Hsin-Zu and A-Men (Hsieh) L.; children: Cinderella, Richard. BS, Nat. Taiwan U., Taipei, 1964; PhD, UCLA, 1969. Fellow Rockefeller U., NYC, 1970-73, asst. prof., 1973-74, Okla. State U., Stillwater, 1974-78, assoc. prof., 1978-82, prof., 1982-85; prof. biochemistry Nat. Taiwan U., Taipei, 1985—, assoc. dean, 1988-91, dir. Inst. Ctr., 1991-95, dir. Inst. Biochem., 1996—. Grantee NIH, 1975-80, Nat. Sci. Coun. Taiwan, 1985—. Mem. AAAS, The Protein Soc., Am. Soc. for Biochemistry and Molecular Biology, Taiwan Soc. for Biochemistry and Molecular Biology (pres. 1999—), Rotary (past pres. Taipei Southsea). Office: Nat Taiwan Univ Coll Medicine No 1 Sec 1 Jen-Ai Rd Taipei Taiwan

LIAO, WAYNE CHANG, medical educator; b. Taipei, Oct. 10, 1965; BS, Nat. Cheng Kung U., 1989; PhD, U. Tenn., Knoxville, 1999. Assoc. prof. Chang Gung Inst. Tech., 2007—. Gen. mgr. Polylife Biomaterials, 2004—07. Mem.: ACS, AIChE, ASABE. Avocation: writing. Office: 2 Chia-Pu Rd W Putz Putz Chia-Yi County 630 Taiwan Office Fax: (886) 5-362-8866. Business E-Mail: bio.liao@msa.hinet.net.

LIAO, XIAOYUN, pathologist; b. Chongqing, China, Oct. 15, 1968; MD, Beijing Med. U., 1992; PhD, U. Hong Kong, 2008. Resident pathologist Peking U. People's Hosp., 1992—97, attending pathologist, 1997—2002, assoc. chief pathologist, 2002—. Recipient Scholar-in-Tng. award, Am. Assn. Cancer Rsch., 2008. Mem.: Chinese Med. Assn. Avocations: travel, music, reading, hiking. Home: Che Gong Zhuang Xi Lu 20# Bldg 11# Beijing 100044 China Personal E-mail: xiaoyliao@yahoo.com.

LIAO, YEN-HSIUNG, public health service officer, educator; b. Chunghua, Taiwan, Mar. 9, 1962; s. Ming-Shan and Yen-Lin Liao; m. Shu-Fang Lin, Feb. 25, 1992; children: Yu-Ing, Yu-Sam. BS, Kaohsiung Med. U., 1986, MS, 1989. Professional in Waste Water Treatment, Environ. Protection Adminstrn./Taiwan, 1995, Professional of Waste Removal, Environ. Protection Adminstrn./Taiwan, 1995, Professional of Disposal Organization, Environ. Protection Adminstrn., 1995; License Medical Technician Dept. of Health /Taiwan, 1987. Rsch. asst. Kaohsiung Med. U., Taiwan, 1987—89, tchg. asst., 1991—92, lectr. occupl. and environ. health, 1992. Leader Health promotes in Puli, Puli, Taiwan, 2000—03; adv. boards Health promotes in Nantou, Nantou, Taiwan, 2000—03; cons. in environ. protection services Small and Medium Enterprise Adminstrn., Taipei, Taiwan, 2000. Contbr. articles to profl. jours. Toilet equipment investigation of primary and jr. h.s. EPA, Kaohsiung, Taiwan, 1994—95, pub. toilet equipment investigation and improvement, 1994—95. Lt. Marine Corps, 1989—91, Taichung. Recipient Prize of profl. tchg., Kaohsiung Med. U., 1997. Mem.: Internat. Assn. of Search and Rescue (assoc.). Christian. Avocations: travel, jogging, climbing. Office: Kaohsiung Med Univ No100 Shih-Chuan 1st Road Kaohsiung 807 Taiwan Office Fax: 88673110811. Business E-Mail: m765025@cc.kmu.edu.tw.

LIAW, YUNG-PO, epidemiologist, researcher; b. Taiwan, June 30, 1962; s. Chia-Yao Liaw and Ye-Zen Zian; m. Chieh-Ying Huang Liaw, July 8, 1989; children: Yi-Ching, Yi-Chia. BS in Horticulture, Nat. Taiwan U., 1986, MS in Biostatistics, 1989; PhD in Epidemiology, Nat. Taiwan U., Taipei, 2000. Dir. dept. pub. health Chung Shan Med. U., Taichung, Taiwan, 2004—, chmn. Inst. Pub. Health, 2005—. Author: Atlas of Cancer Mortality in Taiwan 1972-2001, 2003, Atlas of Cancer Incidence in Taiwan 1995-1998, 2003, (CD) Electric Atlas of Cancer Mortality and Incidence in Taiwan, 2003. Recipient Rsch. award, Nat. Sci. Coun., 2000. Mem.: Chinese Nutrition Assn., Taiwan Pub. Health Assn., Chinese Statis. Assn. Office: Chung Shan Med U Chien-Kuo N Rd Taiwan Taichung 402 Taiwan Office Fax: 886-4-23248179. Business E-Mail: liawyp@csmu.edu.tw.

LIBBY, PETER, cardiologist, medical researcher; b. Berkeley, Calif., Feb. 13, 1947; s. Henry and Vivian (Green) Libby; m. Beryl Rica Benacerraf, Nov. 22, 1975; children: Oliver, Brigitte. BA, U. Calif., Berkeley, 1969; MD, U. Calif., San Diego, 1973; MA (hon.), Harvard U., 1996. Diplomate Am. Bd. Internal Medicine and Cardiovasc. Disease. Intern Peter Bent Brigham Hosp., Boston, 1973-74, resident, 1974-76; fellow Harvard Med. Sch., Boston, 1976-79; asst. Prof. Tufts U. Sch. Sch. Medicine, Boston, 1980-86, assoc., 1986-90; asst. physician New England Med. Ctr., Boston, 1980-87, physician, 1987-90; fellow Brigham and Women's Hosp., Boston, 1979-80, dir. vascular medicine and atherosclerosis unit, 1990-97, physician, 1992—, chief cardiovasc. medicine, 1998—; assoc. prof. medicine Harvard Med. Sch., Boston, 1990-96, prof. medicine, 1996—, Mallinckrodt prof. medicine, 1998—. Mem. ad hoc peer rev. com. NIH, Bethesda, Md., mem. pathology A study sect., 1988—92; mem. advisor W.W. Charitable Trust, Phila., 1985—88; mem. peer rev. com. Am. Heart Assn., Mass., 1982—88, chmn., 1992—94, chmn. rsch. com., 1994—96, George Lyman Duff meml. lectr., 1998; mem. bd. sci. counselors Nat. Heart, Lung, and Blood Inst., 1996—2001; inaugural basic sci. lectr. European Soc. Cardiology, Birmingham, England, 1996; E.B. Raftery meml. lectr. Royal Coll. Physicians, London, 1996; Durrer Meml. lectr. Acad. Med. Ctr., Amsterdam, 1997; Teichman Meml. lectr. Tel Aviv U., 1997; E.F. Bernstein meml. lectr. Scripps Clinic, La Jolla, Calif., 1999; H.J.C. Swan lectr. Cedars-Sinai Med. Ctr., UCLA, 1999; Lord Rayner meml. lectr. Royal Coll. Physicians, London, 1999; Nobel Forum lectr., Karolinska Rsch. Lecture Series Karolinska Inst., Stockholm, 1999, Michel Mirowski lectr. Johns Hopkins U. Cardiovasc. Inst., Balt., 2000; 17th Edward Massie lectr. Wash. U. Sch. Medicine, St. Louis, 2001; Franz M. Groedel lectr., Presdl. Plenary Session, 50th Ann. Scientific Session Am. Coll. Cardiology, Orlando, Fla., 2001; 38th ann. Martin E. Rehfuss lectr. Jefferson Med. Coll., Thomas Jefferson U., Phila., 2001; Herrick lectr. Am. Heart Assn., Chgo., 2001, Russell Ross meml. lectr. in vascular biology, Anaheim, Calif., 01; Frank N. Wilson vis. prof. U. Mich. Health Sys., Ann Arbor, 2002; 18th ann. Lorenzini lectr., Plenary Session 6th Internat. Symposium on Global Risk of Coronary Heart Disease and Stroke, Florence, Italy, 2002; ann. meml. lectr. Fernandez-Cruz Found. XXI Anniversary, Madrid, 2002; 29th ann. Arvilla Berger lectr. N.Y. Cardiological Soc., NYC, 2002. Recipient Established Investigator award, Am. Heart Assn., 1986—91, MERIT award, Nat. Heart, Lung, Blood Inst., 1993—; fellow, Med. Found., Inc., Boston, 1980—82, Coun. Arteriosclerosis, Am. Heart Assn. and Coun. on Circulation; S.A. Levine fellow, Am. Heart Assn., Mass., 1976—77. Fellow: Am. Coll. Cardiology; mem.: Assn. Profs. Cardiology, Internat. Soc. and Fedn. Cardiology, N. Am. Vascular Biology Orgn., Am. Assn. Immunologists, Am. Soc. Cell Biology, Assn. Am. Physicians, Am. Physiol. Soc., Am. Soc. Clin. Investigation. Home: 111 Perkins St Jamaica Plain MA 02130-4313 Office: Brigham & Women's Hosp 75 Francis St Boston MA 02115-6106

LIBERATI, EMILIO, psychology doctor, sociologist, consultant; b. Rome, Dec. 1, 1972; s. Nazzareno Liberati and Rosa-Maria Armonioso. Degree in Acctg., ITC Alessandro Farnese, Rome, 1992; degree in Sociology, Yorker Internat. U., NYC, 2003; PhD in Psychology, U. Le Bon Samaritaine, 2004. Ofcl. Italian Govt., Capranica, Italy, 1992—97; mgr. Advt. Plus, Rome, 1998—2000, Sinergie Aziendali, Rome, 2000—01; CEO Am. Schs., Capranica, Italy, 2007—. Author: Motivation Psychology, 2001. Mem. ANC, Capranica, Italy, 2004, PDL, Capranica, Italy, 2008. Mem.: Am. Psychol. Assn., James Randi Found., CSI, Internat. Positive Psychology Assn., Am. Sociol. Assn., Comitato Italiano Controllo Affermazioni Paranormale (com. skeptical inquiry), Italian Assn. Formatori, Italian Soc. Positive Psychology, Centre Applied Positive Psychology, European Network Positive Psychology, Internat. Coach Fedn., Nat. Assn. Sociology. Roman Catholic. Avocations: football, reading, films. Office: Am Schs Via Montecolle 1012 Capranica VT Italy Office Phone: 00393394397341. Business E-Mail: emilio_liberati@libero.it.

LIBERMAN, M. CHARLES, otolaryngologist, educator; AB in Biology, Harvard Coll., 1972; PhD in Physiology, Harvard U., 1976. Prof. otology, laryngology, health sciences & technol. Harvard Med. Sch. Mass. Eye & Ear Infirmary. Mem.: Am. Assn. Advancement Sci., Soc. for Neuroscience, Assn. for Rsch. in Otolaryngology. Office: 77 Massachusetts Ave E25-519 Cambridge MA 02139 Office Phone: 617-573-3745. E-mail: mcl@epl.meei.harvard.edu.

LICHLITER, WARREN EUGENE, surgeon, educator; b. Murphysboro, Ill., Jan. 24, 1952; s. Gene Estel and Dorothy Colleen (Williams) L.; m. Carol Jane Loftin, Nov. 3, 1979; children: Gary Edward, Christopher Warren, Adrienne Leigh, Abigail Meredith. BA, U. Tenn., 1974; MD, U. Tex., Galveston, 1978. Intern and resident in gen. surgery Baylor U. Med. Ctr., Dallas, 1979-83, resident in colon rectal surgery, 1983-84, mem. attending staff dept. colon rectal surgery, 1984—, assoc. dir. surg. edn., 1984—, program dir. dept. colon rectal residency, 2000—, chief dept. colon rectal surgery, 2000—; clin. asst. prof. surgery health sci. ctr. U. Tex., Dallas, 1990—. Fellow: ACS (pres. North Tex. chpt. 2007, gov.-at-large), Am. Soc. Colon Rectal Surgeons; mem.: Dallas County Med. Soc. (sec.-treas. 2001—02, pres. 2004), Dallas Soc. Surgeons, Tex. Surg. Soc., Alpha Omega Alpha. Avocations: running, bicycling, sailing, kayaking, swimming. Office: 3409 Worth St Ste 500 Dallas TX 75246-2057 Office Phone: 214-824-1730. Business E-Mail: warrenl@baylonhealth.edu.

LICHSTEIN, EDGAR, cardiologist; b. NYC, Nov. 27, 1936; s. Joseph and Ruth (Weisner) L.; m. Marilyn Dorf, June 19, 1966; children: Adam Robert, Amy Ruth. AB, Columbia Coll., 1957; MD, SUNY, Bklyn., 1961. Diplomate Am. Bd. Internal Medicine, Am. Bd. Cardiovascular Disease. Intern Lenox Hill Hosp., NYC, 1961-62, resident in medicine, 1962-63, NYU, NYC, 1963-64; fellow in cardiology NYU-Nat. Heart Inst., 1964-66; chief cardiology Mt. Sinai Med. Services Elmhurst, NYC, 1971-77; dir. cardiology Maimonides Med. Ctr., Bklyn., 1977-89, chmn. dept. medicine, 1989—; prof. medicine SUNY Downstate, 1980—2004, Mt. Sinai Sch. Medicine, 2004—08, SUNY Downstate, 2009—. Bd. dirs. Maimonides Rsch. and Devel. Found., Bklyn., N.Y. Heart Assn. Author: Hemodynamict's Reference File, 1971; contbr. articles to profl. jours. Mem. New Rochelle (N.Y.) Sch. Bd., 1977-81; bd. dirs. New Rochelle Youth Soccer League, 1976. Served to capt. USAF, 1966-68. Fellow ACP, Am. Coll. Cardiology, Am. Coll. Chest Physicians, Coun. Clin. Cardiology; mem. N.Y. Heart Assn. (chmn. coun. cmty. programs, bd. dirs. 1983—). Jewish. Avocation: swimming. Office: Maimonides Med Ctr 4802 10th Ave Brooklyn NY 11219-2844 Office Phone: 718-283-7074. Business E-Mail: clichstein@maimonidesmed.org.

LICHTEN, MICHAEL J., microbiologist, researcher; b. Chgo., Feb. 7, 1954; BS with honors in Biology, Haverford Coll., 1975; PhD, MIT, 1982. Sr. staff fellow Lab. Biochemistry and Molecular Biology, Ctr. Cancer Rsch., Nat. Cancer Inst., 1987, sr. investigator, 1995, chief, 2001—, head DNA Recombination in Yeast Sect.; mem. Sr. Biomedical Rsch. Svc. USPHS, 2000—. Office: Lab Biochemistry Ctr Cancer Rsch 37 Convent Dr Bldg 37 Rm 6124 Bethesda MD 20892-4255 Office Phone: 301-496-1760. Office Fax: 301-402-3095. E-mail: lichten@helix.nih.gov. *

LICHTENFELD, JAY LEONARD, internist, oncologist; b. Phila., Pa., July 23, 1946; m. Sandra Reed. Grad., U. Pa.; MD, Hahnemann U. Med. Coll. (now Drexel U. Coll. Medicine), Phila., 1971. Cert. Internal Medicine, Oncology. Intern, medicine Temple U. Hosp., Phila., 1971—72; resident, oncology John Hopkins Hosp., Balt., 1976—77, med. instr.; fellow Balt. Cancer Rsch. Ctr., 1972—75; hosp. appointment Sinai Hosp.; private practice Thomasville, Ga.; dep. chief med. officer, nat. office Am. Cancer Soc. Spkr. in field. Master: ACP; mem.: Am. Med. Assn., Alpha Omega Alpha. Office: 103 Hiding Pl Thomasville GA 31792-8829 Address: Am Cancer Soc 1599 Clifton Rd NE Atlanta GA 30329

LICHTENSTEIN, ALICE HINDA, nutritional biochemist; b. NYC; d. Armand and Adelaide (Goldstein) L.; m. Barry R. Goldin: children: David Aaron Lichtenstein Goldin, Rachel Bella Lichtenstein Goldin. BS, Cornell U., 1971; MS, Pa. State U., 1973, Harvard U., 1975, DSc, 1979. Rsch. assoc. Boston U., 1982-83, asst. prof., 1983-88; scientist II Jean Mayer USDA Human Nutrition Rsch. Ctr. on Aging, Boston, 1988-94, scientist I, 1994—; assoc. prof. sch. nutrition Tufts U., Boston, 1994-98, prof. sch. nutrition, 1998—, Stanley N. Gershoff Prof. Nutrition Sci. and Policy, Dorothy R. Friedman Sch. Nutrition Sci. and Policy. Bd. dirs. Edinformer, Marblehead, Mass. Mem. editl. bd. Womens' Letter, 1990-91, Jour. Nutrition, 1993-99; contbr. articles to profl. jours. Mem. Am. Inst. Nutrition (new mems. com. 1994-98), Am. Soc. Clin. Nutrition, Am. Heart Assn. (basic sci. coun. 1984—, arteriosclerosis coun. 1980—, nutrition com. 1993—, bd. dirs. Greater Boston chpt. 1983-86, rsch. grant peer rev. com. Mass. chpt. 1988-90, chair task force on heart health edn. in young 1986-89, chair sub task force on evaluation task force on heart-health sch. lunch 1992-93), Phi Kappa Phi, Kappa Omicron Nu. Office: Tufts Univ HNRCA USDA 711 Washington St Boston MA 02111-1524 E-mail: alice.lichtenstein@tufts.edu.

LICHTENSTEIN, GARY R., gastroenterologist, educator; BA, U. Pa.; MD, Mt. Sinai Sch. of Medicine. Diplomate Am. Bd. Internal Medicine, 1987, Am. Bd. Internal Medicine-gastroenterology, 1987. Resident Duke Univ. Med. Ctr.; fellow Hosp. Univ. Pa., physician, dir. Inflammatory Bowel Disease Ctr.; assoc. prof. medicine dept. Univ. Pa. Co-author: MRI Evaluation of Crohn's Disease Activity, 2000; author: Chemokines and Cytokines in Inflammatory Bowel Disease. And Their Application to Disease Management, 2000, Introduction: Inflammatory Bowel Disease. Seminars in Gastrointestinal Diseases, 2010. Named recognized, Best Doctors in America, 2005—06, 2007—08, 2009—10, 2010; named one of the Top Doctors, Phila. Mag., 2004—11, the Top Doctors in America, 2007—08. Mem.: ACP, Am. Coll. Gastroenterology, Am. Gastroent. Assn., Am. Soc. of Gastrointestinal Endoscopy. Office: Hospital of the University of Pennsylvania 3400 Spruce St Philadelphia PA 19104 Office Phone: 215-662-4000. Business E-Mail: grl@mail.med.upeen.edu.

LICHTENSTEIN, STEVEN JAY, ophthalmologist; b. Phila., July 29, 1952; s. Albert and Mildred Lichtenstein; m. Pamela Ann Davenport, Aug. 31, 1997; children: Adam Kenton Elder, Ariana Ronit Turner, Andrew (Drew) Gregory. BA, La Salle Coll., Phila., 1976; MS in Anatomy, U. Louisville, 1979, MD, 1983. Bd. cert. Am. Bd. Ophthalmology, 1990. Intern U. Louisville, Sch. Medicine, Dept. Internal Medicine, 1983—83; resident Yale U. Sch. Medicine, Dept. Ophthalmology and Visual Sciences, New Haven, 1984—87, Harvard Med. Sch., Boston Children's Hosp., 1987—88; pediatric ophthalmologist pvt. practice, Louisville, 1988—89; chief of pediatric ophthalmology Louisville Children's Eye Specialists, P.S.C., Louisville, 1990—2005; pediatric ophthalmologist Ill. Eye Ctr., Peoria,

2005—; clin. assoc. prof. U. Ill. Coll. Medicine, Depts. Surgery and Pediat., 2005—; chief pediat. ophthalmology Childrens Hosp. Ill., 2011—. Del. Ill. State Med. Soc. Congress; mem. Drug and Therapeutics Com. Ill. State Med. Soc., Exec. Com. Ill. Soc. Prevent Blindness, 2009—11; mem., pediatric adv. com. Prevent Blindness Am., Chgo., 2002—08; pres. Peoria Med. Soc., 2009—10. Contbr. articles to profl. jours. and monographs. Bd. mem. Joint Commn. Allied Health Pers. Ophthalmology Found., 2005—09; mem. Louisville Zoo Found., 1988—90; v.p. Joint Commn. Allied Health Pers. Ophthalmology Found., 2009—; lead ophthalmologist, med. mission Romania NW Med. Teams, Portland, 1994—94; vol. ophthalmologist Louisville Zoo, 1988—2005. Recipient Physician's Recognition award, AMA, 1989, 1992, 1998, 2001, 2004, Physician's Recognition award with commendation, 2007, Golden Apple award, Jefferson County Pub. Schs., 1993, Lifelong Edn. Ophthalmologist award, Am. Acad. Ophthalmology, 1997, 2000, 2004, Honor award, Am. Assn. Pediatric Ophthalmology and Strabismus, 2004. Fellow: ACS, Am. Acad. Pediat. (mem. exec. com. sect. ophthalmology 1996—2002, chair sect. ophthalmology 2002—04, mem. surg. adv. panel 2002—06), Am. Acad. Ophthalmology (mem. leadership devel. program 2002—03, mem. councilor 2002—04, mem. ophthalmic tech. assessment com. 2006—); mem.: Peoria Med. Soc. (chair program com. 2005—08, program chair, bd. dirs. 2005—, bd. dirs. 2006—, pres. 2009—10, exec. com. mem. 2009—), Ill. State Med. Soc. (mem. coun. membership & advocacy 2005—07), Am. Assn. Pediatric Ophthalmology and Strabismus (chair bylaws com. 2004—06, internet website com. mem. 2008—). Achievements include research in pediatric population of Levofloxacin ophthalmic antibiotic; pediatric population of Moxifloxacin ophthalmic antibiotic; bevacizumab for treatment of retinopathy of prematurity; patents in field. Office: Illinois Eye Center 8921 North Wood Sage Rd Peoria IL 61615 Office Phone: 309-243-2400. Office Fax: 309-243-5376.

LICHTER, ALLEN S., oncologist, medical association administrator; BS, U. Mich., 1968, MD, 1972. Intern St. Joseph Hosp., Denver; resident U. Calif., San Francisco, 1976; former dir. radiation therapy sect. radiation oncology br. Nat. Cancer Inst.; dir. breast oncology program Comprehensive Cancer Ctr., U. Mich., Ann Arbor, 1984-91, chmn. dept. radiation oncology, 1984-97, interim dean Med. Sch., 1998-99, prof. radiation oncology, 1999—2006, dean Med. sch., 1999—2006; exec. v.p., CEO Am. Soc. Clin. Oncology, Alexandria, Va., 2006—. Bd. dirs. Accreditation Coun. for Grad. Med. Edn. Assoc. editor Jour. Clin. Oncology; editl. bd. Jour. Nat. Cancer Inst., Internat. Jour. Radiation Oncology; co-editor Clinical Oncology, 1995, 2d edit., 1999. Mem.: Am. Soc. Therapeutic Radiology and Oncology (bd. dirs.), Am. Soc. Clin. Oncology (pres. 1998—99, chmn. ASCO Found. bd. dirs. 1999—2002, exec. v.p. and CEO 2006—). Achievements include research in effective breast cancer treatment. Office: Am Soc Clin Oncology 2318 Mill Rd Ste 800 Alexandria VA 22314 Office Phone: 571-483-1300.

LICHTER, STEPHEN MARC, oncologist; b. NYC, Feb. 13, 1949; MD, Univ. Health Scis./Chgo. Med. Sch., 1975. Diplomate Am. Bd. Internal Medicine, Am. Bd. Med. Oncology. Intern Brookdale Hosp. Med. Ctr., NY, 1975—76, resident NY, 1976—78, fellow NY, 1978—80; assoc. chief hematology/oncology Beth Israel Med. Ctr., Bklyn.; asst. clin. prof. mediicine SUNY Health Sci. Ctr., Bklyn. Fellow: ACP; mem.: NY State Soc. Med. Oncologists, Kings County Med. Assn., NY State Med. Assn., Am. Soc. Hematology, Am. Coll. Clin. Oncology. Office: 2935 Avenue S Brooklyn NY 11229-3231 Home Phone: 516-678-2584; Office Phone: 718-616-0801. Business E-Mail: lichter@hemoncare.com.

LICHTIG, LEO KENNETH, health economist; b. Bklyn., Oct. 20, 1953; s. Samuel and Alyne Norma (Strauss) L.; m. Susan Mary Walsh, May 15, 1977; children: Brielle Joy, Danica Jill. BS, MS, Rensselaer Poly. Inst., 1974, PhD, 1976. Asst. prof. SUNY, Albany, 1976—77; project specialist, econometrician N.J. State Dept. Health, Trenton, 1977—82; dir. utilization econs. and rsch. Empire Blue Cross/Blue Shield, Albany, 1982—90; v.p. rsch. and demonstration Health Care Rsch. Found., Albany, 1982—90; v.p. Network, Inc., Randolph, NJ, 1990—94, sr. v.p., chief info. officer Somerset, NJ, Latham, NY, 1994—2002; v.p. life sci. group Aon Consulting, Inc., Somerset, 2002—. Nat. diagnosis related group steering com. health care fin. adminstrn. Yale U., Washington, 1979-81; adj. faculty Russell Sage Grad. Sch. Health Adminstrn., Albany, 1986-94, Union Coll. Grad. Mgmt. Inst., Schenectady, NY, 1991-92; expert reviewer Health Care Financing Adminstrn., Washington, 1987, 89; mem. Nat. Database Nursing Quality Indications Methods Devel. Adv. Panel, 2009-; mem. tech. expert panel Medicare Diagnosis Related Groups refinement RAND Corp., 2006-07; cons. in field. Author: Hospital Information Systems for Case Mix Management, 1986; contbg. editor (newsletter) Nat. Report on Computers & Health, 1982-85; contbr. articles to profl. jours. Mem. tech. adv. com. Statewide Planning and Rsch. Coop. Sys., N.Y. State Dept. Health; mem. N.Y. State Universal Data Set Specifications Task Force, 1998-2002, N.Y., State Uniform Billing Com., 2002—, N.Y. State Data Protection Rev. Bd., 2003-. Mem. Am. Statis. Assn. (com. on privacy and confidentiality 1981-84, subcom. on quality and productivity measures 1988-90), Acad. for Health Svcs. Rsch. and Health Policy, Healthcare Fin. Mgmt. Assn., Internat. Arthurian Soc. (N.Am. br.). Office: Aon Consulting Inc 400 Atrium Dr Somerset NJ 08873 Business E-Mail: lichtl@rpi.edu.

LICHTIN, LEON (JUDAH LEON LICHTIN), retired pharmaceutical educator; b. Phila., Mar. 5, 1924; s. Aaron and Rosa (Rosenberg) L.; m. Beverly I. Cohen, Aug. 6, 1950; children— Benjamin Lloyd, Alan Eli. BS in Pharmacy, Phila. Coll. Pharmacy and Sci., 1944, MS in Pharmacy, 1947; PhD in Pharm. Chemistry, Ohio State U., 1950. Asst. prof. pharmacy U. Cin., 1950-51, assoc. prof., 1951-64, prof., 1964-71, Andrew Jergens prof. pharmacy, 1971-91, Andrew Jergens prof. pharmacy emeritus, 1991—. Cons. in cosmetic sci. Composer string music, vocal music, prodr. (CDs) JuChriLam in Celebration of Jerusalem 3000, Ezekiel, Chapter 37, Verses 1-14 "The Valley of Dry Bones, Zichronot Gimal-Remembrances III String Quintet; contbr. articles to pharm. jours. Past pres. No. Hills Synagogue, Cin. Fellow AAAS, Soc. Cosmetic Chemists; mem. Rho Chi. Achievements include patents in field. Home: 801 Cloverview Ave Cincinnati OH 45231-6017 Office Phone: 513-522-6688. Business E-Mail: leon.lichtin@uc.edu.

LICHTINGER, MOISES, obstetrician, gynecologist; arrived in U.S., 1976; s. Kuba Lichtinger and Teresa Waisman-Lichtinger; m. Rina B. Lichtinger, Nov. 26, 1978; children: Liza, Alexis. BS, Escuela de la Ciudad de Mexico, Mexico City, 1969; MD, Nat. U. Mexico, Mexico City, 1975. Ho. officer ob-gyn. Gynccobstretras S.Q., Mexico City, 1976; intern Jackson Meml. Hosp., Miami, Fla., 1976, resident dept. ob-gyn., 1976—80, fellow dept. ob-gyn. divsn. oncology, 1980—82; instr. dept. ob-gyn. U. Miami, 1980—81, jr. attending in gynecology and gynecologic oncology, 1981—82, asst. prof. dept. ob-gyn., 1982—86, 1982—87, asst. prof. dept. oncology, 1984—87; asst. prof. dept. med. oncology U. Miami Sch. Medicine, 1982—87, clin. asst. prof. dept. med. oncology, 1986—87, clin. asst. prof. dept. ob-gyn., 1986—90, vol. faculty, 1990—93; physician in charge gyn-oncology Mt. Sinai Med. Ctr., Miami Beach, 1986—87, assoc. attending dept. ob-gyn., 1986—88; chmn. peer rev. ob-gyn. Holy Cross Hosp., Ft. Lauderdale, Fla., 1998—2001, chmn. dept. ob-gyn., 2002—. Chmn. ob-gyn. dept. Holy Cross Hosp., Ft. Lauderdale; rschr. in field; presenter in field. Contbr. articles to profl. jours. Named Best Med. Student of Mexico, Pres. Luis Ecteravia, 1976, Best Chief Resident Tchr., U. Miami Sch. Medicine, 1980. Mem.: BCMA, ACOG (2nd best video on gynecol. surgery award 2002), ACS, Philharmonic Soc., Opera Soc. (Father of Yr. award). Avocation: yoga instructor. Office: Holy Cross Med Group 4701 N Federal Hwy Fort Lauderdale FL 33308

LICHTMAN, DAVID MICHAEL, orthopedist, health facility administrator, educator, retired military officer; b. Bkyln., Jan. 14, 1942; s. Harry S. and Frances (Rubin) L.; m. Frances Lubin; children: James Matthew, Elisabeth Jill. Student, Tufts Coll., 1962; MD, SUNY, Bklyn., 1966. Diplomate Am. Bd. Orthop. Surgery. Intern U. Minn. Hosp., 1966-67, Naval Aerospace Med. Inst., Pensacola, Fla., 1967; commd. lt. USN, 1967, advanced through grades to rear adm., 1988, flight surgeon Air Wing 3, 1968-69; mem. staff orthop. svc. Nat. Naval Med. Ctr., Bethesda, Md., 1974-77, chmn. dept. orthop. surgery, head, hand surgery svc., 1984-87, dir. orthop. residency program, 1984-87, asst. chmn. dept. orthop. surgery, 1975-77, chmn. dept. orthop. surgery, head hand surgery svc., dir. orthop. residency program, 1984-87; chmn. dept. orthop. surgery and rehab. Naval Hosp., Oakland, Calif., 1977-83, dir. orthop. residency program/dir. navy hand fellowship, 1977-83, head hand and microsurgery svc., 1977-83, mem. staff orthop. surgery, sr. hand/microsurgery cons., 1988-91, commdg. officer, 1989-91; comdr. San Francisco Med. Command, Oakland, 1988-91; promoted to Rear Adm. (lower half), 1989; Rear Adm. (upper half), 1991; ret. USN, 1994; John Dunn prof. orthop. hand surgery Baylor Coll. Medicine, Houston, 1994-98; chmn. dir. orthop. residency tng. John Peter Smith Hosp., Ft. Worth, 1998—; clin. prof. orthop. Southwestern Coll. Medicine, Dallas, 1998—2005; chmn. Dept. Orthop. Surgery Health Scis. Ctr. U. North Tex., Ft. Worth, 2005—, chmn. Dept. Orthop. Surgery, 2006—, prof. Dept. Orthop. Surgery, 2006—. Cons. orthop. surgery asst. sec. def. for health affairs Dept. Def., Washington, 1988-94; specialty advisor naval surgeon gen. for orthop. surgery and hand surgery Bur. Medicine and Surgery Dept. Navy, Washington, 1983-86; prof. surgery and head divsn. orthop. surgery Uniformed Svcs. U. of Health Scis., Bethesda, 1984-94, ex-officio mem. bd. regents, 1991-94' examiner Am. Bd. Orthopaedic Surgery. Editor: The Wrist and Its Disorders, 1988, 2d edit., 1997, Hand and Wrist Sect. Current Opinion in Orthopaedics; contbr. articles to profl. jours. Mem. ACS (bd. govs. 1987-96), Am. Acad. Orthop. Surgeons, Am. Soc. Surgery of Hand (coun. 1999-2002, pres. 2005-06, AMA del. 2001-), Am. Orthop. Assn. (hon.), Mil. Surgeons U.S. (Philip Hench award 1982), Tex. Med. Assn. (del. Tarrant County 2003), Soc. Naval Flight Surgeons, Soc. Med. Consultants to the Armed Forces (coun. 1994—, pres. 2002-03), Soc. Mil. Orthop. Surgeons (bd. dirs. 1987-90), Orthopaedic RRC of the ACGME, Fedn. Ctrl. and N.Am. Hand Surgery and Therapy Soc. (pres.-elect 2007). Home: 4958 Overton Woods Ct Fort Worth TX 76109-2433 Office: John Peter Smith Hosp Dept Orthopedic Surgery 1500 S Main St Fort Worth TX 76104-4917 Office Phone: 817-920-6903. Business E-Mail: dlichtma@jpshealth.org.

LICHTMAN, MARSHALL ALBERT, hematologist, medical educator, research scientist; b. NYC, June 23, 1934; s. Samuel and Vera Lichtman; m. Alice Jo Maisel, June 23, 1957; children: Susan, Joanne, Pamela. AB, Cornell U., 1955; MD, U. Buffalo, 1960. Diplomate Am. Bd. Internal Medicine. Resident in medicine Strong Meml. Hosp., 1960-63; surgeon USPHS, 1963-65; postdoctoral rsch. assoc. Sch. Pub. Health, U. N.C., 1963-65; chief resident, instr. medicine Strong Meml. Hosp., 1965-66; sr. instr. medicine, rsch. trainee in hematology U. Rochester (NY) Sch. Medicine, 1966-67, asst. prof. medicine, 1968-70, spl. NIH postdoctoral rsch. fellow hematology, 1968-70, assoc. prof. medicine and biophysics, 1971-74, prof. medicine and biophysics, 1974—95, prof. medicine, biochemistry and biophysics, 1996—, chief hematology unit dept. medicine, 1975-77, co-chief, 1977-89, sr. assoc. dean for acad. affairs and rsch., 1979-89, dean Sch. Medicine and Dentistry, 1990-95; exec. v.p. rsch. and med. affairs Leukemia & Lymphoma Soc., 1996—2007. Mem. sci. coun. Am. Nat. Red Cross, 1987-95; coun. deans, Assn. Am. Med. Colls., 1990-1995, vis. prof. univs.; trustee SUNY, 2010-11; lectr. in field. Editor: Abnormalities of Granulocytes and Monocytes, 1975, Hematology for Practitioners, 1978, Hematology and Oncology, 1980; editor: (with W.J. William, E. Beutler, A.J. Erslev) Hematology, 3d edit., 1983, 4th edit., 1990; editor: (with E. Beutler, B. Coller and T.J. Kipps) Williams Hematology, 5th edit. 1995, 6th edit. 2001; editor: (E. Beutler, T.J. Kipps and others) 7th edit., 2006; editor: (with K. Kaushansky, J.T. P., U. S., E. B., T. J. K.) 8th edit., 2011; editor: (with H.J. Meiselman and P.L. LaCelle) White Cell Mechanics: Basic Science and Clinical Aspects, 1984; editor: Hematology: Landmark Papers of the Twentieth Century, 2000; editor: (with E. Beutler, T.J. Kipps, W.J. Williams) Williams Manual of Hematology, 2003; editor: (with J. Shafer, R. Felgar, N. Wang) Lichtman's Atlas of Hematology, 2007; mem. editl. bd.: Blood Cells, 1978—84, Stem Cells, 1981—83, 1993—, Blood, 1983—87, Internat. Jour. Cell Cloning, 1983—92, Exptl. Hematology, 1990—93, Blood Cells, Molecules and Diseases, 1995—, editor-in-chief:, 2000—, Am. Jour. Hematology, 2000—07; contbr. articles to profl. jours. Bd. dirs., Am. Red Cross Blood Svcs., Rochester Region, 1982-1990; NY State Coun Grad. Med. Edn., 1991-1993, bd. govs. ARC, 1990-96, chair sci. coun., 1987-95. Scholar Leukemia Soc. Am., 1969-74; recipient contracts U.S. Army Rsch., 1972-78, U.S. Dept. Energy, 1972-80; USPHS grantee, 1971-95, disting. Alumnus award, U. Buffalo Sch. Medicine and Biomed. Scis., 2001, Cert. Merit, Rochester Acad. Medicine, 2006. Master ACP; mem. NIH (hematology study sect. 1982-86), AAAS, Am. Fedn. Med. Rsch., Am. Soc. Hematology (pres. 1989), Internat. Soc. Hematology, N.Y. Acad. Scis., Am. Soc. Clin. Investigation, Assn. Am. Physicians, Am. Assn. for Cancer Rsch., Am. Physiol. Soc., Soc. Leuk Biology, Am. Soc. Cell Biology. Office: U Rochester Med Ctr Box 610 601 Elmwood Ave Rochester NY 14642-0001 Office Phone: 585-275-2205. Business E-Mail: mal@urmc.rochester.edu.

LICHTMAN, STEVEN W., physiologist; b. Brooklyn, NY, May 20, 1956; s. Emanuel Lichtman, Gertrude Lichtman; m. Laura Allain; children: Kevin, Ryan. BA, Queens Coll., CCNY, 1978; MEd, Am. U., 1980; EdD, Columbia U., 1992. Dir. exercise prescription program NYU, NYC, 1984—87; rsch. coord. St. Lukes/Roosevelt Hosp. Ctr., 1988—91; dir. cardiopulmonary outpatient svcs. Helen Hayes Hosp., West Haverstraw, 1991—; asst, prof. Mercy Coll., Dobbs Ferry, 1995—. Pres. Monroe Woodbury Soccer Club, Monroe, NY, 1997—2000. Fellow: Am. Assn. Cardiovascular and Pulmonary Rehab. (pres. 2011—); mem.: Am. Heart Assn., NY Acad. Scis. (rsch. mentor 1996), NY Assn. Cardiac and Pulmonary Rehab. (v.p. 2000—01). Avocations: sports, travel, photography. Office: Helen Hayes Hosp Rte 9W West Haverstraw NY 10993 Office Phone: 845 786-4486. Office Fax: 845 786-4781. Business E-Mail: lichtman@helenhayeshosp.org. *

LICHTMAN, STUART MARVIN, oncologist, educator; b. Bklyn., June 1, 1955; MD, Mt. Sinai, 1980. Physician, prof. medicine Meml. Sloan-Kettering Cancer Ctr., 2004—. Fellow: ACP; mem.: SIOG, ABIM, AGS, ASCO. Office: 650 Commack Rd Commack NY 11725 Office Fax: 631-864-3827. Business E-Mail: lichtmas@mskcc.org.

LIDDINGTON, ROBERT C., biomedical researcher, educator; PhD, U. York, England, 1986. Postdoctoral training Harvard U.; asst. prof. Dana-Farber Cancer Inst & Harvard Med. Sch., 1990; prof. & chmn. macromolecular crystallography U. Leicester Dept. Biochemistry, England; co-dir. cell adhesion & extracellular matrix biology program Burnham Inst. for Med. Rsch., 1999—2004, prof. & dir. infectious disease program. Office: 10901 N Torrey Pines Rd La Jolla CA 92037 Office Phone: 858-646-3136. Office Fax: 858-646-3196. E-mail: rlidding@burnham.org.

LIDOFSKY, STEVEN DAVID, medical educator; b. Bklyn., Jan. 19, 1954; s. Leon Julian and Eleanor Helen (Liebman) L.; m. Elisabeth Tang Barfod, May 3, 1982; children: Benjamin Barfod, Anna Barfod. BA, Columbia U., 1975, PhD, 1980, MD, 1982. Diplomate Am. Bd. Internal Medicine, Am. Bd. Gastroenterology. Intern U. Colo., Denver, 1982-83, resident, 1983-85, chief med. resident, 1985-86; fellow in gastroenterology U. Calif., San Francisco, 1986-90, asst. prof. medicine, 1990-97; assoc. prof. medicine and pharmacology, dir. hepatology U. Vt., Burlington, 1997—, dir. MD-PhD program, 2001—, prof. med. and pharmacology, 2008—. Contbr. articles to profl. jours. Recipient Liver Scholar award Am. Liver Found., 1990-93, Rsch. award Am. Diabetes Assn., 1996. Mem. Am. Assn. for Study of Liver Diseases, Am. Gastroenterol. Assn. (Fiterman Found. Rsch. award 1994), Calif. Acad. Medicine, Western Soc. Clin. Investigation. Avocations: cartooning, cooking, running. Office: U Vt Smith 251 MFU Burlington VT 05401 Office Phone: 802-847-2554. E-mail: steven.lidofsky@uvm.edu.

LIEBELT, ERICA LYNN, pediatrician, educator; BS, Duke U., 1983; MD, U. Cin., 1987. Asst. prof. pediat. Yale U., New Haven, 1994—96, Johns Hopkins, Balt., 1998—2001; assoc. prof. pediat. U. Ala., Birmingham, 2003—. Dir. med. toxicology svcs. U. Ala. Hosps., Birmingham, 2003—. Mem. editl. bd.: Jour. Toxicology - Clin. Toxicology; editor: Current Opinion in Pediatrics. Fellow: Am. Acad. Pediat., Am. Coll. Med. Toxicology (bd. dirs. 1998); mem.: Soc. Acad. Emergency Medicine. Office: Childrens Hosp 1600 7th Ave S MC 205 Birmingham AL 35233

LIEBER, H. STEPHEN, health association executive; BA in Psychology, U. Ark.; MA, U. Chgo. Asst. adminstr., rsch. & statistics Ark. Social Services; v.p. ops. Ill. Hosp. Assn.; sr. budget analyst Ill. Bur. of the Budget; CEO Emergency Nurses Assn.; v.p. divsn. of personal membership groups American Hosp. Assn.; pres., CEO Healthcare Information and Mgmt. System Soc., 2000—, bd. dirs. One of the founders of the Certification Commn. for HIT and Health Information Technology Standards Panel; spkr. and contributor to corp. strategic planning efforts, govt.-sponsored policy efforts, private sector initiatives & other non-profit organizations. Mem.: American Soc. of Healthcare Risk Mgmt. (hon. life), American Hosp. Assn. (hon. life), Assn. Forum of Chicagoland, American Soc. of Assn. Executives, Cert. Assn. Exec. Office: Healthcare Information and Management Systems Soc 33 W Monroe St Ste 1700 Chicago IL 60603-5616 Office Phone: 312-664-4467.

LIEBER, RICHARD LOUIS, biomedical engineering scientist, educator; b. Walnut Creek, Calif., Dec. 14, 1956; s. Richard and Janet Elizabeth (Stone) L.; children: Katelyn Suzanne, Kristin Michelle; m. Dina Lieber, Oct. 2004. BS with honors, U. Calif., Davis, 1978, PhD, 1982. Sr.rsch. career scientist VA Med. Ctr., San Diego, 1983—; prof. orthopaerics & bioengring. U. Calif., 1985—. Cons. Pref Med. Products Inc., 1987—. Contbr. sci. papers to profl. publs.; inventor surgical myometor, 1985, adaptive muscle stimulator, 1987. Faculty advisor Inter-Varsity Christian Fellowship, San Diego, 1984—. Recipient Presdl. award Am. Acad. Cerebral Palsy, 1984, Nicolas Andry award Am. Bone & Joint Inst., 1998; State of Calif. Gov.'s scholar, 1974 Mem. IEEE, Orthopaedic Rsch. Soc., Biophys. Soc. (Talbot award 1981), Rehab. Engring. Soc. N.Am., Soc. Neursci., Am. Soc. Biomechanics (Giovani Borellj award), Am. Physiol. Soc. Republican. Achievements include patent for surgical myometer; development of techniques used involving computer controlled muscle contraction and optical sensors for structure monitoring; research on skeletal muscle properties in normal and diseased muscles. Home: 10471 Mira Montana Dr Del Mar CA 92014 Office: UCSD 9500 Gilman Dr Mc 0863 La Jolla CA 92083 Office Phone: 858-552-8585 x 7016, 858-822-1344. Business E-Mail: rlieber@ucsd.edu.

LIEBERMAN, ERIC B., cardiologist; Attended, Emory U., 1987. Diplomate Am. Bd. Internal Medicine, Am. Bd. Internal Medicine-cardiovasc. disease, Am. Bd. Internal Medicine-interventional cardiology, lic. Md. Resident internal medicine Johns Hopkins Hosp., 1990; resident cardiovasc. disease Duke Univ. Med. Ctr., fellow, 1993; cardiologist Assocs. in Cardiology PA, Md.; physician Washington Adventist Hosp. Fellow: Am. Coll. Cardiologists. Office: Associates in Cardiology PA Ste 200 1400 Forest Glen Rd Silver Spring MD 20910 Office Phone: 301-681-5700. Office Fax: 301-681-5599.

LIEBERMAN, JAY R., orthopedist, surgeon; MD, Albany Med. Coll., NYC, 1984. Assoc. prof. UCLA Med. Ctr., 1991—. Recipient Cap CURE Rsch. award, Cap CURE, 1998—2001, Frank Stinchfield award, Hip Soc., 1999, Russel Hibbs award, Scoliosis Rsch. Soc., 1998, Sumner Koch award, Am. Soc. for Surgery of the Hand, 1998; grantee Physician Scientist award, NIH, 1994—99; fellow ABC Traveling fellow, Am. Orthop. Assn., 1997. Mem.: Hip Soc. (assoc.),

Am. Orthop. Assn. (assoc.). Achievements include research in development of gene therapy to enhance bone repair; understanding the pathophysiology of bone metastasis; deep vein thrombosis prophylaxis after total joint replacement. Office: 263 Farmington Ave Farmington CT 06032

LIEBERMAN, JUDY, immunologist, hematologist, medical educator; b. Boston, Sept. 5, 1947; d. Herman and Beatrice (Goldfarb) L.; m. Edward H. Greer, Dec. 19, 1970; children: Paul, Eric. AB summa cum laude, Harvard U., 1969; PhD in Theoretical Physics, Rockefeller U., 1974; MD, Harvard Med. Sch. and MIT, 1981. Cert. internal medicine and hematology. Mem. Sch. Nat. Scis. Inst. for Advanced Study, Princeton, NJ, 1974-76; rsch. assoc., theoretical physics Fermilab, Batavia, Ill., 1976-77; intern to resident, internal medicine Tufts-New England Med. Ctr., Boston, 1981—84, asst. prof., dept. medicine, 1987—95, clin. fellow, hematology-oncology, 1986—87, asst. physician, divsn. hematology-oncology, 1988—95; postdoctoral fellow Ctr. for Cancer Rsch., MIT, Cambridge, Mass., 1984-86; asst. prof., dept. pediat. Harvard Med. Sch., Boston, 1996—98, assoc. prof., dept. pediat., 1998—2004, dir., divsn. AIDS, 2005—, prof., dept. pediat., 2004—; dir., Pathogenesis prog. Harvard Med. Sch. Ctr. for AIDS, Boston, 2003—. Trustee Assn. of Mems.-Inst. for Advanced Study, Princeton, 1982-92; vis. scientist Ctr. for Cancer Rsch., MIT, Cambridge, 1987-89; mem. AIDS Clin. Trial Group Working Group on Immune Based Therapy, Washington, 1993—, Project Inform Immune Restoration Think Tank, San Francisco, 1993-, mem. steering com. 1995-; program dir., Strategic Program in Innovative Rsch. for AIDS Theraphy, New Eng. Med. Ctr., Mass. Gen. Hosp. and Ctr. for Blood Rsch, 1994-99; mem. Office of AIDS Rsch., AIDS Rsch. Evaluation Working Group, 1995-96, mem. vaccine rsch. planning group, 1998, mem. therapeutics rsch. planning group, 1998-; sr. investigator Ctr. Blood Rsch. (now called The CBR Inst. for Biomedical Rsch.), Harvard Med. Sch., 1995-; cons. in medicine, divsn. hematology-oncology, Children's Hosp., Boston, 1995-; mem. PhD program in immunology, divsn. med. scis., Harvard Med. Sch., 1996-, PhD program in virology, 2004-; mem. sci. adv. com., Am. Found. for AIDS Rsch., 1997-; mem. exec. com., Harvard Divsn. AIDS, 2004-. Nat. Merit Scholar, 1965-69; Damon Runyon-Walter Winchell Cancer Fund Postdoctoral Rsch. Grant, 1984-86; Recipient Clin. Investigator award Nat. Cancer Inst., NIH, Bethesda, Md., 1990-95, Pew Scholar award Pew Found., San Francisco, 1991-95. Fellow: Leukemia Soc. Am. (spl.), Am. Acad. Arts & Scis.; mem.: Am. Assn. Physicians, AAAS (mem. electorate nominating com., sect. med. scis. 2005—), Am. Soc. Gene Therapy (mem. Oligonucleotide Based Therapics Com. 2004—), Interurban Clin. Club. Achievements include immune based therapy for HIV infection. Office: CBR Inst Biomedical Rsch 200 Longwood Ave Boston MA 02115 Office Phone: 617-278-3106. Office Fax: 617-278-3134. Business E-Mail: lieberman@cbr.med.harvard.edu.

LIEBERMAN, KENNETH, pediatric nephrologist, educator; BSE in Computer Sci., Princeton U., 1969—73; MD, Albert Einstein Coll. of Medicine Yeshiva U., 1974—77. Diplomate Am. Bd. Pediatrics, Am. Soc. Pediatric Nephrology-pediatric nephrology. Resident pediat. Mount Sinai Hosp., NY, 1977—79; fellow nephrology NY Hosp.-Cornell, 1979—81; chief pediatric nephrology Mount Sinai Med. Ctr., 1981—2001, Hackensack Univ. Med. Ctr., 2001— Prof. pediat. Univ. of Med. and Dentistry NJ. Office: Hackensack University Medical Center 30 Prospect Ave Hackensack NJ 07601 Office Phone: 201-996-2000.

LIEBERMAN, SEYMOUR, biochemist, educator; b. NYC, Dec. 1, 1916; s. Samuel D. and Sadie (Levin) L.; m. Sandra Spar, June 5, 1944; 1 child, Paul B. BS, Bklyn. Coll., 1936; MS, U. Ill., 1937; PhD (Rockefeller scholar 1939-41), Stanford U., 1941; Traveling fellow, U. Basle, Switzerland, Eidgenoess. Tech. Hochschule, Zurich, Switzerland, 1946-47. Chemist Schering Corp., 1938-39; spl. rsch. assoc. Harvard U., 1941-45; assoc. Sloan-Kettering Inst., 1945-50; prof. biochemistry Columbia Coll. Physicians and Surgeons, 1950-87, prof. emeritus, 1987—, vice provost, 1988, assoc. dir. office sci. and tech., 1991-99; assoc. dean Columbis U. Inst. Health Scis. St. Luke's Roosevelt Hosp. Ctr., 1981-97, pres., 1981-97. Syntex lectr. Mexican Endocrine Soc., 1970; mem. Am. Cancer Soc. panel steroids, 1945-49, hormones, 1949-50, mem. com. pathogenesis of cancer, 1957-60; mem. endocrine study sect. NIH, 1959-63, chmn., 1963-65, mem. gen. clin. research centers, 1967-71; med. adv. com. Population Council, 1961-73; mem. endocrinology panel Cancer Chemotherapy Nat. Svc. Ctr., 1958-62; cons. WHO human reprodn. unit, 1972-74, Ford Found., 1974-77; hon. pres. Internat. Congress on Hormonal Steroids, 1982. Mem. editl. bd. Jour. Clin. Endocrinology and Metabolism, 1958-70, Jour. Biol. Chemistry, 1975-80; contbr. articles to profl. jours. Pfizer Traveling fellow McGill U., 1968; recipient Disting. Alumnus award Bklyn. Coll., 1971, Disting. Svc. award Columbia U., 1991. Fellow N.Y. Acad. Scis., NAS; mem. Am. Soc. Biol. Chemists, Am. Chem. Soc., Internat. Soc. Endocrinology (U.S. del. central com. 1964-76), Endocrine Soc. (Ciba award 1952, Koch award 1970, council 1970-73, pres. 1974-75, Roussel prize 1984, Dale medal 1986, Boehringer-Mannheim award lectr. 1992 Gregory Plucus medal, 2009), Harvey Soc. Home: 515 E 72nd St New York NY 10021-4032 Office: 432 W 58th St New York NY 10019-1102 Office Phone: 212-523-7148. Business E-Mail: sl22@columbia.edu.

LIEBERMANN-MEFFERT, DOROTHEA MARIA IRENE, surgeon, researcher; b. Rastatt, Germany, May 6, 1936; d. Karl Peter and Irene (Wrede) Meffert; m. Eduard Karl Heinz Liebermann; children: Marie-Ann, Martin, Julia, Valeria. MD, U. Freiburg, 1958. Resident Dist. Hosp., Bad Sackingen, Germany, 1958, Pediatric Surgery U., Zurich, 1959, Diakonie Hosp., Freiburg, Germany, 1960—64; sr. resident, assoc. prof. Anatomy U. Inst., Freiburg, Germany, 1965—69; assoc. prof. U. Hosp. gen. surgery, Basel, Switzerland, 1970—87; prof. surgery TU., Munchen, Germany, 1987—2002; prof. clin. surgery U. So. Calif., LA, 2003—04; prof. surgery TU Munchen, Germany, 2004—. Author, editor: Anatomy, Physiology, Pathology and Surgery of the Greater Omentum, 1983, Rudolph Nissen, world revolution of Fundoplication, 1999, History of the Internat. Soc. Surgery, 2002; author book chpts. of chief stress on esophagus and stomach; contbr. over 250 articles to profl. jours and author of numerous articles to renowned surg. European and US handbooks. Recipient prize Internat. Gastric Cancer Soc., 1995, Outstanding Woman Achievement award ABI, 1998, 21st century award for outstanding achievement Medicine/surgery, diploma of honor, Cambridge, Eng., 2003. Fellow Am. Coll. Surgery (councilor German chpt.); mem. Royal Soc. Medicine, Am. Gastroent. Assn., Collegium Internat. Chirurgiae Digestivae, Internat. Soc. Diseases of the Esophagus, Internat. Soc. Surgery (prize 1985), Internat. Assn. Surgery Trauma Surg. Intensive Care, Study Group Dysphagia (Tech. U. München), Internat. Gastric Cancer Assn., ACS, Esophageal Surgery Club US, German Soc. Surgery (prize 1976-77), Swiss Soc. Gastroenterology, german Soc. Surgery, Internat. Soc. Surgery, Clin. Rehab. Assn.(Spin Coord., 1995). Avocations: history, art, water sports, winter sports. Office: Klinikum Rechts der Isar Dept Surgery FACS Ismaningerstr 22 D 81675 Munich Germany Personal E-mail: dliebermann-meffert@t-online.de.

LIEBHABER, MYRON I., allergist; b. Denver, Dec. 28, 1943; married; children: Zak, Sam, Abe. MD, U. Ariz., 1972. Diplomate Am. Bd. Pediat., Am. Bd. Allergy Immunology. Allergist Coll. Hosp., Santa Barbara, Calif. Assoc. vis. clin. prof. UCLA, med. dir. Sansum Rsch. Founder and med. dir. Camp Wheez, 1977; bd. mem. Cttage Health Sys., 1996—2007; del. Calif. Med. Assn., 1996—2003. Mem.: AMA, Staff Physician Cottage Hosp., CMA, Santa Barbara County Med. Soc. (pres. 2002), Sansum Clinic. Democrat. Jewish. Avocations: magic, music. Office: Sansum Med Found Clinic 215 Pesetas Ln Santa Barbara CA 93110-1416 Office Phone: 805-681-7635, 805-681-7635. Business E-Mail: mliebhab@sansumclinic.org.

LIEBMANN, JEFFREY M., ophthalmologist, surgeon, educator; BA magna cum laude, Boston U., 1979, MD, 1983; attended, U. Tex., 1986. Lic. Nat. Bd. of Med. Examiners, 1983, Univ. of the State of NY, 1984, State of NJ, 1996, diplomate Am. Bd. of Ophthalmology, 1989. Intern St. Luke's-Roosevelt Hosp. Ctr., NY, NY, 1983—84; resident Brooklyn / Downstate Med. Ctr., 1984—87, chief resident, 1986—87; fellow The NY Eye and Ear Infirmary, NY, NY, 1987—88, Am. Coll. of Surgeons, Am. Acad. of Ophthalmology, NY Acad. of Medicine; asst. dir. glaucoma svc. The NY Eye and Ear Infirmary, 1988—91, assoc. adjunct surgeon, 1988—94, assoc. attending surgeon, 1994—2005, attending surgeon, 2006—, assoc. dir. glaucoma svc., 1991—2002; clin. instr. ophthalmology NY Med. Coll., Valhalla, NY, 1988—89, clin. asst. prof., 1990—93, clin. assoc. prof. ophthalmology, 1993—99, prof. clin. ophthalmology, 1999—2002; dir. glaucoma svc. Manhattan Eye, Ear, and Throat Hosp., 2002—, NY Univ. Med. Ctr., 2002—; clin. prof. ophthalmology NY Univ. Sch. of Medicine, 2002—. Adjunct prof. ophthalmology NY Med. Coll., Valhalla, NY, 2002—. Recipient Sr. Achievement award, Am. Acad. of Ophthalmology, 2003, Honor award, 1994, The John S. Hermann, M.D., Meml. award For Excellence in Tchg., NY, 1991, Resident Tchg. award, The NY Eye and Ear Infirmary, NY, NY, 1989. Mem.: AMA, Am. Glaucoma Soc. (by-laws com. 2000—08, edn. and communication com. 2001—04, vice chair 2005—06, chair 2007—08, exec. com. 2007—, treas. 2008—), Manhattan Ophthal. Soc., Ophthalmic Laser Surg. Soc. (program dir. 1998—2000), NY County Med. Soc., Bklyn. Opthal. Soc., State Univ.-Kings County Ophthalmology Alumni Assn., NY State Acad. of Sciences, NY State Opthal. Soc., NY Soc. for Clin. Ophthalmology (exec. bd. 1994—2002, pres. 1999—2000, exec. bd. 2006—08), Assn. for Rsch. in Vision and Ophthalmology (glaucoma sec. program planning com. 2000—04, profl. devel. & edn. com. 2001—04, chair 2002—03), Am. Soc. for Cataract and Refractive Surgery (chair 2005, program com. 2005—06), Am. Acad. of Ophthalmology (program chair 1999—2000). Office: The New York Eye and Ear Infirmary 310 East 14th St New York NY 10003 Office Phone: 212-979-4000.

LIEBOWITZ, DANIEL S.F., retired medical educator; b. NYC, Nov. 26, 1921; s. David and Emily Liebowitz; m. Florence Evans Liebowitz, 1978 (dec. Feb. 2006); children: Peter(dec.), Sylvie, Danny P. BA, Columbia U., 1943; MD, NYU, 1946. Diplomate internal medicine. Postgrad. tng. Goldwater Meml. Hosp., NY, Crile VA Hosp., Case We. Res. U., Cleve., 1950—52; clin. prof. medicine emeritus Stanford U. Sch. Medicine, 1963—96; dir. med. edn. emeritus Sequoia Hosp., Redwood City, Calif., 1963—99. Lectr. in field. Author: (novels) The Lion and The Flame, 1992, (biography) The Physician and the Slave Trade, The Livingstone Expeditions and the Crusade Against Slavery in East Africa, 1999; co-author: Cook to Your Heart's Content on a Low Fat Low Salt Diet, 1970; co-author: (with Charles Pearson) The Last Expedition - Stanley's Mad journey Through the Congo, 2005; contbr. articles to profl. jours. Capt. US Army, 1949—50. Fellow: ACP, Royal Geog. Soc.; mem.: AMA, Am. Soc. Gastrointestinal Endoscopy, Am. Gastroenterology Assn., Explorers Club. Avocations: hiking, camping, photography, exploration. Personal E-mail: eminpasha@aol.com, eminpasha@yahoo.com.

LIEBOWITZ, NEIL ROBERT, psychiatrist; b. Feb. 5, 1956; s. Harold and Gertrude Liebowitz; m. Judith Linda, Oct. 21, 1952; children: Sarah Michelle, Daniel Geoffery BA, U. Va., 1978; MD, SUNY, Stony Brook, 1982. Cert. Am. Bd. Psychiatry and Neurology; cert. in clin. psychopharmacology Am. Soc. Clin. Psychopharmacology. Intern Greenwich Hosp. Assn., Greenwich, Conn., 1982-83; psychiatry fellow Yale Dept. Psychiatry, New Haven, 1982-86; chief resident psychiatry Yale New Haven Hosp., 1985-86; dir. consultation liaison psychiatry Newington VA Med. Ctr., Newington, Conn., 1986-87, chief mental hygiene clinic, 1986-88; asst. prof. psychiatry U. Conn., Farmington, 1986-92, asst. clin. prof. psychiatry, 1993—; dir. inpatient psychiatry Newington VA Med. Ctr., 1988-89; dir. ambulatory psychiatry John Dempsey Hosp., Farmington, 1989-91. Cons. psychiatrist Rocky Hill (Conn.) Vets. Home and Hosp., 1987-88; attending New Britain Gen. Hosp., 1992—; dir. Conn. Anxiety & Depression Treatment Ctr., Farmington, 1994—; founding mem., bd. dirs. PsychCare, Inc., 1996-98; bd. dirs. Psych Mgmt Author: Psychiatry in Techno Colors: A Psychiatrist's Memoir of Lessons Learned, 2011; contbr. articles to profl. jours.; co-investigator clin. research Clin. Psychopharmocology, 1988—; mem. Integrated Neurosci., Inc., 1999-2002 Fellow Am. Psychiat. Assn., Conn. Psychiat. Soc., Conn. Acad. Arts & Scis., Hartford Psychiat. Soc. (pres. 1997), Phi Beta Kappa. Office: Conn Anxiety & Depression Treatment Ctr Farmington CT 06032

LIEBSCHER, GREGORY J., plastic surgeon; Grad., U. Notre Dame, 1983; MD, Bowman Gray Sch. Medicine, Wake Forest U., Winston-Salem, NC, 1987. Cert. Gen. Surgery Am. Bd. Surgery, 1993, Am. Bd. Plastic Surgery, 1996. Gen. surgery resident St. Louis U. Med. Ctr., 1987—92; plastic & reconstructive surgery fellow Mayo Clinic, Rochester, Minn., 1992—94; pvt. practice Colorado Springs, Colo. Named El Paso County's "Top Doc, Plastic Surgery", Colo. Springs Bus. Jour., 2004. Fellow: Am. Coll. Surgery. Office: Gregory J Liebscher Md 5901 Corporate Dr Colorado Springs CO 80919-1941 Office Phone: 719-634-2503. Office Fax: 719-634-2686.

LIED, GÜLEN ARSLAN, physician; b. Turkey, Sept. 27, 1974; MD, U. Ankara, Med. Sch., 1995; PhD, U. Bergen, Haukeland Hosp., Norway, 2004. Physician divsn. gastroenterology Haukeland U. Hosp., 2006—. Office: Haukeland University Hosp Dept Medicine Bergen Hordaland 5021 Norway Business E-Mail: gulen.arslan@med.uib.no.

LIEKWEG, RICHARD J., hospital administrator; married; 1 child. BA in Economics, U. Va., Charlottesville, 1983; M in Health Services Adminstrn., U. Mich., Ann Arbor, MBA. Joined as an adminstr. fellow Duke U. Health Sys., NC, 1987, adminstrv. dir. dept. pediat., asst. COO children's and women's services; sr. assoc. COO Duke U. Hosp.; COO Durham Regional Hosp., NC, 1999—2000, CEO, 2000—03; CEO, assoc. vice chancellor U. Calif. San Diego Med. Ctr., 2003—09; group pres. BJC Healthcare, 2009—; pres. Barnes-Jewish Hosp. and Barnes-Jewish West County Hosp., St. Louis, 2009—. Bd. dirs. Novation LLC, Irving, Tex. Named City Medicine Amb., Durham Health Partners, 2003, Vol. of Yr., Durham YMCA, 2003; named a Modern Healthcare Up & Comer, 2001. Office: Barnes-Jewish Hosp One Barnes-Jewish Hosp Plz Saint Louis MO 63110 *

LIEM, DENNIS, orthopedist; MD in Medicine, U. Muenster, NRW, 2003. Resident ATOS Clinic, Shoulder and Elbow Svc., Heidelberg, Baden-Württemberg, Germany, 2004—05, U. Muenster, 2003—04, 2005—08, attending physican, 2008—. Contbr. articles to profl. jours. Office: Univ Muenster Orthopaedics Albert-Schweitzer-Str. 33 48149 Muenster Germany Office Fax: 49-251-8347989. Business E-Mail: dennis.liem@ukmuenster.de.

LIEN, JIH CHING, retired biomedical researcher; s. Ching Jung Lien and Pao Yu Yeh; m. Pao Kuei Chien, Dec. 20, 1929; children: Sio Mei, Pai Pin, Pai Yu, Chi Hung. Degree in Med. Scis., Nagasaki U., Japan, 1969. Adj. prof. Nat. Taiwan U., Taipei, 1973—. Project leader Anti-Malaria Control Project, Agua Grande, Sao Tome and Principe, 2003—06. Achievements include first to rapid control of malaria.

LIEN, SHAO-HUNG, internist; b. Taipei, Taiwan, Nov. 17, 1974; s. Hsi-Ju Lien and Lee-Chin Huang. MD, Nat. Def. Med. Ctr., Taipei, Taiwan, 1999. Med. officer Chinese Marine Corps Sch., Kaohsiung, Taiwan, 1999—2001; resident Tri-Service Gen. Hosp., Taipei, 2001—04, chief resident, 2004—05, attending physician dept. pediatric, 2005—. Contbr. articles to profl. jours. Lt. Chinese Mil., 1999. Mem.: Taiwan Soc. Critical Care Medicine, Soc. Pediatric Pulmonology R.O.C, Soc. Neonatology R.O.C, Taiwan Pediatric Assn., Taipei Med. Assn. Office: Tri-service Gen Hosp No 325 Sec 2 Chenggong Road Taipei 114 Taiwan Office Fax: 886-2-87927293. Personal E-mail: liannshaohung@yahoo.com.tw.

LIEN, WAN-CHING, emergency physician; b. Keelung, Taiwan, Sept. 18, 1973; MD, Nat. Taiwan U., 1998. Vis. physician Nat. Taiwan U. Hosp., 2003—, lectr., 2003. Mem.: Taiwan Soc. Internal Medicine, Taiwan Soc. Ultrasound in Medicine (award 2007—10), Taiwan Soc. Emergency Medicine (Ann. Conf. award 2008—10, Winter Conf. award 2009). Avocations: reading, exercise. Office: 8 Chung-Shan S Rd Taipei 100 Taiwan Office Fax. 886-2-23223150. Business E-Mail: wanchinglien@ntu.edu.tw.

LIEW, HUI P., researcher; b. Malaysia, June 10, 1974; PhD, Miss. State U., 2009. Rsch. fellow Social Sci. Rsch. Ctr., 2005—. Office: Social Sci Research Ctr 103 Research Blvd Starkville MS 39759 Business E-Mail: hpl13@msstate.edu

LIEWEHR, FREDERICK RUSSELL, endodontist, educator; b. Chgo., June 18, 1951; s. Frank Edward and Mary Elizabeth Liewehr; m. Michelle Bernardette Gonzales, Nov. 27, 1970; children: Scott Christopher, Mary Benedicta, Virginia Rose. BS, U. Iowa, Iowa City, 1973, DDS, 1981; MS, Med. Coll. Ga., Augusta, 1993. Cert. in endodontics Am. Bd. Endodontics, 1998. Dental officer U.S. Army, 1979—2003; prof., grad. program dir. Va. Commonwealth U., Richmond, 2004—06, chmn. dept. endodontics, 2004—06; pvt. practice, 2007—. Endodontic cons. McGuire Hunter Holmes VA Med. Ctr., Richmond, 2005—. Col. US Army, 1981—2003, Ft. Gordon, Ga. Decorated Order of Mil. Med. Merit OTSG, US Army, Surgeon General's A Designator, Legion of Merit US Army. Fellow: Internat. Coll. Dentists; mem.: ADA, Am. Acad. Oral Medicine, Am. Assn. Oral Biologists, Am. Assn. Endodontists, Torch Club Internat. R-Conservative.

LIEWENDAHL, BO KRISTIAN, retired pathologist, nuclear medicine physician; b. Helsinki, Aug. 21, 1941; s. Ernst August and Irina (Semenov) Liewendahl; 1 child, Kari Peter Nikolai. MD, U. Helsinki, 1966, PhD, 1968. Diplomate. Resident in clin. chemistry Helsinki U. Hosp., 1966-69, resident in medicine, 1969-72, cons. lab. dept., 1974-82; asst. prof., lectr. U. Helsinki, 1977-96, prof., 1996; chief physician divsn. nuclear medicine Helsinki U. Hosp., 1983-99; NIH fellow U. Calif., San Francisco, 1972-73. Vis. scientist U. Wis., Madison, U. Va., Charlottesville, 1982; dir. nuc. medicine rsch. group Minerva Inst. Found., Helsinki, Finland, 1977—2002; sec. gen. Minerva Found., 1997—2002, bd. dirs., 2002—04; pres. European Nuc. Medicine Congress, Helsinki, 1984, Scandinavian Congress Nuc. Medicine, Helsinki, 1998; chmn. European Congress Clin. Chemistry, Tampere, Finland, 1995; del. nuc. medicine sect. European Union Med. Spltys., 1994—2002; del. European Bd. Nuc. Medicine, 1995—2002. Author, editor: Scandinavian Jour. Clin. Lab. Investigation, 1986—96; mem. editl. bd. European Jour. Nuclear Medicine, 1991—2002; author: (autobiography) Memories of a Nuclear Physician (in Swedish), 2009, 1st illustrated edit., 2011; co-editor (with Esko Vanninen): History of Nuclear Medicine in Finland (in Finnish and Swedish), 2008; contbr. articles to profl. jours. Recipient J. W. Runeberg prize, Finnish Med. Soc., 1969, Ann. Lecture prize, 1973, T. Heiskanen Meml. prize, Finnish Radiol. Soc. and Finnish Nuc. Medicine Soc., 1985, Gold medal, Minerva Found., 1989. Mem.: Russian Nobility Soc. Finland. (sec. 2002—11), NY Acad. Scis., Soc. Nuc. Medicine NY, World Fedn. Nuc. Medicine and Biology (del. 1988—2003, organizing com. 8th World Congress, Santiago, Chile 2002), Finnish Soc. Nuc. Medicine (pres. 1996—98), European Thyroid Assn. (sec. Helsinki congress 1976), European Assn. Nuc. Medicine (del. 1988—95, mem. organizing com. Copenhagen congress 1996, v.p. organizing com. Helsinki congress 2004, Congress prize 1991). Lutheran. Achievements include research in thyroid function tests, particularly accurate assays for free thyroid hormone concentrations in blood, nuclear medicine procedures for diagnosis of oncological, hematological and neurological diseases. Avocation: history.

LIFSON, JEFFREY D., pathologist, researcher; MD, Northwestern U., 1982. Resident, rsch. fellowship Dept. Pathology, Stanford U. Sch. Medicine, Calif.; head retroviral pathogenesis sect. Ctr. Cancer Rsch., Nat. Cancer Inst., NIH, Frederick, Md., 1995—, dir. AIDS and Cancer Virus Program (formerly AIDS Vaccine Program), 2002—. Office: SAIC-Frederick Inc NCI-Frederick Bldg 535 Ste 510 Frederick MD 21702-1201 Office Phone: 301-846-1408. Office Fax: 301-846-5588. E-mail: lifsonj@mail.nih.gov. *

LIFTON, RICHARD P., medical educator, researcher; b. 1953; BA summa cum laude in Biology, Dartmouth Coll., Hanover, NH, 1975; MD, Stanford U., Palo Alto, Calif., 1982, PhD in Biochemistry, 1986. Diplomate Am. Bd. Internal Medicine. Resident internal medicine Brigham and Women's Hosp., Boston, 1983—86, chief med. resident, 1986—87; instr. medicine Brigham and Women's Hosp. and Harvard Med. Sch., 1987—91, asst. prof., 1991—93; asst. prof. medicine and genetics Yale U., New Haven, 1993—94, assoc. prof., 1994—97, prof. medicine, genetics and molecular biophysics & biochemistry, 1997—, chmn. dept. genetics, 1998—; asst. investigator Howard Hughes Med. Inst., 1994—96, assoc. investigator, 1997—; dir. cardiovasc. genetics prog. Boyer Ctr. Molecular Medicine, 1996—; dir. NIH Specialized Ctr. Rsch. in Hypertension, 1996—. Contbr. articles to profl. jours. Recipient SmithKline-Beecham Young Investigator award, Internat. Soc. Hypertension, 1994, Homer Smith award, Am. Soc. Nephrology, 1998, Novartis award, Am. Heart Assn., Med. Rsch. award, Pasarow Found., Earnest H. Starling Disting. lectureship, Am. Physiol. Soc., 2002, Alfred Newton Richards award, Internat. Soc. Nephrology, 2007. Mem.: NAS, Inst. Medicine (coun. mem.). Office: Lifton Lab Yale U Sch Medicine BCMM 147 295 Congress Ave New Haven CT 06510 Office Phone: 203-737-4420, 203-737-1091. E-mail: richard.lifton@yale.edu.

LIGGETT, STEPHEN B., pharmacologist, educator; BS in Physics, Ga. Inst. Technol., 1977; MD, U. Miami Sch. Medicine, 1982. Intern & resident Barnes Hosp. & Wash. U. Sch. Medicine, 1982—85; fellow Wash. U. Sch. Medicine, 1985—88, Duke U. Med. Ctr. Howard Hughes Med. Inst, 1988—90; asst. prof. medicine Duke U. Med. Ctr., 1989—92, asst. prof. pharmacology, 1989—92; assoc. prof. medicine, molecular genetics & pharmacology U. Cin. Med. Ctr., 1992—, dir. pulmonary/critical care medicine, 1992—, prof. medicine, molecular genetics & pharmacology, 1995—. Office: University of Cincinnati Division of Pulmonary, Critical Care & S 231 Albert Sabin Way Cincinnati OH 45267-0564

LIGHT, JIMMY A., surgeon, director; b. Ohio, Nov. 3, 1938; BS, Bowling Green State U., 1960; MD, U. Mich., 1964. Dir. transplant svc. Walter Reed Army Med. Ctr., 1974—83, Wash. Hosp. Ctr., 1983—. Adv. bd. dirs. Nat. Kidney Found. Nat. Capital Area, 1974—; bd. dirs. MidAtlantic Renal Coalition, 1987—2010, United Network Organ Sharing, 2008—10. Recipient John J. Lynch Moral Courage award, Wash. Hosp. Ctr., Recognition award, Georgetown Transplant Inst. Fellow: ACS; mem.: Nat. Kidney Found. NCA, Am. Soc. Transplant Surgeons, Am. Soc. Transplantation. Avocation: tennis. Office: Washington Hosp Ctr 110 Irving S Washington DC 20010 Office Fax: 202-877-6581. Business E-Mail: jimmy.a.light@medstar.net.

LIGHT, TERRY RICHARD, orthopedic hand surgeon; b. Chgo., June 22, 1947; BA, Yale U., 1969; MD, Chgo. Med. Sch., 1973. Diplomate in orthopedic surgery and in hand surgery Am. Bd. Orthopaedic Surgery. Asst. prof. Yale U., New Haven, 1977-80, Loyola U., Maywood, Ill., 1980-82, assoc. prof., 1982-88, prof., 1988-90, Dr. William M. Scholl prof., chmn. orthop. surgery and rehab, 1991—. Attending surgeon Hines (Ill.) VA Hosp., 1980—, Shriner's Hosp., Chgo., 1981—, Foster McGaw Hosp., Maywood, 1980—; hand cons. Chgo. White Sox, 1986-2003; bus. mgr. Jour. Hand Surgery, 1995-99. Editor Am. Acad. Orthop. Surgeons Hand Surgery Update, 1999, 2d edit. V.p. Frank Lloyd Wright Home and Studio Found., Oak Park, Ill., 1985-88, pres., 1988-90; chmn. bd. Fairfield Pub. Gallery, Sturgeon Bay, Wis., 1998-99; bd. dirs. Loyola U. Health Sys., 1999—. Fellow: ACS, Am. Acad. Orthop. Surgeons (editor Instrnl. Cruise Lects. vol. 55 2006); mem.: Am. Orthop. Assn. (2d v.p. 2004—05, 1st v.p. 2005—06, pres. 2006—), Ill. Orthop. Soc. (v.p. 1995, pres.-elect 1996, pres. 1997), Twenty-First Century Orthop. Assn. (pres. 1979—), Acad. Orthopaedic Soc. (pres. 2001—02), Chgo. Soc. for Surgery of Hand (sec. 1985—87, pres.-elect 1987—88, pres. 1988—89), Am. Assn. Hand Surgery (bd. dirs. 1989—91), Am. Soc. for Surgery of Hand (chair Jour. Hand Surgery com. 1995—99, treas. 1999—2002, v.p. 2002—03, pres. 2004—05), Alpha Omega Alpha. Avocation: collecting American arts and crafts and pottery. Office: Loyola U Med Ctr 2160 S 1st Ave Maywood IL 60153-3304 Office Phone: 708-216-4570. Personal E-mail: tlight1320@aol.com. Business E-Mail: tlight@lumc.edu.

LIGOTTI, EUGENE FERDINAND, retired dentist; b. NYC, June 10, 1936; s. Eugene A. and Lee (D'Agata) L.; m. Corbina Theresa Loscalzo, Nov. 21, 1959; children: Gina Maria Ligotti Aliperti, Lisa Anne Ligotti Liberatoscioli. BA, Adelphi U., 1958; DDS, NYU, 1962. Pvt. practice, Huntington, N.Y., 1962-92; instr. operative dentistry NYU, NYC, 1962-65. Author historic fiction, mystery novels, and screenplays; contbr. articles to profl. jours. and mags.; inventor ValueVac. Founder, pres. Upper Bay Civic Assn., Inc., Huntington, 1979—2001. Recipient Cmty. Leader of America, 1969. Mem.: ADA, Suffolk County Dental Soc., N.Y. State Dental Soc., Huntington Hist. Soc. (emeritus trustee), German Shepherd Dog Club (pres. 1971—75), Chi Sigma, Xi Psi Phi (founder alumni chpt. 1981—82). Republican. Roman Catholic. Avocations: travel, writing. Home (Summer): Box 866 Windham Ridge Rd Windham NY 12496 Personal E-mail: eligotti@optonline.net.

LIHONG, JIA, medical educator; b. Shenyang, China, May 1, 1963; PhD, China Med. U., 1987. Prof. China Med. U., 2007—. Office: 92 North Er Heping Dist Shenyang Liaoning 110001 China Business E-Mail: lhjia@mail.cmu.edu.cn.

LIKENS, GENE ELDEN, biology and ecology educator; b. Pierceton, Ind., Jan. 6, 1935; s. Colonel Benjamin and Josephine (Garner) L.; m. Phyllis Craig; children: Kathy, Gregory, Leslie. BS, Manchester Coll., Ind., 1957, DSc (hon.), 1979; MS, U. Wis., 1959, PhD, 1962; DSc (hon.), Rutgers U., 1985, Plymouth State Coll., U. N.H., 1989, Miami U., 1990; LHD (hon.), Union Coll., 1991; DSc (hon.), U. Bodenkultur, Vienna, Austria, 1993, Marist Coll., 1993, Wageningen Agrl. U., Netherlands, 1998, U. Conn., 2004. Asst. zoology Manchester Coll., 1955-57; grad. tchg. asst. U. Wis., 1957-59, vis. lectr., 1963; instr. zoology Dartmouth Coll., 1961, instr. biol. scis., 1963, asst. prof., then assoc. prof., 1963-69; mem. faculty Cornell U., 1969-83, prof. ecology, 1972-83, Charles A. Alexander prof. biol. scis., 1983, adj. prof., 1983—; v.p. N.Y. Bot. Garden, 1983-93; founding dir. Inst. Ecosystem Studies, Millbrook, NY, 1983—2007, pres., 1993—2007, pres. emeritus, 2007—; G. Evelyn Hutchinson chair in ecology Inst. Ecosys. Studies, Millbrook, NY, 2000—05; dir. Mary Flagler Cary Arboretum, 1983—93; prof. biology Yale U., 1984—; prof. grad. field of ecology Rutgers U., 1985—; hon. prof. Jinan U., Guangzhou, 2009—. Vis. prof. Ctr. Advanced Rsch., dept. environ scis. U. Va., Charlottesville, 1978-79, SUNY, Albany, 2004-; vis. disting. rsch. prof. U. Conn., Storrs, 2005—; chmn. New Eng. divsn. task force conservation aquatic ecosystems U.S. Internat. Biol. Program, 1966-67; vis. assoc. ecologist Brookhaven Nat. Lab., 1968; C.P. Snow lectr. Ithaca Coll., 1979, 89; Rilett vis. scholar Ill. State U., 1985; vis. scholar James Madison U., 1988; Class of 1960 vis. scholar, Williams Coll., Williamstown, Mass., 1988; William V. Kaesar Meml. scholar U. Wis., Madison, 1991; vis. disting. ecologist, Colo. State U., 1994; Walker Ames prof., U. Wash., Seattle, 2001; Miegunyah fellow U. Melbourne, Australia; lectr., State U. NY, Oneonta, 2007, Einstein professorship Chinese Acad. Scis., 2009-; cons., panelist, lectr. in field Contbr. articles to profl. jours. Recipient Conservation award Am. Motors Corp., 1969, 75th Anniversary award U.S. Forest Svc., 1980, Disting. Achievement award Lab. Biomed. and Environ. Studies, UCLA, 1982, Regents medal SUNY, 1984, NY Acad. Scis. award, 1986, Internat. ECI prize for Limnetic Ecology, 1989, Disting. Svc. award N.Y. Bot. Garden, 1989, Am. Inst. Biol. Scis., 1990, Lifetime Accomplishment award, 2000, Disting. Svc. award Hudson River Environ. Soc., 1997, The Garden Club Am. Spl. Citation, 1992, Tyler World Environment prize U. So. Calif., 1993, Australia prize, 1994; Sr. fellow NATO, 1969, Guggenheim fellow, 1972-73, Flagship fellow, CSIRO, Canbera, Australia, Commonwealth Environ. Rsch. Facilities fellowship, Australia Nat. U., Canbera, 2008-09; grantee NSF, EPA, Dept. Energy, USDA Forest Svc., NOAA, Disting. Svc. award Hudson River Environ. Soc., Inc., 1997, Vollenweider award and lecturship, Canada Ctr. for Inland Waters, Nat. Water Rsch. Inst., 1998, Storm King award Scenic Hudson Inc., 1998, Excellence award Nat. Coun. State Garden Clubs Inc., 1999, Nat. Medal Sci., 2001, Blue Planet prize, 2003; Miequnyah Disting. fellow U. Melbourne, Australia, 2004. Fellow: AAAS, Am. Philos. Soc.; mem.: NAS (chmn. sect. 27 1986—89), Inst. Biology (London), Royal Danish Acad. Sci., Am. Inst. Biol. Scis. (pres. 2002—03, Lifetime Accomplishment award 2000, Huxley medal, Inst. Biology (UK) 2001), Austrian Acad. Scis., Australian Soc. Limnology, Internat. Water Resources Assn. (charter), Internat. Assn. Gt. Lakes Rsch., Freshwater Biol. Assn., Internat. Water Acad. (life), Am. Water Resources Assn. (hon.), Brit. Ecol. Soc. (hon. E.G. Stillman award, Black Rock Forest Consortium 2008), Explorers Club, Am. Polar Soc., Royal Swedish Acad. Scis., Internat. Assn. Theoretical and Applied Limnology (v.p. 1998, pres. 2001—04, 2004—07, Naumann-Thienemann medal 1995), Am. Soc. Limnology and Oceanography (v.p. 1975—76, pres. 1976—77, 1st G.E. Hutchinson award for excellence in rsch. 1982), Ecol. Soc. Am. (chmn. study com. 1971—74, v.p. 1978—79, pres. 1981—82, Eminent Ecologist award 1995), Am. Acad. Arts and Scis. (Flagship fellowship, Commonwealth Sci. and Indsl. Rsch. Orgn. 2008—10, Commonwealth Environ. Rsch. Facilities fellowship, Australia 2008—), Sigma Xi, Phi Sigma, Gamma Alpha. Methodist. Office: Inst Ecosys Studies Box AB Millbrook NY 12545

LIKENS, JAMES DEAN, economics professor; b. Bakersfield, Calif., Sept. 12, 1937; s. Ernest LeRoy and Monnie Jewel (Thomas) L.; m. Janet Sue Pelton, Dec. 18, 1965 (div.); children: John David, Janet Elizabeth; m. Karel Carnohan, June 4, 1988 (div.); m. Christine Irons, Feb. 8, 2003. BA in Econs., U. Calif., Berkeley, 1960, MBA, 1961; PhD in Econs., U. Minn., 1970. Analyst Del Monte Corp., San Francisco, 1963; economist 3M Co., Mpls., 1968-71; asst. prof. econs. Pomona Coll., 1969-75, assoc. prof. econs., 1975-83, prof. econs., 1983-85, Morris B. and Gladys S. Pendleton prof. econs., 1989—, dept. chair, 1998-2001. Vis. asst. prof. econs. U. Minn., 1970, 71, vis. assoc. prof., 1976-77; pres., dean Western CUNA Mgmt. Sch., Pomona Coll., 1975—; chmn. bd. First City Credit Union, 1978—; coord. So. Calif. Rsch. Coun., LA, 1980-81, 84-85; adv. coun. Western Corp. Fed. Credit Union, 1993—; cons. in field. Author: (with Joseph LaDou) Medicine and Money, 1976, Mexico and Southern California: Toward A New Partnership, 1981, Financing Quality Education in Southern California, 1985; contbr. articles to profl. jours. Served with USCG, 1961-67; dir. Centennial, Pomona Coll., 1987-88. Recipient Leo H. Shapiro Lifetime Achievement award, Calif. Credit Union League, 2001, Herb Wegner Lifetime Achievement award, Nat. Credit Union Found., 2005; named Dir. of Yr., Calif. Credit Union League, 1997, Credit Union Exec. Soc., 2001; grantee rsch. grantee HUD-DOT, Haynes Found. Mem.: ABA, Western Econ. Assn., Am. Econ. Assn. Avocations: guitar, clarinet, golf. Home: 725 W 10th St Claremont CA 91711-3719 Office: Pomona Coll Dept Econs Claremont CA 91711 Office Phone: 909-821-8998. Business E-Mail: jlikens@pomona.edu.

LIKER, HARLEY RUSSELL, physician; b. Boston, Dec. 28, 1962; MD, Albert Einstein Coll. Medicine, 1992; MBA, UCLA, 2001. CEO Liker Consulting, Inc., 2000—. Assoc. clin. prof. medicine David Geffen Sch. Medicine, UCLA, 2010. Mem.: Alpha Omega Alpha. Office: 9675 Brighton Way Ste 350 Beverly Hills CA 90210-5188 Office Fax: 310-205-5595. Business E-Mail: hliker@likerconsulting.com.

LILIKAKIS, ANASTASIOS, orthopedic surgeon; b. Athens, Greece, May 4, 1970; s. Kyriakos and Ioanna Lilikakis; m. Agapi Papaioannou, May 10, 2002; 2 children. MD, Med. Sch. Kapodistriakon U., Athens, 1994; MSc In Orthop. Engring., Cardiff U., UK, 2006. Cons. orthop. surgeon Euroclinic Hosp., Athens, 2007—, Bank Greece, Athens, 2008—; cons. surgeon Heraeus Med., 2008. Contbr. articles to profl. jours. Scholar Bequest Ioannis Papadakis, Nat. and Kapodistrian U. Athens, 1993, Award for Physics and Chemistry Saris Bequest, Varvakios Model Sch., 1988; Travelling fellowship, European Fedn. Orthopaedics & Traumatology, 2003, Vis. fellowship, Hellenic Soc. Orthopaedic & Traumatology, 2004. Mem.: Internat. Soc. Orthopaedic And Traymatologic Rsch., European Hip Soc., Hellenic Assn. Orthopaedic Surgery & Traumatology. Office: Private Practice 4 Dionysiou Aiginitou Athens 11528 Greece Home: 70 Ethnilis Amums St Athens 15669 Greece Office Phone: 00302107292002. Personal E-mail: alilikakis@yahoo.com.

LILLEHOFF, PIPER, psychiatrist; d. Harvest and adopted d. Foster Eubank. BA in Psychology, U. Calif., Irvine, 1989; MD, Drexel U., Phila., 1996. Resident adult psychiatry Oreg. Health Scis. U., Portland, 1996—99; fellow child psychiatry U. Calif., Irvine, 1999—2001; child and adolescent psychiatrist County of Orange, Health Care Agy., Costa Mesa, Calif., 2002—; pvt. practice Irvine, 2007—10. Mem. physician content rev. bd. Healthcasts/Profl. TV Network, NYC, 2005—. Author poetry. Mem. Universalist-Unitarian Ch., Laguna Beach, Calif., 2006. Recipient Youth Leadership award, Hugh O'Brien Found.; finalist Flute Competition, Calif. Music Tchrs. Assn.; scholar, Mills Coll., U. Calif., Irvine; Rock Sleyster scholar for Outstanding Med. Student Performance in Psychiatry, AMA. Mem.: Physician's Com. For Responsible Medicine, Am. Psychiat. Assn., Am. Acad. Child and Adolescent Psychiatry, Internat. Libr. Poetry (hon.; Am. amb. poetry), Phi Beta Kappa, Psi Chi. Avocations: flute, poetry, dance, yoga. Personal E-mail: pprlhf@yahoo.com.

LILLY-HERSLEY, JANE ANNE FEELEY, nursing researcher; b. Palo Alto, Calif., May 31, 1947; d. Daniel Morris Sr. and Suzanne (Agnew) Feeley; children: Cary Jane, Laura Blachree, Claire Foale; m. Dennis C. Hersley, Jan. 16, 1993. BS, U. Oreg., 1968; student, U. Hawaii, 1970; BSN, RN, Sacramento City Coll., 1975. Cert. ACLS, BCLS. Staff and charge nurse, acute rehab. Santa Clara Valley Med. Ctr., San Jose, Calif., staff nurse, surg. ICU and trauma unit; clin. project leader mycophenolate mofetil program team Syntex Rsch., Palo Alto. Pres. Rsch. Consultation Inc., Santa Cruz, Calif, cons. med. rsch. pharmaceutical rsch. Featured in BBC documentary, appearances nat. TV and radio broadcasts, pub. presentations; contbr. articles to profl. publs. Co-founder, CFO, dir. scientific rsch. Citizens United Responsible Environmentalism, Inc., (CURE), Wild Bird Rescue. Mem. AACN, Nature Conservancy, Nat. Wildlife Fedn., Monterey Bay Aquarium, World Wildlife Fund., Smithsonian Assn., Nat. WWII Mus. (charter mem.), Nat. Sludge Alliance. Achievements include research and education in mold exposure and human mycotoxicoses; research in WWII letters, diaries and historical documents. Personal E-mail: janelh_temp@comcast.net, jhersley@comcast.net.

LIM, ADRIAN C., dermatologist; b. Malaysia, June 14, 1965; MBBS, U. Melbourne, 1988. Ptnr. Sydney Skin and Vein Clinic, 1998—2011; assoc. St George Dermatology and Skin Cancer Ctr., 2005—11; med. dir. Urepublic Cosmetic Dermatology, 2007—. Grant, Fred Bauer, Australian Dermatology Rsch. & Edn. Found. Fellow: Internat. Acad. Cosmetic Dermatology, Am. Acad. Dermatology, Australasian Coll. Phlebology (dir. tng. 2011—), Australasian Coll. Dermatologists (dir. tng. 2010—, dir. mentorship program 2005—10); mem.: Australian Med. Assn. Avocations: exercise, filmmaking. Home: 124/169 Phillip St Waterloo NSW 2017 Australia Home Fax: 612 9264 2166. Business E-Mail: adrian@urepublic.com.au.

LIM, ALAN YOUNG, plastic surgeon; b. St. Louis, Apr. 11, 1953; MD, U. Calif., San Diego, 1979. Plastic surgeon Sutter Med. Group, Sacramento. Assoc. clin. prof. U. Calif. Davis Office: Plastic Surg 1020 29th Ste 600 Sacramento CA 95816 Office Phone: 916-733-9588. Business E-Mail: limay@sutterhealth.org.

LIM, ALEXANDER RUFASTA, neurologist, clinical investigator, neurophysiologist, educator, writer; b. Manila, Philippines, Feb. 20, 1942; s. Benito Pilar and Maria Lourdes (Cuyegkeng) Lim; m. Norma Sue Hanks, June 1, 1968; children: Jeffrey Allen, Gregory Brian, Kevin Alexander, Melissa Gail. Student, U. Santo Tomas, Manila, 1959, MD, 1964. Intern Bon Secours Hosp., Balt., 1964-65; resident in internal medicine Scott and White Clinic Tex A&M U., Health Sci. Ctr. Coll. Medicine, Temple, Tex., 1965-67; resident in neurology Cleve. Clinic, 1967-69, chief resident in neurology, 1969-70, fellow clin. neurophysiology, 1970-71; clin. assoc. neurologist Cleve. Clinic Hosp., 1971-72; neurologist-in-chief, co-founder, co-mng. ptnr. Neurol. Clinic, Corpus Christi, Tex., 1972—; pres., CEO Neurology, P.A., Corpus Christi, 1972-92. Chief neurology dept. Meml. Med. Ctr., Corpus Christi, Tex., 1975—90, Spohn Hosp., Corpus Christi, 1974—90, Reynolds Army Hosp., Ft. Sill, Okla., 1990—91; clin. assoc. prof. sch. medicine U. Tex. Health Sci. Ctr., San Antonio, 1992—2002; cons., reviewer Tex. Medicine, 1995—. Mem. editl. bd. Coastal Bend Medicine, 1988—95, NEURO Ctrl., 1999—. Active mentorship program for gifted and talented srs. South Tex. Area HS; forum contbr. Corpus Christi Caller-Times. Lt. col. med. corps US Army, 1990—91, Desert Shield/Desert Storm. Decorated Army Commendation medal, Nat. Def. medal US Army; recipient Best doctors in Am., 1988, 1989, 1990, Am. Top Physicians, 2005; named one of Best Poems & Poets, Internat. Library Poetry, 2003, 2005, 2007. Mem.: KC, AMA, Physicians Com. for Responsible Medicine (book reviewer), Tex. Neurol. Soc. (sec. 1986—88, pres. 1989—90), Tex. Med. Assn. (chmn. neurology 1985—86), Soc. Behavioral and Cognitive Neurology, Am. Acad. Immunotherapy, Am. Clin. Neurophysiology Soc., Am. Epilepsy Soc. (editl. bd. mem. Neurocentral), Am. Acad. Neurology (spkr's. bur. mem.), Internat. Soc. Poets, Acad. Am. Poets, Internat. Platform Assn. Republican. Roman Catholic. Avocations: tennis, stamp collecting/philately, essay and poetry writing, skiing, bonsai. Home: 4821 Augusta Cir Corpus Christi TX 78413-2711 Office: Neurol Clinic Corpus Christi Med Towers 1521 South Staples St Ste 402 Corpus Christi TX 78404 Home Phone: 361-992-2261; Office Phone: 361-883-1731. Office Fax: 361-883-1440. Personal E-mail: anlim8@hotmail.com. Business E-Mail: lima@neurologypa.com.

LIM, BENG-HAI, hand surgeon, educator; b. Penang, Malaysia, Nov. 11, 1958; m. Florence Siew Ching Lim; children: Nicole Mayee, Derek Zwingli, Kevin Wangli, Michelle Shuyee. MB BChir, Nat. U. Singapore, 1985. Lic. hand surgery. Chief, sr. cons. hand surgeon Nat. U. Hosp., Singapore, 2000—, vice chmn. med. bd.; assoc. prof. Nat. U. of Singapore, 2000—. Specialist tng. committee hand surgery Ministry of Health. Author: Six Strand Flexor Tendon Repair, 1996, reconstruction for drug instability, Lateral Forearm Flap - Vascular Anatomy, 2000, (surgery) Double Vascularised Joint Transfer on One Pedicle, 1996, Digital Replantation Surgery, 2001. Fellow: Royal Coll. of Surgeons Edinburgh; mem.: Internat. Fedn. for Surgery of the Hand, Singapore Orthopaedic Assn., Harold Keinert Soc., Asian Pacific Fedn. of Socs. for Surgery of the Hand (coun. mem. 1999—2001), Singapore Soc. for Hand Surgery (pres. 1999—2001). Office: Nat Univ Hosp 5 Lower Kent Ridge Rd Singapore 119074 Singapore Office Phone: 65 67725549. Office Fax: 65 67732558. E-mail: doslimbh@nus.edu.sg.

LIM, C.C. TCHOYOSON, radiologist, researcher; s. K.C. Lim and C.K. Wong; m. A. Tan; children: C., E. MBBS, Nat. U. Singapore, 1988, MMed in Diagnostic Radiology, 1995. Assoc. cons. Tan Tock Seng Hosp./Nat. Neurosci. Inst., Singapore, 1998—2000; cons. Nat. Neurosci. Inst., Singapore, 2000—05, sr. cons., 2005—. Vis. radiology fellow U. Calif., San Francisco, 1997—98; cons. Gen. Electric Med. Sys. Picture Archive and Comm. Sys. Global and Asian Adv. Bd., Waukesha, Wis., 2000—; adj. assoc. prof. Yong Loo Lin Sch. Medicine, Nat. U. Singapore, 2004—; cons. Gerson Lehrman Group, NYC, 2004—. Contbr. articles to profl. jours. Grantee, Nat. Med. Rsch. Coun., Biomedical Rsch. Coun., NHG and SHS Group Endowment Fund, 1996, 1999, 2001, 2002, 2003, 2004, 2005; fellow, Ministry of Health, Singapore, 1995, Health Manpower Devel. Plan, 1997; Pres. scholar, Ministry of Edn., Singapore, 1983. Fellow: Acad. Medicine Singapore, Royal Coll. Radiologists; mem.: Singapore Radiol. Soc. (sec. 2004—05, Best Scientific Paper & Poster prize 2000, 2002, 2004), Soc. Magnetic Resonance in Medicine, Am. Roentgen Ray Soc. Achievements include patents for method and apparatus for building a multi-discipline and multi-media personal medical image library; method and apparatus for creating radiological teaching files from clinical image archive; research in radiology information technology and picture archive and communication systems; neuroimaging: MRI, MR spectroscopy in brain tumor, ischemia, infection and metabolic disease. Avocation: travel. Office: Nat Neurosci Inst 11 Jalan Tan Tock Seng Singapore 308433 Singapore Office Fax: 65-63581259. Personal E-mail: tchoyoson@gmail.com. Business E-Mail: tchoyoson_lim@nni.com.sg.

LIM, DANIEL VAN, microbiology educator; b. Houston, Apr. 15, 1948; s. Don H. and Lucy (Toy) L.; m. Carol Lee, Sept. 2, 1973. BA in Biology, Rice U., 1970; PhD in Microbiology, Tex. A&M U., 1973. Postdoc. fellow Baylor Coll. Medicine, 1973-76; asst. prof. U. South Fla., Tampa, 1976-81, assoc. prof. microbiology, 1981-87, chmn. dept. biology, 1983-85, prof., 1987—, disting. univ. prof., 2006—. Pres. Micro Concepts Rsch. Corp; dir. Inst. Biomolecular Sci., 1988-93; co-dir. Ctr. Excellence, 2007-; cons. and expert witness in field. Author: Microbiology, 1989, 98, 2003, Introduction to Microbiology, 1995. Recipient Outstanding Contbn. in Sci. and Tech. award Fla. Gov., Christopher Columbus Fellowship Found. award Homeland Security, 2004. Fellow Am. Acad. Microbiology; mem. Inter-Am. Soc. Chemotherapy (v.p. 1983-88), Am. Soc. Microbiology (pres. southeastern br. 1990-91, mem. coun. 2000—06, mem. career devel. com., 1999—2008, branch orgn. com. mem., 2008-, Carski award com. 1983-86, Margaret Green Outstanding Tchr. award, P.R. Edwards award, Ivan Roth award). Achievements include invention of bacteriological broth. Office: University South Fla Dept Cell Biology Microbiology & Molecular Biology BSF 218 4202 E Fowler Ave Tampa FL 33620-5150 Office Phone: 813-974-1618. Business E-Mail: lim@usf.edu.

LIM, DENNIS T H, surgeon; Grad., Nat. U., Singapore, 1987, M of Medicine in Surgery, 1992. Surg. fellowship Royal Coll., Edinburgh, 1992, Glasgow, 1992; tng. under prof. Abu Rauff and prof. Rajmohan Nambiar; fellowship Meml. Sloan-Kettering Cancer Centre, NY, 1997; pvt. practice Mt. Elizabeth Hosp.; former cons. surg. oncologist Nat. Cancer Centre; gen. surgeon Singapore Gen. Hosp.; surgeon DennisLim Surgery, Singapore. Office: DennisLim Surgery Mt Elizabeth Medical Centre 3 Mt Elizabeth Number 11-09 Singapore 228510 Singapore Office Phone: 6568365167. Office Fax: 6568265165. *

LIM, DO-SUN, cardiologist, educator; s. Jin Chol Jung; m. Hyun mi Ryu, Jan. 30, 1988; children: Jung Ook, Jung Hoon. PhD in Med. Sci., Med. Sch. Korea U., Seoul, Republic of Korea, 1998. Cert. Korean Circulation Bd. Ministry Health, Walfare & Family Affairs, 1997. Rotating internship Korea U. Med. Ctr., Seoul, 1989—90, residency internal medicine, 1990—94, cardiology fellowship, 1994—; assoc. prof. Korea U. Med. Sch., Seoul, 1998—2006, prof., 2006—. Rsch. fellow Baylor Coll. Medicine, Houston, 1999—2000, U.Tex., Houston, 2000—01. Co-author: (textbook) The Textbook of Cardiovascular Medicine. Dir. Social welfare Soc., Seoul, 2008. Lt. Navy Korean Army, 1986—89, Republic of Korea. Recipient 1st Pl., Young Investigator award, Korean Soc. Circulation, 1995. Master: Korean Soc. Lipidology & Atherosclerosis (assoc.; chmn. internat. relationship com. 2009—), Korean Soc. Interventional Cadiology (assoc.; bd. dirs. 2008), Korean Soc. Lipidology & Atherosclerosis (assoc.; chmn. med inst. & llegislation com. 2007); mem.: Korean Soc. Hypertension (assoc.; mem. rsch. com. 2007), Korean Soc. Circulation (assoc.; mem. rsch. com. 2006—08, mem. publish com. 2002—04, mem. sci. com. 2004—06). Achievements include development of dual promoter-driven reporter systems & their application in simultaneous tracing of mesenchymal stem cells differentiating into the cardiomyogenic or the endothelial cell lineage. Office: Korea Univ Med Ctr 126-1 5th St Anam-dong Sungbuk-ku Seoul 136-705 Republic of Korea Office Phone: 82-2-920-5445. Office Fax: 82-2-927-1478. Business E-Mail: dslmd@kumc.or.kr.

LIM, EVI, medical researcher; b. Indonesia, Feb. 9, 1983; BS, UW, Stevens Point, 2006. Rsch. assoc. UW, Madison, 2007—. Office: 1300 University Ave MSC Bldg SMI-24 Madison WI 53726 Office Phone: 608-263-2250. E-mail: elim@medicine.wisc.edu.

LIM, HENRY WAN-PENG, dermatologist; b. Bandung, Indonesia, July 19, 1949; s. Budiman Ruslim and Nietje Tedjasuryani; m. Mamie Wong, July 20, 1975; children: Christopher T., Kevin T. BS in Biochemistry with honors, McGill U., 1971; MD cum laude, SUNY, Bklyn., 1975. Diplomate Am. Bd. Dermatology, Nat. Bd. Med. Examiners. Intern Albert Einstein Coll. Medicine, Bronx, NY, 1975-76; resident dept. dermatology NYU Sch. Medicine, NYC, 1976-79, NIH fellow in dermatology, 1979, Dermatology Found. fellow, 1979-80, from instr. to assoc. prof. dermatology, 1979-93, prof. dermatology, 1993-97, asst. dean vet. affairs, 1993-97; chmn., Clarence S. Livingood chair dermatology Henry Ford Hosp., Detroit, 1997—, dir. acad. programs, 2002—03, v.p. acad. affairs, 2003—08, sr. v.p. acad. affairs, 2008—; assoc. dean Wayne State U./Henry Ford Health Sys., Wayne State U. Sch Medicine, Detroit, 2004—. Chief dermatology svc. N.Y. VA Med. Ctr., NYC, 1985—94, chief staff, 1993—97, staff physician dermatology svc., 1994—97; prof. pathology Sch. Medicine Wayne State U., Detroit, 2003—. Editor: Photodermatology, Photoimmunology & Photomedicine, 2000—03; assoc. editor: Jour. Investigative Dermatology, 2003—09; mem. editl. bd. Jour. Am. Acad. Dermatology, 1993—2008, Archives Dermatology, 2009—. Recipient numerous awards; scholar, McGill U., 1968—70. Mem.: AMA, AAAS, Skin Color Soc. (bd. dirs. 2010—), Am. Bd. Dermatology (dir. 2004—, pres. elect. 2010—11, pres. 2011—), Internat. Union Photobiology (v.p. 2004—09, pres. 2009—), Photomedicine Soc. (pres. 1992—99), Am. Assn. Immunologists, Am. Soc. Photobiology (councilor 1998—2001, pres. 2002—03, chair sci. program com. 2003—04), Am. Fedn. for Clin. Rsch., Assn. Profs. Dermatology (bd. dirs. 2000—03), Am. Dermatol. Assn. (chair membership com. 2002—03, bd. dirs. 2006—, program com. 2007—08, chair), Dermatology Found. (trustee 2003—09), Soc. Investigative Dermatology, Am. Acad. Dermatology (bd. dirs. 2002—06, exec. com. 2004—08, v.p. 2007—08), Alpha Omega Alpha. Avocation: travel. Office: Henry Ford Med Ctr New Ctr One Dept Dermatology 3031 W Grand Blvd Dept Ste 800 Detroit MI 48202-2689 Office Phone: 313-916-4060. Business E-Mail: hlim1@hfhs.org.

LIM, HYO SOON, radiologist; married. MD, PhD, Chonnam Nat. U., Gwang ju, South Korea. Cert. Radiologist South Korea, 2003. Fellow Chonnam Nat. U. Hosp., 2003—04, clin. instr., 2004—06; asst. prof. Chonnam Nat. U. Hwasun Hosp., Hwasun gun, Republic of Korea, 2006—. Recipient Cert. Merit award, Radiologic soc. North Am., 2003. Achievements include research in breast imaging. Office: Chonnam Nat Univ Hosp Ilsim Ri 160 519-809 Jeollanam-do Republic of Korea Office Fax: 82-61-379-7133.

LIM, HYUN-SUL, medical educator; b. Iksan-si, Jeonbuk-do, Republic of Korea, July 15, 1952; s. Ik-Doo Lim and Suk-In Oh; m. Hae-Gyeong Kim, Mar. 22, 1980; children: Jae-Yoon, Song-I. MD, Seoul Nat. U., 1978, PhD, 1986, MPH, 1981. Med. practicing lic. Korea Ministry Health and Welfare, 1978, bd. cert. in preventive medicine Korea Ministry Health and Welfare, 1983, bd. cert. in family medicine Korea Ministry Health and Welfare, 1989, bd. cert. in occupl. medicine Korea Ministry Health and Welfare, 1997, lic. Korean Soc. Preventive Medicine. Asst. prof. Coll. Medicine, Dongguk U., Gyeongju-si, Republic of Korea, 1990—94, assoc. prof. Gyeongju-si, 1994—99, full prof. Gyeongju-si, 1999—, chief preventive medicine Gyeongju-si, 2001—, chmn. Dept. Preventive Medicine Gyeongju-si, 2001—, head med. inst. Gyeongju-si, 2002—04; dean sch. medicine Dongguk U., 2011—. Vis. scientist Environ. Epidemiology Svcs., Dept. Vets. Affairs, Washington, 1999—2000. Author: (book) Environmental Epidemiology, 2005, From Glassfiber Wastes to Avian Influenza, 2005, Preventive Medicine and Public Health, 2011. Mem. Prevention of Zoonosis in Korea Communicable Disease Control and Prevention, Seoul, 1998—2006, Reform Mass Screening, Korea Min. Health and Welfare, Seoul, 2002—06; dir. Korean Fedn. AIDS Prevention, Seoul. Maj. Korean Army, 1983—86. Recipient Presdl. Citation, Korea Govt., 2003, Govt. Svc. Merit medal. Master: Korean Assn. Agrl. Medicine and Cmty. Health (licentiate; v.p. 2003—06, pres. 2007—09), Korean Soc. Epidemiology (licentiate; pres. 2004—06); mem.: APHA (licentiate), Korean Soc. Preventive Medicine (licentiate; pres. 2011—), Korean Soc. Zoonoses (licentiate; v.p. 2006—09), Nat. Acad. Medicine Korea (licentiate). Home: 102-207 Samsung Apt Gyeongju-si Gyeongbuk 780-922 Republic of Korea Office: 707 Sookjang Dong Gyeongju Si Gyeongsangbuk-do 780-714 Republic of Korea Office Phone: 82-54-770-2401. Office Fax: 82-54-770-2438. Business E-Mail: wisewine@dongguk.ac.kr.

LIM, JUNGHA, child development professor; b. Seoul, Republic of Korea, Sept. 18, 1971; PhD, Korea U., 2004. Assoc. rsch. prof. SUNY, Buffalo, 2006—07; assoc. prof. Korea U., 2007—. Mem.: APA, Korean Assn. Human Devel. Office: Korea University Coll Edn Seoul 136701 Republic of Korea Business E-Mail: jhlim@korea.ac.kr.

LIM, KYOUNG AH, medical educator; b. Yeongcheon-si, Gyeongbuk, Republic of Korea, July 31, 1969; M, Ewha Womans U., Seoul, Republic of Korea, 2000, PhD, 2008. Asst. prof., dept. pediat. CHA Gangnam Med. Ctr., CHA U., 2004—. Med. counsel com., cons. Planned Population Fedn. Korea, 2007—08. Recipient Young Investigator award, Asian Soc. Pediat. Rsch., Il-dong Rsch. award, Korean Pediat. Soc. Mem.: Korean Birth Defect Forum, Korean Soc. Hypertension, Korean Soc. Cardiology, Korean Pediat. Heart Assn., Korean Pediat. Soc. Avocations: piano, jogging. Office: 650-9 Yeoksam-1 dong Gangnam-gu Seoul 135-913 Republic of Korea Business E-Mail: kaleem@hanmail.net.

LIM, KYUNG-JOON, medical educator, professor, anesthesiologist; b. Republic of Korea; MD, Chosun U., Gwangju, Republic of Korea, 1987; PhD, Chonbuk Nat. U., Chonju, Republic of Korea, 1997. Dir. pain clinic Chosun U. Hosp., Gwangju, 2000—, dir., Internat. Med. Assistance Ctr., 2009—10, chair dept. anesthesiology and pain medicine, 2009—; gen. mgr. Chosun U. Med. Rsch. Inst., 2005—07. Dir. pub. rels. Chosun U. Hosp., Gwangju, 2007—09; cons. Korean Food and Drug Adminstrn., Seoul, 2002—04. Mem.: World Inst. Pain (FIPP regular mem. 2010—), Korean Pain Rsch. Soc. (dir. 2005—), Internat. Assn. Study Pain (regular mem. 1993—), Gwangju Med. Assn. (rep. 2008—), Korean Soc. Thermology (vice chmn. 2009—), Korean Pain Soc. (councilman 2001—, dir. judgment 2005—, chmn. Honam chpt. 2008—10), Korean Soc. Complimentary and Alternative Medicine (vice chmn. 2009—), Korean Med. Assn. (com. mem. 2003—07), Korean Soc. Anesthesiologists (councilman 2003—04, editor Jour. Anesthesia and Pain Medicine 2006—09, councilman 2010—). Office: Chosun University Hosp 588 Seosuk-Dong Gwangju 501-717 Republic of Korea Business E-Mail: kjlim@chosun.ac.kr.

LIM, LESLIE ENG CHOON, psychiatrist, senior consultant; s. Kay-Kok and Alice Lim; m. Cindy Chin; 1 child, Leanne. MBBS, Nat. U. Singapore, 1980. FRCPsych Royal Coll. Psychiatrists, 1988, FAMS Acad. Medicine Singapore, 1993, cert. FRCPsych 2009; LRSM Royal Sch. Music, 1970. Ho. officer Singapore Gen. Hosp., 1981—82; med. officer Singapore Armed Forces, 1982—83; registrar St. George's Hosp., London, 1984—88; sr. registrar St. Bartholomew's Hosp., London, 1989, Kingston Hosp., London, 1990, registrar Inst. Mental Health, Singapore, 1990—92, sr. registrar, 1992—95, cons., 1996—2001, sr. cons., 2001—03; vis. cons. psychiatrist Mil. Medicine Inst., Singapore, 2002—05; sr. cons., head dept. psychiatry Singapore Gen. Hosp., 2003—06; vis. sr. cons. psychiatrist Nat. Cancer Ctr., Singapore, 2003—; sr. cons., dept. psychiatry Singapore Gen. Hosp., 2006—. Examiner Nat. U. Singapore, 1996—, clin. tchr., 1996—2000, lectr., supr., examiner cognitive behaviour therapy course, Singapore, 1999—2005, adj. assoc. prof., 2000—04, clin. assoc. prof., 2004—, chief examiner, 2006—, adj. assoc. prof. Duke NUS Grad. Med. Sch. Duke, 2008; vis. cons. Mil. Medicine Inst., 2002—05. Editor: (books) I'm Not Mad, 2001; author: Mental Illness or Demonisation, 2007, Depression: The Misunderstood Illness, 2008; contbr. chapters to books, articles to profl. jours. Chmn. Mental Health Network, Nat. Coun. Social Svc., Singapore, 2003—06; bd. mem. Met. YMCA, Singapore, 1996—. Capt. Combat Support Hosp., 1995—2000. Recipient Long Svc. award, Inst. Mental Health, 2002, MCDS, 2004, Singapore Gen. Hosp., 2004, NCSS, 2007, MCYS, 2008, Svc. Quality award, Singapore Gen. Hosp., 2006, Excellent Svc. Star award, 2008; grantee, Singhealth Found., 2005. Fellow: Acad. Medicine Singapore (hon.; sec. 1994, 2007); mem.: Singapore Assn. Mental Health (pres. 1997—), Singapore Psychiat. Assn. Avocations: violin, reading. Office: Singapore General Hosp Dept Psychiatry Outram Rd Singapore 169608 Singapore Office Fax: 65 63214015. Business E-Mail: gdmlec@sgh.com.sg.

LIM, OH-KYUNG, medical educator; b. Seoul, Republic Of Korea, July 26, 1962; d. Soo-sung Lim and Eun-ji Bae; m. Young-kyu Yoo; children: Mi-rim Yoo, Sang-jong Yoo. D, Catholic U. Medicine, Seoul, 2001. Cert. Bd. Rehab. Seoul, 1988. Prof. Gachon U. Gil Med. Ctr., Incheon, Republic of Korea, 2007—. Dir. Paralympic Inst. Med. Part, Seoul, 2006—08, Health Conv. Gilhospital, Incheon, Republic of Korea, 2006—08. Achievements include research in rehabilitation. Office: Gachon Univ Gil Med Ctr 1198 Guweol-dong Namdong-gu Incheon 405-760 Republic of Korea Office Phone: 032-460-3722. Office Fax: 032-460-3722. Business E-Mail: phmed@gilhospital.com.

LIM, PIN, physician, consultant; b. Penang, Malaysia, Jan. 12, 1936; m. Shirley Loo-Lim, Mar. 21, 1964; children: Jui, Jiun, Elaine Hsuen. MBBChir, U. Cambridge, 1963, MA, 1964, MD, 1970; DSc (hon.), U. Hull, 1999. Registrar diabetic dept. King's Coll. Hosp., London, 1965; med. officer Ministry Health, Singapore, 1965-66; lectr. to assoc. prof. medicine Nat. U. Singapore, 1966-77, prof., head dept. medicine, 1978-81, dep. vice-chancellor, 1979-81, vice-chancellor, 1981-2000, prof., sr. cons. endocrinologist, 2000—. Chmn. Nat. Wages Coun., Bio-ethics Adv. Com., chmn. Tropical Marine Sci. Inst.; Commonwealth Med. fellow Royal Infirmary, Edinburgh, Scotland, 1970, dir. Raffles Med. Group, co chair ETH Singapore SEC Ltd, 2010, Tum Create Ctr., governing bd. mem. Lee Kuan New Sch. Pub. Policy (NUS). Founder, pres. Endocrine and Metabolic Soc. Singapore; overseas advisor Royal Coll. Physicians London; chmn. bd. trustees Ang Mo Kio Hosp., Nat. Univ. Hosp. Endowment Fund, chmn. Nat. Longevity Ins. Com., Singapore-MIT Alliance Rsch. & Tech., Singapore Millenium Found. Ltd., Spl. Needs Trust Co., Chmn., bd. trustees NUH Patientcare Charity Fund.; dep. chmn., Lee Kwan Yew Water Prize Coun. Decorated Disting. Svc. Order (Republic of Singapore), 2000; recipient Republic Singapore Pub. Adminstrn. gold medal, 1984, Republic Singapore Meritorious Svc. award, 1990, Friend Labour award Nat. Trade Union Congress, 1995, Nat. U. Singapore Outstanding Svc. award, 2003; Eisenhower fellow, 1982; Queen's scholar, 1957. Fellow ACP, Royal Coll. Physicians, Acad. Medicine Singapore, Royal Australasian Coll. Physicians, Royal Coll. Surgeons Edinburgh (hon.), Coll. Gen. Practitioners Singapore (hon.), Royal Australian Coll. Ob-Gyn. (hon.), Royal Coll. Physicians and Surgeons Glasgow (hon.), Royal Coll. Dentists (U.S.A.), Royal Coll. Surgeons Edinburgh (hon.); mem. Singapore Med. Assn., Acad. Medicine (past master), British Med. Assn., Singapore Profl. Centre. Office: National University Singapore Department Medicine 1E Kent Ridge Rd NUHS Tower Block Level 10 Singapore 119228 Singapore E-mail: mdcplim@nus.edu.sg.

LIM, RAMON (KHE-SIONG LIM), neuroscience educator, researcher; b. Cebu City, Philippines, Feb. 5, 1933; came to U.S., 1959, naturalized, 1973; s. Eng-Lian and Su (Yu) L.; m. Victoria K. Sy, June 21, 1961; children: Jennifer, Wendell, Caroline. AB, U. Santo Tomas, Manila, 1953; MD cum laude, U. Santo Tomas, 1958; PhD in Biochemistry, U. Pa., 1966. Diplomate Am. Bd. Psychiatry and Neurology. Rsch. neurochemist U. Mich., Ann Arbor, 1966-69; asst. prof. biochemistry U. Chgo., 1969-76, assoc. prof. Brain Rsch. Inst., 1976-81; prof. dept. neurology U. Iowa, Iowa City, 1981—2005, dir. divsn. neurochemistry and neurobiology, 1981—2005, prof. emeritus, 2005—. Career investigator VA, 1983; adv. internat. writing program U. Iowa, 2002—05. Author: (non-sci. book) An Anthology of Literary and Artistic Works of RAMON LIM, 2008; mem. editl. bd. Internat. Jour. Devel. Neurosci., 1984-91, Neurochem. Rsch., 1997—2006, Handbook of Neurochemistry and Molecular Neurobiology, 2005-; contbr. numerous articles to sci. jours. Grantee NIH, 1971—, NSF, 1979—, VA, 1981—; recipient 3d prize Art Assn. Philippines, 1957, 3d prize 8th Internat. Calligraphy Competition, Shanghai, China, 2005; named Outstanding Overseas Young Chinese, Fedn. Overseas Chinese Orgns., 1961, Outstanding Med. Alumni award U. Santo Tomas, Manila, 2008. Mem. Am. Soc. Biochem. Molecular Biology, Internat. Soc. Neurochemistry (vis. lectureship 1986), Am. Soc. Neurochemistry, Soc. Neurosci., Am. Soc. Cell Biology. Achievements include research in isolation and characterization of regulatory brain proteins; growth and differentiation of brain cells; brain chemistry and molecular biology. Avocations: calligraphy, painting, writing, music. Home: 118 Richards St Iowa City IA 52246-3516 Office: U Iowa Iowa City IA 52242 Office Phone: 319-335-8527. E-mail: ramon-lim@uiowa.edu.

LIM, SABINA, medical educator; m. Young-Hong Kim, Oct. 30, 1988; children: Dong-sub Kim, Myung-sub Kim. BA in Korean Medicine, Kyunghee U., 1987, MA in Korean Medicine, 1989, PhD in Korean Medicine, 1993. Lic. MD Ministry Health and Welfare Korea, 1987. Asst. dept. meridian and acupuncture Coll. Korean Medicine, Kyunghee U., Seoul, Republic of Korea, 1987—91, part-time tchg. fellow, 1991—93, assoc. prof., 2000—04; prof. Kyunghee U., Seoul, 2004—; instr. Coll. Korean Medicine, Kyunghee U., Daegu, Republic of Korea, 1993—95, asst. prof., 1995—99, assoc. prof., 1999—2000; chief dept. meridian and acupuncture Kyung Hee East-West Med. Rsch. Inst., WHO Collaborating Ctr., Seoul, Republic of Korea, 2000—; planning chairperson, Industry Original Tech. Roadmap Ministry of Knowledge Economy, Seoul, 2009, expert advisor, Total Tech. Blue Print, 2010; chief Dept. Menolian & Acupoint, Deagu, 1993—2000, Dept. Menolian & Acupoint Kyung Hee U., 2000—06; chair person Coll. Korean Medicine Kyung Hee U., 2010—11. Evaluator Korea Sci. and Engring. Found., Ministry Sci. and Tech., Seoul, 1999—; evaluator R&D Evaluation Team Korea Inst. Sci. and Tech. Evaluation and Planning (KISTEP), Ministry Sci. and Tech., Seoul, 1999—. mem. advisor bd. Sci. and Tech. Policy of 'Scientists and Parliament', Ministry Sci. and Tech., Seoul, 2005—; examiner Korea Rsch. Found., Seoul, 2000—; expert advisor Korean Techno-Venture Found., Seoul, 2000—; mem. practical affairs com. Health Tech. Planning and Evaluation Bd., Korea Health Industry Devel. Inst., Seoul, 2000—, mem. tech. devel. and planning evaluation com., 2000—, planning advisor Korean Med. Therapeutics Rsch. and Developing, 2001—, advisor tech. classification and disease analysis, 2001—; com. mem. exam question devel. Nat. Health Pers. Licensing

Exam. Bd., Seoul, 2002—; editl. bd. mem. Jour. Exptl. and Clin. Medicine, 2008. Contbr. articles to profl. jours.; mem. editl. bd.: Evidence-based Complementary and Alternative Medicine, 2004—. Recipient Honoring award, Ministry Edn. and Human Resources Devel., 1981, Kohwang Med. award, Kohwang Fund, 2002, 2005. Mem.: Korean Oriental Medicine Soc. (classification com. mem. 2002—04, mem. oriental medicine terminology establishment com. 2002—04), Soc. Meridian and Acupoint (mem. mgmt. com. 1999—, dir. internat. acad. com. 2002), Korean Soc. Lab. Animal Sci. (licentiate), Korean Inst. Herbal Acupuncture (licentiate), Korean Acupuncture and Moxibustion Soc. (licentiate), Assn. Korean Medicine (licentiate), Women's Bioscience Forum (life; dir. fin. com. 2004—). Achievements include patents for nelumbo nucifera gaertn; lonicera japonica thunb; acanthopanacis cortex; drug delivery device for using ultrasonic energy; automatic massage physical therapy device by one sided movement of ultrasonic horn; anti-inflammatory and anti-nociceptive effect of Cinnamomum Loureirii branches extract and pharmaceutical preparations containing the same; anti-inflammatory and anti-nociceptive effect of Alpinia officinarum rhizome extract and pharmaceutical preparations containing the same; anti-inflammatory and anti-nociceptive effect of Cinnamomum loureirii extract and pharmaceutical preparations; invention of the system of ultrasonic acupuncture for the stimulation of acupoint. Office: Kyunghee University 1 Hoeki-dong Dongdaemoon-ku Seoul 130-701 Republic of Korea Office Fax: 82-2-961-7831. Business E-Mail: lims@khu.ac.kr.

LIM, SABINA, psychiatrist, director; b. Seoul, Republic of Korea, Apr. 22, 1972; MPH, Columbia U. Sch. Pub. Health, 1992; MD, SUNY Buffalo Sch. Medicine, 1997. Attending psychiatrist Yale-New Haven Psychiat. Hosp., 2005—10, assoc. med. dir., 2009—11, exec. dir., 2011—. Asst. prof., psychiatry Yale U. Sch. Medicine, 2005—11, asst. clin. prof., psychiatry, 2011. Mem.: Am. Psychiat. Assn. Office: Yale-New Haven Psychiatric Hosp 184 New Haven CT 06519 Business E-Mail: sabina.lim@ynhh.org.

LIM, SEUNG PYUNG, medical educator; b. Seoul, Republic Of Korea, Aug. 25, 1950; s. Yong Whan Lim and Jung Hee Lee; m. Myung Hee Kim, May 27, 1978; children: Jee Sun, Sung Kyu. PhD, Seoul Nat. U., 1987. Cert. chest surgery Korean Nat. Health & Welfare Adminstrn., 1981, clin. trial profl. KFDA, 2006. Trainee Seoul Nat. U. Hosp., 1976—81; clin. fellow Green Ln. Hosp., Auckland, New Zealand, 1988—89; instr. Chungnam Nat. U., Daejeon, Republic of Korea, 1984—86, asst. prof., 1986—90, assoc. prof., 1990—95, prof., 1995—, assoc. dean, coll. medicine, 1999—2001; vis. prof. U. BC, Vancouver, Canada, 1996—98; head, dept. edn. & rsch. Chungnam Nat. U. Hosp., Daejeon, 2002—04, head, clin. rsch. & med. inst., 2002—06; v.p. Assn. Korean Thoracic & Cardiovasc. Surgery, Seoul, 2007—09, Korean Assn. Study Lung Cancer, 2009—; dir. Daejeon Regional Cancer Ctr., 2009—. Head Korean Cath. Med. Assn., Daejeon, 2006—08. Army capt. (chest surgeon) Capital Armed Forces Gen. Hosp., 1981—84. Home: Seogu Samchondong 991 Daejeon Republic of Korea Office: Chungnam Nat Univ Hosp Munwha-Ro Joong-Ku 33 301-721 Daejeon Daejeon Republic of Korea Home: 206 201 Kyungnam Honors Ville Yongsan dong Youseong Ku Daejeon Republic of Korea Office Phone: 82-42-280-7376. Office Fax: 82-42-280-7373. Business E-Mail: splim@cnu.ac.kr.

LIM, SEUNG-MIN, orthodontist; b. Seoul, Republic of Korea, Sept. 28, 1972; s. Kab-Sun and Jung-Rye Lim; m. Angie Eun-Ji Hong; children: Aston Seung Min, Martin Seung Min. DDS, Seoul Nat. U., 1998. Cert. Korean Assn. Orthodontists, 2002. Mem. Korean Assn. Orthodontists, Seoul, 1992—; founding mem. & instr. Korean Assn. Lingual Orthodontists, Seoul, 2008—. Contbr. articles to profl. jours. Chorister Dental Chorus, Seoul, 1993—97. Fellow, Asan Med. Ctr., 2002. Mem.: World Soc. Lingual Orthodontics. Home: Tower Palace F-1902 Seoul 135-272 Republic of Korea Office: Kagirunee Pvt Orthodontic Clinic 139-30 Seoul 156-090 Republic of Korea Office Fax: 82-2-541-6228. Personal E-mail: sm720928@hotmail.com. Business E-Mail: sm720928@hanmail.net.

LIM, SUNG-CHUL, medical educator; b. Seosan City, Chung Nam, South Korea, Jan. 18, 1963; s. Byung-pal Lim and Garb-dong Hahn; m. Hae-jeong Kim, Sept. 18, 1988; children: Hye-rin, Dahrin, June-hyuk. MD, Chosun U., Kwangju City, Korea, 1987; PhD, Chung-nam Nat. U., Daejeon City, Korea, 1993. Lic. physician Dept. of Pub. Health and Welfare, 1987, diplomate Board of Anatomical Pathologists Dept. of Pub. Health and Welfare, 1991, cert. qualified Cytopathologist in edn. Korean Soc. for Cytopathology, 1997, diplomate Board of the Toxicologic Pathologist The Korean Soc. of Toxicologic Pathology, 2003. Instr. Coll. of Medicine Chosun U., Kwangju City, Republic of Korea, 1994—96, asst. prof., 1996—2000, assoc. prof., 2000—05, prof., 2005—. Dir., divsn. rsch. Chosun U. Sch. Medicine, Kwangju City, Republic of Korea; vis. prof. U. of Tex., MD Anderson Cancer Ctr., Houston, 2000—01; vice dir. Rsch. Ctr. for Resistant Cells/Korean Sci. and Engring. Found. Contbr. articles to profl. jours. Grantee, Korea Rsch. Found., 2003—. Avocations: hiking, travel. Home: Poong-am Dong 1101 Seo Ku Gwangju 501322 Republic of Korea Office: Chosun Univ Hosp Dept Pathology Seosuk Dong Dong Ku 588 501-140 Gwangju Republic of Korea Office Fax: 82-62-234-4584. Personal E-mail: sclim42@hotmail.com. E-mail: sclim@chosun.ac.kr.

LIM, SUNG-JIG, medical educator; b. Republic of Korea, Oct. 28, 1965; D, Kyung Hee U., 2003. Prof. Kyung Hee U., 2006—. Mem.: Korean Soc. Pathologists. Office: 149 Sangil-Dong Gangdo-Gu Seoul 134-727 Republic of Korea Personal E-mail: sungjig@yahoo.co.kr.

LIM, YOUNG AE, hematologist; b. Seoul, Republic of Korea, June 15, 1965; d. Jongdo Lim and Seunghee Lee; m. Sinwhan Choi, Sept. 14, 1991; 1 child, Jonghoon Choi. MD, Chung Ang U., Seoul, 1990, PhD, 1997. Lic. med. dr. Ministry Health and Welfare, 1990, cert. med. specialist lab. medicine Ministry Health and Welfare, 1995. Instr. Sch. Medicine Ajou U., Suwon, 1996—97, asst. prof., 1998—2003, assoc. prof., 2004—. Transfusion specialist Ajou U. Hosp., Suwon, 1995—; vis. scientist Scripps Rsch. Inst., La Jolla, Calif., 2003—04. Mem. mgmt. subcom. blood and blood components Ministry of Health, Seoul, 2005. Recipient Most Outstanding Oral Presentation, Korean Soc. Clin. Pathologist, 2002, Most Outstanding Column, Korean Assn. Quality Assurance Clin. Lab., 2003; grantee, Korea Rsch. Found., 2005, Korea Health Industry Devel. Inst., 2005. Mem.: Korean Soc. Hematology (licentiate), Korean Soc. Blood Transfusion (life Most Outstanding Poster 2005), Korean Soc. Lab. Medicine (life). Achievements include research in effects of transfusion, blood usage and platelet functions. Office: Ajou Univ Hosp San 5 Wonchon-dong Gyeonggi-do Suwon 443-721 Republic of Korea Office Fax: +82-31-219-5778.

LIM, YOUNG JIN, medical researcher; b. Seoul, Chongno-Gu, Republic of Korea, Apr. 19, 1953; s. Nam Soo Lim and Keum Ae Kim; m. Kyung Hee Kim, Jan. 12, 1980; children: Seung Hoon, Ji Eun. B, Coll. Sci, Yonsei U., Seoul, 1975, Kyunghee U., 1982, MD, 1984, M, 1986. Intern Coll. Medicine, Kyunghee U., 1982—83, resident, 1983—87, clin. fellow, dept. Neurosurgery, 1987—, instr., 1988—91, asst. prof., 1991—2000, chmn., 1991—, prof., 2000—; vis. fellow Karolinska Inst., Stockholm, 1994—95; dir. Kyung Hee University Med. Ctr., 2010—. Com. mem. med. affair Korea Football Assn., Seoul, 1996—; local com. mem. Internat. Steriotactic Radiosurgery Soc.; ins. com. chmn. Korean Neurosurg. Soc.; judging com. mem. Health Ins. Rev. & Assessment Svc.; organizing com. mem. World Fedn. Neurosurg. Soc.; acad. com. chmn. Asia Gamma Knife Radiosurgery, Korean Soc. Radiosurgery; bd. mem. Korean Soc. Skull Base Surgery; sec. gen. Korean Soc. Geriatric Neurosurgery; bd. mem. Korean Soc. of Neurotraumatology, Korean Soc. Cerebrovasc. Surgery; steering com. mem. Korean Soc. Pediatric Neurosurgery; com. mem. Ethical Judgement, Hanyang U.; examiner Jour. Korean Oriental Med. Soc., Korean Acad. Med. Sci., Korean Soc. Emergency Medicine; team dr. Korean Nat. Football Team, Seoul; head coach Korean Med. Football Assn., Korean Neurosurg. Soc. Footbal Team; ins. com. chmn. Korean Neurosurg. Soc.; judging com. mem. Helath Ins. Rev. & Assessment Svc.; organizing com. mem. World Fedn. Neurosurg. Soc., Nyon, Vaud, Switzerland; acad. com. chmn. Asia Gamma Knife Radiosurgery. Lt. Korean Army. Recipient Silver medal, 2005, Grand Prix Miwon Med. award, 2007—08. Mem.: Korean Med. Football Fedn. (pres. 2010—), Korean Neuro-Intensive Care Soc. (sec. gen. 2010—). Home: Pyung chang-Dong Seoul Chong no-Gu 110-848 Republic of Korea Office: Kyunghee Univ Med Ctr Hoegi-Dong 1 Bunji Seoul Dongdaemun-Gu 130-702 Republic of Korea Office Fax: 81-2-958-8380.

LIM, YOUNG MI, nursing educator; b. Seoul, Sept. 14, 1959; PhD, U. Ariz., 1993. Asst. prof. Kwandong U., 1995—97; prof. dept. nursing Yonsei U. Wonju Coll. Medicine, Kangwon, Republic of Korea, 1998—. Editl. bd. mem. Jour. Korean Gerontol. Nursing, 2008—10, Korean Acad. Psychiatric and Mental Health Nursing, 2011. Mem.: Korean Soc. Nursing Sci. Office: Yonsei University Wonju Coll Medicine #162 Ilsan-dong Wonju Kangwon 220-701 Republic of Korea Business E-Mail: youngmi@yonsei.ac.kr.

LIM, YOUNG WOON, microbiologist, educator; b. Daejeon, Republic of Korea, May 18, 1969; PhD, Seoul Nat. U., 2001. Dir. Ministry of Environment, 2007—11; prof. Seoul Nat. U., 2011—. Recipient Excellence award, 1st Pl., Soc. Wood Sci. and Tech. Mem.: Microbiol. Soc. Korea, Korean Soc. Mycology, Mycol. Soc. America. Avocations: fly fishing, singing, soccer. Office: 599 Gwanak-ro Gwanak-gu Seoul 151-747 Republic of Korea Business E-Mail: ywlim@snu.ac.kr.

LIM, YUN JEONG, medical educator; b. Daegu, Republic Of Korea, Oct. 28, 1970; m. Sung Vin Yim; children: Hyo Jin Yim, Hyo Ju Yim. MD, Kyungbuk U., South Korea, 1995; PhD, Sungkyunkwan U. Diplomate Korea, 2004. Internship, residency Asan Med. Ctr., Ulsan U. Hosp., Seoul, Republic of Korea, 1995—2000; clin. fellowship, clin. instr. Samsung Med. Ctr., Sung Kyun Kwan U. Hosp., Seoul, 2000—05; assoc. prof. Dongguk U. Ilsan Hosp., Dongguk U. Coll. Medicine, Goyangsi, Republic of Korea, 2005—. Recipient Young Investigator's award, APDW, 2007—08. Mem.: Korean Soc. Gastroent., Korean Soc. Gastroent. Endoscopy, Am. Gastroent. Assn. Office: Dongguk Univ Ilsan Hosp Siksadong Ilsandonggu 814 410-773 Kyunggido Goyang-si Republic of Korea Office Phone: 821025336288. Office Fax: 82319617141. Personal E-mail: drlimyj@gmail.com. Business E-Mail: limyj@duih.org.

LIMA, ALBERT DICKSON, ophthalmologist, researcher; b. Natal, Rio Grande do Norte, Brazil, Apr. 18, 1972; s. Teresinha Oliveira and Damião Batista Lima; m. Hilkea Carla Medeiros, July 2, 1976. Ophtalmologist Med., Universidade Fed. do Rio Grande do Norte, Natal, 1992—97. Diplomate Universidade Fed. do Rio Grande do Norte, 1997, cert. Ophtalmologist Hosp. de Olhos de Pernanbuco, 2000, Curso Basico de Oftalmologia Universidade de PR, 2000, Fellow de cornea e diseases external Fundação Altino ventura, 2000. Auditor fiscal do tesouro estadual Governo do Rio Grande do Norte, Natal, Rio Grande do Norte, Brazil, 1994—2002. Recipient The best rsch. in corneal simposium, Simposio Brasileiro de cornea, 1988, The best rsch. in sinposium, Universidade Fed. do Rio Grande do Norte, 1994, The best rsch. in north of Brazil, Congresso Brasileiro de Cegueira e Reabilitação Visual, 2000; scholar Curso basico de PR, Associacion Panamericana de oftalmology, 2000. Mem.: Associação Panamericana de Oftalmologia (assoc.), Sociedade Brasileira de Oftalmologia (assoc.), Conselho Brasileiro de oftalmologia (assoc.), Sociedade Brasileira para o desenvolvimento da Pesquisa em Cirurgia (assoc.), Associação medica do Rio Grande do Norte (assoc.). Achievements include research in Effects Of Aloe Vera And Hialuronate Sodium In Corneal Healing. Home: Avenue Senador Salgado Filho 1786 Rio Grande do Norte Natal 59063000 Brazil Office: Albert Dickson Clinic 1786 Senador Salgado Filho avenue Natal 59063000 Brazil Office Fax: 084 6110661; Home Fax: 084 6110661. Business E-Mail: albertlima@dr.com.

LIMA, JOÃO A.C., cardiologist, educator; b. Salvador, Brazil, Oct. 24, 1951; s. Antonio B. and Dinora C. (Costa) Lima; m. Sandra D. Dorsey, Aug. 5, 1983; children: Michael, Jonathan. MD, U. Bahia Sch. Medicine, Brazil, 1977. Diplomate Am. Bd. Internal Medicine, cert. in Cardiovasc. Disease. Intern Hosp. Cardiologique Univ. Claude Bernard, Lyon, France; post-doctoral fellow cardiology divsn. U. Calgary Med. Sch., Canada; resident internal medicine Bayview Med. Ctr., Johns Hopkins U., Balt., 1986—88; fellow cardiology Johns Hopkins Hosp., 1988—90; asst. prof. medicine U. Pa., Phila., 1990-92, Johns Hopkins U., 1992—97, assoc. prof. medicine and radiology, 1997—. Dir. cardiovasc. imaging Johns Hopkins Hosp.; co-dir. intraoperative echocardiography prog. Donald W. Reynolds Cardiovasc. Clin. Rsch. Ctr. Contbr. articles to profl. jours. Named one of 25 Most Influential Movers and Shakers, RT Image Mag., 2006; fellow NIH, 1980—82. Mem.: AAAS, Soc. Magnetic Resonance Imaging, Am. Coll. Cardiology, Am. Heart Assn. Democrat. Roman Catholic. Achievements include research in the development and application of imaging and technology to address scientific and clinical problems involving the heart and vascular system; first to document the mismatch between myocardial dysfunction and ischemia/infarction after coronary occlusion and it's response to changes in loading conditions. Avocations: soccer, bossa nova music. Office: Johns Hopkins Hosp 600 N Wolfe St Blalock 524D1 Baltimore MD 21287-0005 Office Phone: 410-614-1284. Business E-Mail: jlima@jhmi.edu.

LIMA, MARGARIDA MARIA DE CARVALHO, physician, educator; b. Vila Nova de Gaia, Portugal, June 21, 1962; MD, Inst. Ciências Biomédicas Abel Salazar, U. Porto, 1986, PhD, 2004. Clin. dir. asst. Hosp. Santo António, Centro Hosp. Porto, 2005—09, head cytometry lab, clin. dept. hematology, 1992—2011, head dept. edn. & rsch., 2006—. Prof. integrated master medicine Inst Ciências Biomédicas Abel Salazar, U. Porto, 2007—11, prof. doc. program pathology & molecular genetics, 2008—11; prof. clin. analysis & pub. health Inst. Ciências Saúde U. Católica Portuguesa, 2008—11; mem. Portuguese Ethics Com. Clin. Rsch., 2011. Recipient prize, Iberian Soc. Cytometry, 1995—97, Portuguese Soc. Hematology, 1999—2000, 2004—05, 2010. Mem.: Portuguese Ethical Com. Clin. Rsch., Multidisciplinary Unit Biomedical Rsch. (rsch. group coord.), Portuguese Ctrl. Govt. Health Sys. (ACSS) (mem. com. immunology), Portuguese Group Cutaneous Lymphomas (founding mem. 2010—), Clin. Immunology Group (HSA/CHP unit mem.). Avocations: poetry, painting. Office: Hosp Santo António Porto 4099-001 Portugal Business E-Mail: mmc.lima@clix.pt.

LIMA COSTA, MA FERNANDA, epidemiologist, researcher, educator; b. Barbacena, Brazil, June 24, 1951; d. Fernando Victor de Lima e Costa and Nadyr Furtado de Lima e Costa. MD, Fed. U. Minas Gerais, Belo Horizonte, Brazil, 1976, MSc, 1980, PhD, 1984. Med. diplomate. Prof. Fed. U. Minas Gerais Sch. Medicine, Belo Horizonte, 1977—; postdoctoral fellow Johns Hopkins Sch. Hygiene and Pub. Health, Balt., 1987-88, London Sch. Hygiene and Tropical Medicine, London, 1991-92; chair Oswaldo Cruz Found., Belo Horizonte, 1996—. Pres. 2d Brazilian Congress on Epidemiology, Belo Horizonte, 1992; postgrad. program coord. MPH, Belo Horizonte, 1993-96; UN Devel. Program, Brasilia, Brazil, 1994; collaborative rsch. ctr. coord. Brazilian Ministry of Health Collaborative Ctr. on Epidemiology of Aging, Belo Horizonte. Assoc. editor Reports in Public Health, 1993—99, Brazilian Jour. Epidemiology, 1998—, Ciencia E Saude Coletiva, cons. referee Social Sci. and Medicine, 2000—, Pan Am. Jour. Pub. Health, Ciência e Saúde Coletiva; contbr. articles to profl. jours. Recipient Best Work award, Oswaldo Cruz Found.-Rene Rachou Rsch. Inst., 1997, Best Work in Gerontology award, Brazilian Soc. Geriatry and Gerontology, 2000; named postdoctoral fellow, Fulbright Found., 1987—88, rsch. fellow scholar, WHO, 1991—92, sr. rschr. scholar, Brazilian Rsch. Coun., 1992—. Mem. Internat. Epidemiol. Assn., Brazilian Assn. Pub. Health (Honor award 1998), Nat. Commn. Epidemiology. Roman Catholic. Avocation: photography. Home: 921/1103 Rua Rio Grande do Norte Belo Horizonte 30130140 Brazil Office: Oswaldo Cruz Found Av Augusto de Lima 1715 Belo Horizonte Brazil Office Fax: 55-31-3295-3115. E-mail: lima-costa@cpqrr.fiocruz.br.

LIMA-MAROBONA, JANICE, dermatologist, cosmetics executive; Attended, Nova Southeastern U., Fort Lauderdale, 1993. Diplomate Am. Osteo. Bd. of Dermatology. Intern Met. Gen. Hosp., Clearwater; resident Sun Coast Hosp., Largo; hosp. affiliations Miami Children's Hosp., Mercy Hosp.; dermatologist Bay Pointe Dermatology and Cosmetic Ctr. P.A. Office: Bay Pointe Dermatology and Cosmetic Center PA Ste 104 3850 Bird Rd Miami FL 33146 Office Phone: 305-669-8337. Office Fax: 305-856-4883.

LIMBRUNO, UGO, cardiologist; b. Rome, Jan. 5, 1961; s. Alfonso and Adriana (Delfico) L.; m. Cristina Fioretti; 1 child, Luca. MD, U. Rome, 1985; PhD, Scuola Superiore, Pisa, Italy, 1989. Resident cardiology U. Pisa, 1988, interventional cardiologist, 1992—. Contbr. articles to profl. jours. Vol. ARC, Rome, 1983. Fellow European Soc. Cardiology, Italian Soc. Cardiology. Avocation: sailing. Office: Cathelerization Lab Livorno Hosp ASL6 57100 Livorno Italy E-mail: ulimbru@tin.it.

LIMDI, JIMMY K., gastroenterologist, consultant, medical researcher, educator; s. Kakubhai C. and Manorama Kakubhai Limdi; m. Sonali Limdi, Nov. 25, 1997. Student, Jaihind Coll. Sci., Bombay, 1985—87; MBBS, U. Pune, India, 1994. Cert. internal medicine and gastroenterology United Kingdom, 2006. Resident Jaslok and P.D. Hindju Hosps., Bombay, 1995—97; internal medicine Dewsbury Dist. Hosp., West Yorkshire, England, South Manchester U. Hosps., England; specialist registrar in gastroenterology N.W. Deanery Nat. Health Svc., Manchester, England, 2001—; clin. lead, inflammatory bowel diseases Pennine Acute Hosps. NHS Trust, Manchester. Examiner 3rd and 5th yr. U. Manchester, England; examiner Queen Mary U., London; presenter to internat. profl. mtgs. Author (co-editor): The PLAB and Beyond-A Survivor's Handbook, 2002; author: Guidelines in Gastroenterology, 2003; contbr. articles to profl. jours. (First of top 10 articles Postgraduate Med. Jour., 2004). Fellow: RCP (Edinburgh); mem.: RCP (London), Am. Soc. Gastroenterology Endoscopy, Am. Coll. Gastroenterology, Am. Gastroenterology Assn., Brit. Soc. Gastroenterology, Brit. Med. Assn. Avocations: tennis, reading, singing, public speaking. Office: Fairfields Hosp Pennine Acute Hosps NHS Trust Manchester & Beaumont Hosp Bolton 241 Fairfield House Bury Lancashire BL9 7TD England Office Phone: 0044 161 7782642.

LIMIN, ZHU, ophthalmologist; b. Jiangxi, China, Dec. 20, 1975; M, Tianjin med. U., 2006. Physician Tianjin Med. U. Eye Ctr., 2008—. Office: Rd FuKang 251 Tianjin Nankai 300384 China Personal E-mail: zlmjojo@163.com.

LIMING, YANG, agricultural studies educator; b. Anhui Province, Oct. 10, 1974; D, Nanjing Agrl. U., 1997. Assoc. prof. Huaiyin Normal U., 2010—. Office: 111 Changjiang West Rd Huaian Jiangsu 223300 China Business E-Mail: yanglm@hytc.edu.cn.

LIMMROTH, VOLKER, neurologist, educator; MD, Göttingen U., Germany, 1990, PhD in Pharmacology, 2002. Cert. German Bd. Neurology, 1998. Resident U. Hosp., Essen, Germany, 1990—93, cons. neurologist, 1998—2001, vice-chmn. Dept. Neurology, 2002—05; postdoctoral fellow Mass. Gen. Hosp., Boston, 1993—96; chmn. Dept. Neurology Cologne (Germany) City Hosps., 2006—. Author (editor): Neurology for Practitioners, 2d edit. (German Pain award, 1996), 2d edit., 2006; author: Pain-disorders of the head and face: Current knowledge of pathophysiology, diagnosis and therapy, 2006; co-author: Therapeutic guidelines: Multiple Sclerosis, 2d edit.,

2003, Pocket-atlas Multiple Sclerosis, 2004, Neurology - 1000 Questions for the Boards, 2006; contbr. 60 chpts. to book;, editor 10 books; contbr. over 200 articles to profl. jours. Achievements include research in pathophysiology of pain and headache syndromes, multiple sclerosis; development of drugs against pain syndromes and stroke. Office: Klinikum Köln - Merheim Ostmerheimer Str 200 Köln 51109 Germany Office Fax: +49 221 8907 3772. Business E-Mail: limmrothv@kliniken-koeln.de.

LIMON, AGENOR, research scientist; b. Puebla, Sept. 5, 1973; Degree in Chemistry & Pharmacobiology, Benemerita U. Autonoma de Puebla, 1998; PhD, Inst. Physiology, BUAP, 2004. Postdoc. rschr. U. Calif., Irvine, 2005—09, asst. project scientist II, 2010—. Adj. prof. Inst. Physiology, BUAP, 2001—04, Benemerita U. Autonoma de Puebla, 2002—04. Recipient Merit award, Pres., Mex., Maximiliano Ruiz Castañeda, Benemerita U. Autonoma de Puebla, George E. Brown award, UCMexus-Conacyt, 2002; fellowship, Grass Found. Fellow: Alumni Internat. Brain Rsch. Orgn.; mem.: Sistema Nacional de Investigadores Mex., Acad. Advancement Sci., Soc. Neurosci. Avocation: singing. Office: 2205 McGaugh Hall Irvine CA 92697 Business E-Mail: alimonru@uci.edu.

LIMPEROPOULOS, CATHERINE, occupational therapist, researcher; BS in Occupational Therapy, McGill U., MS, PhD in Rehabilitation Sci. Asst. prof. dept. physical & occupational therapy McGill U.; researcher Montreal Children's Hosp. Office: McGill University Davis House 3654 Promenade Sir William Osler Montreal PQ Canada H3G 1Y5 E-mail: catherine.limperopoulos@mcgill.ca.

LIM QUAN, KATHERINE, dermatologist; MD, Northwestern U., 1992. Diplomate Am. Bd. Dermatology, 2006. Resident dermatology Mayo Clinic, Rochester, Minn., 1993—96, fellow mohs surgery, 1996—97; hosp. affiliation include Chandler Regional Med. Ctr. Office: Chandler Regional Medical Center Ste 223 1100 S Dobson Rd Chandler AZ 85286 Office Phone: 480-214-0388.

LIN, BLOSSOM YEN-JU, healthcare educator, researcher; b. Taichung, Taiwan, Nov. 15, 1970; d. Wen-Hung and Shu-Jang Lin. BS in Pharmacy, China Med. U., Taichung, 1993; MS in Biochemistry, Nat. Taiwan U., Taipei, 1995; PhD in Health Svcs. Orgn. & Rsch., Va. Commonwealth U., 1999. LCSW nat. pharmacist Taiwan, 1993. Dir., dept. quality control Shin-Phon Pharm. Co., Taichung, 1996; asst. prof., health care adminstrn. Chang Jung U., Tainan, Taiwan, 1999—2002; asst. prof., health svc. adminstrn. China Med. U., Taichung, 2002—07, assoc. prof. health svc. adminstrn., 2008—. Conf. spkr. several univs. and hosps., Taiwan, 1999—2008; rsch. cons. Taichung Hosp., Dept. Health, 2000—05; coordinative investigator, rsch. project Taichung Vet. Gen. Hosp., 2001; acad. cons. Sin Lau Hosp., 2003; prin. investigator, rsch. project Nat. Sci. Coun., Taiwan, 2000—, Nat. Health Rsch. Inst., Taiwan, 2003—05, Dept. Health, Exec., Yuan, Taiwan, 2004—09, Bur. Health Promotion, Dept. Health, Taiwan, 2005; project reviewer Taiwan Nat. Sci. Coun., 2003—10; project cons. pharmacy mgmt. and policy Taichung County Pub. Health Bur., 2007—08. Translator: Financial Management of Health Care Organizations, 2002, 2nd edit., 2006, Healing Environments: Design For The Body, Mind & Spirit, 2007; author: (book) Integrated Care and Management:Creating Values for Health Care Organizations, 2007; jour. paper reviewer: Jour. Healthcare Mgmt. (Chinese), 2002—08, Internat. Jour. Nursing Studies, 2008, Jour. Med. Sys., 2008; contbr. numerous articles to profl. jours.; reviewer: conf. papers. Recipient Rsch. award, Nat. Sci. Coun., 2000, Silver prize, Chuang Yi-ckou Found., 2008; grantee, Taiwan Nat. Sci. Coun., 2000—, Taiwan Nat. Health Rsch. Inst., 2003—05, China Med. U., 2003—04;, Dept. Health, Exec. Yuan, Taiwan, 2004—05, Bur. Health Promotion, Dept. Health, ROC, 2005. Mem.: Am. Coll. Healthcare Execs., Acad. Mgmt. Avocations: reading, travel, movies. Office: China Med Univ 91 Hsueh Shih Rd Taichung 404 Taiwan Office Fax: 886-4-22076923. Personal E-mail: yenju1115@hotmail.com.

LIN, CHEN, medical educator; b. Fuzhou, China, Sept. 1, 1965; PhD, Rice U., 1990. Rsch. scientist Mayo Clinic, 1999—2006; asst. prof. Ind. U. Sch. Medicine, 2006—. Mem.: AAPM, ISMRM. Office: 950 W Walnut St R2 E124 Indianapolis IN 46202 Business E-Mail: clin1@iupui.edu.

LIN, CHENG-CHIEH, geriatrician, educator; b. Taiwan, Oct. 5, 1957; PhD, U. SC, 2002; degree in Health Adminstrn., Sch. Pub. Health, 2002. Attending physician China Med. U. Hosp., Taiwan, 1989—, adminstrv. vice supt., 1995—2001, supt., 2001—09; chmn. Grad. Inst. Health Care Adminstrn. China Med. U., Taiwan, 2001—03, prof., 2002, dean Coll. Medicine, 2009—. Chief editor Jour. Mid-Taiwan, Jour. Medicine, 1997—2003; pres. Taiwan Coll. Family Physicians, 2006—09, Old Five Old Found., 2009. Recipient Disting. Alumni award, Michael E. and Saundra P. Samuels, U. SC, Asia Travel award, Internat. Soc. Quality Life Rsch. Master: Alumni Assn. Taiwan Sch. Pub. Health U. SC; mem.: Jour. Open Access Med. Stats., Jour. Clin. Medicin Geriat., Taiwan Assn. Family Medicine, Taiwan Assn. Gerontology and Geriat., Delta Omega. Avocations: travel, tennis. Office: 2 Yu-Der Rd Taichung 404 Taiwan Business E-Mail: cclin@mail.cmuh.org.tw.

LIN, CHIH-LUNG, medical educator; b. Xin Ying, Tainan, Taiwan, Jan. 15, 1965; s. Qing-Yun and Huang-Yan Lin; m. Li Hui Lu, Feb. 21, 2009. Dr., Nat. Ctrl. U., Jhongli City, Taoyuan, Taiwan, 2003. Asst. rschr. Chung- Shan Inst. Sci. and Tech., Long Tan, Taoyuan, 1989—2002, project mgr., 2002—07, maj. Decorated Bao Xing medal Ministry of Nat. Def., Zhong Qin, Jing Feng medal, Ji Xue medal. Achievements include development of a fiber communication system for an anti-aircraft missile system. Office: Chung Yung Christian Univ 200 Chung Pei Rd Chung Li Taoyuan County 32023 Taiwan Office Fax: 886-3-2654799. Business E-Mail: linclr@yahoo.com.tw.

LIN, CHUN CHIH, biotechnologist, educator; b. Kaohsiung, Taiwan, Aug. 26, 1972; PhD, Nat. Tsing-Hua U., 2003. Assoc. prof., dept. natural biotechnology Grad. Inst. Natural Healing Scis., Nanhua U., 2003—. Fellow: Taiwanese Applied Radiation and Isotopes Soc., Internat. Acad. Natural Medicine (chmn.); mem.: Phi Tau Phi Scholastic Honor Soc. Avocation: tai chi. Office: Rm 5319 55 Nanhua Rd Dalin Jiayi 62248 Taiwan Business E-Mail: cclin@mail.nhu.edu.tw.

LIN, CHUN-FAN DANIEL, information technology executive; b. Australia, Aug. 28, 1981; B in Aero. Engring. with honors, U. Witwatersrand, 2004; PhD, U. Sydney, 2009. Rsch. assoc. U. Sydney, 2009; IT specialist IBM, 2011—. Avocations: reading, weightlifting, movies. Home: 6/48 Denison Rd Lewisham Sydney NSW 2049 Australia Personal E-mail: dlin1981@yahoo.com.au.

LIN, DAHANG, medical physicist; arrived in U.S., 1985; s. Meitan Lin and Wenzhen Zhang; m. Qixian Zhang; children: Gang, Xia. Diploma, Tsing Hua U., 1967, MS Physics, 1982; MA Physics, Bklyn. Coll., 1989; PhD Physics, CUNY, 1992. Lic. med. physicist N.Y. Instr. Hubei Coll. Traditional Chinese Medicine, Wuhan, 1974—78, Wuhan Poly. Inst., China, 1981—85; tchg. asst. Bklyn. Coll., 1985—92; med. physicist, assoc. dir. Elmhurst Hosp. Ctr., NY, 1992—. Contbr. articles to profl. jours. Bd. dirs. N.Y. Chinese Am. Assn., Flushing, 1998—. Mem.: Am. Assn. Physicists in Medicine, Soc. Nuc. Medicine. Avocations: travel, photography, fishing, sports. Home: 40-11 Murray St Flushing NY 11354 Office: Elmhurst Hosp Ctr 79-01 Broadway Elmhurst NY 11373 Business E-Mail: lind@nychhc.org.

LIN, DANIEL W., urologist, oncologist, educator; b. Cleve. BS in Biology, Stanford U., Calif., 1989; MD, Vanderbilt U. Sch. Medicine, Nashville, 1994. Diplomate Am. Bd. Urology. Surgery intern U. Wash. Sch. Medicine, Seattle, 1994—95, surgery resident, 1995, urology resident, 1996—99, chief resident dept. urology, 1999—2000, acting asst. prof. dept. urology, 2001—03, asst. prof., 2003—08, assoc. prof., chief divsn. urologic oncology, 2008—; urologic oncology fellowship Meml. Sloan-Kettering Cancer Ctr., 2000—01. Clin. staff Vet.'s Affairs Puget Sound Health Care Sys., Seattle, 2001, Harborview Med. Ctr., Seattle, 2001—, Seattle Children's Hosp. & Regional Med. Ctr., 2006—; rsch. assoc. divsn. human biology Fred Hutchinson Cancer Rsch. Ctr., Seattle, 2002—06, affiliate divsn. pub. health scis., 2004—06, asst. mem. cancer prevention program, 2006—; assoc. clin. staff Seattle Cancer Care Alliance, 2003—. Assoc. editor Advances in Urology, 2006—, Jour. Med. Case Reports, 2007—, UroToday Internat. Jour., 2008, reviewer Jour. Urology, 2002—, Asian Jour. Andrology, 2003—, Urologic Oncology, 2005—, Brit. Jour. Urology Internat., 2006—, Cancer, 2006—, European Urology, 2006—, Cancer Rsch., 2006—, Jour. Cellular & Molecular Medicine, 2007—, Urology, 2008—, Prostate, 2008—, World Jour. Urology, 2008—, Therapeutic Advances in Urology, 2009—; contbr. articles to profl. jours. Recipient Julian S. Ansell Faculty Tchg. award, 2008. Mem.: AMA, Urol. Rsch. Socc., Soc. Basic Urol. Rsch. (Young Investigator award 2007), Northwest Urologic Soc., Soc. Urologic Oncology (mem. exec. bd., program com. 2009—, Young Investigator award 2009), Wash. State Urol. Soc. (mem. exec. bd. 2007—), Am. Urol. Assn. (Earl F. Nation Resident Scholarship 1998), Alpha Omega Alpha. Office: U Wash Med Ctr Dept Urology 1959 NE Pacific St Box 356510 Seattle WA 98195 Office Phone: 206-221-0797. Business E-Mail: dlin@u.washington.edu. *

LIN, ERICA P., anesthesiologist, educator; b. Houston, May 4, 1979; MD, U. Tex. Med. Sch., Houston, 2004. Asst. prof. dept. anesthesiology Cin. Children's Hosp. Med. Ctr., 2008—. Office: 3333 Burnet Ave MLC 2001 Cincinnati OH 45229 Business E-Mail: erica.lin@cchmc.org.

LIN, FANG-YUE, hospital administrator; b. July 8, 1950; Grad., Nat. Taiwan U., 1975, PhD, 1989. Internship Nat. Taiwan Univ. Hosp. 1974—75, residentship gen. surgery and cardiovasc. surgery, 1977—81, attending cardiovasc. surgeon, 1981—2009, chief divsn. cardiovasc. surgery, 1996—98, chmn. dept. emergency medicine, 1997—2000, supt., 2004—08; fellowship Hosp. Henri-Mondor, Paris, 1983—84, Hosp. Broussais, Paris, 1984, Kanazawa Univ. Hosp., Japan, 1989; asst. prof. coll. medicine Nat. Taiwan Univ., 1991—95, prof. coll. medicine, 1995—2009, vice supt., 1999—2004; supt. Taipei Veterans Gen. Hosp., Taiwan, 2009—. Recipient Award of Outstanding Young Investigator, Chin-Shin Med. Coun., Taipei, Taiwan, 1990, Award of Young Investigator, Eric K. Fernstrom Found., Sweden, 1993, Best Tchrs. award of Nat. Taiwan Univ. Med. Sch., North America Alumni Assn., 1999. Office: Taipei Veterans General Hospital 201 Sec 2 Shih-Pai Rd Taipei Taiwan Office Phone: 886228712121. *

LIN, HORNG-CHYUAN, thoracic medicine physician, educator; b. Hsin-Chu, Taiwan, Apr. 24, 1964; m. Yuan-Chun Fu. Attending physician dept. thoracic medicine Chang Gung Meml. Hosp., Taipei, Taiwan, 1994—; chief dept. thoracic medicine II Lin-Kou Med. Ctr. of Chang Gung Meml. Hosp., Taipei, 2003—05; assoc. prof. Chang Gung U., Lin-Kou, Taiwan, 2005—. Dir. Rsch., Edn. and Devel. Ctr., dept. thoracic medicine Lin-Kou Med. Ctr. of Chang Gung Meml. Hosp., 2005—. Recipient award of biosci. rsch., Nat. Sci. Coun., 1998, 1999, 2000. Achievements include research in airway inflammation, critical care medicine. Office: Chang Gung Meml Hosp 199 Tun-Hwa N Rd Taipei 105 Taiwan Office Fax: 886-3-3272474. Business E-Mail: lin53424@ms13.hinet.net.

LIN, HSIN-CHING, otolaryngologist; b. Kaohsiung City, Taiwan, July 8, 1968; s. San-Lang Lin and Chu-Huan Lin Kuo; m. Pei-Wen Lin, Sept. 26, 1995; children: Chung-Wei, Chung-Hsin, Chung-Yi. MB, China Med. U., 1994. Lic. med. dr. Dept. Health, Exec. Yuan, Taiwan, otolaryngologist Dept. Health, Exec. Yuan, Taiwan. Resident in otolaryngology Chang Gung Med. Ctr., Kaohsiung County, Taiwan, 1996—99, chief resident in otolaryngology, 1999—2000, attending in otolaryngology, 2000—; asst. prof. Chang Gung Meml. Hosp. Chang Gung U. Kaohsiung Med. Ctr., 2005—. Lectr. Fooyin U., Kaohsiung County, 2001—02, Chang Gung Meml. Hosp., 2003—, Chang Gung U., 2004—. Med. officer Taiwanese mil., 1994—96. Recipient 1995 Best Mil. Med. Staff award, Med. Affairs Bur., Ministry of Nat. Def., Taiwan, 1995, Best Clin. Rsch. award, Taiwan Otolaryn. Soc., 2000, Best Oral Presentation award, Taiwan Soc. Sleep Medicine, 2008. Fellow: Taiwan Assn. Endoscopic Surgery (life; instr. 2006—), Taiwan Sleep Soc. (life), Taiwan Otolaryn. Soc. (life); mem.: Am. Acad. Sleep Medicine (life), Taiwan Assn. Med. Edn. (life), Am. Rhinologic Soc. (life), Am. Acad. Otolaryngology-Head and Neck Surgery Found. (life). Achievements include development of new surgical modality for allergic rhinitis by radiofrequency; research in Kikuchi's disease. Avocations: opera, tennis, classical music, model airplanes, travel. Office: Chang Gung Meml Hosp Chang Gung U Dept Otolaryngology Kaohsiung Med Ctr No 123 Ta-Pei Rd Kaohsiung 833 Taiwan Office Phone: 886-7-7317123 ext. 2533. Office Fax: 886-7-7318762; Home Fax: 886-7-7318762. Business E-Mail: hclin@adm.cgmh.org.tw.

LIN, HWAI JENG, physician; b. Ping-Tung, Taiwan, May 15; m. Linna Wang, Nov. 3, 1961; children: Betty, Alex. MD, Taipei Med. U., 1979. Resident VGH-Taipei, 1979—84, intern, 1978—79, attending physician, gastroenterology, 1986—.

LIN, JAMES, medical educator; b. Dec. 4, 1974; MD, Va. Commonwealth U., 2000. Asst. prof. LSU Health Scis. Ctr., 2008—. Home: 420 Homestead Ave Metairie LA 70005 Personal E-mail: jimlinoto@gmail.com.

LIN, JAMES CHIH-I, biomedical and electrical engineer, educator; b. Dec. 29, 1942; m. Mei Fei, Mar. 21, 1970; children: Janet, Theodore, Erik. BS, U. Wash., 1966, MS, 1968, PhD, 1971. Engr. Crown Zellerbach Corp., Seattle, 1966-67; asst. prof. U. Wash., Seattle, 1971-74; prof. Wayne State U., Detroit, 1974-80, U. Ill., Chgo., 1980—, head dept. bioengring., 1980-92, dir. robotics and automation lab., 1982-89, dir. spl. projects Coll. Engring., 1992-94, rsch. chair NSC, 1993-97. Vis. prof., Beijing, Rome, Shan Dong, Taiwan Univs.; lectr. short courses, 1974—; cons. Battelle Meml. Inst., Columbus, Ohio, 1973-75, SRI Internat., palo Alto, Calif., 1978-79, Arthur D. Little Inc., Cambridge, Mass., 1980-83, Ga. Tech. Rsch. Inst., Atlanta, 1984-86, Walter Reed Army Inst. Rsch., 1973, 87, 88, Naval Aerospace Med. Rsch. Labs., Pensacola, 1982-83, U.R.S. Corp., San Francisco, 1985-87, CBS Inc., N.Y., 1988, U. Va., 1991-92, ACS Inc., Santa Clara Calif., 1989-90, Luxtron Corp., Mountainview, Calif., 1991-92, Commonwealth Edison, Chgo., 1991-95, Lucent Tech./Bell Labs., 1998-2000, Biopac, Santa Barbara, Calif., 2006-07; program chmn. Frontiers of Engring. and Computing Conf., Chgo., 1985; chmn., convener URSI Jt. Symposium Electromagnetic Waves in Biol. Sys., Tel Aviv, 1987, Internat. Conf. on Sci. and Tech., 1989-91; chmn. Chinese-Am. Acad. and Profl. Conv., 1993; mem. Congrl. Health Care Adv. Coun., 13th dist., Ill., 1987-99; panelist NSF Presdl. Young Investigator award com., Washington, 1984, 89; mem. NIH diagnostic radiology, 1981-85, chmn. spl. study sect., 1986—2004; mem. U.S. Nat. Commn. for URSI, NAS, 1980-82, 90-99, chair Commn. K., 1990-99, Extremely Low Frequency Field monitoring com., 1995-97; mem. Internat. Commn. on Nonionizing Radiation Protection, 2004—; mem. Pres. Com. Nat. Medal of Sci., 1992-93; mem. Nat. Coun. Radiation Protection and Measurement, 1992—, chmn. radio frequency sci. com., 1995—, v.p. 2005-07; chmn. Internat. Union of Radio Scis. Commn., Electromagnetics in Biology and Medicine, 1996-99; chmn. Internat. Sci. Meeting on Electromagnetics in Medicine, 1997; chmn. Chinese Am. Academic and Profl. Convention, 1993; chmn. Internat. Conf. Wireless Mobile Communication and Healthcare, 2010; mem. citizens adv. coun. Hinsdale Ctrl. H.S., 1988-93 Author: Microwave Auditory Effects and Applications, 1978, Biological Effects and Health Implications of Radiofrequency Radiation, 1987, Electromagnetic Interaction with Biological Systems, 1989, Mobile Comm. Safety, 1996; editor: Advances in Electromagnetic Fields in Living Systems, 1994—, EMB Mag., 1997—99, Wireless Networks, 1996—97; editor in chief: Bioelectromagnetics, 2006 ; contbr. articles to profl. jours., columns to mags. Recipient Nat. Rsch. Svcs. award 1982, Disting. Svc. award, Outstanding Leadership award Chinese Am. Acad. and Profl. Assn. MidAm., 1989. Fellow AAAS, AIMBE, IEEE (tech. policy coun. 1990-91, chmn. com. on man and radiation, 1990-91, assoc. and guest editor transactions on biomed. engring., guest editor transaction on microwave theory and techniques, disting. lectr. engring. in medicine and biology 1991—, com. chair 2007-, Transaction Best Paper award 1975); mem. Biomed. Engring. Soc. (sr. mem.), Robotics Internat. (sr. mem.), Am. Soc. Engring. Edn., Bioelectromagnetics Soc. (charter, pres.-elect 1993-94, pres. 1994-95, chmn. ann. meeting 1994, d'Arsonval medal 2003), Marconi Found. (sci. com. 1996—), Golden Key, Sigma Xi, Phi Tau Phi (v.p.), Tau Beta Pi. Office: U Ill Coll Engring 1030 SEO MC/154 851 S Morgan St Chicago IL 60607-7042 Office Phone: 312-413-1052. Business E-Mail: lin@uic.edu.

LIN, JIN-DING, healthcare educator, consultant; b. Ping Dong County, Taiwan, June 7, 1964; s. Wu-Chiu Lin and S. I. Hwang; m. Chia-Ling Wu, Dec. 25, 1992; 1 child, Tzu-Kuan. BSc, Nat. Def. Med. Ctr., Taipei, Taiwan, 1988, MPH, 1990; PhD, Griffith U., Brisbane, Australia, 2000. Healthcare Executive Profession Taiwan Healthcare Exec. Coll., 2001. Dir. Health Sta., Marine Corps, Ping-Gong County, Taiwan, 1990—92; teching asst. Nat. Def. Med. Ctr., Taipei, 1992—94, lectr., 1994—96, asst. prof., 2000—02, assoc. prof., 2003—06, prof., 2007—09, dean, 2010—; IEHDAP rsch. fellow Griffith U., Brisbane, Australia, 1997—2000, adj. assoc. prof., 2005—, adj. prof., 2006—; disting. prof. gerontol. health Taiwan Gerontol. Health Soc., 2005—. Adv. bd. mem. Taipei City Govt. Med. Dispute Resolution, 2001—04, Chinese Consumer Found. - Health Com., Taipei, 2001—05, Taiwan Accreditation Com. on Disability Institutions, Taipei, 2003—; bd. dirs. Taiwan Assn. Health Promoting Hosps., 2007—; cons. in field; prof. dean SPH NDMC, 2010—. Author: Health Planning for the Disabled, 2004; editor-in-chief: Jour. Disability Rsch., 2003—, Taiwan Jour. Gerontol. Health, 2010. Recipient Outstanding Mil. Med. Pers., Ministry of Def., 1991, Disting. Alumnus award, Nat. Def. Med. Ctr., Taiwan, 2008, NDMC, Taipei, 2008; Dr. R.H. Liu Meml. scholar, Nat. Def. Med. Ctr., 2002, Nat. Def. Med. Ctr., Taiwan, 2003. Fellow: Chinese Assn. on Mentally Handicapped; mem.: Internat. Assn. Sci. Study on Intellectual Disability, Taiwan Healthcare Exec. Coll., Taiwan Pub. Health Assn. Buddhist. Achievements include Set up the first research center Research Center for Intellectual Disability Taiwan; research in field of disability to advocate the health rights of people with a disability; development of a 'Health Promoting Center for Persons with Disabilities Living in Institutions in Taiwan' to improve the quality of life for persons with disabilities. Avocations: swimming, jogging. Office: Nat Def Med Ctr 161 Min-Chun E Rd Sec 6 Taipei 114 Taiwan Home: 6F 235 Min-Chun St Sansia Dist New Taipei City Taiwan Office Fax: 886-2-87923147; Home Fax: 886-2-23648108. Business E-Mail: a530706@ndmctsgh.edu.tw.

LIN, JIUNN-LEE, cardiologist, researcher; b. Chi-San, Taiwan, Jan. 31, 1953; s. Chun-Huei Lin and Tsai-Mein Ong-Lin; m. Huei-Jen Tu-Lin, Dec. 6, 1981; children: Chia-Hsuan, Connie, Brian. MD, Nat. Taiwan U. Coll. of Medicine, 1979, PhD, 1991. Board of Internal Medicine Taiwan Soc. of Internal Medicine, 1986, Board of Adult Cardiologist Taiwan Soc. of Cardiology, 1985. Prof. medicine Nat. Taiwan U. Coll. of Medicine, 2001—; dir., cardiac electrophysiology and pacing svc. Nat. Taiwan U. Hosp., 1999—, vice chmn., dept. of internal medicine, 2004—. Exec. bd. mem. Taiwan Soc. of Cardiology, 2003—, Taiwan Soc. of Hypertension, 2005—. Author: (book) Radiofrequency Catheter Ablation of Cardiac Arrhythmia. Sponsor World Vision-Taiwan, 2000. Grant, Nat. Sci. Coun., Taiwan,

1992—95. Fellow: Am. Coll. of Cardiology; mem.: Taiwan Soc. of Hypertension (exec. bd. 2005—), Taiwan Soc. of Cardiology (exec. bd. 2003—). Office: Dept of Internal Medicine NTUH 7 Chun-Shan S Rd Taiwan Taipei 100 Taiwan Office Fax: 886-2-23951841. E-mail: jiunn@ha.mc.ntu.edu.tw.

LIN, JULIE, nephrologist, educator; b. Chiayi, Taiwan, June 8, 1970; MD, Columbia U., 1996; MPH, Harvard Sch. Pub. Health, 2003. Asst. prof. medicine Harvard Med. Sch., 2001. Fellow: Am. Soc. Nephrology; mem.: Internat. Soc. Nephrology (mem. young nephrologists com.). Avocations: violin, viola. Office: Brigham and Women's Hosp Renal Divsn Boston MA 02115 Business E-Mail: jlin11@partners.org.

LIN, KANT, plastic surgeon, educator; b. NYC, Feb. 9, 1959; s. Samuel Pao-Hsi and Joanna Tu Lin; children: Samantha, Michelle. BA, U. Pa., 1980; MD, Mt. Sinai Sch. Medicine, 1984. Diplomate Am. Bd. Plastic Surgery. Itern Hosp. U. Pa., 1984—85, resident, 1985—91; fellow Hosp. Sick Children U. Toronto, 1991—92; asst. prof. U. Va., Charlottesville, 1992—98, assoc. prof., 1998—2006, full prof., 2007—. Author, editor: Craniofacial Surgery: Science and Surgical Technique, 2001. Named one of Am.'s Top Physicians, Consumers Rsch. Coun. Am. Fellow: ACS, Am. Assn. Plastic Surgeons, Am. Soc. Plastic Surgeons; mem.: Alpha Omega Alpha, Phi Beta Kappa. Office: Univ VA Box 800376 Charlottesville VA 22908 Home: 1105 Hilltop Rd Charlottesville VA 22903 Business E-Mail: kyl5s@virginia.edu. *

LIN, KAO-CHANG, neurologist; b. Kaohsiung, Taiwan, Sept. 5, 1959; s. Yan-Kuo Lin and Yue-shong Shiu; m. Kao-Chang Lu, Sept. 19, 1999. MPH, Cheng-Kung U. Coll., Tainan, 2003. Lic. Taiwan Neurology Bd., 1991. Attending physician, neurologist Chi-mei Med. Ctr., Tainan, Taiwan, 1991—2005. Chief dir. Environ. Protection Allied, Tainan, 1997—2005. Mem.: Taiwan Headache Soc. (bd. dirs.), AAN (assoc.). Office: Chi-Mei Med Ctr Jon-Hwa Rd Tainan 886 Taiwan Office Fax: 886-6-2828928. Business E-Mail: gaujang@mail2000.com.tw.

LIN, LI-CHING, oncologist; b. Kaohsiung, Taiwan, Jan. 9, 1962; s. Chi-An Lin and Li-Hsuang Su; m. Yi-Mei Wu; children: Yu-Hsuan, Yu-Fan. MD, Chung Shan Med. U., Taichung, 1988. Cert. Taiwan Soc. Therapeutic Radiation Oncology, 1994. Resident physician Vet. Gen. Hosp., Taipei, Taiwan, 1990—94, Kaohsiung, 1990—94, attending physician, 1994—96, Chimei Found. Med. Ctr., Tainan, Taiwan, 1996—2000, chief, 2008—. Contbr. articles to profl. jours. Business E-Mail: 8508a6@mail.chimei.org.tw.

LIN, LI-JEN, physician; b. Kaohsiung City, Aug. 31, 1960; MB, Nat. Yang-Ming U., 1987, MPH, 1996. Dir. Health Bur. Kaohsiung County, 1998—2003; chief family medicine divsn. E-Da Hosp., 2005—07; dir. fifth br. dept. health Ctrs. Disease Control, Taiwan, 2007—. Recipient Best Civil Servant, Exec. Yuan, Taiwan, 2001. Office: 180 Tz-You 2nd Rd Kaohsiung City 81358 Taiwan Office Fax: 886-7-5563717. Business E-Mail: gp.lin@cdc.gov.tw.

LIN, MAO-TSUN, physiologist, educator; b. Taipei, China, July 1, 1942; m. Hai-Chuan Chou, Dec. 1, 1968; 3 children. DDS, Nat. Def. Med. Ctr., 1968; PhD, Yale U., 1977. Prof. Nat. Def. Med. Ctr., 1981-86, Nat. Cheng-Kung U., Tainan, Taiwan, 1986-96, Nat. Yang-Ming U., Taipei, 1996—2002; chair prof. dept. med. rsch. Chi-Mei Med. Ctr. U Tainan, Yung Kang, Taiwan, 2000—; chair prof. Taipei Med. U., China, 2009—, Southern Tainan U., 2009—. NIH fellow, 1973-76, Alexander von Humboldt Found. fellow, 1980. Fellow Internat. Coll. Dentists; mem. Chinese Physiol. Soc. (pres. 1990-93), Chinese Neurosci. Soc. (pres. 1993-97), Internat. Soc. Cerebral Blood Flow & Metabolism. Office: Chi Mei Med Ctr Dept Med Rsch Yung Kang U Tainan 910 Taiwan China Office Phone: 886 6 2812811 ext. 52657. Business E-Mail: mtlin@ym.edu.tw, 891201@mail.chimei.org.tw.

LIN, MARIE MA-LI, molecular anthropologist, pathologist, educator, immunohematologist; b. I-Lan, Taiwan, May 30, 1938; d. Sing-Chen Lin and Makino Yoshitake; children: Thomas Wei-Tao Chu, Steven Wei-Song Chu; m. Theodore Kay. MD, Kaohsiung Med. Coll., Taiwan, 1964; MS, Nat. Taiwan U., Taipel, 1967; Dr of Taiwan Culture honoris causa, Taiwan Cultural Coll., 2001. Resident pathology Nat. Taiwan U. Hosp., Taipei, 1964-69, instr. pathology, 1969-76, assoc. prof. pathology, 1976-78; resident pathology Med. Branch U. Tex., Galveston, 1972-73, 78-81; dir. med. lab. Mackay Meml. Hosp., Taipei, 1981-98, dir. Immunohematology Reference Lab. and Transfusion Med. Lab, 1992—2005, dir. Transfusion Med. Lab, Molecular Anthropology Lab., 2005—10; cons. Transfusion Med. Lab. Molecular Anthropology Lab, 2010—. Prof. Taipei Med. U., 1987-, Nat. Taiwan U. Hosp., 2004-, Kaohsiung Med. Coll., 1988-2000, Nat. Taiwan U. Med. Coll., 2005-; pres. Taiwan Soc. Blood Transfusion, Taipei, 1990-96; mem. blood transfusion adv. com. Dept. Health, Taipei, 1988-2007. Author: Procedure Manual for Blood Banks, 1983, Transfusion Medicine, 1990, 3d edit, 2005, Cosmos in the Wind, 2005, We Are Having The Different Blood, 2010; contbr. articles to profl. jours. Artist Greenfield Art Assn., Taipei, 1964-78, Homerun Art Assn., Taipei, 1990—2000. Recipient Su-Wei award Ministry Edn., Taipei, 1980, Wang Ming-Ning Found. award, 1992, Helena Rubinstein award for women of sci. nominee, 1998, Outstanding Alumni award Kaohsiung Med. U., 2010; grantee Nat. Sci. Coun. and Dept. Health, 1984—. Fellow Coll. Am. Pathologists (diplomate); mem. Internat. Soc. Blood Transfusion (councilor London 1992-96, pres. 10th regional congress western pacific region, 1999, hon. pres. 22nd regional congress western pacific region, 2011). Avocations: painting, writing, music. Office: Mackay Meml Hosp 92 Sec 2 Chung-San N Rd Taipei Taiwan Office Phone: 886-228094661-2380.

LIN, MING-JEN, economics professor; b. Tainan, Taiwan, Aug. 7, 1970; PhD, U. Chgo., 2002. Prof. Nat. Taiwan U., 2010—. Recipient Wu Da-You Meml. award, Nat. Sci. Coun., Taiwan, Jr. Rsch. Investigation award, Acad. Sinica, Taiwan. Achievements include research in Hepatitis B and sex ratio of offspring, fetal origin hypothesis, low birth weight and future developmental outcome. Office: 21 Hsu-Chow Rd Taipei 100 Taiwan Business E-Mail: mjlin@ntu.edu.tw.

LIN, SHIE-JEA, food scientist; b. Taipei, July 23, 1960; M, Tokyo U., 1991, PhD, 1996. Rsch. scientist Food Industry R & D Inst., 1997—. Dir. En Qing Found. Anti-Cancer, 2010—. Mem.: Taiwan Assn. Food Sci. and Tech. Home: Ming Hu Rd 648 Ln 121 Hsinchu 30062 Taiwan Home Fax: 886-3-5290886. Business E-Mail: lsj@firdi.org.tw.

LIN, SHIH-HUA, medical researcher; b. Taipei, Taiwan, Nov. 16, 1963; s. Tsan-Tan and Lee-Shih Lin; m. Yi-Chien Tan; children: Alan, Tina, Willian, Eric. MD, Nat. Def. Med. Ctr., Taipei, 1988. Lic. physician Ministry of Edn., Taiwain, 1988. Lectr. Tri-Svc. Gen. Hosp., Nat. Def. Med. Ctr., Taipei, 1995—2000, assoc. prof., 2000—03, prof., 2004—; rsch. fellow St. Michael's Hosp., U. Toronto, Ont., Canada, 1996—97. Assoc. editor Nat. Def. Med. Ctr., Taipei, 2001—. Contbr. articles to profl. jours. Recipient 2d class honor award, Nat. Def. Med. Ctr., 1988, Best Tchr. award, Tri-Svc. Gen. Hosp., Taipei, 1994—96, Young Investigator award, Tri-Svc. Gen. Hosp., 1996, 1998, Rsch. award, 1997—99, Soc. of Nephrology, 1996, 1998, 2000, 2002, Travel award, NDI Found., 2000. Mem.: European Renal Assn., Internat. Soc. for Renal Nutrition and Metabolism (corr.; USA 1995), Internat. Soc. of Nephrology (corr.; USA 1994—98), European Dialysis Transplant Assn. (corr.; Europe 1996), Am. Soc. of Artificial Internal Organs (ASAIO) (corr.; USA 1994—2001, Lippinott Reaven award 1996, Willem J Kolff Young Investigator award and Lippincott-Reaven award 1996), Am. Soc. of Nephrology (corr.; USA 1994). Achievements include first to identify the thiazide-sensitive sodium chloride mutations in Taiwan and design the rapid clincal diagnosis and treament in patients with hypokalemic periodic paralysis. Avocations: ping pong/table tennis, golf, Japanese culture, travel. Office: Tri-Service Gen Hosp NO 325 Sect 2 Cheng-Kung Rd Neihu Taipei 114 Taiwan Office Fax: 886-2-87927134. E-mail: l521116@ndmctsgh.edu.tw, shihhualin@yahoo.com.

LIN, SHIU RU, medical association administrator, researcher; PhD, Kaohsiung Med. U., Taiwan, 1992. Cert. med. technologist Exam. Yuan Taiwan, 1985. Dir. Medico-Genomics Rsch. Ctr., 2000—06; dir., Biomed. Innovation Incubation Ctr. Kaohsiung Med. U., Taiwan, 2006—08, chief R & D, 2008; dir. Biomed. Tech. Devel. Ctr., 2008—09; v.p. academic rsch. Fooyin U., Kaohsiung, 2008—09; dir., divsn. med. rsch. Fooyin U. Hosp., 2008—. Recipient Rsch. award, 1995, 1997, 1999—2000, Tech. Transfer award, Nat. Sci. Coun., Taiwan, 2003, Merck, Sharpe & Dome award for Best Rsch., 1999, Outstanding Faculty award in Med. Rsch., 2002, 2004—06, Excellent Achievement in Tech. Transfer, Kaohsiung Med. U., Taiwan, 2004—06. Achievements include patents pending for automatic system of isolating and incubating circulating tumor cells; automatic gene chip array diagnosing apparatus; patents for method for biochip detecting limited cells; genes for diagnosing colorectal cancer. Office: Fooyin Univ 151 Jinsyue Rd Daliao Dist Kaohsiung City 831 Taiwan Office Fax: 886-8-8339046. Business E-Mail: srlin@ms2.hinet.net.

LIN, SYH-JAE, pediatrician, educator; b. Taipei, Taiwan, Mar. 31, 1964; s. Der-Tsong Lin and Rei-Hwa Tseng; m. Yu-Che Pong, Feb. 25, 1967; children: Hsing-Yi, Jia-Wei, Cheng-Ray. MD, Nat. Taiwan U., Taipei, 1988. Resident dept. pediat. Nat. Taiwan U. Hosp., Taipei, 1991—94; attending pediatrician Chang Gung Children's Hosp., Kweishan, Taoyuan, Taiwan, 1994—; assoc. prof. Chang Gung U., Kweishan, 2004—. Chief divsn. pediatric allergy, asthma and rheumatology Chang Gung Children's Hosp., Kweishan, 1998—; post doctoral fellow in allergy/immunology Nat. Taiwan U. Hosp., 1994; post doctoral fellow dept. pediat. UCLA Med. Ctr., 1996. Recipient Schering-Plough Academic award, Taiwan Soc. Pediat. Allergy, Asthma and Immunology, 2000, 2005, Mead Johnson Academic award, 2005, Nestle Academic award, Taiwan Pediat. Assoc., 2001. Office: Chang Gung Children's Hosp 5 Fu Hsing St Kweishan Taoyuan 333 Taiwan Office Phone: 886-3-3281200 x8969. Office Fax: 886-3-3288957. Business E-Mail: sjlino@adm.cgmh.org.tw.

LIN, VIVIAN KWANG-WEN, healthcare educator; b. Taipei, Taiwan, China, Sept. 22, 1955; d. Andrew Wen-chan and Helen Tai Lin; m. G. David Wilmoth, Sept. 14, 1979; children: Maya Gui, Sasha Lin-jia Wilmoth, Kina Xin Lin-Wilmoth. BA, Yale U., 1977; MPH, U. Calif., Berkeley, 1979; DPH, U. Calif., 1985. Dir. New South Wales Health Dept., Sydney, Australia, 1984—90, Worksafe Australia, Sydney, 1987—88, Health Dept. Victoria (and successors), Melbourne, Australia, 1990—97; exec. officer Nat. Pub. Health Partnership, Melbourne, 1997—2000; prof. pub. health, head of sch. La Trobe U., Bundoora, Australia, 2000—. Cons. WHO, Manila, 1988—, World Bank, Wash., DC, 1994—, AusAID, Canberra, Australia, 1999—, Dept. Internat. Devel., London, 1999—; bd. mem. Chinese Health Found. Australia, Melbourne, 1994—2010, Dairy Food Safety Victoria, Melbourne, 2000—03, Working Women's Health, Melbourne, 2001—03, Coop. Rsch. Ctr. Aboriginal Health, Darwin, Australia, 2003—10; temp. advisor Kobe Ctr. WHO, Japan, 2000—08; pres. Chinese Medicine Registration Bd., Melbourne, 2000—09; pub. health com. Australian Med. Assn., Canberra, 2003—06; chair Australian Network Academic Pub. Health Instns., 2006—08; bd. dirs. Australia-China Coun., 2006—; assoc. editor Internat. Jour. Pub. Health, 2010—; mentor World Econ. Forum, Global Agenda Coun. Health Care, 2011—. Rev. editor: Australia New Zealand Jour. Pub. Health, 2001—08; adv. editor Health Policy, Social Sci. and Medicine, 2006—, mem. editl. bd. Australia New Zealand Health Policy, 2004—, Health Edn. Rsch., 2006—. Recipient Traveling fellowship, U. Calif. Alumni Ho., 1982, Women's Studies fellowship, Woodrow Wilson Found., 1985. Mem.: APHA (Drotman award 1982), Asian Studies Assn. of Australia, AcademyHealth, Inst. of Pub. Adminstrn. Australia, Internat. Union Health Promotion and Edn. (v.p. sci. affairs 2007—), Health Svc. Rsch. Assn. of Australia and New Zealand (chair, third conf. 2002—03), Pub. Health Assn. Australia (policy convenor 1995—99). Office: La Trobe Univ Sch of Public Health 3086 Bundoora Australia Office Fax: 61394791783. Business E-Mail: v.lin@latrobe.edu.au.

LIN, WAN-YU, physician, researcher; b. Hsinchu, Taiwan, May 22, 1962; s. Hsang-Win Lin, Lan-Mei Win; married. MD, Chinese Med. Coll., Taichung, Taiwan, 1988. Resident physician Taichung (Taiwan) Vets. Gen. Hosp., 1990—95, attending physician, 1995—2004, dir. dept. nuc. medicine, 2004—. Contbr. articles to profl. jours. Lt. Taiwan's Navy, 1988—90. Recipient Important Contbn. to Rsch. award, Kaohsiung Jour. Med. Scis., 1994, Rsch. award, Nat. Sci. Coun., 1994, 1995, 1996, 1997, 1998, Vets. Gen. Hosp., Taiwan, 1998, 2000—03, 2006. Mem.: European Assn. Nuc. Medicine, Soc. Nuc. Medicine. Achievements include invention of method for preparation of Re-188 microsphere; method for preparation of Re-188 sulfur colloid. Office: Taichung Vets Gen Hosp 160 Sec 3 Taichung Harbor Rd Taichung 407 Taiwan Office Phone: 886 423741349. Office Fax: 886 423741348. Personal E-mail: wy6172@pchrome.com.tw. Business E-Mail: wylin@vghtc.gov.tw.

LIN, WEI-HSIANG, cardiologist; s. Chung-Cheng Lin and Tuan Wang; m. Mei-Shia Chen, Sept. 17, 1996; children: Yu-Tao, Yu-Pu. MD, Nat. Def. Med. Ctr., 1992. Diplomate Dept. Health, Taiwan, 1992. Attending physician Tri-Svc. Gen. Hosp., Taipei, Taiwan, 1999—, directorship clin. electrophysiology, 2005—; postdoc. rschr. rheumatology UCLA, 2004—05; lt. col Taiwan Army, 2000—. Contbr. articles to profl. jours. Mem.: Heart Rhythm Soc. Achievements include research in pulmonary vein morphology, non-pulmonary vein catheter ablation. Office: Tri-Svc Gen Hosp No 325 Sec 2 Cheng-Kung Rd Taipei 114 Taiwan Office Fax: 886-2-66012656. E-mail: wslin545@ms27.hinet.net.

LIN, XIAOXI, physician, surgeon, educator; b. Fuzhou, Fujian Province, China, Nov. 4, 1969; s. Qiqiu Lin and Renchen He; m. Jie Zhang; 1 child, Yuanshan. MD, Shanghai Med. U. (now Fudan U. Med. Sch.), 1992; PhD, Shanghai Second Med. U. (now Shanghai Jiaotong U. Med. Sch.), 1997. Cert. mentor PhD candidates Shanghai Second Med. U., 2003. Resident Dept. Plastic Surgery Shanghai 9th People's Hosp., Shanghai Jiaotong U. Sch. Medicine, 1992—97, asst. prof. plastic surgery Dept. Plastic Surgery, 1997—99, assoc. prof. plastic surgery Dept. Plastic Surgery, 1999—2003, prof. plastic surgery Dept. Plastic Surgery, 2003—. Editor: Chinese Jour. Plastic Surgery, 2000—, Chinese Jour. Practical Aesthetic and Plastic Surgery, 2001—, Jour. Tissue Engring. and Reconstructive Surgery, 2004—, Chinese Jour. Med. Aesthetics and Cosmetology, 2006—; corr. editor: Chinese Jour. Surgery, 2001—. Recipient Clin. Achievements award, Shanghai Second Med. U., 2003, Chinese Med. Sci. and Tech. award, 2004, Shanghai Sci. and Technol. Advancement award, 2004, Shanghai Med. Sci. and Tech. award, 2004, Chinese Med. Sci. and Tech. award, Chinese Med. Assn., 2004, Shanghai Sci. and Tech. Advancement award, Shanghai Mcpl. Sci. and Tech. Commn., 2004, Shanghai Med. Sci. and Tech. award, Shanghai Med. Assn., 2004; grantee, Shanghai Sci. and Technol. Coun., 1998, 2002, 2004, Shanghai Govt., 2002, Shanghai San. Bur. Found., 2002, Chinese Nat. Sci. Found. Coun., 2004. Mem.: Soc. Aesthetic Medicine (vice-chmn. 2001—), Chinese Assn. Reconstructive Surgery (com. mem. 2001—), Chinese Assn. Aesthetic Surgery, Chinese Soc. Popular Sci. (com. mem. 1998—), Chinese Soc. Maxillofacial Surgery (com. mem. vascular anomalies 2003—). Achievements include research in Qiming Star project; post Qiming Star project; New Star project; cosmetic and sequential plastic procedures for hemangioma and vascular malformation; proliferative mechanism of hemangioma and vascular malformation and its clinical application; cosmetic and plastic surgery in Asians; Shuguang scholar project. Office: Shanghai Jiaotong U Sch Medicine Shanghai 9th People's Hosp 639 Zhizaoju Rd Shanghai 200011 China Personal E-mail: linxiaoxi@126.com, linxiaoxi@yahoo.com.

LIN, XIUKUN, medical educator; b. China, Nov. 2, 1957; PhD, Peking Union Med. Coll., China, 1996. Prof. Inst. Oceanology, Chinese Acad. Scis., 2003—. Mem.: Assn. Anticancer Agents China. Office: 7 Nanhai Rd Qingdao Shandong 266071 China E-mail: linxiukun@yahoo.com.

LIN, YUH LING, medical researcher, educator; b. Taichung, Taiwan, Mar. 8, 1960; d. Yao Qing Lin and Luan Yu LinYe; children: Li Qi Wang, Yue Xun Wang, Yao Ting Wang. PhD, Nat. Tsing-Hua U., Hsin-Chu, 1993. Investigater Ever-Life Pharm. Factory, Taipei, 1993—94; asst. investigator Acad. Sinica, Taipei, Taiwan, 1986—88; postdoctoral rschr. Chang-Gung U., Tao-Yuan, Taiwan, 1994—97; asst. prof. Taipei Med. U., 1997—2001, assoc. prof., 2001—02, Fu-Jen Cath. U., Taipei, 2003—07, vice dir. med. dept., 2004—, prof., 2007—. Cons. Microbio Biotech. Co., Taipei, Taiwan, 2000—08. Taoism. Avocations: reading, travel, music. Office: Fu-Jen Univ Dept Medicine 510 Chung-Cheng Rd Taipei-Hsien Hsinchu 24205 Taiwan Office Phone: 886-2-29053463. Office Fax: 886-2-29052096. Business E-Mail: med0018@mail.fju.edu.tw.

LINCHAK, RUSLAN, cardiologist; b. Russia, Nov. 7, 1972; MD, Mil. Med. Acad., 1997. Head, dept. cardiology Pirogov Med. Surg. Ctr., 2007—. Sr. lectr., dept. internal medicine Inst. Physician, 2005. Mem.: Europian Soc. Cardiology. Avocation: football. Office: N Pervomajskaja 70 Moscow 105203 Russia Office Fax: 7 (499) 461-20-55. E-mail: ruslanlinchak@mail.ru.

LIN-CHAO, SUE DUAN, molecular microbiologist, educator, researcher; b. Taichung, Taiwan, Sept. 20, 1955; d. Gung Shin and Jow (Wu) L.; m. Ching Kuey Chao, Sept. 20, 1981. BS, Nat. Changhua U. Edn., Taiwan, 1977; MS, U. Tex., Dallas, 1984, PhD, 1987. Tchr. DarAn Jr. HS, Taichung, 1978—79, Wutsi Jr. HS, Taichung, 1979—82; postdoctoral fellow dept. genetics Stanford U. Sch. Medicine, Calif., 1987—90; assoc. rsch. fellow Academia Sinica Inst. Molecular Biology, Taipei, Taiwan, 1990—97, rsch. fellow, 1997—2008, Distinguished, 2008—. Assoc. dir. Inst. Molecular Biology, 2004-2006; dir., Internat. Affairs Office, Akademic Sinica, adj. assoc. prof. to prof. Inst. Biochemistry Nat. Yang-Ming U., Taipei, 1991—, Nat. Def. Med. Ctr., 1992—, Taipei, Inst. Molecular Medicine Nat. Taiwan U., Taipei, 1993—, Grad. Inst. Med. Scis. Taipei Med. U., 1999-; vice-chair Taiwan Internat. Grad. Prog., Academia Sinica, 2005—, dir. Internat. Affairs Office Academia Sinica, 2007-. Contbr. articles to profl. jours. Recipient Excellent Rsch. award Nat. Sci. Coun., Taiwan, 1993, Ann. Republic of China Ten Outstanding Young Persons award Republic of China Jr. Chamber Internat., 1995, Outstanding Rsch. award Nat. Sci. Coun., 1996, 98, 2000, 02, 03. Mem. Soc. Chinese Bioscientists Am. (life), Am. Soc. Microbiol., Am. Soc. Biochemistry and Molecular Biology, Asia-Pacific Internat. Molecular Biology Network, Sigma Xi Avocations: aerobic dancing, classical music, hiking. Office: Inst Molecular Biology Academia Sinica Nankang Taipei 11529 Taiwan Business E-Mail: mbsue@gate.sinica.edu.tw.

LINCOLN, THOMAS L., pathologist, educator; b. Pitts., Jan. 4, 1929; s. John J. and Jean Gregg Lincoln; m. Nancy, Apr. 15, 1956 (dec. Feb. 1971); children: Elizabeth, John; m. Catherine Delaprée., May 30, 1972; 1 child, Iris. BS, Yale U., 1955, MD, 1960. Diplomate Nat. Bd. Med. Examiners, Am. Bd. Anat. Pathology. Intern in pathology Yale U., New Haven, 1960-61, resident, 1961-63; asst. prof. Inst. for Fluid Dynamics and Applied Math., U. Md., 1963-66; assoc. clin. prof., dept. pathology U. So. Calif. Cancer Ctr., LA,

1975-77, assoc. prof., 1977-87, prof. rsch. pathology, 1987-96; prof. emeritus U. So. Calif.; sr. scientist Sunquest Info. Sys., Tucson, 1995-96, Rand Corp., Santa Monica, Calif., 1967—2010; prof. Coll. Health and Human Devel. Scis., U. Ill., Chgo., 1997—2000, cons., 1985—2009. Vis. prof. dept. clin. epidemiology and social medicine, St. Thomas's Hosp. Med. Sch., London, 1972; cons., rschr. in field. Contbr. articles to profl. jours. Fellow Pathology, Johns Hopkins, 1963—65. Mem. AMA, IEEE, Johns Hopkins Med. Soc., Leukemia Soc. Am. (patient advisor, L.A., 1970-82), Cosmos Club (Washington), Coll. Am. Pathologists, Am. Informatics Asn., Am. Coll. Med. Informatics, others. Episcopalian. Avocations: history, politics, calendar algorithms, computers, psychology. Home: 802 Franklin St Santa Monica CA 90403-2318 Office: Rand Corp 1776 Main St Santa Monica CA 90401-3297

LIND, LAWRENCE R. (L. LIND), obstetrician, gynecologist, urologist; Grad., Cornell U., 1990. Diplomate Am. Bd. Ob-Gyn. Resident North Shore Univ. Hosp., 1991—94, physician; fellow gynecologic urology Univ. of Calif. LA Med. Ctr., 1994—96; with St. Mary's Hosp. Children. Office: North Shore University Hospital Ste 202 865 Northern Blvd Great Neck NY 11021 Office Phone: 516-622-5114. Office Fax: 516-622-5045.

LINDBERG, DONALD ALLAN BROR, federal agency administrator, library director, pathologist; b. NYC, Sept. 21, 1933; s. Harry B. and Frances Seeley (Little) Lindberg; m. Mary Musick, June 8, 1975; children: Donald Allan Bror, Christopher Charles Seeley, Jonathan Edward Moyer. AB, Amherst Coll., Mass., 1954, ScD (hon.), 1979; MD, Columbia U. Coll. Physicians & Surgeons, NYC, 1958; ScD (hon.), SUNY, 1987, U. Health Sci. Med. Informatics & Tech., Austria, 2004; LLD (hon.), U. Mo., Columbia, 1990. Diplomate Am. Bd. Pathology, Am. Bd. Med. Examiners. Rsch. asst. Amherst Coll., 1954-55; intern pathology Columbia-Presbyn. Med. Ctr., 1958-59, asst. resident pathology, 1959-60, Columbia U. Coll. Physicians & Surgeons, 1958-60; dir. Diagnostic Microbiology Lab., U. Mo. Sch. Medicine, 1960-63, instr. pathology, 1962-63, asst. prof., 1963-66, assoc. prof., 1966-69, prof., 1969-84, dir. med. ctr. computer program, 1962-70, exec. dir. health affairs, 1968-70, prof., chmn. dept. info. sci., 1969-71; dir. Nat. Libr. Medicine NIH, Bethesda, Md., 1984—. Adj. prof. pathology U. Md. Sch. Medicine, 1988—; clin. prof. pathology U. Va., 1992—; mem. exec. bd. Am. Bd. Med. Examiners, 1987—91; dir. Nat. HPCC Coord. Office (High Performance Computing & Comm.), 1992—95; bd. dirs. Am. Med. Info. Assn., 1992—, Health on the Net Found., Gorgas Meml. Inst. Tropical & Preventive Medicine. Author: The Computer and Medical Care, 1968, Computers in Life Science Research, 1975, The Growth of Medical Information Systems in the United States, 1979; editor: Methods of Info. in Medicine, 1970—83, Computer Applications in Medical Care, 1982; mem. editl bd. for various med. pubs.; contbr. articles to profl. jours. Recipient Walter C. Alvarez award, Am. Med. Writers Assn., 1989, Surgeon Gen.'s Medallion, USPHS, 1989, Nathan Davis award, AMA, 1989, Outstanding Svc. Medal, Uniformed Svcs. U. Health Scis., 1992, Computers in Healthcare Pioneer award, 1995, Silver award, US Nat. Commn. Libraries & Info. Sci., 1996, Pres.'s award, Med. Libr. Assn., 1997, Morris F. Collen, M.D. award of excellence, Am. Coll. Med. Informatics, 1997, Ranice W. Crosby Disting. Achievement award, Johns Hopkins U. Sch. Medicine, 1998, Lila A. Wallis Women's Health award, Am. Med. Women's Assn., 2005, US Medicine Frank Brown Berry Prize, 2005, Meritorious Svc. award, HHS, Presdl. Sr. Exec. Rank award; Simpson Fellow, Amherst Coll., 1954—55, Markle Scholar in academic medicine, 1964—69. Fellow: AAAS, NY Acad. Medicine (Info. Frontier award 1999), Am. Acad. Arts & Scis.; mem.: Am. Med. Informatics Assn. (pres. 1988—91), Am. Assn. Med. Systems & Informatics (bd. dirs. 1982, internat. com. 1982—89), Assn. Computing Machines, Mo. Med. Assn., Coll. Am. Pathologists, Cosmos Club, Sigma Xi. Democrat. Avocations: photography, riding. Office: National Library of Medicine Bldg 38 Rm 2E 17B 8600 Rockville Pike Bethesda MD 20894-0002 Office Phone: 301-496-6221. Office Fax: 301-496-4450. Business E-Mail: donald.lindberg@nih.gov. *

LINDE, LUCILLE MAE (LUCILLE JACOBSON), motor-perceptual specialist; b. Greeley, Colo., May 5, 1919; d. John Alfred and Anna Julia (Anderson) Jacobson; m. Ernest Emil Linde, July 5, 1946 (dec. Jan. 27, 1959). BA, Colo. State Coll. of Edn., 1941, MA, 1947; EdD, U. No. Colo., 1974. Cert. tchr. Calif., Colo., Iowa, N.Y.; cert. ednl. psychologist; guidance counselor. Dean of women, dir. residence C.W. Post Coll. of L.I. Univ., 1965-66; asst. dean of students SUNY, Farmingdale, 1966-67; counselor, tchr. West High Sch., Davenport, Iowa, 1967-68; instr. grad. tchrs. and counselors, univ. counselor, researcher No. Ariz. U., Flagstaff, 1968-69; vocat. edn. and counseling coord. Fed. Exemplary Project, Council Bluffs, Iowa, 1970-71; sch. psychologist, counselor Oakdale Sch. Dist., Calif., 1971-73; sch. psychologist, intern Learning and Counseling Ctr., Stockton, Calif., 1972-74; pvt. practice rsch. in motor-perceptual tng. Greeley, 1975—. Rschr. ocumeter survey Lincoln Unified Sch. Dist., Stockton, 1980, 81, 82, Manteca (Calif.) H.S., 1981; spkr. Social Sci. Edn. Consortium, U. Colo., Boulder, 1993; mem. Monday Morning steering com. House Spkr. Newt Gingrich, 1997-98; mem. Attention Disorder Advocacy Group, 1997-2001; mem. Ltd. Rep. Nat. Com., 2011; instr. seminars for ADD and ADHD, alleviating lag/dysfunction in neural system noted, 1997-98, 1998-99, presenter seminars in field. Author: Psychological Services and Motor Perceptual Training, 1974, Guidebook for Psychological Services and Motor Perceptual Training (How One May Improve in Ten Easy Lessons!), 1992, Manual for the Lucille Linde Ocumeter: Ocular Pursuit Measuring Instrument, 1992, Motor-Perceptual Training and Visual Perceptual Research (How Students Improved in Seven Lessons!), 1992, Effects of Motor Perceptual Training on Academic Achievement and Ocular Pursuit Ability, 1992, Teaching University of Northern Colorado Laboratory Students and Greeley District 6 Students Motor-Perceptual Training Seminar, 2001; inventor ocumeter, instrument for measuring ocular tracking ability, 1989, ocutarget for use, 1991, cure for oculomotor dysfunction noted; patentee in field. Mem. Rep. Presdl. Task Force, 1989-96, trustee, 1991-92, charter mem., 1994—, life mem., 1994-95; mem. Rep. Nat. Com., 1990, 93-2008, Rep. Nat. Com. on Am. Agenda, 1993, Nat. Rep. Congl. Com., 1990, 92, 93, 95-2008, Nat. Fedn. Rep. Women, Greeley Rep. Women, 1996-2008; advisor Senator Bob Dole for Pres.; charter mem. Rep. Newt Gingrich's Speaker's Task Force, Senator Phil Gramm's Presdl. Steering Com.; at-large del. Rep. Platform Planning Com.; team leader Nat. Rep. Rapid Response Network, Campaign America, 1996; active Heritage Found. (certificate as honored mem. leadership adv. bd., 1998-2000), Christian Bus. Men's Assn., Friends U. N.C. Librs., Citizens Against Govt. Waste, 1996-2008, Concerns of Police Survivors, 1996-98, Nat. Assn. of Police Orgn., elected to Libr. of Congress Nat. membership, 1997-2001; mem. WW II Vets. Com., 2000-03, Rep. Gov.'s Assn., 2001; mem. Rep. Gov.'s Policy Commn. Recipient Presdl. medal of merit and lapel insignia, 1990, Nat. Rep. Senatorial Com., 1991-2008, cert. of appreciation Nat. Rep. Congl. Com., 1992, 95, lapel pin Rep. Senatorial Inner Circle, 1990-96, Rep. Presdl. commemorative honor roll, 1993, Rep. Senatorial Freedom medal, 1994, Rep. Legion of Merit award, 1994, 96, Rep. Congl. Order of Freedom award, 1995, Senatorial Inner Cir. Lapel Pin, 1998, Lapel Pin award RNC, 1996, Leadership citation Rep. Senatorial Inner Cir./ Rep. Nat. Conv., 1996, Legion of Merit Rep. Presdl. exec. com., 1996, Honor cert. House Spkr. Newt Gingrich, 1996, Rep. Presdl. Legion of Merit medallion and matching lapel pin, 1994, Order of Merit, 1996, Conservative Leadership award Young Am.'s Found., 1999, Nat. Rep. Congl. Com. Rep. of the Yr. from Colo. award, 2000, Majority Leader's Commn. Cert., 2001, 2001 Conservative Patriot award The Pres., Ron Robinson and Bd. of Dirs. of The Young America's Found., Congl. Order Merit, Nat. Rep. Congressman Senancintheny, 2006; named to Rep. Nat. Hall of Honor, 1992. Mem. AAUP, NAFE, Nat. Assn. Sch. Psychologists and Psychometrists (spkr. conf. 1976), Rep. Senatorial Inner Cir. (name engraved on Ronald Wilson Reagan Eternal Flame of Freedom, 1995, on the Nat. Rep. Victory Monument, Washington, 1996, Rep. Sen. Inner Cir. (Conv. Medallion 1996, RNC Mems. Only pin 1996), 20th Century Rep. Leader, Rep. Sen. Inner Cir., 1998, The Smithsonian Assocs., Ronald Reagan Presdl. Libr. and Mus., Bush Presdl. Libr. and Mus., Nat. Trust for Hist. Preservation, Physicians Adv. Bd. to Pres. Bush (Pioneer Healthcare award, 2004), Internat. Platform Assn. (sec. gen. United Cultural Convention, 2007—), Independence Inst., Assn. Children Learning Disabilities (spkr. internat. conv. 1976), Libr. of Congress Assn., 1999, Children and Adults with Attention Deficit Disorder, Learning Disabilities Assn. Colo., Order of Merit (life), Nat. Fragile X Found., Fraxa Rsch. Found., Pi Omega Pi, Pi Lambda Theta. Avocations: music, architecture. Home: 1954 18th Ave Greeley CO 80631-5208 Office Phone: 970-353-0592. Personal E-mail: dlcinclmlinde@cs.com.

LINDEMANN, MONIKA, lab administrator; b. Aachen, NRW, Germany, Dec. 16, 1967; d. Hermann-Josef and Lucie Lindemann. MD in Immunogenetics Lab Work, U. Hosp., Essen, Germany, 1992. Specialist in lab. medicine Ärztekammer Nordrhein, 2001, specialist in tng. qualification lab. medicine 2004, cert. venia legendi in immunology U. Duisburg-Essen Med. Sch., 2006, specialist in immunogenetics & immunology, Fachimmunologin DGI German Soc. Immunogenetics, 2007, specialist in immungenetics, Fachimmungenetikerin DGI German Soc. Immunology, 2007. AiP internal medicine, dept. endocrinology and nephrology U. Hosp., 1994—95, lab. supr., Inst. Immunology, 1996—2007, lab. supr., Inst. Transfusion Medicine, Transplantation Diagnostics and R&D, 2008—. Chmn. confs. German Soc. Immunogenetics, Munich, Essen, 2007—08. Contbr. scientific papers, to poster presentation (Poster award, 2007). Recipient H. Behçet award, 1997; grantee, DFG, 2004—. Mem.: German Soc. Immunology, German Working Group Bone Marrow and Peripheral Blood Stem Cell Transplantation, German Soc. Immunogenetics (mem. tng. com. 2005, chmn. tng. com. 2006, exec. bd. sec. 2009). Office: University Hosp Essen Virchowstraße 179 Robert-Koch-Haus Essen 45147 Germany Business E-Mail: monika.lindemann@uk-essen.de.

LINDEN, R. MICHAEL, medical educator; b. Zurich, Switzerland, Dec. 19, 1958; PhD, U. Zurich, 1990. Prof. King's Coll. London, 2007—. Adj. prof. Mt. Sinai Sch. Medicine, 2007—11. Rsch. Grant, Med. Rsch. Coun. Office: King's College London Guy's Hosp London SE1 9RT England Business E-Mail: michael.linden@virology.ch.

LINDENFELD, JOANN, physician, educator; b. Benton Harbor, Mich., Feb. 11, 1948; d. Nelson Albert and Viola C. Lindenfield. MD, U. Mich., 1973. Diplomate in internal medicine, cardiology and critical care medicine Am. Bd. Internal Medicine. Asst. prof. medicine U. Colo., Denver, 1980-85, assoc. prof. medicine, 1985-90, prof. medicine, 1990—. Mem. cardiovenal adv. panel FDA, Washington, 1995—; cons. for pharm. firms. Author: Geriatric Internal Medicine, 1995, 99; contbr. articles to profl. jours. Recipient numerous awards U. Colo., Denver. Fellow Am. Coll. Cardiology, Am. Heart Assn. (clin. coun. rep.); mem. Internat. Soc. Heart and Lung Transplant, Am. Soc. Transplant Physicians. Avocations: hiking, poetry, gardening, writing. Office: Univ Colo Health Scis Ctr 1635 Aurora Ct F 749 Rm 7083 Aurora CO 80045 Home Phone: 303-733-4352; Office Phone: 720-848-0850.

LINDLEY, JAMES GUNN, JR., neurosurgeon; b. Key West, Fla., Jan. 23, 1956; s. James Gunn Lindley Sr. and Jane Kennedy Lindley; m. Stephanie Curl, July 3, 1999; children: Jennifer Anne, James Gunn III. BS in Chemistry, East Carolina U., Greenville, NC, 1979; MD, Med. U. SC, Charleston, 1984. Diplomate Am. Bd. of Neurol. Surgeons, 1993. Intern in gen. surgery Wake Forest U. Med. Ctr., 1984, resident in neurol. surgery, 1985—90; neurosurgeon Neurol. Inst. of Savannah, Ga., 1990—. Chief of surgery St. Joseph's Hosp., Savannah, Ga., 2003—05, vice chief of staff, 2005—07, chief of staff, 2007—09. Fellow: Am. Coll. Surgeons; mem.: AMA, N.Am. Spine Soc., Spine Arthroplasty Soc., Am. Acad. of Spine Physicians, Ga. Med. Soc., Med. Assn. of Ga., Ga. Neurosurgical Soc. (sci. program chmn. 1998—99), So. Neurosurgical Soc. (v.p. 2001—02), Congress of Neurol. Surgeons, Am. Assn. of Neurol. Surgeons. Republican. Episcopalian. Office: Neurol Inst Savannah 4 Jackson Blvd Savannah GA 31405 Office Phone: 912-355-1010.

LINDNER, PAUL GARY, allergist, immunologist; MD, SUNY, Buffalo, 1985. Diplomate Am. Bd. Internal Medicine, Am. Bd. Allergy and Immunology. Intern Sch. medicine and biomedical sciences SUNY, 1986; resident in internal medicine Stamford Hosp., 1987—89, hosp. affiliation includes; fellow in allergy and immunology Nassau Univ. Med. Ctr., 1989—91. Named one of Top Doctors, NY Metro Area, Best Doctors, NY Mag., 2010. Office: Stamford Hospital 22 15th St Stamford CT 06905 Office Phone: 203-978-0072. Office Fax: 203-978-1393.

LINDOR, KEITH D., dean, gastroenterologist, researcher, hepatologist; b. Morris, Minn., June 21, 1953; m. Noralane Morey Lindor, July 16, 1977; children: Carl (CJ), Rachel. BS in Chemistry, U. Minn., 1975; MD, Mayo Med. Sch., Rochester, Minn., 1979. Diplomate Am. Bd. Internat. Medicine. Resident Bowman Gray Sch. Medicine, Winston-Salem, NC, 1979—82; asst. prof. medicine Mayo Clinic Coll. Medicine, Rochester, Minn., 1986—91, assoc. prof. medicine, 1991—96, assoc. vice chair practice dept. medicine, 1997—99, cons. divsn. gastroenterology/hepatology, 1986—, prof. medicine, 1996—, chair divsn. gastroenterology. hepatology, 1999—2005, dean Mayo Med. Sch., 2005—. Reviewers res. NIH, Bethesda, Md., 2003—; spkr. in field. Editor: (book) Primary Biliary Cirrhosis: From Pathogenesis to Clinical Treatment, 1997; contbr. articles to profl. jours. Grantee NIH, 2001—06. Mem.: Am. Liver Found. (vice chair med. affairs 1999—), Am. Coll. Physicians, Am. Coll. Gastroenterology, Am. Assn. for Study of Liver Disease (chair edn. com. 1997—99). Avocation: landscape gardening. Office: Mayo Clinic Coll Medicine 200 First St SW Rochester MN 55905 *

LINDQUIST, SUSAN LEE, biology and microbiology professor; b. June 5, 1949; BA in Microbiology with honors, U. Ill., 1971; PhD in Biology, Harvard U., 1976. Asst. prof. dept. molecular biology University of Chicago, 1978-84, assoc. prof., 1984—99, full prof., 1988, Albert D. Lasker prof. med. sciences, 1999—2001, investigator Howard Hughes Med. Inst., 1988—2001; dir. Whitehead Institute Biomedical Research, Cambridge, Mass., 2001—04, mem., 2001—; prof. biology MIT, Cambridge, Mass., 2001—; investigator Howard Hughes Medical Institute, 2006—. Mem. com. genetics, com. devel. biology U. Chgo., 1999—; cons. Mus. Sci. & Industry, Chgo., 1983-87; vis. scholar Cambridge U., 1983; cons., prin. in film Lights Breaking, 1985; mem. sci. adv. com. Helen Hay Whitney Found., 1997—; bd. dirs. Johnson & Johnson, 2004-; lectr. in field. Co-editor: The Stress Induced Proteins, 1988, Heat Shock, 1990; assoc. editor The New Biologist, 1991-93; mem. editl. bd. Cell Regulation, 1989—, Molecular and Cell Biology, 1984—, Gene Expression, 1994-95, Cell Stress and Chaperones, 1995—, Current Biology, 1996—, Molecular Biology of the Cell, 1996—; monitoring editor Jour. Cell Biology, 1993—; contbr. articles to profl. jours. Teaching fellow Harvard U., 1973-74, Postdoctoral fellow Am. Cancer Soc., 1976-78, U. Chgo.; recipient Novartis Drew award in Biomedical Rsch., 2000, Dickson prize in Medicine, 2003, Sigma Xi William Procter prize for Scientific Achievement, 2006, Emil Christian Hansen Gold medal, 2006, U. Ill. Alumni Achievement award, 2006, Nat. Medal Sci. The White House, 2010; named one of Top 50 Women Scientists, Discover Mag., 2002. Fellow Am. Acad. Microbiology, AAAS, NAS, Am. Acad. Arts and Sci.; mem. Am. Soc. Cell Biology, Am. Soc. Microbiology, Fedn. Am. Scientists for Exptl. Biology, Genetics Soc. Am. (former sec.), Molecular Medicine Soc., Inst. Medicine. Achievements include research in the impact of protein-conformational changes on diverse processes in cellular and organismal biology. Office: Whitehead Inst Nine Cambridge Ctr Cambridge MA 02142-1479 Office Phone: 617-258-5184. E-mail: lindquist_admin@wi.mit.edu.

LINDQVIST, RIKARD, health facility administrator; b. Skelleftea, Sweden, Apr. 12, 1966; s. Torsten and Karin Lindqvist; m. AnnaMaria Thunman, June 15, 1991; children: Lukas Thunman-Lindqvist, Esther Thunman-Lindqvist. Cert. in Gen. Nursing, Umeå vårdhögskola, 1987, BS in Social Sci., Stockholm U., 1998; PhD in Health Systems Rsch., Karolinska Inst., Stockholm, 2005. RN Sweden, 1987. Asst. staff nurse Råcksta Hosp., Stockholm, 1987—89; sr. programme officer Pub. Health and Med. Svc. Com., Stockholm County Coun., 1990—96; cons. Enator Inc., Stockholm, 1996; sr. cons. Sinova Mgmt. Cons. AB, Stockholm, 1997—98; head centre Centre for Patient Classification Systems, Stockholm, 1999—2006; dir. vice-chancellor office Ersta Skondal U. Coll., Stockholm, 2006—. Mem.: Patient Classification Systems Internat. Office: Ersta Skondal Univ Coll Box 11189 100 61 Stockholm Sweden Business E-Mail: rikard.lindqvist@esh.se.

LINDSAY, BRUCE DUNCAN, cardiologist; b. Kansas City, Mo., 1951; BS, Eckerd Coll., St. Petersburg, Fla., 1973; MD, Jefferson Med. Coll., Phila., Pa., 1977. Diplomate Am. Bd. Internal Medicine, Am. Bd. Cardiovascular Disease. Resident in internal medicine U. Mich., Ann Arbor, 1977-80; fellowship in cardiology Wash. U. Sch. Medicine, Barnes Hosp., St. Louis, 1983-85; med. dir., Nat. Health Svc. Corps. East Jordan Family Health Ctr., Mich., 1980-83; hosp. staff Barnes-Jewish Hosp., St. Louis, 1985—2008, dir. clin. cardiac electrophys., 1994—2008; assoc. prof. medicine Wash. U Sch. Medicine; dir. electrophys. Cleve. Clinic Heart & Vascular Inst., Cleve., 2008—. Contbr. chapters to books, several articles to profl. jours. Named one of Best Doctors in America, Best Doctors, Inc., 2003, 2005, 2006, America's Top Doctors, Castle Connolly Med. Ltd., 2003—06. Fellow Am. Coll. Cardiology (chmn. bd. govs., bd. trustee, mem. exec. com.); mem. N.Am. Soc. of Pacing and Electrophysiology (bd. trustee) Office: Cleve Clinic Heart & Vascular Inst 9500 Euclid Ave Cleveland OH 44195 Office Phone: 216-445-9288.

LINDSAY, ROBERT, internist, educator; s. William G. and Agnes M. Lindsay; m. Amy Merrill Conovitz, Dec. 15, 1958; children: Avril Cunningham, Nigel Gareth, Emma Kate, Liliane Margaret. BSc, Glasgow U., 1966, MB, BChir, 1968, PhD, 1972. Lectr. medicine Glasgow U. Med. Sch., 1972—79; prof. clin. medicine Columbia U., Coll. Physicians and Surgeons, NYC, 1979—; chief internal medicine Helen Hayes Hosp., West Haverstraw, NY, 1980—2003. Pres. Nat. Osteoporosis Found., Washington, 1992—99; mem. adv. coun. Nat. Inst. Arthritis, Musculskeletal and Skin Diseases, NIH, Washington. Contbr. articles to profl. jours. Recipient Bartter award, Am. Soc. for Bone and Mineral Rsch., 1997, Disting. award, Internat. Soc. for Clin. Densitometry, 1998, Disting. Achievement award, N.Am. Menopause Soc., 2001; fellow, Nutrition Soc., 1993. Fellow: Am. Acad. for Clin. Endocrinology, Royal Coll. Physicians. Office: Helen Hayes Hospital Route 9W West Haverstraw NY 10993 Personal E-mail: lindsayr@helenhayeshosp.org. E-mail: lindsayr@helnhayeshosp.org.

LINDSEY, JENNIFER H., pediatrician; MD, U. Va. Diplomate Am. Bd. Pediatrics, Am. Bd. Pediatrics-pediatric cardiology. Pediatric tng. Univ. NC, Chapel Hill, Univ. Va., fellow in pediatric cardiology; pvt. practice Child Cardiology Assocs., Va. Named to Hall of Fame, Nat. Coll. Athletes. Fellow: Am. Coll. of Cardiology (pediat. sect.), Am. Acad. of Pediatrics; mem.: Am. Acad. of Pediatrics (cardiology sect.). Office: Child Cardiology Associates 8316 Arlington Blvd Ste 500 Fairfax VA 22031 Office Phone: 703-876-8410.

LINDSEY, MARGARET A., psychiatrist; children: Jenna, Abigail. BA, Trinity U., San Antonio, 1972; BS, Columbia U., NYC, 1975; postgrad., Cornell U., Ithaca, NY, 1981; MD, Case Western Res. U., Cleve., 1988. Lic. physician N.Y., 1989, diplomate Am. Bd. Psychiatry; RN N.Y., 1975. From resident to sr. instr. child psychiatry U. Rochester, NY, 1988—95, sr. instr. child psychiatry, 1995—; pvt.

practice Rochester, 1996—; with, forensic divsn. Monroe County Children's Ctr., 2003—. Cons. in field. Vol. Genessee Valley Women's Found., Rochester, 2000—05. Mem.: APA, Am. Acad. Child and Adolescent Psychiatry. Presbyn. Office: 2505 East Ave Apt 108 Rochester NY 14610-3155

LINDSEY, ROBERT J., medical association administrator; BA in Psychology, St. Bonaventure U., NY, MEd. Exec. dir. Allegany County Coun. on Alcoholism and Substance Abuse, Inc., Wellsville, NY, 1975—80; unit mgr., therapist Spofford Hall Mediplex Facility, NH, 1980—82; exec. dir. NY State Coun. on Alcoholism and Other Drug Addictions, Inc., Albany, NY, 1982—90; dir. cmty. rels. Betty Ford Clinic Eisenhower Med. Ctr., Rancho Mirage, Calif., 1990—94; v.p. Longview Associates, White Plains, NY, 1994—2005; pres. Nat. Coun. on Alcoholism and Drug Dependence, NYC, 2006—. Bd. chmn. St. Joseph's Rehab. Ctr., Inc., Saranac Lake, NY. Mem.: Employee Assistance Professionals Assn., Soc. Human Resource Mgmt. Office: Nat Coun on Alcoholism and Drug Dependence Inc 244 E 58th St 4th Fl New York NY 10022 Office Phone: 212-269-7797. Office Fax: 212-269-7510. *

LINDSLEY, CAROL BETLACK, pediatric rheumatologist; d. Otto and Ruth Betlack; m. Herbert Benzinger Lindsley, June 12, 1966; children: Erik, Greg. MD, U. Washington, Seattle, 1968. Cert. Pediat. Am. Bd. of Pediat., 1973. Dir. Mid-America Pediat. Rheumatology Program, Kans., 1983—; prof. pediat. U. Kans. Med. Ctr., Kansas City, 1989—. Directorship Am. Coll. of Rheumatology, Atlanta, 2002—05; dir. Am. Bd. of Pediat., Chapel Hill, NC, 2005—. Author numerous jours. articles, (textbbook) Pediatric Rheumatology. Leadership group Arthritis Found., Atlanta, 2006—08. Recipient Cassidy award, Am. Acad. Pediat., 2006. Master: Am. Coll. Rheumatology (Master 2006). Avocations: travel, swimming, music. Office: Univ Kansas Medical Center 39th and Rainbow Kansas City KS 66160-7330

LINDSTROM, ERIC EVERETT, ophthalmologist; b. Helena, Mont., Nov. 28, 1936; s. Everett Harry and Nan Augusta (Johnson) L.; m. Nancy Jo Alexander, July 24, 1960; children: Laura Ann, Eric Everett. BS, Wheaton Coll., 1958; MD, U. Md., 1963; MPH, Harvard U., 1966. Diplomate Am. Bd. Preventive Medicine, Am. Bd. Ophthalmology. Intern Madigan Army Med. Ctr., Tacoma, 1963-64; resident in aerospace medicine Sch. Aerospace Medicine, Brooks AFB, Tex., 1966-68; resident in ophthalmology Brooke Army Med. Ctr., Ft. Sam Houston, Tex., 1972-75; surgeon 12th combat aviation group U.S. Army, Vietnam, 1968-69; chief profl. svcs. and aviation medicine Beach Army Hosp., Ft. Wolters, Tex., 1969-72; asst. chief ophthalmology clinic Madigan Army Med. Ctr., Tacoma, 1975-76; with Lindstrom Eye Clinic, 1987—; med. dir. Palo Pinto County (Tex.) Mental Health Clinic, 1970-72; ret. Cons. Tex. State Rehab. Com., 1971-72; chmn. bd. trustees South Ctrl. Regional Med. Ctr., 1982-2001; sr. aviation med. examiner, FAA; flight surgeon Miss. Air N.G. (ret.). Deacon First Bapt. Ch., Laurel, Miss., 1978—; bd. dirs. Laurel Salvation Army, Good Shepherd Clin., Laurel. Decorated Bronze Star, Air medal with 2 oak leaf clusters, Meritorious Svc. medal. Fellow ACS, Am. Coll. Physician Execs., Am. Coll. Preventive Medicine, Aerospace Med. Assn. (assoc.), Am. Acad. Ophthalmology; mem. AMA, Am. Acad. Cataract and Refractive Surgery, New Orleans Acad. Ophthalmology, Miss. Med. Assn. (pres.), South Miss. Med. Soc., So. Med. Assn. (pres.), Flying Physicians Assn., Soc. Mil. Ophthalmologists, Soc. USAF and US Army Flight Surgeons, Alliance Air N.G. Flight Surgeons, Mil. Officers Assn. Am., Aircraft Owners and Pilots Assn., Kiwanis, Nu Sigma Nu. Home: 809 Cherry Ln Laurel MS 39440-1651 Office: Lindstrom Eye Clinic PO Box 407 Laurel MS 39441-0407 Office Phone: 601-426-9454. Business E-Mail: drelindstrom@gmail.net.

LINDSTRÖM, MIKAEL STIG, medical educator; b. Stockholm, Aug. 18, 1975; MS, Karolinska Inst., 1999, PhD, 2004. Postdoc. rschr. U. NC, Chapel Hill, 2004—07, Karolinska Inst., 2007—09, asst. prof., 2009—, assoc. prof., 2011—. Postdoc. Rsch. fellowship, Swedish Rsch. Coun., 2005—06, Swedish Cancer Soc., 2007—10. Mem.: Am. Assn. Cancer Rsch. Avocation: bird watching, fishing, mountain climbing. Office: Karolinska Inst Dept OnkPat Stockholm SE17176 Sweden Office Fax: 0046 8 321047. Business E-Mail: mikael.lindstrom@ki.se.

LINDSTROM, TORSTEN AXEL, mathematician; b. Turku, Finland, Apr. 5, 1965; s. Stig Arne and Brita Dorothea L.; m. Dagmar Elisabeth Patsch, Aug. 26, 1995; children: Arne Michael, Axel Matthias, Algot Markus, Anton Martin, Arthur Manfred. MSc, Abo Academi U., 1989; PhD, Luleå, 1995. Sr. lectr. U. Orebro, Sweden, 1995-96; asst. prof. U. Oslo, Norway, 1996-99; from sr. lectr. to assoc. prof. Linnaeus U., Sweden, 1999—. Office Phone: 46 480 497082. E-mail: torsten.lindstrom@lnu.se.

LINDVALL, PETER, neurosurgeon; b. Umeå, Sweden, Sept. 19, 1971; s. Jörgen and Elvy Lindvall; m. Erika Marie Louise Sund; 1 child, Ally Maria Helena. Degree in medicine, Umeå U., 1997. Cert. physician Swedish Nat. Bd. Health and Welfare. Resident dept. neurosurgery Umeå Univ. Hosp., 1999—2005, specialist in neurosurgery, 2005—. Contbr. articles to profl. jours. Achievements include research in hypofractionated conformal stereotactic radiotherapy of arteriovenous malformations and brain metastases. Avocations: sailing, hunting. Office: Dept Neurosurgery Umeå Univ Hosp 901 85 Umeå Sweden

LINEHAN, WILLIAM MARSTON, urologist, researcher; b. Tulsa, Okla., June 25, 1947; s. John Marston and Ella Marie (Bourg) L.; m. Tracey Ann Rouault, Sept. 29, 1979; children: Erin Louise, Emily Pauline. AB, Brown U., 1969; MD, U. Okla., Okla. City, 1973. Diplomate Am. Bd. Urology. Intern medicine U. Okla., 1973-74; intern and resident surgery Duke U., 1974-76, fellow cancer rsch., 1976-78, resident urologic surgery, 1978-82; chief Urologic Oncology Br. Nat. Cancer Inst., NIH, Bethesda, Md., 1982—. Mem. urology interagy. coord. com. NIH, Bethesda, 1987—. Mem. editl. bd. Jour. Urology, 1990—; assoc. editor Jour. Nat. Cancer Inst., 1992—; contbr. articles to Nature Science, P.N.A.S., New Eng. Jour. Medicine, Jour. Nat. Cancer Inst. Recipient Gold Cystoscope award 1992 and Disting. Contribution award 2001, Am. Urological Assn., Nathan Davis award for Outstanding Govt. Svc., AMA, 2008, SUO Medal 2004 and Huggins medal 2009 Soc Urologic Oncology, Barringer medal, Am. Assn. Genitourinary Surgeons 2005, NIH Merit award 2006 and Dir.'s award 1995 Nat. Inst.s Health, Joseph H. Burchenal Memorial award for Outstanding Achievement in Clinical Cancer Rsch. AACR 2009, Disting. Alumnus award, Duke U. Sch. Medicine Alumni Ass 2009, Wick R. Williams Memorial award, Fox Chase Cancer Ctr., 2010 Fellow mem. Inst. Medicine, Am. Urol. Assn., Am. Assn. Cancer Rsch., Am. Assn. Genitourinary Surgeons. Achievements include co-discovery of kidney cancer disease gene in sporadic renal cell carcinoma as well as in the familial renal cell carcinoma associated with von Hippel Lindau syndrome; co-discovery of hereditary papillary renal carcinoma gene; co-discovery of the BHD kidney cancer gene; detailing of molecular genetic changes associated with initiation and progression of kidney cancer; evaluation of new anti-neoplastic agents for patients with advanced prostate carcinoma. Office: Ctr Cancer Rsch NCI NIH Urologic Oncology Br 10 Center Dr MSC 1501 10/2B47 Bethesda MD 20892 Office Phone: 301-496-6353. Office Fax: 301-402-0922. E-mail: linehanm@mail.nih.gov. *

LINET, TEDDY, physician; b. Mantes-La-Jolie, France, June 04; MD, Nantes U., 2004. Chef de clinique CHU de Nantes, 2004—06. Avocations: computers, tennis, languages. Office: 4 Rue Jean de la Fontaine Nantes PDL 44000 France Office Fax: 33218460406. Personal E-mail: teddy.linet@free.fr.

LING, BAO-DONG, medical educator, researcher; b. Wanxian, China, Sept. 1, 1956; BS, North Sichuan Med. Coll., 1978; MD, Sichuan U., 1988. Disting. prof. North Sichuan Med. Coll., 1997—, bd. dirs., 1997—2011. Recipient Sci. and Tech. award, Sichuan Province, China Govt. Mem.: Chinese Pharmacological Soc. Office: 234 Fujiang Rd Nanchong Sichuan 637007 China Office Fax: 86-817-2242761. Business E-Mail: bdling@nsmc.edu.cn.

LING, BOOI CIE, prosthodontist, educator; b. Sitiawan, Malaysia, May 2, 1943; s. Chu Kai Ling and Ciu Lieng Ding; m. Sang Lim Teh, Aug. 17, 1972; children: Daniel Wan En, Rebekah Wan Hong. B in Dental Surgery, U. Singapore, 1969; MSc in Prosthetic Dentistry, U. London, 1977. Dental ho. officer Gen. Hosp., Penang, Malaysia, 1969—70; dental officer Dist. Hosp., Jerantut, Malaysia, 1970—71, Lumut, Malaysia, 1971—74; lectr. U. Malaya, Kuala Lumpur, Malaysia, 1974—82, assoc. prof., 1982—98, prof., 1998—2000, U. Kebangsaan Malaysia, Kuala Lumpur, 2000—. Head of dept. U. Malaya, 1990—98; mem. Dental Coun. Malaysia, Kuala Lumpur, 1997—2000. Contbr. articles to profl. jours.; hon. editor Dental Jour. Malaysia, 1983—85, mem. editl. bd. Jour. Asian Acad. Aesthetic Dentistry, 1991—. Fellow: Royal Australasian Coll. Dental Surgeons; mem.: Internat. Assn. Dental Rsch., Malaysian Dental Assn. (editor 1983—85, coun. 1982—85), Brit. Gen. Dental Coun., Dental Coun. Malaysia. Achievements include development of new techniques and use of magnetic retention units in sectional (2-part) dentures; new 3-appointment method instead of the usual 5-visit technique in complete denture construction; new techniques in personnel identification, denture, laser, ID-disk labeling. Avocations: jogging, collecting fountain pens, clocks. Office: U Kebangsaan Malaysia Faculty of Dentistry Jalan Raja Muda Abdul Aziz 50300 Kuala Lumpur Malaysia Office Phone: (603) 40405744. Fax: (603) 40405779.

LING, FENG, neurologist, educator; b. Hebei, China, Oct. 1, 1951; BA, 3rd Mil. Med. U. PLA, 1973; PhD, Med. Grad. Coll. PLA, 1989, MD; BA, U. Paris, 1983. Resident, cons., dep. chief Dept. Neuosurgery Gen. Hosp. PLA, 1977—92; prof., chief, dir., dept. neurosurgery Rsch. Ctr. Interventional Neuroradiology Beijing Hosp., 1992—2000; prof., chair, dir., exec. dir., dean Ctr. Interventional Neuroradiology Xuanwu Hosp., China Internat. Neurosci. Inst., 2006—, Neurointerventional Grad. Sch. Capital U., 2011—. Dir. Nat. Tng. Ctrs. Yasargi Microneurosurgery, Samii Skull Base, Spine Surgery, Endoscopic Surgery, Interventional Neuroradiology, 2002; editor-in-chief Chinese Jour. Cerebrovasc. Diseases, 2004; group leader Regime & Lic. Regulating Body Neurointerventional Practice China Health Ministry, 2010. Recipient 2nd class State award, Chinese Govt., prize, Zhou Guangzhao Found., Ministerial award, Chinese Med. Doc. award, Nat. Tole Model Med. Ethics; named one of Top 10 Best Doctors, Beijing Mcpl. Govt. Master: Cerebral Vascular Com. WFNS (vice chair), Women Neurosurgery World Fedn. Neurol. Surgeons (pres.), Chinese Congress Neurosurgeons (pres.), Asia-Australasian Fedn. Interventional Theraputic Neuroradiology (life; pres.); fellow: World Fedn. Interventional Theraputic Neuroradiology; mem.: Internat. Soc. Mini Invasive Neurosurgery (v.p.). Avocations: swimming, philosophy, calligraphy. Office: 45 Changchun St Beijing 100053 China Office Fax: 8610-8316 3245.

LING, FRANK W., obstetrician, gynecologist; b. Evanston, Ill. B, Wabash Coll., Crawfordsville, Ind., 1970; MD, U. Tex. Southwestern, 1974. Intern Wilmington Medical Ctr., 1975; resident U. Tenn., Memphis, 1978, student clerkship dir., asst. dean student affairs, residency dir., dir. gynecology, chair, dept. gynecology, 1994—2003; ptnr. Women's Health Specialists, Germantown, Tenn. Fellow: Soc. Gynecologic Surgeons, Central Assn. Obstetricians and Gynecologists, American Coll. Obstetricians and Gynecologists; mem.: Assn. Professors Gynecology and Obstetrics (Career Achievement award 2005), American Bd. Obstetrics and Gynecology (examiner 1989—, pres. 2006—). Office: Womens Health Specialists 7800 Wolf Trail Cove Germantown TN 38138

LING, HENRY T., internist; MD, Thomas Jefferson U. Diplomate Am. Bd. Internal Medicine. Intern Lankenau Hosp., resident; hosp. affiliation includes Lankenau Med. Ctr.; attending physician. Named one of the Top Doctor, Phila. Mag., 2011. Office: Lankenau Medical Center MOB W Ste 140 100 Lancaster Ave Wynnewood PA 19096 Office Phone: 610-642-6990. Office Fax: 610-642-6723.

LINGEGOWDA, VIJAYKUMAR, nephrologist; b. Mysore, July 7, 1972; MBBS, Mysore Med. Coll., 1997; MSEd, U. Toledo, 1999. Cons. nephrologist, owner Srishti Kidney Ctr., 2011—. Internist Dakota Clinic Ltd., Jamestown, ND, 2002—04; hospitalist Fremont Med. Ctr., Las Vegas, Nev., 2004—07; cons. Kantor Nephrology, Las Vegas, 2009—10. Fellow: Am. Soc. Nephrology. Avocations: Karate, cricket. Office: Srishti Kidney Ctr 826 New Kantharaj Urs Rd Mysore Karnataka 08123 829242 India E-mail: vgowda2@yahoo.com.

LINGL, FRIEDRICH ALBERT, psychiatrist; b. Munich, Apr. 4, 1927; came to U.S., 1957, naturalized, 1962; s. Friedrich Hugo and Marie Luise (Lindner) L.; m. Leonore E. Trautner, Nov. 15, 1955; children— Herbert F., Angelika M. MD, Ludwig-Maxim U., Munich, 1952. Diplomate Am. Bd. Psychiatry and Neurology); cert. mental health adminstr. Intern Edward W. Sparrow Hosp., 1957-58; resident internal medicine City Hosp., Augsburg, Germany, 1953-54; resident psychiatry Columbus (Ohio) State Hosp., 1958-61; supt. Hawthornden State Hosp., Northfield, Ohio, 1963-66; dir. Cleve. Psychiat. Inst., 1966-72; pvt. practice, 1972-92; med. dir. Windsor Hosp., 1976-92, med. dir. emeritus, 1992—. Asst. clin. prof. Case Western Res. U., Cleve., 1970-97. Contbr. articles to med. jours. Fellow Am. Psychiat. Assn. (disting. life); mem. AMA, Ohio Med. Assn., Ohio Psychiat. Assn., Cleve. Psychiat. Soc. Address: 40 Farwood Dr Chagrin Falls OH 44022-6848

LINK, MARK S., cardiac electrophysiologist, educator; MD, Tufts U., 1986. Diplomate Am. Bd. Internal Medicine, 1989, Am. Bd. Internal Medicine-cardiovasc. disease, 2007, Am. Bd. Internal Medicine-clin. cardiac electrophysiology, 2008. Intern internal medicine Columbia-Presbyn. Med. Ctr., NY, resident internal medicine NY, 1986—89; fellow cardiovasc. disease New Eng. Med. Ctr., 1993—96, fellow cardiac electrophysiology, 1996—97; prof. medicine Tufts Univ.; co-dir. Cardiac Electrophysiology and Pacemaker Lab. Tufts Med. Ctr., co-dir. Hypertrophic Cardiomyopathy Ctr., dir. Ctr. for the Evaluation of Heart Disease in Athletes, dir. Adult Heart Sta. Co-author: (publs.) Implantable cardioverter—defibrillator therapy for prevention of sudden death in patients with arrhythmogenic right ventricular cardiomyopathy/dysplasia., 2003, Evidence that Hypertrophic Cardiomyopathy is a Disease Characterized by Predominantly Left Ventricular Outflow Tract Obstruction., 2006, Prevention of sudden cardiac death and selection of patients for implantable cardioverter-defibrillators in hypertrophic cardiomyopathy., 2007, numerous publs. Recipient Charlton Rsch. award, 1998, Oliver Smith award, New Eng. Med. Ctr., 1999—2007, Faculty Recognized for Excellence in Tchg., Tufts Univ., 2002—03; named one of The Best Doctors in Boston, Boston Mag.; finalist Young Investigators's award, 47th Annual Am. Coll. of Cardiology Sessions, 1998. Office: Tufts Medical Center 800 Washington St Box 197 Boston MA 02111 Office Phone: 617-636-5902.

LINKE, REINHOLD PAUL, immunologist; s. Josef and Hedwig Emilie Linke; m. Katharina Barbara Linke; children: Norbert Matthias, Anne Katharina Maria. MD, U. Münster and Tübingen; PhD in Immunology, U. Munich. Rsch. fellow NYU, NYC; vis. assoc. NIH, Edn. and Welfare, Bethesda, Md.; asst. U. of Tübingen; asst. prof. immunology U. Munich, 1978—2005; guest-scientist Max-Planck-Institut für Biochemie, Martinsried, Germany, 1990—2005. Organizer med. confs. Amyloidforum, 1978—2001; lectr. in field. Recipient Tosse-Prize in Juvenile Rheumathology, Tosse Co., 1996; grantee, Deutsche Forschungsgemeinschaft, 1975—2005. Mem.: Internat. Soc. Amyloidosis, German Soc. Amyloid Diseases (pres. 1993—2001). Office Phone: 0049 (0) 89-520 12 638. Business E-Mail: linke@amymed.de.

LINKLATER, JAMES M., radiologist; b. Sydney, Jan. 5, 1965; MBBS, U. NSW, 1989. Clin. dir. Castlereagh Sports Imaging, 1999—. Fellow: RANZCR. Office: 286 Pacific Hwy Crows Nest NSW 2065 Australia Office Fax: 0299066233. Business E-Mail: linklj@bigpond.com.

LINKONIS, SUZANNE NEWBOLD, retired counselor; b. Phila., Aug. 24, 1945; d. William Bartram and Kathryn (Taylor) Newbold; m. Bertram Lawrence Linkonis, May 29, 1966; children: Robert William, Deborah Anne, Richard Anthony. AA in Psychology, Albany Jr. Coll., Ga., 1979; BA in Psychology, Albany State U., Ga., 1981; MS in Indsl. Psychology, Va. Commonwealth U., 1986. Office mgr., media buyer Long Advt. Agy., Richmond, Va., 1981-84; media mgr. Clarke & Assocs., Richmond, 1984-85; human resources asst. Continental Ins., Richmond, 1985; rsch. assoc. Signet Bank, N.A., Richmond, 1986-87; program coord. Med. Coll. Va., Richmond, 1988; personnel mgr. Bur. Microbiology, Richmond, 1988-89; pers. specialist Va. State Dept. Corrections, Richmond, 1989-90; human rights adv. Va. State Dept. Youth and Family Svcs., Richmond, 1990-92, rehab. counselor, 1992-94, sr. rehab. counselor, 1994; pre-trial case mgr./counselor Henrico County Govt., Richmond, 1994-97, cmty. corrections case mgr., counselor, 1997-2000, sr. county probation officer, counselor, 2001—06. Future dir., cons. Mary Kay Cosmetics, Springfield, Va., 1975-77, cons., New Bern, NC, 2007-. Republican. Roman Catholic. Avocations: walking, reading, boating, fishing, genealogy. Home: 6206 Bent Tree Pl Chester VA 23831

LINN, CAROLE ANNE, dietician; b. Portland, Oreg., Mar. 3, 1945; d. James Leslie and Alice Mae (Thorburn) L. BS, Oreg. State U., 1967. Intern U. Minn., 1967—68; nutrition cons. licensing and cert. sect. Oreg. State Bd. Health, Portland, 1968-70; chief clin. dietitian Rogue Valley Med. Ctr., Medford, Oreg., 1970—; clin. faculty, dietetic internship program Oreg. Health Scis. U., Portland, 2000—. Cons. Hillhaven Health Care Ctr., Medford, 1971-83; lectr. Local Spkrs. Bur., Medford. Mem. Am. Soc. Parenteral and Enteral Nutrition, Am. Dietetic Assn., Am. Diabetic Assn., Oreg. Dietetic Assn. (sec. 1973-75, nominating com. 1974-75, Young Dietitian of Yr. 1976), So. Oreg. Dietetic Assn., Alpha Lambda Delta, Omicron Nu. Democrat. Mem. Christ Unity Ch. Avocations: sewing, needlecrafts, cooking, swimming, skiing. Office: Rogue Valley Med Ctr 2825 E Barnett Rd Medford OR 97504-8332

LINS, BRUNO TESTONI, surgeon, educator; b. Rio de Janeiro, Jan. 6, 1975; DVM, Coll. Vet. Medicine, U. Brasília, 2001; PhD, Inst. Orthopedics, U. São Paulo, 2011. Prof. small animal surgery and orthop. Anhembi Morumbi U., 2007—. Surgeon Brazilian Coll. Vet. Surgeons and Anesthetists, 2010. Mem.: AOVET. Avocations: Judo, running. Home: Rua Diogo Jácome n 1030 Apt 24 São Paulo 04512-001 Brazil Home Fax: 55(011)27904642. Personal E-mail: bt_lins@yahoo.com.br.

LINTHICUM, FREDERICK HAMILTON, lab administrator; b. LA, July 2, 1921; BA, Pomona Coll., 1943; MD, U. South Calif., 1946. Assoc. House Ear Clinic, 1957—70; dir. histopathology temporal bone lab. House Rsch. Inst., 1960—. Clin. prof. surgery, otolaryngology Keck Sch. Medicine, U. South Calif., 1958. Mem.: Pacific Coast Oto-Ophthomologic Soc., Am. Triological Soc., Am. Otol. Soc., Politzer Soc., Collegium Oto-Rhino-Laryngologicum Amicittae Sacrum. Avocation: fly fishing. Office: 210 West Third St Los Angeles CA 90057 Office Fax: 213-413-6739. Business E-Mail: flinthicum@hei.org.

LINTON, WILLIAM A., JR., medical products executive; s. Marion and William Linton. BS, U. Calif., Berkeley, 1970. Founder, chmn., CEO Promega Corp., 1978—. Bd. dirs. Bruker BioSciences Corp., 2000—, lead dir., 2004—; bd. dirs. High Throughput Genomics,

2003—. Bd. dirs. Med. Coll. of Wis. Cardiovascular Ctr., Wisconsin Tech. Coun. Mem.: Analytical & Life Sci. Systems Assn. (chmn. 2004—). Office: Promega Corp 2800 Woods Hollow Rd Madison WI 53711

LINZ, ANTHONY JAMES, osteopathic physician, consultant, educator; b. Sandusky, Ohio, June 16, 1948; s. Anthony Joseph and Margaret Jane (Ballah) Linz; m. Kathleen Ann Kovach, Aug. 18, 1973; children: Anthony Scott, Sara Elizabeth. BS, Bowling Green State U., 1971; D.O., Des Moines U., 1974; MPH, NW Ohio Consortium for Pub. Health, 2006. Diplomate Nat. Bd. Osteo. Examiners; bd. cert., diplomate Am. Osteo. Bd. Internal Medicine, Internal Medicine, Med. Diseases of Chest and Critical Care Medicine. Internship South Pointe Hosp., Cleve. Clinic Sys., Brentwood Hosp., Cleve., 1974—75, resident internal medicine Brentwood, 1975-78, chief resident, 1977-78; subsplty. fellow in pulmonary diseases Riverside Meth. Hosp., Columbus, Ohio, 1978-80; med. dir. pulmonary svcs. Sandusky Meml. Hosp., Ohio, 1980-85; med. dir. cardio-pulmonary svcs. Firelands Regional Med. Ctr., Sandusky, 1985—. Cons. staff dept. medicine Good Samaritan Hosp., 1982—85, sect. internal medicine specializing pulmonary diseases; cons. pulmonary, critical care and internal medicine Firelands Regional Med. Ctr., 1985—, active staff sect. internal medicine, chmn. dept. medicine, head div. pulmonary medicine, 1985—; cons. pulmonary, critical care, and internal medicine Providence Hosp., Sandusky, Mercy Hosp., Willard, Ohio; clin. prof. pulmonary and critical care med.,internal med. Ohio U. Coll. Osteo. Medicine; clin. prof. medicine Univ. Health Scis. Coll. Osteo. Medicine, Kansas City, Mo.; clin. asst. prof. med. Med. Coll. of Ohio at Toledo; adj. prof. applied scis. Bowling Green State U., adj. prof. pub. health, mem. respiratory tech. adv. bd. Firelands Campus, Northwest Ohio Consortium pub. health supporting faculty, 1983—, med. dir. respiratory care tech. program, 1984—; clin. prof. pulmonary and critical care med. Des Moines U.; rep. Pub. Health Adminstrn., 2001—; exec. bd. pub. health student orgn. N.W. Ohio Consortium for Pub. Health; med. dir., cons. physician O.E. Meyer Corp., 2003—. Contbr. articles and abstracts to profl. jours. Water safety instr. ARC, 1965—; med. dir., clin. rsch. investigator, bd. trustees Stein Hospice, 1986-90, chmn., 2000-; mem. adv. bd. Ams. with Disabilities Act, City of Sandusky, Ohio, chmn., 2001-; mem. LPN adv. bd. Sandusky Career Ctr., 2005-; med. dir. in residence Camp Superkids Asthma Camp, 1984-97 Recipient Edward Ruff Cmty. Svc. award Am. Lung. Assn., 1985, Master Clinician award Ohio U. Coll. Osteopathic Medicine, 1987, Golden Rule award J.C. Penney, 1990, Disting. Alumna/Alumnus award Firelands Coll., Bowling Green State U., 1995. Fellow: ACP-Am. Soc. Internal Medicine (Ohio chpt.), Am. Coll. Osteo. Internists (master) (Grover Gillum Soc. Master Fellows), Am. Coll. Critical Care Medicine, Am. Coll. Chest Physicians; mem.: AAAS, Ohio Lung Assn. (N.W. regional adv. bd.), Found. Critical Care (mem. Founder's Cir.), Ohio Pub. Health Assn., Am. Soc. Internal Medicine, So. Critical Care Medicine, Ohio Soc. Respiratory Care (med. adviser/dir. 1982—), Nat. Assn. Med. Dirs. Respiratory Care, Sandusky Yacht Club (corr.), Am. Lung Assn. (bd. dirs. Ohio's So. Shore sect. 1984—, pres., exec. bd. dirs., 1st v.p., med. adv. bd. chmn., bd. dirs. Ohio Norwest Region), Ohio Thoracic Soc., Am. Thoracic Soc., Am. Heart Assn., Ohio Osteo. Assn. (fifth dist. past pres., past v.p., past sec.-treas., acad. trustees 5th dist. acad.), Am. Osteo. Assn., European Thoracic Soc., Phi Kappa Phi, Atlas Med. Fraternity, Pi Kappa Alpha, Beta Beta Beta, Alpha Epsilon Delta. Roman Catholic. Office Phone: 800-372-5560. Personal E-mail: doclinz@aol.com.

LIOSIS, GEORGE THEODOROS, physician, educator; b. Attica, Greece, June 6, 1952; Degree, U. Thessaloniki, 1977; PhD, U. Ioannina, 1984. Registrar U. Ioannina, 1981—84, Nicu Agia Sofia Hosp. Athens, 1984—85, Neonatal Unit King's Coll. Hosp. London, 1987—88; signor registrar Gen. Hosp. Pireus, 1985—89; cons. Helenas Venizelou Perinatal Ctr. Athens, 1989—. Adj. prof. Technol. U. Athens, 2003—. Mem.: European Soc. Hematology and Immunol ogy, Neonatal Soc. Greece, Nat. Breast Feeding Orgn. Greece. Avocation: singing. Home: Megalou Alexandrou 125 Thracomacedones Attica 13676 Greece Home Fax: 0302106467165. Personal E-mail: agelios1@otenet.gr.

LIOSSIS, STAMATIS, rheumatologist, educator; b. Hamilton, Ont., Can., Feb. 26, 1962; MD, U. Patras Med. Sch., 1985, PhD, 1998. Asst. prof. medicine, rheumatology U. Patras Med. Sch., 2007—. Fellow: Am. Coll. Rhematologists. Office: Patras University Hosp Rion Achaia 26500 Greece E-mail: sliossis@hotmail.com.

LIOU, HORNG-HUEI, neurologist, educator; b. Taiwan, Oct. 21, 1957; MD, Nat. Taiwan U., PhD, 2007. Prof. Dept. Neurology and Pharmacology, Coll. Medicine, Nat. Taiwan U., 2008—. Recipient Bruce S. Schoenberg Internat. award, Am. Acad. Neurology, 1996, Outstanding Tchr. award, Coll. Medicine, Nat. Taiwan U., 2004, 2007. Mem.: ILAE. Office: 7 Chung-Shan S Rd Taipei 100 Taiwan Business E-Mail: hhl@ntu.edu.tw.

LIOU, YIING-MEI, nurse; b. Taipei, Taiwan, Jan. 11, 1963; m. Tao-Yeuan Wang; children: Tzer-Jenn Wang, Tzer-Wey Wang. PhD, Nat. Taiwan U., 2004. RN, Dept. of Health, Taiwan, 1985. Chief Health Promotion Divsn., Yang-Ming Exercise Health Sci. Inst., Taipei, Taiwan, 1998—2004; coun. mem. Formosa Active Life Assn., Taipei, Taiwan, 2002—06, Sigma Theta Tau Internat. Honor Soc. Nursing, Taipei, 2004—; asst. prof. Inst. of Cmty. Health Nursing, Nat. Yang-Ming U., Taipei, 2005—. Contbr. articles to profl. jours. Con. Ministry of Edn., Taiwan, 2003—. Recipient Academic award, Ministry of Def., 1985, Outstanding award of Undergraduate Student, Exec. Yuen, 1984; grant, Buebera of Health Promotion, 2002—06. Home: 6F 9-4 Aly16 ln81 Sec7 ZhongShan N R Taipei 111 Taiwan Office: National Yang- Ming University Taiwan 155 Li-Nong St Sec 2 Pai-Tou Taipei 112 Taiwan Office Fax: 886-2-28202372. Business E-Mail: ymliou@ym.edu.tw.

LIP, GREGORY YH, cardiologist; b. Ipoh, Malaysia; s. Stephen Lip and Philomena Ong; m. PeckLin Woo; children: Philomena, Aloysius. MD, Univ. Glasgow. FRCP (London, Edinburgh, Glasgow) Royal Coll. of Physicians, UK. Prof. of cardiovasc. medicine U. of Birmingham, England, 2001—; dir. - haemostasis thrombosis and vascular biology unit U. Dept of Medicine, City Hosp., Birmingham, England, sr. lectr., 1996—99, reader medicine, 2000—01, prof., 2001—. Cons. cardiologist. Contbr. over 1000 pubs. in med. lit., books, etc. Peer reviewer of nat. guidelines, rsch. grants, rsch. papers. Fellow: Royal Coll. Physicians and Surgeons Glasgow, Royal Coll. Physicians of Edinburgh, Am. Coll. Cardiology, European Soc. Cardiology, Royal Coll. Physicians of London. Achievements include research interest and papers in thrombosis, atherosclerosis, vascular biology etc. in cardiovascular disease and stroke; clinical research into atrial fibrillation, hypertension, heart failure, etc. Office: University Birmingham Ctr Cardiovascular Scis City Hospital Dudley Road B18 7QH Birmingham England

LIPKIN, IAN (WALTER IAN LIPKIN), epidemiologist, neurologist, educator; BA, Sarah Lawrence Coll., 1974; MD, Rush Med. Coll., 1978. Cert. American Bd. Internal Medicine, 1981, American Bd. Neurology & Psychiatry, 1986. Intern medicine U. Pitts.; resident medicine U. Wash.; resident neurology U. Calif., San Francisco, asst. prof. to prof. neurology, anatomy & neurobiology, and microbiology and molecular genetics Irvine, 1990—2002; fellow Scripps Rsch. Inst.; prof. Sch. Basic. Med. Svcs. Beijing U.; with Columbia U. College of Physicians & Surgeons, 2002—, prof. neurology & pathology; prof. epidemiology Columbia U. Mailman Sch. Pub. Health, dir. Ctr. for Infection & Immunity, John Snow Prof. Epidemiology; dir. Northeast Biodefense Ctr. Spl. advisor to China for Rsch.; spl. advisor to Internat. Cooperation in Infectious Diseases; prin. investigator Autism Birth Cohort; Dalldorf Affiliated Rsch. Physician, Wadsworth Ctr., NY State Dept. Health; vis. prof. Japanese Human Sci. Found., 1999; found. lectr. American Soc. of Microbiology, 2001—03. Contbr. of several articles to profl. publications. Pew Scholar, 1991, Ellison Med. Found. Sr. Scholar in Global Infectious Disease, 2001. Fellow: NY Acad. Sciences. Achievements include first to identify a microbe using molecular tools; led the team that identified West Nile Virus in NY in 1999; development of as assay for SARS infection in 2003. Hand carried 10,000 test kits to Beijing at the height of outbreak. Office: Center for Infection and Immunity 722 W 168th St Rm 1801 New York NY 10032 Office Phone: 212-342-9033. Office Fax: 212-342-9044. E-mail: wil2001@columbia.edu. *

LIPKIN, MARTIN, medical scientist and educator; b. NYC, Apr. 30, 1926; s. Samuel S. and Celia (Greenfield) Lipkin; m. Joan Schulein, Feb. 16, 1958; children: Richard Martin, Steven Monroe. AB, NYU, 1946, MD, 1950. Diplomate Nat. Bd. Med. Examiners. Mem. staff NY Hosp., Meml. Hosp. for Cancer and Allied Diseases, 1972-96; prof. medicine Cornell U. Med. Coll., 1978—2009, prof. Grad. Sch. Med. Scis., 1978—2009; mem. and attending physician Meml. Sloan-Kettering Cancer Ctr., 1985-96; dir. clin. rsch. Strang Cancer Prevention Ctr., NYC, 1996—2008. Vis. physician Rockefeller U. Hosp., 1981—2006; nominator Nobel Prize for Physiology and Medicine, 1982; medallion Nat. Cancer Ctr. Res. Inst., 1976; Chao disting. lectr. U. Calif., 2000. Editor: (textbooks) Gastrointestinal Tract Cancer, 1978, Inhibition of Tumor Induction and Development, 1981, Gastrointestinal Cancer: Endogenous Factors, 1981, Calcium, Vitamin D and Prevention of Colon Cancer, 1991, Cancer Chemoprevention, 1992; contbr. articles to profl. jours. Bd. dirs., officer Med. Ednl. and Sci. Found. NY; bd. dirs. Internat. Soc. Cancer Chemoprevention. Officer USN, 1953—55. Recipient NIH Career Devel. award, 1962—71, Albert F.R. Andresen award, NY State Med. Soc., 1971, medallion, U. Padua, Italy, 1978, Elise Strang L'Esperance Leadership award, NY, 2005. Fellow: ACP, Am. Coll. Gastroenterology; mem.: Am. Gastroenterol. Assn., Am. Assn. Cancer Rsch., Am. Physiol. Soc., Am. Soc. Clin. Investigation, Med. Soc. State of NY (chmn. sci. program com. 1990—91, chmn. edn. com. 1991—99). Achievements include introducing computers into medicine; first identification of DNA synthesis and the cell cycle in humans; expansion of chemoprevention clinical trials worldwide; the first human intervention study of dietary calcium as a chemopreventive agent against colon cancer. Business E-Mail: mal2019@med.cornell.edu.

LIPKIND, MICHAEL AHARON, molecular biologist, philosopher; b. Moscow, Feb. 5, 1934; s. Aharon Solomon and Roza (Kogan) L.; m. Inessa Kluyeva, June 3, 1958 (div. Sept. 1964); 1 child, Tamara; m. Ludmila Shenderey, Sept. 12, 1970; children: Dina, Gabriel. MD, Moscow Med. Inst., 1958; PhD, Inst. Virology, Moscow, 1967. Pediatrician Dist. Hosp., Siberia, Russia, 1959—62; virologist Inst. Virology, Moscow, 1969—71, Vet. Acad., Moscow, 1971—74, Tel-Aviv U. Med. Sch., 1975—76, Kimron Vet. Inst., Beit Dagan, Israel, 1976—. Trade union rschr. Kimron Vet. Inst., Beit Dagan. Contbr. articles to profl. jours. Lt. Soviet Army, 1972. Grantee WHO, Geneva, 1978, U.S.-Israel Binat. Agrl. Rsch. Fund, Washington, 1979, 80, U.S.-Israel Coop. Devel. Rsch. Fund, Washington, 1991, 94. Fellow Israel Soc. Microbiology, Am. Soc. Virology, Internat. Soc. Study Subtle Energies, Assn. Sci. Study Consciousness; mem. Internat. Inst. Biophysics (directorial bd. Kaiserslautern 1987-95, directorial bd. Neuss-Hombroich 1995—). Avocations: classical music, kayaking, hiking, gardening. Home: Dafna 28 44810 Shaarey-Tikva Israel Office: Kimron Vet Inst 50200 Bet Dagan Israel Office Phone: 572549294173, 972-3-9688940. Personal E-mail: michael@lipkind.info.

LIPMAN, DAVID J., medical association administrator, researcher; BA with honors, Brown U., Providence, RI, 1976; MD, SUNY, Buffalo, 1980. Rsch. fellow math. rsch. br. Nat. Inst. Diabetes, Digestive & Kidney Diseases; dir. Nat. Ctr. Biotechnology Info., Bethesda, Md., 1989—, exec. sec. Bd. Sci. Counselors; editor-in-chief Biology Direct. Contbr. articles to profl. publs. Recipient 3 Pub. Health Svc. Outstanding Svc. medals, Dir.'s award, NIH, Sr. Scientist Accomplishment award, Internat. Soc. Computational Biology (ISCB), 2004. Fellow: Am. Acad. Arts and Sciences, Am. Coll. Med. Informatics; mem.: NAS Inst. Medicine. Achievements include development of FASTA biol. sequence comparison prog., 1985; Basic Local Alignment Search Tool (BLAST), 1990; contributed to some of the most important tools in gene sequence analysis. Office: Nat Ctr Biotechnology Info Bldg 38A Rm 8N807 8600 Rockville Pike Bethesda MD 20894 Office Phone: 301-496-2475. Office Fax: 301-480-9241. E-mail: lipman@ncbi.nlm.nih.gov.

LIPMAN, MARVIN MATTHEW, physician, medical educator, editor, writer; b. NYC, Nov. 6, 1928; s. Louis B. and Bertha L.; m. Naomi L. Lipman, June 17, 1951; children: Barry D., Amy F., Mark A., Harry W. AB, Columbia Coll., 1949; MD, Columbia Coll. of Phys. & Surg., 1954. Intern, asst. resident Columbia-Presbyn. Med. Ctr., 1954-56; sr. resident Mass. Gen. Hosp., 1959-61; chief of endocrinology N.Y. Med. Coll., Valhalla, 1967—81, White Plains (N.Y.) Hosp. Ctr., 1980—85, chief of medicine, 1985—90; prof. clin. medicine N.Y. Med. Coll., Valhalla, 1986—. Bd. trustees U.S. Pharmacopeia, 2000-05; chief med. adviser Consumers Union, Yonkers, N.Y., 1967—. Author: The Medicine Show, 1972, The Best of Health, 1998, Guide to a Healthy Heart, 2003; med. editor: Consumer Reports Mag., 1967—, Consumer Reports on Health, 1989—. Capt. US Army, 1956—58. Recipient Gold medal, Assn. Alumni of Columbia U. Coll. Physicians and Surgeons. Fellow: Am. Coll. Endocrinology, ACP; mem.: Physicians for Social Responsibility, Physicians for a Nat. Health Program, Am. Assn. Clin. Endocrinologists, Endocrine Soc., Am. Fedn. Med. Rsch., Am. Diabetes Assn., Alpha Omega Alpha. Avocations: theater, opera, chamber music, squash. Office: Scarsdale Med Group 259 Heathcote Rd Scarsdale NY 10583 Office Phone: 914-723-8100. Business E-Mail: mml83@columbia.edu.

LIPMAN, RICHARD PAUL, pediatrician; b. Cambridge, Mass., Aug. 1, 1935; s. Hyman Zelig and Betty (Likovsky) L.; m. Mary Alice Wilcox, Aug. 25, 1963; children: Gregory, Susan; m. Lora H. Higgins, July 6, 1996; children: Sarad, Michael Tomlinson. AB magna cum laude, Harvard U., 1957; MD cum laude, Tufts U., 1961. Diplomate Am. Bd. Pediatrics. Intern Boston Floating Hosp., 1961-62, jr. resident, 1962-63, sr. resident, 1963-64, chief resident, 1964; rsch. fellow infectious disease Med. Sch. U. N.C., Chapel Hill, 1967-69; practice pediatrics Peabody and Salem, Mass., 1969—. Mem. staff Mass. Gen. Children's Hosp. at NSMC, Salem, Mass., assoc. chief of staff, 1974-76, pres., chief of staff, 1976-79, chief of medicine, 1979-83, trustee, 1980-84, corporator, 1985-86; mem. staff Boston Children's Hosp., Mass Gen. Children's Hosp. NSMC, Beverly Hosp., Melrose-Wakefield Hosp., Salem Hosp.; clin. instr. pediatrics Tufts U. Sch. Medicine, Boston, 1969-74, asst. clin. prof., 1974-78, assoc. clin. prof., 1978—; bd. dirs. Tufts Assoc. Health Maintenance Orgn., 1988-95, North Shore Health Systems, Inc., 1995-96. Contbr. articles to profl. jours. Capt. M.C., AUS, 1964-66. Fellow Am. Acad. Pediatrics; mem. Am. Soc. Microbiology, Mass. Med. Soc., Tufts Alumni Assn., Nat. Assn. Watch and Clock Collectors. Office: 10 Centennial Dr Peabody MA 01960

LIPORACE, JOYCE, neurologist; MD, John Hopkins U., Balt., 1988. Diplomate Am. Bd. Psychiatry and Neurology, 1993. Intern Univ. Pa Sch. Medicine, resident; fellow John Hopkins Univ. Sch. Medicine; neurologist ctr. for neuroscience Riddle Meml. Hosp. Co-author: Concerns regarding Lamotrigine and breastfeeding, 2004, A Dissociation between Implicit and Explicit Verbal Memory in Left Temporal Lobe Epilepsy, 2004, Frequency of catamenial seizure exacerbation in women with localization-related epilepsy, 2004, "Seizure-alert" dogs: observations from an inpatient video/EEG unit, 2005, Mortality after epilepsy surgery, 2005, various others. Office: Riddle Memorial Hospital HCC II Ste 2205 1088 W Baltimore Pike 2205 Media PA 19063 Office Phone: 610-744-2960. Office Fax: 610-744-2420.

LIPP, MARILDA NOVAES, psychologist; d. Moacyr Mendes and Gilda Emmanuel Novaes; m. Darci Sassi, Sept. 5, 1993; children: Daniel Moacyr Novaes, Louis Mario Novaes. PhD in Psychology, George Washingotn U., DC, 1977. Instr. George Washingotn U., 1977—79; psychologist Gt. Oaks Ctr., Md., 1978—80; rsch. prof. PUC Campinas, Sao Paulo, Brazil, 1981—; dir. Ctr. Psicologico de Controle do Stress, Campinas, 1985—. Chief editor Estudos de Psicologia Jour., Brazil, 2005—. Author: (book) O Stress do Professor, Stress e o turbilhao da raiva, Como enfrentar o stress infantil, Stress no Brasil, Crianças estressadas, Mecanismos neuropsicofisiológicos do stress, Relaxamento para todos, Stress, Hipertensao arterial e qualidade de vida, Stress ao Longo da Vida. Financing grants, CNPq, 1986—2008. Mem.: APA, Assn. Brasileira de Stress (pres. 2005—08, coord. 2005—08). Achievements include patents for psychological test to measure stress in adults (ISSL). Home: Am Con Gen APO AA 34030-5000 Office: Cath Univ Campinas PUCC Rua Tiradentes 289 Conj 91 Guanabara Sao Paulo 013023-190 Brazil Home Fax: 055 19 3871 8572. Personal E-mail: mlipp@uol.com.br.

LIPPA, CAROL FRANCES, neurologist; b. Erie, Pa., Aug. 19, 1955; d. John Winn and Dorothy Marie (Zarembski) Ryan; m. Robert Leo Lippa, July 1982; children: Sara Marie, Alex Mitchell, Adam Lee. BA, McGill U., 1978; MD, U. Mass., 1983. Diplomate Am. Bd. Psychiatry and Neurology, Am. Bd. Neurorehab., cert. in geriat. neurology UCNS, 2009. Intern St. Vincent Hosp., Worcester, Mass., 1983—84; resident in neurology U. Mass. Med. Ctr., Worcester, 1984—86, chief resident, 1986—87, resident in neuropathology, 1987—88, fellow neurobiology of aging, 1988—89, asst. prof. neurology, 1989—95, dir. brain donation program, 1993—, investigator clin. drug trials, 1992—; physician neurorehab. svc. Fairlawn Rehab. Hosp., 1992—96; prof. neurology Drexel U. Coll. Medicine, Phila., 1996—; chief neurology svc. Med. Coll. Pa.-Hahnemann U., Phila., 2000—03, dir. Memory Disorders Ctr., 1996—. Contbr. more than 150 to 200 abstracts and articles to profl. jours. Recipient 2d prize residents and fellows presentation, Boston Soc. Neurology and Psychiatry, 1985. Mem.: Phila. Neurol. Soc. (pres. 2004—05), Am. Neurol. Assn., Am. Soc. Neurorehab., Soc. Neurosci., Am. Acad. Neurology, Alpha Omega Alpha. Home: 16 Radcliff Rd Bala Cynwyd PA 19004-2631 Office: Hahnemann Hosp Mailstop 423 245 N 15th St Philadelphia PA 19102 Business E-Mail: clippa@drexelmed.edu.

LIPPE, PHILIPP MARIA, neurosurgeon, academic administrator, educator; b. Vienna, May 17, 1929; came to U.S., 1938, naturalized, 1945; s. Philipp and Maria (Goth) L.; m. Virginia M. Wiltgen, 1953 (div. 1977); children: Patricia Ann Marie, Philip Eric Andrew, Laura Lynne Elizabeth, Kenneth Anthony Ernst; m. Gail B. Busch, Nov. 26, 1977. Student, Loyola U., Chgo., 1947-50; BS in Medicine, U. Ill. Coll. Medicine, 1952, MD with high honors, 1954. Diplomate Am. Bd. Neurol. Surgery, 1965, Nat. Bd. Med. Examiners, 1955, Am. Bd. Pain Medicine, 1992. Rotating intern St. Francis Hosp., Evanston, Ill., 1954-55; asst. resident gen. surgery VA Hosp., Hines, Ill., 1955, 58-59; asst. resident neurology and neurol. surgery Neuropsychiat. Inst., U. Ill. Rsch. and Ednl. Hosps., Chgo., 1959-60, chief resident, 1962-63, resident in neuropathology, 1962, postgrad. trainee in electroencephalography, 1963; resident in neurology and neurol. surgery Presbyn.-St. Luke's Hosp., Chgo., 1960-61; practice medicine, specializing in neurol. surgery/pain medicine San Jose, Calif., 1963—93; clin. prof. neurosurgery Stanford U., Calif., 1996—; exec. v.p. Am. Bd. of Pain Medicine, 1994—; exec. med. dir. Am. Acad. of Pain Medicine, 1996—. Instr. neurology and neurol. surgery U. Ill. 1962-63; clin. instr. surgery and neurosurgery Stanford U., 1965-69, clin. asst. prof., 1969-74, clin. assoc. prof., 1974-96, clin. prof., 1996—; staff cons. in neurosurgery O'Connor Hosp., Santa Clara Valley Med. Ctr., San Jose Hosp., Los Gatos Cmty. Hosp., El Camino Hosp. (all San Jose area); chmn. divsn. neurosurgery Good Samaritan Hosp., 1989-97, chmn. dept. clin. neuroscis., 1997-99; founder, exec. dir. Bay Area Pain Rehab. Ctr., San Jose, 1979—; clin. adviser to Joint Commn. on Accreditation of Hosps.; mem. dist. med. quality rev.

com. Calif. Bd. Med. Quality Assurance, 1976-87, chmn., 1976-77; cons., med. expert Med. Bd. Calif., 1996—; participant, moderator of numerous profl. seminars and sessions. Assoc. editor Clin. Jour. Pain; contbr. articles to profl. jours. Fellow ACS, Am. Coll. Pain Medicine (bd. dirs. 1991-94, v.p. 1991-92, pres. 1992-93, exec. med. dir.); mem. AMA (ho. of dels. 1981-, CPT editl. panel 1995-99, sr. adv. panel Guides to the Evaluation of Permanent Impairment 1997—, chair pain and palliative medicine splty. sect. coun. 2006-), Am. Coll. Physician Execs., Calif. Med. Assn. (ho. of dels. 1976-80, sci. bd., coun. 1979-87, sec. 1981-87, Outstanding Svc. award 1987), Santa Clara County Med. Soc. (coun. 1974-81, pres. 1978-79, Outstanding Contbn. award 1984, Benjamin J. Cory award 1987), Chgo. Med. Soc., Congress Neurol. Surgeons, Calif. Assn. Neurol. Surgeons (dir. 1974-82, v.p. 1975-76, pres. 1977-79, Pevehouse Disting. Svc. award 1997), San Jose Surg. Soc., Am. Assn. Neurol. Surgeons (chmn. sect. on pain 1987-90, dir. 1983-86, 87-90, Disting. Svc. award 1986, 90), Western Neurol. Soc., San Francisco Neurol. Soc., Santa Clara Valley Profl. Stds. Rev. Orgn. (dir., v.p., dir. quality assurance 1975-83), Fedn. Western Socs. Neurol. Sci., Internat. Assn. for Study Pain, Am. Pain Soc. (founding mem.), Am. Acad. Pain Medicine (sec. 1983-86, pres. 1987-88, Philipp M. Lippe Disting. Svc. award 1995, exec. med. dir. 1996—), Am. Bd. Pain Medicine (pres. 1992-93, exec. v.p. 1994—), Am. Soc. Law, Medicine, and Ethics, Alpha Omega Alpha, Phi Kappa Phi. Achievements include pioneer in medical application of centrifugal force using flight simulator; pioneer in the developing medical specialty of pain medicine. Avocations: photography, travel, computers, raising animals. Office: PO Box 41217 San Jose CA 95160-1217 Address: Am Acad Pain Medicine 4700 W Lake Glenview IL 60025 Personal E-mail: pmlippe@att.net.

LIPPINCOTT, JAMES ANDREW, retired biochemistry and biological sciences educator; b. Cumberland County, Ill., Sept. 13, 1930; s. Marion Andrew and Esther Oral (Meeker) L.; m. Barbara Sue Barnes, June 2, 1956; children— Jeanne Marie, Lisa Ellen, John James. AB, Earlham Coll., 1954; A.M., Washington U., St. Louis, 1956, PhD, 1958. Lectr. botany Washington U., 1958-59; Jane Coffin Childs Meml. fellow Centre Nat. de la Recherche Scientifique, France, 1959-60; asst. prof. biol. scis. Northwestern U., Evanston, Ill., 1960-66, assoc. prof., 1966-73, prof., 1973-81, prof. biochemistry, molecular biology and cell biology, 1981-94, prof. emeritus Evanston, Ill., 1994—, assoc. dean biol. scis., 1980-83; ret., 1994. Vis. assoc. prof. U. Calif., Berkeley, 1970-71; vis. prof. Inst. Botany U. Heidelberg (Germany), 1974. Contbr. articles to profl. jours. Grantee NIH, NSF, Am. Cancer Soc., USDA. Mem. Am. Soc. Biol. Chemists, Am. Soc. Plant Physiologists, Bot. Soc. Am., Am. Soc. Microbiology

LIPPMAN, MARC ESTES, oncologist, educator, medical researcher; b. Bklyn., Jan. 15, 1945; BA magna cum laude, Cornell U., 1964; MD, Yale U., 1968. Intern Osler med. svc. Johns Hopkins Hosp., Balt., 1968-69, asst. resident, oncology, 1969-70; clin. assoc. leukemia svc. Nat. Cancer Inst., NIH, Washington, 1970-71, clin. assoc. lab. biochemistry, 1971-73, sr. investigator med. br., 1974-88, head med. breast cancer sect., 1976-88; clin. prof. medicine and pharmacology Uniformed Svcs. U. Health Scis., 1978-88; dir. Vincent T. Lombardi Cancer Rsch. Ctr. Georgetown U., Washington, 1988—2001, prof. medicine and oncology, 1988—2001, also chair, dept. oncology, chief, divsn. hematology/oncology; John G. Searle prof. and chair, dept. internal medicine U. Mich. Health Sys., 2001—07; Kathleen & Stanley Glaser prof., chmn., dept. medicine Leonard M. Miller Sch. Medicine, U. Miami, 2007—. Mem. merit rev. bd. oncology Vet. Adminstrn. Med. Rsch. Svc., 1977-81, endocrine treatment com. Nat. Surg. Adjuvant Breast Project, 1977-86; cons. dept. pharmacology George Washington Sch. Medicine, 1978-89; co-chmn. Gordon Rsch. Conf. on Hormone Action, 1984, chmn., 1985; treas. Internat. Congress Hormones & Cancer, 1984—; mem. med. adv. bd. Nat. Alliance Breast Cancer Orgn., 1986—; mem. stage III monitoring com. Nat. Surg. Adjuvant Project Breast & Bowel Cancers, 1987-89; bd. trustees Am. Cancer Soc., Washington, 1989-92; mem. sci. adv. bd. Coordinated Coun. Cancer Rsch., 1989—; hon. dir. Y-ME, Nat. Orgn. Breast Cancer Info. & Support, 1990—; Woodward vis. prof., mem. Sloan-Kettering, 1990; Sidney Sachs Meml. lectr. Case Western Reserve, 1985, D.R. Edwards lectr. Tenovus Inst., Wales, 1985, Gosse lectr. Dalhousie U., Halifax, N.S., 1987, Transatlantic lectr. Brit. Endocrine Socs., 1989, Barofsky lectr. Howard U., 1990, Rose Kushner Meml. lectr. Long Beach Meml. Med. Ctr., 1990, Constance Wood Meml. lectr. Hammersmith Hosp., Eng., 1991; adj. prof. internal medicine, U. Mich. Med. Sch., Ann Arbor, Mich., 2007-; mem. clin. adv. bd., Raven Biotechnologies, Inc.; mem. scientific adv. bd., Seattle Genetics, 2000-, Perseus-Soros Fund; bd. dir. Ascenta Therapeutics; co-founder Oncologix (sold to Aronex), Peregrine Biotechnology (sold to Techniclone); invited spkr. in field. Contbr. articles to profl. jours., chapters to books. Endocrinology fellow Yale Med. Sch., 1973-74; recipient Mallinckrodt award Clin. Radioassay Soc., 1978, D.R. Edwards medal Tenovus Inst., 1985, Transatlantic medal Brit. Endocrine Socs., 1989, Tiffany award of Distinction, Komen Found., 1989, Brinker Internat. prize for Basic Rsch. in Breast Cancer. Fellow ACP, Am. Fedn. Clin. Rsch.(Clin. Investigator prize), Am. Soc. Cell Biology, Am. Assn. Cancer Rsch. (program com. 1986, Richard and Hinda Rosenthal Found. award, 1994), Am. Soc. Clin. Oncology (program com. 1987-89, chmn. local organizing com. 1989-90), Endocrine Soc. (pub. affairs com. 1980-81, Edward B. Astwood Lecture award, 1991), Metastasis Rsch. Soc.; mem. Assn. Am. Physicians, Am. Soc. Clin. Investigators (program com. 1988), Am. Soc. Biol. Chemists, Alpha Omega Alpha. Achievements include research in growth regulation of cancer, breast cancer, cancer endocrinology, growth factor receptors. Office: U Miami Dept Medicine Room 1001 MSTL 1430 NW 11th Ave Miami FL 33101 Office Phone: 305-243-9120. Business E-Mail: mlippman@med.miami.edu.

LIPPMAN, SCOTT MICHAEL, oncologist, educator; b. Columbia, SC, Apr. 2, 1955; s. Melvyn and Nanette (Gwirtzman) Lippman; m. Mary Elizabeth Marsh, Feb. 27, 1987; children: Kyle Andrew, Elizabeth Pauline. BS in Biol. Sci., magna cum laude, U. Calif., Irvine, 1977; MD, Johns Hopkins U. Sch. Medicine, Balt., 1981. Diplomate Am. Bd. Internal Medicine, cert. in Hematology, Med. Oncology, lic. Calif., Ariz., Tex. Intern in internal medicine Johns Hopkins Hosp., 1981—82; resident internal medicine Harbor-UCLA Med. Ctr., 1982—84; resident hematology Stanford U. Sch. Medicine, Calif., 1984—85; fellow med. oncology U. Ariz. Cancer Ctr., Tucson, 1985—87; clin. dir., faculty mem. cancer prevention/control prog. U. Ariz., 1987-88; asst. prof. medicine U. Tex. M.D. Anderson Cancer Ctr. & Grad. Sch. Biomed. Scis., Houston, 1988-92, assoc. prof. medicine, 1992-96, clinic chief head & neck medical oncology, 1994—96, prof. medicine, chair dept. clin. cancer prevention, 1996—. Mem. Am. Fedn. Clin. Rsch., 1982, Gulf Coast Hematology Soc., 1989, Am. Assn. Cancer Edn., 1989—99, Am. Soc. Preventive Oncology, 1989—99; chmn. chemoprevention subcom. Radiation Therapy Oncology Group, Phila., 1990—98; mem. numerous spl. rev. coms./panels Nat. Cancer Inst., Bethesda, Md., 1991—; vis. prof. U. Calif. Cancer Ctr., Irvine, 1991, Cancer Therapy & Rsch. Ctr., San Antonio, 1993, Orlando Cancer Ctr., Fla., 1993, Vancouver Cancer Ctr., Canada, 1997; cons. FDA, 1999. Assoc. editor Cancer Prevention Internat., 1993—95, Jour. of Nat. Cancer Inst., 1994—, Cancer Epidemiology Biomarkers & Prevention, 1998—, Clin. Cancer Rsch., 1999—, mem. editl. bd. Investigational New Drugs, 1995—97, 1997—, Jour. Cancer Edn., 1996—, Jour. Oncology: Index & Reviews, 1996—2000, Jour. Cellular Biochemistry, 1997—99, Cancer Therapeutics, 1997—99, Breast Cancer, 1998—, Internat. Jour. Oncology, 2002—, Head & Neck, 2003—, Oral Oncology, 2005—; contbr. articles to profl. jours., chapters to books. Recipient Tchg. award, Am. Acad. Family Physicians, 1987, Career Development award, Am. Cancer Soc., 1989—92, Sci. Writers award, 1990, 1994, Faculty Achievement award for cancer prevention, U. Tex., 1998; grantee NIH, 1980. Fellow: ACP, Internat. Acad. Oral Oncology (founding fellow), Am. Coll. Nutrition; mem.: AMA (cons. divsn. drugs/toxicology 1994), Internat. Assn. for Study of Lung Cancer, Soc. Head & Neck Surgeons (membership com. 1994), Am. Soc. Hematology, Am. Assn. Cancer Rsch. (prog. com. 1993—2002, awards com. 2000—03, pubs. com. 2002—07), Am. Soc. Clin. Oncology (cancer prevention/control com. 1993—96, edn. com. 2000—03, mem. Breast Cancer Risk Reduction Update Panel 2005—, Travel award 1985), Am. Chem. Soc., Harris County Med. Soc., Tex. Med. Assn. Avocation: tennis. Office: U Tex MD Anderson Cancer Ct Cancer Prevention Bldg CPB6 3468 1155 Pressler Houston TX 77030-4009 Office Phone: 713-745-3672. Office Fax: 713-794-4679. Business E-Mail: slippman@mdanderson.org.

LIPPMAN, SHARON ROCHELLE, art historian and therapist, filmmaker; b. NYC, Apr. 9, 1950; d. Emanuel and Sara (Goldberg) L. Student, Mills Coll., Columbia U., 1968; BFA, New Sch. Social Rsch., 1970, CCNY, 1972; MA in Cinema Studies, NYU, 1976, postgrad., 1987. Cert. secondary tchr., N.Y.; cert. in nonprofit orgn. mgmt. Instr., dir., founder Sara Sch. of Creative Art, Sayville, NY, 1976-85; founder, exec. dir., tchr. Art Without Walls, Inc., Sayville and NYC, 1985—; hon. bench mem. Art Without Walls Inc., 2009; curator art exhbn. Mus. Without Walls Heckscher State Park, East Islip, NY, 1985-87; exec. dir., curator Profl. Artist Network for Artists Internationally, 1991—; founder Art Without Walls, Inc., 1985—, Mus. Without Walls, Ctrl. Park, NYC, 2005; with Hon. Bench Art Without Walls Inc.; founder, vol. Bethdage state Pk., Long Island, NY; with Moods Southwest Art Exhibition, 2009, West Islip Pub. Libr., NYC; founder Sharon Lippman LI Hall of Fame Vol. Svc. Organizer Profl. Artist Network for Nat./Internat. Artists, 1994; curator Pub. Art in Pub. Spaces,Scott Landoll Art Exhbn., West Islip; instr. art therapy sessions Maryhaven Ctr. Pub. Libr., Port Jefferson, N.Y., 2004, Mus. Without Walls - Rhapsody in Art, 2006; head art therapy project Mary Haven Ctr., Port Jefferson, N.Y., 2004; origami zoo art therapist Southside Hosp., Bayshore, N.Y., 2005; with 9/11-City-Country-Memories Art/Writting Expo, Battery Pk., NYC, 2007. Author: Patterns, 1968, College Poetry Press Anthology, 1970, America at the Millennium, 2000; exhibited in group shows at LI Children's Mus., Garden City, NY, 1995-97, Suffolk County Legislature, Hauppauge, NY, 1997, Bayport-Bluepoint Libr., 1997, East Islip Libr., 1997-98, U.S. Dept. Interior, Ft. Wadsworth, NY, 2001, Ellis Island Immigration Mus., NY, 2002, West Islip Libr., 2000-01, 07, Battery Park, NYC, 2002, Central Park, NYC, 2003, Spirit Walk Gallery, Sayville, NY, 2003, Within These Walls, Nassau County Detetion Ctr., Westbury, NY, 2003, South St. Seaport, NYC, 2004, 06, Southside Hosp., Bayshore, NY, 2005, West Islip Libr., 2005, 07, South Country Libr., Bellport, NY, 2005, 2010, Cuisine Cuisine, Museum Without Walls, Battery Pk., NYC, 2008, Memories 9/11 City Country, 2009, Mus. Without Walls-Ctr. Pk., NYC, 2005-06, 07, South County Libr., Bellport, 2005, Nassau County Detention Ctr., 2005, Nassau Denention Ctr., Westbury, 2006, West Sayville Firehouse, NY, 2007, Into The Woods, South Country Lib, 2008, Artists at Work, Art Exhbn., Ctrl. Pk., 2011; pub. art mural History of LI-NY Baymen, 1987, Immigration on the NYS Waterways, 2001, Leadership Tng. Inst., Hempstead, NY, 2003, Nassau County Detention Ctr., 2003, Southside Hosp., Bay Shore, 2004, Mary Haven Ctr., Port Jefferson Station, NY, 2004, Miko Mus. Art Therapy, 2006, West Islip Pub. Libr., NY, 2006-07; represented in permanent collection Devel. Disabilities Inst., Suffolk County Legis. Bldg., Polish Consulate, NY, West Islip Pub. Libr., East Islip Pub. Libr., Ctrl. Park Zoo, Coll. Art Assn. Bull. Conv. NY, Gerald Ginsburg Artist with Disabilities West Islip, 2010, Mus. without Walls-War-peace-Space and H2O, Intrepid Sea, Air & Space Mus., 2010, Peter Klubek & Maria Petrovaskaya, South County Pub. Libr., Bellport, NY, 2010, War and Peace, Am. War Vets., NYC, 2010, Three: 3 Artists-3 Views, Art Exhbn., South Coontry Libr., Bellport, NY, 2010, Peter Klubek, Maria Petrovaskaya and Gerald Ginsburg Art Exhbn., South Country Libr., Bellport, NY, 2010, Mus. W Thout Walls: War-Peace-Space-H20, Bryant Pk., NYC, 2010; Robert Moses State Park, NY, Smith Haven Mall Lake Grove, Garden City Mall, NY, Southside Hosp., Bayshore, Connections-Outsider Art, South Country Pub. Libr., Bellport, NY, 2007, Rhapsody in Art, Nassau Detention Ctr., Westbury, 2006, West Islip Pub. Libr., NY, 2007, Pen to Brush, 2008, Bryant Park, NYC, 2007, health program West Sayville Firehouse, NY, 2008,Cuisine -Cuisine Museum Without Walls Batterypark NYC, 2008, Memories 9/11 City Country Museum Without Walls Batterypark NYC, 2009, Art Without Walls INC, Lone Artist Art Exhibition West Islip Lib., NY,2009, Gerald Gins Burg: Artist Disability Art Program South Country Lib.Bellport,2009, Gerald Ginsburg Outsider Artist-Art Exhbn.-ISLIP Pub. Libr., 2010, Scottish Castles Art & Writing Art Therapy Good Samartan Hospital Pediatric Word West Iship, 2009, Moods of the Southwest, 2009, Bones & Bugs Art Exhbn., 2010-11, Kim Turner Artist Disabilities Art Exhbn. West Island Pub. Libr., 2011, South Country Pub. Libr., Bellport, NY, 2011, Safari Adventure Art Therapy Game NYU Pediat. Ward U. Hosp. NYC, 2011, Mus. Without Walls Art Am. Vets. & Vets. Without Vets. Disabilities, Art Exhbn., Battery Pk., 2011, People, Animals, Magic, Kim Turner-Artist Art Exhbn., Ctrl. Pk, NYC, 2011, South Country Libr., Bellport, NY, 2011. Vol. Good Samaritan Hosp., 1984, Southside Hosp., 1983, U. Stony Brook Hosp., 1985, Schneider Children's Hosp., New Hyde Park, N.Y., 1992, New Light-AIDS Patients, Smithtown, N.Y., 1993, Gerald Ginsburg, Artist, Helen Keller Svcs. for the Blind, Hempstead, N.Y., 1993-94, St. Charles Hosp. and Rehab. Ctr., 1996, Nat. Health Bill Pub. Forum, Sayville Mid. Sch., 1996, Art Puzzles-Art Therapy Geriatrics Ward, Brookhaven (N.Y.) Meml. Hosp., 1990,South Country Libr., Bellport, 2009, Art Therapy Program Original Dept. Disabilities, Suffolk County, N.Y., 1988, Din-o-Soar Art Therapy Southside Hosp.-Pediatrics Ward, Bayshore, N.Y., 1999, Scotish Castles, Art & Writing Art Therapy, Good Samaritan Pediatric Ward, West Iship, Ny, 2009, Art Box-Art Therapy, Pediat. Ward Southside Hosp., Bayshore, 2000, It Takes Two Art Therapy, St. Charles Hosp., Port Jefferson, N.Y., 2000; mem. Whitney Mus., Guggenheim Mus., Mus. Modern Art, Met. Mus. Art, Jewish Mus., Mus. of the City of N.Y., Art in Am., Art News, Am. Artist, Mus. Without Walls-Cuisine-Cuisine, Art Expo Battery Pk. Inc., 2008; trustee Sayville Libr. Bd., 1996; bd. dirs. Friends of the Arts St. Joseph's Coll., N.Y., 1997. Gen. MWW Army - TEST. Recipient Suffolk County New Inspiration award, 1990, 2006, Am. Artist Art Svc. award Am. Artists mag., 1993, Suffolk County Legis. proclamation, 1993, Newsday Leadership Vol. award Newsday newspaper, 1994, Nat. Women's Month award Town of Islip, 1996, Disting. Women's award Town of Islip, 1996, Nat. Poetry Press award, 1996, Cmty. Action award Suffolk County Ret./Sr. Vol. Program, 2002; named to L.I. Vol. Hall of Fame for Cultural Arts, 2004, Hall of Fame; Inspiration award Suffolk County News, 2005. Mem. Orgn. Through Rehab. and Tng., Coll. Art Assn., Met. Mus. Art, Mus. Modern Art Univ. Film Assn., Sayville C. of C. American Heritage. Achievements include honorary bench installed in Bethpage State Park, NY. Avocations: art, reading, politics. Office: Art Without Walls Inc PO Box 2066 New York NY 10185-2066 also: Art Without Walls Inc PO Box 341 Sayville NY 11782 Office Phone: 631-567-9418. Personal E-mail: artwithoutwalls@msn.com. Business E-Mail: artwithoutwalls3@webtv.net.

LIPPY, KAREN DOROTHY FETHE, nurse psychotherapist; b. Balt., July 2, 1946; d. Vernon Harold and Dorothy Margaret (Wirth) Fethe; m. Robert Eugene Lippy, July 29, 1972; 1 child, Jarrod Blaire. BS in Nursing, U. Md., Balt, 1972, MS in Nursing, 1975. Cert. clin. specialist in adult psychiat./mental health nursing, master addictions counselor, critical incident stress mgmt., eye movement desensitization and reprocessing, diplomate Am. Coll. Profl. Mental Health Practitioners; cert. nursing adminstrn.-advanced. Clin. nurse specialist Springfield Hosp. Ctr., Sykesville, Md., 1975-79, asst. dir. nursing, 1979-86, dir. nursing, 1986-97; nurse psychotherapist Reentry Mental Health Svcs., Westminster, Md., 1983—; mem. Carroll County Criticial Incident Stress Mgmt. Team, 1999—. Task force on RN stds. practice Md. State Bd. Nursing; patient rights, classification, RN job specification, and credentialing/privileging task forces Md. Mental Hygiene Adminstrn. Recipient Gov.'s Citation for Excellence, State of Md., Achievement in Nursing Adminstrn., Md. Dept. Mental Hygiene. Mem. ANA, Md. Nurses Assn. (dist. bd. dirs.), Internat. Critical Incident Stress Found., EMDR Internat. Assn., Sigma Theta Tau, Phi Kappa Phi. Home: 2519 Bird View Rd Westminster MD 21157-8309 Office: 40 S Church St Ste 105 Westminster MD 21157-5414 Office Phone: 410-848-9244.

LIPSHUTZ, LAUREL SPRUNG, psychiatrist; b. Easton, Pa., Dec. 11, 1946; d. Joseph A. and Helen A. (Rochlin) S.; m. Robert M. Lipshutz, June 15, 1975; 1 child, Jonathan. BA, U. Pa., 1968; MD, Albany Med. Coll. of Union U., 1972. Diplomate Am. Bd. Psychiatry and Neurology. Resident in psychiatry Johns Hopkins Hosp., Balt., 1972-75; unit chief psychiat. inpatient unit Phila. Gen. Hosp., 1975-77; dir. psychiat. inpatient svc. Pa. Hosp., Phila., 1977-96; assoc. dir. residency tng. Inst. of Pa. Hosp., Phila., 1983-96; coord. psychiat. clerkship for U. Pa. med. students Pa. Hosp., Phila., 1982-95; psychiatrist, 1995—; pvt. practice, psychiatry and psychotherapy, 1996—. Sr. examiner Am. Bd. Psychiatry and Neurology, 1979—; sr. attending psychiatrist Inst. Pa. Hosp., Phila., 1989-97, psychiatrist, 1984—; clin. assoc. prof. psychiatry U. Pa. Sch. Medicine, Phila., 1997—, Thomas Jefferson Med. Coll., Phila. 1994-97. Fellow: Am. Psychiat. Assn. (life, disting.); mem. Am. Soc. Psychoanalytic Physicians, Pa. Psychiat. Assn. (com. on women), Phila. Psychiatry Soc., Assn. Acad. Psychiatry (region III Excellence in Tchg. award 1995). Office: The Curtis Ctr 601 Walnut St Ste 960W Philadelphia PA 19106 Office Phone: 215-923-7851. Office Fax: 215-592-7853. Personal E-mail: lslipshutz@comcast.net.

LIPSITT, DON RICHARD, psychiatrist, educator; b. Boston, Nov. 24, 1927; s. Joseph (None) and Anna Naomi Paeff Lipsitt; m. Merna Maxine Pilot, Aug. 9, 1953; children: Eric David, Steven Daniel. BA, NYU, NYC, 1949; MA, Boston U., 1951; MD, U. of Vt., 1956; MA (hon.), Harvard U., 1990. Cert. psychoanalyst Boston Psychoanalytic Inst./Mass., 1969. Med. intern Albert Einstein Med. Ctr., Bronx, 1956—57, psychiatry resident, 1957—58, NIMH, Bethesda, Md., 1959—60, Beth Israel Hosp., Boston, 1960—62; candidate Boston Psychoanalytic Inst., 1961—68; rsch. psychiatrist Clin. Neuropharmacology Rsch. Ctr., St. Elizabeths Hosp., Washington, 1958—60; sr. asst. surgeon USPHS, Washington, 1958—60; dir. med. psychology and cons.-liaison psychiatry Beth Israel Hosp., Boston, 1962—69, founding dir. integration clinic, 1962—69; founding chmn. dept. psychiatry Mt. Auburn Hosp., Cambridge, Mass., 1969—99; asst. prof. psychiatry Harvard Med. Sch., Boston, 1969—74, assoc. prof. psychiatry, 1974—90, clin. prof. psychiatry, 1990—. Founding editor-in-chief Psychiatry in Medicine, Baywood, NY, 1969—79, Gen. Hosp. Psychiatry, Elsevier, St. Louis, 1979—2004; founding dir. Integration Clinic, Beth Israel Hosp., Harvard Med. Sch.; pres. Inst. for Integrated Healthcare. Author: (textbook (hart publications) Your Self: An Introduction to Psychology; editor: (textbook (oxford university press) Psychosomatic Medicine: Current Trends and Clinical Applications, (textbook) Handbook of Studies on General Hospital Psychiatry (Elsevier); editor: (author) Hypochondriasis: Modern Perspectives on an Ancient Malady (Oxford Press); contbr. over 100 articles to profl. jours., chapters to books. Mem. Gov.'s Com. on Alzheimer's Disease, Boston, 1985—86, Blue Ribbon Commn. on Inpatient Mental Health Svcs., Boston, 1979—81; cons. Dukakis for Pres. Com. on Health Resources, Boston, 1987—89; dir. Health Planning Coun. Greater Boston, 1978—81. Recipient Psyche Award for Innovation in Integrated Behavioral Health Care, Dorothy and Nicholas Cummings Found., 1999, Thomas P. Hackett Award for Lifetime Contbn. to Consultation-Liaison Psychiatry, Acad. of Psychosomatic Medicine, 2000, Robert Kellner Meml. Lectureship, U. N.M. Psychiatry Dept., 2003, First Milton Rosenbaum Lecture, U. of N.Mex, 1995, Outstanding Contribn. to Consultation-Liaison Psychiatry award, Soc. of Liaison Psychiatry, 1994, Pres. award, Am. Psychiat. Assn., 2009, Lifetime Achievement Presdl. award, Mass. Psychiatric Soc., 2010; fellow, Internat. Coll. of Psychosomatic Medicine, 1972. Fellow: World Psychiat. Assn. (mem. psychosom. sect., chair gen. hosp. psychiatry sect., co-chair psychiat. medicine and primary care sect., jour. editl. advisor), Internat. Coll. Psychosomatic Medicine (pres. 1999—2001), Am. Psychiat. Assn. (disting. life fellow 2003—, Spl. Presdl. Commendation award, 53rd Convocation 2009), Am. Coll. Psychiatrists (life; publs. com. 1987—88, emeritus); mem.: Boston Psychoanalytic Soc. (ethics com. 2001), Assn. for Academic Psychiatry (exec. sec. 1985—2001, disting. life fellow 2006—, Lifetime Achievement award 2001), Am. Psychosomatic Soc. (life; coun. 1986—89), Inst. for Integrated Health Care (pres. 2005—, founder), Am. Assn. Gen. Hosp. Psychiatrists (pres. 1991—93, founding charter mem.), Mass. Psychiat. Soc. (pres. 1991). Avocations: travel, music, reading, sailing. Home and Office: 15 Griggs Rd Brookline MA 02446-4782 Office Phone: 617-734-2825. Business E-Mail: don_lipsitt@hms.harvard.edu.

LIPSITT, LEWIS PAEFF, psychology professor; b. New Bedford, Mass., June 28, 1929; s. Joseph and Anna Naomi (Paeff) L.; m. Edna Brill Duchin, June 8, 1952; children: Mark, Ann. BA, U. Chgo., 1950; MS, U. Mass., 1952; PhD, U. Iowa, 1957; Doctorate (hon.), U. Athens, Greece, 2006. Lic. Psychologist RI, 2010. Instr. dept. psychology Brown U., Providence, 1957, asst. prof., 1958-61, assoc. prof., 1961-66, prof., 1966-96, dir. Child Study Ctr., 1967-92, Wriston lectr., 1993—96, prof. emeritus psychology, med. sci. and human devel., 1996—, rsch. prof. psychology, 1996—. Mem. Gov.'s Adv. Commn. on Mental Retardation, 1963-66; cons. Nat. Inst. Health; edn. task force Model Cities Program, Providence, 1969-71; fellow Stanford Ctr. for Advanced Study in Behavioral Scis., 1979-80; vis. scientist Nat. Inst. Mental Health, 1986-87; chair steering com. nat. child care project Nat. Inst. Child Health and Human Devel., 1994-99, adv. com., 1999-2001. Co-author: Child Development, 1979; founder, editor: Infant Behavior and Devel., 1978-82; founding co-editor: Advances in Child Development and Behavior, 1963-70, 78-82; co-editor: Research Readings in Child Psychology, 1963, Experimental Child Psychology, 1971, Advances in Infancy Research, 1981-99, Self-regulatory Behavior and Risk Taking, 1991, Progress in Infancy Research, 1991-99; contbr. articles to profl. jours. Bd. dirs. Providence Child Guidance Clinic, 1960-63, bd. mem. RI Kids Count Bd., 2003-07, chmn., 2004-07; trustee Butler Hosp., Providence, 1965-84, 2006—; mem. bd. sci. counselors Nat. Ins. Child Health and Human Devel., 1984-88; nat. co-dir. Lee Salk Family Ctr., Kidspeace, Allentown, Pa., 1993-2008; participant White House Conf. on Child Care, 1998. With USAF, 1952—54, clin. psychologist USAF, 1952—54, Lackland AFB. Recipient Mentor Lifetime Achievement award, AAAS, 1995, Profl. Achievement citation, U. Chgo., 1995, James McKeen Cattell award, 1979, Lifetime Achievement Child Studies award, Internat. Soc. Infant Studies, Japan Soc. Baby Studies, 2006; USPHS Spl. Rsch. fellow, 1966, Guggenheim fellow, 1972—73, USPHS fellow, 1973. Fellow AAAS, APA (exec. com. divsn. devel. psychology 1967-70, pres. divsn. devel. psychology 1980-81, bd. sci. affairs 1985-88, exec. dir. for sci. 1990-91, sci. officer 1991-92, Nicholas Hobbs award 1990, exec. com. divsn. gen. psychology 1997-01, coun. of reps. 1997-00, pres. divsn. gen. psychology 1999-00, exptl. psychology coun. of reps. 2001-, Ernest R. Hilgard award for life achievement in gen. psychology 2004, Urie Bronfenbrenner award for studies in child devel. 2004, Lee Salk award for contribution to pediatric psychology 2010), Internat. Soc. Infant Studies (founding mem. 1978-, citation lifetime achievement studies on babies 2006); mem. AAUP, Soc. Rsch. in Child Devel., Internat. Soc. Study Behavioral Devel. (membership sec. 1981-83, exec. com. 1984-89), Am. Psychol. Soc. (founding mem., charter fellow, bd. dirs. 1989-90), Can. Inst. for Advanced Rsch. (chair adv. com. human devel. group 1995-2003, mem. adv. com. human devel. and population health 2000-04), RI Psychol. Assn. (bd. dirs. 1995-98, Mental Health Svc. award 1998), Eastern Psychol. Assn. (bd. mem., 1991-94, 2010-, pres., 1992-93). Jewish. Home Phone: 401-272-0828; Office Phone: 401-863-2332. Business E-Mail: Lewis_Lipsitt@brown.edu.

LIPSON, JONATHAN MARK, psychologist; s. Sheldon Robert and Joan B. L.; m. Yvonne Marie Lipson, Sept. 19, 1998. BA, Queen's U., Kingston, Ont., Can., 1984; MS, Okla. State U., 1988, PhD, 1993. Psychologist Saginaw (Mich.) Psychol. Svcs., 1993-95; postdoctoral fellow Genesys Regional Med. Ctr., Flint, Mich., 1995-97; dir. behavioral scis. Swedish Family Medicine Residency, Littleton, Colo., 1997—2002; ind. practice Lakewood, Colo., 2002—. Cons. Physicians for Social Responsibility, Denver, 1997-98; citizen amb. del. People to People Internat., Eastern Europe, 1992. Contbr. chpt. to book, articles to profl. jours. Med. Explorer advisor Boy Scouts Am., Flint, 1996-97. Named Explorer Post of Yr., Tall Pine coun. Boy Scouts Am., 1997. Mem. APA, Colo. Psychol. Assn. Avocations: hiking, camping, skiing, bicycling. Office: 1746 Cole Blvd Bldg 21 Ste 295 Lakewood CO 80401 Office Phone: 303-916-1952. Personal E-mail: jlipsonphd@aol.com.

LIPTON, LESTER, ophthalmologist, entrepreneur; b. NYC, Mar. 14, 1936; s. George and Rita (von Steinbaum) L.; m. Harriet Arfa, June 25, 1960; children: Sherri, Brandi, Shawn BA, NYU, 1959; MD, Chgo. Med. Sch, 1964. Rsch. fellow Chgo. Med. Sch., 1959-60; intern Brookdale Hosp. Ctr., Bklyn., 1964-65; resident Harlem Eye and Ear Hosp., NYC, 1965-68; assoc. attending Polyclinic French hosps., NYC, 1968-75; asst. attending physician, ophthalmologist, surg. instr. St. Clare's Hosp., NYC, 1975—; attending ophthalmologist Cabrini Med. Ctr., NYC, 1982—, St. Vincent's Hosp., NYC, 1995—. Founder Lipton Eye Clinic, N.Y.C., 1981—; v.p. Van Arfa Realty, N.Y.C., 1984-88; pres. H&L Realty, Suffern, N.Y., 1981—; mem. bd. dirs. Salisbury (Conn.) Pub. Health Nursing Assn. Mem. U.S. Congl. Adv. Bd.; former mem. bd. deacons Congregationalist Ch., mem. Presbyn. Ch.; With AUS, 1956-58. Named Internat. Amigo, OAS; recipient Presdl. Citation for outstanding community svc., 1991 Mem. N.Y. Med. Soc., Am. Assn. Individual Investors, Bronx High Sch. Sci. Alumni Assn., Sharon Country Club, United Shareholders Assn., Internat. Platform Assn., Wider Quaker Fellowship, Vanderbilt U. Cabinet Club, Fairhope Yacht Club, Lakewood Golf Club. Republican. Home: 55 Interlaken Estates Box 1923 Lakeville CT 06039 Mailing: PO Box 1923 Lakeville CT 06039 Office: Lipton Eye Clinic PO Box 1923 Lakeville CT 06039 Personal E-mail: hslipton@sbcglobal.net.

LIPTZIN, BENJAMIN, psychiatrist; b. NYC, Sept. 17, 1945; s. David Murray and Mollie (Brody) L.; m. Sharon Leslie Rothstein, June 10, 1968; children: Shoshanna, Daniel, Deborah. BA, Yale U., 1966; MD, U. Rochester, NYC, 1971. Diplomate Am. Bd. Psychiatry and Neurology. Resident in psychiatry U. Va. Hosp., Charlottesville, 1971-74; med. officer NIMH, Rockville, Md., 1974-78; dir. geriatric psychiatry McLean Hosp., Belmont, Mass., 1978-89, asst. gen. dir., 1989-90; chief dept. psychiatry Baystate Med. Ctr., Springfield, Mass., 1990—; prof., dep. chmn. dept. psychiatry Tufts U. Sch. Medicine, 1990—. Contbr. articles to profl. jours. With USPHS, 1972-78. Recipient Acad. award NIMH, 1983, Jact Weinberg award, APA. Fellow Am. Psychiat. Assn. (comtee-at-large 1992-95, Disting. life mem.); mem. AMA, Am. Coll. Psychiatrists, Am. Assn. Geriatric Psychiatry (sec., treas. 2007—08), Group Advancement Psychiatry (chmn. com. aging). Democrat. Jewish. Office: Baystate Med Ctr Dept Psychiatry 759 Chestnut St Springfield MA 01199-1001 Office Phone: 413-794-4235. E-mail: benjamin.liptzin@bhs.org.

LIS, CHRISTOPHER G., public health service officer; b. Chgo., Sept. 29, 1969; BS, U. Ill. Urbana Champaign, 1993; PhD, MPH, U. Ill. Med. Ctr., 2011. V.p. r & d Cancer Treatment Ctrs. America, 2003—08, chief strategy officer, v.p., r & d, 2008—11, chief outcomes rsch., v.p. market insights, 2011—. Invited expert reviewer, referee Am. Jour. Managed Care, Cancer Am. Cancer Soc., 2008—11; invited expert reviewer, interdivsn. innovation rsch. program Netherlands Orgn. Sci. Rsch., 2010. Recipient award, US Pub. Health Svc. Mem.: Bain & Co. Exec. NPS Forum, Comparative Effectiveness Rsch. (hon.; mem. editl. adv. bd.). Avocations: soccer, baseball. Office: 500 E Remington St Schaumburg IL 60173 Business E-Mail: christopher.lis@ctca-hope.com.

LISAK, ROBERT PHILIP, neurologist, researcher, educator; b. Bklyn., Mar. 17, 1941; s. Irving Arthur and Sylvia Lillian (Kadish) L.; m. Deena Freda Penchansky, Aug. 2, 1964; children: Ilene Ann, Michael Loren. BA, NYU, 1961; MD, Columbia U., 1965; MA (hon.), U. Pa., 1976. Diplomate Am. Bd. Neurology. Intern in medicine Montefiore Hosp. and Med. Ctr., Bronx, 1965-66; rsch. assoc. NIMH, Bethesda, Md., 1966-68; resident in medicine Bronx Mcpl. Med. Ctr., 1968-69; resident in neurology Hosp. of the U. of Pa., Phila., 1969-72; with Sch. of Medicine U. Pa., Phila., 1972-87, prof. neurology Sch. of Medicine, 1980-87, vice chmn. dept. neurology Sch. of Medicine, 1985-87; prof., chmn. dept. neurology Sch. of Medicine Wayne State U., Detroit, 1987—. Mem. adv. bd. Guillain-Barre Syndrome Internat., Wynnewood, Pa., 1985—; mem. med. adv. bd. Myasthenia Gravis Found., Mpls., 1988—, Nat. Multiple Sclerosis Soc., N.Y.C., 1988—. Co-author: Myasthenia Gravis, 1982; mem. editl. bd. Jour. Neuroimmunology, 1984-98, Muscle and Nerve Jour., 1981-86, 92-95, 98-2002, Neurology, 1981-86, Annals of Neurology, 1990-95, Jour. Peripheral Nervous Sys., 1995-2006, Clin. Neuropharm., 1997—; editor-in-chief Jour. Neurol. Sci., 1998—; contbr. articles to profl. jours. With USPHS, 1966-68. Fulbright rsch. scholar, London, 1978-79; recipient Disting. Teaching award U. Pa., 1985, Drs. award Myasthenia Gravis Found., 1991. Fellow Am. Acad. Neurology (sci. issues com. 1987-93, chair elect, sect. multiple sclerosis, 2008-), Royal Coll. Physicians, London; mem. Am. Neurol. Assn. (membership com. 1989-91, chmn. 1990-91, sci. program com. 1994-96, councillor 2002 05), Internat. Soc. Neuroimmunology (exec. com. 1987-91, 95-2001, sec.-treas. 1991-95), Am. Assn. Immunologists, Soc. for Neurosci., Norwegian Neurol. Assn., Royal Soc. Medicine. Office: Wayne State U Sch Medicine 8D-UHC 4201 St Antoine Detroit MI 48201 Home Phone: 248-646-2974. Business E-Mail: rlisak@med.wayne.edu.

LISBERGER, STEPHEN G., physiologist, educator; BA in Math., Cornell U.; PhD in Physiology, U. Wash. Investigator Howard Hughes Med. Inst., 1997—; prof. physiology U. Calif., San Francisco, dir. W.M. Keck Found. Ctr. Integrative Neuroscience, co-dir. Sloan Ctr. Theoretical Neurobiology. Recipient McKnight Scholar award, Distinction in Tchg. award, U. Calif. San Francisco, McKnight Investigator award. Fellow: Am. Acad. Arts and Sciences; mem.: AAAS, Soc. Neuroscience (Young Investigator award). Office: UCSF Dept Physiology Box 0444 513 Parnassus Ave San Francisco CA 94143-0444 Office Phone: 415-476-1062. Office Fax: 415-502-4848. E-mail: sgl@keck.ucsf.edu.

LISBONA BAÑUELOS, ANA M., psychology professor; b. Zaragoza, Spain, July 9, 1976; d. Juan J. Lisbona and Ana M. Bañuelos; m. Francisco J. Palací, Sept. 30, 2001; 1 child, Carmen Palaci. PhD in Psychology, UNED, Madrid, 2007. Asst. prof. UNED, 2003—, Ministry of Edn., Spain, 2007. Office: UNED C/Juan del Rosal 10 Madrid 28005 Spain Business E-Mail: amlisbona@psi.uned.es.

LISH, BRUCE JARED, dentist; b. June 27, 1969; s. Jerome and Marion Lish; m. Cindy Michelle Rosenblum-Lish, Aug. 15, 1993; children: Matthew, Jessica. BA Biology, NYU, 1991, DDS, 1994. Cert. dental oral surgery Brookdale U. Hosp. Med. Ctr. Pvt. practice gen. dentistry, Bklyn., 1995—; clin. asst. prof. NYU Coll. Dentistry, NYC, 1996—98; residency dir. gen. practice program Brookdale U. Hosp. Ctr., Bklyn., 1998—2000; dir. divsn. dentistry St. Luke's-Roosevelt Hosp., NYC, 2000—; surg. course instr. IMTEC Implants; clin. asst. prof. Columbia U. Coll. Dentistry; clin. asst. prof. dept. pediatric dentistry NY U. Dentistry, 2008—. Creator: (ednl. dental program) Dr. Molar Magic Show, 1993—; pub.: Magic Builder's Monthly, 2000—03. Performer, provider cmty. svc. Clown Dr. Program, 1994—; bd. dirs. Hebrew Ednl. Soc., Bklyn., 1998—2003, Dr. Molar Magic Found., 2005—. Mem.: Am. Soc. Dentistry for Children (sec./treas. 2000—01), Am. Acad. Implant Dentistry, Soc. Am. Magicians (chpt. pres. 1998). Jewish. Office: 7224 Ave T Brooklyn NY 11234 Home Phone: 718-264-1727; Office Phone: 718-763-1817. E-mail: blish@chpnet.org.

LISI, DEBORAH JEANNE, performance improvement coordinator; b. Providence, Apr. 10, 1949; d. Henry Joseph and Alice Deborah Brown; m. Robert Guido Lisi, Nov. 6, 1971; 1 child, Sheryl Lisi Cheal. BS, Boston U., 1971; MS, U. RI, 1977. Cert. diabetes educator U. RI Coll. Pharmacy, 2005, cardiovasc. outpatient educator RI Dept. Health, 2010. Asst. prof. nursing Cmty Coll. RI, Lincoln, RI, 1972—81; sales assoc. Uptown Baby, E. Greenwich, RI, 1994—96; mgr., cons. Cinderella's Bridal, E. Greenwich, 1996—2000; staff nurse RI Renal Inst., Warwick, RI, 2000—01, Pawtucket Valley Urgent, Coventry, RI, 2001—04; adj. instr. New England Inst. of Tech., Warwick, RI, 2003—; nurse supervisor CCAP Family Health Svc., Cranston, RI, 2004—08. Mem. med. adv. com. Family Planning Dept. Health, RI, 2004—08; performance improvement coord. CCAP Family Health, 2008—. Founder Outreach Quilters, E. Greenwich, RI, 1989—97; mem. Our Lady of Mercy Outreach Steering Com., E. Greenwich, 1992—98; agy. leader Nat. Health Disparities Collaborative, 2006—, RI Chronic Care Collaborative, 2005—, mem., planning com., 2011. Mem.: ANA, Am. Assn. Diabetes Educators, Cert. Diabetes Outpatient Educators (fin. officer 2007, bd. mem. 2005—08, bd. dirs., mem. credentialing com.), Boston U. Alumni, R.I. State Nurses Assn. Cath. Avocations: quilting, embroidery, knitting, reading, exercise. Home: 147 Wunnegin Cir East Greenwich RI 02818 Office: CCAP Family Health Svcs 1090 Cranston St Cranston RI 02920 Office Phone: 401-943-1981, 401-427-4085. Personal E-mail: deborah_lisi@hotmail.com. Business E-Mail: dlisi@comcap.org.

LISOWSKA, BARBARA, anesthesiologist, educator; b. Warsaw, Feb. 19, 1954; Degree in Higher Edn., Med. U. Warsaw, 1979. Assoc. prof. Inst. Rheumatology, 2010—. Office: Spartanska 1 Warsaw Mazowsze 02-637 Poland Office Phone: 0048228444241 ext. 216. E-mail: blisowska19@gmail.com.

LISTER, GEORGE, pediatrician; b. Miami, May 8, 1947; BA in Psych., Religious Studies, Brown U., Providence, 1969; MD, Yale U. Sch. Medicine, New Haven, 1973. Diplomate Am. Bd. Pediat., Nat. Bd. Med. Examiners, cert. Pediat. Cardiology, Neonatal-Perinatal Med., Pediat. Critical Care Med. Resident pediat. med. Yale U. Sch. Medicine, 1973—75; fellowship pediat. cardiology and neonatology U. Calif. Cardiovasc. Rssc. Inst., San Francisco, 1975—78; asst. to full prof. pediat. and anesthesiology Yale U. Sch. Medicine, 1978—2003; Robert L. Moore chair pediat. and prof. pediat. Southwestern Med. Sch., Dallas, 2003—. Sect. chief pediat. critical care medicine, dir. pediat. ICU Yale U. Sch. Medicine, 1978—2003; former editor-in-chief Pediat. Rsch.; sr. editor Rudolph's Pediat.; editor Rudolph's Pediat. Online. Contbr. articles to profl. jours. Recipient Established Investigator award, Am. Heart Assn., 1985; named one of Best Doctors Am., 1992;, Fulbright fellowship, 1990. Mem.: Inducted to Ist. Medicine (IOM), Acad. of Medicine, Engring. & Sci. Tex., Am. Bd. Pediat. (chair bd. dirs. 2004), Soc. Pediat. Rsch. (pres. 1993, Maureen Andrew Mentor award 2004), Internat. Pediat. Rsch. Found., Am. Pediat. Soc. (pres. 2008—09), Am. Acad. Pediat. (Disting. Career award, sect. on critical care 1999). Office: UT Southwestern Med Ctr 5323 Harry Hines Blvd Dallas TX 75390-9063 Office Phone: 214-648-3563. Business E-Mail: george.lister@utsouthwestern.edu.

LITCHMAN, MARK, allergist, immunologist, educator; MD, Rush U., 1984. Diplomate Am. Bd. Internal Medicine, Am. Bd. Internal Medicine-rheumatology, Am. Bd. Allergy and Immunology. Intern Greenwich Hosp., Conn., resident in internal medicine, 1985—87; fellow in allergy and immunology Yale-New Haven Hosp., 1987—89, fellow in rheumatology, 1987—89; assoc. clin. prof. medicine Yale Univ., hosp. affiliation includes Stamford Hosp.; active med. staff Greenwich Hosp. Named one of Best Doctors, NY Mag., 2010. Office: Greenwich Hospital 5 Perryridge Rd Greenwich CT 06830 Office Phone: 203-863-3000.

LITERÁTI-NAGY, BOTOND, physician; b. Budapest, Sept. 4, 1976; MD, 2002; degree in Internal Medicine, Med. Health & Sci. Centre, U. Debrecen, Hungary, 2007; degree in clinicopharmacology, U. Szeged, Hungary, 2010. Clin. physician, 1st dept. internal medicine Med. Health & Sci. Centre, U. Debrecen, 2002—07; investigator Drug Rsch. Ctr. Ltd, 2008. Mem.: Hungarian Soc. Osteporosis & Osteoarthrology, Hungarian Diabetes Assn., EASD. Avocations: tennis, sailing, skiing. Office: Ady E 12 Balatonfured Veszprem 8230 Hungary E-mail: botond.literati@drc.hu.

LITLE, VIRGINIA R., surgeon, educator; b. Boston, Mar. 26, 1963; BS, U. Vt., 1985; MD, Dartmouth-Brown, 1990. Asst. prof., surgery Mt. Sinai Hosp., 2004—08; assoc. prof., surgery U. Rochester Med. Ctr., 2008—. Fellow: ACS, Am. Coll. Chest Physicians. Home: 1470 Clover St Rochester NY 14610 Personal E-mail: vlitle@gmail.com.

LITMAN, GEORGE IRVING, physician, educator; b. Mass., Oct. 15, 1939; children: Scott, Amy, Kimberly, Megan. BS, Boston Coll., 1960; MD, Boston U., 1964. Intern Phila. Gen. Hosp., 1964-65; resident Univ. Hosp., Boston, 1965-66, Boston Vet.'s Hosp., 1966-67; fellow cardiology Emory U., Atlanta, 1967—69; unit head cardiology Genessee Hosp., Rochester, NY, 1969-71; assoc. physician Morton F. Plant Hosp., Clearwater, Fla., 1971-72; chief cardiology Akron Gen. Med. Ctr., Akron, Ohio, 1972—, med. dir. The Heart and Vascular Ctr., 2002—; prof. medicine NE Ohio U., Rootstown, Ohio, 1982—, chmn. dept. internal medicine, Coll. Medicine & Pharmacy, 2007—, chief cardiology emeritus, 2008; physician laurates Am. Coll. Physicians State Ohio, 2010. Recipient Disting. Svc. award Ohio Heart Assn., 1988, Physicians Laughts award, ACP, Ohio Chapt., 2010 Fellow Am. Coll. Cardiology, ACP, Am. Coll. Chest Physicians; mem. AMA, Summit County Med. Soc., Am. Heart Assn. (trustee Ohio 1974—, research rev. com. 1975—, chmn. 1981-83), Ohio Heart Assn. (Disting. Service award 1983), Akron Heart Assn. (Sauvageot Vol. Services award 1984). Office: Akron Gen Med Ctr 400 Wabash Ave Akron OH 44307-2463 Home Phone: 330-666-2220; Office Phone: 330-344-2132. Business E-Mail: glitman@agmc.org.

LITMAN, ROBERT BARRY, physician, writer, television and radio commentator; b. Phila., Nov. 17, 1947; s. Benjamin Norman and Bette Etta (Saunders) L.; m. Niki Thomas, April 21, 1985 (dec. April 4, 2011); children: Riva Belle, Nadya Beth, Caila Tess, Benjamin David (dec.). BS, Yale U., New Haven, Conn., 1968, MD, 1970, MS, MPhil in Anatomy, 1972. Diplomate Am. Bd. Family Practice, Am. Bd. Family Medicine, 2008. Postdoct. rsch. fellow Am. Cancer Soc. Yale U., New Haven, 1970-73, USPHS fellow, 1974-75; resident in gen. surgery Bryn Mawr Hosp., Pa., 1973-74; pvt. practice in medicine and surgery Ogdensburg, NY, 1977-93, San Ramon, Calif., 1993—; mem. staff A. Barton Hepburn Hosp., 1977-93, John Muir Med. Ctr., 1993—, San Ramon Regional Med. Ctr., 1993—, also chmn. med. edn., chmn. dept. family practice, 1998-99, chmn. med. edn., 2004—06. Commentator Family Medicine Stas. WWNY-TV and WTNY-Radio, TCI Cablevision, Contra Costa T.V.; moderator Ask the Dr.; clin. preceptor dept. family medicine State U. Health Sci. Ctr., Syracuse, 1978—. Author: Wynnefield and Limer, 1983, The Treblinka Virus, 1991, Allergy Shots, 1993; contbr. articles to numerous profl. jours. Pres. No. NY chpt. AHA. Fellow Life Ins. Med. Rsch. Fund, U. Coll. Hosp., U. London, 1969-70; recipient We. Access Video Excellence award, 1998, 2001, Bay Area Cable Excellence award, 1999, Telly award, 1999-2005, 06-08. Fellow Am. Coll. Allergy, Asthma, and Immunology, Am. Acad. Family Physicians; mem. AMA (Physicians Recognition award 1970—), Calif. State Med. Assn., Alameda-Contra Costa County Med. Assn., Joint Coun. Allergy and Immunology, Nat. Assn. Physician Broadcasters (charter), Acad. Radio and TV Health Communicators, Book and Snake Soc., Gibbs Soc. Yale U. (founder), Sigma Xi, Nu Sigma Nu, Alpha Chi Sigma. Home and Office: PO Box 1857 San Ramon CA 94583-6857

LITMAN, THOMAS, medical educator, researcher; b. Lublin, Poland, Aug. 28, 1967; s. Zygmunt and Lucyna Litman; m. Minna

Henriette Jensen, Dec. 31, 1993; children: Jacob, Joachim. MS in Human Biology, U. Copenhagen, 1991; MS in Chemistry, Tech. U. Denmark, 1992; PhD, U. Copenhagen, 1996. Weimann assoc. rsch. prof. U. Copenhagen, 2002—04, asst. prof. bioinformatics, 2003—. Mem. study bd. masters program bioinformatics U. Copenhagen, 2003—. Recipient Glaxo Wellcome Oncology Scholar award, Glaxo Wellcome, 1998; fellow, Fogarty, NIH, 1997—99, The Weimann Found., 2002—04. Mem.: AAAS (assoc.), Nordic Cancer Chemoresistance Group (assoc.), Am. Assn. Cancer Rsch. (assoc.), Danish Soc. Cancer Rsch. (assoc.). Achievements include discovery of MXR (ABCG2) The Mitoxantrone Resistance Associated Protein. Office: U Copenhagen Universitetsparken 15 2100 Copenhagen Denmark Office Fax: +45 3532 1300. E-mail: tlitman@binf.ku.dk.

LITNIEWSKI, JERZY, medical educator; b. Warszawa, Feb. 23, 1953; Cert. IPPT, 2009. Prof. IPPT, 2007—. Office: Pawinskiego Warszawa 02-991 Poland Business E-Mail: jlitn@ippt.gov.pl.

LITRENTA, FRANCES MARIE, psychiatrist; b. Balt., June 25, 1928; d. Frank P. and Josephine (DeLuca) L. AB, Coll. Notre Dame Md., 1950; MD, Georgetown U., 1954. Diplomate Am. Bd. Psychiatry and Neurology. Intern St. Agnes Hosp., Balt., 1954-55, asst. resident in psychiatry, 1955-56; fellow psychiatry Univ. Hosp., Balt., 1956-57; fellow child psychiatry Georgetown U. Hosp., Washington, 1957-59; clin. instr. psychiatry Med. Ctr. Georgetown U., Washington, 1959-63, clin. asst. prof. Med. Ctr., 1963-72, clin. assoc. prof. psychiatry Med. Ctr., 1972-87; pvt. practice Balt., 1959—. Cons. St. Vincent's Infant Home, Balt., 1965-75; mem. coun. to dean Georgetown U. Sch. Medicine, 1977-93. Recipient Georgetown U. Alumni Assn. John Carroll award, 1998. Fellow Am. Acad. Child and Adolescent Psychiatry, Am. Orthopsychiat. Assn. (life); mem. Am. Psychiat. Assn. (life), Md. Psychiat. Soc. (life), Georgetown Med. Alumni Assn. (nat. comm. chair 1987-90, class co-chair 1974-87, class comm. chair 1987—, bd. dirs. 1989—, gov. 1989-95, senator 1995—), Georgetown U. Alumni Assn. (Founder's award 1994, John Carroll award 1998). Office: 6110 York Rd Baltimore MD 21212-2697 Office Phone: 410-435-6340.

LITTIG, LAWRENCE WILLIAM, psychologist, educator; b. Madison, Wis., June 30, 1927; s. Lawrence Victor and Elsie Louise (Rosanske) L.; m. Iris Mark, June 15, 1957; children— Eve Alexandra, Amy Victoria, Sharon Elizabeth. BS, U. Wis., 1950, MS, 1955; PhD, U. Mich., 1959. Instr. dept. psychology U. Mich., Ann Arbor, 1958-59; asst. prof. psychology U. Buffalo, 1959-62; asst. program dir. instl. programs NSF, Washington, 1962-63; social psychologist W.E. Upjohn Inst. Employment Research, Washington, 1963-65; prof. social psychology Howard U., Washington, 1965-92, prof. emeritus social psychology, 1992—; prof. psychology Md. Inst. Coll. of Art, Balt., 1993—. Fulbright prof. U. Nottingham, 1961-62; vis. scholar U. London, 1971-72; cons. Brookings Instn., 1968-70, Dept. Labor, 1968-70; vis. prof. U. Wis., 1970 Cons. editor: Jour. Cross Cultural Psychology, 1969-74; contbr. articles to profl. jours. Mem. Annapolis Bd. Port Wardens, 1994—. U.S. Office Edn. grantee, 1965-70; NIMH research grantee, 1968-69; NSF research grantee, 1961-62; Nat. Inst. Child Health and Human Devel. grantee, 1971-73 Fellow: APA, AAAS, Soc. for Personality and Social Psychology, Am. Psychol. Soc.; mem.: Brit. Psychol. Soc., Psychonomic Soc., Annapolis bd. Port Wanders, Chesapeake Area Profl. Capts. Assn., Fleet Reserve Club, Cosmos Club (Washington), Eastport Yacht Club (Annapolis, Md.), Annapolis Yacht Club, Amateur Fencing Club (London), Sigma Xi. Home: 2 Wells Lndg Annapolis MD 21403-2316 Office: Howard U Dept Psychology Washington DC 20059-0001 Personal E-mail: llittig@comcast.net. *

LITTLE, ALAN BRIAN, gynecologist, educator; b. Montreal, Que., Canada, Mar. 11, 1925; emigrated to U.S., 1951, naturalized, 1959; s. Herbert Melville and Mary Lizette (Campbell) L.; m. Nancy Alison Campbell, Aug. 20, 1949 (div.); children: Michael C. (dec.), Susan MacF. and Deborah MacF. (twins), Catherine E., Jane A., Mary L.; m. Bitten Stripp, Mar. 31, 1983 BA, McGill U., 1948, MD, CM, 1950. Intern Montreal Gen. Hosp., 1950-51; resident Boston Lying-in and Free Hosp. for Women, 1951-55, asst. obstetrician, asso. obstetrician and gynecologist, 1955-65; teaching fellow, asst. prof. Harvard Med. Sch., 1952-65; prof. ob-gyn, then Arthur H. Bill prof. ob-gyn Case Western Res. U. Sch. Medicine, Cleve., 1965-82, chmn. dept. reproductive biology, 1972-82; prof. gynecology McGill U., Montreal, 1983—, chmn. dept. ob-gyn., 1983-94, prof. emeritus, 2009; clin. prof. ob-gyn. U. Medicine and Dentistry N.J., Newark, 1994—. Dir. dept. ob-gyn. Univ. Hosps., Cleve., to 1982, Royal Victoria Hosp., Montreal, 1983-94; mem. nat. adv. com. Nat. Inst. Child Health and Human Devel. Author: (with B. Tenney) Clinical Obstetrics, 1962; editor: (with others) Gynecology and Obstetrics-Health Care for Women, 1975, 2d edit., 1982; (with D. Tulchinsky) Maternal Fetal Endocrinology, 2d edit., 1994; contbr. articles to profl. jours. Served with RCAF, 1943-45. Fellow: ACS, Am. Coll. Obstetricians and Gynecologists, Royal Coll. Surgeons Can.; mem.: Soc. Ob-Gyn. Can., Soc. Gynecol. Investigation, Assn. Profls. Ob-Gyn., Am. Gynecol. and Obstet. Soc. Office: UMDNJ MSB E506 185 S Orange Ave P O Box 1709 Newark NJ 07101-1709 Business E-Mail: littleb1@umdnj.edu.

LITTLE, ANGELA CAPOBIANCO, nutritional science educator; b. San Francisco, Jan. 12, 1920; d. Alfredo Agosto and Elizabeth (Kruse) Capobianco; m. George Gordon Little, Nov. 8, 1947; 1 child, Judith Kristine. BA, U. Calif., Berkeley, 1940, MS, 1954, PhD, 1969. Specialist jr. to asst. to assoc. U. Calif., Berkeley, 1958-69, food scientist, 1969-85, assoc. prof. to prof, 1977-85, prof. emeritus, 1985—, acad. ombudsman, 1985-87, 89-91. Cons. in field; v.p., bd. dirs. Math/Sci. Network, Berkeley; vis. scholar U. Wash., Seattle, 1976-77, Kans. State U., Manhattan, 1972; mem. faculty Fromm Inst., U. San Francisco, 1992-96; pres. bd. dirs. Laguna Heights Co-op Corp., 1999-2001. Author: Color of Foods, 1962. Nutritional adv. bd. Project Open Hand, San Francisco, 1989—91, vol., 1988—91, UNICEF, San Francisco, 1986—89, Saint Francis Hosp., 1992—; bd. dirs. Museo Italo-Am., 2004—; mem. San Francisco Mus. Modern Art, Calif. Palace of the Legion of Honor, Asian Art Mus. Rsch. grantee Robert Woods Johnson Found., 1989-90, others 1960-85. Mem. AAUW, San Francisco Acad. Sci., San Francisco Mus. Soc., U. Calif. Berkeley Emeritii Assn. (pres. 1991-93), Am. Assn. for History of Medicine, Exploratorium, Bay Area History of Medicine Club (pres. 1995-97), Laguna Heights Co-op Corp. (pres., bd. dirs. 1999-2001), Sigma Xi. Avocations: music, books, travel, exercising, walking. Home: 85 Cleary Ct Apt 3 San Francisco CA 94109-6518 Office: U Calif Dept Nutritional Scis Berkeley CA 94720-0001 Business E-Mail: aclittle@berkeley.edu.

LITTLE, JOHN BERTRAM, radiologist, educator, researcher; b. Boston, Oct. 5, 1929; s. Bertram Kimball and Nina (Fletcher) L.; m. Francoise Cottereau, Aug. 4, 1960; children: John Bertram, Frederic Fletcher AB in Physics, Harvard U., 1951; MD, Boston U., 1955. Diplomate Diplomate Am. Bd. Radiology. Intern Johns Hopkins Hosp., Balt., 1955—56; resident in radiology Mass. Gen. Hosp., Boston, 1958-61; fellow Harvard U., Cambridge, Mass., 1961-63; from instr. to assoc. prof. radiobiology Harvard Sch. Pub. Health, Boston, 1963-75, prof., 1975—, chmn. dept. physiology, 1980-83, James Stevens Simmons prof. radiobiology, 1987—, chmn. dept. cancer cell biology, 1997—2002, dir. Ctr. Radiation Scis. and Environ. Health, 1998—2006; dir. Kresge Ctr. Environ. Health, Boston, 1982-98. Cons. radiology Mass. Gen. Hosp., Boston, 1965—, Brigham and Women's Hosp., Boston, 1968—2000; chmn. bd. sci. counsellors Nat. Inst. Environ. Health Sci., 1982—84; bd. sci. counsellors Nat. Toxicology Program, 1988—92; mem. sci. coun. Radiation Effects Rsch. Found., Hiroshima, Japan, 1992—98, chmn., 1996—98; bd. dirs. on radiation effects rsch. NAS, 1992—98, chmn., 1996—98; mem. Coun. Internat. Assn. for Radiation Rsch. Mem. editorial bd. numerous nat. and internat. jours.; contbr. chpts. to books and articles to profl. jours. Mem. coun. Nat. Coun. on Radiation Protection and Measurements, 1993—; trustee various hist. and cultural orgns. Capt. U.S. Army, 1956-58. Recipient numerous rsch. and tng. grants, NIH, 1968—; named one of Outstanding Investigator grantee, Nat. Cancer Inst., 1988—; grantee, Am. Cancer Soc., 1965—68. Mem. AAAS (coun. in med. scis. 1988-91), Radiation Rsch. Soc. N.Am. (pres.-elect 1985, pres. 1986-87), Am. Assn. Cancer Rsch., Am. Physiol. Soc., Health Physics Soc., Am. Soc. Photobiology, Internat. Assn. Radiation Rsch. (coun.). Natl. Assoc. mem., Natl. Acad. of Sci. Avocations: music, architecture. Office: Harvard U Dept Cancer Cell Biology 665 Huntington Ave Boston MA 02115-6021

LITTLE, MICHELLE, medical educator; b. NY, Dec. 24, 1966; BA, Yale U., 1990; PhD, Temple U., 2006. Rsch. data analyst Mass. Gen. Hosp., 1995—98; nimh postdoc. rsch. fellow Prevention Rsch. Ctr., Ariz. State U., 2006—08; asst. prof. U. Tex., San Antonio, 2008—. Instr. Ariz. State U., 2005—06. Recipient Sloboda-Bukoski Soc. Prevention Rsch. prize, Soc. Prevention Rsch., 2006. Mem.: Soc. Rsch. Child Devel. Office: University Tex One UTSA Cir San Antonio TX 78249 Business E-Mail: michelle.little@utsa.edu.

LITTLEFIELD, JOHN WALLEY, geneticist, cell biologist, pediatrician; b. Providence, Dec. 3, 1925; s. Ivory and Mary Russell (Walley) Littlefield; m. Elizabeth Lascelles Legge, Nov. 11, 1950; children: Peter P., John W., Elizabeth I. MD, Harvard U., 1947; MHS, Johns Hopkins U, 1992. Diplomate Am. Bd. Internal Medicine. Intern Mass. Gen. Hosp., Boston, 1947-48, resident in medicine, 1948-50, staff, 1956-74, chief genetics unit children's service, 1966-73; assoc. in medicine Harvard U. Med. Sch., 1956-62, asst. prof. medicine, 1962-66, asst. prof. pediatrics, 1966-69, prof. pediatrics, 1970-73; prof., chmn. dept. pediatrics Johns Hopkins U. Sch. Medicine, Balt., 1974-85; pediatrician-in-chief Johns Hopkins U. Hosp., 1974-85; prof., chmn. dept. physiology Johns Hopkins U. Sch. Medicine, Balt., 1985-92. Author: Variation, Senescence and Neoplasia in Cultured Somatic Cells, 1976; co-author (with Edward A. Parks, Henry M. Seidel, Lawrence S. Wissow): The Harriet Lane Home, A Model and a Gem, 2006. With USNR, 1952—54. Fellow Guggenheim, 1965—66, Josiah Macy Jr. Found., Oxford U., 1979. Mem.: NAS, Assn. Am. Physicians, Am. Pediatric Soc., Am. Soc. Human Genetics, Soc. Pediatric Rsch., Tissue Culture Assn., Am. Soc. Clin. Investigation, Am. Soc. Biol. Chemists, Am. Acad. Arts and Scis., Phi Beta Kappa, Delta Omega, Alpha Omega Alpha. Office: Johns Hopkins U Sch Medicine Dept Physiology Baltimore MD 21205 Home: 13801 York Rd APT P6 Cockeysville MD 21030-1893 Personal E-mail: jlittlefield@comcast.net.

LITTLEFIELD, LYN, medical association administrator; Head, Sch. Psychological Sci. La Trobe Univ.; inaugural dir. Victoria Parenting Ctr., Australia; exec. dir. Australian Psychological Soc., Melbourne, 2001—. Fellow: Australian Inst. Mgmt., Australian Inst. of Company Dir. Office: Australian Psychological Soc PO Box 38 8009 Melbourne VIC Australia Business E-Mail: l.littlefield@psychology.org.au. *

LITTLEJOHN, CHARLES EUGENE, colon and rectal surgeon, educator; b. New York City; Grad., Darthmouth Coll., Hanover, NH; MD, Dartmouth Med. Sch., Hanover, NH, 1978. Diplomate Am. Bd. Colon and Rectal Surgery, 1985. Pvt. practice colorectal surgery, 1984; resident surgery Univ. Rochester Affiated Hosps., NY, 1979—80; resident surgery Univ. Medicine and Dentistry NJ Med. Ctr. Robert Wood Johnson Med. Ctr., Newark, 1980—83, fellow colon & rectal surgery Univ. Medicine and Dentistry NJ Med. Ctr., 1983—84; asst. clin. prof. surgery Columbia Univ. Coll. Physicians and Surgeons; attending colon-rectal surgeon Stamford Hosp., Conn. Mem.: Am. Coll. Surgeons (pres. Conn. chapter), Am. Soc. Colon and Rectal Surgery (chair young surgeons com., exec. coun. mem.). Office: Stamford Hospital 70 Mill River St Stamford CT 06902 Office Phone: 203-323-8989. Office Fax: 203-975-9904.

LITTLETON, JESSE TALBOT, III, radiology educator; b. Corning, NY, Apr. 27, 1917; s. Jesse Talbot and Bessie (Cook) L.; m. Martha Louise Morrow, Apr. 17, 1943 (dec. 1994); children: Christine, Joanne, James, Robert, Denise; m. Mary Lou Durizch, Mar. 25, 1995. Student, Emory and Henry Coll., 1934-35, Johns Hopkins U., 1935-39; MD, Syracuse U., 1943. Diplomate Am. Bd. Radiology. Intern Buffalo Gen. Hosp., 1943; resident in medicine, surgery and radiology Robert Packer Hosp., Sayre, Pa., 1946-51, assoc. radiologist, 1951-53, chmn. dept. radiology, 1953-76; prof. radiology U. South Ala., Mobile, 1976-87, prof. emeritus, 1987—. Cons. in field. Author 4 textbooks; contbr. chpts. to books and articles to profl. jours., sci. exhibits to profl. confs. Served with M.C., U.S. Army, 1944-46, PTO. Fellow Am. Coll. Radiology; mem. AMA, Radiol. Soc. N.Am., Am. Roentgen Ray Soc., Ala. Acad. Radiology, Med. Assn. Ala., French Soc. Neuroradiology, Country Club of Mobile, Sigma Xi, Alpha Omega Alpha. Republican. Methodist. Achievements include research on conventional tomography, physical principles, equipment development and testing and clinical applications; transportation and radiology of acutely ill and traumatized patient; development of patient litter with removable top leading to placement of backboards in ambulances; development of dedicated trauma x-ray machine; angiography, development of first sheet film serialograph; development of equipment for sectional radiographic anatomy with Durizch. Home: 5504 Churchill Downs Ave Theodore AL 36582-9601 Office: U South Ala Med Ctr 2451 Fillingim St Mobile AL 36617-2238 Office Phone: 251-471-7674. E-mail: littletonjtandml@aol.com.

LITTLETON, NAN ELIZABETH FELDKAMP, psychologist, educator; b. Covington, Ky., Oct. 23, 1942; AAS, No. Ky. U., Highland Heights, 1976, BS, 1978; MACE, Morehead State U., Ky., 1981; MA, U. Cin., 1986, PhD in Psychology, 1995. Prof. No. Ky. U., Highland Heights, 1976—, dir. Counseling and human svcs. program, 1989—. Officer, pres. Holly Hill Children's Home, Cold Spring, Ky., 1980-86; cons. Attituding Healing Ctr., Cin., 1990-94; treas. ADO Nat. Honor Soc., 2004-. Treas., editor So. Orgn. Human Svcs. Edn. Link, 1997-2002. Bd. dir. Coun. Stds. in Human Svc. Edn., Chgo., 1990-98—, Cancer Family Care, Cin., 1992-96, Sr. Svcs. Northern Ky., 2005-. Mem. APA, Am. Psychol. Soc., Nat. Orgn. Human Svc. Edn., Am. Coun. Assn., So. Orgn. Human Svc. Edn. (state rep. 1991-2007, treas., 1999-2002), Nat. Women's Studies Assn., Assn. Humanistic Psychologists, Alpha Delta Omega (treas. 2003—). Home: 333 W 17th St Covington KY 41014-1007 Business E-Mail: littleton@nku.edu.

LITTMAN, EDWARD, physician; b. NYC, Mar. 4, 1935; s. Morris and Gertrude (Goldberg) L.; m. Elaine Becker, Aug. 10, 1961; children: Jay, Karen. BA, Cornell U., 1957; MD, Chgo. Med. Sch., 1961. Intern Michael Reese Hosp., Chgo., 1961-62; resident Jersey City (N.J.) Med. Ctr., 1962-63, Montefiore Hosp., Bronx, 1965-66; fellow in renal disease Mt. Sinai Hosp., NYC, 1963-65; physician Norwalk (Conn.) Med. Group, 1968-86, pvt. practice, Norwalk, 1986—; chief sect. nephrology Norwalk Hosp., 1970—2005, dir. dialysis unit, 1972—2005, sr. attending, 1975—2005, cons. sect. nephrology, 2006—10; med. dir. DaVita Dialysis, 2005—10. Bd. trustees Norwalk Hosp., 1986-91; clin. instr. Yale U., New Haven, Conn., 1976-77, asst. clin. prof., 1977-81, assoc. clin. prof., 1981—09; lectr. Chgo. Med. Sch., 1987—2003. Contbr. articles to profl. jours. Vice chmn. adv. bd. Kidney Found., Conn., 1978-81, chmn. med. adv. bd., 1981-84; chmn. ESRD Network Coord. Coun., Conn., 1979-81. Capt. U.S. Army, 1966-68. Fellow ACP, ASN. Avocations: white water rafting, scuba diving, skiing, rock-mountain climbing, tennis. Office Phone: 203-853-2042. Personal E-mail: elittman@gmail.com. *

LITTMAN, RICHARD ANTON, psychologist, educator; b. NYC, May 8, 1919; s. Joseph and Sarah (Feinberg) L.; m. Isabelle Cohen, Mar. 17, 1941; children— David, Barbara, Daniel, Rebecca. AB, George Washington U., 1943; postgrad., Ind. U., 1943-44; PhD, Ohio State U., 1948. Faculty U. Oreg., 1948—, prof. psychology, 1959—, chmn. dept., 1963-68, vice provost acad. planning and resources, 1971-73, prof. emeritus, 1990. Vis. scientist Nat. Inst. Mental Health, 1958-59 Contbr. articles to profl. jours. Sr. postdoctoral fellow NSF, U. Paris, 1966-67; sr. fellow Nat. Endowment for Humanities, U. London, 1973-74; Ford Found. fellow, 1952-53; recipient U. Oreg. Charles H. Johnson Meml. award, 1980. Mem. APA, Western Psychol. Assn., Am. Psychol. Soc., Soc. Research and Child Devel., Psychonomics Soc., Animal Behavior Soc., Soc. Psychol. Study of Social Issues, Internat. Soc. Developmental Psychobiology, History of Sci. Soc., Am. Philos. Assn., AAUP, Sigma Xi. Home: 3625 Glen Oak Dr Eugene OR 97405-4736 Office: U Oreg Dept Psychology Eugene OR 97403 Business E-Mail: rlittman@uoregon.edu.

LITVACK, FRANK, medical products executive; MD, McGill U. Attending cardiologist Cedars-Sinai Medical Center, 1985—, co-dir., Cardiovascular Intervention Ctr, 1986—2000; founder, bd. dirs. Progressive Angioplasty Sys., Inc. (acquired by United States Surgical Corp.), 1989—97; founder, dir. Immusol Inc., 1992; prof., med. UCLA, 2000—; chmn. Savacor, Inc. (acquired by St. Jude Medical, Inc.), 2000—05, Conor MedSystems, Inc., Menlo Park, Calif., 2002—07, CEO, 2003—07. Bd. dirs. Nile Therapeutics, Inc, 2009—. Office: Nile Therapeutics Inc Ste 310 115 Sansome St San Francisco CA 94104 Office Phone: 510-281-7700. Office Fax: 510-288-1310.

LITVINTSEV, ALEXANDER NIKOLAEVICH, medical educator; b. Irkutsk, Russia, Dec. 21, 1928; s. Nikolai Philipovich Litvintsev and Phekla Ivanovna Litvintseva; married, Oct. 6, 1952. Cand. Med. Sci., Irkutsk State Med. U., Russia, 1970; Dr.Med.Sci., Irkutsk State Med. U., 1985. Sr. lectr. Irkutsk State Med. U., 1977—85, head of nutrition study, 1985—, prof., 1986—, dep. chmn. union orgn., 1980—85. Author: Medical Protection of East Siberian Natural Reservoir in the Developed Industrial Regions; contbr. articles to profl. jours. Recipient Medal of Labour Veteran, Russian Govt., Moscow, 1981, Medal of the 50th Ann. of the Victory, Patriotic War, Moscow, 1995, Medal for Valiant Labor, 2005. Mem.: Internat. Sci. Acad. of Ecology and Safety and Nature (corr.). Avocations: fishing, hunting, cultivating flowers, reading. Home: Marshal Zurovs Ave House 58 Flat 371 664057 Irkutsk Russia Office: Irkutsk State Medical Univ ul. Krasnogo Vosstaniya 1 664003 Irkutsk Irkutskaya obl. Russia Personal E-mail: jetlion@rol.ru.

LITWINISZYN-KRZEWICKA, KATARZYNA, pediatrician, educator; b. Krakow, Poland, June 10, 1946; d. Jerzy and Halina Litwiniszyn; m. Jerzy Krzewicki; children: Lukasz, Karolina Romera. MD, Med. Acad., Krakow, 1970, PhD, 1984, Specialist in Paediats., 1978, Specialist in Oncology, 1996. Lectr. Med. Acad., 1974—91, Swietokrzyska Acad., Kielce, Poland, 2005—; head dept. Pediat. Oncology Dept. Med. Acad., 1991—2007. Mem.: Polish Pediat. Soc. (head 1991). Home: Ul. Artura Grottgera 16 25-441 Kielce Poland

LIU, CHANG-CHIA, medical researcher; b. Taiwan, Jan. 29, 1977; PhD, U. Fla., 2008. Rsch. fellow Johns Hopkins U., 2008—. Avocations: reading, music, travel. Office: 600 N Wolfe St Meyer 5-110 Baltimore MD 21287 Business E-Mail: iamjeff@ufl.edu.

LIU, CHAU TANG, obstetrician, gynecologist; b. Taichung, Taiwan, Republic of China, Nov. 28, 1943; s. King Sheu and Mei Yue (Chang) L.; m. Tsai Sheu Chen, Sept. 23, 1943. MB, Taipei Med. Sch., 1969. Diplomate Republic of China Bd. Ob-Gyn. Resident Taipei (Republic of China) Choun-Shin City Hosp., 1971-72; chief resident Hsu Chien-Tien Hosp., Taipei, 1973-75; dean Huii-Yin Ob-Gyn. Pvt. Clinic, Taipei. Cons. China Radio Broadcasting Co., 1989-94, Taipei City Broadcasting, 1991-93; mem. Com. of Ob-Gyn. of the Republic of China, 1996—. Lt. China Air Force, 1969-70. Avocations: climbing, swimming, gardening, singing. Home: 10F 306 Sec 2 Zen-Kaou S Rd Taipei 106 Taiwan Office: Huii-Yin Obs/Gyn Pvt Clinic 2F 5&6 62 Chang Chun Rd Taipei 104 Taiwan Mailing: 50 Chungsiao West Rd Sect 1 24F-24 Taipei 100 Taiwan Office Phone: 886-02-23886731.

LIU, CHIUN-MING, engineering educator; b. Tainan, Taiwan, Jan. 4, 1951; PhD, Va. Tech., 1988. Rsch. asst. Taiwan Forest Rsch. Inst., 1976—83, Va. Tech., 1985—88; prof. Feng Chia U., 1989—, curriculum dir., 1999—2002, dept. head, 2004—08. Cons. Inst. Chun Shen

Tech., 1989—90, Pochen Group, 2003—05; vis. prof. Ga. Tech., 2003—04, W.Va. U., 2008—09. Recipient Outstanding Tchg. award, Feng Chia U., Outstanding Rsch. award, Presdl. award, Nat. Taiwan U. Mem.: Chinese Inst. Indsl. Engring., INFORMS, Ops. Rsch. Soc. Taiwan (coun. mem. 2007—10). Avocations: hiking, travel, classical music. Office: 100 Wenhwa Rd Taichung 407 Taiwan Office Phone: 0920129023. Office Fax: 886424510240. Business E-Mail: cmliu@fcu.edu.tw.

LIU, DAVIS, physician, writer; Grad. summa cum laude, Wharton Sch. Bus.; MD, U. Conn. Sch. Medicine. Resident Glendale Adventist Family Practice; family physician Permanente Med. Group, 2000—. Author: Stay Healthy, Live Longer, Spend Wisely, 2008. Office: 1001 Riverside Ave Roseville CA 95678 Office Phone: 916-784-4050.

LIU, DEDING, physician; b. Jiao Zuo, Henan, China, Feb. 23, 1984; PhD, 2nd Mill. Med. U., 2010. Physician in charge Changhai Hosp., 2007—11. Office: Chang Hai Rd Yangpu Dist Shanghai 454000 China Personal E-mail: liudeding@126.com.

LIU, DEPEI, academic administrator, molecular biologist, educator; b. China, May 4, 1950; Grad., Chinese Acad. Med. Sciences, Peking Union Med. Coll.; PhD in molecular biology, U. Calif., San Francisco, 1990. Assoc. prof. Chinese Acad. Med. Sciences and Peking Union Med. Coll., Beijing, 1989—92, prof. and investigator, 1992—, vice. dir. Inst. Basic Med. Sciences, 1997—98, asst. to pres., 1998—99, dep. dean grad. sch., 1998—99, v.p., 1999—2001, pres., 2001—; v.p. Chinese Acad. Engring., 2006—. Mem.: Inst. Medicine (fgn. assoc.), Chinese Med. Assn., Chinese Acad. Engring., Soc. Chinese Bioscientists in America, Am. Soc. Hematology, Chinese Soc. Biochemistry and Molecular Biology. Office: Nat Lab Med Molecular Biology Chinese Acad Med Sciences 5 Dong Dan San Tiao 100005 Beijing China E-mail: liudp@95777.com.

LIU, HUNG-HUAN, engineering educator; b. Penghu, Taiwan, Dec. 12, 1968; m. Chia-Tian Yu; children: Paul, Arwen. PhD, Nat. Taiwan U. Sci. and Tech., Taipei, 2003. Lectr. and asst. prof. Nat. Penghu U. Sci. & Tech., 2000—04; asst. prof. Chung Yuan Christian U., Chung Li, Taiwan, 2004—. Mem.: IEEE, SIGCOMM, ACM. Achievements include way guiding system for people with severe mental illness in Taipei rapid transit system, sensor network and smart life technologies, radio resource management and allocation for wireless networks, research in sensor network and smart life technologies, radio resource management and allocation for wireless networks. Office: Chung Yuan Christian University EL 200 Chung Pei Rd Chung Li 32023 Taiwan Office Phone: 886-3-2654624. Business E Mail: hhliu@cycu.edu.tw.

LIU, ISAAC KUO-KANG, education educator, researcher; b. Tainan, Taiwan, Aug. 1, 1962; PhD in Chem. Eng., Imperial Coll., London, Eng., 1995. Assoc. prof. Nanyang Technol. U., Singapore, 1998—2003; sr. lectr. Inst. of Sci. & Tech. in Medicine, Keele U., Stoke-on-Trent, Staffordshire, 2003—. Author scientific journal publications. Conf. chmn. 1st Biennel Meeting of the European Tissue Engring. Soc. Recipient y Best Paper Award in the 11th Internat. Conf. on Biomedical Engring., Singapore, 2002; scholar Life Sci. Scholarship, Ministry of Edn. (Taiwan), 1992-1996. Mem.: AIChE, IEEE Engring. in Medicine and Biology Soc. (conf. chmn.). Achievements include research in Groundbreaking discoveries on cell mechanics and adhesion (20 publications in top scientific journals). Office: Inst Sci and Tech in Medicine Sch Medicine Keele Univ Staffordshire Stoke-on-Trent ST4 7QB England Home Fax: +44 (0)1782 711597. Personal E-mail: kksyliu@yahoo.co.uk. E-mail: i.k.liu@keele.ac.uk.

LIU, JENG-FEN, dentist, educator; b. Taipei, Taiwan, Aug. 14, 1958; d. Shen-Wei and Yu-Yu Chiu Liu; m. Chung-Ming Hung, Mar. 12, 1989; children: Owen Hung, Cheng-Hung Hung. MS, U. Medicine and Dentistry NJ, 1991. Diplomate Taiwan Acad. Pediat. Dentistry, 1998, 2008. Chair Taichung Vets. Gen. Hosp., Taiwan, 1995—. Asst. prof. Nat. Yang Ming U., Taipei, Taiwan, 2007—. Master: Taiwan Acad. Pediat. Dentistry (pres. 2008—, 1st award 2006). Buddhist. Avocations: hiking, swimming, bicycling, travel. Home: 329 Chung Ming Rd Taichung 40466 Taiwan Office: Taiwan Acad Pediat Dentistry 160 Sec 3 Taichung Harbor Rd Taichung 40705 Taiwan Office Phone: 886-4-23592525 ext. 5571. Office Fax: 886-4-23595837. Personal E-mail: jengfen1124@yahoo.com.tw. Business E-Mail: jengliu@vghtc.gov.tw.

LIU, JIA-JIA, immunologist, educator; b. Chongqing, China, Dec. 18, 1957; s. Cao-dong Liu and Mei-feng Duan; m. Fu-lan Zhen Liu, Dec. 30, 1955; children: Yi-lan, Yi-jia. MD, Luzhou Med. Coll., 1982. Lectr. immunology Luzhou (China) Med. Coll., 1985—87, assoc. prof., 1991—97, prof. immunology, 2001—; vis. scholar Shimane Med. U., Izuimo, Japan, 1988—90; vis. prof. Kitasato U., Kanagawa, Japan, 1998—2000. Contbr. articles to profl. jours. Grantee, Nat. Nature Sci. Fund, 2003. Avocations: reading, movies, music. Home and Office: Central Lab Luzhou Med Coll Zhong-shan 20 Luzhou 646000 China

LIU, JIEN-WEI, infectious-disease physician, epidemiologist, educator; MD, Chung Shan Med. U., Taichung, Taiwan. Resident physician, dept. of internal medicine Nat. Cheng Kung U. Hosp., Tainan, Taiwan, 1991—94, chief resident physician, divsn. of infectious diseases, 1994—96; attending physician, divsn. of infectious diseases Chang Gung Med. Ctr., Kaohsiung, Kaohsiung, Taiwan, 1996—99, chief, divsn. of infectious diseases, 1999—; asst. prof. Chang Gung U., Taiwan, Taoyuan, Taiwan, 2001—. Investigator Asian Network for Surveillance of Resistant Pathogens, Seoul, 1998—. Achievements include designing study identifying patients who are at high risk for acquisition of concurrent bacteremia among adult patients suffering from dengue hemorrhagic fever; being a major person in designing and implementation of an infection control program successful in containment of a SARS nosocomial outbreak in a large medical center in Taiwan 2003. Office: Chang Gung Med Ctr Kaohsiung 123 Ta Pei Rd Taiwan Niao Sung Hsiang, Kaohsiung Hsien 833 Taiwan Office Fax: 886 77322402. Business E-Mail: 88b0@adm.cgmh.org.tw.

LIU, JING, pathologist, educator; b. Beijing, Sept. 28, 1957; d. Songtao and Suru Liu; m. David Youdong Tong, July 9, 1983; children: Lawrence Guoxin Tong, Brian Alexander Tong. MD, Capital U. Med. Sci., Beijing, 1982; PhD, Tex. A&M U., College Station, 1992. Diplomate Am. Bd. Pathology, 1999. Pediatric cardiologist Beijing Childrens' Hosp., Beijing, 1985—87; asst. prof. U. Tex., S.W. Med. Sch., Dallas, 1999—2000, U. Tex. Med. Sch., Houston, 2000—05, dir. cytopathology, 2004—, assoc. prof., 2005—. Contbr. articles to profl. jours. Recipient Sci. and Technol. Advance award, Beijing Pub. Health Bur., 1986, Travel award, Fifth World Congress for Microcirculation, 1991, Am. Soc. Investigative Pathology, 1995. Fellow: Am. Soc. Clin. Pathology, Coll. Am. Pathologists; mem.: Tex. Soc. Cytology, US and Can. Acad. Pathology, Am. Soc. Cytopathology, Phi Kappa Phi. Achievements include research in immunocytochemistry, mechanisms of myogenic enhancement by norepinephrine research, utility of doppler echocardiography. Office: Univ Tex 6431 Fannin St Rm 2136 Houston TX 77030 Office Fax: 713-500-0732. Business E-Mail: jing.liu.1@uth.tmc.edu.

LIU, JING, cardiologist, educator; b. China, Jan. 29, 1973; MD, Peking U., 2000. Chief physician, prof. Peking U., 2009—. Quaker fellowship, World Heart Fedn., 2010, grant, Japanese Soc. Hypertension, 2010. Mem.: Vascular Biology Working Group, Internat. Soc. Hypertension. Office: 11 xizhimen South St Xicheng Beijing 100044 China Personal E-mail: heartcenter@163.com.

LIU, LIN, ophthalmologist; b. Shenyang City, Liaoning, China, June 8, 1963; B in Medicine, Second Mil. Med. U., Shanghai, 1985, M in Ophthalmology, 1988. Vice chmn. Chinese PLA Ophthalmologic Soc., 2003—06; supr. Shanghai Changhai Hosp., 2005—. Standing com. mem. Chinese Ophthalmologic Immunology Soc., 2001—11. Mem.: Chinese Assn. Ophthalmology. Avocations: chess, swimming. Home: Rm 502 27 Ln 395 Shuangyangbei Rd Shanghai 200433 China Personal E-mail: linliu@sh163.net.

LIU, MINETTA CHUNG-SUI, oncologist, educator; b. Mpls., Minn., Dec. 6, 1968; AB, Princeton U.; MD, Jefferson Med. Coll. Phila., 1995. Cert. Internal Medicine, Med. Oncology. Intern, medicine Georgetown U. Hosp., 1995—96, 1996, resident, internal medicine, 1996—2001, fellow, 1998—2001; joined breast cancer program Lombardi Comprehensive Cancer Ctr., Georgetown U., Washington, 2001—, chief fellow, asst. prof. medicine and oncology. Office: Lombardi Comprehensive Cancer Ctr Podium B Georgetown U 3800 Reservoir Rd NW Washington DC 20057 Office Phone: 202-444-3677, 202-444-2988. Business E-Mail: liumc@georgetown.edu.

LIU, NINGFEI, surgeon, educator; b. Nanjing, China, May 1, 1952; MD, Shanghai Jiao Tong U., 1973, PhD, 1990. Prof. plastic surgery Surg. Shanghai 9th People's Hosp., Shanghai Jiao Tong U. Sch. Medicine, 1994—, dir. lymphology ctr., 2002. Internat. cons. Angio pediatria Ctr., Argentina, 2008; prof. hon. Argentina Med. Assn. Grad. Sch., 2008. Recipient Chinese Med. Progress prize, Shanghai Chinese Med. Assn., Achievement award, Polish Acad. Scis. Mem.: Internat. Confederation Plastic Reconstructive and Aesthetic Surgery, Chinese Medicine Assn., Internat. Soc. Lymphology. Avocations: music, travel, reading. Office: 639 Zhi Zao Ju Rd Shanghai 200011 China Office Fax: 86-21-53078128. Personal E-mail: liuningfei@126.com.

LIU, QIANG QUENTIN, medical scientist; b. Anqing, Anhui, China, Jan. 22, 1968; s. Honghua Liu and Ying Zhou. PhD, U. Ill., Urbana-Champaign, 1997, MD, 2000. Diplomate bd. cert. 2000. Rsch. assoc. Harvard Med. Sch., Boston, 2003—05; prof. Cancer Ctr., Sun Yat-sen U., Guangzhou, Guangdong, China, 2006—. Clin. resident Mt. Sinai Hosp., NYC, 2000—03. Contbr. scientific papers (Nat. Rsch. Svc. award, NIH fellowship, 2004). Recipient Outstanding Young Scientist Fund, Nat. Natural Sci. Found. China, 2008. Achievements include anti-cancer molecular targeting therapy; research in leukemia treatment, cancer prevention, drug discovery. Home: 80 Xingang Rd E Guangzhou Guangdong China Office: Cancer Ctr Sun Yat-sen Univ 602 651 Rm Dongfeng Rd E 510060 Guangzhou Guangdong China Personal E mail: liuqlab@yahoo.com. Business E-Mail: liuq9@mail.sysu.edu.cn.

LIU, SHANGQIN, hematologist, director; b. Hubei, Sept. 5, 1963; PhD, Yamaguchi U., 2005. Dir., dept. hematology Zhonnan Hosp. Wuhan U., 2010—. Office: 169 Donghu Rd Wuhan Hubei 430071 China E-mail: ubeliu@yahoo.com.cn.

LIU, SHU-YING, microbiologist, educator; b. Taichung, Taiwan, June 20, 1962; d. Ping-Huei Liu and Weng-Chi Chuang; m. Kou-Cheng Peng, Mar. 10, 1993; 1 child, I Peng. BS in Botany, Chung Hsing U., Taiwan, 1984, MS in Botany, 1987; PhD, U. Ga., Athens, 1995. Postdoctoral assoc. Chang Gung U., Lin Ko, Taiwan, 1996—98, Tsing Hua U., HsinChu, Taiwan, 2000—01; asst. prof. Da-Yeh U., Dah Tsuen, Taiwan, 2002—09, assoc. prof., 2010—. Contbr. articles to profl. jours. Grantee, Nat. Sci. Coun., Taiwan, 2002—04, 2007—. Mem.: Chinese Soc. Microbiology. Home: 88 Wu Ying St Yang Mei Taoyuan 326 Taiwan Office: Da Yeh University 168 University Rd Dacun Changhua 515 Taiwan Home Phone: 886 3 8630315; Office Phone: 886-4-8511888-4256. Office Fax: 886-4-8511326. Business E-Mail: syliu@mail.dyu.edu.tw.

LIU, SIMIN, epidemiologist, educator; b. Guangzhou, China, 1967; MD, Jinan U., 1991; MPH, Harvard U., DSc, 1998. Asst., assoc., adj. prof. Harvard Sch. Pub. Health, 2001—07; epidemiologist Brigham and Women's Hosp., Harvard Med. Sch., 1998—2005; prof., dir. UCLA, 2005—, bd. mem., med. rev. bd. 1, 2010—. Cons. Ctrs. Disease Control and Prevention, 1999—2006; study sect. mem. NIH, 2002—10; bd. mem. Whole Grain Couns., 2005; sci. bd. mem. NHLBI Global Health Initiative, 2009—11. Recipient Applied Rsch. award, Whole Grain Rsch. Submit; Physician Scientist Devel. grant, NIH. Fellow: Am. Soc. Clin. Nutrition, Am. Heart Assn.; mem.: AAAS, Am. Soc. Human Genetics, Am. Diabetes Assn. Avocations: soccer, travel, ping pong/table tennis. Office: 71-265 CHS PO Box 951772 650 Charles E Young Dr Los Angeles CA 90095-1772 Office Fax: 310-206-6039. Personal E-mail: drsiminliu@gmail.com.

LIU, TAI-FENG, physiologist; b. Shenyang, Liaoning, China, May 22, 1930; s. Dingbin and Cunyi (Yao) L.; m. Hui Lan Li, Aug. 6, 1956; children: Li, Jian, Rong. Bachelor, Peking U., 1953. Asst. Peking U., Beijing, 1953-60, lectr., 1960-79, assoc. prof., 1979-85, prof., 1985—. Head sect. of physiology Peking U., 1986-90; chmn. com. of degree Coll. Life Scis., 1993-98; adv. coun. mem. Internat. Biographical Ctr, Eng., 1998-; rsch. fellow Am. Biographical Inst., 2005-. Author: Electrophysiology of Myocardium, 1988 (Prize for Textbook 1989), Electrophysiology of Myocardiac Cells, 2000, Electrophysiology of Myocardiac Cells: Ionic Channels, Transporters and Currents, 2005, Cardiac Ion Channels and Channelopathy, 2006; co-editor: Antiarrhythmic drugs and cardiac ion channels, 2008. Mem. Internat. Soc. for Heart Rsch. (coun. Chinese sect. 1988-96), Methods and Findings in Exptl. and Clin. Pharmacology (contbg. editor 1991—), N.Y. Acad. Scis. Avocation: reading. Office: Coll of Life Scis Peking Univ Beijing 100871 China Home: Peking U 410 42 Bldg Apt Zhong Guan Yuan Beijing 100193 China Mailing: 2-102 Bldg 9 Qicaihuayuan Xianghuangqi Beijing 100193 China Home Phone: (010) 6275-5379; Office Phone: (010) 6275-9054. Business E-Mail: cardiac@pku.edu.cn.

LIU, TE HUA, retired neuroradiologist; b. Shanghai, Dec. 21, 1924; arrived in US, 1978; m. Chi-Chien Kao, Apr. 16, 1950; children: Diana K. Chu, Frank Kao, Winifred K. Seda. MD, Nat. Shanghai Med. Coll., 1950. Diplomate Am. Bd. Radiology, 1982. Resident 1st Red Cross Hosp. Med. Sch., Shanghai, 1950—54; attending physician radiology Shanghai Med. Sch. Hua-San Hosp., 1954—60, chairperson Dept. Radiology, 1960—78; resident radiology Roosevelt and St. Lukes Hosp., NYC, 1980—82; fellow radiology Columbia U., NYC, 1982—83; attending physician neuroradiology, asst. prof. radiology Temple U. Sch. Medicine, Phila., 1983—86, chief neuroradiology, 1986—94, assoc. prof. radiology, 1986—90, prof. radiology and neurosurgery, 1990—96; ret., 1996. Author (co-editor): Diagnostic Radiology, 1978; co-author: MRI & CT of Muscular-Skeletal Systems, 1984; contbr. articles to profl. jours. Mem.: Ea. Neuroradiological Soc., Assn. Prog. Dirs. Radiology, Radiol. Soc. N.Am., Am. Soc. Neuroradiology (sr.). E-mail: sinocow@comcast.net.

LIU, TING, physical education educator; b. China, Sept. 16, 1971; PhD, U. Tex., Austin, 2006. Asst. prof. Tex. State U., 2009—. Mem.: N.Am. Soc. Psychology Sport and Phys. Activity, Nat. Assn. Sport and Phys. Edn. (Lolas E. Halverson Motor Devel. and Learning Young Investigator award), Am. Alliance for Health, Phys. Edn., Recreation and Dance (phys. activity cons. 2009—, Lolas E. Halverson Motor Devel. and Learning Young Investigator award). Office: Dept Health & Human Performance San Marcos TX 78666 Personal E-mail: tingliuzhou@yahoo.com.

LIU, XIAOWEI, plastic surgeon; b. China, Sept. 14, 1982; MSc, Peaking Med. Coll., 2009. Plastic surgeon Chongqing Xinqiao Hosp., 2006—. Office: Xinqiaozheng St Shapinba Dist Chongqing 400037 China

LIU, YEN-CHIN, physician, educator; b. Taiwan, May 5, 1967; MD, Nat. Yang Ming U., PhD, 1994. Physician Nat. Cheng Kung U. Hosp., 2004—. Assoc. prof. Nat. Cheng Kung U., 2010—. Office: Nat Cheng Kung University Med Hosp Dept Anesthesiology 138 Sheng Li Rd Tainan 704 Taiwan Business E-Mail: inp1965@mail.ncku.edu.tw.

LIU, YIJUN, medical educator; b. Nanjing, Jan. 7, 1963; PhD, U. Tex., 1999. Prof. U. Fla., 1999—. Home: 3217 SW 98th Dr Gainesville FL 32608 Personal E-mail: yjliufl@gmail.com.

LIU, YI-XUN, reproductive biologist, academician, researcher, educator; b. Si-An-Tai, Shandong, China, May 5, 1936; s. Si-Pong Liu and Gua-Zhen Zhou; m. Xue-Kun Zhao; 1 child, Guo-Li. Bachelor's degree, Fudan U., Shanghai, China, 1963; PhD, Academia Sinica, Beijing, 1966. Rsch. assoc. Inst. Zoology, Beijing, 1967-73; postdoctoral fellow Imperial Cancer Rsch. Fund, London, 1974 76; from asst. to assoc. prof. Inst. Zoology, Acad. Sinica, Beijing, 1977-90; postdoctoral prof. U. Calif., San Diego, 1984-86; prof. Acad. Sinica, Beijing, 1990—. Vis. prof. U. Umeå, Sweden, 1989-92, 98-99, Babraham Inst., Leicester U., 1995-97, 99-2001; prof., cons. mem. Nat. Natural Sci. Found. China, Beijing, 1993-98, 2000-02; dir., prof. State Key Lab. Reproductive Biology for Family Planning, Beijing, 2000-; mem. sci. com. Nat. Commn. of Family Planning; project holder, advisor initiative implantation rsch. WHO/Rockfeller Found., 1999-2004; chmn. academic com. Key Lab. Reproductive Medicine, 2002-, Liao-Ning Key Lab. Reproductive Health, 2004-, Ning-Xian Province Genetic and Reproductive Biology Key Lab., 2006, Shangdon Province Reproductive Health Key Lab., 2006 , Shen Young Environ. Pollution and Human Health Key lab., 2007-; chmn. academic com. edn., Dept. Human Supplemental Fertility Tech. Key Lab., Beiking U., 2011, Dept. Reproductive Endocrinology Key Lab., Shandong U., 2011, Dept. Reproductive Genetics Key Lab., Zhejiang U., 2011, mem. rev. com. Tan Kah Ken; advisor sci. and tech. Ning-Xian; sci. advisor She-Young City, 2007-. Mem. editl. bd.: Human Reproduction (Cambridge), 1995-2001, Archives of Andrology (US), 2000—09, Endocrine (US), 2007—; mng. editor Frontier in Biosci., 2004—; assoc. editor: Developmental and Reproductive Biology, 1991-2004, Asia Jour. Andrology, 2004—11; mem. editl. bd.: Sci. in China, Acta Physiol. Sinica, Jour. Reproductive Medicine, Reproduction and Contraception, Andrology, Basic Med. Scis. and Clinics; contbr. over 250 articles to profl. jours. including Jour. Biol. Chemistry, Exptl. Cell Rsch., Human Molecular Reproduction, Human Reproduction, Fertility and Sterility, Jour. Clin. Endocrinol. Metabolism, Biology of Reproduction. Recipient 2d Grade of Natural Sci. award Chinese Acad. Scis., 1984, 85, 92, 93, 95, 97, 1st grade of Natural. award, 1997, China Population Sci. and Tech. prize, 2004, 06, China Population prize, 2005, China Population and Family Planning Achievement prize, 2006; named Disting. Internat. Referee of Stature, U. Leicester; postdoctoral fellow Rockefeller Found., NY Population Coun., 1984-86, prof. fellow Swedish Med. Rsch. Coun., 1989-90, Royal Soc. UK, 1995-97, 99-2001. Fellow Chinese Acad. Scis. (chair acad. com. state key lab. reproductive biology 1999--); mem. Chinese Soc. for Reproductive Biology (vice-chmn. 1990-99, chmn. 2000—), Nat. Com. Endocrinology, Reproduction and Metabolism (vice-chmn. 1995—), Soc. for Study of Reproduction (US), NY Acad. Scis. Achievements include coordinating gene expression of tissue type plasminogen activator by granulosa cells and its inhibitor-type-1 by theca cells in the ovary induces ovulation. Office: Inst Zoology Academia Sinica State Key Lab Reproductive Biol 5 Da-Tun Lu Chao-Yang Qu Beijing 100101 China Business E-Mail: liuyx@ioz.ac.cn.

LIU, YOUNG KING, biomedical engineering educator; b. Nanjing, China, May 3, 1934; came to U.S., 1952; s. Yih Ling and Man Fun (Teng) L.; m. Nina Pauline Liu, Sept. 4, 1964 (div. July 1986); children— Erik, Tania; m. Anita Beeth, Aug. 14, 1994 (div. Aug. 2000). BSME, Bradley U., 1955; MSME, U. Wis.-Madison, 1959; PhD, Wayne State U., 1963. Cert. acupuncturist, Calif. Asst. prof. Milw. Sch. of Engring., 1956—59; instr. Wayne State U., Detroit, 1960—63; lectr. then asst. prof. U. Mich., Ann Arbor, 1963—69; assoc. prof. then prof. Tulane U., New Orleans, 1969—78; prof. biomed. engring., dir. dept. U. Iowa, Iowa City, 1978—93; pres. U. No. Calif., Petaluma, 1993—; interim pres., CEO Calif. Coll. Podiatric Medicine, 2000—01. COO, 3DMetrics, Inc., 2001—03; emeritus chmn. bd. Ossen Therapeutics Inc., 2006—10. Contbr. articles to profl. jours., chpts. to books NIH spl. research fellow, 1968-69; recipient Research Career Devel. award NIH, 1971-76 Mem. Internat. Soc. Lumbar Spine (exec. com., ctrl. U.S. rep. 1983-88), Orthopedic

Research Soc., Sigma Xi. Democrat. Home Phone: 707-843-7372; Office Phone: 707-636-5964. Personal E-mail: ykingliu@yahoo.com. Business E-Mail: ykingliu@uncm.edu.

LIU, YUNGANG, medical educator; b. Luzhou, China, Jan. 21, 1964; MD, Chongqing Med. U., China, 1985; PhD, West China Med. U., 1995. Prof. Southern Med. U., China, 2009—. Physician occupl. diseases Luzhou Sanitation & Anti-epidemic Sta., China, 1985—87; lectr. Guangzhou Med. Coll., 1995—98, assoc. prof., 1999—2000; guest scientist German Inst. Human Nutrition, 2000—03; postdoc. rsch. U. Iowa, 2003—09. Postdoc. scholarship, German Academic Exch. Svcs. (DAAD). Mem.: Chinese Assn. Environ. Mutagens, Chinese Assn. Toxicology. Avocation: singing. Office: 1838 N GuangzhouDaDao Guangzhou Guangdong 510515 China Office Fax: 86-20-61648324. Personal E-mail: yungang1@hotmail.com.

LIU, YUNG-TIEN, engineering educator, researcher; b. Taichung, Taiwan, May 10, 1961; s. Ren-De and Li Zhan Liu; m. Mei-Yun Wu, Oct. 19, 1960; children: Chia-Yu, Ting-Ju. B in Mech. Engring., Nat. Taiwan Inst. Tech., Taipei, 1983; M in Precision Machinery Engring., U. Tokyo, 1993, DEng, 1999. Foreman China Steel Corp., Kaohsiung, Taiwan, 1985—90, mech. engr., 1993—96; rschr. Inst. of Phys. and Chem. Rsch. (RIKEN), Saitama, Japan, 1999—99; asst. prof. Nat. Kaohsiung First U. of Sci. and Tech., Kaohsiung, Taiwan, 1999—2003, assoc. prof., 2003—. Assoc. prof. Ministry of Edn., 2003; vis. scientist Inst. of Phys. and Chem. Rsch. (RIKEN), Saitama, 2006. Author: Encyclopedia of Sensors, Nano-Positioning and Sensing Technologies; contbr. articles to profl. jours. Second lt. arty. Army, 1983—85. Recipient writing awards, Machinery Monthly, 2004; grantee, Nat. Sci. Coun., 2000-2005; scholar, Ministry of Edn., 1996-1999, Panasonic Taiwan Co., Ltd. (PTW), 1990-1993; Rsch. grant, Nat. Sci. Coun., 2000—06, Electro Mechanic Tech. Advancing Found., Japan, 2001, Mitutoyo Assn. for Sci. and Tech. (MAST), Japan, 2004. Mem.: The Japan Soc. for Precision Engring., PA, Chinese Automatic Control Soc. Achievements include patents for Multi-Degree-of-Freedom of Precision Positioning Device Using Spring-mounted Electromechanical Actuators; High-precision Pneumatic Positioning Method Using Piezoelectric Actuator; invention of The Combined Piezo-pneumatic Actuator. Avocation: travel. Office: Natl Kaohsiung First Univ Sci&Tech No1 University Rd Kaohsiung 824 Taiwan Office Fax: 886-7-6011066. Business E-Mail: ytliu@ccms.nkfust.edu.tw.

LIU, ZENGLI, medical educator, director; b. Shandong Anqiu, Sept. 7, 1965; MD, Suzhou Med. Coll., 1999. Prof., dir., dept. nuc. medicine 2nd Affiliated Hosp. Soochow U., 2004—. Office: 1055 Sanxiang Rd Suzhou Jiangsu 215004 China Business E-Mail: liuzengli@126.com.

LIU, ZHENGCHUN, chemistry professor; b. Hunan, China, Jan. 28, 1974; BS in Chemistry, Xiantan U., 1991, MS in Chemistry, 1998; PhD in Biomed. Engring., SE U., 2003. Postdoc. rschr. Seoul Nat. U., 2004—06, U. Houston, 2006—07; prof. Ctrl. South U., 2007—. Recipient Young Skeleton Tchr. award, Dept. Edn., Hunan. Mem.: Chinese Chem. Soc. Avocation: badminton. Office: Yule Dist 932 Changsha Hunan 410083 China

LIUJUN, ZHAO, medical educator; b. China, Dec. 9, 1974; D, Zhejiang U. Traditional Chinese Medicine, 2008. Assoc. prof. Ningbo 6th Hosp., 2007—11. Office: 1059# Zhongshan Dong Rd Ningbo Zhejiang 315040 China Business E-Mail: zhaoliujun555@sina.com.cn.

LIVERSAGE, RICHARD ALBERT, cell biologist, educator; b. Fitchburg, Mass., July 8, 1925; s. Rodney Marcellus and Hazel Mildred (Huntting) L.; m. June Patricia Krebs L., June 19, 1954; children: John Walter, Robert Richard, James Keith, Ross Andrew. BA, Marlboro Coll., 1951; A.M., Amherst Coll., 1953; A. M., Princeton U., 1957, PhD, 1958. Fellow Bowdoin Coll., Brunswick, Maine, 1953-54; instr. Amherst Coll., 1954-55, Princeton, 1958-60; mem. faculty U. Toronto, 1960—, prof. cell and sys. biology, 1969—, grad. sec. dept., 1975-77, asso. chmn. grad. affairs dept., 1978-84, acting chmn., 1980-81. Investigator Huntsman Marine Lab., St. Andrews, N.B., Can., 1968-71; vis. prof. Strangeways Rsch. Lab., Cambridge, Eng., 1972. Contbr. numerous articles on role of nerves and endocrine secretions and the genetic basis of vertebrate appendage regeneration to sci. jours. Served as flight engr. B-24 liberators 8th USAAF, 1943-45. Recipient 5 combat decorations. Mem. Royal Can. Inst., Sigma Xi (exec. com., v.p., pres. U. Toronto chpt.). Home: PO Box 651 Bobcaygeon ON Canada K0M 1A0 Office: Univ Toronto Dept Cell and Sys Biology Ramsay Wright Bldg Toronto ON Canada M5S 3G5 Business E-Mail: rliversage@nexicom.net.

LIVINGSTON, DAVID MORSE, internist, biomedical researcher; b. Cambridge, Mass., Mar. 29, 1941; s. Arthur Joshua and Phyllis Freda (Kanters) Livingston; m. Jacqueline Gutman, June 23, 1963 (div. 1983); m. Emily Rabb, Jan. 25, 1986; children: Catherine Ellen, Julie. AB cum laude, Harvard U., Cambridge, Mass., 1961; MD magna cum laude, Tufts U., Medford, Mass., 1965. Diplomate Am. Bd. Internal Medicine. Intern, resident Peter Bent Brigham Hosp., Boston, 1965—67; rsch. assoc., sr. staff fellow, sr. investigator NCI-NIH, Bethesda, Md., 1967—69, 1971—73; rsch. fellow in biol. chemistry Harvard Med. Sch., Boston, 1969—71, asst. prof. medicine, 1973—76, assoc. prof. medicine, 1976—82, prof. medicine, 1982—92, Emil Frei prof. medicine, 1992—, chmn. exec. com. rsch., 1995—2000, 2005—; v.p. Dana-Farber Cancer Inst./Harvard Med. Sch., Boston, 1989—91, dir., physician-in-chief, 1991—95, dep. dir., mem. exec. com., 1999—. Mem. editl. bd. Virology, 1989—97, MOI & Cell Biology, 1998—2000; editor: BBA Revs. on Cancer, 1988—2001; contbr. articles to profl. jours. Vice chmn. sci. adv. com. Pezcoller Found., Trento, Italy, 1994—; mem. sci. adv. bd. Inst. Cancer Rsch., Fox Chase, Pa., 1991—96, Lineburger Comprehensive Cancer Ctr., U. NC, Chapel Hill, 1993—95, MIT Cancer Ctr., 1994—; mem. ext. adv. com. Fred Hutchinson Cancer Rsch. Ctr., 1992—96, Ctr. Cancer Rsch. MIT, 1994—; chmn. bd. sci. advisers, mem. exec. com. NCI/NIH, 1995—99; mem. sci. adv. com. Damon Runyan-Walter Winchell Cancer Fund, NYC, 1988—92, chmn. sci. adv. com., 1989—92, bd. dirs., 1992—97, bd. dirs., vice-chmn. sci. programs; pres. bd. Cancer Rsch. Fund, 1997—. Comdr. USPHS, 1967—73. Recipient Claire & Richard Morse award for Rsch., Dana-Farber Cancer Inst., 1991, Baxter award, AAMC, 1997, Brinker award, Susan Komen Found., 1997, Lila Gruber award, 2001, Clowes Meml. award, Am. Assn. Cancer Rsch., 2005, Boveri award for molecular cancer genetics, German Cancer Soc., 2005. Fellow: Am. Acad. Arts and Scis.; mem.: NAS, Am. Acad. Microbiology, Inst. Medicine of NAS, Am. Soc. Virology, Am. Soc. Biol. Chemistry and Molecular Biology, Assn. Am. Physicians, Am. Soc. for Clin. Investigation, Harvard Club (NYC, Boston), St. Botolph Club, Met. Club Washington, Alpha Omega Alpha. Achievements include discovery of important aspects of the neoplastic transforming process and of the mechanisms governing control of the mammalian cell cycle. Office: Dana-Farber Cancer Inst 44 Binney St Smith Bldg Rm 870 Boston MA 02115-6084 Office Phone: 617-632-3074. Office Fax: 617-632-4381. Business E-Mail: david_livingston@dfci.harvard.edu.

LIVSHITS, ARKADY, neurosurgeon; b. Baku, Azerbaijan, USSR, Oct. 12, 1937; arrived in Israel, 1993; s. Vladimir and Esphire Livshits; m. Tsilia Dinkin, July 28, 1959; children: Vadim, Irina. MD, Medical Inst., Baku, 1960; PhD, Inst. of Gen. Surgery Acad. of Medical Scis., 1964; DM, Inst. of Gen. Surgery, Acad. of Medical Scis., 1969. Cert. prof. neurosurgery 1978. Surgeon specialist Gen. Hosp., Murom, Russia, 1960—65; sci. specialist Inst. of Gen. Surgery, Moscow, 1965—69, chief of neurosurgery dept., 1969—77; dir./gen. neurosurgeon All-Union Ctr. of Spinal Neurosurgery, Moscow, 1977—93; sci. dir. Inst. of Neurosurgery, Head of Medical Scis., Moscow, 1990—93; prof. Spinal Care Unit, Israel, 1993—. Prof. Inst. Neurosurgery, Moscow, 1978—93; vis. prof. Belgrad U., Yugoslavia, 1985; lectr. Minneapolis U., 1981, U. Buenes Aires, 1990; sr. investigator Tel Aviv U. Faculty Medicine, 2002—. Author of over 156 scientific articles; author, editor (book) Electrostimulation of the Bladder, 1973, Surgery of the Spinal Cord, 1991; contbr. chapters to books. Recipient Devel. of med. tech. gold medal, 1972, Devel. of med. tech. bronze medal, 1980—81. Fellow: Internat. Soc. of Spinal Cord; mem.: Internat. Functional Electrostimulation Soc. (internat. mem.), Medico Technic Soc. (bd. dirs. 1970—93). Jewish. Achievements include patents in field. Office: Spinal Care Unit Meir Gen Hosp 44201 Kefar Sava Israel Home: Rothshield Str 65/1 44100 Kefar Sava Israel

LIWSZYC, GUILLERMO ELI, physician, researcher, interpreter; b. Buenos Aires, May 18, 1958; arrived in Finland, 1988; s. Aaron Leon and Teresa (Jramoy) L.; m. Maria Alejandra Vaz, Aug. 5, 1983 B in Bus., Escuela Superior, Buenos Aires, 1975; MD, U. Buenos Aires, 1983. Asst. physician Hosp. Mcpl., Merlo, Argentina, 1984-88; guest scientist dept. pathology U. Helsinki, Finland, 1988—. Asst. physician Hosp. Mcpl., Buenos Aires, 1985-90; first asst. Hosp. J. Fernandez, Univ. Buenos Aires, 1986; cons. Flexigom, Buenos Aires, 1995-2001; mgr., spkr. radio broadcast Moliendo Cafe, 1995—2000; mem. tech. and health com. Internat. Assn. Conf., 1997-2000, pres., 1998-2000, coun. mem. 2000—; lectr. Ctr. Transl. and Interpretation U. Turku, Finland, 1997—; lectr. Romanic langs. dept. U. Turku, Finland, 1997—; specialist in internal medicine U. Buenos Aires, Argentina, 1990. Contbr. articles to profl. jours. Treas. Circulo de Estudio Latino, Helsinki, 1995. Grantee Ministry Edn. Finland, 1988, 90, Finnish Acad. Scis., 1993. Mem.: N.Y. Acad. Scis., Internat. Assn. Conf. Interpreters (pres. tech. and health com. 1998, European Commn. 1997—). Avocations: travel, tennis, swimming, music, cinema. Office: U Helsinki Haartmaninkatu 3 00140 Helsinki Finland Home: Eriksgatan 50 B 37 180 Helsinki Finland Fax: 358 9 685 2375.

LIZAMA SOBERANIS, BEATRIZ EUGENIA, health facility administrator, researcher; b. Mexico City, Dec. 26, 1969; d. José Manuel Lizama Velázquez and Beatriz Eugenia Soberanis Villafana; m. Carlos Vázquez Arriaga, Jan. 22, 1994; 1 child, Javier. B in Chemistry, U. Autonoma del Estado de Mexico, Toluca, Mex., 1993; MBA, Inst. Tecnológico y de Estudios Superiores de Monterrey, Toluca, 1997; PhD in Engring., U. Autonoma de Querétaro, Mex., 2001. Cert. mktg. specialist. Chemist Syntex, Cuernavaca, Mexico, 1992-95; lab. head ININ, Toluca, 1995-97; lab. head faculty quimica UAEM, Mexico, 1997—2002; quality assurance mgr. Plastiesteril-Baxter Health Care Corp., Atlacomulco, Mexico, 2002—03; applied rsch. head U. del Valle de Mexico, Toluca, Mexico, 2003—07; cons. Qualitygenia, 2003—; technosci. regional head U. del Valle de Mexico, Mexico City, 2007—; evaluator Health Care Govt., Nat. Rsch. Sys. Candidate Level Qualitygenia Group, Mex. City, 2009—. Contbr. articles to profl. jours. Mem.: Am. Assn. Cereal Chemistry, Assn. Analytical Chemistry, Am. Chem. Soc. Avocations: reading, movies, cooking, gardening. Home Phone: 525553438301. Personal E-mail: bels_a@yahoo.com.mx. Business E-Mail: beatriz.lizamas@uvmnet.edu.

LIZARRAGA, WILLIAM ANTHONY, physician; b. Tenn., Apr. 16, 1978; BS, Vanderbilt U., 2000; MD, U. Tenn., 2005. Internal medicine resident Brown U., Lifespan Hosps., 2005—08, chief med. resident, 2008—09; physician The Frist Clinic, 2009—. Med. dir. Gentiva Home Healthcare Svcs., Nashville, 2010—. Recipient Gerald I. Plitman award, U. Tenn., Resident Rsch. award, Brown Internal Medicine Residency. Mem.: AMA, ACP. Office: 2400 Patterson St Ste 400 Nashville TN 37203 Office Fax: 615-342-5947. E-mail: tonylizarraga@hotmail.com.

LIZIO, GIUSEPPE, research scientist; b. Messina, Italy, May 11, 1972; Grad. in Dentistry, U. Messina, 1996; degree in Oral Surgery, U. Florence, 2001; M in Prosthodontics, U. Chieti, Italy, 2003; M in Oral surgery, Periodontology. Rsch. asst. U. Bologna, 2008—. Avocations: swimming, painting, literature. Office: Via S Vitale 59 Vicolo Bolognetti 11 Bologna 40125 Italy Office Fax: 0039 051 225208. Business E-Mail: giuseppelizio@libero.it.

LJUBIMOV, ALEXANDER V., molecular biologist, cell biologist, researcher; b. Moscow, Oct. 27, 1952; s. Vladimir V. Ljubimov and Margarita S. Ljubimova; m. Julia Y. Savchenko, Apr. 1, 1989; children: Anna A., Vladimir A. PhD, Russian Cancer Rsch. Ctr., Moscow, 1979. Staff scientist Russian Cancer Rsch. Ctr., 1979—93; rsch. scientist Cedars Sinai Med. Ctr., LA, 1993—2002, dir. Ophthalmology Rsch. Labs., 2002—, prof., 2009, UCLA Sch. Medicine, 2003—. Mem. editl. bd.: Frontiers in Biosci., Exptl. Eye Rsch., ISRN Ophthalmology, The Open Ophthalmology Journal, Brain Rsch. Bull., The Vascular Cell; mem. editl. bd. Experimental Biology and Medicine; contbr. articles to profl. jours. Grantee, NIH, 1998—. Fellow: Assn. Rsch. in Vision and Ophthalmology; mem.: Internat. Soc. Eye Rsch., Am. Diabetes Assn., Assn. UICC Fellows. Achievements include patents for cancer research and angiogenesis. Office: Cedars Sinai Med Ctr Ste SSB-363 8700 Beverly Blvd Los Angeles CA 90048 Office Phone: 310-248-8583. E-mail: ljubimov@cshs.org.

LJUBOJEVIC, SUZANA, physician; b. Zagreb, Croatia, Nov. 30, 1971; MD, U. Zagreb, 1996, PhD, 2005. Physician, dept. dermatology and venereology Sch. Medicine U. Hosp. Ctr. Zagreb, 2001—. Home: Dobri Dol 48 Zagreb 10000 Croatia Personal E-mail: suzana.ljubojevic@zg.t-com.hr.

LLAURADO, JOSEP G., nuclear medicine physician, researcher; b. Barcelona, Catalonia, Spain, Feb. 6, 1927; s. José and Rosa (Llaurado) Garcia; m. Catherine D. Entwistle, June 28, 1958 (dec.); children: Thadd, Oleg, Montserrat; m. Deirdre Mooney, Nov. 9, 1966; children: Raymund, Wilfred, Mireya. BS, BA, Balmes Inst., Barcelona, 1944; MD, Barcelona U., 1950, PhD in Pharmacology, 1960; MSc in Biomed. Engring., Drexel U., 1963. Diplomate Am. Bd. Nuclear Medicine. Resident Royal Postgrad. Sch. Medicine, Hammersmith Hosp., London, 1952-54; fellow M.D. Anderson Hosp. and Tumor Inst., Houston, 1957-58, U. Utah Med. Coll., Salt Lake City, 1958-59; asst. prof. U. Otago, Dunedin, New Zealand, 1954-57; sr. endocrinologist Prizer Med. Rsch. Lab., Groton, Conn., 1959-60; assoc. prof. U. Pa., Phila., 1963-67; prof. Med. Coll. Wis., Milw., 1970-82, Marquette U., Milw., 1967-82; clin. dir. nuc. medicine svc. VA Med. Ctr., Milw., 1977—82; chief nuc. medicine svc. VA Hosp., Loma Linda, Calif., 1983—; prof. dept. radiation scis. Loma Linda U. Sch. Medicine, 1983—. U.s. rep. symposium dynamic studies with radioisotopes clin. medicine and rsch. IAEA, Rotterdam, Netherlands, 1970, Knoxville, Tenn., 74. Hon. editor: Internat. Jour. Biomed. Computing, dep. editor: Mgmt. Environ. Quality (now Mgmt. Environ. Quality: an Internat. Jour.); contbr. articles to profl. jours. Merit badge counselor Boy Scouts Am., 1972—; pres. Hales Corners (Wis.) Hist. Soc., 1981—83. Recipient Commendation cert., Boy Scouts Am., 1980, Joan d'Alos prize, Cardiovasc. Ctr. St. Jordi, Barcelona, 1999, XII Batista-Roca prize, Inst. Exterior Projection Catalan Culture, 2000. Fellow: Am. Coll. Nutrition; mem.: IEEE (life), Calif. Med. Assn. (mem. sci. adv. panel nuc. medicine 1993—), Soc. Catalana Biologia, Am. Soc. Nuc. Cardiology, Endocrine Soc., Soc. Math. Biology (founding), Am. Soc. Pharmacology and Exptl. Therapeutics, Am. Physiol. Soc., Biomed. Engring. Soc. (charter), IEEE Medicine and Biology Soc. (mem. nat. adminstrv. com. 1986—89), Soc. Nuc. Medicine (computer and acad. couns.), Royal Acad. Medicine Catalonia/Barcelona, Casal dels Catalans Calif. (pres. 1989—91). Roman Catholic. Office: VA Hosp Nuclear Med Svc Rm 115 11201 Benton St Loma Linda CA 92357-0001 Office Phone: 909-583-6102.

LLEDO, ALBERTO, neurologist; b. Madrid, May 31, 1960; s. Emilio Lledo and Montserrat Macau; married; children: Montserrat, Martin. MD, U. Complutense; PhD, U. Complutense, Madrid, 1984; student, Cajal Inst. CSIC, Madrid, 1992—95. Resident neurology Hosp. U., Madrid, 1987—91, cons. neurologist, 1991—92, 1995—96; rsch. physician Lilly Rsch. Ctr., 1996—2007, sr. med. fellow, 2007—. Fellow neuroimmunology U. Chgo., 1993—94. Recipient Premio Extraordinario de Doctorado, U. Complutense, 2005. Office: Lilly Rsch Ctr - Lilly SA Calle Santa Tecla 1 8012 Barcelona Spain Business E-Mail: lledo_alberto@lilly.com.

LLERANDI PHIPPS, CARMEN GUILLERMINA, nutritionist and dietitian; b. Aguadilla, PR., Jan. 6, 1958; came to U.S., 1979; d. Pablo Manuel Llerandi Alum and Carmen Estela (Santana Phipps) Llerandi; m. June 21, 1981 (div. 1990); 1 child, Paul Gabriel Vallejo Llerandi. BA, Glasboro Coll., NJ, 1984; postgrad., Loma Linda U., Calif., 1994—. Lic. and registered dietitian. Pub. health nutritionist Sa Lantic Health Svc., Hammonton, N.J., 1989-90; clin. mgmt. dietitian Clifton T. Perkins Psychiat. Hosp., Jessup, Md., 1990-91; adminstrv. clin. dietitian Brownsville (Tex.) Med. Ctr., 1991-93; clin. dietictan, pediatric outpatient clin. dietitian Loma Linda U. Childrens Hosp., 1993-95; nutrition cons. Rio Grande Valley Midway House, Inc., Harlingen, Tex., 1993—; chief adminstrv. sect. Jerry L. Pettis VA Med. Ctr., Loma Linda, 1995—. Mem. bd. dietetic and nutrition depts. U. Tex., 1991-93. Mem. Am. Dietetic Assn., Am. Assn. Diabetes Educators, Seventh Day Adventist Dietetic Assn., Nutrition Edn. Assn. Office: Valley Baptist Health Systm 2101 Pease St Harlingen TX 78551 Home: 14 Sanctu Spiritus Brownsville TX 78526 Office Phone: 909-825-7084 x 2104. E-mail: llerandic1@aol.com.

LLEWELLYN, GWYNNYTH M., dean, educator; b. Arncliffe, NSW, Australia, May 31, 1946; PhD, U. Sydney, 1995. Dean, prof. U. Sydney, 2005—. Dir. Australian Family and Disability Studies Rsch. Collaboration, 2000; bd. dir. Royal Rehab. Ctr. Sydney, 2004, found. dir., 09; expert mem. Australian Collaborating Ctr. World Health Orgn. Family Internat. Classifications, 2010; mem. Rschr. Network Intellectual and Devel. Disability, 2010. ARC Discovery Project grant, Schizophrenia fellowship, grant, Dept. Family Cmty., Housing & Indigenous Affairs, ARC Linkage Projects Scheme grant. Mem.: Jour. Applied Rsch. Intellectual Disability (assoc. editor), IASSID Spl. Interest Rsch. Group Parents and Parenting Intellectual Disabilities, Internat. Assn. Sci. Study Intellectual Disabilities (exec. com.), IASSID Asia Pacific SINGA Scholarship Com. (expert mem.). Office: 75 East St Lidcombe NSW 2141 Australia Business E-Mail: fhs.dean@sydney.edu.au.

LLINÁS, RODOLFO RIASCOS, neuroscientist, researcher; b. Bogota, Colombia, Dec. 16, 1934; came to U.S., 1959, naturalized, 1973; s. Jorge Enrique (Llinas) and Bertha (Riascos) L.; m. Gillian Kimber, Dec. 24, 1965; children: Rafael Hugo, Alexander Jorge. BS, Gimnasio Moderno, Bogota, 1952; MD, U. Javeriana, Bogota, 1959; PhD, Australian Nat. U., 1965; MD (hon.), U. Salamanca, Spain, 1985; PhD (hon.), U. Barcelona, Spain, 1993, U. Nacional Bogota, Colombia, 1994; D, Univ. Complutense, Madrid, 1997. Research fellow Mass. Gen. Hosp.-Harvard U., 1960-61; NIH research fellow in physiology U. Minn., Mpls., 1961-63, assoc. prof., 1965-66; assoc. mem. AMA Inst. Biomed. Research, Chgo., 1966-68, mem., 1970, head neurobiology unit, 1967-70; assoc. prof. neurology and psychiatry Northwestern U., 1967-71; guest prof. physiology Wayne State U., 1967-74; professorial lectr. pharmacology U. Ill.-Chgo., 1967-68, clin. prof., 1968-72; prof. physiology, head neurobiology div. U. Iowa, 1970-76; prof., chmn. physiology and biophysics NYU, NYC, 1976—, Thomas and Suzanne Murphy prof. neurosci., 1985—. Mem. neurol. sci. research tng. com. Nat. Inst. Neurol. Diseases and Stroke, NIH, 1971-73; mem. neurology A study sect. div. research grants NIH, 1974-78; assoc. neurosci. research program MIT, 1974-83; mem. U.S. Nat. Com. for IBRO, 1978-81; acting chmn. U.S. Nat. Com. For IBRO, 1982, chmn., 1983-89, exec. com., 1985—; mem. sci. adv. bd. Max-Planck Inst. for Psychiatry, Munich, 1979-83; professorial lectr. Coll. de France, Paris, 1979, Nat. Poly. Inst., Mexico City, 1981; IBRO internat. lectr., S.Am., 1982; McDowall lectr. King's Coll.,

London, 1984 Author: (with Hubbard and Quastel) Electrophysiological Analysis of Synaptic Transmission, 1969; editor: Neurobiology of Cerebellar Evolution and Development, 1969, (with W. Precht) Frog Neurobiology: A Handbook, 1976; chief editor: Neurosci., 1974—1999; mem. editorial bd.: Jour. Neurobiology, 1980—; mem.: Pfluegers Archives, 1981—, Jour. Theoretical Neurobiology, 1981—. Recipient John C. Krantz award U. Md., 1976, Einstein Gold medal UNESCO, 1991, Signoret award in cognition, Fondation Ipsen La Salpâtrière, Paris, 1994. Mem. NAS, Soc. For Neurosci. (council 1974-78), Am. Physiol. Soc. (Bowditch Lectr. 1973), Am. Soc. Cell Biology, Biophys. Soc., Harvey Soc., Internat. Brain Research Orgn., N.Y. Acad. Scis., Am. Acad. Arts & Scis., Am. Philosophical Soc., Real Academia Nacional de Medicina, Nat. Deafness and Other Communication Disorders, Nat. Inst. of Health (adv. coun.), Alpha Omega Alpha (hon.), French Acad. Scis.

LLOMBART-BOSCH, ANTONIO, pathologist, educator; b. San Sebastian, Spain, Spain, 1935; m. Nadine Cussac Llombart-Bosch, 1964; children: Antonio, Patricia, Javier, Beatriz. MD in Medicine & Surgery, U. Valencia, Spain, 1959; PhD, 1965. Prof., pathology U. Valencia, 1975—2005, dean, med. sch., 1980—83, 1990—93, dir., pathology dept., 1983—90, 1993—99; prof. emeritus Faculty Medicine U. Valencia, 2009—; invited prof. Faculty Medicine U. Norte, Barranquilla, Colombia, 2009—, Inst. Superior Ciencias Medicas, Harbana, Cuba, 2009—. Former pres. & chmn. Several Nat. and Internat. Pathology Orgns., prin. investigator & organizer; rschr. U. Ciencia, 2005—07; with FIS Project, Madrid, 2005—08; pres. Fundacion Inst. Valenciano Oncologia, 2009—; sci. advisor Assn. Ligas Latinoamericanas Contra Cancer, 2009—. Contbr. chpts. in 27 sci. publs., numerous articles to nat. and internat. jours. Exec. com. mem. & treas. European Orgn. Cancer Insts., 2001—07; pres., ednl. com. Valencia Med. Assn., 2006—; advisor Ecole Formation Europeenne Cancerologie, France, 2009—. Recipient Order of French Legion of Honor, France, 2002, Santiago Ramon Cajal award, Spanish Soc. Pathology, 2007, Golden medal, City Valencia, 2007; Rsch. grant, European Consortium, 2005—08. Achievements include research in human urological and renal carcinogenesis; biopathology of undifferentiated sarcomas and liver cancer; cytogenetics and molecular biology; human and experimental neoplasms. Office: Univ Valencia Facultad Medicina Odontologia Dept Patologia Ave Blasco Ibanez 17 Valecia 46010 Spain Office Fax: 34 963 864 173. E-mail: antonio.llombart@uv.es.

LLOYD, DAVID, biochemist, educator; b. Tonypandy, Wales, Nov. 26, 1940; s. Frederick Lewis and Annie Mary Lloyd; m. Margaret Jones, Apr. 5, 1969; children: Alun Lewis, Siôn Huw. BSc, Sheffield U., Eng., 1961, DSc, 1972; PhD, U. Coll. Cardiff, Wales, 1964. ICI rsch. fellow U. Coll. Cardiff, 1964-66, MRC rsch. asst., 1966-69, lectr., 1969-76, sr. lectr., 1976, reader, 1976-78, prof., 1978-82, Cardiff U., 1982—, head microbiology dept., 1982—87. Leverhulme rsch. fellow U. Pa., 1971; vis. prof. U. NSW, 1998. Author: (book) The Mitochondria of Microorganisms, 1974, The Cell Division Cycle, 1982; editor: The Eukaryotic Microbial Cell, 1980, Ultradian Rhythms in Life Processes, 1992, Metabolic and Cellular Engineering, 2002, Ultradian Rhythms from Molecular to Mind: a New Vision of Life, 2008. Mem.: Am. Soc. Protozoologists, Soc. Gen. Microbiology, Biochemical Soc. Avocations: opera, walking, bicycling. Business E-Mail: lloydd@cf.ac.uk.

LLOYD, DOUGLAS SEWARD, physician, public health administrator; b. Bklyn., Oct. 16, 1939; s. Heber Hughes and Virginia Seward (Chamberlin) L. AB in Chemistry, Duke U., 1961, MD, 1971; postgrad., Old Dominion U., 1965-67, MPH in Health Planning, U. N.C., 1971. Diplomate Am. Bd. Preventive Medicine. Intern Duke U., Durham, NC, 1971-72, clin. scholar, 1972, resident in family practice, 1972-73; commr. health Conn. Dept. Health Services, 1973-87; assoc. med. dir. Nat. Med. Rsch. Corp., Hartford, Conn., 1987-89; pres. Doug Lloyd Assocs., Farmington, Conn., 1989-92; dir. Ctr. Pub. Health Practice Health Resources and Svcs. Adminstrn., Rockville, Md., 1992-98; with Assn. Schs. Pub. Health, Washington, 1999—2001. Lectr. Yale U., Conn., 1973-87; chmn. bd. Pub. Health Found., 1984-87. Contbr. articles to profl. jours. Capt. USNR, ret. Recipient Lange Publ. award, 1971, McCormick award for excellence in pub. health, 1987, Ervin award for creative vision, The Pub. Health Found., 2001. Fellow Am. Coll. Preventive Medicine; mem. AMA, Am. Pub. Health Assn., Assn. State and Territorial Health Ofcls. (past pres.). Home: 10804 Bird Song Path Columbia MD 21044-3693 Office Phone: 301-854-3646. Personal E-mail: drdoug.lloyd@comcast.net. Business E-Mail: dLloyd@hrsa.gov.

LLOYD, MARGARET ANN, psychologist, educator; b. Weiser, Idaho, Sept. 14, 1942; d. Laurance Henry and Margaret Jane (Patch) L. BA, U. Denver, 1964; MS in Edn., Ind. U., 1966; MA in Psychology, U. Ariz., 1972, PhD in Psychology, 1973. Asst. prof. psychology Suffolk U., Boston, 1973-76, assoc. prof., 1976-79, prof., 1979-88, chair dept., 1981-88; prof. Ga. So. U., Statesboro, 1988—2004, head dept., 1988—93, prof. emerita and chair, 2004—. Author: Adolescence, 1985; author: (with others) Psychology Applied to Modern Life, 1991, 1994, 1997, 2000, 2003, 2006, 2009; contbr. articles to profl. jours. Mem. AAUP, APA (bd. ednl. affairs 2000-2002, sec.-treas. divsn. 2, 1990-93, pres. 1994-95, coun. rep. 2003-08), New Eng. Psychol. Assn. (steering com. 1984-86), Mass. Psychol. Assn. (sec. 1979-81, chair bd. acad. and. sci. affairs 1981-82), Coun. Undergrad. Psychology Programs (chmn. 1990-91). Home: 3288 Palo Pkwy Boulder CO 80301-3708 Personal E-mail: mlloyd@georgiasouthern.edu. *

LLOYD, STEVEN GLEN, cardiologist; b. Geneva, Ala., Apr. 17, 1968; BS, Auburn U., 1990; MD, PhD, Emory U., 1997. Asst. prof. medicine U. Ala., Birmingham, 2004—09, head sect. cardiovasc. magnetic resonance, scientist Diabetes Rsch. & Tng. Ctr., Nutrition Obesity Rsch. Ctr., Ctr. Cardiovasc. Biology, 2004—11, assoc. prof. medicine, 2009—. Recipient Editor's Recognition award, Radiology; US Presdl. scholar, Dept. Edn. Fellow: Am. Coll. Cardiology (Gov.-elect Ala. Chpt. 2011—, mem. publs. com. 2011—, chair edn. and imaging com. Ala. chpt. 2005—11, Career Devel. award, Outstanding Chpt. Vol. award); mem.: Am. Heart Assn. (Scientist Devel. grant). Avocations: reading, gardening. Office: D-101 UAB Cardiac MRI 1808 7th Ave Birmingham AL 35294 Office Phone: 205-934-9736. Office Fax: 205-934-9730. Business E-Mail: sglloyd@uab.edu.

LLOYD, WILLIAM C., III, ophthalmologist; b. Red Bank, NJ, Jan. 3, 1953; m. Mary Lloyd. BS, US Mil. Acad.; MD, Uniformed Svcs. U., 1980. Diplomate Am. Bd. Ophthalmology. Intern, ophthamology Brooke Army Med. Ctr., Fort Sam Houston, Tex., 1980—81, resident, ophthalmologic pathology, 1981—84, hosp. appointment in ophthamology; fellow, anatomical pathology Wills Eye Hosp., Phila., 1988—89; clin. prof. U. Tex. Health Sci. Ctr., San Antonio; prof. ophthalmology & pathology U. Calif. Davis Med. Ctr. Founder M3W Media Inc.; contbr. & cons. WebMD. With Corp. Engrs. US Army. Decorated Order of Mil. Merit US Army; recipient Physician's Recognition award, AMA. Fellow: Am. Acad. Ophthalmology, Am. Coll. Surgeons.

LO, HSIAO-FENG, horticulturist, educator; b. Taichung, Taiwan; d. Peng-Fei Lo and Feng-Yuan Lee; m. Long-Fang Chen; 1 child, Ing-Gin Chen. BS, Nat. Chung-Hsing U., 1977; MS, Nat. Taiwan U., 1980; PhD, Miss. State U., 1986. Cert. prof. Ministry Edn. Taiwan, 1995. Assoc. rschr. dept. agronomy Chia-Yi Agrl. Expt. Sta., Taiwan, 1986—87; assoc. prof. dept. horticulture Chinese Culture U., Taipei, Taiwan, 1987—95, prof., 1995—, chmn. dept. horticulture, 1999—2009; prof. dept. horticulture Nat. Taiwan U., 2009—. Contbr. articles to profl. jours. Tchr. children bible sch. Nangang Bapt. Ch., Taipei, 2000—05. Mem.: Taiwan Flower Devel. Soc. (bd. dirs. 2002—09), Chinese Hort. Assn. (life; bd. mem. 2007—). Home: 75 2d Fl Academia Rd Sect 2 Nangang Taipei 115 Taiwan Office Fax: 886-2-23625542. Personal E-mail: hflochen26@hotmail.com. Business E-Mail: hflo@ntu.edu.tw.

LO, HSIU-JUNG, biomedical science investigator; b. Taoyuan, Taiwan, Apr. 25, 1965; d. Chin-Kang and Shui-Mei (Chang) Lo; m. Yun-Liang Yang, Feb. 16, 1989; children: Summer Yang, Nova Yang. BS, Nat. Chung-Hsing U., Taichung, Taiwan, 1987; PhD, Ind. U., Bloomington, 1995. Postdoctoral fellow Whitehead Inst. Biomedical Rsch., Chambridge, Mass., 1995—98; asst. investigator Nat. Health Rsch. Inst., Taipei, Taiwan, 1999—2004, assoc. investigator, 2004—, acting dir. divsn. infectious disease, 2008—09; assoc. edior BMC Microbiology, 2008—. Mem.: Internat. Soc. Human and Animal Mycology, Am. Soc. Microbiology. Achievements include patents for regulation of fungal gene expression; research in non-fiamentous Candida albicans mutants are avirulent; reduced-susceptibility to fluoroquinolones. Office: Nat Health Rsch Inst 35 Keyan Rd Miaoli Taiwan Office Fax: 886 37 586 457. Business E-Mail: hjlo@nhri.org.tw.

LO, JUNG-HUA, engineering educator; b. Yilan, Taiwan, Jan. 3, 1971; PhD, Nat. Taiwan U., 2003. Asst. prof. Lan-Yang Inst. Tech., 1998—2006, Dept. Applied Informatics, 2006—08, assoc. prof., 2008—10, assoc. prof., chmn., 2010—. Mem.: IEEE. Avocation: rugby. Office: 160 Linwei Rd Jiaosi Yilan County 26247 Taiwan Business E-Mail: jhlo@mail.fgu.edu.tw.

LO, KWOK MING STEVE, medical oncologist, educator; BA, Harvard Coll.; MD, Harvard U., 1985. Diplomate Am. Bd. Internal Medicine, Am. Bd. Internal Medicine med. oncology, Am. Bd. Internal Medicine hematology. Clin. fellow in med. oncology Dana Farber Cancer Inst., fellow in autologus bone marrow transplantation; intern Brigham and Women's Hosp., Mass., 1986, resident, 1988; asst. clin. prof. physicians and surgeons coll. Columbia Univ.; med. oncologist Bennett Cancer Ctr. Stamford Hosp., Conn. Recipient Physician Scientist award, NIH. Office: Stamford Hospital Bennett Cancer Center 30 Shelburne Rd Stamford CT 06904 Office Phone: 203-325-2695.

LO, PATRICK PUNCHUK, physician; b. Hong Kong, Nov. 26, 1952; came to U.S., 1972; s. Yuen and City-Yu (Cheung) L.; m. Daisy Yawluan Sim, Dec. 19, 1982; 1 child, Jeffrey. BS in Pharmacy, U. Okla., 1977; DO, Okla. State U., 1982. Diplomate Am. Bd. Osteo. Gen. Practice; registered pharmacist, Okla. Intern Hillcrest Health Ctr., Oklahoma City, 1982-83; physician Corn Med. Clinic, Oklahoma City, 1983—. Mem. Am. Osteo. Assn., Okla. Osteo. Assn., Am. Coll. Gen. Practice, Lions. Office: Corn Med Clinic 1506 S Agnew Ave Oklahoma City OK 73108-2432 Office Phone: 405-235-3933.

LO, WEN-LIN, dermatologist; b. Kaohsiung, Taiwan, Jan. 1, 1958; s. Jhi-Yuan and Chung-Hwa (Wang) L.; m. Yung-Jung Ho, March 7, 1987. MD, Nat. Yang-Ming Med. Coll., 1982. Resident in dermatology Vets. Gen. Hosp., Taipei, 1984-89, attending physician, 1989-91, Chutong (Taiwan) Vets. Hosp., 1991-93, sect. chief, 1993-94; pvt. practice Taipei, 1994—. Lectr. Nat. Yang-Ming Med. Coll., Taipei, 1989-91. Assoc. editor: Dermatologica Sinica, 1990; contbr. articles to profl. jours. 2nd lt. Chinese Army, 1982-84. Fellow Am. Acad. Dermatology; mem. Asian Dermatol. Assn., Internat. Soc. Dermatology, Chinese Dermatol. Soc. (Rsch. paper award 1986, 87), Laser Medicine Soc. Office: 2/F # 2 Ln 14 Chung Shan N Sec 7 Taipei 111 Taiwan Home Phone: 886-2-2872-1550; Office Phone: 886-2-2874-3223. E-mail: loskin@ms17.hinet.net.

LOARIE, THOMAS MERRITT, healthcare executive; b. Deerfield, Ill., June 12, 1946; s. Willard John and Lucile Veronica (Finnegan) L.; m. Stephanie Lane Fitts, Aug. 11, 1968 (div. Nov. 1987); children: Thomas M., Kristin Leigh Soule. BSME, U. Notre Dame, 1968; student, U. Minn., 1969—70, U. Chgo., 1970—71, Columbia U., 1978. Registered profl. engr., Calif. Prodn. engr. Honeywell, Inc., Evanston, Ill., 1968-70; with Am. Hosp. Supply Co., 1970—83, pres. Heyer-Schulte divsn., 1979—83; pres. and COO Novacor Med. Corp., Oakland, Calif., 1984—85, bd. dir.; pres. ABA Bio Mgmt., Danville, 1985—87; chmn., CEO Keravision, Inc., Fremont, 1987—2001, Mercator MedSystems, Inc., San Leandro, 2005—08, 2005—08, exec. chmn., 2008—; chmn. Silicon BioDevices, Inc., Palo Alto, 2010—; founder, chmn., med. device CEO Roundtable, 1993—2002; co-founder, chmn. CardioProfile, Inc., Berkeley, 2002—05; bd. dirs. SinoMed, Hong Kong, 2010—, ME2, Inc, Scotts Valley, Calif., 2010—. Asst. prof. surgery Creighton U. Med. Sch., Omaha, 1986-94; guest lectr. Anderson Sch. Mgmt., UCLA, 2001-2003, Haas Sch. Bus., U. Calif., Berkeley, 2002-03; trustee Grad. Theol. Union, Berkeley, Calif., 2003—; mem. adv. bd. Occulogix, Inc., Tampa, 2001-03, Uptake Med. Inc., Seattle, 2003-2006; program dir. Catholics at Work, Oakland Diocese, 2005-; bd. dirs. Clarity Med. Sys., Inc., Pleasanton, Calif.; mem. external adv. bd., dept. mech. engring. U. Calif., Berkeley, 2007-, chmn., 2008-; spkr. in field Contbr. articles on med. tech. and pub. policy to Wall St. Jour., Jour. Retractive Surgery, others; columnist Cath. Bus. Jour., 2007—. Bd. dir. Marymount Sch. Bd., 1981-84; bd. dir. United Way Santa Barbara, 1981-84, assoc. chair, 1982-83, treas., 1983. Named One of 50 Rising Stars: Exec. Leaders for the 80's Industry Week mag., 1983. Mem. Assn. Rsch. in Vision and Ophthalmology, Contact Lens Assn. Ophthalmology, Health Industry Mfrs. Assn. (spl. rep. bd. dirs. 1993-96, 2006—, bd. dirs. 1997-2001, exec. com. 1997-2001, treas. 1998-2000, chmn.-elect 2000-01), Am. Entrepreneurs for Econ. Growth, Med. Tech. Leadership Forum, Calif. Healthcare Inst. (bd. dirs. 1998-2001, exec. com. 1999-2001), Diablo Venture Alliance. Roman Catholic. Achievements include leading development of Intacs corneal ring segments for treatment of nearsightedness (named One of Top 10 Medical Advances by Health Magazine/CNN 1999). Notre Dame Col. Prep, Wall of Fame, 2009. Office: Mercator Med Sys Inc Bldg 4 1640 Alvarado St San Leandro CA 94577 Personal E-mail: tloarie@mercatormed.com.

LOA ZAVALA, NASHYIELA, psychiatrist; b. Mex., Mar. 11, 1973; Degree in Adolescent Psychiatry, U. Nacional Autónoma de Mex., 2005. Psychoanalyst Asociación Psicoanalitica Mexicana, 2005—10. Office: Bosques de Caobas 67 Mexico City 11700 Mexico E-mail: nashyiela@yahoo.com.

LOBACH, KATHERINE S., retired pediatrician; b. Akron, June 2, 1927; d. Titus Breinig and Katherine M. (Slawik) L.; m. Richard Joseph Kaufman, Oct. 10, 1953; children: James Lobach, Susan Elizabeth, John Roger. AB, Smith Coll., 1948; MD, Columbia U., 1952. Diplomate Am. Bd. Pediats. Instr. pediats. Southwestern U. Sch. Medicine, Dallas, 1955-57; from instr. to prof. emerita pediats. Albert Einstein Coll. Medicine, Bronx, NY, 1957—2003, prof. emerita pediats., 2003—; asst. commr. for child health City of N.Y. Dept. Health, 1987-94; dir. Child Health Clinics N.Y.C. Health and Hosps. Corp., 1994-98, ret., 1998. Mem. health profl. adv. bd. March of Dimes of Greater NY, 1980—2001; mem. health svcs. adv. com. The Children's Aid Soc., NYC, 1992—; chmn. adv. com. Infant, Child Health Assessment Program, NYC, 1992—2002; mem. adv. coun. Citizen's Com. for Children of NYC, 1998—2004, bd. dirs., 2005—. Contbr. chapters to books, articles to profl. jours. Co-chmn. City Wide Coalition for Immunization Initiatives, NYC, 1992—2001; bd. dirs. Westchester Children's Assn., 2000—, pres., 2004—06; active Mayoral Commn. on future of Child Health in NYC, NYC, 1987—89; bd. dir. Bronx Com. Health Network, 1998—, Statewide Youth Advocacy, 2000—04. Recipient Sloan Pub. Svc. award Fund for City of N.Y., 1993, Haven Emerson award Pub. Health Assn. of N.Y.C., 1993, Martha May Eliot award, 2005, Charles Loring Brace medal Children's Aid Soc., NYC, 2004; named Hon. Alumna, Albert Einstein Coll. Medicine, 2001. Fellow Am. Acad. Pediats. (pres. N.Y.C. chpt. 1985-88, chair nat. nominating com. 1997, Child Advocacy award sr. sect. 2006), N.Y. Acad. Medicine (chmn. pediats. sect. 1994-96); mem. Ambulatory Pediat. Assn. (pres. 1973-74), Am. Pediat. Soc., Phi Beta Kappa, Sigma Xi. Avocations: reading, travel, tennis, gardening, music. Home: 238 Kensington Oval New Rochelle NY 10805-2917 Office Phone: 718-920-6497.

LOBO, RAIMUNDO NONATO BRAGA, animal science educator, researcher; b. Cedro, Ceará, Brazil, Dec. 18, 1969; s. Edivá de Aquino and Terezinha Braga de Oliveira Lobo; m. Maria Auxiliadora Braga de Oliveira Lobo, Mar. 13, 1996 (div. Feb. 13, 2003); 1 child, Amanda Braga de Oliveira; m. Ana Maria Bezerra Oliveira, Sept. 29, 2004. BS in Vet. Sci., State U. Ceará, Fortaleza, Ceará, 1992, Lic. vet. Federal Coun. Vet. Medicine, 1993. Prof. State U. Ceará, 1993—96; vis. rschr. Fed. U. Ceará, Fortaleza, 1997—2000; rschr. Embrapa Caprinos, Sobral, Ceará, 2001—, Nat. Coun. Sci. and Technol. Devel., Brasília, 2004—; postgrad. prof. Fed. U. Ceará, Fortaleza, Ceará, 2005—, Fed. U. Piauí, Teresina, Piauí, Brazil, 2006—. Cons. Brazilian Jour. Animal Sci., Viçosa, Minas Gerais, Brazil, 2001—, Agri. Rsch. Corp. Rio Grande do Norte, Natal, Rio Grande do Norte, Brazil, 2003—; asst. rschr. chief Embrapa Caprinos, Sobral, 2005—06; exec. sec. Goat and Sheep Sectorial Cameral Productive Chain, Brasília, 2005—07; cons. Brazilian Jour. Vet. Rsch. and Animal Scis., Belo Horizonte, Minas Gerais, Brazil, 2005—, Brazilian Jour. Agrl. Rsch., Brasília, 2007—, Found. Support Sci. and Tech. State Pernambuco, Recife, Pernambuco, Brazil, 2007—, Found. Support Devel. Edn. Sci. and Tech., Campo Grande, Mato Grosso do Sul, Brazil, 2007—. Office: Embrapa Caprinos Ovinos Estrada Sobral Groaíras km 4 Ceará Sobral 62011-970 Brazil Office Fax: 55 88 3112 7487. Business E-Mail: lobo@cnpc.embrapa.br.

LOBO, ROGERIO ARNALDO, obstetrician, gynecologist; b. Hong Kong, 1949; MD, Georgetown U., 1974. Diplomate Am. Bd. Ob-Gyn. Intern U. Chgo. Hosps., 1974-75, resident in obstetrics, 1975-78; fellow in reproductive endocrinology L.A. County-U. So. Calif. Med. Ctr., 1980; physician Presbyn. Hosp., NYC, 1995—; dir. Sloane Hosp. for Women, Columbia Univ. Med. Ctr., NYC, 1995—2002; Willard C. Rappleye prof. and chmn. ob-gyn. Columbia Coll. Physicians and Surgeons, NYC, 1995—2002. Editor Jour. Soc. for Gynecol. Investigation, 1993-06. Mem. ACOG, Am. Soc. Reproductive Medicine, Endocrine Soc., Soc. Gynecol. Investigation (past pres.). Office: Columbia Univ Med Ctr 622 W 168th St Rm 16 64 New York NY 10032-3720 Office Phone: 212-305-6337.

LOBUE, ANGE JOSEPH, psychiatrist, writer, pharmacologist, neuroscientist; s. Joseph Vincent Lobue; m. Chantal Madeleine Giebert, Dec. 24, 2000; children: Robert Kent Jr., Sandrine Kent. BS in Pharmacy, U. Miss. Sch. Pharmacy, Oxford, 1960; MD, La. State U. Sch. Pharmacy, New Orleans, 1964; MPH Health Care Adminstrn., UCLA Sch. Pub. Health, 1968. Diplomate Am. Bd. Psychiatry and Neurology, 1980. Med.-surg. intern So. Pacific Meml. Hosp., San Francisco, 1964-65; resident in preventive medicine, dept. preventive and social medicine UCLA Sch. Medicine, 1968-71, resident in psychiatry and neorology dept. psychiatry, 1969-72, asst. clin. prof., 1972-92; instr. sch. cinema-TV U. So. Calif., LA, 1987—89; pvt. practice Santa Rosa & Mendocino, Calif., 1988—97, Century City, Iowa, 1972—77, Long Beach, Calif., 1977—88; psychiatric cons. Redwood Coast Regional Ctr., 1998—, Humboldt State U., Student Health Svc, 2009; bd. dirs. La Compagnia de Colombari Performance Group, 2006—. Vis. fellow U. Belgrade, Yugoslavia and Fed. Inst. Pub. Health, U. Edinburgh, Scotland and Ministry Health, 1969, St. Thomas Hosp. and Ministry Health, London, 1969; vis. scholar, spl. asst. to adminstr. Health Svcs. and Mental Health Adminstrn., HEW, Wash., 1970; med. dir. health info. and edn. Hoffman La-Roche, Inc., Roche Labs., 1977-85; vis. scholar, asst. to pres. NYC Health and Hosps. Corp., 1970-71; registered pharmacist, mgr. Briargrove Pharmacy, Houston, Tex., 1960; writer, spkr., lectr., numerous workshops, hosps., colls., univs., TV, assns.; apptd. staff Santa Rosa Meml. Hosp., UCLA Ctr. Health Scis., Warrack Hosp., Santa Rosa, Sutter Coast Hosp., Cresent City, Calif., 1998-. Editor: Psychiatry and the Media, 1983; contbr. articles to profl. jours. Sr. pub. health physician Venice Youth Clinic, LA, 1969; commr. APA joint commn. on pub. affairs, 1985-88. Capt. med. corps. US Army, 1965—67, commdr. 133th Med.

Detachment US Army, 1965—66, Vietnam. Recipient Blue Ribbon, Prime Time Emmy Awards Panel, Acad., TV Arts & Scis., 1995, award, Humboldt Arts Coun., 2001. Fellow Acad. Psychosomatic Medicine, Am. Coll. Preventive Medicine (assoc.), Am. Geriatrics Soc. (founding), Royal Soc. Health; mem. Kappa Psi Pharm. Fraternity (Hon Citation Order Golden Mortar, 2006), MENSA (life), Am. Film Inst. Alumni Assn., Am. Med. Writers Assn., Biofeedback Cert. Inst. Am., Mendocino-Lake County Med. Soc., Nat. Thespian Soc. (Best Actor award), Physicians Coun. on Drug Dependence, Sonoma County Med. Assn., Acad. TV Arts & Scis., UCLA Alumni Assn., Delta Omega. Avocations: music, literature, art, theater, gardening. Office: 1301 Northcoast Ste A Crescent City CA 95531 Office Phone: 707-444-1616. Personal E-mail: trinidadca@gmail.com.

LOCASCIO, JOSEPH A., surgeon, educator; b. May 8, 1949; Ophthalmologist Med. and Surgical Direct Ctr. Sight of HIMG; assoc. clin. prof. West Va. U., Sch. Medicine; clin. prof. ophthalmology Marshall U. Office: 5170 US Rte 60 E Huntington WV 25705 Office Phone: 304-522-1055.

LOCKE, EDWIN ALLEN, III, retired psychologist, educator; b. NYC, May 15, 1938; s. Edwin Allen and Dorothy (Clark) Locke; m. Cathy Durham, Apr. 13, 2001. BA, Harvard U., 1960; MA, Cornell U., 1962, PhD, 1964. Assoc. research scientist Am. Inst. Research, 1964-66, research scientist, 1966-70; asst. prof. psychology U. Md., College Park, 1967-69, assoc. prof., 1969-70, assoc. prof. bus., mgmt. and psychology, 1998—2001, dean's prof. of leadership & motivation, 1984—96; chmn. faculty mgt. and orgn. Coll. Bus. and Mgmt. U. Md., College Park, 1984-96, prof. emeritus, 2001. Author: A Guide to Effective Study, 1975, The Prime Movers: Traits of the Great Wealth Creators, 2000, 2nd edit., 2008; co-author: Goal Setting: A Motivational Technique That works, 1984, A Theory of Goal Setting and Task Performance, 1990, The Essence of Leadership, 1991; editor: Generalizing from Laboratory to Field Settings, 1986, Handbook of Principles of Organizational Behavior, 2000, 2nd edit., 2009, Postmodernism in Management: Pros Cons and the Alternative, 2003, Selfish Path to Romance, 2011; contbr. articles to profl. jours. Office Naval Research grantee, 1964, 79; NIMH grantee, 1967; Army Rsch. Inst. grantee, 1993. Fellow APA, Acad. Mgmt. (Lifetime Achievement award, Disting. Sch. Contbn. award), Soc. Indsl. and Orgnl. Psychology (Disting. Sci. Contbn. award 1993, Career Contbn. award 2005), Assn. Psychol. Sci. (J.M. Cattell award). E-mail: elocke@rhsmith.umd.edu.

LOCKE, WILLIAM, retired endocrinologist; b. Morden, Man., Can., Mar. 16, 1916; s. Corbet and Ruby Louise (Brown) L.; m. Katherine Elizabeth Acer Russell, Sept. 29, 1945 (dec.). MD, U. Man., Winnipeg, 1938; MS in Medicine, U. Minn., Rochester, 1947. Diplomate Am. Bd. Internal Medicine. Intern Winnipeg Gen. Hosp., Manitoba, Canada, 1937-38; fellow in medicine Mayo Found., Rochester, Minn., 1938-40, 46-48; rsch. fellow Harvard U., Boston, 1948-50; staff Ochsner Clinic, New Orleans, 1950-2000, sr. cons., 1987-2000, head sect. of endocrinology, 1968—76, 1986—89; clin. prof. medicine Tulane U., New Orleans, 1968-86, prof. emeritus, 1986—, ret., 2000. Sec. Alton Ochsner Med. Found., New Orleans, 1976—81; pres. med. staff Ochsner Found. Hosp., New Orleans, 1954—55, trustee, 1978—2003, councillor, 2003—, cons. in endocrinology, 1998—. Author, co-editor: Hypothalmus and Pituitary in Health and Disease, 1972; contbr. chpts. to books and articles to profl. jours. Chief med. cons. Atlantee Command, 1946; lt. comdr. RCNVR, 1940-46. NIH grant, 1958-62. Fellow ACP; mem. Am. Diabetes Assn., Endocrine Soc., Sigma Xi. Republican. Episcopalian. Home: 701 Poydras St Ste 5000 New Orleans LA 70139-7758

LOCKEY, RICHARD FUNK, allergist, immunologist, educator; b. Lancaster, Pa., Jan. 15, 1940; s. Stephen Daniel and Anna (Funk) L.; m. Carol Lee Madill, July 3, 1982; children: Brian Christopher, Keith Edward. BS, Haverford Coll., 1961; MD, Temple U., 1965; MS, U. Mich., 1972. Diplomate Am. Bd. Internal Medicine, Am. Bd. Allergy and Immunology. Intern Temple U. Med. Sch., Phila., 1965-66; asst. resident internal medicine Univ. Hosp. U. Mich., Ann Arbor, 1966-67, resident, 1966-68, fellow in allergy and immunology, 1969-70; asst. prof. medicine U. South Fla. Coll. Medicine, Tampa, 1973-77, assoc. prof. medicine, 1977-83, asst. dir. divsn. allergy and immunology, 1979-82, dir. allergy and immunology, 1982—, prof. medicine, 1983—, prof. pediat., 1983—, prof. pub. health, 1987—; asst. chief sect. allergy and immunology VA Hosp., Tampa, 1973-82, chief sect. allergy and immunology, 1983—, Joy McCann Culverhouse endowed chair allergy and immunology, 1997. Mem. allergenic adv. com. FDA, 1985-89. Editor: Allergy and Clinical Immunology, 1980, World Allergy Orgn. website, 2005—; co-editor: (with S.C. Bukantz) Fundamentals of Immunology and Allergy, 1987, (with S.C. Bukantz) Principles of Immunology and Allergy, 1987, JAMA Primer on Allergic and Immunologic Diseases, 1987, (with S. C. Bukantz) Allergen Immunotherapy, 1991, (with M. Levine) Monograph on Insect Allergy, 1995, (with S. Bukantz) Allergens and Allergen Immunotherapy, 1999, (with D. Ledford) Immunotherapy: A Practical Review and Guide, 2000, (with S. Kemp) Diagnostic Testing of Allergic Disease, 2000, (with S. Bukantz) Allergens and Allergen Immunotherapy Allergic Diseases, 4th edit., 2004, (with M. Levine) Insect Allergy, 4th edit., 2004; mem. editl. bd. Jour. on Allergy and Immunology, 1999-04; contbr. more than 500 articles to profl. jours. and chpts. to books; author monographs. Hon. chmn. R.I. chpt. Asthma and Allergy Found., 2004. Served as maj. USAF, 1971-73. Rrecpient Alumni Achievement award Temple U. Sch. of Medicine Alumni Assn., 1990, Outstanding Leadership in Chpt. Devel. and Patient Support, Nat. Asthma and Allergy Found. of Am. award, 1992, Cert. of Appreciation Fla. Med. Assn., 1992, medalist Fla. Acad. Scis., 2000, Disting. Svc. award Univ. S. Fla., 2001, Alumni award McCaskey HS, 2007; Named Outstanding Med. Specialist, Town and Country Mag., 1989, Claude P. Brown Meml. lectr. Assn. Clin. Scientists, ADA, 1981, Disting. Visitor Ann. Meeting of Coll. of Medicine, Republic of Costa Rica, 1979, spl. mem. Internat. Sci. Bd. Pharmacia Allergy Rsch. Found., 1992—. Fellow ACP, AAAS, AMA, Am. Coll. Chest Physicians, Am. Acad. Allergy and Immunology (chmn. com. on insects 1978-81, chmn. undergrad. and grad. edn. com. 1982-88, com. on occupl. lung disease 1982—, chmn. com. on standardization of allergenic extracts 1983-86, exec. com. mem. at large 1986-88, historian 1988-89, sec. 1989-90, treas. 1990-91, pres.-elect 1991-92, pres. 1992-93, Am. Bd. Allergy and Immunology (bd. dirs. 1993-98), World Allergy Orgn. (bd. dirs. 1997—, editor web page, 2004, treas. 2006—, pres. elect, 2008-09), Soc. Allergy and Immunology of Cordoba, Argentina (hon.), John M. Sheldon U. of Mich. Allergy Soc. (councilor 1977-80, pres. 1980-82), Fla. Allergy and Immunology Soc. (sec.-treas. 1979-80, pres. 1981-82, Disting. Svc. award 2002), Southeastern Allergy Assn., Hillsborough County Med. Assn., Joint Coun. Allergy and Immunology, Clin. Immunology Soc., Fla. Thoracic Soc., Univ. Club, Tampa Yacht Club. Avocations: antique cut glass, antique tools, hunting, fishing. Home: 2708 W Marlin Ave Tampa FL 33611 Office: U So Fla VA Hosp 13000 Bruce B Downs Blvd 111D Tampa FL 33612 Office Phone: 813-972-7631.

LOCKHEAD, GREGORY ROGER, retired psychology professor; b. Boston, Aug. 8, 1931; s. John Roger and Ester Mae (Bixby) L.; m. Jeanne Marie Hutchinson, June 9, 1957; children: Diane, Elaine, John. BS, Tufts U., 1958; PhD, Johns Hopkins, 1965. Psychologist rsch. staff IBM Research, Yorktown Heights, NY, 1958-61; rsch. assoc., instr. Johns Hopkins U., Balt., 1961-65; asst. prof. psychology Duke U., Durham, NC, 1965-68, assoc. prof., 1968-71, prof., 1971-2001, chmn. dept. exptl. psychology, 1991-97, prof. dept. psychol. and brain scis., 2001—06; prof. emeritus, 2006—. Scholar Stanford U.; rsch. assoc. U. Calif., Berkeley, 1971-72; fellow Wolfson Coll., Oxford (Eng.) U., 1980-81; scholar Fla. Atlantic U., 1981; cons. in human engrng. Cons. editor: Perception and Psychophysics, 1972-92; contbr. articles to profl. jours., co-author, editor chpts. in books. With USN, 1951-55. NSF grantee, 1966-69, 79-84, USPHS grantee, 1963-69, 70-79, Air Force Office Sci. Rsch., 1983-91. Fellow APA, Am. Psychol. Soc., Soc. Exptl. Psychologists; mem. Psychonomic Soc., Internat. Soc. Psychophysics, Sigma Xi, Phi Beta Kappa (hon.). Home: 37 Gardenia Ct Durham NC 27705 Business E-Mail: greg@psych.duke.edu.

LOCKSHIN, MICHAEL DAN, rheumatologist; b. Columbus, Ohio, Dec. 9, 1937; s. Samuel Dan and Florence (Levin) L.; m. Jane Toby Roberts, Sept. 2, 1965; 1 child, Amanda. AB, Harvard U., 1959, MD, 1963. Cert. in Internal Medicine, 1969, Rheumatology, 1972; Diplomate Am. Bd. Internal Medicine. Resident in internal medicine Bellevue Hosp., NYC, 1966—68; fellow in rheumatology Columbia-Presbyn. Hosp., NYC, 1968—70; from asst. prof. to prof. Cornell U. Weill Med. Coll., NYC, 1970-89; attending physician Hosp. for Spl. Surgery and N.Y. Hosp., NYC, 1970-89; dir. extramural program Nat. Inst. Arthritis & Musculoskeletal Skin Diseases/NIH, Bethesda, Md., 1989-97, acting dir., 1994-95; dir. Barbara Volcker Ctr. Hosp. for Spl. Surgery, NYC, 1997—. Prof. Cornell U. Med. Coll., N.Y.C., 1997—. Editor: Arthritis & Rheumatism, 2005-; contbr. over 150 articles to jours., chpts. to books. Mem. Am. Rheumatism Assn. (2d v.p. 1984-85), La Sociedad Chilena de Reumatologica (hon.), Alpha Omega Alpha. Achievements include research in Lupus/SLE; Antiphospholipid Syndrome; Pregnancy-Rheumatic Disease. Office: 535 E 70th St New York NY 10021-4872 Home Phone: 212-588-0028; Office Phone: 212-606-1461. Business E-Mail: volckerctr@hss.edu.

LOCKWOOD, CHARLES JOSEPH, obstetrician, gynecologist, medical educator; b. Norwood, Mass., Nov. 22, 1954; s. Charles William and Emma (Barletta) Lockwood; m. Nancy Lou Jones, Sept. 18, 1985; 1 child, Sarah Elizabeth. BS in Devel. Biology, magna cum laude, Brown U., Providence, 1977; MD, U. Pa. Sch. Medicine, 1981; MS, Harvard Sch. Pub. Health, 2009. Diplomate American Bd. Ob-Gyn., cert. in maternal-fetal medicine. Intern, resident in ob-gyn Pa. Hosp., Phila., 1981-85; fellow in maternal-fetal medicine Yale-New Haven Hosp., 1985—89; postdoc. rschr. Mt. Sinai Sch. Medicine, NYC, 1989—91; faculty, chair ob-gyn. NYU, 1999—2002; Anita O'Keeffe Young prof. & chair dept. ob-gyn. and reproductive scis. Yale U. Sch. Medicine, 2002—. Examiner American Bd. Ob-Gyn., 1996—2009; vis. prof. U. Belgrade, Serbia, 2003. Editor-in-chief Contemporary OB/Gyn; contbr. articles to profl. jours., chapters to books. Med. missionary work, Kingston, Jamaica, 2002—04. Recipient Jesse H. Neal Nat. Bus. Journalism award, American Soc. Bus. Publ. Editors, 2005, 2007, Adv. Com. Svc. award, FDA Ctr. Drug Evaluation & Rsch., 2007. Mem.: Inst. Medicine, Soc. Gynecologic Investigation (pres. 2007—08), American Coll. Ob-Gyn., Alpha Omega Alpha, Sigma Xi. Roman Catholic. Achievements include research in the prevention of recurrent pregnancy loss, preterm delivery and maternal thrombophilias; credited with helping to develop fetal fibronectin, the first biochemical predictor of prematurity. Avocation: sailing. Office: Obstetrics Gynecology & Reproductive Scis Yale Univ Sch Medicine PO Box 208063 New Haven CT 06520 Office Fax: 203-688-2806. E-mail: charles.lockwood@yale.edu. *

LODDE, GORDON MAYNARD, retired health physics consultant; b. Lafayette, Ind., Aug. 19, 1933; s. Herman Morris and Eva Grace (Robinson) Lodde; m. Nancy Jean Caldwell, Aug. 21, 1955 (dec. Aug. 2006); children: Gordon A., Bruce C., Melissa J. BS, Purdue Univ., 1958; MS, Univ. Rochester, 1964. Health physist U.S. Army, 1959-79; health physics cons. Porter Cons., Ardmore, Pa., 1979-84; cons. engr. GPU Nuclear, Middletown, Pa., 1984-94; health physics cons. Mt. Joy, Pa., 1994—. Contbr. Handbook for Management of Radiation Protection Programs, 1992; contbg. author Ency. Occupl. Health and Safety, 1997. Scoutmaster Boy Scouts Am., White Sands, N.Mex., 1967—70, Edgewood, Md., 1975—79, post adv., 1976—80. With Med. Svc. Corp US Army, 1959—79. Decorated Commendation medal with two oak leaf clusters,,, Legion of Merit; recipient Merit award, Boy Scouts Am., 1976, Silver Beaver award, 1978. Fellow: Health Physics Soc.; mem.: Am. Conf. of Gov. Hygienists, Am. Nuc. Soc. Home: 742 Ferndale Rd Mount Joy PA 17552-9384 Personal E-mail: gml-hpc@msn.com.

LODER, ELIZABETH WENTZ, neurologist, educator; d. Thomas Arthur Wentz and Janet Marie Neff; m. John Mark Loder, June 1, 1985; children: Thomas Andrew, Stephen Albert Charles. BS in Biology, Harvard Coll.; MPH, U. Mass.; MD, U. ND Sch. Medicine, Grand Forks, 1985. Diplomate Am. Bd. Internal Medicine, cert. headache medicine United Coun. Neurologic Subspecialties. Resident internal medicine Faulkner Hosp., Boston, 1985—89; fellow Graham Headache Ctr., 1989—90; instr. neurology Harvard Med. Sch., 1994—2003, asst. prof. neurology, 2003—06, assoc. prof. neurology, 2006—. Med. dir. pain & headache mgmt. programs Spaulding Rehab. Hosp, Boston, 1996—2006; chief divsn. headache & pain, dept. neurology Brigham & Women's/Faulkner Hospitals, 2006—. Clin. editor Brit. Med. Jour.; contbr. articles to profl. jours. Mem.: Am. Headache Soc. (bd. dirs.). Office: Faulkner Hosp 1153 Ctr St Boston MA 02130 Office Phone: 617-573-2493. Office Fax: 617-573-7119. E-mail: eloder@partners.org. *

LODGE, HENRY SEARS, physician; b. Oct. 20, 1958; BA, U. Pa., 1981; MD, Columbia U., 1985. Diplomate Am. Bd. Internal Medicine. Intern Columbia U. Presbyterian Med. Ctr., NYC, residency; attending physician N.Y. Presbyterian Hosp., 1988—; assoc. clin. prof. medicine Coll. Physicians and Surgeons Columbia U., NYC, 1989—; pvt. practice specializing internal medicine and prevention NYC. Chmn., CEO N.Y. Physicians LLP; past pres. Presbyn. Hosp. Alumni Assn., N.Y. Clin. Soc., Soc. Practitioners of Columbia Presbyn. Med. Ctr. Mem. Am. Coll. Physicians. Office: 635 Madison Ave New York NY 10022-1009

LODWICK, GWILYM SAVAGE, radiologist, educator; b. Mystic, Iowa, Aug. 30, 1917; s. Gwylim S. and Lucy A. (Fuller) Lodwick; m. Maria Antonia De Brito Barata; children from previous marriage: Gwilym Savage III, Philip Galligan, Malcolm Kerr, Terry Ann. Student, Drake U., 1934—35; BS, State U. Iowa, 1942, MD, 1943. Resident in pathology State U. Iowa, 1947—48, resident in radiology, 1948—50; fellow, sr. fellow radiologic and orthop. pathology Armed Forces Inst. Pathology, 1951; asst., then assoc. prof. State U. Iowa Med. Sch., 1951—56; prof. radiology, chmn. dept. U. Mo. at Columbia Med. Sch., 1956—78, rsch. prof. radiology, 1978—83, interim chmn. dept. radiology, 1980—81, chmn. dept. radiology, 1981—83, prof. bioengring., 1969—83, acting dean, 1959, assoc. dean, 1959—64; assoc. radiologist Mass. Gen. Hosp., 1983—88, radiologist, 1988—91, hon. radiologist Boston, 1991—; vis. prof. dept. radiology Harvard Med. Sch., 1983—93. Vis. prof. Keio U. Sch. Medicine, Tokyo, 1974; chmn. sci. program com. Internat. Conf. on Med. Info., Amsterdam, 1983; trustee Am. Registry Radiologic Technologists, 1961—69, pres., 1964—65, 1968—69; mem. radiology tng. com. Nat. Inst. Gen. Med. Scis., NIH, 1966—70; com. radiology NAS-NRC, 1970—75; chmn. com. computers Am. Coll. Radiology, 1965, Internat. Commn. Radiol. Edn. and Info., 1969—73; cons. to health care tech. divsn. Nat. Ctr. for Health Svcs., Rsch. and Devel., 1971—76; dir. Mid-Am. Bond Tumor Diagnostic Ctr. and Registry, 1971—83; adv. com. mem. NIH Biomed. Image Processing Grant Jet Propulsion Lab., 1969—73; nat. chmn. MUMPS Users Group, 1973—75; mem. radiation study sect. divsn. rsch. grants NIH, 1976—79, mem. study sect. on diagnostic radiology and nuc. medicine divsn. rsch. grants, 1979—82, chmn., 1980—82; mem. bd. sci. counselors Nat. Libr. Medicine, 1985, chmn., 1987—89; dir. radiology Spaulding Rehab. Hosp., 1986—92; cons. in field. Adv. editl. bd.: Radiology, 1965—86, cons. to editor:, 1986—91, adv. editl. bd.: Current/Clin. Practice, 1972—88, mem. editl. bd.: Jour. Med. Systems, 1976—, Radiol. Sci. Update divsn. Biomedia, Inc., 1975—83, Critical Revs. in Linguistic Imaging, 1990, mem. cons. editl. bd.: Skeletal Radiology, 1977—92, Contemporary Diagnostic Radiology, 1978—80, assoc. editor: Jour. Med. Imaging, 1988—. Served to maj. US Army, 1943—46, ETO. Decorated Sakari Mustakallio medal Finland; recipient Sigma Xi Rsch. award, U. Mo., Columbia, 1972, Gold medal, XIII Internat. Conf. Radiology, Madrid, 1973, Founder's Gold medal, Internat. Skeletal Soc., 1990, Disting. Alumni Achievement award, U. Iowa, 2002; named Most Disting. Alumnus in Radiology, State U. Iowa Centennial, 1970. Fellow: AMA (radiology rev. bd. coun. med. edn., coun. rep. on residency rev. com. for radiology 1969—74), Am. Coll. Radiology (co-chmn. ACR-NEMA standardization com. 1983—90, NEMA Med. Tech. Leadership award 1995); mem.: Phila. Roentgen Ray Soc., Ind. Roentgen Soc., Tex. Radiol. Soc., Salutis Unitas, Mo. Radiol. Soc. (1st pres. 1961—62), Finnish Radiol. Soc. (hon.), Portuguese Soc. Radiology and Nuc. Medicine (hon.), Assn. Univ. Radiologists, Radiol. Soc. N.Am. (3d v.p. 1974—75, chmn. ad hoc com. representing assoc. scis. 1979—87, chmn. assoc. scis. com. 1981—87), Nat. Acad. Practice in Medicine, Am. Coll. Med. Informatics (founding), NAS Inst. Medicine, Cosmos, Harvard of Boston Club, Rotary, Alpha Omega Alpha. Home: 3900 Galt Ocean Dr Apt 307 Fort Lauderdale FL 33308-6622 Personal E-mail: lodwickmd@aol.com.

LOEB, JOHN NICHOLS, physician, educator; b. NYC, Dec. 17, 1935; s. Robert Frederick and Emily Guild (Nichols) L. AB summa cum laude, Harvard Coll., 1957; MD summa cum laude, Harvard Med. Sch., 1961. Intern in medicine Mass. Gen. Hosp., Boston, 1961-62; asst. resident in medicine Presbyn. Hosp., NYC, 1962-63, chief resident in medicine, 1965-66, asst. physician, 1966—67, asst. attending physician, 1967-73, assoc. attending physician, 1973-79, attending physician, 1979—98, secy. medical bd., 1976—77; attending physician NY-Presbyn. Hosp., 1998—; rsch. assoc. lab. of molecular biology Nat. Inst. Arthritis and Metabolic Diseases, NIH, Bethesda, Md., 1963-65; NIH trainee in metabolism Columbia U. Coll. Phys. and Surg., 1966—67; instr. medicine Columbia U., NYC, 1965—66, asst. prof. medicine, 1967—73, assoc. prof. medicine, 1973-79, prof. medicine, 1979—2004, prof. emeritus medicine, 2005—, spl. lectr. in medicine, 2005—, assoc. chmn. rsch. dept. medicine, 1997—2003, vice chmn. for acad. affairs, 2003—04. Vis. chief resident Mass. Gen. Hosp., Boston, Mass., 1966; asst. vis. physician Harlem Hosp., NYC, 1968-73; adj. asst. prof. Rockefeller U., NYC, 1970-75, adj. assoc. prof., 1975-83; vis. prof. dept. internal medicine Pahlavi U., Shiraz, Iran, 1974, 77; vis. prof. dept. medicine U. Cape Town, 1982; sec. med. bd. Presbyn. Hosp., 1976-1977; mem. Med. Coun. of the Iran Found., 1974-75; councillor Harvard Med. Alumni Assn., 1982-85; bd dir. Royal Soc. Medicine Found., NY, 1984-95; praktikant Friedrich Miescher Inst., Basel, Switzerland, 1986. Contbr. articles to profl. jours. Elder Presbyn. Ch., 1982—; ruling elder Madison Ave. Presbyn. Ch., NYC, 1983-88; mem., bd. dirs. Amateur Chamber Music Players, Inc., 1984-99, vice chmn., 1985-99, mem. adv. coun., 1999-2006. Lt. comdr. grade surgeon USPHS, 1963-65. Recipient Boylston medal Harvard U., 1961, P&S Club Tchg. award, 1969, Career Scientist award Irma T. Hirschl Charitable Trust, 1973-77, Disting. Tchr. award, Coll. of Physicians and Surgeons, Columbia U., 1974, Tchg. award citation, 1975, House Staff Recognition award Presbyn. Hosp., 2004, Disting. Svc. award, Coll. Physicians and Surgeons, Columbia U., 2007; grantee NIH, 1967-99, MERIT award, 1988-99. Fellow AAAS, ACP, NY Acad. Medicine, Royal Soc. Medicine; diplomate Am. Bd. Internal Medicine; mem. Assn. Am. Physicians, Practitioners' Soc. NY (sec. 1973, 74, pres. 1985, 86), Am. Soc. Clin. Investigation, Am. Fedn. Clin. Rsch., Harvey Soc., Am. Clin. and Climatological Assn., Century Assn., Soc. for Exptl. Biology and Medicine, Endocrine Soc., Soc. Gen. Physiologists, Peripatetic Club (councillor 1987-94), Interurban Clin. Club, Charaka Club (pres. 1984-85), Am. Philos. Soc. (councillor 2006—), Phi Beta Kappa, Alpha Omega Alpha. Presbyterian. Achievements include research in mechanisms of hormone action, physical chemistry of receptor-ligand interactions and their quantitative relationship to biological response, and regulation of glucose and monovalent cation transport. Home: 80 Haven Ave New York NY 10032-2617 Office: Columbia Univ Dept Medicine 630 W 168th St New York NY 10032-3702

LOEPP, DANIEL J., insurance company executive; b. Detroit, July 1, 1957; m. Renee Farhat; children: Danielle, Michael, Patrick. BA in Comm., Wayne State U., Detroit, 1982, MA in Polit. Comm., 1986. Staff mem. US Congressman Dennis Hertel, 1981—84; comm. dir. to Mich. Atty. Gen. Frank Kelley, 1984—87; CEO Svc. Sta. Dealers Assn. Mich., 1987—92; chief of staff Mich. Spkr. the House Curtis Hertel, 1993—98; with Karoub Assocs., 1998—99; v.p. govtl. affairs Blue Cross and Blue Shield Mich., 2000, sr. v.p., chief of staff, exec. v.p., CEO designate, 2005—06, pres., CEO, 2006—. Bd. dirs. Accident Fund Ins. Co. America, Blue Care Network Mich.; chair Mackinac policy conf. Detroit Regional Chamber, 2007, chmn., 2007—08. Author: Sharing the Balance of Power: An Examination of Shared Power in the Michigan House of Representatives, 1993-94, 1999. Bd. dirs. Greater Detroit C. of C., Coun. Affordable Healthcare, Detroit Econ. Growth Corp., Detroit Renaissance, New Detroit, The Parade Co., Blue Cross and Blue Shield Assn., plans holding corp. bd., health policy and legis. com., emerging issues bd., chmn. adminstrv. com. Office: Blue Cross and Blue Shield of Michigan 600 E Lafayette Blvd Detroit MI 48226 Office Phone: 313-225-9000. Office Fax: 313-225-6764. Business E-Mail: dloepp@bcbsm.com. *

LOESCHER, RICHARD ALVIN, retired gastroenterologist; b. Brockton, Mass., Feb. 6, 1940; s. Vernon Alvin and Anna Marie (Good) Loescher; m. Linda Rockwell Clifford, June 5, 1965 (div. Jan. 1982); children: Steven Clifford, Laura May. BA, DePauw U., Greencastle, Ind., 1961; MD cum laude, Harvard U., Boston, 1965. Diplomate Am. Bd. Internal Medicine, 1972, Am. Bd. Gastroenterology, 1973. Chief med. svc. USPHS Hosp., Lawton, Okla., 1967-69, chief med. staff, 1968-69, svc. unit dir., 1969, attending physician Seattle, 1970-71, Univ. Hosp., Seattle, 1970-71; active staff Sacred Heart Med. Ctr., Eugene, Oreg., 1973—2005, Eugene Hosp., Oreg., 1972—88; courtesy staff McKenzie-Willamette Hosp., Springfield, Oreg., 1982—2004. Recipient Rector scholarship DePauw U., 1957-61, Maimonides award Harvard Med. Sch., 1965. Mem. AMA, ACP-Am. Soc. Internal Medicine, Lane County Med. Soc., Oreg. Med. Assn., Am. Soc. for Gastrointestinal Endoscopy, Alpha Omega Alpha, Phi Beta Kappa. Democrat. Unitarian Universalist. Avocations: physical fitness, personal growth, magic, dance. Home: 2345 Patterson St Apt 34 Eugene OR 97405-2974

LOFLAND, GARY KENNETH, cardiac surgeon; b. Milford, Del., Mar. 5, 1951; s. Joseph Sudler and Doris Louise (Peters) L.; m. Janice Marie Show, Feb. 3, 1979; children: Kiernan Sudler, Glennis Kathleen. BA cum laude, Boston U., 1969, MD cum laude, 1975. Diplomate Am. Bd. Surgery, Am. Bd. Thoracic Surgery; lic. physician, Va., N.Y., Mont., N.C. Intern, jr. asst. resident in surgery Duke U. Med. Ctr., Durham, NC, 1975-81, rsch. fellow dept. surgery, 1979-81, sr. asst. resident in surgery, 1981-84, chief resident in surgery, 1984-85, teaching scholar in cardiac surgery, 1985-86; sr. registrar in cardiothoracic surgery Hosp. for Sick Children, London, 1986-87; dir. cardiovascular surgery Children's Hosp. of Buffalo, 1987-88, asst. prof. surgery SUNY, Buffalo, 1987-88; assoc. prof. surgery/pediatrics, Med. Coll. Va., Richmond, 1988-94, dir. pediatric cardiac surgery/med. dir. cardiac surgery ICU, 1988-94; clin. prof. surgery Georgetown U., Washington, 1994-97; dir. Columbia/HCA Ctr. Congenital Heart Disease, Richmond, 1994-97; dir. cardiovascular surgery Children's Mercy Hosp., Kansas City, Mo., 1997—; prof. surgery U. Mo. Kansas City Sch. Medicine, 1997—, Joseph Boon Gregg chair sect. cardiac surgery. Editor (in chief): Progress in Pediat. Cardiology, 2002—; mem. editl. rev. bd.:, —, Year Book of Thoracic Surgery, —; contbr. articles to profl. jours. Pres. Am. Heart Assn., Richmond; mem. bd. trustees Transplant Found. Lt. comdr. USPHS, 1977-79. Recipient Univ. Hosp. Trustees award, Boston, 1975; HEW/USPHS commendation medal, 1979. Mem. AMA, Am. Heart Assn., Am. Surgions Assn., Am. Assn. Thoracic Surgery, Assn. for Acad. Surgery, Internat. Soc. for Heart Transplantation, Med. Soc. Va., Richmond Acad. Medicine, Richmond Surg. Soc., So. Thoracic Surg. Assn., Soc. for Thoracic Surgeons, Congenital Heart Surgeons Soc., Alpha Omega Alpha. Home: PO Box 126 Crozier VA 23039-0126 Office: Children's Mercy Hosp Divsn Cardiovascular Surgery 2406 Gillham Rd Kansas City MO 64108 Office Phone: 816-234-3580. Business E-Mail: glofland@cmh.edu.

LOFT, LLOYD MARK, otolaryngologist; b. NYC, Aug. 5, 1960; MD, N.Y. Med. Coll., 1986. Diplomate Am. Bd. Otolaryngology. Intern St. Vincent's Hosp. Med. Ctr., NYC, 1986-88; resident in otolaryngology Manhattan Eye Ear & Throat Hosp., NYC, 1991—, attending surgeon, 1991—; mem. staff Lenox Hill Hosp., NYC; pvt. practice. Asst. prof. otolaryngology Weill med. coll. Cornell U., NY, Presbyn hosp., NYC, 1994-; asst. attend. surgeon. Fellow Am. Coll. Surgeons, Am. Acad. Otolaryngology-Head and Neck Surgery; mem. Am. Rhinol. Soc., Med. Soc. State NY, NY County Med. Soc. Office: 115 East 57th St Ste 600 New York NY 10022 Office Phone: 212-832-1699.

LOFTON, KEVIN EUGENE, medical facility administrator; b. Beaumont, Tex., Sept. 29, 1954; BS, Boston U., 1976; M Health Care Adminstrn., Ga. State U., 1979. Adminstrv. resident Meml. Med. Ctr., Corpus Christi, Tex., 1978-79; adminstr. emergency svcs. Univ. Hosp., Jacksonville, Fla., 1979-80, adminstr. material mgmt., 1980-81, asst. exec. dir. ambulatory care, 1981-82, asst. v.p. ambulatory svcs., 1982-83, v.p. profl. svcs., 1983-86; exec. v.p. Univ. Med. Ctr., Jacksonville, 1986-90; exec. dir. Howard Univ. Hosp., Washington, 1990-93, U. Ala. Hosp., Birmingham, 1993-98; group pres. Cath. Health Initiative, Louisville, 1998-99, COO Denver, 1999—2003, CEO, 2003—. Contbr. articles to profl. publs. Fellow Am. Coll. Health Care Execs. (R.S. Hudgens award 1993); mem. Am. Hosp. Assn. (bd. dirs.), Nat. Assn. Health Svcs. Execs. (past pres., bd. dirs.). *

LOGAN, JOHN A., III, hospital administrator; b. Dec. 16, 1937; BS, Western Ky. U., 1958; MD, Vanderbilt U., 1961. Intern Toledo Hosp., 1961-62; pvt. practice Henderson, Ky., 1962-86; chief of staff Meth. Hosp., Henderson, 1967-86, med. dir., 1986—. Author: Innovation, 1992. Pres. YMCA, Henderson. Named Citizen of Yr., Henderson C. of C., 1993. Mem. Rotary (pres.). Address: 1305 N Elm St # 48 Henderson KY 42420-2783 Office Phone: 270-827-7353. Business E-Mail: jalogan@methodisthospital.net.

LOGAN, JOHN WELLS, pediatrician; b. Chattanooga, Feb. 19, 1964; BS in Mech. Engring., NC State U., 1989; MD, Med. U. SC, 1995. Resident physician Med. Coll. Ga., 1995—98; pediatrician Cape Fear Pediat., 1998—2004; postdoc. fellow, neonatology Duke U. Med. Ctr., 2004—07; neonatologist East Carolina U., Brody Sch. Medicine, 2007—08, Coastal Carolina Neonatology, 2008—. Dir., neonatal follow-up Betty H. Cameron Women's and Children's Hosp., New Hanover Regional Med. Ctr., 2008—. Contbr. articles to profl. publs. Fellow: Am. Bd. Pediat., Am. Acad. Pediat. Avocations: reading, history, literature, basketball. Home: 5164 Somersett Ln Wilmington NC 28409 Personal E-mail: wellslogan@usa.net.

LOGGIE, JENNIFER MARY HILDRETH, retired physician, educator; b. Lusaka, Zambia, Feb. 4, 1936; arrived in U.S., 1964, naturalized, 1972; d. John and Jenny (Beattie). M.B., B.Ch., U. Witwatersrand, Johannesburg, South Africa, 1959. Intern Harare Hosp., Zimbabwe, 1960-61; gen. practice medicine Lusaka, Zambia, 1961-62; sr. pediatric house officer Derby Children's Hosp., also St. John's Hosp., Chelmsford, England, 1962-64; resident in pediatrics Children's Hosp., Louisville, 1964, Cin. Children's Hosp., 1964-65; fellow clin. pharmacology Cin. Coll. Medicine, 1965-67; mem. faculty U. Cin. Med. Sch., 1967—, prof. pediatrics, 1975-98, assoc. prof. pharmacology, 1972-77, prof. emeritus pediatrics, 1998—; ret., 1998. Contbr. articles to med. publs.; editor Pediatric and Adolescent Hypertension, 1991. Grantee, Am. Heart Assn., 1970—72, 1989—90. Mem. Am. Pediatric Soc. (Founder's award 1996), Midwest Soc. Pediatric Rsch. Episcopalian. Home: 1133 Herschel Ave Cincinnati OH 45208-3112

LOGOTHETIS, NIKOS KONSTANTINOS, neuroscientist, researcher; b. Istanbul, Turkey, Nov. 5, 1950; came to U.S., 1985; s. Kostas N. and Thalia K. (Mumgi) L.; m. Yanna G. Karagianni, Jan. 11, 1981. BS in Math., U. Athens, Greece, 1969-77; BS in Biology, U. Thessaloniki, Greece, 1977-80; PhD in Human Neurobiology, Ludwig-Maximilians U., Munich, 1985. Rsch. asst. U. Thessaloniki, 1977-80, U. Munich, 1982-85; postdoctoral fellow, brain and cognitive scis. dept. MIT, Cambridge, 1985-88, sr. scientist, 1988-90; rsch. assoc. prof., divsn. neuroscience Baylor Coll. Medicine, Houston, 1990—97; dir., dept. physiology of cognitive processes Max Planck Inst. for Biol. Cybernetics, 1997—. Adj. prof. neurobiology Salk Inst., San Diego, 1992—; adj. prof. ophthalmology Baylor Coll. Medicine, Houston, 1995—; assoc. Neurosciences Inst., San Diego, 1995—; sr. vis. fellow U. Coll., London, 1995—; coun. sec., chair nominating com. Human Brain Mapping; adv. bd. mem. McGovern Inst., MIT, Brain and Cognitive Scis., MIT, Centre of Excellence in Systems Neuroscience and Neuroimaging Acad. Finnland in Helsinki, Posit Sci. Corp., San Francisco, ICM, Paris, Hebrew U., Weizmann Inst., Israel. Contbr. several articles to profl. jours. Recipient DeBakey award for Excellence in Sci., Golden Brain award, Minerva Found., Louis-Jeantet prize medicine, 2003, Zülch-Price for Neuroscience, IPSEN Found. prize on Neuronal Plasticity. Mem.: German Acad. Natural Scientists Leopoldina, Math. Assn. America, Am. Math. Soc., Soc. Indsl. and Applied Math., NY Acad. Sciences, Assn. for Rsch. in Vision and Ophthalmology, AAAS, European Neuroscience Assn., Soc. Neuroscience, Am. Acad. Arts & Scis. (fgn.) (hon.), Rodin Remediation Acad. Office: Max Planck Inst for Biological Cybernetics Dept Logothetis Rm L103 Postfach 2169 72012 Tübingen Germany Office Phone: 49 7071 601 651 Office Fax: 49 7071 601 652. Business E-Mail: nikos.logothetis@tuebingen.mpg.de.

LOGUE, JAMES NICHOLAS, epidemiologist; b. Duryea, Pa., June 18, 1946; s. James and Lucille (Polen) L.; m. Mary Frances Carey, Nov. 25, 1972; children: Melissa, Jimmy, Jeffrey. BS, Kings Coll., 1968; MPH, U. Mich., 1971; DrPH, Columbia U., 1978. Statistician Warner Lambert Co, Morris Plains, NJ, 1969-70, 71-73; sr. med. biostatistician Ciba-Geigy Co., Summit, NJ, 1973-78; epidemiologist GEOMET Technologies, Inc., Rockville, Md., 1978-80; supervisory epidemiologist US FDA, Rockville, 1980-82; dir. divsn. environ. health epidemiology Pa. Dept. Health, Harrisburg, 1982—; acting dir. Bur. Epidemiology, 2004—07. Personal E-mail: epidoc@comcast.net.

LOGUE, JUDITH FELTON, psychoanalyst, educator; b. Phila., Aug. 21, 1942; d. Martin and Laura (Goldman) Kirshenbaum; m. Stephen Felton, Feb. 8, 1966 (div. Aug. 1989); 1 child, Jane Jennifer; m. A. Douglas Logue, Feb. 14, 1990. AB in Govt., Wheaton Coll., Mass., 1963; MSW, Rutgers U., 1966, PhD, 1983; grad., NY Ctr. Psychoanalytic Tng., 1978. Diplomate Am. Bd. Psychotherapy, Am. Bd. Forensic Medicine, Am. Bd. Examiners Clin. Social Worker, Am. Bd. Forensic Examiners, Am. Bd. Psychol. Specialties, cert. profl. coach, mentor coach. Clin. social worker VA, Newark, 1967; psychotherapist Santa Barbara (Calif.) Mental Health Svcs., 1967-69; supr. Santa Barbara Counselling Ctr., 1967-69; pvt. practice psychoanalysis, 1969—; pres. Goldilox Co. Inc., 1997—, Shairing Co., 2001—. Psychoanalyst, therapist Fifth Ave. Ctr. for Psychotherapy, NYC, 1969-72; instr. Marymount Manhattan Coll., 1971; psychotherapy supr. clin. faculty, dept. psychiatry Rutgers Med. Sch., New Brunswick, NJ, 1972-75, tchg. asst. Grad. Sch. Social Work, 1974-76; vis. lectr. Bryn Mawr Coll. Sch. Social Work and Social Rsch., 1980; faculty NY Ctr. for Psychoanalytic Tng., 1980—, NJ Inst. Psychoanalysis and Psychotherapy, 1982—; adv. bd. Am. Bd. Forensic Social Workers, 1999—, chair adv. bd., 2000; pres. Goldilox Co., Inc., 1997, ShAIRing, Inc., 2000; faculty So. NJ Psychoanalytic Inst., Brigantine, 2004—, bd. dirs. Mem. editl. bd. jour Current Issues in Psychoanalytic Practice, 1983-93; contbr. articles to profl. jours. Bd. dirs. N.Y. Ctr. for Psychoanalytic Tng., Inst. for Psychoanalysis and Psychotherapy N.J. Faculty, 1982—. Recipient Disting. Faculty award Atlantic County Psychoanalytic Soc., 1987; NIMH fellow, 1965. Fellow N.J. Soc. for Clin. Social Work; mem. AAUP, NASW, APA (pres. divsn. 39 2003-04, bd. dirs. 2005—, com. psychoanalytic psychotherapists, bd. dirs. divsn. 39 2006—), Nat. Assn. for Advancement of Psychoanalysis, Acad. Cert. Social Workers, Soc. for Psychoanalytic Tng. (bd. dirs. 1983-90, dir. social sci. program 1983-86), Am. Coll. Forensic Examiners Internat. (mem. editl. bd. jours. 1999—, Outstanding Svc. award 2000), Internat. Coach Fedn.; mem. APA (pres. div. 39 sec. III, 2003-04), Am. Psychoanalytic Assn. (psychotherapy task force, psychoanalysis and undergrad. edn. task force, com. on psychotherapist assocs. 2003—), Am. Coll. Forensic Social Workers (chair 2000-01), Women in Aviation Internat, 99's Internat. Orgn. Women Pilots, Nat. Bus. Aviation Assn, Rutgers U. Alumni Assn. (bd. dirs. 2003-05), So. NJ Psychoanalytic Inst. (faculty mem. 2004-06, bd. dirs. 2004-06). Home and Office: 159 Valley Rd Princeton NJ 08540-3442 Home Phone: 609-921-0828; Office Phone: 609-921-0828. Personal E-mail: judith@judithlogue.com.

LOH, HORACE H., pharmacology educator; b. Canton, Republic of China, May 28, 1936; BS, Nat. Taiwan U., Taipei, Republic China, 1958; PhD, U. Iowa, 1965. Lectr. dept. pharmacology U. Calif. Sch. Medicine, San Francisco, 1967; assoc. prof. biochem. Wayne State U., Detroit, 1968-70; lectr., rsch. assoc. depts. psychiatry, pharmacology Langley Porter Neuropsychiatric Inst. U. Calif. Sch. Medicine, San Francisco, 1970-72, assoc. prof. depts. psychiatry, pharmacology Langley Porter Neuropsychiatric Inst., 1972-75, prof. depts. psychiatry, pharmacology Langley Porter Neuropsychiatric Inst., 1975-88; prof., head dept. pharmacology U. Minn. Med. Sch., Mpls., 1989—, Frederick and Alice Stark prof., head dept. pharmacology, 1990—. Chmn. ann. meeting theme com. on receptors Fedn. Am. Socs. for Exptl. Biology, 1984; mem. exec. com. Internat. Narcotic Rsch. Conf., 1984—87, chair sci. program ann. meeting, 1986; mem. adv. com. Nat. Tsing Hua U. Inst. Life Scis., Taiwan, China, 1985—89; mem. exec. com. Com. on Problems of Drug Dependence, Inc., 1985—88; mem. sci. adv. coun. Nat. Found. for Addictive Diseases, 1987—; cons. U.S. Army R & D Dept. Def., 1980—84. Mem. editl. adv. bd. Life Scis., 1978—, Substance and Alcohol Abuse, 1980—, Neurochemistry Internat., 1980—88, Neuropharmacology, 1992—, Neurosci. Series, 1982—83, Ann. rev. Pharmacology and Toxicology, 1984—89, Jour. Pharmacology and Exptl. Therapeutics, 1987—, assoc. editor CRC Critical Rev. in Pharmacol. Scis., 1987—88, Ann. Rev. Pharmacology and Toxicology, 1990—95; contbr. 56 chpts. in books, 300 articles to profl. jours. Recipient Career Devel. award, USPHS, 1973—78, 1978—83, Rsch. Scientist award, 1983—88, 1989—94, Humboldt award for sr. U.S. scientists, 1977. Mem.: We. Pharmacology Soc. (councilor 1980—83, pres. 1984—85), Soc. Chinese Bioscientists in Am. (pres. 1985—86), Am. Soc. Pharmacology and Exptl. Therapeutics (program com. 1976—86, trustee bd. publs. 1987—93, com. on confs. 1990—93), Am. Coll. Neuropsychopharmacology (honorific awards com. 1988—). Office: U Minn Med Sch Dept Pharmacology 6-120 Jackson 321 Church St SE Minneapolis MN 55455-0217 Office Phone: 612-626-4460, 612-625-9997. Business E-Mail: lohxx001@umn.edu.

LOHMANN, GEORGE YOUNG, JR., neurosurgeon, health facility administrator, artist; b. Scranton, Pa., Aug. 9, 1947; s. George Young Lohmann and Elizabeth (Nichols) Frantzen; m. Joette Calabrese, May 15, 1973 (div. 1981); m. Rosemary Ei-Ling Ma, Sept. 24, 1988 (div. 1998); 1 child, Norelle Christa Victoria. AB in Chemistry with honors, Hobart Coll., 1968; MD, SUNY, Buffalo, 1972. Diplomate Am. Bd. Neurol. Surgeons, Am. Acad. Pain Specialists, Am. Bd. Forensic Medicine, Am. Acad. Disability Analysts. Resident gen. surgery Wesley Meml. Hosp., Chgo., 1972-73; asst. med. dir. West Side Orgn., Chgo., 1973-74; emergency physician St. James Hosp., Chicago Heights, Ill., 1973-74; from jr. resident to chief resident neurosurgery Georgetown U. Hosp., Washington, 1975-79; chief resident neurosurgery Washington Vets. Hosp., 1978; pvt. practice Baton Rouge, 1979-81, 81-84; dir. dept. neurosurgery Brookdale Hosp. Med. Ctr., Bklyn., 1984-93; pres. Bklyn. Neurosurg. Svcs., Inc., 1985—; pvt. practice Midland, Tex., 1994-96; founding pres. Dragongate Adoption Cons., Inc., 1999—; CEO Doc Mktg. LLC, 2008—. Mem. Med. Dir. Com., Risk Mgmt. Com., Exec. Quality Assurance Com., 1987-93; mem. Med. Bd. Com., 1985-93, Exec. Bd. Com., 1984-93, Pain Mgmt. Com., 1988-91; regional dir. Tex. Physicians Resource Coun., 1996-97. Editl. bd. Computerized Radiology, 1975—85, assoc. editor, 1975—85; contbr. articles to profl. jours.; actor: (in amatur theatre) Mem. adv. bd. Ctr. Latin Affairs, Baton Rouge, 1982-84; mem. Senatorial Inner Cir., 1988, mem. presdl. roundtable, 1991; mem. Presdl. Roundtable, 1992; trustee Christian Victory Ctr., Hempstead, N.Y., 1986-88; vol. Appalachian Project, 1970; mem. transition team for Pres. Ronald Reagan, 1980-81. Named to Compton-Connolly Guide to Best Physicians in the N.Y. Met. Area, Best Surgeons America, 2007-10, Guide to America's Top Surgeons-Neurol. Surgery, Consumer's Rsch. Coun. America, 2007-09; selected by peers as one of Best Doctors in America Ctrl. Region, 1996-97. Fellow ACS, Am. Coll. Pain Mgmt., Am. Coll. Forensic Examiners, Am. Coll. Disability Analysts, Lohman Found. (dir.); mem. AMA, Am. Assn. Neurol. Surgeons (sect. intensive care), Christian Med. and Dental Soc., Am. Assn. Neurologic Surgeons, N.Y. State Neurosurg. Soc., N.Y. Soc. Neurosurgery, Congress Neurologic Surgeons (spine sect., sect. on trauma, sect. on intensive care), Tex. State Med. Soc., So. Med. Soc. Presdl. Roundtable (presdl. transition team 1980-81), NRA (life), West Tex. Cigar Soc., Physicians Resource Coun. (Tex. regional dir.), Cmty. Resource Coun. troubled Youth West Tex., Mission Bd. China, 2005; Argentier Honoraire Confrerie de la Chaine des Rotisseurs, Bailli Foundateur de Midland-Confrerie de la Chaine des Rotisseurs, Midland Confrerie de la Chaine des Rotisseurs (Bailli Honoraire), Chaine des Rotisseurs (comdr.), Consul de L'Ordre Mondial des Gourmets Degustateurs, Brilliat-Savarin Soc., Shanhai Tiffin Club, Donyin Sister City Assn., Midland Arts Assn., Midland C. of C., Midland-Odessa Symphony and Choral Soc. Achievements include patents in field. Avocations: skiing, painting, poetry, music, cooking.

LOHNER, RONALD A., plastic surgeon; B in Chemistry and German, Dartmouth Coll.; attended, U. of Medicine and Dentistry of NJ-Rutgers. Diplomate Am. Bd. Surgery-gen. surgery, 1992, Am. Bd. Plastic Surgery-plastic/reconstructive surgery, 1995. Gen. surgery residency U. Conn-Hartford Hosp., chief resident gen. surgery; tng. Hosp. of the Univ. of Pa., Children's Hosp., Phila.; with Bryn Mawr Hosp., 1993—, chief plastic surgery, 2005—; with Bryn Mawr Rehab. Hosp., Lankenau Med. Ctr., 1993—; instr. Univ. of Conn. Sch. of Medicine; trains residents Univ. of Pa. Sch. of Medicine; with Paoli Hosp., 2002—. Recipient Dr. Robert W. Painter award, Edward Weck Inc.; named Alpha Mega Alpha. Fellow: ACS; mem.: Robert H. Ivy Soc. of Plastic Surgeons, Northeastern Soc. of Plastic Surgeons, Am. Soc. for Aesthetic Plastic Surgery, Am. Soc. of Plastic Surgery. Office: Dr Ronald Lohner Bryn Mawr Plastic Surgeon Bldg 1 Ste 200 919 Conestoga Rd Bryn Mawr PA 19010 Office Phone: 610-717-0332.

LOHR, JACOB ANDREW, pediatrician, educator; b. Lexington, NC, Aug. 15, 1940; s. Dermot and Blanche (Grimes) L.; m. Elizabeth Waite, June 19, 1967 (div. 1978); m. Lura Galloway, Nov. 27, 1993; children: Jason Merrill, Lara Jane Parker (dec.), Jonathan Waite, Elizabeth Brice. AB, U. N.C., 1962, MD, 1967. Diplomate Am. Bd. Pediats. Chief resident dept. pediat. U. Va., Charlottesville, 1969-70, prof., 1984-90, divsn. chief, assoc. chair, 1976-90; prof. dept. pediat. U. NC, Chapel Hill, 1990—, divsn. chief, assoc. chair, 1990—98, vice chair dept. pediat., 1998—2000, disting. prof. pediat., 2006—; pediatrician-in-chief NC Children's Hosp., Chapel Hill, 1999—2000, sr. clinician, 2000—02; exec. dir. Gov.'s Inst. Alcohol and Substance Abuse, 1998—2007. Cons. to task force on urinary tract infections Am. Acad. Pediats., 1992-99, WHO Com. on Hospitalized Children at Risk, Geneva, 1999-2000; McLemore Birdsong disting. prof. U.Va., 1984-90. Editor: Pediatric Outpatient Proceedings, 1992, Guidelines for Nurse Practitioners, 1994, 5th edit., 1999, Essence of Pediatrics, 2000; med. editor Am. Bd. pediats., 1996—; contbr. articles to profl. jours. Bd. dirs. Head Start, Charlottesville, 1973-76, Ronald Mc-

Donald House, 1980-82, Orange County Ptnrship. for young Children, Chapel Hill, 1994-96; trustee Bowman Fund, U. Va., 1972—. Lt. comdr. USN, 1970-72. Recipient H. Fleming Fuller award, U. NC Healthcare Sys. Fellow Am. Acad. Pediats.; mem. Am. Soc. for Microbiology, Ambulatory Pediat. Assn., Pediat. Infectious Disease Soc., Infectious Disease Soc. Lutheran. Avocations: golf, boating. Office: U NC Dept Pediat 231 Mac Nider Chapel Hill NC 27517-6208 Office Phone: 919-966-2504. Office Fax: 919-966-3852. Business E-Mail: jacob_lohr@med.unc.edu.

LOIKE, JOHN DAVID, director; b. Stockholm, Mar. 13, 1950; BA, Yeshiva U., 1971; PhD, Albert Einstein Coll. Medicine, Yeshiva U., 1976. Dir. spl. programs, ctr. bioethics Columbia U. Coll. Physicians and Surgeons, 2005—. Recipient Revel award, Yeshiva U.; Rsch. grant, Dept. Def., NSF, grant, NY State. Mem.: Am. Soc. Cell Biology. Office: 630 W 168th St PS 11- 444 New York NY 10032 Office Fax: 212-305-5775. Business E-Mail: jdl5@columbia.edu.

LOIZZO, ALBERTO, retired medical researcher; b. Cosenza, Italy, Mar. 9, 1941; MD, U. Roma La Sapienza, 1966. Rsch. dir., sect. endocrine pharmacology Inst. Superiore di Sanita, 1981—2002, rsch. dir., sect. pediatric pharmacology, 2002—08. Cons. European Medicines Evaluation, 1995—2002; contract prof. U. Bologna, 2005—08. Office: Via Regina Elena 299 Rome 00161 Italy Personal E-mail: alberto.loizzo@gmail.com.

LOKE, JOAN TSO FONG, respiratory therapist; b. Hong Kong, Nov. 29, 1950; d. Choong Shee and Elsie L.C. Loke; m. Fabian Chan, Dec. 2, 1975 (div. July 1993); children: Jeffrey Chan, Jeremy Chan. BS in Biology, U. Puget Sound, 1973, BS in Med. Tech., 1974; AS in Respiratory care, Kapiolani C.C., 1995. Cert. respiratory therapy technician, registered respiratory technologist; lic. respiratory therapist Lobbied, 2011. Med. technologist Harborview Med. Ctr., Seattle, 1975—76; EKG technologist St. Francis, Honolulu, 1987—94, oxygen technologist, 1994—95, respiratory therapist, 1995, Kapiolani Med. Ctr., Honolulu, 1995—2002, Kaiser Permanent, Honolulu, 1995—, Tripler Med. Ctr., Honolulu, 2002—06. Mem.: AARC (pact team mem. 2002—, pub. rels. chair 2002—03), HSRC (v.p. 2000, bd. dirs. 2000, pres. 2001—03). Avocations: Karate (black belt), swimming, tennis, piano, singing. Office: Kaiser Permanente 3288 Moanalua Rd Honolulu HI 96819 Home: 2586A Kekuanoni St Honolulu HI 96813 E-mail: catnap@hawaii.rr.com.

LÖKER, ALTAN, retired electrical engineer, psychologist; b. Kutahya, Turkey, Nov. 6, 1927; s. Hakki Idris and Muazzez (Hatice) L. MSEE, Tech. U. Istanbul, Turkey, 1951; MS in Physics, Stevens Inst. Tech., 1957. Elec. engr., project mgr., subcontractor, contractor in Turkey; elec. engr. in U.S., Can., Saudi Arabia; non-lic. vol. psychotherapist Turkey. Author: Film and Suspense, 1976, 2nd edit., 2005, Dreams and Psychosynthesis, 1987, Cognitive-Cybernetic Theory and Therapy of Mental Disorders, 1993, Dreams, Migraine, Facial Neuralgia, 1993, Cognitive-Behavioral Cybernetics of Symptoms, Dreams, Lateralization: Theory Interpretation Therapy, 2001, 2d edit., 2002, Migraines and Dreams, 2003, Theory Construction and Testing in Physics and Psychology, 2007; contbr. articles to profl. jours. Lt. signal corps, Turkish mil., 1952-54. Achievements include explanation of complete method of theory constrn. which is used in physics and has to be used also in psychology but is not found anywhere in literature and constitutes the blind spot of some disciplines of sci.; constrn. of theory of automatic responses, such as symptoms of primary mental disorders and dreams, which exposes the precise adaptive, self-protective functions of those responses; and the resulting definitive cure of many mental disorders by very fast psychotherapy, including migraine and tension headaches and facial neuralgia. Home: Lalasahin 19 (23) 5 Feriköy Istanbul 80260 Turkey Office Phone: 90-0212-230 51 81. Personal E-mail: alloker@superonline.com.

LOKHMATKINA, NATALIA V., neurologist, educator, researcher; b. Vladivostok, Russia, June 24, 1964; MD, Vladivostok State Med. Inst., Russia, 1988; PhD in Clin. Psychology, St. Petersburg Med. Acad. Postgrad. Studies, Russia, 2010. Neurologist Far Eastern Regional Hosp., Vladivostok, 1997—2006; dir. NGO Women's and Children's Crisis Ctr., Vladivostok, 2000—06; chief neurologist Closed Joint Stoke Co. Modern Med. Techs., 2009—; asst. prof. St. Petersburg Med. Acad. Postgrad. Studies, 2009—. Cons. St. Petersburg Govt. Task Force Stop Gender-Based Violence, 2007—; rschr. WONCA Spl. Interest Group Family Violence, 2010—. Fellowship, Ford Found. Internat., Inst. Internat. Edn., USAID, IREX, Alumni Small grant, Cmty. Connections fellowship, grant, US Congress. Mem.: St. Petersburg Assn. Family Medicine, European Acad. Tchrs. Gen. Practice. Avocations: exercise, reading, languages. Home: 32 Utinaya Ap 116 Saint Petersburg 197375 Russia Office Phone: 7-812-448-54-68. Home Fax: 7-812-448-94-69. Personal E-mail: lokhmatkinan@yahoo.com. Business E-Mail: lohmatkina@dchmt.com.

LOKHOV, PETR GENRIEVICH, research scientist; b. Moscow, Aug. 23, 1973; MD, Russian State Med. U., 1996; PhD, Russian Acad. Med. Scis., 2001. Sr. scientist Inst. Biomed. Chemistry, 1996—. Home: Chernomorskii bulvard 23/1-45 Moscow 117452 Russia Personal E-mail: lokhovpg@rambler.ru.

LOLLAR, KEVIN, otolaryngologist; b. Helena, Ark., Dec. 6, 1979; MD, U. Ark. Med. Scis., 2006. Otolaryngologist head & neck surgeon Hannibal Regional Med. Group, U. Mo., Columbia, 2011—. Physician. Office: 1 Hospital Dr MA313 Columbia MO 65212 E-mail: kevinlollar@yahoo.com.

LÖLLGEN, HERBERT HANS, cardiologist; b. Bonn, Germany, Jan. 5, 1943; s. Artur and Maria (Decker) L.; m. Inge Horres, Nov. 18, 1969; children: Ruth, Deborah, Noëmi, Eva. MD, U. Bonn, 1967; PhD, U. Mainz, Germany, 1979. Asst., intern U. Mainz Med. Sch., 1970-72, asst., 1976-78; asst. med. dept. Hosp., Moers, Germany, 1973-75; rsch. fellow Aug Krogh Inst., Copenhagen, 1975; vice-head dept. cardiology U. Freiburg, Germany, 1978-82; head dept. cardiology Acad. Hosp., Limburg, Germany, 1983-85; head dept. medicine and cardiology Mcpl. Hosp., Acad. Hosp., Remscheid U., Bochum, Germany, 1986—2008; pvt. practice cardiology, 2008. Chmn. Working Group on Ergometry, 1985-93; mem. med. bd. German and Esa Astronauts, Cologne, 1980—; cardiol. cons. ESA, 2004-. Author: Cardio-Pulmonary Diagnosis, 1983, Arrhythmias, 1983, ECG in Practice, 1984, 90; editor (with E. Erdmann) Ergometry, 1990, 3rd edit., 2009, Progress in Ergometry: Quality Control and Test Criteria, 1984, Catecholamines in the ICU, 1989, Cardiopulmonary Function, 4th edit., 2005, Advances in Ergometry, 1990, Resuscitation, 2nd edit., 1995; mem. editl. bd., contbr. articles to nat. and internat. sci. jours Mem. Sci. Med. Coun. of German Army. Served with German Army, 1970. Fellow Am. Coll. Cardiology, Am. Heart Assn.; mem. Nordrhein (pres 1986-2006), German Soc. Sports Medicine and Preventive Medicine (pres. 2006—), German Coun. on Resuscitation. Roman Catholic. Avocations: sports, opera, collecting old medical books. Home and Office: Bermesgasse 32 b D-42897 Remscheid Germany Home Phone: 0049 219165354; Office Phone: 00492191231455. Personal E-mail: herbert.loellgen@gmx.de, loellgen@dgsp.de.

LOMBARDI, JOSEPH V., vascular surgeon; MD, Jefferson Med. Coll. Diplomate Am. Bd. Surgery-vascular surgery. Intern Pa. Hosp. (UPHS), resident; fellow vascular gene therapy Univ. of Pa. Hosp., fellow Vascular Surgery; dir. Cooper Aortic Ctr. Cooper Univ. Hosp.; physician Cooper Univ., head vascular and endovascular surgery divsn., program dir. vascular surgery fellowship; assoc. prof. Cooper. Univ. Named one of the Top Doctor, Phila. Mag., 2011. Mem.: Soc. for Clin. Vascular Surgery, Soc. of Vascular Surgery, Eastern Vascular Soc., Peripheral Vascular Surgery Soc., Del. Valley Vascular Soc. Office: Cooper University Hospital Bldg OneSte G 900 Centennial Blvd Voorhees NJ 08043 Office Phone: 856-342-2151.

LOMBARDO, FREDRIC ALAN, pharmacist, educator; b. New Castle, Pa., May 11, 1948; s. Valentine Frank and Clara Eleanor (Cugini) Lombardo; m. Loretta D. Patts, May 22, 1971; children: Alan John, Lauren Beth, Leslie Anne. BS in Pharmacy, Duquesne U., Pitts., 1971, PharmD, 1974; MS, Fla. Inst. Tech., Melbourne, 1979. Lic. pharmacist Pa., Va., D.C., Tex., cert. Am. Coll. Clin. Pharmacists. Resident in hosp. pharmacy Mercy Hosp., Pitts., 1973; commd. 2nd lt. US Army, 1974, advanced through grades to lt. col., 1993; chief clin. pharmacy support svc. Brooke Army Med. Ctr., Ft. Sam Houston, Tex., 1980-85; chief outpatient pharmacy svc. Walter Reed Army Med. Ctr., Washington, 1985-86, chief cancer treatment sect., chief hematol.-oncol. pharmacy, 1986-92; resigned active duty entered US Army reserve, 1993; sr. clin. pharmacy supr. Nat. Heart, Lung and Blood Inst., NIH, Bethesda, Md., 1992-95; assoc. prof. clin. and adminstrv. pharmacy sci. Howard U., Washington, 1995—, assoc. prof. psychiatry Coll. Medicine, assoc. prof. cmty. medicine and family practice, dept. infectious diseases, assoc. prof., neurology, adv. com. mem.; assoc. prof. U. Md. Adj. ordinary prof. pharmacology Cath. U., Washington, 1995—; assoc. prof. pharmacology H. Lee Med. Sch., USPHS, Bethesda, Md., 1995—; assoc. prof. pharmacology Cancer Ctr., Ctr. Sickle Cell Disease Howard U., 1995—, asst. dir. Cancer Ctr., 1997; adj. assoc. prof. neurology Howard U., Coll. Medicine; prof. Found. Advancement Edn. Sci., Grad. Sch. NIH, 1996—; mem. Mid-Atlantic Oncology Adv. Group, Washington, 1997; mem. coun. experts com. Oncologic Diseases USP; mem. faculty, cons. Comprehensive AIDS Tng. Initiative and Nat. Minority AIDS Edn. and Tng. Ctr.; cons. faculty Nat. Minority AIDS Edn. and Tng. Ctr. Faculty Comprehensive AIDS Tng. Inst.; mem. DC Medicare Pharmacy and Therapeutics Com., Washington, 2007; mem. pharmacy and therapeutics com. Medicade Assistance Agy., Washington; cons. Comprehensive Psychiatric Emergency Program, DC Govt., Washington. Co-host Ask the Pharmacy Doctor program Sta. WRC-980, Washington, 1997—, guest various TV and radio programs; editor: Jour. of Hosp. Ethics. Active Urban Health U., Urban Family Inst., Washington, 1996—97; mem. Medicaid Adv. Bd. DC Govt. Lt. col. USAR, 1993—. Named Pharmacist of Yr. 2006, Washington Met. Assoc. Health Sys. Pharmacists, 2007; Rsch. grant, Ortho-McNeil Pharm., Washington, 1996—97. Fellow: Am. Soc. Cons. Pharmacists; mem.: Gen. Clin. Res. Ctr., Med. Assistance Agy. DC Govt. (adv. com. mem.), Gen. Clin. Rsch. Com., DC Govt. (adv. bd.), Medicinal Adv. Com., Nat. Pharm. Assn., Am. Soc. Health Professions, Am. Pharm. Assn. (bd. cert. in pharmacotherapy nutrition support, oncology, psychopharmacology, and geriatrics), KC, Am. Legion. Democrat. Roman Catholic. Avocations: military history, mathematics. Home: 13503 Apple Barrel Ct Herndon VA 20171-4006 Office: Howard U Sch Pharmacy and Coll Medicine 2300 4th St NE Washington DC 20002

LOMBARDO, MARCO, ophthalmologist, researcher; b. Reggio Calabria, Italy, July 9, 1975; s. Mario Lombardo and Giuliana Zaffino. Degree in Medicine and Surgery, U. Rome "La Sapienza", Italy, 1999; PhD in Biomed. Engring., U. Magna Graecia, Catanzaro, Italy, 2007. Diplomate ophthalmology specialization Cath. U. Rome, 2003. Rsch. fellow IRCCS Found, 2010. Named Best and youngest grad. in Medicine and Surgery, Calabria and Sicily, Italy, 2000. Mem.: Assn. Rsch. Vision and Ophthalmology, Optical Soc. Am., European Soc. Cataract and Refractive Surgery (assoc.). Roman Catholic. Achievements include research in biophysics of the cornea; human optics wavefront sensing and adaptive optics for vision science. Avocations: cooking, reading, classical music, soccer. Office: Vision Engineering Rome Italy Home: via Nizza 46 Rome 00198 Israel Office Phone: 393313438300. Home Fax: 39068840971. Personal E-mail: mlombardo@visioeng.it.

LOMBARDO, PETER CHARLES, dermatologist; b. Rochester, NY, Dec. 4, 1935; s. Charles J. and Constance R. (Inguaggiato) L. BA, U. Rochester, 1955; MD, Union U., 1959. Diplomate Am. Bd. Dermatology., cert. voluntary, 2009. Intern Mary Imogene Bassett Hosp., Cooperstown, N.Y., 1959-60; resident in dermatology Columbia Presbyn. Med. Ctr., NYC, 1962-65; resident in internal medicine St. Luke's Hosp. Ctr., NYC, 1965-66; pvt. practice NYC, 1966-97; with Sutton Pl. Dermatology, NYC, 1997—. Faculty dept. dermatology Coll. Physicians and Surgeons Columbia U., N.Y.C., 1966-97, assoc. clin. prof. dermatology, 1997—; case rev. Med. Liability Mutual Ins. Co., N.Y.C., 1985—, Office of Profl. Med. Conduct Dept. Health N.Y. State, N.Y.C., 1995—, independent physician review orgn., 2004- Author: (with others) Clinical Geriatrics, 1979, Dermatology and Person Threatening Diseases, 1996; manuscript rev. Jour. Am. Acad. Dermatology, 1986; contbr. articles to profl. jours. Del. Govs. Conf. on Librs., Albany, N.Y., 1978. With USNR. Named Best Drs. in NY, NY Mags., 1991, Castle Connelly Guide, 1998—. Am. Acad. Dermatology (adv. coun. 1992—, mem. ethics com. 1995—, mem. exec. com. rep. N.Y. 1997—), Med. Soc. County N.Y. (grievance com. peer rev. 1992—, chair grievance com. 1997—2005), bd. dirs, 2008-, v.p. 2010-2011, pres. elect 2011-), Med. Soc. State NY (del. 2006-), Am. Med. Assn., NY State Soc. Dermatology (bd. dirs. 1992—), Individual Practice Assn. Met. N.Y. (credentials com. 1995—), NY State Soc. Dermatology (bd. dirs. 1992-, pres. 2005-2007), N.Y. Acad. Medicine (Fred Wise Meml. award 1965), chair, sect. on dermatology, 2003 N.Y. Dermatol. Soc. (bd. dirs. 1992—, pres. 1993), Manhattan Met. Dermatol. Soc., NY Athletic Club. Office: Sutton Pl Dermatology 445 E 58th St New York NY 10022-2302 Office Phone: 212-838-0270. Personal E-mail: pclmd@aol.com.

LOMBARDO, ROBIN ANN, therapeutic recreation director, educator; b. Mineola, NY, July 28, 1956; d. John Donald and Irene (Pepe) Alexander; m. Ralph John Lombardo, Dec. 30, 1980 (div. Feb. 2010); children: Jason Alexander, Jessica Janine. BA, SUNY, Stony Brook, 1978; MS in Recreation Edn., CUNY, 1985. Cert. therapeutic recreation specialist; cert. leisure profl. Activities aide A. Holly Patterson Home, Uniondale, N.Y., 1975-76; activities asst. Franklin Park Nursing Home, Franklin Square, N.Y., 1977; recreation leader Brunswick Hosp. Nursing Home, Amityville, N.Y., 1978-80; dir. recreational therapy Brunswick Hosp. Ctr. Rehab., Amityville, N.Y., 1980-86; recreation therapist Kings Park (N.Y.) Psychiat. Ctr., 1986-87, VA Med. Ctr., Northport, 1988-91; dir. therapeutic recreation L.I. State Vets. Home, Stony Brook, 1991-93; adj. asst. prof. Suffolk County C.C., Selden, N.Y., 1985—. Asst. prof. St. Joseph's Coll., Patchogue, N.Y., 1994—; cons. N.Y. State civil Svc. Exam. Bd., N.Y.C., 1984; vol. med. staff N.Y. State Games for the Physically Challenged, East Meadow, N.Y., 1984-86; participant Internat. Roundtable on Aging, Oxford (Eng.) U., 2005. Pres. Masons, Westbury, N.Y., 1973-74. Named one of Outstanding Young Women of Am., 1985. Fellow Nat. Recreation & Park Asns., N.Y. State Recreation & Park Soc., Inc.; me. L.I. Recreation, Parks & Leisure Svcs. Assn. (exec. bd. mem., pres.-elect 1989-90, Citation 1989, 91). Episcopalian. Avocations: entertainer, dance, music, shows, concerts. Office: Alzheimers Assoc Long Island 45 Park Ave Bay Shore NY 11706 Business E-Mail: robin.lombardo@alz.org.

LOMHOLT, NIELS FINSEN, retired pharmacologist; b. Copenhagen, Mar. 16, 1932; s. Svend and Gudrun (Finsen) Lomholt; m. Bodil Elizabeth Parkes, June 29, 1955 (div. Nov. 1978); children: Margrethe Lomholt Kemp, Thorkild Finsen; m. Hanne Dorthe Graabek Jensen, Nov. 25, 1978 (dec. Apr. 1993); 1 child, Trine; m. Hanne Flinker, Mar. 15, 1997. MD, U. Copenhagen, 1961. With dept. anesthesiology U. Copenhagen, 1963—65, asst. prof. dept. pharmacology, 1968—99, sr. scientist, 2000—10. Scholar Dept. Anesthesiology scholar, U. Copenhagen, 1965—68. Achievements include patents for in field. Home: Lars Nielsens Vej 4 2970 Horsholm Denmark

LOMONACO, CECÍLIA, biology educator; b. Uberlândia, Oct. 8, 1962; MSc, U. Estadual Rio de Janeiro, 1987; PhD, U. Estadual Campinas, 1994. Tchr. U. Fed. de Uberlândia, 1987—. Office: Rua Princesa Isabel 274 Uberlândia Minas Gerais 38 400-129 Brazil Business E-Mail: lomonaco@ufu.br.

LONDERO, FRANCO, retired gynecologist; b. Gemona, Udine, Italy, Jan. 7, 1947; s. Pietro and Domenica Londero; m. Nevia-Agnese Garzitto, Mar. 8, 1975 (dec. 2005); 1 child, Ambrogio-Pietro; m. Volga Bonacic karelovic (Mar 2, 2011). Degree in medicine and surgery, U. Trieste, Italy, 1974, diploma in ob-gyn, 1978, diploma in nephrology, 1988; diploma in oncology, U. Ancona, Italy, 1982; resident, Inst. Dexeus, Barcelona, 1990. Registrar Gen. Hosp., San Vito, Pordenone, Italy, 1976-77, San Bonifacio, Verona, 1977-78, Gemona, 1978-89, sr. registrar, 1989-97, coord. perinatal medicine, 1993—, Monfalcone, 1998—2007; ret., 2007. Co-author: Our History, 1990, The Fortresses of North-East, 1992, The Birth of Fascism, 1998, War Memories-Cephalonia 1943, 2004, Early Middle Ages Fortresses in Friuli, 2005; contbr. articles to profl. jours. Town councillor City of Artegna, Udine, 1985-90; councillor Cmty. of Gemona, 1985-90. Mem. Storie Dai Longobarz, Italian Assn. Hosp. Gynecology and Obstatrics, Italian Assn. Uro-Gynecology, Italian Assn.Invalid and Mutilated by Work. Avocations: archaeology, history. Home: c/o Borgo Aplia 8 Dubrovnik-Ragusa (HR) Getaldiceva 12 Artegna Italy also: via Brunner 2 Trieste 34125 Italy Personal E-mail: londero.franco@libero.it.

LONDON, IRVING MYER, physician, educator; b. Malden, Mass., July 24, 1918; s. Jacob A. and Rose (Goldstein) London; m. Huguette Piedzicki, Feb. 27, 1955; children: Robert L.J., David T. B in Jewish Edn., Hebrew Coll., 1938; AB summa cum laude, Harvard U., 1939, MD, 1943; DSc (hon.), U. Chgo., 1966. Sheldon Traveling fellow Harvard U., 1939—41, Delamar rsch. fellow med. sch., 1940—41; intern Presbyn. Hosp., NYC, 1943, asst. resident, 1946—47, asst. physician, 1946—52, assoc. attending physician, 1954—55; Rockefeller fellow in medicine Coll. Physicians and Surgeons, Columbia U., 1946—47; instr. Columbia U., 1947—49; assoc. in medicine Coll. Phys. and Surg., Columbia U., 1949—51; asst. prof. Coll. Phys. and Surg., Columbia, 1951—54, assoc. prof., 1954—55; prof., chmn. dept. medicine Albert Einstein Coll. Medicine, NYC, 1955—70, vis. prof. medicine, 1970—; dir. med. svc. Bronx Mcpl. Ctr., 1955—70; prof. biology MIT, 1969—89, prof. emeritus, 1989—; vis. prof. medicine Harvard Med. Sch., 1969—72, prof. medicine, 1972—89, prof. emeritus, 1989—; founding dir. divsn. health scis. and tech. Harvard and MIT, 1969—85, prof. medicine, 1972—, Grover M. Hermann prof. health scis. and tech., 1977—89, prof. emeritus, 1989—; dir. Whitaker Coll. Health Scis., Tech. and Mgmt., MIT, 1978—83. Delta Epsilon lectr. U. Colo., 1962, Harvey lectr., 61; Jacobaeus lectr., Stockholm, 64; vis. scientist Pasteur Inst., Paris, 1962—63; Commonwealth Fund fellow, 1962—63; Alpha Omega Alpha lectr. Yale, Boston U., Columbia, SUNY Downstate Med. Ctr., U. Chgo.; Harry L. Alexander vis. prof. Wash. U., St. Louis, 1968; Alpha Omega Alpha vis. prof. Johns Hopkins U., 1970; Eugene A. Stead Jr. vis. lectr. Duke Med. Ctr., 1970; cons. to Surgeon Gen. AUS, 1957—60; chmn. metabolism study sect. USPHS, 1961—63; Med. fellowship bd. NAS, NRC, 1955—64; mem. bd. sci. cons. Sloan Kettering Inst., 1960—72; bd. sci. counselors Nat. Heart Inst., 1964—68; exec. com. Health Rsch. Coun., City N.Y., 1958—63; mem. sci. adv. coun. Pub. Health Rsch. Inst., NYC, 1958—63; mem. adv. com. to dir. NIH, 1966—70, nat. cancer adv. bd., 1972—76; physician Brigham and Women's Hosp., 1972—83, sr. physician, 1983—; chmn. rsch. grp. Nat. Commn. on Arthritis, 1975—76; chmn. adv. com. Divsn. Health Scis., Inst. Medicine, 1979—82; mem. Bd. Sci. Counselors, NIH and NIADDK, 1979—83; bd. dirs., cons. Johnson and Johnson, 1982—89; founder Genetix Pharms., 1996. Assoc. editor: Jour. Clin. Investigation, 1952—57, mem. editl. bd.: Am. Jour. Medicine, 1965—79. Bd. overseers Hebrew Coll., 2000—; bd. dirs. Philippe Found. Capt. US Army, 1944—46. Recipient Bloomfield medal and lectr., Lady Davis Inst., 1986. Fellow: Am. Acad. Arts and Scis., Am. Assn. Advancement Scis. (Theobald Smith award in med. scis. 1953); mem.: NAS (med. bd. medicine 1967—70, founding mem. Inst. Medicine 1970—), Assn. Am. Physicians, Internat. Soc. Hematology, Am. Soc. Hematology, Am. Soc. Clin. Investigation (pres. 1963—64), Am. Soc. Biol. Chemists, Alpha Omega Alpha, Phi Beta Kappa. Office: Harvard U-MIT Div Health Scis and Tech 77 Massachusetts Ave Cambridge MA 02139-4301 E-mail: imlondon@mit.edu.

LONDON, RAY WILLIAM, mediator, consultant, arbitrator, researcher; b. Burley, Idaho, May 29, 1943; s. Loo Richard and Maycelle Jerry (Moore) L. AS, Weber State Coll., 1965, BS, 1967; MSW, U. So. Calif., 1973, PhD, 1976, Exec. MBA, 1989; postgrad. cert. dispute resolution, Pepperdine Law Sch., 1993; LLM, Strathcylde Sch. Law, 2000. Diplomate: Am. Bd. Psychol. Hypnosis (dir. 1984-97, pres. 1989-97, forensic and ethics divsn.), Am. Acad. Behavioral Med., Internat. Acad. Med. and Psychol. (dir. 1981-90, pres. 1981-85), Am. Bd. Profl. Neuropsychology, Am. Bd. Adminstrv. Psychol., Am. Bd. Examiners Clinic Social Work, Am. Bd. Profl. Psychol., NASW Clin. Social Work Bd., Am. Bd. Psychol. Specialties, Am. Bd. Forensic Med., Am. Acad. Pain Mgmt., Am. Acad. Experts in Traumatic Stress, Am. Bd. Forensic Examiners, Cyberlex. Global Info. Tech. Law Forum; cert. Soc. Med. Analysts; cert. mgmt. cons., profl. cons. to mgmt.; registered internat. cons. Registry of Arbitrators. Congl. asst. U.S. Ho. of Reps., 1964-65; rsch. assoc. Bus. Advs., Inc., Ogden, Utah, 1965-67; dir. counseling and cons. svcs. Meaning Found., Riverside, Calif., 1966-69; mental health and mental retardation liason San Bernandino (Calif.) Cmty. Social Svcs., 1968-72; clin. trainee VA Outpatient Clin., LA, 1971-72, Childrens Hosp. of LA, 1972-73, clin. fellow, 1973-74; clin. trainee Reiss David Child Study Ctr., LA, 1973-74, LA Cmty. - U. So. Calif. Med. Ctr., 1973; group facilitator conflict resolution Benjamin Rush Ctr., Orange, Calif., 1973-75; psychologist Orange Police Dept., 1974-80; COO London Assocs. Internat., 1974-80; clin. and consulting psychology postdoctoral intern Orange Cmty. Mental Health, 1976-77; postdoctoral fellow U. Calif., Irvine-Calif. Coll. Med., 1978; cons. to pub. schs., agys., hosps., bus. Nat. and Internat., 1973—; cons. qualitative-quantitative rsch., dispute resolution and assessment Santa Ana, Calif., 1974—; pres. bd. govs. Human Factor Programs, 1976-86; CEO Human Studies Ctr., 1987—; pres., CEO London Consult Orgn. Behavioral-Crisis-Devel. Info. and Knowledge, Conflict Resolution, Change and Rsch. Cons., 1980—. Prof. Argosy U., Sch. Bus. and Info. Tech., 2000—, dean, 2004; rsch. affiliate Ctr. for Crisis Mgmt., U. So. Calif. Grad. Sch., Bus. Adminstrn., 1988-90; presenter nat. and internat. lectures, seminars and workshops; mem. faculty UCLA, U. So. Calif., Calif. State U., U. Calif., Irvine, Calif. Coll. Medicine, Internat. Cong. of Psychosomatic Medicine, Internat. Coll., U. Strathclyde Sch. of Law, Argosy U., U. Phoenix; Arbitration Trained World Intellectual Property Orgn.; rsch. assoc. Nat. Commn. for Protection of Human Subjects of Biomed. and Behavioral Rsch., 1976; rschr. E commerce, info. tech., info. security, intellectual property, defective software law, liability in info. age, Internet telecom. law U. Strathclyde Sch. Law, 1998-2000, Harvard Law Internet Seminar, 2001-02; mem. arbitration panel EEOC, Ford. Author: Encyclopedia of Telecommunications Regulation and Policy; editor: Internat. Bull. Med. and Psychol., 1980—90, A.B.C.D. Report, 1988—, Behavioral Med., Australian Jour., 1980, Internat. Bull. Conflict Resolution, 1993—, Internat. Jour. of Info. Tech. Policy and Practice, 2001—; editor-in-chief LondonConsult.com, 1993—; adv. editor: Internat. Jour. Clin. and Exptl. Hypnosis, 1981—92, mng. editor:, 1991—97, assoc. editor:, 1992—97; cons. editor Internat. Jour. Psychosomatics, 1984—90, Experimentalle und Klinische, 1987—, pub. London Behavioral Med. Assessment, 1982, A Behavioral-Crisis-Devel. newsletter, ABCD newsnote; prodr.: (TV series) Being Human, 1980; contbg. author: World Book Ency. and books; contbr. articles to profl. jours. Recipient Congl. recognition U.S. Ho. of Reps., 1978, Morton Prince award, 1993; named scholar laureate Erickson Advanced Inst., 1980. Fellow: Soc. Clin. and Exptl. (bd. dirs. 1985—87, treas. 1987—89), Am. Coll. Forensic Psychol., Soc. Clin. Social Work (dir. 1979—80), Royal Soc. Health, Inst. for Social Influence Studies, Inst. for Soc. Scientists Rsch. Coun.; mem.: ABA (assoc., ethics and tech. coms.), Acad. Legal Studies in Bus., Am. Arbitration Assn., Internat. Dispute Resolution Ctr., London Ct. of Internat. Arbitration, Profl. Mediation Assn., Calif. Dispute Resolution Coun., So. Calif. Mediation Assn., Soc. Profls. in Dispute Resolution, Qualitative Rsch. Cons. Assn., Soc. for Computers in Psychology, Assn. Internet Rschrs., Toastmasters, Lamda Iota Tau, Pi Rho Phi, Tau Kappa Alpha, Delta Sigma Rho, Phi Delta Kappa. Office: CDEPRO Inst Internat 665 S Main St Ste 200-402 Orange CA 92868 Office Fax: 714-285-9197. E-mail: rwl@londonconsult.com.

LONG, EDWIN TUTT, surgeon; b. St. Louis, July 23, 1925; s. Forrest Edwin and Hazel (Tutt) L.; m. Mary M. Hull, Apr. 16, 1955; children: Jennifer Ann, Laura Ann, Peter Edwin. AB, Columbia U., 1944, MD, 1947. Diplomate Am. Bd. Surgery, Am. Bd. Thoracic Surgery. Rotating intern Meth. Hosp., Bklyn., 1947—48; surg. intern U. Chgo. Clinics, 1948-49, resident in gen. surgery, 1952-55, resident in thoracic surgery, 1955-57; asst. prof. surgery U. Chgo., 1957-59; thoracic and cardiovasc. surgeon Watson Clinic, Lakeland, Fla., 1960-69, chief surgery dept., 1969; dir. Watson Clinic Rsch. Found., 1965—69; assoc. prof. surgery U. Pa., Phila., 1970-73; attending thoracic and cardiovasc. surgeon Allegheny Cardiovasc. Surg. Assocs., Pitts., 1973-88; exec. v.p. Mailings Clearing House and Roxbury Press, Inc., 1988-90, pres., 1990-96, chmn. bd. dirs., 1991—; regent Rockhust U., 2002—10. Disting. lectr., curriculum advisor Healthcare Leadership Program, Helzberg Sch. Mgmt., Rockhurst U., 2001-10, mem. dean's adv. com., 2004-10; nat. adv. panel Ctr. for Practical Health Reform, 2003-2008, regional co-chair Kansas City chpt., 2003—. Author: (book) Life Liberty And The Pursuit of Health Care, 2008. Capt. USAF, 1950—52. Pressure Vectorography Rsch. grant Alfred P. Sloan Found., 1963; Nelson-Atkins Mus. fellow, 1997—. Fellow Heart Rhythm Soc.; mem. AMA, ACS, Am. Coll. Cardiology, Soc. for Vascular Surgery, Allegheny Vascular Soc. (pres. 1987), Ea. Vascular Soc., Soc. Thoracic Surgery, Ctr. for Practical Bioethics, Kansas City Consensus, Woodside Club, Rotary Club, Carriage Club, Sigma Xi, Beta Theta Pi. Achievements include patents for gas sterilizer. Home: 4550 Warwick Blvd # 1204 Kansas City MO 64111-7725 Office: 4550 Warwick Blvd # 1209 Kansas City MO 64111 also: MCH Strategic Data 601 E Marshall St Sweet Springs MO 65351-0295 Office Phone: 816-753-0089. E-mail: elongmd@kc.rr.com.

LONG, JEAN-ALEXANDRE, urologist; b. Bourg de Peage, France, Feb. 27, 1975; MD, Grenoble U., 2005. Praticien hospitalier Grenoble U. Hosp., 2006—. Mem.: Assn. Française D'urologie. Office: Urology Dept CHU Grenoble Rhône-Alpes 38043 France Business E-Mail: jalong@chu-grenoble.fr.

LONG, KIMBERLY A., biologist, educator; d. Kathie E. and Carl B. Weihrer; m. Scott D. Long, Sept. 27, 2003. BS in Biology, Millersville U., Pa., 1999; MS in Biology, Bucknell U., Lewisburg, Pa., 2001. Environ. trainee Pa. Dept. Environ. Protection, Norristown, 2001—02, water pollution biologist, 2002—06, watershed mgr., 2006—07; assoc. scientist FirstEnergy Corp., Reading, Pa., 2007—09; environ. specialist Exelon Corp., Kennett Square, Pa., 2009—. Instr. Montgomery County CC, Pottstown, Pa., 2007—. Vol. Relay for Life Pottstown - Am. Cancer Soc., Pa., 1997—; mem. open space planning com. West Pottsgrove Twp., 2010—, mem. planning commn., 2011—; com. mem. Pottstown Rumble Volleyball Tournament, Pa., 2001—. Office: Exelon Corp 300 Exelon Way Kennett Square PA 19348 Business E-Mail: kimberly.long@exeloncorp.com.

LONG, SARAH ELIZABETH BRACKNEY, physician; b. Sidney, Ohio, Dec. 5, 1926; d. Robert LeRoy and Caroline Josephine (Shue) Brackney; m. John Frederick Long, June 15, 1948; children: George Lynas, Helen Lucille Corcoran, Harold Roy, Clara Alice Lawrence, Nancy Carol Sieber. BA, Ohio State U., 1948, MD, 1952. Intern Grant Hosp., Columbus, Ohio, 1952—53; resident internal medicine Mt. Carmel Med. Ctr., Columbus, 1966—69, chief resident internal medicine, 1968—69; med. cons. Ohio Bur. Disability Determination, Columbus, 1970—. Physician student health Ohio State U., Columbus, 1970-73; sch. physician Bexley City Schs., Ohio, 1973-83; physician advisor to peer rev. Mt. Carmel East Hosp., Columbus, 1979-86, med. dir. employee health, 1981-96; physician cons. Fed. Black Lung program U.S. Dept. Labor, Columbus, 1979-98. Mem.: AMA, Gerontol. Soc. Am., Columbus Med. Assn., Ohio State Med. Assn., Ohio Hist. Soc., Phi Beta Kappa, Alpha Epsilon Delta. Home: 2765 Bexley Park Rd Columbus OH 43209-2231

LONG, SARAH SUNDBORG, pediatrician, educator; b. Portland, Oreg., Oct. 31, 1944; MD, Jefferson Med. Coll., 1970. Diplomate Am. Bd. Pediat. Intern St. Christopher Hosp. for Children, Phila., 1970-71, resident, 1971-73, fellow pediat. and infectious diseases, 1973-75, staff, 1975—2002; prof. pediat. Drexel U. Coll. Medicine, 2002—. Chief editor: Principles and Practice of Pediatric Infectious Diseases, 1997; assoc. editor Jour. Pediatrics, 1997—; contbr. over 100 articles to med. jours. Mem. Am. Acad. Pediat., Soc. for Pediat. Rsch., Am. Pediat. Soc., Pediatric Diseases Soc. (pres. 1999 2001). Office: St Christopher Child Hosp Sect Infectious Diseases Erie Ave at Front St Philadelphia PA 19134

LONG, STEPHEN GEOFFREY, epidemiologist; b. Oxford, Eng., Jan. 12, 1962; BA, Yale U., 1983; MD, Tex. Tech. Health Sci. Ctr., 1997. Epidemiologist Houston Health & Human Svcs., 2001—. Mem.: APHA. Avocation: singing. Home: 5353 Institute Ln #11 Houston TX 77005 Home Fax: 832-393-5232. Personal E-mail: long_stephen@att.net.

LONG, TERESA C., city health department administrator; m. Tom Denune; 1 child, Katherine. MD, U. Calif., San Francisco; MPH, U. Calif., Berkeley. Med. dir., asst. health commr Columbus Health Dept., Ohio, 1986—2002, commr., 2002—; clin. assoc. prof. Ohio State U., Coll. Medicine and Pub. Health. Chair Ctrl. Ohio Med. Dirs. Coalition, Columbus Area Asthma Coalition; co-chair Healthy Columbus Adv. Bd. Recipient Elizabeth Blackwell award for Pioneering Efforts to Improve Women's and Cmty. Health. Mem.: Columbus Med. Assn. (past pres., past pres., bd. trustees found.). Office: Columbus Health Dept 240 Parsons Ave Columbus OH 43215

LONG, THOMAS LAWRENCE, English educator; b. Washington, Jan. 29, 1953; s. Thomas Lawrence Sr. and Lucy Ann (McVey) L. BA in English, Cath. U. Am., 1975, MA in Theology, 1981; MA in English, U. Ill., 1977; PhD in English, Indiana U. of Pa., 1997. Pastoral intern Cath. Diocese Richmond, Va., 1977-81, pastor Va., 1981-88; from asst. prof. to Chancellors commonwealth prof. English Thomas Nelson C.C., Hampton, Va., 1989—2005, Chancellors commonwealth prof. English, 2005—, head English dept., 2000—. Chmn. Cath. Comm., Richmond, 1981-87, Rescuing Reading Project, Thomas Nelson C.C., 2005—; pres. Writing Program Assocs., Norfolk, 1991-93; vis. prof. Coll. William & Mary, 1999-2000, Old Dominion U., 2003-04 Author: Children's Catechumenate, 1988, 1997, AIDS and American Apocalypticism, 2005; prodr., dir. (video) Voyagers to a New World, 1985, writer, prodr. (theater performance) Our Kind, 1977; editor: Harrington Gay Men's Fiction Quar., 2000—. Sec. Lesbian and Gay Pride Coalition, Norfolk, Va., 1989-93, pres., 1993-94; mem. Virginians for Justice, Richmond, 1990—; bd. mem., adv. coun. Tidewater AIDS Taskforce, Norfolk, 1994—. Mem. MLA, Nat. Coun. Tchrs. English, Assn. Tchrs. Tech. Writing, Modern Lang. Assn./Gay Caucus Avocations: travel, cooking, gardening, music. Office: Thomas Nelson CC PO Box 9407 Hampton VA 23670-0407 Office Phone: 757-825-3663. Business E-Mail: longt@tncc.edu.

LONGAKER, MICHAEL T., plastic surgeon, educator; BS, Mich. State U.; MD, Harvard Med. Sch.; MBA, U. Calif.-Berkeley/Columbia U., 2003. Resident in surgery U. Calif., San Francisco, post-doctoral rsch. fellow in fetal treatment and radiology; resident in plastic surgery NYU; craniofacial fellow UCLA; John Marquis Converse prof. plastic surgery NYU Sch. Medicine Inst. Reconstructive Plastic Surgery, dir. surg. basic sci. and plastic surgery rsch.; dir. children's surg. rsch. Stanford U. Sch. Medicine, 2000—, Deane P. and Louise Mitchell prof., 2003—, dep. dir. Inst. Stem Cell Biology and Regenerative Medicine. Recipient Dr. Bernd Spiessl award, Am. Soc. Maxillofacial Surgeons, Maxillofacial Found., 1999. Mem.: Inst. Medicine, Am. Soc. Clin. Investigation, Am. Surg. Assn., Soc. U. Surgeons (past pres.). Office: PRSL Bldg MC 5148 257 Campus Dr Stanford CA 94305 Office Phone: 650-736-1707. Office Fax: 650-736-1705. E-mail: longaker@stanford.edu.

LONGFIELD, WILLIAM HERMAN, retired health products executive; b. Chgo., Aug. 8, 1938; s. William A. and Elizabeth (Beringer) L.; m. Nancy Shofstall, June 10, 1961; children: William, Scott. BS, Drake U., 1960; grad. bus. mgmt. program, Northwestern U., 1972. Pres. Convertors divsn. Am. Hosp. Supply, Evanston, Ill., 1961-82; exec. v.p., dir. Lifemark, Inc., Houston, 1982-83; pres., CEO Cambridge Group, Inc., Dallas, 1983-89; chmn., CEO C.R. Bard, Inc., Murray Hill, NJ, 1989—2003, also bd. dirs.; ret., 2003. Bd. dirs. Atlantic Health Sys., Manor Care, Inc., Toledo, West Pharm. Svcs., Pa., Horizon Health Corp., Dallas; bd. dirs. Internat. Non-Wovens Assn., N.Y.C., 1975-82; chmn. AdvaMed; bd. dirs. Applera., Applied Biosystems, 2008-, C.R. Bard, Inc. Chmn., bd. dirs. Deerfield Youth Orgn., 1975-80. Recipient Pres.' award Nat. Nurse Cons. Assn., 1980. Mem. Baltrusol Golf Club, Metedeconk Country Club, Hamilton Farm Golf Club, Bull Bay Golf Club. Republican. Presbyterian. Avocations: golf, tennis. Office: Applied Biosystems Inc Bd Directors 850 Lincoln Centre Dr Foster City CA 94404 Office Phone: 650-638-5800. Office Fax: 650-638-5998. E-mail: wlongfield@applera.com. *

LONGNECKER, DAVID EUGENE, anesthesiologist, educator; b. Kendallville, Ind., 1939; MD, Ind. U., 1964, MA in Anesthesiology, 1968. Diplomate Am. Bd. Anesthesiology. Intern Blodgett Meml. Hosp., Grand Rapids, Mich., 1964—65; resident in anesthesiology U. Ind., 1965—69; asst. prof. dept. anesthesiology U. Mo., 1970—73; assoc. prof. dept. anesthesiology U. Va., Charlottesville, 1974—78, prof., 1978—88; Robert D. Dripps prof., chmn. dept. anesthesia U. Pa., Phila., 1999—2002, sr. v.p., corp. chief med. officer, 2002—04, Robert D. Dripps prof. anesthesia emeritus, 2005—; dir. Assn. Am. Med. Coll., 2005—. With USPHS, 1968—70. Mem.: Inst. Medicine, Am. Soc. Anesthesiologists. Office: AAMC 2450 N St NW Washington DC 20037-1127 Office Phone: 202-862-6113. Business E-Mail: dlongnecker@aamc.org.

LONGO, ANTONIO, surgeon; b. Tusa, Sicily, Mar. 4, 1953; Degree in Medicine & Surgery, U. Palermo, Italy, 1978, degree in Gen. Surgery, 1984. Resident U. Palermo, 1979; pvt. practice, 2000—. Fellow: SIUCP. Home: Via Maqueda 8 Palermo 90134 Italy Business E-Mail: alongo@neomedia.it.

LONGO, DAN LOUIS, internist, researcher, oncologist; b. St. Louis, Apr. 25, 1949; s. Dominic L. and Alene V. (Bratcher) L.; m. Nancy Kay Schiffman, May 29, 1971; children: Jennifer Alene, Adam Daniel, Paul Anthony. AB, Washington U., St. Louis, 1970; MD cum laude, U. Mo., 1975. Diplomate Am. Bd. Internal Medicine, Am. Bd. Oncology, Nat. Bd. Med. Examiners. Resident in medicine Peter Bent Brigham Hosp., Boston, 1975-77; fellow in oncology Nat. Cancer Inst., Bethesda, Md., 1977-78; postdoctoral fellow in immunology Nat. Inst. Allergy and Infectious Diseases, Bethesda, 1978-80; sr. investigator Medicine Br. Nat. Cancer Inst., Bethesda, 1980—85; assoc. dir. Biolog. Response Modifiers Program Nat. Cancer Inst., Frederick, Md., 1985-95; sci. dir. Nat. Inst. on Aging, Balt., 1995—2010; dep. editor New England Jour. Medicine, 2010—. Mem. editl. bd. Critical Reviews in Oncology/Hematology; editor: Clin. Oncology Alert, 1985—2000, Cancer Chemotherapy and Biol. Response Modifiers Annual, 1987—2000, Cancer Chemotherapy and Biotherapy, 1994—, Harrison's Principles of Internal Medicine, 1995—, Hot Topics on Oncology, 2007—10, Harrison Manual of Oncology, 2008—; asst. editor Am. Jour. Clin. Nutrition, 1981—91, assoc. editor Jour. Nat. Cancer Inst., Clin. Cancer Rsch., Jour. Immunology, Clin. Immunology, Blood, Jour. Gerontology, Med. Sci.; contbr. chpts. to textbooks, over 750 articles to profl. jours.; editor: Harrison's Hematology and Oncology, Harrison's Gastroenterology and Hepatology. Rear adm. USPHS, 1977—2006. Recipient Harvard Book award, 1965, Young Physician award U. Mo. Alumni Assn., Citation of Merit, 1997, Tovi Comet-Walerstein award Bar-Ilan Univ., Israel, 1992. USPHS Commendation medal, 1987, Outstanding Svc. medal, 1992 and 2005, NIH Merit award, 1993, NIH Dir. award 1996, 2010. Master: ACP (MKSAP IX Oncology Subsplty. Com. 1989—91, MKSAP 12 1999—2001, MKSAP 13 2002—04); fellow: AAAS, Molecular Medicine Soc.; mem.: Assn. Am. Physicians, Am. Soc. Blood and Marrow Transplantation, Am. Soc. Clin. Pharm. and Theraputics, Am. Soc. Cell Bio., Am. Geriatrics Soc., Internat. Cytokine Soc., Soc. Leukocyte Bio., N.Y. Acad. Scis., Assn. Am. Physicians, Clin. Immunology Soc. (councilor 1987—90), Am. Soc. Cell Biology, Am. Soc. Clin. Investigation, Am. Soc. Hematology (subcom. on Neoplasia 1989—91, chmn. 1990, program com. 1994, chmn., Hematology in Aging Com. 2008—), Am. Assn. Cancer Rsch. (program com. 1986), Am. Assn. Immunologists, Am. Soc. Clin. Oncology (edn. com. 1992—94), Am. Soc. Clin. Nutrition (award com. 1989—91, program com. 1990), Am. Inst. Nutrition, Am. Soc. Microbiology, Am. Fedn. Clin. Rsch., Alpha Omega Alpha, Phi Kappa Phi, Sigma Xi. Achievements include 11 patents in field. Office: New England Jour Medicine 10 Shattuck St Boston MA 02115 Home Phone: 301-942-7176; Office Phone: 617-487-6573. Business E-Mail: dlongo@nejm.org.

LONGO, GERNON MATTHEW, surgeon; b. Omaha, Aug. 12, 1970; BA, Coll. Holy Cross, 1992; MD, U. Nebr., 1996. Chief, sect. vascular surgery U. Nebr. Med. Ctr., 2005—. Office: University Nebr 985182 Nebraska Med Ctr Omaha NE 68198-5182 Office Fax: 402-559-8985. Business E-Mail: glongo@unmc.edu.

LONGO, LAWRENCE DANIEL, physiologist, obstetrician, gynecologist, educator; b. LA, Oct. 11, 1926; s. Frank Albert and Florine Azelia (Hall) L.; m. Betty Jeanne Mundall, Sept. 9, 1948; children: April Celeste, Lawrence Anthony, Elisabeth Lynn, Camilla Giselle. BA, Pacific Union Coll., 1949; MD, Coll. Med. Evangelists, Loma Linda, Calif., 1954. Diplomate Am. Bd. Ob-Gyn. Intern L.A. County Gen. Hosp., 1954-55, resident in ob-gyn., 1955-58; asst. prof. ob-gyn UCLA, 1962-64; asst. prof. physiology and ob-gyn U. Pa., 1964-68; prof. physiology and ob-gyn Loma Linda U., 1968—; dir. ctr. for perinatal biology Loma Linda U. Sch. Medicine, 1974—, Bernard D. Briggs disting. physiology prof. Perinatal biology com. Nat. Inst. Child Health, NIH, 1973-77; co-chmn. reprodn. scientist devel. program NIH; NATO prof. Consiglio Nat. delle Rsch., Italian Govt. Editor: Respiratory Gas Exchange and Blood Flow in the Placenta, 1972, Fetal and Newborn Cardiovascular Physiology, 1978, Charles White and A Treatise on the Management of Pregnant and Lying-in Women, 1987; co-editor: Landmarks in Perinatology, 1975-76, Classics in Obstetrics Gynecology, 1993, Dearest G..., Yours W.O., William Osler's Letters from Egypt to Grace Revere Osler, 2003, William Osler's Man's Redemption of Man, 2003, Our Lords the Sick..., 2004; editor classic pages in ob-gyn. Am. Jour. Ob-Gyn.; contbr. articles to profl. jours. Served with AUS, 1945-47. Founder Frank A. and Florine A. Longo lectureship in faith, knowledge, and human values Pacific Union Coll., 1993. Fellow Royal Coll. Ob-Gyns., Am. Coll. Ob-Gyns.; mem. Am. Assn. History Medicine (coun.), Am. Osler Soc. (bd. govs., sec.-treas., pres.), Am. Physiol. Soc., Assn. Profs. Ob-Gyn., Perinatal Rsch. Soc., Soc. Gynecologic Investigation (past pres.), Neurosci. Soc., Royal Soc. Medicine. Adventist. Office: Loma Linda U Sch Medicine Ctr Perinatal Biology Loma Linda CA 92350-0001 Office Phone: 909-558-4325. Business E-Mail: llongo@llu.edu.

LONGO, MARIE CRISTIANA, research scientist; b. Adelaide, Australia, Sept. 28, 1974; d. Donato and Lynette Jean Longo; m. Ian Michael Roach. BA in Psychology with honors, U. Adelaide, 1993, PhD, 2001. Project officer rd. accident rsch. unit U. Adelaide, 1995; project officer safety and strategy sect. Transport SA, Adelaide, 1996—97; project officer clin. policy and rsch. Drug and Alcohol Svcs. South Australia, Adelaide, 2001—03, sr. rsch. officer amphetamine use disorders rsch. group, pharmacotherapies rsch. unit, 2003—08; project mgr. Queensland U., 2008—. Cons. Royal Adelaide Hosp. Designer Drug Academic Rsch. Group, 2003—, Vt. Alcohol Rsch. Ctr./Addiction Rsch. Inst., Burlington, Vt., 2002—. Contbr. articles to profl. jours., chapters to books. Lifeline tel. counselor Adelaide Ctrl. Mission, 2003; translator, interpreter Italian C. of C. and Industry, Adelaide, 1993; cultural com. Molinara Social and Sports Club, Adelaide, 1993—94. Recipient E.H. Ryan Prize for Italian, 1990, D.J. Symonds prize for lang. and math., 1990, Annie Montgomerie Martin prize for French, 1991, Alliance Française prize for French, 1991; scholar, Fed. Office of Rd. Safety, Canberra, Australia, 1998—2001; Postgraduate Travelling fellow for biomed. rsch., U. Adelaide, 1999, Rsch. grant, Transport SA, Adelaide, 2001. Avocations: reading, travel, music, movies, exercise. Office: University of Queensland School of Population Health Brisbane QLD 4072 Australia Business E-Mail: marie.longo@health.sa.gov.au.

LÖNNROTH, EMMA-CHRISTIN, dentist, researcher; b. Barkåkra, Skåne, Sweden, Feb. 22, 1947; d. Ingrid Pavlovna Lönroth; children: Peter Lennart Tuleby(dec.), David Daouda Diaw, Daniel Salim Diaw. DDS, U. Gothenburg, Sweden, 1981; MPH, Nordic Sch. Pub. Health, Gothenburg, 1996; Licentiate Engr., Luleå U. Tech., Sweden, 1996, PhD, Dr. Tech., Dr. Odontology, 1999. Dentist County Coun. Norrbotten, Jokkmokk, Sweden, 1981—91; asst. prof. ergonomics, human work sci. Luleå U. Tech., 1999—2002, assoc. prof. human work sci., 2002—07, rschr., 2005—; dentist pvt. clin., Norway, 2005—. Dir. internat. master program ergonomics Luleå U. Tech., 2000—02, dir. rsch. sch. in arena lifestyle, health and tech., 2003—05; editl. bd. mem. Internat. Jour. Occupl. Safety and Ergonomics, 2009—. Contbr. more than 30 articles to profl. jours. Grantee, Scandinavian Inst. Dental Materials, 1998, 1999, 2000, 2001. Mem.: Internat. Acad. Oral Medicine and Toxicology Sweden (assoc.). Achievements include research in dental restorative materials; med. gloves toxicity, irritation potential of deutal materials, work environment in dental clinics. Personal E-mail: dr.emmachristin@yahoo.se, dr.emmachristin@hotmail.com.

LONSDALE, HOWARD CHARLES, physician; b. Berlin, Sept. 24, 1933; s. Henry and Hilda M. Lonsdale; children: Lauren, Elizabeth, Henry, Geraldine. BA, Princeton U., 1955; MD, U. Ark., 1960. Chief Physician Ear Nose & Throat Clin., Calif., 1966—99; bd. dir. Village Gen. Hosp., Calif., 1971—74, Broadway Hosp., Calif., 1972—74, pres.; mem. Calif. Med. Soc., 1972, chairman Calif., 1970; staff Broadway Hosp., 1971. Pres. Comprehensive Health Planning assn., 1966—74; dir. World Martial Art Assn., 1997—2001. Pres. Valley'o Symphony, 1969—70. Capt. USAF, 1964—66. Recipient award, C of C Vallejo Calif., 1968, Lifetime Achievement award, Unified Martial Arts, 2001; named Man of the Yers's. Fellow: Am. Acad. Laryngology. Avocations: history, music, sports, reading.

LONSDALE, TOM, veterinarian, writer; b. Hargrave, Eng., Sept. 14, 1949; s. Thomas and Lilian Lonsdale; m. Jie Liu, Dec. 17, 2005; children: Luke Bentley, Thomas Robert, William John. B Vet. Medicine, U. London, 1972. Vet. pvt. practice, London, 1972—80, prin. Sydney, 1981—97; dir. Rivetco P/L, 1997—. Author: Raw Meaty Bones: Promote Health, Work Wonders: Feed your dog raw meaty bones. Mem.: Royal College Vet. Surgeons. Achievements include first to Cybernetic hypothesis of periodontal disease in mammalian carnivores. Avocations: veterinary reform, cricket, travel. Office: Rivetco P/L PO Box 6096 Windsor NSW 2756 Australia Home: PO Box 6096 2756 Windsor NSW Australia Office Phone: 61 2 4577 7061. Office Fax: 61245777019. Business E-Mail: tom@rawmeatybones.com.

LOO, JASMINE MAY YEE, psychology professor; b. Kuala Lumpur, Malaysia, Nov. 15, 1984; PhD in Psychology, 2011. Guest lectr. Queensland U. Tech., 2008—10; tutor, rsch. asst. U. Queensland, 2007—11; lectr. HELP U. Coll., 2011—. Recipient Rsch. Excellence award, U. Queensland, Tutor Excellence award. Avocations: yoga, cooking. Office: Level 8 Wisma HELP Jalan Dungun Dama Kuala Lumpur Wilayah Persekutuan 50490 Malaysia Personal E-mail: jlmy84@yahoo.com.

LOO, KEK KHEE, pediatrician, educator; b. Singapore, Dec. 9, 1968; BA, Johns Hopkins U., 1991; MD, U. Chgo. Pritzker Sch. Medicine, 1996. Assoc. prof. Geffen Sch. Medicine UCLA, 2001—, med. dir. intervention program, fellow program dir. devel. behavioral pediat., 2009—11. Recipient Career Devel. award, NIH. Fellow: Am. Acad. Pediat.; mem.: Western Soc. Pediatric Rsch., Soc. Rsch. Child Devel., Soc. Devel. and Behavioral Pediat. Avocations: hiking, running, reading. Office: 300 UCLA Med Plz Ste 3300 Los Angeles CA 90095 E-mail: kloo@mednet.ucla.edu.

LOO, MARCUS HSIEU-HONG, urologist, physician, educator; b. NYC, Aug. 12, 1955; s. David Wei and Patricia (Pai) L.; m. Donna C. Wingshee, Oct. 3, 1987; children: Christopher, Courtney. BSEE with distinction, Cornell U., 1977, MD, 1981. Diplomate Am. Bd. Urology. Attending urologist NY Hosp. Presbyn. Hosp., NYC, 1988—; clin. asst. prof. urology Cornell U. Med. Coll., NYC, 1994-2000, clin. assoc. prof. urology, 2000—05, clin. prof. urology, 2005—. Admissions com. Cornell U. Med. Coll.; mem. univ. coun. Cornell U.; mem. operating bd. Columbia Cornell Care, LLC.; cons. Chinatown Health Cilnic; clin. dir. Asian Am. Cancer Awareness Rsch. and Tng. grant. Author: The Prostate Cancer Source Book, 1998. Mem. Univ. Coun. Cornell U., 2002—, trustee, 2003—11, trustee emeritus, 2011—, presdl. councillor, 2011—. Fellow: ACS; mem.: IEEE, AMA, Fedn. Chinese Am. and Chinese Can. Med. Socs. (bd. dirs., v.p.), Chinese Am. Med. Soc. (pres., bd. dirs. 1990—97), Soc. Internat. d'Urologie, Am. Urological Assn., Am. Assn. Clin. Urologists, Cornell U. Med. Coll. Alumni Assn. (bd. dirs.), Tau Beta Pi, Phi Tau Phi, Eta Kappa Nu. Office: 449 E 68th St New York NY 10021-4941 Office Phone: 212-925-8388.

LOOK, JANET K., psychologist; b. Bklyn., Mar. 11, 1944; d. Harry and Isabelle (Chernoff) Kaplan; m. Willian Marel; children from previous marriage: Howard, Erika(dec.). AB, NYU, 1964; EdM, Rutgers U., 1967, EdD, 1976. Lic. psychologist. Asst. examiner Ednl. Testing Svc., Princeton, NJ, 1964-66; instr. Rutgers U., New Brunswick, NJ, 1968-69; psychologist Seattle Pub. Schs., 1991—2006; pvt. practice Seattle, 1993—. Lectr. U. Conn., Waterbury, 1973-91; appearances on various TV and radio shows including the Today Show; interviews include Litchfield County Times, 1987, Waterbury Rep.-Am., 1983-87, Manchester Jour. Inquirer, 1986, Danbury News-Times, 1985, NW Cable News, 2010; presenter So. Conn. State U., New Haven, 1989, Nation's Concern and Its Response, U. Wis., Milw., 1991, Nat. Assn. Sch. Psychologists, Dallas, 1991, Seattle, 1994, Divorce Issues Inst. Author: (with others) The Troubled Adolescent, 1991; contbr. articles to newspapers, including N.Y. Times, MSNBC. With Examing Bd. Psychologists, Wash., 2010. Mem. APA (presenter, 1991), Wash. State Psychol. Assn. (presenter, 1995, 2007), Wash. State Assn. Sch. Psychologists (area rep., bd. dirs. 1991-93). Avocations: sailing, fishing, hiking, bicycling, travel, cooking. Office: 3626 NE 45th St 301 Seattle WA 98105

LOOMIS, REBECCA C., psychologist; b. New London, Conn., Nov. 9, 1959; d. Aubrey Kingsley and Marillyn Louise (Dirks) Loomis; m. DeWitt Montgomery Smith, Nov. 24, 1984 (div. Sept. 1997); children: Adrienne Kingsley Smith, Walker Loomis Smith; m. Jack G. Gental, July 9, 2005; stepchildren: Alexander Gentul, Robert Gentul. BA in Sociology and Polit. Sci., Vanderbilt U., 1981; MEd, U. Houston, 1990, PhD in Counseling Psychology, 2004. Lic. psychologist NY, NJ. Group rep. Home Life Ins., Houston, 1981—83; sr. account exec. CNA Ins. Co., Houston, 1983—87; rsch. asst. dept. ednl. psychology U. Houston, 1988—90, 1991—93, tchg. asst., 1993, rsch. asst. Clearwater, Tex., 1993; acad. advisor Montclair (N.J.) State U., 2001—02; psychology intern Assn. Help of Retarded Children, NYC, 2002—03; prin. investigator St. Luke's-Roosevelt Hosp. Manhattan Ctr. for Pain Mgmt., 1999—2004; clinician Assn. for Help of Retarded Children, NYC, 2003—07; pvt. practice Morristown, NJ. Group facilitator children div. parents, counselor Houston Child Guidance, 1990; counselor learning support svcs. U. Houston, 1990, counselor counseling and testing svcs., 1994—95; facilitator mentorship program Wildwood Elem. Sch., Mountain Lakes, NJ, 1996; pvt. practise, Morristown, NJ. Contbr. articles to various profl. jours. Hospice aid Casa de Ninos Hospice, Houston, 1986—87; vol. Houston Area Women's Ctr., 1992—93, 1994—95; cmty. aid Mountain Lakes, 1999—2000; vol. organizer grief workshop for September 11, 2001 attacks Cmty. Ch. Mem.: APA, N.J. Psychol. Assn. Democrat. Home and Office: 249 Morris Ave Mountain Lakes NJ 07046 Address: 44 Elm St Morristown NJ 07960 Personal E-mail: beckyloomis@earthlink.net.

LOOMIS, SALORA DALE, psychiatrist, educator; b. Peru, Ind., Oct. 21, 1930; s. S. Dale Sr. and Rhea Pearl (Davis) L.; m. Carol Marie Davis, Jan 3, 1959; children: Stephen Dale, Patricia Marie Black. AB in Zoology, Ind. U., 1953, MS in Human Anatomy, 1955, MD, 1958. Diplomate Am. Bd. Psychiatry and Neurology. Intern Cook County Hosp., Chgo., 1958-59; resident in psychiatry Logansport (Ind.) State Hosp., 1959-60, Ill. State Psychiat. Inst., Chgo., 1960-62; staff psychiatrist Katharine Wright Psychiat. Clinic, Chgo., 1962-65, dir., 1965-92. Cons. Ill. Youth Commn. 1962-64; instr. psychiatry Northwestern U. Med. Sch., Chgo., 1962-64, assoc. 1964-67; asst. dir. Northwestern U. Psychiat. Clinics, Chgo., 1963-65; attending psychiatrist St. Joseph Hosp., Chgo., 1964—; lectr. psychiatry and neurology Loyola U. Med. Sch. Chgo., 1964-65, assoc. 1965, asst. prof. 1965-73, lectr. 1980-89, clin. assoc. prof., 1989-2002, clin. prof., 2002—; psychiat. cons. Ill. Dept. Pub. Health, 1967-92; sr. attending psychiatrist, chmn. dept. psychiatry Ill. Masonic Med. Ctr., Chgo. 1970-92, chmn. emeritus, 1992—; clin. assoc. prof. psychiatry U. Ill. Coll. Medicine, Chgo., 1973—. Mem. U. Club Chgo., 1970—. Fellow Am. Coll. Psychiatrists (emeritus), Am. Psychiat. Assn. (disting. life), Acad. Psychosomatic Medicine; mem. AMA, Ill. State Med. Soc. (chmn. council on mental health and addiction 1974-75, chmn. joint peer rev. com. 1975-76), Ill. Psychiat. Soc. (chmn. ethics com. 1974-75, chmn. peer rev. com. 1976-78), Chgo. Med. Socs, Chgo. Acad. Medicine. Avocations: opera, classical music. Office Phone: 312-343-7313. Personal E-mail: sdaleloomis@mac.com.

LOONEY, CLAUDIA ARLENE, health facility administrator; b. Fullerton, Calif., June 13, 1946; d. Donald F. and Mildred B. Schneider; m. James K. Looney, Oct. 8, 1967; 1 child, Christopher K. BA, Calif. State U., 1969. Dir. youth YWCA No. Orange County, Fullerton, Calif., 1967-70; dir. dist. Camp Fire Girls, San Francisco, 1971-73, asst. exec. dir. LA, 1973-77; asst. dir. cmty. resources Childrens Hosp., LA, 1977-80; dir. cmty. devel. Orthopaedic Hosp., LA, 1980-82; sr. v.p. Saddleback Meml. Found./Saddleback Meml. Med. Ctr., Laguna Hills, Calif., 1982-92; v.p. planning and advancement Calif. Inst. Arts, Santa Clarita, Calif., 1992-96; pres. Northwestern Meml. Found., Chgo., 1996-99; sr. v.p. Childrens Hosp., LA, 1999—. Instr. U. Calif., Irvine, Univ. Irvine; mem. steering com. U. Irvine. Steering com. United Way, LA, 1984-86, bd. mem. Woodmark Group, 2004-, chair, 2010-, sec., 2005-2008, chair-elect, 2008- Recipient Orange County Woman of Achievement award, YWCA, 2004. Fellow Assn. Healthcare Philanthropy (nat. chair-elect, chmn. program Nat. Edn. Conf. 1986, regional dir. 1985-89, 98, fin. com. 1988—, pres., com. chn. 1987—, Give To Life com. chmn. 1987-91, mid-west regional conf. chmn. 1998, Orange County Fund Raiser of Yr. 1992, LA County Fund Raiser of Yr. 1996); mem. Am. Assn. Fundraising Profls. 1996, Woodmark Group (bd. mem. 2005-, vice chair 2008-, chair, 2010) Nat. Soc. Fund Raising Execs. Found. (cert., vice chmn. 1985-90, chair 1993-96, mem. Chgo. conf. com. 1997, 98), So. Calif. Assn. Hosp. Devel. (past pres., bd. dirs.), Profl. Ptnrs. (chmn. 1986, instr. 1988—), Philanthropic Ednl. Orgn. (past pres.), Assn. for Healthcare Profls. (regional conf. co-chmn. 2003), Assn. Fundraising Profls. (mem. internat. ethics com. 2003—), Orange County Women of Achievement, Regency Club Los Angeles (bd. mem. 2008-). Avocations: swimming, sailing, photography. Office: Children's Hosp LA 4650 Sunset Blvd Ste 29 Los Angeles CA 90027

LOPES, LUIZ AUGUSTO FREIRE, gynecologist; b. Recife, PE, Brazil, Mar. 28, 1947; PhD, Faculdade Ciencias Medicas Pernambuco, 1972; MD, Escola Paulista de Medicina, 2006. Physician gynecology oncology Hosp. Servidor Publico Estadual Estado de Sao Paulo, 1996—2010; physician gynecology U. Fed. da Grande Dourados, 2010—, adj. prof., 2010. Avocations: hunting, fishing, travel. Home: Rua Franca 385 Dourados 79826-420 Brazil Personal E-mail: luizfreire1947@yahoo.com.br.

LOPES, NEUZA, cardiologist, educator; b. Pinheiro, Maranhao, Brazil, Mar. 13, 1966; d. Jose Augusto and Iolanda Lopes. MD, Med. Sch. U. Marahao, Sao Luis, 1991; PhD, Med. Sch. U. Sao Paulo, Brazil, 1998. Diplomate Brazilian Bd. Cardiovascular, 1993, Brazilian Bd. Internal Medicine, 1993. Postdoc. rschr. Ohio State U., 1999—2000, Duke U., 2000—02; asst. prof., medicine Heart Inst. Inc. Divsn. Cardiology U. Sao Paulo, 2002; assoc. prof., cardiology Med. Sch. U. Sao Paulo, 2008—. Cons. Gerson Lehrman Group Coun., Austin, Tex., 2008—. Contbr. scientific papers. Home: Rua Alves Guimaraes 733 Apt 72 Sao Paulo 5403000 Brazil Office: Inst Coracao FMUSP Rua Dr Eneas Carvalho Aguiar 44 54030-00 Sao Paulo Brazil Office Fax: 5511-30695188. Personal E-mail: neuzalopes@hotmail.com. Business E-Mail: neuza.lopes@incor.usp.br.

LOPES, THUCYDIDES RODRIGUES, plastic surgeon; b. Lajeado, Rio Grande do Sul, Brazil, Nov. 11, 1970; s. Marco Antonio Rodrigues and Beatriz Scherer Lopes. MD, Cath. U. Pelotas, Pelotas, Rio Grande do Sul, 1999; Gen. Surgery, U. do Extremo Sul Catarinense, Santa Catarina, Brazil, 2002; Visceral Surgery, U. Fed. de Santa Catarina, Florianopolis, Brazil, 2004; Plastic, Reconstructive & Asthetic Surgery, Hand Surgery, Joseph Fourier U., Grenoble, France, 2007; Degree in Microsurgery, U. Claude Bernard Lyon I, France, 2007. Lic. dr. Rio Grande do Sul, 1999. Gen. physician Brasilian Army, Alegrete, Brazil, 1999—2000; med. resident gen. surgery St. Joseph Hosp., Criciuma, Brazil, 2000—02; med. resident visceral surgery U. Santa Catarina's Hosp., Florianopolis, Brazil, 2003—04; emergency physician Hosp. Nossa Senhora da Conceiçao, Urussanga, Brazil, 2001—04, Hosp. Azambuja, Brusque, Brazil, 2003—04; med. resident plastic & recontructive surgery, hand surgery CHU, Grenoble, France, 2004—07. Author: (memoire) Latissimus Dorsi Flap - Breast Reconstruction: Technical Aspects, Free Gracilis Flap Conclusion Microsurgery Formation, (book) Conclusion of Simus Donsi Fisp Prothesis in Breast Truction: Technical From CHU-Grenoble; contbr. articles to profl. jours. Lt. Healthcare, 2000, 13 Regiment Mechanized Engring., Alegrete, Brazil. Peace And Freedom. Roman Catholic. Achievements include invention of modified Thomas's local cutaneous fat flap technique; breast reconstruction. Avocations: bicycling, skiing, volleyball, windsurfing, running. Office: Avenida Carlos Gones 1610 CJ 304 Porto-Alegro RS Rio Grande Sol CEP 92220 220 Brazil Personal E-mail: thucy99@yahoo.com.

LOPEZ, CAROLYN CATHERINE, physician; b. Chgo., Oct. 13, 1951; d. Joseph Compean and Angela (Silva) L. BS, Loyola U., Chgo., 1973; MD, U. Ill., 1978. Diplomate Am. Bd. Family Practice. Intern, resident Rush/Christ Hosp., Chgo., 1978-81; med. dir. Wholistic Health Ctr., Oak Lawn, Ill., 1981-82; clin. dir. Anchor HMO, Oak Brook, Ill., 1982-84, assoc. med. dir., 1984-87; med. dir. Chgo. Pk. Dist., 1987-91; v.p. Rush Access HMO, Chgo., 1992-93; asst. dean Rush Med. Coll., 1990-93; med. dir. Rush Access HMO, Chgo., 1991-93, v.p., 1992-93; v.p. for profl. affairs Rush Anchor HMO, 1993; sr. v.p. and chief med. officer Rush-Prudential Health Plans, 1993-95; chair dept. family practice Cook County Hosp., 1996—2007; med. dir. North Health Svc. Corp., 2009—. Pres. Inst. Medicine, Chgo., 2006—; interim co-chief Cook County Bur. Health, 2006. Mem. Chgo. Bd. Health, 2004—; bd. govs. Inst. Medicine, Chgo., 2003—. Primary Care Policy fellow USPHS, 1993. Fellow: Inst. Medicine Chgo. (bd. govs. 2003—, pres. 2006—, 2006—); mem.: AMA, Am. Med. Women's Assn., Ill. Acad. Family Physicians (bd. dirs. 1987—89, spkr. 1990—91, bd. chair 1990—91, pres.-elect 1991—92, pres. 1992—93), Am. Acad. Family Physicians (alt. del. 1992—95, del. 1996—99, vice-spkr. 1999—2002, spkr. 2002—04). Roman Catholic. Avocations: swimming, cooking. Office: Cook County Hosp Dept Family Practice 1900 W Polk St Chicago IL 60612-3736 *

LÓPEZ, JOSÉ M., ophthalmologist; b. Santiago, Chile, Jan. 3, 1967; MD, Pontificia U. Católica Chile, 1992; degree in Ophthalmology, U. Chile, 1995. Chief Vitreo retinal unit Pontificia U. Católica Chile, 1999—2010, asst. prof., 2001—08, assoc. prof., 2008—10; staff mem. Fundación Oftalmológica Los Andes, 2010. Mem.: Chilean Soc. Opothalmology, Am. Acad. Ophthalmology. Avocations: reading, tennis. Office: Av Las Hualtatas 5951 Vitacura Santiago Metropolitan Region 0000 Chile Office Fax: (56-2)371-8934. Business E-Mail: jmlopez@manquehue.net.

LOPEZ, MARIANO BELZA, internist, cardiologist; b. Mandaluyong City, Metro Manila, Philippines, Feb. 21, 1956; s. Felix Sarmiento and Adela Belza Lopez; m. Josephine Alcantara Lopez, Dec. 12, 1981; children: Marian Joy, Marian Jasmine, Marian Johanna. BS in Zoology magna cum laude, U. Philippines, Quezon City, 1976; MD, U. Philippines, Manila, 1980. Clin. asst. prof. Coll. Medicine U. Philippines, Manila, 1987—97, clin. assoc. prof. Coll. Medicine, 1997—; chmn. dept. internal medicine Rizal Med. Ctr., Pasig City, Philippines, 1988—, med. specialist III, 1998—; mgr. and scientist II med. affairs div. United Laboratories, Inc., Mandaluyong City, 1993—2000; head sect. cardiology Victor R. Potenciano Med. Ctr., Mandaluyong City, Philippines, 1993—; med. dir. Therapharma, Inc., San Juan, Philippines, 2001—. Founder and med. adviser Love Your Heart Found., Inc., Pasig City, 1990—. Recipient Insular Life Leadership award, Lourdes Sch. Mandaluyong, 1972, Mosby Book award, U. Philippines Coll. Medicine, 1977; named Most Outstanding Alumnus in field of medicine, Lourdes Sch. Mandaluyong, 1989; named one of Top Ten in Academic Excellence, U. Philippines Coll. Medicine, 1976—80; Bailon Dela Rama Scholarship grantee, 1976—77. Fellow: Philippine Coll. Pharm. Medicine (sec. 2006—07), Philippine Soc. Exptl. and Clin. Pharmacology, Am. Coll. Cardiology, Philippine Soc. Echocardiography (pres. 2008—), Philippine Coll. Physicians (regent PCP bd. mem. 2008, Disting. fellow 2000), Philippine Coll. Cardiology (Francisco F. Tangco Young Investigator award 1986, 1987); mem.: Philippine Heart Assn. (pres. 2005—06, Cathay Rsch. award 1984, Francisco F. Tangco Cardiology fellow 1984—85), Philippine Med. Assn. (vice chmn. commn. on continuing med. edn. 1994—98, Most Outstanding Resident/Fellow in Cardiology 1985, ABBOTT Rsch. award 1987, Raul J. Rivas Meml. award for rsch. 1988, Dr. Hermogenes A. Santos Meml. award for continuing med. edn. 1994, first hon. mention), Pasig Pateros Taguig Med. Soc. (pres. 1991—92), U. Philippines Coll. Medicine Class 1980 Alumni (pres. 1990—). Office: Therapharma Inc 3F Bonaventure Plaza Ortigas Ave Greenhills San Juan Manila 1500 Philippines Home: 7 Tulip St Greenwoods Exec Village 1900 Rizal Calabarzon Philippines Office Fax: 632-858-1238. Business E-Mail: mblopez@unilab.com.ph.

LOPEZ, RALPH IVAN, pediatrics educator; b. San Juan, Jan. 3, 1942; s. Ralph and Aida (Miranda) L.; m. Paula, July 30, 1964; 1 child, Abigail AB cum laude, Fordham Coll., 1963; MD, NYU, 1967.

Intern pediatrics NYU Bellevue Hosp., NYC, 1967-68, resident pediatrics, 1968-69, Boston Children's Hosp., Harvard Med. Ctr., 1969-70; asst. prof. pediatrics N.Y. Hosp., NYC, 1973-79, assoc. prof. pediatrics, 1979-83, clin. assoc. prof. pediatrics, 1983—2007; clin. prof. pediat. Weill Med. Coll., Cornell U., 2007—. Cons. physician Dalton Sch., NYC, 1973-86, Nightingale Bamford, NYC, 1986-90. Editor: Adolescent Medicine Topics, 1976, 2d edit. 1980; author: The Teen Health Book, 2002; contbr. articles to profl. jours. Bd. dirs. Louis August Jones Found., Rhinebeck, NJ, 1973-91, chmn. bd. dirs., 1990—; bd. dirs. Covenant House, NYC, 1990-92; chmn. Ind. Doctors of NY; nominating com. Girl Scouts U.S., NYC, 1991. Lt. comdr. USNR, 1971-73 Mem. Phi Beta Kappa. Office: 418 E 71st St New York NY 10021-4894 Office Phone: 212-772-8989.

LOPEZ, SUSAN NORDSTROM, hospital administrator; BA in Bus. Adminstrn., U. Notre Dame; MA in Hosp. and Health Adminstrn., U. Iowa. With Advocate Ill. Masonic Med. Ctr., 1982—90, pres., CEO, 2003—, St. Anthony Med. Ctr., Crown Point, Ind.; with Grant Med. Ctr., Edgewater Med. Ctr., West Suburban Hosp. and Med. Ctr. Office: Advocate Illinois Masonic Medical Center 836 W Wellington Ave Chicago IL 60657 Office Phone: 773-975-1600.

LOPEZ, VIOLETA, nursing educator; b. Philippines, Dec. 11, 1947; PhD, U. Sydney, 1997. Prof. Chinese U. Hong Kong, 1997—2005; head sch. nursing Australian Cath. U., 2005—08; prof. Australian Nat. U., 2009—. Dir. rsch. ctr. nursing and midwifery practice ACT Health, 2008—; vis. prof. Hubei Med. U., China, 2006—. Recipient Internat. Rsch. Excellence award, Beta Nu Delta; Edn. Program grant, Australian Govt. Dept. Fgn. Affairs and Trade, Rsch. grant, Invacare. Fellow: Royal Coll. Nursing Australia; mem.: Cancer Nurses Soc. Australia. Avocations: opera, tennis, travel. Office: RCNMP TCH Bldg 6 Level 3 Yamba d Garran 2605 Australia Office Fax: 612 62442375. Business E-Mail: violeta.lopez@anu.edu.au.

LÓPEZ-ARCAS, JOSÉ M., oral surgeon; Degree in Medicine, Autónoma de Madrid, 2003; degree in Oral and Maxillofacial Surgery, Hosp. La Paz, Madrid, 2009. Faculty oral and maxillofacial surgery dept. Ruber Internat. Hosp., 2009—, Hosp. Sanitas Sanchinarro, 2009. Grant, European Union, Spanish Soc. Oral and Maxillofacial Surgery, 2008—09. Fellow: Spanish Soc. Oral and Maxillofacial Surgery, European Assn. Craniomaxillofacial Surgery, Internat. Assn. Oral Maxillofacial Surgeons. Avocations: sports, music. Office: Bravo Murillo 151 4° C Madrid 28020 Spain Office Fax: 34 91 4490896. E-mail: odinson32@gmail.com.

LOPEZ-BARCENA, JOAQUIN, physician, educator; b. Mex., Apr. 6, 1947; MD, U. Nacional Autónoma Méx., 1971. Cert. internal medicine specialist U. Nacional Autónoma Méx., 1976. Prof. medicine U. Nacional Autónoma Méx., Faculty Medicine, 1976, gen. sec., 2003—. Fellow: ACP; mem.: ASMEE, Colegio De Medicina Interna De Mex. Avocations: reading, exercise, travel. Office: Magdalena 434 Mexico City 03100 Mexico Business E-Mail: joaloh@unam.mx

LOPEZ-JARAMILLO, PATRICIO, physician, educator, researcher; b. Quito, Pichincha, Ecuador, Feb. 10, 1953; s. Jose and Fanny (Jaramillo) Lopez; m. Marisol Lopez Pico, Nov. 21, 1991; children: Jose Patricio, Maria Cristina. BS in Biology, Colegio Benalcazar, Quito, 1971; MD, Ctrl. U., Quito, 1978; MS, São Paulo U., 1983, PhD, 1987. Specialist endocrinology Colegio Medicode Pichincha, Quito, 1984, specialist in clinical hypertension Guadalajara U., Mexico, 2004. Prof. Ctrl. U., Quito, 1978—99; rsch. dir. Health Ministry, Quito, 1994—98; sr. rschr. Wellcome Labs., London, 1998—99; prof. U. Indsl. Santander, Bucaramanga, Colombia, 2000—03; rsch dir. Cardiovascular Found., Bucaramanga, 2000—09; rsch. dir. Med. Sch., Santander U., Bucaramanga, 2005—, Found. Talmologica Santander, Clinica CarlosArdilla Lulle Foscal, 2010—. Postdoctoral fellow Hosp. Enfant Malade, Paris, 1988-89; dir. Nat. Inst. Rsch.-MSP, Quito, 1990-98; cons. Pan Am. Health Orgn., Quito, 1998—99; sci. dir. Colombian Inst. Biomed. Rsch., Bucaramanga, 1999—2003. Author: Biochemistry and Physiology of Vascular Endothelium, 1991 (Ctrl. U. award 1993), Pregnancy-Induced Hypertension: Pathophysiology and Prevention, 1992 (Enrique Garces award 1993), The L-Arginine-Nitric Oxide Pathway: From Discovery to Clinical Use, 1995 (Ciba award 1996). Pres. Nat. Coun. Micronutrients, Ministry Public Health, Quito, Ecuador, 1997—98. Recipient Kabi award Endocrinology Soc., Caracas, Venezuela, 1991, Simon Bolivar award Endocrinology Soc., 1993, Congress award Pharmacol. Soc., Montreal, Can., 1994, Gold medal and Honor Diploma, Met. Coun. and Mayor, Quito, 1997, XII Aventis award, Nat. Acad. Medicine, Bogota Colombia, 2001, Nat. award, Colombian Assn. Advance Scis., Bogota, 2006. Fellow Interam. Med. and Health Assn.; mem. AAAS (internat.), Pan Am. Endothelium Coll., Colombian Soc. Cardiology, Venezuelan Soc. Medicine, Ecuadorian Soc. Medicine. Avocations: soccer, volleyball, music, tennis, cooking. Office: Univ de Santander Lagos de Cacique Bucaramanga Colombia Home: Ruitoque Gold House 44 Bucaramanga Colombia Office Phone: 57 7 638600 ext. 2510. Business E-Mail: jplopezj@hotmail.com, investigaciones@foscal.com.co.

LOPEZ MORENO, JOSE LUIS, radiologist; b. Barcelona, Apr. 20, 1948; MD, U. Barcelona, 1973. Chief ICS, 1992—2011. Assoc. prof. U. Barcelona, 1995—2011. Mem.: ACRAM, SERAM, ECR, RSNA. Office: Feixa Llarga S/N Hospitalet De Llobregat 08907 Spain Business E-Mail: jllm@bellvitgehospital.cat.

LOPEZ-POUSA, ANTONIO, physician; b. Santiago, Apr. 10, 1954; MD, U. Santiago, 1976. Physian Hosp. Sant Pau, Barcelona, 1979—, clin. head, 2004—. Mem.: ASCO. Office: Mas Casanovas 90 Barcelona 08041 Spain Business E-Mail: alopezp@santpau.cat.

LÓPEZ-POUSA, SECUNDINO, neurologist, director; b. Santiago de Compostela, Spain, Jan. 31, 1948; PhD, U. Santiago, 1972. Neurologist U. Autónoma de Barcelona, 1976; dir., memory, assessment and investigation svc. Inst. d'Assistència Sanitària Girona, 1990—. Master: Royal Medicine Acad. Catalonia; mem.: Catalan Neurologist Acad., Spanish Neurologist Acad. Avocations: drawing, politics. Office: C/Dr Castany s/n Salt Girona 17190 Spain Office Fax: 0034972189017. Business E-Mail: uvamid@ias.scs.es.

LOPEZ-SANCHEZ, PEDRO, pharmacologist, educator; b. Mex. City, Oct. 18, 1965; MD, Nat. Poly. Inst., 1988, PhD, 1999. Rsch. prof. Nat. Poly. Inst., 1992—, ESM, PhD program coord., 2009—. Mem.: Mexican Soc. Physiol. Scis., Mexican Pharmacological Soc., Am. Physiol. Soc., Am. Soc. Pharmacology and Exptl. Therapeutics. Avocations: reading, music. Office: Plan de San Luis y Diaz Miron s/n Casco Mexico City 11340 Mexico Office Fax: 5255-57296300 ext 62745. Personal E-mail: pelosa651018@yahoo.com.

LOPEZ-VELEZ, ROGELIO, epidemiologist; b. Madrid, Dec. 9, 1956; MD, U. Autonoma Madrid, 1980; PhD, U. Alcalá Henares Madrid, 1992. Clin. fellow McGill U., Montreal, Canada, 1985—86; specialist internal medicine & infectious diseases St. Joseph Cath. Hosp., Monrovia, Liberia, 1987—88; head tropical medicine & clin. parasitology infectious diseases dept. Hosp. Ramon y Cajal, Madrid, 1989—. Assoc. prof. medicine U. Alcala de Henares, Madrid, 1998; expert adv. panel on internat. health regulation WHO, 2009, expert adv. panel on parasitic diseases, 09; mem. expert pannel for leishmaniasis Idsa & Astm, 2010. Recipient Honor award, CDC; grant, Fundación para la Investigación Biomedica del HRC, 2009. Mem.: EuroTravNet, ISTM (mem. migration health com.), GeoSentinel, Global Surveillance Network ISTM & CDC, TropNetEurop. Avocations: tennis, travel, skiing. Office: Carretera de Colmenar km 9 100 Madrid 28034 Spain Business E-Mail: rlopezvelez.hrc@salud.madrid.org.

LOPICCOLO, JOSEPH, psychologist, educator, author; b. LA, Sept. 13, 1943; s. Joseph E. and Adeline C. (Russo) Lo P.; m. Leslie Joan Matlen, June 20, 1964 (div. 1978); 1 child, Joseph Townsend; m. Cathryn Gail Pridal, Dec. 20, 1980; 1 child, Michael James. BA with highest honors, UCLA, 1965; MS, Yale U., 1968, PhD, 1969. Asst. prof. U. Oreg., Eugene, 1969-73; assoc. prof. U. Houston, 1973-74; prof. SUNY, Stony Brook, 1974-84, Tex. A&M U., College Station, 1984-87; prof. psychol. scis. U. Mo., Columbia, 1987—, prof. emeritus psychol. sci., 2010, chmn. dept., 1987-90. Vis. scholar Cambridge (Eng.) U., 1991. Author: Becoming Orgasmic, 1976, 2d edit., 1988, also book chpts., editor: Handbook of Sex Therapy, 1970; contbr. numerous articles to profl. jours. Woodrow Wilson Found. fellow; NIH rsch. grantee, 1973-84 Fellow Am. Psychol. Assn.; mem. Internat. Acad. Sex Rsch., Soc. for Sci. Study of Sex (pres. 1983-84, Alfred Kinsey Meml. Rsch. award), Soc. for Sex Therapy and Rsch. (Masters and Johnson Rsch. award 1997), Phi Beta Kappa, Sigma Xi. Office: Univ Mo Dept Psychol Scis 26 McAlester Hall Columbia MO 65211-2500 Office Phone: 573-882-7752. Business E-Mail: LoPiccoloJ@missouri.edu.

LOPRINZI, CHARLES LAWRENCE, oncologist, educator; b. Vancouver, Wash., Mar. 26, 1953; s. Philip George and Claire Elizabeth Loprinzi; m. Margie D. Dufour, Feb. 4, 1984; children: Caitlin Elizabeth, Philip Lawrence, Chelsea Elise. MD, Oreg. Health Sci. U., Portland, 1979. Physician, scientist Mayo Clinic, Rochester, Minn., 1985—, regis prof. brest cancer rsch. Co-dir. Mayo Cancer Ctr. Prevention & Ctrl. Program. Recipient Brinker award for Sci. Distinction, Susan G. Komen Found., 2002, Outstanding Svc. award, Cancer Care, 2003, Prof. Survivorship award, Susan G. Komen Breast Cancer Found., 2003, Clin. Rsch. award, Assn. of Cmty. Cancer Ctrs., 2005, Vasomotor Symptoms Rsch. award, North Am. Menopausal Soc. (NAMS), 2006. Mem.: North Ctrl. Cancer Treatment Group (dir., cancer control program 1987—). Office: Mayo Clinic 200 First St SW Rochester MN 55905 Business E-Mail: cloprinzi@mayo.edu. *

LOPUS, MANU, biologist; b. Kottayam, Kerala, India, May 25, 1970; s. George Lopus and Mary George. BSc in Chemistry, Botany, Zoology, M.G. U., Kerala, 1998, MSc in Zoology, 2000; PhD in Biotech., Indian Inst. Tech., Mumbai, 2007. Rsch. scholar Indian Inst. Tech., 2006; postdoctoral scholar U. Calif., Santa Barbara, 2006—. Reviewer Free Radical Biology & Medicine, Biologics: Target & Therapy, Cancer Letters. Vol. Nat. Svc. Scheme, Kottayam, Kerala, India, 1995, Group for Rural Activities, Mumbai, 2001—06; senate mem. Indian Inst. Tech., 1995, gen. sec., sch. biosci., 2004—05. Recipient Best Rsch. Scholar award, IIT Bombay, 2006. Fellow: Royal Microscopical Soc. (London), Ministry Human Resource Devel.; mem.: NY Acad. Scis. (assoc. editor biol. & biomed. reports), Am. Assn. Cancer Rsch. (assoc.), Assn. Scientists Indian Origin America (Jr. Scientist award), Am. Soc. Cell Biology. Avocations: tennis, drums, philosphy of science, popular articles. Office: Univ Calif 1203 Wilson Lab MCDB Life Sci Bldg Santa Barbara CA 93106-9610 Home Phone: 805-280-6223. Personal E-mail: lopus@sigmaxi.net. Business E-Mail: lopus@lifesci.ucsb.edu, manu.lopus@gmail.com.

LORCH, YAHLI DEBORAH, medical educator; b. LA; d. Netanel and Erika (Frost) Lorch; m. Roger Kornberg; children: Guy, Maya, Gil. BA, Hebrew U., 1978, PhD, 1983. Assoc. prof. Stanford U., 1985—. Contbr. articles to profl. jours. With Israel Def. Forces, 1973—75. Recipient Woman of Distinction award, Am. Friends Hebrew U., 2010. Office: Dept Structure Bio Stanford Med Sch Stanford CA 94305 Home Phone: 650-854-1935; Office Phone: 650-723-2707. Business E-Mail: lorch@stanford.edu.

LORD, CATHERINE E., psychology professor; b. Inglewood, Calif., Dec. 28, 1950; d. Earle Newton and Marjorie Wilson Lord; m. Frederick J. Morrison, May 5, 1973; children: Janina Lord Morrison, Anthony Hayden Morrison. BA, UCLA, 1971; PhD, Harvard U., 1976. Lic. clin. psychologist Mich., Ill., NC. Prof. pediat. U. Alta., Edmonton, Canada, 1989—91; clin. dir., Greensboro Tchg. Ctr. U. NC, Chapel Hill, 1989—93; clin. psychologist Glenrose Hosp., Edmonton, 1989—99; prof. psychiatry U. Chgo., 1993—2001; dir. U. Mich. Autism & Comm. Disorders Ctr., Ann Arbor, 2001—; prof. psychology & psychiatry U. Mich., Ann Arbor, 2001—11; interim dir. Asperger Inst. NYU Child Study Ctr., NYU, 2010—; dir. Inst. for Brain Devel. NY-Presbyterian Hosp., White Plains, 2011—. Author: (diagnostic instruments for autism) Autism Diagnostic Observation Schedule, Autism Diagnostic Interview; author: (chair) (nrc/nas report on autism intervention) Educating Children with Autism. Recipient Irving B. Harris Early Childhood Lecture award, 2004, Patricia Buehler Legacy award for Clinical Innovation, American Coll. Occupational Therapy, 2011; grantee, NIH, Dept. of Edn., Can. Med. Rsch. Coun., 1981—. Fellow: APA. Office: The Asperger Institute NYU Child Study Center 145 E 32nd St New York NY 10016 Office Phone: 212-652-1952. *

LORD, RICHARD S., chemist; b. Atlanta, Nov. 14, 1942; BS in Chemistry, Ga. State U., 1965; PhD in Chemistry, U. Tex., Austin, 1970. Chief sci. officer Metametrix Clin. Lab., 1989—. Clin. biochemistry edn. U. Bridgeport, 2010—. Office: 3425 Corporate Way Duluth GA 30096 Office Fax: 678-638-2941. Business E-Mail: rslord@metametrix.com.

LORD, ROGER JOHN, immunologist, biochemist, researcher; b. Mt. Isa, Queensland, Australia, Mar. 26, 1966; s. John Russell and Noela Mary (Roberts) L.; m. Jane Fiona Corlis, Sept. 19, 1992 (div. Aug. 2005). Assoc. Diploma in Applied Sci. with distinction, Queensland U. Tech., 1987, B in Applied Sci., 1992; PhD, Dokkyo U., Tokyo, 1996. Chartered biologist. Rsch. asst. Queensland Inst. Med. Rsch., Brisbane, 1986-92; rsch. officer U. Queensland, Brisbane, 1993-96; rsch. fellow U. Wales Coll. Medicine, Cardiff, 1997-2000; lectr., lab. head, disciple of surgery U. Tasmania, Hobart, Australia, 2000—05; pvt. practice, 2006; lectr. med. sci., lab head protein biochemistry rsch. Sch. Nursing and Midwifery, Australian Cath. U., Banyo, Brisbane, 2007—. Contbr. articles to profl. jours. Br. officer Australian Aid for Ireland, Brisbane, 1990-92. Named Young Queenslander of Yr., State Govt., Brisbane, 1991, Young Achiever award for Sci. and Tech., Dept. Bus., Industry and Regional Devel., 1992; recipient Young Investigator award Sandoz Pharm., Sydney, 1996. Mem. Australian Inst. Biology (credentials com. 1994-95), NY Acad. Scis., Transplantation Soc. Australia & New Zealand, Australian Soc. Biochemistry and Molecular Biology, Inst. Biology (UK). Labor. Methodist. Avocations: photography, reading, travel, entomology, bush walking. Office: Australian Cath Univ Po Box 456 Virgina 4014 Queensland Queensland Australia Office Phone: 61736237240. Business E-Mail: roger.lord@acu.edu.au. E-mail: roger.lord@bigpond.com.

LORELL, BEVERLY H., medical products executive, consultant; BA with distinction, Stanford U., 1971; MD, Stanford Sch. Medicine, 1975. Intern to resident physician Stanford U. Hosp.; clin. rsch. fellowship, cardiology Mass. Gen. Hosp., Harvard Med. Sch.; dir., program in heart failure, also mem. interventional cardiology team Besth Israel Deaconess Med. Ctr.; prof., medicine Harvard U. Med. Sch.; v.p., chief med. tech. officer Guidant Corp., Indpls., 2003—06; sr. med. and policy advisor King & Spalding LLP, Washington, 2006—. Served as an advisor to the fed. govt., including svc. on study sect. of the NIH and Cardiovascular and Renal Drugs Adv. Com. of the FDA; lectr. at various heart conf. and symposiums around the world. Contbr. articles to profl. jours. Mem.: Besth Israel Intervention Cardiology Team, Am. Coll. Cardiology, Heart Failure Soc. of Am., Am. Heart Assn., Guidant Compass Bd. Office: King & Spalding LLP Ste 200 1700 Pennsylvania Ave, NW Washington DC 20006-4706 Office Phone: 202-383-8937. Office Fax: 202-626-3737. E-mail: blorell@kslaw.com.

LORENTZEN, JAMES CLIFFORD, radiologist; b. Ardmore, Okla., Apr. 15, 1957; s. Clifford Leslie and Doris Lorraine (Thompson) L.; m. Tracey J. Smith, Apr. 4, 1992; children: Abigail, Andrew. BA, Baylor U., 1979; MD, Baylor Coll. Med., 1983. Diplomate Am. Bd. Internal Medicine, Am. Bd. Radiology. Intern Baylor Coll. of Medicine, 1983-84, resident, 1984-86; staff physician Okla. City Clinic, 1986-92; resident Health Sci. Ctr. U. Okla., 1992-96; pvt. practice radiology, 1997—. Clin. asst. in medicine Med. Sch. U. Okla., 1987-92. U. Okla. fellow, 1996-97. Mem. AMA, Am. Coll. Radiology, Radiol. Soc. N.Am., Phi Beta Kappa, Alpha Omega Alpha, Pi Kappa Alpha. Republican. Baptist. Avocations: music, literature, flying. Office: Coastal Radiology 720 Newman Rd New Bern NC 28562 Home: 711 Cove Harbor New Bern NC 28562 Personal E-mail: LorentzenJ@aol.com.

LORENZ, HERMANN PETER, plastic surgeon; b. Sacramento, Calif., May 19, 1961; BS in Biology, UCLA, 1983; MD, U. Mich. Sch. Medicine, 1987. Cert. Am. Bd. Surgery, Am. Bd. Plastic Surgery. Intern U. Calif. Med. Ctr., San Francisco, 1987—88, resident, gen. surgery, 1988—95, rsch. fellow, Fetal Treatment Ctr.; asst. prof., dept. surgery, divsn. plastic and reconstructive surgery UCLA, resident, plastic and reconstructive surgery, 1995—97, assoc. prof., dept. surgery, divsn. plastic and reconstructive surgery, 2001; fellow Stanford U.Med. Ctr., Calif., 1998; craniofacial surgery fellow Lucile Packard Children's Hosp and Stanford U. Hosp.; prof., plastic and reconstructive surgery Stanford Sch. Medicine, Calif.; svc. chief, plastic surgery Lucile Packard Children's Hosp., 2006—. Dir. Scarless Skin Repair Lab, Children's Surgical Rsch. Program. Contbr. several articles to profl. jours. Mem.: Am. Soc. Plastic Surgeons, Calif. Soc. Plastic Surgeons, Plastic Surgery Rsch. Coun. Office: Lucile Packard Childrens Hosp Stanford Dept Surgery 770 Welch Rd Ste 440 MC 5715 Stanford CA 94305 Office Phone: 605-723-5824.

LORENZ, MARK A., orthopedist; MD, Univ. Vienna. Assoc., clin. dir., applied biomechanics and kinesiology lab. Rehab. Rsch. Devel. Ctr. Edward Hines Hosp.; consul. Edward Hines Hosp.; clin. assoc. prof., dept. orthopaedics and rehab. Loyola Univ. Med. Ctr.; staff physician Hinsdale Hosp., Good Samaritan Hosp., Provena St. Joseph's Med. Ctr.; ptnr. Hinsdale Orthopaedic Associates, S.C. Intern Gersthof, Vienna, Cook Co. Hosp., Chgo.; resident Loyola Univ. Med. Ctr., Maywood, Ill.; fell., spinal surgery Univ. Toronto, Canada. Mem.: Internat. Soc. Study Lumbar Spine, Scoliosis Rsch. Soc., Chgo. Orthopaedic Soc., DuPage Co. Med. Soc., Orthopaedic Rsch. Soc., No. Am. Spine Soc., Ill. State Med. Soc., Chgo. Trauma Soc., Am. Acad. Orthopaedic Surgeons. Office: Hinsdale Orthopaedic Assoc 550 W Ogden Ave Hinsdale IL 60521

LORENZEN, ROBERT FREDERICK, ophthalmologist; b. Toledo, Mar. 20, 1924; s. Martin Robert and Pearl Adeline (Bush) L.; m. Lucy Logdson, Feb. 14, 1970; children: Roberta Jo, Richard Martin, Elizabeth Anne. BS, MD, Duke U., 1948; MS, Tulane U., 1953. Intern Presbyn. Hosp., Chgo., 1948-49; resident Duke U. Med. Ctr., 1949-51, Tulane Grad. Sch., 1951-53; practice medicine specializing in ophthalmology Phoenix, 1953—. Bd. dirs. St. Vincent de Paul Eye Clinic; mem. staff St. Joseph's Hosp., St. Luke's Hosp., Good Samaritan Hosp., Surg. Eye Ctr. of Ariz. Pres. Ophthalmic Scis. Found., 1970-73; chmn. bd. trustees Rockefeller and Abbe Prentice Eye Inst. of St. Luke's Hosp., 1975—. Editor in chief Ariz. Medicine, 1963-66, 69-70. Recipient Gold Headed Cane award, 1974; named to Honorable Order of Ky. Colls. Fellow ACS, Internat. Coll. Surgeons, Am. Acad. Ophthalmology and Otolaryngology, Pan Am. Assn. Ophthalmology; mem. Am. Assn. Ophthalmology (sec. of ho. of dels. 1972-73, trustee 1973-76), Ariz. Ophthal. Soc. (pres. 1966-67), Ariz. Med. Assn. (bd. dirs. 1963-66, 69-70), Royal Soc. Medicine, Rotary (pres. Phoenix 1984-850). Republican. Office: 3333 E Camino Sin Nombre Paradise Valley AZ 85253

LORENZI, MARA, medical educator, researcher; b. Bordighera, Italy, Nov. 19, 1946; MD, U. Turin, Italy, 1971. Asst. prof., dir. diabetes clinic U. Calif., San Diego, 1980—87; sr. scientist, prof. Harvard Med. Sch. Schepens Eye Rsch. Inst., 1987—, dir., juv. diabetes rsch. found. ctr. diabetic retinopathy, 2000—05. Vis. prof. U. Vita- Salute San Raffaele, Milan, 2006—. Recipient Beretta-

Anguissola prize, U. Rome La Sapienza; named one of America's Top Physicians, Consumers' Rsch. Coun. America. Mem.: AAAS, Am. Diabetes Assn. Avocations: tennis, music, travel. Office: Schepens Eye Research Inst 20 Staniford St Boston MA S2114 Business E-Mail: mara.lorenzi@schepens.harvard.edu.

LORENZO, RINO, VII, surgeon; s. Felipe and Peregrina Lorenzo. BS in Med. Tech., U. Santo Tomas, med. degree. Cert. bd. cert. Philippine Regulatory nat. Med. Bd. Exam, 1999, cert. part 1 Philippine Bd. of Plastic Surgery, 2006, cert. part 2 Philippine Bd. of Plastic Surgery, 2008; bd. cert. in plastic surgery. Tng. in gen. surgery Philippine Gen. Hosp. Med. Ctr. (PGH); tng. in plastic surgery Univ. Philippines Sect. of Plastic and Reconstructive Surgery, chief resident surgery dept., 2005; med. internship Sto. Tomas Univ. Hosp.; GS residency Univ. Philippines-Philippine Gen. Hosp. Med. Ctr., gen. plastic residency, burn chief resident, chief resident dept. of surgery, reconstructive plastic tng.; burn surgery residency Univ. Philippines-Philippine Gen. Hosp. Burn Ctr., burn chief resident; cosmetic plastic tng. Cardinal Santos Med. Ctr.; cosmetic plastic cons. Philippine Cosmetics. Fellow: Philippine Assn. of Plastic Reconstructive and Aesthetic Surgeons (PAPRAS); mem.: Philippine Bank of Mercy, Operation Smile Philippines Inc., Quezon City Med. Soc. (mem. 1999—), Philippine Med. Assn. (mem. 1999—), Philippine Coll. of Surgeons, Philippine Bd. of Plastic Surgery (diplomate). Achievements include research in Inhalation Injury: A regression analysis of factors affecting outcome a Philippine burn center experience; Glandular Odontogenic Cyst Presenting as a Lateral Mandibular Mass in a 2-Year Old Female. Office: Philippine Cosmetics MD Eastwood 3rd Fl Cybermall Tower One Eastwood City Quezon City Philippines Business E-Mail: drrinolorenzo@gmail.com. *

LORES, LUIS, pneumologist, consultant; b. Madrid, Sept. 5, 1968; s. Jose Luis Lores and Maria Pilar Obradors; m. Mariluz Benavente, Sept. 14, 1996; 1 child, Carmen; m. Rosa-Maria Morales. Med. degree, Valencia U., Spain, 1992; MD, Barcelona U., 2003. Specialist in pneumology Germans Tras i Pujos Hosp. Med. resident Germans Tras i Pujos Hosp., Barcelona, 1995—96; physician Emergency Med. Sys., Barcelona, 1997—98; with clinic for pneumology Hosp. Sant Boi, 1998—2001, chief dept. pneumology, 2002—. Cons. Inst. Univ. Dexeus, Barcelona, 1997—2002. Author: (book) Tratado de Med. Interna Farrenos Medicine, Advances in Pneumology, 1997. Mem.: Medicos Sin Fronteras, Catalan Soc. Pneumology, Spanish Soc. Pneumology. Avocations: writing, reading. Office: Hosp Sant Boi Bonaventura Calopa 13 08830 Sant Boi Spain Home: Calle Pomaret 1-9 8017 Barcelona Spain Fax: 0034 93 6306175. E-mail: luislores@wanadoo.es.

LORI, FRANCO, medical researcher, educator; b. Salsomaggiore Terme, Parma, Italy, Sept. 23, 1958; s. Renato Lori and Filomena Carretta; m. Emanuela Montagna; children: Rodolfo, Eugenio. MD magna cum laude, U. Parma, 1983; PhD in Hematology magna cum laude, U. Pavia, Italy, 1986. Intern in medicine U. Parma, 1979—83, vol. asst. Inst. Med. Pathology, 1983—86; guest rschr. lab. tumor cell biology Nat. Cancer Inst., NIH, Bethesda, Md., 1989—90; sci. co-dir., founder Rsch. Inst. For Genetic And Human Therapy, Washington, 1994—; 1st level dir. Fondazione Irccs Policlinico San Matteo, Pavia, 1995—2007; pres., chmn. bd. Virostatics, Sassari, Italy, 2007—. Mem. adminstrv. coun. U. Parma, 1979—83; adj. assoc. prof. microbiology and immunology George Washington U., Washington, 1996—; mem. sci. adv. bd. Global Healthcare Orgn., 2001—; mem. rev. bd. XIV Internat. AIDS Conf., Barcelona, 2002. Recipient Internat. Travel award USA-Italy Coop. Treaty Tech. Transfer award, Nat. Cancer Inst., 1989, AIDS Rsch. award, Ministry Health Italy, 1990—93, Tech. Transfer award, NIH, 1993, Heroes in Medicine award, Internat. Assn. Physicians In Aids Care, 2000. Mem.: AAAS (assoc.). Office: RIGHT at Fondazione IRCCS Policlinico San Matteo Ple Golgi 2 27100 Pavia Italy Office Fax: 390382502988. Business E-Mail: rightpv@tin.it.

LORI, NICOLAS FRANCISCO, physicist, researcher; s. Roberto Dante Lori and Maria Eduarda Gavino Silva e Sousa. Degree in physics, Coimbra U., Portugal, 1993; PhD in physics, Washington U., 2001. Rsch. assoc. Svc. Hospitalier Frederic Soliot/Commissariat a' l'Energie Atomique, Orsay, France, 2001—03, Washington U., St. Louis, 2003—. Contbr. articles to profl. jours. Fulbright fellow, U.S. Govt., 1995. Mem.: Internat. Soc. for Magnetic Resonance in Medicine. Home: 4615 Lindell Saint Louis MO 43108 Office: Washington Univ - MIR 4525 Scott Saint Louis MO 63110 Office Fax: 314-362-6911. E-mail: nlori@npg.wustl.edu.

LORKOWSKI, STEFAN, biochemist, molecular biologist, cell biologist; b. Marl, Germany, Jan. 1, 1973; s. Hubert and Inge Lorkowski. MS, U. Münster, 1997, PhD, 2001. Head rsch. group Leibniz Inst. Arteriosclerosis Rsch., Münster, 2003—08, asst. prof. biochemistry and cell biology, 2006—08; assoc. prof. Friedrich Schiller U., Jena, 2008—. Editor: (textbook) Analysing Gene Expression. A Handbook of Methods: Possibilities and Pitfalls; contbr. numerous articles in internat. peer-reviewed jours. Recipient E. Betz award for Arteriosclerosis Rsch., German Soc. Arteriosclerosis Rsch., 2001, Young Chemists prize, Internat. Union Pure and Applied Chemistry, 2002, Sibylle Hahne award, 2007. Fellow: Soc. Biology (life); mem.: Soc. Leukocyte Biology, European Macrophage & Dendritic Cell Soc. (life), German Soc. Nutrition (life), Soc. German Scientists and Physicians (life), Soc. German Chemists (life), Soc. Clin. Biology and Bioanalytics (life), Soc. Chem. Tech. and Biotechnology (life), Soc. Biochemistry and Molecular Biology (life), Royal Soc. Chemistry (life), German Soc. Arteriosclerosis Rsch. (life), Union German Biologists and Bioscientific Soc. (life), German Soc. Cell Biology (life). Office: Inst Nutrition Friedrich Schiller Univ Dornburger Str 25 Jena 07743 Germany Office Fax: 49-3641-949712. Business E-Mail: stefan.lorkowski@uni-jena.de.

LORUSSO, DOMENICA, gynecologist, educator; b. Gravina In Puglia, Bari, Mar. 9, 1971; MD, Cath. U. Rome, 1995, degree in Ob-Gyn., 1999. Physician Cath. U. Rome, 2003—, rschr., 2007. Office: Catholic University Rome Largo Gemelli 8 Rome 00168 Italy Office Phone: 390630154979. Office Fax: 390630156332. Business E-Mail: kettalorusso@libero.it.

LOSCALZO, JOSEPH, cardiologist, biochemist; b. Camden, NJ, Oct. 26, 1951; s. Joseph and Dolores Rita (Ventura) L.; m. Anita Beth Sendrow, Mar. 10, 1974; children: Julia, Alexander. AB summa cum laude, U. Pa., 1972, MD and PhD, 1978. Diplomate in internal medicine and cardiovasc. disease Am. Bd. Internal Medicine. Postdoctoral fellow U. Pa., Phila., 1978; resident in internal medicine Brigham and Women's Hosp., Boston, 1978-81, clin. fellow cardiology, 1981-83, chief med. resident, 1983-84, instr. medicine, 1983-85, chair, dept med., 2005—, physician-in-chief, 2005—; clin. fellow medicine Harvard Med. Sch., Boston, 1978-81, asst. prof. medicine, 1985-88, assoc. prof., 1989-93, Hersey prof., Theory and Practice Physics, 2005—; chief cardiol. sect. Brockton West Roxbury VA Med. Ctr., Boston, 1989-93; prof. biochemistry Boston U., 1994—2005, disting. prof. medicine, 1994—97, dir. Whitaker Cardiovasc. Inst., Sch. Medicine, 1994—2005, vice chmn. dept. medicine, chief cardiovasc. medicine, 1994-96, Wade prof., chmn. dept. medicine, 1997—2005; Hersey prof. theory and practice medicine Med. Sch. Harvard U., 2005—; chmn. dept. medicine Brigham and Women's Hosp., 2005—. Mem. rsch. rev. com. Am. Heart Assn., 1988—, chmn., 2000—02; rsch. rev. coms. Nat. Heart, Lung and Blood Inst., Bethesda, Md., 1990—, mem. bd. sci. counselors, 2000—04, chair, 2001—04, mem. adv. coun., 2005—; dir. NIH Specialized Ctr. Rsch. in Ischemic Heart Disease, 1995—2005; chair cardiovsasc. disease bd. Am. Bd. Internal Medicine, 1999—2003. Author, or editor 26 books on vascular biology, medicine, thrombosis and hemostasis; editor-in-chief Circulation, 2004-; assoc. editor New Eng. Jour. Medicine, 1995-2004; contb. mem. editl. bd. Circulation, Circulation Rsch., Jour. Am. Coll. Cardiology, Jour. Thrombosis and Thrombolysis, Vascular Medicine, Am. Jour. Cardiology, Jour. Am. Coll. Cardiology; contbr. over 500 articles to profl. jours. Recipient Med. Scientist Tng. award NIH, 1972-77, Rsch. Career Devel. award, 1989-94, Clin. Scientist award Am. Heart Assn., 1983-88, Disting. Scientist award Am. Heart Assn., 2004, Merit award, 2004-, Rsch. Achievement award Am. Heart Assn., 2006, Outstanding Investigator award Internat. Soc. Heart Rsch., 2006. Fellow ACP, Am. Coll. Cardiology; mem. Am. Fedn. Clin. Rsch., Am. Soc. Clin. Investigation, Assn. Am. Physicians, Assn. Univ. Cardiologists, Am. Soc. Biol. Chemistry, Inst. Medicine of Nat. Acads., Phi Beta Kappa, Alpha Omega Alpha. Achievements include 31 patents related to nitric oxide congeners. Office: Brigham and Womens Hosp 75 Francis St Boston MA 02115 Address: Dept Medicine Brigham and Womens Hosp New Rsch Bldg Rm 630 77 Avenue Louis Pasteur Boston MA 02115

LOSEE, JOSEPH E., plastic surgeon; MD, U. Rochester, 1994. Diplomate Am. Bd. Plastic Surgery. Resident gen. surgery Strong Memorial Hosp., Rochester, NY, 1997, resident plastic surgery, 1999; fellow Hosp. of the Univ. of Pa., 2000, Children's Hosp. of Phila.; hosp. affliation include/s Magee-Womens Hosp. of UPMC, Children's Hosp. of Pitts. of UPMC, UPMC Mercy, UPMC Presbyterian, UPMC Children's Surgery Ctrs.; assoc. prof. surgery and pediatrics Univ. of Pitts.; program dir. plastic surgery residency Univ. of Pitts. Med. Ctr.; chief pediatric surgery Children's Hosp. of Pitts.; dir. Pitts. Cleft-Craniofacial Ctr. Recipient Establishment of The Joseph E. Losee MD Teaching award, 2003. Mem.: Am. Assn. of Pediatric Plastic Surgeons, Am. Soc. of Craniofacial Surgeons, Am. Soc. of Plastic Surgeons. Office: Childrens Hospital of Pittsburgh of UPMC 1 Childrens Hospital Drive 4401 Penn Ave Pittsburgh PA 15224 Office Phone: 412-692-7949. Office Fax: 412-692-5263. E-mail: joseph.losee@chp.edu.

LOSICK, RICHARD M., biology professor; BA in Chem., Princeton Univ.; PhD in Biochem., MIT. Past. chmn. dept. molecular and cellular biology Harvard Coll., Maria Moors Cabot prof. biology. Former vis. scholar Phi Beta Kappa Soc.; sci. adv. bd. Tularik Tex. Corp., 1995—; chair, sci. adv. bd. Cumbre; rsch. prof. Howard Hughes Med. Inst., 2002—. Contbr. articles to sci. jours.; mem. editl. bd.: Science, Cell. Recipient Howard Hughes Med. Inst. grant, 2002, Selman A. Waksman award, Nat. Acad. Scis., 2007, Gairdner Found. Internat. award, 2009. Fellow: Am. Acad. Microbiol., AAAS, Am. Acad. Arts and Scis.; mem.: NAS (Selman A. Waksman award in Microbiol. 2007). Office: Biology Dept Harvard Coll Rm 3023 16 Divinity Ave Cambridge MA 02138 Office Phone: 617-495-4905. E-mail: losick@mcb.harvard.edu. *

LOSONCZY-MARSHALL, MARTA ELIZABETH, psychologist, educator; b. Budapest, Hungary, June 1, 1956; arrived in U.S., 1961; d. John Ambrosio and Martha Ambrosio Losonczy. BA in Philosophy, Salisbury U., 1978; MA in Clin. Psychology, Towson U., 1986; PhD in Devel. Psychology, George Washington U., 2001. Early childhood tchr. Relay Children's Ctr., Md., 1979—86; psychologist Balt. Assn. Retarded Citizens, 1986—88; instr. psychology Wor-Wic C.C., Salisbury, Md., 1992—94; bereavement counselor Coastal Hospice, Salisbury, 1993—94; lectr. Salisbury U., 1994—2001, asst. prof., 2001—07, assoc. prof., 2007—. Bereavement support group facilitator Coastal Hospice, Salisbury, 1994—2002. Vol. Joseph Ho. Ministries, Salisbury, 1993—95; religious edn. tchr. St. Francis De Sales Ch., Salisbury, 1994—95, eucharistic min., 1997—, sacristin, 1999—. Grantee, Fulton Sch. Liberal Arts, 2000, 2002, 2003, 2006, 2008, 2009. Mem.: World Assn. Infant Mental Health, Internat. Soc. Infant Studies, Soc. Rsch. Child Devel., Eastern Psychol. Assn. Democrat. Roman Catholic. Achievements include research in emotional development in infants and young children. Avocations: fishing, hiking, reading, knitting, needlepoint. Office: Salisbury U Psychology Dept 1101 Camden Ave Salisbury MD 21801 Home: 803 Gretman Dr Salisbury MD 21804 E-mail: melosonczy@salisbury.edu.

LOSORDO, DOUGLAS WILLIAM, cardiologist, educator; b. Bklyn., Dec. 20, 1957; s. Dominic and Louise (Ascione) Losordo. BA, U. Vt., 1979; MD, U. Vt. Coll. Medicine, 1983. Diplomate Nat. Bd. Med. Examiners, Am. Bd. Internal Medicine, cert. in cardiovasc. disease. Intern internal medicine St. Elizabeth's Hosp., Boston, 1983-84, resident, 1984-86, fellow in cardiology, 1986-88, rsch. fellow in interventional cardiology, 1988-89, staff physician, divs. cardiovascular medicine rsch., 1989—2001, chief cardiovasc. rsch., 2001—06; instr. medicine Tufts U. Sch. Medicine, Boston, 1983-89, asst. prof. medicine, 1989—2006; prof. medicine, Eileen M. Foell prof. heart rsch. Northwestern U. Feinberg Sch. Medicine, Chgo., 2006—, dir. Feinberg Cardiovasc. Rsch. Inst., 2006—. Assoc. editor Circulation Rsch., mem. editl. bd. Circulation, Stem Cells, Vascular Medicine; contbr. articles to profl. jours. Mem.: AAAS, ACP, Am. Heart Assn., Am. Fedn. Clin. Rsch., Am. Coll. Chest Physicians, Am. Coll. Cardiology. Office: Feinberg Cardiovasc Rsch Inst Northwestern U 303 E Chicago Ave Tarry 14 725 Chicago IL 60611 *

LOSOWSKY, MONTY SEYMOUR, physician, medical educator; b. London, Aug. 1, 1931; s. Myer and Dora (Gottlieb) L.; m. Barbara Malkin, Aug. 15, 1971; children: Kathryn, Andrew. MB, ChB with honors, Leeds U., Eng., 1955, MD, 1961. House officer Leeds Gen. Infirmary, 1955-56; registrar St. Margaret's Hosp., Epping, 1957-59; asst. externe Hosp. St. Antoine, Paris, 1960-61; rsch. fellow, med. unit Harvard U., Boston, 1961-62; from lectr. to reader in medicine, univ. dept. medicine Leeds Gen. Infirmary, 1962-69; prof. medicine, head dept. medicine U. Leeds, 1969-96, dean sch. medicine, 1989-94;, 1989-94. Gov., chmn. med. adv. bd. Brit. Liver Trust, 1969-2005; gov., chmn. med. adv. coun. Coeliac Soc., Eng.; sci. gov. Brit. Nutrition Found.; mem. gen. med. coun., 1990-95. Co-author: Malabsorption in Clinical Practice, 1974, The Liver and Biliary System, 1984, Gastroenterology, 1988, Getting Better: Stories from the History of Medicine, 2007; contbg. editor Gut Defences in Clinical Practice, 1986, others. Exec. chmn., bd. trustees Thackray Med. Mus., Leeds. Fellow Royal Coll. Physicians (Watson Smith lectr. 1995, Simms lectr. 1996); mem. Brit. Soc. Gastroenterology (coun. mem., edn. com. 1991-94, nominations com. 1991-94, pres. 1993-94), Royal Soc. Medicine, Assn. of Physicians of Great Britain and Ireland. Avocations: golf, watching cricket, walking, medical history. Office: Thackray Mus Beckett ST Leeds LS9 7LN England

LÖSSL, ANDREAS G., biotechnologist; b. Traunstein, Germany, Feb. 27, 1965; s. Bruno Anton and Anita Dora Lössl; m. Elke Katrin Zwerenz, Jan. 11, 2003; children: Jonas Isaia children: Johanna Christine. D, U. of Tech. Munich, 1996. Rsch. asst. Ludwig-Maximilians-U. Munich, 2000—04; asst. prof. U. of Natural Resources, Vienna, 2004—. Co-author: Research on Plant Secondary Metabolites, Pharmaceuticals, 2008, 2010—11; contbr. articles to profl. jours. Achievements include research in plant derived vaccines and trans-activation system for inducible expression of transgenes in chloroplasts. Home: Schiessstattgraben 10 3400 Klosterneuburg Austria Personal E-mail: loessl@grains-of-faith.org. E-mail: andreas.loessl@boku.ac.at.

LOSTY, PAUL DAMIEN, pediatric surgeon, educator; b. Belfast, No. Ireland, Sept. 25, 1959; s. Francis Brendan and Agatha Catherine Losty; m. Carmel Patricia Noonan, Sept. 12, 1987; children: Harry Patrick, Anna Louise, Ciara Jane. MD, U. Coll. Dublin, Ireland, 1985. Registrar in pediat. surgery Our Lady's Hosp. for Sick Children, Dublin, 1991—92; pediat. surgery rsch. fellow Mass. Gen. Hosp., 1992—94; clin. lectr./hon. sr. registrar Royal Liverpool Children's Hosp., England, 1994—97, sr. lectr. in pediat. surgery, 1997—2002; assoc. prof., reader U. Liverpool, 2002—04, prof. pediatric surgery, 2004—. Guest lectr. Japanese Soc. Pediat. Surgeons, 2003. Recipient Matti Sulamma medal and lectr., Finnish Assn. Pediat. Surgeons, 2003; fellow Traveling fellow, Stephen L. Gans Internat., 1998, GAR Surg. fellow, Mass. Gen. Hosp./Harvard Med. Sch./, 1992—94. Fellow: Royal Coll. Surgeons Ireland; mem.: Brit. Assn. of Pediat. Surgeons (coun. mem. 1997, prize 1993). Avocations: skiing, golf, swimming. Office: Univ Liverpool Alder Hey Hospital Eaton Road L12 2AP Liverpool England E-mail: paul.losty@liv.ac.uk.

LOTANO, VINCENT E., thoracic surgeon; MD, U. Medicine and Dentistry of NJ, 1993. Diplomate Am. Bd. Surgery, Am. Bd. Thoracic Surgery, lic. NJ, 1994. Resident gen. surgery Cooper Univ. Hosp., 1999; fellow cardiothoracic surgery Univ. Mo. Hosps. and Clinics, 2002; hosp. affiliations includes Pa. Hosp. Named one of Best Doctors in America, 2009—10, Top Doctors, Phila. Mag., 2010—. Fellow: ACS; mem.: Soc. of Thoracic Surgeons, Am. Coll. of Chest Physicians. Office: Pennsylvania Hospital Garfield Duncan Bldg Ste 305 700 Spruce St Philadelphia PA 19106 Office Phone: 800-789-7366.

LOTFIPOUR, SHAHRAM, medical educator; b. Tehran, Iran, July 20, 1970; Degree in Medicine, U. Iowa, 1995; MPH, U. Calif., LA, 2006. Prof., emergency medicine and pub. health U. Calif. Irvine Sch. Medicine, 2002—, assoc. dean, clin. sci. edn., 2010. Recipient Excellence Tchg. award, U. Calif. Irvine Sch. Medicine, Excellence Physician award, Orange County Med. Assn. Fellow: Am. Coll. Emergency Physicians, Am. Acad. Emergency Medicine. Office: 101 City Dr Rt 128-01 Orange CA 92868 Business E-Mail: shl@uci.edu.

LOTT, IRA TOTZ, pediatric neurologist; b. Cin., Apr. 15, 1941; s. Maxwell and Jeneda (Totz) L.; m. Ruth J. Weiss, June 21, 1964; children: Lisa, David I. BA cum laude, Brandeis U., 1963; MD cum laude, Ohio State U., 1967. Intern Mass. Gen. Hosp., Boston, 1967, resident in pediatrics, 1967-69, resident in child neurology, 1971-74; clin. assoc. NIH, Bethesda, Md., 1969-71; from clin. rsch. fellow to asst. prof. Harvard Med. Sch., Boston, 1971-82; clin. dir. Eunice Kennedy Shriver Ctr. for Mental Retardation, Waltham, Mass., 1974-82; assoc. prof. U. Calif., Irvine, 1983-91, prof., 1992—, chmn. dept. pediat., 1990-2000, dir. clin. neurosci. devel., 2000—03; assoc. dean for clin. neuroscis. U. Calif. Irvine Health Sys., 2003—. Chmn. dept. pediat. U. Calif., Irvine, 1990-2000, dir. pediat. neurology, 1983—, clin. neuroscience devel., 2000-01, assoc. dean clin. neurosciences, 2002—; pres. Prof. Child Neurology, Mpls., 1992—. Editor: Down Syndrome-Medical Advances, 1991; contbr. articles to profl. jours. Sec., treas. Child Neurology Soc., Mpls., 1987-90. Lt. comdr. USPHS, 1969-71. Recipient Career Devel. award Kennedy Found., 1976, Spotlight award Outstanding Svc. People with Devel. Disabilities as Health Care Provider, Regional Ctr. Orange County, 2005; NIH grantee, 1974—. Fellow Am. Acad. Neurology; mem. Am. Pediatric Soc., Am. Neurol. Assn., Nat. Down Syndrome Soc. (sci. acad. bd. 1985—, chmn. sci. adv. bd., 2005—, dir. sci. adv. bd. 2005, Rsch. award, 2004, Christian Puschel Meml. Rsch. award, 2005), Western Soc. for Pediatric Rsch. (councillor 1989-91). Achievements include research in relationship of Down Syndrome to Alzheimer's disease, neurometabolic disease. Office: Univ Calif Irvine Med Ctr Dept Pediat 101 City Dr S # 2C 4482 Orange CA 92868-4482 Office Phone: 714-456-5333. Business E-Mail: itlott@uci.com, itlott@uci.edu.

LOTUFO, PAULO A., epidemiologist, educator; b. Sao Paulo, Brazil, Jan. 19, 1957; MD, U. Sao Paulo, 1980, D in Pub. Health, 1996. Dir. Hosp. U. Sao Paulo, 2001—03; assoc. prof. internal medicine Sch. Medicine, U. Sao Paulo, 2002—06, prof. epidemiology and health economics, 2006—. Sci. dir. Sao Paulo Med. Assn., 1999—2005; med. editor Sao Paulo Med. Jour., 1999—2005. Grant, Estudo Longitudinal de Saude do Adulto. Office: av Lineu Prestes 2565 Sao Paulo 05508-000 Brazil Business E-Mail: palotufo@hu.usp.br.

LOU, HANS CHRISTENSEN, pediatric neurologist; b. Frederiksberg, Denmark, Jan. 26, 1939; s. Regnar Christensen and Margrethe Lou; m. Louise Lange, 1963 (div. 1967); 1 child, Thora; m. Hanne R. Køser, Mar. 9, 1969; children: Niels, Astrid, Ida. MD, U. Copenhagen, 1963, DSc, 1973. Bd. qualified in neurology and pediat. Chmn. dept. neurology Roskilde Hosp., Denmark, 1979—83; chmn. dept. neuropediatrics J.F. Kennedy Inst., Copenhagen, 1983—2001; prof. devel.

neurology U. Copenhagen, 1993—98; prof. PET Ctr. Aarhus (Denmark) U., 2002—. Vis. asst. prof. pediatric neurology U. Calif., San Francisco, 1981; cons. Rsch. Coun. Switzerland, 1990, NIH, 1992. Author: Developmental Neurology, 1983; editor: Brain Lesions in the Newborn, 1994; contbr. articles to profl. jours. Bd. dirs. Elsass Found. Recipient Segawa award, Japanese Neuropediatric Soc., 1994. Fellow: Royal Soc. Medicine (London); mem.: Child Neurology Soc. (meritorious mem.), European Pediatric Neruology Soc. (bd. dirs. 1994—97), Internat. Child Neurology Assn. (bd. dirs. 1982—94). Avocations: music, tennis, skiing, history of art and science. Office: PET Ctr Aarhus Univ Hosp 8000-DK Aarhus Denmark Home: Christiansgave 43 2960 Rungsted Denmark Personal E-mail: hans.lou@webspeed.dk. Business E-Mail: hl@ipm.regionh.dk.

LOUBRIEU, GEORGES LOUIS, radiologist, neurologist, consultant; b. Limoges, France, June 20, 1948; s. Jean and Marie Therese (Leniaud) L.; 1 child, Johanne. MD, U. Tours, France, 1976; diploma, U. Paris-Sud, 1988. Resident neurology, gen. medicine, neurosurgery Hosp. Tours, 1973-77; substitute chief svc. Hosp. Ctr. Dreux, France, 1977-78; asst. neurology svc. Regional Hosp. Tours, 1977-81, asst. neuroradiology svc., 1981, asst. prof., 1977-81, med. attaché, 1981-86; physician Centre Hospitalier, Bourges, France, 1986—, chief radiology, 1995—. Presenter numerous confs. Contbr. articles to med. jours., including French Pediatric Archives, Rev. Internal Medicine, Annals Surgery. Mem. ext. Mus. d'Histoire Naturelle Bourges; pres. Intrnationalist Musique Electroacoustique Bourges. Mem. French Radiology Soc., French Neuroradiology Soc., Western soc. Radiol. Imagery. Office: Centre Hospitalier 145 Ave F Mitterrand 18016 Bourges France also: 4 Ave Jean Jaurés 18000 Bourges France Home Phone: 0-66-333-0451; Office Phone: 0248484926. E-mail: georgesloubrieu@msn.com.

LOUDON, KAREN LEE, physical therapist; b. Kansas City, Mo., July 25, 1958; d. Walter Raymond and Clarice Frances (Washburn) L. BS in Edn., U. Kans., 1980; BS in Phys. Therapy, U. Kans. Med. Ctr., 1985; MS in Edn., U. Kans., 1987; MS in Orthop. Manual Phys. Therapy, Ola Grimsby Inst. Consortium, 1997. Registered phys. therapist, Kans., Mo.; cert. clin. specialist in orthop. phys. therapy. Phys. therapist Watkins Ctr. U. Kans., Lawrence, 1985—. Athletic trainer, Sunflower State Games, Lawrence, 1990-92; clin. instr. U. Kans. Med. Ctr., Lawrence, 1987—; presenter in field. Contbr. articles to profl. jours. Mem. Am. Phys. Therapy Assn. (mem. Kans. legis. com. 1983-84, Kans. Disting. Clin. Svc. award 1995), Nat. Athletic Trainer Assn., Am. Coll. Sports Medicine, Phi Kappa Phi. Avocations: golf, biking, softball, hiking. Office: Watkins Health Ctr U Kans Lawrence KS 66045-0001

LOUGEAY, DENRUTH COLLEEN, clinical psychologist, educator; b. Chgo., Nov. 7, 1943; d. Denzil Gordon Barre and Ruth Marion (Bergstrom) Larsen; m. Denis Howard Lougeay, Aug. 14, 1965; children: Stace Michael, Gregg Christopher. BS, U. Ill., Urbana, 1965, MEd, U. Ill., 1968; PhD, U.S. Internat. U., San Diego, 1986. Lic. clin. psychologist, Calif. Tchr. spl. edn. Urbana Pub. Schs., Ill., 1965-68; ednl. diagnostician Clin. Classroom Joliet Pub. Schs., Ill., 1968-69; counselor Women's Resource Ctr., San Luis Rey, Calif., 1980-82; psychologist Delmont Prt. Hosp., Victoria, Australia, 1982-83; group therapist Parents United East and North San Diego County, 1982-84; psychologist Palomar Coll., San Marcos, Calif., 1984-87; pvt. practice, Encinitas, Calif., 1988—. Disaster Mental Health officer ARC, San Diego, 1993-96. Recipient State ARC Leadership award, 1991—97, Lou Liay Spirit award, U. Ill., 2008. Fellow San Diego Psychol. Assn. (pres. 1998), mem. APA (Calif. state coord. Disaster Response 1995—, nat. adv. bd. Disaster Response 1998-2001, Presdl. Citation 2000), Calif. Disaster Mental Health Coalition (charter), Calif. Psychol. Assn. (state chair Disaster Mental Health 1995-2010, chair emeritus 2011, Silver Psi award 1998, Disting. Humanitarian award, 2006), Soc. Mental Health Profls. (pres. 1989-90, bd. dirs.), Assn. Psychol. Type (sec. San Diego chpt. 1988-90, bd. dirs.), Mensa, Illini Club San Diego County (bd. dirs. 1987—). Avocations: hot air ballooning, genealogy, travel. Office: Arrow Psychol Svc 404 Alviso Way Encinitas CA 92024-2616

LOUGHEED, PETER, lawyer, former Canadian premier; b. Calgary, Alta., Can., July 26, 1928; s. Edgar Donald and Edna (Bauld) L.; m. Jeanne Estelle Rogers, June 21, 1952; children— Stephen, Andrea, Pamela, Joseph. BA, U. Alta., 1950, LL.B., 1952; MBA, Harvard U., 1954. Bar: Alta 1955. With firm Fenerty, Fenerty, McGillivray & Robertson, Calgary, 1955-56; sec. Mannix Co., Ltd., 1956-58, gen. counsel, 1958-62, v.p., 1959-62, dir., 1960-62; individual practice law, from 1962; formerly mem. Alta. Legislature for Calgary West; formerly leader Progressive Conservative Party of Alta., 1965-85; premier of Alta., 1971-85; ptnr. Bennett Jones, Calgary, 1986-99, counsel, 1999—. Named an inductee, Canadian Med. Hall of Fame, 2001. Office: Bennett Jones LLP 855 2nd St SW 4500 Bankers Hall Calgary AB Canada T2P 4K7 Office Phone: 403-298-3456.

LOUGHLIN, GERALD M., pediatrician, educator; b. 1947; m. Barbara Loughlin; children: Ceila, Shaye. BS, U. Notre Dame, South Bend, Ind., 1969; MD, U. Rochester Sch. Medinine & Dentistry, NY, 1973; MS in Bus. Health Care Fin. & Adminstrn., Johns Hopkins U. Sch. Profl. Studies, Md., 1998. Diplomate Am. Bd. Pediat., Am. Bd. Pediat. Pulmonology. Intern pediat. Ariz. Med. Ctr., Tuscon, 1974—75, resident pediat., 1974—75, pulmonary fellow, 1975—77; faculty dept. pediat. U. Fla.; dir. divsn. pediat. respiratory scis. Johns Hopkins U., 1984—2002; Nancy C. Paduano prof. pediat., pediatrician-in-chief Weill Cornell Med. Coll., NY, 2002—. Past v.p. med. affairs Mt. Wash. Pediat. Hosp., Balt.; assoc. dir. pediat. clin. rsch. Johns Hopkins U., 1991—99; chmn. dept. pediat. Weill Cornell Med. Coll. Contbr. articles to profl. jours. Recipient Outstanding Tchr. award, U. Fla. dept. pediat., 1979, Schaffer Award for the Outstanding Tchr., Johns Hopkins Children's Ctr., 1985, George Will Comstock award, Am. Lung Assn. Md., 1998. Mem.: Am. Thoracic Soc. (bd. dirs.). Office: Weill Cornell Med Coll 525 E 68th St New York NY 10065 Office Phone: 212-746-4111. Office Fax: 212-746-8117. Business E-Mail: gml2001@med.cornell.edu.

LOUIE, BRIAN E., surgeon; b. Edmonton, Alberta, Can., Jan. 16, 1967; MD, U. Toronto, 1996; MPH, U. Alta.; MHA, U. Ottawa. Surgeon Swedish Cancer Inst. and Med. Ctr., 2005—, dir., thoracic rsch. and edn., 2005—, co-dir., minimally invasive thoracic surgery program, 2005—. Fellow: ACS, Royal Coll. Physicians and Surgeons, Can.; mem.: Am. Soc. Gastrointestinal Endoscopy, Western Thoracic Surg. Assn., Soc. Thoracic Surgeons. Office: Ste 850 1101 Madison St Seattle WA 98104 Office Fax: 206-215-6801. Business E-Mail: brian.louie@swedish.org.

LOUILOT, ALAIN ERIC, neurobiologist; b. Lyon, France, Dec. 1, 1957; s. Lucien and Michèle (Pétillot) L. M of Sci. and Techniques, U. Poitiers, France, 1979; PhD, U. Bordeaux, France, 1983, DScs, 1990. In charge rsch. 2d class Nat. Ctr. Sci. Rsch., Bordeaux, 1988-92, in charge rsch. 1st class, 1992-97, Strasbourg, France, 1998—. Cons. Synthélabo, France, 1984, Roussel-Uclaf, France, 1986, Servier, France, 1992; specialist mem. univ. coms. Bordeaux, Toulouse, Paris, 1992—95; specialist mem. Inst. Nat. de la Santé et de la Rsch. Med. Com., Paris, 1998—99; mem. sci. coun. Inst. Fed. Rsch. Neurosci., Strasbourg, France, 2000—; mem. bd. Faculty Medicine, Strasbourg, France, 2001—, mem. rsch. com., 2001—. Editor: Monitoring Molecules in Neuroscience, 1994; contbr. articles to profl. jours. Recipient E.D.F. Found. award, 2001; grantee, Lilly-CNRS, 1998. Mem. French Soc. Neurosci., Internat. Brain Rsch. Orgn., Am. Soc. Neurosci., N.Y. Acad. Scis.; Assoc. Behavioral and Brain Scis. Achievements include discovery of method of in vivo recording in freely-moving animals; demonstration of an interdependent functioning between mesencephalic neuronal subgroups; involvement of dopaminergic neurons in affective perception and latent inhibition; differential involvement of dopaminergic neurons in latent inhibition. Office: U Louis Pasteur INSERM U666 & Inst Physio 11 Rue Humann 67085 Strasbourg France Business E-Mail: alouilot@alsace.u-strasbg.fr.

LOUIS, STEVEN, orthopedist; MD, Northwestern Med. Sch., Chgo. Cert. Orthopaedic Surgery. Ptnr. Hinsdale Orthopaedic Assoc., 1997—; instr., faculty mem. Assn. for the Study of Internal Fixation. Clin. instr. Loyola Univ. Med. Ctr.; dir., orthopaedic trauma Good Samaritan Hosp.; staff physician Hinsdale Hosp., Hinsdale Surgery Ctr., Salt Creek Surgery Ctr. Mem.: DuPage Co. Med. Soc., Ill. Orthopaedic Soc., AMA, Orthopaedic Trauma Assn., Assn. Bone and Joint Surgeons, Am. Acad. Orthopaedic Surgeons. Office: Hinsdale Orthopaedic Assoc 550 W Ogden Ave Hinsdale IL 60521

LOURENCO, ANDREZZA VIVIANY, pharmacist; b. Ponta Grossa, July 29, 1977; M, AC Camargo Hosp., 2010. Cert. pharmacist UEPG, 2001. With ISPON, 2002. Mem.: ISOPP. Office: Francisco Ribas 638 Ponta Grossa Parana 84010-260 Brazil Office Fax: 55 42 3026-5400. Business E-Mail: andrezza@ispon.com.br.

LOURIA, DONALD BRUCE, retired medical educator; b. Bklyn., July 11, 1928; s. Milton and Lucy (Littauer) Louria; m. Barbara Watson, May 21, 1955; children: Dana, Charles, Anne Ludes. BS cum laude, Harvard U., Cambridge, Mass., 1949; MD cum laude, Harvard Med. Sch., Boston, 1953. Cert. internal medicine, epidemiology, Am. Bd. Internal Medicine, 1959, Am. Coll. Epidemiology, 1982. Resident The NY Hosp., 1953—55; asst. surgeon NIH, Bethesda, Md., 1955—57, instr. Cornell U. Med. Sch., NYC, 1958—60, assoc. prof., 1964—69, asst. prof., 1960—64; chmn. dept. preventive medicine NJ Med. Sch., Newark, 1969—99, prof., 1999—2008. Bd. mem. Poly Prep County Day Sch., Bklyn., 1973—76, Nuc. Policy Rsch. Inst., Washington, 2003—07; mem. adv. bd. Quantia Comm., Cambridge, Mass., 2006—. Author: (books) The Drug Scene, 1968, Overcoming Drugs, A Program for Action, 1971, Your Healthy Body, Your Healthy Life. How to Take Control of Your Medical Destiny, 1989; author: (and co-author) 350 articles in med. jours. 90 chpts. in monographs or books, and 2 short stories; author: rethink: A Twenty First Century Approach to Preventing Societal Catastrophes, 2009. Pres. N.Y. State Coun. on Drug Addiction, 1965—72; pres. NJ chpt. World Future Soc., NJ, 1984—94; pres. N.Y. Young Rep. Club, 1965; pres. N.J. chpt. Physicians Social Responsibility, Newark, 1982—85. Recipient Golden Apple Tchg. award, N.J. Med. Sch., 1972, 1980, 1981, 1982, Gov.'s Clara Barton, N.J., 1991, Med. Svc. award. Master: Am. Coll. Physicians (Rosenthal Found. award 1991); fellow: Infectious Diseases Soc. Am., Am. Coll. Epidemiology; mem.: Am. Coll. Preventive Medicine, World Future Soc., Am. Soc. Clin. Investigation. D-Liberal. Mem. Soc. Of Friends. Achievements include creating Healthful Life Program now law in New Jersey as the Health Wellness Promotion Act. Avocations: squash, photography. Home: 61 Overleigh Rd Bernardsville NJ 07924-1509 Home Phone: 908-766-2184. Personal E-mail: dlouria@msn.com.

LOURIDO, JUAN ALBERTO, neurosurgeon, consultant; b. Cedeira, Galicia, Spain, Nov. 24, 1971; s. Jesus and Maria Angeles (Garcia) Lourido. Bachelor's degree, Santo Domingo/Nordonia HS, La Coruña, Spain and Ohio, 1989; MD, U. Navarra, Spain, 1995, U. Louvain, Belgium; diploma in neurosurgery, European Assn. Neurosurgical Socs., 2005. Lic. U. Navarra, Spain, 1995, specialist in neurosurgery Canary Islands U. Hosp., Spain, 1997, neurosurgery cons. Servicio Canario Salud, Spain, 2004. Emergency svc. dr. Servicio Galego Saude, Ortigueira, Galicia, Spain, 1995; navy med. officer Armada Española, Ferrol, Galicia, 1995—96; neurosurgery resident Canary Islands U. Hosp., Tenerife, 1997—2002; neurosurgeon Candelaria U. Hosp., Tenerife, 2002—05; neurosurgery cons. U. Insular and Women and Children Hosps., Las Palmas Gran Canaria, Canary Islands, 2005, Gran Canaria U. Hosp., Canary Islands, 2006; neurosurgery dir. USP Hosp., Costa Adeje, Tenerife, 2007—. Vis. trainee of residence Lund/Harvard/Zurich and Melbourne U. Hosps., Lund, Boston, Zurich, Melbourne, Sweden, US, Switzerland, Australia, 1997—2002; nat. rep. Spain European Assn. Neurosurgical Socs. Young Neurosurgeon Com., 2004—; mem. European Assn. Neurosurgical Socs. Website Com., 2004—. Recipient Prin., Chemistry and Physics awards, Nordonia HS, 1988. Mem.: Sociedad Española Medicina Aeroespacial, Am. Assn. Neurosurgeons, European Assn. Neurosurgery, Soc. Neurooncology, European Assn. Neurooncology, Spanish Neurosurg. Soc., Real Aeroclub Tenerife (assoc.), Real Club Náutico Coruña (assoc.). Roman Catholic. Avocations: sailing, diving, private pilot, archery, music. Office: USP Hosp Costa Adeje Neurosurgery Dept 38600 San Eugemo Tenerife Spain Personal E-mail: juanlourido@hotmail.com.

LOURWOOD, DAVID LEE, JR., pharmacotherapist, educator; b. St. Louis, Mo., Nov. 20, 1956; s. David Lee Sr. and Nancee Joan (Spradling) L.; m. Betty Jane McClure, May 19, 2001. BS in Pharmacy, St. Louis Coll. Pharmacy, 1979; PharmD, Wayne State U., 1982. Bd. cert. pharmacotherapy specialist, 1992. Pharmacy intern Jewish Hosp., St. Louis, 1976-79; pharmacist Hutzel Hosp., Detroit, 1980-81; clin. pharmacist Cook County Hosp., Chgo., 1981-85, clin. pharmacy coord., 1985-89; asst. dir. pharmacy Edgewater Med. Ctr., Owen Healthcare Inc., Chgo., 1989-90; pharmacotherapist Columbia/Michael Reese Hosp. and Med. Ctr.-Columbia/HCA, Chgo., 1990-97; clin. pharmacy coord. St. James Hosp. Health Ctr., Chicago Heights, Ill., 1997—99; clin. pharmacist Corum Healthcare, 1999—2001; dir. pharmacy Kindred Hosp., St. Louis, 2002—03; clin. pharmacy coord. Jefferson Meml. Hosp., Crystal City, Mo., 2003—05; clin. pharmacist Poplar Bluff Regional Med. Ctr., Mo., 2005—. Clin. asst. prof. dept. pharmacy practice Coll. Pharmacy, U. Ill., Chgo., 1990-99, clin. asst. prof. dept. pharmacy practice Chgo. Coll. Pharmacy, Midwestern U., 1998-2002, St. Louis Coll. Pharmacy, 1999-, Drake U., 2004-05, U. Mo., Kansas City, 2006—, U. Ark., 2006—; Southern Ill. U., 2008-, cons. Profl. Drug Systems, Inc., St. Louis, 1982—. Author: Antibiotic Drug Interactions in Evaluations of Drug Interactions, 1982—; mem. editl. bd. Annals of Pharmacotherapy, 1986-94, Jour. Am. Pharm. Assn., 1999-2003. Dist. commr. Boy Scouts Am., Oak Park, Ill., 1982-85, La Grange, Ill., 1985-89; pres. Lombard (Ill.) Park Dist. Swim and Dive Team, 1994-96, chmn. water park adv. com., 1996-99. O.J. Cloughly Grad. fellow St. Louis Coll. Pharmacy, 1979; fellow, Am. Coll. Clin. Pharmacy, 2006. Mem.: Shriners (Whiffer), Mo. Soc. Health-Systems Pharmacists, Am. Pharm. Assn., Am. Coll. Clin. Pharmacy, Am. Soc. Health-Systems Pharmacists, St. Louis Coll. Pharmacy Alumni Assn., Scottish Rite Accepted Masons. Republican. Avocations: personal computers, baseball, science fiction, jogging. Office: Poplar Bluff Regional Med Ctr 2620 N Westwood Blvd Poplar Bluff MO 63901 Home: 2815 Karmen Ave Poplar Bluff MO 63901-2085 Office Phone: 573-686-5989. Personal E-mail: drdave6@mycitycable.com.

LOVE, SUSAN MARGARET, surgeon, educator; b. Long Branch, NJ, Feb. 9, 1948; d. James Arthur and Margaret Connick (Schwab) Love; life ptnr. Helen Sperry Cooksey, Sept. 18, 1982; 1 child, Katherine Mary. BS, Fordham U., Bronx, NY, 1970; MD, SUNY, NYC, 1974; MBA, UCLA, 1998; DSc (hon.), Northeastern U., 1991, Simmons Coll., 1992, SUNY, 1998, Trinity Coll., 1999; LHD (hon.), U. RI, 1997. Surgery intern Beth Israel Hosp., Boston, 1974—75, surg. resident, 1975—79, chief resident, 1979, clin. fellow in pathology, 1980, asst. in surgery, 1980—87, dir. breast clinic, 1980-88, assoc. surgeon, 1987—92; clin. fellow in surgery Harvard Med. Sch., Boston, 1977-78, clin. instr., 1980-87, asst. clin. prof. surgery, 1987-92; clin. assoc. in surg. oncology Dana Farber Cancer Inst., Boston, 1981-92; dir. Faulkner Breast Ctr., Faulkner Hosp., Boston, 1988-92; assoc. prof. clin. surgery UCLA Med. Sch., 1992-96, adj. prof. divsn. gen. surgery, 1996—2002; dir. Revlon/UCLA Breast Ctr., 1992-96; clin. prof. divsn. gen. surgery UCLA David Geffen Sch. Medicine, 2002—. Med. dir. Santa Barbara Breast Cancer Inst., 1983—2000; prin. investigator Nat. Surg. Adjuvant Breast & Bowel Project, 1985—96; founder, bd. dirs. Nat. Breast Cancer Coalition, 1991—; adv. com. Women's Health Initiative Program, Washington, 1993—95; adv. coun. Breast & Cervical Cancer Program/Breast Cancer Early Detection Program, Calif. State Dept. Health Svcs., 1994—98; mem. Nat. Action Plan on Breast Cancer, HHS, 1994—2000, pres., med. dir. Dr. Susan Love Rsch. Found., 1995—, co-founder with Avon Found. for Women, Army of Women, 2008; Presdl. appointee Nat. Cancer Adv. Bd., 1998—2004; founder, sr. ptnr., dir. LLuminari, Inc., 2000—; nat. adv. environ. health sci. coun. NIH, 2003—04. Author: Dr. Susan Love's Breast Book, 1990, Atlas of Techniques in Breast Surgery, 1996, Dr. Susan Love's Menopause and Hormone Book: Making Informed Choices About Menopause, 1997; contbr. articles to profl. jours. Bd. dirs. Lesbian Health Found., 1992—, Soc. Menstrual Cycle Rsch., 2000—, Y-ME Nat. Breast Cancer Orgn., 2001—. Recipient Rose Kushner award, Am. Med. Writers Assn., 1991, Achievement award, Am. Assn. Physicians for Human Rights, 1992, Women Making History award, US Senator Barbara Boxer, 1993, Woman of Yr. award, YWCA, 1994, Frontrunner award, Sara Lee Corp., 1994, Women of Distinction award, Nat. Coun. Aging, 1994, Spirit of Achievement award, Albert Einstein Coll., Yeshiva U., 1995, Abram L. Sachar medallion, Brandeis U., 1996, Bicentennial honoree, U. Louisville, 1997, Walker prize, Boston Mus. Sci., 1998, Alumni Achievement award, SUNY Coll. Medicine, 1999, Radcliffe medal, Harvard U., 2000, Humanitarian of Yr. award, Western U. Health Sci., Pomona, Calif., 2001, Excellence in Cancer Awareness award, Cancer Rsch. Found. America, 2002, Dir.'s award, Nat. Cancer Inst., 2004; named to Internat. Women's Forum Hall of Fame, 2006. Fellow: ACS; mem.: Assn. Women Surgeons, Am. Coll. Women's Health Physicians, Am. Assn. Cancer Rsch., N.Am. Menopause Soc., Boston Surg. Soc., LA Med. Soc., Am. Soc. Preventive Oncology, Soc. Study of Breast Disease, Am. Med. Women's Assn. (Lila Wallis Women's Health award 2004). Office: Dr Susan Love Rsch Found 2811 Wilshire Blvd Ste 500 Santa Monica CA 90403-0846 Office Fax: 310-828-5103. Business E-Mail: slove@earthlink.net. *

LOVETT, JUANITA PELLETIER, clinical psychologist; b. Youngstown, Ohio, Mar. 9, 1937; d. Joseph Arcadia and Alice Beatrice (Davis) Pelletier; children: Laura Ann, James Emmett. BA summa cum laude with honors in Psychology, Fairleigh Dickinson U., 1975; MPhil, Columbia U., 1978, MA, 1979, PhD, 1980. Freelance fashion cons., 1958-70; psychology fellow Westchester divsn. NY Hosp.-Cornell Med. Ctr., White Plains, 1977-80; program dir. inpatient svc. Fair Oaks Hosp., Summit, NJ, 1980-82; pvt. practice Summit, 1980—; asst. dir. med. rsch. CIBA-GEIGY Pharms., Summit, 1982-83; cons. AT&T Bell Labs., Murray Hill, NJ, 1983, Lucent Techs., 1996—2004. Adj. asst. prof. psychology and edn., Dept. Psychology, Tchrs. Coll., Columbia U., NYC, 1980-84; field supr. grad. sch. applied profession psychology Rutgers U., 1981-83; assoc. prof. Polytechnic, NY, 1988-91. Union County Mental Health Bd. mem., 1974-76; bd. dirs. Wye River Group on Healthcare, Am. Found. for Healthcare Policy. Author: (book) Solutions for Adults With Aspergers Syndrome, 2005; contbr. articles to profl. jours. Recipient Laurie Shavel award, 1975; Mennen scholar, 1975. Mem. APA, NY Acad. Scis., NJ Psychol. Assn., Sigma Xi, Phi Omega Epsilon. Office: No2 The Cloisters 25 Norwood Ave Summit NJ 07901-3647 Home Phone: 908-277-9596; Office Phone: 908-273-5147. Personal E-mail: jplovett@comcast.net.

LOVIN, physician; b. Iasi, Romania, Oct. 11, 1974; MD, Iasi U., Romania, 1999, PhD, 2010. Physician Railways Hosp. Galati, Romania, 2007—11, Ctr. Hospitalier Salon de Provence, France, 2011—. Asst. U. Lower Danube, Galati, 2007—11. Grant, European Respiratory Soc. Mem.: Romanian Soc. Pneumology, European Sleep Rsch. Soc., European Respiratory Soc. Office: 207 Ave Julien Fabre Salon de Provence 13300 France Office Fax: (0033) 4 90 56 61 45. Personal E-mail: sinziana_lovin@yahoo.com.

LOW, CZE HONG, ophthalmologist; b. Singapore; s. Cheng Kim Low and Siow Lung Seah; m. Shuit Hung Ho; 1 child, Jonathan, Mensian. MBBS, U. Singapore, 1971; med. student, Monash U., Australia. Mem., sr. cons. ophthalmologist chmn. Eye Surg. Ctr. Mt. Elizabeth Hosp., Singapore, 1983—. Cons. 3M, 1984—89, St. Andrew's Mission Hosp., Singapore, 1994—; bd. dirs. Singapore Nat. Eye Ctr., vis. sr. ophthalmologist, 1990—2008, chmn. exec. laser com.; med. dir. Asia Medic Eye Ctr., Singapore, 1997—; chmn. Asia Medic Specialist Ctr., Singapore; vis. prof. Tianjin Med. U., China, 1996—; course dir. Internat. Congress Ophthalmology, Sydney, 2002; adv. Visx, 2004—06, global adv., 2007—; pres. Singapore Soc. Ophthalmology, 1995—97; head presbyopic lasik surgery Asia Medic Ctr. for Presbyopia Correction; physician trainer in Custom Vue Lasik and Presbyopic Lasik, Advanced Medical Optics; pres. elect Rotary Club Raffles City. Founding mem. half percent charity club, 2001—. Capt. Singapore Armed Forces, 1971-83. Recipient Gold medal SNEC, 1997, Grand award for cmty. svc. Singapore Govt., 2005, Genius Laureaute of Singapore, 2005; Cmty Svc. medal Ministry Cmty. Devel. and Prime Min.'s Office, Singapore; Commonwealth scholar in ophthalmology, 1975-77. Fellow ACS, Royal Coll. Surgeons (Eng.), Royal Coll. Surgeons (Glasgow and Edinburgh), Internat. Coll. Surgeons, Acad. Medicine, Royal Coll. Ophthalmologists; mem. Singapore Med. Assn., Am. Soc. Cataract and Refractive Surgeons, Am. Acad. Ophthalmology, Internat. Soc. Refractive Surgery (internat. coun., Singapore rep.), Singapore Med. Alumni, Barraquer Inst. (hon.; Man of Yr. 2001, 03, 04, 05, 06, 07, 08, 09, 2010), European Soc. Cataract & Refractive Surgeons. Achievements include first to introduce Presbyopic Lasik and topical phacoemulsification surgery in Singapore; pioneer in Singapore refractive surgery, RK, PRK, Lasik wavefront lasik phakic 10L, Wavescan and Customvue Presbyopic Lasik; Presbyopic vision correction, bioptics, posterior vitrectomy under topical anesthesia; phacovitrectomy under topical anesthesia; adult and pediatric multifocal 10L implantation ambulatory day surgery facility; Advanced Medical Optics intralase custom-vue bladeless Lasik surgeon in South East Asia. Avocations: travel, computers, photography, art and oil painting collector, sports cars. Office: Specialist Eye Surg Ctr 3 Mt Elizabeth #16-01/02 Singapore 228510 Singapore Office Phone: 65-67346685, 6734 6684. Personal E-mail: dr_eaglevision@yahoo.com. Business E-Mail: eyesurgery2020@gmail.com.

LOW, DONALD E., thoracic surgeon; MD, Queens U., 1981. Head thoracic surgery and thoracic oncology Va. Mason Med. Ctr., 1999—. Head esophageal ctr. excellence Digestive Disease Inst. Va. Mason Med. Ctr., 2006—11. Recipient Aust award, Western Surg. Assn. Fellow: ACS. Avocation: woodworking. Office: 1100 Ninth Ave Seattle WA 98111 Office Phone: 206-223-6164. Office Fax: 206-625-7245. Business E-Mail: gtsdel@vmmc.org.

LOW, JAMES A., physician; b. Toronto, Ont., Can., Sept. 22, 1925; s. Donald M. and Doris V. (Van Duzer) L.; m. Margery Una, Oct. 5, 1952; children: Donald E., Margeret P., Norman I. MD, U. Toronto, 1949. Intern Toronto Gen. Hosp., 1949-50; resident in ob-gyn U. Toronto, 1950-54; fellow ob/gyn Duke U., 1955; clin. instr. dept. ob-gyn U. Toronto, 1955-65; prof. and chmn. dept. ob-gyn Queens U., Kingston, Ont., Canada, 1965-85, prof., 1985—. Exec. dir. Mus. Health Care at Kingston, 1995—. Mem. editl. bd. Ob-Gyn., 1986-89, Am. Jour. Ob-Gyn., 1995-99. Served with Can. Navy, 1943-45. Recipient Pres. award, SOCG, 1985, Spl. Recognition award, Kingston Gen. Hosp., 1997, William B. Spaulding Cert. of Merit, AOIE Found., 1999, Disting. Svc. award, Queen's U., 2007, First Capital Honorable Achievement award, Kingstone, 2010. Fellow: Royal Coll. Obstetricians and Gynecologists, Royal Coll. Physicians and Surgeons Can. (chmn. splty. com. 1976—82, chmn. manpower com. 1984—92); mem.: Can. Soc. Clin. Investigation, Soc. Obstetricians and Gynecologists Can., Soc. Gynecol. Investigation, Am. Gynecol. and Obstet. Soc., Assn. Profs. Ob-Gyn. Can. (sec.-treas. 1972—80, pres. 1983—84). Office: Queens U Dept Ob Gyn Kingston ON Canada K7L 3N6 Home: 185 Fairway Hill Cres Kingston ON Canada K7M 2B5 Home Phone: 613-548-8381. Business E-Mail: lowj@kgh.kari.net.

LOW, MALCOLM JAMES, research scientist; b. Edinburgh, Aug. 25, 1955; s. George Duncan Low and Jessie Forbes Morton; m. Gaye Thomas, Dec. 26, 1981; children: Nicholas Duncan Thomas-Low, Jacob Armon Thomas-Low. BS, Rensselaer Poly. Inst., 1975; MD, Albany Med. Coll., 1979; PhD, Tufts U., 1987. Diplomate Am. Bd. Internal Medicine, 1982, Am. Bd. Endocrinology and Metabolism, 1985. Intern, resident in internal medicine Michael Reese Hosp., Chgo., 1979—82; neuroendocrinology fellow New Eng. Med. Ctr., Boston, 1982—85; asst. prof. medicine Tufts U., Boston, 1986—89; asst. scientist Oreg. Health & Sci. U., Portland, 1990—94, asst. prof. biochemistry and molecular biology, 1991—95, scientist, 1995—2009, assoc. prof. biochemistry and molecular biology, 1996—2002, prof. behavioral neurosci., 2002—09, sr. scientist, 2003—09; prof. physiology U. Mich. Med. Sch., Ann Arbor, 2009—. Mem. endocrinology and IPOD study sect. Ctr. for Sci. Rev., NIH, Bethesda, Md., 2001; assoc. dir. Ctr. for Study Weight Regulation & Assoc. Disorders, 2005—. Contbr. articles to profl. jours. Recipient Pfizer Scholar award, Pfizer Pharmaceuticals, 1988—90; grantee, NIH, 1988—; fellow Individual Nat. Rsch. Svc. award, 1983—84, Physician-Scientist award, 1984—89. Mem.: AAAS, Assn. Am. Physicians, Pituitary Soc., Soc. Neurosci., Endocrine Soc., Alpha Omega Alpha. Achievements include development of transgenic mice with fluorescent proopiomelanocortin neurons for physiological studies of neuronal function; invention of immortalized pituitary melanotroph cell line; ß-endorphin knockout mice; dopamine D2 receptor knockout mice; dopamine D4 receptor knockout mice; human follicle stimulating hormone ß-subunit transgenic mice and conditional neuron specific POMC knockout mice; patents for mammalian melanocortin receptors and uses; upstream control elements of the proopiomelanocortin gene and their use; modification of feeding behavior; assessment of neurons in the arcuate nucleus to screen for agents that modify feeding behavior. Avocations: travel, model railroading. Office: Dept Molecular and Integrative Physiology University Mich 6116 Brehm Tower 100 Wall St Ann Arbor MI 48105 Office Phone: 734-647-1350. Business E-Mail: mjlow@umich.edu.

LOW, MORTON DAVID, retired neuroscientist, healthcare educator, consultant; b. Lethbridge, Alta., Can., Mar. 25, 1935; s. Solon Earl and Alice Fern (Litchfield) L.; m. Cecilia Margaret Comba, Aug. 22, 1959 (div. 1983); children: Cecilia Alice, Sarah Elizabeth, Peter Jon Eric; m. Barbara Joan McLeod, Aug. 25, 1984; 1 child, Kelsey Alexandra MD, C.M., Queen's U., 1960, M.Sc. in Medicine, 1962;

PhD with honors, Baylor U., 1966. From instr. to asst. prof. Baylor Coll. Medicine, Houston, 1965-68; assoc. prof. medicine U. B.C., Vancouver, Can., 1968-78, prof. medicine, 1978-89, clin. assoc. dean, 1974-76, assoc. dean rsch. and grad. studies, 1977-78, coord. health scis., 1985-89, creator Health Policy Rsch. Unit, 1987; Alkek-Williams Disting. Prof. and pres. U. Tex. Health Sci. Ctr., Houston, 1989-2000, disting. mem. faculty Grad. Sch. Biomed. Scis., 1989—2004, dir. Health Policy Inst., 1990—2000; Rockwell chair in soc. and health, dir. Ctr. Soc./Population Health U. Tex., Houston, 2000—04; prof. neurology U. Tex. Med. Sch., Houston, 1989—2001; prof. health policy and mgmt. Sch. Pub. Health U. Tex., 1989—2004, prof. emeritus, 2005—. Cons. in neurology U. Hosp. Shaughnessy site, Vancouver, 1971—89, U. B.C. site, Vancouver, 1970—89; dir. dept. diagnostic neurophysiology Vancouver Gen. Hosp., 1986—87; cons. in EEG, 1987—89; exec. dir. Rsch. Inst., 1981—86; med. sci. adv. com. USIA, 1991—93; adj. prof. Health Informatics Sch. Allied Health Scis.; adj. prof. psychology Simon Fraser U., 2004—; adj. prof. cmty. health scis. U. Calgary, 2005—; mem. Premier's Adv. Coun. on Health, Alta., Canada, 2000—02; strategic adv. Calgary Regional Health Auth., 2002—; spl. advisor to the pres. on pub. health program devel. U. Calgary, 2005—07. Mem. editorial bd. numerous jours.; contbr. articles to profl. jours Bd. dirs. Tex. Inst. for Rehab. and Rsch. Found., Greater Houston Ptnrship., 1994-2000, Episcopal Health Charities Found., 1997-2004, Houston Ind. Sch. Dist. Found., 2002-04; governing bd. Houston Mus. Natural Sci., 1991-97; trustee Kinkaid Sch., Houston, 1991-2004, Meml.-Herman Hosp. Sys., 1997-2000 Med. Rsch. Coun. Can. grantee, 1968-80; recipient Tree of Life award Jewish Nat. Fund, 1995, Caring Spirit award Inst. Religion, 1995 Fellow Am. EEG Soc., Royal Coll. Physicians (Can.), Royal Soc. Medicine (London); mem. AMA, Tex. Med. Assn. (coun. on med. edn. 1990-2000), Tex. Found. Soc. & Health (founding chmn. 1999), Can. Soc. Clin. Neurophysiology, Internat. Fedn. Socs. for EEG and Clin. Neurophysiology (rules com. 1977-81, sec. 1981-85), Assn. Acad. Health Ctrs. (task force on access to care and orgn. health svcs. 1988-95, chmn. 1992, task force on instnl. values 1989-95), Harris County Med. Soc., Am. Coun. Edn., Forum Club of Houston Avocations: sailing, photography, soccer, skiing, flying.

LOW, MURRAY, physiologist; BA, MS, CUNY: Hunter Coll.; EdD in applied physiology, Columbia U. Prof. emeritus physical edn. and gerontol. services CUNY: York Coll.; prog. dir. cardiac rehab. Sound Shore Med. Ctr. of Westchester, NY, 1987—, Burke Rehab. Hosp., White Plains, NY, 2007—, Stamford Hosp., Conn. Fellow: Am. Coll. Sports Medicine, Am. Assn. Cardiovascular and Pulmonary Rehab. (pres. 2008—09, Disting. Svc. award 2006); mem.: NY State Assn. Cardiovascular and Pulmonary Rehab. (pres. 1993—94), Westchester/Putnam County Am. Heart Assn. Mailing: 15 Springdale Rd Scarsdale NY 10583-7320 Office Phone: 914-584-9694. Office Fax: 914-825-9787. E-mail: murray.low@verizon.net. *

LOW, RANDALL, internist, cardiologist; b. San Francisco, June 24, 1949; s. Huet Hee and Betty Tai (Quan) L.; m. Dorothy Fung, May 4, 1975; children: Audrey, Madeleine, Jennifer. AA, City Coll., San Francisco, 1969; BA, U. Calif., Berkeley, 1971; MD, U. Calif., Davis, 1975. Diplomate Am. Bd. Internal Medicine, Nat. Bd. Med. Examiners, Am. Bd. Cardiovascular Diseases. Intern Hosp. of Good Samaritan, LA, 1975-76, resident, 1976-77, chief med. resident, 1977-78, fellow in cardiology, 1979-81; mem. staff St. Francis Meml. Hosp., San Francisco, 1981—, chmn. dept. cardiology, 1995—; pvt. practice internal medicine and cardiology San Francisco, 1981—; mem. staff Chinese Hosp., San Francisco, 1981—, chief of medicine, 1991-92; asst. clin. prof. U. Calif., San Francisco, 1994-2000. Courtesy staff St. Mary's Hosp., San Francisco, 1981—, Calif. Pacific Med. Ctr., San Francisco, 1990—; cardiology cons. Laguna Honda Hosp., San Francisco, 1981—. Home health quality assurance com. Self Help for Elderly, San Francisco, 1991—; bd. trustees San Francisco Health Authority, 2000—; bd. dirs. Youth Advocates, San Francisco, 1992-99, Chinese Hosp. San Francisco, 2008-, Chinese Cmty. Health Plan, 2008-, vice chmn. bd., San Francisco Hon. Authority, 2008-. Recipient Hearst Pub. Svc. award U. Calif.-Berkeley, 1970, Homecare Recognition award Self Help for Elderly, 1993. Mem. ACP, Am. Soc. Internal Medicine, Am. Coll. Cardiology, Am. Heart Assn. (bd. govs. 1983-90), Calif. Acad. Medicine, Calif. Med. Soc., San Francisco Med. Soc. (bd. dirs. 1999-2005), Assn. Chinese Cmty. Physicians (sec.-treas. 1986-89), Chinese Cmty. Health Care Assn. (pres. 1991-96, 99-2002), Fedn. Chinese Am. and Canadia Med. Soc. (pres. 2005-06, chmn. bd., acting exec. v.p., 2007-). Office: 728 Pacific Ave Ste 501 San Francisco CA 94133-4449

LOW, REGINALD INMAN, cardiologist; b. Stockton, Calif., June 1, 1947; MD, U. Calif. Davis, 1975. Cert. Internal Medicine 1978, Cardiovascular Disease 1981, Interventional Cardiology 1999. Intern in internal medicine U. Calif. Davis Med. Ctr., 1975—76, resident in cardiology, 1976—78, fellow in cardiology, 1978—80, chief cardiovascular medicine, 2000—, dir., Heart Ctr.; dir. coronary catherization lab. and coronary care unit U. Ky. Med. Ctr., VA Med. Ctr.; dir. Mercy Heart Inst. Mercy Gen. Hosp., Sacramento, 1989—97; prof. medicine U. Calif. Davis Sch. Medicine, 2000—. Mem., divsn. med. quality Med. Bd. Calif., Dept. Consumer Affairs, 2006—. Recipient Disting. Alumni award, U. Calif. Davis, 2007. Office: U Calif Davis Med Ctr Div Cardiology 4860 Y St Ste 2820 Sacramento CA 95817 Office Phone: 916-734-5191.

LOW, RUSSELL NORMAN, physician; b. Stockton, Calif., Apr. 11, 1953; s. Loren Irving and Rose Low; m. Carolyn Hesse-Low, Apr. 27, 1980; children: Ryan, Robert. BS, U. Calif., Santa Barbara, 1975; DDS, U. Calif., LA, 1979; MD, U. Calif., San Diego, 1990. Resident diagnostic radiology U. Calif., San Francisco, 1986—90; fellow body imaging Stanford U. Med. Ctr., Palo Alto, Calif., 1990—91; physician San Diego Diagnostic Radiology, San Diego, 1991—. Med. dir. Sharp and Children's MRI Ctr., Calif., 1992—. Contbr. 40 articles to profl. and med. jours. on clin. applications for MRI of the abdomen and pelvis. Named David Carroll Med. Intern of Yr., St Mary's Med. Ctr. San Francisco, 1986, One of Best Drs. in Am., Best Drs. Inc., 2003. Mem.: Internat. Soc. Magnetic Resonance in Medicine, Am. Coll. Radiology (bd. cert. 1990), Radiologic Soc. N.Am., Phi Beta Kappa. Office: Sharp and Children's MRI Ctr 7901 Frost St San Diego CA 92123

LOWE, CAMERON ANDERSON, dentist, endodontist, educator; b. Alcester, SD, Dec. 19, 1932; s. Richard Barrett and Emma Louise Lowe; m. Doris Teresita Franquez, Dec. 23, 1957; children: Barrett, Steven, Leslie. Student, George Washington U., 1951-53, U. Va., 1955-56; DDS, Georgetown U., 1956-60; cert. residency in endodon-

tics, U.S. Naval Dental Sch., 1967-69. Commd. lt. (j.g.) U.S. Navy Dental Corps, 1960, advanced through grades to capt., 1976, ret., 1978; pvt. practice endodontist Newport News, Va., 1978-81; assoc. prof. dentistry emeritus Old Dominion U., Norfolk, Va., 1991, asst. chair Sch. Dental Hygiene, 1985-89. Adj. asst. prof. Med. Coll. Va.-Va. Commonwealth U. Sch. Dentistry, Richmond, 1979-81. Contbr. articles to profl. jours. and to book: Oral Pathology, 3d edit., 1989. Tutor adult literacy, 1994-99; coord. Neighborhood Watch, 1994-98; pack and troop chmn. Boy Scouts Am., Guam, 1969-72, Virginia Beach, Va., 1972-78. With USN, 1953-55. Mem. Assn. Mil. Surgeons of U.S., Am. Assn. Endodontists, Am. Acad. Oral Medicine, Am. Dental Assn., Va. Acad. Endodontics, USN Assn. Endodontists, Peninsula Dental Soc., Sigma Alpha Epsilon, Delta Sigma Delta, Sigma Phi Alpha (Dental Hygiene Honor Soc.). Methodist. Avocations: tennis, drawing, carving, reading, sculpting. Home: 1497 Wakefield Dr Virginia Beach VA 23455-4541

LOWE, DALE S., health facility administrator; b. Wilmington, Del., Jan. 29, 1960; BSN, Wilmington Coll., 1999; M in Health Care Adminstrn., Wilmington U., 2008. Dir., preventive medicine, rehab. inst. Christiana Care Health Sys., 2005—. Bd. dirs. DE Sleep Disorders Ctr., 2009—. Vol. Boys Scouts America. Mem.: Nat. Assn. Health Care Quality, Am. Coll. Health Care Execs. Office: 3506 Kennett Pike Wilmington DE 19807 Office Phone: 302-661-3061. Office Fax: 302-661-3010. E-mail: dlowe@christianacare.org.

LOWENBERG, DAVID A., pharmaceutical executive; Pres. Healthcare Devel. Consulting; sr. v.p., dir. site ops. Express Scripts, Inc., Md. Heights, Mo., 1993—99, exec. v.p., COO, 1999—2006, CEO CuraScript, Inc., 2006—; dep. dir. Ariz. Health Care Cost Containment Sys. Bd. dirs. Logos Sch. Office: CuraScript 1 Express Way Saint Louis MO 63121

LOWENBERG, MARC GREGORY, dentist; b. NYC, Mar. 2, 1946; m. Joan Levy Finkelstein; children: Terrence, Tara. BA in Psychology, Am. U., Washington, 1968; DDS, NYU Coll. Dentistry, 1972. Gen. practice intern Met. Hosp., NYC, 1972—73; co-founder, dentist Lowenberg and Lituchy, NYC. Cons. ABC's Extreme Makeover; adv. bd. cancerandcareers.org; guest Oprah Winfrey Show, Good Morning Am., The View. Mem.: ADA, Dental Soc. State NY, Am. Acad. Implant Dentistry, Internat. Congress Oral Implantologists, Am. Acad. Cosmetic Dentistry, Acad. Gen. Dentistry. Office: Lowenberg and Lituchy 230 Central Park S New York NY 10019 Office Phone: 212-586-2890. Office Fax: 212-586-2889. Business E-Mail: info@lowenberglituchy.com.

LOWENSTEIN, ARLENE JANE, nursing educator, health facility administrator; b. Phila., Oct. 10, 1936; d. Nathan Morris and Rae (Greenburg) Needleman; m. Manfred Lowenstein, June 9, 1957; children: Jay David, Russell Scott. Diploma in nursing, Hosp. of U. Pa., Phila., 1957; BSN, Fairleigh Dickinson U., 1969; MA, NYU, 1974; PhD, U. Pitts., 1985. Staff and tchg. nurse Albert Einstein Med. Ctr., Hosp. U. Pa., 1957-59; instr. Middlesex County Coll., Edison, NJ, 1969-71; staff nurse Vis. Nurse Svc., NYC, 1970-72; supr. obstet. and pediat. Middlesex Gen. Hosp., New Brunswick, NJ, 1972-74; dir. ambulatory & cmty. health Peter Bent Brigham Hosp., 1974-79, dir. nurse practitioner program, 1974-81; dir. surg. nursing Brigham and Women's Hosp., Boston, 1980—81; acting dir. nursing Peter Bent Brigham Hosp., Boston, 1978-80; assoc hosp. dir., dir nursing svc. U. Ky. Med. Ctr., Lexington, 1981-83; asst. prof. U. Pitts., 1983-85; prof. nursing, dept. chair. Med. Coll. Ga., Augusta, 1985-95; prof., dir. grad. program in nursing Mass. Gen. Hosp. Inst. of Health Professions, Boston, 1995—2003, prof. emeritus, 2003—; mentor Thomas Edison State Coll., 2007—. Dir. health professions edn. doctoral, Simmons Coll., 2005—. Author textbooks; contbr. articles to profl. jours. Bd. dirs. Sr. Citizens Coun. of Ctrl. Savannah River Area, Augusta, 1982-95; coord. vols. Opera Boston. Recipient Outstanding Tchg. award, Book of Yr. award, Am. Jour. Nursing, 2009, Excellence Nursing Adminstrn. award, Sigma Theta Tau, Theta Chptr. Mem. ANA, Coun. Grad. Edn. for Nursing Adminstrs. (chair 1990-92), Sigma Xi, Sigma Theta Tau. Avocations: opera, music, art. Home: 312 Lewis Wharf Boston MA 02110-3905 Office Phone: 617-521-2305. Business E-Mail: arlene.lowenstein@simmons.edu.

LOWENTHAL, DENNIS ALAN, medical oncologist; MD, Boston U., 1979. Diplomate Am. Bd. Internal Medicine, Am. Bd. Internal Medicine-med. oncology, Am. Bd. Internal Medicine-hematology, lic. NJ, 1986. Intern in internal medicine Cleve. Clinic, 1980; resident in internal medicine Montefiore Med. Ctr., Bronx, NY, 1982, fellow in hematology, 1983; blood bank dirs. tng. fellow NY Blood Ctr., 1984; fellow in med. oncology Meml. Sloan-Kettering Cancer Ctr., 1986, chief fellow in med. oncology, 1986, spl. clin. fellow, 1986; asst. med. dir. cancer ctr. Overlook Hosp., NJ, co-chair thoracic panel, sect. chief hematology/oncology. Office: Overlook Hospital Overlook Oncology Center 99 Beauvoir Ave Summit NJ 07902 Office Phone: 908-608-0078. Office Fax: 908-608-1504.

LOWER, ELYSE E., physician, educator; b. Salem, Ohio, Mar. 28, 1953; d. John E. and Joyce E Lower; m. Robert P. Baughman, May 26, 1984. BS, Baylor U., Waco, Tex., 1975; MA, Baylor U., 1977; MD, U. Cin., 1981. Fellow in hematology-medical oncology U. Cin., 1984—87, asst. prof. internal medicine, 1987—92; assoc. prof., 1992—99, prof. internal medicine, 1999—; ptnr. Oncology-Hematology Care, Inc., Cin., 1999—. Recipient award of hope, Greater Cin. Breast Cancer Alliance, 1996, honoree, Speaking of Women's Health, 2000, Leading Women Honoree, Cin. Bus. Courier, 2001; named Health Care Hero, 1999. Fellow: ACP (fellow 1999); mem.: Am. Soc. Clin. Oncology (life). Office: U Cin Holmes Rm 1001 Eden and Bethesda Cincinnati OH 45267-0565

LOWERY, ROBERT CHESLEY, thoracic surgeon, educator; b. Columbus, Oct. 7, 1949; s. Robert Lowery and Rutha Mae Whiteside; m. Nancy Lowery, July 19, 1986 (div. Dec. 9, 2002); 1 child, Jason. At. State U. of Calif. at LA, 1969—72; MD, U. Calif., San Francisco, 1976. Cert. Nat. Bd. of Med. Examiners, 1978, Am. Bd. of Surgery, 1984, Am. Bd. of Thoracic Surgery, 1986. Dir. sickle cell screening and testing, student nat. med. ctr. U. Calif., San Francisco, 1974—75; acting chief divsn. of cardiothoracic surgery Howard U., Washington, 1987—88; chmn. med. adv. com. Washington Regional Transplant Consortium, 1987—89; co-founder Cardiovasc. and Thoracic Surgery Assoc., Washington, 1994; prof. surgery SUNY Downstate Sch. of Medicine, Bklyn., 2002—06; chief divsn. of cardiothoracic surgery, Downstate Sch. of Medicine SUNY, Bklyn., 2002—06; pvt. practice Washington, 1989—2002. Pres. Stillwild Photography, Washington,

1995—; mem. bd. med. dirs. Life Link MD, Washington, 2000—05. Contbr. articles to profl. jours. Fundraiser DC Pub. Sch., Washington, 2002. Recipient commendation, NY Health and Hosp. Corp., 1979, Patient Choice award, Washington Hosp. Ctr., 1997—2001, Top Dr., Washingtonian mag., 1999. Mem.: Cosmos Club, Sigma Alpha, Epsilon Boulé chpt. Roman Catholic. Achievements include development of new vascular procedure. Avocations: skiing, scuba diving, photography, hiking, wine collecting. Office: Washington Regional Cardiac Surgery PC 110 Irving St NW Ste 1E3 Washington DC 20010 Office Phone: 202-291-1430. Personal E-mail: clowery1@mac.com. Business E-Mail: rlowery@downstate.edu, robert.lowery@medstar.net.

LOWMAN, JOHN D., JR., physical therapist, researcher; m. Mary (Beth) E. Lindsay, Aug. 17, 1996. BS in Edn., Va. Poly. Inst. and State U., 1993; MS, Duke U., 1995; PhD, Va. Commonwealth U., 2004. Lic. phys. therapist N.C. Bd. Phys. Therapy Examiners, 1995, Ala. State Bd. Phys. Therapists, 2005, bd. cert. cardiovasc. and pulmonary phys. therapy clin. specialist 1999. Phys. therapist Vencor Hosp., Greensboro, NC, 1995—96, Interim Healthcare, Durham, 1996—97, Duke U. Med. Ctr., 1996—2005; grad. rsch. and tchg. asst. Va. Commonwealth U., Richmond, 2000—04; postdoctoral assoc. Va. Commonwealth U. Med. Ctr., Richmond, 2005; asst. prof. dept. phys. therapy U. Ala., Birmingham, 2005—, Am. Bd. Phys. Therapy Specialties, 2010—. Phys. therapist asst. exam. devel. com. Fedn. State Bds. Phys. Therapy, Alexandria, Va., 2004—09, chair, 2007—09, cardiovasc. and pulmonary specialization acad. content experts and speciality coun., 2003—; adj. instr. New River C.C., Dublin, 1993. Asst scoutmaster Boy Scouts Am. Troop 45, Dublin, 1989—93, Boy Scouts Am. Troop 430, Richmond, 2001—02; asst. scoutmaster Boy Scouts Am. Troop 736, Glen Allen, Va., 2003—05. Recipient Disting. Svc. award, Va. Tech., Cardiac Therapy and Intervention Ctr., 1992, Outstanding Sr. of Yr., Va. Tech Coll. Edn., 1992—93, Paul Gunsten Leadership award, Va. Tech., Health and Phys. Edn. Dept., 1993, Outstanding Acad. Achievement award, Va. Tech., Coll. Edn., 1993, U. Outstanding Svc. award, Va. Commonwealth U., 2004, U. Outstanding Leadership award, 2004, Outstanding Svc. award, Fedn. State, Bd. Physical Therapy, 2008; scholar, Va. Tech., Health and Phys. Edn. Dept., 1993, Found. Phys. Therapy, 2003—04; Andrea Walnes Meml. scholar, Va. Tech., Coll. Edn., 1992—93. Mem.: Am. Assn. Cardiovasc. and Pulmonary Rehab., Am. Physiol. Soc., Am. Phys. Therapy Assn. Avocations: bicycling, hiking, backpacking, rock climbing. Office: University Ala Dept Phys Therapy Sch Health Pro SHPB 344 1530 3d Ave S Birmingham AL 35294-1212 Personal E-mail: jdlowman@charter.net. Business E-Mail. jlowman@uab.edu.

LOWMAN, ROBERT PAUL, psychology professor, academic administrator; b. Lynwood, Calif., Jan. 23, 1947; s. Hubert Alden and Martha Guynn (Howard) L.; m. Kathleen Marie Drew, June 25, 1972; children: Sarah Guynn, Amy Katherine. AB, U. So. Calif., 1967; MA, Claremont U., 1969, PhD, 1973. Asst. prof. U. Wis., Milw., 1972-76; adminstrv. officer APA, Washington, 1976-81; asst. dean Kans. State U., Manhattan, 1981-86, assoc. dean grad. sch., 1986-90, assoc. vice provost, 1990-91; dir. rsch. svcs. U. NC, Chapel Hill, 1991—2002, adj. assoc. prof., psychology, 1991—2006, rsch. prof., psychology, 2006—, assoc. vice chancellor, rsch., 1994-96, 2001—, assoc. vice provost, rsch., 1996-2001. Owner Lowman Pub. Co., Arroyo Grande, Calif., 2006—. Editor: APA's Guide to Rsch. Support, 1981; contbr. over 30 articles to profl. jours. Recipient numerous grants. Mem. AAAS, Soc. Psychologists in Mgmt. (newsletter editor 1994-96, bd. dirs. 1996-01, pres. 2000), Nat. Coun. U. Rsch. Adminstrs. (mag. co-editor 2006-08, profl. devel. com. 2006-08, bd. dirs. 2009-10), NC Assn. Biomed. Rsch. (bd. dirs. 2010-), Phi Beta Kappa (exec. sec. Alpha NC chpt. 2005—), Phi Kappa Phi, Phi Eta Sigma, Psi Chi. Democrat. Methodist. Home: 104 Chesley Ln Chapel Hill NC 27514-1459 Office: Univ NC Office Vice Chancellor Rsch & Econ Devel CB # 4100 Chapel Hill NC 27599-4100 E-mail: lowman@unc.edu.

LOWMAN, WARREN, microbiologist; MBBCh, U. Witwatersrand, 2002, MMed in Microbiology, 2011. Rschr. Nat. Health Lab. Svcs., 2008—. Mem.: Am. Soc. Microbiologists, South African Soc. Microbiologists. Avocation: golf. Office: 7 York Rd Parktown Johannesburg Gauteng 2193 South Africa Business E-Mail: warren.lowman@wits.ac.za.

LOWRY, ALAIRE HOWARD, psychologist; b. Phila., June 4, 1943; d. Lorn Lambier and Etha Johannaber Howard; m. Thomas Wells Lowry, Apr. 20, 1963; children: Michael Andrew, Thomas Ethan. BA in Music with high honors, So. Meth. U., Dallas, 1965; MusM in Conducting, U. Tex., Austin, 1969, Dr.Mus.Arts, 1972, PhD in Psychology, 1988. Diplomate in group psychology Am. Bd. Profl. Psychology; lic. psychologist Tex., 1990. Harpist Dallas Symphony Orch., 1962—65, 1967; tchr. 2d grade St. Mary's Cathedral Sch., Austin, 1965—66; tchr. Ursuline Acad., Dallas, 1966—67; tchg. asst. U. Tex., Austin, 1967—72; instr. Southwestern U., Georgetown, Tex., 1972—73; from asst. to assoc. prof. U. Tex., Austin, 1973—82; psychologist in pvt. practice Austin, 1988—. Asst. scoutmaster, Philmont Trek leader Boy Scouts Am., Austin, 1988—90; chair Psy-Pac, Tex., 1993—94; adminstrv. bd. chair Univ. United. Meth. Ch., Austin, 2001—03; v.p. bd. dirs. Capital Area Mental Health Ctr., Austin, 1992—94; bd. dirs. Am. Group Psychotherapy Found., 2000—01. Fellow: Am. Bd. Profl. Psychology (bd. dirs. 2008—11), Am. Group Psychotherapy Assn. (ann. meeting mktg. chair 2006); mem.: Am. Acad. Group Psychology (bd. dirs. 2008—11), Southwestern Group Psychotherapy Soc. (sec., inst. chair, tng. chair, newsletter editor, mem. chair), Austin Mental Health Int. Practice Assn. (sec. bd. dirs. 1996—97), Tex. Psychol. Assn. (bd. trustees 1998—2001), Phi Beta Kappa. Democrat. Methodist. Avocations: travel, reading, photography, hiking, skiing, knitting. Office: 8140 N Mopac Bldg 2 Ste 200 Austin TX 78759 Office Phone: 512-346-2332. Business E-Mail: dr_lowry@mac.com.

LOWY, ANDREW M., oncologist, surgeon; BS, Johns Hopkins U.; MD, Cornell U. Med. Coll. Resident Cornell Med. Ctr., Memorial Sloan Kettering Cancer Ctr.; fellow U. Tex. MD Anderson Cancer Ctr.; surgical oncologist UCSD Moores Cancer Ctr. Editorial bd. mem. Jour. Clinical Oncology, Annals of Surgical Oncology; surgical liaison Southwest Oncology Group Pancreas & Hepatobiliary com. Achievements include development of HIPEC treament for advanced abdominal cancer. Office: Moores UCSD Cancer Center 3855 Health Sciences Dr La Jolla CA 92093 Office Phone: 858-822-6243.

LOWY, DOUGLAS RONALD, oncologist, researcher; b. NYC, 1942; MD, NYU, 1968. Intern Stanford Med. Ctr., Calif., 1968—69, resident in internal medicine, 1969—70; rsch. assoc. lab. viral diseases Nat. Inst. Allergy and Infectious Diseases, NIH, 1970—73; resident in dermatology Yale-New Haven Med. Ctr., 1973—75; with Lab. Cellular Oncology Nat. Cancer Inst., NIH, Bethesda, Md., 1975—, chief Lab. Cellular Oncology, 1983—, dep. dir. Ctr. Cancer Rsch., chief Basic Rsch. Lab. Recipient Wallace Rowe award for virus rsch. Mem.: Inst. of Medicine. Office: Nat Cancer Inst Lab Cellular Oncology 37 Convent Dr Bldg 37 Rm 4106C Bethesda MD 20892 Office Phone: 301-496-9513. Office Fax: 301-480-5322. E-mail: dl60z@nih.gov. *

LOYKE, HUBERT FRANK, internist, cardiologist; b. Cleve., Sept. 9, 1923; s. Frank Alex and Casimer Marie (Malczewski) L.; m. Ellen Marie Eynon, June 16, 1951; children: Thomas F., Christopher J. BS, John Carroll U., 1944; MD, St. Louis U., 1948; postgrad., U. Mich., 1952. Intern St. Alexis Hosp., Cleve., 1948-49; resident St. John Hosp., Cleve., 1949-51; fellow in hypertension U. Mich., 1951-52; sch. physician Pub. Health Dept., Cleve., 1952-54; chief Hypertension Clinic, Cleve., 1957-95; dir. Hypertension Lab., Cleve., 1957-95; internist, cardiologist St. Vincent Charity Hosp., Cleve., 1957-95; med. examiner FAA, Washington, 1961-63; chief cardiology St. John Hosp., Cleve., 1962-65; chief of staff St. Augustine Manor, Cleve., 1971-72; chief medicine Langley AFB Hosp. Med. advisor ARC, Cleve., 1982-92, Lee County, 1996—, cancer com. Southwest Reg. Hosp., 2004—; physician mem. Sr. Friendship Ctr., Ft. Myers, Fla., 1997—. Reviewer 6 med. jours., 1972-95; contbr. over 50 articles to profl. jours. Vol. ARC, Ft. Myers, Fla., 1997—. Capt. USAF, 1955-57. Grantee NIH, 1959-71, Kidney Found., 1977-78, Morison Found., 1980-81, Vol. of Yr. award, Lee Meml., 2011. Mem. AMA, Internat. Soc. Hypertension, Coun. High Blood Pressure Rsch., Soc. Airlace Hist. Republican. Roman Catholic. Achievements include identification of effect of altitude on Sickle Cell disease, liver blood pressure effect, diseases which lower blood pressure, elements which affect blood pressure; alcohol's effect of blood pressure, demonstrated lowering blood pressure by animal ACE blockade. Office: St Vincent Charity Hosp 2351 E 22d St Cleveland OH 44115-3111 Home: 1441 Graham Cir Lehigh Acres FL 33936 Office Phone: 440-886-0921.

LOZANO, FRANCISCO S., surgeon, educator; b. Zamora, Spain, Aug. 14, 1953; s. Francisco and Emilia Sanchez; m. Alix Lozano, Nov. 26, 1977; children: Pablo Sanchez, Teresa Sanchez. MD with honors, Salamanca U., Spain, 1977, PhD with honors, 1982; cert. in stats., Barcelona U., 1980; MA in Clin. Mgmt., UNED, Madrid, 2003. Cert. vascular surgery Spain. Resident Clinic Hosp., Salamanca, 1978—82; surgeon Multizonale Hosp., Varese, Italy, 1988, Milan U. Hosp., 1988, U. Md. Hops., Balt., 1993, Barnes Hosp., St. Louis, 1996; sec. Nat. Commn. Surg. Infections, Spain, 1986—2000; staff Nat. Commn. Vascular Surgery, Spain, 1990—. Prof. surgery Salamanca U., chmn. dept. surgery, 1992—98, subdirector Investigation Biomedical Inst., 2000—, collaborator Cochrane Libr., 2000—. Author: 9 books; contbr. articles to profl. jours. Chair commn. PLANCIR vascular surgery Ministry Health, Spain, 1997—2000, expert Health Tech. Spain Agy., 2002—. Med. officer Spanish Army, 1979—80. Fellow: ICA, ICS, ACS; mem.: Soc. Catile-Lyons Vascular Surgery (pres. 2003—). Roman Catholic. Office: U Salamanca Dept Cirugia Alfonso X El Sabio s/n 37007 Salamanca Spain Business E-Mail: lozano@usal.es.

LOZANO, JOSE, nephrologist; b. San Vicente, El Salvador, Feb. 11, 1941; arrived in USA, 1968, naturalized; s. Jose E. and Transito Maria (Mendez) L.; m. Hilda Berganza, Jan. 27, 1965; children: Jose E., Claudia Maria. MD, U. El Salvador, 1965. Diplomate Am. Bd. Internal Medicine, Am. Bd. Nephrology. Rotating intern Nat. Med. Ctr., San Salvador, El Salvador, 1963-64; asst. resident in internal medicine Rosales Hosp., San Salvador, 1965-66, resident in internal medicine, 1966-67, chief resident in internal medicine, 1967-68; resident in internal medicine Baylor U. Affiliated Hosps., Houston, 1968-70, fellow in nephrology, 1970-71, 73-74; asst. prof. medicine U. El Salvador, 1971-72; internist and nephrologist Social Security Hosp., San Salvador, 1971-72; instr. in medicine Baylor Coll. Medicine, Houston, 1974-75, asst. prof. medicine in nephrology, 1975-76, clin. asst. prof. medicine, 1976-80; mem. staff internal medicine St. Elizabeth Hosp., Beaumont Med./Surg. Hosp., Bapt. Hosp., Beaumont, Tex., 1976; med. dir. Golden Triangle Dialysis Ctr., Beaumont, 1977-98, BMA Jasper, Jasper, Tex., 1986-98, BMA Orange, Orange, Tex., 1987-90, Kidney Ctr., Beaumont, Tex., 2001—, Jasper, 2001—. Med. dir. Jasper Dialysis Ctr., 1986-98, Kidney Ctr. of Jasper, 2001-, Beaumont Kidney Ctr., 2001-; mem. Kidney Health Care Adv. Com., 1981-82; pesenter in field. Contbr. articles to profl. publs. Fellow ACP, Am. Soc. Nephrology; mem. AMA, Internat. Soc. Nephrology, Tex. Med. Assn., Harris County Med. Soc., Jefferson County Med. Soc., Physicians for A Nat. Health Plan. Office: 2955 Harrison Ste 100 Beaumont TX 77702 E-mail: bmtnp410@aol.com.

LOZANO, MIGUEL, hematologist, consultant; b. Algar, Cádiz, Spain, June 14, 1959; s. Manuel Lozano and Paquita Molero; m. Gloria Carbassé, Jan. 2, 1960; children: Oriol, Mireia. MD with honors, U. Barcelona, Spain, 1984, PhD, 1992. Rsch. fellow U. Hosp. Utrecht, Netherlands, 1990—91; med. dir. Immuno, Barcelona, 1991—92; staff hematologist Hosp. Clínico Barcelona, Barcelona, 1992—. Pres. Catalan Soc. of Blood Transfusion, Barcelona, 2000—04; v.p. Spanish Soc. Blood Transfusion, Madrid, 2002—; spkr. in field. Contbr. over 60 articles to profl. jours. Grantee, Spanish FIS, 1999—2000. Mem.: Internat. Soc. Blood Transfusion, Am. Assn. Blood Banks, Internat. Soc. Thrombosis and Haemostasis, Spanish Soc. Hematology and Hemotherapy. Office: Hosp Clínico Barcelona Villarrocl 170 08036 Barcelona Spain Home Phone: +34 932 055 036; Office Phone: +34 932 275 448. Office Fax: + 34 932 279 369. Business E-Mail: mlozano@clinic.ub.es.

L. R. KUMARASWAMY NAIK, dental educator; b. Lakshmipura, Karnataka, India, Apr. 15, 1978; B in Dental Surgery, Bapuji Dental Coll. and Hosp., Davangere, Karnataka, 1999; M in Dental Surgery, A. B. Shetty Meml. Inst. Dental Scis., Mangalore, Karnataka, 2005. Reader Maharana Pratap Coll. Dentistry & Rsch. Ctr., 2008—. Mem.: IAOMP. Avocations: cricket, yoga, gardening. Home: Door 1974/51 15th Cross Anjaney Davangere Karnataka 5977004 India Personal E-mail: drkumarswamylr@rediffmail.com.

LU, AMY SHIRONG, media specialist, educator; b. Beijing, Feb. 1, 1980; MA, U. NC, Chapel Hill, 2004, PhD, 2009. Postdoc. assoc. Baylor Coll. Medicine, 2009—10; asst. prof. Ind. U. Sch. Informatics, 2010—. Mem.: APHA, Internat. Soc. Behavioral Nutrition and Phys. Activity, Assn. Edn. in Journalism and Mass Comm., Nat. Comm. Assn., Internat. Comm. Assn. Avocations: piano, painting, ballet. Office: 535 W Michigan St IT 461 Indianapolis IN 46202 Office Fax: 317-278-7669. Business E-Mail: amylu@iu.edu.

LU, CHENG-HSIEN, neurologist, educator; b. Fengshan, Taiwan, Jan. 27, 1966; s. Fu-Tien Lu and Chiu-Chu Luling; m. Yu-Han Huang, Dec. 5, 1999; children: Pin-Ying, Yen-Ting. MD, Chung Shan Med. U., Taichung, 1992; MS, Chang Gung U., Linko, 2002. Diplomate Nat. Bd. Neurologist, 1996. Resident Chang Gung Meml. Hosp., Kaohsiung, Taiwan, 1992—96, med. fellow, 1996—97, vis. staff, 1997—99, lectr., 1999—2002, asst. prof., 2002—05, assoc. prof., 2005—. Contbr. articles to numerous profl. jours. Mem.: Taiwan Soc. Critical Care Medicine, Soc. Ultrasound in Medicine ROC, Taiwan Stroke Soc., Formosan Med. Assn., Taiwan Neurol. Soc., Am. Acad. Neurology. Buddhist. Avocations: jogging, mountain climbing. Office: Chang Gung Meml Hosp 123 Ta Pei Rd Niao Sung Hsiang Kaohsiung Hsien 833 Taiwan Personal E-mail: chlu99@ms44.url.com.tw.

LU, CHRISTINE YI-JU, pharmacist, researcher; b. Taoyuan, Taiwan, Mar. 5, 1977; d. Alex Shaw-Wu Lu and Olga Shou-Hwa Wu. B of Pharmacy, U. Sydney, 1997; MS in Biopharms., U. NSW, 2002, postgrad. in Clin. Pharmacology, 2003—06. Registered pharmacist NSW, 1999. Pharmacist-in-charge Chatswood Sta. Pharmacy, NSW, Australia, 1999—2001, Sta. Med. Ctr. Pharmacy, 1999—2001, Curry Chemist, Hornsby, 1999—2000, Med. Ctr. Pharmacy Chatswood, 2001—07; rsch. assoc. Population Health and Use Medicines Unit, U. NSW & St Vincent's Hosp. Sydney, Sydney, 2004—06; clin. trial asst. St Vincent's Clin. Trials Centre, St Vincent's Hosp. Sydney, Darlinghurst, 2005—06; rsch. fellow Harvard Med. Sch., 2007—. Cons. pharmacist M-TAG Pty Ltd, Sydney, 1999. Contbr. articles to profl. jours. Mem. postgrad. bd. U. NSW, 2004. Grantee, Australasian Soc. Clin. and Exptl. Pharmacologists and Toxicologists, 2004, U. NSW, Sch. Med. Scis., 2005, 2006, Am. Statis. Health Policy Stats. Sect., 2005, Australian Rheumatology Assn., 2006, Internat. Soc. Pharamacoepidemiology, 2006; fellow, Harvard Med. Sch., 2007; scholar, Nat. Health & Med. Rsch. Coun., 2005, 2006. Mem.: Internat. Soc. for Pharmacoecons. and Outcomes Rsch., Australian Pharm. Sci. Assn., Australasian Soc. Clin. and Exptl. Pharmacologists and Toxicologists, Soc. Hosp. Pharmacists Australia. Evangelical. Achievements include contribution to the debate concerning arrangements for access to high cost biologic medicines via the Australian Pharmaceutical Benefits Scheme by publishing and presenting the results of our research. Avocations: music, travel, tennis, jogging, movies. Home: 26 Nicholson St Chatswood NSW 2067 Australia Office Fax: 612 83822724. Personal E-mail: y.christine.lu@gmail.com.

LU, CHUAN HUA, pharmacist; b. Hefei, China, Nov. 4, 1960; M, Anhui U., 1988. Mem. Chinese Pharm. Assn., 2000. Office: Meishan Rd Hefei Anhui 230038 China Office Fax: 86-0551-5169146. Business E-Mail: lch@ahtcm.edu.cn

LU, CHUN-YI, epidemiologist, researcher; b. Taipei, Taiwan, Jan. 4, 1967; m. Ling-Ling Tsai, Jan. 1, 1999; children: Jonathan, Vincent. MD, China Med. U., 1981; PhD, Nat. Taiwan U., 2000. Lic. paediat. specialist Taiwan Paediatrics Assn., 1998, infectious disease specialist Infectious Disease Soc., Taiwan, 2000. Intern Nat. Taiwan U. Hosp., Taipei, Taiwan, 1990—91, resident dept. pediatrics, 1994—97, fellow divsn. of infectious disease dept. pediatrics, 1997—99, attending physician, 2000—, lectr., 2005—; postdoctoral fellow NIH, Bethesda, Md., 2002—03. Reviewer Jour. Microbiology, Imunology and Infection, Taipei, 2003—, Jour. Formasan Med. Assn., Taipei, 2003—. Contbr. articles to profl. jours. Grantee, Nat. Sci. Coun., Taiwan, 2003, Nat. Taiwan U. Hosp., 2005; fellow, NIH, 2002; scholar, Rotary Club, Taiwan, 2004. Mem.: Infectious Disease Soc., Taiwan Pediatric Assn., Taiwan Med. Assn. Achievements include research in long-term immunity of HBV vaccine; blocking SARS replication by siRNA technology; enterovirus 71 and apoptosis. Office: National Taiwan University Hospital 7 Chung-Shan South Road Taipei 100 Taiwan

LU, GUOCHENG, retired medical educator; b. China; d. Yanying Lu and Dehua Wang. Grad., Beijing Med. Coll., 1953. Cert. in tchg. Beijing Mcpl. Commn. Edn., 1997. Lectr. Beijing Med. Coll., 1960—79, assoc. prof., 1979—87; prof. Beijing Med. U., 1987—95, prof. ret., 1995—2000, Health Sci. Ctr., Peking U., Beijing, 2000—11. Com. mem. 1st, 2nd and 3rd Nat. Com. Health Std. Tech., Ministry of Pub. Health, Beijing, 1979—96, Specialized Com. Rare Earth Environ. Protection, 2nd Exec. Coun. Chinese Rare Earth Soc., Beijing, 1991—95; 1st, 2nd and 3rd editl. com. mem. Jour. Chinese Rare Earth Soc., 1987—2000. Translator: (book) Methodological Approaches in Deriving Environmental and Occupational Health Standard; contbr. chapters to books, scientific papers, articles to many sci. jours. (Sci. and Tech. award, Beijing City Govt., 2005). Recipient Med. Sci. and Tech. award, Chinese Med. Assn., 2005; Rsch. grants, Ministry of Sci. and Tech., China, 1981, Ministry of Pub. Health, China, 1982, Nat. Natural Sci. Found. China, 1986, 1995, 1998. Mem.: Chinese Preventive Medicine Assn. (Beijing). Achievements include discovery of that children living in ion-adsorptive light rare earths mining area were rare earths exposed high risk group; toxicological and epidemiological studies, rare earths contents in human scalp hair has been identified as a biomarker of their exposure; hormetic effect of cerium at low dose level per os; sperm toxicity of yttrium per os and itra-peritoneal; research in the standard setting of rare earths content in surface water body resulted in the derivation of the recommended value of Cerium; developing two certified reference materials for ultra-trace analysis of 15 rare earth elements in biological samples. Office: Peking Univ Health Sci Ctr Xueyuan Rd Beijing 100191 China Office Fax: 086 010 82801176. Personal E-mail: guochlu@yahoo.com.cn.

LU, GUOHUA, research scientist; b. China, Feb. 17, 1976; PhD, Sch. Biomed. Engring., 2005. Rsch. scientist Fourth Mil. Med. U., 2005—. Office: 17 ChangLe West St Xian Shaanxi 710032 China Business E-Mail: lugh1976@fmmu.edu.cn.

LU, JANG-JIH, pathologist; b. Pingtong City, Taiwan, Oct. 13, 1956; m. Yin-Chuan Lee, Oct. 12, 1984; children: Christine, Ezekiel, Patrick. MD, Nat. Def. Med. Ctr., 1982; PhD, Ind. U. Sch. Medicine, 1995. Board certified in Clinical Pathology Taiwan, ROC, lic. MD Dept. of Health, 1982. Resident Divsn. Clin. Pathology, Dept. Pathology Tri-Svc. Gen. Hosp., Taipei, Taiwan, 1984—87, chief resident Divsn. Clin. Pathology, Dept. Pathology, 1987—88, attending physician Divsn. Clin. Pathology, Dept. Pathology, 1988—, chief

Divsn. Clin. Pathology, Dept. Pathology, 2003—; prof. Dept. Pathology Nat. Def. Med. Corps., Taipei, 2001—. Counselor Taiwan Soc. of Clin. Pathologists, 2003—, Taiwan Assn. of Lab. Medicine, 2003—, Taiwan Com. for Clin. Lab. Standards, 2004—, Taiwan Assn. of Histocompatibility Immunogeneity, 2003—, Taiwan Soc. of Microbiology, 2001—04. Christianity Canaan fellowship, Taipei, Taiwan, 1982—2005. Col. Taiwanese Army, 2002—. Recipient Rsch. awards, Inst. of Biomedical Sciences, Academia Sinica, 1999—2000, Excellent Physician, Tri-Service Gen. Hosp., 1997, Rsch. award, Nat. Def. Med. Ctr., 1995, 1999, Tri-Service Gen. Hosp. 1997, 1998, 1998, Excellent Tchr., Nat. Def. Med. Ctr. 1998, 2000; grant, Nat. Sci. Coun., 1996—2005, Dept. of Health, 1995—2005. Mem.: Taiwan Assn. of Histocompatibility Immunogeneity (assoc.), Taiwan Com. for Clin. Lab. Standards (assoc.), Formosa Med. Assn. (assoc.), Taiwan Assn. of Lab. Medicine (assoc.), Taiwan Soc. of Microbiology (assoc.), Taiwan Soc. of Clin. Pathologists (assoc.), European Congress of Clin. Microbiology and Infection Disease (assoc.), Assn. of Molecular Pathology, USA (assoc.), Am. Soc. for Microbiology (assoc.). Home: 114 Taiwan Office: Tri-Service Genl Hosp (TSGH) No325 Sec 2 Chengkung Road Neihu Chiu Taipei 114 Taiwan Office Fax: 886-2-8792-7226; Home Fax: 886-2-8792-7226. Business E-Mail: jjl@mail.ndmctsgh.edu.tw.

LU, MONG-LIANG, psychiatrist; b. Nantou, Taiwan, Dec. 16, 1968; s. Zhu-Ging Lu and Mei-Hui Zheng; m. Kuei-Fen Lee, Nov. 6, 1996; children: Cheng-Yu, Hong-Jun. MD, Nat. Taiwan U., Taiwan, 1986—93, MS, 1993—95. Res. phys. Taipei City Psychiat. Ctr., Taipei, Taiwan, 1995—99; staff psychiatrist Shin Kong Wu Ho-Su Meml. Hosp., Taipei, Taiwan, Taiwan, 1999—2000, Taipei Med. University-Wan Fang Hosp., Taipei, Taiwan, Taiwan, 2000—; instr. Taipei Med. U., Taipei, Taiwan, Taiwan, 2001—05, asst. prof., 2005—. Mem.: Taiwanese Soc. of Psychiatry (Tsai Shi-Jin award 2005, Schizophrenia Rsch. award 2005). Office: Taipei Med Univ Wan Fang Hosp No 111 Hsin Long Rd Sec 3 Taipei 116 Taiwan

LU, YUN (LUCY LU), pharmacist, educator; b. China, Dec. 3, 1967; MS, Tongji Med. U., 1992; PharmD, U. Minn., 1998. Clin. pharmacist, cardiology Hennepin County Med. Ctr., 1998. Clin. assoc. prof. Coll. Pharmacy, U. Minn., 1998. Recipient Cheers award, ISMP, 2010. Mem.: Am. Pharmacist Assn., Am. Coll. Clin. Pharmacy, Bd. Pharmacy Splty., Am. Heart Assn. Office: 701 Park Ave Minneapolis MN 55415 Business E-Mail: yun.lu@hcmed.org.

LU, ZHONG XIAN, pathologist, educator; b. China, May 20, 1964; MD, Guangzhou Med. Coll., 1987; PhD, Monash U., 2000. Chem. pathologist Melbourne Pathology, 2007—. Adjunct lectr., dept. medicine Monash U., 2006—. Fellow: Royal Coll. Pathologists Australasia. Office: 103 Victoria Pde Collingwood Victoria 3066 Australia Business E-Mail: zhong.lu@mps.com.au.

LÜß, HARTMUT, clinical pharmacologist, researcher; b. Greifswald, Mecklenburg-Vorpommern, Germany, Dec. 20, 1964; s. Klaus-Dieter Horst Wolfgang and Hanne Lore Lüß; m. Iva Maria Kocianova; children: Anne-Marie, Katharina. MD, U. Rostock, Germany, 1990; Habil, U. Muenster, Germany, 2004. Cert. toxicologist; clin. pharmacologist, pharmacologist. Rsch. fellow Dept. of Pharmacology, Kiel, Schleswig-Holstein, Germany, 1991, Inst. of Pharmacology and Toxicology, U. Rostock, 1992—93; rsch. assoc. Dept. of Surgery, U. of Pitts., 1993—95; asst. prof. Inst. of Pharmacology and Toxicology, U. Münster, Germany, 1995—2002; clin. rsch. scientist CardioPep Pharma, Hannover, Niedersachsen, Germany, 2002—. Tchr. in pharmacology Nurse Sch. at Tilbeck, Havixbeck, Nordrhein-Westfalen, Germany, 1998—2002. Contbr. chpts. to book, Drug Profiles for Drug Therapy, 1998. Roman Catholic. Avocations: cycle riding, swimming. Office: CardioPep Pharma Karl-Wiechert-Allee 76 Niedersachsen Hannover D-30625 Germany Home Phone: 49-511-51069-84; Office Phone: 49-511-53045-15. Office Fax: 49-511-53045-10. Personal E-Mail: lussis@web.de. E-Mail: luess@cardiopep.de.

LUBAWSKI, JAMES LAWRENCE, businessman and consultant; b. Chgo., June 4, 1946; s. Harry James and Stella Agnes (Pokorny) L.; m. Kathleen Felicity Donnellan, June 1, 1974; children: Kathleen N., James Lawrence, Kevin D., Edward H. BA, Northwestern U., 1968, MBA, 1969, MA, 1980. Asst. prof. U. Northern Iowa, Cedar Falls, 1969-72; instr. Loyola U., Chgo., 1974-76; dir. market planning Midwest Stock Exchange, Chgo., 1976-77; dir. mktg. Gambro Inc., Barrington, Ill., 1977-79; mktg. mgr. Travenol Labs., Deerfield, Ill., 1979-82; dir. mktg. Hollister Inc., Libertyville, Ill., 1982-84; pres., chief exec. officer Neomedica Inc., Chgo., 1984-86; v.p. bus. devel. Evangl. Health Svcs., Oak Brook, Ill., 1986-87; pres., chief exec. officer Cath. Health Alliance Met. Chgo., 1987-95; mng. dir. Ward Howell Internat., Chgo., 1995-98; v.p. A.T. Kearney, Chgo., 1998-2000; pres. Zwell Internat., Chgo., 2000—02; founder Lubawski & Assocs., Northfield, 2002—09; chief operating officer Felician Svcs. Inc., 2009—. Author: Food and Man, 1974, Food and People, 1979; co-editor: Consumer Behavior in Theory and in Action, 1970. Trustee Madonna U., 2010—, Felician Coll., 2010, Villa Mavia Coll., 2010. Mem. Evanston Golf Club (pres. 2000-02, 2009). Avocations: golf, fishing. Office: 3800 W Peterson Ave Chicago IL 60659 Office Phone: 773-463-3806. Personal E-Mail: Jim@Lubawski.com.

LUBBERS, ALICE DIANNE, operating room nurse; b. Spokane, Wash., Nov. 10, 1956; d. Donald Lee and Dianne B. (Engstrom) L. BS, U. Idaho, 1979; BSN, Ctr. for Nursing Edn., 1985; grad, U.S. Army Command and Gen. Staff Coll., 1999; MS in Bus. Orgn., U. La Verne, Calif., 2002. RN, Wash.; cert. oper. rm. nurse. Commd. U.S. Army, 1988, advanced through grades to lt. col.; oper. rm. nurse Kootenai Med. Ctr., Coeur d'Alene, Idaho; psychiatric nurse Sacred Heart Med. Ctr., Spokane; neurosurg. head nurse operating room Madigan Med. Ctr., U.S. Army Nurse Corps., Ft. Lewis, Wash., 1988—90; head nurse dept. urology Madigan Army Med. Ctr., 1990—91; head nurse oper. rm. and ctrl. supply Bassett Army Cmty. Hosp., Ft. Wainwright, Alaska, 2000—04; head nurse ctrl. supply 47th Combat Support Hosp., Operation Iraqi Freedom, 2003; chief oper. room and ctrl. supply Bayne Jones Army Cmty. Hosp., Ft. Polk, La., 2004—06; head nurse or Madigan Army Med. Ctr., Ft. Lewis, Wash., 2006—08. Clin. staff perioperative nurse 47th Combat Support Hosp., Operation Desert Shield/Desert Storm, 1991; head nurse OR/CMS 18th MASH, 1991-92; head nurse same day surgery/OR, Bayne-Jones Army Cmty. Hosp., Ft. Polk, La., 1993-96; OR edn. coord./laser safety officer Madigan Army Med. Ctr., Ft. Lewis, Wash., 1997-2000. Decorated Meritorious Svc. medal (3), Army Achievement medal (6), Army Commendation medal (6), Southwest Asia medal with 3 combat stars, Kuwait Liberation medal, Saudi Arabia liberation medal, Nat.

Defense medal (2), Meritorious Unit Citation medal (2), Global War on Terrorism Epiditionary medal with one combat star, Global War on Terrorism Svc. medal, Overseas medal, Humanitarian Svc. medal, Iraqui Freedom medal. Mem. Assn. Oper. Rm. Nurses, Am. Soc. Laser Medicine and Surgery, Laser Inst. Am. Home: PO Box 213 Pahrump NV 89041 Personal E-mail: alicelubbers@att.net.

LUBIC, RUTH WATSON, innovative health facility administrator, nurse midwife; b. Bucks County, Pa., Jan. 18, 1927; d. John Russell and Lillian (Kraft) Watson; m. William James Lubic, May 28, 1955; 1 child, Douglas Watson. Diploma, Sch. Nursing Hosp. U. Pa., 1955; BS, Columbia U., 1959, MA, 1961, EdD in Applied Anthropology, 1979; cert. in nurse midwifery, SUNY, Bklyn., 1962, DSc (hon.), 1993; LLD (hon.), U. Pa., 1985; Dlaw (hon.), U. Medicine and Dentistry, NJ, 1986; LHD (hon.), Coll. New Rochelle, 1992, Pace U., 1994, U. Mass., 2009; DSc with honors, U. Mass. Med. Coll., Worcester, 2009. Staff nurse through head nurse Meml. Hosp. for Cancer and Allied Disease, NYC, 1955-58; clin. assoc. Grad. Sch. Nursing NY Med. Coll., NYC, 1962-63; parent educator, cons. Maternity Ctr. Assn., NYC, 1963-67, gen. dir., 1970-95, dir. clin. projects, 1995-97; project dir. Nat. Assn. of Childbearing Ctrs., Washington, 1997-99; pres., CEO DC Developing Families Ctr., 1998—2002, founder, pres. emeritus, 2003—; pres., CEO Family Health and Birth Ctr., Washington, 1998—2007; founder, chair emeritus DC Birth Ctr., 2007—. Cons. in midwifery, nursing and maternal and child health Office Pub. Health and Sci. HHS, 1995—97; adj. prof. divsn. nursing NYU, 1995—; bd. dirs., v.p. Am. Assn. World Health U.S. Com. WHO, 1975—94, pres. Am. Assn. World Health U.S. Com., 1980—81; mem. bd. maternal child and family health NRC, 1974—80; mem. bd. Commn. Grads. Fgn. Nursing Schs., 1979—83, v.p., 1980—81, treas., 1982—83; bd. govs. Frontier Nursing Svc., 1982—92; bd. dirs. Pan Am. Health Edn. Found., pres., 1987—88; vis. prof. King Edward Meml. Hosp., Perth, Australia, 1991; Kate Hanna Harvey vis. prof. cmty. health nursing Frances Payne Bolton Sch. Nursing Case Western Res., 1991; Lansdowne lectr. U. Victoria, B.C., Canada, 1992; adj. prof. Sch. Nursing, Georgetown U., 1997—; Therese Dondero lectr. Am. Coll. Nurse-Midwives Found., 1995; Andrea Printy Meml. lectr. U. Minn., 1998; Kemble lectr. Sch. Nursing, U. NC, Chapel Hill, 2000; Hugh P. Davis lectr. Emory U. Sch. Nursing, 2004. Author (with Gene Hawes): (book) childbearing: A Book of Choices, 1987; contbr. articles to profl. jours. Recipient Martha May Eliot award, Am. Pub. Health Assn., 2006, Letitia White award, Sch. Nursing Hosp. U. Pa., 1955, Florence Nightingale medal, 1955, Nursing Practice award, U. Pa., 1980, Rockefeller Pub. Svc. award, 1981, Hattie Hemschemeyer award, 1983, Alumnae award, Sch. Nursing U. Pa., 1986, McManus medal, Tchrs. Coll. Columbia U., 1992, Disting. Svc. award, Francis Payne Bolton Sch. Nursing, 1993, Hon. Recognition, NY State Nurses Assn., 1993, Nurse-Midwifery Faculty award, Columbia U., 1993, Spirit of Nursing award, Vis. Nurses Svc. NY, 1994, Maes-Macinnes award, Divsn. Nursing NYU, 1994, Hon. Recognition, ANA, 1994, Carola Warburg Rothschild award, Maternity Ctr. Assn., 1997, Healthy Babies Project award, 1998, Woman of Distinction award, Nat. Assn. Women in Edn., 1999, Never Say Die award, DC Primary Care Assn., 2001; named Maternal-Child Health Nurse of the Yr., ANA, 1985, Disting. Alumna, U. Pa., 1992; named to Nursing Hall of Fame, 1999; Irving Harris vis. scholar, Coll. Nursing U. Ill., 1999, MacArthur fellow, 1993. Fellow: AAAS, Soc. for Applied Anthropology, Am. Acad. Nursing (Living Legend award 2001); mem.: APHA (mem. com. on internat. health, sec. maternal and child health coun. 1982, mem. governing coun. 1986—89, mem. nominating com. 1987, mem. action bd. 1988—90), Densford Ctr. U. Minn. Summit (SAGE award 2009), UNFPA (award 2010), Nat. Rsch. Ctr. Women Families (Fore Mother award 2010), Vis. Nurse Svc. of NY (Lillian Wald award 2003), Herman Biggs Soc. (sec.-treas. 1989—90), Am. Assn. Colls. Nursing (McGovern lectr. 1997), Nat. Assn. Childbearing Ctrs. (pres. 1983—91, Lifetime Achievement award 2005), Inst. of Medicine of NAS (Lienhard award 2001), Am. Coll. Nurse Midwives (v.p. 1964—66, pres.-elect 1969—70), NY Acad. Medicine, Alpha Omega Alpha (hon.). Home Phone: 212-749-8590; Office Phone: 202-398-2007. Personal E-Mail: rlubic@aol.com.

LUBIN, MICHAEL FREDERICK, physician, educator; b. Phila., Mar. 20, 1947; BA, Johns Hopkins U., 1969, MD, 1973. Resident Emory U. Affiliated Hosp., Atlanta, 1973-76; asst. prof. medicine Emory U. Sch. Medicine, Atlanta, 1976-82, assoc. prof. medicine, 1982—2001, dir. div. gen. medicine, 1989-95; dir. preoperative clinic Grady Hosp., Atlanta, 1995—; intern. housestaff evaluation com. dept. medicine Emory U. Sch. Medicine, 1985—2001, dir. geriatrics assessment clinic, 1998—, prof. medicine, 2001—; vis. prof. U. Tokyo, 2008. Chmn. univ. adv. coun. tchg. Emory U., 2004—08. Editor: Medical Management of the Surgical Patient, 1982, 4th edit., 2006, Med. Rounds, 1988—90; mem. editl. bd. I-M: Internal Medicine, 1992—95; contbr. to Med. Knowledge Self Assessment Program X, 1994. Chmn. univ. adv. coun. on tchg. Emory U.; mem. alumni coun. Johns Hopkins U., 1995—2001; mem. Cmty. Supporters of Atlanta Symphony Orch., 1996—98, bd. dirs., 1996—97. Scholar Hartford scholar in Geriatrics, UCLA, 1984—85, Ctr. for Medicare & Medicaid Svcs. Health Policy scholar, 2003. Fellow: ACP, Phi Beta Kappa (bd. dirs. Met. Atlanta chpt. 1996—2000, v.p. 2000—05, bd. dirs. 2005—, nat. nominating com. mem. 2010—); mem.: Soc. Gen. Internal Medicine (edn. com. 2003—), Am. Geriat. Soc., Alpha Omega Alpha, Fellows of Phi Beta Kappa (bd. dirs. 2002—), Phi Lambda Upsilon. Office: Emory U Sch Medicine 49 Jesse Hill Jr Dr Atlanta GA 30303 Office Phone: 404-778-1607.

LUBY, ELLIOT DONALD, psychiatrist, educator; b. Detroit, Apr. 3, 1924; m. Ideane Maura Levenson, June 28, 1950; children: Arthur, Howard, Joan. Student, U. Chgo., 1943-44; BS, U. Mo., 1945-47; MD, Wash. U., St. Louis, 1947-49. Clin. dir. Lafayette Clinic, Detroit, 1957-74; chief psychiatry Harper Hosp., Detroit, 1978-91. Prof. psychiatry and law Wayne State U., 1965—, endowed chair in psychiatry, 2005; pres. Comprehensive Psychiatry Svcs., Southfield, Mich., 1972-98. Contbr. numerous articles to various publs., also several book chpts. Served to lt. USPHS, 1950-52. Recipient Gold Medal award Am. Acad. Psychosomatic Medicine, 1962, Career Achievement award Mich. Mental Health Assn., 1999 Endowed Chair award Wayne State U., 2005. Fellow Am. Psychiat. Assn. (disting. life), Am. Coll. Psychiatrists; mem. AMA, N.Y. Acad. Sci., Sigma Xi. Jewish. Office: 28800 Orchard Lake Rd Ste 250 Farmington Hills MI 48334-2922 Home: 27540 Lakehills Dr Franklin MI 48025-1742 Office Phone: 248-932-2500. Business E-Mail: blyot10@aol.com.

LUCAS, ALEXANDER RALPH, child psychiatrist, educator, writer; b. Vienna, July 30, 1931; came to U.S., 1940, naturalized, 1945; s. Eugene Hans and Margaret Ann (Weiss) L.; m. Margaret Alice Thompson, July 6, 1956; children: Thomas Alexander, Nancy Elizabeth Watson, Alexander Eugene, Peter Clayton. BS, Mich. State U., 1953; MD, U. Mich., 1957. Diplomate Am. Bd. Psychiatry and Neurology (psychiatry and child and adolescent psychiatry), Am. Bd. of Med. Specialties. Intern U. Mich. Hosp., 1957-58; resident in child psychiatry Hawthorn Ctr., Northville, Mich., 1958-59, 61-62, staff psychiatrist, 1963-65, sr. psychiatrist, 1965-67; resident in psychiatry Lafayette Clinic, Detroit, 1959-61, rsch. child psychiatrist, 1967-71, rsch. coord., 1969-71; asst. prof. psychiatry Wayne State U., 1967-69, assoc. prof., 1969-71; cons. child and adolescent psychiatry Mayo Clinic, 1971-97; assoc. prof. Mayo Med Sch., 1973-76, prof., 1976-97; emeritus prof., 1998—; head sect. child and adolescent psychiatry Mayo Clinic, Rochester, Minn., 1971-80, emeritus cons., 1998—. Dir. com. on certification in child and adolescent psychiatry Am. Bd. Psychiatry and Neurology, 1997-2001; residency rev. com. Accreditation Coun. for Grad. Med. Edn., 1999-2001. Author (with C. R. Shaw): The Psychiatric Disorders of Childhood, 1970; author: Demystifying Anorexia Nervosa, 2004, 2008. Recipient Eating Disorders Scientific Achievement award, 1998. Fellow Am. Acad. Child and Adolescent Psychiatry (life, editl. bd. jour. 1976-82), Am. Orthopsychiat. Assn. (life), Am. Psychiat. Assn. (life); mem. Minn. Soc. Child and Adolescent Psychiatry (pres. 1993-95), Soc. Profs. Child and Adolescent Psychiatry (pres. 2000-02), Sigma Xi Achievements include research in biol. aspects of child psychiatry, psychopathology, psychopharmacology, eating disorders, psychiat. treatment of children, adolescents, and young adults. Office: Mayo Clinic 200 1st St SW Rochester MN 55905-0002 Office Phone: 507-284-2691.

LUCAS, CESAR DE PAULA, neurosurgeon; b. Goiania, Nov. 23, 1965; MD, U. Goias, 1989; degree in Neurosurgery, U. Minas Gerais, 1993; MS, PhD, U. Sao Paulo. Vasc. neurosurgeon Goiania Neurol. Inst., 1997—. Adj. prof. Cath. U. Goias, 2009—. Mem.: Am. Assn. Neurosurgeons. Office: Av T1 140 St Bueno Goiania Goias 74250-210 Brazil Office Fax: 55 62 32857130. Business E-Mail: cesar.lucas@uol.com.br.

LUCE, EDWARD ANDREW, plastic surgeon; b. Syracuse, NY, Mar. 5, 1940; s. Edward Andrew and Constance Faith (Jones) L.; m. Rebecca Sue Wall (div.); children: Darcie, Michael, Caitlin. BS, U. Dayton, 1961; MD, U. Ky., 1965. Diplomate Am. Bd. Surgery, Am. Bd. Plastic Surgery (chmn. 1990-91). Resident in surgery Barnes Hosp., St. Louis, 1965-71; resident in plastic surgery Johns Hopkins Hosp., Balt., 1971-73, asst. prof. plastic surgery, 1973-75; assoc. prof. plastic surgery U. Ky., Lexington, 1975-87, prof. plastic surgery, 1987-95, chief plastic surgery, 1975-95, VA Hosp., 1975-95; Kiehn-DesPrez prof. surgery Case Western Reserve U., Cleve., 1995—2004; chief plastic surgery U. Hosps. of Cleve., 1995—2004, VA Hosp., Cleve., 1995—2004; prof. plastic surgery U. Tenn., Memphis, 2004—; pvt. practice Plastic Surgery Group of Memphis, 2004—. Attending plastic surgeon St. Joseph Hosp., Lexington, 1975-95, Good Samaritan Hosp., Lexington, 1978-95, Humana Hosp., Lexington, 1982-95; Kiehn-DesPrez Prof. and Chief of Plastic Surgery, Case Western Reserve U. and Univ. Hosps. of Cleveland; pres. Assn. Acad. Chmn. of Plastic Surgery, 1989-90, Am. Soc. Maxillofacial Surgeons (pres. 1990-91), Southeastern Soc. Plastic and Reconstructive Surgeons (pres. 1992-93) Pres. U. Ky. Med. Alumni Assn., 1977-78; pres. John Hoopes Plastic Surgery Found., 1993. Recipient Clinician of Yr., Am. Assn. Plastic Surgeons, 1990, Prejidential citation Am. Soc. Head and Neck Surgeons, 2000, Dist. Svc. award Am. Soc. Plastic Surgeons, 2000 Mem. Plastic Surgery Ednl. Found. (pres. 1993-94), Am Coll. Surgeons, Am. Surg. Assn., So. Surg. Assn., Am. Assn. Plastic Surgeons (pres. 2000-2001), Am. Soc. Plastic and Reconstructive Surgeons (pres. 2001-2002), Soc. Head and Neck Surgeons. Avocations: clinical photography, military history of small, obscure wars, collecting old and rare medical books. Home Phone: 901-374-9184; Office Phone: 901-761-9030. Personal E-Mail: edluce@yahoo.com.

LUCE, JOHN MORSE, physician, educator; b. San Francisco, May 13, 1942; s. Raymond Philip Luce and Berenice Nudd; m. Judith Christine Aldridge; m. Caroline Elizabeth, Michael Aldridge. BA, Stanford U., 1963; MD, U. Calif., San Francisco, 1974. Diplomate Am. Bd. Internal Medicine, Am. Bd. Pulmonary Diseases, Am. Bd. Critical Care Medicine. Asst. prof. medicine U. Calif., San Francisco 1981-87, assoc. prof. medicine, 1987-93, prof. medicine, 1993—. Co-author: Love Needs Care, 1971, To Your Health, 1976, Intensive Respiratory Care, 1984, Critical Care Medicine, 1988. V.p. bd. dirs. Hamlin Sch., San Francisco, 1990-96, Cate Sch., Carpinteria, Calif., 1987—. Fellow ACP, Am. Coll. Chest Physicians, Am. Coll. Critical Care Medicine; mem. CUm Laude Soc., Phi Beta Kappa, Alpha Omega Alpha. Democrat. Avocations: writing, reading, tennis, skiing. Home: 3015 Baker St San Francisco CA 94123-2401 Office: San Francisco Gen Hosp 1001 Potrero Ave San Francisco CA 94110-3594 E-mail: john_luce@sfgh.org.

LUCENA, ELKIN E., physician, director; b. Medellin, Colombia, June 22, 1939; MD in Surgery, U. Javeriana, 1963; degree in Ob-Gyn., U. Hosp. Militar Ctrl., 1968. Sci. dir. CECOLFES, 1976—. Prof. U. San Jose FUCS Bogota, 1969, U. San Martin Bogota, 2000; founder, bd. dirs. Soc. Colombiana de Fertilidad y Esterilidad, 1978—81; cons., various pvt. clinics in ctrl. & S.Am., 1990. Decorated Order of Democracy Colombian Congress; recipient Grand Ofcl. Degree award, Internat. Peace prize, United Cultural Conv. USA, Chevalier de Merite award, Le Prince Grand Maitre Gen. Hereditaire. Mem.: ASRM, ESHRE. Avocations: travel, movies, reading. Office: Calle 102 14A-15 Bogota Cundinamarca 56769 Colombia Office Phone: 57-1-7420505. Business E-Mail: cecolfes@cecolfes.com.

LUCEY, CATHERINE REINIS, medical educator, department chairman; b. Edwardsville, Ill., Oct. 1, 1958; d. Gedeminas Joseph and Patricia (Wetzel) Reinis; m. Daniel Richard Lucey, June 18, 1988; children: Alexander Daniel, Abraham Gedeminas. BSc in Medicine, Northwestern U., Evanston, Ill., 1980; MD with distinction, Northwestern U. Coll. Medicine, Chgo., 1982. Diplomate Am. Bd. Internal Medicine, 1985, geriat. Am. Bd. Internal Medicine, 1994. Intern resident U. Calif., San Francisco, 1982—85; chief resident San Francisco Gen. Hosp., 1985—88; staff physician Harvard Comm. Health Plan, Boston, 1986—88; asst. prof. medicine UTHSC-SA, San Antonio, 1988—90; staff physician WRAMC, Washington, 1990—92; assoc. program dir. Wash. Hosp. Ctr., 1990—2002; vice dean edn. Ohio State U. Coll. Medicine, Columbus, 2002—, interim dean, 2010—; assoc. v.p. health sciences edn. Ohio State U. Office

Health Sciences, Columbus. Coun. mem. Soc. Gen. Internal Medicine, 1994—97, Assn. Program Dir. Internal Medicine, 2004—; bd. dirs. Am. Bd. Internal Medicine, Phila., 2005—. Fellow: Am. Coll. Physicians (Master Tchr. 2003). Office: Ohio State Univ Coll Medicine 209 Means Hall 1654 Upham Dr Columbus OH 43221 Business E-Mail: catherine.lucey@osumc.edu. *

LUCEY, JEROLD FRANCIS, pediatrician; b. Holyoke, Mass., Mar. 26, 1926; s. Jeremiah F. and Pauline A. (Lally) L.; m. Ingela Barth, Oct. 7, 1972; 1 child, Patrick; children by previous marriage: Colleen, Cathy, David. AB in Zoology, Dartmouth Coll., NH, 1948; MD, NYU Coll. Medicine, 1952. Intern, Children's Med. Svc. Bellevue Hosp., NYC, 1952-53; sr. and asst. resident Columbia-Presbyn. Med. Ctr., Babies Hosp., 1953-55; rsch. fellow, pediat. Harvard Med. Sch., Children's Med. Sch., 1955-56; rsch. fellow, biol. chemistry Harvard Med. Sch., 1960—61; instr., pediat. U. Vt. Coll. Medicine, Burlington, Vt., 1956—57, asst. prof., pediat., 1957—60, assoc. prof., pediat., 1961—66, prof., pediat., 1967—, U. scholar, 1989—, Harry Wallace Professorship, neonatology, endowed chair, 1995—, Jerold F. Lucey endowed chair neonatology. Rsch. fellow in biol. chemistry Harvard Coll., 1960—61; cons. NIH; vis. prof. Royal Soc. Medicine, England, 1980; mem. senate U. Vt., 2000—. Expert adv. panel on pediat. periodicals, Internat. Pediat. Assn., 1980-88; mem. editl. bd., Jour. Perinatal Medicine, 1971-, Oxford Database Perinatal Trials, Oxford U. Press, 1988-92, European Jour. Perinatal Medicine, 1980-; Editor-in-chief Pediatrics 1974-2009, editor-in-chief emeritus 2009-; contbr. articles on neonatology, phototherapy and transcutaneous oxygen to profl. jours. With USN, 1944—46. Recipient C.V. Mosby Book prize, NYU Coll. Medicine, 1952, Nu Sigma Nu Tchr. of Yr. award for Excellence in Tchg., 1960, Duro Test-Great Am. Yr. award, 1974, Humbolt Sr. Am. Scientist award, Bonn, Germany, 1978, United Cerebral Palsy Rsch. award, 1984, Humboldt Travel award, 1985, Ronald McDonald Charities Rsch. award, 1990, Gov. Vt. award in Excellence, 1991, Am. Lung Assn. Gold Medallion for Humanitarianism, 1991, Alumnus of Yr. award, Columbia Presbyn. Med. Ctr., 1995, Advances in Clin. Practice and Rsch. award, March of Dimes, 2002, Best Doctors, Inc. award, 2001-2002, Lucey Exclusive Gift from Prof. A. Kappas for a Med. Student Rsch. award, 2002, Vt. Physician of Yr., 2005, Dupont award, 2007-08, Pediat. Legends award, 2008, J.F. Lucey Chair U. Vt., 2008, Howland award, Am. Pediat. Soc., 2009, 10, APA, 2009, Butterfield award NICHD, 2010; named one of the Best Doctor in U.S.A., 1980, Best Med. Specialists for Children, Harpers Bazaar, 1980, Best Doctors in Am. (Nat. Poll), 1991, 1994, 1998, Best Doctors-New Eng. Region, 1996-97; Bowen-Brooks Scholarship, NY Acad. Medicine, 1953, Named in Legends in Pediat. Pediatrix, 2008, John and Mary R. Markle Scholar in Med. Sci., 1959-64, Humbolt scholar, 1978, Univ. scholar, 1991. Fellow Am. Acad. Pediat. (Grulee award 1981, Apgar award, 1993, Neonatal Edn. award, perinatal sect., 1997, Lifetime Achievement award 1997, mem. com. on fetus and newborn, 1963-66, chmn. com. on fetus and newborn, 1966-72, mem. scientific program com., 1965-71, cons. 1974-96, Howland award), Royal Soc. Pediatrics (hon.), Brit. Pediat. and Child Health Assn (hon.); mem. Royal Soc. Medicine, Am. Assn. for Study Liver Diseases, Am. Pediat. Soc. (Highest award 2009), Soc. Pediat. Rsch., New Eng. Pediat. Soc. (coun. mem 1968-70), Vt. State Med. Soc., Second World Congress Pediat. (hon. pres. 1993), Indian Pediat. Soc. (hon., Gold medal 1994), Inst. Medicine (sr. mem.), Finnish Pediat. Soc. (hon.), Peruvian Pediat. Soc. (hon.), Irish Am. Pediat. Soc., Chilean Pediat. Soc. (hon.), Vt. Acad. Sci., AMA Chittenden County Med. Soc. (v.p., 1961-63), Alpha Omega Alpha, Cosmos Club, Coun. Biology Editors. Home: 32 Overlake Park Burlington VT 05401 Office: U Vt Coll Medicine Dept Pediatrics Given Bldg D201 89 Beaumont Ave Burlington VT 05405-0068 Home Phone: 802-762-7272. Business E-Mail: jerold.lucey@uvm.edu.

LUCHETTE, FREDERICK ALBERT, surgeon; b. Sharon, Pa., Aug. 9, 1954; s. Albert and Rosemary (Songer) L.; m. Barbara Ann O'Brien, Aug. 31, 1985; children: Richard, Matthew, Claire, Katherine. BA, Thiel Coll., 1976; MS, U. Louisville, 1978, MD, 1981. Diplomate Am. Bd. Surgery. From clin. instr. to asst. prof. surgery SUNY, Buffalo, 1981-93; assoc. prof. surgery U. Cin., 1994—. Fellow Am. Coll. Surgeons; mem. Am. Assn. Surgery of Trauma, Am. Trauma Soc., Eastern Assn. Surgery of Trauma, Soc. Critical Care Medicine, Surgical Infection Soc., Soc. Univ. Surgeons. Roman Catholic.9 Avocations: jogging, reading, travel. Office: Loyola Univ Medical Ctr 2160 S First Ave Maywood IL 60153

LUCHI, CARLO, medical educator, researcher; b. Lucca, Italy, Apr. 2, 1967; Degree in Medicine and Surgery, U. Pisa, 1996, degree in Ob-Gyn., 2003; MD, AOUP, PhD, 2003. Rschr. AOUP, 2003, med. dirigent and splty. prof., 2008. Home: Via Paolina Bonaparte 132 Viareggio Lucca 55049 Italy Home Fax: 3358485247. Business E-Mail: c.luchi@unipi.it.

LUCHINS, DANIEL JONATHAN, psychiatrist; b. NYC, July 1, 1948; s. Abraham Samuel and Edith (Hirsch) L.; children: Kerith, Matthew. BSc, McGill U., Montreal, Que., Can., 1971, MD, 1973. Diplomate in psychiatry and geriatric psychiatry Am. Bd. Psychiatry and Neurology. Vis. scientist NIMH, Washington, 1977-81; assoc. prof. U. Chgo., 1981—; med. coord. mental health Ill. Dept. Mental Health, Chgo., 1989-91; chief of adult psychiatry U. Chgo., 1991-93; chief clin. svcs. Office Mental Health, Ill. Dept. Human Svcs., Chgo., 1995—2005; chief pub. psychiatry U. Chgo., 1996; chief, Mental Health Rsch. Ctr. Jesse Brown VAMC, 2007—. Dir. SGA Youth and Family Svcs., 2001—. Contbr. articles to profl. publs. Recipient A.E. Bennett award Soc. Biol. Psychiatry, Geriatric Mental Health acad. award NIMH, 1984-87, Exemplary Psychiatrist award NAMI, 1998. Fellow Am. Psychiat. Assn. (disting.); mem. Ill. Psychiat. Assn. (councillor 1989-91, pres. 1995, Am. Psychiat. Assn. rep.). Jewish. Achievements include development of criteria for hospice care for demented patients. Office: Jesse Brown VAMC 820 S Damen Ave 116A Chicago IL 60612 Home Phone: 773-667-5947; Office Phone: 312-567-8072. Business E-Mail: daniel.luchins@va.gov.

LUCHS, JODI IAN, ophthalmologist; b. NYC, May 26, 1965; s. Saul Myron and Marjorie Ellen Luchs; children: Ethan, Evan, Elana. BA, U. Pa., Phila., 1987; JD, Albert Einstein Coll. Medicine, Bronx, NY, 1991. Diplomate Am. Bd. Ophthalmology. Intern Mt. Sinai Med. Ctr., NYC, 1991—92; resident LI Jewish Med. Ctr., New Hyde Park, NY, 1992—95; Cornea fellow Wills Eye Hosp., Phila., 1995—96; ophthalmologist South Shore Eye Care, Wantagh, NY, 1996—; dir. dept. refractive surgery LI Jewish/North Shore U. Health Sys, Great Neck, NY, 2006—. Clin. instr. cornea svc. LI Jewish Med. Ctr.; adj. clin. asst. prof. surgery NY Coll. Osteo. Medicine; clin. trials in field; presenter, lectr. in field; mem. staff North Shore U. Hosp., Manhasset, Syosset, Plainview, LE Jewish Med. Ctr., New Island Hosp, Queens Hosp. Author (with C.J. Rapuano and T. Kim): The Requisites in Ophthalmology: Anterior Segment, 2000; contbr. articles to profl. jours. Mem. med. adv. bd. Eye Bank for Sight Restoration, NYC. Fellow: ACS, Nassau County Med. Soc., Am. Acad. Ophthalmology; mem.: LI Ophthalmol. Soc. (asst. sec./treas. 2006, sec./treas. 2007), Nassau Acad. Medicine (trustee), Am. Soc. Cataract and Refractive Surgeons, Med. Soc. State NY, NY State Ophthalmol. Soc., Internat. Soc. Refractive Surgery, Alpha Omega Alpha. Office: South Shore Eye Care 2185 Wantagh Ave Wantagh NY 11793 Office Phone: 516-785-3900. Personal E-mail: jluchs@aol.com.

LUCHT, ANDREAS, laboratory medicine physician, microbiologist; b. Herford, Germany, Sept. 30, 1968; s. Horst and Ingrid Lucht. MD, U. Ulm, Münster, Germany, 1996; MSc in Epidemiology, U. Mainz, Germany, 2011. Lt. col. MC, 1988—2004; physician Mil. Hosps., Hamm, Germany, 1996—97, Ulm, Germany, 1997—98, Ctrl. Inst. Garching, Hochbrück, Germany, 2003—04; rschr. Bundeswehr Inst. Microbiology, Munich, 1999—2003; lab. physician Labor Dr. Krone Ptnr., Bad Salzuflen, Germany, 2004—. Cons. World Health Orgn., Brazzaville, Republic of the Congo, 2003. Contbr. articles to profl. jours. Mem.: German Soc. Mil. Medicine, German Soc. Clin. Chemistry and Lab. Medicine, German Soc. Tropical Medicine. Achievements include development of diagnostic assay for detection of Ebola virus antigens. Office: Labor Dr Krone Ptnr Siemensstrasse 40 Bad Salzuflen 32105 Germany Personal E-mail: andreaslu@gmx.de. Business E-Mail: alucht@labkr.one.de.

LUCIA, MARILYN REED, physician; b. Boston; m. Walter M. Dickie Jr., 1951 (div. 1958); m. Salvatore P. Lucia, 1959, (dec. 1984); m. C. Robert Russell, 1985 (dec. 2000); children: Elizabeth, Walter, Salvatore, Darryl. AB with highest honors, U. Calif., Berkeley, 1951; MD, U. Calif., San Francisco, 1956. Cert. in psychiatry and child psychiatry Am. Bd. Psychiatry and Neurology. Intern Stanford U. Hosp., 1956-57; NIMH fellow, resident in psychiatry Langley Porter, U. Calif., San Francisco, 1957-60; NIMH fellow, resident in child psychiatry Mt. Zion Hosp., San Francisco, 1964-66; NIMH fellow, in cmty. psychiatry U. Calif., San Francisco, 1966—68, clin. prof. psychiatry, 1982—. Founder, cons. Marilyn Reed Lucia Child Care Study Ctr., U. Calif., San Francisco; cons. Cranio-facial Ctr., U. Calif., San Francisco; No. Calif. Diagnostic Sch. for Neurologically Handicapped Children; dir. children's psychiat. svc. Contra Costa County Hosp., Martinez. Fellow Am. Psychiat. Assn. (disting. life), Am. Acad. Child Psychiatry; mem. Am. Cleft Palate Assn., San Francisco Med. Soc., Phi Beta Kappa. Office: 350 Parnassus Ave Ste 602 San Francisco CA 94117-3608

LUCIER, GREGORY THOMAS, medical technology executive; b. Plainfield, NJ, May 9, 1964; s. Thomas Edward and Ann (Rivinus) L.; m. Marilena Cieri, June 4, 1988; children: Ross Edward, Grant Michael, Allana Marie. BS in Indsl. Engring., Pa. State U., 1986; MBA, Harvard U., 1990. Product mgr. International Paper Co., Memphis, 1986-88; v.p. opers. Morrison Knudsen Corp., Boise, Idaho, 1990-95; gen. mgr. bus. devel. General Electric Co., 1995; pres., CEO GE-Harris Rlwy. Electronics, 1996-99; v.p. global svcs. GE Med. Sys. Tech., 2000—03; pres., CEO GE Med. Systems, Info. Tech., 2000-01; CEO Invitrogen Corp., Carlsbad, Calif., 2003—08, chmn., 2004—08; chmn., CEO, Life Technologies Applied Biosystems, Inc., 2008—. Cons. in field. Fundraising organizer Arthritis Found., Boise, 1992; instr. Jr. Achievement, Memphis, 1986-88; vol. Project Outreach, Boston, 1989-90. Mem. Inst. Indsl. Engrs., Railway Suppliers Assn., Idaho Total Quality Mgmt. Inst., Harvard Club of Wis., Tau Beta Pi. Republican. Roman Catholic. Avocations: golf, tennis, skiing. Office: Life Technologies Corp 5791 Van Allen Way Carlsbad CA 92008 Office Phone: 760-603-7200. *

LUCKSTEAD, EUGENE FREDDIE, SR., medical educator, consultant; b. Wyoming, Iowa, Nov. 20, 1938; s. Freddie William and Velda Edwina Luckstead; m. Margaret Ann Dandl, June 24, 1961; children: Eugene Freddie, Ann Marie Gosdin, Erik Louis. BA in Liberal Arts, U. Iowa, Iowa City, 1960; MD, U. Iowa, Coll. Medicine, 1963. Tchr Med. Sch., Kans., Okla., Va., Iowa; exec. med. dir. King's Daughters Children's Hosp., Norfolk, Va., 1996—2000; prof. pediat., cardiology Tex. Tech U. Health Scis. Ctr., Amarillo, 2000—. Med. dir. Cook Children's Med. Ctr., Ft. Worth, 1988—96. Served with USN, 1963—68, Calif. Fellow: Am. Acad. Pediat. (Young Investigator of Yr., sect. cardiology 1970, Thomas Shaffer award, sports medicine 2004). Home: 7108 Rochelle Ln Amarillo TX 79109

LUCY, DENNIS DURWOOD, JR., neurologist, educator; b. Little Rock, July 3, 1934; s. Dennis Durwood and Ann Louise (Besiegel) L.; m. Patricia Wilch, Nov. 26, 1958; children: Stephen H., Vincent A., Denise D., David D. BS, MD, U. Ark., 1959. Diplomate: Am. Bd. Psychiatry and Neurology. Intern U. Ark. Med. Scis., 1959-60, resident in internal medicine, 1960-62, resident in psychiatry, 1962-63; resident in neurology U. Iowa Hosp., 1963-64, 65-66; from instr., acting head dept. neurology to prof. U. Ark., 1964—74, prof., 1974—; chmn. Coun. Departmental Chmn., 1980—81; chief of staff Univ. Hosp., 1973—76; chmn. acad. senate U. Ark. for Med. Scis., 2002—03. Bd. dirs. Ark. chpt. Multiple Sclerosis Soc., 1965-78; mem. Ark. Council Devel. Disabilities, 1971-74; bd. dirs. Ark. chpt. Epilepsy Soc., 1972-76; bd. dirs. Holy Souls Cath. Sch., 1974-77, pres. bd., 1976-77. Recipient Golden Apple award U. Ark., 1968-69 Mem. Am. Acad. Neurology, Alpha Omega Alpha. Roman Catholic. Home: 17 Robinwood Dr Little Rock AR 72227-2241 Office: 4301 W Markham St Little Rock AR 72205-7101 Office Phone: 501-686-5135.

LUDDY, PAULA SCOTT, nursing educator; b. Plymouth, Mass., May 29, 1945; d. James Bernard Scott and Margaret Elizabeth Legge Scott; m. Robert Thomas Luddy, May 20, 1944; children: Scott, Shawn. BSN, Bowie State U., 1993, MSN, 1996. RN Mass., 1966, Md., 1970. Educator Group Health Assn., Washington, 1983—87; ob/lactation cons. Dr. Rafiq Mian, Cheverly, Md., 1984—94; childbirth educator Childbirth Edn. Assn., Washington, 1971—95; staff nurse Prince George Hosp. Ctr., Cheverly, Md., 1981—87, patient educator, 1987—2002; coord./home interviewer Prince George Med. Soc., Prince George County, 1994—2002. Mem. nursing faculty dept. nursing Prince George's C.C., 1997—. Recipient Award of Excellence in Health Care, Assn. Women's Health Obstetric Neonatal Nurses, 2000, Hero for Babies, March of Dimes, 2002, Excellence in Edn. award, Prince George's C. of C. Bd. Edn., 2001. Home Phone: 301-474-1253. Personal E-mail: lastnerbob@aol.com.

LUDER, ELISABETH, medical educator; b. Switzerland; US; BS, U. Zurich, Switzerland, 1958; MS in Nutrition & Pub. Health, Columbia U., 1976; PhD in Nutrition, New York U., 1986. Cert. Am. Dietetic Assn. Tchg. assoc. pediat. Pediatric Pulmonary Ctr., Mount Sinai Sch. Medicine, NY, 1978—85, edn. coord., MCHB Funded Interdisciplinary Training Program, 1978—90, dir. Clinical Nutrition Training Program, 1980—, asst. dir., 1985—90, instructor pediat., 1986—89, asst. prof. pediat., 1989—94, dir. MCH Funded Interdisciplinary Training Program, 1990—, assoc. dir., 1990—93, co-dir., 1993—, assoc. prof. pediat., 1994—2006, prof. pediat., clinical/educator track, 2006—; adj. asst. prof. Sch. Edn.,NYU, 1987—94, adj. assoc. prof., 1994—. Chair NYC Maternal and Child Health, Nutrition Task Force Maternal and Child Health Bureau, DHHS, 1984—87; co-chair Rsch. and Awards Com., Pediatric Nutrition Practice Group Am. Dietetic Assn., 1989—90, chair, 1990—91; pres. Greater NY Dietetic Assn., 1989—90, bd. dirs., 1994—99; tech. assistance com. mem. Nat. Ctr. for Youth with Disabilities Maternal and Child Health Bureau, DHHS, 1987—99; com. mem. Pub. Health New York Acad. Medicine, 1987—; adv. com. mem. Pub. Health Nutrition Program Inst. Human Nutrition Columbia U., 1993—94; steering com. mem. Pediat. Pulmonary Ctr. Training Program Maternal and Child Health Bureau, DHHS, 1991—; chair Maternal and Child Health Nutrition Network, Region II Maternal and Child Health Bureau, DHHS, 1992—; mem. Infant Formula Task Force State New Jersey Dept. Health, 1996—; adv. bd. Office the Regional, Health Administr., 2009; consensus com. Nutrition North Am. Cystic Fibrosis Found., 1990; with numerous other coms. Contbr. articles to numerous jours. Grantee, NIH, NHLB, NIAID, US Environ. Protection Agency, 2000, GlaxoSmithKline, Solvay Pharmaceuticals, Inc., Cystic Fibrosis Found. Mem.: Phi Delta Kappa. Office: Dept Pediatrics/Pediatric Pulmonary Divsn Mount Sinai Sch Medicine One Gustave L Levy Pl New York NY 10029 Business E-Mail: elisabeth.iuder@mssm.edu.

LUDMERER, KENNETH MARC, medical educator; b. Long Beach, Calif., Jan. 13, 1947; s. Sol and Norma (Helfer) L.; m. Loren Rae Starobin, Aug. 9, 1987. AB, Harvard U., 1968; MA, Johns Hopkins U., 1971, MD, 1973. Med. resident, fellow Washington U., St. Louis, 1973-78; chief resident internal medicine Barnes Hosp., St. Louis, 1978-79; asst. prof. medicine, asst. prof. history Faculty Arts and Scis. Washington U., St. Louis, 1979-86, assoc. prof. medicine, assoc. prof. history, 1986-92, prof. medicine, prof. history, 1992—2010, Mabel Dorn Reeder disting prof. medicine & history medicine, 2010—. Clin. scholars adv. com. mem. Robert Wood Johnson Found., Princeton, N.J., 1988-92; new pathway program evaluation com. mem. Assn. Am. Med. Colls., 1986-88; mem. nat. adv. com. Robert Wood Johnson Found. Clin. Scholars Program, Princeton, N.J., 1988-92; mem. adv. bd. Culpeper Found. Program in Med. Humanities, Stanford, Conn., 1992-93; mem. task force on med. edn. Acadia Inst.-Med. Coll. Pa., Phila., 1992-96; mem. vis. com. Harvard Med. Sch., Boston, 2000-2002, North Shore-L.I. Jewish Health Sys., Manhasset, N.Y., 2003—; bd. mem. Nat. Bd. Med. Examiners, 2011-, Accreditation Coun. Grad. Med. Edn., 2011-; med. edn. cons. numerous schs., hosps., profl. orgns., state govts., 2000-, Inst. Med. Com. on Resident Duty Hours, 2007-08. Author: Genetics and American Society: A Historical Appraisal, 1972, Learning to Heal: The Development of American Medical Education, 1985, Time to Heal: American Medical Education from the Turn of the Century to the Era of Managed Care, 1999 (William Welch medal 2004), Am. Assn. History Medicine, 2004 (William Welch medal); mem. editl. bd. Am. Jour. Medicine, 1981-96, Jour. History Medicine, 1981-83, 88-90, The Pharos, 1986—, History Edn. Quar., 1993-96, Annals Internal Medicine, 1993-. Med. adv. com. St. Louis Sci. Ctr., 1985-87, trustee Mo. Hist. Soc., St. Louis, 1987-93, St. Louis History Mus., 1987-93, Jewish Fedn. St. Louis, 2002—, Sommers Children's Welfare Bur., St. Louis, 2000—; chair cmty. rsch. peer rev. com. St. Louis Heart Assn., 1988-89, bd. mem. Nat. Bd. Med. Examiners, 2011-, bd. trustees, 2011-. Faculty scholar gen. internal medicine Henry Kaiser Family Found., 1981-86; recipient Rsch. award Joseph Macy Jr. Found., 1989-96, J. Abraham Flexer award for Distinguished Svc., Assn. Am. Med. Coll., 2003, Daniel Tosteson award for Leadership Med. Edn., Harvard Med. Coll., 2001, Nicholas Davies award, Am. Coll. Physicians, 1997. Master ACP (com. on publ. policy 1988-93, Tchg. and Rsch. scholar 1980-83); fellow AAAS, Am. Acad. Arts and Scis. (Midwest coun.); mem. Assn. Am. Physicians, Am. Clin. and Climatol. Assn., Am. Assn. History Medicine (coun. 1984-87, 2000—, v.p. 2000-02, pres. 2002-04), Am. Fedn. for Clin. Rsch., History Sci. Soc., Am. Osler Soc. (bd. govs. 1988-96, v.p. 1992-94, pres. 1994-95), Phi Beta Kappa, Alpha Omega Alpha, Sigma Xi. Avocations: music, running, travel. Home: 42 Rio Vista Dr Saint Louis MO 63124-1745 Office: Washington U Sch Medicine Dept Medicine Box 8066 660 S Euclid Ave Saint Louis MO 63110 Business E-Mail: kludmere@dom.wustl.edu.

LUDWIG, DAVID S., endocrinologist; b. LA, Calif., Dec. 24, 1957; PhD, Stanford U. Sch. Medicine, Calif., 1988, MD, 1990. Cert. Pediatrics, Endocrinology. Intern, pediatrics Children's Hosp. Boston, Mass., 1990—91, resident, pediatrics Mass., 1991—93, fellow, pediatric endocrinology Mass., 1993—95, attending physician Mass., 1995—, dir. obesity program Mass., 1998—, assoc. prof. pediatrics Mass., 2003—. Developed Optimal Weight for Life Program; serves as prin. or co-investigator of several epidemiological and clin. studies to identify dietary factors that contribute to obesity. Contbr. articles to profl. jours., author. Ending the Food Fight: Guide Your Child to a Healthy Weight in a Fast Food/Fake Food World, 2007. Office: Childrens Hosp Boston Divsn Endocrinology LO-624 300 Longwood Ave Boston MA 02115 Office Phone: 617-355-5159, 617-355-4878. Office Fax: 617-730-0505.

LUDWIG, EDWARD J., medical technology executive; Grad., Holy Cross Coll., Columbia U. Bus. Sch. In mgmt. Becton, Dickinson & Co., Franklin Lakes, NJ, 1979—87, corp. planning & devel. mgr., 1987—89, pres. diagnostics divsn. Balt., 1989—94, sr. v.p. fin., CFO Franklin Lakes, NJ, 1995—99, exec. v.p., 1998—99, pres., 1999—2000, pres., CEO, 2000—02, chmn., pres., CEO, 2002—08, chmn., CEO, 2009—11, exec. chmn. of bd., 2011—. Bd. dirs. Aetna; chmn. HealthCare Inst. of NJ. Trustee Johns Hopkins U.; mem. adv. bd. Johns Hopkins Bloomberg Sch. of Public Health; trustee Hackensack U. Medical Ctr., Coll. of Holy Cross; bd. dirs. US Fund for UNICEF. Mem.: Advanced Medical Tech. Assn. (chmn.-elect, chair bd. comt. tech. and regulation). Office: BD 1 Becton Dr Franklin Lakes NJ 07417-1815 *

LUDWIG, KIRK ALLEN, colon and rectal surgeon, educator; b. Cin., Oct. 2, 1962; BS, John Carroll U., 1984; MD, U. Cin., 1988. Vernon O. Underwood prof., chief, divsn. colorectal surgery Med. Coll. Wis., 2008—. Office: 9200 W Wisconsin Ave Milwaukee WI 53226 Office Fax: 414-454-0152. Business E-Mail: kludwig@mcw.edu.

LUDWIG, STEPHEN, pediatrics and emergency medicine educator; b. Phila., Nov. 12, 1945; m. Zella Wolgin, 1968; children: Susannah, Elisa, Aubrey. BA with honors, Pa. State U., 1966, BS, 1967; MD, Temple U., 1971. Diplomate Am. Bd. Pediat., Nat. Bd. Med. Examiners; cert. pediat. emergency medicine, CPR advanced life support, ATLS instr., PALS. Intern and resident pediat. Children's Hosp. Nat. Med. Ctr., Washington, 1971-74, chief resident, 1973-74; assoc. pediat. Phila. Gen. Hosp. U. Pa. Sch. Medicine, 1974-76, asst. prof. pediat., 1976-83, assoc. prof. pediat., 1983-89, prof. pediat., 1989—, prof. emergency medicine, 1994—; assoc. physician-in-chief med. edn., emergency medicine attending physician Children's Hosp. Phila. Asst. physician The Children's Hosp. Phila., 1974-76, sr. physician, 1979—, divsn. chief gen. pediat., 1988-95, assoc. physician-in-chief for med. edn. dept. pediat., 1995—, sec. med./dental staff, 1986-88, v.p. med./dental staff, 1988-90, exec. com. dept. pediat., 1993—,; attending physician, dir. in-patient svcs. Phila. Gen. Hosp., 1974-76, asst. chief svc. pediat. dept., 1989—; lectr. in field. Editor-in-chief Children's Doctors, 1995—; co-editor-in-chief Pediat. Emergency Care, 1985—; mem. editl. bd. Pediat. Emergency and Critical Care, 1987—, Jour. Ambulatory Pediat. Assn., 1998—; adv. editl. bd. Pediat. Emergency Trends, 1986—; contbg. editor Yearbook of Emergency Medicine, 1988-93; reviewer Clin. Pediat., 1979-93, Pediat., 1980—, Jour. AMA, 1986—, Yearbook Pediat., 1990—, Annals Emergency Medicine, 1990—, Archives Pediat. and Adolescent Medicine, 1992—; contbr. chpts. to books and articles to profl. jours. Grantee Robert Wood Johnson Found., 1982-83, 82-84, 85-87. Mem. Internat. Soc. Child Abuse and Neglect, Am. Acad. Pediat. (chmn. emergency medicine sect. 1984-86, chmn. com. on pediat. emergency medicine 1988-92, exec. bd. sect. on child abuse, membership chmn. 1988-90, Career Achievement award sect. pediat. emergency medicine 1992), Am. Pediat. Soc., Am. Pediat. Assn. (exec. bd. 1989-92, founding mem. pediat. emergency medicine interest group 1989—), Am. Bd. Pediat. (program dirs. com.), Am. Profl. Soc. Against Child Abuse, Am. Coll. Emergency Physician (co-chmn. edn. com. Pa. chpt. 1980-88, treas., co-chmn. edn. com. Pa. chpt. 1986-89), Ambulatory Pediat. Assn. (Nat. Tchg. award 1988), Phila. Emergency Physicians Soc. (steering com.), Phila. Pediat. Soc., Univ. Assn. for Emergency Medicine, Soc. Tchrs. Emergency Medicine, Phila. Trauma Consortium, Pediat. Emergency Medicine Fellowship Dirs. (chmn. 1984-87), Soc. for Pediat. Trauma (charter), Soc. for Pediat. Emergency Medicine (charter), Assn. Pediat. Program Dirs., Helfer Soc. (founder). Office: Childrens Hosp Phila 324 S 34th St, #9557 Philadelphia PA 19104 Office Phone: 215-977-9779, 215-590-2162. E-mail: ludwig@email.chop.edu.

LUE, TOM F., urologist, educator; b. Taiwan, Dec. 26, 1947; MB, Kaohsiung Med. Coll., 1972. Prof. urology U. Calif., San Francisco, 1992—. Recipient Innovative Rsch. award, Am. Found. Urol. Diseases, Merit award, NIH. Fellow: ACS; mem.: Sexual Medicine Soc. N.Am., Internat. Soc. Sexual Medicine, Am. Assn. Genitourinary Surgeons, Am. Urol. Assn. (Gold Cystoscope award). Office: 400 Parnassus Ave A633 San Francisco CA 94143-0738 Office Fax: 415-476-8849. Business E-Mail: tlue@urology.ucsf.edu.

LUEDEMAN, GERALD WARREN, radiologist; b. Kansas City, Mo., Jan. 17, 1941; s. Clarence Henry and Hazel McClure Luedeman; m. Brenda Jane Kvamme, Sept. 1, 1984; children: Robert Warren, Richard Brandt. AB cum laude, Harvard Coll., Cambridge, Mass., 1962; MD, George Washington U., Washington, 1966. Diplomate Am. Bd. Radiology, 1974, Am. Bd. Nuc. Medicine, 1976. Intern Grady Meml. Hosp., Atlanta, 1966—67; resident radiology Med. Coll. Va., Richmond, 1970—73; radiologist Ventura County Cmty. Hosp., Calif., 1973—75; pvt. practice Radiology Cons. PA, Winter Haven, Fla., 1975—2009, Sunshine Radiology, 2009—. Capt. US Army, 1967—69. Mem.: Radiol. Soc. N.Am., Am. Inst. of Ultrasound in Medicine, Roentgen Ray Soc., Masons Lake Region Yacht and Country Club. Avocations: travel, reading, golf. Office Phone: 863-299-1155.

LUEDKE, PATRICIA GEORGIANNE, microbiologist; b. Milw., May 4, 1956; m. Michael Andrew Luedke, July 15, 1978; children: Christopher M., Sean P. BS, Marquette U., 1978, postgrad., 1981—82. Registered med. technologist; registered microbiologist; specialist microbiology; lic. pvt. investigator. Med. technologist Med.-Surg. Clinic, Milw., 1978—79, Milw. County Hosp., 1979, Fort Atkinson Meml. Hosp., Fort Atkinson, Wis., 1979—88, Wheaton Franciscan Lab., Wauwatosa, Wis., 1988—, Sherlock Donatello and Co., Oconomowoc, Wis., 2004—. Cons. Forensic Rsch. Assocs., Oconomowoc, Wis., 1978—. Mem. Am. Soc. Microbiology, Am. Soc. Clin. Pathologists, Anaerobe Soc. Am., N.Y. Acad. Scis. Home: 739 Elizabeth St Oconomowoc WI 53066-3703

LUEPKER, RUSSELL VINCENT, epidemiology educator; b. Chgo., Oct. 1, 1942; s. Fred Joseph and Anita Louise (Thornton) L.; m. Ellen Louise Thompson, Dec. 22, 1966; children: Ian, Carl. BA, Grinnell Coll., 1964; MD with distinction, U. Rochester, 1969; MS, Harvard U., 1976; PhD (hon.), U. Lund, Sweden, 1996. Intern U. Calif., San Diego, 1969-70; resident Peter Bent Brigham Hosp., Boston, 1973-74; cardiology fellow Peter Bent Brigham Hosp./Med., Boston, 1974-76; asst. prof. divsn. epidemiology med. lab. physiol. hygiene U. Minn., Mpls., 1976-80, assoc. prof., 1980-87, prof. divsn. epidemiology and medicine, 1987—, dir. divsn. epidemiology, 1991—2004, Mayo prof. pub. health, 2000—; with Def. Health Bd. USDOD, 2007—. Cons. NIH, Bethesda, Md., 1980—, U. So. Calif., L.A., 1985—, Armed Forces Epidemiology Bd., 1993-97; vis. prof. U. Goteborg, Sweden, 1986, Ninewells Med. Sch., Dundee, Scotland, 1995. With USPHS, 1970—73. Harvard U. fellow, 1974-76, Bush Leadership fellow, 1990; recipient Prize for Med. Rsch. Am. Coll. Chest Physicians, 1970, Nat. Rsch. Svc. award Nat. Heart, Lung and Blood Inst., Bethesda, 1975-77, Disting. Alumni award Grinnell Coll., 1989, Sci. Advocate of Yr., AHA, 2008. Fellow ACP, Am. Coll. Cardiology, Am. Heart Assn. (chmn. coun. on epidemiology 1992-94, chair program com. sci. sessions 1995-97, award of merit 1997), Am. Coll. Epidemiology; mem. Am. Epidemiol. Soc., Am. Soc. Preventive Cardiology (Joseph Stokes award 1999), Delta Omega Soc. (Nat. Merit award 1988). Office: Univ Minn Sch Pub Health Div Epidemiology 1300 S 2nd St Minneapolis MN 55454-1087 Home Phone: 612-729-2659; Office Phone: 612-624-6362. Business E-Mail: luepker@epi.umn.edu.

LUFTMAN, DEBRA, dermatologist, educator; married; 2 children. Grad., U. Calif., San Diego; MD, Tufts U. Diplomate Am. Bd. Dermatology, 1996, Am. Bd. Medical Specialties. Fellow St. Andrew Univ., Scotland; resident internal medicine and dermatology UCLA, prof. Skin Surgery and Gen. Dermatology; owner Therapeutix; pvt. practice dermatologist LuftmanMD Dermatology, Beverly Hills, Calif. Co-author: (book) The Beauty Prescription, 2008; co-editor: Glycolic Acid Peels. Mem. Skin Cancer Found.; with Clear Up Skin Program; mem. Step Up Women's Network. Mem.: San Fernando Valley Dermatology Soc., LA Metroderm, Am. Acad. of Dermatology. Office: LuftmanMD Dermatology Ste 100 416 N Bedford Dr Beverly Hills CA 90210 Office Phone: 310-275-1170.

LUGG, MARLENE MARTHA, research scientist, immunization coordinator, health information systems specialist, health planner; b. Wauwatosa, Wis., Mar. 6, 1938; d. Armand Werner and Elise (Kuehni) Heinrich; m. Richard S.W. Lugg, June 11, 1966 (div. Dec. 1976); children: Jennifer Elsie, William Thomas Armand. BS in Gen. Sci., U. Wis., Milw., 1960; MPH in Med. and Hosp. Adminstrn., U. Pitts., 1966, DrPH in Health Svcs. Rsch. and Planning, 1981. Dep. chair Nat. Com. on Health and Vital Stats., Canberra, Australia, 1973-83; dir. State Ctr. for Health Stats. and Planning Health Dept. Western Australia, Perth, 1966-83; dir. health info. systems program UCLA, 1983-88; vis. prof. pub. health Calif. State U., Northridge, 1987—2000; health info. systems specialist Kaiser-Permanente-So. Calif., Pasadena, Calif., 1988-98; immunization coord., sr. rschr. Panorama City Med. Ctr. Kaiser Permanente, Calif., 1998—2009, rsch. scientist Pasadena, 2010—; chair curriculum com. West Coast U., 2003—10, prof., 2003—. Co-founder Australian and New Zealand Soc. for Epidemiology and Cmty. Health, Sydney, 1966-68, Pub. Health Assn. Australia, Canberra, 1968-83; examiner LA Civil Svc. Commn., 1986-88; vis. prof. Pasadena City Coll., 1992-98; mem. Calif. State Health Info. Policy Interagy. Com., 1992-94; mem. Calif. Health Data Coordinating Coun., 1995-2000; bd. dirs. Pub. Health Found. Enterprises, LA, 1994-2006, sec., 1995-97; co-chmn. LA Immunization Coalition, 2000-2001, chmn., 2002—; steering com. Calif. Adult Immunization Coalition, 2001-07; mem. adv. bd. Calif. Coalition for Childhood Immunization, 2000-07, Nat. Network Immunization Nurses and Assocs., 2001—; adv. bd. Calif. Immunization Coalition, 2007-; apptd. CDC Vaccine VAERS Reporting Group, 2003-2005, CDC/AIRA Immunization Practice Com., 2005—; CDC/AIRA Immunization Data Workgroup, 2006—; Am. Red Cross Nat. Emergency Response Bd., 2007; Am. Red Cross Nat. Wilderness First Aid Bd., 2009-10, reviewer Vaccine, 2011-; cons. in field, mem., IEA Epidemiology Supercoarse, 2011-. Author: Medical Manpower in Western Australia, 1978; contbg. editor Australian Health Rev., 1998-2004, IEA Epidemiology Supercourse, 2011-; contbr. articles on injury, health data systems, immunization, air quality and illness, injury control and Pub. Health Conf. stats./records to profl. jours. Leave No Trace Master Educator, 1998—, Tread Lighty master tread Trainer, 2011-; leader, trainer Girl Scouts USA, Milw., Pitts., LA, 1956—, Australian Girl Guides, Perth, Australia, 1966-82; instr., trainer ARC, Milw., Pitts., LA, 1959-, Girl Scouts USA, 1995—; explorer leader, trainer Boy Scouts Am., Western LA and Verdugo Hills, 1983-99; venturer leader, trnr. Boy Scouts Am., Verdugo Hills, 1999—; del. Girl Scouts Nat. Coun., 1996-2002. Recipient Broughton award Izaak Walton League Am., Wis., 1966, Fisher award Am. Med. Technologists, 1971, Outstanding Young Person award Western Australian Jaycees, Perth, Australia, 1977, Take Pride in Am. award US Govt., Washington, 1990, 2007, Wm. T. Hornaday Gold medal Boy Scouts Am., 1991, Silver Beaver Boy Scouts Am., 1999, Venturer Adult Leadership award, 1999, Thanks Badge Girl Scouts USA, 1990, Thanks Badge II, 2000, Outstanding Family award Girl Scouts San Fernando Valley, 1992, UN Environ. Conservation award, 1992, Wm. Spurgeon award, 1995, Nat. Vohs Quality award Kaiser Permanente, 1995, Outstanding Cmty. Svc. Alumni award U. Wis., Milw., 1997, Spotlight on Leadership award Kaiser Permanente, 1999, Innovations in Immunization award Am. Assn. Health Plans, 2001, Margaret Gloninger Alumni Cmty. Svc. award U. Pitts., 2004, Venturer Leader Merit award, 2005, Disting. Alumni award U. Pitts., 2006, Natalie J. Smith M.D. Meml. Immunization Champion award Calif. Coalition for Childhood Immunization, 2006, Disting. Alumni award U. Wis., Milw., 2010; named Woman of Yr. Western Australia, 1976, Career Woman of Yr., Daily News, 1983, Woman of the Year San Fernando Valley Girl Scouts, 1995; Nat. Health and Med. Rsch. Coun. pub. health fellow, Australia, 1978. Fellow APHA, Australian Coll. Health Execs. (state bd. dirs. 1977-82), Royal Soc. Health, London; mem. Internat. Epidmiological Assn., Am. Coll. Forensic Examiners (cert. level III homeland security), So. Calif. Pub. Health Assn. (bd. dirs. 1987-95), NY Acad. Scis., Wilderness Med. Soc., Delta Omega. Lutheran. Achievements include research in serial section microcinematography, large linked databases, and vaccine safety studies. Office: Kaiser-Permanente Southern Calif 100 S Los Robles 2nd Fl Pasadena CA 91101 Business E-Mail: mmhlugg@alumni.pitt.edu.

LUGINBUEHL, MARSHA L., psychologist; d. Harley W. and Betty Marie Knapp; m. Peter Luginbuehl, Dec. 28, 1973; children: Nicole Sitter, Matthew, Kellie Goode. BA in Psychology, U. Kans., 1974; PhD, U. South Fla., 2003. Cert. Nat. Assn. Sch. Psychologists, 1992, lic. sch. psychologist Dept. Health, Fla., 1996. Sch. psychologist Pasco County Sch. Dist., Land 'O Lakes, Fla., 1987—2006, Lincoln County Sch. Dist., Wyo., 2006—; pres. Child Uplift, Inc., 1997—, Fairview, Wyo., 2006—; pres. & CEO Provider of Workshops for Professionals on Sleep Disorders in Students. Expertise in universal sleep screenings for students. Sec., chmn. Action Youth Care Fla., 1993—98. Named Fla. Student Svcs. Person of Yr., Pasco County, 2004. Mem.: APA (Oustanding Dissertation of Yr. award 2003), Am. Acad. Sleep Medicine, Wyo. Assn. Sch. Psychologists, Nat. Assn. Sch. Psychologists. Achievements include invention of sleep disorders inventory for students; expertism in universal sleep disorders screening for children and adolescents. Mailing: PO Box 146 Fairview WY 83119 Home and Office: Child Uplift Inc 92 Moose Manor Dr Fairview WY 83119 Office Fax: 307-886-9093. Personal E-mail: mllugin@aol.com. Business E-Mail: childuplift@aol.com.

LUGNIER, CLAIRE, pharmacologist, researcher; d. Jean-Charles Moreau and Suzanne Carrez; m. Claire Moreau, Mar. 21, 1970; children: Vincent, Hélène. PhD, U. Strasbourg, 1979. Rschr. Euratom, Mol, Belgium; rsch. dir. CNRS, Strasbourg, France, Illkirch, 1990—. Editor: (book) Phosphodiesterase Methods and Protocols. Recipient awards, Found. Dr Antonio Esteve, 1992—93. Mem.: AAHA, Soc. Biology Strasbourg. Roman Catholic. Avocations: cooking, gardening, singing. Office Phone: 33368854264. Office Fax: 33368854313; Home Fax: 33388605487. Personal E-mail: claire@unistra.fr. Business E-Mail: claire.lugnier@pharma.u-strasbg.fr.

LUI, TUN HING, surgeon, director; s. Yuk Sai Lui and Yuk Wan Ip; m. Man Wai Lee; children: Pun Lok, Pun Ho. MBBS, U. Hong Kong, 1990. Dir. foot and ankle svc. North Dist. Hosp., Hong Kong, 1998—, cons., dept. orthopaedics and traumatology, 2008—. Tng. dir. Hong Kong Coll. Orthopaedic Surgeon, Hong Kong, 2007—. Contbr. articles to profl. jours. Fellow: Hong Kong Acad. Medicine, Royal Coll. Surgeon (Edinburg), Hong Kong Coll. Orthopedic Surgeon. Office: North Dist Hosp 9 Po Kin Rd Hong Kong China Office Fax: 852-26837576. E-mail: luithderek@yahoo.co.uk.

LUIZ, OLINDA DO CARMO, medical researcher; b. Brazil, Apr. 2, 1962; Degree in Medicine, UNIFESP, 1987; PhD, U. São Paulo, 2004. Sci. rschr. Faculdade Medicina U. São Paulo, 2009—. Prof. Faculdade Medicina do ABC, 1998—2009. Recipient award, Incentivo em Sci. Tech. para o SUS. Mem.: Assn. Brasileira Pós-Graduação em Saúde Coletiva. Avocation: embroidery. Office: Av Dr Arnaldo 455 - Dep Med Prev São Paulo 01246903 Brazil Office Fax: 55 11 30618466. Business E-Mail: olinda@preventiva.fm.usp.br.

LUIZA, SPIRU, medical educator; b. Calarasi, Romania, Aug. 5, 1962; PhD, Carol Davila U. Medicine & Pharmacy, 1997. Prof. Carol Davila U. Medicine & Pharmacy, 1990—. Named one of Women of Yr., Am. Biog. Inst. Office: P-ta M Kogalniceanu 1 Sc 1 Apt 17 Bucharest 050064 Romania Office Phone: 40 21 3124696, 40 724232849. Office Fax: 40 21 3124696. Business E-Mail: lsaslan@brainaging.ro.

LUK, KEITH DIP-KEI, medical educator; m. O'Hoy Luk. MBBS, U. Hong Kong, 1977; MCh in Orthopaedics, U. Liverpool, Eng., 1984. Med. & health officer Dept. Health, Hong Kong Govt., 1978—80; lectr. Dept. Orthop. & Traumatology, U. Hong Kong, 1980—87, sr. lectr., 1987—92, reader, 1992—96, prof., 1996—2000, chair prof., 2000—. Fellow: RCS (Glasgow), RCS (Edinburgh), Hong Kong Acad. Medicine, Hong Kong Coll. Orthopaedic Surgeons. Achievements include patents for intervertebral disc transplantation. Office: Univ Hong Kong Dept Orthop & Traumatology Pokfulam Hong Kong

LUKASZKIEWICZ, JACEK, pharmacologist, educator; b. Siedlce, Mar. 10, 1946; M, U. Warsaw, 1969; PhD, Polish Acad. Sci., 1982. Asst. prof. Med. U. Warsaw, Pharmacy Faculty, 2000—, adj. prof., head dept., 2005. Grant, Ministry Sci. Fellow: Metabolic Bone Disease Children and Adolescents. Achievements include research in vitamin D metabolism and supplementation, bone metabolism, genotyping. Avocations: photography, motorcycling. Home: Hirszfelda 16 m 20 Warsaw Mazovia 02-776 Poland Business E-Mail: jacekluk@farm.amwaw.edu.pl.

LUKE, JOHN ANDERSON, JR., paper, packaging and chemical company executive; b. Nov. 24, 1948; s. John Anderson Luke Sr. and Joy (Carter) Luke; m. Kathleen Allen, June 30, 1984; children: Lindsay Allen, Elizabeth Carter, John A. III. BA, Lawrence U., 1971; MBA, U. Pa., 1979. Unit sales mgr. Procter & Gamble Co., 1974—77; corp. assoc. Westvaco Corp., NYC, 1979—81, sr. fin. analyst, 1981—82, asst. treas., 1982, treas., 1983—86, v.p., treas., 1986, sr. v.p. mktg., internat. and Brazilian subsidiary, 1987—90, exec. v.p., 1990—92, pres., 1992—2002, chmn., 1996—2002; CEO Westvaco Corp. (now MeadWestvaco Corp.), Stamford, Conn., 1992—; chmn. MeadWestvaco Corp., Stamford, Conn., 2002—. Dir. FM Global, The Timken Co.; trustee Am. Enterprise Inst. for Pub. Policy Rsch.; chmn. Am. Forest Found., Nat. Assn. Mfr.; vice chmn. Sustainable Forestry Bd.; bd. dirs. Bank of N.Y., The Tinker Found., Ams. Soc., Bank of N.Y.; bd. trustees Lawrence U.; mem. President's Export Coun. Bd. govs. NCASI; dir. United Negro Coll. Fund. Officer USAF, 1971—74, S.E. Asia, Vietnam conflict. Mem.: Am. Forest and Paper Assn. (dir., exec. com.), The Commonwealth Club, The Links, Univ. Club. Office: Meadwest Vaco 501 S 5th St Richmond VA 23219-0501 *

LUKE, ROBERT GEORGE, nephrologist, medical educator; b. Sept. 4, 1935; s. Henry and Jemima (McCracken) L.; m. Catriona Mary MacDonald, Mar. 10, 1964; children: Colin Henry, Margaret Ann M.B., Ch.B., U. Glasgow, Scotland, 1959. Intern, then resident Univ. Hosps., U. Glasgow, 1959-63; Dir. renal div. U. Ky. Med. Ctr., Lexington, 1968-79; dir nephrology rsch. and tng. ctr. U. Ala., Birmingham, 1979-88; chmn. dept. medicine U. Cin. Med. Ctr., 1988—2004. Contbr. articles to profl. jours. Grantee NIH, 1972-91; fellow Yale U. Med. Ctr., 1964-65. Master ACP (bd. regents 2004—, chmn.-elect 2009, chmn. 2010); fellow Royal Coll. Physicians; mem. Assn. Am. Physicians, Am. Soc. Clin. Investigation, Nat. Kidney Found., Am. Soc. Nephrology (past pres.), Clin. and Climatol. Assn. (past pres.). Presbyterian. Avocation: tennis. Business E-Mail: robert.luke@uc.edu.

LUKE, SHARAZ ANAND, pharmaceutical executive; b. Swindon, England, Dec. 27, 1977; s. Shamime Alice Luke. BS in Biotechnology (hon.), U. Westminster, London, 1999. Cert. Project Mgmt. Open U., 2006. Antigen prodn. technician Intervet UK Ltd., Milton Keynes, England, 1999—2003, antigen prodn. team leader, 2003—06. Achievements include development of mycoplasma production (veterinarian). E-mail: sharaz.luke@intervet.com.

LUKHARD, KENNETH W., hospital administrator; MPA, U. San Francisco; BA in Theology, Azusa Pacific U.; MA in Counseling, Wheaton Coll. Pres., CEO Lake Cumberland Regional Hosp., Princeton Hosp.; exec. v.p., COO St. Mary, pres.; exec. v.p., COO SSM St. Joseph Hosp. West, pres., Advocate Health Care Corp. Office: Advocate Christ Medical Center 4440 W 95th St Oak Lawn IL 60453 Office Phone: 708-684-8000.

LUKSAMIJARULKUL, PIPAT, healthcare educator; m. Soavalug Luksamijarulkul; 1 child, Nicha. Diploma, Mahidol U., Bangkok, MSc, 1983. Cert. pub. health rsch. WHO, Mahidol U., 1987. Assoc. prof. Faculty Pub. Health Mahidol U., Bangkok, 1991—, dep. dean,

1991—, cons., 1991—. Contbr. scientific papers. Mem.: Rsch. Ctr. Health Risk. Office: Faculty Pub Health Mahidol Univ Ratchavithi Bangkok 10400 Thailand Office Fax: 66 026409835. Personal E-mail: luksamijarulkul@yahoo.com.

LUM, JOHNNY, physician assistant, consultant; b. Kowloon, Hong Kong, Oct. 3, 1954; arrived in US, 1955; s. So Hong Lum and Shok Hing Yuen; m. Nancy Virginia Caron, May 13, 1995. Cert. in Respiratory Therapy, Bay City Coll., 1978; BA in Physician Asst., Trevecca Nazarene U., 1986; cert. in Surg. Tech., Bridgeport Hosp. Sch. Nursing, Conn., 2001. Physician asst. Bapt. Med. Ctr., Jacksonville, Fla., 1986—87, Correctional Med. Systems, Inc., Reidsville, Ga., 1987—92, Beth Israel Med. Ctr., NYC, 1992—96, The Vein Treatment Ctr., NYC, 1996—97, Arthritis Ctr. Conn., Waterbury, Conn., 1997—2003, Danbury (Conn.) Internal Medicine Assocs., 2003—, Waterbury Hosp., Conn., 2004—. Cons. Pfizer, Miami, 2003—; lead project designer world Trade Ctr. Site Meml. Competition Lower Manhattan (N.Y.) Devel. Corp., NYC, 2003—. Mem.: Soc. Physician Asst. Rheumatology, Conn. Acad. Physician Assts., Am. Acad. Physician Asst. Home: 4-6 Union Avenue 20 Norwalk CT 06851 Office: Waterbury Hosp 64 Robbins St Waterbury CT 06708 Personal E-mail: jlum090@aol.com.

LUM, MILTON SIEW WAH, obstetrician, gynecologist; b. Kuala Lumpur, Malaysia; s. Kin Tuck Lum and Sun Lin Chan; m. Patricia Sok Ai Ng. MBBS, U. Malaya, 1973. House officer Univ. Hosp., Kuala Lumpur, 1973-74; med. officer Gen. Hosp., Klang and Kuala Lumpur, 1974-76; sr. house officer Royal Infirmary, Edinburgh, 1976-77; registrar Newcastle Gen. Hosp., Newcastle upon Tyne, 1977-79; rsch. fellow U. Hosp. South Manchester, Manchester, 1979-82; cons. ob-gyn Tung Shin Hosp., Kuala Lumpur, 1983—93, Taman Desa Hosp., Kuala Lumpur, 1997—2003, Assunta Hosp., Petaling Jaya, Malaysia, 1994—2011, Alpha Specialist Ctr., Petaling, Jaya, Malaysia, 2011—. Vis. prof. Fedn. Gynecology and Obstetrics, 1996; dir. Nat. Heart Inst., Kuala Lumpur, 1997—2010, Assunta Hosp., Petaling Jaya, 1998—2006, Social Security Orgn., 2001—09, Med. Defence Malaysia, 2004—, Nanyang Press Found., 2006—, Tung Shin Hosp., 2006—. Columnist: The Star Newspaper, 2002—. Mem. Malaysian Med. Coun., 1995—, Nat. Econ. Consultative Coun., 1999—2000; coun. mem. U. Tunku Abdul Rahman, 2001—; mem. Malaysian Coun. for Healthcare Stds., 2001—, Nat. Patient Safety Council, 2003—; chmn. Commonwealth Med. Trust, 2005—; mem. exec. com. Malaysian Mental Literacy Movement, 2006—, dep. chmn., 2009—. Recipient Johan Setia Mahkota award King of Malaysia. Fellow: Acad. Medicine of Malaysia, Royal Coll. Ob-Gyn. (chmn. Malaysia rep. com. 2000—05); mem.: ASEAN Ob-Gyn. Socs. (treas. 1995—98), Fedn. Pvt. Med. Practitioners Assn. Malaysia (pres. 1991—95), Acad. Medicine (dep. scribe 1998—2002), Commonwealth Med. Assn. (v.p. 1998—2001), Ob-Gyn. Soc. Malaysia (pres. 1994—95), Malaysian Med. Assn. (pres. 1997—98), Internat. Fedn. Ob-Gyn. (mem. exec. bd. 1994—2003). Office: Alpha Specialist Ctr [illegible] Petaling Jaya 47810 Malaysia

LUMB, WILLIAM VALJEAN, veterinarian; b. Sioux City, Iowa, Nov. 26, 1921; m. Lilly Carlson, 1949; 1 child, John W. DVM, Kans. State U., 1943; MS, Tex. A&M U., 1953; PhD in Vet. Medicine, U. Minn., 1957; DSc (hon.), Ohio State U., 1999. Intern, resident Angell Meml. Animal Hosp., Boston, 1946—48; from instr. to assoc. prof. medicine and surgery Tex. A&M U., 1949—52; asst. prof. clin. surgery Colo. State U., 1954—58; assoc. prof. surgery and medicine Mich. State U., 1958—60; assoc. prof. medicine Coll. Vet. Medicine, Colo. State U., Ft. Collins, 1960—63, dir. surg. lab., 1963—79, prof. surgery, 1963—81, emeritus prof., 1981—; prof. Ross U., St. Kitts, West Indies, 1986. Pres., CEO The Lubra Co., 1972—99. Author: Small Animal Anesthesia, 1963; author: (with E.W. Jones) Veterinary Anesthesia, 1973, 1984, Veterinary Anesthesia, Japanese and Spanish translations, 1979; editor: Vet Surgery, 1982; contbr. over 150 articles to profl. jours.; patentee in field. With Vet. Corps US Army, 1943—46, major Air Force. Recipient Gaines medal, 1965, Ralston Purina Rsch. award, 1980, Disting. Svc. award, Kans. State U., 1982, Jacob Markowitz award, 1986, Glover Disting. Faculty award, Colo. State U., 2004, ACVS Founders award, 2008; named Colo. Vet. of Yr., 1981. Mem.: NAS, AAAS, AVMA, Nat. Acads. of Practice, Am. Assn. Vet. Clinicians, N.Y. Acad. Sci., Am. Coll. Vet. Surgeons (founding diplomate, pres., chmn. bd. 1974—75, Founders award 1965), Am. Coll. Vet. Anesthesiologists (founding diplomate, Svc. award 1982). Address: 1905 Mohawk St Fort Collins CO 80525-1501

LUMBRAZO, MARIA CONSTANCE, adult nurse practitioner; b. Niagara Falls, NY, Nov. 30, 1960; BSN, Upstate Med. U. Coll. Nursing, 2005, MS, 2009, FNP-C. Registered nurse SUNY Upstate Med. U. Hosp., 1983—93, nurse adminstr. neuroscis., 1993—2000, clin. quality investigator dept. risk mgmt., 2000—10, stroke program coord., 2010—. Family nurse practitioner adult medicine & urgent care Syracuse Cmty. Health Ctr., 2009—. Mem.: Am. Heart Assn., Nurse Practitioner Assn., Am. Acad. Nurse Practitioners, Sigma Theta Tau. Avocation: swimming. Home: 8397 Shoveler Ln Liverpool NY 13090 Personal E-mail: mlumbrazo1@aol.com.

LUMPKIN, JOHN ROBERT, public health physician, state official; b. Chgo., July 28, 1951; s. Frank and Beatrice (Shapiro) L.; m. Mary S. Blanks, Jan. 28, 1984; children: Alia, John R. Jr. BS, Northwestern U., Evanston, Ill., 1973; MD, Northwestern U., Chgo., 1974; MPH, U. Ill., Chgo., 1985. Diplomate Am. Bd. Emergency Medicine. Intern U. Chgo. Hosps., 1975, resident in anesthesiology, 1976-78, vice-chmn. emergency medicine, 1981-84; asst. prof. U. Chgo., 1978-84; asst. dir. emergency medicine South Chgo. Hosp., 1984-85; staff physician St. Mary of Nazareth Hosp., Chgo., 1985; assoc. dir. Ill. Dept. Pub. Health, Springfield and Chgo., 1985-90, dir., 1990—2003; sr. v.p. Robert Wood Johnson Found., Princeton, NJ, 2003—, dir. Health Care Group, 2003—. Cons. Egyptian Ministry Health, Cairo, 1986-90; chmn. Nat. Com. on Vital & Health Stats., 1996-, mem. sec.'s adv. com. on injury control Ctrs. for Dis. Control, Atlanta, 1989-93. Recipient Arthur MacCormack Excellence & Dedication in Pub. Health award, Assn. State & Territorial Health Officials, Jonas Salk Health Leadership award, Ill. Pub. Health Assn., Leadership in Pub. Health. Fellow Am. Coll. Med. Informatics, Am. Coll. Emergency Physicians (bd. dirs. 1987-93); mem. Soc. Tchrs. Emergency Medicine (pres. 1981-82), Ill. Coll. Emergency Physicians (pres. 1982-83, Bill B. Smiley award 1986), Assn. State and Territorial Health Ofcls. (pres. 1995-96), Inst. Medicine. Avocations: racquetball, model trains, football, computers. Office: Robert Wood Johnson Found PO Box 2316 College Rd E & Rt 1 Princeton NJ 08543 Business E-Mail: jlumpkin@rwjf.org.

LUMPKIN, THOMAS RILEY, retired physician; b. Tuskegee, Ala., Jan. 4, 1926; s. William Clifford and Harriet Graham (Riley) L.; m. Jean D. Perry, June 10, 1955; children: Leah, Ry, Mary Lyman, Cliff BS, U. Ala., 1949; MD, Med. Coll. Ala., 1958. Diplomate Am. Bd. Family Physicians. Pvt. practice, Tuskegee, Ala., 1959—65, Enterprise, Ala., 1965—74; asst. prof. Coll. Cmty. Health Scis., Tuscaloosa, Ala., 1974—77; assoc. prof. U. Ala., Tuscaloosa, 1977—81, prof. family medicine, 1981—91, prof. emeritus, 1991—93; interim dean Coll. Cmty. Health Scis. Capstone Med. Ctr., Tuscaloosa, 1979—80. Councilman City of Tuskegee, 1962-64; active Leadership Ala. Class III, 1992-93; bd. dirs. free med. care for under and non-insured Good Samaritan Clinic, 1999; chmn. bd. trustees Tuscaloosa Dist. Meth. Bd, 2003-07. With USAAC, 1946, inf., sgt. 1st class AUS, 1951-52 Mem. Ala. Acad. Family Physicians (pres. 1968-69), Med. Assn. State of Ala. (pres. 1990-91), Rotary Internat. (pres. Enterprise Club 1968-69, pres. Tuscaloosa 1993-94, dist. gov. 1997-98, vice chmn. world cmty. svc., 2004-06, Polio Plus award 2003, Disting. Svc. award 2004-05), U. Ala. Sch. Med. Alumni Assn. (pres. 2001-03), Rotary (Dist. 6860 Outstanding Svc. award 2005, Found. Dist. Svc. award 2004-05), Pillar West Ala. Cmty. (Disting. Svc. award 2009), Kappa Alpha, Alpha Omega Alpha Methodist. Avocations: travel, hunting, reading. Home: 2 Ridgeland Tuscaloosa AL 35406-1607 Business E-Mail: snakedoc.lumpkin@gmail.com. *

LUMSDEN, ANDREW GINO, neurobiologist, researcher; b. Beaconsfield, Berkshire, Eng., Jan. 22, 1947; s. Edward Gilbert and Stella Pirie (Lumsden) Sita; m. Anne Farrington Roberg, Nov. 20, 1970 (div. 1997); children: Ailsa, Isobel; m. Kathleen Marie Wets, Feb. 2, 2002. BA with hons., Cambridge U., Eng., 1968, MA, 1972; PhD, London U., 1978. Lectr. anatomy Guy's Hosp. Med. Sch., London, 1972—78, sr. lectr., 1978—86; reader craniofacial devel. United Med. Dental Sch. Guy's and St. Thomas Hosps., London, 1986—89, prof. devel. neurobiology, 1989—; dir. MRC Centre dept. devel. neurobiology Kings Coll., London, 1999—. Mem. neurosci. bd. Med. Rsch. Coun., 1994-98, neurosci. panel Wellcome Trust Med. Rsch. Coun., 1997-2000; mem. Human Frontier Sci. Program Brain Functions rev. com., 1998-2001. Author: The Developing Brain, 2001; contbr. articles to profl. jours. Grantee Wellcome Trust Med. Rsch. Coun., 1978—; Internat. Rsch. scholar Howard Hughes Med. Inst., 1992-98. Fellow Royal Soc. Avocations: natural history, mechanical engineering, bridge, lotus 7s. Home: 16 Elephant Ln London SE16 4JD England Office: Guy's Hosp/Devel Neurobiol King's Coll London SE1 1UL London England Office Phone: +44 207848-6520. E-mail: andrew.lumsden@kcl.ac.uk.

LUNA, JAIME R., physician assistant; b. San Pablo de Lago, Imbabura, Ecuador, Nov. 14, 1956; Came to U.S., 1986; s. Jaime Sebastian Luna and Martha Feliza Cordova; m. Andrea E. Picchi, Sept. 26, 1986 (div. 1990); m. Dianne Figueroa, Aug. 17, 1996; children: Sebastian, Elizabeth. MD, Ctrl. U. Ecuador, 1983; grad. Psychiatric Technician, Valley Vocat. Coll., 1992; grad. physician asst., Charles Drew U., 1997. Resident El Corazon Health Hosp. Ctr., Pangua, Ecuador, 1983-84, Eugenio Espejo Hosp., Quito, Ecuador, 1985-86; lab. technician Northview Pacific Lab., Berkeley, Calif., 1987-88, med. asst. Oakland Assocs., Oakland, Calif., 1988-90; pharmacy asst. Fairview Devel. Ctr., Costa Meza, Calif., 1991-92; psych. technician Lanterman Devel. Ctr., Pomona, Calif., 1992-98, U. Calif., Orange, Calif., 1993-96; physician asst. City of Hope Nat. Med. Ctr., Duarte, Calif., 1998; house call physicians South Coast Pediatrics, Santa Ana, 1998—; physician Urgent Care, Newport Beach, Calif., 2006. Bd. dirs. missionary svcs. Saint Columbus. Fellow Am. Inst. Ultrasound Med.; mem. Calif. Assn. Psychiatric Tech., Am. Assn. Physician Assts., Consortium Physicians Latin Am., Calif. Assn. Physicians Assts, Alcon Labs. Spkrs. Bur. Avocations: swimming, bicycling. Office: South Coast Pediatrics 2650 S Bristol St # 101-103 Santa Ana CA 92704-5766 also: South Coast Pediatrics 1619 N Spurgeon St Santa Ana CA 92701-2328 Personal E-mail: toqui@earthlink.net.

LUNA, MARTA, biologist; b. Barcelona, June 8, 1975; B, U. Barcelona, 1998; degree in Human Reproduction, U. Autónoma de Barelona, 2001. Biologist Inst. U. Dexeus, 2004—. Recipient award, Comissió de Docència Inst. U. Dexeus. Mem.: Spanish Soc. Fertility, ASEBIR, ESHRE. Home: Avda Gaudí 33 5° 1a Barcelona 08025 Spain Business E-Mail: marlun@dexeus.com.

LUNDBERG, GEORGE DAVID, II, medical editor-in-chief, pathologist; b. Pensacola, Fla., Mar. 21, 1933; s. George David and Esther Louise (Johnson) Lundberg; m. Nancy Ware Sharp, Aug. 18, 1956 (div.); children: George David III, Charles William, Jean Carol; m. Patricia Blacklidge Lorimer, Mar. 6, 1983; children: Christopher Leif, Melinda Suzanne. AA, North Park Coll., Chgo., 1950; BS, U. Ala., Tuscaloosa, 1952; MS, Baylor U., Waco, Tex., 1963; MD, Med. Coll. Ala., Birmingham, 1957; ScD (hon.), SUNY, Syracuse, 1988, Thomas Jefferson U., 1993, U. Ala., Birmingham, 1994, Med. Coll. Ohio, 1995. Cert. anatomic, clinical Am. Bd. Pathology, 1962. Intern Tripler Hosp., Hawaii; resident Brooke Hosp., San Antonio; assoc. prof. pathology U. So. Calif., LA, 1967—72, prof., 1972—77; assoc. dir. labs. L.A. County-U. So. Calif. Med. Ctr., 1968—77; prof., chmn. dept. pathology U. Calif.-Davis, Sacramento, 1977—82; v.p. scientific info., editor Jour. AMA, Chgo., 1982—99, editor in chief scientific publ., 1991—95; editor-in-chief AMA Sci. Info. and Multimedia, Chgo., 1995—99, Medscape, 1999—2001, editor-in-chief emeritus, 2001—03; editor Medscape Gen. Medicine, 1999—; editor-in-chief and exec. v.p. Medicalogic/Medscape, 2000—02; spl. healthcare advisor to CEO WebMD, 2002—03; editor-in-chief Medscape Core, 2005—, eMedicine, 2006—. Vis. prof. U. London, 1976, Lund U., Sweden, 1976; prof. clin. pathology Northwestern U., Chgo., 1982—2009; adj. prof. health policy Harvard U., Boston, 1993—2008, vis. prof. pathology, 1994—96; sr. fellow Northwestern U., 1999—2004; cons. prof. health policy Stanford U., Palo Alto, Calif., 2005—; pres., chief bd. dirs. Ludberg Inst., Berkeley, Calif., 2009—. Author, editor Managing the Patient Focused Laboratory, 1975, Using the Clinical Laboratory in Medical Decision Making, 1983, 1951, Landmark Articles in Medicine, 1984, AIDS From the Beginning, 1986, Caring for the Uninsured and Underinsured, 1991, Violence, 1992, 100 Years of JAMA Landmark Articles, 1997, Severed Trust: Why American Medicine Hasn't Been Fixed, 2001, paperback edit., 2002; contbr. articles to profl. jours. Lt. col. M.C. US Army, 1956—67. Fellow: Am. Soc. Clin. Pathologists (past pres.); mem.: Inst. Med., N.Y. Acad. Scis., Am. Acad. Forensic Sci., Alpha Omega Alpha. Democrat. Episcopalian. Office Phone: 312-560-0290. Personal E-mail: glundberg@gmail.com.

LUNDBERG, PER OLOV MAGNUS, neurology educator; b. Vänersborg, Sweden, Apr. 12, 1931; s. Ernst Magnus and Lilly (Wallgren) L.; m. Kerstie Sjöberg, Dec. 4, 1960; children: Ann Charlotte Lotta, Eva Maria. MD, Uppsala U., Sweden, 1957, PhD in Anatomy, 1960. Lic. physician, specialist in clin. sexology. Rsch. asst. anatomy U. Uppsala, 1950-58, jr. physician, asst. prof. neurology, 1958-74, prof., head neurology dept., 1974-96, med. dir. univ. hosp., 1978-83. Med. adviser Nat. Bd. Health and Welfare, Sweden, 1975-2000; adv. bd. Med. Products Agy., Uppsala, 1981-98; advisor Swedish Inst. Infectious Disease Control, 2001-05; reviewer WHO Collaborating Ctr. Internat. Drug Monitoring, 2001—. Editor: Sexology, 1994, 2d edit., 2002, 3rd edit., 2010; editor in chief Scandinavian Jour. Sexology, 1997-2001. Mem. Uppsala County Coun., 1974-85; pres. Selander Found., Sweden. Recipient Dr. Herman Musaph prize, Med. Sexology, 1997, Gold medal, World Assn. for Sexology, Paris, 2001. Mem. Scandinavian Migraine Soc. (founder, former pres.), Internat. Acad. Sex Rsch. (charter mem.; pres. 1991-93), Nordic Assn. Clin. Sexology (founder, pres. 1997-99), Acad. Sci. Sexuologicae Polonia (hon.), Soc. Sexuologica Bohemica (hon.), Swedish Migraine Soc. (hon.), European Fedn. Neurol. Socs. (chmn. task force for neurosexology), Albert Schweitzer World Acad. Medicine. Mem. Moderata Samlings Partiet. Avocation: ornithology. Home: Tallbacksvägen 19 S 756 45 Uppsala Sweden Office: U Hosp Dept Neurology S 751 85 Uppsala Sweden Home Phone: 46 18 309397; Office Phone: 46 18 6115026. Business E-Mail: po.lundberg@neurologi.uu.se.

LUNDBLAD, ROGER LAUREN, biotechnology consultant; b. San Francisco, Oct. 31, 1939; s. Lauren Alfred and Doris Ruth (Peterson) L.; m. Susan Hawly Taylor, Oct. 15, 1966 (div. 1985); children: Christina Susan, Cynthia Karin. BSc, Pacific Luth. U., 1961; PhD, U. Wash., 1965. Rsch. assoc. U. Wash., Seattle, 1965-66, Rockefeller U., NYC, 1966-68; asst. prof. U. NC, Chapel Hill, 1968-71, assoc. prof., 1971-77, prof. pathology and biochemistry, 1977-91, adj. prof., 1991—; dir. sci. tech. devel. Baxter-Hyland/Immuno, Duarte, Calif., 1991-99; biotech. cons., 2000—. Vis. scientist Hyland divsn. Baxter Healthcare, Glendale, Calif., 1988-89. Author: Applications of Solution Protein Chemistry to Biotechnology, 2009, Chemical Reagents for Protein Modification, 1984, 2d edit., 1990, 3d edit., 2004, The Evolution of Protein Chemistry to Proteomics, 2005, Compendium for Biochemistry and Molecular Biology, 2007, Applications of Solutions Protein Chemistry to Biotechnology, 2009, Approaches to the Conformational Analysis of Biopharmaceuticals, 2010, Development and Application of Biomarkers, 2010; editor: Chemistry and Biology of Thrombin, 1977, Chemistry and Biology of Heparin, 1980, Techniques in Protein Modification, 1994; editor-in-chief: Biotechnology and Applied Biochemistry, 1996-2003, Internet Jour. Genomics and Proteonics, 2005-10; contbr. articles to profl. jours. Mem. Am. Soc. Biochem. Molecular Biology. Office: PO Box 16695 Chapel Hill NC 27516-6695 Office Phone: 919-929-5082. Personal E-mail: lundbladr@bellsouth.net.

LUNDQUIST, DANA RICHARD, health facility administrator; b. Mpls., Sept. 12, 1941; s. R. Dana and Mary Jane (Norton) L.; children: Brenda A., Sheila R. BA, Valparaiso U., 1963; postgrad., U. Hawaii, 1963-64, U. Colo., 1963; MBA, U. Chgo., 1966. Adminstrv. asst. U. Chgo. Hosps. and Clinics, 1966—67, asst. supt., 1967—68, asst. dir., 1968—70, officer, bd. dirs. affiliates Hamot Health Systems, Inc., Erie, Pa., 1970—92, pres. parent co., 1981—92, cons., 1992—97; sr. v.p. Highmark Blue Cross Blue Shield, 1993—97; exec. v.p. Hardware Hawaii, 1997—98. Lectr. grad. program in hosp. adminstrn. U. Chgo., 1967-70; mem. Erie County Hosp. Coun., 1978-92, pres., 1982; bd. dirs. Hosp. Coun. Western Pa., 1978-92, vice chmn.; exec. com. Pa. Coun. Tchg. Hosps., 1986-90; adv. coun. risk mgmt. Pa. Hosp. Ins. Co., 1982-90, bd. dirs. Vol. Hosps. Am. of Pa., 1983-92, mem.; bd. visitors The Behrend Coll., Pa. State U., 1990-92; bd. dirs. Pa. Med. Coll., 1991-92. Mem. Erie Conf. on Community Devel., 1981-92, bd. dirs., 1988-92; bd. dirs. N.W. Pa. Buy Right Coun., 1986-92, United Way Erie County, 1983-92; mem. pres.'s coun. Villa Maria Coll., Erie, 1981-90, bd. incorporators Gannon U., Erie, 1981-92; mem. governing bd. St. Paul's Luth. Ch., Erie, 1973-78, v.p., 1974-78; mem. Erie Down Town Coalition Steering Com., 1990-92, chmn., 1991-92, numerous other activities. Fellow Am. Coll. Healthcare Execs. (mem. regents adv. coun. Pa.); mem. Am. Hosp. Assn. (governing coun. sect. met. hosps. 1987, alt. ho. of dels. 1988), Hosp. Assn. Pa. (polit. action com. 1981-92), Pa. C. of C., U. Chgo. Hosp. Alumni Assn. (exec. com. 1967-70, 87-92, sec.-treas. 1988, pres. 1990-91), Rotary. Lutheran. Home and Office: 207 E Ohio St # 423 Chicago IL 60611 Personal E-mail: danalundquist@yahoo.com.

LUNSFORD, W. BRUCE (WILLIAM BRUCE LUNSFORD), former health facility administrator and products executive; b. Kenton County, Ky., Nov. 11, 1947; s. Amos and Billie Lunsford; m. Becky Lunsford, Aug. 29, 1970; children: Amy, Cindy, Brandy. BA in Polit. Sci., U. Ky., 1969; JD, Salmon P. Chase Coll. Law, 1974. CPA Ky., Ohio; bar: Ky. 1974, Ohio 1974. With Alexander Grant & Co., CPA, Cin., 1969—74, Keating, Muething and Klekamp Attys., Cin., 1974—79; dep. sec. Devel. Cabinet and Gov.'s Legis. Liaison State of Ky., 1980—81, sec. commerce, 1981—83; of counsel Greenebaum Doll & McDonald, Louisville, 1984—91; chmn., pres., CEO Vencor Inc., Louisville, 1985—99; pres., CEO Ventas Inc., Louisville, 1998, chmn., 1998—2003. Bd. trustees U. Ky., 1983—87, Centre Coll., 1992—97, Shakertown at Pleasant Hill, Ky., Inc., 1992—; bd. trustees., sec. Bellarmine Coll., 1991—97; bd. govs. Salmon P. Chase Coll. Law, 1983—87; bd. dirs. Greater Louisville Fund for the Arts, 1990—97, Ky. Ctr. for the Arts Endowment Fund, Inc., 1992—97, Ky. Econs. Devel. Corp., 1989—, chmn., 1996—; bd. dirs., exec. com. Nat. City Bank, Ky., 1991—; bd. dirs. Res-Care, Inc., 1992—, Churchill Downs, Inc., 1995—, Nat. City Corp., 1995—; Fedn. Am. Health Sys., 1996—; bd. dirs. exec. com. Greater Louisville Econ. Devel. Partnership, 1992—. Named Entrepreneur of the Yr., Ky. and So. Ind., 1988, U. Ky. Bus. Leader of Yr., 1994; named to Kentuckiana Bus. Hall of Fame, 1993. Mem.: AICPA (Outstanding CPA in bus. and Ind. 1996), Omicron Delta Kappa. Democrat.

LUNTZ, MAURICE HAROLD, ophthalmologist; b. Capetown, South Africa, July 27, 1930; came to US, 1978; s. Montague Bernard and Sarah Miriam (Friedman) L.; m. Angela June Myerson, June 21, 1956; children: Melvyn Howard, Caryn Susan, David Sean. B Medicine B Surgery, Capetown U., 1952; MD, U. Witwatersrand, Johannesburg, South Africa, 1974. Diplomate Am. Bd. Ophthalmology. Lectr. ophthalmology Oxford U., England, 1960-62; prof., chmn. ophthalmology U. Witwatersrand, 1964-78; dir. ophthalmology Beth Israel Med. Ctr., NYC, 1978-88; chief glaucoma svc. Manhattan Eye, Ear & Throat Hosp., NYC, 1992—2002, bd. surgeon dir., 1993-95, pres. bd. surgeon dir., 1995—98; clin. prof. Mt. Sinai Sch. Medicine, NYC, 1978—2005, clin. prof. emeritus, 2005—; clin. prof. NYU, NYC, 2000—07. Adj. prof. NYU, 2007—; cons. Merck, Sharp & Dohme, NJ, 1980-82; chmn. Internat. Com. Ophthalmic Edn., 1974-90; mem. Internat. Coun. Ophthalmology, 1972-80. Author: Uveitis, 1983, Glaucoma Surgery, 1984, 2d edit., 1995, Innovations in Diagnosis and Management of the Glaucomas, 2002; mem. editl. bd. Highlights Ophthalmology, Panama, 1970—2008, pres., 2002—07; contbr. articles to profl. jour.; prodr. film Glaucoma Surveys, 1970. Bd. mem. The Glaucoma Found., NYC. Fellow Royal Coll. Surgeons (Edinburgh), Coll. Surgeons South Africa (hon.), Royal Coll. Ophthalmologist; mem. Academia Ophthalmologica Internationalis, Order St. John Jerusalem (comdr. 2001—). Office: 550 Pk Ave New York NY 10021 Office Phone: 212-832-9228. Personal E-mail: juneboy193@aol.com.

LUO, CHWAN YAU, cardiologist, surgeon; b. Taichung, Oct. 24, 1960; m. Ruey Ling Huang; children: Kevin, Luo. MD, Kaohsiung Med. Coll., 1986; MSc in Perimental Surgery, McGill U., 2004. Cons. surgeon Nat. Cheng Kung U. Hosp., Tainan, Taiwan, 1993—; assoc. dir. Surgical Intensive Unity Nat. Cheng Kung U. Hosp., 1995—98; cons. surgeon Chi Mai Found. Hosp., 1993—97, Chia Yi Christian Hosp., 1994—99, Provincial Tainan Hosp., 1997—99; chief of cardiovascular surgery Nat.Cheng Kung U. Hosp., 2002—. Lt. Army Surgeon, 1986—88, Taiwan. Mem.: Internat. Soc. Artheriosclerosis, Formosa Med. Assn., Surgery Soc. of Critical Care Medicine, Soc. of Thoracic and Cardiovascular Surgery, Soc. of Cardiology, Soc. of Surgery. Avocations: classical music, art, literature, violin. Office: Nat Cheng Kung U Hosp Dept Surgery 138 Sheng Li Rd Taiwan 704 China Business E-Mail: luochwy@mail.ncks.edu.tw.

LUO, GUANGHUA, molecular biologist, director; b. Changzhou, China, July 2, 1972; MS, Soochow U., 2003. Dir. Comprehensive Lab., 3rd Affiliated Hosp. Soochow U., 2006—. Editl. bd. mem. World Jour. Hepatology. Recipient Sci. and Tech. Achievement 1st prize, Changzhou City, Sci. and Tech. Achievement 2nd prize, Jiangsu Province. Avocation: fishing. Office: 85 Juqian St Changzhou Jiangsu 213003 China Business E-Mail: shineroar@163.com.

LUO, YAN-LING, biology professor; b. Weinan, Shaanxi, China, Nov. 7, 1962; M, East China U. Sci. and Tech., 1995. Prof. Shaanxi Normal U., 1985—. Recipient 2nd award, SINOPEC, 3rd award, 2nd award, Shanghai Mcpl. People's Govt. Avocations: travel, ping pong/table tennis. Office: 199 South Chang'an Rd Xi'an Shaanxi 710062 China Office Fax: 86-29-85307774. Business E-Mail: luoyanl@snnu.edu.cn.

LUONG, KHANH VINH QUOC, nephrologist, researcher; b. Cantho, Vietnam, Oct. 20, 1952; s. Hien Vinh Luong and Lieu Thi Huynh; m. Lan Thi Hoang Nguyen, Oct. 15, 1981. MD, U. Kans., 1981. Diplomate Am. Bd. Internal Medicine, Am. Bd. Nephrology, Nat. Bd. Med. Examiners, Am. Coll. Ethical Physicians. Intern in internal medicine St. Elizabeth Med. Ctr., Northeastern Ohio U., Youngstown, 1981; resident internal medicine Tulane U. Hosp. Program, New Orleans, 1982-83, City of Faith Med. and Rsch. Ctr., Oral Roberts U., Tulsa, Okla., 1986-87; fellow in nephrology Cedars-Sinai Med. Ctr., UCLA Program in Nephrology, LA, 1987-90; pvt. practice Westminster, Calif., 1990—; clin. assoc. prof. family medicine U. So. Calif., Keck Sch. Medicine, LA, 2002—. Vis. asst. prof. medicine UCLA, 1989—90; clin. assoc. prof. family medicine Keck Sch. Medicine, U. So. Calif., LA, 2002—; presenter at nat. and internat. meetings. Contbr. articles to profl. jours. Nat. Kidney Found. So. Calif. fellow, 1989-90. Fellow ACP, Am. Coll. Endocrinology, Am. Coll. Allergy, Asthma and Immunology, Am. Coll. Nutrition, Am. Bd. Hosp. Physicians (diplomate), Am. Soc. Nephrology, Am. Assn. Clin. Endocrinologists, Am. Coll. Chest Physicians, Endocrine Soc., Am. Soc. Bone and Mineral Rsch., Assn. Vietnamese Physicians of the Free World, Vietnamese Med. Assn. in U.S., Vietnamese Am. Med. Rsch. Found. (pres.). Office: 14971 Brookhurst St Westminster CA 92683-5556 Office Phone: 714-839-5898.

LUPIANI, DONALD ANTHONY, psychologist; b. NYC, June 7, 1946; s. Louis and Josephine (Boccia) L.; m. Linda Moyik, June 20, 1970; 1 child, Jennifer. BA, Iona Coll., 1968; MA, Columbia U., 1971, PhD, 1973; post-doctoral, Behavior Therapy Inst., White Plains, NY, 1976. Lic. psychologist, N.Y.; diplomat Am. Bd. Profl. Psychology, Am. Bd. Psychotherapy, Am. Acad. Behavioral Medicine, Internat. Acad. Behavioral Medicine, Internat. Acad. Behavioral Medicine. Clin. assoc. Columbia U., NYC, 1974-85, Fordham U., Bronx, NY, 1979-81; dir. psychology and spl. edn. svcs. Riverdale Country Sch., Bronx, 1973-87; chief psychologist Franciscan Order of Priests, NYC, 1983—; pvt. practice Yonkers, NY, 1975—. Dir. spl. svcs. Riverdale Country Sch., Bronx., 1973-87; bd. dirs. St. Ursula Learning Ctr., Mt. Vernon, N.Y. Contbr. articles to profl. jours. Bd. dirs., mem. The St. Ursula Learning Ctr. Fellow Am. Orthopsychiat. Assn., Am. Coll. Psychology, Am. Acad. Sch. Psychology; mem. APA, N.Y. State Psychol. Assn., Westchester County Psychol. Assn. (chmn. ethics com. 1980-87). Roman Catholic. Avocations: woodworking, painting, drawing. Home and Office: 227 Mile Square Rd Yonkers NY 10701-5369

LUPIANI, JENNIFER LYNNE, school psychologist; b. Bronx, NY, Mar. 24, 1975; d. Donald Anthony and Linda Lupiani. BA, Boston Coll., 1993—97; MS in edn., Fordham U., 1997—2001, profl. diploma, 1997—2001, PhD, 1997—2004. Cert. school psychologist NY, 2001. Sch. psychologist Astor Child Guidance Ctr., Bronx, NY, 2001—02, Croton Harmon Sch. Dist., Croton-on-Hudson, NY, 2002—04; asst. psychologist Ind. Practice, Yonkers, NY, 1999—; sch. psychologist Putnam No. Westchester BOCES, Yorktown Heights, NY, 2002—, Hendrick Hudson Sch. Dist., Cortlandt Manor, NY, 2004—. Field specialist for applied behavior analysis Fordham U., New York, NY, 2001—02. Recipient Ted Bernstein award, NY Assn. of Sch. Psychologists, 2004, Lambda Xi Chpt. of Kappa Delta Pi, Fordham U., 2000, Golden Key Nat. Honor Soc., Boston Coll., 1995, Psi Chi, 1996. Mem.: NASP, NY Assn. of Sch. Psychologists, APA. Avocations: sewing, knitting, painting, swimming, travel. Home: 227 Mile Square Rd Yonkers NY 10701 Office: Furnace Woods Elementary Sch 239 Watch Hill Rd Cortlandt Manor NY 10567 Personal E-mail: jlupiani@aol.com.

LUPO, ANTONIO, medical educator; b. Francavilla Fontana, Italy, Aug. 8, 1948; Degree in Medicine, Padova U., 1972. Prof. nephrology U. Verona, 2003—. Office: Piazzale Aristide Stefani Verona Veneto 37126 Italy Business E-Mail: antonio.lupo@univr.it.

LUPSKI, JAMES R., medical geneticist, educator; b. Hicksville, NY, Feb. 22, 1957; BA, NYU, 1979, PhD, 1984; MD, NYU Sch. Medicine, 1985. Diplomate Am. Bd. Pediat., Am. Bd. Med. Genetics, cert. in molecular genetics and clin. molecular genetics. Intern med. genetics Tex. Children's Hosp./Baylor Coll. Medicine, Houston, 1986—87, resident pediat., 1987—89, fellow med. genetics, 1989—91; attending physician Tex. Children's Hosp., 1989—; prof. dept. molecular and human genetics Baylor Coll. Medicine, 1995—, Cullen endowed chair molecular genetics. Attending physician Ben Taub Gen. Hosp., Houston, 1989—. Contbr. articles to profl. jours. Fellow: AAAS; mem.: AMA, Harris County Hosp. Soc., Tex. Med. Assn., Am. Fedn. Med. Rsch., Am. Acad. Pediat., Am. Soc. Microbiology, Am. Soc. Human Genetics (Curt Stern award 2002), Genetics Soc. America, Soc. Pediatric Rsch., Inst. Medicine, Am. Soc. Clin. Investigation, Am. Neurol. Inst. Office: Baylor Coll Medicine Dept Molecular & Human Genetics One Baylor Plz MS BCM225 Houston TX 77030 Office Phone: 713-798-6530. Office Fax: 713-798-5073. E-mail: jlupski@bcm.edu. *

LUPULESCU, AUREL PETER, medical educator, researcher, physician; b. Manastiur, Banat, Romania, Jan. 1, 1923; came to US, 1967, naturalized, 1973; s. Peter Vichentie and Maria Ann (Dragan) L. MD magna cum laude, Sch. Medicine, Bucharest, Romania, 1950; MS in Endocrinology, U. Bucharest, 1965; PhD in Biology, U. Windsor, Ont., Can., 1976. Diplomate Am. Bd. Internal Medicine. Chief lab. investigations Inst. Endocrinology, Bucharest, 1950-67; rsch. assoc. SUNY Downstate Med. Ctr., 1968-69; asst. prof. medicine Wayne State U., 1969-72, assoc. prof., 1973—. Vis. prof. Inst. Med. Pathology, U. Rome, 1967; cons. VA Hosp., Allen Park, Mich., 1971-73; sr. cancer rsch. scientist Wayne State U., 1991—. Author: Steroid Hormones, 1958, Advances in Endocrinology and Metabolism, 1962, Experimental Pathophysiology of Thyroid Gland, 1963, Ultrastructure of Thyroid Gland, 1968, Effect of Calcitonin on Epidermal Cells and Collagen Synthesis in Experimental Wounds As Revealed by Electron Microscopy Autoradiography and Scanning Electron Microscopy, 1976, Hormones and Carcinogenesis, 1983, Hormones and Vitamins in Cancer Treatment, 1990, Cancer Cell Metabolism and Cancer Treatment, 2001; reviewer various sci. jours.; contbr. chpts., numerous articles to profl. publs. Recipient Lifetime Sci. Achievement award, Internat. Biographical Ctr., 2003. Fellow Fedn. Am. Socs. for Exptl. Biology; mem. AMA, AAAS, Electron Microscopy Soc. Am., Soc. for Investigative Dermatology, NY Acad. Scis., Am. Soc. Cell Biology, Soc. Exptl. Biology and Medicine. Republican. Achievements include research on hormones and tumor biology; studies regarding role of hormones and vitamins in cancer treatment and prevention. Office: Wayne State U Sch Medicine 540 E Canfield St Detroit MI 48201-1928

LURIA, MARTIN JAY, endocrinologist; b. Bklyn., Apr. 19, 1946; MD, NYU, 1971. Diplomate Am. Bd. Internal Medicine, Am. Bd. Endocrinology. Intern Kings County Hosp.-SUNY Downstate Med., 1971—72, resident in medicine, 1972—74; fellow in endocrinology Mt. Sinai Hosp., NYC, 1974—76; chief sect. endocrinology Monmouth Med. Ctr., Long Branch, NJ, 1976—. Attending physician dept. medicine Riverview Med. Ctr., Red Bank, NJ, 1976—; mem. courtesy staff Bayshore Cmty. Hosp., Holmdel, NJ, 1976—; consulting physician in endocrinology Ctrl. State Hosp., Freehold, NJ, 1976—. Named one of Top Drs., N.J. Monthly Mag., 2003, 2005, Castle Connolly, 2003, 2005. Fellow: Am. Coll. Diabetes (specialist), Am. Coll. Endocrinology. Office: 170 Morris Ave Ste F Long Branch NJ 07740-6660 Home Phone: 732-222-1070; Office Phone: 732-222-8874.

LURIE, NICOLE L., federal agency administrator, former health science association administrator; b. June 19, 1953; BA, U. Pa., 1975, MD, 1979; MPH, UCLA, 1982. Resident UCLA, 1982, asst. prof. medicine; asst. to assoc. prof. U. Minn., prof. medicine and pub. health, 1985-98, dir. primary care rsch. and edn., dir. divsn. gen. and internal medicine; prin. dep. asst. sec. for health & sci. US Dept. Health & Human Services, Washington, 1998—2001, asst. sec. for preparedness & response, 2009—, medical dir. regular corps. Pub. Health Svc., 2009—; Paul O'Neil Alcoa prof. policy analysis, sr. natural scientist RAND Corp., Washington, 2002—09, assoc. dir. RAND Ctr. Domestic & Internat. Health Security, 2002—09. Recipient Henry J. Kaiser Found. Faculty Scholar award, 1987, Nellie Westerman Prize for Rsch. in Ethics, 1987, Young Investigator award Assn. Health Svcs., 1990, Heroine in Health Care award Minn. Women's Consotium, 1994, award Am. Soc. Clin. Investigation, 1995, Article of Yr. Assn. Health Svcs., 1996, spl. recognition for Physical-Led Rsch. Minn. Physicians, 1997. Mem.: Soc. Gen. Internal Medicine (coun., treas., pres.), Inst. of Medicine. Office: US Dept Health & Human Services 200 Independence Ave SW Rm 638G Washington DC 20201 Office Phone: 202-205-2882. E-mail: Nicole.Lurie@hhs.gov, ASPR@hhs.gov. *

LUSHER, JOANNE MARIE, psychologist, researcher, lecturer; b. Harlow, Essex, Eng., Dec. 15, 1974; d. Peter Lusher and Carol Giffin. BSc with honors, Middlesex U., London, 1997; MSc, Inst. Psychiatry, London, 1998; PhD in Addictions, London Met. U., 2005. Chartered health psychologist 2005; postgrad. certificate in tchg. and learning in higher edn. 2004. Care mgr. Pathways CDP, Annapolis, Md., 1997—98; rsch. asst. Inst. Psychiatry, 1998; rsch. psychologist London Met. U., 1999—, sr. lectr., 2003—. Contbr. articles to profl. jours. Mem.: Brit. Psychol. Soc. Avocations: travel, reading, food, exercise. Office: London Metropolitan Univ Old Castle St London E1 7NT England Business E-Mail: j.lusher@londonnet.ac.uk.

LUSHNIAK, BORIS D., federal official, public health service officer; b. Chgo. married; 2 children. BS in Med. Scis., Northwestern U., 1981, MD, 1983; MPH, Harvard U., 1984. Diplomate American Bd. Preventive Medicine, American Bd. Dermatology. Intern, resident family medicine St. Joseph Hosp., Chgo., 1984—87; lt., Epidemic Intelligence Svc., Nat. Inst. Occupl. Safety & Health (NIOSH), Centers Disease Control & Prevention (CDC), Cin., 1988—90, sr. med. officer divsn. surveillance, hazard evaluations & field studies, 1990—2004; chief med. officer, Office Counterterrorism Policy & Planning, FDA, Washington, 2004—05, asst. commr. counterterrorism policy, dir. Office Counterterrorism & Emerging Threats, 2005—10; dep. surgeon gen. US Dept. Health & Human Services, 2011—. Officer Commissioned Corps, USPHS, 1988—, rear adm., asst. surgeon gen., 2006—. Recipient Outstanding Svc. Medal (2), USPHS, Achievement award (2), Commendation Medal. Mem.: AMA (Dr. William Beaumont award in medicine 2006), Ukrainian Med. Assn. North America, Assn. Mil. Surgeons US (Sustaining Mem. Lectr. award), American Contact Dermatitis Soc., American Dermatological Assn., American Acad. Dermatology. Office: Office Surgeon General 5600 Fishers Ln Rockville MD 20857 Office Phone: 301-443-3574. *

LUSKIN, FREDERIC MICHAEL, psychologist, educator; b. NYC, May 5, 1954; BA, Binghamton U., 1976; MS, San Jose State, 1987; PhD, Stanford U., 1999. Cert. Lic. psychologist, marriage & family therapist, ednl. psychologist. Sch. psychologist, 1986—93; dir. Stanford Forgiveness Project Stanford U., 1996—2011; sr. cons. HLTH Promo, 2008—11; full prof. Inst. Transpersonal Psychology, Palo Alto, Calif., 2003—11. Author: Forgive for Good, 2002, Stress Free for Good, 2005, Forgive for Love, 2007. Office: Institute of Transpersonal Psychology 1069 East meadow Circle Palo Alto CA 94303 Personal E-mail: learningtoforgive@comcast.net. Business E-Mail: fredl@stanford.edu.

LUSTIG, SUSAN GARDNER, occupational therapist; b. Beloit, Wis., Apr. 27, 1942; d. James and Sally Howell; m. Karl Lustig, Aug. 16, 1969 (div. 1997); children: Kurt, Daniel, Benjamin, David, Amy, Richard, Lauren. BS with distinction, U. Minn., 1965. Lic. occupl. therapist. Occupl. therapist Minn. State Hosp., Hastings, 1965—66; occupl. therapy cons. Hawaii Divsn. Vocat. Rehab., Honolulu, 1966—67; occupl. therapist Kaneohe State Hosp., Kaneohe, Hawaii, 1967, Minn. VA Hosp., Mpls., 1967—68, unit supr., 1968—70; chief occupl. therapist, mgr. occupl. therapy dept. Avery Health Care Sys., Newland, NC, 1997—2000, AOTA Sponsored Trip, Russia; established occupl. therapy depts. Autumn Care Marion.Autumn Care, Drexel, NC, 2000—01, occupl. therapist, 2001—05, Yancey County Schs., 2005—07, Rehab. Sys. & Carolina Therapy Svcs., 2005—, Avery County Schs., 2007—11. Mem. Nat. Bd. for Cert. Occupl. Therapy, 1997—, NC Bd. Occupl. Therapy, 1997—2011, Occpl. Therapy Collaboration Group, 2009—11; team mem. Avery County ADDS Interdisciplinary Team Assessment Students with Autism Spectrum Disorder, 2007—11; invited del. to Russia People to People Amb. Program; manual reviewer Social Comm. and Symbolic Play Intervention for Preschoolers with Autism, 2008; mem Cow Camp Cmty. Svc. Group. Pres. LaSalle County Med. Aux., Ill., 1976—78; tutor, mentor Burke County Elem. Sch. Students; with Buck Hill Evangelical Presbnyn. Ch.; organist New Life Bapt. Ch., Newland, NC, 2003—11, Crossmore 1st Bapt. Ch., NC, 1999—2001; organist, pianist, dir. of music Linville River Bapt. Ch., NC; organist, Sunday sch. tchr. Long Ridge Bapt. Ch., 2001—03; bd. dirs. Harrison County Sheltered Workshop, 1971—72, Ottawa Pub. Health Nursing, Ill., 1976—78, Cooking for Christ, 1998—2002, Heartland Christian Acad. Sch., 1986—88, Diversified Industries, Port Angeles, Wash., 1980—82. Mem.: N.C. Occupl. Therapy Assn., Nat. Bd. for Cert. of Occupl. Therapists, Am. Occupl. Therapy Assn. Republican. Presbyterian. Avocations: organ, gardening, travel, ice skating, reading. Home: 101 E Country Club Dr Allyn WA 98524

LUTHER, THOMAS WILLIAM, retired dermatologist; b. Milw., Feb. 27, 1925; s. Elmer Charles and Ida Martha (Sohrweide) L.; m. Warrene E. Luther; children: Brian Thomas, Siri Karen Luther Witt. BS, U. Wis., 1947, MD, 1950. Diplomate Am. Bd. Dermatology. Intern West Suburban Hosp., Oak Park, Ill., 1950-51; resident VA Hosps., 1951-52, 55-56, U. Pa., 1954-55. Lt. USN, 1943-54. Fellow Am. Acad. Dermatology; mem. AMA, Wis. Med. Soc., Wis. Dermatologic Soc., Appleton Rotary. Avocations: archaeology, genealogy. Home: 1936 Palisades Dr Appleton WI 54915-1023 Personal E-mail: tomandwarrene@aol.com.

LUTHRA, SILKY, audiologist; b. Khurja, Uttar Pradesh, India, Nov. 4, 1985; MA in Audiology, Speech Lang. Pathology, Post Grad. Inst. Med. Edn. & Rsch., 2010. Rschr. JNMCH, Aligarh Muslim U., 2009, Hear n Speck Clin., 2011—. Mem.: Indian Speech & Hearing Assn. Avocations: reading, writing. Home: B-52 Ram Villa Panchawati Colony Jun Khurja Uttar Pradesh 203131 India Personal E-mail: silkyluthra@gmail.com.

LUTINS, JAY ALLAN, urological surgeon; MD, Med. Coll. of Va. Diplomate Am. Bd. of Urology-urological surgery. Intern Univ. of Pitts. Med. Ctr., resident; chief divsn. of urology The Western Pa. Hosp., The Western Pa. Hosp.-Forbes Regional Campus; physician St. Clair Hosp. Office: St. Clair Hospital 1145 Bower Hill Rd Ste 105 Pittsburgh PA 15243 Office Phone: 412-661-3400.

LUTS, ALAIN, psychiatrist, educator; b. Brussels, Mar. 10, 1959; s. Willy Luts and Monique Temmerman; m. Simy Luts. MPhil, Cath. U. Louvain, 1984, MD, 1987. Cons. Neurologic Inst., Belgium, 1992—95; assoc. clin. chief Cliniques U. St-Luc, Brussels, 1996—. Contbr. articles to publs. Mem.: Am. Psychatric Assn., European Assn. Psychotherapy, Italian Soc. Psychiatrists, European Assn. Psychiatrists. Office: Cliniques U St-Luc avenue Hippocrate 10 1200 Brussels Belgium

LUTSKY, MIKHAIL, neurologist; b. Magnitogorsk, Russia, July 1, 1944; MD, Zaporozhsky State Med. Inst., 1969; PhD in Med. Sci., Voronezh State Med. Acad., 2002. Head neurology dept. Voronezh N.N. Burdenko State Med. Acad., 2003—. Cons. Voronezh Regional Clin. Hosp., 2003. Mem.: Russian Soc. Neurologists. Avocations: literature, classical music. Office: Studencheskaya St 10 Voronezh 394 036 Russia Office Fax: 7-473-2579673. Business E-Mail: fo_sekr@vsma.ac.ru.

LUTZ, TAMARA JEAN, nursing consultant; d. Edward and Dorothy Lutz. AA, Kirkwood CC, Cedar Rapids, Iowa, 1983; B of Nursing, U. Iowa, 1985; M of Nursing, U. Wash., 1995. RN Iowa, registered Level I-II Neonatal Nurse. Commd. 2d lt. US Army, 1986, advanced through grades to maj., 1996; nurse methods analyst Gen. Leonard Wood Army Cmty. Hosp., Ft. Leonard Wood, Mo., 2002—04, joint commn. on accrediation of hospitals coord., 2004—05; behavioral mental health program developer US Army, Ft. Leonard Wood, Mo., 2005—06; case mgr. Prin. Fin. Group, 2006—. Cons. in field. Decorated Army Svc. Ribbon US Army, Nat. Def. Svc. medal with Bronze Star U.S. Army, Overseas Svc. Ribbon US Army, Achievement medals, Commendation medals, Humanitarian Svc. medal, Joint Svc. Commendation medal, Global War on Terrorism Svc. medal, Meritorius Svc. medal, Mil. Outstanding Vol. Svc. medal. Mem.: Nat. Assn. Healthcare Quality (cert.), Mo. League Nursing (assoc.), Sigma Theta Tau. Lutheran. Avocations: travel, reading, cross stitch. E-mail: tamara.lutz@yahoo.com.

LUUKANEN-KILDE, RAUNI-LEENA TELLERVO, public health and tropical medicine physician; b. Värtsilä, Carelia, Finland,

Nov. 15, 1939; arrived in Norway, 1991; d. Erkki William and Eeva Tellervo (Halmetoja) Valve; m. Mauri Mikael Luukanen, Apr. 24, 1965 (div. May 1975); m. Sverre Kilde, Feb. 28, 1987 (div. Nov. 1994). B Medicine, U. Turku, Finland, 1964, MD, 1967; diploma in tropical medicine, Karolinska Inst., Sweden, 1970; diploma in pub. health, Nat. Bd. Health, Finland, 1974, diploma in health adminstrn., 1980. Cert. in social medicine Nordic Sch. Pub. Health/ Goteborg, Sweden. Intern and resident U. Hosp. Turku, City Hosp. Turku, Regional Hosp. Salo; chief physician Pelkosenniemi-Savukoski Hosp.; physician United Christian Hosp., Lahore, Pakistan, 1968; acting surgeon gen. Finland, 1978; acting dir. Dept. Environ. Health and Health Edn., Finland, 1978; chief med. officer Lapland, 1975-87; mem. staff various hosps. Finland, 1969-75. Chief med. adviser Internat. Red Cross, Malaysia, Indonesia, 1979; del., chief del. Govt. Finland WHO/Tropical Medicine, Geneva, 1978—79; mem. com. Arctic med. rsch. Nordic Coun., 1981—84; mem. adv. bd. Internat. Assn. Near-Death Studies, Conn., 1983—; cons., Mufon, Tex., 1991—98; v.p. Acad. Clin. Close Encounter Therapists, Calif., 1994—2002. Author: There Is No Death, 1982 (Lit. award, 1983), Messenger From the Stars, 1991, Who Am I, 1993, Child of the Universe, 1995, Our Secret Worlds, 2007. Mem. Security Coun., Lapland, 1975—87; bd. dirs. Red Cross Lapland, 1976—79; pres. Nursing Coll., Lapland, 1976—87. Recipient medal with gold broach for civil defence, Finland, 1991, Anniversary medal, UN Parapsychology Soc., 1992, hon. diploma, Citizens Against Human Rights Abuse, 1999; Travel grantee, Nat. Bd. Health Finland, 1979—81. Mem.: First Scandinavian Conf. Extraterrestrial Intelligence and Human Future (pres. 1996), Am. Soc. Psychical Rsch., NY Acad. Scis., Parapsychol. Assn. Lapland (pres. 1981—85, hon. pres. 2001—), Finnish Med. Assn., US Psychotronic Assn. (assoc.). Avocations: ufology, parapsychology, reindeer herding, mind control research. Home and Office: Feierbakken 30 1555 Son Norway Office Phone: +47 6495 8999. Personal E-mail: rauni.kilde@yahoo.com.

LUVIANO, DAMIEN M., ophthalmologist; BA in Biology with honors, U. Tex., Austin, 1997; MD, U. Tex. Southwestern Med. Sch., Dallas, 2003. Bd. cert. ophthalmologist, diplomate Am. Bd. Ophthalmology, Am. Bd. Quality Assurance & Utilization Rev. Physicians, Am. Bd. Physicians Specialties. Med. software cons. Skyscape, Hudson, Mass., 2001—; postdoc. intern in gen. surgery Meth. Hosp. Dallas, 2004, Charles R. Drew Sch. Medicine and Sci., 2007; chief ophthalmology Joslin Diabetes ctr. Sr. editor ethics Pearls of Ophthalmology; editl. bd. mem. Soc. Clin. Ophthalmology; jour. reviewer Jour. Diabetes, Jour. Ophthalmic Surgery Lasers and Imaging, Jour. Nature, Jour. Lancet, New Eng. Jour. Medicine, Am. Jour. Ophthalmology, Jour. Ophthalmology, Jour. Diabetes Care. Author: Wills Eye Manual for Pocket PCs and PDAs, 2002; contbr. articles to profl. jours., scientific papers. Vol. physician Lions Club Internat., 2007—; chair U. Tex., Tex. Exes, Physician and Healthcare Network, 2010—. Named one of America's Top Surgeon, 2009. Fellow: ACS, Am. Inst. Health Quality, Am. Acad. Ophthalmology; mem.: Osler Inst. Opthalmology, World Ophthalmology Physician Soc., Am. Retina Found., Am. Acad. Ophthalmology, Am. Diabetes Assn. Achievements include research in diabetes & macular edema. Office: SETMA 3570 College St # 100 Beaumont TX 77701

LUVIRA, USANA, nephrologist; b. Smutsakorn, Thailand, Sept. 16, 1942; d. Tang Hui and Lim Ear; m. Unnop Luvira, Mar. 28, 1969; children: Eliza, Anita, Apinunt. MD, Mahidol U., Thailand, 1967. Diplomate Am. Bd. Internal Medicine, Bd. Nephrology Thai Med. Coun. Intern Buffalo Gen. Hosp., NY, 1969—70; resident in gen. medicine Flushing Hosp., NY, 1970—71, resident in internal medicine, 1971—73; fellow in nephrology Henry Ford Hosp., Mich., 1974; nephrologist, instr. neprology divsn. Phramongkutklao Med. Coll., Bangkok, 1975—2000, sr. cons. nephrologist, 1989—. Sr. cons. nephrologist Vibhavadi Hosp., Bangkok, 1986—. Editor: Renal Replacement Therapy in Thailand, 1992, Critical Care Medicine in Thailand, 1999; contbr. articles to profl. jours. Mem. sci. com. Kidney Found. of Thailand, 2000—03; mem. scientific com. Organ Donation Ctr. of Thai Red Cross Soc., 2000—03. Maj. gen. Thailand Mil., 1999—2003. Master: Nephrology Soc. Thailand (pres. 1994—98); fellow: Royal Coll. Physicians of Thailand; mem.: Thai Transplantation Soc. (pres. 2000—03). Avocations: cooking, travel. Home: 386/4 Soi Chalermsuk Chatuchak Bangkok 10900 Thailand Home Phone: 6625132894; Office Phone: 6625611260. E-mail: usaualu@hotmail.com.

LUXENBERG, MALCOLM NEUWAHL, ophthalmologist, educator; b. Philipsburg, Pa., July 29, 1935; s. Maurice and Henrietta (Neuwahl) L.; m. Sandra Diane Rosen, June 16, 1957; children: Steven Neuwahl, Cathy Ann. Student, Tulane U., 1953-56; MD, U. Miami, Fla., 1960. Diplomate: Am. Bd. Ophthalmology. Intern Cin. Gen. Hosp., 1960-61; resident in neurology U. Vt. Affiliated Hosps., Burlington, 1961-63; resident in ophthalmology Bascom Palmer Eye Inst., U. Miami-Jackson Meml. Hosp., Miami, Fla., 1963-66; asst. prof. ophthalmology Coll. Medicine, U. Iowa, Iowa City, 1968-70; chief ophthalmology service VA Hosp., Iowa City, 1968-70; practice medicine specializing in ophthalmology West Palm Beach, Fla., 1970-72; clin. asst. prof. ophthalmology Bascom Palmer Eye Inst., Sch. Medicine, U. Miami, 1971-72; prof., chmn. dept. ophthalmology Med. Coll. Ga., Augusta, 1972-2000, prof. emeritus, 2000—. Cons. ophthalmology VA Hosp., Augusta, 1972-2011; sr. surgeon USPHS, 1966-68; mem. Residency Review Com. Ophthalmology, 1987-92, Am. Bd. Ophthalmology, 1987-94. Mem. editl. bd.: Archives of Ophthalmology, 1986-94. Recipient Outstanding Civilian Service Medal Dept. of Army, 1986. Mem. AMA, Am. Acad. Ophthalmology (hon. award 1986), Am. Ophthalmol. Soc., Assn. Univ. Profs. in Ophthalmology (pres. 1982-83), Ga. Soc. Ophthalmology, Med. Assn. Ga., Richmond County Med. Soc. Office: Med Coll Ga Dept Ophthalmology Augusta GA 30912

LU-YAO, GRACE, epidemiologist; d. George Lu and Jessica Yao; m. Siu-Long Yao; children: Kaelan Yao, Haley Yao. BS with honors, SUNY, Stony Brook, 1986; MPH, Yale U., New Haven, 1988, PhD, 1990. Biostatistician Biostatistics Consults Unit, New Haven, 1987—90, Pfizer Pharmas., 1989—90; asst. prof. Ctr. Evaluative Clin. Scis., 1990—94; staff divsn. health info. and outcomes Office Rsch. and Demonstration, 1995—96; dir. Health Stats., 1997—2004; assoc. prof. Cancer Inst. U. Medicine and Dentistry NJ, New Brunswick, 2004—, assoc. prof. Sch. Pub. Health Piscataway, NJ, 2007—10, prof. medicine, Robert Wood Johnson Med. Sch., 2010—. Contbr. articles to profl. med. jours. Recipient Nat. Rsch. Svc. award, 1989—90, Henry Christian award, 1994. Fellow: Am. Coll. Epidemiology; mem.: Am. Assn. Cancer Rsch., Am. Soc. Clin. Oncology. Avocations: travel, music. Office: The Cancer Inst of New Jersey 195 Little Albany St New Brunswick NJ 08901 Business E-Mail: luyaogr@umdnj.edu.

LUZIO, J. PAUL, research scientist, educator; b. Aug. 15, 1947; married; 1 child. BA, Clare Coll., U. Cambridge, 1968, PhD, 1974. Lectr. med. biochemistry Welsh Nat. Sch. Medicine, 1974—77; sr. rsch. assoc. Dept. Clin. Biology, Cambridge U., 1977—79, lectr., 1979—96, reader molecular membrane biology, 1996—2001, prof. molecular membrane biology, 2001—; dir., Univ. chair clin. biochemistry Cambridge Inst. Med. Rsch., England, 2002—. Master St. Edmund's Coll., Cambridge, 2004—. Fellow: Acad. Med. Sci., Royal Coll. Pathologists. Office: Cambridge Inst Med Rsch Wellcome Trust/MRC Bldg Addenbrookes Hosp Hills Rd Cambridge CB2 2XY England Office Phone: 01223 762322. Office Fax: 01223 762323. Business E-Mail: jpl10@cam.ac.uk. *

LYALL, DAVID GRIFFIN, nuclear medicine scientist, educator, director; b. Taree, NSW, Australia, Sept. 21, 1971; s. Alastair Clarence and Gael Lyall; children: Natasha Josephine, Victoria Grace. Diploma in applied sci. (nuc. medicine), U. Newcastle, Australia, 1994; degree in applied sci. (nuc. medicine), U. Sydney, 1998. Accredited nuc. medicine scientist Australian and New Zealand Soc. Nuc. Medicine, 1997. Nuc. medicine scientist Hunter Imaging Group, Newcastle, NSW, 1993—99; lectr., convenor nuc. medicine program U. Newcastle, 1999—. Program convenor (nuc. medicine) U. Newcastle, 1999—2006; acad. rep. Pub. Image Alliance, Sydney, 2003—04. Rsch. scholar, Australian Inst. Radiography, 2005. Mem.: Australian and New Zealand Soc. Nuc. Medicine (mem. edn. adv. coun. 1999—). Avocations: breeding cattle and horses, polocrosse. Office: U Newcastle Sch Health Scis Faculty Health University Dr Callaghan 2308 Australia Office Phone: 0249215083. Office Fax: 0249217053.

LYCKE, JAN, neurologist; b. Stockholm, June 15, 1956; PhD, Sahlgrenska Acad., 1993. Registered assoc. prof. Sahlgrenska Acad., 2001. Cons. neurology Sahlgrenska U. Hosp., 1999. Dir. dept. neurology MS Ctr., 2001. Office: Sahlgrenska University Hospital Gothenburg Västra Götaland 413 45 Sweden Business E-Mail: jan.lycke@neuro.gu.se.

LYDER, COURTNEY HARVEY, dean, nursing educator; b. Port of Spain, Trinidad & Tobago, June 8, 1966; arrived in USA, 1981; s. Ormond and Jean Peters. BA, Beloit Coll., Wis., 1989; BS, Rush U., Chgo., 1989; MS, Rush U., 1990, D in Nursing, 1991. Asst. prof. St. Xavier U. Sch. Nursing, Chgo., 1991—94; from asst. to assoc. prof. Yale U. Sch. Nursing, 1994—97, assoc. prof., 1997—2002; endowed prof. nursing, prof. internal medicine and geriatrics U. Va. Sch. Nursing, Charlottesville, 2003—08, dir. diversity initiatives, 2006—08; prof., dean UCLA Sch. Nursing, 2008—. Sr. cons. US Health Care Financing Adminstrn., Washington, 1997—; bd. dirs. Nat. Pressure Ulcer Adv. Bd., Washington, 1997. Contbr. articles to profl. jours., chapters to books. Fellow Am. Acad. Nursing; mem. Gerontol. Soc. America, Ea. Nursing Rsch. Soc., Sigma Theta Tau. Avocations: travel, reading, scuba diving. Office: UCLA Sch Nursing 2-256 Factor Bldg Los Angeles CA 90095 Office Phone: 310-825-9621. Office Fax: 310-206-7433. Business E-Mail: clyder@sonnet.ucla.edu.

LYDON, NICHOLAS B. (NICK LYDON), biochemist, pharmaceutical executive, researcher; b. Feb. 27, 1957; BSc, U. Leeds, Eng.; PhD in Biochemistry, U. Dundee, Scotland, 1984. With Schering Plough, Paris and Lyon, France, 1982—85; oncology rsch. team Ciba-Geigy AG (now Novartis Pharmaceuticals AG), 1985—97; founder, pres., CEO Kinetix Pharmaceutical Inc. (acquired by Amgen, Inc.), Medford, Mass., 1997—2000; v.p. small molecule drug discovery Amgen, Inc., Thousand Oaks, Calif., 2000—02; with Verizon Pharmaceutical Co., Calif., 2002; founder Granite Biopharma LLC, Jackson Hole, Wyo. Past mem. Novartis Oncology Mgmt. Com.; bd. dirs., scientific adv. bd. Ambit Biosciences, AnaptysBio, Inc. Biosciences; advisor Avalon Ventures. Recipient Sci. Prize, Warren Alpert Found., 2001, Bruce F. Cain Meml. award, Am. Assn. Cancer Rsch., 2002, Charles F. Kettering prize, GM Cancer Rsch. Found., 2002, Bruce F. Cain Meml. award, Am. Assn. Cancer Rsch., 2002; co-recipient Lasker-DeBakey Clin. Med. Rsch. award, Lasker Found., 2009. Achievements include development of leukemia drug, Gleevac, that effectively treats chronic megelogenous leukemia and other forms of cancer. Office: Avalon Ventures 1134 Kline St La Jolla CA 92037-4565 *

LYERLY, HERBERT KIM, oncology researcher, surgery educator; b. San Diego, Aug. 26, 1958; s. Albert Elliot and Mitsu (Kinoshita) L.; m. Anne Drapkin. BS, U. Calif., Riverside, 1980; MD, UCLA, 1983. Diplomate Am. Bd. Surgery. Intern, surgery Duke U. Med. Ctr., Durham, NC, 1983—84, resident, surgery, 1984—85, 1987—90, rsch. fellow, 1985—87; asst. prof., surgery Duke U., Durham, NC, 1990—94, assoc. prof., surgery, 1994—97, asst. prof. pathology, 1991-98, clin. dir. molecular therapeutics, 1993-97, asst. prof. immunology, 1995-97, prof. surgery, 1997—, clin. dir. Ctr. for Molecular and Cellular Therapy, 1997-98, assoc. prof. pathology, 1998—, dir. SPORE in breast cancer, 2002—; dir. Duke Comprehensive Cancer Ctr., Durham, NC, 2003—. Editor: Surgical Intensive Care, 2d edit., 1989, co-editor: Surgical Intensive Care, 3d edit., 1991, Companion Textbook of Surgery, 1992, Essentials of Surgery, 1994; co-editor Textbook of Surgery, 15th edit., 1997, Companion Textbook of Surgery, 2d edit., 1997; contbr. several articles to profl. jours. Mem. ACS, Assn. Acad. Surgery, Soc. Surg. Oncology, Soc. Univ. Surgeons, Am. Soc. Clin. Oncology, Am. Assn. Cancer Rsch. Office: Duke U Hosp PO Box 3843 DUMC 2714 Durham NC 27710 Office Phone: 919-668-5613. Office Fax: 919-684-5653.

LYJAK CHORAZY, ANNA JULIA, retired pediatrician, retired health facility administrator; d. Walter and Cecilia (Swiatkowski) Lyjak; m. Chester John Chorazy, May 6, 1961; children: Paula Ann Chorazy, Mary Ellen Chorazy-Cuccaro, Mark Edward Chorazy. BS, Waynesburg Coll., 1958; MD, Women's Med. Coll. Pa., 1960. Diplomate Am. Bd. Pediat. Intern St. Francis Gen. Hosp., Pitts., 1960-61; resident in pediat., tchg. fellow Children's Hosp. Pitts., 1961-63, pediatrician, devel. clinic, 1966-75; pediat. house physician Western Pa. Hosp., Pitts., 1963-66; med. dir. Rehab. Instn. Pitts., 1975-98, Children's Inst., Pitts., 1998—2001, interim med. dir., 2002—03. Clin. asst. prof. pediat. Children's Hosp. Pitts. and U. Pitts. Sch. Medicine, 1971—94, clin. assoc. prof. pediat., 1994—2001; pediat. cons. Children's Home Pitts., 1985—2001. Author chpts. to books. Co-chmn. EACH Joint Planning and Assessment, Pitts., 1980-85; mem. adv. com. 10th Nat. Conf. on Child Abuse, Pitts., 1993. Recipient Miracle Maker award, Children's Miracle Network, 1995, Disting. Alumni award, Waynesburg Coll., 2002. Fellow Am. Acad. Pediat.; mem. Pitts. Pediat. Soc. Avocations: reading, theater, music, opera. Home: 131 Washington Rd Pittsburgh PA 15221-4437 *

LYKENS, KRISTINE ANN, healthcare educator; d. Joann Margaret Martin; 1 child, Lawrence Hadley Kenslow. PhD, U. Tex. Dallas, Richardson, Tex., 1999. Assoc. prof. UNT Sch. Pub. Health, Fort Worth, Tex., 2000—; program analyst U.S. HHS, Dallas, 2007—09. Contbr. articles to rsch. jours. Program svcs. com. mem. Mar. Dimes North Tex. Region, Dallas, 2000—03; adv. com. mem. Tex. Health & Health & Human Svc. Dept., Arlington, 2003—08; adv. ONE.org, Washington, 2005—11. Named Outstanding Faculty Advisor, UNT Pub. Health Students Assn., 2003, Outstanding Faculty Rschr., UNT Sch. Pub. Health, 2004; Vibhooti Shukla Fellowship, U. Tex. Dallas, Sch. Social Scis., 2005—06. Mem.: Assn. Policy Analysis & Mgmt., Acad. Health. Liberal. Methodist. Avocations: reading, swimming, photography. Office: University North Tex Sch HSC 3500 Camp Bowie Blvd Fort Worth TX 76107 Home: 1011 Switchyard St #3215 Fort Worth TX 76107 E-mail: kristine.lykens@unthsc.edu.

LYKISSAS, MARIOS GEORGE, orthopedist; MD, Nat. and Kapodistrian U. Athens, Sch. Medicine, Greece, 2000. Resident, orthopaedics U. Ioannina, Sch. Medicine, Greece, 2006—. Contbr. scientific papers to profl. jours. and others. Avocation: sailing. Office: Univ Ioannina Med Sch Panepistimioupoli 451 10 Ioannina Greece Home Phone: 00302661052057; Office Phone: 00302651097515. Office Fax: 00302651097018, 00302651097891. Personal E-mail: mariolyk@yahoo.com.

LYKO, FRANK, molecular biologist; b. Heidelberg, Germany, July 16, 1970; Diploma in biology, U. Heidelberg, 1994, PhD in biology, 1998; postdoctoral rsch., Whitehead Inst. Biomedical Rsch., 1998—2000. Group leader epigenetics German Cancer Rsch. Ctr., 2001—04, divsn. head epigenetics, 2004—; prof. epigenetics U. Heidelberg, 2006—. Contbr. articles to profl. jour. Recipient Heinz Maier-Leibnitz award, 2002, Karl Freudenberg award, 2003, Pharma. Rsch. award, Novartis Found., 2007; named one of Top 100 Young Innovators, MIT Tech. Review, 2004. Office: Deutsches Krebsforschungszentrum Im Neuenheimer Feld 280 Heidelberg 69120 Germany

LYMAN, GARY HERBERT, epidemiologist, cancer researcher, educator; b. Buffalo, Feb. 24, 1946, s. Leonard Samuel and Beatrice Louise Lyman; children: Stephen Leonard, Christopher Henry. BA, SUNY, Buffalo, 1968, MD, 1972; MPH, Harvard U., 1982. Diplomate Am. Bd. Internal Medicine, Am. Bd. Oncology and Hematology. Resident in medicine U. NC, Chapel Hill, 1972-74; fellow in oncology Roswell Park Meml. Inst., Buffalo, 1974-77; rsch. instr. medicine SUNY Med. Sch., Buffalo, 1974-77; mem. faculty U. South Fla. Coll. Medicine, Tampa, 1977-2000, assoc. prof. medicine, 1980-06, prof. medicine, 1986-2000, dir. divsn. med. oncology, 1979-93, chief medicine H. Lee Moffitt Cancer and Rsch. Inst., 1985—93, prof. epidemiology and biostats., 1988-2000; Thomas Ordway prof. medicine divsn. hematology and oncology Albany (NY) Med. Coll., Union U., 2000—02, dir. Cancer Ctr., 2000—02; prof. biometry and stats SUNY Sch. Pub. Health, 2000—02; prof. medicine, dept. medicine U. Rochester (NY) Sch. Medicine and Dentistry, 2002—07, Duke U., 2007—, dir., 2002—07; dir. comparative effectness and outcomes rsch. Duke Comprehensive Cancer, 2007—; sr. fellow Duke Ctr. Clin. Health Policy Rsch., 2007—. Vis. prof. med. stats. London Sch. Hygiene and Tropical Medicine, 1997—98; editor-in-chief Cancer Investigation, 2006—. Editor: Geriatric Oncology, 1998, Comprehensive Geriatric Oncology, 1997, 2d edit., 2004, Breast Cancer: Transitional Therapeutic Strategies, 2007, Cancer Supportive Care-Advances in Therapeutic Stragies, 2009, Hematopoietic Growth Factors, 2011; contbr. chpts. to books, mre than 400 articles to profl. jours. Spl. fellow Leukemia Soc. Am., 1976-77; postdoctoral fellow biostats. Harvard U., 1981-82; spl. clin. rellow Roswell Park Meml. Inst., 1975-76, Statesman award Am. Soc. Clin. Oncology, 2010. Fellow ACP, Am. Coll. Preventive Medicine, Am. Coll. Clin. Pharmacology, Royal Coll. Physicians (Edinburgh); mem. Am. Soc. Clin. Oncology (statesman). Achievements include research in cancer clinical trials, biostatistics, epidemiology and clinical decision analysis. Home: 103 Regiment Way Durham NC 27705-6466 Office: Duke Univ Med Ctr 2424 Erwin Rd Ste 205 Durham NC 27705 Office Phone: 919-681-1604. Business E-Mail: gary.lyman@duke.edu.

LYNCH, CAROL, psychologist, minister; d. Joseph Louis and Ellen (Birish) Dobkowski; 1 child, Eric Alexander. BA, William Paterson Coll., 1966; MA, NYU, 1970, PsyD, 1984. Lic. psychologist, N.J., N.Y. Tchr. Bloomfield (N.J.) Pub. Schs., 1966-68, psychologist, 1970-87; dir. spl. svcs. Waldwick (N.J.) Pub. Schs., 1987—2008, acting supt. schs., 1995-96, 98. Adj. clin. prof. NYU, N.Y.C., 1983-86 adj. prof. Montclair (N.J.) State Coll., 1984-85; mem. Bergen County Assn. Lic. Psychologists, 1991-93. Mem. prof. alumni coun. Sch. Edn., Health and Nursing, NYU, 1989—91; alumni coun. chair Sch. Edn., NYU, 1991—93; bd. trustees First Church Religious Sci., 2001, sec., 2002—05, lic. practitioner, 2004; v.p. First Church of Religious Sci., 2006, staff minister, 2007—; NYU fellow, 1981-82; recipient Best Practice award N.J. State Dept. Edn. for Fast Families Program, 1995, Disting. Grad. Brian E. Tomlinson Meml. award NYU, 1995, Exemplary Practice award N.J. Adminstrs. Assn./N.J. Sch. Bds. "Crisis Response Initiative," 2002. Mem. APA (sch. psychology task force 1989-90), N.J. Psychol. Assn. (treas. 1985-86, Sch. Psychologist of Yr. 2003), Nat. Assn. Sch. Psychologists (del. 1984-88), N.J. Assn. Sch. Psychologists (pres. 1982-83, Sch. Psychologist of Yr. 2003), Ea. Ednl. Rsch. Assn. (pres. 1993-95), NYU Sch. Psychology Alumni Assn. (founder 1988-92), Ramapo Valley Adminstrs. (v.p. 1996-98, pres. 1998—). Avocations: skiing, antiques, tennis, gourmet cooking. Home: 124 Frank Ct Mahwah NJ 07430-2963 Office: 1st Ch Religious Sci 14 E 48th St New York NY 10017 Office Phone: 212-688-0600. Personal E-mail: drcarollynch@msn.com.

LYNCH, DENNIS JAMES, retired plastic surgeon; b. Bayonne, NJ, Aug. 5, 1939; s. Dennis J. Lynch and Eileen Mallon; m. Mary; children: Dennis, David, Sarah. BS, Villanova U., 1961; MD, Georgetown U. Med. Ctr., 1965. Diplomate Am. Bd. Surgery, Am. Bd. Plastic Surgery. Resident U. Pa., Phila., 1965—74; plastic surgeon Scott & White Clinic, Temple, Tex., 1974—2007; with Ctrl. Tex. Vet. Admin. Health Sci. Ctr. Dir. divsn. plastic surgery Tex. A&M Med. Sch., Temple, 1974-87, chair dept. surgery, 1990-2004; bd. dirs. Scott & White Clinic, 1981-95, part time plastic surgeon Ctrl. Tex. Vets. Health Care Sys. Mem. AMA, Am. Coll. Surgeons, Am. Cleft Palate

Assn., Am. Assn. Plastic Surgeons, Tex. Soc. Plastic Surgeons, Am. Soc. Plastic & Reconstructive Surgeons (pres. elect 1996—, pres. 1997), Am. Bd. Plastic Surgery. Roman Catholic. Avocations: tennis, sailing. Business E-Mail: djlynch154@msn.com.

LYNCH, GARRY WILLIAM, medical researcher; s. William Stanley Lynch and Joyce Veronica Kane. BSc, Flinders U., Adelaide, Australia, 1976, BSc with honors, 1977; PhD, Monash U., Melbourne, Australia, 1985. Cert. med. technician South Australian Inst. Tech., 1974. Rsch. fellow pathology Beth Israel Hosp., Harvard Med. Sch., Boston, 1983—85; rsch. assoc. pathology U. N.Mex, Albuqurque, 1985—86; rsch. assoc. cellular and molecular physiology Dana Farber Cancer Inst. Harvard U. Med. Sch., Boston, 1987—90; rsch. assoc. cellular and molecular biology Boston Biomed. Rsch. Inst. Harvard U. Med. Sch., 1990—92; sr. scientist, virology dept. Westmead Hosp., Sydney, NSW, 1992—96; sr. rsch. scientist and head HIV-protein interactions lab. Westmead Millenium Inst., Westmead Inst. Health Rsch., Sydney, 1996—2002; sr. rsch. fellow, faculty medicine U. Sydney; sr. rsch. transfusion med. scientist Australian Red Cross Blood Svc., Sydney, 2004—07; conjoint sr. lectr., faculty medicine U. Sydney, 2005—07; rschr. biosafety, immunology, global health & pandemic infections rsch. Faculty Medicine U. Sydney, Camperdown, NSW, 2006. Adj. sr. rsch. fellow U. NSW, Sydney, 2005—; vis. rsch. scholar, cellular and molecular pathology rsch. unit, faculty denistry U. Sydney, 2002—07, hon. sr. lectr. faculty medicine, 2008—, adj. sr. lectr. faculty dentistry, 2008—, sr. rsch. fellow, faculty vet. sci., 2008—. Achievements include research in discovery of covalent dimer and novel monomer isoform structures of the immunology and HIV receptor, CD4; identification of cross-reactive human antibodies to Avian H5N1 influenza in an unexposed general population; biosafety, immunology, global infections & pandemic infections research. Office: University Sydney Faculty Vet Sci Rm 551 RMC Gunn Bldg Camperdown NSW 2006 Australia Office Fax: 61-2-93513957. Personal E-mail: garry_lynch@optusnet.com.au. Business E-Mail: garry.lynch@sydney.edu.au.

LYNCH, GORDON STUART, physiologist, researcher; b. Melbourne, Victoria, Australia, Sept. 27, 1964; s. Gordon Francis Lynch, Hilda Rose Lynch; m. Toni De Giorgio, Aug. 4, 1991; children: Ethan Francis children: Nicholas James. PhD, U. Melbourne, 1992; BSc with honors, La Trobe U., Victoria, 1988. Postdoctoral U. Mich., Ann Arbor, Mich., 1995—97; rsch. asst. U. Melbourne, 1991, rsch. officer, 1992—94, C.J. Martin rsch. fellow, 1995—98, lectr., 1999—2001, sr. lectr., 2001—03, sr. rsch. fellow Ctr. for Neurosci., 2001—05, assoc. prof., reader, 2003—08, prof., 2008—, dep. head physiology, 2004—06; sr. rsch. fellow Melbourne Neuromuscular Rsch. Inst., 1999—2005, head dept. chair, 2011—. Co-founder, chmn. rsch. mgr. fitness2live.co.au Health 1st Pty Ltd, Melbourne, Victoria, Australia, 2000—09; councilor Australian Physiological Soc., 2005—08; editl. bd. mem. jour. Applied Physiology, 2003—; bd. mem. Expo Opinion Engrng. Drugs. Recipient Nat. Journalism award, Nat. Asthma Coun., 2002, travel award, Ian Potter Found., 2003, Citation award, Australian Learning & Tchg. Coun., 2009; finalist Eureka award, Australian Govt., 2006; R.D. Wright Rsch. fellow, Nat. Health & Med. Rsch. Coun., 1998, Australian rsch. fellow, Australian Rsch. Coun., 1998. Fellow: Am. Coll. Sports Medicine; mem.: F. Hoffmann-La Roche Ltd (Switzerland), Merck & Co. Inc., Pfizer Inc. USA, Assn. Francaise Contre Les Myopathies France, Muscular Dystrophy Assn., Australian Rsch. Coun., Nat. Health & Med. Rsch. Coun., Gerontological Soc. America, Australian Soc. Med. Rsch., Australian Strength and Conditioning Assn. (mem. level 1 Australian coaching coun. 2002), Sports Medicine Australia, Nat. Strength and Conditioning Assn. (cert. specialist 2000—), Biophys. Soc., Am. Physiol. Soc., Australian Physiol. Soc. (Student prize-Best Spkr. 1992, A.K. McIntyre Young Investigator award 1995). Achievements include research in muscular dystrophy, sarcopenia, cancer cachexia, muscle injury and repair. Avocation: exercise. Office: Basic & Clin Myology Lab Dept Physiology University Melbourne 240 Grattan St 3010 Melbourne VIC Australia Office Phone: 613-8344-0065. Office Fax: 613-8344-5818. Business E-Mail: gsl@unimelb.edu.au.

LYNCH, JOHN BROWN, plastic surgeon, educator; b. Akron, Ohio, Feb. 5, 1929; s. John A. and Eloise Lynch; m. Mary Joyce Burrus, Dec. 1, 1994; children: John Brown, Margaret Frances Lynch Callihan. Student, Vanderbilt U., Nashville, Tenn., 1949; MD, U. Tenn., Memphis, 1952. Diplomate Am. Bd. Plastic Surgery. Rotating intern John Gaston Hosp., Memphis, 1953—54; resident gen. surgery U. Tex. Med. Br., Galveston, 1956—59, resident plastic surgery, 1959—62, instr., 1962, asst. prof. surgery, 1962—67, assoc. prof., 1967—72, prof., 1972—73; prof., plastic surgery, chmn. dept. plastic surgery Vanderbilt U. Med. Ctr., 1973—. Co-editor (with S.R. Lewis): Symposium on the Treatment of Burns, 1973; contbr. articles to porfl. jours. Capt. USAF, 1954—56. Fellow: ACS; mem.: AMA, Am. Surg. Assn., Southern Surg. Assn., Am. Soc. Maxillofacial Surgeons, Nashville Surg. Soc., Jr. Soc., H. William Scott, Southeastern Surg. Soc., Southeastern Soc. Plastic Surgeons, Tenn. Soc. Plastic Surgeons, Nashville Acad. Medicine, Tenn. Med. Assn., Southern Med. Assn. (pres.-elect 1983—84), Am. Cancer Soc. (pres. Galveston County, Tex., Chpt. 1968), Pan Am. Med. Assn., Internat. Burn Assn., Soc. Head and Neck Surgeons, Am. Burn Assn., Am. Cleft Palate Assn., Plastic Surgery Rsch. Coun., Am. Assn. Plastic Surgeons, Am. Soc. Plastic and Reconstructive Surgeons (pres. 1983—84), Singleton Surg. Soc. (pres. 1982—83), Sigma Xi. Home: 5810 Hillsboro Pike Nashville TN 37215-4602 Office: Vanderbilt Hospital Nashville TN 37232-0001 Personal E-mail: jblynchsr@bellsouth.net.

LYNCH, PETER JOHN, retired dermatologist; b. Mpls., Oct. 22, 1936; s. Francis Watson and Viola Adeline (White) L.; m. Barbara Ann Lanzi, Jan. 18, 1964; children: Deborah, Timothy. Student, St. Thomas Coll., 1954-57; BS, U. Minn., 1958, MD, 1961. Intern U. Mich. Med. Ctr., 1961-62, resident in dermatology, 1962-65, asst. prof., then assoc. prof. dermatology, 1968-73; clin. instr. U. Minn., 1965; chief dermatology and venereal disease Martin Army Hosp., Columbus, Ga., 1966-68; asso. prof. to prof. dermatology U. Ariz., Tucson, 1973-86, chief sect. dermatology, 1973-86, asso. head dept. internal medicine, 1977-86; prof., head dermatology U. Minn. Med. Sch., Mpls., 1986-95; med. dir. ambulatory care U. Minn. Health Sys., 1993-95; prof., chmn. dept. dermatology U. Calif., Davis, 1995-2000, prof. emeritus, 2000—, tng. program dir., 2001—08, Frederick G. Novy, Jr. prof., 2005—. Co-author: (with S. Epstein) Burckhardt's Atlas and Manual of Dermatology and Venereology, 1977, Dermatology for the House Officer, 1982, 3rd edit., 1994, (with W.M. Sams) Principles and Practice of Dermatology, 1992, 2nd edit., 1996, (with I.E. Edwards) Genital Dermatology, 1994, (with M. Black, C. Ambros-Rudolph & L. Edwards) Obstetric and Gyneacologic Dermatology, 2008, (with L. Edwards)Genital Dermatology Atlas, 2011. With AUS, 1966-68. Decorated Army Commendation Medal; recipient Disting. Service award for faculty U. Mich., 1970, Disting. Faculty award U. Ariz., 1981 Mem.: Am. Acad. Dermatology (hon., bd. dirs. 1974-78, v.p. 1991-92, Pearson Tchg. award, 2009), Assn. Profs. Dermatology (bd. dirs. 1976-80, pres. 1994-96), Internat. Soc. Study of Vulvar Disease (bd. dirs. 1976-79, pres. 1983), Soc. Investigative Dermatology, Am. Bd. Dermatology (bd. dirs. 1984-89), Gougerot Soc. (Bronze medal award), Alpha Omega Alpha. Democrat. Roman Catholic. Home: 425 Hartnell Pl Sacramento CA 95825-6615 Office: U Calif 3301 C St #1400 Sacramento CA 95816

LYNCH, PRISCILLA A., nursing educator, psychotherapist; b. Joliet, Ill., Jan. 8, 1949; d. LaVerne L. and Ann M. (Zamkovitz) L. BS, U. Wyo., 1973; MS, St. Xavier Coll., Coll., 1981. RN, Ill. Staff nurse Rush-Presbyn.-St. Luke's Med. Ctr., Chgo., 1977-81, psychiat.-liaison cons., 1981-83, asst. prof. nursing, unit dir., 1985—2008. Mgr. and therapist Oakside Clinic, Kankakee, Ill., 1987—; mem. adv. bd. Depressive and Manic Depression Assn., Chgo., 1986—; mem. consultation and mental health unit Riverside Med. Ctr., Kankakee, 1987—; speaker numerous nat. orgns. Contbr. numerous abstracts to profl. jours., chpts. to books. Bd. dirs. Cornerstone Svcs., ARC of Ill. Recipient total quality mgmt. award Rush-Presbyn.-St. Luke's Med. Ctr., 1991, named mgr. of the quarter, 1997, Wayne Lerner Leadership award, 1998. Mem. APNA, ISPN, Ill. Nurses Assn. (coms.), Coun. Clin. Nurse Specialists, Profl. Nursing Staff (sec. 1985-87, mem. coms.). Presbyterian. Home: 606 Darcy Ave Joliet IL 60436-1673 Office Phone: 312-942-5100, 815-933-2240.

LYNCH, THOMAS JAMES, medical oncologist, educator; BS, Yale U., 1982, MD, 1986. Diplomate Am. Bd. Internal Medicine, 1989, Am. Bd. Internal Medicine-med. oncology, 2003. Intern Mass. Gen. Hosp., 1987, resident in internal medicine, 1989; fellow in med. oncology Dana Farber Cancer Inst., 1991; medicine prof. Harvard Univ.; chief hematology/oncology cancer ctr. Mass. Gen. Hosp., dir. thoracic cancer ctr., dir. med. oncology thoracic oncology ctr.; physician-in-chief Smilow cancer hosp. Yale-New Haven Hosp., Conn., Richard Sackler and Jonathan Sackler prof. internal medicine, cancer ctr. dir. Author: various publs. Named one of Best Doctors, NY Mag., 2010. Achievements include development of therapeutics and in defining the optimal treatment for patients with lung cancer; pioneered the use of molecular testing for mutations in the epidermal growth factor receptor gene to select patients who can benefit from targeted lung cancer therapies. Office: Yale-New Haven Hospital Cancer Center 20 York St New Haven CT 06510 Office Phone: 203-688-4242.

LYNGBYE, JØRGEN, hospital advisor, researcher; b. Andst, Denmark, July 23, 1929; arrived in Norway, 1988, permanent resident; s. Knud and Estrid Marie Schou (Nielsen) Lyngbye; m. Ulla von Holstein, July 15, 1967 (div. 1982); 1 child, Rie; m. Jintana Detwilaiphong, Jan. 3, 1994. MD, U. Copenhagen, 1956; PhD, U. Arhus, Denmark, 1969. Asst. U. Arhus, 1957-65; asst. prof. U. Copenhagen, 1966-72; sr. cons. Regional Hosp., Frederiksborg, Denmark, 1973-83, Førde, Norway, 1983—88; prof. molecular biology, 1988—89; prof. U. Thailand, 1990—91; dir. Regional Hosp., Molde, Norway, 1991—98; sci. advisor Copenhagen, 1999—. Author: Clinical Biochemistry, 1986, Twins--A Unique World Scenario, 1995, Norwegian Handbook of Laboratory Medicine, 1999, Danish Textbook of Laboratory Medicine, 2001, 2010, Niels Finsen, A Danish Nobel Prize Laureate, 2003, Ole Roemer, The Scientist, A Biography, 2004; editor: (book) Maskinen Skabt I Menneskets Billede, 2010; contbr. articles to sci. jours. and newspapers. Sec. Danish Polit. Orgn., Copenhagen, 1977-81. Lt. Danish Army, 1951-66. Decorated WEO Order (Thailand); recipient prize Danish Sci. Soc., 1978, Prix Scientifique, France, 1980, prize Danish Soc. for Protection of Animals, 1987, Applied Physics award, 1993. Mem. Danish Med. Assn. (rep. 1978-83), Ole Roemer Soc. Avocations: philosophy, mathematics, nuclear physics, music. Home Phone: 45-32576477. Personal E-mail: jin@c.dk.

LYNGDOH, TOIJAM SONI, pediatrician; b. Imphal, Aug. 28, 1973; MS, Postgrad. Inst. Med. Edn. & Rsch., Chandigarh, 2003; MCh, Postgrad. Inst. Med. Edbn. & Rsch., Chandigarh, 2011. Sr. resident dept. gen. surgery Postgrad. Inst. Med. Edn. & Rsch., 2003—05, physician, 1998—; jr. specialist Tura Civil Hosp., West Garo Hills, Meghalaya, 2005—09. Mem.: Indian Assn. Pediatric Surgeons, Assn. Minimal Access Surgeons India, Assn. Surgeons India. Avocations: football, surfing. Office: Dept Pediatric Surgery APC Bldg Chandigarh 160012 India Office Fax: 01722743577. Personal E-mail: sonilyngdoh@rediffmail.com.

LYNN, D. JOANNE, physician, researcher; b. Oakland, Md., July 2, 1951; d. John B. and Mary Dorcas (Clark) Harley; m. Barry W. Lynn; children: Christina, Nicholas. BS with summa cum laude, Dickinson Coll., 1970; MD with cum laude, Boston U., 1974; MA in Philosophy and Social Policy, George Washington U., 1981; MS Clin. Evaluative Scis., Dartmouth Coll., 1995. Diplomate Am. Bd. Internal Medicine. Resident internal medicine George Washington U. Med. Ctr., 1974—77; emergency rm. physician, triage physician Washington VA Hosp., 1977—78; faculty assoc. medicine and humanities divsn. experimental programs George Washington U., Washington, 1978—81, dir. divsn. aging studies, 1988—92, prof. health care scis. and medicine, 1991—92, assoc. chairperson dept. health care scis., 1990—92, dir Ctr. to Improve the Care Dying, 1995—2000; prof. medicine, cmty. and family medicine, sr. assoc. Ctr. Evaluative Clin. Scis. Dartmouth-Hitchcock Med. Ctr., Hanover, NH, 1992—95, assoc. dir. Ctr. Aging, 1992—95; dir. RAND Ctr. Improve Care Dying, Arlington, Va., 2000—02, Washington Home Ctr. Palliative Care Studies, Arlington, 2002—05; pres. Ams. Better Care of the Dying, 1995—2005; sr. natural scientist RAND, 2005—06; med. officer Ctr. Medicine and Med. Svcs., 2006—08; bur. chief, cancer & chronic diseases Dept. Health, Washington, 2008—10; clin. improvement expert Colo. Found. Med. Care, 2010—. Sr. fellow Ctr. Health Policy Rsch., 1991-92; asst. dir. med. studies The Pres. Commn. for Study of Ethical Problems in Medicine and Biomed. and Behavioral Rsch., 1981-83; med. dir. The Washington Home, 1983-89, Hospice Washington, 1979-91, George Washington Cancer Home Care Program and Home Health Svcs. Washington Home, 1990-92, staff physician, 1979-92; fellow Hastings Ctr., 1984—; mem. working group on guidelines for care of terminally ill, 1985-87, rsch. project on ethical issues in care and treatment of chronically ill, 1985-87, working group on new physician-patient relationship, 1991-94, v.p., 1987, chair fellows nominating com., 1991; mem. coordinating coun. on life-sustaining med. treatment decision making by cts. Nat. Ctr. State Cts., 1989-93; fellow Kennedy Inst., 1991; mem. geriat. and gerontology adv. com. Dept. Vet. Affairs, 1991-97; mem. bioethics com. Vets. Health Adminstrn., 1991-93; active Washington Area Seminar on Sci., Tech., and Ethics, 1982-92, Nat. Clin. Panel on High-Cost Hospice Care, Washington, 1991; presenter in field: mem. editl. bd. The Ency. Bioethics, 1994-95; mem. adv. editl. bd. Biolaw, 1983, The Hospice Jour., 1984—, Med. Ethics for the Physician, 1985-92, Med. Humanities Rev., 1986—, Cambridge Quar., 1991-95 Co-Author: (with A. Kabenell and J. Lynch Schuster) Improving Care for the End of Life: A Sourcebook for Health Care Managers and Clinicians, 2000, Sick to Death and Not Going to Take It Any More, 2004; author chpts. to books; contbr. articles, revs. to profl. jours. Dr. Bertha Curtis prize Boston U. Med. Sch., 1974, Nat. Bd. award Med. Coll. Pa., 1992. Master ACP (mem. subcom. on aging 1986-91), Am. Geriatrics Soc. (mem. com. public policy 1983-98, mem. ethics com. 1988, chair subcom. on ethics and policy 1986, chair ethics com. 1991-98, bd. dirs. 1991-97); mem. AAAS, APHA, Am. Fedn. Clin. Rsch., Am. Health Care Assn. (mem. task force on AIDS 1987-89), Am. Hosp. Assn. (mem. spl. com. on biomedical ethics 1983-85, 89-94), Am. Med. Dirs. Assn., Am. Soc. Law and Medicine, Am. Coll. Health Care Adminstrs. (mem. nat. adv. com. wandering patients 1987-88), Nat. Inst. on Aging (mem. senile dementia Alzheimer's type, mem. rsch. ethics task force 1981-82, Am. Geriatrics Soc. rep. 1984-86), Soc. Health and Human Values (mem. gov. coun. 1981-84), Inst. Medicine (mem. com. on future issues in med. tech. devel. 1992-94), N.H. Med. Soc., Soc. Health and Human Values (mem. gov. coun. 1981-84), Internat. Hospice Inst. (mem. physician's adv. com. 1984-86), Med. Soc. D.C. (mem. legis. affairs com. 1985-92, vice chairperson 1991-92), Soc. Gen. Internal Medicine (mem. editl. adv. bd. Jour. 1988-91), Inst. Medicine, Americans for Better Care of the Dying (pres. 1994-2005) Home and Office: 2318 Ashboro Dr Chevy Chase MD 20815-3055 Business E-Mail: drjoannelynn@gmail.com.

LYNN, MORTON DANIEL, orthopedist; b. Paterson, NJ, Apr. 4, 1939; s. Allan A. and Sophie (Schwartz) L.; m. Susan Z. Zeller, July 3, 1966; children: Allison, Elizabeth, Sarah, Geoffrey (dec.). AB, Dartmouth Coll., 1961; MD, Cornell U., 1965. Diplomate Nat. Bd. Med. Examiners, Am. Bd. Orthopedic Surgeons. Intern, resident in surgery U. Hosp., Cleve., 1965-67; resident in orthopedics Vanderbilt U. Hosp., Nashville, 1967-70; pvt. practice New Eng. Orthopedic Surgeons, Springfield, Mass., 1972—. Emeritus staff Baystate Med. Ctr., Springfield, 1972—, Mercy Hosp., Springfield, 1982-2006, Shriners Hosp., Springfield, 1973-2006; asst. clin. instr. orthopedics N.Y. Med. Coll., N.Y.C., 1970-72, Boston U. Med. Sch., 1972-82, clin. asst. prof. orthopedics, 1982-2005; v.p. med. staff Baystate Med. Ctr., 1989, 90, pres., 1991, 92; clin. instr. Tufts Med. Sch., 2005—. Author: Morton Daniel Lynn, 1972; Contbr. articles to profl. jours. Bd. mem. Ctr. for Human Devel.; grant reviewer The Cmty. Found. Lt. comdr. USPHS, 1970—72. Mem. Mass. Med. Soc., New Eng. Orthopedic Soc., Am. Orthop. Foot and Ankle Soc., Am. Acad. Orthop. Surgeons. Achievements include research in triplane distal tibial epiphyseal fracture. Avocations: tennis, piano, fishing, skiing, golf. Office: New Eng Orthopedic Surgeons 300 Birnie Ave Springfield MA 01107-2316 Business E-Mail: morton.lynn@neortho.com.

LYNN, PAUL, health facility administrator; MD, La. State Sch. Med. Sch. Intern Charity Hosp., New Orleans, 1968; dir. San Francisco Preventive Med. Group. Fellow: Internat. Coll. Applied Nutrition; mem.: Price Pottenger Nut. Found., Rheumatoid Disease Found., Am. Longevity Assn., Orthomolecular Med. Soc. Office: San Francisco Preventive Med Group 345 W Portal Ave San Francisco CA 94127

LYNN, THOMAS NEIL, JR., retired medical center administrator, physician; b. Ft. Worth, Feb. 14, 1930; s. Thomas Neil and Florence Van Zandt (Jennings) L.; m. Virginia Carolyn Harsh, July 26, 1952; children: Thomas Neil, Leslie Elizabeth, Kathryn Barry. BS, U. Okla., 1951, MD, 1955. Diplomate: Am. Bd. Internal Medicine, Am. Bd. Preventive Medicine. Intern Barnes Hosp., St. Louis, 1955-56, resident, 1956-57; clin. asso Nat. Heart Inst. NIH, Bethesda, Md., 1957-59; chief resident medicine U. Okla. Hosps., 1959-61; med. staff U. Hosps. and Clinics, 1970-72; staff Okla. Children's Meml. Hosp., Presbyn. Hosp., VA Hosp., Oklahoma City; instr. asst. prof. community health Okla. Med. Center, 1961-63, asso. prof., 1963-67, prof., chmn. dept., 1970-76; acting dean U. Okla. Coll. Medicine, 1974-76, dean, 1976-80; v.p. for med. staff affairs Bapt. Med. Ctr., Oklahoma City, 1980-95. Med. expert Office Hearings and Appeals of Social Security Adminstrn., 1980—; mem. governing bd. Okla. Physician Manpower Tng. Commn., 1974-80, Ambulatory Health Care Consortium, Inc., 1977-78, T.N. Lynn Inst. for Healthcare Rsch., 1996—; mem. Okla. Bd. Medicolegal Examiners. Contbr. articles to profl. jours. Bd. dirs. Okla. Arthritis Found., 1978-82, v.p., 1981-82; bd. dirs. North Care Mental Health Ctr., 1981-87, pres., 1986-87, Oklahoma City Community Coun., 1982-90; med. dir. Okla. Organ Sharing Network, 1989-90; mem. Bd. Health Oklahoma City-County Health Dept., 1983-85; bd. dirs. Okla. chpt. Am. Heart Assn., 1984-86; mem. Nat. Commn. on Cert. Physician Assts., 1987-90; bd. dirs. Quail Creek Homeowners Assn., 1998-2000. Fellow Am. Coll. Preventive Medicine; mem. AMA, Okla. Med. Assn. (trustee 1981-87, chmn. bd. trustees 1986-87), Oklahoma County Med. Soc. (trustee, pres. 1982), Thomas N. Lynn Inst. Healthcare Rsch. (bd. dirs. 1996-), Sigma Xi, Alpha Omega Alpha, Phi Sigma, Alpha Tau Omega. Presbyterian. Home: 3136 Pine Ridge Rd Oklahoma City OK 73120-5918 *

LYON, MARY FRANCES, retired medical researcher; b. Norwich, England, Sept. 15, 1925; BA, Cambridge U., 1946, DSc, 1968. Head genetics sect. Med. Rsch. Coun. (MRC) Radiobiology Unit, Harwell, England, 1962—86, ret., 1990. Recipient Mauro Baschirotto award in human genetics, 1994, Wolf Found. prize for medicine, Israel, 1997, Amory prize, 1997. Fellow: Royal Soc.; mem.: NAS (fgn. assoc.), Am. Acad. Arts & Scis. (fgn. hon.). Achievements include discovery of X-chromosome inactivation (1961). Mailing: c/o Royal Soc 6 9 Carlton House Terrace London SW1 5AG England Office Phone: 66 1235 841000. Business E-Mail: m.lyon@har.mrc.ac.uk. *

LYONS, THOMAS PATRICK, economics professor; b. Groton, Conn., Sept. 8, 1953; BA in Asian Studies, Cornell U., 1979, MA in Econs., 1982, PhD in Econs., 1983. Asst. prof. econs. Dartmouth Coll., Hanover, NH, 1983-87; vis. asst. prof. Cornell U., Ithaca, NY, 1986-88, asst. prof., 1988-91; assoc. prof., 1991-2000; dir. East Asia program Cornell U., Ithaca, NY, 1991-94, dir. undergrad. studies, econs., 1995—, prof., 2000—. Author: Economic Integration and Planning in Maoist China, 1987, China's War on Poverty, 1992,

Economic Geography of Fujian: A Sourcebook, vols. 1 and 2, 1995, China Maritime Customs and China's Trade Statistics 1859-1948, 2003, Townships in Fujian, 1997-2003: Digital Maps and Data, 2006; contbr. articles to profl. jours. With USN, 1972—76. Grantee, Ford Found., 1987. Mem.: Assn. Am. Geographers, Assn. Asian Studies, Am. Econ. Assn. Office: Cornell U Dept Econs Uris Hall Ithaca NY 14853-7601 Business E-Mail: tpl4@cornell.edu.

LYRAS, DIMITRIS NIKOLAOS, surgeon; b. Chios, Greece, Feb. 7, 1971; DVM, Vet. Sch. Thessaloniki; MD, Med. Sch. Alexandroupolis, 2002; PhD, U. Thrace, Greece, 2010. Specialist registrar trauma and orthop. surgery Amalia Fleming Gen. Hosp., Athens, 2006—09; clin. fellow Royal Manchester Children's Hosp., 2009—10; trauma fellow Poole, NHS Hosp., UK, 2010—. Scholarship, Greek Nat. Found. Master: Nat. Kapodistrian U. Athens; mem.: Hellenic Orthop. Assn. Avocations: sports, music. Home: Flat 8 Aqua Lifeboat Quay Poole Dorset BH15 1LS England Office: Dimitris Lyras Leros Hosp Leros Island Greece Office Phone: 0030-6949-313155. Personal E-mail: dimitrislyras@yahoo.gr.

LYSLE, DONALD T., psychology professor, department chairman; BS in Anthropology-Psychology, magna cum laude, U. Pitts., 1979, MS in Biol. Psychology, 1983, PhD in Biol. Psychology, 1986. Grad. rsch asst. & tchg. fellow, dept. psychology U. Pitts., 1980—86, post-doctoral rsch. assoc., Western Psychiatric Inst. and Clinic, 1986—87, rsch. asst. prof., dept. pathology & adj. asst. prof., dept. psychology, 1988—90; grad. faculty, curriculum in neurobiology U. NC, 1990—, asst. prof., dept. psychology, 1990—93, assoc. prof., dept. psychology, 1993—97, dir. biol. psychology program, 1995—2004, prof., dept. psychology, 1997—, Gillian T. Cell disting. term prof., 2004—05, assoc. chmn. dept. psychology, 2004—07, Kenan disting. prof., 2005—, chmn. dept. psychology, 2007—. Contbr. articles to profl. jours. Mem.: APA, Am. Psychol. Soc., Eastern Psychol. Assn., Internat. Soc. Neuroimmunomodulation, Psychoneuroimmunology Rsch. Soc., Psychonomic Soc., Soc. Neuroscience, Soc. NeuroImmunePharmacology, Sigma Xi. Office: Dept Psychology Behavioral Neurosci Program Davie Hall CB 3270 Univ NC Chapel Hill NC 27599-3270 Office Phone: 919-962-3374. Office Fax: 919-962-2537. Business E-Mail: dlysle@email.unc.edu.

LYTLE, BRUCE WHITNEY, cardiovascular surgeon; b. Mpls., Sept. 10, 1945; s. Francis Theodore and Dorothy L. (Whitney) L.; m. Ellen Suzanne Baker, Feb. 1970; children: Francis Theodore, Medora Suzanne. BA with great distinction, Stanford U., 1967; MD cum laude, Harvard Med. Sch., 1971. Diplomate Am. Bd. Surgery, Am. Bd. Thoracic Surgery. Surg. intern Mass. Gen. Hosp., Boston, 1971-72, third asst. resident in gen. surgery, 1972-73, second asst. resident, 1973-74, fourth yr. resident, 1974-75; sr. registrar in cardiothoracic surgery Shotley Bridge Hosp., No. Regional Health Authority, Eng., 1975-76; fifth yr. resident in surgery Mass. Gen. Hosp., Boston, 1976, chief resident in cardiovascular surgery, 1977; assoc. staff Dept. Thoracic and Cardiovascular Surgery The Cleve. Clinic Found., 1978-79, profl. staff Dept. Thoracic and Cardiovascular Surgery, 1979—, chmn., Heart and Vascular Inst., 2004—. Contbr. over 200 articles to profl. med. jours. Named Dana A. Hamel Chair for Heart Disease Rsch., 2006. Mem. ACS, AMA, Am. Coll. Cardiology, Am. Heart Assn., Ohio Chpt. ACS, Ohio State Med. Assn., Am. Assn. for Thoracic Surgery (pres. 2006 07), Cleve. Acad. Medicine, Soc. Thoracic Surgeons, Am. Surg. Assn. Avocations: fly fishing, motorcycling. Office: Cleve Clinic Found 9500 Euclid Ave # F25 Cleveland OH 44195-0002

LYTLE, IAN FRAZIER, plastic surgeon; m. Marija Grahovac. Attended, Alma Coll.; MD, Wayne State U., 2002. Diplomate Am. Bd. Plastic Surgery. Resident in gen. surgery Univ. Hosp. Cin., Ohio; resident in plastic surgery Univ. of Mich. Med. Ctr., rsch. fellow in plastic surgery; hosp. affiliation include Oakwood Hosp.; staff St. Joseph Mercy Ann Arbor Hosp., St. Joseph Mercy Livingston Hosp., St. Joseph Mercy Saline Hosp.; plastic sugeon Ctr. for Plastic and Reconstructive Surgery. Mem.: ACS. Avocations: painting, sculpting. Office: Center for Plastic and Reconstructive Surgery PO Box 994 5333 McAuley Dr Suites 5001 and 5008 Ann Arbor MI 48106 Office Phone: 734-712-2323. Office Fax: 734-712-2312.

LYTTON, BERNARD, urology educator; b. London, June 28, 1926; came to U.S., 1962; s. Morris and Pearl (Zuckerberg) L.; m. Norma M. Mendle, Oct. 28, 1963; children: Sharon, Simon, Timothy, Jennifer. MB, BS, U. London, 1948, FRCS, 1955. House officer, sr. registrar Royal London Hosp., 1948-50, 58-61; prof., chief urology Yale Univ. Sch. Medicine, New Haven, 1967-87, Donald Guthrie prof. surgery, 1987—96, prof. emeritus, 1996—, dir. Henry Koerner Ctr. Emeritus Faculty, 2001—; Master Jonathan Edwards Coll. Yale U., 1987-97. Squadron leader Royal Airforce Med. Br., Eng., 1950-52. Fellow, Kings Coll. Hosp., 1961—63. Fellow ACS; mem. Am. Urol. Assn. (Hugh Hampton Young award 1985, pres. New Eng. sect. 1974), Am. Assn. Genito-Urinary Surgeons (v.p. 2006, pres. 2008-09), Korean Emeritus Ctr. Yale U.(dir. 2003-), Clin. Soc. Genito-Urinary Surgeons (pres. 2000-01), Soc. Pelvic Surgeons. Avocations: tennis, skiing, history, hiking. Home: 21 Autumn St New Haven CT 06511-2220 Office: Yale U Sch Medicine Sect Urology PO Box 208041 New Haven CT 06520-8041 Office Phone: 203-432-8227, 203-785-2815. Business E-Mail: bernard.lytton@yale.edu.

MA, C-M (CHARLIE), physicist, educator; b. Heilongjiang, China, Aug. 28, 1956; s. Defu Ma and Haibo Zhang; m. Lili Chen, Jan. 1, 1983; children: Caroline, Glenn. PhD, U. London, 1992. Diplomate Am. Bd. Radiology. Prof., vice chair radiation oncology, dir. radiation physics Fox Chase Cancer Ctr., Phila., 2001—; assoc. prof. Stanford U., Calif., 2000—01, asst. prof., 1996—99; rsch. assoc. NRC, Ottawa, Ont., Canada, 1993—95; postdoctoral fellow Inst. Cancer Rsch./Royal Marsden Hosp., Sutton, Surrey, England, 1992—93. Mem. adv. bd. Physics Med. Biology Internat., 2002—. Grantee R01 (two cycles), NIH, 1999—; Idea grantee, U.S. Army Breast Cancer Rsch. Program, 1998—2001, Seed grantee, Radiological Soc. N.Am., 1997—98, New Concept grantee, 2010—. Fellow: Am. Coll. Med. Physics, Inst. Physics, Am. Assn. Physicists in Medicine (computer com. 1996—2001, pub. edn. com. 1996—2001, radiation therapy com. 2000—03, pres. Del. chpt. 2004, calibration laboratory accreditation subcom. 1999—2005, Asian oceanic affairs subcom. 2006—, sci. program track chair 2006, sci. program dir. 2007, Summer Sch. scholarships subcom. chair 2008—, bd. dirs. 2008—10, Med. Physics Travel award 2000); mem.: Med. Dosimetry (adv. editor 2005—), Phys. Med. Biology (internat. adv. bd. 2002—), Am. Soc. Therapeutic Radiology and Oncology (Best Paper in Basic Sci. 1999), European Soc. Therapeutic Radiology and Oncology, Can. Orgn. Med. Physicists (Best Poster award 1999). Achievements include development of clinical implementation of Monte Carlo techniques for radiotherapy dose calculation; research in energy and intensity-modulated electron therapy (MERT) and image-guided radiation therapy; MR guided high-intensity focused ultrasound therapy and surgery; development of laser-accelerated proton (ion) beams for radiation therapy; patents in field. Avocations: reading, gardening, music, writing, volleyball. Office: Fox Chase Cancer Center Radiation Oncology Dept Rm P0069 333 Cottman Ave Philadelphia PA 19111 Business E-Mail: charlie.ma@fccc.edu.

MA, HUI, medical educator; b. Ningxia, China, May 28, 1972; MD, Shanghai Med. U., 1995, Chongqing Med. U., 2001. Prof. Ningxia Med. U. Hosp., 2008—. Office: Shenglinanjie 804 YinChuan Ningxia 750004 China Personal E-mail: blackcat0528@hotmail.com.

MA, RUJIAN, chemist, educator; b. Jianhu, Jiangshu, China, Aug. 26, 1969; s. Yiqing Ma and Wenying Li; m. Zhuoping Li, July 23, 1970; 1 child, Yujie. D, Tokushima U., Japan, 2001. Tchr. East China U. Sci. and Tech., Shanghai, 1995—97; rschr. U. Tokushima, Japan, 1997—98; assoc. dir. chemistry WuXi PharmaTech Co., Ltd., Shanghai, 2001—02, dir. chemistry, 2002—03, sr. dir. chemistry, 2004—. Contbr. articles to profl. jours. Scholar, Shanghai BAO Steel Co. Ltd., 1994. Fellow: Japanese Soc. for Promotion of Sci. Achievements include 9 patents. Office: WuXi PharmaTech Co Ltd No1 Bldg 288 FuTeZhongLu Shanghai 200131 China Office Fax: 0086-21-50461000. Business E-Mail: marj@pharmatechs.com.

MA, WEI-GUO, cardiac surgeon educator; b. China, Oct. 13, 1971; MD, Peking Union Med. Coll., 2001. Assoc. prof. Fu Wai Hosp., Peking Union Med. Coll., 2005—. Cons. Gerson Lehrman Group Couns., 2007—11. Translator: Surgery for Congenital Heart Defect, 3rd Edit. Recipient Tech. Innovation award, Chinese Acad. Med. Scis. Fellow: Chinese Assn. Health Mgmt. Young Councilors. Avocations: music, philosophy, history. Home: 2 405 Da long Gongyu 6 Xinghua Rd Beijing 100013 China Office Phone: 86 10 6445 6496. Personal E-mail: wgma@yahoo.com.

MA, WENXUE, medical scientist; s. Shumin Ma and Xiuqin Liu; m. Chunyang Hou, Dec. 12, 1992; children: Duli, Yiming. MS, Zhejiang Med. U., Hangzhou, China, 1997, MD, 1989; PhD, Zhejiang U., Hangzhou, 2002. Fellow U. Nebr. Med. Ctr., Omaha; rsch. assoc. U. Wis., Madison, 2004—05; with U. Calif., San Diego, 2005—. Mem.: AAAS (assoc.), Am. Assn. for Cancer Rsch. (assoc.), Sigma Xi (assoc.). Achievements include patents pending for transmembrane superantigen staphylococcal enterotoxin A. Office: Univ Calif San Diego 3855 Health Sciences Dr #0820 La Jolla CA Office Fax: 858-534-7061. Personal E-mail: mawenxue@hotmail.com. E-mail: wma@ucsd.edu.

MA, XIANG-YANG, medical educator; b. Yiyang, China, June 8, 1970; D, Nanfang Med. U., 2004. Prof. Guangzhou Liu Hua Qiao Hosp., 2004 . Office: 111 Liu Hua Rd Guangzhou Guangdong 510010 China Personal E-mail: maxy1001@126.com.

MA, ZHANFANG, chemistry professor; b. Changchun, China, Sept. 29, 1965; PhD, Inst. Photographic Chmistry Chinese Acad. Scis., 2000. Prof., dept. chemistry Capital Normal U., 2006— Office: Xi San Huan N Rd Beijing 100048 China Personal E-mail: mazhanfang@yahoo.com.

MA, ZHENJUN, engineering educator; b. China, July 28, 1978; PhD, Honng Kong Poly. U., 2008. Lectr. U. Wollongong, 2011—. Office: Hung Hom Kowloon Hong Kong Hong Kong Personal E-mail: zhenjun_ma@hotmail.com.

MA, ZHIZHONG, medical educator; s. Baozeng Ma and Guixin Liu; m. Jie Wang, Sept. 19, 1990; children: Miaohan, Qianxiang. M, PLA Postgraduate Med. Coll., Beijing, China, 1983. Lic. physician Liaoning Province Health Care Bur., 1976. Prof. ophthalmology PLA 301 Gen. Hosp., Beijing, 1991—2001, mentor dr. degree, 1998—2001, dir. eye dept., 1998—2001; mentor dr. degree Peking U. Third Hosp., Beijing, 2001—; prof. ophthalmology Peking U. Eye Ctr., Beijing, 2001—. Chmn. ocular trauma, ocular plastic and orbit group Chinese Ophthalmology Soc., Beijing, 1998—; china rep. Internat. Soceity of Ocular Trauma, 1999—; mem. Am. Acad. Ophthalmology, China, 1994—2001; chmn. PLA Ophthalmology Soc., Beijing, 1996—2001; editor Chinese Ophthalmology Jour., Beijing, 2001—; dep. dir. Peking U. Eye Ctr., Beijing, 2001—; editor Chinese Jour. Ocular Fundus Diseases, Chengdu, Xichuan Province, China, 2002—, Am. Jour. Ophthalmology, Chinese Edit., 2007—. Contbr. scientific papers. Achievements include development of new surgical approaches to "wet" AMD are being developed by Dr. Ma, which achieved unprecedented success in improving patients' vision. Office: Peking Univ Eye Ctr No 49 Hua Yuan Bei Lu Beijing 100191 China Office Fax: 8610-82089951. Business E-Mail: puh3_yk@bjmu.edu.cn.

MAAS, COREY S., plastic surgeon; BS in Bio., Fla. St. Univ., Tallahassee, 1982; MD with hon., Univ. Fla. Coll. Med., Gainesville, Fla., 1986. Cert. Nat. Bd. Med. Examiners, 1987, Miss., 1987, Calif., 1991, Fla., 1996, Am. Bd. Otolaryngology, 1992, Am. Bd. Facial Plastic and Reconstructive Surgery, 1996. Gen. surg. intern St. Louis Univ. Med. Clinic, 1986—87, otolaryngology-head neck surgery resident, 1987—90, chief resident, 1990—91; fell. facial plastic and reconstructive surgery divsn. UC San Francisco Med. Clinic, 1991—92; private practice plastic surgeon San Francisco; founder, dir. Maas Clinic, 2001—. Clin. instr., divsn. plastic surgery UC, San Francisco, 1991, assoc. clin. prof., 1992—; dir., facial plastic surgery tng. fell. Am. Acad. Facial Plastic and Reconstructive Surgery, 2000. Recipient Gold Key Scholastic Leadership honor, FSU, 1982, Sir Harold Delf Gilles Rsch. award, Am. Acad. Facial and Plastic Surgery, 1992, Nat. Cmty. Svc. award, 1994. Fellow: Triologic Soc., Am. Coll. Surgeons, Am. Acad. Otolaryngology - Head and Neck Surgery, Am. Acad. Facial Plastic and Reconstructive Surgery; mem.: Calif. Soc. Facial Plastic Surgery, World Aesthetic Surgery Soc., San Francisco Med. Soc., Calif. Soc. Otolaryngology - Head and Neck Surgery, Calif. Med. Assn., Am. Rhinologic Soc., AMA. Office: The Maas Clinic 2400 Clay St San Francisco CA 94115 Office Phone: 415-567-7000. Office Fax: 415-567-7011.

MAAS, WERNER KARL, microbiology educator; b. Kaiserslautern, Germany, Apr. 27, 1921; came to U.S., 1936, naturalized, 1945; s. Albert and Esther (Meyer) M.; m. Renata Diringer, Oct. 15, 1960; children— Peter, Andrew, Helen. AB, Harvard U., 1943; PhD, Columbia U., 1948. Postdoctoral fellow Calif. Inst. Tech., Pasadena, 1946-48; commd. officer USPHS, Tb Research Lab., Cornell U. Sch., NYC, 1948-54; asst. prof. pharmacology NYU, 1954-57, assoc. prof. microbiology, 1957-63, prof., 1963-94, prof. emeritus, 1994—, chmn. dept. basic med. scis., 1974-81. Career grantee, USPHS, 1962—94. Mem.: Am. Soc. Microbiology, Genetics Soc. Am., Am. Soc. Biol. Chemists. Home: 86 Villard Ave Hastings On Hudson NY 10706-1821 Office: 550 1st Ave New York NY 10016-6402 Home Phone: 914-478-1839; Office Phone: 212-263-5322. E-mail: werner.maas@nyumc.org.

MABEE, JOHN RICHARD, physician assistant, educator; b. San Francisco, Sept. 18, 1956; s. Robert John and Mary Sachiko (Nose) M.; m. Cheryl Ann Saxton, June 24, 1978 (div. Aug. 1995); children: Jonathan, Alan; m. Carol Mendez, 1998. BS, Regents Coll., 1981; MS, Calif. State U., LA, 1991; PhD, Union Inst., Cin., 2001. Cert. physician asst., Nat. Commn. Cert. Physician Assts. Physician asst. resident dept. emergency medicine LA County/U. So. Calif. Med. Ctr., 1984-85, emergency medicine physician asst., 1985—. Rsch. asst. dept. biology Calif. State U., LA, 1987—88, lectr., 1988—91, physician asst., 1992; rsch. physician asst. U. So. Calif. Emergency Medicine Assocs., LA, 1993—95, clin. instr. dept. emergency medicine, 1994—, conscious sedation adv. com., 1995—, lectr. sch. medicine, 1995—2000, asst. prof. clin. family medicine, 2001—. Contbr. articles to profl. jours. Named Alumnus of Yr., Emergency Medicine Physician Asst. Residency, 1994. Fellow Am. Acad. Physician Assts., Calif. Acad. Physician Assts. (Educator of Yr. 1998); mem. AAAS, N.Y. Acad. Scis., Soc. Emergency Medicine Physician Assts. (founding, election com., 1988—). Democrat. Avocations: reading, watching videos, horseback riding, chess, cooking, Tae Kwon Do. Office: U So Calif Keck Sch Medicine 1000 S Fremont Ave Bldg 6 Alhambra CA 91803 Home: 10561 Cliota St Whittier CA 90601 Business E-Mail: mabee@usc.edu.

MACALPIN, REX NERE, physician, educator; b. Glendale, Calif., Apr. 25, 1932; s. Frederic and Christine Capitola (Wright) MacA.; m. Carol Elizabeth White, June 22, 1957; children: David Ian, Anne Louise. Student, Harvard Coll., 1949-51; BA, Pomona Coll., Claremont, Calif., 1953; MD, U. Calif., San Francisco, 1957. Diplomate Am. Bd. Internal Medicine, Am. Bd. Cardiovasc. Disease. Med. intern, resident U. Calif. Sch. Medicine, San Francisco, 1957-60; cardiology fellow UCLA Sch. Medicine, 1960-61, prof. medicine, cardiology, 1963-88, prof. emeritus, 1988—. Contbr. over 100 articles to profl. publs. Lt. cmdr. USNR, 1961-63. Mem. Am. Heart Assn. (Svc. award 1981-84). Achievements include contribution to knowledge of the role of vasomotion in producing myocardial ischemia in coronary disease. Office: UCLA Divsn Cardiology 10833 Le Conte Ave Los Angeles CA 90095-1679 Office Phone: 310-206-5068. Business E-Mail: rmacalpi@ucla.edu. *

MACAREZ, REMI JACQUES, military ophthalmologist; b. Setif, Algeria, Dec. 9, 1961; s. Jacques Albert and Isabelle Dominique Macarez; m. Anne-Beatrice Bernadette Clarou, Mar. 14, 1987; children: Pierre Thibault, Thibault Benoît, Marie-Camille Sabine, Anne-Constance Béatrice. BS, Haffreingue-Chanlaire, Boulogne sur mer, 1980; MD, Universite Claude Bernard, Lyon I, 1988. Cert. specialist French Army Health Svc., 2000. Intern French Army Hosp., 1994. Contbr. articles to profl. jours. Capt. French Med. Svc. Corps., 1980—, France. Decorated French Legion of Honor, French Nat. Order of Merit; recipient Young Rschr. prize, Brest Med. U. Hosp. Ctr., 1998. Mem.: French Ophthalmology Soc. Achievements include research in the long term effect of iterative diving on visual system. Office: Hospl Clermont Tonnerre Rue Colonel Fonferrier Bp 41 Brest Armees F-29240 France Business E-Mail: remi.macarez@wanadoo.fr.

MACARIN-MARA, LYNN, psychotherapist, consultant; b. Queens, NY, Feb. 27, 1948; d. David and Grace Macarin; m. Marvin Weingast, Sept. 2, 2000; 1 child, Leah Mara. MA, NYU, 1972; MSW, Hunter Sch. Social Work, 1980. Cert. psychoanalytic psychotherapy, hypnotherapy and hypnoanalysis. With Greenwich Inst. Psychotherapy and Psychoanalysis, 1984-87; pvt. practice, 1987—; pres. Face to Face Psychotherapy Svcs., Metuchen, N.J., 1987—; dir. family and children svcs. Ednl. Alliance, Inc., NYC, 1990-95. Adj. prof. SUNY, Staten Island, N.Y., 1972-73, New Sch. for Social Rsch., N.Y.C., 1980-81. Contbr. articles to profl. jours. Chairperson membership com. Temple Emanu-El, Edison, N.J., 1998-2001. Mem. N.J. Soc. for Clin. Social Work (newsletter editor 1997-99). Democrat. Jewish. Avocations: travel, dance, writing, painting. Office: Face to Face Psychotherapy Svcs 2 Blair Ave Metuchen NJ 08840 also: 633 Close Rd Staten Island NY 10310 also: 915 Broadway Ste 1200 New York NY 10010

MACARIO, ALBERTO JUAN LORENZO, physician; arrived in US, 1974, naturalized, 1980; s. Alberto Carlos and Maria Elena (Giraudi) M.; m. Everly Conway, Mar. 16, 1963; children: Alex, Everly. MD, Nat. U. Buenos Aires, 1961. Cert. physician 1976. Intern Ramos Mejia Hosp., Buenos Aires, 1958—60, resident, 1960, Rivadavia Hosp., Buenos Aires, 1961—62, physician-hematologist, 1962—64; fellow NRC Argentina, Buenos Aires, 1964—69; head dept. radioactive isotopes Inst. Hematol. Investigations Nat. Acad. Medicine, Buenos Aires, 1967—69; Eleanor Roosevelt fellow Internat. Union Against Cancer Dept. Tumor Biology Karolinska Inst., Stockholm, 1969—71; mem. sci. staff Lab. Cell Biology NRC Italy, Rome, 1971—73; head lab. immunology Internat. Agy Rsch. on Cancer WHO, Lyons, France, 1973—74; rsch. scientist Brown U., Providence, 1974—76; rsch. scientist divsn. labs. and rsch. N.Y. State Dept. Health, Albany, 1976—79, chief hematology clin. lab. ctr., 1979—81; dir. clin. and exptl. immunology sect. Lab. Medicine Inst., 1981—83, rsch. physician, 1981 83; rsch. physician Wadsworth Ctr. N.Y. State Dept. Health, 1981—2006; rschr. U. Md. Biotechnology Inst., Balt., 2006—10; adj. prof. dept. microbiology & immunology Sch. Medicine, U. Md., 2010—; group head Inst. Euro-Mediterranean Sci. Tech., Palermo, Italy, 2010—. Prof. dept. biomed. scis. Sch. Pub. Health, SUNY, Albany, 1985-2006, adj. prof. 2006-09, mem. senate, 1989-94; adj. prof. pathology and lab. medicine Albany Med. Coll., 1991-2004; mem. structural and cell biology program Albany Univs. and Colls.; grant reviewer for nat. and internat. agys.; manuscript reviewer for sci. jours. Editor multivolume treatise Monoclonal Antibodies Against Bacteria and treatise Gene Probes for Bacteria; contbr. chpts. to books and encys. and articles to profl. jours. Past mem. Scandinavian Soc. Immunology, Italian Assn. Immunologists, French Soc. Immunology. Recipient Diploma de Honor prize Nat. U. Buenos Aires, 1961, Bernardino Rivadavia prize Nat. Acad. Medicine

Argentina, 1967, Ciencia e Investigation prize Argentinian Soc. Advancement Sci., 1967; Ford Found.-NAS travel fellow, 1968, Eleanor Roosevelt fellow, 1969. Mem. Internat. Soc. Microbial Ecology, Cell Stress Soc. Internat., Am. Assn. Immunologists, Am. Soc. Microbiology (sect. editor Manual of Clin. Lab. Immunology 4th and 5th edits. 1989-97), Am. Soc. Investigative Pathology, Assn. Internat. Union Against Cancer. Achievements include patents in field; discovered primary myeloperoxydase deficiency in leucocytes, and oscillations of antibody affinity during maturation of immune responses; developed method for immunologic identification of bacteria (archaea) that produce methane gas; discovered antigenic diversity of these microbes in natural and manufactured ecosystems; described structural topography of methanogenic archaea and population dynamics in granular microbial consortia; found novel multicellular forms of archaea; isolated for the first time ABC-transporter genes and the genes in the hsp70(dnak) locus from an archaebacterium (archaeon); devised and constructed the first integration vector for genetically engineering a methanogen useful for waste bioconversion; discovered a uni-celled organism with the main four chaperoning systems in its cytosol; found two new chaperonins in archaea; developed concept of sick chaperone or chaperonopathy as a factor contributing to the aging process and disease; discovered that archaeal hsp70 genes belong to various evolutionary lineages; elucidated the entire set of hsp70 genes in the human genome; characterized the whole complement of cct-Hsp60 genes in the human genome. Office: Sch Medicine University Md Columbus Ctr IMET 701 E Pratt St Baltimore MD 21202 Office Phone: 410-234-8871. Personal E-mail: macarioster@gmail.com.

MACASKILL, ANN, healthcare educator; d. Kenneth James and Jane Ann Kelly; m. Norman Duncan Macaskill, Sept. 25, 1970; children: Sean, Fiona. MA in Psychology with honors, U. Aberdeen, Scotland, 1974, PhD, 1977. Chartered health psychologist Brit. Psychol. Soc., 1990. Postdoc. rschr. U. Edinburgh, 1977—99; lectr. U. Aberdeen, Grampian, Scotland, 1980—82; part time rschr. U. Sheffield, South Yorkshire, England, 1982—85, lectr., Sheffield Hallam U., 1987—2002, sr. lectr., prin. lectr., reader, prof. health psychology, 2005—. Mem. gen. qualifications and accreditation com. Brit. Psychol. Soc., London, 1999—2004; com. mem. assn. heads Assn. Heads UK Psychology Depts., London, 1998—2001; com. mem., academic adv. group Nat. Health Svc., Sheffield, South Yorkshire, United Kingdom, 2003—; mem. admissions com. Brit. Psychol. Soc., 2006—; sci. com. mem. Internat. Congress Psychology, Cape Town, South Africa, 2008—. Contbr. articles to profl. jours. Voluntary advisor Sheffield Family Svcs. Unit, 1990—96, mem. mgmt. com.; mem. bd. trustees YMCA, Sheffield, 2006; govt. advisor Sci. & Trust Expert Group., Dept. Bus. & Skills, 2009—10; city ctr. counselling svc. Sheffield Anglican Cathedral, South Yorkshire, England, 1990—94. Fellow: UK Higher Edn. Acad. Bd., Brit. Psychol. Soc.; mem.: Brit. Assn. Christians Psychology, Inst. Rational-Emotive Therapy (assoc.). Avocations: walking, gardening, cooking, travel, theater. Office: Sheffield Hallam Univ Unit 1 Sci Pk Howard St Sheffield South Yorkshire S11WB England Business E-Mail: a.macaskill@shu.ac.uk.

MACAULAY, WILLIAM B., orthopedist, surgeon, educator; BS in Biochemistry, Trinity Coll., 1986; MD, Columbia U., 1992. Cert. Nat. Bd. of Med. Examiners, diplomate Am. Bd Orthopaedic Surgery. Intern dept. of gen. surgery Univ. of Pitts. Med. Ctr., 1992—93, clin. instructorship, 1997—98; resident dept. of orthopaedic surgery Musculoskeletal Inst.; clin. fellow adult reconstruction surgery Hosp. for Spl. Surgery, 1998—99; prof. orthopaedic surgery Columbia Univ.; with NY-Presbyn. Hosp. Co-author: (publs.) Peripheral neuropathies following total hip arthroplasty, 1994, Understanding economic evaluations: a review of the knee arthroplasty literature, 1999, Hybrid Total Hip Replacement, 2000, and numerous other publications. Chmn. joint walk com. Arthritis Found., 1999—2002, mem. adv. bd. Hudson Valley branch NY, 2000—05; mem. Mus. of Natural History, 2001—04, Nat. Geographic Soc., 2001—05; and numerous other organizations. Recipient Marion Merrill Dow Biomedical Rsch. prize, 1992, Am. Orthopaedic Assn.-Zimmer award, 1996, and numerous other awards.; scholar Brittenstool Scholar, 1991, Gillespie Scholar, 1991, Louis and Rachel Rudin Found. Scholar, 1992. Mem.: Am. Orthopaedic Assn., Orthopaedic Trauma Assn., Am. Assn. of Hip and Knee Surgeons, Frank Stinchfield Soc., NYS Soc. of Orthopaedic Surgeons, Eastern Orthopaedic Assn., AMA, Orthopaedic Rsch. Soc., Am. Acad. of Orthopaedic Surgeons, Allegheny County Med. Soc., Pa. Med. Soc. Achievements include research in Developed an assay scheme to determine the relative tyrosine hydroxylation activity of tyrosinase and tyrosine hydroxylase within a crude tissue homogenate; Synthesized analogs of glucagon via solid phase methodology, Purified these products via self-designed preparative HPLC set-up, and studied structure/function relationships via circular dichroism, biological assays and molecular modeling; Completed pilot project examining cytoplasmic peptide fragment transport/presentation in J774 murine macrophages; Studied potential biochemical markers of osteoarthritis and developed an improved sandwich ELISA for keratan sulfate. Office: NewYork-Presbyterian Hospital Herbert Irving Pavilion 2nd Fl 161 Fort Washington Ave New York NY 10032 Office Phone: 212-305-6959. Office Fax: 212-305-4024.

MACAVINTA-TENAZAS, GEMORSITA, physician; b. Numancia, Aklan, Phillippines, Dec. 18, 1938; arrived in U.S., 1967; d. Dominador Zalazar and Georgina Estrada (Tabanera) Macavinta; m. Salvador Torrefiel Tenazas Jr., Apr. 18, 1963; children: Alan, Alex, Albert, Alfred. BA, Far Ea. U., Manila, 1959, MD, 1964. Diplomate Am. Bd. Family Practice. Intern North Gen. Hosp., Manila, 1963-64; pvt. practice Manila, 1965-67; extern Chinese Gen. Hosp., Manila, 1965-67; with St. Joseph Med. Ctr., Burbank, Calif., 1967-69; chief cytotechnologist Cancer Screening Svcs., North Hollywood, Calif., 1969-73; resident in family practice medicine Health Scis. Ctr., Tex. Tech. U., Lubbock, 1974-75; staff physician VA Outpatient Clinic, LA, 1975—. Recipient physician recognition awards AMA, 1973-85, 92-94; named Mrs. Aklan, 1986, Disting. Alumna, Aklan Acad., Philippines, 1991, Most Outstanding Parent award Builders Lions Club, 1995, Citizen of Yr. Builders Lions Club, 1996, Outstanding Physician Club Filipino, 1996; named one of Ams. Top Family Drs. Consumers Rsch. Counc. Am., 2007; named to Asian Acad. Hall Distinction, Asian Leaders Assn., US Capital, 2007. Fellow Am. Acad. Family Physicians (bd. govs. 2003-05); mem. Philippine-Am. Assn. Family Physicians (bd. govs. 1996, 2003, 05-07, sec. 1998, sec. 1998-2002, Outstanding Leader award 2000, Mrs. Philippine Am. 2000), Am. Assn. Family Physicians (bd. govs., Phillipines 1996-), Calif. Acad. Family Physicians, Filipino Asian-Pacific VA Employees Soc. (pres. LA chpt. 1988—), Assn. Philippine Physicians in Am. (bd. govs. 2004, named Mrs. Mindanao 2002), Aklanons of Am. (pres. 1988—90, bd. govs. 1998-2000, 04-06, bd. dirs. 1990—, 1st Mrs. Aklan 1986-89), Far Ea. U. Med. Alumni Assn. (life mem., asst. sec. 1988—), Far Ea. U. Dr. Nicanor Reyes Alumni Found. (life). Roman Catholic. Avocations: dance, singing, sewing, piano playing, gardening. Office: VA Outpatient Clinic 351 E Temple Los Angeles CA 90012 Office Phone: 213-253-2677 ext. 4417. Business E-Mail: tenazas@va.gov.

MACCARTHY, PHILIP ANDREW, medical educator, consultant; m. Ruth Diane McLaren; children: Tobias James, Hannah Mae. BSc with honors, Bristol U., 1988, B.Medicine with honors, 1991; PhD, U. Wales Coll. Medicine, 2000. Clin. tng. fellow Med. Rsch. Coun., U. Wales Coll. Medicine, Cardiff, 1996—99; sr. registrar King's Coll. Hosp., London, 2000—03, cons. cardiologist, 2003—; sr. lectr. Guy's, King's and St. Thomas' Sch. Medicine, London, 2003—. Editl. bd. mem. Heart Journ., London. Contbr. chapters to books, articles to profl. jours. Grantee Project grant, British Heart Found., 1999, Advanced Tng. Scholarship, 2002. Fellow: Royal Coll. Physicians; mem.: British Cardial Soc. Ch. Of England. Office: Kings Coll Hosp Denmark Hill London SE5 9RS England Office Phone: 0044 20 7234 2971. Business E-Mail: philip@maccarthy.co.uk.

MACCHIARINI, PAOLO, surgeon; b. Basel, Switzerland, Aug. 22, 1958; s. Renzo Macchiarini and Rosa DiMeo. MD, U. Pisa Med. Sch., Italy, 1986; diploma in Gen. Surgery, U. Pisa, Italy, 1991; PhD, U. Franche-Compte, 1993—97. Resident, gen. surgery U. Pisa, Pisa, Italy, 1986—91; fellow thoracic surgery U. Birmingham, Birmgingham, Ala., 1989-90; fellow, cardiothoracic U. Paris-Sud, Paris, 1991—93, rsch. dir., 1998; head, dept. thoracic and vascular surgery Heidehaus Hosp., Hannover Med. Sch., 1999—2004; head, dept. gen. thoracic surgery Hospital Clinico de Barcelona, U. Barcelona; prof. regenerative surgery Karolinska Inst., Stockholm. Contbr. articles to profl. jours. Recipient Biomedica Rsch. award Italian Assn., Pisa, 1986-88, Internat. award U. Ala., Birmingham, 1989; oncology fellow Europe, 1990. Mem. European Assn. Cancer Rsch., European Soc. Surgical Oncology, Internat. Assn. Study Lung Cancer, Am. Assn. Thoracic Surgery, Cardiothoracic Surgery Network, European Assn. for Cardio-Thoracic Surgery, German Soc. for Thoracic and Cardiovascular Surgery, Spanish Soc. for Thoracic and Cardiovascular Surgery, Soc. Thoracic Surgeons. Achievements include performing the first transplant of a trachea grown from stem cells, 2008; performing the first transplant of a synthetic trachea grown from stem cells, 2011. Office: Dept Clin Sci Intervention and Tech Karolinska Inst 171 77 Stockholm Sweden Office Fax: 46 760 503 213. Business E-Mail: paolo.macchiarini@ki.se. *

MACCHIONE, NICK, city health department director; b. Catanzarro, Italy, Feb. 14, 1968; came to U.S., 1969; BA, Rutgers State U., 1990; MS, NYU, 1994; MPH, Columbia U., 1997. Program dir. Newark Dept. of Health and Human Services, 1993-97; chief, dir. Office AIDS Coord. County San Diego Dept. Health, 1997-98; gen. mgr. through dep. dir. & dir. County of San Diego Health and Human Services Agy., 1998—. Faculty mem. Grad. Sch. Pub. Health San Diego State Univ. John J. Hanlon Scholar, Pub. Health Leadership Scholar, Centers for Disease Control & Prevention. Fellow: Am. Coll. Healthcare Executives; mem.: Delta Omega of the Sigma (hon.). Avocations: domestic and international travel, chess, wine collecting. Office: San Diego HHSA Rm 207 MS-P501 1700 Pacific Hwy San Diego CA 92101 Office Phone: 619-515-6555.

MACCIONI, FRANCESCA, radiobiologist, educator; b. Rome, Feb. 11, 1963; MD, U. Sapienza, Rome, 1987. Radiologist Dept. Radiol. Scis., U. Sapienza, 1992—2001, prof., 2001—, gastroenterologist, 2005. Mem.: SIRM, ECR, ESGAR. Office: Ave Medical G via S Alberto Magno Rome 00153 Italy Business E-Mail: francesca.maccioni@uniroma1.it.

MACCONI, DANIELA, biomedical researcher; b. Bergamo, Italy, June 5, 1957; d. Giacomo Macconi and Lucia Raffaini; children: S. Breviario, L. Breviario. D in Biol. Sci., U. Milan. Fellow, assn. bergamasca per lo studio delle malattie renali Divsn. Nephrology and Dialysis, Ospedali Riuniti di Bergamo, 1982—83; postdoc. fellow, dept. Pathology U. Mich. Med. Sch., Ann Arbor, Mich., 1984—85; postdoc. fellow Mario Negri Inst. Pharmacological Rsch., Bergamo, 1985—89, scientist, 1989—94, head unit inflammatory mediators leukocyte origin, 1994—2000, head lab. renal biophysics, dept. biomedical engring., 2000—. Office: Mario Negri Inst Ctr Anna Maria Asteri Sci & Tech Pk Kilametro Rosso via Stezzano Bergamo 87-24126 Italy Office Phone: 0039-0354213310. Business E-Mail: daniela.macconi@marionegri.it.

MACDONALD, DOUGLAS ANDREW, psychologist, educator; b. Barrie, Can., June 2, 1967; s. David James and Rachel Marie MacDonald; children: Moriah, Sarah. BA in Psychology (hon.), U. Windsor, Ont., Can., 1990, MA in Psychology, 1992, PhD in Psychology, 1998. Practicum student Guelph Assessment and Treatment Unit, Ont., Canada, 1991; intern U. Windsor Psychol. Svc. Clinic, 1992—93, Windsor Regional Hosp., 1994—95; behavioral cons. Essex County Dist. Sch. Bd., Ont., Canada, 1995—97; psychologist Greater Essex County Dist. Sch. Bd., Windsor, 1997—2004; prof. psychology U. Detroit, 2000—; dir. clin. MA program U. Detroit Mercy, 2003—. Rsch. asst. U. Windsor, 1987—88; faculty Saybrook Grad. Sch., San Francisco, 2001—; clin. cons. Glengarda Child Family Svc., 2004—. Co-editor: (novels) Approaches to Transpersonal Measurement and Assessment, 2002; editor (rsch. assoc.): Jour. Humanistic Psychology, 2002; co-editor: Humanistic Psychologist, 2003, Internat. Jour. Transpersonal Studies, 2003—06; assoc. editor: Jour. Transpersonal Psychology, 2001, consulting editor: Australian Gestalt Jour. Cons., bd. dirs. Glengarda Child & Family Svc., Windsor, Ontario, Canada, 2000—04. Grantee, Floraglades Found., 2000—04. Mem.: APA (Carmi Harari Early Career award 2006), Can. Psychol. Assoc. Achievements include research in expression, measurement, and devel. of spirituality and assessment tools. Avocations: gardening, music, martial arts. Home: 470 Frontenac Ave N9E1M1 Windsor ON Canada Office: U Detroit Mercy Dept Psychology 4001 W McNichols Rd Detroit MI 48221 Home Phone: 519-250-4723. Business E-Mail: macdonda@udmercy.edu.

MACDONALD, JOEL D., medical educator; b. Dec. 27, 1963; BA, U. NC, 1985, degree, 1989. Asst. prof. U. Ariz., 1996—99; assoc. prof. U. Utah, 1999—. Mem.: Soc. Neurol. Surgeons, Western Neurosurg. Soc., Rocky Mountain Neurosurg. Soc., Am. Assn. Neurol. Surgeons, Congress Neurol. Surgeons. Office: 175 N Medical Dr E Salt Lake City UT 84132 E-mail: vasospaz@aol.com.

MACDONALD, KAREN CRANE, occupational therapist, geriatrics services professional; b. Denville, NJ, Feb. 24, 1955; d. Robert William and Jeanette Wilcox (Crane) M.; m. Geno Piacentini, Oct. 22, 1993. BS, Quinnipiac U., 1977; MS, U. Bridgeport, 1982; PhD, NYU, 1998. Cert. occupl. therapist. Occupational therapist, coord. of spl. care unit Jewish Home for the Elderly, Conn., 1987-92, N.Y. Inst., NYC, 1984-86; pvt. practice Fairfield County, Conn., 1977-88; occupl. therapist Rehab. Assocs., Fairfield, Conn., 1993-96. Instr. NYU, 1985—89, Quinnipiac CU, 1986—92, Housatonic CC, Bridgeport, Conn., 2002—, Sacred Heart U., Fairfield, Conn., 2006—; lectr., cons. in field. Contbr. articles to profl. jours. Youth leader, deacon Union Meml. Ch., Stamford, Conn., 1980-88; deacon Southport Congl. Ch., 1992-94; chair consumer com. Alzheimer's Coalition of Conn., 1991-92. Teaching fellow NYU, 1983-86. Mem.: NOW, AAUW, PEO, AAAS, NY Acad. Scis., Am. Bd. Disability Analysts, Conn. Occupl. Therapy Assn. (gerontology liaison 1980—83), Am. Occupl. Therapy Assn. (coun. edn., scholar 1985), World Fedn. Occupl. Therapy, Grange, Toastmasters Internat., Pi Lambda Theta. Avocations: poetry writing, quilting. Home: 198 Glenbrook Rd Bridgeport CT 06610-1149 Personal E-mail: genokaren@aol.com.

MACDOUGALL, IAIN C., nephrologist, consultant; b. Glasgow, Scotland, Mar. 24, 1958; s. Alasdair Iain and Mary Couper (Cumming) Macdougall; m. Penny Ackland, Jan. 10, 2001; children: Jennifer, Alan, Daniel, Inigo, Ella, Nancy. BSc in Pharmacology with 1st class honors, U. Glasgow, 1980, MB, BChir, 1983, MD, 1991. Renal registrar, rsch. fellow Cardiff (Wales) Royal Infirmary, 1988—91; sr. registrar nephrology St. Bartholomew's Hosp., London, 1991—96; cons. nephrologist King's Coll. Hosp., London, 1996—. Author: Renal Anaemia, 2004; contbr. chapters to books. Recipient Watson prize, Royal Coll. Physicians Glasgow, 1989. Fellow: Royal Coll. Physicians London; mem.: Am. Soc. Nephrology, European Renal Assn. (coun. mem. 2004—). Avocations: tennis, snooker, squash, windsurfing. Office: King's Coll Hosp Renal Unit Denmark Hill SE5 London England

MACDOUGALL, JOHN DUNCAN, thoracic surgeon; b. Indpls., Mar. 4, 1925; s. Duncan Campbell and Beulah Stewart (Ward) MacDougall; m. Inga Margaretha Tranberg, Oct. 6, 1951 (div. 1980); children: Duncan Campbell, Stewart Andrew, Eric Matthew, Victoria Suzanne MacDougall Oehmen; m. Barbara Lee Mayse, Nov. 1, 1980; children: Katherine Jane, James William. BS, Ind. U., Bloomington. Ind., 1948, MD, 1951. Diplomate Am. Bd. Surgery, Am. Bd. Thoracic Surgery. Pvt. practice, Indpls., 1957-93; pres. med. staff St. Francis Hosp., Beech Grove, Ind., 1975, pres. adv. bd., 1993-95, mem. governing bd. trustees, 2003—, chmn. governing bd. trustees, 1995—2003. Chmn. bd. dirs. Med. Assurance Ind., Indpls., 1987—2000, med. cons., 1993—. Mem. Ind. Gov.'s Task Force Organ Transplantation, Indpls., 1986—89; bd. dirs. Ind. Med. History Mus., 1989—2000, 2006—; active Ind. Hist. Soc., Indpls. Mus. Art; pres. Ind. Med. Polit. Action Com., Indpls., 1992—98; mem. exec. com. dean's coun. Ind. U. Sch. Medicine, Indpls., 1988—, mem. adv. com., 1989—96, pres. dean's coun., 1992—95; pres. English Speaking Union, 1987—2001. With US Army, 1943—46, ETO. Decorated Bronze Star. Fellow: ACS; mem.: AMA (del., chmn. Ind. delegation 1994—2003), Nat. Med. Vets. Assn. (bd. dirs. 1992—2004), Orgn. State Med. Assn. Pres. (pres. 1994—95), Indpls. Med. Soc. (pres. 1978—79), Ind. State Med. Assn. (pres. 1987—88), Purdue U. Pres.'s Coun., Ind. U. Sch. Medicine J. O. Ritchery Soc., Ind. U. Arbutus Soc., Meridian Hills Country Club, Contemporary Club, Indpls. Lit. Club, Masons (33d degree), Am. Legion (comdr. Paul Coble Post #26 1999—2007), Soc. Ind. Pioneers. Republican. Episcopalian. Avocations: woodworking, golf, fishing. Home: 7202 Dean Rd Indianapolis IN 46240-3628

MACDOUGALL, ROBERT HUGH, oncologist; b. Dundee, Scotland, Aug. 9, 1949; s. John David MacDougall and Isabella Williamson Craig; m. Moira Jean Gray, July 21, 1977; children: John, Elsie, Ellen. MBChB, U. of St. Andrews, Scotland, 1972; DMRT, U. Edinburgh, Scotland, 1979. Cons. Tayside Health Bd., Dundee, Lothian Health Bd., Edinburgh; clin. dir. Western Gen. Hosp., Edinburg, 1991—99; prof. and dean medicine U. St. Andrews, 2002—. Hon. cons., clin. oncologist Edinburgh Cancer Ctr., Lothian U. Hosps., 1986—. Author (contbg): (book) Oxford Text Book of Palliative Medicine, 1997. Fellow: Royal Coll Surgeons Edinburgh, Royal Coll Radiologists London, Royal Coll Physicians Edinburgh; mem.: New Club Edinburgh. Office: University St Andrews Fife Medicine Sch KY16 9TS Saint Andrews Scotland

MACE, JOHN WELDON, pediatrician; b. Buena Vista, Va., July 9, 1938; s. John Henry and Gladys Elizabeth (Edwards) M.; m. Janice Mace, Jan. 28, 1962; children: Karin E., John E., James E. BA, Columbia Union Coll., 1960; MD, Loma Linda U., 1964. Diplomate: Am. Bd. Pediatrics, Sub-bd. Pediatric Endocrinology. Intern U.S. Naval Hosp., San Diego, 1964-65, resident in pediatrics, 1966-68; fellow in endocrinology and metabolism U. Colo., 1970-72; asst. prof. pediatrics Loma Linda (Calif.) U. Med. Ctr., 1972-75, prof., chmn. dept., 1975—2003. Med. dir. Loma Linda U. Children's Hosp., 1990-92, physician-in-chief, 1992—2003. Contbr. articles to profl. jours. Treas. Found. for Med. Care San Bernandino County, 1979-80, pres., 1980-82; mem. Congl. Adv. Bd., 1984-87; pres. So. Calif. affiliate Am. Diabetes Assn., 1985-86, dir., 1987-89; chmn. adv. bd. State Calif. Children's Svcs., 1986—; bd. dirs. So. Calif. Children's Cancer Svcs., 1993-94, Loma Linda Ronald McDonald House, 1991—2003, Aetna Health Plans of Calif., 1993-95; bd. dirs. Loma Linda U. Health Care, 1995—2003, elder, at Trinity Evangelical Ch. With USN, 1962—70. Recipient Shirley N. Pettis award, 2002, Contrbn. to Medicine award, San Bernardino County Med. Soc., 2003; named Alumnist of Yr., Loma Linda U. Sch. Medicine, 1994; named one of Best Doctors in Am., 1998, America's Top Pediatricians, 2006. Mem. AAAS, N.Y. Acad. Sci., Calif. Med. Soc. (adv. panel genetic diseases State Calif., 1975—, chmn. acad. practice forum 1997—), Western Soc. Pediatric Rsch., Lawson Wilkens Pediatric Endocrine Soc., Assn. Med. Pediatric Dept. Chmn., Am. Acad. Pediatrics, Sigma Xi, Alpha Omega Alpha.

MACEDO, GUILHERME DE OLIVEIRA, dental educator; b. Aracaju, SE, May 20, 1975; Degree in Dentistry, UFS, 1998; PhD in Periodontology, USP, 2009; MMS. Prof. titular UNIT, 2010—. Home: Av Acrisio Cruz 147 ed Morea ap 702 Aracaju Sergipe 49020-210 Brazil Personal E-mail: gniacedo75@yahoo.com.br.

MACER, DARRYL RAYMUND JOHNSON, biology educator; b. Christchurch, New Zealand, July 22, 1962; s. John Owen and Eileen Rose (Johnson) M.; m. Nobuko Yasuhara, Nov. 23, 1987; 1 child, Manna Kalon. BS with honors, U. Canterbury-Lincoln Coll., Christchurch, 1983; PhD, U. Cambridge, Eng., 1987; PhD (hon.), U. Kumamoto, Japan, 2009. Sr. Rouse Ball scholar Trinity Coll., Cambridge, 1987-89; scientist Dept. Sci. Indsl. Rsch., Lincoln, New Zealand, 1990; fgn. prof. U. Tsukuba, Japan, 1990-95, assoc. prof., 1995—2005; dir. Eubios Ethics Inst., New Zealand, 1990—; regional advisor social and human scis. Asia and Pacific UNESCO, Bangkok, 2004—. Vis. prof. UN Univ., 2001—09, sr. vis. rsch. fellow., 2010—. Author: Shaping Genes, 1990, Attitudes to Genetic Engineering: Japanese and International Comparisons, 1992, Bioethics for the People by the People, 1994, Bioethics is Love of Life, 1998, A Cross Cultural Introduction to Bioethics, 2006, Moral Games for Teaching Bioethics, 2008; editor: Unesco/IUBS/Eubios Bioethics Dictionary, 2002. Recipient Cambridge Commonwealth Prince of Wales award, 1984-87. Mem. UNESCO (internat. bioethics com. 1993-98), Human Genome Orgn. (ethics com. 1995—), Internat Union Biological Sci. Bioethics (program dir. 1997-2007), Internat. Assn. Bioethics (bd. dirs. 1999-2007). Avocations: gardening, music. Office: UNESCO Bangkok 920 Sukumvit Rd 10110 Prakanong Thailand Office Phone: 66 2 391 0577. Business E-Mail: d.macer@unesco.org.

MACER, GEORGE ARMEN, JR., orthopedic hand surgeon; b. Pasadena, Calif., Oct. 17, 1948; s. George A. and Nevart Akullian M.; m. Celeste Angelle Lyons, Mar. 26, 1983; children: Christiana Marilu, Marina Lynn, Emily Sue. BA, U. So. Calif., 1971, MD, 1976. Diplomate Am. Bd. Med. Examiners; diplomate in orthop. surgery and hand surgery Am. Bd. Orthop. Surgery. Intern Meml. Hosp. Med. Ctr., Long Beach, Calif., 1976; Joseph Boyes Hand fellow, 1982; resident Orthop. Hosp./U. So. Calif., 1977-81; pvt. practice Long Beach, 1983—; vol. clin. faculty orthops. U. So. Calif., LA, 1983-89, 90—; cons. hand surgery svc. Rancho Los Amigos Hosp. Downey, 1990—. Cons. Harbor UCLA Med. Ctr., Torrance, 1983—; asst. clin. prof. U. Calif. Irvine, 2004-. Mem. AMA, Calif. Med. Assn., Los Angeles County Med. Assn., Calif. Orthop. Assn., Western Orthop. Assn., Am. Soc. for Surgery of Hand, Am. Acad. Orthop. Surgery, So. Calif. Soc. Surgery of Hand (pres. 2004-06). Republican. Avocations: boating, skiing, scuba diving, carpentry. Office: The Hand & Wrist Ctr 3918 Long Beach Blvd Ste 100 Long Beach CA 90807 Office Phone: 562-424-9000. Personal E-mail: macer4337@aol.com. Business E-Mail: george@handwristcenter.com.

MACFARLANE, PETER WILSON, medical researcher, educator; s. Robert Barton Macfarlane and Dinah Wilson; m. Irene Grace Muir, Oct. 8, 1971; children: Alan James Robert, David Peter. BSc with honors, U. Glasgow, 1964, PhD, 1970, DSc, 2000. Asst lectr. med. cardiology U. Glasgow, 1967—70, lectr. med. cardiology, 1970—74, sr. lectr. med. cardiology, 1980—84, reader med. cardiology, 1984—91, prof. med. cardiology, 1991—95, prof. electrocardiology, 1995—2010, emeritus prof., 2010—. Author: (monograph) An introduction to automated electrocardiogram analysis, 1974, 12 Lead Vectorcardiography, 1995, (book) Computer Techniques in Clinical Medicine, 1985; editor: (textbook) Comprehensive Electrocardiology, 2010. Recipient Rijlant Found. prize, Royal Acad. Medicine, Belgium, 1996—98. Fellow: Royal Soc. Edinburgh, Brit. Computer Soc., European Soc. Cardiology, Royal Coll. Physicians; mem.: Computing in Cardiology (bd. pres. 2008—), Internat. Soc. Electrocardiology (pres. 2007—09). Achievements include development of software used worldwide for analysis of electrocardiograms. Office: Univ Glasgow Section of Electrocardiology Royal Infirmary Glasgow G31 2ER Scotland Office Phone: 44 141 211 4724.

MACGINITIE, WALTER HAROLD, psychologist, educator; b. Carmel, Calif., Aug. 14, 1928; s. George Eber and Nettie Lorene (Murray) MacG.; m. Ruth Olive Kilpatrick, Sept. 2, 1950; children: Mary Catherine, Laura Anne. BA, UCLA, 1949; A.M., Stanford U., 1950; PhD, Columbia U., 1960. Tchr. Long Beach (Calif.) Unified Sch. Dist., 1950, 1955-56; mem. faculty Columbia U. Tchrs. Coll., 1959-80, prof. psychology and edn., 1970-80; Lansdowne scholar, prof. edn. U. Victoria, B.C., Canada, 1980-84. Research assoc. Lexington Sch. Deaf, N.Y.C., 1963-69; mem. sci. adv. bd. Ctr. for Study of Reading, 1977-80, chmn. 1979-80. Co-author: Gates-MacGinitie Reading Tests, 1965, 78, 89, 2000, Psychological Foundations of Education, 1968; Editor: Assessment Problems in Reading, 1972; co-editor: Verbal Behavior of the Deaf Child, 1969. Life mem. Calif. PTA. Served with USAF, 1950-54. Fellow APA, AAAS, Assn. Psychol. Sci., Nat. Conf. Rsch. on Lang. and Literacy, N.Y. Acad. Scis.; mem. Internat. Reading Assn. (pres. 1976-77, Spl. Svc. award 1981), Reading Hall of Fame (pres. 1989-90). Home and Office: PO Box 1789 Friday Harbor WA 98250-1789 *

MACGREGOR, GRAHAM ALEXANDER, medical educator, physician, researcher; b. St. Albans, Eng., Apr. 1, 1941; s. Alexander Brittan and Sybil Philip (Hawkey) MacG.; m. Christiane Bourquin, Feb. 11, 1968; children: Annabelle, Vanessa, Christopher. Student, Marlborough Coll., Wiltshire, Eng., 1955-59; BA, MA, Cambridge U., 1964; MB, BChir, Middlesex Hosp., London, 1967. House physician Middlesex Hosp. and Hammersmith Hosp., London, 1967-69; lectr. St. Thomas' Hosp., London, 1970-73; sr. registrar Charing Cross Hosp., London, 1973-79, sr. lectr., 1979-89; prof., cardiovasc. medicine St. George's Hosp., London, 1989—2010, Barts and London, 2010—. Author: Hypertension in Practice, 1987, 3d edit., 1999, Low Salt Diet Book, 1989, 2d edit., 1992, Salt, Diet and Health, 1998; contbr. sci. papers to profl. publs. Fellow Royal Coll. Physicians; mem. Brit. Hypertension Soc. (pres.), Internat. Soc. Hypertension, Assn. Physicians, Am. Soc. Hypertension. Office: Wolfson Inst Preventive Medicine Charterhouse Square London EC1M 6BQ England Office Phone: (44) 207 882 6217. Business E-Mail: g.macgregor@qmul.ac.uk.

MACGREGOR, JAMES THOMAS, toxicologist, consultant; b. NYC, Jan. 14, 1944; s. James and Phyllis (Bowman) MacG.; m. Judith Anne Anello, July 12, 1969; 1 child, Jennifer Lee. BS in Chemistry, Union Coll., Schenectady, NY, 1965; PhD in Toxicology, U. Rochester, 1971. Diplomate Am. Bd. Toxicology, 1980—. Postdoctoral fellow U. Calif., San Francisco, 1970-72; dir. food safety rsch. USDA, Berkeley, Calif., 1972-88; assoc. prof. U. Calif., Berkeley, 1978-88; pres. Toxicology Consulting Svcs., Danville, Calif., 1988-90; dir. toxicology and metabolism lab. SRI Internat., Menlo Park, Calif., 1990-97; dir. Office of Testing and Rsch. FDA Ctr. for Drug Evaluation and Rsch., Rockville, Md., 1997-2001; dep. dir. Washington ops. FDA Nat. Ctr. for Toxicological Rsch., Rockville, Md., 2001—04; prin. Toxicology Consulting Svcs., Arnold, Md., 2004—. Mem. numerous nat. and internat. profl. coms. and working groups. Mem. editl. bd.: Environ. Molecular Mutagenesis, N.Y.C., 1986-88, Mutation Res., Amsterdam, 1989-91, 97-2006, Mutagenesis, Oxford, 1989-93. Recipient Alexander Hollaender award, 1995, Genetic Toxicology Assn. Excellence in Sci. award, 2010. Mem. Assn. Govt. Toxicologists (pres. 2003-04), Soc. Toxicology (v.p. regulatory and safety evaluation splty. sect. 2004-06, pres. 2006-07), Environ. Mutagen Soc. (treas. 1986-89, pres. 1992-93), Genetic Environ. Toxicology Assn. No. Calif. (pres. 1982), Genetic Toxicology Assn., Am. Assn. Advancement Sci. Personal E-mail: jtmacgregor@earthlink.net.

MACGREGOR, JENNIFER L., dermatologist, educator; Grad. with honors, Georgetown U. Sch. of Medicine. Diplomate Am. Bd. Dermatology. Resident dermatology Columbia Univ. Med. Ctr., NY; fellow laser, cosmetic, and dermatologic surgery Boston; asst. prof. dermatology Georgetown Univ. Hosp., dir. laser, surg. and cosmetic dermatology ctr. Reviewer (journals) Dermatologic Surgery. Mem.: AMA, Women's Dermatologic Soc., Am. Soc. for Laser Medicine and Surgery, Am. Soc. for Dermatologic Surgery, Am. Acad. of Dermatology, Alpha Omega Alpha nat. med. honor soc. Office: Georgetown University Hospital 3800 Reservoir Rd NW Washington DC 20007 Office Phone: 202 444 2000.

MACHADO, FELIPE SALLES NEVES, psychiatrist; b. Petropolis, May 28, 1982; Degree, Fameca, Michel, Fameca, Michel, 2007; attending, Iamspe-Hspe, 2011. Physician, psychiatry IAMSPE-HSPE, 2009—. Office: Avenida Ibirapuera 981 São Paulo Brazil Business E-Mail: felipemac@msn.com.

MACHADO, MARCIA M. TAVARES, nursing educator, researcher; b. Ceara, Brazil, Jan. 3, 1963; Degree in Nursing, U. Fed. Ceara, 1985. Prof., DRA U. Fed. Ceara, 1997—; postdoc. Harvard Sch. Pub. Health, 2011. Contbr. articles to profl. jours. Avocations: reading, writing. Office: Professor Costa Mendes 1609 5° Andar Fortaleza Ceara 60430120 Brazil Business E-Mail: marciamachado@ufc.br.

MACHADO, MARIA APARECIDA, speech language pathologist, educator; b. Bebedouro, São Paulo, Bebedouro, Dec. 21, 1955; U., Pontifícia U. Católica do Paraná, 1990; PhD, U. de São Paulo, 2003—03. Prof. Brazilian Inst., 2004—06; specialist, dept Otolaringology Fed Univ Parana, 2004—05; specialist public health Prefeitura Mcpl. de Araucária, 1990—99; adj. prof. Pontifícia U. Católica do Paraná, 1996—2003; prof. U. São Paulo, 2006. Mem.: Ctr. Studies and Law Enforcement Protection for Women, Internat. Assn. Logopedics and Phoniatrics, Graduation Health Public Brazilian Assn., Speech Brazilian Soc. Avocations: travel, skydiving, movies. Home: Caetano Sampieri 1-25 ap93 São Paulo Bauru 17012 460 Brazil Home Phone: 55 (14) 8135 5202. Home Fax: 55 (14) 3234 34 73. Business E-Mail: cidamachado@usp.br.

MACHADO, WELLINGTON MONTEIRO, medical educator; b. Teresina, Brazil, May 23, 1948; MD, Fed. U. Rio de Janeiro, 1972; postdoc., U. Sheffield, 1998. Asst. prof. medicine State U. São Paulo, 1989, Coord. lab. gastroenteroloy U. Hosp. Botucatu-Unesp, 2003. Mem.: Functional Brain-Gut Rsch. Group, Brazilian Fedn. Gastroenterology. Avocations: music, history, movies. Home: Rua Matheus Damato 118 Botucatu São Paulo 18610-350 Brazil Home Fax: 55 14 38822238. Business E-Mail: wmachado@fmb.unesp.br.

MACHER, JEAN-PAUL, psychiatrist, educator, foundation administrator; b. Basel, Switzerland, Dec. 15, 1946; m. Christiane Macher. MD, U.Paris Necker Med. Sch., 1974. Cert. doctor Paris, 1974, psychiatrist Paris, 1977. Tchr., asst. Faculté des Saints-Pères, Lab. Pr. André Delmas, Paris, 1970—83; tchr. U. Paris Necker Med. Sch., France, 1976—83; head dept. Psychiat. Hosp., Rouffach, France, 1981—2006; founder Clin. Data Mgmt., MT3D. Mem. bd. dirs. Assn. Argile, 1983—2002; co-founder, sci. dir. Found. Applied Neurosci. Rsch. Psychiatry Hosp. Ctr., Rouffach, 1986—2005; founder Clin. Data Mgmt., MT3D: Mgmt. Therapeutic Drug Discovery; editor-in-chief Dialogues Clin. Neurosci., 1995—. Pres. Found. Mental Health and Neurosciences, Geneve, Switzerland, 1996—2008; pres. sci. adv. bd. Clin Data Mgmt. and MT3D. Mem.: WHO, WPA (assoc.; chair sect. rsch. methods in psychiatry). Achievements include experience as main investigator in psychopharmacological studies; development of a hospital unit for psychophysiological exploration; a unit for the study of normal and abnormal aging of the brain; activities in phase 0,I,II,III,IV-microdosing and others pharmacological studies. Office: BP 30 68250 Rouffach France Personal E-mail: jpm@jpmacher.fr.

MACHIDA, CURTIS A., research molecular neurobiologist, molecular virologist, oral biologist, educator; b. San Francisco, Apr. 1, 1954; AB, U. Calif., Berkeley, 1976; PhD, Oreg. Health Scis. U., 1982. Postdoctoral scientist Oreg. Health Scis. U., Portland, 1982-88; asst. sci. div. neurosci. Oreg. Nat. Primate Rsch. Ctr., Beaverton, 1988-95, assoc. scie. divsn. neurosci., 1995—2002; assoc. rsch. prof. integrative biosciences Sch. Dentistry Oreg. Health Scis. U., Portland, 2002—05, rsch. prof. integrative bioscis., 2005—07, tenured prof. integrative biosci., 2008—, adj. prof. pediat. dentistry, 2010. Rsch. asst. prof. biochemistry and molecular biology Oreg. Health Sci. U., 1989-95, mem. faculty neurosci. and molecular and cell biology grad. programs, 1989—, adj. assoc. prof. biochemistry and molecular biology, 1995—; mem. grad. faculty biochemistry and biophysics Oreg. State U., Corvallis, 1997-01; mem. Institutional Ethics oversight com., Institutional Biosafety com., faculty bylaws com., preclin. curriculum com.; mem. Dental Sch. Rsch. Task Force, promotion & tenure com. mem.; mem. biotech. program adv. com. Portland C.C. Editor Adrenergic Receptor Protocols, 1997-99, Viral Vectors for Gene Therapy: Methods and Protocols, 2000-03; mem. editl. bd. Molecular Biotechnology, Frontiers in Biosci., Internat. Jour. Biomed. Sci., World Medicine; ad-hoc reviewer Endocrinology, Molecular Pharmacology, Biochimica et Biophysica Acta, Am. Jour. Physiology, Lab. Animal Sci., NSF, BioTechs., Brain Rsch.; contbr. articles, revs., and abstracts to profl. jours. and internat. confs. Recipient Leukemia Assn. award, 1981, Tartar award Med. Rsch. Found. Oreg., 1980; NIH fellow, 1980-82, 85-87, grantee, 1989, 95, 98, 2002, 05; rsch. grantee, Am. Assn. Endodontists Found, Med. Rsch. Found. Oreg., Wills Found., Nat. Parkinson Found., Collins Med. Trust, Murdock Charitable Trust and Rsch. Corp., Nat. Am. Heart Assn. Mem. AAAS, Am. Soc. Biochemistry and Molecular Biology, Am. Soc. Microbiology, Soc. Neurosci., Am. Heart Assn. (basic scis. coun., established investigator 1994-99), Am. Soc. Gene Therapy, U.S.-Israel Binational Sci. Found. (reviewer). Achievements include patent on dopamine receptor and genes; cloning of several adrenergic receptor genes and simian retroviral infectious genomes; depositor, nucleotide sequence to EMBL and GenBank databases, and clones to American Type Culture Collection. Office: Oreg Health Sci U Sch Dentistry Dept Integrative Biosciences 611 SW Campus Dr Portland OR 97239-3097 E-mail: machidac@ohsu.edu.

MACHOVEC, FRANK J., psychologist; b. Balt., May 16, 1930; s. James Joseph and Theresa Anna MacH.; m. Evelyn Mary Stultz, May 5, 1951; 1 child, Frank. BA, U. Md., 1964; MA, Loyola U., Balt., 1965; PhD, Fielding Inst., 1979. Diplomate Am. Bd. Psychol. Hypnosis, Am. Bd. Med. Psychotherapy; lic. clin. psychologist. Psychologist Victoria Hosp., Winnipeg, Man., Canada, 1975—76, Alta. Mental Health, Lethbridge, Canada, 1976—78, Alaska Psychol. Inst., Anchorage, 1978—80, State Hosp. South, Blackfoot, Idaho, 1979-81; dir. psychol. svcs. South Va. Mental Health Inst., Danville, 1981-86; dir. quality assurance Va. Dept. Mental Health, 1986-90; supr. psychology Va. Juvenile Corrections, 1991-95, ret., 1995. Prof. Piedmont Va. Com. Coll.; instr. Jefferson Inst. Author: Hypnosis Complications, 1986, Expert Witness Survival Manual, 1987, Humor Theories, History, 1988, Interview and Interrogation, 1989, Cults and Personality, 1989, Becoming Street Smart, 1994, Spiritual Intelligence, 2002, Light from the East, 2005, Private Investigative and Security Science, 2006, Divine Spark, 2007, Buddha, Tao, Zen, 2007, Lead and Manage, 2007, Whats Funny, Psychology of Humor, 2008, Cults and Terrorism, Zen Classics, 2009. With USMC, 1950—52. Avocations: writing, travel, teaching.

MACIAS, MIGUEL ANGEL, neurologist, researcher; b. Inglewood, Calif., Mar. 2, 1959; s. Miguel Macias and Victoria Islas; m. Alejandra Contreras, Nov. 21, 1987; children: Angela Monserrat, Sofia Alejandra, Daniela Isadora. MS, U. Guadalajara, 1995, PhD, 1997. Bd. Certificate Consejo Mexicano de Neurología, 2000. Resident in clin. neurology Inst. Mexicano Seguro Social, Guadalajara, Jalisco, Mexico, 1986—89, head neurology dept., 1997—; titular prof. U. Guadalajara, 2000—. Dir. Multiple Sclerosis Mexican Study Group, Guadalajara, 2000—02. Contbr. articles to profl. jours. Recipient Alzheimer's Disease award, Mexican Alzheimer Assn., 2003. Mem.: Mexican Acad. Neurology (corr.). Achievements include founding a multiple sclerosis Mexican study group; co-founding a Latin American committe for research and treatment of multiple sclerosis. Avocations: music, travel. Home: Millet 70 La Estancia Jalisco Zapopan 45030 Mexico Office: Dept Neurociencias CUCS UdeG Sierra Mojada 950 Jalisco Guadalajara 44340 Mexico Personal E-mail: miguelangelmacias@hotmail.com.

MACIEIRA-COELHO, ALVARO D'ARAUJO, retired medical educator, researcher; b. Lisbon, Portugal, May 26, 1932; arrived in France, 1967; s. Eduardo Carneiro and Matilde Dias (D'Araujo) Macieira-C.; m. Ana Maria Vieira Da Cruz, Aug. 4, 1962; children: Goncalo, Lourenco, Alexandre, Carlota. MD, U. Lisbon, 1958, PhD, U. Uppsala, Sweden, 1967; D Honoris Causa (hon.), U. Linköping, Sweden, 1991. Rsch. assoc. Wistar Inst., Phila., 1961-64, U. Uppsala, 1965-67; head dept. Inst. Cancerology, Villejuif, France, 1968-86; rsch. dir. Nat. Inst. Health, Versailles, France, 1973-97; ret., 1997. Vis. prof. Med. Sch. U. Linköping, 1987-89; mem. cons. coun. U. Paris, 1970-71; mem. nat. coun. CNRS, France, 1976-79, mem. coun. European Tissue Culture Soc., 1984-88; internat. Johananoff vis. prof. Inst. Mario Negri, Milan, Italy, 1982. Author: Biology of Cell Aging, 1988; editor, author: Cancer and Aging, 1990, Molecular Basis of Aging, 1995, Progress in Molecular and Subcellular Biology Growth Inhibitors, 1998, Progress in Molecular and Subcellular Biology, Cell Immortalization, 1999, Progress in Molecular and Subcellular Biology, Signaling Through the Cell Matrix, 2000, Progress in Molecular and Subcellular Biology, Biology of Aging, 2003, Progress in Molecular and Subcellular Biology Developmental Biology of Neoplastic Growth, 2005, Progress in Molecular and Subcellular Biology, Asymmetric Cell Division, 2007; contbr. more than 150 articles to profl. jours. Recipient Fritz-Verzar prize U. Vienna, 1988, Seeds Sci. prize, Career award, Portugal Avocation: sailing. Home: 73 Bis Rue du Marechal Foch 78000 Versailles France Personal E-mail: macieiracoelho@orange.fr.

MACIEJEWSKI, MATTHEW LEONARD, education educator, researcher; b. Rochester, NY, June 26, 1969; s. Norman Thomas and Barbara Theresa Maciejewski; m. Donna Elaine Cook, Oct. 12, 2002. PhD, U. Minn., Mpls., 1998. Rschr. VA Puget Sound Health Care Sys., Seattle, 1998—2006; asst. prof. U. Wash., Seattle, 1998—2005, assoc. prof., 2005—06; rschr. Durham VA Med. Ctr., NC, 2006—; assoc. prof. U. NC, Chapel Hill, 2006—08, Duke U. Med. Ctr., 2007—. Contbr. scientific papers to profl. jour. Fellow AHCPR Doctoral Thesis Grant, Agy. for Health Care Policy and Rsch., 1996-1998. Mem.: Internat. Health Econ. Assn., Acad. Health. Avocations: soccer, travel, cooking. Office: HSRD Durham Med Ctr Durham NC 27705 also: Ctr for Health Svcs Rsch in Primary Care Durham VA Med Ctr 508 Fulton St Durham NC 27705

MACINA, LUCY, geriatrician; Attended, Loyola U., 1978, Roger Williams Gen Hosp. Diplomate Am. Bd. of Internal Medicine, Am. Bd. of Internal Medicine-geriatric medicine. With Winthrop Univ. Hosp.; resident VA Hosp., 1979—80, Loyola Univ. Stritch Sch. Medicine, Providence, 1980—82; fellow Roger Williams Hosp. Mem.: Met. Area Geriat. Soc., Am. Geriat. Soc., Am. Coll. of Physicians. Office: Winthrop University Hospital 259 1st St Mineola NY 11501 Office Phone: 516-663-0333.

MACINTYRE, NEIL ROSS, JR., medical educator; b. San Diego, Nov. 21, 1946; s. Neil Ross and Rebecca (Torrey) MacI.; m. Suzanne Artusio, June 20, 1970; children: Catherine, Neil III, Douglas, Charles, Elizabeth, Stephen. BS cum laude, U. San Francisco, 1968; MD, Cornell U., 1972. Diplomate Am. Bd. Internal Medicine, Pulmonary Disease, Critical Care Medicine; lic. physician, NC. Intern, jr. resident, sr. resident medicine Cornell U. Med. Ctr., N.Y. Hosp., NYC, 1972-75; fellow pulmonary diseases U. Calif., San Francisco, 1978-81; med. dir. respiratory care svcs., pulmonary function lab. Duke U. Med. Ctr., Durham, N.C., 1981—, asst. prof. medicine, 1981-89, assoc. prof., 1989-95, prof., 1995—. Editor:

Complications of Mechanical Ventilation, 1992, Comprehensive Respiratory Care, 1994, Respiratory Care Principles and Practice, 2002; editorial bd. Respiratory Care, 1986—, chmn., 1990-92, edtl. bd. chief, 2005-; assoc. editor, 2000-, co-editor in chief Problems in Respiratory Care, 1988-91; med. editor Arkos, The Jour. of Mechanical Ventilation, 1989; editorial bd. Critical Care Medicine, 1992—, sci. editor, 1997-, editor Mechanical Veatilation Elsevier, Ist Edit, 2001, 2nd, 2009; contbr. articles to profl. jours., chpts. to books. Trustee Am. Respiratory Care Found., 1988—, vice chmn., 1990—. With USN, 1975-78. Recipient Forrest Bird award, 2002, Jimmy Young award, 2008. Fellow Am. Coll. Chest Physicians; mem. Am. Thoracic Soc. (pres. NC chpt. 1989, lab. stds. com. 1992—), Am. Assn. Respiratory Care (chmn. bd. med. advisors 1990), Am. Lung Assn. (pres. Rsch. Triangle region 1988), Am. Heart Assn. (chmn. emergency cardiac care com. 1989-90, Silver Svc. medal 1978), Soc. Critical Care Medicine, Nat. Assn. Med. Dirs. Respiratory Care (pres. 1991-93), NC Soc. Respiratory Care (hon.), Alpha Omega Alpha. Office: Duke U Med Ctr PO Box 3911 Durham NC 27710-0001

MACKALL, CRYSTAL L., medical researcher; BS/MD, Northeastern Ohio Universities Coll. Medicine, 1984. Medicine/pediatrics resident Northeastern Ohio U. Coll. Medicine, Akron, Ohio, 1984—88; clin. assoc. Pediatric Oncology Br., Ctr. Cancer Rsch., Nat. Cancer Inst., NIH, 1989—92, rschr., 1996—, acting chief, 2005—08, chief Pediatrics Oncology Br., head Immunology Sect., 2008—; postdoctoral sci. training Exptl. Immunology Br. Nat. Cancer Inst., 1990—96. Office: Nat Cancer Inst Bldg 10-CRC, Rm 1W-3750 10 Center Dr, MSC 1104 Bethesda MD 20892-1104 Office Phone: 301-402-5940. Office Fax: 301-451-7052. Business E-Mail: cm35c@nih.gov. *

MACKAY, JAMES ROBERT (JIM MACKAY), state legislator, social worker; b. Medford, Mass., May 8, 1930; s. James Alexander and Julia (MacNaught) MacK. BA, Tufts U., 1952, MA, 1954; MSW, Boston U., 1958; PhD, Union Inst., 1987. Social worker Peter Bent Brigham Hosp., Boston, 1958-60; dir. alcoholism NH Dept. Health & Welfare, Concord, 1960-63; dir. cmty. mental health State of NH, Concord, 1963-64; pvt. practice psychotherapy Concord, 1964-97; exec. dir. Merrimack Valley Assistance Program, Concord, 2002; adj. faculty U. N.H., Durham, 1995—2001; mem. Merrimack Dist. 24 NH House of Reps., 2001—02, mem. Merrimack Dist. 39, 2002—04, mem. Merrimack Dist. 11, 2004—08, 2011—. Mem. bd. examiners mental health practice State of N.H., 1995-97; city councilman, City of Concord, 1980-92, mayor, 1987-88, 90-91; sr. lectr. psychotherapy Franklin Pierce Law Center, Concord, 1978; lectr. U. Conn. Grad. Sch. Social Work, 1981-88; adv. com. City of Concord Airport, 1992—. Contbr. articles on alcoholism, addiction, and juvenile delinquency to profl. jours. Chmn. N.H. Coun. Aging, 1969-83; chmn. Merrimack Valley AIDS Program, 2000-2002, treas., 2003-; pres. N.H. Social Welfare Coun.; chmn. N.H. del. to White House Conf. Aging, 1974, 80; chmn. N.H. Com. Older Am. Act, 1968-69; mem. Concord City Coun., 1980-91; chmn. Concord Pub. Transp. Adv. Bd., 1982-86; del. N.H. Rep. Conv., 1982; del. N.H. Constl. Conv., 1984; chmn. City of Concord Rep. Com.; mem. exec. com. State Rep. Com.; pres. Concord Outright Inc., 2000-02; commr. Christa McAuliffe Planetarium, 2001-; chmn. N.H. Mental Health Commn., 2006-08. Recipient Ann. award N.H. Social Welfare Coun., 1970, Vaughn award Activities in Aging, N.H., 1974; named Social Worker of Yr., State of N.H., 1997, Legislator of the Yr., NASW, 2003. Mem. NASW (pres. N.H. chpt. 1995-97), AAUP, Nat. League Cities (human devel. policy com. 1986). Democrat. Office: NH House of Representatives 139 N State St Concord NH 03301-6414 Office Phone: 603-224-0623. Business E-Mail: james.mackay@mygait.com.

MACKAY, PATRICIA MCINTOSH, retired psychotherapist; b. San Francisco, Sept. 12, 1922; d. William Carroll and Louise Edgerton (Keen) McIntosh; m. Alden Thorndike Mackay, Dec. 15, 1945 (dec. June 2002); children: Patricia Louise, James McIntosh, Donald Sage; m. Richard John Rihn, July 26, 2003. AB in Psychology, U. Calif., Berkeley, 1944, elem. tchg. credential, 1951; MA in Psychology, John F. Kennedy U., Orinda, Calif., 1979; PhD in Nutrition, Donsbach U., Huntington Beach, Calif., 1981. Cert. marriage, family and child counselor. Elem. tchr. Mt. Diablo Unified Sch. Dist., Concord, Calif., 1950-60; exec. supr. No. Calif. Welcome Wagon Internat., 1960-67; wedding cons. Mackay Creative Svcs., Walnut Creek, Calif., 1969-70; co-owner Courtesy Calls, Greeters and Concord Welcoming Svcs., Walnut Creek, 1971-94; marriage, family and child counselor, nutrition cons., Walnut Creek, 1979—2011. Coord. Alameda and Contra Costa County chpts. Parents United Internat., 1985—, pres. region 2, bd. dirs., 1992; bd. dirs. New Directions Counseling Ctr., Inc., 1975-81, founder, pres. aux., 1977-79. Bd. dirs. Ministry in Marketplace, Inc.; founder, dir. Turning Point Counseling; active Walnut Creek Presbyn. Ch.; bd. dirs., counseling dir. Shepherd's Gate, shelter for homeless women and children, 1985-92, Contra Costa County Child Care Coun., 1993-95. Recipient award New Directions Counseling Ctr., 1978, yearly awards Neo-Life Co. Am. Prestige Club, 1977-856, Cmty. Svc. award Child Abuse Prevention Coun., 1990, 92, 94. Mem. AAUW, Am. Assn. Marriage and Family Therapists, U. Calif.-Berkeley Alunni Assn. (sec. 1979-94), Walnut Creek C. of C., Prytanean Alumnae, Soroptimists (bd. dirs. Walnut Creek 1976, 86), Delta Gamma. Republican. Home: 1101 Scots Ln Walnut Creek CA 94596-5432 Home Phone: 925-933-3126.

MACKAY, WILLIAM JAMES, geneticist, educator; s. Bernard M. and Shirley M. Mackay; m. Annette Marie DelCimmuto, May 29, 1982; 1 child, Caroline Marion. PhD, Carnegie-Mellon U., 1984. Asst. prof. Angelo State U., San Angelo, Tex., 1996—99; assoc. prof. Edinboro U. Pa., 1999—. Mem.: Soc. Toxicology (treas. Allegheny-Erie chpt. 2000—), Tex. Acad. Sci. Home: 12800 Kline Rd Edinboro PA 16412-1733

MACKENZIE, DONALD MURRAY, health facility administrator; b. Toronto, Ont., Can., June 5, 1947; s. Donald Alexander and June Cameron MacKenzie; m. Marilyn Adele McNaughton, Jan. 3, 1970; children: Jennifer, Katherine, Kenneth. BA in Econs., U. Toronto, 1968, MA in Polit. Sci., 1970, D Health Adminstr., 1974. Exec. asst. Mt. Sinai Hosp., Toronto, 1974-76, successively asst. exec. dir., assoc. exec. dir., v.p., 1974-89; pres. North York Gen. Hosp., Toronto, 1989—2002; asst. prof. U. Toronto, 1989—; internat. healthcare cons., 2002—. Chair Cardiac Care Network Ont., 2001-2002; founding dir. OH Africa, The Seeing Eye, North York Family Health Team. Editor: History of Canadian Hospitals, 1972; contbr. articles to profl. jours. Bd. dirs. Cancer Care Ont., 1989-99. Mem. Can. Coll. Health Svc. Execs. (cert., various coms.), Can. Cancer Soc. (hon. life, pres. Ont. div. 1989-91, award of merit 1988), Ont. Hosp. Assn. (chmn. 1999-2000), York Club. Anglican. Avocations: golf, tennis, canoe tripping. Personal E-mail: mmackenzie55@hotmail.com.

MACKENZIE, KENNETH, otolaryngologist; b. Greenock, Scotland, Nov. 26, 1954; s. Alasdair Macrae and Jenny MacKenzie; m. Karin Leslie Gane, Aug. 6, 1983; children: Katherine, Gillian, Kenneth, Finlay. MBChB, Dundee, Scotland, 1978. Pre-registration ho. officer medicine and surgery, Dundee, 1978—79; anatomy lectr. U. Glasgow, 1979—80; sr. ho. officer pediatric surgery Royal Hosp. Sick Children, 1979—80; sr. ho. officer ENT Hosp., Newcastle, 1980—81, registrar Glasgow, 1981, Glasgow Royal Infirmary, Glasgow, 1981—83; sr. registrar Glasgow Hosps., Glasgow, 1983—89; cons. otorhinolaryngologist, head and neck surgeon Glasgow Royal Infirmary, Scotland, 1989—. Author: Case Presentations in Otolaryngology, 1992. Fellow: Royal Coll. Surgeons of Edinburgh. Office: Glassgow Royal Infirmary 16-18 Alexandra Parade G31 2ER Scotland Office Phone: 0141 211 0484.

MACKENZIE, RICHARD G., internist, educator; MD, McGill U., Montreal, 1966. Intern Royal Victoria Hosp., Montreal, resident internal medicine, 1966—69; assoc. prof. pediat. and medicine Univ. of Southern Calif.; fellow adolescent medicine Chidren's Hosp. LA, 1969—70, dir. adolescent medicine program, physician. Pres. Soc. for Adolescent Medicine, LA Pediatric Society. Mem.: Bd. of the Internat. Ctr. for Child, Youth and Family Studies, Internat. Assn. of Adolescent Medicine, Soc. of Adolescent Medicine, Am. Acad. of Pediat. Office: Children's Hospital Los Angeles 5000 Sunset Blvd Fl 4 Los Angeles CA 90027-5861 Office Phone: 323-361-2153. Office Fax: 323-361-2153. E-mail: rmackenzie@chla.usc.edu.

MACKILL, DAVID JAMES, geneticist; b. San Diego, Mar. 26, 1954; s. James Richard and Geraldine Ann (Busch) M.; m. Alita Obusan, June 11, 1983. BS in Plant Sci., U. Calif., Davis, 1976, MS in Agronomy, 1978, PhD in Genetics, 1981. Rsch. fellow Internat. Rice Rsch. Inst., Los Baños, Philippines, 1978-81, plant breeder, 1982—91, head plant breeding, genetics and biotechnology, 2001—, program leader, Genetic Resources Conservation, Evaluation and Gene Discovery, 2001—; postdoctoral fellow Internat. Crops Rsch. Inst. for Semi Arid Tropics, India, 1981—82; rsch. geneticist USDA-Agrl. Rsch. Svc., 1991—2001; adj. prof. dept. agronomy range sci. U. Calif., Davis, 1991—2001. Vis. rsch. fellow Regional Rice Rsch. Sta., Punjab Agrl. U., Kapurthala, India, 1980; vis. asst. prof. U. Philippines at Los Baños, 1982—. Contbr. articles to profl. jours., chapters to books; editor: Theoretical and Applied Genetics; assoc. editor: Crop Sci. Recipient USDA Nat. Rsch. Initiative Discovery award for work on submergence tolerant rice, 2008. Fellow Crop Sci. Soc. Am.; mem. Am. Soc. Agronomy, AAAS, Soc. for Advancement of Breeding Rsch. in Asia and Oceania (sec.-gen.), Sigma Xi. Baha'I. Achievements include with colleagues genetically engineering rice for resistance to diseases and flooding. Office: Internat Rice Rsch Inst 7777 Dapo Box 1444 Metro Manila National Capital Region Philippines E-mail: D.Mackill@cgiar.org.

MACKINNON, RODERICK, neuroscientist, educator; b. Burlington, Mass., Feb. 19, 1956; married. BA, Brandeis U., Waltham, Mass., 1978; MD, Tufts U., Medford, Mass., 1982, PhD (hon.), 2002. Postdoc. fellow Beth Israel Hosp., Harvard U., Boston, 1985—86, Brandeis U., 1986—89; asst. prof. to prof. dept. neurobiology Harvard Med. Sch., 1989—96; John D. Rockefeller Jr. prof. Rockefeller U., NYC, 1996—. Investigator Howard Hughes Med. Inst., Chevy Chase, Md., 1997—. Recipient Young Investigator award, Biophysical Soc., 1995, Newcomb Cleveland prize, AAAS, 1998, Albert Lasker award for basic med. rsch., 1999, Lewis S. Rosentiel award for disting. work in basic med. sci., 2000, Gairdner Found. Internat. award, 2001, Nobel prize for chemistry, 2003, Louisa Gross Horwitz prize, Columbia U., 2003. Mem.: NAS, Alpha Omega Med. Honor Soc. Avocation: kayaking. Office: Rockefeller U Lab Molecular Neurobiology & Biophysics 1230 York Ave New York NY 10065 also: Howard Hughes Med Inst 4000 Jones Bridge Rd Chevy Chase MD 20815-6789 Office Phone: 212-327-7288. Business E-Mail: Roderick.MacKinnon@rockefeller.edu. *

MACKINNON, SUSAN, plastic surgeon; b. Can., Jan. 31, 1950; married; 4 children. MD, Queen's U., Kingston, Can., 1975. Cert. in plastic surgery. Surgery residency Queen's U., 1978; surgery residency divsn. plastic surgery U. Toronto, 1980, neurosurgery fellowship dept. surgery, 1981; hand surgery fellowship Union Meml. Hosp., Balt., 1982; Shoenberg prof., surgery chief divsn. plastic and reconstructive surgery Wash. U. Sch. Medicine. Surgeon Barnes-Jewish Hosp., St. Louis Children's Hosp.; with Barnes-Jewish West County Hosp. Contbr. chapters to books, articles to profl. jours. Recipient Medal award in surgery, Royal Coll. Physicians and Surgeons Can., 1988, Outstanding Clinician award, Wash. U. Sch. Medicine III Humanity Program; named a Top Dr., Wash. U.; named to, Best Doctors in America, 2002, 2005, 2006. Mem.: Inst. Medicine, Am. Assn. Plastic Surgeons (treas. 2003—05, v.p. 2005, pres. 2007—, awards com. chair), Am. Assn. Hand Surgery (v.p. 2003, pres.-elect 2004, pres. 2005). Achievements include completing the first donor nerve allotransplant, a procedure that can restore function to severely injured limbs that previously were considered irreparable; research in peripheral nerve surgery in hand/upper extremity and lower extremity; carpal tunnel syndrome; tarsal tunnel syndrome; thoracic outlet syndrome; nerve transplant; facial palsy. Office: Wash U Sch Medicine 600 S Euclid Ave Campus Box 8238 Saint Louis MO 63110 also: Plastic and Reconstructive Surgery Ctr Ctr for Advance Medicine 4921 Parkview Pl Ste G Fl 6 Saint Louis MO 63110 Office Phone: 314-362-4586. Office Fax: 314-362-4536.

MACKLIN, MARTIN RODBELL, psychiatrist; b. Raleigh, NC, Aug. 27, 1934; s. Albert A. and Mitzi (Robdell) M.; m. Ruth Chimacoff (div.); children: Meryl, Shelley; m. Anne Elizabeth Warren, May 25; children: Alicia, Aaron. BME, Cornell U., 1957, M in Indsl. Engring., 1958; PhD in Biomed. Engring., Case Western Res. U., 1967, MD, 1977. Diplomate Am. Bd. Psychiatry and Neurology; cert. in alcoholism and other drug dependencies Am. Soc. Addiction Medicine. Investigator Am. Heart Assn., Cleve., 1969-74; vis. fellow U. Sussex, Brighton, England, 1970; assoc. prof. biomed. engring. Case Western Res. U., 1972-81, asst. prof. psychiatry, 1981—; clin. dir. Horizon Ctr. Hosp., Warrensville Township, Ohio, 1981-83; adminstrv. dir. Riverview Psychiat. Assocs., 1983-94; med. dir. Woodside Hosp., 1989-94; v.p. med. affairs UHHS Geauga Regional Hosp., Chardon, Ohio, 1994—2007; physician surveyor The Joint Commn., 2007—. Psychiat. cons. Glenbeigh Hosp., Ohio and Fla.; chair quality intervention panel Ohio State Med. Bd.; cons. in field. Contbr. articles to profl. jours; patentee in field. NIH rsch. grantee Kellogg Found., Cleve., 1967-81; Laughlin fellow Am. Coll. Psychiatry, 1980. Mem. Am. Psychiat. Assn., Am. Coll. Physician Execs., Cleve. Psychiat. Soc., AMA. Avocations: woodworking, gardening. Home: 843 Haywood Dr South Euclid OH 44121 Home Phone: 216-691-5950. E-mail: martin.macklin@sbcglobal.net.

MACKLIN, RUTH, bioethics educator; b. Newark, Mar. 27, 1938; d. Hyman and Frieda (Yaruss) Chimacoff; m. Martin Macklin, Sept. 1, 1957 (div. June 1969); children: Meryl, Shelley Macklin Taylor. BA with distinction, Cornell U., 1958; MA in Philosophy, Case Western Res. U., 1966, PhD in Philosophy, 1968. Instr. in philosophy Case Western Res. U., Cleve., 1967—68, asst. prof., 1968—71, assoc. prof., 1971—76; assoc. for behavioral studies The Hastings Ctr., Hastings-on-Hudson, NY, 1976—80; vis. assoc. prof. Albert Einstein Coll. Medicine, Bronx, NY, 1977—78, assoc. prof., 1978—84, prof. dept. epidemiology and social medicine, 1984—. Cons. NIH, 1986—; advisor WHO, Geneva, 1989—; mem. White House Adv. Com. on Human Radiation Experiments, Washington1994; chair ethical rev. com. UNAIDS, Geneva, 1996—2001. Author: Man, Mind and Morality, 1982, Mortal Choices, 1987, Enemies of Patients, 1993, Surrogates and Other Mothers, 1994, Against Relativism, 1999, Double Standards in Medical Research, 2004; contbr. articles to ethics, law and med. jours. Fellow: APHA, Am. Soc. Law, Medicine and Ethics, Inst. Medicine NAS, The Hastings Ctr., Am. Philosophs. Assn. (life); mem.: Am. Soc. Bioethics and Humanities (bd. dirs. 1997—99), Internat. Assn. Bioethics (bd. dirs., pres. 1999—2001). Democrat. Office: A Einstein Coll Medicine Dept Epidemiology Population Health 1300 Morris Park Ave Bronx NY 10461-1926 E-mail: macklin@aecom.yu.edu.

MACKLIS, ROGER MILTON, physician, educator, researcher; b. Stratford, Conn., Mar. 12, 1956; m. Carol Clark, July 25, 1987; children: Andrew Clark, Paul Clark. BS, MS, Yale U., 1978; MD, Harvard U., 1983. Diplomate Am Bd Radiation Oncology. Instr. Harvard Med. Sch., Boston, 1988-89, asst. prof. radiation oncology, 1989-93; dep. div. chief Children's Hosp., Boston, 1990-93; chmn. dept. radiation oncology Cleve. Clinic Found., 1993—. Biomedical consult, Boston, 1989—; assoc prof hist med Case Western Res Univ, 1995—; prof. medicine Cleve. Clin. Lerner Coll. of Medicine, 2004—. Author: (book) Manual of Introductory Clinical Medicine, 1984; contbr. articles to profl jours. Recipient Resident Research Award, ASTRO, 1988, Jr Faculty Research Award, Am Cancer Soc, 1990. Mem.: Soc Chairs of Acad Radiation Oncology Programs (treas, vpres, pres), Am Soc Therapeutic Radiology and Oncology, Am Soc Clin Oncology (Young Investigator Award 1987), Radiation Research Soc. Achievements include research in research on new approaches to cancer treatment involving radioactively labeled molecules and novel technologies for minimizing medical errors in oncology. Office: Cleve Clinic Found Dept Radiation Oncology 9500 Euclid Ave Cleveland OH 44195-0001 Office Phone: 216-444-5576. Business E-Mail: macklir@ccf.org. *

MACKOOL, RICHARD J., ophthalmologist, educator; BA, MD, Boston U., 1968. Diplomate Am. Bd. of Ophthalmology, 1975. Intern L.A. County / U.S.C. Med. Ctr., 1968—69; resident NY Eye and Ear Infirmary, 1970—73, dir. residency tng., 1973—74, attending surgeon corneal svc., 1974—78, sec. med. bd., 1980—83, attending surgeon, 1974—96, sr. attending surgeon, 1996—; clin. asst. prof. ophthalmology MY Med. Coll., 2000—; dir. The Mackool Eye Inst., 1983—. Editl. bd. mem. Video Jour. of Ophthalmology, 1990—, Eyecare Tech., 1994—; editl. adv. bd. mem. Phaco and Foldables, 1996—. Recipient Mem. in Good Standing award, NY State Ophthal. Soc. Inc., 1995, Internation Soc. of Refractive Surgery, 1996, Honor award, AAO, 1997, Gift of Sight award, Order of the Sons of Italy Found., Bethpage, NY, 1997, Honor award, Am. Acad. of Ophthalmology, 1997; named one of Best Ophthalmologist in America, Ophthalmology Times, 1996, Best Doctors in America, Woodward/White, Inc., 1996—97, Best Doctors in NY, NY Mag., 1991, 1996, 1998—99. Mem.: AMA, Vitreous Soc., Refractive Surgery Interest Group, Outpatient Ophthalmic Soc., NY State Ophthal. Soc., NY Soc. for Clin. Ophthalmology, NY County Med. Soc., Internat. Soc. of Refractive Surgery, Am. Soc. of Cataract and Refractive Surgery, Am. Coll. of Eye Surgeons, Am. Assn. of Physicians and Surgeons, Am. Acad. of Ophthalmology. Office: The New York Eye and Ear Infirmary 310 East 14th St New York NY 10003 Office Phone: 212-979-4000.

MACKY, TAMER AHMED, medical educator; b. Cairo, Aug. 9, 1970; s. Ahmed Abdel Rheem Macky and Tayseer Mohamed El Anany; m. Dina Mohamed Kadry; children: Mariam Tamer, Yasmin Tamer. MBBCH, Cairo U., 1993, M in Ophthalmology, 1997, PhD in Ophthalmology, 2002. Asst. lectr. Cairo U. Hosps., 1998—2002, lectr., 2002—07, asst. prof., 2007—, dir. rsch. diagnostic laser unit, 2003—; vitreoretinal fellow Storm Eye Inst., Med. U. SC., Charleston, 1999—2000, ocular pathology fellow, 2000—01. Med. missions Prevent Blindness Group, Cairo U. and Al Nour Eye Hosp., 2002—08. Recipient 1st prize, Congress Am. Soc. Cataract and Refractive Surgery, 2001, 2nd prize, Congress European Soc. Cataract and Refractive Surgery, 2001, Best of Show award, Am. Acad. Ophthalmology Ann. meeting, New Orleans, LA, 2001, Rsch. award, Cairo U., 2008—09; grantee Retina fellowship, Internat. Coun. Ophthalmology, 2004; Travel grant, 2004. Fellow: RCS (Edinburgh); mem.: Am. Acad. Ophthalmology, Assn. for Rsch. and Vision Ophthalmology, Egyptian Vitreoretinal Soc. Office: Cairo Univ Hosps 61 Nahda St Maadi Cairo 11431 Egypt Home: 29th 13th St Apt #11 Maadi 11431 Cairo Egypt Office Phone: 20127892888, 20225391191. Office Fax: 20233388742. Personal E-mail: tamermacky@gmail.com.

MACLAYTON, DAREGO OPUNABO, pharmacist, educator; b. Tallahassee, Fla., Aug. 2, 1979; PharmD, Tex. Southern U. Coll. Pharmacy & Health Scis., 2003. Assoc. prof. Tex. Southern U., 2005—. Clin. pharmacist specialist Micheal E. Debakey Va. Med. Ctr., 2005. Mem.: Am. Coll. Clin. Pharmacy. Avocations: reading, travel, golf. Office: 3100 Cleburne Ave Gray Hall Houston TX 77004 Business E-Mail: maclaytondo@tsu.edu.

MAC LEAN, LLOYD DOUGLAS, surgeon; b. Calgary, Alta., Can., June 15, 1924; s. Fred Hugh and Azilda MacL.; m. Eleanor Colle, June 30, 1954; children: Hugh, Charles, Ian, James, Martha. B.Sc. (Viscount Bennett scholar), U. Alta., 1947, MD (Viscount Bennett scholar), 1949; PhD, U. Minn., 1957. Resident U. Minn. Hosp., Mpls., 1950-56; instr. dept. surgery U. Minn., Mpls., 1956-58, asst. prof.

surgery, 1958-59, asso. prof., 1959-62; prof. McGill U., Montreal, Que., Canada, 1962—, chmn. dept. surgery, 1968-73, 77-82, 87-88. Surgeon-in-chief Ancker Hosp., St. Paul, 1957-62, Royal Victoria Hosp., Montreal, 1962-88; Edward Archibald prof. surgery McGill U., 1988-93, prof. surgery 1993—. Contbr. numerous articles on surgery, shock, host resistance and transplantation to profl. jours. Decorated officer Order Can. Fellow Royal Soc. Can.; mem. ACS (pres. 1993-94), Am. Surg. Assn. (pres. 1993), Ctrl. Surg. Assn. (pres. 1982-83), Am. Physiol. Soc., Am. Assn. Thoracic and Cardiovasc. Surgery, Soc. Surgery of Alimentary Tract. Home: # 1402-80 Berlioz Montreal PQ Canada H3E 1N9 Personal E-mail: lloydm@vdn.ca.

MACLENNAN, BERYCE WINIFRED, retired psychologist; b. Aberdeen, Scotland, Mar. 14, 1920; came to U.S., 1949, naturalized, 1965; d. William and Beatrice (MaCrae) Mellis; m. John Duncan MacLennan, Nov. 29, 1944. BSc with honors, London Sch. Econs., 1947; PhD, London U., 1960. Diplomate Am. Bd. Clin. Psychology, cert. group therapist, trauma specialist. Group psychotherapist, youth specialist cons., NYC and Washington, 1949-63; dir. Ctr. for Prevention Juvenile Delinquency and New Careers, Washington, 1963-66; sect. chief NIMH, Mental Health Study Ctr., Adelphi, Md., 1967-70, chief, 1971-74; regional adminstr. Mass. Dept. Mental Health, Springfield, 1974-75; sr. mental health adv. GAO, Washington, 1976-90; pvt. practice, specialist psychotherapy Bethesda, Md., 1990—2010. Clin. prof. George Washington U., 1970-2002; group therapy cons. DC Mental Health Svcs., 1993-2002, Washington Assessement and Therapy Svcs., 1992-2006; lectr. Montgomery CC, 1988-91, Washington Sch. Psychiatry Geropsychiatric Program, 1997—; tech. adv. com. Prince George's County Mental Health Assn., 1968-84; cons. Washington Bus. Group on Health, 1990-91, KOBA, 1991; leader Trauma Psychotherapy Groups, 2002-03, Hebrew Home Rsch. Inst. Elder Housing Socialization and Memory Improvement Groups, 2000-02. Mem. NIMH Prevention Intervention Rsch. Task Force, 1990-91, Montgomery County Victims Assistance Programs, 1990-95; v.p. Compliance, Federally Employed Women, 1979-81; pres. Glenecho chpt. Older Women's League, 1993-94; mem. Montgomery County Disaster Outreach Team, 2004—. Recipient Hon. award, Wash. Sch. Psychiatry, 2011. Fellow APA; disting. fellow Am. Group Psychotherapy Assn. Democrat.

MACLENNAN, CALMAN ALEXANDER, immunologist, clinician, researcher; b. Taplow, Buckinghamshire, Eng., May 25, 1968; s. Ian Calman Muir and Pamela MacLennan; m. Jennifer Mary Green, Sept. 23, 1994, children: Robert Calman, James Peter, Michael Stephen, James Stewart. BA, U. Oxford, Eng., 1989, BM, BCh, 1992, DPhil, 1996. Pre-registration house officer Oxford Radcliffe Hosp., Oxford, 1996—97, sr. house officer, 1997—99; ward paediatrician Kilifi Dist. Hosp., Kenya, 1999—2000; specialist registrar immunology Birmingham Heartlands Hosp., England, 2000—03; clin. lectr. immunology U. Birmingham, 2003—08, clin. sr. rsch. fellow, 2008—; welcome trust rsch. fellow clin. tropical medicine Malawi-Liverpool-Wellcome Trust Clin. Rsch. Programme, Blantyre, Malawi, 2003—07; hon. lectr. microbiology and genito-urinary medicine U. Liverpool, England, 2003—; hon. lectr. microbiology Coll. Medicine, U. Malawi, 2004—, hon. cons. immunologist U. Hosp. Birmingham, 2008—. Contbr. articles to profl. jours. Clin. Tropical Medicine fellowship, Wellcome Trust, 2003—07, Clin. Rsch. fellowship, GlaxoSmithKline, 2007—. Fellow: Higher Edn. Acad. (London), Royal Coll. Pathologists, (London), mem.: Am. Assn. Microbiologists, Brit. Soc. Immunology, Royal Coll. Physicians, (London). Achievements include research in mechanisms of immunity to tropical infectious diseases, especially salmonella, HIV and malaria, affordable diagnostics in HIV medicine. Avocations: mountain climbing, running, cycling, rowing, surfing. Office: Univ Birmingham/Inst Biomedical Rsch Med Sch B15 2TT Birmingham England Office Phone: 44 121 415 8013. Office Fax: 44 121 414 3599.

MACLENNAN, ROBERT, epidemiologist, educator; b. Brisbane, Queensland, Australia, Jan. 3, 1931; MBBS, Queensland, 1954; MS in Epidemiogy, Tulane U., New Orleans, 1966. Asst. prof. epidemiology Tulane Med. Sch. & Sch. Pub. Health, 1965—67, assoc. prof. epidemiology, 1968—71; epidemiologist Internat. Agy. Rsch. Cancer, Lyon, France, 1971—78; assoc. prof. epidemiology Commonwealth Inst. Health, U. Sydney, 1979—81; prof. Queensland Inst. Med. Rsch. & U. Queensland, 1982—. Mem.: RCP (London), Coun. Queensland Inst. Med. Rsch., Internat. & Australasian Epidemiol. Assn., Pub. Health Assn. (Australia) (life). Avocation: classical music. Home: 16 Lindsay Rd Mount Glorious Queensland 4520 Australia Business E-Mail: bobm@qimr.edu.au.

MACLENNAN, SHEILA, hematologist, consultant; b. Staffordshire, Eng., June 27, 1955; MBBS, U. London, 1979. Cons. in transfusion medicine NHS Blood and Transplant, 1995—. Profl. dir., com. transfusion UKBTS-HPA Joint Profl. Adv. Com., 2008; clin. dir. NHS Blood and Transplant, 2008. Fellow: Royal Coll. Pathologists; mem.: Internat. Soc. Blood Transfusion, Am. Assn. Blood Banks, Brit. Soc. Hematology, Brit. Blood Transfusion Soc. Office: Leeds Blood Ctr Bridle Path Leeds West Yorkshire LS15 7TW England Office Fax: 44 113 2148696. Business E-Mail: sheila.maclennan@nhsbt.nhs.uk.

MACLEOD, ANGUS, retired internist; b. Romford, Essex, Eng., Apr. 24, 1943; came to U.S., 1967; s. Malcolm Macleod and Jean (Littlefair) McKean; m. Gwynne Louise Grellner, May 23, 1969 (div. Aug. 1987); children: Kenneth, Anne, Stephen; m. Betty Durante (Dees), Oct. 23, 2009. MB, ChB, Glasgow U., 1967. Diplomate Am. Bd. Internal Medicine. Intern Luth. Hosp., St. Louis, 1967—68; resident in internal medicine St. Louis U., 1969, 1971—73, fellow in cardiology, 1973—74; physician Grandel Med. Group, St. Louis, 1974—2000, ret., 2000. Instr., then asst. prof. medicine St. Louis U.; chmn. dept. medicine Lutheran Hosp., St. Louis; pres. Grandel Med. Group, St. Louis. Capt. U.S. Army, 1969-71. Decorated Bronze Star. Fellow: ACP; mem.: St. Louis Met. Med. Soc., Mo. State Med. Soc. Personal E-mail: corvus1745@yahoo.com.

MACLEOD, GORDON C., surgeon; b. Quincy, Mass., July 12, 1930; AB, Harvard U., Cambridge, Mass., 1952, MD, 1956. Diplomate Am. Bd. Surgery. Intern Madigan Army Hosp., Tacoma, 1956-57; resident Brigham-Childrens Hosps., Boston, 1957-59; surg. resident Boston Univ. Hosps., Boston, 1959-61; staff surgeon USAF Hosp., Tachi-Kawa AB, Japan, 1961-64, surgeon Westover AFB, Mass., 1964-68, David Grant USAF Med. Ctr., Calif., 1968-74; chmn. surgery USAF Med. Ctr., Scott AFB, Ill., 1974-76; active staff Washington Hosp., Fremont, Calif., 1976—2002, med. dir. oper. rm., 1998-2000. Instr. surgery Boston U., 1960-61; instr. U. Calif., Davis, 1969-71, asst. clin. prof. surgery, 1971-74; with US Air Force, 1956-76, colonel. Mem. ACS, AMA. Business E-Mail: gcmacleodmd56@post.harvard.edu. *

MACLEOD, RODERICK DUNCAN, medical educator, researcher; b. York, Eng., Jan. 16, 1952; s. Angus and Agnes MacLeod; m. Bridget Simpson, July 9, 2007; children: Katherine, Lucy, Sally. MBChB, U. Dundee, Scotland, 1976, MMedEd, 1992; PhD, U. Glamorgan, Wales, 2002. Prin. gen. practice Holt Group Practice, Norfolk, England, 1980—89; med. dir. physician palliative medicine Dorothy House Found., Bath, England, 1989—94; dir. palliative care Mary Potter Hospice Found., Wellington, New Zealand, 1994—2003; south link health prof. palliative care U. Otago, Dunedin, New Zealand, 2003—05; hon. clin. prof. gen. practice and primary health care U. Auckland, New Zealand, 2003—; med. dir. Northshore Hospice Takapuna, Auckland. Contbr. articles to profl. jours., chapters to books. Mem. Hospice New Zealand Exec., Wellington, 1997—2005, clin. advisor, 2011—. Inaugural Lloyd Morgan Charitable Trust fellowship, 2000. Fellow: Royal Australasian Coll. Physicians (mem., edn. com. 2004—08); mem.: NZ Ministry Health Palliative Care (adv. group mem. 2011—, mem. chpt. com. 2011—), Royal Coll. Gen. Practitioners (fellow), Lions Clubs New Zealand. Office: Univ Auckland Tamaki Campus Glen Innes Auckland New Zealand Business E-Mail: rd.macleod@auckland.ac.nz.

MAC MAHON, THOMAS P., pharmaceutical executive; b. 1946; BS in Mktg., St. Peter's Coll. NJ, 1968; MBA in Mktg., Fairleigh Dickinson U., 1972. Joined as mktg. rsch. analyst Roche Biomedical Labs., 1969; v.p., pub. affairs and planning Hoffmann-La Roche, Inc., 1982—83, v.p., gen. mgr. diagnostics sys. unit, 1983—86, sr. v.p., 1993—97; pres. Roche Diagnostics Group, 1988—96, mem. exec. com., 1988—96; with HLR (Hoffman-La Roche) Holdings Inc., 1988—95; vice-chmn. Laboratory Corp. of America Holdings, 1995—96, chmn., 1996—2009, pres., CEO, 1997—2006; chmn. Pharmerica Corp., 2007—. Bd. dirs. Roche Diagnostics Group, 1988—96, Lab. Corp. of America Holdings, 2009—, Golden Pond Health Care, Inc., Express Scripts, Inc., 2001—. Named to The Pinnacle (highest award), Fairleigh Dickinson U., 2001. Mem.: Am. Clin. Lab. Assn. (chmn.). Office: PharMerica Corp 1901 Campus Pl Louisville KY 40299 Office Phone: 502-627-7000. Business E-Mail: tmacmahon@pharmerica.com. *

MACMILLAN, STEPHEN P., medical products executive; b. July 19, 1963; married; 2 children. BA in econ., Davidson Coll.; grad. advanced mgmt. program, Harvard Bus. Sch. Various mktg. positions Procter & Gamble Co.; with over the counter div. McNeil Consumer and Specialty Pharm. Johnson & Johnson Corp., mktg. dir. J&J/Merck over-the-counter franchise worldwide England; mgr. dir. Johnson & Johnson MSD (Merck), England, 1995; v.p., mktg. and profl. sales McNeil Consumer and Splty. Pharm. Johnson & Johnson Corp., 1997; pres. Johnson & Johnson Merck Consumer Pharmaceuticals; sector v.p. global splty. ops. Pharmacia & Upjohn, 1999—2003; COO Stryker Corp., 2004—05, pres., CEO, 2005—10, chmn., pres., CEO, 2010—. Office: Stryker Corp 2725 Fairfield Rd Kalamazoo MI 49002 *

MACMILLEN, RICHARD EDWARD, biological sciences educator, researcher; b. Upland, Calif., Apr. 19, 1932; s. Hesper Nichols and Ruth Henrietta (Golder) MacM.; m. Ann Gray, June 12, 1953 (div. 1975); children: Jennifer Kathleen, Douglas Michael; m. Barbara Jean Morgan, Oct. 23, 1980, 1 child, Ian Richard. BA, Pomona Coll., Claremont, Calif., 1954; MS, U. Mich., 1956; PhD, UCLA, 1961. From instr. to assoc. prof. Pomona Coll., Claremont, Calif., 1960-68, Wig Disting. prof., 1965; assoc. prof., then prof. U. Calif., Irvine, 1968—, chair dept. population and environ. biology, 1972-74, chair dept. ecology and evolutionary biology, 1984-90, prof. emeritus, 1993—. Award panel NSF, Washington, 1976-80; coord. U. Calif. Multi-Campus Supercourse in Environ. Biology, White Mountain Rsch. Sta., 1996-97, tchg. participant, 1998—; rev. panel, EPA Star grad. fellowship program, 2002, 04; budget com., Jackson County Fire Dist. 5, 2001—; Alumni Admissions vol., Pomona Coll., 2001—; SMART vol. Talent Elem. Sch., 2007-; vol. morphologist US Fish and Wildlife Svc. Forensics Lab., 2004—. Contbr. numerous articles to profl. jours; co-author: (with Barbara MacMillen) Meandering in the Bush: Natural History Explorations Outback Australia, 2007, 2nd edit., 2009. Chair sci. adv. bd. Endangered Habitats League, 1991-93. Recipient Rsch. award NSF, 1961-83; Fulbright-Hays Advanced Rsch. fellow Monash U., Australia, 1966-67. Fellow AAAS; mem. Am. Soc. Mammalogists (life), Ecol. Soc. Am. (cert. sr. ecologist), Am. Ornithologists Union (life), Cooper Ornithol. Soc. (life, bd. dirs. 1982-84). Democrat. Avocations: fly fishing, camping, hiking, nature photography. Home: 705 Foss Rd Talent OR 97540-9758 Home Phone: 541-512-9884. Business E-Mail: bidmac@jeffnet.org.

MACMURREN, HAROLD HENRY, JR., psychologist, lawyer; b. Jersey City, Sept. 18, 1942; s. Harold Sr. and Evelyn (Almone) MacM.; m. Margaret Bartro, Nov. 21, 1970. BA, William Paterson Coll., Wayne, NJ, 1965; MA, Jersey City Coll., 1973; EdD, St. Johns U., NYC, 1985; JD, Rutgers U., 1989. Cert. secondary tchr., N.J.; Bar: N.J. 1989. Instr. Wanaque (N.J.) Bd. Edn., 1965-66, cons. psychologist, 1983-84; instr. Elmwood Park (N.J.) Bd. Edn., 1967-70; coll. faculty mem., psychologist Assoc. Clinic, Jersey City, 1971-72; cons. psychologist Rockaway (N.J.) Bd. Edn., 1972-83; intern lawyer Environ. Law Clinic, Newark, 1988-89; cons. psychologist Pequannock (N.J.) Bd. Edn., 1984—; pvt. practice law, 2000—. Coord. child study team Sandyston Walpack Sch. Sys.; adj. prof. William Paterson U.; spkr., writer in field. Mem. ABA, NEA, N.J. Edn. Assn., N.J. Psychologists Assn., N.J. Bar Assn., Sierra Club, Phi Delta Kappa. Avocations: reading, travel, skiing, hiking. Home: 4 Systema Pl Sussex NJ 07461-2833 Office: 293 Rt 519 Sussex NJ 07461 Office Phone: 973-948-3500.

MACOVSKI, ALBERT, electrical engineer, educator; b. NYC, May 2, 1929; s. Philip and Rose (Winogr) Macovski; m. Adelaide Paris, Aug. 5, 1950; children: Michael, Nancy. BEE, City Coll. N.Y., 1950; MEE, Poly. Inst. Bklyn., 1953; PhD, Stanford U., 1968. Mem. tech. staff RCA Labs., Princeton, NJ, 1950—57; asst. prof., then assoc. prof. Poly. Inst. Bklyn., 1957—60; staff scientist Stanford Rsch. Inst., Menlo Park, Calif., 1960—71; fellow U. Calif. Med. Center San Francisco, 1971—; prof. elec. engring. and radiology Stanford U., 1972—, endowed chair, Canon USA prof. engring., 1991—. Dir. Magnetic Resonance Sys. Rsch. Lab.; cons. to industry. Recipient award for color TV cirs., Inst. Radio Engrs., 1958; spl. fellow, NIH, 1971. Fellow: IEEE (Zworykin award 1973), Internat. Soc. Magnetic Resonance in Medicine (trustee 1991—94, gold medal 1997), Optical Soc. Am., Am. Inst. Med. Biol. Engring.; mem.: NAE, Am. Assn. Physicists in Medicine, Inst. Medicine, Eta Kappa Nu, Sigma Xi. Jewish. Achievements include patents in field. Office: Stanford Univ Dept Elec Engring Stanford CA 94305 Home: 620 Sand Hill Rd Apt 407B Palo Alto CA 94304 Office Phone: 650-723-2708. Business E-Mail: macovski@stanford.edu.

MACPHAIL, THERESA, anthropologist; b. Mar. 27, 1972; BA, U NH, 1990; attending, UC-Berkeley, 2011—. Med. anthropologist UC-Berkeley, 2006—. Cons. Chancellor's Multi-Yr. fellowship, U. Calif. Mem.: Soc. Applied Anthropology, Soc. Social Studies Sci., Am. Anthrop. Assn. Achievements include research in global public health, disease surveillance, information-sharing technology, infectious disease, and biosecurity. Office: 232 Kroeber Hall Berkeley CA 94720 Business E-Mail: tmacphail@berkeley.edu.

MACRIS, JACK ACHILLES, surgeon; b. Highland Park, Mich., Nov. 3, 1924; MD, U. Mich., 1950. Diplomate Am. Bd. Surgery. Intern Grace Hosp., Detroit, 1950-51; resident in surgery U. Mich. Hosp., 1951-52, 1952-55, fellowship in surgery, 1955; hosp. staff mem. St. Anthonys Hosp., St. Petersburg, Fla. Fellow ACS (past pres. Fla. chpt.); mem. Fla. Med. Assn. (past pres.), Frederick A. Coller Surg. Soc. (past pres.), Fla. Surg. Soc. (past pres.). Home: # 822 555 5th Ave NE Saint Petersburg FL 33701 *

MACTAGGART, PATRICIA JOY, research scientist; b. Breckenridge, Minnesota, June 19, 1951; BA, Moorhead State U., 1973; MBA, Met. State U., 1988, MMA. Med. dir., multi-divsn. dir., asst. dir., supr., cons. Minn. Dept. Human Svcs., 1985—97; sr. advisor, divsn. dir., group dir. Ctr. Medicare & Medicaid Svcs., 1997—2003; exec. state & local govt. east region, client exec., vp gov. solutions EDS, 2003—06; prin. Health Mgmt. Assoc., 2006—07; lead rsch. scientist George Wash. U., 2007—. Pub. policy com. HIMSS, Mar. Dimes, CAHMI, 2005—; bd. dirs. AHIMA Found., HIMSS NCA Capital, Ctr. Health Policy Devel., 2008—; hit interest group Acad. Health, 2008—11; cons. IOM, 2009—11; adv. com. HIT-UP, Nat. Health Collaboratiave, e-HIE, Connecting Health HIE, 2011—. Mem.: Found. Assoc. Women Bus. Leaders US Health Care Industry Found., Women Bus. Leaders Am., NASI. Office: 2021 K St Washington DC 20006 Business E-Mail: patricia.mactaggart@gwumc.edu.

MADARA, JAMES LEE, medical association administrator, pathologist; b. Altoona, Pa., Sept. 16, 1950; s. Daniel Rodman and Margaret Jane (Hauser) M.; m. Victoria Mollenkopf, May 14, 1975; children: J. Maxwell, Alexis Lindsy. BA, Juniata Coll., 1971; MD, Hahnemann Med., 1975. Cert. anatomic and clin. pathology. Intern Deaconess Hosp., Boston, 1975—76, resident in pathology, 1976—78; fellow in internal medicine Harvard Med. Ctr., Boston, 1978—80; instr. pathology Harvard Med. Sch., Boston, 1980-81, asst. prof. pathology, 1981-85, assoc. prof. pathology, 1985-91, prof. pathology, 1993-97; assoc. prof. of health scis. and tech. Harvard-M.I.T., Boston, 1986-91; Timmie prof., chmn. dept. pathology & lab. medicine Emory U. Sch. Medicine, Atlanta, 1997—2002; dean, v.p. for medical affairs U. Chgo. Pritzker Sch. Medicine, 2002—06, Sara & Harold Lincoln Thompson Disting. svc. prof., 2002—11; dean Biological Sciences Divsn. U. Chgo. Med. Ctr., 2002—09, CEO, 2006—09; sr. adv. Leavitt Partners LLC, Salt Lake City, 2009—11; exec. v.p., CEO AMA, Chgo., 2011—. Assoc. editor Gastroenterology, 1986-91, mem. editl. bd. Jour. Clin. Investigation, 1987—, editor-in-chief American Jour. Pathology, 2000; contbr. over 160 articles to profl. jours. Grantee NIH, 1980—. Mem. American Soc. for Clin. Investigation (elected), American Soc. for Cell Biology, American Gastroenterological Assn. (rsch. coun. 1988-90, Ross Rsch. scholar award 1982), American Physiol. Soc., American Assn. Pathology (Parke/Davis award 1990), Assn. American Physicians. Achievements include description of functional sequellae of neutrophil-epithelial cell interactions; recognition that tight junctions between epithelial cells are regulated under physiological conditions. Office: American Medical Association 515 N State St Chicago IL 60654 Office Phone: 800-621-8335. *

MADDEN, BRENDAN PATRICK, cardiothoracic medicine professor; b. Dublin, June 29, 1961; arrived in Eng., 1988; s. Denis J. and Joan M. (Redmond) M.; m. Aileen Peake, 1998; children: Aisling, Aoife, Niamh, Roisin Ronan. MB, BCh and BAO, all with honors, Univ. Coll., Dublin, 1984, MD, 1991; MSc, Brunel U., London, 1992. Cert. cons. cardiothoracic and transplant physician, instr. advanced life support, advanced trauma life support, in cardiac advanced life support, in care of critically ill surgical patient. Dir. pulmonary hypertension and endobronchial intervention programs; registrar Meath Hosp., Dublin, 1987-88; cardiothoracic registrar Harefield Hosp., Middlesex, 1988-90; sr. registrar Harefield and Brompton Hosps., London, 1990-93; sr. registrar, tutor Brompton Hosp., London, 1993-94; cons. thoracic, intensive care and transplant physician St. Georges Hosp., London, 1994—. Med. advisor USA Cystic Fibrosis Trust, Washington, 1996, French Transplant and Cystic Fibrosis Soc., 1992—, Transplant Ctrs. in Brazil and Argentina, 1992—, U.K. Cystic Fibrosis Trust, 1992—; lectr. in field; examiner Royal Coll. Surgeons Eng., 2000—. Author book chpts. on thoracic surgery, ARDS, intensive care, cystic fibrosis, pulmonary rehab., lung transplantation; contbr. numerous articles and sci. papers to profl. jours. Dir. Med. Students Overseas Relief, Kenya, 1983. Scholar Univ. Coll., 1980, 82; grantee Brit. Heart Found., 1996, 97, 99. Fellow Royal Coll. Physicians Ireland, Royal Acad. Medicine of Ireland, Royal Coll. Physicians London; mem. Brit. Thoracic Soc. Roman Catholic. Avocations: french, skiing, scuba diving, music, foreign travel. Office: St Georges Hosp Cardiothoracic Unit Blackshaw Rd SW17 0QT London SW17 0QT England Office Phone: 0044-02087251094. Business E-Mail: brendan.madden@stgeorges.nhs.uk.

MADDEN, ROBERT EDWARD, surgeon, educator; b. Oak Park, Ill., Sept. 16, 1925; s. Joseph Edward and Gertrude Celelia (McGowan) M.; m. Susan Ann Hale, May 24, 1958; children: Robert Joseph, Lisa Marie, Karen Louise, Kevin Francis. BS in Medicine, U. Ill., Chgo., 1950, MS in Biochemistry, 1952, MD, 1952. Diplomate Am. Bd. Surgery, Bd. Thoracic Surgery. Assoc. in surgery U. Ill. Coll. Medicine, Chgo., 1957-58; sr. surgeon Nat. Cancer Inst., Bethesda, Md., 1959-60; asst. prof. surgery N.Y. Med. Coll., NYC, 1961-66, assoc. prof., 1966-71, prof. Valahlla, 1971—2001, emeritus, 2009—. Mem. N.Y. State Health Rsch. Coun., Albany, 1976—; med. coord. N.Y. State Dept. Health, 1998—2007. Author: (with Lippincott) Problems In General Surgery, 1988; editor: Gastrointestinal Bleeding, 1987; editor-in-chief N.Y. Med. Quarterly, 1979-90; contbr. articles to profl. jours. With U.S. Army, 1943-46. Recipient Borden Undergrad. Rsch. award, 1952; postdoctoral fellow Am. Cancer Soc., 1958-59. Fellow ACS (com. on cancer 1993-97); mem. Am. Soc. for Vascular Surgery, Soc. Internat. Chirurgie, Am. Assn. Cancer Edn. (pres. 1979), N.Y. Cancer Soc. (pres. 1975-76), N.Y. State Cancer Programs Assn. (pres. 1975-76), Knights of Holy Sepulchre, Knights of the Order of Malta, Pi Gamma Mu. Republican. Roman Catholic. Home: 6 Crows Nest Rd Bronxville NY 10708-4802 Office: NY Med Coll Munger Pavilion Valhalla NY 10595 Office Phone: 914-493-7615. E-mail: remadden@verizon.net. *

MADDEN, SLOANE, psychiatrist; b. Sydney, Aug. 10, 1967; MBBS with honor, U. Sydney, 1993. Sr. staff specialist Children's Hosp. Westmead, Westmead, 2000—11, head dept. psychol. medicine, 2010—. Clin. lectr. U. Sydney, 2006—11; steering com. chair nat. eating disorder collaboration Australian Govt. Dept. Health and Ageing, 2009—11. Rsch. grant, Nat. Health and Med. Rsch. Coun. Fellow: Acad. Eating Disorders, Royal Australian and New Zealand Coll. Psychiatry; mem.: Australian and New Zealand Acad. Eating Disorders. Avocations: bicycling, reading. Office: Children's Hosp Westmead Cnr Hawkesbury Rd Westmead Sydney NSW 2145 Australia Office Phone: 61298452005. Business E-Mail: sloanem@chw.edu.au.

MADDI, SALVATORE R., medical educator; b. NYC, Jan. 27, 1933; BA, Bklyn. Coll., MA, 1956; PhD, Harvard U., 1960. Diplomate Am. Bd. Forensic Examiners. Prof. U. Chgo., 1959—86, U. Calif., Irvine, 1986—. Disting. wellness lectr. U. Calif. HealthNet; founder, pres. Hardiness Inst., 1984, individual counsellor, orgnl. cons., 84. Fulbright fellowship. Fellow: APA (Master Lectr. award, RHR Internat. award, Henry Murray award), Am. Coll. Forensic Examiners, Soc. Personology, Internat. Network Pers. Meaning, Am. Psychol. Soc. Avocations: writing, painting, woodworking. Office: University Calif Irvine 4201 SBS Gateway Irvine CA 92697 Home Phone: 949-494-0109; Office Phone: 949-824-7045. Office Fax: 949-252-8087. Business E-Mail: srmaddi@uci.edu.

MADDREY, WILLIS CROCKER, medical educator, internist, academic administrator, consultant, researcher; b. Roanoke Rapids, NC, Mar. 29, 1939; s. Milner Crocker and Sara Jean (Willis) M.; m. Ann Marie Matt; children: Jeffrey, Gregory, Thomas. BS, Wake Forest U., 1960; MD, Johns Hopkins U., 1964. Diplomate: Am. Bd. Internal Medicine. Intern Osler Med. Service Johns Hopkins Hosp., Balt., 1964-65, asst. resident, 1965-66, 68-69, chief resident, 1969-70; fellow in liver disease Yale U., 1970-71; asst. prof. medicine Johns Hopkins U., Balt., 1971-75, assoc. prof., 1975-79, prof., 1980—82, asst. dean Sch. Medicine, 1975-79, assoc. dir. dept. medicine, 1979-82; prof., chmn. dept. medicine Jefferson Med. Coll., Phila., 1982-90; v.p. clin. affairs U. Tex. Southwestern Med. Ctr., Dallas, 1990-93, exec. v.p. clin. affairs, 1993—2010, pres. asst., 2010—. Assoc. editor: Medicine, 1972-82, Hepatology, 1988-95, mem. editl. bd., 1981-84, 86-87, Gastroenterology, 1982-87, Am. Jour. Medicine, 1978-88; contbr. articles to profl. jours. Bd. dirs. Am. Liver Found., 1978-81, Dallas County Med. Soc., 1996-98; trustee Magee Rehab. Hosp., Phila., 1982-87. With USPHS, 1966-68. Mem. ACP (bd. regents 1986-92, pres. 92-93), Am. Soc. Clin. Investigation, Am. Gastroenterol. Assn., Am. Assn. Study Liver Disease (pres. 1981). Republican. Office: U Tex Southwestern Med Ctr 5323 Harry Hines Blvd Dallas TX 75390-8570 Office Phone: 214-648-2024.

MADESKA, VALERIE GAY, biology educator; b. Bethpage, NY, Mar. 1, 1959; d. Arthur Lincoln and Theresa Van Dyke; m. Christopher Joseph Madeska, Aug. 24, 1982; children: Christopher Arthur, Thomas Michael, Joseph Daniel. AS, SUNY, Farmingdale, 1979; BS, SUNY, 2009. Cert. Nat. Credentialing Agy. for Lab. Pers. Part-time tech. asst. SUNY, Farmingdale, 1981—83, full time tech. asst., 1983—88, instrnl. support tech., 1988—2001, instrnl. support specialist, 2001—, lab. mgr., 2001—08, lab. mgr. biology dept., 2008—. Sec. med. lab. tech. dept. adv. bd. SUNY, Farmingdale, 1997—2007; v.p. for profls. United Univ. Professions, Farmingdale, 2000—07, sec., 2007—09, 2009—11. Democrat. Methodist. Office: Farmingdale State Coll NY 2350 Broadhollow Rd Farmingdale NY 11735 Office Phone: 631-420-2511. Business E-Mail: madeskv@farmingdale.edu.

MADGULKAR, ASHWINI R., pharmacist, educator; b. Pune, India, May 15, 1966; PhD, U. Pune, 2008. Prin. AISSMS Coll. Pharmacy, 2009—. Head, bd. studies pharmaceutics U. Pune, 2011. Mem.: Indian Pharm. Assn., Maharashtra State Pharmacy Coun., Assn. Pharm. Tchrs. India. Achievements include patents in field. Avocation: reading. Office: AISSMS Coll Pharmacy Kennedy Rd Pune Maharashtra 411001 India Office Phone: 912026058208. Personal E-mail: ashwini.madgulkar@indiatimes.com.

MADHAVAN, SETHU M., nephrologist, researcher; b. Thazhakkara, India, May 17, 1979; MD, All India Inst. Medical Scis., 2006. Scientist, nephrologist Case Western Reserve U., Cleve., 2009—. Fellow: Am. Soc. Nephrology; mem.: Am. Medical Assn., Am. Coll. Physicians, Am. Physicain Scientist Assoc., Am. Bd. Internal Medicine. Office: 2500 Metrohealth Dr Cleveland OH 44109 Business E-Mail: smadhavan@metrohealth.org.

MADHAVAN, SUNDARESWARAN SURESH, pharmacologist, educator; b. Kalyan, India, Apr. 4, 1959; MBA, Symbiosis Inst. Mgmt., 1982; PhD, Purdue U., 1988. Prof., chair, pharm. sys. and policy W.Va. U. Sch. Pharmacy, 1988—. Prin. investigator and dir. W.Va. Collaborative Health Outcomes Rsch. Therapies and Svcs. Ctr., 2006; editl. bd. mem. Jour. Am. Pharmacists Assn. Recipient Nat. award, Coun. State Govt., award, W.Va. U. Health Scis. Ctr., Acad. Excellence Tchg. and Learning, Excellence Rsch. award, W.Va. U. Sch. Pharmacy Bd. Advisors; grant, Agy. Healthcare Rsch. and Quality, W.Va. CoHORTS Ctr. Fellow: Am. Assn. Colls. Pharmacy, Am. Pharmacists Assn.; mem.: Acad. Pharm. Rsch. and Scis., Agy. Healthcare Rsch. and Quality (HCQER study sect. mem.), Internat. Soc. Pharmacoeconomics and Outcomes Rsch. Achievements include research in health services research and health policy, with particular emphasis on improving access to and quality of health and preventive care services. Avocations: woodworking, travel, reading, sports. Office: 1129 HSCN Medical Center Dr Morgantown WV 26506-9510 Office Fax: 304-293-2529. Business E-Mail: smadhavan@hsc.wvu.edu.

MADHOUN, MOHAMMAD FAROUQ, gastroenterologist, researcher; b. Taif, Saudi Arabia, July 13, 1978; MD, Jordan U. Scis. and Tech., 2003. Gastroenterology rsch. fellow U. Okla. Health Scis. Ctr., 2008—11. Recipient Dean's Honor List, Jordan U. Scis. and Tech.; fellowship, Salix Program, grant, Am. Coll. Gastroenterology. Mem.: AMA, Am. Coll. Gastroenterology, Am. Gastroent. Assn., Am. Soc. Gastrointestinal Endoscopy, Alpha Epsilon Lambda, Phi Kappa Phi Academic Honor Soc. Avocations: billiards, swimming. Home: 124 NW 16th St #107 Oklahoma City OK 73103 Personal E-mail: moar78@yahoo.com.

MADI, NADA MOHAMMED, virologist, educator; b. Kuwait, Oct. 22, 1972; MSc, Kuwait U., 1999, PhD, 2008. Tchr. Faculty Medicine, Kuwait U., 2000—, v.p., rsch. Recipient Grad. Rsch. award, Kuwait U. Mem.: European Soc. Clin. Virology. Office: Kuwait University Faculty Medicine PO Box 24923 Safat 12345 Kuwait Business E-Mail: madi@hsc.edu.kw.

MADISON, GRACE LENORE, retired medical/surgical nurse, psychologist, educator; b. Albert Lea, Minn., July 29, 1924; d. Ernest and Gertrude Abbie (Gordy) Clubb; m. Eldon Harold Madison, June 15, 1946; children: Paul Ernest, Curtis John, Roger Dale, Carol Ann. BA in Psychology, So. Ill. U., Edwardsville, 1969, MA in Psychology, 1971. RN Minn., 1945; cert. clin. psychologist Ill., 1973. Pediat. staff nurse Sacramento City Hosp., 1945; spl. duty surg. nurse U. Minn. Hosp., 1945—46, nurse technician x-ray therapy, 1946—48, spl. duty heart surgery nurse, 1951—53; guest lectr. Coll. Home and Scis., Lahore, Pakistan, 1958; tchr. English Dacca, Bangladesh, 1959—60; staff nurse Mpls. Gen. Hosp., 1961—63, Alton Meml. Hosp., Ill., 1964; grad. rsch. asst. So. Ill. U., 1969—70, grad. tchr. asst., asst. project dir. Sch. Nursing, 1971—72. Psychology instr. Florissant Valley CC, Mo., 1973—77, Belleville Area Coll., Ill., 1974—75. Unitarian. Achievements include patent for Empathy Game. Avocations: travel, writing. Home: 1828 Stanford Pl Edwardsville IL 62025-2633

MADJIROVA, NADEJDA PETROVA, psychiatrist, educator; b. Plovdiv, Bulgaria, Nov. 7, 1945; d. Peter Todorov and Ivanka Nikolova (Kostova) M.; m. Petko Tanev Valkov, Oct. 31, 1940; 1 child, Stoyanka. MD, Higher Med. Inst., Plovdiv, 1971; PhD, Med. Acad., Sofia, Bulgaria, 1985; DMS student in Psychiatry, 2007—. Psychiatrist Psychiat. Hosp., Radnevo, Bulgaria, 1971-76; asst. prof. Higher Med. Inst., Plovdiv, 1976-85, chief asst. prof., 1985-89, assoc. prof., 1989—2001, pres. ethics com., 2001—02; head dept. psychiatry and med. psychology Med. U., Plovdiv, 2002—, U. Sant Georgy, Plovdiv, 2003—08, prof. psychiatry, 2010—. DGS Ethics com. mem., 2000—08; lectr. in field. Author: Manual of Psychiatry for General Practice, 2005, Manual for Seminary of Medical Psychology, 2005; co-author: Psychiatry, 2005, A Course of Lectures in Clinical Psychology, 2001,; contbr. articles to profl. jours.; author monographs: Chronobiological Aspects in Psychiatry, 1995, Child Complexes, 1996, Pharmacological Management of Children's Behavior at the Dental Office, 2005; (in English) Medical Psychology, 2001, Psychopathology of Childhood, 2003, Common and Special Physcophysiology, 2003; editor: (monograph) Chronobiology & Biometeorology in Bulgarian Medicine, 2001; A Practical Manual for Seminaries of Medical Psychology, 2nd edit., 2007, A Textbook for Psychiatry for Students in Dental Medicine, 2007. Mem. Psychiat. Soc. in Bulgaria, Chronobiol. Soc., Bulgarian Chronobiology and Biometeorology Soc. (pres. 1998—). Avocations: pen and ink drawing, wood carving. Home: Peter Stoev 123 4004 Plovdiv Bulgaria Office: Med Univ Plovdiv Vasil Aprilov 15-A 4002 Plovdiv Bulgaria

MADKOR, HAFEZ RAGAB, medical educator; b. Egypt, Nov. 1, 1974; BSc, Coll. Pharmacy Assiut U., Egypt, 1997—2007, PhD, 2004. Asst. prof. Coll. Clin. Pharmacy King Faisal U., 2005—. Rsch. grant, King Faisal U. Office: Khaldia PO Box 400 Hofuf Al-Ahsa 31982 Saudi Arabia Office Fax: 00966-3-5817174. Personal E-mail: hmadkor@yahoo.com.

MADLOCK, YVONNE, city health department administrator; m. Lawrence Madlock; 3 children. BS, Wellesley Coll.; MAT, Wesleyan U., Middletown, Conn.; studied, U. Tex. Sch. Pub. Health. Adminstr., bur. personal health svcs. Shelby Co. Divsn. Health Svcs., Memphis, dir., 1995—. Bd. pres. Cmty. Inst. for Early Childhood; bd. dirs. W. Tenn. Area Health Edn. Ctr., Memphis Leadership Inst., Cmty. Found. of Greater Memphis, Shelby Co. Ground Water Quality Control Bd. Mem.: Nat. Assn. City and County Health Officials (bd. dirs.). Office: Shelby Co Divsn Health Svcs 814 Jefferson Ave Memphis TN 38103 Business E-Mail: HealthDirector@co.shelby.tn.us.

MADOFF, DAVID CRAIG, radiologist; b. Queens, NY, Oct. 12, 1967; s. Lawrence and Marilyn Madoff; m. Esa Robbin Smith, June 6, 1999; children: Samuel Isaac children: Emma Grace, Benjamin Aaron. BA in Psychology, Emory U., 1989; MD, U. Pitts., 1995. Diplomate Am. Bd. Radiology, 2000, cert. in vascular and interventional radiology. Instr. radiology U. Tex. M. D. Anderson Cancer Ctr., Houston, 2001—02, asst. prof. radiology, 2002—07, assoc. prof. radiology, 2007—11; chief interventional radiology NY-Presbyterian Hosp./Weill Cornell Med. Ctr., NYC, 2011—; prof. radiology Weill Cornell Med. Coll., NYC, 2011—. Dep. editor Jour. Vascular Interventional Radiology, 2007; edtl. bd. Techniques Vascular Interventional Radiology, 2007. Appt. editl. and adv. bd.: Jour. Vascular and Interventional Radiology, 2004. Recipient Excellence Rsch. award, U. Pitts., Sch. Medicine, 1993, Disting. Reviewer award, Jour. Vascular and Interventional Radiology, 2004—07; grantee, U. Pitts., Sch. of Medicine, 1992, 1993, Cardiovasc. and Interventional Radiology Rsch. and Edn. Found., 2003; elected fellow, Soc. Interventional Radiology. Mem.: American Hepato-Pancreato-Biliary Assn., Internat. Hepato-Pancreato-Biliary Assn., Soc. Interventional Radiology, Radiol. Soc. North America, American Roentgen Ray Soc., American Coll. Radiology, Cardiovasc. & Interventional Radiology Soc. of Europe (corr.). Achievements include research in improved techniques for portal vein embolization; development of technique to improve hepatic encephalopathy after transjugular intrahepatic portosystemic shunt (TIPS) creation. Office: NY-Presbyterian Hospital 525 E 68th St Payson 5-518 New York NY 10065 Office Phone: 212-746-2602. Office Fax: 212-746-8463. *

MADOFF, ROBERT D., colon and rectal surgeon, educator; Grad., Roxbury Latin Sch., West Roxbury, 1971; BA in Biological Sciences magna cum laude, Harvard U., Cambridge, 1975; MD, Columbia U., NY, 1979. Diplomate Am. Bd. Colon and Rectal Surgery, 2002. Intern in surgery Univ. Minn. Hosps., Mpls., 1979—80, resident in surgery, 1980—81, 1983—87, resident in medicine, 1981—82, fellow in colon and rectal surgery, 1987—88; prof. surgery Univ. Minn., chief colon and rectal surgery divsn., Stanley M. Goldberg endowed chair in colon and rectal surgery. Co-author: The incidence of dysplasia and adenocarcinoma in surgical patients, 2006, The status of radical proctectomy and sphincter-sparing surgery in the United States, 2007, Population-based analyses of lymph node metastases in colorectal cancer, 2006, Female Sexual Dysfunction after Ileal Pouch-Anal Anastomosis, 2008, Anal Dysplasia in Kidney Transplant Recipients, 2008, various others. Office: University of Minnesota Colon and Rectal Surgery Division 420 Delaware St SE Minneapolis MN 55455 Office Phone: 612-625-7992. Office Fax: 612-625-4406.

MADORY, JAMES RICHARD, hospital administrator, retired military officer; b. Staten Island, NY, June 11, 1940; s. Eugene and Agnes (Gerner) M.; m. Karen James Clifford, Sept. 26, 1964; children: James E., Lynn Anne, Scott J., Elizabeth Anne, Joseph M. (dec.). BS, Syracuse U., 1964; MHA, Med. Coll. Va., 1971. Enlisted USAF, 1958; x-ray technician Keesler Area Med. Ctr., Biloxi, Miss., 1959-62; commd. 2d lt. USAF, 1964, advanced through grades to maj., 1979—; x-ray technician Keesler Area Med. Ctr., Biloxi, Miss., 1959-62; adminstr. Charleston (S.C.) Clinic, 1971-74, Beale Hosp., Calif., 1974-77; assoc. adminstr. Shaw Regional Hosp., S.C., 1977-79; ret. USAF, 1979; asst. adminstr. Raleigh Gen. Hosp., Beckley, W.Va., 1979-81; adminstr., dir., sec. bd. Chesterfield Gen. Hosp., Cheraw, S.C., 1981-87; pres., CEO Grand Strand Hosp., Myrtle Beach, S.C., 1987-95, trustee, 1987-95; elected vice chairman Horry County Planning Commn., 1996-98; cons. Healthcare Adminstrn., 1995—. Adv. bd. Cheraw Nursing Home, 1984-85. Contbr. articles to profl. jours. Chmn. bd. W.Va. Kidney Found., Charleston, 1980-81; chmn. youth bd. S.C. TB and Respiratory Disease Assn., Charleston, 1972-73; county chmn. Easter Seal Soc., Chesterfield County, S.C., 1984-85; campaign crusade chmn. Am. Cancer Soc., Chesterfield County, 1985-86; chmn. dist. advancement com. Boy Scouts Am., 1987-90; bd. dirs. Horry County United Way, 1989-95, Horry County Access Care, 1989-91; trustee Cheraw Acad., 1982-85, Grand Strand Gen. Hosp., 1987-94, Coastal Acad., 1988-90; commr. Horry County Planning Commn., 1995-97, vice chmn., 1996-97; mem. Myrtle Beach AFB Redevel. Authority, 1997—; chmn. Horry County Boys & Girls Clubs Am., 1998-99, bd. dirs., 1998-2000; apptd. Myrtle Beach Air Base Redevel. Authority, 1998, Waccamaw Regional Workforce Investment Bd., 1998-01, vice-chmn., 1998—01; vice-chmn. Horry County Republican Party, 1998-99; S.C. fin. steering com.; campaign chmn. McCain 2000 for Pres., 1999-2000, Harry County. volunteer med. missionary Haiti Hosp. Lumieer, 2002, mem. Parish Coun., St. Mary Help Christians RC Ch., Auban, SC, 2007-. Decorated Bronze Star, Vietnamese Cross of Gallantry, Vietnamese Medal of Honor; named to S.C. Order of Palmetto Gov. David Beasley, 1995. Fellow Am. Coll. Hosp. Adminstrs., Am. Coll. Health Care Execs; mem. S.C. Hosp. Assn. (com on legislation 1984-86, trustee 1989-94), Am. Acad. Healthcare Adminstrs., Cheraw C. of C. (bd. dirs. 1982-83), Rotary (pres. 1984-85). Republican. Roman Catholic. Home and Office: 341 Implement Dr Aiken SC 29803-6293 E-mail: jmadory@yahoo.com. *

MADRID, CIRILO L., health facility administrator; b. Clint, Tex., Mar. 18, 1945; s. Leandro L. and Felicitaz L. Madrid; m. Grace Avila Madrid, Jan. 23, 1971; children: Michelle, Melinda, Jesus. AA, Glendale CC, 1967; BA, Ariz. State U., 1969; MEd, U. Tex., El Paso, 1981; PhD, Hamilton U., 2002. Psychiat. tech. St. Mary's Hosp., Tucson, 1970—71; CEO Aliviane No-Ad, Inc., El Paso, 1971—, Family Reintegration Tex., El Paso, 1995—2000, New Beginnings of Tex., El Paso, 2000—. Mem. Lt. Gov. Drug Bd. State of Tex., Austin, 1978—81, Nat. Drug Coun. Ctr. Substance Abuse Tex., Wash., 2003—. Author: Mi India, 1981, Changing Heart of America, 2002; contbr. articles various profl. jours. Mem. Eastside Polit. Action Com., El Paso, 1995—; leg. chair. ASAP of Tex., Austin, 2002—; elected off. Ysleta Sch. Bd., El Paso, 1976—81. Combat medic US Army, 1969—70, South Vietnam. Recipient Carlos Finlay award, Pub. Health Svc., 1996, TCADA award, State of Tex., 1997, Tex. Chem. Found. award, 2000. Mem.: VFW, Tex. Assn. Drug Abuse Counselors, Assn. of Substance Svcs. Roman Catholic. Achievements include development of promising chem. dependence prevention approaches; evident based treatment approaches for hispanic addicts; chem. dependence training approaches for ethnic minorities. Avocations: running, weight training, poetry, comedy. E-mail: cmadrid@aliviane.org.

MADSEN, JANET JEAN, pharmacist; b. Glenwood, Minn., Nov. 10, 1953; BS in Pharmacy, U. Minn., 1978; PharmD, U. Ga., 1987. Hosp. pharmacy tng. and knowledge mgr. Fairview Health Svcs., 1988—. Mem.: Am. Soc. Health-Sys. Pharmacists, Minn. Soc. Health-Sys. Pharmacists (named Minn. Outstanding Pharmacist 2006). Avocation: gardening. Office: Fairview Pharmacy Services 711 Kasota Ave Minneapolis MN 55414 Business E-Mail: jmadsenl@fairview.org.

MADURA, JAMES ANTHONY, surgeon, educator; b. Campbell, Ohio, June 10, 1938; s. Anthony Peter and Margaret Ethel (Sebest) M.; m. Loretta Jayne Sovak, Aug. 8, 1959; children: Debra Jean, James Anthony II, Vikki Sue. BA, Cogate U., 1959; MD, Western Res. U., 1963. Diplomate Am. Bd. Surgery. Intern in surgery Ohio State U., Columbus, 1963—64, resident in surgery, 1966—71; asst. prof. surgery Ind. U., Indpls., 1971—76, assoc. prof. Surgery, 1976—80, prof. Surgery, 1980—, J.S. Battersby prof. surgery, 2001—. Dir. gen. surgery Ind. U. Sch. Medicine, Indpls., 1985—, vice-chmn., 1985—. Contbr. articles to profl. jours. Bd. dir. Indpls. Opera. Capt. med. corps US Army, 1965—66, Vietnam, 85th Evacuation Hosp. Fellow Am. Coll. Surgeons; mem. Cen. Surg. Assn., Western Surg. Assn., Soc. Surgery Alimentary Tract, Midwest Surg. Assn., Internat. Biliary Assn., Assn. Acad. Surgeons, The Columbia Club. Republican. Roman Catholic. Home: 9525 Copley Dr Indianapolis IN 46260-1422 Personal E-mail: jmadura1@comcast.net. Business E-Mail: jmadura@iupui.edu.

MADUREIRA, SOFIA, psychotherapist; b. Lobito, Angola, July 29, 1969; Degree in Clin. Psychology, Inst. Superior Psicologia Aplicada, Lisboa, 1995; MS in Neuroscis., Faculdade Medicina Lisboa, 2005. Clin. rschr. Faculdade Medicina Lisboa, Dept. Neuroscis. and Mental Health, 1995—. Office: Hosp Santa Maria Neurologia Piso 6 Lisbon 1649-035 Portugal Business E-Mail: pmadureira@fm.ul.pt.

MAEBA, RYOUTA, biochemist, educator; b. Gifu, Japan, Apr. 7, 1957; s. Shouzou and Sugiko Maeba; m. Noriyo Satou, Nov. 7, 1963; children: Keita, Yu-ki, Nozomi. B, Ngoya U., 1976—80; PhD, Teikyo U. Sch. of Medicine, 1986—95. Rschr. Terumo Co., Tokyo, 1980—85, Teikyo U. Sch. of Medicine, Tokyo, 1985—. Local chief acad. dept. Sokagakkai Internat. (SGI), Tokyo, 2000—03. Recipient Oleo Sci., Japan Oil Chem. Found., 2003. Buddhism. Achievements include research in bioscience of lipids. Avocations: reading, travel, music, soccer. Office: Teikyo Univ Sch Medicine 2-11-1 Kaga Itabashi-Ku Tokyo 173-8605 Japan Office Fax: +81-3-5248-3588. E-mail: maeba@med.teikyo-u.ac.jp.

MAEDA, HIDEFUMI, dentist, researcher; b. Saga, Japan, Nov. 1965; DDS, PhD, Kyushu U., 1994; postgrad., U. Tex. Health Sci. Ctr., San Antonio, 1999—2001. Rsch. assoc. Kyushu U., Fukuoka, Japan, 1995—2004, asst. prof., 2004—. Office: Kyushu U 3-1-1 Maidashi Fukuoka 812-8582 Japan Office Fax: 81-92-642-6366. Business E-Mail: hide@dent.kyushu-u.ac.jp.

MAEDA, HIROSHI, medical educator, researcher; b. Hyogo-ken, Japan, Dec. 22, 1938; s. Muraji and Yoshiko Maeda; m. Norico Soma, Oct. 1, 1967; children: Jun-ichiro, Kei. BS, Tohoku U., Sendai, Japan, 1962; MS, U. Calif., Davis, 1964; PhD, Tohoku U., 1967, MD, 1972. Rsch. assoc. Sidney Farber Cancer Inst., Harvard U., Boston, 1967-71; assoc. prof. Med. Sch., Kumamoto U., 1971-80, prof., chmn., 1980—2004, prof. emeritus, 2004—; prof. Sch. Pharmacy, Sojo U., Kumamoto, 2004—. Lichfield lectr. John Radcliffe Med. Sch., Oxford U., Eng., 1990. Pioneer in macromolecular anti-cancer agt. discovery, cancer treatment methods, viral disease rsch. Fulbright fellow, 1962; recipient Internat. Career Tech. Transfer award Internat. Union Against Cancer, Geneva, 1974, Sapporo Life Sci. Rsch. award, 1983, Princess Takamatsu Cancer Rsch. Found. Acad. Merit prize, 1997, Commemorative Gold medal E.K. Frey E. Werle Found. Germany, 1998, Nishi-nippon Culture award Nishi-nippon Shimbun, Japan, 2010, Yoshida Tomiso award Japan Cancer Assn., 2011, Nagai award Japan DDS Soc., 2011; named Hon. Mayor of San Antonio, Hon. Citizen of Okla. State. Mem. Japanese Biochem. Soc., Japanese Cancer Assn., AAAS, Am. Assn. Cancer Rsch., Am. Chem. Soc., N.Y. Acad. Sci., Japan Soc. Bacteriology (hon.; Asakawa award 1995), Am. Soc. Microbiology, Soc. Exptl. Biology Med., Japan Soc. Virology, Soc. for Controlled Release (Nagai Innovation award 2003), Biodynamic Rsch. Found. (founder, dir.), Internat. Nitric Oxide Soc. (pres. 2001-03), Nitric Oxide Soc. Japan (pres. 2003), Japan Bacteriol. Soc. (pres. 2003). Home: Kotoh 3-21-24 Kumamoto 862-0909 Japan Office Phone: 81-96-326-4114. Business E-Mail: hirmaeda@ph.sojo-u.ac.jp. *

MAEDA, KAZUO, retired obstetrician, gynecologist, educator; b. Kirishima, Kagoshima-ken, Japan, Jan. 5, 1925; s. Sumi and Nao Maeda; m. Mariko Fuchiwaki Maeda; 1 child, Mahiro. MD, Kyushu Imperial U., Fukuoka, Japan, 1947, PhD, 1955. Diplomate Ministry of Health and Welfare, Japan, 1949, Specialist in Obstetrics and Gynecology Japan Soc. Obstetrics and Gynecology, 1997, Board Certified Fellow Japan Soc. Med. Ultrasound. Asst. prof. Kyushu U., 1957—58; chmn., prof. dept. obstetrics and gynecology Tottori U., Yonago, Japan, 1968—90; head U. Hosp., 1976—80; pres. 4th Asia-Oceania Congress Perinatology, 1986, 3d Internat. Congress The Fetus as a Patient, 1987, 2d Internat. Congress Computers Care Mother, Fetus and Newborn, 1989, 5th World Congress Ultrasound Ob-Gyn., 1995. Cons. Seirei Hospitals, Hamamatsu, Japan, 1990—97. Dir. Japanese Ian Donald Sch. Med. Ultrasound, Japan, 1998—2008. Recipient William Liley medal, Internat. Soc. Fetus as Patient, 2001. Mem.: Croatian Acad. Med. Sci., Ian Donald Interuniversity Sch. Med. Ultrasound (Japan dir. 1998—2008), World Assn. Perinatal Medicine, Internat. Acad. Perinatal Medicine (organizer 2010), Japan Soc. Med. Ultrasound (chmn. working group 1983—90), Japan Soc. Med. Biol. Engring. (chmn. working group 1983—90), Japan Soc. Perinatology (pres. 1984), Japan Soc. Ob-Gyn. (mem. council 1971—75, chmn. com. on med. engring. 1971—90, mem. council 1983—85), Croatian Soc. Ultrasound in Medicine and Biology (hon.), Am. Inst. Ultrasound Medicine (sr.; sr. fel.). Achievements include invention of Doppler fetal actocardiograph, 1984. Avocations: photography, vintage camera, computer works, classical music. Home: 125 3-Chome Nadamachi Yonago Tottori 683-0835 Japan Personal E-mail: maedak@mocha.ocn.ne.jp.

MAEDA, MASANOBU, physiology educator, researcher; b. Osaka, Japan, Aug. 24, 1952; s. Shunichirou and Misao Maeda; m. Eiko Ikeuchi, June 12, 1982; children: Akiko, Ayako, Satoko, Eiichi. MD, Osaka City U., 1979, PhD, 1985. Resident Osaka City U. Hosp., Japan, 1979—81; instr. Osaka City U. Med. Sch., 1985—91, asst. prof., 1991—92; assoc. prof. sys. physiology U. Occupl. Environ. Health, Kitakyushu, Japan, 1993—2000; prof. physiology Wakayama Med. U., Japan, 2000—. Vis. prof. U. Medicine and Dentistry of N.J., N.J. Med. Sch., Newark, 1989-91. Contbr. articles to profl. jours. Grantee Ministry Edn., Sci., Sports and Culture of Japan, 2011. Fellow Physiol. Soc. Japan; mem. Am. Physiol. Soc., Soc. for Neurosci., Internat. Soc. for Autonomic Neurosci., Am. Heart Assn. (circulation coun.). Avocations: music, mountain climbing. Office: Wakayama Med U Sch Medicine Dept Physiol 811-1 Kimiidera Wakayama 641-8509 Japan

MAEDA, NOBUAKI, biochemist, educator; b. Yokohama, Kanagawa, Japan, Mar. 12, 1959; s. Masayoshi and Sumie (Murayama) M. BS, Nagoya U., Japan, 1981, MS, 1983; PhD, Osaka U., Japan, 1988. Postdoctoral fellow Inst. for Protein Rsch., Osaka, 1988-90; rsch. assoc. Inst. Devel. Rsch., Aichi, Japan, 1990-92, Nat. Inst. Basic Biology, Aichi, 1992-97; asst. prof. Grad. U. Advanced Studies, Aichi, 1993-97; assoc. prof. Nat. Inst. for Basic Biology, Aichi, 1997—2001, Grad. U. for Advanced Studies, Kanagawa, 1999—2001; lab. head Tokyo Met. Inst. for Neurosci., 2001—11; project leader Tokyo Met Inst. Med. Sci., 2011—. Contbr. articles to profl. jours. Recipient postdoctoral fellowship Japan Soc. Promotion of Sci., 1988-90, award Takeda Sci. Found., 2002, award Brain Sci. Found., 2002, award Mizutani Found. Glycosci., 2004, Uehara Meml. Found., 2004, Naito Found., 2007. Mem. Japanese Biochemistry Soc., Japanese Soc. Neurosci., Am. Soc. Biochemistry and Molecular Biology. Office: Tokyo Met Inst Med Sci 2-1-6 Kamikitazawa Setagaya Tokyo 156-8506 Japan Home: 2-22-39 Renkoji Tama Tokyo 206-0021 Japan Business E-Mail: maeda-nb@igakuken.or.jp.

MAEDA, SHINICHIRO, pharmacist, educator; b. Kagawa, Japan, Mar. 13, 1978; MS, Osaka U., 2002. Pharmacist dept. pharmacy Osaka U. Hosp., 2002; asst. prof. Grad. Sch. Pharm. Scis., Osaka U. Hosp., 2009—. Office: Yamadaoka 2-15 Suita Osaka 565-0871 Japan Business E-Mail: maeda313@hosp.med.osaka-u.ac.jp.

MAEDA, TAKESHI, spine surgeon; b. Kitakyushu, Fukuoka, Japan, Oct. 11, 1961; s. Toshiharu and Sachiko Maeda; m. Tomoko Inoue; children: Kyoko, Moeko, Eriko. MD, Kyushu U., Fukuoka. Cert. in orthop. surgery Japanese Orthop. Assn. Bd., 1994, in spine surgery Japanese Soc. Spinal Surgery and Related Rsch. Bd., 2003. Hosp. resident Kyushu U., 1986—88, rschr., 1990—94, assoc. prof., 1998—2007; med. stuff Hiroshima Red Cross Hosp., Japan, 1988—89, Karatsu Red Cross Hosp., Saga, Japan, 1989—90; chief med. stuff Spinal Injuries Ctr., Iizuka, Fukuoka, 2007—. Office: Spinal Injuries Ctr 550-4 Igisu Iizuka Fukuoka 820-8508 Japan Business E-Mail: maeken@ortho.med.kyushu-u.ac.jp.

MAEDE, YOSHIMITSU, retired veterinarian educator; b. Japan, Feb. 22, 1944; DVM, Hokkaido U., 1967, PhD, 1980. Prof. Grad. Sch. Vet. Medicine Hokkaido U., 1987—2007, dean, 1996—99; v.p. Hokkaido U., 1999—2001, dir. Vet. Tchg. Hosp., 2001—03. Mem. bd. dirs. Japan Vet. Med. Assn., 1990—92. Recipient Vet. Sci. prize, Japan Vet. Med. Assn. Fellow: Japanese Soc. Vet. Sci. (mem. bd. dirs. 2002—05, Vet. Sci. prize). Avocations: fishing, birdwatching, writing. Home: Akebono-4-1-3-8 Teine-ku Sapporo Hokkaido 006-0834 Japan

MAEHARA, KAYOKO, medical researcher; b. Japan, Feb. 21, 1967; MD, Hamamatsu U. Sch. Medicine, 1996. Resident physician Hamamatsu U. Sch. Medicine, 1991—92; postdoc. scientist Nat. Inst. Longevity Scis., 1996—2002, Paterson Inst. Cancer Rsch., Christie Hosp. NHS Trust, 2002—04; asst. prof. Inst. Life Sci., Kurume U., 2005—10; chief Nat. Rsch. Inst. Child Health and Devel., 2010—. Fellow Domestic Rsch. fellowship, Japan Sci. and Tech. Corp.; Grant-in-Aid, Japan Soc. Promotion Sci., rsch. grant, Ichiro Kanehara Found. Promotion Med. Scis. and Med. Care, Postdoc. fellowship, Assn. Internat. Cancer Rsch., fellowship, Japan Found. Aging and Health. Mem.: Japan Soc. Obstetrics & Gynecology, Japan Soc. Biomedical Gerontology, Molecular Biology Soc. Japan, ASM. Avocations: walking, swimming, movies. Office: 2-10-1 Okura Tokyo Setagaya 157-8535 Japan Office Fax: 81-3-3417-2864. Business E-Mail: kmaehara@nch.go.jp.

MAEKAWA, TOSHIHIKO, psychiatrist, educator; b. Okinawa, Japan, July 12, 1964; MD, Kyushu U., 1996, PhD, 2006. Asst. prof. Grad. Sch. Med. Scis., Kyushu U., 2006—09, 2011—, Kyuhshu U. Hosp., 2010—11; postdoc. fellow Harvard Med. Sch., 2009—11. Mem.: Japanese Soc. Biol. Psychiatry, Japan Epilepsy Soc., Japan Clin. Neurophysiology, Japanese Soc. Gen. Hosp. Psychiatry, Japanese Soc. Schizophrenia Rsch. Office: Maidashi3 1 1 Higashiku Fukuoka 812-8582 Japan Office Fax: 81-92-642-5644. Business E-Mail: t-mae@npsych.med.kyushu-u.ac.jp.

MAELAND, JOHAN ANDREAS, retired microbiologist, researcher; b. Hordaland, Norway, Feb. 22, 1934; s. Nils and Hilda Maeland; divorced; children: Frode, Njall, Dag. MD, U. Bergen, Norway, 1959, PhD, 1969. Cert. specialist in med. microbiology. Intern Haugesund (Norway) Hosp., 1959-60, U. Hosp., Bergen, Norway, 1961-63, resident, 1963-74; asst. prof. U. Buffalo, 1971-72; head dept. microbiology Regional Hosp., Trondheim, Norway, 1971—2001, ret., 2002, prof. emeritus, 2004—, Prof. U. Trondheim, 1975—, dean med. faculty, 1978-80; bd. dirs. Norwegian Rsch. Counsel, 1980-86. Contr. 120 articles to profl. jours. and sci. publs. Lt. Norwegian Air Force, 1961. Recipient Schering Corp. prize, 1984. Mem. ESCMID, Am. Soc. Microbiology, Scandinavian Nat. Med. Socs. Mem. Conservative Party. Lutheran. Avocations: travel, music, literature. Office: Univ Hosp Olav Kyrresg 17 N 7006 Trondheim Norway Home: Havstadvegen 15A 7021 Trondheim Norway Personal E-mail: joanmael@online.no. Business E-Mail: johan.meland@ntnu.no.

MAENG, SUNGHO EDDIE, medical educator; b. Toronto, Can., June 10, 1968; MD, Konkuk U., 1992; PhD, Seoul Nat. U., 2001. Vis. fellow Nat. Cancer Inst. NIH, 2001—05, vis. fellow NIMH, 2005—07; rschr. Maria Biotech. Co., 2007—10; asst. prof. Kyung Hee U., Grad. Sch. East-West Med. Sci., 2010—. Mem.: Korean Soc. Pharmacology, Soc. Neurosci. Home: Sucho-gu Sucho dong Sampoong AP 16-705 Seoul 137-779 Republic of Korea Personal E-mail: jethrot@hotmail.com.

MAENO, SHINICHI, physician; b. Nagoya, Aichi, Japan, July 2, 1972; MD, Keio U. Sch. Medicine, 1997, PhD. Assoc. prof. Shioya Hosp., Internat. U. Health & Welfare, 2011—. Mem.: Japanese Orthopaedic Assn. Home: 1-14-13 Tsuganodai Wakaba-ku Chiba-city 264-0033 Japan Home Fax: 81-43-287-5426. Personal E-mail: maenoshin@gmail.com.

MAES, MICHAEL, psychiatrist, educator; b. Ghent, Belgium, Mar. 10, 1954; came to U.S., 1991; s. Leo and Jeanne (Delfosse) M.; life partner: Olga Mikhaleva; children: Annabel, Eveline, Xenia. MD, RUG Univ., Ghent, 1979; Psychiatrist, U. Antwerp, Belgium, 1986, PhD, 1991. Dir. dept. U. Antwerp, 1986—91; asst. prof. psychiatry Case Western Res. U.-Univ. Hosp. Cleve., 1991—95; dir. Clin. Rsch. Ctr. Mental Health, Antwerp, 1996—; adj. prof. psychiatry Vanderbilt U., Nashville, 1997—; prof. psychiatry U. Maastricht, Netherlands, 1999—; dir. MCare4U Outpatient Clinics, Belgium. Cons. psychiatrist IRCCS, Brescia, Italy, 1997—2004; invited lectr. over 200 internat. confs.; editor Acta Neuropsychiatrica. Contbr. numerous articles to profl. jours. Dir. Art Gallery Ediver, Lanaken, Belgium. Mem. AAAS, Soc. Biol. Psychiatry, Internat. Brain Rsch. Assn., World Psychiat. Assn. (sec. sects.), European Coll. Neuropsychopharmacology, Internat. Soc. Psychoneuroendocrinology, European Assn. Psychiatrists, N.Y. Acad. Scis. Achievements include research in psychoneuroendocrinology and immunology of severe depression in man. Home Phone: 0032-15-3309777. E-mail: crc.mh@telenet.be.

MAES, PAUL JOEL, dentist; b. Bozeman, Mont., Mar. 29, 1952; s. Joseph Paul Maes and Alice Mae Ehlman; m. Nancy Susan Gallagher, Dec. 21, 1975 (div. Feb. 2001); children: Jacob Paul, Joshua William, Jeffrey Gallagher, Justin Timothy; m. Stephanie Patton Hilger, Apr. 11, 2008; stepchildren: Mackenzie, Taylor, Sam. BA, U. Mont., Missoula, 1974; BS in Dentistry, U. Minn., Mpls., 1976, DDS, 1978. Dentist USN, San Diego, 1978—81; pvt. practice Helena, Mont., 1981—2006; group practice South Hills Dental, Helena, 2006—; regional v.p. Acad. Gen. Denstry, 1994—96. Trustee Shodair Hosp., Helena, 1990—2001; co-founder Helena Coop. Dental Clinic, 1991, chmn. dental adv. bd., 1992—; pres. Mont. chpt. Donated Dental Svcs., 1996—; founder Shodair Classic All Star Soccer Game, Mont., 2000; bd. dirs. Holter Mus. Art, Helena, 2006—08. Lt. comdr. USNR, 1978—81. Master: Acad. Gen. Dentistry (Nat. Humanitarian award 1999); fellow: Internat. Coll. Dentists, Am. Coll. Dentists; mem.: ADA, Cmty. Health Assn. Mountain/Plains States (Outstanding Vol. award 2002), Mont. Dental Assn. (Clin. execellence award 2000), Mont. Dental Assn., Mont. Study Club. Avocations: backpacking, photography, bicycling. Office: South Hills Dental 2480 Tracy Dr Helena MT 59601 Office Phone: 406-443-2780. Office Fax: 406-443-5902.

MAESTRO, MARIO ALVAREZ, urologist; b. Madrid, July 23, 1978; Degree in Urology, Hosp. U. La Paz, 2003. Lic. in medicine and surgery U. Complutense Madrid, 2002; cert. Nat. Langs. Sch. Nat. commn. officer European Soc. Residents Urology, 2006—, database mgr.; attending urologist Dept. Urology Hosp. U. Infanta Sofia, 2009—. Mem. editl. bd. Annals Urology, Archivos Espaholes de Urologia, Actas Espaftolas de Urologia and Jour. Med. Reports. Contbr. articles to jours. publs. Fellow: European Bd. Urology; mem.: European Assn. Transluminal Surgery, Endourology Soc., Internat. Soc. Sexual Medicine, European Soc. Sexual Medicine, Madrid Urological Soc., Am. Urology Assn., European Assn. Urology, Spanish Assn. Urology. Personal E-mail: malvarezmaestro@hotmail.com.

MAETANI, IRURU, medical educator; b. Tokyo, Mar. 10, 1958; s. Teruji and Sadako (Saeki) M.; m. Haruko Hayashi, Jan. 11, 1961. M of Med. Sci., Toho U., Tokyo, 1982, MD, 1982. Instr. 3d dept. internal medicine Toho U., Tokyo, 1982-87, instr., 1987-97, asst. prof., 1997—2006, prof., chmn., 2006—. Contbr. articles to profl. jours. Office: Toho U Ohashi Med ctr 2-17-6 Ohashi Meguro-ku 153-8515 Tokyo Japan Office Phone: 81-3-3468-1251. Business E-Mail: mtnir50637@med.toho-u.ac.jp.

MAEYAMA, AKIRA, medical educator; b. Fukuoka City, Japan, Sept. 1, 1976; MD, Fukuoka U., PhD, 2002. Asst. prof., dept. orthop. surgery Sch. Medicine Fukuoka U., 2010. Office: 7-45-1 Nanakuma Jonan-ku Fukuoka 814-0180 Japan Personal E-mail: akira.maeyama0713@joy.ocn.ne.jp.

MAFFEO, ALPHONSE A., anesthesiologist; b. 1947; MD, SUNY Syracuse, 1972. Diplomate Am. Bd. Anesthesiology. Intern Harrisburg Hosp., 1972-73; res. anesthesiology Mass Gen. Hosp., Boston, 1973-75; physician Lehigh Valley Hosp., Allentown, Pa., 1977—, chmn. anesthesiology, 1990-2001. Clin. assoc. prof., assoc. chmn. anesthesiology Pa. St. U. Hershey Med. Ctr., 1994—2001. Fellow ABA, Am. Coll. Anesthesiologists, mem. Am. Soc. Anesthesiologists. Office: Allentown Anesthes Assn Inc 1245 S Cedar Crest Blvd Ste 301 Allentown PA 18103-6258

MAFFIA, JASON, health services administrator; b. NYC, June 23, 1977; s. Anthony and Gerri Maffia, Anthony and Gerri Maffia. MS in Psychology, Iona Coll., New Rochelle, NY, 2002. Diplomate cert. expert traumatic stress, cert. emergency crisis response, acute traumatic stress mgmt. Am. Acad. Experts Traumatic Stress, NY, cert. in health cons. Therapist Goodwill Industries, Queens, NY, 2002—03; applied behavior sci. specialist AHRC Nassau County, Brookville, NY, 2004—06; health svcs. adminstr., clin. supr. critical incident stress mgmt. team GEO Group Inc, Queens Pvt. Detention Facility, Jamaica, NY, 2006—, Team coord., mental health profl. Regional EMS Coun. NYC: Critical Incident Response Team; team leader, mental health profl. Nassau County Critical Incident Stress Mgmt. Team; team mem. Nassau County Cmty. Emergency Response Team: Office Emergency Mgmt.; presenter in field. Contbr. articles to profl. jours. Recipient Pioneering Sprit award, ICISF, 2009. Mem.: Nat. Scholars Honor Soc., Nat. Honor Soc. Psych., Nat. Ctr. Crisis Mgmt.: Premier Speakers Bur., Disaster Preparedness Emergency Response Assn., Internat. Critical Incident Stress Found., Am. Acad. Experts Traumatic Stress. Republican. Home: 722 Willow Rd Franklin Square NY 11010 Personal E-mail: jmaff72653@aol.com.

MAGAL, MEIR, physical education educator; b. Tel-Aviv, Mar. 19, 1971; PhD, U. Southern Miss., 2002. Assoc. prof. exercise sci. NC Wesleyan Coll., 2002—. Fellow: Am. Coll. Sports Medicine. Home: 7333 Brighton Hill Ln Raleigh NC 27616 Business E-Mail: mmagal@ncwc.edu.

MAGALHÃES, EDUARDO, physical therapist; b. São Paulo, Brazil, Dec. 21, 1982; Degree, U. Guarulhos, 2004; M, Fed. U. São Paulo, 2010. Head Eduardo Magalhães Inst., 2006—. Invited prof. Santa Casa de Misericórdia de São Paulo, 2007; editl. mem. Word Jour. Orthopedics, 2011. Recipient Excellence Rsch. award, Jour. Orthop. & Sports Phys. Therapy, 2010, Rsch. award, Internat. Soc. Arthroscopy, Knee Surgery and Orthop. Sports Medicine, 2011. Master: Fed. U. São Paulo. Avocation: soccer. Office: Domingos de Moraes n°2243 São Paulo 04035000 Brazil Personal E-mail: emresearch@hotmail.com.

MAGALHÃES, FERNANDA OLIVEIRA, endocrinologist, educator; b. Uberaba, Brazil, May 24, 1966; d. José Aluízio and Marília José de Oliveira Magalhães; children: João Lucas Magalhães Hueb Menezes, Carolina Magalhães Hueb Menezes. MD, Triangulo Mineiro Fed. U., Uberaba, Brazil, 1988; PhD, São Paulo U., Brazil, 1996. Lic. physician Faculdade Medicina do Triângulo Mineiro, 1988. Residency Triangulo Mineiro Fed. U., 1991—94; physician Faculdade Medicina Triangulo Mineiro, 1995—2000, prof., 1998—2000, Uberaba U., 2000—, rschr., 2002—. Coord. diabetes academic league Uberaba U., 2005—, coord. rsch. and post grad. group primary attention, 2007—; cons. in field. Med. dir. Diabetes Assn. Uberaba and Vale do Rio Grande, Uberaba, 1996—99, sec., 1999—2002. Recipient Best Rsch. on IX Diabetes award, Brazilian Congress, 1993. Mem.: Endocrinology Brazilian Soc. (assoc.). Messianic. Achievements include research in diabetes and obesity. Avocations: travel, walking, movies, music. Office: Afonso Ratto 415 Uberaba Minas Gerais 38060-040 Brazil Office Fax: 55-34-33335758. Personal E-mail: fefef@terra.com.br. Business E-Mail: fernanda.magalhaes@uniube.br.

MAGALHÃES, ROSANA, researcher; b. Rio de Janeiro, Sept. 9, 1959; PhD, UERJ, 1999. Cert. nutritionist UFRJ, 1982. Rschr. Oswaldo Cruz Found., 1889—. Mem.: ABRASCO. Avocations: tennis, travel, swimming. Office: Rua Leopoldo Bulhões 1480 Rio de Janeiro 21940120 Brazil Office Fax: 21 25982779. Business E-Mail: rosana@ensp.fiocruz.br.

MAGALLONA, EDWIN PAUL V., surgeon; b. Quezon City; BS in Biology major in Cell Biology, U. Philippines, Los Banos, 1990; grad. in Medicine, DeLa Salle U., 1994. Cert. cosmetic reconstructive and plastic surgeon Philippine Bd. of Plastic Surgery. Intern Makati Med. Ctr.; specialized in gen. surgery Univ. East Ramon Magsaysay Meml. Ctr., Philippines; subspecialized in plastic, reconstructive and aesthetic surgery Consortium I Program (UERMMMC, Makati Med.

Ctr., Veterans Meml. Med. Ctr., Rizal Med. Ctr.); surgeon Philippine Cosmetic Plastic Surgery. Fellow: Philippine Assn. of Plastic, Reconstructive and Aesthetic Surgeons (PAPRAS), Philippine Coll. of Surgeons (PCS); mem.: Oriental Soc. of Aesthetic Plastic Surgery (OSAPS), Philippine Bd. of Plastic Surgery (diplomate). Office: Med Central Medical Clinics and Diagnostic Center L/1 Food Blvd Robinson's Galleria EDSA Corner Ortigas Ave Quezon City Philippines Office Phone: 636334567. *

MAGAREY, MARY ELIZABETH, physical therapist, educator; b. Adelaide, Australia, Oct. 11, 1952; Diploma in Physiotherapy, South Australian Inst. Tech., 1971; PhD, U. South Australia, 1999. Sr. tutor South Australian Inst. Tech., 1976—80; lectr. U. South Australia, 1980—96, sr. lectr., 1996—. Chmn. academic stds. com. Manipulative Physiotherapists Assn. Australia, 1986—99. Fellow: Australian Coll. Physiotherapists (v.p. 2009—11); mem.: Sports Medicine Australia, Sports Physiotherapy Australia, Musculoskeletal Physiotherapy Australia, Australian Physiotherapy Assn. Avocations: sports, reading. Office: University South Australia N Ter Adelaide South Australia 5000 Australia Office Fax: 61883022977. Business E-Mail: mary.magarey@unisa.edu.au.

MAGAZINE, CYNTHIA PENROSE, retired health care consultant; b. Manila, Philippines, Nov. 24, 1939; d. Douglas Lee Lipscomb Cordiner and Jane (Sturgeon) Edises; m. Douglas Francis Penrose, July 11, 1959 (div. 1981); children: Vicki, Lee Douglas; m. Alan Harrison Magazine, Aug. 30, 1984. BA, U. Calif., Berkeley, 1963; MBA, U. Santa Clara, 1977. LCSW. V.p., dir. employment Resource Ctr. for Women, Palo Alto, Calif., 1973-78; bus. planner Raychem Corp., Menlo Park, Calif., 1979; adminstrv. mgr. Electric Power Rsch. Inst., Palo Alto, 1979-83; sr. ptnr. MB Assocs., Washington, 1983—85; dir. ops. Utility Data Inst., Washington, 1985—86, Randmark, Inc., 1986-87; coord. market devel. for Mid-Atlantic states Kaiser Found. Health Plan, Washington, 1987-88, asst. to assoc. regional mgr., 1988-94; market planner MetraHealth, Vienna, Va., 1995; exec. staff asst. United HealthCare, Vienna, 1995, dir. strategic planning, splty. cos., 1996-97; dir. spl. projects MetraComp subs. United HealthCare, Vienna, 1997, v.p. regulatory affairs and compliance, 1997-99; ptnr. Penrose Mag. LLC, 2000—01; ret., 2001. Bd. dirs., treas. Unique Enterprises, Washington, 1985-87; sec. Wesley Property Mgmt. Co., 1987-89; bd. dirs. Wesley Housing Devel. Corp., 1988-89. Chair vol. com. Habitat for Humanity, No. Va., 2002—03, bd. dirs., 2003—06, chair Restore adv. com., 2003—05, v.p., exec. com., 2005—06; mem. Affirmative Action Adv. Com., Palo Alto, 1975—76; bd. dirs., sec. Am. Hospice Found., 1995—97, treas., 1998—2000; bd. dirs. Nat. Inst. for Med. Options, 1999—2001; bd. dirs., v.p. LWV, Berkeley, 1966—72, Palo Alto, 1972—73; chmn. program adv. com. Resource Ctr. for Women, Palo Alto, 1980—83. Mem. Peninsula Profl. Women's Network (v.p. 1981-82), U. Calif. Alumni Assn., AAUW (Bicentennial br. sec. 1986-88), Scottsdale, Ariz. (2008-), Fountain Hills, Ariz. (2007-), 4 Peaks Women's Club, Fountain Hills (2007-09), Fountain Hills Libr. Assn. (bd. dir. & mem. chair 2009-), Restore Com. Habitat Humanity Desert Foothills (chair 2009-), Capitol Area Soc. Healthcare Planning and Mktg., Nat. Capital Healthcare Execs., LWV. Democrat. Episcopalian. Avocations: nutrition and health, reading. Home: 16449 E Bainbridge Ave Fountain Hills AZ 85268 Home and Office: 16449 E Bainbridge Ave Fountain Hills AZ 85268 Home Phone: 480-219-6279. Personal E-mail: ccpenrose@cox.net.

MAGEE, BERNARD DALE, obstetrician, gynecologist; b. Niagara Falls, NY, June 8, 1950; s. Bernard Dale and Rose (Roffle) Magee; m. Melanie Ann Ciszek, Aug. 31, 1974; 1 child, Ryan. Student, SUNY, Buffalo, 1968-71; MD, SUNY, Syracuse, 1975; MS, Dartmouth Coll., 1998. Diplomate Am. Bd. Ob-Gyn., Am. Bd. Med. Examiners. Resident Case Western Res., 1975—79; obstetrician-gynecologist Fallon Clinic, Worcester, Mass., 1979-83; pvt. practice Shrewsbury, Mass., 1983-96, U. Mass. Cmty. Physicians, Shrewsbury, 1996—2001, Shrewsbury Ob-Gyn, 2001—; med. dir. Ctrl. MA Ind. Physicians Assn., 2004—05, bd. trustees, 2009—; commr. pub. health Worcester, Mass., 2011—. Chmn. ob-gyn. com. Ctrl. Mass. Health Care, Worcester, 1990—97, trustee, 1993—95. Fellow: ACOG; mem.: AMA, Ctrl. Mass. Ind. Physicians Assn. (med. dir. 2004—05), Worcester Dist. Med. Soc. (tras. 1988—94, pres. 1995—96), Mass. Med. Soc. (chmn. com. quality med. practice 1997—2000, 2004—, v.p. 2005—05, pres. 2007—08), Maddox Soc. (pres. 1992—94). Avocation: medical history. Office: 604 Main St Shrewsbury MA 01545-5639

MAGEE, ELAINE, dietician, consultant; BS in Nutrition, San Jose State U.; MPH in Nutrition, U. Calif., Berkeley. Registered Dietitian. Nutrition instr. Diablo Valley Coll.; nutrition mktg. specialist Calif. Dept. Health; host Light Cooking segment KSBW-TV NBC, Salinas, Calif.; nutrition expert & writer WebMD, SilverPlanet; nutrition expert & writer for nationally syndicated newspaper column The Recipe Doctor. Author: Eat Well for a Healthy Menopause, 1996, The Good News Eating Plan for Type II Diabetes, 1997, Someone's in the Kitchen with Mommy: 100 Easy Recipies and Fun Crafts for Parents and Kids, 1997, The Flax Cookbook: Recipes and Strategies for Getting the Most From the Most Powerful Plant on the Planet, 2003, Fry Light, Fry Right: Fried Food Flavor Without Deep Frying, 2004, The Change of Life Diet & Cookbook, 2004, Food Synergy: Unleash Hundreds of Powerful Healing Food Combinations to Fight Disease and Live Well, 2008, (med. nutrition series) Tell Me What to Eat If I Have...; regular contbr. to Women's Day and All You, written articles and recipes are featured in American Girl Mag. and Cooking Light, guest appearances on CBS Evening News, CNN, Caryl & Marilyn Real Friends, Good Morning NY and Debra Duncan Show.

MAGEE, KATHLEEN S., foundation executive; b. NJ; m. William Preston Magee, Jr.; 5 children. BSN, Coll. Misericordia, Pa.; MEd, U. Md.; MSW, Norfolk State U. Nurse, social worker; co-founder (with William P. Magee, Jr.) Operation Smile, 1982, pres., bd. dir. Featured guest Montel Williams, guest appearances Dateline NBC, CBS Sunday Morning, 48 Hours, NBC Nightly News. Bd. gov. World of Children; adv. bd. World Healing Inst.; founder, organizer World Journey of Hope, 1999. Recipient Conrad N. Hilton Humanitarian prize, 1996, Servants of Peace award, 1997, Golden Plate award, Am. Acad. Achievement, 1999, Kellogg's Hannah Neil World of Children award, 1999, Lifetime Volunteer Achievement award, Operation Smile, 2005; co-recipient Common Wealth Disting. Svc. award, 2001; named one of America's Best Leaders, US News & World Report, 2009; named to Med. Mission Hall of Fame, 2004. Office: Operation Smile 6453 Tidewater Dr Norfolk VA 23509

MAGEE, THOMAS HENRY, radiologist, educator; b. Newport, RI, Nov. 26, 1958; s. Francis Robert and Anne Louise (Moriarty) M.; m. Christina Marie (Lapolla), June 7, 1987. BA, Wesleyan Univ., 1977-81; MD, NY. Med. Coll., 1982-86. Diplomate Am. Bd. Radiology. Staff radiologist Bethesda Naval Hosp., Md., 1991-94; asst. prof. medicine Uniformed Svc. Sch. of Med., Bethesda, Md., 1991-94, Kans. U. Sch. of Med., Kans. City, Kans., 1994—; staff radiologist Menorah Med. Pk., Overland Pk., Kans., 1994—; asst. prof. radiology U. Mo., Kans. City, Mo., 1997—2006; clin. prof. radiology U. Miami, 2006—. Pres. Rockhill Radiology, 1999; bd. examiner Am. Bd. Radiology; reviewer prof. jours., Am. Coll. Radiology. Contbr. articles to profl. jours. including Radiology, Jour. of Computer Assisted Tomography, Am. Jour. Roentgenology. Lt. comdr. USNR, 1991-94. Recipient: Jonas N. Muller Award, NY Med. Coll., 1986. Fellow Am. Coll. Radiology; mem. Am. Roentegen Ray Soc., Radiol. Soc. N.Am. (moderator, cert. of merit 1990); Kansas City Roentegen Ray Soc. (pres.), Internat. Skeletal Soc., Am. Bd. Radiology (bd. examiner, 2005). Avocations: stamp collecting/philately, tennis. Home: 235 Lansing Island Dr Indian Harbor Beach FL 32937 Office: Neuroskeletal Imaging Melbourne FL Personal E-mail: tmageerad@cfl.rr.com.

MAGEE, WILLIAM PRESTON, JR., plastic surgeon; b. NJ; m. Kathleen S. Magee; 5 children. BS, Mt. St. Mary's Coll., Maryland; DDS, U. Md.; MD, George Washington U. Resident gen. surgery U. Va. Med. Sch.; resident plastic surgery Ea. Va. Grad. Sch. Medicine; pvt. practice Norfolk, Va.; co-founder (with Kathleen S. Magee) Operation Smile, 1982, CEO; co-dir. Inst. Craniofacial and Plastic Surgery Children's Hosp. of King's Daughters, chmn. Plastic Surgery Dept.; assoc. prof. plastic surgery Ea. Va. Med. Sch. Contbr. chapters to books, articles to med. jours.; guest appearances NBC Nightly News, Dateline NBC, Fox News, Leeza, The Rosie O'Donnell Show, Hour of Power, 48 Hours, CBS Sunday Morning, Touched by an Angel. Bd. dirs. Operation Smile; founder, organizer World Journey of Hope, 1999; bd. dirs. talksurgery.com. Recipient Conrad N. Hilton Humanitarian prize, 1996, Servants of Peace award, 1997, Golden Plate award, Am. Acad. Achievement, 1999, Frank Annunzio award, Christopher Columbus Fellowship Found., 2002; co-recipient Common Wealth award disting. svc., 2001; named one of America's Best Leaders, US News & World Report, 2009; named to Med. Mission Hall of Fame, 2003. Mem.: Am. Soc. Plastic Surgeons (Disting. Svc. award 1998), Va. Soc. Plastic and Reconstructive Surgeons (pres. 1991—93), AMA (Pride in the Profession award 2000). Office: Operation Smile 6435 Tidewater Dr Norfolk VA 23509

MAGID, STEVEN K., rheumatologist, educator; MD, Cornell U., 1976. Diplomate Am. Bd. Internal Medicine, Am. Bd. Internal Medicine-rheumatology. Intern Weill Cornell Med. Coll.; resident internal medicine New York Hosp., 1977—79; fellow rheumatology Hosp. for Spl. Surgery, 1979—81, assoc. attending physician; with NY Presbyn. Hosp. Assoc. clin. prof. medicine Weill Cornell Med. Coll. Fellow: ACP, Am. Coll. of Rheumatology. Office: Hospital for Special Surgery 535 E 70th St New York NY 10021 Office Phone: 212-606-1060. Office Fax: 212-794-2543.

MAGILL, ALAN JON, preventive medicine physician; b. Craig, Colo., Nov. 26, 1953; s. Reese Arnett and Rose (Zaccardo) M.; m. Janiine Grace Babcock, June 10, 1984; children: Lara, Sarah. BS in Biology, Chemistry, Environ. Sci., Lamar U., 1976; MS in Zoology, U. R.I., 1978; MD, Baylor U., 1984. Intern internal medicine Tripler Army Med. Ctr., Honolulu, 1984-85, resident, internal medicine, 1985-87; staff physician, internal medicine 5th Gen. Hosp., Bad Canstaat, Germany, 1987-89; fellow infectious diseases Walter Reed Army Med. Ctr., Washington, 1989-92, infectious disease officer dept. immunology, 1992-94, asst. chief, immunology, 1994—96, attending physician; chief dept. parasitology Naval Med. Rsch. Ctr. Detachment, Lima, Peru, 1996—99; head clin. rsch., malaria vaccine devel. unit NIH, 1999—2001; dir. divsn. exptl. therapeutics Walter Reed Army Inst. Rsch., Silver Springs, Md., rsch. coord., Leishmania rsch. program and anti-Malaria drug R&D program, Mil. Infectious Disease Rsch. Program. Assoc. prof. medicine and preventive medicine and biometrics Uniformed Services U. the Health Scis., Bethesda, Md. Asst. editor: Hunter's Tropical Medicine, 1995; contbr. articles to profl. jours., books. Maj. U.S. Army, 1984—. Fellow Am. Coll. Physicians; mem. Am. Soc. Tropical Medicine and Hygiene (pres. clin. group), Infectious Disease Soc. America, Royal Soc. Tropical Medicine and Hygiene, Internat. Soc. Travel Medicine (pres.). Avocations: mountain climbing, skiing. Office: Walter Reed Army Inst Rsch 503 Robert Grant Ave Silver Spring MD 20910-7500

MAGLACAS, A. MANGAY, nursing researcher, educator; BSN, Vanderbilt U.; MPH, U. Minn.; DPH, Johns Hopkins U.; DSc (hon.), U. Ill.; DSc (hon.), St. Paul U., Tuguegarao City, Philippines. Former chief sci. for nursing devel. health manpower divsn. WHO, Geneva, Switzerland, 1976-89, regional nurse adviser Southeast Asia Office Delhi, India, 1972-75. Internat. health/nursing cons., 1989—; adj. prof. Coll. Nursing, U. Ill., Chgo., 1990-2000; various vis. prof. positions in several countries, 1990—. Former mem., bd. dirs. Internat. Coun. Nurses, 1989-93; fgn. assoc. NAS Inst. Medicine, 1988—. Rockefeller fellow, 1964-67; Fulbright-Smith-Mundt scholar, 1952-54; recipient Outstanding alumni award Vanderbilt U., 1986, Internat. Pub. Health Leadership award Johns Hopkins U., 1992, Outstanding Profl. award for Nursing, Profl. Regulation Commn. of Philippines, 2000, Profl. Recognition award U. Philippines, 1989, Disting. Achievement award Philippine Nurses Assn., 1989, Outstanding Alumni award U. Philippines Sch. Nursing, 1987, Disting. Leadership award USA Commn. on Grads. of Fgn. Nursing Schs., 2002; named Woman of Yr. Am. Rsch. Inst. Bd. Internat. Rsch., 1988, named Most Outstanding Paulinian St. Paul's U., Philippines, 2002. Fellow Royal Coll. Nursing U.K. (hon.). Office: 147 Panay Ave 1103 Quezon City Philippines Home Phone: 6324358894. Personal E-mail: amelia_maglacas@yahoo.com.ph.

MAGLIONE, MANUEL, general and transplant surgeon; b. Bolzano, Italy, Nov. 7, 1978; Degree, Franziskanergymnasium, 1997; MD, Innsbruck Med. U., 2003. Rsch. fellow, dept. surgery U. Pa., 2002; postdoc. fellow Innsbruck Med. U., Daniel Swarovski Rsch. Lab., 2003—05; physician, dept. visceral, transplant and thoracic surgery Innsbruck Med. U., Ctr. Operative Medicine, 2005—, sr. resident, 2005. Recipient award, Austrotransplant Soc., Biotest award; grant, Tiroler Wissenschaftsfond, 2008, Medizinischer Forschungsfond Tirol, European Soc. Organ Transplantation, 2009. Mem.: European Assn. Endoscopic Surgery, Internat. Soc. Pteridinology, Austrian Soc. Surgery, European Liver and Intestine Transplant Assn., European Soc. Transplantation. Avocations: poetry, mountain climbing, travel. Office: Anichstr 35 Innsbruck Tirol 6020 Austria Business E-Mail: manuel.maglione@i-med.ac.at.

MAGNAN, SANNE, health care company executive, former public health service officer; b. NC, Oct. 5, 1951; m. David Magnan; children: Grace, Hannah. BS in Pharmacy, U. NC, 1974; PhD in Medicinal Chemistry, U. Minn., 1978, MD, 1983. Cert. gen. internist. Staff physician various clinics; staff physician Lino Lakes Correctional Facility; lead physician Adult Care Clinic at Ramsey Clinic, Minn.; v.p., med. dir., consumer health Blue Cross Blue Shield Minn.; clin. asst. prof. medicine U. Minn.; staff physician, TB clinic St. Paul-Ramsey County Dept. Pub. Health, Minn.; pres. Inst. Clin. Systems Improvement, Bloomington, Minn.; commr. Minn. Dept. Health, St. Paul, 2007—11; pres., CEO Inst. for Clinical Systems Improvement, Bloomington, Minn., 2011—. Contbr. articles to profl. jours. Named one of 100 Influential Health Care Leaders, Minn. Physician, 2004, 2008; grantee Bush Fellowship, U. Minn., 1974—77. Office: Institute for Clinical Systems Improvement (ICSI) 8009 34th Ave S Ste 1200 Bloomington MN 55425 Office Phone: 952-814-7075. E-mail: Sanne.Magnan@icsi.org. *

MAGNANO, BRIAN J., physical therapist; b. Dec. 17, 1976; BS in Sports Medicine, U. Conn., 1999, MS in Phys. Therapy, 2002. Phys. therapy mgr. Bristol Orthops. Phys. Therapy, 2005—. Avocation: basketball. Office: 641 Clark Ave Ste A Bristol CT 06010 Personal E-mail: bmags45@yahoo.com.

MAGNARELLI, LOUIS ANTHONY, medical entomologist, microbiologist; b. Syracuse, NY, Mar. 27, 1945; s. David and Jennie Magnarelli; m. Sharon Dishaw, June 28, 1969. BS, SUNY, Oswego, 1967; MS, U. Mich., 1968; PhD, Cornell U., 1975. Asst. entomologist Conn. Agrl. Experiment Sta., New Haven, 1975-78, assoc. entomologist, 1978-81, scientist, 1981-87, state entomologist, chief scientist, 1987—2004, vice-dir., 1992—2004, dir., 2004—. Co-inventor in field. Named Edmund Niles Huyck Rsch. fellow, N.Y., 1974. Mem.: Conn. Acad. Scis. and Engring.

MAGNES, HARRY ALAN, physician; b. Orange, NJ, Dec. 3, 1948; s. Sam and Shirley (Daniels) Magnes; m. Patricia Bruce, Mar. 25, 1989; 1 child, Carlos Fontiveros. AB in Biology magna cum laude, Brown U., Providence, 1970; MD, Yale U., New Haven, Conn., 1974; M in Med. Mgmt., Tulane U., New Orleans, 1998; cert. in med. mgmt., Am. Coll. Physician Execs., 1997. Diplomate Am. Bd. Internal Medicine. Intern, resident internal medicine U. Iowa Hosps. and Clinics, 1974—77; ptnr., med. dir., pres., CEO Gallatin Med. Clinic, Downey, Calif., 1997—2001; pres., CEO Gallatin Med. Corp., Downey, Calif., 1992—94; med. dir., bd. dirs. Gallatin Med. Found., Downey, Calif., 1993—2001; chief med. officer Gallatin Med. Group, 2000—01, Physician Assocs. of Greater San Gabriel Valley, Pasadena, Calif., 2001—05; CEO Lovelace Med. Group, Albuquerque, 2005—07; pres., CEO ABQ Health Ptnrs. Endoscopy Ctr., 2008—, ABQ Health Ptnrs. Med. Group, 2007—. Staff physician Downey Cmty. Hosp., 1977—96, Presbyn. Intercmty. Hosp., 1992—2001; clin. instr. Rancho Los Amigos Hosp., Downey, 1981—83; chairperson bd. dirs. Primehealth of So. Calif., 1997—99; sec.-treas. Calif. Health Network, 1998—99; project adv. bd. VA/UCLA/RAND Calif. Med. Group, IPA Governance Project, 1997—98; prin. investigator Reach Asthma Rsch. Project, 2002; bd. dirs. Calif. Health Network; bd. govs. Lovelace Clinic Found., 2006—, Lovelace Med. Ctr., 2006—07, ABQ Health Ptnrs., 2007—, Med. Group Holding Co., 2007—; steering coms. N.Mex. Health Info. Collaborative, 2007—. Author: Rheumatic Fever in Connecticut, 1974. Bd. dirs. N.Mex. Symphony Orch., 2007—10, Wells Fargo Cmty. Bd., 2010—, Albuquerque C. of C., 2010—, Kirkland Partnership Com., 2011—. James Manning scholar Brown U., 1968; named one of Top Performing CEOs NM Bus. Week, 2009. Mem.: Greater Albuquerque Med. Assn., N.Mex. Med. Soc., Med. Group Mgmt. Assn., Am. Med. Group Assn. (policy com. 1994—98, legis. com. 1997—2000), Sigma Xi, Phi Beta Kappa, Delta Omega. Office Phone: 505-262-3085. Business E-Mail: harry.magnes@abqhp.com.

MAGNONI, SANDRA, anesthesiologist; b. Cles, Trento, Jan. 16, 1971; Degree, Med. Sch., Parma U., Italy, 1996; specialist in Anesthesia & Intensive Care, Milan U., 2003. Intensivist U. Hosp. Ca'Granda Policlinico, Milan, 2004—. Mem.: Am. Nat. Neurotrauma Soc., Italian Resuscitation Coun. Avocation: sports. Office: Via SForza 35 Milan 20122 Italy Business E-Mail: smagnoni@policlinico.mi.it.

MAGOON, PATRICK MICHAEL, hospital administrator; b. Chgo., Mar. 9, 1953; s. Albert George and Elizabeth Jane (Nolan) M.; m. Robin L. Gaeski, June 4, 1977. BA, Western Ill. U., 1976; MS in Urban Policy and Planning, U. Ill., Chgo., 1978. Asst. planner Children's Meml. Hosp., Chgo., 1977-78, adminstrv. svcs. mgr., 1978-80, dir. adminstrv. svcs., 1980-81, asst. v.p., 1981-83, v.p. adminstrn., 1983-90, v.p. adminstrn. ambulatory and satellite svcs., 1990, exec. v.p. corp. svcs., pres., CEO, 1998—. Bd. dirs. Nr. North Health Svcs. Corp., Chgo.; mem. profl. adv. com. Pediatric Excellence Program, Westchester, Ill., 1990—; chmn., Nat. Assn. Children's Hospitals and Related Instns., 2005-. Mem. Am. Hosp. Assn., Nat. Assn. Children's Hosp. and Related Instns., Ill. Hosp. Assn., Soc. for Ambulatory Care Profls, Met. Chgo. Healthcare Coun. (bd. dirs.), Comml. Club, Econ. Club, Exec. Club, City Club Chgo. Office: Children's Meml Hosp 2300 N Childrens Plz Chicago IL 60614-3394 *

MAGOVERN, GEORGE J., JR., thoracic surgeon, educator; MD, U. Pitts. Diplomate Am. Bd. Thoracic Surgery, Am. Bd. Thoracic Surgery-critical care surgery. Intern Johns Hopkins Hosp., resident; practice McGinnis Thoracic and Surgical Assocs.; prof. cardiovascular and thoracic surgery Drexel Univ.; chmn. dept. of thoracic and cardiovascular surgery Allegheny Gen. Hosp. Named one of Top Doctors, Pitts. mag., 2011. Office: Allegheny General Hospital 320 E N Ave Pittsburgh PA 15212 Office Phone: 412-359-3131. Office Fax: 412-359-4108.

MAGRAMM, IRENE, ophthalmologist; b. NYC, Jan. 24, 1955; BA, Columbia U. Barnard Coll., NYC, 1977; MD, Cornell U. Med. Coll., 1981. Diplomate Am. Bd. Ophthalmology, cert. Nat. Bd. Medical Examiners, lic. NY. Intern St. Luke's Hosp., NYC, 1981—82; resident ophthalmology North Shore U. Hosp., Manhasset, NY, 1982—85; fellowship pediat. ophthalmology, strabismus Manhattan Eye, Ear & Throat Hosp., NYC, 1985—86, asst. attending surgeon, 1986—89, assoc. attending surgeon, 1989—. Resident. instr. Manhattan Eye, Ear & Throat Hosp., 1986—90, resident selection com., 1987—93, asst.

dir. Pediat. Ophthalmology Clinic, 1987—, quality assurance com., 1990—, continuing edn. com., 1996—; clin. instr. ophthalmology Weill Med. Coll. Cornell U., 1989—2000, clin. asst. prof., 2000—; asst. attending ophthalmologist NY Hosp. Cornell Med. Ctr., 1989—; assoc. adj. ophthalmologist NY Eye Ear Infirmary, 1999—. Contbr. articles to profl. jours. Fellow: Am. Acad. Medicine, Am. Acad. Ophthalmology; mem.: NY Soc. Clin. Ophthalmology, NY Soc. Pediat. Ophthalmology & Strabismus, Am. Assn. Pediat. Ophthalmology & Strabismus, NY State Ophthalmological Soc. Office: Irene Magramm MD 225 E 64th St New York NY 10065 Office Phone: 212-644-5100. Office Fax: 212-644-2520.

MAGRUDER, JOAN R., hospital administrator; married; 3 children. B, Hamilton Coll.; MBA, U. Pa. With Devereux Found. Ctr. for Head Trauma; adminstr. surgery dept. Johns Hopkins Hosp., dir. outpatient svcs., transplantation program, physician group practice; joined BJC HealthCare, 2000, v.p. bus. devel., physician services, alternate care sites, dir. strategic planning, physician svcs. and market rsch. in affiliated hosps.; pres. Missouri Bapt. Med. Ctr., 2006—. Named one of 25 Women in Healthcare, Modern Healthcare mag., 2011. Mem.: Mo. Hosp. Assn. (bd. dirs. mgmt. svcs. corp., dist. pres.). Office: Missouri Baptist Medical Center 3015 N Ballas Rd Saint Louis MO 63131 Office Phone: 314-996-5000.

MAGUIRE, CHARLOTTE EDWARDS, retired pediatrician; b. Richmond, Ind., Sept. 1, 1918; d. Joel Blaine and Lydia (Betscher) Edwards; m. Raymer Francis Maguire, Sept. 1, 1948 (dec.); children: Barbara, Thomas Clair II (dec.). Student, Stetson U., 1936—38, U. Wichita, 1938—39; BS, Memphis Tchrs. Coll., 1940; MD, U. Ark., 1944; LHD (hon.), Fla. State U., 2002. Intern, resident Orange Meml. Hosp., Orlando, Fla., 1944—46, med. staff., 1944—69, instr. nurses, 1947—57; resident Bellevue Hosp. and Med. Ctr., NYU, NYC, 1954—55; staff mem. Fla. Santarium and Hosp., Orlando, 1946—56, Holiday House and Hosp., Orlando, 1950—62; mem. courtesy and cons. staff West Orange Meml. Hosp., Winter Garden, Fla., 1952—67; active staff, chief dept. pediat. Mercy Hosp., Orlando, 1965—68; med. dir. childrens med. svcs., asst. sec. Fla. Dept. Health and Rehab. Svcs., 1969—71, med. dir. med. svcs. and basic care, 1975—84; med. exec. dir., med. svcs. divsn. worker's compensation Fla. Dept. Labor, Tallahassee, 1984—87; chief of staff physicians and dentists Ctrl. Fla. divsn. Children's Home Soc. Fla., 1947—56; dir. Orlando Child Health Clinic, 1949—58; pvt. practice Orlando, 1946—68; asst. regional dir. HEW, 1970—72; ret., 1987. Asst. dir. health and sci. affairs Dept. Health Edn. & Welfare, Atlanta, 1971-72, Washington, 1972-75; pediat. cons. Fla. Crippled Children's Commn., 1952-70, dir., 1968-70; med. dir. Office Med. Svcs. and Basic Care, sr. physician Office of Asst. Sec. Ops., Fla. Dept. Health and Rehab. Svcs.; clin. prof. dept. pediat. U. Fla. Coll. Medicine, Gainesville, 1980-87; mem. Fla. Drug Utilization Rev., 1983-87; real estate salesperson Investors Realty, 1982-2003; bd. dirs. Stavros Econ. Ctr. Fla. State U., Tallahassee, pres.'s coun. Fla. State U., U. Fla., Gainesville; Charlotte Edwards Maguire eminent scholar chair and scholarships for qualified students, 1999. Mem. profl. adv. com. Fla. Ctr. for Clin. Svcs. at U. Fla., 1952-60; del. to Mid-century White House Conf. on Children and Youth, 1950; U.S. del from Nat. Soc. for Crippled Children to World Congress for Welfare of Cripples, Inc., London, 1957; pres. of corp. Eccleston-Callahan Hosp. for Colored Crippled Children, 1956-58; sec. Fla. chpt. Nat. Doctor's Com. for Improved Med. Svcs., 1951-52; med. adv. com. Gateway Sch. for Mentally Retarded, 1959-62; bd. dirs. Forest Park Sch. for Spl. Edn. Crippled Children, 1949-54, mem. med. adv. com., 1955-68, chmn., 1957-68; mem. Fla. Adv. Coun. for Mentally Retarded, 1965-70; dir. ctrl. Fla. poison control Orange Meml. Hosp.; mem. orgn. com., chmn. com. for admissions and selection policies Camp Challenge, participant 12th session Fed. Exec. Inst., 1971; del. White House Conf. on Aging, 1980; dir. Stavros Econ. Ctr. Fla. State U.; trustee Fla. State U. Found., 1998—, mem. campaign com. Charlotte Edwards Maguire Eminent Scholarship named in her honor Fla. State U., Charlotte Edwards Maguire MLS Med. Libr., Fla. State U. Coll. Medicine named in her honor, 2005; named Outstanding Woman in Our Cmty. AAUW, Tallahassee, 2002; recipient David M. Solomon Disting. Pub. Svc. award Am. Geriatric Soc., 2005, Torch award Fla. State U., 2005. Mem. AMA (life), Nat. Rehab. Assn., Am. Congress Phys. Medicine and Rehab., Fla. Soc. Crippled Children and Adults, Ctrl. Fla. Soc. Crippled Children and Adults (dir. 1949-58, pres. 1956-57), Am. Assn. Cleft Palate, Fla. Soc. Crippled Children (trustee 1951-57, v.p. 1956-57, profl. adv. com. 1957-68), Mental Health Assn. Orange County (charter mem.; pres. 1949-50, dir. 1947-52, chmn. exec. com. 1950-52, dir. 1963-65), Fla. Orange County Heart Assn., Am. Med. Women's Assn., Am. Acad. Med. Dirs., Fla. Med. Assn. (life, chmn. com. on mental retardation), Orange County Med. Assn., Orange Med. Soc. (life), Fla. Pediat. Soc. (pres. 1952-53), Fla. Cleft Palate Assn. (counselor-at-large, sec.), Nat. Inst. Geneal. Rsch., Nat. Geneal. Soc., Assn. Profl. Genealogists, Tallahassee Geneal. Soc., Fla. State U. Found. Inc. (bd. dirs. Stavoris Ctr. for Econ. Edn.), Capital City Tiger Bay Club, Fla. Econs. Club, Francis Eppes Soc. Fla. State U., Econ. Club Fla., Governors Club. Home: 4158 Covenant Ln Tallahassee FL 32308-5765

MAGUIRE, JAMES HARVEY, physician; b. Easton, Pa., Nov. 25, 1948; s. James I. and Elizabeth C. (Updegrove) Maguire. AB, Princeton U., 1970; MD, Harvard U., 1974, MPH, 1978. Cert. internal med, infectious disease. Rsch. assoc. Harvard Sch. Pub. Health, Boston, 1978-81; instr. in medicine Harvard Med. Sch. Pub. Health, 1982-85; asst. prof. Medicine Tropical Pub. Health, Boston, 1985-92, assoc. prof. medicine, 1992-2001; physician, clin. dir. infectious disease Brigham Womens Hosp., Boston, 1992-2001; chief parasitic disease br. Ctrs. for Disease Control and Prevention, Atlanta, 2001—05; prof., dir. internat. health divsn. U. Md. Sch. Medicine, Balt., 2005—08; prof. medicine Harvard Md. Sch., 2008—; sr. physician divsn. infectious diseases Brighham and Womens Hosp., Boston. Editor: Parasitic Diseases, 1993; sect. editor: Am. Jour. Tropical Medicine and Hygiene, 2002—. Mem.: Am. Epidemiol. Soc., Infectious Disease Soc. Am., Am. Soc. Tropical Medicine and Hygiene (councillor 2000—04, Ben Kean medal 2001). Avocation: tennis. Business E-Mail: jmaguire@partners.org.

MAGUIRE, JOSEPH I., ophthalmologist; Grad., Williams Coll., 1979; MD, Jefferson Med. Coll., 1983. Diplomate Am. Bd. Ophthalmology, 1990. Resident Wills Eye Hosp., 1987, fellow retina-vitreous, 1987—89; attending surgeon wills retina svc. Wills Eye Inst.; fellow Moorfields Hosp., 1989—90; intern Thomas Jefferson Univ. Hosp.; assoc. prof. ophthalmology Thomas Jefferson Univ. Retina svc. pres. Eye Rsch. Inst. (ERI); prin. investigator VEGF-trap clin. trial Nat. Insts. of Health. Author of multiple jour. articles and book chapts.; editor: (articles) 5-Minute Consult in Ophthalmology; co-editor: Yearbook of Ophthalmology; reviewer (jours.) Retina, Archives of Ophthalmology, Ophthalmology, American Journal of Ophthalmology, British Journal of Ophthalmology. Fellow: ACP; mem.: Am. Acad. of Ophthalmology, Associated Soc. of Vitreoretinal Surgeons, Retina Soc. Office: Wills Eye Institute 10th Fl 840 Walnut St Philadelphia PA 19107 Office Phone: 215-928-3300. Office Fax: 215-825-2443.

MAGUN, ARTHUR M., gastroenterologist, educator; MD, Mt. Sinai Sch. Medicine, NY, 1977. Diplomate Am. Bd. Internal Medicine, Am. Bd. Internal Medicine-gastroenterology. Intern internal medicine Columbia-Presbyn. Med. Ctr., NYC, resident internal medicine, 1978—80, fellow gastroenterology, 1980—83; asst. prof. medicine Columbia Univ., NYC, 1983—90, assoc. clin. prof. medicine, 1990—2000, clin. prof. medicine, 2000—, interim chief digestive and liver disease divsn., 2002—04; attending physician NY-Presbyn. Hosp., 1983—. Office: New York-Presbyterian Hospital Ste 3-338 161 Fort Washington Ave New York NY 10032 Office Phone: 212-305-5287. Office Fax: 212-305-1005.

MAHABIR, RAMAN CHAOS, plastic surgeon, educator; b. New-castle, NB, Canada, Aug. 14, 1975; s. Ray and Joan Ellen Mahabir. BSc, U. NB, Fredericton, 1996; MD, U. BC, Vancouver, Canada, 2000, MSc, 2001. Lic. Med. Coun. Can., 2002, cert. plastic surgeon Royal Coll. Physicians & Surgeons, Can., 2006. Clin. rsch. fellow Okanagan Plastic Surgery Ctr., Kelowna, British Columbia, Canada, 2000—01; plastic surgery resident U. Calgary, Alberta, Canada, 2001—05, chief plastic surgery resident, 2005—06; clin. asst. prof. U. Nev., Sch. Medicine, Las Vegas, 2006—07, aesthetic & breast surgery fellow, 2006—07, hand & microsurgery fellow, 2006—07; asst. prof. Tex. A&M and Scott & White, Temple, 2007—, chief microsurgery, 2007—, rsch. dir., 2007—, elective adminstr., 2008—. Contbr. articles to profl. jours. (Gaspar Anastasi award, 2004). Surgeon Las Vegas Med. Mission Philippines, Nev., 2007—09. Recipient Meml. Endowment award, U. BC, 2006; Can. Millennium scholarship, Govt. Can., 2000. Fellow: Royal Coll. Physicians & Surgeons, Can.; mem.: AMA, Can. Med. Assn., Am. Soc. Plastic Surgeons, Can. Soc. Plastic Surgeons, Alpha Omega Alpha. Office: Scott & White Dept Surgery 2401 S 31st St Temple TX 76504

MAHADEVAPPA, MANJUNATHA, engineering educator; b. Mysore, India, Jan. 22, 1968; MTech, SJCE, 1994; PhD, Indian Inst. Tech., Chennai, 2001. Asst. prof. SMST, Indian Inst. Tech., Kharagpur, India, 2007—. Mem., reviewer Int. Jour. Therapy and Rehab., 2009—. Mem.: IEEE Engring. Medicine and Biology Soc. Avocation: swimming. Home: 2BR/F-20 IIT Campus Kharagpur West Bengal 721302 India Home Fax: 91-3222-282220. Personal E-mail: mmaha2@gmail.com.

MAHAFFEY, JOHN CHRISTOPHER, medical association executive; b. Jefferson City, Mo., July 20, 1953; s. Fred Turner and Betty Cord (Woodfill) Mahaffey; children: Michael, Katherine. BA, Western Ill. U., Macomb, 1975; MS, DePaul U., 1999. Cert. assn. exec. Legis. aide Congressman Harold R. Collier, Washington, 1972-73; legis. asst. Nat. Assn. Retail Druggists, Washington, 1975-76; dir. Commn. and Meetings Nat. Assn. Bds. of Pharmacy, Chgo., 1976-80; pres., CEO Assn. Forum, Chgo., 1980—2002; exec. dir. Am. Coll. Foot and Ankle Surgeons, Park Ridge, Ill., 2002—. Bd. dirs. Healthcare Assocs. Credit Union, 2003—. Commr. City of Park Ridge (Ill.) Econ. Devel. Commn., 1990—94, 1996—2000, mem. exec. com. Chgo. Convention and Tourism Bur., Chgo., 1993—2002. Recipient Disting. Alumni award, Western Ill. U., Macomb, 1993, Shapiro award, Assn. Forum, 2002. Fellow: Am. Soc. Assn. Execs. (Key award 1994); mem.: U.S. C. of C., Assn. Com. 100. Presbyn. Office: Am Coll Foot and Ankle Surgeons 8725 W Higgins Rd Chicago IL 60631 Office Phone: 773-693-9300. Business E-Mail: mahaffey@acfas.org.

MAHAJAN, AJAY, dental educator; b. India, Jan. 5, 1981; MDS, King George's Med. U., 2003. Asst. prof. Himachal Pradesh Govt. Dental Coll. & Hosp., 2011—. Office: Dept Periodontics Himachal Pradesh Gov Dental Coll & Hosp Shimla HP 171001 India Personal E-mail: julius05@rediffmail.com.

MAHAJAN, MUKESH K., pharmacologist; b. Amritsar, Apr. 28, 1977; PhD, Mass. Coll. Pharmacy and Health Scis., 2006. Prin. scientist GlaxoSmithKline, 2006—. Office: 1250 S Collegeville Rd UP1250 Collegeville PA 19426 Business E-Mail: mukesh.k.mahajan@gsk.com.

MAHAJAN, PRASHANT, pediatrician, educator; b. Nagpur, India, June 30, 1967; MD, KEM Hosp., 1988; MPH, U. Mich. & U. Amherst, Mass., 2002, MBA. Prof. pediat., divsn. chief Childrens Hosp. Mich., 2010—. Rsch. dir. Divsn. Pediatric Emergency Medicine, 2005. Fellow: Am. Acad. Pediat. Office: 3901 Beaubien Detroit MI 48201 Business E-Mail: pmahajan@dmc.org.

MAHAJAN, PREETAM BHALCHANDRA, primary care physician, educator; b. Goa, India, Aug. 3, 1979; MD, GMC, PSM, 2005. Physician Indira Gandhi Med. Coll. & Rsch. Inst., 2005—, asst. prof., 2009—. Named Emerging Young Scientist, Internat. Diabetes Fedn., Pfizer. Office: Indira Gandhi Medical College & R I Comm Pondicherry 605005 India Personal E-mail: preetammahajan_2002@yahoo.com.

MAHAJAN, SUPRIYA SUDHAKAR, pharmacist, educator; b. Pune, Maharashtra, India, Dec. 28, 1955; MSc in Tech., Inst. Chem. Tech., Mumbai, 1982; PhD in Pharm. Chem. Tech., Bombay Coll. Pharmacy, 1992. Asst. prof., lectr. pharm. chemistry Bombay Coll. Pharmacy, Mumbai U., 1982—97; prof. pharm. chemistry C. U. Shah Coll. Pharmacy, 1997—. Mem. experts panel All India Coun. Tech. Edn., 2009; mem. editl. bd. Indian Drugs Mfrs. Assn., 2010; mem. ad-hoc bd. studies chemistry S. N. D. T. Women's U., 2009, mem. ad-hoc bd. studies pharmacy, 10; with Governing Bd. Pharmacy Coll., Nashik, 2011. Recipient 1st prize, Assn. Indian U. Fellow: Rsch. Jour. Chemistry and Environment; mem.: Assn. Pharmacy Tchrs. India, Indian Pharm. Assn. Avocations: reading, surfing. Office: C U Shah Coll Dept Pharmacy Santacruz W Mumbai Maharashtra 400 049 India Office Fax: 91-22-26603968. Personal E-mail: supriya_ma2@yahoo.com. Business E-Mail: supriya.ma2@gmail.com.

MAHÉ, GUILLAUME, physician; b. Pontivy, France, Apr. 7, 1979; A-level, La Mennais, France, 1997; MD, Faculty Medicine, Rennes, France, 2007; PhD student in Integrated Neurovasc. and Mitochondrial Biology, INSERM, 2008—. Physician U. Hosp., 2007—. Asst. Hosp. U. Faculty Medicine Angers, France, 2010. Mem.: French Vascular Soc. Avocation: golf. Office: 4 Rue Larrey Angers Maine et Loire 49933 Cedex 9 France

MAHER, EAMONN RICHARD, medical geneticist; s. Richard and Edna Maher; m. Helen Marie Jackson, July 19, 1980; children: Siobhan Maria, Kieran Michael, Caitlin Helen, Conor Patrick, Aine Ciara. BSc with highest honors, U. Manchester, Eng., 1977, MBChB with honors, 1980, MD, 1988; MA (hon.), U. Cambridge, Eng., 1996. Ho. officer in medicine and surgery Manchester Royal Infirmary, 1980—81; sr. med. ho. officer Addenbrooke's and Papworth Hosps., Cambridge, England, 1981—82; tutor in medicine U. Leeds, England, 1982—83; med. registrar Univ. Coll. Hosp., London, 1983—85; rsch. fellow Charing Cross Hosp. Med. Sch., London, 1985—87; registrar Royal Free Hosp., London, 1987—88; clin. lectr. U. Cambridge, London, 1988—91, lectr. med. genetics England, 1991—96; prof. med. genetics, head dept. med. and molecular genetics U. Birmingham Sch. Medicine, West Midlands, England, 1996—. Author: A Practical Guide to Human Cancer Genetics, 1993, 3d edit., 2007; contbr. over 250 articles to profl. jours.; editor-in-chief Jour. Med. Genetics, 1998—. Fellow: Acad. Med. Scis., Royal Coll. Physicians. Achievements include research in co-discoverer of genes for inherited human diseases (e.g. VHL, SDHB, VPS33B, RAB3GAP1, RAB3GAP2, CHRNG, PLA2G6, NALP2 & SLC29A3, SLC6A3). Office: Univ Birmingham Sch Medicine Institute Of Biomedical Research B15 2TT Birmingham B15 2TT England Office Fax: 44 121 2618. Business E-Mail: e.r.maher@bham.ac.uk.

MAHER, TIMOTHY JOHN, pharmacologist, educator; b. Boston, Nov. 24, 1953; s. Robert Daniel and Veronica Irene (Cody) M.; m. Barbara Jean Walz, Aug. 20, 1977; children: Andrew Michael, Matthew Edward, Elizabeth Irene, Jonathan Daniel. BS, Boston State Coll., 1976; PhD, Mass. Coll. Pharmacy, 1980. Asst. prof. Mass. Coll. Pharmacy, Boston, 1980-83, assoc. prof., 1983-87, prof., 1987—, chmn., 1987-93, dir. pharm. scis., 1994-99, chmn., 2009—, Sawyer prof. pharm. scis., 1994—, dean, grad. studies, 2010—. Postdoctoral fellow MIT, Cambridge, 1983-88, lectr., 1988—2010, bd. dirs. Mass. Soc. Med. Rsch., Chelmsford, 1985-2003; adv. bd. Mass. Poison Control System, Boston, 1990-2006. Contbr. more than 250 articles to profl. jours. Roman Catholic. Achievements include 4 patents, involving the use of L-Tyrosine to enhance/supplement the pharmacological activity of various sympathomimetic amine drugs. Office: Mass Coll Pharmacy 179 Longwood Ave Boston MA 02115-5804 Office Phone: 617-732-2940. Business E-Mail: timothy.maher@mcphs.edu.

MAHESH, VIRENDRA BHUSHAN, endocrinologist; b. India, Apr. 25, 1932; came to U.S., 1958, naturalized, 1968; s. Narinjan Prasad and Sobhagyawati; m. Sushila Kumari Aggarwal, June 29, 1955; children: Anita Rani, Vinit Kumar. BSc with honors, Patna U., India, 1951; MSc in Chemistry, Delhi U., India, 1953, PhD, 1955; DPhil in Biol. Sci, Oxford U., 1958. James Hudson Brown Meml. fellow Yale U., 1958-59; asst. rsch. prof. endocrinology Med. Coll. Ga., Augusta, 1959-63, assoc. rsch. prof., 1963-66, prof., 1966-70, Regents prof., 1970-86, Robert B. Greenblatt prof., 1979-99, chmn. endocrinology, 1972-86, chmn., Regents prof. physiology and endocrinology, 1986-99, chmn. physiology and endocrinology, 1986-99, regents prof., chmn. emeritus physiology and endocrinology, 1999—, Robert B. Greenblatt prof. emeritus endocrinology, 1999—. Dir. Ctr. for Population Studies, 1971-99; mem. reproductive biology study sect. NIH, 1977-81, mem. human embryology and devel. study sect. NIH, 1982-86, 90-93, chmn., 1991-93. Contbr. articles to profl. jours., chpts. to books; editor: The Pituitary, a Current Review, Functional Correlates of Hormone Receptors in Reproduction, Recent Advances in Fertility Research, Hirsuitism and Virilism, Regulation of Ovarian and Testicular Function, Excitatory Amino Acids: Their Role in Neuroendocrine Function; mem. editl. bd. Steroids, 1963—, Jour. of Clin. Endocrinology and Metabolism, 1976-81, Jour. Steroid Biochemistry and Molecular Biology, 1991—, Assisted Reproductive Tech./Andrology, 1993-98, Endocrinology, 1999-2003; mem. adv. bd. Maturitas, 1977-81; editor-in-chief Biology of Reprodn., 1999-2004, cons. editor, 2004-09. Recipient Rubin award Am. Soc. Study Sterility, 1962, Billings Silver medal, 1965, Best Tchr. award freshman class Sch. Medicine, Med. Coll. Ga., 1969, Outstanding Faculty award Sch. Medicine, 1992, Outstanding Faculty award Sch. Grad. Studies, 1981, 94, Disting. Tchg. award, 1988, Excellence in Rsch. award Grad. Faculty Assembly, 1987-91, 93-95, Disting. Scientist award Assn. Scientist Indian Origin in Am., 1989, Lifetime Achievement award Sch. Medicine, 1997, Lifetime Achievement award Med.Coll. Ga. Rsch. Inst., 2006; rsch. grantee NIH, 1960-2000. Mem. Fedn. Am. Soc. Exptl. Biology (bd. dirs. 2004-07, 2008-), AAUP, Chem. Soc. (Eng.), Soc. Biochem. and Molecular Biol., Soc. Neurosci., Endocrine Soc., Soc. for Gynecologic Investigation, Internat. Soc. Neuroendocrinology, Soc. for Study Reproduction (Carl G. Hartman award 1996, Disting. Svc. award 2005), Am. Physiol. Soc. (chmn. endocrinology and metabolism sect. 2004-06), Internat. Soc. Reproductive Medicine (pres. 1980-82), Soc. Exptl. Biology and Medicine, Am. Fertility Soc., Am. Assn. Lab. Animal Sci., NY Acad. Scis., Sigma Xi. Business E-Mail: vmahesh@georgiahealth.edu.

MAHESHWARI, RADHA KANT, healthcare educator; b. Kasganj, India, Jan. 1, 1951; MSc, BITS, Pilani, 1970; PhD, Kanpur U., 1974. Prof. Uniformed Svcs. U. Health Scis., 1981—. Adj. prof. BITS, 1990—. Recipient Exceptional Svc. medal, Uniformed Svcs. U. Health Scis. Office: Uniformed Svcs University Health Scis 4301 Jones Bridge Rd Bethesda MD 20814-4799 Office Fax: 301-295-1640. Business E-Mail: rmaheshwari@usuhs.mil.

MAHLER, HALFDAN THEODOR, physician, health organization executive; b. Vivild, Denmark, Apr. 21, 1923; s. Magnus and Benedicte (Suadicani) M.; m. Ebba Fischer-Simonsen, Aug. 31, 1957; children: Per Bo, Finn. MD, U. Copenhagen, 1948, degree in pub. health; LLD (hon.), U. Nottingham, Eng., 1975; MD (hon.), Karolinska Inst., Stockholm, 1977; Docteur, U. Scis. Sociales de Toulouse, France, 1977; DPH (hon.), Seoul Nat. U., 1979; ScD (hon.), U. Lagos, Nigeria, 1979, Emory U., 1989; MD (hon.), Warsaw Med. Acad., 1980; LHD (hon.), U. Nat. Federico Villareal, Lima, Peru, 1980, U. Gand, Belgium, 1983, CUNY, 1989; MD (hon.), Charles U., Prague, 1982, Mahidol U., Bangkok, Thailand, 1982, Aarhus U., Denmark, 1988, U. Copenhagen, 1988, Aga Khan U., Pakistan, 1989; LHD (hon.), U. Nat. Autonoma de Nicaragua, 1983; PhD (hon.), Semmelweis U., Budapest, Hungary, 1987; LLD (hon.), McMaster U., Can., 1989; DSc (hon.), SUNY, 1990; MD (hon.), U. Newcastle Upon Tyne, 1990; LLD (hon.), U. Exeter, 1990, U. Toronto, 1990; DPH (hon.), U. Goteborg, 2005. Specialized tng. in TB; active field of internat. pub. health work; planning officer mass Tb campaign Ecuador, 1950-51; sr. officer nat. Tb program WHO, India, 1951-61, chief Tb unit, Hdqrs., Geneva, 1962-69, sec. to expert adv. panel on Tb, 1962-69, dir. project systems analysis, 1969-70, asst. dir.-gen. div. health services and div. family health, 1970-73, dir.-gen., 1973-88, dir. gen. emeritus, 1988; sec. gen. Internat. Planned Parenthood Fedn., 1989-95. Contbr. articles to profl. jours. Decorated Grand Officier de l'Ordre Nat. du Benin, 1975, Grand Officier de l'Ordre Nat. du. Voltaique, Upper Volta, 1978, comdr. de l'Ordre Nat. du Mali, 1982, Grand Officer de l'Ordre du Merite de la Rep. du Senegal, 1982, comdr. 1st class Order White Rose (Finland), Grand Officier de l'Ordre nat. malgache, Madagascar, 1987, Grand Cross Icelandic Order of the Falcon, 1988, Grand Cordon of Order Sacred Treasure, Japan, 1988, Bourgeoisie d'Honneur, Geneva, Switzererland, Grand Croix De L'Ordre De Merite, Luxenbourg, 1990, Grand Cross Ordem do Merito Medico, Brazil, 2003; recipient Jana Evangelisty Purkyne medal (Presdl. award) Prague, 1974, Comenius U. Gold medal Bratislava, 1974, Carlo Forlanini gold medal Federazione Italiana contro la Tubercolosi et le Malattie Polmonari Sociali Rome, 1975, Ernest Carlsens Found. Prize Copenhagen, 1980, Georg Barfred-Pedersen prize Copenhagen, 1982, Hagedorn medal and prize Denmark, 1986, Freedom From Want medal Roosevelt Inst., 1988, Storkors Af Dannebrogsordenen, Denmark, 1988; hon. prof. U. Nat. Mayor de San Marcos, Lima, Peru, U. Chile Faculty of Medicine, Beijing Med. Coll., Rep. of China, Shanghai Med. U.; Bartel World Affairs fellow Cornell U., 1988; U.N. Population award, 1995, Andrija Stampar award, 1995. Fellow Royal Coll. Physicians (London), Faculty Community Medicine of Royal Colls. Physicians U.K. (hon.), Indian Soc. for Malaria and other Communicable Diseases (hon.), Royal Soc. Medicine (London) (hon., U.K.-U.S. Hewitt award 1992), London Sch. Hygiene and Tropical Medicine (hon.); mem. Med. Assn. Argentina (hon.), Latin Am. Med. Assn. (hon.), Italian Soc. Tropical Medicine (hon.), Belgium Soc. Tropical Medicine (assoc.), Societe medicale de Geneve (hon.), Union Internat. contre la Tuberculose (hon.), Soc. Francaise d'Hygiene, de Medecine sociale et de Genie sanitaire (hon.), Uganda Med. Assn. (hon. life), Coll. Physicians and Surgeons, Bangladesh Royal Coll. Gen. Practitioners (ad eundem), List of Honour of the Internat. Dental Fedn., Am. Pub. Health Assn. (hon.), Nat. Acad. Medicine Mex. (hon.), Nat. Acad. Buenos Aires (hon.), Swedish Soc. Medicine (hon.), Brit. Medal Assn. (hon. fgn. corr. 1990), Inst. Medicine (NAS U.S.A.). Achievements include research in epidemiology and control of Tb, polit., social, econ, and technol. priorities in health sector, application of systems analysis to health care problems. Home and Office: Chemin de Pont-Céard 12 CH-1290 Versoix Switzerland Office Fax: 022 755 26 10. Business E-Mail: halfdan.mahler@bluewin.ch.

MAHMOUD, ADEL A., physician, molecular biologist, educator; b. Cairo, Aug. 24, 1941; arrived in US, 1972; s. Abdel Fattah and Fathia (Osman) Mahmoud; m. Sally L. Hodder, Jan. 31, 1993. Grad., Cairo U., 1958, MD, 1963; PhD, U. London, 1971. Asst. lectr. Ain Shams U., Cairo, 1965—68; WHO fellow U. London, 1969—72; rsch. assoc., prof. Case Western Res. U., Cleve., 1973—87, prof., chmn. dept. medicine, 1987—98; physician-in-chief Univ. Hosps., Cleve., 1987—98; pres. vaccines Merck & Co. Inc., Whitehouse Sta., NJ, 1998—2006; prof. dept. molecular biology and Woodrow Wilson Sch. Princeton U., 2007—. Editor: The Eosinophil in Health and Disease, 1979, Tropical and Geographical Medicine, 1990, Schistosomaisis, Tropical Medicine Sci. and Practice, Vol. 1, 2001, Biological Threats and Terrorism: Assessing the Science and Response Capabilities, 2002. Fellow: Infectious Diseases Soc. Am.; mem.: Inst. Medicine, Assn. Am. Physicians, Am. Soc. Clin. Investigations. Office: Princeton Univ 228 Lewis Thomas Lab Princeton NJ 08544 Office Phone: 609-258-8557. Business E-Mail: amahmoud@princeton.edu.

MAHMOUD, NAJJIA N., colon and rectal surgeon, educator; MD, Cornell U., 1993. Diplomate Am. Bd. Surgery, Am. Bd. Colon and Rectal Surgery, lic. Pa., 2001. Intern in gen. surgery NY Presbyn. Hosp., resident in gen. surgery, 1999; fellow in colon and rectal surgery Univ. Minn. Med. Ctr., Mpls., 2001; asst. prof surgery Hosp. Univ. Pa., surgeon. Named one of Best Doctors in America, 2006, 2008, 2010, Top Doctors, Phila. Mag., 2010. Fellow: ACS; mem.: Am. Soc. of Colon and Rectal Surgeons. Office: Hospital of the University of Pennsylvania Perelman Center for Advanced Medicine 4th Fl W Pavilion 3400 Civic Center Blvd Philadelphia PA 19104 Office Phone: 800-789-7366.

MAHNKE, KURT LUTHER, psychotherapist, clergyman; b. Milw., Feb. 18, 1945; s. Jonathan Henry and Lydia Ann (Pickron) M.; m. Dana Moore, Mar. 19, 1971; children: Rachel Lee, Timothy Kurt, Jonathan Roy. BA, Northwestern Coll., Watertown, Wis., 1967; MDiv, Wis. Luth. Sem., 1971; MA, No. Ariz. U., 1984. Lic. profl. counselor, marriage and family therapist, ind. clin. social worker, cert. trauma counselor. Pastor Redeemer/Grace Luth. Chs., Phoenix & Casa Grande, Ariz., 1971-75, St. Philips Luth. Ch., Milw., 1975-78, 1st Luth. Ch., Prescott, Ariz., 1978-82; counselor NAU Counseling/Testing Ctr., Flagstaff, Ariz., 1983-84, Wis. Luth. Child & Family Svc., Wausau, Wis., 1984-86, area adminstr. Appleton, Wis., 1986-89; founder, psychotherapist Family Therapy & Anxiety Ctr., Menasha, Wis., 1989—. Part-time min. St. Paul Luth. Ch., Appleton, 1993-94; presenter Nat. Police Week, Washington, 1995—, 13th Nat. Conf. on Anxiety Disorders, Charleston, S,C., 1993; cons. editor Northwestern Pub. House, Milw., 1990-97; adj. faculty Fox Valley Tech. Coll., Appleton, 1993—; on-call critical incident stress debriefer, U.S. Marshall's Svc., 1999—; critical incident stress cons., Appleton Police Dept., Brillion Police Dept., Menasha Police Dept., Neenah Police Dept., Two Rivers Police Dept., Outagamie County Sheriff's Dept., 1999—, New London Police Dept., Winnebago County Sheriff's Dept., 2000—, Green Bay Police Dept., 2009-. Cons. editor Counseling at the Cross, 1990; contbr. articles to profl. publs. Cons. Wis. Evang. Luth. Synod, Milw., 1986—; Brillion Police Dept., New London Police Dept., Winnegago County Sheriff's Dept., U.S. Marshall's Office, 1999—; crisis counselor, clin. dir. Critical Incident Stress Debriefing Team, Fox Cities, 1991—2011, U.S. Atty.'s Office, 1995-99; victim crisis response coord. Appleton Police Dept., 1996-99, Neenah Police Dept., Menasha Police Dept., Town of Menasha Police Dept., 1997-99. Mem. Internat. Critical Stress Found., Nat. Anxiety Found., Obsessive Compulsive Found. Republican. Lutheran. Office: Family Therapy Anxiety Ctr 3701 E Evergreen Dr Ste 200 Appleton WI 54913-7889 Office Phone: 920-729-6780. Personal E-mail: klmahnke@aol.com.

MAHOMED, SURREYA, physical therapy educator; b. Pretoria, South Africa, Jan. 25, 1955; BSc in Physiotherapy, U. Durban Westville, 1979; DEd, U. South Africa, 1998. Educator U. Southern Africa, 1981—85, U. Witatersrand, South Africa, 1986, Kuwait U., 1987—. Clin. cons. orthop. phys. therapy Phys. Therapy Practice, 2005—11. Recipient Cert. of Appreciation, Ministry of Health, Adminstrn. Phys. Therapy Svcs. Mem.: Kuwait Phys. Therapy Assn., Chartered Soc. Phys. Therapy. Office: Kuwait University Dept Physical Therapy PO Box 31470 Sulaibekhat 31470 Kuwait Office Fax: 00965-24983841. Business E-Mail: surreya@hsc.edu.kw.

MAHONEY, DAVID L., former pharmaceutical wholesale and healthcare management company executive; b. Brighton, Mass., June 24, 1954; s. Thomas H.D. and K. Phyllis (Norton); m. Winn Canning Ellis, Sept. 26, 1992. AB in English, Princeton U., 1975; MBA, Harvard U., 1981. Asst. gen. mgr. Ogden Food Svc. Corp., LA, 1975-76, concessions mgr. East Boston, Mass., 1976-77, gen. mgr., 1977-78, ops. analyst, 1978-79; assoc. McKinsey & Co., San Francisco, 1981-86, prin., 1986-90; v.p. strategic planning McKesson Corp., San Francisco, 1990-94, pres. HDS, Inc., 1994-95, pres. pharm. svcs., 1995-97, group pres. pharm svcs. & internat. group, 1997-99; exec. v.p., CEO pharm. svcs. bus. McKesson HBOC, 1999, co-CEO, 1999-2001; CEO iMcKesson, 2000-01. Bd. dirs. Symantec Corp., Corcept Therapeutics, KQED, Live Oak Sch., SFMOMA, Mercy Corps., Adamas Pharmaceuticals. Mem.: Young Pres. Orgn. Avocations: outdoor activities, photography. Office: Pier 5 The Embracadero Ste 102 San Francisco CA 94111

MAHONEY, DONALD H., JR., pediatrician, educator; b. Jacksonville, Fla., Sept. 12, 1946; s. Donald H. and Doris Ann Mahoney; m. Mary Jane Scherberger, Dec. 27, 1970; children: Donald H. III, Michael Joseph, Timothy Ryan, Lauren R. Flynn. MD, Tulane U., New Orleans, 1972. Lic. Tex., 1977. Prof. Baylor Coll. Medicine, Houston, 1979—. Dir. hematology svc. Tex. Children's Cancer Ctr., Houston, 1980—. Lt comdr. USNR, 1975—77. Office: Tex Children's Cancer Ctr 6621 Fannin Houston TX 77030 Personal E-mail: jmahoney3@comcast.net. Business E-Mail: dhmahone@txccc.org. *

MAHONEY, MAURICE JEREMIAH, medical educator; b. Washington, Aug. 4, 1935; s. Maurice Mahoney and Julia Johnson; m. Blanche Katz, May 23, 2004; children: Tatyana Renner, Karen, Cydney, Matthew, Allison, Linnea. AB, Cornell U., 1957; MD, U. Pitts., 1962; JD, U. Conn., 1994. Bar: Conn. 1994; diplomate Med.Genetics Am. Bd. of Med. Genetics, 1982, Pediats. Am. Bd. of Pediat., 1967. Prof. of genetics Yale U., New Haven, 1970—; dir. human investigation com. Yale U. Sch. of Medicine, 2000—. Editl. bd. Am. Jour. of Med. Genetics, NYC, 1977—94, Fetal Diagnosis and Therapy, Basel, Switzerland, 1984—, Jour. of BioLaw & Bus., Denville, NJ, 1997—; bd. dirs. Am. Soc. of Human Genetics, Bethesda, Md., 1981—84, Soc. for Inherited Metabolic Disorders, Washington, 1984—87; fellow Am. Pediat. Soc., The Woodlands, Tex., 1983—, Am. Coll. of Med. Genetics, Bethesda, Md., 1993—. Editor: (medical text book) Medicine of the Fetus & Mother. Capt. US Army, 1966—68, Ft. McClellan, AL USA. Fellow, AAAS, 1998—2005. Avocations: kayaking, opera. Home: 526 Riverdale Dr Stratford CT 06615 Office Fax: 203-785-7673. Personal E-mail: maurice.mahoney@yale.edu.

MAHONY, SUSAN (SUE MAHONY), pharmaceutical company executive; BS, Aston U., PhD in Pharmacy; MBA, London Bus. Sch., 1998. Sales and mktg. positions Amgen, Bristol-Myers Squibb Co., Schering-Plough; joined Eli Lilly & Co., global mktg. & new product devel. positions, sr. v.p. human resources & diversity, 2009—11, sr. v.p., 2011—, gen. mgr. Lilly Canada, 2008—09, pres. Lily Oncology, 2011—. Office: Eli Lilly & Co Lilly Corp Ctr Indianapolis IN 46285 *

MAHOWALD, ANTHONY PETER, geneticist, developmental biologist, educator; b. Albany, Minn., Nov. 24, 1932; s. Aloys and Cecilia (Maus) Mahowald; m. Mary Lou Briody, Apr. 11, 1971; children: Maureen, Lisa, Michael. BS, Spring Hill Coll., 1958; PhD, Johns Hopkins U., 1962. Asst. prof. Marquette U., Milw., 1966-70; asst. staff mem. Inst. Cancer Rsch., Phila., 1970-72; assoc. prof. Ind. U., Bloomington, 1972-76, prof., 1976-82; Henry Willson Payne prof. Case Western Res. U., Cleve., 1982-90, chmn. dept. anatomy, 1982-88, chmn. dept. genetics, 1988-90; Louis Block prof., chmn. dept molecular genetics and cell biology U. Chgo., 1990—2002, Louis Block prof. emeritus, 2002—. Chmn. Com. Devel. Biology U. Chgo., 1991-99. Woodrow Wilson Found. fellow, 1958, NSF fellow, 1958-62. Fellow AAAS, Am. Acad. Arts and Scis., Soc. Scholars Johns Hopkins U.; mem. Nat. Acad. Scis., Genetics Soc. Am. (sec. 1986-88), Soc. Devel. Biology (pres. 1989, editor-in-chief jour. 1980-85), Am. Soc. Cell Biology (coun. mem. 1996-98). Office: U Chgo Dept Molec Genet/Cell Biol 920 E 58th St Chicago IL 60637-5415 Business E-Mail: am29@uchicago.edu.

MAHOWALD, MARY BRIODY, humanities educator; b. NYC, Mar. 24, 1935; d. Thomas Michael and Mae Angela Briody; m. Anthony Peter Mahowald, Apr. 11, 1971; children: Maureen Elise, Lisa Marie, Michael Anthony. BA, St. Francis Coll., Bklyn., 1965; MA, Marquette U., Milw., 1967; PhD, Marquette U., 1969. Tchr. parochial schs., NYC, 1955—65; asst. prof. St. Joseph's Coll., Bklyn., 1969—70, Villanova U., Villanova, Pa., 1970—72; asst. prof./assoc. prof. Ind. U., Indpls., 1972—82; assoc. prof. to prof. Case Western Res. U., Cleve., 1982—90; prof. to prof. emeritus U. Chgo., 1990—. Cons. NIH, Washington, 1995, 2000—03, U.S. Dept. Def., Washington, 1993—97, Pres.'s Coun. on Bioethics, Washington, 2003. Author: Women and Children in Health Care, 1993, Genes, Women, Equality, 2000; contbr. articles to profl. jours. Adult lit. tutor Blue Gargoyle, Chgo., 2000—; hospice vol. Chgo., 1997—98. Grantee, NIH, 1992—97, U.S. Dept. Energy, 1995—98, Am. Coun. Learned Socs., 1997—98. Mem.: Am. Soc. Social Philosophy (pres. 1998), Am. Soc. for Bioethics and Humanities, Am. Philos. Assn. Avocations: reading, needlepoint. Office: University of Chicago 5841 S Maryland Ave Chicago IL 60637

MAÏDI, HOUARI, psychologist, psychotherapist; b. Nanterre, Paris, France, Sept. 28, 1954; s. Ahmed Maïdi, Aicha Bentlahcen; m. Sylvia Colli Maïdi, July 1, 1987. Diploma of deepen's studies, U. Lille III, France, 1979; PhD, U. Lille III, 1983; Diploma of deepen's studies into psychoanalyse, U. Paris 13, 1993. Psychologist/psychotherapist Ctr. d'Observation Placement Soins, Hauboudin, France, 1980—89, Inst. Médico-Educatif, Villeneuve d'Ascq, France, 1984—95, Ctr. d'Aide Travail, Armentieres, 1983—. Faculty U. Paris X, Nanterre, 1997—; cons. Ct. of Justice, Arras, France, 1990—94. Contbr. articles to profl. jours. Past pres., founder GREEP Paris Hosp. Trousseau, 1996—. Mem.: L'Evolution psychiatique, Internat. Soc. Adolescent Psychiatry and Psychology, Soc. Française Psychiatrie l'Enfant et de l'Adolescent. Avocations: reading, jogging, travel, art galleries. Home: 8 Avenue de la Marne 59700 Marcq en Baroeul France Office: 1027 bis avenue de la République 59700 Marcq en Baroeul France

MAIER, DONNA MARIE, psychologist; b. Somerville, NJ, July 22, 1959; d. Donald Victor and Patricia Norma (Ledwith) Maier. BS in Biology, Youngstown State U., 1980; respecialization cert. in Clin. Psychology, U. Cin., 1992; PhD in Psychology, Rutgers U., 1986. Cert. prof. qual. in psycho. Assn. State and Provincial Psycho. Bds., 1996. Grad. fellow, tchg. asst. Rutgers U., New Brunswick, NJ, 1981—86; rsch. fellow Armed Forces Radiobiology Rsch. Inst., Wash., 1986—89; psycho. intern. VA Hosp., Lexington, Ky., 1991—92; clin. psychologist Comprehensive Care N. Ky., Covington, 1992—95, Group Health Assoc., Dayton, Ohio, 1995—2003, Maier Psychol. Svcs., Cin., 2003—. Inst. Montgomery Coll., Rockville, 1988—89, U. Cin., Psycho. Dept., Cin., 1989—91, No. Ky. U., Highland Heights, 1990—91. Contbr. articles various profl. jours. Mem.: Nat. Register Health Svc. Providers in Psychology, Cin. Acad. Profl. Psychology, Feminists for Life, Amnesty Internat. Office: Maier Psychological Svcs 4301 State Rt 725 Bellbrook OH 45305 Office Phone: 513-739-8705, 937-848-9858 25. Personal E-mail: donnamaier@hotmail.com.

MAIER, RONALD VITT, surgeon, researcher, educator; b. Wheeling, W.Va., Oct. 23, 1947; BS, U. Notre Dame, 1969; MD, Duke U., 1973. Intern Parkland Meml. Hosp., Dallas, 1973-74; resident U. Wash. Hosps., Seattle, 1974-78; rsch. assoc. Scripps Rsch. Found., La Jolla, Calif., 1978-81; surgeon-in-chief HMC, Seattle, 1993—; vice chair U. Wash., Seattle, 1994—, Jane and Donald D. Trunkey prof., 2005—. Office: Dept Surgery 359796 Harborview Med Ctr 325 9th Ave Seattle WA 98104-2499 Office Phone: 206-744-3564. Business E-Mail: ronmaier@uw.edu.

MAIESE, KENNETH, neurologist, neuroscientist; b. Audubon, NJ, Dec. 5, 1958; s. Charles and Margaret (Fioretti) M. BA summa cum laude, U. Pa., 1981; MD, Cornell U., 1985. Intern N.Y. Hosp., 1985—86, resident neurology, 1986—89, asst. attending physician, 1989—94; asst. prof. Cornell U. Med. Coll., NYC, 1989—94; assoc. prof. dept. neurology, anatomy and cell biology Ctr. Molecular Toxicology and Medicine Wayne State U., Detroit, 1994—99, dir. lab. molecular and cellular cerebral ischemia Ctr. Molecular Toxicology, 1994—, prof. dept. neurology, anatomy, cell biology Ctr. Molecular Toxicology, 1999—; prof. Barbara Ann Karmanos Cancer Inst., 2005—; prof., chair neurology & neurosci. UMDNJ, 2010—. Dir. neurol. diagnosis NY Hosp., 1991—94; chmn. nat. brain/stroke consortium Am. Heart Assn., 2000—01, exec. coun., 2001—, nat peer rev. steering com., 2002—, mem. rsch. com., 2003—; mem. study sect. cell death and injury NIH/CDIN, 2003—; mem. neurobiology study sect. Vet.'s Adminstrn., 2004—; spkr. in field. Author: Neurology and General Medicine, 1989, Neurological and Neurosurgical ICU Medicine, 1988; editor-in-chief Current Neurovascular Rsch., 2002—, Oxidative Stress and Cellular Longevity, 2007—; editor: Neuronal and Vascular Plasticity, 2003, Neurovascular Medicine, 2008-, Forkhead Transcripttion Factors, 2009, Aging & Oxidative Stress, 2009-; mem. editl. bd. Letters in Drug Design and Discovery, 2002—, Histology and Histopathology, 2002—, Jour. Histological Histopathology, 2002—, Drug Design Revs., 2003—, Medicinal Chemistry, 2004—, Current Drug Targets-Heme Agts., Jour. Heart Digest, 2005—, Internat. Jour. Molecular Medicine, 2005—, Ctrl. Nervous Sys. Agts., Medicinal Chemistry, 2006—, Open Neurosci. Letters, 2007—, Open Biochem. Jour., 2007—, Current Bioactive Components, 2007-, Open Neurology Jour., 2007-, Jour. Epithelial Biology and Pharmacology, 2008-, Jour. Interferon & Cytokine, 2008-, Jour. Coll Death, 2008-, Jour. Breast Cancer, 2009-, World Jour. Stem Cells, 2009-, World Jour. Diabetes, 2009-, World Jour. Gastrointestinal Pathology, 2009-, Jour. Nuc. Energy & Power Generation Techs., 2010-, Jour. Molecular Biomarkers & Diagnosis, 2010-, Jour. Diabetes & Metabolism, 2010-; editl. bd. contbr. The Merck Manual Profl. Home Edit., 2007; contbr. articles to profl. jours. Joseph Collins scholar, 1981-85, Grupe Found. scholar, 1985; grantee NIH, 1990—, Nat. Stroke Assn., 1992-94, Alzheimer's Assn., 1994—, Am. Heart Assn., 1995—, United Cerebral Palsy Found., 1995—, Janssen Found., 1995—; recipient Young Scientist award Jours. Cerebral Blood Flow, 1991, Hoechst Investigator award, 1993, Robert G. Siekert award in stroke, 1994, Johnson and Johnson Disting. Investigator award, 1996-98, Maiese Lab. Neurosci. Tng. award J & J/Janssen, 1998, Boehringer Investigator award, 1999, NIH/NIEHS award, Learn Found. award, 2002-03, MI Challenge award, Bugher Found. award, 2005, Am. Diabetes Assn. award, 2006, NIH/NIA award, 2007, NIH/NINDS/NIA award, 2009, NIH/NINDS/ARRA award, 2010, ADA award, 2010; named one of Am.'s Top Physicians, 2005-11, Best of US Physicians, 2006-11, Top Dr. 2009-. Mem. NIH (minority edn. tng. 2002—, spl. emphasis cellular pathophysiologyspl., emphasis panel cellular degeneration 2004—), Am. Acad. Neurology, NY Acad. Scis., Assn. for Rsch. in Nervous and Mental Diseases, Am. Neurol. Assn. (elected), Soc. Neurosci., Internat. Acad. Cardiology (sci. com. 2003-, Bugher Found. award 2005-), Am. Diabetes Assn. (Sr. Investigator award 2006, award, 2010), Alzheimer's Soc. UK, Diabetes Found. UK, Rsch. Coun. Hong Kong, Rsch. Coun. Spain, NIH Applied Metabolom Techs., Austrian Sci. Fund., Nat. Swiss Sci. Found., Wellcome Trust, UK, Alzheimers Rsch. Trust, UK, NMRC, Singapore, Natural Scis. & Engring. Rsch. Coun. Can, Am. Diabetes Assn. Rev. Roman Catholic. Achievements include rsch. in imidazole receptors, cerebral ischemia, nitric oxide toxicity, growth factor neuroprotection, signal cellular transduction mechanisms, metabotropic glutamate receptors, gene regulation, and gene therapy, patents in field. Home: Apt 66 177 East Hartsdale Ave Hartsdale NY 10530 Office: Cuncer Ctr F 1220 205 S Orange Ave Newark NJ 07101

MAIKON, MARC STEVEN, podiatrist; BA, Grinnell Coll., 1980; BS, U. Iowa, 1982; DPM, U. Osteo. Medicine, Des Moines, 1989. Cert. Am. Coun. Cert. Podiatric Physicians and Surgeons. Podiatrist, owner Family Foot Care Ctr. PLC, Cedar Rapids, Iowa, 1991—. Mem. Am. Coll. Foot Surgeons, Am. Podiatric Med. Assn., Iowa Podiatric Med. Soc., C. of C. Cedar Rapids, Rotary Internat. Office: Family Foot Ctr 3359 Center Point Rd NE Cedar Rapids IA 52402-5568 Home: 3359 Center Point Rd Ne Cedar Rapids IA 52402-5568

MAINGOT, STEVE GORDON ALNATON, health researcher, consultant; b. Kingstown, St. Vincent, Nov. 12, 1954; arrived in U.K., 1973; s. Patrick McDonald and Elise Elaine (Hazell) M.; m. Jacqueline Fernandez, Dec. 17, 1977; children: Stefan, Candice, Fabian, Elise. BSc with honors, U. East London, 1979; MSc, City of London Poly., 1981; MBA, Middlesex U., Eng., 1989. Justice of the peace. Regional buyer Northwest Thames Regional Health Authority, London, 1979-82; supplies mgr. Wntrita, London, 1982-84, R & D mgr., 1984-85, nat. contracts mgr., 1985-90; with mgmt. info. svcs. dept. Ealing Hammersmith and Hounslow, London, 1990-93, info. mgr. Southall, U.K., 1993-95; facilitation cons. Nat. Health Svc. Exec. on Info. Mgmt. and Tech. Projects, 1995—; head info. mgmt. and tech. Benenden Hosp. Trust, Cranbrook, Kent. Ind. cons., Middlesex; cons. Trintime, London, 1982-84, Med. Assocs., Kingstown, St. Vincent, 1985-87, London, 1990, SMI Moscow, 1990-92; non-exec. dir. Parkside Health WHS Trust St. Charles Hosp., London, Brent Tchg. Primary Care Trust, 2002-07; trustee Southside Partnership, Clapham, London, bd. chmn.; co. sec., trustee African Caribbean Health Edn. Cache, London; dir. health informatics Smith Manchester U. Hosp., 2003-05; dep. clin. lead advisor BTCCA, 2004-06; health informatics cons. R2 Design Pathology Team, 2006-; participant health informatics projects, NHS relationship dir. Contbr. articles to profl. jours. Chmn. St. Mary's Sch., West London, 1994, Our Lady of Dolours, London, 1994; trustee Trust for Youth Edn., 2005-, chair, trustee, Southside Partnership, vice chair, trustee, Gratitude Interim Head Patients Safety Analysis & Feedback Unit, Nat. Patient Safety Unit, dir., 2005-; mem. Commonwealth Magistrates Assn., 2007-; dir. Commissioning Svcs., London. Fellow Royal Soc. Arts, Royal Soc. Medicine; mem. Inst. Health Svcs. Mgmt., Chartered Inst. for Purchasing and Supply (pro. Ctrl. London chpt. 1992). Roman Catholic. Avocations: music, bicycling, swimming, tennis. also: Steve Maingot Cons 140 Wyld Way Wembley HA9 6PU England Home: Sudbury Ct Estate 37 Abbotts Drive HA0 3SB Wembley England Office: HumanEurope LD 25 St George St Wrayfair London WIS IFS England Office Phone: 02089312886, 07759094773, 44 (0) 7759. Personal E-mail: smain62239@btinternet.com, smain@totalise.co.uk, steve.maingot@gmail.com.

MAINI, SIR RAVINDER NATH, rheumatologist, educator; b. Ludhiana, Punjab, India, Nov. 17, 1937, arrived in U.K., 1955; s. Amar Nath and Saheli Ram (Mehra) M.; m. Marianne Pentz Gorm, 1963 (div. 1986); children: Mala, Ashwin, Nikul (dec.); m. Geraldine Rainier Walden Room, May 22, 1987; children: Alexander, Justin. BA, U. Cambridge, Eng., 1959; MB, BChir, U. Cambridge, 1962; Doctor (hon.), U. René Descartes, Paris, 1994; DSc (hon.), U. Glasgow, 2004. Jr. hosp. staff Guy's Hosp., Brompton Hosp., Charing Cross Hosp., London, 1962-70; cons. physician Charing Cross Hosp., West London Hosp., St. Stephen's Hosp., London, 1970-79; prof., head dept. immunology rheumatic diseases Charing Cross and Westminster Med. Sch., London, 1979—89, prof., head dept. rheumatology, 1989—2002; head divsn. clin. immunology Kennedy Inst. Rheumatology, London, 1979—2002, dir., 1990—2002, prof. rheumatology, 1989—2002, emeritus prof. rheumatology, 2002—; mem. faculty of medicine Imperial Coll, U. London, 2000—02. Hon. cons. physician Charing Cross Hosp., London, 1970—2007, Hammersmith Hosps., London; European Union Med. Specialists Bd. in Rheumatology, 1994 98; past chmn. standing com. for investigative rheumatology European League Against Rheumatism (EULAR); mem. organizing com. European Workshop Rheumatology Rsch related European Workshops; trustee found. bd. Deutsches RheumaForschungsZentrum, Berlin, mem. sci. coun. Karolinska Hosp., Stockholm; mem. arthritis rsch. campaign Brit. Soc. for Rheumatology Clin. Trials Com., others; spkr. Nobel Assembly symposium for inauguration of Ctr. Molecular Medicine, Karolinska Hosp., Stockholm, 1997; inaugural Morris Ziff lectr. U. Tex. Health Scis., Dallas, 2001; Langdon Brown Lecture, Royal Coll. Physicians, 2005. Author (with D.N. Glass, J.T. Scott): Immunology of the Rheumatic Diseases, 1977; Modulation of Autoimmune Disease: The Penicillamine Experience, 1981; co-editor (with M. Feldmann, J.N. Woody): T-Cell Activation in Health and Disease: Disorders of Immune Regulation, Infection and Autoimmunity, 1989; co-editor: (with J.R. Kalden, J.S. Smolen) Rheumatoid Arthritis: Recent Research Advances, 1992; co-editor: (with W.V. van Venrooij) Manual of Biological Markers of Disease, 1996; co-editor in chief: Arthritis Rsch. & Therapy, 1999—; mem. editl. bd. Jour. Immunol. Methods, Annals Rheumatic Diseases, mem. adv. bd. Rheumatology Internat., Japanese Jour. Rheumatology, Scandinavian Jour. Rheumatology; contbr. articles to profl. jours. Recipient Disting. Investigators award, Am. Coll. Rheumatology, 1999, Crafoord Prize in Polyarthritis, Royal Swedish Acad. Scis., 2000, Outstanding Achievement in Clin. Rsch. award, Inst. Clin. Rsch., 2004, Fothergillian medal, Med. Soc. London, 2004, Cameron prize (with Prof. Feldmann), U. Edinburgh, 2004, Ambuj Nath Bose prize, Royal Coll. Physicians, 2005, Courtin-Clarins Prix award, 2000, Meritorious Svc. award in rheumatology, European League Against Rheumatism, 2005, Galen medal, The Worshipful Soc. Apothecaries London, 2006, RA award, Japan Rheumatism Found. Internat., 2007, Dr. Paul Janssen award, 2008; co-recipient Carol Nachman prize, Germany, 1999, Albert Lasker Clin. Med. Rsch. award, Lasker Found., 2003, EULAR Meritorious Svc. award in rheumatology, 2005, Ernst Schering prize (with Prof. Marc Feldmann), 2010; named Freyburg lectr. Hosp. for Spl. Surgery, NYC; 1993, Croonian Lectr. award, Royal Coll. Physicians, London, 1995, Lumleian Lectr. award, 1999; named to Knighthood, Queen Elizabeth II, 2003; Hon. fellow, Sidney Sussex Coll., U. Cambridge, 2004. Master: Am. Coll. Rheumatology (hon.); fellow: Royal Coll. Physicians London, Royal Coll. Physicians Edinburgh, Brit. Soc. Rheumatology (Heberden Oration medal 1988), Royal Soc. UK, Slovakian Rheumatology Soc., Royal Soc. Medicine, Acad. Med. Scis.; mem.: NAS (fgn. assoc.), Royal Soc. Medicine (Samuel Hyde lectr. 1999), Norwegian Soc. Rheumatology (hon.), European League Against Rheumatism (hon.), Australian Rheumatism Assn. (hon.), Hellenic Rheumatology Soc. (hon.), Assn. Clin. Profs., Mexican Soc. Rheumatology (hon.), Scandinavian Soc. Immunology (hon.), Hungarian Rheumatology Soc. (hon.), Assn. Physicians Gt. Britain and No. Ireland, Brit. Soc. Immunology, 1942 Club, Reform Club, Antibody Club. Avocations: music appreciation, walking. Office: Kennedy Inst Rheumatology Imperial Coll ARC Bldg 65 Aspenlea Rd London W6 8LH England Office Phone: 44 (0) 20 8383 4403. Business E-Mail: r.maini@imperial.ac.uk. *

MAINIGI, SUMEET, cardiac electrophysiologist, educator; BS in Biomedical Engring., Johns Hopkins U., 1992—96; MD, NYU, 1996—2000. Diplomate Am. Bd. Cardiology, Am. Bd. Internal Medicine, Am. Bd. Internal Medicine-clin. cardiac electrphysiology. Intern Hosp. of the Univ. of Pa., resident internal medicine, 2000—03, fellow cardiology, 2003—05, fellow electrophysiology, 2005—07; assoc. dir. electrophysiology Albert Einstein Med. Ctr., 2007—; asst. prof. medicine Jefferson Med. Coll., 2008—. Mem.: Heart Rhythm Soc. Office: Albert Einstein Medical Center 4th Fl Willowrest Bldg 5501 Old York Rd Philadelphia PA 19141 Office Phone: 215-456-7022. Office Fax: 215-456-1432.

MAIOCCO, KENNETH JOSEPH, dermatologist; b. Bridgeport, Conn., Oct. 3, 1941; s. John Paul Maiocco and Jane Marie Pilgoste; m. Maxine Marie Gormley, Dec. 7, 1967; children: David, Mark, Dana, Adam. BS, Fairfield U., Conn., 1963; MD, U. Rochester, NY, 1967. Diplomate Am. Bd. Dermatology, 1976. Dir. pub. health Trumbull Health Dept., 1976—2006. Vol. skin cancer screening clinic Health Dept. Trumbull, Trumbull and Westport, Colo. Maj. US Army, 1971—73. Decorated Commendation medal; named Top Dr. for Women, Conn. Mag., 2002, Best Dr. in America, 2000—09, Top Dr. NY Metro Area, 2000—09. Mem.: Conn. Dermatology and Dermatol. Surgery Soc., Fairfield County Med. Assn., Conn. State Med. Soc., Am. Acad. Dermatology, Dermatology Found. Scholar's Cir., Gaelic Am. Club, Brooklawn Country Club. Avocations: golf, boating, skiing, model trains. Office: 4639 Main St Bridgeport CT 06606-1838 Office Phone: 203-374-5546.

MAIORANO, DOMENICO, biologist, researcher; b. Vibo Valentia, Italy, Nov. 10, 1966; s. Leonardo Maiorano and Vincenzina Pasquino; m. Hélène Guillon, Aug. 23, 2003; children: Valentina children: Gabriel. Laurea in biology cum laude, U. Milan, 1990; PhD in Genetics and Cell Biology, U. Oxford, Eng., 1995. Rsch. asst. U. Oxford, 1995—96; postdoctoral fellow Nat. Ctr. Sci. Rsch., Paris, 1997—98, staff rschr. Montpellier, France, 2001—, lab. head, 2007—. Tutor U. Oxford, England, 1991, U. Montpellier, 1998—; adj. prof., devel. biology U. Insubria, Italy, 2000—; reviewer of sci. jours. Contbr. articles to profl. jours. Grantee European Cmty., Biomedicine and Health, 2000—02, Rsch. grant, French Assn. Cancer Rsch., 2006—08, Nat. Inst. Cancer, 2007—, Rsch. grant, French Med. Rsch. Found., 2008—. Mem.: Faculty 1000 Biology, Am. Assn. Advancement Sci., French Soc. Cell Biology, Trinity Coll. (life). Achievements include discovery of two oncogenes; patents pending for use of new Mini Chromosome Maintenance genes in pharmaceutical compositions; DNA replication modulating peptides, nucleic acids composing them and their use in pharmaceutical compositions. Avocations: swimming, travel, music, art. Office: Nat Ctr Sci Rsch 141 Rue de la Cardonille Montpellier 34396 France Office Fax: 33 4 99619901; Home Fax: 33 4 99619901. Personal E-mail: domenico.maiorano@laposte.net. Business E-Mail: domenico.maiorano@igh.cnrs.fr.

MAISEL, WILLIAM HOWARD, cardiologist, internist; b. Mar. 26, 1966; BS in Biology, MIT, Cambridge, Mass.; MPH, Harvard Sch Pub. Health, Boston, Mass.; MD, Cornell U., 1992. Cert. Am. Bd. Internal Medicine, 1995. Intern, internal medicine Brigham & Women Hosp., Boston, 1992—93, resident, internal medicine, 1993—95, fellow, cardiovascular, 1996—99, fellow, cardiac electrophysiology; clin. fellow, medicine Harvard Med. Sch., Boston, asst. prof. medicine; attending staff physician, cardiovascular divsn. Beth Israel Deaconess Med. Ctr., Boston. Chmn. circulatory system med. devices adv. panel FDA. Ad hoc reviewer Am. Jour. Cardiology, Annals Internal Medicine, Circulation, Jour. Am. Coll. Cardiology, Jour. Cardiovascular Electrophysiology, Jour. Interventional Cardiac Electrophysiology, New England Jour. Medicine, Pacing and Clin. Electrophysiology; contbr. articles to profl. jours., chapters to books. Mem.: AMA, Heart Rhythm Soc., Am. Heart Assn., Am. Coll. Cardiology, Mass. Med. Soc. Office: Beth Israel Deaconess Med Ctr 185 Pilgrim Rd Baker 4 Boston MA 02215 Office Phone: 617-632-7457. Office Fax: 617-632-7620.

MAISIN, JEAN RENÉ SIMON, medical researcher, educator; b. Leuven, Belgium, May 25, 1928; m. Claudine Derrider, Sept. 18, 1958; 3 children. MD, Cath. U. Louvain, 1954, dipl. Electro-Radiology, 1958, specialist in Pathology, 1959. Head radiobiology dept. CEN/SCK, Mol, Belgium, 1960-87; lectr., prof. Cath. U. Louvain, 1973-93, prof. emeritus, 1993—. Spkr. in field. Contbr. over 300 articles to sci. publs. Sec.-gen. European Late Effects Project Group, 1970-85, chmn. 1985-95, hon. mem., 1996—; mem. governing bd., v.p. Internat. Coun. Lab. Animal Sci., 1991, acting chmn., 1994-95, chmn. 1995-99, hon. mem., 1999—; rep. UN Sci. Com. on Effects Atomic Radiation, 1985—2008, pres. sessions, 1991-92; chmn. European Soc. Radiation Biology, 1986-88, hon. chmn., 1996-2003. Decorated gt. officer Order of Crown, comdr. Order of Leopold II, and officer Order of Leopold, Hanns-Langendorff Medaille, 1994; recipient Bacq and Alexander award, 1997. Mem. European Soc. Lab. Animal Sci. (former mem. governing bd.) European Assn. Late Effects (chmn. 1983-95), Internat. Assn. Late Effects. (former chmn.), Belgian Soc. Lab. Animal Sci. (hon.) Belgian Soc. Radiation Biology (former chmn.). Roman Catholic. Home: Ave du Manoir 55 B-1410 Waterloo Belgium Office: Unite Imre UCL-IMRE 54/69 Ave Hippocrate S4 1200 Brussels Belgium also: Unite Radiobiol Radioprotec IMRE 54 Gb UCL avenue Hippocrate 55 1200 Brussels Belgium Office Phone: 32027645431. Personal E-mail: jrmaisin@skynet.be. Business E-Mail: maisin@rbnt.ucl.ac.be.

MAITIN, IAN, physiatrist; BA in Biochemistry, Rutgers U., 1983; MD, Jefferson Medical Coll., 1989; MBA, Temple U., 2002. Intern, internal medicine Bryn Mawr Hosp., Bryn Mawr, Pa., 1989—90; resident, physical medicine and rehab. Robert Wood Johnson Rehab. Inst. UMDNJ, 1990—93, chief resident, 1993; assoc. prof. physical medicine and rehab. Temple U., 1993—, acting chair physical medicine and rehab., 2003—06, chair physical medicine and rehab., 2006—. Fellow: American Academy Physical Medicine and Rehab., American Assn. Electrodiagnostic Medicine; mem.: Assn. Academic Physiatrists. Office: Temple U 3420 N Broad St Philadelphia PA 19140 Office Phone: 215-707-2997. Business E-Mail: maitin@temple.edu.

MAIZE, JOHN CHRISTOPHER, dermatologist, educator; b. Elizabeth, NJ, July 23, 1943; s. Donald Adam and Caroline Marie (Costanzo) Maize; m. Janice Lee Bentley, May 21, 1966; children: Sandra Kristine Tolly, John C. Jr., Jennifer Lee. MD, U. Mich., 1968. Cert. Am. Bd. Dermatology. Intern U. Mich., Ann Arbor, 1968—69, residency in dermatology, 1968—72; asst. prof. dermatology SUNY, Buffalo, 1972—77, assoc. prof., 1977—80, Med. U. SC, Charleston, 1980—83, prof., 1983—89, prof., chmn. dept. dermatology, 1989—2003, clin. prof., 2003—. Author: Pigmented Lesions of the Skin, 1987, Cutaneous Pathology, 1998; editor-in-chief Am. Jour. Dermatology, 1986—90. Fellow: Am. Soc. Dermapathology (pres. 1995), Am. Acad. Dermatology; mem.: Am. Bd. Dermatology (dir. 1990—99, pres. 1999), S.C. Dermatol. Assn. (pres. 2001), S.C. Med. Assn., Internat. Soc. Dermatopathology (sec. 1987—89, pres. 1989—91), Am. Dermatol. Assn. Roman Catholic. Avocations: fishing, golf, travel. Office: 266 W Coleman Blvd Unit 101 Mount Pleasant SC 29464 Home Phone: 843-881-1007; Office Phone: 843-388-6911. E-mail: jmaizesr@ameripath.com.

MAJ, MARIO, psychiatrist, educator; b. Naples, Italy, June 20, 1953; s. Federico and Olga (Imperato) M. MD, U. Naples, 1977, diploma in psychiatry, 1981; PhD in Behavioral Scis., U. Umeå (Sweden), 1985. Prof. mental health U. Naples, 1985-92; coord. neuropsychiatric sect. global program on AIDS World Health Orgn., Geneva, 1989-91; prof., chmn. dept. psychiatry U. Naples, 1992—. Dir. Italian Ctr. for Mental Health World Health Orgn., 1997—. Editor: Mental Disorders in HIV Infection and AIDS, 1993; co-editor: (jour.) European Psychiatry, 1991—; contbr. articles to profl. jours. Mem. Italian Soc. Biol. Psychiatry (pres. 1991—), Italian Psychiat. Assn. (pres.), Italian Soc. Neurosci. (nat. councillor), European Psychiat. Assn. (past pres.), World Psychiat. Assn. (pres.). Avocations: poetry, listening to chamber music. Home: Corso Europa 72 80127 Naples Campania Italy Office: U Naples Dept Psychiatry Largo Madonna Delle Grazie 80138 Naples NA Italy

MAJALI, MUSTAFA MOHD, physicist; b. Sobak, Jordan, Jan. 14, 1966; s. Mohd AbdelMuhdi Majali and Fatmeh Safr Hadad; m. Reem Ali Majali, May 17, 1996; children: Mais Mustafa, Abdullha Mustafa, Lana Mustafa. Degree in physics, U. Jordan, 1988, degree in med. physics, 1990; PhD, Czech Tech. U., Prague, 2004. Cert. nuc. engring., Czech Republic, 2004. Radiation protection Ministry of Energy, Amman, Jordan, 1990—2001; head health physics dept. Jordan Atomic Energy Commn., Amman, 2004—. Author: (book) Quality Assurance in Diagnostic Radiology, Radiation Protection-Principle and Applications. Achievements include design of software for sheilding calculation; software for digitizing the radiographic image. Home: Mustafa Al Turk St Amman PO Box141350 Amman11814 Jordan Office: Jordan Atomic Energy Commn PO Box 70 Shafa Badran Amman 11934 Jordan Personal E-mail: mustafamajali@hotmail.com.

MAJAVA, HEIKKI TAPIO, psychiatrist; b. Helsinki, Finland, Jan. 4, 1939; s. Oiva Tapio and Ida Margareta Majava; m. Marja Katriina Virkki, Dec. 1, 2001; m. Mirjam Lundberg (div.); 1 child, Antti Juhana; m. Lcenz Soininen Majava (div.). MSc, Helsinki U., Finland, 1968. Cert. psychiatrist Helsinki U. Ctrl. Hosp., 1976. Asst. physician U. Psychiat. Clinic, Helsinki, 1968—71; specialist Child&Family Clinic, Helsinki, 1977—79; dr. in chief SE Ctr. Mental Hosp., Joutseno, Finland, 1979—2003. Chief editor Med. Student Orgn., Helsinki, 1966—67, chief editor Therapia Fennica, 1968—69; editor psychotherapy theory & practice Therapeia Soc., Helsinki, 1979—80, chief editor, Psykoterpia Jour., 1985—89; chair SC Psychotherapy Soc., Lappeenranta, Finland, 1985—; county coun. mem., Joutseno city, 2001—08; med. adviser & cons. Tiuru Emigrant Asuly, Joutseno. Musician: (jazz pianist) Old Time Jazz Band, 1960—65. Abourd of local adminstr. Green Party, Joutseno, 2001—08; mem. European Union Parliament Election. Sub-lt. NAVY, 1957—58, Suomenlinna. Mem.: Finnish Med. Joga Soc., Soc. Poets, Finnish Semiotic Soc. (adminstr.), Finnish Med. Assn. Green Party. Evangel Lutherian. Avocations: piano, jazz. Home: Lääkäritie 21 Joutseno 55330 Finland Office: Taide&Terapia Käännekohta Kirkkokatu 14 A 10 Lappeenranta 53100 Finland

MAJDAK, EWA J., plastic surgeon; d. Kaz Majdak and Jolanta Studencka; m. Jorge Luis Paredes. MD, Med. U. Gdansk, Poland, 2000. Rschr. Lab. Surg. Rsch. & Transplantology, U. Antwerp, Belgium, 1999—2000; internship Med. U. Gdansk, 2000—01, PhD fellow human genetics, 2001—04; surg. resident Princess Royal U. Hosp., Orpington, 2003—06; resident plastic & reconstructive surgery City Hosp., Birmingham & St. Thomas Hosp., London, 2006—. PhD fellow human genetics Leiden U. Med. Ctr., Netherlands, 2002—03; reviewer in field. Contbr. articles to profl. jours. Co-recipient Rsch. award, Med. U. Gdansk, 2006; grantee, European Commn. Cancer Rsch., Eurogendis & Dutch Cancer Inst., 2002; Marie Curie fellowship, Karolinska U. Sweden, 2002. Fellow: Royal Coll. Surgeons Edinburgh (assoc.); mem.: European Assn. Cancer Rsch. (assoc.), Brit. Assn. Plastic, Reconstructive & Aesthetic Surgeons (assoc.).

MAJESKI, JAMES ANTHONY, surgeon, research scientist; b. Newark, Jan. 29, 1945; s. Anthony Andrew and Irene Teresa Majeski; m. Elizabeth Watts Durst, June 16, 1973; children: Elizabeth, James Anthony, Marie. BS, Citadel, 1966; MS, USC, Columbia, 1968, PhD, 1971; MD, Med. U. SC, Charleston, 1974. Intern surgery U. Cin., 1974—75, resident surgery, 1975—80, fellow transplantation and vascular surgery, 1980—81, instr. surgery, 1979—81; asst. prof. surgery Med. USC, 1981—99, assoc. prof., 1999—2005, prof. surgery, 2005—. Editor transplantation surgery sect. Reference and Index Services, Inc., 1976—90; mem. editl. bd. J.S.C. Med Assn., 2003—. Contbr. more than 125 articles to profl. jours. First lt. USAFR, 1966—71. Recipient Jefferson award, SC Acad. Sci., 1972, Roe award, 1990, Silver Beaver award, 2001, Eagle award, 1957, Spurgeon award, 1998; fellow, NSF, 1968. Fellow: ACS, ICS; mem.: AMA, Assn. Acad. Surgery, Am. Soc. Transplant Surgeons, SC Med. Assn., Sigma Xi. Home: 274 Copahee Rd Mount Pleasant SC 29464 Office: 900 Bowman Rd Ste 100 Mount Pleasant SC 29464 Home Phone: 843-881-0099; Office Phone: 843-884-7991. Personal E-mail: drmajeski@aol.com.

MAJORS, NELDA FAYE, physical therapist; b. Houston, Aug. 3, 1938; d. Columbus Edward and Mary (Mills) M. Cert. in Phys. Therapy, Hermann Sch. Phys. Therapy, Houston, 1960; BS, U. Houston, 1963. Lic. phys. therapist, Tex. Staff therapist Tex. Med. Ctr. Hermann Hosp., Houston, 1960-61; phys. therapist Chelsea Orthopedic Clinic, Houston, 1961-63; dir. phys. therapy Meml. Hosp. Southwest, Houston, 1963-75; owner, pres. Nelda Majors, Inc., Houston, 1975—. Profl. adv. bd. Logos Home Health Agy., Houston, 1985-86; adv. dir. Prime Bank, Houston; sec.-treas., bd. dirs. Dominion Media Corp.; realtor, State of Ariz., 2005-. Ptnr. Houston Proud Ptnr., 1986—; founder, pres. Instnl. Safety Advs. Inc., 1994—; bd. dirs. Texans for the Improvement of Long Term Care Facilities, 1995—; mem. founders cir. Crosswalk Am. Christian Orgn., 2006. Named All Am. Softball Pitcher, Amateur Softball Assn., 1964, All-Regional and All-State Pitcher, Tex. Amateur Softball Assn., 1954-70; named to

Houston Amateur Softball Assn. Softball Hall of Fame, 1994, Houston Softball Legends Hall of Fame, 2002. Mem. Am. Phys. Therapy Assn. (pvt. practice sect.), Ams. for Separation of Ch. and State, Tex. Phys. Therapy Assn., U. Houston Alumni Assn., Nat. Assn. Realtors, E. Cullen Soc. (U. Houston), Crosswalk Am. (founders circle), Rotary Club (Houston, Meml. Spring br.), Phi Kappa Phi. Clubs: U. Houston Cougar. Avocations: softball, bicycling, travel, golf, reading.

MAJRA, J. P., medical educator; b. Majra, May 3, 1965; MD, MBA, 1986. DIT 1986. Prof. Yenepoya Med. Coll., 2010—. Home: 7 B Delta Ct, S.L. Mathias Rd Mangalore Karnataka 575001 India Personal E-mail: jpmajra@hotmail.com.

MAJUMDAR, SANJIB, research scientist; b. West Bengal, Feb. 2, 1976; PhD, IIT Mumbai, 2009. Sci. officer Bhabha Atomic Rsch. Ctr., 1999—2011. Faculty mem. Homi Bhabha Nat. Inst., 2010—11. Recipient Young Scientist award, Indian Sci. Congress Assn. Avocations: soccer, football. Home: Anushaktinagar Mumbai Maharashtra 400085 India Business E-Mail: sanjib@barc.gov.in.

MAK, LINDA L., dermatologist; BSc with honors, U. Wis.; PhD, Johns Hopkins U. Contbr. articles to profl. jours. Mem.: Am. Acad. Pediats., Johns Hopkins Med. and Surg. Assn., Am. Acad. Cosmetic Surgery, Royal Coll. Surgeons Eng. Achievements include research in HIV vaccine development and gene therapy.

MAKARCHIKOV, ALEXANDER FEDOROVICH, biologist, educator; b. Shchuchin, Grodno region, Belarus, Dec. 13, 1964; s. Fedor Filippovich Makarchikov and Nina Adamovna Makarchikova; m. Irina Frantsevna Podzelinskaya, Mar. 17, 1964; 1 child, Igor Alexandrovich. Degree, Grodno State Agrl. U., 1987; postgrad., Inst. Biochemistry NAS Belarus, Grondo, 1992; PhD in Biology, Smolensk State Med. U., 1993; D in Biol. Sci., Highest Cert. Commn., Belarus, 2009. Cert. asst. prof. Highest Cert. Commn., 2004. Jr. rschr. Inst. Biochemistry NAS Belarus, 1993—94, rschr., 1995—97, sr. rschr., 1998—99, head lab. enzymology, 2000—05; asst. prof. Grodno State Agrl. U., 2006—09, prof., 2010, head, chem. dept., 2011—. Grantee grant, Belarusian Rep. Found. Fundamental Rsch., 2003—05;, 1995—96, 1998—2000, 2005—07, NAS Belarus, 1999—, Belgian FNRS, 2001—02, 2005-2006. Achievements include discovery of adenylated thiamine triphosphate as well as the enzyme of its biosynthesis. Avocations: reading, cooking, exercise. Home: Tavlaya 34/1 Apt 11 Grodno 230005 Belarus Office: Grodno State Agrl Univ Tereshkovoi 28 Grodno 230008 Belarus Office Fax: 0152 721365. Personal E-mail: a_makarchikov@yahoo.com.

MAKAROUN, MICHEL S., surgeon; MD, Am. U. Beirut, Lebanon. Diplomate Am. Bd. Surgery, Am. Bd. Surgery-vascular surgery. Intern Am. Univ. of Beirut, Lebanon; resident Univ. of Pitts. Med. Sch., fellow; physician, divsn. vascular surgery UPMC Presbyterian, UPMC Shadyside; hosp. affiliations include Magee-Womens Hospital of UPMC, UPMC McKeesport, UPMC Mercy, UPMC Passavant, UPMC St. Margaret. Office: University of Pittsburgh Shadyside Division of Vascular Surgery Ste 307 5200 Centre Ave Pittsburgh PA 15232 Office Phone: 412-623-3333.

MAKAROVA, SVETLANA, medical researcher; b. Kaluga, Russia, Aug. 24, 1963; Degree, Med. Inst., Moscow, 1987, Inst. Nutrition, 1992. Rsch. officer Inst. Nutrition Russian Acad. Med. Scis., 1992—2000, Russian Acad. Med. Scis. Rsch. Ctr. Children's Health, 2000—08, sr. rsch. officer, 2008. Mem.: Russian Soc. Children's Allergy and Immunology. Avocations: dance, painting, travel, skiing, scuba diving. Home: Kedrova 21-2-44 Moscow 117036 Russia Personal E-mail: sm27@yandex.ru.

MAKHIJA, MOHAN, nuclear medicine physician; b. Bombay, Oct. 1, 1941; came to US, 1969; m. Arlene Zambito, Nov. 11, 1978. MD, Bombay U., 1965. Diplomate Am. Bd. Nuc. Medicine, Am. Bd. Radiology; cert. spl. competence in nuc. radiology. Resident in radiology Morristown Meml. Hosp., NJ, 1972—75; resident in nuc. medicine Yale-New Haven Hosp., 1975; fellow Yale U. Sch. Medicine, New Haven, 1976—77; jr. attending physician Helene Fuld Med. Ctr., Trenton, NJ, 1977—78; acting dir. dept. nuc. medicine Monmouth Med. Ctr., Long Branch, NJ, 1978, dir. nuc. medicine sect., 1979—2000, asst. attending radiology, 1978—80, assoc. attending radiology, 1980—83, attending radiologist, 1983—2000, St. Peter's U. Hosp., New Brunswick, NJ, 2001—, Robert Wood Johnson U. Hosp., New Brunswick, 2001—. Sr. instr. Hahneman U., Phila., 1978-80, clin. asst. prof., 1980-83, clin. assoc. prof., 1983-91, clin. prof., 1991-94, clin. prof. radiologic scis. Med. Coll. Pa. and Hahnemann U., 1994-2000; clin. prof. radiology U. Medicine and Dentistry NJ-Robert Wood Johnson Med. Sch., 2002—; radiol. cons. to NJ State Bd. Med. Examiners., 1994. Contbr. articles to profl. jours. Mem. NJ Commn. on Radiation Protection, 2004—. Fellow: ACP (spkr. ho. of dels. 1992—93), Am. Coll. Radiology, Am. Coll. Nuc. Physicians; mem.: Med. Soc. NJ (trustee 2003—), Assn. Med. Specialties NJ (sec. 2001—02, pres. 2003—04), Soc. Nuc. Medicine (bd. govs. Gt. NY chpt. 1992—98), Indo-Am. Soc. Nuc. Medicine (pres. 1992—92), Radiol. Soc. NJ (chmn. nuc. medicine 1988—94, treas. 1994—95, sec. 1995—96, v.p. 1996—97, pres.-elect 1997—98, pres. 1998—99, chmn. nominting com. 2001—02, chmn. fellowship com. 2002—), Monmouth County Med. Soc. (pres. 1991—92). Home: 5 High Ridge Rd Ocean NJ 07712-3460 Office: St Peter's U Hosp 254 Easton Ave New Brunswick NJ 08901 Personal E-mail: mmakhija@aol.com.

MAKI, DENNIS G., epidemiology educator; b. River Falls, Wis., May 8, 1940; m. Gail Dawson, 1962; children: Kimberly, Sarah, Daniel. BS in Physics with honors, U. Wis., 1962, MS in Physics, 1964, MD, 1967. Diplomate Am. Bd. Internal Medicine, Am. Bd. Infectious Diseases, Am. Bd. Critical Care Medicine. Physicist, computer programmer Lawrence Radiation Lab., AEC, Livermore, Calif., 1962; intern, asst. resident Harvard Med. unit Boston City Hosp., 1967-69, chief resident, 1972-73; with Hosp. Infections sect. Ctrs. for Disease Control, USPHS, Atlanta, 1969-71; acting chief nat. nosocomial infections study Ctr. for Disease Control, USPHS, Atlanta, 1970-71; sr. resident dept. medicine Mass. Gen. Hosp., 1971-72, clin. and research fellow infectious disease unit, 1973-74; asst. prof. medicine U. Wis., Madison, 1974-78, assoc. prof., 1978-82, prof., 1982—; hosp. epidemiologist, U. Wis. Hosp. and Clinic, Madison, 1974—; Ovid O. Meyer prof. medicine U. Wis., Madison, 1975—, head sec. infectious diseases, 1979—2007, attending physician Ctr. for Trauma and Life Support, 1976—. Clinician, rschr., educator in field; mem. program com. Intersci. Conf. on Antimicrobial Agts. and Chemotherapy, 1987-94; mem. Am. Bd. Critical Care Medicine, 1989-95. Sr. assoc. editor Infection Control and Hosp. Epidemiology, 1979-93; mem. editl. bd. Jour. Lab. and Clin. Investigation, 1980-86, Jour. Critical Care, 1985-96, Jour. Infectious Diseases, 1988-90, Critical Care Medicine, 1989-94, 97—, Mayo Clinic Procs., 2002-07; contbr. articles to med. jours. Recipient 1st award for disting. rsch. in Antibiotic Rev., 1980, Internat. CIPI award, 1994, SHEA lectr., 1999, numerous tchg. awards and hon. lectrs. Master ACP; fellow Infectious Diseases Soc. Am. (coun. 1993-96, citation 2000), Am. Acad. Microbiology, Am. Soc. for Critical Care Medicine, Surg. Infection Soc., Wis. Acad. Scis., Arts and Letters; mem. Soc. Hosp. Epidemiologists Am. (pres. 1990), Ctrl. Soc. for Clin. Rsch., Am. Soc. Microbiology, Am. Fedn. Clin. Rsch., Alpha Omega Alpha (nat. bd. dirs. 1983-89). Office: U Wis Hosp and Clinics H4/574 Madison WI 53792 Office Phone: 608-263-7367. Fax: 608-833-0327. Personal E-mail: dgmaki@yahoo.com. Business E-Mail: dgmaki@medicine.wisc.edu.

MAKKAT, SMITHA, physician, researcher; d. Madhavan and Devaki Namboodiri; m. Madhu Kumar Krishnan Bhattathiri, July 2, 1995; children: Gayathri Bhattathiri, Ambika Bhattathiri. MBBS, U. Calicut, Keral, 1995; MS in Med. and Pharm. Rsch., Vrije U. Brussel, Belgium, 2002, PhD, 2008. Med. house officer Calicut Med. Coll., Kerala, India, 1994—95; hon. rsch. asst. U. Hosp. Antwerp, Edegem, India, 1998—2000; rschr. Vrije U. Brussel, 2000—08, postdoc. rschr., 2008—. Business E-Mail: smitha.makkat@vub.ac.be.

MAKKER, SUDESH PAUL, physician; b. Sargodha, Punjab, India, June 8, 1941; came to U.S., 1966; s. Manohar Lal and Daya Wati (Kharbanda) M.; m. Donna Mae Stohs, Feb. 15, 1969; children: Vishal, Kirin. Fellow of Sci., Panjab U., 1959; MD, All India Inst. med. Scis., New Dehli, 1964. Bd. cert. Am. Bd. Pediatrics, Am. Bd. Pediatric Nephrology. Intern in internal medicine All India Inst. of Med. Scis., New Dehli, 1965, resident in internal medicine, 1966; rotating intern Queens Gen. Hosp., NYC, 1966-67; resident in pediatrics U. Chgo. (Ill.) Hosps., 1967-69; rsch. fellowship in pediatric nephrology Case Western Res. U., 1969-71; fellowship in pediatric nephrology U. Calif., San Francisco, 1971; instr. to asst. prof. pediatrics Case Western Res. U., Sch. Medicine, Cleve., 1971-76, assoc. prof., div. head pediatric nephrology, 1976-83; prof., div. head pediatric nephrology U. Tex. Health Sci. Ctr., San Antonio, 1983-91; prof., sect. chief pediatric nephrology U. Calif., Davis Sch. Medicine, Davis, 1991—. Mem. ad hoc com. on nat. standards for dialysis and transplantation in children Am. Soc. Pediatric Nephrology; ad hoc com. on hypertension in the young Am. Heart Assn., N.E. Ohio Chpt.; mem. end stage renal disease program Crippled Children Svcs. State of Ohio; mem. rsch. grants com. and pub. edn. com. Kidney Found. of Ohio; vis. prof. U. Pa. Children's Hosp., Phila., 1981, U. So. Calif., L.A., 1981, U. Calif. Sch. Medicine, San Francisco, 1982, U. Mich., Ann Arbor, 1990, and many others. Editor: (textbook) Pediatric Nephrology, 1992, 2006; editorial bd.: Internat. Jour. Pediatric Nephrology, Indian Jour. Pediatrics; contbr. over 110 articles to profl. jours. Mem. AAAS, Am. Soc. Investigative Pathology, Am. Acad. Pediatrics, Am. Soc. Nephrology (elected fellow, 2004), The Soc. for Exptl. Biology and Medicine, Am. Assn. Immunologists, Soc. for Pediatric Rsch., Am. Pediatric Soc., Sigma Chi, Sigma Xi. Avocations: tennis, hiking, reading, photography. Office: Univ Calif Davis Med Ctr Pediatric Nephrology 2516 Stockton Blvd Sacramento CA 95817-2208 Office Phone: 916-734-8118. Business E-Mail: spmakker@ucdavis.edu. *

MAKOUS, NORMAN, retired internist, cardiologist, educator; b. Chgo., July 22, 1924; s. Lawrence Alonzo and Ruth (Luehring) M.; m. Dorothy Murl Bowlin, Sept. 25, 1948 (dec. July 25, 2003); children: David, Bruce, Catherine, Monte, Joseph, Martin, John, Virginia, Dorothy, Margaret; m. Eleanor B. Sullivan Feb. 21, 2004. BS, U. Wis., Madison, 1945, MD, 1947. Diplomate in internal medicine and cardiovascular diseases Am. Bd. Internal Medicine. Mixed intern Rsch. Hosp., Kansas City, Mo., 1947—48, resident in internal medicine, 1948—50; fellow in cardiovasc. disease U. Vt., Burlington, 1950—51; resident in internal medicine U.S. Naval Hosp., Camp Lejeune, NC, 1951—52; dir. cardiac catheterization lab. Kansas City, Mo., 1955—56; fellow in cardiovasc. disease Pa. Hosp., Phila., 1953—54, assoc. cardiologist, assoc. physician to hosp., 1960—72, cardiologist, physician to hosp., 1972—2000, cons., 2000—01; pvt. practice Kansas City and Independence, Mo., 1956—59, Phila., 1959—2001; assoc. in medicine U. Pa., Phila., 1959—71, asst. prof. clin. medicine, 1971—74, clin. asst. prof. medicine, 1974—94; clin. asst. prof. medicine Thomas Jefferson U., Phila., 1994; ret., 2006. Physician advisor Keystone Profl. Rev. Orgn., 1986-93; mem. cons. Pa. Bur. Disability Determination, 1981-2001; cardiology cons. Phila. City Solicitor's Office, 1986-2005; mem. peer rev. panel Jour. Cardiopulmonary Rehab., 1990; mem. adv. group Greater Delaware Valley Regional Med. Program, 1971-75. Author: Time to Care: Personal Medicine in the Age of Technology, 2010; contbr. articles to med. jours., chpts. to books. Founder, acting chmn. Southeastern Pa. Regional High Blood Pressure Control Program, 1978-80; mem. interim bd. Health Sys. Agy. Southeastern Pa., 1975-77, chmn. adv. coun., 1979-80; trustee Edna B. Kynett Meml. Found., Phila., 1963—, v.p., 1994-96, pres., 1997—2004; pres. Home and Sch. Assn., Our Lady of Lourdes Parish, Phila., 1972-73, mem. parish pastoral coun., 1991-95, co-chmn., 1993-95; trustee Vis. Nurse Assn. Greater Phila., 1997-2000. Lt. USNR, 1943-45, 50-52, Res., 1952-62. Recipient Legion of Honor, Chapel of Four Chaplains, 1980, Spl. Achievement award Southeastern Pa. Regional High Blood Pressure Control Program. Fellow ACP, Am. Coll. Cardiology, Am. Soc. Internal Medicine; mem. AMA, Pa. Med. Soc. (chmn. profl. liaibility ins. appeals com. 1986-91), Phila. County Med. Soc. (standing com. Med. Econs., 1979-86, pres. Center City br. 1980-81, sec. 1990-91, chmn. membership and orgn. com. 1991-2000, Cristol award 1994), Am. Heart Assn. (fellow coun. clin. cardiology, pres. Southeastern Pa. affiliate 1988-89, bd. govs., program chmn. 1988-92, pres. Pa. affiliate 1981-82, Disting. Svc. award Pa. affiliate 1982, Disting. Achievement award Pa. affiliate, 1986, Disting. Achievement award Southeastern Pa. affiliate 1988, Vol. of Yr. award Southeastern Pa. affiliate 1988), Pa. Soc. Internal Medicine (pres. 1983-84). Avocations: tennis, cinematography. Office: 243 Freedom Blvd Coatesville PA 19320 Office Phone: 610-466-9441. Personal E-mail: drnmakous@aol.com.

MAKOV, ISRAEL, pharmaceutical executive; BSc in Agrl., Hebrew U., 1963, MSc in Economics, 1965. Chmn. Axiom Ltd., 1987—91; CEO Yachin Hakal Ltd., 1991—93, Gettex, 1993—95; v.p. bus. devel. Teva Pharms., Petach Tikva, Israel, 1995—99, exec. v.p., 1999—2001, COO, 2001—02, pres., CEO, 2002—07; chmn. Given Imaging Ltd, 2007—. Bd. dirs. Bank Hapoalim Ltd., 2002—. Dir. of Ramol Tel Aviv U. Ltd., 2001—; founder, dir. INNI-Israel Nat. Nanotechnology Initiative, 2003—. Office: Given Imaging Ltd 2 Hacarmel St New Industrial Park 20692 Yoqneam Israel

MAKRIS, PANTELIS PE, retired hematologist, educator; b. Thessaloniki, Sept. 25, 1939; MD, Med. Sch. Thessaloniki, 1978. Prof. hematology- hemostasis Sch. Thessaloniki, 2000; emeritus prof. hematology -hemostasis Aristotle U. Thessaloniki, 2007. With hemostasis unit 1st Med. Propaedeutic Clinic Med. Sch., 1982—2007; dir. PE MAKRIS. Mem.: Panhellenic Soc. Hematology, Internat. Soc. Angiology, Internat. Soc. Hematology, Internat. Soc. Thrombosis and Hemostasis. Avocations: photography, chess, music. Home: Epiktitou 3 Thessaloniki Macedonia 54351 Greece Home Fax: 00302310905960. Business E-Mail: pemakris@med.auth.gr.

MALACH, MONTE, physician; b. Jersey City, Aug. 15, 1926; s. Charles and Yetta (Pascher) M.; m. Ann Elaine Glazer, June 15, 1952 (dec. June 1989); children: Barbara Sandra, Cathie Tara, Matthew David. BA, MD, U. Mich., 1949. Diplomate Am. Bd. Internal Medicine, Nat. Bd. Med. Examiners. Intern Beth Israel Hosp., Boston, 1949-50, resident, 1950-51, chief resident, 1951-52; chief med. resident Kings County Hosp., Bklyn., 1954-55; practice medicine specializing in internal medicine and cardiology Bklyn., 1955—2001; dir. CCU Bklyn. Hosp., 1965-91, dir. emeritus CCU, 1991—; med. dir., clin. coord. Medicare IPRO Downstate N.Y., 1990—2005; cardiology cons., 2005—; pres. Residents Coun. Hallmark, Battery Pk. City, 2009—. Pres. profl. staff Bklyn. Hosp., 1966-69, chmn. med. bd., 1971-72; attending staff Caledonian Hosp., pres. profl. staff, 1984-85; pres. profl. staff Bklyn. Hosp.-Caledonian Hosp., 1987-89, chmn. med. bd., 1988-89; cons. Kings County Hosp.; tchg. fellow Tufts U. Med. Sch., 1951-52; instr. medicine Downstate Med. Ctr., Bklyn., 1955-59, clin. asst. prof. medicine, 1959-68, clin. assoc. prof., 1969-76, clin. prof., 1976—; clin. prof. medicine NYU Med. Ctr., 1994—; bd. dirs. Bay St. Landing One Owners Corp., 1985-87; v.p. Ocean View Condos, 1989-90, pres., 1990-95; med. dir. IPRO Medicare Rev., N.Y. State, 1990—, IPRO N.Y. State Peer Rev., 1990-2006. Kings County committeeman Dem. Party, 1964, 65; pres. Resident Coun. Hallmark., Battey Pk., 2009-10. Served with USNR, 1944-46, to 1st lt. M.C. U.S. Army, 1952-54. Recipient 1st Prize for Crisis Mgmt. Habitat Mag., 1987. Fellow Am. Coll. Chest Physicians, ACP (master, Laureate award 2000), Am. Coll. Cardiology (task force Health Care Quality Improvement Initiative 1996—); mem. AMA (chmn. sect. coun. internal medicine 1980), N.Y. Heart Assn., Am. Soc. Internal Medicine (master, trustee 1975-79, sec.-treas. 1979—, pres. elect 1981, pres. 1982-83, chmn. investment com. 1985-93), N.Y. State Soc. Internal Medicine (pres. 1973-74, dir. 1966-84, chmn. Bklyn. chpt., v.p. 1971, award of merit 1978), Bklyn. Soc. Internal Medicine (mem. council 1965, pres. 1969-72), Med. Soc. State of N.Y. (chmn. sect. internal medicine 1976, chmn. med. care ins. com. 1988-93), Federated Council for Internal Medicine (chmn. 1979-80), Med. Soc. County Kings (censor 1985-91). Office: President Resident Coun Hallmark Battery Park City New York NY 10282 Office Phone: 917-522-1201. Office Fax: 917-522-1201. Personal E-mail: mmmdmacpl@gmail.com.

MALAFRONTE, DONALD, health planning consultant; b. Bklyn., Dec. 16, 1931; s. Pasquale and Amalia (Castaldo) M.; m. Diane Freedenberg, Jan. 7, 1960 (dec. Nov. 14, 1970); children: Philip, Victor.; m. Hillary Demby, Oct. 30, 1982. BS, NYU, 1954. Reporter L.I. Daily Press, 1956-58; reporter, editor Newark Star-Ledger, 1958-65, art columnist, 1963-70; adminstrv. asst. to mayor of Newark, 1965-70; dir. Newark Model Cities Program, 1967-70, Newark Community Devel. Adminstrn., 1968-70; chief urban field operations N.J. Regional Med. Program, 1970-73; pres. Urban Health Inst., Roseland, NJ, 1973—. Cons. to hosps., local govts., 1970— Author articles in field. Served with AUS, 1954-56. Recipient Joyce Kilmer fiction prize NYU, 1953 Office: Urban Health Inst 101 Eisenhower Pky Roseland NJ 07068-1028 Home: 1056 5th Ave New York NY 10128-0112 Office Phone: 973-228-9000. Business E-Mail: dmalafronte@uhi.org.

MALAKOFF, STACEY L., hospital administrator; children: AJ, Allie. BSBA, Wash. U., 1985. CPA 1987. With NY Times; mgr. audit divsn. Ernst & Young LLP; dir. reimbursement dept. Hosp. for Spl. Surgery, 1990, contr., 1992, v.p. fin., 1996, treas., exec. v.p. and CFO. Mem.: AICPA, Healthcare Fin. Mgmt. Assn., Greater NY Hosp. Assn. (fiscal policy com. mem.). Office: Hospital for Special Surgery 535 E 70th St New York NY 10021 Office Phone: 212-606-1196. Office Fax: 212-794-1309.

MALANGONI, MARK ALAN, surgeon, educator; b. East Chicago, Ind., Nov. 3, 1949; s. Roland G. and Cornelia (Marza) M.; m. Nancy Knapp, Aug. 12, 1972; children: Joseph, Michael, Jonathan. AB in Zoology cum laude, Ind. U., 1971, MD, 1975. MD; diplomate Am. Bd. Surgery. Asst. prof. surgery Med. Coll. Wis., Milw., 1980-84, assoc. program dir., gen. surgery, 1981-84; assoc. prof. Surgery U. Louisville, 1984-90, chief surgery Humana Hosp., 1985-90; prof. surgery Case Western Res. U., Cleve., 1990—. Chmn. dept. surgery MetroHealth Med. Ctr., Cleve., 1990-2010. Merit Rev. grantee VA, Louisville, 1985-88. Fellow Am. Coll. Surgeons; mem. Cen. Surg. Assn., So. Surg. Assn., Am. Surg. Assn., Phi Beta Kappa, Alpha Omega Alpha. Office: MetroHealth Med Ctr 2500 Metrohealth Dr # 914 Cleveland OH 44109-1998 Office Phone: 216-778-4558.

MALANI, ASHOK K., physician; b. Jadcharla, India, Dec. 17, 1969; s. Jugal K. and Kamala Malani; m. Hemalata Malani, Feb. 1, 1972; children: Khushi, Gyan. MBBS, Osmania Med. Coll., 1992; MS in Gen. Surgery, Postgraduate Inst. Med. Edn. and Rsch., 1996; MD in Internal Medicine, 2003. Jr. resident in gen. surgery Postgraduate Inst. Med. Edn. and Rsch., Chandigarh, India, 1993—96, sr. resident in surgery, 1996; sr. resident in surg. oncology Nizams Inst. Med. Scis., Hyderabad, India, 1996—97; resident in surgery and oncology Leighton Hosp., Crewe, England, 1998; resident in breast and surg. oncology Royal Free Hosp., London, 1998—2000; resident in internal medicine Coney Island Hosp., Bklyn., 2000—03, alt. del., com. interns and residents, 2001—03, mem. grad. med. edn. com., 2003, mem. quality control exec. com., 2003; attending physician, internal medicine St. Mary Hosp., Kankakee, Ill., 2003—05, mem. continuing med. edn., libr. and cancer com., 2004; attending physician, internal medicine Riverside Med. Ctr., Kankakee, 2003—05; pvt. practice Momence, Ill., 2003—05; hospitalist in hematology, oncology Heartlands Regional Med. Ctr., St. Joseph, Mo., 2005—. Hematology com. mem. US Oncology, Dallas, 2005—, US Oncology Rsch., Houston, 2005—. Contbr. scientific papers, abstracts, publs. in field. Com.

mem. Coney Island Hosp., Bklyn., 2000—03, edn. com., quality control com., alt. del. com. of interns and residents New York, NY, 2001—03. Master: Post Grad. Inst. (life); fellow: Royal Coll. Surgeons, Royal Coll. Physicians and Surgeons of Glasgow (life); mem.: AMA (assoc.), ACP (assoc.). Office: St Joseph Oncology Inc 902 N Riverside Rd Saint Joseph MO 64507 Home: 2247 Legacy Trl Irving TX 75063-3846 Personal E-mail: drmalani@yahoo.com.

MALATACK, JAMES JEFFREY, pediatrician, liver transplant specialist; m. Catherine Malatack. BS in Physics, Villanova U., Pa., 1971; MD, Med. Coll. Pa., Phila., 1976. Diplomate Am. Bd. Pediat. Intern pediat. Children's Hosp., Pitts., 1976—77, resident, 1977—79, fellow, 1979—80, Phila., 1986—87; staff mem. St. Christopher's Hosp. for Children, Phila.; prof. Temple U. Sch. Medicine, Phila., dir. diagnostic referral svc., 1992—2000; chief pediat. diagnostic referral svc. Thomas Jefferson U. Sch. Medicine, Phila., 2000—. Dir. med. liver transplantation AI DuPont Hosp. Children, Wilmington, Del., 2006—. Dir. Malatack Meml. Scholarship, Muhlenberg Coll., Allentown, Pa., 2005. Recipient Thomas K. Oliver award, U. Pitt. Sch. Medicine, Victor C. Vaughn Tchg. award, Temple U. Sch. Medicine, Miracle Worker award, Children's Miracle Network, Residents Tchg. award, Thomas Jefferson Sch. Medicine, 2001; named Top Dr., Phila. Mag., 2001; named one of Best Drs. in Del., Del. Today Mag., 2005. Fellow: Am. Acad. Pediat.; mem.: Am. Bd. Pediat. Avocation: swimming. Office: AI duPont Hosp for Children 1600 Rockland Rd Wilmington DE 19803 Office Phone: 302-651-5638.

MALAVE, ANDRES, pharmacologist, educator; b. San Juan, Puerto Rico, Nov. 18, 1949; s. Andres Malave, Adela Nevarez; m. Lillian Arce, July 28, 1972; children: Jose A., Jaime E., Josue I., Jessica M. BS in Pharmacy, U. P.R., 1972; MS, Purdue U., 1981, PhD, 1983. Registered pharmacist P.R. Instr. U. P.R., San Juan, 1975—78, asst. prof., 1984—87, assoc. prof., 1988—91; prof., chmn. Nova Southeastern U., Ft. Lauderdale, Fla., 1992—2001, assoc. dean, 2001—04, dean Coll. Pharmacy, 2004—. CEO Malave Consulting Svcs., Inc., Ft. Lauderdale, 2001—04; dean coll. pharmacy U. P.R., 1987—91. Recipient Bristol Meyers/Squibb Faculty Devel. award, 1991—92; scholar, Fulbright, 2001. Mem.: Am. Assn. Pharm. Scientist, Peruvian Acad. of Pharmacy, N.Y. Acad. Sci., Soc. Neurosci., Am. Assn. Coll. Pharmacy. Achievements include development of simple non-radioactive assay for estimating protein kinase C and protein phosphatase-1. Avocations: sports, racquetball, basketball, music, guitar. Home: 224 La Costa Way Weston FL 33326 Office Phone: 954-262-1304. E-mail: amalavc@nova.edu, copdean@nova.edu.

MALBON, CRAIG CURTIS, pharmacology educator, scientist, ethicist, dean; s. Elroy Willis and Edith Roberta (Curtis) M.; children: Lindsey Gei Sook Coffin, Hailey Sook Yee; m. Hsien-yu Wang, June 26, 1993. BA, Worcester State U., 1972; PhD in Biochemistry, Case Western Res. U., Cleve., 1975; MDiv in Christian Ethics, Union Theol. Seminary, NYC, 2010. Cert. clin. pastoral edn. NIH postdoctoral fellow sect. physiological chemistry Brown U., Providence, 1976-77, research assoc. sect. physiological chemistry, 1977, asst. prof. research sect. physiological chemistry, 1978; asst. prof. dept. pharmacology SUNY Sch. Medicine, Stony Brook, 1978-83, assoc. prof., 1983-90, prof., 1990—, leading univ. prof. Sch. Medicine SUNY, Stony Brook, 1993—, vice chmn. dept. pharmacology, 1988-89, prof. dept. pharmacology Stony Brook, 1990—, assoc. dean biomed. scis. Sch. Medicine, 1989-93, v.p. rsch., 1993-97; vice dean Univ. Hosp. and Med. Ctr. SUNY, Stony Brook, 1993—2005; lectr. Union Theol. Seminary, NYC. Bd. dir. diabetes & metabolic diseases rsch. program NIH, Stony Brook, NY, 1986—, mem. cell biology & physiology study sect., Bethesda, Md., 1981—86; founder Diabetes & Metabolic Diseases Res. Ctr., 1986, Office Sci. Affairs, 1997, LI Cancer Ctr., NY, 2000, Ctr. Molecular Medicine & Biology Learning Lab., 2004; bd. dir. LI High Tech. Incubator, NY; mem. sci. adv. bd. Brookhaven Nat. Lab. DOE, 1998—2005; assoc. pastor Wading River Congregational Church-UCC, Wading River, NY; mem. United Ch. Christ Com. Ethics & Social Justice, 2010. Mem. editl. bd. Am. Jour. Physiology, 1985—, assoc. editor, 1993-99; mem. editl. bd. Jour. Biol. Chemistry, 1988-93; contbr. articles to profl. jours. Mem. Marine Biol. Lab., Inc., Woods Hole, Mass., 1986; bd. dirs. Faculty/Student Assn., Inc., Stony Brook, 1979-82. Recipient nat. rsch. svc. award NIH, 1976-80, career devel. award, 1981-86; rsch. award Am. Cancer Soc., 1998; Leading Prof., bestowed by Bd. Trustees, SUNY, 1993- pres.; Recipient, Louis Harris award Med. Coll. Virginia, 1995; Recipient, Am. Cancer Soc.- Excellence in Rsch. award, 1997; Honorary Mem., Biochem. Soc. (United Kingdom), 1999-pres.; Recipient, Am. Cancer Soc. award Outstanding Achievement & Contributions to Cancer Rsch. for Decade, 2003; U. Nominee, NIH Pioneer award, 2004; Vis. Scholar, Princeton Theological Seminary, 2006-2007; Recipient, 2008 Goodman & Gilman award ASPET; Traveling fellowship, Union Theol. Sem. NYC, 2010. Fellow AAAS; mem. Biophys. Soc., NY Acad. Scis., Am. Physiol. Soc. (editl. bd. 1986, assoc. editor 1990), Am. Soc. for Biochemistry and Molecular Biology (editl. bd. 1988), Biochem. Soc. (U.K.) (hon.), Harvey Soc., Am. Acad. Religion, Soc. Christian Ethics (Am.), InterNat. Bonhoeffer Soc., Sigma Xi. Independent. Congregationalist. Achievements include isolate mammalian beta1-adrenergic receptor; development of Frizzleds as G protein-coupled receptors; research in link overexpression and hyperphosphorylation of Erk1, 2 in human breast cancer; patents for tissue-specific promoters; patents in field. Home: PO Box 2726 East Setauket NY 11733-0852 Business E-Mail: craig@pharm.stonybrook.edu.

MALBON, LOUISE, nursing educator, hypnotherapist; b. Fayetteville, NC, Feb. 13, 1956; d. Margaret Bess and John Bullard, Fletcher Bess (Stepfather); children: Lessel Malbon, III, Lawrence A., Leslie. Assoc. Applied Scis., Excelsior Coll., 1987. Cert. CPR instr., ACLS instr.; RN; cert. clin. hypnotherapist. Clin. resource nurse educator DC Gen. Hosp., Washington, 2001—02; ambulatory svs. coord. Wash. Hosp. Ctr., Washington, 2002. ACLS instr. Wash. Adventist Hosp. Tng. Ctr., Takoma Park, 2002—. Author: Caring Enough to Change, 2002. Cmty. activist 8th Precinct Civic Assn., Chillum, 1987—2002. Named 100 Extra Ordinary Nurses, Sigma Theta Tau Internat. Honor Soc. Nursing, 2001. Mem.: Emergency Nurses Assn. Democrat. Baptist. Home and Office: Fresh Start Hypnotherapy and Pub 5405 13th Avenue Chillum MD 20783 Personal E-mail: lsmlb@aol.com.

MALCHAU, HENRIK, orthopedic surgeon; b. Stockholm, Feb. 27, 1951; m. Britt Inger Malchau; children: Emma Louise Carlsen, Sara Sofia, Eric Christian. MD, U. Aarhus, Denmark, 1977; PhD, U. Goteborg, Sweden, 1995. Resident Uddevalla Hosp., Sweden; asst. prof. dept. orthopedics Sahlgrenska U. Hosp., Goteborg U., 1983—95, asst. clin. head orthopedics, 1991—2002, assoc. prof. dept. orthopedics, 1995—2002, clin. head orthopedics, 1996—2004, prof. orthop. surgery, 2002—04; vis. prof. orthopedic surgery Harvard Med. Sch., Boston, 2004—05, assoc. prof. dept. orthopaedics, 2006—. Co-dir. Swedish Nat. Total Hip Replacement Register, Goteborg, 1989—2004; external expert Nat. Bd. Health & Welfare, Stockholm, 1993—95; vis. rschr. orthopedic biomechanics & biomaterials lab. Mass. Gen. Hosp., Boston, 2000—01, staff surgeon dept. orthopedics, 2004—; co-dir. Harris Biomaterials & Biomechanical Lab. Mass Gen. Hosp., Boston, 2004—; dir. Nat. Competence Ctr. Orthopedics, Stockholm, 2003—04; pres. Internat. Soc. Registries, Stockholm, 2007—. Mem.: Am. Hip Soc., Orthopaedic Rsch. Soc., Swedish Med. Assn., Nordic Orthop. Fedn., Danish Orthop. Soc., Swedish Orthop. Soc., Hip Soc. (adj. mem. 2006—08), Internat. Hip Soc. (nominating com. mem. 2003—08, sec. 2006—08), Am. Acad. Orthop. Surgeons (internat. affiliate mem. 2001—08, Otto Aufranc award 2004), Goteborg Med. Assn. Achievements include patents for a radial impaction grafting system; screw anchored joint prosthesis. Office: Mass Gen Hosp 55 Fruit St YAW 3922 Boston MA 02114-2696 Office Phone: 617-643-1322, 617-724-7548. Office Fax: 617-726-8770. Business E-Mail: hmalchau@partners.org. *

MALDONADO, CARLOS MANUEL, surgeon; b. Barcelona, Sept. 25, 1938; came to U.S., 1964. MD, U. Barcelona, 1964. Diplomate Am. Bd. Surgery. Intern Columbia Hosp., Milw., 1964—65; resident gen. surgery Marquette Affiliate Hosps., Milw., 1966—68; fellow thoracic cardiac surgery Newark Beth Israel Med. Ctr., 1969—70, resident gen. surgery, 1972—75. Mem. staff Martin Meml. Hosp., Stuart, Fla., Martin Meml. Hosp. South, Ft. Salerno, Fla., 1975—, chief surgery, 1983-85, chmn. quality coun., 1994— Fellow ACS; mem. AMA, Fla. Med. Assn., Internat. Soc. Cardiovasc. Surgery, Southeastern Surg. Congress, Martin County Med. Soc. (pres. 1999) Republican. Roman Catholic. Home: 2392 SE Ocean Blvd Stuart FL 34996-4230 Office Phone: 772-286-0050. Business E-Mail: carlosmmaldonado@bellsouth.net. *

MALDONADO FERNANDEZ, MIGUEL, otolaryngologist; b. Oviedo, Asturias, Spain, June 25, 1972; s. Marciano Maldonado Cuesta and Teresa Fernandez Garcia. MD, U. Oviedo, Spain, 1996, PhD, 2005. Otolaryngology Spanish Ministry of Health, 2002, Fellowship in Rhinology Spanish Soc. of Otolarynology, 2004. Med. officer Spanish Army, Ibiza, Baleares, Spain, 1997—97; ear nose throat resident Hosp. Ctrl. de Asturias, Oviedo, Asturias, Spain, 1998—2002; vis. resident Harvard Med. Sch./ Mass. Eye and Ear Infirmary, Boston, 2001; med. bd. mem. Curso Intensivo MIR Asturias, Oviedo, 1998—; fellow in rhinology Hosp. Clinic, Barcelona, Barcelona, 2002—05; cons. Pvt. Practice, Oviedo, Asturias, Spain, 2005—; prof. Curso Intensivo MIR Asturias, Asturias, 2005—; cons. Hosp. Alvarez Buylla, Asturias, 2005—. Reviewer Chest (The Am. Coll. of Chest Physicians), Northbrook, Ill., 2005—. Author: Gastroenterology: Repaso Iconográfico, 1998, Care and Rehabilitation del Paciente Traqueotomizado, 2000, Anatomy, 2000, 2nd edit., 2001, 3rd edit., 2002, 4th edit., 2003, 5th edit., 2004, 6th edit., 2005, Preventative Medicine, Biostatistics & Epidemiology, 2005. Grantee, European Acad. of Allergy and Immunology, 2003. Mem.: European Acad. of Allergy and Immunology, Spanish Soc. of Otolaryngology. Office: Private Practice Uría 60 1°A Asturias Oviedo 33003 Spain Home: Oviedo 12 33405 Salinas 33405 Spain Personal E-mail: mmaldonadof@mixmail.com.

MALECI, ALBERTO, neurosurgeon; b. Padua, Italy, Oct. 15, 1954; Degree, U. Florence, 1980; PhD, U. Rome, 1989. Chmn. neurosurgery U. Cagliari, 1997—. Mem.: AO Spine, Italian Soc. Neurosurgery. Avocation: sailing. Home: Via Cavour 36 Quartu Sant'Elena (CA) 09045 Italy Home Fax: 39 0708635090. Personal E-mail: amaleci@unica.it.

MALECK, WOLFGANG HELMUT, anesthesiologist; b. Mannheim, Germany, Mar. 21, 1960; s. Helmut and Margot (Klein) Maleck; m. Katharina Patricia Koetter, June 29, 1998; children: David, Justus. MD/ARZT, U. Heidelberg, 1988. Diplomate Bd. Anesthesiology. Physician City Hosp., Frankenthal, Germany, 1989, Deaconess Hosp., Speyer, Germany, 1989-90, Med. Acad., Dresden, Germany, 1990, Ev. Stift, Koblenz, Germany, 1991-92, City Hosp., Ludwigshafen, Germany, 1992—2002, Spital Grenchen, Switzerland, 2003—05, Spital Menziken, Switzerland, 2005—08, Spital Aarberg, Aarberg, Switzerland, 2008, Spital Langenthal, Switzerland, 2008—. Mem. City Parliament, Mannheim, 1986-89. Mem. Reformed Ch. Office: Spital Langenthal St Urban Str CH-4900 Langenthal Switzerland Office Phone: 41-62-916-3111.

MALENKA, ROBERT C., psychiatrist, educator; b. Boston, June 21, 1955; PhD in Neuroscis., MD, Stanford U., 1983. Resident in psychiatry Stanford Sch. Medicine; postdoctoral work U. Calif., San Francisco, asst. prof. psychiatry and physiology, prof. psychiatry and physiology; dir. Ctr. for Neurobiology of Addiction; assoc. dir. Ctr. for Neurobiology and Psychiatry; Pritzker prof. psychiatry and behavioral scis., dir. Pritzker Lab. Stanford U. Sch. Medicine, 1999—; lectr. in field. Scientific adv. bd. Renovis, Inc., 2000—, Merck, Inc., 2000—; Wendy and Stanley Marsh lectr., 2002. Mem. editl. bd. jours.; co-author: (textbook) Molecular Neuropharmacology: A Foundation for Clinical Neuroscience, 2001; contbr. articles to profl. jours. Mem. Nat. Adv. Coun. on Drug Abuse. Recipient Alfred P. Sloan rsch. fellowship, 1990, Young Investigator award, Nat. Alliance for Rsch. in Schizophrenia and Depression, 1990, 1992, Scholars award in neurosci., McKnight Endowment Fund for Neurosci., 1990, Investigator award in neurosci., 1997, Soc. for Neurosci. Young Investigator award, 1993, Daniel H. Efron award, Am. Coll. Neuropsychopharmacology, 1998, Dargut and Milena Kemali Found. Internat. prize in neurosci., 2000, MERIT award, NIMH, 2001—11, Basic Neuroscience Rsch. award, Collegium Internationale Neuropsychopharmacologicum, 2002. Fellow: Am. Acad. Arts & Sciences; mem.: NAS, Inst. Medicine of Nat. Academies, American Coll. Neuropsychopharmacology, Soc. for Neurosci. (program com.). Office: Stanford U Sch Medicine Psychiatry and Behavioral Scis MSLS P104 Mail Code 5485 Stanford CA 94305-5485 E-mail: malenka@stanford.edu. *

MALHOTRA, MADHU BALA, psychiatrist; b. New Delhi, June 10, 1951; arrived in U.S., 1974; d. Faqir Chand and Krishna Khandpur; m. Amjed Hussain; 1 child, Saira H. Amjed. MBBS, India. Dir. Out Patient Dept. Psychiatry Brookdale U. Hosp. and Med. Ctr., NY. Mem.: Am. Assn. Psychiatrists from India, Am. Psychiat. Assn.

MALHOTRA, NEERAJ, medical educator; b. Meerut, Uttar Pradesh, India, May 18, 1981; B in Dental Surgery, Manipal Coll. Dental Scis., Mangalore, 2004; M in Dental Surgery, Manipal Coll. Dental Scis., 2008. Asst. prof. Manipal Coll. Dental Scis. Mangalore Manipal U., 2008—. Reviewer Malaysian Dental Jour., 2010—11. Recipient Excellence award, MCODS, Mangalore. Mem.: Indian Soc. Periodontics, Restorative Dentistry and Prosthodontics, Fedn. Operative Dentist India. Avocations: swimming, dance, acting. Office: Light House Hill Rd Mangalore Karnataka 575001 India Office Fax: 91-0824-2422653. Personal E-mail: nmalhotra81@gmail.com.

MALICAY, MANUEL ALABAN, physician; b. Zamboonga City, The Philippines, Aug. 13, 1947; arrived in US, 1973; s. Bernardino Malicay Agan and Juliana (Alaban) Malicay; m. Lourdes V. Manzano, Jan. 12, 1974; children: Mark, Marlo, Brian, Michael, Margaret. BS, Far Eastern U., Manila, 1967, MD, 1972. Rsch. and tchg. fellow Far Eastern U., Manila, 1972-73; intern St. Francis Hosp., Evanston, Ill., 1973-74; resident in internal medicine Vets. Hosp., Hines, Ill., 1974-76; pvt. practice Bolingbrook, Ill., 1976—; physician Hinsdale (Ill.) Hosp., 1976-97, 1976—, Good Samaritan Hosp., Downers Grove, Ill., 1977—, vice chmn. dept. medicine, 1998—2001, chmn. Clin. Quality Coun., 1999-2001; asst. prof. in medicine Rush Med. Coll., Chgo., 2004—. Chmn continuing med educ comt IPMS, 1998—; prin. clin. investigator Dynacirc Assessment Trial Analysis, 1990, The Safety and Efficacy of Cardizem SR as anti-anginal medication, 1991, Comparative Outcome Study of Metformin vs. conventional approach, 1996, Lantus GOAL AIC Clin. Trials, 2003, REACH Registry, 2004—; spkr., bureau mem. Novartis Pharm. Corp., 2003, Abbott Pharm. Editor: IPMS Today, 1989—91. Trustee Far Ea. U. Sch. Med. Alumni Found., 1993—2001, v.p., 2002—04; pres. Class of 1972 Far Ea. U. Dr. N. Reyes Med. Alumni Found.; chmn. continuing med. edn. Far Ea. U. DNR Sch. Med. Alumni Found., 2005—; co-chmn. physician adv. bd. Nat. Rep. Congl. Com., 2002—. Recipient Leadership award, Feu-Med. Alumni Assn. Northern Ill., 2009, Physician Recognisation Excellence award, Advocate Physician Ptnrs. Exemplary, 2010; named Most Outstanding Silver Jubilarian, Far Eastern U. Dr N Reyes Med. Alumni Found., 1997, Physician of Yr., Nat. Rep. Congl. Com., 2003. Fellow: ACP; mem.: AMA, Far Eastern U. Med. Alumni Assn. Ill. (pres. 1991—93, co-chair conv. ann. reunion and sci. seminar 1993, Oustanding Alumnus 1995), Assn. Philippine Physicians Am. (co-chair 25th ann. conv. and sci. seminar 1996, gov. 1996—2001), Ill. Med. Soc. (del. 1990—, coun. on econs. com. 2002—), DuPage County Med. Soc. (bd. dirs. 1986—), Ill. Philippine Med. Soc. (seminar program dir. 1994, pres. 1994—96, chmn CME comt 1998—, program dir. Primary Care Update 1999, 2001, Disting Leadership Award 1996, Disting Physician Award Organized Med 1999, Disting Serv Award 2001, Presdl. award 2009, Recognition Excellence award, named Exemplary Physician 2010). Avocations: tennis, dance. Home: 2 S 676th Ave Vendome Oak Brook IL 60521 Office: 402 W Boughton Rd Bolingbrook IL 60440-1872 also: 430 Sherwood Rd La Grange Park IL 60526-1968 Office Phone: 630-759-3782. Personal E-mail: mmalicaymd@hotmail.com.

MALICH, ANSGAR CHRISTOPH BERNHARD, radiologist, b. Halle, Sachsen-Anhalt, Germany, Nov. 22, 1970; s. Burkhard and Christa Malich; m. Juliana Müller, Nov. 3, 1995; children: Leander Adrian, Helena Rebecca, Victoria Johanna, Fiona Regina. MD, Martin Luther U., Halle-Wittenberg, 1996; PhD, Friedrich Schiller U., Jena, Thuringia, Germany, 2003. Surgeon tng. St. Barbara Hosp., Halle, 1996—97, Hosp. Bergmannstrost, Halle, 1997—98; radiologist Friedrich Schiller U., 1998—2003, asst. prof., 2003—05; chief radiologist Suedharz Hosp., Nordhausen, Thuringia, 2005—. Reviewer European Radiology, 2001—03, IEEE, 2002, Rocfo, 2002, European Jour. Radiol., 2003—, Jour. of Digital Imaging, 2004—, Sheffield Hosp. Charitable Trust, 2003, AJR, 2007—, Phys. Meors, 2008—; asst. prof. U. Jena, 2004. Contbr. scientific papers. Vice head Jugend des Demokratischen Aufbruchs, Berlin, 1990—91; counselor Halle, 1990—92. Soldier, 1989—90, Sondershausen. Recipient Poster prize, German Radiologic Meeting, 2005, Best Sci. Presentation award, European Congress Radiology, 2006, Gold medal, Lessing, Bronze medal, Herder, Poster award, European Congress Radiology, 2009. Mem.: Adenauer Found., DRG, ESR (subcom. mem.). Roman Catholic. Avocations: soccer, hockey. Home: Wiesenweg 33 Nordhausen Thuringia 99734 Germany Office: Suedharz Hosp Nordhausen Dr.-Robert-Koch-Str. 39 99734 Nordhausen Germany Office Fax: 03631412195. Business E-Mail: ansgar.malich@shk-ndh.de.

MALICKA, IWONA, physical education educator; b. Wroclaw, Poland, Apr. 25, 1974; PhD in Phys. Edn., Wroclaw U., 2003. Educator, rsch. scientist, physiotherapy and phys. activity, breast cancer Wroclaw U. Sch. Phys. Edn., 2003. Office: Al IJ Paderewskiego 35 Wroclaw Dolnoslaskie 51-612 Poland Business E-Mail: iwona.malicka@awf.wroc.pl.

MALIFRANDO, FRANK, healthcare executive, theater producer, consultant, film producer, international real estate investor, publisher; b. NYC, Feb. 16, 1954; s. Frank Malifrando and Michele Michelin Kuhn. BS, Southwest U., LA, 1986, MS in Health Scis., 2004. Cert. media comm. Boston U., 1991. CEO Spring Fed Corp., NYC, 1982—88, Kalanakila Prodns., Hawaii, 1985—91, Thunder Key Inc., 1982—89; mktg. dir. Mus. Edits. West, LA, 1988—91; dir. of devel. No. Calif. Svc. League, 1997—99; exec. dir. Keith Haring AIDS Interfaith Chapel, 1994—2000, Grace Cathedral, San Francisco; dir. devel. Life Lines Ministries, San Francisco, 1997—98; dir. of career svcs. Computer Learning Ctr., 1999—2001; project dir., designer Career Acceleration Mentor Program, 2000—01; exec. dir. fundraising arm Seton Med. Ctr., Seton Med. Ctr. Coastside, Dau. Charity Healthcare Sys., Seton Health Svcs. Found., Daly City, Calif., 2001—04, Sutter Marin-Marin Gen. Hosp., Novato Cmty. Hosp., Marin Cmty. Health Found., San Rafael, Calif., 2004—, regional exec. dir., 2007—08; owner Restaurant Spring Fed., NYC; personal mgr. of photographer Kenn Duncan; mem. Marin Gen. Hosp. found. bd.; mem. com. north and south Sutta Marin Found. Bd. Dir. of programs Alma DelFina Group, San Francisco, 1995—2000; CEO Artist Alliance Against AIDS, 1996; bd. dirs. Bethany Ctr., bd. vice chair, 2007; regional exec. dir. Sutter Marin Region, Marin Gen. Hosp., 2008—, Sutter Chartaible Found., Sutter Solano Med. Ctr., Sutter Regional Med. Found. Prodr.: Red Shoes, Kenn Duncan, 1984, (fine art reproductions) Hula Kahiko Series, 1986 (Pele Award of Excellence, 1986), Dance Cos., 1984 (Nat. Ann. Print award and Comm. Arts award, 1984); prodr., dir.: (documentaries) Poets and Painters, A Night at the Palace, 1994; Willie by Madaglia Cruz, starring Sean San Jose, 1996; In Conversation with David Henry Hwong, 1996; Awakening New Futures (behind bars), 1997; The making of an event: Charity Ball-150 Years for Daughters of Charity Seton Medical Center, 2001. Exec. dir., bd. mem. Marin Cmty. Health Found.; bd. dirs. Seton Health Svcs. Found., Bethany Ctr.; mem. adv. bd. Philanthropy Leadership Coun., Washington; chair CAPP; overseer Sutter Solano Charitable Found. Recipient Radiant Baby Gold Pin, Keith Haring Found., 1995, Canon Pastor award, Grace Cathedral, San Francisco, 1995, Pele award for excellence, Advertising Assn. of Hawaii, 1984, Cert. of Design Excellence, Print's Regional Design Annual, 1986, Black and White award, Assn. Honolulu Artist, 1987, Resolution recognition, State of Calif., 2003. Mem.: Dir.'s Coun. Devel.-Sutter Health, San Francisco C. of C., Seniors RSVP/San Francisco (adv. bd.), Brisbane C. of C., Half Moon Bay C. of C., Daly City C. of C. Achievements include creator and founder of the AIDS Interfaith Chapel in Grace Cathedral, San Francisco. Address: 4000 Civic Ctr Dr Ste 150 San Rafael CA 94903 Office: Sutter Marin-Marin Gen Hosp Found 4000 Civic Ctr Dr Ste 150 San Rafael CA 94903 Office Phone: 415-492-4735. E-mail: malifrf@sutterhealth.org.

MALIHA, GABRIEL M, academic administrator, medical educator, internist, nephrologist; s. Michael N Maliha and Juliette V Zreik; m. Maggie E Yazbeck, Mar. 25, 1987; children: Nicole J, Peter G. MD, Northwestern U., 1978—82, PhD, 1987—90. Internal Medicine Am. Bd. Internal Medicine, 1986, Nephrology Am. Bd. Nephrology, 1989. Assoc. prof. Lebanese Am. U., Sch. Pharmacy, 1996—99, dean, prof., 1999—. Contbr. articles to profl. jours. Exec. coun. mem. Greek Orthodox PA, Tripoli, Lebanon, 1996—2003. Recipient Gratitude and Appreciation, Kuwait Soc. of Dermatologists, 2003, Gratitude, Lebanese Order of Pharmacists, 2001. D-Liberal. Greek Orthodox. Avocations: travel, reading.

MALIK, AAMIR SAEED, science educator, researcher; b. Jessore, Pakistan, Nov. 18, 1969; s. Mohammad and Husna Sher; m. Humaira Nisar, Oct. 1995; children: Umama Aamir, Reham Aamir. BEE, U. Engring. & Tech., Taxila, Pakistan, 1993; MS in Nuc. Engring., Quaid-i-Azam U., Islamabad, Pakistan, 1995; MS in Info. & Comm., Gwangju Inst. Sci. & Tech., Republic of Korea, PhD in Mechatronics, 2008. Cert. in tchr. tng. IBM, Pakistan, 2001. Vis. prof. Hamdard U., Islamabad, 2000—04; project dir. IBM Advanced Ctr. Edn., Islamabad, 2000—04, sr. instr., sr. analyst; asst. prof. Yeugnam U., Republic of Korea, 2008—09, Hanyang U., Republic of Korea, 2009—. Contbr. articles to profl. jours. V.p. Flag Carriers, Islamabad, 1990—93; vol. SOS Village (Orphanage), RawalPindi, Pakistan, 1989—2004, Edhi Trust, Islamabad, 1988—95. Recipient Presedl. award, Fed. Bd. Islamabad, 1985, Mugunghwa award, IITA, 2007, Dasan award, 2007. Mem.: IEEE, Pakistan Engring. Coun., SPIE. Islam. Achievements include design of depth estimation algorithm for 3D shape recovery using image focus; development of an algorithm for classification of honeycombed HRCT lung images; technique to improve SNR and resolution for fMRI. Avocations: swimming, travel, badminton, movies, mountain climbing. Office: Sch EE & CS Hanyang Univ 1271 Sa-3 dong Sangnok-Gu Ansan Gyeonggi-do 426-791 Republic of Korea Home Phone: 82-10-5802-8968; Office Phone: 82-31-400-5664. Personal E-mail: aamirmalik@hotmail.com. Business E-mail: aamir@hanyang.ac.kr.

MALIK, ABID, psychiatrist; s. Naimat K. Malik and Riaz Begum. MD, Dow Med. Coll., Karachi, 1995. Diplomate Am. Bd. Addiction Medicine, 2010, Am. Bd. Psychiatry & Neurology, 2009, cert. in psychiatry, psychosomatic medicine and sleep medicine Am. Bd. Psychiatry & Neurology, 2009, in psychiatry ABPN, 2008, in psychosomatic medicine ABPN, 2009, in sleep medicine ABPN, 2009, in addiction medicine ABAM, 2010. Psychiatry resident Albany Med. Ctr., NY, 2003—07; chief resident psychiatry, 2006—07; staff psychiatrist Area Mental Health Ctr., Garden City, Kans., 2007—10; psychiatrist South Seminole Hosp., Behavior Health, 2010—; asst. prof. psychiatry U. Ctrl. Fla., Coll. Medicine, 2010—. Contbr. rsch. papers to profl. publs. Asst. prof. psychiatry U. Ctrl. Fla., Coll. Medicine, 2010—. Recipient Scholarly paper award, Albany Med. Coll. Dept. Psychiatry Residency Program, 2007, Alan M. Kraft M.D. award, 2007. Mem.: AMA, Am. Acad. Sleep Medicine, Am. Psychiat. Assn. Personal E-mail: the_abid@hotmail.com.

MALIK, ANUSHREE, biotechnologist, educator; b. Indore, July 19, 1969; PhD, Indian Inst. Tech. Delhi, 2000. Assoc. prof. Indian Inst. Tech., 2004—. Recipient award, Japan Soc. Promotion Sci., Govt. Japan. Mem.: Biotechnol. Rsch. Soc. India. Avocations: literature, reading. Office: Applied Microbiology Lab CRDT Indian I New Delhi Delhi 110 016 India Office Fax: 91-11-26591121. Business E-mail: anushree@rdat.iitd.ac.in.

MALIK, JAN, physician; b. Prague, Sept. 24, 1968; MD, Charles U. Prague, 1993, PhD, 2000. Physician faculty medicine Charles U. Prague, 1993—. Master: Vascular Access Soc. Avocations: art, travel. Office: U nemocnice 1 Prague 12808 Czech Republic Business E-Mail: malik.jan@vfn.cz.

MALIN, HOWARD GERALD, podiatrist; b. Providence, Dec. 2, 1941; s. Leon Nathan and Rena Rose (Shapiro) M. AB, U. R.I., 1964; MA, Brigham Young U., 1969; BSc, Calif. Coll. Podiatric Medicine, 1969, DPM, 1972; MSc, Pepperdine U., 1978; MD (hon.), Internat. U. Sch. Medicine, Winnipeg, Man., Can., 2001. Diplomate Am. Bd. Podiatric Pub. Health, Am. Bd. Podiatric Orthops. Extern in podiatry VA Med. Ctr., Wadsworth, Kans., 1971-72, Marine Corps Res. Dept., San Diego, 1972; resident in podiatric medicine and surgery N.Y. Coll. Podiatric-Medicine, NYC, 1972-73; resident in podiatric surgery, instr. in podiatric surgery N.Y. Coll. Podiatric Medicine, NYC, 1973-74; pvt. practitioner in podiatric medicine and surgery Bklyn., 1974-77; mem. staff Prospect Hosp., Bronx, NY, 1974-77; chief podiatry service, mem. staff, cons. sports medicine David Grant U.S. Air Force Med. Ctr., Travis AFB, Calif., 1977-80; chief podiatric sect. VA Med. Ctr., Martinsburg, W.Va., 1980—2009. Instr. ednl. devel. program VA Med. Ctr., Martinsburg, W.Va., 1980—84; emeritus clin. prof. med. sci. Alderson-Broaddus Coll., U. Osteopathic Medicine and Health Scis.; emeritus adj. faculty Barry U. Sch. Podiatric Medicine; emeritus adj. clin. prof. Ohio Coll. Podiatric Medicine; emeritus clin. asst. prof. surgery W.Va. U. Sch. Medicine. Mem. editl. rev. bd. Jour. Contemporary Podiatric Physician, 1991—. Lt. Col. USAFR, ret. Fellow Am. Soc. Podiatric Dermatology (past archivist)(life), Am. Coll. Foot Orthopedics (emeritus), Am. Coll. Podiatric Physicians, Am. Coll. Podiatric Radiology (archivist, past pres.)(life), Am. Soc. Podiatric Medicine (asst. exec. dir. emeritus, past pres., archivist, life), Am. Podiatric Med. Writers Assn. (pres., archivist), Am. Coll. Foot and Ankle Pediat. (past pres., archivist, historian, life), Royal Soc. for

Promotion Health, Royal Soc. Medicine (life); mem. Am. Acad. Podiatric Sports Medicine (assoc.), Assn. Mil. Surgeons US (life), Am. Coll. Podiatric Surgery (life), Am. Hosp.& Healthcare POD,Am. Podiatric Med. Assn. (life), Phi Kappa Theta, Phi Kappa Psi, Phi Delta Kappa (life). Home and Office: 2250 Bear Den Rd Ste 210 Frederick MD 21701-9408

MALININA, ELENA, psychiatrist, educator; b. Novosibirsk, Russia, Oct. 13, 1958; Degree, Med. Acad., 1981. Prof. State Med. U. Chelyabinsk, 2006—, Head child psychiatry, 2007—. Fellow: Russians Soc. Psychiatry. Avocations: music, poetry, travel. Home: Engelsa 95 -128 Celyabinsk 454048 Russia Business E-Mail: malinina.e@rambler.ru.

MALITS, BELLA, pain medicine physician; Grad., Columbia U., 1986; MD, NY Med. Coll., 1990. Diplomate Am. Bd. Anesthesiology, 1995, Am. Bd. Nuc. Medicine, 1995, Am. Bd. Nuc. Medicine-pain mgmt., 1996, Am. Bd. Nuc. Medicine-pain mgmt., 2007. Intern in internal medicine St. Vincent Med. Ctr., 1991; resident anesthesiology Mt. Sinai Med. Ctr., 1991—95, fellow pain mgmt., 1995—96; physician Mt. Kisco Med. Group. Office: Mount Kisco Medical Group 34 South Bedford Rd Mount Kisco NY 10549 Office Phone: 914-241-1050.

MALKASIAN, GEORGE DURAND, JR., obstetrician, educator; b. Springfield, Mass., Oct. 26, 1927; s. George Dur and Gladys Mildred (Trombley) M.; m. Mary Ellen Koch, Oct. 16, 1954; children: Linda Jeanne, Karen Diane, Martha Ellen. AB, Yale U., 1950; MD, Boston U., 1954; MS, U. Minn., 1963. Diplomate Am. Bd. Ob-Gyn. Intern Worcester (Mass.) City Hosp., 1954-55; resident in ob-gyn Mayo Grad. Sch. Hosp., Rochester, Minn., 1955-58, 60-61; mem. faculty Mayo Med. Sch., 1962—, prof. ob-gyn, 1976—, chmn. dept. ob-gyn, 1976-86. Author articles in field. Served to lt. comdr. M.C., USNR, 1958-60. Named Tchr. of Yr., Mayo Grad. Sch. Medicine, 1973, 77, Alumnus of Yr., Boston U. Sch. Med., 1990. Fellow Royal Coll. Obstetricians and Gynecologists (ad eundum); mem. ACS, Am. Coll. Ob-Gyn (pres. 1989-90), Am. Ob-Gyn Soc., Am. Radium Soc., Soc. Ob-Gyn, Assn. Profs. Ob-Gyn., N.Am. Ob-Gyn. Soc., Ctrl. Assn. Ob-Gyn, Minn. Soc. Ob-Gyn, Internat. Fedn. Ob-Gyn (v.p. 1997-2000), Zumbro Valley Med. Soc. (exec. dir. 1996-2002). Home: 211 NW 2nd St #503 Rochester MN 55901 Office: Mayo Clinic 200 1st St SW Rochester MN 55905-0001

MALKIN, STANLEY LEE, neurologist; b. Pitts., Nov. 11, 1942; s. Maurice and Bessie Beatrice (Serbin) M.; m. Candace N. Conard; children: Justin Ross, Keith Richard. BA with honors, U. Pa., 1964; MD, U. Pitts., 1968. Diplomate Am. Bd. Psychiatry and Neurology, Nat. Bd. Med. Examiners. Intern Montefiore Hosp., Pitts., 1968-69; resident in neurology Columbia-Presbyn. Med. Ctr., NYC, 1969-72; chief neurology svc., Wright-Patterson AFB, Dayton, 1972-74; practice medicine specializing in neurology NYC; attending staff Mt. Sinai Hosp.; former dir. Neuro-Diagnostic Lab., Englewood; assoc. clin. prof. neurology Mt. Sinai Sch. Medicine; founder Bergen-Passaic Tomography Ctr., Fairlawn, N.J. Neurology cons. Regent Hosp.; med. dir. Pain Suppression Labs., Inc.; med. dir. Efficient Health Systems, Inc.-N.Y.C. Healthline; founder, med. dir., exec. v.p. Hosp. Diagnostic Equipment Corp., 1987—; pres. Cancer Treatment Holdings, Inc, 1993-95, dir. 1993-94, sr. med. dir. 1995-97; founder Montvale Med. Imaging Assocs. (N.J.), N.Y. Med. Imaging, N.Y.C., Hosp. Diagnostic Equipment Corp.; ptnr. Sall/Myers Med. Assocs., prin. 1995—; mem. Edgewater Rent Control Bd., 1978. Maj. M.C. USAF, 1972-74. Recipient Comdr.'s Recognition award for care of repatriated prisoners of war, 1973, award Am.'s Top Physicians Consumers' Rsch. Coun. Am., 2004-05, Conn. Vets. Wartime Svc. medal, 2008. Fellow Royal Soc. Medicine; mem. Am. Acad. Neurology, Am. Assn. Electrodiagnostic Medicine, Am. Soc. Neuro-Imaging (charter), EEG and Clin. Neurosci. Soc., Am. Headache Soc. (rev. bd.), Nat. Headache Found., Internat. Headache Soc., Nat. Neurotrauma Soc., N.Y. Acad. Scis., NYU Bellevue Psychiat. Soc., European Fedn. Neurol. Socs. Home: 36 W 44th St Ste 1208 New York NY 10036-8104

MALKINSON, FREDERICK DAVID, retired dermatologist; b. Hartford, Conn., Feb. 26, 1924; s. John Walter and Rose Malkinson; m. Una Zwick, June 15, 1979; children by previous marriage: Philip, Carol, John. Student, Loomis Inst., 1937-41; 3 yr. cert. cum laude, Harvard U., 1943, DMD, 1947, MD, 1949. Intern Harvard-Beth Israel Hosp., Boston, 1949-50; resident in dermatology U. Chgo., 1950-54, from instr. to assoc. prof. dept. dermatology, 1954-68; prof. medicine and dermatology U. Ill., Chgo., 1968-71; chmn. dept. dermatology Rush Med. Coll. and Rush-Presbyn.-St. Luke's Med. Ctr. (now Rush U. Med. Ctr.), Chgo., 1968-92, Clark W. Finnerud, M.D. prof. dept. dermatology, 1981-95, 95—; trustee Sulzberger Inst. Dermatol. Comm. and Edn., 1976-96; pres. Sulzberger Inst. Dermatol. Communication and Edn., 1983-88, 93-96; prof. Rush U. Med. Ctr., Chgo., 2000—10; emeritus prof., 2010—. Editor: Year Book of Dermatology, 1971-78; chief editor: AMA Archives of Dermatology, 1979-83; bd. editors, 1976-84, Jour. AMA, 1979-83; editorial cons. World Book Medical Encyclopedia, 1991-2000; contbr. articles to profl. jours., chpts. to books. Active Evanston (Ill.) Libr. Bd., 1988-94, pres., 1993-94. With M.C. USNR, 1950-52. Grantee, U.S. Army, 1955—61, USPHS, 1962—70. Fellow AAAS; mem. Am. Acad. Dermatology (v.p. 1987-89, dir. 1964-67), Am. Dermatol. Assn., Soc. Investigative Dermatology (v.p. 1978-79, dir. 1963-68), Am. Fedn. Med. Rsch., Cen. Soc. Clin. Rsch., Radiation Rsch. Soc., Assn. Profs. of Dermatology (dir. 1982-85), Dermatology Found. (exec. com., trustee 1980-93, pres. 1983-85, Lifetime Career Educator award 2006), Nat. Coun. on Radiation Protection and Measurements (mem. com. on cutaneous radiobiology 1986-92), Chgo. Dermatol. Soc. (pres. 1964-65, Gold Medal award 1992, established ann. lectureship, 2004), Chgo. Lit. Club (v.p. 1997-99, 2000-03, pres. 1999-2000).

MALKOWICZ, STANLEY BRUCE, urologist; b. Passaic, NJ; s. Stanley Jacob and Jeanne (iracki) m.; m. Denise Elaine Ewald, Sept. 22, 1985. BA, U. Vt., 1977; MD, U. Pa., Phila., 1981. Intern in surgery Hosp. U. Pa., Phila., 1981-82, resident in surgery, 1982-83, resident in urology, 1983-86, chief resident in urology, 1986-87; fellow in urologic oncology U. So. Calif., LA, 1987-88, Hosp. U. Pa., Phila., 1988-90, asst. prof. surgery, 1990-95, assoc. prof., 1995—2003, prof. urology, 2003—; chief urology Phila. VA Med. Ctr. Assoc. scientist Wistar Inst. Anatomy and Biology, Phila., 1988—; Nat. Kidney Found. rsch. fellow, 1983-84; Am. Found. Urologic Disease rsch. scholar, 1988-90. Contbr. articles to profl. jours. Mem. AAAS, Am. Urologic Assn., Am. Assn. GU Surgeons, Am. Soc. Clin. Oncology, Soc. Univ. Urologists, Urodynamics Soc., Assn. Academic

Surgeons, Soc. Pelvic Surgeons (treas.-sec.), Soc. Urologic Oncology, Urol. Rsch. Soc., Phila. Urol. Soc. (pres.), S.E. Pa. Am. Cancer Soc. (pres.), Sigma Xi. Presbyterian. Avocations: camping, reading, cooking. Office: Hosp U Pa Philadelphia PA 19104-4206 Home Phone: 610-525-0117; Office Phone: 215-662-7330.

MALLAH, HUSAM, pediatrician; b. Jeddah, Saudi Arabian, Nov. 11, 1977; MD, Damascus U., 2003. Pediat. gastroenterologist Luth. Med. Group, 2010—. Office: 7230 Engle Rd Ste 340 Fort Wayne IN 46804 Business E-Mail: husam_mallah@urmc.rochester.edu.

MALLAK, CRAIG T., pathologist; Chief, Armed Forces Med. Examiner Sys. Armed Forces Inst. Pathology. Capt. med. corps. USN. Mem.: Am. Acad. Forensic Sci. Office: Armed Forces Medical Examiners Systems 1413 Research Blvd Bldg 102 Rockville MD 20850 Office Phone: 301-319-0000. Office Fax: 301-319-0635. E-mail: mallak@afip.osd.mil.

MALLALIEU, NAVITA LUTHRA, pharmacologist, director; d. Jawahar and Indu Luthra; m. Hugh Luthra, June 18, 1994; children: Nina, Natessa. PhD, Rutgers U., NJ, 1994. Sr. scientist, DMPK Hoffmann-La Roche, Nutley, NJ, 1999—2006, assoc. dir. clin. pharmacology, 2006—. Mem.: Am. Soc. Microbiology, Am. Diabetes Assn., Am. Assn. Pharm. Scientists. Office: Hoffmann-La Roche 340 Kingsland Ave Nutley NJ 07110

MALLELA, KRISHNA M.G., chemistry professor, researcher; BSc, P. B. Siddhartha Coll. Arts and Sci., Vijayawada, India, 1991; MSc, U. Hyderabad, India, 1993; PhD, Tata Inst. Fundamental Rsch., Mumbai, 1999. Postgrad. rschr. biophysics, Dept. Medicine and Physiology, Cardiovasc. Rsch. Inst., U. Calif., San Francisco, 1998—99; postdoc. rsch. assoc. biophysics and biochemistry, Dept. Biochemistry and Biophysics, Sch. Medicine, U. Pa., Phila., Colo., 1999—2003, rsch. asst. prof. biophysics and biochemistry, 2003—07; asst. prof. biophysical chemistry, Dept. Pharm. Sciences, Sch. Pharmacy U. Colo. Denver, Aurora, 2007—. Contbr. articles to rsch. jours. Mem.: AAAS, The Protein Soc., Internat. Union Pure and Applied Chemistry, Am. Chem. Soc. Office: Univ Colo Denver 12700 E 19th Ave C238-P15 Rsch 2 Aurora CO 80045

MALLIA, MARIANNE, medical writer; b. Davenport, Iowa, Feb. 14, 1948; d. Norman Bramblett and Mary Jane (Hilkemeyer) Hagar; 1 child from previous marriage, Lindsay Sharyn. BA in English, U. Iowa, 1970. Cert. tchr., editor in life sci. Tchr. tech. writing Houston Ind. Sch. Dist., 1970—76; med. writer Tex. Heart Inst., Houston, 1976—; editl. cons. Tex. Heart Inst. Jour., Houston, 1977—87, head sci. publ., 1986—, sr. med. writer, 1994—. Instr. Sch. Allied Health Sci. and Sch. Pub. Health U. Tex., 1990—94. Editor: Techniques in Cardiac Surgery, 1984; editor: (with Denton A. Cooley) Surg. Treatment of Aortic Aneurysms, 1985; editor: (essays) Reflections and Observation, Denton A. Cooley, MD, 1985; author: (handbook) Heart Owner's Handbook, 1995; bd. editors: Life Sci., 2002. Fellow: Am. Med. Writers Assn. (core curriculum cert. 1984, instr. 1985—, advanced curriculum cert. 1989, honor roll workshop leader 1992—, bd. dir., exec. com. 1996—2005, pres. 2002—03, writer advanced core curriculum, Award Tchg. Excellence 1998, Golden Apple award 1998, Swanberg Disting. Svc. award 2010); mem.: Women in Comm. (Matrix award 1996—2000), Coun. Biology Editors, Pi Beta Phi. Avocation: classic cars. Office: Tex Heart Inst PO Box 20345 Houston TX 77225-0345 Office Phone: 832-355-6776. Business E-Mail: mmallia@heart.thi.tmc.edu.

MALLIKAARJUN, SURESH, pharmaceutical executive, clinical pharmacologist; b. Bangalore, Karnataka, India, 1956; arrived in U.S., 1982; m. Kusuma Rajasekharaiah, 1987. BPharm, U. Bombay, Mumbai, India, 1978; PhD, Va. Commonwealth U., 1987. Clinical Pharmacology Am. Bd. Clin. Pharmacology, 2003. Pharmacokinetic reviewer FDA, Rockville, Md., 1988—93; sr. scientist Proctor and Gamble Pharmaceuticals, Cincinnati, Ohio, 1993—96; sr. dir. Otsuka Md. Rsch. Inc, Rockville, Md., 1996—. Vice chair Am. Assn. Indian Pharm. Scientists, Wash. Chpt., Bethesda, Md., 2004—. Contbr. articles in field, chapters to books. Recipient Commendable Achievement, FDA, 1992, 1990; fellow A D Williams Fellowship, Va. Commonwealth U., 1982. Fellow: Am. Coll. Clin. Pharmacology; mem.: Am. Soc. Clin. Pharmacology and Therapeutics, Am. Assn. Pharm. Scientists. Achievements include Clin. devel. of Abilify(R); Clin. Devel. of Pletal.(R).

MALLING, HEINRICH VALDEMAR, retired geneticist; b. Copenhagen, Apr. 21, 1931; came to US, 1963; s. Henry August Valdemar and Jenny Bolette (Hansen) M.; m. Bodil Jensen, June 15, 1955 (div. June 1968); children: Tove, Soren, Jakob, Mikael; m. Martha Hale Shackford, July 18, 1969; children: Richard, Kevin, Kirsten. PhD, U. Copenhagen, 1957, Lic. Sci., 1962. Rsch. staff Leo Pharm., Copenhagen, 1957—58; postdoctoral fellow Inst. Genetics U. Copenhagen, 1958—61, assoc. prof. Inst. Genetics, 1961—63; rsch. staff mem. Oak Ridge Nat. Lab., Tenn., 1963—72; sect. head Nat. Inst. Environ. Health Sci., Research Triangle Park, NC, 1972—76, 1982—2004, lab. chief, 1976—82; dir. HVMutagen LLC, 2004—; ret., 2004. Adj. prof. NC State U., Raleigh, 1972-78, U. NC, Chapel Hill, 1976—; dir. Environ. Mutagen Info. Ctr., Oak Ridge, 1968-72; vis. prof. Flinders U., 2004-05; CEO HVMutagen, 2005— Editorial bd. Environ. and Molecular Mutagenesis, 1989—, Mutation Rsch., 1971—; contbr. articles to profl. jours. Nation chief YMCA Indian Guides, Knoxville, Tenn, 1970, Raleigh, 1974. Recipient Sci. award Environ. Mut. Soc., Washington, 1980; Grad. fellow U. Copenhagen, 1953-57, postdoctoral fellow NSF, 1958-61. Mem. Environ. Mutagen Soc. (com. 1989—), Med. Rsch. Coun. (Can., grant revs. 1987—). Democrat. Lutheran. Achievements include patent in transgenic mice for study of mammalian mutagenesis; first to demonstrate mammalian liver microsomes can active non-mutagenic carcinogens to mutagens, first to develop transgenic mutation systems based on recoverable vectors. Office: Nat Inst Environ Health Sci PO Box 12233 Durham NC 27709-2233 Mailing: PO Box 16663 Chapel Hill NC 27516 Home: PO Box 16663 Chapel Hill NC 27516 Office Phone: 919-541-3378. Personal E-mail: hvmalling@nc.rr.com. Business E-Mail: malling@niehs.nih.gov.

MALLO, FEDERICO, medical educator, director; b. Aug. 25, 1963; Degree in Medicine, Surgery, U. Santiago Compostela, 1987, PhD in Endocrinology, 1991. Dir., master nutrition U. Vigo, 2008—, full prof., physiology, endocrinology, 2009—. Bd. dirs. Biomed. Rsch. Inst. Vigo, 2009—; mem. Health Coun. Galicia, Autonomous Region

Spain, 2009—. Avocation: soccer. Office: Faculty Biology Campus Vigo University Vigo Pontevedra 36310 Spain Office Fax: 34 986812556. Business E-Mail: fmallo@uvigo.es.

MALLONE, ROBERTO, research scientist; b. Turin, Italy, Nov. 20, 1973; MD, U. Turin Med. Sch., 1999, degree in Internal Medicine, 2004, PhD, 2007. Resident, internal medicine I Divsn. Internal Medicine, U. Turin, 1999—2002; postdoc. fellow Benaroya Rsch. Inst., Va. Mason, Seattle, 2002—04; vis. assoc. prof. Paris Descartes U., Necker Hosp., Paris, 2005—06; vis. scientist Autoimmunity and Transplantation Divsn., Walter and Eliza Hall Inst. Med. Rsch., Melbourne, Victoria, Australia, 2007; sr. rsch. scientist INSERM U561, Hôsp. St. Vincent Paul, Paris, 2008—. Steering com. mem. Immunology Diabetes Soc. T Cell Workshop, 2007—; ad hoc reviewer JClinInvest, Diabetes, DiabetesCare, EurJImmunol, JClinImm, HumImmunol, JImmunol Methods, JAutoimmun, 2005—; mem. Diabetes Trial Net, 2007—. Contbr. articles to med. jours. Recipient Rsch. award, Italian Soc. Internal Medicine, 2001, Italian Soc. Immunology, 2001, Fgn. Rschr. award, Med. Rsch. Found., 2007, Rising Star award, EASD, 2008, Avenir INSERM, 2008; fellow Postdoc. Fellowship award, Am. Diabetes Assn., 2003; grants, Juvenile Diabetes Rsch. Found., 2007—, European Assn. Study Diabetes, 2007—. Mem.: IDS, European Assn. Study Diabetes, Am. Assn. Immunologists, Fedn. Am. Soc. Exptl. Biology. Achievements include research in diabetes autoimmunity. Office: INSERM U561 Saint Vincent de Paul Hosp 82 avenue Denfert Rochereau 75674 Paris France Office Phone: 33-1-40-48-82-47. Business E-Mail: roberto.mallone@inserm.fr.

MALLUCHE, HARTMUT HORST, nephrologist, medical educator; b. Jan. 1, 1943; arrived in U.S., 1975, naturalized, 1985; s. Harald E. and Renate (Muenzberg) M.; children: Nadine, Danielle, Tiffany. Abitur, Albertus Magnus Coll., Koenigstein, Germany, 1963; postgrad., Phillips U., Marburg/Lahn, Fed. Republic Germany, 1963—65, U. Innsbruck, Austria, 1965—66, U. Vienna, 1966; MD, J.W. Goethe U., Frankfurt, Fed. Republic Germany, 1969. Diplomate German Bd. Internal Medicine. Intern County Hosp., Aichach, Germany, 1969—70; resident in internal medicine, fellow in nephrology Cen. Internal Medicine, Univ. Hosp., Frankfurt Am Main, Germany, 1970—75; asst. prof. medicine U. So. Calif., Calif., 1975—78, assoc. prof., 1978—81; prof., dir. divsn. nephrology, bone and mineral metabolism U. Ky. Med. Ctr., Lexington, 1981—. Cons. NIH, FDA; mem. Va. Merit Rev. Bd. Nephrology; program dir. Gen. Clin. Rsch. Ctr. Author: (monograph) Atlas of Mineralized Bone Histology, 1986; editor-in-chief Clinical Nephrology; contbr. articles to profl. jours. and books. Grantee, NIH, 1982—, Shriner's Hosp. for Crippled Children. Fellow: ACP; mem.: AAAS, Internat. Soc. Bone Morphometry (founder), Internat. Soc. Nephrology, Am. Fedn. Clin. Rsch., European Dialysis and Transplantation Assns., Am. Soc. Physiol. endocrinology Am. Soc. Bone and Mineral Rsch., Am. Soc. Clin. Investigation, Am. Soc. Nephrology. Office Phone: 859-323-5049 221.

MALM, JAMES ROYAL, surgeon; b. Cleve., Sept. 7, 1925; s. Royal Dinsmore and Theodora (Drumont) M.; m. Constance Brooks, July 8, 1950; children— Martha, Melissa, Karen, Sarah. AB, Princeton, 1947; MD, Columbia, 1949. Diplomate: Am. Bd. Thoracic Surgery, Am. Bd. Surgery. Intern Pa. Hosp., Phila., 1949-51; surg. resident Presbyn. Hosp., NYC, 1953-57, thoracic surg. resident, 1957-59, attending surgeon, 1967-90, instr. surgery Columbia, 1959-60, asst. prof., 1960-63, assoc. prof., 1963-67, prof. clin. surgery, 1967-88, prof. surgery, 1988-90, prof. surgery emeritus, 1991—. Served to lt., M.C. USNR, 1951-53. Mem. ACS, N.Y. Heart Assn. (dir.), AMA, Internat. Cardiovascular Soc., Am. Assn. Thoracic Surgery (past pres.), N.Y. Soc. Cardiovascular Surgery, N.Y. Soc. Thoracic Surgery (past pres.), Asian Thoracic and Cardiovascular Soc. (hon.), Soc. Thoracic Surgeons, Soc. U. Surgeons, Soc. Vascular Surgeons, Am. Surg. Assn. Pioneer in use of tissue valves for heart valve replacement and surgery for congenital heart disease; leader in improving the quality of thoracic training in the U.S. Office: Milstein Bldg 7GN-435 177 Fort Washington Ave New York NY 10032-3713 *

MALM, TORSTEN, cardiac surgeon; b. Luleå, Sweden, May 12, 1952; s. Ingemar and Maj Malm; m. Margareta Malm, May 25, 1980; children: Alexander, Lukas. Cand med, U. Kiel, Germany, 1976; MD, Med. U. Lübeck, Germany, 1980; PhD, U. Uppsala, Sweden, 1991. Cert. physician Nat. Bd. Health and Welfare, Sweden, 1983, specialist in cardiothoracic surgery 1989. Internship County Hosp., Gävle, Sweden, 1981—83, residency, dept. surgery, 1983—84; residency Dept. Cardiothoracic Surgery U. Hosp., Uppsala, 1984—89, staff surgeon, 1989—91; cardiac surgery fellowship Dept. Pediat. Cardiac Surgery Royal Childrens Hosp., Melbourne, Australia, 1991—93; cons., pedicat. cardiac surgery unit U. Hosp., Lund, Sweden, 1993—; assoc. prof. Lund U., 2009. Med. dir. Lund Tissue Bank U. Hosp., 1995—; bd. mem. Nat. Coun. Organ and Tissue Donation, Stockholm, 2005—11; assoc. prof. Lund U. Mem.: Scandinavian Assn. Thoracic and Cardiovasc. Surgery, Swedish Soc. Thoracic Surgery, Swedish Med. Soc. Office: Univ Hosp Pediat Cardiac Surgery Unit 221 85 Lund Sweden

MALMQUIST, CARL PHILLIP, psychiatrist; b. St. Paul, Mar. 10, 1934; s. Phillip C. and Lillian Viola (Kahler) M.; m. Arlyn Virginia Bodal (dec. 1984); children: Derek, Jay. BA summa cum laude, U. Minn., 1954, MD, 1958, MS in Philosophy of Sci., 1961. Diplomate Am. Bd. Psychiatry and Neurology, Am. Bd. Child Psychiatry, Am. Bd. Adult Psychiatry; cert. forensic psychiatry, added qualification in forensic psychiatry. Intern Columbia Med. Ctr., NYC, 1963—64, U. Minn., Mpls., 1962—63; assoc. prof. dept. psychiatry U. Mich., 1965—67; assoc. prof. Inst. Child Devel. U. Minn., 1967—70, prof., dir. child and adolescent psychiatry, 1971—72, prof. criminal justice, 1972—80, prof. social psychiatry, dept. sociology, 1980—. Cons. Hennepin County Dist. Ct., Mpls., 1967—; mem. commn. of mentally disabled ABA, 1985. Author: Handbook of Adolescence, 1980 (Guttmacher award 2007), Homicide: Psychiatric Perspectives, 1996, 2d edit., 2006; mem. editl. bd. Psychiat. Anns., 1981; contbr. articles to profl. jours. Fellow Am. Psychiat. Assn. (disting. sr.; commn. on jud. action 1994—, Isaac Ray award 2011), Am. Coll. Psychiatrists, Am. Orthopsychiat. Assn., Am. Acad. Child Psychiatry, Am. Acad. Psychiatry and Law (Segmour Pollock Disting. Achievement award 2004), Am. Coll. Forensic Psychiatry; mem. Group for Advancement Psychiatry, Am. Psychopathol. Assn. Episcopalian. Home: 5010 Bruce Ave Minneapolis MN 55424-1318 Office Phone: 612-624-4300, 952-926-6654. E-mail: malmq001@umn.edu.

MALNICK, STEPHEN DAVID HOWARD, internist, director; b. London, Aug. 7, 1958; MA, Oxford U., 1980; MBBS, U. London, 1985. Dir., internal medicine C Kaplan Med. Ctr., 1999—. Mem.: Am. Gastroent. Assn. Office: Kaplan Med Ctr Dept Internal Medicine C Rehovot 76100 Israel Office Fax: 97289441852. Business E-Mail: stephen@malnick.net.

MALONE, DONALD ANTHONY, psychiatrist, educator; b. Cleve., May 9, 1961; BS, Youngstown State U., 1981; MD, Northeastern Ohio Univs. Coll. Medicine, 1985. Staff psychiatrist Cleve. Clinic, 1989, dir. Ctr. Behavioral Health, 2008, bd. govs., 2009, prof., chair dept. psychiatry and psychology, 2009—. Bd. dirs. Internat. Soc. ECT and Neurostimulation, 2008; pres. Assn. Convulsive Therapy, 2006—08. Fellow: Am. Psychiat. Assn., Am. Coll. Psychiatrists (Laughlin fellowship); mem.: Alpha Omega Alpha. Office: 9500 Euclid Ave Desk P57 Cleveland OH 44195 Office Fax: 216-445-0127. Business E-Mail: maloned@ccf.org.

MALONE, JOHN DUDLEY, epidemiologist; b. Cleve., Ohio, June 21, 1953; MD, Ohio State Med. Sch., 1975; MPH, Uniformed Svcs. U., 2005. Program mgr., Ctr. Biol. Monitoring and Modeling Pacific NW Nat. Lab., 2006—08, instl. rev. bd., 2008—11; liaison, Armed Forces Health Surveillance Ctr. Ctr. Disaster and Humanitarian Assistance Medicine, 2008—10; sexually transmitted disease clinic physician San Diego County Pub. Health Dept., 2010—. Prof. medicine Uniformed Svcs. U., 2001—11. Contbr. articles to profl. publs., chapters to books. Ret. capt. Med. Corps. USN, 2004. Decorated Legion of Merit USN, Def. Meritorious Svc. medal, Meritorious Svc. medal. Fellow: ACP (exec. mem.), Infectious Diseases Soc. America; mem.: ACP. Avocation: rowing. Home: 45 Delaport Way Coronado CA 92118 Personal E-mail: jmalone001@san.rr.com.

MALONEY, MILFORD CHARLES, retired internal medicine educator; b. Buffalo, Mar. 15, 1927; s. John Angelus Maloney and Winifred Hill; m. Dione Ethyl Sheppard. BS, Canisius Coll., 1947, postgrad., 1947-49; MD, U. Buffalo, 1953. Diplomate Am. Bd. Internal Medicine. Rsch. chemist Buffalo Electrochem. Co., 1947-49; intership Mercy Hosp./Georgetown U., 1953-54; med. residency Buffalo VA Hosp., 1954-56; cardiology fellow Buffalo Gen. Hosp., 1956-57; chmn. dept. medicine Mercy Hosp., 1969-94, program dir., internal medicine residency Buffalo, 1972-89; with steering com. Assn. Program Dirs. in Internal Medicine, 1976, coun. mem., 1977-80; clin. prof. medicine SUNY, Buffalo, 1981-94; trustee Am. Soc. Internal Medicine, 1984-90, edn. leader, European seminar, 1987, edn. leader, So. Am. seminar, 1988; faculty instr. Christopher Wren Assn. Coll. William and Mary, Williamsburg, Va., 1997—2008. Bd. dirs. Internal Medicine Ctr. for Advancement and Rsch. Edn., Ctr. Excellence in Aging and Geriatric Health, Williamsburg, Va., Heart Assn. Western NY, Buffalo, 1969; sr. cancer rsch. physician Roswell Park Meml. Cancer Inst., 1959-62; mem. internal medicine liaison com. NY State, 1980-90; faculty instr., mem. curriculum com. Christopher Wren Assn. Coll. William & Mary, Williamsburg, Va., 1997-99. Editor newsletter N.Y. State Soc. Internal Medicine, 1972-78. Bd. dirs. Health Sys. Agy. Western N.Y., Buffalo, 1981; mem. exec. com., bd. dirs. Blue Cross Western N.Y., Buffalo, 1987-1994; mem. bd. regents Canisius Coll., Buffalo, 1987—; mem. pres. assocs. SUNY, Buffalo; founding mem. Greater Williamsburg Va. Symphony Soc., 1998; bd. dirs. Va. Symphony, Norfolk, 2001; bd. dirs., dir. devel. Williamsburg Ctr. for Excellence in Aging and Geriatric Health, 2004. Capt. M.C., U.S. Army, 1957-59. Recipient award of merit N.Y. State Soc. Internal Medicine, 1980, Man of Yr. award Heart Assn. Western N.Y., 1982, ann. honoree award Trocaire Coll., 1986, Disting. Alumni award Canisius Coll., 1991, Berkson Excellence award in tchg. and art of medicine, SUNY at Buffalo, 1992, Outstanding Med. Tchg. Attending award Mercy Hosp./SUNY Med. Residents, 1994, Lifetime Career Achievement award Med. Alumni Assn. SUNY, Buffalo, 2005, Heritage award Mercy Hosp. Found., Buffalo, N.Y., 2005; named to Sports Hall of Fame, Canisius Coll., 1978. Master ACP (pres. emeritus, Upstate Physician Recognition award 1989); fellow Am. Coll. Cardiology; mem. AMA (SUNY rep. 1986-94, rep. to sect. med. schs. at ann. meetings 1984-94, chmn. sect. on internal medicine 1990-91), Am. Soc. Internal Medicine (bd. dirs. Internal Medicine Ctr. for Advancement of Rsch. Edn. 1988-91, trustee 1984-90, pres. 1990-91, chmn. long range planning com., rep. to Federated Coun. on Internal Medicine 1990-91, rep. nat. practice parameters and guidelines com. 1989-91, Scroll of Honor benefactor for Internal Medicine Ctr. for Advancement of Rsch. and Edn. 1991), Va. State Soc. Internal Medicine (ex officio mem. exec. com., bd. dirs.), N.Y. State Soc. Internal Medicine (pres. 1974-75), Alumni Assn. SUNY (pres. 1975), Med. Soc. County Erie (pres. 1991-82), Va. Soc. Internal Medicine (hon.), Greater Williamsburg Va. Symphony Soc. (founding mem. 1998, editor newsletter 1998-2003). Home: 3000 Earls Ct Unit 1211 Williamsburg VA 23185-3873 E-mail: m.c.maloney@cox.net.

MALONEY, PATSY LORETTA, nursing educator; b. Murfreesboro, Tenn., Feb. 19, 1952; d. Buford Leon Browning and Ina (Bush) DuBose; m. Richard J. Maloney, July 26, 1975; children: Katherine Nalani, Nathaniel Allen, Elizabeth Maureen. BS in Nursing, U. Md., 1974; MA, Cath. U., DC, 1984, MS in Nursing, 1984; EdD, U. So. Calif., 1994. Commd. 1st lt. U.S. Army, 1974, advanced through grades to lt. col., 1989; asst. chief nurse evenings and nights DeWitt Army Hosp., Ft. Belvoir, Va.; chief nurse, tng. officer 85th EVAC Hosp., Ft. Lee, Va.; clin. head nurse emergency rm./PCU Tripler Army Med. Ctr., Honolulu, chief nursing edn.; chief surg. nursing sect. and acute care nursing sect. Madigan Army Med. Ctr., Tacoma, 1991-94; dir. Ctr. for Continued Nursing Learning Pacific Luth. U., Tacoma, 1994—. Asst. prof., dir. continuing nursing edn. Pacific Luth. U., Tacoma, 1994—2000, assoc. prof., 2000—08, prof., 2008—. Mem. Emergency Nurses Assn., Nat. Nursing Staff Devel. Orgn., Acad. Med. Surg. Nurses, Sigma Theta Tau, Phi Kappa Phi. Home: 7002 53rd St W Tacoma WA 98467-2214 Office: Pacific Luth U Continuing Nursing Edn Tacoma WA 98467 Business E-Mail: malonepl@plu.edu.

MALONEY, ROBERT KELLER, ophthalmologist, medical educator; b. May 1, 1958; AB in Mathematics summa cum laude, Harvard U., 1979; MA in Philosophy, Politics and Econs., Oxford U., Eng., 1981; MD, U. Calif., San Francisco, 1985. Diplomate Am. Bd. Ophthalmology. Rsch fellow dept. physiology Cambridge (Eng.) U., 1985; intern U. Calif., LA, 1985-86; resident Wilmer Ophthal. Inst. Johns Hopkins Hosp., Balt., 1986-89; Heed fellow cornea and refractive surgery Emory U., Dept. Ophthalmology, Atlanta, 1989-91; clin. prof. ophthalmology Jules Stein Eye Inst. Sch. Medicine U. Calif., 2005—, assoc. prof. ophthalmology Jules Stein Eye Inst. Sch. Medicine, 1991—2004; dir. Maloney Vision Inst., LA, Calif., 1998—. Bd. dirs. Lasik Inst., Calhoun Vision; cons. in field. Contbr. numerous articles to profl. jours.; presenter and spkr. in field; assoc. editor (N.Am.) Jour. Refractive and Corneal Surgery, 1991-95; internat. editl. bd. European Jour. Implant and Refractive Surgery, 1995; reviewer Am. Jour. Ophthalmology, Ophthalmology, Archives of Ophthalmology, Jour. Cataract and Refractive Surgery, Ophthalmic Surgery and Lasers; editl. bd. Ophthalmology Times. Rhodes scholar, 1979, Heed Found. fellow, 1989-90, Heed/Knapp fellow, 1990-91, John Harvard scholar, 1978; recipient Detur and Edward Whitaker prizes, Harvard U., Rsch. to Prevent Blindness Career Devel. award, 1992, Mericos Whittier award, 1997, VISX Star Surgeon award, 1999, 2000. Mem. Am. Acad. Ophthalmology (long-range planning com. 1989-92, quality of care com. 1987-91, retina preferred practice pattern subcom., refractive errors preferred practice pattern subcom.; chmn. ann. meeting program com. for young ophthalmologists, 1990-92; adv. group to ad hoc com. on orgnl. design 1991, young ophthalmologists' com. 1992-94; Honor award 1993, 97, Sr. Achievement award 2002, Secretariat award 2003), Assn. Rsch. in Vision and Ophthalmology, Internat. Soc. Refractive Surgery (Disting. Lans Refractive Surgery award 2001), Calif. Assn. Ophthalmology, Max Fine Corneal Soc., Phi Beta Kappa. Office: Maloney Vision Inst Ste 900 10921 Wilshire Blvd Los Angeles CA 90024 Office Phone: 310-208-3937. Business E-Mail: info@maloneyvision.com.

MALONEY, WILLIAM JAMES, dentist, educator; b. White Plains, NY, Feb. 16, 1967; BS, Siena Coll., Loudonville, NY, 1989; DDS, NYU, 1992. Faculty NYU Coll. Dentistry, NY, 2000—. Contbr. articles to profl. jours.; Spoting News Magazine, Detroit free Press. Fellow, Acad. of Dentistry Internat., Pierre Fauchard Acad. Mem.: ADA. Office: 12 Ellis Pl Ossining NY 10562 Business E-Mail: maloneydentistry@aol.com.

MALPESO, JAMES V., interventional cardiologist, educator; MD, Yeshiva U., 1975. Diplomate Am. Bd. Internal Medicine, Am. Bd. Internal Medicine-cardiovascular disease, Am. Bd. Internal Medicine-interventional cardiology, Am. Bd. Internal Medicine-cardiovascular computed tomography, lic. NY. Resident in internal medicine Kings County Hosp., Brooklyn, NY, 1976—78; fellow in cardiovascular disease St. Vincent's Hosp., 1978—80; asst. prof medicine SUNY; cardiologist Staten Island Univ. Hosp. Office: Staten Island University Hospital 501 Seaview Ave Ste 300 Staten Island NY 10306 Office Phone: 718-663-7000.

MALPHUS, EDWARD WILSON, pediatric gastroenterologist; b. Miami, Fla., Sept. 19, 1950; MD, U. South Fla. Coll. Medicine, Tampa, 1975. Diplomate Am. Bd. Pediat., cert. Pediat. Gastroenterology, lic. Calif. Intern pediat. Martin Luther King Jr. Gen. Hosp., LA, 1975—76, resident pediat. gastroenterology; fellowship Baylor U., Houston, 1980—82; pvt. practice in pediatric gastroenterology San Francisco. Contbr. articles to profl. jours. Avocations: boating, fishing, skiing. Office: Pvt Practice 2021 Santa Monica Blvd Ste 612 E Santa Monica CA 90404 Office Phone: 310 829-4403. Office Fax: 310-829-3279.

MALTZ, ALLEN P., insurance company executive; B in Math., SUNY, Albany, NY. Actuary Travelers Ins. Co.; various sr. strategic, fin., and actuarial positions Aetna US Healthcare; CFO Blue Cross Blue Shield Mass., Inc., Boston, 2001—, exec. v.p. Bd. dirs. United Way of New Eng., Neighborhood Health Plan, Crohn's & Colitis Found., Goodwill Industries of Boston, Treasurers Club of Boston. Fellow: Soc. Actuaries; mem.: American Acad. Actuaries. Office: Blue Cross Blue Shield Massachusetts Landmark Center 401 Park Dr Boston MA 02215 Office Fax: 617-832-4832. *

MALTZ, ROBERT, surgeon; b. Cin., July 21, 1935; s. William and Sarah (Goldberg) M.; m. Sylvia Moskowitz, Aug. 24, 1958; children: Mark Edward, Deborah Lynn, Steven Alan, David Stuart. BS in Zoology, U. Cin., 1958, MD, 1962. Diplomate Am. Bd. Otolaryngology. Intern Cin. Gen. Hosp., 1962-63; resident Barnes Hosp., St. Louis, 1965-69; asst. prof. surgery Stanford U. Med. Ctr., Palo Alto, Calif., 1969-71; asst. prof. otolaryngology U. Cin. Med. Ctr., 1971-75, assoc. prof. otolaryngology, 1975—; dir. dept. otolaryngology Jewish Hosp., Cin., 1992—. Chief divsn. head and neck surgery, dept. otolaryngology and maxillofacial surgery U. Cin. Med. Ctr., 1972-76; bd. dirs. Cancer Control Coun., U. Cin. Med. Cntr.; cons. Bur. Crippled Children's Svcs., State of Ohio; on staff Univ. Hosp., Cin., Jewish Hosp., Cin., Children's Hosp. Med. Ctr., Bethesda Hosp., Cin.; del. to numerous profl. confs.; mem. health affairs adv. com. Cmty. Mut. Ins. Co.; mem. mng. bd. PIE Mut. Ins. Co.; bd. dirs. UCATS, 1995-98; trustee Health Found. Greater Cin., 1997-2006, vice-chmn., 2000-01, chmn. 2001-03, chmn. program com., 2000-01; instr. short term courses in field; pres.-elect alumni exec. coun. U. Cin. Coll. Medicine, 1998-2000, pres., 2000-02. Contbr. articles to profl. jours. Bd. dirs. Jewish Cmty. Rels. Coun.; bd. trustees Cin. Art Acad., 1998-2007; faculty adv. com. U. Cin.; trustee Health Found. Fund, 2002-09, vice-chmn., 2002-03, chmn., 2003—05. Capt. USAF, 1963-65. USPHS fellow, 1968-69; Eli Lilly Co. grantee, 1971-76, Burroughs Wellcome Co., 1972. Fellow ACS, Am. Acad. Facial and Reconstructive Surgery (edn. com. 1972, future plans com. 1973-75, sci. program com., budget and fin. com. 1975, chmn. credentials com., no. sect. 1980-85), Royal Soc. Health, Internat. Cosmetic Surgeons, Am. Acad. Cosmetic Surgeons, Am. Assn. Cosmetic Surgeons (sec.-treas. 1976-81); mem. Am. Acad. Otolaryngology and Head and Neck Surgery, Am. Coun. Otolaryngology, Soc. Univ. Otolaryngologists, Pan-Am. Assn. Oto-Rhino-Laryngology and Broncho-Esophagology, Ohio State Med. Assn., Cin. Acad. Medicine (trustee 1992-98, treas. 1993-95, pres. 1996-97, chmn. pub. rels. com. 1980, chmn. comm. com. 1994-96, chmn. sply. soc. com. 1995, legis. com. 1985, editl. bd. 1994-96, jud. com. 1995—2004, chmn. managed care med. dirs. com. 1997-2002), U. Cin. Alumni Assn. (bd. govs., sec. 1994, fin. v.p. 1995, 1st v.p. 1996, pres. 1997-98), Acad. Medicine Found. (bd. dirs., v.p., pres. 2002-2004), Cin. Ear, Nose and Throat Soc., Losantiville Country Club (bd. govs. 1996-2002, pres. 1999-2001), Omicron Delta Kappa, Sigma Sigma, Sigma Alpha Mu. Avocations: tennis, golf, travel. Home: 2601 Willowbrook Dr Cincinnati OH 45237-3725 Office: 11135 Montgomery Rd Cincinnati OH 45249 Office Phone: 513-793-9600.

MALTZMAN, IRVING MYRON, psychology professor; s. Israel and Lillian (Mass) M.; m. Diane Seiden; children— Sara, Kenneth, Ilaine. BA, NYU, 1946; PhD, State U. Iowa, 1949. Mem. faculty UCLA, 1949—, assoc. prof., 1957—60, prof. psychology, 1961—94, chmn. dept., 1970—77, prof. emeritus, 1994—. Co-author: Handbook of Contemporary Soviet Psychology, 1969, Alcoholism: A Review of its' Characteristics, Etiology, Treatments, and Controversies, 2000, author: Alcoholism: Its Treatments and Mistreatments, 2008. Fellow: APA, AAAS; mem.: Psychonomic Soc., APS, Phi Beta Kappa, Sigma Xi. Office Phone: 310-825-2907.

MALTZMAN, JONATHAN S., physician, educator; b. London, Aug. 8, 1967; BS in Biology, MIT, 1989; MD, U. Pa., PhD, 1997. Asst. prof. U. Pa. Sch. Medicine, 2006—. Office: 754 BRB II/III 421 Curie Blvd Philadelphia PA 19104 Business E-Mail: maltz@mail.med.upenn.edu.

MALYAPA, ROBERT, oncologist, educator; b. India, May 12, 1955; MD, All India Inst. Med. Scis., 1987; PhD, Hiroshima U., 1992. Diplomate Am. Bd. Radiology. Asst. prof. Wash. U., Dept. Radiation Oncology, 2003—05, U. Fla. Proton Therapy Inst., 2005—. Recipient Simon Kramer New Investigator award, RTOG, Rsch. Award, Radiol. Soc. N.Am., Young Oncologist Essay award, Am. Radium Soc.; named Intern of Yr., St. Luke's Hosp., Internal Medicine, St. Louis; Travel fellowship, 43rd Particle Therapy Coop. Group Meeting, Travel grant, Am. Radium Soc. Mem.: Soc. Neuro-Oncology, Am. Soc. Therapeutic Radiology and Oncology, North Am. Skull Base Soc. Office: 2015 N Jefferson St Jacksonville FL 32206 Office Fax: 904-588-1300. Business E-Mail: cleone@floridaproton.org.

MAMELAK, ADAM N., neurosurgeon, educator; b. Phila., July 25, 1963; BS, Tufts U., 1985; MD, Harvard Med. Sch., 1990. Sect. head, neurosurgery City of Hope Cancer Ctr., 1997—2005; porf., neurosurgery Cedars-Sinai Med. Ctr., 2005—. Cons. Transmolecular Inc, 2000—05, VCA Animal Hosps., 2008, Karl Storz Endoscopy, 2011; sci. adv. bd. mem. Epinano Techs., 2009. Recipient Sirgay Sanger award, Harvard Med. Sch., Top Surgeon award; named one of America's Top Dr., Castle Connely; Best Translational Rsch. award, Nat. Brain Tumor Found. Award, Pasadena Neuroscis. fellowship, HHMI, Calif. Inst. Tech. Fellow: ACS, Am. Assn. Neurol. Surgeon (Young Clinician Investigator award); mem.: Internat. Soc. Pituitary Surgeons, Pituitary Soc., Congress Neurol. Surgeons. Office: 8631 W 3rd St Ste 800E Los Angeles CA 90048 Business E-Mail: mamelaka@cshs.org.

MAMMEN, JENS SKAUN, psychologist, educator; b. Copenhagen, Feb. 26, 1942; s. Jens Holger and Kirsten Mammen; m. Anne Bjerg, Feb. 17, 1967; children: Annette Bjerg, Christian Bjerg. Mag.art. in Psychology, U. Copenhagen and Aarhus, 1969; PhD, U. Aarhus, Denmark, 1983. Asst. prof. U. Aarhus, 1969—70, assoc. prof., 1970—2000, prof., 2000—08. Chmn., faculty bd. psychology U. Aarhus, 1980—83, dep. dean, faculty social sciences, 1980—83, mem., com. good sci. practice, 1999—2008, head dept., inst. psychology, 2001—06; mem. Danish Com. Sci. Dishonesty, Ministry Rsch., Copenhagen, 2006—07; chmn. governing bd. Danish Rsch. Sch. Psychology, Copenhagen, 2008; prof. U. Aalborg, 2009—. Co-organizer Forum Theology and Psychology, Aarhus, 1995—2000. None NONE. Home: Vestergade 39 Aarhus DK 8000 Denmark Office: Univ Aarhus Jens Chr Skous Vej 4 Aarhus DK 8000 Denmark Business E-Mail: jens@psy.au.dk.

MAMORU, FUKUDA, medical researcher; b. Tokyo, Dec. 21, 1971; s. Toshiharu and Masako Fukuda; m. Mihoko Togashi; 1 child, Misato Fukuda. PhD, Chiba U. Cert. pharmacist Tokyo, 1994. Vis. scientist U. Tex., Austin, 2003—05; mgr. Kyorin Pharm. Co., Ltd., Tochigi, Japan, 1996—. Recipient awards, Internat. Jour. Pharmaceutics Highest Cited Original Rsch., 2006. Office: Kyorin Pharm Co Ltd 1848 Nogi Nogi-machi Shimotsuga-gun Tochigi 329-0114 Japan Personal E-mail: mamoru1221@hotmail.com.

MAN, DANIEL, plastic surgeon; married; 3 children. MD, Tel Aviv U., 1973. Lic. Maine, 1976, Del., 1976, Ky., 1978, Fla., 1981, diplomate in Plastic and Reconstructive Surgery Am. Bd. Plastic Surgery, 1981. Intern in gen. surgery Tel Hashomer Hosp., Ramat Gan, Israel, 1972—73; resident in gen. surgery Montefiore Hosp., Bronx, NY, 1974—76; resident in surgery Wilmington Gen. Hosp., Del., 1976—78; resident in plastic and reconstructive surgery U. Louisville, 1978—80; pvt. practice Boca Raton, Fla., 1981—. Presenter in field; profl. interviewed various mags., newspapers, and TV programs. Author: The Art of Man: Faces of Plastic Surgery, 1998, The New Art of Man: Faces of Plastic Surgery, 2002, Man at Work: A Photographic of Plastic Surgery and Art, 2010; contbr. books, anthologies, and profl. jours. in field. Recipient Humanitarian of Yr. award, Palm Beach County Victim Svcs., 2001, Letter of Recognition for Humanitarian Contbns., Fla. State Senator M. Mandy Dawson, 2001, Fla. State Senator Tom Rossin, 2001, US Congressman Robert Wexler, 2001, US Senator Bill Nelson, 2001, US Senator Bob Graham, 2001, Gov. Jeb Bush, Fla., 2001, US Atty. Gen. Nat. Crime Victim Rights Week Svc. award, 2009; named Dr. Man Day in his honor, Boca Raton, Fla., 2001; Hand fellowship, U. Louisville, 1978—80, Microvascular fellowship, 1980. Fellow: Am. Soc. Laser Surgery and Medicine; mem.: AMA, Y-ME Fla. (founding bd. mem. 1982—87, med. advisor 1982—87), Lipolysis Soc. N.Am., Broward County Soc. Plastic Surgeons, Palm Beach County Soc. Plastic Surgeons, Palm Beach County Med. Soc., Am. Soc. Aesthetic Plastic Surgery, Am. Soc. Plastic Surgeons. Office: 851 Meadows Rd Ste 222 Boca Raton FL 33486 Office Phone: 561-395-5508.

MANAMPERI, ARESHA, molecular biologist, educator; b. Colombo, Sri Lanka, Dec. 8, 1968; d. Wollie Manamperi and Esme De Silva; m. Channa Unantenne, June 11, 2003; 1 child, Ranaali Unantenne. BSc, U. Colombo, Sri Lanka, 1994, MSc, 1997, PhD, Inst. Pasteur, Paris, 2002. Head sr. lectr. Molecular Medicine Unit, Faculty Medicine, U. Kelaniya, Ragama, Sri Lanka, 2003—. Cons. molecular biologist Durdans Hosp., Colombo, Sri Lanka, 2007—; tech. assessor quality assurance med. labs. Sri Lanka Accreditation Bd., Colombo, 2008. Contbr. articles to profl. jours. Recipient Prof. Stanley Wijesundera Meml. award, 1995, Devel. Co-operation prize, 2004, Vice Chancellors award, 2005, 2008, Presdl. award, 2006, Best Sci. Paper award, 2008, Presdl. award for sci. rsch., 2010. Mem.: Sri Lanka Assn. Advancement Sci. (life; com. mem. gen. rsch. com. 2008—09). Achievements include development of molecular technology based diagnostics applicable in infectious diseases; research in genetic polymorphism in malaria parasites and research activities related to other infectious diseases. Office: University of Kelaniya Faculty of Medicine Thalagolla Rd 11010 Ragama Sri Lanka Office Fax: 94112958337.

MANAPPALLIL, JOHN JOY, prosthodontist; b. Kuwait City, Sept. 6, 1967; s. John Joy Manappallil and Gracy Joy; m. Divya Susan Thomas; children: Reuben Manappallil John, Jordan John. BS in Dental Surgery, Coll. Dental Surgery, Manipal, India, 1990; MS in Dental Surgery, Bapuji Dental Coll., Davengere, India, 2005. Gen. dentist J. J. Dental Clinic, Kottayam, Kerala, India, 1990—91; sr. house officer St. John's Med. Coll., Bangalore, Karnataka, India, 1991; asst. prof. Yenepoya Dental Coll., Mangalore, Karntaka, 1995—96, Coll. Dental Surgery, Mangalore, 1996—98; registrar Al Jahra Dental Ctr., Kuwait, 1998—2008; registrar dentist Ministry of Health, Bneid Al Gar Dental Ctr., Kuwait City, 2008—. Author: (book) Basic Dental Materials, Complete Denture Prosthodontics; contbr. articles to numerous rsch. jours. Mem.: RCS (Ireland) (trainer, MFDRCSI KU program, faculty dentists, Kuwait 2000—08), Indian Dental Assn., Indian Prosthodontic Soc., Kuwait Dental Assn., Indian Dentists Alliance Kuwait (cultural and entertainment sec. 2006—08), Dental Students Assn., Coll. Dental Surgery (Manipal) (pres. 1988—89). Avocations: boating, badminton, writing, music, fishing. Home: Manappallil Joy Villa PO Box Mavelikara Kunnam Kerala 690108 India Office: Bneid Al Gar Dental Ctr Bneid Al Gar Kuwait City Kuwait Address: Flat 12 Bldg 7 St 2 Block 1 Riggai Kuwait City Kuwait Personal E-mail: jonsbin@yahoo.com.

MANASIA, ANTHONY, surgeon, educator; b. NYC, Oct. 9, 1952; MD, U. Turin, Italy, 1987. Assoc. prof. medicine and surgery Mt. Sinai Sch. Medicine, 1989—. Dir. surg. critical care rsch. Mt. Sinai Med. Ctr., 1993—2011. Recipient Thomas J. Iberti Rsch. award, Mt. Sinai Dept. Surgery, Divsn. Surg. Critical Care. Mem.: Shock Soc., Am. Coll. Chest Physicians, Soc. Critical Care Medicine. Office: 1468 Madison Ave Guggenheim Pavilion New York NY 10029 Office Fax: 212-860-3669. Business E-Mail: anthony.manasia@mountsinai.org.

MANASSE, HENRI RICHARD, JR., pharmaceutical executive; b. Amsterdam, The Netherlands, Nov. 27, 1945; came to U.S., 1954, naturalized, 1963; s. Henri David and Janny Lynn (Borst) M.; m. Arlynn Hem, Aug. 9, 1969; children: Bryan, Sheralynn. BS in Pharmacy, U. Ill., Chgo., 1968; MA, Loyola U., Chgo., 1972; PhD, U. Minn., 1974; DSc (hon.), Campbell U., 1997, Union U., 1997, Mercer U., 1998, LI U., NY, 2004, U. Salamanca, Spain, 2010. Lic. pharmacist, Ill. Rsch. pharmacist Xttrium Labs., Chgo., 1968-69; asst. to dean Coll. Pharmacy U. Ill., Chgo., 1969-72, asst. prof. pharmacy adminstrn., 1974-77, assoc. dean, 1977-80, acting dean, 1980-81, dean, prof., 1981-93, interim vice chancellor for health svcs., 1992-93; prof. coll. pharmacy and medicine U. Iowa, v.p. for health scis., 1993-96; exec. v.p.-designate Am. Soc. Health-Sys. Pharmacists, 1996—, CEO, exec. v.p., 1997—. Sr. policy fellow Ctr. on Drugs and Pub. Policy, U. Md., 1988—; mem. Ill. Bd. Pharmacy, Springfield, 1982-94; pub. mem. Am. Soc. Hosp. Pharmacists Commn. on Credentialling, Bethesda, Md., 1984-86; chair bd. dirs. Nat. Patient Safety Found., 1999-2001, chair bd. govs., 2006; mem. adv. bd. PEW Found. Health Professions Edn. Reform Commn.; bd. dirs. Am. Soc. Cons. Pharmacists Rsch. and Edn. Found.; pres. Coun. on Credentialing in Pharmacy, 1998—02; mem. quality quest prize selection com. Am. Hosp. Assn.; co-chair safe practices steering com. Nat. Quality Forum, 2001-04, adv. com. on exec. leadership; mem. sentinel events adv. com. JCAHO Sentinel, 2002—; cons. FDA Adv. Com. on Risk Mgmt. and Drug Safety, 2003-07; expert on patient safety Bd. Pharmacy Practice, profl. sec., 2005—, Internat. Pharm. Fedn., fellow, 2008; JCAHO mem. Internat. Adv. Com. on Patient Safety, with joint commn. resources, 2008-. Mem. editl. bd. Am. Jour. Hosp. Pharmacy, 1990-92; contbr. chpts. to books and articles to profl. jours. Pres. Downers Grove Sch. Bd. Caucus, Ill., 1984-85; bd. dirs. med. svc. Westside Holistic Ctr., Chgo., 1979-89. Recipient Lederle Faculty award Lederle Pharm. Co., 1975, Outstanding Achievement award U. Minn., 1998; named Alumnus of Yr., U. Ill. Alumni Assn., 1983. Jesse E Stewart Svc. award, U. of Illinois, 2004, Harvey A.K. Whitney Lecture award Am. Soc. Health Sys. Pharmacists, 2007. Fellow: Inst. Medicine Chgo.; mem.: NAS, AHRQ (ctrs. on edn. & rsch. therapeutics adv. com. mem. 2009—), Am. Soc. Assn. Execs., Am. Pharm. Assn., Inst. Medicine, Am. Soc. Health Sys. Pharmacists (H.A.K. Whitney award 2007), Am. Assn. Colls. Pharmacy (pres., adminstrv. bd. 1982—86, bd. dirs. 1984—86, pres. 1988—89). Baptist. Avocations: computers, international travel. Home: 10118 Vanderbilt Cir Rockville MD 20850-4674 Office: ASHP 7272 Wisconsin Ave Bethesda MD 20814 Office Phone: 301-657-3000, 301-664-8890. Business E-Mail: hrmjr@ashp.org.

MANASWI, ANSHUMAN, surgeon; b. India, May 13, 1971; MBBS, Jipmer, Pondicherry, 1992; MCh, G.S. Med. Coll., Mumbai, 2002. Cons. cancer & plastic surgeon Jawaharlal Nehru Cancer Hosp., Bhopal, 2002—04; pvt. practice, 2004—08; cons., plastic, cosmetic surgeon Bombay Hosp. & Med. Rsch. Ctr., 2008—. Dir. Transformation, 2010—11. Recipient Bihar Gaurav award, Indian Soc. Creative Arts. Mem.: Assn. Plastic Surgery India. Avocations: writing, music. Office: Transformation 201 Sakib Bldg A Bandra Mumbai Maharashtra 400050 India Personal E-mail: dramanaswi@yahoo.com.

MANCALL, ELLIOTT LEE, retired neurologist, educator; b. Hartford, Conn., July 31, 1927; s. Nicholas and Bess Tuch M.; m. Jacqueline Sue Cooper, Dec. 27, 1953; children: Andrew Cooper, Peter Cooper. BS, Trinity Coll., Hartford, 1948; MD, U. Pa., 1952. Diplomate Am. Bd. Psychiatry and Neurology. Intern Hartford Hosp., 1952-54; clk. in neurology Nat. Hosp. Nervous Disease, London, 1954-55; asst. resident neurology Neurol. Inst. NY, 1955-56; resident in neuropathology Mass. Gen. Hosp., 1956-57, clin. and rsch. fellow, 1957-58; tchg. fellow neuropathology Harvard Med. Sch., 1956-57; from asst. prof. neurology to assoc. prof. Jefferson Med. Coll., 1958-65; prof. medicine Hahnemann Med. Coll. and Hosp., 1965-76; prof. neurology Med. Coll. Pa.-Hahnemann U., 1993-95; prof. neurology, chmn. dept. Hahnemann Med. Coll. and Hosp., 1976-93; prof. neurology Jefferson Med. Coll., Phila., 1995—, interim chmn. dept. neurology, 1997—2003; prof. emeritus, 2006—. Dir. Hahnemann U. ALS Clinic, 1985-95; chmn. bd. dirs. Phila. Profl. Stds. Rev. Orgn., 1981-84. Author: (with others) The Human Cerebellum: A Topographical Atlas, 1961; (with B.J. Alpers) Clinical Neurology, 1971, Essentials of the Neurological Examination, 1971, 81; editor Gray's Clinical Neuroanatomy, 2010; contbr. articles to profl. jours. With USN, 1945—47. Recipient Christian R. and Mary F. Lindback award, 1969, Oliver Meml. prize ophthalmology U. Pa., 1952. Fellow Am. Acad. Neurology (alt. del. to AMA 1982-86, gen. editor CONTINUUM 1991-2003, A.B. Baker award for excellence in neurol. edn. 1997, Presdl. award 2003); mem. Am. Neurol. Assn., Am. Assn. Neuropathology, Assn. Rsch. in Nervous and Mental Diseases, Soc. Neurosci., AAUP, Pa. Med. Peer Rev. Orgn. (dir. 1979-84), Phila. Neurol. Soc., Alpers Soc. Clin. Neurology, Coll. Physicians Phila., Sydenham Coterie, Phila. County Med. Soc., Pa. State Med. Soc., AMA (sec.-treas. sect. coun. neurology 1983-86), Am. Med. Soc. on Alcoholism, Neurology Intersoc. Liaison Group, Intersoc. Com. Neurol. Resources, Assn. Univ. Prof. Neurology (pres. 1988-90), Soc. for Exptl. Neuropathology, Am. Bd. Med. Specialities (exec. bd., chmn. com. study of evaluation procedures, 1992-99, rep. accreditation com. continuing med. edn. 1998-2004, chair accredidation coun., 2003-05), Am. Bd. Psychiatry and Neurology (v.p. 1990, del. to Am. Bd. Med. Spltys., dir. 1983-91, emeritus dir. 1991—, cons. 2004-), Pa. Blue Shield (profl. adv. coun. 1991-98). Democrat. Jewish. Home: PO Box 498 Lafayette Hill PA 19444-0498 Office: Ste 200 900 Walnut St Philadelphia PA 19107 Office Phone: 215-955-0707. Business E-Mail: elliott.mancall@jefferson.edu.

MANCHIKANTI, PADMAVATI, biology professor; b. Durgapur, Mar. 23, 1971; MSc in Biotech., U. Hyderabad, 1993, PhD, 1999. Scientist Monsanto Rsch. Ctr., 1999—2001, sr. scientist, 2001—03; sr. scientist, cons. Ocimum Biosolutions, 2005—07; asst. prof. Indian Inst. Tech., Kharagpur, 2006—. Recipient Outstanding Young Faculty award, Microsoft India, Spl. Recognition award, Monsanto Rsch. Ctr., Fast Track Scientist award, Dept. Sci. & Tech., Govt. of India. Mem.: Internat. Patent User Group, Biotech Consortium India Ltd., Food Safety Stds. Authority of India. Avocations: singing, dance. Office: Rajiv Gandhi Sch IP Law IIT Kharagpur Kharagpur West Bengal 721302 India Office Fax: 91-3222-282238. E-mail: mpadma@rgsoipl.iitkgp.ernet.in.

MANCINI, MARY CATHERINE, cardiothoracic surgeon, researcher; b. Scranton, Pa., Dec. 15, 1953; d. Peter Louis and Ferminia Teresa (Massi) M. BS Chemistry, U. Pitts., 1974, MD, 1978; PhD Anatomy and Cellular Biology, La. State U. Med. Ctr., New Orleans, 2000; M Med. Mgmt., U. Tex. Southwestern, Dallas, 2005. Diplomate Am. Bd. Surgery (speciality cert. critical care medicine), Am. Bd. Thoracic Surgery, cert. Med. Mgmt. U. Tex. Southwestern, 2000. Intern surgery U. Pitts., 1978—79, resident surgery, 1979—87; fellow pediat. cardiac surgery Mayo Clinic, 1987—88; asst. prof. surgery, dir. cardio-thoracic transplantation Med. Coll. Ohio, Toledo, 1988—91; assoc. prof. surgery, dir. cardio-thoracic transplantation La. State U. Health Scis. Ctr., Shreveport, 1991—98, prof. surgery, chief cardiothoracic surgery, 1999—2002; dir. cardiovasc. rsch. Willis Knighton Med. Ctr., 1991—2004; chief cardiothoracic surgery LSUHSC, Shrevepost, 2008—. Med. advisor Total Artificial Heart Devel., ABIOMED Corp. Author: Operative Techniques for Medical Students, 1983; editor-in-chief: Cardiothoracic Surgery and Transplantation EMedicine Textbooks; contbr. articles to profl. jours. Mem. physicians adv. bd. Rep. Com. Recipient Pres. award, Internat. Soc. Heart Transplantation, 1983, Charles C. Moore Tchg. award, U. Pitts., 1985, Internat. Order of Merit award, 1995, Nina S. Braunwald Career Devel. award, Thoracic Surgery Found., 1996—98, Nat. Leadership award, Rep. Com., 2000, Disting. Alumni award, U. Pitts. Dept. Chemistry, 2002, Tchg. award, dept. surgery La. State U. Health Sci. Ctr., 2005; named Am. Top Surgeons, Consumers Rsd Coun. America, 2009, 2011; named one of Am.'s Top Thoracic Surgeons, Consumer's Rsch. Coun. Am., 2006, Am. Top Surgeon, 2007—09, America's Top Surgeons, Consumers' Rsch Coun. America, 2007—08; grantee Am. Heart Assn., 1988, Whittaker, 1998, NIH, 2000. Fellow ACS, AHA, Am. Coll. Chest Physicians, Internat. Coll. Surgeons (councillor 1991—); mem. Assn. Women Surgeons, Am. Surg. Assn., Am. Assn. Thoracic Surgery, Am. Physiol. Soc., So. Surg. Assn., Rotary (gift of life program 1991), Beta Gamma Sigma, Gamma Sigma Gamma. Roman Catholic. Achievements include first multiple organ transplant in La; first pediatric heart transplant in La., 1993. Office: La State U Med Ctr 1501 Kings Hwy Shreveport LA 71103-4228 Office Phone: 318-675-6154. Personal E-mail: mcmmd@hotmail.com. Business E-Mail: mmanci@lsuhsc.edu.

MANCUSO, GIUSEPPE, dermatologist; b. Modena, Italy, Feb. 27, 1950; s. Salvatore Mancuso and Adele Bandeli; m. Renza Maria Berdondini; children: Mauro, Alessandra. MD, Bologna, Italy, 1975; diploma in dermatology. Vol. asst. Dermo Clinic, Bologna, 1975-80; asst. dir. dept. dermatology Mcpl. Hosp., Lugo, Italy, 1980-99, dir. dept. dermatology, 1999—2007; pvt. practice, 2008—. Contbr. articles to sci. and profl. jours. Lt. Italian Infantry, 1977-78. Achievements include research in area of occupational contact dermatitis. Home: Via Federico Pescantini 33 48022 Lugo RA Italy Home Phone: 054530319. Personal E-mail: mavelabs@hotmail.com.

MANCUSO, JOSEPH EDWARD, medical psychotherapist; b. Rockford, Ill., Dec. 1, 1955; s. Robert and Anne Mancuso. Student, Bradley U., Peoria, Ill., 1974-76; BA in Psychology, Marquette U., 1984, MEd in Ednl. Psychology, 1987. Diplomate Am. Bd. Med. Psychotherapists; WI. LCSW, LPC, CCSAC, CICS. Child care worker Community Care Svcs. Inc., Milw., 1978—79; day care dir. Mich. Street Day Care, Milw., 1979—80; adminstrv. unit clk. Milw. Jewish Nursing Home, 1980—81; day care tchr. St. Mary's Children's Sch., Milw., 1983—84; psychotherapist Wis. Correctional Svcs., Milw., 1984—90; coord. alcohol and other drug abuse St. Mary's Psychiat. Hosp., Milw., 1990-92; pvt. practice Lighthouse Clinic, Milw., 1993—2004; emergency rm. social worker Sinai Samaritan Med. Ctr., Milw., 1994-99; intake psychotherapist psychiat. svcs. Behav. Health Intake Ctr.-Sinai Samaritan Med. Ctr., Milw., 1999-2000; childrens psychotherapist Sinai Samaritan Med. Ctr., Milw., 2000—02, adult psychotherapist, 2002—03, geriatric psychotherapist, 2003; program psychotherapist Aurora Psychiat. Hosp., Wauwatosa, Wis., 2003—. Cons., presenter in field. Cartoonist, published and shown in galleries throughout Milw. Mem. APA, Wis. Psychol. Assn. (assoc.). Avocations: hiking, drawing, birdwatching, writing. Home: 1612 E Hartford Ave Milwaukee WI 53211-3036 Office: Aurora Psychiat Hosp 1220 Dewey Ave Wauwatosa WI 53213 Office Phone: 414-454-6695.

MANDAL, AMIT KEIRAN JOHN, cardiologist; MB, BChir, Imperial Coll., London, 1996. House physician Charing Cross Hosp., London, 1996—97; sr. house physician Harefield Hosp., 1998—99; cardiology rsch. fellow Imperial Coll., London, 2001—04; specialist registrar cardiology Royal Brompton Hosp., London, 2000—. Contbr. numerous articles to profl. jours. Mem.: Royal Coll. Physicians (Edinburgh), Royal Coll. Physicians (UK), Royal Soc. Medicine (licentiate). Achievements include research in prevalence, pathogenesis, treatment of anemia in heart failure; invention of modified cannula for thoracocentesis. Home: 8 Averill St London W6 8EB England Office: Royal Brompton and Harefield NHS Trust Sydney St London SW3 6NP England E-mail: akjm@mac.com.

MANDAL, ANIL KUMAR, ophthalmologist; b. Calcutta, India, Jan. 2, 1958; s. Manick Chandra and Jaya Laxmi (Barman) M.; m. Vijaya Kumari Gothwal, Aug. 4, 1995. MB BS, N.R.S. Med. Coll., Calcutta, India, 1983; MD, All-India Inst. Med. Scis., New Delhi, India, 1987. Diplomate Nat. Bd. for Practice of Ophthalmology. House surgeon N.R.S. Med. Coll., Calcutta, India, 1983-84; jr. resident A.I.I.M.S., New Delhi, India, 1984-86, sr. resident, 1987-90; cons. L.V. Prasad Eye Inst., Hyderabad, India, 1990—; rsch. fellow Doheny Eye Inst., Calif., 1992; jr. ophthalmologist L.V. Prasad Eye Inst., Hyderabad, 1990-93, asst. ophthalmologist, 1991-94, assoc. ophthalmologist, 1994—, in charge Children's Eye Care Ctr., 1997-98, clin. prof. ophthalmology, 1998—. Vis. prof. Duke U. Eye Ctr., Durham, N.C., 1995; book rev. editor for Indian Jour. of Ophthalmology, 1993-96. Contbr. numerous articles to profl. jours. Recipient Best Resident award Ophthalmic Rsch. Assn., 1990. Mem. All-India Ophthal. Soc. (Best Thematic Film award 1997, Prof. P. Siva Reddy Gold medal 1997), Am. Acad. Ophthalmology (Achievement award 2000), Assn. for Rsch. and Vision in Ophthalmology (S.S. Bhatnager award 2003, Med. Excellence Apollo award 2005, Sr. Achievement award 2008). Avocations: reading literary books, music, poetry, swimming, cooking. Office: L V Prasad Eye Inst Rd No 2 Banjara Hills 500 034 Hyderabad India Business E-Mail: mandal@lvpei.org.

MANDAL, NRIPENDRANATH, biochemist, educator; b. Kantagore, West Bengal, India, Jan. 14, 1959; MSc in Biochemistry, U. Calcutta, 1982, PhD in Biochemistry, 1990. Postdoc. assoc. dept. biology MIT, Cambridge, 1989—92; postdoctoral trainee fellow (NIH) dept. molecular microbiology & immunology St. Louis U. Health Scis. Ctr., St. Louis, 1994—96; sr. lectr. Bose Inst., Immunotechnology Sect., Kolkata, West Bengal, 1997—2005, asst. prof., 2005—08; assoc. prof. divsn. molecular medicine Bose Inst., 2008—. Vis. prof. biotechnology, genetics & molecular biology Calcutta U., North Bengal U., Ctrl. Inst. Fishery Edn. and Bose Inst., 1997—2011; examiner, question setter M degree exam. IIT, Kharagpur, Calcutta U., Genetics Dept., North Bengal U, Zoology Dept., North-Eastern Hill U., 2001—11; reviewer DBT, MoES, CSIR, ICMR, Govt. India, 2001—08, Plant Foods Human Nutrition, JCIM, BMC-CAM, e-CAM, 2005—11. Contbr. articles to profl. jours. Recipient Rajiv Gandhi Excellence award, India Internat. Friendship Soc., Bharat Jyoti award. Mem.: Internat. Inst. Success Awareness (New Delhi) (Glory Of India Gold medal), Asiatic Soc. (Kolkata), Swadeshi Sci. Movement India (New Delhi), Soc. Biol. Chemist (India). Avocation: music. Office: Bose Inst P-1/12 CIT Rd Scheme VII M Kolkata West Bengal 700054 India Office Fax: 91-33-2355-3886. Personal E-mail: mandaln@rediffmail.com.

MANDALAKAS, ANNA MARIA, medical association administrator, educator; b. Greensburg, Pa., Apr. 15, 1968; BA, Case Western Res. U., 1990; MD, Hahnemann U., 1994. Assoc. prof. Case Western Res. U., 2000—; Med. dir. Cuyahoga County Bd. Health, 2000—. Recipient Burtris Burr Breese award, Pediatric Infectious Disease Soc., Career Devel. award, NIH, Young Investigator award, Academic Pediatric Assn.; named Triad Adv. of Yr., Adoption Network Cleve.; scholarship, Fulbright Commn., US State Dept. Fellow: Am. Acad. Pediat.; mem.: Internat. Union Against TB & Lung Disease, Academic Pediatric Assn. Avocations: running, skiing, bicycling. Home: 8119 Forestdale Dr Kirtland OH 44094 Business E-Mail: anna.mandalakas@case.edu.

MANDALI, SWARNA L., healthcare educator; b. India, May 14, 1966; PhD, Okla. State U., 2001. Prof. U. Ctrl. Mo., 2001. Named Outstanding Dietetics Educator, Mo. Dietetic Assn. Mem.: Am. Soc. Clin. Nutrition, Am. Dietetic Assn. Home: 21772 Spoon Creek Rd Edgerton KS 66021 Home Fax: 660-543-8847. Business E-Mail: mandali@ucmo.edu.

MANDAVA, RAJESWARI, engineering educator; b. India, June 15, 1955; MTech, Indian Inst. Tech., Kanpur, India, 1980; PhD, U. Wales, 1995. Assoc. prof. U. Sains Malaysia, 1982—. Recipient MSC Malaysia Asia Pacific ICT award; fellow, Assn. Commonwealth U., CICHE fellowship, Brit. Coun., VCC fellow, Japan Soc. Promotion Sci. Mem.: IEEE, MICCAI, ACM. Avocations: reading, tennis. Office: University Sains Malaysia Sch Computer Scis Penang 11800 Malaysia Business E-Mail: mandava@cs.usm.my.

MANDEL, JOEL EMANUEL, orthopedist; b. NYC, Mar. 1, 1930; s. Morris and Minnie Mandel. BA, N.Y. U., 1951; MS, Ga. Inst. Tech., 1952; MD, Chgo. Med. Sch., 1956. Diplomate Am. Bd. Med. Examiners, Am. Bd. Orthop. Surgery, Am. Bd. Profl. Disabled Cons. Intern D.C. Gen. Hosp., 1956—57; resident in gen. surgery VA Hosp., 1957—58; resident in orthopedic surgery D.C. Gen. Hosp., 1958—60, N.Y. U., Bellevue, 1960—61; pres., founding ptnr. The New City (N.Y.) Orthopedic Group, P.C., 1961—85; med. dir. Post-Trauma Med. Svcs., New Windsor, NY, 1985—. Host weekly radio program Today Med. Soc., 1973—80. Mem. editl. bd. Jour. Disability, 1990—93, Disability, 1995—96. Bd. govs. Rockland County (N.Y.) Health Complex, 1977—88; mem. coord. coun. Rockland County Emergency Med. Svc., 1977—81; bd. dirs. Rockland County Coun. Arts, NY, 1981—90. Recipient Rockland County Dist. Svc. award, 1973. Fellow: ACS, NY State Soc. Surgeons, Am. Acad. Orthop. Surgeons, Internat. Coll. Surgeons, Am. Acad. Disability Evaluating Physicians (bd. dirs. 1988—93, sec. 1990—93); mem.: Rockland County Med. Soc. (dir. pub. rels. 1967—73, exec. com. 1967—76, peer rev. com. 1973—85, pres. 1974—75, chmn. bd. censors 1975—76), Orange County Med. Soc. (peer rev. com. 1987—, exec. com. 1994—), Ea. Orthop. Assn., NY State Soc. Orthop. Surgeons (bd. dirs. 1976—82). Republican. Jewish. Avocations: astronomy, sailing, windsurfing. Office: Post-Trauma Med Svc PC 833 Blooming Grove Tpk New Windsor NY 12553 Office Phone: 845-561-2000. Business E-Mail: jmandelmd@hvc.rr.com.

MANDEL, SHELDON LLOYD, dermatologist, educator; b. Mpls., Dec. 6, 1922; s. Maurice and Stelle R. M.; m. Patricia E., Oct. 15, 1978; 1 child, Melissa A. BA, U. Minn., Mpls., 1943, BS, 1944, BM, MD, U. Minn., Mpls., 1946; MA, St. Thomas U. Diplomate Am. Bd. Dermatology, 1953. Intern U. Okla., 1946-47; resident Valley Forge (Pa.) Gen. Hosp., 1947—49, VA Hosp., Mpls., 1949—51, VA Hosp. and U. Minn., Mpls., 1949—51; pvt. practice dermatology Mpls., 1951—; prof. clin. dermatology U. Minn., Mpls., 1970—. Contbr. articles to profl. jours. Capt. MC, U.S. Army, 1947-49. Fellow Royal Soc. Medicine (Britain), Am. Acad. Dermatology (life); mem. AMA, Minn. Med. Soc., Noah Worcester Dermatol. Soc. (bd. dirs. 1988-91), Internat. Dermatol. Soc. Office: Downtown Dermatology PA 7300 France Ave S Ste 400 Minneapolis MN 55435-4544 Office Phone: 952-374-5595. Personal E-mail: concha8@earthlink.net.

MANDEL, SUSAN JENNIFER, physician, educator; b. NYC, May 25, 1960; AB, Harvard U., 1982; MD, Coll. Physicians and Surgeons, Columbia U., 1986. Prof. medicine, dir. clin. endocrinology & diabetes U. Pa., 2007—. Pres. Assn. Program Dirs. Endocrinology, Diabetes and Metabolism, 2009—11; coun. mem. Endocrine Soc., 2009—. Recipient Disting. Educator award, Endocrine Soc., 2011, Louis Duhring Outstanding Clin. Specialist award, Penn Medicine. Fellow: ACP, Am. Assn. Clin. Endocrinologists; mem.: Am. Thyroid Assn. Office: Penn Endocrinology Perelman Ctr W Pavilion Philadelphia PA 19104 Office Fax: 215-614-1949. Business E-Mail: susan.mandel@uphs.upenn.edu.

MANDELBAUM, DAVID EZRA, pediatric neurologist; b. NYC, Oct. 24, 1952; s. Bernard Mandelbaum and Judith Louise Werber; m. Elana Katz, June 24, 1975 (div. Aug. 1992); 1 child, Danya Judith; m. Alison Speckman, Aug. 29, 2004. BA, Columbia U., 1974, MD, PhD, Columbia U., 1980. Diplomate Am. Bd. Pediatrics, Am. Bd. Psychiatry and Neurology; cert. child neurology, clin. neurophysiology, neurodevel. disabilities. Intern Yale-New Haven Hosp., 1980-81, resident in pediat., 1981-82; resident in neurology Neurol. Inst. Columbia-Presbyn. Med. Ctr., NYC, 1982-83, fellow pediat. neurology, 1983-85; dir. divsn. child neurology U. Med. & Dentistry N.J., New Brunswick, 1985—2003, asst. prof. pediat. and neurology, 1985-91, assoc. prof., 1991-2001, prof., 2001—03; prof. clin. neuroscis. and pediatrics Brown U., Providence, 2003—; dir., divsn. child neurology, dept. neurology R.I. and Hasbro Children's Hosps., 2003—; dir. Children's Neurodevel. Ctr., Hasbro Children's Hosp., 2005—. Chief child neurology svc. Robert Wood Johnson U. Hosp., New Brunswick, 1985-2003, St. Peters U. Hosp., New Brunswick, 1985-2003; chmn. profl. adv. bd. Epilepsy Found. N.J., 2002-03 cons., lectr. and presenter in field. Mem. editl. bd. Jour. Child Neurology, Pediatric Neurology; contbr. articles to profl. jours. Bd. dirs. YM/YWHA Raritan Valley, Highland Park, N.J., 1997-2001, Princeton (N.J.) Pro Musica, 1998. Grantee NIH, 1974-80, U. Medicine and Dentistry N.J. Found., 1986-88, Ortho-McNeil Pharm. Corp./Johnson & Johnson, 1997-98, Parke-Davis Corp., 1998, Nat. Alliance for Autism Rsch., 2002-04. Mem. Profs. Child Neurology, Child Neurology Soc., Am. Acad. Pediat., Am. Epilepsy Soc.; fellow: Am. Acad. Neurology. Jewish. Avocations: music, swimming. Office: Prof Office Bldg Ste 342 Providence RI 02906 Home Phone: 401-453-2570; Office Phone: 401-444-4345. Fax: 401-444-3236. E-mail: David_Mandelbaum@brown.edu, dmandelbaum@lifespan.org.

MANDELL, GERALD A., nuclear medicine physician; b. Phila., Dec. 20, 1943; s. Samuel Philip and Ida (Slutsky) M.; m. Susan Perilstein, June 13, 1964 (div. 1989); children: Nathan, Joshua, Geoffrey, Samantha, m. Joanna DiRenzo, Mar. 29, 1991; children: Christian Fermant, Brianne Bailey, Kyle Bailey. BA in Biology, U. Pa., 1965; MD, Jefferson Med. Coll., 1969. Diplomate Am. Bd. Radiology, Am. Bd. Nuclear Medicine, cert. added qualification Am. Bd. Pediatric Radiology. Intern in medicine Albert Einstein Med. Ctr., Phila., 1969-70; resident in diagnostic radiology Thomas Jefferson U. Hosp., Phila., 1970-73; fellow in pediatric radiology Thomas Jefferson U. Hosp./St. Christopher's Hosp. Children, Phila., 1973-74; fellow in nuclear medicine U. Pa. Hosp., 1981-83; assoc. dir. med. imaging A.I. duPont Inst., Wilmington, Del., 1983-93, chief nuclear medicine, 1993—2002; pediat. radiologist Phoenix Children's Hosp., 2002—. Instr. in radiology U. Pa., Phila., 1974-76, asst. prof., 1976-77, adj. assoc. prof. radiology, 1984-92, adj. prof. radiology, 1992-2007; assoc. prof. radiology, assoc. prof. pediatrics Hahneman Med. Coll. and Hosp., Phila., 1979; prof. radiology Jefferson Med. Coll., 1990-2002, prof. radiation therapy and nuclear medicine, 1991-2002; assoc. radiologist Children's Hosp. Phila., 1974-77, dir. radiology residency tng. program, 1974-77, assoc. staff dept. radiology, 1990-03; lectr., presenter in field. Co-author: Imaging Strategies in Pediatric Orthopaedics, 1990; editor Clin. Nuclear Medicine, 1996—; reviewer Jour. Nuclear Medicine, 1987, 94, 99-2001; contbr. numerous articles to profl. publs., chpts. to books. Trustee Samuel P. Mandell Found.; bd. dirs. Del. Guidance Svcs., Wilmington. Recipient Best Doctors in Am. award-N.E., 1997, Best Doctors in Del. award, 1997, Best Doctors in Am., 1998-2002, 2006-08, Top Doctors for Kids Phila. mag., 2001; grantee Soc. for Pediat. Medicine, 1991, Am. Heart Assn., 1991, Mallinckrodt Critical Care, 1992-93. Fellow ACP, Am. Acad. Pediatrics, Am. Coll. Radiology; mem. AMA, Pediatric Radiol. Soc., Soc. Nuclear Medicine (sec.-treas. pediat. coun. 1993, mem. healthcare com. 1993-2001, pres. pediat. coun. 1994-96, past-pres. pediat. coun. 1996-98, mem. ho. dels. 1996-98, Alavi-Mandell prize), Internat. Skeletal Soc., NY Acad. Scis., Phila. Roentgen Ray Soc., Del. Soc. Nuclear Medicine, New Castle County Med. Soc., Del. Radiol. Soc., Del. Med. Soc. (alt. del. 1993-2002). Jewish. Achievements include discovery of isotope method of scanning patients with neurofibromatosis. Home Phone: 602-237-6171; Office Phone: 602-546-1207. Personal E-mail: gmandell@phoenixchildrens.com.

MANDELL, GERALD LEE, internist, educator; b. NYC, Aug. 20, 1936; s. Herman and Sylvia (Keller) M.; m. Judith Rensin Mandell, Dec. 22, 1960; children: James, Pamela, Scott. BA, Cornell U., 1958; MD, Cornell U., NYC, 1962. Diplomate Am. Bd. Internal Medicine. Intern, resident NY Hosp. Cornell Med. Ctr., NYC, 1965-67; instr. Med. Coll., Cornell U., NYC, 1968-69; asst. prof. U. Va., Charlottesville, 1969-71, assoc. prof., 1972-75, prof., 1976—, Owen R. Cheatham prof. sci., 1981—, chief infectious diseases, 1970—2002. Editor: Principles and Practice of Infectious Diseases, 1979, 6th edit., 2005. Lt. comdr. USPHS, 1963-65. Recipient MERIT award NIH, 1986; named Outstanding Alumnus, Cornell Med. Coll, 2002. Master ACP; fellow AAAS, Infectious Diseases Soc. Am. (pres. 1994, Maxwell Finland award 2000), Nat. Inst. Allergy and Infectious Diseases (adv. coun.), Inst. Medicine; mem. Assn. Am. Physicians, Am. Soc. Clin. Investigation (emeritus prof. 2006—), Phi Beta Kappa, Alpha Omega Alpha, Coun. Am. Climatology Soc. (pres. elect 2009). Avocations: photography, tropical fish, sculling.

MANDELL, JAMES, health facility executive, urologist, educator; b. SI, NY, Feb. 20, 1945; s. Gustave and Rose (Zimmerman) M.; m. Valerie Steele, Jan. 20, 1967; children: Joshua Lindstrom, Jeremy Hill, Bethany Shalom. AA, U. Fla., 1965; MD, U. Fla. Coll. Medicine, 1970; MS, Union U., 1999. Am. Bd. Diplomate Urology 1979. Intern U. Fla. Sch. Medicine, Gainesville, 1970-71, resident in surgery, 1971-72; resident in urology U. NC Sch. Medicine, Chapel Hill, 1974-77, fellow in pediatric urology, 1977-78, asst. prof. surgery and pediatrics, 1979-84, assoc. prof., 1984-85; dir. pediatric urology NC Meml. Hosp., Chapel Hill, 1979-85; instr. surgery Harvard U. Med. Sch., Boston, 1978-79, asst. prof. surgery (urology), 1985-90, assoc. prof. surgery, urology, 1990-94, prof. surgery (urology); prof. surgery and pediat., chief divsn. urology, exec. med. dir. Albany Med. Coll., NY, 1994-97, dean NY, 1996-2000; fellow in surgery (urology) Children's Hosp., Boston, 1978-79, asst. in surgery (urology), 1985-90, sr. assoc. surgery, 1990-94, CEO, pres., 2000—. Contbr. numerous articles to med. jours., chpts. to books. Lt. comdr. M.C., USNR, 1972-74. Fellow ACS, Am. Acad. Pediatrics; mem. Am. Urol. Assn. (New England sec.), Soc. Pediatric Urology (exec. com. 1988-92), Soc. Univ. Urologists (pres. 2001-02). Avocations: fishing, skiing, tennis. Office: Children's Hosp Boston Dept Urology Hunnewell 3 300 Longwood Ave Boston MA 02115-5724 Office Phone: 518-355-2080, 617-355-6000. Office Fax: 617-730-0474. Business E-Mail: james.mandell@childrens.harvard.edu.

MANDELL, MARSHALL, pediatrician, allergist, consultant; b. NYC, Feb. 4, 1922; s. Albert and Beatrice (Roth) M.; m. Thelma Sylvia Cantor, Aug. 1, 1944 (div. 1974); children: Joan Arlene, Steven Marshall, Nori Lyn; m. Blanca Aurora Abrego, June 22, 2001. BA in Zoology, U. Conn., 1943; MD, L.I. Coll. Medicine, 1946. Diplomate Am. Bd. Pediat., Pediat. Allergy, Am. Bd. Allergy and Immunology, Am. Bd. Environ. Medicine. Intern in pediat. Yale U. Med. Sch./New Haven Hosp., 1946—47; jr. resident in pediat. St. Louis Children's Hosp./Washington U. Med. Sch., 1949-50; resident in pediat. Gen. Hosps. #1 and #2, Kansas City, Mo., 1950-51; instr., clin. asst. N.Y. Med. Coll., 1955-58, asst. prof. allergy, 1958-80. Adj. prof. nutrition and allergy U. Bridgeport, Conn., 1976—90; cons. in allergy and bio-ecologic disorders in mental illness Fuller Meml. Sanitarium, South Attleboro, Mass., 1972—76; cons. in cerebral allergy Ctr. Neurol. Rehab., Morton, Pa., 1980—; lectr. in field. Author: 5-Day Allergy Relief System, 1979, Lifetime Arthritis Relief System, 1983, It's Not Your Fault You're Fat Diet, 1983; co-author Brian Injury, 1986, The Unsuspected Brain Allergy Connection, 2003; editor: Let's Have Healthy Children, 1981; creator and pub. large print edit. Tom Sawyer; contbr. more than 35 articles to profl. jours. Capt. U.S. Army, 1947-49. Recipient Founders medal demonstrating the role of brain allergy in schizophrenia, Huxley Soc., 2 awards Citizens Commn. Human Rights showing the role of nervous sys. sensitivity to dietary and environ. factors in mental and behavioral disorders. Fellow: Internat. Acad. Nutrition and Preventive Medicine, Acad. Orthomolecular Medicine and Psychiatry (Spl. Commendation for Contbns. to Mental Illness), Am. Acad. Environ. Medicine (Jonathan Forman Gold medal), Am. Coll. Allergy, Asthma and Immunology (mem. com. nervous sys. allergy); mem.: Am. Acad. Allergy, Lions (pres. Norwalk club 1956—58), Phi Sigma Delta (pres. 1941—43). Avocations: medical writing, woodcarving, gardening, swimming. Home and Office: 112 Canterbury Ln Laredo TX 78041 Office Phone: 956-753-0305. Personal E-mail: mmandell@stx.rr.com.

MANDERNACH, DIANNE, medical products executive, former state agency administrator; married; 4 children. Attended, Coll. St. Theresa; BA, Univ. Minn. Cert. Nursing Home Adminstrn. Jr. high sch. teacher, 1976—87; positions through dir. human resources & assoc. adminstr. Mercy Hosp. & Health Care Ctr., Moose Lake, Minn., 1987—94, CEO, 1994—2003; commr. Minn. Dept. Health, Saint Paul, 2003—07; CEO SISU Med. Systems, Duluth, Minn., 2007—. Bd. dir. Minn. Hosp. & Healthcare Partnership. Fellow: Am. Coll. Health Care Executives. Office: SISU Med Systems 5 W 1st St Ste 200 Duluth MN 55802 Office Phone: 218-529-7900. Office Fax: 218-529-7920.

MANDERS, KARL LEE, neurosurgeon; b. Rochester, NY, Jan. 21, 1927; s. David Bert and Frances Edna (Cohan) Mendelson; m. Ann Laprell, July 28, 1969; children: Karlanna Butler, Maidena Fulford-;children from previous marriage: Karl, Kristine Myers, Kerry. Student, Cornell U., 1946; MD, U. Buffalo, 1950. Diplomate Am. Bd. Neurol. Surgery, Am. Bd. Clin. Biofeedback, Am. Bd. Hyperbaric Medicine, Am. Bd. Pain Medicine, Nat. Bd. Med. Examiners. Intern U. Va. Hosp., Charlottesville, 1950-51, resident in neurol. surgery, 1951-52, Henry Ford Hosp., Detroit, 1954-56; pvt. practice Indpls., 1956—. Med. dir. Cmty. Hosp. Rehab. Ctr. Pain, 1973—92; chief hosp. med. and surg. neurology Cmty. Hosp., 1983, 93; coroner Marion County, Ind., 1977—85, 1992—96; with Ind. Med. Om Bund Sman, 2009. With USN, 1952—54, Korea. Recipient cert. Achievement, Dept. Army, 1969, Disting. Physician award, Cmty. Hosp., 1997, Cert. of Distinction, Ind. State Med. Assn., Am.'s Top Surgeon award, Cosumers Rsch. Coun. Am., 2002. Fellow: ACS, Harvey Cushing Soc., Am. Acad. Neurology, Internat. Coll. Surgeons; mem.: AMA, Med. Expert Soc. Sec. Adminstrn., Marion County Med. Soc., Ind. Med. Soc., James McClure Surg. Soc., Am. Bd. Med. Psychotherapists (mem. profl. adv. coun.), James A. Gibson Anat. Soc., Internat. Soc. Aquatic Medicine, Interurban Neurosurg. Soc., Ctrl. Neurol. Soc., Am. Acad. Pain Medicine, Midwest Pain Soc. (pres. 1988), Am. Pain Soc., Nat. Assn. Med. Examiners, Royal Soc. Medicine, Ind. Coroners Assn. (pres. 1979), Soc. Computerized Tomography and Neuroimaging, Am. Soc. Stereotaxic and Functional Neurosurgery, N.Am. Spine Soc., Internat. Back Pain Soc., Pan Am. Med. Assn., Acad. Psychosomatic Medicine, Biofeedback Soc. Am., Pan Pacific Surg. Assn., Soc. Cryosurgery, Am. Assn. Biofeedback Clinicians, Am. Acad. Forensic Sci., Undersea Med. Soc., Am. Holistic Med. Assn. (co-founder), Am. Soc. Contemporary Medicine and Surgery, Am. Coll. Angiology, NY Acad. Scis., Am. Assn. Study Headache, Internat. Assn. Study Pain, Congress Neurol. Surgery, Am. Legion, Sci. Tech. Club, Brendonwood Country Club, Highland Country Club, Phi Chi Med. Fraternity (mem. vol. medicine). Home and Office: 5845 High Fall Rd Indianapolis IN 46226-1018 Office Phone: 317-546-6691. Personal E-mail: karllmandersmd@hotmail.com.

MANDERS, STEVEN M., dermatologist, educator; Attended, UMDNJ-Robert Wood Johnson Med. Sch., Piscataway, NJ. Diplomate Am. Bd. Dermatology, Am. Bd. Dermatology-pediatric dermatology. Intern Robert Wood Johnson Univ. Hosp., New Brunswick, NJ; resident dermatology Univ. Cin. Med. Ctr., Cin.; prof. medicine and pediat. Cooper Univ. hosp. UMDNJ-Robert Wood Johnson Med. Sch.; dir. pediatric dermatology Cooper Univ. Hosp. Named Top Doctor, Phila. Mag., NJ Monthly, South Jersey Mag. Mem.: Soc. of Pediatric Dermatology, Am. Acad. of Dermatology. Office: Heymann Manders Green LLC Ste 306 100 Brick Rd Marlton NJ 08053 Mailing: Cooper University Hospital Ste 200 Camden NJ 08103 Office Phone: 856-596-0111, 856-342-2001. Office Fax: 856-596-7194, 856-968-8318.

MANDERSCHEID, RONALD WILLIAM, program administrator; s. William Joseph and Norene Elsine (Batteen) M.; m. Frances Elizabeth Fedkiw, Sept. 1, 1973; children: William Derrick, Kristen Elizabeth, Erika Marie. BA maxima cum laude, Loras Coll., 1965; MA, Marquette U., 1967; PhD, U. Md., 1975; Cert., Fed. Exec. Inst., 1986. Rsch. asst. U. Md., College Park, 1970—72; rsch. assoc. NIMH, Adelphi, Md., 1972—75, sr. rsch. sociologist, 1975—80, chief evaluation rsch. sect. Rockville, Md., 1980—81, chief stats. rsch. br., 1981—92; acting dir. divsn. state and cmty. sys. devel. Ctr. Mental Health Svcs., Rockville, 1992—93, chief survey & analysis, 1992—2006; sr. prin., dir. mental health and substance use program Global Health Sector/SRA, Rockville, 2006—11; exec. dir. Nat. Assn. County Behavioral Health and Devel. Disability Dirs., 2009—. Cons. George Washington U., Washington, 1978-83, WHO, 1993—, Pan Am. Health Orgn., 1995—, Columbia U., 1998-2001; mem. Internat. Consortium Mental Health Policy & Rsch., 2000—; adj. prof. dept. mental health Bloomberg Sch. Pub. Health, Johns Hopkins U., Balt., 2006—; HHS Sec.'s Adv. Group Health People 2020, 2008-; bd. mem. Frameworks Inst., 2010-. Author, editor: Mental Health in the United States, 1987, 90, 92, 94, 96, 98, 2000, 02, 04; editor: System Science and the Future of Health, 1976; prodr.: Making the Numbers Work for You, 1987; spl. editor Jour. of Washington Acad. Scis., 2000, Internat. Jour. Mental Health, 1998, 2005, 07, 08; contbr. articles to profl. jours. Active West Montgomery Citizens Assn., Potomac, Md., 1983—. With U.S. Army, 1967-69. Decorated Army Commendation medal; recipient Disting. Alumni award, Loras Coll., 1998, Sec. Disting. Svc. award, Dept. Health and Human Svcs., 1999, Dept. Health and Human Sevcs., 2004, 2005, 2006, 2008, Mental Health Stats. Improvement Program Leadership award, 2001, Dept. Health and Human Svcs., 2006, Irving Blumberg Humanitarian award, Am. Assn. for Psychosocial Rehab., 2002, Stuart A. Rice award, DC Sociol. Soc., 2011. Fellow Washington Acad. Scis. (life, pres. 1987-88), World Acad. Art and Sci.; mem. APHA (chair mental health 1997-98, Mental Health Sect. award 2000, Mental Health Chairperson's Disting. Svc. award 2001, Consumer Leadership award 2003, governing coun. 2007-10), NY Acad. Scis., Am. Sociol. Assn. (chmn. various coms. 1983-91), chmn. com. fed. stds. sociologists 1983-88), Soc. for Gen. Sys. Rsch. (chmn. Washington chpt. 1976—2010), Ea. Sociol. Soc. (exec. com. 1979-84, chmn. various coms., Peter Gellman award 1984), D.C. Sociol. Soc. (pres. 1992-93), Fed. Exec. Inst. Alumni Assn. (exec. bd. 1997-2005, chair policy issues com. 1995-2000, pres. 2003, pres. found. 2003—11, Meritorious Svc. award 1999), Soc. Applied Sociology (Nat. Sociol. Practice award 1995), Nat. Assn. State Mental Health Program Dirs. (Disting. Svc. tribute 2006), Am. Coll. Mental Health Adminstrs. (Saul Feldman Lifetime Achievement award 2003, Disting. Svc. award 2006, exec. bd. 2007-11, pres. 2011-), Nat. Coun. Cmty. Behavioral Healthcare (Pub. Svc. award 2006), Cosmos Club, Farmington Country Club, Alpha Kappa Delta (pres. 1972-73), Delta Epsilon Sigma, Phi Kappa Phi. Avocations: coin collecting/numismatics, reading. Office: Nat Assn County Behavioral Health and Devel Disability Dirs Ste 500 25 Massachusetts Ave NW Washington DC 20001 Office Phone: 202-942-4296. Office Fax: 202-661-8871. Business E-Mail: rmanderscheid@nacbhd.org.

MANDERSON, EASTON L., orthopedist, surgeon; arrived in U.S., 1963; s. Caleb Sterling and Beatrice Anita Manderson; m. Lois Constance Manderson; children: Tanya Michelle, Mario Sean, Keisha Anita Rochelle. BS cum laude, Howard U., 1967, MD, 1971. Diplomate Am. Bd. Orthopedic Surgery, Am. Bd. Ind. Med. Examiners. Rotating intern Freedmen's Hosp., Howard U., 1971—72; orthop. resident Howard U., 1972—75; pediat. orthop. fellow/resident Johns Hopkins U. Med. Sch.; med. officer DC Gen. Hosp., Washington, 1975—2001, chief orthopedic surgery, 1995—2001; pvt. practice Riggs Orthopedic Clinic, Washington, 1978—. Clin. instr. Howard U. Med. Sch., Washington, 1975—90, asst. prof., 1990—. Contbr. articles to profl. jours. Fellow: ACS, Am. Acad. Orthopedic Surgeons. Achievements include patents for extra medullary rod fixateur for long bone fracture; sub muscular and incision technique; jigless intra medullary nail with easy locking; intra medullary screw for fusion of ankles with complex deformities. Avocations: jogging, weightlifting, reading. Office: Riggs Orthopaedic Clinic 1140 Varnum St NE Washington DC 20017 Office Phone: 202-526-5300.

MANDIL, AHMED MA, epidemiologist, educator; b. Alexandria, Egypt, July 28, 1958; MBChB, Alexandria U., 1981; DPH, UCLA Sch. Pub. Health, 1991. Prof. epidemiology & pub. health Alexandria U. - High Inst. Pub. Health, Egypt, 2002—08; prof. epidemiology, coord. cmty. medicine unit King Saud U. - Coll. Medicine, Saudi Arabia, 2008—. Dean, Coll. Health Scis. U. Sharjah, United Arab Emirates, 2004—06; cons. WHO, Health Action Crises, Geneva, 2006—07. Recipient award, Model Studentof U., U. Alexandria. Mem.: Egyptian Med. Syndicate, Egyptian Pub. Health Assn., Internat. Epidemiol. Assn. (sec. 2002—11). Avocations: reading, accordion, sports. Home: 38 Ismailiah St Mostafa Kamel Alexandria 00127 Egypt Home Fax: (203)5467576. Personal E-mail: ahmed.mandil@yahoo.com.

MANDLER, GEORGE, psychologist, educator; b. Vienna, June 11, 1924; came to U.S., 1940, naturalized, 1943; s. Richard and Hede (Goldschmied) M.; m. Jean Matter, Jan. 19, 1957; children: Peter Clark, Michael Allen. BA, NYU, 1949; MS, Yale U., 1950, PhD, 1953; post grad., U. Basel, Switzerland, 1947-48; PhD (hon.), U. Vienna, 2009. Asst. prof. Harvard U., 1953-57, lectr., 1957-60; prof. U Toronto, 1960—65; prof. psychology U. Calif., San Diego, 1965-94, chmn. dept. psychology, 1965-70, disting. prof. emeritus, 1994—; dir. Ctr. Human Info. Processing, U. Calif., San Diego, 1965-90. Hon. rsch. fellow Univ. Coll. London., 1977-78, 82-90, vis. prof., 1990—. Author: Mind and Emotion, 1975, (German edit.), 1980, Mind and Body, 1984, (Japanese edit.), 1987, Cognitive Psychology, 1985, Japanese edit., 1991, Human Nature Explored, 1997, Interesting Times, 2001, Consciousness Recovered, 2002, A History of Modern Experiemental Psychology, 2007; co-author: (with W. Kessen) The Language of Psychology, (Italian edit.), 1959, (with J.M. Mandler) Thinking: From Association to Gestalt, 1964; contbr. articles and revs. to profl. jours.; editor: Psychol. Rev., 1970-76. Served with U.S. Army, 1943-46. Fellow Ctr. for Advanced Study in Behavioral Scis., 1959-60; vis. fellow Oxford U., Eng., 1971-72, 78; Guggenheim fellow, 1971-72. Fellow AAAS, Am. Acad. Arts and Scis.; mem. AAUP, Am. Assn. Advancement Psychology (1974-82); Psychonomic Soc. (governing bd., chmn. 1983), Am. Psychol. Soc., Am. Psychol. Assn. (pres. div. exptl. psychology 1978-79, pres. div. gen psychology 1982-83, mem. coun. reps. 1978-82, William James prize 1986), Internat. Union Psychol. Scis. (U.S. com. 1985-90), Soc. Exptl. Psychologists, Fedn. Behavioral Psychol. and Cognitive Scis. (pres. 1981). Home: 1406 La Jolla Knoll La Jolla CA 92037-5236 Office: U Calif San Diego Dept Psychology La Jolla CA 92093-0109 also: 3 Perrins Lane London NW3 1QY England Business E-Mail: gmandler@ucsd.edu.

MANDLER, JEAN MATTER, psychologist, educator; b. Oak Park, Ill., Nov. 6, 1929; d. Joseph Allen and May Roberts (Finch) Matter; m. George Mandler, Jan. 19, 1957; children: Peter Clark, Michael Allen. Student, Carleton Coll., 1947-49; BA with highest honors, Swarthmore Coll., 1951; PhD, Harvard U., 1956. Rsch. assoc. lab. social rels. Harvard U., 1957-60; rsch. assoc. dept. psychology U. Toronto, Ont., Canada, 1961-65; assoc. rsch. psychologist, lectr. U. Calif. at San Diego, La Jolla, 1965-73, assoc. prof., 1973-77, prof. psychology, 1977-88, co-founder dept. cognitive sci., 1986, prof. cognitive sci. La Jolla, 1988—96, disting. prof., 1996—2000, disting. rsch. prof., 2000—; mem. adv. com. memory and cognitive processes NSF, 1978-81. Hon. rsch. fellow U. Coll., London, 1978-89, vis. prof., 1990—; hon. mem. Med. Rsch. Coun. Cognitive Devel. Unit, 1982-98. Author: (G. Mandler) Thinking: From Association to Gestalt, 1964, Stories, Scripts and Scenes, 1984, The Foundations of Mind: Origins of Conceptual Thought, 2004 (APA Divsn. 7 Eleanor Maccoby Book award 2005, Cognitive Devel. Soc. Best Authored Book award 2006); assoc. editor Psychol. rev., 1970-76; mem. editl. bd. Child Devel., 1976-89, Discourse Processes, 1977-94, Jour. Exptl. Psychology, 1977-85, Text, 1979-97, Jour. Verbal Learning and Verbal Behavior, 1980-88, Lang. and Cognitive Processes, 1985-2008, Cognitive Devel., 1990-99, Jour. Cognition and Devel., 1999-2008; contbr. articles to profl. jours Pres. San Diego Assn. Gifted Children, 1968-71; v.p. Calif. Parents for Gifted, 1970-71; mem. alumni council Swarthmore Coll., 1975-78. Recipient Disting. Scientific Contrbn. award, Am. Psychol. Assn., 2007; NIMH research grantee, 1968—81, NSF research grantee, 1981—99. Fellow: APA (mem. exec. com. divsn. 3 1983—85), Am. Acad. Arts and Scis.; mem.: Soc. Exptl. Psychologists, Cognitive Devel. Soc., Cognitive Sci. Soc., Psychonomic Soc. (mem. governing bd. 1982—87, chmn. 1985—86), Phi Beta Kappa. Office: U Calif San Diego Dept Cognitive Sci 9500 Gilman Dr La Jolla CA 92093-0515 Business E-Mail: jmandler@ucsd.edu.

MANDREKAR, PRANOTI, science educator; b. Mumbai, Aug. 11, 1964; PhD, U. Bombay, 1991. Asst. prof. U. Mass. Med. Sch., 2002—08, assoc. prof., 2008—. Grantee Basic Rsch. award, Dept. Def.; grant, NIH. Mem.: AAAS, Soc. Leukocyte Biology, Rsch. Soc. Alcoholicm. Office: 364 Plantation St Worcester MA 01605 Business E-Mail: pranoti.mandrekar@umassmed.edu.

MANDSAGER, RICHARD, hospital administrator; MD. Ret. asst. surgeon gen. USPHS Commissioned Corps; staff pediatrician South-central Found.; dir., Anchorage svc. unit Alaska Native Med. Ctr., dir., med. dir., pediatric svc. ctr. Anchorage, 2000—04; dir. Public Health Alaska Dept. Health & Social Svc., Juneau, 2004—06; exec. dir. Children's Hosp. at Providence, Anchorage, 2006—. Office: Children's Hosp 3200 Providence Dr Anchorage AK 99508 Office Phone: 907-561-2211.

MANDY, STEPHEN HOWARD, dermatologist, educator; b. Balt., Jan. 6, 1943; s. Arthur Jennings and Sylvia Bliss Mandy; 1 child, Ashley Jacqueline. BA, George Washington U., 1962, MD, 1966. Cert. dermatology Am. Bd. Dermatology, 1972. Intern U. Fla., Gainesville, 1966—67; resident ob-gyn. Sinai Hosp., Balt., 1967—68; resident dermatology Johns Hopkins, Balt., 1968—69, U. Miami, Fla., 1969—71; pvt. practice South Miami, 1973—91, Aspen, Colo., 1991—2003, South Miami Beach, Fla., 2003—; chmn. bd. and founder DVM Pharm., 1976—92; clin. prof. dermatology U. Miami, Fla., 1982—; chmn. bd. Sirius Pharm., 2005—. Chmn. bd. Dermatologics For Vet. Medicine, Miami, 1976—92; pres. Am. Soc. for Dermatologic Surgery, Rolling Meadows, Ill., 2000—01. Contbr. articles to profl. jours. Maj. USAF, 1971—73. Jewish. Avocations: skiing, travel, photography. Office: South Beach Dermatology 555 Washington Ave Ste 210 Miami Beach FL 33139 Office Fax: 305-673-6422. *

MANE, ARATI KISHOR, research scientist; b. Pune, Apr. 23, 1978; MBBS, Bj Med. Coll., Pune, 2001, MD in Microbiology, 2005. Asst. prof. Bj Med. Coll., 2005—07; scientist B Nat. Aids Rsch. Inst., 2007—. Mem.: Indian Assn. Med. Microbiologists. Avocations: horseback riding, swimming, reading. Office: National Aids Research Inst 73 G Block MIDC Bhosari Pune Maharashtra 411026 India E-mail: arati2478mane@rediffmail.com.

MANENTI, LUCIO, nephrologist; b. Salo-Brescia, Italy, Dec. 7, 1969; MD, U. Parma, 1995. Nephrology specialist U. Parma, 1999. Physician Hosp. Parma, 2001—. Splty. prof. U. Parma, 2011. Mem.: Italian Soc. Nephrology. Office: Via Gramsci 14 Parma 43125 Italy Business E-Mail: lmanenti@ao.pr.it.

MANESS, LISA RENA, microbiologist; b. NC, Apr. 19, 1974; MS in Biology, U. NC, Greensboro, 2003; degree in Energy and Environ. Sys., NC A&T State U., 2010. Postdoc. rschr. NC A&T State U., 2001—. Med. technologist Solstas Lab., 1997; adj. prof. Winston-Salem State U., 2003; HS tchr. Guilford County Schs., Winston-Salem Forsyth County Sch., 2005. Mem.: Am. Soc. Microbiology. Avocations: motorcycling, reading, tennis. Home: 2001 Whites Mill Rd High Point NC 27265 Business E-Mail: lmwishon@ncat.edu.

MANFREDINI, DANIELE, dentist, researcher; b. Carrara, Italy, Nov. 5, 1975; s. Pierluigi Manfredini and Dania Ferretti; m. Debora Rossi; children: Aurora, Giacomo. D in Dentistry, U. Pisa, 1999, M in Occlusion and Temporomandibular Disorders, 2001. Board Certified Diplomate Italian Soc. Prosthetic Dentistry, 2003, Italian Soc. Temporomandibular Disorders, 2003. Rsch. fellow Dept. Neuroscience; U. Pisa, 1999—2001, rsch. asst., 2001—03; head of rsch. activities Sect. Prosthetic Dentistry, Dept. Neuroscience, U. Pisa, 2003—; dir. Orofacial Pain Clinic, Marina di Carrara, Italy, 2004—. Cons. Novartis Pharma, Switzerland, 2003—, Nat. Inst. Healthcare Advisors, 2004—, Biomax, Italy, 2004—, Italian Nat. Inst. Health, Rome, 2004—, Legal Medicine Italian Com., Rome, 2005—, Intra-Lock, Italy, 2005—; vis. prof. Sect. Prosthetic Dentistry, Dept. Neuroscience, U. Pisa, 2006—, Dept. Oral and Maxillofacial Surgery, U. Padua, Italy, 2006—; chief editor Archives Legal Medicine and Dentistry, 2007—. Contbr. articles to profl. jours. Recipient First Pl. Winner, Am. Acad. of Orofacial Pain, 2005, First Pl. Winner (TMD), Italian Universities Ann. Meeting, 2004, 2002, Second Pl. Winner (TMD), 2005, 2001, Third Pl. Winner (Sci. Contbn. on TMD), 2003. Mem.: Italian Soc. Oral and Maxillo-Facial Surgery (assoc.), Italian Soc. Temporomandibular Disorders (assoc.), Italian Soc. Prosthetic Dentistry (assoc.). Achievements include research in masticatory muscles EMG activity. Avocations: exercise, sports. Office: Orofacial Pain Clinic Via Ingolstadt 3 Ms Marina di Carrara 54036 Italy Home: Viale XX Settembre 298 54036 Marina di Carrara MS Italy Office Fax: 0039 0585 630964. E-mail: daniele.manfredini@tin.it.

MANGAN, KENNETH F., hematologist; MD, George Wash. U., 1973; Clin. and Rsch. Subspecialty training in Hematology, Tufts-New England Med. Ctr., Boston, Mass., 1976—79. Diplomate Am. Bd. Internal Medicine, 1976, Am. Bd. Internal Medicine-hematology, 1978. Intern George Wash. Univ., resident; faculty mem. Albany Med. Coll., Pitts. Univ., 1981; Fox Chase temple mem. Fox Chase Cancer Ctr.; pres. Hematology- Oncology Soc., 1995—98; prof. medicine Temple Univ., assoc. prof. microbiology and immunology; dir. temple bone marrow transplant program Temple Univ. Hosp. Pub. (180 journ. articles, book chapters and/ or abstracts). Fellow Nat. Leukemia Associated Fellowship. Office: Temple University Hospital 2450 W Hunting Park Ave Philadelphia PA 19129 Office Phone: 215-707-2000.

MANGANARO, AGATINO, physician, educator; b. Messina, Italy, June 15, 1951; MD, U. Messina, 1976. Prof. cardiovasc. diseases U. Hosp., Messina, 1998—. Mem.: Italian Soc. Angiology and Vascular Pathology, Italian Soc. Cardiology. Home: via Michele Mari 7 Messina Sicilia 98122 Italy Home Fax: 090712092. Personal E-mail: manganaro51@unime.it.

MANGANO, SALVATORE NICHOLAS, retired surgeon; b. Cambridge, Mass., 1922; s. Santo and Rose (Costa) M.; m. Anna Barney Stevenson, Apr. 28, 1956; children: Paul Stephen, John Joseph, Mary Ellen (dec.). AB, Harvard U., 1944; MD, Tufts U., 1947. Diplomate Am. Bd. Surgery. Intern Cambridge City Hosp., 1947-48, resident in surgery, 1949-51; resident Carney Hosp., Boston, 1948-49; pvt. practice gen. and colon-rectal surgery, 1953-90; cons. Mass. Dept. Correction, 1990—2007. Surgeon Lemuel Shattuck, Boston; asst. clin. prof. surgery Tufts U. Sch. Medicine, 1994—. Capt. USAF, 1951-53. Fellow ACS; mem. Am. Soc. Colorectal Surgery, Nat. Bd. Med. Examiners, Mass. Bd. Registration in Medicine (sec. 1984-87), Fedn. State Med. Bds. (cert. of appreciation 1987), Middlesex Dist. Med. Soc. (exec. sec. 1970-2007). Roman Catholic. Personal E-mail: snmangano@gmail.com. *

MANGER, WILLIAM MUIR, internist, educator, writer, research scientist; b. Greenwich, Conn., Aug. 13, 1920; s. Julius and Lilian (Weissinger) M.; m. Lynn Seymour Sheppard, May 30, 1964; children: William Muir, Jr., Lilian Wade (Mrs. Porter Fleming), Stewart Sheppard, Charles Seymour. BS, Yale U., 1944; MD, Columbia U., 1946; PhD, Mayo Found., U. Minn., 1958. Diplomate Nat. Bd. Med. Examiners, Am. Bd. Internal Medicine. Intern Presbyn. Hosp., NYC, 1946-47, resident, 1949-50, asst. physician, 1957—2001; fellow internal medicine Mayo Found., 1950-55; dir. Manger Rsch. Found., 1961-77; clin. asst. attending physician Columbia divsn. Bellevue Hosp., 1964-68; asst. attending physician NYU Bellevue Hosp., 1969-77, assoc. attending physician, 1977-83, attending physician, 1983—; instr. medicine Columbia U. Coll. Physicians and Surgeons, 1957-66, assoc. medicine, 1966-70, lectr. emeritus, 1991—. Asst. attending physician Presbyn. Hosp., 1966—68; asst. clin. prof. medicine NYU Med. Ctr., 1968—75, assoc. clin. prof. medicine, 1975—83, clin. prof. medicine, 1983—; mem. devel. com. Mayo Clinic, 1981; vice chmn. bd. Manger Hotels, Inc., 1957—73, 1990—2004; former mem. nat. high blood pressure edn. program NIH. Co-author: Chemical Quantitation of Epinephrine and Norepinephrine in Plasma, 1959, Pheochromocytoma, 1977, Clinical and Experimental Pheochromocytoma, 1996, 100 Questions and Answers About Hypertension, 2001, Our Greatest Threats, 2006; author: Catecholamines in Normal and Abnormal Cardiac Function, 1982; editor, co-author: Hormones and Hypertension, 1966; editor: Am. Lecture Series in Endocrinology, 1962-75; guest editor First Irvine H. Page Internat. Hypertension Rsch. Symposium, 1990; contbr. articles to profl. and lay jours. Mem. bd. govs. St. Albans Sch., Washington, 1958-64, 83-89, chmn., 1962-64, 67-69; trustee Found. Rsch. in Medicine and Biology, 1971-77, Buckley Sch., 1975-85, Lycee Francais, NY, 1996-98, Found. for Advancement Internat. Rsch. in Microbiology, 1977-82, Thyroid Found., 1980-85; mem. bd. visitors Boston U. Med. Sch., 1992—; trustee Found. for Depression and Manic Depression, 1978-89, pres., 1980-89; elder Presbyn. Ch., 1968-70, 92-93, trustee, 1962-67, 80-84, deacon, 1959-61; founder Values Initiative Tchg. About Lifestyle program to combat obesity, 2002. Lt. (j.g.) MC, USNR, 1947-49. Recipient Mayo Found. Alumni award for Meritorious Rsch., 1955, Disting. Alumnus award, 1992, Alumni Svc. award St. Albans Sch., 2007. Fellow ACP, Acad. Psychosomatic Medicine, Am. Geriatric Soc., Coun. on Geriatric Cardiology, NY Acad. Medicine (admission com. 1976-78, edn. com. 1979-92) Am. Coll. Cardiology, Am. Coll. Clin. Pharmacology, Royal Soc. Health, Am. Inst. Chemists; Nat. Hypertension Assn. (founder, trustee, chmn. 1977—), AMA, Am. Soc. Internal Medicine, NY State Med. Soc., NY County Med. Soc., Am. Heart Assn. (fellow coun. on circulation and coun. for high blood pressure rsch.), Inter-Am. Soc. Hypertension, Internat. Soc. Hypertension, Am. Soc. Hypertension (designated hypertension specialist), Am. Thoracic Soc., NY Acad. Sci., AAAS, Am. Physiol. Soc., Am. Chem. Soc., Am. Soc. Pharmacology and Exptl. Therapeutics, Am. Soc. for Clin. Pharmacology and Therapeutics, Clin. Autonomic Rsch. Soc., Am. Autonomic Soc., Med. Strollers, NYC, Endocrine Soc., Pan Am. Med. Assn., Harvey Soc., Soc. Exptl. Biology and Medicine, Rsch. Discussion Group (founding mem., sec.-treas. 1958-80), Am. Fedn. Clin. Rsch. Am. Soc. Nephrology, Royal Soc. Medicine (affiliate), Fellows Assn. Mayo Found. (v.p., pres. 1953), Mayo Alumni Assn. (v.p. 1981-82, exec. com. 1981-89, pres. elect 1982-85, pres. 1985-87), Chatecholamine Club (founder, sec.-treas. 1967-80, pres. 1981-82), Pheochromocytom Rsch. Support Orgn. (pres. and treas. 2005—), Drs. Mayo Soc., Plummer Soc., Albert Gallatin Assocs., The 1941 Soc., New Eng. Soc., SAR (chmn. admissions com 1959-67, bd. mgrs. 1959-67, 69-70), Soc. Colonial Wars, Soc. of the Cin., Sigma Xi, Nu Sigma Nu, Phi Delta Theta, Explorers, Meadow (L.I., NY), Univ. Club, NY Athletic Club (NYC), Southampton Bathing Corp. Achievements include research on the mechanism of salt-induced hypertension, the mechanism whereby potassium lowers blood pressure and prevents stroke, and on pheochromocytoma. Home: 8 E 81st St New York NY 10028-0201 Home Phone: 212-772-3068; Office Phone: 212-689-0873. Fax: 212-447-7032. Personal E-mail: nathypertension@aol.com.

MANGO, CHRISTINA ROSE, psychiatric art therapist; b. Garden City, NY, May 13, 1962; d. Camillo Andrew and Dorothy Mae (Harrison) Mango; m. Keith Hurdman, Sept. 11, 1993 (div. 2001); children: Clarissa Rose Hurdman, Andrew James Hurdman. BFA summa cum laude, Coll. of New Rochelle, 1984; MA, NYU, 1987. Lic. Creative Arts Therapist, Registered art therapist; bd. cert. structural family therapy tng.; cert. psycho-edn. multi family therapy tng. Art therapist Bronx Mcpl. Hosp. Ctr., 1984-88; clin. supr. Fordham-Tremont Cmty. Mental Health Ctr., Bronx, 1988-98, unit dir., 1998—2009; asst. dir. rehab. svc. Bronx Fegs, 2009—10; art dir. PROS, 2010—. Art therapy fieldworker Bronx State Hosp., 1984, art therapy intern Bronx Children's Hosp., 1985, Saint Lukes Hosp., N.Y.C., 1986. Contbr. articles to profl. jours. Mem. N.Y. Art Therapy Assn., No. N.J. Art Therapists Assn., Am. Art Therapy Assn. Home: 234 Garfield St Haworth NJ 07641-1420 Office: FEGS 3600 Jerome Ave Bronx NY 10456 Office Phone: 718-881-7600 ext 397. Personal E-mail: crm07641@yahoo.com.

MANGONI, MARCELLINA, hematologist, director; b. Salsomaggiore, July 22, 1946; Chief Haematology Unit Bone Marrow Transplantation ctr., 2000—10, head, 2010, dir. Sch. U. Parma, 2010—. Tchr. med. sch. Parma U., 1975—. Rsch. Activity grant, CNR MIUR. Mem.: Italian Soc Exptl. Hematology SIES, Italian Soc Hematology SIE, Ebmt Iseh. Avocation: music art gardening. Office: Via Gramsci 14 Parma 43126 Italy Office Fax: 30 521033264. Business E-Mail: marcellina.mangoni@unipr.it.

MANGUN, CLARKE WILSON, JR., public health physician, consultant; b. Iowa Falls, Iowa, Feb. 12, 1919; s. Clarke Wilson and Vallie Hazel (Hoffman) M.; m. Edith Lauretta DuBois, May 13, 1945; children: Edith Ann, Nancy June, Laura Jane. BS, U. Iowa, 1940, MD, 1943; MPH, Columbia U., 1947. Diplomate Am. Bd. Preventive Medicine. Commd. officer USPHS, 1945-66; med. adminstr. Am. Hosp. Assn., Chgo., 1966-67, Chgo. Heart Assn., 1967-68, AMA, Chgo., 1969-80; long-term cons. Abbott Labs., North Chicago, Ill., 1980—2004. Recipient award Nat. Bd. Med. Examiners, 1944. Fellow APHA, Am. Coll. Preventive Medicine; mem. AMA (Physician's Recognition award, 1970—). Avocations: photography, travel, gardening. Home: 14001 W 92s St Apt 322 Lenexa KS 66215 Home Phone: 913-495-9995.

MANHEIMER, ERIC, medical researcher; Lab rsch. asst. dept. physiology U. Md. Sch. Medicine, 1993—95, database mgr & rsch. asst. dept. epidemiology, 1995—97, fellow Baltimore Cochrane Ctr., 1997—98, rsch. assoc. Ctr. for Integrative Medicine, 2003—; intern CDC Pub. Health Program Office, 1995; program analyst & intern NIH Office of Dietary Supplements, 1996—97; coord. & methodologist Brown U. New England Cochrane Ctr., 1998—2002; adminstr. Cochrane Collaboration Complementary Medicine Field, 2003—. Office: Kernan Hospital 2200 Kernan Dr Baltimore MD 21207-6997 Office Phone: 410-440-6071. Office Fax: 410-448-6875. E-mail: emanheimer@compmed.umm.edu.

MANHOLD, JOHN HENRY, dental educator, consultant; b. Rochester, NY, Aug. 20, 1919; s. John Henry and Helen Martha (Shulz) Manhold; m. Beverly Schecter, 1953 (div. 1969); 1 child; m. Enriqueta Andino, Mar. 20, 1971. BA, U. Rochester, 1940; MD, Harvard U., 1944; MA, Washington U., 1956. Instr. Coll. Medicine Tufts U., Boston, 1948—50; asst. prof., chmn. gen. and oral pathology Coll. Dentistry U. Washington, St. Louis, 1954—56; from asst. prof. to prof., chmn. dept. gen. and oral pathology Seton Hall Coll. Medicine and Dentistry (now U. Medicine and Dentistry NJ), Newark, 1956—87; med. dir. Woog Internat., 1987—89; ret., 1989. Cons. Johnson & Johnson, New Brunswick, NJ, 1960—70, Richardson-Vicks, Shelton, Conn., 1981—87, Los Produits Associes, Geneva, 1965—87, Health Care Devel. Group NJ, 1990—2005, Health Care Devel. Group Pa., 1990—2005, Consumer Comm. Network NY, 1990—2005, Consumer Comm. Network Conn., 1990—2008; lectr. in field. Author: Introductory Psychosomatic Dentistry, 1956, Outline of Pathology, 1960; editor: Clinical Oral Diagnosis, 1965; author: Tissue Respiration and Oxigenating Agents, 1977, Practical Dental Management: Patients and Practice, 1984; author: (in 4 langs.) Illustrated Dental Terminology: A Lexicon for the Dental Profession, 1985; author: (with others) Handbook of Pathology, 1987; author: (novels) El Tigre, 2007, The Elymais Coin, 2008, Lobo, 2009; editor: Clinical Preventive Dentistry Jour., 1979—92; contbr. articles to profl. jours. Recipient Pres. award, Alumni Assn. U. Medicine and Dentistry NJ, 1980, Letter Appreciation, Asara Mihara former min. Japan, 1980, Cert. Achievement, U. Md., 1965, Hist. category book award, Nat. Indie Excellence, 2008, Western Category Book award, 2008, Best Book award, 2008, Suspense Category Book award, 2009, Book award, 2010, Lifetime Achievement award, 2009; named Disting. Alumni, Harvard U., 1989; named to Sr. Soc. Harvard Sch. Dental Medicine, 1984. Fellow: Acad. Psychosomatic Medicine (sec. 1975—76, treas. 1976—77, pres. 1977—78), Internat. Coll. Dentists, Am. Coll. Dentists; mem.: APA, AZ Authors, Fla. Writers Assn., AZ Book Pub. Assoc., Western Writers of Am., Internat. Assn. Dental Rsch., Am. Soc. Clin. Pathologists, St. Petersburg Yacht Club, Sigma Xi. Home and Office: 13844 Wood Duck Cir Lakewood Ranch FL 34202-8297 Personal E-mail: kupferce@cox.net.

MANIACI, MICHAEL JOSEPH, medical educator; b. Mo., Jan. 1, 1976; MD, St. Louis U., 2003. Asst. prof., medicine Mayo Clinic, Fla., 2007—. Office: 4500 San Pablo Rd Jacksonville FL 32224 Business E-Mail: maniaci.michael@mayo.edu.

MANIATIS, THEODORE, pulmonologist, educator; Attended, SUNY Med. Ctr., 1980. Diplomate Am. Bd. Internal Medicine-pulmonary disease medicine, Am. Bd. Internal Medicine-critical care medicine, Am. Bd. Internal Medicine-geriatric medicine, Am. Bd. Internal Medicine. Splty. tng. Univ. Medicine and Dentistry, NJ, fellow in pulmonary disease NJ, 1983—85; asst. clin. prof. medicine SUNY Downstate; intern SI Univ. Hosp., NY, resident in internal medicine, 1981—83, dir. critical care svc., assoc. chmn. medicine dept.; physician Pulmonary Assocs. P.C. Office: Staten Island Pulmonary Associates 501 Seaview Ave Staten Island NY 10305 Office Phone: 718-980-5700. Office Fax: 718-980-5499.

MANIS, MELVIN, psychologist, educator; b. NYC, Feb. 18, 1931; s. Alex and Hanna (Oyle) M.; m. Jean Denby, May 28, 1954; children: Peter Eugene, David Denby. AB in Psychology, Franklin and Marshall Coll., 1951; PhD, U. Ill., 1954. Instr. psychology U. Pitts., 1956-58; rsch. psychologist Ann Arbor VA Med. Ctr., Mich., 1958-89; prof. psychology U. Mich., Ann Arbor, 1966-98, assoc. chmn. dept., 1990-91; ret., 1998. Author: Cognitive Processes, 1966, An Introduction to Cognitive Psychology, 1971; editor Jour. Personality and Social Psychology, 1980-84. With USPHS, 1954—56. Mem.: APA, Soc. Exptl. Social Psychology, Racquet, Phi Beta Kappa. Democrat. Jewish. Home: 1937 Boulder Dr Ann Arbor MI 48104-4165 Home Phone: 734-975-0172. Business E-Mail: Melmanis@umich.edu.

MANJI, HUSSEINI K., pharmaceutical company executive, neuropsychopharmacologist; BS, MD, U. BC. Fellow in psychopharmacology NIMH, Bethesda, Md.; fellow in cellular and molecular biology Nat. Inst. Diabetes and Digestive and Kidney Diseases; prof. psychiatry and behavioral neurosciences Wayne State U. Sch. Medicine; sr. investigator NIMH, 2000—08, chief Lab. Molecular Pathophysiology Bethesda, dir. Mood and Anxiety Disorders Prog., 2005—08; v.p. ctrl. nervous system and pain Johnson & Johnson Pharmaceutical Rsch. and Devel., Titusville, NJ, 2008—. Recipient A.E. Bennett award for Neuropsychiatric Rsch., Ziskind-Somerfeld award for Neuropsychiatric Rsch., Falcone prize, Nat. Alliance for Rsch. on Schizophrenia and Depression (NARSAD), 1999, Mougens Schou Disting. Rsch. award, Henry and page Laughlin Disting. Tchr. award, Disting. Rschr. award, Brown U. Sch. Medicine, Mentor of the Yr. award, NIHM, Supr. of Yr. award, Excellence in Clin. Care and Rsch. award. Fellow: Am. Coll. Neuropsychopharmacology (Joel Elkes award); mem.: Inst. Medicine, Soc. Biol. Psychiatry. Office: Johnson & Johson Pharmaceutical Rsch and Devel 1125 Trenton Harbourton Rd Titusville NJ 08560

MANKOFF, DAVID ABRAHAM, nuclear medicine physician; b. July 10, 1959; BS in Physics summa cum laude, Yale U., 1981; MD, PhD in Bioengring., U. Pa., 1988. Diplomate Am. Bd. Internal Medicine, Am. Bd. Nuclear Medicine. Rsch. scientist UGM Med. Sys., Phila., 1988-89, dir. engring., 1989-90; rsch. assoc. nuclear medicine sect. U. Pa., Phila., 1988-90; resident in internal medicine U. Wash., Seattle, 1990-92, resident in nuclear medicine, 1992-96, asst. prof. radiology, 1996—2001, assoc. prof. radiology, 2001, assoc. prof. medicine, 2002—06, assoc. prof. bioengring., 2005—06; prof. radiology, medicine, and bioengring. Seattle Cancer Care Alliance, 2006—.

MANLEY, AUDREY FORBES, retired academic administrator, pediatrician, military officer; b. Jackson, Miss., Mar. 25, 1934; d. Jesse Lee and Ora Lee (Buckhalter) Forbes; m. Albert Edward Manley, Apr. 3, 1970. AB with honors (tuition scholar), Spelman Coll., Atlanta, 1955; MD (Jesse Smith Noyes Found. scholar), Meharry Med. Coll., 1959; MPH, Johns Hopkins U.-USPHS traineeship, 1987; LHD (hon.), Tougaloo Coll., Miss., 1990, Meharry Med. Coll., Nashville, 1991, LLD (hon.), Spelman Coll., 1991, Tskegee U., 1998; DSc (hon.), Coll. New Rochelle, 1998, Morehouse Coll., 2002, U. Del., 2002. Diplomate: Am. Bd. Pediatrics. Intern St. Mary Mercy Hosp., Gary, Ind., 1960; from jr. to chief resident in pediatrics Cook County Children's Hosp., Chgo., 1960—62; NIH fellow neonatology U. Ill. Rsch. and Ednl. Hosp., Chgo., 1963—65; staff pediatrician Chgo. Bd. Health, 1963—66; practice medicine specializing in pediatrics Chgo., 1963—66; assoc. Lawndale Neighborhood Health Ctr. North, 1966—67; asst. med. dir., 1967—69; asst. prof. Chgo. Med. Coll., 1966—67; instr. Pritzker Sch. Medicine, U. Chgo., 1967—69; asst. dir. ambulatory pediatrics, asst. dir. pediatrics Mt. Zion Hosp. and Med. Center, San Francisco, 1969—70; med. cons. Spelman Coll., 1970—71, med. dir. family planning program, chmn. health careers adv. com., 1972—76; med. dir. Grady Meml. Hosp. Family Planning Clinic, 1972—76; commd. officer, advanced though grades to rear adm. USPHS, 1976—97; chief genetic diseases services br. Office Maternal and Child Health, Bur. Community Health Services, Rockville, Md., 1976—81; acting assoc. adminstr. clin. affairs Office of Adminstr. Health Resources and Services Adminstrn., 1981—83, chief med. officer, dep. assoc. adminstr. planning, evaluation and legis., 1983—85; sabbatical leave USPHS Johns Hopkins Sch. Hygiene and Pub. Health, 1986—87; dir. Nat. Health Service Corps.; asst. surgeon gen. US Dept. Health & Human Services, 1988, dep. asst. sec. for health, 1989—93, acting asst. sec. health, 1993, dep. asst. sec. health & intergovtl. affairs, 1993—94, dep. surgeon gen., acting dep. asst. sec. for minority health, 1994—95, acting surgeon gen., 1995—97; pres. Spelman Coll., 1997—2002, pres. emerita, 2003—. Mem. U.S. del. UNICEF, 1990-94, Am. Acad. Family Physicians (pub. adv. bd.), Am. Coun. Learned Socs., Am. Med. Assn. Minority Affairs Consortium (sr. advisor), Ctrs. for Disease Control Found. (bd. visitors), Morehouse Sch. Medicine (clin. Prof. Pediats., Pub. Health Lectr.), Rollins Sch. Pub. Health Emory U (Commrs., Adv. Coun., Ga. Leadership Commn. Organ, Tissue, Blood Marrow donation amont African Ams. Author numerous articles, reports in field; artist permanent collections Nat. Acads. Sci., Spelman Coll. Alumnae Hall of Fame, 2005. Trustee Spelman Coll., 1966-70; The Coll. Fund (UNCF com. Archives, Hist. Govtl. Affairs Com.), Coun. Fgn. Rels., bd. dirs. coun. Ind. Colls.; bd. dirs. March of Dimes, 1998, Nat. Merit Scholarship Corp., Nat. Minority Mil. Mus. Found. Edl. Adv. Coun., Am. Cancer Soc. Found., CDC Found., Compas Compact, Downtown Atlanta Chpt. Rotary, Atlanta 2000 Adv. Com., Quality Edn. for Minorities; adv. bd. Atlanta Regional Health Summit, Commerce Club, Ga. Found. Ind., Food and Drug Adv. Com., publ. advisory bd. Am. Acad. Family Physicians, sr. advisor AMA Minority Affairs Consortium, bd. visitors CDC Found., hon. advisor coun., charter mem. The Children's Inn at NIH, mem. Coun. on Fgn. Rels., Adv. Com., vaccine and biologics com. Food and Drug Adminstrn., mem. Health Careers Exploring Advisory Com., Tribal Colls.; chair, advisory group Univ. S.Carolina Rural Health Initiative. Rear adm. USPHS, ret. USPHS. Recipient Meritorious Svc. award USPHS, 1981, Mary McLeod Bethune award Nat Coun. Negro Women, 1979, Dr. John P. McGovern Ann. Lectureship award Am. Sch. Health Assn., Disting. Alumni award Meharry Med. Coll., 1989, Spelman Coll. 108 Founder's Day Convocation, 1989, Disting. Svc. medal USPHS, 1992, Hildrus A. Poindexter award OSG/PHS, 1993, numerous other svc. and achievement awards; named to African Americans in Sci., Engring., and Medicine Portrait Collection, Nat. Acads., 2005. Fellow Am. Acad. Pediatrics; mem. Nat. Inst. Medicine of Nat. Acad. Sci., Nat. Med. Assn., APHA, AAUW, AAAS, Coun. Fgn. Rels., Spelman Coll. Alumnae Assn. (Hall of Fame 2005), Meharry Alumni Assn., African Am. Collection Portraits of NAS, Operation Crossroads Africa Alumni Assn., Atlanta C. of C., Rotary, Delta Sigma Theta (hon.), Phi Beta Kappa. Mailing: 5820 Hannah Brook St Ardiente North Las Vegas NV 89081 Personal E-mail: amanley009@aol.com. *

MANN, CINDY, federal agency administrator; Grad., Cornell U.; JD, NYU Sch. Law. Dir. fed. & state health policy work Ctr. Budget & Policy Priorities, Washington; dir. family & children's health programs Health Care Financing Adminstrn. (Centers Medicare & Medicaid Svcs.), 1999—2001; rsch. prof., exec. dir. Ctr. Children & Families, Georgetown U. Health Policy Inst.; dep. adminstr. Centers Medicare & Medicaid Services (CMS), US Dept. Health & Human Services, 2009—, dir. Ctr. Medicaid, CHIP and Survey & Certification, 2009—. Assoc. commr. Kaiser Commn. on Medicaid and the Uninsured. Contbr. articles to profl. jours. Office: Ctrs for Medicare and Medicaid Svcs 7500 Security Blvd Baltimore MD 21244 *

MANN, DOUGLAS LOWELL, cardiologist; b. Oct. 31, 1951; MD, Temple U., 1979. Cert. Internal Medicine 1982, Cardiovascular Disease 1985. Resident in internal medicine Temple U. Hosp., Phila.; fellow in cardiology U. Calif., San Diego; rsch. fellow Mass. Gen. Hosp., Boston; chief cardiology divsn. Baylor Coll. Medicine, Houston, dir. Winters Ctr. Heart Failure Rsch. Office: Baylor Coll Medicine FC 9-83 1 Baylor Plz Houston TX 77030 Office Phone: 713-798-2545, 713-798-0285. Office Fax: 713-798-0270. E-mail: dmann@bcm.edu.

MANN, ERICA L., pharmaceutical executive; b. Vereeniging, South Africa; Undergrad. in Analytical Chemistry; grad. in Mktg. Mgmt., Inst. of Mktg. Mgmt., Johannesburg, South Africa. Pres. Pfizer, gen. mgr.; mng. dir. Wyeth, Australia, New Zealand, mng. dir. pharm. bus. South Africa, CEO pharm. bus.; pres. healthcare's consumer care divsn. Bayer, 2011—, mem. healthcare exec. com.; bd. dirs. Internat. Infant Food Mfrs. Assn. (IFM); with Lederle Labs., Johnson and Johnson, Eli Lilly and Co. Mem.: Medicines Australia, South African Pharm. Mfrs.' Assn. Office: Bayer HealthCare LLC 36 Columbia Rd Morristown NJ 07962-1910 Office Phone: 973-254-5009. Office Fax: 973-254-4862.

MANN, HELMUT, experimental medicine educator, researcher; b. Cologne, Germany, Feb. 18, 1938; s. Max and Else (Wessel) M.; m. Kook-Ja Park, June 10, 1974; children: Daniel, Julia, Lilian. MD, U. Cologne, 1963, postgrad., 1973, U. Aachen, Germany, 1986. Prof. exptl. medicine Tech. U. Aachen, 1986—; CEO Inst. Applied Nephrology. Author: Therapie der Chronischen Niereninsuffizienz. Served with German Navy. Mem. Deutsche Arbeitsgemeinschaft Klinische Nephrologie, Verband Deutscher Nierzuzentien (hon.), Europ. Dialysis Transplant Assn., Am. Soc. Artificial Internal Organs, NY Acad. Scis., Internat. Soc. Artificial Organs., Bulgarian Soc. Nephrology (hon.), European Soc. Artifical Organs, Soc. Francophone Dialyse, Fach Pselischaft fuv eruahrungs therapies und Prevention. Roman Catholic. Home: Fuchserde 7 52066 Aachen Germany Office: Schurzelter Str 564 52074 Aachen Germany Office Fax: 49241872578.

MANN, J. JOHN, medical educator; b. Australia, Jan. 23, 1948; MD, Melbourne U., 1971. Prof. Columbia U., 1994—. Recipient Morselli medal, Internat. Acad. Suicide Rsch. Fellow: Am. Coll. Neuropsychopharmacology. Office: NYSPI Box 42 1051 Riverside Dr Bronx NY 10471 Business E-Mail: jjm@columbia.edu.

MANN, OSCAR, retired physician, internist, educator; b. Paris, Oct. 13, 1934; arrived in U.S., 1953; s. Aron and Helen (Biegun) Mann; m. Amy S. Mann, July 19, 1964; children: Adriana, Karen. AA with distinction, George Washington U., 1958; MD cum laude, Georgetown U., 1962. Diplomate Am. Bd. Med. Examiners, Am. Bd. Internal Medicine, Am. Bd. Cardiovasc. Disease, cert. advanced achievement in internal medicine. Intern Georgetown U. Med. Ctr., Washington, 1962-63, jr. asst. med. resident, 1963-64, clin. fellow in cardiology with Proctor Harvey program, 1965-66; sr. asst. resident in medicine Georgetown svc. D.C. Gen. Hosp., Washington, 1964-65; clin. prof. medicine Georgetown U. Sch. Medicine, 1985—; nat. chmn. med. alumni fund Georgetown U. Med. Sch., Washington, 1993-95; pvt. practice internal medicine and cardiology, Washington, 1966-99. Mem. med. nursing com. Georgetown U. Med. Ctr., mem. adv. com. CME, mem. tchg. adv. com., opthalmology dept. rev. com., surgery dept. rev. com., faculty com., search com. for a new dean for acad. affairs; appointed coun. to the dean Georgetown U. Sch. Medicine, 1977—; mem. Instnl. Self Study Task Force. Author: A Journey of Hope, 2005; contbr. articles to profl. jours. Nat. chmn. med. alumni fund Georgetown U., 1997—99. With US Army, 1953—55, with US Army, 1953—55. Recipient Mead Johnson Postgrad. Scholar ACP, 1964—65, Physicians Recognition award, AMA, 1987—96, Advanced Achievement in Internal Medicine, 1987, John Carroll award, Georgetown U., 1999, Founder's Gold medal, Georgetown U. Sch. Medicine, 2010. Fellow: ACP, Am. Coll. Chest Physicians, Am. Coll. Cardiology; mem.: AMA, Med. Soc. D.C., Am. Heart Assn. (coun. clin. cardiology), Am. Soc. Internal Medicine, Georgetown U. Alumni Assn. (bd. govs. 1993—, chair med. alumni bd. 1995—, nat. chmn. med. alumni fund 1997—99), Phi Delta Epsilon, Alpha Omega Alpha. Home: 5137 Yuma St NW Washington DC 20016 E-mail: oscarmann@comcast.net.

MANN, RICHARD ALAN, physician, educator; b. Bklyn., Dec. 18, 1952; s. Daniel Isaac and Claire Ethel (Spiller) M.; m. Judith Fleischer, Aug. 6, 1977; 1 child, David Michael Mann. BS in Math., Union Coll., Schenectady, NY, 1973; MS in Biophysics, SUNY, Buffalo, 1975; MD, Albert Einstein Coll. Medicine, The Bronx, NY, 1979. Diplomate Am. Bd. Internal Medicine. Intern Grad. Hosp. U. Pa., Phila., 1979-80; resident Temple U. Hosp., Phila., 1980—82; clin. nephrology fellow Hosp. U. Pa., Phila., 1982—83, rsch. fellow, 1983—86; asst. prof. medicine Rutgers U. Med. Sch., New Brunswick, NJ, 1986—93; assoc. prof. medicine, microbiology and molecular genetics; physician Robert Wood Johnson Med. Sch., New Brunswick, 1993—, med. dir. Kidney/Pancreas Transplant Program, 1999—; mem. grad. program in microbiology and molecular genetics Rutgers U., Piscataway, NJ, 1989—. Antiviral drug adv. com. FDA, Rockville, Md., 1993—; spl. study sect. NIH, Bethesda, Md., 1994; NIH Reviewers Res.; State Dept. Task Force, Operation Desert Storm, 1991. Contbr. over 50 articles, chpts. and abstracts to profl. jours. Recipient Young Investigator award Nat. Kidney Found., 1987, Nat. Med. award Kidney and Urology Found. Am., 2004, named one of Best Drs. in Am., 1996-2010, Guide to Americas Top Physicians, Top Docs. in NJ, NJ Monthly Mag., njtopdocs.com, others; grantee NIH, 1988-93, William Lightfoot Schultz Found., 1987-88, UMDNJ Found., 1987-88. Mem. Am. Soc. Nephrology (co-chair basic immunology free comm. session 1989, 90), Am. Fedn. for Clin. Rsch., Am. Heart Assn. (Coun. on the Kidney in Cardiovascular Disease), Nat. Kidney Found., Nephrology Soc. N.J., Am. Assn. for Lab. Animal Sci., Am. Soc. Transplantation, Alpha Omega Alpha (Acad. Excellence and Outstanding Tchg. award 1995). Office: UMDNJ Robert Wood Johnson Med Sch Acad Health Sci Ctr CN-19 New Brunswick NJ 08903 Business E-Mail: mannri@umdnj.edu.

MANN, ROBERT WALTER, forensic anthropologist; b. Thacker, W.Va., Nov. 12, 1949; PhD, U. Hawaii, 2001. Dep. dir. pathology Shelby County Morgue, U. Tenn., dir. dept. pathology, morgue Memphis, 1987; anthropologist Smithsonian Instn., 1988—92; anthropologist, dep. sci. dir. Joint POW/MIA Acctg. Command, 1992—2008; dir. Forensic Sci. Acad., 2008—. Adj. instr. Chaminade U. Honolulu, 2002—11; lectr. U. Hawaii, West Oahu, 2007—11; overseas vis. scientist Khon Kaen U. Med. Sch., Thailand, 2009—11. Decorated Dept. Army Commendation Cert. US Army; recipient Dept. Army Civilian award, 1998, 2001. Mem.: Calif. Coroner's Assn., President's Subcom. Forensic Sci. (mem. dept. edn. & tng.), Am. Acad. Forensic Scis. Avocations: guitar, writing. Office: Joint POW/MIA Acctg Command (CIL) Ctrl Identification Lab Joint Base Pearl Harbor-Hickam Hickam AFB HI 96853-5530 Business E-Mail: robert.mann@jpac.pacom.mil.

MANN, TRUE SANDLIN, psychologist, consultant; b. Longview, Tex., Aug. 4, 1934; d. Bob Murphy and Stella True (Williams) Sandlin; m. Jack Matthewson Mann, Sept. 4, 1954 (div. Dec. 1989); children: Jack Matthewson Jr., Bob Sandlin, Daniel Williams, Nathaniel Currier. BS, Stephen F. Austin State U., Nacogdoches, Tex., 1973, MA, 1977; PhD, East Tex. State U., 1982. Lic. psychologist, Tex., Ark. Instr. Stephen F. Austin State U., 1975-76, vis. asst. prof. psychology, 1986-87; instr. East Tex. State U., Commerce, 1980-81; postdoctoral fellow Southwestern Med. Sch., Dallas, 1982-83; pvt. practice, Longview, Tex., 1983-92; psychologist dept. family practice U. Tex. Health Sci. Ctr., Tyler, 1990-92; dir. psychol. svcs. St. Michael's Hosp., Texarkana, Tex., 1992-93; cons. psychologist, Longview, 1993—. Weekly newspaper columnist HARBUS, Cambridge Mass., 1959-60; cons. Made-Rite Co., Longview, 1989—. Mem. candidate com. Assoc. Reps. Tex., Austin, 1990—; bd. dirs. Mental Health Assn. Tex., 1977-82, 84-92, Longview Symphony, 1995-99, Dallas Opera Guild, 1999—, Longview Mus. of Art, 1995; mem. Leadership Tex., 1988—. Mem. APA, Tex. Psychol. Assn., N.E. Tex. Field Ornithologists. Episcopalian. Avocations: photography, travel, history. Home: 1906 N 4th St Longview TX 75601-3202 Office: 1203 Montclair St Longview TX 75601-3565

MANNICK, JOHN ANTHONY, surgeon; b. Deadwood, SD, Mar. 24, 1928; s. Alfred and Catherine Elizabeth (Schuster) M.; m. Alice Virginia Gossard, June 9, 1952; children— Catherine Virginia, Elizabeth Eleanor, Joan Barbara. BA, Harvard U., 1949, MD, 1953. Diplomate: Am. Bd. Surgery (dir. 1971-77). Intern Mass. Gen. Hosp., 1953-54, resident in surgery, 1956-60; instr. in surgery to asst. prof. Med. Coll. Va., 1960-64; asso. prof. to prof. surgery Boston U., 1964-76, chmn. div. surgery, 1973-76; Moseley prof. surgery Harvard U., 1976-94, Moseley Disting. prof. surgery, 1994—2008; dir. ednl. programs Harvard Med. Internat., 1994-96; chmn. dept. surgery Peter Bent Brigham Hosp. and Brigham and Women's Hosp., Boston, 1976-94. Mem. surgery, anesthesiology and trauma study sect. NIH, 1978-82, mem. medicine study sect., 1967-70; rsch. com. Med. Found., Inc., 1970-76. Author: (with others) Modern Surgery, 1970, Core Textbook of Surgery, 1972, Surgery of Ischemic Limbs, 1972, The Cause and Management of Aneurysms, 1990; mem. editorial bd. AMA Archives of Surgery, 1973-84, Clin. Immunology and Immunopathology, 1972-84, Surgery, 1982-97, Brit. Jour. Surgery, 1982-92, European Jour. Vascular Surgery, 1988-96, Shock, 1997—; mem. editl. bd. Advances in Surgery, 1979—, editor, 1984-86; mem. editl. bd. Jour. Vascular Surgery, 1984-97, assoc. editor, 1990-97; also articles. Served to capt. M.C. USAF, 1954-56. Markle scholar in acad. medicine, 1961-66. Fellow ACS (gov.), Royal Coll. Surgeons (hon., Eng.), Royal Coll. Surgeons (hon., Edinburgh), Royal Coll. Surgeons (hon. Ireland), Vascular Soc. Gt. Britain and Ireland (hon.); mem. Am. Fedn. Clin. Rsch., Am. Assn. Immunologists, Am. Soc. Exptl. Pathology, Soc. Clin. Investigation, Soc. Clin. Surgery, Soc. Univ. Surgeons (Lifetime Achievement award 2005), Soc. Surg. Chmn. (sec. 1985-87, pres. 1987-88), Am. Surg. Assn. (pres. 1989-90), Internat. Cardiovascular Soc. (recorder N.Am. chpt., 1973-76, pres. N.Am. chpt. 1991-92, internat. v.p. 1993, Disting. Svc. award 2002), Soc. Vascular Surgery (pres. 1981), N.E. Surg. Soc., (Nathan Smith Disting. award, 1999), New Eng. Soc. Vascular Surgery (pres. 1994-95), Royal Coll. Surgeons (hon., Australasia) So. Surg. Assn., So. Soc. Vascular Surgery (hon.), Surg. Infection Soc.(Sci. Leadership award, 2008), Halstead Soc., Lifeline Found. (pres. 1997-2002), Shock Soc. (Sci. Achievement award 2000), Uniformed Svcs. U. Health Scis. (dr. mil. medicine and surgery, Hon. 2003), Phi Beta Kappa. Home: 81 Bogle St Weston MA 02493-1056

MANNING, ROBERT THOMAS, internist, educator; b. Wichita, Kans., Oct. 16, 1927; s. Thomas Earl and Mary Francis (Schlegel) M.; m. Jane Bell, July 29, 1949; children: Mary Kay Fausch, Phillip Trenton, Susan Ann Shiba. AB, Wichita U., 1950; MD, Kans. U., 1954; DHL, Med. Coll. Hampton Rds., 1991. Diplomate Am. Bd. Internal Medicine. Intern Kansas City (Mo.) Gen. Hosp., 1954-55; resident Kans. U., Kansas City, 1955-58; from asst. prof. to prof. Kans. U. Med. Ctr. Sch. of Medicine, Kansas City, 1958-71, assoc. dean students, 1969-71; dean Eastern Va. Med. Sch., Norfolk, Va., 1971-74, chmn., prof. internal medicine, 1974-77; prof. internal medicine U. Kans. Sch. of Medicine, Wichita, 1977-93; prof. emeritus U. Kans. Sch. Medicine, Wichita, 1993—; assoc. dean, clin. affairs U. Kans. Sch. of Medicine, Wichita, 1985-89; chmn. internal medicine U. Kans. Sch. Medicine, Wichita, 1987—89, prof. emeritus, 1994; pres. Wesley Med. Rsch. Inst., 1986-88. Nat. cons. surgeon gen. USAF, 1973-78. Author: Major's Physical Diagnosis, 9th edit., 1982; contbr. articles to profl. jours. Pres. Kans. Health Ethics, Inc., 1994-96. With US Army Air Corps, 1945—47. Recipient Advanced Achievement award Am. Bd. Internal Medicine, 1987. Fellow ACP (laureate Kans. chpt., bd. govs. Kans. 1984-88); mem. Am. Fedn. Clin. Rsch., Cen. Soc. Clin. Rsch., Am. Assn. Study Liver Disease, Sigma Xi, Alpha Omega Alpha. Presbyterian. Avocations: woodworking, golf. Home: 126 Trail Of The Flowers Georgetown TX 78633-4814 Personal E-mail: rmannsun@suddenlink.net.

MANNINO, J(OSEPH) ROBERT, retired medical educator; b. Altoona, Pa., May 6, 1941; s. Joseph Robert and Helen La Rue (Menza) M.; m. Rosemary Kathleen McGrath, Apr. 8, 1978; 1 child, Angela Christine. BS, Juniata Coll., 1963; MA, East Carolina U., 1965; PhD, Colo. State U., 1974; DO, Kansas City Coll. Osteo. Med., 1971. Diplomate Am. Osteo. Bd. Family Practice. Intern Rocky Mountain Hosp., Denver, 1971-72; physician pvt. practice, Denver, 1972-77; dir. med. edn.nt Kansas City Coll. Osteo. Medicine, 1977-80; prof. family medicine Ohio U. Coll. Osteo. Medicine, Athens, 1981-94, Nova Southeastern U., Coll. Osteo. Medicine, North Miami Beach, Fla., 1994—2000. Teaching asst. physiology East Carolina U., 1965; coord. rsch. Phila. Coll. Osteo. Medicine, 1966-67; asst. dir. med. edn. Rocky Mountain Hosp., Denver, 1972-73, dir. med. edn., 1975-77, bd. trustees, 1975-77; dir. gen. practice residency Drs. Hosp., Columbus, 1980-94; dir. med. edn. & program dir. family practice residency North Broward Hosp. Dist., Ft. Lauderdale, Fla., 1994-96; clin. assoc. Cleveland Clinic, Ft. Lauderdale, 1996-2000; regional med. dir., Wexfold Health Sources, Ft. Lauderdale, Fla., 2002—2003; cons. in field. Contbr. articles to profl. jours. Rsch. fellow Colo. State U., 1968-69. Fellow Am. Coll. Osteo. Family Practice, Am. Soc. Colposcopy & Cervical Pathology, Am. Soc. Laser Medicine & Surgery; mem. Am. Osteo. Assn., Am. Coll. Cyrosurgery, N.Y. Acad. Scis., Fla. Soc. Osteo. Medicine, Fla. State Soc. Am. Coll. Osteo. Family Physicians, Broward County Acad. Fla. Soc. Osteo. Medicine, Endocrine Soc., Chi Beta Phi. Republican. Roman Catholic. Avocation: restoring antique cars.

MANNIS, MARK J., ophthalmologist, director; b. Atlanta, Dec. 5, 1946; MD, U. Fla., 1975. Prof., chair UC Davis Eye Ctr., Health Sys. U. Calif., 1980—, dept. chair dept. ophthalmology & vision sci., 2006. Editor in chief Jours. Cornea & Vision Pan-America. Contbr. articles to profl. jours. publs. Recipient R Townley Paton award, Eye Bank Assn. America. Mem.: Am. Acad. Ophthalmology, Am. Ophthal. Soc., Pan Am. Assn. Ophthalmology, Cornea Soc. Avocation: bagpipes. Office: 4860 Y St Ste 2400 Sacramento CA 95817 Office Fax: 916-703-5076. Business E-Mail: mjmannis@ucdavis.edu.

MANNON, PETER, medical educator; b. NY, Aug. 20, 1959; BA, Boston U., 1983, MD. Prof. medicine UAB, 2008—. Office: 1825 University Blvd SHEL613 Birmingham AL 35294 Office Fax: 205-934-3411. Business E-Mail: pmannon@uab.edu.

MANOCHA, ANSHU, pharmacology educator; b. Delhi, India, Oct. 10, 1971; d. Chander Prakash and Savitri Manocha. BPharm, Jamia Hamdard U., Delhi, 1994, MPharm, 1997; PhD, Delhi U., 2001. Jr. rsch. fellow Indian Inst. Tech., Jamia Hamdard U., 1994-95; sr. rsch. fellow Coun. Sci. and Indsl. Rsch., U. Coll. Med. Sci. and Guru Teg, Bahadur Hosp., 1996-99; asst. prof. Jamia Hamdard U., 2000—04, sr. asst. prof., 2005—. Contbr. articles to profl. jours., including Indian Jour. Pharmacology, Indian Jour. Exptl. Biology, Pharm. Biochem. Behavior (Young Investigator's award 1999); presenter papers at profl. confs. Mem. Indian Pharmacol. Assn. (life), Indian Pharm. Assn. (life). Achievements include investigation of role of various opioid receptors in convulsive disorders. Office: Jamia Hamdard Dept Pharmacology New Delhi 110062 India Office Phone: 0091-11-22514073. Personal E-mail: anshumanocha@hotmail.com.

MANOLIO, TERI A., physician; d. Henry and Mary Jo Manolio. BS in Biochemistry, U. Md., Balt., 1976, MD, 1980; MHS in Epidemiology, Johns Hopkins Sch. of Hygiene and Pub. Health, Balt., 1987, PhD in Human Genetics and Genetic Epidemiology, 2001. Diplomate Nat. Bd. of Med. Examiners, 1981, Nat. Bd. of Internal Medicine, 1984, License to Practice Medicine Dept. of Health and Mental Hygiene/Md., 1987. Resident Boston City Hosp., 1980—84; chief resident DC General, 1983—84; fellow, divsn. internal medicine John Hopkins Hosp., 1984—87; med. officer, epidemiology and biometry program Nat. Heart, Lung, and Blood Inst., Bethesda, Md., 1987—94, dir., epidemiology and biometry program, divsn. epidemiology and clin. applications, 1994—2005; dir., office population genomics Nat. Human Genome Rsch. Inst., NIH, Bethesda, Md., 2005—, sr. advisor to the dir. for population genomics, 2005—. Prof. of preventive medicine and biometrics and clin. prof. of medicine Uniformed Services U. of the Health Sciences, Bethesda, Md., 1987—; active appointment, in-patient med. svcs. Nat. Naval Med. Ctr.; spkr. in field. Author several scientific research presentations, several book chapters; contbr. several sci. rsch. papers to profl. publs. Instr. NIH Tae Kwon Do Club, Bethesda, Md., 1996—2003. Recipient Presdl. Rank Award for Meritorious Svc., Pres., U.S., 2001, Phi Kappa Phi Honor Soc., U. Md., Coll. Pk., 1974, Phi Beta Kappa Honor Soc., 1976. Fellow: ACP, Am. Heart Assn. Office: Nat Human Genome Rsch Inst NIH Bldg 31 Rm 4B09 31 Center Dr MSC 2152 Bethesda MD 20892-2152 Office Phone: 301-402-2915. Office Fax: 301-402-4831. E-mail: manolio@nih.gov.

MANOWITZ, PAUL, biochemist, researcher, educator; b. Monticello, NY, Dec. 13, 1940; s. Jacob M. and Rose (Levine) M.; m. Joyce L. Swartz, June 16, 1968; children: Neal J., Lauren H. BA in Chemistry with honors, Cornell U., 1962; PhD in Biochemistry, Brandeis U., 1967. Fellow NYU Sch. Medicine, 1967-70, instr., 1970-72; asst. prof. psychiatry U. Medicine and Dentistry N.J. Robert Wood Johnson Med. Sch., Piscataway, 1972-78, assoc. prof. psychiatry, 1978-96, prof. psychiaty, 1996—. Rsch. cons. VA Med. Ctr., Lyons, N.J., 1987—. Mem. editl. bd. Jour. of Studies on Alcohol, 1993—2003; contbr. articles to profl. jours. Mem. AAAS, Internat. Soc. for Biomed. Rsch. on Alcoholism, Am. Soc. Human Genetics, Am. Soc. Neurochemistry, Soc. Biol. Psychiatry, Rsch. Soc. Alcoholism. Home: 7 Guernsey Ln East Brunswick NJ 08816-3506 Office: U Medicine and Dentistry NJ Robert Wood Johnson Med Sch 671 Hoes Ln Piscataway NJ 08854-5627 Office Phone: 732-235-4347. Business E-Mail: manowitz@umdnj.edu.

MANSBACH, CHARLES, gastroenterologist, researcher; b. Norfolk, Va., Aug. 21, 1937; m. May Lynn Mansbach; children: Samuel Ross, Jonathan children: Harry. BA, Yale U., New Haven, 1963; MD, NYU, NYC, 1963. Lic. internal medicine Am. Bd. of Internal Medicine, gastroenterology Am. Bd. of Internal Medicine. Assoc. prof. of medicine Duke U. Med. Ctr., Durham, NC, 1970—86; prof. of medicine and physiology U. of Tenn., Memphis, 1986—. Lt. cdr. USNR, 1968—70. Recipient Merit Rev. grant, VA, 1971—2006; NIH rsch. grantee, 1975—. Achievements include research in Identified the pre-chylomicron transport vesicle. Office: University Tenn Rm H210 956 Court Ave Memphis TN 38163 Business E-Mail: cmansbach@uthsc.edu. *

MANSEL, ROBERT EDWARD, surgery educator, researcher; b. Carmarthen, Wales, Feb. 1, 1948; s. Regnier Ranulf and Germaine Mary (Littlewood) M.; m. Elizabeth Clare Skone, Sept. 19, 1960; children: Joanna, Juliet, Jemma, Charlotte, Rhys, Courtenay. MB, BS, U. London, 1971, MS, 1989. Lectr. surgery Welsh Nat. Sch. Medicine, Cardiff, Wales, 1979-82; UICC scholar U. Tex., San Antonio, 1982-83; sr. lectr. surgery U. Wales, Cardiff, 1983-89; prof. surgery Cardiff U., 1992—, U. Manchester, Eng., 1989-92. Mem. sci. com. Cancer Rsch. Campaign, London, 1993-2002; hon. sec. Surg. Rsch. Soc., UK, 1993-98; sr. v.p. Brit. Assn. Surg. Oncology, 1991-93., pres. 2004-. Author: Textbook of Benign Breast Disease, 3d edit., 2009, Wolfe Atlas of Breast Disease, 1994. Decorated comdr. Brit. Empire; recipient Charles Gros award Internat. Senology Assn., 1988; Hamilton Bailey fellow Internat. Coll. Surgeons, 1981, Churchill fellow Winston Churchill Trust, 1982, James IV fellow James IV Assn., 1989. Fellow Royal Coll. Surgeons (Eng.), Royal Coll. Physicians (licentiate), Royal Coll. Surgeons of Edinburgh (hon.), Brit. Med. Assn., British Breast Group (chair 2010-), Welsh Surg. Soc. (pres. 2010-11). Avocations: salmon fishing, rugby, travel. Office: Cardiff Univ Dept Surgery Heath Park Cardiff CF14 4XN Wales Office Phone: 44 2920 742749. Office Fax: 44 2920 742896. Business E-Mail: ManselRE@cf.ac.uk.

MANSFIELD, SIR PETER, physicist, educator; b. London, Oct. 9, 1933; s. Sidney George and Rose Lilian (Turner) Mansfield; m. Jean Margaret Kibble, Sept. 1, 1962; 2 children. BSc, Queen Mary Coll., U. London, 1959, PhD, 1962; D (hon.), U. Strasbourg, France, 1995, U. Kent, Canterbury, Eng., 1996, Jagellonian U. Physics, Krakow, Poland, 2000. Rsch. assoc. dept. physics U. Ill., 1962—64; lectr. dept. physics U. Nottingham, England, 1964—68, sr. lectr., 1968—70, reader dept. physics, 1970—79, prof., 1979—83, 1988—94, emeritus prof., 1994—; profl. fellow Med Rsch. Coun., London, 1983—88. Sr. visitor Max Planck Inst. Med. Rsch., Heidelberg, Germany, 1972—73. Co-author: NMR Imaging in Biomedicine, 1982; editor: MRI in Medicine, 1995, NMR Imaging, 1991. Recipient Antoine Beclere medal, Internat. Radiol Soc./Antoine Beclere Inst. Physics, 1989, Gold medal, European Assn. Radiology, 1995, Garmisch Partenkirchen prize, Germany, 1995, Rank prize, 1997, Nobel prize in physiology/medicine, 2003, MRC Millennium medal, London, 2009; named to Nat. Inventors Hall of Fame, 2007. Fellow: Acad. Med. Scis., Soc. Magnetic Resonance, Royal Coll. Physicians (hon.), Inst. Physics (hon. Duddel medal 1988), Royal Soc. (Mullard medal 1990), Royal Coll. Radiology (hon.); mem.: European Soc. Magnetic Resonance in Medicine & Biology, Soc. Magnetic Resonance in Medicine (pres. 1987—88, Gold medal 1983), Soc. Magnetic Resonance Imaging (hon.), British Inst. Radiology (hon. Barclay medal 1993). Achievements include pioneering work with magnetic resonance imaging (MRI), discovering how the signals emitted by the body in response to the magnetic field could be mathematically analyzed to produce a clear image; discovering how fast imaging could be possible by developing the MRI protocol called echo-planar imaging, allowing weighted images to be collected many times faster than previously possible. Office: U Nottingham Sch Physics & Astronomy 1 University Park NG7 2RD Nottingham England Office Phone: 01159 514740. *

MANSKE, PAUL ROBERT, orthopedic hand surgeon, educator; b. Ft. Wayne, Ind., Apr. 29, 1938; s. Alfred R. and Elsa E. (Streufert) M.; m. Sandra H. Henricks, Nov. 29, 1975; children: Ethan Paul, Claire Bruch, Louisa Hendricks. BA, Valparaiso U., 1960, DSc (hon.), 1985; MD, Washington U., St. Louis, 1964. Diplomate Am. Bd. Surgery. Intern U. Wash., Seattle, 1964-65, resident in surgery, 1965-66; resident in orthopedic surg. Washington U., St. Louis, 1969-72; hand surgery fellow U. Louisville, 1971; instr. orthopedic surgery Washington U. Med. Sch., St. Louis, 1972-76, asst. prof. orthopedic surgery, 1976-83, prof., 1983—, chmn. dept., 1983-95. Editor-in-chief Jour. Hand Surgery, 1996—; contbr. over 215 articles to profl. jours. Lt. comdr. USN, 1966-69, Vietnam. Fellow AMA, Am. Acad. Orthopaedic Surgery (Elizabeth Winston Lanier award, 1985Am. Orthopaedic Assn.; mem. Am. Soc. Surgery of the Hand, Alpha Omega Alpha. Office: Washington Univ Sch Medicine Dept Orthop Surgery Box 8233 660 S Euclid Ave Saint Louis MO 63110-1036

MANSKE, ROBERT C., physical therapist, educator; b. Topeka, Kans., Sept. 16, 1966; s. Robert Warren and Judith Lynn (Kimbell) Manske; m. Julia Oler, Jan. 25, 1992; children: Rachael Elizabeth, Halle Grace, Robert Tyler. B in Phys. Edn., Wichita State U., Kans., 1991, M in Phys. Therapy, 1994, EdM, 2000; D in Phys. Therapy, Mass. Gen. Inst., 2005. Cert. athletic trainer, nat. strength and conditioning cert. Mem. staff Via Christi Regional Med. Ctr., Wichita, 1994—97, mem. staff phys. therapy dept., 1998—; mem. staff Gundersen Luth. Sports Medicine, LaCrosse, Wis., 1997—98; mem. staff dept. phys. therapy Wichita State U., 1998—2005; with Dept. Mass. U. Hosp. Inst. Health Processing, 2005—. Contbr. articles to profl. jours. Mem.: Nat. Strength and Conditioning Assn., Nat. Athletic Trainers Assn., Kans. Phys. Therapy Assn. (named Instr. of Yr. 2003), Am. Phys. Therapy Assn. (bd. splty. cert. 2002), Alpha Eta. Office: Wichita State U Dept Phys Therapy 1845 N Fairmount Wichita KS 67260 Home: 2623 Keywest Ct Wichita KS 67204 Office Phone: 316-978-3702. Business E-Mail: robert.manske@wichita.edu.

MANSON, BONITA YVONNE, nutritionist, educator; b. Decatur, Ala., Sept. 14, 1950; d. Will Henry and Joan Ann Jones; m. Tony James Manson, May 27, 1972; children: Tony James Jr., Gregory Keith. BSc, Wayne State U., 1975; MSc, Tex. So. U., 1984; PhD, Kans. State U., 1998. Nutrition splist. City of Riverside, Calif., 1986-95; program rep. U. Calif. Coop. Extension, Riverside, Calif., 1986-96; adj. instr. Chaffey Coll., Rancho Cucamonga, Calif., 1993-95; tchg. asst. Kans. State U., Manhattan, Kans., 1995-98; asst. prof. Austin Peay State U., Clarksville, Tenn., 1999, Middle Tenn. State U., Murfreesboro, 2000—01, SC State U., Orangeburg, 2002, 2007—, interim chair dept. family and consumer scis., 2006—07. Author: Downsizing Issues, 2000, Let's Take a Look at Gender Equity in the Classroom Teacher Education Preparation for Diversity.; author: (with T.J. Manson) The Teacher Education Program: Is There a Vision and Can They Accomplish It. Teacher Education Preparation for Diversity, 2002; contbr. chapters to books; author: Downsizing Issues: The Impact on Employee Morale and Productivity, 2004. Mem.: Assn. Fin. Counseling. Planning, Edn., Nat. Coun. Family Rels., Am. Edn. Rsch. Assn., Am. Assn. Family and Consumer Scis., Am. Dietetic Assn., Phi Delta Kappa, Kappa Omicron Nu. Democrat. Roman Cath. Office: SC State Univ 300 College St NE Orangeburg SC 29117 Office Phone: 803-536-7179. Business E-Mail: bmanson@scsu.edu.

MANSON, JOANN ELISABETH, endocrinologist; b. Cleve., Apr. 14, 1953; d. S. Stanford and Therese (Palay) M.; m. Christopher N. Ames, June 12, 1979; children: Jennifer, Jeffrey, Joshua Simon. AB magna cum laude, Harvard U., 1975; MD, Case Western Res. U., 1979; MPH, Harvard Sch. Pub. Health, 1984, DPH, 1987. Bd. cert. internal medicine; bd. cert. in subspecialty of endocrinology and metabolism. Intern and resident internal medicine NEDH, Harvard

Med. Sch., Boston, 1979-82; fellowship in endocrinology U. Hosp. Boston, Mass., 1982-84; rsch fellow in medicine Brigham and Women's Hosp., Boston, 1984-87, co-dir. women's health, divsn. preventive medicine, 1993—, chief divsn. preventive medicine, 1999—; staff physician, consulting endocrinologist Harvard Vanguard Med. Assocs., Peabody, Mass., 1986—2003; prof. medicine Harvard Med. Sch., Boston, 1999—, Elizabeth Brigham prof. women's health, 2003—. Mem. editl. bd.: Jour. Women's Health, 1996—, Menopause, 2004—; contbr. chapters to books, more than 700 articles to profl. jours.; author, editor: several books and textbooks. Vol. physician Lynn (Mass.) Shelter for the Homeless, 1989-93; med. adv. bd. Harvard Health Letter, Boston, 1992—, Greater Boston (Mass.) Diabetes Soc., 1993—, Harvard Women's Health Watch, Boston, 1993—; vol. Am. Heart Assn., 1992—. Recipient Connors award for oustanding leadership in women's health, 1999—, Woman in Sci. award, Am. Med. Women's Assn., 2003, Henry I. Bowditch award for excellence in pub. health, Mass. Med. Soc., 2002, Women's Profl. Achievement award, Harvard Coll., 2006; named Hero in Women's Health, Am. Health for Women Mag., 1997; named one of Top 10 Champions of Women's Health, Ladies Home Jour., 2000, Top Docs for Women, Boston mag., 2001. Fellow ACP, ACE; mem. AMA, Am. Med. Women's Assn., Am. Heart Assn., Am. Diabetes Assn., Women's Health Initiative (mem. steering com.), Assn. Am. Physicians, Alpha Omega Alpha. Avocations: reading, hiking, music, travel. Home: 14 Washington St Beverly MA 01915-5820 Office: Brigham and Women's Hosp 900 Commonwealth Ave E Fl 3 Boston MA 02215-1204 Home Phone: 978-927-6764; Office Phone: 617-278-0871. Business E-Mail: jmanson@rics.bwh.harvard.edu.

MANSON, PAUL NELLIS, plastic surgeon, educator; b. Kansas City, Mo., Dec. 28, 1943; s. Nellis Emanuel and Alice Winifred (Olson) Manson; m. Kathryn Garland, 1968; children: Ted, Jenner. BA in Chemistry, Northwestern U., 1965, MD, 1968. Cert. Gen. Surgery, 1978, Plastic Surgery, 1979. Intern gen. surgery Boston City Hosp., Mass., 1968—69; resident plastic surgery New England Deaconess Hosp., 1968—71, 1973—74; fellow Lahey Clinic, Boston, 1974—75; resident gen. surgery Johns Hopkins U., Balt., 1976—78; staff mem. Johns Hopkins Hosp. and Health Sys., 1987—, chief plastic surgery; prof., chmn. plastic surgery Johns Hopkins U. Sch. Medicine, 1990—. Maj. US Army, 1970—73. Republican. Presbyterian. Office: 8152 F McElderry Wing 601 N Caroline St Baltimore MD 21287-0981 Office Phone: 410-955-9477. Office Fax: 410-614-1296. Business E-Mail: pmanson@jhmi.edu.

MANSOUR, AHMAD M., ophthalmologist, educator; b. Beirut, Dec. 1, 1955; MD, Am U. Beirut, 1981. Clin. prof. Am. U. Beirut, 2000—. Assoc. prof. U. Tex. Med. Br., 1992—93; chair, dept. ophthalmology Rafic Hariri U. Hosp., 2004. Recipient Cedar Legion, Pres. Lebanon, award, Shouman Found., Amman, Jordan, Debs Found. Fellow: Am. Soc. Retina Specialist (hon.), Am. Acad. Ophthalmology (hon.); mem.: Euroretina, Assn. Vision & Ophthalmology. Avocation: reading. Office: Am University Beirut A/Aziz 31 Beirut 1136044 Lebanon Business E-Mail: dr.ahmad@cyberia.net.lb.

MANSOUR, MAHMOUD AHMED, biochemistry educator; b. Shebin El-Kome, Egypt, Sept. 29, 1960; s. Ahmed Ali Mansour and Nafisa Mohamed Hussein; m. Hanan Hassan El-Saban; children: Ahmed Mahmoud, Mostafa Mahmoud. BSc in Pharmacy, Al-Azhar U., Cairo, 1984, diploma in biochemistry, 1986, MSc, 1989, PhD, 1992. Demonstrator Al-Azhar U., 1984-89, asst. lectr., 1989-92, lectr., 1993-96, assoc. prof., 2000—; prof. King Saud U., Riyadh, 2005—. Recipient Nat. Encouragement award Govt. Egpyt, 1998. Avocations: tennis, football, swimming, reading. Office: King Saud U P.O. Box 2457 11451 Riyadh Saudi Arabia Office Phone: 966-1-4675492. Office Fax: 966-1-4677200. Personal E-mail: mansour1960us@yahoo.com. Business E-Mail: mahmedm@ksu.edu.sa.

MANSOUR, MOHAMMED H. M., oral and maxillofacial surgeon; MBBS, Cairo U., 1990, MS in Otolaryngology, 1994, MD in Otolaryngology, 1998; B in Dentistry, Sydney U., 2004. Resident ENT surgeon, 1992—94; ENT surgeon, 1995—99; dentistry student, part time general medicine practitioner, 2000—04; registrar oral and maxillofacial surgeon, 2005—08; oral and maxillofacial surgeon, 2009—. Staff mem. Cairo U., 1995—; sr. lectr. Queensland U., 2009—. Mem.: Internat. Assn. Oral and Maxillofacial Surgeons, Royal Australasian Coll. Dental Surgeons. Muslim. Avocation: deep sea fishing. Office: 3/113 Wickham Ter Brisbane Queensland 4000 Australia Personal E-mail: mman0896@optusnet.com.au.

MANSUE, AMY, hospital administrator; s. Russell and Barbara Beaulieu. BS, MSW, U. Ala. Dep. commr. of state Dept. Human Svcs., 1989—92; v.p. Cablevision, NJ; sr. v.p. corp. devel. HIP, NY, pres., CEO NJ; dep. chief of staff to Gov. James McGreevey, NJ; pres., CEO Children's Specialized Hosp., Mountainside, 2003—. Bd. mem. Children's Specialized Hosp., 1995—99. Bd. mem. Planned Parenthood of Ctrl. NJ, Organ and Tissue Sharing Network, NJ Cmty. Devel. Corp. Recipient NJ Woman of Achievement award, NJ Fedn. Women's Clubs, 2007, Leadership award, Brain Injury Assn., 2007; named Garden State Women Leader in Non-Profits, Garden State Woman Mag., 2007. Office: Children's Specialized Hosp 150 New Providence Rd Mountainside NJ 07092

MANSY, SOHEIR SAIID, pathologist; MBBCh, Cairo U., 1978, MSc in Pathology, 1983, PhD in Pathology, 1988. Med. tech. specialist Theodor Bilharz Rsch. Inst., Cairo, 1981—84, asst. rschr to rschr., 1984—93, assoc. prof. pathology, 1993—98, prof. pathology, 1998—, chief electron microscopy rsch. dept., 1994—2006; deputy Clin. Labs. Divsn. TBRI, 2006—; com. mem. Promotion TBRI, 2008—; head Sci. Tech. Office TBRI, 1999—. Editl. sec. Egyptian Jour. Schistosomiasis & Infectious & Endemic Diseases, 1999—2005; contbr. articles to profl. jours. Recipient Ideal Dr. of Yr., Theodor Bilharz Rsch. Inst., 1983, Excellence award for disting. mgmt. of dept. and link of rsch. to cmty. svcs., 2003. Mem.: European Soc. Pathology (soc. mem.), Soc. Ultrastructural Pathology, Com. Promotion TBRI, Egyptian Soc. Pathology, Egyptian Soc. Lab. Medicine (mem. electron microscopy working group database), Internat. Acad. Pathology, Arab divsn. Achievements include invention of a technique for the simultaneous processing of urine cytology for light and electron microscopic examination, proving effective by increasing the sensitivity of urine cytology for the detection of low grade malignant cells; founding member of the electron microscopy research department at Theodor Bilharz Research Institute, which also introduced the technique of immunoelectron labeling. Avocations: drawing, reading, stamp collecting/philately. Office: Theodor Bilharz Rsch Inst ElNile WarrakElhadar Imbaba PO Box 30 Giza 12411 Egypt Office Fax: 202 5408125. Business E-Mail: soheir_mansy@tbri.sci.eg.

MANTERO-ATIENZA, EMILIO, psychiatrist, epidemiologist; b. Seville, Spain, Jan. 23, 1958; came to U.S., 1984; s. Jose Mantero and Marina Atienza. MD, U. Seville, Spain, 1981; MPH in Epidemiology, U. Miami Sch. Medicine, Fla., 1988; PhD, U. Seville Grad. Sch., Spain, 1990. Diplomate Am. Bd. Psychiatry and Neurology; lic. Fla. Staff physician Spanish Health Ctrs., Madrid, Seville, 1981-84; rsch. coord. Clin. Pharmacology Assocs., Miami, Fla., 1984-85; rsch. assoc. dept. pharmacology U. Miami, Fla., 1985-87, Am. Heart Assn. fellow dept. pharmacology, 1987-88, rsch. asst. prof. dept. epidemiology, 1989-91, clin. asst. prof. dept. epidemiology and pub. health, 1991—; resident in psychiatry Jackson Meml. Hosp. U. Miami Sch. of Medicine, Fla., 1991-94; attending physician alcohol disorders rsch. unit dept. psychiatry U. Miami Sch. of Medicine, Fla., 1995—; med. dir. St. Thomas Comty. Mental Health Ctr., Coral Gables, Fla., 1995—. Hosp. privileges at Mt. Sinai Med. Ctr., Cedars Med. Ctr., South Miami Hosp., Mercy Hosp., Deering Hosp., Miami Heart Inst., Coral Gables Hosp.; seminar conductor Dept. Pharmacology U. Miami Sch. of Medicine, 1986-88; lectr. in basic nutrition Trinity Sr. H.S., Dade County, Fla., lectr. in nutrition, Fla. Internat. U., 1987-89, Metro-Dade Police Dept., Miami, 1988-89; instr. Pub. Health Nutrition, U. Miami Sch. of Medicine, 1989-93, Geriatic Edn. Ctr. Dept. Psychiatry, U. Miami Sch. Medicine. Contbr. articles to profl. jours., chpts. to books; over 60 abstracts from scientific proceedings and confs. Vol. AIDS Watch South Fla., 1989; AIDS Epidemiology Rsch. Cable-TAD Program; seminar conductor on Chronic Fatigue Syndrome to comty. based orgns., 1989, 90; mem. Cure AIDS Now, 1989, 91; vol. Body Positive Resource Ctr., 1989, 92, Biopsychosocial Ctr. for Studies on AIDS, 1991, 92, 93, 94. Recipient NIH postdoctoral fellowship, 1987, Clinician Sci. award, Am. Heart Assn., 1987-88, 88-89; grantee: NIH, 1986-91, 1988-91, 1988-93, 1989-92, Am. Heart Assn. Fla. Affiliate 1987-88, 87-89, 88-89, NIH and Fogarty Internat. Ctr., 1988-93, Human Health Svcs., 1988-91, Fla. Cystic Fibrosis Found., 1988-89, 1988-89., NIAAA, 1993-95. Fellow So. Assn. Geriatric Medicine, Am. Coll. Clin. Pharmacology; mem. AMA, Am. Soc. Clin. Nutrition, So. Med. Assn., Am. Inst. Nutrition, N.Y. Acad. Sci., Am. Psychiat. Assn., Fla. Psychiat. Assn., Am. Soc. Addiction Medicine, Fla. Pub. Health Assn., Am. Coun. on Sci. and Health, Physicians for a Nat. Health Program, Nat. Coun. for Internat. Health, Soc. Latinoam. de Nutricion, Fla. Med. Assn., Southeastern Med. Soc. Home: 278 Palm Ave Miami Beach FL 33139-5142 Office: 444 Brickell Ave Ste 701 Miami FL 33131-2406 *

MANTHEY, FRANK ANTHONY, retired physician, director; b. NYC, Dec. 2, 1933; s. Frank A.J. and Josephine (Roth) M.; m. Douglas Susan Falvey, Sept. 14 1958 (div. 1979, dec. 1989); children: Michael P., Susan M., Peter J.; m. Doris Jean Pulley, Oct. 11, 1979. BS, Fordham U., 1955; MD, SUNY, Syracuse, 1958. Diplomate Am. Bd. Anesthesiology, Am. Bd. Med. Examiners. Intern Upstate Med. Ctr., Syracuse, 1958-59; resident in anesthesiology Yale-New Haven Med. Ctr., 1962-64; physician Yale-New Haven Hosp., 1964-75; pvt. practice medicine Illmo, Mo., 1975-79; dir. Manthey Med. Clinic, Elkton, Ky., 1979—2011. Clin. instr. anesthesiology Yale U. Med. Sch., New Haven, 1964-69, asst. clin. prof. anesthesiology, 1969-75; cons. Conn. Dept. Aeros., Hartford, 1969-70; sr. med. examiner Fed. Aviation Adminstrn., Illmo, 1975-79. Contbr. articles to profl. jours. Chmn. gen. works Little Folks Fair, Guilford, Conn., 1967-71; mem. Rep. Town Com., Guilford, 1969-75; chmn. Guilford Sch. Bldg. Com., 1973-75; mem. Todd County (Ky.) Bd. of Health, 1999—. Capt. USAF (M.C.), 1956-62. Mem.: Flying Physicians Assn. (v.p. NE chpt. 1973—75, v.p. nat. 1974—75, 1979—80, bd. dirs. 1970—73, 1975—78, bd. dirs. nat. 1975—78), Aerospace Med. Assn. (assoc. fellow 1973—75), Ky. Med. Assn., Aircraft Owners and Pilots Assn., Mercedes Benz ClubAm., Alpha Kappa Kappa. Avocations: stamp collecting/philately, coin collecting/numismatics, aviation, auto restoration, skiing. Home: 105 Sunset Dr Elkton KY 42220-9257

MANTOVANI, JOHN F., pediatric neurologist; b. St. Louis, Jan. 17, 1949; s. John F. and Marinelle Mantovani; children: John R. and Ann Marie. BA cum laude, U. Evansville, 1971; MD, U. Mo., 1974. Diplomate Am. Bd. Pediat., Am. Bd. Psychiatry and Neurology in child neurology and in neurodevel. disabilities. Resident pediat., neurology, fellow child neurology Washington U.-St. Louis Children's Hosp., 1974-79; practitioner adult and child neurology Dean Clinic, Madison, Wis., 1979-84; dir. child devel. Mercy Children Hosp., St. Louis, 1984—, chief med. officer, 2006—. Clin. asst. prof. neurology U. Wis., Madison, 1980-84; instr. clin. pediatrics and neurology Washington U., 1985-95, asst. prof., 1995-99, assoc. prof., 1999—; past chmn. neurodevel. disabilities com. Am. Bd. Psychiatry and Neurology. Mem. editl. bd., Dev. Med. and Child Neurology; Contbr. articles to profl. jours. Fellow Am. Acad. Cerebral Palsy and Devel. Medicine (bd. dirs. 1994-2003, v.p. 1997-98, pres.-elect 1999, pres. 2000); mem. AMA, Am. Acad. Neurology, Child Neurology Soc., Alpha Omega Alpha. Office: St John's Mercy Med Ctr 621 S New Ballas Rd Ste 5009 Saint Louis MO 63141-8232

MANTZELL, BETTY LOU, school nurse practitioner, consultant; b. Brookville, Pa., Oct. 16, 1938; d. Elmer William and Wilda Mae (Enterline) M. Diploma, Ind. Hosp. Sch. Nursing, Pa., 1959; BSN, Case We. Res. U., Cleve., 1969, MA, 1978; cert. supr. ednl. adminstrn., Cleve. State U., 1983; cert. supr., John Carroll U., University Heights, Ohio, 1989. RN Ohio, Pa.; cert. supr. Ohio Dept. Edn. Oper. room nurse Univ. Hosps. of Cleve., 1963—69; sch. nurse various locations Cleve. Pub. Schs., 1969—85, coord. sch. nurses, 1976—85, acting asst. supr. health svcs., 1985—86, supr. health svcs., 1986—98, sch. nurse, 1998—, John Hay HS Buhrer Dual Lang. Sch., Cleve. Met. Schs. Former adv. com. to baccalaureate nursing program Cleve. State U.; prevention of blindness adv. com. Cleve. Sight Ctr.; active All Kids Count Consortium Cleve. Dept. Pub. Health; sch. health com. Acad. Medicine Cleve.; Frances Payne Bolton Sch. Nursing, mem. alumni assn.; clin. instr. cmty. health nursing Case We. Res. U., Cleve., 1988-90, women's connection; coun. econ. opportunities Greater Cleve.; adv. com. Headstart Health Svcs.; ind. health care provider Met. Life Ins. Co., 2004-06; cons. in field. Recipient pres. award, Case Sch. Nursing Alumni. Assn., 2009. Mem. Am. Sch. Health Assn., Nat. Assn. Sch. Nurses, Ohio Assn. Sch. Nurses, Northeastern Ohio Assn. Sch. Nurses, Case Sch. Nursing (alumni bd. 2006-10), Cleve. Coun. Adminstrs. and Suprs., Cleve. Med. Libr. Assn., Cleve. Tchrs. Union Local 279, Order Ea. Star. Avocations: swimming, water-skiing, reading. Office: John Hay High Sch 2075 Stokes Blvd Cleveland OH 44106 also: Buhrer Dual Language Sch 1600 Buhrer Ave Cleveland OH 44109 Office Phone: 216-744-2811, 216-229-0113.

MANTZOROS, CHRISTOS SOCRATES, internist, endocrinologist; b. Nafplion, Greece, May 28, 1963; MD, U. Athens, Greece, 1987, DSc, 1996; MSc in Med. Sci., Clin. Epidemiology, Harward Sch. Health, 1997. Diplomate Am. Bd. Internal Medicine, Am. B. Endocrinology, Diabetes and Metabolism, Am. Bd. Nutrition. Intern Wayne State U., Detroit, 1990-91, resident in internal medicine, 1991-93; fellow Harvard U. Med. sch., Boston, 1993-96, instr. medicine, 1996-98, asst. prof., 1998—2003, assoc. prof., 2003—09, prof., 2009—, Harvard Sch. Pub. Health, 2010—; chief, endrocrinilogy VA Boston Heathcare Sys. Recipient Wilhelm Friedrich Bessel award, Humboldt Found., Germany, 2005, award, Am. Assn. Clin. Endocrinology Frontiers Sci., 2005, Novartis, 2005, Lilly award, North Am. Assn. Study Obesity, 2006, HypoCCS award, 2006, Mead Johnson award, Am. Soc. Nutrition, 2007, Outstanding Investigator award, Am. Fedn. Med. Rsch., 2008. Office: Divsn Endocrinology Beth Israel Deaconess Med Ctr Boston MA 02215 Business E-Mail: cmantzor@bidmc.harvard.edu.

MANYAK, MICHAEL JOHN, urologist, expedition medicine educator, researcher; b. Flint, Mich., Mar. 25, 1951; m. Rebecca Bruning; children: Rachel, Susannah, Timothy. BA, U. Notre Dame, 1973; MD, U. of East, Manila, 1979. Resident in gen. surgery Booth Meml. Med. Ctr., Flushing, NY, 1980-82; resident in urology George Washington Univ. Med. Ctr., Washington, 1982-84, instr. urology, 1988—89, asst. prof., 1989—91, assoc. prof., 1991—95, prof. urology engring. microbiology and tropical medicine, 1996—; v.p. med. affairs Cxtogen Corp., 2005—09; sr. med. advisor Global Rescue Inc.; chief med. officer Triple Canopy, Inc., 2010—; exec. dir., global med. leader GlaxoSmithKline, 2011—. Mem. adv. bd. Nat. Kidney and Urological Disease, 1992—. Contbr. articles to profl. jours. Adv. bd. aerospace medicine NASA. Biotech. fellowship Nat. Cancer Inst., 1985-88; scholar Am. Urol. Assn., 1986-88. Fellow Explorers Club (nat. bd. dirs. 1996-06, chmn. sci. adv. bd., Sweeney medal); mem. Am. Urol. Assn. (chmn. tech. coun. 1995).

MANYAM, BALA VENKATESHA, medical researcher, neurology educator; arrived in US, 1972, naturalized, 1980; s. Kolar Venktesha and Swarnam (Venktesha) Iyer; m. Rani Manyam; 1 child, Shaila. MBBS, Bangalore Med. Coll., 1967. Diplomate Am. Bd. Psychiatry and Neurology. With Thomas Jefferson U., Phila., 1974—84, asst. prof. pharmacology, 1981—83, assoc. prof. pharmacology, 1983—84; staff neurologist VA Med. Ctr., Wilmington, Del., 1975—80, asst. chief neurology, 1982—84; assoc. prof. neurology Sch. of Medicine Southern Ill. U., Springfield, 1984—92, prof., 1992—99, dir. neurology residency program, 1993—99; prof., dir. Plummar Movement Disorder Ctr., Scott & White Clinic, Tex. A&M U. HSC Coll. Medicine, 1999—2005; disting. rsch. prof. Hindu U. Am., 2006—08; clin. prof. dept. neurology Pa. State U., 2008—. Founding dir. Parkinson's Disease & Movement Disorders Clinic, Springfield, 1984—99; mem. NIH/NCCAM Coun., 2004—07; mem. editl. bd. Phytotherapy Rsch. Jour. Contbr. numerous articles to profl. jours. Grantee grants, Various Founds.; grant, NIH, various founds., Va. Fellow Am. Acad. Neurology; mem. Am. Neurologic Assn., Am. Assn. Physicians Indian Origin, Fla. Assn. Physicians Indian Origin, World Assn. Vadic Studies. Hindu. Achievements include research in drug development from herbs for neurological diseases; patents in field. Avocations: creative writing, photography, art, history, coin collecting/numismatics. Personal E-mail: balavmanyam@yahoo.com.

MANZI, JIM P., investment company executive; b. NYC, Dec. 22, 1951; s. Walter Edward and Ann (Smirka) M.; m. Glenda Baugh, May 20, 1978 BA, Colgate U., 1973; MAL.D., Fletcher Sch., Tufts U., 1979. Editl. asst. Nat. Rev. Mag., NYC, 1973-74; news reporter Gannet Newspapers, Port Chester, 1974-77; cons. McKinsey & Co., LA, Boston and NYC, 1979-83; v.p. mktg. and sales Lotus Devel. Corp., Cambridge, Mass., 1983-84, pres., 1984-86, 89-1996, CEO, 1986-1996; pres., CEO Industry Net, 1996; chmn. StoneGate Capital Group, LLC, Stanford, Conn., 1995—; bd. dirs. ThermoFisher Scientific, Inc., Waltham, Mass., 2000—, chmn., 2004—06, 2007—. Recipient In-Depth Reporting award AP, N.Y., 1976, 77, Investigative Reporting award N.Y. State Pubs. Assn., 1976, 77 Office: ThermoFisher Sci Inc 81 Wyman St Waltham MA 02454-9046 also: StoneGate Capital Group LLC 20 Stanford Dr Farmington CT 06032 *

MANZI, SUSAN M., rheumatologist; MD, U. Pitts., 1985. Diplomate Am. Bd. Internal Medicine, Am. Bd. Internal Medicine-rheumatology, lic. Pa., 1988. Intern Duke Univ. Hosp., Durham, NC, resident, 1988; fellow Univ. Pitts. Med. Ctr., 1991; chmn. dept. medicine West Penn Allegheny health system The Western Pa. Hosp., dir. Lupus ctr. of excellence, hosp. affiliations include, Allegheny Gen. Hosp., Forbes Regional Hosp. Named one of Top Doctors, Pitts. Mag., 2011. Office: The Western Pennsylvania Hospital 4800 Friendship Ave Pittsburgh PA 15224 Office Phone: 412-578-1152. Office Fax: 412-605-6669.

MANZKE, HERMANN GUSTAV, pediatrician, consultant; b. Stettin, Pomerania, Germany, May 13, 1933; s. Hermann Wilhelm and Elisabeth Margarete (Hollmichel) Manzke; m. Traute Behrmann, Aug. 30, 1963; children: Holger Christian, Jens Martin. MD, U. Kiel, Germany, 1959, privatdozent habilitation, 1970, prof., 1975. Resident, Kiel and Essen, Germany, 1959—61; staff Univ. Hosp. for Children, Kiel, 1962—68, dep. dir., 1975—86; med. dir. Kaiser-Friedrich Hosp., Norderney, 1987—95; chief dr. Fachklinikum, Borkum, Germany, 1997—2002; ret., 2002. Cons. Fachklinikum, Borkum, 2001—. Author: (books) Entwicklungsprognose von Kindern mit perinatalen Risikofaktoren, 1984, Entscheidet die Geburt uber das Schicksal?, 1998, August Steffen (1825-1910), Nestor and Spiritus rector of Pediatrics in Germany and Central Europe, 2005, History of Pediatrics, 2005; contbr. articles to profl. jours. Mem.: European Respiratory Soc. Home: Roesoll 13 Heikendorf 24226 Germany

MANZONI, DIEGO, medical educator; b. Milan, Nov. 14, 1955; Degree in Biol. Scis., U. Pisa, 1978; diploma, Scuola Normale Superiore, 1978. Vis. asst. prof. Dept. VCAPP, WSU, Wash., 1988—89; rschr. Scuola Normale Superiore Pisa, Italy, 1981—85, U.

Pisa Italy, 1985—92, assoc. prof., 1992—2011. Mem.: Collegium Orlas Barany Soc. Home: via Legnano 52 Lavagna Genova Liguria 16033 Italy Home Fax: 050 2213527. Personal E-mail: manzoni@dfb.unipi.it.

MAO, FRANK C., science educator; s. Wen-Bin Mao and Don-Tso Yen; m. Su-Fang Lin, Dec. 20, 1989; children: Huei-Yun, Jin-Yun, Chi-Yun, Chian-Yun. BS, Nat. Taiwan U., Taipei, 1984; MS, U. Wis., Madison, 1988, PhD, 1991. Assoc. prof. Nat. Chung Hsing U., Taichung, Taiwan, 1991—2004, prof., 2004—, chmn. dept. vet. med., 2006—09; dean coll. vet. med., 2009—. Chief cons. Maxluck Biotech Corp., Taipei, 1999—. Recipient Excellent Rsch. Achievement award, Nat. Chung Hsing U., 2004. Mem.: Taiwan Assn. of Vet. Medicine (life), Chinese Soc. of Vet. Sci. (life Excellent Tchg. award 2002). Achievements include patents for trivalent chromium complex compound and milk product containing the same; patents pending for composition for preventing and treating cardiovascular disorders; composition for reducing blood lipids. Avocations: travel, music, art. Home: 12F-5 No 108 sec 2 Han-Ko Rd Taichung 407 Taiwan Office: National Chung Hsing Univ 250 Kuo-Kuang Rd Taichung 402 Taiwan Office Fax: 886-4-22862073; Home Fax: 886-4-23116932. Business E-Mail: fcmao@nchu.edu.tw.

MAO, GUANG-PING, orthopedist, researcher; s. Jin-han Mao and Gui-zhen Tao. PhD, Fukushima Med. U., Japan, 1998. Diplomate Ministry Pub. Health China, 1990. Surgeon Nanjing Traffic Hosp., China, 1981—86, Nanjing Dongnan U. Hosp., 1990—93; asst. Fukushima Med. U., Japan, 1993—98; staff Fuxing Hosp. Orthops., Beijing, 1998—2000, Jinling Hosp. Orthops., Nanjing, 2001—. Adj. prof. Nanjing U. Jinling Hosp., China, 2003—. Manuscript editor: Chinese Jour. Clin. Rehab. Mem.: Japanese Soc. Lumbar Spine Disorders. Achievements include patents pending in field; patents in field. Avocations: swimming, travel, music, gardening, tropical fish. Home: Zhongshandonglu 305 Jiangsu Nanjing 210002 China Office: Nanjing Univ Jinling Hosp Zhongshandonglu 305 Jiangsu Nanjing 210002 China Office Fax: 86 25-84806263. Business E-Mail: maogp@sohu.com.

MAO, HUI JUAN, physician; b. Nanjing, Jan. 13, 1972; MD, Nanjing Med. U., 1989. Physician Jiangsu Province Hosp., 1989. Office: Guangzhou Rd 300 Nanjing Jiangsu 210029 China Business E-Mail: huijuanmao@126.com.

MAPEL, DOUGLAS WAYNE, epidemiologist, educator, pulmonologist, critical care specialist; b. Torrejon U.S. AFB, Madrid, Spain, Apr. 14, 1961; children: Xena, Sierra. BS in Chemistry, U. Tex., Arlington, 1984; MD, U. Tex., Galveston, 1988; MPH, U. N.Mex., 1996. Diplomate Am. Bd. Internal Medicine, Am. Bd. Pulmonary Diseases, Am. Bd. Critical Care Medicine. Resident Tex. Tech. U., Lubbock, 1988—92; fellow U. N.Mex., Albuquerque, 1992—96, asst. prof., 1996—2000, clin. prof., 2001—; med. dir. Lovelace Respiratory Rsch. Inst., Albuquerque, 2001—03, Lovelace Clinic Found., Albuquerque, 2003—; sr. ptnr. Progressive Med. Intensivists, 2003—06; founding ptnr. Critical Care Cons. of Ariz., 2006—, Northern Ariz. Pulmonary Assn. Co-author: (book) Rom's Occupational Medicine, 1998, Occupational Disorders of the Lung, 2001; contbr. articles to profl. jours., scientific papers. Fellow: ACP, Am. Coll. Chest Physicians (Clin. Rsch. award 2004); mem.: Am. Thoracic Soc. Home: PO Box 67038 Albuquerque NM 87193 Office: Lovelace Clin Found 2309 Renard Pl SE Ste 103 Albuquerque NM 87106 Office Phone: 505-938-9900. Business E-Mail: doug.mapel@lcfresearch.org.

MAPLESDEN, CAROL HARPER, marriage and family therapist, music educator; b. Phila., Aug. 27, 1947; d. Emmitt Dewain and Helen Esther (Davison) Harper; m. James Paul Maplesden, May 27, 1967, (dec. Apr. 14, 2008); children: Andrew James, Elizabeth Elvira. BA, Holy Family Coll., Phila., 1979; MA, La Salle U., Phila., 1984. Cert. counselor Nat. Bd. Cert. Counselors, lic. profl. counselor of mental health Del., Pa. Child, youth and family therapist People Acting To Help, Phila., 1983—86, Benjamin Rush Cmty. Mental Health, Phila., 1987-88; clin. dir. N.E. Treatment, Phila., 1988-89; outpatient supr. Interact Com. Mental Health, Phila., 1989; program supr. Cath. Charities Christopher House, Trenton, N.J., 1989-90; dir. Carden Family Inst., Phila., 1984—, CEO, 1984—, instr. keyboard, organist, vocal performer, vocal choir and handbell choir dir. Carden music div., 1993—. Seminar lectr. in Phila. area. Author: (piano course and audio tape) Young Beginnings Piano Course, Part I, 1993. Mem.: DAR, APA, DAC, Internat. Assn. Marriage and Family Counselors, Daus. Am. Colonists (chpt. regent 2006—), Daughters Union Vets. Civil War (Pa. state pres. 2001—02). Methodist. Avocations: history studies, genealogy, crafts. Office Phone: 215-741-4234.

MARAMOROSCH, KARL, virologist, educator; b. Vienna, Jan. 16, 1915; came to U.S., 1947, naturalized, 1952; s. Jacob and Stefanie Olga (Schlesinger) M.; m. Irene Ludwinowska, Nov. 15, 1938; 1 dau., Lydia Ann. MS magna cum laude in Entomology, Agrl. U., Warsaw, Poland, 1938; student, Poly. U. Bucharest, Rumania, 1944-46; fellow, Bklyn. Bot. Garden, 1947-48; PhD (predoctoral fellow Am. Cancer Soc. 1948-49), Columbia, 1949. Civilian internee, Romania, 1939—46; asst., then assoc. Rockefeller U., NYC, 1949-61; sr. entomologist Boyce Thompson Inst., Yonkers, NY, 1961-74, program dir. virology and insect physiology, 1962-74; disting. prof. microbiology Waksman Inst., Rutgers U., New Brunswick, NJ, 1974—85; prof. entomology Cook Coll., Rutgers U., New Brunswick, 1985—, Robert L. Starkey prof., 1983—; vis. prof. agr. U. Wageningen, Netherlands, 1953, Cornell U., 1957, Rutgers U., 1967-68, Fordham U., 1973, Hokkaido U., Sapporo, Japan, 1980, Justus Liebig U., Giessen, Ger., 1983. Mendel lectr. St. Peters Coll., Jersey City, 1963; virologist FAO to Philippines, 1960; Disting. Vis. prof. Fudan U., Shanghai, 1982; cons. FAO-UN, World-wide survey, 1963; chmn. U.S.-Japan Coop. Seminar, 1965, 74, 85; mem. panel food and fiber Nat. Acad. Scis., 1966; cons. rice virus diseases AID-IRRI, Hyderabad, India, 1971; cons. UNDP, Bangalore, India, 1978-79; virologist FAO/UNDP, Sri Lanka, 1981, 82, 83, Mauritius, 1985; AIBS lectr., 1970-72, Found. Microbiology Nat. lectr., 1972-73, Fulbright Disting. prof., Yugoslavia, 1972, 78; mem. tropical medicine and parasitology study sect. NIH, 1972-76; chmn. 1st-3d Internat. Confs. Comparative Virology, 1969, 73, 76. Author: Comparative Symptomatology of Coconut Diseases of Unknown Etiology, 1964; editor: Biological Transmission of Disease Agents, 1962, Insect Viruses, 1968, Viruses, Vectors and Vegetation, 1969, Comparative Virology, 1971, Mycoplasma Diseases, 1973, Viruses, Evolution and Cancer, 1974, Invertebrate Immunity, 1975, Legume Diseases in the Tropics, 1975, Invertebrate Tissue Culture: Research Applications, 1976, Invertebrate Tissue Culture: Applications in Medicine, Biology and Agriculture, 1976, Aphids as Virus Vectors, 1977, Insect and Plant Viruses: An Atlas, 1977, Viruses and Environment, 1978, Practical Tissue Culture Applications, 1979, Leafhopper Vectors and Plant Disease Agents, 1979, Vectors of Plant Pathogens, 1980, Invertebrate Systems in Vitro, 1980, Vectors of Disease Agents, 1981, Mycoplasma Diseases of Trees and Shrubs, 1981, Mycoplasma and Allied Pathogens of Plants, Animals and Human Beings, 1981, Plant Diseases and Vectors: Ecology and Epidemiology, 1981, Invertebrate Cell Culture Applications, 1982, Pathogens, Vectors and Plant Diseases: Approaches to Control, 1982, Subviral Pathogens of Plants and Animals, 1985, Viral Insecticides for Biological Control, 1985, Biotechnology Advances in Insect Pathology and Cell Culture, 1987, Mycoplasma Diseases of Crops, 1988, Invertebrate and Fish Tissue Culture, 1988, Biotechnology for Biological Control of Pests and Vectors, 1991, Viroids and Satellites: Molecular Parasites at the Frontier of Life, 1991, Plant Diseases of Uncertain Etiology, 1992, Insect Cell Biotechnology, 1994, Arthropod Cell Culture Systems, 1994, Forest Trees and Palms: Diseases and Control, 1996, Invertebrate Cell Culture: Novel Directions and Biotechnology Applications, 1997, Invertebrate Cell Culture: Looking Toward the XXI Century, 1997, Biotechnology and Plant Protection in Forestry Sci., 1998, Maintenance of Human, Animal, and Plant Pathogen Vectors, 1999; Methods in Virology, 1964-84, Advances in Virus Research, 1972—, Archives of Virology, 1973-78, Intervirology, 1973-77, Advances in Cell Culture, 1979-89, Jour. Virological Methods, 1980-; editor in chief Jour. NY Entomol. Soc, 1972-84; assoc. editor: Virology, 1964-68, 75-79. Recipient Sr. Rsch., Lalor Found., 1957, Nat. Ciba-Geigy award in agr., 1976, Wolf prize in agr., Wolf Found., Israel, 1980, Jurzykowski prize in biology, 1980, Disting. Svc. award, Am. Inst. Biol. Scis., 1983, Khailshanker Durlabhji award, Jaipur, 1993, Lifetime Achievement award, Soc. In Vitro Biology, 2001, Gold Shield award, Egyptian Soc. Biol. Control, 2007, Naydu Lifetime Achievement award, Tirupati U., India, 2010. Fellow AAAS (hon., Campbell award 1958), Entomol. Soc. Am. (hon., L.O. Howard Disting. Achievement award 2006), Am. Phytopath. Soc., NY Acad. Scis. (A. Cressy Morrison prize natural sci. 1951, chmn. divsn. microbiology 1956-60, rec. sec. 1960-61, v.p. 1962-63), Nat. Acad. Scis. India (hon.); mem. Harvey Soc., Growth Soc., Phytopath. Soc., Indian, Japan, Can. phytopath. socs., Leopoldina Acad., Internat. Com. Virus Nomenclature, Electron Microscopy Soc., Am. Soc. Microbiology (Waksman award 1978), Soc. In Vitro Biology (Tissue Culture Assn., pres. N.E. br. 1978-81, pres. history br. 1988-90, Disting. Lifetime Achievement award 2001), Soc. Invertebrate Pathology (hon., founder's lectr., Adelaide 1990, Founder's honoree Sapporo 1998, hon. mem. Warwick, 2008), Internat. Assn. Medicinal Forest Plants (pres. 1989—), Am. Soc. Virology, Sigma Xi (pres. Rugers chpt. 1978). Home: 17 Black Birch Ln Scarsdale NY 10583-7456 Office: Rutgers U Dept Entomology New Brunswick NJ 08901 Office Phone: 848-932-9329. Personal E-mail: karlmaramorosch@yahoo.com. Business E-Mail: maramors@rci.rutgers.edu, maramorosch@aesop.rutgers.edu.

MARÃO, HELOISA FONSECA, dentist, researcher; b. Araçatuba, São Paulo, Brazil, July 5, 1982; DD, São Paulo State U., 2005, attending, 2008—. Rsch. fellow, dept. surgery and integrated clinics Sch. Dentistry Araçatuba, UNESP São Paulo State U., Araçatuba, Brazil, 2008—. Home: Afonso Pena Araçatuba São Paulo 16015040 Brazil Personal E-mail: heloisafonsecamarao@yahoo.com.br.

MARASCO, WAYNE A., oncologist, educator; PhD, U. Conn. Sch. Medicine, 1980; MD, U. Mich. Med. Sch., 1986. Assoc. prof. Harvard Med. Sch.; assoc. prof. cancer immunology & AIDS Dana-Farber Cancer Inst. Founder Nat. Found. Cancer Rsch. Ctr. for Therapeutic Antibody Engring. Office: Dana-Farber Cancer Institute 44 Binney St Jimmy Fund 824 Boston MA 02115 Office Phone: 617-632-2153. Office Fax: 617-632-3889. E-mail: wayne_marasco@dfci.harvard.edu.

MARAZITA, MARY LOUISE, genetics researcher; b. Cheboygan, Mich., June 13, 1954; m. Richard T. McCoy, 1984; 5 children. BS, Mich. State U., East Lansing, 1976; PhD in Genetics, U. NC, Chapel Hill, 1980. Fellow U. So. Calif., 1980-82; statistician, instr. UCLA, 1982-86; asst. prof. human genetics Med. Coll. Va., 1986-93; dir. Cleft Palate-craniofacial Ctr. U. Pitts., 1993-00, dept. chair oral biology, 1999—, asst. dean for rsch. Sch. Dental Medicine, 2000-2001, assoc. dean rsch., 2001—. Instr. biomath. U. Calif., 1984-86; asst. prof. dentistry Med. Coll. Va., 1992-93; assoc. prof. human genetics and oral biology U. Pitts., 1993-97, prof. human genetics and oral and maxillofacial surgery, 1997—, prof. psychiatry, 2003—. Fellow Am. Coll. Med. Genetics, Am. Cleft Palate Assn., Am. Soc. Human Genetics, Internat. Genetic Epidemiol. Soc., Internat. Assn. Dental Rsch. Achievements include research in genetics of cleft lip, cleft palate and other craniofacial anomalies, including statistical genetic analysis and gene mapping studies. Office: Univ Pitts Dept Oral Biology/Genetics Ste 500 Bridgeside Point 100 Technology Dr Pittsburgh PA 15219 Business E-Mail: marazita@pitt.edu.

MARCAL, WILMAR SACHETIN, veterinarian, educator; b. Londrina, Parana, Brazil, Mar. 22, 1959; PhD, UNESP, 1996. Veterinarian U. Londrina, 1981, adj. prof., 1987—, pres., 2006—10. Named Educator of Yr., Brazilian Assn. Tng. and Devel., 2010. Mem.: Londrina Acad. Scis., Parana Acad. Vet. Medicine, Elos Club Londrina. Avocation: soccer. Office: Rua Sao Bernardo Do Campo 234 Londrina Parana 86062150 Brazil Business E-Mail: wilmar@uel.br.

MARCDANTE, KAREN JEAN, medical educator; b. Milw., Sept. 15, 1955; d. Willard Karl and Beth Elaine (Maule) Kohn; m. Mark Wendelberger, Aug. 5, 1978 (div. Sept. 1985); m. Anthony Marcdante, Oct. 17, 1998. Student, Marquette U., Milw., 1973-76; MD, Med. Coll. Wis., Milw., 1980. Diplomate Am. Bd. Pediat. & Pediat. Crit. Care. Resident in pediat. Med. Coll. Wis. affiliated hosps., Milw., 1980-83; instr. pediat. Med. Coll. Wis., Milw., 1983-85, asst. prof. pediat., 1987-94, assoc. prof. pediat., 1994-2000, prof. pediat., 2000—, assoc. dean curriculum, 1997—2003, vice-chair edn. dept. pediat., 1994—, sr. assoc. dean edn., 2010—; fellow in pediatric critical care U. Calif., San Francisco, 1985-87; vice chief staff Children's Hosp. Wis., Milw., 1995-97; chair rank and tenure com. Med. Coll. Wis., 2007—09. Dir. Respiratory Care Svcs., 1992-98, Transport Program, 1998-2008; chief dept. pediat. Children's Hosp. Wis., 1991-95, dept. critical care 1993-95, mem. numerous coms., including care mgmt. steering com., 1994-1999, critical care com., 1991—2011, pres.-elect, 2003-05; pres. med. dental staff, 2005-07. Contbr. numerous articles to profl. jours. Recipient New Investigator award Assn. Am. Med. Colls., 1992, Cert. Leadership award YWCA and Marquette Electronics Found., 1992, Laureate award Ctrl. Group Ednl. Affairs, 2004, Disting. Svc. award, 2009; grantee Dept. HHS, 1996—. Mem. Am. Acad. Pediat. (pub. rels. chair Wis. chpt. 1988-91, sec.-treas. 1990-95, v.p. 1995-96, chair careers and opportunities 1996-2001), Soc. Critical Care Medicine (chair task force on quality improvement pediat. 1994-96, quality indicator devel. work group 1997-98, Presdl. citation 1996, 97), Coun. on Med. Student Edn. in Pediat. (co-chair task force on tchg. methods 1991-96, nominating com. 1993-95, exec. com. 1996-99, sec.-treas. 1997-99). Business E-Mail: kwendel@mcw.edu.

MARCHASE, RICHARD BANFIELD, cell biologist, educator, research administrator; b. Sayre, Pa., Mar. 12, 1948; s. Nicholas and Vivian H. (Banfield) M.; m. Gail C. Andrews, Sept. 2, 2006; children: Nicholas Darrow, Allison Elizabeth. BS in Engring., Cornell U., 1970; PhD in Biophysics, Johns Hopkins U., 1976; postgrad., Duke U., 1978. Muscular Dystrophy Assn. postdoctoral fellow divsn. neurology Duke U. Med. Ctr., 1976-77, USPHS postdoctoral fellow dept. anatomy, 1977-78, asst. prof. anatomy, 1978-86; assoc. prof. cell biology U. Ala.-Birmingham, 1986—90, prof., 1990—, chmn., 1992—2000, sr. assoc. dean biomed. rsch., 2000—06, v.p. rsch. and econ. devel., 2004—. Contbr. chpts. to books, articles to profl. jours. Recipient Hamilton Watch award Cornell U., 1970, award Juvenile Diabetes Found., 1995-2002; Grad. fellow NSF, 1970-73, Danforth Found. grad. fellow, 1973-76; Nanaline H. Duke scholar, 1982-85; grantee USPHS 1979-, NSF, Presdl. Young Investigator grant, 1982-87. Mem. AAAS, Am. Soc. Cell Biology, Am. Soc. Zoology, Assn. of Anatomy, Cell Biology, and Neurobiology Chairpersons (pres. 1995-96), Am. Assn. Anatomists, Fed. Am. Soc. Exptl. Biology (bd. dirs. 2000— v.p. sci. policy, 2005, pres.-elect 2007), Sigma Xi. Office: U Ala Birmingham 720 AB Birmingham AL 35294-0001 Home: 4012 Lenox Rd Birmingham AL 35213 Office Phone: 205-934-1294. Business E-Mail: marchase@uab.edu.

MARCHESINI REGGIANI, LEONARDO, orthopedist; b. Bologna, Italy, June 6, 1976; Degree in Medicine, U. Bologna, 2002, degree in Orthops. & Traumatology, 2007. Asst. Inst. Orthop. Rizzoli, 2007—. SITOP fellow, 2000 Euros. Avocation: cycling. Office: Inst Rizzoli segr Chir Ped Bologna 40136 Italy Office Fax: 390516366837. E-mail: lmarchesinireggiani@gmail.com.

MARCIKIĆ, MLADEN, pathologist; b. Osijek, Slavonija, Croatia, Mar. 5, 1953; s. Žarko and Emilija (Stanković) M.; m. Marija Vuković, Jan. 22, 1983; 1 child, Marina. MD, U. Zagreb, Croatia, 1978, MS, 1988. Lic. pathologist, forensic pathologist, Croatia. Gen. practitioner Primary Health Svc., Osijek, 1980; specialist Inst. Forensic Medicine U. Zagreb, 1980-85; specialist Inst. Pathology Clin. Hosp. Rebro, Zagreb, 1990-92; chief dept. forensic medicine Clin. Hosp., Osijek, 1993—; prof. med. faculty U. Osijek, Croatia. Expert forensic medicine Ct. Justice, Osijek, 1985; sr. instr. forensic medicine U. Zagreb Sch. Medicine, 1993; prof. med. faculty U.Osijek, Croatia, 2004. Contbr. articles to profl. jours. Lt. Croatian Med. Corps, 1984. Jr. state champion Rowing Assn., Lake Bled, 1971. Mem. Croatian Soc. Ct. Experts. Avocation: rowing. Home: Sjenjak 36 31000 Osijek Slavonija Croatia Office: Clin Hosp Dept Forensic Med J Huttlera 4 31000 Osijek Croatia Home Phone: 385 31 573 679; Office Phone: 385 31 511 858. Business E-Mail: mladen.marcikic@os.t-com.hr.

MARCINIAK, WITOLD LUKASZ, orthopaedic surgeon; b. Poznan, Poland, Oct. 18, 1929; s. Justyn and Jadwiga (Kubanek) M.; m. Zofia Fedorczyk, Jan. 4, 1955 (div. 1973); 1 child, Wojciech; m. Krystyna Bogumila Alwin, Aug. 18, 1980 MD, K. Marcinkowski Med. Sch., Poznan, 1954. Intern, resident, fellow dept. orthop. K. Marcinkowski Med. Sch., Poznan, 1954—60, adj., 1960—75, docent, 1975—89, prof., 1989—90, prof. dept. pediat. orthop., 1990—2000; ret., 2001. Dir. Inst. Orthop. and Rehab., Poznan, 1988-97; head dept. orthop., Poznan, 1988-89, head dept. pediat. orthop., 1989-00; regional cons. Ministry Health, Poland, 1995-98 Author: Club Foot, 1976, Dega's Orthopeadics and Rehabilitation, 2003; editor: Early Conservative Treatment of Club Foot, 1993 Mem.: Polish Soc. Orthop. and Traumatology (hon.; pres. pediat. orthop. divsn. 1997—2000). Roman Catholic. Avocations: sightseeing, recreational activities, gardening. Home: Ul. Grunwaldzka 29A/18 60-783 Poznan Poland

MARCOM, PAUL KELLY, oncologist; MD, Baylor Coll. Medicine, Tex., 1989. Resident, medicine Duke U. Med. Ctr, 1989—92, resident, hematology and oncology, 1992—95, post-doctoral fellow, 1995—97, with med. oncology dept., 1997—. Contbr. several articles to profl. jours. Office: Duke U Med Ctr Box 3395 Med Ctr DUMC 3147 Durham NC 27710 Office Phone: 919-684-3877. Office Fax: 919-681-0874.

MARCOS, LUIS, physician, researcher; b. Lima, Peru, Mar. 16, 1978; MD, U. Peruana Cayetano Heredia, 2003. Internal medicine resident U. Tex. Health Sci., Houston, 2006—09; clin. infectious diseases fellow Wash. U., St. Louis, 2009—. Recipient Abeefe Bristol-Myers Squibb Med. Rsch. award, 2001, 2004, Procter & Gamble award, 2002. Mem.: ACP (Rsch. and Clin. award 2007—09), Am. Soc. Tropical Medicine and Hygiene, Infectious Diseases Soc. Am. Home: 1031 Highlands Plz Dr Apt 410 Saint Louis MO 63110 Personal E-mail: marcoslrz@yahoo.com.

MARCOTTE, PAUL JOHN, neurosurgeon, educator; b. Ottawa, Ont., Can., Oct. 15, 1958; (parents Can. and Am. citizens); s. Paul John and Elinor Ann (Simeone) M. BSc, U. Ottawa, 1980, MD, 1984. Intern Ottawa Civic Hosp., 1984-85; resident U. Ottawa, 1985-90, asst. prof., 1990-92; fellow in spinal surgery Barrow Neurol. Inst., Phoenix, 1991-92; assoc. prof. U. Pa., Phila., 1993—. Contbr. articles to profl. jours., chpts. to books. Fellow: ACS, Royal Coll. Physicians and Surgeons (Can.); mem.: Can. Congress Neurol. Surgeons, Am. Assn. Neurol. Surgeons, Congress Neurol. Surgeons. Roman Catholic. Avocations: hockey, model railroading, automobiles. Office: Hosp U Pa 3400 Spruce St Philadelphia PA 19104-4206

MARCUS, ABIR A., psychiatrist; arrived in US, 1995; d. Assaad Aziz Abdel-Sayed and Nadra Nassry Sourial; divorced; 1 child, Gina Marie. MD with honors, Ain Shams U., Cairo, 1991. Diplomate Am. Bd. Psychiatry and Neurology, Am. Bd. Med. Specialties, lic. psychiatrist NJ, NY. Intern Ain Shams Med. Sch., Cairo, 1992—93, instr. forensic medicine and toxicology, 1994—95; resident in psychiatry NJ Med. Sch., Newark, 1996—2000; fellow, asst. prof. Robert Wood Johnson, Piscataway, NJ, 2000—01; pvt. practice Little Silver and NYC, 1999—. Adj. asst. prof. Robert Wood Johnson Med. Sch., Piscataway, 2001—; task force com. for curriculum devel. in psychotherapy tng. for residents U. Medicine and Dentistry NJ Med. Sch., Newark, 1999—2000; cons. CPC Behavioral Health Care, Red Bank, NJ, 2001—; cons. in field. Contbr. articles to profl. jours. Recipient Physician's Recognition award, AMA, 1999, 2005; scholar, Nat. Inst. Drug Abuse. Mem.: Am. Psychoanalytic Assn. (assoc. mem.), Neurosci. Edn. Inst., Am. Soc. Clin. Psychopharmacology, NJ Psychiat. Assn. (pres. resident chpt. 1999, pres. 2000, early career psychiatry com., pub. edn. com., disaster preparedness com., resident and med. student com.), Am. Psychiat. Assn., Am. Acad. Addiction Psychiatry, Am. Soc. Addiction Medicine. Avocations: reading, travel, ballroom dancing, salsa dancing. Office: 34 Sycamore Ave # 2C Little Silver NJ 07739 Office Phone: 732-530-3122. Personal E-mail: doctor.marcus@hotmail.com. Business E-Mail: drmarcus@birovenusmedicalspa.com.

MARCUS, CAROLE LESLEY, pediatric pulmonologist, educator; MB, BChir, U. Witwatersrand, 1982. Diplomate Am. Bd. Pediatrics-pediatric pulmonology, Am. Bd. Pediatrics-sleep medicine, lic. Pa., 2003. Intern pediatrics Schneider Children's Hosp., 1983; resident pediatrics Li Jewish Hosp., 1984, Univ. Hosp. of Bklyn., 1986, State Univ. NY Downstate Med. Ctr., 1986; fellow pediatric pulmonology Children's Hosp. of LA, 1991; co-program dir. Clin. and Translational Sci. Awards; co-dir. Clin. and Translational Rsch. Ctr.; assoc. dir. Inst. for Translational Medicine and Therapeutics; prof. pediat. Univ. of Pa., Children's Hospital of Phila., dir. sleep ctr. Dep. editor Sleep. Co-author: (publs.) Cortical processing of respiratory occlusion stimuli in children with central hypoventilation syndrome, 2008, Rapid eye movement latency in children and adolescents, 2008, Effect of sleep stage on breathing in children with central hypoventilation, 2008, and other numerous publications. Named one of Top Doctors, Phila. Mag., 2011. Mem.: Am. Acad. of Pediatrics, Am. Thoracic Soc., Sleep Rsch. Soc. Office: Children's Hospital of Philadelphia Division of Pediatric Pulmonology Wood Bldg 5th Fl 34th & Civic Ctr Blvd Philadelphia PA 19104 Office Phone: 267-426-5842. Office Fax: 215-590-3500. E-mail: marcus@email.chop.edu.

MARCUS, DEVRA JOY COHEN, internist; b. Bronx, NY, Sept. 5, 1940; d. Benjamin and Gertrude (Siegel) Cohen; m. Robert A. Marcus, Apr. 1963 (div. 1974); children: Rachel, Adam; m. Michael J. Horowitz, Mar. 2, 1975, 1 child, Naomi. BA, Brandeis U., 1961; MD, Stanford U., 1966. Diplomate Am. Bd. Internal Medicine. Intern Stanford U., 1966-67, resident in internal medicine, 1967-68; gen. internist D.C. Dept. Pub. Health, 1968-69, Cardozo Neighborhood Health Ctr., Washington, 1969-73; med. dir. East of the River Health Assn., Washington, 1973-75; fellow in infectious disease Washington Hosp. Ctr., 1975-77; gen. internist Police and Fire Clinic, Washington, 1977-78; pvt. practice Washington, 1977—; assoc. clin. prof. medicine George Washington U. Med Ctr., Washington, 1978—; gen internist World Bank, Washington, 1978-81; ptnr. Traveller's Med. Svc. D.C., 1980-82; gen. internist Community of Good Hope Med. Clinic, Washington, 1984-85; assoc. clin. prof. medicine Georgetown U. Med. Ctr., Washington, 1987—; internist, physician So Others Might Eat, 2011. Preceptor Georgetown U. Hosp., 1986—; med. missions to Honduras, 2001, Romania, 2002, Dominican Republic, 2004, 05, 06, 10, 11, China, 2005. Contbr. articles to profl. jours. Exec. com. Woodley Park Citizen's Assn., 1979-80; chair mayor's adv. com. on prevention, 1982-83; bd. dirs. Exodus Youth Svcs., 1987-89; vol. med. work Arlington Free U., 2010. Named Best Physicians of Washington, Washingtonian Mag., 1999, 2005 Fellow: ACP; mem.: AMA (Physicians Recognition award 1981, 1984, 1987, 1990, 1993, 1996, 1999, 2002, 2005, 2008), Physicians for Human Rights (asylum applications), Med. Soc. D.C. (founder com. on women 1983, pres. com. on women 1985—87, med. ethics and judiciary com. 1987—91, judiciary coun. 1992—96, credentials com., communicable disease com.). Home: 1205 Crest Ln Mc Lean VA 22101-1837

MARCUS, ERIC ROBERT, psychiatrist; b. NYC, Feb. 16, 1944; s. Victor and Pearl (Maddow) M.; m. Eslee Samberg, Nov. 24, 1985; children: Max, Pia. AB, Columbia U., 1965; MD, U. Wis., 1969. Diplomate Am. Bd. Psychiatry and Neurology. Intern med. ctr. Bellevue hosp. NYU, 1969-70; resident NY state psychiat. inst. Columbia Presbyn. Med. Ctr.st., 1972-75; from co-dir. to dir. neuropsychiat//diagnostic treatment unit Columbia-Presbyn. Med. Ctr., NYC, 1975-84; dir. St. Marks Free Clinic, NYC, 1971-75; dir. med. student edn. in psychiatry coll. physicians and surgeons Columbia U., NYC, 1981—2007, bd. govs. student health, 1986—2003, supervising tng. analyst ctr. psychoanalytic training and rsch., 1994—, clin. prof. psychiatry and social medicine coll. physicians and surgeons, 1995—, dir. ctr. psychoanalytic tng. and rsch., 2007—, prof. clin. psychiatry, 2008—. Author: Psychosis and Near Psychosis, 1992, 2d edit., 2003; mem. editl. bd.: The Psychoanalytic Study of Society, 1989—94, Jour. Clin. Psychoanalysis, 1998—2002; co-editor: Psychiatry, 1998, 2nd edit, 2010; contbr. articles to profl. jours. Recipient Weber Rsch. award Columbia U. Psychoanalytic Ctr., 1991, O'Connor Tchg. award, 1995, Columbia U. Presdl. award for Outstanding Tchg., 1999. Fellow: NY Acad. Medicine, Am. Coll. Psychoanalysts, Am. Psychiat. Assn. (pres. NY County Dist. 2002—03, Roeske award 1991); mem.: Assn. Psychoanalytic Medicine (pres. 1999—2001), Am. Psychoanalytic Assn. (chmn. com. on univ. and med. edn. 1999—2005, mem. editl. bd. Jour. 2000—03, Sabshin award 2003). Avocations: classical music, photography, swimming, reading. Office: Columbia U Dept Psychiatry 1051 Riverside Dr New York NY 10032-1013 Office Phone: 212-427-0543.

MARCUS, FRANK ISADORE, cardiologist, educator; b. Haverstraw, NY, Mar. 23, 1928; s. Samuel and Edith (Sattler) M.; m. Janet Geller, June 30, 1957; children: Ann, Steve, Lynn. BA, Columbia U., 1948; MS, Tufts U., 1951; MD cum laude, Boston U., 1953. Diplomate Am. Bd. Internal Medicine (subspecialty cardiovasc. diseases). Intern Peter Bent Brigham Hosp., Boston, 1953-54, asst. resident, 1956-57, research fellow in cardiology, 1957-58; clin. fellow in cardiology Georgetown U. Hosp., 1958-59, chief med. resident, 1959-60; chief of cardiology Georgetown U. Med. Service, D.C. Gen. Hosp., Washington, 1960-68; instr. medicine Georgetown U. Sch. Medicine, 1960-63, asst. prof., 1963-68, assoc. prof., 1968; prof. medicine, chief cardiology sect. U. Ariz. Coll. Medicine, Tucson, 1969-82, disting. prof. internal medicine (cardiology), 1982-99, emeritus prof., 1999—, dir. electrophysiology, 1982—2001; prin. investigator multidisciplinary study of right ventricular dysplasia Nat. Heart, Lung and Blood Inst., 2001—08. Cons. cardiology VA Hosp., Tucson, 1969, USAF Regional Hosp., Davis-Monthan AFB, Tucson, 1969; mem. panel drug efficacy study, panel on cardiovascular drugs Nat. Acad. Scis.-NRC, 1967-68; chmn. undergrad. cardiovascular tng. grant com. HEW-NIH, 1970; dir. Arrhythmia Svcs., 1996-2001. Editor: Modern Concepts of Cardiovascular Disease, 1982—84; mem. editl. bd. Circulation, 1974—81, Current Problems in Cardiology, 1975—79, Cardiovascular Drugs and Therapy, 1986—2000, New Trends in Arrythmias, 1984—, Jour. Am. Coll. Cardiology, 1983—87, 1996—2000, Am. Jour. Cardiology, 1984—, Jour. Cardiovasc. Drugs and Therapy, 1991—2000, Pacing and Clin. Electrophysiology, 1995—, Annals of Noninvasive Electrocardiology, 1996—, Cardiology, 2000—, Jour. Electrocardiology, 2005—; contbr. articles to profl. jours. Chmn. Washington Heart Assn. High Sch. Heart Program, 1966-68. Capt. USAF, 1954-56. Recipient Career Devel. award NIH, 1965, Student AMA Golden Apple award Georgetown U. Sch. Medicine, 1968, Disting. Alumni award Boston U. Sch. Medicine, 2003, Master Clinician award Coun. Clin. Cardiology, 2005; Mass. Heart Assn. fellow, 1957-58; John and Mary Markle scholar, 1960-65; grantee Nat. Heart, Lung and Blood Inst., 2001—08. Fellow Coun. on Clin. Cardiology Am. Heart Assn., ACP (Ariz. laureate award 1987), Am. Coll. Cardiology (bd. govs. Ariz. 1984-87, asst. sec. 1987-89, trustee); mem. Assn. Univ. Cardiologists, Inc. (v.p. 1989-90, pres. 1990-91), Ariz. Heart Assn. (dir. 1970, v.p. 1972-73, chmn. rsch. com. 1970-72), So. Ariz. Heart Assn. (dir. 1969), Heart Rhythm Soc.(Pioneer Facial & Electrophysiology award 2011, Outstanding Achievement award, Pacing & Electrophysiology award), Electrocardiac Arrhytamia Soc., Alpha Omega Alpha. Home: 4949 E Glenn St Tucson AZ 85712-1212 Office: U Ariz Univ Med Ctr 1501 N Campbell Ave Tucson AZ 85724-0001 Home Phone: 520-327-1339; Office Phone: 520-626-1416. Business E-Mail: fmarcus@u.arizona.edu.

MARCUS, JUDITH R., pediatrician, hematologist, oncologist; Studied, NYU, 1971. Diplomate Am. Bd. of Pediatrics, cert. pediatric hematology-oncology. Intern Albert Einstein coll. of medicine, resident, 1972—74; fellow Meml. Sloan-Kettering Cancer Ctr., 1977—79; with White Plains Hosp. Ctr., Morgan Stanley Children's Hosp.; clin. prof. coll. of physicians and surgeons Columbia Univ. Med. Ctr. Office: Columbia University Medical Center 161 Ft Washington Ave 7th Fl New York NY 10032

MARCUS, LINDA SUSAN, dermatologist; b. Bklyn. d. Nathaniel and Eugenia (Portnay) Marcus; m. Ronald Carlin, July 5, 1976; children: Robert Adam, Neal Marc. BS, Adelphi U., Garden City, NJ, 1970; MD, Downstate Med. Sch., Bklyn., 1975. Diplomate Am. Bd. Dermatology. Intern Long Island (N.Y.) Jewish Med. Ctr., 1975-76; resident in dermatology Columbia-St. Luke's, NYC, 1976-77, Boston U.-Tufts U., 1977-79; pvt. practice Wyckoff, NJ, 1980—. Dir. dermatology Valley Hosp., Ridgewood. Contbr. articles to profl. jours. Chair Nat. Psoriasis Found., NJ. Mem. Am. Acad. Dermatology (editor pamphlet editl. bd.), Am. Soc. Dermatol. Surgeons, Internat. Soc. Dermatol. Surgeons, NJ Dermatol. Soc. (program dir.), NJ North Dermatol. Soc. (co-chair, pres.), Dermatol. Soc. NJ (pres.). Avocations: swimming, ice skating. Office: 271 Godwin Ave Wyckoff NJ 07481-2037 Office Phone: 201-891-1373. Personal E-mail: sexyderm@verizon.net.

MARCUS, MARY ELLEN, nursing educator, marketing public relations educator; d. Douglas Raymond and Genevieve Marie Marcus. B, U. Mass., Boston, 1977; M, Goddard Coll., Plainfield, Vt., 1986, studied with Mary Belenky; PhD, Harvard U. RN Bellevue Hosp. NY, 1967; cert. in acting Am. Conservatory Theater, 1976, Drama Studio, 1978, psychotherapist Psychosynthesis Inst. NY, 1986. Adj. faculty St Johns River CC, Orange Pk., Fla., 2009—; consulting nursing dir. Substance Abuse Rehab., Jacksonville, Fla., 2010—. Contbr. articles to profl. jours. Citizen adv. bd. Saratogian Newspaper, NY, 2001—02; bd. dirs. HOA bd., Middleburg, Fla., 2010—. Grant, Saratoga Springs, NY, 1988—2008. Mem.: AFTRA. Avocation: travel. Home: 2711 Woodsdale Dr Middleburg FL 32068

MARCUS, MICHAEL, pediatrician, pulmonologist, educator; Attended, State U. NY. Diplomate Am. Bd. of Pediatrics, Am. Bd. of Pediatrics-pediatric pulmonology, Am. Bd. Allergy and Immunology. Resident Nassau County Med. Ctr.; fellow Children's Hosp. of Phila.; assoc. prof. pediat. Suny Downstate. Office: Maimonides Medical Center 4820 10th Ave Brooklyn NY 11219 Office Phone: 718-283-6000.

MARCUS, RANDALL EVAN, orthopaedic surgery educator; b. NYC, Feb. 10, 1950; s. Irwin and Dorthy (Mann) Marcus; m. Anne Mulligan, June 2, 1984; 1 child, Blair Mulligan. BS in Biochemistry, magna cum laude, Tulane U., 1972; MD, La. State U. Sch. Medicine, 1975. Diplomate Am. Bd. Orthopaedic Surgery, lic. Ohio. Fellow Nufield dept. orthopaedic surgery Oxford U., England, 1980-81; internat. fellow dept. surgery U. Basle, Switzerland, 1981; sr. fellow dept. orthopaedics U. Wash. Harborview Med. Ctr., Seattle, 1981; rotating surg. intern Case Western Res. U. Sch. Medicine, Cleve., 1975-76, asst. resident gen. surgery, 1976-77, resident orthopaedics, 1977-79, chief resident, 1979-80, postdoctoral fellow, 1977-80, instr. orthopaedic surgery, 1981-82, asst. prof., 1982-83, 86-91, assoc. prof., 1992-97, prof., 1998—. Dir. divsn. foot and ankle surgery Case Western Res. U. Sch. Medicine. Contbr. articles to med. jours. Recipient Tchg. Excellence award, Case Western Res. U. Sch. Medicine, 1996—97; named one of America's Top Surgeons, Consumers Rsch. Coun., 2001—07. Fellow: ACS, Am. Acad. Orthopaedic Surgeons; mem.: Pasteur Club Cleve., Cleve. Aesculapian Med. Soc., Innominatum Med. Soc. Cleve., Cleve. Orthopaedic Soc. (bd. dirs. 1986—89), Twentieth Century Orthopaedic Soc., Orthopaedic Trauma Assn., Am. Orthopaedic Foot & Ankle Soc., Assn. Bone & Joint Surgeons (pres. 2007—08), Am. Orthopaedic Assn., Am. Bd. Orthopaedic Surgery (pres. 2007—08, bd. dirs.). Achievements include patents for a multi-use femoral intramedullary nail. Avocations: golf, tennis, skiing. Office: Case Sch Med Dept Orthopaedic Surgery 11100 Euclid Ave Cleveland OH 44106 Office Phone: 216-844-3041.

MARDER, MICHAEL ZACHARY, dental educator, researcher; b. NYC, Aug. 30, 1938; s. Jospeh Theodore and Rhea (Greenspun) M.; (widowed); children: Sherri Ellen, Robert Whitney. Student, Tufts U., 1959; DDS, Columbia U., 1963. Diplomate: Am. Bd. Oral Medicine. Practice dentistry, NYC, 1963-66, 68—; asst. Sch. Dental and Oral Surgery, Columbia U., NYC, 1963-66, instr., 1968, asst. clin. prof., 1968-72, assoc. clin. prof., 1972-76, NYC clin. prof. dentistry, 1976—, rschr., 1963—; dir. oral medicine, 1972-84; dir. clin. cancer tng., 1993—; attending dental surgeon Presbyn. Hosp., 1972-76; assoc. attending dentist, 1976-82; attending dentist, 1982—; cons. Good Samaritan Hosp., Suffern, NY. Lectr. field. Author 2 textbooks in dental medicine; contbr. chpts. to med. and dental textbooks articles to profl. jours. Served to capt. US Army, 1966-68. Recipient Cert. Achievement US Army, 1968. Fellow NY Acad. Dentistry; mem. ADA, Internat. Assn. Dental Rsch., Am. Acad. Oral Medicine, Frist Dist. Dental Soc. NY, Omicron Kappa Upsilon, Sigma Xi. Office: 119 W 57th St New York NY 10019-2303 Office Phone: 212-265-8291. Business E-Mail: mzm2@columbia.edu.

MARDIKIAN, JACKIE, medical librarian; married. BA, York U., Toronto, Ont., Can., 1969; MLS, Western Mich. U., Kalamazoo, 1980. Cert. Acad. Health Info. Profls., Med. Libr. Assn., Chgo. Reference libr. Borgess Med. Ctr., Kalamazoo, 1981—83, dir., libr. svcs., 1983—85; collection devel., reference libr. SUNY Health Sci. Ctr., Syracuse, 1985—90; med. scis. libr. Rutgers State U. NJ, Piscataway, 1991—. Contbr. articles to libr. lit. jours. Mem.: Health Sci. Libr. Assn. NJ (pres. 1994—95). Office: Rutgers State Univ NJ 165 Bevier Rd Piscataway NJ 08854 Office Fax: 732-445-5703. Business E-Mail: mardikia@rolmail.rutgers.edu.

MARDIS, ELIZABETH WILLIAMS, occupational health nurse; b. Colbert County, Ala., July 31, 1953; d. Bobby Joe and Nell Elizabeth (Cochran) Williams; m. Danny Richard Mardis, Dec. 18, 1976; children: Paige, Patrick. Diploma nursing, Sanford U., 1973; BS in Nursing, U. North Ala., 2004. Cert. occupl. health nurse; cert. occupl. hearing conservationist. Occupl. health mgr. Huntsville Hosp., Ala., Goodyear Dunlop Tire Corp., Huntsville, Ala.; occupl. health nurse Delphi Automotive Systems, Athens, Ala.; dir. case mgmt. Parkway Med. Ctr., Decatur, Ala., emergency rm. supr.; asst. dir. nursing svcs. Lawrence County Hosp., Moulton, Ala.; patient edn. and infection control nurse Humana Hosp., Russelville, Ala. Instr. prepared childbirth. Mem. Am. Assn. Occupl. Health Nurses, Case Mgmt. Soc. Am., Assn. Occupl. Health Profls. in Healthcare. Home: 2006 Cotaco Valley Trl SE Decatur AL 35603-5145 Office Phone: 256-265-8046. Business E-Mail: eliza093@hhsys.org, elizabeth.mardis@hhsys.org.

MARDJUADI, ADIWIRAWAN, rheumatologist; b. Jakarta, Indonesia, Sept. 27, 1948; MD, Cath. U. Leuven, Belgium, 1974; PhD in Medicine, U. Amsterdam, Netherlands, 1999. Mem. Asian Pacific League Against Rheumatism, 1985; editl. bd. Internat. League Against Rheumatism, 2002; vis. cons. rheumatology Nat. Devel. U. Indonesia, Jakarta, 2007; cons. field rheumatology Team Dr. Pres. Indonesia, 2007—10; rheumatologist dept. fgn. affair Indonesian Rheumatologist Assn., 1985—. Mem.: Am. Coll. Rheumatologie, Koninklijke Belgishe Verening voor Reumatologie. Avocations: reading, writing, languages, travel, bicycling. Home: Taman Pulo Asem Utara No2 Rawamangun Jakarta Timur 13220 Indonesia Home Fax: 62-21-4721601. Personal E-mail: reuma@cbn.net.id.

MARDONES, RODRIGO MARCELO, orthopedist; b. Santiago, Chile, Dec. 26, 1973; MD, U. Chile, 1998. Orthop. surgeon Pontificia U. Cath. Chile, 2001. Adult reconstructive surgery fellow Clinica Las Condes, 2002—, Dept. Orthops. Rsch. Mayo Clinic, 2003—04, rsch. fellow, 2003; chief, reconstructive surgery hip Hosp. Militar Santiago, 2007—10; dir. Lab. Ingeniería Tejidos para Ortop. y Traumatología, 2010—. Dir., orthop. rsch. Pontificia U. Cath. Chile, 2004—07; asst. prof., orthops. dept. U. Chile, 2007—. Recipient Frank Stinchfield award, Hip Soc. Open Meeting., 2005, E. W. Johnson, Jr. Physician Tng. award, XXXIII Ann. Meeting Mid Am. Orthop. Surgeon Soc., 2005, Best Sci. award, AAOS, 2006; grant, Proyecto CORFO INNOVA. Clinica Las Condes. Mem.: Internat. Cartilage Repair Soc., Orthop. Rsch. Soc., Soc. Chilena Medicina del Deporte, Chilean Soc. Orthops. Surgeons, Internat. Soc. Hip Arthroscopy. Avocations: golf, skiing. Office: Lo Fontecilla 441 Las Condes Santiago 7591046 Chile Office Fax: 562 6108689. Business E-Mail: rmardones@clc.cl.

MARECEK, JEANNE, psychologist, educator; b. Berwyn, Ill., May 28, 1946; d. Frank J. and Josephine (Serio) M. BS, Loyola U., Chgo., 1968; MS, Yale U., 1971, PhD, 1973. Asst. prof. to prof. psychology Swarthmore (Pa.) Coll., 1972—2010, chmn. dept., 1986—91, 1994—95, 1998—99, head women's studies program, 1996—99. Fulbright sr. lectr., Sri Lanka, 1988. Co-author: Making a Difference: Psychology and the Construction of Gender, Gender & Culture in Psychology: Theories & Practices, 2010; contbr. numerous articles to profl. jours. and chpts. to books. Bd. dirs. Women in Transition, Phila., 1980-86; vice patron Nest, Hendala, Sri Lanka, 1995—; bd. dirs. Women's Therapy Ctr., Phila., 1996-2004, CHOICE, Phila., 2006-10. Fellow Swedish Collegium for Advanced Study in Social Scis., 1997; various fed. research grants. Fellow: APA (internat. rels. psychology com., 2007-09, chair 2009), Assn. Asian Studies, Am. Inst. Sri Lanka Studies (sec. 1995-2000, pres. 2001-07), Am. Overseas Rsch. Ctrs. (mem. exec. coun. 2002-09, chair 2011), Ctr. Advanced Study Oslo. Office: Swarthmore Coll Dept Psychology 500 College Ave Swarthmore PA 19081-1306 Business E-Mail: jmarece1@swarthmore.edu.

MAREN, STEPHEN, neuroscientist, psychologist, educator; PhD, U. Southern Calif. Prof. psychology U. Mich., dir. neuroscience grad. program. Assoc. editor various Neuroscience Jours. Fellow: Am. Psychological Assn. (Disting. Scientific award 2001). Office: Univ of Michigan Dept of Psychology 530 Church St 4046 East Hall Ann Arbor MI 48109-1043 Office Phone: 734-647-6980. E-mail: maren@umich.edu.

MARES, ABRAHAM JACOB, pediatric surgeon; b. Bucharest, Romania, May 15, 1935; arrived in Israel, 1941; s. Samuel and Pauline (Bercovici) M.; m. Ofra Disatnik, May 3, 1962; children: Eyal, Sharon Mares-Klauzner, Michal Mares-Yoel. MD, Hadassah-Hebrew U., 1962. Intern Beilinson Med. Ctr., Petach Tiqva, Israel, 1961, resident, 1963-65, Beth Israel Hosp., Boston, 1965-68; chief resident Children's Hosp., LA, 1968-69; chief physician, surgeon Pondville State Cancer Hosp., Walpole, Mass., 1969-70; sr. staff surgeon Soroka Med. Ctr., Be'er Sheba, Israel, 1970-71, chief dept. pediatric surgery, 1971-2000. Sr. lectr. Ben Gurion U., Faculty Health Scis., Be'er Sheba, 1974-81, assoc. prof., 1981-89, vice dean, 1984-86, prof. surgery, 1989—2002, prof. emeritus, 2002. Contbr. articles to profl. jours. Maj. Israeli Defence Forces Res., 1963-89. Fellow ACS; mem. British Assn. Pediatric Surgeons, Israeli Soc. Pediatric Surgeons (founding mem., 1st chmn. 1976-90), Asian Assn. Pediat. Surgeons. Avocations: classical music, gardening. Home and Office: 3 Arava St 84965 Omer Israel Home Phone: 972-8-6460525. Fax: 972-8-6469303. Personal E-mail: profmaresh@bezeqint.net.

MARESCA, ALESSANDRA, orthopedist; b. Rome, June 25, 1974; MD, La Sapienza U. Rome, 1999; degree in Orthop. and Traumatology, Rizzoli Inst. Alma Mater U. Bologna, 2004. Orthop. surgeon, med. dirigent I level Maggiore Hosp., 2005—. Award, Best Young Comm. C.I.O., 2000, Alma Mater U. Bologna. Mem.: SICSeG,

SIGASCOT, SIA, SIOT. Avocations: running, flute, travel. Office: Lgo Nigrisoli 2 Bologna Emilia Romagna 40133 Italy Business E-Mail: alexandre_m@libero.it.

MARGALHO, CLÁUDIA ISABEL, forensic specialist; b. Coimbra, Portugal, Mar. 13, 1968; Degree in Biochemistry, U. de Coimbra, 1992, M in Forensic Medicine, 2005. Superior specialist, forensic medicine Inst. Nat. de Medicina Legal I.P., 1998—. Avocations: gymnastics, bicycling, reading. Office: Largo da Sé Nova Coimbra 3000-213 Portugal Business E-Mail: claudiamargalho@iol.pt.

MARGALIT, ALON A. P., physician; s. Yehoshua and Ruty Margalit; life ptnr. Aviva M Elad; children: Osher Y., Tali. MD, Ben Gurion U., Beer Sheba, Israel, 1982, PhD in Med. Psychology, 1982. Med. dir. Talk2doc - Teleconsultation, Zichron Yacov, Israel, 1995—; dir., biopsychosocial clinic Meuhedet, Tel Aviv, 2005—. Personal E-mail: alon@talk2doc.net.

MARGESSON, LYNETTE JOAN, dermatologist; b. Toronto, Ont., Can., Feb. 6, 1947; MD, U. Western Ont., 1970. Asst. prof. Queen's U. Dept. Medicine Appointments, 1976—97; adj. asst. prof. obstetrics-gyn.& medicine dermatology Dartmouth Med. Sch., 1999—2011. Recipient First Gold award, St Clement's Sch. Toronto Can. Fellow: RCPC, Internat. Soc. Study Vulvovaginal Disease (internat. chairperson patient info. 2001—06, treas. 2005—11); mem.: New Eng. Dermatologic Soc., Women's Dermatologic Soc., Am. Dermatology Assn., Can. Dermatology Assn. Avocations: skiing, horseback riding, travel. Office: Dartmouth Med Sch 721 Chestnut St Manchester NH 03104-3002 Office Fax: 603-647-0017. Personal E-mail: ljmderm@hotmail.com.

MARGETIC, BRANIMIR, psychiatrist; b. Derventa, Bosnia-Herzegovina, Nov. 17, 1963; s. Josip and Olga Margetic; m. Branka Aukst Margetic; 1 child, Luka. MD, U. Zagreb, Med. Sch., 1989. Head dept. Neuropsychiatric Hosp. Dr Ivan Barbot, Popovaca, Croatia, 2001—. Contbr. articles to prof. med. jours. Lt. Med. Svc. Corps., 1991—92. Achievements include research in clinical investigations. Office: Neuropsychiatric Hosp Dr Ivan Barbot Jelengradska 1 Popovaca 44317 Croatia Home: Ulica Vjekoslava Heinzela 47B 10-000 Zagreb Croatia Personal E-mail: branimir.margetic@zg.t-com.hr. Business E-Mail: branimir.margetic@npbp.hr.

MARGILETH, ANDREW MENGES, physician, former naval officer; b. Cin., July 17, 1920; s. Elmer C. and Bertha (Menges) M.; m. Catherine Lanier, Oct. 31, 1994; children: R. Lynn, Andrew C., Elle C., David Lanier. BA, Washington and Jefferson Coll., 1943; BS, MIT, 1944; MD, U. Cin., 1947. Diplomate Am. Bd. Pediat. Commd. ensign USN, 1943, advanced through grades to capt., 1963; intern, then residen in pediat. Nat. Naval Med. Ctr., 1947-49; resident in pediat. Johns Hopkins Hosp., 1949-50; chief pediat. U.S. Naval Hosps., Corona, Calif., 1953-57, Chelsea, Mass., 1957-63, Bethesda, Md., 1963-67; prof. Uniformed Svcs. U. Health Scis., 1979-90; clin. prof. U. Va. Health Scis. Ctr., 1990-95, Mercer U. Sch. Medicine, 1995—2010, U. Fla., Jacksonville, 2001—. Mem. coun. Nat. Inst. Child Health and Human Devel., 1963-67; sr. attending physician Childrens Hosp., Washington; assoc. clin. prof. pediat. Med. Sch., Howard U.; adj. prof. pediat. Med. Sch., George Washington U., 1967-79. Contbr. chpt. to Current Pediatric Therapy, 1970, 72, 74, 76, 80, 83, 85, 90, 93, 95; contbr.: (textbooks) Neonatology, 1975, 81, 86, 94, 99, Pediatrics, 1977, 81, 86, 91, 95, 96, 2001, 2003, Medicine, 1978, 82, 86, 88, 91, Current Therapy Medicine, 1996, 99, Current Therapy of Infectious Disease, 1996, 2000, Pediatric Dermatology, 1978, 86, 88, Neurological Presentation of Cat Scratch Disease, 2007; also 160 articles to profl. jours.; co-editor Clin. Procs. of Children's Hosp. Nat. Med. Ctr., 1970-79; co-editor: An Atlas of Pediatric Infectious Diseases, 1998. Fellow ACP, Am. Acad. Pediat.; mem. Assn. Mil. Surgeons, Am. Pediat. Soc., Soc. Pediat. Dermatologists (Alvin H. Jacob MD Soc. Pediat. Dermatology award, 2007), Soc. Pediat. Infectious Diseases, Alpha Omega Alpha. Address: 515 W 6th St Jacksonville FL 32206 Office Phone: 904-253-2703. Personal E-mail: catmargileth@bellsouth.net.

MARGO, KATHERINE LANE, family physician, educator; d. Warren Wilson and Virginia (Penney) Lane; m. Geoffrey Myles Margo, Apr. 20, 1980; 1 child, Benjamin stepchildren: Jenny, Judy. BA, Swarthmore Coll., 1974; MD, SUNY Health Sci. Ctr., Syracuse, 1978. Cert. in family medicine. Resident physician St. Joseph's Hosp., Syracuse, 1979-82; attending physician Health Svcs. Assn., Syracuse, 1982-90, asst. med. dir. for quality assurance, 1985-90; asst. prof. family medicine SUNY-HSC at Syracuse, 1990-94; mem. residency faculty Harrisburg (Pa.) Hosp., 1994-2000; med. dir. Harrisburg Kline Family Practice Ctr., 1996-2000; assoc. residency dir. Harrisburg Family Practice Residency, 1997-2000; predoctoral dir., dept. family medicine & cmty. health U. Pa., 2000—, asst. prof., assoc. dir. family practice residency, 2000—, assoc. prof., 2009. Clin. assoc. prof. Allegheny Med. Sch., 1997—2000. Contbr. articles to profl. jours. Bd. trustees Pt. Choice, Syracuse, 1993—94; chair med. com. Planned Parenthood, Syracuse, 1984—94; bd. dirs. Planned Parenthood Susquehanna Valley, 1996—2000; active Friends of Chamber Music, Syracuse, 1985—94; keyboard player Old World folk Band. Recipient Exemplary Tchg. award, Pa. Acad. of Family Practice, 2003, Penn Pearls Tchg. award, U. Pa. Sch. Medicine, 2004. Mem.: Am. Acad. Family Practitioners (v.p. Syracuse chpt.), Soc. Tchrs. of Family Medicine (chair group on predoctoral edn. 2003—04). Democrat. Avocations: music, theater, gardening, birdwatching. Home: 426 Carpenter Ln Philadelphia PA 19119-3040 Office: Univ Pa Dept Family Practice Community Medicine 2 Gates 3400 Spruce St Philadelphia PA 19104 Office Phone: 215-662-8941. E-mail: margok@uphs.upenn.edu.

MARGOLIN, FRANCES MONGIN, clinical psychologist, educator; b. Montgomery County, Pa. d. Harry and Dorothy (Blanc) Mongin; m. Elias L. Margolin, Mar. 12, 1944; children: Janice, John, Carol, Paul. BA, Temple U., 1948; MA, Ohio U., 1955; PhD, US Internat. U., 1973. Lic. psychologist, marriage and family therapist Calif., diplomate Am. Bd. Clin. Psychology. Clin. psychologist Dayton State Hosp., Ohio, 1948—53; pvt. practice clin. psychology Dayton, 1953—55, La Jolla, Calif., 1974—; marriage counselor San Diego County Superior Ct., San Diego, 1955—74. V.p. AAUW, Dayton, 1954; asst. prof. psychology San Diego State U., 1975—76; prof. LaVerne Coll., San Diego, 1976—78, Chapman Coll., San Diego, 1978—88; chair psychology com. Harbor View Hosp., SD, 1985—88. Mem.: APA, San Diego Acad. Psychology, SD Nurses Coun. (Woman of Wisdom Leader 2004), Am. Women Psychology (San Diego rep. 1982—90), Assn. Psychologists Pvt. Practice, Calif. Psychol. Assn., Psi Chi. Home and Office: The Patrician 4025 Pulitzer Pl Rm 231 San Diego CA 92122 *

MARGOLIS, DAVID MICHAEL, medical educator; b. New Haven, Aug. 23, 1959; AB, Harvard Coll., Cambridge, Mass., 1981; MD, Tufts U. Sch. Medicine, Boston, 1985. Asst. prof. medicine, microbiology & immunology U. Md. Sch. Medicine and Inst. Human Virology, Balt., 1994—99; prof. medicine, microbiology & immunology U. Tex. Southwestern Med. Ctr., Dallas, 1999—2005; prof. medicine, microbiology & immunology, epidemiology U. NC, Chapel Hill, 2005—. Mem. AIDS Rsch. Adv. Com., DAIDS, NIH, Bethesda, 2004—08. Fellow: ACP, Infectious Diseases Soc. Am.; mem.: Am. Soc. Clin. Investigation. Achievements include research in demonstration of the role of HDACs in HIV latency. Office: Univ NC Sch Medicine 3302 Michael Hooker Res Ctr CB #7435 Chapel Hill NC 27599-7435 *

MARGOLIS, GERALD JOSEPH, psychiatrist, psychoanalyst; b. Bronx, NY, May 7, 1935; s. Max and Sophie (Siegel) M.; m. June Edelman Greenspan, July 13, 1976; children: David J., Peter S., Steven J. AB, U. Rochester, 1957; MD, U. Chgo., 1960; postgrad., Inst. Phila. Assn. Psychoa., 1972. Diplomate in psychiatry Am. Bd. Psychiatry and Neurology. Intern to resident in psychiatry Upstate Med. Ctr. SUNY, Syracuse, 1960-64, instr. psychiatry, 1966-67; from instr. to clin. prof. psychiatry Med. Sch. U. Pa., Phila., 1967—. Practice medicine specializing in psychiatry and psychoanalysis, Cherry Hill, NJ; tng. and supervising analyst Inst. of the Psychoanalytic Ctr. Phila. Contbr. articles to profl. jours. Served with M.C., USAF, 1964-66. Mem.: AMA, Internat. Psychoanalytic Assn., Med. Socl N.J., Camden County Med. Soc., Psychoanalytic Ctr. Phila. (tng. and supervising analyst), Am. Psychiat. Assn., Am. Psychoanalytic Assn. (cert.), B'nai B'rith, Phi Beta Kappa. Office: One Mall Dr Ste 930 Cherry Hill NJ 08002-2194 Office Phone: 856-667-1055.

MARGOLIS, MARC, thoracic surgeon, educator; BM, BChi, U. Cape Town. Diplomate Am. Bd. General Surgery. Rotating intern gen. surgery, internal medicine and obstetrics and gynecology Groote Schuur Hosp.; intern general surgery Mt. Sinai Hosp., NY; resident general surgery NY Meth. Hosp.; fellow cardiothoracic surgery George Wash. Univ. Med. Ctr., clin. assoc. prof. Fellow: ACS; mem.: AMA, Southern Thoracic Surg. Assn., Soc. of Thoracic Surgeons. Mailing: The George Washington University Hospital 900 23rd St NW Washington DC 20037 Office Phone: 202-715-4000.

MARGOLIS, PHILIP MARCUS, psychiatrist, educator; b. Lima, Ohio, July 7, 1925; s. Harry Sterling and Clara (Brunner) M.; m. Nancy Nupuf, July 26, 1959; children: Cynthia, Marc, David, Laurence. BA magna cum laude, U. Minn., 1945, MD, 1948. Diplomate Am. Bd. Psychiatry and Neurology, 1966 (examiner 1973—1999, 2003-), recert. com., 1998-2004. Intern Milw. County Hosp., 1948-49; resident VA Hosp. and U. Minn., 1949-52, Mass. Gen. Hosp. and Harvard U., Boston, 1952-54; instr. U. Minn., Milw., 1953-55; asst. prof. dept. psychiatry Med. Sch., U. Chgo., 1955-60, assoc. prof., 1960-66; prof. psychiatry Med. Sch. U. Mich., 1966—, prof. cmty. mental health, 1968—; prof. psychiatry emeritus L.S.A., 1997—, instr., 1977-97; chief psychiat. inpatient service U. Chgo. Hosps. and Clinics, 1956-66; dir. Civil Forensic Tng. Program, 1997—, Forensic Psychiatry, 1998—; cons. psychiatrist, co investigator Measuring Psychiatric Problems Mich. Correctional Facilities: Independent Study Mental Health & substance Abuse, 2009—; chair therapeutic U. Mich. Depression Ctr. Innovation Fund, 2009—; mem. Mich. Dept. State Med. Adv. Bd., 2009—. Cons. Forensic Psychiat. Ctr., State of Mich., 1972—, mem. dept. state med. adv. bd., 2009-, coord. med. student edn. program, 1975-78, dir., 1978-82; cons. Turner Geriatric Clin., 1978-86, cons. Breast Cancer Clinic, 1988, Powertrain subs. Gen. Motors, 1984—, Dept. Mental Health, U.S. Dept. Justice; assoc. chief clin. affairs U. Mich. Hosps., 1981-85, chair legis. govt. com., 1996—, chmn. ethics com.; profl. rev. com. PSRO Area VII, 1982-86, PROM, 2003—; mem. Mich. State Bd. Medicine, 1986-94, chmn. 1992-94, senate adv. com. Univ. Affairs., 1986-89; spl. com. on profl. conduct and ethics Fedn. of State Med. Bds., 1998—, Mich. del., 1988-96, FLEX Com. Nat. Bd. Med. Examiners, 1988-98; civil liberties bd. U. Mich., 1995-2004, chmn., 1996-2002, gen counsel adv. com., 2002-08; dir. Forensic Tng. Program, 1999—. Author: Guide for Mental Health Workers, 1970, Patient Power: The Development of a Therapeutic Community in a General Hospital, 1974; also articles.; cons. editor: Community Mental Health jour, 1967—. Recipient Commonwealth Fund fellow award, 1964, Career Svc. award, 1992, Resident Appreciation award, 1991. Fellow: Am. Coll. Psychiatrists (chmn. bylaws com. 1997—, newsletter editor, Lifers 2003—), Am. Psychiat. Assn. (life; chmn. membership com. 1979—83, cons. ethics com. 1983—86, trustee 1985—88, sec. 1989—91, chmn. ethics appeals bd. 1989—, cons. steering com. on practical guidelines 1991—, budget com. 1991—, mem. assembly 1992, coun. med. edn. and career devel. 1993—, pres. Lifers 1994—, recertification com. 1998—, mem. pub. funding com. 2001—, assembly rep. 2003—, newsletter editor 2003—, cons. mem. com. 2004—, mem. audit com. 2004—, annual Lifers award 1999); mem.: Am. Acad. Psychiatry and Law (com. on psychoanalytic edn. 1995—, edn. com. 1998, treas. midwest chpt. 1998—2000, forensic tng. com. 2000—, pres. 2001—02), Am. Acad. Psychoanalysis, Mich. State Med. Soc. (bioethics com. 1989—, com. on med. licensure and discipline 1995—, mental health liaison com. 1995—, legis. and regulations com. 1995—, liaison com. Gen. Motors 1998—, chair 2000—, chair com. on med. licensure and discipline 2000—), Mich. Psychiat. Soc. (pres. 1980—81, chmn. ethics com. 1983—86, chmn. legislation and govt. com. 1996—2005, resolutions officer student rights responsibilities 1996—, v.p. 2000—, chmn. mem. com. 2004—, Career Achievement award 2000), Washtenaw County Med. Soc. (exec. coun. 1982—, chmn. ethics com. 1983—87, pres. 1987—88, editl. bd. 1995—, chair legis. commn. 1999—). Home: 228 Riverview Dr Ann Arbor MI 48104-1846 Office: 4250 Plymouth Rd Ann Arbor MI 48109 Office Phone: 734-647-8762. Business E-Mail: margolis@umich.edu.

MARGOLIS, THOMAS IRA, vitreoretinal ophthalmologist; s. Herbert and Barbara M.; m. Robin Deborah Small, Mar. 12, 1989; children: Rebecca, Joshua, Jennifer. BA summa cum laude, U. Pa., 1984; MD magna cum laude, Harvard U., 1989. Cert. Am. Bd. Ophthalmology. Intern Cedars Sinai Med. Ctr., LA, 1989-90; resident Wills Eye Hosp., Phila., 1990-93; fellowship (vitreoretinal) Tufts U.-New Eng. Eye Ctr., Boston, 1993-95. Instr. ophthalmology Tufts U. Med. Sch., Boston, 1993-96; hosp. staff AtlantiCare Regional Med. Ctr., Shore Meml. Hosp., Somers Point, N.J.; prin. investigator Multi Ctr. Clin. Trials. Contbr. sci. articles to profl. jours. and chpt. to book. Pres. Atlantic County Med. Soc., 2007—08. Recipient Benjamin Franklin scholar U. Pa., 1980-84, Laurence B. Ellis scholar Harvard Med. Sch., 1987; named one of Top Docs, NJ Monthly, 2003, 05, Phila. Mag., 2004, 05, 06, 07, 08, 09, 10, NJ Life, 2005, fellowship Harvard U., Mass. Eye and Ear Infirmary, Boston, 1987-88 Mem. AMA, Am. Acad. Ophthalmology, N.J. Acad. Ophthalmology, N.J. Med. Soc., Wills Eye Hosp. Soc., N.J. Retina Soc., Am. Soc. Retina Specialists, Phi Beta Kappa. Jewish. Avocations: running, skiing, golf, tennis, travel. Office: Retinal and Ophthalmic Cons PC 1500 Tilton Rd Northfield NJ 08225-1827 also: 2466 E Chestnut Ave Vineland NJ 08360 also: Ste 102 211 S Main St Cape May Court House NJ 08210 Office Phone: 609-646-5200. Business E-Mail: vitrector@gmail.com.

MARGREITER, MARKUS, urologist, educator; b. Vienna, Apr. 17, 1976; MD, Med. U. Vienna, 2000. Rsch. fellowship Weill Cornell Urology, 2005—06; clin. fellowship Johns Hopkins Urology, 2008—09; asst. prof. urology Med. U. Vienna, 2006—. Recipient Pfizer Young Andrologist award, Spl. Achievement award, Med. U. Vienna. Fellow: European Bd. Urology; mem.: Austrian Med. Assn., Austrian Soc. Urology, European Assn. Urology, Am. Urol. Assn. Avocations: literature, travel, running. Office: Waehringer Guertel 18-20 Vienna A-1090 Austria Business E-Mail: markus.margreiter@meduniwien.ac.at.

MARGULIS, ALEXANDER RAFAILO, physician, educator; b. Belgrade, Yugoslavia, Mar. 21, 1921; arrived in U.S., 1946; s. Rafailo and Olga (Weiss-Belic) Margulis; m. Hedvig Hricak, Feb. 26, 1983; 1 child, Peter Hricak. Student, U. Belgrade, 1939—41, student, 1945—46; MD, Harvard U., 1950; Doctorate (hon.), Aix-Marseille U., 1980, Med. Coll. Wis., 1986, Cath. U. Louvain, 1986, Karolinska Inst., Stockholm, 1986, U. Munich, 1987, U. Toulouse, 1987, U. Montpellier, 1993, U. Novi Sad, 2005. Diplomate Am. Bd. Radiology. Intern Henry Ford Hosp., Detroit, 1950—51; resident in radiology U. Mich. Hosps., 1951—53; jr. clin. instr. U. Mich., 1953—54; instr., then asst. prof. U. Minn., 1954—59; asst. prof. sch. medicine Washington U., St. Louis, 1959—60, assoc. prof. to prof., 1960—63; prof. radiology, chmn. dept. U. Calif., San Francisco, 1963—89, dir. magnetic resonance Sci. Ctr., assoc. chancellor spl. projects, 1989—93, spl. cons. to vice chancellor, 1993—2000; clin. prof. radiology Cornell U. Weill Med. Coll., NYC, 2000—; radiologist N.Y.-Presbyn. Med. Ctr., 2000—. Radiologist in chief U. Calif. Hosps., 1963—89; cons. VA Hosp., Letterman Gen. Hosp., San Francisco, U.S. Naval Hosp., Oakland, Calif.; cons. in radiology Office Surgeon Gen., 1967—71. Author (with others): Roentgen Diagnosis of Abdominal Tumors in Childhood, 1957; editor: Modern Alimentary Tract Radiology, Opinion in Radiology, 1988—91; co-editor: Alimentary Tract Roentgenology; editl. bd. Calif. Medicine, 1964—74, Radiology, 1975—93, assoc. editor Investigative Radiology, 1980—89; author: Be in Charge: A Leadership Manual, 2002, The Road to Success (How to get to the top of your profession), 2006. Capt. US Army, 1957—59. Recipient Cannon medal, Soc. Radiol., 1977, Gold medal, Am. Roentgen Ray Soc., 1988, J.P. Allyn medal, P. Roberts Rsch. Inst., 1989, Gold medal, Am. Coll. Radiology, 1999, UCSF medal, 2000; named to Hall of Honor, U. Mich. Med. Sch., 2006. Fellow: Internat. Soc. Mgmt. Res. Medicine, Hongkong Coll. Radiol., Royal Coll. Radiologists (hon.); mem.: AMA (cons. drugs 1961—), Radiol. Soc. Korea, Internat. Soc. Strategic Studies in Radiology (founding pres. 1995—), Royal Coll. Radiologists of Thailand, Polish Soc. Radiology, Thai Coll. Radiology, Chinese Radiol. Soc., Russian Radiol. Soc., Royal Coll. Surgeons Ireland, French Radiol. Soc., Swiss Radiol. Soc., Italian Radiol. Soc., Russian Acad. Scis. (fgn.), Serbian Acad. Scis. (fgn.), Soc. Magnetic Resonance in Medicine (pres. 1983—84), Calif. Acad. Medicine (pres. 1978), San Francisco Radiol. Soc. (pres. 1973—74), Radiol. Soc. N.Am. (Gold medal 1983), Rocky Mountain Radiol. Soc. (hon.), German Radiol. Soc. (hon.), Japan Radiol. Soc. (hon.), Soc. Chmn. Acad. Radiology Depts. (pres. 1968—69), Am. Gastroenterology Assn., Assn. Univ. Radiologists (pres. 1966—67, chmn. adv. com. acad. radiology 1971, pres. 1971), Roentgen Ray Soc., NAS-Inst. Medicine, U. Mich. Med. Sch. Hall Honor. Business E-Mail: arm2001@med.cornell.edu.

MARIANO, ANA VIRGINIA, retired pathologist; b. Baguio City, The Philippines, Nov. 20, 1938; came to US, 1963; d. Celestino Chuongco and Ana (Tanseco) Juan; m. Gregorio Torres Mariano, June 4, 1966; children: Joel, Eric, Greg, Anita. AA, U. St. Tomas, Manila, 1957, MD, 1962. Bd. cert. in anatomic pathology and clin. pathology Am. Bd. Pathology; lic. physician, NY, Pa. Med. intern Youngstown Hosp., Ohio, 1963; pathology resident I RI Hosp., Providence, 1964; pathology resident II-IV Wayne State U. Med. Sch., Detroit, 1965-68; assoc. pathologist Newark-Wayne Cmty. Hosp., Newark, NY, 1979-83; interim pathologist Clifton Springs Hosp., NY, 1983; lab. dir. and acting lab. dir. VA Med. Ctr., Altoona, Pa., 1995—97, staff pathologist, 1997-99. Locum tenens Altoona Hosp., Pa., 1999-2001; mem. courtesy med. staff Newark-Wayne Cmty. Hosp., 1983-92, Clifton Springs Hosp., NY, 1983-89; mem. adv. bd. Cath. Physicians Guild, Rochester, NY, 1991-92; cons. in pathology VA Med. Ctr., Altoona, 1993-96. Tchr. religious edn. St. Michael's Ch., Newark, 1978-80, 82-84. Fellow Am. Soc. Clin. Pathologists, Coll. Am. Pathologists. Roman Catholic. Avocations: swimming, aerobics, gardening.

MARICICA, STOICA, research scientist; b. Botesti, Vaslui, Romania, Jan. 18, 1969; D, 2010. Rschr. Dunarea Joos U. Galati, 2009—. Recipient award, Postdoc. Sch. Applied Biotechnologies With Impact Romanian Bioeconomy; grant, Lifelong Learning Program - Erasmus Tchg. Program. Mem.: Internat. Soc. Electrochemistry (Laussane, Switzerland). Home: Rosiori St Galati 800055 Romania Home Fax: 40236464056. Business E-Mail: maricica.stoica@ugal.ro.

MAŘÍK, IVO ANTONÍN, health facility administrator, physician; b. Prague, Czech Republic, Feb. 6, 1950; s. Antonín and Olga (Kuncová) M.; children: Olga, Radka, Helena; m. Alena Korinková, Nov. 26, 1994; children: Antonín, Jan. MD, Charles U., Prague, 1975; PhD, Charles. U., Prague, 1986; specialization in pediat., 1979, specialization in orthop., 1982. Resident in pediat. Beroun (Czech Republic) Hosp., 1976-80; resident in orthop. surgery Orthop. Clin. 2d Med. Faculty, Charles U., 1980-82, rsch. fellow, 1982-86, sr. rsch. worker, 1988-91, asst. prof., 1991-94; head Ambulant Ctr. Defects Locomotor Apparatus, Prague, 1994—. Lectr. dept. anthropology and human genetics Charles. U., 1998—, dept. anatomy and biomechanics, 2005-; assoc. prof. faculty sci., 2003-; cons. dept. rehab. Kostelec Hosp., 1991-96, dept. orthop. Pribram Hosp., 1994—. Founder, editor,

editor-in-chief Locomotor Sys.-Advances in Rsch., Diagnostics and Therapy, 1994—; contbr. over 100 articles to profl. jours. Founder The Mařík Fdn., 1992-94. Capt. Czech Air Force Res., 1975-76. Mem. Czech Soc. Surgery of Hand and Rehab. (founding mem.), Czech Soc. Connective Tissue Rsch. and Biol. Use (founding mem., chmn. 2004-05), Soc. Connective Tissue, Czech Med. Assn. J.E. Purkyne (founding mem., chmn. 2005-), Czech Soc. Prosthetics and Orthotics, Czech Med. Assn. J.E. Purkyne (founding mem., mem. com. 2002-05, rsch. sec. 2005—), Czech Soc. Accidental Surgery, Czech Pediat. Soc., Czech Soc. Orthopaedics and Traumatology, Assn. Med. Genetics, Internat. Soc. Musculoskeletal and Neuronal Interactions, Internat. Skeletal Soc., Czech Soc. Biomechanics, Fedn. European Soc. Surgery Hand. Avocations: rowing, bicycling. Home: Žitomírská 39 101 00 Prague Czech Republic Office: Ambulant Ctr Locomotor Def Olsanská 7 130 00 Prague 3 Czech Republic Office Phone: 420 222 582 214. Business E-Mail: ambul_centrum@volny.cz.

MARIN, ARTURO REYES, nephrologist; b. El estado de Chihuahua, Chihuahua, Mex., Oct. 14, 1960; MD, UNAM-Medicine, 1985; MS, Inst. Politécnico Nacional, Mex., 2009. Cert. specialist in internat medicine and nephrology INNSZ-UNAM, 2009. Nephrologist Hosp. ISSEMYM-Satelite, 1991—2011, Hosp. Juarez de Mex., 1996—. Adj. prof. UNAM, 2007—11. Author: (book) Acute Kidney Injury, 2005. Rsch. grant, ISSEMYM. Mem.: Nephrology Coll. Mex., IMIN-Mex., Internat. Peritoneal Dialysis, Internat. Soc. Nephrology, Am. Soc. Nephrology. Avocations: swimming, tennis, computers. Home: Calle Grieta 32 Colonia Ampliacion V Mexico City 54080 Mexico Home Fax: 53437393. E-mail: artmar@prodigy.net.mx.

MARIN, DEBORAH B., psychiatrist, educator; b. Cleve., Oct. 9, 1957; d. Emanuel and Klara Blumenthal; m. Michael Marin; children: Lea, Max. BA, Wellesley Coll., 1979; MD, Mt. Sinai Med. Sch., 1984. Cert. American Bd. Psychiatry and Neurology. Resident in psychiatry Mt. Sinai Hosp., NYC, 1984—88; fellowship in psychiatry Cornell U. Med. Coll., NY, 1988—92; joined Mt. Sinai Med. Ctr., NYC, 1992—, assoc. prof. psychiatry, assoc. prof. geriatrics and palliative medicine, chief geriatric psychiatry, med. dir. dept. psychiatry, exec. v.p. strategic devel., chief med. officer, dean clin. rsch. Office: Mt Sinai Med Ctr 1425 Madison Ave New York NY 10029 E-mail: deborah.marin@mssm.edu. *

MARINELLI, LUCIO, neurologist; b. Termoli, Sept. 2, 1974; MD, U. Genova, 1999, PhD, 2008. Postdoc fellow U. Genova, 2008—. Mem.: Soc. Italiana Neurologia. Avocation: computers. Office: Largo Daneo 3 Genova Liguria 16132 Italy Business E-Mail: lucio.marinelli@unige.it.

MARINER, WILLIAM MARTIN, chiropractor; b. Balt., Jan. 2, 1949; s. William Joseph and Ellen (Dexter) M. AA, Phoenix Coll., 1976; BS in Biology, L.A. Coll. of Chiropractic, 1980, D Chiropractic summa cum laude, 1980; DD (hon.), Universal Life Ch., Modesto, Calif., 1986. Health food restaurant mgr. Golden Temple of Conscious Cookery, Tempe, Ariz., 1974-75; health food store mgr. Guru's Grainery, Phoenix, 1975, physical therapist A.R.E. Clinic, Phoenix, 1975-76; research dir., founder G.R.D. Healing Arts Ctr., Phoenix, 1974-77; aminstrv. asst., acad. dean L.A. Coll. Chiropractic, Whittier, Calif., 1977-80; faculty Calif. Acupuncture Coll., LA, 1978 80; ednl. cons. Avanti Inst., San Francisco, 1985-91; found, dir., head clinician Pacific Healing Arts Ctr., Del Mar, Calif., 1980-93, Mt. Shasta, Calif., 1993—. Ednl. cons. John Panama Cons., San Francisco, 1991-99. Patentee in field. Co-dir. We Care We Share Charitable Orgn., San Diego, 1985-86. Named Outstanding Sr., L.A. Coll. Chiropractic, 1980. Mem. Calif. Chiropractic Assn., Am. Chiropractic Assn., Internat. Coll. Applied Kinesiology, Holistic Dental Assn., Brit. Homopathic Assn. Avocations: personal growth, natural healing methods, cooking. Office: Pacific Healing Arts Ctr PO Box 192 Mount Shasta CA 96067-0192 Office Phone: 530-926-6448. Personal E-mail: wmariner@jps.net.

MARINI, GIOVANNI, retired medical educator, researcher; b. Bergamo, Italy, June 2, 1930; s. Stefano Marini and Orsolina Folonari; m. Eva Klosova, Dec. 28, 1971; children: Eva Maria, Janamaria. Med. doctor, U. Med. Sch., Milano, Italy, 1954. Resident in neurosurgery Columbia U., NYC, 1957-61; assoc. prof. U. Med. Sch., Milano, 1961-70, prof. neurosurgery Brescia, Italy, 1971—; ret., 2006. Mem. Rotary (pres. 1974-76). Roman Catholic. Avocations: travel, hunting. Home: Via San Gottardo 20 25123 Brescia BS Italy Office Phone: 390303365696. Personal E-mail: giovanni.marini@alice.it.

MARINI, IDA, dentist, researcher; b. Brescia, Italy, Jan. 28, 1956; d. Lionello Marini, Pierangiola Boni; m. Domenico Russo; 1 child, Pierluigi Russo. MD, U. Milan, 1980. Cert. medical dentist 1984. Resident tutor U. Brescia, 1979—82; rschr. U. Chieti, Italy, 1982—91; asst. prof. U. Bologna, Italy, 1991—. Author: (Book) Myofascial Pain - trigger points, 1987, And Rapid Maxiller Expansion Craniomandibular Disorder: Physiotherapy. Mem.: Internat. Myopain Soc., Internat. Assn. Dental Rsch., Internat. Study Pain. Home: via S Angela Merici 60 25123 Brescia Italy Office: Studio dentistico Ida e Federico Marini via Rossini 16 25089 Villanuova sul Clisi Italy Home Phone: 0039-030-361188; Office Phone: 0039-0365-34787. Personal E-mail: idmarini@tin.it.

MARINO, ROBERT A., insurance company executive; b. Newark; m. Lorraine Marino; 2 children. BA in Economics, Rutgers U. Asst. v.p. profl. benefits adminstrn. Empire Blue Cross Blue Shield, NYC, v.p. nat. accounts; v.p. nat. market divsn. Horizon Blue Cross Blue Shield NJ, sr. v.p. market bus. units, 1997, COO, exec. v.p., 2008—11, CEO, 2011—. Bd. dirs. Nat. Inst. for Health Care mgmt. (NIHCM), Blue Cross Blue Shield Assn., Interplan programs com. mem., bd. dirs. Nat. Inst. for Health Care Mgmt.; trustee St. Benedict's Prep. Sch.; past chmn. Newark Regional Bus. Partnership, exec. com. mem., Partnership for a Drug-Free NJ, Nat. Account Svc. Co. (NASCO); bd. visitors John F. Welch Coll. of Bus. Sacred Heart Univ., Fairfield, Conn.; bd. mem. Newark Alliance, Choose NJ, Essex County Heart Assn., United Way Essex and West Hudson, chmn. ann. campaigns, 1997, 98. Office: Horizon Blue Cross Blue Shield of New Jersey 3 Penn Plz East Newark NJ 07105 Office Phone: 973-466-4000. Office Fax: 973-466-4317. *

MARINO, WILLIAM J., retired insurance company executive; m. Paula Marino; 4 children. BS in Economics, St. Peter's Coll. Various positions Prudential Ins. Co. America, 1968-91, Horizon Blue Cross Blue Shield of NJ Inc., Newark, 1991-94, pres., CEO, 1994—2011, chmn., 2010—11. Ind. dir. Sun Bancorp, Inc., Sealed Air Corp.; corp. bd. dirs. Digital Solutions, Inc. Past chmn. bd. trustees United Way of Essex and West Hudson, NJ, campaign chmn., 1993-94; past chmn. bd. dirs., mem. exec. com. Regional Bus. Partnership; trustee NJ Network Found., chmn. cmty. adv. coun. NJ Network; bd. dirs. St. Peter's Coll., Newark Mus., NJ State C. of C., NJ Symphony Orchestra, NJ Performing Arts Ctr. 1999-, chmn. 2009-; mem. coun. of predsl. advisors Fairleigh Dickinson Univ.; mem. chief justice com. on efficiency for the NJ Jud. Sys.; past trustee Kessler Inst. for Rehab. Inc.; mem. Gov.'s Coun. for a Drug-Free Workplace; bd. trustee Cmty. Theatre of Morristown, Newark Mus. Recipient Ellis Island medal of honor, 1997. Mem. Blue Cross and Blue Shield Assn. (BCBSA)(bd. dirs.), Health Ins. Assn. of America (bd. dirs.), Nat. Inst. for Health Care Mgmt (past chmn.). *

MARION, JAMES F., gastroenterologist, educator; b. Rochester, NY, Apr. 17, 1963; BA, U.C. Berkeley, 1985; MD, Columbia P&S, 1989. Assoc. clin. prof. Mt. Sinai Sch. Medicine, 1995—. Cons. gastroenterology Present, Chapman, Marion & Steinlauf, 1995—. Fellow: AGA; mem.: Am. Coll. Gastroenterology, Charaka Club. Office: 12 E 86th St Ste 1 New York NY 10028 Office Fax: 212-628-3648. Business E-Mail: james.marion@mssm.edu.

MARION, ROBERT W., clinical geneticist, educator; Grad., Yeshiva U., 1979. Diplomate Am. Bd. Pediatrics, cert. clin. genetics. Resident pediatrician Montefiore Med. Ctr., Bronx, NY, 1980—82, fellowships, 1982—84; prof. pediat. Albert Einstein Coll. Med., prof. obstetrics & gynecology and women's health dept., chief sect. child devel. pediat. dept., chief sect. genetics pediat. dept., dir. children's evaluation and rehab. ctr. Office: Albert Einstein College of Medicine Rose F Kennedy Center 1410 Pelham Pky South Room 237 Bronx NY 10461 Office Phone: 718-430-8521. Office Fax: 718-904-1162. Business E-Mail: robert.marion@einstein.yu.edu.

MARIOTTI, ERIC, plastic surgeon; BS in Biol. Sciences, U. Calif., Davis, 1984—89; MD, Thomas Jefferson U., 1989—93. Diplomate Am. Bd. Plastic Surgery. Surg. resident Univ. of Conn., Farmington, 1993—97; resident plastic surgery Univ. of Louisville, 1997—99, chief resident plastic surgery, 1998—99; chmn. plastic surgery divsn. John Muir Med. Ctr., Concord, Calif., hosp. affiliations include Walnut Creek, Calif., Premier Surgery Ctr., Concord, Calif., Doctors Med. Ctr., San Pablo, Calif.; pvt. practice plastic and reconstructive surgery, 1999—. Vol. Orthopaedic Overseas, Thimpu, Bhutan, 1992, Philippine and Am. Group of Educators and Surgeons (P.A.G.E.S.)/Operation Hope, Santa Maria, Bulacan, Philippines, 1999, Overseas Health Outreach, 1990. Mem.: AMA, Overseas Health Outreach (co-founder and organizer), Calif. Med. Assn., Calif. Soc. of Plastic Surgeons, Am. Soc. of Aesthetic Plastic Surgery, Am. Soc. of Plastic Surgery, Hobart Amory Honor Soc. Office: 2222 East St Ste 310 Concord CA 94520 Office Phone: 925-685-4533.

MARIOTTO, ALDO, physician, medical researcher; b. Venice, Italy, Sept. 6, 1958; s. Italo Mariotto and Elide Wally Bellonio; m. Paola Ghidoni, July 30, 1987; 1 child, Carlotta. Specialty in Hygiene, Preventive Medicine and Hosp. U. Ferrara, Italy, 1992. Med. dir. Geriatric Hosp., Italy, 1995—99; head, tech. assessment and quality assurance svc. Italy, 1999—2000; head, cmty. medicine svc. Pordenone, 2000—01, Gorizia, 2002—03. Tenent Carabinieri, Health Care body, 1987—88, Vicenza. Recipient Knight of the merit of Italian Republic, Pres. Republic and Premier, 1997. Avocations: travel, music, soccer. Home: Via Delle Palme 15 35137 Padua PD Italy Personal E-mail: pghid@libero.it.

MARIS, JOHN M., pediatric oncologist; BS in Biology, Wheeling Coll., W.Va.; MD, U. Pa. Sch. Medicine, Phila., 1989. Diplomate Am. Bd. Pediat., cert. in pediatric hematology-oncology. Resident pediat. Children's Hosp. Phila., hematology-oncology fellowship, 1992—95, attending physician oncology clinic, 1995—, Giulio D'Angio endowed chair neuroblastoma rsch., 2004—, acting chief oncology divsn., 2008—09, chief oncology divsn., 2009—, also dir. Ctr. Childhood Cancer Rsch. Assoc. prof. pediat. U. Pa. Sch. Medicine, mem. Abramson Family Cancer Rsch. Inst. Mem. editl. bd. Pediatric Blood & Cancer, 2004—, Jour. Clin. Oncology, 2005—; contbr. articles to profl. jours. Recipient Clin. Oncology Career Devel. award, Am. Cancer Soc., 1996, Ethel Brown Foerderer Fund award, 2000, Leonard Berwick Meml. Tchg. award, U. Pa. Sch. Medicine, 2009. Mem.: AAAS, Am. Soc. Clin. Investigation, Soc. Pediatric Rsch., Am. Soc. Pediatric Hematology/Oncology (Young Investigator award 1998, Oski award 2007), Am. Soc. Clin. Oncology (Merit award 1995, Young Investigator award 1996, Career Devel. award 1997), Am. Assn. Cancer Rsch., Interurban Clin. Club, Alpha Omega Alpha. Office: Childrens Hosp Philadelphia 324 S 34th St Philadelphia PA 19104 E-mail: maris@chop.edu. *

MARK, HARRY HORST, ophthalmologist, researcher; b. Breslau, Germany, Jan. 21, 1931; came to U.S., 1957; s. Lothar and Ruth Mark. MD, U. Vienna, Austria, 1957. Diplomate Am. Bd. Ophthalmology. Intern George Washington U., Washington, 1957; resident Boston U., 1958-60, SUNY, Bklyn., 1960-62; pvt. practice New Haven, 1963—; attending ophthalmologist Yale-New Haven Hosp., 1963—, St. Raphael Hosp., New Haven, 1963—. Author: Optokinetics, 1982, 2008; contbr. articles to profl. jours. Fellow: Am. Coll. Surgeons. Avocations: optics, history, sailing. Office: 16 Broadway North Haven CT 06473-2301 Office Phone: 203-234-2212. Personal E-mail: iiMD@aol.com.

MARK, HON FONG LOUIE, cytogeneticist; m. Roger Mark; children: Yvonne, Roger Jr., Seamus. PhD, Brown U. Diplomate Am. Bd. Med. Genetics. Postdoctoral fellow in med. genetics R.I. Hosp., Providence, asst., assoc. dir. cytogenetics, fellow molecular biology, dir. cytogenetics, 1990-99, clin. cytogeneticist Cancer & Leukemia Group B, 1990—99; pres., CEO KRAM Corp., 1994—; dir. human genetics RIDOH, 1999—2001; exec. dir. RIACA, 2001—02; dir. cytogenetics dept. Presbyn. Lab. Svcs., Charlotte, NC, 2002—04; dir. cytogenetics Boston U. Sch. Medicine, 2004—07, clin. prof., 2004—07. Instr. pathology Brown U., Providence, asst. prof. pathology; clin. prof. Brown Med. Sch., 1998-2009; emeritus prof. Warren Alpert Med. Sch., Brown U., 2009-; assoc. mem. Maine Toxicology Inst., 1993-96; chair grants rev. com. mem., prenatal diagnosis com., chair cancer genetics com., steering com., NERGG; grant reviewer NIH, U.S. Army Breast Cancer Rsch. Program, U.S. Army Prostate Cancer Rsch. Program; reviewer numerous other panels. Author: Medical Cytogenetics, 2000; mem. editl. rev. bd. Applied Cytogenetics, Pathobiology, Exptl. and Molecular Pathology, Cancer Genetics and Cytogenetics; contbr. 200 articles to profl. jours. Recipient award Time Mag. Essay Writing Contest, Balfour award, Award R.I. Found.; NSF rsch. grantee Brown U., co-grantee Dept. Energy; Florence Seibert postdoctoral fellowship AAUW Ednl. Found.; North Providence Citizens scholar, Fruithill Jr. Women's Club scholar; others. Fellow Am. Coll. Med. Genetics; mem. AAAS, Am. Soc. Human Genetics, Assn. Genetic Technologists, Sigma Xi.

MARK, JAMES B. D., surgeon, educator; b. Nashville, June 26, 1929; s. Julius and Margaret (Baer) M.; m. Jean Rambar, Aug. 18, 1955; children: Jonathan, Michael, Margaret, Elizabeth, Katherine. BA, Vanderbilt U., 1950, MD, 1953. Intern, resident in gen. and thoracic surgery Yale-New Haven Hosp., 1953-60; instr. to asst. prof. surgery Yale U., 1960-65; assoc. prof. surgery Stanford U., 1965-69, prof., 1969-97, prof. emeritus, 1997—, Johnson and Johnson prof. surgery, 1978—97, head div. thoracic surgery, 1972-97, assoc. dean clin. affairs, 1988-92; chief staff Stanford U. Hosp., 1988-92. Governing bd. Health Systems Agy., Santa Clara County, 1978-80; sr. Fulbright-Hays fellow, vis. prof. surgery U. Dar es Salaam, Tanzania, 1972-73 Mem. editl. bd.: Jour. Thoracic and Cardiovasc. Surgery, 1986-94, World Jour. Surgery, 1995-2003, The Pharos, 2002-11; contbr. numerous articles to sci. jours. Bd. dirs. Stanford U. Hosp., 1992-94. With USPHS, 1955-57. Fellow ACS (pres. No. Calif. chpt. 1980-81), Am. Coll. Chest Physicians (pres. 1994-95); mem. Am. Assn. Thoracic Surgery, Am. Surg. Assn., Western Surg. Assn., Pacific Coast Surg. Assn., Halsted Soc. (pres. 1984), Western Thoracic Surg. Assn. (pres. 1992-93), Calif. Acad. Medicine (pres. 1978), Santa Clara County Med. Soc. (pres. 1976-77). Office: Stanford U Med Ctr CVRB Stanford CA 94305 Home: 81 Pearce Mitchell Pl Stanford CA 94305-8535 Office Phone: 650-723-6649. Business E-Mail: jbdm@stanford.edu.

MARK, MELVIN M., psychology professor, department chairman; b. Grand Island, Nebr., 1953; BA in Psychology, U. Nebr., Lincoln; MA in Social Psychology, Northwestern U., Evanston, Ill., PhD in Social Psychology, 1979. Prof. psychology Pa. State U., sr. scientist, Inst. Policy Rsch. and Evaluation, head, dept. psychology. Co-author (with G. Henry and G. Julnes): Realist Evaluation, 1998, Evaluation: An Integrated Framework for Understanding, Guiding, and Improving Policies and Programs, 2000; editor emeritus: Am. Jour. Evaluation; contbr. articles to profl. jours. Named Outstanding Tchr., Pa. State U. Coll. Liberal Arts, 2000. Mem.: Am. Evaluation Assn. (pres. 2006). Office: Dept Psychology Pa State Univ 407 Monroe Bldg University Park PA 16802-3106 Office Phone: 814-863-1755. Office Fax: 814-863-7002. Business E-Mail: m5m@psu.edu.

MARKEL, GAL, immunologist; s. Shlomo and Ariela Markel; m. Lee Raz. BSc, Hadassah Med. Sch., Jerusalem, 1999, PhD, 2004, MD, 2006. Lic. physician Israel Ministry Health, 2006. Ind. investigator Sheba Med. Ctr., Israel, 2005—07, chief scientist Ella Inst. Melanoma, Cancer Rsch. Ctr., 2008—; lectr. dept. clin. microbiology & immunology Sackler Sch. Medicine, Tel Aviv U., Israel, 2007—. Med. officer Israeli Def. Forces, 2006—. Recipient Wolf prize, Wolf Found., 2002, Cancer Rsch. prize, KKL Found., 2003, Faculty Medicine prize of Excellence, Hebrew U., 2005, Shlmiuk prize for Distinction, 2005, Cert. of Merit for Cmty. Svc., Internat. Inner Wheel - Golden Wheel Fund, 2006, Tsur award, Israel Soc. Plastic Surgery, 2006, 2008, Pfizer prize for best rsch. in oncology, Israel Soc. Clin. Oncology and Radiation Therapy, 2007; fellow, Foulkes Found. UK, 2002—04; Physician Rschr. grantee, Sheba Med. Ctr., 2005, Cancer rsch. grantee, Israel Cancer Rsch. Found., 2006—, Israel Cancer Assn., 2006—, Golda Meir fellow, Hebrew U. Jerusalem, 2002—04. Mem.: NY Acad. Scis. (assoc.), Am. Assn. Immunologists (assoc.). Achievements include discovery of novel regulatory mechanism of immune system; patents for immunomodulation with implementations in cancer treatment and diagnosis; cardiovascular broadband monitoring; immunomodulation with implementations in treatment and prevention of infectious diseases. Avocations: travel, sports, piano. Office: Ella Inst Melanoma Cancer Rsch Ctr Sheba Med Ctr 52621 Tel Hashomer Israel Office Phone: 972 3 530 4591. Office Fax: +97235304922. E mail: markel@post.tau.ac.il.

MARKEL, HOWARD, physician, educator; b. Detroit, Apr. 23, 1960; s. Samuel and Bernice Markel; m. Marcia Deborah Gordin, Sept. 20, 1987 (dec. Oct. 1988); m. Kate Gelya Levin, Aug. 17, 1997; children: Bess Rachel, Samantha Louise. AB in English Lit. summa cum laude, U. Mich., 1982, MD cum laude, 1986; PhD in History of Sci., Medicine & Tech., Johns Hopkins U., 1994. Diplomate Am. Bd. Pediat., 1989. Intern, resident Johns Hopkins Hosp. & Sch. Medicine, Balt., 1986-89, fellow, gen. pediat. and adolescent medicine, 1989—91, fellow, history medicine, 1989—93; asst. prof. pediatrics, communicable diseases U. Mich., Ann Arbor, 1993-98, assoc. prof. pedicatrics, communicable diseases, 1998—2002, George E. Wantz disting. prof. history medicine, 2000—, prof. pediat. and communicable diseases, prof. history, 2002—, prof. pub. health, psychiatry, 2004—. Dir. Ctr. for History of Medicine, U. Mich., 1996—. Author: The H.L. Mencken Baby Book, 1990, The Portable Pediatrician, 1992, The Portable Pediatrician, 2nd edit., 2000, The Practical Pediatrician, 1996 (Child Mag. Book of Yr., 1997), Quarantine! East European Jewish Immigrants and the New York City, 1997 (Arthur Viseltear prize, APHA, 2003), When Germs Travel, 2004. Recipient Nat. Rsch. Svc. award, NIH, 1991, James A. Shannon Dirs. award, 1996, Burroughs Wellcome Fund 40th Ann. History Medicine award, 1996, History of Medicine award, Nat. Libr. Medicine, NIH, 2005—, Woodward award, Am. Clin. and Climatol. Assn., 2008; scholar Robert Wood Johnson Found., 1996—2000, 2008—. Fellow: Am. Acad. Pediat.; mem.: Inst. Medicine Nat. Academies Sci., Am. Pediat. Soc., Soc. Pediat. Rsch., Am. Assn. History Medicine (exec. coun. 1994—97). Democrat. Jewish. Office: U Mich Ctr for History of Medicine 100 Simpson Meml Inst 102 Observatory Ann Arbor MI 48109-0725 Office Phone: 734-647-6914. Business E-Mail: howard@umich.edu.

MARKENROTH BLOCH, KARIN, physicist; b. Växjö, Feb. 27, 1973; MSc in Engring. Physics, Chalmers U. Tech., 1996, PhD, 2001. Clin. physicist MR Hvidovre Hosp., 2001—03; clin. scientist MR Philips Healthcare, 2003—. Grant, Swedish Found. Strategic Rsch. Mem.: European Soc. Magnetic Resonance Medicine and Biology, Soc. Cardiovasc. Magnetic Resonance, Internat. Soc. Magnetic Resonance Medicine. Avocations: reading, crossword puzzles. Office: MR Dept University Hosp Lund Lund Scania 22185 Sweden Business E-Mail: karin.markenroth@philips.com.

MARKENSON, JOSEPH ARON, physician, educator; b. Lincoln, Nebr., Jan. 2, 1943; MS in Physiology, Biochemistry, Rutgers U., 1966; MD, SUNY, Downstate, 1970. Attending physician Hosp. Spl.

Surgery, NY Presbyn. Hosp., 1975—; prof. clin. medicine Weill Med. Coll. Cornell U., 1976—. Master: Am. Coll. Rheumatology; fellow: ACP, Am. Soc. Immunology. Avocations: photography, travel, golf. Office: Hosp Special Surgery 535 E 70th St New York NY 10021 Office Fax: 212-535-6183. Business E-Mail: markensonj@hss.edu.

MARKEVICH, NIKOLAI I., biology professor; b. Perm, Russia, Oct. 15, 1952; MS, Rostov U., 1974; PhD, Inst. Biol. Physics, 1983. Rsch. asst. prof., dept. pathology, anatomy and cell biology Thomas Jefferson U., 2000—. NIH K-25 grant, 2011. Avocation: mountain climbing. Office: 1020 Locust St Rm 212E Philadelphia PA 19107 Business E-Mail: nikolai.markevich@jefferson.edu.

MARKEY, WILLIAM ALAN, health facility administrator, consultant; b. Cleve., Dec. 29, 1927; s. Oscar Bennett and Claire (Feldman) M.; m. Irene Nelson, Oct. 31, 1954; children: Janet Ellen Markey-Hisakawa, Suzanne Katherine Markey-Johnson. Student, Case Inst. Tech., 1945—48; BA, U. Mich., 1950; MS, Yale U., 1954. Resident in hosp. adminstrn. Beth Israel Hosp., Boston, 1953-54; asst. dir. Montefiore Hosp., Pitts., 1954-56; asst. adminstr. City of Hope Med. Ctr., Duarte, Calif., 1956-57, adminstrv. dir., 1957-66; assoc. dir. cancer hosp. project, instr. pub. health U. So. Calif. Sch. Medicine, 1966-67, asst. clin. prof. pub. health and cmty. medicine, 1968-70, asst. prof., 1970-75, dep. dir. regional med. programs, 1967-71; adminstr. Health Care Agy., County of San Diego, 1971-74, health svcs. cons., 1974-75; dir. Maricopa County Dept. Health Svcs., Phoenix, 1975-79, cons., 1979-80; adminstr. Sonoma Valley Hosp., Calif., 1980—83. Lectr. pub. health Sch. Pub. Health, UCLA, 1969-74; lectr. cmty. medicine Sch. Medicine, U. Calif., San Diego, 1973-75; cons. LA County Dept. Hosps., 1966-71, cons. Hosp./Health Svcs., 1983—; CEO Chinese Hosp., San Francisco, 1985-86, 90-91; adj. instr. Golden Gate U., 1992-96. Mem. bd. edn. Duarte Unified Sch. Dist., 1967-72, pres., 1970-72; bd. dir. Hosp. Coun. So. Calif., 1963-67, sec., 1966-67, Duarte Pub. Libr. Assn., 1965-72, Duarte-Bradbury chpt. Am. Field Svc., 1965-72, Duarte-Bradbury Cmty. Chest, 1961-68, Ctrl. Ariz. Health Svcs. Agy., 1975-80, Vis. Nurse Assn. The Redwoods, Santa Rosa, Calif., 1985-86, Sonoma Greens Homeowners Assn., 1990-95, 2002-05, Sonoma City Opera, 1987, 93, United Way, Sonoma, 1996—; com. chmn. Sonoma County Bd. Realtors, 1990-92; active Sonoma County Multiple Listing Svc., 1987-97; mem. Sonoma County Human Svcs. Commn., 2003-. With AUS, 1950-52. Fellow Am. Coll. Health Care Execs. (life); mem. Am. Hosp. Assn. (life), APHA, Royal Soc. Health, Calif. Hosp. Assn. (trustee 1966-69, dir. 1966-69), Internat. Fedn. Hosps., Hosp. Coun. No. Calif. (dir. 1981-83), Kiwanis, Rotary (past pres. Duarte). Home: 2901 Loveland Way Bakersfield CA 93309-5414 *

MARKIC, DEAN, urologist; b. Rijeka, Croatia, May 31, 1972; MD, Sch. Medicine Rijeka, Croatia, 1997, PhD, 2010. Staff urologist U. Hosp. Rijeka, Croatia, 2002—. Mem.: European Assn. Urology. Office: Tome Striica 3 Rijeka 51000 Croatia Office Fax: 385 51 218 861. Business E-Mail: dean.markic@ri.htnet.hr.

MARKISON, BRIAN A., pharmaceutical executive; BS, Iona Coll., 1982. Various mktg. and sales positions Bristol-Myers Squibb Co., 1982—98, sr. v.p., neuroscience/infectious disease, pres. neuroscience/infectious disease/dermatology, v.p., operational excellence and productivity, 1998—2001; pres. Bristol-Myers Squibb's Oncology, Virology and Oncology Therapeutics, 2001—04; COO King Pharmaceuticals, Inc., Bristol, Tenn., 2004, pres. & CEO, 2004—07, chmn., pres., CEO, 2007—11; pres., CEO Nycomed US Inc., 2011—. Bd. dir. King Pharm., Inc., Bristol, Tenn., 2004—11. Office: Nycomed US Inc 60 Baylis Rd PO Box 2006 Melville NY 11747 Office Phone: 631-454-7677. *

MARKMANN, DANIEL P., plastic surgeon; BA in Biology, La Salle U.; grad. in Biomedical Engring., Drexel U.; MD, Thomas Jefferson U. Diplomate Am. Bd. Plastic Surgery. Intern gen. surgery The Union Meml. Hosp., Balt., resident gen. surgery; fellow burn care and plastic surgery John Hopkins Univ., Balt.; fellow plastic surgery Rush Univ., Chgo.; surgeon Metamorphosis, Md.; hosp. affiliations include Ellicott City Surgery Ctr., Md., NW Hosp. Ctr., Randallstow, Md. Mem.: Northeastern Soc. of Plastic Surgeons, Am. Soc. for Laser Medicine and Surgery, John Staige Davis Soc. of Plastic Surgeons of Md., Am. Soc. of Plastic Surgeons, Am. Bd. of Plastic Surgery. Office: Metamorphosis North Ridge Profl Bldg Ste 202 2850 North Ridge Rd Ellicott City MD 21043 Office Phone: 410-465-3600.

MARKOVIC, VINKO, nuclear medicine physician, educator; b. Sinj, Croatia, Apr. 18, 1955; MD, Med. Faculty Zagreb, 1979; PhD, Med. Faculty Split, 2007. Nuc. medicine specialist, dept. nuc. medicine U. Hosp. Split and U. Split Med. Faculty, 1989, assoc. prof., dept. nuc. medicine, 1989. Mem.: EANM. Office: Spinciceva 1 Split 21000 Croatia Office Fax: 0038521556622. Business E-Mail: vinko.markovic@mefst.hr.

MARKOVICS, SHARON BECKER, allergist, immunologist, educator; MD, Yeshiva U., 1975. Diplomate Am. Bd. Pediatrics, Am. Bd. Allergy and Immunology, registered NY, 1976. Intern Bellevue Hosp. Ctr., NY, 1976, resident in pediat., 1977; fellow in allergy and immunology Montreal Children's Hosp., Canada, 1977—79; pediat. asst. clin. prof. medicine sch. NYU; hosp. affiliations include LI Jewish Med. Ctr., North Shore Univ. Hosp., NY. Named one of Best Doctors, NY Mag., 2010. Office: North Shore University Hospital 1129 Northern Blvd Ste 300 Manhasset NY 11030 Office Phone: 516-365-6077. Office Fax: 516-365-6137.

MARKOWITZ, DAVID D., gastroenterologist, educator; MD, Columbia U., 1985. Diplomate Am. Bd. Internal Medicine, Am. Bd. Internal Medicine-gastroenterology. Intern internal medicine Columbia-Presbyn. Med. Ctr., NYC, resident internal medicine, 1986—88, fellow gastroenterology, 1988—91; assoc. prof. medicine Columbia Univ., NYC; attending physician NY-Presbyn. Hosp. Office: New York-Presbyterian Hospital Ste 853 161 Fort Washington Ave New York NY 10032 Office Phone: 212-305-1024. Office Fax: 212-305-1039.

MARKOWITZ, PHYLLIS FRANCES, retired mental health services professional, retired psychologist; b. Malden, Mass., Sept. 2, 1931; d. Abraham and Rose (Kaplan) Kalishman; children: Gary Keith, Carol Diane Donnelly. AB, Harvard U., 1972, EdM, 1974; EdD, Boston U., 1987. Lic. psychologist Health Svc. Provider; LCSW Mass. Rsch. asst. Boston Coll., Newton, Mass., 1971-73; social worker Combined Jewish Philanthropies, Boston, 1973-74; instr. Harvard U., Cambridge, Mass., 1974-75, sr. counselor Bur. of Study Counsel, 1974-79; supr. Dept. Social Svcs., Newton and Marlborough, Mass., 1979-88; area dir. case mgmt. and tng. Dept. Mental Health, Boston, 1988-94, area coord. medically-mentally ill, 1988—, chair consumer/family empowerment project, 1992-96. Area dir. Svcs. Integration, 1994—95, Clin. Affairs and Rehab., 1995—2000; project dir. Supported Employment Svcs., 1994—95; area Am. with Disabilities coord. Dept. of Mental Health, Boston, 1995—2000; instr. human devel. U. Mass., Boston, 1990—97. Grantee, Radcliffe Inst., 1972; Rsch. scholar, Boston U., 1981—82. Mem.: Mass. Psychol. Assn. Avocations: music, opera, writing.

MARKS, CHARLES, surgeon, educator; b. Kiev, Ukraine, Jan. 28, 1922; came to U.S., 1963; s. Abe and Sonia (Beck) M.; m. Joyce Wernick, Dec. 11, 1949; children: Malcolm, Peter, Ian, Anthony. MD, U. Cape Town, South Africa, 1945; MS, Marquette U., 1966; PhD, Tulane U., 1973. Intern and surg. resident Groote Schuur Hosp., Cape Town, 1946-49; surg. resident Royal Coll. Surgeons Affiliated Hosps., London, 1950-53; cons. surgeon Salisbury (Rhodesia) Gen. Hosp., 1953-63; assoc. prof. surgery Marquette U. Med. Sch., Milw., 1963-67; dir. dept. surgery Mt. Sinai Hosp., Cleve., 1967-71; assoc. clin. prof. surgery Case Western Res. U. Sch. Medicine, Cleve., 1967-71; prof. surgery La. State U. Sch. Medicine, New Orleans, 1971-88; sr. attending surgeon Charity, VA, Touro and Hotel Dieu Hosps., New Orleans, 1971—88; med. exec. dir. Fla. Dept. Corrections, Charlotte, Fla., 1994-97. Cons. cardiothoracic surgeon Ministry of Health, Govt. Zimbabwe, Harare, 1989-94; Hunterian prof. Royal Coll. Surgeons, 1956. Mem. bd. govs. Drs. Hosp. Sarasota, 1997-2004, chmn. bd. govs., 2001—; mem. inner senatorial com. Rep. Party, Washington, 1997—. Recipient Schlieder Rsch. award, 1975. Fellow ACS, Royal Coll. Physicians Edinburgh, Am. Coll. Cardiology; mem. Internat. Cardiovasc. Soc., Am. Transplantation Soc., New Orleans Surg. Soc. (pres.). Republican. Avocations: tennis, golf, travel. Home: # 1517 988 Blvd of the Arts Sarasota FL 34236 Personal E-mail: colray1963@yahoo.com.

MARKS, GERALD, surgeon, educator; b. Bklyn., Apr. 14, 1925; s. Maurice and Lee (Leib) M.; m. Barbara Ann Hendershot, Nov. 25, 1950; children: Richard M., James M., John H. Grad., Villanova U., 1945; MD, Jefferson Med. Coll., 1949. Diplomate: Am. Bd. Surgery, Am. Bd. Colon and Rectal Surgery (examiner). Intern Jefferson Med. Coll. Hosp., Phila., 1949-51, resident in surgery, 1952-57, resident in proctology, 1953-54, asst. dir. Tumor Clinic, 1959-68; practice medicine specializing in gen. and colorectal surgery Phila., 1957—; asst. chief surgery Phila. Gen. Hosp., 1957-70, chief Proctology Clinic, 1968-70, coordinator student surg. edn. Jefferson Surg. Service, 1960-70; attending physician in surgery Thomas Jefferson U. Hosp., 1957-95, sec. med. staff, 1974-77, dir. Comprehensive Rectal Cancer Ctr., Colorectal Surgery Residency Program, exec. dir. Colorectal Surgical Found., 1984-95, co-dir. Colorectal Cancer Genetics Ctr.; dir. div. internat. surg. edn. and practice Ctr. for Research in Med. Edn. and Health Care; instr. surgery Jefferson Med. Coll., 1958-67, assoc. in clin. surgery, 1967-68, clin. assoc. prof. surgery, 1974-78, prof., 1978-95; chief sect. colorectal surgery, cons. in colon-rectal surgery Pa. Hosp.; cons. in colon-rectal surgery VA Hosp., Coatesville, Pa., 1959—, San Juan, P.R., 1968—, Wilmington, Del., 1977—; cons in colon-rectal surgery USN Regional Med. Ctr., Phila., 1977—; Edgar Deissler prof. surgery Allegheny U. Health Scis., 1995—2001, dir. comprehensive rectal cancer ctr., 1995—98, dir. GI surg. endoscopy, 1995. Adj. prof. surgery U. Pa. Sch. Medicine; sr. investigator, Lankenan Inst. for Med. Rsch.; dir. Internat. Network Comprehensive Rectal Cancer Ctrs., 1997-; chmn. Marks Colorectal Surg. Found.; clin. prof. surgery Drexel U. Sch. Medicine, 2001; Deissler prof. surgery and founding dir. divsn. colorectal surgery Hahnemann Med. Coll. of Allegheny U., 1995-2000, dir. annual, Internat. Rectal Cancer Consensus Construct Lankeuau Med. Ctr. Sr. editor Surg. Endoscopy, Ultrasound and Interventional Techniques Jour.; assoc. editor Diseases of the Colon and Rectum Jour., 1977—; cons. editor Pa. Medicine; editl. cons. bd. mem. Gen. Surgery News, 1991, Jour. Surg. Techn.; contbr. articles to profl. jours.; developed colonscopic colon teaching model; solo artist exhbn. in watercolor painting in Italy and U.S Chmn. Marks Colorectal Surg. Rsch. Found. Served with USN, 1943-46; served to capt. M.C. USAF, 1951-52, co-dir. Multidisciplinary Internat. Recital Cancer Soc., exec. bd. mem. Internat. Fedn. Socs. Eudoscopic Surgeons, founding chmn. sr., adv. bd., multidisciplinary, Internat. Rectal Cancer Soc., 2011. Recipient 7th Ann. Jonathan M. Wainwright award, Moses Taylor Hosp., Scranton, Pa., 1989; Ann. Alumni Achievement award, Jefferson Med. Coll.; named Professorship, Jefferson Med. Coll., Thomas jefferson U., 1992, Annual Graveld Marks Rector Cancer Lectureship Lakeman Med. Ctr., 1992, Man of the Yr., Jewish Nat. Fund, Lifetime Achievement award Northeast Soc. of Colon and Rectal Surgeons, 2004, award, Annual Gerald Marks Leadership Pa. Soc. Colon & Rectal Surgeons, 2011. Mem. ACS (rep. to bd. govs. 1983, council Met. Phila. chpt.), AMA, Pa. Soc. Colon and Rectal Surgery (pres. 1981-82), Am. Soc. Colon and Rectal Surgeons (v.p. 1989), Am. Soc. Clin. Oncology, Internat. Soc. Univ. Colon and Rectal Surgeons, Coll. Physicians Phila., Internat. Fedn. Socs. Endoscopic Surgeons (founding pres. 1991-2000), Royal Soc. Medicine (affiliate), Ea. Surg. Soc., Phila. Acad. Surgery (mem. council), Pa. Med. Soc., Phila. County Med. Soc. (bd. dirs., v.p., chmn. publs. com., pub. affairs com., v.p. 1986—; Stritmatter award 2009), Soc. Surgery Alimentary Tract, Am. Soc. Gastrointestinal Endoscopy, Italian Soc. Gastrointestinal Endoscopy (hon.), Soc. Am. Gastrointestinal Endoscopic Surgeons (founder, pres. 1980, bd. govs., honoree Annual Gerald Marks Lectureship, former chmn. internat. rels. com., Dist. Svc. award, 1997, Lifetime Achievement award, 2004), Italian Soc. Surgery (hon.), Northeastern Soc. Colon and Rectal Surgeons (past pres.), Jefferson Vol. Faculty Assn. (pres. 1973-74, Brady Cancer Rsch. Inst. award, 1997), Am. Soc. Colon and Rectal Surgeons (v.p. 1989—), Abruzzi Surg. Soc. (hon.), European Assn. Endoscopic Surgeons, Endolaparoscopic Surgeons of Asia, Puerto Rico Chpt. Am. Coll. Surgeons, Alpha Omega Alpha Home: 45 Fairview Rd Narberth PA 19072-1328 Office: 100 Lancaster Ave # 3-west Wynnewood PA 19096-3411 Home Phone: 610-896-5901; Office Phone: 610-645-9093. E-mail: marksg@mlhs.org.

MARKS, ISAAC MEYER, psychiatrist; b. Cape Town, South Africa, Feb. 16, 1935; arrived in the UK, 1960; s. Morris N. and Anna (Janowsky) Marks; m. Shula E. Winokur, May 31, 1957; children: Lara V., Raphael C. MD, DPM, U. Cape Town, South Africa, 1973. Intern, resident Groote Schuur Hosp., Cape Town, 1957-59; prof. Inst. Psychiatry Bethlehem-Maudsley Hosp., London, 1978-2000; prof. emeritus Kings Coll., London, 2000—; med. dir. CCBT Ltd., 2006—. With Imperial Coll., London, 2000—04; vis. prof. Vrije U. Amsterdam, 2004—07; coord. Common Lang. Psychotherapy Procedures. Author: 17 books; contbr. 470 articles to profl. jours. Med. advisor to self-help charities. Fellow Royal Coll. Psychiatrists. Business E-Mail: Isaac.Marks@kcl.ac.uk.

MARKS, JAMES GARFIELD, JR., dermatologist; b. Trenton, NJ, May 19, 1945; s. James Garfield and Lavinia May (Ellis) M.; m. Joyce Lynne Turner, Aug. 9, 1969; 1 child, Shannon. BA, Wilkes Coll., 1967; MD, Temple U., Phila., 1971. Intern Geisinger Med. Ctr., Danville, Pa., 1971-72; resident Wilford Hall USAF Med. Ctr., San Antonio, 1975-78; clin. instr. dermatology U. Tex. Health Sci. Ctr., San Antonio, 1978-80; staff dermatologist Pa. State U. Coll. Medicine, Hershey, 1980—, asst. prof., 1980-85, assoc. prof., 1985-91, prof. dermatology, 1991—; chair dept. dermatology Hershey Med. Ctr. Team leader Cosmic Ingredient Rev. Expert Panel; co-dir. Caribbean and Coastal Dermatology Symposia. Author: Atlas of Differential Diagnosis in Dermatology, 1998, Principles of Dermatology, 2006, Handbook of Contact Dermatitis, 2000, Contact and Occupational Dermatology, 2002, Principles and Practice of Dermatology, 1990, 2d edit., 1996, Occupational Skin Diseases, 1999, Conn's Current Therapy, 1988, 2d edit., 1989; author: (with others) Principles of Clinical Diagnosis, 1992, Dermatology, 2008; contbr. articles to profl. jours. Bd. dirs. Braun Sta. East Cmty., 1976. Maj. USAF, 1972-80. Decorated Meritorious Svc. Commendation meadl; Am. Acad. Dermatology Exch. fellow, 1984; recipient Roerig Pharms. Challenges in Dermatology Ednl. award, 1982. Mem. Am. Acad. Dermatology, Am. Contact Dermatitis Soc. (v.p. 1993, pres. 2001), N.Am. Contact Dermatitis Group, Pa. Acad. Dermatology, Phila. Dermatology Soc., European Soc. Contact Dermatitis, Soc. Investigative Dermatology, Assn. Mil. Dermatologists, Dermatology Found., Lions (v.p. 1982, pres. 1983). Office: Hershey Med Ctr 500 University Dr # 850 Hershey PA 17033-2360 Office Phone: 717-531-8307. Business E-Mail: jmarks@psu.edu.

MARKS, JAMES S., public health service administrator; b. Buffalo, May 13, 1948; AB cum laude, Williams Coll., 1969; MD, SUNY, Buffalo, 1973; MPH, Yale U., 1980. Diplomate Am. Bd. Pediatrics. Intern in pediat. U. Calif., San Francisco, 1973-74, resident in pediat., 1974-75, chief resident pediatric outpatient dept., 1975-76; fellow Robert Wood Johnson Clin. Scholars Program Yale U., New Haven, 1978-80; resident in preventive medicine Ctrs. for Disease Control, Atlanta, 1977-78, 1981-82, chief epidemiology and rsch. br., nutrition divsn., 1982-84, asst. dir. preventive medicine residency program, 1985-87, dir. divsn. reproductive health, 1987, coord. for chronic disease control activities, 1987-88, acting dir. divsn. diabetes transl., 1988-89, acting dir. divsn. chronic disease control, 1990-91, dir. divsn. reproductive health, 1992-95, dir. Nat. Ctr. Chronic Disease Prevention/Health Promotion, 1995—2004, acting dir., 2004; sr. v.p., dir. health group Robert Wood Johnson Found., 2004—. Clinic physician Planned Parenthood of San Francisco Teen Clinic, 1975-76; cons. physician Ohio Dept. Health Bur. Preventive Medicine, 1978-79; cons. PAHO Consultative Group on Perinatal Care, Washington, 1982, WHO Malaysia Ministry of Health, 1982, 83, WHO Maternal and Child Health Unit Geneva, 1983, World Bank China Program Third Health Project, 1988, 1991, World Bank Poland, Health Promotion/Chronic Disease Prevention, 1992, World Bank China, Seventh Health Project, 1993; adj. assoc. prof. Emory U. Sch. Pub. Health; asst. surgeon general, 1996—. Editor Chronic Disease Notes and Reports, 1989-92; contbr. articles to profl. jours, chpts. to books. Exec. sec. Diabetes Tech. Adv. com., 1989-92; liaison mem. Nat. Diabetes Adv. Bd., 1988-89; mem. Diabetes Mellitus Interagy. Cording. com., 1988-89; mem. subcom. adult edn., Am. Cancer Soc., 1987-92; staff White House Task Force on Infant Mortality, 1989; presenter in field. Epidemic Intelligence Svc. Officer USPHS Field Svcs. Divsn., 1976-78. Recipient Alexander D. Langmuir award, 1978, CDC Group award, 1984, Commendation Medal USPHS, 1984, and many other awards and citations. Fellow Am. Coll. Epidemiology; mem. APHA (active in com. work), Inst. Medicine, Am. Epidemiol. Soc., Soc. Epidemiol. Rsch., Am. Acad. Pediat. (com. pediatric rsch. 1994-95), Internat. Epidemiol. Assn., Physicians for Social Responsibility, Soc. on Med. Decision Making, Epidemic Intelligence Svc. Alumni Assn., Sigma Xi. Home: 15 Houghton Rd Princeton NJ 08540-3300 Office: Robert Wood Johnson Found PO Box 2316 College Rd East and Rte 1 Princeton NJ 08543

MARKS, JOHN H., colon and rectal surgeon, educator; MD, Thomas Jefferson U., 1989. Lic. Pa., 1991, diplomate Am. Bd. Colon and Rectal Surgery, 1997, Am. Bd. Surgery, 2004. Resident in gen. surgery Thomas Jefferson Univ. Hosp., 1994, resident in colon and rectal surgery, 1995, fellow in minimally invasive surgery, 1996; asst. clin. prof. surgery sch. medicine Hahnemann Univ., Pa.; hosp. affiliations include Bryn Mawr Hosp., 1999—, Paoli Hosp., 1999—, Lankenau Med. Ctr., 1999—; chief colorectal surgery. Author: (articles) Radical Sphincter Preservation Surgery With Coloanal Anastomosis Following High-Dose External Irradiation for the Very Low Lying Rectal Cancer, 1998, High-Dose Preoperative Radiation and the Challenge of Sphincter Preservation Surgery for Cancer of the Distal 2cm of the Rectum, 1998, Colorectal Cancer: Look to the Future, 2001, Transanal Endoscopic Microsurgery in the Treatment of Select Rectal Cancers or Tumors Suspicious for Cancer, 2003. Named one of Top Doctors, Phila. Mag., 2007, 2010. Fellow: ACS; mem.: Soc. of Surgical Oncology, Soc. of Am. Gastrointestinal and Endoscopic Surgeons, Soc. for Surgery of the Alimentary Tract, Assoc. for Academic Surgery, Am. Soc. of Colon and Rectal Surgeons. Office: Lankenau Medical Center Marks Colorectal Surgical Associates Mob W Ste 330 100 Lancaster Ave Wynnewood PA 19096 Office Phone: 886-225-5654.

MARKS, LAWRENCE EDWARD, psychologist, educator; b. NYC, Dec. 28, 1941; s. Milton and Anne (Parnes) M.; m. Joya Ellen Cazes, Dec. 24, 1963; children: Liza, Laura. AB, Hunter Coll., NYC, 1962; PhD, Harvard U., Cambridge, Mass., 1965; PhD honoris causa, Stockholm U., 1994. Rsch.-assoc. prof. Yale U., New Haven, 1966-84; asst.-assoc. fellow John B. Pierce Lab., New Haven, 1966-84; prof. epidemiology and psychology Yale U., New Haven, 1984—; fellow John B. Pierce Lab., New Haven, 1984—, dir., 1999—2009. Author: Sensory Processes: The New Psychophysics, 1974, The Unity of the Senses, 1978. Named to Hall of Fame, Hunter Coll., N.Y.C., 1985; recipient Jacob Javits award NIH, Washington, 1987. Fellow AAAS, Am. Psychol. Assn., Am. Psychol. Soc., N.Y. Acad. Sci. Democrat. Jewish. Achievements include elucidation of common principles underlying sensory processes in various sense modalities; development of validational scheme for quantifying magnitudes of sensory experience; indication of role of cross-modal (synesthetic) perception in relation to language and literature. Home: 48 Maplevale Dr Woodbridge CT 06525-1118 Office: John B Pierce Lab 290 Congress Ave New Haven CT 06519-1403 Home Phone: 203-393-1565; Office Phone: 203-562-9901. Business E-Mail: marks@jbpierce.org.

MARKS, MELVIN I., physician, educator, hospital administrator, consultant; b. Montreal, July 30, 1940; came to U.S., 1979; s. Irving and Kate Marks; div. March 1999; children: Suzanne, Jennifer, Daniel. BSc, McGill U., 1961, MD CM, 1965; Cert. in Exec. Mgmt., UCLA, 1990. Diplomate Am. Bd. Pediat., Am. Bd. Pediat. Infectious Disease. Intern Montreal Gen. Hosp., 1965-66; resident in pediat. Montreal Children's Hosp., 1966-68; fellow in pediat. infectious diseases U. Colo. Med. Ctr., 1968-70; asst. prof. McGill U., Montreal, 1970-75, assoc. prof., 1975-79; prof. U. Okla., Oklahoma City, 1979-86; prof., vice-chmn. dept. U. Calif., Irvine, 1986—2009; clin. prof. U. So. Calif., 1997-99. Author: Pediatric Infectious Disease for the Practitioner, 1985; editor: Cystic Fibrosis, 1996. Bd. dirs. Starlight Found., L.A., 1995—2009; bd. trustees, 2009-. Office: Miller Childrens Hosp 2801 Atlantic Ave Long Beach CA 90806-1737 Home Phone: 714-402-3027; Office Phone: 562-933-9701. E-mail: mmarks@memorialcare.org. *

MARKS, PAUL ALAN, oncologist, cell biologist, educator; b. NYC, Aug. 16, 1926; s. Robert R. and Sarah (Bohorad) Marks; m. Joan Harriet Rosen, Nov. 28, 1953; children: Andrew Robert, Elizabeth Susan Marks Ostrer, Matthew Stuart. AB with gen. honors, Columbia U., 1945, MD, 1949, DSc (hon.), 2000; D in Biol. Sci. (hon.), U. Urbino, Italy, 1982; PhD (hon.), Hebrew U., Jerusalem, Israel, 1987, U. Tel Aviv, 1992; DSc (hon.), Ben Gurion U., Be'er Sheva, Israel, 2003. From fellow to prof. Coll. Physicians and Surgeons Columbia U., NYC, 1952—67, prof. medicine Coll. Physicians and Surgeons, 1967—82, dean faculty of medicine, v.p. med. affairs Coll. Physicians and Surgeons, 1970—73, dir. Comprehensive Cancer Ctr. Coll. Physicians and Surgeons, 1972—80, v.p. health scis. Coll. Physicians and Surgeons, 1973—80; prof. cell biology and genetics Coll. Medicine Cornell U., NYC, 1980—, prof. medicine Grad. Sch. Med. Scis., 1983—; pres., CEO Meml. Sloan-Kettering Cancer Ctr., NYC, 1980—99, pres. emeritus, 2000—. Instr. Sch. Medicine George Wash. U., 1954—55; cons. VA Hosp., NYC, 1962—66; attending physician Presbyn. Hosp., NYC, 1967—82; bd. dirs. Pfizer Inc., 1978—96, Shape Pharm., 2009—; attending physician Meml. Hosp. for Cancer and Allied Diseases, 1980—; prin. investigator, Devel. Cell Biology Sloan-Kettering Inst. for Cancer Rsch., 1980—; adj. prof. Rockefeller U., 1980—; vis. physician Rockefeller U. Hosp., 1980—; bd. sci. counselors divsn. cancer treatment Nat. Cancer Inst., 1980—83; hon. staff N.Y. Hosp., 1981—; steering com. Frederick Cancer Rsch. Facility Nat. Cancer Inst., 1982—86; chmn. prog. adv. com. Robert Wood Johnson Found., 1983—89; adv. com. on NIH to Sec. HHS, 1989—90, 1993—98; external adv. com. Intramural Rsch. Prog. Rev. NIH; gov. com. NYPRHA, 1996; tech. adv. grp. UN Assn. U.S.; coun. biol. scis. Pritzker Sch. Medicine U. Chgo., 1977—88; William Dameshek vis. prof. hematology Mt. Sinai Med. Ctr., 1985; nat. vis. com. CUNY Med. Sch., 1986—89; trustee Feinberg Grad. Sch. Weizmann Inst. Sci., Rehovot, Israel, 1986—; vis. prof. Coll. de France, 1988; Alpha Omega Alpha vis. prof. N.Y. Med. Coll., 1990; Mario A. Baldini vis. prof. Med. Sch. Harvard U., 1991; sci. adv. bd. City Hope Nat. Med. Ctr., Duarte, Calif., 1987—92, Raymond and Beverly Sackler Found., Inc., 1989, Jefferson Cancer Inst., Phila., 1989, PTC Biotech., Inc., 2002—, Ikonysis, 2004—08, Merck, Inc., 2004—05; mem Found. Biomed. Rsch., 1989—; sci. adv. com. Imperial Cancer Rsch. Fund, 1994—2003; sr. adv. Lazard Freres, 2000—; co-founder, sec. and vice chmn. Aton Pharma, Tarrytown, NY, 2001—04, co-founder, chmn. bd.dir., 2006—; internat. adv. coun. Singapore Econ. Devel. Bd., 2000—03; dir. Dreyfus Mutual Funds, NC, 1998—2005; lectr. Nobel Forum, Karolinska Inst., Sweden, 2004; pres. Pres. Cancer Panel, 1975—78, Commn. Investigates Release Reactor Tree Mile Island, 1978. Author: 11 books; mem. editl. bd.: Blood, 1964—76, editor-in-chief:, 1978—82, mem. editl. bd.: Jour. Clin. Investigation, 1970—71, editor-in-chief: Jour. Clin Investigation, mem. editl. bd.: Cancer Treatment Revs., 1981—, Japanese Jour. Cancer Rsch., 1985—, Molecular Reprodn. and Devel., 1988—, Cancer Preventions, 1989, Sci., 1990, Current Opinion Oncologic Endocrine and Metabolic Drugs, 1998; mem. editl. bd. WTL Jour. Cell Biology; expert analyst: Chemistry and Molecular Biology edit. of Chemtracts, 1990—92, mem. adv. bd.: Internat. Jour. Hematology, 1992, Stem Cells, bd. contbg. editors: Blood Cells, Molecules and Diseases, 1994, Comité des Sages, 1994; contbr. over 400 articles to profl. jours. Trustee St. Luke's Hosp., 1970—80, Roosevelt Hosp., 1970—80, Presbyn. Hosp., 1972—80, Metpath Inst. Med. Edn., 1977—79, Hadassah Med. Ctr., Jerusalem, 1996; mem. jury Albert Lasker Awards, 1974—82; bd. dirs. Revson Found., 1976—91, Am. Found. for Basic Rsch. Israel, Israel Acad. Scis., 1991; mem. tech. bd. Milbank Meml. Fund, 1978—85; bd. govs. Friends of Sheba Med. Ctr., Tel Hashomer; mem. commn. sci. and tech. Mayor, NYC, 1984—87; mem. commn. Shoreham Nuc. Plant Gov., NYC, 1983; mem. task force biomed. rsch. and tech. Mayor, NYC, 1999. Recipient Stevens Triennial prize, 1960, Swiss-Am. Found. award, 1965, Centenary medal, Inst. Pasteur, 1987, Found. for Promotion of Cancer Rsch. medal, Japan, 1984, DSM, Robert Wood Johnson Found., 1989, Outstanding Achievement award, U. Innsbruck, 1991, Pres.'s Nat. Medal Sci., 1991, Japan Found. for Cancer Rsch. award, 1995, Lifetime Achievement award, Greater N.Y. Hosp. Assn., 1997, Am. Italian Cancer Found., 1999, Humanitarian award, Breast Cancer Rsch. Found., 2000, Disting. Lifetime Achievement award, Healthcare Chaplaincy, NY, 2001, John Stearns award, NY Acad. Medicine, 2002, Annie Blount Storrs Humanitarian award, Calvary Hosp., NY, 2002; fellow Commonwealth Fund fellow, Pasteur Inst., 1961—62; Ayrey fellow, 1985. Master: ACP, Coll. Physicians and Surgeons (Gold medal 1994); fellow: AAAS, Pasteur Inst. Paris (Commonwealth Fund fellow 1961—62), Am. Acad. Arts and Scis., Royal Soc. Medicine; mem.: NAS (chmn. Acad. Forum Adv. Com. 1980—81, chmn. sect. med. genetics, hematology and oncology 1980—83, coun. 1984—87, del. biol. warfare com. Internat. Security and Arms Control 1986—89, bd. dirs. 2002), Am. Philos. Soc., NY Acad. Sci. (bd. dirs. 2002), European Acad. Scis., UN Assn. (tech. adv. grp.), Weizmann Inst. Sci. (gov. emeritus, Israel), Third World Acad. Scis. (adv.), Soc. Study Devel. and Growth, Japan Soc. Hematology (Disting. lectr. 1989), Soc. Devel. Biology, Internat. Soc. Devel. Biologists, Harvey Soc. (pres. 1973—74), Assn. Am. Physicians, Am. Soc. Hematology (pres.-elect 1983, pres. 1984, chmn. adv. bd. 1985), Soc. Cell Biology, Assn. Am. Cancer Insts. (bd. dirs. 1983—88), Am. Assn. Cancer Rsch., Am. Soc. Human Genetics (past mem. prog. com.), Italian Assn. Cell Biology and Differentiation (hon.), Chinese Anti-Cancer Assn. (hon.), Japanese Cancer Assn. (hon.), Am. Soc. Biol. Chemists, Am. Soc. Clin. Investigation (pres. 1972—73), Am. Fedn. Clin. Rsch. (past councillor Ea. dist.), Red Cell Club (past chmn.), Inst. Medicine (coun. 1973—76, chmn. com. study resources clin. investigation with NAS 1988), Univ. Club, Soc. Interurban Clin. Club, Century Assn., Alpha Omega Alpha. Office: Meml Sloan-Kettering Cancer Ctr 1275 York Ave New York NY 10065-6094 Office Phone: 212-639-6568. Business E-Mail: marksp@mskcc.org.

MARKS, STANLEY M., internist; MD, U. Pitts. Diplomate Am. Bd. Internal Medicine, Am. Bd. Internal Medicine-hematology. Resident Univ. Pitts.; fellow Dana Farber Cancer Inst., Harvard Univ.; hosp. affiliations include Univ. Pitts. Med. Ctr. Presbyn., Pa., Univ. Pitts. Med. Ctr. Shadyside, Univ. Pitts. Med. Ctr. Hillman Cancer Ctr. Office: University of Pittsburgh Medical Center Hillman Cancer Center 5115 Centre Ave Pittsburgh PA 15232 Office Phone: 412-235-1020.

MARKS, STEPHEN J., neurologist, educator; b. Bklyn., Aug. 30, 1953; s. Ansel R. Marks and Frances L. Carpenter; m. Cindy G. Marks, Mar. 27, 1994; children: Jordan, Avery. BA, Colgate U., 1979. Diplomate Am. Bd. Neurology & Psychiatry. Intern Lenox Hill Hosp., NYC; resident Mt. Sinai Hosp., NYC; assoc. prof. N.Y. Med. Coll., Valhalla, 1987—. Team neurologist N.Y. Jets, Hempstead, 1986. Co-author: (chapter) Principle & Practice of Emergency Medicine, 1992, (book), 1997. Fellow: Am. Heart Assn. (mem. stroke coun.); mem.: Soc. Neuroscience, Nat. Stroke Assn., Am. Acad. Neurology. Avocations: skiing, windsurfing. Office: Dept Neurology Munger Pavilion, NYMC Valhalla NY 10595

MARKWARDT, FRITZ, pharmacologist, educator; b. Magdeburg, Germany, Dec. 3, 1924; s. Friedrich and Else (Hallupp) Markwardt; m. Gertrud Vogler, June 12, 1952; children: Maria Bronisch, Fritz Jr. PhD, U. Greifswald, 1951, MD, 1960; MD (hon.), Med. Acad. Erfurt, 1991. Asst. rsch. and tchg. Inst. Pharmacology, Greifswald, Germany, 1952—56; lectr. Inst. Pharmacology and Toxicology, Greifswald, 1956—60, prof., 1960, head Erfurt, Germany, 1961—90; sr. advisor Inst. Thrombosis and Vascular Diseases, Frankfurt, Germany, 1992—. Vis. prof. Loyola U., Chgo., 1988—98, U. Milan, Italy, 1985—88. Author (textbook): Antithrombotica, Pharmacology, Clinical Use, 1986; author: (editor) Exptl. Pharmacology, Anticoagulantian, 1971, Exptl. Pharmacology Fibrinolytica, Antifibrinolytica, 1978. Recipient Nat. award, Berlin, 1956, Sixth Biann. award for Contbns. to Hemostatis, NY, 1993, Schmiedeberg award, Berlin, 2000. Mem.: German Soc. Pharmacology and Toxicology, Academia Europea, Deutsche Akademie Naturforscher, German Soc. Hemostasis Thrombosis Rsch. (hon.). Achievements include development of novel groups hemostyptic and antithrombotic drugs, such as antifibrinolytic agents, synthetic inhibitors of clotting enzymes and anticoagulant agents from bloodsucking animals. Home: Das Queirgfeld 3 D 99192 Frienstedt Germany E-mail: f.markwardt@t-online.de.

MARKWELL, SUSAN JANE, physiotherapist, educator, writer; b. Melbourne, Australia, June 8, 1951; d. William Anthony Jesser-Coope and Mavis Proctor Sandford; m. James Stuart Markwell, Apr. 28, 1972 (div. Oct. 6, 1996); children: Alexandra Louise, Anthony Stuart, Timothy Scott; m. Paul David Oates, June 5, 1999. B in Physiotherapy, U. Queensland, Brisbane, Australia, 1973. Registered physiotherapist Australia, U.K. Gen. physiotherapist Repatriation Gen. Hosp., Melbourne, 1973—75; sr. physiotherapist Queen Victoria Hosp., Melbourne, 1975—77; clin. tutor, grad. asst. dept. physiotherapy U. Queensland, 1977—78; ante-natal educator, pvt. practice in women's health Lilian Cooper Ctr. for Women, N.W. Hosp., Brisbane, 1979—2003; specialist physiotherapist depts. gastroenterology and physiotherapy Royal Brisbane Hosp., 1992—2007. Reviewer Cochrane Collaboration, Australia and U.K., 1997; specialist physiotherapist to profl. bd. assessors State Govt. Queensland, Brisbane, 2000—; rschr. muscle dysfunction in Bosindicus stud cattle U. Queensland Vet. Sch., 2003—. Author, editor Let's Get Things Moving, Overcoming Constipation, 1992, 2d edit., 2003, Women's Health, A Textbook for Physiotherapists, 1997. Rsch. grantee, Dept. Health and Aged Care, Commonwealth Govt. Australia, 2001—06. Mem.: Droughtsmaster Soc. Australia, Australian Continence Found., Australian Physiotherapy Assn. (clin. rsch. grantee 1994, 1996, Best Invited Spkr. award 1996). Achievements include research in pelvic floor dysfunction, including defecation; development of clinical program of abdominal/pelvic floor retraining for all forms of bowel and bladder dysfunction; treatment protocol for pelvic and perineal pain, including vulvovestibulitis. Avocations: breeding and showing Droughtmaster stud beef cattle, farming, antique restoration, genealogy. Home and Office: 205 Bunjurgen Rd 4310 via Boonah QLD Australia Office Phone: 07-5463-4383. Business E-Mail: boonah.vista@bigpond.com.

MARLETT, JUDITH ANN, nutritional sciences educator, researcher; b. Toledo; BS, Miami U., Oxford, Ohio, 1965; PhD, U. Minn., 1972; postgrad., Harvard U., 1973-74. Registered dietitian. Therapeutic and metabolic unit dietitian VA Hosp., Mpls., 1966-67; spl. instr. in nutrition Simmons Coll., Boston, 1973-74; asst. prof. U. Wis., Madison, 1975-80, assoc. prof. dept. nutritional scis., 1981-84, prof. dept. nutritional scis., 1984—2010, emeritus prof. dept. nutritional scis., 2010—. Cons. U.S. AID, Leyte, Philippines, 1983, Makerere U., Kampala, Uganda, 2005; acting dir. dietetic program dept. Nutritional Scis. U. Wis., 1977-78, dir., 1985-89; cons. grain, drug and food cos., 1985—, adv. bd. U. Ariz. Clin. Cancer Ctr., 1987-95; sci. bd. advisors Am. Health Found., 1988—; reviewer NIH, 1982-2004; vis. prof. Makerere U., Kampala, Uganada, 2005; spkr. in field. Mem. editl. bd. Jour. Sci. of Food and Agrl., 1989—, Jour. Food Composition and Analysis, 1994-2000, Jour. of Nutrition, 2002-08; contbr. articles to profl. jours. Mem. NIH (Diabetes amd Digestive and Kidney Disease spl. grant rev. com. 1992-96), Am. Soc. Nutrition, Am. Dietetic Assn. Achievements include research on human nutrition and disease, dietary fiber and gastrointestinal function. Office: U Wis Dept Nutritional Sci 1415 Linden Dr Madison WI 53706-1527 Home Phone: 623-972-5221; Office Phone: 623-972-5221. Business E-Mail: jmarlett@nutrisci.wisc.edu.

MARLETTA, MICHAEL A., chemistry professor; b. Rochester, NY, Feb. 12, 1951; m. Margaret Gutowski, 1991. BA, SUNY, Fredonia, 1973; PhD in Pharm. Chemistry, U. Calif., San Francisco, 1978. NIH postdoctoral fellow, dept. chem. MIT, Cambridge, 1978-80, from asst. prof. to assoc. prof. toxicology, 1980-87; assoc. prof. med. chemistry U. Mich., Ann Arbor, 1987-91, assoc. prof. biol. chemistry, 1989-91, John G. Searle prof. med. chemistry, prof. biol. chemistry, 1991—2001; prof., chemistry, biochemistry & molecular biology U. Calif., Berkeley, 2001—, Aldo DeBenedictis Disting. prof., chmn. dept. chemistry, 2005—10, Joel Hildebrand Disting. prof. chem., 2005—. Investigator Howard Hughes Med. Inst., 1997—2001; Miller vis. rsch. prof. U. Calif., Berkeley, 2000. Recipient George H. Hitchings award for innovative methods in drug discovery & design, 1991, Faculty Recognition award, U. Mich., 1992, Outstanding Achievement award, SUNY, Fredonia, 1993, Disting. Faculty Leadership award in biomed. rsch., U. Mich. Med. Sch., 2000, Disting. Faculty Achievement award, U. Mich., 2000, Emil Thomas Kaiser award, Protein Soc., 2007; named State of Mich. Scientist of Yr., 2000; named a MacArthur fellow, John D. and Catherine T. MacArthur Found., 1995; named to Alumni Honor Roll, SUNY, 1996. Fellow: Am. Acad. Arts and Scis., Mich. Soc. Fellows (sr.); mem.: NAS, Inst. Medicine, Am. Chem. Soc. (Repligen award in chemistry of biol. processes 2007, Esselen award for chemistry in pub. interest 2007), Am. Soc. Biochem. and Molecular Biology. Achievements include research in protein/structure function with a particular interest in enzyme reaction mechanisms and molecular mechanisms of signal transduction, study of nitric oxide synthase, guanylate cyclase and related enzymes in this signaling system. Office: Univ Calif Chemistry Dept 570 Stanley Hall Berkeley CA 94720-1460 Office Phone: 510-666-2763. Office Fax: 510-666-2765. Business E-Mail: marletta@berkeley.edu.

MARLOWE, SHARON NALINI SINGH, epidemiologist; b. Georgetown, Guyana, Oct. 10, 1970; d. Doodnauth and Savitri Singh; m. Simon James Lee, Oct. 9, 2004; 1 child, Lucia Elizabeth Kaikuchi Lee. MBChB, U. Bristol, Eng., 1994—94; PhD, U. London, 2002. House physician Southmead Hosp., Bristol, 1994—95; house surgeon Cheltenham Hosp., England, 1995; sr. house physician Dryburn Hosp., Durham, England, 1995—96, Frenchay Hosp., Bristol, 1996—98; med. registrar Trafford Hosp. & U., Manchester, England, 1998; med. cons. & lectr. Jimma Hosp. & U., Ethiopia, 1999; clin. rsch. fellow & tropical diseases registrars London Sch. Hygiene & Tropical Medicine & Hosp. Tropical Diseases, 1999—2002; med. specialist registrar Flinders Hosp., Adelaide, Australia, 2002; sr. lectr. & cons. Flinders U. & Hosp., 2003; clin. lectr. & specialist registrar infectious diseases & microbiology U. Bristol & Hosps. Bristol, 2003—05; specialist registrar respiratory & TB medicine West Midlands Hosps., Birmingham, England, 2005—07; specialist registrar infectious diseases, tropical medicine & gen. internal medicine North Manchester Hosp., 2007—09, Southmead Hosp., Bristol, 2009—. Cons. & dir. Ethiopian HIV pub. health project Dept. Internat. Devel., London, Addis Ababa, 2000—01. Contbr. articles to profl. sci. jours. Organizer antiapartheid benefit concert U. Bristol, 1990; fin. charity mycobacterial rschr. Robert Cochrane Fund Leprosy, London, 2003; rep. Brit. Med. Assn., Bristol, 1996—97, Assoc. Med. Microbiologists, Bristol, 2004—05. Grant, Luxembourgh Govt., 1999—2002. Mem.: RCP (UK), Internat. Soc. Infectious Diseases, Brit. Assn. Sexual Health & HIV, Brit. Infection Soc., Royal Soc. Tropical Medicine & Hygiene (advisor women in medicine 2008—), Brit. Med. Assn. (rep. 1996—97). Achievements include research in new treatment for leprosy; lack of efficacy of leprosy & antiretoviral therapy in africans. Office: Southmead Hosp ID Dept Southmead Rd Westbury-on-Trym Bristol BS10 5NB England

MARMER, ELLEN LUCILLE, pediatrician, cardiologist; b. Bronx, NY, June 29, 1939; d. Benjamin and Diane (Goldstein) M.; m. Harold O. Shapiro, June 5, 1960; children: Cheri, Brenda. BS in Chemistry, U. Ala., 1960; MD, U. Ala., Birmingham, 1964. Cert. Nat. Bd. Med. Examiners; diplomate Am. Bd. Sports Medicine, Bd. Pediat., Bd. Qualified and Eligible Pediatric Cardiology, Bd. cert. sports medicine. Intern Upstate Med. Ctr., Syracuse, NY, 1964-65, resident, 1965-66; fellow in pediatric cardiology Columbia Presbyn. Med. Ctr.-Babies Hosp., NYC, 1967-69; pvt. practice Hartford, Vernon, Conn., 1969—. Examining pediatrician child devel. program Columbia Presbyn. Med. Ctr.-Babies Hosp., N.Y.C., 1967, instr. pediat., 1967-69; dir. pediatric cardiology clinic St. Francis Hosp., Hartford, 1970-80; asst. state med. examiner, Tolland County, Conn., 1974-79; sports physician Rockville (Conn.) High Sch., 1976—; advisor Cardiac Rehab. com., Rockville, 1984-90; mem. bd. examiners Am. Bd. Sports Medicine, 1991—, chmn. credentials com., 1991-93. Mem. Vernon Town Coun., 1985-89; bd. dirs. Child Guidance Clinic, Manchester, Conn., 1970—; life mem. Tolland County chpt. Hadassah, v.p., 1969-70, pres., 1970-72, bd. dirs., 1973-74; mem. B'nai Israel Congregation and Sisterhood, Vernon, 1969—, chmn. youth commn., 1970-72; mayor Town of Vernon, 2003-05, 05-. Recipient Outstanding Svc. award Indian Valley YMCA, 1985, Outstanding Contribution award, Am. Heart Assn. Conn. Affiliate, Inc., 1988, Outstanding Vol. award, 1989, Outstanding Svc. award, 1992, Indian Valley YMCA, 1987, Dedicated Svc. award, 1984, 1991, Outstanding Contribution award, 1992, Vernon Town Coun. Gratitude & Appreciation award, 1989, Golden Rule award, Child Guidance Clinic, 1990, Spl. Mem. award, Vernon Vol. Ambulance, 1990, Vol. Physician award, US Olympic Tng. Ctr., Lake Placid, 1997, Spl. Physician Recognition award, Nurse & Health Svcs. Conn., Inc., 1998, Rsch. award, AHA, 2001-, Top Physician award, Guide of Americas Top Physician, 2004-05, Top Cardiologist award, 2008, Thomas F. Burpee award, 2007, Helen Butler Terry Cmty. Svc. award, U. Ala. Med. Alumni Assn., 2010. Fellow Am. Acad. Pediat., Am. Coll. Cardiology, Am. Coll. Sports Medicine; mem. Conn. Med. Soc., Am. Heart Assn. (mem. coun. cardiovasc. disease in young 1969—, chmn. elect New Eng. regional heart com. 1990-91, mem. Heritage affiliate 1998—), Conn. Heart Assn. (bd. dirs. 1974-75, 83-84, pres. 1986-88), Heart Assn. Greater Hartford (bd. dirs. 1970-89, mem. exec. com. 1972-73, 79-84, pres. 1982-84), Tolland County Med. Assn. (sec. 1971-72), Vis. Nurse and Cmty. Care Tolland County, LWV (state program chairperson Vernon chpt. 1971-73). Democrat. Jewish. Avocation: sports. Office: 520 Hartford Tpke Vernon Rockville CT 06066 Office Phone: 860-870-9366.

MARMO, FRANCESCO, embryologist, medical consultant; b. San Rufo, Italy, Feb. 14, 1934; s. Orazio Marmo and Rosa Santoro; m. Isabella Bianconi, Sept. 2, 1967; children: Fabrizio, Valerio, Francesca-Rosa, Silvia. MD summa cum laude, U. Naples, Italy, 1959. Diplomate Bd. Otorhinolaryngology. Asst. prof. gen. biology U. Naples, 1960—62, asst. prof. genetics, 1963—71, prof. anatomy, 1968—76, asst. prof. gen. biology, 1969—80, 1971—78, asst. prof. histology and embryology, 1978—80, prof. histology and embryology, 1980—. Contbr. Histology, 1981, articles to profl. publs. Mem.: Pontaniana Acad. Naples, NY Acad. Sci., Unione Zoologica Italiana, Italian Soc. Otorhinolaryngology, Gruppo Embriologico Italiano. Achievements include discovery of carbonic anhydrase role on otolith morphogenesis. Home: Donizetti 11 00198 Rome Italy Office: U

Naples Federico II Mezzocannone 8 80134 Naples Italy Home Phone: 39 06 8416027; Office Phone: 39 081-2535012. Office Fax: 39 081 2535000. Business E-Mail: francesco.marmo@unina.it.

MARMOR, MICHAEL FRANKLIN, ophthalmologist, educator; b. NYC, Aug. 10, 1941; s. Judd and Katherine (Stern) M.; m. C. Jane Breeden, Dec. 20, 1968; children: Andrea K., David J. AB, Harvard U., Cambridge, Mass., 1962, MD, 1966. Diplomate Am. Bd. Ophthalmology. Med. intern UCLA Med. Ctr., 1967; fellow neurophysiology NIMH, 1967-70; resident in ophthalmology Mass. Eye and Ear Infirmary, Boston, 1970-73; asst. prof. ophthalmology U. Calif. Sch. Medicine, San Francisco, 1973-74; asst. prof. surgery (ophthalmology) Stanford U. Sch. Medicine, Calif., 1974-80, assoc. prof. Calif., 1980-86, prof. Calif., 1986—, head. div. ophthalmology Calif., 1984-88, chmn. dept. Calif., 1988-92, dir. Basic Sci. Course Ophthalmology Calif., 1993—2005. Faculty mem. program in human biology Stanford U., 1982—; chief ophthalmology sect. VA Med. Ctr., Palo Alto, Calif., 1974-84; mem. sci. adv. bd. No. Calif. Soc. to Prevent Blindness, 1984-92, Calif. Med. Assn., 1984-92, Nat. Retinitis Pigmentosa Found., 1985-95; affiliate Stanford Ctr. for Biomedical Ethics, 2008-. Author: The Eye of the Artist, 1997, Degas Through his own Eyes, 2002, The Artists' Eyes, 2009; editor: The Retinal Pigment Epithelium, 1975, The Effects of Aging and Environment on Vision, 1991, The Retinal Pigment Epithelium: Function and Disease, 1998; editor-in-chief Doc. Ophthalmologica, 1995-99; history and TimeOph editor: Survey of Ophthalmology; contbr. more than 250 articles to peer-reviewed jours., 50 chpts. to books. Mem. affirmative action com. Stanford U. Sch. Medicine, 1984-92. Sr. asst. surgeon USPHS, 1967-70. Recipient Svc. award Nat. Retinitis Pigmentosa Found., Balt., 1981, Rsch. award Alcon Rsch. Found., Houston, 1989; rsch. grantee Nat. Eye. Inst., Bethesda, Md., 1974-94. Fellow Am. Acad. Ophthalmology (bd. councillors 1982-85, pub. health com. 1990-93, rep. to NAS com. on vision 1991-93, mus. com. 2004—, Honor award 1984, Sr. Honor award 1996, Lifetime Achievement award 2009), Cogan Ophthalmology Hist. Soc. (pres. 2003—06), Assn. Rsch. Vision & Ophthalmology; mem. Internat. Soc. Clin. Electrophysiology of Vision (v.p. 1990-98, dir. stds.), Internat. Soc. for Eye Rsch., Retina Soc. (Award of Merit, named Charles L. Scheques Lectr. 2011), Macula Soc. (Green lectr. 2007). Democrat. Avocations: tennis, bicycling, art, history, clarinet. Office: Byers Eye Inst at Stanford 2452 Watson Ct Palo Alto CA 94303-5353

MARMUR, ELLEN S., dermatologist, educator; Grad. with highest honors, U. Calif., San Francisco; MD with distinction, Albert Einstein Coll. Diplomate Am. Bd. Dermatology. Intern internal medicine Mt. Sinai Hosp.; resident dermatology Cornell University Med. Ctr.; assoc. prof. Mt. Sinai Med. Ctr., NYC, chief dermatologic and cosmetic surgery; dir. Procedural Dermatology Fellowship; co-dir. Mt. Sinai Cosmetic Dermatology Fellowship. Author numerous articles; guest editor Your Health Now mag., featured in (newspaper) NY Times, The NY Post, The NY Daily News, (mags.) Vogue, Marie Claire, People. Recipient award for Outstanding Rsch. in Melanoma Vaccines, award for Excellence in Clin. and Academic Medicine, Leading Health Professionals of the World, numerous awards. Mem.: Am. Soc. for Laser Medicine and Surgery, Am. Coll. of Mohs Micrographic Surgery and Cutaneous Oncology, Am. Med. Women's Assn., Womens Dermatologic Soc., NY Dermatologic Soc., Am. Acad. of Dermatology, Am. Soc. of Dermatologic Surgery. Office: Dermatology Associates 5 East 98th St 5th Fl New York NY 10029 Office Phone: 212-241-7092.

MARNEY, SAMUEL ROWE, JR., retired allergist, immunologist, educator; b. Bristol, Va., Feb. 15, 1934; m. Elizabeth Ann Bingham, Oct. 1, 1966; children: Samuel Rowe III, Annis Morison. BA in Chemistry, U. Va., 1955, MD, 1960. Diplomate Am. Bd. Internal Medicine, Am. Bd. Allergy and Immunology; cert. in Diagnostic Lab. Immunology, 1988. Staff physician VA Hosp., Nashville, 1968—69, clin. assoc., 1969—71, clin. investigator, 1971—74, staff physician, infectious disease and allergy cons., 1974—; asst. prof. medicine Med. Ctr. Vanderbilt U., Nashville, 1971—76, assoc. prof., 1976—2008, dir. allergy and immunology, 1974—2008. Vis. investigator Scripps Clinic and Rsch. Found., La Jolla, Calif., 1973-74. Capt. USAF, 1962—64, Korea. Fellow ACP, Am. Acad. Allergy and Immunology, Am. Coll. Allergy and Immunology; mem. Southeastern Allergy Assn. (pres. 1986-87, Hal M. Davison Meml. award, 1981, 99), Tenn. Soc. Allergy and Immunology. Home: 4340 Sneed Rd Nashville TN 37215-3242 Personal E-mail: smarney@att.net.

MAROCCO, ARMANDO, psychologist, researcher; b. July 9, 1922; s. Luiz and Antonia Marocco. BA, Pontificia U., Port Alegre, Brazil, 1960; Psychology, U. Montreal, Can., 1972; M Psychology, U. Montreal, 1977, PhD Psychology, 1991. Vocat. counsellor U. do Vale do Rio dos Sinos Unisinos, Sao Leopoldo, Brazil, 1973—2011. Vocat. counsellor state & pvt. schs., Brazil; rschr. psychol. values, interests. Editor: Unisinos, 1977, 1993, Sagra, 1984, Nova Harmonia, 2007; contbr. articles pub. to profl. jour. Founder and pres. Fundacao Estadual do Bem-estar do Menor, 1967—70. Mem.: APA, Internat. Assn. of Applied, Assn. Brasileira de Orientaçao Profl., Soc. Interamericana de Psicologia. Achievements include research in educational activity with adolescents and young male delinquents according to treatment for the untreatable. Avocations: piano, organ. Home: R Aloysio Sehnem 186 93001 970 São Leopoldo Brazil

MARON, DAVID JOEL, cardiologist, educator; b. Nov. 1, 1954; Undergraduate degree, Stanford Univ.; MD, U. Southern Calif. Sch. Medicine, 1981. Cert. Internal Medicine, Cardiovascular Disease. Intern, internal medicine UCLA Med. Ctr., 1981—82; resident, medicine, 1982—84; fellow, cardiology Stanford U., 1989—91; staff mem. St. John's Hosp., Santa Monica, 1991—93, Santa Monica Hosp., 1991—93, Vanderbilt Univ. Hosp., Nashville, 1993; clin. instr. Stanford U., 1984—89, UCLA, 1992—93; asst. prof. medicine Vanderbilt Univ. Med. Ctr., Nashville, 1993—2002, assoc. prof. medicine, 2002—10; med. dir. Dayani Ctr. for Health Promotion, prof. medicine, 2010—. Co-founder Cardiovascular Services of Am. Contbr. articles to profl. jours. Office: Vanderbilt University Med Ctr 1215 21st Ave S 5th Fl MCE Nashville TN 37232

MARONI, DONNA FAROLINO, biologist, researcher; b. Buffalo, Feb. 27, 1938; d. Enrico Victor and Eleanor (Redlinska) Farolino; m. Gustavo Primo Maroni, Dec. 16, 1974. BS, U. Wis., 1960, PhD, 1969. Project assoc. U. Wis., Madison, 1960-63, 68-74; Alexander von Humboldt fellow Inst. Genetics U. Cologne, Fed. Republic Germany, 1974-75; Hargitt fellow Duke U., Durham, NC, 1975-76, rsch. assoc., 1976-83, rsch. assoc. prof., 1983-87; sr. program specialist N.C. Biotech. Ctr., Research Triangle Park, 1987-88, dir. sci. programs div., 1988-92, v.p. for sci. programs, 1992-94, ret., 1995. Mem. adv. com. MICROMED at Bowman Gray Sch. Medicine, Winston-Salem, NC, 1988—94; mem. sci. adv. bd. NC Biosci. Fund, LLC, 1998—99, Minority Sci. Improvement Alliance for Instrn. and Rsch. in Biotech, Ala. A&M U., Normal, 1990—91. Contbr. articles to profl. jours. Grantee NSF, 1977-79, NIH, 1979-82, 79-83, 82-87. Mem. Genetics Soc. Am., N.C. Acad. Sci., Inc. (bd. dirs. 1983-86), Sigma Xi (mem. exec. com. Duke U. chpt. 1989-90). Achievements include research in electron microscopy, evolution of chromosomes, chromosome structure, evolution of mitosis, and mitosis and fungal phylogeny. Home: 355 Carolina Meadows Villa Chapel Hill NC 27517 Personal E-mail: maroni.donna@gmail.com.

MAROTO, MYRIAM, dentist, researcher; b. Madrid, Dec. 26, 1975; d. Francisco Javier Maroto and Mercedes Edo; life ptnr. Sergio De Pablo. Licentiate in Dentistry, Complutense U., Madrid, 1998, M in Pediatric Dentistry, 2000, M, 2001, PhD, 2003. Titular dentist specialist pediatric dentistry Pvt. Dental Clinic, Madrid, 1998—; rschr. different investigation lines pediatric dentistry attention program Complutense U., 1998—, asst. tchr. master progam pediatric dentistry, 2000—; rschr. investigation program about spl. dental care handicapped children Nat. Pub. Health Sys. and Complutense U., 2003—; rschr. investigation program about low-weight new borned children Nat. Pub. Health Sys., 2004—; assoc. tchr. Complutense U., 2003—. Joint dir. investigation lines MD program pediatric dentistry Complutense U., 2001—, coord. MD program pediatric dentistry, 2004—. Co-author: (scientific book) Atlas of Pediatric Dentistry; contbr. articles to profl. jours. Grantee, Socrates-Erasmus U., Program Dentistry, Faculty Oslo, Norway, 1998, Complutense U., 2003—05. Mem.: Pediatric Dentistry Spanish Soc. (assoc.). Avocations: reading, languages (english, french, italian), travel, scuba diving, movies. Office Fax: 913941944. Personal E-mail: myriammaroto@yahoo.com. Business E-Mail: mmaroto@odon.ucm.es.

MAROTTA, JOSEPH THOMAS, medical educator; b. Niagara Falls, NY, May 28, 1926; emigrated to Can., 1930; s. Alfred and Mary (Montemuro) M.; m. Margaret Hughes, Aug. 31, 1953; children: Maureen, Patricia, Margaret, Fred, Thomas, Jo Anne, Michael, Martha, John, Virginia. MD, U. Toronto, 1949. Trainee in internal medicine U. Toronto, 1949-52; trainee in neurology Presbyn. Hosp., NYC, 1952-55, U. London, Eng., 1955-56; mem. faculty U. Toronto, 1956—, prof. medicine, 1969—; former assoc. dean clin. affairs U. Toronto Faculty of Medicine, 1981-89; hon. prof. of neurology U. Western Ont., 1990—. Fellow Royal Coll. Physicians (Can.); mem. Alpha Omega Alpha, Phi Chi. Home and Office: 46 Carnforth Rd London ON Canada N6G 4P6 Office Phone: 519-642-4698.

MAROTTA, TEODORO, internist, researcher; b. Salerno, Italy, July 7, 1957; Grad. in Medicine and Surgery cum laude, U. Naples Federico II, Italy, 1982, postgrad. in Internal Medicine, 1982—87, PhD in Clinics of Vascular Diseases, 1993; postdoctoral student in Lipid Metabolism, U. Umea, Umea, Sweden, 1995—96. Lic. MD Italy, 1982. Rsch. asst. dept. clin. exptl. medicine Med. Sch. U. Naples, 1982—98; cons. internal medicine Nat Health Svc., Maiori, Amalfi, Italy, 1992—, Naples, Italy, 1996—; hypertension specialist European Soc. Hypertension, 2008—, mem., 2009—. Mem., reader panel Jour. Nature, 2010. Contbr. articles to profl. jours. Mem. Assn. Medicine-Dialogue-Communion, Rome, 2003—, Focolare Movement, Rome, 1977—. Mem.: European Soc. Hypertension, Italian Soc. Arterial Hypertension, Società Italiana dell'Ipertensione Arteriosa. Roman Catholic. Avocations: swimming, history, literature. Office: ASL Via Cesare Battisti 15 Naples 80134 Italy Home: Salita Sant Antonio Ai Monti 13 80135 Naples NA Italy Office Phone: 390812545511. Office Fax: 390812543594; Home Fax: 390815645496. Personal E-mail: teodoro.marotta@libero.it.

MARQUES, JUAN ALBERTO, cardiologist; b. Caracas, Distrito Federal, Venezuela, Nov. 17, 1960; s. Alfredo Marques and Capitulina Augusta de Marques; m. Nancy del Valle Mejias de Marques; children: Juan Eduardo, Maria Andreina, Maria Gabriela. MD, Ctrl. U. Venezuela, 1984; M in Pharm. Medicine, Hibernia Coll., Ireland, 2007. Cert. cardiologist Ctrl. U. Venezuela, 1990. Prof. Ctrl. U. Venezuela, Caracas, 1991—; med. dir. Parke Davis, Caracas, Venezuela, 1991—94, Hoechst, Caracas, 1994—95, Hoechst Marion Roussel, Caracas, 1997—99, Aventis, Caracas, 2000—05, Pfizer, Caracas, 2004—. Cardiologist Policlinica Santiago de León, Caracas, 1991—. Co-author: (book) Atherosclerosis in the 90's, Update in Atherosclerosis II; contbr. articles to med. jours. Pres. Associação de Médicos Luso-Venezuelanos, Caracas, 2003. Recipient Young Investigator Award, Interamerican Soc. Cardiology, 1989, 1992. Fellow: European Soc. Cardiology, Am. Soc. Cardiology; mem.: Colegio Venezolano de Endotelio (assoc.), Venezuelan Soc. Cardiology (assoc. High Blood Pressure award 1990, Electrophysiology and Arrhythmias award 1990, High Blood Pressure award 1991, Cardiology Nat. award 2006—07). Catholic. Achievements include research in in arrhythmias, Chagas disease, sudden death, and cardiovascular risk factors. Avocations: travel, soccer, golf.

MARQUES, LUANA, psychologist; b. Governador Valadares, Brazil, Aug. 28, 1977; PhD in Clin. Psychology, SUNY Buffalo, 2007. Asst. prof. psychiatry Harvard Med. Sch., 2011; clin. asst., psychology Mass. Gen. Hosp., 2007; dir. psychotherapy rsch. & tng. program Ctr. Anxiety and Traumatic Stress Disorders Mass. Gen. Hosp., 2011—. Dir. MGH Hispanic Clin. and Rsch. Program, 2010, Cognitive Therapy Gateway, 2011. Grant, NIMH. Mem.: Assn. Behavioral & Cognitive Therapies, MGH Psychiatry Diversity Com., Anxiety Disorders Assn. America. Office: One Bowdoin Sq 6th Fl Boston MA 02114 Business E-Mail: lmarques@partners.org.

MARQUES, OTAVIO AUGUSTO VUOLO, biologist, researcher; b. Sao Paulo, Sao Paulo, Brazil, Apr. 13, 1964; s. Euclydes Fontegno and Maria Nilda (Vuolo) M.; m. Wânia Duleba, March 20, 1993; 1 child, Isabela. Diploma in Biology, U. Sao Paulo, 1987, Masters, 1992, PhD, 1998. Rschr. Butantan Inst., Sao Paulo, 1993—. Avocations: photography, jogging, swimming. Office: Butantan Inst Av Vital Brazil 1500 05503900 Sao Paolo Brazil

MARQUEZ, VICTOR E., retired medical researcher; naturalized, US, 1987; BS in pharmacy, Ctrl. U. of Venezuela, Caracas, 1966; MS in medicinal chemistry, U. Mich., Ann Arbor, 1968, PhD, 1970. Postdoctoral training Nat. Cancer Inst., NIH, 1970—71; positions in pvt. industry Venezuela, 1971—76; vis. scientist Nat. Cancer Inst., NIH, 1977—87, granted tenure, 1987, chief Lab. Medicinal Chemistry, Ctr. Cancer Rsch., 2001—09, head Organic Chemistry Sect., scientist emeritus Chem. Biology Lab., 2009—. Achievements include holding over 20 US patents. Office: Nat Cancer Inst 376 Boyles St, Rm 104 Frederick MD 21702-1201 Office Phone: 301-846-5954. Office Fax: 301-846-6033. E-mail: marquezv@dc37a.nci.nih.gov. *

MARQUEZINI, MÔNICA VALERIA, research scientist; b. Pirassununga, São Paulo, June 10, 1961; Degree in Biol. Sci., U. Metodista de Piracicaba, 1983; PhD, U. Fed. de São Paulo, 1996. Sci. rschr. Fundação Pro Sangue Hemocentro de São Paulo, 1991—, Faculdade de Meedicina da U. de São Paulo, 2010. Cons. European Cmty., Beacon - Brazilian European Consortium, 2007—10, Endeavour - Erasmus Mundus, 2008—10. Recipient award, Conf. Stockholm, 2003. Avocation: cooking. Office: Ave Dr Arnaldo 455 São Paulo 01246903 Brazil E-mail: marquezinissa@uol.com.br.

MÁRQUEZ-MURILLO, MANLIO, cardiologist, researcher, physiologist; s. Manlio Márquez-Oramas and Elena Murillo-Monge; m. Ana Rosa Abraham, June 26, 1999. MD, U. Nacional Autonoma de Mex., Mexico City, 1992. Lic. med. Sec. Edn. Pub., Mex., 1992, internal medicine Nat. Inst. Nutrition, Mexico City, 1996, cert. cardiologist Mexican Bd. of Cardiology, 1999. Med. staff Nat. Heart Inst. Ignacio Chávez, Mexico City, 2000—; clin. rsch. scientist Nat. Health Insts., Nat. Investigators Sys., Mexico City, 2002—. Author: (medical research) Arch Cardiol Mex (Manuel Vaquero Young Investigator award clin. investigation, 2001); contbr. scientific papers, articles to profl. jours. including Am. Heart Jour., Jour. Internat. Medicine, Jour. Electrocardiology. Fellow: ACP, Am. Coll. Chest Physicians; mem.: North Am. Soc. Pacing and Clin. Electrophysiology. Home: Planicie 5 DF Mexico City 14010 Mexico Office: Inst Nacional de Cardiologia Juan Badiano 1 Seccion XVI Tlalpan DF Mexico City 14080 Mexico Office Fax: (5255) 55730994. E-mail: manliomarquez@yahoo.com.

MARQUIS, ROBERT EDWARD, microbiologist, educator; b. Sarnia, Ont., Can., Jan. 21, 1934; s. Louis Joseph and Margaret Ellen (Mulvale) M.; m. Diana Elizabeth Mears, June 7, 1956; children: Linda, Heather, André. BS, Wayne State U., 1956; MS, U. Mich., 1958, PhD, 1961. Biologist Parke, Davis & Co., Rochester, Mich., 1955-56; NATO fellow U. Edinburgh, Scotland, 1961-62, NSF fellow, 1962-63; asst. prof. microbiology and immunology U. Rochester, NY, 1963-70, assoc. prof., 1970-78, prof., 1978—, dir. program in biology and medicine, 1982-87, now assoc. chair and prof. microbiology and immunology and prof. biology; USPHS Spl. Rsch. fellow Scripps Inst. Oceanography, La Jolla, Calif., 1970-71. Mem. rev. panel NSF, Washington, 1975-78; mem. study sect. NIH, 1987—; mem. adv. bd. U. Rochester Press, 1994—; cons. Fonds de la Recherche en Santé du Québec, Montreal, 1995. Editor: Current Perspectives in High Pressure Biology, 1987, Basic and Applied High Pressure Biology, 1994. Mem. Am. Soc. Microbiology (sect. chair 1991-92), Internat. Assn. for Dental Rsch. Office: U Rochester Sch Medicine and Dentistry Box 672 601 Elmwood Ave Rochester NY 14642 Office Phone: 585-275-1674. E-mail: mutansst@aol.com.

MARRA, GUIDO, orthopedist, educator; b. Olympia Fields, Ill., Sept. 20, 1966; BS, Cornell U., 1988; MD, U. Ill., Abraham Lincoln Sch. Medicine, 1992. Assoc. prof. Loyola U. Health Sys., 1998—, dir., shoulder and elbow surgery, mem. edn. com., dept. orthop., 2007, dir., resident recruitment, orthop. dept., 2010. Recipient Patient's Choice award, Ill., 2008; named one of Best Dr. in Ill., 2009; finalist New Investigator Recognition award, Orthop. Rsch. Soc., Atlanta, 1996; Sofield Traveling fellowship, C.M. Craig Rsch. fellowship, 1997. Mem.: Am. Acad. Orthop. Surgeons (internat. com. mem., Achievement award 2010), Assn. Bone and Joint Surgeons (membership com. mem.), Am. Shoulder and Elbow Surgeons (program com. mem., chair, elbow curriculum com., mem., com. upper extremity surgery edn.). Office: Loyola University Health System 2160 S 1st Ave Maywood IL 60153 Office Fax: 708-216-5858. Business E-Mail: gmarra@lumc.edu.

MARRACK, PHILIPPA CHARLOTTE, immunologist, researcher; b. Ewell, Eng., June 28, 1945; m. John Kappler, 1974; children: Kate, Jim. BA, U. Cambridge, 1967, PhD in Biology, 1970. Post-doctoral fellow, lab. rschr. U. Calif., San Diego, 1971-73; post-doctoral rschr. fellow U. Rochester, NY, 1973-79, assoc. rschr. NY, 1974-75, asst. prof. immunology NY, 1975-79, assoc. prof. NY, 1980-85; prof. dept. microbiology and immunology U. Colo. Health Scis. Ctr., Denver, 1988—94, prof. integrated dept. of Immunology, 1994—, prof., dept. biochemistry and molecular biology, prof. medicine; head, div. of basic immunology Nat. Jewish Ctr. for Immunology and Respiratory Medicine, Denver, 1988—90; prof. dept. biophysics, biochemistry and genetics U. Colo. Health Scis. Ctr., Denver, 1985-88; head, div. of Basic Immunology Nat. Jewish Medical and Rsch. Ctr., Denver, 1998—99, sr. faculty mem., Integrated Dept. of Immunology; investigator Kappler and Marrack Rsch. Lab. Howard Hughes Med. Inst., Chevy Chase, Md., 1986—. Mem. dept. medicine Nat. Jewish Hosp. and Rsch. Ctr., Denver, 1979—. Contbr. articles to profl. jours.; mem. editl. bds. Cell, Science, and Journal of Immunology. Served on panels for Am. Cancer Soc., US NIH, Burroughs Wellcome Fund. Recipient Feodor Lynen medal, 1990, William B. Coley award Cancer Rsch. Inst., 1991, Wellcome Found. lecturer Royal Soc., 1990, Paul Ehrlich and Ludwig Darmstädter prize, 1993, Louisa Gross Horwitz prize, 1994, Women's Excellence Scis. award Fedn. Am. Socs. Exptl. Biology, 1995, Women in Sci. award, L'Oreal-UNESCO, 2004. Mem. NAS, Inst. Medicine, Royal Soc., Am. Assn. Immunologists (pres. 2000-2001, Lifetime Achievement award, 2003), Brit. Soc. Immunology, Internat. Union of Immunological Societies (past pres.). Office: Howard Hughes Med Inst Natl Jewish Med and Rsch Ctr 1400 Jackson St 5th fl Goodman Bldg Denver CO 80206

MARRETT, CORA B., federal official, science educator; b. Richmond, Va., June 15, 1942; d. Horace Sterling and Colra Ann (Boswell) Bagley; m. Louis Everand Marrett, Dec. 24, 1968. BA, Va. Union U., 1963; MS, U. Wis., 1965, PhD, 1968. Asst. prof. U. NC, Chapel Hill, 1968-69; from asst. to assoc. prof. Western Mich. U., Kalamazoo, 1969-73; from assoc. prof. to full prof. U. Wis., Madison, 1973-97; asst. dir. for social, behavioral, & econ. sciences NSF, Arlington, Va., 1992-96; provost, vice chancellor for acad. affairs U. Mass., Amherst, 1997—2001; sr. v.p. for acad. affairs U. Wis. System, 2001—07; asst. dir. for edn. & human resources NSF, Arlington, Va., 2007—09, acting dep. dir., 2009—11, acting dir., 2010, dep. dir., 2011—. Mem. sci. adv. panel US Army, Washington, 1976—77; mem. Naval Rsch. Adv. Com., Washington, 1978—81, Pres. Commn. on the Accident at Three

Mile Island, 1979; bd. govs. Argonne Nat. Lab., Ill., 1983—90, Ill., 1996—99. Editor: Research in Race and Ethnic Relations, 1988, Gender and Classroom Interaction, 1990. Resident fellow, NAS, 1973—74, fellow, Ctr. for Advanced Study in Behavioral Scis., 1976—77. Mem.: ASA, AAAS, Phi Kappa Phi. Avocations: reading, travel, film appreciation. Office: National Science Foundation Suite 1205N 4201 Wilson Blvd Arlington VA 22230 Office Phone: 703-292-8001. Office Fax: 703-292-9232. E-mail: cmarrett@nsf.gov. *

MARRIN, CHARLES AINSWORTH STAVELEY, cardiovascular and thoracic surgeon, educator; b. Santa Monica, Calif., Dec. 19, 1947; s. Charles Ainsworth and Cecilia Margaret (Staveley) M.; m. Marian Anthon Bruen, Apr. 19, 1976; 1 child, Minet A. B. MB, BS, U. London, Royal Free Hosp. Sch. Medicine, London, 1971. Ho. physician Willesden Gen. Hosp., London, 1971, Royal Free Hosp., London, 1972; resident in gen. surgery St. Luke's Hosp. Ctr., NYC, 1973-76, chief resident, 1976-77, fellow in cardiovasc. surgery, asst. physician, 1977; fellow in cardiovasc. surg. rsch. Coll. Physicians and Surgeons, Columbia U., NYC, 1978; resident in cardiovasc. and thoracic surgery Columbia-Presbyn. Med. Ctr., NYC, 1979-80, chief resident, 1980; staff surgeon Hitchcock Clinic and Dartmouth-Hitchcock Med. Ctr., Lebanon, N.H., 1981—; prof. surgery Dartmouth (N.H.) U. Med. Sch., 2000—. Author chpts. to books; contbr. articles to profl. jours. Co-prin. investigator Am. Heart Assn., 1993—; co-investigator U.S. Agy. for Health Care Policy and Rsch., 1993—. Fellow ACS, Am. Coll. Cardiology, Am. Coll. Chest Physicians; mem. AMA, Am. Assn. Thoracic Surgery, Soc. Thoracic Surgeons.

MARSALA-CERVASIO, KATHLEEN ANN, medical/surgical nurse; b. Mar. 22, 1955; d. James Patrick and Kathleen (McLoughlin) Waters. AAS with honors, S.I. Coll., 1974, BS in Nursing with honors, 1984; MSN with honors, CUNY, 1986; PhD in Pub. Adminstrn., Kensington U., 1997; EDd, North Central U. RN, N.Y.; cert. CS, CCRN, CNAA. Staff nurse USPHS Hosp., SI, 1974-80; head nurse MICU-critical care unit-surg. ICU Bayley Seton Hosp., N.Y., 1980-82; staff nurse surg. ICU, MICU, critical care unit East Orange (N.J.) VA Med. Ctr., 1982-86, critical care nurse specialist; clin. specialist, cons. Med. Ctr. Bklyn. VA Med. Ctr., 1989-95; dir. nursing svcs., asst. prof. nursing U. Hosp./SUNY Health Sci. Ctr., Bklyn., 1990-2000; mem. faculty L.I. U., 2001—. Asst. clin. prof. Met. Jewish Healthcare Sys.; adj. prof. Touro Coll., 2006. Mem. AACN, Sigma Theta Tau. Home: 8898 16th Ave Brooklyn NY 11214-5804

MARSCHALL, HANNS-ULRICH, gastroenterologist, consultant; b. Ibbenbüren, Germany, Feb. 15, 1954; s. Friedrich and Elisabeth Marschall; children: Andrea, Hannah. MSc, Aachen Tech. U., Germany, 1982; MD, Aachen Tech. U., Germany, 1994; PhD, Karolinska Inst., Stockholm, 1994. Cons. dept. internal medicine Univ. Hosp., Aachen, 1985—96; cons. dept. internal medicine divsn. gastroenterology and hepatology Karolinska Inst., 1996—; assoc. prof. medicine Aachen Tech. U., Germany, 1998—; prof. Karolinska Inst., 2007; prof. clin. hepatology Sahlgrenska Acad., U. Gothenburg, 2010. Office: University Gothenburg Sahlgrenska Univ Hosp Gothenburg 41345 Sweden Office Phone: +46-31 3429587. Business E-Mail: hanns-ulrich.marschall@gu.se.

MARSDEN, HARUE JEAN, optometrist, educator; b. Oceanside, Calif., Sept. 25, 1960; d. Bruce D. and Fujiko Y. Marsden. D in Optometry, So. Calif. Coll. Optometry, Fullerton, 1987; MS in Physiologic Optics, U. Houston, 1991. Diplomate, Cornea and Contact Lens Section Am. Acad. of Optometry, 2002. Resident in family practice U. Houston, 1989; assoc. prof. So. Calif. Coll. Optometry, Fullerton, Calif., 1989—; chief of cornea and contact lens svc. Eye Care Clinic Fullerton, 2000—. Fellow: Am. Acad. Optometry; mem.: Am. Optometric Assn. Avocations: travel, scrapbooking. Office: So Calif Coll Optometry 2575 Yorba Linda Blvd Fullerton CA 92831 E-mail: hmarsden@scco.edu.

MARSH, DAVID RAYMOND, pediatrician; b. Salem, Mass., Feb. 21, 1949; BA, Williams Coll., 1971; MD, U. Rochester, 1975. Pediatrician Gallup Indian Med. Ctr., USPHS, 1979—84, Kaiser Permanente Med. Group, 1984—89; asst. prof. Aga Khan U. Med. Coll., 1990—95; sr. advisor, child survival Save the Children, 1995—. Recipient Excellence Leadership award, PVO CORE Group, Wash., Commendations, Save the Children. Mem.: Sigma Xi. Avocations: literature, bicycling, stamp collecting/philately. Home: 31 Wildflower Dr Amherst MA 01002 Home Fax: 413-256-6805. Business E-Mail: dmarsh@savechildren.org.

MARSH, ELLA JEAN, pediatrician; b. Chgo., Dec. 16, 1941; d. Charles and Eleanor (Canfield) M. BA, St. Mary of Woods Coll., Ind., 1963; DO, Chgo. Coll. Osteo. Medicine, 1971. Diplomate Am. Coll. Osteo. Pediatricians (chmn. evaluating com. 1981-89), Nat. Osteo. Bds., Am. Bd. Pediats., Am. Bd. Osteopathic Pediatricians. Intern Doctor's Hosp., Columbus, Ohio, 1971-72; resident in pediatrics Chgo. Coll. Osteo. Medicine, 1972-74, asst. prof., 1974-78, assoc. prof. pediatrics, 1978-82; assoc. prof. W.Va. Coll. Osteo. Medicine, 1975-86; clin. assoc. prof. pediatrics South Eastern Osteo. Sch. Medicine, 1984-96, chmn. pediatric and newborn nursery, 1982-94; assoc. dir. med. edn. Orlando (Fla.) Gen. Hosp., 1985-88. Mem. staff Arnold Palmer Children's Hosp., Fla. Hosp., Health Ctr.; pediatric cons. Nat. Bd. Osteo. Examiners; lectr., cons. in field. Alumni bd. dirs. St. Mary of Woods Coll., 1992-95, Ctrl. Fla. Primary Care, 1994-97. Donald Bucknar Moore scholar, 1963. Fellow Am. Coll. Osteo. Pediatricians (v.p. 1986, pres. 1988), Am. Coll. Pediatricians, Am. Acad. Pediats.; mem. AMA, Am. Osteo. Assn., Fla. Osteo. Assn., Fla. Med. Soc., Orange County Med. Soc., Cen. Fla. Pediatric Soc., Chgo. Coll. Osteo. Medicine Alumni Assn., Am. Coll. Osteo. Pediatricians, Am. Acad. Pediatricians, Irish Am. Pediatric Soc., Am. Acad. Osteopathy Roman Catholic. Home: 8210 Imber St Orlando FL 32825-8233

MARSH, HAROLD MICHAEL, anesthesiologist; b. Sydney, Mar. 7, 1939; came to U.S., 1974; m. Elizabeth Eleanor. BSc in Medicine, U. Sydney, 1956, MBBS, 1963. Intern Royal Prince Alfred Hosp., Sydney, 1964, resident, 1965—68, Mayo Grad. Sch. Medicine, Rochester, Minn., 1969—71; clin. assoc. dept. anesthesiology Toronto We. Hosp., 1971; dir. dept. intensive care Royal Prince Alfred Hosp., 1972—74; instr. anesthesiology Mayo Med. Sch., Rochester, 1975—76, asst. prof. anesthesiology, 1976—83; assoc. prof. anesthesiology Mayo Grad. Sch., Rochester, 1981—89, prof. anesthesiology, 1989; chmn. dept. anesthesiology Henry Ford Hosp., Detroit, 1989—98; prof. chmn. dept. anesthesiology Wayne State U., 1998—; spec.-in-chief anesthesiology Detroit Med. Ctr., 1998—2007; chief, anesthesia svc. Karmanos Cancer Inst., 2006—; anesthesiologist John D. Dingell VAMC, 2007—. Part-time lectr., tutor faculty medicine U. Sydney, 1972-74; cons. anesthesiology Mayo Clinic, 1974-89, med. dir. surg. and respiratory intensive care units, 1977-81, dir. critical care svcs., 1981-83, 87-89, assoc. dir. critical care svcs., 1984-87, chmn. divsn. intensive care & respiratory therapy, 1985-89; vis. prof. dept. anesthesia U. Pa., 1976, Nat. Naval Med. Sch., 1981, Northwestern U., 1982, 89, Royal Prince Alfred Hosp., 1983, Sir Charles Gairdner Hosp., 1984, U. Md., 1987, Sloan-Kettering Inst., 1990, Rush-Presbyn.-St. Luke's Med. Ctr., Chgo., 1991, U. Hosp., London, Ont., 1993; invited lectr. dept. anesthetics IV Pan Am. Congress of Diseases of Chest, Caracas, Venezuela, 1987, Uniformed Svcs. U. Health Scis. Med. Sch., Bethesda, Md., 1987, Walter Reed Amry Med. Ctr., 1987, Naval Hosp., 1987, Bethesda, World Congress Intensive Care, Kyoto, Japan, 1989, Uddevalla (Sweden) Hosp., 1993, Karolinska Hosp., Stockholm, Sweden, 1993, Nat. Inst. Cardiology, Mexico City, Mexico, 1993; presenter in field. Contbr. chpts. to books and articles to profl. jours. With Australian Mil., 1958-61. Faculty of Anaesthetists, Royal Australasian Coll. Surgeons fellow, 1968. Fellow Am. Coll. Chest Physicians; mem. AAAS, Am. Bd. Anesthesiology, Am. Coll. Anesthesiologists, Wayne County Med. Soc. (pres. 2002). Achievements include research on general anesthesia and the lung, acute lung injury, metabolism, epidemiology in critical care, anesthesia education, anesthetic drugs and neurochemistry. Office: Detroit Med Ctr DRH/UHC Dept Anesthesiolog 4201 Saint Antoine St Detroit MI 48201-2153 Office Phone: 313-745-4300.

MARSH, JAMES WILLIS, surgeon, educator; MD, U. Ark. Diplomate Am. Bd. Surgery. Resident St. Paul Med. Ctr., Dallas; fellow renal transplant Mayo Clinic Rochester, Minn.; fellow liver transplant Univ. of Pitts. Med. Ctr., dir. advanced liver surgery; faculty dept. surgery; Thomas E. Starzl transplantation inst. Univ. of Pitts.; hosp. affiliations include UPMC Mercy, UPMC Passavant, UPMC Shadyside, UPMC St. Margaret. Co-author: (publs.) Microdissection-based allelotyping discriminates de novo tumor from intrahepatic spread in hepatocellular carcinoma, 2003, Genotyping of hepatocellular carcinoma in liver transplant recipients adds predictive power for determining recurrence-free survival, 2003, Liver organ allocation for hepatocellular carcinoma: Are we sure?, 2003, Role of liver transplantation for hepatobiliary malignant disorders, 2004, Use of alemtuzumab and tacrolimus monotherapy for cadaveric liver transplantation: with particular reference to hepatitis C virus, 2004. Mem.: Am. Soc. of Transplant Surgeons, Soc. of Surg. Onocology, Ctrl. Surg. Soc. Office: University of Pittsburgh Medical Center Presbyterian 7 N 3459 Fifth Ave Pittsburgh PA 15213 Office Phone: 412-692-2033. E-mail: marshw@upmc.edu.

MARSH, MARTHA H., board member, retired hospital administrator; BS, U. Rochester; MPH, MBA, Columbia U. Pres. and CEO Matthew Thornton Health Plan, Dartmouth Hitchcock Med. Ctr., 1986—94; sr. v.p., profl. svcs. and managed care and v.p, managed care U. Pa. Health Sys., 1994—98; COO U. Calif.-Davis Health Care Sys., 1999—2002; dir., Hosp. and Clinics U. Calif.-Davis Medical Ctr., 1999—2002; pres. and CEO Stanford Hosp. and Clinics, 2002—10; ret., 2010. Bd. dirs. Calif. Healthcare Assoc., Integrated Healthcare Assoc., Blue Cross of Calif. Hosp. Relations Com., AMN Healthcare, Inc., San Diego, 2010—. Presdl. appointee Nat. Infrastructure Adv. Coun., 2003. Office: AMN Healthcare Inc Bd Directors 12400 High Bluff Dr San Diego CA 92130 *

MARSHAK, DANIEL R., health and science products company executive; BA in Biochemistry & Molecular Biology, Harvard U., Cambridge, Mass.; PhD, Rockefeller U., NYC. Postdoctoral rsch., pharmacology Vanderbilt U. Sch. Medicine, Nat. Inst. of Health; sr. staff investigator Cold Spring Harbor Lab., 1986—94; sr. v.p., chief sci. officer Osiris Therapeutics, Inc., 1999—2000; v.p., rsch. & devel., BioSciences Group Cambrex Corp., 2000—02, v.p., chief tech. officer, biotechnology, 2002—06; v.p. PerkinElmer, Inc., Wellesley, Mass., 2006—08, sr. v.p., chief sci. officer and pres., greater China, 2008—. Adj. assoc. prof., oncology & molecular biology & genetics John Hopkins U. Sch. Medicine; mem., working group, ethics of stem cell rsch. AAAS; advisor PharmaFrontiers Corp., Ortec Internat., Inc.; mem., sci. adv. bd. Dystonia Med. Rsch. Found. Contbr. articles to profl. jours.; mem. editl. bd. Journal Biological Chemistry. Achievements include patents for stem cell research. Office: PerkinElmer Inc 940 Winter St Waltham MA 02451 Office Phone: 781-663-6900. Office Fax: 781-663-5985. Business E-Mail: dmarshak@perkinelmer.com. *

MARSHAK, HARRY, plastic surgeon; b. LA, Oct. 1, 1961; s. Herbert and Pearl (Engelson) M. BS, U. Calif., Riverside, 1981; MD, UCLA, 1984. Diplomate Am. Bd. Surgery, Am. Bd. Plastic Surgery. Pvt. practice, Beverly Hills, Calif., 1991—. Fellow ACS (hon.), Internat. Coll. Surgeons; mem. Am. Soc. Plastic Surgeons, Calif. Soc. Plastic Surgery, Am. Soc. for Aesthetic Plastic Surgery, Am. Soc. Pediat. Plastic Surgeons. Republican. Avocation: sports. Office: 421 N Robeo Dr Penthowe 1 Beverly Hills CA 90210 Office Phone: 310-657-7600.

MARSHAK, HILARY WALLACH, psychotherapist, small business owner; b. NYC, May 27, 1950; d. Irving Isaac and Suni (Fox) Wallach; m. Harvey Marshak, Jan. 1, 1981; children: Emily Fox, Jacob Randall. BA, U. Conn., Storrs, 1973; MSW, N.Y.U., 1992; cert., Inst. for Study of Culture and Ethnicity, NYC, 1994. Lic. clin. social worker, N.Y.; qualified clin. social worker; cert. secondary English tchr., N.Y. Tchr. English, Glastonbury (Conn.) H.S., 1973; instr. English, U. Autonoma de Guerrero, Acapulco, Mexico, 1974; adminstrv. asst. 4M Pub. Svcs. Corp., NYC, 1975, bus. mgr.; exec. v.p. Vitalmedia Enterprises Inc., NYC, 1977-87, pres., CEO, 1987-2001; psychotherapist Fifth Avenue Ctr. Counseling and Psychotherapy, NYC, 1992-95; pvt. practice, NYC, 1992—; co-dir. Inst. for Advanced Thinking, NYC, 2000—; asst. dir. adult undergrad. admissions Pace U., NYC, 2003—07, asst. dir. enrollment mgmt., 2007—. Mktg. cons. Frana Ltd., London, 1988-89; infertility counselor; v.p. Think Impossible, 2000—; adj. faculty Pace U., 2005-07; founder, owner, pres. MyDonor.net, 2007-. Editor: Before the Bar, 1978-80, Guide to Higher Edn., 1980; reviewer vol 32, The Jour. of Sex Rsch. Founder Women's Radical Caucus, U. Conn., 1970; broadcaster Sta. WHUS; bd. dirs. N.Y. Theater Ballet, 1990—, Am. AIDS Assn., 1992-97. Mem. NASW (qualified clin. social worker), Soc. for Sci. Study of Sex, Sex Edn. and Info. Coun. of U.S., Nat. Coun. Family Rels., Am. Fertility Assn., Am. Soc. for Reproductive Medicine, Resolve. Jewish. Avocations: gardening, birdwatching, cooking, reading. Home: 103 W 108 New York NY 10011 Office Phone: 212-349-0011, 212-691-6600. Office Fax: 212-349-0011. Personal E-mail: hilarymarshak@hotmail.com. Business E-Mail: hmarshak@mydonor.net.

MARSHAK, ROBERT REUBEN, retired dean, medical educator, veterinarian; b. NYC, Feb. 23, 1923; s. David and Edith (Youselovsky) Marshak; m. Ruth Emilie Lyons, Dec. 4, 1948 (div. 1983); children: William Lyons, John Ball, Richard Best; m. Margo Post Marshall, June 25, 1983. Student, U. Wis., 1940—41; DVM, Cornell U., 1945; DVM (hon.), U. Bern, 1968; MA (hon.), U. Pa., 1971. Diplomate Am. Coll. Vet. Internal Medicine (charter). Practice vet. medicine, Springfield, Vt., 1945—56; prof., chmn. dept. medicine Sch. Vet. Medicine, U. Pa., Phila., 1956—58; prof. medicine Grad. Sch. Medicine, 1957—64; chmn. dept. clin. studies Sch. Vet. Medicine, 1958—73; dir. Bovine Leukemia Research Center, 1965—73; dean Sch. Vet. Medicine, 1973—87; co-dir. Center on Interactions Animals and Soc., 1975—79, also mem. grad. group com. in comparative med. scis.; prof. medicine, chief sect. epidemiology and pub. health Sch. Vet. Medicine U. Pa., 1990—93, prof. medicine emeritus, 1993—, dean emeritus, 1987—. Adv. bd. Pa. Dept. Agr., 1973—87; chmn. Gov.'s STudy Group on Horse Racing Industry in Pa., 1979; del. to evaluate vet. med. and rsch. Chinese Ministry Agr.; adv. com. Stround Water Rsch. Ctr., 1992; adv. coun. Coll. Vet. Medicine, Cornell U., 1993—; animal use and care com. Calif. Inst. Tech., 2003—. Contbr. articles to profl. jours. Sci. adv. bd. Sch. Vet. Medicine The Hebrew U., Jerusalem, 1984—, rev. com., 1997—; trustee Upland Country Day Sch., 1988—91; animal adv. com. City of Phila., 1989—93; pres. rev. com. Koret Sch. Vet. Medicine Hebrew U. Jerusalem, 1997—98, bd. dirs. Humane Soc. U.S., 1978—82, Bide-a-wee Home Assn., 1980—85. With US Army, 1943—44. Recipient Disting. Vet. award, Pa. Vet. Med. Assn., 1984, Barnraiser award, Pa. Farmers Assn., 1987. Fellow: Phila. Coll. Physicians; mem.: Pa. Vet. Med. Assn., Am. Vet. Med. Assn., Nat. Acad. Inst. Medicine (sr.), John Morgan Soc. (pres. 1967—68), Phila. Zool. Soc. (bd. dirs. 1986—87), James A. Baker Inst. for Animal Health (mem. adv. coun. 1977—), Westminster Kennel Club, Phi Zeta, Sigma Xi. Personal E-mail: rmarshak@caltech.edu.

MARSHALL, BARRY JAMES, microbiologist, educator; b. Kalgoorlie, Western Australia, Australia, Sept. 30, 1951; arrived in US, 1986; s. Robert William and Marjory Jean (Donald) Marshall; m. Adrienne Joyce Feldman, Dec. 27, 1972; children: Luke, Bronwyn, Caroline, Jessica. MB, BChir, U. Western Australia, Perth, 1974. Diplomate Am. Bd. Internal Medicine, cert. in gastroenterology. Intern Sir Charles Gairdner Hosp., Perth, 1975-76, resident Ala., 1976-77, registrar medicine, 1977-78, Royal Perth Hosp., 1979-82, Nat. Health & Med. Rsch. Coun. rsch. fellow in gastroenterology, 1985—86; gen. physician, acting supt. Port Hedland Regional Hosp., 1982—83; sr. registrar medicine Fremantle Hosp., 1983—85; rsch. fellow divsn. gastroenterology U. Va., Charlottesville, 1986—96, asst. prof. medicine, 1988—92, assoc. prof., 1992—92, prof., 1993—2001, clin. prof., 1993—96, prof. rsch. in internal medicine, 1996—2007; clin. prof. medicine U. Western Australia, 1997—, Burnet fellow, 1998—2003, clin. prof. microbiology, 1999—, co-dir. Marshall Ctr. Infectious Diseases Rsch. & Training, 2006—. Med. dir. TRI-MED Distributors Pty Ltd, Western Australia, 1990—. Contbr. articles to profl. jours. Svc. with Citizen Mil. Forces, Western Australia, 1969—71. Decorated Companion, Order of Australia; recipient Warren Alpert prize, Harvard U., 1995, Albert Lasker award for basic med. rsch., 1995, John Scott award, Phila., 1995, Gairdner Found. Internat. award, Can., 1996, Paul Ehrlich prize, Germany, 1997, Australian Achiever award, 1998, Heineken prize for medicine, Netherlands, 1998, Florey Medal, Australia, 1998, Buchanan Medal, Brit. Royal Soc. Medicine, 1998, Benjamin Franklin Medal for life sci., Franklin Inst., Phila., 1999, Clunies Ross Nat. Sci. & Tech. award, Australia, 2001, Prince Mahidol award, Thailand, 2001, Keio Med. Sci. prize, Japan, 2002, Australian Centenary Medal, 2003, Nobel prize for physiology/medicine, 2005; named Western Australian Citizen of Yr., 2006, Western Australian of Yr., 2007. Fellow: Australian Acad. Sci., Brit. Royal Soc., Royal Australian Coll. Physicians; mem.: Am. Soc. Clin. Investigation, Am. Fedn. Clin. Rsch., Am. Gastroenterological Assn. (Disting. Achievement award 1995, William Beaumont prize 2006), Australian Med. Assn. (Med. Rsch. award 1995), Am. Coll. Gastroenterolgy, Australian Gastroenterological Soc. (Disting. Rsch. prize 1998). Achievements include first to prove that the bacterium Helicobacter pylori is the cause of most peptic ulcers, reversing decades of medical doctrine which held that ulcers were caused by stress, spicy foods, and too much acid. Avocations: computer hardware and software, photography, skin diving, american cuisine. Office: TRI-MED Distributors Pty Ltd 105 Hay St Subiaco 6008 Australia Mailing: TRI-MED Distributors Pty Ltd Locked Bag 15 Subiaco 6904 Australia Office: Helicobacter pylori Rsch Lab Rm 1 11 L Block Qeii Med Ctr 6009 Nedlands WA Australia Office Phone: 61 8 9346 4815. Office Fax: 61 8 9346 4816. E-mail: bmarshall@hpylori.com.au. *

MARSHALL, FREDERICK J., neurologist, educator; BA in Psychology, Swarthmore Coll., 1983; MD, Harvard Med. Sch., 1989. Fellow Brigham & Women's Hosp. Harvard Med. Sch., 1986; resident Harvard-Longwood Neurological Training Program; assoc. prof. dept. neurology U. Rochester Med. Ctr., 1997—. Mem.: Nat. Alzheimer's Assn., Huntington Disease Soc. America (Leadership award 2000), Alpha Omega Alpha, Sigma Xi, Phi Beta Kappa. Office: 919 Westfall Rd Bldg C Ste 220 Rochester NY 14618 Office Fax: 585-760-6236.

MARSHALL, GAILEN DAUGHERTY, JR., allergist, educator; b. Houston, Sept. 9, 1950; s. Gailen D. and Evelyn C. (Gresham) M.; m. Elizabeth M. Marek, Nov. 5, 1978; children: Sarah Elizabeth, Jonathan David, Rebecca Marie. BS, U. Houston, 1972; MS, Tex. A&M U., 1975; PhD, U. Tex., 1979, MD, 1984. Rsch. sci. U. Tex., Galveston, 1981-84; rsch. fellow U. Iowa, Iowa City, 1985-86; lab. dir. Biotherapeutics Inc., Memphis, 1986-88; chief med. resident Bapt. Meml. Hosp., Memphis, 1988-89; assoc. dir. Rsch. for Health Inc., Houston, 1989-90; dir. divsn. allergy and immunology U. Tex., Houston, 1990—2004, clin. asst. prof. medicine, 1990-91, asst. prof. medicine, 1991—98, assoc. prof. medicine and pathology, 1998—2003, prof., 2003—04; vice chair medicine, dir. divsn. clin. immunology and allergy U. Miss. Med. Ctr., Jackson, Miss., 2004—, prof. medicine and pediatrics. Mem. sci. adv. com. Carrington Labs., Dallas, 1992-94; mem. Merck Rhinitis Adv. Bd., 2002-05, Genentech/Novartis Adv. Bd., 2003—. Mem. editl. bd. Molecular Biotherapy, 1992-93, Cancer Biotherapy, 1994-96, Allergy Procs., 1994-2003, Annals Allergy, Asthma and Immunology, 1995-99, Jour.

Interferon Cytokin Rsch., 1999-2005, Clin. Immunology, 2001-05, Jour. Clin. Immunology, 2002-05, Cellular Molecular Allergy, 2003-05; editor-in-chief Annals of Allergy, Asthma and Immunology, 2006—; contbr. articles to profl. jours. Judge Greater Houston Sci. Fair, 1992—; adv. bd. Merck Rhinitis, 2002-04, Grenentech Worch's, 2003-05. Fellow ACP, Am. Coll. Allergy and Immunology, Am. Acad. Allergy-Immunology (chair com.); mem. Tex. Allergy-Immunology Soc. (chair com., bd. dirs. 1999-2002), Greater Houston Allergy Soc. Republican. Baptists. Avocations: classical music, fishing. Office: U Miss Med Ctr 2500 N State St Jackson MS 39216 Home Phone: 601-899-1793; Office Phone: 601-815-5527. Business E-Mail: gmarshall@medicine.umsmed.edu.

MARSHALL, GRAYSON WILLIAM, JR., materials scientist, biomedical engineer, health sciences educator, dentist; b. Balt., Feb. 12, 1943; s. Grayson William and Muriel Marie Marshall; m. Sally Jean Rimkus, July 4, 1970; children: Grayson W. III, Jonathan Charles. BS in Metall. Engring., Va. Poly. Inst., 1965; PhD in Materials Sci., Northwestern U., 1972, DDS, 1986; MPH, U. Calif., Berkeley, 1992. Cert. dentist. Rsch. assoc., design and devel. ctr. Northwestern U., Evanston, Ill., 1972-73, NIH fellow, 1973, instr. Dental and Med. Schs. Chgo., 1973-74, asst. prof. Dental Sch., 1974-78, assoc. prof. Dental Sch. and Grad. Sch., 1978-87; prof. preventive and restorative dental scis. U. Calif., San Francisco, 1987—2009, disting. prof., 2009—, chief biomaterials sect. San Francisco, 1988-92, chmn. biomaterials and bioengring. divsn., 1992—, vice chmn. rsch. preventive and restorate dental scis., 2005—. Chmn. oral and craniaofacial scis. program U. Calif., San Francisco, 2002-07, UCSF Grad. Coun., 2003-05, UCSF Inst. Regenerative Medicine, 2007-; guest scientist Lawrence Livermore Nat. Lab., 1989-2000, Lawrence Berkeley Nat. Lab., 1989—; cons. oral biology and medicine study sect. NIH, 1988-92; dir. Clin. Rsch. Unit, 1992-96, Dentist-Sci. Award Program, 1996-2004, Integrated DDS-PhD Program, 1996—2009, Comprehensive Oral Health Rsch. Tng. Program, 2001-08. Contbr. articles to profl. jours. and books. Mem. City of Larkspur Heritage Preservation Bd., 1998—, chmn., 2006—08, mem. centennial com., 2007—08. Recipient Spl. Dental Rsch. award Nat. Inst. Dental Rsch., 1975, Rsch. Lectr. award U. Calif., San Francisco, 1994, IADR Wilmer Souder Disting. Scientist award, 2007, ADM Founders award, 2009; vis. fellow U. Melbourne, Australia, 1981. Fellow: AAAS, Acad. Dental Materials (exec. sec. 1983—85, chmn. credentials 1984—91, bd. dirs. 1985—93, pres. 1991—93), Am. Coll. Dentists, Internat. Coll. Dentists (mem. editl. bd. Scanning Microscopy 1987—93, Cells and Materials 1992—2000, sect. editor 1993—2000, Jour. Oral Rehab. 1994—2010, Dent Mater 1998—, Am. Jour. Dentistry 2004—); mem.: APHA, ADA (assoc. editor Jour. ADA 2002—05), U.S. Power Squadrons, U.S. Naval Inst., Calif. Pub. Health Assn.-North, Calif. Acad. Scis., N.Y. Acad. Scis., Am. Assn. Dental Rsch. (bd. dirs. 1996—98, San Francisco coun. 1997—2007, v.p. 2007—08, pres. elect 2008—09, pres. 2009—10), Microscopy Soc. Am., Am. Coll. Sports Medicine, Internat. Assn. Dental Rsch. (Chgo. sect. officer 1978—80, dental materials coun. 1990—96, pres. 1998—99), Soc. Biomaterials, Am. Dental Edn. Assn. (sect. officer 1981—83), Omicron Kappa Upsilon, Sigma Gamma Epsilon, Sigma Xi, Alpha Sigma Mu. Avocations: swimming, sailing, hiking, travel. Office: U Calif Dept Preven & Restor Dental Scis San Francisco CA 94143-0758 Business E-Mail: gw.marshall@ucsf.edu, gwmarshall@lbl.gov.

MARSHALL, IAN N., pediatric endocrinologist, educator; MD, U. Cape Town, So. Africa, 1991. Diplomate Am. Bd. Pediatrics. Intern Schneider Children's Hosp., NY, resident pediat., 1996—98; fellow pediatric endocrinology NY Presbyn. Hosp., NYC, 1999—2002; asst. prof. pediat. Robert Wood Johnson Med. Sch., NJ; pediatric endocrinology Robert Wood Johnson Univ. Hosp., NJ. Office: Robert Wood Johnson Medical School 89 French St New Brunswick NJ 08903 Office Phone: 732-253-9378. Office Fax: 732-235-5002.

MARSHALL, JANET GARDNER, nursing educator; b. Hillsville, Va., Jan. 13, 1959; d. Emmett Conner and Mary Lorene (Martin) Gardner; m. Anthony V. Marshall, Sept. 4, 1982. BSN, U. Va., 1981; MSN, U. N.C., Greensboro, 1990. RN, Va., N.C. Instr. nursing Wytheville (Va.) C.C., 1981; charge nurse Pulaski County Hosp., Pulaski, Va., 1981; staff nurse Montgomery County Hosp., Blacksburg, Va., 1981-82, Va. Tech. Student Health, Blacksburg, 1983; charge nurse Meml. Hosp., Danville, Va., 1984; coord. family planning program Danville Health Dept., 1984-88, pub. health nurse, 1989; instr. clin. nursing Rockingham C.C., Wentworth, N.C., 1989-90; instr. nursing Piedmont C.C., Roxboro, N.C., 1990—. Mem. ANA, NAACOG, Va. State Nurses' Assn., Sigma Theta Tau. Avocations: reading, writing, travel, animals. Home: 2901 Whittington Dr Tallahassee FL 32309-8219

MARSHALL, JO TAYLOR, social worker; b. NYC; BA, Sarah Lawrence Coll., Bronxville, NY, 1957; MSW, Columbia U., NYC, 1959. Cert. clin. social worker, NY, NJ; bd. cert. diplomate. Caseworker Youth Cons. Svcs., 1960-62; program cons. Social Work Recruiting Ctr., 1962-63; casework supr. Louise Wise Svcs., 1963-68; faculty field instr. sch. social work Columbia U., NYC, 1968-70; coord. social work vol. and student tng. programs St. Lukes/Roosevelt Hosp. Ctr., 1970-75; asst. dir. fieldwork, faculty lectr. in health care Columbia U., NYC, 1975-78; dir. social work and psychiat. emergency svcs. Morristown Meml. Hosp., 1978—95; social worker pvt. practice, 1995—2002; ret., 2002. Adj. prof. Columbia U.; adv. bd., faculty Nat. Discharge Planning Inst. SUNY, Buffalo; prin. speaker, cons. Hosp. Assn. Pa., 1983, Mid-Atlantic Health Congress, 1985, VA, East Orange, N.J., 1986, Hosp. Assn. Tenn., 1987; adv. com. Rutgers GGrad. Sch. Social Work; mem. multidisciplinary state rev. com. for discharge planning standards in NJ. Contbr. articles to profl. jours.; produced and cons. on numerous film and TV prodns. Named Dir. of Yr., NJ Hosp. Social Work, 1989-90. Mem.: NASW, Acad. Cert. Social Workers, Soc. Hosp. Social Work Dirs. (pres. NJ chpt. 1988—89, exec. bd., chmn. nat. media task force). Achievements include The Welcome Terrace at Columbia Grad. Sch. of Social Work named in her honor in 2004. Home (Winter): 1230 Hillsboro Mile Hillsboro Beach FL 33062-1344 Home (Summer): PO Box 40 Far Hills NJ 07931-0040 Office Phone: 908-553-5444. Personal E-mail: jomase@msn.com.

MARSHALL, JOHN CROOK, internal medicine educator, researcher; b. Blackburn, Lancashire, Eng., Feb. 28, 1941; came to US, 1976; s. Albert Acey and Marion Miller (Crook) M.; m. Marilyn Dallas Parry, Sept. 20, 1969; children: Samantha Jane, Susannah Crook. BS, Victoria U., Manchester, Eng., 1962, MB, ChB, 1965, MD, 1973. Diplomate Am. Bd. Internal Medicine, Am. Bd. Endocrinology and Metabolism. Intern Manchester Royal Infirmary, 1965-66; resident Brompton Hosp., Nat. Heart Hosp., Nat Hosp. Queen Sq., London, 1966-69, Hammersmith Hosp., London, 1966-69, rsch. fellow, 1969-72; lectr. U. Birmingham, Eng., 1972-76; assoc. prof. internal medicine U. Mich., Ann Arbor, 1976-79, prof., 1979-91, chief endocrinology and metabolism, 1987-91; prof. U. Va., Charlottesville, 1991—, dir. Ctr. for Rsch. in Reprod., 1996—. Sci. counselor NIH, Bethesda, Md., 1983-84. Editor: Endocrinology Jour., 1979-84, Endocrinology Text, 1990—; contbr. articles to profl. jour. Grantee NIH, 1977-. Fellow ACP, Royal Coll. Physicians, Royal Soc. Medicine; mem. Ctrl. Soc. for Clin. Rsch. (coun. 1983—), Assn. Am. Physicians, Am. Soc. for Clin. Investigation, Am. Clin. and Climatological Soc. Anglican. Avocations: vintage racing cars, golf. Office: U Va Sch Medicine Dept Internal Medicine Charlottesville VA 22908-0001 Business E-Mail: jcm9h@virginia.edu.

MARSHALL, THOMAS A., medical association administrator; Dir. pub. rels. pvt. high sch., Ill.; sr. mgmt. positions Am. Soc. Safety Engrs., Second Harvest Nat. Foodbank Assn.; divsn. dir., mktg., comm. Am. Soc. Plastic Surgeons, 1989—99; assoc. exec. dir., programs Am. Assn. Neurol. Surgeons, Rolling Meadows, Ill., 1999—2001, exec. dir., 2001—. Office: Am Assn Neurol Surgeons 5550 Meadowbrook Dr Rolling Meadows IL 60008-3852 Office Phone: 847-378-0502. *

MARSHALL, VINCENT DE PAUL, industrial microbiologist, researcher; b. Washington, Apr. 5, 1943; s. Vincent de Paul Sr. and Mary Frances (Bach) M.; m. Sylvia Ann Kieffer, Nov. 15, 1986; children from previous marriage: Vincent de Paul III, Amy. BS, Northeastern State Coll., Tahlequah, Okla., 1965; MS, U. Okla. Health Sci. Ctr., Oklahoma City, 1967, PhD, 1970. Rsch. assoc. U. Ill., Urbana, 1970, postdoctoral fellow, 1971-73; rsch. scientist The Upjohn Co., Kalamazoo, Mich., 1973-74, rsch. head, 1975, sr. rsch. scientist, 1976-91, sr. scientist, 1991-2000; cons., 2000—. Mem. editl. bd. Jour. of Antibiotics, 1990-2001, Jour. Indsl. Microbiology, 1989-2001, Devels. in Indsl. Microbiology, 1990; contbr. numerous articles to profl. jours., chpts. to books; patentee in field. Served with U.S. Army Nat. Guard, 1960-65. NIH predoctoral fellow, 1967-70; NIH postdoctoral fellow, 1971-73. Fellow Am. Acad. Microbiology; mem. Soc. for Indsl. Microbiology (membership com. 1988-90, co-chair edn. com. 1989-93, local sects. com. 1991-96, chair nominating com. 1993-94, mem. nominating com. 1999-2000, co-chair program com. 1993-94, dir. 1994-96, pres. So. Great Lakes sect. 1992-95), Am. Soc. Microbiology, Am. Soc. Biochemistry and Molecular Biology, Internat. Soc. for Antimicrobial Activity of Non-Antibiotics (sci. adv. bd.), Sigma Xi. Republican. Lutheran. Home and Office: 203 Paisley Ct Kalamazoo MI 49006-4359 Home Phone: 269-349-3795; Office Phone: 269-349-3795. E-mail: vince3795@aol.com.

MARSHALL, WAYNE KEITH, anesthesiology educator; b. Richmond, Va., Feb. 9, 1948; s. Chester Truman and Lois Ann (Tiller) M.; m. Dale Claire Reynolds, June l8, 1977; children: Meredith Reynolds, Catherine Truman, Whitney Wood. BS in Biology, Va. Poly. Inst. and State U., 1970; MD, Va. Commonwealth U., 1974. Diplomate Am. Bd. Anesthesiology, Nat. Bd. Med. Examiners; bd. cert. in pain mgmt. Surg. intern U. Cin., 1974-75, resident in surgery, 1975-77; resident in anesthesiology U. Va. Coll. Medicine, Charlottesville, 1977-79, rsch. fellow, 1979-80; asst. prof. anesthesia Pa. State U. Coll. Medicine, Hershey, 1980-86, assoc. prof., 1986-95, assoc. clin. dir. oper. rm., 1982-95, dir. pain mgmt. svc., 1984-95, chief divsn. pain mgmt., 1992-95; prof., chmn. dept. anesthesiology Med. Coll. Va., Richmond, 1995-99; med. dir. operating rms. MCV Hosp., 1995-99; prof. anesthesiology Coll. Medicine Pa. State U., Hershey, 1999—2004; pvt. practice, 2004—. Moderator nat. meetings. Mem. editorial bd. Am. Jour. Anesthesiology, 1987-99, Jour. Neurosurg. Anesthesiology, 1988—2004; contbr. articles and abstracts to med. jours. Recipient Antarctic Svc. medal NSF, 1980. Mem. AMA, Soc. Neurosurg. Anesthesia and Critical Care (sec.-treas. 1985-87, v.p. 1987-88, pres. 1989-90, bd. dirs. 1985-91), Assn. Univ. Anesthetists, Am. Soc. Anesthesiologists (del. ASA ho. of dels. 1990-92), Internat. Anesthesia Rsch. Soc., Pa. Soc. Anesthesiology. Republican. Baptist. Personal E-mail: wmarsh2723@aol.com.

MARSHALL, WILLIS HENRY, psychiatrist; b. Covington, Ky., Nov. 28, 1936; s. Willis Henry Sr. and Pauline Elizabeth (Murphy) M.; m. Carolyn Mae Kowalski; children: Louann Lorinda Marshall Johnson, John Willis. AB cum laude, U. Evansville, Ind., 1958; MD, Ind. U., Bloomington, 1961. Cert. psychiatry Am. Assn. Psychiat. Medicine, 2005. Intern Detroit Meml. Hosp., 1961-62; resident psychiatry Mental Health Inst., Cherokee, Iowa, 1965-67, 69-70, staff psychiatrist, 1967-69, Mental Health Ctr., Muskegon, Mich., 1970-71; pvt. practice psychiatry Madison, Tenn., 1974-85, Bowling Green, Ky., 1987-98; staff psychiatrist chief admission svc., staff psychiatrist treatment unit Mid. Tenn. Mental Health Inst., Nashville, 1981—85, staff psychiatrist evaluation unit forensic svcs. div., 1985—87, chief of staff, 1986-87; forensic psychiatrist State of Tenn., 1981—87; staff psychiatrist Moccasin Bend Mental Health Inst., Chattanooga, 1998—2003; staff psychiatrist, med. dir. Crisis Stabilization Unit Vol. Behavioral Health Svcs. Ctr., Chattanooga, 2003—05, outpatient psychiatrist, 2005—. Part-time staff psychiatrist Ottawa County Mental Health Ctr., Grand Haven, Mich., 1971-73, Tenn. Dept. Mental Health and Mental Retardation Mid. Tenn. Mental Health Inst., Nashville, 1981-87, Lifeskills, Inc., Glasgow, Ky., Franklin, Ky., 1987-89; psychiat. cons. Allegan County Mental Health Ctr., Allegen, Mich., 1973; med. svcs. cons. dept. of forensic svcs. Mid. Tenn. Mental Health Inst., Nashville, 1983-84; clin. asst. prof. psychiatry dept. allied health Trevecca Nazaraene Coll., Nashville, 1985-87; part-time pvt. practice psychiatry, Muskegon, Mich., 1970-74, Madison, Tenn., 1974-87; assoc. clin. dir. mental health unit Med. Ctr., Bowling Green, Ky., 1987-91; preceptor, asst. clin. prof. resident physician asst. program U. Ky., 1988-91; acting med. dir. Rivendell Children's Psychiat. Hosp., Bowling Green, 1989; med. dir. adult mental health unit Rivendell of Ky., 1992-94. Prin. works include several sculptures and paintings. Commd. officer, surgeon USPHS, 1962-65. Recipient AMA Physicians Recognition award, 1969, 79, 83, 86, 89, 92, Exemplary Psychiatrist award Nat. Alliance for Mentally Ill, 1993; named to Am. Top Psychiatrists, 2007, 08. Mem. Am. Psychiat. Assn. (life, art assn. 1976—), Ky. Med. Assn., Warren County Med. Soc., Am. Profl. Practice Assn., Am. Acad. Clin. Psychiatrists, Am. Assn. of Psychiat. Medicine, Am. Physicians Art Assn., NRA, Nat. Geog. Soc., AAA Automobile Club, Gallatin Gun Club, Alpha Omega Alpha. Republican. Adventist. Avocations: sculpture, photography, painting, hunting, fixing old guns. Home: 5115 Silver Ln Apison TN 37302-9594 Office: 420 Bell Ave Chattanooga TN 37405 also: Pub Consumers Rsch Coun Am 2020 Pennsylvania Ave NW Ste 300-A Washington DC 20006

MARSIK, FREDERIC JOHN, microbiologist; b. Camden, NJ, June 22, 1943; s. Ferdinand Vincent and Helen (Reidl) Marsik; m. Pamelia Ehlers; children: Terri Jean Lehman, Kristi Ann Marsik McCann. BA, Lebanon Valley Coll., 1965; MS, U. Mo., 1970, PhD, 1973. Diplomate Am. Bd. Med. Microbiology. Clin. microbiology staff Hartford Hosp., Conn., 1973-76; asst. prof. U. Va. Sch. Medicine, Charlottesville, 1976-80; tech. dir. microbiology and serology Children's Hosp. Wis., Milw., 1980-84; assoc. prof. microbiology and internal medicine Oral Roberts U. Sch. Medicine, Tulsa, 1984-87; dir. microbiology Crozer-Chester Med. Ctr., Upland, Pa., 1987-88; dir. R&D Becton Dickinson Microbiology Sys., Cockeysville, Md., 1988-96; microbiology team leader FDA, Rockville, Md., 1996—. Mem. adv. com. Milw. Area Tech. Coll., Milw., 1983-84, Tulsa Jr. Coll., 1985-87. Contbr. chpts. to textbooks. Alumni amb. Lebanon Valley Coll., 1991—. Lt. col. USAR. Recipient Carmean award, Lebanon Valley Coll., 2002. Mem. Am. Soc. Microbiology, Am. Soc. Med. Tech., N.Y. Acad. Scis. Congregationalist. Avocations: fishing, camping, basketball. Home: 244 E Main St New Freedom PA 17349-9213 Office: FDA HFD 520 WO22 Rm 6108 10903 New Hampshire Ave Silver Spring MD 20903 Office Phone: 301-796-0756. Business E-Mail: frederic.marsik@fda.hhs.gov.

MART, CHRISTOPHER ROBIN, cardiologist, educator; b. Tucson, Ariz., Apr. 27, 1955; BS, U. Ark., Little Rock, BA, 1982; MD, U. Ark. Sch. Medicine, 1986. Assoc. prof. pediat., pediatric cardiology U. Utah, Primary Children's Med. Ctr., 2003—. Fellow: Am. Coll. Cardiology. Avocation: swimming. Office: University Utah Primary Children's Med Ctr 100 N Mario Capecchi Dr Salt Lake City UT 84113 Office Fax: 801-662-5404. Business E-Mail: christopher.mart@imail.org.

MARTA, DAWN RENEÉ, clinical psychologist; b. Ottawa, Ill., Sept. 10, 1963; d. Bruce Roger Rooks and Marsha Ann (Meade) Monroe; m. David Lee LeBeau (div. Oct. 1987); 1 child, Nicholas Scott LeBeau; m. Scott Kennedy Echols (dec. Feb. 1996); m. Anthony John Marta, Dec. 21, 2001. Student, Fla. C.C., Jacksonville, 1990—93; AA in Medicine, Ctrl. Fla. C.C., Ocala, Fla., 1994; student, Santa Fe C.C., Gainesville, 1994; BA in Philosophy with high honors, U. Fla., 1997; MDiv in Theology, Duke U., 2000; postgrad., George Fox U., 2000; D in Psychology, Argosy U., 2004. Cert. personal trainer Am. Coun. Exercise. Membership dir. Duval County Med. Soc., Jacksonville, Fla., 1987—93; emergency rm. admissions rep. Munroe Regional Med. Ctr., Ocala, Fla., 1993—94; admissions rep. Shands Hosp. U. Fla., Gainesville, 1994; adminstr. Covenant Presbyn. Ch., Gainesville, 1994—95; chaplain Duke U. Med. Ctr., Durham, NC, 1998—2000; personal trainer Ottawa, Elgin, 2000—04; resident Meridian Behavioral Health Svcs., 2004—05; clin. psychologist, owner, operator Ctr. Human Flourishing, Andrews, 2005—. Usher First United Meth. Ch., Chgo., 2002, Elgin, 2003—04, trustee edn. com., 2003—04; mem. Andrews Methodist Ch, Andrews, NC. Mem.: Nat. Alliance Profl. Psychology Providers, Potters Touch, Nat. Health Svc. Corp. Avocations: bodybuilding, bicycling, hiking, kayaking, travel. Office: Ctr Human Flourshing 34 First St Box 2462 Andrews NC 28901 Office Phone: 828-321-9900. E-mail: drmarta11@frontier.com.

MARTELLA, ORESTE, urologist; b. Bologna, Italy, Mar. 23, 1976; Degree in Medicine and Surgery, L'Aquila U. Med. Sch., 2004, degree in Urology, 2009. Exec. urologist, 2009; cons. Inst. Calabrese, 2009. Avocations: painting, skiing, swimming. Home: Via kennedy 38 Puglia Tiggiano Lecce 73030 Italy Personal E-mail: oreste.martella@virgilio.it.

MARTELLI, EUGENIO, surgeon; b. Palermo, Italy, Mar. 2, 1968; Degree in Medicine, U. Rome Tor Vergata, 1992. Rsch. vascular fellow Mayo Clinic & Found., Rochester, Minn., 1996—97; resident, vascular surgery U. Rome Tor Vergata, 1997, rschr., vascular surgery, 1999—2011, sr. staff vascular surgeon, 1999—, assoc. prof., vascular surgery, 2011; medecin attachè Ctr. Hospitalier U. Trousseau, Tour, France, 1998. Mem.: Italian Soc. Vascular and Endovascular Surgery, Mayo Clinic Alumni Assn. Home: Via Arenula 16 Rome 00186 Italy Business E-Mail: martelli@uniroma2.it.

MARTELLI, GABRIELE, physician, researcher; b. Novara, Italy, Aug. 23, 1957; s. Aristide Martelli and Alda Forni; m. Marina Fumagalli, Feb. 15, 1997; children: Riccardo, Davide. MD, U. Turin, Italy, 1983. Cert. specialization in oncology U. Genoa, 1987, specialization in gen. surgery U. Milan, 1994. Fellowship MD Anderson Cancer Ctr., Houston, 1984, Dept. Surgery, U. Pitts., 1989; grant holder Istituto Tumori, Genoa, 1984—87; med. asst. prof. Istituto Nazionale Tumori, Milan, 1987—. Mem.: Nat. Task Force Against Breast Cancer, Nat. Acad. Cuisine. Roman Catholic. Avocations: tennis, movies. Home: Via Buschi 12 20131 Milan Italy Office: Istituto Nazionale Tumori Via Venezian 1 20131 Milan Italy Home Phone: 0039022664843; Office Phone: 00390223903436. Office Fax: 00390223902194. Business E-Mail: gabriele.martelli@istitutotumori.mi.it.

MARTELLO, ANTHONY, medical sales executive, consultant; BS in Biol. Scis., Calif. Poly U., San Luis Obispo, 1993—98. Cert. post-rehab. specialist Am. Acad. Health Fitness & Rehab., Calif., 1999; personal trainer Am. Coun. Exercise, Calif., 1999. Cert. personal trainer, post-rehab. specialist Los Gatos Athletic Club, Calif., 1998—2000; sales exec. Siemens Med. Solutions, Mt. View, 2000—05; sales rep. Omnicell, Inc., Mt. View, 2005—10; bus. devel. exec. Wave Mark Inc., 2011—. Dir. spl. events, coord. health fairs, sales exec. Health Coun. Grp. Polit. action com. mem. Siemens Polit. Action Com., Malvern, Pa., 2001—05. Recipient Cmty. Svc. award, San Luis Obispo Co., Calif. Poly. U., 1998, Outstanding Sales award, Acuson/Siemens Med. Solutions, 2000—01; named Top Sale Exec., Omnicell, 2005—10. Mem.: Am. Coun. Exercise (assoc.). Office: Wave Mark Inc One Month Dr Littleton MA 01460 Office Phone: 408-384-9461. Personal E-mail: tony.martello@comcast.net. Business E-mail: meddevicepro@gmail.com.

MARTEN, TIMOTHY JAMES, plastic surgeon; b. Kingstown, RI, Jan. 7, 1956; MD, U. Calif., Davis, 1982. Cert. Plastic Surgery, 1993. Intern surgery Kaiser Found. Hosp., Oakland, Calif., 1982—83, resident plastic surgery, 1983—87; resident U. Ill., Chgo., 1987—89; staff mem. Calif. Pacific Med. Ctr., San Francisco, 1990—, St. Mary's Hosp. Med. Ctr., San Francisco, 1990—, St. Francis Hosp. Med. Ctr., San Francisco, 1990—; pvt. practice Marten Clinic of Plastic Surgery,

San Francisco. Office: Marten Clinic Of Plastic Surgery 450 Sutter St Rm 2222 San Francisco CA 94108-4201 Office Phone: 415-677-9937. Office Fax: 415-677-9473. E-mail: info@martenclinic.com.

MARTENS, LUC CONSTANT, pediatrician, dental educator; m. Martine Helene Athur Withouck, Oct. 24, 1981; children: Lies, Ine. DDS, Ghent U., Belgium, 1980, MSc in Pediat. Dentistry, 1986, PhD in Dentistry, 1987. Cert. in inhalation sedation ACTA-Amsterdam, Netherlands, 1994. Asst. and assoc. prof. dept. operative dentistry Ghent U., 1980—91, prof. and chair pediat. dentistry and spl. care, 1991—, sec. faculty medicine, 1994—99, dean, Dental Sch., 2003—07; dir. dental clinic U. Hosp., Ghent, 2003—07. Cons. Flemish Dental Assn., Brussels, 1985—; external examiner, dept. pediat. dentistry ACTA-Amsterdam, 1997—, vis. prof., 2007—; external examiner Leeds Dental Sch., 1998—2000; pres. Internat. Assn. Disabilty and Oral Health (iADH), 2006—08; external examiner Dept. Pediat. Dentistry, Kuala Lumpur, Malaysia, 2008—. Contbr. scientific papers. Recipient Academician award, World Congress Microdentistry, 2000, VBTGG Corsodyl award, Dutch Soc. Oral Health and Disability, 2000. Mem.: Hellenic Soc. Pediat. Dentistry, Belgian Acad. Pediat. Dentistry (founding pres. 1998—2002), European Acad. Pediat. Dentistry (pres. 1998—2000), Internat. Assn. Pediat. Dentistry, Am. Acad. Pediat. Dentistry. Office: Dept Pediat Dentistry (UZG-P8) De Pintelaan 185 Gent 9000 Belgium Office Fax: 32 9 332 3851. Business E-Mail: luc.martens@ugent.be.

MARTENS, WILLEM HENDRIKUS, psychologist, director; b. Zevenaar, Gelderland, Netherlands, July 21, 1950; s. Harry Martens and Ida Roncken; m. Ineke Adriana Tuijten, Nov. 22, 1997; children: Miriam Elisabeth, Joshua Maria. MA in Philosophy (hon.), Amsterdam U., The Netherlands, 1972, MD (hon.) in Psychopathology, 1975; PhD Forensic Psychiatry (hon.), Tilburg U., The Netherlands, 1997. Diplomate in psychoanalysis Soc. Psychanalytique de Paris, France, 1985, lic. forensic psychologist Nat. Registration The Netherlands, 1997. Sr. rschr. psychology Nijmegen U., Gelderland, Netherlands, 1975—85; sr. rschr. forensic psychiatry Forensic Psychiat. Hosp., Nijmegen, 1975—85; pvt. practice Utrecht, Netherlands, 1985—94; dir. W. Kahn Inst. of Theoretical Psychiatry and Neuroscience, Elst, Utrecht, Netherlands, 1985—, exec. rschr. forensic psychiatry, 1985—, chair, 2001—. Apptd. advisor psychiatry European Commn. Leonardo da Vinci, Brussels, 2004—; scientific adv. BBC documentaries "How to Make a Psychopath" and "How to Cure a Psychopath", 2007. Author: Psychopathy and Maturation, 1997; mem. editl. bd.: Medicine and Law, mem. expert review panel: Jour. Med. Ethics, Jour. Contemporary Psychotherapy; contbr. articles to profl. jours.; musician: Orch. of U. of Wageningen, 1995—2002. Recipient 21st Century Achievement award, 2005, 2007, Internat. Profl. Yr. award, 2006, Outstanding Scientist of 21st Century award, 07, Outstanding Scientists Worldwide medal, 2007, Archimedes Medal of Honor, 2007, Scientist of Yr., IBC Cambridge, 2009; named Internat. Health Profl. of Yr., 2007, Internat. Scientist of Yr., 2007, Outstanding Scientist of Yr., IBC Cambridge, 2008—09, Great Mind of 21st Century, Am. Biographical Inst., 2006—07; named to Internat. Profiles Accomplished Leaders, 2008—09; nominee Internat. Dan David prize, 2004, Jean Delay prize, World Psychiatric Assn., 2005. Jewish. Achievements include invention of new therapeutic models for antisocial and psychopathic patients; new explanation models for mental disorders. Avocations: music, art, botany, literature. Home and Office: H v Tienhovenstraat 67 JB Nijmegen 6543 Netherlands Personal E-mail: wimkahn1@hotmail.com, willem.martens@gmail.com.

MARTENSEN, ROBERT LAWRENCE, emergency physician, educator, historian, ethicist, writer; b. Lake County, Ohio, Jan. 1, 1947; s. Lorenz Thomas and Bernice Helen (Sommer) M.; m. Phoebe Cutler (div.); m. Anne Carver (div.); children: Bayard Cutler, Charles Carver, Robert Maxwell. BA, Harvard U., 1969; MD, Dartmouth Coll., 1974; PhD, U. Calif., San Francisco, 1993. House officer U. Calif., San Francisco, 1974-77; staff physician Calif. Pacific Med. Ctr., San Francisco, 1977-93; asst. prof. Harvard Med. Sch., Cambridge, Mass., 1993, faculty mem., dept. social medicine; prof., chair, history and philosophy of medicine dept. U. Kansas Med. Ctr., dir., Clendening Libr. and Mus. of History of Medicine; James A. Knight Chair in Humanities and Ethics in Medicine, prof. surgery Tulane U. Sch. Medicine; dir. Office NIH History, Office of Intramural Rsch., 2007—. Invited presenter in field. Author The Brain Takes Shape: An Early History, 2004, A Life Worth Living: A Doctor's Reflections on Illness in a High-Tech Era, 2008, assoc. editor: Surgical Palliative Care: A Resident Guide, 2009; Contbr. articles to profl. jours., chpts. to books. Med. advisor on disaster planning, San Francisco, 1977-79, adv. bd. Sci. Translational Medicine, 2010-, Canniff Dixon Found., 2007- Guggenheim Fellowship, 2002. Mem. History of Sci. Soc., Am. Assn. for the History of Medicine Office: Office NIH History National Institute Health Bldg 45 3AN38 MSC 6330 Bethesda MD 20892-6330 Office Phone: 301-496-6610. Business E-Mail: martensenr@mail.nih.gov.

MARTER, JOYCE BRINKMAN, psychotherapist; b. 1972; BA in Psychology, Ohio State U., 1994; MA in Counseling Psychology, Northwestern U., 1996. Lic. clin. profl. counselor 1998. Intern The Family Inst.; clin. supr. Counseling Psychology Program Northwestern U.; acct. mgr. Employee Resource Systems, 1998—2002; psychotherapist Joyce Marter & Associates, 1998—; co-owner, psychotherapist Urban Balance LLC, Chgo., 2003—. Recipient Distinguished Alumni award, Nothwestern Univ., 2008; named one of The 40 Under 40, Crain's Chgo. Bus., 2010. Mem.: ACA, Ill. Counseling Assn., Ill. Mental Health Counselors Assn. Office: Urban Balance LLC 2550 Crawford Ave Suite 22 Evanston IL 60201 Office Phone: 888-726-7170. Office Fax: 847-492-1255. *

MARTH, WILLIAM S., pharmaceutical executive; BSc in Pharmacy, U. Ill., 1977; MBA, Keller Grad. Sch. of Mgmt., Chgo. Ill., 1989. Various positions with Apothecon Divsn. of Bristol-Myers Squibb; v.p., sales and mktg. Teva Pharm. USA, North Wales, Pa., 1999—2002, exec. v.p., 2002—05, pres., CEO, 2005—08, Teva Pharm. N.Am., 2008—10, Teva Pharm. Americas, 2010—. Office: Teva Pharm USA 1090 Horsham RD POB 1090 North Wales PA 19454 *

MARTHAN, ROGER, medical educator; b. Fes, Morocco, June 13, 1957; MD, U. de Bordeaux, 1983, PhD, 1989. Prof. U. de Bordeaux, 1993—. Staff specialist, head Tchg. Hosp. Bordeaux, 1993. Mem.: Am. Physiol. Soc. Office: Universite de Bordeaux 146 Rue Léo Saig Bordeaux Gironde 33076 France Office Fax: 33-5-57-57-16-95. Business E-Mail: roger.marthan@u-bordeaux2.fr.

MARTI-CRUCHAGA, PABLO, gastroenterologist, surgeon; b. Pamplona, Spain, Jan. 20, 1979; Degree, U. Navarra, 2002. Gastrointestinal surgeon Clinica U. Navarra, 2003—. Office: Pio XII 36 Pamplona Navarra 31008 Spain Office Fax: 34948296500. Business E-Mail: pamartic@unav.es.

MARTIKAINEN, A. HELEN, retired health specialist educator; b. Harrison, Maine, May 11, 1916; d. Sylvester and Emma (Heikkinen) M. AB, Bates Coll., 1939, DSc (hon.), 1957; MPH, Yale U., 1941; DSc, Harvard U., 1964; DSc (hon.), Smith Coll., 1969. Health edn. sec. Hartford TB and Pub. Health Assn., 1941; cons. USPHS, 1942—49; chief health edn. WHO, Geneva, 1949—74; ret., 1974; chair internat. affairs AAUW-NC, 1986—94, rep. to NC Coalition on Aging, 2001—, bd. dirs., 2001—08; mem. NC Health Adv. Bd. Aging, 2001—08. Hon. trustee Bridgton Acad., North Bridgton, Maine; mem. NC Women's Forum, 1984—; bd. dirs. NC Ctr. of Laws Affecting Women, Inc.; bd. dirs. West Triangle chpt. UNA-USA; chair residents health and social svcs. com., residents coun., residents com. for cmty. rels. Carol Woods. Recipient Delta Omega award Yale U., Nat. Adminstrv. award Am. Acad. Phys. Edn., Key award Bates Coll., Internat. Svc. award, France, 1953, Prentiss medal, 1956, Spl. medal, cert. for internat. health edn. svc. Nat. Acad. Medicine for France, 1959, Profl. award Soc. Pub. Health Educators, 1963, Benjamin Elijah Mays award Bates Coll. Alumni Assn., 1989, Legacy of Leadership honoree Pines of Carolina coun. Girl Scouts U.S., 2002; named to Bridgeton Acad. Hall of Fame, Maine, 2003. Fellow APHA (chmn. health edn. sect., Excellence award 1969); mem. AAUW, LWV, Women's Internat. League for Peace and Freedom, U.S. Soc. Pub. Health Educators, Internat. Union Health Edn. (Parisot medal, tech. adviser), Acad. Phys. Edn. (assoc.), NC Coun. Women's Orgns. (mem. coun. assembly 1988-92, Women of Distinction award 1989), Phi Beta Kappa. Home: 13127 Carol Woods 750 Weaver Dairy Rd Chapel Hill NC 27514-1443

MARTIN, ANTONIO D., hospital administrator; M in Health Svc. Adminstrn. and Policy, New Sch. U., NYC. Dep. dir. network behavioral health NYC Health and Hosp. Corp., Brooklyn; exec. dir. East NY Neighborhood Family Care Ctr., Brooklyn, 1990—98; COO Queens Hosp. Ctr., 1999, exec. dir., 2002; sr. v.p. Ctrl. Brooklyn Family Health Network, 2009—; exec. dir. Kings County Hosp. Ctr., Brooklyn, 2009—. Recipient, Congressman Gregory Meeks, NYC Comptr. William C. Thompson Jr., Lawrence R. Bailey Sr. Cmty. Svc. Award, NAACP - Jamaica Br., Awards for Leadership and Svc., Clin. Soc. of Queens and LI, Aesclepius Med. Soc. Inc. Mem.: Am. Diabetes Assn. (chairperson 2007—08). Office: Kings County Hospital Center 451 Clarkson Ave Brooklyn NY 11203 Office Phone: 718-245-3131.

MARTIN, BENJAMIN GAUFMAN, ophthalmologist; b. Louisville, Aug. 18, 1937; s. Benjamin and Catherine L. Martin; m. Caroline Sue Martin, May 25, 1973; children: Benjamin, Lori, Tamara, Farrell, Steven, David. BME, U. Louisville, 1954, M. Engring., 1973; MD, U. So. Calif., 1964. Design engr. Philco/Ford, Palo Alto, Calif., 1957-60; rsch. engr. N.Am./Rockwell, Inglewood, Calif., 1961 63; intern Wright Patterson Med. Ctr., Dayton, Ohio, 1964-65; ophthalmology resident Wilford Hall Med. Ctr., San Antonio, 1968-71; commd. USAF, 1963, advanced through grades to col., ret., 1980; CEO Cape Coral (Fla.) Eye Ctr., 1980—. With USN, 1954-57. Decorated Legion of Merit, DFC, Bronze Star, Air medal. Mem.: DFC Soc., Daedalions, Elks, Shriners, Masons. Republican. Lutheran. Office: Cape Coral Eye Ctr 4120 Del Prado Blvd S Cape Coral FL 33904-7165 Home Phone: 239-481-8071; Office Phone: 239-542-2020.

MARTIN, CHARLES NEIL, JR., surgical hospital company executive; b. Florence, Ala., Dec. 11, 1942; s. Charles Neil Sr. and Hazel Lucy (Hawkins) M. BS, So. Coll., Chattanooga, 1964. Adminstr. El Reposo Nursing Home, Florence, 1964-66, Parkwood Convalescent Ctr., Chattanooga, 1966-67; project dir. Tenn. Hosp. Assn., Nashville, 1967-68, asst. dir., 1968-69; v.p. Gen. Care Corp., Nashville, 1969-76, exec. v.p., 1976-79, pres. & COO, 1979-80; sr. v.p. HCA, Inc., Nashville, 1980-85, exec. v.p., 1985-87, also bd. dirs.; pres., chief oper. officer HealthTrust, Inc., Nashville, 1987—92; chmn., pres., CEO OrNda HealthCorp., 1992—97; chmn., CEO Vanguard Health Sys., Inc., Nashville, 1997—. Bd. dirs. Equicor, Nashville, 1986—. Bd. dirs. Cystic Fibrosis Found., Nashville, 1987. Office: Vanguard Healthcare Systems Inc Ste 100 20 Burton Hills Blvd Nashville TN 37215 Office Phone: 615-665-6000. Office Fax: 615-665-6099. Business E-Mail: c.martin@vanguard.com. *

MARTIN, DALE, health facility administrator; b. NYC, May 10, 1935; d. Byron Pink Molter and Ruth Nobel; m. Robert A. Wishart, Dec. 13, 1985; children from previous marriage: Elizabeth, Devon. BS, U. Conn., 1957. RN, cert. case mgr., disability mgmt. specialist, lic. rehab. counsellor, Mass. Dental asst., Hempstead, NY, 1951; with Wesson Maternity Hosp., Springfield, Mass., 1957—58, Huntington Hartford Meml. Hosp., Pasadena, Calif., 1958—59; mgr. office Indsl. By Products Inc., Kalamazoo, 1969—72, contr. Chgo., 1970—74; cons. Mgmt. Resources Inc., Broomall, Pa., 1978—81; cons., owner Martin-Collard Assocs., Inc., Monmouth Beach, NJ, 1980—84; cons., owner, chmn. bd. dirs. MCA, Inc., St. Helena Island, SC, 1984—. Bd. dirs. Consortium Advantage, Inc., St. Helena Island, Silvers Assocs., Plymouth, Mass., Low Country Human Devel. Ctr., Beaufort, SC, mentor program dir., 2001—04, exec. com., steering com., chmn. vol. program, 2001—04; cons. Viewfinder, Old Chatham, NY, 1987—99, Phoenix Inc., Global Explorations, Inc., 1987—99, Fallon Inc., Dr. Martens Shoe Distbr., 1998—2000, Retail Swap.com, 2000—02, shoespot.com, 2001—02; chmn. Okatie Acad. Tennis Benefit; NJ state girls gymnastic judgenn, 1985—89. Contbr. articles to profl. jours., 2001. Bd. govs. Rumson-Fair Haven HS, NJ, 1976—78; mem. corp. fundraising com. Beaufort Orch., SC, 2003—04; mem. Beaufort Orch. League, 2004—; benefit tennis co-chair Jordan Hosp.-White Cliffs County Club; vol. Habitat Humanity Fundarising, 2007—. Mem.: Coastal Carolina Tennis Assn. (communication & med. dir. 2011—), Dataw Island Feline Found. Inc., Cappuccino Tennis Group (founder), Tennic Ctr. Found. Comm., Case Mgmt. Soc. Am., Mass. Nurses Assn. (chmn. image com. 1984—85, pub. info. com. 1986—89), Individual Case Mgmt. Assn., Internat. Assn. Psychosocial Rehab. Specialists, Nat. Rehab. Assn. (pvt. sector group), Nat. Assn. Rehab. Profls. in Pvt. Sector (forensic sect., past rep. region 1 to bd. dirs.), Jr. League, Dataw Island Club (tennis assn. social chmn. 2001—04, chmn. visual arts 2003—04, mem. recreation com. 2003—, bd. dir. 2003—, pres. 2005—07, tennis ctr. fundraising com. 2005—, capt. 3.5 womans USTA team 2006—08, chmn. clubhouse pub. art 2006—08, membership com. 2009—, exec. dir. 2010—, found. collaborator), Jr. Women's Club, Town Club (v.p.), Miles Grant Country Club (bd. dirs. Tennis Assn. 1997—2001, pres. 1998—2000), Mountain Lakes Ski Club (founder), Alpha Delta Pi, Sigma Theta Tau. Avocations: painting, tennis, croquet, kayaking.

MARTIN, DANIEL C., surgeon, gynecologist, educator; b. St. Louis, Apr. 7, 1946; s. Dan Allen and Ruth Keel (Fields) M.; m. Glenn Ann Blakemore, July 7, 1970; children: Josh, Adam. BS in Physics, Emory U., Atlanta, 1968, MD, 1972. Diplomate Am. Bd. Ob-Gyn. Rsch. asst. physics and radiology Emory U., Atlanta, 1968-69; intern, resident, fellow, instr. The Johns Hopkins Med. Instns., Balt., 1972-77; from asst. prof. to clin. asst. prof. U. Tenn., Memphis, 1977-90, clin. assoc. prof., 1990—2005, clin. prof., 2005—06, prof., 2006—, fed. senate, Health Sci. Ctr., 2010—11; surgeon Reproductive Surgery, P.C., Memphis, 1977—2006, UT Med. Group, Memphis, 2006—. Gynecologist, reproductive surgeon Bapt. Meml. Hosp., 1977—; Axel Munthe presenter, Naples, Italy, 1992; guest spkr.Annual Japanese Endometrosis Symposium, Osaka, 1994, 2004; dir. gynecologic laser and endoscopy workshops, 1982-93. Editor: (textbooks) Lasers in Endoscopy, 1990, Laparoscopic Appearance of Endometriosis, 1990, Manual of Endoscopy, 1990, Atlas of Endometriosis, 1993, Endoscopic Management of Gynecologic Disease, 1996. Picker Found. fellow Emory U., 1969; Tex. Assn. Ob-Gyn. hon. fellow, 1989; recipient Bridges trophy for athletics Emory U., 1968, Codman surg. award, 1982, 83, Video award Am. Fertility Soc., 1992, Physician Recognition awrd Endometriosis Assn., 1995, APGO Tchg. award, 2010; named one of Best Drs. Am. Woodward and White Inc., 1992, 94, 96, 98, 00, 02, 04, 06, 08, 10; Hon. mem. Australian Gynecol. Endoscopy Soc., 1993, named to Sports Hall of Fame, Emory Coll., 2002; named one of Memphis Mag. Top Drs., 2010-2011. Mem. ACOG (sect. chair jr. fellows Md.), Tenn. Med. Assn., Memphis and Shelby County Med. Soc. (comm. com.), Am. Nat. Std. Inst. (subcom. on laser safety in med. facility), Am. Assn. Gynecol. Laparoscopists (pres. 1990-91, Videoendoscopy award 1993), Gynecologic Surgery Soc. (pres. 1994-96, chmn. bd. 1996-98), Australian Gynecol. Endoscopy Soc. (hon.), Argentinian Ob-Gyn. Soc. (hon.), Alpha Omega Alpha. Office Phone: 901-347-8331. *

MARTIN, DAVID EDWARD, health sciences educator; b. Green Bay, Wis., Oct. 1, 1939; s. Edward Henry and Lillie (Luckman) M. BS, U. Wis., 1961, MS, 1963, PhD, 1970. Ford Found. research trainee Wis. Regional Primate Ctr., Madison, 1967-70; asst. prof. health scis. Ga. State U., Atlanta, 1970-74, assoc. prof., 1974 80, prof., 1980-91, regents prof., 1992—2000, regents prof. emeritus, 2000—. Affiliate scientist Yerkes Primate Rsch. Ctr., Emory U., Atlanta, 1970—98; US rep to Internat. Olympic Acad., 1978; sport medicine rsch. assoc. US Olympic Com., 1981—84; chmn. sports scis. USA Track and Field; mem. coaching staff US teams to world championships in distance running, Rome, 1982, Gateshead, England, 83, Budapest, Hungary, 94, Vilamoura, Portugal, 2000, Fukuoka, Japan, 06, head coach, Paris, 1980, Madrid, 84, Hiroshima, Japan, 85, Warsaw, 87, Antwerp, Belgium, 91; mem. Olympic med. support group Atlanta Olympic Games. Author: Laboratory Experiments in Human Physiology, 4th edit., 1980, The Marathon Footrace, 1979, La Corsa Di Maratona, 1982, The High Jump Book, 1982, The High Jump Book, 2d edit., 1987, Respiratory Anatomy and Physiology, 1987, Training Distance Runners, 1991, Training Distance Runners, 2d edit., 1997, Training Distance Runners, German edit., 1992, Training Distance Runners, Spanish edit., 1995, Training Distance Runners, Japanese edit., 2001, The Olympic Marathon, 2000. Trustee Ga. Found. for Athletic Excellence. Named Disting. prof. Ga. State U., 1975, 81, 85 Fellow Am. Coll. Sports Medicine; mem. Internat. Soc. Olympic Historians, Am. Physiol. Soc., Atlanta Track Club. Home: 510 Coventry Rd Apt 13A Decatur GA 30030-5038 Office: Ga State U Dept Respiratory Therapy Atlanta GA 30303 Office Phone: 404-413-1272. Business E-Mail: drdavexy@gmail.com.

MARTIN, DAVID HUBERT, internist, epidemiologist, educator; b. Detroit, Mar. 24, 1943; s. Hubert Cillis and Mable Anita (Stewart) M.; m. Jane Ellen Schlichtemeier, Nov. 22, 1970; children: Jennifer, Jason. BA with distinction, U. Kans., 1965; MD cum laude, Harvard Coll., 1969. Diplomate Nat. Bd. Med. Examiners, Am. Bd. Internal Medicine, Infectious Disease Subspecialty Bd. Am. Bd. Internal Medicine. Intern Bronx (N.Y.) Mcpl. Hosp. Ctr., 1969-70; staff assoc. Nat. Inst. Allergy and Infectious Diseases, Mid. Am. Rsch. Unit, NIH, Panama Canal Zone, 1970-73; med. resident U. Wash. Affiliated Hosps., 1973-75; sr. fellow in infectious diseases U. Wash., 1976-78; chief resident in medicine USPHS Hosp., Seattle, 1975-76, staff internal medicine clinic, 1975, attending physician internal medicine, 1976-78, staff dept. internal medicine New Orleans, 1979-81; staff Hotel Dieu Hosp., New Orleans, 1982-94; clin. asst. prof. medicine La. State U. Med. Sch., New Orleans, 1979-81, asst. prof. medicine divsn. infectious diseases, 1981-82, assoc. prof. medicine divsn. infectious diseases, 1982-88, assoc. prof. microbiology, 1986-88, prof. internal medicine and microbiology, 1988, asst. chief sect. infectious diseases, 1988-89, chief sect. infectious diseases, 1990—, Harry E. Dascomb M.D. prof. of medicine, 1990—. Instr. dept. medicine U. Wash. Sch. Medicine, Seattle, 1975-78, acting asst. prof. medicine, 1978-79; chmn. infection control com., chmn. instnl. rev. bd. human rsch. com., chmn. antibiotic utilization com., sec. rsch. and editl. com., sec. animal welfare com. USPHS Hosp., New Orleans, 1979-81, dep. chief clin. rsch. dept., 1979-81, chmn. credentials com., 1980-81; mem. infection control com. Hotel Dieu Hosp., New Orleans, 1983-84, chmn. pharmacy and therapeutics com., 1988-94, mem. infection control com., 1990-94; vis. physician Charity Hosp. (now Med. Ctr. of La. at New Orleans), New Orleans, 1982—, chmn. antibiotics com., 1982—, dir. infection control program, 1993—, chmn. infection control com., 1993—, vice chmn. pharmacy and therapeutics com., 1995—; chmn. comprehensive medicine head search com. La. State U. Med. Sch., 1989-90, dept. medicine faculty promotion com., 1988—, AIDS policy com., 1992; adv. bd. La. State Labs., 1993—, State La. Pub. Health Lab. Adv. Com., 1994—, U.S. Pub. Health Region 6 Infertility Prevention Adv. Com., 1995—; mem. nat. STD treatment guidelines com. Ctrs. Disease Control, 1993, 98, nat. Chlamydia and gonorrheadiagnosis guidelines com., 1997—; dir. La. STD/HIV rsch. ctr., 2001-04, Gulf South STI/TM Collaborative Rsch. Ctr., 2004—. Peer reviewer various jours. including Sexually Transmitted Diseases, The Jour. of Infectious Diseases, The Am. Jour. of the Med. Scis., Archives of Internal Medicine, Clin. Infectious Diseases, New Eng. Jour. Medicine, Annals Internal Medicine, Jour. AMA; contbr. chpts. to books and articles to profl. jours. Dir. La. STD/HIV Rsch. Ctr., 2002—. With USPHS, 1970-82. Fellow ACP (La. chpt. program chmn. 1994-95), Infectious Diseases Soc. Am.; mem. Internat. Soc. for Sexually Transmitted Disease Rsch. (bd. dirs. 1991-99, chmn. 1995 meeting organizing com., pres. 1993-95, sec.-treas. 1999—), Am. Fedn. for Clin. Rsch., Am. Sexually Transmitted Diseases Assn. (v.p. 1992-94, pres. 1994-96), Am. Soc. for Microbiology, European Soc. for Clin. Microbiology and Infectious Diseases, So. Soc. for Clin. Investigation, La./Miss. Infectious Diseases Soc. (bd. dirs., sci. program chmn. 1993, pres. 1997-99), Phi Beta Kappa. Achievements include research in the effect of sexually transmitted microorganisms on pregnancy outcome, antibiotic treatment of sexually transmitted diseases and in particular C. trachomatis, epidemiology of C. trachomatis in normal populations, chancroid and other genital ulcer diseases; establishment of first chlamydia laboratory in the Gulf South. Office: La State U Med Sch 1542 Tulane Ave New Orleans LA 70112-2825 Office Phone: 504-568-5031.

MARTIN, DAVID JULIAN, medical association administrator; Cert. Assn. Exec. Positions related to acctg. and bus. mgmt.; with Bands of America; asst. exec. dir. Am. Assn. Neurol. Surgeons; exec. dir. Urban and Regional Info Systems Assn., Park Ridge, Ill.; CEO, exec. v.p. Soc. Critical Care Medicine. Mem.: Assn. Forum Chicagoland, Am. Assn. Med. Soc. Execs., Coun. Engring. and Sci. Soc. Execs., Am. Soc. Assn. Execs. Office: Soc Critical Care Medicine 500 Midway Dr Mount Prospect IL 60056 Office Phone: 847-827-6869. Office Fax: 847-827-6886. Business E-Mail: dmartin@sccm.org. *

MARTIN, DENISE ANN, safety and environmental health manger; d. Richard Frank and Jeannine Carol Salisbury; m. Gerald Lee Martin, June 10, 1972; children: Katrina Ann Martin Davenport, Brett Lee. BS, Colo. State U., Ft. Collins, 1974. Rsch. assoc. Colo. State U., Ft. Collins, Colo., 1988—91; microbiologist Ctrs. Disease Control, Ft. Collins, Colo., 1991—2005, alternate responsible official select agts. program, 2005—; responsible official select agt. program Ctrs. for Disease Control, 2009—. Contbr. articles to profl. jours. including Jour. Virology (Charles C. Shepard Sci. award, 2002, James Nakano Citation, 2002). Recipient Spl. Recognition award, USPHS, 1994, Honor award, Nat. Ctr. for Infectious Diseases, 1994, Group award, 1996, 2003, Spl. Act of Svc. award, 1996, 2001, Sec.'s Disting. Svc. award, DHHS, 1997, 2000—01. Achievements include research in West Nile diagnostic serology techniques. Avocations: singing, sewing, travel, reading, music. Office: Ctrs for Disease Control & Prevention Foothills Campus 1300 Rampart Rd Fort Collins CO 80522 Business E-Mail: dzm9@cdc.gov.

MARTIN, DONALD KEITH, ophthalmologist, educator; b. Grafton, Australia, Nov. 26, 1957; PhD, U. NSW, 1985. Chaire d'excellence, prof. Found. Nanoscis. and U. Joseph Fourier, 2008—. Head, R & D Seagull Tech. Pty Ltd., 2005. Sr. Chaire d'Excellence fellow, Found. RTRA Nanoscis., France. Mem.: Assn. Rsch. Vision and Ophthalmology. Avocations: clarinet, skiing, squash, tennis. Office: Universite Joseph Fourier TIMC-IMAG La Tronche Rhone-Alpes 38706 France E-mail: don.martin@imag.fr.

MARTIN, ERIC C., radiologist; b. Eng., Aug. 7, 1942; BA, Oxford U., 1963, MA, BMBCh, Oxford U., DM, 1967. Dir. cardiovasc. & interventional radiology Columbia Presbyn. Med. Ctr., 1980—99; sr. attending radiologist St. Luke's Roosevelt Hosp. Ctr., 2000—. Prof. radiology Coll. Physicians and Surgeons Columbia U., 1985. Fellow: RCP, Am. Coll. Cardiology, Soc. Interventional Radiology (Gold medal), Royal Coll. Radiology. Office: St Luke's Roosevelt Hosp 1000 10th Ave New York NY 10019 Office Fax: 212-523-7483. Business E-Mail: emartin@chpnet.org.

MARTIN, GRACE BURKETT, psychologist; b. Sumter, SC, Aug. 27, 1939; d. John Hazel and Grace Thomasine (Briggs) Burkett; m. H. Russell Jr. Martin, Oct. 9, 1957; children: H. Russell, Carolyne, Melinda. BA magna cum laude, Armstrong State Coll., 1976; MS, Fla. State U., 1979, PhD, 1980. Lic. psychologist. Hist. preservationist, 1962—; dir. Christian Edn. St. Thomas Parish, Savannah, Ga., 1970—74; prof. psychology Armstrong State Coll., Savannah, 1980—2001, prof. emeritus, 2002—, dept. head psychology, dir. gen. studies degree program, head. divsn. social and behavioral scis.; interim dean arts and scis.; pres. Orgn. Cons.; lectr.; radio and TV appearances; author, collaborator nat. and cross-nat. studies of women and work; cons. editor Jour. Supplementary Abstract Svc., 1980—81. Bd. dirs. Coastal Empire YMCA, 1972—75; mem. Savannah Symphony Soc.; mem. commn. mission Episcopal Diocese Ga., 1972—74, mem. liturg. commn., 1972—74, lic. lay reader; pres. Operation Return, 1972—76. Named Mrs. Ga., 1962. Mem.: Ga. Ednl. Research Assn., Commerce Club Savannah (charter mem.), Ga. Assn. Women Deans and Adminstrators, Nat. Assn. Women Deans & Administrators, Am. Mgmt. Assn., Soc. Indsl. Organizational Psychology, Southeastern Psychol. Assn., Am. Psychol. Soc. (charter mem.), Am. Psychol. Assn. Home: 50 Shipwatch Rd Savannah GA 31410-2950 Personal E-mail: martingrace@comcast.net.

MARTIN, JACK, physician; b. Northport, Ala., Aug. 11, 1927; s. Marvin Oscar and Glenavis (Rice) M.; m. Ann Inman, Apr. 7, 1957; children: Sarah, Richard, Charles Randall, Robert. BS, U. Ala., 1949; MD, Vanderbilt U., 1953. Intern Charity Hosp., New Orleans, 1953-54; resident in adult and child psychiatry Cin. Gen. Hosp., 1954-58; dir. child psychiatry U. Tex. Health Scis. Ctr., Dallas, 1958-67, clin. prof. child psychiatry, 1967—; med. dir. Shady Brook Rsch. Ctr., Richardson, Tex., 1963-81; physician pvt. practice, Dallas, 1981—. With USNR, 1945-47. Independent. Episcopalian. Avocations: bridge, golf. Home: 8020 Frankford Rd Apt 314 Dallas TX 75252-6862 Personal E-mail: jam4757@aol.com. *

MARTIN, JAMES GRUBBS, healthcare consultant, former Governor of North Carolina, former United States Representative from North Carolina; b. Savannah, Ga., Dec. 11, 1935; s. Arthur Morrison and Mary Julia (Grubbs) M.; m. Dorothy Ann McAulay, June 1, 1957; children: James Grubbs, Emily Richey, Arthur Benson. BS, Davidson Coll., 1957; PhD, Princeton U., 1960. Assoc. prof. chemistry Davidson (N.C.) Coll., 1960-72; mem. US Congress from 9th N.C. Dist., 1973-85; gov. State of N.C., 1985-92; v.p. Carolinas HealthCare System, Charlotte, NC, 1993—2008. Mem. Mecklenburg (NC) Bd. County Commrs., 1966-72, chmn., 1967-68, 70-71; pres. NC Assn. County Commrs., 1970-71; tuba player Charlotte Symphony, 1961-66; bd. dirs. Family Dollar Stores, Inc., Palomar Med. Techns., Inc. Chmn. Global TransPark Found., 1993—; trustee Davidson Coll., 1998-2005; trustee Union Theol. Sem., Va., 2002-07. Danforth fellow, 1957—60. Mem. Beta Theta Pi (v.p., trustee 1966-69, pres. 1975-78), Masons (33 deg., Grand Cross), Shriners. Presbyterian. Office: Carolinas Med Ctr PO Box 32861 Charlotte NC 28232-2861 Office Phone: 704-355-5310. E-mail: jgmartin@carolinas.org.

MARTIN, JAMES LARENCE, dentist, educator; b. Dubuque, Iowa, Sept. 3, 1940; s. James Larence and Ada Virginia (Boone) M.; m. Willie Mae Walker, Jan. 23, 1941; children: Linda Gail, James Larence III, John Lance. BS, Loras Coll., Dubuque, 1959, LittD, 1982; MS, Tenn. State U., 1960; DDS, Meharry Med. Coll., 1966; MPH, U. Mich., 1975. Dental dir. children and youth Meharry Med. Coll., Nashville, 1967-72, acting dir. children and youth program, 1972-73, dir. primary dental svcs., 1973-75, coord. dental component Ctr. for Health Care Rsch., 1975-77, prof., 1981—; owner Martin Dental, Nashville, 1980—. Dental cons. Medically Dedicated, Washington, 1992—; pres. faculty senate Meharry Med. Coll., 1989-93, mem. pres.'s exec. mgmt. team, 1989-93, dir. divsn. dental public health 1999—, chmn. dept. dental pub. health, 1999—. Contbr. articles to profl. jours., chpts. to books. Bd. regents Loras Coll., 1997—. Recipient Meritorious Svc. award Acad. Oral Medicine, 1977. Mem. ADA, Am. Pub. Health Assn. (med. com.), Am. Assn. Pub. Health Dentistry, Nat. Assn. Cmty. Health Ctrs., Am. Acad. Goil Foil Operators, Soc. of the Upper 10th, Nashville Area C. of C., Beta Kappa Chi, Phi Sigma. Achievements include discovery of leukoedema in childrem. Avocations: reading, swimming, photography. Home: 3515 Geneva Cir Nashville TN 37209-2524 Office: 908 34th Ave N Nashville TN 37209-2502 Personal E-mail: jmarti3817@aol.com.

MARTIN, JAMES NELLO, JR., gynecologist, educator; b. Bethesda, Md., Feb. 14, 1947; MD, U. NC Sch. Medicine, 1973. Prof. ob-gyn., chief MFM divsn. U. Miss. Med. Ctr., 1981—. Pres. ACOG, 2011—. Recipient HOPE award, Preeclampsia Found. Avocations: reading, model building. Office: Umc Dept Ob-gyn 2500 N State St Jackson MS 39216 Business E-Mail: jnmartin@umc.edu.

MARTIN, JAY HERBERT, psychoanalyst, researcher, literature professor, political science professor; s. Sylvester K. and Ada M. (Smith) M.; m. Helen Bernadette Saldini, June 9, 1956; children: Helen E., Laura A., Jay Herbert. AB with honors, Columbia U., 1956; MA, Ohio State U., 1957, PhD, 1960; PhD in Psychoanalysis, So. Calif. Psychoanalytic Inst., 1983. Instr. English Pa. State U., 1957-58; instr., then asst. to assoc. prof. English and Am. Studies Yale U., New Haven, 1960-68; prof. English and comparative culture U. Calif., Irvine, 1968-79; asst. prof. psychiatry and human behavior, clin. supr. residency program Calif. Coll. Medicine Calif. Coll. Medicine U. Calif.-Irvine, 1978—96; Leo S. Bing prof. English and Am. lit. U. So. Calif., LA, 1979-96, dir. undergrad. program in Am. studies, 1968-69, dir. program in comparative culture, 1969-71, dir. edn. abroad program, 1971-75; prof. govt., Edward S. Gould prof. humanities Claremont McKenna Coll., 1996—; dir. civilization program Claremont (Calif.) McKenna Coll., 1996—2000, acting dir. Gould Ctr. for Humanistic Studies, 1998-2000, prof., English, grad. sch., 2004—. Instr. psychoanalysis So. Calif. Psychoanalytic Inst., 1984-96; Bicentennial prof. Am. lit. and culture Moscow State U., USSR, 1976, Dai Ho Chun (Wisdom) chair Prof. U. Hawaii, 2000-01; dir. NEH summer sems., 1976, 77; mem. evaluation com. dept. pvt. post-secondary edn. State of Calif., 1986; lectr. in field; cons. in field Author: (criticism and biography) Conrad Aiken: A Life of His Art, 1962, Harvests of Change: American Literature 1865-1914, 1967, Nathanael West: The Art of His Life, 1970 (U. Calif. Friends Libr. award), Robert Lowell, 1970, Always Merry and Bright. The Life of Henry Miller, 1978, (U. Calif. Friends of Libr. award, Phi Kappa Phi Best Faculty Publ. prize U. So. Calif., transl. in French, Japanese and German), (fiction) Winter Dreams: An American in Moscow, 1979, Who Am I This Time, Uncovering the Fictive Personality, 1988 (trans. Portuguese), Burlington No. Found. award 1989); Swallowing Tigers Whole, 1996, A Corresponding Leap of Love: Henry Miller, 1996, Henry Miller's Dream Song, 1996, Journey to Heavenly Mountain, 2002 (ForeWord mag. Book of Yr. prize), The Education of John Dewey, 2003; author Baseball Magic (short stories) 2008, Live All You Can: Alexander Joy Cartwright And the Invention of Modern Baseball, 2009, Territoriality and Terror: A Biological Basis for Terrorism, 2011, one hour radio drama, William Faulkner. Sound Portraits of Twentieth-Century Humanists, starring Tennessee Williams, Glenn Close, Colleen Dewhurst, Nat. Pub. Radio, 1980; author one-act docudrama Trial Days in Coyocoan, Antioch Rev., 2001; author sects. 24 books including most recently American Writing Today, vol. I, 1982, The Haunted Dusk: American Supernatural Fiction, 1820-1902, 1983, Frontiers of Infant Psychiatry, vol.II, 1986, Centenary Essays on Huckleberry Finn, 1985, Robert Lowell: Essays on the Poetry, 1987, William Faulkner: The Best from American Literature, 1989, The Homosexualities: Reality, Fantasy and the Arts, 1991, Life Guidance Through Literature, 1992, Biography and Source Studies, 1995, William Faulkner and Psychology, 1995, Psychotherapy East and West, 1996, Readings on Huckleberry Finn, 1999, John Fante: A Critical Gathering, 2000, Uncollected Works By...Paul Laurence Dunbar, 2000, American Literature of the Civil War, 2004, Blackwell Companion to Modernist Literature and Culture, 2004,Cases as Catalysts, 2005, Only God: A Biography of Ramsuratkumar, 2005, International Research on Global Affairs, 2005, Psychoanalytic Rev., Contemporary Psychoanalysis Jour., Am. Imago; editor: Winfield Townley Scott (Yale series recorded poets), 1962, Twentieth Century Interpretations of the Waste Land: A Collection of Critical Essays, 1968, Twentieth Century Views of Nathanael West, 1972, A Singer in the Dawn: Reinterpretations of Paul Laurence Dunbar (with intro.), 1975, Economic Depression and American Humor (with intro.), 1986; mem. edit. bd. Am. Lit., 1978-81, Humanities in Society, 1979-1983; editor-in-chief Psychoanalytic Edn., 1984-89; editor Humanitas/Communitas, 1998-2000; appearances on TV and radio including Connie Martinson Talks Books, Barbara Brunner Nightline, Sonya Live in LA, Oprah Winfrey Show, C-SPAN, 1988-89; contbr. numerous articles and revs. to profl. jours., bulls. Pres. Friends of Irvine Pub. Libr., 1974-75; mem. Com. for Freud Mus. Recipient Fritz Schmidl Meml. prize for rsch. applied psychoanalysis Seattle Assn. Psychoanalysis, 1982, Marie H. Briehl prize for child psychoanalysis, 1982, Franz Alexander prize in psychoanalysis, 1984, Disting. Writers award Antioch Rev., 2004; Morse rsch. fellow, 1963-64, Am. Philos. Soc. fellow, 1966, J.S. Guggenheim fellow, 1966-67, Rockefeller Found.humanities sr. fellow, 1975-76, Rsch. Clin. fellow So. Calif. Psychoanalytic Soc. 1977-81, Rockefeller fellow, Bellagio, Italy, 1983, NEH sr. fellow, 1983-84; Durfee Found. fellow to China, 2004; fellow Bogliasco Found. Liguria Ctr. for Arts and Humanities, 2004. Mem. So. Calif. Am. Studies Assn. (pres. 1969-71), Am. Studies Assn. (exec. bd. 1969-71, del. to MLA Assembly 1974, chmn. Ralph Gabriel prize com. 1975-77), MLA (chmn. prize com. Jay B. Hubbell Silver medal in Am. lit. 1978-84), Nat. Assn. Arts and Letters (prize com. 1987-88), Nat. Humanities Faculty (advisor to Valhalla High Sch., El Cajon, Calif. 1979-81), Nat. Am. Studies Faculty, Internat. Psychoanalytic Assn., Internat. Assn. Empirical Aesthetics, Internat. Assn. U. Profs. English, Internat. Karen Horney Soc., Newport Psychoanalytical Inst., Phi Beta Kappa. Home: 748 Via Santo Tomas Claremont CA 91711-1569 Home Phone: 909-624-8155; Office Phone: 909-398-0193. Personal E-mail: helenjay@ca.rr.com.

MARTIN, JOHN C., pharmaceutical company executive; b. Easton, Pa., 1951; BS in Chemical Engring., Purdue U., 1973; MBA in Mktg., Golden Gate U., 1974; PhD in Organic Chemistry, U. Chgo., 1977. With Syntex Corp., 1978-84; dir. antiviral chemistry Bristol-Myers Squibb Co., 1984-90; v.p. R&D Gilead Sciences, Inc., Foster City, Calif., 1990-95, COO, 1995-96, pres., CEO, 1996—2008, chmn., CEO, 2008—. Bd. dirs. Gilead Sciences, Inc., 1996—, Gen-Probe Inc., 2007—; chmn. Bay Area Bioscience Ctr., 1999—2001; mem. Nat. Inst. Allergy & Infectious Diseases Coun., 2000—03, Presdl. Advisory Coun. on HIV/AIDS, 2005—; bd. dirs. Calif. Healthcare Inst., 2003—, chmn. bd., 2005—06, 2008—. Bd. trustee U. Chgo., Golden Gate U. Recipient Isbell award, Am. Chemical Soc., Gertrude B. Elion award for Scientific Excellence, Internat. Soc. for Antiviral Rsch.; named to Nat. Acad. Engring. Nat. Academies, 2008. Mem.: Internat. Soc. for Antiviral Rsch. (pres. 1998—2000). Office: Gilead Scis Inc 333 Lakeside Dr Foster City CA 94404 *

MARTIN, JOSEPH BOYD, neurologist, educator, retired dean; b. Bassano, Alta., Can., Oct. 20, 1938; s. Joseph Bruce and Ruth Elizabeth (Ramer) Martin; m. Rachel Ann Wenger, June 18, 1960; children: Bradley, Melanie, Douglas, Neil. BSc, Eastern Mennonite Coll., Harrisonburg, Va., 1959; MD, U. Alta., 1962; PhD in Anatomy, U. Rochester, NY, 1971; MA (hon.), Harvard U., 1978; ScD (hon.), McGill U., 1994, U. Rochester, 1996, U. Wis., 1997, U. Alta., 1998, U. Montreal, 2007. Mem. faculty McGill U. Faculty Medicine, Montreal, Canada, 1970—78, chair, dept. neurology and neurosurgery, 1977—78; prof. medicine and neurology, neurologist-in-chief Montreal Neurol. Inst., 1976—78; Bullard prof. neurology, chief dept. neurology svc. Mass. Gen. Hosp., Boston, 1978—89; Julieanne Dorn prof. neurology Harvard U. Med. Sch., 1984; dean Sch. Medicine U. Calif., San Francisco, 1989—93; chancellor U. Calif., San Francisco, 1993—97; dean faculty medicine Harvard U. Med. Sch., Boston, 1997—2007, Lefler prof. neurobiology, 2007—. Editor: Harrison's Principles of Internal Medicine, 1980—99. Recipient Moshier Meml. gold medal, U. Alta. Faculty Medicine, 1962, John W. Scott gold med. award, 1962, Abraham Flexner award, AAMC, 1999, Henry Friesen Internat. prize, 2006. Fellow: Am. Acad. Arts and Scis.; mem.: NAS, Inst. of Medicine, Assn. Am. Physicians, Soc. Neurosci., Am. Neurol. Assn. (pres. 1990). Office: Department of Neurobiology Goldenson Bldg Long Wood Ave Boston MA 02115 Office Phone: 617-432-7197. E-mail: joseph_martin@hms.harvard.edu.

MARTIN, JOSEPH VINSON, neuroscientist, educator; b. Boston, Sept. 17, 1952; s. James Cullen and Mary Louise (Echols) M.; m. Jean Ann Rusteberg, Apr. 27, 1989; 1 child, Lara Jean. BA, Northwestern U., Evanston, Ill., 1973; PhD, U. So. Calif., 1987. Chemist NIMH, Bethesda, Md., 1982—87; postdoctoral rsch. assoc. SUNY, Stony Brook, 1987—88, rsch. instr.; asst. prof. Biology Dept., Rutgers U., Camden, NJ, 1989—95, assoc. prof., 1995—2004, prof., 2004—, chair, 2006—, acting dir. ctr. computational and integrative biology, 2007—09. Manuscript reviewer European Jour. Pharmacology, Hormones and Behavior, Neuroendocrinology, Pharmacology Biochemistry and Behavior, Sleep; lectr. in field. Contbr. articles to profl. jours. NIMH Predoctoral Rsch. fellowship, 1977-78, NSF grantee, 1994-97, 98-2001, 2002-04, 2004—08, 07-, Dean's Citation, UMDNJ. Mem. AAAS, Assn. Profl. Sleep Socs., Internat. Brain Rsch. Orgn., NJ Acad. Sci., NY Acad. Scis., Sleep Rsch. Soc., Soc. for Neuroscience. Business E-Mail: jomartin@camden.rutgers.edu.

MARTIN, KEITH ROBERT GRAHAM, ophthalmologist, researcher; b. Portadown, Northern Ireland, Apr. 4, 1969; s. Graham and Mabel Martin; m. Susan Harden, Sept. 21, 1996; children: Natalie, Peter, Andrew. MA, U. Cambridge, Eng., 1990; BMBCh, U. Oxford, Eng., 1993, DM, 2004. Cert. ALCM London Coll. Music, 1986. Med. intern John Radcliffe Hosp., Oxford, 1993—94, med. resident, 1995—95, Nat. Hosp. Neurology and Neurosurgery, London, 1994—94, Hammersmith Hosp., London, 1994—95; resident ophthalmology Hillingdon and Western Eye Hosps., London, 1995—96, Cambridge U. Tchg. Hosps. NHS Found. Trust, 1996—2000, sr. resident ophthalmology, cons. ophthalmologist, 2005—; rsch. fellow Wilmer Eye Inst., Johns Hopkins U., Balt., 2000—02; clin. fellow Moorfields Eye Hosp. and Inst. Ophthalmology, London, 2003—04, rsch. fellow; lectr. Cambridge U. Ctr. Brain Repair, 2005, prin. investigator; prof., ophthalmology U. Cambridge, 2010—. Co-chair basic sci. program com. World Glaucoma Congress, Singapore, 2007. Basic sci. sect. editor: Jour. Glaucoma, 2006—; contbr. scientific papers to profl. jours. Recipient Sir William Lister award, Royal Coll. Ophthalmologists, 2000, John Cairns Meml. prize, U. Cambridge, 2000, Arnall Patz Rsch. award, Wilmer Eye Inst., 2001, Glaucoma Fellows Merit award, Alcon USA, 2002, Clin. Excellence award, NHS, 2007, NC3R prize, 2009, AVRO Camras Translational Rsch. award, 2010, Sr. Clinician Scientist award, World Glaucoma Assn., 2011; Clinician Scientist fellowship, GSK, 2005—, Radcliffe Travelling fellowship, U. Oxford, 2000—02, Travelling fellowship, TFC Frost Trust, 2000—02, UK and Eire Glaucoma Soc., 2000—02. Fellow: Royal Coll. Ophthalmologists (Foulds trophy 2003); mem.: World Glaucoma Assn. (treas. 2009—), Am. Acad. Ophthalmology, Assn. Rsch. Vision and Ophthalmology, Royal Coll. Physicians. Avocations: piano, tennis, skiing, windsurfing, travel. Office: Cambridge Univ Ctr Brain Repair Forvie Site Robinson Way Cambridge CB2 0PY England Business E-Mail: krgm2@cam.ac.uk.

MARTIN, LEVINE S., physician; Studied, A.T. Still U. Health Sciences, 1980. Diplomate Am. Bd. Family Practice. Resident family medicine Kennedy Meml. Hosp.; with Bayonne Med. Ctr., Steinbaum Levine Assocs. LLC; physician Christ Hosp.; assoc. clin. prof. family medicine Seton Hall Univ. Sch. Health and Med. Sciences. Office: Christ Hospital 789 Ave C Bayonne NJ 07002 Office Phone: 201-339-2620. Office Fax: 201-339-2785.

MARTIN, MARCELLA EDRIC, retired community health nurse; b. Rosedale, Miss., Jan. 25, 1930; d. Amos and Alma Allen; m. Reuben Clifton Martin, Jan. 25, 1969; children: Brunetta, Jacqueline, Cornell, Constance. Student, Marygrove Coll., Detroit, 1971; ADN, Highland

Park Sch. Nursing, Mich., 1979; ThB, Cmty. Bible Coll., Detroit, 1968. Lic. LPN. Nurse VA Hosp., Ann Arbor, Mich., Crittendon Hosp., Detroit, Vis. Nurses Assn., Detroit. Instr. Charles H. Mason Bible Sch., Detroit, 1991—95; mem. C.O.G.I.C. Bus. owners Assn., 1982—. Author: Women Who Struggle, 2001; prodr.: (plays) And Didn't Those Knees Bow, 2004. Founder Prime of Life Adult Foster Care Home, 1979, Somebody's Got To Care Min., 2003; mem. Nat. Campaign Tolerance-The Wall of Tolerance, 2003; missionary over women Chs. of God in Christ, 1986—2002; vol. Redford Geriatric Home, Mich., 1999—. Recipient Spirit of Detroit award, City of Detroit, 1978, 2000, 2002, Disting. Citizen of Detroit award, 1980, Testimonial Resolution award, 1985; named to Wall of Tolerance, New Civil Rights Meml. Ctr., Montgomery, Ala., 2003. Mem.: Detroit Writers Guild. Democrat. Pentecostal Ch. Avocations: reading, writing. Home: 9610 Winthrop St Detroit MI 48227-1620 Personal E-mail: reumarone@comcast.net.

MARTIN, PETER ROBERT, psychiatrist, pharmacologist; b. Budapest, Hungary, Sept. 6, 1949; came to U.S., 1980; s. Nicholas M. and Eva (Horvat) M.; m. Barbara Bradford, Dec. 23, 1985; 1 child, Alexander Bradford. BSc with honors, McGill U., Montreal, Que., Can., 1971, MD, CM, 1975; MSc, U. Toronto, Ont., Can., 1978. Diplomate Am. Bd. Psychiatry and Neurology, Psychiatry, Addiction Psychiatry. Resident in internal medicine U. Toronto, 1975-76, resident in psychiatry, 1978-80; fellow clin. pharmacology Addiction Rsch. Found., Toronto, 1976-78; chief sect. clin. sci. Nat. Inst. on Alcohol Abuse & Alcoholism, Bethesda, 1983-86; assoc. prof. Vanderbilt U. Sch. Medicine, Nashville, 1986-92, prof., 1992—, dir. divsn. addiction psychiatry, 1986—, dir. addiction ctr., 1994—; dir. Vanderbilt Inst. for Coffee Studies, 1999—. Vis. scientist Lab. of Clin. Sci., NIMH, Bethesda, Md., 1980-83; investigator John F. Kennedy Ctr. for Rsch. on Human Devel., Nashville, 1993—. Fellow Royal Coll. Physicians (Can.), Am. Psychiat. Assn. (disting.), Am. Acad. Addiction Psychiatry (disting.); mem. AAAS, Rsch. Soc. on Alcoholism, Internat. Soc. Biomed. Rsch. in Alcoholism. Office: Vanderbilt Psychiat Hosp Ste 3068 1601 23rd Ave South Nashville TN 37212 Office Phone: 615-322-3527. E-mail: peter.martin@vanderbilt.edu.

MARTIN, RICHARD JAY, medical educator; b. Detroit, May 16, 1946; s. Peter Aaron and Tillie Jean (Munch) M.; m. Helene Iris Horowitz, Dec. 23, 1967; children: Elizabeth Hope, David Evan. BS, U. Mich., 1967, MD, 1971. Diplomate Am. Bd. Internal Medicine and Pulmonary Disease. Intern, Ariz., 1971-72; resident Tulane U., New Orleans, 1974-76; pulmonary fellow, 1976-78; asst. prof. medicine U. Okla., Okla. City, 1978-80, U. Colo., Denver, 1980-85, assoc. prof., 1985-92, prof., 1992—. Dir. Cardiorespiratory Sleep Rsch., Nat. Jewish Health, Denver, 1980-89, staff physician, 1980-, head divsn. pulmonary medicine, 1993-2005, vice-chair dept. medicine, 1997-2004, acting chair dept. medicine, 2004-2005, chair dept. medicine, 2006— . Author: Cardiorespiratory Disorders During Sleep, 1984, 2d edit., 1990, (with others) Current Therapy in Internal Medicine, 1984, Clinical Pharmacology and Therapeutics in Nursing, 1985, Interdisciplinary Rehabilitation of Multiple Sclerosis and Neuromuscular Disorders, 1984, Drugs for the Respiratory System, 1985, Current Therapy in Pulmonary Medicine, 1985, Abnormalities of Respiration During Sleep, 1986, Mitchell's Synopis of Pulmonary Medicine, 1987, Pulmonary Grand Rounds, 1990, Asthma and Rhinitis, 1994, The High Risk Patient: Management of the Critically Ill, 1995, Manual of Asthma Management, 1995, 2000, Severe Asthma: Pathogenesis and Clinical Management, 1995, Curret Pulmonology, 1995, Pulmonary and Respiratory Therapy Secrets, 1996, (book chpts.) Lung Biology in Health and Disease, 1995, 3d edit., 2000, Allergy, 1997, Asthma, 1997, Emergency Asthma, 1999, Difficult Asthma, 1999, Asthma and Rhinitis, 1999, Imaging of Diffuse Lung Disease, 2000, Manual of Asthma Management, 2000, Severe Asthma, 2001, Asthma Critical Debates, 2002, Inhaled Steroids in Asthma, 2002, The Merck Manual, 2002, Current Review of Asthma, 2003; editor: Nocturnal Asthma: Mechanisms and Interventions, 1993, Cardiothoracic Interrelationships in Clinical Practice, 1997; author, editor: Nocturnal Asthma: Mechanisms and Treatment, 1993, Combination Therapy for Asthma and Chronic Obstructive Pulmonary Disease, 2000; mem. editl. bd. Chronobiology Internat., 1997—, Am. Jour. Respiratory and Critical Care Medicine, 1994-98, Bronchial Asthma: Index and Review, 1996-97; assoc. editor: Clinical Care for Asthma, 1995-97; contbr. articles to profl. jours. Pres. Congregation Rodef Shalom, Denver, 1984-85; regional v.p. United Synagogues of Am., Denver, 1988-89. Recipient Best Paper in Internal Medicine award, Okla. Soc. Interna. Medicine, 1977—78, U. Okla. Gastroenterology sect, 1977, Amb. award, Nat. Jewish Med. and Rsch. Ctr., 2002; named Disting. Lectr., Royal Coll. Physicians and Surgeons Can., 1998, Cardio-Pulmonary Congress, Argentina, 1998, Assn. Argentina Allergy and Immunology, 2001; grantee Am. Lung Assn., Va., U. Okla. Lung Assn., NIH, Parker B. Francis Found.; Pulmonary fellow, Am. Lung Assn., 1977—79, James F. Hammarsten Outstanding fellow, U. Okla. Health Scis. Ctr., 1978. Mem. ACP, Am. Thoracic Soc., Am. Fedn. for Clin. Rsch., Am. Coll. Chest Physicians (Disting. scholar in respiratory health 2003-07, Colorado Pulmonary Hall of Fame, 2007), Colo. Trudeau Soc., Western Soc. Clin. Investigation. Avocations: biking, golf, Karate. Office: Nat Jewish Health 1400 Jackson St Denver CO 80206-2761 Office Phone: 303-398-1095. Business E-Mail: martinr@njhealth.org.

MARTIN, ROBERT B., dean, medical educator; B, Rutgers Coll., NJ; MD, Phila. Coll. Osteopathic Medicine. Cert. American Osteo. Bd. Phys. Medicine and Rehab., American Bd. Phys. Medicine and Rehab., American Bd. Neuromuscular and Electrodiagnostic Medicine. Residency tng. St. Vincent's Hosp. and Med. Ctr., NYC, sr. attending physician dept. phys. medicine and rehab.; prof., chmn. dept. rehab. medicine Phila. Coll. Osteopathic Medicine; clin. assoc. prof. rehab. medicine NY Med. Coll., Valhalla, NY; prof. phys. medicine Touro Coll. Osteopathic Medicine, NYC, former assoc. dean. cmty. med. affairs and advocacy, dean, 2008—. Former chmn. Coun. State Soc. Presidents; co-chmn. Carrier adv. com. Centers Medicare and Medicaid Services. Mem.: American Osteopathic Assn. (former pres. Coll. Rehab.), NY County Med. Soc. (former pres., former chmn. bd. trustees, former chmn. managed care task force), American Acad. Phys. Medicine and Rehab (former chmn. profl. med. practice com.), Med. Soc. of State of NY (pres. 2007). Office: Touro Coll Osteopathic Medicine Office of Dean 230 W 125th St New York NY 10027 Office Phone: 646-981-4534. *

MARTIN, THIERRY, immunologist, researcher; b. Montbeliard, Doubs, France, Jan. 24, 1958; MD, Strasbourg U., PhD, 1982. Cert. prof. French Ministery Edn., 1995. Postdoc. fellow UCSD, San Diego, 1989—90; head clin. immunology ward Strasbourg U. Hosp., Bas-Rhin, France, 1995—; dir. UPR CNRS 9021, Strasbourg, 2001—. Mem.: French Soc. Immunology. Achievements include research in many works on autoimmune diseases. Office: Strasbourg Univ Hosp NHC 1 Place De L'Hopital Strasbourg Bas-Rhin 67091 France Office Fax: 33 369 550 396.

MARTIN, THOMAS JOHN, pediatrician, sports medicine physician; b. Greensburg, Pa., July 4, 1934; s. John William and Mary DeTar Martin; m. Lois Darlene Miller, June 20, 1992; children: Jack T., Susan L. O'Malley, James S., David S. BS, Franklin and Marshall Coll., Lancaster, Pa., 1956; MD, U. Pitts., 1960. Diplomate Am. Bd. Pediats. Gen. practice medicine, Slippery Rock, Pa., 1961—62, 1964—65; pediat. resident Children's Hosp. of Pitts., 1965—67; assoc. in pediats. Geisinger Med. Ctr., Danville, Pa., 1967—75, chmn. pediats., 1975—95; dir. inpatient pediats. Aultman Hosp., Canton, Ohio, 1995—97; team physician, prof. Pa. State U., University Park, 1997—2004, clin. prof. pediats., Milton S. Hershey Med. Ctr., 2005—; assoc. program dir. family practice residency The Williamsport (Pa.) Hosp., 2004—; prof. emeritus dept. orthop. and rehab. Hershey Med. Ctr., 2005—; dir. pediat. hosp. level II nursery svc., 2004—; vice chmn. pediat., 2008—; dir. pediat. edn. Commonwealth Med. Coll., 2010—. Adj. clin. assoc. prof. Jefferson Med. Coll., Phila.; team physician football, wrestling Pa. State U., University Park, 1997—2004; courtesy staff Lewistown (Pa.) Hosp., 1999—2004; active staff Nittery Med. Ctr., State College, Pa., 1997—2004, Children's Hosp. Med. Ctr. of Akron, Ohio, 1995—97; lectr. in field. Contbr. articles to profl. jours. Pres. Riverside Home and Sch., Pa., 1968—69, coach, organizer Danville H.S. Swim Team, 1974; pres. Riverside Home and Sch. Assn., 1968—69; mem. global mission com. Upper Susquehanna Synod Coun., 1999—2003; fin. com. Pine St. Luth. Ch., Danville, 1994—96, coun. mem., 1993—95, chmn. religious com., 1993—95; bd. dirs. Sunbury Area YMCA, Pa., 1976—84. Capt. US Army, 1962—64. Recipient Honors for Exceptional Svc. to Children and Youth, Nat. Child Labor Com., N.Y.C., 1995, Best Tchg. award, 2009; named Citizen of the Yr., Elks, 1995; named to Geisinger's Pediat. Wall of Fame, 2005. Mem.: AMA, Nat. Wrestling Coaches Assn., Pa. Med. Soc. (continuing med. edn. accreditation surveyor 1988—93), Am. Coll. Sports Medicine, Am. Acad. Pediats. (com. on sports medicine and fitness 1998—2004, exec. com. sect. on sports medicine 1997—2003, chpt. chmn. 1980—82), Lycoming County Med. Soc., Am. Bd. Pediats. Lutheran. Avocations: running, skiing, swimming. Home: 23 E Hayes Crossing Belleville PA 17004 Office: Susquehanna Health System 777 Rural Ave Williamsport PA 17701 Office Phone: 570-321-2810. Business E-Mail: tmartin@susquehannahealth.org.

MARTIN, THOMAS REED, medical educator, medical association administrator; BA in Chemistry, Macalester Coll., St. Paul, 1969; MD, U. Pa., 1973. Cert. in internal medicine, pulmonary medicine critical care medicine. Intern, pulmonary medicine U. Wash., Seattle, 1973—74, resident, 1974—77, fellow, pulmonary and critical care medicine, 1978—80, asst. prof. medicine, 1982-85, assoc. prof. medicine to prof. medicine, 1985—91, prof. medicine, 1991—, dir., Pulmonary Rsch. Training Prog., 1990—99, vice chair dept. medicine, 2000—; chief medicine svc. VA Pugent Sound Health Care Sys., Seattle, 2000—. Vis. scientist, dept. immunology Scripps Rsch. Inst., La Jolla, Calif., 1989—90; vis. scientist, dept. biochemsitry Geneva Biomedical Rsch. Inst. & Hosp. U. Geneva (Switzerland), 1997—98. Contbr. several articles to profl. jours. Mem. NIH Rsch. Fund, Va Rsch. Fund; bd. dirs. ABIM, 2006—10; sci. dir. Parker B. Francis Fellowship Program, 2008—. Mem.: Am. Thoracic Soc. (former pres.). Office: Va Puget Sound Med Ctr Hosp and Splty Medicine 1660 S Columbian Way Seattle WA 98108 Office Phone: 206 764-2345, 206-764-2219. Office Fax: 206-768-5289. Business E-Mail: trmartin@u.washington.edu.

MARTIN, VINCENT THOMAS, internist, educator; b. May 11, 1958; MD, U. Cin., 1984. Diplomate Am. Bd. Internal Medicine, cert. in headache medicine. Residency/fellowship gen. medicine U. Cin. Med. Ctr.; prof. dept. internal medicine U. Cin. Coll. Medicine. Bd. dirs. Nat. Headache Found. Assoc. editor Jour. Headache; contbr. articles to profl. jours. Named a Top Doctor, Cin. Mag., 2010. Mem.: ACP, Internat. Headache Soc., Am. Headache Soc. (bd. dirs. 2002—08). Office: U Cin Physicians 222 Piedmont Ave Ste 6000 Cincinnati OH 45219 Office Phone: 513-475-7880. Office Fax: 513-475-8766.

MARTIN-CONTE, ERICA L., physiologist, researcher; b. Hamilton, Ont., Can., Aug. 31, 1978; BSc in Physiology with honor, U. Western Ont., 2001, PhD in Physiology, 2006. Postdoc. fellow U. Turin, Italy, 2006—11, rschr., 2011—. Postdoc. fellowship, Can. Inst. Health Rsch. Office: Cso Dogliotti 14 Anestesiologia & Rian Turin 10126 Italy Office Fax: 390116960448 Business E-Mail: ericaleanne.martin@unito.it.

MARTINELLI, VINCENZO, medical educator, researcher; b. Naples, Italy, Oct. 13, 1954; Degree in Medicine and Surgery, U. Naples Federico, 1980; degree in Hematology, U. Catania, 1984. Med. rschr. gen., clin., pediatric nursing sci. U. Naples Federico, 2004—11, assoc. prof., 2006—. Mem.: Soc. Italiana di Ematologia. Avocations: sailing, rock climbing. Office: Via Pansini 5 Naples 80131 Italy Office Fax: 0817462165. Business E-Mail: vincenzo.martinelli@unina.it.

MARTINEZ, BELINDA, health insurance company executive; MBA, U. Southern Calif.; MPH, Loma Linda U. Joined Delta Dental Ins. Co., 1988, dir., acct. svcs., Delta Dental, sr. v.p., mktg.; COO Delta Dental Insurance Co., 2003—; v.p., profl. svcs. PMI Dental Health Plan Delta Insurance Co., v.p., underwriting & fin., 1999—2001, sr. v.p., COO, 2001—. Named one of Top 10 Latinos in Healthcare, LatinoLeaders mag., 2004. Office: Delta Dental Insurance Co 100 1st St Fl 4 San Francisco CA 94105 Office Phone: 415-972-8400. Office Fax: 415-972-8429. Business E-Mail: bmartinez@deltadental.com.

MARTÍNEZ, LEANDRO MANUEL, pediatrician; b. Ciudad Victoria, Oct. 27, 1980; Degree in Pediat., UANL, 2009; degree in Pediatric Pneumology, UNAM, 2011. Resident Hosp. U. UANL, 2006—09, Inst. Nat. Pediatria UNAM, 2009—11. Home: Carretera Nacional 6501 Col La Estanzu Monterrey Nuevo Leon 64988 Mexico Personal E-mail: drleandromtz@hotmail.com.

MARTINEZ, LUPE, psychologist, director; b. Madrid, June 16, 1967; MD, Autonoma Madrid, 1991; degree in Psychiatry, Hosp. Rodriguez Lafora, Madrid, 1996. Med. affairs dir. psychiatry Janssen, Pharm. Cos. J & J, 2008—. Avocations: ice skating, movies. Home: Santa Hortensia 35 5A Madrid 28002 Spain Personal E-mail: lupecia1967@gmail.com.

MARTINEZ, MARIA DOLORES, pediatrician; b. Cifuentes, Cuba, Mar. 16, 1959; d. Demetrio and Alba Silvia (Perez) M. MD, U. Navarra, Pamplona, Spain, 1984. Med. diplomate. Resident in pediatrics Moses Cone Hosp., Greensboro, NC, 1986-89; pvt. practice Charlotte, NC, 1989-93, Mooresville, NC, 1993-96; pediat. pulmonary fellow Univ. Med. Hosp., Tucson, 1996-99; pediatric pulmonologist, also in sleep medicine/transplants Duke U., Durham, NC, 1999—, dir. pediat. lung transplant svcs., assoc. dir. sleep medicine lab., 2000—, St. Joseph's Hosp., Phoenix, 2004. Mem. AMA, Am. Acad. Pediat. Republican. Roman Catholic. Avocations: horseback riding, travel. Office: St Joseph s Hosp and Med Ctr 222W Thomas Rd Ste 410 Phoenix AZ 85013 Office Phone: 602-406-4645. Personal E-mail: maria.martinez2@chw.edu.

MARTINEZ, MIGUEL ACEVEDO, urologist, consultant, lecturer; b. Chihuahua, Mex., Aug. 18, 1953; came to US, 1956; s. Miguel Nuñez and Velia (Acevedo) M. AB, Stanford U., 1976; MD, Yale U., 1983. Diplomate Am. Bd. Urology. Intern U. SC Med. Ctr., 1983—84; resident, urology White Meml. Med. Ctr., LA, 1984-89, urologist, 1989—, treas. & sec. staff, 2009—10. Cons., lectr. physician asst. program U. So. Calif., LA, 1990—, clin. instr.; patient edn. cons. ICI Pharm., Del., 1991—, Zeneca's Speaker Forum; patient edn. and med. cons., lectr. Abbott Labs., 1991—; mem. edn.cons. several radio/TV stas., 1991—; mem. subcom. for diseases on kidney and transplantation NIH, Washington, 1991; mem. nat. Hispanic adv. bd. Pfizer Pharms., Inc., 1998—; mem. adv. bd. Glaxo Smith Kline, 2002—; cons. spkrs. bur. Pfizer, Bayer/ESK. Author: Intercellular Pathways, 1981; editor, contbg. writer: Optimizing the Treatment of Design Prostatic Hyperplasia in African American And Latin American Men the American Journal Medicine, supplement, 2008. Polit. cons. Xavier Becerra, US Congress, 1992, Martin Gallegos, Gil Cedillo, Calif. State Assembly, 1993, others; bd. dirs. Latino Ctr. for Prevention and Action in Health, Orange County, calif.; bd. govs., sec., rep. Zeneca Urology Econ. Summit, Washington, 1993; mem. Pfizer Nat. Hispanic Adv. Bd. Named Nat. Male Outstanding Teenage of Am., 1971, America's Top Physician, 2007-10, Best Dr. Pasadena Mag. Ann. Survey, 2010, One of Outstanding Young Men of Am., 1981; named one of America's Top Physicians, 2005, 06-09, Top Drs. San Gabriel Valley, Pasadena, Mag. Calif.; recipient Philanthropic Leadership award Philanthropic Svc. Instns., 2006; Nat. Hispanic Med. Assn. Pub. Policy fellow, 2000-01. Mem. AMA, Nat. Hispanic Med. Assn. (public policy fellow), Am. Urological Assn., Calif. Med. Assn. (polit. action com. bd. dirs. 1997—, del.), LA Med. Assn. (polit. action com. 1992—), LA County Med. Assn., Yale Alumni Assn., Stanford Alumni Assn., LA Athletic Club. Office: 1701 Cesar Chavez Ave Ste 500 Los Angeles CA 90033 Office Phone: 323-224-6202, 323-261-0108. Personal E-mail: uromd53@gmail.com.

MARTINEZ, ROSE MARIE, health science association administrator; DSc, Johns Hopkins Sch. Hygiene and Pub. Health. Directing rsch. studies Regional Health Ministry of Madrid, Spain, 1982—88; asst. dir. health financing and policy U.S. Gen. Acctg. Office, 1988—95; sr. health rschr. Mathematica Policy Rsch., 1995—99; dir., Health Promotion and Disease Prevention Bd. Inst. of Medicine-Nat. Academics, 1999— . Office: Institute of Medicine 500 Fifth St NW Keck 855 Washington DC 20001 Office Phone: 202-334-2655.

MARTÍNEZ-CARPIO, PEDRO ANTONIO, physician; b. Barcelona, 1966; s. Benito Martínez and María Luisa (Carpio). MD, U. Autónoma de Barcelona, 1991, PhD cum laude, 1999. Prof, clin. chemistry U. Barcelona, 1994—98; prof. human physiology U. Autónoma de Barcelona, 1999—; dir. rsch. unit Ctr. Oftalmológico Bonafonte, Barcelona, 2003—, dir. gen. medicine unit, dir. lasser medicine and surgery unit, 2003—. Avocations: music, astronomy, paleontology. Office: Centro de Oftalmología Bonafonte Pasaje Méndez Vigo 6 08009 Barcelona Spain Home: Gran Via Corts Catalanes 275 3 8a Izq 8014 Barcelona Spain

MARTINEZ-CONDE, SUSANA, neurologist, researcher; married. PhD in Neuroscience, U. Santiago de Compostela, Spain, 1996. Fellow Harvard Med. Sch.; dir. & prin. investigator Visual Neuroscience Lab. Barrow Neurological Inst. Founding mem. & executive chmn. Neural Correlate Soc. Mem.: Assn. for Scientific Study of Consciousness. Office: Barrow Neurological Institute St Josephs Hospital 350 W Thomas Rd Phoenix AZ 85013

MARTINEZ-LOPEZ, JORGE IGNACIO, internist, educator, cardiologist, consultant, b. Santurce, PR, Oct. 5, 1926; s. Jorge Martinez-Rivera and Dolores (Lopez) Martinez; m. Mona Hagan, June 12, 1950 (div. 1982); children: Jorge Alan, Anthony James, Ricardo, Matthew Joseph; m. Glenda Gayle Tomlinson, Mar. 4, 1983. MD, La. State U., 1950. Diplomate Am. Bd. Internal Medicine, Am. Bd. Cardiovascular Diseases. Intern Arecibo Dist. Hosp., PR, 1950-51; resident in internal medicine La. State U. Medicine Svc., Charity Hosp. La., New Orleans, 1954-57; trainee in cardiology, instr. dept. medicine La. State U. Med. Ctr., 1957-59, asst. prof., 1960-63, assoc. prof., 1963-70, prof., 1970-86, prof. emeritus, 1986—; clin. prof. dept. internal medicine Tex. Tech. U. Health Scis. Ctr., Lubbock, 1988; prof. dept. internal medicine Tex. Tech. U. Health Sci. Ctr., El Paso, 1988—; mem. staff R. E. Thomason Gen. Hosp., U. Med. Ctr., El Paso. Cardiologist Heart Sta., Charity Hosp. La., 1960-75, dir. dept. cardiology, 1975-86, vis. physician, 1957-64, sr. vis. physician, 1964-86; cardiologist Hotel Dieu, New Orleans, 1961-86, dir. cardiology dept., 1970-75; dir. cardiac work evaluation unit Delgado Rehab. Ctr., New Orleans, 1967-86; cons. cardiology Edward F. Hebert Meml. Hosp., USN, Gretna, La., 1977-78; bd. govs. Orleans Parish Med. Soc., 1974-76; v.p. New Orleans Acad. Internal Medicine, 1969-70, pres., 1970-71. Contbr. more than 300 articles to profl. jour. Col. U.S. Army, 1951-53, 86-88, res. 1953-88, ret. Scholar Govt. P.R., 1947-50. Fellow Am. Coll. Cardiology, Am. Coll. Chest Physicians, Am. Coll. Physicians, Am. Heart Assn., Coun. Clin. Cardiology; mem. Am. Heart Assn. (fellow Coun. Clin. Cardiology, La. bd. dir. 1965-86, v.p. 1972-73, pres.-elect 1973-74, pres. 1974-75, El Paso div. pres.-elect 1989-90, pres. 1990-91, bd. dir. 1989—), Assn. Army Cardiology, La. State Med. Soc., Res. Officers Assn. (La. dept. surgeon 1963-69, 74-75, pres. Chpt. 19, 1963-69), Mil. Officers Assn. Am. Avocations: photography, music, painting. Office: Tex Tech U Health Science Ctr 4800 Alberta Ave El Paso TX 79905-2709 *

MARTINEZ-MALDONADO, MANUEL, academic administrator, medical and science educator; b. Yauco, PR, Aug. 25, 1937; s. Manuel and Josefa Maldonado (Josefa Maldonado) Martinez; m. Nivia Elena Rivera, Dec. 18, 1959; children: Manuel, David, Ricardo, Pablo. BS, U. PR, 1957; MD, Temple U., 1961. Diplomate Am. Bd. Internal Medicine, Am. Bd. Nephrology. Intern St. Charles Hosp., Toledo, 1961—62; resident VA Hosp., San Juan, 1962—65, chief resident, 1964—65, chief med. svcs., 1973—90, co-dir. renal metabolic lab., 1973—90; instr. U. Tex. Southwestern Med. Sch., Dallas, 1967—68; from asst. prof. to prof. medicine, co-dir. renal sect. Baylor Coll. Medicine, Houston, 1968—73; prof. medicine U. PR Sch. Medicine, 1973—90, prof. physiology, 1974—90; prof. medicine U. Caribbean, Bayamon, PR, 1980—90; prof., vice chmn. dept. medicine Emory U. Sch. Medicine, 1990—98; chief med. svcs. and clin. affairs Atlanta VA Med. Ctr., 1990—98; v.p. for rsch., prof. medicine Oreg. Health Scis. U., Portland, 1998—99, v.p. rsch., 1999—2000; pres., dean, prof. medicine and physiology Ponce Sch. Medicine, 2000—06; prof. medicine, pharmacology, toxicology U. Louisville, 2007—, exec. v.p. rsch., 2007—. Assoc. mem. nephrology com. Am. Bd. Internal Medicine, 1982—86; nat. adv. bd. gen. medicine B study sect. Nat. Inst. Arthritis, Metabolism and Digestive Diseases NIH; bd. sci. counselors, sci. advisors com. Nat. Heart, Lung and Blood Inst., NIH. Author: La Voz Sostenida, 1984, Palm Beach Blues, 1986, Por Amor al Arte, 1989, Hotel Maria, 1989, Isla Verde, 1999, Novela de Mediodia, 2003; film critic: El Reportero, 1983—86, El Mundo, 1987—90, editor/co-editor: in field, mem. editl. bd.: U. P.R. Press; editor: Am. Jour. of Med. Scis., 1994—98, Am. Jour. Kidney Disease, 1997—2002; contbr. over 200 articles to profl. jours. Com. mem. 500th Anniversary of Discovery Am., PR, 1987—92; pres. bd. trustees Inst. Puerto Rican Culture and Performing Arts Ctr., 2001—05; trustee Corp. Musical Arts, 2001—05, Inst. Puerto Rican Lit., 2001—05; chair culture and recreation panel PR 2025; health com. Popular Dem. Com., PR, 1982—84; bd. dirs. Alliance for PR, Inc., bd. sec., 2004—06. Recipient Lederle Internat. award, Lederle Corp., 1966—67, Macy Faculty Scholar award, The Josiah Macy Jr. Found., 1979—80, Grand Mobil prize medicine, Mobil Oil Corp., 1981, Disting. Alumnus award, Temple Med. Sch., 1988, Presdl. award, Nat. Kidney Found., 1988, Donald W. Seldin award, 1994, Disting. Physician award, PR Hosps. Assn., 1988, Orden del Cafetal award, Municipality of Yauco, 1989, Abelardo Díaz Alfaro award, Medicine & Humanites Acad. of Family Medicine, 2002, Svc. Exec. award, PR Mfrs. Assn., 2005, Svc. Exec. of Yr. award, PR Mfrs. Assn. (So. region), 2006; named one of Outstanding Young Men, PR C. of C., 1976. Master: ACP; fellow: AAAS, Am. Heart Assn. (hypertension rsch. coun.), Coun. for High Blood Pressure Rsch.; mem.: Am. Acad. Arts and Scis. (hon. fgn.), Nat. Kidney Found. (chmn. pub. policy com. 1992—94, chmn. sci. adv. com. 1987—91, Pub. Svc. medal, Donald W. Seldin award), Consortium Southeastern Hypertension Ctrs. (bd. dirs.), Assn. Am. Physicians, Inter-Am. Soc. Hypertension Assn. (bd. govs., chmn. 8th Sci. Congress 1989, U.S. Pharmacopeial Conv. Cardio Renal Drugs com. 1990—96), L.Am. Soc. Nephrology (v.p. 1987—91, pres.-elect 1991—94, pres. 1994—96, Miatello award 1999), Am. Soc. for Clin. Investigation, So. Soc. Clin. Investigation (sec.-treas. 1983—85, pres. 1985—86, Founders medal 1990), Am. Soc. Nephrology (legis. liaison com., chmn. audit com. 1988), Inst. Medicine of NAS (com. on human rights 1987—92), Alpha Omega Alpha. Roman Catholic. Achievements include research in kidney physiology and pathophysiology, treatment of clinical disturbances of blood composition, clinical use of diuretics, mechanisms of the devel. of hypertension. Avocations: theater, art, music, poetry, films. Office: U Louisville Rm 200 Jouett Hall 2310 S Third St Louisville KY 40292 Office Phone: 502-852-8373. Business E-Mail: m0mart10@louisville.edu. *

MARTINEZ MONCADA, RODNEY ALBERTO, health products executive, researcher; b. Caracas, Libertador, Venezuela, Apr. 27, 1951; s. Alberto Pedro Martinez Arbona and Maria Celia Moncada de Martinez; m. Maria de los Santos Rodriguez, July 7, 1973; children: Marianella Martinez Rodriguez, Rodney Alberto Jr. Martinez Rodriguez, Roman Alberto Martinez Rodriguez, Reyner Eduardo Martinez Rodriguez. B in Adminstrn., Instituto Superior Universitario, Caracas, Venezuela, 1980; D (hon.), Yorker Internat. U., Florence, Italy, 2006. Pres., CEO, founder Producciones Rodeneza, C.A., Caracas, 1984—, Notisalud, C.A., Libertador, 1991—, Pubes Publicidad, C.A., 1998—; founder, pres. Asesores Regimar, C.A., 2002—; founder Laboratorios Rodeneza Europas, S.L., Madrid, 2300—; founder, pres. Ropenezaticr, S.A., San Jose, Costa Rica, 2004—. Mag. editor NOTISALUD, Caracas, 1991—; health and leadership lectr. various hosps., Caracas, 1994—. Hon. mem. Nursing Coll., Caracas, Venezuela, 2002, Coro, Venezuela, 2002. Recipient Gt. Comdr. Order Liberator Simon Bolivar, Brazilian Acad. Culture, History and Sciences, 2004, Nat. Prestige, Venezuelan Managerial Assn., 1990. Mem.: Nursing Coll. Coro (hon.), Nursing Coll. Caracus (hon.), Venezuelan Assn. Med. Instruments Manufacturers (assoc.; pres. 2000—04), Los Canales de Rio Chico Golf Club (assoc.), Magnum City Club (assoc.). Roman Catholic. Achievements include invention of medical and surgical disinfectant GERDEX - 1987; Surgical Brush GER-SOLAB - 1992; Soap NEAT - 1993; Moist Towellete FLORENS - 1994; detergent - Disinfectant KHAM - 1997. Avocations: golf, travel, diving, music, reading. Office: Producciones Rodeneza CA Lecuna St Rodeneza Bldg Boleita sur Miranda 1071 Caracas Venezuela Fax: 58212 2376260. Business E-Mail: presidencia@rodeneza.com.ve. E-mail: rodeneza@cantv.net.

MARTINEZ-SAID, HECTOR, oncologist, consultant; b. Mex. City, May 12, 1968; MD, U. Anahuac, 1991; PhD student, Inst. Poly. Nat. Surg. oncologist, Melanoma Clinic Inst. Nat. Cancerología, 2002—, pres. med. soc., 2009—10; pres., melanoma chpt. Soc. Mexicana de Oncología, 2005—09. Office: Puente de Piedra # 150 S1 Col Toriell Mexico City 14050 Mexico Office Fax: 52 55 5424 7210. Personal E-mail: mtzsaid@hotmail.com.

MARTÍNEZ-SALAMANCA, JUAN IGNACIO, urologist; b. Madrid, Oct. 4, 1976; Degree, U. Complutense, Madrid, 2000; degree in urology, Gregorio Marañon Hosp. Gen. U. Madrid., 2006. Attending urologist Hosp. U. Puerta De Hierro-majadahonda, Madrid, 2007—. Editor newsletter European Soc. Sexual Medicine, 2009. Rsch. grant, Prostate Cancer Found., 2006, Endourological Soc. Gyrus Acmi Corp., 2006—07, Mutua Madrileña Med. Found. Mem.: Spanish Assn. Urology, European Assn. Urology, Am. Urology Assn. Home: Cerro del Castañar 8C Madrid 28034 Spain Home Fax: 34915348983. Personal E-mail: msalamanca99@hotmail.com.

MARTINEZ-SANCHIS, SONIA, psychotherapist, educator; b. Valencia, Spain, Sept. 4, 1967; d. Miguel Martinez Fuster and Concepcion Sanchis Raga; m. Antonio Torregrosa Maicas, Dec. 20, 2003; 1 child, Antonio Torregrosa Martinez. Degree in Psychology, U. Valencia, 1990, MD, 1995. Assoc. lectr. U. Valencia, 1995—2002, lectr., 2002—. Cons. psychotherapist, Valencia, 1995—2005. Contbr. scientific papers. Fellow, U. Valencia, 1994—95. Avocations: reading, mountain climbing, travel. Office: Facultad de Psicologia Psicobiologia Blasco Ibañez 21 Valencia 46010 Spain Office Fax: 34 963864668. Business E-Mail: sonia.mtnez-sanchis@uv.es.

MARTIN-FARDON, REMI, pharmacologist; b. Montpellier, France, Apr. 12, 1968; PhD, U. Montpellier II, 1996. Staff scientist The Scripps Rsch. Inst., 2004—. Mem.: Rsch. Soc. Alcoholism, Internat. Brain Rsch. Orgn., Am. Soc. Pharmacology and Exptl. Therapeutics, Coll. Problems Drug Dependence, Soc. Neurosci. Avocations: running, movies. Office: The Scripps Research Inst 10550 N Torrey Pines Rd SP30-2120 La Jolla CA 92037 Business E-Mail: rmartinf@scripps.edu.

MARTÍN FERNÁNDEZ, PILAR, biologist; b. Madrid, Aug. 22, 1973; B in Biol. Scis., U. Complutense Madrid, 1996, PhD in Immunology, 2001. Postdoc. rsch. fellow Consejo Superior de Investigaciones Científicas, 2001—02, rsch. scientist of i3p program, 2002—06; rsch. scientist. ramón y cajal program. Nat. Ctr. Cardiovasc. Rsch., 2007—10, head lab., 2010—. Reviewer, cons. Agencia Nacional de Evaluación y Prospectiva, Spain, 2008; peer-reviewer Blood, 2008, Molecular Medicine, 2010, Immunotherapy, Future Sci. Group, 2011; mem. editl. bd. Am. Jour. Cardiovasc. Disease, 2011. Named one of Best Rsch. Scientist I3P program, NRC, Spain; Rsch. fellowship, Comunidad de Madrid Govt. Mem.: Spanish Soc. Immunology. Avocations: mountain climbing, sports, dance. Office: Melchor Fernández Almagro 3 CNIC Madrid E-28029 Spain Business E-Mail: pmartinf@cnic.es.

MARTINO, PABLO EDUARDO, research scientist, educator; b. La Plata, Buenos Aires, Dec. 19, 1956; s. Juan José Martino and Nelly Edith Galli; m. Mirta Alicia Prestia. Degree in Med. Vet., La Plata U., 1979, PhD, 1985; MS in Biology (hon.), Middlcham U., North Yorkshire, Eng., 2006. Sci. rschr. CIC, Buenos Aires Rsch. Coun., La Plata, 1987—; asst. prof. Vet. Scis. Coll., UNLP, La Plata, 1993—. Cons. FADEPEL, Buenos Aires, 1981—96. Contbr. rsch. articles to sci. jours. Directive Assn. Argentina Zoonosis, Buenos Aires, 2005—08. Mem.: NY Acad. Scis. Office: CIC Scientific Rsch Coun Calle 526 e/ 10 y 11 La Plata Buenos Aires 1900 Argentina

MARTINO, ROBERT SALVATORE, retired orthopedic surgeon; b. Clarksburg, W.Va., May 31, 1931; s. Leonard L. and Sarafina (Foglia) M.; m. Lenora Cappellanti, May 22, 1954; children: Robert S. Jr., Leslie L. Reckziegel. AB, W.Va. U., 1953, postgrad., 1955-56, BS in Medicine, 1958; MD, Northwestern U., 1960. Diplomate Am. Bd. Orthop. Surgery; lic. Ill., Calif., Ind. Intern Chgo. Wesley, 1960-61; resident dept. orthopaedic surgery Northwestern U., 1961-65, Chgo. Wesley Meml., 1961-62, Am. Legion Hosp. for Crippled Children, 1962-63, Cook County Hosp., Chgo., 1964, 64-65; orthop. surgeon Gary, Ind., 1965-67, Merrillville, Ind., 1967—2010. Fellow Nat. Found. Infantile Paralysis, 1956, Office of Vocat. Rehab., Hand Surgery, 1965; chief of staff St. Mary Med. Ctr., 1976, chief of surgery, 1974-85; chief of staff Gary Treatment Ctr./Ind. Crippled Children's Svcs., 1974-84; adj. asst. prof. anatomy Ind. U., 1978, clin. asst. prof. orthop. surgery, 1980, emeritus asst. prof. anatomy and cell biology Ind. U., 2003, emeritus clin. asst. prof. orthop. surgery, 2003; mem. Zoning Bd., 1989-90. Chmn. Planning Bd. Town of Dune Acres, 1992-96; bd. dirs. United Steel Workers Union Health Plan, 1994—, St. Mary's Med. Ctr., Hobart, Ind.; com. on Health Care Reform. Capt. infantry US Army, 1953—55, active duty USAR, 1955—58. Fellow ACS (emeritus), Am. Acad. Orthop. Surgery (emeritus); mem. AMA, NRA, Ind. Med. Soc., Ill. Med. Soc., Chgo. Med. Soc., Ill. Orthop. Soc., Ind. Orthop. Soc., Mid-Am. Orthop. Assn., Tri-State Orthop. Soc., Clin. Orthop. Soc., Tri-State Sons Italy. Republican. Roman Catholic. Home: 22 Oak Dr Chesterton IN 46304-1016 Personal E-mail: beutabobm@aol.com.

MARTINO, SAL, medical association administrator; 3 children. BA in Polit. Sci., CUNY: Queens Coll., Flushing; grad., NY Hosp. Sch. Radiography, 1976; M in Hosp. Adminstrn., 1979; M in Health Edn., CUNY: Lehman Coll., Bronx, 1986; M in Higher Edn., Columbia U., NYC, 1989, EdD, 1991. Cert. Am. Soc. Assn. Execs., 2005. Darkroom tech. Queens Gen. Hosp.; asst. prof. to prof. radiologic tech. CUNY: Hostos CC, NYC, 1979—99, dir. radiologic tech. program, chmn. allied health dept., assoc. dean academic affairs; dir. edn. Am. Soc. Radiologic Technologists, Albuquerque, 1999—2000, v.p. edn. rsch., 2000—01, COO, Edn. Rsch. Found., 2001—, exec. v.p., chief academic officer, 2001—08, CEO, 2008—. Bd. dirs. NYC Soc. Radiologic Technologists, 1982—86; bd. trustees Am. Registry Radiologic Technologists, 1987—95; vice chmn. exam com. Am. Soc. Assn. Execs., mem. health care cmty. com. Fellow: Am. Soc. Radiologic Technologists; mem.: Commn. Accreditation Allied Health Edn. Programs, Acad. Radiology Rsch. Office: Am Soc Radiologic Technologists 15000 Ctrl Ave SE Albuquerque NM 87123-3909 *

MARTINO, SILVANA, osteopath, medical oncologist; b. Guardia Piemontese, Italy, Sept. 7, 1948; came to U.S., 1958; d. Antonio and Elena (Iannuzzi) M. BS in Psychology, Wayne State U., 1970; DO, Mich. State U., 1973. Bd. cert. internal medicine and med. oncology. Intern Detroit Osteo. Hosp., 1973-74; resident in internal medicine Botsford Hosp., Farmington, Mich., 1974-77; fellow in oncology Wayne State U. Sch. Medicine, Detroit, 1977-79, asst. prof. med., 1979-88, assoc. prof., 1988-93; med. dir. Westlake Comprehensive Breast Ctr., Westlake Village, Calif., 1993-97, Breast Ctr., Van Nuys, Calif., 1997-99; med. oncologist John Wayne Cancer Inst., Santa Monica, Calif., 1999—; dir., Breast Cancer Program, Angeles Clinic & Rsch. Inst., 1999—2011, Breast Cancer Rsch. and Edn., Angeles Clinic Found., 2011. Full-time staff Harper-Grace Hosps., Detroit, 1979-93, coord. oncology housestaff 1979-83; univ. affiliate, sect. of oncology, dept. medicine, Hutzel Hosp., Detroit, 1979-93; clin. advisor breast cancer prognostic study Mich. Cancer Found., Detroit, 1981-86; univ. affiliate dept. medicine Detroit Receiving Hosp., 1983-93; adj. faculty dept. medicine Wayne State U. 1989-92; mem. oncology drug adv. com. FDA, 2002—, chair, 2005—, dir., Cancer Program LA Clinic & Rsch. Inst., 1994-2011, Breast Cancer Edn. & Rsch., The Angeles Clinic Found., 2011-; spkr. in field. Co-author: Diet & Cancer: Markers, Prevention and Treatment, 1994; contbr. articles to profl. jours., chpt. to book. Bd. dir. Wellness Cmty., Conjeo Valley/Ventura, Calif., 1995-99; bd. dir. ACS Greater Conjeo Valley Unit, Thousand Oaks, Calif., 1994-99. Fellow Am. Coll. Osteo. Internists; mem. AAAS, Am. Osteo. Assn., Am. Soc. Clin. Oncology, Internat. Assn. Breast Cancer Rsch., Am. Soc. Preventive Oncology, Am. Assn. for Cancer Rsch., Inc., Southwest Oncology Group (chair breast com. 1992-2000, co-chair cancer control rsch. com. 87-92, oncology drug adv. com. 2002-2006, chmn. com. 2005-06). Office Phone: 310-582-7900. Business E-Mail: smartino@theangelesclinic.org.

MARTINS, FERNANDO GONINI, physician; b. Londrina, July 6, 1962; Degree in Medicine, U. Sao Paulo Med. Sch., 1986, MS in Medicine, 2008. Med. asst. Hosp. Ipiranga, 1993—. Mem.: Brazilian Urol. Soc., Am. Urol. Assn. Home: Alameda Arapanes 1084 ap 81 Sao Paulo 04524-001 Brazil Personal E-mail: martinsfg@uol.com.br.

MARTINS, GUSTAVO MAMORÉ, research scientist, educator; b. Campo Grande, Mar. 20, 1984; Engenheiro Agrônomo, Mato Grosso do Sul State U., 2006; PhD, São Paulo State U., 2011. Rschr. Nat. Coun. Sci. & Technol. Devel., 2007—08, Coordination Improvement Higher Edn. Pers., 2009—10; asst. prof. Mato Grosso do Sul State U., 2010—, cons., rsch. divsn., 2010—. Recipient Merit award, Mato Grosso do Sul State U. Mem.: Brazilian Region Internat. Biometric Soc., Entomol. Soc. America. Office: Passeio Monção 408 Ilha Solteira São Paulo 15385000 Brazil E-mail: gustavomamore@hotmail.com.

MARTINS, HUGO LIMA, medical researcher; b. Recife, Sept. 17, 1975; PhD, U. Fed. Pernambuco, 2000. Rschr. U. Fed. Pernambuco, 2008—. Office: Josefa Miranda de Farias 33 Surubim Pernambuco 55750-000 Brazil Office Fax: 81-36341727. Business E-Mail: hugomt2001@yahoo.com.br.

MARTINS-GREEN, MANUELA, cell biologist; b. Luso, Moxico, Angola, Dec. 30, 1947; came to U.S., 1973; d. Joaquim P. and Maria Alice (Marques) Martins; m. Harry W. Green, II, May 15, 1975; children: Alice, Harry, Maria Green. BS, U. Lisbon, 1970; MS, U. Calif., Riverside, 1975; PhD, U. Calif., Davis, 1987. Chief scientist EM lab Agronomical Sta., Oeiras, Portugal, 1970-73; electron microscopist, dept. ophthalmology U. Calif., Davis, 1975-82; postdoctoral researcher Lawrence Berkeley Lab., U. Calif., 1987-88, rsch. scientist, 1992-93; adj. asst. prof. Rockefeller U., 1991-92; asst. prof. cell biology U. Calif., Riverside, 1993-2000, assoc. prof. cell biology, 2000—06, prof. cell biology, 2006—; vis. prof. Stanford U., 2007—08, Ohio State U., 2011. Vis. lectr. U. Wuhan, China, 1988; vis. scientist Lab. Molecular Immunoreg. Nat. Cancer Inst., Frederick, 2000, pres. UCR Faculty, 2004-06 Contbr. articles to profl. jours., books. Recipient Nat. Rsch. Svc. award, 1988-91, NIH traineeship, 1986-87; Fulbright Travel grantee Internat. Exch. Scholars, Riverside, 1973, NIH grantee, 1992-98, Am. Heart Assn. grantee, 2000—, Tobacco Related Disease Rsch. Program grantee, 2001—, Disting. Svc. award, UCR, 2008, Innovatives Teaching award, 2008. Fellow AAAS; mem. Wound Healing Soc., Am. Soc. for Cell Biology, Am. Soc. Devel. Biology, Cytokine Soc., Women for Cell Biology, Wound Healing Soc., Phi Kappa Phi. Avocations: travel, hiking. Office: U Calif Dept Cell Biology Neuros 900 University Ave Riverside CA 92521-0001 Business E-Mail: manuela.martins@ucr.edu.

MARTINSON, IDA MARIE, retired medical/surgical nurse, physiologist; b. Mentor, Minn., Nov. 8, 1936; d. Oscar and Marvel (Nelson) Sather; m. Paul Varo Martinson, Mar. 31, 1962; children: Anna Marie, Peter. Diploma, St. Luke's Hosp. Sch. Nursing, 1957; BS, U. Minn., 1960, M.N.A., 1962; PhD, U. Ill., Chgo., 1972. Instr. Coll. St. Scholastica and St. Luke's Sch. Nursing, 1957—58, Thornton Jr. Coll., 1967—69; lab. asst. U. Ill. at Med. Ctr., 1970—72; lectr. dept. physiology U. Minn., St. Paul, 1972—82, asst. prof. Sch. Nursing, 1972—74, assoc. prof. rsch., 1974—77, prof., dir. rsch., 1977—82; prof. dept. family health care U. Calif., San Francisco, 1982—2003, chmn. dept., 1982—90. Vis. rsch. prof. Nat. Taiwan U., Def. Med. Ctr., 1981; vis. prof. nursing Sun Yat-Sen U. Med. Scis., Guang Zhou, China, Ewha Women's U., Seoul, Republic of Korea, Frances Payne Bolton Sch. Nursing, Case Western Res. U., Cleve., 1994—96; chair, prof. dept. health scis. Hong Kong Poly. U., 1996—2000. Author: Mathematics for the Health Science Student, 1977; editor: Home Care for the Dying Child, 1976, Women in Stress, 1979, Women in Health and Illness, 1986, The Child and Family Facing Life Threatening Illness, 1987, Family Nursing, 1989, Home Health Care Nursing, 1989, Home Health Care Nursing, 2d edit., 2002; contbr. chapters to books, articles to profl. jours. Active Am. Cancer Soc. Recipient Book of Yr. award, Am. Jour. Nursing, 1977, 1980, 1987, 1990, Humanitarian award for pediat. nursing, 1993; fellow, Fulbright Found., 1991. Mem.: ANA, Inst. Medicine, Am. Acad. Nursing, Coun. Nurse Rschrs., Sigma Theta Tau, Sigma Xi. Lutheran. Address: 12149 E Movil Lake Rd NE Bemidji MN 56601

MARTINSON, VJOLLCA, marriage and family therapist; b. Albania, May 12, 1971; PhD, Brigham Young U., 2005. Clin. therapist Provo Canyon Sch., 2001—. Rsch. fellowship, Brigham Young U. Avocations: tennis, bicycling. Office: 763 North 1650 West Springville UT 84663 Business E-Mail: vjollca.martinson@uhsinc.com.

MARTINS-PINGE, MARLI CARDOSO, physiologist, researcher; d. José de Matos and Deolinda Alves Cardoso Martins; m. Phileno Pinge-Filho, June 23, 1989; children: Philipi Martins Pinge, João Lucas Martins Pinge. Degree, PUCCAMP, Campinas, SP, 1986; PhD, Fed. U. São Paulo, 1998. Assoc. prof. State U. Londrina, Paraná, Brazil, 1998—, chair dept. physiological scis., 2007—. Fellow, NIH, 2003—04. Mem.: Am. Physiol. Soc. Achievements include research in rostral ventrolateral medulla and cardiovascular control in conscious animals. Office: State Univ Londrina Rodovia Celso Garcia Cid km 380 Londrina Paraná 86051-990 Brazil

MARTINY, KLAUS PER JUUL, psychiatrist, researcher; b. Holstebro, Denmark, Mar. 27, 1961; s. Per Juul and Karen Martiny; m. Birgitte Handberg Nielsen, Mar. 11, 1989; children: Frederik Handberg Juul, Johannes Handberg Juul, Karen Anna Handberg. MD, U. Aarhus, Denmark, 1988; PhD, U. Copenhagen, 2004. Cert. specialist in psychiatry Danish Med. Agy. Acting cons. Forensic Psychiatry, Copenhagen, 2000—02; dep. supt. Psychiat. Rsch. Unit, Hilleoed, Denmark, 2001—04; pvt. practice psychiatrist Frederiksberg, Denmark, 2003—. Fellow: Internat. Soc. Affective Disorders (assoc.); mem.: Com. on Chronotherapeutics in Affective Disorders (assoc.). Achievements include research in the use of light treatment for non-seasonal depression; psychometric properties of self-report and interview scales; methods to accelerate antidepressant response;

development of new antidepressant therapies (light and sleep deprivation). Office: Psychiat Rsch Unit Dyrehavevej 48 3400 Hilleroed Denmark Office Fax: 45 48 26 38 77. Business E-Mail: kmar@fa.dk.

MARTIROSIAN, GAYANE, microbiologist, educator; b. Tbilisi, Jan. 3, 1954; MD, Yerevan Med. Sch., 1977; PhD, Warsaw Med. U., 1996. Prof., head dept. med. microbiology Med. U. Silesia, 2002—. Prof. dept. histology Warsaw Med. U., 1991. Rogosa award, ASM. Mem.: Polish Soc. Microbiology. Avocations: literature, music. Office: Medyków 18 Katowice Silesia 40-752 Poland Office Fax: 48-32-252-6075. Business E-Mail: gmartir@sum.edu.pl.

MARTOF, MARY TAYLOR, retired nursing educator; b. Charlotte County, Va., Feb. 8, 1935; d. James Russell and Ella (Lipscomb) Palmer; m. John Laning Taylor III, Oct. 3, 1959 (div. 1971); children: Tara, Laura; m. Steven Martof, Apr. 7, 1979. BSN, U. Md., 1973, MS in Nursing, 1976; EdD, N.C. State U., 1984. Clin. nurse Clin. Ctr., NIH, Bethesda, Md., 1969—73, nursing educator, 1973—79; instr. U. N.C., Chapel Hill, 1979—81; asst. prof. Tex. Christian U., Ft. Worth, 1984—88, U. Southwestern La., Lafayette, 1988—92; assoc. prof. nursing La. State U., New Orleans, 1992—2001, chmn. critical thinking Sch. Nursing, 1994—2000; mem. grad. coun. Sch. Nursing La. State U. Health Sci. Ctr., New Orleans, 2000—01, ret., 2001. Cons. nephrology nursing NIH, 1974-79; chmn. profl. edn. Am. Cancer Soc., New Orleans, 1990-96; chmn. rsch. com. Sch. Nursing, La. State U., 1995-98; reviewer/rschr. various pubs.; coord. oncology grand rounds La. State U. Med. Ctr., 1995-2001; judge for Rsch. Day, La. State U. Sch. Medicine, 1999-2001. Author: What Every Adult Facing Surgery Should Know, 2003, Crisis: The Story Behind the Nursing Shortage, 2010; contbr. articles to profl. jours., chpts. to books. Faculty Am. Cancer Soc., Cancer Update, Ochsner Hosp., 1996-98; coord. blood drive Holy Trinity Episcopal Ch., Clemson, SC, 2007-; vol. Clemson Free Clinic, Lake Cheohee Homeowners Assn.(treas., 2009-11) Recipient Merit award NIH, 1977, plaque Am. Cancer Soc., 1991-93. Mem. Sigma Theta Tau (Disting. Writer) Independent. Episcopalian. Avocations: hiking, writing, cooking, gardening. Personal E-mail: smartof@hughes.net.

MARTON, LAURENCE JAY, clinical pathologist, researcher, educator; b. Bklyn., Jan. 14, 1944; s. Bernard Dov and Sylvia (Silberstein) M.; m. Marlene Lesser, June 27, 1967; 1 child, Eric Nolan. BA, Yeshiva U., 1965, DSc (hon.), 1993; MD, Albert Einstein Coll. Medicine, 1969. Intern Los Angeles County-Harbor Gen. Hosp., 1969-70; resident in neurosurgery U. Calif.-San Francisco, 1970-71, resident in lab. medicine, 1973-75, asst. research biochemist, 1973-74, asst. clin. prof. depts. lab. medicine and neurosurgery, 1974-75, asst. prof., 1975-78, assoc. prof., 1978-79, prof., 1979-92, asst. dir., divsn. clin. chemistry, dept. lab. medicine, 1974-75, dir., 1975-79, acting chmn. dept., 1978-79, chmn. dept., 1979-92; dean med. sch. U. Wis., 1992-95, prof. pathology and lab. medicine and oncology, 1992-2000, prof. dept. human oncology Madison, 1993-95. Interim vice chancellor Ctr. Health Scis., U. Wis., 1993-94; adj. prof. dept. lab medicine U. Calif., San Francisco, 1992—; pres., CEO SLIL Biomed. Corp., 1998-2000, chief sci. and med. officer, 2000—04; chief sci. officer Cellgate, 2004-08, chief Sci. Office Progen Pharm., 2008-. Co-editor: Polyamines in Biology and Medicine, 1981; Liquid Chromatography in Clinical Analysis, 1981; Clinical Liquid Chromatography, vol. 1, 1984, vol. 2, 1984 Served with USPHS, NIH, 1971-73 Recipient Rsch. Career Devel. award Nat. Cancer Inst., Disting. Alumnus award Albert Einstein Coll. Medicine, 1992. Mem. Am. Assn. Cancer Rsch., AAAS, Acad. Clin. Lab. Physicians and Scientists, Am. Soc. Investigative Pathology, Alpha Omega Alpha. Jewish. Avocations: photography, art, music, travel. Home: 581 Military Way Palo Alto CA 94306 Office: Progen Pharm Chief Sci Officer 2479 E Bayshore Rd Ste 709 Palo Alto CA 94303 Home Phone: 650-494-1818; Office Phone: 650-610-7800. Personal E-mail: ljmarton@gmail.com. Business E-Mail: laurencem@progen-pharma.com.

MÁRTONYI, CSABA LÁSZLO, retired ophthalmic photographer; b. Budapest, Hungary, Mar. 23, 1941; came to U.S., 1951; s. Louis Péter and Magda (Gyürky) M.; m. Elnajean Beyst, Sept. 4, 1976; 1 child, Erika Lyn. Cert. retinal angiographer. Chief photographer U. Mich. Photog. Svcs., Ann Arbor, 1967—71; dir. ophthalmic photography, dept. ophthalmology U. Mich., Ann Arbor, 1971—75, instr. dept. ophthalmic photography, 1975—80, asst. prof., 1980—83, assoc. prof., 1983—2000, assoc. prof. emeritus, 2000—. First author: Clinical Slit-Lamp Biomicroscopy and Photo Slit-Lamp Biomicrography, 1985; author, artist exhibit of eye images Landscapes of the Eye, 1993; author sci. exhibits. With U.S. Naval Air Res., 1965-67. Recipient Disting. Tchg. award Joint Commn. on Allied Health Pers. in Ophthalmology, 1997, Csaba L. Martonyi award, Ophthalmic Photographers Soc. Fellow Ophthalmic Photographers Soc. (parliamentarian 1988—, chair hon. life membership com. 1991—, fellowship com., pres. 1978-80, chair bd. certification 1978-84, chmn. editl. com. 1987-89, awards including top award for outstanding contbns. to ophthalmic photography), Am. Acad. Ophthalmology (assoc., Honor award 1984, Sr. Honor award 2001). Personal E-mail: martonyi1@msn.com.

MARTY, RAYMOND, nuclear physician; b. Oct. 26, 1929; s. Harry Kenneth and Pearl (Bailin) M.; m. Carole M. Perry, Jan. 25, 1960. BA, UCLA, 1952; MD, U. Lausanne, Switzerland, 1959. Intern Hosp. Good Samaritan, LA, 1960-61; resident in diagnostic radiology Albert Einstein Sch. Medicine, Bronx, N.Y., 1962; fellow radiation therapy Stanford Med. Sch., 1962-63; dir. out patient clinic St. Joseph's Hosp., San Francisco, 1963-65; fellow Tumor Inst., Seattle, 1965-66, mem. staff, 1966—, dir. nuclear medicine/ultrasound, 1967—. Assoc. clin. prof. nuclear medicine tech. Seattle U. Med. Sch., 1972—; asst. clin. prof. nuclear medicine U. Wash. Med. Sch., Seattle, 1974—. Contbr. articles to profl. jours. Fellow Am. Coll. Radiology, Am. Coll. Nuc. Medicine; mem. AMA, Radiol. Soc., N. Am. Soc. Nuclear Medicine, Seattle Yacht Club, Columbia Tower (Seattle) Club, La Chaine des Rotisseurs. Home: 4607 103rd Ln NE Kirkland WA 98033-7638 Personal E-mail: rbmarty@earthlink.net.

MARUKAWA, KAZUSHI, radiologist; b. Hiroshima, Japan, Feb. 15, 1967; s. Takuma and Mitsuko Marukawa; m. Hiromi Tsujiyama, Feb. 20, 1994; 1 child, Masaki. MD, Hiroshima U., Hiroshima, 1991; PhD, Hiroshima U., 2002. Cert. radiology specialist Japan Radiol. Soc., 1996. Resident Kure Nat. Hosp., Kure, Japan, 1992—94; staff Kure Med. Assn. Hosp., Kure, Japan, 1994—96; chief Kitakyushu Gen. Hosp., Japan, 1996—98; vice-chief Hiroshima City Hosp., 1998—2007; asst. prof. Hiroshima U. Avocations: driving, music. Office: Dept of Radiology Hiroshima U 1-2-3 kasumi Minami-ku Hiroshima 734-8551 Japan Business E-Mail: k-maru@ra2.so-net.ne.jp.

MARUNO, HIROTAKA, radiologist, researcher; MD, Chiba U., Japan, 1989. Diplomate Japanese Bd. Nuc. Medicine, 2000. Chief dr. dept. of radiology Toranomon Hosp., Tokyo, 2000—. Office: Toranomon Hosp 2-2-2 Toranomon Minato-ku Tokyo 1058470 Japan

MARUPUDI, SAMBASIVA RAO, surgeon, educator; b. Chintalapudi, India, July 1, 1952; arrived in US, 1976; s. Venkateswarlu and Nagendramma (Gaddipati) M.; m. Usha Nandipati, Mar. 25, 1976; children: Neena, Neelima. MB, BS, Guntur Med. Coll., India, 1974. Diplomate Am. Bd. Surgery, Am. Bd. Colon and Rectal Surgery. Rotating internship St. Clare's Hosp., Schenectady, NY, 1976-77; resident in gen. surgery St. Agnes Hosp., Balt., 1977-78, Franklin Sq. Hosp., Balt., 1978-82; fellow in colon and rectal surgery U. Tex. Health Scis. Ctr., Houston, 1982-83; pvt. practice Amarillo, Tex., 1983—. Clin. asst. prof. dept. surgery Tex. Tech. U. Health Scis. Ctr., Amarillo, 1984—. Fellow ACS, Am. Soc. Colon and Rectal Surgeons, Internat. Coll. Surgeons; mem. AMA, Tex. Med. Assn., Potter-Randall County Med. Soc. (past pres.), Tex. Soc. Colon and Rectal Surgeons (past pres.). Republican. Hindu. Office: 800 Quail Creek Dr # 103 Amarillo TX 79124-1634 Home: 8800 Blackhawk Rd Amarillo TX 79119 Office Phone: 806-358-7911. Personal E-mail: smarupudi@aol.com, drmarupudi@hotmail.com.

MARUSZEWSKI, MARCIN, surgeon, researcher; b. Tarnowskie Gory, Poland, Nov. 11, 1975; m. Ewa Wanda Bialy; 2 children. MD, Med. U. Silesia, Zabrze, Poland, 2001. Resident cardiac surgery Silesian Ctr. Heart Diseases, Zabrze, 2002—; transplant fellow (spr) Royal Brompton & Harefield NHS Trust, Harefield, Uxbridge, England, 2007—08; vis. scholar Med. U., Innsbruck, Tirol, Austria, 2003—06, Stanford U., Calif., 2008—. Clin. prodn. liaison Cytograft Tissue Engring., Novato, Calif., 2006—. Contbr. scientific papers. Business E-Mail: marcinm@stanford.edu.

MARUYAMA, HIROKI, internist, researcher; b. Shibata, Niigata, Japan, Feb. 7, 1957; s. Mankichi and Masu Maruyama; m. Yoshiko Seki, Sept. 28, 1986; 1 child, Kiyofumi. MD, Asahikawa Med. Coll., 1984. Cert. Medical doctor Ministry of Health, Labour, and Welfare, Japan, 1984, bd. cert. nephrologist Japan Soc. Nephrology, 1996. Internist Niigata U., Niigata, Niigata, Japan, 1984—85, Tsuruoka City Shonai Hosp., Yamagata, 1985—86, Kouseiren Itoigawa Sougou Hosp., Itoigawa, Niigata, 1986, Niigata U., 1986, Kouseiren Chuo Sougou Hosp., Nagaoka, Niigata, Japan, 1987, Niigata U., 1987—89, Niigata, 1990, Shinrakuen Hosp., Niigata, 1989, Niigata Prefectural Muikamachi Hosp., Muikamachi, Niigata, 1990—93; internist, rschr. Niigata U., 1993—97, assoc. prof. Internal Medicine, rschr. gene therapy, renal failure, 1997—. Author: (journal) Human Gene Therapy, 2000, 2002, Gene Therapy, 2001, 2003, Am. Jour. Nephrology, 2003, Journal of Gene Medicine, 2002, 2004, Biochemical and Biophysical Research Communications, 2004, Molecular Biotechnology, 2004, numerous others; assoc. mem. (editl. bd.) Gene Therapy and Molecular Biology, 2004; contbr. articles to profl. jours. Fellow: Japanese Soc. Internal Medicine; mem.: Japan Soc. Nephrology (attending nephrologist 1996), Japanese Soc. Dialysis Therapy (sr. mem. 1994, Young Investigator's award 1990). Achievements include patents pending for Method of regulating the activity of expression product of gene transferred into living body; Method of kidney-targeted gene transfer by retrograde injection into the renal vein. Home: 2-10-1-706 Igakucho-dori Niigata 951-8124 Japan Office: Niigata Univ 1-757 Asahimachi-dori Niigata 951-8120 Japan Office Fax: +81-25-227-0775. E-mail: hirokim@med.niigata-u.ac.jp.

MARUYAMA, KOSHI, pathologist, educator; b. Sapporo, Hokkaido, Japan, Feb. 19, 1932; s. Kotaro and Oe (Nakamura) M.; m. Rumy Misawa, May 6, 1961; children: Nariyuki, Narihiro, Yumie. MD, U. Hokkaido, 1957, PhD, 1962. Diplomate Japanese Bd. Pathology. Staff pathologist Nat. Inst. Leprosy Rsch., Tokyo, 1962-65, Nat. Cancer Ctr. Rsch. Inst., Tokyo, 1965-67; assoc. prof., assoc. virologist U. Tex. M.D. Anderson Hosp. and Tumor Inst., Houston, 1967-75; dir. dept. pathology Chiba (Japan) Cancer Ctr. Rsch. Inst., 1975-97. Vis. prof. Dalian Med. U., China, 1995—2001; cons. Immunobiology Labs. Co., Gunma, 1997—; dir. geriatric health svcs. facility Heart Village, Hasunuma, Japan, 2000—01; mem. dept. internal medicine Sakura Koseien Hosp., Nissan Koseikai, Japan, 2006—07; internist Sakura FOYER, Nissan Koseikai Geriat. Health Svcs. Facility, Japan, 2007—08, dir., 2009—. Mem. bd. editors Japanese Jour. Cancer Clinic, 1978—, Cancer Bull., 1978-89, The Year Book of Cancer, 1979; contbr. articles to profl. jours. Trustee Tex. Gulf Coast chpt. Leukemia Soc. Am., Houston, 1973-75. Scholar Leukemia Soc. Am., 1968; named hon. prof. Liaoning Cancer Hosp. and Inst., Shenyang, China, 1992; recipient Culture Promotion award Tsuchiya Found., 1995, Disting. Svc. award Dalian Med. U., 1997, Sci. Tech. and Edn. Promotion award Liaoning Edn. Com., China, 1998. Fellow: Japanese Soc. Lymphoreticular Tissue, Japanese Cancer Assn. (emeritus), Japanese Soc. Pathology (coun. internat. exch. 1997—98, emeritus), N.Y. Acad. Scis., Molecular Medicine Soc. (emeritus); mem.: AAAS (emeritus), Internat. Acad. Pathology (bd. dirs. Japan divsn. 1995—98, emeritus mem. 2010, Disting. Svc. award 2002), Internat. Assn. Comparative Rsch. on Leukemia and Related Diseases (world com. 1993—99), Japan Assn. Hosp. Pathologists, Am. Assn. Investigative Pathology, Microscopy Soc. Am. (emeritus), Am. Soc. Microbiology (emeritus), Am. Assn. Cancer Rsch. (emeritus), Soc. Welfare Corp. Sakura Kosei Kai (bd. dir. 2008—), U. Tex. Japan Exes (trustee 1996—).

MARUYAMA, MITSUNORI, physiologist; b. Tokyo, Feb. 6, 1970; married. MD, PhD, Nippon Med. Sch., Tokyo. Contbr. scientific papers. Office: Nippon Med Sch 1-1-5 Sendagi Bunkyo-ku Tokyo 113-8603 Japan Office Fax: 81-3-5685-0987. Business E-Mail: maru@nms.ac.jp.

MARUYAMA, SEITARO, endocrinologist, chemist; s. Kohtaro and Toshiko (Otobe) Maruyama. BS, Aoyamgakuin U., Tokyo, 1988; MD, Niigata U., Japan, 1996, PhD, 2002. Intern Internat. Med. Ctr. Japan, Tokyo, 1996—98; resident Niigata U. Hosp., 1998—2002; staff physician Tsubame Rosai Hosp., Niigata, 2002—03, Nat. Sagamihara (Japan) Hosp., 2003—05, Yokohama Brick Ave. Clin., Yokohama City, Japan, 2005—. Mem.: Endocrine Soc., Am. Diabetes Assn. Avocations: skiing, travel, tennis, gardening. Office: Yokohama Brick Ave Clin Kaneko Bldg Shin Yokohama Shin Yokohama 2 3 9 Kouhohu ku Yokohama 222 0033 Japan Office Phone: +81-50 5526 3953. E-mail: brick_ave_clinic@yahoo.co.jp.

MARX, ROBERT G., orthopedic surgeon, educator; b. May 1, 1965; BSc in Biology, U. Montréal, 1987; MD, McGill U., 1991; MSc in Clin. Epidemiology, U. Toronto, 1996. Cert. Am. Bd. Orthop. Surgery, Royal Coll. Surgeons Can. Resident U. Toronto; fellow, sports medicine/shoulder and knee surgery Hosp. Spl. Surgery, assoc. attending orthop. surgeon; dir., Foster Ctr. for Clin. Outcome Rsch. Hosp. for Spl. Surgery, Weill Med. Coll., Cornell U.; assoc. prof. orthop. surgery Weill Med. Coll., Cornell U., assoc. prof. pub. health. Orthop. dir. Sports Medicine Inst. for Young Atheletes; invited lectr. or vis. prof. in the field. Contbr. several articles to profl. jours., chapters to books; mem. editl. adv. bd. Muscle and Fitness Mag. Recipient O'Donoghue Sport Injury Rsch. award, Am. Orthop. Soc. for Sports Medicine, 2003; Royal Coll. Physicians and Surgeons Can. Detweiler Traveling Fellowship, Am. Acad. Orthop. Surgeons Health Services Rsch. Fellowship. Mem.: Knee Surgery and Orthop. Sports Medicine (mem. scientific adv. com.), Canadian Orthop. Assn., Am. Orthop. Soc. for Sports Medicine, Am. Acad. Orthop. Surgeons, Internat. Soc. Arthroscopy (mem. scientific adv. com.). Office: 519 E 72nd St New York NY 10021 Address: Hosp Spl Surgery 535 E 70th St New York NY 10021 Office Phone: 212-606-1645. Office Fax: 212-774-7822. Business E-Mail: MarxR@HSS.EDU.

MARYA, CHARU MOHAN, dental educator; b. Rohtak, Haryana, India, Jan. 24, 1969; BDS, Govt. Dental Coll., Rohtak, 1998; MDS, Kles Inst. Dental Scis., Belgaum, 1998. Prof., head Sudha Rustagi Coll. Dental Scis. & Rsch., Faridabad, 1998—. Mem.: Indian Assn. Pub. Health Dentistry. Avocations: reading, writing. Home: House 986 Sector 15 Faridabad Haryana 121007 India Personal E-mail: maryacm@yahoo.co.uk.

MARYMONT, JESSE HENRY, anesthesiologist, educator; b. Tacoma, Wash., July 10, 1957; MD, St. Louis U., 1983. Attending anesthesiologist NorthShore U. Health Sys., 1987—. Assoc. prof. U. Chgo. Pritzker Sch. Medicine, 2010. Named Attending Physician of Yr., NorthShore U. Health Sys. Sch. Nurse Anesthesia. Fellow: Am. Soc. Echocardiography, Am. Coll. Cardiology. Home: 288 Auburn Ave Winnetka IL 60093 Office Phone: 847-570-1926. Business E-Mail: jmarymont@northshore.org.

MARZOUK, YOSEF, retired microbiologist, pharmacist, consultant; b. Cairo, Dec. 21, 1928; s. Lictto Eliahoo and Rashell (Menashe) Marzouk; m. Ora Lemkin, Aug. 15, 1991; children: Moshe, Avneir; m. Miriam Daissy (dec.). BSc in Pharmacy, Faculty Pharmacy, Cairo, 1952; MSc in Microbiology, Tel Aviv U., 1966; DSc in Environ. Sci., Technion U., Haifa, 1974. Cert. quality engr. Head hosp. pharmacy Israel Def. Army, Haifa, 1954—57; pharmacist Sick Fund, Haifa, 1957—58; indsl. pharmacist Taro, Haifa, 1958—59; staff cell culture dept. Central Virus lab. Ministry Health, Jaffa, 1959—78, staff environ. virology dept., 1978—85, dir. Inst. for Ctr. Pharm. Jerusalem, 1985—93; ret., 1993. Lectr. in field. Achievements include research in environ. virology. Home: 7, Jabotinsky 47100 Ramat Hasbaron Israel Office Phone: 972-3-5497970. Personal E-mail: marzouk@netvision.net.il.

MASAAKI, HORI, radiologist, educator; b. Suginami, Tokyo, Mar. 2, 1971; m. Kumiko Hatori, July 7, 1999; children: Hori Yukina, Hori Wakana. Instr. U. Yamanashi, Chuou, Japan, 2004—. Office: Yamanashi Univ Hosp 1110 Shimokato Yamanashi Chuou 4093898 Japan E-mail: masahori-tky@umin.ac.jp.

MASAAKI, TAKAHASHI, pharmacist; b. Mie, Dec. 5, 1964; PhD, Gifu Pharm. U., 1990. Sr. pharmacist Nat. Hosp. Orgn. Nagoya Med. Ctr., 2003—. Office: 4-1-1 Sannomaru Naka Ku Nagoya Aichi 460-0001 Japan Business E-Mail: masaakit@nnh.hosp.go.jp.

MASAFUMI, TAKAHASHI, physician; b. Miyazaki, Aug. 28, 1972; Degree in medicine, Kumamoto U., 1997. Head physician, ctr. digestive and liver diseases Miyazaki Med. Ctr. Hosp., 2010—. Office: Takamatsu-cho 2-16 Miyazaki 880-0003 Japan

MASALOVA, OLGA OLEGOVNA, medical educator; b. Leningrad, Russia, May 18, 1979; MD, St. Petersburg State Pediatric Med. Acad., 2002; PhD, Inst. Exptl. Medicine NWB RAMS, 2002. Rsch. worker Inst. Exptl. Medicine NWB RAMS, 2003—09; educator St. Petersburg Med. Tech. Sch., 2009—. Office: Volkovskiy pr 106 Saint Petersburg 192102 Russia Office Fax: 7(812)7660540. Personal E-mail: molga@mail15.com.

MASAMITSU, HINATA, physician; b. Adachi, Tokyo, Dec. 23, 1971; MD, Fukushima Med. Coll., 1997; grad student, Fukushima Med. U., Sch. Medicine, 2001—04; PhD, Fukushima Med. U., 2004. Resident dept. internal medicine Toranomon Hosp., 1997—2001; dir. Med. Affairs Sect., Fukushima Prison, 2004—07, Ichiyokai Hosp., 2007—. Office: 15-27 Yashima-cho Fukushima 960-8136 Japan Office Phone: 81-24-534-6715. Office Fax: 81-24-531-0427. E-mail: mhinata@hotmail.com.

MASARU, IWASAKI, physician, researcher; b. Shizuoka, Japan, May 3, 1947; MD, U. Tokyo, PhD, 1973. Asst. prof. surg. dept. Yamanashi Med. U., 1883—1993; mgr. dept. med. affairs R&D, Hoechst Japan, 1993—96; devel. head R&D, Hoechst-Marion-Russel Japan, 1996—2000; head clin. rsch. devel. divsn. Aventis Pharma Japan, 2000—05; v.p., head, devel. & med. affairs divsn. GlaxoSmithKline, Japan, 2005—11; prof., medicine Yamanashi U., 2011—. Adj. prof. med. faculty, Oita U., 2010—11. Mem.: DIA, Japanese Soc. Surgery, Japanese Soc. Clin. Pharmacology & Therapeutics, ASCO. Avocations: golf, cello. Office: 1110 Shimogato Chou City Yamanashi 409-3898 Japan Office Phone: 81-55-273-1266. Office Fax: 81-55-273-1262. Business E-Mail: miwasaki@yamanashi.ac.jp.

MASATO, TAKAO, orthopedist, educator; b. Japan, Oct. 24, 1963; D, Shimane Med. U., 1989. Asst. prof. Simane U. Sch. Medicine, 2004—05, assoc. prof., 2005—07; prof. Teikyo U. Sch. Medicine, 2007—. Travelling fellow, JOSSM/KOSSM/GOTS. Mem.: JOA, SICOT, AAOS, IFFAS, ISAKOS. Avocations: golf, fishing, horseback riding. Office: 2-11-1 Kaga Itabashi Tokyo 173-8605 Japan Office Fax: 81-3-5375-6864. Business E-Mail: mtakao@med.teikyo-u.ac.jp.

MASCARENHAS, LEO, oncologist; b. Bangalore, India, July 17, 1967; MBBS, St. John's Med. Coll., 1990; MS, U. Southern Calif., 2008. Assoc. prof. pediat. Keck Sch. Medicine, U. Southern Calif.

Children's Hosp., LA, 1998—, prin. investigator children's oncology group, dir., clin. trials office Children's Ctr. Cancer and Blood Diseases, 2008—. Mem. certification and continuing edn. com., program com., devel. com. mem. Am. Soc. Pediat. Hematology and Oncology, 2007—; bd. dirs. Pablove Found., 2009. Recipient Bristol Myers Squibb award, NY Med. Coll., Philip E. Rothman Meml. award, Children's Hosp. LA, Walter Laug Disting. Tchg. award, Best Drs. in America, Southern Calif. Super Drs. Mem.: Internat. Soc. Pediat. Oncology, Am. Soc. Hematology, Am. Soc. Clin. Oncology, Am. Soc. Hematology and Oncology, Soc. Pediat. Rsch. Avocations: music, travel, reading. Office: Children's Hosp LA 4650 Sunset Blvd Los Angeles CA 90027 Office Fax: 323-361-8174. Business E-Mail: lmascarenhas@chla.usc.edu.

MASCI, JOSEPH RICHARD, physician; b. New Brunswick, NJ, Nov. 27, 1950; s. Joseph Nicholas and Delfina (Musa) M.; m. Elizabeth Bass, May 21, 1993; 1 child, Jonathan Samuel. BA, Cornell U., 1972; MD, NYU, 1976. Diplomate Am. Bd. Internal Medicine, Am. Bd. Infectious Diseases. Instr. medicine Boston U. Sch. Medicine, 1979—80, Mt. Sinai Sch. Medicine, NYC, 1982—84, asst. prof. clin. medicine, 1984—88, asst. prof. medicine, 1988—90, assoc. prof. medicine, 1990—2003, prof. medicine, 2003—, prof. preventive medicine, 2006—; assoc. dir. medicine Elmhurst Hosp. Ctr., NY, 1987—2002, chief, infectiious disease, 1999—2002, dir. medicine, 2002—. Peer reviewer NIH, 1994—. Author: Primary and Ambulatory Care of the HIV-Infected Adult, 1992, Outpatient Management of HIV-Infection, 2nd edit., 1996, 3rd edit., 2001, 4th edit., 2011, Bioterrorism: A Guide for Hospital Preparedness, 2005. Recipient Dr. Linda Laubenstein award for Excellence in AIDS Care, 2002, Presdl. Voluntary Svc. Gold award, Ruth Abramsm award, NY State Aids Inst., 2006, Faculty Counsel Academic Excellence award, Mt. Sinai Sch. Medicine, 2008. Fellow NY Acad. of Medicine, ACP; mem. Am. Soc. Microbiology, Assn. Program Dirs. Internal Medicine, Assn. Profs. of Medicine, US Agy. Internat. Devel., Royal Soc. Medicine. Office: Elmhurst Hosp Ctr 79-01 Broadway Elmhurst NY 11373-1329 Office Phone: 718-334-3446.

MASCITELLI, LUCA, cardiologist; b. Chieti, Italy, July 6, 1966; s. Carlo Mascitelli and Annamaria Meaolo; m. Francesca Pezzetta, Oct. 27, 1996; children: Jacopo, Chiara, Francesco. MD, U. Florence, 1992. Specialist in cardiology and sport medicine. Lt. col., physician Comando Brigata alpina Julia, Italian Army, Udine, 1994—, cardiologist. Office: Casa di Cura Città di Udine Viale Venezia 410 Udine 33100 Italy Home: Via Alessandro Manzoni 34 33019 Tricesimo UD Italy Home Fax: 0039 0432852577. Personal E-mail: lumasci@libero.it.

MASCULO, FRANCISCO SOARES, engineering educator; b. Rio de Janeiro, Apr. 27, 1954; Degree in Engring., Rio de Janeiro Fed. U., 1976; PhD, NYU, 1991; MSc in Operations Mgmt., Coppe Rio Saneiro Fed. U. Assoc. prof. Paraiba Fed. U., 1978—; sci. dir. Brasilian Soc. Production Engring. Master: Brasillian Assn. Prodn. Engring. Avocation: volleyball. Home: Edvaldo S Brandao 181 Apt 101 Joao Pessoa 58037-215 Brazil Home Fax: 55 - 83 - 3216 7549. Business E-Mail: masculo@ct.ufpb.br.

MASEK, TOMISLAV, veterinarian, educator; b. Karlovac, Croatia, Dec. 7, 1975; DVM, U. Zagreb, PhD, 2001. Asst. prof. U. Zagreb, Faculty Vet. Medicine, 2010—. Home: Heinzelova 55 Zagreb 10000 Croatia Personal E-mail: tomislav.masek@vef.hr.

MASERU, NOBLE A.W., city health department administrator; b. Detroit; BS, Wayne State U.; MPH, Emory U. Sch. Medicine; PhD in Health Policy, Atlanta U. Founding dir., master of pub. health program Morehouse Sch. Medicine, Atlanta; health policy scientist Morehouse Coll., Pub. Health Scis. Inst.; v.p., cmty. health Greater Detroit Area Health Coun. Inc., 1998—2000; dir. and health officer Detroit Dept. Health and Wellness Promotion, 2003—06; health commr. City of Cin. Health Dept., 2006—. Office: Cin Health Dept 3101 Burnet Ave Cincinnati OH 45229 Office Phone: 513-357-7280.

MASHIACH, ROY, gynecologist; b. Israel, May 14, 1968; MD, Tel Aviv Med. Sch., 1994. Sr. gynecologic surgeon Haim Sheba Med. Ctr., 2005—. Chief gynecologic simulation MSR Israeli Med. Simulation Ctr., 2009—11. Recipient award, Hotel Dieu -CHU de Clermont Ferrand France. Mem.: AAGL's Spl. Interest Group Reproductive Surgery (Daniel F Kott award), Israeli Gynecol. Endoscopic Soc. (bd. mem.). Avocation: motorcycling. Office: 18 Reiness St Tel Aviv 64220 Israel Office Fax: 97235239996. Business E-Mail: rmashiach@013.net.

MASHIKO, RYOTA, neurosurgeon; s. Osamu and Hisayo Mashiko; m. Masae Mashiko; children: Kyo, Nao, Kazu. MD, Fukui Med. Sch., Japan, 1996; PhD, U. Tsukuba. Cert. neruosurgeon Japan Neurosurgical Soc., Tokyo, 2002, neurologist Japan Stroke Soc. Tokyo, 2011. Physician Kitaibaraki Mcpl. Gen. Hosp., Ibaraki, Japan, 2002—05; chief physician Hata Hosp., Hitachi, Ibaraki, 2006—10, Tsukuba Med. Ctr. Hosp., Tsukuba, Japan, 2010—. Contbr. articles to jour.; editor: Neurology India, 2006—, Yonsei Med. Jour., 2006. Office: Tsukuba Med Ctr Hosp 1-3-1 Amakubo Tsukuba Ibaraki 305-8558 Japan Business E-Mail: mashimashi@par.odn.ne.jp.

MASHIMA, TETSUO, medical researcher; b. Tokyo, May 29, 1969; PhD, U. Tokyo, 1999. Staff scientist, Cancer Inst. Japanese Found. Cancer Rsch., 2010—. Office: 3-8-31 Ariake Koto-ku Tokyo 135-8550 Japan Business E-Mail: tmashima@jfcr.or.jp.

MASHIN, JACQUELINE ANN COOK, health facility consultant; b. Chgo., May 11, 1941; d. William Hermann and Ann (Smidt) Cook; m. Fredric John Mashin, June 7, 1970; children: Joseph Glenn, Alison Robin. BS, U. Md., 1984; BSN, Cath. U., Washington, 1993. Cert. realtor. Adminstrv. asst. CIA, Washington, 1963-66; asst. to mng. dir. Aerospace Edn. Found., Washington, 1966-74; exec. asst. to asst exec. dir. Air Force Assn., Washington, 1974-79; v.p., ptnrship. owner Discount Linen Store, Silver Spring, Md., 1979-81; asst. regional polit. dir. Office of Pres.-elect, Washington, 1980-81; confidential asst. to dir. Office of Personnel Mgmt. (US), Washington, 1981-83; spl. asst. to dep. dir. Office of Mgmt. and Budget, Washington, 1983-86; dir. internat. communications and spl. asst. to commr. Dept. of the Interior, Washington, 1986-89, cons., 1989-93; with Washington Hosp. Ctr., 1993—2009. Chmn., vol. coord. Mo. County Rep. Party, 1999; chmn. Bayclub, Mo. County Fedn. Rep. Women, 1999, 2000. Pres. Layhill Civic Assn., Silver Spring, Md., 1980; state chmn. Md.'s Reagan Youth Delegation, Annapolis, Md., 1980; state treas., office mgr. Reagan-Bush State Hdqrs. of Md., Silver Spring, 1980; mem. Women's Com. Nat. Symphony Orch.; pres. Rock Creek Women's Rep. Club, 1998, Montgomery County Rep. Party, 1999, Montgomery County Fedn. Rep. Women, 1999—; steering com. Wheaton Redevel. Program, 2001—07; gov.'s adv. bd. Md. Bd. Health and Mental Hygiene Balt., 2003- Mem.: White House Vols., Air Force Assn. (life), U.S. Capital Hist. Soc., Aux. Salvation Army (life). Republican. Avocations: golf, horseback riding. Home and Office: 2429 White Horse Ln Silver Spring MD 20906-2243 Office Phone: 301-871-6063. Personal E-mail: Jaguar041@aol.com.

MASI, ALFONSE THOMAS, medical educator; b. NYC, Oct. 29, 1930; s. Antonio and Mary (Genese) M.; m. Nancy Ann Bouton, Aug. 27, 1960; children: Anthony Mark, Christopher Maurice, Maria Lisa, Amy Elizabeth. BS, CUNY, 1951; MD, Columbia U., 1955; Dr.P.H., Johns Hopkins U., 1963. Intern Johns Hopkins Hosp., 1955-56; resident Johns Hopkins Hosp. and UCLA Med. Ctr., 1958-60; practice medicine specializing in rheumatology; asst. prof. epidemiology Johns Hopkins Sch. Hygiene, 1963-65, asso. prof., 1965-67; prof. medicine, dir. div. connective tissue diseases Coll. Medicine, U. Tenn., Memphis, 1967-78, prof. dept. health care scis., 1967-78; prof. dept. medicine U. Ill. Coll. Medicine-Peoria, 1978—, head dept. medicine, 1978-85; prof. epidemiology U. Ill. Sch. Pub. Health, Chgo., 1978—. Cons. various divs. NIH, 1971—; com. mem. various projects NRC, 1972— Served with USPHS, 1956-58. Sr. investigator Arthritis Found., 1966-71; also Russell L. Cecil fellow. Fellow ACP, APHA, Am. Coll. Epidemiology, Am. Coll. Rheumatology (master), Am. Rheumatism Assn. Home: 6710 N Skyline Dr Peoria IL 61614-3127 Office: U Ill Coll Medicine-Peoria Dept Medicine One Illini Dr Box 1649 Peoria IL 61656-1649 Office Phone: 309-671-8428. Business E-Mail: amasi@uic.edu.

MASIHA, SAID, physician; b. Shiraz, Iran, Aug. 25, 1967; MD, Uppsala U. Hosp. Physician Uppsala U. Hosp., 1999—. Avocations: pottery, music. Home: Fanstav Uppsala 75350 Sweden E-mail: said.masiha@medsci.uu.se.

MASIUK, MAREK, pathologist, educator; s. Stanislaw and Maria Masiuk; m. Magdalena Baskiewicz-Masiuk. MD, Pomeranian Med. U., Szczecin, Poland, 2000, PhD, 2004. Cert. pathologist Nat. Med. Exam. Ctr., Poland, 2007. Assoc. prof., pathology Pomeranian Med. Acad., Szczecin, 2007—08, cons., pathology Clin. Hosp. No.1, 2007—09; cons., pathology Voivodeship Hosp. Szczecin, Poland. Postdoc. Vis. fellow, Nat. Insts. Health, LIP, Postdoc. Vis. fellowship, Nat. Inst. Allergy & Infectious Diseases, 2007—09. Mem.: Polish Biochem. Soc., Polish Soc. Pathology, Am. Soc. Hematology. Achievements include research in nucleolin expression in human breast cancer and its relation to some pathologic features and clinical data. Office: Voivodeship Hosp Szczecin Lab Pathology Ul. Arkonska 4 71-455 Szczecin Poland Office Phone: 48-91-813-9520.

MASKATI, QURESH B., ophthalmologist, consultant; b. Mumbai, Nov. 13, 1956; s. Badar T. and Mariam B. Maskati; m. Sajeda Quresh Heptulla, Dec. 25, 1981; children: Merzia Q., Shaista Q. MS, Seth G.S. Med. Coll., Mumbai, 1983; MS in Surgery, Maharashtra Med. Coun., 1983. Cons. eye surgeon Habib Hosp., Mumbai, 1986—, Saifee Hosp., Mumbai, 1987—. Cons. eye surgeon Sight Savers Internat., Mumbai, 1998—2006. Past pres. Rotary, Bombay North, Rotary Internat., 1995—96. Recipient Gold Medal, Indian Implant and Refractive Soc., 2007. Mem.: All India Ophthalmic Soc. (mem., mng. com. 1999—2002). Avocations: swimming, travel. Office: Maskati Eye Clinic 23 M Karve Rd Mumbai 400004 India Office Fax: 00912223885822. Business E-Mail: qureshmaskati@gmail.com.

MASO, GIUSEPPE, physician, educator; b. Mirano, Venezia, Italy, Oct. 20, 1952; s. Dario Maso and Argenide Tomaello; m. Antonella Livieri; 1 child, Dario Giuseppe. Maturità scientifica, Liceo Scientifico Giordano Bruno, Venezia, 1971; MD in Chirurgia, U. Padova Italy, 1977. Cert. in nephrology U. Padova, 1980, in internal medicine U. Padova, 1986. Clinician, tchr. Inst. Internal Medicine, Padua, Italy, 1978—84; chief med. officer Battaglione Lagunari, Venezia, Italy, 1979—80; family physician Local Health Unit, Mirano, 1979—; contract prof. family medicine Udine U., Italy, 1999—. Rschr. cme facilitator Veneto Region, Venezia, 1985—; pres. Soc. Italiana Medicina Generale, Venezia, 1987—91, leader cancer registry, 1988—93, nat. bd. mem., 1991—93; tchr. nephrology nursing sch. Italian Order Malta, Venice, Venezia, 1993—96; pres. Italian Acad. Family Physicians, Milan, 2000—03; tutor family medicine U. Padova, 2005—; editor in chief Italian Jour. Primary Care, Bari, 2009—. Author: (book) Registro Tumori per la Medicina Generale, La Disciplina Invisibile. Migliorare la Medicina di Famiglia per Migliorare la Salute di Tutti, Il Progetto RTMG Simg Venezia, RTMG Venezia Fase Operativa, Registro Tumori, La Ricerca in Medicina di Famiglia; editor: The European Textbook of Family Medicine; author: Le Età della Vita. Appunti di Medicina di Famiglia, la Gionata del Medico di Famiglia Italiano, Infermiera e medica di Famiglia. Dep. pres. Lega Italiana Contro i Tumori Venezia, Italy, 1990—92. Lt. Italian Army, 1979—80. Mem.: Italian Acad. Family Physicians, Am. Acad. Family Physicians. Office: Studio Medico Dr GMaso Via Sabbiona 68 30034 Oriago-Mira VE Italy Office Phone: 0039 0415630405. Office Fax: 0039 0415630405. Business E-Mail: giuseppe.maso@gmail.com.

MASOKO, PETER, research scientist; b. Tweelaaagte, May 28, 1974; PhD, U. Pretoria, 2006. Rschr. U. Limpopo, 2006—. Postdoc. fellow, Nat. Rsch. Found., scholarship, Nat. Dept. Agr. South Africa, Bursary grant, Ernst and Ethel Eriksen Trust. Mem.: Internat. Soc. Devel. Natural Products, Indigenous Plant Use Forum, Molecular and Cell Biology Group, South African Soc. Biochemistry and Molecular Biology, Profl. Natural scientist. Avocations: soccer, cricket, music. Office: University Limpopo Pvt Bag X1106 Polokwane Sovenga 0727 South Africa Office Fax: 27-15-268-3012. Business E-Mail: peter.masoko@ul.ac.za.

MASON, DEAN TOWLE, cardiologist; b. Berkeley, Calif., Sept. 20, 1932; s. Ira Jenckes and Florence Mabel (Towle) M.; m. Maureen O'Brien, June 22, 1957; children: Kathleen, Alison. BA in Chemistry, Duke U., Durham, NC, 1954; MD, Duke U., 1958. Diplomate Am. Bd. Internal Medicine, Am. Bd. Cardiovasc. Diseases, Nat. Bd. Med. Examiners. Intern, then resident in medicine Johns Hopkins Hosp., 1958-61; clin. assoc. cardiology br., sr. asst. surgeon USPHS, Nat. Heart Inst., NIH, 1961-63, asst. sect. dir. cardiovascular diagnosis, attending physician, sr. investigator cardiology br., 1963-68; prof. medicine, prof. physiology, chief cardiovascular medicine U. Calif. Med. Sch., Davis-Sacramento Med. Center, 1968-82; dir. cardiac ctr. Cedars Med. Ctr., Miami, Fla., 1982-83; physician-in chief Western Heart Inst., San Francisco, 1983—2000; chmn. dept. cardiovascular medicine St. Mary's Med. Ctr., San Francisco, 1986-99, hon. med. staff, 2000—. Co-chmn. cardiovascular-renal drugs U.S. Pharmacopeia Com. Revision, 1970—75; mem. life scis. com. NASA; med. rsch. rev. bd. VA, NIH; prof. medicine (hon.) Peking Med. U., China, 1987; vis. prof. numerous univs.; cons. in field. Editor-in-chief Am. Heart Jour., 1980—96; contbr. chapters to books, articles. Recipient rsch. award, Am. Therapeutic Soc., 1965, Theodore and Susan B. Cummings Humanitarian award, Dept. State-Am. Coll. Cardiology, 1972, 1973, 1975, 1978, Skylab Achievement award, NASA, 1974, U. Calif. Faculty Rsch. award, 1978, Symbol of Excellence, Tex. Heart Inst., 1979, Disting. Alumnus award, Duke U. Sch. Medicine, 1979, award of Honor, Wisdom Soc., 1997, Medal of Honor, Winston Churchill Soc., 1998, Armand Hammer Creative Genius award, 1998, Dwight D. Eisenhower Admirable Am. of Achievement award, 1998, Eternal Jesus Christ award, 1998, Blessed Lord's Prayer award, 1998, Dean Towle Mason Eminent Physician of Wisdom award, 1998, Dean Towle Mason, M.D. Medal of Wisdom award, 2001, Cardiologist of the Century Wisdom award, 2001, Albert Schweitzer world Humanitarian of Wisdom award, 2002, Jonas Salk award for med. rsch., 2003, Albert Einstein Sci. Rsch. award, 2003, John Wayne Pioneer of Am. award, 2003, Ernest Hemingway award for maj. contbns. to med. lit., 2003, Will Durant Philosopher-Physician award, 2004, Paul Dudley White award for disting. svc. in cardiovasc. medicine, 2004, Newton Kugelmass Children's Cardiology Crusader award, 2004, Norman Vincent Peale Healing Power of Prayer award, 2005, Lifetime Achievement award, U. Calif., Davis, 2008. Master Am. Coll. Cardiology (pres. 1977-78); fellow ACP, Am. Heart Assn., Am. Coll. Chest Physicians, Royal Soc. Medicine; mem. Am. Soc. Clin. Investigation, Am. Physiol. Soc., Am. Soc. Pharmacology and Exptl. Therapeutics (Exptl. Therapeutics award 1973), Am. Fedn. Clin. Research, NY Acad. Scis., Am. Assn. U. Cardiologists, Am. Soc. Clin. Pharmacology and Therapeutics, We. Assn. Physicians, AAUP, We. Soc. Clin. Rsch. (past pres.), El Macero Country Club, Phi Beta Kappa, Alpha Omega Alpha. Republican. Methodist. Home: 44725 Country Club Dr El Macero CA 95618-1047 Office: Western Heart Inst St Marys Med Ctr 450 Stanyan St San Francisco CA 94117-1079

MASON, EDWARD EATON, surgeon; b. Boise, Idaho, Oct. 16, 1920; s. Edward Files and Dora Bell (Eaton) M.; m. Dordana Fairman, June 18, 1944; children— Daniel Edward, Rose Mary, Richard Eaton, Charles Henry. BA, U. Iowa, 1943, MD, 1945; PhD in Surgery, U. Minn., 1953. Intern, resident in surgery Univ. Hosps., Mpls., 1945-52; asst. prof. surgery U. Iowa, 1953-55, asso. prof., 1956-60, prof., 1961-91, prof. emeritus, 1991—, chmn. gen. surgery, 1978-91. Cons. VA Hosp.; trainee Nat. Cancer Inst., 1949-52 Author: Computer Applications in Medicine, 1964, Fluid, Electrolyte and Nutrient Therapy in Surgery, 1974, Surgical Treatment of Obesity, 1981; developer gastric bypass and gastroplasty for treatment of obesity; contbr. articles profl. jours. Served to lt. (j.g.) USNR, 1945-47. Fellow ACS; mem. AMA, Am. Surg. Assn., Western Surg. Assn., Soc. Univ. Surgeons, Internat. Soc. Surgery, Ctrl. Surg. Assn., Soc. Surgery Alimentary Tract, Am. Thyroid Assn., Am. Soc. Bariatric Surgery, Sigma Xi, Alpha Omega Alpha. Republican. Presbyterian. Home: 5 Melrose Cir Iowa City IA 52246-2013 Office: Univ Hosp Dept Surgery Iowa City IA 52242 Business E-Mail: edward-mason@uiowa.edu.

MASON, GREGG CLAUDE, orthopedic surgeon, researcher; b. Schenectady, NY, July 28, 1958; s. George and Maureen (Murphy) M.; m. Dina Marie Sokolowski, June 16, 1990. BS in Chemistry magna cum laude, Allegheny Coll., 1980; MD, U. Pitts., 1984. Diplomate Am. Bd. Orthop. Surgery, Nat. Bd. Med. Examiners. Gen. surgery intern U. Colo./U. Colo. Med. Ctrs., Denver, 1984-85; orthopaedic rsch. fellow U. Pitts., 1985-86, resident in orthopaedic surgery, 1986-89; orthopedic surgeon U.S. Naval Hosp., Okinawa, Japan, 1989-92; pvt. practice, Erie, 1992—. Active staff St. Vincent Med. Ctr., St. Vincent Surgery Ctr., Hamot Med. Ctr., Union City Meml. Hosp.; lectr. in field. Contbr. articles to profl. jours. Comdr. M.C. USNR, 1980—. Recipient Outstanding Student Rsch. award U. Pitt. Sch. Medicine, 1984, Harold Henderson Sankey Orthop. award, 1984; rsch. grantee Competitive Med. Rsch. Fund., Presbyn.-Univ. Hosp. of Pitts., 1986-87, U. Pitts. Rsch. Devel. Fund, 1986-87. Disting. Alden scholar 1977, 78, 79, 80, Sandra Doane Turk scholar, 1979, Armed Svcs. Health Professions scholar, 1981-84. Fellow ACS, Internat. Coll. Surgeons, Mil. Soc. Orthop. Surgeons, Am. Acad. Orthop. Surgeons (tchg. seal 1993); mem. AMA, Pa. Orthop. Soc. (Best Rsch. Paper 1987, 88), Erie Orthop. Soc., U. Pitts. Med. Ctr. Orthop. Alumni., Am. Orthop. Soc. of Sports Medicine (Cabaud award 1988), Ea. Orthop. Assn. (Founders award 1988), Phi Beta Kappa. Office: Orthopaedic Surgeons Inc 204 W 26th St Erie PA 16508-1898 Office Phone: 814-454-2401.

MASON, JAMES OSTERMANN, retired public health administrator, former federal agency administrator; b. Salt Lake City, June 19, 1930; s. Ambrose Stanton and Neoma (Thorup) Mason; m. Lydia Maria Smith, Dec. 29, 1952; children: James, Susan, Bruce, Ralph, Samuel, Sara, Benjamin. BA, U. Utah, 1954, MD, 1958; MPH, Harvard U., 1963, DPH, 1967. Diplomate Am. Bd. Preventive Medicine. Intern Johns Hopkins Hosp., Balt., 1958—59; resident in internal medicine Peter Bent Brigham Hosp.-Harvard Med. Service, Boston, 1961—62; chief infectious diseases Latter-day Saints Hosp., Salt Lake City, 1968—69; commr. Health Services Corp., Ch. of Jesus Christ of Latter-day Saints, 1970—76; dep. dir. health Utah Div. Health, 1976—78, exec. dir., 1979—83; chief epidemic intelligence service Ctr. Disease Control, Atlanta, 1959, chief hepatitis surveillance unit epidemiology br., 1960, chief surveillance sect. epidemiology br., 1961, dep. dir. bur. labs., 1964—68, dep. dir. of Ctr., 1969—70; dir. Ctrs. for Disease Control, Atlanta; adminstr. Agy. for Toxic Substances and Disease Registry, 1983—89; acting asst. sec. for health US Dept. Health & Human Services, Washington, 1985, asst. sec. for health, 1989—93; asst. prof. dept. medicine and preventive medicine U. Utah, Salt Lake City, 1968—69; acting surgeon gen. US Dept. Health & Human Services, Washington; assoc. prof., chmn. div. community medicine, dept. family and community medicine U. Utah, 1978—79; v.p. planning, devel., prof. preventive medicine and biometrics Uniformed Svcs. U. Health Scis., 1993—94; 2nd quorum of Seventy LDS Ch., 1994—2000; pres. & CEO Avalon Health Care Inc., Salt Lake City, 2005—07; mem. Nat. Vaccine Adv. Com., 2008—; bd. mem. Nat. Coun. Cmty. Behavioral Healthcare, 2008—09. Physician, cons. to med. svcs. Salt Lake VA Hosp., 1977—83; clin. prof. dept. family and cmty. medicine U. Utah Coll. Medicine, 1979—83, clin. prof. dept. pathology, 1980—83; clin. prof.

cmty. health Emory U. Sch. Medicine, 1984—86; chmn. joint residency com. in preventive medicine and pub. health Utah Coll. Medicine, 1975—80; mem. Utah Cancer Registry Rsch. Adv. Com., 1976—83; mem. adv. com. Utah Ctr. Health Stats., 1977—79; chmn. bd. Hosp. Coop. Utah, 1977—79; chmn. exec. com. Utah Health Planning and Resource Devel. Adv. Group, 1977—79; chmn. Utah Gov.'s Adv. Com. for Comprehensive Health Planning, 1975—77; mem. recombinant DNA adv. com. NIH, 1979—83; mem. Gov.'s Nuclear Waste Repository Task Force, 1980—83, chmn., 1980—82; bd. dirs. Utah Health Cost Mgmt. Found., 1980—83; mem. adv. com. for programs and policies CDC, 1980; mem. com. on future of local health depts. Inst. Medicine, 1980—82; mem. exec. com., chmn. tech. adv. com. Thrasher Rsch. Found., 1980—89; mem. Robert Wood Johnson Found. Program for Hosp. Initiatives in Long-Term Care, 1982—84; mem. sci. and tech. adv. com. UNDP-World Bank-WHO Spl. Programme for Rsch. and Tng. in Tropical Diseases, 1984—89; mem. Utah Resource for Genetic and Epidemiologic Rsch., 1982—85, chmn. bd., 1982—83; U.S. rep. WHO Exec. Bd., 1990—93. Author (with H.L. Bodily and E.L. Updyke): Diagnostic Procedures for Bacterial, Mycotic and Parasitic Infections, 1970; author: (with M.H. Maxell, K.H. Bousfield and D.A. Ostler) Funding Water Quality Control in Utah, Procs. for Lincoln Inst., 1982; contbr. articles to profl. jours. Mem. nat. scouting com. Boy Scouts Am., 1974—78. Recipient Roche award, U. Utah, 1957, Wintrobe award, 1958, Disting. Alumni award, 1973, Adminstr. of Yr. award, Brigham U., 1980, spl. award for outstanding pub. svc., Am. Soc. Pub. Adminstrn., 1984, DSM, USPHS, 1988, Legacy of Life award, LDS Hosp. Deseret Found., 1992, Gorgas Medal and Scroll, 1993. Mem.: APHA (task force for credentialing of lab. pers. 1976—78, program devel. bd. 1979—81), AMA, Utah Pub. Health Assn. (pres. 1980—82, Beatty award 1979), Utah Acad. Preventive Medicine (pres. 1982—83), Utah State Med. Assn. (trustee 1979—83), Inst. Medicine of NAS, Rotary, Delta Omega, Alpha Omega Alpha, Phi Kappa Phi, Alpha Epsilon Delta, Sigma Xi. Mem. Lds Ch. *

MASON, JOAN ELLEN, nurse; b. Reading, Pa., June 29, 1947; d. Richard Lenhart and Mary Jane (Miller) Fritz; m. W. Davis Mason, Feb. 12, 1977 (dec. Jan. 2002). RN, Temple U. Hosp. Sch. Nursing, 1968; BS in Nursing Edn., Temple U., 1971, EdM in Health Edn., 1981; postgrad., U. Pa. Staff nurse Temple U. Hosp., Phila., 1968-71; nursing instr. Phila. Gen. Hosp. Sch. Nursing, 1971-76; coord. staff devel. Meml. Hosp., Roxborough, Pa., 1976-84; clin. editor Springhouse Corp., Pa., 1984-94; nurse cons. Kelly Sci. Resources, 1995-98; adminstrn., profl. nurse Bed and Breakfast Inn, Cape May, NJ, 1982—2003; nurse cons. Reading, 1999—2003, Orwigsburg, 2003—05. Mem. exhibit com. Mus. Nursing History, Inc., 1988-2001. Editor Congl. Free Ch. of Chirst newsletter; devel.: Bible Fellowship Group; contbr. articles to profl. jours. Vol. Reading Mus., Berks Arts Coun. Mem. Mid-Atlantic Ctr. for Arts, Orwigsburg Women's Libr. Soc. Republican. Home: 225 Eisenhower Dr Orwigsburg PA 17961-1605

MASON, JOEL BERNARD, internist, gastroenterologist; b. Syracuse, NY, June 17, 1955; B in General Biology, U. Ill.-Urbana, 1977; MD, U. Chgo.-Pritzker Sch. Medicine, 1981. Cert. internal medicine, gastroenterology, nutrition. Intern. gastroenterology U. Iowa Hosps., Iowa City, 1981—82, resident, 1982—84; fellow U. Chgo. Hosp., 1984—86; gastroenterologist Tufts-New England Med. Ctr., Boston; assoc. prof. medicine and nutrition Tufts Sch. Medicine; dir., vitamins and carcinogenesis lab., USDA Human Nutrition Rsch. Ctr. Tufts U. Cons. Mead-Johnson Nutritional; editorial bd. Jour. Parenteral & Enteral Nutrition. Mem.: Am. Soc. for Nutritional Sciences. Office; Tufts-New England Med Ctr Medicine Clin Nutrition 711 Washington St Boston MA 02111-1524 also: Tufts New England Med Ctr Medicine Gastroene 750 Washington St #218 Boston MA 02111 Office Phone: 617-556-3194. Office Fax: 617-556-3234. E-mail: joel.mason@tufts.edu.

MASON, JOHN WAYNE, psychoneuroendocrinologist, retired medical educator; b. Chgo., Feb. 9, 1924; s. John Ralph and Frances Elsie (Swedman) Mason; m. Joyce Ann Towne; children: John Mark, Victoria Joyce, Peter Brooke. AB, Ind. U., Bloomington, 1944; MD, Ind. U., Indpls., 1947; MA (hon.), Yale U., New Haven, 1977. Diplomate in pathol. anatomy Am. Bd. Pathology. Surg. intern NY Hosp.-Cornell Med. Ctr., NYC, 1947—48, resident in pathology, 1948—50; chief dept. neuroendocrinology Walter Reed Army Inst. Rsch., Washington, 1953—74; prof. emeritus psychiatry Yale U. Sch. Medicine, New Haven, 1977—. Cons. and dir. psychoendocrine lab. Adult Psychiatry br. NIMH, Bethesda, Md., 1960—65; sci. advisor, neuropsychiatry br. Walter Reed Army Inst. of Rsch., Washington, 1974—77; dir. psychoendocrine lab. Nat. Ctr. for PTSD, VA Med. Ctr., West Haven, Conn., 1977—2000; lectr. and invited lectr. in field. Contbr. more than 170 sci. rsch. publs. to profl. jours., 24 chpts. to books, also revs. in field; author: (monograph) Organization of Psychoendocrine Mechanisms, 1968 (Med. Lit. Citation Classic award). Website builder Finishingofourfauty Dot Com; faculty sponsor, Campus Crusade for Christ ministry Yale U., 1983; Bible tchr. Trinity Evang. Free Ch., Woodbridge, Conn., 1978—2009. Served to maj. M.C. US Army, 1948—53. Recipient Rsch. Scientist Career award, NIMH, 1981-1991, medal, Pavlovian Soc., 1985, Meritorius Civilian Svc. award, Dept. of Army, 1960, Sustained Superior Performance Civil Svc. awards, 1960, 1966, 1969, Lifetime Achievement award, 21st Century Traumatology Conf., Georgetown U. Med. Ctr. Founds., 1996; grantee, NIMH, 1989-2000. Mem.: Assn. Psychosomatic Medicine (editl. bd. mem. 1963—91), Internat. Soc. Psychoneuroendocrinology (Lifetime Achievement award 2005), Endocrine Soc., Am. Psychosomatic Soc. (pres. 1969—70, Pres.'s award 2000), Alpha Omega Alpha, Phi Beta Kappa. Achievements include long term systematic basic and clinical research on the importance of psychosocial influences upon a wide range of endocrine systems in relation to stress and stress-related clinical disorders; major pioneering contributions to the development of the field of psychoneuroendocrinology and to exploring its far-reaching clinical implications for psychiatry and medicine; development of psychoendocrine strategies using concurrent hormonal and psychological measurements providing new leverage for the interdisciplinary study of; intrapsychic processes including emotional states, psychological defenses and coping styles; established that psychosocial and physical stress stimuli produce broadly organized multihormonal patterns of change involving many interdependent endocrine systems; received national and international recognition as a leader providing landmark experimental and conceptual contributions in the fields of psychoendocrinology and stress research; development of an unusual profile of thyroid hormonal alterations in PTSD patients, which provides compelling leads concerning the pathogenesis and possible treatment of this disorder. Home: 3701 International Dr Apt 709 Silver Spring MD 20906-1574 Personal E-mail: jwmason@pol.net.

MASON, MALCOLM DAVID, oncologist, researcher; b. London, May 31, 1956; s. Seymour and Marion (Grant) M.; m. Lee-Anne Isaacs, Mar. 27, 1983; children: Danielle Cynthia, Jenna Frances. MB, BS, U. London, 1979, MD, 1991. Registrar Royal Marsden Hosp., London, 1984-87; Bob Champion clin. rsch. fellow Inst. Cancer Rsch., Sutton, Eng., 1988-89; lectr. clin. oncology Royal Marsden Hosp., Sutton, 1989-91; cons. clin. oncologist Velindre Hosp., Cardiff, Wales, 1992-96; Cancer Rsch. Wales prof. clin. oncology U. Cardiff, Wales, 1997—. Dir. rsch. Velindre Cancer Centre, Cardiff, 1996; chmn. UK Nat. Cancer Rsch. Inst.'s Prostate Cancer Clin. Studies Group, 2009-; dirs. Wales Cancer Bank. Contbr. articles to profl. cancer jours., chpt. to Oxford Textbook of Oncology, 1994; asst. editor jour. Clin. Oncology, 1994-99. Fellow Royal Coll. Radiologists, Royal Coll. Physicians, Royal Soc. Medicine (sec. oncology sect. 1997-98, pres. 1999-2000), UK TNM Com. (chmn., mem., UICC TNM Core Group 2008-). Avocations: music, art. Office: Velindre NHS Trust Velindre Rd Whitchurch Cardiff CF14 2TL Wales E-mail: masonmd@cardiff.ac.uk.

MASON, ROBERT J., physician; b. Milw., Nov. 25, 1940; MD, Western Res. U., 1966. Prof. Nat. Jewish Health, 1981—. Recipient Sci. Achievement award, Am. Thoracic Soc. Fellow: ACP. Avocation: reading. Office: Nat Jewish Health Smith Bldg 459 Denver CO 80206 Business E-Mail: masonb@njhealth.org.

MASON, TERRY, hospital administrator, urologist; b. Washington; BS, Loyola U., 1974; MD, U. Ill. Abraham Lincoln Sch. Medicine, 1978. Pres., ptnr. Prairie Med. Associates; chief Dept. Urology Mercy Hosp., Chgo.; asst. prof. surgery Abraham Lincoln Sch. Medicine U. Ill.; commr. Chgo. Dept. Pub. Health, Ill., 2006—09; chief medical officer Cook County Health & Hosp. Sys. (CCHHS), Chgo., 2009—11, interim CEO, 2011—; ptnr. Urolpartners, 2005—10. Host radio prog. Doctor in the House WVON, Chgo., 2001—11. Author: Making Love Again, Renewing Intimacy & Helping Your Man Overcome Impotence, 1988. Recipient Physician of the Year, Nat. Med. Assn., 1999, Black Enterprise Best in Medicine award, 2001, C.A.R.E.S. award, Resurrection Health Care, 2010. Fellow: American Coll. Surgeons; mem.: World Impotence Assn. (regional dir.), American Urological Assn., Nat. Med. Assn. (nat. chmn.), AMA, Saltpond Redevelopment Inst., Ghana West Africa, NAACP. Office: Cook County Health & Hospital System (CCHHS) 1900 W Polk St Chicago IL 60612 Office Phone: 312-864-4800. *

MASON, WILLIAM A(LVIN), psychologist, educator, researcher; b. Mountain View, Calif., Mar. 28, 1926; s. Alvin Frank and Ruth Sabina (Erwin) M.; m. Virginia Joan Carmichael, June 27, 1948; children: Todd, Paula, Nicole, Hunter. BA, Stanford U., 1950, MS, 1952, PhD, 1954. Asst. prof. U. Wis.-Madison, 1954-59; research assoc. Yerkes Labs. Primate Biology, Orange Park, Fla., 1959-63; head dept. behavioral sci. Delta Primate Research Ctr., Tulane U., Covington, La., 1963-71; prof. psychology, research psychologist U. Calif., Davis, 1971-91, leader behavioral biology unit Calif. Primate Rsch. Ctr., 1972-96, prof. emeritus, 1991. Bd. dirs. Jane Goodall Inst., 1978-92, Karisoke Rsch. Ctr., 1980-86. Mem. Editorial bd. Animal Learning and Behavior, 1973-76, Internat. Jour. Devel. Psychobiology, 1980-92, Internat. Jour. Primatology, 1980-90; contbr. numerous articles to profl. jours., chpts. to books. With USMC, 1944-46. USPHS spl. fellow, 1963-64. Fellow AAAS, APA (pres. divsn. 6 1982, disting. sci. contbn. award 1995), Am. Psychol. Soc., Animal Behavior Soc.; mem. Internat. Primatological Soc. (pres. 1976-80, 81-84), Am. Soc. Primatologists (pres. 1988-90, disting. primatologist award), Internat. Soc. Devel. Psychobiology (pres. 1971-72, Best Paper of Yr. award 1976), Sigma Xi. Home: 2809 Anza Ave Davis CA 95616-0257 Office: U Calif Regl Primate Rsch Ctr 1 Shields Ave Davis CA 95616 Home Phone: 530-756-2479. Business E-Mail: wamason@ucdavis.edu.

MASOPUST, VÁCLAV, neurosurgeon; b. Mladá Boleslav, Aug. 21, 1971; MD, Charles U., 1995. Neurosurgeon Ctrl. Mil. Hosp., 1995. Mem.: Neurosurgery & Pain Treating Assn. Avocation: golf. Home: Nad Hradním Vodojemem Prague 16200 Czech Republic Personal E-mail: masopust.vaclav@gmail.com.

MASS, MYRON FRANK, allergist, immunologist; b. Phila., Feb. 24, 1945; m. Marilyn Halpern, June 12, 1966; children: Ellis, David. Student, U. Fla., 1963; BA, Brandeis U., 1966; MD, U. Fla., 1970; postgrad., U. Colo., Albany, NY, 1972, U. Colo., Denver, 1975. Intern Albany Med. Ctr., NY, 1970-71, residency, 1971-72; sr. residency U. Colo. Med. Ctr., Denver, 1972-73, postgrad. fellow/allergy-immunology, 1973-75; assoc. clin. prof. medicine U. Fla., Jacksonville, 1977—. Past chmn. dept. medicine Meml. Med. Ctr., Jacksonville; prin. investigator Jacksonville Ctr. for Clin. Rsch. Inventor skin chamber. Chmn. Duval County Environ. Protection Bd.; trustee Fla. CC at Jacksonville, 1999-2007, also bd. trustees. Maj. USAF, 1975-77. Health Professions scholar U. Fla. Fellow ACP, Am. Acad. Allergy and Immunology, Am. Coll. Allergy; mem. Duval County Med. Soc. (v.p., pres.-elect, pres.). Office Phone: 904-733-8200. E-mail: massjax@comcast.net.

MASSA, FERNANDO, dentist; b. Caxias do Sul, Rio Grande do Sul, Brazil, Feb. 22, 1960; Degree in Dentistry, Fed. U. Rio Grande do Sul, 1982; MS in Prosthodontics, U. Luterana do Brasil, Canoas, 2003. Pvt. practice, 1983. Adj. prof. dept. prosthodontics U. Luterana do Brazil, 1996—2006. Avocations: music, exercise, movies. Office: Rua Dr Montaury 1471 rm 504 Caxias do Sul Rio Grande so Sul 95020-190 Brazil Business E-Mail: massafernando@terra.com.br.

MASSE, LOUIS M.F., epidemiologist; b. Rilly-la-Montagne, France, Feb. 26, 1925; s. Edouard and Lucie (Charlot) M.; m. Genevieve Mayer, Oct. 16, 1951; children: Jean-Remi, Anne. MD, U. Paris, 1951; MPH, Harvard U., 1959, DPH, 1966; Dr.esL., U. Sorbonne, 1963. Med. resident hosps., France, 1949-52; rsch. asst. U. Dakar, Senegal, 1953-63; prof. Nat. Sch. Pub. Health, Rennes, France, 1963-88; dir. Inter-State Sch. Pub. Health, Brazzaville, Congo, 1988-90; vice chmn. Univ. Hosp., Rennes, 1990—2007. Panelist WHO, Geneva, Switzerland, 1967-89; vis. lectr. Pasteur Inst., Paris, 1970-99. Co-author: Data Handling in Epidemiology, 1970, Epidemiology: A Guide to Teaching Methods, 1972, Health Care and Epidemiology, 1978, Environmental Epidemiology, 1982, Health Information Systems, 1984. Roman Catholic. Avocations: windsurfing, home repair. Office: Ecole Nat de la Sante Pub 35 043 Rennes Cedex France

MASSEY, ROBERT UNRUH, internist, educator, dean; b. Detroit, Feb. 23, 1922; s. Emil Laverne and Esther Elisabeth (Unruh) M.; m. June Charlene Collins, May 28, 1943 (dec. July 2005); children: Robert Scott (dec.), Janet Charlene. Student, Oberlin Coll., 1939-42, U. Mich. Med. Sch., 1942-43; MD, Wayne State U., 1946. Intern, resident in internal medicine Henry Ford Hosp., Detroit, 1946-50; assoc. Lovelace Clinic, Albuquerque, 1950-68, chmn. dept. medicine, 1958-68, bd. govs., 1957-68; dir. med. edn. Lovelace Found. for Med. Edn. and Research, 1960-68; clin. assoc. U. N.Mex. Sch. Medicine, 1961-68; prof. medicine U. Conn. Sch. Medicine, Farmington, 1968-92, prof. emeritus, 1992—, assoc. dean for grad edn., 1968-71, dean Sch. Medicine, 1971-84, currently prof. emeritus dept. community medicine and health care, acting univ. v.p. for health affairs, 1975-76. Chief staff Newington VA Hosp., Conn., 1968-71; trustee Am. Assn. Med. Clinics, 1966-68; exec. com., regional adv. group Conn. Regional Med. Program, 1971-76; trustee, v.p. Capitol Area Health Consortium, 1974-78, pres., 1980-81. Editor-in-chief Conn. Medicine, 1986-99; editor Jour. of the History of Medicine and Allied Scis., 1987-91. Bd. dirs. Health Planning Coun., Inc., 1974-76; bd. dirs. Hartford Inst. for Criminal and Social Justice, 1976-80, Conn. Easter Seal Soc., 1977-85, Hospice Inst. Edn., Tng. and Rsch., 1979-81. With AUS, 1955-57; maj. Res. Fellow ACP; mem. Am. Group Practice Assn. (accreditation commn. 1968-78), Assn. Am. Med. Colls., Am. Assn. History of Medicine, Hartford County Med. Assn., AMA, Conn., Hartford med. socs., Am. Osler Soc., Beaumont Med. Club, Soc. Med. Adminstrs., Twilight Club (Hartford), Acorn Club, Sigma Xi, Alpha Omega Alpha. Roman Catholic.

MASSIMO, LUISA MARIA ELENA, pediatrician; b. Genova, Italy, Dec. 22, 1928; d. Diodato F. and Ada G.M. (Nicola) Massimo. MD cum laude, U. Genova, 1953, spec. in pediatrics cum laude, 1955, PhD in Pediatrics, 1962, PhD in Child Health, 1965. Asst. U. Genova, 1955-65, asst. prof. pediatrics, 1965-72, faculty Sch. Splzn. in Pediatrics, Hematology, Oncology, 1972—97. Dir. dept. pediatric hematology and oncology Inst., G. Gaslini Children's Hosp., Genova, 1972-97, emeritus, 1997—; expert Priority Area Life Sci. and Tech. Com. NATO, 1997-2001; expert European Union, 2000—. Contbr. articles to profl. jours. Pres. Nat. Sci. Cancer Inst., Genova, 1986—94. Recipient prize Accademia Nat. dei Lincei, 1971, Barbara Bohen Pfeifer, NY, 1991, Gold medal Italian Republic, 2004, Gold medal 2011; fellow Centre Internat. de l'Enfance, 1959, Basel, Switzerland, 1960 Mem. Internat. Soc. Pediatric Oncology, European Soc. Pediatric Hematology and Immunology. Société Suisse de Pediatrie, Associazione Ital. di Ematologia e Oncologia Pediatrica, N.Y. Acad. Scis., Internat. Coll. Pediatrics, Societa Italiana di Pediatria, Soroptimists. Roman Catholic. Office: 5 L go Gerolamo Gaslini Quarto 16148 Genoa Italy Home: Viale Brigata Bisagno 8 16129 Genoa GE Italy Home Phone: 39 010 561218; Office Phone: 39 010 591788. Personal E-mail: luisamassimo@yahoo.it. Business E-Mail: luisamassimo@ospedale-gaslini.ge.it.

MASSIN, EDWARD KRAUSS, physician; b. Houston, 1939; MD, Washington U., St. Louis, 1965; BA, Rice U., 1961. Intern Barnes Hosp., St. Louis, 1965-66, resident, 1966-67; with St. Lukes Episcopal Hosp., Houston. Clin. prof. Baylor Coll. Medicine. Cardiology fellow U. Colo. Med. Ctr., 1969-71. Fellow Am. Coll. Cardiology Office; Cardiology Cons Houston 6624 Fannin St Ste 2310 Houston TX 77030-2335 Office Phone: 713-796-2668. *

MASSOF, ROBERT WILLIAM, neuroscientist, educator; b. Minn., Jan. 2, 1948; m. Patricia Massof; children: Eric, Allison. BA, Hamline U., 1970; PhD, Ind. U., 1975. Postdoctoral fellow in ophthalmology Johns Hopkins U. Sch. Medicine, Balt., 1975-76, instr. ophthalmology, 1976-78, from asst. prof. to assoc. prof., 1978-91, prof. ophthalmology, 1991—, prof. neurosci. Lectr. in field. Mem. editl. bd. Clin. Vision Scis., N.Y.C., 1986-94, Eye Care Technology/Computers in Eye Care, Folsom, Calif., 1992-96, Opthalmic Epidemiol., London, 2008-; patentee in field (5); contbr. articles to profl. jours. Recipient Manpower award, 1989, Tech. Transfer award NASA, 1993, Popular Mechanics Design and Engring. award, 1994, EyeCare Tech. Lifetime Achievement award, 1995, Richard E. Hoover Svc. award, 1995, Humanitarian award Lions, 2000, Disting. Svc. in Vision award Am. Pub. Health Assn., William Feinbloom award Am. Acad. of Optometry, 2000, Alfred W. Bressler prize Jewish Guild for the Blind, 2004, Alcon Rsch. Inst. award, 2009, Pigart award, Lighthouse Int., 2009, RPB Sr. Investritor award, 2009. Fellow Optical Soc. Am. (chmn. edn. coun. 1993-95, bd. dirs. 1993-95), Am. Acad. Optometry; mem. Assn. Rsch. in Vision and Ophthalmology. Office: Johns Hopkins Univ Lions Vision Ctr 550 N Broadway Fl 6 Baltimore MD 21205-2020 Office Phone: 410-502-6246. Business E-Mail: rmassof@lions.med.jhu.edu.

MASSONE, CESARE, dermatologist, educator; b. Alessandria, Italy, May 22, 1971; s. Luigi Massone and Antonietta Bello Massone. MD, U. Genoa, Italy, 1996. Asst. dept. dermatology U. Genoa, 1998—2002; fellow in dermatopathology Med. U. Graz, Austria, 2001—04, asst. prof. dept. dermatology, 2005—08, assoc. prof. dermatology, 2008—; fellow Inst. Tropical Medicine-Manaus & RDTC-MOSHIE, Tanzania, Brazil. Moderator www.telederm.org, Med. U. Graz, 2003—; coord. dermoscopy courses Internat. Dermoscopy Soc., 2004—05. Contbr. articles to profl. jours. Recipient Best Case in Cutaneous Mycology award, Novartis Farma, 1998, L. Bertellotti award, ADOI, 2000, 2004, AESCA award, 2005, award, French Soc. Dermatology, 2005, Steigleder, 2005; grantee, SIDeMaST, 2004. Master: Internat. Dermoscopy Soc. (corr.), Internat. Soc. Dermatopathology (corr.), Internat. Soc. Teledermatology (corr.). Achievements include development of a DermOnline community in teledermatology, T-REGS in leprosy; research in classification and definition of CD30 negative cutaneous lymphomas; definition of the criteria for the diagnosis of early mycosis fungoides (cutaneous T-cell lymphoma); definition and classification of subcutaneous T-cell lymphomas; definition of the criteria for the diagnosis of lupus erythematosus panniculitis; early diagnosis of melanoma through dermoscopy; telediagnosis in dermatopathlogy; assessment of disease activity in cutaneous lupus erythematosus; autoimmune antibodies in lichen planus; biologics in psoriasis; imported leprosy in Italy. Office: Med Univ Graz Dept Dermatology Auenbruggerplatz 8 Graz A-8036 Austria Office Fax: 0043-316-385-12466. Business E-Mail: cesare.massone@klinikum-graz.at.

MASTEJ, J. MICHAEL, retired hospital administrator; b. Detroit, Mar. 19, 1949; s. Joseph Albert and Bertha A. (Toleikis) Mastej; m. Laura Thtatcher Wright, Dec. 28, 1975 (div. 1983); 1 child; m. Lucy Shafer Mastej, July 28, 1984. BBA in Acctg., U. Notre Dame, 1971.

Group dir., dir., devel. Universal Health Svcs., Inc; medicare and medicaid auditor Mich. Blue Cross; asst. contr. Emma L. Bixby Hosp., Adrian, Mich., 1973—75; CEO, acute care hosps. Humana, Inc., reimbursement specialist, 1975—77; exec. dir. Humana Hosp., Ft. Walton Beach, Fla., 1981; assoc. exec. dir. Llano Estacado Med. Ctr., Hobbs, N.Mex., 1977—78, The Wellington Hosp., 1978—79; exec. dir. Garden State Cmty. Hosp., Marlton, NJ, 1979—81; bd. advisor Okaloosa County Emergency Med., 1984; v.p., acquisitions Health Management Associates, Inc., 2001—05, CEO, Collier Regional Med. Ctr. Naples, Fla., 2005—07. V.p. Okaloosa Symphony; bd. dirs. Okaloosa chpt. Am. Heart Assn. Recipient Humana Mgmt. Club award, Louisville, 1981—82; named King of Hearts, Am. Heart Assn., Okaloosa County, 1985. Mem.: Greater Ft. Walton Beach C. of C. (v.p. 1985), Am. Coll. Hosp. Adminstrs., Rotary (program chmn. 1985). Republican. Episcopalian. Avocations: sailing, skiing, golf. *

MASTERS, JOHN CHRISTOPHER, psychologist, educator; b. Terre Haute, Ind., Oct. 25, 1941; s. Robert William and Lillian Virginia (Decker) M.; m. Mary Jayne Capps, June 6, 1970; children—Blair Christopher, Kyle Alexander. AB, Harvard Coll., 1963; PhD, Stanford U., 1967. Asst. prof. Ariz. State U., Tempe, 1968-69; from asst. prof. to prof. U. Minn., Mpls., 1969-79; assoc. dir. Inst. Child Devel., 1974-79; Luce prof. pub. policy and the family, prof. psychology Vanderbilt U., Nashville, 1979-87, interim chair dept. psychology, 1986-88; pres. Profl. Mgmt. Group, Inc., 1991—; dir. Master Ventures, 1989—, Master Travel, 1989—. Assoc. editor: Child Development, 1973-76, Behavior Therapy: Techniques and Empirical Findings, 1974, 79, 88; editor: Psychol. Bull., 1987-89. Home: 4923 Old Oakleaf Dr Sarasota FL 34233-3947 Office Phone: 800-767-6162.

MASTERSON, LISA M., gynecologist, obstetrician; married; 1 child. Grad., Mt. Holyoke Coll.; MD, U. So. Calif. Pvt. practice, Santa Monica, Calif.; founder, med. dir. Ocean Oasis Med. Spa, Santa Monica, Calif.; staff mem. Cedars-Sinai Med. Ctr., LA. Med. expert The Doctors, 2008—. Founder Maternal Fetal Care Internat. (MFCI). Office: Ocean Oasis Med Spa 1333 Ocean Ave Santa Monica CA 90401 Office Phone: 310-451-9900. *

MASTROROBERTO, PASQUALE, cardiovascular surgeon; b. Matera, Lucania, Italy, Dec. 20, 1959; s. Giuseppe and Giovanna Battista (Passarella) M.; m. Francesca Vista, Mar. 31, 1990 MD, U. Naples, Italy, 1984. Diplomate Italian Bd. Thoracic and Cardiovascular Surgery. Postgrad. fellow dept. cardiovascular surgery U. Naples, 1984-89; asst. prof. Med. Sch. U. Catanzaro, Italy, 1990-91, 94—, prof. Sch. Cardiac Surgery, 1994—; resident surgeon Thoracic and Cardiovascular Dept., Monte Carlo, Monaco, 1992-93. Cons. Sch. Pediatrics, Catanzaro, 1995—. Fellow Internat. Coll. Angiology, Am. Coll. Angiology (assoc.); mem. N.Y. Acad. Scis. Home: Corso Vittorio Emanuele 58 84123 Salerno Italy

MASUD, FAISAL, cardiologist; b. Pakistan, Jan. 21, 1965; MBBS, Rawalpindi Med. Coll., 1988. Assoc. prof. clin. anesthesiology, Weil Cornell Med. Coll. Meth. Hosp., Meth. DeBakey Heart & Vascular Ctr., 1997, vice chair qulality & patient safety, med. dir., CVICU, 1997—. Recipient Fulbright & Jaworski Faculty Excellence award, Baylor Coll. Medicine. Fellow: Am. Coll. Chest Physician; mem.: Acad. Disting. Educators, Assn. Profl. Infection Control & Epidemiology (named Hero in Infection Prevention 2010), Soc. Cardiovasc. Anesthesiologists, Soc. Critical Care Medicine (Alan I Fields award, Tex. chpt. 2010). Avocations: basketball, cricket. Office: 6565 Fannin St B452 Houston TX 77030 Business E-Mail: fmasud@tmhs.org.

MASUDA, GOHTA, retired physician, educator; b. Tokyo, Nov. 21, 1940; s. Ryota and Chiyo (Ikeuchi) M.; m. Mitsuko Taguchi, May 14, 1983. MD, Keio U., 1966, PhD, 1977. Intern Keio U., Tokyo, 1967-74, 76-78; asst. prof. Kitasato U., 1974-76; chief dept. infectious diseases Tokyo Met. Komagome Hosp., 1978-95, dir. dept. infectious diseases, 1995-2001; pres. Tokyo Met. Kiyose Children's Hosp., 2001—03, Tokyo Met. Kita Med. and Rehab. Ctr., 2003—05. Asst. prof. Toho U., Tokyo, 1985—, Keio U., Tokyo, 1986; dir. NPO: Biomed. Sci. Assn., 2008—. Home: 1-25-15 Honkomagome Bunkyo-ku Tokyo 113-0021 Japan

MASUDA, NORIKAZU, oncologist, surgeon; b. Matsubara-city, Osaka, Japan, Mar. 13, 1969; s. Kunihiko and Etsuko Masuda; m. Kimie Takai, Dec. 25, 2001. MD, Osaka U., 1993, PhD, 2001. Cert. med. specialist Japan Surg. Soc., Japanese Breast Cancer Soc., Japan Soc. Clin. Oncology. Resident Osaka U. Med. Sch., Suita-city, 1993—94; physician Osaka Teishin Hosp., Osaka-city, 1994—97; chief physician breast oncology Sakai Mcpl. Hosp., Sakai-city, Japan, 2001—03, Osaka Nat. Hosp., Osaka-city, Japan, 2003—. Councilor Japanese Breast Cancer Soc., 1998—, Japanese Breast Cancer Screening Soc., 2003—. Recipient 7th award of bounty for rsch., Japanese Breast Cancer Soc., 2001. Avocations: travel, tennis, cooking. Office: Osaka Nat Hosp Chuou-ku 2-1-14 Hoenzaka Osaka 540-0006 Japan Office Phone: 81-6-6942-1331. Office Fax: +81-6-6946-3608. Business E-Mail: nmasuda@alpha.ocn.ne.jp.

MASUDA, YUKIHIRO, otolaryngologist; b. Nagano, Japan, May 12; s. Kazuyo Masuda; 1 child, Miyu. PhD (hon.), Nat. Def. Med. Coll., Tokorozawa city Saitama, Japan, 1995. Cert. in ENT doctor Nat. Def. Med. Coll., 2006. Maj. Japan Nat. Def. Med. Coll., 1995—2006. Contbr. articles to profl. jours. Office: Sayama ENT Clinic Chuou 3-3-25 Sunpales 1F Sayama Saitama 350-1308 Japan

MASUDA, YUKITAKA, cardiologist, educator; b. Hofu, Yamaguchi, Japan, Mar. 22, 1951; s. Itsuo and Yasuko Masuda; m. Junko Fujii; children: Adjusa, Yuki. MD, Yamaguchi U., Japan, 1975, undergrad. Diplomate Japanese Soc. Internal Medicine. Intern, resident Internat. Med. Ctr. of Japan, 1975—77; rsch. assoc. Mt. Sinai Med. Ctr., Cleve., 1977—85; instr. Dokkyo U. Sch. Medicine, Mibu, Japan, 1986—91; asst. prof. Dokkyo U. Sch. of Medicine, Mibu, Japan, 1991—97; dir. Utsunomiya (Japan) Ctrl. Hosp., 1993—94; head dept. medicine Tashirodai Hosp., Mitou, Japan, 1997—2008; dir. Masuda Health Promotion Ctr., Aiofutajima, Japan, 2008—. Contbr. monograph Encyclopedia of Neuroscience, monograph Simulation and control of the cardiac system. USPHS grantee, NIH, 1983—89. Mem.: Japanese Circulation Soc. (corr.; diplomate in cardiology), Am. Heart Assn. (corr.). Office Fax: 81 839872066. Personal E-mail: yuknrepi@c-able.ne.jp.

MASUI, YOSHIO, zoology educator; b. Kyoto, Oct. 6, 1931; arrived in Can., 1969; s. Fusa and Toyo Masui; m. Yuriko Masui, May 9, 1959; children: Sayuri, Hitoshi. BSc, Kyoto U., 1953, MSc, 1955, PhD, 1961; DSc (hon.), U. Toronto, 1999. Asst. prof. Konan U., Kobe, Japan, 1965; rsch. staff biologist Yale U., New Haven, 1966-69, lectr., 1969; assoc. prof. U. Toronto, Ont., 1969-78, prof. Ont., 1978-97, prof. emeritus, 1997—, Konan U., 1999—. Recipient Manning award Manning Found., Calgary, Alta., 1991, Gairdner Internat. award Gairdner Found., Toronto, 1992, Albert Lasker award for Basic Med. Rsch., Lasker Found., 1998; named Officer, Order of Canada, 2003. Fellow Royal Soc. London., Royal Soc. Can. Achievements include discovery of Maturation Promoting Factor (MPF) and Cytostatic Factor (CSF) and their roles in cell divison control. Office: Univ Toronto Dept Cell and Sys Biology 25 Harbord St Toronto ON Canada M5S 3G5 Home Phone: 647-343-0497; Office Phone: 416-978-3493. Business E-Mail: masui@rogers.com. *

MASUO, KAZUKO, medical educator, director; d. Kazuhiko and Kieko Masuo. MD, PhD, Osaka U. Postgrad. Sch. Med., Japan, 1983. Assoc. med. dir., Nucleus Network Ltd. Baker IDI Heart & Diabetes Inst., Melbourne, Victoria, Australia, 2007—, acad. fellow, 2010—; assoc. prof. Monash U. Sch. Med., Melbourne, 2008—. Contbr. articles to med. jours. Recipient JSH Novartis award, 2008; Future Forum Rsch. grant, NIH, 2006, NHMRC Project grant, Australian Govt., 2007. Fellow: Japanese Soc. Endocrinology, Japanese Soc. Nephrology, Japanese Soc. Internal Med., Am. Heart Assn. (New Investigator award, Coun. High Blood Pressure Rsch. 2002), Japanese Soc. Hypertension (faculty mem.). Office: Baker IDI Heart & Diabetes Inst 75 Commercial Rd Melbourne Victoria 3004 Australia Business E-Mail: kazuko.masuo@bakeridi.edu.au.

MASUO, YOSHINORI, biomedical researcher; b. Yanagawa, Japan, Aug. 10, 1956; s. Yoshikatsu and Takako (Kitagawa) Masuo; m. Hiromi Akagi, June 15, 1986; 1 child, Hiroaki. BS, Toho U., 1983; M in Med. Sci., Tsukuba U., Japan, 1986; PhD in Neurosci., U. Paris 6, 1990; PhD in Medicine, U. Tokyo, 1994. Asst. rsch. fellow Nat. Ctr. Neurology and Psychiatry, Nat. Inst. Neurosci., Kodaira Tokyo, 1982-83; rsch. fellow dept. neurology U. Tsukuba, 1983-84; fgn. rschr. INSERM U. 114 Coll. de France, Paris, 1986-87, INSERM U. 55 Hosp. St. Antoine, Paris, 1987-90; rschr. Tsukuba Rsch. Labs. Takeda Chem. Industries, 1990-93; assoc. rsch. head Discovery Rsch. Labs. I Takeda Chem. Industries, 1993-97; rsch. assoc. dept. physiology Toho U. Sch. Medicine, 1997-2000; rschr. Nat. Inst. Biosci. and Human Tech., 2000—01; chief asst. Internat. Patent Organism Depositary, Nat. Inst. Advanced Indsl. Sci. and Tech., 2001—04; rschr. class A New Energy and Indsl. Tech. Devel. Orgn., 2001—04; rschr. Human Stress Signal Rsch. Ctr. Nat. Inst. Advanced Indsl. Sci. and Tech., 2004—05, with Health Tech. Rsch. Ctr., 2008—10; prof. lab. neurosci., dept. biology Faculty of Sci., Toho U., 2010—; team leader mentak stress team Human Stress Signal Rsch. Ctr. Nat. Inst. Advanced Indsl. Sci. & Tech., 2005—08. Guest rschr. Nat. Inst. Environ. Studies, 2001—05; guest prof. U. Louis Pasteur, Strasbourg, 2006. Contbr. articles to profl. jours. Fellow, INSERM, 1988; Vis. Rsch. fellow, Canon Found. Europe, 1990. Mem.: Japan Soc. Endocrine Disrupters Rsch., Japanese Soc. Neurochemistry, Physiol. Soc. Japan, Internat. Brain Rsch. Orgn., Japan Neurosci. Soc., Soc. for Neurosci., NY Acad. Scis. Avocations: skiing, scuba diving, tennis. Office: Lab Neuroscis Dept Biology Faculty Sci Toho University 2-2-1 Miyana Funabashi Chiba 274 8510 Japan Office Phone: 81474725257.

MASUR, HENRY, internist; b. NYC, Mar. 8, 1946; s. Jack and Barbara (Forsch) Masur; m. Grace Steinacker, Jan. 14, 1979; children: Carrie, Jack, Julia. AB, Dartmouth Coll., 1968; MD, Cornell U., 1972. Diplomate Am. Bd. Internal Medicine, Am. Bd. Infectious Diseases. Intern, resident N.Y. Hosp., 1972—74; resident Johns Hopkins Hosp., Balt., 1974—75; asst. prof. Cornell Med. Coll., NYC, 1978—82; asst. chief critical care medicine NIH, Bethesda, Md., 1982—83, dep. chief critical care medicine, 1983—89, chief critical care medicine, 1989—. Clin. prof. George Washington U. Med. Sch., Washington. Mem.: Infectious Diseases Soc. Am. (pres. 2006—07), Assn. Am. Physicians, Am. Soc. Clin. Investigation. Office: NIH Rm 2C145 9000 Rockville Pike Bethesda MD 20892-1662 Home Phone: 301-229-1111. Business E-Mail: hmasur@nih.gov. *

MASYS, DANIEL RICHARD, medical educator, department chairman; b. Columbus, Ohio, Mar. 6, 1949; s. Paul John and Jane Marie (Mollenauer) M.; m. Linda Suzanne Bross, June 2, 1974; 1 child, Christopher. AB in Biochemistry, Princeton U., 1971; MD, Ohio State U., 1974. Diplomate Am. Bd. Internal Medicine. Staff hematologist, oncologist U.S. Naval Hosp., San Diego, 1980-84; chief ICRDB br. NIH, Bethesda, Md., 1984-86; dir. Lister Hill Nat. Ctr. Nat. Libr. Medicine, Bethesda, Md., 1986-94; dir. biomed. informatics, prof. Sch. Medicine U. Calif., San Diego, 1994—2004; prof., chair dept. biomedical informatics Vanderbilt U., 2005—. Assoc. editor Acad. Medicine jour., 1988-91, Jour. Am. Med. Informatics, Assn., 1994-2004. Mem. high performance computing White House Office of Sci., Washington, 1991-94; rep. Fed. Networking Coun., Washington, 1991-94. Capt. USPHS, 1984-94; NASA Adv. Aerospace Medicine, 2004-. Fellow: ACP, Am. Coll. Med. Informatics (exec. com. 1989—92, pres. 2006—); mem.: Nat. Acad. Scis., Inst. Medicine, Am. Med. Informatics Assn. (bd. dirs. 1992—95, assoc. editor jour. 1993—2004, Pres.'s award 1992), Alpha Omega Alpha. Office: Vanderbilt Univ 416 EBL 2209 Garland Ave Nashville TN 37232-8340

MATALLANA, LYNNE, patient advocacy association administrator; BA in Polit. Sci., UCLA, 1977; MA in Internat. Politics, London Sch. Economics & Polit. Scis., 1985. Former ptnr. advt. agy., Calif.; co-founder, pres. Nat. Fibromyalgia Assn., Calif., 1997—; cmty. devel. coord, adminstrative asst. City Ont., 1980—83; v.p. mktg. devel Cmty. Sys. Assocs. Inc., 1983—84; mktg. dir. Main Place Mall, JMB Inc.; gen. mgr. Mission Viejo Mall, Edward J. DeBartolo Corp., 1986—89; dir. promotions & pub. relations Raging Waters Amusement Inc., 1989—90; ptnr, v.p. Diversified Mktg. Concepts Inc.; pres. Cause Mktg. LLC, 2005—. Mem. FDA Ctr. for Drug Evaluation Rsch., Arthritis Adv. Com., Nat. Inst. Arthritis & Musculoskeletal & Skin Diseases Coalition. Pub., editor-in-chief Fibromyalgia AWARE mag, 2002—; author: The Complete Idiot's Guide: Fibromyalgia, 2005, 2nd edit., 2008. Office: National Fibromyalgia Association 2121 S Towne Centre Pl Ste 300 Anaheim CA 92806-6124 Office Phone: 714-321-0150. Office Fax: 714-921-6920. *

MATARASSO, ALAN, plastic and reconstructive surgeon; b. NYC, Oct. 19, 1953; s. Daniel and Ethel M. BA magna cum laude, Boston U., 1975; MD, U. Miami Sch. Medicine, Miami, Fla., 1979. Diplomate Nat. Bd. Med. Examiners, 1980, Am. Bd. Plastic Surgery, 1986. Intern, dept. gen. surgery Albert Einstein Coll. Med., Montefiore Med. Ctr., Bronx, NY, 1979-80, resident, dept. gen. surgery, 1980—83, chief resident, dept. gen. surgery, 1982—83, resident and chief resident dept. of plastic surgery, 1983—85; fellow aesthetic surgery Manhattan Eye, Ear and Throat Hosp., 1985, asst. attending surgeon, 1985—, attending surgeon, 1986—, NY Eye and Ear Infirmary, 1986—, Beth Israel North Hosp., 1988—; surgeon St. Luke's/Roosevelt Hosp. Ctr., 1986—; asst. attending surgeon Lenox Hill Hosp., 2000—; clin. prof. plastic surgery Albert Einstein Coll. Medicine, 1996—. Expert cons., State NY, Dept. Health, Office of Profl. Med. Conduct. Contbr. chpt. Encyclopedia of Flpas, Mastery in Plastic Surgery; instrnl. course vol. Plastic Surgery Ednl. Found.; editor Clinics in Plastic Surgery on Non Operative Techniques for Facial Rejuvenation and Liposuction and Body Contouring for Operative Techniques in Plastic Surgery; sr. sci. editor Aesthetic Surgery Jour.; numerous profl. presentations; contbr. several articles to profl. jours.; quoted in numerous mags. and newspapers including NY Times, Wall Street Jour., Vogue, Elle, Marie Claire, Hapers Bazaar, Ladies Home Jour., Self, InStyle, GQ, Newsweek, Time and Economist; featured on TV broadcasts including 20/20, Lifetime LIVE, Fox 5 TV, CNN and others. Bd. dirs. Sephardic Home For The Aged, Bklyn.; NE reg. coord., Ultrasonic Assisted Lipoplasty Reg. Workshops, 1996-98. Recipient Physicians Recognition award AMA, 1994, 2004; named one of Best Drs. in Am. Am. Health Mag., 1996, Best Doctors in N.Y., N.Y. Mag., 1996, 98-2005, Castle-Connolly Guide to the Best Drs., NY Metro Area. Fellow ACS, NY Acad. Medicine, Internat. Coll. Surgeons (USA) in Plastic Surgery; mem. Am. Assn. Plastic Surgeons (chair videotape com., 1996-99, symposium com., 1997-99, mem. teaching course subcom., 1996-, vice chair, 1998-99, program com., 1996-, Strategic Planning com., 1999-, travelling prof., 1999-2001, edu. commn., 1999-2000, time and place com., 2000-, chair, corp. sponsorship com., 2000-, rep. to products/svcs. workshop, 2000, parliamentarian, 2001-2002); mem. Am. Soc. Aesthetic Plastic Surgery (bd. dirs.), Fla. Soc. Plastic and Reconstructive Surgeons (corr. mem.), Internat. Soc. Aesthetic Plastic Surgeons (pub. edu. com., 2000), Nat. Endowment for Plastic Surgery, Lipoplasty Soc. N.Am., Assn. for Academic Surgeons, Northeastern Soc. Plastic Surgeons (chmn., aesthetic symposium, 1998-99, bd. dirs.), NY Reg. Soc. of Plastic and Reconstructive Surgery (treas., sec., program chair, pres.), Soc. for Acad. Surgeons, Royal Soc. Medicine, England Oversee Fellow, Am. Cleft Palate Assn., Pan Am. Med. Soc. (mem., sect. on Plastic and Reconstructive Surgery), Pan Pacific Surgical Assn., NY County Med. Soc. (Young Physician's Com., 1992-94, peer review com. I & II, 1993-, grievance com., 1993-, media com., 1993-), Med. Soc. State NY (social discipline com., 1994-, state legis. com., 1994-96), NY Reg. Soc. Plastic Surgeons, (exec. com. 1988-, sci. com. med. program chair, 1988-), NY State Soc. Surgeons, Rhinoplasty Soc. (bd. dirs., historian, pres. elect, 2008), Soc. of Laparoendoscopic Surgeons, So. Med. Assn., AMA, Am. Soc. Plastic Surgeons (Young Plastic Surgeons, 1987-89, Plastic Surgery Product Assessment Commn., 1991-92, CPT/ICD 9 Coding Workshop, 1991-96, Ad Hoc Com. 1992, mktg. com, 2000), Plastic Surgery Edu. Found. (Computerized Exam, 1989, EF Teleplast, 1992-95, vis. scholar, 1993-94, Edu. Assessment, 1992, Internat. Symposia, 1993, chair, Resource Book Subcom. of Resident Information Com., 1995-98, rep. on Domsestic Clin. Symposia, 1997-, In-service Examination Com., Aesthetic and Breast Subcom., 2000, Device and Technique Assessment Com., 2000, Domestic Clin. Symposia Com., 2000), Aesthetic Surgery Edu. and Rsch. Found. (charter mem.), Skin Cancer Found. (med. adv. com., 1986-), Cancers and Careers.org (adv. bd. 2000), Northeastern Soc. Plastic Surgeons. Developed a new technique of muscle tightening and liposuction for flattening the stomach. Office: Manhattan Eye Ear and Throat Hosp 1009 Park Ave New York NY 10028-0936 Home Phone: 212-628-0900; Office Phone: 212-249-7500. Office Fax: 212-628-5000. Personal E-mail: matarasso@aol.com.

MATARASSO, SETH L., dermatologic surgeon; b. Oct. 12, 1957; MD, U. Buffalo, 1984. Intern Beth Israel Med. Ctr., NYC, 1984-85; resident Baylor Coll. Medicine, Houston, 1985-88; fellowship U. Calif. Sch. Medicine, San Francisco, 1989-90; clin. prof. dermatology Sch. Medicine U. Calif., San Francisco, 1990—. Lectr. in field. Contbr. articles to profl. jours. Fax: 415-362-7745. Business E-Mail: marlena@dmgsf.com.

MATARAZZO, JOSEPH DOMINIC, psychologist, educator; b. Caiazzo, Italy, Nov. 12, 1925; (parents Am. citizens); s. Nicholas and Adeline (Mastroianni) M.; m. Ruth Wood Gadbois, Mar. 26, 1949; children: Harris, Elizabeth, Sara. Student, Columbia U., 1944; BA, Brown U., 1946; MS, Northwestern U., 1950, PhD, 1952. Fellow in med. psychology Washington U. Sch. Medicine, 1950-51; instr. Washington U., 1951-53, asst. prof., 1953-55; rsch. assoc. Harvard Med. Sch., assoc. psychologist Mass. Gen. Hosp., 1955-57; prof., head med. psychol. dept. Oreg. Health Scis. U., Portland, 1957-96, prof. behavioral neurosci., 1996—2007, prof. emeritus behavioral neurosci., 2007—. Mem. behavioral medicine study sect. NIH; nat. mental health adv. coun. NIMH; bd. regents Uniformed Svcs. U. Health Scis., 1974-80. Author: Wechsler's Measurement and Appraisal of Adult Intelligence, 5th edit., 1972, (with A.N. Wiens) The Interview: Research on its Anatomy and Structure, 1972, (with Harper and Wiens) Nonverbal Communication, 1978; editor: Behavioral Health: A Handbook of Health Enhancement and Disease Prevention, 1984; mem. editl. bd.: Jour. Clin. Psychology, 1962-96; cons. editor: Contemporary Psychology, 1962-70, 80-93, Intelligence: An Interdisciplinary Jour, 1976-90, Jour. Behavioral Medicine, 1977—2005, Profl. Psychology, 1978-94, Jour. Cons. and Clin. Psychology, 1978-85; editor: Psychology series Aldine Pub. Co, 1964-74; editor Williams & Wilkins Co, 1974-77; contbr. articles to profl. jours. With USNR, 1943-47, res. USNR, 1947-88; capt. Res. Recipient Hofheimer prize Am. Psychiat. Assn., 1962 Fellow AAAS, APA (pres. 1989-90, divsn. health psychology 1978-79, mem. coun. reps. 1982-91, bd. dirs. 1986-90, Ann. Disting. Profl. Contbn. award 1991, Ann. Gold Medal for Life Achievement in the Application of Psychology 2001); mem. Western Psychol. Assn. (pres. 1986-97), Am. Assn. State Psychology Bds. (pres. 1963-64), Nat. Assn. Mental Health (bd. dirs.), Oreg. Mental Health Assn. (bd. dirs., pres. 1962-63), Internat. Coun. Psychologists (bd. dirs. 1972-74, pres. 1976-77), Am. Psychol. Found. (pres. 1994-2000). Home: 1934 SW Vista Ave Portland OR 97201-2455 Office: Oreg Health Scis U Sch Medicine 3181 SW Sam Jackson Park Rd Portland OR 97239 Home Phone: 503-228-3215; Office Phone: 503-494-8644. Office Fax: 503-494-5972. Business E-Mail: matarazz@ohsu.edu.

MATARAZZO, RUTH GADBOIS, behavioral neuroscience and psychiatry professor emerita; b. New London, Conn., Nov. 9, 1926; d. John Stuart and Elizabeth (Wood) Gadbois; m. Joseph D. Matarazzo, Mar. 26, 1949; children: Harris, Elizabeth, Sara. AB with honors, Brown U., 1948; MA, Washington U., St. Louis, 1952, PhD, 1955. Diplomate in clin. psychology and clin. neuropsychology Am. Bd. Examiners Profl. Psychology; cert. in bus. adminstrn. Harvard Radcliffe Program, 1949. Rsch. fellow pediat. Washington U. Med. Sch., 1954-55; rsch. fellow psychology Harvard U. Med. Sch., 1955-57; asst. prof. med. psychology Oreg. Health Scis. U., Portland, 1957-63, assoc. prof., 1963-68, prof. dept. med. psychology, 1968—, prof. emerita, 1997. Woman liaison officer to Assn. Am. Med. Coll.s, 1979—90; cons. Tillamook Job Corps, Oreg. Bd. Med. Examiners, Social Security Adminstrn., Portland Ctr. Hearing and Speech. Author (E. Greif): (book) Behavioral Approaches to Rehabilitation: Coping with Change, 1982; contbr. chapters to books, articles to profl. jours., book reviews to jours. Bd. dirs. Portland Opera Assn., Portland Mental Health Assn., Morrison Child Guidance Clinic, Portland Chamber Orch., Neskowin Valley Sch.; fin. chair Hoover-Minthorn House Mus.; gov. Soc. of Mayflower Desc. Oreg. Fellow: APA (mem. policy and planning bd., mem. edn. and tng. bd., vice-chair accreditation bd., chair accreditation task force, site visitor APA accreditation of grad. programs, Oreg. rep. to coun. rep., Annual Presdl. award 2007), Oreg. Psychol. Assn. (past pres.), We. Psychol. Assn. (bd. dirs.); mem.: AAAS, Nat. Soc. Colonial Dames Oreg. (treas., fin. chair, bd. dirs., v.p.), Portland Psychol. Assn. (past pres.), Sigma Xi. Home: 1934 SW Vista Ave Portland OR 97201-2455 Business E-Mail: matarazr@ohsu.edu.

MATCHAR, DAVID B., physician, researcher; b. Balt., Sept. 29, 1955; s. Joseph Charles and Evelyn M.; m. Barbara Fran Goldfinger, May 4, 1980; children: Emily Ruth, Benjamin Jacob, Daniel William. MD, U. Md., 1980. Diplomate Am. Bd. Internal Medicine. Prof. medicine Duke U. Med. Ctr., Durham, NC, 1985—, dir. Duke Ctr. Clin. Health Policy Rsch., 1985—; dir., program health svcs. rsch. Duke Nat. U. Singapore Grad. Med. Sch., 2008—. Fellow ACP, Soc. Gen. Internal Medicine (pres. so. sect. 1988), Am. Heart Assn., Soc. for Med. Decision Making (editl. bd., chair 1993 ann. meeting, trustee), Am. Acad. Neurology, Svoke Coun. Office: Duke Ctr Clin Health Policy Rsch 2400 Pratt St # 311 Durham NC 27705-3976 Office Phone: 919-286-3399. Business E-Mail: david-matchar@duke-nus.edu.sg. *

MATECZUN, JOHN MATTHEW, career military officer; b. Albuquerque, Aug. 29, 1946; s. Alfred Joseph and Margaret Ellen Mateczun; m. Elizabeth Kathleen Holmes; children: Erin Johnson, Adam Johnson, Laura. MD, U. N.Mex., 1978; MPH, U. Calif., Berkeley, 1982; JD, Georgetown U. Law Ctr., 1988. Diplomate Am. Bd. Psychiatry & Neurology, cert. in forensic psychiatry. Asst. divsn. surgeon, divsn. psychiatrist 3rd Marine Divsn., USN, Okinawa, Japan, 1982—83, med. staff, Nat. Naval Med. Ctr. Bethesda, Md., 1983—85, intern adv, dir. transitional internship, 1985—87, chmn. dept. psychiatry, 1989—90, dir. med. svcs., 1990—91, force surgeon, USMC Forces Pacific Camp Smith, Hawaii, 1991—94, chmn. dept. psychiatry, Naval Regional Med. Ctr. Portsmouth, Va., 1987—89, dir. TRICARE Region 1 Washington, 1994—95, prin. dir. clin. svcs., office asst. sec. of def. (health affairs), 1995—97, chief med. officer Tricare Mgmt. Activity, 1997—98, commdg. officer Naval Hosp. Charleston, SC, 1998—2000, asst. chief ops., Bur. Medicine & Surgery Washington, 2000—01, chief staff, Bur. Medicine & Surgery, 2003, comdr. Naval Med. Ctr. San Diego, 2003—05, dep. surgeon gen., 2005—07, vice chief, Bur. Medicine & Surgery, 2005—07, comdr. Joint Task Force Nat. Capital Region Med., 2007—. Assoc. prof. clin. psychiatry Uniformed Svcs. U. Health Scis. Contbr. chapters to books. Decorated Navy Disting. Svc. medal, Def. Superior Svc. Medal with Oak Leaf Cluster, Legion Merit with three gold stars, Bronze Star, Def. Meritorious Svc. medal, Meritorious Svc. medal with gold star, Navy/Marine Corps Commendation medal, Army Commendation medal, Navy/Marine Corps Achievement medal. Fellow: APA (disting.); mem.: Am. Coll. Physician Execs., Am. Acad. Psychiatry & Law, Assn. Mil. Surgeons of US (life). Office: Joint Task Force CAPMED Bldg 27 8901 Wisconsin Ave Bethesda MD 20889

MATEJU, JOSEPH FRANK, hospital administrator; b. Cedar Rapids, Iowa, Oct. 18, 1927; s. Joseph Frank and Adeline (Smid) M. BA, U. N.Mex., 1951; MA, N.Mex. State U., 1957. Sr. juvenile probation officer, San Diego County, 1958-64; adminstr. Villa Solano State Sch., Hagerman, N.Mex., 1965-67; state coord. on mental retardation planning N.Mex. Dept. Hosps. and Instns., Santa Fe, 1969-70; adminstr. Los Lunas (N.Mex.) Hosp. and Tng. Sch., 1968-69, 70-85. Pres. Intercare, bd. dirs. With USAF, 1946—47. Fellow Am. Assn. Mental Deficiency, Am. Coll. Nursing Home Adminstrs.; mem. Am. Assn. Retarded Children (v.p.), Albuquerque Assn. Retarded Citizens, N.Mex. Hosp. Assn., Pi Gamma Mu. Home: 405 Fontana Pl NE Albuquerque NM 87108-1168

MATELES, RICHARD ISAAC, biotechnologist; b. NYC, Sept. 11, 1935; s. Simon and Jean (Phillips) M.; m. Roslyn C. Fish, Sept. 2, 1956; children: Naomi, Susan, Sarah. BS, MIT, 1956, MS, 1957, DSc, 1959. USPHS fellow Laboratorium voor Microbiologie, Technische Hogeschool, Delft, The Netherlands, 1959-60; mem. faculty MIT, 1960-70, assoc. prof. biochem. engring., 1965-68; dir. fermentation unit Jerusalem, 1968-77; prof. applied microbiology Hebrew U., Hadassah Med. Sch., Jerusalem, 1968-80; vis. prof. dept. chem. engring. U. Pa., Phila., 1978-79; asst. dir. rsch. Stauffer Chem. Co., Westport, Conn., 1980, dir. rsch., 1980-81, v.p. rsch., 1981-88; sr. v.p. applied scis. IIT Rsch. Inst., Chgo., 1988-90; proprietor Candida Corp., Chgo., 1990—. Editor: Jour. Chem. Tech. and Biotech., 1972—2008; editor: (N.Am. edit.) Biotech., 2001—08; editor: Penicillin: A Paradigm for Biotechnology, 1998, Directory of Toll Fermentation and Cell Culture Facilities, 2005; contbr. articles to profl. jours. Mem. Conn. Acad. Sci. Engring., 1981—; mem. vis. com., dept. applied biol. sci. MIT, 1980-88; mem. exec. com. Coun. on Chem. Rsch., 1981-85. Fellow Am. Inst. Med. and Biol. Engring.; mem. AICE, SAR, Am. Chem. Soc., Inst. Food Technologists, Union League. Home: 222 E Chestnut St Apt 10B Chicago IL 60611 Office: Candida Corp Ste 1616 77 W Washington St Chicago IL 60602 Office Phone: 312-346-3335. Business E-Mail: rmateles@candidacorp.com.

MATEOS MANTECA, MARÍA-VICTORIA, hematologist; b. Zamora, Spain, Oct. 4, 1969; MD, U. Valladolid, 1993; PhD, U. Salamanca, 2000. Physician hematology U. Hosp. Salamanca, 1997—. Mem.: Internat. Myeloma Working Group. Office: Paseo San Vicente 58-182 Salamanca Castilla-León 37007 Spain Office Fax: 34923294624. Business E-Mail: mvmateos@usal.es.

MATERA, CRISTINA, gynecologist, educator; b. Englewood, NJ, Sept. 29, 1960; MD, NYU, 1986. Cert. in ob-gyn. and reproductive endocrinology and infertility. Resident ob-gyn. Columbia Presbyn. Med. Ctr./Presbyn. Hosp., NYC, 1986—90, fellow, 1990—92; asst. prof. Columbia P&S, 1990—. Office: 50 E 77th St New York NY 10075 Office Phone: 212-639-9122. E-mail: cmaterand@mac.com.

MATERIA, KATHLEEN PATRICIA AYLING, nurse; b. Jersey City, Nov. 7, 1954; d. Donald Anthony and Muriel Cecilia (Joyce) Ayling; m. Francis Peter Materia, June 5, 1983; children: Christopher Michael, Donna Nicole. BSN, Fairleigh Dickinson U., 1976. RN, N.J. Critical care nurse Palisades Gen. Hosp., North Bergen, N.J., 1976-87; grad. nurse, 1976-77; nurse critical care unit North Hudson Hosp., Weehawken, NJ, 1977-78. Mem. Alpha Sigma Tau. Democrat. Avocations: bowling, dance.

MATERN, ULRICH, surgeon, researcher, consultant; b. Bad-Godesberg, Germany, Nov. 25, 1962; s. Norbert and Annemarie Matern; m. Daniela Matern, 1992; children: Jessica, Theresa. MD, Tech. U., Munich, Germany, 1992. Resident dept. gen. surgery Tech. U., Munich, 1991—92; fellow dept. gen. surgery U. Freiburg, Germany, 1992—2002; dir. ergonomy, minimally invasive surgery sect. U. Tuebingen, Germany, 2003—05; dep. dir. Steinbeis Transfer Ctr. Health Care Tech., Tuebingen, 2003—05; dir. exptl. OR and ergonomics U. Tuebingen, 2005—. Contbr. articles to med. jours. Recipient Eleonore and Fritz Hodeige Stiftung award, 2000. Mem.: German Soc. for Surgery, European Assn. Endoscopic Surgery, Human Factors and Ergonomic Soc. Achievements include patents for new ergonomic surgical instruments and devices. Office: Exptl-OR and Ergonomics Eberhard-Karls U Tuebingen Ernst-Simon-Str 16 72072 Tübingen Germany Office Phone: 0049-0177-5417357.

MATERSON, BARRY JON, physician, educator; b. Phila., May 17, 1938; s. Alfred L. and June (Slakoff) Materson; m. Biruta Donins, Sept. 8, 1963; children: Sandra E. Materson Vidal, Debra M. Rosenthal. BS, U. Miami, Fla., 1959; MD, U. Miami, 1962, MBA Health Care, 1993. Diplomate Am. Bd. Internal Medicine, Am. Bd. Nephrology, cert. specialist in hypertension Am. Soc. Hypertension. Intern Los Angeles County Hosp., 1962—63; resident internal medicine Jackson Meml. Hosp., Miami, Fla., 1963, 1965—67; fellow nephrology Miami VA Med. Ctr., 1967—68; rsch. and edn. assoc. VA Med. Ctr., Miami, 1969—72, asst. chief med. svc., 1972—86, acting chief, 1987—88, assoc. chief, 1988—89, assoc. chief staff edn., 1989—95; med. dir. for managed care U. Miami Med. Group, 1995—2005, dir. self-ins. program, 2003—05; physician liaison Office Patient Protection and Risk Prevention, 2005—09; chief acad. mentor, Divsn. Hosp. Medicine, 2008—. Assoc. prof. medicine U. Miami, 1974—83, prof., 1983—, nat. bd. dirs., chmn. pharmacy and therapy rev. com., 1987—2003; chmn. budget and subcom. VA Med. Ctr., 1980—87, mem. JNC-7 Exec. Commn., 2002—03; assoc. editor Jour. Am. Soc., 2011—. Contbg. author: Hypertension, 1989, Cardiovascular Drug Therapy, 1990; contbr. articles to profl. jours. Capt. M.C. USAF, 1963—65. Recipient Lifetime Achievement award, Consortium of Southeastern Hypertension Control (COSEHC). Fellow: ACP, Am. Soc. Hypertension (sec. 2003—), Am. Heart Assn. (coun. high blood pressure rsch.); mem.: Internat. Soc. Hypertension. Achievements include research in antihypertensive agents regarding beta-adrenergic blocking agents as possible first line therapy; low-dose captopril; hypertension in the elderly; monotherapy of hypertension and race by age interactions as determinants of response to antihypertensive drug therapy, combination therapy. Business E-Mail: bmaterson@med.miami.edu

MATES, LAWRENCE A., JR., medical company executive; b. Toledo, Oct. 10, 1954; s. Lawrence A. and Phyllis A. (Thomas) M.; m. Ulrike D. Heermann, Dec. 23, 1977; children: Lawrence A. III, Jessica M. BS in Mktg. cum laude, Princeton U., 1976, MBA, 1977. Sales mgr. Technicare Corp., Cleve., 1977-80; dist. sales mgr. Siemens Med. Systems, Iselin, NJ, 1980—85; regional sales mgr. Digital Equipment Corp., Detroit, 1985-88; v.p. sales Cemax, Inc., Fremont, Calif., 1988—92; exec. v.p. Philips Electronics, Cin., 1992-2000; sr. v.p. Siemens, 2000—. Bd. dirs. Provident Nat. Bank. Bd. dirs. Cin. City Planners, 1994—, United Way, 1985-86, 92-96, Am. Cancer Soc., 1997-99; mem. Ea. Pa. Planning Commn., 2006—; v.p. West Chester Citizen's Bd., 2006—; mem. banker's bd., Malvern, Pa., 2006—, Chaster City Hosp., 2005-. Mem. Med. Researchers Assn., Am. Hosp. Assn., Toledo Bus. Assn. (v.p. 1984-85), Ohio Young Men's Bus. Assn. (pres. 1985, chmn. 1992-93), Cin. Profl. Bus. Assn. (v.p. 1993—), Cin. Health Profls. (dir. 1994-95), Cin. Investors Ltd. (dir. 1994-98), Toledo Investors Ltd. (pres. 1986, 92), Cin. Bankers Club, Cin. Club, Univ. Club (v.p. 1993-96, pres. 1998-02), Sycamore Athletic Boosters (pres. 1996-98, bd. dirs. 1996—). Republican. Roman Catholic. Avocations: swimming, travel, wine collecting, automobiles, golf. Office Phone: 610-350-9112. Personal E-mail: lmates@aol.com.

MATES, SUSAN ONTHANK, physician, educator, musician, writer; b. Oakland, Calif., Aug. 8, 1950; d. Benson and Lois (Onthank) M.; m. Joseph Harold Friedman, Dec. 10, 1978; children: Rebecca, Deborah, William. Student, Juilliard Sch. Music, 1967-69; BA magna cum laude with distinction, Yale Coll., 1972; MD, Albert Einstein Coll. Medicine, 1976. Cert. Am. Bd. Internal Medicine, Nat. Bd. Med. Examiners. Intern Boston City Hosp., 1976-77; fellow in gen. medicine Coll. of Physicians and Surgeons-Columbia U., NYC, 1977-78; resident/fellow in infectious diseases Montefiore Hosp., Bronx, 1978-82; asst. prof. medicine Brown U., Providence, 1982-85, asst. prof. biochemistry, 1985-86, clin. assoc. prof. medicine, 1993-98, vis. lectr., 2006; staff mem., former dir. R.I. State Tb Clinic, R.I. Dept. Health, Providence, 1986-96, cons. Tb program, 1987-96. Judge short story contest Providence Jour., 1994, 98; mem. jury R.I. Coun. Arts Fellowship; contbg. editor Pushcart Prize, Pushcart Press, 1995, 96, 97, 98, 99. Author: (fiction) The Good Doctor, 1994 (John Simmons Short Fiction Award, U. Iowa Press, 1994); contbr. sci. articles to profl. jours., stories to revs. and jours. and anthologies. Recipient Recognition award for young scholars AAUW, 1985, Clin. Investigator award NIH, 1984, R.I. Found. award, 1983; McDowell Colony fellow, 1995, Yaddo fellow, 1996; Symposium scholar in lit. and medicine for 21st Century, Brown U., 1997. Mem. Am. Med. Women's Assn., Poets and Writers, Alpha Omega Alpha.

MATHAI, SHEILA SAMANTA, pediatrician, neonatologist; b. Liverpool, Eng., Aug. 3, 1961; d. Birinchi Prosad and Rita Samanta; m. Khalil Isaac Mathai, Aug. 24, 1985; 1 child, Shreya Anne. MBBS, Pune U., 1983; MD, Mumbai U., 1991, DM in Neonatology, 2000. Diplomate Nat. Bd. Examinations, 1990. Med. officer, surgeon capt. Indian Navy, Mumbai, Maharashtra, India, 1983—91, graded specailist Port Blair, Andamans, India, 1992—95; assoc. prof. & neonatologist Indian Naval Hosp. Ship, Mumbai, 1995—2005; prof., pediat. & neonatologist Armed Forces Med. Coll., Pune, Maharashtra. Organizing sec. neocon 2007 Nat. Neonatology Forum, Pune, Maharashtra, India, 2006—07. Decorated Chief Naval Staff Commendation Indian Navy. Mem.: Maharashtra State Chpt. Nat. Neonatology Forum (India) (sec.), Royal Coll. Pediatrics & Child Health (vis. fellow), Nat. Neonatology Forum (editor, state br. 2007—, sec. Maharashtra state br. 2009—). Avocations: writing, photography, aerobics. Home: 20/1 Carriappa Enclave Pune Maharashtra 411040 India Office: Armed Forces Med Coll Wanowrie Pune Maharashtra 411040 India

MATHAS, STEPHAN, oncologist, researcher; 4 children. Studied in Human Medicine, U. Cologne, Germany, 1990—97, U. Rene Descartes, France, 1994, Hammersmith Hosp., England, 1996. Lic. MD. Physician Charite U. Hosp., Hematology, Oncology, Berlin, 1997—; rschr., scientist Max Delbruek Ctr. Molecular Medicine, Hematology, Oncology, Molecular Biology, Berlin, 1998—. Contbr. scientific papers. Recipient C.G. Schmidt award, W. German Tumor Ctr., 2004, Karl Mushoff Poster award, German Hodgkin Study Group, 2004, Hodgkin's Lymphoma award, 2010, Curt-Meyer award, Berlin Cancer Soc., 2007, Pappenheim award, German Assn. Hematology and Oncology, 2010; grantee, German Acad.c Exch. Svc., 1993—94; Student grant, German Nat. Acad. Found., 1992—97. Avocations: music, beekeeping, piano, violoncello. Office Phone: 0049 30 9406 3519. Office Fax: 0049 30 9406 3124. Business E-Mail: smathas@mdc-berlin.de.

MATHAVAN, VINEY KUMAR, physician; b. Jammu & Kashmir, India, Dec. 14, 1970; MBBS, Govt Med. Coll. Jammu, 1995; MS, PGI Chandigarh, 2000. Physician Nagan, Arregui and Davis MDs, 2009—. Named one of Best Resident of Yr., Huron Hosp., Cleve. Clinic Hosp. Mem.: ACS, Soc. Am. Gastrointestinal and Endoscopic Surgery, Soc. Robotic Surgery. Avocations: travel, reading, music. Home: 3822 Steeplechase Dr Carmel IN 46032 Office Phone: 317-872-1158. Personal E-mail: vinmathavan@yahoo.com.

MATHENY, ADAM PENCE, JR., child psychologist, educator, consultant, researcher; b. Stanford, Ky., Sept. 6, 1932; s. Adam Pence and Dorotha (Steele) Matheny; m. Ute I. Debus, July 10, 1962 (div.); m. Mary P. Tolbert, June 24, 1967 (div.); children: Laura Steele, Jason Gaverick. BS, Columbia U., 1958; PhD, Vanderbilt U., 1962. Sr. human factors engr. Martin Aerospace divsn., Balt., 1962—63; instr. Johns Hopkins U. Med. Sch., Balt., 1963—65, staff fellow Nat. Inst. Child Health and Human Devel., 1965—67, from asst. prof. to prof. pediat. U. Louisville Med. Sch., 1967—75; assoc. dir. to dir. Louisville Twin Study, 1986—. Mem. rev. panel NIH, 1991—95. Co-author: Genetics and Counseling in Medical Practice, 1969; contbr. articles to profl. jours. With USN, 1951—55. Recipient Outstanding Rsch. medal, U. Louisville. Fellow: APA, Am. Psychol. Soc., Am. Assn. Applied and Preventive Psychology, Internat. Soc. Twin Studies; mem.: AAAS, Internat. Soc. Infant Study, Internat. Soc. Behavior Devel., Behavior Genetics Assn., Soc. Rsch. Child Devel., Sigma Xi, Phi Beta Kappa. Office Phone: 502-634-0050. Business E-Mail: apmathol@louisville.edu. E-mail: adammatheny@aol.com.

MATHER, ELIZABETH VIVIAN, healthcare executive; b. Richmond, Ind., Sept. 19, 1941; d. Willie Samuel and Lillie Mae (Harper) Fuqua; m. Roland Donald Mather, Dec. 26, 1966. BS, Maryville Coll., Tenn., 1963; postgrad., Columbia U., 1965-66. Tchr. Richmond Cmty. Schs., 1963-67, Indpls. Pub. Schs., 1967-68; systems analyst Ind. Blue Cross Blue Shield, Indpls., 1968-71, Ind. Nat. Bank, Indpls., 1971; med. cons. Ind. State Dept. Pub. Welfare, Indpls., 1971-78, cons. supr., 1978-86; systems analyst Ky. Blue Cross Blue Shield, Louisville, 1988-89; contracts specialist Humana Corp., Louisville, 1989—. Active Rep. Cen. Com. Montgomery County, Crawfordsville, 1976-86, Centenary Meth. Ch., adminstrv. bd., 1990. Mem. DAR (treas. 1963-66, sec. 1978-86). Avocation: designing and sewing clothes. Home: 6106 Partridge Pl Floyds Knobs IN 47119-9427 Office: 500 W Main St Fl 6 Louisville KY 40202-2946 Office Phone: 502-580-2519. Business E-Mail: emather@humana.com.

MATHER, PAUL J., cardiologist; BA, U. Pa., 1984; MD, Temple U., 1988. Diplomate Am. Bd. Internal Medicine, Am. Bd. Internal Medicine-cardiovasc. disease. Intern Temple Univ. Hosp., 1991, resident internal medicine, 1991, fellow cardiovasc. diseases, 1994; dir. advanced heart failure and cardiac transplant ctr. Thomas Jefferson Univ. Hosp. Author: Numerous articles in professional journals and book chapters on heart failure, echocardiography and related topics. Named one of Top Doctors, Phila Mag., 2010—11. Mem.: Am. Coll. of Cardiology (mem. congestive heart failure task force), Alpha Omega Alpha Med. Honor Soc. (alumni honoree), Am. Soc. of Transplantation, Heart Failure Soc. of America (with care standards com., with mech. circulatory support database com.), Internat. Soc. of Heart and Lung Transplantation (heart failure coun.), Am. Soc. of Echocardiography, Am. Coll. of Cardiology. Office: Thomas Jefferson University Hospital 925 Chestnut St Philadelphia PA 19107 Office Phone: 215-955-2050. Office Fax: 215-503-0052.

MATHES, DOROTHY JEAN HOLDEN, occupational therapist; b. Paterson, NJ, Mar. 13, 1953; d. Cornelius Fred and Dorothy Johanna (Ferguson) Holden; m. Clayton Derald Mathes, May 26, 1973 (div. Dec. 1984); children: Christy, Carl, Chuck, Chad; m. Elie Youssef Hajjar, Oct. 4, 1989 (dec. Dec. 1996). BS in Occupational Therapy, Tex. Woman's U., Denton, Tex., 1988; MA in Occupational Therapy, Tex. Woman's U., 1995. Lic. occupational therapist, Tex. Mem. Lakes Regional-SOCS Early Childhood Intervention, 1988-97; occupational therapy cons. Denton (Tex.) State Sch., 1997—, Rehab. Svcs. Unlimited, 2003—05, Rehab Care, 2005—10; occupl. therapy cons. Xtreme Therapy Staffing, 2007—10, Heritage Gardens Rehab. & Health Care, 2010—. Mem. Am. Occupational Therapy Assn., Tex. Occupational Therapy Assn. Avocations: gardening, reading, swimming. Home: 2608 Woodhaven St Denton TX 76209-1340 Office: 2135 N Denton Rd Carrollton TX 75006 Personal E-mail: djmathes1@verizon.net.

MATHEW, ANITA S., physician, researcher; b. Trivandrum, Kerala, India, May 29, 1980; MBBS, Thirumala Devaswom Med. Coll., Alappuzha, 2006; MD, La. State U., 2011. Rsch. fellow Biomedical

Rsch. Inst., Shreveport, La., 2007—08; house officer La. State U. Health Scis. Ctr., 2008—; chief resident dept. internal medicine La. State U. Reviewer Bentham Sci. Pub. Mem.: AMA, ACP, Internat. Soc. Clin. Densitometry, Am. Soc. Bone and Mineral Rsch., Am. Coll. Rheumatology. Office: 1501 Kings Hwy PO Box 33932 Shreveport LA 71130 Personal E-mail: amathew29@yahoo.com.

MATHEW, JOE PRASAD, zoologist; b. Alapuzha, Kerala, India, May 28, 1970; s. K. Joseph and Molly Mathew; m. Priya Joseph, June 24, 2000; 1 child, Seethal Maria Joe. BSc in Zoology, Mahatma Gandhi U., Kerala, India, 1991, MSc in Zoology, 1993, PhD in Zoology, 1999. Lectr. St. Berchmans' Coll., Changanacherry, Kerala, 1998—2002; rsch. assoc. Sacred Heart Coll., Thevara, Kochi, Kerala, 2002—03; assoc. head dept. bioscience M.A. Coll., Thiruvalla, 2003—04; sr. lectr. St. Berchmans' Coll., Changanacherry, 2004—08, asst. prof., 2008—. Contbr. articles to profl. jours. Recipient Swadeshi Sci. Puraskaram, 9Th Swadeshi Sci. Congress, 1999. Mem.: Zool. Soc. Kerala (life). Roman Catholic. Achievements include research in selenite cataractogenesis attenuated by vitamin E. Avocation: stamp collecting/philately. Office: Dept Zoology St Berchmans Coll Changanacherry 686101 India Home: Kaippadasseril Muttar Po 689 574 Alapuzha 689574 India Business E-Mail: jopmat@rediffmail.com. E-mail: jopmat@gmail.com.

MATHEW, OOMMEN P., medical educator; b. India, June 29, 1948; MBBS, JIPMER, 1973. Prof. pediat. Ga. Health Scis. U., 2003—. Fellow: Am. Acad. Pediat. Office: 1120 15th St BIW 6033 Augusta GA 30912 Business E-Mail: omathew@georgiahealth.edu.

MATHEWS, BARBARA EDITH, gynecologist; b. Oct. 5, 1946; d. Joseph Chesley and Pearl (Cieri) Mathews. AB, U. Calif., 1969; MD, Tufts U., 1972. Diplomate Am. Bd. Ob-Gyn. Intern Cottage Hosp., Santa Barbara, Calif., 1972-73, Santa Barbara Gen. Hosp., 1972-73; resident in ob-gyn Beth Israel Hosp., Boston, 1973-77; clin. fellow in ob-gyn Harvard U., Boston, 1973-76, instr., 1976-77; gynecologist Sansum Med. Clin., Santa Barbara, 1977-98; sr. scientist Sansum Med. Rsch. Inst., 1998—; med. dir., gynecologist Women's Health Svcs., Santa Barbara, 1998—. Faculty mem. ann. postgrad. course Harvard Med. Sch.; bd. dirs. Sansum Med. Clinic, 1989-96, vice chmn. bd. dirs., 1994-96; dir. ann. postgrad course UCLA Med. Sch. Bd. dirs. Meml. Rehab. Found., Santa Barbara, Channel City Club, Santa Barbara, Music Acad. of the West, Santa Barbara, St. Francis Med. Ctr., Santa Barbara; mem. citizen's contg. edn. adv. coun. Santa Barbara C.C.; moderator Santa Barbara Cottage Hosp. Cmty. Health Forum. Author: (with L. Burke) Colposcopy in Clinical Practice, 1977; contbg. author Manual of Ambulatory Surgery, 1982. Bd trustees Furman U., Greenville, SC, 2005—, bd. dirs., 2005—. Fellow ACOG, ACS; mem. AMA, Am. Soc. Colposcopy and Cervical Pathology (dir. 1982-84), Harvard U. Alumni Assn., Tri-counties Obstet. and Gynecol. Soc. (pres. 1981-82), Birnam Wood Golf Club (Santa Barbara), Phi Beta Kappa. Home: 2105 Anacapa St Santa Barbara CA 93105-3503 Office: 2235 De La Vina St Santa Barbara CA 93105-3815 Office Phone: 805-687-7778. Office Fax: 805-687-0012.

MATHEWS, JOAN HELENE, pediatrician; b. Manchester, NH, Feb. 3, 1940; d. John Barnaby and Helen A. Wlodkoski; m. Ernest Stephen Mathews, June 1, 1965; 3 children. BS, U. N.H., 1961; MD, Columbia U., 1965. Diplomate Am. Bd. Pediatrics. Med. intern Roosevelt Hosp., NYC, 1965-66; pediatric resident Babies Hosp. Columbia Presbyn. Med. Ctr., NYC, 1966-68, pediatric endocrine fellow Babies Hosp., 1968-70; instr. clin. pediat. Columbia U. Coll. Physicians and Surgeons, NYC, 1973-77; asst. prof. pediat. Cornell U. Med. Coll., NYC, 1977-81; clin. instr. pediat. Harvard Med. Sch., Boston, 1985—2003, clin. asst. prof. pediat., 2003—; clin. assoc. children's svc. Mass. Gen. Hosp., Boston, 1985—. Fellow: Am. Acad. Pediat.; mem.: Phi Beta Kappa. Office: 777 Concord Ave Cambridge MA 02138-1053 Office Phone: 617-876-6800. Office Fax: 617-876-5713. E-mail: joan.mathews@childrens.harvard.edu.

MATHEWS, PEGGY ANNE, nurse, consultant; b. Oakdale, La., Sept. 10, 1941; d. Howard Douglas and Huldah Mary (Hicks) Tyler; children: Joseph, Mark, Debra. A in Nursing, La. State U., Alexandria, 1975; BSN, Northwestern State U., La. Cert. Legal Nurse Cons. Inst., Houston; RN La. Nurse intensive care unit St. Frances Cabrini Hosp., Alexandria, 1975—80, staff educator nurse edn. dept., 1978—80, nurse edn. dept., 1979—80, dir. noninvasive cardiology dept., 1980—85, dir. cardiology, 1980—, established cardiac rehab. program, 1982; dir. Cardiac Catheterization Lab.; med. dir. TRACE Detection Svcs. Mem.: Am. Heart Assn., Am. Assn. Critical Care Nurses. Democrat. Roman Catholic. Avocations: dance, fishing, horseback riding, gardening, hunting. Home: 122 Cedar Point Ln Boyce LA 71409-8798 Office: St Frances Cabrini Hosp 3330 Masonic Dr Alexandria LA 71301-3899 Personal E-mail: pmrn41@yahoo.com.

MATHEWS, RADHA K., medical/surgical nurse, midwife; b. Alleppey, Kerala, India, Jan. 1, 1948; d. T. Venkiteswara and Sumithra (Bai) Kini; m. Andrew J. Mathews, July 16, 1973; children: Michelle M., Christian A. BSN, ETC Med. Coll. Hosp., Kolar, Mysore, India, 1968; student, Albany Med. Coll. Hosp., 1973, SUNY, Albany. Cert. psychiat. and pediatric nursing Albany Med. Coll. Hosp., 1974, ICU, CCU Albany Med. Coll. Hosp., 1976; RN U.K., 1969, State of N.Y., 1997. Staff nurse Bahrain Govt. Med. Dept., 1967—71; charge nurse Albany Med. Ctr., NY, 1972—78, St. Peter's Hosp., Albany, 1974—76; RN Northeast Nursing Svcs., Glenmont, NY, 1979—; med. data coder, analyst St. Peter's Hosp., Albany, 1989—94; RN Green Corrections Facility, Coxsackie, NY, 1993—94; charge nurse, asst. head nurse Our Lady of Hope, Latham, NY, 1994—2000; charge nurse Daughters of Sarah Nursing Home, Albany, 1995—, Staffing By Priority Inc., Niskayuna, NY, 2000—. Vol. nurse ambulance svc. North Colonie Sr. Citizen Club, North Colonie Dist. 4; founder Silver Line Sr. Citizen Club. Mem.: ANA, Am. Med. Records Assn. Home: 7515 255TH ST Glen Oaks NY 11004-1136

MATHIAS, CHRISTOPHER JOSEPH, physician, educator, researcher, consultant; b. Mangalore, India, Mar. 16, 1949; arrived in the U.K., 1972; s. Elias Salvadore and Hilda Frances (Pereira) M.; m. Rosalind Margaret Jolleys, July 31, 1977; children: Sarah, James, Timothy. MB, BChir, Bangalore U., India, 1972; DPhil, U. Oxford, Eng., 1976; DSc, U. London, 1995; PhD (hon.), U. Lisboa, 2007. Hon. rsch. officer, registrar Dept. Neurology, Oxford, 1972-76; sr. house officer dept. medicine Royal Postgrad. Med. Sch., London, 1976-77; registrar dept. medicine, Portsmouth and renal unit Southampton (Eng.) U., 1977-79; Wellcome Trust sr. clin. rsch. fellow St. Mary's Hosp. and Med. Sch., London, 1979-84; Wellcome Trust sr. lectr. St. Mary's Hosp. and Med. Sch. and Nat. Hosp. Inst. Neurology, London, 1984-91; prof. neurovascular medicine St. Mary's/Imperial Coll., Nat. Hosp., Inst. Neurology, U. Coll., London, 1991—. Chmn. rsch. com. World Fedn. Neurology on Autonomic Disorders, 1993-97; chmn. sci. panel European Fedn. Neurol. Soc., 1994-99; guest lectr. Thailand Neurol. Soc., 1995; Nimmo vis. prof. U. Adelaide, Australia, 1996; mem. sci. com. Internat. Spinal Rsch. Trust, 1996-2008; Allan Birch Meml. lectr., London, 1997, Abbie Meml. lectr. U. Adelaide, Australia, 1999, Dr. J. Thomas lectr. St. Johns Med. Coll., U. Bangalore, 1988, Lord Florey Meml. lectr. U. Adelaide, 1991, Sir Hugh Cairns Meml. lectr., Adelaide, 1996, Coll. lectr. Royal Coll. Physicians, London, 2001, Sir Robert Menzics Meml. Found. lectr., Sydney, Australia, 2001, Wahler meml. lectr. London Jewish Med. Soc., 2002, inaugural lectr. Portuguese Autonomic Soc., Lisbon, 2002, Prof. Muller lectr. U. Erlangen, Germany, 2002, 4th Athasit Yejajiva lectr., Bangkok, Thailand, 2003, Sir Gordon Holmes lectr., London, 2004, Sir Roger Bannister lectr., First Joint European and Am. Anatomic Soc. Congress, 2004, keynote lectr. 58th Congress of Japan Neuroregulative Soc., 2005, Prof. K. Srinivas orator, 2005, Valsalva lectr., Bologna, Italy, 2006; vis. prof. U. Hawaii, 1999; chmn. Dr. P.M. Shankland Pushpa Chopra Trust Prize Fund, 1998—; patron Anat. Disorders Assn. Sarah Matheson Trust, 1997—, vis. prof. U. Hong Kong, 2008. Co-editor (with M. Weber) Book on Mild Hypertension, 1984, (with P. Sever) Concepts in Hypertension, 1989, (with Sir Roger Bannister) Autonomic Failure: A Textbook of Clinical Disorders of the Autonomic Nervous System, 3d edit., 1992, 4th edit., 1999, reprinted, 2002; contbr. chpts to books and articles to profl. jours.; found. editor-in-chief Clin. Autonomic Rsch. Official Jour. Am. Autonomic Soc., Clin. Autonomic Rsch. Soc. and European Fedn. Autonomic Socs. of Gt. Britain, 1991—; mem. editl. bd. various internat. med./sci. jours. Named Rhodes scholar U. Oxford, 1972-75; recipient Prof. Ruitinga award and vis. professorship U. Amsterdam, The Netherlands, 1988. Fellow Royal Coll. Physicians (London, Brit. Petroleum lectr. 1992, lectr. 2001), Royal Soc. Medicine, Acad. Med. Scis.; mem. Am. Antonomic Soc. (bd. dirs., 1996-2004), Royal Coll. Physicians and Surgeons (licentiate Glasgow and Edninburg), Assn. Physicians Gt. Britain, Physiol. Soc., Assn. Brit. Neurologists, Am. Neurol. Assn., Brit. Pharm. Soc., Clin. Antonomic Rsch. Soc. (chmn. 1987-90, found. sec. 1982-86), Brit. European and Internat. Hypertension Soc., Royal Instn. Movement Disorders Soc., European Fedn. Autonomic Socs. (pres. 1999-2004), Internat. Fedn. Neurorehabilitation (chmn. spl. interest group 2004—), Am. Acad. Neurology, Boston, Internat Jour. Evidence Based Healthcare (mem. edtl. bd.), Parkinsonian and Related Disorders. European Fedn. Neurological Socs. Orthostatic Intolerance(lead task force), West London Mental Health Trust (non-executive dir.) Avocations: gardening, watching cricket and football, observing human and canine behavior. Office: St Marys Hosp Imperial Coll Sch Medicine Neurovascular Medi Unit Praed St London W2 1NY England Home: Meadowcroft West End Ln SL2 4NE Bucks SL2 4NE England E-mail: c.mathias@imperial.ac.uk.

MATHIAS, ROBERT S., pediatric nephrologist; b. Bklyn., Mar. 22, 1955; MD, Rush U. Med. Coll., Chgo., 1983. Diplomate Am. Bd. Pediat., cert. Am. Bd. Pediat. Nephrology. Intern pediat. U. Calif. Med. Ctr., San Diego, 1983—84, resident pediat., 1984—85, resident pediat. nephrology, 1986—87; fellowship Children's Hosp., Boston, 1987; clin. prof. Children's Renal Ctr. U. Calif. Med. Ctr. Contbr. articles to profl. jours. Mem.: Am. Acad. Pediat. Office: UCSF Med Ctr 533 Parnassus Ave Rm U585 S San Francisco CA 94143 Office Phone: 415-476-2423. Business E-Mail: rmathias@peds.ucsf.edu.

MATHIEU, THIERRY, biologist; b. Lille, France, Sept. 16, 1958; s. Jacques Mathieu and Anne Parmentier; children: Thibault, Cédric, Alexandre. M.Immunology, Faculty Of Sci., Lille, 1983; MD, Faculty Medicine, Lille, 1988. Cert. pathologist, biologist Ordre des medecins (France), 1990, hygienist Faculty of Medicine (Paris), 1999, specialist in PMA (Procreation medicalement assistee) Faculty of Medicine (Paris), 2001. Interne des hopitaux Centre Hospitalier Regional, Lens, 1983—89; CEO Laboratoire d'analyses de biologie médicale, Roubaix, 1990—96; pres. and CEO Laboratoire d'analyses de biologie medicale, Lens, Pas-de-Calais, 1996—. Dir., european leader of diagnostics analysis Med. de LABCO SAS, 2004—; bd. dirs. PMA Lab., Lens, Pas-de-Calais, 2001—. Health counseling Mairie, Roubaix, Nord, 1992—96. Capitaine Armée de terre, 1990—96, Lille. Fellow: Round Table; mem.: N.Y. Acad. of Scis. (licentiate), Société Nationale Francaise de Médecine Interne (assoc.). Achievements include first to creation of the first virtual reality place in France named CYBERIA (1992-1996). Avocation: tennis. Office: Laboratoire de Biologie Médicale 19 Rue Du 11 Novembre Pas-de-Calais Lens 62300 France Office Fax: (33)3.21.79.33.69. Personal E-mail: thierrym4@wanadoo.fr.

MATHIS, LISA, federal agency administrator; Assoc. dir. & pediatric & maternal staff FDA Office of New Drugs. Office: 10903 New Hampshire Ave Rm 6414 Silver Spring MD 20903 E-mail: lisa.mathis@fda.hhs.gov.

MATHIS, REMY RENE, orthodontist educator; b. Muttersholtz, Alsace, France, Feb. 3, 1949; s. Rene and Jenny (Sigwalt) M.; m. Odile Marie Grolet, Mar. 11, 1972; children: Charles-François, Juliane D Dentistry, Strasbourg U., France, 1974; DSc, Strasbourg U., 1983. Asst. prof. Dental dept. Strasbourg U., 1979—84, prof. Dental dept., 1984—. Cons. Nat. Health Ins., Strasbourg, 1977— Mem. European Begg Soc., N.Am. Study Soc. Orthodontics, Nat. Tchrs. Assn. (vice sec.), French Orthodontic Soc., French Begg and Tip Edge Soc Avocations: skiing, old-timers. Office: 2 Rue du Sand 67600 Selestat France Home Phone: 03 8882 1169; Office Phone: 03 8892 8660. E-mail: o.r.mathis@wanadoo.fr.

MATHISEN, DOUGLAS J., thoracic surgeon; b. Spring Valley, Ill., 1948; MD, U. Ill. Diplomate Am. Bd. Thoracic Surgery, Am. Bd. Surgery. Thoracic surgeon Mass. Gen. Hosp., Boston, 1995—; prof. thoracic surgery Harvard U. Med. Sch., 1989—99, Hermes C. Grillo prof. thoracic surgery, 1999—; chief cardiac thoracic surgery Mass. Gen. Hosp. Fellow Am. Coll. Surgeons; mem. AMA, ACCPA, Am. Assn. Thoracic Surgery, Soc. Thoracic Surgery (bd. mem., 2nd v.p.), Cardiothoracic Surgery Network, Thoracic Surgery Directors Assn., Thoracic Surgery Found. for Rsch. & Edn., Soc. Thoracic Surgeons (treas.). Office: Mass Gen Hosp Thoracic Surgery Blake 1570 55 Fruit St Boston MA 02114 Office Phone: 617-726-6826. Business E-Mail: dmathisen@partners.org.

MATHOG, ROBERT HENRY, otolaryngologist, educator; b. New Haven, Apr. 13, 1939; s. William and Tiby (Gans) M.; m. Deena Jane Rabinowitz, June 14, 1964; children: Tiby, Heather, Lauren, Jason. AB, Dartmouth Coll., 1960; MD, NYU, 1964. Diplomate Am. Bd. Facial Plastic and Reconstructive Surgery. Intern Duke Hosp., Durham, NC, 1964-65, resident surgery, 1965-66, resident otolaryngology, 1966-69; practice medicine, specializing in otolaryngology Mpls., 1971-77, Detroit, 1977—; chief of otolaryngology Hennepin County Med. Center, Mpls., 1972-77; asst. prof. U. Minn., 1971-74, asso. prof., 1974-77; prof., chmn. dept. otolaryngology Wayne State U. Sch. Medicine, 1977—. Chief otolaryngology Hennepin County Hosp., Mpls., 1972-77, Harper-Grace Hosps., Detroit, 1977—, Detroit Receiving Hosp., 1977-92; cons. staff VA Hosp., Allen Park, Minn., 1977—, Children's Hosp., Detroit, 1977—, Hutzel Hosp., Detroit, 1966, St. Joseph Mercy Hosp., Oakland, Mich., 2001; mem. adv. coun. Nat. Inst. Deaf and Other Communicable Disorders NIH, 1992-96; chief otolaryngology, head and neck surgery June Hosp., 1994-95. Author: Otolaryngology Clinics of North America, 1976, Textbook of Maxillofacial Trauma, 1983; editor in chief Videomed. Edn. Systems, 1972-75; editor: Atlas of Craniofacial Trauma, 1992; contbr. articles to med. jours. Bd. dirs. Bexer County Hearing Soc., 1969-71; adv. coun. WIDCB, 1993; pres. and chmn. Lions Hearing Ctr., 1999-, Mich. Maj. USAF, 1969-71. Recipient Valentine Mott medal for proficiency in anatomy, 1961, Recognition award Wayne State Bd. Govs. Faculty, 1993; Deafness Rsch. Found. grantee, 1979-81, NIH grantee, 1986, 92, 96, Lawrence M. Weiner Alumni award Wayne State U. Sch. Med., 1999. Fellow ACS, Am. Acad. Otolaryngology, Head and Neck Surgery (Cert. award 1976, Cert. of Appreciation 1978), Am. Soc. Head and Neck Surgery, Triological Soc. (v.p. 1995-96, mtg. guest of honor 2002, Vice Presdl. Citation award 2004), Am. Otol. Soc., Am. Acad. Facial Plastic and Reconstructive Surgery (v.p. 1980), Am. Neurotology Soc.; mem. AMA, Am. Laryngol. Soc. (coun. 1994—), Am. Laryngol. Assn., Mich. Med. Soc., Am. Head and Neck Soc., Soc. Univ. Otolaryngologists (pres. 1995), Assn. Acad. Depts. Otolaryngology, Assn. Rsch. Otolaryngology (pres. 1981). Home: 27115 Wellington Rd Franklin MI 48025-1329 Office: 43494 Woodward Ste 210 Bloomfield Hills MI 48312 Also: Wayne State U Sch Med 540 E Canfield St Detroit MI 48201-1928

MATHUR, MANJULA, scientific researcher; d. Ishwar Dayal and Pushpa Lata Mathur; m. Lalit Kumar Mathur, Feb. 1, 1979; children: Mala, Anuj. BSc, Lucknow U., India, 1973, MSc, 1975; MPhil, Inst. Advanced Studies, Meerut, India, 1977. 21st Barc Tng. Sch., Physics Bhabha Atomic Rsch. Ctr., 1977. Lectr. Kanya Gurukul Khanpur Kalan, Haryana, India, 1975—76; sci. officer Mol. Bio. Div., Bhabha Res. Ctr, Mumbai, Maharashtra, India, 1978—, cons., 1994—. Contbr. articles to jour. Mem.: Protein Soc., Indian Soc. Radiation Biology (life), Indian Photobiology Soc. (life), Indian Women Scientists Assn. (life), Hindi Vigyan Parishad (life), Lions Club (pres. 2004—05). Hindu. Avocations: travel, music, drawing, painting, playing musical instruments. Office: Mol Biol Div Bhabha At Res Ctr Mod Lab Ctrl Ave Trombay Maharashtra Mumbai 400085 India Business E-Mail: bioinf@barc.ernet.in.

MATHUR, SHOBHIT, radiologist; b. India, Apr. 19, 1985; MBBS, Baroda Med. Coll., 2008. Resident radiodiagnosis S.S.G.Hos., Vadodara, India, 2008—. Contbr. articles to profl. jours. Recipient Gold medal, Maharaja Sayajirao U. Baroda, Nat. Merit Cert., Ministry Edn. and Welfare, Govt. India, New Delhi., Spl. Merit Cert., United Schs. Orgn. India. Avocations: reading, movies. Home: D-38 Sector-I Petrochemicals Township Vadodara Gujarat 391345 India Personal E-mail: drshobhitmathur@yahoo.co.in.

MATHY, ROBIN MICHELLE, writer, researcher; b. Portsmouth, Va., July 21, 1957; BS with honors in sociology with honors summa cum laude, Ariz. State U., 1985; MA, Ind. U., Bloomington, 1989; MSW, U. Minn., 2003; M in Internat. Rels., U. Cambridge, 2004; MS in Evidence Based Health Care, U. Oxford, 2005. Author: Male Homosexuality in Four Societies: Brazil, Guatemala, the Philippines, and the United States (Best Book in Print, NY Times Rev. of Books, 2002); contbr. articles to profl. jours., chapters to books; editor: Lesbian and Bisexual Women's Mental Health, 2004. Pres. GLBT&Q Suicide Prevention Coalition, Washington, 2003.

MATIA, IVAN, surgeon; s. Ivan Matia and Jolana Matiová; m. Adriána Matia. PhD in Exptl. Surgery, Charles U., Prague, 2008—. Diplomate Slovak Republic, 2002. Faculty of medicine Pavol Jozef Safárik U., Kosic, Slovakia, 1996—2002; mem. transplant surgery dept. Inst. Clin. and Exptl. Medicine, Prague, 2002—. Office: Inst Clin Exptl Medicine Transplant Surgery Dept Vídenská 1958/9 Prague 140 21 Czech Republic Business E-Mail: ivan.matia@ikem.cz.

MATIN, MADJID, dental educator; Grad., U. Houston; DMD, Boston U. Post-doctoral tng. priodontology-treatment of the gums Boston Univ.; lectr.; spkr. Nat. Capital Dental Symposium; dentist Washington Ctr. for Dentistry. Fellow: Am. Soc. of Osseo Integration; mem.: ADA, Northern Va. Implant Soc., DC Dental Soc., Internat. Congress of Oral Implantology, Am. Coll. of Oral Implantology, Am. Acad. of Periodontology, Washington Iranian Dental Study Club, DC Millennium Dental Study Club, Alpha Epsilon Delta Premedical Honor Soc. Office: Washington Center for Dentistry 8th Fl 1430 K St NW Washington DC 20005 Office Phone: 202-223-6630.

MATITO, ALMUDENA, allergist; b. Madrid, May 14, 1979; MD, U. Complutense Madrid, 2003. Allergist Inst. Estudios de Mastocitosis de Castilla La Mancha, 2008—. Office: Carretera de Cobisa Toledo 45071 Spain Business E-Mail: amatito@sescam.jccm.es.

MATLAK, MICHAEL EDWARD, pediatric general surgeon; b. Chgo., Jan. 30, 1944; MD, Loyola U., 1968. Cert. Am. Bd. Surgery, Am. Bd. Pediatric Surgery. Intern, gen. surgery Cook County Hosp., Chgo., 1968—69; resident, gen. surgery Mayo Clinic, Minn., 1971—75; resident, pediatric surgery Children's Nat. Med. Ctr., Washington, 1975—77; staff mem., divsn. pediatric gen. surgery U. Utah Health Sciences Ctr., Salt Lake City, prof. surgery (clin.), pediatrics; program dir. pediat. surgery fellow AIC Kijabe Hosp., Kenya, 2010—11. Mem.: Pacific Assn. Pediatric Surgeons, Am. Pediatric Surgical Assn., Am. Coll. Surgeons, Am. Acad. Pediatrics. Address: U Utah Health Sciences Ctr 50 N Medical Dr Salt Lake City UT 84132 Office: Primary Childrens Med Ctr Ste 2600 100 N Mario Capecchi Dr Salt Lake City UT 84113-1103 Office Phone: 801-662-2950. *

MATLES, HARLAN, physician; b. Portugal, June 14, 1972; MD, Georgetown U., 1999. Attending physician Menlo Med. Clinic, 2002—. Mem.: Alpha Omega Alpha Honor Soc. Office: 1300 Crane St Menlo Park CA 94025 Office Fax: 650-324-4816. Business E-Mail: hmatles@stanfordmed.org.

MATLOCK, DAVID LOUIS, obstetrician, gynecologist, reconstructive surgeon; b. St. Louis, Mo. BA in Chemistry, Coll. St. Louis Univ., Mo., 1974; MD, St. Louis Univ. Sch. Medicine, Mo., 1978; MBA, U. Calif. Irvine Grad. Sch. Mgmt., 2000. Lic. Bd. Med. Quality Assurance, 1979, cert. Am. Bd. Obstetrics and Gynecology, 1987, re-cert. Am. Bd. Obstetrics and Gynecology, 1997. Intern, internal medicine U. So. Calif. Med. Ctr., LA, 1978—79, King/Drew Med. Ctr., LA, 1980, resident, obstetrics & gynecology, 1980—83; private practice Ross Loos, Torrance, Calif., 1979—80, Calif., 1985—; dept. chmn., obstetrics and gynecology Mission Hosp., Huntington Park, Calif., 1984—85; med. dir. Women's Ctr., LA, 1986—88; dir., laser surgery program Marina Hills Hosp., LA, 1988—89; med. dir. Beverly-Wilshire Surgery Ctr., 1990—90, dir., laser surgery program, 1991; med. dir. Beverly Hills Ambulatory Surgery Ctr., Inc., 1995—, So. Calif. Surgery Ctr., LA, Beverly Hills Sunset Surgery Ctr.; CEO, founder Laser Vaginal Rejuvenation Inst. Med. Associates, Inc. Resident coun. on admissions So. Calif. Med. Ctr., 1978; resident program evaluation, obstetrics & gynecology King/Drew Med. Ctr., 1982; presenter in field. Contbr. articles to profl. jours.; author: (book) Sex By Design; featured on Dr. 90210. Fellow: Am. Acad. Cosmetic Surgery, Am. Coll. Obstetricians and Gynecologists; mem.: Am. Soc. Gynecological Laparoscopists, LA County Med. Assn., Calif. Med. Assn., AMA, Am. Soc. Liposuction Surgery. Avocations: tennis, jogging, publishing, travel, entrepreneurial healthcare. Office: Lasar Vaginal Rejuvenation Inst LA 9201 Sunset Blvd Ste 406 Los Angeles CA 90069 Office Phone: 310-859-9052. Office Fax: 310-859-7792. Business E-Mail: drmatlock@drmatlock.com.

MATOS, ANDRÉ COSTA, urologist; b. Salvador, Bahia, Brazil, Aug. 30, 1980; MD, Fed. U. Bahia, 2004. Urol. surgeon Faculty Med. Scis. Santa Casa São Paulo, 2005—10, Brazilian Inst. Cancer Control, 2010—. Med. asst. Albert Einstein Hosp., 2011. Fellow: Braziliam Urol. Assn. (First Pl. award). Avocations: movies, horseback riding, travel. Home: Alameda Barros 66 Apt 142 Sao Paulo 01232-000 Brazil Personal E-mail: andrecostamatos@yahoo.com.br.

MATOS, JEFFREY A., cardiac electrophysiologist; married; 2 children. Grad., Columbia U.; MD, Harvard Med. Sch., 1975. Diplomate Am. Bd. Internal Medicine, Am. Bd. of Internal Medicine-cardiovasc. disease, Am. Bd. of Internal Medicine-clin. cardiac electrophysiology, lic. New York State. Intern Beth Israel Med. Ctr.; cardiovascular fellow Peter Bent Brigham Hosp., electrophysiology fellow. Fellow: Am. Coll. of Cardiology; mem.: Heart Rhythm Soc. (HRS). Office: Lenox Hill Heart and Vascular Institute of New York Interventional and Clinical Cardiology 130 East 77Th St 9Th Fl New York NY 10021 Office Phone: 212-434-2606. Office Fax: 212-434-2610.

MATOUSEK, JOSEF, immunogeneticist; b. Ujezd u Chocne, Czech Republic, Mar. 12, 1925; s. Jan and Marie (Ricarova) M.; m. Vladimira Dvorakova, Mar. 27, 1941; children: Karel, Vladimira, Marie. Degree, U. Agriculture, 1951, DSc, Acad. Scis. Prague, 1954; PhD, Inst. Animal Breeding, 1955. Doctoral student Inst. Animal Breeding, Prague, 1951-55; rsch. worker Lab. Reproduction, Libechov, Czech Republic, 1955-62, Lab. Animal Genetics, Libechov, 1962-72, Inst. Animal Genetics, Libechov, 1972—. Editor: Blood Groups of Animals, 1965; contbr. profl. jours. Mem. Internat. Soc. Animal Genetics, Czech Acad. Agrl. Scis., Slovak Acad. Agrl. Scis., Am. Chem. Soc. Roman Catholic. Avocations: bicycling, working out. Home: V rokli 277 21 Zelizy Czech Republic Office: Rumburska Acad Scis Inst Animal Phys/Genetics 277 21 Libechov Czech Republic Home Phone: 420315697211; Office Phone: 420315639539. Business E-Mail: matousek@iapg.cas.cz.

MATOUSEK, MICHAEL, geriatrician, researcher; b. Plzen, Czechoslovakia, June 3, 1960; arrived in Sweden, 1968; s. Milos M. and Alena Lukesova Hanson; m. Louise Anna Maria Tottie, Oct. 12, 1996; 2 children; Beatrice Sophie, Amelie Josefine. MD, Göteborg U., Sweden, 1984, PhD in Medicine, 1995. Cert. specialist in somatic long-term care and geriatric medicine. Physician Sahlgren's and Vasa Hosp., Göteborg, 1984-91, tutor, dept. geriatric medicine, 1991-96, physician, 1996—. Author: Movement Performance in the Elderly, 1995. Named Hon. Citizen Upper Dublin Twp., Montgomery County, Pa., 1978. Mem. Swedish Med. Soc. Avocations: tennis, sailing, history, skiing. Office: Mölndals Hosp Dept Geriatric Medicine 431 80 Mölndal Sweden Business E-Mail: michael.matousek@swipnet.se.

MATROS, RICHARD K., real estate company executive; b. Queens, NY; m. Adrienne Matros; children: Carly, Chelsea, Alex. BA in Psychology, Alfred U.; MA in Gerontology, U. S.C. Facility adminstr. Extended Care Inc., Catered Living Inc.; regional adminstr., v.p. We. Ops. Beverly Enterprises, Inc.; exec. v.p. ops. Care Enterprises, 1988—91, pres., COO, 1988—91, 1991—94, pres., CEO, 1994; pres., COO Regency Health Svcs. Inc., 1994—95, pres., CEO, 1995—97, Bright Now! Dental, 1998—2000; chmn., CEO Sun Healthcare Group, Inc., 2001—10, Sabra Health Care REIT, Inc., 2010—. Office: Sabra Health Care REIT Inc 18500 Von Karman Ave Ste 550 Irvine CA 92612 *

MATSEN, FREDERICK ALBERT, III, orthopedic educator; b. Austin, Tex., Feb. 5, 1944; s. Frederick Albert II and Cecilia (Kirkegaard) M.; m. Anne Lovell, Dec. 24, 1966; children: Susanna Lovell, Frederick A. IV, Laura Jane Megan. BA, U. Tex., Austin, 1964; MD, Baylor U., 1968. Intern Johns Hopkins U., Balt., 1971; resident in orthopaedics U. Wash., Seattle, 1971-74, acting instr. orthopaedics, 1974, asst. prof. orthopaedics, 1975-79, assoc. prof. orthopaedics, 1979-82, prof., 1982-85, 86—, adjunct prof. Ctr. Bioengring., 1985—, dir. residency program orthopaedics, 1978-81, vice chmn. dept. orthopaedics, 1982-85, acting chmn. dept. orthopaedics, 1983-84, prof., chmn. dept. orthopaedics, 1981—. Mem. Orthopaedic Residency Rev. Com., Chgo., 1981-86. Author: Compartmental Syndromes, 1980; editor: The Shoulder, 1990; contbr. articles to profl. jours., chpts. to textbooks; assoc. editor Clin. Orthopaedics, Jour. Orthopaedic Rsch., 1981—. Lt. comdr. USPHS, 1969-71. Recipient Traveling fellowship Am. Orthopaedic Assn., 1983, Nicholas Andry award Assn. Bone and Joint Surgery, 1979, Henry Meyerding Essay award Am. Fracture Assn., 1974. Mem. Am. Shoulder and Elbow Surgeons (founding, pres. 1991—), Am. Acad. Orthopaedic Surgeons (bd. dirs. 1984-85), Orthopaedic Rsch. Soc., Western Orthopaedic Assn., Phi Beta Kappa. Office: U Wash Dept Orthopaedics RK 10 1959 NE Pacific St Seattle WA 98195-0001 Office Phone: 206-543-3690. Business E-Mail: matsen@u.washington.edu.

MATSUBARA, KEIICHI, medical educator; MD, Ehime U., Shitsukawa, Japan, 1988, PhD, 1994. Cert. med. specialist ob-gyn. Japan Soc. Ob-gyn., 1998. Asst. dept. ob-gyn. Ehime U. Sch. Medicine, Toon, 1994—95, 1996—98; physician dept. ob-gyn. Nomura Town's Hosp., Higashi-Uwa, Ehime, Japan, 1995—96; asst. prof. maternity and perinatal care unit Ehime U. Hosp., Toon, 1998—2005, assoc. prof. maternity and perinatal care unit, 2005—; dir. dept. ob-gyn. Ehime Prefectural Ctrl. Hosp., Matasuyama, Japan, 2010—. Vis. asst. prof. dept. ob-gyn. U. Wis. Med. Sch., Madison, 2001—02. Recipient Young Scientist award, Asia and Oceania Fedn. Ob-gyn., 2005. Home: 12-25 Kiyacho Matsuyama 790-0821 Ehimo Japan Office: Dept Ob Gyn NTT Matsuyama Hosp 1 7 1 Kiyomachi Matsuyama Ehime 790 0802 Japan Office Fax: 81-897-41-2900. Business E-Mail: keiichi@m.ehime-u.ac.jp.

MATSUBARA, MIYAO, endocrinologist; b. Hachinohe, Japan, July 22, 1950; s. Hisashi and Shige Matsubara; m. Ayumi Kappai Matsubara, Aug. 6, 1989; children: Yuuka, Mitsuya. MD, Hokkaido U., Japan, 1976, PhD, 1985. Med. staff Hokkaido U. Hosp., Sapporo, Japan, 1976—85; med. dir. Otaru City Gen. Hosp., Hokkaido, 1985—2001, head med. dept., 2001—05; dir. Matsubara Endocrinology and Metabolism Clinic, Otaru, 2006—. Contbr. articles to profl. jours. Mem.: Lipoprotein and Metabolism Rsch. Soc. (mgr.), Hokkaido Endocrine Soc. (trustee), Japan Endocrine Soc. (rep.). Office: Matsubara Endocrinology and Metabolism Clinic Inaho 2-11-13 Otaru 047-0032 Japan

MATSUBARA, SHIGEKI, obstetrician, educator; b. Tokyo, May 29, 1954; MD, Jichi Med. U., 1979, PhD, 1988. Prof., dept. ob-gyn. Jichi Med. U., 2002—, v.p., 2002—. Contbr. scientific papers. Named Tchr. of Yr. Master: Soc. Tochigi Maternal Health. Office: 3311 Yakushiji Shimotsuke Tochigi 329-0498 Japan Office Fax: 81-285-44-8505. Business E-Mail: matsushi@jichi.ac.jp.

MATSUBAYASHI, HIROYUKI, gastroenterologist; b. Tokyo, Mar. 30, 1968; MD, Tokyo Med. U., 1992; PhD, Niigata U., Japan, 1996. Physician, rsch. fellow Tokyo Med. U., 1992—93; postdoctoral rsch. fellow, mem. faculty Tokyo Med. U. Hosp., 1997—2002; postdoctoral rsch. fellow Johns Hopkins Med. Inst., Balt., 2002—. Contbr. articles to profl. jours. Recipient Sankyo Life Sci. Found. award, 2002. Mem.: Japan Pancreas Soc., Japan Gastroenterology Assn. (award 1999), Japan Internal Medicine Assn. Avocations: eating, sports. Office: Johns Hopkins Med Instns Ross Bldg 632 Rutland Ave Baltimore MD 21205 E-mail: hmatsub1@jhmi.edu.

MATSUDA, MASAMI, healthcare educator; b. Kobe, Japan, Mar. 12, 1954; BSc in Health Sci., U. Tokyo, 1977, PhD in Health Sci., 1986. Dir., internat. tng. Rsch. Inst. TB, 1990—97; prof., health care sys. U. Shizuoka, 1997—2010; prof., pub. health Tokyo Kasei-Gakuin U., 2010—. Bd. editors Internat. Jour. Nursing Ethics, 2003—; dep. dir. Yadokari Inst. Cmty Mental Health, 2009—. Recipient Internat. Cooperation Rsch. Promotion award, APIC. Mem.: APHA, JSPH. Avocation: movies. Office: Tokyo Kasei-gakuin University Sanban tyo Chiyoda Tokyo 1028341 Japan Business E-Mail: matsuda@kasei-gakuin.ac.jp.

MATSUDA, SEIJI, medical educator; b. Higashihiroshima, Hiroshima, Japan, Apr. 12, 1955; s. Hiroyoshi and Takako Matsuda; m. Akiko Kataoka; children: Kenji, Masao. PhD, Ehime Univ Grad. Sch. Med, 1984. Lic. MD Japan, 1980. Prof. Ehime U. Grad. Sch. Med, Toon, Japan, 1997—. Aikido tchr., Matsuyama, Ehime, 1984—2008. Mem.: IBRO. Home: 1979-3 Ehime Toon 791-0212 Japan Office: Ehime Univ Graduate Sch Medicine Shitsukawa Toon Ehime 791-0295 Japan Office Fax: 089-960-5233. Personal E-mail: matsuda@m.ehime-u.ac.jp.

MATSUDA, TADAMITSU, medical educator; b. Japan, Mar. 13, 1978; PhD, Tokyo Met. U., 2009. Instr. Ryotokuji U., 2007—. Avocation: surfing. Office: 5-8-1 Akemi Urayasu Chiba 279-8567 Japan Business E-Mail: matsuda@ryotokuji.u.ac.jp.

MATSUDA, TADASHI, urologist; b. Mie, Japan, Apr. 7, 1953; MD, Kyoto U., 1978, DMS, 1990. Prof., chmn. dept. urology and andrology Kansai Med. U., 1995—. Bd. dirs. Japan Assn. Endocrine Surgeons, 2000, Endourol. Soc., 2008, Japan Soc. Endoscopic Surgery, 2010; pres. Japanese Soc. Endourology, 2010, 29th World Congress Endourology and SWL, 2011. Mem.: Urol. Rsch. Soc., Am. Urol. Assn., Japanese Urol. Assn. Office: Shinmachi 2-3-1 Hirakata Osaka 573-1191 Japan Office Fax: 81-72-804-2068. Business E-Mail: matsudat@takii.kmu.ac.jp.

MATSUDA, TAKAYOSHI, surgeon, educator, biomedical researcher; b. Tonan, Japan, 1937; came to U.S., 1965; MD, Keio Gijuku U., Tokyo, 1963. Diplomate Am. Bd. Surgery. Rotating intern Cook County Hosp., Chgo., 1965-66, resident in surgery, 1966-71, dir. burn ctr., 1975-93; asst. prof. surgery Kyorin U., Tokyo, 1971-75; asst. prof. U. Ill., Chgo., 1977—; pres. TM & Assocs., Oak Park, Ill., 1994—. Cons. alternative medicine, cons. leadership devel., fin. freedom; investigator renewable energy; spkr. in field. Editl. bd. Jour. Burn Care Rehab., 1987-93; contbr. articles to profl. publ., chpt. to books. Recipient Jerry and Thelma Stergios award for Excellence in Basic Rsch., U. Ill. at Chgo., 1979, The Superior Pub. Serv. award, County of Cook, State of Ill., 1993. Fellow ACS; mem. Internat. Soc. Surgery, Internat. Soc. Burn Injuries, Am. Burn Assn., Am. Assn. Surgery Trauma, Soc. Critical Care Medicine, Surg. Soc. Achievements include research in and devel. of a novel approach for the production of electricity without pollution; established the first human skin bank in the State of Illinois at the Burn Unit of Cook County Hospital, 1977. Office: TM & Assocs Alternative Medicine Cons 103 Bishop Quarter Ln Oak Park IL 60302-2672 Office Phone: 708-386-2522. Personal E-mail: takimatsuda@hotmail.com.

MATSUDA, WAKOTO, neurosurgeon, researcher; b. Onomichi, Hiroshima, Japan, Apr. 6, 1968; s. Tadao and Fujiko (Makihata) Matsuda; m. Kiyoe Nakazawa, Mar. 22, 1991; children: Shin, Nako, Tei. MD, U. Tsukuba, Japan, 1996; PhD, Kyoto U., Japan, 2009. Diplomate in neurosurgery Japan Neurosurg. Soc., 2002; bd. cert. physician Japanese Soc. Travel Medicine, 2010. Resident dept. neurosurgery Tsukuba U. Hosp., 1996—2002; clin. fellow dept. neurosurgery Tsukuba Med. Ctr. Hosp., 2002—03; postgrad. dept. morphological brain sci. Grad. Sch. Medicine, Kyoto U., 2003—06; asst. prof. divsn. anatomy and cell biology, dept. anatomy Shiga U. Med. Sci., 2006—. Recipient Best Resident award, Inst. Clin. Medicine, U. Tsukuba, Dept. Neurosurg., 2002; scholar, Iwadare Scholarship Found., 2003; grant, Gen. Ins. Assn. Japan, 2009, Zenkyoren, 2010, Shiga Prefecture Rehab Ctr., 2010—11, Mitsui Sumitomo Insurance Welfare Found., 2010. Mem.: Soc. Neuroscis., Japanese Assn. Anatomists, Japan Neuroscience Soc., Japanese Congress Neurological Surgeons, Japan Neurosurg. Soc. Office: Shiga Univ Med Sci Divsn Anatomy Cell Biology Dept Anatomy Tsukinowa-cho Seta Otsu Shiga 520-2192 Japan Office Fax: 81-77-548-2139. Personal E-mail: wako@mua.biglobe.ne.jp. Business E-Mail: matsuda2@belle.shiga-med.ac.jp.

MATSUI, IKUO, research scientist; b. Joetsu, Niigata, Japan, Jan. 5, 1954; PhD, Tokyo U., 1985. Rschr. Nat. Inst. Advanced Sci. and Tech., 1985. Recipient award, Ministry of Sci. and Tech. Japan. Office: Higashi 1-1-1 central 6-9 Tsukuba Ibaraki 305-8566 Japan Business E-Mail: ik-matsui@aist.go.jp.

MATSUI, JUNJI, pharmacist; b. Japan, Oct. 24, 1973; PhD, Osaka U., 1999. Prin. scientist Eisai Co., Ltd., 1999—. Home: 2410A 6th St Fort Lee NJ 07024 Business E-Mail: j2-matsui@hhc.eisai.co.jp.

MATSUI, KAZUHIRO TANGO, pharmaceutical executive, director; b. Osaka, Japan, Sept. 29, 1961; D, Kyoto U., 1985, Soka U., 1985. Sr. rsch. scientist Tsuruga Inst. Biotech., Toyobo Co. Ltd, 1990—2003, Summit Biosci. Corp., 2005—06; owner, pres. Palmgen Inc.-Palm Corp, 1996—; group leader Summit Glycorsch. Corp, 2007—09; dir. Summit Pharm. Internat. Corp., 2007—. Mem.: Japanese EDCs Soc., Japanese Isotope Assn., Japanese Chem. Soc. Avocations: travel, reading, tennis. Home: #201 Bijou AOI 3-32-1 AOI Adachi Tokyo 120-0012 Japan Personal E-mail: kazumatsu39@mail.goo.ne.jp.

MATSUI, YOSHIRO, surgeon; b. Sapporo, Japan, July 29, 1954; s. Katsuhiro and Michiko Matsui, Yoshio (Stepfather) and Keiko Hanada (Stepmother); m. Mikiko Hanada, May 26, 1959; children: Yuki, Ayumi. MD, Hokkaido U. of Medicine, Sapporo, Japan, 1974—80, PhD. MD Ministry of Health, Labour and Welfare, Japan, 1980. Contbr. articles pub. to profl. jour. Achievements include first to New surgical treatment to severe heart failure. Home: Chuo ku N3W29 Hokkaido Sapporo 0640823 Japan Office: Hokkaido Univ Hosp Dept Cardiovascular Surgery Sapporo N14W5 Japan Office Fax: 81-11-708-8885. Business E-Mail: ymatsui@med.hokudai.ac.jp.

MATSUISHI, TOYOJIRO, medical educator; s. Eiko Matsuishi; m. Naoko Soda, June 10, 1985; children: Sae, Toshiya, Yuki, Kazuya. MD, Japan Med. Lic., PhD, 1975. Prof. & chmn. dept. pediat. Kurume U. Sch. Medicine, Japan, 2001—; dir. Cognitive and Molecular Rsch. Inst. Brain Disease, Kurume, 2004—08. Dir. Rsch. Inst. Med. Mass Spectrometry, Kurume, 2006—. Contbr. articles to profl. jours. Com. nat. bd. med. exam. Nat. Lic. MD, Tokyo, 2003—07. Mem.: Japan Pediat. Soc. Buddhism. Achievements include patents for treatment drug for spinocerebellar degeneration. Avocations: music, exercise, travel, chess. Home: Tsubuku-imamachi299-8 Kurume 830-0061 Japan Business E-Mail: tmatsu@med.kurume-u.ac.jp.

MATSUKAWA, TOSHIYOSHI, physician, researcher; b. Yokohama, Japan, Jan. 12, 1958; MD, Yokohama City U., 1982, DMS, 1986. Physician, 2nd dept. internal medicine Yokohama City U. Hosp., 1986—92; asst. prof. Rsch. Inst. Environ. Medicine, 1992—2011; vis. rsch. mem., faculty sci. Japan Woman's U., 2011—. Fellow: Japan Autonomic Soc., Japan Physiol. Soc.; mem.: Japan Soc. Endocrinology, Japan Soc. Internal Medicine. Home: 458-2-304 Noborito Shin-machi Tama-ku Kawasaki Kanagawa 214-0013 Japan Personal E-mail: toshichao2006@yahoo.co.jp.

MATSUKI, NORIO, medical educator; b. Nagano, Japan, Mar. 4, 1952; PhD, U. Tokyo, 1979. Assoc. prof. U. Tokyo, 1988—97, prof., 1997—. Mem.: Soc. Neurosci., Japanese Pharmacological Soc., Pharm. Soc. Japan (Young Investigator award). Office: Hongo 7-3-1 Bunkyo-ku Tokyo 113-0033 Japan Business E-Mail: matsuki@mol.f.u-tokyo.ac.jp.

MATSUKURA, NORIO, surgeon; b. Kashima, Ibaraki, Japan, Jan. 18, 1948; s. Shoji and Tomiko (Hara) M.; m. Tokiko Mikasa; children: Mitsuru, Kaori, Seiko. MD, Nippon Med. Sch., Tokyo, 1974, PhD, 1979. Resident surgery dept. Nippon Med. Sch., Tokyo, 1975-79; staff mem., sect. chief Nat. Cancer Ctr. Rsch. Inst., Tokyo, 1979-81; expert Nat. Cancer Ctr. NIH, Bethesda, Md., 1988-89; staff surgery dept. Nippon Med. Sch., Tokyo, 1982-87, 89-91, asst. prof. surgery dept., 1992-99, assoc. prof. surgery dept., 2000—03; dir. Matsukura Ctrl. Clinic, 2004—. Author: Monographs on Pathology, 1985, World Cancer Report, 2003. Recipient Tamiya award, 1980. Avocation: golf. Home: Chuo-ku 1-14-13-1107 Tsukishima Tokyo 104-0052 Japan Office: Matsukura Ctrl Clinic 786-16 Kazu Kashima Imbaraki 311-2215 Japan Office Phone: 81-299-90-9222. E-mail: matsun@nms.ac.jp.

MATSUKURA, TOSHIHIKO, virologist; b. Kamakura, Kanagawa, Japan, Dec. 10, 1943; s. Youzou and Yoshi Matsukura; m. Fumiko Matsukura; children: Keisuke, Kano. PhD in Vet. Sci., Hokkaido U., Japan, 1967. Cert. in vet. medicine Hokkaido U., 1965. Rschr. Nat. Inst. Infectious Diseases, Tokyo, 1965—2004; ret., 2004. Contbr. articles to profl. jours.

MATSUMOTO, HIROAKI, hospital administrator; b. Kobe, Japan, Nov. 5, 1975; s. Masahiro and Nobuko Matsumoto; m. Yuriko Okabayashi, July 26, 1976; children: Asuka, Ayaka, Momoka Matsumoto. MD, Ehime U., Toon, Japan, 2000; PhD, Ehime U., 2007. Cert. specialist Japan Neurosurgical Soc., 2007, Japan Stroke Soc. Asst. prof. Ehime U., 2007—08; sect. mgr. Ehime Prefectural Ctrl. Hosp., Matsuyama, Japan, 2008—. Recipient prize, Ehime U., 2008. Avocations: basketball, travel. Office: Eishokai Yoshida Hosp Daikaidori 9-2-6 Kobe 562-0803 Japan Business E-Mail: hiroaki-matsu@umin.ac.jp.

MATSUMOTO, HIROYUKI, biochemistry professor, researcher; b. Izuhara, Nagasaki, Japan, May 5, 1948; arrived in US, 1977; s. Masayuki and Yuriko (Heima) M.; m. Makiko Ohnishi; 1 child, Masaomi. BS, Kyoto U., Japan, 1972, PhD, 1977. Jr. rschr. U. Hawaii, Honolulu, 1977-79; ass. rsch. scientist Purdue U., West Lafayette, Ind., 1980-85; from asst. asst. prof. to assoc. prof. U. Okla. Health Sci. Ctr., Oklahoma City, 1985-97; prof. Health Sci. Ctr., U. Okla.,

Oklahoma City, 1997—. Mem. study sect. NIH, 1998—; dir. Epscor Okla. biotech. network laser mass spectrometry facility NSF. Contbr. articles to profl. jours. including Nature, Science. Rsch. grantee NSF, 1980-88, NIH, 1985—. Mem. Assn. Rsch. Vision and Ophthalmology, Am. Soc. Biol. Chemists, Protein Soc., Am. Soc. for Mass Spectrometry, Am. Soc. for Photobiology, Japanese Soc. Zoology, Sigma Xi. Achievements include prediction of beta-ionone ring binding pocket in rhodopsin; discovery of phosphorylated homologs of arrestin; research in molecular mechanism of vision, biological mass spectrometry, and ocular proteomics, beneficial effect of omega-3 polyunsaturated fatty acids (fish oil) in health & disease. Office: U Okla Health Sci Ctr 940 Stanton L Young Blvd Oklahoma City OK 73104-5020 Home: 1821 Danfield Dr Norman OK 73072-3000 Office Phone: 405-271-2227. Business E-Mail: hiro-matsumoto@ouhsc.edu.

MATSUMOTO, KAZUHIKO, medical educator; b. Nagano, Japan, Nov. 28, 1955; MD, Shinshu U. Sch. Medicine, 1982, PhD, 1991. Resident Shinshu U. Hosp., 1982—83, instr., 1983—94, asst. prof., 1994—2004, vice dir., clin. trial rsch. ctr., 2003—11, assoc. prof., 2004. Fellow: Japanese Skin Cancer Soc.; mem.: Japanese Soc. Immunology, Japanese Cancer Assn., Japanese Soc. Clin. Pharmacology and Therapeutics, Japanese Dermatol. Assn. Avocation: baseball. Office: 3-1-1 Asahi Matsumoto Nagano 390-8621 Japan Office Fax: 81-263-37-3460. Business E-Mail: climatsu@shinshu-u.ac.jp.

MATSUMOTO, MITSUYUKI, medical researcher; b. Yokohama, Japan, Mar. 4, 1965; PhD, U. Tokyo, 1997. CNS group leader Astellas Rsch. Inst. America LLC, 2008—. Adj. prof. Northwestern U., 2010. Mem.: Soc. Biol. Psychiatry, Soc. Neurosci. Avocation: rugby. Office: 8045 Lamon Ave Skokie IL 60077 E-mail: mitsuyuki.matsumoto@us.astellas.com.

MATSUMOTO, NORIHITO, pharmacist; b. Kobe, Japan, Jan. 22, 1965; BS, Kobe U., 1987, PhD, 2002. Head Ono Pharm. Co., Ltd., 1987—. Mem.: Japanese Soc. Alternative to Animal Experiments, Japanese Soc. Toxicology, Soc. Toxicology. Avocation: fishing. Home: 13-11-15 Higashinakano Sakai-cho Sakai Fukui 919-0544 Japan Personal E-mail: no.matsumoto@ono.co.jp.

MATSUMOTO, TAKAFUMI, pharmacologist; b. Kyoto, July 22, 1969; PhD, Fukuoka U., 2009. Sr. rsch. scientist Dainippon Sumitomo Pharma. Co., Ltd., 1994—. Office: 3-1-98 Kasugade-naka Konohana-ku Osaka 554-0022 Japan Office Fax: 81-6-6466-5182. Business E-Mail: takafumi-matsumoto@ds-pharma.co.jp.

MATSUMOTO, YOSHIHIRO, nephrologist; b. Kochi, Apr. 16, 1962; MD, Nagoya U. Sch. Medicine, 1988, PhD. Head nephrology, dialysis dept. Shizuoka City Hosp., 2003—. Office: 10-93 Ohtemachi Aoi-ku Shizuoka 420-8630 Japan Business E-Mail: matsumoto16@aol.com.

MATSUMURA-TAKEDA, KUNIKO, pharmaceutical executive, researcher; b. Japan, Aug. 31, 1966; MS, Kyusyu U., 1991; PhD, Tokushima U., 2008. Part-time lectr. Fukuoka Women's U., 1990—91; rschr. Otsuka Pharm. Co., Ltd., 1991—2010, sect. chief, 2010—. Mem.: Japanese Soc. Immunology. Avocation: reading. Home: Takezuka 87-5 Kawauchi-cho Tokushima 771-0141 Japan Business E-Mail: kuniko_m_t@research.otsuka.co.jp.

MATSUNAGA, TADAHARU, medical doctor; b. Miyama, Mie Prefecture, Japan, Mar. 26, 1956; m. Yuka Kurihara; children: Atsushi, Masanao. MD, Tokyo Med. U., PhD, 1984. Diplomate Japan Breast Cancer Soc., 1998, Japan Surg. Soc., 1985, Japanese Soc. Clin. Cytology, 2003. Chief Tokyo Met. Cancer Detection Ctr., Chiyodaku, 1989—2002; dir. Minami-Aoyama Breastopia Clinic, Minatoku, Tokyo, 2003—06; prof. Tokyo Med. U. Hachioji Med. Ctr., 2006—09; dir. Akasaka Breast Internat. Clinic. Author: (text book) Diagnosis of Mammography. Dir. duty Japanese Soc. Breast Cancer Imaging, Minatoku, Tokyo, 2007—08. Office: Akasaka Breast Internat Clinic 4F 1-7-1 Akasaka Minato-ku Tokyo Japan Office Fax: 81362346276; Home Fax: 81-3-3483-3440. E-mail: thm3@yc4.so-net.ne.jp.

MATSUO, ATSUSHI, medical educator; b. Japan, June 2, 1974; PhD, Kobe U., 2011. Assoc. prof. Kio U., 2009. Office: 4-2-2 Umaminaka Koryocho Kitakatsuragigun Nara 635-0832 Japan Office Fax: 81-745-54-1600. E-mail: a.matsuo@kio.ac.jp.

MATSUO, EIICHI, pathologist; b. Seoul, Mar. 9, 1937; s. Nagahide and Toshiko Matsuo; m. Kazuko Satoh, Dec. 4, 1966; children: Hideko, Noriko. MD, Nihon U., Tokyo, 1962, DSc in Medicine, 1967. Chief investigator Sankyo Pharm. Co., Tokyo, 1967-72; asst. rschr. U. Hawaii Sch. Medicine, Honolulu, 1972—76; assoc. prof. Kyorin U. Sch. Medicine, Tokyo, 1976—88, prof., chmn. 1st dept. pathology, 1988—98; dir. Leprosy Rsch. Ctr., Nat. Insts. Infectious Diseases, Tokyo, 1998—2004. Mem. U.S.-Japan Coop. Med. Sci. Program, 1981-98, pathologist Matsuo Med. Lab, 2004- Contbr. articles to profl. jours. Recipient Appreciation award Am. Leprosy Missions, Inc., 1976. Mem. AAAS, N.Y. Acad. Sci., Japanese Leprosy Assn. (councilor 1992—, editor-in-chief 1994-2000, gen. mgr. 2000-03), Japanese Soc. Pathology (councilor 1972—), Japanese Soc. Nephrology (councilor 1981-98), Am. Chem. Soc. Buddhist. Personal E-mail: yix11344@nifty.com.

MATSUO, HIROAKI, educator, researcher; b. Sakai, Osaka, Japan, Jan. 8, 1970; s. Masayuki and Chieko Matsuo; m. Miho Kobayashi, Oct. 17, 1999; children: Taichi, Sakurako. BS, Hiroshima U., Japan, 1993, MS, 1995, PhD, 1998. Rschr. Wakunaga Pharm. Co. Ltd., Osaka, Japan, 1998—2002; asst. prof. faculty medicine Shimane U., Izumo, Japan, 2002—06; assoc. prof. graduate sch. of biomed. sci. Hiroshima U., 2006—. Recipient 6th Galderma award, 2005. Achievements include research in wheat allergy. Office: Hiroshima U Faculty Pharmacy 1-2-3 Kasumi Minami-ku Hiroshima 734-8551 Japan Office Fax: +81-82-257-5299. Business E-Mail: hmatsuo@hiroshima-u.ac.jp.

MATSUO, KAZUHIRO, lab administrator; b. Okayama, Japan, Dec. 31, 1957; M, Nagoya U., 1982, D, 1990. Head, R & D dept. Japan BCG Lab., 2009—. Avocation: travel. Office: 3-1-5 Matsuyama Kiyose Tokyo 204-0022 Japan Business E-Mail: matsuo@bcg.gr.jp.

MATSUOKA, HIROFUMI, urologist, educator; b. Yamaga, Kumamoto, Japan, June 15, 1957; s. Yasuhiro and Fumie Matsuoka; m. Masako Murawaki; children: Masahiro, Yoshinori. MD, Fukuoka U., Japan, 1985. Diplomate Ministry Health and Welfare Japan, 1985. Assoc. prof. Fukuoka U. Faculty Medicine, Fukuoka, Fukuoka, Japan, 1996—; dir. Aso Iizuka Hosp., Iizuka, Fukuoka, 1999—2005.

MATSUSAKI, MICHIYA, engineering educator; b. Kagoshima, Japan, June 12, 1976; PhD in Engring., Kagoshima U., 2003. Asst. prof. Osaka U., 2006—. Recipient award, Materials Rsch. Soc. Japan, 2010; grant, Japanese Soc. Artificial Organs, 2006. Mem.: Japanese Soc. Biomaterials, Soc. Polymer Sci. (Japan) (Young Scientist Lectr. award 2006), Am. Chem. Soc., Chem. Soc. Japan (Young Scientist Lectr. award 2008, Young Chemists award 2010). Avocation: movies. Office: 2-1 Yamada-oka Suita Osaka 565-0871 Japan Office Fax: 81-6-6879-7359. Business E-Mail: m-matsus@chem.eng.osaka-u.ac.jp.

MATSUURA, TETSUYA, orthopedist, educator; b. Tokushima, Japan, Sept. 5, 1968; s. Hiroaki and Yoko Matsuura; m. Yoko Henmi, June 15, 2003; 1 child, Yufu. MD, U. Tokushima, PhD, 1992. Asst. prof. U. Tokushima, 2008—. Mem.: Am. Acad. Orthopaedic Surgeons. Achievements include research in baseball elbow, muscle injury. Office: Univ Tokushima 3-18-15 Kuramoto Tokushima 770-8503 Japan

MATSUYAMA, HIDEYASU, urologist, educator; b. Fukuoka, Prefecture, Japan, Mar. 17, 1957; m. Naomi Kawamura. MD, PhD, Yamaguchi U., Japan, 1987, Karolinska Inst., Sweden, 1996. Diplomate med. Health, Labor & Welfare Ministry, Japan, 1981. Chief urologist Yamaguchi Red Cross Hosp., 1996—2001; assoc. prof. Yamaguchi U., Ube, 2001—, prof., 2008—. Exec. dir. Yamaguchi Prefectural Med. Assn., 2004—08. Recipient 32nd award, Sojinkai Alumni Assn. Yamaguchi U., 2003, Excellent Presentation award, Japan Soc. Clin. Oncology, 2007; grantee, Ministry Edn., 1995, Japan Soc. Promotion Sci., 2002—, Japanese Found., 2004, Japan Sci. & Tech. Agy., 2006; fellow New Frontier Project, Grad. Sch. Medicine, Yamaguchi U., 2007. Mem.: Japan Urol. Assn., Am. Urol. Assn., Am. Assn. Cancer Rsch. Achievements include patents pending for novel detection system using centrosome amplification predicting for tumor progression in bladder cancer. Home: 2466-17 Nishikiwa Ube Yamaguchi Prefecture 755-0151 Japan Office: Dept Urology Yamaguchi Univ Grad Sch Medicine 1-1-1 Minami-kogushi Ube 755-8505 Japan Office Phone: 81-836-22-2276. Office Fax: 81-836-22-2276; Home Fax: 81-836-54-0066. Business E-Mail: hidde@yamaguchi-u.ac.jp.

MATTERA, GIOVAN GIUSEPPE, pharmacologist, researcher; b. Ischia, Napoli, Italy, Oct. 14, 1961; s. Rosario Mattera and Concetta Di Meglio; life ptnr. Daniela Marcozzi; children: Valerio, Sara. MB ChB, U. Pisa, Italy, 1988; PhD in Pharmacology, Italian Republic, 1992. Cert. MD Italian Republic, 1988. Rschr. Lab. Guidotti, SpA, Pisa, 1989—93; head lab. cardiovasc. pharmacology Sigma Tau, SpA, Pomezia, Italy, 1993—. Avocations: literature, philosophy, travel. Home: Via Saffo 12 Rome 00125 Italy Office: Sigma Tau SpA Via Pontina Km 30 400 000 40 Pomezia RM Italy Office Fax: +390691393988. Business E-Mail: giovanni.mattera@sigma-tau.it.

MATTERSON, JOAN MCDEVITT, physical therapist; b. Bryn Mawr, Pa., Feb. 24, 1949; d. William J. and Wanda Jean (Edwards) McD.; children: Brian, Jennie, Kira. BS in Biology, St. Joseph's U., Phila., 1973; cert. in Phys. Therapy, U. Pa., 1974. Assoc. pharmacologist, rschr. immunology and arthritis Prog. Phys. Therapy, P.A., Wilmington, Del., 1976-93, pediatric phys. therapist, 1974-81, pres., 1976-95; rehab. dir. Achievement Rehab.; phys. therapist Liberty Home Health, 1995—; rehab. dir. Office of Joan Matterson, 1995—, Integrated Health Svcs.- Kent, Smyrna, Del., 1996—; dir. rehab. Keystone Care Therapies, Media, Pa., 1997—, with Pain Mgmt. Ctr. Chester, Pa., 1999; with Hands on Health, Wilmington, 1999—2000; phys. therapist Hickory House Nursing and Rehab. Ctr., Honeybrook, Pa., 2000—; pvt. practice Wilmington, 2000—. Lectr. in field of low level laser therapy. Dep. gov. Am. Biog. Rsch. Inst.; mem. adv. bd. Internat. Biog. Rsch. Inst., Cambridge, Eng. Mem. NAFE, Am. Soc. Laser Medicine and Surgery, Internat. Platform Assn., Am. Acad. Pain (assoc.), Inst. Noetic Sci., Am. Bd. Forensic Examiners, N.Am. Assn. Laser Therapy, Internat. Exec. Service Corp. Avocations: dance, skiing, cooking. Office Phone: 610-457-9158. Personal E-mail: jnmttrsn711@aol.com.

MATTESON, KARLA J., medical geneticist, educator, former health science association administrator; BS in Chemistry, Beloit Coll., Wis., 1969; MS in Chemistry, Marquette U., 1976; PhD, Med. Coll. Wis., 1981. Postdoctoral fellow Baylor Coll. Medicine, Houston, 1981—83; former asst. dir. U. Tenn Devel. and Genetic Ctr., Knoxville; assoc. prof. med. genetics and pathology U. Tenn., Knoxville, 1986—, dir. biochem. and molecular genetics lab., 1986—; bd. dirs. Am. Bd. Med. Genetics, 1998—2001, exec. dir., 2001—09. Fellow: Am. Coll. Med. Genetics; mem.: AAAS, Soc. for Inborn Metabolic Disorders. Office: U Tenn Grad Sch Medicine Ste 435 1930 Alcoa Hwy Knoxville TN 37920-1514 *

MATTHEWS, ALEXANDER, health facility administrator; b. NYC, Sept. 8, 1924; s. Matthew and Helen (Tertis) Fotopoulos; m. Ann Koutsatsa Matthews (dec.); m. Linda Kay Warren, Dec. 30, 1999; children: Andrew Philip, Lydia Ann. BA, Boston U., 1948; MD, SUNY, 1952. Diplomate Am. Bd. Surgery, Bd. Thoracic Surgery. Pvt. practice, 1960—90; med. dir. Des Moines Med. Exchange Program, Stavropal, Russia, 1990—95; chief med. officer Mil. Entrance Processing Sta., Des Moines, 1995—. Chief surgery, med. staff, bd. dirs. Iowa Luth. Hosp., Des Moines, 1962—90. Comdr. USPHS, 1952—59. Fellow: ACS, Am. Coll. Chest Physicians; mem.: Soc. Thoracic Surgeons. Home: 505 Glenview Dr Des Moines IA 50312 Office: Mil Entrance Processing Sta Dept Defense 2500 U Ave West Des Moines IA 50266-1480 *

MATTHEWS, BRIAN W., molecular biology educator; b. Mount Barker, Australia, May 25, 1938; arrived in US, 1967; s. Lionel A. and Ethlinda L. (Harris) Matthews; m. Helen F. Denley, Sept. 7, 1963; children: Susan, Kristine. BS, U. Adelaide, Australia, 1959, PhD, 1964, DSc, 1986. Staff MRC Lab. Molecular Biology, Cambridge, England, 1963-66; vis. assoc. NIH, Bethesda, Md., 1967-69; prof. molecular biology U. Oreg., Eugene, 1969—, chmn. dept. physics, 1985-86, dir. Inst. Molecular Biology, 1980-83, 90-92, Disting. prof. physics. Mem. US Nat. Commn. Crystallography, 1980—86, 1988—90; investigator Howard Hughes Med. Inst., 1989—2008; Drummond lectr. U. Calgary, Canada, 1995; adj. prof. biochemistry and molecular biology Oreg. Health & Sci. U., Portland. Editor: Protein Sci., 2007—. Recipient Career Devel. award, NIH, 1973, Faculty Excellence award, Oreg. Bd. Edn., 1984, Discovery award, Oreg. Med. Rsch. Found., 1987, Vollum award, Reed Coll., Portland, 1994; fellow Alfred P. Sloan Found., 1971, John Simon Guggenheim Meml. Found., 1977. Mem.: AAAS, NAS (coun. mem. 2009—), Biophysical Soc., Protein Soc. (pres. 1995—97, Stein & Moore award 2009), Am. Chem. Soc., Crystallographic Assn. Office: U Oreg Inst Molecular Biology Willamette Hall Rm 376 Eugene OR 97403 Office Phone: 541-346-2572. E-mail: brian@uoregon.edu, brian@uoxray.uoregon.edu.

MATTHEWS, DENNIS J., physiatrist; B, Regis Coll., Denver, Colo.; MD, U. Colo. Sch. Medicine, 1975. Resident dept. physical medicine and rehab. U. Minn.; prof., chair dept physical medicine and rehab. U. Colo. Sch. Medicine, Fischahs chair pediatric rehab. medicine; chmn. dept. rehab. The Children's Hosp., Denver. Authored or co-authored: over 50 journal articles or chapters on pediatric rehab. Fellow: American Academy Pediatrics; mem.: American Bd. Physical Medicine and Rehab. (diplomate 1979—, bd. dirs. 2000—, chair 2007—), Academy Cerebral Palsy and Developmental Medicine, Gait and Clinical Movement Analysis Soc., Assn. Academic Physiatrists, American Academy Physical Medicine and Rehab. Office: Children's Hosp Rehab Medicine B285 13123 E 16th Ave Aurora CO 80045

MATTHEWS, IREN LINDBAK, pediatrician, consultant; b. Norway, Apr. 28, 1966; MBChB, U. Manchester, Eng., 1992; PhD, U. Oslo, 2009. Sr. house officer St. Mary's Hosp. Women and Children, Manchester, 1993—94, Royal Manchester Children's Hosp., 1994—95; jr. physician Oslo U. Hosp., 1995—2003, cons. pediatrician, 2003—. Recipient Voksentoppen Rsch. prize, Manchester Pediat. Club prize. Mem.: Norwegian Med. Assn. Achievements include research in pediatric pulmonology, particular congenital abnormalities and pulmonary problems secondary to advanced medical treatment such as transplantations; infant lung function testing. Avocations: travel, bicycling, reading. Office: Rikshospitalet Sognsvannsveien 20 Oslo 0027 Norway Personal E-mail: iren.l.matthews@gmail.com.

MATTHEWS, JOHN DAVID, psychiatrist, educator; b. Holly, Mich., May 24, 1945; MD, Loma Linda U., 1976; MSc, U. Mich., 1972. Assoc. med. dir. Pembroke Hosp., 1992—94; med. dir., inpatient psychiatry Mass. Gen. Hosp., 1998—2004, dir., inpatient rsch. and tng., 2004—; asst. prof. Harvard Med. Sch., 2005—. Recipient Exemplary Psychiatrist award, Nat. Alliance Mentally Ill., Recognition award, Alliance Mentally Ill., Plymouth, Mass., Am. Psychiat. Assn. Mem.: Alpha Omega Alpha Honor Med. Soc. Avocations: classical music, piano, boating. Office: 55 Fruit St Warren 1220 Boston MA 02114 Office Fax: 617-724-9155. Business E-Mail: jmatthews@partners.org.

MATTICK, JOHN STANLEY, molecular biologist; b. Sydney, NSW, Australia, Apr. 26, 1950; s. Wilfred Stocker and Mary Patricia (Brady) M.; m. Toni Marie Antalis, Jan. 24, 1981 (div. Dec. 1995); 1 child, John Stocker Antalis Mattick; m. Louise Ellen O'Gorman, June 10, 1996. BS with honors, U. Sydney, 1972; PhD, Monash U., 1977. Rsch. assoc. Baylor Coll. Medicine, Houston, 1977-79, instr., 1980-81; rsch. scientist CSIRO, Sydney, 1982-84, sr. rsch. scientist, 1984-87, prin. rsch. scientist, 1987-88; found. prof. molecular biology, dir. Ctr. Molecular Biology and Biotech. U. Queensland, Brisbane, Australia, 1988—2011; exec. dir. Garvan Inst., Sydney, 2012—. Bd. dirs. ANGIS, Sydney, 1991-2000, Lorne Genome, Inc., Sydney, Australian Proteome Analysis Facility; dir. Australia Genome Nat. Rsch. Facility. Mem. Australian Health Ethics Com., Queensland Biotechnology Adv. Coun.; mem. rsch. com. NHMRC, Australia; found. mem. Internat. Molecular Biology Network, Asia-Pacific. Decorated Officer in the Order Australia; recipient Pharmacia-LKB Biotechnology medal, Australian Biochemical Soc., 1989, Eppendorf Achievement award, Lorne Genome Conf., 2000. Mem. Australian Soc. Molecular Biology and Biochemistry (recipient Pharmacia-LKB Biotechnology medal 1989), Australian Soc. Microbiology, Genetics Soc. Australia. Office: Garvan Inst 384 Victoria St Darlinghurst Sydney NSW 1210 Australia *

MATTOX, JOHNNY LYNN, biologist, educator; b. Corinth, Miss., Apr. 13, 1951; s. Oliver Lee Mattox Jr. and Margaret Joyce Mills; m. Glenda Jean Eaton, Aug. 11, 1973; children: Jason Lynn, Jenny Amanda, Julia Elizabeth. AA, NE Miss. C.C., Booneville, 1971; BA Edn., U. Miss., Jackson, 1973, MCS, 1974, PhD, 1979. Tchr. sci. Kossuth HS., Miss., 1973—74; instr. sci. Itawamba CC, Fulton, Miss., 1975—80; instr. Biology NE Miss. CC, Booneville, 1981—2005; HEADWAE faculty rep. Blue Mountain Coll., Miss., 2008—09, assoc. prof. Biology, 2005—10, prof. biology, 2010—. Adj. asst. prof. Miss. U. Women, Columbus, 1984—2000, U. Miss., University, 1991—93, 1996—, U. Tenn. Martin, Selmer, 2000—; prof. biology; chair dept. math. and natural scis. Blue Mountain Coll., 2007—; vice chair, sci. edn. div. Miss. Acad. Scis. Chmn. Sci. Edn. divsn. Miss. Acad. Sci., 1980—81, vice chmn. sci. edn. dvsn., 2008—09; deacon Union Bapt. Ch., Kossuth, 1963—, treas., 1963—, organist, 1963—. Named Outstanding Coll. Sci. Tchr., MS Sci. Tchrs. Assn., 2008. Mem.: NSTA, SAR (Booneville chpt.), Assn. Southeastern Biologists, Miss. Acad. Scis., Miss. Sci. Tchrs. Assn. (Outstanding Coll. Sci. Tchr. award 2008—09), Nat. Assn. Biology Tchrs., Alcorn County Hist. Soc. (pres. 1982—83), Kossuth Hist. Soc. (pres. 1996—98), Kappa Delta Pi, Phi Theta Kappa (advisor 1979—2005, Regional Alumnus of Yr. award 2011, Outstanding Alumnus MS/LS Region award 2011), Phi Kappa Phi. Baptist. Office Phone: 662-685-4771 ext. 164. Business E-Mail: jmattox@bmc.edu.

MATTSSON, ULF, dentist; b. Borås, July 7, 1955; DDS, U. Gothenburg, 1979; PhD, Sahlgrenska Acad. Gothenburg, 1996. Head dentist Folktandvården I Värmland, 1996—. Assoc. prof. Faculty Odontology. Sahlgrenska Acad., Gothenburg, 2005. Mem.: European Assn. Oral Medicine, Swedish Dental Assn. Avocations: music, golf. Home: Clinic Oral & Maxillofacial Surgery Karlstad Värmland 652 30 Sweden Home Fax: 56 54 156086. Personal E-mail: ulf.karin.mattsson@telia.com.

MATUSZEK, JOHN MICHAEL, JR., environmental scientist, educator, consultant; b. Worcester, Mass. s. John Michael and Felicia Martha (Shandruk) M.; m. Roberta Eva Coonan, Nov. 30, 1957; children: Debra-Jane Y., John Michael III, Kevin P., Jennifer R. BS in Chemistry with distinction, Worcester Poly. Inst., 1957; PhD in Nuclear Chemistry, Clark U., 1962. Dept. mgr. Teledyne Isotopes, Westwood, NJ, 1964-71; rsch. scientist in nuclear chemistry, radioactive waste mgmt., radiological health, environ. radioactivity and radiation N.Y. State Health Dept., Albany, 1971-2000; cons., owner

JMM Cons. Svcs., Delmar, NY, 1992—2010. Adj. prof. Rensselaer Poly. Inst., Troy, N.Y., 1977-2003; prof. SUNY, Albany, 1996-99. Lt. comdr. USPHS, 1962-64. Mem.: Internat. Commn. Radionuclide Metrology. Avocations: skiing, music. Home: JMM Cons Svcs 10 Fieldstone Dr Delmar NY 12054

MATYAS, GARY R., medical researcher; b. Berwick, Pa., Apr. 30, 1956; BS, Pa. State U., 1978; PhD, Purdue U., 1985. Sect. chief, vaccine devel., dept. adjuvant and antigen rsch. Walter Reed Army Inst. Rsch., 1988—. Mem.: AAAS, Internat. Soc. Vaccines, Internat. Liposome Soc., Am. Soc. Microbiology, Am. Assn. Immunologists. Office: 1600 East Gude Dr Rockville MD 20850 Office Phone: 301-251-5089. Business E-Mail: gmatyas@hivresearch.org.

MATZ, DIETER RUDOLF, clinical neurologist, educator; b. Witten/Ruhr, Germany, June 9, 1946; s. Paul and Charlotte (Noetzel) M.; m. Radegundis Matz, Apr. 6, 1973; children: Ansgar, Felix. MD, U. Münster, Germany, 1973, Habilitation, 1981. With U. Münster, 1974; asst. Neurology Clinic, Münster, 1975-77; asst. in physiol. chemistry Psychiat. Clinic, Essen, Germany, 1977-78; asst. med. dir. Neurology Clinic, Münster, 1976-82; prof. neurology U. Münster, Germany, 1982—; med. dir. dept. neurology Evangelisches Krankenhaus, Lippstadt, Germany, 1983—. Author: Schwindel, 1985, 2d edit. 1992, Therapiehandbuch, 1983-92, Epilepsien u. Neurotransmission, 1985. Kreisverbandsarzt Deutsches Rotes Kreuz, 1982. Fellow German EEG Soc., NY Acad. Sci., Internat. Liga gegen Epilepsie. Mem. Evangelical Ch. Avocations: golf, surrealistic art. Home: Gerhart-Hauptmann Str 9 Lippstadt D-59555 Germany Office: Neurology Ev Krankenhaus Wiedenbrücker Str 33 Lippstadt D-59555 Germany Home Phone: +49-2941-62034, 492948940808; Office Phone: +49-2941-67-1700. E-mail: profmatz@aol.com.

MAUDGAL, DHARAM PAL, gastroenterologist; b. Tewar, Punjab, India, Sept. 19, 1943; arrived in Eng., 1971; d. Ratti Ram and Poorna Devi (Vashisht) Sharma; m. Malkito Sanghera Maudgal, Oct. 28, 1973 (div. 1994); 1 child, Davinder Dharam. FSc, D.A.V. Coll., Ambala City, India, 1961; MBBS, Govt. Med. Coll., Patiala, India, 1967; PhD in Medicine, St. George's Med. Sch., London, 1981. House officer Rajenara Hosp., Patiala, India, 1967-68; med. registrar Med. Coll. Hosp., Rohtak, 1968; med. officer State Electricity Bd., Haryana, 1968-70; sr. house officer Coventry & Warks Hosp., England, 1971-72, Gen. Hosp., South Shields, 1972-73, Tynemouth Infirmary, North Shields, 1973-74; med. registrar Salford Royal Hosp., 1974-75; from rsch. fellow to sr. med. registrar St. George's Hosp., London, 1975-83; cons. physician Manor House Hosp., 1983-99; cons. gastroenterologist Edgware Comm. Hosp., 1995—2009, Barnet Gen. Hosp., 1995—2009, head dept. gastroenterology Sathya Sai Inst. Higher Med. Scis., Prasanthi Gram, AP, India, 2009—. Med. dir. London Med. Bur., 1984-89; hon. assoc. cons. gastroenterologist St. George's Hosp. Med. Sch., London, 1986-95; hon. cons. gastroenterologist Northwick Park Hosp., Harrow, Eng., 1987-95; dir. Dharam P. Maudgal & Co. Ltd., Edgware, 1999—. Author: Hypothermia, Medical and Social Aspects, 1987; contbr. articles to profl. jours. Instr. meditation in cmty. Recipient Gold medals, Punjabi U., India, 1967, Silver medal, Govt. Med. coll., 1967, Merit scholarship, Punjab U., 1959. Fellow Royal Coll. Physicians London, Royal Soc. Medicine; mem. Brit. Soc. Gastroenterology, Brit. Med. Assn., Assurance Med. Soc., Indian Med. Assn. U.K. Hindu. Avocations: tennis, swimming, current affairs, ayurvedic holistic therapy. Office: Sathya Sai Inst Higher Med Scis Prasanthi Gram AP 515134 India

MAUDGAL, PRABHAT CHANDER, ophthalmologist; b. Tewar, India, May 15, 1948; arrived in Belgium, 1973; s. Rati Ram and Poorna Devi (Vashishth) Sharma; m. Marleen Alice Victoria De Meulemeester, Oct. 29, 1975; children: Krishan, Gayatri, Manou Mohan. MBBS, Panjab U., 1971; DSc, Cath. U., 1977. Asst. in ophthalmology Cath. U. Louvain, Belgium, 1976—81, 1st asst. ophthalmology, 1982, work leader ophthalmology SD, Belgium, 1983—85; chief polyclinic ophthalmology Free U., Amsterdam, Netherlands, 1986—87; prof. Cath. U. Louvain, 1989—. Head clinic U. Hosp., 2001—. Author: Superficial Keratitis, 1979; editor: Herpetic Eye Diseases, 1985; inventor in field. Mem. Belgium Soc. Ophthalmology (mem. mgmt. bd. 1995—), Internat. Soc. Antiviral Rsch., Internat. Soc. Eye Rsch. Hindu. Avocation: gardening. Office: UZ St Rafael Kapucijnenvoer 33 B-3000 Leuven Belgium Office Phone: 3216332372.

MAUGER, JOHN W., dean, pharmacy educator; BS, Albany Coll. Pharmacy, NY, 1965; MS in Pharmaceutics, U. RI, 1968, PhD, 1971. Former faculty mem. U. Nebr. Med. Ctr., W.Va. U. Coll. Pharmacy; prof. dept. pharmaceutics & pharm. chemistry, dean U. Utah Coll. Pharmacy, Salt Lake City, 1994—. Bd. trustees US Pharmacopeia Conv. (USP), Washington, chmn. bd. trustees, 2005—09; USP rep. European Directorate Quality of Medicines, Strasbourg, France, 2007, World Health Professions Alliance, Geneva, 2008. Mem. editl. bd. Pharm. Devel. & Tech.; contbr. articles to profl. jours., chapters to books. Fellow: AAAS; mem.: Am. Coun. Pharm. Edn. (past pres.). Office: U Utah Coll Pharmacy 30 S 2000 E Salt Lake City UT 84112 Office Phone: 801-581-6731. Office Fax: 801-581-3716.

MAUGHAN, KAREN LESLEY, physician, educator; b. Peterborough, Can., Oct. 8, 1963; BSc, U. Waterloo, 1987; MD, McGill U., 1991. Assoc. prof. U. Va., 2006—. Attending physician. Mem.: Am. Acad. Family Physicians, Va. Acad. Family Physicians, Soc. Tchrs. Family Medicine. Office: University Va Heath Sys PO Box 800729 Charlottesville VA 22908 Office Fax: 434-243-2916. Business E-Mail: kmaughan@virginia.edu.

MAUPIN, JOHN E., JR., hospital administrator; b. LA, Oct. 28, 1946; m. Eilene; three children. Diploma, San Jose State Coll.; DDS, Meharry Med. Coll., 1972; MBA, Loyola Coll., Balt., 1979; DSc (hon.), Morehouse Sch. Medicine, 1995; LLD (hon.), Va. Union U., 1996. Chmn. LifePoint Hosps.; CEO Southside Healthcare, Inc., Atlanta; dentistry resident Provident Hosp., Balt., 1973; dentist, capt. & lt. col. U.S. Army Dental Corps/Walter Reed Med. Ctr., Washington, 1974-97; various health/dental positions including dep. commr. Balt. City Health Dept., 1981-87; pres. Meharry Med. Coll., Nashville, 1994—2006; exec. v.p. Morehouse Sch. Medicine, Atlanta, pres., 2006. Mem. adv. groups Nat. Com. on Fgn. Med. Edn. and Accreditation, Bd. of Scientific Counselors, Nat. Ctr. for Infectious Diseases, Managed Care Task Force; bd. dirs. Monarch Dental Corp., Am. Gen. Series Portfolio Co., U.S. Life Mut. Funds, HealthSouth Corp. Exec. coun. Boy Scouts of Mid. Tenn.; bd. dirs. Nashville Cmty. Found., BellSouth Sr. Classic at Opryland; former chair bd. dirs. United Way of Mid. Tenn.; former mem. bd. govs. Nashville Area C. of C. Recipient A.B. Cooper award North Ga. Dental Soc., 1994, Dentist of Yr. award, 1991, Mayor's Citation for outstanding pub. svc., Balt., 1987, others. Mem. Nat. Dental Assn. (past pres.), Nat. Med. Assn., Ga. State Med. Assn., Nat. Assn. Cmty. Health Ctrs., Nat. Assn. Health Care Execs., others. Office: LifePoint Hospitals Inc 103 Powell Ct Ste 200 Brentwood TN 37027 Office Phone: 614-372-8500. E-mail: john.maupin@lpnt.net. *

MAUPOME, GERARDO, dental educator; b. Mexico City, Sept. 1, 1961; DDS, U. Nacional de Mex., 1985; PhD, U. London, 1991. Prof. Ind. U., 2005—. Sect. editor BMC Pub. Health, 2011—. Mem.: Internat. Assn. Dental Rsch. Office: 415 Lansing St Indianapolis IN 46202 Office Fax: 317-274-5425. Business E-Mail: gmaupome@iupui.edu.

MAURER, HAROLD MAURICE, pediatrician; b. NYC, Sept. 10, 1936; s. Isador and Sarah (Rothkowitz) M.; m. Beverly Bennett, June 12, 1960; children: Ann Maurer Rosenbach, Wendy Maurer Linsky. AB, NYU, 1957; MD, SUNY, Bklyn., 1961. Diplomate Am. Bd. Pediatrics, Am. Bd. Pediatric Hematology-Oncology. Intern pediatrics Kings County Hosp., NYC, 1961-62; resident in pediatrics Babies Hosp., Columbia-Presbyn. Med. Center, NYC, 1962-64; fellow in pediatric hematology/oncology Columbia-Presbyn. Med. Center, 1966-68; asst. prof. pediatrics Med. Coll. Va., Richmond, 1968-71, asso. prof., 1971-75, prof., 1975—, chmn. dept. pediatrics, 1976-93; dean U. Nebr. Coll. Medicine, Omaha, 1993-98; chancellor U. Nebr. Med. Ctr., Omaha, 1998—. Chmn. Intergroup Rhabdomyosarcoma Study, 1972-98; exec. com. Pediatric Oncology Group. Editor: pediatrics, 1983, Rhabdomyosarcoma and Related Tumors in Children and Adolescence, 1991; mem. editorial bd. Am. Jour. Hematology, Journal Pediatric Hematology and Oncology, Medical and Pediatric Oncology, 1984-99; contbr. articles to profl. jours. Mem. Youth Health Task Force, City of Richmond., Gov.'s Adv. Com. on Handicapped., Gov.'s Homeland Security Policy Group, Nebr., 2002-; mem. coun. biodefense Assn. Academic Health Ctr., 2003—, coun. global health, 2003—, gov.'s homeland security policy group 2002—; mem. nat. com. on childhood cancer Am. Cancer Soc., bd. dirs. Va. divsn.; bd. dirs. Nebr. Med. Ctr., 1997—, Friends of Nat. Inst. Nursing Rsch., 2004-05; adv. com. Lisstratcom, 2004—. Served to lt. comdr. USPHS, 1964-66. Recipient Midlander of Yr., Omaha World Herald Newspaper, 2004, Face on the Barroom Floor award, Omaha Press Club, 2007, honor, Omaha, 2008; named Ak-Sar-Ben King C IX, 2005; named to Hall of Fame, 2009; grantee, NIH, 1974—98. Mem. Am. Acad. Pediatrics (com. oncology-hematology), Am. Soc. Hematology, Soc. Pediatric Rsch., Am. Pediatric Soc., Va. Pediatric Sic. (exec. com.), Assn. Med. Sch. Pediatric Dept. Chmn., Internat. Soc. Pediatric Oncology, Am. Soc. Clin. Oncology, Va. Hematology Soc., Am. Assn. Cancer Rsch., Am. Cancer Soc., Am. Soc. Pediatric Hematology-Oncology (v.p. 1990-91, pres. 1991-93, Lifetime Achievement award children's oncology group 2003), Sigma Xi, Coun. Deans AAMC, Gov.'s Blue Ribbon Commn., Alpha Omega Alpha. Republican. Jewish. Home: 9822 Ascot Dr Omaha NE 68114-3848 Office: U Nebr Med Ctr 986605 Nebraska Med Ctr Omaha NE 68198-6605 Business E-Mail: hmmaurer@unmc.edu.

MAURI, DAVIDE, biomedical researcher, director; b. Merate, Italy, June 9, 1969; s. Carlo Mauri and Elia Iafrate. MD, Faculty of Medicine, U. of Milan, Italy, 1995. Bioethics Sch. of Medicine & Human Sci., S. Raffaele, Milan, Italy, 1990, ESMO Junior mem. European Soc. for Med. Oncology, Switzerland, 2005. Trainee urology U. Genova, Italy, 1995—97; second lt., med head ambulatory and infirmary dept. Italian Airforce, Rivolto Base, Italy, 1997—98; trainee internal medicine Gen. Hosp. of Lixouri, Greece, 1999—2000, Gen. Hosp. of Chania, Greece, 2000—01; trainee haematology U. Hosp. Patra, Greece, 2002—02; trainee med. oncology U. Hosp. Ioannina, Greece, 2002—. Sci. dir. PACMeR: Panhellenic Assn. for Continual Med. Rsch., Athens, Greece, 2002—. Achievements include development of SESy Europe: standardized three components multilanguage database for the comprehensive assessment of European cancer screening practices. Home: Thoma Pashidi 31 Greece Ioannina TK 45445 Greece Office: PACMeR Karolou 28 Athens Greece Home Fax: +30 26510 99394. Personal E-mail: dmauri@otenet.gr.

MAURICE, PAUL DAVID LAWRENCE, dermatologist; b. London; m. Ruth Mary Ashworth. MB,BChir, Cambridge U. and Westminster Med. Sch., Eng., 1977. Ho. officer in medicine and surgery Westminster and Watford Gen. Hosps., London, 1977—78; sr. ho. officer in pathology Westminster Hosp., 1978—79; sr. ho. officer in medicine Northwick Pk. Hosp., London, 1979—81; sr. ho. officer in dermatology St John's Hosp., London, 1981—82; registrar in dermatology Univ. Hosp., Nottingham, England, 1982—85; sr. registrar in dermatology St John's Hosp. and Charing Cross Hosp., London, 1985—89; cons. in dermatology West Hertfordshire Hosps. NHS Trust, St Albans and Hemel Hempstead, England, 1989—2004, Christchurch (New Zealand) Hosp., 2004—. Clin. sr. lectr. in dermatology Christchurch Sch. Medicine and Health Scis., 2004—. Contbr. articles to profl. jours. Recipient Sturges prize in medicine, Westminster Med. Sch., 1975; fellow Merrell-Dow Travelling scholar, 1987; scholar, Cambridge U., 1973; travelling fellow, Royal Soc. Medicine, 1988. Fellow: Royal Coll. Physicians; mem.: New Zealand Dermatol. Soc., Brit. Assn. Dermatologists. Achievements include research in inflammatory mediators in psoriasis.

MAURICIO, DI SILVIO, surgeon, researcher; b. Oaxaca, Mexico, Mar. 15, 1961; s. Rolando Di Silvio Bianchi and Gloria Lopez Maldonado; m. Fatima Pardo Soto Mayor, Apr. 8, 2005. MD, U. Anahuac, Huixquilucan, Mex., 1985; degree in gen. surgery, Universidad Nacional Autonoma de Mex., Mexico City, 1989. Bd. cert. Consejo Mexicano de Cirugia Gen., cert. Consejo Mexicano de Gastroenterologia. Rsch. fellow dept. surgery U. Pitts., 1990—93; clin. resident, dir. rsch. program Instituto de Seguridad y Servicios Sociales de los Trabajadores del Estado, Mexico City. Pres. Asociación Mexicana de Cirugia Exptl., 2004—, Sociedad Mexicana de Investigación Biomédica, 2004—; sec. Mexican Surg. Bd., 2005—; nat. rschr. level 1 Sistema Nacional de Investigadores, Mexico City, Mexico, 2003—. Transplant coord. Centro Medico Nacional 20 de Noviembre ISSSTE, Mexico City, 2001—05. Recipient diploma and medal, Liderazgo Anahuac en Medicina, 2004, Norman Rich Vascular Surgery award, 2004. Fellow: ACS (assoc.); mem.: Am. Gastroenterology Assn. (assoc.). Achievements include research in angiogenesis; collagen and wound repair; obesity; Rotenone pesticide inducing oxidative stress and dopaminergic neuron damage after chronic exposure to light. Home: AV PALMAS 805 Edif 2 depto 10-2 Distrito Federal Mexico City 11000 Mexico Office: Grupo Medico Sierra Nevada Sierra Nevada 779 Lomas de Chapultepec Distrito Federal Mexico City 11000 Mexico Office Fax: 55200604; Home Fax: 55754879. E-mail: mdisilvio@issste.gob.mx.

MAURIN, MAX, medical educator, clinical microbiologist; b. Aubagne, France, Jan. 9, 1962; s. Maurice and Colette Maurin; m. Sophie Gasquet, Oct. 26, 1996; children: Cédric, Thomas, Camille. B, Aix-Marseille U., France, 1979, student, 1980—86, MD, 1991; M, U. Paris VII, 1991, PhD, 1994. Cert. cert. Ministry Edn., France, 2002. Intern U. Hosp., Aix-Marseille U., 1986—90, clin. microbiologist, 1991—2002, asst. prof., 1996—2002; prof. U. Hosp. Grenoble, Joseph Fourier U., 2002—, clin. microbiologist, 2002—. Postdoctoral fellow Johns Hopkins Hosp., Balt., 2000—01. Mem.: French Soc. Microbiology, Am. Soc. Microbiology. Achievements include research in antibiotic susceptibility of intracellular bacteria. Office: Centre Hospitalier U Bp 217 Grenoble 38043 France Office Fax: 33 4 76 76 59 12. Personal E-mail: max.maurin38@orange.fr. Business E-Mail: mmaurin@chu-grenoble.fr.

MAURIN, NORBERT, nephrologist, researcher; b. Moenchengladbach, Germany, May 22, 1952; s. Hans and Hannelore Maurin; m. Monika Hoerletsberger, Feb. 10, 1979; children: Maria Teresa, Anna Caterina. MD, RWTH U. Aachen, Germany, 1978. Cert. prof. in internal med. 1994. Sr. physician RWTH U., Aachen, 1984—96; med. supt. St. Johannes-Hosp., Bonn, Germany, 1997—2005; head KfH Kidney Ctr., Neuwied, Germany, 2006—. Contbr. scientific papers. Mem. Lions Club, Bonn, Germany, 1997. Maj. Med. Svc., 1977—79, German Army. Roman Catholic. Home: Von-Kuegelgen-St 10 Bonn D-53125 Germany Office: KfH Kidney Ctr Neuwied Engerser Landstr 78 Neuwied D-56564 Germany Office Fax: 49 0 2631 390315; Home Fax: 49 0 228 2436651. Personal E-mail: maurin@t-online.de. Business E-Mail: norbert.maurin@kfh-dialyse.de.

MAURO, CRAIG, orthopedist; b. Pitts., Dec. 6, 1977; BA, Cornell U., 2000; MD, U. Pitts. Sch. Medicine, 2004. Clin. instr. U. Pitts. Med. Ctr., 2011—. Mem.: Am. Orthop. Soc. Sports Medicine, Arthroscopy Assn. N.Am., Am. Acad. Orthop. Surgeons. Office: 200 Delafield Rd Ste 4010 Pittsburgh PA 15215 Office Fax: 412-784-5776. Business E-Mail: maurocs@upmc.edu.

MAURO, MATTHEW ANTHONY, radiologist, educator; b. White Plains, NY, Apr. 4, 1951; s. Anthony Joseph and Rosalie Mauro; m. Patricia Marchase, Aug. 21, 1976; children: Lauren Ann, David Matthew. BS, Cornell U., 1973; MD, Cornell Med. Coll., 1977. Specialty cert. Am. Bd. of Radiology, subspecialty cert. Am. Bd. of Radiology. Prof. radiology and surgery, chmn. radiology dept. U. N.C., Chapel Hill, 1991—; chmn. Cardiovasc. and Interventional Radiology Rsch. and Ednl. Found., 2002—. Contbr. articles to med. jours. Fellow: Soc. Interventional Radiology (pres. 1999—2000), Am. Coll. of Radiology (bd. of chancellors 2003—); mem.: Am. Bd. Radiology (trustee).

MAURYA, PAWAN KUMAR, biotechnologist; b. Rae Bareli, Oct. 10, 1980; PhD, Allahabad U., 2008. Postdoc. rschr. Taipei Med. U., 2011—. Sr. lectr. Amity U., 2008. Office: Amity Inst Biotech Gautam Buddha Nagar Noida Uttar Pradesh 201303 India Business E-Mail: pawan@tmu.edu.tw

MAUSER, MANFRED ALBERT, cardiologist; b. Florence, Italy, June 11, 1956; s. Wolfram and Annemarie Mauser; m. Karin John, Aug. 29, 1986; children: Ingo, Vera, Leonie. MD, U. Tübingen, Germany, 1981. Med. intern Universitätsklinik, Tübingen, Germany, 1983—93, prof. U. Tirbingen, 1992; head catheterization lab Klinikum Lahr, Germany, 1993—2004, chief, dept. cardiology, 2004—. Rsch. fellow, Max-Planck Inst. Exptl. Cardiology, 1981—83. Office: Klinikum Lahr Klostenstr 19 Lahr 77933 Germany

MAUVAIS-JARVIS, FRANCK, physician, researcher; b. Paris, Mar. 3, 1965; s. Pierre Mauvais-Jarvis and Anne Bergue; m. Rachel Webb, Feb. 26, 2003. MD, Paris V Sch. of Medicine, 1991; PhD, U. of Paris XI, 2002. Cert. Medicine/Endocrinology French Bd. of Medicine, 1996. Resident Paris Tchg. Hosps., 1991—94, clin. fellow endocrine svc., 1994—96; rsch. fellow Joslin Diabetes Ctr., Harvard Med. Sch., Boston, 1996—99; instr. St. Louis/Lariboisiere Med. Ctr., Paris, 1999—2003; asst. prof. medicine Baylor Coll. of Medicine, Houston, 2003—. Office: Baylor Coll Medicine One Baylor Plz BCMA 700B Houston TX 77030 Office Fax: 713-798-3810. Business E-Mail: fmjarvis@bcm.tmc.edu.

MAVES, MICHAEL DONALD, former medical association administrator; b. East St. Louis, Ill., Oct. 14, 1948; BS, U. Toledo, Ohio, 1970; MD, Ohio State U., 1973; MBA, U. Iowa, 1988. Diplomate American Bd. Otolaryngology, lic. physician Iowa, Mo., Ill., DC. Rsch. fellow Ohio State U. Coll. Medicine, Columbus, 1977; head & neck surgery fellowship Columbia-Presbyn. Med. Ctr., NYC, 1978, U. Iowa Hosp. & Clinics, Iowa City, 1980-81, asst. prof. otolaryngology, head & neck surgery, 1984-87, assoc. prof., 1987-88; asst. prof. otolaryngology, head & neck surgery Ind. U. Sch. Medicine, Indpls., 1981-84; chmn. dept. otolaryngology St. Louis U. Sch. Medicine, 1988-94; exec. v.p. American Acad. Otolaryngology, Head & Neck Surgery, Alexandria, Va., 1994—2001; pres. Consumer Healthcare Products Assn., Washington, 1999—2001; exec. v.p., CEO AMA, Chgo., 2002—11. Contbr. articles to profl. jours. Capt. US Army, 1974—76. Named one of The 400 Best Cancer Doctors in America, Good Housekeeping mag., 1992. Mem.: American Acad. Facial & Plastic Reconstructive Surgery, American Cancer Soc. *

MAVRIKAKIS, IOANNIS, ophthalmologist; b. Athens, Greece, Nov. 5, 1973; s. Myron Mavrikakis and Angeliki Diamanti. MUDr, 3rd Faculty Medicine, Charles U., Prague, Czech Republic, 1997; PhD, U. Athens, 2005. Cert. specialist qualification in Ophthalmology U. Athens, Greece, 2004. Clin. rsch. fellow ophthalmology Queen Victory Hosp., East Grinstead, England, 1999—2000; ophthalmology resident Eastbourne Dist. Gen. Hosp., England, 2000—01, Brighton and Sussex U. Hosp., Brighton, England, 2001—03, Royal Berkshire Hosp., Reading, England, 2003—04; oculoplastic and lacrimal fellow Brighton and Sussex U. Hosp., England, 2004, Queen Victoria Hosp., East Grinstead, 2004—05; orbital fellow U. BC, Vancouver, Canada, 2005—06; oculoplastic lacrimal and orbital surgeon U. Athens Med. Sch., 2006—. Course instr. Am. Acad. Ophthalmology, 2003—; presenter in field. Contbr. scientific papers to profl. jours. Mem.: Am. Soc. Ophthalmic Plastic and Reconstructive Surgery, Am. Acad. Ophthalmology, Hellenic Soc. Ophthalmic Plastic and Reconstructive Surgery, Hellenic Ophthalmologic Soc., Brit. Oculoplastic Surgery

Soc., European Soc. Ophthalmic Plastic and Reconstructive Surgery. Greek Orthodox. Avocations: swimming, skiing, water-skiing, travel. Office: Solonos 18 Kolonaki 106 73 Athens Greece Office Fax: 302103619339. Personal E-mail: jmavrikakis@yahoo.com.

MAVROCORDATOS, PHILIPPE, anesthesiologist, pain physician, researcher; b. Athens, Greece, Mar. 29, 1962; s. Loucas and Line Mavrocordatos; m. Alejandra Maria Blatter, Feb. 17, 1995; children: Barbara Xenia, Pablo Thanos. MD, Lausanne U., Switzerland, 1988. Diplomate Anesthesiology Bd. FMH Switzerland, 1995, pain practice fellow diploma 2006. Anesthesiologist, chief de clinique Centre Hospitalier Universitaire Vaudois, Lausanne, 1994—95; pain mgmt. clin. and rsch. fellow Royal N. Shore Hosp., Sydney, NSW, 1996—97; head anesthesiology dept. Centre Hospitalier Nord Vaudois, Yverdon, Vaud, Switzerland, 1998—2002; dir. Centre Interdisciplinaire de la Douleur, Clinique Cecil, Lausanne, 1999—; médecin-anocie Hôpitaux Universitaire de Genève, Geneva, 2007—; pain medicine Bangkok U., 2007—; assoc. prof. Mahidol Univ., Bangkok, 2007—. Cons. Debiopharm, Lausanne, 2006—, EISAI Pharmaceutics, Tokyo, 2006—, Medtronic Inc., Minn., 2007—. Pres. Pain Found., Pully, Vaud, Switzerland, 2003—07. Mem.: Swiss Soc. Interventional Pain Medicine (pres. 2004—), World Inst. Pain (chmn. Swiss chpt.), Internat. Assn. Study Pain. Office: Clinique CECIL avenue Louis-Ruchonnet 53 1003 Lausanne 1009 Switzerland Office Phone: 0041213105530. Office Fax: 0041213105442. Personal E-mail: pmavroco@worldcom.ch.

MAVROUDIS, IOANNIS ASTERIOS, medical researcher; b. Thessaloniki, Jan. 24, 1979; PhD, Med. Sch. Aristotle U., Thessaloniki, 2004. Rsch. fellow Lab. Neuropathology & Electron Microscopy, Aristotle U., 2005—; resident, dept. gen. surgery Gen. Hosp. Chalkidiki, 2006—07; physician Greek Army, 2007—08; resident, dept. internal medicine Psychiat. Hosp. Thessaloniki, 2009—10; resident, psychiatry dept. Papanikolaou Gen. Hosp., 2010—. Dir. & editor jour. 'peri politeias' Cultural Assn. Chalkidiki, 2003—05, dir. & editor monthly newspaper 'contemporary culture', 2003—05, pres. adminstrv. coun., 2003—05. Recipient Hon. award, Ednl. Assn. 'Apollon Arnaias' Chalkidiki, 2005, Basketball Assn. Chalkidiki, 2009. Mem.: Cultural Assn. Chalkidiki, Internat. Soc. Ameriolation Life Chronic Neurologic Patients, Greek Neurol. Soc. Avocation: basketball. Home: Sana Chalkidikis Chalkidiki 63073 Greece Personal E-mail: iamav79@hotmail.com.

MAX, ERNEST, surgeon; b. Vienna, Mar. 3, 1936; m. Silvia Neger, Mar. 18, 1964; children: Yvette Rosa, Oliver Fredrick. MD, U. Chile, 1961. Diplomate Am. Bd. Surgery, Am. Bd. Colon and Rectal Surgeons, Am. Bd. Laser Surgery. Intern Hosp. San Borja, Santiago, Chile, 1960-61, resident, 1962-63; fellow in gen. surgery, colon and rectal surgery Lahey Clinic Found., Boston, 1969-70; resident Sinai Hosp., Balt., 1971-72, The Western Pa. Hosp., Pitts., 1972-74; resident in colon and rectal surgery Hermann Hosp., Houston, 1974-75, staff, 1975—, Park Plz. Hosp., 1975—, Meml. Hosp. Southwest, 1975—, Meml. NW Hosp., 1975—, Diagnostic Ctr. Hosp., 1975—, The Methodist Hosp., 1976—, Meml. City Hosp., 1976—, Houston NW Med. Ctr., 1976—, St. Luke's Episcopal Hosp., 1981—, Cypress Fairbanks, 1983—; chief of staff Meml. Hosp., 1983; staff HCA Med. Ctr., 1986—; CEO Colon and Rectal Clinic PA, 1989—. Clin. assoc. prof. surgery Baylor Coll. Medicine; clin. instr. surgery U. Tex. Med. Sch., Houston. Author: (with others) Current Diagnosis, 1971. Recipient Walter A. Fansler Travel Edn. award Am. Soc. Colon and Rectal Surgeons, 1974, Harriet Cunningham award Tex. Med. Assn., 1988, Best of the Best award Tex. Med. Assc., 1989; The Purdue Fredrick fellow Am. Soc. Colon and Rectal Surgeons, 1974. Mem. Am. Coll. Surgeons, Tex. Med. Soc., Harris County Med. Soc., Tex. Soc. Colon and Rectal Surgeons (pres. 1982-83), Am. Soc. Laser Medicine and Surgery, Internat. Soc. Univ. Colon and Rectal Surgeons, Lahey Clinic Alumni Assn., Am. Soc. Colon and Rectal Surgeons, Tex. Gulf Coast Colon and Rectal Surgical Soc. (sec. treas. 1992—), Colombian Soc. Colo-Proctology (hon. mem.). Office: Colon & Rectal Clinic PA 6550 Fannin St Ste 2307 Houston TX 77030-2723 Office Phone: 713-790-9250. Business E-Mail: emax@crchouston.com.

MAXFIELD, ROGER A., pulmonologist, educator; AB, Brown U., Providence, RI, 1974; MD, Brown U. Sch. Medicine, 1977. Diplomate Am. Bd. Internal Medicine-pulmonary disease, Am. Bd. Internal Medicine. Intern Georgetown Univ. Hosp., resident in internal medicine, 1977—80; fellow in pulmonary disease Bellevue Hosp. Ctr., 1983—85, Manhattan V.A. Hosp., 1983—85; clin. prof. pulmonary, allergy and critical care medicine divsns. Columbia Univ. Med. Ctr.; pulmonologist NY Presbyn. Hosp., Columbia. Co-author: (publs.) Gastric carcinoid: two unusual presentations, 1983, Respiratory failure in patients with acquired immunodeficiency syndrome and Pneumocystis carinii pneumonia, 1986, Lung Volume Reduction Surgery for Pulmonary Emphysema: Improvement of the Body Mass Index, Airflow Obstruction, Dyspnea, and Exercise Capacity Index after One Year, 2007, numerous other publs. Recipient Nat. Health Svc. Corps award, USPHS; named one of the Top Doctors: NY Metro Area, Best Doctors in NY, NY Mag., 2000; fellow, Am. Coll. Physicians, Am. Coll. Chest Physicians. Office: New York Presbyterian 16 E 60th St Ste 320 New York NY 10022 Office Phone: 212-326-8415. Office Fax: 212-326-8496.

MAXSON, LINDA ELLEN, biologist, educator; b. NYC, Apr. 24, 1943; d. Albert and Ruth (Rosenfeld) Resnick; m. Richard Dey Maxson, June 13, 1964; 1 child, Kevin. BS in Zoology, San Diego State U., 1964, MA in Biology, 1966; PhD in Genetics, San Diego State U./U. Calif., Berkeley, 1973. Instr. biology San Diego State U., 1966-68; tchr. gen. sci. San Diego Unified Sch. Dist., 1968-69; instr. biochemistry U. Calif., Berkeley, 1974; asst. prof. zoology, dept. genetics and devel. U. Ill., Urbana-Champaign, 1974-76, asst. prof. dept. genetics, devel. and ecology, ethology & evolution, 1976-79, assoc. prof., 1979-84, prof., 1984-87, prof. ecology, ethology and evolution, 1987-88; prof., head dept. biology Pa. State U., State College, 1988-94; assoc. vice-chancellor acad. affairs/dean undergrad. acad. affairs, prof. ecology and evolutionary biology U. Tenn., Knoxville, 1995-97; dean Coll. Liberal Arts & Scis., prof. biol. scis. U. Iowa, Iowa City, 1997—. Exec. officer biology programs Sch. Life Scis., U. Ill., 1981-86, assoc. dir. acad. affairs, 1984-86, dir. campus honors program, 1985-88; vis. prof. ecology and evolutionary biology U. Calif., Irvine, 1988; mem. adv. panel rsch. tng. groups behavioral biol. scis. NSF, 1990-94; rsch. assoc. Smithsonian Instn. Author: Genetics: A Human Perspective, 3d edit., 1992; mem. editl. bd. Molecular Biology Evolution; exec. editor Biochem. Sys. & Ecology, 1993-2001; contbr. numerous articles to scientific jours. Recipient Disting. Alumni award, San Diego State U., 1989, Disting. Herpetologist award, Herpetologists' League, 1993. Fellow: AAAS; mem.: Soc. Molecular Biology and Evolution (treas. 1992—94, sec. 1992—95), Soc. Study Evolution, Soc. for Study of Amphibians and Reptiles (pres. 1991), Am. Men and Women in Sci., Phi Beta Kappa. Office: U Iowa 240 Schaeffer Hall Iowa City IA 52242-1409 Business E-Mail: linda-maxson@uiowa.edu.

MAXWELL, GEORGE PATRICK, plastic surgeon; b. Selma, Ala., July 15, 1946; married; 1 child. MD, Vanderbilt U., Nashville, 1972. Cert. Am. Bd. Plastic Surgery, 1981. Intern gen. surgery Johns Hopkins Hosp., Balt., 1972—73, resident plastic surgery, 1973—76, resident microsurgery, 1976—79; fellow Davis Med. Ctr., San Francisco, 1975; with Baptist Hosp., Nashville; asst. clin. prof. Vanderbilt U.; founder Inst. Aesthetic and Reconstructive Surgery, Nashville, 1989; with Nashville Plastic Surgery. Med. advisor Inamed Corp., Santa Barbara, Calif.; founder, chmn. Inamed Acad.; co-founder, exec. v.p., chief surg. officer Diversified Specialty Insts.; founder, bd. mem. Aspen Ctr. Integrative Health. Contbr. articles to med. jours.; featured: newspapers New York Times, magazines Departures, 1997, Town & Country, 1999, Good Housekeeping, 1999, W, 2000, 2001, Redbook, 2001, New York Times Mag., 2005, More. Mem.: Southeastern Soc. Plastic Surgeons, Am. Soc. Aesthetic Plastic Surgery (Walter Scott Brown award), Am. Assn. Plastic Surgeons (James Barrett Brown award), Am. Soc. Plastic Surgeons (Presdl. award 2005, Robert H. Ivy Soc. award), Am. Coll. Surgeons, South African Soc. Plastic Surgery (hon.), Japanese Soc. Plastic Surgery (hon.), Can. Soc. Plastic Surgery (hon.). Achievements include patents in field.

MAXWELL-JACKSON, CRISPIN FOX (MAX MAXWELL-JACKSON), medical communications executive; b. Kampala, Uganda, Sept. 29, 1961; s. George and Amanda C. Maxwell-J.; m. Teresa Moore, Jan. 24, 1988 (div. 1993); children: Joe Brian, Lucy Fox. BSc, U. Auckland, New Zealand, 1981, MSc, 1984. Flotilla skipper Sunsail Ltd., Turkey, 1989-90; sales and mktg. exec. Schering-Plough Ltd., Eng., 1991-92; account mgr. Advt. and Design Assocs., London, 1993-94; account dir. The Medicus Group, London, 1995; dir. strategic and client svcs. FSP Internat. (formerly Franklin Sci. Projects), London, 1996-98; mng. dir. FSP Internat. (formely Franklin Sci. Projects), London, 1999—2001; regional pres. Europe The Medicus Group, London, 2002; pres. Europe Publicis Healthcare Group, London, 2003—04, CEO, pres., 2004—06, pres. emerging markets and businesses, 2007—. Co-creator (web site) Awakenings, 1997; developer MERCURA strategic planning process. Lt. Royal New Zealand Navy, 1984-88. Fellow Inst. Direct Mktg., Pharm. Mktg. Soc. (mem. Inst. Dirs.) Avocations: sailing, scuba diving, skiing, music, paragliding. Office: Publicis Health Group Pembroke Building Avonmore Road W14 8DG London England E-mail: max.jackson@medicusgroup.com.

MAXWELL-JOLLY, DAVID, public health service officer, state official; b. 1949; BA in History & Polit. Sci., Ind. U., Bloomington; MPH, U. Mich.; PhD in Pub. Policy, Frederick S. Pardee RAND Grad. Sch. Project analyst Kaiser Permanente Med. Care Program; supervising analyst Office of the Calif. Legis. Analyst, 1982—86; prin. cons. health and human services issues Calif. State Senate, 1986—99; dep. sec. Calif. Health & Human Services Agency, Sacramento, 1999—2002, project dir. Calif. Child Support Automation Sys., 2002—04, chief dep. dir. Dept. Child Support Services, 2005—07, dir. Dept. Child Support Services, 2007—09, dir. Dept. Health Care Services, 2009—11, under sec., 2011—. Democrat. Office: California Dept Health & Human Services Avency 1600 Ninth St, Room 460 Sacramento CA 95814-6439 Office Phone: 916-654-3454. *

MAY, DONALD ROBERT LEE, ophthalmologist, educator, academic administrator, farmer; b. Spring Valley, Ill., Nov. 26, 1945; BS in Liberal Arts and Scis. with high honors and distinction, U. Ill., 1968, MD, 1972. Diplomate Am. Bd. Ophthalmology, Nat. Bd. Med. Examiners. Rsch. fellow dept. ophthalmology U. Ill. Eye and Ear Infirmary, Chgo., 1971—72; intern Northwestern U. Sch. Medicine Meml. Hosps., Chgo., 1972—73; resident in ophthalmology U. Ill. Eye and Ear Infirmary, Chgo., 1973—76, instr. dept. ophthalmology, 1974—77, attending surgeon dept. ophthalmology, 1976—77, fellow in diabetic retinopathy study, diabetic retinopathy vitrectomy study, and retina and vitreous surgery, 1976—77; founder, dir. retina svc., dept. ophthalmology Wilford Hall USAF Med. Ctr., San Antonio, 1977—79; asst. prof. ophthalmology, founder, dir. Retina/Vitreous/Ocular Trauma Svc. U. Calif. Davis Sch. Medicine, Calif., 1979—81; assoc. prof., dir. retina, vitreous and ocular trauma svc. U. Calif. Sch. Medicine, Davis, 1981—84; prof. ophthalmology Tulane U. Sch. Medicine, New Orleans, 1984—89, dir. med. student edn. dept. ophthalmology, 1985—89, dir. ophthalmology Charity Hosp., 1985—89; prof. Tex. Tech U. Health Scis. Ctr., Lubbock, Tex., 1989—2001, chmn. dept. ophthalmology and visual scis., 1989—94, prof. dept. health orgn. mgmt., 1993—2001, assoc. dean Sch. Medicine, 1994—96; del. 19th Congaessional Dist. to Repulican Nat. Convention, Tex. Co-investigator in the intraocular gentamicin prophylaxis study Govt. Erskine Hosp., Madurai, India, 1975, Dept. Ophthalmology, Audie Murphy VA Hosp., San Antonio, 1977—79, Martinez VA Hosp., Calif., 1979—84, VA Hosp., New Orleans, 1984—89, VA Med. Ctr., Big Spring, Tex., 1989—93, 1996—2001, VA Ctr., Lubbock, Tex., 1989—92, Lubbock, 1996—2001; vis. prof., Germany, 1984, Switzerland, 87; pres. US Eye Injury Registry, 1994—96; founder, med. dir. Tex. Eye Injury Registry, 1991—2001; cons. in field; co-owner Fullanime Cos., Lubbock, Tex., Selenium Ltd. Concert Lighting Internat., Compliance Svcs. Group Internat.; ptnr. Concert Lighting Internat.; with Brit. Parliament & Royal Family, Et al. Contbg. editor: Outcome/Fragmatome Newsletter, 1978—81; assoc. editor: Vitreorentinal Surgery and Tech., 1989—98, mem. editl. bd.: Jour. Eye Trauma, 1996—2001; contbr. articles to profl. jours.; appeared in numerous TV and radio programs. Com. mem. Sch. Medicine U. Calif., Davis, Tulane U. Sch. Medicine, New Orleans, Sch. Medicine Tex. Tech. U. Health Scis. Ctr.; bd. dirs. Lubbock Internat. Cultural Ctr., Inc., 1997—, pres. bd. dirs., 2005—07; planning com., chmn. medicine and history com., liaison Vatican Mus. Exhbn. Found., 2001—02; bd. trustees Nat. Exhibits Assn. Mus., Post, Tex., 2007—; Tex. del. 19th Congl. Dist. to Rep. Nat. Convention, 2008. Maj. USAF, 1973—80. Decorated Air Force Commendation medal. Mem.: AMA, ACS, Mil. Officers Assn. of Am., Mil. Officers Assn. Am. (bd. dirs. Greater Lubbock chpt. 2007—), Ill. Farm Bur., Ill. Agrl. Assn., Am. Farm Bur. Fedn., Soc. Med. Cons. Armed Forces, Vitreous Soc. (charter), Retina Soc., Schepens Internat. Soc., Tex. Tech. Rsch. Found. (bd. dirs. 1993—96), Tex. Ophthal. Assn. (chair edn. com. 1990—93, coun. 1990—93, nominating com. 1991—93), So. Retina Study Group, Tex. Med. Assn. (com. continuing edn. 1993—96, bd. dirs. TEXPAC 2000—02), So. Med. Assn. (vice-chmn. sec. ophthalmology 1995—96, chmn. sec. ophthalmology 1996—97), Christian Med. Assn., Assn. Rsch. Vision and Ophthalmology (pub. rels. com. 1997—2000), Am. Acad. Ophthalmology (bylaws and rules com. 1990—95, com. internat. ophthalmology 1991—95), Lubbock C. of C., Am. Legion, Sigma Xi (sec. Tex. Tech. chpt. 1990—91, v.p., pres.-elect 1999—2000, pres. 2000—01). Republican. Lutheran. Avocations: travel, photography, bicycling, hiking. Office: PO Box 1678 Lubbock TX 79408-1678

MAY, HAROLD LOUIS, retired surgeon, not-for-profit developer; s. Arthur Earnest and Margaret Jestina May; m. Agnes Martens, Apr. 26, 1960; children: Jeannette Elizabeth, Alison Gabrielle, Margaret May Jenkins. MD, Harvard Med. Sch., Boston, 1951, MPH, 1974. Lic. physician Mass., 1959, diplomate Am. Bd. of Surgery, 1965. Med. intern U. Minn. Hosps., Mpls., 1951—52; med. asst. resident Boston City Hosp., 1952—53; surg. resident Mass. Gen. Hosp., Boston, 1953—59; chief of surgery Albert Schweitzer Hosp., Deschapelles, Haiti, 1960—70; dir. Divsn. Cmty. Health and Med. Care Peter Bent Brigham Hosp., Boston, 1970—75; assoc. surgery Peter Bent Brigham Hosp. and Brigham and Women's Hosp., Boston, 1970—94; asst. prof. surgery Harvard Med. Sch., 1970—94; dir. med. svcs. Wrentham (Mass.) Devel. Svcs., 1975—94, ret., 1994. Exec. com. Boston-Brookline (Mass.) Health Resources Orgn., 1970—73; chmn. Region VI Emergency Med. Svcs. Com., Mass., 1972—74. Editor (author): Emergency Medicine, 1984; editor: Emergency Procedures, 1984; editor in chief: Emergency Medicine, 2d edit., 1992. Founder and pres. FAMILY, Inc., Boston, 1997; co-founder Ecole La Providence Primary Sch., Deschapelles, Haiti, 1962; founder FAMILY Tuskegee Inst., Haiti, 2010. Aviation cadet US Army Air Corps, 1945. Recipient Excellence in Tchg. Faculty prize, Harvard Med. Sch., 1987, 1992, Congl. Gold medal, 2008, Living Legends award, Mus. African Am. History, Boston. Fellow: ACS; mem.: MGH Surg. Soc., Tuskegee Airmen, Boston Surg. Soc. Avocations: music, painting. Home and Office: FAMILY Inc 80 Waban Hill Road Newton MA 02467 Business E-Mail: haroldmay@familysystem.net.

MAY, JAMES WARREN, JR., plastic surgeon; b. Lexington, Ky., 1943; MD, Northwestern U., 1969. Cert. gen. surgery Am. Bd. Surgery, 1975, plastic surgery Am. Bd. Plastic Surgery, 1977. Intern gen. surgery Mass. Gen. Hosp., Harvard Medical Sch., 1969, surg. resident Boston, 1969—74; resident plastic surgeon Harvard Medical Sch., 1974—75; fellow, hand and Microsurgery U. Louisville, 1975, U. Melbourne, Australia, 1975—76; assoc. prof. clin. surgery Harvard Med. Sch., Boston; chmn. Am. Bd. Plastic Surgery; chief, plastic, reconstructive surgery Mass. Gen. Hosp. Cancer Ctr., Boston; prof. surgery Harvard Medical Sch.; chmn. plastic and Reconstructive Surgery Mass. Gen. Hosp., 1982—. Named one of Top Cancer Specialists for Women, Good Houskeeping mag., 1999, Top Breast Cancer Doctors, Redbook mag., 2002, Boston's Top Doctor's, Boston mag., 2006. Mem.: Royal Coll Physicians and Surgeons (hon. fellow 2008), Am. Assn. Plastic Surgeons (pres. 2007), Am. Assn. Hand Surgery (pres. 1996), Am. Assn. Acad. Chmn. Plastic Surgery (pres. 1995), Am. Bd. Plastic Surgery (chmn. 1992), New England Soc. Plastic Surgeons (pres. 1990), Northeastern Soc. Plastic Surgeons (pres. 1990), Plastic Surgery Rsch. Coun. (chmn. 1987), Mass. Soc.Plastic Surgeons (pres.), Am. Assn. Plastic Surgeons (pres.-elect 2006, pres. 2007). Office: MA Gen Hosp Divsn Plastic Surgery WACC 435 55 Parkman St Boston MA 02114-3117

MAY, JOHN RAYMOND, clinical psychologist; b. Rahway, NJ, Jan. 31, 1943; s. John Y. and Aline (Eichorn) M.; m. Brenda Lee Berg, June 17, 1967; children: Stacey Anne, John Jeffrey. BA in Psychology, Colgate U., 1965; PhD in Clin. Psychology, U. N.C., 1970. Clin. intern U. Wis. Med. Ctr., 1967—68; staff psychologist to chief, clin. svcs. divsn. Nat. Security Agy., Ft. Meade, Md., 1969—72; cons., 1972—92, 2003—; pvt. practice Columbia, Md., 1972—. Exec. dir. Psychol. Health Svcs., Inc., Columbia, 1976—84, 1993—2001, Columbia Psychol. Svcs., 1984—91, Cmty. Counseling Assocs., 1991—; co-dir. Columbia Addictions Ctr., 1994—98; adj. prof. Loyola Coll., 1970—72. Co-author films on mental health tng., articles in profl. jours. and manuals. Recipient Wallach award U. N.C., 1969, Humanitarian award Citizens Against Spousal Assault, 1989; USPHS fellow, 1966-69; VA fellow, 1965-66. Mem. APA, Md. Psychol. Assn. (exec. coun., various coms. 1977-91, treas. 1985-88, pres.-elect 1988, pres. 1989-90, past pres. 1990-91, Outstanding Profl. Contbn. to Psychology award 1993), Am. Bd. Sexology (diplomate), Assn. Advancement of Psychology, Am. Soc. Clin. Hypnosis, Am. Assn. Sex Educators, Counselors, and Therapists (cert. sex. therapist), Anxiety Disorders Assn. Am., Howard County Psychol. Soc. (pres. 1975-76). Home: 1310 Harmony Ln Annapolis MD 21409-5719 Personal E-mail: john.may@crossroadspsych.net.

MAY, LINDA KAREN CARDIFF, occupational health nurse, safety engineer, consultant; b. San Mateo, Calif., Oct. 26, 1948; d. Leon Davis and Jane Vivian (Gallow) Cardiff; m. Donald William May, Dec. 7, 1969 (div. Feb. 1988); children: Charles David, Andrew William. At, So. Ill. U., 1969; post grad., Ill. Wesleyan U., 1989; AAS, Parkland Coll., 1977; BS in Pub. Health and Safety Engring. with honors, U. Ill., Urbana, 1987; BSN, Lakeview Coll., 1990. RN Ill., Ind., Mo., N.Mex., Tex., Wis., registered profl. nurse; nat. registered EMT Ill., accredited instr. constrn. safety and health OSHA. Indsl. nurse C.S. Johnson Co., Champaign, Ill., 1979—84; safety engr. Clinton Nuclear Power Plant Ill. Power Co., 1984—86; occupl. safety and health specialist Danville Vet.'s Med. Ctr., 1986—; pres.CEO Waileler Ill. Co. With LKM Health and Safety Cons., Inc., Champaign, Ill. Active Mercy Hosp. Aux., Covenant Hosp Aux., 1977—, Champaign County Task Force on Arson, 1981—; alumni assn. liason Parkland Coll. Found. Bd., 1993; mem. Champaign County Crime Prevention Coun., 1978—83, bd. dir., 1980—82. Ill. State Gen. Assembly scholar, 1967. Mem.: APHA (occpl. health and safety sect.), AACN, Lakeview Coll. Nursing Alumni Assn., N.Y. Acad. Sci., Ill. EMTs Assn., Pre-Hosp. Care Providers Ill., Associated Ill. Milk, Food and Environ. Sanitarians, Ill. Soc. Pub. Health Educators, Ill. Environ. Health Assn., Nat. Registry EMT, Am. Assn. Occupational Health Nurses, Am. Nuc. Assn. (mem. biology and medicine divsn., mem. radiopharm. and isotope product stds. com.), Am. Soc. Safety Engrs. (vice chair Ctrl. Ill. sect. 1985—86), Ill. Wesleyan U. Alumni Assn., U. Ill. Alumni Assn. (life), Parkland Coll. Alumni Assn. (life; bd. dir. 1987—, v.p. 1992—), Eta Sigma Gamma. Methodist. Achievements include patents in field. Home: PO Box 3954 Champaign IL 61826-3954 Personal E-mail: lmay4111@aol.com.

MAY, ROBERT M., retired obstetrician, gynecologist, educator; b. Camberg, Germany, Feb. 17, 1926; came to U.S., 1940; s. Herman and Flora May; m. Anita S. Wynne, Sept. 6, 1953; children: Harvey, Ann, Julie. MD, La. State U., 1948. Diplomate Am. Bd. Ob-Gyn. Intern Touro Infirmary, New Orleans, 1948-49, resident in ob-gyn., 1949-53; practice medicine specializing in gynecology Birmingham, Ala., 1954-97; mem. staff Bapt. Med. Ctr., pres. med. staff, 1985-86, chmn. dept. ob-gyn., 1980-86; assoc. clin. prof. ob-gyn. U. Ala., Birmingham, 1975-97. Served to capt. USAFR, 1950-52. Mem. Ala. Med. Soc., Am. Soc. Study Infertility, Am. Coll. Ob-Gyn.

MAY, ROBERT MCCREDIE (LORD MAY OF OXFORD), biology educator; b. Sydney, Jan. 8, 1936; s. Henry W. and Kathleen (McCredie) M.; m. Judith Feiner, Aug. 3, 1962; 1 child, Naomi Felicity. BSc, Sydney U., 1956, PhD, 1959; DSc (hon.), City U. London, 1989, Uppsala U., 1990, Yale U., 1993, Heriot-Watt U., 1994, U. Edinburgh, 1994; DSC (hon.), U. Sydney, 1995. Gordon Mackay lectr. applied math Harvard U., Cambridge, Mass., 1959—61, mem. vis. faculty, 1966; theoretical physics lectr. Sydney U., 1962—64, reader, 1964—69, personal chair, 1969—73; prof. biology Princeton U., NJ, 1973—88; Royal Soc. rsch. prof. U. Oxford, England, 1989—, fellow Merton Coll., 1989—. Vis. faculty Calif. Inst. Tech., 1967; vis. prof. UKAEA Culham Lab., 1971, Magdalen Coll., 1971, Imperial Coll., England, 1975—95; chief sci. adviser to U.K. Govt., head U.K. Office Sci. and Tech., 1995—2000. Editor: Stability and Complexity in Model Ecosystems, 1973, Population Biology of Infectious Diseases, 1982, Theoretical Ecology: Principles and Applications, 1976, Perspectives in Ecological Theory, 1989, Infectious Diseases of Humans: Dynamics and Control, 1991, Extinction Rates, 1995. Trustee Nuffield Found., Cambridge U. Gates Trust; chmn. emeritus bd. trustees Natural History Museum; bd. mem. UK Sport Institute. Decorated Order of Australia, Knighthood; recipient MacArthur award, 1984, Linnean Medal, Linnean Soc., 1991, Christian Marsh prize, 1992, Frink medal, 1995, Crafoord prize in Biosciences, Royal Swedish Acad. Sciences, 1996, Balzan prize, 1998, Blue Planet prize, Asahi Glass Found., 2001, Life Peerage, Ho. of Lords Appointments Commn., 2001, Order of Merit, 2002. Fellow Royal Soc. (pres. 2000-2005, Copley medal, 2007), Am. Acad. Arts and Scis.; mem. NAS, Athenaeum Club. Office: The Royal Society 6-9 Carlton House Terrace SW1Y 5AG London England E-mail: robert.may@zoo.ox.ac.uk.

MAY, STERLING RANDOLPH, biology professor, department chairman; b. Muskogee, Okla., Dec. 27, 1946; s. William Sterling and Mary Catherine (Griffith) May. BA with honors, U. Kans., 1968, MS, U. Mich., 1969, PhD, 1977; M in Bus., Johns Hopkins U., 1995, MBA, 2000. Coord. Skin Bank St. Agnes Med. Ctr., Phila., 1977-79, assoc. dir. Burn Rsch., 1980, dir. Burn Rsch., 1981-83; dir. Southeastern Burn Rsch. Inst., Augusta, Ga., 1983-87; v.p. LifeCell Corp., The Woodlands, Tex., 1987-91; chief oper. officer ARC Nat. Hdqs., Arlington, Va., 1991-2000; pres. Health Care Rsch., Arlington, 2000—04; assoc. prof. biology and genetics, chmn. dept. math. and sci. Brenau U., Gainsville, Ga., 2004—09; prof. biology and genetics, Richard & Phyllis Leet disting. chair, biol. sci., dir. Anna Thomas Biosci. Ctr., 2009—. Rsch. asst. prof. Hahnemann U. Sch. Medicine, Phila., 1979-82, rsch. assoc. prof., 1983; assoc. clin. prof. Med. Coll. Ga., 1984-87; adj. prof. U. Tex. Med. Sch., Houston, 1987-91. Editor: Care of the Burn Wound, 1985; author 84 published articles in biomed. lit., 1974—; mem. editorial bd. Jour. Burn Care and Rehab., 1982-90, Burns, 1985-92, Cryobiology, 1987-93. Mem. Soc. for Cryobiology (pres. 1989-91, chmn. 23d ann. meeting, 1986), Am. Burn Assn. (chmn. rsch. com. 1998-2000), Internat. Soc. For Burn Injuries (mem. gen. coun. 1982-90), Am. Assn. Tissue Banks (sec. 1991-93, v.p. 1993-95, pres. 1995-97, bd. govs. 1989-93), Sigma Xi, Phi Kappa Phi (chartered mem., founding mem. Brenau U. chpt.). Avocations: antique furniture, music. Home: 2318 River Cliff Dr Gainesville GA 30501-1685 Office: Dept Math and Sci Brenau Univ 500 Washington St NE Gainesville GA 30501 Home Phone: 770-536-9171; Office Phone: 770-534-6278. Business E-Mail: rmay@brenau.edu.

MAYA, IVAN DARIO, internist, interventional nephrologist; b. Bogota, Colombia, May 3, 1961; s. Ivan and Agustina (Cortes) M.; m. Patricia Alvarado, Aug. 10, 1985; children: Joanna, Nancy, Jessica. MD, Juan N. Corpas Sch. Medicine, Suba, Colombia, 1983. Diplomate in internal medicine and nephrology Am. Bd. Internal Medicine. Intern, resident U. Ala. Birmingham, Montgomery, 1994—97; staff Bapt. Med. Ctr., Montgomery, 1997—2002; instr. medicine internal medicine U. Ala. Birmingham, 1998—2002; fellow in nephrology U. Ala., Birmingham, 2002—04, asst. prof. medicine and radiology Dept. Nephrology, 2004—10, assoc. prof. medicine and radiology Dept. Nephrology, 2008—10; attending physician UAB Univ. Hosp., 2004—10; asst. scientist Nephrology Rsch. Tng. Ctr. U. Ala. Birmingham, 2005—10, assoc. dir. interventional nephrology sect., dept. nephrology, 2004—08, dir. internat. nephrology sec., 2008—10, assoc. prof. medicine & radiology, 2008—; assoc. prof. U. Ctrl. Fla., 2011—. Phys. asst. Dept. Def., Eglin AFB, Fla., 1990-94; med. officer VA Hosp., Montgomery, 1995-2000; attending physician Bapt. Med. Ctr., Montgomery, 1997-2002; contract clin. dir. FPC Maxwell, Montgomery, 1997-98; instr. medicine Montgomery internal medicine residency program U. Ala., Birmingham, 1998-2002. Recipient awards Fed. Bur. Prisons, 1991, 92, 93. Fellow ACP, Am. Soc. Internal Medicine; mem. AMA, Med. Assn. State Ala., Am. Soc. Nephrology, Am. Soc. Diagnostic Interventional Nephrology. Roman Catholic. Avocations: reading, music. Office: Univ Alabama Dept Nephrology Birmingham AL 35242 Office Fax: 205-996-6465. Personal E-mail: ivmaya@hotmail.com. Business E-Mail: imaya@nacfla.com.

MAYBERG, HELEN SUSAN, neurologist, educator; b. Orange, Calif., Jan. 2, 1956; BA in psychobiology, UCLA, 1976; MD, U. Southern Calif., 1981. Cert. Neurology, 1987. Resident in medicine LA County-U. Southern Calif. Med. Ctr., LA, 1981—82; resident in neurology Columbia-Presbyn. Med. Ctr., NYC, 1982—85; fellow in nuclear medicine Johns Hopkins Med. Inst., Balt., 1985—87, staff, 1987—91; asst. prof. neurological psychiatry Johns Hopkins Sch. Medicine, Balt., 1987—91; assoc. prof. U. Tex. Health Sci. Ctr., San Antonio, 1991—98; prof. psychiatry and neurology U. Toronto, 1999—2003, Sandra Rotman chair neuropsychiatry; staff Baycrest Hosp., Toronto, 1999—2004; prof. psychiatry, behavioral sciences, and neurology Emory U. Sch. Medicine, Atlanta, 2003—, Dorothy C. Fuqua chair psychiatric neuroimaging and therapeutics. Recipient Arnold Pfeffer prize, Jour. Neuropsychoanalysis, 2001. Fellow: Royal Coll. Physicians of Can.; mem.: NARSAD (Young Investigator award 1991, Independent Investigator award 1995, Disting. Investigator award 2002, Falcone prize for Outstanding Achievement in Mood Disorders Rsch. 2007), Inst. Medicine, Am. Coll. Neuropsychopharmacology, Am. Neurological Assn., Alpha Lambda Delta. Office: Emory U Sch Medicine WMB 4313 101 Woodruff Cir Atlanta GA 30322 Office Phone: 404-727-6740. Office Fax: 404-727-6743. E-mail: helen.mayberg@emory.edu.

MAYER, JONATHAN DAVID, medical educator; b. Chgo., Sept. 4, 1955; BA, U. Rochester, 1973; PhD, U. Mich., 1977. Prof. epidemiology, geography, medicine U. Wash., 1977—. Pres. Health Improvement and Promotion Alliance, 2004. Nat. fellowship, WK Kellogg Found. Office: Dept Epidemiology Box 353550 Seattle WA 98195 Business E-Mail: jmayer@uw.edu.

MAYER, LLOYD F., gastroenterologist, immunologist, educator; MD, Mt. Sinai Sch. Medicine, 1976; BS in Biology, Union Coll., 1996. Diplomate Am. Bd. Internal Medicine, Am. Bd. Internal Medicine-gastroenterology. Resident internal medicine NYU Med. Ctr., 1977—79; fellow gastroenterology Mt. Sinai Hosp., NYC, 1979—81; prof. microbiology Mt. Sinai Sch. Medicine, NYC, prof. medicine gastroenterology, prof. medicine clin. immunology, co-dir. immunology inst., 2007—. Named one of Best Doctors, NY Mag., 2009. Office: Mount Sinai Medical Center Department of Medicine 5 E 98th St 11th Fl New York NY 10029 Office Phone: 212-241-0764. Office Fax: 212-534-0971.

MAYER, MICHAEL, general practitioner, pediatrician, researcher; b. Linz, Upper Austria, May 10, 1980; married. D, Med. Sch. Innsbruck, Austria, 2004. Sci. asst. Dept. Physiology, U. Innsbuck, Tyrol, 2000—01, Landes- Frauen- und Kinderklinik Linz, 2005—09, pediat. resident, 2009—; intern, resident AKH Linz, 2005—09. Contbr. articles to profl. med. jours. Recipient Internat. Health Profession of Yr., 2010; grant, Pfizer Inc., 2005. Achievements include research in neonatology, especially birth measurements, infantile hemangioma, growth hormone deficiency, Seckel syndrome and APGAR score. Office: Landes- Frauen- und Kinderklinik Linz Krankenhausstraße 26 Linz Upper Austria 4020 Austria Office Fax: 43-732-6923-22004. Business E-Mail: dr.michael.mayer@gmx.at.

MAYER, NATTHANIEL H., physiatrist, educator; MD, Yeshiva U., NYC. Diplomate Am. Bd. Physical Medicine and Rehab. Intern Mt. Auburn Hosp., Cambridge; resident Temple Univ. Sch. of Med., fellow, with tchg. appointment; fellow Yeshiva Univ., NYC, Drexel Univ. Sch. of Med.; co-dir. neuro-orthpaedic program Moss Rehab. Hosp., dir. motro control analysis lab. Named one of the Top Doctors, Phila. Mag., 2011. Office: Moss Rehab Hospital 60 Township Line Rd Elkins Park PA 19027 Office Phone: 215-663-6681. Office Fax: 215-663-6685.

MAYER, RICHARD EDWIN, psychology professor; b. Chgo., Feb. 8, 1947; s. James S. and Bernis (Lowy) M.; m. Beverly Linn Pastor, Dec. 19, 1971; children: Kenneth Michael, David Mark, Sarah Ann. BA with honors, Miami U., Oxford, Ohio, 1969; MS in Psychology, U. Mich., 1971, PhD in Psychology, 1973. Vis. asst. prof. Ind. U., Bloomington, 1973-75; asst. prof. psychology U. Calif., Santa Barbara, 1975-80, assoc. prof., 1980-85, prof., 1985—, pres., chmn. dept., 1987-90. Vis. scholar Learning Rsch. and Devel. Ctr., U. Pitts., 1979, Ctr. for Study of Reading, U. Ill., 1984. Author: Foundations of Learning and Memory, 1979, The Promise of Cognitive Psychology, 1981, Thinking, Problem Solving, Cognition, 1983, 2d edit., 1992, BASIC: A Short Course, 1985, Educational Psychology, 1987, The Critical Thinker, 1990, 2d edit., 1995, The Promise of Educational Psychology, Vol. I, 1999, Vol. II, 2002, Multimedia Learning, 2001, Learning and Instruction, 2003, (with R. Clark) E-Learning and the Science of Instruction, 2004, Cambridge Handbook of Multimedia Learning, 2005; editor: Human Reasoning, 1980, Teaching and Learning Computer Programming, 1988; editor jours. Instructional Sci., 1983-87, Educational Psychologist, 1983-89. Sch. bd. officer Goleta (Calif.) Union Sch. Dist., 1981—. Grantee, NSF, 1975—88, 1991—. Fellow APA (divsn. 15 officer 1987—, G. Stanley Hall lectr. 1988, E.L. Thorndike award 2000), Am. Psychol. Soc.; mem. Am. Ednl. Rsch. Assn. (divsn. C officer 1986-88, 2007-), Psychonomic Soc. Democrat. Jewish. Avocations: computers, hiking, bicycling, reading, dogs. Office: U Calif Dept Of Psychology Santa Barbara CA 93016 Home Phone: 805-964-5936. Business E-Mail: mayer@psych.ucsb.edu.

MAYER, ROBERT J., oncologist, gastroenterologist, educator; MD, Harvard Med. Sch., 1969. Fellow Nat. Cancer Inst., Dana Farber Cancer Inst.; dir. Ctr. for Gastrointestinal Oncology Dana-Farber Cancer Inst., dir. Partners CancerCare's Fellowship Training Program in Hematology & Medical Oncology, vice chmn. acad. affairs dept. medical oncology; prof. medicine Harvard Med. Sch.; sr. physician Beth Israel Deaconess Med. Ctr.; attending physician MGH Cancer Ctr. Mass. Gen. Hosp. Mem.: Am. Soc. Clinical Oncology (pres. 1997). Office: Dana-Farber Cancer Institute 44 Binney St Dana 1602 Boston MA 02115 Office Phone: 617-632-3474. Office Fax: 617-632-2260.

MAYER, STEPHAN ANTHONY, neurologist; b. NYC, Sept. 22, 1962; s. Roman Henry Mayer and Karin (Lehmkuhl) Ludewig; m. Elizabeth Alcott Webster, Sept. 11, 1993; children: Philip Brett, Catherine Weld. AB, Brown U., 1984; MD, Cornell U. Med. Coll., 1988. Diplomate Am. Bd. Psychiatry and Neurology. Intern Columbia-Presbyn. Med. Ctr., NYC, 1988-89, resident in neurology, 1989-92, clin. fellow, 1992—94, dir. neurol. ICU, 1995—; asst. prof. neurology and neurosurgery Columbia U. Coll. Physicians & Surgeons, NYC, 1995—2001, assoc. prof. clin. neurology and neurosurgery, 2001—; with Neurol. Inst., NYC, 1989—. Co-author: On Call-Neurology, 1997; co-founder, assoc. editor Neurocritical Care; co-author Ropper; contbr. several articles to profl. jours., chapters to books; ad-hoc reviewer for many journals. Rsch. Fellow Nat. Stroke Assn., 1993; Am. Heart Assn. grant, 1997; named one of America's Top Doctors. Fellow Am. Heart Assn. (stroke coun.); mem. Am. Acad. Neurology, Soc. Critical Care Medicine (Neuroscience award, 2003), Am. Neurol. Assn.; founding mem. Neurocritical Care Soc. Office: Neurol Inst 710 W 168th St Critical Care New York NY 10032 Office Phone: 212-305-7236. Office Fax: 212-305-2792. E-mail: sam14@columbia.edu.

MAYER, SUSAN LEE, nurse, educator; b. NYC, Feb. 10, 1946; d. Hans and Frieda (Schein) Abramson; m. Steven Mayer, June 24, 1973; children: Jason, Stuart, Richard, Deborah. BSN, Hunter Coll., NYC, 1968; MA, NYU, 1974; EdD, Columbia U., NYC, 1996; postgrad., Yeshiva U., NYC, 1986, Adelphi U., Garden City, NY, 1987. RN, NY; cert. in gerontology; cert. tchr., NY. Staff nurse ICU-CCU Montefiore Hosp., Bronx, N.Y., 1968; organizer CCU Jewish Meml. Hosp., NYC, 1968; supr., adminstr. Morrisania City Hosp., NYC, 1969-76; instr. Adelphi U., Garden City, N.Y., 1977-78; substitute nurse Great Neck (N.Y.) Pub. Schs., 1980-90; rsch. asst. to dean Adelphi U. Sch. Nursing, 1987-88; network dir. nursing ambulatory North Bronx Healthcare Network, 2001—. Staff nurse Winthrop U. Hosp., Mineola, NY, 1987—90, per diem nurse, 1987—90; instr. dept. nursing edn. Bronx Mcpl. Hosp. Ctr. (now Jacobi Med. Ctr.), 1990—96; asst. prof. Helene Fuld Coll. Nursing, 1996—2001; adj. instr. Bronx C.C., 1992, Queensborough C.C., 1987—89; adj. asst. prof. Iona Coll. Sch. Nursing; adj. assoc. prof. Tchrs. Coll./Columbia U., 1997—; field nurse coord. RN Home Care Winthrop U. Hosp., Mineola, 1996—2001; lectr. and presenter in field. Contbr. articles to profl. jours. including Nursing and Health Care. Bd. dirs. Great Neck Synagogue, 1981-91, v.p. Sisterhood, 1978-79, pres., 1979-81; former bd. dirs. Russell Gardens Assn.; founder Work for Share Zedek Hosp., 1977—; pres., past fin. sec. Hadassah Nurse Coun. NY State Regents scholar, 1963. Mem. Am. Assn. Ambulatory Care Nurses, NY State Nurses Assn. (dist. 13 bd. dirs., past chmn. nurse practice com., past treas., past chair coun. ethical practice), NY Assn. Ambulatory Care, Am. Assn. for History of Nursing, Nurses Edn. Alumni Assn. (past historian), Sigma Theta Tau, Kappa Delta Pi. Democrat. Office Phone: 718-515-1438. Business E-Mail: susan.mayer@nbhn.net.

MAYERS, MARGUERITE M., pediatrician, educator; MD, Albert Einstein Coll. Medicine, 1971. Diplomate Am. Bd. Pediatrics, Am. Bd. Pediatrics-pediatric infectious disease. Clin. prof. pediat. Albert Einstein Coll. Medicine; resident in pediat. Montefiore Hosp. Med. Ctr., Bronx, NY, 1972—74, fellow infectious disease, 1974—76, pediatrician Henry and Lucy Moses divsn. Office: Montefiore Hosp. Medical Center 3444 Kossuth Ave Bronx NY 10467 Office Phone: 718-920-5871. Office Fax: 718-652-5707.

MAYERS, STANLEY PENROSE, JR., public health service officer, educator; b. Phila., Nov. 9, 1926; s. Stanley Penrose and Margaret Amelia (Thorpe) M.; m. Virginia Lee Lytle, Aug. 25, 1951 (dec. Oct. 1990); children: Douglas Lytle, Kenneth Stanley, Daniel John, Andrew William; m. Patricia Ann Harne Hulsey, Mar. 6, 1993. BA, U. Pa., 1949, MD, 1953; MPH, Johns Hopkins U., 1958. Diplomate Am. Bd. Preventive Medicine. Intern Phila. Gen. Hosp., 1953-54; resident Arlington County Health Dept., Va., 1954-55; health dir. Henry-Martinsville-Patrick Health Dist., Martinsville, Va., 1955-57; regional dir. Va. State Health Dept., Richmond, 1958-59; dist. state health officer N.J. State Dept. of Health, Trenton, 1959-62; asst. prof. and asst. dean Johns Hopkins Sch. Hygiene and Pub. Health, Balt., 1962-65; dir. Arlington County Dept. of Human Resources, Arlington, Va., 1965-71; prof. health policy and adminstrn. Pa. State U., University Park, 1971-97, prof. emeritus, 1997—, chmn., 1979 88, assoc. dean undergrad. studies Coll. Health and Human Devel., 1989-92, assoc. dean acad. studies Coll. Health and Human Devel., 1992-95, assoc. dean emeritus, 1997—. Interim dir. internat. edn. programs and studies Pa. State U., 2000-2001; faculty assoc. Johns Hopkins U. Sch. Hygiene and Pub. Health, Balt., 1965-75; clin. assoc. prof. Georgetown U. Sch. Medicine, Washington, 1965-71; cons. VA, 1985—. Contbr. articles to profl. jours. Pres. Arlington Optimist Club, 1970-71; bd. dirs. Centre County Family Planning Svcs., Bellefonte, Pa., 1972-79, vice chmn., Ctr. County Hosp. Commn., 2005-; With USN, 1945-46. Recipient Outstanding Achievement award Dept. Community Medicine, Georgetown U. Sch. Medicine, 1968, Saubel award Coll. of Human Devel., Pa. State U., 1985, Pioneer Achievement award Frankford H.S., Phila., 1999. Fellow Am. Coll. Preventive Med., APHA (chmn. membership com. health officer's sect. 1968-70, mem. nominating com. health adminstrn. sect. 1970 72, chmn. com. to draft a statement on local health agy. responsibilities 1973-74); mem. AMA, Arlington County Med. Soc. (Wellborn award 1971), Centre County Med. Soc. (pres. 1978), Med. Soc. Va., Met. Washington Health Officers Assn. (sec. 1967-71), Am. Assn. Pub. Health Physicians (pres. Va. chpt. 1970-71), Pa. Med. Soc. (mem. Ho. of Dels. for Centre County 1974-76, 81-97, treas. 1973-74, 85—, sec. 1974-76, v.p. 1976, pres. elect 1977, pres. 1978), Mt. Nittany Soc., Univ. Club (State College, Pa.), Phi Beta Kappa. Episcopalian. Avocations: fishing, boating, hiking. Home: 648 Wiltshire Dr State College PA 16803-1450 Office: Pa State U Human Devel Bldg Rm 115 University Park PA 16802 Business E-Mail: spm1@psu.edu.

MAYES, THOMAS C., pediatrician, department chairman; B magna cum laude, Baylor U.; MD cum laude, Georgetown U. Sch. Medicine. Cert. in pediatrics and pediatric critical care medicine. Full-time faculty mem. U. Tex. Health Sci. Ctr., San Antonio, 1994—, prof., chmn. dept. pediatrics, assoc. dean clin. affairs, interim dean sch. medicine, 2005—06; pres. & CEO U. Tex. Medicine San Antonio, 2009—; physician-in-chief CHRISTUS Santa Rosa Children's Hosp. Served with Med. Corps USAF. Office: University Tex Health Sci Ctr San Antonio Dept Pediatrics 7703 Floyd Curl Dr MSC 7802 San Antonio TX 78229-3900 Office Phone: 210-567-5200. Office Fax: 210-567-6921. Business E-Mail: pedschair@uthscsa.edu. *

MAYFIELD-CLARKE, ANN BERNADETTE, speech, language pathologist; d. Bobby Clarence and Johnnie Lee Mayfield; m. Don Lazaro Clarke, June 24, 1989. BSc, Marquette U., Milw., 1976; MSc, Howard U., Washington, 1978, PhD, 1998. Cert. in clin. competence Am. Speech Lang. Hearing Assn., Md., 1983. Spl. edn. program specialist DC Pub. Schs. State Edn. Agy., Washington, 1986—88; speech lang. pathologist Morena Valley Pub. Sch. Sys., Calif., 1988—89, Locomotion Therapy Co., San Gabriel, Calif., 1992—94, Suzanne Barnes & Assocs., Sierra Madre, Calif., 2000—02; instr. Calif. State U. Northridge, 1994—96, clin. faculty supr., 1994—96, adj. prof., 1998—99, asst. prof., 1999—2002; contractor, speech lang. pathologist Berman Peverley & Assocs., Silver Springs, Md., 1996—98, Posh Rehab. U. South Calif. Hosp., LA, 1998—2002; dir., speech lang., pathology & audiology Therapeutic Comprehensive Svcs., Mission Hills, Calif., 1998—2000; assoc. prof. NC A & T State U., Greensboro, 2002—, program dir., 2002—. Contbr. scientific papers. Adv. bd. mem. State Employees Credit Union, Stoney Creek, NC, 2005—. Recipient Outstanding Svc. award, NC A & T State U., 2003—08, Academic Advising Excellence award, NC A & T State University, 2009, Mentor award, Nat. Black Assn., 2009. Fellow: Am. Speech Lang. Hearing Assn. (Continuing Edn. award 2003—09); mem.: Nat. Acad. Pre-profl. Programs Comm. Disorders, Southeastern U. Clin. Educators, Coun. Academic Program Comm. Scis. & Disorders (Diversity Incentive award 2006), Nat. Black Assn. Speech

Lang. & Hearing (bd. dirs. 2005—, convention program chair 2005—07), Phi Kappa Phi (com. mem. bylaws 2005), Delta Sigma Theta. Personal E-mail: bc62489@sbcglobal.net.

MAYHEW, ERIC GEORGE, medical researcher, educator, consultant; b. London, June 22, 1938; came to U.S., 1964; s. George James and Doris Ivy (Tipping) M.; m. Barbara Doe, Sept. 28, 1966 (div. 1976); 1 child, Miles; m. Karen Caruana, Apr. 1, 1978 (div. 1994); children: Ian, Andrea; m. Ludmila Khatchatrian, June 29, 1995. BS, U. London, 1960, MS, 1963, PhD, 1967, DSc, 1993. Rsch. asst. Chester Beatty Rsch. Inst., London, 1960—64; cancer rsch. scientist Roswell Pk. Meml. Inst., Buffalo, 1964—68, sr. cancer rsch. scientist, 1968—72, assoc. cancer rsch. scientist, 1979—83, dep. dir. exptl. pathology, 1988—93; prin. scientist The Liposome Co., Princeton, NJ, 1993—99, May Pharm Consulting, 2000—. Assoc. rsch. prof. SUNY, Buffalo, 1979-93; ad-hoc mem. NIH study sects., 1982-94; cons. to industry, 2000-. Editor jour. Selective Cancer Therapeutics, 1989-91; contbr. articles to Jour. Nat. Cancer Inst., Cancer Rsch. and many other profl. jours. Grantee NIH, Am. Heart Assn., and pvt. industry, 1972-93. Mem. Am. Assn. Cancer Rsch., N.Y. Acad. Sci. Achievements include development of liposomes for drug delivery and patents for new chemical entities and liposome delivery. Office: May Pharm Consulting 1782 S Seaview Ave Coupeville WA 98239 Home Phone: 360-678-2175.

MAYHEW, MARY C., public health service officer, state official; b. 1964; BA in Polit. Sci., U. Ark. Ptnr. Hawkes & Mayhew, Augusta, Maine; mgr. state govt. rels. Equifax Corp., Atlanta; legis. asst. for Rep. William Alexander US House of Reps., Washington; v.p. Maine Hosp. Assn.; sr. health policy advisor to Gov. Paul LePage State of Maine, Augusta, Maine; commr. Maine Dept. Health & Human Services, Augusta, 2011—. Democrat. Office: Maine Department of Health and Human Services 221 State St Augusta ME 04333 Office Phone: 207-287-3707. Office Fax: 207-287-3005. *

MAYLAHN, CHRISTOPHER M., epidemiologist; b. Phila., Feb. 6, 1952; s. Frances (Scott) M.; m. Katherine M. Scharff, May 27, 1989; children: Michael, David, Juliana. BA, U. Vt., 1975; MPH, Yale U., 1978. Epidemiologist Vt. Heart Assn., Rutland, 1978-80, N.Y. State Health Dept., Albany, 1980—. Mem. APHA, Assn. State and Territorial Chronic Disease Program (chmn. sci. and epidemiology com. 1997—, pres. 2000), Coun. State and Territorial Epidemiologists. Office: NY State Dept Pub Health Svc 2565 Tower Empire State Plz Albany NY 12237-0001 Home: 112 Cobble Hill Dr Gansevoort NY 12831-2532

MAYNARD, CHARLES DOUGLAS, radiologist; b. Atlantic City, Sept. 11, 1934; m. Mary Anne Satterwhite; children: Charles D., Deanne, David. BS, Wake Forest U., 1955, MD, 1959. Diplomate Am. Bd. Radiology (trustee 1987-99, sec.-treas., v.p. 1992-94, pres. 1994-96, guest examiner). Intern U.S. Army Hosp., Honolulu, 1959—60; resident N.C. Baptist Hosp., 1963—66; dir. Nuclear Medicine Lab., 1966—77; asst. dean admissions Bowman Gray Sch. Medicine, 1966—71, asso. dean student affairs, 1971—75, prof. radiology, chmn. dept., 1977—2000. Mem. Am. Bd. Med. Specialists; acting dean Wake Forest U. Sch. Medicine, 2001—02. Author: Clinical Nuclear Medicine, 1969; mem. editl. bd.: Yearbook of Diagnostic Radiology, Contemporary Diagnostic Radiology. Mem. Leadership Winston-Salem, Triad Leadership Network; bd. dirs. Downtown Devel. Corp., 1995—2000, Winston-Salem Bus., Inc., 1995—99, Forsyth Tech. CC, 1997—2005, pres., 2004—05; bd. dirs. Va. Tech. Coll. Engring., 2002—06, Wake Forest U. Health Scis., 2003—. Mem.: AMA, Greater Winston-Salem C. of C. (bd. dirs.), Acad. Radiology Rsch. (pres. 1999—2001), Soc. Chairmen Radiology Depts. (past pres.), Assn. Univ. Radiologists, Radiol. Soc. N.Am. Rsch. and Edn. Found. (chmn. bd. 1999), Radiol. Soc. N.Am. (pres. 1999—2000), Am. Coll. Radiology (past bd. chancellors, past chmn. commn. on nuc. medicine), Soc. Nuc. Medicine (past pres.). Office: Wake Forest U Sch Medicine Dept Radiology Medical Center Blvd Winston Salem NC 27157-1088

MAYNARD, KENNETH IRWIN, pharmaceutical executive, medical educator, researcher; b. San Fernando, Trinidad, Jan. 17, 1963; Student, Howard U., 1982; BSc with honors, Univ. Coll., London, 1986, MSc, 1987, PhD, 1991. Cert. design and conduct of clin. trials. Postdoctoral rsch. assistantship Univ. Coll., London, 1991; postdoctoral rsch. fellow Stroke Rsch. Lab. Neurosurg. Svc. Mass. Gen. Hosp., Harvard Med. Sch., Boston, 1991—93, postdoctoral rsch. fellow neurophysiology lab. Neurosurg. Svc., 1993—97; tchg. fellow dept. neurobiology Harvard Med. Sch., Boston, 1992, instr. in surgery, 1995—98, asst. prof., 1998—2001; asst. neuroscientist Mass. Gen. Hosp., 1998—2001; section head, cerebrovascular disorders Aventis Pharms., Inc., 2000—02, prin. sci., 2002—04; project dir. Sanofi-Aventis, Inc., 2005—. Ad hoc reviewer Jour. Vascular Rsch., 1991, Neurosci. Letters, 1995, Vision Rsch., 1996, Neurosurgery, 1998, others; presenter in field; tutor dept. of neurobiology, 1998—2000; asst. prof. surgery, 1998; steering com. Boston Area Neurosci. Group, 1998—2000; ad hoc reviewer Ministry of Health, Internal Grant Agy., Czech Republic, 1998; med. rsch. grant program Jewish Hosp. Found., 2000; cons. neurosurgery Mass. Gen. Hosp., 2001—02; lectr. Harvard U. Med. Sch., 2001—02. Contbr. articles to med. jours. including Neurosci. Letters, articles to med. jours. including Stroke, articles to med. jours. including Exptl. Neurology, articles to med. jours. including Jour. Neurol. Rsch. Mem. parish pastoral coun. St. Joseph's Cath. Ch., Boston, 1992—95, chmn. stewarship commn., 1997; advisor regional com. ctrl. region on stewardship Archdiocese of Boston, 1995—97. Recipient Travel fellowship for minority neuroscientists, Nat. Inst. Neurol. Disease and Stroke, 1995, travel award, FASEB MARC, 1998; scholar, Autumn Sch. Caen France, 1996, Tokyo, 1998. Fellow: Am. Heart Assn. (minority scientist devel. award 1996, nat. affiliate brain/stroke study sect. 1999—, stroke coun. 2002, minority affairs com.); mem.: AAAS, Am. Acad. Neurology, Internat. Soc. Cerebral Blood Flow and Metabolism (Young Scientist Bursary award 1993), Congress of Neurosurg. Surgeons, Am. Assn. Neurosurg. Surgeons (adj. assoc. mem. joint sect. on cerebrovascular surgery 1995), Soc. for Neurosci. (minority neurosci. fellowship program 2000—02, minority edn., tng. and profl. advancement com. 2000—03, membership com. 2002—07, fin. com. 2007—), N.Y. Acad. Sci., Am. Stroke Assn. (affiliate brain rsch. peer rev. group 1999—2003). Roman Catholic. Office: Sanofi Aventis Inc 200 Crossing Blvd BX2-309A Bridgewater NJ 08807 Office Phone: 908-304-6352. Business E-Mail: kenneth.maynard@sanofi-aventis.com.

MAYO, CLYDE CALVIN, psychologist, educator; b. Robstown, Tex., Feb. 2, 1940; s. Clyde Culberson and Velma (Oxford) Mayo; m. Jeanne Lynn McCain, Aug. 24, 1963; children: Brady Scott, Amber Camille. BA, Rice U., Houston, 1961; BS, U. Houston, 1964, PhD, 1972; MS, Trinity U., 1966. Lic. psychologist Tex., La. Mgmt. engr. LWFW, Inc., Houston, 1966-72, sr. cons., 1972-78, prin., 1978-81; ptnr. Mayo, Thompson, Bigby, Houston, 1981-83; founder Mgmt. and Pers. Systems, Houston, 1983—. Counselor Interface Counseling Ctr., Houston, 1976—79; dir. Mental Health HMO Group, 1985—87; instr. St. Thomas U., Houston, 1979—90, U. Houston Downtown Sch., 1972, 2002—06, U. Houston, Clear Lake, 1983—88, U. Houston-Ctrl. Campus, 1984—; dir. mgmt. devel. insts. U. Houston Woodlands and West Houston, 1986—91; adj. prof. U. Houston, 1991—; mem. 50th reunion com. Rice U., 2011. Author: LWFW Annual Survey of Manufacturers, 1966—81, Bi/Polar Inventory of Strengths, 1978. Coach, mgr. Meyerland Little League, 1974—78, So. Belles Softball, 1979—80, S.W. Colt Baseball, 1982—83, Friends of Fondren Libr. Rice U., 1988—; charter mem. Holocaust Mus. Mem.: APA, Rice U. Hist. Soc. (reunion com. 1986—), Houston Area Indsl. Orgnl. Psychologists (bd. dirs. 1989—92, orgnl. renewal com. 2010—, bd. dirs. 2011—), Am. Psychol. Soc., Tex. Psychol. Assn., Houston Psychol. Assn. (membership dir. 1978, sec. 1984, bd. dirs. 2010—), Tex. Indsl. Orgnl. Psychologists (founder, bd. dirs. 1995—, pres. 1999—2002), Soc. Indsl. Orgn. Psychologists, Found. Contemporary Theology (bd. dirs. 2005—, chair youth recruitment com. 2006—), Romeo, Meyerland Club (bd. dirs. 1988—92, pres. 1991), Forum Club. Home: 8723 Ferris Dr Houston TX 77096-1409 Office: Mgmt and Personnel Systems 4545 Bissonnet St Bellaire TX 77401-3121 Office Phone: 713-667-9251.

MAYOR, SATYAJIT, research scientist; b. Baroda, India, Jan. 26, 1963; PhD, Rockefeller U., 1991. Prof. Nat. Centre for Biol. Sci., 2003—; dean Nat. Centre for Biol. Sciences, 2008—11. Dean Nat. Centre for Biol. Sci., 2008—11. Recipient TWAS Prize in Biology, 2010. Fellow: Indian Nat. Sci. Acad., Indian Acad. of Sci.; mem.: Am. Soc. of cell biology. Avocations: reading, sport, cricket. Office: Bellary Road Karnataka Bangalore 560065 India Office Phone: +918023666260. Office Fax: +918023626662. E-mail: mayor@ncbs.res.in.

MAYORAL, FLOR A., dermatologist; MD, U. Fla., Gainesville. Diplomate Am. Bd. Dermatology. Resident Univ. of Miami, assoc. clin. prof. dept. of dermatology; leader Flor A. Mayoral M.D. Dermatology Group. Mem.: Dade County Med. Assn., Am. Acad. of Dermatology, AMA, Miami Dermatol. Soc. Mailing: Flor A. Mayoral MD Dermatology Group Ste 314 Plz San Remo 6705 Red Rd Miami FL 33143 Office Phone: 305-665-6166. Office Fax: 305-662-4649.

MAYOUX-BENHAMOU, MARIE-ANNE, anatomist, educator; d. Jacques Mayoux and Jeanne Soupat; m. Maurice Benhamou, Aug. 29, 1979; children: Guillaume Jacques Benhamou, Pierre Benjamin Benhamou. MD, Med. Sch. Necker-Enfants Malades, Paris, 1984; MS in Biol. and Med. Scis., U. Paris Descartes (formerly U. Paris V), 1987; PhD in Live Scis., U. Paris XI, 1992. Cert. in rheumatology Nat. Coun. Med. Drs., 1989, hosp. physician Assistance Publique-Hopitaux de Paris, 1990, in maitre confs. U. Paris Descartes, 1990, in rehab. European Bd. Phys. Medicine and Rehab., 1998, autorization to direct rsch. efforts U. Paris Descartes, 1997. Prof. in anatomy U. Paris Descartes (formerly U. Paris V), 1990—2009; hosp. practitioner, rehab. Assistance Publique-Hôpitaux de Paris, Hôsp. Cochin, Paris, 1990—2009. Cons. Haute Autorité de la Santé, Paris, 2007—08. Author: (book) Halte aux rhumatismes. Collection Guide Pratique, Lexique Anatomique Français-Anglais: Nomenclatures Anatomiques. Recipient award, Palmes Académiques, 2009.

MAYR, AGNES, hematologist; b. Bruneck, Italy, Oct. 23, 1949; MD, U. Innsbruck, 1974. Specialist in hematology clinic and lab. U. Modena, Italy, 1979. Chief cons. Hosp. Bruneck Lab. Clin. Pathology and Transfusion Therapy, 1987—. Med. dir. Hosp. Bruneck, 1993—99. Mem.: Soc. Hematology, SIMEL (Italy), SIBIOC (Italy). Avocations: mountain climbing, music, gardening. Home: St Nikolausstrasse 9 Bruneck Bozen 39031 Italy Personal E-mail: agnes.mayr@alice.it.

MAYRING, PHILIPP ANSELM EBERHARD, psychologist; b. Munich, June 7, 1952; s. Lothar Philipp and Elsbeth (Braun) M.; m. Ursula Reuter, Mar. 25, 1983; children: Jakob, Laura. MA, U. Munich, 1978; PhD, U. Augsburg, Germany, 1985, habilitation, 1990. Rsch. asst. U. Munich, 1978-85; asst. prof. U. Augsburg, 1985-93; prof. Univ. Edn., Ludwigsburg, Germany, 1993—2002, U. Klagenfurt, Austria, 2002—. Dir. dept. applied psychology and rsch. in methods, Ctr. Evaluation and Rsch. Cons. U. Klagenfurt, vis. prof., 1993—94, U. Fribourg, Switzerland, 1996—2000, U. Vienna, Austria, 1998—99. Author: Psychology of Happiness, 1991, Introduction into Qualitative Research, 5th edit., 2002, Learning Emotions, 2003, Mixed Methods, 2007, Qualitative Content Analysis, 10th edit., 2008. Mem.: APA, Austrian Assn. Psychology, German Assn. Psychology DGPs, German Assn. Gerontology, German Assn. Ednl. Sci. Office: Inst Psychol U Klagenfurt Universitaetsstrasse 65 A 9020 Klagenfurt Austria Office Phone: 43-463-27001671. Business E-Mail: philipp.mayring@uni-klu.ac.at.

MAYRON, LEWIS WALTER, clinical ecology consultant; b. Chgo., Sept. 20, 1932; s. Max and Florence Minette (Brody) M.; m. Sondra Mayron; children: Leslie Hope Mayron Coff, Eric Brian. BS in Chemistry, Roosevelt U., 1954; MS in Biol. Chemistry, U. Ill., 1955, PhD in Biol. Chemistry, 1959. Rsch. assoc. dept. biochemistry and nutrition U. So. Calif., LA, 1959-61; asst. biochemist dept. biochemistry Presbyn.-St. Luke's Hosp., Chgo., 1961-62; instr. dept. biol. chemistry U. Ill., Chgo., 1961-62; biochemistry group leader Tardanbek Labs., Chgo., 1962-63; sr. devel. chemist Abbott Labs., Chgo., 1963-64; asst. attending physician, mem. spl. staff Michael Reese Hosp. and Med. Ctr., Chgo., 1964-66, rsch. assoc. Dept. Allergy Rsch., 1964-66; asst. prof. in biochemistry and physiology Sch. Dentistry Loyola U., Chgo., 1968-71; guest investigator Argonne (Ill.) Nat. Lab., 1973-79; rsch. chemist V.A. Hosp., Hines, Ill., 1968-79; chief clin. radiobiochemist nuclear medicine svc. V.A. Wadsworth Hosp. Ctr., LA, 1979-83; cons. in clin. ecology, 1980—. Contbr. articles to profl. jours. Mem. AAAS, Am. Assn. Clin. Chemists, Soc. for Exptl. Biology and Medicine, Sigma Xi. Home: 823 S 1850 West Cedar City UT 84720-8237

MAYS, MARYANN, neurologist; Grad., Marquette U.; MD, Med. Coll Ohio, Toledo, 1993. Cert. clinical neurophysiology. Intern Cleveland Clinic, 1993—97, fellow, staff neurologist, 1998—, dir. neurology residency program, 2005—. Mem.: Assn. U. Professors Neurology, Am. Acad. Neurology, Nat. Headache Found., Am. Headache Soc., Alpha Omega Alpha. Office: Clevland Clinic 9500 Euclid Ave Mail Code S91 Cleveland OH 44195 Office Phone: 216-445-3616.

MAYTAL, JOSEPH, pediatrician, neurologist; Grad., Tel Aviv U. Lic. NY, 1987, diplomate Am. Bd. of Pediatrics, Am. Bd. Psychiatry and Neurology. Resident pediatric neurology Albert Einstein Coll. of Medicine, Bronx, NY, fellow; chief divsn. of pediatric neurology Steven and Alexandra Cohen Children's Med. Ctr., dir. neurophysiology lab., Long Island Jewish Med. Ctr. Prof. clin. neurology & clin. pediatrics Albert Einstein Coll. of Medicine. Office: Steven and Alexandra Cohen Children's Medical Center Suite 105 410 Lakeville Rd New Hyde Park NY 11040 Office Phone: 516-465-5255.

MAYUMI, TOSHIHIKO, medical educator; b. Nagoya, Japan, May 21, 1960; MD, Nagoya U., 1985, PhD, 1996. Asst. prof. Nagoya U. Grad. Sch. Medicine, 1999—. Office: Dept Emergency & Critical Care Nagoya Aichi 466-8560 Japan Office Fax: 81-52-744-2978. Business E-Mail: mtoshi@med.nagoya-u.ac.jp.

MAZARIS, EVANGELOS, urologist, consultant; s. Michael Mazaris and Violetta Mazari. MD, Athens Med. Sch., 1999; MSc, Imperial Coll. London, 2005, PhD, 2008. Lic. to practice medicine Athens Prefecture, 1999. Gen. physician Evdilos Health Ctr., Evdilos, Ikaria, Greece, 2001—02; gen. surgery resident KAT Hosp., Athens, 2002—03; sr. house officer Norfolk and Norwich U. Hosp., England, 2004—05; clin. fellow, transplantation surgery Hammersmith Hosp., London, 2004—05; urology chief resident Sismanoglio Hosp., Athens, 2005—09; uro oncology sr. clin. fellow Lister Hosp., Stevenage, England, 2009—11, cons. urologist, 2011—. Resident rep. Hellenic Urol. Assn., Athens, 2006—08. Lt. MC, 2000—01, Greece. Decorated Hellenic Army. Mem.: Greek Urol. Assn., European Assn. Urology, Athens Med. Assn., Endourol. Soc., Gen. Med. Coun. Achievements include research in NSAIDs after radical retropubic prostatectomy and ethical issues in live donor kidney transplantation. Avocations: swimming, travel, stamp collecting/philately. Office Phone: 00447788930668. Personal E-mail: evmazaris@yahoo.gr.

MAZER, MIKE, cardiologist, retired nephrologist, artist; b. Boston, May 17, 1936; s. Louis and Belle Mazer; m. Marilyn Wood, Feb. 26, 1987; children: Mark, Pamela. BS cum laude, Boston U., Mass., 1958; MD, U. Cin., 1962. Diplomate in internal medicine Am. Bd. Internal Medicine, 1970, in nephrology Am. Bd. Nephrology, 1978, in cardiology Am. Bd. Cardiology, 1979. Fellow gastrointestinal disease U. Cin., 1962—64; fellow renal and metabolic studies Med. Ctr. Boston U., 1964—65; fellow cardiovasc. disease West Roxbury VA Hosp., Boston, 1967—68; dir. acute hemodialysis Goddard Meml. Hosp., Stoughton, Mass., 1968—90, chief Echocardiography and Noninvasive Vascular Lab, 1977—94, chief cardiology, 1986—94; chief of nephrology Cardinal Cushing Hosp., Brockton, Mass., 1968—94; pvt. practice Bridgewater Goddard Pk. Med. Assocs., Mass., 1968—98; co-dir. Brockton- Goddard Hemodialysis Unit, Brockton, 1992—97; chief cardiology Good Samaritan Med. Ctr., Brockton, 1994—97, chief Echocardiography and Noninvasive Vascular Lab, 1994—97; med. dir. Pk. Cardiographics, Taunton, Mass.; dir. Cardiac Ultrasonography and Transtelephonic Monitoring Nat. Med. Co, Taunton; dir. Cardiac Rehab. Ctr. Striar Jewish Cmty. Ctr., Stoughton, 1994—97; artist Mattapoisett, Mass., 1997—. Splash 9: Watercolor Secrets, 2006, Solo New Bedford Art Mus., Mass., 2006, Splash 10: Passionate Brush Strokes, 2008, The Artistic Touch 4, 2010, Contemporary American Marine Art, 2003—04; co-author: Principles of Interpretation in Echocardiography, 1985; editor: Jour. Diagnostic Med. Sonography, 1985—87; over 500 exhbns. & 10 awards, collections, US Coast Guard, Wash., Tabor Acad., Marion, Mass., New Bedford Free Pub. Lib., Commonwealth Mass, Dept. Environ. Protection, Lakeville, Mass., Marion Art Ctr., exhibitions include Zeeland Maritime Mus., Vlissingen, 2009, internat. exhbn., Maritime Mus., Vlissingen, Holland, one-man shows include New Bedford Art Mus., 2006, Cape Cod Art Museum, Dennis, Mass., 2009, New Bedford Whaling Mus., 2009—10, Represented in permanent collections Cape Cod Mus. Art, New Bedford Art Mus., Represented in permanent collections New Bedford Whaling Mus., Mass. Maritime Acad.; contbr. articles to profl. publs. Recipient Top Money Water Media award, Am. Artists Profl. League, Grand Nat. Exhibitions, 1999, 2004, Best in Show award, Stoughton Art Assn., 2002, 2004, Miss. Grand Nat. Exhbn., 2003, Excellence award, North Shore Arts Assn. Gloucester, 2009, 1st pl., Marina Bay Guincy, Mass., Watercolor Northshore Arts Assn., 2009, Marina Bay Art Affair, 2009; named Top 100, Paint America Exhbn., 2007—10; nominee Top 100 award, 2008—11. Fellow: Am. Artists Profl. League; mem.: Nat. Watercolor Soc., Phila. Watercolor Soc., New Eng. Watercolor Soc. (pres. 2004—07), Canton (Mass.) Art Assn. (dir. edn. 1997—2007), Coast Guard Artist Program, Cape Cod Art Assn., Audubon Artists, Inc, Allied Artists of Am., Academic Artists Assn., Am. Soc. of Marine Artists, R.I. Watercolor Soc. (Best in Show award 2004), North Shore Arts Assn., Phila. North East Watercolor Soc., Tex. Watercolor Soc., Pa. Watercolor Soc., Nat. Soc. of Artists, Mo. Watercolor Soc., Internat. Guild of Realism (assoc.), Miss. Watercolor Soc., Mont. Watercolor Soc., Internat. Soc. of Marine Painters, Hudson Valley Art Assn., Ga. Watercolor Soc., The Salmagundi Club, Alpha Omega Alpha, Watercolor U.S.A. Honor Soc. Achievements include development of the first acute hemodialysis on the South Shore of Massachusetts, 1968; discovery of a Left Ventricular Myxoma by ultra sonography, 1984. Home: 7 Holly Woods Rd Mattapoisett MA 02739

MAZID, MD. ABDUL, pharmacist, educator; b. Jhenaidah, Bangladesh, Apr. 6, 1973; s. Md. Abdul and Shahana Aziz; m. Shamima Jahan, Sept. 24, 2003; 1 child, Rania Mehnoor. BPharm in Pharmacy with honors, U. Dhaka, Bangladesh, 1996, MPharm, 1999, MPhil in Pharmacy, 2003; PhD in Molecular and Cellular Biology, Tottori U., Japan, 2007. Cert. pharmacist Pharmacy Coun. People's Republic of Bangladesh. Pharmacist Kuwait Army Hosp., 1999—2000; lectr. U. Asia Pacific, Dhanmondi, Dhaka, 2001—03, Dept. Pharm. Chemistry, U. Dhaka, 2003—07, asst. prof., 2007—, assoc. prof., 2010—; postdoc. fellow European Molecular Biology Orgn., Nat. Health Rsch. Inst., Miaoli, Taiwan, 2009, Inst. Protein Biochemistry, Nat. Rsch. Coun., Naples, Italy, 2010; guest instr., pharmacy courses Armed Forces Medical Inst., Dhaka. Contbr. articles to sci. profl. jours. Fellowship, Nat. Sci. and Tech., Ministry Sci. and Tech., Govt.

Bangladesh, 2001, Japanese Govt. Monbukagakusho scholarship, 2003—06, Travel grant, Internat. Congress Cell Biology, 2008, Internat. Union Biochemistry and Molecular Biology, 2008, fellowship, European Molecular Biology Orgn., 2009—, Nat. Sci. Coun., Taiwan ROC, 2009, Youth Travel grant, Fed. European Biochem. Soc., 2010. Mem.: Italian Soc. Biochemistry and Molecular Biology, Japanese Us. Alumni Assn. Bangladesh, Pharmacy Grad. Assn. (Bangladesh), Bangladesh Pharm. Soc., Bangladesh Chemi. Soc. (life). Muslim. Home: Village-Rishkhali PO Rishkhali Upozilla-Horinakunda Jhenaidah 7200 Bangladesh Office: University Dhaka Faculty Pharmacy 1000 Dhaka Bangladesh Office Phone: 88028612069. Office Fax: 8808612069, 88028615583. Personal E-mail: mazid_ma@hotmail.com.

MAZIN, AOUF, engineering educator; b. Sydney, Nov. 13, 1981; MS with honors, U. Western Sydney, 2011; degree, U. Sydney, 2006. Lectr. U. Western Sydney, 2008—. Avocation: sports. Home: 9 Caroline St Guildford NSW 2161 Australia Personal E-mail: m.aouf@uws.edu.au.

MAZLEN, ROGER GEOFFREY, internist, pharmacologist; b. Bklyn., Nov. 23, 1937; s. Henry Gershwin and Ann Kurland (Shapero) M.; m. Sandra Phyllis Kuritzky, Aug. 7, 1960; children: James Edward, Vivien Gayle. BS in Biology, Rensselaer Poly. Inst., 1959; MD, SUNY, Bklyn., 1963. Intern maimonides Med. Ctr., Bklyn., 1963-64, resident in medicine, 1964-65; rsch. assoc. NIH, Bethesda, Md., 1965-67; resident in med. ophthalmology Mt. Sinai Med. Ctr., NYC, 1967-69; assoc. med. dir. Pfizer Inc., NYC, 1970-71; asst. dir. clin. rsch. Ayerst Labs., NYC, 1971-75; assoc. dir. clin. rsch. Schering Corp., Bloomfield, NJ, 1975-78; adj. asst. prof. medicine N.Y. Med. Coll.; sr. clin. asst. prof. Mt. Sinai Sch. Medicine; sr. faculty, sr. attending div. endocrinology and metabolism Mt. Sinai Med. Ctr., 1972—2008. Mem. cons. Profl. Children's Sch.; cons. in clin. nutrition and metabolism South Oaks Hosp; chief sci. officer Biomolecular Sci., Inc., 2000-07. Author: A New Manifesto for Middle America, 1972; author: (with others) Nutrition and Health Care; contbr. (chpt.) Quick Reference to Clinical Nutrition. Founder, chmn. Queens County (N.Y.) Common Cause, 1972—75, vice chmn. for N.Y. State, 1974—75; bd. dirs. Bayside Hills Civic Assn., 1970—80; adv. mem. bd. dirs. U.S.A., Inc., 1970—72; chmn. hyperalimentation com. Astoria (N.Y.) Gen. Hosp.; former dir. Clin. Rsch. N. Am. Immunotec Ltd., Montreal; nutrition dir. Cernitin Am. Nutritional, 1983—88. With USPHS, 1965—67. Fellow: Am. Coll. Nutrition (chmn. coun. on nutrition and cardiovasc. diseases 1976—85, sec.-treas.); mem.: N.Y. State Soc. Internal Medicine, Soc. for Natural Immunity, Am. Coll. Cardiology (constituent mem. N.Y. State chpt.), Am. Soc. Clin. Pharmacology and Therapeutics (Good Doctors List award CFIDS), Muhammad Ali Internat. Sport Youth Athletic Found. Inc. (bd. dirs.). Republican. Office: 30 Middledeck Rd Roslyn NY 11576 Home Phone: 718-631-4908; Office Phone: 516-869-0717. Personal E-mail: rgm1@aol.com.

MAZUMDAR-SHAW, KIRAN, biotechnology company executive; b. Bangalore, India, Mar. 23, 1953; m. John Shaw. Graduate in Zoology, Bangalore Univ., India, 1973; graduate Master Brewer, Ballarat Univ., Australia, 1975; PhD in Sci. (hon.), Ballarat Univ.; PhD (hon.), Manipal Academy Higher Edn. Chmn., mng. dir. Biocon Ltd. Recipient PADMASHRI, Pres. India, 1989, Padma Bhushan, 2005, MV Meml. award; named Businesswoman of Yr., ET, Model Employer, Ernst & Young; named one of The 50 Most Powerful Women, Fortune Mag., 2005, The 100 Most Powerful Women, Forbes mag., 2008, 2009, The 100 Most Influential People in the World, TIME mag., 2010. Office: Biocon India Electronics City Hosur Road 560 011 Bangalore 560 100 India

MAZUMDER, AVIJIT, pharmacist, educator; b. Kolkata, India, Jan. 23, 1971; s. Kamal Kumar and Late Anita Mazumder; m. Rupa Sarkar, Feb. 25, 1994; 1 child, Avishek. BS in Pharmacy, Jadavpur U., 1992, MS in Pharmacy, 1994; MBA, U. Lucknow, 1996; PhD, Jadavpur U., 2005. Lectr. Inst. Pharmacy & Tech., Salipur, India, 1996—98; sr. lectr. Birla Inst. Tech., Mesra, India, 1999—. Sect. incharge Stancert Lab., Ranchi, India, 2003—; presenter in field. Mem. editl. bd.: Ethiopian Jour. Pharm. Scis., Advances in Pharmacology and Toxicology, Jour. Indian Chem. Soc.; contbr. chapters to books, over 70 articles to profl. jours. Scholar, Govt. India, 1998—. Fellow: Indian Chem. Soc. (life mem. editl. bd. 2005); mem.: Indian Assn. Hosp. Pharmacist (life), Assn. Pharmacy Tchrs. India (life), Indian Pharm. Assn. (life), Inst. Chemists. Hinduism. Achievements include research in pharmaceuticals, pharmacology and microbiology. Avocations: travel, playing. Home: 19P Baishnab Ghata Bye Lane Po Naktala West Bengal 700047 India Office: Scs Birla Instt Of Tech Dept Of Pharm Mesra Ranchi 834 021 Jharkhand Ranchi India Office Fax: 06512275401. Personal E-mail: avijitmazum@yahoo.com.

MAZUMDER, RUPA, medical educator; b. Kolkata, India, Aug. 30, 1970; M in Pharm., 1995, PhD, 2005. Lectr. Inst. Pharmacy & Tech., Cuttack, 1996—98; reader, dept. pharm. scis., hostel warden, coop. com. mem. Birla Inst. Engring. & Tech., 1998—2007; prof., sch. pharm. tech. & mgmt. Nmims U., Mumbai, 2007—09; prof., dean, R & D dept. pharm. tech. Noida Inst. Engring. & Tech., Greater Noida, 2009—. Recipient Merit award, All India Sci. Tchrs. Assn., 1986; Nat. scholarship, Govt. of India, 1987—88. Mem.: Assn. Pharm. Tchrs. India, Indian Pharm. Assn., Bioinformatics Inst. India, Indian Chem. Soc., Inst. Chemists. Avocations: reading, music, art, crafts. Office: Noida Inst Engineering & Tech 1 Greater Noida Uttar Pradesh 201306 India Personal E-mail: rupa_mazumder@rediffmail.com.

MAZUR, LEONARD L., pharmaceutical company executive; b. Ansbach, Germany, Jan. 23, 1945; came to U.S., 1949; s. Walter and Maria (Zatwarnitsky) M.; m. Helena Maria Olijnyk, Nov. 1966; children: Maria, Michael, Irene. BA, Temple U., 1968, MBA, 1975. Mktg. mgr. Cooper Labs., Inc., Fairfield, N.J. and Palo Alto, Calif., 1971—81; dir. product mgmt. Knoll Pharm. Corp. divsn. BASF, Whippany, NJ, 1981—84; v.p. ICN Pharm. Corp., Costa Mesa, Calif., 1984—88; pres., COO Chantal Pharm. Corp., LA, 1988—89; exec. v.p. Medicis Pharm. Corp., NYC, 1989—93; vice chmn. Cabot Labs., Inc., NYC, 1994—96; chmn., CEO Genesis Pharm., Inc., Parsippany, NJ, 1996—2006; COO, co-founder Triax Pharms., LLC, Cranford, NJ, 2006—, vice chmn., co-founder, 2008—; COO, co-founder Akrimax Pharms. LLC. Ptnr. Mazier Ptnrs. LLC, Morristown, NJ, 1995-05. Adv. bd. Manor Coll., Jenkintown, Pa., 1972-78, trustee, 2000-06, 2007-; ind. observer Referendum for Independence, Ukraine, 1991; bd. visitors Coll. Liberal Arts Temple U., 2006—. With USMC, 1965—71. Recipient Temple U. Diamond Achievement award, 2005; named to West Cath. HS Hall of Fame, 2009. Achievements include patents in field. Office: Triax Pharms LLC 11 Commerce Dr Cranford NJ 07016

MAZUR, ROBERT A., physician; b. Bayonne, NJ, Dec. 20, 1958; BS, USMA, West Point, 1992; MD, Uniformed Svcs. U., 1992. Physician GEA, 2008. Home: 125 Dunnyveg Rd Richmond Hill GA 31324 Business E-Mail: bobmazur@pol.net.

MAZZA, DAVID S., pediatric allergist, immunologist; b. Burlington, Vt., Dec. 10, 1947; s. Frank, Jr. and Margret Alice (Fuller) Mazza. BA, U. Vt., Burlington, 1969, MA in Math., 1971; MD, U. Vt. Coll. Med., Burlington, 1977. Diplomate Am. Bd. Pediats., lic. NY. Resident pediats. NYU-Bellevue Hosp., NYC, 1977—80, fellow in ambulatory pediats., 1980—82, attending staff emergency svc., 1982—. Instr. NYU, 1982—84; dir. ambulatory svcs. Booth Meml. Med. Ctr., NYC, 1982—, dir. fellowship program, 1985; attending staff North Shore U. Hosp., NY, 1985—, Cornell U., 1985—. Campaign vol. City Coun., NYC, 1985. Mem.: AAAS, NY Acad. Sci., Am. Acad. Pediats., Nature Conservancy Group, Defenders of Wildlife, Sierra Club. Democrat. Avocations: swimming, bicycling, travel. Office: David S Mazza MD 7 Lexington Ave #3 New York NY 10010 Office Phone: 212-677-7170.

MAZZA, DOMENICO, orthodontist; b. Rimini, Italy, Nov. 16, 1935; s. Dino and Flora (Morri) M.; m. Valeria Berger, July 30, 1970; children: Maddalena, Francesco, Stefano. MD, U. Bologna, 1960, DDS, 1964. Pvt. practice dentistry, Rimini, 1964—. Med. dental cons. City Ct., Rimini, 1970-71. Translator: (book) Biomechanics in Orthodontics, 1993; contbr. articles to profl. jours. Mem. W.W.F., Rimini, 1970-72, Movement for Earth Conservation, Rimini, 1972-74. Lt. Italian Mil. Corps, 1961-62. C.H. Tweed Internat. Found. for Orthodontic Rsch. fellow, 1970-74. Fellow Italian Dental Assn., Italian Assn. Orthodontists; mem. Rotary. Achievements include development of a highly non-linear software for the calculation of ortodontic springs; Identification of a general procedure for clinical application of calculated springs in edgewise orthodontics. Avocations: swimming, canoeing, reading. Home: Via C Colombo 6 Rimini RN47900 Italy Office: Via Tempio Malatestiano 12 47921 Rimini RN Italy Office Phone: 39 541 22902. Office Fax: 39 541 23563.

MAZZAFERRI, ERNEST LOUIS, endocrinologist, educator; b. Cleve., Sept. 27, 1936; s. Joseph and Nanetta (Marinelli) M., m. Florence Mildred Marolt, Nov. 23, 1957; children: Patricia Marie Atchison, Michael Louis, Sharon Lynne Brown, Ernest Louis. BS cum laude, John Carroll U., 1958; MD, Ohio State U., 1962. Diplomate Am. Bd. Internal Medicine. Intern Ohio State U. Hosps., Columbus, 1962-63, resident, 1963-64, 66-68; asst. prof. medicine Ohio State U., 1968-70, assoc. prof., 1973-76, prof., 1976-79, dir. div. endocrinology and metabolism, 1975-78; acting dean U. Nev., Reno, 1979-81, prof., chmn. dept. medicine, 1978-84, prof. physiology, 1982-84; prof., chmn. dept. medicine, prof. physiology Ohio State U., Columbus, 1984-99, prof. emeritus, 1999—; pres. Dept. of Medicine Found., 1986-99; chmn. bd. Ohio State Practice Group, 1996-99, clin. prof. medicine U. Fla., Gainesville, 2001—. Bd. dirs. The Ohio State U. Hosps., 1997—99; mem. com. on exposure of Am. people to I-131 from Nev. atomic bomb tests Nat. Acad. Sci. Inst. of Medicine, 1997—99, mem. com. on health effects assoc. with exposures experienced during the Gulf War, 1999—2000; mem. com. guidelines for thyroid cancer screening Inst. Medicine, 1997—99; chmn. Nat. Cancer Ctr. Network Com. on Thyroid Cancer Guidelines; mem. com. on health effects associated with exposures during the Gulf War Inst. of Medicine Nat. Academies of Sci., 1999—2000. Author: Endocrinology Case Studies, 3d edit., 1985, Internal Medicine Pearls, 1993; editor: Textbook of Endocrinology, 3d edit., 1986, Contemporary Internal Medicine, 1988, 3d edit., 1990, Advances in Endocrinology and Metabolism, Vol. 6, 1995, Endocrine Tumors, 1993, Morning Report, 1999, Yearbook of Endocrinology, 1999 ; Endocrine editor Yearbook of Medicine, 1999—; editor: Practical Management of Thyroid Cancer: A Medical Disciplinary Approach, 2005, Essentials of Thyroid Cancer Management, Kluwer Acad. Publishers, 2005-; editor-in-chief: Clinical Thyroidology; mem. sci. adv. bd. Western Jour. Medicine, 1993; mem. editl. bd. Jour. Lab. Clin. Medicine, 1987-97, Hosp. Practice, Jour. of Clin. Endocrinology and Metabolism, Thyroid, 1999—; contbr. articles to profl. jours. Chmn. Gov.'s Com. on Radiation Fallout in Nev., 1980-84, hosp. ethics com. Ohio State U., 1994-98; mem. Sec. of Energy Dose Assessment Adv. Com., 1980-84, Agy. for Health Care Policy, Rsch. Cataract Guideline Com., 1991-92, Inst. of Medicine Guideline for Thyroid Cancer Screening com., 1997-99; mem. rsch. coun. com. on expense of Am. People to I-131 from Nev. Atomic Bomb Tests: Implications for Public Health, 1997-99,editor in chief Clin. Thyroidology. Capt. USAF, 1964, maj. USAF, 1968, lt. col. USAF, 1968—73, col. USAR, 1984—91. Recipient Earl N. Metz Disting. Physician award, Ohio State U., 1998, Light of Life award, Light of Life Found. N.Y., 1999, Graves' award, Thyroid Soc. for Rsch. and Edn., 2001, Disting. Svc. award, Ohio State U., 2009, 2010. Master: ACP (gov. for Nev. 1984—85, chmn. clin. efficacy assessment program com. 1992—95, edn. policy com. 1992—95, mem. health and pub. policy com.); mem.: AMA, Ohio State U. (Disting. Svc. award), Am. Coll. Clin. Endocrinology (bd. dis. 1995—96, Disting. Clinician award 2002), Ctrl. Soc. Clin. Rsch., Am. Clin. and Climatol. Assn., Endocrine Soc. (Disting. Educator award 2005), Am. Diabetes Assn. (pres. Ohio affiliate 1988—89), Am. Thyroid Assn. (pres.-elect 2004—05, pres. 2005—, Paul Star award, Disting. Svc. award), Am. Bd. Internal Medicine (chmn. Endocrinology and Metabolism 1999—2003, bd. dirs. 1999—2003, cert. in endocrinology and metabolism, gen. internal medicine, cert. in geriatrics, continuous profl. devel.), Alpha Omega Alpha. Roman Catholic. Achievements include research in thyroid cancer. Home: 4020 SW 93rd Dr Gainesville FL 32608-4653

MAZZEI, MARIA ANTONIETTA, radiologist, educator; b. Paola, Cozensa, Italy, May 13, 1975; Degree in Medicine, 1999, degree in Diagnostic Imaging, 2003. Radiologist Azienda Ospedaliera U. Senese, 2003—08; asst. prof. radiology U. Siena, Italy, 2008—. Mem.: European Soc. Radiology, Soc. Italiana Radiology Medica. Avocation: piano. Office: viale Bracci 16 Siena 53100 Italy Office Fax: 57744496.

MAZZIO-MOORE, JOAN L., retired radiology educator, physician; b. Belmont, Mass., Oct. 26, 1935; d. Frank Joseph and Maria L. Mazzio; children: Hon James Thomas Moore, Edwin Stuart Moore. BA in Chemistry and Theology, Emmanuel Coll., 1957; MA in Genetics and Physiology, Wellesley Coll., Mass., 1961; PhD candidate in Genetics, Bryn Mawr Coll., Pa.; DO in Medicine Surgery, Phila. Coll. Medicine, 1977, MSc in Radiology, 1981. Instr. organic chemistry Gwynedd Mercy Coll., 1962—64; instr. in genetics Holy Family Coll., Phila., 1964—65; instr. in anatomy Phila. Coll. of Medicine, 1971—77, assoc. prof., 1977—84; prof. W.Va. Sch. of Medicine, 1984—2003, ret., 2004; rotating intern Phila. Coll. of Medicine Hosp., 1977—78, resident in radiology and radiation therapy, 1978—81, mem. hosp. staff, 1981—84; consulting radiologist Byrd Clinic, Lewisburg, W.Va., 1984—2004; med. dir. Anthony Correctional Ctr., 1986—99; pvt. practice, 1986—2004. Author (with Dr. Gino DiVirgilo): Essentials of Neuropathology, 1974. Treas. Hist. Soc. of Frankford, Phila., 1968—75, Treas. Mother's Assn., Devon, Pa., 1980—81; vol. mem. Ct. Appts. Spl. Adv. for Children, 2000—; parlamentarian Greenbrier Com. on Aging, 2000—07; bd. trustees Lake Erie Coll. Medicine and Pharmacy, Erie, Pa., Bradenton, Fla.; organist Ch. of Incarnation, W.Va., St. Charles Borromeo Ch., White Sulphur Springs, W.Va., 2000—10; lector St. Ann's Cath. Ch., Phoenixville, Pa., 1981—84. Lt. Col. MC USAR, 1984—2002. Recipient Pres.'s award, LECOM, 2010. Mem. AAUP, Am. Assn. Women Radiologists, Am. Med. Women's Assn., Am. Osteo. Coll. Radiology (life), Am. Soc. Clin. Oncology, Am. Soc. Therapeutic Radiologists, Hist. Soc. Lewisburg (life), Pa. Osteo. Med. Assn., Radiol. Soc. N.Am., Radiation Rsch. Soc., Res. Officers Assn. (life), W.Va. Soc. Osteo. Medicine, Greenbrier Valley Med. Soc., NRA (life), W.Va. Assn. Ham Radio Operators. Home: PO Box 97 Frankford WV 24938 Home Fax: 304-497-2752. Personal E-mail: drjoanlmoore@yahoo.com.

MAZZIOTTI, GHERARDO, endocrinologist, researcher; b. Celso di Pollica, Salerno, Italy, June 17, 1969; s. Mario Mazziotti and Marianna Diana; m. Alessandra Russo, Dec. 27, 2003. Grad. medicine, 2d U. Naples, 1995, specialization in endocrinology, 2000. Clin. fellw Sch. Endocrinology 2d U. Naples, Italy, 1988—95, rsch. fellow doctorate in endocrine disease, 2000—. Recipient Leonardo di Capua grant, 2002. Home: Via Pietro Mazziotti 34 84050 Celso di Pollica-SA Italy Office: 2d U Naples Via Pansini 5 Pad 16 80131 Naples Italy Office Fax: 0039 0815666632. E-mail: gherardomazziotti@hotmail.com.

MAZZOCCHIO, RICCARDO CALOGERO VITO, neurologist, researcher; b. Trapani, Sicily, Italy, Nov. 27, 1959; s. Orazio Alfio and Anna (Tipa) M.; m. Donatella Donati, July 5, 1986; children: Cecilia Costanza, Enrica Alberta, Daria Caterina. MD, Faculty of Medicine, Siena, Italy, 1984, PhD in Neurosci., 1994. Med. diplomate. Lt. Mil. Hosp., Padua, Italy, 1985-86; visitor Inst. Physiology, Milan, 1987-88; rsch. fellow Inst. Neurology, Siena, 1989-91; guest investigator Brit. Med. Rsch. Ctr., London, 1991-92; cons. neurologist Pub. Health Svc., Siena, 1992—. Cons. rschr. dept. neurology U. Siena, 1992—; cons. neurophysiologist Pub. Health Svc., Siena, 1994—, asst. prof. human physiology Univ. Inst. Physiology, Siena, 1995—.; rsch fellow, Nat. Inst. Neurological Disorders and Stroke, Bethesda, 2001-03; Chief, motor control and Posture labs, EVIP Sect., Clinical Neurophysiology Unit 2003-; asst. prof., neurology and neurorehabilitation, 2003- Contbr. articles to profl. jours. Mem. World Wildlife fund, Italy, 1986, Nat. Geog. Soc., Italy, 1990. Fellow Human Frontier Sci. Program Orgn., France, 1991; grantee Brit. Coun., 1992, Nat. Rsch. Coun., Italy, 1993. Mem. Italian Soc. Neurosci., Italian Soc. Clin. Neurophysiology. Avocations: music, windsurfing, skiing. Home: Strada di Piaggiano 13 53100 Siena Italy Office: U Siena Clin Neurophysiology Viale Mario Bracci 53100 Siena SI Italy Business E-Mail: mazzocchio@unisi.it.

MAZZOLENI, LUIZ EDMUNDO, medical educator; b. Getulio Vargas, Brazil, July 8, 1953; PhD, U. Federal do Rio Grande do Sul, 2003. Prof. Hosp. De Clínicas De Porto Alegre, 1991—. Adj. prof. U. Federal do Rio Grande do Sul, 1991—2011. Master: U. Federal do Rio Grande do Sul. Home: Rua Pedro Chaves Barcelos 987 1003 Porto Alegre 90450-010 Brazil Home Fax: 51 33328531. Personal E-mail: lemazzoleni@yahoo.com.br.

MAZZOTTA, COSIMO, ophthalmologist, researcher; b. Copertino, Le, Italy, Sept. 13, 1970; m. Paola Preite, Sept. 21, 2002. BSc, Med. Sch., 1997; MD, U. Siena, Italy; PhD in Ocular Pathology, U. Siena, 2006. Cert. specialist diploma in ophthalmology 2001. Rschr., dept. ophthalmolgy Siena U., 2001—, nat. sci. coord.ophthalmology, 2004—06. Contbr. articles to profl. jours. Recipient Best Rsch. of Yr., Italian Soc. Ophthalmology, 2004. Achievements include first to in Vivo confocal microscopy of crosslinked corneas in keratoconus; invention of CBM X linker solid state UV A illuminator; introduce the corneal cross linking in Italy in 2004. Home: Via Chiantigiana 52 Siena Si 53100 Italy Office: Siena Univ Dept Ophthalmology Viale Mario Bracci 53100 Siena SI Italy Office Phone: 39 0577 23 33 60. Office Fax: 39 0577 586162. Business E-Mail: cgmazzotta@libero.it.

MAZZUCCO, ALESSANDRO, cardiologist, educator; b. Venice, Italy, Feb. 4, 1944; MD, U. Padova, 1968. Cert. in cardiovascular surgery U. Turin, 1977. Asst. prof. surgery U. Padova, 1975—80, assoc. prof. pediatric cardiac surgery, 1980—91; assoc. prof. cardiac surgery U. Verona, 1991—95, prof. cardiac surgery, 1995—. Pres. U. Of Verona, 2005. FETCS fellow, European Bd. Cardiothoracic Surgery. Mem.: European Assn. Cardiothoracic Surgery, Italian Soc. Cardiac Surgery. Avocations: literature, music, art. Home: Piazza Del Porto 17 Verona Veneto 35124 Italy Home Fax: 0459492438. Personal E-mail: alessandro.mazzucco@univr.it.

MBEUNKUI, FLAUBERT, medical researcher; b. Cameroon, Aug. 7, 1968; PhD, U. Stuttgart, Germany, 2003. Postdoc. rsch. assoc. Mitchell Cancer Inst., U. South Ala., 2004—06; rsch. assoc. NC State U., 2006—, mgr. mass spectrometry lab., 2009—. Mem.: Am. Soc. Mass Spectrometry. Avocations: soccer, jogging, travel. Office: 600 Laureate Way Kannapolis NC 28081 Business E-Mail: fmbeunk@ncsu.edu.

MBEWU, ANTHONY DAVID, cardiologist, educator; b. Durban, South Africa, Jan. 15, 1960; Sr. house officer Tchg. Hosps., Manchester, 1985—86; pres. South African Med. Rsch. Coun., Cape Town, 2005—, CEO, exec. dir., rsch., 1996—; vis. prof., cardiology U. Cape Town, 2004—; cons. cardiologist Cardiac Clinic Groote Schuur Hosp., U. Cape Town Med. Sch., 1994—96; pres. South African Med. Rsch. Coun., 2005—. Fellow: Royal Coll. Physicians; mem.: Inst. Medicine, Assoc. Mem. Coll. Medicine South Africa (fgn. assoc.), Med. Protection Soc., South African Heart Assn., South African Med.

Assn., Gen. Med. Coun., Health Professions Coun. South Africa. Office: South African Med Rsch Coun Francie van Zijl Drive 7505 Parow Valley South Africa Office Fax: 270219380201.

MBULAITEYE, SAM, medical researcher; s. Daniel F. and Elizabeth S. Mbulaiteye; m. Annet N Nagadya; children: Daniel E., Delma E., Donna E. MB, Makerere U. Kampala, Uganda, 1990; MPhil in Epidemiology and Biostatistics, U. Cambridge, England, 1994; M.Med, Makerere U., 1996. Lic. med. practice Uganda Med. and Dental Practitioners Coun., 1991. Intern med. officer St. Mary's Hosp. Lacor, Gulu, Uganda, 1990—91; med. officer Mulago Hosp., Kampala, 1991—92, sr. ho. officer, 1993—96; med. officer, spl. grade Uganda Cancer Inst., Kampala, 1996—98; project leader Uganda Virus Rsch. Inst. Med. Rsch. Coun., Entebbe, 1998—2000; rsch. fellow Nat. Cancer Inst., Bethesda, Md., 2000—05, prin. investigator, 2005—; rev. editor Frontiers Cancer Prevention Rsch., 2011—. Dir., cmty. svcs. Rotaract Club Mengo, Kampala, 1992—96; edtl. bd. mem. Internat. Jour. Cancer, 2009—; nat. rep. World Fedn. Scientists, 2010; co-editor-in-chief Infectious Agents and Cancer; review editor Frontiers Cancer Epidemiology & Prevention, 2011—. Promoter Uganda Cancer Rsch. Found., 2007. Recipient Dir's Intramural Innovation award, Nat. Cancer Inst., 2008, Individual Merit award, NIH, 2008, Elective Bursary, Common Wealth Trust, 1989. Fellow: Darwin Coll. Soc., Cambridge Common Wealth Trust; mem.: Uganda Acad. Scis., Uganda Med. Assn., African Orgn. Rsch. and Tng. Cancer. Independent. Achievements include research in significant declines in HIV incidence; risk of transmission of human herpesvirus 8 with history of blood transfusion; mother-to-child transmission of human herpesvirus 8 infection within families; first to feasibility of using registry record-linkage methods to study HIV/AIDS-associated cancers; research in extremely high levels of Epsterin-Barr virus, linked to Burkitt lymphoma, in the saliva and peripheral blood of children and their mothers; discovery of age-related variants of Burkitt's lymphoma. Avocations: travel, jogging, bicycling, water-skiing. Office Phone: 301-496-8115.

MCABEE, THOMAS ALLEN, psychologist; b. Spartanburg, SC, Mar. 31, 1949; s. Thomas Walker and Doris Lee (Gillespie) McA. Student, Ga. Inst. Tech., 1967-69; BA, Furman U., 1971; MA, U. SC, 1975, PhD, 1979. Clin. counselor Adolescent Inpatient Svc. William S. Hall Psychiat. Inst., Columbia, SC, 1971-73; counselor children's therapeutic camp Columbia Area Mental Health Ctr., 1974; co-dir. cmty. problems survey Eau Claire Cmty. Project, Columbia, 1975; asst. aging svcs. planner Ctrl. Midlands Regional Planning Coun., Columbia, 1976; instr. U. SC, 1976; NSF intern SC State Legislature, 1978; rsch. dir. SC Legis. Gov.'s Com. Mental Health and Mental Retardation, Columbia, 1979-80; co-dir. Children's TV project "Feelings Just Are" Columbia Area Mental Health Ctr., 1980-89; psychologist SC Dept. Mental Retardation, 1982-93, SC Dept. Disabilities and Spl. Needs, 1993—2003, SC Vocat. Rehab. Dept., 2004—. Cons. SC Protection and Advocacy System for Handicapped Citizens, 1980, 81, SC Dept. Mental Health, 1981; mem. deinstitutionalization task force SC Developmental Disabilities Coun., 1979-80; mem. subcom. State Commr.'s Ad Hoc Com. to Study and Develop Work/Lodge System for SC, SC Dept. Mental Health, 1979-80; mem. Media Task Force of Gov.'s Adv. Com. on Early Childhood Devel. and Edn., 1980-81; chmn. primary prevention public media com. SC Dept. Mental Health, 1979-81; adj. faculty U. SC, Spartanburg, 2003; treas. Direct Client Svcs. Divsn. SC Vocat. Rehab. Assn., 2006-08; chmn. Workforce Readiness Com., Spartanburg Human Resources Assn., 2008-2009; pres. Victor Mill Cmty. Assn., 2009-10. Recipient Palmetto Pictures Photography award, 1977; NIMH fellow, 1976-77. Mem. APA, SC Psychol. Assn., Zoning Appeals Bd., City of Greer, SC. Home: 310 Snow St Greer SC 29651-4006 Office Phone: 864-249-8030. Business E-Mail: tmcabee@scvrd.state.sc.us.

MCAFEE, ROBERT ELWOOD, retired surgeon; b. Portland, Maine, Aug. 25, 1935; BS Biology, Bates Coll., 1956; MD, Tufts U., 1960. Diplomate Am. Bd. Surgery. Intern Maine Med. Ctr., Portland, 1960-61, resident in gen. surgery, 1961-65, mem. staff, 1965-96; assoc. prof. surgery U. Vt., Burlington, 1965-96; ret., 1996. Sr. cons. Am. Med. Accreditation Program. Mem.: AMA (pres. 1994—95), ACS, New Eng. Cancer Soc., New Eng. Surg. Soc. Home: 158 Clinton St Portland ME 04103-3228 Personal E-mail: rmcafee1@maine.rr.com. *

MCALINDON, MARY NAOMI, retired nursing consultant; b. Ebensburg, Pa., Oct. 16, 1935; d. S. David and Genevieve (Little) Solomon; m. James Daniel McAlindon, Nov. 25, 1961; children: Robert, Donald, James, Peter, M. Catherine. BSN, Georgetown U., 1957; MA, U. Mich., 1979; EdD, Wayne State U., 1992. RN, Mich. Staff nurse Georgetown U. Hosp., Washington, 1957-59; instr. St. Joseph Hosp., Flint, 1959-62; clin. instr. Mott. C.C., Flint, 1980-81; asst. DON McLaren Hosp., Flint, 1980-89, adminstrv. asst., 1989-92, asst. v.p., 1992-95; clin. informatics mgr. McLaren Health Care Corp., Flint, 1995-97; pres. McAlindon Assocs., 1997-99, ret., 1999. Asst. prof. U. Mich., Flint, Mich., 1992—2001. Trustee United Way Genesee County, Flint, Mich., 1988—95, Cmty. Found. Greater Flint, 1997—2001, chmn. personnel com., 2000—01; trustee McLaren Home Health, 1996—2001. Mem.: Nursing Honor Soc. U. Mich. (pres. 1996—98), ANA (exec. com. 1991—93), Dist. Nurses Assn. (pres. 1993—96), Vis. Nurses Assn. (pres. 1988—90, bd. dir. 1984—96), Mich. Nursing Informatics Network, Am. Med. Informatics Assn. (chmn. nursing group 1993—94), Sigma Theta (pres. Pi Delta chpt. 1998—2001). Home and Office: 8230 Sawgrass Trl Grand Blanc MI 48439-1874 Home Phone: 810-577-1160. Personal E-mail: mmcalind@comcast.net.

MCALLISTER, ANITA M., medical educator; b. Stockholm, May 8, 1955; B in Speech and Lang. Pathology, Karolinska Inst., 1985, MD, 1997. Speech and lang. pathologist Danderyd Hosp., 1986—2003; asst. prof. Linköping U., 2003—. Mem.: Tallkrogen Garden Soc., Vaxholm Soroptimist Club (Stockholm). Avocations: singing, gardening, hunting. Home: Maratonvägen 29 Enskede Stockholm 12240 Sweden Personal E-mail: anita.mcallister@liu.se.

MCALLISTER, TODD, biomedical engineer; PhD in biomedical engrng., U. Calif., San Diego. Co-founder Cytograft Tissue Engrng., Inc., Novato, Calif.; co-dir. Ctr. Regenerative Medicine St. Joseph's Translational Rsch. Inst., Atlanta. Achievements include development of Lifeline vascular graft. Office: Cytograft Tissue Engring Inc Ste 220 3 Hamilton Landing Novato CA 94949 also: Ctr Regenerative Medicine St Josephs Translational Rsch Inst 5673 Peachtree Dunwoody Rd NE Ste 675 Atlanta GA 30342 Office Phone: 415-506-0260, 678-843-6500. E-mail: contact@cytograft.com.

MCALPINE, FREDERICK SENNETT, anesthesiologist; b. Monessen, Pa., June 16, 1929; s. Karl Sennett and Kathryn Helen (Schuerhoff) McA.; m. Barbara Ellen Adams, June 23, 1956; children: Christopher, Daniel, Karen. AB with honors, St. Vincent Coll., Latrobe, Pa., 1950; MD, U. Pitts., 1954. Diplomate Am. Bd. Anesthesiology. Rotating intern U.S. Naval Hosp., Bethesda, Md., 1954-55; resident in anesthesia Mass. Gen. Hosp., Boston, 1955-57, chief resident anesthesia, 1957; asst. chief anesthesia Bethesda Naval Hosp., 1957-60; staff anesthesiologist Lahey Clinic, Boston, 1960-95, chmn. dept. anesthesiology, 1971-82, sr. staff anesthesiologist, 1962-95; retired, 1995. Contbr. chpts. to books on nerve injuries. Del. Am. Soc. Anesthesiologists, 1970-74. Lt. comdr. USN. Mem. Mass. Med. Soc. (sr. physicians program 1996—), Mass Soc. Anesthesia Med. Malpractice (tribunal mem. 1985—), Mass. Soc. Anesthesiologists (pres. 1971-72, spkrs. bur. 1995—). Republican. Roman Catholic. Home: 2 Lookout Farm Rd Natick MA 01760-5641 Personal E-mail: fsmbam@comcast.net.

MCANDREWS, LAWRENCE A., medical association administrator; married; 2 children. BA in psychology, Vanderbilt U.; Master's in health adminstrn., George Washington U. V.p. professional affairs Lafayette Gen. Hosp., La.; adminstrv. asst. MacNeal Meml. Hosp., Berwyn, Ill.; adminstr. Inst. Psychiatry Northwestern Meml. Hosp., Chgo., adminstr. Prentice Women's Hosp.; pres., CEO Children's Mercy Hosp., Kansas City, Mo., 1986—92; exec. pres., CEO Nat. Assn. Children's Hospitals and Related Institutions, Alexandria, Va., 1992—. Vice-chair Generations United. Fellow: Am. Coll. Health Care Executives; mem.: Am. Hosp. Assn. Office: Nat Assn Childrens Hosps and Related Instns 401 Wythe St Alexandria VA 22314 E-mail: lmcandrews@nachri.org. *

MCANENY, BARBARA L., oncologist; b. Kansas City, Mo., 1952; BA in Math., magna cum laude, U. Minn., Mpls., 1973; MD, U. Iowa Coll. Medicine, Iowa City, 1977. Diplomate American Bd. Internal Medicine, cert. in hematology-oncology, lic. N.Mex. Resident internal medicine U. Iowa Coll. Medicine, 1977—80; fellow hematology-oncology U. N.Mex. Sch. Medicine, Albuquerque, 1980—82, Univ. physician/instr. medicine, 1982—84; pvt. practice Hematology Oncology Assocs., Albuquerque, 1983—87, N.Mex. Oncology Hematology Consultants, Ltd., Albuquerque, 1987—; mng. ptnr., CEO N.Mex. Cancer Ctr., Albuquerque, 2002—. Investigator Response Oncology Rsch. Network, Albuquerque, 2000—01. Mem. Practicing Physicians Adv. Com., HHS, 2002—06; pres. N.Mex. Med. Found., 2001—07. Recipient Ayerst-Wyeth award for Medicine, 1992, Gov.'s award for Outstanding Women in N.Mex., 1996, Top Doc award, Albuquerque Mag., 2004, 2005. Fellow: ACP; mem.: AMA (mem. Coun. Med. Svc. 2003—, chair Coun. Med. Svc. 2009—10, bd. trustees 2010—), American Soc. Hematology, N.Mex. Med. Soc. (pres. 2000—01), American Soc. Clin. Oncology (bd. dirs. 2005—08). Office: New Mexico Cancer Ctr 4901 Lang Ave NE Albuquerque NM 87109 Office Phone: 505-842-8171. *

MCANINCH, JACK WELDON, urological surgeon, educator; b. Merkel, Tex., Mar. 17, 1936; s. Weldon Thomas and Margaret (Canon) McA.; m. Barbara B. Buchanan, Dec. 29, 1960 (div. Aug. 1972); m. Burnet B. Sumner, Dec. 29, 1987; children: David A., Todd G., Brendan J. BS, Tex. Tech U., 1958; MS, U. Idaho, 1960; MD, U. Tex., 1964. Diplomate Am. Bd. Urology (trustee 1991-97, pres. 1996-97). Commd. capt. U.S. Army, 1964-66, advanced through grades to col., 1977, ret., 1977; col. USAR; intern then resident Letterman Army Med. Ctr., San Francisco, 1964-69; chief urol. surgery San Francisco Gen. Hosp., 1977—; prof. urol. surgery U. Calif., San Francisco, 1977—. Editor: Urogenital Trauma, 1985, Urologic Clinics of North America, 1989, Smith's gen. Urology, 1995; section editor: Early Care of Injured Patient, 1990, Traumatic and Reconstructive Urology, 1996. Col. US Army, 1964-72. Recipient Disting. Alumnus award Tex. Tech U., 1994; named Disting. Alumnus U. Idaho, 1997. Fellow ACS (govt. 1992-97, regent 1998—); mem. Am. Urol. Assn. (pres. we. sect. 1992-93, bd. dirs. 1990—, pres. 1996-97), Genitourinary Reconstructive Surgeons (pres.), Am. Assn. Surgery Trauma (v.p.), Soc. U. Urologists, Am. Bd. Urology (pres. 1996-97). Office: San Francisco Gen Hosp Dept Urology 1001 Potrero Ave San Francisco CA 94110-3594 Home Phone: 415-282-1149; Office Phone: 415-476-3372. Business E-Mail: jmcaninch@urology.ucsf.edu.

MCARTHUR, JUSTIN C., neurologist; b. Reigate, Eng., Feb. 20, 1956; m. Julie Helen Luebbe, Sept. 11, 1982; 1 child, Heather. MB, BS, U. London, 1979; MPH, Johns Hopkins U., 1988. Diplomate Am. Bd. Internal Medicine, Am. Bd. Neurology and Psychiatry. Asst. prof. neurology Johns Hopkins U., Balt., 1985-90, assoc. prof., 1990—, assoc. prof. epidemiology, 1992—, dir. med. clerkship, 1988-95, dir. neurology residency program, 1995—. Advisor World Health Orgn., 1988-89, Pres.'s Commn. on AIDS, 1988; chmn. neurology com. AIDS Clin. Trials Group, 1994-96. Author: AIDS and Neurology, 1995; contbr. articles to profl. jours., chpts to books. Sci. adv. com. Am. Found. AIDs Rsch., 1988—. Mem. Am. Acad. Neurology, Am. Neurol. Assn., Alpha Omega Alpha. Office: Johns Hopkins U 6109 Moyer Ave Baltimore MD 21206-2354

MCAVOY, JOHN MARTIN, plastic surgeon; b. White Plains, NY, Jan. 8, 1947; s. Joseph Patrick and Claire Margaret (Boucher) McAvoy; m. Laurel Ann Streeter, June 21, 1969; children: Holly, Ian. BS in Biology, Tufts U., Medford, Mass., 1968; MD, Tufts U., Boston, 1972. Cert. Am. Bd. Surgery, Am. Bd. Plastic Surgery, Nat. Bd. Med. Examiners, ACLS. Resident dept. surgery UCLA Med. Ctr., 1972—77, chief resident dept. surgery, 1976—77; resident plastic surgery U. Colo. Med. Ctr., Denver, 1977—79, chief resident plastic surgery, 1978—79; chief plastic surgery Santa Rosa Meml. Hosp., Calif., 1986—91; pvt. practice Santa Rosa, Calif., 1979—. Presenter in field. Contbg. editor: Hosp. Physician mag., 1976—81; contbr. articles to profl. jours. Youth baseball coach Santa Rosa Babe Ruth Rincon Valley Little League, 1992—96. Reinach-Turnesia Caddie scholar, Westchester County, 1964. Fellow: ACS; mem.: Am. Soc. Plastic Surgeons (membership com.), Calif. Soc. Plastic Surgeons (ins. mediation com.), Am. Soc. for Aesthetic Plastic Surgery. Avocations: woodworking, gardening, poetry. Office: 4773 Hoen Ave Santa Rosa CA 95405 Office Phone: 707-526-2276. Personal E-mail: dr.jmcavoy@yahoo.com. Business E-Mail: jmcavoy@sonic.net.

MCAVOY, ROGERS, educational psychology educator, consultant, educational psychology educator, consultant; b. Webster Springs, W.Va., Dec. 28, 1927; s. Ellis McLaughlin and Carolyn (McIntosh) McA.; m. Anne T. Limpe, Dec. 19, 1956 (div.); children: Carol Ann, Philip Ellis, Karen Lynelle; m. Irma Jean Tingler, July 7, 1973. BA, Fairmont State Coll., 1951; MA, W.Va. U., 1954; PhD, Ind. U., 1966. Tchr. biology Petersburg HS, W.Va., 1951-53; asst. dir. admissions Marshall U., Huntington, W.Va., 1953-55; registrar Glenville State Coll., W.Va., 1955-56; rsch. asst., asst. to dean Ind. U., Bloomington, 1956-61; asst. prof. ednl. psychology W.Va. U., Morgantown, 1961-65, assoc. prof., 1967-72, prof., 1973-97, prof. emeritus, 1997—. Cons. state and county ednl. systems, W.Va., others, 1965-89; cons. follow through program Stanford Rsch. Inst., 1969-72. Contbr. articles to profl. jours. Mem. Phi Delta Kappa (Disting. Svc. award 1982, 25-yr. svc. award 1990). Avocations: writing, book collecting, restoring houses, photography, reading. *

MCBRIDE, ANGELA BARRON, nursing educator; b. Balt., Jan. 16, 1941; d. John Stanley and Mary C. (Szczepanska) Barron; m. William Leon McBride, June 12, 1965; children: Catherine, Kara. BS in Nursing, Georgetown U., Washington, 1962; MS in Nursing, Yale U., New Haven, Conn., 1964; PhD, Purdue U., West Lafayette, Ind., 1978; doctorate of Pub. Svc. (hon.), U. Cin., 1983; LittD (hon.), Purdue U., 1998; LLD (hon.), Ea. Ky. U., 1991; LHD (hon.), Georgetown U., 1993; DSc (hon.), Med. Coll. Ohio, 1995; LHD (hon.), U. Akron, 1997. Asst. prof., rsch. asst. inst. Yale U., New Haven, 1964-73; assoc. prof., chairperson Ind. U. Sch. Nursing, Indpls., 1978-81, 80-84, prof., 1981-92, assoc. dean rsch., 1985—91, interim dean, 1991—92, univ. dean, 1992—2003, disting. prof., 1992—2005, disting. prof., univ. dean emerita, 2006—; sr. v.p. acad. affairs, nursing Clarian Health Ptnrs., 1997—2003; Am. Acad. Nursing, Am. Nurses Found. scholar-in-residence Inst. Medicine, 2003—04; Helene Denne Schulte vis. prof. U. Wis., Madison, 2006; cons. prof. Duke U. Sch. Nursing., 2008—09. Mem. Nat. Adv. Mental Health Coun., 1987—91; adv. com. NIH Office of Women's Health Rsch., 1997—2001, NIH Office of Women's Health Rsch. Specialized Ctrs. Rsch. on Sex and Gender Factors, 2003—06; coun. mem. Yale U. Coun., 1999—2005; ext. acad. advisor Sch. Nursing, Hong Kong Poly. U., 2000—06; adv. bd. Meth. Health Found., 2000—; advisor U. Hong Kong, 2004—06, Hong Kong Soc. Nursing Edn., 2004—; appointed to Old Master Program Purdue U., 2007. Author: The Growth and Development of Mothers, 1973 (Best Book award 1973), Living with Contradictions, A Married Feminist, 1976, How to Enjoy A Good Life With Your Teenager, 1987, The Growth and Development of Nurse Leaders, 2010; editor: Psychiatric-Mental Health Nursing: Integrating the Behavioral and Biological Sciences, 1996 (Best Book award 1996); compiler: Nursing and Philanthropy, 2000. Adv. bd. Women's Fund Indpls., 2000—05; chair Nat. Adv. Com. Nurse Faculty Scholars Program Robert Wood Johnson Found., 2007—; bd. dirs. United Way of Ctrl. Ind., 2002—06, Clarian Health Ptnrs., 2004—, chair quality and patient safety com.; mem. Yale U. Sch. Nursing Adv. Bd., 2006—, chair, 2007—09. Recipient Disting. Alumna award Yale U., Disting. Alumna award Purdue U., Univ. Medallion, U. San Francisco, 1993, Hoosier Heritage award, 2000, Disting. Nurse Educator award Coll. Mt. St. Joseph, Cin., 2000, Ross Pioneering Spirit award Am. Assn. Critical-Care Nurses, 2004, Lifetime Achievement award Assn. Fundraising Profls., Ind., 2005, Woman of Achievement award, Ball State U., 2005 Torchbearer award Ind. Commn. for Women, 2005, Melva Jo Hendrix Leadership award Internat. Soc. Psychiat. Nursing, 2006; named Influential Woman in Indpls., Indpls. Bus. Jour./Ind. Lawyer, 1999, HealthCare Hero Indpls. Bus. Jour., 2003, Adele Herwitz Disting. scholar Commn. Fgn. Nursing Schs., 2005, Harold Burdette award Behavioral Coop. Oncology Group, 2007; Kellogg nat. fellow; Am. Nurses Found. scholar, Salute to Women award Indpls. YMCA, 1999, Sagamore of Wabash, 1999, medal Yale Sch. Nursing, named to Hall of Fame, 2008. Fellow: Nat. Acads. Practice, Am. Acad. Nursing (dir. leadership devel. bldg. acad. geriatric nursing capacity program 2000—, past pres., Living Legend 2006), APA (Nursing and Health Psychology award divsn. 38 1995); mem.: MNRS Found. (trustee 2007—09), Soc. for Women's Health Rsch. (bd. mem. 2007—10), Nat. Acad. Scis., Inst. of Medicine (mem. bd. health policy ednl. programs and fellowships 2006—), Soc. for Rsch. in Child Devel., Midwest Nursing Rsch. Soc. (Disting. Rsch. award 1985), Sigma Theta Tau (past pres., Mentor award 1993, disting. lectr 1995—99, Melanie Dreher award for contbns. as a dean 2001), Chi Eta Phi (hon.). Home: 744 Cherokee Ave Lafayette IN 47905-1872 Home Phone: 765-474-9187; Office Phone: 317-278-9076. Business E-Mail: amcbride@iupui.edu.

MCBRIDE, SANDRA TEAGUE, psychiatric nurse; b. Corinth, Miss., Sept. 13, 1958; d. Clarence R. and Alice (Ingram) T. AAS, Shelby State Community Coll., 1983; BSN, U. North Ala., 1987; MSN, Union U., 2001. RN, Miss., Tenn. Nurse supr. Alcorn County Care, Inc., Corinth, Miss., 1985-87; staff nurse Bolivar (Tenn.) Cmty. Hosp., 1988-90; shift supr. Tenn. Dept. of Corrections, West Tenn. High Security Facility, Ripley, 1990-91; staff nurse U.S. Med. Ctr. for Fed. Prisoners, Springfield, Mo., 1991-92, Western Mental Health Inst., Bolivar, 1992—.

MCBURNEY, ELIZABETH INNES, dermatologist, physician, educator; b. Lake Charles, La., Dec. 24, 1944; d. Theodore John and Martha (Caldwell) Innes; divorced, 1980; children: Leanne Marie, Susan Eleanor. BS, U. Southwestern La., 1965; MD, La. State U., 1969. Diplomate Am. Bd. Internal Medicine, Am. Bd. Dermatology. Intern Pensacola (Fla.) Edn. Program, 1969-70; resident in internal medicine Boston U. and Carney Hosps., 1970-72; resident in dermatology Charity Hosp., New Orleans, 1972-74; staff physician Ochsner Hosp., New Orleans, 1974-80; assoc. head of dermatology Ochsner Clinic, New Orleans, 1974-80; clin. asst. prof. La. Health Scis., New Orleans, 1976-79, clin. assoc. prof., 1979-90, clin. prof., 1990—; clin. asst. prof. Tulane Health Scis., New Orleans, 1976-88, clin. assoc. prof., 1988-91, clin. prof., 1991—. Courtesy staff Northshore Regional Med. Ctr., Slidell, La., 1985—; staff Slidell Meml. Hosp., 1988—, chmn. CME courses, 1988—, pres.-elect med. staff, 2000-01, pres., 2001—02; regional dir. Mycosis Fungoides Study Group, Balt., 1974-94. Contbr. articles to profl. jours. Bd. dirs. Slidell Art Coun., 1988—, Camp Fire, New Orleans, 1979-83, Cancer Assn. New Orleans, 1978-83; juror Art in Pub. Places, Slidell, 1989; councilman St. Tammany Art Coun., 2003-06, with Dermatology fdn. Exec. Comm., 2008- Recipient Disting. Woman Physician award AMA, 1999, Thomas Pearson edn. meml. award, 2004. Fellow ACP; mem. Am. Soc. Dermatologic Surgery (treas. 1991-94, bd. dirs. 1988-91, pres. elect 1995-96, pres. 1996-97), Women's Dermatol. Soc. (pres. 2006—07, Samuel Stegman award 2000, Pub. Svc. award, 2001), Am.

Acad. Dermatology (bd. dirs. 1994-98), Am. Bd. Laser Medicine and Surgery (bd. dirs. 1991-96), La. Dermatologic Soc. (pres. 1989-90), Am. Dermatologic Soc. (pres. 2007-08), St. Tammany Med. Soc. (pres. 1988), Phi Kappa Phi, Alpha Omega Alpha. Avocations: reading, gardening, fine art, music, films. Office: 1051 Gause Blvd Ste 460 Slidell LA 70458-2985 Office Phone: 985-649-5880.

MCCABE, EDWARD R. B., hospital administrator, educator, physician; b. Balt., Mar. 26, 1946; BA in Biology, Johns Hopkins U., 1967; PhD in Pharmacology, U. So. Calif., 1972, MD, 1974. Diplomate Am. Bd. Pediatrics. Resident in pediatrics U. Minn. Hosps., Mpls., 1974—76; pediatric metabolism fellow Sch. Medicine U. Colo., Denver, 1976—78, instr., asst. prof., assoc. prof. pediatrics Sch. Medicine, 1978—86; from assoc. prof. to prof. genetics, pediatrics Baylor Coll. Medicine, Houston, 1986—94; exec. prof., chmn. dept. pediatrics David Geffen Sch. Medicine UCLA, 1994—. Physician-in-chief Mattel Children's Hosp. UCLA, 1995—; mem. med. genetics residency rev. com. Accreditation Coun. Grad. MEd. Edn., 1993—97; chmn. conf. gaucher disease NIH, Bethesda, Md., 1994—96; mem. NICHD Coun., 1995—99. Editor: Biochem. and Molecular Medicine, 1990—97, Molecular Genetics and Metabolism, 1998—. Chair sci. adv. bd. HEreditary Disease Found., LA, 1998—99; chmn. Basil O'Connor award March Dimes, White Plains, NY, 1997—99. Mem.: Inst. Medicine, Soc. Pediatric Rsch. (E. Mead Johnson award 1993), Am. Coll. Med. Genetics (chair sec.'s adv. com. genetics, health and society 2002—, maternal and child health bur. 1999—2000, pres. 2001—02, co-chair newborn screening screening task force), Am. Soc. Biochem. and Molecular Biology, Am. Pediatric Soc., Am. Fedn. Clin. Rsch., Am. Soc. Human Genetics, Am. Bd. Med. Genetics (bd. dirs. 1992—97, pres. Bethesda 1995—96, diplomate), Am. Acad. Pediatrics (chmn. com. genetics Elk Grove Village, Ill. 1987—91, co-founder, chmn. sect. genetics Elk Grove Village 1990, 1993—95), Alpha Omega Alpha, Sigma Xi, Phi Kappa Phi. Achievements include First to describe the Continguous Gene Syndrome Complex Glyverol Kinase Deficiency; first to extract DNA from blood in newborn screening blotters; first to set up molecular genetic diagonosis for sickle cell disease as part of newborn screening; development of concept of molecular genetic triage of bacterial infection. Office: UCLA Pediatrics Box 951752 22-412 MDCC Los Angeles CA 90095 Office Phone: 310-825-5095. E-mail: emccabe@mednet.ucla.edu.

MCCABE, JOHN B., emergency physician, health science association administrator; MD, SUNY Upstate Medical Coll., Syracuse, NY, 1979. Cert. American Bd. Emergency Medicine. Resident emergency medicine Wright State U. Sch. Medicine, Dayton, Ohio; prof., founding chair dept. emergency medicine SUNY Upstate Medical U., Syracuse, NY, 1991—, interim CEO, sr. v.p. clinical affairs, 2009—. Mem.: American Bd. Emergency Medicine (trustee), American Bd. Medical Specialties (vice chair). Office: SUNY Upstate 911 Jacobsen Hall 750 E Adams St Syracuse NY 13210

MCCAFFERTY, LEO RAYMOND, plastic surgeon; b. Pitts., Nov. 24, 1953; s. Leo Garvey and Virginia Catherine (Ballard) McC.; m. Susan Mary Kimball, July 31, 1992; children: Leo Thomas, Kristin Rae, Kimberly Lynn. BS, Pa. State U., 1975; MD, Temple U., 1981. Diplomate Am. Bd. Plastic Surgery. Resident in gen. surgery Cedars-Sinai Med. Ctr., LA, 1981-85; resident in plastic surgery Jackson Meml. Hosp. U. Miami (Fla.), 1985-87, asst. prof. plastic surgery, 1987-90; pvt. practice, vol. asst. prof. Plastic Surgery U. Pitts., Pitts., 1990—. Asst. clin. prof. Plastic Surgery U. Pitts. Sch. Medicine, Pitts., 1990—. Contbr. articles to profl. jours. Med. practitioner Govt. Jamaica, Jamaica, 1987. State Sen. scholar Temple U., 1977-78, Measey scholar Temple U., 1977-78. Mem. Am. Soc. Plastic Surgeons, Am. Soc. Maxillofacial Surgeons, Am. Cleft Palate Assn., Am. Burn Assn., Greater Pitts. Plastic Surgery Soc. Avocations: athletics, art, music. Office: Plastic Surgery 211532 S Aiken Ave Pittsburgh PA 15232

MCCAFFREE, MARY ANNE WIGHT, pediatrician, neonatal-perinatal specialist, educator; b. Guatemala City, Dec. 9, 1945; m. Robert McCaffree; 2 children. MD, U. Okla. Coll. Medicine, 1971. Diplomate American Bd. Pediat., cert. in neonatal-perinatal medicine. Intern pediat. Bethesda Nat. Naval Med. Ctr., Md., 1971—72; resident neonatal perinatal Medicine Children's Hosp. Nat. Med. Ctr., Washington, 1972—74, fellow, 1973—75; prof. pediat. U. Okla. Health Sciences Ctr.; co-dir., Infantile Apnea Diagnostic Ctr. Children's Hosp. Okla. Named Physician of Yr., U. Okla. Coll Medicine, 1996, Alumnus of Yr., 2006. Mem.: AMA (mem. Commn. on Unity 1998—2000, bd. trustees 2008—, past chair Coun. Sci. & Pub. Health, mem. pediat. sect. coun.), Okla. State Med. Assn. (pres. 1998—99, Ed. L. Calhoon MD Leadership in Medicine award 2005, Women in Medicine award 2007), American Acad. Pediat. (Abraham Jacobi award 2005). Office: U Okla Childrens Physicians PO Box 26307 Oklahoma City OK 73126 *

MCCALL, CHARLES BARNARD, retired health facility administrator; b. Memphis, Nov. 2, 1928; s. John W. and Lizette (Kimbrough) McCall; m. Carolyn Jean Rosselot, June 9, 1951 (dec. Feb. 2002); children: Linda, Kim, Betsy, Cathy; m. Ernestine Mann, Jan. 5, 2004. BA, Vanderbilt U., 1950, MD, 1953. Diplomate Am. Bd. Internal Medicine, Am. Bd. Pulmonary Diseases. Intern Vanderbilt U. Hosp., Nashville, 1953-54; clin. assoc., sr. asst. surgeon USPHS, Nat. Cancer Inst., NIH, 1954-56; sr. asst. resident in medicine U. Ala. Hosp., 1956-57, chief resident, 1958-59; fellow chest diseases Nat. Acad. Scis.-NRC, 1957-58; instr. U. Ala. Med. Sch., 1958-59; from asst. prof. to assoc. prof. medicine U. Tenn. Med. Sch., 1959-69, chief pulmonary diseases, 1964-69; mem. faculty U. Tex. Sys., Galveston, 1969-75, prof. med. br., 1971-73; assoc. prof. medicine Health Sci. Ctr., Southwestern Med. Sch., Dallas, 1973-75, also assoc. dean clin. programs, 1973-75; dir. Office Grants Mgmt. and Devel., 1973-75; dean, prof. medicine U. Tenn. Coll. Medicine, 1975-77, Oral Roberts U. Sch. Medicine, Tulsa, 1977-78; interim assoc. dean U. Okla. Tulsa Med. Coll., 1978-79; clin. prof. medicine U. Colo. Med. Sch., Denver, 1979-80; prof. medicine, assoc. dean U. Okla. Med. Sch., 1980-82; exec. dean and dean U. Okla. Coll. Medicine, 1982-85; v.p. patient affairs, prof. medicine U. Tex. M. D. Anderson Cancer Ctr., 1985-94; chief of staff VA Med. Ctr., Oklahoma City, 1980-82; ret., 2004. Exec. dir. Worldwide Healthcare Svcs., Inc., Waco, Tex., 1998—2002; clinic dir. Claremore Family Medicine, 2002—04, cons., 2002; bd. dirs. Amigos Internacionales, Inc. Contbr. articles to med. jours. Fellow: ACP, Am. Coll. Chest Physicians; mem.: AMA, Am. Fedn. Clin. Rsch., So. Thoracic Soc. (pres. 1968—69), Am. Thoracic Soc., Sigma Xi, Alpha Omega Alpha. Baptist. Home: 1392 Forest Lake Dr Branson West MO 65737 Personal E-mail: mccallcharles@centurytel.net.

MCCALL, SHEDRICK DWIGHT, psychologist; b. Richmond, Va., Apr. 24, 1970; s. Roslyn Annette and Shedrick Dwight McCall; m. Nancy Adelle Swann, July 25, 1992. B, Maryville Coll., 1995; M, Liberty U., 2000; D, Argosy U., 2005. Ceo Youth Pathways, LLC, Richmond, Va., 2000—. Mem. NCAAP, Chesterfield, Va., 1997. Minority scholarship, Maryville Coll., 1989—95. Mem.: Kappa Alpha Psi (assoc.; asst. keeper of exchequer 2004—). Office: Youth Pathways LLC PO Box 34003 Richmond VA 23234 Office Fax: 804-674-1021; Home Fax: 804-674-1021. Personal E-mail: shedrickmccall@verizon.net.

MCCALLISTER, BEN D., internist, cardiologist, educator; b. Fort Worth, Tex., 1932; s. Clarence Dee and Agnes (Horton) McC.; m. Virginia McCallister, Aug. 20, 1956; children: Ben Jr., Scott, John, Tom, Katherine. BA, U. Kans., 1954; MD, U. Kans., Kansas City, 1957. Intern Tripler Army Hosp., Honolulu, 1957-58; resident cardiology and internal medicine Mayo Clinic, Rochester, Minn., 1960-65, cons., 1965-70, St. Lukes Hosp., Kansas City, 1970—; dir. cardiovasc. rsch., endowed chair Mid-Am. Heart Inst., Kansas City, 1996—2007, dir. emeritus, CV rsch.; emeritus prof. medicine Univ. Mo.-Kans. City Sch. Medicine; mentor Am. Coll. Cardiology, 2007. Prof. medicine U. Mo., Kansas City. Recipient Nobel award for leadership potential, Mayo Found., 1965, W.F. Yates Medallion for Disting. Svc. in Medicine, William Jewell Coll., 1989, named a Kans. City Super Doctor, Kans. City mag., 2007. Fellow ACP, Am. Coll. Cardiology (treas., bd. trustees), Clin. Coun. Cardiology, Soc. Cardiac Angiography & Intervention; mem. AMA., Am. Heart Assn., Kans. City Heart Assn., Mo. Heart Assn., Am. Fedn. Clin. Rsch., Ctrl. Soc. Clin. Investigation, Met. Med. Assn. Kans. City, SW Clin. Soc., Mo. Med. Assn., Phi Beta Kappa, Sigma Xi, Office: MidAm Heart Inst 4401 Wornall Rd Kansas City MO 64111-3220

MCCALLISTER, MICHAEL B., insurance company executive; b. Indpls., May 27, 1952; m. Charlene Gray, 1985; children: Megan, Ryan. BA, La. Tech. U., 1974; MBA, Pepperdine U., 1983. Fin. specialist Humana, Inc., Louisville, 1974—75, exec. dir. fin. Cmty. Hosp. Springhill, La., 1975; exec. dir. Humana Hosps. in, Huntington and West Anaheim, Calif., 1978—85, Humana Hosp. West Hills, Canoga Park, Calif., 1985—88; pres. Humana Hosp. Phoenix, 1988—89, v.p. Humana Health Care Plans, Phoenix, 1989—92, San Antonio, 1992—96, pres. divsn. 1 with responsibility for Tex., Fla. and P.R., 1996—97; sr. v.p. health sys. mgmt. Humana, Inc., Louisville, 1997—99, sr. v.p., office chmn., 1999—2000, pres., CEO, 2000—10, chmn., CEO, 2010—. Bd. dirs. Humana Inc., 2000—. Recipient Tower Medallian Award, La. Tech., 2003. Mem.: Am. Assn. Health Plans (bd. dirs.). Office: Humana Inc 500 W Main St Ste 300 Louisville KY 40202-4268 *

MC CALLUM, CHARLES ALEXANDER, academic administrator; b. North Adams, Mass., Nov. 1, 1925; s. Charles Alexander and Mabel Helen (Cassidy) McC.; m. Alice Rebecca Lasseter, Dec. 17, 1955; children: Scott Alan, Charles Alexander III, Philip Warren, Christopher Jay. Student, Dartmouth Coll., 1943-44, Wesleyan U., Middletown, Conn., 1946-47; DMD, Tufts U., 1951; MD, Med. Coll. Ala., 1957; DSc (hon.), U. Ala., 1975, Georgetown U., 1982, Tufts U., 1988, Chulalongkorn U., Thailand, 1993, U. Medicine and Dentistry, NJ, 1993. Diplomate Am. Bd. Oral Surgery (pres. 1970). Intern oral surgery Univ. Hosp., Birmingham, Ala., 1951-52, resident oral surgery, 1952-54, intern medicine, 1957-58; mem. faculty U. Ala. Sch. Dentistry, 1956-96, prof., chmn. dept. oral surgery, 1959-65, dean sch., 1962-77; prof., dept. surgery U. Ala. Sch. of Medicine, 1965-96; v.p. for health affairs, dir. U. Ala. Med. Center, Birmingham, 1977-87; pres. U. Ala., Birmingham, 1987-93, chief sect. oral surgery Sch. Dentistry, 1958-65, 68-69; prof., 1959-93; disting. prof., 1992-2000; disting. prof. emeritus, dean emeritus, 2000—. Mem. nat. adv. dental rsch. coun. NIH, 1968-72; mem. Joint Commn. on Accreditation of Hosps., 1980-91, vice chmn., 1985, chmn., 1986-88. Fellow Am. Coll. Dentists, Internat. Coll. Dentists; mem. ADA (council on dental edn. 1970-76), Am. Assn. Dental Schs. (pres. 1969), Ala. Acad. of Honor, AMA, Am. Soc. Oral Surgeons (trustee 1972-73, pres. 1975-76), Southeastern Soc. Oral Surgeons (pres. 1970), Inst. of Medicine of Nat. Acad. of Scis., Assn. Acad. Health Ctrs. (chmn. bd. dirs. 1984-85), Omicron Kappa Upsilon, Phi Beta Pi. Home: 2328 Garland Dr Birmingham AL 35216-3002 Home Phone: 205-822-8445. Personal E-mail: cmccallum@charter.net.

MCCALLUM, GERALD CHRISTOPHER, clinical psychologist; s. William Robert and Helen Frances (Kaullen) McCallum. BS in Psychology, U. Ill., Champaign, 1984; MS in Clin. Psychology, U. Memphis, 1991, PhD in Clin. Psychology, 1992. Lic. clin. psychologist Ill. Technician Forest Hosp., Des Plaines, Ill., 1983—86; clin. therapist, rschr., instr. U. Memphis, 1986—91; clin. intern Ark. Children's Hosp., U. Ark. Med. Scis., Little Rock, 1991—92; postdoctoral fellow U. Tenn., Memphis, 1992—93; clin. psychologist, program coord. Alexian Bros. Med. Ctr., Elk Grove, Ill., 1993—98; instr. Chgo. Sch. Profl. Psychology, 1995; clin. psychologist DuPage Psychol. Assocs., Naperville, Ill., 1995—. Mem.: APA, Nat. Eagle Scout Assn., Mensa, Ill. Psychol. Assn., Nat. Register Health Svc. Providers in Psychology. Roman Catholic. Avocations: reading, gardening, woodworking, travel, running. Home: PO Box 4345 Naperville IL 60567 Office: DuPage Psychol Assocs 1112 S Washington St Ste 217 Naperville IL 60540 Office Phone: 630-355-4070.

MCCANCE, ANDREW MURRAY, orthodontist; b. Glasgow, Scotland, Apr. 4, 1956; s. Andrew Maltman McCance and Olivia (Mackay) Parkes; m. Ann Roff, Sept. 11, 1982; children: Alistair, Stuart. BS, Glasgow U., 1978; MSc, U. London, 1988; PhD, U. Coll. London, 1992. Sr. house officer St. Georges, London, 1985-86; registrar Guys Hosp., London, 1986-88; sr. registrar GRT Ormondst, London, 1989-92, sr. lectr., 1992-94; sr. clinician East Grinstead (Eng.) Orthodontic Ctr., 1994—. Edn. advisor Royal Coll. London, 1992-94; rschr. U. Coll. London, 1989—; dir., chmn. Rochester Orthodontic Ctr., 1998; lectr. in field. Contbr. articles to profl. jours. Chmn. PTA, Chevening Ch. of Eng. Primary Sch., 1989-97. Grantee, UCL, 2002—07. Fellow Royal Coll. Surgeons Glasgow, Royal Coll. Surgeons Eng.; mem. Open London Orthodontie Soc. Sussex Mem. Labour party. Mem. Ch. of Eng. Achievements include patents in field. Avocations: golf, sailing, garden, music, tennis. Home: Hilden Farm Oast London Rd Hildenborough Kent TN10 3DH England Office: Rochester Orthodontic Ctr 227 Frindsbury Hill Rochester England also: East Grinstead Orthodontic 67-69 Cantelupe Road RH19 3BL East Grinstead England Personal E-mail: egorthodontics@btconnect.com.

MCCANN, BIFF (RAYMOND BIFF MCCANN), plastic surgeon; b. Fayetteville, Ark., Dec. 24, 1966; BS (cum laude) in Natural Scis., U. Ark., Fayetteville, 1989; MD, U. Ark. for Med. Scis., Little Rock, 1993. Intern, gen. surgery U. Ark. for Med. Scis., Little Rock, 1993—94, resident, gen. surgery, 1994—96; fellow, plastic surgery Scott & White Clinic, Temple, Tex., 1996—98; staff plastic surgeon U. Med. Ctr., Las Vegas, Nev., Mountain View Hosp., Las Vegas, Nev., Sunrise Hosp., Las Vegas, Nev.; chief, plastic surgery Valley Hospital, Las Vegas, Nev.; private practice Ctrl. Tex. to practice in Las Vegas, Nev., 1998—. Guest appearances on Plastic Surgery Before and After. Recipient Best Scientific Presentation by Resident Candidate, Am. Soc. for Aesthetic Plastic Surgery Ann. Mtg., NYC, 1997, Am. Soc. for Aesthetic Plastic Surgery Ann. Mtg., Dallas, Tex., 1999; named one of Las Vegas Top 10 Plastic Surgeons. Mem.: Golden Key, Gamma Beta Phi, Alpha Epsilon Delta. Office: 241 N Buffalo Dr Las Vegas NV 89145 Office Phone: 702-360-9500.

MCCANN, PETER DAMIAN, orthopedist, surgeon, educator; AB, Columbia U., 1971—75, MD, 1976—80. Lic. NY State, 1981, diplomate Am. Bd. Orthopaedic Surgery, 1988. Intern gen. surgery St. Vincent's Hospital, 1980—81, resident gen. surgery, 1981—82; asst. resident orthopaedic surgery Columbia-Presbyn. Med. Ctr., 1982—84, resident and jr. Annie C. Kane fellow, 1984—85, co-chief resident orthopaedic surgery, 1984—85, sr. Annie C. Kane fellow shoulder and elbow surgery, 1985—86, attending orthopaedic surgeon, 1987—91; vis. clin. fellow orthopaedic surgery Columbia Univ., 1985—86, dir. orthopaedic surgery dept., asst. prof. orthopaedic surgery, 1987—91; attending orthopaedic surgeon Helen Hayes Hosp., 1986—87, chief of svc. orthopaedic surgery dept., 1987—91, pres. med. staff, 1988—89, chair med. exec. com., 1988—89; program dir. and fellow in adult reconstruction Insall Scott Kelly Inst. for Orthopaedics and Sports Medicine, 1991—2004; vis. prof. Brown U., 1993; assoc. chair orthopaedic surgery dept. Beth Israel Med. Ctr., 1996—, chair singer divsn. exec. com., 2000, assoc. med. ctr., 2000—04, chair orthopaedic surgery dept., 2004—; assoc. clin. prof. surgery Albert Einstein Coll. of Medicine, 2006—. Consulting reviewer Journ. of Shoulder and Elbow Surgery, 1996; mem. IX internat. shoulder meeting com. Am. Shoulder and Elbow Surgeons, 2004; editor in chief Am. Jour. of Orthopedics, 2006; jour. editors group Am. Acad. of Orthopaedic Surgery, 2006. Recipient NY Orthopaedic Hosp. Tchg. award, Columbia Presbyn. Med. Ctr., 1991, Orthopaedic Fellowship award, Arthritis Found., 2004—05. Fellow: Am. Acad. of Orthopaedic Surgeons; mem.: Am. Orthopedic Assn., Am. Shoulder and Elbow Surgeons, AMA, NY County Med. Soc. Office: Beth Israel Medical Center Ste 3M 10 Union Sq E New York NY 10003 Office Phone: 212-844-6735.

MCCANN, PETER PAUL, biology researcher, educator; s. Peter F. and Kathleen (Burnett) McC.; m. Danielle Soury, July 31, 1971. AB in Zoology, Columbia U., 1965; PhD, Syracuse U., 1970. Fellow NIH, Bethesda, Md., 1970-73, sr. scientist Ctr. of Rsch. Merrell Internat., Strasbourg, France, 1973-79; sr. biochemist Merrell Dow Rsch. Ctr., Cin., 1979-82; rsch. assoc. scientist Merrell Dow Rsch. Inst., Cin., 1982-84, dir. scientific and acad. liaison, 1984-90, dir. sci. adminstrn., 1988-90; prof. U. Cin. Coll. Medicine, 1981—, sr. dir., ctr. dir. Marion Merrell Dow Inc., Indpls., 1990-93; pres. Brit. Biotech Inc., Annapolis, Md., 1993-98; interim pres. U. Md. Biotech. Inst., College Park, Md., 1998-99; pres., CEO Oncostasis, Inc., 1999—2001, Mymetics Corp., 2001—03; GG; ptnr. Profl. Fin. Assoc., 2004—07, registered rep. MetLife, 2008—. Co-vice chmn. Gordon Rsch. Conf. on Polyamines, 1987, co-chmn., 1989. Chief editor, co-author Inhibition of Polyamine Metabolism, 1987; co-editor, co-author. Enzymes as Targets for Drug Design, 1989; contbr. articles to profl. jours. Mem. Am. Soc. Cell Biology, Am. Soc. Tropical Medicine and Hygiene, Am. Soc. Biochemistry and Molecular Biology, Biochem. Soc. (editl. adv. bd. 1986-92, editor 1992-99), Soc. Protozoologists (editl. bd. reviewers 1989-95), Am. Philat. Congress, Inc. (pres. 1990-95), Am. Philat. Soc. (v.p. 1995-99, pres. 1999-2003, Fédération Internat. De Philatélie (v.p. 2004—). Achievements include patents for method of inhibiting the growth of protozoa, method of controlling phytopathogenic fungus. Personal E-mail: p103226706@cs.com.

MCCARBERG, BILL HAROLD, physician; b. Seattle, Apr. 4, 1948; s. Harold Carl and Elizabeth Ann Mehlberg; m. Peggy J. McCarthy McCarberg. BA summa cum laude, U. Calif., Berkeley, 1972; MD, Northwestern U., 1976. Diplomate Am. Bd. Family Practice, Am. Coll. Pain Medicine; cert. in geriatrics. Residency Highland Hosp., Rochester, NY, 1979; physician in charge Kaiser Permanent, Escondido, Calif., 1982—2003; asst. clin. prof. U. Calif. Sch. Medicine, San Diego, 1983—; coord. pain svcs. Kaiser Permanent, San Diego, 1974—2002, dir. chronic pain mgmt. program, 1984—2003; founding mem. managed care task force Am. Pain Soc., 1990—. Author: (monograph) Chronic Pain Management: Perspective for Primary Care Physicians, 1998, (book chpt.) A Sample of Existing Managed Care Organizations Pain Programs, 1999; contbr. articles to profl. jours. Recipient K Star for Outstanding Svc., Kaiser Permanente, San Diego, 1985, 92, Award of Excellence Southern Calif. Cancer Pain Initiative, L.A., 1999. Mem. Am. Acad. Pain Medicine, Am. Pain Soc. (chair managed care com. 2000—, bd. dirs., Elizabeth Narcessian award 2003), Western Pain Soc. (chair program 1999—, pres. 1998-), Appraisal Physician Svcs., Phi Beta Kappa. Avocations: running, guitar, golf. Office: Kaiser Permanente 732 N Broadway Escondido CA 92025

MCCARGAR, JASON, cosmetic dentist; BA in Journalism, U. Nev.; D in Dental Medicine, U. Pitts. Lic. Ariz., Tex. With hospital-based dentistry, Ctrl. Phoenix, Ariz.; owner, dentist Scottsdale Dental Arts, 2007—. Mem.: ADA, Ctrl. Ariz. Dental Assn., Ariz. Dental Assn., Am. Acad. of Cosmetic Dentistry. Office: Scottsdale Dental Arts 9751 N 90th Pl Scottsdale AZ 85258 Office Phone: 480-860-8282.

MCCARROLL, KATHLEEN ANN, radiologist, educator; b. Lincoln, Nebr., July 7, 1948; d. James Richard and Ruth B. (Wagenknecht) McC.; m. Steven Mark Beerbohm, July 10, 1977 (div. 1991); 1 child, Palmer Brooke; m. Lawrence Arthur Weis, Aug. 28, 2004 BS, Wayne State U., 1974; MD, Mich. State U., 1978. Diplomate Am. Bd. Radiology. Intern/resident in diagnostic radiology William Beaumont Hosp., Royal Oak, Mich., 1978-82, fellow in computed tomography and ultrasound, 1983, dir. divsn. emergency radiology, 2001—; radiologist, dir. radiologic edn. Detroit Receiving Hosp., 1984-2001, vice-chief dept. radiology, 1988-96, chief dept. radiology, 1996-2001; prof. radiology Oakland U., William Beaumont Sch. Medicine, 2011. Pres.-elect med. staff Detroit Receiving Hosp., 1992-94, pres., 1994-96; mem. admissions com. Wayne State U. Coll. Medicine, Detroit, 1991-2001; trustee Detroit Med. Ctr., 1996-2001, dir. med. staff consolidation, 1996-97, mem. consol. med. exec. com., 1998-2001, chmn. credentials com., 1998-99, joint conf. com., 1998-99; officer bd. dirs. Dr. L. Reynolds Assoc., P.C., Detroit, 1991-94, 96-2001; presenter profl. confs.; assoc. prof. radiology Wayne State U. Sch. Medicine, Detroit, 1995—; health care cons./med. staff affairs, 1998-2006. Editor: Critical Care Clinics, 1992; mem. editl. bd. Emergency Radiology, 1998-2006; contbr. articles to profl. publs. Named to Crain's Bus. Detroit, Detroit's 100 Most Influential Women, 1997. Mem.: AMA, Wayne/Oakland County Med. Soc., Mich. State Med. Soc., Am. Soc. Emergency Radiologists (bd. dirs. 1996—2001, exec. com. 1998—2001, bylaws com. 2001—05), Am. Roentgen Ray Soc., Radio. Soc. N.Am., Am. Coll. Radiology (Mich. chpt. sec. 1995—98, alt. councilor 1999—2002, councilor 2002—08, plain film and fluoroscopy accreditation com. 2003—05), Phi Beta Kappa. Avocations: travel, skiing, reading. Office: Wm Beaumont Hosp Dept Diag Radiology 3601 W 13 Mile Rd Royal Oak MI 48073

MCCARTER, KATHERINE SAUTER, association executive; b. Nov. 12, 1942; d. William Charles and Josephine Rosina (Schoenle) Sauter; m. Robert James McCarter, Dec. 6, 1969; 1 child, Emily Katherine. BA in Biology, Cedar Crest Coll., Allentown, Pa., 1964; MHA (EPA trainee), Johns Hopkins U., 1973. Chmn. sci. dept. Arundel (Md.) Jr. H.S., 1964—68; assoc. career devel. program Am. Lung Assn., NYC, 1968; air conservation cons. Mass. Lung Assn., 1968—69; exec. dir. Met. Boston Citizen's Coalition Clean Air, 1968—69; cmty. health educator Environ. Health Adminstrn., Md. Dept. Health, 1971—76; dir. govt. rels. APHA, Washington, 1976—80, asst. exec. dir., 1980—83, assoc. exec. dir., 1984—97; exec. dir. pub. Ecol. Soc. Am., Washington, 1997—. Mem. nat. air pollution manpower devel. adv. com. EPA, 1973—76. Mem. editl. adv. bd.: The AIDS Reference Guide, 1987. Bd. dirs. Nat. Coalition Health and Environment, 1980—82, Coalition for Health Funding, 1983—, treas., 1983—86, v.p., 1987—88, pres., 1989—94, past pres., 1994—97. Mem.: APHA, Nat. Ecol. Obs. Network (bd. dirs. 2010—), Coun. Engring. and Sci. Soc. Execs. (bd. dirs. 2003—, sec. 2007—08, v.p. 2008—09, pres. 2009—, past pres. 2010—11). Home: 9027 Billow Row Columbia MD 21045-2343 Office: 1990 M St NW Ste 700 Washington DC *

MCCARTHY, DENIS M., medical educator; b. Galway, Ireland, July 16, 1938; s. Michael Denis and Mary Beatrice McCarthy; m. Sallie Susan Schirmer; children: Michael, Kevin, Anne, Brian, Jessica, Ben. MB BCh, BAO, U. Coll. Dublin, Ireland, 1962, MD, 1970; BSc in Physiology and Biochemistry with 1st Class honors, U. Coll. Cork, Ireland, 1963, MSc in Physiology, 1965. Cert. E.C.F.M.G. Exam., 1970, bd. eligible ABIM, 1973, in FLEX exam. State Bd., Md., 1974; gastroenterologist Md., 1975, registered Eng., 1963, Ireland, 1963, Calif., 1976, Washington, 1977, Va., 1977, lic. N.Mex., 1980. Attended U. Coll. Dublin, Med. Sch., 1956—62; med. internship Mater Misericordial Hosp., Dublin, 1962—63, sr. med. registrar, gastroenterology, 1969—70; asst. lectr. physiology U. Coll. Cork, 1963—65; med. residency London U., Royal Postgrad. Med. Sch. Fedn., Hammersmith, Dept. Gastroenterology, 1966—69, Brompton Hosp. Diseases Chest, Cardio-Pulmonary and Pediat. Cardiology Dept., London, 1966—69, Royal Free Hosp., Gastroenterology Dept., London, 1967—69; postdoc. rsch. fellow, biochemistry and gastroenterology U. Calif. Med. Ctr., San Francisco, 1970—74, asst. prof. medicine, gastroenterology, Vet. Adminstrn. Hosp., 1973—74; vis. scientist NIH, Bethesda, Md., 1974—77, attending physician, clin. ctr., 1974—80, supr., clin. rsch. digestive diseases, 1974—80, sr. investigator, Digestive Disease Br., 1977—80, capt., USPHS, 1977—80, dir., 2006; prof. medicine, GI U. N.Mex., Sch. Med., Albuquerque, 1980—, adj. prof. biochemistry, adv. com., NIH clin. rsch., exec. com., chief gastroenterology, 1988—2000, dir., GI fellowship tng. program, 1988—2001; chief gastroenterology Vets. Adminstrn. Health Care Svc., N.Mex. Regional Fed. Med. Ctr., 1980—2002, hepatologist, 2007, adj. prof., sect. gastroenterology and hepatology. Mem. US Food and Drug Adminstrn., cons., gastrointestinal and arthritis adv. com., 1985—92. Contbr. scientific papers to profl. med. jours., chapters to books. Recipient Leonard prize, Mater Hosp., Dublin, 1962, Gold medal, 1962, Irish Nat. Maternity Hosp., 1962; named one of Am. Top Physicians, Consumer Rsch. Coun. America, 2007. Master: RCP (fellow specialty bds., Ireland 1975, fellow specialty bds., London 1998); fellow: ACP; mem.: Am. Digestive Disease Soc. (exec. com. 1975—80, v.p. 1978—80, bd. mem. 1980—84), NY Acad. Scis., Western Assn. Physicians, NY Acad. Scis., Western Soc. Clin. Investigation, Brit. Soc. Gastroenterology, Gastroent. Rsch. Group, Am. Gastroent. Assn. (fellow 2006—, Disting. Mentorship award, Am. Digestive Health Found. 2005). Democrat. Roman Catholic. Avocations: music, history, travel, mountain climbing, skiing. Office: NM Vets Adminstrn Health Care Svc Med Ctr 111F Dept Vet Affairs 1501 San Pedro Blvd SE Albuquerque NM 87108 also: Univ NM HSC Divsn Gastroenterology MSC10 5550 Albuquerque NM 87131 Home: 3808 Oxbow Village LN NW Albuquerque NM 87120-1180 Office Fax: 505-256-2803; Home Fax: 505-256-5751. Business E-Mail: denis.mccarthy2@med.va.gov, bmccarthy@salud.unm.edu.

MCCARTHY, EDITH A., pediatrician, educator; b. Elizabeth, NJ, Sept. 22, 1964; BA in biology with honors, NYU; MD, U. Medicine and Dentistry NJ, Robert Wood Johnson Med. Sch., 1992. Cert. Pediat., 1997, Neonatal-Perinatal Medicine, 2005. Resident pediat. Cornell Med. Ctr.-NY Hosp., 1992—95, fellowship neonatology, 1997—2000, instr. pediat., child protection rep., clin. dir. Children's Advocate Ctr. of Manhattan; pvt. practice Watchung Pediat., NJ, 1996—97; asst. prof. pediat. to clin. asst. prof. NYU Sch. Medicine; attending NYU Med. Ctr.; mem. NYU Neonatology Assocs.; staff Bellevue Hosp. Ctr.; founder Care Intensive Pediatrics, PLLC, NYC. Contbr. articles to med. jours. Office: Care Intensive Pediat 244 E 32nd St New York NY 10016 Office Phone: 212-726-0005. Office Fax: 212-726-9073. E-mail: info@careintensivepediatrics.com.

MC CARTHY, FRANK MARTIN, oral surgeon, educator; b. Olean, NY, Aug. 27, 1924; s. Frank Michael and Joan (Quinn) McC.; m. Julia Richmond, Nov. 24, 1949; children: Robert Lee, Joan Lee. BS, U. Pitts., 1943, DDS, 1945, MD, 1949; MS in Oral Surgery, Georgetown U., 1954; ScD (hon.), St. Bonaventure U., 1956. Med. intern Mercy Hosp., Pitts., 1949-50; practice oral surgery LA, 1954-75; tchg. fellow Georgetown U., 1952-53; rsch. fellow NIH, 1953-54; prof. oral surgery U. So. Calif. Sch. Dentistry, 1966-75, prof., chmn. sect. anesthesia and medicine, 1975-90, prof. emeritus, 1990—, chmn. dept. surg. scis., 1979-84, assoc. dean adminstrv. affairs, 1977-79, asst. dean hosp. affairs, 1979-84. Dir. anesthesiology U.So. Calif. oral surgery sect. L.A. County Hosp., 1958-89; clin. supr., lectr. dental hygiene program Pasadena City Coll., 1992—; v.p. Am. Dental Bd. Anesthesiology, 1984-89; lectr. in field; mem. adv. panel on dentistry sect. anesthesizing agts. Nat. Fire Protection Assn., 1971-79; mem. Am. Nat. Stds. Com., 1974-86, 95—; cons. in field. Author: Emergencies in Dental Practice, 1967, rev., 1972, 79, Medical Emergencies in Dentistry, 1982, Safe Treatment of the Medically Compromised Patient, 1987, Essentials of Safe Dentistry for the Medically Compromised Patient, 1989; mem. editorial bd.: Calif. Dental Assn. Jour; contbr. articles to profl. publs. Bd. councilors Sch. Dentistry, U. So. Calif., 1972-75. Served as lt., M.C. USNR, 1950-52. Recipient Lifetime Achievement award, So. Calif. Orofacial Acad., Palm Springs, Calif., 2006. Fellow Internat. Assn. Oral Surgeons (founder), Am. Coll. Dentists, Internat. Coll. Dentists; mem. ADA (editl. bd. jour.), Am. Dental Soc. Anesthesiology (Heidbrink award 1977), Am. Assn. Oral-Max Surgeons (chmn. anesthesia com. 1971), So. Calif. Soc. Oral Surgeons (pres. 1974), Calif., L.A. County Dental Assns., Delta Tau Delta, Psi Omega, Phi Rho Sigma, Omicron Kappa Upsilon. Home and Office: 480 S Orange Grove Blvd Apt 11 Pasadena CA 91105-1720

MCCARTHY, JOSEPH GERALD, plastic surgeon, educator; b. Lowell, Mass., Nov. 28, 1938; s. Joseph H. and Eva (Murphy) McC.; m. Karlan von L. Sloan, June 6, 1964; children: Cara, Stephen. AB, Harvard U., 1960; MD, Columbia U. Coll. Physicians and Surgeons, 1964. Diplomate: Am. Bd. Surgery, Am. Bd. Plastic Surgery. Intern, gen. surgery Columbia-Presbyn. Med. Ctr., 1964—65, resident, plastic surgery, 1967—71, NYU Med. Ctr., NYC, 1971—73, dir., Inst. Reconstructive Plastic Surgery; Lawrence D. Bell prof. plastic surgery NYU Sch. Medicine, NYC, 1981—; attending physician Univ. Hosp.; vis. plastic surgeon Bellevue Hosp.; attending surgeon Manhattan Eye, Ear and Throat Hosp., N.Y.C. VA Hosp. Editor: Symposium on Diagnosis and Treatment of Craniofacial Anomalies, 1979, Plastic Surgery, 1990; assoc. editor Reconstructive Plastic Surgery, 1977, Jour. Plastic and Reconstructive Surgery, Jour. Craniofacial, Genetics and Developmental Biology; contbr. several articles to peer-reviewed jours.; cotbr. chpts. to books. Bd. trustee Nat. Found. for Facial Reconstruction; founding chmn. med. adv. bd. Smile Train. Lt. comdr. USPHS, 1965—67. Recipient Joseph Garrison Parker prize Columbia U., 1964, 1st prize Plastic Surgery Edn. found., 1980, James Barret Brown prize, 1991, 1st prize Am. Soc. Maxillofacial Surgeons, 1991, 93, 94, Surgical Pioneer award, U. Zurich, 2003, Clin. Excellence award, Castle Connolly Med. Ltd., 2007; Am. Cancer Soc. fellow Presbyn. Hosp., N.Y.C., 1969-70, prin. investigator NIH, 1974. Fellow ACS; mem. Am. Soc. Plastic and Reconstructuve Surgeons, Assn. Acad. Chairmen Plastic Surgery (pres. 1988-89), N.Y. Regional Soc. Plastic and Reconstructive Surgeons (pres. 1984-85), Am. Assn. Plastic Surgeons (historian 1990-93), Internat. Soc. Craniomaxillofacial Surgeons (pres. 1989-91), Northeastern Soc. Plastic Surgeons. Achievements include first to the concept of craniofacial distraction. Mailing: NYU Langone Med Ctr TCH 1 148 550 1st Ave New York NY 10016 Office: 722 Park Ave New York NY 10021 Office Phone: 212-263-5208. Office Fax: 212-988-7230.

MCCARTHY, SHERRI NEVADA, psychologist, educator, consultant; b. Topeka, June 2, 1958; d. Wallace Gene and Lois Elaine (McDyson) McCarthy; m. Scott Newlin Tucker, Feb. 14, 1983 (div. Feb. 2001); children: Colin Apollo, Chrysallis Altair; m. Brian David Ewing, Feb. 5, 2006. AA in Liberal Arts, Phoenix Coll., 1981; BA in Psychology, Ariz. State U., 1984, BEd in English Lit., 1985, MA in Spl. Edn., 1987, PhD in Ednl. Psychology, 1995. Cert. kindergarten -12 spl. edn., gifted edn., ESL, Ariz. Mng. editor Scottsdale (Ariz.) Free Press, 1977-78; lit. instr. CTY program Johns Hopkins U., 1985; gifted specialist Fountain Hills (Ariz.) Schs., 1985-87; writing instr. Ariz. State U. Ctr. Acad. Precocity, 1986; tchr. ESL Chandler-Gilbert C.C., Chandler, Ariz., 1986-87; tchr. of gifted Chandler (Ariz.) Unified Schs., 1987-90; psychology tchr., cons. Maricopa County C.C., Tempe, Ariz., 1988-96; prof. ednl. psychology No. Ariz. U., Yuma, 1993—. Freelance writer, 1974—; spl. edn. tchr., sch. psychologist Hawaii Dept. Edn., 1990-91; faculty assoc. ednl. psychology Ariz. State U., Phoenix, 1992-96; tchr. English Mesa (Ariz.) C.C., 1993-96; advisor, asst. honors coord. Phi Theta Kappa, 1994-96; gifted ednl. specialist Kyrene Pub. Schs., Chandler, Ariz., 1995-96; vis. prof. adolescent psychology Fed. U., Porto Alegre, Brazil, 2002-06, U. Malaya, 2008-09; sr. lectr., rschr. Vologola State U., Russia, 2003-04. Author: Metamorphosis-A Collection of Poems, 1975, Speed Communication, 1979, A Matter of Time, 1980, A Death in the Family, 1988, Coping with Special Needs Classmates, 1993, Preventing Adolescent Aggression, 2005, Tchg. Psychology Around World, 2007, Vol. 2, 2009, Teaching Psychology Around the World, vol. III, 2011, Building Asian Families and Communities in the 21st Century, 2010; staff writer: Ariz. Hwy. Patrolman mag., Phoenix, 1979-82; newsletter editor: Ednl. Opportunity Ctr., Tempe, Ariz., 1982-83; contbr. articles to profl. jours. Bd. dirs. Young Astronauts, Fountain Hills, 1985-87. US Fulbright scholar, US State Dept. to Russian Fedn., 2003—04, Rsch. scholar, U. Fed. Rio Grande do Sul, 2004—06. Fellow APA (CIRP liaison 1992—), Internat. Coun. Psychologists (bd. dirs. 1998—), Internat. Coun. Psychology Educators (conf. organizer 2000—), Asian Psychol. Assn (bd. dirs. 2006-), Women's Leadership Inst.; mem. Ariz. Ednl. Rsch. Orgn. (bd. dirs. 1997—2004), Ariz. English Tchrs. Assn. (bd. dirs. 1998—2009), Odyssey of the Mind (mem. bd. govs. 1987-89, Creativity award 1986, 87). Avocations: writing, guitar, camping, travel, piano. Office: No Ariz U PO Box 6236 Yuma AZ 85366-6236 Business E-Mail: sherri.mccarthy@nau.edu.

MCCARTHY, SHIRLEY M., radiologist, educator; b. NY, 1950; m. Johan Gallalee; 2 children. PhD, Cornell U., 1975; MD, Yale U., 1979. Diplomate Am. Bd. Radiology, 1983. Resident diagnostic radiology Yale-New Haven Hosp., New Haven, 1980—83, diagnostic radiology; fellow cross sectional imaging Univ. of Calif. Med. Ctr., San Francisco, 1983—84; prof. diagnostic radiology Yale Univ., New Haven, prof. obstetrics, gynecology and reproductive sciences. Office: Yale-New Haven Hospital 2nd Fl S Pavilion 20 York St New Haven CT 06510 Office Phone: 203-688-2433. Office Fax: 203-688-9258.

MCCARTHY-ALLEN, MARY FRANCES, medical foundation administrator, not-for-profit fundraiser, consultant; b. Washington, Apr. 16, 1937; d. Joseph Francis and Frances (Oddi) McGowan; m. Charles M. Sappenfield, Dec. 14, 1963 (div. June 1990); children: Charles Ross, Sarah Kathleen; m. Daniel Fendrich McCarthy, Jr., Aug. 25, 1990 (dec. Apr. 1999); m. Cary Walter Allen, Nov. 30, 2002. BA, Trinity Coll., Washington, 1958; cert. in bus. adminstrn., Harvard U.-Radcliffe Coll., 1959; MA, Ball State U., Muncie, Ind., 1984. Systems engr. IBM, Cambridge, Mass., 1959-61; editl. asst. Kiplinger Washington Editors, 1961-63; feature writer pub. info. dept. Ball State U., 1984-85, coll. editor Coll. Bus., 1985-86, coord. alumni and devel., 1986-88, dir. major gift clubs and donor rels., 1988-90; dir. devel. Sweet Briar (Va.) Coll., 1990-91; adminstr. St. Mary's Hosp. and Med. Ctr. Found., Grand Junction, Colo., 1991—. Editor: A History of Maxon Corporation, 1986, Managing Change, 1986, Indiana's Investment Banker, 1987; assoc. editor Mid-Am. Jour. Bus., 1985-86. Participant Leadership Lynchburg, 1990, Jr. League; regional dir. IX Assn. for Healthcare Philanthropy, 1996—98, found. bd., 1997—; bd. dirs. Sr. Companions, Grand Junction, 1992—; mem. steering com. Mesa County Health Cmtys., 1992—; bd. dirs. Grand Junction Musical Arts, 1997—; trustee Women's Found. of Colo., 2000—; bd. dirs. Grand Valley Hospice, 2002—; mem. Mesa County Health Assessment, 1994—. Recipient Golden Broom award Muncie Clean City, 1989; svc. of distinction award Ball State U. Coll. Bus., 1990. Mem. Coun. for Advancement and Support of Edn., Assn. of Healthcare Philanthropy (regional 9 cabinet 1992—, bd. dirs. 1997—), Nat. Soc. Fundraising Execs. (cert., Colo. chpt. bd. dirs. 1994—), Rotary. Republican. Avocations: biking, walking, cross country skiing, gardening.

MCCARTY, RICHARD CHARLES, psychology professor, provost; b. Portsmouth, Va., July 12, 1947; s. Constantine Ambrose and Helen Marie (Householder) McC.; m. Sheila Adair Miltier, July 15, 1965; children: Christopher Charles, Lorraine Marie, Ryan Lester, Patrick James. BS in Biology, Old Dominion U., 1970, MS in Zoology, 1972; PhD in Pathobiology, Johns Hopkins U., 1976. Rsch. assoc. NIMH, Bethesda, Md., 1976-78; asst. prof. U. Va., Charlottesville, 1978-84, assoc. prof., 1984-88, prof., 1988-2001, chair psychology, 1990-98, chair Coun. of Grad. Depts. Psychology, 1996-97; exec. dir. sci. directorate APA, Washington, 1998-2001; dean arts and sci. Vanderbilt U., Nashville, 2001—08, provost, 2008—. Mem. editl. bd. Behavioral and Neural Biology, 1985—90, Physiology and Behavior, 1989—2007, editor-in-chief Stress, 1995—99; editor: Am. Psychologist, 2000—01. Lt. comdr. USPHS, 1976—78. Recipient Rsch. Scientist Devel. award, NIMH, 1985—90; sr. fellow, Nat. Heart Lung Blood Inst., NIH, 1984—85. Fellow AAAS, APA, Assn. Psychol. Sci. Roman Catholic. Office: Office of the Provost Vanderbilt Univ 205 Kirkland Hall Nashville TN 37240 Business E-Mail: richard.mccarty@vanderbilt.edu.

MCCASKEY, RAYMOND F., retired health insurance company executive; b. 1944; m. Judy McCaskey. With Continental Assurance Co., Chgo., 1963-73; assist v.p. Health Care Service Corp., 1973—79, chief actuary, 1979—82, CFO, 1982—91, pres., COO, 1991—98, pres., CEO, 1998—2008. Bd. dirs. Health Care Service Corp. Former bd. chmn. Lincoln Found. for Bus. Excellence.

MCCAULEY, LINDA A., dean, nursing educator; BSN, U. NC; Master's in child health nursing, Emory U., 1979; PhD in environ. health and epidemiology, U. Cin., 1988. Nightingale prof. nursing U. Pa. Sch. Nursing, Phila., assoc. dean rsch.; dean Nell Hodgson Woodruff Sch. Nursing Emory U., Atlanta, 2009—. Fellow: Am. Acad. Nursing; mem.: ANA, Inst. Medicine, Am. Coll. Occupational and Environ. Medicine, Internat. Soc. Environ. Epidemiology, Am. Assn. Occupational Health Nurses, Am. Pub. Health Assn., Sigma Theta Tau. Office: Nell Hodgson GA Woodruff Sch Nursing Emory U 1520 Clifton Rd NE Atlanta GA 30322-4207 Office Phone: 404-727-7976. Office Fax: 404-727-9800. E-mail: dean@nursing.emory.edu.

MCCAWLEY, AUSTIN, psychiatrist, educator; b. Greenock, Scotland, Jan. 17, 1925; arrived in U.S., 1954; s. Austin and Anna Theresa (McBride) McC.; m. Gloria Klein, Feb. 15, 1958; children: Joseph, Tessa. MBCHB, U. Glasgow, 1948. Diplomate Am. Bd. Psychiatry and Neurology; DPM Royal Coll. London. Intern Glasgow Royal Infirmary, Scotland, 1948; resident Inst. Living, Harford, Conn., 1954-57, clin. dir., 1960-66; med. dir. Westchestor br. St. Vincent's Hosp., NYC, 1966-72; dir. psychiatry St. Francis Hosp., Hartford, 1972-88; prof. psychiatry U. Conn. Med. Sch., Farmington, 1983-93; pvt. practice, West Hartford, Conn., 1988—. Dir. psychiatry Kaiser Permanente of Conn., 1996-99. Author: A Comb for a Bald Man: A Psychiatrist's Experience, 2009; co-author: The Physician, 1983; contbr. articles to profl. jours. Chmn. Bd. Mental Health, State of Conn., 1981-84, Search Com. for Commr. Mental Health, Conn., 1981; mem. Gov.'s Spl. Task Force on Mental health Policy, Conn., 1982. With RAF, 1948-50. Fellow: Conn. Psychiat. Soc. (pres. 1978—79), Am. Coll. Psychiatry (charter fellow, founder), Am. Psychiat. Assn. Democrat. Roman Catholic. Avocation: music. Home and Office: 6020 Piney Grove Way Gainesville VA 20155-6670 Office Phone: 571-248-0277. Business E-Mail: amccawley@olviasart.com.

MCCLELLAN, MARK BARR, think-tank executive, former federal agency administrator; b. Austin, Tex., June 26, 1963; m. Stephanie McClellan; 2 children. BA in English & Biology, U. Tex., Austin, 1985; MA, MPA in Regulatory Policy, Harvard U., 1991, MD, 1992; PhD in Economics, MIT, 1993. Resident in internal medicine Brigham and Women's Hosp., Boston; cons. The Rand Corp., Santa Monica, Calif., 1989—91; rsch. assoc. Harvard Med. Sch. Dept. of Health Care Policy, Boston, 1991—95; attending physician Stanford U. Health Services; assoc. prof. economics Stanford U., 1995—99; assoc. prof. medicine Stanford Med. Sch., dir. program on health outcomes rsch.; dep. asst. sec. for econ. policy US Dept. Treasury, Washington, 1998—99; mem. Coun. Econ. Advisors Exec. Office of the Pres., Washington, 2001—02; commr. FDA, Rockville, Md., 2002—04; adminstr. Centers for Medicare & Medicaid Services US Dept. Health & Human Services (HHS), Washington, 2004—06; sr. rsch. fellow American Enterprise Inst.-Brookings Joint Ctr. for Regulatory Studies, Washington, 2006—07; dir., Leonard D. Schaeffer Chair in Health Policy Studies, sr. fellow econ. studies Engelberg Ctr. for Health Care Reform, The Brookings Inst., Washington, 2007—. Co-editor (with Daniel P. Kessler): A Global Analysis of Technological Change in Health Care: Heart Attacks, 2002; co-editor: (with Joshua S. Benner) Implementing Comparative Effectiveness Research: Priorities, Methods, and Impact, 2009. Recipient Kenneth J. Arrow award for Outstanding Rsch. In Health Economics, 1997, Career Devel. award, Nat. Inst Aging, 1999, Vision, Innovation, Dedication & Advocacy (VIDA) award, Nat. Alliance for Hispanic Health, 2003, Indispensable Person in Health Rsch. award, Alliance for Aging Rsch., 2003, King David award for Pub. Leadership, The Jerusalem Fund, 2004,

Cancer Leadership award, Friends of Cancer Rsch., 2004, Joseph F. Boyle award for Disting. Pub. Svc., 2005, Pub. Svc. Leadership award, Nat. Coalition for Cancer Survivorship, 2005, Booker T. Washington award, Nat. Minority Health Month Found., 2006, Surgeon General's Medallion for Outstanding Commitment & Dedication to the Health & Welfare of All People & Exemplary Svc. in the Pub. Trust, 2006, Star of Tex. Healthcare award, 2008, Presdl. Citation in Recognition of Contributions to Promoting High Quality Innovative & Affordable Health Care, The American Coll. of Cardiology, 2008. Mem.: Inst. Medicine. Office: The Brookings Instn 1775 Massachusetts Ave NW Washington DC 20036 Home: 4900 Chesapeake St NW Washington DC 20016-4335

MCCLELLAN, MARY ANN, pediatric nurse practitioner; b. Mar. 29, 1942; BS, Tex. Woman's U., 1964; MN, U. Wash., 1968-69; cert., U. Tex., Arlington, 1997. Cert. family life educator, CPNP, pediatric nurse practitioner; advanced RN practitioner, Okla. Charge nurse Baylor U. Med. Ctr., Dallas, 1964—65; pub. health staff nurse Dallas County Health Dept., Dallas, 1965—68; supervising nurse Okla. State Dept. Health, Oklahoma City, 1969—70, maternal-child health nurse cons., 1971; asst. prof. U. Okla. Coll. Nursing, Oklahoma City, 1971—72; from instr. to asst. prof. Harris Coll. Nursing Tex. Christian U., Ft. Worth, 1972—75; asst. prof. continuing edn. U. Okla. Coll. Nursing, Oklahoma City, 1976—79, asst. prof. baccalaureate program, 1979—96, mem. grad. faculty, 1991—. Cons. and lectr. in field. Contbr. chpts. to books, articles to profl. jours. Mem. Nat. Coun. on Family Rels., Okla. Family Resources Coalition, Nat. Assn. Pediatric Nurse Assocs. and Practitioners, Assn. Faculty of Pediat. Nurse Practitioner Programs, Okla. Coun. on Family Rels., Sigma Theta Tau., Phi Kappa Phi. Office: U Okla Coll Nursing PO Box 26901 Oklahoma City OK 73126-0901

MCCLELLAN, ROGER ORVILLE, toxicologist; b. Tracy, Minn., Jan. 5, 1937; s. Orville and Gladys (Paulson) McC.; m. Kathleen Mary Dunagan, June 23, 1962; children: Eric John, Elizabeth Christine, Katherine Ruth. DVM with highest honors, Wash. State U., 1960; M of Mgmt., U. N.Mex., 1980; DSc (hon.), Ohio State U., 2005. Diplomate Am. Bd. Vet. Toxicology, Am. Bd. Toxicology. From biol. scientist to sr. scientist Gen. Electric Co., Richland, Wash., 1957-64; sr. scientist biology dept. Pacific N.W. Labs., Richland, Wash., 1965; scientist med. rsch. br. divsn. biology and medicine AEC, Washington, 1965-66; asst. dir. rsch., dir. fission product inhalation program Lovelace Found. Med. Edn. and Rsch., Albuquerque, 1966-73; v.p., dir. rsch. adminstrn., dir. Lovelace Inhalation Toxicology Rsch. Inst., Albuquerque, 1973-76, pres., dir., 1976-88; chmn. bd. dirs. Lovelace Biomed. and Environ. Rsch. Inst., Albuquerque, 1988-96; pres., CEO Lovelace Respiratory Rsch. Inst., Triangle Park, NC, 1988-99; pres. emeritus Hamner Inst. Health Sci., Triangle Park, NC, 1999—; pvt. advisor Toxicology and Human Health Risk Analysis, 1999—. Mem. rsch. com. Health Effects Inst., 1981-92, mem. future techs. com., 2000—; bd. dir. Toxicology Lab. Accreditation Bd., 1982-90, treas., 1984-90; adj. prof. Wash. State U., 1980-95, U. Ark., 1970-88; clin. assoc. U. N.Mex., 1971-85, adj. prof. toxicology, 1985—; adj. prof. toxicology and occupl. and environ. medicine Duke U., 1988—; adj. prof. toxicology U. N.C., Chapel Hill, 1989-2000; adj. prof. toxicology N.C. State U., 1991-2008; cons. faculty Colo. State U., 2002—; regents lectr. UCLA, 1999-2000; mem. dose assessment adv. group U.S. Dept. Energy, 1980-87, mem. health and environ. rsch. adv. com., 1984-85, 1999-2004; mem. exec. com. sci. adv. bd. EPA, 1974-95, mem. environ. health com., 1980-83, chmn., 1982-83, chmn. radionuclide emissions rev. com., 1984-85, chmn. Clean Air Sci. Adv. Com., 1987-92, Diesel Exhaust Panel, 1996-2001, chmn. rsch. strategies adv. com., 1992-94, mem. Particulate Matter Panel, 1993-97, 99-2006; mem. com. toxicology NAS-NRC, 1979-87, chmn., 1980-87; mem. com. risk assessment methodology for hazardous air pollution NAS-NRC, 1991-94, com. biol. effects of Radon NAS NRC, 1994-98, com. rsch. priorities airborne particulate matter, 1998-2004; mem. Environ. Roundtable, Inst. Medicine, 1998-2002; mem. com. on environ. justice Inst. of Medicine, 1996-99, trustee toxicology excellence in risk assessment, 2000-07, chmn. bd. trustees, 2002-04, mem. coord. com. strengthening sci.-based decision making, 2002—; pres. Am. Bd. Vet. Toxicology, 1970-73; mem. adv. coun. Ctr. for Risk Mgmt., Resources for the Future, 1987-2001; mem. Nat. Coun. Radiation Protection Measurements, 1970-2001, disting. emeritus fellow, 2002—; bd. dirs. NC Assn. Biomed. Rsch., 1989-91, N.C. Vet. Med. Found., 1990-95, pres., 1993-94; bd. govs. Rsch. Triangle Inst., 1994-2001; mem. adv. com. alternative toxicol. methods Interagy. Ctr. Evaluation Alternative Methods, Health and Human Svcs., 1998-2001, mem. sci. adv. com. on Alternative Toxic and Logical Methods Nat. Inst. Environ. Health Scis., 2006-; mem. sci. adv. bd. strategic environ. rsch. strategies program Dept. Def./Dept. Energy/EPA, 1997-99; mem. adv. com. Ctr. for Environ. Health, Agy. for Toxic Substances and Disease Registry, CDC, 2002-04, lunar dust toxicity panel NASA, 2005—; mem. bd. sci. counselors Ctr. for Environ. Health/Agy. Toxic Substances Disease Registry, 2004-06; mem. sci. adv. com. alternative toxicol. methods Nat. Inst. Environ. Health Scis., 2006-08. Jour. Toxicology, 1984—89, assoc. dir., 1987—89; editor: Critical Revs. in Toxicology, 1987—; mem. editl bd.: Regulatory Toxicology and Pharmacology, 1993—, Risk Analysis, 1998—, Ullman's Ency. of Indsl. Chemistry, 1999—2008, Non-Linearity in Biology-Toxicology-Medicine, 2003—08; contbr. articles to profl. jours. Trustee Wash. State U. Found., 2001—; mem. bd. of vis. Wash. State Univ., Coll. Sci., 2002—; mem. dean's adv. coun. Coll. Vet. Medicine Wash. State U., 2003—, chair dean's adv. coun., 2003—05. Recipient Herbert E. Stokinger award Am. Conf. Govtl. Indsl. Hygienists, 1985, Alumni Achievement award Wash. State U., 1987, Disting. Assoc. award Dept. Energy, 1987, 88, Arnold Lehman award Soc. Toxicology, 1992, Disting. Vet. Medicine Alumnus award Wash. State U., 1999, Regents Disting. Alumnus award, 2008, N.Mex. Disting. Pub. Svc. award, 2006; co-recipient Frank R. Blood award Soc. Toxicology, 1989, Merit award Soc. Toxicology, 2005, Founders award, 2009, Disting. Pub. Svc. award N.Mex., 2006,; named Robert Leader Meml. lectr. Mich. State U., 1999, H.M. Parker Meml. lectr. H.M. Parker Found., 1999; named to Hall of Fame Robert O. Anderson Schs. of Mgmt., U. N.Mex., 2002; fellow Internat. Aerosol Rsch. Assembly, 1998. Fellow: AAAS, Acad. Toxicol. Sci., Gesellschaft fur Zerosol Forschung, Health Physics Soc. (chmn. program com. 1972, fellow 1997, Elda E. Anderson award 1974), Soc. Risk Analysis (fellow 1992), Am. Vet. Med. Assn., Am. Acad. Vet. and Comparative Toxicology; mem.: Internat. Soc. Aerosols in Medicine (Thomas Mercer Joint prize for Aerosol Rsch. 1997), Am. Assn. Aerosol Rsch. (bd. dir. 1982—94, treas. 1986—90, v.p. to pres. 1990—93, fellow 2008), Toxicology Edn. Found. (founding pres. 1990—91), Internat. Congress Toxicology VII (treas. 1995), Soc. Toxicology (chmn. 1983—85, inhalation splty. sect. v.p. to pres. 1983—86, bd. publs. 1983—86, v.p.-elect to pres. 1987—90, Amb.mid-Atlantic chpt. 1995, founding chair endowment fund bd. 2006—09), Am. Conf. Govtl. Indsl. Hygienists, Internat. Regulatory Pharmacology and Toxicology (Internat. Achievement award 1999), Am. Assn. Cancer Rsch., Am. Thoracic Soc., Radiation Rsch. Soc. (chmn. fin. com. 1979—82, sec.-treas. 1982—84), Inst. Medicine (elected mem. 1990, chair other health professions sect. 1999—2001), Am. Chem. Soc., Phi Zeta, Phi Kappa Phi, Sigma Xi. Republican. Lutheran. E-mail: roger.o.mcclellan@att.net.

MCCLELLAND, JAMES LLOYD, psychologist, educator, cognitive neuroscientist; b. Cambridge, Mass., Dec. 1, 1948; s. Walter Moore and Frances (Shaffer) McClelland; m. Heidi Marsha Feldman, May 6, 1978; children: Mollie S., Heather Ann. BA in Psychology, Columbia U., 1970; PhD in Cognitive Psychology, U. Pa., 1975. Asst. prof. dept. psychology U. California, San Diego, 1974-80, assoc. prof., 1980-84, Carnegie-Mellon U., Pitts., 1984-85, prof. psychology, 1985—2006, co-dir. Ctr. for Neural Basis of Cognition, 1994—2006, univ. prof., 2001—06, Walter Van Dyke Bingham chair in psychology and cognitive neurosci., 2002—06; prof. psychology, dir. Ctr. Mind, Brain and Computation Stanford U., Calif., 2006—, dept. chair, 2009—, Lucie Stern prof. in social scis., 2009—. Rev. panel for cognition, emotion and personality NIMH, 1983-87, Cognitive Functional Neurosci., 1995-99, chair 1997-99; mem. Nat. Adv. Mental Health Coun., 2000-2003; mem., bd. trustees Ctr. Advanced Study in Behavioral Scis., 2006-; chair, sci. adv. bd. NSF Temporal Dynamics Learning Ctr., 2007-. Author: (with others) Parallel Distributed Processing: Explorations in the Microstructure of Cognition, Vols. I, II, 1986; co-author: A Handbook of Models, Programs, and Exercises, 1988, Semantic Cognition: A Parallel-Distributed Processing Approach, 2004; contbr. numerous articles, reports, book chpts. to profl. publs.; sr. editor Cognitive Sci., 1988-91; sect. editor (Cognitive Neuroscience), Internat. Ency. of The Social and Behavioral Sciences; mem. numerous jour. edit. bds. Recipient William W. Cumming prize, Columbia U., 1970, Rsch. Scientist Career Devel. award, NIMH, 1981—86, 1987—97; co-recipient Grawemeyer prize in psychology, 2002; grantee, NSF, 1976—79, 1980—84, 1986—87, 1988—, Office Naval Rsch., 1982—87; fellow, NSF, 1970—73. Fellow: APA (Disting. Sci. Contbn. award 1996), AAAS, Am. Psychol. Soc. (William James Fellow award 2003—04); mem.: NAS, Am. Philos. Soc., Fedn. Assns. in Behavioral & Brain Scis. (pres. elect 2008—09, pres. 2010—11), Soc. Exptl. Psychologists (Warren medal 1993), Internat. Assn. for Study Attention and Performance (lectr. 1986, governing bd. 1986-94), Psychonomic Soc., Cognitive Sci. Soc. (governing bd. 1988—93, chmn. 1991, Rumelhart prize 2010), Phi Beta Kappa. Office: Stanford Univ Dept Psychology Jordan Hall Bldg 420 450 Serra Mall Stanford CA 94305-2130 Business E-Mail: mcclelland@stanford.edu. *

MCCLELLAND, ROBERT NELSON, surgeon, educator; b. Gilmer, Tex., Nov. 20, 1929; s. Robert Hilton and Verna Louise (Nelson) McC.; m. Connie Logan, May 5, 1958; children: Robert Christopher, Alison, Julie. BA, U. Tex., Austin, 1952; MD, U. Tex., Galveston, 1954. Diplomate Am. Bd. Surgery. Rotating intern U. Kans. Med. center, 1954-55; resident in gen. surgery Parkland Hosp., Dallas, 1957-59, 60-62; instr. surgery Southwestern Med. Sch., U. Tex., Dallas, 1962-63, asst. prof., 1963-67, asso. prof., 1967-71, prof., 1971—, Alvin Baldwin prof. surgery, 1977—. Examiner Nat. Bd. Med. Examiners Editor Audio Jour. Rev. Gen. Surgery, 1971-82, Selected Readings in Gen. Surgery, 1974—2005; contbr. numerous articles to profl. jours., chpts. to books. Served to capt. M.C. USAF, 1955-57. Fellow ACS (mem. grad. edn. com.); mem. AMA, Am. Surg. Assn., Western Surg. Assn., Soc. Surgery of Alimentary Tract, Am. Gastroent. Assn., Southwestern Surg. Soc., So. Surg. Assn., Dallas Soc. Gen. Surgeons (pres. 1987-88), Tex. Surg. Soc., Tex. Med. Assn., Dallas Country Med. Soc., Soc. Internatale de Chiurgie (bd. dirs. Am. chpt.), Phi Beta Kappa, Alpha Omega Alpha. Republican. Methodist. Office: 5323 Harry Hines Blvd Dallas TX 75390-7208 Home: 2848 Woodside St Dallas TX 75205

MCCLELLAND, SHEARWOOD JUNIOR, orthopaedic surgeon; s. Shearwood and Zenobia McClelland; m. Yvonne Shirley Thornton, 1974; children: Shearwood III, Kimberly. AB, Princeton U., 1969; MD, Columbia U., 1974, MPH, 1996. Diplomate Am. Bd. Orthopaedic Surgery., Nat. Bd. Med. Examiners, 1975. Intern St. Luke's Hosp., NYC, 1974—75; resident St. Luke;s Hosp., 1975—76; asst. resident in orthop. surgery N.Y. Orthop. Hosp., 1976—79; lt. comdr. USNR, 1979—82; staff orthop. surgeon Nat. Naval Med. Ctr., Bethesda, Md., 1979—82; asst. prof. surgery Uniformed Svcs. U. Health Scis., 1980—82; acting chief orthop. surgery Harlem Hosp. Ctr., 1983—84, assoc. dir. orthop. surgery, 1985—92, acting dir., 1992—94, dir., 1994—; asst. prof. clin. orthop. surgery Columbia U., 1983—94, assoc. prof. clinic, 1994—. Oral examiner Am. Bd. Othopaedic Surgery, 1993—; mem. N.Y. State Bd. of Profl. Med. Conduct, 1989-98. Annie C. Kane fellow in orthopaedic surgery, 1978-79; fellow in total joint implant surgery Ohio State U., 1982. Recipient Alumni Fedn. medal, Columbia U., 2005, P&S Gold medal, 2006, Am. Leading Dr., Black Enterprise Mag., 2001; named America's Leading Physician, 2001, 2008; fellow, Nat. Assn. Pub. Hosps., 2005. Fellow ACS, AMA, Am. Acad. Orthop. Surgeons, N.Y. Acad. Medicine, Nat. Assn. Pub. Hosps.; mem. Assn. Mil. Surgeons U.S., Am. Coll. Phys. Execs., N.Y. Orthop. Hosp. Alumni Assn., Mensa, No. N.J. Princeton Alumni Assn., Columbia P&S Alumni Assoc. (pres. 2002-04, Alumni Fedn. medal 2005), Columbia Alumni Assn. (bd. mem.), Columbia U. 1754 Soc., Princeton U. Maclean Soc. Office: Harlem Hosp Ctr Dept Orthopaedic Surgery 506 Lenox Ave New York NY 10037-1802 Office Phone: 212-939-3510. E-mail: sjm2@columbia.edu.

MCCLINTOCK, RICHARD POLSON, dermatologist; b. Lancaster, NH, Dec. 16, 1933; s. Richard P. and Dorothy Grace McClintock; m. Barbara Wyatt, June 1959 (div. Mar. 1970); children: Peter, Pamela; m. Mary Joy Fitzgerald, Mar. 21, 1970; children: Wayne, Patrick. BA, Dartmouth Coll., 1956; MD, Harvard U., 1960. Diplomate Am. Bd. Dermatology, Am. Bd. Dermatopathology. Intern in medicine U. N.C., Chapel Hill, 1960-61; resident in dermatology Stanford U., Palo Alto, Calif., 1964-67; pvt. practice Ukiah, Calif., 1967—; clin. instr. dermatology Stanford U., Palo Alto, 1967-78, clin. asst. prof., 1978-86, assoc. clin. prof., 1986-92, lectr., 1992-98, adj. assoc. clin. prof., 1998—. Mem. hosp. staff Ukiah Valley Med. Ctr., chief of staff, 1974. Contbr. articles to profl. jours. Trustee Found. for Med. Care for Mendocino and Lake Counties, 1990-2008, pres., 1992-94. Lt. Med. Corps, USN, 1961-64. Mem. San Francisco Dermatol. Soc. (Practitioner of Yr. 2004), Pacific Dermatol. Assn., Am. Acad. Dermatology, Calif. Med. Soc., Mendocino Lake County Med. Soc.(pres., 1975), Internat. Soc. Dermatopathology. Office: 723 S Dora St Ukiah CA 95482-5335 Office Phone: 707-462-1401. E-mail: fitzmac@pacific.net.

MCCLINTOCK, WILLIAM THOMAS, healthcare consultant; b. Pittsfield, Mass., Oct. 23, 1934; s. Ernest William and Helen Elizabeth (Clum) M.; m. Wendolyn Hope Eckerman, June 22, 1963; children: Anne Elizabeth, Carol Jean, Thomas Daniel. BA, St. Lawrence U., Canton, NY, 1956; MBA, U. Chgo., 1959, MHA, 1962. Prodn. planner Corning Glass, NY, 1959-60; adminstrv. resident Alameda County Med. Instns., Oakland, Calif., 1961-62; adminstrv. asst. Univ. Hosps. of Cleve., 1962-65; asst. adminstr. Presbyn. Hosp., Whittier, Calif., 1965-68; regional asst. Kaiser Found. Hosps., Oakland, 1968-70; assoc. dir., exec. dir. Conn. Hosp. Planning Commn., New Haven, 1970-75; project dir., lectr. sch. health studies U. NH, Durham, 1975-77; regional mgr. Tex. Med. Found., Austin, 1977-81; adminstr. Schick Shadel Hosp., Ft. Worth, 1981-87; mgmt. cons. George S. May Internat. Co., Park Ridge, Ill., 1987-88; mgr. Nat. Ctr. Rsch. Programs Am. Heart Assn., Dallas, 1988-89; adminstr. Ambulatory Svcs. Health Care of Tex., Ft. Worth, 1990-92; CEO Boundary Cmty. Hosp., Bonners Ferry, Idaho, 1992-2000; healthcare cons., 2000—02; exec. dir. Oceanview Convalescent Ctr., Long Beach, Wash., 2002—06, Gilroy Healthcare and Rehab. Ctr., Calif., 2006. 1st lt. US Army, 1957. Fellow Am. Coll. Health Care Execs. (life, Sr.-Level Healthcare Exec. Regent's award 2000); mem. Am. Hosp. Assn. (life), Am. Heart Assn. (bd. dirs. Idaho/Mont. affiliate 1993-95), Idaho Hosp. Assn. (bd. dirs. 1995-2000, sec.-treas. 1998, chmn. bd. dirs. 1999, Recognition of Retirement award 2000), Masons, Rotary (pres. 2010-11). Avocations: book collections, gardening, photography, fly fishing. Mailing: PO Box 1226 Bonners Ferry ID 83805 Office Phone: 208-267-2570. Personal E-mail: wtmcclintock@earthlink.net. *

MCCLOUD, MELODY T., obstetrician, gynecologist, surgeon, media consultant, health care strategist; BA, Boston U., 1977, MD, 1981. Intern Emory U. Affiliated Hosps., Atlanta, 1981-82, resident in ob-gyn., 1982-85; pres., founder, med. dir. Atlanta Women's Health Care, Coll. Women's, 1985—; founder McCloud Renaissance LLC, 2008—; health expert Tom Joyner Morning Show, 2010—. Bd. dirs. Vis. Nurses Health Sys., Atlanta; spkr. Nat. Dental Assn.-Atlanta Bus. League, 1995, Speaking of Women's Health, Universal Sisters, Nat. Coalition 100 Black Women, Congl. Black Caucus-Women, others; cons. health WXIA-TV, Atlanta, 1995, 99; owner McCloud Renaissance, LLC, pres., med. editor Nat. Orgn. African-Am. Women Author: Medical Bloopers!! Amusing, Amazing Stories, 1994, The Health Diary for Women, 1999, Blessed Health, 2003, Melodies of the Heart, 2004, Living Well, Despite Catching Hell, 2010; med. advisor Body and Soul, 1994. Med. support group Com. Olympic Games, Atlanta, 1996; chair selection com. YWCA Acad., Atlanta, 1992 Inductee Leadership Atlanta, YWCA Acad. for Women Achievers; named Bus. Woman of Yr. Am. Bus. Women's Assn., Atlanta's Top 100 Black Women of Influence Atlanta Bus. League, 2008; recipient Cmty. Health Svc. award Black Pages. Mem. Med. Assn. Ga., Ga. Ob-Gyn Soc., Med. Assn. Atlanta, Atlanta Med. Assn., Soc. Laparoendoscopic Surgeons. Baptist. Avocations: tennis, bowling, water sports, theater, travel. Office: Melody T McCloud MD PO Box 344 Roswell GA 30077-0344 Office Phone: 770-921-6038. E-mail: mtm@drmccloud.com.

MCCLUNG, JOHN ARTHUR, cardiologist; b. Oneonta, NY, Mar. 18, 1949; s. Charles Harvey and Ruth Steiner (Voegtly) McC.; m. Jane Giles, June 29, 1985; children: Daniel James, Timothy John. AB, Johns Hopkins U., 1971; MD, N.Y. Med. Coll., 1975. Diplomate Am. Bd. Internal Medicine with specialties in cardiovascular disease, critcal care medicine, Nat. Bd. Echocardiography. Instr. in clin. medicine NY Med. Coll., Valhalla, 1979-82, asst. prof. medicine, 1982-89, assoc. prof. medicine, 1989—2006, prof. medicine, 2006—, founder, divsn. clin. ethics, 1990—, dir. Inst. Human Values Med. Ethics, 1993-98, dir. cardiovascular fellowship program, 2001—; chief critical care sect. Westchester Med. Ctr., Valhalla, 1982—, asst. dir. cardiac catheterization lab., 1987—99; dir. Noninvasive Cardiology Lab., 2006—, Westchester Med. Ctr. Regional corr. Soc. Bioethics Consultants, Cleve., 1992-94; dir. cardiovasc. fellowship program NY Med. Coll., 2001—; bd. dirs. Physicians Home, 2009-. Contbr. articles to profl. jours. Fellow: Am. Heart Assn. (coun. clin. cardiology), Am. Coll. Physicians, Am. Coll. Cardiology, Am. Soc. Echocardiography; mem.: Alpha Omega Alpha (N.Y. Iota chpt.). Episcopalian. Office: Westchester Med Ctr 19 Bradhurst Ave Ste 3750 Hawthorne NY 10532-2140 Office Phone: 866-962-4327. *

MCCLUSKEY, LEO FRANCIS, neurologist, educator; b. Paterson, NJ, Nov. 9, 1954; BS, Boston Coll., 1976; MD, Columbia U., 1980. Assoc. prof. neurology U. Pa., 1986—, med. dir. ALS Ctr. Pa., 1999—. Mem.: Am. Acad. Neurology. Office: Pa Comprehensive Neurosci Ctr Philadelphia PA 19104 Office Fax: 215-829-6606. Business E-Mail: lfmcclusky@pahosp.com.

MC COIN, JOHN MACK, social worker; b. Sparta, NC, Jan. 21, 1931; s. Robert Avery and Ollie (Osborne) McC. BS, Appalachian State Tchrs. Coll., Boone, NC, 1960; MS in Social Work, Richmond Profl. Inst., Va., 1962; postgrad., U. NC, 1959—60; PhD, U. Minn., 1977. Lic. master social worker; cert. social worker, NY. Social svc. worker Broughton State Hosp., Morganton, NC, 1958-59, John Unstead State Hosp., Butner, NC, 1960-61; clin. social worker Dorothea Dix State Hosp., Raleigh, NC, 1962-63; child welfare case worker Wake County Welfare Dept., Raleigh, 1963-64; psychiat. social worker Toledo Mental Hygiene Clinic, 1964-66; sr. psychiat. social worker NY Hosp.-Cornell U. Med. Ctr. Westchester divsn., White Plains, 1966—68; social worker VA Hosp., Montrose, NY, 1968-73; also vol. mental health worker Westchester County Mental Health Assn. and Mental Health Bd., White Plains; seminar instr. Grad. Sch. Social Work U. Minn., Mpls., 1973-74; social worker F.D.R. VA Health Care Facility, Montrose, 1975-77; asst. prof. social work U. Wis., Oshkosh, 1977-79, chmn. dept. cmty. liaison com., 1978-79; assoc. prof. social work Grand Valley State Colls., Allendale, Mich., 1979-81; social worker VA Med. Ctr., Battle Creek, Mich., 1981-83, supr. social worker dept. Leavenworth, Kans., 1983-94. Cons. 44th Gen. Hosp., USAR, Menasha, Wis., 1978-79, 5540th Support Command, USAR, Grand Rapids, Mich., 1979-83; cons. in field; adj. faculty social scis. dept. Kansas City CC, 1985-89, St. Mary Coll., 1984, Kellogg CC, Battle Creek, 1981-83; adj. faculty sch. social welfare U. Kans., Lawrence, 1992; presenter in field. Author: Adult Foster Homes: Their Managers and Residents, 1983; founder (with Human Scis. Press), editor Adult Foster Care Jour., 1987-88, Adult Resdl. Care Jour., 1989-91, ind. jour., 1992-96; contbr. articles to profl. jours. With USMC, 1948-52, USMCR, 1957-72; lt. col. USAR, 1972-91. Recipient Outstanding Performance award VA, 1971, 83, Superior Performance award, 1982; grantee NIMH, 1974. Mem. NASW (social action com. West Mich. br. 1980-81), Alpha Delta Mu. Democrat. Baptist. Avocations: golf, jogging, genealogy, military history. Home and Office: 4913 Colonial Way Lawrence KS 66049-3599 Home Phone: 785-842-1386.

MCCOLLOUGH, NEWTON CLARK, III, orthopaedic surgeon; b. Butler, Pa., July 17, 1934; s. Newton C. and Margaret Elizabeth (Mattocks) McC.; m. Mary Eva Semanski, Feb. 22, 1968; children: Peter Scott, Amy Marie. BA, Duke U., 1956; MD, U. Pa., 1959. Diplomate: Am. Bd. Orthopaedic Surgery. Intern Jackson Meml. Hosp., Miami, Fla., 1959-60, resident in orthopaedic surgery, 1960-64; dir. orthopaedic resident edn. Orange Meml. Hosp., Orlando, Fla., 1965-66; asst. prof. orthopaedics and rehab. U. Miami Sch. Medicine, 1968-72, assoc. prof., 1972-76, prof., vice chmn. dept., 1976-78, prof., chmn. dept., 1978-86; dir. rehab. Jackson Meml. Hosp., Miami, 1972-82, chief orthopedics and rehab., 1978-86; dir. med. affairs Internat. Shriners Hosps. Children, Tampa, Fla., 1986-2001, 2001—, mem. med. adv. bd., 2001—09, dir. med. affairs emeritus, 2001—, med. adv. bd. mem., 2001—10. Dir. Am. Bd. for Certification in Prosthetics/Orthotics, 1974-77; mem. Health Planning Council So. Fla. Task Force on Long Term Patient Care, 1974-77; asst. med. dir. Div. of Children's Med. Services, State of Fla., 1975-86; chmn. Statewide Com. for Spinal Cord Injury, 1976-78 Trustee Jour. Bone and Joint Surgery, 1992-98, vice chmn., 1996-98; contbr. articles to med. jours. Served to lt. comdr. M.C. USNR, 1966-68. Decorated Legion of Merit. Mem. ACS, AMA, Am. Acad. Orthopaedic Surgeons (bd. dirs. 1978-79, 87-92, 2d v.p. 1987-88, 1st v.p. 1988-89, pres. 1989-90), Am. Burn Assn. (Disting. Achievement award 2001), Fla. Orthopaedic Soc. (mem. exec. com. 1978-79), Miami Orthopaedic Soc. (v.p. 1978-79), Am. Acad. Orthotists and Prosthetists (hon.), Fla. Med. Soc. Hillsborough County Med. Assn., Am. Congress Rehab. Medicine, Nat. Rehab. Assn., Scoliosos Rsch. Soc., Internat. Soc. Prosthetics and Orthotics, Am. Orthopaedic Assn., Orthopaedic Rsch. and Edn. Found. (trustee 1991-97, sec. 1995-97), Internat. Soc. Prosthetics and Orthotics (dir. 1980-83), Assn. Children's Prosthetic and Orthotic Clinics (pres. 1983-84), Rehab. Engring. Soc. N.Am. (dir. 1980-83), Am. Spinal Injury Assn., Internat. Med. Soc. Paraplegia, Pediatric Orthopaedic Soc. (dir. 1983-84, pres. 1984-85, Disting. Achievement award 2000), 20th Century Orthopaedic Assn. (treas. 1984-89), Am. Acad. Pediatrics, Phi Beta Kappa, Alpha Omega. Republican. Lutheran. Office: 602 Juan Anasco Dr Longboat Key FL 34228 Office Phone: 941-383-6146. Personal E-mail: newt3md@gmail.com.

MCCOLLUM, JEAN HUBBLE, medical technician; b. Peoria, Ill., Oct. 21, 1934; d. Claude Ambrose and Josephine Mildred (Beiter) Hubble; m. Everett Monroe Patton, Sept. 4, 1960 (div. Jan. 1969); 1 child, Linda Joanne; m. James Ward McCollum, Jan. 2, 1971; 1 child, Steven Ward. Student, Bradley U., Ill. Cen. Coll. Stenographer Caterpillar Tractor Co., Peoria, 1952-53, supr. stenographer pool, 1953-55, adminstrv. sec., treas., 1955-60, sec., asst. dept. mgr., 1969-71; med. staff sec. Proctor Cmty. Hosp., Peoria, 1978-82; med. asst. Drs. Taylor, Fox and Morgan, Peoria, 1982-84; freelance med. asst. Meth. Hosp. and numerous physicians, Peoria, 1984-89; office mgr. bus. office Dr. Danehower, McLelland and Stone, Peoria, 1989—2006. Vol. tutor Northmoor Sch., Peoria, 1974—78; bd. dirs., mem. exec. com., chmn. patient rels. com., com. chmn. Planned Parenthood, Peoria, 1990—92; judge Region 2 Ill. State History Fair, Bradley U., 2004—06. Recipient Outstanding Performance award Proctor Hosp., 1981, also various awards for svc. to schs., ch. and hosps. for mentally ill. Mem. Nat. Wildlife Fedn., Mensa Internat. (publs. officer, scholarship com., editor 1987-89, scholar com. 1993), Mothers League (treas. 1977), Willow Knolls Country Club (social com. 1989-90), Nature Conservancy (Seasons of the River event com. 2000—), World Wildlife Fund, Forest Park Found., Nat. Trust for Historic Preservation, Natural Resources Def. Coun., Religious Coalition for Reproductive Rights, USO, Am. Indian Educators Found. (hon., scholar com. 2004). Methodist. Avocations: reading, travel, theater, yoga. Home: 6501 N Brookwood Ln Peoria IL 61614-2401

MCCONNELL, BRIGHT, III, orthopaedic surgeon; b. Augusta, Ga., Mar. 3, 1953; s. Bright McConnell, Jr. and Elizabeth Custer McConnell; m. Pam Hollings, Oct. 14, 1978; children: Elizabeth Anne, Bright McConnell, IV, Ian Deryck. BS, Davidson Coll., NC, 1971—75; MD, Med. Coll. Ga., Augusta, 1975—79. Lic. orthopaedic surgeon Am. Bd. Orthopaedic Surgery, 1987, cert. clin. densitometrist Internat. Soc. Clin. Densitometry, 2001. Residency in orthopaedic surgery U. Fla., 1984; fellowship in sports medicine Kerlan-Jobe Orthopaedic Clinic & Nat. Athletic Health Inst., 1985; orthopaedic surgeon, ptnr. Orthopaedic Specialists of Charleston, SC, 1985—2002; CEO Prevecare, Charleston, 2002—05; pvt. practice Daniel Island, SC, 2005—. Bd. dir. Internat. Ctr. Birds of Prey, Awendaw, SC, 2000—. Named to Best Doctors in Am., 2006. Fellow: Am. Acad. Orthopaedic Surgery; mem.: Charleston County Med. Soc., Am. Orthopaedic Soc. Sports Medicine, Aircraft Owners & Pilots Assn. Avocations: aerobatics, fishing, flying. Home: 8863 Hwy 17N Mc Clellanville SC 29458 Office: 900 Island Park Dr Ste 105 Charleston SC 29492 Office Fax: 843-284-5201. Personal E-mail: makaira1@aol.com. Business E-Mail: drbrightmcconnell@yahoo.com, pmcconnell@charlestonsportsmed.com. *

MCCONNELL, MICHAEL V., medical educator, researcher; b. NYC; SB, MIT, 1983, SM in Elec. Engring., 1985; MD, Stanford U., 1990. Intern medicine Brigham and Women's Hosp., Boston, 1990-91, jr. asst. resident in internal medicine, 1991-92, cardiology fellow, 1992-96, assoc. physician medicine, 1996—; cardiovasc. imaging fellow Brigham and Women's Hosp., Beth Israel Hosp., Boston, 1995-96; clin. fellow in medicine Harvard Med. Sch., Boston, 1990-93, rsch. fellow in medicine, 1993-96, instr. medicine, 1996—. Tech. intern pacing rsch. divsn. Medtronic, Inc., 1982, 83; bioengring. apprentice Micro-Med, Paris, 1985. Contbr. articles to profl. jours. Recipient Undergrad. Rsch. award Uniroyal, 1981, Individual Nat. Rsch. Svc. award NHLBI, 1994, fellowship award for rsch. in cardiac imaging Bracco Diagnostics, Inc.-Soc. for Cardiac Angiography and Interventions, 1995. Mem. Am. Coll. Cardiology, Am. Heart Assn. Coun. Clin. Cardiology (student rsch. fellow 1987, clinician scientist award 1996), Internat. Soc. Magnetic Resonance Medicine, Mass. Med. Soc., Eta Kappa Nu, Sigma Xi, Tau Beta Pi. Achievements include research in magnetic resonance angiography of coronary artery disease, magnetic resonance imaging of atherosclerotic plaque. Office: Standford University School of Medicine 300 Pasteur Dr Rm J2157 Stanford CA 94305 *

MCCONNELL, WILLIAM F., JR., medical products executive; b. LaGrange, Ill. BS in sys. analysis, Miami U., Oxford, Ohio, 1971. CPA. Staff mem. Arthur Andersen LLP, Indpls., 1971—75, mgr., 1975—81, ptnr., 1981—83, mng. ptnr., bus. cons., 1983—89, re-joined, 1997; CFO Resort Condo. Internat., 1989—90, COO, 1990—96, info. officer, worldwide, 1996—97; v.p., COO Guidant Corp., Indpls., Ill., 1998—2006; sr. v.p. adminstrn. Boston Scientific Corp., Natick, Mass., 2006—. Bd. dir. Global Healthcare Exchange, Vesalius Ventures. Former chmn. Children's Mus. of Indpls., Am. Red Cross of Greater Indpls., Red Cross of Conner Prairie; former bd. mem. Acordia Personal Ins. Svcs.; hon. trustee Children's Mus. of Indpls.; bd. gov. Nat. Am. Red Cross; chmn. bd. trustee Trustee Leadership Development; bd. mem., info. tech. com. Cmty. Hosp. of Indpls., Inc., Ind. U. Info. Tech. Advancement Coun. Office: Boston Scientific Corp One Boston Scientific Pl Natick MA 01760 *

MCCORD, CLINTON D., JR., oculoplastic surgeon; b. Dec. 10, 1935; married; 2 children. BA, Emory U., Ga., 1957; MD, Emory Sch. Medicine, 1961; MS in Physiology, Emory U., Ga., 1963. Cert. Am. Bd. Ophthalmology, diplomate Am. Acad. Ophthalmology, lic. Ga. Resident, ophthalmology Emory U., Ga., 1963—66; Heed fellowship, oculoplastic Manhattan Eye and Ear Hosp., 1966—67; mem. USAF Keesler AFB (Biloxi, Miss.) & Andrews AFB (Washington, DC), 1967—69; private practice Atlanta, 1969—79; chief of staff Metropolitan Eye and Ear Hosp., 1974; prof., ophthalmology Emory U. Sch. Medicine, Ga., 1979—80, assoc. clin. prof., plastic surgery Ga., 2002—; private practice Paces Plastic Surgery, Atlanta, 1980—; clin. prof., ophthalmology Emory U., 1980—2002. Invited spkr. in field; vis. professorship at nat. universities and institutions. Contbr. chapters to books, several articles to profl. jours.; co-author: (textbooks) Optical Techniques, 1971; author: Oculoplastic Surgery, 1981, Oculoplastic Surgery, 2nd edit., 1987, Oculoplastic Surgery, 3rd edit., 1994, Eyelid Surgery, Standard and Advanced, 1996; co-author: Color Atlas of Cosmetic Oculofacial Surgery, 2004. Med. missions Interplast Mission Nicaragua (Managua)-Oculoplastica Jornada, 2003, Tanzanian Project (Moshi, Tanzania) Surgical Lectures-Surgical Demonstrations, Kilimanjari Christian Med. Ctr., 2007. Recipient Montague Boyd award, Best Physician Book award, Piedmont Hosp., Atlanta, Oculoplastic Surgery-2nd edit., 1988, Best Clin. Paper of the Yr.-Midfacial Rejuvenative Surgery, Am. Soc. Aesthetic Surgery, NYC, 1997; co-recipient Best Resident's Paper (with Hisham Seify)-Quantitating Ptosis Surgery, 2007; named one of Best Doctors in US, 1979, 1981, The Doctor's Doctors, Atlanta Mag., 1988, Top Docs, Atlanta's most trusted specialists, 2005, Outstanding Med. Specialists in the US, Town and Country Mag., 1989, Best Doctors in America, 1992, Best 200 Ophthalmologist in America, Ophthalmology Times, 1996; named to Guide to the 1,500 Best Doctors in America, Town and Country Mag., 1984, America's Top Doctors, Castle Connolly Med. Inc, 2004, NY Times Beauty Supplement Edit., Best Three Cosmetic Eyelid Surgeons in US, 2005. Fellow: ACS (program chmn. 1975); mem.: Med. Assn. Atlanta, Med. Assn. Ga., Internat. Orbital Soc., Am. Acad. Ophthalmology (Ednl. Honor award 1980), Atlanta Ophthal. Soc. (pres. 1978), Ga. Soc. Ophthamology (program chmn. 1978, coun. mem. 1983—87), Am. Soc. Ocularists (program chmn. 1978), Am. Soc. Ophthalmic Plastic Surgery and Reconstructive Surgery (program chmn. 1982, pres. 1989, chmn. adv. bd. 1990, mem. adv. bd. 1991—99, with Am. Acad. Ophthalmology, Wendell Hughes Lecture Coun. 1995—2000, Lester Jones Surgical Anatomy award, Best Clin. Presentation of Anatomy 1984), Byron Smith Study Club. Avocations: hiking, mountaineering. Office: Paces Plastic Surgery 3200 Downwood Cir Ste 640 Atlanta GA 30327 Office Phone: 404-351-0051. Office Fax: 404-351-0632.

MCCORMACK, TIFFANY DANTON, plastic surgeon; married; 2 children. BS in Psychology, Ariz. State U., 1993; MD, U. Ariz., 1997. Diplomate Am. Bd. Plastic Surgery, lic. Calif., Nev. Intern in gen. surgery Stanford Univ. Med. Ctr., 1997—98, resident in plastic and reconstructive surgery, 1998—2003; hosp. affiliations include Sequoia Hosp., Redwood, Calif., Menlo Surgical Hosp., Menlo Pk., Santa Clara Valley Med. Ctr.; resident representative Interplast; owner McCormack Plastic Surgery, Nev., plastic surgeon. Co-editor: Stanford Plastic Surgery Anthology; guest reviewer Jour. of Hand Surgery; author: various publs. Named one of 10 Most Dependable Plastic Surgeons of the West, Forbes Mag., Best Plastic Surgeons in Nev., Newsweek Mag., Best of 2010, Reno Mag., various others. Fellow: ACS; mem.: Calif. Med. Assn., Washoe County Med. Assn., Washoe County Med. Soc., Am. Soc. of Bariatric Plastic Surgeons, Am. Soc. for Aesthetic Plastic Surgery, Am. Soc. of Plastic Surgeons. Office: McCormack Plastic Surgery 10685 Professional Cir Ste B Reno NV 89521 Office Phone: 775-284-2020.

MCCORMICK, BERYL A., radiation oncologist, educator; MD, U. Medicine and Dentistry of NJ-Sch. Health Related Prof, 1973. Prof. radiation oncology Cornell Univ-Weill Coll.; attending physician NY Presbyn. Hosp./Weill Cornell; resident in therapeutic radiology Meml. Sloan Kettering Cancer Ctr., NY, 1974—77, clin. dir. Named one of Castle Connolly America's Top Doctors, 2011, Castle Connolly America's Top Doctors for Cancer, 2011, Castle Connolly Top Doctors: NY Metro Area, 2011. Mem.: Am. Soc. for Therapeutic Radiology and Oncology, Am. Soc. of Clin. Oncology. Office: Memorial Sloan-Kettering Cancer Center 1275 York Ave. New York NY 10065

MCCORMICK, CHAD DONALD, otolaryngologist; b. Sandpoint, Idaho, Apr. 19, 1972; BS, Washington State U., Pullman, 1994; MD, U. Utah, Salt Lake City, 1999. Diplomate Am. Acad. Otolaryngology, 2005. Otolaryngology head & neck surgeon Ohio State U., Columbus, 1999—2004, Ear, Nose and Throat, Coeur d'Alene, Idaho, 2004—. Mem.: Idaho Med. Assn., Am. Acad. Otolaryngic Surgery, Am. Acad. Otolaryngology Head & Neck Surgery. Cath. Avocations: fly fishing, hunting, skiing. Office: Kootenai Ear Nose Throat And Allergy 700 Ironwood Dr Ste 236 Coeur D' Alene ID 83814 Business E-Mail: cdaent@yahoo.com.

MCCORMICK, FRANK, research scientist, biology professor; BSc in Biochemistry, U. Birmingham, Eng., 1972; PhD in Biochemistry, U. Cambridge, Eng., 1975. Postdoc. fellow SUNY, Stony Brook, 1975—78, Imperial Cancer Rsch. Fund, London, 1978—81; dir. molecular biology Cetus Corp., 1981—90, v.p. rsch., 1990—91, Chiron Corp., 1991—92; founder, chief sci. officer Onyx Pharm., 1992—96; prof. dept. microbiology & immunology U. Calif., San Francisco, 1997—, David A. Wood disting. prof. tumor biology & cancer rsch., E. Dixon Heise disting. prof. oncology, dir. UCSF Cancer Rsch. Inst., 1997—2009, assoc. dean, dir. UCSF Helen Diller Family Comprehensive Cancer Ctr., 1997—. Mem. sci. adv. bd. Iconix Pharm. Contbr. articles to profl. jours. Recipient G.H.A. Clowes Meml. award, Am. Assn. Cancer Rsch., 2002, Novartis Drew award in Biomed. Rsch., 2002, Shubitz award, U. Chgo. Cancer Rsch. Ctr., 2003. Fellow: Royal Soc.; mem.: Inst. Medicine. Office: UCSF Comprehensive Rsch Ctr Box 0128 San Francisco CA 94143-0128 Office Phone: 415-502-1710. Office Fax: 415-502-1712. Business E-Mail: director@cc.ucsf.edu.

MCCORMICK, JAMES THOMAS, surgeon, researcher; s. James Nagel and Jean C McCormick; m. Tricia Kuhar McCormick, July 22, 1994; children: Marnie children: Moira, Clara. BA in Biology, Canisius Coll., Buffalo, 1992; DO, Lake Erie Coll. of Osteo. Medicine, Erie, PA, 1998. Gen. surgery resident Temple U. Sch. Medicine Clin. Campus Western Pa. Hosp., Pitts., 1998—, chief adminstrv. resident, 2003—; colorectal surgery residency U. Tex., Dallas. Curriculum com. rep. Lake Erie Coll. Osteo. Medicine, Erie, Pa., 1994—98; co-founder and coord. Bridging the Gaps/Erie Cmty. Health Internship, Pa., 1995; founder and pres. Erie Med. Student Sect. AMA, Pa., 1995; grad. med. edn. com. rep. The Western Pa. Hosp., Pitts., 1999—, resident rep. gov.'s bd., 2003—, mem. surg. exec. com., 2003—. Contbr. articles to internat. jours. in surg. scis., including Annals of Thoracic Surgery, Burns, Am. Jour. Surgery, Surg. Endoscopy, Abdominal Surgery. Recipient Laparoscopic Achievement award, Soc. for Laparoendoscopic Surgery, 2001; scholar, NY State Bd. of Regents, 1987, Pa. Osteo. Med. Assn. Found., 1996. Mem.: ACS, Am. Soc. Gen. Surgeons, Soc. Am. Gastrointestinal Endoscopic Surgeons, Am. Soc. Colon and Rectal Surgeons, Psi Sigma Alpha. Achievements include research in the use of routine chest x-ray films after chest tube removal in postoperative cardiac patients; effect of diagnosis and treatment of sinusitis in critically ill burn victims; laparoscopic revision of failed open bariatric procedures; laparoscopic management of complications following laparoscopic Roux-en-Y gastric bypass for morbid obesity; fine needle aspiration biopsy of the thyroid: an outcome study at a community hospital; management of a complex enterocutaneous fistula using cadaver skin; prospective study to determine if orocecal transit time can be used as a prognosticator of weight reduction in patients undergoing Roux-en-Y gastric bypass for morbid obesity; effect of gum chewing on bowel function and hospital stay after laproscopic and open colestomy: rectal prolapse, preoperative evaluation for colorectal cancer. Avocations: exercise, sailing. Office: West Penn Hosp Dept Surgery 4800 Friendship Ave Pittsburgh PA 15224

MCCORMICK, MARIE CLARE, pediatrician, educator; b. Winchester, Mass., Jan. 7, 1946; d. Richard John and Clare Bernadine (Keleher) McC.; m. Robert Jay Blendon, Dec. 30, 1977. BA magna cum laude, Emmanuel Coll., 1967, LHD (hon.), 2006; MD, Johns Hopkins U., 1971, ScD, 1978; MA, Harvard U., 1991; D of Humane Letters (hon.), Emmanuel Coll., Boston, 2006. Diplomate Am. Bd. Pediat. Pediatric resident, fellow Johns Hopkins Hosp., Balt., 1971-75, rsch. fellow, 1972-75; asst. prof. U. Ill. Schs. Medicine & Pub. Health, Chgo., 1975-76; pediat. instr. Johns Hopkins Med. Sch., Balt., 1976-78; asst. prof. healthcare orgn. Johns Hopkins Sch. Hygiene & Pub. Health, 1978-81; asst. prof. pediat. U. Pa., Phila., 1981-86, assoc. prof. pediat., 1986-87, Harvard Med. Sch., Boston, 1987-91, prof. pediat., 1992—, 1st Sumner and Esther Feldberg prof. maternal/child health, 1996—; prof. Harvard Sch. Pub. Health, Boston, 1992—2003, chair maternal and child health, 1992—2003, prof. Soc., Human Devel. and Health, 2003—. Adj. assoc. prof. pediat. U. Pa., 1987-92; active attending physician, Johns Hopkins Hosp., 1976-81, asst. physician Children's Hosp. Phila., 1981-84, assoc. physician, 1984-86, sr. physician, 1986-87, assoc. pediatrician Brigham & Women's Hosp., 1987—; sr. assoc. in medicine Children's Hosp., 1987—; sr. assoc. in pediat. Beth Israel Deaconess Med. Ctr., 1987—; vis. prof. Wash. U., St. Louis, 1993; editl. bds. Health Svcs. Rsch., 1985-94, Pediat. in Rev., 1986-91, Pediat., 1993-99; assoc. editor Jour. Academic Pediatric Assn., 1999—; adv. coun. Ctr. Perinatal & Family Health Brigham & Women's Hosp., 1991—; cons. to numerous coms., orgns. and bds. Contbr. articles to profl. jours. Adv. The David and Lucile Packard Found., 1993-95; bd. dirs. Family Planning Coun. S.E. Pa., 1984-87; chair com. child health Mayor's Commn. Phila., 1982-83. Recipient Johns Hopkins U. Soc. Scholars award, 1995, award, Nat. Assn. of Nat. Acads., 2001, David Rall award, Inst. Medicine, 2005, Knisely Lecture award, U. Pa., 2008; named Henry Strong Denison scholar, Johns Hopkins Sch. Medicine, 1971, Leonard Davis Inst.; Health Econs. fellow, U. Pa., 1984. Fellow Am. Acad. Pediat.; mem. AAAS, Inst. Medicine of NAS, Academic Pediat. Assn. (Rsch. award 1996), Soc. Pediatric Rsch. (sr., Douglas K. Richardson award 2006), Am. Pediatric Soc., Am. Pub. Health Assn., Internat. Epidemiol. Assn., Assn. Health Svcs. Rsch., Ea. Soc. Pediatric Rsch., Soc. Pediatric Epidemiologic Rsch., Assn. Tchrs. Maternal and Child Health, Mass. Med. Soc., Mass. Med. Soc.(Henry Bowditch Pub. Health award, 2008), Norfolk Dist. Med. Soc., Mass. Pub. Health Assn., Johns Hopkins U. Soc. Scholars, Nat. Vaccine Adv. Com., Vaccine Safety Working Group (co-chair 2009-), HINI Vaccine Safety Risk Assessment Working Group (chair 2009-), Maternal, Infant and Early Childhood Home Vis. Program Evaluation (mem. sec.'s adv. com.). Office: Harvard Sch Pub Health 677 Huntington Ave Boston MA 02115-6096 Business E-Mail: mmccormi@hsph.harvard.edu.

MCCORMICK, WAYNE C., geriatrician, educator; b. St Louis, Mo., Aug. 21, 1952; m. Elizabeth C. White, May 22, 1983. MD., Wash. U., 1983. Diplomate Am. Bd. Internal Medicine, 1986, Am. Bd. Internal Medicine-public health & general preventive medicine, 1992, Am. Bd. Internal Medicine-geriatric medicine, 2002. Intern Michael Reese Hosp., 1984, resident internal medicine, 1984—87; fellow in geriatric medicine Univ. Wash. Med. Ctr., 1987—90, hosp. affiliations include, Evergreen Hosp. Med. Ctr., Harborview Med. Ctr., VA Puget Sound Health Care Sys., Va. Mason Med. Ctr.; asst. prof. medicine Univ. Wash. Office: Harborview Medical Center 325 9th Ave Seattle WA 98104-2499 Office Phone: 206-744-3300.

MCCOY, SHERILYN S. (SHERI MCCOY), pharmaceutical executive; b. Quincy, Mass., 1958; married; 3 children. BS in Textile Chemistry, U. Mass., Dartmouth, 1980; MChemE, Princeton U., NJ, 1982; MBA, Rutgers U., NJ, 1988. Various positions of increasing responsibility from assoc scientist to v.p. Johnson & Johnson, New Brunswick, NJ, 1982—96, v.p. R&D, 1996—2000, v.p. mktg. skin care franchise, 2000—02, global pres. baby & wound care franchises, 2002—05, company group chmn., franchise chmn. med. devices & diagnostic products Latin America, 2005—08, worldwide chmn. surg. care group., 2008—09, mem. exec. com., 2008—, worldwide chmn. pharmaceuticals divsn., 2009—11, vice chair exec. com., 2011—. V.p. Montgomery Twp. Edn. Found., NJ; mem. Rutgers U. Pres.'s Bus. Leaders Cabinet; bd. dirs. For Inspiration & Recognition of Sci. & Tech. (FIRST). Named one of The 50 Most Powerful Women in Bus., Fortune mag., 2008, 2009, 2010, The World's 100 Most Powerful Women, Forbes mag., 2009. Office: Johnson & Johnson 1 Johnson & Johnson Plz New Brunswick NJ 08933 *

MCCOY, SUE, retired surgeon, biochemist, bioethicist; b. Charlottesville, Va., Nov. 14, 1935; d. Hulburt Christopher and Evelyn (Savage) McC. AB, Radcliffe Coll., 1957; PhD, Johns Hopkins U., 1964; MD, U. Va., 1980, postgrad., 2001—. Diplomate Am. Bd. Surgery. Fellow in physiol. chemistry Johns Hopkins U., Balt., 1964-67; asst. prof. chemistry U. South Fla., Tampa, 1967-69; asst. prof. orthopedics U. Va., Charlottesville, 1969-73, asst. prof. surgery, 1973-78; resident in surgery Hosp. U. Pa., Phila., 1980-83; resident in surgery Cooper Hosp. Rutgers U. Med. Sch., Camden, N.J., 1983-85, asst. prof. surgery, 1985-86, East Tenn. State U., Johnson City, 1986-91, assoc. prof., 1991-2000, prof., 2000—01; ret., 2001. Fellow: ACS; mem.: Assn. for Women Surgeons, Southeastern Surg. Congress, Shock Soc., Assn. for Acad. Surgery, Royal Soc. Chemistry, N.Y. Acad. Sci., Am. Chem. Soc., Sigma Xi. Achievements include research in hemorrhagic shock, aging, oxygen transport. Home: 8658 Batesville Rd Afton VA 22920

MCCRACKEN, JAMES T., child and adolescent psychiatrist, educator; MD, Baylor Coll. Medicine, 1980. Resident psychiatry Duke Univ. Med. Ctr., Durham, 1981—84; fellow child & adolescent psychiatry UCLA Neuropsychiatric Inst., 1984—85; prin. investigator NIMH Rsch. Ctr.; faculty UCLA, 1987; Joseph Campbell prof. child psychiatry UCLA NPI-Semel Inst. (formerly Neuropsychiatric Inst.), dir. divsn. child and adolescent psychiatry. Editl. bd. Jour. Child and Adolescent Psychopharmacology. Recipient several honors and awards; named one of Best Doctors in America. Mem.: Soc. Neuroscience, Internat. Soc. Psychoneuroendocrinology, Internat. Soc. Rsch. Child and Adolescent Psychopathology, Am. Acad. Child and Adolescent Psychiatry, APA, Am. Psychiatric Assn. (Young Psychiatrist Rsch. award). Office: University of CAlifornia Los Angeles Medical Center 760 Westwood Plz Los Angeles CA 90024 Office Phone: 310-825-0470. Business E-Mail: jmccracken@mednet.ucla.edu.

MCCRADY, BARBARA SACHS, psychologist, educator; b. Evanston, Ill., May 7, 1949; d. James Frederick and Margaret Maxine (Miller) Sachs; m. Dennis D. McCrady, June 13, 1969; 1 child, Eric Paul. BS, Purdue U., 1969; PhD, U. R.I., 1975. Lic. clin. psychologist. Clin. project evaluator Butler Hosp., Providence, 1974-75, chief psychol. assessment program, 1975-76, chief problem drinkers' project, 1976-83; assoc. prof. psychology Rutgers U., Piscataway, NJ, 1983-89, prof. psychology, 1989-2000, prof. II, 2000—07. From instr. to assoc. prof. psychiatry Brown U., Providence, 1975—83; reviewer Nat. Inst. on Alcohol Abuse and Alcoholism, Washington, 1979—82, extramural sci. adv. bd., 1989—93; cons. Inst. Medicine, Washington, 1988—89; acting dir. Rutgers Ctr. Alcohol Studies, Piscataway, 1990—92, dir. clin. tng. dept. psychology, 1993—2005, chair dept. psychology, 2005—07; dir. Ctr. on Alcoholism, Substance Abuse, and Addictions U. N. Mex., Albuquerque, 2007—, prof. dept. psychol., 2007—, disting. prof. psychology, 2008—. Author: The Alcoholic Marriage, 1977; editor: Marriage and Marital Therapy, 1978, Directions in Alcohol Abuse Treatment Research, 1985, Research on Alcoholics Anonymous: Opportunities and Alternatives, 1993, Addictions: A Comprehensive Guidebook, 1999, Overcoming Alcohol Problems: A Couples-Focused Program, 2009. Grantee Nat. Inst. on Alcohol Abuse and Alcoholism, 1979-83, 1988—. Fellow Am. Psychol. Assn. (past pres. divsn. addictions); mem. Assn. for Advancement Behavior Therapy, Rsch. Soc. on Alcoholism (bd. dirs., 1999-2003). Avocations: horseback riding, piano. Office: Univ N Mex CASAA 2560 Yale Blvd SE MSCII 6280 Albuquerque NM 87106 Home Phone: 505-856-1161; Office Phone: 505-925-2388. Business E-Mail: bmccrady@unm.edu. *

MCCRAVEN, EVA STEWART MAPES, health service administrator; b. LA, Sept. 26, 1936; d. Paul Melvin and Wilma Zech (Ziegler) Stewart; m. Carl Clarke McCraven, Mar. 18, 1978; children: David Anthony, Lawrence James, Maria Lynn Mapes. ABS magna cum laude, Calif. State U., Northridge, 1974; MS, Cambridge Grad. Sch. Psycholoy, 1987, PhD, 1991. Dir. spl. projects Pacoima Meml. Hosp., 1969—71, dir. health edn., 1971—74; asst. exec. dir., v.p. Hillview Cmty. Mental Health Ctr., Lakeview Terrace, Calif., 1974—99, exec. dir., 1999—2004, CEO and pres., 2004—. Past dir. dept. consultation and edn. Hillview Ctr., developer, mgr. long-term residential program, 1986-90; former program mgr. crisis residential program, transititional residential program and day treatment program for mentally ill offenders, past dir. mentally ill offenders svcs.; former program dir. Valley Homeless Shelter Mental Health Counseling Program; dir. Integrated Svcs. Agy., Hillview Mental Health Ctr., Inc., 1993-98, dir. clin. programs, 1996-99, exec. dir. 1999—; mem., steering com., prevention and each intervation manpat death, Svc. Act Planning, LA County Svc. Area, 2009; mem. at large, bd. dir., Calif. Coun. Cmty. Mental Death Agys. Former pres. San Fernando Valley Coordinating Coun. Area Assn., Sunland-Jujunga Coordinating Coun.; bd. advisors Pacoima Sr. Citizens Multi-Purpose Ctr.; bd. dirs. N.E. Valley Health Corp., 1970-73, Golden Gate Cmty. Mental Health Ctr., 1970-73 Recipient Resolution of Commendation State of Calif., 1988, Commendation award, 1988, Spl. Mayor's plaque, 1988, Cmty. Svcs. Commendation awards City of L.A., 1989, County of Los Angeles, 1989, Calif. Assembly, 1989, Calif. Senate, 1989, award Sunland-Tujunga Police Support Coun., 1989 Mem. Health Svcs. Adminstrn. Alumni Assn. (past v.p.), Sunland-Jujunga Bus. and Profl. Women (Women of Achievement award 1990), LWV, Valley Philharm. Soc Office: Hillview Cmty Mental Health Ctr 11500 Eldridge Ave Lake View Terrace CA 91342-6523 Office Phone: 818-896-1161 ext. 211. Business E-Mail: esm@hillviewmhc.org, lmecraven@hillviewmhc.org, esmecraven@hillviewmhc.org.

MCCREDIE, JANET, retired medical educator; b. Sydney, Mar. 14, 1935; d. Harold Andrew McCredie and Marjorie Clare Dalgarno. MBBS, U. Sydney, 1959, MD, 1979. Staff radiologist Royal Prince Alfred Hosp., Sydney, 1965—75, vis. radiologist, 1975—2000; sr. lectr. surgery U. Sydney, 1975—80, assoc. prof. radiology, 1980—90, chair coun. Womens Coll., 1993—98, 2002—05, hon. fellow, 2007. Author: (book) Beyond Thalidomide- Birth Defects Explained, 2007; contbr. articles to profl. jours. Grantee, Australian Govt., 1974—. Fellow: Royal Australian and New Zealand Coll. Radiologists. Achievements include discovery of site and mode of action of Thalidomide; neuropathic birth defects; birth defects due to neural crest injury. Avocations: travel, music, art, theater, gardening. Home: 2A/27 Sutherland Crescent Darling Point 2027 Sydney NSW Australia Personal E-mail: janetmccredie@ozemail.com.au.

MCCRYSTAL, ANN MARIE, community health nurse, administrator; b. Jersey City, Jan. 5, 1937; d. Robert W. and Sybilla M. (Koenig) Bouse; m. Hugh K. McCrystal, Sept. 14, 1963; children: Carolyn, Hugh K., Kelly Ann. BSN, U. Miami, 1959. Chmn. bd. Vis. Nurse Assn. of the Treasure Coast, Vero Beach; nurse Task Force Indian River Med. Ctr., Adv, Bd. Indian River Med. Ctr. Found., Indian River Med, Ctr. Cancer Svcs. Task Force. Chmn. Vis. Nurse Assn. Treasure Coast Found., 1991, adv. coun. Vis. Nurse Assn. of Am., 1994; chmn. bd. dirs. Vis. Nurse Assn./Hospice Found. Named Indian River County Woman of Distinction, Girl Scouts Am., 1998, Vol. Fundraiser of Yr., Treasure Coast Nat. Soc. Fundraising Execs., 1999, Book of Golden Deeds award Exch. Club Vero Beach, 2000; recipient C. of C. Cmty. Svc. award, 2000, Nat. award for Cmty. Svc., Nat. Soc. Colonial Dames VXII Cadbury, 2005, Dan Richardson Humantarian award, Gifford Youth Activities Ctr., 2010. Mem. Fla. Nurses Assn. (Dist. 17 Nurse of Yr. 2004), Am. Urol. Assn. Allied, Am. Cancer Soc. (life hon.), Vis. Nurse Assn. Am. (chmn. bd. dirs. 1995—, adv. coun., edn. com., Vol. of Yr. 1991), Sigma Theta Tau. Home: 511 Bay Dr Vero Beach FL 32963-2163 Personal E-mail: ammccrystal@yahoo.com.

MCCUISTION, PEG OREM, retired health facility administrator; b. Houston, July 28, 1930; d. William Darby and Dorothy Mildred (Beckett) Orem; m. Palmer Day McCuistion, Sept. 4, 1949 (div. 1960); 1 child, Leeanne E. BBA, Southwest Tex. State, 1963; MBA, George Washington U., 1968; EdD, Wayne State U., 1989. Patient care adminstr. Holy Cross Hosp., Silver Spring, Md., 1968-79; exec. dir. Hospice of S.E. Mich., Southfield, 1979-86, Hospice Austin, Tex., 1987-94; CEO EMBI, Inc., Arlington, Tex., 1994—98; gen. mgr. Hospice Home Care, San Antonio, 2001—04, ret., 2004. Bd. dirs. Cmty. Home for the Elderly, Austin, 1989-92. Fellow Am. Coll. Health Care Execs. (membership com.); mem. Internat. Hospice Inst. (assoc.), Nat. Hospice Orgn. (chair standards and accreditation com.), Tex. Hospice Orgn. (pres. 1993-94), exec. com., standards and ethics com., edn. com., chair legis. com.), Mich. Hospice Orgn. (chair edn. com., bd. dirs.). Personal E-mail: pegomc@txwinet.com.

MCCUISTION, ROBERT WILEY, hospital administrator, management consultant, lawyer; b. Wilson, Ark., June 15, 1927; s. Ed Talmadge and Ruth Wiley (Bassett) McC.; m. Martha Virginia Golden, June 11, 1949 (dec. Nov. 1991); children: Beth, Dan, Jed.; m. Sudola M. Getz, Feb. 12, 1994. AB in History, Hendrix Coll., Conway, Ark., 1949; JD, U. Ark., 1952. Bar: Ark. 1952, U.S. Dist. Ct. (we. dist.) Ark. 1953. Practice in, Dermott, Ark., 1952-57; dep. pros. atty. 10th Jud. Dist. Ark., 1952-57; bus. mgr. St. Mary's Hosp., Dermott, 1953-56, asst. adminstr., 1956-57; adminstr. Stuttgart (Ark.) Meml. Hosp., 1957-60, Forrest Meml. Hosp., Forrest City, Ark., 1960-68; assoc. adminstr. St. Edward Mercy Hosp., Ft. Smith, Ark., 1968-70; pres. Meml. Med Center, Corpus Christi, Tex., 1970-79; adminstr. Methodist Hosp., Mitchell, SD, 1979-85, cons., 1985-86; mgmt. cons., owner Creative Leadership Concepts, Arlington, Tex., 1985—, adminstr. Cen. United Meth. Ch., Fayetteville, 1986-91. Sec. Ark. Hosp. Adminstrs. Forum, 1958-59, pres., 1959-60; pres. Ark. Hosp. Assn., 1964-65, Areawide Health Planning, 1970; pres. Ark. Conf. Cath. Hosps., 1970; chmn. Twin City Hosp. Coun. West Ark., 1968; v.p. Ark. Assn. Mental Health, 1966-70. Feature writer, make up editor, editor Wiesbaden Post, Germany, 1946—47; editor: Air Force Publ. Div. chmn. Forrest City United Cmty. Svcs., 1961, Corpus Christi United Way Cmty. Svcs., 1972, DeSoto coun. Boy Scouts Am., Explorer advisor, 1954-57; vice-chmn., sec. ofcl. bd. Meth. Ch., 1957, lay del. S.D. ann. conf., 1980-85, cert. lay spkr., 1960—, Stephen minister, 1995-; trustee Midwest Hosp. Conf., Kansas City, Mo., 1964-1966. With USAAF, World War II. Recipient Eminent Leadership award DeSoto Area council Boy Scouts Am., 1956 Mem. Am. Assn. Hosp. Accts. (pres. Ark. chpt. 1957), S.D. Hosp. Assn. (dist. chmn. 1980-81), Am. Coll. Health Execs. (life), Rotary (pres. Forrest City 1964-65, Internat. Order of St. Luke (grief counselor, Stephen min.). Home and Office: 2401 St Gregory St Arlington TX 76013 Home Phone: 817-275-8378. Personal E-mail: sudobobm@tx.rr.net.

MCCULLOCH, MARTI, health science association administrator; b. Rock Springs, Wyo., June 6, 1970; BSc, U. Houston, Clearlake, 2004; MBA, U. St. Thomas, Houston, 2008. Chief cardiac sonographer U. Tex. Med., Galveston, 1995—2001; sr. rsch. coord. Baylor Coll. Medicine, 2002—03; mgr., echocardiography & electrocardiography Meth. Hosp., 2003—05, dir., cardiac & vascular imaging, 2005—08, dir., Meth. Debakey heart & vascular ctr., 2008—. Adv. bd. dirs. Alvin CC, Diagnostic Cardiovasc. Sonography, 1998—2011; editl. bd. mem. Cardiac Ultrasound Today, 2000—11. Fellow: Am. Soc. Echocardiography (editl. bd. mem. 2002—05, chair, sonogrpher coun. bd. 2009—11, sec., exec. bd. dirs. 2011—, Cardiovasc. Sonographer Disting. Tchr. Award); mem.: Am. Inst. Ultrasound Medicine, Greater Houston Soc. Echocardiography, Am. Coll. Healthcare Execs., Soc. Diagnostic Med. Sonographers. Avocations: writing, tennis, skiing, rollerblading. Office: 6565 Fannin F9-093 Houston TX 77030 Office Fax: 713-793-7798.

MCCULLOCH-COX, ANNA MARY KNOTT, pharmacy technician; b. Riverdale, Md., Aug. 29, 1964; d. Samuel Eugene and Jean M. (Schildt) Knott; m. Richard Sears McCulloch, Nov. 6, 1988 (dec. 2004); children: John Austen II, Anna Rebecca; m. Michael L. Cox, June 18, 2005. Student, W.Va. U., 1982-84; cert., Children's Inst. Lit., 1987. Cert. nat. med. asst. AAMA. Pharmacy technician Montgomery Gen. Hosp., Olney, Md., 1981-92; med. asst., sec. Dr. Arthur Lomant, Eldersburg, Md., 1986-87; pharmacy technician Frederick (Md.) Meml. Hosp., 1991-95. With Clin. Lab Aid, Frederick CC Med. Asst. Program, 2011—. Mem. Assn. Pharmacy Technicians, Stringband Am., Inc. (v.p. Eldersburg chpt. 1989-90), Md. State Soc. Chpt., Am. Assn. Med. Assts. Roman Catholic. Avocation: teaching music. Home: PO Box 54 Sabillasville MD 21780-0054 E-mail: mccullochanna@hotmail.com.

MCCULLOUGH, DAVID LEGARDE, urologist; b. Chattanooga, 1938; MD, Bowman Gray, 1964. Intern U. Hosps. Case Western Res. U., Cleve., 1964-65, resident in surgery, 1965-66; fellow urology Baylor U. Coll. Medicine, Houston, 1968-69; resident in urology Mass. Gen. Hosp., Boston, 1969-72; chief urologist N.C. Bapt. Hosp., Winston-Salem, 1983—; prof., former chmn. urology Wake Forest U. Coll. Medicine, Winston-Salem. Past pres. Am. Bd. Urology. Mem. ACS, AMA, Am. Urol. Assn. (past pres. southeastern sect., past pres., bd. dirs., chair for edn.), Am. Assn. Genitourinary Surgeons (past pres.), Clin. Soc. Urol. Surgeons, Halsted Soc. Office Phone: 336-217-9242. Business E-Mail: dmcullough@allianceurology.com.

MCCULLOUGH, ROBERT DALE, II, osteopath; b. Tulsa, June 2, 1937; s. Robert Dale and Roberta Maud (Purdy) McC.; m. Lindell Arlene Wilcox, Sept. 28, 1963(dec. Jan. 08, 2010); children: Robert Mark, Lori Lindell. Student, Wheaton Coll., Ill., 1955-57; BS, N.E. Mo. State U., 1958; DO, Kans. City Coll. Osteopathy, Mo., 1958-62. Diplomate in internal medicine and med. oncology Am. Osteo. Bd. Internal Medicine. Gen. practice McCullough Clinic, Tulsa, 1963-68; internal medicine resident Detroit Osteo. Hosp., 1968-71; internal medicine Baker-Todd-McCullough-Sutton, Tulsa, 1971-74; fellow med. oncology M.D. Anderson Hosp., Houston, 1974-75; internal medicine-med. oncology Baker-Todd-McCullough-Sutton, Tulsa, 1975-90; pvt. practice Tulsa, 1990-93; attending staff mem. VA Outpatient Clinic, Tulsa, 1993-94; assoc. med. dir. Blue Cross/Blue Shield of Okla., Tulsa, 1994—2005. Trustee Tulsa Regional Med. Cttr., 1983-88, 90-93; bd. dirs. Okla. Blue Cross Blue Shield, Tulsa, 1983-92, vice chmn., 1991-92; mem. adv. coun. Okla. State U. Coll. Osteo. Medicine, 1988-94, chmn., 1988-90; part-time worker VA and Indian Health Svc. Mem. bd. editors Patient Care Magazine, Montvale, N.J., 1988-93. Mem. Okla. State Bd. Health, Oklahoma City, 1983—87, Tulsa City/County Bd. Health, 1988—95, chmn., 1993; bd. mem. Cmty. Health Found., 1997—, chmn., 2003—05. Mem. Nat. Osteo. Found. (trustee 1993-00, treas. 1998-00), Am. Osteo. Assn. (vice speaker Ho. of Dels. 1986-92, trustee 1993-00), Am. Coll. Osteo. Internists, Okla. Osteo. Assn. (pres. 1982-83), Tulsa Downtown Lions Club, Soc. for Preservation and Encouragement of Barbershop Quartet Singing in Am. Republican. Southern Baptist. Avocation: barbershop quartets. Home: 5803 E 75th Pl Tulsa OK 74136-7255 Home Phone: 918-481-8725. Personal E-mail: RMccull207@aol.com.

MCCURDY, HARRY WARD, otolaryngologist; b. Branchton, Pa., Aug. 15, 1918; s. Adam Oscar and Sarah Fern (Hindman) McC.; m. Joan Jacqueline Talty, Dec. 10, 1955; children: Bridget Elizabeth, Peter Adam. AB, Allegheny Coll., 1940; MD, U. Pa., 1943. Diplomate Am. Bd. Otolaryngology. Intern Geisinger Meml. Hosp., Danville, Pa., 1944, resident in otolaryngology, 1944-45, 48-49; resident in pathology Hamot Hosp., Erie, Pa., 1945-48; mem. staff Geisinger Med. Center, Danville, 1948-50; commd. 2d lt. U.S. Army, 1945, advanced through grades to col., 1962-74; mil. cons. Surgeon Gen., U.S. Army, 1964-74; ret., 1974; exec. v.p. Am. Acad. Otolaryngology-Head and Neck Surgery, Washington, 1974-84; mem. staff Walter Reed Army Hosp. Resources coun. Gallaudet Coll., 1975-80; nat. adv. coun. Sertoma Found., 1976-84; chmn. FDA Panel on Otolaryngologic Med. Devices, 1974-78, cons., 1978-84 Mem. ACS, AMA, Royal Soc. Medicine (U.K.), Am. Acad. Otolaryngology, Mil. Surgeons Assn., Am. Soc. Assn. Execs., Soc. Med. Consultants to Armed Forces, AAAS, Am. Soc. Facial Plastic Surgery, Soc. Mil. Otolaryngologists, Am. Acad. Facial Plastic and Reconstructive Surgery, Am. Laryngol., Rhinol. and Otol. Soc., Anglo-Am. Med. Soc., Am. Audiology Soc., Royal Soc. Health, Osler Med. Soc., Acad. Medicine, Soc. Univ. Otolaryngologists, Am. Council Otolaryngology, Pan-Am. Soc. Bronchoesophagology., Internat. Fedn. Otolaryngol. Socs. (sec. gen. 1981—), Soc. Mil. Cons. to Armed Forces (sec. 1993—). Clubs: Army Navy, Press, Mil. Attaches of London, Les Chevaliers du Tastevin. Republican. Methodist. Home and Office: 6006 Dellwood Pl Bethesda MD 20817-3812

MCCURDY, LAYTON, medical educator; b. Florence, SC, Aug. 20, 1935; m. Gwendolyn A. McCurdy, 1958; children: Robert Jr., David Barclay. BS, U. NC, 1956; MD, Med. U. SC, 1960. Resident in psychiatry NC Meml. Hosp., Chapel Hill, 1961—64; with psychiatry tng. br. NIMH, Bethesda, Md., 1964—66; asst. prof. dept. psychiatry Sch. Medicine Emory U., Atlanta, 1966—68; prof., chmn. dept. psychiatry and behavioral scis. Med. U. SC, 1968—82, v.p. med. affairs, dean, 1990—2001, dean emeritus, disting. prof., 2001—; prof. psychiatry Sch. Medicine U. Pa., Phila., 1982—90; psychiatrist-in-chief Inst. of Pa. Hosp., Phila., 1982—90. Vis. colleague Inst. Psychiatry, U. London, 1974—75; nat. adv. mental health coun. NIMH, 1980—83; apptd. Pa. Adv. Com. for Mental Health and Mental Retardation, 1984—87. Recipient Disting. Alumnus award, Med. U. SC, 1988, Earl B. Higgins Diversity Achievement award, 1999, Disting. Alumnus award, George C. Ham. Soc., 1990, Humanatati award, La Soc. Francaise, 2002. Fellow: Am. Coll. Psychiatrists (pres. 1993—94, Bowis award 1997); mem.: Am. Bd. Psychiatry and Neurology (pres. 1993), Assn. Academic Psychiatry (pres. 1970—71), SC Commn. on Higher Edn. (chmn. 2005—), Royal Coll. Psychiatrists (UK), Am. Psychiat. Assn. (joint commn. pub. affairs 1981—84, chmn. com. on diagnosis and assessment 1988—94), Cosmos Club. Office: Med Univ SC Inst Psychiatry PO Box 250861 Charleston SC 29425 Home Phone: 843-723-1186; Office Phone: 843-792-2084. Business E-Mail: mccurdy@musc.edu.

MCDANIEL, DAVID HENRY, physician; b. Clarksburg, W.Va., May 12, 1952; s. Hubert Harold and Ada Virginia (Henry) McD.; m. Sheila Marie Travis, Sept. 17, 1994. BS in Chemistry cum laude, W.Va. U., Morgantown, 1974, MD, 1978. Diplomate Am. Bd. Dermatology, 1983. Emergency physician Monongalia Gen. Hosp., Morgantown, 1979—82; dir. McDaniel Lasu & Cosmestic Ctr., Va. Beach, 1982—; asst. prof., clin. dermatology Eastern Va. Med. Sch., Norfolk, 1991—, asst. prof., clin. plastic surgery, 1992—2010; command cons., dept. plastic surgery Naval Med. Ctr., Portsmouth, Va., 1994—2005; dir., rsch. and innovation Light BioSci. LLC, 2002—09. Adj. asst. prof., dept. biol. scis. Old Dominion U., 2001-; pres. The Ctr. for Disfigurement, Virginia Beach, 1993-, McDaniel Inst. Anti Aging Rsch., Va. Beach, 1995-; co-dir. Skin Color Rsch. Inst. Hampton U., 2008-; adj. prof., sch. sci., 2008-. Contbr. numerous articles to sci. jours. Named one of Best Drs. in America, 1994—2011. Fellow Am. Acad. Dermatology, Am. Soc. Laser Medicine and Surgery, Am. Soc. Dermatologic Surgery (com. practice mktg. and pub. rels. 1993-96, chair 1996); mem. Tidewater Dermatology Soc. (pres. 1987-88), Space Dermatology Found. (founding), Va. Space Bus. Roundtable (charter), Phi Lambda Upsilon. Avocations: nature and wildlife photography, bicycling, gardening, hiking, church and charitable activities. Office: Laser & Cosmetic Ctr 125 Market St Virginia Beach VA 23462 Office Phone: 757-437-8900. Business E-Mail: mail@lsvcv.com.

MCDANIEL, REUBEN ROOSERVELT, healthcare educator; b. Petersburg, Va., 1936; BS, Drexel U., 1962; EdD, Ind. U., 1971. Dir. ednl. svcs. Baldwin Wallace Coll., 1964—69; Charles and Elizabeth Prothro regents chair health care mgmt. U. Tex., Austin, 1972—. Recipient Heman Sweatt Legacy award, U. Tex. Austin, Civitatus award, Myron Fottler Svc. award, Acad. Mgmt. Avocation: singing. Home: 3910 Knollwood Dr Austin TX 78731 Business E-Mail: reuben.mcdaniel@mccombs.utexas.edu.

MCDANIELS, AUDREY EVELYN, retired microbiologist; b. Grants Pass, Oreg., Feb. 11, 1928; d. Charles Pixley and Ruby Clark Best; divorced; 1 child, David Douglas. BS in Microbiology, Oreg. State U., 1950; BS in Edn., U. Wash., 1964; MS in Gen. Scis., Oreg. State U., 1965; PhD in Environ. Sci., U. Mich., 1980. Jr. scientist GE, Hanford, Wash., 1950-53; microbiologist City of Seattle, 1954-57, Wash. State Pub. Health, Seattle, 1957-60; 4th grade tchr. Amity (Oreg.) Elem., 1965-68; biology tchr. Rainier (Oreg.) H.S., 1968-72; microbiologist EPA, Cin., 1980—2008. Home: 1029 Fashion Ave Cincinnati OH 45238 Personal E-mail: scam952@aol.com.

MCDERMOTT, JAMES ADELBERT, United States Representative from Washington, psychiatrist; b. Chgo., Dec. 28, 1936; m. Therese Hansen; 2 children. BS, Wheaton Coll., Ill., 1958; MD, U. Ill. Med. Sch., Chgo., 1963. Intern Buffalo Gen. Hosp., 1963-64; resident adult psychiatry U. Ill. Hospitals, Chgo., 1964-66; resident child psychiatry U. Wash. Hospitals, 1966-68; asst. clin. prof. dept. psychiatry U. Wash., Seattle, 1970-83; mem. Dist. 43 Wash. State House of Reps., 1971-72, Wash. State Senate, 1975-87, chmn. ways and means com., 1983—87; regional med. officer US Fgn. Svc., Kinshasa, Zaire, 1987-88; mem. US Congress from 7th Wash. dist., 1989—. Cons. divsn. juvenile rehabilitation Wash. State Dept. Social & Health Services, 1972—79; cons. Wash. State Dept. Labor & Industries, 1972—83; chief psychiatrist Seattle/King County Jail, 1978. Mem. Wash. State Arts Commn., Wash. Coun. Prevention Child Abuse & Neglect. Lt. comdr. Med. Corps USN, 1968—70. Mem.: King County Med. Soc., Wash. State Med. Assn., Am. Psychiat. Assn. Democrat. Episcopalian. Office: US House Reps 1035 Longworth House Office Bldg Washington DC 20515 also: 1809 7th Ave Ste 1212 Seattle WA 98101 Office Phone: 202-225-3106. *

MC DERMOTT, JOHN FRANCIS, psychiatrist, physician; b. Hartford, Conn., Dec. 12, 1929; s. John Francis and Camilla R. (Cavanaugh) McD.; m. Sarah N. Schemm, Dec. 27, 1958; children: Elizabeth C., John Francis III. AB, Cornell U., 1951; MD, N.Y. Med. Coll., 1955. Diplomate in psychiatry and child psychiatry Am. Bd. Psychiatry and Neurology. Intern Henry Ford Hosp., Detroit, 1955-56; resident in psychiatry U. Mich. Med. Center, 1956-58, resident in child psychiatry, 1960-62; practice medicine, specializing in psychiatry and child and adolescent psychiatry Honolulu, 1969-95; instr., asst. prof., asso. prof. psychiatry U. Mich. Sch. Medicine, 1962-69; prof., chmn. dept. psychiatry U. Hawaii Sch. Medicine, 1969-95, prof. emeritus, 1995—; scholar-in-residence Rockefeller Found. Study Ctr., Bellagio, Italy, 1985, 92. Chmn. com. cert. in child psychiatry Am. Bd. Psychiatry and Neurology, 1974-78, bd. dirs., 1983-91, chmn. R&D com., 1985-91; sr. vis. scientist dept. exptl. psychology Oxford (Eng.) U., 1993; sr. vis. fellow Inst. Criminology Cambridge U., Eng., 1998, 2000; vis. prof. numerous univs.; cons. in field. Author: Psychiatry for the Pediatrician, 1970, Childhood Psychopathology, 1972, Mental Health Education in New Medical Schools, 1973, Roles and Functions of Child Psychiatrists, 1976, Psychiatric Treatment of the Child, 1977, New Directions in Childhood Psychopathology, vol. I, 1980, vol. II, 1982, Raising Cain (and Abel Too), 1980: People and Cultures of Hawaii, 1980, Culture Mind and Therapy: An Introduction to Cultural Psychiatry, 1982, Japanese edit., 1984, The Complete Book on Sibling Rivalry, 1987, German edit., 1991, People and Cultures of Hawaii: The Evolution of Culture and Ethnicity, 2011; editor Jour. Am. Acad. Child and Adolescent Psychiatry, 1987-97; contbr. over 150 articles to profl. jours.; mem. editorial bds. numerous psychiat. jours. Served with USN, 1958-60. Named Disting. Alumnus N.Y. Med. Coll., 1976. Fellow Cambridge Univ. Clare Hall (Eng.) (life), Am. Psychiat. Assn. (disting. life, Agnes Purcell McGavin award 1998), Am. Orthopsychiat. Assn. (life), Am. Acad. Child and Adolescent Psychiatry (life)(Jeanne Spurlock award and Lectr. for Culture and Diversity, 2008), Am. Coll. Psychiatrists, World Psychiat. Assn. (chmn. child and adolescent psychiatry 1977-89), Benjamin Rush Soc. (sec.-treas. 2000-02, v.p. 2002-04, pres. 2004-06), Cosmos Club, Outrigger Canoe Club.

MCDERMOTT, MARGARET, hospital administrator; m. Michael McDermott. BS in Biochemistry, U. Ill.; MBA in Fin. and Ops., De Paul U. Dir. and materials mgmt. Mercy Hosp. (Sisters of Mercy), Chgo.; asst. v.p. instl. svcs. Northwestern Meml. Hosp., Chgo.; divsn. dir. McNeal Hosp., Berwyn, Ill.; COO and v.p. ops. St. Joseph Hospital (Ascension Healthcare), Chgo.; COO Catholic Health Ptnrs. (St. Joseph and Columbus Hosps.), Chgo.; exec. v.p. and CEO St. Elizabeth Hosp./Resurrection Healthcare; CEO Sts. Mary and Elizabeth Med. Ctr., 2003—. Marillac House/St. Vincent DePaul Ctr. chairperson and bd. trustees, Chgo.; mem. Big Shoulders Program, Chgo. Mem.: Horizon Hospice, Cook County Bur. of Health Svcs., Met. Chgo. Healthcare Coun. (chairperson, CAPES (Clin., Adminstrv., Profl. and Emergency Svcs.) com.), Ill. Hosp. Assn. Office: Saints Mary and Elizabeth Medical Center Saint Mary Campus 2233 W Division St Chicago IL 60622 Office Phone: 312-770-2000.

MCDERMOTT, MARY ANN, nursing educator; b. La Junta, Colo., June 23, 1938; d. George O. and Alice Agnes (Nohelty) Kelley; m. Dennis J. McDermott; children: Dennis, Michael, Sarah, William. BSN, Loyola U., 1960, MSN, 1969; EdD, No. Ill. U., 1980. RN, Ill. Staff nurse Evanston (Ill.) Vis. Nurse Assn., 1960-63, St. Francis Hosp., Sch. Nursing, Evanston, 1963-67; nurse, tchr. Head Start, Chgo. Bd. Edn., 1967-68; faculty mem. Niehoff Sch. Nursing Loyola U., Chgo., 1969—2004, prof. emeritus, 2004—06, dir., Ctr. Faith and Mission, 1998—2002, assoc. dir., Ctr. Faculty Profl. Devel., 2006—, faculty liaison Evoke project, 2006—; pres., nursing and humanities Hecktoen Inst. Medicine, Chgo. Bd. dirs. Park Ridge Ctr. Study Health, Faith and Ethics; adv. coun. Chgo. Dept. Aging, 1995—99; prin. Quality Life Tng., 2002—. Co-editor: Parish Nursing: The Developing Practice, 1990, Parish Nursing: Promoting Whole Person Health Within Faith Communities, 1998, Parish Nursing: Development, Education, Preparation and Administration, 2005. Adv. bd. St. Scholastica Acad., Chgo., 1996-2005; adv. coun. Chgo. Schweizer Urban Fellows, 1996-99; chair Civic Affairs com. U. Club. Chgo., 2001-03; bd. dir. Loyola Gen. Hosp., Park Ridge, 1985-95, chair 1994-95; bd. dir. Adv. Health Care, Oak Brook, Ill., 1995-2003, chair, 1998-2000. Recipient Ill. Nurse Leader/Power of Nursing award, 2002. Fellow: Am. Acad. Nursing; mem.: ANA, Health Ministries Assn. (adv. bd. 1989—99), Ill. Nurses Assn., Am. Hosp. Assn. (nominating com. 1995—97). Democrat. Roman Catholic. Office: Loyola U Sch Nursing Damen Hall 6525 N Sheridan Rd Chicago IL 60626-5344 Office Phone: 773-508-2904. Personal E-mail: maryannmcdermott@msn.com. Business E-Mail: mmcderm@luc.edu.

MCDERMOTT, PATRICIA ANN, nursing administrator; b. Bklyn., July 10, 1943; d. John J. and Lillian J. (Sweeney) Skelly; m. Joseph Kevin McDermott, Oct. 5, 1963; children: Colleen Mary, John Joseph. Diploma, Kings County Hosp Sch. Nursing, Bklyn., 1963; BS in Health Care Adminstrn., St. Francis Coll., Bklyn., 1979. Staff nurse Kings County Hosp., Bklyn., 1963-66, head nurse outpatient dept., 1966-74; evening supr. Park Nursing Home, Rockaway Park, N.Y., 1974-83; day supr. Hyde Park Nursing Home, Staatsburg, NY, 1984-85, DON, 1985—96, Victory Lake Nursing Ctr., Hyde Park, N.Y., 1996-97. NY State evaluator for nurses aides, 1988—2009; PRI assessor; MDS coord. Active local Girl Scouts U.S.A., 1971-78, Boy Scouts Am., 1978-82, Stella Maris Parents Club, 1978-82, St. Francis de Sales Altar and Rosary Soc., 1970-83; active St. Francis de Sales Little League, 1978-80, also softball coach, 1974-77; elected tax collector Town of Clinton, N.Y., 1999—, GOP com. mem.; dance com. chair St. Peter's, Hyde Park, N.Y., 1998-2002. Dutchess County Salute to Women honoree, 1997. Mem.: Town of Clinton Ladies Rep. Club, Town of Clinton Hist. Soc. Home: 184 Shadblow Ln Clinton Corners NY 12514-2834 Home Phone: 845-266-3592.

MCDERMOTT, RAYMOND, JR., physician; b. Chgo., Apr. 20, 1924; s. Raymond A. and Helen (Furlong) M.; m. Audrey H. Bergt, Feb., 1995; children: Kathy, Mary Anne, Raymond III, Thomas, Laura, Sharon, Jean, Michael, Trish. MD, Loyola U., 1947. Bd. cert. Obstertrics and Gynocology. Assoc. attending Cook County Hosp., Chgo., 1954-61; asst. prof. obgyn. Northwestern U. Med. Sch., Chgo., 1958—; med. reviewer Healthcare Compare, Oakbrook, Ill., 1978-88, CIMRO, Champaign, Ill., 1988—2003; med. dir. Wellmark (Health Network), Oakbrook, 1992—2002. Staff pres. Grant Hosp. Chgo., 1976-78, staff v.p., 1974-76. Lt. U.S. Navy, 1941-53. Avocation: sailing. Home: 3950 W Bryn Mawr Ave Chicago IL 60659-3156 Office Phone: 312-346-6330. *

MCDONAGH, THOMAS JOSEPH, physician; b. NYC, Feb. 29, 1932; s. John and Delia (Lee) McD.; m. Helen Marie Drury, May 18, 1957; children: Kevin T., Eileen D., Thomas J., Brian P., Patricia M. BS, CCNY; MD, Columbia U. Diplomate Am. Bd. Internal Medicine, Am. Bd. Preventive Medicine-Occupational Medicine. Intern Bronx Mcpl. Hosp., NYC, 1957-58, resident, 1958-60; fellow in medicine, trainee in gastroenterology Albert Einstein Coll. Medicine, Bronx, 1960-62; pvt. practice internal medicine Coatesville, Pa., 1962-64; sr. physician Exxon Corp., NYC, 1964-69, asst. med. dir., 1969-79; dir. medicine and environ. health Exxon Chem. Co., Darien, Conn., 1979-80, dir. medicine and environ. affairs, 1980-81; v.p. medicine and occupational health Exxon Corp., Dallas, 1981-97; dir. medicine and environ. health Exxon Co. Internat., Florham Park, NJ, 1983-97; bd. dirs. Nat. Assn. Drug Abuse Problems, NYC, 1981-92. Bd. dirs. Nat. Fund Med. Edn., San Francisco, 1983-95. Contbr. articles to med. jours. Chmn. bd. appeals Inc. Village of Bellerose, N.Y., 1977-84, trustee, 1965-77, dep. mayor, 1975-77. Fellow ACP, Am. Coll. Occupational and Environ. Medicine (bd. dirs. 1989-92); mem. AMA. Roman Catholic.

MCDONALD, CAPERS WALTER, biomedical engineer, manufacturing executive, entrepreneur, educator; b. Georgetown, SC, Nov. 29, 1951; s. WalBern and Cecilia (Lockwood) McD.; m. Marion Elizabeth Kiper, Aug. 23, 1975; 1 child, Adam Capers. BS in Engring. magna cum laude, Duke U., 1974; MS in Mech. Engring., MIT, 1976; MBA, Harvard Bus. Sch., 1983. Dir. mktg. Becton Dickinson Co., Sunnyvale, Calif., 1978-81; cons. Booz, Allen & Hamilton, San Francisco, 1982-84; v.p. Siegen Corp., Mountain View, Calif., 1984, HP Genenchem, South San Francisco, Calif., 1984-87; bio-analytic systems mgr. Hewlett-Packard Corp., Palo Alto, Calif., 1986—87; v.p. Orion Instruments, Inc., Redwood City, Calif., 1987-89, Spectroscopy Imaging Systems Corp., Fremont, Calif., 1989-90, pres., bd. dirs., 1991—92; pres., CEO, bd. dirs. BioReliance Corp., Rockville, Md., 1992—2004; pres., CEO Magenta Corp., Rockville, 1993—2000; chmn., dir. Magenta Svcs., Ltd., Stirling, Scotland, 1994-2000; dir. BioReliance Holdings GmbH, Heidelberg, Germany, 1996—2004, Q-One Biotech Group Ltd., Glasgow, Scotland, 2003—04; exec. in residence, faculty mem. Johns Hopkins U., 2004—. Bd. dirs. Expion, Inc., Olney, Md.; bd. visitors U. Md. Biotech Inst., 1996-00, Duke U. Sch. Engring., 2001-10, chmn. edn. and student affairs com., 2005-09; bd. advisors Md. Partnership for Workforce Quality, 1996-98, Washington Bus. Jour., 2003-05; vice chmn. High Tech. Coun. Md., 1998-01; chmn. Tech. Coun. Md., 2001-04; mem. industry adv. bd. Chesapeake Bay Area chpt. ISPE, 1998-2000; mem. mfg. extension partnership nat. adv. bd. US Dept. Commerce, 2007-10, mem. MBA exec. bd., Carey Bus. Sch. Johns Hopkins U., 2007-09; lectr. in field. Contbr. chpts. to books; patentee flow microfluorometer; contbr. articles to profl. jours. Asst. scoutmaster Boy Scouts Am., Georgetown, SC, 1965-66; trustee Bethesda Acad. Performing Arts, 1998-01; mem. oversight bd. advanced tech. consortium Montgomery Coll., 1998-01; mem. steering com. Biotech. Industry Orgn., 2003 Ann. Meeting, 2002-03; mem. econ. adv. coun. Montgomery County, 1998-05; mem. founding exec. bd. Greater Washington Regional Partnership, 1998-01; mem. leadership coun. Treatment and Learning Ctrs., 1998-2000; with Capstone Co., Johns Hopkins U., 2003-04; mem. Md. Advanced Tech. Bus. Devel. Commn., 2003; state planning com. for postsecondary edn. Md. Higher Edn. Commn., 2004; chmn. Md. Adv. Tech. del. to Peoples Republic China, 2004; chmn. Eagle Career Day, Greater Washington, 2002-03. Angier B. Duke Scholar, Duke U., 1970-74, MIT scholar, 1974-76; hon. fellow NSF, 1974; recipient Leadership in Tech. award Md. High Tech. Coun., 1996, Employer of Yr. award Md. Pvt. Industry Coun., 1996, Region's Most Admired Bosses award Washington Techway Mag., 2000, Good Scout award Nat. Capital Area Coun., 2000, Nat. Disting. Eagle Scout award Boy Scouts Am., 2001, Export award Scottish Coun. Devel. and Industry, 2001, Stevie award Am. Bus. Awards, 2003, Disting. Alumnus award Pratt Sch. Engring., Duke U., 2005, Endowed Ann. award, Excellence in Mentoring and Advising, 2005; named Greater Washington Entrepreneur of Yr. in Life Scis., 2002. Mem. AAAS, ASME, Acad. Mgmt., Biomed. Engring. Soc., NC Acad. Sci., Md. C. of C. (bd. dirs. 1996-00), Soc. Cin. (endowment com., 2008-09, lib. com. 2008-, comm. com., vice chmn., 2010-, mem. standing com. Md. Soc., 2010-), Order Founders and Patriots Am. (SC soc. founding sec. 2007-10, gov., 2010-, founding editor SC Clarion 2010-), St. Andrews Soc. of Washington, Order Magna Charta (Nat. Surety, 2010-), First Families SC, Hugnenot Soc. SC, Gen. Soc. Colonial Wars, Soc. Sons Am. Revolution, Harvard U. Alumni Assn., Duke U. Alumni Assn., MIT Alumni Assn., Johns Hopkins Club, Iron Dukes, Congl. Country Club, Sigma Xi, Tau Beta Pi (chpt. pres. 1973-74, nat. fin. devel. com. 2007-10), Phi Eta Sigma, Pi Mu Epsilon. Methodist. Avocations: fishing, travel. Office: Johns Hopkins Univ 9601 Med Ctr Dr Rockville MD 20850 Business E-Mail: capersmcd@jhu.edu.

MC DONALD, CHARLES J., dermatologist, educator; b. Tampa, Fla., Dec. 6, 1931; s. George B. and Bertha C. (Harbin) McDonald; m. Maureen McDonald; children: Marc S. McDonald, Norman D. McDonald, Eric S. McDonald. BS magna cum laude, A and T Coll., NC, 1951; MS, U. Mich., 1952; MD with highest honors, Howard U., Washington, DC, 1960. Diplomate Am. Bd. Dermatology. Rotating intern Hosp. St. Raphael, New Haven, 1960-61, asst. resident in medicine, 1961-63; asst. resident, dermatology Yale U., 1963-65, spl. USPHS rsch. fellow, chief resident dermatology, 1965-66, instr. medicine, pharmacology, 1966-67, asst. prof. medicine, pharmacology, 1967-68; asst. prof. med. sci. Brown U., Providence, 1968-69, assoc. prof., 1969-74, prof., 1974—, dir. dermatology program, 1970-74, head subsect. dermatology, 1974-82, dir. divsn. dermatology, 1982—96, chair dept. dermatology, 1996—; dir. dermatology Roger Williams Gen. Hosp., 1968-97; physician in chief, dept. dermatology RI Hosp., 1989—. Mem. com., task force, chmn. task force minority affairs Am. Acad. Dermatology, 1975—80; mem. dermatology adv. panel Fed. Drug Adminstrn., 1975—78, cons., 1978—; chmn. com. pub. edn., dir., v.p. RI divsn. Am. Cancer Soc., 1978—83, bd. dir. nat. soc., 1983—90, nat. dir. at large, 1990—95, mem. nat. exec. com., 1991—99, nat. officer, 1995—2001, pres. elect, 1997—98, pres., 1998—99; mem. pharm. scis. rev. commn. NIH, 1979—83; mem. residency rev. com. dermatology ACGME, 1992—97, mem. bd. accreditation appeals dermatology, 1999—; vice chmn. RRC dermatology, 1996—97; mem. adv. com. Arthritis, Muscular, Skeletal, Skin Disease Inst., NIH, 1993—95. Editor: Post Grad. Med. Jour., 1970—85; mem. editl. bd.: Jour. of Am. Acad. Dermatology, 1981—86; contbr. numerous articles to med. publs. Bd. trustees Citizens Bank of RI, 1975—97, chair cmty. reinvestment com., 1991—97; trustee Howard U., 1993—, chair health affairs com., 1994—98, mem. exec. com., 1994—98; chair adv. bd. Howard U. Cancer Ctr., 2005—; chair bd. advisors Sch. Medicine, 1998—2005; founding mem., bd. dirs. Providence Health Care Found., 1968—76, chmn. mem. adv. com., 1976—87; bd. dirs. Providence Fund for Edn., 1986—90; mem. bd. dirs. Providence Pub. Libr., 1971—2000, sec., 1977—2000; bd. dirs. R.I. Cancer Coun., 1999—2001; mem. bd. dirs. Lifespan Hosp. Consortium, RI, 2001—; mem. R.I. State Bd. Edn., 1970—72. Maj. USAF, 1952—56. Recipient Disting. Svc. award, Hosp. Assn., RI, 1971, Disting. Alumni award, Howard U. Coll. Medicine, 1983, St. George medal, Nat. Divsn. award, Am. Cancer Soc., 1992, WW Keen award, Brown Med. Alumni, 2002, Candle award, Morehouse Coll., 2005, Disting. Alumni award for medicine and cmty. affairs, Howard U., 2005, Cmty. Svc. and Medicine award, RI Black Heritage Soc., 2005. Mem.: Assn. Profs. Dermatology (bd. dirs. 1991—94), Dermatology Found. (chmn. sci. com. 1972—76), New Eng. Dermatology Soc., Am. Soc. Clin. Oncology, Nat. Med. Assn. (chmn. sect. dermatology 1973—75), Am. Acad. Dermatology (bd. dirs. 1987—91), Am. Fedn. Clin. Rsch., Soc. Investigative Dermatology, Noah Worcester Dermatol. Assn. (bd. dirs. 1983—86), RI Dermatol. Assn., Am. Cancer Soc. New Eng. (Lifetime Achievement award 2007), New Eng. Dermatol. Soc. (v.p. 1983—84, pres. 1984—85), Am. Dermatol. Assn. (bd. dirs. 1995—2000, pres elect 2002, pres. 2003—04), AAAS, Am. Acad. Derm (hon.), Beta Kappa Chi, Alpha Kappa Mu, Alpha Omega Alpha, Sigma Xi. Democrat. Office: RI Hosp Dept Dermatology 593 Eddy St Providence RI 02903-4971 Office Phone: 401-444-7137. Business E-Mail: cmcdonald@lifespan.org, charles_mcdonald@brown.edu.

MCDONALD, CRAYDON DEAN, psychologist; b. Denver, Dec. 22, 1946; s. Donald D. and Irene (Dunlavy) McDonald; children: Ian, Brendan, Tavis, Morgynne. BFA, Parsons Sch. Design, NYC, 1970; MDiv cum laude, St. Paul Sch. Theology, Kansas City, Mo., 1979; D of Ministry, Wesley Theol. Sem., Washington, 1982; PhD, Boston U., 1987. Diplomate Am. Bd. Profl. Psychology, lic. psychologist Mass., Wis., Ill., Ariz., approved supr. Am. Assn. Marriage and Family Therapy; ordained to ministry United Meth. Ch., 1982. Psychologist Worcester (Mass.) Pastoral Counseling Ctr., 1982-87; chief psychologist Dr. McDonald & Assocs., Inc., 1982—; assoc. prof., asst. program dir. Loyola U., Chgo., 1987-88; clin. psychologist Lake Geneva, Wis., 1987-93; psychology faculty No. Ariz. U., 1993—2007. Examiner Am. Bd. Profl. Psychology. Author: Personality and Cognitive Theology, 1982, Type A Coronary Prone Behavior and Narcissism, 1987. Fellow: Acad. Family Psychology; mem.: APA (mem. program com. divsn. 43), Am. Assn. Pastoral Counselors, Human Factors Soc. Democrat. Home and Office: 1105 E Fern Dr N Phoenix AZ 85014-3244 Office Phone: 602-234-4719.

MCDONALD, DOUGLAS JOEL, orthopedic surgeon, educator; b. Thief River Falls, Minn., Aug. 4, 1956; BS in Biology, St. John's U., Collegeville, Minn., 1978; MD, U. Minn., Mpls., 1982; MS in Orthop. Surgery, Mayo Grad. Sch. Medicine, Rochester, Minn. Cert. Am. Bd. Orthop. Surgery, 1990. Resident orthop. surgery Mayo Grad. Sch. Medicine, 1987, fellow orthop. oncology, 1987; fellow orthop. surgery Istituto Ortopedico Rizzoli Universita Di Bologna, Italy, 1988; prof., vice chmn., residency program dir. dept. orthop. surgery St. Louis U.; prof. orthop. surgery Washington U., St. Louis, chief orthop. oncology. Contbr. articles to med. jours., chapters to books. Named one of Am.'s Top Drs., Castle Connolly Med. Ltd., 2005—08. Fellow: Am. Acad. Orthop. Surgeons; mem.: Internat. Soc. Limb Salvage, Internat. Skeletal Soc., Mid-Am. Orthop. Assn., Musculoskeletal Tumor Soc., Am. Orthop. Assn., Acad. Orthop. Soc. Office: Washington U Sch Medicine Dept Orthop Surgery Campus Box 8233 660 S Euclid Ave Saint Louis MO 63110 Office Phone: 314-747-2563. E-mail: mcdonaldd@wustl.edu.

MCDONALD, H. RICHARD, ophthalmologist, educator; b. NYC, Apr. 24, 1954; BA, Stanford U., 1976; MD, U. of Calif. LA, 1980. Pres. West Coast Retina Med. Group, 1985—. Clin. prof., ophthalmology Calif. Pacific Med. Ctr., 2005—, dir., vitreoretinal fellowship program, 2005—; dir. San Francisco Retina Found., 2007—. Mem.: San Francisco Med. Soc., Am. Acad. Ophthalmology, Am. Soc. Retina Specialists, Retina Soc., Macula Soc. Avocation: golf. Office: 185 Berry St #130 San Francisco CA 94107 Office Fax: 415-975-0999. Business E-Mail: hrmcdonald@westcoastretina.com.

MCDONALD, JOSEPH VALENTINE, neurosurgeon; b. NYC, June 7, 1925; m. Carolyn Alice Patricia Petersen, Apr. 30, 1955; 5 children. AB, Coll. Holy Cross, 1946; MD, U. Pitts., 1949. Intern St. Vincent's Hosp., NYC, 1949-50; rsch. fellow neuroanatomy Vanderbilt U., 1950-51; gen. surgery asst. resident Cushing VA Hosp., Boston, 1951-52; neurology extern Lenox Hill Hosp., 1952; asst. resident neurosurgery Johns Hopkins Hosp., 1953-55, resident neurosurgeon, 1955-56; practice medicine specializing in neurol. surgery Rochester, NY, 1956—; emeritus prof. neurosurgery U. Rochester Med. Sch. Mem. Soc. Neurol. Surgeons, A.C.S., Am. Assn. Neurol. Surgeons, Congress Neurosurgeons. Home: 800 Allens Creek Rd Rochester NY 14618-3412

MCDONALD, KATHRYN MACK, health facility administrator; b. Evanston, Ill., Feb. 12, 1962; BS, Stanford U., 1984; MM, Northwestern U., 1992, MBA. Sr. rsch. scholar, exec. dir. Stanford Health Policy, 1998—. Past pres. Soc. Med. Decision Making, 2008—. Office: 117 Encina Commons Stanford CA 94305-6019 Business E-Mail: kathy.mcdonald@stanford.edu.

MCDONALD, L. CLIFFORD, epidemiologist; Epidemiologist CDC Divsn. Healthcare Quality Promotion. Office: 1600 Clifton Rd Atlanta GA 30333 Office Phone: 404-639-3311.

MCDONALD, ROBERT ALAN (BOB MCDONALD), consumer products company executive; b. Gary, Ind., June 20, 1953; s. Ray Wellington and Froso (Manolios) McD.; m. Diane Janine Murphy, Dec. 31, 1977; children: Jennifer Elizabeth, Robert Wade. BS in Engring., U.S. Mil. Acad., 1975; MBA, U. Utah, 1978. Asst. Solo brand Procter & Gamble Co., Cin., 1980-81, asst. mgr. Dawn brand, 1981-82, asst. mgr. Cascade brand, 1982-83, mgr. Cascade brand, 1983-84, mgr. Tide brand, 1984—86, assoc. advt. mgr., 1986—89, mgr. laundry prod. P&G Canada, 1989—91, gen. mgr. P&G Far East, 1991—94, v.p., gen. mgr. P&G Far East, 1994—96, regional v.p. Japan, P&G Asia, 1996—99, v.p. NE Asia, 1999, pres. NE Asia, 1999—2001, pres. global fabric care & home care, 2001—04, vice chmn. global ops., 2004—07, COO, 2007—09, pres., CEO, 2009, chmn., pres., CEO, 2010—. Instr. economics, Meth. Coll., Golden Gate U., Campbell U., Fayetteville, N.C., 1979-80; bd. dirs. Xerox Corp., 2005-, The Procter & Gamble Co., 2009-. Deacon Knox Presbyn. Ch., Cin., 1982-85, Mt. Washington Presbyn. Ch., Cin., 1986; mem. bd. vis. Fuqua Sch. Bus., Duke Univ.; mem. bd. adv. Northwestern Integrated Mktg. Communications. Advanced through grades to capt. US Army, 1975—80. Fellow Royal Soc. of Arts of London (Silver medal 1975); mem. Phi Kappa Phi, Beta Gamma Sigma, Commonwealth Club. Republican. Avocations: reading, running, painting. Office: Procter & Gamble 1 Procter And Gamble Plz Cincinnati OH 45202-3393 Mailing: Procter & Gamble PO Box 599 Cincinnati OH 45201-0599 Office Phone: 513-983-1100. Office Fax: 513-983-4381. Business E-Mail: mcdonald.r@pg.com. *

MCDONALD, THERESA BEATRICE PIERCE (MRS. OLLIE MCDONALD), church official, minister; b. Vicksburg, Miss., Apr. 11, 1929; d. Leonard C. Pierce and Ernestine Morris Templeton Pierce; m. Ollie McDonald, Apr. 23, 1966. Student, Tougaloo Coll., 1946-47, U. Chgo. Indsl. Rels. Ctr., 1963-64; BA in Sociology with deptl. honors, Roosevelt U., 1997; student, Chgo. Theol. Sem., 1997—. Ordained to Gospel Ministry, 1997. Vol. rep. Liberty Bapt. Ch., Am. Legion Aux., VA West Side Hosp., Chgo., 1971-73; nat. instr. ushers dept. Prog. Nat. Bapt. Conv. Inc., Washington, 1973-75, nat. sec. ushers dept., 1975-76, v.p. at large, 1980-82, chmn. pers. com., 1982-84; mem. faculty Congress of Christian Edn., 1978-85; mem. pub. rels. staff Liberty Bapt. Ch., Chgo., 1973-79, trustee, 1987-91; asst. Christian edn. dir. Maryland Ave. Bapt. Ch., Chgo., 1995-99; assoc. min. Md. Ave. Bapt. Ch., Chgo., 1997—; Tchr. Tng. Instr., 1998, 2000; dir. Christian edn. Md. Ave. Bapt. Ch., Chgo., 2000—02. Cons., lectr. in field; Sunday ch. sch. tchr.; bible class instr.; guest speaker TV and radio programs. Participant White House Regional Confs., 1961. Recipient Christian Svc. award Prog. Nat. Bapt. Conv. Inc., 1986, 92, 94, Disting. Svc. award, 1990-94, Dedicated Svc. award, 1998. Mem. VFW (life mem. Hunt aux. 2024), Bethlehem Bapt. Dist. Assn. Chgo. (asst. sec. 1982-84), Ch. Women United in Greater Chgo. (Ecumenical Actions com. 1981-83), Am. Legion (Outstanding Svc. award 1972, 73), Bapt. State Conv. Ill. (life), Order Ea. Star. Address: 9810 S Calumet Ave Chicago IL 60628-1432

MCDONALD, THOMAS LEE, medical educator; b. Milford, Iowa, Oct. 29, 1943; BS, SD State U., 1966; MS, Wash. State U., PhD, 1973. Prof. U. Nebr. Med. Ctr., 1980—. Recipient Excelence in Tchg. award, UNMC. Avocation: gardening. Office: 986495 Nebraska Med Ctr Omaha NE 68198-6495 Business E-Mail: tmcdonal@unmc.edu.

MCDONALD, TRACEY THERESE ANNE, nursing educator; d. James Nicholas Burton and Pearl Elizabeth Toole; children: Iain Patrick Crawford, Duncan John. Diploma in Nurse Edn., Cumberland Coll. Health Sci., Sydney, 1976; B in Health Adminstrn., U. NSW, Kingsford, 1988; MS with honor, U. Wollongong, NSW, Australia, 1994, PhD, 2003. Cert. in nursing, in Nursing Prince Henry Hosp., St Vincent's Hosp., 1969, in gen. nursing, NSW Registration Bd., 1969; Midwifery NSW Registration Bd., 1983. Nurse educator St Vincent's Hosp., Sydney, 1974—78; educator, sr. educator Prince Henry Hosp., 1978—80, continuing edn. coord., 1980—82, cmty. liaison, discharge planner, 1983—84, asst. don, 1984—85; cons. - policy and practice Various Svc. and Govt. Depts., Sydney, Canberra, 1987—89; lectr. U. Wollongong, 1993—95, sr. lectr., 1990—95, 1997—99; head, sch., nursing Monash U., Melbourne, Australia, 1995—97; mgr., profl. svcs. NSW Nurses' Assn., Sydney, 1999—2003; mgr., rsch., policy, profl. svcs. Australian Nursing Homes Extended Care Assn. NSW, Sydney, 2003—05; prof. Chair Ageing, Australian Cath. U., Sydney, 2005—. Inaugural pres. Cmty. Liaison and Discharge Planners Assn., Sydney, 1984—85; listed mem. Nursing Tribunal Standards Com., Nurse Registration Bd. NSW, Sydney, 1998—; pres. Australian Nurse Teachers' Soc., Sydney, 1993—95; dir. Health Industry Group Tng. Bd., Sydney, 2000—03, Welfare Rights Bd., Sydney, 2000—03; chair Cmty. Svcs. and Health Industry Tng. Adv. Bd. NSW, Sydney, 2000—02; rep. Nat. Aged Care Alliance, Canberra, Australia, 2003—, Aged Care Funding Instrument Industry Reference Group and Tech. Reference Groups, Canberra, 2003—; world expert group social policy ageing UN, NYC, 2008; editor, rev. Internat. Jour. Nursing and Health Scis., Yamaguchi, Ube, Japan, 2007—, Internat. Jour. Care Svcs. Mgmt., London, 2009—; world expert group rights older persons UN, NYC, 2009; chair, faculty health, wellness ageing Royal Coll. Nursing Australia, Canberra, 2009—; advisor Dem. Nurses South Africa (DENOSA), Durban, South Africa, 2009—. Justice peace Atty. General's Office, Sydney, 1999—; with 45th Patricia Chonley Orator, 2011; chair Cmty. Services and Health Industry Tng. Bd. NSW, Cmty. Services and Health Industry Tng. Adv. Bd. NSW, Sydney, 2000—02; dir. Health Industry Group Tng. Adv. Bd. NSW, Sydney, 2000—03, Welfare Rights Bd. NSW, Sydney, 2000—03; listed mem. Australian Nursing & Midwifery Accreditation Coun., Sydney, 1998—, assessor, 2011. Recipient Notable Achievement ERT award, U. Wollongong, 1990, Vice Chancellor's award, 1991, Ethyo Hayton Trophy Outstanding Contbn. award, 1994; named Nurse of the Yr., NSW and Australian Capital Ter., Lions Found., 1977. Fellow: Coll. Nursing NSW, Royal Coll. Nursing Australia; mem.: Aged Care Standards and Accreditation Agy. (Australia) (judge, quality panel 2005—10), World Alliance Patient Safety, World Health Organisation, UN Network Ageing, Winston Churchill Meml. Trust. Office: Australian Cath University 40 Edward St North Sydney NSW 2059 Australia Office Fax: 61 2 9739 2009. Business E-Mail: tracey.mcdonald@acu.edu.au.

MCDONOUGH, DAVID M., insurance company executive; b. Simsbury, Conn. B, Ctrl. Conn. State U., New Britain; MS, U. Mass., Amherst; MA, Trinity Coll., Hartford, Mass. Career mktg., fin. services and risk mgmt. profl.; exec. v.p., COO Assurant Health, Milw.; pres., COO Trustmark Companies, Lake Forest, Ill., CEO, 2005—. Chmn. Ill. Life Ins. Coun.; bd. dirs. America's Health Ins. Plans, mem. exec. strategy task force. Bd. dirs. Lake Forest Grad. Sch. Mgmt. Office: Trustmark Companies 400 Field Dr Lake Forest IL 60045 Office Phone: 847-615-1500. Office Fax: 847-615-3910. *

MCDONOUGH, KENNETH LEE, pharmaceutical company medical administrator; b. Buffalo, Apr. 7, 1953; s. Sidney Lee and Jeanne Francis (Sheets) McD.; children: Jameson, Laurel, Meghan; m. Connie Kay Staley; stepchildren: Audrey, Kelsie. BS, U. Minn., 1975, MD, 1979, MS, 1986. Diplomate Am. Bd. Quality Assurance and Utilization Rev. Physicians. Resident in occupl. medicine U. Calif., San Francisco, 1984; v.p. Indsl. Health and Hygiene Group, Mpls., 1982-86; pvt. practice occupl. medicine, 1985—92, v.p. Am. Gen. Ins., Dallas, 1986-88, Mut. of Omaha Ins., Omaha, 1988-91, sr. v.p., 1991-95; med. dir. Stuart Disease Mgmt. Svcs. Inc., Wilmington, Del., 1995-98; asst. clin. prof. dept. preventive medicine and pub. health Creighton U. Sch. Medicine, 1994—; med. dir. AstraZeneca Pharms., Wilmington, Del., 1998—2009; instr. Monmouth (NJ) U., 2004—; payer rels. dir. Bristol-Myers Squibb, 2009—. Instr. nursing Gustavus Adolphus Coll. Nursing, St. Paul, 1984-86; instr. astronomy Met. State U., St. Paul, 1982-83; prin. rsch. into cost effectiveness of Dr. Dean Ornish's coronary reversal program in collaboration with Harvard Med. Sch., 1992-95. Author and designer of computer software. Inst. Sci. Mus. of Minn., St. Paul, 1982. Recipient Design Excellence award Seako, Inc., 1987, 3M Creativity award Minn. Mining & Mfg., 1971; recipient acad. scholarships. Mem. Am. Coll. Med. Quality, Am. Coll. Occupl. and Environ. Medicine, Nat. Assn. Managed Care Physicians, Gt. Plains Occupl. Medicine Assn. (nominating com. 1990-91), Am. Lung Assn. Nebr. (bd. dirs. 1995—), Disease Mgmt. Assn. Am. (bd. dirs. 2005—), Phi Kappa Phi. Avocations: genealogy, travel, astronomy, history. Home: 9 Devonshire Ct Greenville DE 19807-2572 Office: Bristol Meyers Squibb 9 Devonshile Ct Greenville DE 19807 Office Phone: 302-999-9264. Business E-Mail: kenneth.mcdonough@bms.com, rumster@verizon.net.

MCDOUGAL, WILLIAM SCOTT, urology educator; b. Grand Rapids, Mich., 1942; s. William Julian and Verna Wilma (Pasma) McD.; m. Mary Stuart Logan, Sept. 19, 1992; 1 child, Molly Katherine. AB, Dartmouth Coll., 1964; MD, Cornell U., 1968. Intern in surgery U. Hosps., Cleve., 1968-69, resident in surgery, 1969-75, attending urologist, 1977-80; postdoctoral fellow in physiology Yale U., New Haven, 1971-72; postdoctoral fellow in surgery Case-Western Res. U., Cleve., 1972-75; chief, burn study div. Inst. Surg. Rsch. Brooke Army Med. Ctr., Ft. Sam Houston, 1975-77; instr. surgery U. Tex., San Antonio, 1975-77; asst. prof. urology Case Western Res. U., Cleve., 1977-78, assoc. prof., 1978-80, Dartmouth Coll., Hanover, NH, 1980-84, chmn. dept. urology, 1982-84; prof., chmn. dept. urology Vanderbilt U., Nashville, 1984-90; Walter S. Kerr Jr. prof. urology Harvard Med. Sch., 1996—; chief urology Mass. Gen. Hosp., Boston, 1990—. Office: Mass Gen Hosp Dept Urology Fruit St Boston MA 02114

MCDOUGALL, IAIN ROSS, nuclear medicine educator; b. Glasgow, Scotland, Dec. 18, 1943; came to U.S., 1976; s. Archibald McDougall and Jean Cairns; m. Elizabeth Wilson, Sept. 6, 1968; children: Shona, Stewart. MB, ChB, U. Glasgow, 1967, PhD, 1973. Diplomate Am. Bd. Nuclear Medicine (chmn. 1985-87), Am. Bd. Internal Medicine (gov. 1984-86). Lectr. in medicine U. Glasgow, 1969-76; fellow Harkness-Stanford Med. Ctr., 1972-74; assoc. prof. radiology and medicine Stanford U., Calif., 1976-84, prof. radiology and medicine, 1985—. Contbr. numerous articles to sci. jours. Fellow Royal Coll. Physicians (Glasgow), Am. Coll. Physicians; mem. Am. Thyroid Assn., Soc. Nuclear Medicine, Western Assn. for Clin. Research. Office: Stanford U Med Ctr Divsn Nuclear Medicine Stanford CA 94305 Office Phone: 650-725-4711. Business E-Mail: rossmcdougall@stanford.edu.

MCDOWELL, DAVID MICHAEL, psychiatrist, educator, researcher; b. Middletown, Conn., Mar. 16, 1963; s. Arthur Vanall and Jacqueline Larson McDowell. MD, Columbia Coll. Physicians and Surgeons, 1989. Bd. cert. psychiatry Am. Bd. Psychiatry and Neurology, 1993, cert. addiction psychiatry Am. Bd. Psychiatry and Neurology, 1996. Fellow in addiction psychiatry NYU Med. Ctr., NYC, 1993—95; instr. psychiatry Bellevue Hosp./NYU Med. Ctr., NYC, 1995—; asst. prof. clin. psychiatry Columbia U. Coll. Physicians and Surgeons, NYC, 1995—; dir. buprenorphine program Columbia U.; founder, med. dir. STARS the Substance Treatment and Rsch. Svc. Columbia U., NYC, 1997—. Cons. Malinkrodt Pharmaceuticals, St. Louis, 2002—; cons. psychiatrist The Actors Fund. Author: (textbook) Substance Abuse: From Principles to Practice; contbr. chapters to books, articles to profl. jours. Bd. mem. The Three Dollar Bill Theater Co., NYC, 1995—99. Named one of Best Dr.'s in Am.; grantee, NIH/Nat. Inst. on Drug Abuse, 2000—. Fellow: APA (sr. disting.), Am. Psychiat. Assn. (vice chair sci. program com. 2000—, disting.); mem.: Charaka Club. Achievements include Advisor for Creative work including the Golden Globe Award winning film Quills, and other plays and film scripts. Avocations: cooking, singing. Office: 37 West 57th St 6B New York NY 10019 Home: 160 W 86th St # 6 B New York NY 10027 Office Phone: 212-750-7801. Personal E-mail: drdave@bway.net.

MCDOWELL, ELIZABETH MARY, retired pathology educator; b. Kew Gardens, Surrey, Eng., Mar. 30, 1940; arrived in U.S., 1971; d. Arthur and Peggy (Bryant) McD. B Vet. Medicine, Royal Vet. Coll., London, 1963; BA, Cambridge U., 1968, PhD, 1971. Gen. practice vet. medicine, 1964-66; Nuffield Found. tng. scholar Cambridge (Eng.) U., 1966-71; instr. dept. pathology U. Md., Balt., 1971-73, asst. prof., 1973-76, assoc. prof., 1976-80, prof., 1980-96, ret., 1996. Co-author: Biopsy Pathology of the Bronchi, 1987; editor: Lung Carcinomas, 1987; contbr. over 120 articles to sci. jours., chpts. to books. Rsch. grantee, NIH, 1979—92. Avocations: gardening, swimming.

MCDOWELL, WILBUR BENEDICT, retired chemist, consultant; b. Omaha, Feb. 27, 1920; s. Samuel Brownlee and Rose Gwendolen (Benedict) McDowell; m. Jean Erskine Clapp, Aug. 9, 1947 (dec. Aug. 1996); children: Linda Jane, Wendy Sue, Bruce Benedict. BSc, Ohio State U., 1941, MSc, 1942, PhD, 1944. Asst. Ohio State U., Columbus, 1942—43, tchg. fellow, 1943—44; rsch. assoc. The Squibb Inst., New Brunswick, NJ, 1944—52, section head, 1953—58, sr. rsch. assoc., 1958—66; mgr. prof. svc. dept. Squibb Corp., NYC, 1966—69, Princeton, NJ, 1970—85; ret., 1985. Cons., archivist Squibb Corp., 1985—89, Bristol-Myers Squibb Co., Princeton, 1989—99, New Brunswick, NJ, 2000—. Mem., v.p., pres. BOE, East Brunswick, NJ, 1957—65. Fellow: AAAS; mem.: Soc. Nuclear Medicine, Am. Chem. Soc., Sigma Xi. Achievements include wartime research on penicillin; 8 patents in field of manufacturing processes for phamaceuticals. Personal E-mail: benmcdowell@comcast.net.

MCELVANY, ROCKY, state agency administrator; BS in Chemistry, U. Ctrl. Okla., Edmond; MS in Environ. Sci., U. Okla., Norman. Lab. analyst Okla. State Environ Lab., supr., environ. monitoring lab.; svc. chief Okla. Occupl. Licensing and Consumer Health Services; dep. commr., protective health svc. Okla. State Dept. Health, 2004—06, COO, 2006—, interim commr. health, 2009. Okla. dept. health rep. Okla. Emergency Mgmt. Divsn. Named Lloyd Pummill Sanitarian of Yr., 1986. Mem.: Okla. Soc. Environ. Health Profls., Okla. Pub. Health Assn. (chmn., environ. sect.). Office: Okla State Dept Health 1000 NE 10th St Rm 305 Oklahoma City OK 73117-1299 Office Phone: 405-271-5600.

MCELVEEN-HUNTER, BONNIE, international relief organization executive; b. SC, Jan. 1945; m. Bynum Merritt Hunter, Sr.; 1 child, Bynum Merritt Hunter Jr. Grad., Stephens Coll., Columbia, Mo., 1972; LHD (hon.), NC State U., 2006; LLD (hon.), Pepperdine U., Graziadio Sch. Bus. and Mgmt., 2008. Founder, pres., CEO, owner Pace Mag (now Pace Comm.), Greensboro, NC, 1973—; US amb. to Finland Dept. of State, Helsinki, 2001—03; nat. chair Am. Red Cross, Washington, 2004—. Chmn. Alexis de Tocqueville Soc., United Way Greater Greensboro, NC; bd. mem. United Way Am., chair nat. women's leadership giving campaign; chair Women in Philanthropy Summit, Washington; internat. bd. mem. Habitat for Humanity; bd. mem. Internat. Women Build Habitat for Humanity, Habitat for Humanity First Ladies Build; founder $1 Billion dollar Women's Leadership Initiative. Recipient Dr. Carl Christian Rosenbroijer award, Woman Entrepreneur of the Yr. award, Nat. Found. for Women Legislatures, Nat. Athena award for bus. and civic contbn., US C. of C., Trailblazer of the Yr. award, Women Leaders Forum, Outstanding Bus. Leader award, Northwood U., Nat. Alexis de Tocqueville Soc. award, United Way, 2004, Ellis Island Medal of Honor, 2005, Appeal Conscience award Pub. Svc. award, 2006; named Comdr. Grand Cross Order of Lion, Pres. of Finland; named to Jr. Achievement Bus. Hall of Fame, 2004. Achievements include being the first woman to be selected as Chairman to the American Red Cross in it's 126-year history. Office: American Red Cross National Headquarters 2025 E St NW Washington DC 20006 also: Pace Comm 1301 Carolina St Greensboro NC 27401 Office Phone: 202-737-8300.

MCELWEE, DORIS RYAN, psychotherapist; d. Dennis M. and Emma A. (Klockau) Ryan; m. Charles B. McElwee, Feb. 6, 1959; children: Brent, Gregg, Cynthia; m. Craig A. Thomson, May 6, 1988. BA, Millikin U., Decatur, Ill.; MA, U. Ariz.; PhD, U. So. Calif., UCLA, Temple U. Officer, pyschiat. divsn. LA County Superior Ct., Mental Health Dept.; counselor LA Co. Mental Health Dept., 1956—60; sr. therapist Am. Inst. Family Rels., Burbank, Calif., 1969—2000, grad. faculty, 1972-85; psychotherapist in pvt. practice Burbank and Arcadia, Calif., 1970—; grad. faculty Chapman U., 1973-75, Pepperdine U., LA, 1975-78; psychotherapist Calif. Family Study Ctr., Burbank, 1985-90. Guest expert Phil Donahue Show. Co-author: Techniques of Marriage and Family Counseling, Suicide Prevention for College Students, A Place to Rest Your Heart; contbr. articles to Ladies Home Jour. Bd. dirs. NOW, Pasadena, Calif.; mem. Arcadia Assistance League, Las Alas Orgn. Recipient Merit award, Millikin U., 1983. Mem.: Self Esteem Task Force, So. Calif. Assn. Marriage and Family Therapy, Calif. Assn. Marriage and Family Therapists, Am. Assn. Marriage and Family Therapy, Group Psychotherapy Assn. So. Calif. (v.p., exec. bd. dirs.), Panhellenic Assn., Psi Chi, Pi Beta Phi. Republican. Lutheran. Avocations: travel, gardening.

MCEVOY, LORRAINE KATHERINE, oncology nurse; b. S.I., NY, Mar. 24, 1950; d. Edward Donald and Josephine (Boyle) McMahon; children: Kelly Ann, Kevin Michael. RN, St. Vincent's Sch. Nursing, 1970; BSN, Seton Hall U., 1994; MSN, Kean U. N.J., 1997. RN, N.J. Staff nurse St. Joseph's Hosp. and Med. Ctr., Paterson, N.J., 1981-88, nurse mgr. oncology, bone marrow transplant, 1988—, cons., educator devel. bone marrow, stem cell and cord blood transplant programs, 1995-98. Adj. prof. Kean U., 1997-98. Recipient Disting. Alumni award Kean U., 1999; Susan G. Komen Breast Cancer Found. grantee, 1997, 98, 99. Mem. Oncology Nursing Soc., Transcultural Nursing Soc., Tri-State Bone Marrow Transplant Nurses Assn., Breast Cancer Connection, Sigma Theta Tau. *

MCEWEN, JAMES, physician; b. Stirling, Scotland, Feb. 6, 1940; s. Daniel and Elizabeth Wells (Dishington) McEwen; m. Elizabeth May (Archibald), Oct. 24, 1964; children: Daniel Mark, Ruth Elizabeth. MBChB, U. St. Andrews, 1963; DSc (hon.), Glasgow Caledonian U.,

2008. Asst. med. officer of health Dundee Corp., Scotland, 1965-66; lectr. social and occupational medicine U. Dundee, Scotland, 1966-74; sr. lectr. cmty. health U. Nottingham, England, 1975-81; chief med. officer Health Edn. Coun., England, 1981-82; prof. cmty. medicine Kings Coll., U. London, 1982-89; Henry Mechan prof. pub. health U. Glasgow, Scotland, 1989—2000, prof. pub. health Scotland, 2000—02, prof. emeritus pub. health, 2002—, pres. faculty pub. health medicine, 1998—2001; chmn. U.K. Voluntary Register Pub. Health Specialists, 2003—09; chair Pharmacy Health Link, 2004—08; chmn. Health Protection Advisory Group, Scotland, 2005—. Contbr. chpts. to books and articles to profl. jours. Fellow Acad. Med. Scis., Royal Coll. Physicians London, Faculty Pub. Health, Faculty Occupl. Medicine, Royal Coll. Surgeons Eng. (fellow dental surgery), Royal Coll. Physicians Ireland (hon. faculty pub. health medicine). Episcopalian. Avocations: gardening, theater. Home: Auchanachie AB54 4SS Ruthven Huntly Scotland E-mail: j.mcewen@tiscali.co.uk.

MCFADDEN, DENNIS, psychologist, educator; b. Oakland, Calif., Oct. 2, 1940; s. Samuel John and Evelyn (Dinnerson) McF.; m. Nancy L. Wilson, Dec. 28, 1960; children: Tracie Ann, Devin James. BA, Sacramento State Coll., 1962; PhD, Ind U., 1967. Asst. prof. U. Tex., Austin, 1967-72, assoc. prof., 1972-77, prof., 1977—, Piper prof., 1987, Ashbel Smith prof., 1998—2011, prof. emeritus, 2011—. Contbr. articles to profl. jours. Recipient Jacob K. Javits Neurosci. Investigator award, NIH, 1984-89, Claude Pepper award of Excellence, 1989-91; NIH grantee. Fellow AAAS, Acoustical Soc. Am., Am. Psychol. Soc.; mem. Assn. for Rsch. in Otolarynology, Com. Hearing, Bioacoustics and Biomechanics (NAS-NRC com. on hearing, bioacoustics and biomechanics), Soc. Neurosci., Soc. for Behavioral Neuroendocrinology, Internat. Acad. for Sex Rsch., Orgn. for Study of Sex Differences. Avocations: jogging, bicycling, birdwatching, travel. Office: U Tex Dept Psychology 1 University Station Seay Bldg A 8000 Austin TX 78712-0187 Business E-Mail: mcfadden@psy.utexas.edu.

MCFADDEN, P. MICHAEL, surgeon; b. Hobbs, N.Mex., June 16, 1946; s. Paul Marion and Venita Lenora (Bowen) McF.; m. Jennifer Marie James, Apr. 8, 1990; children: Heather Anne, Jennifer Suzanne, Bryn Ellen, Callan Michael. BS, La. State U., 1968; MD, Tulane U., 1974. Diplomate Am. Bd. Surgery, Am. Bd. Thoracic Surgery. Surg. intern, resident Tulane U. Sch. Medicine, New Orleans, 1974-79, instr. surgery, 1974-79, clin. prof. surgery, 1991—; resident in thoracic surgery Ochsner Clinic, New Orleans, 1979-81, cardiovascular and thoracic surgeon, 1991—2006, surg. dir. lung transplantaion, 1991—2006, dir. thoracic surgery program, 1998—2006; cardiovascular and thoracic surgeon Stanford U. Hosp., Calif., 1981-91; chief cardiovascular surgery Palo Alto Med. Clinic, Calif., 1983-91; prof. cardiothoracic surgery, surg. dir. lung transplantation Keck Sch. Medicine, U. So. Calif., 2006—; thoracic surgery sect. head Huntington Hosp., Pasadena, Calif.; thoracic surgery sect. head expert Heart & Lungs Transplant. Contbr. articles to profl. jours. Bd. dirs. YMCA, Palo Alto area, 1988-91; bd. dirs. U. Tulane Health Svcs., 2006—2010, bd. Govs., Tulane Med. Sch., 2010-. Capt USNR, 1984-94, bd. gov. Tulane U. Sch. Medicine, 2010-, chmn. One Legacy OPO, LA, thoracic surgery divsn. chair Huntington Meml. Hosp. Fellow ACS, Am. Coll. Cardiology, Am. Coll. Chest Physicians; mem. AMA, Alton Ochsner Surg. Soc., Am. Assn. for Thoracic Surgery, Am. Soc. Vascular Surgery, Soc. Vascular Surgeons, Am. Soc. Transplant Surgeons, Am. Heart Assn. (coun. on cardiovascular surgery), Assn. Mil. Surgeons U.S., Internat. Soc. for Cardiovascular Surgery, Internat. Soc. for Heart and Lung Transplantation, Norman E. Shumway Surg. Soc., Pacific Coast Surg. Assn., So. Surg. Assn., So. Thoracic Surg. Assn., Thoracic Surgery Found., Tulane Surg. Soc., Tulane U. Med. Alumni Assn., Western Thoracic Surg. Assn., Alpha Omega Alpha, Alpha Epsilon Delta, Nu Sigma Nu, Kappa Alpha. Republican. Presbyterian. Office: Dept Cardiothoracic Surgery U So Calif Keck Sch Medicine 1520 San Pablo St Ste 4300 Los Angeles CA 90033 Home: 4359 Shepherds Ln La Canada Flintridge CA 91011 Office Phone: 323-442-5849. Business E-Mail: mmcfadden@surgery.usc.edu.

MCFEE, ARTHUR STORER, physician; b. Portland, Maine, May 1, 1932; s. Arthur Stewart and Helen Knight (Dresser) McF.; m. Iris Goeschel, May 13, 1967. BA cum laude, Harvard U., Cambridge, Mass., 1953, MD, 1957; MS, U. Minn., Mpls., 1966, PhD, 1967. Diplomate: Am. Bd. Surgery. Intern U. Minn. Hosp., 1957-58, resident in surgery, 1958-65; asst. prof. surgery U. Tex. Med. Sch., San Antonio, 1967-70, asso. prof., 1970-74, prof., 1974-2001, ret., 2001, prof. emeritus, 2001—. With U. Health Sys., Bexar-County, 1968-; spl. cons. on emergency med. care text to AAOS. Contbr. articles to profl. jours. Served with USNR, 1965-67. Fellow ACS; mem. AMA, Am. Assn. History of Medicine, Assn. Acad. Surgery, Tex. Med. Assn., Bexar County Med. Soc., Tex. Surg. Soc., Western Surg. Assn., San Antonio Surg. Soc., Soc. Surgery Alimentary Tract, So. Med. Assn., N.Y. Acad. Scis., Royal Soc. Medicine, So. Surg. Assn., Internat. Surg. Soc., Halsted Soc., J. Bradley Aust Surg. Soc., Am. Surg. Assn. Home: 131 Brittany Dr San Antonio TX 78212-1721 Office: MC 7842 7703 Floyd Curl Dr San Antonio TX 78229-3900 Office Phone: 210-567-5730, 210-567-5726. Business E-Mail: mcfee@uthscsa.edu.

MCGAHEE, THAYER W., nursing educator; b. Chattanooga, Aug. 8, 1956; BSN, Vanderbilt U., 1978; PhD, Med. Coll. Ga., 1998. Educator Med. Coll. Ga. Health Inc., 1998—2005; assoc. prof. nursing U. SC. Aiken, 2005—. Recipient Excellence Tchg. award, U. SC Aiken, Excellence Pub. Writing award, Pi Lambda Chpt. Sigma Theta Tau Internat. Mem.: Sigma Xi, Sigma Theta Tau Internat. Honor Soc. Nursing. Office: 471 University Pky Sch Nursing Aiken SC 29801 Office Fax: 803-641-3725. Business E-Mail: thayerm@usca.edu.

MCGARRY, KELLY, physician, educator; b. Providence, Jan. 2, 1965; BS, Brown U., 1987; MD, Yale U., 1992. Assoc. prof. medicine U. Medicine Found., Warren Alpert Med. Sch. Brown U., 1996—. Fellow: ACP. Avocations: running, bicycling. Office: Jane Brown Bldg 593 Eddy St Providence RI 02903 Office Fax: 401-444-3056. Business E-Mail: kmcgarry@lifespan.org.

MCGAUGHEY, CHARLES GILBERT, retired biochemist; b. San Diego, Sept. 8, 1925; s. Gilbert Arthur and Louisa Ellen (Inskeep) McG. BA, U. Calif., Berkeley, 1950; MA, U. So. Calif., 1952. Diplomate Am. Inst. Oral Biology. Scientist radiol. hazards evaluation U.S. Naval Radiol. Def. Lab., San Francisco, 1952; rsch. biochemist VA Med. Ctr., Long Beach, Calif., 1953-81; prin. investigator studied dental caries, plaque and oral cancer Oral Diseases Rsch. Lab., 1978-81. Contbr. articles to profl. jours. Grantee Nat. Inst. Dental Rsch., 1965. Home: PO Box 14617 Long Beach CA 90853

MCGAVIN, DAVID DOUGLAS MURRAY, ophthalmologist, consultant; s. David and Margaret Keir McGavin; m. Ruth Nicola Brash Bonsall, Oct. 4, 1969; children: David Charles Murray, Andrew Stuart Brash, Caroline Margaret Anne. MBChB, U. Glasgow, Scotland, 1962, MD with Honours, 1974; diploma in Child Health, U. Glasgow, 1966. Diploma DObstRCOG: Royal Coll. Obstetricians and Gynaecologists 1964. Project & med. dir. NOOR Eye Inst., Kabul, Afghanistan, 1976—81, Herat Ophthalmic Ctr., Herat, Afghanistan, 1976—81; founder editor, jour. cmty. eye health Internat. Ctr Eye Health, London, 1988—2003; med. dir. Internat. Resource Ctr. Prevention Blindness, London, 1990—2003; exec. dir. & founder Internat. Cmty. Trust Health & Ednl. Svcs., Glasgow, Scotland, 1999—2008; founder, editl. cons. Cmty. Ear & Earing Health, 2003—11; founder, editl. cons. Cmty. Dermatology Dev. Mental Health, 2003—11. Consulting WHO, Occasional - to developing countries, Help the Aged & HelpAge Internat., London, 1989—2001; dir. & chmn., Scottish com. Christian Blind Mission, Glasgow, Scotland, 2003—07, Cambridge, England, 2003—07. Editor: (online textbook) A Global Review for the Prevention of World Blindness; contbr. chapters to books, articles to profl. jours. Recipient MBE New Yrs. Hon. award, 2010. Fellow: Royal Coll. Physicians, Royal Coll. Ophthalmologists, Royal Coll. Surgeons Edinburgh, Royal Geog. Soc. Mem. Christian Ch. Avocations: sports, music, travel. Home: West Hurlet House Glasgow Rd Glasgow G53 7TH Scotland

MCGEE, WILLIAM TOBIN, intensivist; b. Port Chester, NY, May 23, 1957; s. James R. and Mary (Delzotto) McG.; m. Sarah McGrath; children: Erin, Kelly, Mary, Kate. BA in Physics, Dartmouth Coll., 1979; MD, N.Y. Med. Coll., 1983; M in Health Adminstrn., Clark U., 1997. Diplomate Am. Bd. Internal Medicine with spl. qualifications in Critical Care. Resident in internal medicine Baystate Med. Ctr., Springfield, Mass., 1983-86, intensivist, acting dir. surg. ICU, 1990-95; fellow in critical care St. Louis U./St. John's Mercy Med. Ctr., St. Louis, 1986-88; intensivist critical care divsn. Baystate Med. Ctr., Springfield, Mass., 1990-98, dir. ICU quality improvement, 1998—. DeWitt Wallace fellow rehab. medicine Rusk Inst. NYU Med. Ctr. Fellow Coll. Chest Physicians (Cecile Lehman Mayer award 1993); mem. AMA, Soc. Critical Care Medicine (presdl. citation 2000, internal medicine specialty award 2000), Am. Soc. Parenteral and Enteral Nutrition. Roman Catholic. Avocations: skiing, biking, hiking, sailing, windsurfing. Office: Baystate Med Ctr 759 Chestnut St Springfield MA 01199-1001

MCGEEHIN, FRANK C., III, cardiologist, educator; MD, Temple U. Diplomate Am. Bd. Internal Medicine, Am. Bd. Internal Medicine-interventional cardiology, Am. Bd. Internal Medicine-cardiovasc. disease. Resident Lankenau Hosp., fellow; staff Lankenau Med. Ctr., 1985; assoc. cardiology dept. Lankenau Hosp.; staff Bryn Mawr Hosp., 1997, Riddle Hosp., 2008; clin. asst. prof. medicine Thomas Jefferson Univ.; sec. chief clin. cardiology Main Line Health. Team cardiologist Phila. 76ers; pres. coun. Mt. Saint Mary's Coll.; exec. com. bd. govs. Main Line Health; bd. trustees Jefferson Health System; credentials com. Lankenau Hosp., med. edn. com.; bd. dirs. Cardiovasc. Alliance of the Del. Valley; pres. Cardiology Assocs. of Southeastern Pa. Mem.: ACP, Montgomery County Med. Soc., Pa. Med. Soc., The Coll. of Physicians of Phila., Soc. for Cardiac Angiography & Interventions, Am. Coll. of Cardiology. Office: Lankenau Medical Center MOB E Ste 356 100 Lancaster Ave Wynnewood PA 19096 Office Phone: 866-225-5654.

MCGEER, EDITH GRAEF, retired neurological scientist; b. NYC, Nov. 18, 1923; d. Charles and Charlotte Annie (Ruhl) Graef; m. Patrick L. McGeer, Apr. 15, 1954; children: Patrick Charles, Brian Theodore, Victoria Lynn. BA, Swarthmore Coll., 1944; PhD, U. Va., 1946; DSc (hon.), U. Victoria, 1987, U. B.C., 2000; DSc, Shiga U., 2006. Rsch. chemist E.I. DuPont de Nemours & Co., Wilmington, Va., 1946—54; rsch. assoc. divsn. neurol. sci. U. B.C., Vancouver, Canada, 1954-74, assoc. prof., 1974—76, prof., acting head, 1976—83, prof., head, 1983—89, prof. emerita, 1989—. Author: (with others) Molecular Neurobiology of the Mammalian Brain, 1978, 2d edit., 1987; editor: (with others) Kainic Acid as a Tool in Neurobiology, 1978, Glutamine, Glutamate, and GABA, 1983; contbr. articles to profl. jours. Decorated officer Order of B.C., Order of Can.; recipient citation, Am. Chem. Soc., 1958, Rsch. award, Clarke Inst., 1992, Lifetime Achievement award, Sci. Coun. B.C., 1995, Hon. Alumnus award, 1996, cert., Internat. Sci. Inst., 2001, medal of svc., Dr. Cam Coady Found., 2003, Lifetime Achievement award, U. B.C. Med. Faculty, 2006. Fellow Can. Coll. Neuropsychopharmacology, Royal Soc. Can.; mem. Can. Biochem. Soc., Internat. Brain Rsch. Orgn., Internat. Soc. Neurochemistry, Soc. Neurosci., Am. Neurochem. Soc. (councilor 1979-83), North Pacific Soc. Neurology and Psychiatry (hon. fellow), Lychnos Soc., Sigma Xi, Phi Beta Kappa. Office: U BC Divsn Neurol Sci 2255 Wesbrook Mall Vancouver BC Canada V6T 1Z3 Business E-Mail: mcgeer@interchange.ubc.ca.

MC GHAN, WILLIAM FREDERICK, pharmacist, educator; b. Sacramento, July 6, 1946; s. Roy William and Nelleen (Zischang) McG.; children: Monica, Matthew, Brian, Brent; m. Marilyn Dix Smith. Pharm.D., U. Calif., San Francisco, 1970; PhD, U. Minn., 1979. Clin. intern U. Calif. Med. Center, San Francisco, 1969-70, clin. resident, 1970-71; pharmacy coordinator Appalachian Student Health Project, 1970; staff dir. Student Am. Pharm. Assn., Washington, 1971-74, chmn. community health, 1969-70; staff dir. Project SPEED, nat. drug edn. program, 1971-73; assoc. dir., 1973-74; staff dir. Acad. Pharm. Scis., Washington, 1974-76, mem. pub. policy com., 1974-78, chmn. publs. com., 1975-76; grad. fellow, instr. Coll. Pharmacy, U. Minn., 1976-78; asst. prof. Sch. Pharmacy, U. So. Calif., 1978-82; prof., coord. div. adminstrv. and behavioral scis. Coll. Pharmacy U. Ariz., Tucson, 1982-89; founder, sr. rschr. Inst. for Pharm. Econs., 1989—2000; prof. Phila. Coll. Pharm., U. Scis., 1989—; dir. pharmacy adminstrn. grad. program Phila. Coll. Pharm., 1990—. Membership com. mem. Nat. Coord. Coun. for Drug Edn., 1974-75; mem. steering com. Am. Pharm. Assn. Drug Interactions Program, 1973-76; Acad. Pharm. Scis. liaison to NAS-NRC, 1975-76. Editor Student Am. Pharm. Assn. News, 1971-74; editor Acad. Reporter, 1974-76; contbr. over 200 profl. articles and book chpts. Recipient Archambault award Am. Soc. Cons. Pharm., 1987; cmty. scholar, Jackson, Calif., 1964. Fellow Am. Found. for Pharm. Edn., Am. Assn. Pharm. Sci. (chmn. econs. sect. 1988); mem. Am. Pharmacy Assn., Acad. Pharm. Rsch. and Sci. (chmn. econ., social and adminstrv. scis. sect. 1987-88, pres. 1988), Am. Soc. Hosp. Pharmacists, Am. Assn. Colls. Pharmacy (bd. dirs. 1995-97, chmn. pharm. adminstrn. sect. 1989-90, chmn. coun. of faculties 1995-96, co-recipient Lyman award 1989), Internat. Soc. Pharmacoecons. and Outcomes Rsch. (founding trustee; founding pres. 1995-96), Delta Sigma Phi, Rho Chi, Phi Kappa Phi, Sigma Xi Office: Phila Coll Pharmacy Univ of the Scis 600 S 43rd St Philadelphia PA 19104-4418 Business E-Mail: w.mcghan@usciences.edu.

MCGILL, HENRY COLEMAN, JR., pathologist, educator, researcher; b. Nashville, Oct. 1, 1921; s. Henry Coleman and Thursa (Lowry) McG.; m. Cloace Laurite Ferguson, Sept. 12, 1945; children: Margaret Ann, Laurilynn, Elizabeth Gail. BA, Vanderbilt U., 1943, MD, 1946. Intern Vanderbilt Hosp., Nashville, 1946-47; asst. prof. pathology La. State U. Med. Ctr., New Orleans, 1950-55, assoc. prof., 1955-61, prof., chmn. dept., 1961-66; prof. pathology U. Tex. Health Sci. Ctr., San Antonio, 1966-92, chmn. dept., 1966-72; sci. dir. S.W. Found. for Biomed. Rsch., San Antonio, 1978-92, sr. scientist, 1992-96, sr. scientist emeritus, 1996—. Contbr. articles to med. jours. Capt. M.C., U.S. Army, 1948-50. Mem. Phi Beta Kappa, Sigma Xi, Alpha Omega Alpha. Home: 4102 Fawnridge Dr San Antonio TX 78229-4212 Office: PO Box 760549 San Antonio TX 78245-0549 Business E-Mail: hmcgill@txbiomed.org.

MCGILL, KENNETH, JR., mental health services professional; b. Paterson, NJ, Aug. 22, 1965; s. Kenneth and Shirley A. McG.;m. Barbara Joan, Dec. 27, 1989; children: Megan Elizabeth, Shannon Eileen BA, William Paterson Coll., 1989; MA in Edn., Seton Hall U., 1995; Ednl. Specialist, 1999. Social Worker N.J., cert. Hypnotherapist Am. Bd. Clin. Hypnotherapy, lic. Marriage and Family Therapist. Mental health worker Wayne (N.J.) Gen. Hosp., 1989-90; case supr. N.J. Superior Ct. Essex County, Newark, 1990-95; adj. prof. psychology William Paterson U., Wayne, 1995—; asst. dir. admissions, evalns., 1996-99; marriage and family therapist St. Mary's Counseling Svcs., Pompton Lakes, N.J., 1998—; owner, pres., therapist Bergen-Passaic Psychol. Assocs., LLC, North Haledon, N.J., 1999—. Bd. dirs. Apraxia Network Bergen County, Paramus, N.J., 2000—. Reviewer books. Asst. soccer coach North Haledon Soccer Assn., 2000. Mem. APA, ACA, Am. Assn Marriage and Family Counselors, Mental Health Assn. Passaic County (bd. dirs. 1993-96, 2000—), Assn. Christian Counselors, KC (1st, 2nd degree 1995, 3rd degree 1996, Knight of the Month 1997), Ancient Order Hibernians, Psi Chi. Democrat. Roman Catholic. Avocations: mountain biking, hiking, sketching, writing. Office: Bergen Passaic Psychological 125 Terrace Ave North Haledon NJ 07508-2617 E-mail: mcgillkb@bellatlantic.net.

MCGILLICUDDY, JOAN MARIE, psychotherapist, consultant; b. Chgo., June 23, 1952; d. James Neal and Muriel (Joy) McG. BA, U. Ariz., 1974, MS, 1976; PhD, Walden U., 1996. Cert. nat. counselor. Counselor ACTION, Tucson, 1976; counselor, clin. supr. Behavioral Health Agy. Cen. Ariz., Casa Grande, 1976-81; instr. psychology Cen. Ariz. Coll., Casa Grande, 1978-83; therapist, co-dir. Helping Assocs., Inc., Casa Grande, 1982—, v.p., sec., 1982—; cert. instr. Silva Method Mind Devel., Tucson, 1986—. Active Mayor's Com. for Handicapped, Casa Grande, 1989-90, Human Svcs. Planning, Casa Grande, 1985-95, Pinal Gila Srs. Coun. Found., 2005—. Named Outstanding Am. Lectr. Silva Mind Internat., 1988-99; recipient Gov. Special Recognition award, 2006. Mem. ACA. Avocations: jogging, singing. Office: Helping Assocs Inc 1901 N Trekell Rd Casa Grande AZ 85222-1706 Office Phone: 520-836-1029. Business E-Mail: jmcgillicuddy@helpingassociates.com.

MCGINN, JOSEPH T., thoracic surgeon, educator; b. Brooklyn; MD, SUNY, 1981. Diplomate Am. Bd. Surgery, Am. Bd. Surgery-surgical critical care, Am. Bd. Thoracic Surgery. Resident surgery Downstate Med. Ctr., Brooklyn, 1981—85; resident thoracic surgery Long Island Jewish Med. Ctr., New Hide Park, NY, 1986—87, fellow cardiothoracic surgery, 1987—88; dir. Heart Inst. SI; dir. cardiothoracic surgery SI Univ. Hosp., NY; clin. assoc. prof. NY Med. Coll., NY; clin. asst. prof. health sci. ctr. SUNY, Brooklyn. Named one of Best Doctors, NY Mag. Mem.: NY State Med. Assn., Am. Coll. of Chest Physicians, Soc. of Thoracic Surgeons, ACS. Office: Staten Island University Hospital 475 Seaview Ave Staten Island NY 10305 Office Phone: 718-226-9000.

MCGINNIES, ELLIOTT MORSE, psychologist, educator; b. Buffalo, Sept. 19, 1921; BA, SUNY, Buffalo, 1943; MA, Brown U., 1944; PhD, Harvard U., 1948. Tchg. fellow Harvard U., 1944—47; asst. prof. U. Ala., 1947—52; from assoc. prof. to prof. U. Md., 1952—70; prof., chmn. Dept. Psychology American U., Washington, 1970—86, prof. emeritus, 1987. Vis. prof. U. Calif., Berkeley, 1987—88; Fulbright prof. Nat. Taiwan U. Author: Social Behavior: A Functional Analysis, 1970, The Reinforcement of Social Behavior, 1971, Attitudes, Conflict and Social Change, 1972, Perspectives on Social Behavior, 1994. Fellow: Am. Psychol. Assn.; mem.: Psychonomic Soc., Eastern Psychol. Assn., Harvard Club DC, Nat. Press Club, Sigma Xi.

MCGINNIS, JAMES MICHAEL, physician; b. Columbia, Mo., July 12, 1944; s. Leland Glenn and Lillian Ruth (Mackler) McG.; m. Patricia Anne Gwaltney, Aug. 4, 1978; children: Brian, Katherine AB, U. Calif., Berkeley, 1966; MA, MD, UCLA, 1971; M.P.P., Harvard U., 1977. House officer in internal medicine Boston City Hosp., 1971-72; internat. med. officer HEW, 1972-74; dir. Office for Asia and Western Pacific, 1974-75; state coordinator smallpox eradication program WHO, India, 1974-75; fellow Harvard Center for Community Health and Med. Care, Boston, 1976-77; cons. to sec. HEW, Washington, 1977, dep. asst. sec. for health, dir. office disease prevention, 1977-95, asst. surgeon gen., 1980-95, acting dir. office of rsch. integrity, 1992-93; scholar-in-residence NAS, Washington, 1995-99; sr. cons. Robert Wood Johnson Found., Princeton, 1996—99, sr. v.p., dir. Health Grp., 1999—2004, counselor to pres., 2004—05; sr. scholar, Inst. Medicine NAS, 2005—. Instr. medicine George Washington U. Med. Sch., 1973-75; adj. prof. pub. policy Duke U., 1979-81, 99—; chair, sec. task force on smoking and health; chair exec. com. HHS Environ. Health Policy Com.; mem. U.S. Japan Leadership program; chair World Bank/European Commn. Task Force on Reconstrn. of Health Sector, Bosnia, 1996-97; sr. scholar Assn. of Acad. Health Ctrs., 1997-99. Mem. editl. bd. Jour. Med. Edn., 1975-78, Jour. Preventive Medicine, 1987—, Jour. Health Promotion, 1992-98; editor-in-chief: Healthy People, Healthy People 2000, Surgeon General's Report on Nutrition and Health, Determining Risks to Health,

Food Marketing to Children and Youth. Bd. dirs. United Way of Nat. Capital, Nemours Found. With USPHS, 1972—75, with USPHS, 1977—95. Recipient Arthur S. Flemming Pub. Svc. award, 1979, USPHS Disting. Svc. medal, 1989, Surgeon Gen.'s medallion, 1995, Fed. Profile in Leadership award, 1989, Wilbur Cohen award, 1995, award for excellence APHA, 1995, Health Leader of Yr. award, 1996. Fellow Am. Coll. Epidemiology, Am. Coll. Preventive Medicine; mem. Inst. Medicine/NAS. Office: 500 5th St NW Washington DC 20001 Office Phone: 202-334-3963. Business E-Mail: mcginnis@nas.edu.

MCGIRR, DAVID WILLIAM JOHN, pharmaceutical executive; b. Glasgow, Scotland, May 19, 1954; arrived in US, 1991, naturalized, 2004; s. Edward McCombie and Diane Curzon (Woods) McG.; m. Margaret Joslin Richardson, May 9, 1981; children: William David, Katherine Joslin, Lucy Ann, Elizabeth Margaret. BSc (hon.), U. Glasgow, 1976; MBA, U. Pa., 1978. Assoc. S.G. Warburg & Co. Ltd., London, 1978—80, exec. dir., 1981—86; mng. dir. S.G. Warburg & Co. Inc., NYC, 1991—95, CFO, 1992—95; assoc. Warburg Paribas Becker Inc., NYC, 1980—81; exec. dir. S.G. Warburg Securities, London, 1986—87; CEO S.G. Warburg Securities Ltd., Toronto, Ont., Canada, 1987—89; COO, CFO Bunting Warburg Inc., Toronto, 1989—91; pres. GAB Robins North Am. Inc., Parsippany, NJ, 1996—99, CEO, 1997—99; COO hippo, Inc., New Haven, 1999—2002, pres., 2001—02; sr. v.p., CFO Cubist Pharm., Inc., Lexington, Mass., 2002—, treas., 2002—03. Selection com. Thouron Scholarship, 1989-2009 Bd. dirs. Friends of Glasgow U., Inc., 2003—08; bd. dirs., chmn audit com. Lifecell Corp., 2007—08. Thouron scholar, 1976-78. Mem. Apawamis Club (Rye, N.Y.). Avocations: collecting cars, golf, classic wooden boats. Office: 65 Hayden Ave Lexington MA 02421 Home Phone: 203-629-5607; Office Phone: 781-860-8526. Business E-Mail: david.mcgirr@cubist.com.

MCGLASHAN, THOMAS HAMEL, psychiatrist, educator; b. Rochester, NY, Oct. 20, 1941; 2 children. BA in Chemistry magna cum laude, Yale U., 1963; MD, U. Pa., 1967. Diplomate in psychiatry Am. Bd. Psychiatry and Neurology. Intern Mary Hitchcock Meml. Hosp., Hanover, NH, 1967-68; resident, chief resident psychiatry Mass. Mental Health Ctr., 1968-71; officer in psychiatry, sr. asst. surgeon USPHS, 1971-73; chief clin. rsch. unit psychiat. assessment sect. NIMH, Adult Psychiatry Br., Bethesda, Md., 1973-75; staff psychiatrist Chestnut Lodge, Rockville, Md., 1975-90, dir. adult studies Rsch. Inst., 1977-81, dir. rsch., 1982-90; prof. dept. psychiatry Yale U. Sch. Medicine, 1990 ; exec. dir. Yale Psychiat. Inst., New Haven, 1990-2000; prof. psychiatry Yale U. Sch. Medicine; attending psychriatist Conn. Mental Health Ctr. New Haven. Spl. and invited faculty, supr. Washington Sch. Psychiatry, 1978, 81, 82, 83; instr. Washington Psychoanalytic Inst., 1982-89, Western New Eng. Psychoanalytic Inst., 1992-93; clin. assoc. prof. dept. psychiatry Uniformed Svcs. U. of the Health Scis., 1983-88, clin. prof. dept. psychiatry, 1988-90; rsch. prof. dept. psychiatry U. Md. Sch. Medicine, 1986-90; bd. dirs. Parents Found. for Transitional Living, 1991-97; cons. and grant cons. in field; presenter in field; many others. Author: The Documentation of Clinical Psychotropic Drug Trials, 1973, The Borderline: Current Empirical Research, 1985, Schizophrenia: Treatment, Process and Outcome, 1989. Early Intervention in Psychosis, 2001, A Developmental Model of Borderline Personality Disorder, 2003; editl. cons.: Schizophrenia Bull., 1980-82, 84 , Archives of Gen. Psychiatry, 1982—, Am. Jour. Psychiatry, 1982—, Hosp. and Cmty. Psychiatry, 1984—, Jour. Personality Disorders, 1987—, Schizophrenia Rsch., 1987—, Acta Psychiatrica Scand., 1999—, Jour. Abnormal Psychology, 1988, Psychiatry Rsch., 1988—, others, mem. editl. bd.: Jour. Personality Disorders, 1989—, Schizophrenia Bull., 1989—; contbr. chpts. to books, over 400 articles to profl. jours. Recipient Gary Morris Rsch. award Washington Psychoanalytic Soc., 1980, Presdl. award for rsch. Nat. Assn. Pvt. Psychiat. Hosps., 1988, Silvano Arieti award Am. Acad. Psychoanalysis, 1990, Psychiat. Inst. Am. Found. award for rsch. devel. in hosp. psychiatry, 1990, Alexander Granlick award Am. Psychiat. Found., 1997, Americas Top Doctors, 2004-, Stanley Dean award, Am. Coll. Psychriatists, 2008, Richard Wyatt award, Early Psyliosis Internat. Early Psychosis Assn., 2008, Am. Psychiatry Assn. award, 2010, Established Investigator award Nat. Alliance Rsch. Schizophrenia & Depression, 1997-98; grantee Fund for Psychoanalytic Rsch. Am. Psychoanalytic Assn., 1978, 79, NIMH, 1996—, Norwegian Rsch. Coun., 1997—. Fellow Am. Psychiat. Assn., Am. Psychopathol. Assn.; mem. Western New Eng. Psychoanalytic Inst. and Soc., Soc. for Psychotherapy Rsch., Assn. for Clin. Psychosocial Rsch., Psychiat. Rsch. Soc., Internat. Soc. Study Personality Disorders, Internat. Early Psychosis Assn. Business E-Mail: thomas.mcglashan@yale.edu.

MCGLYNN, ELIZABETH A., health policy analyst; b. 1955; BA in Internat. Polit. Economy, Colo. Coll.; MPP, U. Mich. Gerald R. Ford. Sch. Pub. Policy; PhD in Pub. Policy, RAND Grad. Sch., 1988. Assoc. dir. RAND Health, Santa Monica, Calif.; dir. Ctr. Rsch. on Quality in Health Care, Santa Monica, Calif., Kaiser Permanente Ctr. for Effectiveness & Safety Rsch. (CESR), 2011—. Adv. com. Nat. Com. for Quality Assurance (NCQA), Nat. Quality Forum (NQF), Coun. Accountable Physician Practices, American Med. Group Assn.; editorial bd. Health Services Rsch., Milbank Meml. Fund Quarterly. Mem.: Inst. Medicine. Achievements include development of QA Tools. Office: Kaiser Permanente 280 West MacArthur Blvd Oakland CA 94611 Office Fax: 510-752-1000. *

MCGOLDRICK, JOHN LEWIS, medical products executive, lawyer; b. Plainfield, NJ, Mar. 2, 1941; s. John Leslie and Sarah (Walker) McGoldrick; m. Ann Chapman Puffer, Oct. 1, 1966; children: Scott Runyon, Jennifer Winslow. BA cum laude, Harvard U., 1963, LLB, 1966. Bar: N.J. 1966, N.Y. 1985. Ptnr. McCarter & English, 1974—95; sr. v.p. Bristol-Myers Squibb Co., 1995—98, pres. Med. Devices Group, 1998—2000, gen. counsel, 2000—05, exec. v.p., 2000—06; sr. v.p. International AIDS Vaccine Initiative, 2006, exec. v.p. external strategy devel., 2006—09, sr. advisor, 2009—; chmn. Zimmer, Inc., 2007—. Vice-chmn., bd. dirs. N.J. Transit Corp., Newark, 1979—2005. Mem. HealthCare Inst. NJ; trustee Essex-Newark Found. Legal Svcs. NJ Montclair State U.; bd. dirs. NJ Network Found., Regional Plan Assn.; mem. Harvard Malaria Initiative Adv. Coun.; mem. com. to visit The Coll., mem. com. to visit Sch. Pub. Health Harvard U. Fellow: Am. Acad. Appellate Lawyers, Am. Bar Found., Am. Coll. Trial Lawyers; mem.: ABA, Am. Arbitration Assn., Nat. Panel Arbitrators, Aspen Inst. World Economy, Coun. Chief Legal Officers, Assn. Gen. Counsel, Am. Law Inst., Assn. Fed. Bar N.J. (former pres.), Assn. Bar City of N.Y., N.Y. Bar Assn., N.J. Bar Assn., World Econ. Forum, Coun. U.S. and Italy, Harvard Law Sch. Assn. N.J. (former pres.). Office: Zimmer Holdings Inc 345 E Main St Warsaw IN 46580 Office Fax: 574-372-4988.

MCGOLDRICK, KATHRYN ELIZABETH, anesthesiologist, educator, writer; b. Worcester, Mass., 1946; MD, Cornell U., NYC, 1970. Diplomate Am. Bd. Anesthesiology, 1975. Intern N.Y. Hosp.-Cornell Med. Ctr., 1970—71; resident anesthesiology Peter Bent Brigham Hosp., Boston, 1971—73; fellow pediat. anesthesiology Children's Hosp. Med. Ctr., Boston, 1973—74; prof. anesthesiology Yale U., New Haven, 1992—2001; prof., chmn. dept. anesthesiology N.Y. Med. Coll., Valhalla, 2001—. Med. dir. ambulatory surgery Yale-New Haven Hosp., 1991—2001; bd. dirs. Found. Anesthesia Edn. and Rsch., 2005—; mem. editl. bd. Current Reviews in Clin. Anesthesia, 2011—. Editor-in-chief Survey of Anesthesiology, 1995—. V.p., trustee Wood Libr.-Mus. Anesthesiology, 1998—2001, pres., 2001—04. Fellow Am. Coll. Anesthesiology; mem. Am. Soc. Anesthesiologists, Conn. State Soc. Anesthesiologists (pres. 1998-2000), Assn. Univ. Anesthesiologists, Acad. Anesthesiology (v.p., 2008-09, pres. elect 2009-10, pres. 2010-11), Soc. Ambulatory Anesthesia (pres-elect 2003, pres. 2004-05), NY State Soc. Anesthesiologists., Alpha Omega Alpha, Acad. Anesthesiology (pres., 2010-11) Office: Dept Anesthesiology NY Med Coll Valhalla NY 10595 Office Phone: 914-493-7693.

MCGONAGLE, DUNCAN FRANCIS, mental health nurse, substance abuse counselor; b. Bklyn., May 6, 1939; s. John and Kathleen (Rooney) McGonagle; m. Gloria Maria Carrubba, Dec. 5, 1987. AA, Allan Hancock, 1964; AAS in Nursing, CUNY, 1992. Cert. psychiat. and mental health nurse, addictions RN. Substance abuse counselor Pritikin Longevity Ctr., Santa Monica, Calif., 1978-84; paramedic N.Y.C. Emergency Med. Svc., 1987-92; psychiatric nurse Bellevue Hosp. Ctr., NYC, 1992-99; adminstr. Methadone Maintenance Treatment Program, St. Barnabas Hosp., Bronx, NY, 1999—2001; nurse mgr. Methadone Maintenance Treatment Program, Beth Israel Med. Ctr., NYC, 2001—. Founder Methadone Anonymous, NY; pvt. practice, specializing in addiction and recovery svcs. Aux. police officer N.Y.C. Police Dept., 1985—. With USN, 1956-60, 1961-62, Vietnam. Recipient Nat. award for Clin. Excellence in Nursing, Nat. Nurses Soc. on Addictions, 1995. Mem. Blue Knights, Knights of Life, Rolls Royce Owners Club, Harley Owners Group. Roman Catholic. Avocations: computers, sailing, motorcycling, antique autos. Home: 73 Verona St Brooklyn NY 11231-1612 Office: Beth Israel Med Ctr 160 Water St New York NY 10038-4922 E-mail: duncan73@aol.com.

MCGOVERN-SCATURO, DIANE JOAN, psychotherapist; d. Francis Michael and Joan Veronica (Quinn) McCarthy; m. Thomas Joseph McGovern (dec.); children: Judith Ann McGovern, Robert Thomas McGovern; m. Christopher John Scaturo, Aug. 1, 1992. BA, Trinity U., Washington, 1953; MEd, U. Pitts., 1956; MS in Edn., St. Bonaventure U., NY, 1992. Lic. mental health counselor N.Y. State Edn. Dept., cert. group psychotherapist Nat. Registry Cert. Group Psychotherapists, credentialed Alcoholism and Substance Abuse Counselor N.Y. State Office Alcoholism Substance Abuse Svcs., cert. rational marriage and family therapists Nat. Assn. Cognitive Behavioral Therapists, rational addictions counselor Nat. Assn. Cognitive Behavioral Therapists. Family svcs. coord. Cattaraugus County Coun. on Alcoholism and Substance Abuse, Olean, 1987—92, behavioral health therapist Charter Behavioral Health Sys. Winston-Salem, NC, 1994—96; behavioral health therapist, group psychotherapist Olean Gen. Hosp. Behavioral Health Unit, 2000—. Oral panel examiner Credentialled Alcoholism Counselor Exam., Credentialling Application Svcs., Albany, NY, 1992. Mem., bd. dirs. Olean Gen. Hosp. Found., 2000—09, sec., bd. dirs., 2005; mem., adv. bd. Salvation Army, Olean, 1959—86, chmn., adv. bd., 1972 77. Fellow: Am. Psychotherapy Assn.; mem.: ACA, Am. Group Psychotherapy Assn. (clin. mem.), Rochester Group Psychotherapy Soc. Avocations: golf, downhill skiing. Office: Olean Gen Hosp Behavioral Health Unit 515 Main St Olean NY 14760

MCGRATH, GLENN A., endocrinologist; MD, Pa. State U., 1987. Diplomate Am. Bd. Internal Medicine, Am. Bd. Internal Medicine-endocrinology, diabetes and metabolism. Hosp. affiliations include Doylestown Hosp., Abington Meml. Hosp. Author: (publs.) New technique for quantitation of pituitary adenoma size: use in evaluating treatment of gonadotroph adenomas with a gonadotropin-releasing hormone antagonist., 1993, Incidentalomas of the parathyroid gland multiple presentations, variable function, and review of the literature., 2006. Named one of The Top Docs, Phila. Mag., 2010—11. Mem.: Am. Assn. of Clin. Endocrinologists, Hormone Found. Office: Abington Memorial Hospital 1200 Old York Rd Abington PA 19001 Office Phone: 215-481-2000.

MCGRATH, MARY HELENA, plastic surgeon, educator; b. NYC, Apr. 12, 1945; d. Vincent J. and Mary M. (Manning) McG.; children: Margaret E. Simon, Richard M. Simon. BA, Coll. New Rochelle, 1966; MD, St. Louis U., 1970; MPH, George Washington U., 1994. Diplomate Am. Bd. Surgery, Am. Bd. Plastic Surgery, lic. physician Calif. Resident in surg. pathology U. Colo. Med. Ctr., Denver, 1970-71, intern in gen. surgery, 1971-72, resident in gen. surgery, 1971-75; resident in plastic and reconstructive surgery Yale U. Sch. Medicine, New Haven, 1976—78, chief resident plastic and reconstructive surgery, 1977-78; fellow in hand surgery U. Conn.-Yale U., New Haven, 1978; instr. in surgery divsn. plastic and reconstructive surgery Yale U. Sch. Medicine, New Haven, 1977-78, asst. prof. plastic surgery, 1978-80; attending in plastic and reconstructive surgery Yale-New Haven Hosp., 1978-80, Columbia-Presbyn. Hosp., NYC, 1980-84, George Washington U. Med. Ctr., Washington, 1984-2000, Children's Nat. Med. Ctr., Washington, 1985-2000, Loyola U. Med. Ctr., 2000—02, Hines VA Hosp., 2001—02, U. Calif., San Francisco, 2003—, San Francisco VA Ctr., 2003—, San Francisco Gen. Hosp., 2003—; asst. prof. plastic surgery Columbia U., NYC, 1980-84; assoc. prof. plastic surgery Sch. Medicine, George Washington U., Washington, 1984-87, prof. plastic surgery, 1987-2000, Loyola U. Med. Ctr., 2000—02, U. Calif., San Francisco, 2003—. Bd. dirs. Am. Bd. Plastic Surgery, 1989 95, historian, 1991-95; examiner certifying exam., 1986—; mem. Residency Rev. Com. Plastic Surgery, 2006—; senator med. faculty senate George Washington U., bd. govs. Med. Faculty Assocs.; presenter, cons. in field. Co-editor: (with M.L. Turner) Dermatology for Plastic Surgeons, 1993; assoc. editor: The Jour. of Hand Surgery, 1984-89, Annals of Plastic Surgery, 1984-87, Plastic and Reconstructive Surgery, 1989-95, Contemporary Surgery, 1999-2006, Archives of Surgery, 2004—; Aesthetic Surgery Jour., 2009-, advt. editor Plastic and Reconstructive Surgery, 2003-06; guest reviewer numerous jours.; contbr. chpts. to books and articles to profl. jours. Recipient numerous rsch. grants, 1978—. Fellow ACS (DC chpt. program ann. meeting chmn., 1992, pres. 1994-95, bd. govs. 1995-98, exec. com. 1996-97, chmn. adv. coun. plastic surgery 1995-98, regent 1997—2006, vice-chair bd. regents 2005-06, 1st v.p. 2007-08), Bd Commr., The Jt. Commn. (2009-), mem. AAAS, Am. Surg. Assn., Am. Assn. Hand Surgery, Am. Assn. Plastic Surgeons (trustee 1997-00), Am. Soc. for Aesthetic Plastic Surgery, Am. Soc. Maxillofacial Surgeons, Am. Soc. Plastic and Reconstructive Surgery (chmn. ethics com. 1985-87, chmn. device/tech. evaluation com. 1993-94, chmn. workforce task force 1997-00, bd. dirs. 1994-96, chmn. endowment bd. dirs. 2000-04, trustee 2004—07, chmn. bd. trustees 2006-07, ednl. found. bd. dirs. 1985-96, treas. 1989-92, v.p. 1992-93, pres.-elect 1993-94, pres. 1994-95), Am. Soc. Reconstructive Microsurgery (edn. com. 1992-94), Am. Soc. Surgery of Hand (chmn. 1987 ann. residents' and fellows conf. 1986-87, rsch. com. 1988-90), Assn. Acad. Chmn. Plastic Surgery (bd. dirs. 1999—), Assn. Acad. Surgery, Chgo. Soc. Plastic Surgeons (treas. 2001-02), Calif. Soc. Plastic Surgeons (councilor 2008-), San Francisco Surg. Soc., Chgo. Surg. Soc., Internat. Soc. Reconstructive Surgery, Met. D.C. Soc. Surgery Hand (pres. 1995-97), N.Y. Surg. Soc., Northeastern Soc. Plastic Surgeons (treas. 1993-96, pres. 1997-98), Pacific Coast Surg. Assn., Plastic Surgery Rsch. Coun. (chmn. 1990), Surg. Biology Club III, The Wound Healing Soc, Mem. FDA Gen. & Plastic Surgery Devices Panel (2010-). Office Phone: 415-353-4389. Business E-Mail: mary.mcgrath@ucsfmedctr.org.

MCGRATH, PAMELA DELLA, psychosocial researcher; b. Brisbane, Australia, Oct. 29, 1951; d. Andrew Lloyd and Iris Olive (Allen) Palmer; m. Philip William McGrath, May 13, 1972 (dec. Apr. 1988); children: Amy Beth, Emma Louise, Zoe Marisa, Bo Youn. B of Social Work, U. Queensland, Brisbane, Australia, 1972; MA, Queensland U. Tech., Brisbane, Australia, 1993; PhD, U. Queensland, 1996. Child care officer Dept. Children's Svcs., Brisbane, Australia, 1973—76, supr. child care officer, 1976; resource officer Dept. Family Svcs., Brisbane, Australia, 1989—90; tutor, lectr. Queensland U. Tech., Brisbane, Australia, 1992—94, U. Queensland, Brisbane, Australia, 1994—97; rsch. fellow Queensland U. Tech., Brisbane, 1998, Nat. Health and Med. Rsch., Brisbane, Australia, 1999—2001; sr. rsch. fellow Nat. Health and Med. Rsch. Coun., 2006—; with Griffith U., 2011—. Founder, dir. psycho-social rsch. program Leukaemia Found. Australia, 1997—2000; dir. rsch., founder Internat. Program Psycho-Social Health Rsch., 2006—. Author: A Question of Choice, 1997, Confronting Icarus: A Psycho-Social Perspective on Haematological Malignancies, 1999, Living with Leukaemia and Related Disorders, 2001, The Living Model, 2006, Living With Leukaemia, Lymphoma, Myeloma & Related Disorders, 2008; contbr. chapters to books Spirituality and Palliative Care, 2001, articles to numerous profl. jours.; editl. bd.: Austral-Asian Jour. Cancer, 2000—, reviewer: to numerous internat. jours. Justice of peace, commr. declarations Dept. Justice, Brisbane, 1973—. Grantee rsch. fellow Ctr. Pub. Health Rsch., Brisbane, 1998-99 and other numerous rsch.grants from U. and Industry; recipient Millenium Golden Internat. award Internat. Rsch. Promotion Coun., 1999; named Eminent Scientist of Yr. Asia Pacific chpt. Internat. Rsch. Promotion Coun., 1999. Mem. Palliative Care Assn. Queensland (chair edn. and rsch. sub-com. 1997—2000), Australian Bioethics Assn., Nat. Assn. Rsch. Fellows Avocations: gardening, classical music, art. Office: Internat Program Psycho-Social Health Rsch Griffith University Logan Campus Brisbane 4131 Australia

MCGRAW, DONALD JESSE, biologist, science historian, writer; b. Altadena, Calif., Oct. 27, 1943; s. Jesse E. and Mary L. (Hajostek) McG.; m. Laura Lee Hansen, July 13, 1968; children: Adrienne, Holly, Rachel. BS in Biol. Scis., Calif. State Poly. Coll., 1965; MS, Utah State U., 1967; PhD, Oreg. State U., 1976. Registered microbiologist Am. Acad. Microbiology; CCR fed. registration. Research asst. microbiology Utah State U., 1965-66, teaching asst. food and aquatic microbiology, 1966-67; grad. teaching asst. gen. biology Oreg. State U., 1970-72, instr., 1972-73; tchr. phys. and biol. scis. U.S. Bur. Indian Affairs Boarding Sch., Shonto, Ariz., 1974-75; asst. prof. biology Franklin Coll., Ind., 1975-78; adj. asst. prof. biology Ind. Central U., Indpls., 1977-78; adj. asst. prof. Ind. U.-Purdue U., Columbus, 1978; mem. faculty Yavapai C.C., Prescott, Ariz., 1978-79; assoc. dir. Ute Research Lab., Ft. Duchesne, Utah, 1980-81, dir., 1981-82; asst. prof. biology Coll. St. Thomas, Minn., 1985-87; assoc. provost U. San Diego, 1988—2004, prof., 2001—04; independent fed. contractor USFWS, US Nat. Sci. Found., 2005—. Summer ranger/naturalist U.S. Nat. Park Svc., 1970—79, 1983—86; vis. prof. Bard Coll., NYC, 1984. Author: Andrew Ellicott Douglass and the Role of the Giant Sequoia in the Development of Dendrochonology, 2001, Edmund Schulman and the Living Ruins: Bristlecome Pines, Tree Rings and Radiocarbon Dating, 2007; contbr. articles to profl. jours. Commr. San Diego County Columbian Quincentenary Commn., 1990-93, chmn. edn. com., 1990-93; mem. pres.'s adv. com. San Diego Zool. Soc., 1995-97; trustee Quail Bot. Gardens Found., 1995-98. Capt. (0-6) USPHS Res. Recipient Disting. Alumnus award, Calif. State Poly. U., 1991, Monrovia H.S., 1991, Meritorious Pub. Svc. award USN, 2003; Eli Lilly doctoral grantee Oreg. State U., 1973-74; NSF grantee, 1998. Mem. AAAS, Cabrillo Hist. Assn. (bd. dirs. 1989-94, vice chair 1992, chair 1993, 94), History of Sci. Soc., Tree Ring Soc., Alpha Scholastic Honor Soc. of Franklin Coll. (pres. 1976-78), Sigma Xi (sec. San Diego chpt. 1996-97, v.p. 1997-98, pres. 1999-2000, assoc. dir. S.W. region 2000-02, bd. dirs. 2004-06, Silver medal of achievement San Diego (Calif.) chpt. 2002), Beta Beta Beta. Office Phone: 619-947-5108. Personal E-mail: donaldmcgraw@mac.com.

MCGRAW, PHILLIP CALVIN **See DR. PHIL**

MCGREGOR, DOUGLAS HUGH, pathologist, educator; b. Temple, Tex., Aug. 28, 1939; s. Harleigh Heath and Joyce Ellen (Lambert) McG.; m. Mizuki Kitani, July 6, 1969; children: Michelle Sakuya, David Kenji. BA, Duke U., 1961, MD, 1966; postgrad., U. Edinburgh, Scotland, 1961-62. Diplomate Am. Bd. Pathology. Intern, chief resident in pathology UCLA Med. Ctr., 1966-68; surgeon, lt. comdr. Atomic Bomb Casualty Commn., Hiroshima, Japan, 1968-71; chief resident in pathology Queens Med. Ctr., Honolulu, 1971-73; asst., assoc. prof. pathology U. Kans. Med. Ctr., Kansas City, 1973-82, prof., 1982—. Dir. anat. pathology VA Med. Ctr., Kansas City, Mo., 1975-94, chief pathology and lab. medicine, 1994-2003, dir. surg. pathology, 2003—. Contbr. numerous articles to profl. jours., chpts. to books. Leader YMCA Indian Princess Program, Overland Park, Kans., 1977-79, Indian Guide Program, 1978-80, Cub Scout Am.,

Overland Park, 1980-82, Boy Scouts Am., Leawood, Kans., 1982—. Lt. comdr. USPHS, 1968-71, Japan. Grantee Merck, Sharp and Dohme, 1980. Fellow Coll. Am. Pathologists, Am. Soc. Clin. Pathologists; mem. Am. Assn. Pathologists, Internat. Acad. Pathologists, Soc. Exptl. Biology and Medicine, N.Y. Acad. Scis., AAAS, Kansas City Soc. Pathologists (sec.-treas. 1982-83, pres. 1983-84). Achievements include research in ultrastructure and pathobiology of neoplasms, radiation carcinogenesis, and morphogenesis of atherosclerosis. Home: 9400 Lee Blvd Shawnee Mission KS 66206-1826 Office: VA Med Ctr 4801 E Linwood Blvd Kansas City MO 64128-2226 Business E-Mail: douglas.mcgregor@va.gov.

MCGREGOR, ROBERT SHAYNE, pediatrician, educator; b. Altoona, Pa., Aug. 22, 1955; MD, Pa. State U., 1981. Pediat. resident, chief Pitts. Children's Hosp., 1985; prof., vice chair pediat., residency dir. Drexel U. Coll. Medicine, St. Christopher's Hosp. Children, 1996—. Past pres., bd. mem. Assn. Pediat. Program Dirs., 2000—10; oversight com. Iniative Innovation Pediat. Edn., 2009—; bd. mem. Patnership Pediat. Progress, 2010—. Fellow: Am. Acad. Pediat. (planning com., chair continuing med. edn. program PREP course 2000—), Am. Bd. Pediat.; mem.: Academic Pediat. Assn., APPD (Tunnessen award). Avocations: exercise, running. Office: St Christopher's Hosp Children Philadelphia PA 19134 Office Fax: 215-427-4805. Business E-Mail: robert.mcgregor@drexelmed.edu.

MCGUIGAN, STUART M., pharmaceutical executive; BA, Fairfield Univ., 1982; MS, MPhil, Yale Univ., 1986. Assoc. rsch. scientist Honeywell, 1986—88; dir. info. planning Merck & Co., Inc. (formerly Schering-Plough Corp.), 1988—93; sr. v.p. info. tech. Medco Health Solutions, Inc., 1993—2004; sr. v.p., CIO Liberty Mutual Group, Inc. (subs. of Liberty Mutual Holding Co., Inc.), 2004—08, CVS Caremark Corp., 2008—. Bd. dir. Netscout Systems Inc. Office: CVS Caremark Corp 1 CVS Dr Woonsocket RI 02895

MCGUINESS, LUKE, hospital administrator; BA in Fin., U. Notre Dame, Ind., 1966; MBA in Healthcare Adminstrn., George Wash. U., Washington, 1969. Career healthcare adminstr.; pres., CEO MacNeal Health Network, Berwyn, Ill.; positions including sr. v.p. devel. Vanguard Health Systems, Nashville, 2000—03; pres., CEO Ctrl. DuPage Hosp., Ill., 2003—11; CEO Ctrl. DuPage Hosp.-Delnor Health Sys., 2011—. Past chmn. Met. Chgo. Healthcare Coun. Office: Ctrl DuPage Hosp-Delnor Health Sys 25 N Winfied Rd Winfield IL 60190 Office Phone: 630-933-4833. *

MCGUINNESS, LUKE, hospital administrator; BA in Fin., U. Notre Dame, 1966; MBA in Healthcare Adminstrn., George Wash. U., 1969. Pres. and CEO McNeal Health Network, Berwyn, Ill.; sr. v.p. devel. Vanguard Health Sys., Nashville, 2000—03; pres. and CEO Ctrl. DuPage Hosp., Ill. Mem.: Met. Chgo. Healthcare Coun. (past chmn.). Office: Central DuPage Hospital 25 N. Winfield Rd Winfield IL 60190 Office Phone: 630-933-1600.

MCGUIRE, BRENDAN MARTIN, gastroenterologist, educator; b. Gary, Ind., May 15, 1962; BS in Chem. Engring., U. Notre Dame, 1984; MS in Bioengring., Pa. State U.; degree in Medicine, U. Pitts., 1990. Prof. medicine, med. dir., Liver Transplant Program U. Ala., Birmingham, 1996—. Region 3 liver and intestinal regional rep. United Network for Organ Sharing, 2010—. Recipient Argus award, U. Ala., 2011. Fellow: ACP. Avocation: soccer. Personal E-mail: bmcguire@uab.edu.

MCGUIRE, JOHN ALBERT, dentist; b. Warren, Ohio, June 20, 1950; s. Bernard Leo and Lucille Ann (Guarnieri) McG.; m. Pamela Kay Muter, May 30, 1969; children: John, Jessica. BS, Ohio State U., 1972, DDS, 1975. Dentist, capt. USAF, Bellevue, Nebr., 1975-77; dentist pvt. practice Dayton, Tenn., 1977-83, Knoxville, Tenn., 1983—. Author: (short story) Stirs, 1990, (screenplay) Sonspot, 2000. Mem. Sertoma Club, Knoxville, 1983-86, Jaycees, Dayton, 1978-81; vol. United Meth. Ch., Tilaran, Costa Rica, 1985. Recipient Scholarship, Fred M. Roddy Found., 1990. Mem. Phi Kappa Phi. Avocations: fly fishing, photography, bicycling, music, writing. Home: 301 Grandeur Dr Knoxville TN 37920-6325 Office: Dr John Mcguire PO Box 20548 Knoxville TN 37940-1548

MCGUIRE, MICHAEL FRANCIS, plastic surgeon; b. St. Louis, Oct. 4, 1946; s. Arthur Patrick and Virginia Claribel (Gannon) McG. BA, Columbia U., 1968, MD, 1972. Diplomate Am. Bd. Surgery, Am. Bd. Plastic Surgery. Intern UCLA, 1972-73, resident in gen. surgery, 1973-77, resident in plastic surgery, 1978-80; fellow in plastic surgery rsch. Stanford (Calif.) U., 1977-78; traveling fellow in plastic surgery Gt. Britain, 1980; chief plastic surgery L.A. County-Olive View Med. Ctr., Sylmar, Calif., 1980-85; pvt. practice Santa Monica, Calif., 1980—; chief plastic surgery St. John's Health Ctr., 1990—; asst. clin. prof. surgery UCLA, 1980-97, assoc. clin. prof., 1998—. Bd. dirs. Calif. Med. Rev., Inc., sec.-treas., 1997, v.p., 1997-99, chmn. bd. dirs. 1999-2003; chmn. surg. rev. St. Johns Health Ctr., 1996-98, chief plastic surgery, 1992-; pres. Pacific Coast Plastic Surgery Ctr., 1988—. Charter patron LA Music Ctr. Opera, 1983—; sponsoring patron LA County Art Mus., 1986—2005; patron Colleague Helpers in Philanthropic Svc., Bel Air, Calif., 1987, 93, 95; pres. Found. for Surg. Reconstrn., 1996-2007, LA Philanthropic Com. Arts Bd., 2009-11, Nat. Accred Program Breast Ctrs. Bd., 2009-. Fellow ACS, Royal Soc. Medicine, Am. Assn. Plastic Surgeons, Am. Bd. Plastic Surgery (mem. bd. dirs. 2010-); mem. Am. Soc. Plastic Surgeons (membership chmn. 1997-2000, bd. dirs. 2002-05, sec. 2005-2007, v.p. 2007-08, pres.-elect, 2008-09, pres. 2009-10, chmn. leadership devel. com. 2004-07, chair nominating com. 2010-11, chair internat. com. 2010-), Am. Soc. Aesthetic Plastic Surgery (ethics chmn. 1998-99, bd. dirs. 2004-07, pub. edn. chmn. 2004-05, commr. comm., 2005-2007, publications chair, 2007-09), Am. Health Quality Assn. (bd. dirs. 1999-2005), LA County Med. Assn. (v.p. 1995-97, sec.-treas. 1997-99), Calif. Med. Assn. (del., exec. com., splty. delegation 1994-99), Calif. Soc. Plastic Surgery (exec. com., auditor 1988-89, program chmn. 1990, exec. coun. 1991-94, treas. 1994-97, v.p. 1997-98, acting pres. 1997, pres.-elect 1998-99, pres. 1999-2000, nominating com. chmn. 2000-01, strategic planning com. chmn. 2005-), Am. Assn. Accreditation of Ambulatory Surgery Facilities (ops. com. 1995-96, bd. dirs. 1996-, treas. 1996-98, sec. 1998-2000, v.p. 2000-02, pres. 2002-04), Surgery Facilities Resources (founding pres. 2005-07), Alpha Omega Alpha, Am. Mensa. Avocations: golf, travel, collecting antique glass, opera, art. Office: 1301 20th St Ste 460 Santa Monica CA 90404-2054 Office Phone: 310-315-0121. Business E-Mail: mmcguire@ucla.edu.

MCGUIRE, SANDRA LYNN, nursing educator; b. Jan. 28, 1947; d. Donald Armstrong and Mary Lue (Harvey) Johnson; m. Joseph L. McGuire, Mar. 6, 1976; children: Matthew, Kelly, Kerry. BSN, U. Mich., 1969, MPH, 1973, EdD, 1988, MSN, 1997. Staff nurse Univ. Hosp., Ann Arbor, Mich., 1969; pub. health nurse Wayne County Health Dept., Eloise, Mich., 1969—72; instr. Madonna Coll., Livonia, Mich., 1973; pub. health coord. Plymouth Ctr. for Human devel., Northville, Mich., 1974—75; asst. prof. cmty. health nursing U. Mich., Ann Arbor, 1975—83; asst. prof. U. Tenn., Knoxville, 1983—88, assoc. prof., 1990—2007, prof., 2007—09, coord. gerontol. nurse practitioners program, 1998—2006, chair MSN program Coll. Nursing, coord. gerontology, 2008—09, emeritus prof., 2009; asst. dean Lincoln Meml. U. Sch. Nursing, 2009—. Dir. Kids Are Tomorrow's Srs. Program, 1988—; resource person Gov.'s Com. Unification of Mental Health Svcs. in Mich.; spkr. profl. assns. and workshops; mem. Coun. Accreditation Nurse Anesthesia Ednl. Programs, 2007—10. Author (with S. Clemen-Stone and D. Eigsti): Comprehensive Community Health Nursing, 1981, Comprehensive Community Health Nursing, 5th edit., 1998, Comprehensive Community Health Nursing, 6th edit., 2002; author: Growing Up and Growing Older: Annotated Bibliography of Early Children's Literature, 2009. Bd. dirs. Ctr. Understanding Aging, 1987-93, v.p., 1995; bd. dirs. Mich. chpt. ARC, 1980-83, Knoxville chpt., 1984-85; founder Knoxville Intergenerational Network, 1989; mem. nat. policy coun. AARP, 2006-. Recipient John W. Runyan, Jr. Cmty. Health Nursing award U. Tenn. Memphis, 2002, Outstanding Svc. award U. Tenn. Knoxville Libr. Friends, 2004; USPHS fellow, 1972-73, Robert Woodruff fellow Emory U., 1996-97, Hewlett Innovative Tech. fellow U. Tenn., Knoxville, 1999-00, Profl. Devel. awardee U. Tenn. Knoxville, 1996-97, 99-2000. Mem. ANA, AARP Nat. Policy Coun., Tenn. Nurses Assn., Gerontological Soc. Am., Assn. Gerontology in Higher Edn.(mem. k12 com., 2008-, mem. book awards sumcom., 2008-), Nat. Gerontol. Nursing Assn., Mich. Pub. Health Assn. (chmn. mental health sect. 1976, dir., co-chmn. residential svcs. com. 1976-79, chmn. health svcs. 1979-82), Nat. Assn. Retarded Citizens, Mich. Assn. Retarded Citizens, Nat. Coun. on Aging, Ctr. for Understanding Aging (v.p. 1994-95), Plymouth, Assn. Retarded Citizens (chmn. residential svcs. com. 1975-77), Tenn. Assn. Retarded Citizens, Sr. Citizens Home Assistance Svcs. (bd. mem. 2009-), Sigma Theta Tau, Pi Lambda Theta, Phi Kappa Phi. Home: 11008 Crosswind Dr Knoxville TN 37934 Office: Cumberland Gap Pky Harrogate TN 37752 Office Phone: 800-325-0900. Business E-Mail: sandra.mcguire@lmunet.edu.

MCGUIRE, TREASURE MADELEINE, pharmacist, educator; b. Australia, Oct. 22, 1955; B in Pharmacy, U. Queensland, Australia, 1975, PhD, 2005. Asst. dir. pharmacy Mater Health Svcs., 1996; conjoint sr. lectr., sch. pharmacy U. Queensalnd, 1996; assoc. prof. pharmacology Bond U., Gold Coast, Queensland, 2006—. Chair Royal Brisbane & Royal Women's SSC HREC, 1995. Mem.: Data and Safety Monitoring Com. Meeting Nat. Palliative Care PaCCSC Studies, Australasian Assn. Quality Health Care, Pharm. Soc. Australia (Bowl of Hygeia 1984), Soc. Hosp. Pharmacists Australia (Lilly Internat. fellowship 1983, Sandoz Rsch. fellowship 1993). Avocation: boating. Office: Bond University dept. Health Sci Medicine Gold Coast Queensland 4229 Australia Business E-Mail: tmcguire@bond.edu.au.

MCGUIRE, WILLIAM DENNIS, healthcare consultant, director; b. Glen Ridge, NJ, Sept. 24, 1943; s. John William and Kathleen Mary (Sexton) McG.; m. Nancy Katherine Hoyne, Aug. 13, 1966; children: Kathleen Anne, Colleen Dempsey. BA, U. Notre Dame, 1965; M.H.A., U. Mich., 1968. Asst. adminstr. U. Wis. Hosps., Madison, 1971-74; adminstr. Children's Med. Ctr., Dayton, Ohio, 1974-79; COO Mercy Cath. Med. Ctr., Phila., 1979-80; CEO Wills Eye Hosp., Phila., 1980-85; pres., CEO Mercy Health Care Sys., Scranton, Pa., 1985-89, Mt. Carmel Health, Columbus, Ohio, 1989-92, Incarnate Word Health Svcs., San Antonio, 1992-95, Cath. Med. Ctrs. of Bklyn. and Queens, NYC, 1996—2000, Kaleida Health, Buffalo, 2002—06; pvt. practice San Antonio, 2000—02; dir. HBCS, Wilmington, 2005—, Chair., 2010—; dir. CTG, Buffalo, 2008—, Ziegler, 2010—. Asst. clin. prof. U. Wis., 1971—74, instr., 1972—73; asst. clin. prof. Wright State U. Sch. Medicine, Dayton, Ohio, 1978—79; asst. prof. Ohio State U., 1990—92; adj. faculty dept health care Trinity U., 1992—95, Harvard Bus. Sch. Club, 2003—06; allied health techs. adv. com. Sinclair CC, 1974—79; mem. Dayton Pub. Schs. Lay Adv. Com. on Vocat. Edn., 1974—79; pres. Dayton Area Young Adminstrs. Group, 1977. Trustee Cath. Social Svcs., 1976—79, pres., 1978—79; trustee Cmty. Blood Ctr., 1977—79; pres. elect Greater Dayton Area Hosp. Assn., 1979; mem. Wilkes Coll. Health Adminstrn. Adv. Com., 1988—89; bd. dirs. Coop. Purchasing Corp., 1974—79, Coll. Misericordia Health Care Task Force, 1988—89, Covenant Health Sys., 1992—2003, chmn. fin. com., 2001—03, Fletcher Allen Health Care, 2002—03; with Consol. Cath. Risk Retention Group, 1992—95; consol. Cath. Charities, 1996—2000, Primary Care Devel. Corp., 1997—2000, Buffalo Niagara Partnership, 2002—06, D'Youville Coll., 2004—06, Hosp. Billing & Collection Svc. Ltd., 2004—, chmn., 2010—; with Computer Task Group, 2008—; consol. The Ziegler Co., 2010—; bd. govs. League Vol. Hosps., 1996—2000, sec., 1997—2000; bd. govs. Fidelis Care NY, 1996—2000, Queensbrook Ins. Ltd., 1996—2000, vice chmn., 1996—97, chmn., 1997—2000; active Health Policy Forum, United Hosp. Fund, United Way, ARC. Fellow Am. Coll. Healthcare Execs. (life), NY Acad. Medicine, Royal Soc. Medicine; mem. Acad. for Cath. Health Care Leadership, Mercy Leadership Group. (nat. commn. Cath. health care ministry), Maj. Cath. Health Alliance (sec. 1990-95, chmn. 1997-99), Health Care Fin. Mgmt. Assn. (advanced mem.), Am. Assn. Univ. Profs. Ophthalmology, Am. Soc. Law and Medicine, Am. Hosp. Assn., Am. Assn. Eye and Ear Hosps. (pres.-elect 1984-85), Health Mgmt. Edn. Assn. (pres. 1987-88, 2008-), Hosp. Assn. NY State (bd. dirs. 1998-2000, 02-05), Greater NY Hosp. Assn. (bd. govs. 1997-2000, 02-06), Tex. Hosp. Assn., We. NY Hosp. Assn. (bd. dirs. 2002-05), Ohio Hosp. Assn., Hosp. Assn. Pa., Wis. Hosp. Assn., Cath. Health Assn., Am. Pub. Health Assn., Pa. Pub. Health Assn., Del. Valley Hosp. Council, Pa. Emergency Health Svcs. Coun., Del. County Emergency Health Svcs. Coun., Nat. Union Hosp. and Health Care Employees (plan trustee), Pa. Hosps. Ins. Co. Adv. Coun., 1988-89. C. of C., U. Notre Dame Alumni Assn., U. Mich. Alumni Assn., Pres.'s Soc., U. Wis. Med. Sch. Alumni Assn., Wills Eye Soc., Sorin Soc., Badin Guild, Notre Dame Club (pres. 1971, v.p. 1983-84), Dominion Country Club. Conservative. Roman Catholic. Office: 6 Clubhouse Green San Antonio TX 78257 Home: 6 Clubhouse Grn San Antonio TX 78257-1295 Personal E-mail: billmcg@together.net.

MCGUIRE PORTER, AMY, foundation administrator; B, Kent State U., Ohio. Dir. devel., major gifts Volunteers for America; dir. devel. Nat. AIDS Fund; exec. dir. Found. for NIH, 2001—10; exec. dir., CEO Nat. Osteoporosis Found., Washington, 2010—. Recipient Hon. Alumni award, U. Akron, Ohio, 2008. Office: Nat Osteoporosis Found 1150 17th St NW Ste 850 Washington DC 20036 Business E-Mail: amy.porter@nof.org. *

MCGURGAN, PAUL, obstetrician, gynecologist; b. Antrim, Ireland, Oct. 15, 1970; m. Katrina Calvert, Mar. 30, 2002. MBBCh, U. Dublin, 1995, BA in Obstetrics, 1995. Editor: Conservative Surgery For Menorrhagia, Reviews In Gyn. Practice. Scholar, Trinity Coll. Dublin, 1989; Karl Storz fellow, 1998—2000. Mem.: Royal Coll. Physicians Ireland, Royal Coll. Ob-gyn., Brit. Soc. Gyn. Endoscopy, Brit. Menopause Soc., Brit. Soc. Cervical Colposcopy Pathology. Achievements include research in aetiology and development of endometrial polyps. Personal E-mail: paul_mc_gurgan@hotmail.com.

MCHENRY, MARTIN CHRISTOPHER, physician, educator; b. Feb. 9, 1932; s. Merl and Marcella (Bricca) McH.; m. Patricia Grace Hughes, Apr. 27, 1957; children: Michael, Christopher, Timothy, Mary Ann, Jeffrey, Paul, Kevin, William, Monica, Martin Christopher. Student, U. Santa Clara, 1950-53; MD, U. Cin., 1957; MS in Medicine, U. Minn., 1966. Diplomate Am. Bd. Internal Medicine. Intern Highland Alameda County (Calif.) Hosp., Oakland, 1957-58; resident, internal medicine fellow Mayo Clinic, Rochester, Minn., 1958-61, spl. appointee in infectious diseases, 1963-64; staff physician Henry Ford Hosp., Detroit, 1964-67, Cleve. Clinic, 1967-72, chmn. dept. infectious diseases, 1972-92, sr. physician infectious diseases, 1992-98. Cons. infectious diseases, 1998—2006; asst. clin. prof. Case Western Res. U., 1970-77, assoc. clin. prof. medicine, 1977-91, clin. prof. medicine, 1991—2006; assoc. vis. physician Cleve. Met. Gen. Hosp., 1970-00; cons. VA Hosp., Cleve., 1973-74. Contbr. more than 100 articles to profl. jours., also chpts. to books. Chmn. manpower com. Swine Influenza Program, Cleve., 1976. With USNR, 1961-63. Named Disting. Tchr. in Medicine, Cleve. Clinic, 1972, 90; recipient 1st ann. Bruce Hubbard Stewart award Cleve. Clinic Found. for Humanities in Medicine, 1985, Nightingale Physician Collaboration award Cleve. Clinic Found. Divsn. Nursing, 1995, Clinician of Yr. award Acad. Medicine of Cleve./No. Ohio Med. Assn., 2002. Fellow ACP, Infectious Diseases Soc. Am. (Clinician award 2000), Am. Coll. Chest Physicians (chmn. com. cardiopulmonary infections 1975-77, 81-83), Royal Soc. Medicine of Gt. Britain; mem. Am. Soc. Clin. Pharmacology and Therapeutics (chmn. sect. infectious diseases and antimicrobial agts. 1970-77, 80-85, dir.). Home: 2779 Belgrave Rd Pepper Pike OH 44124-4601 Office: 9500 Euclid Ave Cleveland OH 44195-0001

MCHUGH, PAUL R., psychiatrist, neurologist, educator; b. Lawrence, Mass., May 21, 1931; s. Francis Paul and Mary Dorothea (Herlihy) McH.; m. Jean Barlow, Dec. 27, 1959; children: Clare Mary, Patrick Daniel, Denis Timothy. AB, Harvard U., 1952, MD, 1956. Diplomate: Am. Bd. Psychiatry and Neurology. Intern Peter Bent Brigham Hosp., Boston, 1956-57; resident in neurology Mass. Gen. Hosp., 1957-60, fellow in neuropathology, 1958-59; teaching fellow in neurology and neuropathology Harvard, 1957-60; clin. asst. psychiatry Maudsley Hosp., London, Eng., 1960-61; mem. neuropsychiatry div. Walter Reed Army Inst. Research, Washington, 1961-64; asst. prof. psychiatry and neurology Cornell U., NYC, 1964-68, assoc. prof., 1968-71, prof., 1971; dir. electroencephalography N.Y. Hosp., 1964-68; founder, dir. N.Y. Hosp. Bourne Behavioral Rsch. Lab., 1967-68, clin. dir., supr. psychiat. edn., founder, dir. Weschester divsn. dept. psychiatry, 1968-73; prof., chmn. dept. psychiatry U. Oreg. Health Sci. Center, Portland, 1973-75; Henry Phipps prof. psychiatry Johns Hopkins U. Sch. Medicine, Balt., 1975—2001, chmn. dept. psychiatry, 1975—2001, dir. dept. psychiatry and behavioral sciences, univ. disting. svc. prof. psychiatry, prof. dept. mental hygiene, 1976; psychiatrist-in-chief Johns Hopkins Hosp., 1975—2001, chmn. med. staff, 1983-89, trustee, 1983—89; dir. Blades Ctr. for Clin. Practice and Rsch. in Alcoholism Johns Hopkins Med. Inst., 1992—2001; prof. mental health John Hopkins Bloomberg Sch. Pub. Health. Author: The Perspectives of Psychiatry, 1983, 1998; (with Phillip R. Slavney) Psychiatric Polarities, 1987, Genes, Brain and Behavior, 1990, The Mind Has Mountains: Reflections on Society and Psychiatry, 2006; contbg. author: Cecil-Loeb Textbook of Medicine; mem. editl. bd. Am. Jour. Physiology, Jour. Nervous and Mental Disease, Comprehensive Psychiatry, Medicine, Psychol. Medicine, 1976—, Am. Scholar; contbr. articles to profl. jours. Mem. Md. Gov.'s Adv. Com., 1977—80, U.S. Conf. Cath. Bishops Nat. Rev. Bd. Office of Child and Youth Protection, 2002—07, Pres. Coun. on Bioethics, 2001—; serving on False Memory Syndrome Found.; advisor Assn. for Rsch. in Nervous and Mental Disease. Grantee NIH, 1964-68, 67-70, 70-74, 75-96; recipient William C. Menninger award ACP, 1987. Fellow: Am. Psychiat. Assn., Royal Coll. Psychiatry; mem.: Am. Coll. Psychiatrists (Disting. Svc. award 2002), Pavlovian Soc., Am. Psychopath. Assn. (Joseph Zubin award 1995, Paul Hoch award 2006), Am. Coll. Neuropsychopharmacology (co-chmn., ethics com.), Harvey Soc., Am. Physiol. Soc., Am. Neurol. Assn., Inst. Medicine (Rhonda and Bernard Sarnat Internat. prize in Mental Health 2008), W Hamilton St. Club, Phi Beta Kappa (vis. scholar 2003—04). Home: 3707 St Paul St Baltimore MD 21218-2403 Office: Johns Hopkins Med Insts Meyer 127 615 N Wolfe St Baltimore MD 21205 Office Phone: 410-502-3150. Office Fax: 410-502-3152. Business E-Mail: pmchugh1@jhmi.edu.

MCHUGHEN, ALAN, geneticist, educator; b. Ottawa, Ontario, Can., Apr. 13, 1954; m. Donna Greschner; children: Stephanie, Nicola. PhD, Oxford U., Eng., 1979. Lectr. Yale U., New Haven, 1979—82; prof. U. Saskatchewan, Canada, 1982—2001; prof., botany and plant scis. U. Calif., Riverside, 2002—. Author: Pandora's Picnic Basket (Book of Yr., Can. Sci.Writers Assn., 2000); contbr. articles to profl. jours. Pres. Internat. Soc. for Biosafety Rsch., Riverside, 1988—2004. Fellow, Am. Coll. Nutrition, 2002, Am. Assn. Advancement Sci., 2009. Fellow: AAAS. Achievements include patents in field, including one of the first for a higher lifeform; development of public sector commercial transgenic and conventional crop cultivars. Office: Univ Calif University Ave Riverside CA 92521-0124 Office Fax: 951-827-4437. Business E-Mail: alanmc@ucr.edu.

MCILVAINE, PATRICIA MORROW, physician; b. Pitts., Feb. 4, 1947; d. James Morrow McIlvaine and Virginia Fuller Tucker. BS in Chemistry, Simmons Coll., 1969; MD, U. Utah, 1984. Rsch. technician Mass. Gen. Hosp., Boston, 1969-70, MIT, Cambridge, 1970-75,

Utah State U., Logan, 1975-80; resident in internal medicine U. Mass. Hosp., Worcester, 1984-87; pvt. practice, Monson, Mass., 1987-2001; mem. pvt. group practice Walla Walla (Wash.) Clinic, 2002—. Staff physician Wing Meml. Hosp., Palmer, Mass., 1987-2001. Vol., trainer IRBIS Enterprises, Mongolia, 1998-2004. NFS summer scholar, 1968, Helena Rubinstein scholar Simmons Coll., 1968-69. Mem. ACP/Am. Soc. Internal Medicine, Sigma Xi. Avocations: fiber crafts, international travel, hiking, gardening, sailing. Home: 913 Bonnie Brae Walla Walla WA 99362

MCILWAIN, HARRIS H., physician, researcher; s. Cordelia B. McILwain; m. Linda Fulghum, June 19, 1970; children: Laura E. McILwain, Kimberly L. McILwain, Michael Fulghum McILwain, Daniel E. McILwain, Virginia H. McILwain, Lisa Ann McILwain. MD, Emory U., Atlanta, 1973. Diplomate Am. Bd. Internal Medicine, Am. Bd. Rheumatology, Am. Bd. Geriat. Internal medicine intern Grady Meml. Hosp., Atlanta, 1973—74; resident in internal medicine Emory U., Atlanta, 1974—76, rheumatology fellow, 1976—78; physician Tampa Med. Group, Fla., 1978—. Med. dir. John Knox Village Retirement Ctr., Tampa, 1995—. Contbr. articles to profl. jours. Bd. dirs. Fla. Osteoporosis Bd., Tampa, 1998—2003. Named one of Top Physicians in the US, Town and Country Mag., 1997, Top 100 Physicians in the US, 1998. Mem.: AMA, ACP, Assoc. Profls. in Coll. Pub. Health, Am. Med. Dirs. Assn. (cert.), Fla. Med. Assn., Hillsborough County Med. Assn., Am. Coll. Rheumatology, Alpha Omega Alpha. Avocation: soccer. Office: Tampa Med Group 4700 Habana Ave Ste 303 Tampa FL 33614 Office Phone: 813-875-9742, 813-879-5485. Personal E-mail: hmcil@aol.com.

MC INDOE, DARRELL WINFRED, retired nuclear medicine physician; b. Wilkinsburg, Pa., Sept. 28, 1930; s. Clarence Wilbert and Dorothy Josephine (Morrow) McIndoe; m. Carole Jean McClain, Aug. 23, 1952; children: Sherri L. McIndoe, Wendy L. McIndoe, Darrell B. McIndoe, Ronald S. McIndoe, Holly B. McIndoe. BS, Allegheny Coll., 1952; MD, Temple U., 1956, MS, 1960. Commd. 2d lt. M.C. US Air Force, 1956, advanced through grades to col., 1971; intern Brooke Army Med. Ctr., San Antonio, 1956-57; resident in medicine Temple U. Med. Ctr., Phila., 1957-60; chief internal medicine and Hosp. svc. Norton AFB, 1960-64; chief internal medicine and hosp. services 7520 U.S. Air Force Hosp., England, 1964-68; vis. rsch. fellow Royal Post Grad. Med. Sch., London, 1968-69; chief endocrinology svcs., chmn. dept. nuc. medicine USAF Med. Ctr., Keesler AFB, Miss., 1969-75; dep. dir. Armed Forces Radiobiology Rsch. Inst., Def. Nuc. Agy., Bethesda, Md., 1975-77, dir., 1977-79; staff physician nuc. medicine br., dept. radiology Nat. Naval Med. Ctr., Bethesda, Md., 1979-82; sr. lectr. mil. medicine Uniformed U. of Health Scis., Bethesda, Md., 1975-80; asst. prof. radiology/nuc. medicine and rsch. program coord. Uniformed U. of Health Sci., 1980-82; assoc. divsn. nuc. medicine St. Joseph Hosp., Towson, Md., 1982-91, dir. divsn. nuc. medicine, 1991—2000; ret. 2000. Med. advisor Nev. ops. office Dept. Energy, Las Vegas; cons. in field. Col. med. corp. USAF. Fellow: Am. Coll. Nuc. Medicine, Am. Coll. Nuc. Physicians (regent ea. USA), Fellow royal Soc. Medicine; mem.: AMA, Soc. Med. Cons.'s to Armed Forces, Assn. Mil. Surgeons U.S., Health Physics Soc. (dir. Balt., Washington chpt.), Md. Soc. Nuc. Medicine (past pres.), Soc. Nuc. Medicine (ho. of dels.), Uniformed Svcs. Nuc. Medicine Assn. (pres. 1975), Air Force Soc. Physicians (bd. govs. 1973—77), Alexander Graham Bell Soc. Home: 15510 Foxpaw Trail Woodbine MD 21797-8000

MCINTIRE, LARRY VERN, biomedical engineering educator; b. St. Paul, June 28, 1943; s. James Lawrence and Lenore Vincal (Converse) McI.; m. Suzanne G. Eskin, June 27, 1997. BChemE, MS, Cornell U., 1966; MA, Princeton U., 1968, PhD, 1970. Registered profl. engr., Tex. Asst. prof. Rice U., Houston, 1970-74, assoc. prof., 1974-78, prof. chem. engring., 1978—2003, E.D. Butcher prof., 1983—2003, chmn. dept., 1981-91, chmn. Bioscis. and Bioengring. Inst., 1991—2003, chmn. rsch. coun., 1988-91, dir. biomed. engring. lab., 1980—99, chmn. dept. biomed. engring., 1997—2003; Wallace Coulter prof. Ga. Tech., 2003—. Adj. prof. medicine Baylor Coll. Medicine, Houston, 1982—2007, U. Tex. Med. Sch., Houston, 1982—2007, M.D. Anderson Cancer Ctr., 2001-08; Emory U. Sch. Medicine, 2003-, chmn. blood/materials working group NIH, Bethesda, Md., 1982-85; surgery and bioengring. study sect. NIH, 1984-88, 99-2003; com. bioprocessing NRC, 1991-94; chmn. rheology subcom. Internat. Coun. Thrombosis and Hemostasis, 1985-89; engring. directorate adv. coun. NSF, 2002-05; chmn. Coulter dept. biomed. engring Gal Tech., 2003-. Editor-in-chief: Annals of Biomed. Engring., 2002—; contbr. over 278 articles to profl. jours. Recipient Merit award NIH, 1989; NSF fellow Cornell U., Princeton U., 1965-69, NATO-NSF postdoctoral fellow Imperial Coll., London, 1976-77. Fellow AAAS, Am. Inst. Med. Biol. Engring. (sec., treas. 1993-96, pres. 1997-98), AICHE (officer local sect. 1980-81, 86, Food Pharm. and Bioengring. divsn. award 1992, divsn. chair 1998), Biomed. Engring. Soc. (bd. dirs. 1992-97, pres. 1995-96, Disting. lectr. 1992, Presdl. award, 2004); fellow Am. Heart Assn.; mem. N.Am. Soc. Biorheology (v.p. 1992-94, pres. 1994-96), N.Y. Acad. Scis., Faculty Club Rice U. (bd. dirs., chmn. 1982-84), Sigma Xi (nat. lectr. 1993-96), Nat. Acad. Engring. (editor-in-chief Annals Biomed. Engring., 2002-). Presbyterian. Avocations: tennis, squash, classical music, hiking. Office: Ga Tech Dept Biomed Engring Atlanta GA 30332-0535 Office Phone: 404-894-5057. Office Fax: 404-385-5028. Business E-Mail: larry.mcintire@bme.gatech.edu.

MC INTOSH, J(OHN) RICHARD, retired biologist, educator; b. NYC, Sept. 25, 1939; s. Rustin and Millicent Margaret (Carey) McI.; m. Marjorie Rogers Keniston, Aug. 30, 1961; children— Robert K. (dec.), Elspeth R., Craig T. BA in Physics, Harvard U., 1961, PhD in Biophysics, 1968. Instr. in math. and physics Cambridge Sch., Weston, Mass., 1961-63; asst. prof. biology Harvard U., 1968-70; asst. prof. U. Colo., Boulder, 1970-72, assoc. prof., 1972-76, prof., 1977—2006, chmn. dept. molecular, cellular and devel. biology, 1977-78, dir. Lab for High Voltage Electron Microscopy, 1986—2005, disting. prof., 1999—2006; disting. emeritus prof., 2006—. Mem. editl. bd. Jour. Cell Biology, 1978-82, 1986-90, Cell Motility, 1986-87, Jour. Structural Biology, 1990-97, Molecular Biology Cell, 1995-2006; contbr. articles to profl. jours. Recipient Teaching Recognition award U. Colo., 1974, Scholar award Am. Cancer Soc., 1976, 90; Am. Cancer Soc. grantee, 1971-90, NSF grantee, 1970-82, NIH grantee, 1973-78, 80—; Eleanor Roosevelt Internat. Cancer fellow, 1984; Guggenheim fellow, 1990-91, Fulbright fellow Uganda, 2003-03. Mem. Am. Soc. Cell Biology (coun. 1977-80, 86-89, pres. 1994), Am. Cancer Soc. (cell biology panel 1983-87, rsch. prof. 1994-2005, adv. coun. 1997-2001), NIH (molecular cytology study sect. 1988-92), Nat. Acad. Sci., Am. Acad. Arts and Sci. Home: 870 Willowbrook Rd Boulder CO 80302-7439 Office: U Colo Dept Molec Devel & Devel Bio Boulder CO 80309-0001

MCINTYRE, OSWALD ROSS, physician; b. Chgo., Feb. 13, 1932; m. Helen Whyte; children: Margaret Jean, Archibald Ross, Elizabeth Geary. AB cum laude, Dartmouth Coll., Hanover, NH, 1953, postgrad, 1953-55; MD, Harvard U., Cambridge, Mass., 1957. Intern U. Pa. Hosp., 1957-58; resident in medicine Dartmouth Med. Sch. Affiliated Hosps., 1958-60; instr. medicine Dartmouth Coll., 1964-66, asst. prof. medicine, 1966-69, assoc. prof., 1969-75, prof., 1976—, James J. Carroll prof. oncology, 1980-95, dir. Norris Cotton Cancer Center, 1975-92, prof. emeritus, 1995—; attending physician VA Hosp., White River Junction, Vt., 1964. Cons. in hematology and oncology; acting chmn. dept. medicine Dartmouth-Hitchcock Med. Ctr., 1987-89; chmn. Cancer and Leukemia Group B.; 1990-95. Mem. Am. Soc. Hematology, Am. Assn. Cancer Rsch., Am. Soc. Clin. Oncology, Assn. Cancer Inst. (pres. 1988-89), New Eng. Cancer Soc. (pres. 1989-90). Home: 34 Lamphire Hill Ln Lyme NH 03768-3109

MCKAY-WILKINSON, JULIE ANN, minister, marriage and family therapist; b. Washington, Feb. 26, 1953; d. Charles William and Evelyn Loretta (Starr) McKay; m. Grover Gene Wilkinson, Jan. 13, 1990; 1 child, Angela Starr Gotti. AS, Camden County Coll., 1975; BA, Rowan U., 1978; grad., Unity Sch. Christianity, Lee's Summit, Mo., 1997. Cert. pastoral addictions counselor, and lic. addictions counselor, co-dependency counselor. Probation officer York County Probation, Pa., 1983—86; therapist pvt. practice, York, 1985—90, New Insights, York, 1985—87, Clare Ctr., York, 1987—90; founder, min., therapist Unity Christ Ch., Lubbock, Tex., 1997—2003. Host weekly TV program Spiritual Lifelines. Editor: (monthly newsletter) Spiritual Lifelines, 1997—2003. Chairperson Christmas toy dr. Unity Christ Ch., 1997—2003, founder, Christmas bear dr., 2003—. Mem.: Lubbock Ecimenical Orgn. Democrat. Avocations: gardening, music, movies. Office: Unity Ctr Spiritual Living 7300 Mallard Creek Rd Charlotte NC 28262 Home: 2540 Pickway Dr Charlotte NC 28269 Office Phone: 704-599-1180. Personal E-mail: revjulie3@carolina.rr.com.

MCKEAG, DOUGLAS BRUCE, physician, educator; b. Berwyn, Ill., July 21, 1945; s. Diane (Dolan) McKeag; children: Heather, Kelly, Ian. BS in Zoology, Iowa State U., 1968; MS in Cardiov. Phys., Mich. State U., 1970, MD, 1973. Diplomate Am. Bd. Family Practice & Sports Medicine. Intern Presbyn. Hosp., Pacific Med. Ctr., San Francisco, 1973-74; resident in family practice Grand Rapids Area Med. Edn. Ctr., Mich., 1974-76; fellow in family practice Mich. State U., East Lansing, 1976-77, fellow in adolescent medicine, 1976-77, team physician dept. intercollegiate athletics, 1977—95, assoc. dir., coordinator sports medicine, 1984—95, adj. assoc prof. sch. health edn., 1986—95; dir. Primary Care Sports Medicine, vice chmn. Dept. Family Medicine and Orthopedic Surgery U. Pitts., 1995—99, Arthur J. Rooney Sr. chair for sports medicine, 1995—99; chmn. Dept. Family Medicine Ind. U. Sch. Medicine, 1999—2009, OneAmerica prof. preventive health medicine, 1999—, dir. Ctr. Sports Medicine, 1999—. Mem. com. Nat. Bd. Med. Examiners, 1988—92; mem. drug testing and drug edn. subcom. NCAA, 1988-94; cons. Kuwait U. Faculty of Medicine, Walt Disney Ednl. Svcs., Puerto Rico Olympic Com.; presenter in field. Editor series Primary Care Sports Medicine, 1988—, Basketball (Handbook of Sports Medicine and Science), 2003; assoc. editor: Medicine and Science in Sports and Exercise, 1987; mem. editorial bd. various jours. in field; contbr. articles to profl. publs. Grantee Mich. Heat Assn., 1975-76, NIH, 1980-81, 81-82, 84, 85, Nat. Collegiate Athletic Assn., 1983, 88, Mich. Acad. Family Physicians, 1986; NIH fellow, 1968-70; named one of America's Top Doctors, 2005. Fellow Am. Coll. Sports Medicine (trustee 1987, v.p., 2002), Am. Acad. Family Physicians; mem. N.Am. Primary Care Rsch. Group, Soc. Tchrs. Family Medicine, Soc. Adolescent Medicine(pres., 1994-95), Am. Medical Soc. for Sports Medicine, Am. Bd. of Family Practice, Am. Coll. Sports Medicine, Ind. Acad. Family Physicians. Office: Ind U Dept Family Medicine 1110 W Michigan St Indianapolis IN 46202 Office Phone: 317-278-0360. Business E-Mail: dmckeag@iupui.edu.

MCKEAN, SHERRY LYNN, neurodiagnostic technologist; b. Owosso, Mich., Mar. 3, 1953; d. William Ash and Myrtle Viola (Darling) Salander; m. Brian Patrick McKean, May 31, 1997; 1 child, Jennifer Lynn Bentley. A, John Wesley Coll., 1979; degree, Calif. Coll. Health Scis., 2002. Registered polysomnographic technologist. Neurodiagnostic supr. Dr. Gary Roat, Flint, Mich., 1978—95; neurodiagnostic tech. Flint Osteo. Hosp., 1993—95, Dr. I. Zachar Dyme, Lansing, 1995—, Meml. Healthcare, Owosso, 1995—. Mem.: Assn. Polysomnographic Technologists. Avocations: hiking, travel, reading, sewing, walking. Office: 826 W King St Owosso MI 48867 Home: 2220 West Mason Rd Owosso MI 48867 Office Phone: 989-729-4346.

MCKEAN, THOMAS WAYNE, retired dentist, military officer; b. Adams County, Ind., May 18, 1928; s. Gorman F. and Elmira B. (Staley) McK.; m. Marilyn Kimberlin, Aug. 9, 1952; children: Thomas Wayne, Randall K., Dana K. D.D.S., Ind. U., 1953; grad., Naval Dental Sch., 1963. Diplomate: Am. Bd. Oral Surgery. Commd. ensign Dental Corps USN, 1949—53, advanced through grades to rear adm., 1980; stationed at Naval Tng. Ctr., Great Lakes, Ill., 1953; dental officer U.S.S. Randall, 1953-56; head dental svc., asst. dental officer U.S. Naval Acad./Naval Hosp., Annapolis, Md., 1956-59; dental officer FASRON III; asst. dental officer U.S. Naval Sta., Bermuda, 1959-63; postgrad. student Naval Dental Sch., Bethesda, Md., 1963-64; resident oral and maxillofacial surgery Naval Hosp., Great Lakes, Ill., 1964-66; dental officer U.S.S. America, 1966-68; chief oral surgery Naval Hosp., Orlando, Fla., 1968-70; dir. oral surgery and gen. practice residency tng. programs Naval Regional Med. Ctr., Great Lakes, 1970-74, chmn. dept. dentistry, 1970-74; cons., lectr. U.S. Army, Fort Sheridan, Ill., 1970-74; dir. oral surgery and gen. practice residency tng. programs Naval Regional Med. Ctr., Oakland, Calif., 1974-78, chmn., dept. dentistry, 1974-78; lectr. oral surgery Letterman Army Med. Ctr., San Francisco, 1974-78; clin. lectr. dept. oral surgery U. of Pacific Sch. Dentistry, San Francisco, 1974-78; comdg. officer Naval Regional Dental Ctr., Pensacola, Fla., 1978-80; lectr. oral surgery Pensacola (Fla.) Jr. Coll., 1978-80; cons., lectr. Dwight D. Eisenhower Army Regional Med. Ctr., Augusta, Ga., 1978-80; insp. gen. dental Bur. Medicine and Surgery, Dept. of Navy, Washington, 1980-81; comdg. officer Naval Regional Dental Ctr., San Diego, 1981-82; insp. gen. Naval Med. Command, Washington, 1983-85; ret., 1985—2008. Contbr. articles to profl. jours. Chmn. bd. trustees UMC, Winter Park, 1992, mem. bd. adminstrs. 1995-98; bd. dirs. Circle of Friends Fla. Hosp. Found., 1989-91, Fla. Hosp. Found., 1991—, chmn. bd., 1995-96; bd. dirs., Fla. Hosp. Found., 1991-, chmn., Ctrl. Fla. Veterans, Inc., 2007-, bd. trustees 2008-; chmn. Fla. Hosp. Shares (Internat. Med. Missions), 1994—2010; mem. Fla. Hosp. Cmty. Benefits subcom., 1996-, Leadership Coun. FUMC Winter Pk., 2007-09. Decorated Humanitarian Service medal, Legion of Merit with Gold Star, Meritorious Service medal, Nat. Def. Service medal with star, Vietnam Service medal, Republic of Vietnam Campaign medal with device, others; recipient Alumnus of Yr. award Ind. U. Sch.of Dentistry Alumnus Assn., 1988. Fellow Am. Dental Soc. of Anesthesiology, Internat. Coll. Dentists, Am. Coll. Dentists, Internat. Assn. Oral Surgeons; mem. Am. Assn. Oral and Maxillofacial Surgeons, ADA, Western Soc. Oral Surgeons, Assn. Mil. Surgeons U.S. (medal), Fla. Soc. Oral Surgeons, Delta Sigma Delta, Sigma Chi (Significant Sig award 1983). Home: 557 Village Pl Longwood FL 32779 Home Phone: 407-644-9672. Personal E-mail: tmckean1@cfl.rr.com.

MCKECHNIE, JOHN CHARLES, gastroenterologist, educator; b. Louisville, Feb. 1, 1935; s. Albert Hay and Edna Scott (Johnson) McKechnie; children: Steven Keith, Kevin Stuart. BA, U. Louisville, 1955; MD, Baylor Coll. Medicine, Houston, 1959. Diplomate Am. Bd. Internal Medicine, Am. Bd. Gastroenterology. Intern Jefferson Davis Hosp., Houston, 1959—60; resident internal medicine Baylor Affiliated Program, Houston, 1960—61, 1965—66; gen. practice medicine Benham, Ky., 1964; practice medicine specializing in gastroenterology Houston, 1966—; clin. instr. Baylor Coll. Medicine, Houston, 1966—69, asst. prof., 1969—72, assoc. prof., 1972—77, prof., 1977—. Mem. staff Meth. Hosp., assoc. dir. internal medicine program; cons. Ben Taub Hosp., St. Luke's Episcopal Hosp.; clin. prof. Weill Cornell Med. Coll., NYC. Contbr. articles to profl. jours. Capt. USMC, 1962—64. Fellow: ACP, Am. Coll. Gastroenterology (gov. Tex. chpt. 1979—80, trustee 1981—84); mem.: AMA, Houston Gastroent. Soc. (pres. 1983), Tex. Soc. Gastrointestinal Endoscopy, Am. Soc. Gastrointestinal Endoscopy, Digestive Disease Found., Am. Gastroent. Assn., Tex. Med. Assn., So. Med. Assn., Alpha Omega Alpha. Republican. Presbyterian. Office: Th-Meth Hosp 6560 Fannin St Ste 1630 Houston TX 77030-2734 Office Phone: 713-797-0916.

MCKEE, FRANCIS JOHN, medical association consultant, lawyer; b. Bklyn., Aug. 31, 1943; s. Francis Joseph and Catherine (Giles) McK.; m. Antoinette Mary Sancis; children: Lisa Ann, Francis Dominic, Michael Christopher, Thomas Joseph. AB, Stonehill Coll., 1965; JD, St. John's U., 1970. Bar: N.Y. 1971. Assoc. Samuel Weinberg, Esquire, Bklyn., 1970-71, Finch & Finch, Esquire, Long Island City, NY, 1971-72; staff atty. Med. Soc. of State of NY, Lake Success, NY, 1972-77; of counsel Suffolk County Med. Soc., Hauppauge, NY, 1977—81; exec. dir. Suffolk Physicians Rev. Orgn., East Islip, NY, 1977-81; prin. Francis J. McKee Assocs., Clinton, NY, 1984—2001; exec. dir. NY State Soc. Surgeons, Inc., Clinton, NY, 1981-2000, NY State Soc. Orthopaedic Surgeons, Inc., Clinton, NY, 1981—2000, Upstate NY chpt. ACS, Inc., Clinton, NY, 1981-2000, NY State Ophthalmol. Soc., 1984-92, NY State Soc. Obstetricians and Gynecologists, 1985-2001, Orthopac of NY, 1986-2000, Nat. Com. for the Preservation Orthopaedic Practice, New Hartford, NY, 1989-2000, L.I. Ophthalmol. Soc., 1994-2000. Mgr. Thomas J. McKee and Assocs., LLC, 2005-10; exec. v.p. Thomas J. McKee and Assocs., Inc., 2011-; mgr. Michael C. Mckee and Assoc., 2009-10; exec. v.p. Michael C. Mckee and Assoc., Inc., 2011-. With U.S. Army, 1966-68. Mem.: NY State Bar Assn., Am. Legion, Taberna Country Club, Elks (presiding justice, subordinate order 2007—11). Republican. Roman Catholic. Home and Office: 908 Taberna Cir New Bern NC 28562 E-mail: frank4mets@embarqmail.com.

MCKEE, PATRICK ALLEN, physician; b. Tulsa, Apr. 30, 1937; s. Charles and Estelle Marie McK. Student, U. Tulsa, 1955-58; MD, U. Okla., 1962. Intern, resident Duke Hosp., Durham, NC, 1962—63, 1963—64; rsch. fellow cell biology Duke U. Med. Ctr., 1963—64; chief resident U. Okla. Med. Center, Oklahoma City, 1967-68; clin. assoc. Framingham Heart Program, NIH, Framingham, MA, 1965-67; assoc. medicine dept. medicine Duke U. Med. Center, 1969-70, clin. investigator, 1970-71, asst. prof. medicine, 1970-72, asst. prof. biochemistry, 1971-85, assoc. prof. medicine, 1972-75, prof. medicine, 1975—, dir. outpatient clinic, 1975-85, chief div. gen. medicine, 1976-85; chmn. dept. medicine U. Okla., Health Sci. Ctr., 1985-95; Laureate chair in molecular medicine and prof. medicine, sci. dir. W.K. Warren Medical Rsch. Ctr. U. Okla., 1995—; investigator Howard Hughes Med. Inst., Duke U. Med. Ctr., 1977—85. Cons. thrombosis research Nat. Heart and Lung Inst., 1970-71; mem. hematology study sect. NIH, 1973-77, NASA Aerospace Medicine Occupl. Health Adv. Subcom., 1995-2000. Contbr. numerous articles to profl. jours. Trustee Okla. Sch. Math. and Sci., 1986-90; vice chmn. Okla. Ctr. for Advancement Sci. and Tech., 1987-91. Recipient McGovern Lectr. & medal Am. Osler Soc., 2009; NIH grantee U. Okla. Med. Center, 1968-69, 2003-07; NIH grantee Duke U. Med. Center, 1972-85, 2003-07. Mem. US Pharmacop (coun. experts, 1995-), Hematology and Blood Products Com. (chair, coun. experts, 2005-); fellow Am. Heart Assn., ACP; Assn. Am. Physicians, Am. Soc. Clin. Investigation, So. Soc. Clin. Investigation, Cen. Soc. Clin. Investigation, Am. Fedn. Medical Research, Internat. Soc. Thrombosis and Haemostasis, Am. Soc. Hematology, Am. Soc. Biochem. Molecular Biol., Am. Clin. and Climatol. Soc., Am. Soc. Internal Medicine, Sword and Key, Alpha Omega Alpha, Phi Eta Sigma, Sigma Xi. Roman Catholic. Office: University Okla Health Scis Ctr PO Box 26901 Oklahoma City OK 73126-0901 Office Phone: 405-271-5645. *

MCKEEL, SHERYL WILSON, pharmacist; b. Nashville, Apr. 6, 1957; d. Robert Lewis and Norma Anne (Cox) Wilson; m. Vaughn Allen McKeel, Apr. 22, 2000. BS in Biology, David Lipscomb U., 1979; BS in Pharmacy, Auburn U., 1985. Lic. pharmacist, Tenn. Student extern/intern East Alabama Med. Ctr., Opelika, Ala., 1982-86; staff pharmacist Metro Nashville Gen. Hosp., 1987-95, PharmaThera, Inc., Nashville, 1995-99, Mid. Tenn. Mental Health Inst., Nashville, 1999-2000, Kmart, 2009, Maxim Staffing Solutions, 2010—11. Flutist Nashville Cmty. Concert Band, 1973-97; presch. tchr. Donelson Ch. of Christ, 1988—; active Lipscomb U. Cmty. Chorus, 1998—2008 Mem. Am. Pharm. Assn., Am. Soc. Health Sys. Pharmacists, Am. Soc. Parenteral and Enteral Nutrition, Tenn. Soc. Health Sys. Pharmacists, Nashville Area Pharmacists Assn. Democrat. Avocations: art, music, reading, cooking, sewing. Home: 1439 McGavock Pike Nashville TN 37216-3231 Home Phone: 615-228-7285. Personal E-mail: mckeelv@prodigy.net.

MCKEITH, IAN GRANT, geriatric psychiatrist; b. North Shields, Eng., Aug. 31, 1954; s. George William and Margaret (Grant) McK. MB, BChir, U. Newcastle, Eng., 1977, MD, 1993. Cons. Nat. Health Svc., Newcastle, 1987-89; sr. lectr. Newcastle, 1989-93; clin. scientist Med. Rsch. Coun., Newcastle, 1993-94, prof. old age psychiatry, 1994—; pres. Lewy Body Disease Soc., 2006—10. Head dementias and neurodegensatieve disease rsch. group U. Newcastle, 2005—10; co-dir. UK Dept. Health Dementia and Neurodegenerative Diseases Rsch. Network, 2005—, clin. dir. Inst. Aging. and Health, U. Newcastle. Editor: Dementia with Lewy Bodies, 1996, 2006; contbr. over 350 articles to profl. jours. including Neurology, Lancet, Brit. Med. Jour. Fellow Royal Coll. Psychiatrists (London, Laughlin prize 1981, Roche Traveling prof. 1999, Squibb travel fellow 1985, Lifetime Achievement award 2008), Acad. Med. Scis. Avocations: running, sailing. Office: Newcastle Univ/Aging and Vitality Inst Aging Health/Wolfson Rsch Ctr Newcastle Univ Campus NE4 5PL Newcastle upon Tyne England Office Phone: 44 191 2481313. Business E-Mail: i.g.mckeith@ncl.ac.uk.

MCKELVEY, ROBERT S., child psychiatrist, educator; MD, Dartmouth Med. Sch., Hanover, 1974. Diplomate Am. Bd. Psychiatry and Neurology, 1980, Am. Bd. Psychiatry and Neurology-child psychiatry, 1982. Resident psychiatry Harvard Med. Sch. Cambridge Hosp., 1975—77; resident child psychiatry Harvard Med. Sch. McLean Hosp., 1977—79; prof. child and adolescent psychiatry Oreg. Health and Sci. Univ. Avocations: German, Vietnamese. Office: Oregon Health & Science University 3181 SW Sam Jackson Pk Rd Portland OR 97239-3098 Office Phone: 503-494-6176.

MCKENNA, BARBARA J., clinical pathologist; b. Sept. 21, 1954; BS, Mich. State U.; MD, U. Mich., 1981. Cert. Anatomic Pathology and Clin. Pathology, 1985, Cytopathology, 1996. Resident in anatomic and clin. pathology U. Mich. Med. Sch.; staff physician and assoc. dir. laboratories Saratoga Hosp., NY, 1985—88; dir. laboratories Moses-Ludington Hosp., Ticonderoga, NY, 1985—88; assoc. attending physician St. Peter's Hosp., Albany, 1988—94; joined faculty Albany Med. Coll., 1994—2002; assoc. prof. pathology U. Mich. Med. Sch., 2002—, dir. surg. pathology fellowship prog. Mem.: Am. Soc. Clin. Pathology (pres. 2008—09, George F. Stevenson Disting. Svc. award, Commn. on Continuing Edn. 2003), A. James French Soc. Pathology, Coll. Am. Pathology, US and Can. Acad. Pathology. Office: U Mich Med Sch 2G332 UH 1500 E Medical Center Dr Ann Arbor MI 48109-0054 Office Phone: 743-936-6770. Office Fax: 734-763-4095. E-mail: barbmcke@umich.edu. *

MCKENNA, RICHARD HENRY, financial consultant, health facility administrator; b. Covington, Ky., Dec. 19, 1927; s. Charles Joseph and Mary Florence (Wieck) McK.; m. Patricia M. Macdonald, Jan. 6, 1979; children: Linda Ann, Theresa K., Joan Marie; stepchildren: Stuart J. Goodman, Ann Elizabeth Goodman. BS in Commerce, U. Cin., 1959; MBA, Xavier U., Cin., 1963. Acct. Andrew Jergens Co., Cin., 1947-55; treas., dir. Ramsey Bus. Equipment, Inc., Cin., 1955-59; asst. to pres. Oakley Die and Mfg. Co., Cin., 1959-60, Electro-Jet Tool Co., Inc., Cin., 1959-60; pvt. practice acctg., Cin. and, No. Ky., 1960-62; bus. mgr. St. Joseph Hosp., Lexington, Ky., 1962-66; asst. adminstr. fin. U. Ky. Hosp., Lexington, 1966-70; v.p., CFO, St. Lawrence Hosp., Lansing, Mich., 1970-87; v.p., CFO, asst. sec.-treas. St. Joseph's Hosp., Inc., Savannah, Ga., 1987-95, St. Joseph's Health Ctr., Inc., Savannah, 1987-90; chmn. bd. McKenna & McKenna Assocs., Inc., Savannah, 1983—. Adj. faculty Aquinas Coll., Grand Rapids, Mich., 1980-89, asst. prof.; chmn. bd. North Grand River Coop. Laundry, 1986-87; former mem. adv. com. to commr. of fin. State of Ky., mgr. Diversified Enterprises LLC, 2010-, R's Unlimited Opportunities LLC, 2010-. Chmn. Cath. divsn. Oak Hills Bus. Com.; mem. spkrs. com. Oak Hill Sch. Dist.; bd. dirs. Savannah YMCA, 1992-94, mem. exec. com., 1994-96; bd. dirs. Habersham br. YMCA, 1992-96, chmn. bd. and treas., 1945-66. With U.S. Mcht. Marine, 1945-47, U.S. Army, 1948-51. Mem. AICPA (ret.), Healthcare Fin. Mgmt. Assn. (past dir. Ky. chpt. Follmer award), Am. Mgmt. Assn., Ky. Soc. CPAs, Mich. Hosp. Assn. (former mem. com. on reimbursement), Ga. Hosp. Assn. (com. on fin. and mgmt.), Delta Mu Delta, Alpha Sigma Lambda. Personal E-mail: rhmck118@aol.com.

MCKENNA, SAMUEL JAY, dentist; b. La Jolla, Calif., May 6, 1954; BA in Biology, U. Calif., San Diego, 1976; DDS, UCLA; MD, Vanderbilt U., 1983. Residency program dir. Vanderbilt U. Sch. Medicine, 1992—2007, prof., chmn., oral and maxillofacial surgery, 2008. Co-chair, exam. com. Am. Bd. Oral and Maxillofacial Surgery, 1997—99; bd. dirs. Nashville Interfaith Dental Clinic, 2000—06, pres., bd. directors, 2004—05. Recipient Robert S. McCleery Master Teach award, Vanderbilt U. Sect. Surg. Scis. Fellow: ACS, Am. Assn. Oral and Maxillofacial Surgeons; mem.: ADA, Nashville Acad. Medicine, Tenn. Med. Assn. Avocations: scuba diving, bicycling. Office: 1623 The Vanderbilt Clinic Nashville TN 37232-5225 Business E-Mail: samuel.mckenna@vanderbilt.edu.

MCKENNA, VOLEEN, microbiologist; b. Camden, NJ, Aug. 13, 1962; d. Ross and Julie Bergenstein; m. John McKenna; children: Gary, Gale, Stephen. BS in Chemistry, Wayne State Univ., 1980, MD, 1984; PhD in Pathobiology, Oklahoma State Univ., 1996. Asst. prof. Wayne State U., 1987—91; vis. sci. Oklahoma State Univ., 1992—96; rsch. Meriks Rsch., 1997—2001, chief rsch., 2002—; adj. prof. Univ. of Michigan, 2005—; vis. prof Boston Univ., Boston, 2011—. Contbr. articles to profl. jours. Vol. coach Battle Creek volleyball team, 2005—; bd. dir. Battle Creek Elementary Sch., 2007—. Republican. Jewish. Avocations: aerobics, French horn. Office: Meriks Rsch 5420 A Beckley Rd #10 Battle Creek MI 49015-4123

MCKENZIE, HARRY JAMES, cardiothoracic surgeon, researcher; b. Meyersdale, Pa., Aug. 7, 1960; s. Henry Sadrus and Betty Elaine (Reiber) McK.; m. Judith Palmieri, July 6, 1985; children: Henry James, Anne Christine, Mark Angus. BS, Duquesne U., 1984; postgraduate, U. Pitts., 1986-87; MD, Hahnemann U., 1992. Surg. intern Temple U., Conemaugh Med. Ctr., Johnstown, Pa., 1992-93, surg. resident, 1993-97; cardiothoracic resident Med. Coll. Ga., Augusta, 1997-99. Mem. problem task force Conemaugh Med. Ctr., 1992-93. Contbr. articles to profl. jours.; presenter in field. Hosp. vol. Ctrl. Med. Pavilion, Pitts., 1981-84, Presbyn. Hosp., Pitts., 1986-87; med. exam. officer, Phila. Special Olympics, 1989-90; grad. banquet spkr. Salisbury (Pa.) H.S., 1993. Recipient 3d place rsch. competition award, ACS Region III com. on trauma, Norfolk, Va., 1993; recipient 1st place rsch. competition award ACS-Pa. com. on trauma, Hershey, 1993. Mem. AMA, Am. Soc. Gen. Surgeons, Soc. Am. Gastrointestinal Endoscopic Surgeons, Soc. Thoracic Surgeons. Avocations: skiing, golf, jogging, fishing, hiking. Home: 4130 N Tara Cir Wichita KS 67226-3367

MCKHANN, GUY MEAD, neurologist, educator; b. Boston, Mar. 20, 1932; s. Charles Fremont and Emily (Priest) McKhann; m. Katherine E. Henderson, Nov. 30, 1957 (div. 1983); children: Ian, James, Emily, Guy, Charles; m. Marilyn S. Albert, Sept. 27, 1997; children: Joshua, Katie. Student, Harvard U., 1948—51; MD, Yale U., 1955; MD (hon.), Hebei Med. Coll., Shijiazhuang, China, 1994. Intern N.Y. Hosp., 1955—56; asst. resident pediat. Johns Hopkins Hosp., Balt., 1956—57; clin. assoc. NIH, Bethesda, Md., 1957—60; resident neurology Mass. Gen. Hosp., Boston, 1960—63; asst. and assoc. prof. pediat. and neurology Stanford (Calif.) U., 1963—69; prof. neurology Johns Hopkins, Balt., 1969—, Kennedy prof. neurology, head neurology dept., 1969—88, dir. Zanvyl Krieger Mind Brain Inst., 1988—2000, 2004—; acting dir. for clin. activities Nat. Inst. Neurol. Diseases and Stroke NIH, 2000—01. Prin. investigator Neurologic and Cognitive Outcomes Following Coronary Artery Bypass Grafting; sci.cons. Dana Found.; sci. adv. Brain in the News. Served with USPHS, 1957—60. Recipient Med. Student Teaching Award, Medical Student Teaching Award, Johns Hopkins, 197, 1974, Weinstein-Goldenson Rsch. Award, United Cerebral Palsy, 1978, Undergrad. Teaching Award, Johns Hopkins, 1996; named to Macy Faculty Ward, 1982; scholar in Acad. Medicine, John and Mary R. Markle, 1964—69, Joseph P. Kennedy Jr., 1963—69. Fellow: AAAS, Royal Coll. Physicians; mem.: Inst. Medicine, Soc. Neuroscis., Am. Neurol. Assn. (hon.), Am. Neurochem. Soc., Alpha Omega Alpha. Achievements include research in on normal and abnormal human nervous system. Home: 6526 Montrose Ave Baltimore MD 21212-1023 Office: Zanvyl Krieger Mind/Brain Inst 338 Krieger Hall Johns Hopkins U 3400 N Charles St Baltimore MD 21218-2685 Office Phone: 410-516-8640. E-mail: guy.mckhann@jhu.edu.

MCKIE, LINDA JANE, sociologist, educator, researcher; b. Belfast, Ireland, Sept. 29, 1956; d. James William and Irene (Cowie) McIlroy; 1 child, Laura Louise. BA in Social Policy, U. Ulster, Belfast, No. Ireland, 1981; MSc in Pub. Policy, U. Bath, Eng., 1983; PhD in Sociology, U. Durham, Eng., 1989. Lectr. in Social Policy U. Teesside, Middlesborough, England, 1986—88, U. Glasgow, Scotland, 1989; sr. exec. officer Equal Opportunities Commn., Manchester, England, 1990; sr. lectr. in sociology Queen Margaret U. Coll., Edinburgh, Scotland, 1991—93; sr. lectr. in sociology of health and illness U. Aberdeen, Scotland, 1993—99; prof. sociology Glasgow (Scotland) Caledonian U., 1999—. Trustee Inst. Rural Health, Wales, 1998—, Evaluation Support, Scotland, 2005—; co-opted trustee Eiskine Vets. Charity, Helsinki, 2011—. Author: Families, Violence and Social Change, 2005; co-author (with S. Bowlby, S. Gregory and I. Macpherson): Interdependency and Care Over the Life Cause; editor: Researching Women's Health: Methods and Process, 1996; editor: (with S. Cunningham-Burley) Families in Society: Boundaries and Relationships, 2005; co-editor (with others): Gender, Power and the Household, 1999; co-editor: (with N.Watson) Organizing Bodies: Institutions, Policy and Work, 2000; co-editor: (with K. Backett-Milburn) Constructing Gendered Bodies, 2000; contbr. chapters to books, articles to 100 internat. and U.K. jours.; co-author (with S. Callan): Understanding Facilites. Assoc. Dir. Ctr. for Rsch. on Families and Relationships, 2000—. Fellow Loch Haven U., 2001—02. Fellow: Salzburg Seminar (hon.). Avocations: films, theater, exercise. Office: Glasgow Caledonian University Business Law and Social Scis 70 Cowcaddens Road G4 0BA Glasgow Scotland Office Fax: 0141 331 8211. E-mail: l.mckie@gcu.ac.uk.

MCKINNELL, ROBERT GILMORE, retired zoologist, biology professor, geneticist; b. Springfield, Mo., Aug. 9, 1926; s. William Parks and Mary Catherine (Gilmore) McK.; m. Beverly Walton Kerr (dec.); children: Nancy Elizabeth, Robert Gilmore, Susan Kerr. B in Naval Sci., U. Notre Dame, 1946; AB, U. Mo., 1948; BS, Drury Coll., 1949, DSc (hon.), 1993; PhD, U. Minn., 1959. Rsch. assoc. Fox Chase Cancer Ctr., Phila., 1958-61; asst. prof. biology Tulane U., New Orleans, 1961-65, assoc. prof., 1965-69, prof., 1969-70; prof. zoology U. Minn., Mpls., 1970—76, prof. genetics and cell biology St. Paul, 1976—99, prof. emeritus, 1999—. Vis. scientist Dow Chem. Co., Freeport, Tex., 1976; guest dept. zoology U. Calif., Berkeley, 1979; Royal Soc. guest rsch. fellow Nuffield dept. pathology John Radcliffe Hosp., Oxford U., 1981-82; NATO vis. scientist Akademisch Ziekenhuis, Ghent, Belgium, 1984; faculty rsch. assoc. Naval Med. Rsch. Inst., Bethesda, Md., 1988; secretariat Third Internat. Conf. Differentiation, 1978; organizer, secretariat 6th Internat. Conf. on Pathology of Reptiles and Amphibians, 2001; mem. amphibian com. Inst. Lab. Animal Resources, NRC, 1970-73, mem. adv. coun., 1974; mem. panel genetic and cellular resources program NIH, 1981-82, spl. study sect., Bethesda, 1990. Author: Cloning: Amphibian Nuclear Transplantation, 1978, Cloning, A Biologist Reports, 1979; sr. editor: Differentiation and Neoplasia, 1980, Cloning: Leben aus der Retorte, 1981, Cloning of Frogs, Mice and Other Animals, 1985, (with others) The Biological Basis of Cancer, 1998, 2d edit., 2006, (with D.L. Carlson) Pathology of Reptiles and Amphibians, 2002, Prevention Cancer, 2008, also symposium procs. in field; mem. bd. advisors Marquis Who's Who; contbr. articles to profl. jours. Served to lt. USNR, 1944-47, 51-53. Recipient Outstanding Teaching award Newcomb Coll., Tulane U., 1970; Disting. Alumni award Drury Coll., 1979, Morse Alumni Tchg. award U. Minn., 1992; Rsch. fellow Nat. Cancer Inst., 1956-58, Prince Hitachi award Japanese Found. Cancer Rsch., 1998; Sr. Sci. fellow NATO, 1974. Fellow AAAS, Linnean Soc. (London); mem. Am. Assn. Cancer Rsch. (emeritus), Am. Assn. Cancer Edn. (sr.), Am. Assn. History of Medicine, Indian Soc. Devel. Biology (lifetime emeritus), Internat. Soc. Differentiation (pres. 1994-96), Minn. Acad. Medicine, Gown-in-Town Club, Sigma Xi. Office: 140 Gortner Lab Biochemistry 1479 Gortner Ave Saint Paul MN 55108 Home Phone: 651-646-3690. Business E-Mail: mckin002@umn.edu.

MCKINNEY, ALEXANDER STUART, retired neurologist; b. NYC, Feb. 3, 1933; s. John McDowell and Katherine Elizabeth (Morse) McK.; m. Carolyn Clifton Braman, Aug. 15, 1958 (div. July 1985); children: James, David, Mark; m. Susan Lowe Childress, July 30, 1985; children: Josephine, Mary, Jennifer. AB, Princeton U., 1955; MD, Columbia U., 1959. Diplomate Am. Bd. Neurology. Intern St. Luke's Hosp., NYC, 1959-60; resident N.Y. Neurological Inst., 1960-63; prof. neurology Emory U., Atlanta, 1965-85; pvt. practice Mountain Med. Assocs., Clyde, N.C., 1985-95; chief of staff Haywood County Hosp., Clyde, N.C., 1989-90. Contbr. articles to profl. jours. Served to lt. comdr. USNR, 1963-65. Fellow Am. Acad. Neurology (sr.); mem. N.C. Neurol. Soc. (pres. 1992). Avocations: travel, gardening. Home: 9 Charles Wesley Dr Waynesville NC 28786-3066 Personal E-mail: ssmck@charter.net.

MCKINNON, MCKAY, plastic and reconstructive surgeon; b. Wadesboro, NC, Oct. 20, 1949; BA, U. NC, Chapel Hill; MD, U. NC Sch. Medicine, 1976. Diplomate American Bd. Plastic Surgery. Intern gen. surgery Beth Israel Deaconess Med. Ctr., Boston, 1976—77, resident plastic surgery, 1977—80; fellow plastic surgery Boston Children's Hosp., 1980—81; Mailman fellowship craniofacial plastic surgery U. Miami-Jackson Meml. Med. Ctr., Fla., 1981—83; plastic surgery fellowship Foch Hosp./Belvedere Clinic, Paris, 1983—84; clin. prof. U. Chgo., 1985—2009; plastic & reconstructive surgeon Children's Meml. Hosp., U. Chgo. Med. Ctr. Contbr. articles to profl. jours. Mem.: American Soc. Craniofacial Surgeons, International Soc. Craniofacial Surgeons, American Soc. Maxillofacial Surgeons, American Assn. Plastic Surgeons, American Soc. Plastic Surgeons, Cleft Palate Found. Achievements include since 1985, has led annual missionary surgical teams to Choluteca, Honduras performing cleft lip and palate surgery for more than 500 children at no cost; in 2000, removed a 200 pound tumor during an 18 hour operation on a woman with a large tumor disorder; in 2004, traveled on a special mission to Romania with 12 other doctors to remove an 80 pound tumor from a woman suffering from a genetic disorder causing tumors to grow on her body. Office: Childrens Memorial Hospital 680 N Lake Shore Dr Ste 1208 Chicago IL 60611 Office Phone: 312-335-9566. Office Fax: 312-335-1681. *

MCKINNON, STUART J., ophthalmologist, educator; MD, La. State U. Sch. Medicine, New Orleans, 1990; PhD in Physical Chemistry, U. New Orleans, 1990. Diplomate Am. Bd. Ophthalmology, lic. La., Md., Tex., NC. Resident ophthalmology La. State U. Eye Ctr., 1991—95; glaucoma fellow Wilmer Ophthal. Inst., Johns Hopkins U. Sch. Medicine, Balt., 1995—96; prof. ophthalmology U. Tex. Health Sci. Ctr., San Antonio; assoc. prof. dept. ophthalmology & dept. neurobiology Duke U. Med. Ctr., Durham, NC, 2009—. Mem. editl. bd. Jour. Ocular Pharmacology & Therapeutics; contbr. articles to profl. jours. Com. mem. Am. Health Assistance Found. Mem.: Southern Med. Assn., Am. Glaucoma Soc., Am. Acad. Ophthalmology. Office: Duke U Med Ctr Box 3802 Durham NC 27710 Office Phone: 919-681-3937. Office Fax: 919-681-8267. Business E-Mail: stuart.mckinnon@duke.edu. *

MCKNIGHT, AMY JAYNE, medical educator; b. Belfast, Co. Antrim, Northern Ireland, Oct. 11, 1977; d. Frederick Barry and Cindy Helen Merrilees McKnight. BSc with honors, U. Aberdeen, Scotland, 2000; PhD, Queen's U. Belfast, 2003; MSc with distinction, U. Manchester, Eng., 2007. MBCS Brit. Computer Soc., 2008. Lectr., sch. medicine, dentistry and biomed. scis. Queen's U. Belfast, 2006—. Dir. ABC Sci. Data Svcs., Newtownards, Co. Down, Northern Ireland, 2008—. Mem.: The Renal Soc., European Diabetic Nephropathy Study Group, European Soc. Human Genetics, Am. Soc. Human Genetics, The Kennel Club, Irish Kennel Club (life). Achievements include design of online genetics resource for renal research community; research in first genome-wide, microsatellite-based association screen for diabetic kidney disease; first large-scale candidate-gene based nsSNP scan and genome-wide nsSNP scan for diabetic kidney disease; development of online database for allele frequencies in Northern Ireland. Office: Queen's University Belfast Nephrology Rsch Group Level A Tower Block Belfast City Hosp Belfast Co Antrim BT9 7AB Northern Ireland Office Fax: 44(0)2890236911. Personal E-mail: a.j.mcknight@lineone.net. Business E-Mail: a.j.mcknight@qub.ac.uk.

MCKOWN, CHARLES HENRY, academic administrator, former dean; b. Huntington, W.Va., Dec. 29, 1934; BS, W.Va. U., 1956; MD, Med. Coll. Va., 1960. Intern Med. Coll. Va., 1961; resident in radiology McGuire VA Hosp., 1961—62; fellow NIH, 1964—67; prof. radiology, chmn. dept. radiology Marshall U., Huntington, W.Va., 1975—88, dean Sch. Medicine, 1989—2011, v.p. health scis. advancement, 1989—. Office: Marshall U Joan C Edwards Sch Medicine 1600 Medical Center Dr Huntington WV 25701-3655 *

MCLAFFERTY, ISABELLA (ELLA) HELEN RUTH, nursing educator; b. Scotland, Apr. 20, 1955; BSc with honors, U. Abertay, 1991, PhD, 2002. Sr. lectr. U. Dundee, 2006—. Avocations: reading, swimming. Office: Sch Nursing & Midwifery 11 Ai Dundee DD1 4HJ Scotland E-mail: i.h.r.mclafferty@dundee.ac.uk.

MCLAIN, GINNY, hospital administrator; B in Nursing, Met. State U.; M in Health Care Sys., U. Denver. Nurse; mgr., exec., Colo. Kaiser Permanente, 1995—, v.p. primary care and med. specialties. Recipient Friend of Pharmacy award, Inst. Health Rsch., 2009. Office: Kaiser Permanente 10350 E Dakota Ave Denver CO 80231 Office Phone: 303-338-3800. Office Fax: 303-344-7277. Business E-Mail: G.McLain@KP.org. *

MCLANAHAN, CHARLES SCOTT, neurosurgeon; b. Chgo., Sept. 23, 1946; s. Charles Jackson and Anna Martin (Findley) McL.; m. Mary Ivey, Aug. 23, 1975; children: George, Ward, Matt. BA, Yale U., 1969; MD, Columbia U., 1973. Diplomate Am. Bd. Neurol. Surgery, Am. Bd. Pediat. Neurol. Surgery. Resident in neurosurgery Emory U., Atlanta, 1973-78, instr. neurosurgery, 1979; asst. prof. neurosurgery La. State U. Med. Sch., New Orleans, 1979-80; neurosurgeon Carolina Neurosurgery & Spine Assocs., PA, Charlotte, 1980—. Mem.: Am. Bd. Pediat. Neurological Surgery (bd. dirs. 2004—), N.C. Neurosurg. Soc. (sec.-treas. 1997—99, pres. 1999—2001). Republican. Avocation: reading. Office: Carolina Neurosurgery and Spine Associat 225 Baldwin Ave Charlotte NC 28204-3109 Home Phone: 704-333-4677.

MCLARDY-SMITH, PETER DAVID, orthopedist, consultant; b. July 16, 1951; BA in Physiol. Sci., Wadham Coll., Oxford, 1972; MBBS, St. Bartholomews Hosp., London, 1975. Clin. lectr., orthopedic surgery U. Oxford, 1981—87; specialist asst. Hosp. de Toulouse, France, 1985—86; cons. orthopedic surgeon Nuffield Orthopedic Ctr., Oxford, 1987—; specialist hip and knee arthoritis and revission surgery. Contbr. articles to profl. jours. Fellow: Royal Coll. Surgeons; mem.: Assn. Bone and Joint Surgeons Internat., Girdlestone Orthop. Soc. (pres. 2009—), Internat. Soc. Tech. Orthoplast (pres. 2002—03). Office: Nuffield Orthopaedic Ctr Nhs Trust Windmill Rd Headington Oxford OX3 7LD England Home Phone: 1865361471; Office Phone: 1865738273. Business E-Mail: peter.mclardy-smith@noc.nhs.uk.

MCLARNON, MARY FRANCES, neurologist; b. Montreal, Que., Canada, May 13, 1944; came to U.S., 1969; d. John Francis and Patricia Jessica (Dore) McL.; m. Malcolm Weiner, Dec. 21, 1975; m. Lawrence Zingesser, Oct. 12, 1982; children: Andrea, Eliza. BS, McGill U., 1965, MD, 1969. Intern St. Vincent's Hosp., NYC, 1969-70; fellow seizure unit Boston Children's Hosp., 1970-71; resident in neurology Albert Einstein Coll. Medicine, Bronx, N.Y., 1971-73; resident in radiology N.Y. Hosp.-Cornell Med. Ctr., NYC, 1973-76; pvt. practice. Home: 752 Cove Rd Mamaroneck NY 10543-4324 Office Phone: 917-856-8301. Personal E-mail: mmclmd@hotmail.com.

MCLAUGHLIN, FRANK E., nursing educator; b. Bklyn., Mar. 27, 1935; s. Edward Patrick and Anna (Barr) McL. BS, Adelphi U., 1959; MA, NYU, 1961; PhD, U. Calif., Berkeley, 1968. Lecturer U. Calif., San Francisco, 1961—64, asst. prof., 1968—72, coord. rsch. grad. programs, 1970—72, asst. clin. prof. Davis, 1972—80, assoc. clin. prof. San Francisco, 1975—2004; assoc. prof. San Francisco State U., 1981—84, prof., 1984—2004, assoc. dir. sch. nursing, 1996—2001, prof. emeritus, 2004—. Vis. prof. European Inst. of Med. and Health Rsch., U. Surrey, Inst. of Nursing, Sch. of Medicine, U. Wales, U.K., 1996. Edn. bd. (internat. jour. evaluation in clin. practice, UK). V.p. bd. trustees Cen. City Hospitality House, San Francisco, 1975-78; chmn. Mental Health Adv. Bd. San Francisco, 1979-85; bd. dirs. San Francisco Mental Health Assn., 1985-88. Recipient Outstanding Nurse Leadership award Golden Gate Nurses Assn., 1986. Fellow Am. Acad. Nursing; mem. ANA, Sigma Theta Tau. Avocations: opera, travel, cooking. *

MCLAUGHLIN, TRACEY L., medical educator; b. NYC, Aug. 5, 1966; BA, Stanford U., 1988; MD, U. Calif., San Francisco, 1994. Asst. prof. Stanford U. Sch. Medicine, 2005—. Office: 300 Pasteur Dr Rm S025 Stanford CA 94305-5103 Office Fax: 650-725-7085. Business E-Mail: tmclaugh@stanford.edu.

MCLAWHON, RONALD WILLIAM, pathology educator, biochemist; b. Chgo., Sept. 10, 1957; s. William Columbus and Esther Shirley (Bukowski) McL. AB in Biol. Scis., U. Chgo., 1979, MS in Biochemistry, 1980, PhD in Biochemistry, 1982; MD, Rush Med. Coll., 1986. Diplomate Am. Bd. Pathology. Rsch. assoc. pediat. Joseph P. Kennedy Jr. Mental Retardation Rsch. Ctr., Chgo.; rsch. assoc. pediatrics U. Chgo. Pritzker Sch. Medicine, 1982-83; resident in pathology Rush-Presbyn.-St. Luke's Med. Ctr., Chgo., 1986-87, pathologist, 1987-88; instr. Rush Med. Coll., Chgo., 1986-87, asst. prof., 1987-88; resident in pathology U. Chgo. Med. Ctr., 1988-90; asst. prof. U. Chgo. Pritzker Sch. Medicine, 1990-96, assoc. prof., 1996—2007; dir. clin. chemistry, attending physician U. Chgo. Med. Ctr., 1990—2007; dir. outreach and clin. support svcs. U. Chgo. Hosps. and Health Sys., 1997—98, dir. regional lab. svcs. and med. dir. of hosp. labs., 1998—2007; prof., head divsn. lab. medicine dept. pathology U. Calif. San Diego Sch. Medicine, 2007—; dir. clin. labs., attending physician U. Calif. San Diego Health Sys., 2007—. Contbr. articles to Jour. Biol. Chemistry, Molecular Pharmacology, Jour. Neurochemistry, Jour. Membrane Biology, Procs. of NAS, Am. Jour. Clin. Pathology, Clin. Chemistry. US Pub. Health Predoctoral fellow NIH, 1981-82; James B. Herrick scholar Rush Med. Coll., 1986 87; recipient Young Investigator award Acad. Clin. Lab. Physicians and Scientists, 1990. Fellow: Am. Soc. Clin. Pathologists, Coll. Am. Pathologists, Nat. Acad. Clin. Biochemistry; mem.: AAAS, Am. Soc. Cell Biology, Am. Soc. Biochemistry and Molecular Biology, Am. Soc. Investigative Pathology, Am. Assn. Clin. Chemistry (chair Chgo. sect. 2005, Chgo. Chpt. Past Chmn. award 2006, Albert A. Dietz Svc. award 2008), Fretted Instrument Guild America (v.p. 2006—08, pres. 2008—), Sigma Xi. Achievements include research in biochemistry of cell membrane receptors and signal transduction in the nervous system, molecular pharmacology of opiates and opioid peptides, regulation of complex carbohydrate and lipid metabolism, clinical laboratory automaton and robotics. Office Phone: 619-543-5816. Business E-Mail: rmclawhon@ucsd.edu.

MC LEAN, DONALD MILLIS, microbiologist, educator, pathologist, pediatrician; b. Melbourne, Australia, July 26, 1926; s. Donald and Nellie (Millis) McL.; married. BSc, U. Melbourne, 1947, MB, 1950, MD, 1954. Fellow Rockefeller Found., NYC and Hamilton, Mont., 1955; vis. instr. bacteriology U. Minn., Mpls., 1957; med. officer Commonwealth Serum Labs., Melbourne, 1957; virologist Research Inst., Hosp. for Sick Children, Toronto, Ont., Canada, 1958-67; assoc. prof. microbiology, assoc. in pediatrics U. Toronto Med. Sch., 1962-67; prof. med. microbiology U. B.C. Med. Sch., Vancouver, Canada, 1967-91, prof. emeritus Pathology, 1991—. Author: Virology in Health Care, 1980, Immunological Investigation of Human Virus Disease, 1982, Same-Day Virus Diagnosis, 1984, Virological Infections, 1988, Medical Microbiology Synopsis, 1991, Acute Viral Infections, 1991; contbr. articles to profl. jours. Fellow Royal Coll. Physicians (Can.), Royal Coll. Pathologists; mem. Am. Epidemiological Soc., Am. Soc. Tropical Medicine, Can. Med. Assn., Am. Soc. Virology, Infectious Diseases Soc. Am. Home and Office: 2720 Yukon St Vancouver BC V5Y 3R1 Canada Office Phone: 604-263-9076. Business E-Mail: donaldmclean@shaw.ca.

MCLEAN, GORDON KENNEDY, vascular and interventional radiologist, internist, educator; MD, Dartmouth-Hitchcock Med. Ctr., 1975. Diplomate Am. Bd. Internal Medicine-diagnostic radiology, Am. Bd. Internal Medicine-vascular and interventional radiology, cert. Pa., 1976. Intern Pa. Hosp.; resident Hosp. of the Univ. of Pa., 1979, fellow, 1980; with Allegheny Radiology Assocs. Ltd.; prof. diagnostic imaging Temple Univ.; dir. vascular interventional radiology fellowship program The Western Pa. Hosp., chief. vascular interventional radiology. Named one of the Top Doctors, Pitts. Mag., 2011. Office: The Western Pennsylvania Hospital 4800 Friendship Ave Pittsburgh PA 15224 Office Phone: 412-578-7412. Office Fax: 412-578-4064.

MCLEOD, ALEXANDER CANADAY, physician; b. Fayetteville, NC, Jan. 14, 1935; s. Walter Guy and Vida (Canaday) McLeod; m. Dorothy Venning Woods, Aug. 21, 1965; children: Alexander Woods, Dorothy Seward. Akat., Städische Akad. Tönkunst, 1955; AB, Princeton U., 1956; postgrad., Johns Hopkins U., 1959-60; MD, Duke U., 1960; MBA, Vanderbilt U., 1988. Diplomate Am. Bd. Internal Medicine, Nat. Bd. Med. Examiners. Intern, asst. resident N.Y. Hosp.-Cornell Med. Ctr., NYC, 1960-62; resident in medicine and neurology, fellow Vanderbilt U. Hosp., Nashville, 1964-67; pvt. practice internal medicine Nashville, 1967-98; clin. prof. med. adminstrn. Vanderbilt U., Nashville, 1999—2002, clin. prof. medicine, 1999—2002, clin. prof. medicine emeritus, 2002—, adj. prof. mgmt. Owen Grad. Sch. Mgmt., 1995—2002, faculty coord. health care mgmt. Owen Grad. Sch. Mgmt., 1996-2000. Bd. dirs. Nat. Security Alliance, Inc., 1990—2000; cons. internal medicine student health svc. Vanderbilt U., Nashville, 1991—96, cons. health ins., 1997—99. Presenter papers to various orgns.; contbr. numerous articles to med. jours. Trustee Friends of Heard Libr. Vanderbilt U., Nashville, 1998; past trustee, past chmn. Dunvegan Found.; bd. dirs. Nashville Symphony, 1988—91, Symphony Hall subcom., 2002; bd. dirs. Skye Terrier Found., 1998—2000; bd. dirs. music ensemble, bd. mem. Belle Meade Baroque, 2008—09; former fellow Hugenot Soc. Gt. Britain and Ireland, Soc. Antiquaries Scotland; former mem. St. Andrew's Soc. NC, Nassav Club, Sloane Club, Farmington Country Club, Princeton Club NY, Grolier Club; past music com. mem. Westminster Presbyn. Ch., 1989—91, liturgy com. mem.; past vestryman, jr. warden St. George's Episc. Ch., music. com. mem., 2009—. With USNR, 1962—64. Recipient Physicians Achievement award, AMA, 1971, 1974, 1977, 1981, 1984, 1987, 1990, 1993, 1996, 1999; fellow Summer fellow in neurology, USPHS, 1957—58, Mid. Tenn. Heart Assn., 1966—67. Fellow: ACP; mem.: Nashville Acad. Medicine, Tenn. Med. Assn., Am. Coll. Physician Execs., World War II Study Group, Gaelic Soc. of Inverness, Coun. Scottish Clan Assns., Inc. (former trustee), Heraldry Soc. Scotland, Scottish Soc. Mid. Tenn. (life), Clan MacLeod Soc. (life; past pres.), Associated Clan MacLeod Socs. (pres. 1998—2006, past co-chmn. Alasdair Crotach com., past exec. v.p.), Belle Meade Country Club, Tower Club Princeton, Princeton Club Nashville (past pres. and trustee), Univ. Club Nashville, Skye Terrier Club Am. Independent. Episcopalian. Avocations: reading, music, writing. Home: 203 Evelyn Ave Nashville TN 37205-3307 Office: PO Box 50451 Nashville TN 37205-0451 Office Phone: 615-383-1276. Personal E-mail: acmcl@aol.com.

MCLEOD, ANNE, critical care nurse, educator; d. John and Clare McLeod. BSc in Health Studies (hon.), Inst. Advanced Nurse Edn., RCN, London, 1997; Postgrad. in Critical Care, Anglia Poly. U., Chelmsford, 2003, MSc in Critical Care, 2005; Postgrad. Diploma in Learning and Tchg., Anglia Ruskin U., Chelmsford, 2007. Registered gen. nurse, St Bartholomew's Sch. Nursing and Midwifery, 1989, cert. in neuromed. and neurosurg. nursing, ENB, 1992, in intensive care nursing, S. Bank U., 1999. Staff nurse St Bartholomew's Hosp., London, 1989—90, Westminster Hosp., London, 1990—91, Nat. Hosp. Neurology and Neurosurgery, London, 1991—93, sr. staff nurse, 1993—96, Atkinson Morleys Hosp., London, 1996—97; neuroscience tchg. and devel. sister Barking Havering and Redbridge NHS Trust, Romford, Essex, England, 1997—2003; lectr. critical care City U., London, 2003—09, sr. lectr. critical care, 2009—. Editl. bd. Brit. Jour. Neurosci. Nursing, London, 2004—. Editor (author): (book) Advanced Practice in Critical Care: A Case Study Approach; contbr. book. Office: City University 20 Bartholomew Close W Smithfield London ECIA 7Q2N England Business E-Mail: a.c.mcleod@city.ac.uk.

MCLEOD, STEPHEN D., ophthalmologist, researcher; b. Mandeville, Jamaica, July 9, 1964; arrived in US, 1982; s. Dinsdale St. Ledger and Merle Elethia McLeod; m. Marion Faymonville, Feb. 28, 1998. AB in Biology, Dartmouth Coll.; MD, Johns Hopkins U., 1989. Cert. Am. Bd. Ophthalmology. Intern in internal medicine Beth Israel Med. Ctr., NY, 1989—90; resident in ophthalmology Ill. Eye and Ear Infirmary, U. Ill., Chgo., 1990—93, dir. refractive surgery, 1995—98; fellow in refractive surgery, cornea and external disease U. So. Calif. Doheny Eye Inst., 1993—94; mem. dept. ophthalmology U. Calif., San Francisco, 1998, interim chmn. dept. ophthalmology, 2005—06, prof., 2006—, chmn. dept. ophthalmology, 2006—. Office: U Calif San Francisco Dept Ophthalmology 10 Koret Way K 304 San Francisco CA 94143 Office Fax: 415-476-0336. Business E-Mail: mcleods@vision.ucsf.edu.

MCLEOD, WILLIAM RICHARD, retired medical officer, psychiatrist, professor; b. Melbourne, Victoria, Australia, Mar. 28, 1933; s. Norman Alexander McLeod and Margaret Collister (Watterson) Finlay; m. Margaret Frances Stuckey, Oct. 10, 1960; children: Elizabeth, Fiona, Andrew, Sarah. BA, U. Melbourne, 1958, postgrad., 1963, MD in Psychol. Medicine, 1968, MDBS, 1970. Resident med. officer St. Vincent's Hosp., Melbourne, 1964—65; med. officer Mental Health Adv., Melbourne, 1966—70; assoc. prof. dept. psychiatry U. Auckland, New Zealand, 1971—77, head dept. psychiatry, 1975—77; supt. Royal Pk. Psychiat. Hosp., Melbourne, 1977—82; clin. dean Monash and Melbourne U. Royal Pk. Clin. Sch., Melbourne, 1977—82; pvt. practice psychiatrist Ascot Vale, Australia, 1983—. Censor-in-chief Royal Australian and New Zealand Coll. Psychiatrists, 1979—84. Author: Drug Rehabilitation, 1972-89, Epistemology & constructivism, 1987-89, (with others) Predisposition to Heart Diseases, Biochemistry of Hallucinogens, 1974-89. Mem. coun. Queen's Coll., 1970-71, 88-89; tchr. Pub. Seminars Communication, Melbourne, 1986-89; active drug rehab. programmes, Auckland and Melbourne, 1974—. Decorated knight St. John of Jerusalem of Ams.; Wolfson fellow, 1974. Internat. fellow APA; fellow Academic Medicine and Psychiatry., Royal Australasian Coll. Physicians, Royal Australian and New Zealand Coll. Psychiatrists, Royal Coll. Psychiatrists, Am. Assn. Group Psychotherapy; mem. Collegium Internat. Neuro-Psychopharmacologicum, Am. Group Psychotherapy Assn. Avocations: literature, opera, mythology, altered states of consciousness, meditation, comparative religion. Home: 302 Providence Gully Rd PO Box 151 Newstead VIC 3462 Australia Personal E-mail: wrmcleod@fastmail.fm, wrmcleod@gmail.com.

MCLESKEY, CHARLES HAMILTON, anesthesiologist, educator, pharmaceutical executive; b. Phila., Nov. 8, 1946; s. W. Hamilton and Marion A. (Butts) McL.; m. Nanci S. Simmons, June 3, 1972; children: Travis, Heather. BA, Susquehanna U., 1968; MD, Wake Forest U., 1972. Diplomate Am. Bd. Anesthesiology. Intern Maine Med. Ctr., Portland, 1972-73; resident in anesthesiology U. Wash. Sch. Medicine, Seattle, 1973-76, NIH rsch. trainee, 1974-75; clin. teaching assoc. dept. anesthesiology U. Calif., San Francisco, 1976-78; asst. prof. anesthesiology Wake Forest U. Bowman Gray Sch. Medicine, Winston-Salem, NC, 1978-83, assoc. prof., 1983-84, U. Tex. Med. Br., Galveston, 1985-87; assoc. prof. anesthesiology U. Colo. Health Sci. Ctr., Denver, 1987-91, prof., 1991-93, dir. acad. affairs, 1987-93; prof., chmn. dept. anesthesiology Tex. A&M U., 1993-2000; chmn. dept. anesthesiology, med. dir. perioperative svcs. Scott and White Clin. and Meml. Hosp., Temple, Tex., 1993-2000; assoc. med. dir. Scott and White Health Plan, 1995-2000; sr. dir. clin. devel. Abbott Labs., Abbott Park, Ill., 2000—02, global med. dir., global mktg. dir. anesthesia and sedation, 2002—06; v.p. clin. affairs ZARS, Salt Lake City, 2006—07; leader therapeutic area Global Anesthesia and Critical, Baxter Pharm., New Providence, NJ, 2007—. Cons., lectr. Janssen Pharmaceutica, Piscataway, N.J., 1980-98, Alza Corp., Palo Alto, Calif., 1986-99; cons. Glaxo-Wellcome Co., Research Triangle Park, N.C., Abbott Labs., Chgo., Hoechst, Marion, Roussel, Kansas City, Kans., Aspect Med., Natick, Mass., Baxter Labs., Chgo., Scott Labs., Lubbock, Tex.; lectr. to over 500 nat. and state med. orgns., 1982—; examiner Am. Bd. Anesthesiology; lectr. Ohmeda, Liberty Corner, N.J. Assoc. editor Anesthesiology Rev., Anesthesiology News, Pharmacy Practia News; editor Geriatric Anesthesiology, 1997; contbr. numerous articles to med. jours. Mem. choir Friendswood (Tex.) Meth. Ch., 1985-87; mem. Friendswood Fine Arts Commn., 1985-87; mem. Temple Chamber Arts Adv. Coun., 1997-99. Lt. comdr. M.C., USN, 1976-78. Woodruff-Fisher scholar, 1964-68. Mem.: Temple C. of C., Evergreen Newcomers, Soc. Acad. Anesthesia Chairs (councilman 1996—99), Soc. for Ambulatory Anesthesia (program chair 1999), Internat. Anesthesia Rsch. Soc., Colo. Soc. Anesthesiologists (past pres.), Soc. for Edn. in Anesthesiology (past v.p., past pres., SEA-Duke Edn. prize), Am. Soc. Anesthesiologists (del. 1983—85, 1988—90), Assn. U Anesthetists, Nat. Spkrs. Assn., Internat. Platform Assn., Mensa, Alpha Omega Alpha. Republican. Presbyterian. Avocations: running, fishing, racquetball, squash. Personal E-mail: charles.mcleskey@comcast.net.

MCMAHAN-WONEIS, CELESTINE, integrative medical educator, organizational psychologist, health psychology educator; b. Denver, Jan. 4, 1948; d. Frank McMahan and Jean Dolores Kauno; m. John Thomas Woneis, Nov. 10, 2001 (dec.). BA in Urban Studies, U. Colo., Boulder, 1976, M in Urban and Regional Planning, 1977; MA in Orgnl. Psychology, Calif. Sch. Profl. Psychology, Berkeley, 1997; MS in Med. Gong, Internat. Sch. Med. Qi Gong, 2000; PhD in Orgnl. Psychology, Calif. Sch. Profl. Psychology, Berkeley, 2002; cert. in ednl. therapy, U. Calif., Santa Cruz, 2006; MA in Med. Qigong, Henan U., China, 2006; postgrad. in Nutrition, Hawthorne U. MHNE, 2009. Diplomate, bd. cert. in integrative and alternative medicine Am. Assn. Integrative Medicine, 2010; lic. real estate agt. Colo., bd. cert. in integrative medicine BCIM, cert. ednl. therapy profl. BCET, orgnl. psychology educator, AEIP. Floral design cons. Lehr's Flowers and Alpha Floral, Denver, 1967—70; lic. real estate saleswoman, housing sales coord. Gt. Western United, Colorado City, Colo., 1970—73; archtl. project mgr. facilities planning Stanford U., Calif., 1977—80; designer, facilities planner corp. real estate dept. Sacramento Savs. & Loan, 1980—81; archtl. project mgr., corp. real estate dept. Crocker Bank, San Francisco, 1981—82; project mgr. design and constrn. and real estate, corp. real estate dept. Bank of Am., San Francisco, 1982—96; design cons. McLink, San Francisco, 1985—88; team mgr. design and constrn. Bank of Am., 1986—87; project mgr., design and constrn. cons. Grace Cathedral, San Francisco, 1993—96; mgr. design and constrn., cons. Boudin Bakery & Cafe, San Francisco, 1997—98; exec. coach, complimentary and alternative med. educator and practitioner, orgnl. health psychologist, ednl. therapist Metapatterns, Felton, Calif., 1997—; labyrinth design and constrn. cons. Minn. Hosp., Mpls., 1999, Trinity Cath., Atlanta, 1999, Columbus, Ohio, 2000; sovereign amb. Am. Order of Ambs., 2006; edtl. review bd. Am. Assn. Integrative Medicine. Cons. redeployment team Bank of Am., 1995—96; cons. Veriditas, San Francisco, 1998—99, Parents Helping Parents, Santa Clara Staff Tng., Santa Clara, Calif., 2003—04; ednl. therapy cons. Devel. Learning Solutions, Santa Cruz, 2003—; bus. cons. Inner Voyages, Santa Cruz, 2006—; creativity and innovation cons. Mountain Pks. Found., Felton, 2006—; owner, leadership training for young adults, intergenerational and intercultural comm. Quantum Learning Acad., 2006; owner Wisdom and Wealth and Health, 2008, Quantum Findings LLC, 2010, Wisdom, Health, Wealth Corp., 2010. Interim dir. pks. and recreation City of Edgewater, Colo., 1973; cons., mem. com. Colo. Gov. Lamm's Housing Task Force, Denver, 1975—76; co-founder Aurora Devel. Corp., Calif., 1977; mem. Menlo Pk. Beautification Commn., 1978—79; fundraising cons. Friends of the Arts, San Francisco, 1985; cons. Spirit of Peace Conf., Women's Dream Quest Grace Cath., founder Michaelmas Faire, 1986; cons. Founding of the Labyrinth Project, San Francisco, 1996; docent Henry Cowell & Mountain Pks., Felton, 2006—; trustee Grace Cath.; mem. Internat. Women's Rev. Bd., 2008, 2010; USA cultural attache Cultural World Forum, 2011; bd. dirs. Friends of the Arts, Calif. Lawyers for the Arts, Inst. for Study of Natural Systems. Recipient Sovereign Amb., Am. Order of Ambs., 2006, Internat. Peace award, IBC, 2008, Seat of Wisdom award, 2010; named Citizen of Yr., Hutt River Principality, 1995. Mem.: APA, Internat. Mind, Brain, Edn. Soc., Learning Brain Soc., Coun. for Exceptional Children, Optometric Ext. Program Found., Am. Assn. Clin. Nutritionists, Internat. Assn. Clin. Nutritionists, Assn. for Applied Psychophysiology and Biofeedback, Nat. Assn. Nutritional Profls., Assn. Ednl. Therapists, Am. Holistic Med. Assn., Nat. Assn. Neuropsychologists, Am. Assn. Integrative Medicine (editl. bd. 2010). Avocations: music, art, reenacting. Personal E-mail: quantumfindings@gmail.com.

MCMAHON, JAMES BRISLIN, medical researcher; b. Burlington, Vt., Oct. 9, 1950; s. James William and Margaret Joan (McGarry) McM.; m. Laurie Jean Hinds, Oct. 1, 1983; children: Megan, Michael. BA in Chemistry, U. Vt., 1972, PhD in Cell Biology, 1978. Scientist 1 Frederick Cancer Rsch. Ctr., Md., 1978-81, scientist 2, 1981-83; cancer expert Lab. Exptl. Therapeutics and Metabolism, devel. therapeutics program Nat. Cancer Inst., Bethesda, Md., 1983-88, rsch. biologist program devel. rsch. group, devel. therapeutics program, 1988-90; sr. rsch. biologist Lab. Drug Discovery Rsch. and Devel., devel. therapeutics program Ctr. Cancer Rsch., Nat. Cancer Inst., NIH, Frederick, 1990, dir. Molecular Targets Lab. Contbr. articles to profl. jours.; patentee in field. Pres. Frederick County Alzheimer's Assn., 1987-89; mem. Sci. Curriculum Rev. Com., Frederick, 1990-91. Mem. Am. Chem. Soc., Tissue Culture Assn., N.Y. Acad. Scis., Am. Assn. for Cancer Rsch., Sigma Xi. Avocations: skiing, fishing, photography. Office: Nat Cancer Inst - Frederick Molecular Targets Devel Program PO Box B Bldg 1052 Rm 121 Frederick MD 21702-1201 Office Phone: 301-846-5391. Office Fax: 301-846-6919. E-mail: mcmahon@ncifcrf.gov. *

MCMEEKIN, THOMAS OWEN, dermatologist; b. Shelby, Nebr., Apr. 17, 1945; s. Wallace Walton and Evajane (Taber) McM.; m. Dale Goodwin, 1999(Div. Aug. 15, 2008); children: Michele, Sean. BA with distinction, Stanford U., 1967; MD with honors, U. Rochester, 1971. Intern Beth Israel Hosp., Boston, 1971-72; resident U. Rochester (N.Y.), 1974-76, Mass. Gen. Hosp., Boston, 1976-78; clin. prof. depts. medicine, pediatrics, dermatology U. Rochester Sch. Medicine, 1978—; dermatologist pvt. practice, Rochester, 1978—; clin. asst. prof. SUNY, Buffalo, 1997—. Pres. Geneese Valley Laser Ctr.,

Rochester, 1990—. Capt. USPHS, 1972—74. Kohn fellow U. Rochester, 1980-81; recipient Doren J. Stephens Alumni award U. Rochester, 1971, Brian Flanagan Teaching Svc. award, 1995, 2003. Fellow Am. Acad. Dermatology (Svc. award 1993), Am. Bd. Internal Medicine, Am. Soc. LAser MEdicine (co-chmn. 1993-94), Am. Soc. Dermatologic Surgery (edn. com. 1983—); mem. N.Y. State Dermatological Soc. (v.p. 1993, treas. 1992), Buffalo Rochester Dermatological Soc. (pres. 1990), Rochester Dermatological Soc. (pres. 1980-89), Alpha Omega Alpha. Avocations: golf, tennis, computers. Office: 300 White Spruce Blvd Rochester NY 14623-1606 Office Phone: 585-424-6770. Personal E-mail: 041745@msn.com.

MCMILLAN, COLIN JAMES, cardiologist; b. PEI, Canada; m. Sandy McMillan; children: Andrew, Alexandra, James, Victoria(dec.), Virginia. BA, St. Dunstan's U., 1964; MA, Oriel Coll., Oxford, Eng., 1970; MD, McGill U., Canada, 1972. Pvt. practice, PEI, 1977—. Clin. instr., dept. medicine Dalhousie U.; former dir. Heart and Stroke Rsch. Found. Can. Gov. Nat. Theatre Sch. Canada; bd. dirs. PEI Arts Coun., U. PEI Found., PEI Govt. Confedn. Birthplace Commn., Rhodes Scholarship Selection Com. for Maritimes. Fellow: ACP, Royal Coll. Physicians; mem.: Canadian Med. Assn. (pres. 2006—07), Med. Soc. PEI (pres. 1986—87), Rotary Internat. Avocations: bridge, reading. Office: Parkdale Med Ctr 20 St Peter's Rd Charlottetown PE C1A 5N4 Canada Office Phone: 902-368-7429.

MCMILLAN, JAMES ROBERT, medical educator; b. Liverpool, Eng., Mar. 14, 1969; BSc, U. York, 1989; PhD, Kings Coll. London, 1997. Postdoc. rschr. Kings Coll. London, 1997—2000; postdoc. team leader, rschr. Grad. Sch. Medicine Hokkaido U., Sapporo, Japan, 2000—04; prof., skin tissue engring. Faculty Sci. Hokkaido U., Sapporo, 2004—08; hon. assoc. prof., head, lab. rsch. Ctr. Childrens Burns and Trauma Rsch. U. Queensland, Brisbane, Australia, 2008—. Master: Soc. Cutaneous Ultrastructural Rsch. (pres.). Office: Ctr Childrens Burns Rsch University Queensland Herston Queensland 4029 Australia Business E-Mail: j.mcmillan@uq.edu.au.

MCMILLAN, JULIA A., pediatrician, educator; b. Pinehurst, NC, July 10, 1946; m. Jed Dietz; children: Edith Root, Robert Grant, Elihu Root. BA in English Lit., U. NC, Chapel Hill, 1969, M in Tchg., 1971; MD, SUNY, Syracuse, 1976. Diplomate Nat. Bd. Med. Examiners, 1977, cert. Am. Bd. Pediat., 1981. Intern SUNY Health Sci. Ctr., Syracuse, 1976—77, resident pediat., 1977-78, 79-80, fellow in pediat. infectious diseases, 1979-81, physician co-dir. Pediat. Nurse Practitioner Program, 1978—79, asst. prof. infectious disease sect., 1981—87, asst. prof. Dept. Pathology, 1982—87, co-dir. Univ. Hosp. Virology Lab., 1984—90, residency program dir., 1985—90, assoc. prof. Dept. Pediat. and Pathology, 1987—90; assoc. prof. pediat. John Hopkins U. Med. Sch., Balt., 1991—2001, dep. dir. Dept. Pediat., 1991—95, dir., 1995—, vice chair Edn. and Residency Program, 1995—, prof., 2001—, acting divsn. chief gen. pediat., 2001—02, assoc. dean. grad. med. edn., designated institutional official, 2004—. Lectr. in field. Co-author: The Whole Pediatrician Catalog: A Compendium of Clues to Diagnosis and Management, 1977, The Best of the Whole Pediatrician Catalogs, I-III, 1984, The Portable Pediatrician, 1992, Blueprints in Pediatrics, 1998, Oski's Pediatrics: Principles and Practice, 3d edit., 1999; editor-in-chief Contemporary Pediatrics; contbr. articles to med. jours. Recipient Alexander Schaffer Award, 1999, Walter W. Tunnessen, Jr. MD Award, 2007. Mem.: Am. Pediat. Soc., Infectious Diseases Soc. Am., Pediat. Soc. Onondaga County, Am. Soc. Microbiology, Am. Acad. Pediat., Am. Bd. Pediat. (assoc.). Office: Johns Hopkins Hosp Dept Pediatrics 600 N Wolfe St Baltimore MD 21287-3224 Office Phone: 410-955-2727. Office Fax: 410-955-9850. E-mail: jmcmill@jhmi.edu.

MCMILLAN, ROBERT RALPH, lawyer; b. NYC, May 21, 1932; s. Harry and Vivian (Beatty) McM.; m. Phoebe Parker Bunn, Nov. 2, 1996; children: Robin, Karen, Kenneth. Student, Adelphi U., 1951-52, 55-56; JD, Bklyn. Law Sch., 1960. Bar: N.Y. 1960. Spl. asst. staff of Richard M. Nixon, NY., Washington, 1960, 64-65; counsel Senator Kenneth B. Keating, Washington, 1960-62; govt. rels. advisor Mobil Oil Co., NYC, 1962-63, 65-68; v.p. Avon Products, NYC, 1973-78, 79-85; sr. v.p. A&S Dept. Stores, NYC, 1978-79; counsel Rivkin, Radler, Bayh, Dunne & Bagh, Uniondale, NY, 1986—91; ptnr. McMillan, Rather, Bennett & Farinoci, P.C., Melville, NY, 1991—2003, Fischbein Badillo Wagner Harding, Melville, 2003—05. Chmn. Panama Canal Commn., 1993-94; mem. nat. adv. coun. FannieMae, 1998-2000, co-hosts Face-Off, PBS, NY. News commentator Sta. WLIW-TV, 1993-2007; columnist, Anton Community Newspapers, Long Island; occasional columnist for Newsday. Trustee Adelphi U., 1984-89; bd. dirs. L.I. (N.Y.) Assn.; chmn. L.I. Housing Parntership, 1988-2002. 1st lt. U.S. Army, 1952-54. Decorated Bronze Star; recipient Excellence in Leadership award, Helen Keller Services for the Blind, Humanitarian award, Alzheimer's Assn. Mem.: AMA (bd. trustees 2002—08), Suffolk County Bar Assn., Nassau County Bar Assn. Republican. Avocations: golf, fishing. E-mail: mcmillanr@aol.com.

MCMULLAN, PAUL, cardiologist; Consulting physician cardiology Ochsner St. Anne Gen. Hosp. Office: Ochsner Hospital 1514 Jefferson Hwy New Orleans LA 70121 Office Phone: 985-537-3712. Office Fax: 985-537-3396.

MCMULLEN, MICHAEL KEVIN, herbal medicine specialist; b. Sydney, July 13, 1955; m. Anna Kristina Bergen, Aug. 31, 2002. BA in Psycholigy with honors, U. NSW, Sydney, Australia, 1978; diploma of med. herbalism, So. Cross Herbals, Gosford, Australia, 1987; postgrad., U. Westminster, London, 2004—. Cert. audiology Nat. Acoustics Lab., Commonwealth Dept. Health Australia, 1980. Resident herbalist and nutritionist Alpha Plus, Falun, Sweden, 1989—91; herbalist pvt. practice, Stockholm; principle lectr., founder Nordic Nutrition and Phytotherapy Sch., 1996—2008. Rector and prin. lectr. McMullen's Phytotherapy Sch., Stockholm, 2007. Author: (book) Herbal Medicine - Nature's Healing Power. Recipient Basic Sci. Poster prize, European Assn. Cardiovascular Prevention and Rehabilitation, 2007. Mem.: Nat. Herbalists Assn. Australia. Office: Life Force Box 65 760 40 Väddö Sweden Business E-Mail: research@micmcmullen.se.

MCMURTRY, ROBERT Y., orthopedic surgeon; b. Toronto, Ont., Can., Mar. 6, 1941; s. Roland Roy and Elizabeth McMurtry; m. Jane Macdougall, May 6, 1979; children: Angus, Abbey, Sean, Meghan. MD, U. Toronto, 1965. Fellow Hosp. Sick Children, Toronto, 1972—73; orthopedic surgeon, head dept. emergency svcs., founder and dir. regional trauma unit Sunnybrook Med. Ctr., Toronto, 1975—87; asst. to assoc. prof. U. Toronto, 1976—87; head dept. surgery Foothills Hosp., Calgary, Canada, 1988—92; prof. U. Western (Can.) Ont., Ont., Canada, 1992—, dean faculty medicine, 1992—99, dean faculty medicine and dentistry, 1997—99; cameron chair Health Can., 1999—2000, vis. asst. dep. min. Population and Pub. Health br., asst. dep. min., 2000—02; spl. advisor to commr. Royal Commn. of Health Care in Can., 2002; orthopedic surgeon St. Joesph's Health Centre, Ont.; spl. adviser to Dep. Min. Health, Nanavut, Canada, 2002—03; councillor Health Coun. Can., 2004—07. Worker Mission Hosp./Can. Internat. Devel. Agy., Africa, 1965—70; chmn. dept. surgery, prof. surgery U. Calgary, 1988—92; chmn. provincial com. on role, function and financing acad. health ctrs., 1994—95; reviewer Provincial Cancer Network, 1994—95; vis. prof. Can. and internationally; mem. transition adv. bd. Govt. Ont., 2003; chmn. steering com. Can. Index Well-Being Project, 2003—08; chmn. internat. adv. bd. Alta. (Can.) Bone and Joint Health Inst., 2006—09; founding bd. dirs. Can. Drs. for Medicare, 2006; bd. mem. Physician Svcs. Inc., 2011—; mem. Coll. Physicians and Surgeons, Ontario, 2011—. Editor: Management of Blunt Trauma, 1990; contbr. chapters to books, articles to profl. jours. Named Order of Can., 2011; Am., Brit. Can. Travelling fellow, 1981. Fellow: ACS, Royal Coll. Surgeons Can.; mem.: Royal Coll. Physicians and Surgeons Can. (James H. Graham award 2009), Ont. Med. Assn. (Emergency Medicine award 2010), Can. Med. Assn., Coll. Physicians and Surgeons Ont., Can. Orthopedic Assn. (Presdl. Excellence award 2003). Office: St Joseph's Health Orthopedic Surgery/Hand & Upper Limb 268 Grosvenor St London ON Canada N6A 4L63 Business E-Mail: robert.mcmurtry@sjhc.london.on.ca.

MCNAIR, RUTH P., physician, director; b. Australia, June 12, 1963; MBBS, U. Melbourne, 1986, PhD, 2010. Assoc. prof., dir., gen. practice and primary health care NW node Dept. Gen. Pratice U. Melbourne, 2011—. Bd. dirs. Gay and Lesbian Found. Australia, 2006; gen. practitioner Northside Clinic, 2009—. Recipient 1st prize, U. Melbourne, Cultural Diversity award, Vida Goldstein award, Women's Electoral Lobby Australia; Rsch. scholarship, Nat. Health and Med. Rsch. Coun. Australia. Fellow: Royal Australian Coll. Gen. Practitioners; mem.: Australian Lesbian Med. Assn. Office: 200 Berkeley St Carlton Victoria 3053 Australia Business E-Mail: r.mcnair@unimelb.edu.au.

MCNALLY, DAMIEN, physician; b. Lurgan, Dec. 27, 1967; MB BCh BAO, Queen's U. Belfast, Antrim, Northern Ireland, 1993. GP svc. prin. Ormeau Health Ctr., Belfast, 1993—. Mem.: MRCGP. Office: Ormeau Health Ctr 120 Ormeau Rd Belfast Antrim BT7 2EB Northern Ireland Business E-Mail: damienmcnally@doctors.org.uk.

MCNALLY, DANIEL PATRICK, critical care specialist; MD, U. Conn., 1976. Diplomate Am. Bd. Internal Medicine, 1979, Am. Bd. Internal Medicine- pulmonary disease, 1982, Am. Bd. Internal Medicine- sleep medicine, 1992, Am. Bd. Internal Medicine- critical care medicine, 2007. Resident in internal medicine St. Francis Hosp. and Med. Ctr., Hartford, Conn., 1977—79; fellow in pulmonary disease Univ. Conn. Health Ctr., Farmington, Conn., 1979—80; hosp. affiliation includes Univ. Conn. Health Ctr.- John Dempsey Hosp. Office: University of Connecticut Health Center John Dempsey Hospital 263 farmington Ave Farmington CT 06032-1956 Office Phone: 860-679-3343.

MCNALLY, JAMES RANDY, III, state legislator; b. Dedham, Mass., Jan. 30, 1944; s. James Randy and Margaret McKinna McNally; m. Janice Rebecca Buck, 1967; children: Melissa Kathleen, Margaret Diane. Former rep. fl. leader; house rep. Tenn.; state rep. Dist. 33 Tenn.; state senate Tenn.; bd. dir., cmty. svc. except citizens, 1974—78; treas. Anderson County Rep. Com., Tenn., 1975—78; panel mem. Tenn. Law Enforcement Planning Commn., 1976; campaign chmn., citizens for brock Oak Ridge, 1976; vice chmn. 3rd Dist. young rep., 1977; bd. mem. Elder Citizens Adv. Coun., 1977—, Am. Red Cross, 1978—80; pres. Am. Cancer Soc. Anderson County, 1978—79; pharmacist Meth. Med. Ctr., Oak Ridge, Tenn., 1978—; sec. House-Senate Rep. Joint Caucus, 1979; adv. com. mem. Martin Marietta Energy Sys. Environment, 1985—93; state senator Dist. 5 Tenn., 1987—; chmn., calender com.; chmn., edn. com.; mem. Rules, Gen. Welfare, Health & Human Resources & Tenncare Oversight Coms. Recipient Outstanding Legislator award, Mothers Against Drunk Driving, Tenn., Bird Dog award, Common Cause, 1994, Disting. Svc. award, Am. Coun. Alcohol Problems, 1994, U. Tenn. Coll. Pharmacy, 1996, Vocat. Svc. award, Oak Ridge Rotary Club, 2001, Appreciation award, 2002, Jr. Leagues award, C. of C., Tenn., 2002—03, Svc. award, Sweetwater Fire Dept., 2003, Edn. Persuits award, Internat. Assn. Adminstrv. Profl., 2003, Legislature award, Tenn. Sch. Bds. Assn., 2004, Outstanding Legislature Leadership award, 2005, Outstanding State Senator award, County Ofcl. Assn., 2006; named Young Man of Yr., 1977, Legislator of Yr., Nat. Retail Lumbermen's Assn., 1990, Man of Yr., Sertoma, 1991, Legislator of Yr., Tenn. Devel. Dist. Assn., 1997, Tenn. Men's Health Network, 2004, 2005, Mothers Against Drunk Driving, Tenn.; grantee, Tenn. Dept. Revenue Work to Create Excise Tax on Controlled Substances, 2005; Paul Harris fellow, Rotary Internat., 1996. Mem.: Nat. Conf. State Legislature, Anderson County Pharm. Soc., Tenn. Pharm. Assn., Big Bros & Big Sisters (bd. mem. 1980—), Girls Club, Rotary Club. Republican. Catholic. Office: 307 War Memorial Bldg Nashville TN 37243-0205 also: 94 Royal Troon Cir Oak Ridge TN 37830 Office Phone: 615-741-6806. Office Fax: 615-253-0285. Business E-Mail: sen.randy.mcnally@capitol.tn.gov.

MCNAMARA, ANN DOWD, medical technician; b. Detroit, Oct. 17, 1924; d. Frank Raymond and Frances Mae (Ayling) Sullivan; m. Thomas Stephen Dowd, Apr. 23, 1949 (dec. 1980); children: Cynthia Dowd Restuccia, Kevin Thomas Dowd; m. Robert A. McNamara, June 15, 1985. BS, Wayne State U., 1947. Med. technologist Woman's Hosp. (now Hutzel Hosp.), Detroit, 1946-52, St. James Clin. Lab., Detroit, 1960-62; supr. histo-pathology lab. Hutzel Hosp., Detroit, 1962-72, Mt. Carmel Mercy Hosp., 1972-87, ret., 1987. Docent Domino's Ctr. Architecture & Design, Ann Arbor, Mich. 1988. Mem. Am. Soc. Clin. Pathologists, Am. Soc. Med. Technology, Mich. Soc. Med. Technology, Nat. Soc. Histotechnology, Mich. Soc. Histotechnologists, Wayne State U. Alumni Assn., Smithsonian Assos., Detroit Inst. Arts Founders Soc., Gt. Lakes Rabbit Sanctuary, Irish Genealogy Soc. Mich. Home: 2488 Signature Dr Pinckney MI 48169

MCNEE, ANNE E., physical therapist, researcher; b. Brisbane, Queensland, Australia, July 29, 1974; d. Donald Ak and Margot A. McNee. BA in Physiotherapy, U. Queensland, 1996, MA in Physiotherapy & Paediatrics, 2001; PhD, Kings Coll., London, 2011. Cert. in physiotherapy Australian Physiotherapy Assn., 1996, Chartered Soc. Physiotherapy, 2003. Physiotherapist Royal Brisbane Hosp., Brisbane, Queensland, Australia, 1996—98; paediatric physiotherapist Royal Children's Hosp., Brisbane, 2000—01; rsch. physiotherapist Guy's & St. Thomas' Hosp. Trust, London, 2002—. Contbr. articles to profl. jours. Grantee Rsch. grant, Nancie Finnie Trust, 2006. Mem.: Chartered Soc. Physiotherapy. Office: One Small Step Gait Lab Guy's Hosp St Thomas St London SE1 9RT England Business E-Mail: anne.mcnee@gstt.nhs.uk, anne.mcnee@kcl.ac.uk.

MCNEELY, BONNIE L. (K.W. ROWE JR.), retired internist; b. Cin., Nov. 26, 1930; d. William Vernuel and Lydia LaBelle McNeely; m. Kenneth Wyer Rowe, Jr., Sept. 18, 1969; children: Christopher, Amy, Gregory, Laurel. BS, U. Cin., 1952, MD, 1956. Intern Cin. Gen. Hosp., 1956-57, resident in surgery, 1957-58, resident in internal medicine, 1958-60, fellow in cardiology, 1960-61; mem. faculty, dir. med. ctr. health svc. U. Cin. Coll. Medicine, 1961-88; dir. pers. health and employee health svcs. Conemaugh Meml. Med. Ctr., Johnstown, Pa., 1989-97; ret., 1997. Elder, Seventh Presbyn. Ch., Cin. Republican. Avocations: outdoor activities, reading, gardening.

MCNEILL, ELIZABETH (LIZ MCNEILL), nursing educator, massage therapist; b. Adelaide, South Australia, Oct. 14, 1968; d. Roland Murray and Margaret Jean McNeill. B in Health Sci., Southern Cross U., Lismore, NSW, Australia, 2000; Degree In Tertiary Edn., U. Ballarat, Victoria, 2002; M in Nursing, Flinders U., Adelaide, 2010; Degree in Critical Care Nursing, Coll. Nursing, NSW, 2006; diploma, Remedial Message Health Sch., Australia, 2011. RN South Australia Nurses Bd., 1992. Agy. critical care nurse Nursing Agy. Australia, Adelaide, 1992—; European camping mobile cook Contiki Travel Svc., 1993—95; emergency nurse Royal Prince Alfred Hosp., Sydney, 1996—99; lectr. nursing Ballarat U., 1999—2004, Sch. Nursing & Midwifery, Flinders U., Adelaide, 2003—; pandemic influenza clin. nurse cons., dept health SA Royal Dist. Nursing Soc., Adelaide, 2006—09; sr. first aid trainer Australian Red Cross, First Aid, Health and Safety, Adelaide, 2008—10, Liz McNeill Mobile Massage, 2010—. Mem. Nat. Tertiary Edn. Industry Union, 2003—; founding mem. Ally Network, Sexual Diversity Flinders U., Equal Opportunity Unit, 2004—, Soc. Participatory Medicine, 2009—, Internat. Wellness Profls. Assn., 2009—. Contbr. articles to profl. jours.; exhibitions include life drawings, photography, digital art. Mem. Handball Assn. South Australia, Adelaide, 2008—; vol. KIVA Microfinancing, 2008—, World Police & Fire Games, Australasian Masters Games, Australasian Nat. Beach Handball Championships, New Hope Canbochen Contbr., 2010—; com. mem. - lit. and forums FEAST Festival, Adelaide, 2006—09. Recipient Gold Duke award, Adelade. Mem.: ZooSA, Soc. Partcipatory Medicine, Australian Nurses Fedn. Union, South Australian Orthopaedic Nurse Assn., Australian and New Zealand Orthopaedic Nurse Assn., Renal Soc. Australiasia, Australian Nursing Fedn., Royal Coll. Nursing, Australia. E-mail: liz.mcneill@flinders.edu.au.

MCNEILL, G. DAVID, psychologist, educator; b. Santa Rosa, Calif., Dec. 21, 1931; s. Glenn H. and Ethel G. (Little) McN.; m. Nobuko Baba, Dec. 17, 1957; children: Cheryl, Randall L.B. AB, U. Calif., Berkeley, 1953, PhD, 1962. Research fellow Harvard U., 1962-65; asst. prof. psychology U. Mich., 1965-66, assoc. prof., 1966-68; prof. psychology and linguistics U. Chgo., 1969—2001, chmn. dept. psychology, 1991-97, prof. emeritus, 2001—. Vis. fellow Ctr. for Humanities, Wesleyan U., Middletown, Conn., 1970; mem. Inst. Advanced Study, Princeton, 1973-75; fellow Netherlands Inst. for Advanced Studies, 1983-84; visitor Max Planck Inst. for Psycholinguistics, Nijmegen, Netherlands, 1998-99 Author: The Acquisition of Language, 1970, The Conceptual Basis of Language, 1979, Psycholinguistics: A New Approach, 1987, Gengo Shinrigaku, 1991, Hand and Mind: What Gestures Reveal about Thought, 1992, Gesture and Thought, 2005; editor: Language and Gesture, 2000. Recipient Faculty Achievement award, 1991, Ann. Excellence in Pub. award Assn. Am. Pubs., Gordon G. Laing prize U. Chgo. Press, 1995; Guggenheim fellow, 1973-74; grantee NSF, 1983-89, 97—, Spencer Found., 1979-82, 89-92, 95-99, NIDCD, 1992-96, Advanced Rsch. and Devel. Agy., 2003—. Fellow AAAS, Am. Psychol. Soc.; mem. Internat. Soc. Gesture Studies (v.p. 2002-05, hon. pres. 2007—), Cognitive Sci. Soc., Linguistic Soc. Am., Violoncello Soc., Phi Beta Kappa, Sigma Xi Office: U Chgo Dept Psychology 5848 S University Ave Chicago IL 60637-1515 Business E-Mail: dmcneill@uchicago.edu.

MCNELLY, FREDERICK WRIGHT, JR., psychologist; b. Bangor, Maine, Apr. 14, 1947; s. Frederick Wright and E. Frances (Cutter) McNelly; 1 adopted child, Roger foster children: Joseph, Ronald, Michael, Jeffrey, Jeremy. BA magna cum laude, U. Minn., 1969; MA, U. Mich., 1971, PhD, 1973. Registered clin. psychologist Ill., cert. profl. qualification, state and provincial bds. of psychology. Rsch. coord. NSF project U. Minn., Morris, 1968-69, lab. instr., 1969, trainee USPHS, 1969-70, 72; teaching fellow psychology U. Mich., Ann Arbor, 1970-72; ednl. examiner Ann Arbor Pub. Schs., 1971; dir. psychol. svcs. Childrens Devel. Ctr., Rockford, Ill., 1972—82, program dir., 1982—86; cons. psychologist, 1986—2000; early intervention program provider Ill., 1995—2007. Lectr. Rock Valley Coll., Rockford, 1974—75; part-time pvt. practice psychology, Rockford and Belvidere, Ill., 1980—86, Beloit, Wis., 1985—86; full time, 1986—; mental health cons. Rockford Head Start, 1982—, United Cerebral Palsy, Blackhawk Region, 1986—, Access Svcs., Mendota, Ill., 1992—2000; mem. health svcs. adv. com. human resources dept. City of Rockford, 1985—; presenter state and regional workshops and confs. Contbr. articles to profl. jours. Active Boy Scouts Am., 1978—83, Big Bros./Big Sisters, 2004—09; chmn. spl. edn. regional adv. com. Bi-County Office Edn., Rockford, 1976—78; mem. Nat. and Ill. Com. Child Abuse, 1975—85; co-chmn. Winnebago County Child Protection Assn., 1980; elder Willow Creek United Presbyn. Ch., Rockford, 1980—83; mem. stronghold renovation session com. Presbytery Blackhawk, Oregon, Ill., 1985. Named U.S. Jaycees Outstanding Young Man of 1977. Mem.: Ill. Assn. Infant Mental Health, No. Ill. Alliance Mentally Ill, Nat. Assn. Mentally Ill, Nat. Assn. Disability Examiners, State Provincial Bds. Psychology, Nat. Register Health Svc. Providers Psychology, Coun. Exception Children, No. Ill. Pvt. Practice Mental Health Assn. (v.p. 1993, pres. 1994—95), No. Ill. Psychol. Assn., Ill. Psychol. Assn. Home: 11591 Beverly Ln Belvidere IL 61008-8708 Office: 631 N Longwood St Ste 205 Rockford IL 61107-4263

MCNICOL, EWAN, medical educator, director; b. Glasgow, Oct. 29, 1967; BSc Pharmacy, Strathclyde U., Scotland, 1988; Masters in Pain Rsch. Edn. & Policy, Tufts U. Sch. Medicine, Boston, 2001. Asst. prof. anesthesiology Tufts U. Sch. Medicine, 2007—. Course dir. Tufts U., 2004—; editor Cochrane Collaboration Pain, Palliative & Supportive Care Group, Oxford, 2008—. Mem.: Internat. Assn. Study Pain. Office: Tufts Med Ctr 800 Washington St Box 420 Boston MA 02111 Office Fax: 617-636-4633. Business E-Mail: emcnicol@tuftsmedicalcenter.org.

MCNIFF, JENNIFER MADISON, pathologist, educator; b. Cleve., Feb. 22, 1960; MD, U. Vt. Coll. Medicine, 1960; BA, Swarthmore Coll., 1982. Prof. dermatology and pathology, dir. yale dermatopathology Yale U., 1992—. Mem.: Am. Soc. Dermatopathology (Walter Nickel award). Office: Yale Dermatopathology PO Box 208059 New Haven CT 06520-8059 Office Fax: 203-785-6869. Business E-Mail: jennifer.mcniff@yale.edu.

MCNULTY, KATHLEEN ANNE, social worker, consultant, psychologist; b. Hackensack, NJ, Oct. 6, 1958; d. Alfred Edward and Gertrude Natalie (Currie) McN.; m. Henry Stanislaw Kowal, Sept. 16, 1988. BA, Rutgers U., 1980; MSW, Smith Coll., 1984; postgrad, Fielding Grad. Inst., 2001—09. Lic. marriage and family therapist; lic. clin. social worker; psychologist. Mental health aide Belleville Mental Health Clinic, NJ, 1980-82; clin. social worker Albert Einstein Coll. Medicine, Bronx, NY, 1984-86, Family Guidance Bergen, Hackensack, 1986-87, Cliffwood Mental Health Ctr., Englewood, NJ, 1986-87; pvt. practice Rutherford, NJ, 1987-99, Ridgewood, NJ, 1999—. Cons. Meadowlands Weight Control, Rutherford, 1988—, St. Lukes-Roosevelt Hosp. Ctr., NYC, 1988. Contbr. articles to profl. jours. Mem. Am. Orthopsychiat. Assn., Acad. Cert. Social Workers (cert.), Nat. Assn. Social Workers. Avocations: painting, singing, sports, poetry. Office Phone: 201-444-4010. Personal E-mail: relationsconnect@aol.com.

MCNUTT, PAMELA G., hospital administrator; Attended in Mgmt. Info. Sys., George Wash. U.; BBA in Statistics and Mktg., U. Tex. With Medicus/HBOC, Hermann Hosp.; mem. coun. data initiative exec. com. Dallas Fort Worth Hosp.; mem. hosp. data collection workgroup Info. Coun. Tex. Health Care; joined Meth. Health System, 1993, chief info. officer, sr. v.p. Named John Gall Chief Info. Officer of the Year, 2002, Rising Star to Watch, Healthcare IT News, 2010; named one of Top 25 Women in Healthcare, Modern Healthcare mag., 2011. Fellow: Coll. of Healthcare Info. Mgmt. Execs. (faculty mem. healthcare chief info. officer boot camp 2003—06, trustee 2007—09, chair policy steering com.), Healthcare Info. and Mgmt. Sys. Soc. (dir. nat. bd. 1998—2001, Info. Sys. award 1998, Leadership award 2001); mem.: Healthcare Info. Sys. Execs. Assn. (chair). Office: Methodist Health System PO Box 655999 Dallas TX 75265-5999 Office Phone: 877-637-4297.

MCPARTLAND, PATRICIA ANN, adult education educator; b. Passaic, NJ; d. Daniel and Josephine McP. BA, U. Mo., 1971; MCRP, Ohio State U., 1975, MS in Preventive Medicine, 1975; EdD in Higher and Adult Edn., Columbia U., 1988; cert. distance edn., Tex. A&M U., 2000, cert. distance edn. web pub. cert., 2001. Cert. health edn. specialist, distance edn. web pub., grants specialist; workforce devel. profl. Sr. health planner Merrimack Valley HSA, Lawrence, Mass., 1977—79; planning cons., adminstr. Children's Hosp., Boston, 1979—80; exec. dir. Assn. Workforce Alternatives, Rsch. & Devel., Inc., Marion, Mass., 1980—; dir. adult continuing edn. Upper Cape Cod Regional Tech. Sch., Bourne, Mass., 2005—; with DTM Toastmasters Internat. Area Gov. Advanced Comn. Gold. V.p., cons. New Bedford (Mass.) Cmty. Health Ctr., 1993—94; chmn. edn. and tng. com. Health and Human Svc. Coalition, 1988—89; mem. project expert panel Office of Minority Health, 1997—2003; mem. New Eng. Regional Minority Health Conf. Com., 1997—99; vis. lectr. Bridgewater State Coll.; lectr. in field; project expert panel Office Minority Health's Culturally and Linguistically Appropriate Svcs.; mem. New Eng. Regional Minority Health Conf. Com., 2001—03. Author: Promoting Health in the Workplace, 1991; mem. editl. bd. Jour. Healthcare Edn. and Tng., 1989-93; editor-in-chief, Jour. Walprice Del., 2007-09, mem. editl. bd., editor: Jour. Workforce Devel.; reviewer Qualitative Health Rsch. Jour.; contbr. articles to profl. jours. Vol. spkr. March of Dimes Found., Wareham, Mass., 1992-93; coll.-wide vocat. Cape Cod C.C., Hyannis, Mass., 1989—; planning adv. 2nd Internat. Symposium, Pasco, Wash., 1992; v.p. New Bedford chpt. Am. Cancer Soc., 1985-90. Recipient award Excellence in Continuing Edn. Nat. AHEC Ctr. Dirs. Assn., 1994, 95, 96, 97, Sec.'s awards for Outstanding Progam in Community Health, Nat. Cancer Inst., Washington, 1990. Mem.: APHA, Nat. Assn. Workforce Devel. Profls. (bd. dirs.), Nat. Planning Conf. (mem. com. 1984—87), Southeastern Mass. Health Planning (bd. dirs., sec. 1982—87), Inst. for Disease Prevention (steering com. 1982—). Avocations: writing, acting, dance, theater, travel. Home: PO Box 1116 Marion MA 02738-0020 Office: Upper Cape Tech 220 Sandwich Rd Bourne MA 02532 Office Phone: 508-759-7711 ext. 258. Personal E-mail: pcmcpartland@comcast.net. Business E-Mail: pmcpartland@uppercapetech.org.

MCPHERSON, ALICE RUTH, ophthalmologist, educator; b. Regina, Sask., Can., June 30, 1926; came to U.S., 1938, naturalized, 1958; d. Gordon and Viola (Hoover) McP. BS, U. Wis., 1948, MD, 1951, DSc (hon.), 1997. Diplomate Am. Bd. Ophthalmology. Intern Santa Barbara (Calif.) Cottage Hosp., 1951-52; resident anesthesiology Hartford (Conn.) Hosp., 1952; resident ophthalmology Chgo. Eye, Ear, Nose and Throat Hosp., 1953, U. Wis. Hosps., 1953-55; ophthalmologist Davis and Duehr Eye Clinic, Madison, Wis., 1956-57; clin. instr. U. Wis., 1956-57; fellow retina svc. Mass. Eye and Ear Infirmary, 1957-58; ophthalmologist Scott and White Clinic, Temple, Tex., 1958-60; practice medicine specializing in ophthalmology and retinal diseases Houston, 1960—; pres. Retina Rsch. Found., Houston, 1969—. Staff Meth., St. Luke's, Tex. Children's Hosps., Harris County Hosp. Dist., Houston; clin. asst. prof. Baylor Coll. Medicine, Houston, 1959-61, asst. prof. ophthalmology, 1961-69, clin. assoc. prof., 1969-75, clin. prof., 1975-98, prof., 1998—; cons. retinal diseases VA Hosp., Houston, 1960—, Ben Taub Hosp., Houston, 1960—; mem. adv. com. for active staff appt. sect. ophthalmology Meth. Hosp., 1986-91, mem equipment com., 1993-95, mem. grievance panel, 1997; vol. clin. faculty appts. and promotions com., 1993; bd. dirs. Highlights of Ophthalmology; v.p. N.Am. Highlights of Ophthalmology Internat. Editor: New and Controversial Aspects of Retinal Detachment, 1968, New and Controversial Aspects of Vitreoretinal Surgery, 1977, Retinopathy of Prematurity: Current Concepts and Controversies, 1986. Amb. Houston Ballet, mem. Houston Ballet Found.; mem. pres.'s coun. Houston Grand Opera; condrs. cir. Houston Symphony, mem. Houston Symphony Soc.; mem. campaign for 80s Baylor Coll. Medicine; mem. Assn. for Cmty. TV, BBB, Physicians' Benevolent Fund, South Tex. Diabetes Assn. Inc., Jr. League Houston; bd. dirs. U. Wis. Found., Madison; mem. Bd. Internat. Coun. Ophthalmology Found., 2008, external adv. bd. mem. U. Wis. Eye Rsch. Inst., 2010. Recipient Award of appreciation KT Eye Found., 1978, Woodlands Medal for Outstanding Contbn. to the Econ. Devel. of Cmty., 1988, spl. recognition award Assn. for Rsch. in Vision in Ophthalmology, Crystal award Recognizing Generous Support-Ptnrs. with an Eye for Vision Found. Am. Acad. Ophthalmology, 2000, Benjamin Boyd Humanitarian award Pan Am. Assn. Ophthalmology, 2001, Philip Corboy Meml. award Disting. Svc. Ophthalmology, 2002, Women of Vision Houston Delta Gamma Found., 2002; Alice R. Mc Pherson Lab. for Retina Rsch. dedicated Baylor Ctr. for Biotech., 1988; Alice R. Mc Pherson Day proclaimed in her honor Mayor of City of Houston, Mar. 12, 1988. Fellow: ACS (credentials and Tex. credentials com., com. on applications), Am. Acad. Ophthalmology (2nd v.p. 1979, vice chmn. program devel. found. bd. trustees 1993—, nominating com. subspecialty/specialized sect. of coun. 2001, com. for pub. and profl. rels., bd. dirs. opthalmology ednl. trust fund found., laureate award selection com., mem. coun. representing PAAO, hon. found. bd. dirs., honor award 1956, sr. honor award 1986, guest of honor 1998 meeting, Visionary Soc. Gold Mem.); mem.: AMA, Internat. Coun. Ophthal. Found. (bd. dirs. 2006—), Highlights Ophthal. Internat., Schepens Internat. Soc. (sec. 1986—93, v.p. 1993—95, pres. 1995—97), U. Wis. Ophthal. Alumni Assn. (founding pres. 1990—93, founded Alice R. McPherson lectureship 1994), Assn. Rsch. Surgeons, Pan Am. Assn. Ophthalmology Found., Tex. Ophthal. Assn., So. Med. Soc., Rsch. to Prevent Blindness, Pan Am. Assn. Opthalmology (v.p. 1991—92, pres. elect 1992—95, AJO lectr. 1993, pres. 1995—97, pres. found. 1997, bd. dirs., membership com., Benjamin Boyd Humanitarian award 2001), Macula Soc. (credentialing com. 1992), Internat. Soc. Eye Rsch. (credentials com. 1992), Houston Ophthal. Soc. (pres. 1990—91, credentials com.), Harris County Med. Soc., Am. Bd. Laser Surgery, Am. Soc. Contemporary Ophthalmology (Charles Schepens Hon. award), Internat. Coll. Ocular Surgeons (vice regent 1991), Retina Soc. (v.p. 1976—77, pres. 1978—79, credentials com.), Am. Med. Women's Assn., Internat. Coll. Surgeons (vice regent 1991—), Tex. Med. Assn., Vitreous Soc., Jules Gonin Club. Achievements include research in vision and ophthalmology. Office: 1977 Butler Blvd Houston TX 77030 Office Phone: 713-798-3276.

MCPHERSON, CRAIG A., cardiologist, educator; s. Lester F. and Gloria K. Mcpherson; m. Anita K. Kerbeshian, 1948; children: Marianne E., Christina R. AB, Columbia U., NYC, 1972; MD, Tufts U., Boston, 1976. Lic. internal medicine Am. Bd. of Internal Medicine, cardiovasc. diseases Am. Bd. of Internal Medicine, cardiac electrophysiology Am. Bd. of Internal Medicine, Am. Bd. of Internal Medicine. Asst. prof. of medicine Yale U., New Haven, Conn., 1984—89, assoc. prof. of medicine, 1989—2006, clin. prof. of medicine, 2006—. Dir. cardiac electrophysiology Bridgeport Hosp., Conn., 1992—, dir. cardiology tng., 1995—. Recipient Hands and Heart award, Dept. of VA, 1989; named Tchr. of the Yr., Bridgeport Hosp., 1995, 2005. Fellow: Am. Coll. of Cardiology; mem.: ACP, Am. Heart Assn., Heart Rhythm Soc., Alpha Omega Alpha. Office: Bridgeport Hosp Yale Univ 267 Grant St Bridgeport CT 06610 Business E-Mail: pcmcph@bpthosp.org.

MCQUILLEN, MICHAEL PAUL, neurologist, educator; b. NYC, Sept. 9, 1932; s. Paul and Dorothy Marian (Moore) McQ.; m. Louise Devlin; children: Daniel, Thomas, Patrick, Kathleen. BA cum laude, Georgetown U., 1953, MD, 1957; MA, U. Va., 1994. Diplomate Am. Bd. Psychiatry and Neurology (bd. dirs. 1991-95, exec. com. 1995), added qualification in clin. neurophysiology. Rotating intern Royal Victoria Hosp., Montreal, Que., Canada, 1957—58; resident in neurology Georgetown U. Med. Center, 1958—60; fellow in physiology Johns Hopkins U. Med. Sch. and Hosp., 1960—62, instr. medicine, 1962—65; mem. faculty U. Ky. Med. Center, 1965—74, prof. neurology, 1972—74, prof., chmn. neurology, 1987—93; prof. neurology, chmn. dept. Med. Coll. Wis., Milw., 1974—87; clin. faculty mem. dept. neurology U. Va. Health Sci. Ctr., Charlottesville, 1993—94; prof. neurology U. Rochester, NY, 1995—2005; clin. prof. neurology and neurol. scis. Stanford (Calif.) U., 2006—. Vis. sci. Inst. Neurophysiology U. Copenhagen, 1971-72; vis. prof. U. Ky. Med. Ctr., 1978, Royal Coll. Surgeons, Ireland, 1983. Contbr. articles to profl. jours. Mem. Cath. Commn. on Intellectual Affairs. Recipient Neurology medal Georgetown U. Med. Sch., 1957; Clin. Teaching award Med. Coll. Wis., 1976; Disting. Service award N.Y. Med. Coll., 1983; named to Johns Hopkins Soc. Scholars, 1981, Tchg. award, Stanford U., 2006-10; Lifetime Achievement award, Myasthenia Gravis Found. America, 2011. Fellow Am. Acad. Neurology; mem. AMA, Nat. Myasthenia Gravis Found. (chmn. 1981-83), Am. Neurol. Assn., Wis. Neurol. Assn. (pres. 81-82), Alpha Omega Alpha. Office: Stanford Univ 300 Pasteur Dr Rm H3152 Stanford CA 94305 Home: 3611 Louis Rd Palo Alto CA 94303 Office Phone: 650-723-5297. Personal E-mail: michael_mcquillen@comcast.net. Business E-Mail: mmcquillen@stanfordmed.org.

MCRAE, MARION ELEANOR, cardiovascular surgery nurse; b. Kingston, Ont., Can., Sept. 19, 1960; d. James Malcolm and Madeline Eleanor (MacNamara) McR. BSN, Queen's U., Kingston, 1982; MSN, U. Toronto, 1989, ACNP diploma, 2001. RN, Calif., CCRN; cert. BCLS, ACLS, CMC, CSC, ANA cardiac/vascular; advanced practice RN; bd. cert. acute care nurse practitioner, ACNPC. Staff nurse thoracic surgery Toronto (Can.) Gen. Hosp., 1982-83, staff nurse cardiovascular ICU, 1983-85; nurse clinician critical care St. Michael's Hosp., Toronto, 1985-87; external critical care clin. tchr. Ryerson Poly. Inst., Toronto, 1986-87; staff nurse cardiovascular ICU The Toronto Hosp.-Toronto Gen. Divsn., 1987-89; clin. nurse specialist cardiac surgery The Toronto Hosp., 1989-90; clin. nurse II cardiothoracic ICU UCLA Med. Ctr., 1990-92, clin. nurse III cardiothoracic ICU, 1992-2000; nurse practitioner cardiovasc. surgery Toronto Gen. Hosp., 2000—; adj. faculty nursing U. Toronto, Ont., 2004—; medicolegal nursing cons. Mem. critical care nursing adv. bd. George Brown Coll., Toronto, 1987-88, textbook reviewer. Contbr. articles to profl. nursing jours. Recipient Open Master's fellowship U. Toronto, 1987-88, Nursing Faculty-Staff fellowship, 2010, Yaufong Chang scholarship, 2011, M. Keyes bursary Toronto Gen. Hosp., 1988-89, Nursing fellowship Heart and Stroke Found. Ont., 1988-89, Cardiovascular Nursing fellowship, Frank Gerstein Charitable Found., Lewis Family Fund fellowship, 2010, Outstanding Svc. award UCLA Med. Ctr., 1994, Cardiothoracic ICU Nurse of Yr. award UCLA, 1995, Excellence in Clin. Practice Leadership award, 2010. Mem. AACN, Am. Heart Assn. Coun. on Cardiovascular Nursing., ISACHD. Office: Toronto Gen Hosp 4C 453 585 University Ave Toronto ON Canada M5G 2N2 Business E-Mail: marion.mcrae@uhn.on.ca.

MCSHANE, FRANKLIN JOHN, III, nurse anesthetist; b. Columbia, SC, July 25, 1962; s. Franklin John Jr. and Helga Rita (Fischer) McS.; m. Leesa Ann West, Sept. 24, 1988; children: Amanda Nicole, Hannah Ryan. BSN, U. Mass., 1985; MSN, U. Tex., Houston, 1995; DNP, U. Minn., 2011. RN, Wis.; cert. RN anesthetist ANCC.; cert. ACLS instr., CPR, PALS instr. Am. Heart Assn. Commd. 2d lt. U.S. Army, 1985, advanced through grades to col., 2005; clin. staff nurse oncology unit Letterman Army Med. Ctr., San Francisco, 1985-86, clin. staff nurse surg. ICU and post anesthesia care unit, 1987-90; head nurse emergency room 67th Evacuation Hosp., Würzburg, Germany, 1990-92, infection control nurse, 1992-93; staff nurse anesthetist Walter Reed Army Med. Ctr., Washington, 1996-98, asst. program dir. US Army grad. program anesthesia nursing, 1998-2000; staff nurse anesthetist 2290th Gen. Hosp. (Reserves), Washington, 2000—06; ptnr. Ctrl. Wis. Anesthesia Associates, S.C., Berlin, Wis. Adj. lectr. emergency med. svcs. tract City Colls. Chgo. Europe, 1991-93; adj. clin. faculty U. Tex. Grad. Program in Anesthesia Nursing, Walter Reed Army Med. Ctr., 1996-98, asst. prof. clin. nursing U. Tex. Houston Health Sci. Ctr., 1998-2000, Uniformed Svcs. U. Health Scis., 1998-2000; adj. clin. faculty U. Minn.; presenter in field. Contbr. articles to nursing jours. Mem. ANA, Am. Assn. Nurse Anesthetists, Sigma Theta Tau. Avocations: reading, cooking, triathlon. Office: Ctrl Wis Anesthsia Assocs 225 Memorial Dr Berlin WI 54923-1243 Office Phone: 920-361-5538. Business E-Mail: frank.mcshane@chnwi.org. E-mail: skytrane@charter.net.

MCSORLEY, MARYANN B., pediatrician; MD, U. Pa. Sch. Medicine, 1983. Diplomate Am. Bd. Pediatrics, 1987. Resident, intern Children's Hosp. Phila.; faculty appointment Clin. Assoc. Pediats.; hosp. affiliation includes Pa. Hosp. Named Top Docs, Phila. Mag., 2010, 2011; named one of the Best Doctors in America, 2003—04, 2005—06, 2007—08, 2009—10. Office: Pennsylvania Hospital 800 Spruce St Philadelphia PA 19107 Office Phone: 215-829-3000.

MCSWAIN, BYRDIE ENGLE, laboratory scientist, immunohematologist; b. Ethel, Ark., Oct. 13, 1939; d. James Marvin and Katherine Engle (Martin) McSwain. BS, U. Ark., 1968; BS in Med. Tech., U. Ark. Sch. Medicine, 1969; MS, U. Ctrl. Ark., 1973; Specialist in Blood Banking, U. Ark. Med. Scis., 1976. Cert. in regulatory affairs (RAPS). Supr. blood bank Univ. Ark. Med. Scis., Little Rock, clin. instr.; dir. tech. svcs., dir. product mgmt. ARC Blood Svcs., dir. transplantation svcs., dir. regulatory affairs, South Ctrl. area dir. tech. and regulatory svcs., acting area dir. quality assurance. Contbr. 13 articles to profl. jours. Grad. scholar Am. Soc. Med. Tech.; recipient Omicron Sigma award, Am. Soc. for Med. Tech., Outstanding Svc. award, Disting. Alumni award U. Ark. for Med. Scis. Mem. Ark. Soc. Clin. Lab. Scientists (Med. Technologist of Yr.), Am. Assn. Blood Banks, South Ctrl. Assn. Blood Banks (pres., author, editor), Am. Soc. Clin. Lab. Scientists, Clin. Lab. Mgmt. Assn. (pres. Ark. chpt.), Am. Soc. Clin. Pathologists, Regulatory Affairs Profl. Soc., Am. Soc. Quality Assurance, Phi Beta Kappa.

MCTAGGART, STEVEN JAMES, pediatrician; MB BChir, U. Queensland, Australia, 1991; PhD, U. Melbourne, Australia, 2001. Dir. Child & Adolescent Renal Svc., Brisbane, Queensland, 2001—; sr. rschr. Mater Med. Rsch. Inst., Brisbane, 2002—. Fellow: Royal Australasian Coll. Physicians. Office: Child & Adolescent Renal Svc Herston Rd Herston 4029 Australia Office Fax: 61 7 3636 1704.

MEAD, PHILIP BARTLETT, retired obstetrician, healthcare administrator, educator; b. Poughkeepsie, NY, June 23, 1937; s. Ralph Allen and Altina (Gervin) Mead; m. Ann Elaine Smith, June 27, 1964; children: Ralph Allen II, David Smith. BA, Hamilton Coll., 1959; MD, Cornell U., 1963. Diplomate Nat. Bd. Med. Examiners, Am. Bd. Ob-gyn. Intern in medicine Bellevue Hosp., NYC, 1963-64; resident in ob-gyn. NY Hosp./Cornell Med. Ctr., NYC, 1964-69; asst. prof. U. Vt. Coll. Medicine, Burlington, 1971-76, assoc. prof., 1976-81, prof., 1981—2001, prof. emeritus, 2001—; hosp. epidemiologist Med. Ctr. Hosp. of Vt., Burlington, 1984-93; dir. clin. sys. Vt. Acad. Med. Ctr., Burlington, 1993-95; sr. v.p., med. dir. Fletcher Allen Health Care, Burlington, 1995-97; prof., chmn. ob-gyn. U. Vt. Coll. Medicine, 1997—2001, prof., chmn. emeritus, 2001—; physician leader women's health care svcs. Fletcher Allen Health Care, Burlington, 1997—2001. Lt. comdr. M.C. USN, 1969—71. Fellow: ACOG, Infectious Disease Soc. Am.; mem.: Soc. Hosp. Epidemiologists, Infectious Disease Soc. Ob-Gyn. (pres. 1987—88), Phi Beta Kappa, Alpha Omega Alpha. Home: 203 Pinehurst Dr Shelburne VT 05482-6882 Personal E-mail: pbmeadmd@comcast.net. *

MEADERS, NOBUKO YOSHIZAWA, psychotherapist; b. Kobe, Hyogo-ken, Japan, Mar. 2, 1942; d. Shigenobu and Ayako (Takahashi) Tsuchiya; m. Wilson E. Meaders, Apr. 2, 1976 (div. Apr. 1985); m. Takeshi Yoshizawa, June 15, 1989. AA, Seiwa Coll., Nishinomiya, Japan, 1965, Warren Wilson Coll., Swannanoa, NC, 1967; BA, So. Meth. U., Dallas, 1969; MS in Social Work, U. Tex., Arlington, 1971; cert. psychotherapy-psychoanalysis, Postgrad. Ctr. Mental Health, NYC, 1977, cert. in supervision psychotherapeutic processes, 1979. Cert. social worker N.Y., diplomate Am. Bd. Examiners Clin. Social Work. Psychiat. social worker Killgore Children's Psychiat. Hosp., Amarillo, Tex., 1971-73, Jewish Child Care Assn., Childville div., NYC, 1973-74; supr. social work, social work dept. Bellevue Hosp., NYC, 1974-76; asst. dir. tng. Postgrad. Ctr. Mental Health, NYC, 1979-82, assoc. supr., 1979-82, supr., 1982-85, sr. supr., 1985—, tng. analyst, 1989—; pvt. practice psychotherapy and psychoanalysis NYC, 1976—. Clin. cons. Pace U. Personal Devel. Ctr., NYC, 1987—. Fellow: N.Y. Soc. Clin. Social Work Psychotherapists; mem.: NASW, Acad. Cert. Social Workers. Avocations: sculpting, drawing, gardening, writing. Office Phone: 212-228-6988. Personal E-mail: nobukomeaders@gmail.com.

MEADOR, KIMFORD JAY, neurologist, researcher; b. New Orleans, Apr. 28, 1950; s. John D. and Marion (Pierce) M.; m. G. Maggie Pabon; children: Anthony Shane, Mary Catherine, Adrienne Christin, Kellan Jacob. BS in Applied Biology with high honors, Ga. Inst. of Tech., 1972; MD, Med. Coll. of Ga., 1976. Diplomate Nat. Bd. of Med. Examiners, Am. Bd. Neurology and Psychiatry; lic., Ga., S.C. Rsch. asst. Ctr. Disease Control, Atlanta, 1970, 71; intern diversified psychiatry U. Va. Hosp., Charlottesville, 1976-77; lt. comdr. USPHS,

1977-80; residency in neurology Med. Coll. Ga., Augusta, 1980-83; fellow in behavioral neurology U. Fla., Gainesville; asst. prof. neurology Med. Coll. Ga., Augusta, 1984-88, assoc. prof., 1988-93, prof., 1993, Charbonnier prof. neurology; chair neurology Georgetown U., Washington, 2002—04; Melvin Greer prof. neurology U. Fla., Gainesville, 2004—09; prof. neurology, dir. Emory Epilepsy Ctr. Emory U., Atlanta, 2009—. Reviewer: Annals of Neurology, Archives of Neurology, Epilepsia, Exptl. Jour. of Aging, Jour. Clin. Neurophysiology, Neurology, N.Y. State Jour. Medicine, Psychiatry Rsch.; contbr. over 100 articles to Brain, Epilepsia, Neuropsychology, Neuropsychologia, Neurology, Brain and Cognition, Am. Jour. Neuroradiology, Internat. Jour. Neurosci., Archives of Clin. Neuropsychology and others. Scholastic scholar Ga. Inst. Tech. Fellow Am. Acad. Neurology (essay award, 1989); mem. AAAS, AMA, Internat. Neuropsychol. Soc., Am. Neurol. Assn., Am. Epilepsy Soc., The Soc. for Psychophysiol. Rsch., Behavioral Neurology, Soc., The N.Y. Acad. of Scis., Ga. Neurol. Assn., Phi Kappa Phi, Beta Beta Beta. Achievements include research in perception, cerebral lateralization, neglect syndrome, memory, Alzheimer's disease, epilepsy, psychopharmacology and psychophysiology. Home: 851 Courtenay Dr NE Atlanta GA 30306 E-mail: Meador@Neuro.mcg.edu.

MEADORS, ALLEN COATS, academic administrator, educator; b. Van Buren, Ark., May 17, 1947; s. Hal Barron and Allene Coats (Means) Meadors. AA, Saddleback Coll., 1981; BBA, U. Ctrl. Arki., 1969; MBA, U. No. Colo., 1974; MPA, U. Kans., 1975; MA in Psychology, Webster U., 1979, MA in Health Svcs. Mgmt., 1980; PhD in Adminstrn., So. Ill. U., 1981. Assoc. adminstr. Forbes Hosp., Topeka, 1971-73; asst. dir. health svcs. devel. Blue Cross Blue Shield of Kans., Topeka, 1973-76; asst. dir. Kansas City Health Dept., Mo., 1976-77; program dir., asst. prof. So. Ill. U., Carbondale, 1977—82, Webster U., St. Louis, 1979—82; mem. faculty Calif. State U., Long Beach, 1977-81; assoc. prof., dir. divsn. health adminstrn. U. Tex., Galveston, 1982-84; exec. dir. N.W. Ark. Radiation Therapy Inst., Springdale, 1984-87; mem. grad. faculty Sch. Bus. Adminstrn. U. Ark., Fayetteville, 1984-87; prof., chmn. dept. health adminstrn. U. Okla., Oklahoma City, 1987-90, dean Coll. Pub. Health, 1989—90; dean Coll. Health, Social and Pub. Svcs. Ea. Wash. U., Cheney, 1990—94; chancellor U. NC, Penbroke, 1994—99, Pembroke, 1999—2009; pres. U. Ctrl. Ark., 2009—. Cons. Surgeon Gen. Office and Air Force Sys.; bd. dirs. Lumbar Guartoner Bank, Southeastern Regional Med. Ctr. Contbr. articles to profl. jours. Command bd. dirs. Blair County Hall of Fame, Blair County Hist. Soc., Martin Luther King Hosp., Health Care Svcs. Adv. Bd.; bd. dirs., exec. com. Altoona Symphony Orch.; bd. dirs. Home Health Agy., NC Retirement Fund, Southwestern Regional Med. Ctr. With Med. Svc. Corps USAF, 1969—73. Fellow: Am. Coll. Healthcare Execs.; mem.: Am. Hosp. Assn., C. of C. (v.p.). Office: U Ctrl Ark / Office of Pres Wingo Hall RM 207G 201 Donaghey Ave Conway AR 72035 Office Phone: 501-450-5286. E-mail: ACM@uca.edu.

ME-AE, KIM, hematologist; b. Dae-Gu, Gyeung-Sang Buk-Do, Republic of Korea, Feb. 23, 1965; d. Kim and Yoon; m. Ji-Hong Kim, Feb. 18, 1995; children: Gyeung-Hye Kim, Eun-Cho Kim. PhD, In-Je U. Med. Sch., Seoul, 2002. Cert. lab. medicine Ministry Health and Welfare, Korea. Asst. prof. dept. lab. medicine Gyeongsang Nat. U. Hosp., Jinju, Republic of Korea, 2002—05. Office Fax: 82-41-850-5219. Personal E-mail: givmea2004@yahoo.co.kr.

MEALIE, CARL A., emergency physician, educator; b. Astoria, NY, Jan. 26, 1948; s. Patrick and Natalie (Previti) M.; m. Maureen Frances Maybury, Apr. 24, 1993; children: David, Ian, Daniel. BA, NYU, 1969; MD, N.Y. Med. Coll., 1974. CCRN. Chmn. Dept. Emergency Medicine St. Mary's Hosp., Roswell, N.Mex., 1975-83; emergency dept. attending physician Guadalupe Med. Ctr., Carlsbad, N.Mex., 1979-83, LI Jewish Med. Ctr., New Hyde Park, NY, 1993—, chmn. disaster preparation com., 1991—2010, asst. chief emergency dept., 1989-95, chief clin. ops., 1995; asst. prof. emergency medicine Albert Einstein Coll. Medicine, NYC, 1995—2011, Hofstra North Shore-LIJ Sch. Medicine, 2011, 2011. Mem. ambulance adv. bd. Chavez County Med. Soc., Roswell, 1980-83, ambulance bd., 1981-87. Mem. City Roswell EMS Bd., 1981-93. Fellow Am. Coll. Emergency Physicians (key contact 1987—), NY Acad. Medicine; me. AMA, Am. Acad. Emergency Medicine, NY State Med. Soc., Soc. Acad. Emergency Medicine. Roman Catholic. Avocations: skiing, sailing, hunting, golf. Home: 33 Heights Rd Northport NY 11768-2629 Office: LI Jewish Med Ctr Lakeville New Hyde Park NY 11040 Personal E-mail: carl_mealie@msn.com.

MEANS, ANTHONY ROSS, pharmacology educator; PhD, U. Tex., 1967. Nanaline H. Duke prof., chmn. pharmacology & cancer biology, dep. dir. comprehensive cancer inst. Duke U. Med. Ctr., Durham, NC. Contbr. articles to profl. publs. Fellow AAAS, Am. Acad. Arts and Sci.; mem. Endocrine Soc. (pres. 2004-05, Fred Conrad Koch award 1998), Am. Soc. Pharmacology and Exptl. Therapeutics (Goodman and Gilman award 2006). Office: Duke U Med Ctr PO Box 3813 Durham NC 27710-0001 E-mail: means001@mc.duke.edu.

MEANS, ROBERT TAYLOR, JR., hematologist, educator, researcher; b. Midland, Tex., July 14, 1957; s. Robert Taylor and Anna Therese (Cassidy) M.; m. Stacey W. McKenzie, May 23, 1992; children: Anna, Robert III, Patrick. BA in Biochemistry, Rice U., Houston, 1979; MD, Vanderbilt U., Nashville, 1983. Diplomate Am. Bd. Internal Medicine; cert. in hematology. Resident Baylor Coll. Medicine, Houston, 1983-86; fellow in hematology Vanderbilt U., Nashville, 1986-88, instr. medicine, 1988-90, asst. prof. medicine, 1990-92; assoc. investigator VA Med. Ctr., 1988-91, asst. chief hematology/oncology Cin., 1992-98, chief hematology/oncology Charleston, SC, 1998—2004, prof. internal medicine, 2004—, chief med. svc. Lexington, Ky., 2004—06; assoc. prof. med. U. Cin., 1992-98; prof. med., head hematology, assoc. divsn. chief Med. U. SC, 1998-2000, dir. divsn. hematology-oncology, 2000—04; prof. internal medicine U. Ky., 2004—, assoc. rsch. chair internal medicine, 2004—07, interim assoc. dean, 2004—06, sr. assoc. chair, 2007—11. Interim dir. Markey Cancer Ctr., 2006—09, assoc. dean vets. affairs, 2011—, exec. vice dean, 2011—. Editor (assoc.) Jour. Investigative Medicine; mem. editl. bd. Internat. Jour. Hematology, Hematology, Am. Jour. Med. Sci., Winthrobe's Clinical Hematology, 12th edit.; contbr. chpts. to books, articles to profl. jours. Recipient Career Devel. award Dept. Veterans Affairs., 1988, Henry Christian award Am. Fedn. Clin. Rsch., 1991, Chief Resident's Faculty of Yr. award, U. Ky., 2006. Fellow Am. Coll. Physicians; mem. Am. Soc. Hematology, Internat. Soc. Exptl. Hematology, Am. Fed. Med. Rsch. (v.p. mtgs., programs, 1998-2002), Southern Soc. Clin. Investigation (councillor, 2005-2010, exec. adv. com. 2010-11, pres. elect. 2011-), Phi Beta Kappa. Achievements include being first to report response of anemia of chronic disease to erythropoietin; first description of erythropoietin receptor in polycythemia. Home: 2204 Abbeywood Rd Lexington KY 40515 Office: J525 Ky Clinic 740 S Limestone St Lexington KY 40536 Home Phone: 859-971-8184; Office Phone: 859-257-5116. Business E-Mail: robert.means@uky.edu.

MEARS, JOHN GREGORY, hematologist, educator, oncologist, internist; MD, Columbia U., NYC, 1973. Diplomate Am. Bd. Internal Medicine, Am. Bd. Internal Medicine-hematology. Intern Boston Univ. Med. Ctr., resident internal medicine, 1973—75; fellow hematology and oncology Columbia Presbyn. Med. Ctr., NYC, 1975—78; clin. prof. medicine Columbia Univ., NYC; with NY-Presbyn./Columbia Univ. Med. Ctr., NYC. Office: New York-Presbyterian/Columbia University Medical Center 622 West 168th St New York NY 10032 Office Phone: 212-305-2500.

MEASE, PHILIP, rheumatologist; b. Va., Oct. 4, 1951; BA, Stanford U., 1973, MD, 1977. Dir. Seattle Rheumatology Assocs., 2001—. Clin. prof. U. Wash. Sch. Medicine, 1982; dir. Swedish Rheumatology Rsch., 2001. Mem.: Am. Coll. Rheumatology. Office: 1101 Madison St Ste 1000 Seattle WA 98104 Office Fax: 206-386-2083. Business E-Mail: pmease@nwlink.com.

MECCIA, FRANCIS (FRANK) ANTHONY, physician assistant; s. Aniello J. and Marie Celeste Meccia. AA, Kendall Coll., 1976; BS, Columbus Univ., 1998; MS, Trinity So. U., 2000; cert. physician asst., Cook County Hosp., 1989. Cert. advance cardiac life support. Enlisted U.S. Army, 1976, advanced through ranks to staff sgt., 1985, sr. med. aidmen Spangdahlem, Germany, 1976-80, sr. med. advisor Hdqrs. 2d Inf. White House Washington, 1980-83, med. recruiter Ft. Sheridan, Ill., 1983-87, ret., 1987; physician asst. Montefiore Med. Ctr., Bronx, NY, 1989-91; cardiovasc. physician asst. Murphy Otto and Assocs., Evanston, Ill., 1991-98; sr. physician asst. for cardiovasc. svcs. Resurrection Hosp., Chgo., 1998—; staff physician asst. Our Lady of the Resurrection Med. Ctr., Chgo., 2001—; staff physician asst. for cardiovasc. surgery St. Francis Hosp., Evanston, Ill., 2001—. Preceptor U. Health Scis., Chgo. Med. Sch., North Chgo., 1993-94, Cook County Hosp. Physician Asst. Program, Chgo., preceptor 1993—; bd. trustees Alexian Bros. Bonaventure Ho., Chgo., 2005—, host Castle TV, 2008 Decorated Meritorious Svc. medal USAR, Washington, 1992, Army Commendation medal with oak leaf cluster, 1997; recipient The David award Allied Health Pers., Chgo., 1993. Mem. Am. Assn. Physician Assts. (cert., editor/treas. AAPA caucus GLPA 2003—), Am. Assn. Physician Assts. Surgery, Am. Heart Assn. (cert. advance trauma life support), Assn. Physician Assts. Cardiovasc. Surgery, Ill. Acad. Physician Assts. Avocations: scuba diving, sky diving, skiing. Home: 6219 W Cornelia Ave Chicago IL 60634-4120 Office: Resurrection Hosp 7435 W Talcott Ave Ste 1 Chicago IL 60631-3746 E-mail: frank1906@aol.com.

MECHANIC, DAVID, social sciences educator; b. NYC, Feb. 21, 1936; s. Louis and Tillie (Penn) Mechanic; m. Kathleen Mars Wiltshire; children: Robert Edmund, Michael Alexander. BA, CCNY, 1956; MA, Stanford U., 1957, PhD, 1959. Faculty U. Wis., Madison, 1960—79, prof. sociology, 1965—73, John Bascom prof., 1973—79; dir. U. Wis. (Center for Med. Sociology and Health Services Research), 1971—79, chmn. dept. sociology, 1968—70; prof. social work and sociology Rutgers U., New Brunswick, NJ, 1979—, acting dean faculty arts and scis., 1980—81, Univ. prof., dean faculty arts and scis., 1981—84, Univ. prof. and Rene Dubos prof. behavioral scis., 1984—, dir. Inst. for Health, Health Care Policy and Aging Research, 1985—. Panelist on health svcs. rsch. Pres.'s Sci. Adv. Com., 1971—72; coord. panel Pres.'s Commn. Mental Health, 1977—78; mem. Nat. Adv. Coun. Aging, NIH, 1982—86; treatment com. on reduction of cancer mortality Nat. Cancer Inst., 1984; expert adv. panel on mental health WHO, 1984—89; vice-chmn. com. pain, disability and chronic illness behavior Inst. Medicine-NAS, 1985—86, panel on prevention of disability, 1989—90, panel on new data for an aging world, 1999—2000, com. on capitalizing on social sci. and behavioral rsch. to improve the pubs. health, 1999; health adv. bd. GAO, 1987—95; nat. com. on vital and health stats. HHS, 1988—92; commn. on med. edn. Robert Wood Johnson Found., 1990—92, nat. adv. com. scholars in health policy rsch. program, 1993—, nat. dir. investigators awards in health policy rsch. program, 2000—, tech. adv. com. scholars in health policy rsch. program, 2001—02, nat. adv. com. health and soc. scholar's program, 2003—09; mem. Com. on Prevention of Mental Disorder, 1992—94; panel on tech., ins. and health care sys. Office of Tech. U.S. Congress, 1992—95; commn. on behavioral and social scis. and edn. NRC, 1992—95; adv. com. Picker/Commonwealth Scholars Program, 1992—99; panel on rethinking disability policy Nat. Acad. Social Ins., 1993—96; vis. scholar Kings Fund Inst., London, 1994—95; professionalism adv. com. Am. Bd. Internal Med. Found., 2002—05; bd. dirs. Acad. Health; panel on divergent trends in longevity in high-income countries NAS. Author: Students Under Stress, 1962, 1978, Medical Sociology, 1968, 1978, Mental Health and Social Policy, 1969, 1980, 1989, 1999, 2008, Public Expectations and Health Care, 1972, Mental Health and Social Policy, 2007, Politics, Medicine and Social Science, 1974; author: (with Charles E. Lewis and Rashi Fein) A Right to Health, 1976; author: Growth of Bureaucratic Medicine, 1976, Future Problems in Health Care, 1979, From Advocacy to Allocation: The Evolving American Health Care System, 1986, Painful Choices: Research and Essays on Health Care, 1989, Inescapable Decisions: The Imperatives of Health Reform, 1994, The Truth About Health Care: Why Reform is Not Working in America, 2006; author, editor: Symptoms, Illness Behavior and Help-Seeking, 1982; editor: Handbook of Health, Health Care and the Health Professions, 1983, Improving Mental Health Services: What the Social Sciences Can Tell Us, 1987, General Hospital Impatient Psychiatry, 1997, Managed Behavioral Health Care: Current Realities and Future Potential, 1998; co-editor (with Robert Hauser, Archibald Haller and Tess Hauser): Social Structure and Personality, 1982; co-editor: (with Linda Aiken) Applications of Social Science to Clinical Medicine and Social Policy, 1986; co-editor: Paying for Services: Promises and Pitfalls of Capitation, 1989; co-editor: (with Marian Osterweis and Arthur Kleinman) Pain and Disability: Clinical Behavior and Public Policy Perspectives, 1987; co-editor: (with Carl Taube and Ann Hohmann) The Future of Mental Health Services Research, 1989; co-editor: (with Lynn Rogut, David Colby, and James Knickman) Policy Challenges in Modern Health Care, 2005. Recipient Ward medal, CCNY, 1956, Carl Taube award, APHA, 1990, Rema Lapouse award, 2003, Disting. Investigator award, Assn. for Health Svcs. Rsch., 1991, Disting. Contbn. award mental health sect., Soc. for Study of Social Problems, 1991, Emily Mumford medal, Columbia U., 1991, Investigator award in health policy rsch., Robert Wood Johnson Found., 1995—99, Health Svcs. Rsch. prize, Assn. of U. Programs in Health Adminstrn. and the Baxter Allegiance Found., 1997, Senator Frank R. Lautenberg Ann. award, Sch. Pub. Health, U. Medicine and Dentistry NJ, 2003, Benjamin Rush award, Am. Psychiat. Assn., 2004, First Matilda Riley award and lectr., NIH, 2006, Rhoda and Bernard Sarnat Internat. prize, The National Acads., 2009, Adam Yamolinsky medal, Inst. Medicine. The Nat. Acad., 2008; fellow Ford Behavioral Sci. fellow, 1956—57, NIMH rsch. fellow, 1965—66, Ctr. for Advanced Study in Behavioral Scis., 1974—75, Guggenheim fellow, 1977—78, Disting. fellow, Assn. Health Svcs. Rsch., 1996. Fellow: AAAS (chmn. sect. social, econ. and polit. scis. 1985), Assn. Health Svcs. Rsch. (disting. 1996); mem.: NAS, Nat. Acad. Sciences, Hogg Found. Mental Health (nat. adv. coun. 1987), Nat. Acad. Social Ins. (founding), Am. Acad. Arts and Scis., Inst. Medicine-NAS (governing coun. 1972—74), Sociol. Rsch. Assn. (pres. 1991—92), Am. Sociol. Assn. (chmn. med. sociol. sect. 1969—70, governing coun. 1977—78, chmn. publs. com. 1989—91, chmn. mental health sect. 1992—93, Disting. Med. Sociologist award 1983, Lifetime Achievement award mental health sect. 1994, Disting. Career award 2001, Disting. Career award for Practice of Sociology 2004), Phi Beta Kappa. Home: 5 Overbrook Dr Princeton NJ 08540-3924 Office Phone: 848-932-8415. Business E-Mail: mechanic@rci.rutgers.edu.

MECKLENBURG, GARY ALAN, retired hospital administrator; b. June 17, 1946; m. Lynn Kraemer; children: John, Sarah. BA, Northwestern U., 1968; MBA, U. Chgo., 1970. Adminstrv. resident Presbyn.-St. Luke's Hosp., Chgo., 1969-70, adminstrv. asst., 1970-71, asst. supt., 1971-76, assoc. supt., 1976-77, U. Wis. Hosps., Madison, 1977-80; adminstr. Stanford U. Hosp. Clinics, Calif.; pres., CEO St. Joseph's Hosp., Milw., 1980-85; pres. Franciscan Health Care Inc., Milw., 1985; pres., CEO Northwestern Meml. Hosp., Chgo., 1985—2001, Northwestern Meml. HealthCare, Chgo., 2001—06. Preceptor, guest lectr., mem. adv. bd. Kellogg Sch. Mgmt., Chgo., 1986—; pres., CEO, Northwestern Healthcare Network, 1990-92. Recipient Todd Scout award Boy Scouts Am., 1998, Chgo. Bus. Hall of Fame award Jr. Achievement, 2000, GSB Disting. Pub. Svc./Pub. Sector Alumnus award U. Chgo., 2000. Mem. Am. Hosp. Assn. (sect. met. hosps., governing coun. 1984-92, chmn. 1991, 2001, trustee 1996-2002, exec. com. 1997-2002, chmn., 2001, mem. regional policy bd., #5 1984, 87-89, 91-93, 95-99, chmn. 1996-99, 2001, mem. ho. dels. 1984, 87-89, 91—, mem. com. on med. edn. 1976-80), Ill. Hosp. Assn. (bd. dirs. 1988-95, chmn. 1994, mem. adv. panel coun. tchg. hosps. 1997—), U. Chgo. Hosp. Adminstrn. Alumni Assn. (pres. 1985-86), Econ. Club Chgo., Comml. Club Chgo.

MEDAER, ROBERT, neurologist, researcher; b. Hasselt, Limburg, Belgium, July 1, 1949; s. René Medaer and Jenny Gorissen; m. Reinhilde Leurs, June 1, 1996; children: Jeroen, Pieter, Wouter, Anne, Paquito, Julie. MD, Cath. U. Louvain, 1974. Med. dir. Multiple Sclerosis Clinic, Overpelt, Belgium, 1977-93; neurologist hosp., Bree, Belgium, 1978—2002, Weert, Netherlands, 2002—; pvt. practice Hasselt, Belgium. Cons. Bakhsh Clinic, Jeddah, Saudi Arabia, 1987-90, Biomed. Limburg U., Diepenbeek, Belgium, 1993— Contbr. articles on multiple sclerosis to med. jours. Mem. Lions. Achievements include first to vaccinate MS with success. Office: Ctr for Neurology De Gerlachestraat 4/1 3500 Hasselt Belgium Office Phone: 0032-11222828.

MEDDERS, EMILY ANNA, speech pathology/audiology services professional; d. Emerson C. and Christina Marylene Gillett; children: Gregory, Jeffrey. BS, Phillips U., Enid, Okla., 1980, MS in Speech Pathology, 1982. Cert. clin. competence Am. Speech Lang. Hearing Assn. Speech lang. pathologist Drummond-Lahome Okla. Pub. Sch., 1981—83, Oklahoma City Pub. Sch., 1983—. Mission trip coord. New Covenant Christian Ch., Oklahoma City, 2005—07.

MEDEIROS, ROSEANE PÔRTO, epidemiologist; b. Belém, Oct. 22, 1964; Degree in Medicine, U. Fed. Pará, 1991; MS in Clin. Infectious Diseases, U. Fed. São Paulo, 2001. Physician, clin. infectious diseases Ctr. Referência E Treinamento DST/AIDS, 2002. Postdoc. fellow U. Fed. São Paulo, 1996—2001. Mem.: Soc. Brasileira Infectologia, European Assn. Study Liver. Office: Rua Santa Cruz n 81 São Paulo 04121-000 Brazil Office Fax: (5511) 3262-2031. Business E-Mail: roseporto@uol.com.br.

MEDICH, DAVID S., colon and rectal surgeon, educator; MD, Ohio State U., Columbus, 1987. Diplomate Am. Bd. Surgery, 2004, Am. Bd. Colon and Rectal Surgery, 2006. Resident in surgery Univ. Pitts. Med. Ctr., Pa., 1988—90, rsch. fellow, 1990—93; fellow in colon and rectal surgery Cleve. Clinic, Ohio, 1993—94; assoc. prof. colon and rectal surgery coll. medicine Drexel Univ.; hosp. affiliations include Pitts. Colon and Rectal Surgery Assocs., P.C., Univ. Pitts. Med. Ctr. Presbyn., Univ. Pitts. Med. Ctr. Passavant Cancer Ctr. Office: University of Pittsburgh Medical Center Passavant Cancer Center 9100 Babcock Blvd Ground Fl S Pavillion Pittsburgh PA 15237 Office Phone: 877-684-7189. Office Fax: 412-359-8614.

MEDIETA, CONSTANTINO, plastic surgeon; Attended, Santa Clara U., 1981—82; BS in Psychology, Creighton U., 1985—89, MD, 1985—89. Diplomate Am. Bd. of Plastic Surgery, lic. Fla., 1994, Ga., 1998. Internship gen. surgery Maricopa County Hosp., Phoenix, resident, chief resident; resident plastic & reconstructive surgery Univ. Miami / Jackson Meml. Hosp., 1995—97; fellow The Royal Coll. of Surgeon, Edinburgh, 1994—94, Harvard Med. Sch., 1998—98, Am. Coll. of Surgeons; med. dir. Adams Air Ambulance, 1996—97; flight surgeon, 1996—97. With LA Olympics, 1984; med. volunteer Am. Cancer Soc., 1987, 91, 93; support instr. Advance Trauma Life, 1991—95. Mem.: AMA, Am. Soc. of Plastic Surgeons, Am. Soc. for Aesthetic Plastic Surgery, Dr. D. Ralph Millard, Jr. Soc., Dade County Med. Assn. Office: Constantino G Mendieta MD FACS 2310 & 2320 South Dixie Hwy Miami FL 33133 Office Phone: 305-860-0717. Office Fax: 305-860-0760.

MEDNICK, SHELDON IRA, pharmacist; b. Balt., Apr. 8, 1955; s. Sol Abraham and Doris Asbell Mednick. BSc in Pharmacy, Phila. Coll. Pharmacy, 1979. Registered pharmacist Pa., NJ, Md. Pharmacy intern Cooper U. Hosp., Camden, NJ, 1979—80; staff pharmacist Trenton Psychiat. Hosp., NJ, 1981—86, Phila. Geriatric Ctr., 1986—95, Neighborcare Pharmacy, King of Prussia, Pa., 1997—2001, Girard Med. Ctr., Phila., 2001—. Named one of 2000

Outstanding Scientists, Internat. Biog. Ctr. Cambridge, Eng., 2008—09; Pharmacy fellowship, Am. Biog. Inst., 2009. Mem.: Masons (sr. deacon Burlington lodge 1984—85). Jewish. Avocations: reading, music, travel. Home: 2801 Wingate Ct Edgewater Park NJ 08010

MEDOWS, RHONDA M., healthcare company executive, former public health service officer; married; 3 children. BS, Cornell Univ.; MD, Morehouse Sch. Med., Atlanta. Cert. family medicine. Residency Univ. Hosp., Stony Brook, NY; physician Kaiser Permanente, Atlanta, 1989—93; private practice Mayo Clinic, Jacksonville, Fla., 1993—2000; med. dir. Blue Cross Blue Shield Fla., Jacksonville, 2000—01; sec. Fla. Agy. Health Care Adminstrn., 2001—04; chief med. officer Centers for Medicare & Medicaid Svc. Region IV, Atlanta, 2004—05; commr. Ga. Dept. Cmty. Health, Atlanta, 2005—10; chief med. officer, exec. v.p. Pub. & Senior Markets UnitedHealthcare, 2010—. Instr. Univ. Fla., Fla. State Univ. Mem.: Am. Acad. Family Physicians, Nat. Med. Assn., Am. Coll. Physician Executives, Fla. Med. Assn., Fla. Acad. Family physicians, Nat. Assn. Managed Care Physicians. Office: UnitedHealthcare Suite 300 3720 Davinci Ct Norcross GA 30092 *

MEDVEDEVA, YULIA, geneticist; b. Moscow, Nov. 16, 1977; PhD, GosNII Genetika, 2008. Technician Engelhardt Inst. Molecular Biology, 2003—05; rsch. asst. State Inst. Genetics and Selections Indsl. Microorganisms, 2005—10; rsch. fellow Vavilov Inst. Gen. Genetics, 2011—. Avocations: travel, bicycling, yoga. Office: Gubkina 3 Moscow 117312 Russia Personal E-mail: ju.medvedeva@gmail.com.

MEDVIN, NADEEN BETH, psychologist, consultant; b. Miami, Mar. 22, 1960; d. Daniel and Celia Medvin. BA with high honors, Fla. Internat. U., 1981; MS with honors, U. Ga., 1984; PhD with high honors, Fla. Internat. U., 1993. Cert.: Crisis Mgmt. Internat. (corporate crisis intervention) 1997, Fla. Internat. U./Mediation Tng. Group (mediation and conflict resolution) 2003, Fla. Supreme Ct. (mediator) 2006; lic. psychologist Fla., 1996, diplomate Am. Bd. Psychol. Specialties, Am. Coll. Forensic Examiners, 1998, Am. Coll. Disability Analysts, 2000. Staff psychologist, quality assurance comm. chair N. Miami Cmty. Mental Health Ctr., Miami, 1984—88; psychologist, cons. pvt. practice, 1987—; dir. planning & effectivness Miami-Dade C.C., 1994—96; performance cons., quality com. med. ethics com. Bapt. Health Systems South Fla., 1996—2000; applied psychologist City of Miami, 2000—, tng. and devel. coord. employee assistance program adminstr., 2005—. Adj. prof. applied psychology & bus. Fla. Internat. U., 1988—, Barry U., 1988—, healthcare administrn. grad prog. leadership devel. strategic planning, 1997—2001; adj. prof. applied psychology & bus. U. Miami, Sch. Medicine Leadership Devel. Sensivity Tng. Patient Relations, 1988—, St. Thomas U., 1988—; mem. adv. bd. human resource mgmt./bus. continuing edn. programs U. Miami, 2002—, lectr. in field; cons. in field. Contbr. articles to profl. jours.; mem. adv. bd.: Chief Learning Officer jour., 2004—. Vol. Switchboard of Miami Crisis Counseling, 1984—86, Red Ribbon Coun./Informed Families, 1986—89; adv. bd. mem. Fla. Internat. U. Inst. Govt., Miami, 2002—03; bus. tech. adv. bd. Dade County Pub. Schs., 2005—; med. edn. tng. South Fla. Aids Network, 1987—88. Fellow: Am. Coll. Forensic Examiners; mem.: APA, Am. Coll. Disability Analysts, Soc. Human Resource Mgmt., Soc. Indsl. Orgnl. Psychology, Psi Chi, Phi Kappa Phi. Achievements include development of HR metrics, statistical performance models, organizational culture and climate surveys; psychological tests and measures; wellness and health risk assessments, corporate wellness, leadership development and university training programs; leadership, executive assessment and performance coaching. Office: City of Miami 444 SW 2nd Avenue Miami FL 33130 Office Phone: 305-416-2129, 305-815-1129. Personal E mail: drnadeenmedvin@aol.com.

MEDYANIK, ZOYA, physician; b. Kharkiv, Ukraine, Aug. 17, 1940; arrived in Hungary, 1993; d. Ivan Medyanik and Anna Klyuchnik. Degree in Econ. Engring., Kharkiv U., Ukraine, 1967; MD, Kharkiv Med. Inst., 1977. Rschr. Kharkiv Inst. Radio Electronics, 1970-90; specialist manual therapy Health Ctr., Kharkiv, 1987-93; prin. specialist manual therapy Internat. Ctr. Medium, Kharkiv, 1990-94; dir. Medic BT, Veszprem, Hungary, 1994—. Prin. cons. Folk Healers Acad., Budapest, 1995—. Author: Mysteries of Life, 1997. Recipient Social Innovator USSR, social innovation com., 1990, gold medal Folk Healers Congress, 1995. Mem. Am. Inst. Alternative Medicine (pres. 1998—), Hungarian Union Folk Healers (pres. profl. com. 1995—), N.Y. Acad. Scis. Achievements include research in design and implementation of bioenergetic manual therapy method. Home: Faskert utca 6 8200 Veszprem Hungary Home Fax: 36 88 327030. E-mail: medyanik@gmx.net.

MEDZHITOV, RUSLAN, medical educator, researcher; b. Tashkent, Uzbekistan, Mar. 12, 1966; s. Maksut Medzhitov and Roza Medzhitova. BS, Tashkent State U.; PhD in Biochemistry, Moscow State U., 1993. Postdoc. fellow Yale U. Sch. Medicine, New Haven, 1994—99, asst. prof. immunobiology, 1999—2003, prof., 2003—, David W. Wallace prof. immunobiology, 2008—. Investigator Howard Hughes Med. Inst., 2000—; co-founder VaxInnate Inc., New Haven, 2002. Pvt. USSR Air Force, 1984—86, Russia. Recipient William B. Coley award, Cancer Rsch. Inst., 2002, Howard Taylor Ricketts award, U. Chgo., 2008, Blavatnik award for young scientists, NY Acad. Scis., 2008, Lewis S. Rosenstiel award, Brandeis U., 2010, Emil von Behring prize, Philipps U., Marburg, Germany; co-recipient Shaw Found. Prize in Life Sci./ Medicine, Hong Kong, 2011; Searle scholar, Kinship Found., 2000. Mem.: NAS, American Assn. Immunologists (BD Bioscience Investigator award 2006). Achievements include research in the analysis of the immune system, host-pathogen interactions, inflammation, cell signaling and gene regulation. Office: Yale Univ Dept Immunobiology PO Box 208011 300 Cedar St New Haven CT 06520 Office Phone: 203-785-7541. Personal E-mail: ruslan.medzhitov@yale.edu. *

MEEHAN, JEAN MARIE ROSS, human resources, occupational health and safety management consultant; b. Chgo., Mar. 16, 1954; d. A. Ronald Gonzalez and Barbara Marx Shipley; m. John J. Meehan, 1993; 1 child, Jenna A.; 1 child from previous marriage, Justin L. Ross DC. Diploma in Nursing, St. Mary of Nazareth Hosp., Chgo., 1974; BS in Health Arts with high honors, U. St. Francis, 1988; MPA with honors, Roosevelt U., 2000. Cert. occupl. health nurse specialist COHN-S, cert. pharmacy technician (CPhT); cert. senior professional in human resources SPHR. Staff nurse St. Mary of Nazareth Hosp., Chgo., 1973—75; head nurse ambulatory care Edgebrook Med. Diagnostic Ctr., Chgo., 1975—76; occupl. health nurse Williams Electronics, Inc., Chgo., 1976—84; adminstr. safety and benefits Reliable Power Products, Franklin Park, Ill., 1984—90; dir. corp. human resources MacLean-Fogg Co., Mundelein, Ill., 1990—2005, Navitus Health Solutions LLC, Madison, Wis., 2005—. Pres. Auriel Mgmt. Group, LLC, Island Lake, Ill., 1992—, Claim Masters, LLC, 1998—99; adv. bd. dir. Gt. Lakes Health Care Alliance, 1996—97; spkr. in workshops. Poetry included in Visions of Beauty, 1999 (Editor's Choice award 1999), Tides of Memory, 2000, America at the Millennium—The Best Poems and Poets of the 20th Century, 2000. Guest spkr. local schs. and environ. groups, also I.E.P.A. and U.S. E.P.A. workshops; mem. Ill. Pollution Prevention Adv. Coun., Springfield, Ill., 1993-98; mem. Lake County Employer Coun. Bus./Govt. Partnership, 1996-99; faculty Am. Occupl. Health Conf., 2003-04. Recipient Leadership Civic citation United Way Charities of Lake County, 1993, 94. Mem. AAOHN, Soc. for Human Resources Mgmt., Interventional & Prevention Lake County Employer Coun.(former mem.) Avocations: writing, interior design, reading, arts patronage. Office: Auriel Mgmt Group LLC PO Box 86 Wauconda IL 60084 also: Navitus Health Solutions LLC 2601 W Beltline Hwy Ste 600 Madison WI 53713 Business E-Mail: hrpro@email.com.

MEEHAN, WILLIAM PAUL, pediatrician, educator; b. Medford, Mass., Nov. 27, 1970; BA, Boston Coll., Chestnut Hill, Mass., 1993; MD, Harvard U., Boston, 2002. Physician Children's Hosp. Boston, 2002—, co-founder, concussion and sports clinic, 2008—; instr. pediat. Harvard U., Med. Sch., 2007—, dir. brain injury rsch. Contbr. articles to profl. jours. Inductee Golden Key Nat. Honor Soc, 1992—93; vol. SJ Vol. Corps., Omak, Wash., 1993—94; neighborhood coord. Menino Adminstrn, Boston, 1994—96. Recipient Cmty. Svc. citation, Mass. State Senate, 1996, Mass. House Representatives, 1996, Boston City Coun., 1996, Boston Fire Dept., 1996, Tchg. award, Harvard Med. Sch., 2005; Enrichment Program Rsch. grant, 1999—2000, grant, NIH, Ctr. Imegration Medicine and Innovative Tech. Mem.: Am. Acad. Pediat., Am. Med. Soc. Sports Medicine, Am. Coll. Sports Medicine. Avocation: music. Office: Children's Hosp Boston 300 Longwood Ave Boston MA 02115 Office Phone: 857-218-5508. Office Fax: 617-730-0178.

MEEKERS, DOMINIQUE ARMAND, public health professor, demographer; b. Diepenbeek, Belgium, June 23, 1962; arrived in US, 1987; BA magna cum laude, Free U. Brussels, 1985; MA, U. Pa., 1988, PhD, 1990. Rschr. Free U. Brussels, 1985-87; rsch. assoc. NAS, Washington, 1990-91; asst. prof., rsch. assoc. Pa. State U., University Park, 1992-96; assoc. Johns Hopkins U., Balt., 1996-2001; rsch. dir. Population Svcs. Internat., Washington, 1996—2001; prof. dept. internat. health and devel. Tulane U., New Orleans, 2001—, chair, 2005—10. Cons. John Snow, Arlington, Va., 1992—93, Demographic and Health Surveys, Macro Internat., Calverton, Md., 1993—97, Population Svcs. Internat., 2001—, Hewlett Found., 2003—; invited mem. Com. Reproductive Health, 2000—03, Internat. Union Sci. Study Population; cons. Green Star Social Mktg., 2009. Contbr. articles to profl. publs. Rsch. grantee Spencer Found., 1995, U. Md., 1996, UNICEF, Bucharest, Romania, 1997, UNAIDS, 1997, Deloitte Touche Tohmatsu, 2002, UNICEF, 2002, USAID/Health Comm. Partnership, 2002-2007. Mem. APHA, Population Assn. Am. Office: Tulane U Dept Internat Health and Devel 1440 Canal St Ste 2200 New Orleans LA 70112 Home: 5633 Durham Dr New Orleans LA 70131 Office Phone: 504-988-3655. E-mail: dmeekers@tulane.edu.

MEELIA, RICHARD J., medical products executive; BA, St. Anselm Coll.; MBA, Boston Coll. Sales & mktg. positions Am. Hosp. Supply Corp., pres. Infusaid div. Pfizer Hosp. Products Group, pres. Kendall Co., Mansfield, Mass., 1991—95, Tyco Healthcare, Mansfield, Mass., 1995—2007; pres., CEO Covidien plc, 2007—11, chmn., 2008—. Bd. dir. Aspect Med. Systems; bd. govs. Tufts New Eng. Med. Ctr. Chmn. Employ+Ability Inc.; bd. mem. Chernobyl Children Project, St. Anselm Coll. Office: Covidien 15 Hampshire St Mansfield MA 02048 *

MEENA, MANJU, ophthalmologist; b. Uttar Pradesh, India, Jan. 30, 1980; MS in Ophthalmology, Maulana Azad Med. Coll., 2008. Rsch. fellowship, opthalmic plastics facial aesthetics and ocular oncology L. V. Prasad Eye Inst., 2010, oculoplastic cons., 2011, physician, 2011—. CSIR Fgn. Travel grant, India, Illumina Travel fellowship, Asia ARVO, Singapore, 2011. Mem.: Oculoplastic Assn. India (Best Clin. Video award 2010, Best Slit Lamp Photography award 2010, 1st prize 2010), All India Ophthal. Soc., Andhra Pradesh Ophthalmology Soc., Am. Acad. Ophthalmology, Delhi Ophthal. Soc. Avocations: drawing, photography, music. Office: LVPEI Hanumanthuwaka Junction Vishakhapatnam Andhra Pradesh 530040 India Personal E-mail: mina_manju@yahoo.co.in.

MEENGS, WILLIAM LLOYD, cardiologist; b. Zeeland, Mich., Dec. 23, 1942; s. Lloyd Stanley and Gertrude (Wyngarden) M.; m. Helen Delores Van Dyke, June 10, 1964; children: Michelle Rene, William Lloyd, Lisa Ann. AB, Hope Coll., 1964; MD, U. Mich., 1968. Diplomate Am. Bd. Cardiology, Am. Bd. Interventional Cardiology, Am. Bd. Nuc. Cardiology. Intern in internal medicine U. Hosp., Ann Arbor, Mich., 1968-69, resident in internal medicine, 1971-73, fellow in cardiology, 1973-75; practice medicine specializing in cardiology, interventional cardiology and nuc. cardiology Petoskey, Mich., 1975—. Cardiologist Burns Clinic Med. Center, Petoskey, 1975-99, Mich. Heart & Vascular Specialists, 2004-, chmn. dept. cardiology and cardiac surgery, 1978-89; med. dir. No. Mich. Heart Center, 1989-95; pres. Petoskey Cardiology, P.C., 1999-2004; chief sect. cardiology No. Mich. Hosps., 2000-04; cardiologist Little Traverse Hosp., Petoskey, 1975—, dir. coronary care unit, 1986-89; dir. cardiac catheterization lab. No. Mich. Hosps., Petoskey, 1985-87, 92-2004, adult spl. care units, 1986-89; vice chmn. bd. dirs. Burns Clinic Med. Ctr., 1989-92. Contbr. med. articles to profl. jours. Trustee Mich. Heart Assn., 1979-83. Served as surgeon USPHS, 1969-71. Named one of Best Drs. in America, Best Drs. Inc., 2001—. Fellow: Soc. Cardiovasc. Angiography and Interventions, Am. Coll. Cardiology; mem.: Am. Heart Assn. (fellow Coun. on Clin. Cardiology), Alpha Omega Alpha. Home: 1224 Autumn Ln Petoskey MI 49770-9019 Office: Mich Heart & Vascular Specialists 560 W Mitchell St Ste 400 Petoskey MI 49770-2274 Office Phone: 231-487-2490.

MEENSOOK, CHAROEN, physician, consultant; b. Bangkok, May 20, 1942; s. Song Tiang and Geng Teg (Bae) Ngo; m. Hataya Tantiviwattanapan, Oct. 2, 1976; children: Chayaron, Priya. MD, Siriraj Med. Sch., Bangkok, 1967; diploma of tropical medicine & hygiene, Liverpool U., Eng., 1974. Diplomate Am. Bd. Internal Medicine and Gastroenterology. Med. dir. Thainakarin Hosp., Bangkok, 1993—2010, chief med. officer, 2011—. Named Excellent Citizen of Thai Soc., 2001, Nat. Exemplary Father, 2007; recipient Excellent Hosp. Adminstr. award Assn. Excellent Adminstrs., Thailand, 1996. Fellow Am. Coll. Gastroenterology, Royal Coll. Physicians Thailand, Am. Coll. Physicians. Avocations: jogging, hiking, stamp collecting/philately, coin collecting/numismatics. Office: Chief Med Office Thai Nakarin Hosp Public Co Ltd Bangna Bangkok 10260 Thailand Office Phone: 023612727, 023612828. Business E-Mail: medical@thainakarin.co.th.

MEERE, PATRICK A., orthopedist, surgeon, educator; Attended in Physics, McGill U., MD, 1988. Diplomate Am. Bd. Orthopedic Surgeon. Resident orthopedic surgery McGill Univ., 1989—93; fellow arthritis and adult reconstructive orthopaedic surgery Hosp. for Joint Diseases Orthopaedic Inst., 1993—95; fellow adult total joint reconstructive orthopaedic surgery; assoc. prof. orthopaedic surgery NY Univ. Sch. of Medicine; with NY Univ. Langone Med. Ctr.; chief ortho NY Univ. Hosp. for Joint Diseases, chief adult reconstructive surgery, chmn. quality assurance com., chmn. orthopaedic surgery dept. Mem.: Am. Acad. of Hip and Knee Surgeons, Am. Acad. of Orhopaedic Surgeons. Office: New York University Langone Medical Center FPO Bldg Ste 5J 530 First Ave New York NY 10016 Office Phone: 212-263-2366. Office Fax: 212-263-2365.

MEERSCHAERT, JOSEPH RICHARD, retired physician; b. Detroit, Mar. 4, 1941; s. Hector Achiel and Marie Terese (Campbell) M.; m. Jeanette Marie Ancerewicz, Sept. 14, 1963; children: Eric, Amy, Adam. BA, Wayne State U., 1965, MD, 1967. Diplomate Am. Bd. Phys. Medicine and Rehab., Am. Bd. Pain Medicine. Intern Harper Hosp., Detroit, 1967-68; resident in phys. medicine and rehab. Wayne State U. Rehab. Inst., Detroit, 1968-71; chief divsn. phys. medicine Naval Hosp., Chelsea, Mass., 1971-73; attending physician William Beaumont Hosp., Royal Oak, Mich., 1973—2006, med. dir. rehab. unit, 1979-87; pvt. practice medicine specializing in phys. medicine and rehab. Royal Oak, 1973—2006; pvt. practice specializing in pain medicine, 1990—2006; ret., 2006. Mem. med. adv. bd. Nat. Wheelchair Athletic Assn., 1973—, U.S. team physician VII World Wheelchair Games, Stoke Mandeville, Eng.; clin. instr. Wayne State U., 1973-83, clin. asst. prof. phys. medicine and rehab., 1983—; mem. Mich. Dept. Licensing and Regulation State Bd. Phys. Therapy, 1978-81. Contbr. articles to profl. jours. With M.C. USN, 1971-73. Recipient John Hussey award Mich. Wheelchair Athletic Assn., 1981. Fellow Am. Coll. Pain Medicine; mem. Am. Acad. Phys. Medicine and Rehab. (reviewer, presenter) Am. Congress Rehab. Medicine, Mich. Phys. Medicine and Rehab. Soc., Am. Geriatrics Soc., Am. Assn. Electromyography and Electrodiagnosis, Mich. Rheumatism Soc., Mich. Acad. Phys. Medicine and REhab. (pres. 1986-87, chmn. program com. 1977-78, trustee 1980—, pres. bd. dirs. 1994-97), Oakland County Med. Soc. (bd. dirs. 1991, 97), Alpha Omega Alpha. Roman Catholic.

MEGAHY, DIANE ALAIRE, physician; b. Des Moines, Oct. 12, 1943; d. Edwin and Georgiana Lee Raygor; m. Mohamed H. Saleh Megahy, Sept. 20, 1969; children: Hassan, Hamed, Hala, Heba. MD, U. Alexandria, Egypt, 1981. Diplomate Am. Bd. Family Practice. Intern Univ. Hosp., Alexandria, Egypt, 1982-83; resident Siu Family Practice, Belleville, Ill., 1987—90; physician St. Joseph's Hosp., Highland, Ill., 1988—2001; med. coord. Tri-County Radiation Oncology, 2001—. Mem. steering com. on domestic violence 3d Jud. Cir. Ct., co-chmn. health care subcom. Active Am. Cancer Soc. Mem.: AAUW, AMA (Excellence in Medicine I.M.G. Leadership award 2004), St. Clair County Med. Soc. (pres. 2007—08), Ill. Rural Health Assn., Ill. State Med. Soc. (del. internat. med. grad. com.), So. Ill. Med. Assn. (past pres.), Ill. Coalition for Injury Prevention, Safe Kid Ill. Home: 2 Bay Meadow Pl Belleville IL 62223 Office: 7300 Twin Pyramid Pky Belleville IL 62223 Office Fax: 618-234-1793. Personal E mail: dialmeg@msn.com.

MEGALLI, MAGUID RAMZI, retired health facility administrator, urologist; b. Cairo, Jan. 26, 1942; arrived in U.S., 1969; s. Ramzi and Lydia Megalli; m. Viviane Wassef, Jan. 28, 1968; children: Michael, Mark. MD, Cairo U., 1965; MBA, Pace U., 1988. Lic. Am. Bd. of Urology. Resident in urology Columbia U., NYC, 1970—74; chief of urology St. Joseph Med. Ctr., Yonkers, NY, 1982—88; chief med. officer Cath. Health Care Sys. Resources, 1999—2002; pres. Benifice Advantage, the Self-Insuring Co. for Archdiocese of N.Y., 2002—; exec. v.p., chief med. officer Our Lady of Mercy Med. Ctr., Bronx, NY, 2003—. Founder, chmn. Servitas IPA, NYC, 1994—99. Contbr. articles to profl. publs. (Valantine Fellowship award, 1974). Lt. col. USAR, 1972—84. Fellow: ACS (life). Home: 35 Island Dr Rye NY 10580 Home Fax: 914-967-3613. Personal E-mail: mmegalli@gmail.com.

MEGGS, WILLIAM JOEL, toxicologist, allergist, emergency physician, educator, author; b. Newberry, SC, May 30, 1942; s. Wallace Nat and Elizabeth (Pruitt) M.; m. Susan Nancy Spring, June 11, 1966 (div. June 1998); m. Susan Krause Martin, Apr. 21, 2001; children: Jason Nathaniel, Benjamin Maffey, Thomas Clute. BS, Clemson U., 1964; PhD, Syracuse U., 1969; MD, U. Miami, 1979. Diplomate Am. Bd. Internal Medicine, Am. Bd. Allergy and Immunology, Am. Bd. Emergency Medicine, Am. Bd. Med. Toxicology. Resident in internal medicine Rochester (N.Y.) Gen. Hosp., 1979-82; staff fellow in allergy and clin. immunology Nat. Inst. Allergy and Infectious Diseases, Bethesda, Md., 1982-85; asst. dir. med. edn. emergency dept. Washington Hosp. Ctr., 1985-88; from asst. prof. allergy, immunology to sr. vice chmn. Sch. Medicine E. Carolina U., Greenville, NC, 1988—2004, sr. vice chmn. Sch. Medicine, 2004—; chmn., dir. emergency dept. Lenoir Meml. Hosp., Kinston, NC, 1990-91. Mem. Emergency Svcs. Com. Lenoir Meml. Hosp., Kinston, 1988-92; mem workshop on immune testing, Agy. for Toxic Substances and Diseases Registry, 1992, workshop on equity in environ. health, U.S. EPA, 1992, workshop on multiple chem. sensitivity syndrome, NRC, 1991; mem. rsch. adv. com. on Gulf War illnesses Dept. VA, 2002-; fellow med. toxicology NYU, 1992-96. Co-author: The Inflammation Cure, 2003; co-editor: Health and Safety in Agriculture, 1997; contbr. numerous articles and abstracts to profl. jours. Vol. physician Indigent Clinic E. Carolina U., Pitt County Med. Soc., 1988—, Pitt County Shelter, 1989—; advanced cardiac life support instr. E. Carolina U. Sch. of Medicine, 1988-2000, advanced trauma life support instr., 1991-2002; mem. Pitt County Traffic Injury Prevention Program, 1989-92; bd. dirs. Rachael Carson Coun., 1988—; mem. adv. bd. Pamplico Tar River Found., 1990—. Named Woodrow Wilson Hon. fellow, 1964, NSF post-doctoral fellow, 1969; grantee N.C. United Way, 1988-89, Greer Labs., 1989-90, Am. Lung Assn. N.C., 1992-93, rsch. award Am. Coll. Med. Toxicology Fellow Am. Coll. Emergency Physicians, Am. Coll. Med. Toxicology; mem. AMA, Am. Acad. Allergy and Immunology, Am. Acad. Clin. Toxicology, Pitt County Med. Soc., N.C. State Med. Soc., Soc. for Acad. Emergency Medicine, N.C. Thoracic Soc. (physicians' sect.). Achievements include creator of the biological homing theory of the origins of life. Office: E Carolina U Sch Medicine Dept Emergency Medicine Rm 3ED311 600 Moye Blvd Greenville NC 27858-4300 Office Phone: 252-744-2954. Business E-Mail: meggsw@ecu.edu.

MEGURO, AKIRA, medical researcher; b. Japan, Dec. 5, 1977; PhD, Yokohama City U., 2008. Rsch. assoc., dept. ophthalmology Yokohama City U. Sch. Medicine, 2008—. Office: 3-9 Fukuura Kanazawa-ku Yokohama Kanagawa 236-0004 Japan Personal E-mail: akirameguro2002@yahoo.co.jp.

MEHANDJIEV, TZVETOZAR ROUSSEV, gynecologist, researcher; b. Sofia, Bulgaria, June 28, 1973; s. Rusi Vichov Mehandzhiev and Verginiya Tsakova Mehandzhieva. MD, Med. U., Sofia, Bulgaria, 2000. Intern Med. U., Sofia, Bulgaria, 2000; physician, rschr. Inst. of Sterility and Art, 2000—; resident U. Hosp. Med. U., 2000—03; physician U. Hosp., Sofia, 2002—. Editor: Reproductive Health (Ann. award Bulgarian Assn. Sterility and Reproductive Health, 2003). Founder Nat. Movement Simeon the Second, Sofia, Bulgaria, 2001—. Officer Air forces, 1992—94, Sadovo. Mem.: Bulgarian Assn. Sterility. Achievements include research in IVG/IVM of oocytes. Avocations: skiing, music, soccer. Home: 103 Tzarigradsko Shosse bl115 Sofia 1113 Bulgaria Office: Inst Sterility and Art Ovcha Kupel 2 bl33A App35 Sofia 1632 Bulgaria Office Fax: + 3592 9515961. Personal E-mail: tzvetozar1@yahoo.com.

MEHL, ALBERT L., pediatrician, poet, composer; s. Clinton Mehl and Alberta Wells; m. Annie Kempe, Aug. 4, 1979 (div.); children: Sarah Kempe-Mehl, James Kempe-Mehl. BA, Colo. Coll., Colorado Springs, 1976; MD, U. Colo. Health Scis. Ctr., Denver, 1980. Diplomate Am. Bd. Pediat. Pediatrician Kaiser Permanente, Lafayette, Colo., 1987—. Editl. cons. various publs., Various US states, 1988—; assoc. clin. prof. U. Colo. Health Scis. Ctr., Denver, 2001—. Singer, songwriter: albums Asphalt Cowboy, I'd Rather Be..., writer, performer: albums Cowboy Pottery; contbr. articles to profl. jours. Mem. expert working group effective interventions infants and young children with hearing loss U.S. HHS; gubernatorial appointee Colo. Children's Trust Fund Child Abuse Prevention, Denver, 1992—97, vice chmn., 1995—96; chmn. infant hearing adv. com. Colo. State Dept. Health and Environment, Denver, 1997—. Recipient Peak Performance award, Colo. Acad. Audiology, 1998, Communities Helping Young Children award, Frances Owens, First Lady of Colo., 2005, Antonia Maxon Excellence award, 2010; Boettcher Found. scholar, 1973—77. Fellow: Am. Acad. Pediat. (chmn. nat. task force infant hearing 2005—, appointee U.S. joint com. infant hearing 2005—). Avocations: fly fishing, skiing, golf. Office: Kaiser Permanente Med Offices 280 Exempla Cir Lafayette CO 80026 *

MEHLER, MARK FREDERICK, neurologist, medical educator; b. NYC, 1953; MD, Yeshiva U., 1980. Intern Beth Israel Harvard Med. Ctr., Boston, 1980—81; resident Albert Einstein Coll. Medicine, Bronx, NY, 1981—84, prof. psychiatry & behavioral sciences, 1995—, Alpern Family Found. prof. cerebral palsy rsch., prof., chair Saul R. Korey Dept. Neurology, 2004—; neurology chmn. Montefiore Med. Ctr., 2004—. Contbr. articles to med. jours. Office: Albert Einstein College of Medicine Rose F Kennedy Center 1410 Pelham Parkway South, Room 220 Bronx NY 10461 Office Phone: 718-430-3543. Office Fax: 718-430-8785. E-mail: mark.mehler@einstein.yu.edu. *

MEHLER, PHILIP S., internist; m. Leah Mehler; children: Avi, Ilana, Ben. BA in Biology, U. Colo., Denver, 1979, MD, 1983. Diplomate internal medicine, addiction medicine; cert. eating disorder specialist. Internship and residency U. Colo. Health Sci. Ctr., 1983—87; staff attending physician Denver Health Med. Ctr., Denver, 1987—, chief internal medicine, 1994—2004; assoc. med. dir. Denver Health, 2003—08, chief med. officer, 2008—. V.p. Colo. Prevention Ctr., Denver, 1995—2007; Prof. of Medicine and Glassman endowed prof. Internal Medicine U. Colo. Sch. Medicine, Denver, 2000—. Contbr. articles to profl. jours. Recipient Ciba-Geigy Tchg. award, U. Colo. Sch. Medicine, 1986, Outstanding Faculty award, 1991, Outstanding Tchr. Yr., Denver Health Med. Ctr., 1996, Safety award, NAPH, 1997, Academic Excellence award, Denver Health, 2005, Silver & Gold award, U. Colo. Sch. Medicine, Chair award, Patient Safety Nat. Assoc. Pub. Hosp., 2009; named Best Doctors in Am., 5280 Mag., Editl. Bd. Internat. Jour. of Eating Disorders, Conn. State Bd. Health, 2009—, Patent Safety Adv. Com. NQF. Fellow: Am. Coll. Physicans; mem.: Phi Beta Kappa, Alpha Omega Alpha. Office: Denver Health Med Ctr 660 Bannock St MC0278 Denver CO 80204

MEHLMAN, EDWIN STEPHEN, retired endodontist; b. Hartford, Conn., Nov. 30, 1935; s. Sol Abraham and Rose (Slitt) M.; m. Lesley Judith Lunin, June 13, 1959; children: Jeffrey Cole, Brian Scott, Erik Van. BA, Wesleyan U., 1957; DDS, U. Pa., 1961; cert. endodontics, Boston U., 1965. Diplomate Am. Bd. Endodontists. Instr. oral medicine Sch. Dental Medicine Harvard U., Boston, 1965—67; clin. instr. endodontics Sch. Dental Medicine Tufts U., Boston, 1968—70; lectr. endodontics Sch. Dental Medicine, Harvard U., Boston, 1970—72, asst. clin. prof. endodontics, 1972—2010; staff assoc. Forsyth Dental Ctr., Boston, 1965—2010; asst. prof. endodontics Boston U. Sch. Dental Medicine, 1995—2010; pvt. practice Providence, 1965—. Vis. lectr. dental hygiene U. R.I., Kingston, 1965-71, Community Coll. R.I., Lincoln, 1990—; cons. com. on accreditation of Dentists and Dental Aux. Edn. Programs, 1974-78. Contbr. articles to profl. jours. Pres. Temple Habonim, Barrington, R.I., 1968-70, Bur. Jewish Edn. of R.I., 1980-84; area v.p. Jewish Fedn. R.I., 1975-78; mem. R.I. Legis. Commn. to Study Malpractice Crisis, 1985-86; chmn. R.I. Dental Polit. Action Com., 1987-90. Capt. USAF, 1961-63, bd. dir. New England Dental Soc., 2009-. Recipient Etherington award Six N.E. Dental Assns. for Outstanding Contbns. to Dentistry, Disting. Fellow Internat. Coll. Dentists, 2004, Dist. Alumni award for svc. to dentistry Boston U. Goldman Sch. Dentistry, 2005, Lifetime Achievement award, Indian Dental Soc., 2010 Fellow Am. Coll. Dentists (Vol. Yr. 2004), Internat. Coll. Dentists (dep. regent 1994-98), Pierre Fauchard Acad. (Merit award, Leadership award 2006, Rida Kershaw award for outstanding contbn. to cmty. 2006); mem. ADA (coun. on govt. affairs and fed. dental svcs. 1988-92, vice-chmn. 1991-92, 1st v.p. 1994-95, 1st dist. trustee 1999-2003), Am. Assn. Endodontists (dir. 1988-91), R.I. Dental Assn. (pres. 1986-87), N.E. Dental Assns. (Outstanding N.E. Dentist 1995, Disting. Practitioner 2000), NE Dental Soc. (bd. mem. 2009-), Indian Dental Soc.(US)(Lifetime Achievement award, 2010) Jewish. Avocations: reading, civic activities. Home: 3 Hanley Farm Rd Warren RI 02885-4376

MEHR, SAM S., pediatrician, allergist, immunologist; b. Chalous, Iran, Feb. 26, 1975; MBBS, BmedSci, 1992. Staff specialist Children's Hosp., Westmead, 2006—. Recipient Med. Tchg Excellence award, U. Sydney Med. Program, Anaesthetic prize, U. Melbourne, Dr. William Snowball award, Royal Children's Hosp. Melbourne. Fellow: Royal Coll. Pathologists Australasia, Royal Australasian Coll. Physicians; mem.: Australian Support Network for Eosinophilic Esophagitis, Australasian Soc. Clin. Immunology and Allergy (Poster award 2006). Avocations: football, swimming, fishing. Office: Children's Hosp Westmead Hainworth St Sydney NSW 2145 Australia Business E-Mail: samm@chw.edu.au.

MEHRA, MANDEEP RAJINDER, cardiologist; b. Delhi, Dec. 3, 1964; came to US, 1989; p. Rajinder Pershad and Neeta (Khanna) M.; m. Gayatri Lall, May 5, 1990; children: Anshul, Lushna, Rishka. MD, Nagpur U., 1988. Intern Mt. Carmel Med. Ctr., Ohio State U., Columbus, 1989-90, resident internal medicine, 1990-92; fellow cardiology Alton Ochsner Med. Found., New Orleans, 1992-95; dir. heart failure Ochsner Med. Instns., New Orleans, 1995—2005, dir. ambulatory svcs. advanced heart failure, 1997—2005, sect. head advanced heart failure, cardiac transplant, 1997—2005; Herbert Berger prof., chief cardiology U. Md., 2005—. Sci. reviewer Chest, Jour. Heart and Lung Transplantation, IM-Internal Medicine, ACP Jour. Club, Clin. Cardiology, Evidence Based Medicine; contbr. chpts. to books and articles to profl. jours. Mem. ACP, AMA, Am. Coll. Cardiology, Am. Soc. Internal Medicine, Am. Coll. Chest Physicians, So. Med. Assn., Internat. Soc. Heart and Lung Transplantation, Heart Failure Soc. Am., Am. Soc. Transplant Physicians (Young Investigator award 1995). Office: 22 5th Greene St 53B06 Baltimore MD 21201 Home: 4 Padonia Woods Ct Cockeysville MD 21030 Office Phone: 410-328-7716, 410-328-7716. Office Fax: 410-328-4382. E-mail: mmehra@medicine.umaryland.edu.

MEHRING, NANCY, medical/surgical nurse, administrator; b. Lorain, Ohio, June 13, 1943; d. d. Stacy C. and Mary B. (Sascik) Jezewski; m. Frank Mehring, July 16, 1966; children: Gregory M., Stacey M. Diploma, M.B. Johnson Sch. Nursing, Elyria, Ohio, 1964; BSN, U. Akron, 1984. Staff nurse, asst. head nurse, head nurse Elyria Meml. Hosp., 1964-84, admission coord., mgr., 1984-2000; nurse mgr. P.A.T. and Ambulatory Care Ctr.; onsite mgr. Amherst (Ohio) Hosp., 2000—. Mem. adv. com. U. Akron Outreach Program. Mem. ANA, Ohio Nurses Assn., M.B. Johnson Sch. Nursing Alumni Assn., Lorain County Dist. Nurses Assn., Sigma Theta Tau.

MEHTA, ASHESH, neurologist; MD in Neuroscience, PhD in Neuroscience, Albert Einstein Coll. Medicine. Resident in neurosurgery Cornell U. NY Presbyterian Hosp.; resident in neuro-oncology Memorial Sloan Kettering Cancer Ctr.; dir. epilepsy surgery Long Island Jewish Med. Ctr. Comprehensive Epilepsy Ctr., 2006—. Mem.: Am. Assn. Stereotactic & Functional Neurosurgery, Congress Neurological Surgeons, Am. Assn. Neurological Surgeons, Soc. for Neuroscience, Am. Epilepsy Soc., Epilepsy Found. Long Island (profl. adv. bd.). Office: 270-05 76th Ave New Hyde Park NY 11040

MEHTA, CYNTHIA LEE, dermatologist, educator; BA, Augustana Coll., Sioux Falls, 1988; MD, U. SD, Vermillion, 1993. Diplomate Am. Acad. Dermatology, 1997. Intern in internal medicine U. Wis., 1993—94, resident in dermatology, 1994—97, clin. asst. prof. dermatology Madison, 1997—. Contbr. articles to profl. jours., including Jour. Am. Acad. Dermatology (Nation's Top Doctors, 2003). Fellow: Am. Acad. Dermatology; mem.: AMA, Alpha Omega Alpha Soc. Avocations: travel, music, dance. Office: U Wis 5249 E Terrace Dr Madison WI 53718

MEHTA, DAVENDRA, cardiologist; b. Ajmer, Rajasthan, India, Oct. 30, 1952; arrived in US, 1990; s. Madan Mohan and Rani (Bhirani) Mehta; m. Lakshmi Balakrishnan, June 9, 1981; children: Pooja, Karuna. BSc, Govt. Coll., Ajmer, 1970; MB, BChir, Jawahar Lal Nehru Med. Coll., Ajmer, 1975; MD, Postgrad. Inst. Med. Edn., Chandigarh, India, 1979; PhD, U. London, 1989. Diplomate Am. Bd. Internal Medicine, cert. in cardiovasc. disease. Intern, resident Postgrad. Inst. Med. Edn., Changidarh, 1977—79; resident Regional Cardiac Ctr., Leicester, England, 1983—86; fellow St. Bartholomew's Hosp./St. Georges Hosp., London; rsch. assoc. St. Georges Med. Sch., London, 1986-89; cons. cardiologist Escort's Heart Inst., New Delhi, 1989-91; rsch. assoc. Eastern Heart Inst., Passaic, NJ, 1991-92; asst. prof. medicine Mt. Sinai Sch. Medicine, NYC, 1992—99, assoc. prof., 1999—; dir. Electrophysiology Lab. Mt. Sinai Hosp., 2001—. Contbr. articles to profl. jours., chapters to books. Recipient Am. Heart Assn. rsch. grant, NJ, 1990. Fellow: Am. Coll. Cardiology; mem.: Brit. Pacing & Electrophysiology Group, N.Am. Soc. Pacing & Electrophysiology, Royal Coll. Physicians. Office: Klingenstein Clin Ctr 6th Rm 6N 82 1450 Madison Ave New York NY 10029 also: 5 E 98th St 3rd Fl New York NY 10029-6574 also: Mount Sinai Hosp 1 Gustave 1 Levy Pl New York NY 10029 Office Fax: 212-241-9701. Business E-Mail: davendra.mehta@mssm.edu.

MEHTA, JAWAHAR LAL, cardiologist; b. India, Aug. 10, 1946; arrived in US, 1970; s. Mohan L. and Ishwar D. (Valecha) M.; m. Paulette Smedresman, Oct. 20, 1977; children: Asha, Jason. MD, GN Med. Coll. U. Amritsar, 1968; PhD, Uppsala U., Sweden. Diplomate Am. Bd. Internal Medicine, Am. Bd. Cardiovascular Diseases. Intern N.Y. Med. Coll., Valhalla, NY, 1970, resident in pediat., 1971; resident in internal medicine Mt. Sinai-Beth Israel Hosp., NYC, 1971-73; fellow in cardiology SUNY, NY, 1973-75; from asst. prof. to prof. medicine & physiology U. Fla. Coll. Medicine, Gainesville, 1976-2000; dir. molecular cardiology, Stebbins chair in cardiology U. Ark. Med. Sci., Little Rock, 2000—. Rsch. fellow, instr. in medicine U. Minn., Mpls., 1975—76; staff physician VA Med. Ctr., Gainesville, 1976—2000, clin. investigator, 1980—85; dir. cardiology svcs. Ctrl. Ark. Vets. Healthcare Sys., 2000—. Fellow: ACP, Am. Heart Assn., Am. Coll. Cardiology; mem.: Assn. Univ. Cardiologists, Assn. Am. Physicians, Am. Soc. Clin. Investigation. Office: U Ark for Med Scis Slot 532 Little Rock AR 72205-7199 Business E-Mail: mehtajl@uams.edu.

MEHTA, PRIYANKA, animal scientist, educator; b. Bareilly, Uttar Pradesh, India, Jan. 4, 1979; MSc in Animal sci., M.J.P.R.U., Bareilly, 2002, PhD in Animal sci., 2008. Lectr. dept. animal sci. M.J.P. Rohilkhand U., Bareilly, 2007—. Avocations: reading, badminton. Home: UDIT- 36 A Mahanagar Colony Part One N Bareilly UP 243006 India Personal E-mail: pmsai9@hotmail.com.

MEIER, ANDREAS H., pediatrician, educator; b. Altötting, Germany, May 6, 1963; MD, LMU Munich, 1990; MEd, U. Ill., 2010. Asst. prof., surgery and pediat. Penn. State U., 2002—08; assoc. prof., chair, pediatric surgery Southern Ill. U., 2008—. Recipient Ann. Tchg. award, Dept. Surgery Southern Ill. U. Fellow: ACS, Am. Acad. Pediat. (Surg. Sect.); mem.: Assn. Surg. Edn., SAGES, Am. Pediatric Surgery Assn. Avocations: golf, tennis, philosophy. Office: PO Box 19655 Springfield IL 62794-9655 E-mail: ameier@ahmeier.info.

MEIER, DIANE EVE, geriatrician, researcher, medical educator; b. Princeton, NJ, Apr. 15, 1952; d. Paul and Louise (Goldstone) Meier; m. Warren Sherman; children: Leo William, Anna Helen. BA, Oberlin Coll., 1973; MD, Northwestern U., 1977. Resident Oreg. Health Scis. U., Portland, fellow; prof. dept. geriatrics and adult devel., medicine Mt. Sinai Sch. Medicine, NYC, 1983—, dir. Hertzberg Palliative Care Inst., 1983—, dir. Ctr. to Advance Palliative Care, Catherine Gaisman prof. medical ethics. Recipient Founders Award, Nat. Hospice and Palliative Care Orgn., 2007, Academic Career Leadership Award, Nat. Inst. Aging, Open Soc. Inst.'s Faculty Scholar's Award of the Project on Death in America, Alexander Richman Commemorative Award for Humanism in Medicine, 50th Anniversary Social Impact Award, AARP, 2008, Physician of Yr. Award, Castle Connelly, 2009, Lifetime Achievement Award, Am. Acad. Hospice and Palliative Medicine, 2009; named a MacArthur Fellow, The John D. and Catherine T. MacArthur Found, 2008. Office: 1440 Madison Ave New York NY 10029 Office Phone: 212-659-8552. E-mail: diane.meier@mssm.edu.

MEIER, DOMINIK SIMON, biomedical engineer, researcher; b. Switzerland; arrived in U.S., 1993; s. Hans-Werner Meier and Franziska Peterka. Diploma in engring., Swiss Fed. Inst. Tech., Zurich, 1992; MS, Ohio State U., 1996, PhD, 2000. Grad. rsch. asst. Swiss Fed. Inst. Tech., Zurich, 1991—92; grad. rsch. assoc. Ohio State U., Columbus, 1993—2000; postdoctoral rsch. fellow biomedical engring. Cleve. Clinic Found., 2000—01; postdoctoral rsch. fellow radiology Brigham & Women's Hosp., Boston, 2001—03; instr. Harvard Med. Sch., Boston, 2003—07, asst. prof., 2007—. Mem.: IEEE, Am. Acad. Neurology. Office: Brigham & Women's Hosp 221 Longwood Ave RFB 396 Boston MA 02115

MEIER, JOCHEN CHRISTIAN, professor; b. Neustadt a.d. Weinstrasse, Germany, Oct. 14, 1970; s. Horst and Ingrid Meier; life ptnr. Sabine Jörissen. Student of Biology, Rurpecht Karls U., Heidelberg, 1990—95; PhD Neuroscience (Doctor Rerum Naturalium), U. Pierre et Marie Curie, Paris, 1996—2000; Postdoctoral lecture qualification, Humboldt U. Med. Faculty, Berlin, 2000—05. Postdoctoral lecture qualification Humboldt U. Med. Faculty, 2005. Postdoc Humboldt U. Med. Faculty, Berlin, 2000—02, faculty position, 2003—06. Head of lab. Max Delbruech Ctr Molecular Medicine, Berlin. Fellow Kékulé, Found. of the Chem. Industry, 1996-1998, DAAD Fellowship, NATO, 1998-1999, Centre Internat. des Etudiants et Stagiaires (CIES), French govt., 1999-2000, Grad. program fellowship, Deutsche Forschungsgemeinschaft, 2000-2002. Mem.: Soc. for Neuroscience USA. Avocations: photography, literature, travel. Office: Max Delbrueck Ctr Molecular Medicine Robert Roessle Str 10 Berlin 13092 Germany

MEIER, KATHRYN ELAINE, pharmacologist, educator, academic administrator; b. San Mateo, Calif., Apr. 28, 1953; d. Robert E. and I. Dorothy Hunt; m. G. Patrick Meier, June 16, 1975; children: Adam M., Andrea D. BA in Biology, U. Calif., San Diego, 1975; PhD in Pharmacology, U. Wis., Madison, 1981. Lab. asst., tchg. asst., rsch. fellow U. Calif. San Diego, La Jolla, 1971-75; rsch. asst., fellow U. Wis., Madison, 1975-81; NIH postdoctoral fellow U. Calif. San Diego, La Jolla, 1981-84; assoc., sr. assoc. Howard Hughes Med. Inst., Seattle, 1984-89; rsch. asst. prof. U. Wash., Seattle, 1988-91; asst. prof. Med. U. S.C., Charleston, 1991-96, assoc. prof. pharmacology, 1996—2003; prof. dept. pharm. sci. Wash. State U., Pullman, 2003—, chair dept. pharm. sci., 2003—05, interim asst. dean, 2007, interim-chair nutrition/dietetics, 2007—08, program dir., nutrition & exercise physiology, 2008—. Scientist reviewer Dept. Def., Ft. Detrick, Md., 1996-2005, 2007-11, VA Merit Review, 1999—11; Nat. Sci. Fedn. fellowship reviewer, 2004-11. Mem. editl. bd. Jour. Biol. Chemistry, 1993-98, Am. Jour. Physiology, 1996—11, Jour. Pharmacology and Exptl. Therapeutics, 1998-2000, Molecular Pharmacology, 2004—, mem., Am. Soc. Pharm. & Experimental Therapeutics Bd. Publ. Trustees, 2011-; contbr. articles to profl. jours. Recipient Tchg. Excellence award Med. U. SC, 2001; NIH fellow, 1981-84; Rsch. grantee NIH, 1993-96, 2004—10, Dept. Def., 1998-2006. Mem. Am. Soc. Biochemistry and Molecular Biology, Am. Soc. Pharmacology and Exptl. Therapeutics, Am. Physiological Soc. Office: Washington State Univ Dept Nutrition & Exercise Physiology Spokane WA 99210-1495 Office Phone: 509-335-3573. Business E-Mail: kmeier@wsu.edu.

MEIER-RUGE, WILLIAM ALFRED, pathologist; b. Rudolstadt, Germany, July 28, 1930; s. Artur Robert and Herta (Kruger) M.-R.; m. Jutta Ruge, May 28, 1955; children: Peer, Cora, Tilman, Anja. MD, U. Berlin, 1954. Clin. asst., intern Gen. Hosp., Potsdam-Babelsberg, Germany, 1954-56; rsch. asst. Pathology Inst., U. Berlin, 1956-61; rsch. assoc. Pathology Inst., U. Basel, Switzerland, 1963—, assoc. prof., 1965; head Lab. Exptl. Pathology and Histochemistry dept. biology Sandoz Ltd., Basel, 1967-69, head dept. basic med. rsch., 1969-79, head gerontol. brain rsch. divsn. preclin. rsch., 1979-83; head Lab. Gerontol. Brain Rsch U. Basel, 1984—. Author: Medikamentose Retinopathie, 1967, CNS-Aging and Its Neuropharmacology, 1979, Teaching and Training in Geriatric Medicine, Vol. 1, 1987, Vol. 2, 1990, Vol. 3, 1992, Pathology of Chronic Constipation in Pediatric and Adult Coloproctology, 2005. Recipient Rudolf Virchow prize, Ministry of Health, 1960. Mem. German Soc. Pathology, Swiss Soc. Pathology, German Histochem. Soc., Swiss Gerontol Soc. Home: 12 Oberwilerstrasse CH-4103 Bottmingen Switzerland Office: U Med Sch Basel Dept Pathol Schoenbeinstrasse 40 CH-4003 Basel Switzerland Home Phone: 0041.61.421.5183. Office Fax: 0041.61.421 5191. Business E-Mail: dsc.oberwil@bluewin.ch.

MEINHOLD-HEERLEIN, IVO, gynecologist, consultant; b. Mainz, Rheinland-Pfalz, Germany, Mar. 23, 1969; s. Leo and Heike Meinhold-Heerlein. Diploma in Gymnasium, Bad Kreuznach, Rheinland-Pfalz, 1988; MD, U. Freiburg, 1996. Privatdozent U. Kiel, Schleswig-Holstein, Germany, 2007, ob-gyn. specialist 2006, cert. surgeon German Soc. Gynecol. Endoscopy, 2008. Postdoc. rsch. fellow German Cancer Aid Burnham Inst., La Jolla, Calif.,

1999—2001; acting dir. Kiel Sch. Gynecol. Endoscopy, 2006—08; head, oncological rsch. group, dept. ob-gyn. U. Hosp. Schleswig Holstein Campus Kiel, 2002—08, cons., dept. ob-gyn., 2007—08; cons., acting head, dept. ob-gyn. U. Hosp. Aachen, Germany, 2009—; dir. Endometriosis Ctr. Aachen, 2010—. Contbr. articles to profl. jours. Founder Non-profit Supporting Assn. Rhineland-Palatinate Youth Orch., Bad Kreuznach, 1990, chmn., 1990. Recipient Staude Pfannenstiel award, North German Soc. Gynecology and Obstetrics, 2003, Hans Frangenheim award, German Soc. Gynecol. Endoscopy, 2008, Dr. Rockstroh award, 2010. Mem.: Am. Assn. Gynecol. Laparoscopists, Internat. Soc. Gynecol. Endoscopy, German Soc. Gynecol. Endoscopy, Bd. Gynecol. Oncology, German Cancer Soc., North German Soc. Gynecology and Obstetrics, German Soc. Gynecology and Obstetrics. Lutheran. Office Phone: 49 241 8080076. Home Fax: 49-241-16069016. Personal E-mail: imeinhold@hotmail.com. Business E-Mail: imeinhold@ukaachen.de.

MEINKE, LAURA, pulmonologist, educator; b. San Diego, Oct. 19, 1974; BS, U. Ariz., 1996; MD, Stanford U., 2001. Asst. prof. U. Ariz. Coll. Medicine, 2007—. Fellow: Am. Coll. Chest Physicians; mem.: ACP, Soc. Critical Care Medicine, Am. Thoracic Soc. Office: 1501 N Campbell Ave PO Box 245030 Tucson AZ 85724-5030 Business E-Mail: lmeinke@email.arizona.edu.

MEIR, HADIR MOUSTAFA, oncologist; b. Alexandria, Egypt, June 12, 1959; MB, Alexandria U., BChir, 1985. Cert. in radiotherapy Aachen U., Germany, 1995. Chmn. King Abdull Aziz Hosp. & Oncology Ctr., Jeddah, Saudi Arabia, Ministry of Health, 1985—. Home: PO Box 10001 Jeddah Western 21433 Saudi Arabia Home Fax: 96626637660. Personal E-mail: hadirmeir@hotmail.com.

MEIRELES, JOSÉ ROBERTO CARDOSO, biology professor; b. Salvador, Bahia, Brazil, July 28, 1970; Degree in Biol. Scis., U. Fed. da Bahia, 1998; MS in Genetics, U. Fed. da Paraíba, 2003. Prof. U. Estadual de Feira de Santana, 2005—. Office: UEFS-DCBIO Ave Transnordestina Feira de Santana Bahia 44036900 Brazil Business E-Mail: jrcmeireles@gmail.com.

MEIRELES, MARIA ANGELA DE ALMEIDA, science educator, consultant; b. Campinas, São Paulo, Brazil, Oct. 31, 1953; d. José de Sales and Myrtilla Conforti de Almeida Meireles; m. Maria Angela de Almeida Meireles, Apr. 10, 1976; children: Marcelo Meireles Petenate, Guilherme Meireles Petenate. PhD, Iowa State U., 1982. Cert. in food engring., CREA, 1977. Prof. LASEFI/DEA/FEA/UNICAMP, Campinas, 1983—. Assoc. editor food Brazilian Jour. Medicinal Plants, Botucatu, São Paulo, 2000—, assoc. dir. CPQBA/UNICAMP, Campinas, 2003—05; editl. bd. mem. Jour. Food Process Engring., 2005—, Food and Bioprocess Engring., Open Chem. Engring. Jour., 2007—; editl. bd. mem. open thermodynamics jour. Bentham Sci. Pubs., 2007—, editl. bd. mem. recent patents in engring., 2007—, editl. bd. mem. Open Food Sci. Jour., 2008—. Contbg. mem. Visão Mundial, Belo Horizonte, Minas Gerais, Brazil. Recipient Zeferino Vaz award, 2006. Mem.: SBCTA. Achievements include research in Engineering of Natural Products: volatile oils, pigments, etc. Avocation: reading. Office: LASEFI/DEA/FEA/UNICAMP Rua Monteiro Lobato 80 Campinas São Paulo 13083-862 Brazil Office Fax: 551935214027. Business E-Mail: meireles@fea.unicamp.br.

MEIS, CAMERON MICHAEL, marketing executive; b. Fontana, Calif., June 2, 1984; Degree in Sociology, Calif. State U., 2008. Facility mgr. Epic Mgmt., 2005—. Office: 37558 Yucaipa Blvd Yucaipa CA 92399 Business E-Mail: cmeis@epiclp.com.

MEISLIN, HARVEY WARREN, emergency healthcare physician; b. Rochester, NY, June 19, 1946; s. Milton M. and Celia (Weiner) M.; m. Loretta Marie Bielski, Apr. 30, 1977; children: Justin, Jonathan, Megan. BS in Chemistry, Purdue U., 1968; MD, Ind. U., 1972. Diplomate Am. Bd. Emergency Medicine (chmn.), Am. Bd. Med. Spltys. (del. 1990, fin. com. 1992, exec. com. 1994); cert. cardiac life support, ACLS instr., advanced trauma life support instr. Intern U. Chgo. Hosps. and Clinics, 1973-75, resident, 1975-77, dir. div. emergency medicine, 1975-77; asst. prof. internal and emergency medicine UCLA Emergency Med. Ctr., 1977-80, resident dir. emergency medicine, 1977-80, assoc. dir., 1977-80; assoc. prof. dept. surgery emergency medicine Coll. Medicine, U. Ariz., Tucson, 1980-83, assoc. prof., 1983-85; assoc. head, dept. surgery U. Ariz., Tucson, 1995—; prof. Coll. Medicine, U. Ariz., Tucson, 1985—; chief emergency medicine U. Ariz., Tucson, 1980—; chief sect. emergency medicine dept. surgery Ariz. Health Scis. Ctr., Tuscon, 1980—, dir. emergency svcs. Univ. Med. Ctr., 1980—, dir. Ariz. Emergency Med. Rsch. Ctr., 1990—; med. dir. MEDTRAN-Aeromed. Ambulance Corp., 1985-88. Mem. emergency med. svc. com. Mid-South Health Planning Orgn., Chgo., 1974; coord. Mid-South Disaster Plan, Chgo., 1974; mem. com. revision of Disaster Plan Billings Hosp., 1974-76; mem. faculty Am. Hosp. Assn. Inst. Disaster Preparedness, 1975; vis. prof. dept. emergency medicine Denver Gen. Hosp., 1977; bd. trustees Emergency Med. Found., 1978-81; mem. med. adv. com. L.A. City Fire Dept., 1979-80; chmn.-elect Tuscon Met. EMS Coun., 1983-84, chmn., 1984-85; chmn. Tuscon Pre-Hosp. Care Coun., 1981; mem. trauma steering com. So. Ariz. Regional Trauma Ctr., 1986-88; mem. ETHICON emergency physicians adv. panel Johnson & Johnson Co., 1987-92; presenter and lectr. in field. Editor: Purdue Rivet, 1971-72, abstract sect. Annals Emergency Medicine, 1982-90, EMS sect., 1989-90; guest editor: Topics in Emergency Medicine, 1979; sci. editor: Drug Therapy, 1984—; mem. editorial bd.: Annals Emergency Medicine, 1977-90, Emergency Dept. News, 1979-87, Emergency Dept. and Ambulatory Care News, 1987-90, Digest of Emergency Medicine Care, 1981-87; contbr. articles and revs. to profl. jours. Mem. select med. adv. com. City of Tucson, 1981, med. dir. emergency med. svcs., 1982-83, 84-85; bd. dirs. so. Ariz. divsn. Am. Heart Assn., 1985-90; mem. emergency cardiac care com. so. divsn. Ariz. Heart Assn., 1986-88; mem. med. dirs. commn., dept. health svcs. State of Ariz., 1992—, also mem. Mex. border commn., 1991—; mem. med. direction commn. State of Ariz. (appointed by gov.), 1993—. Recipient Pres. gavel and plaque Am. Bd. Emergency Medicine. Fellow Am. Coll. Emergency Physicians (State of Ill. chpt.): mem. sci. adv. com. 1975, mem. sci. edn. com. 1975-76, mem. grad./undergrad. edn. com. 1976-79, mem. ethics com. 1976-77, mem. surgery/trauma task force bd. cert. exam. 1976-77, bd. dirs. 1976-77, chmn. edn. com. 1976-77; State of Calif. chpt.: mem. hosp. and contract com. 1978-79, mem. EMS and legis. com. 1978-79, mem. spl. task force on emergency dept. distbn. 1979-80, mem. membership com. 1979-80, mem. legis. com. 1979-80, mem. sci. assembly planning com. 1980-81, bd. dirs. 1979-81, mem. rsch. com. 1981; State of Ariz. chpt.: bd. dirs. 1982-92, 92—, chmn. pub. rels. com. 1982-83, v.p. and sec. 1983-84, counselor 1984-87, mem. credentials com. 1986-91, chmn. 1987-90, mem. test com. 1986-87, mem. ad hoc com. for combined tng. 1987-88, chmn. task force on emergency medicine 1987-89, mem. exec. com. 1988—, mem. fin. com. 1988—, sec./treas. 1989-90, mem. EMS com. 1990—, pres.-elect 1990-91, pres. 1991-92, chair stds. com., mem. faculty Nat. Sci. Assembly 1974-76, Cert. Appreciation award 1990); mem. APHA, Am. Coll. Physician Execs., Am. Trauma Soc., Am. Bd. Med. Specialties (mem. fin. com. 1992, mem. exec. com. 1995—, pres., 2004), Ariz. Med. Assn., Pima County Med. Soc. (bd. dirs. 1991—), Phi Rho Sigma. Avocations: racquetball, golf, skiing, automobiles. Office: U Ariz Med Ctr Sect Emergency Med 1501 N Campbell Ave Tucson AZ 85724-0001

MEKITARIAN FILHO, EDUARDO, pediatrician; b. Sao Paulo, Brazil, Oct. 7, 1980; MD, U. Estadual Paulista, 2003; MSc, U. Fed. de Sao Paulo, 2011. Pediatrician U. de Sao Paulo, 2010—. Avocations: music, soccer. Office: Ave Professor Lineu Prestes 2565 Sao Paulo 05508000 Brazil Business E-Mail: emf2002@uol.com.br.

MEKNAS, KHALED, medical educator; b. Aleppo, Dec. 13, 1960; PhD, Silesian U., 1986, U. Tromso Norway, 2010. Assoc. prof. U. Tromsoe, 2008—. Mem.: Norwegian Med. Assn. Office: University Hosp North Norway Tromsø 9038 Norway Business E-Mail: khaled.meknas@unn.no.

MELAMED, YEHUDA DOV, physician, director; b. Israel, Feb. 17, 1943; MD, Tel Aviv U. Med. Sch., 1972; degree in Hyperbaric & Diving Medicine, Chiati Med. Sch. Italy, 1986. Dir. Israeli Neval Med. Inst., 1975—95, Rambam and Elisha Hosps. Hyperbaric and Diving Medicine Ctr., 1996—. Pres., chief diving instr. Israeli Fedn. Underwater Activity, 1975—79; cons. Israeli Health Ministry, 1996; pres. Isreali Hyperbaric Med. and Diving Soc., 1996—98. Recipient Craig Hoffman Meml. Safety award, Internat. Underwater Contractors, Samuel and Paula Alkeles Award, Jewish Nat. Fund, Jerusalem, Comdr. Israeli Navy's award, Boerema award, Undersea Hyperbaric Med. Soc., award, Internat. Hon. Adv. Bd., Ocean Hyperbaric Neurologic Ctr. Mem.: Israeli Soc. Hyperbaric and Diving Medicine and Physiology (founding mem.), EUBS. Avocations: diving, sailing, hiking. Office: 12 Yair Katz Haifa 34636 Israel Office Fax: 9728300055.

MELANI, KENNETH R., insurance company executive; m. Tracy Melani; children: Christine, Carrie, Alyssa, Sofia. B in Chemistry summa cum laude, Washington and Jefferson Coll., Washington, Pa.; MD, Wake Forest U., Winston-Salem, NC, 1979. Diplomate American Bd. Internal Medicine. Pvt. practice in internal medicine; pres., CEO West Penn Cares Inc.; pres. Keystone Health Plan West; corp. med. dir. med. affairs dept. Highmark Inc., Pitts., 1989, bd. dirs., exec. v.p. strategic bus. devel. and health svcs., pres., CEO, 2003—. Bd. dirs. Assn. Health Ins. Plans, Blue Cross and Blue Shield Assn. Bd. dirs. Blue Cross and Blue Shield Assn., Holy Family Inst.; bd. chmn. Pitts. Cultural Trust, Children's Charity Pitts., Wash. and Jefferson Coll. and Variety; bd. dirs. Allegheny Conf. Cmty. Devel., Project for Freedom, Extra Mile, Duquesne Club. Recipient Tony Coelho award, Washington and Jefferson Entrepreneur Yr. award, 2009, Junior Achievement Golden Achievement award, Nat. American Heritage award, The Anti-Defamation League, Allegheny Valley Sch. Dist. Alumni Hall of Fame award, Washington and Jefferson Coll. Alumi award for Achievement, Paul Lackner Person of Vision award, Blind and Vision Rehab. Svcs. Pitts., 2007. Mem.: Am. Coll. of Physician Execs., Am. Soc. of Internal Medicine, Penn. Soc. of Internal Medicine, Am. Med. Assn., Penn. Med. Soc., Allegheny County Med. Soc. Office: Highmark Fifth Avenue Place 120 Fifth Ave Pittsburgh PA 15222-3099 Office Phone: 412-544-7000. *

MELCHER, JENNIFER, otolaryngologist, educator; Assoc. prof. otology & laryngology Harvard Med. Sch. Mass. Eye & Ear Infirmary. Mem.: Assn. Rsch. in Otolaryngology, Am. Assn. Advancement Sci., Soc. for Neuroscience. Office: 77 Massachusetts Ave E25-519 Cambridge MA 02139 Office Phone: 617-573-3745. E-mail: jrm@epl.meei.harvard.edu.

MELE, JOANNE THERESA, dentist; b. Chgo., Dec. 5, 1943; d. Andrew and Josephine Jeanette (Calabrese). Diploma, St. Elizabeth's Sch. Nursing, Chgo., 1964; diploma in dental hygiene, Northwestern U., 1977; AS, Triton Coll., 1979; DDS (hon.), Loyola U., 1983. RN; registered dental hygienist. Staff nurse medicine/surgery St. Elizabeth's Hosp., Chgo., 1964-66, oper. room nurse, 1966-67; head nurse oper. room Cook County Hosp., Chgo., 1967-76, head nurse ICU, 1976-77; dental hygienist Mele Dental Assocs., Ltd., Oakbrook, Ill., 1977-79, practice dentistry, 1983—. Clin. asst. prof. Loyola U., Chgo., 1988-95. Recipient Northwestern U. Dental Hygiene Clinic award, 1977; Dr. Duxler Humanitarian scholar Loyola U., 1982. Mem. Chgo. Dental Soc., Ill. State Dental Soc., Acad. Gen. Dentistry, Acad. Operative Dentistry, Am. Prosthodontic Soc., Internat. Congress Oral Implantologists, Psi Omega (Kappa chpt.). Roman Catholic. Avocations: reading, music, gardening, golf. Office Phone: 630-573-0420. Personal E-mail: joannemere@gmail.com.

MELEIS, AFAF IBRAHIM, dean, nursing educator; b. Alexandria, Egypt, Mar. 19, 1942; d. Abdel Baki Ibrahim and Soad Hussein Hassan; m. Mahmoud Meleis, Aug. 21, 1964; children: Waleed, Sherief. BS magna cum laude, U. Alexandria, 1961; MS, UCLA, 1964, MA, 1966, PhD, 1968; D in Pub. Svc. (hon.), U. Portland, Oreg., 1989; MD (hon.), Linköping U., Sweden, 2007. Instr. U. Alexandria, 1961-62; acting instr. UCLA, 1966-68, asst. prof. nursing, then assoc. prof., 1968-75; assoc. prof., dean Health Inst., Kuwait, 1975-77; prof. nursing U. Calif., San Francisco, 1977—2001, also dir. Study Immigrant Health and Adjustment; Margaret Bond Simon dean of nursing U. Pa. Sch. Nursing, Phila., 2002—, prof. nursing and sociology, dir., WHO Collaborating Ctr. Nursing and Midwifery Leadership. Vis. prof. colls. in Sweden, Brazil, Japan, Saudi Arabia, Kuwait, Egypt; 1st Centennial prof. Columbia U., N.Y.C., 1992-94; cons., speaker in field. Author: Theoretical Nursing: Development & Progress, 1985 (Book of Yr., am. Jour. Nursing, 1985), 2d edit., 1991, 3d edit., 1997; contbr. articles to rsch. and profl. jours. Counsel gen. Internat. Coun. Women's Health Issues; mem. Global Health Coun., Nurses Edn. Fund, Inc., Life Sci. Career Alliance. Recipient Helen Hahm award U. Calif. Sch. Nursing, San Francisco, 1981, Teaching awards U. Calif., San Francisco, 1981, 85, Pres. Hosni Mubarak medal of Excellence, 1990, Chancellor's medal U. Mass., 2000, Global Citizenship award UN Assn. Greater Phila., 2007, Dr. Gloria Twine Chisum award U. Pa., 2007; Kellogg Internat. fellow, 1986-89. Fellow Royal Coll. Nursing, Am. Acad. Nursing, Coll. Physicians Phila.; mem. CARE, Inst. Medicine, Am. Nurses Assn., Coun. Nurse Researchers, Western Soc. Rsch. in Nursing, Pa. Women's Forum, Forum Exec. Women. Avocations: jogging, symphony, reading, politics. Office: Univ Penn Sch Nursing 420 Guardian Dr Rm 465 NEB Philadelphia PA 19104-6096

MELGA, PIERLUIGI, endocrinologist; b. Sanremo, Liguria, Italy, Jan. 8, 1949; s. Stefano and Angela Rosa (Balestra) M.; m. Marilinda Ausonio, Sept. 24, 1973; children: Brigida, Angiola. MD, U. Genoa, Italy, 1973. Specialist in endocrinology U. Genoa, 1976, specialist in internal medicine U. Genoa, 1983. Vol. asst. internal medicine U. Genoa, 1973-75, rschr. metabolic diseases, 1975-80, confirmed rschr., 1980—, lectr. specialization diabetology, 1990-91, lectr. specialization in gerontology, 1991—, lectr. med. sch., 1994—, lectr. specialist in endocrinology, 1999—, cons. in diabetology, 1980—, asst. rector dept. metabolic disease, 1982—. Mem. European Assn. Study Diabetes, Soc. italiana Diabetologia (advisor reg. bd. 1992-96, 2002-06), Assn. Med. Diabetologi (advisor reg. bd. 1990-94, 99—2003, pres. 2002-06). Roman Catholic. Avocations: tennis, travel. Office: DISEM Viale Benedetto XV u 6 16132 Genoa Italy Office Phone: +39 010 3538927. E-mail: melga@unige.it.

MELIKYAN, ARMEN, surgeon; b. Republic of Armenia, Mar. 20, 1961; married; 2 children. MD, Yerevan State Med. Inst., Armenia, 1984. Tng. endo-surgical chair Mich. Univ., 1991; tng. Israel Technion Inst., 1993; asst. of number 3 chair surgical diseases Yeveran State Med. Univ., Armenia, 1987—90, docent, 1990—95, prof., 1995; head surg. svc. Malatya Clinic Hosp., 1990—92. Recipient Vocation For Investing a New Med. Method, 2005. Mem.: NIH (chair endoscopic surgery 1997—98), Russia's Endoscopic Surgeons' Assn., European Endoscopic Surgeons' Assn., Armenian Endoscopic Surgeons' Assn. (founder-pres.), Endoscopic Surgery Ctr. (founder 1992), Olympic Med. Com. of Armenia (editor-in-chief 2002). Prosperous Armenia. Mailing: c/o National Assembly of the Republic of Armenia 19 Baghramyan Yerevan Armenia *

MELIONE, LUIS PAULO RODRIGUES, preventive medicine physician; b. Rio de Janeiro, Mar. 3, 1959; Degree, Sch. Medicine, Rio de Janeiro, 1984; M, Sch. Pub. Health, U. Sao Paulo, 2006. With preventive & social medicine Municipality Sao Jose dos Campos, 1989; occupl. physician Basic Sanitation Co., SABESP, Sao Paulo, 1989—2004, Brazilian Petroleum Corp., PETROBRAS, 2008. Asst. prof. Med. Sch., U. Taubate, Sao Paulo, 2007—08. Mem.: Brazilian Pub. Health Assn. Avocations: photography, literature. Office: Rodovia Presidente Dutra 143 REVAP Sao Jose dos Campos Sao Paulo 12223-900 Brazil Office Fax: 551239386349.

MELIS, MARCOVALERIO, surgeon, educator; b. Cagliari, Italy, Apr. 25, 1970; MD, U. Cagliari, 1994. Asst. prof., surgery NYU Sch. Medicine, 2008—. Fellow: ACS. Office: 423 East 23rd St Rm 4153 N New York NY 10010 Office Phone: 212-686-7500 ext. 7582. Office Fax: 212-951-3238. Business E-Mail: marcovalerio.melis@nyumc.org.

MELLBERG, JAMES RICHARD, retired dental research chemist; b. Manitowoc, Wis., June 3, 1932; s. Millard Filmore Mellberg and Marion Eleanor (Elmer) Zimmerman; m. Gail Maureen Lochning, Sept. 26, 1956 (dec.); children: Eric, Diane, Laura; m. Joan M. Lea, Aug. 6, 2011. BS, Wis. State U., Oshkosh, 1955; MS, Loyola U., Chgo., 1960. Head dental rsch. dept. Kendall Co., Barrington, Ill., 1958-75; assoc. dir. dental rsch. Colgate-Palmolive Co., Piscataway, NJ, 1975-94; ret. Cons. Naval Dental Rsch. Inst., Great Lakes, Ill., 1972-94. Author: Fluoride in Preventive Dentistry, 1983; patentee in field; contbr. over 100 articles in field to sci. publs. Recipient 20 sci. exhibit awards ADA, 1964-87. Mem. Internat. Assn. Dental Rsch. (Disting. Scientist award). Avocations: bicycling, woodworking. Home: 675 Ridge Top Rd Tryon NC 28782 Personal E-mail: mellberg1@windstream.net.

MELLER, JOSE, cardiologist; b. Santiago, Chile, Sept. 29, 1944; MD, Cath. U. Chile, Santiago, 1969. Cert. Internal Medicine, 1973, Cardiovascular Disease, 1975. Intern Elmhurst Gen. Hosp., Queens, NY, 1969—70, resident, 1970—71, Mt. Sinai Hosp., NYC, 1971—74, attending physician, 1974, assoc. attending physician; clin. prof. Mt. Sinai Med. Ctr., NYC. Office: 941 Park Ave New York NY 10028 Office Phone: 212-988-3772. Office Fax: 212-861-4672.

MELLGREN, GUNNAR, endocrinologist, educator; b. Norway, Dec. 12, 1967; MD, U. Bergen, 1992, PhD. Prof. medicine, cons. endocrinologist U. Bergen, 2009—. Fellow: Endocrine Soc. Office: Haukeland University Hosp Bergen N-5021 Norway E-mail: gunnar.mellgren@med.uib.no.

MELLGREN, SVEIN IVAR, neurologist, educator; b. Kristiansand S, Norway, Feb. 26, 1943; MD, U. Oslo, 1968, U. Bergen, 1973. With tng. positions, anatomy, pathology, neurology U. Bergen, 1970—77; lectr. neurology U. Trondheim, 1977—80, prof. neurology, 1980—81; prof. U. Tromsø, 1981—2008, head dept. clin. medicine, prof. faculty health scis., 2008—. Chair European Bd. Exam., Milan, 2009, Geneva, 10. Recipient Monrad-Krohn's prize, U. Oslo, Tchg. prize, U. Tromsø. Master: European Bd. Neurology (v.p.); fellow: Am. Acad. Neurology; mem.: Peripheral Nerve Soc., European Neurol. Soc. Achievements include research in neuroanatomy, multiple sclerosis, peripheral neuropathy. Avocations: travel, running, history. Home: Tomasjordvegen 87 Tromsø N-9024 Norway Personal E-mail: svein.ivar.mellgren@uit.no.

MELLINKOFF, SHERMAN MUSSOFF, medical educator; b. McKeesport, Pa., Mar. 23, 1920; s. Albert and Helen Mussoff Mellinkoff; m. June Bernice O'Connell, Nov. 18, 1944; children: Sherrill, Albert. BA, Stanford U., 1941, MD, 1944; LHD (hon.), Wake Forest U., 1984, Hebrew Union Coll., LA, 1988. Diplomate Am. Bd. Internal Medicine, Am. Bd. Gastroenterology, Am. Bd. Nutrition. Intern asst. resident Stanford U. Hosp., San Francisco, 1944—45; asst. resident Johns Hopkins Hosp., Balt., 1947—49, chief resident, 1950—51, instr. in medicine, 1951—53; fellow in gastroenterology Hosp. of U. Pa., Phila., 1949—50; from asst. prof. to prof. medicine UCLA Sch. of Medicine, LA, 1962—86; dean UCLA Sch. Medicine, LA, 1962—86, emeritus prof. of medicine, 1990—; disting. physician of VA Wadsworth VA Medical Ctr., LA, 1990-93. Mem. sci. adv. panel Rsch. to Prevent Blindness, Inc., NYC, 1975—93; mem. program devel. com. Nat. Med. Fellowships, Inc., NYC, 1984—. Editl. bd.: The Pharos, 1986—2009; contbr. articles to profl. jours. Apptd. by

Gov. of Calif. to McCone Com., 1965. Capt. US Army, 1945—57. Recipient Abraham Flexner award, Assn. Am. Med. Colls., 1981, J.E. Wallace Sterling Disting. Alumnus award, Stanford U. Sch. of Medicine, 1987. Master: ACP; fellow: Royal Coll. of Physicians; mem.: The Johns Hopkins Soc. of Scholars, Am. Acad. of Arts and Scis., Inst. of Medicine of NAS, Assn. Am. Physicians, Am. Gastroenterol. Assn. Assn. Avocation: reading. Office Phone: 310-825-3473.

MELLINS, CLAUDE ANN, psychologist; BA in Psychology, Brown U., 1982; MS in Clin. Psychology, U. So. Calif., LA, 1987; PhD in Clin. Psychology, U. So. Calif., 1990. Full prof., clin. psychology psychiatry, sociomed. scis. Colombia U.; co-dir. and co-founder Spl. Needs Clinic Children & Families Columbia Presbyn., NYC, 1992—; rsch. scientist HIV Ctr. Clin. Behavioral Studies NY State Psychiat. Inst. and Columbia U., NYC, 1994—. Mem. sci. leadership group exec. com. Pediat. HIV AIDS Cohorts Study; v.p. bd. dirs., Ranapo Children, standing mem., NIH Behavioral & Social Consequenses HIV Study Sect., 2009-. Contbr. chpts. to books and articles to profl. jours. Prin. co-investigator, NIH-funded studies. Aaron Diamond Found. fellow. Mem. APA (pediat. psychology subdivsn.).

MELLINS, ROBERT B., pediatrician, educator; b. NYC, Mar. 6, 1928; s. David J. and Ray H. (Hoffman) M.; m. Sue Mendelsohn, Apr. 19, 1959; children: Claude Ann, David Rustin. AB, Columbia U., 1948; MD, Johns Hopkins U., 1952. Intern Johns Hopkins Hosp., 1952—53; mem. epidemic intelligence svc, founder poison control program Ctr. Disease Control, Chgo., 1953—55; resident in pediat. N.Y. Hosp., 1955—56, Presbyn. Hosp., NYC, 1956—57, dir. pediat. ICU, 1970—75; assoc. prof. pediat. Columbia U., NYC, 1970—75, prof. pediat., 1975—, dir. Cystic Fibrosis Ctr., 1976—91, dir. pediat. pulmonary divsn., 1972—97; leloir lectr. USCD, 2008. Christmas Seal prof. Can. Lung Assn., 1979-80; 1st Deans Disting. lectr. in clin. scis. Columbia U. Coll. P&S, 1982; mem. Am. Bd. Pediat., founding mem. sub-bd. on pediat. pulmonology; bd. dirs. A.P. Gold Found. to promote humanism in medicine. Mem. editl. bd. Am. Rev. Respiratory Diseases, 1974-81, assoc. editor, 1984-90; contbr. articles to profl. jours. V.p. Am. Lung Assn., 1987—89; chmn. steering com. multi-ctr. study heart and lung complications of HIV infection in children NIH, 1989—2003; bd. dir. Am. Lung Assn., 1981—83, LA Jonas Found., 1970—78, 1990—, Symphony of UN, 1990—; bd. dirs. Am. Lung Assn. City of N.Y., 2001—05. Recipient Career Devel. award NIH, 1966-71, Career Scientist award Health Rsch. Coun. NYC Health Rsch. Coun., 1975, Stevens Triennial Rsch. award Columbia U., 1980, Health Edn. Rsch. award Nat. Asthma Edn. Program, 1992, Will Ross medal Am. Lung Assn., 1996, 2001, Life & Breath award Am. Lung Assn. NY, Outstanding Alumnus award Babies Hosp., Columbus, 2006, PS Disting. Svcs. award, 2011. Mem.: Louis August Jonas Found. (pres. 2009—, broshe mahorney pres.gov. 2011), Am. Acad. Allergy and Immunology, Soc. Critical Care Medicine, Am. Thoracic Soc. (bd. dir. 1975, 1981—84, nat. pres. 1982—83, v.p., Disting. Achievement award 1996, Founders award 2011, Physicians & Surgeons Disting. Svc. award 2011), Am. Acad. Pediat. (Med. Edn. Lay Edn. award 1995, Kendig award 2003), Am. Soc. Pharmacology and Exptl. Therapeutics, Am. Physiol. Soc., Soc. Pediat. Rsch., Am. Pediat. Soc., Fleischner Soc. (pres. 1995—), Gold Humanism Honor Soc., Alpha Omega Alpha. Office: Childrens Hosp NY-Presbyn 3959 Broadway CHC 746 New York NY 10032 Home: 22 W 66th St Apt 5 New York NY 10023-6207 Office Phone: 212-305-8430. Business E-Mail: rbm3@columbia.edu.

MELLO, CRAIG CAMERON, biologist, educator; b. New Haven, Oct. 18, 1960; BS in Biochemistry, Brown U., Providence, 1982; PhD in Biology, Harvard U., 1990. Postdoc. rsch. fellow Fred Hutchinson Cancer Rsch. Ctr., Seattle, 1990—94; prof. program in molecular medicine U. Mass. Med. Sch., Worcester, 1994—, Blais Univ. chair in molecular medicine, 2003—. Investigator Howard Hughes Med. Inst., 2000—. Contbr. articles to profl. journals. Recipient Wiley prize in biomed. scis., Rockefeller U., 2003, Massry prize, 2005, Lewis S. Rosenstiel award, Brandeis U., 2005, Gairdner Found. Internat. award, 2005, Dr. Paul Janssen award for biomed. rsch., Johnson & Johnson, 2006, Paul Ehrlich & Ludwig Darmstaedter prize, Germany, 2006; co-recipient Nobel prize in physiology/medicine, 2006; Pew scholar, U. Calif., San Francisco, 1995. Fellow: Am. Acad. Arts & Sciences; mem.: NAS (Award in molecular biology 2003). Achievements include discovery of the process now known as RNAi (with Andrew Z. Fire), that double-stranded RNA can quash the activity of specific genes. Office: U Mass Med Sch Biotech Two Ste 219 373 Plantation St Worcester MA 01605 Office Phone: 508-856-1602, 301-215-8500. Office Fax: 508-856-2950. Business E-Mail: craig.mello@umassmed.edu. *

MELLO, ELZA DANIEL DE, medical educator; b. Porto Alegre, Aug. 28, 1961; D, Fed. U. Rio Grande do Sul, 1984, postgrad, 2003. Adj. prof. Fed. U. Rio Grande do Sul, 1993—. Physician Med. Office, 1987; head nutritional support com. Clin. Hosp. Porto Alegre, 2002; cons. Brazilian Soc. Pediat. Nutrology Dept., 2002; chief nutrology svc. Clin. Hosp. Porto Alegre, 2005. Mem.: Brazilian Assn. Nutrology, Brazilian Soc. Pediat. Avocations: travel, movies, reading. Office: Av Taquara 438 / 307 Porto Alegre Rio Grande do Sul 90460210 Brazil Office Fax: 55 51 33317452. Business E-Mail: emello@hcpa.ufrgs.br.

MELNICK, MICHAEL, geneticist, educator; b. NYC, Sept. 24, 1944; s. Lester and Evelyn (Rosenberg) M.; m. Anita Goldberger, June 19, 1966; children: Cliff, Lynn. BA in Biology, NYU, 1966, DDS, 1970; PhD in Genetics, Ind. U., 1978. Instr. oral medicine Ind. U., Indpls., 1973-74, fellow in med. genetics, 1974-77, asst. prof. med. genetics, 1977-78; rsch. assoc. prof. U. So. Calif., LA, 1978-85, assoc. prof., 1985-89, prof. genetics, 1989—. Cons. in human genetics NIH, Bethesda, Md., 1977-88, grant reviewer, 1978—; manuscript referee Am. Jour. Human Genetics, Chgo., 1980—, Am. Jour. Med. Genetics, Helena, Mont., 1980—; MRC vis. prof. McGill U., Montreal, que., 1990. Author, editor 5 books on human genetics; editor-in-chief Jour. Craniofacial Genetics, 1980-2000; contbr. more than 100 articles to profl. jours. Mem. nat. bd. Com. of Concerned Scientists, N.Y.C., 1983—; vice chmn. Youth Towns of Israel, L.A., 1986—. Capt. M.C. U.S. Army, 1970-73. Recipient Ind. U. Disting. Alumnus award, 1984; Warwick James fellow U. London/Guy's Hosp., 1992. Fellow AAAS; mem. Soc. Craniofacial Genetics (pres. 1978-79), Soc. for Developmental Biology, Am. Soc. Human Genetics, Sigma Xi. Achievements include research in delineated major gene causation of cleft lip and palate; delineated insulin-like growth factor, type 2, receptor control of fetal lung, salvary gland and palate development; delineated molecular pathogenesis of viral-induced birth defects; application of probability neural networks and system kinetics to multi-gene analysis; molecular pathology of embryonic CMV infection. Avocations: art, philosophy, chess. Office: Univ So Calif Den 4266 Mc 0641 Los Angeles CA 90089-0641 Business E-Mail: mmelnick@usc.edu.

MELO, SILVANA REGINA, research scientist, educator; b. Uraí, Oct. 13, 1970; Degree in Biol. Sci., Maringa State U., 1990; PhD, São Paulo U., 2000. Prof. Maringá State U., 1991—, rsch. scientist, 2000. Avocation: music. Office: Av Colombo Maringa Paraná 87020900 Brazil Office Fax: 55 44 30114340. Business E-Mail: srmelo@uem.br.

MELONE, CHARLES P., orthopedist, surgeon, educator; Attended, Georgetown U., 1969. Diplomate Am. Bd. Orthopaedic Surgery, 1976, Am. Bd. Orthopaedic Surgery, 1993. Resident gen. surgery Nassau County Med. Ctr., 1970—71, resident orthopaedic surgery, 1971—74; fellow hand surgery Inst. of Reconstructive Plastic Surgery, 1974—75; clin. prof. orthopaedic surgery Albert Einstein Sch. of Medicine; former cons. NY Islanders, NY Yankees; mem. med. adv. bd. NY State Athletic Commn.; bd. mem. of regents Georgetown Univ.; hand surgeon NJ Nets, NJ Devils, Fla. Marlins; hand surgery cons. Pub. Sch. Athletic League; dir. orthopaedic hand surgery NY Univ. Med. Ctr.; with Beth Israel Med. Ctr. Named one of Best Doctors, NY Mag., 2011. Home: Beth Israel Medical Center 1st Fl 321 E 34th St New York NY 10016 Office Phone: 212-340-0000. Office Fax: 212-340-0035.

MELTON, ARTHUR RICHARD, public health administrator; b. Ysleta, Tex., Apr. 28, 1943; s. Francis Charles and Jean (Graham) M.; m. Frances Bay, Aug. 19, 1965; children: David Bay, Amy Elizabeth. BS, U. Utah, 1969; MPH, U. N.C., 1974, D in Pub. Health, 1976. Dir. labs. S.D. Dept. Health, Pierre, 1976-87; microbiologist Utah Dept. Health, Salt Lake City, 1970-73, dir. divsn. lab. svcs., 1987-92, dep. dir., 1992—. Mem.: Assn. State and Territorial Health Ofcls. (pres. elect 1999—2000, pres. 2000—01), SD Pub. Health Assn. (pres. 1980—81, past. pres. 2001—06), Am. Pub. Health Assn. (governing coun. 1980—83). Mem. Lds Ch. Home: 6835 Heather Way West Jordan UT 84084-2304 Office: PO Box 141000 Salt Lake City UT 84114-1000 Office Phone: 801-538-6111. Personal E-mail: dickmelton@yahoo.com. Business E-Mail: dmelton@utah.gov.

MELTON, DOUGLAS A., molecular and cell biology educator; b. Chgo., Sept. 26, 1953; m. Gail Melton; children: Sam, Emma. BS in Biology, with honors, U. Ill., Urbana-Champaign, 1975; BA in Hist. and Phil. of Sci., Cambridge U., Eng., 1977, PhD in Molecular Biology, 1980. Asst. prof, dept. bio chem. and molecular biology Harvard U., 1981—84, assoc. prof., 1984—87, J.L. Loeb assoc. prof. nat. sci., 1987, prof. dept. molecular and cellular biology Cambridge, Mass., 1988—; biologist (med.) Mass. Gen. Hosp., Boston; assoc. mem. Children's Hosp., Boston, 1994—; investigator Howard Hughes Med. Inst., 1994—; Thomas Dudley Cabot prof. Natural Sci. Harvard U., Cambridge, Mass., 1999—; co-dir. Harvard Stem Cell Inst., 2004—. Mem. sci. adv. bd. Genetics Policy Inst. Recipient Richard Lounsbery award, NAS, 1995, George Ledlie prize, 2004, Elliot P. Joslin medal; named Policy Leader of Yr., Scientific Am. mag., 2004; named an 50 Who Matter Now, Bus. 2.0, 2007; named one of The World's Most Influential People, TIME mag., 2007, 2009. Mem.: Internat. Soc. for Stem Cell Rsch. (founding mem.), Inst. Medicine. Office: Harvard Univ Dept Molecular & Cellular Bio Sherman Fairchild 7 Divinity Ave Rm 465 Cambridge MA 02138 Office Phone: 617-495-1812. Business E-Mail: dmelton@biohp.harvard.edu.

MELTON, GARY BENTLEY, psychologist, educator; b. Salisbury, NC, June 4, 1952; s. Harold Sumner Jr. and Marion Adair (Reeves) M.; m. Robin Jo Kimbrough, Aug. 7, 1999; children by previous marriage: Jennifer Lynn, Stephany Beth. BA, U. Va., 1973; MA, Boston U., 1975, PhD, 1978. Asst. prof. psychology Morehead (Ky.) State U., 1978-79, U. Va., Charlottesville, 1979-81; from asst. prof. to full prof. psychology and law U. Nebr., Lincoln, 1981-87, Carl A. Happold prof. psychology and law, 1987-94; prof. neuropsychiatry & behavioral science U. S.C., Columbia, 1994-99, adj. prof. law, pediat. and psychology, 1994-99, dir. Inst. Families in Soc., 1994-99; prof. psychology Clemson U., 1999—. Dir. Inst. Family and Neighborhood Life, Clemson U., 1999—; co-editor Am. Jour. Orthopsychiatry, 09-. Author: Child Advocacy: Psychological Issues and Interventions, 1983; co-author: Community Mental Health Centers and the Courts: An Evaluation of Community-Based Forensic Services, 1985, Psychological Evaluations for the Courts: A Handbook for Mental Health Professionals and Lawyers, 1987, 3d edit., 2007, Pediatric and Adolescent AIDS: Research Findings from the Social Sciences, 1992, Ethical and Legal Issues in AIDS Research, 1995, No Place to Go: Civil Commitment of Minors, 1998; editor numerous books. Mem. U.S. Adv. Bd. on Child Abuse and Neglect, 1989-93, vice-chair, 1991-93. Recipient Frederick Howell Lewis award Psi Chi, 1993, Lynn Stuart Weiss award Am. Psychol. Found., 2000. Fellow: APA (chmn. various coms., cert. recognition for psychology in pub. interest 1981, Disting. Contbn. to Psychology in Pub. Interest award 1985, Nicholas Hobbs award 1992, Harold Hildreth award 1992, Disting. Contbn. to Pub. Svc. award 1999, Disting. Contbn. to Internat. Advancement of Psychology award 2005); mem.: Am. Profl. Soc. on Abuse of Children (Career Achievement in Rsch. award 2005), Prevent Child Abuse Am. (Donna Stone award 1992), Am. Orthopsychiat. Assn. (pres. 2004—05, Blanche F. Ittleson award 2009), Am. Psychology-Law Soc. (pres. 1990—91). Unitarian Universalist. Office: Clemson University Ctr 225 S Pleasantburg Dr Ste B-11 Greenville SC 29607 Office Phone: 864-656-6271. Business E-Mail: gmelton@clemson.edu.

MELTON, KATHY A., medical transcription educator; b. Corpus Christi, Tex., Mar. 30, 1952; d. Thomas Rodman Smith and Dorothy Frances Hays; m. Lynn E. White (div.); children: Robert Jason White, Jerrald Martin White; m. Claude E. Melton, Jan. 21, 2005. Student, East Ctrl. State Coll., Ada, Okla., 1970—72, U. Tex., Austin, 1976—77, Houston Lighthouse for Blind, 1977—78. Med. transcriptionist Meth. Hosp., Houston, 1978—80, Cardiovascular Assoc., Athens, Tex., 1997—2002; owner, med. transcriptionist Accutrans, Houston, 1981—85; legal sec. Law Office of David Hamilton, Paris, Tex., 1986—91; receptionist Criss Cole Rehab. Ctr., Austin, 1991—94; relay agt. Relay Tex., Austin, 1994—97; owner, instr. med. transcription medtransclass.com, Enchanted Oaks, Tex., 2003—. Spkr. in field. Pres. Lake Area Coun. Blind, Athens, 1999—2003; vol. Ark. Enterprises for Blind, 1982—83; chairperson Visually Impaired Transcription Alliance, Assn. Healthcare Documentation Integrity; mem. team Walk to Emmaus, 1998—. Mem.: Assn. Healthcare Documentation Integrity, Lions Club (sec. 1987—90, bd. dirs. 1998—2002). Home and Office: 231 Cedarwood Dr Enchanted Oaks TX 75156 Office Phone: 903-451-2720. Business E-Mail: kathy@medtransclass.com.

MELTZER, ELI OWEN, allergist, immunologist, educator; BA, U. Pa., 1956—60; MD, Thomas Jefferson U., 1960—64. Diplomate Am. Bd. Pediatrics, 1969, Am. Bd. Pediatrics-pediatric allergy, 1969, Am. Bd. Allergy and Immunology, 1969. Intern mixed pediat. Michael Reese Hosp., 1964—65; resident pediat. St. Christopher's Hosp. for Children and Temple Univ., 1965—67; fellow pediatric allergy and clin. immunology Nat. Jewish Med. and Rsch. Ctr. and Univ. of Colo., 1967—69; asst. clin. prof., 1970; assoc. clin. prof., 1974; clin. prof. pediat. dept. and allergy and immunology divsn. Univ. of Calif., 1988—; instl. rev. bd. Rady Children's Hosp. and Health Ctr., 1979—92, with credentials com., 1982—89, chmn. credential com., 1984—89, sr. staff pediat. dept. and allergy divsn., with bioethics com., 1988—90, with physician well being com., 1989—, chmn. physician well being com., 1998—, with children's hosp. vol. faculty com., 2006—; clin. prof. pediat. dept. and allergy and immunology divsn. Univ. of Calif., 1988—; hosp. affiliations include Grossmont Hosp., Scripps Mercy Hosp., Sharp Meml. Hosp., US Naval Hosp. Consulting faculty Calif. Sch. of Prof. Psychology, 1978—79; reviewer Jour. of Allergy and Clin. Immunology, 1984—, Jour. of Pediat., 1986—; editl. bd. Am. Jour. of Rhinology, 1987—, New Eng. and Regional Allergy Procs., 1987—89; editl. adv. bd. Am. Jour. of Asthma & Allergy for Pediatricians, 1987—94; adjunct prof. Coll. of Health and Human Svcs. San Diego State Univ., 1988—93; reviewer Annals of Allergy, 1988—, Jour. of Respiratory Diseases, 1989—; editl. adv. bd. Clin. Advances in Allergic Disorders, 1989—91; reviewer New Eng. Jour. of Medicine, 1990—; cons. Ctr. for Behavioral Epidemiology and Cmty. Health; with pulmonary-allergy drugs adv. com. US Food and Drug Adminstrn., 1993—95; reviewer Jour. of Asthma, 1993—; cons. Ctr. for Drug Evaluation and Rsch. US Food and Drug Adminstrn., 1995—96; reviewer Am. Jour. of Medicine, 1996—, Pharmaco Economics, 1997—, Pediat., 1997—, Jour. of the Am. Med. Assn., 1998—, European Jour. of Allergy and Clin. Immunology, 2000—, Internat. Archives of Allergy and Immunology, 2006—. Co-author: (publs.) Five years survival in a child with thymic dysplasia, 1969, Therapeutic efficacy and equivalence of tablet and syrup formulations of procaterol hydrochloride in childhood asthma, 1985, Comparison of two different techniques for obtaining specimens for nasal cytology: Nose-blowing vs. nasal mucosa scraping, 1991, Mometasone furoate nasal spray reduces nighttime and early morning nasal congestion in patients with seasonal allergic rhinitis, 2010, and other numerous publications. With allergy and immunology fellowship tng. program Scripps Clinic Rsch. Found., 1987—. Lt. comdr. med. corps USNR, 1969—71. Recipient Master in Allergy, Am. Coll. of Allergy, Asthma and Immunology, 1992, Jaros Meml. Lecture, 1994, William Pierson Lecture, Am. Acad. of Allergy, Asthma and Immunology, 2000, Distinguished Clinician, 2002, Jerome Glaser Distinguished Svc., Am. Acad. of Pediat., 2003, Excellence in Patient Satisfaction, Sharp Cmty. Med. Group, 2005, Internat. Distingushed Prof., Mexican Coll. of Clin. Immunology and Allergy, 2009; named one of Best Doctors in America, Woodward-White Inc., America's Top Doctors, Castle Connolly Med. Ltd., Guide to Top Doctors, Ctr. for the Study of Svcs., America's Top Pediatrician, Consumers Rsch. Coun. of America, San Diego Best Doctors, San Diego Mag.; fellow Distinguished Fellow, Am. Coll. of Allergy, Asthma and Immunology, 1993. Fellow: Am. Coll. of Allergy, Asthma and Immunology (with ear, nose and throat com. 1987—90, rep.allergy and immunology joint coun. 1987—91, with rhinitis/rhinosinusitis com. 2003—09, with joint task force, rhinitis measures subcommittee 2007), Am. Acad. of Pediat. (with exec. com. allergy and immunology sect. 1987—90, sec., treas. allergy and immunology sect. 1989—90, with liason com. on drugs 2000—01, vis. prof. program 2000—), Am. Acad. of Allergy (with drugs/pharmacotherapeutics com. 1978—2003, with upper airways allergy com. 1982—92, with undergraduate and grad. edn.com. 1984—87, with liaison com. 1987—91, physicians and pub. svc. coun.and govs. bd. 1988—91, with prof. info. com. and pub. rels. subcommittee 1990—93, with rhinitis com. 1993—2002, with rhinosinusitis com. 1993—, with workforce com. 1994—97, chmn. workforce com. 1994—97, chmn. rhinitis com. 1996—98, with family medicine chief residents program 1996—2001, with ethics/conflict of interest com. 1997—, with advances program design com. 1998, 1998, chmn. ethics/conflict of interest com. 1999—2001, chmn.rhinosinusitis initiatives 2002—06, chmn. seminars com. 2002—06, asthma pharmacotherapeutics com. 2003—05, with seminars com. 2004—05); mem.: Greater San Diego Health Plan (allergy adv. panel 1981—88, chmn. 1985—87, with utilization review and quality assurance adv. com. 1985—87), San Diego Pulmonary Soc., San Diego Allergy Soc. (pres. 1976), San Diego County Med. Soc., Calif. Soc. of Allergy, Asthma and Clin. Immunology (exec. com. 1981—88, sec. and treas. 1984, v.p. 1985, pres. 1986), Calif. Med. Assn. (allergy sci. adv. panel 1984—87, with sci. assembly, allergy sect. 1986, program planner 1986), AMA, Assn. for the Care of Asthma, Am. Assn. of Certified Allergists, WHO, World Allergy Orgn. (with clin. trials in allergy and immunology spl. com. 2008—), Joint Coun. of Allergy, Asthma and Immunology (bd. dirs. 1987—94, pres. 1988—92). Achievements include research in Flunisolide aerosol in pediatric asthmatic patients; a long-term open tria; Terfenadine in the treatment of seasonal allergic rhinitis; A double-blind metered-dose aerosol study comparing terbutaline sulfate with isoproterenol sulfate; and other numerous research. Office: Rady Children's Hospital 3020 Children's Way San Diego CA 92123-4282 Office Phone: 858-576-1700.

MELTZER, PAUL S., geneticist, researcher; BA, Dartmouth Coll., 1967; PhD, Calif. Inst. Tech., 1972; MD, U. Tenn., 1980. Sr. genetics investigator Nat. Human Genome Rsch. Inst., Bethesda, Md.; chief Genetics Br., head molecular genetics sect. Ctr. Cancer Rsch., Nat. Cancer Inst., NIH, Bethesda. Office: Nat Cancer Inst Bldg 37, Rm 6138 37 Convent Dr, MSC 4265 Bethesda MD 20892 Office Phone: 301-496-5266. Office Fax: 301-402-3241. E-mail: pmeltzer@mail.nih.gov. *

MELUZÍN, JAROSLAV, cardiologist; b. Brno, Czech Republic, Feb. 24, 1955; s. Jaroslav and Marta (Součková) M.; m. Hana Kalová, Aug. 1, 1962; children: Martin, Petr. MD, Masaryk's U., Brno, 1980, PhD, 1991. Asst. prof. Masaryk's U., 1986-96, assoc. prof., 1996-2001, chief echocardiographic lab. 1st internal dept., 1998—, prof. internal medicine, 2001—. Contbr. articles to profl. jours. Fellow:

European Soc. Cardiology (working group on echocardiography 1997—). Office: St Anna Hosp Internal Dept Pekařská 53 656 91 Brno Czech Republic Office Phone: 420-5-4318-2224. Business E-Mail: jaroslav.meluzin@fnusa.cz.

MELVILLE, DAVID MURRAY, surgeon; b. Epsom, Surrey, United Kingdom, Oct. 2, 1953; s. John Murray Melville and Joan Cook; m. Sarah Anne Taylor; children: John Edward, Mary Diana, Francis David, Luke. BS, MB, MS, DM, Oxford U. Surgeon St Georges Hosp., London, 1990—2005. Master: Clin. Sect. of Royal Soc. Medicine. (pres. 2005—); fellow: Royal Coll. Surgeons Eng. Achievements include research in papers on Ulcerative Colitis and other intestinal disorders. Home: 18 Caroline Pl London W2 4AN England Office: St Georges Hosp Blackshaw Rd London SW17 0QT England Office Fax: 442087120115; Home Fax: 442087250115. E-mail: david@melville.clara.co.uk.

MELVIN, JOHN LEWIS, physical and rehabilitation physician, educator, administrator; b. Columbus, Ohio, May 26, 1935; s. John Harper and Ruth Eleanor (Wertenberger) M.; m. Carol Ann Pate, Apr. 10, 1991; children from a previous marriage: Megan Marie, Beth Anne, John Patrick, Mia Michelle. BS, Ohio State U., 1955, MD, 1960, M in Med. Sci., 1966. Rotating Intern Mt. Carmel Hosp., Columbus, 1960—61; resident in phys. medicine U. Hosp. Columbus, 1961, 1963—66; asst. prof. Ohio State U., Columbus, 1966—69, assoc. prof., 1969—73; prof., chmn. dept. Med. Coll. Wis., Milw., 1973—91; prof., dep. chmn. dept Temple U., Phila., 1992—98; v.p. med. affairs Moss Rehab. Hosp., Phila., 1991—2002; dept. chmn. Einstein Medical Ctr., Phila., 1991—2002; Michie prof., dept. chmn. rehab. medicine Thomas Jefferson U., 1998—. Contbr. articles to profl. journals; cons. to numerous U.S. govtl. agys., health care insts.; lectr. in field; research assoc. Ohio State Research Found., Columbus, 1966-68; assoc. coordinator Ohio State Regional Med. Program, Columbus, 1969-71; med. dir. Curative Rehab. Ctr., Milw., 1973-91. Bd. dirs. Vis. Nurses Assn., Milw., 1974-83; mem. com. Mental Health Planning Council, Milw., 1974-75, Wis. Council Devel. Disabilities, Madison, 1979-80; mem. planning and evaluation com. Elizabethtown Hosp. for Children and Youth, Pa., 1977; advisor Nat. Multiple Sclerosis Soc., Milw., 1979-87; mem. Wis. Nicaragua Ptnrs., 1982-91; trustee Easter Seal Research Found., vice chmn., 1985, chmn. 1986-88. Served to capt. M.C. US Army, 1961—63. Recipient cert. of appreciation Goodwill Industries, 1972, spl. recognition award Commn. Accreditation Rehab. Facilities, 1977, Performance award Wood VA Med. Ctr., 1978, Goldschmidt award Nat. Rehab. Hosp., 1990, cert. of appreciation Jour. Rehab. Adminstrn., 1982, Alumni Achievement award Ohio State U., 1985; grantee Rehab. Svcs. Adminstrn., 1979-91, Health Care Financing Adminstrn., 1984-85; Ford Found. fellow, 1951-53. Fellow Am. Acad. Cerebral Palsy and Devel. Medicine, Am. Acad. Phys. Medicine and Rehab. (bd. dirs. 1992-2000, pres. 1999, Zeiter Lectr. award 1987, Krusen award 2000, Disting. Mem. award 2007); mem. Am. Bd. Phys. Medicine and Rehab. (Diplomate, chmn. 1988-93, chmn. residency Rev. Com. 1985-88), Am. Bd. Med. Specialists (exec. com. 1990-92), Med. Soc. Milw. 1973-1991, Milw. Acad. Medicine 1979-1991, Wis. Soc. Phys. Medicine and Rehab. 1973-1991, Am. Assn. Electromyography and Electrodiagnosis (pres. 1979-80, Lifetime Achievement award 2007), Am. Congress Rehab. Medicine (pres. 1987-88, gold medal 1971, 78, Gold Key award 1988, Edward Lowman award 1997), Am. Heart Assn., Am. Hosp. Assn. (sect. rehab. hosp., chmn. 1981), AMA (cert. of appreciation 1976, 82), Am. Paraplegia Soc., Assn. Acad. Physiatrists (pres. 1985-87, Disting. Mem. award 2003), Internat. Fedn. Phys. Medicine and Rehab. (exec. com. 1980-1999, hon. sec. 1980-88, pres. elect 1995-99), Internat. Rehab. Medicine Assn. (bd. dirs. 1992-99), Internat. Soc. Phys. and Rehab. Med. (pres. 1999-2002, Flax Lifetime Achievement award 2005), Rehab. Internat. Med. Comm. 1985-1995, Nat. Assn. Rehab. Facilities (pres. 1981-83, bd. dirs.), Coun. of Med. Splty. Socs. (pres. 1989-90), Found. for Phys. Med. and Rehab. (pres. 2005-07), Alpha Omega Alpha, Delta Chi Fraternity-Internat. Hdqs. (Disting. award, 1997, Delta Chi of Yr., 1999). Office: Thomas Jefferson Univ Dept Rehab Med 25 S 9th St Philadelphia PA 19107-5098 Home Phone: 215-238-9708; Office Phone: 215-955-6574. Office Fax: 215-955-2311. Business E-Mail: John.melvin@jefferson.edu.

MELZACK, RONALD, psychology professor; b. Montreal, Que., Can., July 19, 1929; s. Joseph and Annie (Mandel) M.; m. Lucy Birch, Aug. 7, 1960; children: Lauren, Joel. BSc, McGill U., Montreal, 1950, MSc, 1951, PhD, 1954; DLitt (hon.), U. Waterloo, 1992; DLaws (hon.), Dalhousie U., 2004. Lectr. Univ. Coll., London, 1957-58; assoc. prof. MIT, 1959-63; lectr. psychology McGill U., 1953-54, prof., 1963—, E.P. Taylor prof., 1986. Author: The Day Tuk Became a Hunter, and Other Eskimo Stories, 1967, Raven, Creator of the World, 1970, The Puzzle of Pain, 1973, Why the Man in the Moon is Happy, and Other Eskimo Creation Stories, 1977; author: (with P.D. Wall) The Challenge of Pain, 1982, 2d edit., 1996, 3rd edit., 2008; author: Pain Measurement and Assessment, 1983; author: (with P.D. Wall) Textbook of Pain, 1984, 4th edit., 1999; author: (with D.C. Turk) Handbook of Pain Assessment, 1999, with D.C. Turk: 3rd edit., 2011;; author: (with P.D. Wall) Handbook of Pain Management, 2003. Decorated Officer, Order of Can., 1995, Order of Quebec, 2000; recipient Molson prize Can. Coun., 1985, Gaston Labat award Am. Soc. Regional Anesthesia, 1989, J.J. Bonica award VI World Congress on Pain, 1990, Prix du Que. Marie-Victorin, 1994, Disting. Contbn. award, Can. Pain Soc., 1995, Rsch. Recognition award, Canadian Anesthesiology Soc., 1997, Janet Travell award Am. Acad. Pain Mgmt., 1997, Killam prize, 2001; named to Can. Med. Hall of Fame, 2009, Grawemeyer award, 2010 Fellow APA, AAAS, Royal Soc. Can., Can. Psychol. Assn. (Disting. Contbns. to Psychol. Sci. award 1986, hon. pres. 1988-89, gold medal award 2002); mem. Internat. Assn. Study of Pain (past pres.). Home: 7400 Côte Saint Luc Rd Apt 528 Montreal PQ Canada H4W 3J4 Home Phone: 514-342-3283; Office Phone: 514-398-6084. Business E-Mail: rmelzack@mcgill.ca.

MELZER, PETER, neuroanatomist, educator, research scientist; b. Frankfurt am Main, Hesse, Germany, Dec. 9, 1954; m. Thao Phuong Dang, Mar. 17, 1965; children: Audrey children: Henry. PhD, Johann Wolfgang Goethe U., Frankfurt am Main, 1986. Rsch. fellow NIMH, Bethesda, Md., 1989—92, rsch. assoc., 1992—94; rsch. asst. prof. dept. psychology Vanderbilt U., Nashville, 1996—2006; cons. Brain and Mind Inst., Nashville, 2006—. Fogarty fellow, 1989. Mem.: Soc. Neurosci. Home and Office: 109 Woodstock Dr Charlottesville VA 22901 Office Phone: 615-509-6301. Business E-Mail: peter.melzer@brainmindinst.com.

MEMIK, FARUK, gastroenterologist, educator; b. Istanbul, Turkey, Mar. 3, 1938; s. Ali and Fatma M.; m. Oya Kahyaoglu, Feb. 26, 1970; children: Osman, Hakan. MD, Istanbul U., 1962. Intern Kenmore Mercy Hosp., Buffalo, 1963-64; resident in internal medicine Middlesex Gen. Hosp., New Brunswick, N.J., 1964-65, Baroness Erlanger Hosp., Chattanooga, 1965-67; fellow Lahey Clinic, Boston, 1967-68; asst. to assoc. prof. Atatürk U. Med. Sch., Erzurum, Turkey, 1968—79; prof. medicine Uludag U. Med. Sch., Bursa, Turkey, 1979—. Chmn. dept. internal medicine Uludag U. Med. Sch., Bursa, 1981—, head dept. gastroenterology, 1982—, vice-dean, 1991-93; sec. gen. World Inst. Ecology and Cancer, Long Beach, Calif., 1995—. Co-editor: Hepato Gastroenterology, 1994-09; mem. editl. bd. Turkish Jour. Gastroenterolepatology, 1993, Turkish Jour. Endoscopy, 1994, Viral Hepatitis Jour.; contbr. articles to profl. jours. Lt. Turkish Army, 1974-76. Recipient Knight award Ecology and Cancer Inst., Brussels, 1989. Mem. Turkish Soc. Gastroenterology (pres. 1970-), Internat. Gastrosurg. Club. Avocations: hunting, fishing, photography, outdoors. Home: Tilkikaya 15 Çekirge Uludag Yolu Bursa Turkey Office: Uludag U Med Sch Görükle Dept Internal Medicine Kampüs Turkey Personal E-mail: memikf@gmail.com.

MEMON, ABDUL SATTAR, dean; b. Badin, Jan. 27, 1953; MBBS, U. Sindh, 1976. Prof., surgery and cons. Liaquat U. Med. & Health Scis., Jamshoro, 1999—, dean, 2008—. Fellow: ACS, Coll. Physicians and Surgeons Bangladesh, Coll. Physicians and Surgeons Pakistan, Internat. Coll. Surgeons. Office: Dept Surgery and Allied Scis Liaquat University Hyderabad Sindh 71000 Pakistan Office Fax: 92-22-3860057.

MENA, IGNACIO, medical researcher; b. Vigo, Spain, July 15, 1967; BSc in Biology, U. Santiago Compostela, Spain, 1990; PhD in Molecular Biology, U. Autonoma Madrid, 1996. Postdoc Scripps Rsch. Inst., La Jolla, 1996—99, Inst. Pasteur, Paris, 2000—03, Mt. Sinai Sch. Medicine, NYC, 2011—; postdoc rschr. Ramon Y Cajal, Ctr. Investigación en Sanidad Animal, Valdeolmos, Madrid, 2003—11. Grant, Spanish Ministry of Sci., Posdoc. fellowship, EMBO, Fundacion Ramon Areces, Spain, Assn. pour la Recherce sur le Cancer, France. Avocations: Judo, Aikido, birdwatching. Office: 1468 Madison Ave New York NY 10029 Business E-Mail: gmena@inia.es.

MENAKER, MICHAEL, biology professor; b. Vienna, May 19, 1934; came to U.S., 1934; s. William and Esther (Astin) M.; m. Shirley Ann Lasch, June 4, 1955(dec. 2004); children: Ellen Margaret, Nicholas; m. Kazuko Watanabe, 2010. BA in Biology, Swarthmore Coll., 1955; PhD in Biology, Princeton U., 1960; PhD in Math. and Natural Sci. (hon.), U. Groningen, Netherlands, 2009. Asst. instr. Princeton (N.J.) U., 1955-57; postdoctoral fellow Harvard U., Cambridge, Mass., 1960-62; asst. prof. zoology U. Tex.-Austin, 1962-68, assoc. prof., 1968-72, prof., 1972-79; prof. biology U. Oreg., Eugene, 1979-86, dir. interdisciplinary program for neuroscis, 1979-81, dir. Inst. Neurosci., 1981-85; Commonwealth prof. biology U. Va., Charlottesville, 1987—, chmn. dept., 1987-93; dir. Howard Hughes Undergrad. Rsch. Program in Biol. Sci., Charlottesville, 1989-94; core investigator Sci. and Tech. Ctr. in Biol. Timing U. Va., Charlottesville, 1991—. Benjamin Meaker vis. prof. U. Bristol, Eng., 1986. Assoc. editor Behavioral Neurosci., Jour. Biol. Rhythms; contbr. articles to profl. jours. Recipient Lifetime Achievement award Am. Soc. for Photobiology, 2002, Life Achievement in Sci. award Va.'s Outstanding Scientists and Industrialists, 2003, Peter C. Farrell prize Sleep Medicine, 2007, Disting. Scientist award U. Va., 2009; NSF fellow, 1958-59, 60-62; NIH fellow, 1960-62; Guggenheim Found. fellow, 1971-72, ASCHOFF HONMA prize, Biol. Rhythm Rsch., 2009, Fellow AAAS, Am. Acad. Arts and Scis., Japan Soc. Promotion of Scis. (sr.); mem. Soc. Neuroscis., Am. Physiol. Soc., Soc. Rsch. Biol. Rhythms. Avocations: literature, music, sailing. Office: U Va Dept Biology Gilmer Hall PO Box 400328 Charlottesville VA 22904-4328 Office Phone: 434-982-5767. Business E-Mail: mm7e@virginia.edu.

MENASCHÉ, PHILIPPE, cardiovascular surgeon; MD, PhD, U. Paris. Chief, cardiac surgery unit, dir. cell therapy Hospital European George Pompidou, Paris. Mem., med. adv. bd. Regado Biosciences, Inc., Basking Ridge, NJ; prof., Thoracic and Cardiovascular Surgery U. Paris Descartes, France. Bd. dirs. Nat. Inst. of Health and Med. Rsch. (INSERM). Office: 20 Rue Leblanc Paris 75015 France Office Phone: 33 1 56 09 3622. Office Fax: 33 1 56 09 2219. E-mail: philippe.menasche@hop.egp.ap-hop-paris.fr. *

MENDELS, JOSEPH, psychiatrist, educator; b. Cape Town, South Africa, Oct. 29, 1937; came to U.S., 1964; s. Max and Lily (Turecki) M.; m. Ora Kark, Jan. 22, 1960; children: Gilla Avril, Charles Alan, David Ralph. MB, BChir, U. Cape Town, 1960; MD, U. Witwatersrand, Johannesburg, South Africa, 1965. Asst. prof., assoc. prof. psychiatry and pharmacology U. Pa., Phila., 1967-73; prof. U. Pa. and VA Hosp., Phila., 1973-80; med. dir. Fairmount Inst., Phila., 1980-81; hon. prof. psychiatry and human behavior Thomas Jefferson Med. Ctr., 1985—; med. dir. Med. Inst., Phila., 1981-95, Therapeutics PC, Phila., 1981-98. Cons., lectr. in field. Author, editor: Concepts of Depression, 1971, Biological Psychiatry, 1973, Psychobiology of Affective Disorders, 1981; contbr. over 200 articles to med. jours. Fellow Internat. Coll. Neuropsychopharmacology, Am. Coll. Neuropsychopharmacology. Home: 655 Longboot Club Rd #12A Longboat Key FL 34228 Personal E-mail: jos737@mac.com.

MENDELSOHN, FREDERICK ARTHUR, biomedical scientist, physiologist; b. Melbourne, Australia, June 19, 1942; s. Oscar Adolf and Edna Millward (Smale) Mendelsohn; m. Carole Ann Ferguson, Jan. 12, 1967 (div. Nov. 1978); children: Benjamin, David, Thomas; m. Jeannette Milgrom, July 11, 1980 (div. May 1, 2008); children: Natalie, Joshua. BS, MB, Melbourne U., 1965, MD, 1973, PhD, 1972. Resident med. officer Royal Melbourne Hosp., 1966-68; postgrad. med. scholar dept. medicine U. Melbourne, 1969; hon. physician Austin Hosp. & Royal Women's Hosp., Carlton, Australia, 1971; Nuffield Found. traveling med. fellow Middlesex Hosp. Med. Sch., London, 1972-73; Nat. Heart Found. Australia Overseas Med. rsch. fellow, U. Munich Physiologische Inst., Germany, 1974-75; sr. physician Austin Hosp., 1977; asst. dept. medicine U. Melbourne, 1977-81, reader in medicine, 1981-90, personal chair faculty of medicine, 1990-96, R.D. Wright prof. exptl. physiology & medicine, 1997—2009, dir. Howard Florey Inst. Exptl. Physiology & Medicine, 1996—2009. Vis. sci. endocrinology & reprodn. rsch. br. Nat. Inst. Child Health & Human Devel., NIH, Bethesda, Md., 1981—82. Decorated officer Order of Australia. Fellow: Australia Acad. Sci., Royal Australasian Coll. Physicians; mem.: Australian Soc. Neurosci., Soc. Neurosci., Endocrine Soc. Office: Howard Florey Institute C/ University of Melbourn Parkville 3010 Australia Business E-Mail: faom@florey.edu.au.

MENDELSOHN, JANIS S., pediatrician, educator; b. Fort Smith, Ark., Aug. 02; MD, U. Tenn., 1967. Cert. Pediat., 1973. Intern genetics Children's Meml. Hosp., Chgo., 1968—69, resident, 1969—71, fellowship; pediatrician U. Chgo. Med. Ctr., 1972—; assoc. prof. pediat. U. Chgo. Mem.: Am. Acad. Pediat., Chgo. Pediat. Soc. Office: Ctr Advanced Medicine 5841 S Maryland Ave, MC 1057 Chicago IL 60637 Office Phone: 773-702-6169, 773-834-3862, 773-834-3826. E-mail: jmendels@peds.bsd.uchicago.edu.

MENDELSOHN, JOHN, oncologist, hematologist, educator, medical researcher; b. Cin., Aug. 31, 1936; s. Joe and Sarah (Feibel) M.; m. Anne Charles, June 23, 1962; children: John Andrew, Jeffrey Charles, Eric Robert. BA in BioChemical Sciences, Harvard U., 1958, MD, 1963. Diplomate Am. Bd. Internal Medicine, Am. Bd. Hematology, Am. Bd. Med. Oncology. Intern, resident Peter Bent Brigham Hosp., Boston, 1963-65, 67-68; fellow in hematology Washington U. Sch. Medicine, St. Louis, 1968-70; asst. prof. to prof. medicine U. Calif., San Diego, 1970-85, Am. Cancer Soc. prof. clin. oncology La Jolla, 1982-85, dir. Cancer Ctr., 1977-85; prof. medicine, vice-chmn. Cornell U. Med. Coll., NYC, 1985-96; Winthrop Rockefeller chmn. dept. medical oncology, co-head, molecular pharmacology and therapeutics program Meml. Sloan Kettering Cancer Ctr., NYC, 1985-96; pres., prof. medicine U. Tex. M.D. Anderson Cancer Ctr., Houston, 1996—2011, co-dir. Sheikh Khalifa Bin Zayed Al Nahyan Inst. for Personalized Cancer Therapy, 2011—; vice chmn. BioHouston, 2001—. Bd. sci. counselors Nat. Cancer Inst., 1986—90, 1996—2001; cons., mem. sci. adv. bd. Progenics Pharms.; founder, 1st dir. U. Calif. San Diego Cancer Ctr.; mem. Nat. Dialogue on Cancer, 1999, Team on Cancer Rsch., 2001, U. Calif. San Diego External Adv. Com., 2000, Gov.'s Biotech. Panel, Ctr. for Houston's Future; mem. external adv. bd. John Hopkins Oncology Ctr., 1993—; faculty U. Tex. Graduate Sch. Biomedical Sciences. Editor-in-chief: (textbook) The Molecular Basis of Cancer; mem. editl. bd. Growth Factors, Jour. Biol. Response Modifiers, Expert Rev. Anticancer Therapy; editor-in-chief Clin. Cancer Rsch.; founding editor Clin. Cancer Rsch.; contbr. articles to profl. jours. Mem. Gov.'s Cancer Coun., Calif., 1981—85; bd. dirs. Am. Cancer Soc., San Diego, 1981—85, Houston Grand Opera, BioHouston, Ctr. for Houston's Future, Houston Forum; bd. dirs., mem. healthcare task force Greater Houston Partnership, 1997; bd. dirs., mem. exec. com. Houston Tech. Ctr., 1998—, nat. cancer policy bd., 1999—; mem. bd. overseers Harvard Med. Sch.; trustee Houston Grand Opera. Recipient Bourgine award for excellence in cancer rch., Svc. d'Oncologie Med. Pitie-Saltpetriere, 1997, Jill Rose award for oustanding breast cancer rsch., Breast Cancer Rsch. Found., 1999, Gold medal of Paris, 1997, Cancer Rsch. award, Bristol-Myers Squibb, 1997, Joseph H. Burchenal Clin. Rsch. award, Am. Assn. for Cancer Rsch., 1999, Simon Shubitz prize, Univ. Chgo., 2002, David A. Karnofsky award, Am. Soc. of Clin. Oncology, 2002, Freedom to Discover Achievement award in Cancer, Bristol-Myers Squibb, 2004; named Headliner of Yr. in Medicine, San Diego, 1985; Fulbright scholar, U. Glasgow, Scotland, 1958—59. Mem.: ACP, AAAS (electorate nominating com. sect. on med. scis. 2001), Am. Clin. and Climatol. Assn., Harvard Overseers' Com., Royal Netherlands Acad. Arts and Scis., Inst. Medicine U.S. NAS, Century Assn., Am. Soc. Hematology, Am. Assn. Cancer Rsch. (4th Joseph H. Burchenal award 1999), Am. Soc. Clin. Oncology (lectr., David A. Karnofsky award 2002), Am. Soc. Clin. Investigation, Assn. Am. Physicians, Phi Beta Kappa. Achievements include rsch. in establishing inhibition of tumor growth by antibodies against growth factor receptors. Office: University of Texas MD Anderson Cancer Center 1515 Holcombe Blvd # 91 Houston TX 77030-4009 E-mail: jmendelsohn@mdanderson.org. *

MENDELSON, JOEL STUART, allergist, immunologist; b. Bklyn., Nov. 2, 1956; BS, Bklyn. Coll., 1978; MD, U. Ctrl. East Dominican Rep., 1982. Diplomate Am. Bd. Allergy/Immunology, Am. Bd. Pediatrics, Am. Bd. Pediatric Infectious Diseases. Pres. pediatrics St. Lukes Roosevelt Med. Ctr./Columbia U., NYC, 1982-85; fellow allergy, immunology and infectious disease U. Med. and Dentistry N.J., Newark, 1985-87; asst. dir. dept. allergy and immunology Childrens Hosp. N.J., Newark, 1987-88; dir. dept. allergy and immunology Beth Israel Med. Ctr., Newark, 1992—; asst. prof. pediat. St. George U. Med. Sch. Cons. in field. Contbr. articles to profl. jours. Fellow Am. Acad. Allergy and Immunology, Am. Coll. Allergy and Immunology, Am. Acad. Pediatrics; mem. Infectious Disease Soc. N.J. Home: 17 Dartmouth Rd Cranford NJ 07016-1651 Office Phone: 908-233-4477. Personal E-mail: jmendelsonmd@msn.com.

MENDELSON, NEIL H., microbial geneticist, educator; b. NYC, Nov. 15, 1937; s. Michael and Rose (Kutner) M.; m. Joan F. Rintel, July 30, 1959; children: Debora C., Marie D. BS, Cornell U., 1959; PhD, Ind. U., 1964. Postdoctoral fellow microbial genetics rsch. unit Med. Rsch. Coun., Hammersmith Hosp., London, 1965-66; asst. prof. U. Md., Catonsville, 1967-69; assoc. prof. U. Ariz., Tucson, 1969-72, prof., 1972—; prof. emeritus, 2004. Vis. prof. Inst. Pasteur, Paris, 1976-77; vis. scientist Cambridge (Eng.) U., 1984, 91. Author: Collected Papers of Neil. H. Mendelson, 2004, Perfect Mistakes, 2005, Biomimetic Art by and from the Science of Neil Mendelson, 2010, Just Suppose Ideas and Images Neil Mendelson, 2011; (biomimetic artist) Gallery Show, Two Visions of Nature, Studio Viva, Ashland, Oreg., 2008, represented in exhbn. Madrone Kitchen & Wine Tavern, Shady Cove, Oreg., 2010; contbr. over 80 articles to scholarly and profl. jours. Contrebassist So. Ariz. Symphony Orch., Tucson, 1979—, pres., 1983-86, 90-93. Recipient Rsch. Career Devel. award Nat. Inst. Gen. Med. Sci., 1973-77, J.A. Shannon Dir.'s award Nat. Ctr. for Rsch. Resources NIH, 1992; N.H. Mendelson Collection named in his honor Am. Heritage Ctr., U. Wyo., 1986—2011. Fellow AAAS, Am. Acad. Microbiology; mem. Cosmos. Jewish. Achievements include discovery of bacterial macrofibers, producer of bacterial thread and related bionites; invention of helix clock theory. Office: U Ariz Molecular & Cellular Biology LSS Bldg Tucson AZ 85721-0106 Business E-Mail: nhm@u.arizona.edu.

MENDES, MARCIO HENRIQUE, ophthalmologist; Degree, U. Taubaté, 2002; PhD student, U. São Paulo. Physician U. São Paulo, 2009—. Mem.: Alumini Cmty. Harvard Med. Sch., Brazilian Coun. Ophthalmology. Avocations: surfing, tennis, motorcycling. Office: Barata Ribeiro 380 Conjunto 36 São Paulo 01308-000 Brazil Personal E-mail: marciohmendes@yahoo.com.br.

MENDES, MEHMET, agricultural studies educator; b. Elazig, Jan. 10, 1972; Degree, Canakkale Onsekiz Mart U., Turkey, 1995. Agrl. faculty mem. dept. biometry & genetic Canakkale Onsekiz Mart U., 2002. Office: Canakkale Onsekiz Mart University Canakkale 9016100 Turkey Business E-Mail: mmendes@comu.edu.tr.

MENDEZ-NAVARRO, JORGE, gastroenterologist; b. Mex. City, Aug. 2, 1971; MD, La Salle U., 1996; degree in Gastroenterology, Endoscopy, U. Nat. Autónoma México, 2003. Gastroenterologist, staff, gastroenterology dept. Nat. Med. Ctr. Siglo XXI, IMSS, 2004—, clin. coord., gastrointestinal fellow, 2004—11, co-investigator clin. protocols, 2005—11; postdoc. rsch. fellow Mass. Gen. Hosp., 2008—10. Assoc. prof. gastroenterology Nat. Autonomous U. Mex., 2007—11. Recipient 1st Pl., Gen. Hosp. No. 1, San Luis Potosi, IMSS, Outstanding Recognition award, Ministry of Health, Morelos, Mex. Mem.: Mexican Gastroent. Assn., Mexican Assn. Hepatology. Avocations: music, movies. Home: Ave Buenavista 17 Casa 11 Col Pueblo Mexico City 10640 Mexico Home Fax: 52 55 56 60 65 78. Personal E-mail: jmndoc@yahoo.com.

MENDIRATTA, DEEPAK KUMAR, microbiologist, educator; b. Agra, India, Oct. 30, 1952; MBBS, Govt. Med. Coll., Patiala, Punjab, 1977, MD in Med. Microbiology, 1984. Cons., tchr. Mahatma Gandhi Inst. Med. Scis., 1991, prof., head, 2002—. Mem.: Hosp. Infection Soc. (India), Indian Soc. Antibiotic & Chemotherapy, Soc. India Human and Animal Mycologists, Indian Assn. Med. Microbiologists (State chpt., treas., Presdl. Oration award, Hardas Pathak award). Office: Dept Microbiology Mahatma Gandhi Inst Med Scis Sevagram Wardha Maharashtra 442102 India Office Phone: 91-7152-284341 ext 325. Office Fax: 917152284333. Personal E-mail: dkmendiratta@rediffmail.com. E-mail: deepakmendiratta@rediffmail.com.

MENDONÇA, LUCIANA DE MICHELIS, psychotherapist, educator; b. Belo Horizonte, Minas Gerais, Brazil, Dec. 25, 1979; Degree in Physiotherapy, U. Fed. Minas Gerais, 2003, attending, 2011. Prof. Inst. Superior Ciências Saúde, 2006—; physiotherapist Confederação Brasileira Voleibol, 2007, Clube Atlético Mineiro, 2009. Sub-coord., rschr. Lab. Prevenção Reabilitação Lesões Esportivas, 2003—; prof. U. Fed. Minas Gerais - Especialização em Fisioterapia Esportiva, 2010—. Mem.: Academia Brasileira Ciências Médicas Chinesas, Inst. Brasileiro Ciências Esporte, Soc. Nat. Fisioterapia Esportiva. Avocations: martial arts, travel. Office: Ave Presidente Antônio Carlos 6627 Belo Horizonte Minas Gerais 31270-901 Brazil Office Fax: 55 3134092325.

MENDOZA-CARRERA, FRANCISCO, research scientist; b. Villahermosa, Tabasco, Mex., Dec. 30, 1975; Degree in Chemistry, Pharm. Biology, U. Guadalajara, 1999, D in Human Genetics, 2005—05. Associated rschr. Mexican Inst. Social Security, 2005—. Recipient award, Consejo Nat. De Ciencia Tech., Mexican Inst. Social Security; grant, Pedro Sarquis Merrewe Found., Fundación Mexicana para la Salud, Capítulo Jalisco, 2006, Fund. Mexicana para la Salud, 2009. Office: Sierra Mojada 800 Guadalajara Jalisco 44340 Mexico Office Fax: 52 33 36181756. Business E-Mail: francisco.mendozac@imss.gob.mx.

MENEGHINI, LUIGI F., endocrinologist, educator; b. Italy, Apr. 14, 1963; MD, Emory U., 1988; MBA in Healthcare Adminstrn., U. Miami, 2000. Asst. prof. clin. medicine U. Miami Miller Sch. Medicine, 1993—2000, dir., Kosow Diabetes Treatment Ctr., Diabetes Rsch. Inst., 1999—2011, assoc. prof. clin. medicine, 2000—10, prof. clin. medicine, 2010—. Assoc. dir. clin. affairs Diabetes Rsch. Inst., 2001—11; dir., sci. adv. bd. NIPRO Sys., 2004—07; mem. Blue Cross Blue Shield Recognizing Physician Excellence Clin. Adv. Group, 2006—08; program dir., Southeastern Fla. Regional Diabetes Program U. Miami, 2008—11, chair, Continuing Med. Edn. Adv. Com., 2010—11. Recipient Physician's Recognition award, AMA; named Hon. Citizen of Cartagena de Indias, City of Cartagena, Columbia; named one of Best Drs. in America, Castle Connolly Med. Ltd., Best Drs. in America, Inc. Mem.: Am. Assn. Clin. Endocrinologists, European Assn. Study of Diabetes, Am. Diabetes Assn. (Physician's Recognition award). Avocations: languages, winemaking, sports. Office: 1450 NW 10th Ave Miami FL 33136 Office Fax: 305-243-1200. Business E-Mail: lmeneghi@med.miami.edu.

MENELL, JILL SUZANNE, pediatrician; b. NJ, Nov. 26, 1961; BA, Boston U., 1983; MD, SUNY Downstate, 1987. Chief, pediat. hematology, oncology St. Joseph's Children's Hosp., Paterson, NJ, 1999—. Pediat. med. dir. Butterflies Pediat. Palliative Home Care Program, Valley Home Care, Paramus, NJ, 1999—. Mem.: Am. Soc. Hematology, Am. Soc. Pediat. Hematology/Oncology. Office: 703 Main St Xavier 7 Paterson NJ 07503 Office Fax: 973-754-3331. Business E-Mail: menellj@sjhmc.org.

MENENDEZ, JORGE, plastic surgeon; Grad., Southwestern Med. Sch., Dallas. Lic. Tex., Conn., cert. NY. Gen. surgery tng. Parkland Meml. Hosp., Dallas; tng. plastic surgery Mt. Sinai Med. Ctr., NYC; asthetic & craniofacial surgery externship Paris; fellowship in asthetic & craniofacial surgery Internat. Asthetic & Craniofacial Inst., Dallas; asst. attending surgeon plastic surgery dept. Manhattan Eye, Ear and Throat Hosp.; cons. to skincare companies. Mem. Interplast Inc. Office: The Aesthetic Plastic Surgery Center Ste 210 7744 Broadway San Antonio TX 78209 Office Phone: 210-829-7411. Office Fax: 210-829-7899.

MENÉNDEZ, JOSÉ CARLOS, chemical and medical educator, researcher; b. Madrid, June 25, 1960; s. Carlos Menéndez and Mercedes Ramos; m. María Antonia Martín, Dec. 1, 1990; children: Miguel, Pilar. Degree in Pharmacy, U. Complutense, Madrid, 1982, PharmD, 1988; degree in Chemistry, Faculty Ciencias, UNED, Madrid, 1986. Cert. drug analysis specialist Min. Edn. Ciencia, 2002. Prof. ayudante U. Complutense, 1987—89, prof. titular, 1989—2010, prof., 2010, head microanalysis ctrl. svc, 1994; academic visitor Imperial Coll., London, 1988—89; vis. prof. U. Aix-Marseille III, Provence, France, 2007—07. Contbr. articles to profl. jours, chapters to books. Mem. Bd. Experts Chem. Nomenclature, Spanish Pharmacopeia, Madrid, 1995—2005. Recipient Premio FAES award, Real Acad. Farmacia, 1986, Premio Santos Ruiz award, 1988, Premio Carlos Castillo leiva, 2008. Fellow: Real Acad. Farmacia (académico corr. 2004—, award 2004); mem.: Soc. Española Química Terapéutica, Am. Chem. Soc. Roman Catholic. Home: Lérida 9 Madrid 28020 Spain Office: Univ Complutense Facultad Farmacia 28040 Madrid Spain Office Fax: 34-91-3941822. Business E-Mail: josecm@farm.ucm.es.

MENG, QUANFEI, radiologist, educator; b. Jiangxi, China, Dec. 4, 1945; MD, Med. Coll. Beijing U., 1969. Prof. dept. radiology First Hosp., Sun Yat-Sen U., 1995—97, prof., head dept. radiology, 1997—2005, prof., dir. dept. radiology, 2005—. Recipient Gold Pen award, Chinese Jour. Radiology. Fellow: Chinese Med. Assn. (vice chief editor Chinese jour. radiology 2010—); mem.: Chinese Soc. Radiology (vice chmn. 2008—), Internat. Skeletal Soc., RSNA. Avocations: photography, travel. Office: 58 Second Zhongshan Rd Guangzhou Guangdong 510080 China Business E-Mail: cjr.mengquanfei@vip.163.com.

MENGHI, CLAUDIA IRENE, medical educator, researcher; d. Humberto Raimundo Menghi and Nelly Mirta Russo. PhD in Biochemistry, Faculty Pharmacy & Biochemistry, U. Buenos Aires, Argentina, 1981. Tchr. and rschr., parasitology divsn. U. Buenos Aires, 1982—. Editor, staff Assn. Argentina de Microbiologia, Buenos Aires, 2007—. Achievements include research in investigations on transmission of dientamoeba fragilis. Office: Univ Buenos Aires Parasitology AV Cordoba 2351 Buenos Aires Buenos Aires Argentina Business E-Mail: cmenghi@fibertel.com.ar.

MENICK, FREDERICK J., plastic surgeon; b. July 20, 1945; Grad. in Biology, Fordham Coll., NYC, 1966; MD, Yale Med. Sch., New Haven, Conn., 1970. Cert. Am. Bd. Plastic Surgery, lic. Nat. Bd. Med. Examiners, NY, Ariz. Bd. Med. Examiners, Calif. Bd. Med. Quality Assurance, Ark. State Bd. Intern Stanford Med. Ctr., Palo Alto, Calif., 1970—71, resident, gen. surgery, 1974—75, United Hosp., Port Chester, NY, 1974, U. Ariz. Health Scis. Ctr., Tucson, 1975—79, chief resident, 1977—79; resident, plastic surgery U. Calif., Irvine, 1979—81, chief resident, 1980—81; fellowship, aesthetic plastic surgery of the face Bruce F. Connell, MD, Santa Ana, Calif., 1981; reconstructive plastic surgery, sr. house office, sr. registrar, Mark's Fellow Queen Victoria Hosp., East Grinstead, England, 1981—82; congenital, aesthetic and reconstructive surgery, Millard Fellow D. Ralph Millard, MD, U. Miami, Fla., 1982; chief, divsn. plastic surgery Tucson Vet. Adminstrn. Hosp., 1985—98; clin. assoc. prof. U. Ariz. Hosp., 1982—87; clin. lectr. U. Ariz. Sch. Medicine, 1987—90; clin. assoc. prof., dept. surgery U. Ariz. Coll. Medicine, 1991—, chief, sect. plastic surgery, 1991—95; private practice Guam and Micronesia (Western Pacific), the only plastic surgeon in 800,000 square miles of the Western Pacific, 1981, Tucson, 1983—. Assoc. mem. Ariz. Cancer Ctr., 1991—95; chief, dept. surgery St. Joseph's Hosp., Tucson, 1988—90, Tucson, 1990—92, Tucson, 1994—95; chief, divsn. plastic surgery Tucson Med. Ctr., 1994—96; founding mem. Johnson and Johnson Coun. Advisors of Aesthetic Skin Care, 1998. Contbr. several articles to peer-reviewed jours.; co-author: Aesthetic Restoration of the Nose, 1993; editor: Facial Cosmetic Surgery, Clinics in Plastic Surgery, 1992, Aesthetic Surgery on the Face, Clinics in Plastic Surgery, 1997; guest editor Facial and Nasal Reconstruction, Operative Techniques in Plastic and Reconstructive Surgery, 1998; contbr. chapters to books; editor: Nose Sect., Plastic Surgery Book. Medicine Jour. (www.emedicine.com), 2001; manuscript reviewer Annals of Plastic Surgery, 1991—2002, Plastic & Reconstructive Surgery, 1999—2002. Travels overseas frequently to teach and perform reconstructive charity surgery in Brazil, Philippines, Korea and Vietnam. Lt., submarine med. officer, diving med. officer (hon. discharge) USN, 1973, lt., Sch. Submarine Medicine USN, 1971, New London, Conn., lt., Sch. Deep Sea Diving and Salvage, 1971, Washington, DC. Named to Best Doctors in America: Pacific Region, 1996—97, Best Doctors in America (USA), 1999. Mem.: Tucson Surgical Soc. (v.p. 1994, pres. 1995, 1995), Pima Country Med. Soc. (bd. dirs. 1993—99, mem. media com. 1987—92), Millard Soc., U. Miami Dept. Plastic Surgery, Calif. Soc. Plastic Surgeons, Rhinoplasty Soc. (treas. 2003, v.p 2004, pres. 2006), Am. Assn. Plastic Surgeons (James Barrett Brown prize in Plastic Surgery 1990, 2003), Am. Soc. for Aesthetic Plastic Surgery, Am. Soc. Plastic and Reconstructive Surgery (internat. programs com., plastic surgery, ednl. found. 1985—98, mem. socioecomomic com. 1986, mem. plastic surgery product assessment commn. 1989, mem. taskforce on long range planning, plastic surgery endl. found. 1990—92, chmn., internat. program com., plastic surgery ednl. found. (PSEF) 1991—94, bd. dirs., reconstructive surgeons vol. program (RSVP), PSEF 1991—98, v.p., bd. dirs. reconstructive surgeons vol. program, PSEF 1992, mem. internat. symposia com. PSEF 1993—94, vis. scholar com. edn. plastic surgery found. 1993—98, pres., chmn. bd. dirs. reconstructive surgeons vol. program, PSEF 1995, membership com. representing zone #5 1995—97, mem. instructional course com., PSEF 1995—99, mem. domestic clin. symposium com., PSEF 1995—99, 1st Pl. Writing award 1995). Office: 1102 N El Dorado Pl Tucson AZ 85715 Office Phone: 520-881-4525. E-mail: drmenick@drmenick.com.

MENICONI, ROBERTO LUCA, surgeon; b. Rome, Mar. 15, 1983; MD, U. Rome La Sapienza, 2008. Resident gen. surgery U. Rome, 2008—. Mem.: Italian Soc. Surg. Rschrs., Italian Soc. Emergency and Trauma Surgery. Office: Viale del Policlinico 155 Rome 00166 Italy E-mail: roberto.meniconi@gmail.com.

MENIER, ROBERT JOSEPH, physiologist; b. Viroflay, France, June 6, 1935; s. Robert Marie Menier and Elisabeth Ocsenas; m. Nicole Jeanine Bodard, (div. 1991); children: Gwennaelle Benedicte, Marie Salome Audrey; m. Arlette Lallemand, 2002. MD, Med. Sch., Paris, 1962, D of Human Biology, 1975; agrégation, Paris, 1975; laureate (hon.), Acad. Med., Paris, 1976. Attaché, asst. physiology Med. Sch., Paris, 1964-68; asst. biology Paris Hosps., Paris, 1968-75; sr. lectr. physiology Med. Sch., Limoges, 1976-90, full prof., 1991—. Chmn. sports medicine Med. Sch., Limoges, 1989—, chmn. physiology, 1994—; deptl. head functional explorations Univ. Hosp., 1994—; dir. Regional Ctr. Sports Medicine, Limoges, 1996—; cons. in rehab. Med. Ctr. Toki Eder, Cambo, 1984—; sci. coun. Univ. Pres., Limoges, 1977-89. Author: Cinématique de la ventilation spontanée chez l'Homme, 1975 (prize Nat. Acad. Medicine 1976); patentee in field. Decorated chevalier Palmes Acad. (France), Legion of Honor (USA), Internat. Order of Merit, Cambridge. Mem. Soc. Limousine de Med. du Sport (pres. 1994-98), Revue European Biomed. Tech. (mem. sci. com. 1989—), Soc. French Sports Medicine, Soc. Physiology, Soc. Electriciens et des Electroniciens. Achievements include research in clinical respiratory physiology (five compartments lung model-kinematics of spontaneous human ventilation) and in physiology of physical activities; follow-up of effects on physical fitness-graded exercise tests-aerobic endurance indicators-physiol. overwork markers-respiratory rehabilitation by retraining & influence of branched-chain amino acids; research in oral supply in BCAA by a direct action of respiratory centers stimulation, slightly increases ventilation and improves Pa02 at rest, which reduces hypoxemia of chronic obstructive lung diseases; this action of stimulation on respiratory centers might take advantage for the treatment of sleep apneas syndrome or Alzheimer disease and even may be in prevention of sudden death of infants. Avocations: skiing, gardening, travel, reading. Home: 37 Allee de la Garde 87000 Limoges France Office Phone: 33 05 55 05 80 85. Business E-Mail: asp87@wanadoo.fr.

MENIGHAN, THOMAS, medical association administrator; BSPharm, W.Va. U., 1974, ScD (hon.), 2011; MBA, Averett Coll., Danville, Va., 1990; ScD (hon.), U. Charleston, W.Va., 2010. Owner, pharmacist Medicine Shoppe, Huntington, W.Va.; mgmt. positions PharMark Corp.; creator RationalMed; developer CornerDrugstore.com; founder SymRx, Inc.; ptnr. Pharmacy Associates, Inc.; founder, pres. SynTegra Solutions, Inc., Germantown, Md.; exec. v.p., CEO American Pharmacists Assn., Washington, 2008—. Mem.: American Pharmacists Assn. (sr. staff mem. 1987—92, bd. trustees 1995—2003, pres. 2001—02). Office: American Pharmacists Assn 2215 Constitution Ave NW Washington DC 20037 Office Phone: 202-628-4410. Office Fax: 202-783-2351. *

MENINI-STAHLSCHMIDT, CARLA MARTINEZ, surgeon; b. Aug. 14, 1978; CM, PUCPR, 2001. Trauma videolaparoscopic surgeon PUCPR, Hosp. U. Cajuru, resident's preceptor, staff, trauma and gen. surgery divsn., 2004—. Instr. Advanced Trauma Life Support ATLS Program, 2003. Mem.: Colégio Brasileiro Cirurgiões. Avocations: music, sports. Office: Peru 173 Curitiba Paraná 82510140 Brazil Office Phone: 41-88364155, 41-99206061. Business E-Mail: carlamenini@uol.com.br.

MENKEN, JANE AVA, demographer, educator; b. Phila., Nov. 29, 1939; d. Isaac Nathan and Rose Ida (Sarvetnick) Golubitsky; m. Matthew Menken, 1960 (div. 1985); children: Kenneth Lloyd, Kathryn Lee; m. Richard Jessor, Nov. 13, 1992. AB, U. Pa., 1960; MS, Harvard U., 1962; PhD, Princeton U., NJ, 1975. Asst. in biostats. Harvard U. Sch. Pub. Health, Boston, 1962-64; math. statistician NIMH, Bethesda, Md., 1964-66; rsch. assoc. dept. biostats. Columbia U., NYC, 1966-69; mem. rsch. staff Office of Population Rsch. Princeton U., 1969-71, 75-87, asst. dir., 1978-86, assoc. dir., 1986-87, prof. sociology, 1980-82, prof. sociology and pub. affairs, 1982-87; prof. sociology and demography U. Pa., Phila., 1987-97, UPS Found. prof. social scis., 1987-97, dir. Population Studies Ctr., 1989-95; prof. sociology U. Colo., Boulder, 1997—, faculty assoc. Population Program, Inst. Behavioral Sci., 1997—; dir. Population Aging Ctr., 2000—08, Inst. Behavioral Sci., 2001—, disting. prof., 2002—; hon. prof. U. Witwatersrand Sch. Pub. Health, Johannesburg, 2006—. Mem. social scis. and population study sect., NIH, Bethesda, 1978-82, chmn., 1980-82, dirs. adv. com., 1995-2000, Nat. Adv. Child Health and Human Devel. Coun., 1988-91, adv. com. Fogarty Internat. Ctr., 2000-02, population adv. com. Rockefeller Found., NYC, 1981-93, com. on population and demography, NAS, Washington, 1978-83, com. on population, 1983-85, 1996-2002, chair 1998-2002, com. nat. stats., 1983-89, com. on AIDS rsch., 1987-93, chair 1990-93; co-chair panel data and rsch. priorities for arresting AIDS in sub-Saharan Africa, 1994-96, Com. on Behavioral and Social Scis. and Edn., 1991-97, chair, steering com., workshop on aging in Africa, 2003-06, chair, sci. adv. com., INDEPTH network, 2002-; cons. Internat. Centre for Diarrhoeal Disease Rsch., Bangladesh, Dhaka, 1984—. Author: (with Mindel C. Sheps) Mathematical Models of Conception and Birth, 1973, (with Ann Blanc and Cynthia Lloyd) Training and Support of Developing Country Population Scientists, 2002; editor: (with Henri Leridon) Natural Fertility, 1979, (with Frank Furstenberg, Jr. and Richard Lincoln) Teenage Sexuality, Pregnancy and Childbearing, 1981, World Population and U.S. Policy: The Choices Ahead, 1986, (with Barney Cohen) Aging in Sub-Saharan Africa: Recommendations for Furthering Research, 2006; contbr. articles to profl. jours. Bd. dirs. Alan Guttmacher Inst., NYC, 1981-90, 93-2000, African Population and Health Rsch. Ctr., Nairobi, Kenya, 2000—10, chair 2007-10. Nat. Merit scholar, 1957; John Simon Guggenheim Found. fellow, 1992-93, Ctr. for Advanced Study in Behavioral Scis. fellow, 1995-96. Fellow AAAS, Am. Statis. Assn.; mem. NAS, Inst. of Medicine, Am. Acad. Arts and Scis., Population Assn. Am. (pres. 1985, Mindel Sheps award 1982), Am. Pub. Health Assn. (Mortimer Spiegelman award 1975), Am. Sociol. Assn., Soc. for Study of Social Biology, Internat. Union for Sci. Study of Population (coun. 1989-97, Laureate 2009), Sociol. Rsch. Assn. (exec. com. 1991-96, pres. 1996). Office: U Colo IBS 483 UCB Boulder CO 80309-0483 Office Phone: 303-492-8148. Business E-Mail: menken@colorado.edu.

MENLOVE, FRANCES LEE, psychologist; b. Salt Lake City, June 4, 1936; d. Edwin Fred and Pernecy Greaves Anderson; children: Stephen, Lynelle, Spencer, Lauren. BA, Stanford U., Calif.; PhD, U. Mich., 1963; cert. in Profl. Ethics, Pacific Sch. Religion, 1990, MDiv, 1998. Lic. psychologist N.Mex., 1976, Oreg., 1990. Founder, dir. Coun. Alcholism, Los Alamos, N.Mex., 1973—74; chief psychologist U. Calif., Los Alamos, 1974—86, dir. human resources, 1986—96; ethicist Bioethics Consultation Group, Berkeley, Calif., 1997—2000; asst. min. United Ch. Christ Congl., Lincoln City, Oreg., 2002—08. Tchr. ethics U. N.Mex., Los Alamos, 1991—92; trustee Dialogue Jour., Palo Alto, Calif., 1965—72; cons. N.Mex. Dept. Corrections, Albuquerque, 1972—72; dir. Called to Care, Lincoln City, Oreg., 2002—05; psychologist Am. Red Cross, Lincoln City, 2001—; adv. bd. U. N.Mex., Los Alamos, N.Mex., 1993—96. Manuscript editor: Jour. Mormon Thought, 1963—65; author: A Challenge of Honesty, 1966, A Challenge of Honesty-Watershed Articles 35 Years of Dialogue, 2001, Sunstone, 2004; contbr. articles to profl. jours. Recipient Danforth award, Danforth Found., 1954; named Outstanding Young Woman of Yr., New Mex., 1972; fellow, Woodrow Wilson Found., 1959. Mem.: APA (life), Phi Beta Kappa. Avocations: reading, whale watching, travel.

MENNIN, GERALD STANLEY, ophthalmologist; b. NYC, Mar. 20, 1932; children: Danielle, Douglas. BA, NYU, 1954; MD, SUNY, NYC. Intern Beth Israel Hosp., NYC, 1958-59; resident Bronx Mcpl. Hosp. Ctr./Einstein Coll. Medicine, 1050-62; pvt. practice Yonkers; chief ophthalmology Yonkers Gen. Hosp., 1986—. Attending ophthalmologist Montefiore Hosp., Bronx, 1962—, Bronx Mcpl. Hosp., 1962—, St. John's Hosp., Yonkers, 1981—, Yonkers Gen. Hosp., 1962—, Manhattan Eye and Ear Hosp., N.Y.C., 1990—. Fellow ACS, Am. Acad. Ophthalmologists, Nat. Arts Club. Avocation: art. Office: 45 Ludlow St Yonkers NY 10705-1947

MENNINGER, WILLIAM WALTER, psychiatrist; b. Topeka, Oct. 23, 1931; s. William Claire and Catharine Louisa (Wright) Menninger; m. Constance Arnold Libbey, June 15, 1953 (dec. Apr. 13, 2008);

children: Frederick Prince, John Alexander, Eliza Wright, Marian Stuart, William Libbey, David Henry. AB, Stanford U., 1953; MD, Cornell U., 1957; LittD (hon.), Middlebury Coll., 1982; DSc (hon.), Washburn U., 1982; LHD (hon.), Ottawa U., 1986; LLD (hon.), Heidelberg Coll., 1993, Dominican U., 2007. Diplomate Am. Bd. Psychiatry and Neurology, Am. Bd. Forensic Psychiatry. Intern Harvard Med. Svc., Boston City Hosp., 1957-58; resident in psychiatry Menninger Sch. Psychiatry, 1958-61; chief med. officer, psychiatrist Fed. Reformatory, El Reno, Okla., 1961-63; assoc. psychiatrist Peace Corps, 1963-64; staff psychiatrist Menninger Found., Topeka, 1965—2001, coordinator for devel., 1967-69, dir. law and psychiatry, 1981-85, dir. dept. edn., dean Karl Menninger Sch. Psychiatry and Mental Health Scis., 1984-90, exec. v.p., chief staff, 1984-93, CEO, 1993—2001, pres., 1993—96, 1999—2001, chmn. bd. trustees, 2001—; clin. supr. Topeka State Hosp., 1969-70, sect. dir., 1970-72, asst. supt., clin., dir. residency tng., 1972-81; pres. Menninger Clinic, Topeka, 1991-96; staff Stormont-Vail Hosp., Topeka, 1984-94, assoc., 1994—2002. Adj. prof. Washburn U.; mem. Fed. Prison Facilities Planning Coun., 1970—73; mem. adv. bd. Nat. Inst. Corrections, 1975—88, chmn., 1980—84; cons. U.S. Bur. Prisons; mem. adv. bd. US Bank, Topeka, 1999—. Syndicated columnist: In-Sights, 1975—83; author: (book) Happiness Without Sex and Other Things Too Good to Miss, 1976, Caution: Living May Be Hazardous, 1978, Behavioral Science and the Secret Service, 1981, Chronic Mental Patient II, 1987; editor: Psychiatry Digest, 1971—74, Bull. of Menninger Clinic, 2001—; contbr. articles to profl. jours., chpts. to books. Mem. health and safety com. Boy Scouts Am., 1970—, chmn., 1980—85, mem. nat. exec. bd., 1980—90, mem. nat. adv. coun., 1990—; bd. dirs. Nat. Com. Prevention Child Abuse, 1975—83; mem. nat. adv. health coun. HEW, 1967—71; mem. Nat. Commn. Causes and Prevention Violence, 1968—69; rsch. adv. com. U.S. Secret Svc., 1990—2005; pres. Jayhawk coun. Boy Scouts Am., 1998—2001; mem. Kans. Gov.'s Adv. Commn. Mental Health, Mental Retardation and Cmty. Mental Health Svcs., 1983—90, Kans. Gov.'s Penal Planning Coun., 1970; chmn. Kans. Gov.'s Criminal Justice Coun., 1970; mem. Kans. Gov.'s Commn. on Crime Reduction and Prevention/Koch Commn., 1994—98; ruling elder 1st Presbyn. Ch., Topeka, 1992—95; trustee Kenworthy-Swift Found., 1980—; bd. dirs. Police Found., Washington, 1996—, Koch Crime Inst., 1998—2000; trustee Midwest Rsch. Inst., Kansas City, Mo., 1996—. With USPHS, 1959—64. Fellow: ACP, Am. Coll. Psychiatrists, Am. Psychiat. Assn. (chmn. com. chronically mentally ill 1984—86, chmn. Guttmacher award bd. 1990—96); mem.: AMA, Am. Acad. Psychiatry and Law, Am. Psychoanalytic Assn. (chmn. com. psychoanalysis, cmty. and soc. 1984—93), Inst. Medicine NAS, Group Advancement Psychiatry (chmn. com. mental health svcs. 1974—77, 1991—2002), Stanford Assocs. Office: PO Box 4406 Topeka KS 66604-0406 Office Phone: 785-235-3400. Business E-Mail: wmenninger@menninger.edu.

MENON, DIPEN KARUNAKAR, orthopedist, surgeon, consultant; b. Trivandrum, India, Feb. 20, 1962; s. Karunakar and Annu Menon; m. Jayshree Velloor Menon, Nov. 28, 1994; children: Adithya Dipen, Priyanka Durga. MBBS, Madras U., 1986; MS in Orthopaedics, All India Inst. Med. Scis., 1990; MCh in Orthopaedics, U. Liverpool, 1997. Diplomate in orthopedics Nat. Bd. Med. Examinations, New Delhi, India, 1990. Intern JIPMER, 1985—86; resident All India Inst. Med. Scis., 1990; further tng. in Eng. and Scotland, 1993—97; sr. orthop. registrar Queen Alexandra Hosp., Portsmouth, England, 2002—03; cons. Kettering Gen. Hosp., England, 2003—, hon. sr. lectr. med. edn. U. Leicester. Cons. Woodland Hosp., Kettering, 2003—, Three Shires Hosp., Northampton, 2005—, hon. sr. lectr. med. edn. U. Leicester. Contbr. articles to profl. jours. Fellow: Royal Coll. Physicians and Surgeons, Royal Coll. Surgeons, Brit. Orthop. Assn.; mem.: Brit. Orthop. Foot & Ankle Soc., Brit. Assn. Surgery of Knee, Brit. Hip Soc., Assn. for Study of Internal Fixation, Brit. Med. Assn. Office: Kettering Gen Hosp Rothwell Rd Kettering NN16 8UZ England Office Fax: 01536 492563. Business E-Mail: dipen.menon@kgh.nhs.uk.

MENON, MANI, urological surgeon, educator; b. Trichur, Kerala, India; arrived in US, 1972, naturalized, 1977; s. Balakrishna and Sumathie Menon; m. Shameem Ara Begum Menon, Oct. 17, 1972; children: Nisha, Roshen. MBBS, Madras U., India, 1971. Diplomate Am. Bd. Urology. Intern Bryn Mawr Hosp., Pa., 1973—74; resident Brady Urol. Inst., Johns Hopkins Hosp., Balt., 1974—80; asst. prof. urology Wash. U. Med. Ctr., St. Louis, 1980—83, assoc. prof., 1983; prof. urology, chmn. divsn. urology & transplant surgery U. Mass. Med. Ctr., Worcester, 1983—, prof. physiology, 1986—; clin. prof. urology Case Sch. Medicine, U. Toledo, NY U. Contbr. over 300 papers in field robotic surgery, renal transplantation & urolithiasis. Recipient Dr. B.C.Roy award, Pres. India, 2008. Mem.: AAAS, Clin. Soc. Genito Urinary Surgeons, Mass. Soc. Med. Rsch., Mass. Med. Soc., Johns Hopkins Med. & Surg. Assn., Rschrs. Calculus Kinetics, Am. Soc. Transplantation & Vascular Surgery, Am. Fedn. Clin. Rsch., Am. Urol. Assn., Am. Assn. Genito Urinary Surgeons. Avocations: tennis, puzzles, mystery fiction. Office: Henry Ford Hosp Vattikuti Urology Inst 2799 W Grand Blvd Detroit MI 48202 Office Phone: 313-916-2066. E-mail: mmenon1@hfhs.org.

MENON, SURESH KUMAR, medical association administrator; b. India, Mar. 1, 1960; MD, U. Md., Balt., 1997; MHA, U. NSW, Sydney, 2001. Cons. internal medicine Wash. Hosp. Ctr., Washington, 1997—99; med. adminstr. Prince Wales Hosp., Sydney, 1999—2001; founder, prin. cons. Dr S.K. Menon & Assocs., New Delhi, 2001—. Mem.: Royal Australasian Coll. Med. Administrators. Home: 1322 Dr Mukherjee Nagar 2nd Fl New Delhi Delhi 110009 India Personal E-mail: drskmenon@hotmail.com.

MENTER, MARTIN ALAN, dermatologist; b. Doncaster, Eng., Oct. 30, 1941; came to U.S., 1975; s. Harry Menter and Esme (Green) Behr; m. Pamela Mary Williams, Dec. 4, 1966; children: Keith, Colin, Kerith. MB, BChir, U. Witwatersrand, 1966; MMed in Dermatology, U. Pretoria, 1971. Diplomate Am. Bd. Dermatology, 1979. Intern Johannesburg Gen. Hosp., South Africa, 1967, sr. intern, 1968; resident in dermatology U. Pretoria and Pretoria Gen. Hosp., 1968-71; sr. resident in dermatology Guy's Hosp., London, 1972; sr. resident, tutor in dermatology St. John's Hosp. for Disease of Skin, London, 1972-73; cons. dermatologist Pretoria Gen. Hosp., 1973-75; dermatologist Baylor U. Med. Ctr., Dallas, 1975—, chair dermatology, 2010—, chmn. divsn. dermatology, 1992—; dir. Baylor Psoriasis Rsch. Ctr., 2007—; med. dir. Nat. Psoriasis Found. Tissue Bank, Dallas, 1993—99; clin. prof. dermatology U. Tex. Southwestern Med. Sch., 1996—. Fellow dept. dermatology U. Tex. Southwestern Med. Sch., Dallas, 1977-79, assoc. clin. prof. dermatology, 1977-95; med. dir. Psoriasis Ctr., Baylor U. Med. Ctr., Dallas, 1979—, chmn. residency program, 2010-; clin. assoc. prof. dept. periodontics Baylor Coll. Dentistry, Dallas, 1985—; presenter in field. Mem. editl. bd. Jour. Am. Acad. Dermatology, 1993—2003, author 4 books; contbr. numerous articles to profl. jours., chpts. to books. Tex. state chmn. Dermatology Found.; rsch. chmn. Nat. Psoriasis Found., med. adv. bd. exec. com.; coach Rugby football team U. Pretoria, 1974; represented S. Africa Nat. Rugby football team, 1968; coach, commr. Boys Under 12 Classic League Soccer, Dallas, 1978-82; active various local civic organizations and coms. Recipient Clin. Rsch. award Imperial Chem. Industries, 1972-73. Mem. AMA, Acad. Dermatology (mem. com. on psoriasis 1988-93, chmn. 1990-93, mem. com. on stds. care for psoriasis 1988-92, 2007, chmn. 1989-92, 2007, dir. Psoriasis Symposium 1990-93, bd. dirs. 1995-97), Am. Acad. Dermatol. Surgery, Brit. Assn. Dermatology, Dallas County Med. Soc. (mem. med. student rels. com. 1989-94), Dallas Dermatol. Soc. (sec.-treas. 1979, pres. 1980, rep. to adv. coun. Am. Acad. Dermatology 1987-89), Dermatol. Therapy Assn. (pres. 1985), Tex. Dermatol. Soc. (program coord. 1987-93, pres. 1995-96), Tex. Med. Assn. (mem. subcom. on joint sponsorship 1992-95), Internat. Psoriasis Coun. (pres. 2005-10). Home: 5230 Royal Ln Dallas TX 75229-5525 Office: Baylor Rsch Inst Baylor Medical Pavilion 3900 Junius St #125 Dallas TX 75246-1613 Personal E-mail: alanmenter@gmail.com.

MENZ, ROBERT L., psychotherapist, minister; b. Cape Girardeau, Mo., June 29, 1949; s. Robert A. and Vivian Marie Menz; m. Ruth A. Hageman, Jan. 7, 1994; children: Gwendolyn J. Menz Ogle, Shawn E. BS in Edn. and Sci., SE Mo. U., Cape Girardeau, 1975; MDiv, Midwestern Bapt. Sem., Kansas City, Mo., 1979; DMin in Counseling, So. Bapt. Sem., Louisville, 1987. Ordained Am. Bapt. Ch., 1974. Resident chaplain Bapt. Meml. Hosp., Kansas City, 1980—81; chaplain Meml. Med. Ctr., Springfield, Ill., 1981—87; dir. pastoral care Bapt. Home DC, Washington, 1987—91; employee counselor Emerson Climate Techs., Sidney, Ohio, 1991—. Adj. asst. prof. So. Ill. U., Springfield, 1982—87; adj. faculty Edison State Coll., Piqua, Ohio, 1993—. Author: A Memoir of a Pastoral Counseling, 1997, A Pastoral Counselor's Model of Wellness in the Workplace, 2003; editor: Social Change: Vision 2020, 2009. Counsel mem., past pres. Shelby County Cmty. Svcs., Sidney, 1991—; counsel mem. Wilson Home Health Hospice, Sidney, 1998—; bd. dirs., past chmn. Shelby County Counseling Ctr., Sidney, 2002—. With US Army, 1970—71, Vietnam. Decorated Commendation medal US Army. Fellow: Am. Assn. Pastoral Counselors; mem.: Employee Assistance Profl. Assn. (bd. cert.), Am. Psychotherapy Assn. (diplomate 2002—), Nat. Employee Assistance. Avocations: flying, running, mountain climbing, hiking, writing. Home: 1290 Dritwood Trail Sidney OH 45365 Office: Emerson Climate Techs 1650 W Campbell Rd Sidney OH 45365 Office Phone: 937-498-3609.

MENZER, ROBERT EVERETT, retired toxicologist, educator; b. Washington, Dec. 21, 1938; s. Russell Ernest and Ora Taylor (Oates) M.; m. Sara Lee Gribbon, Dec. 29, 1962, children: R. Eric, Paul D., Joan Coleraine. BS in Chemistry, U. Pa., 1960; MS, U. Md., 1962; PhD, U. Wis., 1964. Instr. U. Wis., Madison, 1964; mem. faculty U. Md., 1964-89, asst. prof. entomology, 1964-69, assoc. prof., 1969-73, prof., 1973-89, assoc. dean grad. studies and research, 1974-77, acting dean, 1977-80, chmn. grad. program marine-estuarine-environ. scis., 1978-89, dir. Water Resources Research Ctr., 1981-89; dir. environ. rsch. lab. EPA, Gulf Breeze, Fla., 1989-95, sr. sci. advisor Nat. Ctr. for Environ. Rsch. Washington, 1995—2001; ret., 2001. Prof. emeritus U. Md., 1990—; chmn. hazardous substances data bank rev. panel Nat. Library Medicine, 1973-97, mem. 2008-; cons. in field, 2001-. Contbr. articles to profl. jours. Recipient U. Md. Alumni award, 1974 Fellow Washington Acad. Scis., mem. AAAS, Am. Chem. Soc., Soc. Toxicology, Estuarine Rsch. Fedn., Sigma Xi, Phi Kappa Phi. Clubs: Cosmos (Washington). Republican. Episcopalian. Home: 90 Highpoint Dr Gulf Breeze FL 32561-4014 Personal E-mail: robertmenzer@bellsouth.net.

MENZIES, DONALD, surgeon; b. Johnstone, Scotland, Oct. 22, 1959; s. James and Brenda M.; m. Mel Conway; children: Archibald, Orla, Effie. MBBS, Westminster Hosp. Med. Sch., London, 1983; MS, U. London, 1991. Cert. Certificate of Specialist Tng. in Surgery. Rsch. Fellow Westminster Hosp. Med. Sch., London, 1987—89; registrar in surgery The Royal London Hosp., London, 1988—92; sr. registrar in surgery Addenbrookes Hosp., Cambridge, England, 1992—94; cons. surgeon Essex Rivers Healthcare Trust, Colchester, Essex, England, 1994—. Cons. advisor SCAR - Adhesion Adv. Panel, London, 1997—; vice-chmn. North Essex Ethics Com., Essex, 1999—2000. Author: Laparoscopic Henria Repair, 1996; contbr. articles, chapters to books. Fellow: Royal Coll. Surgeons Eng. (Hunterian Prof. 1990—91); mem.: Internat. Adhesions Soc. (bd. dirs. (hon.) 1997—), Assn. Surgeons Gt. Britain, Brit. Med. Assn., Assn. Upper Gastro-Intestinal Surgeons (coun. 2004—, mem. com. 2004—), Assn. Endoscopic Surgeons Gt. Britain (coun. 1999—, hon. treas. 2003—,), Royal Soc. Medicine. Office: Essex Rivers Healthcare Trust Turner Rd C04 5JL Colchester Essex England Office Fax: 44 1206 742030.

MENZIN, ANDREW, gynecologist; b. Hempstead, Ny, Dec. 31, 1963; m. Lauren Menzin. MD, Ny U. Sch. Medicine. Diplomate Am. Bd. ob-gyn. Physician North Shore U. Hosp., Manhasset, NY, 1995—2008. Achievements include patents for medical instruments. Office: N Shore Univ Hosp 300 Community Dr Manhasset NY 11030 Office Fax: 516-562-2805.

MERCADAL, LUCILE, nephrologist; b. Paris, Feb. 1, 1968; d. Georges Mercadal and Danielle Yvars; children: Maxime, Juliette, Marie Lebourg. PhD, Paris 11 U., MD in Nephrology, 1998. Physician, nephrology dept. Pitié Salpétrière Hosp., Paris, 1998—. Contbr. articles to profl. publs. Office: Pitié Salpétrière Hosp 83 Bd De Hosp Paris 75013 France Office Phone: 33142177211. Business E-Mail: lucile.mercadal@psl.aphp.fr.

MERCANDO, ANTHONY DOMINIC, cardiologist; b. Yonkers, NY, Oct. 6, 1954; s. Dominic and Ida Mercando; m. Lee-Ann Davis, May 3, 1980; children: Michelle, Christina, Andrew, Anne Marie. BSEE, Manhattan Coll., Bronx, 1976; MD, Harvard U., 1980. Lic. physician, N.Y. Med. intern Montefiore Med. Ctr., Bronx, 1980-81, med. resident, 1981-83, cardiology fellow, 1984-86, attending arrhythmia svc., 1986-88; ptnr. Westchester Cardiology Assocs., Scarsdale, NY, 1988—. Founder, pres. Amadeus Multimedia Technologies, Ltd., Irvington, N.Y., 1995—; dir. ACLS Montefiore Hosp., 1991—. Contbr. articles to profl. jours., chpts. to books; computer editor Jour. Pacing and Clin. Electrophysiology, 1993—. Bd. dirs. Home Nursing Assn. Westchester, Tuckahoe, 1994—; tech. com. Irvington Sch. Bd., 1995—. R. Rosen fellow in pacing and electrophysiology N. Am. Soc. Pacing and Electrophysiology, 1986, Sable Meml. Heart fellow United Order Odd Fellows, 1985. Fellow Am. Coll. Cardiology; mem. N.Am. Soc. Pacing and Electrophysiology. Roman Catholic. Avocations: biking, skiing. Office: Westchester Cardiology 688 White Plains Rd # 201 Scarsdale NY 10583-5059 Office Phone: 914-722-6300. Business E-Mail: adm@webaxis.com.

MERCANOGLU, GULDEM OLGUNER, medical educator; b. Erzurum, Turkey, Oct. 11, 1976; d. Fahrettin and Nezihe Olguner; m. Fehmi Mercanoglu; 1 child, Erencan Cemre. Degree in Pharmacy, Hacettepe U., 1997, MSc, 2000; PhD, Istanbul U., 2006. Jr. product mgr. Cankat Drug Co., 1997—98; rsch. asst., dept. radiopharmacy Hacettepe U. Faculty Pharmacy, 1998—2001; rschr., drug rsch. unit Istanbul U. Med. Faculty, 2001—06; asst. prof. Yeditepe U. Faculty Pharmacy, Istanbul, Turkey, 2006—08, instr., dept. pharmacology, 2008—; mfg. mgr. MOLTEK Moleculer Tech. and Rsch. Co., Istanbul, 2008—. Office: Yeditepe Univ 26 Agustos Campus Kayisdagi Istanbul 34350 Turkey Home Phone: 00902125537650. Personal E-mail: guldemiko@yahoo.com.

MERCHANT, JUANITA LYNNE, gastroenterologist, educator; MD, PhD, Yale U., 1984. Cert. Internal Medicine, 1987, Gastroenterology, 1993. Resident Mass. Gen. Hosp., 1987, fellow in gastroenterology, 1990, UCLA, 1991; faculty U. Mich., Ann Arbor, 1991—, prof. internal medicine, prof. molecular and integrative physiology, mem. Cancer Ctr.; investigator Howard Hughes Med. Inst., 1994—2002. Mem.: Inst. Medicine, Am. Soc. Clin. Investigation (Robert and Sally Funderburg award), Am. Soc. Biochemistry and Molecular Biology, Am. Assn. Cancer Rsch., Ctrl. Soc. Clin. Rsch., Midwest Gut Club, Am. Fedn. Clin. Rsch., Am. Gastroenterological Assn. (Outstanding AGA Women in Sci. 2008), Am. Soc. Microbiology, Gastroenterology Rsch. Group, Alpha Omega Alpha. Office: Med Sci Rsch Bldg I Rm 3510 1150 W Med Ctr Dr Ann Arbor MI 48109-0682 Office Phone: 734-647-2944. Office Fax: 734-936-1400. E-mail: merchanj@umich.edu.

MERCHANT, MICHAEL L., medical educator; b. Okla., 1966; PhD, U. Ark., 1994. Asst. prof. medicine U. Louisville, 2006—. Office: 570 South Preston Rm 102S Baxter One Louisville KY 40202 Business E-Mail: mlmerc02@louisville.edu.

MERCHANT, P. GLENN, JR., retired military officer, physician; b. Quonset Point, RI, Jan. 6, 1953; s. Paul Glenn and Mary Jean Merchant; m. Debra Colleene Brown, Nov. 25, 1951; children: Nicholas Ryan, Kaitlin Elizabeth, Joshua Daniel. BS in Biology, The Citadel, 1980—83; MD, Med. U. of SC., 1983—87; BA in Polit. Sci., The Citadel, 1971—75; Masters in Pub. Health and Tropical Medicine, Tulane U. Sch. of Pub. Health & Tropical Medicine, 1991—92. Diplomate Am. Bd. of Preventive Medicine, 1994. Marine aviator VMA-542, Cherry Point, NC, 1975—80; commd. 2d lt. USMC, 1975, advanced through grades to capt., 1980; intern in family medicine Naval Hosp., Charleston, SC, 1987—88; flight surgeon 2d MAW, 1988—91; resident in aerospace medicine Naval Aerospace Med. Inst., Charleston, SC, 1992—94; sr. med. officer USS John C. Stennis (CVN 74), Norfolk, 1994—97; prof. Uniformed Svcs. U., Bethesda, 1997—2005; mem. Dept. Def., Med. Exam. Rev. Bd., USAF Acad., Colo., 2005—11, dir., 2007—11; exec. dir. Am. Bd. Preventive Medicine, 2011—. Chair Am. Bd. Preventive Medicine, Chgo., 2003—07. Recipient Delta Omega Scholastic Honor Soc., Tulane U. Sch. of Pub. Health, 1992, Phi Kappa Phi Honor Soc., The Citadel, 1983. Fellow: Am. Coll. of Preventive Medicine, Aerospace Med. Assn. (v.p. 2001—03); mem.: Am. Bd. Preventive Medicine (chair). Methodist. Office: American Board Preventive Medicine 111 West Jackson Blvd Ste 1110 Chicago IL 60601

MERCHANT, ROLAND SAMUEL, SR., retired health facility administrator, educator; b. NYC, Apr. 18, 1929; s. Samuel and Eleta (McLymont) M.; m. Audrey Bartley, June 6, 1970; children: Orelia Eleta, Roland Samuel, Huey Bartley. BA, NYU, 1957, MA, 1960; MS, Columbia U., 1963, MSHA, 1974. Asst. statistician NYC Dept. Health, 1957-60, statistician, 1960-63, NY Tb and Health Assn., NYC, 1963-65; biostatistician, adminstrv. coord. Inst. Surg. Studies, Montefiore Hosp., Bronx, NY, 1965-72; resident in adminstrn. Roosevelt Hosp., NYC, 1973-74; dir. health and hosp. mgmt. Dept. Health, City of NY, 1974-76; from asst. adminstr. to adminstr. West Adams Cmty. Hosp., LA, 1976; spl. asst. to assoc. v.p. for med. affairs Stanford U. Hosp., Calif., 1977-82, dir. mgmt. and strategic planning Calif., 1982-85, dir. mgmt. planning Calif., 1986-90; v.p. strategic planning Cedars-Sinai Med. Ctr., LA, 1990-94; cons. Roland Merchant & Assocs., LA, 1994—. Clin. assoc. prof. dept. family, cmty. and preventive medicine Stanford U., 1986—88; dept. health rsch. and policy Stanford U. Med. Sch., 1988—90. Author: Passion-Sustained Commitment to Excellence: Family-Oriented Parenting and Training, 2004. With US Army, 1951—53. Fellow, USPHS. Fellow: APHA, Am. Coll. Healthcare Execs. (life); mem.: NY Acad. Scis. Home: 4445 Arcola Ave Toluca Lake CA 91602

MERCIER, FREDERIC, surgeon; b. Marseille, France, Apr. 4, 1966; s. Claude and Christiane Mercier; m. Catherine Yardin Mercier, Dec. 5, 1998; children: Gabrielle, Hortense, Marguerite. MD, U. Paris, 1995. Cert. D.E.A. pathologic infection. Resident in vascular surgery U. Hosp., Paris, 1989—95, chief-asst. surgery, 1995—99; vascular surgeon Clinique Turin rue 75008, Paris, France, 1999—, Hosp. Pitié Salpetriere, Paris, France, 1999—. Fellow: French Soc. Vascular Surgery; mem.: Internat. Soc. Endovascular Specialists, Internat. Soc. Cardiovascular Surgery. Roman Catholic. Avocation: golf. Office: Am Hosp of Paris 67 blvd V Hugo 92000 Neuilly-sur-Seine France Office Phone: 00-39-06-08-60-10-35. Fax: 33 01 43056688. Personal E-mail: dr.f.mercier@wanadoo.fr.

MERCIER, RENEE, pharmacist, educator; b. Can., Sept. 23, 1970; PharmD, Wayne State U., 1995. Assoc. prof. pharmacy and medicine U. N.Mex, 1997—. Office: Coll Pharmacy 2502 Marble NE 250 Albuquerque NM 87131 Office Fax: (505)272-6749. Business E-Mail: rmercier@salud.unm.edu.

MEREDITH, RUBY FRANCES, radiation oncologist, researcher, educator; BA, U. Mo., 1969; MA, Ind. U., 1971, PhD, 1974; MD, Ohio State U., 1983. Diplomate in therapeutic radiology Am. Bd. Radiology. Intern, resident Med. Coll. Va., 1983-87; asst. scientist Allegheny-Singer Rsch. Corp., Pitts., 1978; asst. prof. U. Ala. Sch. Medicine, Birmingham, 1987-92, assoc. prof., 1992—98, prof., 1998—. Audio reviewer Ednl. Revs., Inc., Birmingham, 1989-98

Mem. edn. com. Cancer Supporters, Birmingham, 1990; bd. dirs. Leukemia Soc. Am., Pitts., 1979. Recipient Harold C. Bold rsch. award Am. Inst. Biol. Scientists, 1974, Circle of Excellence award Health Svc. Found., 1997, HSF Health Rsch. award United Way/Health Svcs., Pitts.; named one of Best Drs., 2001-10. Office: U Ala Birmingham Dept Radiation Oncology 619 19th St S Birmingham AL 35233-6832 Office Phone: 205-975-0222.

MEREDITH, THOMAS BRIAN, healthcare consultant; b. Grand Rapids, Mich., Dec. 31, 1957; s. George William and Lucille Francis (Calandrino) M.; m. Colleen Masterson, Oct. 10, 1987; children: Mark Thomas, Brian Christopher. BS in Bus. Adminstrn. Acctg., Ohio State U., 1980. CPA. Acct. Shaker Med. Ctr., Cleve., 1980—83; asst. acctg./budget mgr. Luth. Med. Ctr., Cleve., 1983—85; sr. mgr. KPMG Peat Marwick, Cleve., 1985—95; prin. Advantage Consulting, Inc., Independence, Ohio, 1995—2008; pres. Spectrum Consulting LLC, Cleve., 2008—. Mem. Healthcare Fin. Mgmt. Assn. (Follmer Bronze Merit award 1995, advanced mem., Reeves Silver award 1999), Healthcare Fin. Mgmt. Assn. Northeast Ohio (bd. dirs. 1996-98). Avocations: reading, music, golf.

MERENDINO, K. ALVIN, surgeon, educator; b. Clarksburg, W.Va., Dec. 3, 1914; s. Biagio and Cira (Bivona) M.; m. Shirley Emma Jane Hill, July 6, 1943; children: Cira Anne Watts, Nancy Jane Napuunoa, Susan Hill Mitchell, Nina, Maria King Merendino-Stillwell. BA summa cum laude, Ohio U., Athens, 1936, LLD (hon.), 1967; MD, Yale U., New Haven, Conn., 1940; PhD, U. Minn., Mpls., 1946. Diplomate Am. Bd. Surgery, Am. Bd. Thoracic Surgery. Intern Cin. Gen. Hosp., 1940-41; resident U. Minn. Hosp., Mpls., 1941-45; rsch. asst. Dr. Owen H. Wangensteen, 1942-43; trainee Nat. Cancer Inst., 1943-45; dir. program in postgrad. med. edn. in surgery Ancker Hosp., St. Paul, 1946-48; instr. dept. surgery U. Minn., Mpls., 1944-45, asst. prof. dept. surgery, 1945-48; assoc. prof. dept. surgery U. Wash., Seattle, 1949-55, dir. exptl. surgery labs., dept. surgery, 1950-72, prof. dept. surgery, 1955-81, prof. emeritus, 1981—, prof. and adminstrv. officer dept. surgery, 1957-64, prof., chmn., 1964-72; chmn. dept. surgery King Faisal Specialist and Rsch. Ctgr., Riyadh, Saudi Arabia, 1975—76, dir. med. affairs, 1976-79, chmn. dept. energy, dir. Cancer Therapy Inst., spl. cons. to Coun., supr. for exec. mgmt., assoc. dir. med. affairs Riyadh, Saudi Arabia, 1981-82; dir. ops. King Faisal Med. City, Riyadh, 1981-85. Mem. adv. com. for med. rsch., Boeing Airplane Co., 1959-67, chmn., 1962l cons. Children's Orthopedic Hosp., Seattle, 1972-82; mem. adv. com. on heart disease and surgery for crippled children's svc., Wash. State Dept. Health and Div. Vocational Rehab., 1961; mem. surgery study sect. NIH, 1958-62, subcom. on prosthetic valves for cardiac surgery, chm. 1st Nat. Conf., 1960, mem. adv. com. 2d Nat. Conf. on Prosthetic Heart Valves, 1969, Surgery A study sect. chmn., 1970-72, Nat. Heart and Lung Inst. Tng. Com., 1965-69; cons. VA, Seattle, 1949-59, 65-81; mem. adv. com. on hosps. and clinics, USPHS, 1963-66; mem. surgery test com. Nat. Bd. Med. Examiners, 1963-67; mem. surgery resident rev. com., Conf. Com. on Grad. Edn. in Surgery, 1963-73, vice-chmn., 1972-73; chmn. 2d Saudi Arabian Med. Conf., Riyadh, 1978; mem. com. on postgrad. med. edn., Kingdom of Saudi Arabia Ministry of Health, 1978-79; vis. prof. established open heart surgery program Malaysia U. Hosp., Kuala Lumpur, 1971, edn. and tng. jr. faculty (surg. residents) faculty medicine U. Saigon and Mil. M.C. (army surgeons) Binh Dan Hosp. Saigon, Vietnam. Editor in chief: Prosthetic Valves for Cardiac Surgery, 1961; assoc. editor: Prosthetic Heart Valves, 1969; mem. editorial bd. Am. Jour. Surgery, 1958-83, Jour. Surg. Rsch., 1961-69, Pacific Medicine and Surgery, 1964-68, King Faisal Hosp. Medicine Jour. (renamed Annals of Saudi Medicine), 1981-85; contbr. articles to profl. jours., chpts. to books; producer movies on surgery. Recipient cert. of merit Ohio U. Alumni Assn., 1957, Outstanding W.Va. Italian-Am. award W.Va. Italian Heritage Festival Inc., Clarksburg, W.Va., 1984, Spirit of Freedom award A. James Mancin, Sec. State W.Va., 1984, Disting. W. Virginian award Gov. John D. Rockefeller IV., State of W.Va., 1984, John Baird Thomas Meml. award Ohio U.; named Surgery Alumnus of Yr., U. Minn., 1981, Disting. Citizen Wash. State, Lt. Gov. John Cherberg, 1981, K. Alvin Merendino Day Seattle, Mayor Charles Royer, 1981; NIH grantee, 1951-76; Verdi scholar Yale U., Dr. K. Alvin and Shirley Merendino Professorship, 2008 Fellow ACS (numerous coms., bds.), Soc. of Univ. Surgeons (councilman at large 3 yrs.), Internat. Soc. Surgery; mem. Am. Surg. Assn. (adv. mem. com. 1959-64, v.p. 1972-73), Am. Assn. for Thoracic Surgery, Halsted Soc., Henry N. Harkins Surg. Soc., N. Pacific Coast Surg. Assn., Seattle Surg. Soc. (honored special tribute annual meeting 1997), So. Surg. Soc. (Arthur H. Shipley award 1972), Am. Bd. Surgery 1958-64 (vice chmn. 1962-63, chmn. 1963-64, emeritus 1964—); University Club, Seattle Golf Club, Phi Beta Kappa, Sigma Xi, Beta Theta Pi (sec., pres.), Phi Beta Pi (hon.). Republican. Episcopalian. Avocations: golf, fly fishing, bird hunting, gardening. Home: The Highlands Shoreline WA 98177 Personal E-mail: k.merendinomd@comcast.net.

MERER, DAVID MITCHELL, pediatric otolaryngologist, educator; Grad., Boston U.; MD, Yeshiva U., 1990. Diplomate Am. Bd. Otolaryngology. Intern Montefiore Med. Ctr., NY, resident otolaryngology, 1991—95, fellow pediatric otolaryngology, 1995—96; assoc. prof. otolaryngology NY Med. Coll.; pediatric otolaryngology Westchester Med. Ctr. Author numerous articles and presentations in various areas of Pediatric Otolaryngology. Mem.: Am. Acad. of Pediat., Am. Coll. of Surgeons, Am. Acad. of Otolaryngology/Head & Neck Surgery, Alpha Omega Alpha Med. Honor Soc. Office: Westchester Medical Center Ear Nose and Throat Faculty Practice 1055 Saw Mill River Rd Ste 101 Ardsley NY 10502 Office Phone: 914-693-7636. Office Fax: 914-693-5994.

MERHIGE, MICHAEL EDWARD, cardiologist, director; b. Freeport, NY, Nov. 22, 1951; MS, U. Ky. Coll. Medicine, 1976, MD, 1980. CEO Michael E. Merhige M.D., L.L.C., 2000—11; dir. Heart Ctr. Niagara, 2003—. Clin. assoc. prof. nuc. medicine SUNY, Buffalo, 1996—2011; pvt. practice in cardiology. Named Tchr. of Yr., U. Tex. Health Sci. Ctr., Houston, 1989; named one of 100 Top Drs. in Western NY, Buffalo Spree Mag., 2007, 2009—10. Fellow: Am. Coll. Cardiology; mem.: Am. Soc. Nuc. Cardiology, Alpha Omega Alpha. Avocations: scuba diving, saxophone. Home: 107 Lehn Springs Dr Williamsville NY 14221 Business E-Mail: merhige@buffalo.edu.

MERIDEN, TERRY, physician; b. Damascus, Syria, Oct. 12, 1946; arrived in U.S., 1975; s. Izzat and Omayma (Aidi) Meriden; m. Lena Kahal, Nov. 17, 1975; children: Zina, Lana. BS, Sch. Sci., Damascus, 1968; MD, Sch. Medicine, Damascus, 1972, doctorate cum laude, 1973. Diplomate Am. Bd. Internal Medicine. Resident in infectious diseases Rush Green Hosp., Romford, Eng., 1973; house officer in internal medicine and cardiology Ashford Group Univ. Hosps., England, 1973-74; sr. house officer in internal medicine and neurology Grimsby Group Univ. Hosps., England, 1974; registrar in internal medicine and rheumatology St. Annes Hosp., London, 1974-75; jr. resident in internal medicine Shadyside Hosp., Pitts., 1975-76, sr. resident in internal medicine, 1976-77; fellow in endocrinology and metabolism Shadyside Hosp. and Grad. Inst., Pitts., 1976-77; clin. asst. prof. U. Ill., Peoria, 1979; pres. Am. Diabetes Assn., Peoria, 1982-84; dir. Proctor Diabetes Unit, Peoria, 1984—, 1984—. Adviser Gov. of Ill. on diabetes. Mem. editl. bd. Diabetes Forecast mag., Clin. Diabetes, 1990; contbr. articles to profl. jours. Fellow: ACP, Am. Coll. Endocrinology; mem.: ADA (chmn. profl. edn. and rsch. 1980—, mem. editl. bd., mem. Spanish lit. bd., nat. bd. dirs. 1986—, vice chmn. nat. com. on diabetes edn. and affiliate svcs. 1986—, Outstanding Svc. award 1984, Outstanding Diabetes Educator award 1986), AMA (Recognition award 1985), Am. Coll. Endocrinology, Am. Assn. Clin. Endocrinology (founding), Am. Cancer Soc. (Life Line award 1983), Obesity Found. (Century award 1984, Recognition award 1985). Home: 115 E Coventry Ln Peoria IL 61614-2103 Office: 900 Main St Ste 300 Peoria IL 61602-1049 Office Phone: 309-673-1717. Personal E-mail: tmeriden@aol.com.

MERIGGIOLI, MATTHEW N., neurologist; b. Chgo., June 7, 1960; MD, Chgo. Med. Sch., 1990. Dir. neuromuscular medicine U. Ill., 2004—. Fellow: Am. Acad. Neurology. Office: University Ill 912 S Wood Str Chicago IL 60612 Office Fax: 312-413-3829. Business E-Mail: mmerig@uic.edu.

MERIN, SAUL CVI, ophthalmologist; b. Bedzin, Poland, Aug. 25, 1933; arrived in Israel, 1949; s. Isaac and Gitl (Grun) M.; m. Rachel Siton, May 28, 1958; children: Isaac, David Ofer, Guy. MD, Hebrew U., Jerusalem, 1960. Resident in ophthalmology Hadassah U. Hosp., Jerusalem, 1963-68, specialist in ophthalmology, 1968; fellow U. Toronto, 1970-71; sr. lectr. Hebrew U., Jerusalem, 1972-75, assoc. prof., 1975-79, prof. ophthalmology, 1979—; ophthalmic surgeon Queen Elizabeth Hosp., Blantyre, Malawi, 1965-67; head unit ophthalmology Hadassah Mt. Scopus, Jerusalem, 1979-98. Vis. prof. U. Ill., Chgo., 1983-84. Author: Inherited Eye Diseases, 1991, 2d edit., 2005; contbr. over 100 articles to profl. jours. Chmn. Israel Bd. Ophthalmology, 1989-96. Lt. col. M.C., Israel Def. Forces. Recipient Oscar Hirsch prize Faculty of Medicine Jerusalem, 1960, Jacob Landau prize Sci. Coun. Israel, 1965; numerous rsch. grants, 1973-92. Mem. Israel Ophthalmol. Soc. (pres. 1976-82), Israel Soc. for Eye and Vision Rsch. (pres. 1985-90), Am. Acad. Ophthalmology. Jewish. Office: Hadassah U Hosp 91999 Jerusalem Israel Office Phone: +972-2-677 6337.

MERINO, GRACIA, medical educator; b. Léon, Feb. 28, 1973; PhD in Vet. Medicine, León, 2002. Asst. prof. U. León, 2011—. Office: INDEGSAL Campus de Vegazana León 24071 Spain Office Fax: 34 987291267. Business E-Mail: gmerp@unileon.es.

MERINO-SANJUAN, MATILDE, medical educator; b. Valencia, Spain, May 26, 1960; Degree in Pharmacy, U. Valencia, 1982, PhD, 1987. Assoc. prof. U. Valencia, 1993—. Mem.: Soc. Española de Farmacia Indsl. y Galénica. Office: Avda Vicente Andrés Estelles S/N Burjassot Valencia 46100 Spain Office Fax: 34963544911. Business E-Mail: matilde.merino@uv.es.

MERK, FREDERICK BANNISTER, biomedical educator, researcher; b. Cambridge, Mass., Feb. 21, 1936; s. Frederick and Lois Alberta (Bannister) M.; m. Linda Jean Poole, Oct. 22, 1966 (dec. Dec. 1994); children: John F., R. Daniel; m. Laura Ann Bradford, July 11, 1998; 1 stepchild, Letty A. Bradford. AB, Harvard Coll., 1958; PhD, Boston U., 1971. Asst. prof. pathology Boston U. Sch. Medicine, 1972-73; assoc. prof. dept. pathology Tufts U. Sch. Medicine, Boston, 1973—2002, assoc. prof. dept. anatomy, 1973—2002, emeritus prof. pathology and anatomy, 2002—, part time tchr. anatomy, 2002—, dir. electron microscopy facility, 1975-85. Cons. electron microscopy Mass. Gen. Hosp., Boston, 1964-85; cons. toxicol. testing Transgenic Scis., Worcester, Mass., 1988-91, U.S. Army, 1998-2001. Contbr. more than 60 articles to profl. jours. Trustee Broadway United Meth. Ch., Lynn, Mass., chmn. 1994-2000; lay rep. Grace United Meth. Ch. to ann. New Eng. Conf., 2000—10; trustee Frederick and Paula Anna Markus Found., Audubon Soc., Moultonboro, NH, 2005—. Recipient Disting. Career in Tchr. award, 2002; grantee, NIH, 1994—98. Mem. Am. Soc. Cell Biology, Fedn. Am. Soc. Exptl. Biology, Am. Assn. Anatomists, Microscopy Soc. Am., Boston Cancer Rsch. Assn., Sigma Xi. Achievements include research on biology of cells in target organs responding to hormones with emphasis on benign prostatic hypertrophy (enlargement) and prostate cancer. Avocations: gardening, photography, swimming, scuba diving. Home: 28 Warwick Rd Melrose MA 02176 Office: Tufts Univ Sch Medicine Dept Anatomy 136 Harrison Ave Boston MA 02111-1800 Personal E-mail: fmerk@hotmail.com.

MERKER, EDWARD L., physician; BS, Tufts U., Medford, 1977; MD, Yeshiva U., 1981. Diplomate Am. Bd. Family Medicine, 1984, Am. Bd. Family Medicine, 2005. Resident family medicine Overlook Hosp., 1981—84, chief resident, 1983—84; attending physician Yale Univ. Health Svcs., New Haven, 1983—84; consulting and Supervising physician Pace Univ. Health Svcs., Pleasantville, 1986—90; assoc. physician Family Med. Care P.C., Pleasantville, 1985—2006; mem. utilization rev. com. Phelps Meml. Hosp. Ctr., Sleepy Hollow, 1986—96, dir. dept. of family practice, 1996—2006, mem. family practice appraisal Com., 1989—2007, sr. attending in medicine, 1985—; med. dir. Brandywine Nursing Home, Briarcliff Manor, 2005—; family medicine physician North Star Med. Group P.C., Ossining, 2007—; physician coll. of physicians and Surgeons Columbia Univ., 2008—. Asst. clin. prof. family medicine Albert Einstein Coll. Med. Office: Phelps Memorial Hospital Center 180 Marble Ave Pleasantville NY 10570 Office Phone: 914-769-7300. Office Fax: 914-769-7328.

MERKIN, ALBERT CHARLES, retired pediatrician, allergist; b. Chgo., Sept. 4, 1924; s. Harry A. and Goldie (Lamasky) M.; m. Eunice Aprill, Aug. 22, 1948; children: Audrey, Ellen, Joseph. Student, U. Ill., 1942-44; MD, U. Ill., Chgo., 1949. Diplomate Am. Bd. Allergy and Immunology, Am. Bd. Pediat. Intern, resident Cook County Hosp., Chgo.; resident Children's Meml. Hosp., Chgo.; with Valley Pediatric and Allergy Clinic, Las Vegas, Nev. Capt. USAF, 1950-53. Fellow Am. Acad. Pediatrics (state chmn. Nev. 1961-64, sect. allergy and immunology), Am. Coll. Allergy; mem. Am. Acad. Allergy, Allergy Subsplty. Group of Acad. Pediatrics (cert. pediatric allergist). Avocations: reading, travel. Office Phone: 702-341-8695.

MERLI, GENO J., internist; MD, Jefferson Med. Coll., 1975. Diplomate Am. Bd. Internal Medicine. Intern Thomas Jefferson Univ. Hosp., resident; physician Thomas Jefferson Univ. Named one of the Top Doctor, Phila.Mag., 2010—11. Office: Jefferson University Hospital Gibbon Bldg Ste 6270 111 S 11th St Philadelphia PA 19107 Office Phone: 215-955-6540. Office Fax: 215-503-2203.

MERLINO, ANTHONY FRANK, orthopedist; b. Providence, Jan. 21, 1930; s. Anthony Frank and C. Mildred (Campagna) Merlino; m. Dolores Mary Aucello, Nov. 22, 1956; children: Christa Marianne, Paula Nicole. BS, Providence Coll., 1951; MS, U. Conn., 1952; MD, Jefferson Med. Coll., 1956. Diplomate Am. Bd. Ortho. Surgery. Intern St. Joseph Hosp., Providence, 1956—57; resident orthop. surgery VA Hosp., Phila., 1959—63; orthop. surgeon Phila., 1963—68, Providence, 1968—. Attending orthop. surgeon, pres. med. staff St. Joseph Hosp., Providence, 1974—75, trustee, 1973—76, med. staff, trustee joint conf. com., 1982; attending orthop. surgeon Our Lady of Fatima Hosp., North Providence, RI; vis. orthop. surgeon R.I. State Hosp., Howard, 1968—75; asst. orthop. surgeon Hahnemann Med. Coll., Phila., 1965—69; pediat. orthop. surg. cons. Crippled Children's Program of R.I., 1968—86; cons. orthop. surgeon Roger Williams Gen. Hosp., Providence, 1969—89; v.p. R.I. Orthop. Group, Inc., Providence, 1969—83, pres., 1983—; team physician hockey and basketball teams Providence Coll., 1968—87; mem. R.I. Gov.'s Med. Malpractice Commn., 1975—77, R.I. Bd. Examiners in Chiropractic, 1977—80; mem. study commn. R.I. Med. Rev. Bd., 1977—85; mem. corp. Blue Cross/Blue Shield R.I., 1976—87; physician, adv. R.I. Assn. Med. Assts., 1979—84; mem. R.I. Worker's Compensation Adv. Panel, 1978—88; mem. adv. bd. Cath. Social Svcs., 1981—84; police surgeon Am. Law Enforcement Officers' Assn., 1980; cons. orthop. surgery Am. Assn. Medicolegal Cons., 1980—90. Contbr. articles to profl. jours. Pres. Hindle Bldg. Assocs., 1983—; mem. med. splty. adv. bd. Med. Malpractice Prevention, 1985—90. Capt. med. corp. USAF, 1957—59. Recipient Dr. William McDonnell award, Providence Coll. Alumni Assn., 1981. Fellow: ACS (pres. R.I. chpt. 1982—84), Latin Am. Soc. Orthop. and Traumatology, Internat. Coll. Surgeons, Am. Acad. Orthop. Surgeons; mem.: AMA, Providence Med. Soc., Jefferson Orthop. Soc., R.I. Med. Soc. (commr. profl. rels. 1976, ho. of dels. 1976—82, commr. internal affairs 1982), R.I. Orthop. Soc. (sec.-treas. 1978—80, v.p. 1980—82, pres. 1982—84), Ea. Orthop. Soc., New Eng. Orthop. Assn., Am. Soc. Law and Medicine, Internat. Soc. Rsch. in Orthop. and Trauma, Internat. Soc. Orthop. and Traumatology, Am. Med. Photography Assn., Am. Orthop. Soc. for Sports Medicine, Am. Coll. Sports Medicine, Am. Acad. Compensation Medicine, Am. Profl. Practice Assn., Pan-Pacific Surg. Assn., Am. Fracture Assn., Am. Coll. Legal Medicine, Orthop. Rsch. and Edn. Found. (life), Thomistic Inst. Drs. Guild, R.I. Hist. Soc., 100 of R.I. Club, Mal Brown Club, Boston Orthop. Club. Roman Catholic. Home: 2 Countryside Dr North Providence RI 02904-3419 Office: 655 Broad St Providence RI 02907-1444

MERLINO, GLENN T., medical researcher; BA, Adelphi U., LI, 1975; PhD, U. Mich., Ann Arbor, 1980. Lab. technician NY State Inst. Basic Rsch. in Mental Retardation, 1974—75; grad. fellow cellular and molecular biology dept. U. Mich., 1975—80; postdoctoral fellow Nat. Cancer Inst., NIH, 1980—82, staff fellow lab. molecular biology, 1982—92, sr. investigator, chief lab. cell regulation and carcinogenesis, Ctr. Cancer Rsch., head molecular genetics group, chief lab. cancer biology and genetics, head cancer modeling sect., dep. dir. Ctr. Cancer Rsch. Past adj. asst. prof. Dept. Biochemistry George Washington U.; past adj. assoc. prof. Dept. Pathology Georgetown U. Mem.: AAAS, Am. Soc. Investigative Pathology, Am. Assn. Cancer Rsch. Office: Nat Cancer Inst Ctr Cancer Rsch 37 Convent Dr Bldg 37 Rm 5002 Bethesda MD 20892-4264 Office Phone: 301-496-4270. Office Fax: 301-480-7618. E-mail: gmerlino@helix.nih.gov. *

MERLISS, HARRY, orthopedist, surgeon; b. Russia, July 19, 1921; arrived in US, 1924; s. Eugene and Nettie Merliss; m. Barbara K. Merliss, Jan. 5, 1974; 1 child, Eugenia; m. Evelyn Merliss (div.); children: Andrew, Lois, Teri, Barbara, David. MD, George Washington U., DC, 1943. Diplomate Am. Bd. Orthop. Surgery. Attending orthopaedic surgeon Hackensack U. Med. Ctr., NJ, 1950—65, 1975—98, dir. dept. orthopaedic surgery, 1965—75; ret., 1998. Capt. US Army, 1944—46. Fellow: ACS, Am. Acad. Orthop. Surgeons; mem.: NJ Orthop. Soc. (past pres.). Home: 916 Amaryllis Ave Oradell NJ 07649

MERLO, LARRY J., retail executive; b. 1955; Sr. v.p. stores CVS Pharmacy, Inc., Woonsocket, RI, 1994—98, exec. v.p. stores, 1998—2000, CVS Corp., Woonsocket, 2000—07; exec. v.p. CVS Caremark Corp., Woonsocket, RI, 2007—10, pres., COO, 2010—11, pres., CEO, 2011—; pres. CVS/Pharmacy, Woonsocket, RI, 2007—11. Bd. dirs. CVS Caremark Corp., 2010—; vice chmn. Nat. Assn. Chain Drug Stores (NACDS), 2009—10, chmn., 2010—. Office: CVS Caremark Corp Corp Hdqrs 1 CVS Dr Woonsocket RI 02895 *

MERLOB, PAUL LONY, neonatologist; b. Bucharest, Romania, Apr. 29, 1940; s. Haim and Rachel (Blanc) M.; m. Gila Isler, June 6, 1977; 1 child, Maya. MD, Med. Sch. Bucharest, 1962. Jr. in pediatrics Bucharest Hosp., 1963-66; resident in pediatrics Clinic of Pediatrics, Bucharest, 1966-69; specialist in neonatology Clinic of Ob-Gyn., Filantropia, Bucharest, 1969-73; fellow in neonatology dept. neonatology Beilinson Med. Ctr., Petah Tiqva, Israel, 1974-76, sr. physician dept. neonatology, 1976, head neonatal unit dept. neonatology, 1984, head neonatal dept., 1989—; prof. U. Tel Aviv, 1994. Dir. Israel Birth Defects Monitoring Sys. Internat. Clearinghouse, 1983—, mem. classification com., 1987—, mem. nominating com., vice chairperson, 1996, chairperson 1998; dir. Beilinson Teratology Info. Svc., Petah Tiqva, 1990—. Contbr. chpts. to book: Neonatal Perinatal Medicine, 1990, Neonatal Anthrop., 1984, Issues and Rev. Teratol., 1994, Textbook of Diabetes and Pregnancy, 2003, 2008; contbr. over 320 articles to profl. jours. Lt. Israeli Army, 1976. Mem. Israel Med. Assn., Israel Pediatric Soc., Israel Neonatology Soc., European Network Teratology Info. Svcs., Internat. Clearinghouse, Am. Orgn. Teratology Info. Svcs. Avocations: history of art, stamp collecting/philately. Office: Schneider Childrens Hosp Dept Neonatology 49202 Petah Tiqva Israel

MERLOTTI, DANIELA, internist; b. Siena, Italy, Apr. 7, 1975; d. Giovanni Merlotti and Bonella Nepi. MD, U. Siena, Italy, 2000. Intern Inst. Internal Medicine, Siena, 1997—2000; fellow Dept. Internal Medicine, Siena, 2000—. Contbr. articles to profl. jours. Mem.: Italian Soc. Internal Medicine (Rsch. award 2006), Italian Soc. Pagetic Patients (sec. 2004), Italian Soc. Osteoporosis and Metabolic Bone Disorders (Rsch. award 2002), Am. Soc. for Bone and Mineral Rsch. Home: Via Lippo Memmi 17 53100 Siena Italy Office: Dept Internal Medicine Policlinico le Scotte Viale Bracci 4 53100 Siena Italy Office Fax: +390577233446. Personal E-mail: dmerlotti@yahoo.it.

MEROLLA, MICHELE EDWARD, chiropractor, broadcaster; b. Providence, Feb. 20, 1940; s. Joseph and Viola (Horne) M.; m. Ednamarie G.; children: Michele Edward II, Matthew Joseph, Samantha Joan, Alexandra Marie. BS, Bryant Coll., 1961; DC, Chiropractic Inst. N.Y., 1965; LHD, Logan Chiropractic Coll., St. Louis, 1973. Owner chiropractic clinics chiropractic clinics, New Bedford, Taunton, Somerset, Seekonk, Attleboro, others, Mass., 1965—. Daily Network radio talk show hoset Holistic Hotline; owner radio sta. WJYT-AM, Attleboro, Mass. Editor: New Eng. Jour. Chiropractic. Mem. New Bedford City Coun., 1969-73, Airport Commn., 1972-75, Sch. Com., 1978-86, Recreation Commn., 1983-89, Fairhaven (Mass.) Sch. Com., 2000—; pres. New Bedford Aid Ctr., 1977; bd. dir. Your Theatre Inc. Recipient Svc. award New Eng. Chiropractic Coun., 1973. Mem. Am. Chiropractic Assn., Nat. Assn. Broadcasters, Mass. Assn. Broadcasters, Southeastern Mass. Chiropractic Soc. (bd. dir.), Mass. Chiropractic Soc., NY Acad. Sci., Fla. Chiropractic Soc., New Bedford Preservation Soc. (bd. dir.). Office: 73 Alden Rd Fairhaven MA 02719 Home: PO Box 806 Sandwich MA 02563 Office Phone: 508-888-7122. Personal E-mail: DRMEROLLA@AOL.COM.

MEROPOL, NEAL J., oncologist, researcher; AB, Princeton U., 1981; MD, Vanderbilt U., 1985. Cert. Am. Bd. Internal Medicine, Internal Medicine, Med. Oncology. Intern, resident in internal medicine Case Western Res. U., Cleve., 1985—88; fellow in med. oncology and hematology U. Pa., Phila., 1988—92; asst. prof. medicine Roswell Park Cancer Inst., 1992—98; dir. Gastrointestinal Cancer Program Fox Chase Cancer Ctr., Phila., 1998—, dir., Gastrointestinal Tumor Risk Assessment Program. Prof. medicine Temple U. Sch. Medicine, 2006—. Contbr. articles to profl. publications. Named one of Top Doctors, Phila. mag., 2008. Mem.: Am. Assn. for Cancer Rsch., Am. Soc. Clin. Oncology.

MERRELL, RONALD CLIFTON, surgeon, educator; b. Birmingham, Ala., June 18, 1946; s. Greene Lawrence and Florence (Jones) M.; m. Marsha Karen Cox, Dec. 24, 1966; children: Alexandria, Alison, R. Clifton. BS in Chemistry, U. Ala., 1967, MD, 1970. Diplomate Am. Bd. Surgery. Resident and fellow in surgery Wash. U., St. Louis, 1970-77; asst. prof. surgery Stanford U., Calif., 1979-84; assoc. prof. surgery U. Tex. Med. Sch., Houston, 1984-88, prof. surgery, 1988—93, M.D. Anderson Cancer Ctr., Houston, 1988—93; assoc. dean clin. affairs U. Tex. Med. Sch., Houston, 1988-92, vice dean, 1992-93; Lampman prof. surgery, chmn. dept. surgery Yale U., 1993—99; Stuart McGuire prof. surgery, chmn. dept. surgery Va. Commonwealth U., Richmond, 1999—2003, prof. surgery, 2003—; dir. Med. Informatics Tech. Applications Consortium, 1997—2008. Editor-in-chief Telemedicine and e Health. Contbr. chapters to books, articles to profl. jours. Maj. US Army, 1977—79. Recipient Basil O'Connor award March of Dimes, 1979, Rsch. Career Devel. award NIH, 1979-84, Henry J. Kaiser award Stanford U., 1982, 83, John P. McGovern Outstanding Tchr. award U. Tex. Med. Sch., 1988, Dean's Teaching Excellence award, 1983-89, Pub. Svc. medal NASA, 1998, 2005, 06, Disting. medal as Friend of Democritus, U. Thrace, Greece, 1998; grantee NASA, Dept. Def., Internat. Coop. medal, Russian Space Agy., 2005. Fellow: ACS, Soc. Univ. Surgeons; mem.: Am. Surg. Assn., Am. Assn. Endocrine Surgery, Alpha Omega Alpha. Democrat. Episcopalian. Achievements include research in telemedicine and in the transplantation of islets of Langerhans. Office: Va Commonwealth U PO Box 980480 1200 E Marshall St Richmond VA 23298-0519 Office Phone: 804-827-1031. Office Fax: 804-827-1029. Business E-Mail: rmerrell@mcvh-vcu.edu.

MERRELL, WOODSON C., integrative medicine specialist; Chmn. Dept. Integrative Medicine Beth Israel Med. Ctr.; asst. clinical prof. medicine Columbia U. Coll. Physicians & Surgeons; attending physician St. Luke's-Roosevelt Hosp., Beth Israel Med. Ctr.; past chmn. NY State Bd. Acupuncture; bd. mem. NY State Office Profl. Med. Conduct, 1995—. Author: The Source, 2008. Office: 44 E 67th St New York NY 10065 Office Phone: 212-535-1012.

MERRICK, JOAV, pediatrician, government agency administrator, academic researcher; b. Copenhagen, Sept. 26, 1950; s. Abraham and Yona (Michaelson) Merrick; m. Geula Gadassi; children: Michael Talia, Efrat Miriam, Etai Jaakov, Alona Yona, Amir David, Maya Rachel. MD, MMedSci, U. Copenhagen, 1977, DMSc, 1989. Rotating intern internal medicine and surgery unit Hosp. Rigshospitalet, Copenhagen, 1977—78, resident ambulatory, cmty. and social pediats., 1979—81, sr. resident in pediat., 1983—84, attending physician, dir. sect. ambulatory, cmty. and social pediats., dept. pediat., sr. lectr. cmty. pediat., 1984—86, clin. prof. child health and cmty. pediat., 1986—89, from rsch. pediatrician to dir. Prospective Pediat. Rsch. Unit, 1980—87; intern in internal medicine Vestre Hosp., Copenhagen, 1978—79; resident in gen. pediat. Roskilde County Hosp., Denmark, 1981—82; resident Hosp. for Sick Children, Fuglebakken, Denmark; cons. cmty. pediatrician, dir. child protection team Copenhagen County Dept. Social Svc., 1984—89; attending physician pediat., dir. ambulatory pediat. dept. pediat. Holbaek (Denmark) Ctrl. Hosp., 1986—89; attending physician pediat. Chaim Sheba Med. Ctr., Tel-Hashomer, Israel, 1989—91; dir. Children's House and Nat. Ctr. Prevention Child Abuse and Neglect, Copenhagen, 1987—89; med. dir. divsn. mental retardation Min. Social Affairs, State of Israel, Jerusalem, 1991—; dir. Nat. Inst. Child Health and Human Devel., Jerusalem, 1999—; prof. pediat. U. Ky. Children's Hosp., Lexington, 2007—. Clin. and vis. prof. child health and human devel. U. Copenhagen, U. Chgo., U. Colo., U. Gottenburg, U. Ben Gurion, U. Tel Aviv, 1984—. Author: Children and the Emergency Room, 1980, Child Abuse and Neglect, 1984, The Baby and Child Medical Handbook, 1988, Principles of Holistic Medicine, 2005, 2006; editor: Incest and Child Sexual Abuse, 1983, Child Health and Development. The Scandinavian Textbook on Social and Community Pediatrics, 1984, Children in Alcohol-and-Drug-Abusing Families, 1985, A Scandinavian Textbook on Child Abuse and Neglect, 1985, Suicidal Behavior in Adolescence, 2005, Adolescence and Alcohol, 2006, Alcohol and Suicide, 2007; mem. editl. bd. Jour. Religion Disability and Health, 1999—, editor-in-chief Internat. Jour. Adolescent Med. Health, 2000—, Scientific World Jour., 2003—, Internat. Jour. Disability and Human Devel., 2005—; editor-in-chief: TSW-Holistic Health and Medicine, 2006—, Internat. Jour. Child Health Human Devel., 2008—, Internat. Jour. child Adolescent Health, 2008—, Jour. Pain Mgmt., 2008—. Capt. reserves Israel Def. Forces, 1991—2003. Recipient Peter Sabroe Child award, Danish Child Welfare Found., 1985, Internat. LEGO prize, LEGO Internat, 1987. Mem.: Lego International, Intellectual and Devel. Disabilities, Assn. for Child Psychology and Psychiatry, Internat. Assn. Sci. Study Intellectual Disabilities, Am. Assn. on Mental Retardation, Am. Profl. Soc. and the Abuse of Children, Internat. Soc. for Prevention Child Abuse and Neglect (exec. coun. 1984—86, editl. bd. and rev. internat. jour. 1986—), Israeli Pediat. Soc. Office: Ministry Social Affairs Divsn Mental Retardation Box 1260 91012 Jerusalem Israel Office Fax: 972-15326708275; Home Fax: 972-8-9201917.

MERTA DE VELEHRAD, JAN, safety engineer, psychologist; b. Stare Mesto, Czech Republic, Apr. 24, 1944; arrived in Can., 1968; s. Jan and Marie (Sebkova) M.; m. Margaret; 1 child, Iveta. Diploma, Ucnovská Skola Technická, Slusovice, 1962, Coll. Social Law, Prague, 1968; BS, McGill U., Montreal, Can., 1971; PhD in Psychology, U. Aberdeen, Scotland, 1978. Pres., pub. Jan's Pub. Co., Montreal, 1972-74; deep sea diver, diving supr. North Sea, Mid. East, Africa, 1974-78; dir. R & D Wharton-Williams Ltd., Aberdeen, 1978-79, Oceaneering, Inc., Houston, 1979-81; chief insp. diving Govt. of Can., 1981—2005, insp. officer, health and safety officer. Co-author: Exploring The Human Aura, 1976, Canadian Oil and Gas Diving Regulations, 1989, 99. Chmn. com. for survival suits Can. Gen. Stds. Bd., 1983-96; br. chmn. Czech Assn. of Can., 1986-91; hon. appt. bd. Seneca Coll. Ont., 1983; chmn. com. for diving competency Can. Stds. Assn., 1994-2000; chmn. Z-275 tech. com. Can. Stds. Assn., 2000—. Recipient Spl. Industry award Can. Assn. Diving Contrators, 1985, award for svc. to sub-sea industry, 1988, Internat. Cultural Diploma of Honour, 1989, Commemorative Medal of Honour, 1988, Silver Shield of Valor, 1992, Alta. Centennial medal, 2005; named Pursuivant, Spanish Coll. Arms, 1990, to Internat. Leadership Hall of Fame, 1988, Internat. Hall of Leaders, 1988; named Man of Yr., U.K., 1990, World Intellectual, 1993, One in a Million, U.K., 1992, hon. citizen Town of Modra, Czech Republic, 2001. Fellow Inst. Diagnostic Engrs., Inst. Petroleum; mem. Soc. Fire Protection Engrs., Am. Soc. Safety Engrs., Brit. Psychol. Soc., Internat. Soc. Hyperbaric Medicine (v.p. 1990-96), Undersea Med. Soc., Soc. Petroleum Engrs., Submarine Pilot Assn., Soc. Naval Archs. and Marine Engrs., Am. Soc. Safety Engrs. Achievements include two British patents, 4 patents pending. Address: Tr. Spojencu 29 779 00 Olomouc Czech Republic

MERTINS, JAMES WALTER, entomologist; b. Milw., Feb. 18, 1943; s. Walter Edwin and Harriet Ellen (Sockett) M.; m. Marilee Eloise Joeckel, Dec. 8, 1979. BS in Zoology, U. Wis., Milw., 1965; MS in Entomology, U. Wis., 1967, PhD in Entomology, 1971. Project assoc. dept. entomology U. Wis., Madison, 1971-75, rsch. assoc. dept. entomology, 1975-77; asst. prof. dept. entomology Iowa State U., Ames, 1977-84; entomol. cons. Ames, 1984-89; entomologist Nat. Vet. Svcs. Labs. USDA Animal and Plant Health Inspection Svc., Ames, 1989—. Co-author: (textbook) Biological Insect Pest Suppression, 1977, Russian edit., 1980, Chinese edit., 1988; contbr. articles to profl. jours. NSF Grad. fellow, 1970. Mem. Entomol. Soc. Am. (Insect Photography award 1984, 86, 2003), Entomol. Soc. Can., Mich. Entomol. Soc., Wis. Entomol. Soc. (pres., sec., treas., bd. dirs.), Cyclone Corvettes, Inc. (co-founder, pres. 1978, 79, sec., treas., bd. dirs., Mem. of Yr. 1982), Am. Mensa. Avocations: gardening, movies, photography. Office: USDA Animal and Plant Health Inspection Svc PO Box 844 Ames IA 50010-0844 Business E-Mail: James.W.Mertins@aphis.usda.gov.

MERZENICH, MICHAEL, neuroscientist, educator; m. Diane Merzenich. B in Gen. Sci., U. Portland; PhD, John Hopkins U.; tng., U. Wis. Founder Neuroscience Solutions Corp., 2003; founding CEO, dir. Scientific Learning, Oakland, Calif., 1996—; co-founder, chief scientific officer Posit Science Corp., San Francisco, 2003—; Francis A. Sooy chair of Otolaryngology, Keck Ctr. for Integrative Neurosciences U. Calif. San Francisco, 1998—2007, prof. emeritus otolaryngology, founding mem. Keck Ctr. Integrative Neuroscience. Contbr. several articles to peer-reviewed jours., including Science and Nature, chapters to books, articles to NY Times, Wall Street Jour., Time and Newsweek; editor: Cochlear Implants; guest appearances Sixty Minutes II, CBS Evening News, Good Morning America. Recipient IPSEN prize, Zülch prize, Max-Planck Inst., Thomas Alva Edison Patent award, Purkinje medal. Mem.: Inst. Medicine, NAS. Achievements include patents in field; In the late 1980's, was part of the team that developed the first models of a commercial coclear implant; developed software to help children with dyslexia and other disorders learn how to read; leading pioneer in brain plasticity. Office: Scientific Learning 300 Frank H Ogawa Plz Ste 600 Birds Landing CA 94512-2040 also: U Calif San Francisco Dept Otolaryngology Box 0732 513 Parnassus HSE-828 San Francisco CA 94143-0732 Office Phone: 800-514-3961, 888-665-9707, 415-476-0490. Office Fax: 415-986-2829, 510-444-3580. Business E-Mail: merz@phy.uscf.edu.

MESALLAM, TAMER, physician, educator; b. Egypt, Sept. 27, 1972; MD, Coll. Medicine, Menoufiya U., PhD, 2007. Asst. prof. Coll. Medicine, King Saud U., 2009—. Office: King Abdulaziz University King Abdulaziz Rd Riyadh 11411 Saudi Arabia Personal E-mail: tmesallam@yahoo.com.

MESELSON, MATTHEW STANLEY, biochemist, educator; b. Denver, May 24, 1930; s. Hymen Avram and Ann (Swedlow) M.; m. Jeanne Guillemin, 1986; children: Zoe, Amy Valor. Ph.B., U. Chgo., 1951, D.Sc. (hon.), 1975; PhD, Calif. Inst. Tech., 1957; Sc.D. (hon.), Oakland Coll., 1964, Columbia, 1971, Yale U., 1987, Princeton U., 1988. Asst. prof. chemistry Calif. Inst. Tech., 1958—59, sr. rsch. fellow chem. biology, 1959—60; assoc. prof. molecular biology Harvard U., 1964—76, Thomas Dudley Cabot prof. natural scis., 1976—. Cons. U.S. Arms Control and Disarmament Agency, 1963; adj. scientist Josephine Bay Paul Ctr. Comparative Molecular Biology and Evolution Marine Biol. Lab., Woods Hole, Mass., 2000—. Recipient Eli Lilly award microbiology and immunology, 1964, Alumni medal U. Chgo., 1971; Lehman award 1975, Presidential award 1983, N.Y. Acad. Scis., 1975; Alumni Disting. Svc. award Calif. Inst. Tech., 1975; Leo Szilard award Am. Phys. Soc., 1978; MacArthur fellow, 1984-89, Lasker-Koshland Spl. Achievement award in Med. Sci., Lasker Found., 2004, Mendal medal Genetics Soc., 2008. Fellow AAAS (Sci. Freedom and Responsibility award, 1990); mem. NAS (Molecular Biology prize 1963), Inst. Medicine, Am. Acad. Arts and Scis., Fedn. Am. Scientists (chmn. 1986-88, Pub. Svc. award 1972), Coun. Fgn. Rels., Accademia Santa Chiara, Am. Philos. Soc., Royal Society (London), Académie des Sciences (Paris), Genetics Soc. Am. (Thomas Hunt Morgan medal 1995). Office: Harvard U Fairchild Biochem Bldg 7 Divinity Ave Cambridge MA 02138-2019 *

MESHEL, ELLYN M., emergency physician; b. NY, Mar. 17, 1964; BS in Biology, SUNY, Stony Brook, 1986; MD, UHS, Chgo. Med. Sch., 1990. Er attending physician Midlands Emergency Physicians, 2007—. Fellow: Assn. Emergency Physicians; mem.: ACP. Avocations: boating, water sports. Office: 129 N Washington St Sumter SC 29150 Business E-Mail: emeshel@mac.com.

MESIC, ENISA DZ, physician, department chairman; b. Tuzla, Bosnia-Herzegovina, July 17, 1956; d. Dzemal H. and Samija A. (Cokic) Mesic. Degree, Sarajevo U., 1976—81; PhD, Tuzla U., 1997. Bd. cert. specialist internal medicine Ministry Health Bosnia-Herzegovina, 1988. Physician dialysis dept. U. Hosp., Tuzla, 1984—89, head dialysis dept., 1989—2005; resident U. Hosp. Rebro, Zagreb, Croatia, 1987—88; prof. internal medicine med. faculty Tuzla U., 1997—2005. Author: Standards in Dialysis, 2003, periodicals in profl. jours., Hemodialysis-Handbook for Dialysis Nurses, 2006. Pres. Donor Network of Bosnia and Herzegovina, Tuzla, 2003—05., Mo. U. Hosp., 1997. Mem.: Soc. Nephrology Bosnia and Herzegovina, European Renal Assn., Internat. Soc. Nephrology. Avocations: hiking, rafting, skiing, travel, reading. Office: U Hosp Trnovac bb Tuzla 75000 Bosnia-Herzegovina Home Fax: 387 35 303 104. Personal E-mail: nisa@bih.net.ba.

MESSA, CRISTINA, nuclear medicine physician, educator; b. Monza, Oct. 8, 1961; MD, U. Degli Studi Milan, 1986, degree in Nuc. Medicine, 1989. Physician, prof. U. Milan Bicocca, 2001—. Office: Via Pergolesi 33 Monza 20900 Italy Business E-Mail: nichetti.carmen@hsr.it.

MESSERLE, JUDITH ROSE, retired medical librarian, public relations executive; b. Litchfield, Ill., Jan. 16, 1943; d. Richard Douglas and Nelrose B. Wilcox; m. Darrell Wayne Messerle, Apr. 26, 1968; children: Kurt Norman, Katherine Lynn. BA in Zoology, So. Ill. U., 1966; MLS, U. Ill., 1967. Cert. med. libr. Libr. St. Joseph's Sch. Nursing, Alton, Ill., 1967-71, dir. med. info. ctr., 1971-76, dir. info. svcs., 1976-79; dir. ednl. resources and cmty. rels. St. Joseph's Hosp., 1979-84; dir. Med. Ctr. Libr. St. Louis U., 1985-88; libr. Francis A. Countway Libr. Harvard Med. Sch. and Boston Med. Libr., 1989—2004; ret. Instr. Lewis and Clark Coll., 1975, Med. Libr. Assn.; cons. in field. Bd. dirs. Family Svcs. and Vis. Nurses Assn., Alton, 1976-79. Fellow AAAS, Med. Libr. Assn. (search com. for exec. dir. 1979, dir. 1981-84, pres. 1986-87, legis. task force 1986-90, task force for knowledge and skills 1988-92, nominating com. 1996); mem. OCLC (spl. libr. adv. com. 1994-98), AMA (com. on allied health edn. and accreditation 1991-94), Assn. Acad. Health Sci. Libr. Dirs. (editl. bd. for ann. stats. 1989-94, Region 8 adv. bd. 1992-93, joint legis. task force 1992-96, pres. 1993, charting the future task force 2001-03, scholarly communication task force 2003-05), Am. Med. Informatics Assn. (planning com. 1990, publs. com. 1994-96, ann. mtg. com. 1996-98), Ill. State Libr. Adv. Com., Midwest Health Sci. Libr. Network (divsn. health sci. coun.), St. Louis Med. Librs., Hosp. Pub. Rels. Soc. St. Louis, Nat. Libr. Medicine (biomed. libr. rev. com. 1988-92).

MESSERSMITH, PHILLIP B., biomedical engineer, educator; BS in Life Sciences, U. Ill., Urbana, 1985, PhD in Materials Sci., 1992; MS in Bioengineering, Clemson U., 1987. Asst. prof. restorative dentistry & bioengineering U. Ill. Chgo., 1994—97; asst. prof. divsn. biological materials Northwestern U., 1997—98, asst. prof. dept. physical medicine & rehabilitation, 1998—99, asst. prof. dept. biomedical engring., 2000—03, assoc. prof. dept. biomedical engring, materials sci. & engring., 2003—05, prof. dept. biomedical engring, materials sci. & engring., 2006—. Chief scientific adv. Nerites Corp., 2004; editorial bd. Nanomedicine, 2005, Biointerphases, 2006. Recipient First award, Nat. Inst. Health, 1997. Mem.: Inst. for BioNanotechnology in Advanced Medicine, Implant Dentistry Rsch. & Edn. Found. (scientific adv. bd.). Office: Northwestern University Biomedical Engineering Dept 2145 Sheridan Rd Evanston IL 60208 Office Phone: 847-467-5273. Office Fax: 847-491-4928. E-mail: philm@northwestern.edu.

MESTAN, MIROSLAV, cardiologist; b. Rychnov nad Kneznou, Czech Republic, June 27, 1971; s. Vlastimil Mestan and Dagmar Mestanova; m. Petra Drackova; children: Hana Mestanova, Vit Mestan. MD, Faculty Medicine Hradec Kralove, Charles U. Prague, 1995, PhD, 2006. Asst. prof. Faculty Medicine Hradec Kralove, Czech Republic, 2001—; cardiology cons. U. Hosp., Hradec Kralove, 2002—, dep. dir. med. sect., 2007—. Expert mem. Edn. Clin. Coding & Classification Sys., Czech Republic. Recipient Hlavka's prize, Nadani Josefa, Marie Zdenky Hlavkovych, 1994. Mem.: European Heart Rhythm Assn., European Soc. Cardiology, Czech Soc. Cardiology, Internat. Fedn. Health Info. Mgmt. (assoc.). Avocations: computers, golf, photography, music. Office: University Hosp Sokolska 581 Hradec Králové 500 05 Czech Republic Office Phone: 420495833550. Business E-Mail: mestan@fnhk.cz.

MESZAROS, GYÖRGY, medical educator, director; b. Budapest, Hungary, Dec. 8, 1950; s. Miomír Mészáros and Mészárosné - Konecsny; m. Beáta Mészáros Györgyné - dr Jaranyi; children: Kinga Toman-Mészáros, Ádám Mészáros. PhD, Semmelweis U., Budapest, 1981; med. habilitation, 2008. Diploma chemist Eötvös L. U., Budapest, 1976. Chmn. bd. Pharmafontana Pharms. Holding, Budapest, 1990—95; mem. bd. U. Kútvölgyi Tchg. Hosp., Budapest, 1995—2002, Hungarian Privatisation and State Holding, Budapest, 1998—2002; chmn. bd. Paks Nuc. Power Plant, Hungary, 2000—02; prof., dir. Semmelweis U. Med. Sci. Ctr., Budapest, 2007—. Pres. Pharmafontana Pharm. Holding, 1990—95; chmn., econ. mem., com. mem. Budapest City Parliament, 1990—94; bd. mem. Ednl. Hosp. U., 1995—98, Hungarian Privatisation Ltd., 1998—2002; mem. supervisory bd. Hungarian Electric Co., 1998—2002. Dir.(property com., municipality self-governm): (asset management) Chairman; strategic expert (privatisation & energy politician) Studies, Management Of Projects. Mem. country com. Fidesz, Budapest, 1999—. Fellow

Szechenyi Professorship, Prime Min., Hungary. Roman Catholic. Avocation: swimming. Office: Semmelweis Univ Med Sci Ctr Tüzoltó 37-47 Budapest Europe H-1094 Hungary Business E-Mail: meszaros@eok.sote.hu.

METCALF, DONALD, biomedical researcher; BSc, U Sydney, Sydney, Australia; MB, BS, U Sydney; MD, U. Sydney. Carden fellow, cancer rsch. Walter & Eliza Hall Inst. Med. Rsch., Victoria, Australia, 1954—, head, cancer rsch. unit, asst. dir., 1965—96; emeritus prof. Walter & Eliza Hall Inst. Med. Rsch., Royal Melbourne Hosp., 1996—; rsch. prof., cancer biology U. Melbourne, Australia, 1986—96. Vis. prof., Australia, England, Canada, France, Netherlands, New Zealand, Switzerland, United States. Contbr. articles to profl. jours. Recipient Armand Hammer prize, 1988, Sloan prize, GM Cancer Rsch. Found., Lasker-DeBakey Clin. Med. Rsch. award, Lasker Found., 1993, Louisa Gross Horwitz prize, Columbia U., 1993, Internat. award, Gairdner Found., 1994, Warren Alpert Found. prize, Harvard Med. Sch., 1996, Ernst Neumann award, Internat. Soc. for Exptl. Hematology, 1995, Amgen Australia prize, 1996, Chiron Internat. award, Nat. Acad. Medicine, Italy, 1999, Victoria prize, Australia, 2000, Prime Min.'s prize, 2001, Pres. medal, Australia and New Zealand Soc. for Cell and Devel. Biology, 2002, Centenary medal, Australia, 2003, Mentorship award, Days of Molecular Medicine Found., 2004. Mem.: NAS (fgn. assoc. mem., Jessie Stevenson Kovalenko medal 1994), Assn. Am. Physicians (hon. fgn. mem.), Royal Soc. (Wellcome prize 1986, Royal medal 1995), Polish Soc. Hematology (hon.), Companion Order of Australia, Alpha Omega Alpha (hon.). Achievements include research in clinical use of molecules called colony-simulating factors (CSFs), which control the growth and development of blood cells. Office: Walter and Eliza Hall Inst Med Rsch 1G Royal Parade Parkville VIC 3052 Australia Home Phone: 61-3-9836-1343; Office Phone: 61-3-9345-2555. Business E-Mail: metcalf@wehi.edu.au.

METH, BRUCE, pulmonologist; b. Bridgeport, Conn., Feb. 28, 1956; AB, Harvard U., 1978; MD, NY U. Sch. Medicine, 1982. Physician Springfield Med. Assocs., 1992—. Fellow: ACP, Am. Coll. Chest Physicians; mem.: Am. Coll. Exec. Medicine, Am. Thoracic Soc., Soc. Critical Care Medicine. Office: 2150 Main St Springfield MA 01104 Office Fax: 413-731-9107. Personal E-mail: brmeth@yahoo.com.

METHUKU, NANDA KISHORE, physician; b. Hyderabad, India, July 23, 1980; MD, Osmania Med. Coll., 2003; MPH, Eastern Ky. U., 2005. Physician pub. health Maimonides Med. Ctr., Bklyn., 2005—08, RI Hosp., Providence, 2008—09, Warren Alpert Med. Sch., Brown U., Providence, 2008—09, Maimonides Med. Ctr., Bklyn., 2009—. Contbr. scientific papers to profl. publs. Rsch. grant, Maimonides Rsch. Found. Mem.: AMA, ACP, Indian Med. Assn., Am. Soc. Hematology, Am. Soc. Clin. Oncology. Avocation: chess. Home: 5312 11th Ave Fl 1 Brooklyn NY 11219

METITIERI, TIZIANA, psychologist; b. Switzerland, May 20, 1970; Degree in Psychology, U. Padova, 1996; PhD, U. Verona, 2006. Rschr., neuropsychology and cognitive rehab. Geriatric Rsch. Group, 1997—2002; clin. psychologist Hosp. Ancelle della Carità, Cremona, 1999—2002; cons. neuropsychologist Pediat. Hosp. Anna Meyer, Firenze, 2006—. Contract prof., gen. psychology, faculty polit. scis. U. Firenze, 2010—, contract prof., clin. neuropsychology and devel. assessment, Splty. Sch. Pediat. Neuropsychiatry, 2010—. Mem.: Italian Bd. Psychologists, Italian Assn. Psychology, Internat. Neuropsychol. Soc. Avocation: reading. Home: Via Pescaia 29 Arezzo 52100 Italy Home Fax: 0575401947. Personal E-mail: t.metitieri@iol.it.

METRO, GIULIO, oncologist; b. Rome, July 20, 1978; Degree in Medicine, U. 'La Sapienza', Rome, 2002, degree in Med. Oncology, 2006. Attending physician Divsn. Med. Oncology, Azienda Ospedaliera S. Maria Della Misericordia, Perugia, Italy, 2010—. Office: via Dottori 1 Perugia 06156 Italy Office Fax: 390755784184. Personal E-mail: giulio.metro@yahoo.it.

METRO, MICHAEL J., urologist, educator; MD, U. Pitts. Diplomate Am Bd. Urology. Intern Univ. Pa., resident; fellow Univ. Calif., San Francisco, tchg. appointment includes; hosp. affiliations include Hahnemann Univ. Hosp., Temple Univ. Hosp.; urologist Albert Einstein Med. Ctr. Named Recognized Dr., HealthGrades; named one of the Top Doctors, Phila. Mag., 2011. Fellow: ACS; mem.: Societe Internationale d'Urologie. Office: Albert Einstein Medical Center Klein Bldg Ste 200 5401 Old York Rd Philadelphia PA 19141 Office Phone: 215-456-1177. Office Fax: 215-457-1200.

METRY, DENISE, dermatologist; b. Calif., June 5, 1968; MD, U. Tex. Med. Sch., Houston, 1995. Dermatology resident U. Tex. Med. Sch., 1999; assoc. prof. dermatology and pediat., chief dermatology svc. Baylor Coll. Medicine, Tex. Children's Hosp., 2000—. Office: 6621 Fannin St CC62016 Houston TX 77030 Business E-Mail: dmetry@bcm.edu.

METZ, CHARLES EDGAR, radiology educator; b. Bayshore, NY, Sept. 11, 1942; s. Clinton Edgar and Grace Muriel (Schienke) M.; m. Maryanne Theresa Bahr, July, 1967 (div. 1988); children: Rebecca, Molly. BA, Bowdoin Coll., 1964; MS, U. Pa., 1966, PhD, 1969. Instr. radiology U. Chgo., 1969-71, asst. prof., 1971-75, assoc. prof., 1976-80, dir. grad. programs in med. physics, 1979-85, prof., 1980—, prof. structural biology, 1984-86, prof. med. physics, 2003—. Mem. diagnostic rsch. adv. group Nat. Cancer Inst., 1980-81; mem. sci. com. Nat. Coun. on Radiation Protection and Measurements, 1982-85, 2001-, Internat. Commn. on Radiation Units and Measurements, 1988-96, chmn. sci. com., 1992-99; cons. and lectr. in field. Assoc. editor: Radiology Jour., 1986—91, Med. Physics Jour., 1992—95, mem. editl. bd.: Med. Decision Making Jour., 1980—84; contbr. over 250 articles to sci. jours. and chpts. to books. Recipient L.H. Gray medal, Internat. Commn. on Radiation Units and Measurements, 2005. Fellow Am. Assn. Physicists in Medicine; mem. Radiol. Soc. N.Am., Am. Assn. Physicists in Medicine, Assn. Univ. Radiologists, Phi Beta Kappa, Sigma Xi. Achievements include development of software for ROC analysis used in more than 10,000 labs worldwide. Office: U Chgo Dept Radiology MC2026 5841 S Maryland Ave Chicago IL 60637-1463

METZ, JAMES M., radiation oncologist educator; BS, Juniata Coll., 1989; MS in Clin. Immunology/Microbiology, MCP Hahnemann U., 1991; MD, UMDNJ-Robert Wood Johnson Med. Sch., 1995. Diplomate Am. Bd. Radiology-radiation oncology. Intern internal medicine dept. Cooper Univ. Med. Ctr., Camden, NJ, 1995—96; resident radiation oncology dept. Hops. Univ. of Pa., Phila., 1996—2000, chief resident radiation oncology dept., 1998—99, clin. instr. radiation oncology dept., 1999—2000; asst. prof. radiation oncology Univ. of Pa. Health System, clin. dir. radiation oncology dept. Editor-in-chief (website) www.oncolink.upenn.edu; co-author: (publs.) Cancer Patients Use Unconventional Medical Therapies Far More Frequently Than Standard History and Physical Examination Suggests, 2001, Comparative Treatment Planning Between Proton and X-ray Therapy in Pancreatic Cancer, 2001, Endobronchial Photodynamic Therapy for the Treatment of Lung Cancer, 2001, and numerous others. Office: Perelman Center for Advanced Medicine Concourse Level 3400 Civic Center Blvd Philadelphia PA 19104 Office Phone: 800-789-7366.

METZGER, DENNIS W., medical educator, immunologist, researcher; b. Suffern, NY, Sept. 14, 1951; s. Gertrude Metzger; m. Colleen Walsh, Feb. 14, 1991; children: Jacqueline, Christina, Caroline, Natalie, Gregory. BS in Biology, U. Ill., Champaign, 1973; MS in Microbiolog and Immunology, U. Ill., Chgo., 1976, PhD, 1978. Postdoctoral fellow dept. microbiology UCLA, 1978—80; rsch. assoc. dept. immunology St. Jude Children's Rsch. Hosp., Memphis, 1980—82, asst. mem. dept. immunology, 1982—86, assoc. mem., 1986—90; assoc. prof. microbiology and immunology Med. Coll. Ohio, Toledo, 1990—96, prof. microbiology and immunology, 1996—99, dir. molecular basis of disease grad. program, 1996—99; prof. Theobald Smith Alumni chair, dir. ctr. for immunology and microbial disease Albany Med. Coll., 1999—, prof., dept. medicine, 2011—, prof. dept. medicine, 2011—. Adj. prof. dept. biomed. engrng. Rensselear Poly. Inst., Troy, 2000—; affiliated scientist NY State Dept Health, Wadsworth Ctr., Albany, 2005—. Contbr. scientific papers to profl. jours. Grantee, NIH, 1980—. Mem.: Am. Assn. Immunology. Achievements include patents in field. Home: 504 Windsor Ct Niskayuna NY 12309 Office: Albany Med Coll MC-151 43 New Scotland Ave Albany NY 12208-3478 Office Fax: 518-262-6053. Business E-Mail: metzged@mail.amc.edu.

METZGER, HENRY, federal research institution administrator; b. Mainz, Germany, Mar. 23, 1932; came to U.S., 1938; naturalized, 1945; s. Paul Alfred and Anne (Daniel) M.; m. Deborah Stashower, June 16, 1957; children: Eran D., Renée V., Carl E. MD, Columbia U., 1957. Chief chem. immunology sect. Nat. Inst. Arthritis & Musculoskeletal & Skin Disease/NIH, Bethesda, Md., 1973—2002; br. chief USPHS, Bethesda, 1983-94, sci. dir., 1987-98, med. officer grade VI, 1975-98; scientist Sr. Biomed. Rsch. Svc., 1999—2002, scientist emeritus, 2002—. Carl Prausnitz Meml. lectr., 1982; Ecker Meml. lectr. Case Western Res. U., Cleve., 1984; Harvey Soc. lectr., 1984; Eli Nadel Meml. lectr. St. Louis U., 1987; Rodney Porter Meml. lectr., 1993; Burroughs-Wellcome lectr., 1994; R.E. Dyer lectr., 1995; mem. health rsch. coun. BMFT, German Govt., 1994-97. Editor: Fc Receptors & the Action of Antibodies, 1990; assoc. editor Ann. Rev. Immunology, 1982-96; contbr. numerous articles to profl. jours.; mem. editl. bd. numerous sci. jours. Recipient Meritorious Svc. award USPHS, 1978, Disting. Svc. award, 1985, 97, Joseph Mather Smith prize Columbia U., 1984. Fellow AAAS, Am. Acad. Allergy and Immunology; mem. NAS, Am. Assn. Immunologists (pres. 1991-92), Am. Soc. Biol. Chem. Molecular Biology, Am. Soc. Cell Biology, Internat. Union Immunol. Soc. (pres. 1992-95), Found. for Advanced Edn. in the Scis. (pres. 1990-92, 2005-2008), Alpha Omega Alpha. Home: 3410 Taylor St Chevy Chase MD 20815-4024 Office: NIH Rm 6N216G 10 Center Dr 9000 Rockville Pike Bethesda MD 20892 E-mail: metzgerh@exchange.nih.gov.

METZNER, DAVID MARK, plastic and reconstructive surgeon; b. Cleve., Jan. 16, 1939; children: Damon Hires, Rowan Aliya von Zanthier. AB, U. Mich., 1960; MD, Case Western Res. U., 1964. Diplomate Am. Bd. Otolaryngology, Am. Bd. Plastic Surgery, Nat. Bd. Med. Examiners; lic. MD, Ohio, Calif., Mass., La. Internship Mt. Sinai Hosp., Cleve., 1964-65, residency in gen. surgery, 1965-66; residency in otolaryngology Harvard Med. Sch., Boston, 1966-69; chief of otolaryngology The Cambridge (Mass.) Hosp., 1971-74; residency in plastic and reconstructive surgery La. State U., New Orleans, 1975-76; active staff Lakeside Hosp., Metairie, La., 1977—2007, Highland Pk. Hosp., Covington, La., 1997—2007, Prytania Surgery Ctr., New Orleans, 1986—2007; pvt. plastic surgery New Orleans & Covington, 1977—2007; plastic surgeon Vermont Ctr. Plastic Surgery Dermatology. Active, courtest staff So. Bapt. Hosp., New Orleans, 1977—; courtesy staff St. Tammany Parish Hosp., Covington, 1977—; clin. instr. Harvard Med. Sch., 1971-75; vis. prof. Nassau County, N.Y. Med. Ctr., 1988, Med. Coll. Wis., 1992; vis. lectr. U. Calif. San Diego, 1991; clin. asst. prof. La. State U., 1994-2007; lectr. in field. Recipient AMA Physician's Recognition award, 1981, 84, 87, 90, Appreciation award North Am. Med./Dental Assn.; named one of Top Plastic Surgeons, New Orleans Mag. Mem. Am. Soc. Plastic and Reconstructive Surgeons, Inc., The Am. Soc. for Aesthetic Plastic Surgery (Walter Scott Brown award, 1989), Southeastern Soc. Plastic and Reconstructive Surgeons, Inc., Am. Acad. Facial Plastic and Reconstructive Surgery, Inc., Am. Acad. Otolaryngology-Head and Neck Surgery, Inc., La. Soc. Plastic and Reconstructive Surgeons (pres.), The Double Boarded Soc. (pres.), Southeastern Soc. Plastic and Reconstructive Surgeons, La. Soc. Plastic and Reconstructive Surgeons, La. State Med. Soc., Orleans Parish Med. Soc., Harvard Club La. (pres.). Avocations: art, sculpting, jewelry. Office: 69 Union St PO Box 147 Manchester VT 05254

METZNER, RICHARD JOEL, psychiatrist, psychopharmacologist, educator; b. LA, Feb. 15, 1942; s. Robert Gerson and Esther Rebecca (Groper) M.; children: Jeffrey Anthony, David Jonathan; m. Leila Kirkley, June 26, 1993. BA, Stanford U., 1963; MD, Johns Hopkins U., 1967. Diplomate Am. Bd. Psychiatry and Neurology. Intern Roosevelt Hosp., NYC, 1967-68; resident in psychiatry Stanford U. Med. Ctr., 1968-71; staff psychiatrist divsn. manpower and tng. NIMH-St. Elizabeths Hosp., Washington, 1971-73; chief audiovisual edn. sys. VA Med. Ctr. Brentwood, LA, 1973-79; from asst. prof. psychiatry to assoc. clin. prof. UCLA Neuropsychiat. Inst., 1980-96, clin. prof., 1996—. Lectr. Sch. Social Welfare, 1975-84; pvt. practice medicine specializing in psychiatry, Bethesda, Md., 1972-73, L.A., 1973—, Sedona, Ariz., 1997—; dir. Western Inst. Psychiatry, L.A., 1977—; pres. Psychiat. Resource Network, Inc., 1984-90, chair, Clin. Neuropharmacology, UCLA, 2007. Contbr. articles to profl. jours.; prodr., writer numerous films and videotapes. With USPHS, 1968-71. Recipient 6 awards for film and videotape prodns., 1976-80, Career Achievement award, Psychiat. Clin. Faculty Assn., UCLA 2006 Fellow: Am. Psychiat. Assn. (life Disting.); mem.: UCLA Psychiat. Clin. Faculty Assn. (pres. 2001—02), Mental Health Careerists Assn. (chmn. 1972—73), So. Calif. Psychiat. Soc., Phi Beta Kappa. Democrat. Jewish. Office: 25 Cindercone Cir Sedona AZ 86336 Office Phone: 928-204-5850. E-mail: rmetzner@ucla.edu, rmetzner@earthlink.net.

MEULEMANS, HERMAN, sociologist, educator; b. Wilrijk, Belgium, May 27, 1952; s. Jozef Meulemans and Philomena Wyten; m. Nathalia Bekx, Mar. 27, 1976; children: Stefan, Jeroen. Degree, U. Faculties St. Ignatius Loyola Antwerp, 1972; lic. in Polit. and Social Scis., U. Inst. Antwerp, Antwerp, 1974; PhD, UIA, Antwerp, 1982. Rsch. asst./lectr. U. Inst. Antwerp, 1974—90, assoc. prof., 1990—2003, chair dept. PSW, 1997—99; rsch. assoc. Boston U., 1984—85; prof. U. Antwerpen, Antwerp, 2003—, vice-dean faculty polit. and social scis., 2003—. Mem. gen. meeting Sheltered Workshop Handicapped Persons, Antwerp, 1986—95; bd. dirs. De Ideale Woning, Antwerp. Editor: (book) Tuberculosis in Pakistan, 2000. Recipient Glaxo Prize for Sci. Journalism, Glaxo Belgium NV, Brussels, 1978; Rsch. fellow, NATO, 1984—85. Mem.: European Soc. for Health and Med. Sociology, Vereniging voor Sociologie. Office: Universiteit Antwerpen Fac PSW Universiteitsplein 1 B-2610 Antwerp Belgium Office Fax: 32-3-820.28.82. Business E-Mail: herman.meulemans@ua.ac.be.

MEUNIER, PIERRE JEAN, medical educator; b. Miribel, France, June 5, 1936; s. Marcel Jacques and Marie Ernestine (Ballufin) M.; m. Marie Aimée Loiseleur, July 16, 1961 (div. 1984); children: Gilles, Pascal, Francois; m. Annie Bernadette Mariés, Dec. 27, 1986. B, Lycée Ampère, Lyons, France, 1953; MD, Claude Bernard U., Lyons, France, 1967. Resident Lyons Hosps., 1963-67; asst. prof. Lyons Hosps. Claude Bernard U., 1967-71, head dept. rheumatology and bone disease, 1979—2002, hon. chmn. dept. rheumatology and bone diseases, 2002—, prof. medicine, 1971—; emeritus prof. Lyons 1 U., 2006—; head rsch. unit INSERM 234, 1979-92. Hon. pres. Groupe de Rsch. et d'Info. Osteoporoses, Paris, 1990—; cons. WHO, Geneva; mem. sci. bd. Internat. Osteoporosis Found.; past pres. European Found. for Osteoporosis, 1996—; cons. French Min. of Health, 1997—; hon. pres. Internat. Soc. Bone Morphometry, 2002; cons. in field. Editor-in-chief Bone, 1978-89, Osteoporosis Internat., 1989-2005; contbr. articles to profl. jours., chpts. to books Served with French Navy, 1962-63. Decorated officer Ordre des Palmes Academiques (France); recipient Internat. League Against Rheumatism prize 1989, prize Paget's Disease Found., 1991, John Haddad award Internat. Bone and Mineral Rsch. Soc., 1998, Frederic C. Bartter award Am. Soc. for Bone and Mineral Rsch., 1999, recognition career award Vitamin D Workshop, Nashville, 2000, Pierre Delmas Internat. prize, FLorence, 2010. Mem. European Calcified Tissue Soc. (sec. 1985-91), Nat. Sci. Commn. INSERM, Sci. Coun. Drug Agy., Nat. Coun. Univ. cons. at Minister of Health. Avocation: music. Office: Lieu Dit Chancelades 48130 Aumont France Office Phone: 33 4 66 45 94 26. Personal E-mail: pierre.jean.meunier@cegetel.net. Business E-Mail: pierre.meunier@sante.univ-lyon1.fr, pierre.meunier0896@orange.fr.

MEYER, CARSTEN H., ophthalmologist; b. Goettingen, Germany, May 24, 1965; s. Hans-Jurgen and Borghild Meyer; m. Barbara E. Riedl, May 31, 1967; children: Philipp Marc Louis children: Paula Susi Leonie. D, Albert Ludwigs U., Freiburg, 1990; degree, Ludwig Maximilians U., Munich, 1994. Cert. ophthalmology State Schleswig-Hostein, 1999. Intern Duke U., Eye Ctr., Durham, NC, 1994, fellow vitreoretinal disease, 1999—2001; resident in ophthalmology Med. U. Lübeck, Germany, 1994—98; attending clin. ophthalmology Philipps U., Marburg, Germany, 2001—06; prof. ophthalmology U. Bonn, 2006—11, attending clin. ophthalmology, dept. opthalmology, 2006—11; prof. U. Augenklinik Bonn; vis. prof. U. Sao Paulo, Brazil, 2010; co-head dept. Pallas Clinic, Olten, Switzerland, 2011—. Clin. scientist Dept. Human Genetics, Haunersche Childrens Hosp. U. Munich, 1990—92; cons. dept. applied physics U. Ulm, Germany, 1994—99; rsch. scientist Inspire Pharm. Inc., Durham, 2006; attending clin. dept. ophthalmology U. Bonn. Author: Diagnostic View, 1998, 2nd edit., 2007, Retinal Disease on Optical Coherence Tomography, 2006; editor: Eye and Internal Medicine, 2004. Founding mem. Leo Club, Osnabrueck, Germany, 1984—2003. Lt. Tank Arty., 1985—87, Goettingen. Recipient, Joachim-Ruthlin, 1999; grantee, Pharmacia & Upjohn, 1997—99, Adler Found., 1999—2001, Fehr Found., 2002—05, Pohl Found., 2003—08, Novartis, 2006—, Allergen, 2006—, GSK, 2008. Mem.: Swiss Ophthal. Soc., Retina Soc., EURETINA, Oxford Union Soc., Deutschen Ophthalmologische Gesellschaft, Am. Assn. Rsch. Vision and Ophthalmology, Am. Acad. Ophthalmology, Lions Club, Club Jules Gonin. Achievements include patents pending for posterior vitreous detachment by RGD peptides; patents in field of vitreoretinal internal limiting membrane color enhancer. Avocations: sailing, skiing, hiking. Home: Serturnerstrasse 9 53127 Bonn Germany Office: Pallas Clinic Louis Giroud St 20 Olten 4600 Switzerland Office Phone: 0041(76)4916473. Personal E-mail: meyer_eye@yahoo.com.

MEYER, GEORGE WILBUR, internist, gastroenterologist; b. Calif., Apr. 30, 1941; s. George Wilbur and Emily Fuller (Campbell) M.; m. Carolyn Edwards Garrett, Apr. 8, 1967; children: Robert James, Elizabeth Jackson, Dobro Goodale. BS, MIT, 1962; MD, Tulane Med. Sch., 1966. Intern So. Pacific Hosps. Inc., San Francisco, 1966-67; resident Pacific Presbyn. Med. Ctr., San Francisco, 1969-72; commd. 1st lt. USAF, advanced through grades to col., 1980; fellow in gastroenterology David Grant USAF Med. Ctr., Travis AFB, Calif., 1974-76; asst. chair dept. medicine USAF Med. Ctr., Keesler AFB, Miss., 1976-78; asst. prof. dept. medicine Uniformed Svcs. Univ., Bethesda, Md., 1978-80; chair dept. medicine Wright Patterson AFB, Dayton, Ohio, 1980-82; chief of medicine Wilford Hall USAF Med. Ctr., Lackland AFB, Tex., 1982-86; chief clin. svcs. USAF Acad., Colo., 1986-88; comdr. 1st Med. Group, Langley AFB, Va., 1988-89, 86th Med. Group, Ramstein AFB, Germany, 1989-92; program dir. internal medicine Ga. Bapt. Med. Ctr., Atlanta, 1993-97; assoc. clin. prof. medicine U. Calif., Davis, 1998-2001, clin. prof. medicine, 2001—. Cons. Walter Reed Army Med. Ctr., Washington, 1978-80, Nat. Naval Med. Ctr., Bethesda, 1978-80; assoc. prof. Wright State U. Sch. Medicine, Dayton, 1980-82; cons. Dayton VA Med. Ctr., 1980-82; clin. assoc. prof. medicine U. Tex. Health Sci. Ctr., San Antonio, 1982-86, Med. Coll. Ga., Augusta, 1993-97; cons. dept. corp. med. divsn. State of Calif., 1997-98. Mem. editl. bd. Gastrointestinal Endoscopy, 1993-97, OnLine Jour. of Digestive Health, 1998-2000, Practical Gastroenterology, 1999—; book rev. editor Practical Gastroenterology, 1999-2008, Sierra Sacramento Med. Soc. Jour., 2005—; contbr. articles and revs. to profl. jours. and chpts. to books. Mem. leadership com. Am. Cancer Soc., Ramstein AFB, 1989-93, bd. dirs.

Atlanta City Unit, 1995-97, Ga. divsn. 1996-97, El Paso Teller Unit, Colorado Springs, 1986-88, Bexar Metro Unit, San Antonio, 1984-86; adv. com. United Health Svcs., Dayton, 1980-82. Fellow ACP (Laureate award, AirForce 2001, Northern Calif. 2006), master Am. Coll. Gastroenterology, 2008, Am. Assn. Study Liver Diseases; mem. Am. Soc. for Gastro Endoscopy, Am. Gastrointestinal Assn., Northern Calif. Chpt. Am. Coll. Physicians (gov. North Calif. Chpt. 2009-). Avocations: squash, tennis, scuba diving, stamp collecting/philately. Personal E-mail: geowmeyer1@earthlink.net.

MEYER, HERMANN BELTON PERRIN, retired neonatologist, health facility agency and administrator, bioethicist; b. Stockton, Calif., Apr. 5, 1935; s. Hermann Perrin and Margaret Anna (Kammerer) Meyer; m. Marion Annette Pinkerton, July 2, 1961; children: Paul Belton, Christopher Charles. AA, Sacramento Jr. Coll., Calif., 1955; BA, U. Calif., Berkeley, 1957; MD, U. Calif., San Francisco, 1960; MS, Ariz. State U., Tempe, 1999, PhD, 2006. Diplomate Am. Bd. Pediat., 1969, perinatal medicine Am. Bd. Pediat., 1975. Rotating internship Highland-Alameda County Hosp., Oakland, Calif., 1960—61; sr. pediat. intern U. Calif. Med. Ctr., San Francisco, 1963—64, pediat. residency, 1964—65; fellowship, NIH Newborn Respiratory Physiology Ctr. for Premature Infants, Stanford U., Palo Alto, Calif., 1965—67; med. dir. newborn transport and intensive care Ariz. State Health Dept., Phoenix, 1967—91; med. dir. nurseries Good Samaritan and Phoenix Children's Hosps., Phoenix, 1967—86, 1990—91; med. dir. Ariz. Health Care Cost Containment Sys., Phoenix, 1992—97, ret., 1997. Trustee Ariz. Perinatal Trust, Phoenix, 1980—, trustee emeritus, 2008—; chmn. bioethics com. Good Samaritan Hosp., 1983—89; mem. cmty. bd. St. Joseph's Hosp. and Med. Ctr., Phoenix, 2002—08; sec., adv. com. Cath. Social Svcs., Phoenix, 2003—06; chmn. bioethics com. Phoenix Children's Hosp.; cons. in field. Contbr. articles to profl. jours. Chmn. premature adv. com. Ariz. Health Dept., 1970—73; chmn. bioethics workgroup Kino Inst. Cath. Diocese, Phoenix, 1980—83. Lt. med. corps. USN, 1961—63, med. officer USN, 1961—62, USS Lenawee, asst. med. officer, med. dept. US Naval Air Reserve Training Sta., 1962—63, Los Alamitos, Calif. Recipient various Lifetime Achievement awards, Dr. William Beaumont Outstanding Contbn. by Physician Under 50 award, AMA, 1978. Mem.: SAR (Ariz. and nat. soc. 2006—), Ariz. Med. Assn. (bd. dirs. 1967—74, chmn. govt. svcs. 1983—86, chmn. bioethics 1990—96, A.H. Robins Physician Cmty. Svc. award 1978), Maricopa Med. Soc., Knights Malta (mem. Malta ctr. bd. 1991—98, named Knight Magistral Grace 1991). Democrat. Roman Catholic. Avocations: painting, ceramics, philosophy, reading. Home: 901 West Monte Vista Rd Phoenix AZ 85007 Office Phone: 602-663-1907. Personal E-mail: belhpmar@q.com.

MEYER, JACK EDWARD, radiologist, educator; b. Davenport, Iowa, Oct. 21, 1939; s. Russell and Ellen Meyer; m. Mary Jean Meyer, Jan. 9, 1966; children: Heather, Hilary. BA, Grinnell Coll., Iowa, 1961; MD, Cornell U., 1965; MS (hon.), Harvard U., 1991. Diplomate Am. Bd. Radiology; lic. physician, Mass., Calif., Mich. Intern San Francisco Gen. Hosp., 1965-66; resident in radiology U. Mich., Ann Arbor, 1968-69, Mass. Gen. Hosp., Boston, 1969-71, asst. radiation medicine, 1971-72, head oncologic diagnostic radiology, 1979-85; chief diagnostic radiology Pondville Hosp., Walpole, Mass., 1972-78, chief radiology, chief staff, 1978-79; prof., chmn. dept. radiology U. Louisville, Ky., 1985-87; acting dir. diagnostic radiology Brigham and Women's Hosp., Boston, 1987-88, dir. diagnostic radiology, 1989-99; dir. breast imaging Dana-Farber Cancer Inst., Boston, 2001—. Asst. prof. radiology Boston U., 1972-74, assoc. clin. prof., 1974-79; asst. prof. U. Mass., Boston, 1976-77, assoc. prof. radiology, 1977-79; asst. prof. radiology Harvard Med. Sch., Boston, 1979-82, assoc. prof. radiology, 1982-85, 87-91, prof. radiology, 1991—; dir. diagnostic oncoradiology Dana-Farber Cancer Inst., Boston, 1991-99; dir. breast imaging, Brigham and Womens Hosp, Boston, 1999—2002. Author: (with others) Interventional Radiology, 1981, Cancer: A Manual for Practitioners, 6th edit., 1982, Lymphatic Imaging, 2d edit., 1985; cons. to editorial bd. jours.; contbr. numerous articles and abstracts to profl. jours. Examiner Am. Bd. Radiology, 1992—. Capt. USAF, 1966-68. Fellow: Soc. Breast Imaging, Am. Coll. Radiology; mem.: Radiol. Soc. N. Am., Mass. Radiol. Soc., Mass. Med. Soc. Office: Brigham and Womens Hosp Dept Diagnostic Radiology 75 Francis St Boston MA 02115-6106 Business E-Mail: jmeyer@partners.org.

MEYER, JEAN-PIERRE, psychiatrist; b. Paris, Apr. 3, 1949; s. Henry Jules and Jacqueline Suzanne (Roux).; m. Marie Elisabeth Buisan, June 25, 1977; children: Arnaud Jean, Gauthier Henri. MD, Broussais U., 1975; Cert. of Maritime Medicine, 1976; Cert. of Med. Expertise, Cochin U., 1978; specialist in Psychiatry, Necker U., 1978. Intern Fontainebleau Hosp., France, 1974, Enfants Malades Hosp., 1975, Melun (France) Hosp., France, 1976, Mohamed V Hosp., Rabat, Morocco, 1976, Lagny Hosp., France, 1977; intern psychiatrist infirmary of police Paris, 1977; sole practice medicine, specializing in psychiatry, 1979—. Cons. Paris Hosp., 1986—; expert cons. Securite Sociale, Paris and Creil, 1984—; expert cons. Ct. of Appeals, Paris, 1988; archbishopric, Paris, 1979—. Author: Relaxation Therapeutique, 1986; co-author: Le Projet en Psychotherapie, 1983, Abrege de Neuro-Psychiatrie, Conduites Pratiques de Psychiatrie, 1994. Contbr. articles to profl. jours. V.p. Mutual Ins.'s, Paris, 1972—. Mem. Intergroupe de Formation en Relaxation, Med. Assn. Paris., Soc. Français de Relaxation (treas.). Roman Catholic. Avocations: golf, skiing, surfing. Office: 9 Rue Du Général Delestraint 75016 Paris France Home Phone: 33-1-46-51-51-43; Office Phone: 33-1-40-71-99-15. Fax: 33-1-40-71-99-25. E-mail: meyer@relaxpsy.com.

MEYER, JENS EDUARD, otolaryngologist; s. Gerd Eduard and Renate Elisabeth Meyer; m. Eva Varhegyi, June 12, 1993; children: Joshua Eduard Laszlo, Luis Tamas, Benjamin Tibor. MD with honors, Christian-Albrechts-U., Kiel, Germany, 1997; PhD, Luebeck U., Germany, 2006. Rsch. fellow Yale U., VA Hosp., West Haven, Conn., 1997; subintern Yale U., New Haven, 1998; resident Dept. Otorhinolaryngolgy, Head and Neck Surgery, Kiel, Schleswig-Holstein, Germany, 1998—2003, fellow, 2003—05; attending Dept. Otorhinolaryngolgy, Spl. Head and Neck Surgery, 2005—11, Dept. Otorhinolaryngolgy, Facial Plastic Surgery, Luebeck, 2006—11, vice chmn., 2011—, head dept., 2011—; vis. asst. prof. surgery Yale U., New Haven, 2003—, assoc. prof. otorhinolaryngology, head & neck surgery, 2009—11; chmn., dept. otorhinolaryngolgy, head & neck surgery AK St. George, Hamburg. Lectr. Sch. Speech Therapy, Kiel, 1999—2005; editor Open Jour. Otorhinolaryngology, 2008—; cons. in field. Contbr. articles to profl. jours.; editor: Allergy, 2000—, Open Jour. Otolaryngology, 2009—. Recipient Hensel prize, Christian-Albrechts-U., 2003; grantee, Med. Faculty Christian-Albrechts-U., 2004. Mem.: European Acad. Allergy and Clin. Immunology (licentiate Jr. Mem. Travel award 2003), North German Assn. for Facial Surgery (licentiate), German Otorhinolaryngology, Head and Neck Soc. (licentiate Plester prize 2000), Am. Head and Neck Soc. (corr.), Alumni Club Christian-Albrechts-U. (licentiate). Lutheran. Avocations: Judo, diving, running. Office: Dept Otorhinolaryngology Head Neck Surgery Lohmuehlenstr 5 Hamburg 20099 Germany Office Fax: 49401818853538.

MEYER, JON KEITH, psychiatrist, psychoanalyst, educator; b. Springfield, Ill., May 6, 1938; m. Eleanor Fumie Yamashita, June 6, 1964; children: David Christopher, Laura Tamiko. AB summa cum laude, Dartmouth Coll., 1960; MD, Johns Hopkins U., 1964; grad., Washington Psychoanalytic Inst, 1980. Intern internal medicine Johns Hopkins Hosp., Balt., 1964-65, resident in psychiatry, 1965-67, 69, St. Elizabeth's Hosp., Washington, 1968; spl. asst. to dir. NIMH, Bethesda, Md., 1969-71; asst. prof. psychiatry Johns Hopkins Med. Sch., Balt., 1971-76, assoc. prof., 1976-83; prof. psychiatry Med. Coll. Wis., Milw., 1983—2003, prof. psychoanalysis, 1996—2003, prof. family medicine, 1990—2003, prof. psychiatry and psychoanalysis emeritus, 2003—; tng. and supervising analyst Chgo. Inst. for Psychoanalysis, 1987—2002; vice chmn. Dept. of Psychiatry, 1993—2003; chief psychiatry Froedtert Meml. Luth. Hosp., Milw., 1994-97; tng. and supervising analyst Wis. Psychoanalytic Inst., Milw., 2001—07, Washington Psychoanalytic Inst., 2004—; tchg. analyst Balt.-Washington Psychoanalytic Inst., 2004—11; clin. prof. psychiatry Georgetown U. Sch. Medicine, 2006—. Clin. prof. psychiatry U. Maryland Sch. of Medicine, 2006-, med. dir. Wis., Psychoanalytic Found., Milw., 1987-91, sec. bd. dir., 1988-91; part time assoc. prof. psychiatry Johns Hopkins Med. Sch., 2003-. Author books; editl. bd. Jour. Am. Psychoanalytic Assn., 1991-94; nat. editor: The American Psychoanalyst, 1997-2001; mem. steering com. Psychodynamic Diagnostic Manual; contbr. chpts. to books, numerous articles to profl. jours. Comdr. USPHS, 1967—71. Recipient Dennison Rsch. prize, Johns Hopkins Med. Sch., 1964; Sr. fellow, Dartmouth Coll., 1959—60, Daniel Webster Nat. scholar, 1956—60, Rufus Choate scholar, 1960, Erik Erikson scholar, Austen Riggs Ctr., Stockbridge, Mass., 1991—92, Ctr. Advanced Psychoanalytic Studies, Princeton, NJ, 1998—. Fellow: Am. Coll. Psychoanalysts, Am. Psychiat. Assn. (disting. life fellow), mem.: Task Force Psychoanalysis & Arts, Washington Ctr. Psychoanalysis (bd. dirs. 2007—10), Wash. Psychoanalytic Soc., Balt.-Wash. Psychoanalytic Soc., Can. Psychoanalytic Soc. (hon.), William Alanson White Psychoanalytic Soc. (hon.), Wis. Psychoanalytic Soc. (pres. 1989—91), Assn. Child Psychoanalysis (candidate councilor 2001—03), Am. Psychoanalytic Assn. (exec. councilor 1993—97, chmn. com. on exec. coun. structure and function 1995—98, sec. 1997—2001, chmn. com. on cmty. clinics 1997—2002, exec. com. 1997—2002, adminstrv. bd. Jour. Am. Psychoanalytic Assn. 1997—2002, com. on insts. 1998—2002, com. on bylaws 2001—02, pres.-elect 2002—04, adminstrv. bd. Jour. Am. Psychoanalytic Assn. 2002—06, exec. com. 2002—06, pres. 2004—06, chmn. exec. com. 2004—06, presiding officer exec. coun. 2004—06, chmn. steering com. 2004—06, exploratory subcom. nominating com. 2006—08, exec. councilor 2006—11, chair task force on access to care 2007—08, Edith Sabshin Tchg. award 1999), Internat. Psychoanalytical Assn. (com. on constn. and by-laws 1997—2001, com. on procedural codes 1997—2001, task force on structure and mission 1997—2001, ho. dels. 1998—2001, chair ho. of dels. 1999—2000). Avocations: photography, hiking, kayaking. Office: 2210 Dalewood Rd Lutherville Timonium MD 21093 Office Phone: 410-308-1752, 410-303-2698. Personal E-mail: jkmeyermd@comcast.net.

MEYER, KARIN ZUMWALT, pharmacist, consultant; b. Buffalo, Aug. 17, 1953; d. Robert F. and Mildred (Oswald) Zumwalt; m. Jimmy E. Meyer, Aug. 12, 1994. BS in Pharmacy, Purdue U., 1976; MBA in Healthcare, Cleve. State U., 1987. Registered pharmacist, Ohio. Pharmacist Cleve. Clinic, 1982-87, Caremark, Mayfield Hts., Ohio, 1987-88; dir. pharmacy Careplus, Beachwood, Ohio, 1988-89; pharmacy mgr. Kaiser Permanent, Cleve., 1989-93; dir. pharmacy Homedco Infusion, Valley View, Ohio, 1993-95; relief pharmacist, cons. RPh On the Go, Solon, Ohio, 1995-96; pediat. pharmacist Cleve. Clinic Children's Hosp. for Rehab., 1996—2005; cons. Clin. Edge, 2005—. Adj. instr. Cuyahoga C.C., Cleve., 1990-93; clin. mgmt. team Careplus, Beachwood, 1988-89. Satellite planning com. Cleve. Clinic Found., 1982-87. Mem. USTA, Am. Pharm. Assn., Am. Soc. Health-Sys. Pharmacists (membership com. 1996-97), Cmty. Emergency Response Team, Cleve. Metro Ski Coun., Purdue Club Cleve., Iota Sigma Pi. Avocations: skiing, tennis, windsurfing, travel, music. Home: 8549 Settlers Passage Brecksville OH 44141-1749 Personal E-mail: quagmeyer@sbcglobal.net.

MEYER, RICHARD CHARLES, microbiologist, educator; b. Cleve., May 2, 1930; s. Frederick Albert and Tekla Charlotte (Schrade) M.; m. Carolyn Yvonne Patton, Apr. 6, 1963; children: Frederick Gustav, Carl Anselm. B.Sc., Baldwin-Wallace Coll., 1952; M.Sc., Ohio State U., 1957, PhD, 1961. Teaching and research asst. Ohio State U., 1956-61, research assoc., 1961-62; microbiologist Nat. Cancer Inst., NIH, Bethesda, Md., 1962-64; asst. prof. vet. pathology and hygiene and microbiology U. Ill., Urbana-Champaign, 1965-68, assoc. prof., 1968-73, prof., 1973-89, prof. emeritus, 1989—. Served with C.E. U.S. Army, 1952-54. Mem. Am. Acad. Microbiology, AAAS, Am. Inst. Biol. Sci., Am. Soc. Microbiology, Sigma Xi, Gamma Sigma Delta, Phi Zeta. Republican. Lutheran. Home: 1504 S Buckthorn Ln Mahomet IL 61853-3632 Office: Dept Vet Pathobiology U Ill at Urbana-Champaign Urbana IL 61801

MEYER-BAHLBURG, HEINO F.L., psychology professor; b. Hamburg, Germany, Feb. 26, 1940; came to U.S., 1969; s. Wilhelm and Marie Luise Meyer-B. Vordiplom in Psychology, U. Hamburg, 1963, Diplom Psychology, 1966; D in Natural Scis., U. Düsseldorf, Germany, 1970. Sci. asst. U. Düsseldorf, 1970; rsch. asst., then rsch. assoc. prof. psychiatry and pediat. SUNY Med. Sch., Buffalo, 1970-77; rsch. scientist N.Y. State Psychiat. Inst., NYC, 1977—; from assoc. clin. prof. med. psychology to prof. clin. psychology in psychiatry Columbia U. Coll. Physicians and Surgeons, 1978—; pediat. behavioral endocrinologist Presbyn. Hosp., NYC, 1978-90, prof. psychologist in psychiat. svc., 1990—. Contbr. numerous articles to profl. publs. Recipient Disting. Sci. Achievement award Soc. for Sci. Study of Sex, 1993; grantee NIMH, NICHD. Mem. AAAS, APA, Soc. Pediat. Psychology, Internat. Acad. Sex Rsch., Soc. Sci. Study Sex, Soc. Rsch. Child Devel., Soc. Sexual Therapy and Rsch., Pediat. Endocrine Soc., World Profl. Assn. for Transgender Health. Office: Columbia U Dept Psychiatry 1051 Riverside Dr Unit 15 New York NY 10032 Office Phone: 212-543-5299. Business E-Mail: meyerb@childpsych.columbia.edu.

MEYERHARDT, JEFFREY ABRAHAM, internist, oncologist; b. Englewood, NJ, Oct. 26, 1969; MD, Yale U. Sch. Med., 1997. Resident, internal medicine Beth Israel Deaconess Med. Ctr., Boston, 1997; fellow, med. oncology Dana-Farber Cancer Ctr. Inst., Boston, hosp. appointment, Gastrointestinal Cancer Ctr., dept. med. oncology, 2002—; asst. prof. medicine Harvard Med. Sch., Boston, 2004—. Contbr. articles to profl. jours. Office: Dana-Farber Cancer Inst Mailstop DL 1220 44 Binney St Boston MA 02115 Office Phone: 617-632-6855. Office Fax: 617-632-5370.

MEYEROWITZ, ELLIOT MARTIN, biology professor; b. Washington, May 22, 1951; s. Irving and Freda (Goldberg) Meyerowitz; m. Joan Agnes Kobori, June 17, 1984; 2 children. AB, Columbia U., NYC, 1973; MPhil, Yale U., New Haven, 1975, PhD, 1977; D (hon.), École Normale Supérieure, Lyon, France, 2007. Rsch. fellow Stanford U., Calif., 1977-79; asst. prof. biology Calif. Inst. Tech., Pasadena, 1980-85, assoc. prof., 1985-89, prof., 1989—, George W. Beadle prof. biology, 2002—, chair, divsn. biology, 2000—10. Mem. editl. bd. Trends in Genetics, Current Biology, Genome Biology, Current Opinion in Plant Biology, Jour. Biology; contbr. articles to profl. jours. Recipient Internat. Sci. prize, LVMH Moët Hennessy-Louis Vuitton S.A., France, 1996, Internat. prize for biology, Japan Soc. Promotion of Sci., 1997, Mendel medal, Villanova U., 1997, Wilbur Cross medal, Yale U., 2001, Ross Harrison prize, Internat. Soc. Devel. Biologist, 2005, Balzan prize for plant molecular genetics, Internat. Balzan Prize Found., 2006; Jane Coffin Childs Meml. Fund fellow, 1977—79, Sloan Found. fellow, 1980—82. Fellow: AAAS, Am. Soc. Plant Biologists (Gibbs medal 1995); mem.: NAS (coun. mem. 2006—09, Lounsbery award 1999), Royal Soc., Soc. Devel. Biology (pres. 2005—06), French Acad. Scis. (fgn.), Internat. Soc. Plant Molecular Biology (pres. 1995—97), Genetics Soc. America (pres. 1999, medal 1996), Bot. Soc. America (Pelton award 1994, Centennial award 2006), Am. Acad. Arts & Scis., Am. Philos. Soc. Office: Calif Inst Tech Divsn Biology 156 29 Pasadena CA 91125-0001 Home Phone: 626-844-4555; Office Phone: 626-395-6889. Business E-Mail: meyerow@caltech.edu.

MEYERS, ABBEY S., foundation administrator; b. Bklyn., Apr. 11, 1944; m. Jerrold B. Meyers, Oct. 23, 1966; children: David, Adam, Laura. AAS, N.Y.C. Community Coll., 1962; LHD (hon.), Alfred U., 1994. Comml. artist various advt. agys., NYC, 1962-65; dir. patient svcs. Tourette Syndrome Assn., Bayside, NY, 1980-85; exec. dir., founder Nat. Org. for Rare Disorders, Danbury, Conn., 1985—, pres. U.S. commr. Nat. Commn. on Orphan Diseases, Washington, 1986-89; subcom. human gene therapy NIH, Bethesda, Md., 1989-92, recombinant DNA adv. com., 1992-96; mem. Health Care Payor Adv. Commn. on Conn. Commn. on Hosps. and Health Care, 1992-94; mem. FDA Biol. Response Modifiers Com., 1995-99; DHHS Nat. Human Rsch. Protection Adv. Com., 2000-2002; Partnership for Human Rsch. Protection Pub. Adv. Coun., 2005—. Author: (with others) Orphan Drugs and Orphan Diseases: Clinical Reality and Public Policy, 1983, (with others) Cooperative Approaches to Research and Development of Orphan Drugs, 1985, (with others) Tourette Syndrome: Clinical Understanding and Treatment, 1988, (with others) Physicians Guide to Rare Diseases, 1992. Bd. dirs. Nat. Orphan Drug and Device Found., N.Y.C., 1982-85; leader Coalition to Pass Orphan Drug Act of 1983, 1979-82. Recipient Pub. Health Svc. award HHS, 1985, Commr.'s Spl. citation FDA, 1988. Mem. Nat. Health Coun. (bd. dirs. 1989-94), Alliance of Genetic Support Groups (bd. dirs. 1987-89), European Orgn. for Rare Disorders (hon. pres. 1997—). Avocations: reading, horseback riding. Office: Nat Orgn for Rare Disorders PO Box 1968 Danbury CT 06813-1968 E-mail: orphan@rarediseases.org.

MEYERS, DAVID GEORGE, internist, cardiologist, educator; b. Muscatine, Iowa, Oct. 5, 1950; BS, Loras Coll., 1972; MD, U. Iowa, 1976; MPH, Med. Coll. Wis., 1998. Cert. in cardiology Am. Bd. Internal Medicine, Am. Bd. Preventive Medicine, Am. Bd. Clin. Lipidology. Intern Creighton U., 1976-77, resident medicine, 1977-79; fellow cardiology Med. Coll. Va., 1979-81; from asst. prof. internal medicine to assoc. prof. Neb. U. Med. Ctr., Omaha, 1981-93; mem. faculty U. Kans. Med. Ctr., Kansas City, 1994, prof. internal medicine and preventive medicine, 1994—, dir. of preventive Cardiology, 1994—. Recipient Chancellor's Outstanding Classroom Tchg. award, U. Kans., 1997. Fellow ACP, Am. Coll. Cardiology, Am. Coll. Chest Physicians, Am. Heart Assn., Am. Coll. Preventive Medicine, Nat. Lipid Assn.; mem. Am. Coll. Epidemiology, Am. Soc. Preventive Cardiology, Soc. Civil War Surgeons, Internat. Wine and Food Soc., Am. Inst. for Wine and Food. Office: U Kans Med Ctr 3901 Rainbow Blvd Kansas City KS 66160-0001 Office Phone: 913-588-6015. Business E-Mail: dmeyers@kumc.edu.

MEYERS, LINDA DEE, non-profit administrator, researcher; b. Chgo., Dec. 31, 1945; m. L. Richard Meyers; 2 children. BA in Phys. Edn. & Health with honors, Goshen Coll., 1968; MS in Food and Nutrition, Colo. State U., 1974; PhD in Nutritional Sciences, Cornell U., 1978. Vol., tchr. Swaneng Hill Secondary Sch., Serowe, Botswana, 1968—72; staff Bioteko Rural Coop., Serowe, Botswana, 1972; rsch. asst. dept. food sci. and nutrition Colo. State U., 1973-74; vis. asst. prof. to rsch. assoc. Cornell U., 1979—82; staff officer to sr. staff officer Food and Nutrition Bd., Internat. Nutrition Program, 1982—86; scientist Nat. Ctr. Health Statistics Dept. Health and Human Services, Office Disease Prevention and Health Promotion, Washington, 1976-78, sr. nutrition advisor, 1986—96, dep. dir. and team leader nutrition, environ. health. & sci. coord., 1996—2001; dep. dir., Food and Nutrition Bd. Inst. Medicine-Nat. Academies, Washington, 2001—03, dir., Food and Nutrition bd., 2003—. Contbr. articles to profl. jours. Numerous awards including Sec. Health and Human Services Disting. Svc. award for Healthy People 2010, Surgeon General's Medallion, Disting. Svc. for Nat. Academies. Mem. APHA, IFT, Am. Soc. Nutrition, Omicron Nu, Phi Kappa Phi. Office: Institute of Medicine 500 Fifth St NW Washington DC 20001 Office Phone: 202-334-3153. Business E-Mail: lmeyers@nas.edu.

MEYERS, MARLENE O., retired hospital administrator; m. Eugene Meyers; children: Lori, Lisa, Dean. BSN, U. Sask., 1962; postgrad., U. Oslo, Norway, 1973; MSc, U. Calgary, Alta., Can., 1976; continuing edn., Harvard U., 1980, Banff Sch. Mgmt., 1985, U. Western Ont., Can., 1993; EMT-B, Scottsdale C.C., 2000. RN, Ariz. Various nursing positions, Alta. and B.C., Can., 1962-69; instr., chair Mount Royal

Coll. Allied Health, Calgary, 1969-82; asst. exec. dir. Rockyview Hosp., Calgary, 1982-85; v.p. patient svcs. Calgary Gen. Hosp., 1985-91, pres., CEO, 1991-95, Meyers and Assocs. Health Care Mgmt. Cons., Calgary, 1995—98; clin. nurse Scottsdale Behavioral Health Ctr., 1999—2006. Surveyor Can. Coun. on Health Facilities Accreditation, 1986-97; mem. adv. com. for South Caucasus Health info. project, Can. Adv. Com. Named Calgary Woman of Yr. in field of Health, 1982; recipient Heritage of Svc. award, 1996. Mem. Alta. Assn. RNs (hon.), Can. Coll. Health Svcs. Orgn., Can. Exec. Svcs. Orgn., Can. Soc. for Internat. Health (bd. dirs. 1997-2001, South Caucasus adv. com. 2001—), Rotary Internat. PEO also: 10464 E Cannon Dr Scottsdale AZ 85258-4929

MEYERS, MORTON ALLEN, radiologist, educator; b. Troy, NY, Oct. 1, 1933; s. David and Jeanne Sarah (Dunn) M.; m. Beatrice Applebaum, June 1, 1963; children— Richard, Amy. MD, SUNY, Upstate Med. Coll., 1959. Diplomate Am. Bd. Radiology, 1965. Intern Bellevue Hosp., NYC, 1959-60; resident in radiology Columbia-Presbyn. Med. Ctr., NYC, 1960-63; fellow Am. Cancer Soc., 1961-63; prof. dept. radiology Cornell U. Med. Ctr., NYC, 1973-78; radiologist in chief Stony Brook U. Hosp., 1978—91; prof., chmn. dept. radiology SUNY Sch. Medicine, Stony Brook, 1978-91, prof. dept. radiology, 1991-98, disting. univ. prof., 1998—. Cons. Northport VA Hosp.; vis. investigator St. Mark's Hosp., London, 1976; spkr. in field. Author: Diseases of the Adrenal Glands: Radiologic Diagnosis, 1963, Dynamic Radiology of the Abdomen: Normal and Pathologic Anatomy, 1976, 5th edit., 2000, tranl. in Spanish, 1980, Japanese, 1985, 1991, Italian, 1992, Portuguese, 1999, Iatrogenic Gastrointestinal Complications, 1981; series editor: Computed Tomography of the Gastrointestinal Tract: Including the Peritoneal Cavity and Mesentery, 1986, Neoplasms of the Digestive Tract: Imaging, Staging, and Management, 1998, Happy Accidents: Serendipity in Modern Medical Breakthroughs, 2007, in Japanese, 2010, in Chinese, 2011, founding editor-in-chief: Abdominal Imaging, 1976—, mem. editl. bd.: Iatrogenics; mem. editl. bd. Surg. and Radiol. Anatomy; contbr. chapters to books, articles to profl. jours. Served to capt. M.C. U.S. Army, 1963-65. Recipient Gold medal, U. Leeds, 1980, Radiol. Soc. Republic of China, 1986, Asian-Oceanian Congress Radiology, 1987, European Congress of Radiology, 1995, Indian Radiol. and Imaging Assn., 1999. Fellow: European Soc. Gastrointestinal and Abdominal Radiology, Am. Coll. Gastroenterology, Am. Coll. Radiology; mem.: European Soc. Urogenital Radiology, NY Acad. Gastroenterology, NY Roentgen Ray Soc., Assn. Univ. Radiologists, Israel Radiol. Soc. (hon.), Italian Radiol. Soc. (hon. Medal of honor 1983), Royal Belgian Soc. Gastroenterology (hon.), Spanish Radiol. Soc. (hon.), European Assn. Radiology (hon.), Soc. Gastrointestinal Radiologists (Cannon medal 1993, Hartman medal 1995), Soc. Uroradiology, Am. Gastroenterol. Assn., Am. Roentgen Ray Soc. (Gold medal 1975, 1980), Radiol. Soc. N.Am. (ann. orator 1986), Alpha Omega Alpha. Home: 14 Wainscott Ln East Setauket NY 11733-3816 Office: SUNY Health Scis Ctr Sch Medicine Dept Radiology Stony Brook NY 11794-8460 Office Phone: 631-751-3685. Business E-Mail: jimenez1234@optonline.net.

MEYERS, WAYNE MARVIN, microbiologist, physician; b. Huntingdon County, Pa., Aug. 28, 1924; s. John William and Carrie Venca (Weaver) Meyers; m. Esther Louise Kleinschmidt, Aug. 26, 1953; children: Amy, George, Daniel, Sara. BS in Chemistry, Juniata Coll., Huntingdon, Pa., 1947, DSc (hon.), 1986; diploma, Moody Bible Inst., Chgo., 1950; MS in Med. Microbiology, U. Wis., 1953, PhD in Med. Microbiology, 1955; MD, Baylor Coll. Medicine, 1959. Instr. Baylor Coll. Medicine, 1955-59; intern Conemaugh Valley Meml. Hosp., Johnstown, Pa., 1959-60; staff physician Berrien Gen. Hosp., Berrien Center, Mich., 1960-61; missionary physician Am. Leprosy Missions, Congo/Zaire, Burundi, 1961-73; prof. pathology Sch. Medicine U. Hawaii, Honolulu, 1973-75; chief microbiology divsn. Armed Forces Inst. Pathology, Washington, 1975-89, chief mycobacteriology, 1989—2005, registrar leprosy registry, 1975—2005, asst. to registrar leprosy registry, 2005—11, vis. scientist, 2005—11; mem. leprosy panel US-Japan Coop. Med. Sci. Program, 1976-83; mem. sci. adv. bd. Leonard Wood Meml., 1981-85, sci. cons. dir., 1985-87, sci. dir., 1987-90, cons., 1990—2004; rsch. affiliate Tulane U., 1981—2005. Bd. dirs. Gorgas Meml. Inst. Tropical and Preventive Medicine, Inc., Leonard Wood Meml. Bd. dirs. Jour. Leprosy, 1978—93; contbr. chapters to books, articles to profl. jours. Adv. bd. Damien-Dutton Soc. Leprosy Aid, Inc., 1983—96, corp. bd. dirs., 1996—; adv. bd. Am. Leprosy Missions, Inc., 1979—88, chmn. bd. dirs., 1985—88, program cons. to bd. dirs., 1988—2003, mem. bd. references, 1988—; mem. Hansen's Disease rsch. adv. com. Gillis W. Long Hansen's Disease Ctr., Carville, La., 1985—92, chmn., 1985—92; mem. Buruli Ulcer task force WHO, 1998—2004. With US Army, 1944—46. Allergy Found. Am. fellow, 1957, 1958, WHO Rsch. grantee, 1978—87. Mem.: Internat. Soc. Travel Medicine, Binford-Dammin Soc. Infectious Disease Pathologists (sec.-treas. 1988—91, pres. 1995—96), Am. Soc. Microbiology, Am. Soc. Tropical Medicine and Hygiene, Internat. Soc. Tropical Dermatology, Internat. Acad. Pathology, Internat. Leprosy Assn. (councillor 1978—88, pres. 1988—93), Sigma Xi. Achievements include research in human and experimental leprosy, and other mycobacterial diseases. Office: Armed Forces Inst Pathology Washington DC 20306-6000 Personal E-mail: wmekmeyers@comcast.net.

MEYERS, WILLIAM C., surgeon, educator; BS in History of Sci., Harvard U., 1971; MD, Columbia Coll., 1975; MBA, U. Pa., 2003. Diplomate Am. Bd. Surgery. Intern Duke Univ. Med. Ctr., 1976, rsch. assoc. gastroenterology dept. surgery, 1979, vascular surgery tng., 1982, resident, 1982, fellow gastrointestinal rsch. dept. surgery, 1983, surgical resident Durham, NC, 1983; sr. assoc. dean biotechnology devel. Drexel Univ. Coll. Medicine, prof., chmn. dept. surgery, 2001—10; hosp. affiliations include Hahnemann Univ. Hosp., Abington Meml. Hosp., Durham Regional Hosp. (Duke Univ. Med. Ctr.). Named one of Best Doctors in America, 2009—10, 2011—12. Office: Drexel University College of Medicine Queen Lane Medical Campus 2900 W Queen Lane Philadelphia PA 19129 Office Phone: 215-762-4157. Business E-Mail: William.Meyers@DrexelMed.edu.

MEYER-SIEGLER, KATHERINE L., chemist; b. NYC, June 4, 1959; BS, St. John's U., 1980; PhD, Lehigh U., 1986. Rsch. chemist Dept. Vets. Affairs, 1993. Adj. prof. St. Petersburg Coll., 1999; assoc. prof. U. South Fla., 2008. Grant, Dept. Vets. Affairs. Mem.: Moffitt Cancer Ctr., Soc. Basic Urol. Rsch. Office: Bay Pines VAHCS R&D 151 10000 Bay Pines Blvd Bay Pines FL 33744 Business E-Mail: katherine.siegler@va.gov.

MEYERSON, BJORN A., retired medical educator; b. Stockholm, Feb. 21, 1933; MD, Karolinska Inst., Stockholm, 1964, PhD, 1968. Prof. emeritus Karolinska Inst., Stockholm, 1998—. Cons. prof. Dept. Neurosurgery. Karolinska U. Hosp., 1968—98. Recipient Spiegel and Wycis medal, World Soc. Stereotactic and Functional Neurosurgery, award, Swedish Med. Soc., Karolinska Inst., Umeå U. Mem.: Scandinavian Assn. Study Pain, Int. Assn. Study Pain. Avocations: art, history. Office: Karolinska University Hosp Stockholm SE-171 76 Sweden Office Fax: 46 8 307091. Business E-Mail: bjorn.meyerson@karolinska.se.

MEZENCEV, ROMAN, biomedical scientist, arms control expert, literary translator; b. Kosice, Slovakia, Jan. 20, 1970; s. Vladimir Mezencev and Luboslava Mezencevova; m. Andrea Zatrochova, Sept. 19, 1992; children: Romana Mezencevova, Denis. BS, Pavol Jozef Safarik U., Kosice, MS, 1993, RNDr. in Chemistry, 1999, PhD in Pharmacology, 2007; MS in Biology, Ga. Inst. Tech., Sch. Biology, Atlanta, 2007. Forensic scientist, Inst. Forensic Medicine Pavol Jozef Safarik U., 1993—96, rsch. project cons., faculty sci., 2006—; prin. sci. officer Ministry Economy, Bratislava, Slovakia, 1997—99; clin. rsch. monitor Pharmacia & Upjohn, Bratislava, 1998—2002; insp. roster pers. UNMOVIC, NYC, 2000—07, insp. & biol. team leader & arms control expert, 2002—06; postdoc. rschr. Ga. Inst. Tech., Sch. Biology, 2008—09, rsch. scientist, 2009—. Translator non-fiction and popular sci. books; contbr. scientific papers to profl. jours., chapters to books. Mem.: AAAS, Am. Chem. Soc., Am. Assn. Cancer Rsch. Achievements include patents for metabolomics based identification of disease causing agents. Office: Ga Inst Tech 310 Ferst Dr Atlanta GA 30332 Personal E-mail: romanmez@gmail.com. Business E-Mail: roman.mezencev@biology.gatech.edu.

MEZEY, ESTEBAN, internist, gastroenterologist, educator; b. Vienna, Oct. 12, 1936; came to U.S., 1953; s. Kalman Coloman and Elisabeth (Jaberg) M.; m. Anne Elizabeth Lindeman, June 3, 1962; children: Lillian, Paul Stephen, Marina. BA in Zoology, Yale U., 1958; MD, Harvard U., 1962. Diplomate Am. Bd. Internal Medicine, Am. Bd. Gastroenterology. Intern Pa. Hosp., Phila., 1962-63; resident St. Luke's Hosp. Ctr., NYC, 1963-65, fellow in gastroenterology, 1965-66, NIH postgrad. rsch. fellow, 1966-67, rsch. assoc., 1966-67; Norman Jolliffe fellow in clin. nutrition Columbia U., NYC, 1966-67; from instr. to prof. medicine Sch. Medicine, Johns Hopkins U., Balt., 1968-82, prof., 1982—; mem. staff divsn. gastroenterology Johns Hopkins Hosp., Balt., 1968—, chief hepatology, 1988—, chief clinical gastroenterology, 2002—05. Chief hepatology Francis Scott Key Med. Ctr., Balt., 1968-84, med. dir. alcoholism svcs., 1972-84; med. dir. alcoholism treatment program, phase I, Johns Hopkins Hosp., 1985-87; dir. Johns Hopkins Alcohol Rsch. Ctr., 1985-88; cons. liver diseases VA Hosp., Ft. Howard, Md., 1968-96; med. rsch. svc. merit rev. bd. gastroenterology VA, 1983-87; mem. adv. bd. Liver Ctr., Yale U., New Haven, 1985-93; mem. coms. and subcoms. profl. and ednl. instns. Mem. editl. bd. Alcohol, 1983-87, 93—, Hepatology, 1986—, assoc. editor, 1992-96; mem. editl. bd. Alcoholism: Clin. and Exptl. Rsch., 1988-93, Pharmacology adn Therapeutics; field editor Jour. Alcohol Studies, 1989-92; mem. editl. adv. bd. Biochem. Pharmacology, 1984-96; mem. staff contbrs. Selected Summaries in Gastroenterology, 1974-85; contbr. articles (with others) to profl. jours. Bd. dirs. Balt. Area Coun. on Alcoholism, v.p., 1972-76, pres., 1976-77; bd. dirs. Am. Coun. on Alcoholism, 1980-89; mem. med. adv. bd. Alcoholic Beverage Med. Rsch. Found., 1987-93, chmn., 1992-93; mem. alcoholism adv. coun. to mayor City of Balt., 1987-88; mem. alcoholism rsch. rev. com. biomed. br. Nat. Inst. Alcohol Abuse and Alcoholism, 1979-83, mem. nat. adv. coun., 1985-88, mem. extramural sci. adv. bd., 1990-93, mem. bd. sci. counselors, 1994-98, chmn. 1996—. Fellow ACP; mem. Assn. Am. Physicians, Am. Soc. Clin. Investigation, Am. Assn. for Study of Liver Diseases (pres. 1993, councilor 1989-97, chmn. publs. com. 1986-88), Am. Gastroent. Assn., Internat. Assn. for Study of Liver, Internat. Soc. for Biomed. Rsch. on Alcoholism, Pan Am. Med. Assn. (past counselor alcoholism sect.), Rsch. Soc. on Alcoholism (program com.), Colombian Soc. Gastroenterology (corr.), Argentinian Soc. Pathology, Ibero-Am. Assn. for Study of Problems of Alcoholism, Ea. Gut Club, Am. Liver Found. (bd. dirs. 1995—). Republican. Roman Catholic. Avocations: sailing, swimming. Office: Johns Hopkins U Sch Medicine 720 Rutland Ave Baltimore MD 21205-2109 Business E-Mail: emezey@jhmi.edu.

MEZZANZANICA, DELIA, medical researcher; b. Milan, Feb. 8, 1961; PhD, U. Milan, 1985. Group leader dept. exptl. oncology Fondazione IRCCS Inst. Nat. dei Tumori, Milan, 2006—. Office: Via Amadeo 42 Milan 20133 Italy Business E-Mail: delia.mezzanzanica@istitutotumori.mi.it.

MHLONGO, SAM WYSTAN, physician, educator; b. Tzaneen, Limpopo Province, South Africa, July 30, 1940; arrived in South Africa, 1998; s. Tom Poshela Mhlongo and Tsatsawana Nkuna-Mhlongo; m. Anne Landale, Dec. 16, 1966 (div. Oct. 10, 1977); m. Maria Aparecida Giacomin, June 28, 1980; children: Nandi, Shaka, Zwide. MB BChir, LRCP, MRCS, U. London, 1970, MSc, MD, 1992. Pres. Charing Cross Med. Sch., London, 1974—76; facilitator, dir. African History and Current Affairs Africa Ctr., London, 1980—90; chmn., founder Pfunanani Health Rsch. Trust, South Africa, 2001—; chief specialist, family physician/primary health care physician, head dept. family medicine and primary health care Med. U. So. Africa, Medunsa, South Africa, 1999—. With Charing Cross Hosp., London, Hemel Hempstead Hosp., Hertfordshire, England, Croydon Gen. Hosp., Surrey, England; cardiology resident Mt. Sinai Hosp., NYC, 1976—77; gen. practice, Brent, England; sr. lectr. gen. practice U. London, 1990—98; senate mem. Med. U., South Africa, 1999—; mem., coord. AIDS Adv. Panel, South Africa, 2000—; del. medicine and soc. Second Renaissance, Milan, 2000—; mem., historian Nkuna-Zulu Royal Coun., South Africa, 2002—. Author: Forced Removal of The Mamatola Tribe: BLACK DWARF, 1967, Worker's Strikes in South Africa: New Left Review, 1973, Social Classes in South Africa: Race & Class, 1975, Une analyse des classes en Afrique du Sud: Les Temps Modernes, 1975, Atenolol Post Myocardial infarction: Blackwell Scientific Publication, 1977; co-author: Handbook of Family Practice, 2000; contbr. articles and editorials to profl. jours. Mem. ANC, Johannesburg, 1998—; med. sci. editor African Reclamation Forum, Johannesburg, 1999—. Scholar, UN, 1971—76. Mem.: Royal Coll. Physicians, African-Caribbean Med. Assn. (sec. 1994—98), Royal Coll. Gen. Practitioners U.K. Avocations: soccer, cricket, politics. Home: 13 Central St Houghton Johannesburg South Africa Office: Med U Garankuwa Hosp Box 222 Medunsa South Africa Office Phone: 012 521 4172. Business E-Mail: smmhlong@iafrica.com.

MHYRE, JILL M., medical educator; b. Seattle, Oct. 13, 1972; MD, U. Mich., 1999. Asst. prof. anesthesiology U. Mich. Health Sys., 2005—. Office: University Mich Health Sys L3622 Women's Hospital 1500 E Medical Center Dr Ann Arbor MI 48109-5278 Personal E-mail: jillmhyre@gmail.com.

MIAN, AMIR, oncologist, educator; b. Jan. 1, 1970; MD, AIMC, 1992; MS, UC. Asst. prof. UAMS, 2006. Office: Pediatric Hematology Oncology Little Rock AR 72202 Business E-Mail: mianamir@uams.edu.

MIAO, EDWIN YONG, physical therapist, acupuncturist, consultant; s. Zhong De and Jing Juan Miao; m. Danielle Zhu-DM Miao; children: Miranda Y-M, Fiona Y-C. MB, Shanghai Coll. Traditional Chinese Medicine, 1984; grad. diploma in Cmty. Health, La Trobe U., Melbourne, Australia, 1999. Diplomate physician Bd. Shanghai, 1989, cert. Ofcl. Chinese Radiologist Assn., 1990, diplomate in acupuncture, herbal medicine Chinese Medicine Registration Bd. Victoria, Australia, 2002. Rschr., physician Manipulative Therapy Tuina Rsch. Unit, Yue Yang Hosp., Shanghai, 1984; radiologist Yue Yang Hosp., Shanghai, 1984—89; chief cons. Huang Pu Dist. Acupuncture and Manipulative Therapy Clinic, Shanghai, 1990; chief cons., sr. acupuncturist M. Modern Traditional Chinese Med. Clinic, Melbourne, Victoria, Australia, 1994—. Cons. Prof. Li's Acupuncture Clinic, Melbourne, 1999—2008. Contbr. articles to profl. jours. Fellow: Australian Acupuncture and Chinese Medicine Assn.; mem.: Shanghai Br., Ofcl. Chinese Acupuncturist Assn. Achievements include research in clinical evaluation in low back pain research. Avocations: swimming, travel. Office: M Modern Chinese Med Clinic 54 Part 2 Pitt St Ringwood 3134 Melbourne VIC Australia Office Phone: 61-0425723637. Business E-Mail: edwinmiao2@optusnet.com.au.

MIAO, JINMIN, medical researcher; m. Hongzhang Tao; children: Yufeng Tao, Jin Tao Harmon. MD, Shanghai Second Med. Coll., 1968. Physician Hosps., Zunyi, Guizhou Province, China, 1968—80, Pudin, Guizhou Province; lectr. Zunyi Med. Coll., 1981—86; rschr. JFK Inst., Copenhagen, 1986—88; rschr. asst. Helsinki U. Dept. Med. Genetics, Finland, 1988—99, sr. lab master, 1999—. Contbr. articles to profl. jours. Founder and advisor Chinese Evang. Congregation, Helsinki, 1994. Achievements include research in the gene that responsible for progressive myoclonus epilepsy EPM1. Avocations: travel, swimming, gardening. Office: Helsinki Univ Biomedicum Haartmaninkatu 8 Helsinki 00290 Finland

MIAO, XIANGYANG, agricultural studies educator; b. Laizhou, Shandong, China, Mar. 24, 1963; MSc, Grad. Sch. Chinese Acad. Agrl. Scis., 1988; PhD, China Agrl. U., 2004. Assoc. prof. Inst. Animal Scis. Chinese Acad. Agrl. Scis., 2002—09, prof., 2010—. Evaluation expert Nat. Natural Sci. Found. China, 2002, Natural Sci. Found. Jiangxi, China, 2003, Nat. Basic Rsch. Program China, 2008, Beijing Mcpl. Sci. and Tech. Commn., 2010; cons. Sci. and Tech. Dept. Jiangsu, China, 2011. Recipient Disting. Expert award, Chinese Acad. Agrl. Scis.; Rsch. Fund grant, Nat. Natural Sci. Found. China, Nat. High Tech. Rsch. Devel. Program China, Maj. Sci. and Tech. Project New Variety Breeding of Genetically Modified Organisms. Mem.: Beijing Assn. Lab. Animal Scis. Avocations: music, dance, ping pong/table tennis, basketball, travel, photography. Office: 2 Yuanmingyuan W Rd Haidian Beijing 100193 China Office Fax: 86-10-62895663.

MIAZEK, ARKADIUSZ, medical educator; b. Dzierzoniow, Feb. 25, 1969; PhD, U. Wroclaw, 1997. Assoc. prof. Inst. Immunology and Exptl. Therapy Polish Acad. Scis., 2010—. Fellowship, HFSPO Com. Mem.: ICLAS. Office: Weigla 12 Wroclaw Dolnoslaskie 53-114 Poland Office Fax: 48 71 337 13 82. Business E-Mail: arek@iitd.pan.wroc.pl.

MICA, LADISLAV, surgeon; b. Brno, Czech Republic, Aug. 1974; s. Ladislav Mica and Pavla Mica-Miluska. MD, U. Zürich, Switzerland, 2000, postgrad. in Exptl. Medicine, 2001—03. Specialist in surgery Foederatio Medicorum Helveticorum, 2009. Resident U. Hosp. Zürich, 2000—09; sr. physician U. Zürich, 2010—. Contbr. articles to sci. publs. Master: Go Ju Ryu Karate-Do (3 Dan 2000). Office: University Hosp Zürich Rämistrasse 100 Zürich 8091 Switzerland Business E-Mail: ladislav.mica@usz.ch.

MICHAEL, ALFRED FREDERICK, JR., physician, medical educator; b. Phila. s. Alfred Frederick and Emma Maude (Peters) M.; m. Jeanne Jones; children: Mary, Susan, Carol. MD, Temple U., 1953. Diplomate Am. Bd. Pediatrics (founding mem. sub-bd. pediatric nephrology, pres. 1977-79). Pediat. diagnostic lab. immunology and pediatric nephrology intern Phila. Gen. Hosp., 1953-54; resident St. Christopher's Hosp., Phila., 1954, Children's Hosp. and U. Cin. Coll. Medicine, 1957-60; postdoctoral fellow dept. pediatrics and biochemistry Med. Sch., U. Minn., Mpls., 1960-63, assoc. prof., 1965-68, prof. pediatrics, lab. medicine and pathology, 1968-88, co-dir. pediatric nephrology, 1968—86, Regents' prof., 1986—, head dept. pediatrics, 1986-97, dean, 1996—2002. Established investigator Am. Heart Assn., 1963-68. Past mem. editl. bd. Internat. Yr. Book of Nephrology, Am. Jour. Nephrology, Kidney Internat., Clin. Nephrology, Am. Jour. Pathology; contbr. articles to profl. jours. Physician founder Vikings Children's Fund, Univ. Pediat. Found.; bd. dirs. St. Mary's Health Clinics, Minn. Vikings Children's Fund, No Time For Poetry Haiti. Served with USAF, 1955—57. Recipient Alumni Achievement award Temple U. Sch. Medicine, 1988, John Peters award, 1992, Diehl award, 2003; NIH fellow, 1960-63, Guggenheim fellow, 1966-67, NIH Merit awardee, 1992-2002, Bolles Rogers award, Shotwell award. Fellow AAAS; mem. Am. Soc. Clin. Investigation, Assn. Am. Physicians, Am. Pediat. Soc., Soc. for Pediat. Rsch., Am. Assn. Investigative Pathology, Am. Soc. Cell Biology, Am. Soc. Nephrology (coun., pres.-elect 1992—, pres. 1993, John Peters award), Internat. Soc. Nephrology, Soc. for Exptl. Biology and Medicine, Minn. Med. Assn. Home: 1986 Lower Saint Dennis Rd Saint Paul MN 55116-2820 Office Phone: 612-626-4990. Business E-Mail: micha003@umn.edu.

MICHAEL, DOROTHY ANN, nursing administrator, military officer; b. Lancaster, Pa., Sept. 20, 1950; d. Richard Linus and Mary Ruth (Hahn) M.; m. Juan Roberto Morales, July 15, 1995. Diploma, RN, Montgomery Hosp. Sch. Nursing, Norristown, Pa., 1971; BSN,

George Mason U., 1980; MSN, U. Tex. Health Sci. Ctr., 1985. Commd. ensign USN, 1970, advanced through grades to capt. Nurse Corps, 1994, staff nurse Nat. Naval Med. Ctr. Bethesda, Md., 1971-73, charge nurse Naval Hosp. Guantanamo Bay, Cuba, 1973-74, charge nurse Naval Regional Med. Ctr. Phila., 1974-76, charge nurse Naval Hosp. Keflavik, Iceland, 1977, Bethesda, Md., 1980-84; sr. nurse, asst. officer-in-charge Br. Med. Clinic Naval Weapons Ctr., China Lake, Calif., 1986-89; coord. quality assurance Naval Hosp., Oakland, Calif., 1989-92, assoc. dir. inpatient nursing, 1992-93; divsn. officer USNS Mercy, Persian Gulf, 1990-91; assoc. dir. surg. nursing Naval Hosp., Oakland, 1993-95, dir. nursing svc. Great Lakes, Ill., 1995-98; dep. comdr. Naval Ambulatory Care Ctr., Newport, R.I., 1998-2001; ret. Splty. advisor to dir. Navy Nurse Corp., Navy Med. Command, Washington, 1983-84. V.p. Deepwood Homeowners Assn., Reston, Va., 1978-82; advisor, com. mem. Reston Found., 1979. Decorated Navy Commendation medal, Meritorious Svc. medal, Legion of Merit; recipient R.W. Bjorklund Mgmt. Innovator award, Kern County, Calif., 1988, Comdr.'s award for outstanding professionalism in pub. health support, 1988; named to Hall of Fame, Upper Moreland HS, Pa., 2007. Mem. VFW, Vietnam Vets. Am., Am. Legion, Sigma Theta Tau. Roman Catholic. Home: 3324 Susquehanna Rd Dresher PA 19025 E-mail: dotjuan1@msn.com.

MICHAEL, JERROLD MARK, public health service officer, educator, retired dean; b. Richmond, Va., Aug. 3, 1927; s. Joseph Leon and Esther Leah M.; m. Lynn Y. Simon, Mar. 17, 1951; children: Scott J., Nelson L BCE, George Washington U., 1949; MSE, Johns Hopkins U., 1950; MPH, U. Calif., Berkeley, 1957; DrPH (hon.), Mahidol U., 1983; ScD (hon.), Tulane U., 1984. Commd. ensign USPHS, 1950, advanced through grades to rear adm., asst. surgeon gen., 1966; ret., 1970; dean Sch. Pub. Health, U. Hawaii, Honolulu, 1971-92, prof. pub. health, 1971-95; emeritus prof. pub. health U. Hawaii, Honolulu, 1995—; adj. prof. global health George Washington U., 1997—. Bd. dirs. Nat. Health Coun., 1967-78, Nat. Ctr. for Health Edn., 1977-90; mem. nat. adv. coun. on health professions edn., 1978-81; chmn. bd. dirs. Kuakini Med. Ctr., Honolulu; sec., treas. Asia-Pacific Acad. Consortium Pub. Health; vis. prof. U. Adelaide, 1993, George Washington, 1994; hon. prof. Beijing Med. U., 1994; adj. prof. internat. pub. health Goerge Washington U., 1997- Contbr. articles to profl. jours.; assoc. editor Jour. Environ. Health, 1958-80, Asia-Pacific Jour. of Pub. Health, 1986-95 Pres. Commd. Officers Found., 2000—. Served with USNR, 1944-47 Decorated Meritorious Svc. medal, comdr. Royal Order of Elephant (Thailand); recipient Walter Mangold award, 1961, J.S. Billings award for mil. medicine, 1964, Gold medal Hebrew U., Jerusalem, 1982, San Karcil Gold medal, Malaysia, 1989, Disting. Svc. award Pacific Island Health Officers Assn., 1992, USPHS awards, Commd. Officers Assn. Brutsche awards, 1999, 2009, Founders award Asia-Pacific Acad. Consortium Pub. Health, 2003, U.S. Surgeon Gen.'s medallion, 2005, Michael Ednl. Fellowship, PHS Found., 2007, Adm. Michael PHS Engr. award, 2008, Theta Tau Laureate Alumni Hall Of Fame, others Fellow Am. Public Health Assn.; mem. Am. Acad. Health Adminstrn., Am. Soc. Cert. Sanitarians, Nat. Environ. Health Assn., Am. Acad. Environ. Engrs. Clubs: Masons

MICHAEL, SANDRA DALE, biomedical educator, researcher; b. Sacramento, Jan. 23, 1945; d. Gordon G. and Ruby F. (Johnson) M.; m. Dennis P. Murr, Aug. 12, 1967 (div. 1974). BA, Calif. State Coll., Sonoma, 1967; PhD, U. Calif., Davis, 1970. NIH predoctoral fellow U. Calif., Davis, 1967—70, NIH postdoctoral fellow, 1970—73, asst. rsch. geneticist, 1973—74; asst. prof. Binghamton U., SUNY, 1974—81, assoc. prof., 1981—88, prof. reproductive endocrinology, 1988—2005, disting. svc. prof., 2005—, dept. chair, 1992—2000, dir. grad. studies, 2004—10. Adj. prof. dept. ob-gyn. SUNY Upstate Med. U., Syracuse; mem. NIH Reproductive Endocrinology Study Sect., 1991-95; cons., presenter in field; grant reviewer NIH, NSF, USDA and others. Mem. editl. bd. Reproductive Biology and Endocrinology, Am. Jour. Reproductive Immunology; contbr. articles to profl. jours. Bd. dirs. Tri Cities Opera, Binghamton Summer Music Festival/So. Tier Celebrates; convener Episc. Ch. Network for Sci., Tech. and Faith, 2004—09; vice chair Tri Cities Opera Guild, Binghamton, 1987—90, chair, 1990—92; mem. SUNY Found., Binghamton, 1990—96, Binghamton Forum, Binghamton, 1987—. Fulbright Sr. scholar Czech Republic, 1994; grantee NIMH, 1976-79, Nat. Cancer Inst., 1977-80, 83-87, Nat. Inst. Environ. Health Scis., 1979-80, NSF, 1981-83, NIH, 1987—. Fellow: AAAS; mem.: Reproductive Biology & Endocrinology (editl. bd., founding), AAUP, N.Y. Acad. Sci., Soc. for Exptl. Biology and Medicine, Women in Endocrinology, Am. Soc. for Immunology of Reprodn. (treas. 2005—07, editl. bd.), Soc. for Study of Fertility, Soc. for Study of Reprodn., Endocrine Soc., Sigma Xi. Avocations: golf, bridge, opera, literature, travel. Office: Binghamton U Dept Biol Scis Binghamton NY 13902 Office Phone: 607-777-6517. Business E-Mail: smichael@binghamton.edu.

MICHAELIDES, ANDREAS P., cardiologist, educator; b. Nicosia, Cyprus, Aug. 1, 1946; Degree, U. Athens, Greece, 1972. Assoc. prof. cardiology Hippokration Hosp., Athens, 2002—. Recipient Eight award, Hellenic Soc. Cardiology. Fellow: Am. Coll. Cardiology, European Soc. Cardiology. Home: 66 Thermopylon St Athens Vrilisia 15235 Greece Office Phone: 00302107754495. Business E-Mail: michaelides@freemail.gr.

MICHAELIDES, DOROS NIKITA, internist, medical educator; b. Nicosia, Cyprus, Jan. 7, 1936; came to U.S., 1969; s. Nikita P. and Elpinike (Taliadorou) M.; m. Eutychia J. Loizides, Feb. 27, 1965; children: Nike-Elsie, Joanna-Doris. MD magna cum laude (Royal Greek Govt., Scholar) U. Athens, 1962; DTM and H (Greek State Scholarship, Found. Scholar) U. Liverpool, Eng., 1967; MSc in Clin. Biochemistry (Greek State, Scholarship Found. Scholar), U. Newcastle-upon-Tyne (Eng.), 1969. Diplomate Am. Bd. Family Practice, Am. Bd. Allergy and Immunology; qualified Am. Bd. Internal Medicine; cert. in infectious diseases and immunochemistry, Eng. Clk., intern U. Uppsala, Sweden, 1962; resident Nicosia Gen. Hosp., 1963—66; fellow U. Liverpool Hosps., 1967; fellow internal and clin. medicine Royal Infirmary U. Edinburgh, 1967—68; rsch. fellow Royal Victoria Infirmary U. Newcastle-upon-Tyne, 1968—69; resident internal medicine Bapt. Meml. Hosp., Memphis, 1969—72; fellow in chest diseases We. Okla. Chest Disease Hosp., 1970—71; chief clin. immunology/respiratory care ctr. Erie, Pa.; chief respiratory care ctr. VA Med. Ctr., Erie, 1972—84, acting chief dept. medicine, 1980—81; asst. clin. prof. medicine Hahnemann U. Sch. Medicine, Phila., 1977—, Gannon U., Erie, 1977—. Mem. staff internal medicine Hamot Med. Ctr., immunology and chest diseases Metro Health Ctr., Erie; preceptor medicine St. Vincent's Health Ctr.; affiliate staff Cleveland Clinic Found.; vol. physician Greek Nat. Guard, Cyprus, 1964. Author: The Occurrence of Proteolytic Inhibitors in Heart and Skeletal Muscle, 1969; Blood Gases, Acid-Base and Electrolytes Disturbances, 1980; Immediate Hypersensitivity: The Immunochemistry and Therapeutics of Reversible Airway Obstruction, 1980; The Equivalent Potency of Corticosteroid Preparations used in Reversible Airway Obstruction, 1981; contbr. articles to med. jours. Recipient citation for outstanding svcs. to vets. DAV, 1975, citation Adminstr. U.S. Vets. Affairs, 1978. Fellow ACP (life), Am. Assn. Cert. Allergists, Am. Coll. Allergy and Immunology (com. autoimmune diseases), Am. Assn. Clin. Immunology and Allergy (pulmonary com.), Am. Coll. Chest Physicians (life; critical care com.), Royal Soc. Medicine, Am. Coll. Angiology, N.Y. Acad. Scis., Am. Coll. Clin. Pharmacology, Am. Assn. Cert. Allergists. Greek Orthodox. Home: 4107 State St Erie PA 16508-3129 Office: Doros N Michaelides MD 4107 State St Erie PA 16508-3129 Personal E-mail: dorosmichaelides@yahoo.com. Business E-Mail: dnm777@pol.net.

MICHAELS, DAVID MORRIS, federal agency administrator, epidemiologist; BA in History, CCNY, 1977; MPH, Columbia U., 1981, PhD, 1987. Founder, dir. Epidemiology Unit, Montefiore-Rikers Island Health Svc., 1986—90; asst. sec. for environment, safety & health US Dept. Energy, 1998—2001; rsch. prof., assoc. chmn., dept. environ. and occupl. health, Ctr. for Risk Sci. and Pub. Health George Washington U., Sch. Pub. Health and Health Services, 2001—09, dir., dept. environ. and occupl. health doctoral program, 2001—09, chair, planning com., Project on Scientific Knowledge and Pub. Policy; asst. sec. Occupation Safety & Health Adminstrn. (OSHA) US Dept. Labor, Washington, 2009—. Faculty appointment Albert Einstein Coll. Medicine, Mt. Sinai Sch. Medicine; chief architect Energy Employees Occupl. Illness Compensation Program; mem. Safety and Occupl. Health Study Sect.; lectured on occupl. epidemiology in Columbia, Mexico, and Chile. Author: Doubt Is Their Product: How Industry's Assault on Science Threatens Your Health, 2008, (articles) Jour. AMA, Internat. Jour. Epidemiology, Am. Jour. Pub. Health and other scientific publs.; contbr. editorials in Science Mag. on the stacking of fed. adv. com. and two articles addressing conflict of interest issues in regulatory sci.; guest editor Am. Jour. Pub. Health (spl. issue) on Scientific Evidence and Pub. Policy, editl. bd. Preventative Medicine. Recipient David P. Rall award for Advocacy in Pub. Health, Am. Pub. Health Assn., 2001, Meritorious Svc. Award, US Dept. Energy, 2005 AAAS award for Scientific Freedom and Responsibility, 2006, John P. McGovern Sci. & Soc. award, Sigma Xi, 2009.

MICHAELS, JILLIAN, personal trainer, writer, television personality; b. L.A., Feb. 24, 1974; Grad., Calif. State U., Northridge. Motion picture literary agent ICM, LA; personal trainer; co-owner Sky Sport and Spa, 2004—; co-founder Empowered Media, LLC, 2008—. Radio talk show host KFI AM, LA, 2006—09; celebrity advisor Nat. Day of Dance for Heart Health. Trainer (TV reality series) The Biggest Loser, 2005—11; exec. prodr.: (TV reality series) Losing it with Jillian, 2010—; co-host The Doctors, 2011—, spl. correspondent Dr. Phil, 2011; author: Winning by Losing: Drop the Weight, Change Your Life, 2007, Making the Cut, 2008, Master Your Metabolism, 2009, The Master Your Metabolism Cookbook, 2010, co-author: The Master Your Metabolism Calorie Counter, 2010; host (exercise videos) 30 Day Shred, 2008, No More Trouble Zones, 2009, Banish Fat, Boost Metabolism, 2009, Yoga Meltdown, 2010, (video games) Jillian Michaels' Fitness Ultimatum, 2009, 2010. Amb. Am. Cancer Soc. Office: Empowered Media, LLC 10866 Wilshire Blvd, 10th Fl Los Angeles CA 90024 *

MICHALAK, PETER PAUL, emergency room physician; b. Kingston, Pa., Mar. 21, 1950; s. Alexander J. and Dorothy (Paulik) M.; m. Carla Marie Michalak, May 20, 1987; 1 child, Peter P. Jr. BS in Biology cum laude, King's Coll., 1972; DO, Phila. Coll. Osteo. Medicine, 1976. Diplomate Am. Bd. Emergency Medicine. Intern Tresom Gen. Hosp., 1976-77; dir. emergency medicine Cobre Valley Hosp., Tucson, 1993—. Fellow Am. Coll. Emergency Physicians; mem. Am. Osteo. Assn., Pima Med. Soc. Republican. Roman Catholic. Avocations: fishing, golf, chess, reading. Home: 5520 N Suncrest Pl Tucson AZ 85718-5510 *

MICHALEK, PAVEL, anesthesiologist; b. Pardubice, Czech Republic, Apr. 27, 1968; s. Pavel Michalek and Jaroslava Michalkova, adopted s. Eva Michalkova; m. Michaela Michalkova-Vesela, 2001; children: Eliska Michalkova, Jakub, Adam Kristian. MD, Charles U., Prague, Czech Republic, 1992; PhD, Masaryk U., Brno, Czech Republic, 2001. Diplomate Czech Bd. Anesthesiology and Intensive Care, 2000, Czech Bd. Pain Medicine, 1999, European Soc. Anesthesiology, 2008. Resident, fellow Dist. Hosp., Louny, Czech Republic, 1992—98; cons. Inst. Clin. and Exptl. Medicine, Prague, Czech Republic, 1998—2001; cons., chief dept. cardiovasc. anesthesia and intensive care Na Homolce Hosp., Prague, Czech Republic, 2001—05; cons. Antrim Area Hosp., Northern Ireland, 2005—. Pain cons. Inst. for Postgraduate Med. Edn., Prague, 2001—; hon. sr. lectr. Charles U. Prague, 2001—, assoc. prof. anesthesia & intensive medicine, 2009—. Editor (with P. Kopelent and J. Dutka): (CD-ROM) Techniques of Regional Anesthesia and Analgesia, 2002; editor: (with J. Dutka and V. Masopust) Interventional Pain Management, 2002; editor: (with V. Scigel and L. Hess) Sedation in Dental Practice, 2007; contbr. articles to profl. jours. Master: Czech Royal Soc. Regional Anesthesia; mem.: Difficult Airway Soc., Czech Pain Soc. (bd. mem. 2005—), European Soc. Regional Anesthesia, Czech Soc. Anesthesia & Intensive Care. Evang. Home: Nad Panenskou Prague 16900 Czech Republic Office: Antrim Area Hospital Services Yard 45 Bush Road BT41 2RL Antrim Northern Ireland Personal E-mail: pafkamich@yahoo.co.uk.

MICHALOS, PETER, ophthalmologist, surgeon, educator; Attended, State U. NY, 1986. Diplomate Am. Bd. of Ophthalmology. Intern NY Hosp.-Cornell Med. Ctr.; resident St. Luke's Roosevelt Hosp., 1987—90; fellow Columbia Presbyn. Med. Ctr., 1990—91; assoc. clin. prof. ophthalmology Columbia P&S. Office: Southampton Hospital 240 Meeting House Lane Southampton NY 11968 Office Phone: 631-726-8200.

MICHAUX, GILLES, research scientist; b. Luxembourg, Oct. 23, 1971; Dipl.-Psych., U. Trier, 1999, dr. rer. nat., 2004. Staff scientist U. Luxembourg, 2007—. Pres. Luxembourg Psychol. Soc., 1999—2011. Mem.: Internat. Assn. Study Pain. Avocation: Aikido. Office: 162A av de la Faïencerie Luxembourg 1511 Luxembourg Business E-Mail: gilles.michaux@mac.com.

MICHEL, MARY ANN KEDZUF, retired nursing educator; b. Evergreen Park, Ill., June 1, 1939; d. John Roman and Mary Kedzuf; m. Jean Paul Michel, 1974. Diploma in nursing, Little Company of Mary Hosp., Evergreen Park, 1960; BSN, Loyola U., Chgo., 1964; MS, No. Ill. U., 1968, EdD, 1971. Staff nurse Little Co. of Mary Hosp., 1960-64; instr. Little Co. of Mary Hosp. Sch. Nursing, 1964-67, No. Ill. U., DeKalb, 1968-69, asst. prof., 1969-71; chmn. dept. nursing U. Nev., Las Vegas, 1971-73, prof. nursing, 1975—2008, dean Coll. Health Scis., 1973-90, prof. dean emeritus Coll. Health Scis., 2006—; pres. PERC, Inc.; mgmt. cons., 1993—95; eneritas dean Coll. Health Professions. Mgmt. cons. Nev. Donor Network, 1993; mem. So. Nev. Health Manpower Task Force, 1975; mem. manpower com. Plan Devel. Commn., Clark County Health Sys. Agy., 1977-79, mem. governing body, 1981-86; mem. Nev. Health Coordinating Coun., Western Inst. Nursing, 1971-85; mem. coordinating com. assembly instnl. adminstrs. dept. allied health edn. and accreditation AMA, 1985-88; mem. bd. advisors So. Nev. Vocat. Tech. Ctr., 1976-80; sec.-treas. Nev. Donor Network, 1988-89, chmn. bd., 1988-90. Contbr. articles to profl. jours. Trustee Desert Spring Hosp., Las Vegas, 1976-85; bd. dirs. Nathan Adelson Hospice, 1982-88, Bridge Counseling Assocs., 1982, Everywoman's Ctr., 1984-86; chair Nev. Commn. on Nursing Edn., 1972-73, Nursing Articulation Com., 1972-73, Yr. of Nurse Com., 1978; moderator Invitational Conf. Continuing Edn., Am. Soc. Allied Health Professions, 1978; mgmt. cons. Nev. Donor Network, 1994-95, Donor Organ Recovery Svc., Transplant Recipient Internat. Orgn., SW Eye Bank, SW Tissue Bank. Named Outstanding Alumnus, Loyola U., 1983; NIMH fellow, 1967-68. Fellow Am. Soc. Allied Health Professions, 1991, (chair nat. resolutions com. 1981-84, treas. 1988-90, sec's. award com. 1982-83, 92-93, nat. by-laws com. 1985, conv. chair 1987); mem. AAUP, Am. Nurses Assn., Nev. Nurses Assn. (dir. 1975-77, treas. 1977-79, conv. chair 1978), So. Nev. Area Health Edn. Coun., Western Health Deans (co-organizer 1985, chair, 1988-90), Nat. League Nursing, Nev. Heart Assn., So. Nev. Mem. Hosps. (nursing recruitment com. 1981-83, mem. nursing practice com. 1983-85), Las Vegas C. of C. (named Woman of Yr. Edn.) 1988, Slovak Catholic Sokols, Phi Kappa Phi (chpt. sec. 1981-83, pres.-elect 1983, pres. 1984, v.p. Western region 1989-95, editl. bd. jour. Nat. Forum 1989-93), Alpha Beta Gamma (hon.), Sigma Theta Tau, Zeta Kappa.

MICHEL, PHILIPPE, medical association administrator; b. Paris, Apr. 5, 1961; PhD, Bordeaux U., 2001. Dir. CCECQA Regional Ctr. Quality and Safety, 1996—. Office: Hôpital X Arnozan Pessac Aquitaine 33604 France Business E-Mail: philippe.michel@ccecqa.asso.fr.

MICHEL, WALTER W. P., urologist; b. Oberhausen, Nordrhein-Westfalen, Germany, Mar. 3, 1951; s. Wilhelm and Maria Michel; m. Asuncion Quiamas Michel; children: Marc-André, Angela-Marietta. MD, Ruhr-U. Bochum, Germany, 1980. Surg. resident Knappschafts-Hosp., Bottrop, Nordrhein Westfalen, Germany, 1980—81; urol. resident Ruhr U. Bochum, 1981—86; urologist Knappschafts Hosp., Bottrop, 1986—90; affiliated urologist St. Josef Hosp., Moers, Nordrhein-Westfalen, Germany, 1990—2002; ind. urologist Urologische Gemeinschaftspraxis, Kamp-Lintfort, Nordrhein-Westfalen, Germany, 1990—. Contbr. articles to profl. publs. With Vokalensembl dee Polizei Duisburg, Deutsche Arztechor. Mem.: Berufsverband der Deutschen Urologen., German Soc. Urology, Am. Urol. Assn. Roman Catholic. Home: Monterkampweg 106 Kamp-Lintfort Nordrhein-Westfalen 47475 Germany Office: Urologische Gemeinschaftspraxis Friedrich-Heinrich Allee 2 Kamp-Lintfort Nordrhein-Westfalen 47475 Germany Home Phone: 4928427701; Office Phone: 4928422871. Office Fax: 49284256906, Home Fax: 4928427331. Business E-Mail: drmichel@drwmichel.de.

MICHEL-BRIAND, YVON, microbiologist, educator; b. Besancon, France, May 20, 1934; s. Roger and Liliane (Py) M-B. MD, U. Montpellier, France, 1960, PhD, 1967. Chief of lab. Faculty of Medicine, Montpellier, 1959-62, asst., 1964-68, chief of works Brest, France, 1968-70, prof. bacteriology-virology Besancon, France, 1970-95, prof. emeritus, 1995—. Author: Molecular Mechanisms of Antibiotic Action, 1986 (Nat. Acad. Medicine award 1987), Edvard Munch-Echos and Reflection, 2005, An History of Antibiotic Resistance, 2010, Oskar Kokoschka Echos et Reflets, 2011. Mem. Am. Soc. Microbiology, Brit. Soc. Antimicrobial Therapy, French Soc. Microbiology, French Nat. Acad. Medicine (corr. mem.). Avocation: literature. Office: Faculty Medicine Hosp J Minjoz 25030 Besançon France

MICHELIS, MARY ANN, allergist, immunologist, educator; MD, U. Pittsburgh, 1975. Diplomate Am. Bd. Internal Medicine, Am. Bd. Internal Medicine-diagnostic lab. immunology, Am. Bd. Allergy and Immunology. Intern Lenox Hill Hosp., 1976, resident in internal medicine, 1976—78; fellow in allergy and immunology NY Hosp.-Cornell Med. Ctr., 1976—78; medicine assoc. clin. prof. medicine sch. Univ. of Medicine and Dentistry of NJ; hosp. affiliation includes Hackensack Univ. Med. Ctr., NJ. Author: (article) Rituximab in the treatment of acquired factor VIII inhibitors, 2003. Named one of Best Doctors, NY Mag., 2010. Office: Hackensack University Medical Center 30 Prospect Ave Hackensack NJ 07601 Office Phone: 201-996-2065.

MICHELIS, MICHAEL FRANK, nephrologist; b. Bklyn., Dec. 11, 1938; s. Michael and Gisella (Gammer) M.; m. Mary Ann Wolak, July 28, 1973; children: Elizabeth Ann, Katherine Clare. BA, Columbia U., 1959; MD, George Washington U., 1963. Intern, resident Lenox Hill Hosp., NYC, 1963-65; resident Hosp. Med. Coll. Pa., Phila., 1965-67; fellow in renal disease, dept. medicine U. Pitts. Sch. Medicine, 1969-70, asst. prof. medicine, 1971-75; chief renal diagnostic unit VA Hosp., Pitts., 1971-75; asst. prof. clin. medicine NYU Med. Sch., 1975-93; assoc. prof. clin. medicine N.Y. Med. Coll., 1980-87, prof., 1987-92; assoc. prof. clin. medicine Cornell U. Med. Coll., 1992-93; prof. clin. medicine NYU Med. Coll., 1993—; dir. nephrology sect. Lenox Hill Hosp., NYC, 1975—. Spl. lectr. Georgetown U. Med. Sch., 1973-85; invited spkr., Various Med. Schs. & Socs., 2004-; lectr. Western Pa. Continuing Edn. for Physicians, 1972-75, vis. prof., 1976; mem. merit rev. bd. VA, 1973-76; cons. clin. fellowship rev. com. NIH, 1981-85; mem. exec. com. End Stage Renal Disease Network, N.Y.C., 1981-85; mem. med. adv. bd. Nat. Kidney Found. of N.Y./N.J., 1987-2001; vice-chair med. adv. bd., trustee Kidney and Urology Found. Am., 2001—, v.p., 2005—. Mem. editl. bd. Clin. Nephrology, 1979-89, Geriat. Nephrology, 1986, Jour. Geriatric Nephrology and Urology, 1989—, Am. editor, 1989-98; contbr. articles to profl. jours. Served to maj. M.C., AUS, 1967-69. Decorated

Army Commendation medal; Health, Rsch. and Svcs. Found. grantee, 1970, 72, 74. Mem. AMA (invited lectr. 1973-75), ACP, Am. Fedn. Clin. Rsch., Am. Soc. Nephrology, Internat. Soc. Nephrology, Internat. Soc. for Geriatric Nephrology and Urology (pres. 1999-2003), Ctrl. Soc. Clin. Rsch. Greek Orthodox. Home: 16 Woodland Park Dr Tenafly NJ 07670-3027 Office: 130 E 77 St 5 Fl New York NY 10075-1850 Home Phone: 201-871-3769; Office Phone: 212-988-3506. E-mail: mfmich@ix.netcom.com.

MICHELS, DALE E., physician; b. Wayne, Nebr., Mar. 24, 1948; s. R.B. and Florence A. (Peterson) M.; m. Roylene C. Gustafson, Jan. 25, 1969; children: Gretchen, Sheila, Joel. BA in Medicine, U. Nebr., Omaha, 1969, MD, 1973. Diplomate Am. Bd. Family Practice. Practicing family physician Lincoln (Nebr.) Family Med. Group, 1974—. Med. cons. Comm. Blood Bank of LCMS, Lincoln, 1992-2007; v.p. Wellmark Health Plan of Nebr., Lincoln, 1996-2000; vice-chair bd. trustees Back to the Bible, Lincoln, 1986-2004 chair bd. trustees, 2004—; sec.-treas. Family Care, PC, Lincoln, 1986-97; med. dir. Nebr. Found. for Med. Care, 2001-07; pres. EMS, Inc., 2002-07l med. dir. QualisHealth NE, 2007-. Pres. Lancaster County Med. Soc., Lincoln, 1991-92, Nebr. Acad. of Family Physicians, Omaha, 1987, Nebr. Heart Assn., 1983, Lincoln Christian Sch. Bd., Lincoln, 1990-97. Recipient J.J. Hanigan award Lincoln Lancaster Comm. Health Dept., 1994, Pub. Health Leadership awrd, 2000; named Family Physician of Yr., Nebr. Acad. Family Physicians, 1999, Disting. Svc. award, Nebr. Med. Assn., 2010. Mem. Am. Med. Dirs. Assn. (pres. N.E.), Nebr. Med. Dirs. Assn. (pres. 2006-07), Lancaster County Med. Soc., Nebr. Acad. Family Physicians (Family Physician of Yr. 1999), Christian Med. Dental Soc., Am. Acad. Family Physicians, Nebr. Med. Assn. (pres. 1999-2000). Republican. Avocations: flying, photography, gardening. Office: Lincoln Family Med Group PC 7441 O St Ste 400 Lincoln NE 68510-2466 Home Phone: 402-488-8760; Office Phone: 402-488-7400. E-mail: dale.michels@gmail.com.

MICHELS, GUIDO, internist, cardiologist, neuroscientist, researcher; b. Gerolstein, Rheinland-Pfalz, Germany, Apr. 1, 1971; s. Ernst and Maria Michels; m. Ilona Brueckner, Apr. 15, 1956. MD, U. Cologne, Germany, 2002, habil in Internal Medicine, 2010. Cert. paramedic Emergency Med. Sch., 1994; RN Brother Hosp., Trier, Germany, 1991. Postdoctoral rschr. neurosci. U. Pa., Phila., 2005—07; resident U. Cologne, Nordrhein-Westfalen, Germany, 2002—03, postdoctoral rschr. cardiology, 2003—05, physician and rschr. cardiology, 2007—. Author: (textbooks) Internal Medicine, Repetitorium Notfallmedizin. Grantee, U. Cologne, 2005, German Rsch. Coun., 2006. Mem.: Biophys.Soc. (assoc.). Achievements include research in first direct evidence of cardiac mitochondrial K(ATP) and Ca 2+ channels. Avocations: hiking, travel. Home: Blumenthalstr 9 Nordrhein-Westfalen Cologne 50670 Germany Office: U Hosp Cologne/Cardiology Dept Internal Medicine III Kerpener Str. 62 50937 Cologne 50937 Germany Office Fax: 0049-221-478-32355. Business E-Mail: guido.michels@uk-koeln.de.

MICHELS, ROBERT, psychiatrist, educator; b. Chgo., Jan. 21, 1936; s. Samuel and Ann (Cooper) M.; m. Verena Sterba, Dec. 23, 1962; children: Katherine, James. BA, U. Chgo., 1953; MD, Northwestern U., 1958. Intern Mt. Sinai Hosp., NYC, 1958-59; resident in psychiatry Columbia Presbyn.-N.Y. State Psychiat. Inst., NYC, 1959-62; mem. faculty Coll. Physicians and Surgeons, Columbia U., NYC, 1964-74, assoc. prof., 1971-74; psychiatrist student health service Columbia U., 1966-74; supervising and tng. analyst Columbia U. Center for Psychoanalytic Tng. and Research, 1972—; attending psychiatrist Vanderbilt Clinic, Presbyn. Hosp., NYC, 1964-74; Barklie McKee Henry prof. psychiatry Cornell U. Med. Coll., NYC, 1974-93, chmn. dept. psychiatry, 1974-91, Stephen and Suzanne Weiss dean, 1991-96; provost for med. affairs Cornell U., 1991-96, Walsh McDermott U. prof. of medicine, 1996—, univ. prof. psychiatry, 1996—; psychiatrist-in-chief N.Y. Hosp., 1974-91, attending psychiatist, 1991—. Attending psychiatrist St. Luke's Hosp. Ctr., NYC, 1966—. Co-author: The Psychiatric Interview in Clinical Practice, 1971, 2d edit., 2006; contbr. articles to profl. jours. Served with USPHS, 1962-64. Mem. Am. Psychiat. Assn., Am. Coll. Psychiatrists, NY Psychiat. Soc., Royal Medico-Psychol. Assn., Psychiat. Rsch. Soc., Assn. Rsch. in Nervous and Mental Diseases, Assn. Acad. Psychiatry, Am. Psychoanalytic Assn., Internat. Psychoanalytic Assn., Ctr. Advanced Psychoanalytic Studies, NY Acad. Scis., Alpha Omega Alpha. Office: Cornell U Med Coll 418 E 71st St New York NY 10021-4894 Office Phone: 212-746-6001. E-mail: rmichels@med.cornell.edu.

MICHELSEN, CHRISTOPHER BRUCE HERMANN, surgeon; b. Boston, Aug. 18, 1940; s. Jost Joseph and Ingeborg Elizabeth (Dilthey) M.; m. Kethleen Mary; children: Heidi Elizabeth, Matthew Christopher, Joshua Jost. BA, Bowdoin Coll., 1961; MD, Columbia U., 1969. Diplomate Am. Bd. Orthop. Surgery, Am. Bd. Forensic Medicine. Intern Columbia Presbyn. Med. Ctr., NYC, 1969—70, resident, 1970—71; orthop. resident N.Y. Orthop. Hosp., NYC, 1971—73, jr. Anne C. Kane fellow, 1973—74, sr. Anne C. Kane fellow and hip fellow, 1974—75, traveling fellow, 1975—76; intenrat. A-O fellow, postgrad. fellow in biomechanics Case Western Res. U., NYC, 1975—76, instr. biomed. engring., 1975—76; prof. clin. orthop. surgery, orthop. surgeon Columbia Coll. Physicians and Surgeons, 1976, vice chmn. dept. orthop. surgery, 2002—; chief orthop. svc. Allen Hosp., Columbia Presbyn. Med. Ctr., 1993—; chief orthop. spine surgery svc. Allen Pavillion, Columbia Presbyn. Med. Ctr., 1998—. Col. USAR, ret. Fellow ACS, Am. Assn. for Surgery of Trauma, Am. Orthop. Assn., N.Am. Spine Soc., Am. Acad. Orthop. Surgeons, Internat. Coll. Surgeons, N.Y. Acad. Medicine; mem. AMA, Am. Coll. Physicians Execs., Orthop. Rsch. Soc., Am. Soc. Bone and Mineral Rsch., Royal Soc. Medicine (affiliate). Office: 5141 Broadway New York NY 10034-1159 Home: 10 Rossa Ln Ossining NY 10562-2568

MICHELSON, GARY KARLIN, orthopedic surgeon, inventor; b. Jan. 14, 1949; MD, Hahnemann U., Phila. Cert. Orthopaedic Surgery. Intern, spinal surgery Hahnemann U., Phila., resident, 1971—75; fellow St. Lukes Episcopal Hosp., Houston, 1979; former hosp. appointment Centinela Hosp., Calif.; hosp. appointment Daniel Freeman Hosp., Calif.; founder Karlin Tech. Named one of Forbes 400: Richest Americans, 2006—. Patents and applications covering inventions and techniques related to spinal fusion, surgical implants and surgical techniques. Inventions have revolutionized spinal surgery by introducing minimally invasive devices ans durgical techniques, including widely used threaded and alternative non-threaded spinal interbody implants. The technology has significantly reduced the risks and improved the success of spinal surgery by reducing incision size, shortening the operation, reducing blood loss and improving recovery time; In 2005, Medtronic Inc. paid several billion dollars to settle a patent lawsuit and also to acquire the spine surgery-related patents. *

MICHENER, JAMES LLOYD, medical educator; b. Dec. 19, 1952; m. Gwendolyn Curtis Murphy; children: Rebecca Liane, Joshua Kieran. BA, Oberlin Coll., Ohio, 1974; MD, Harvard Med. Sch., 1978. Diplomate Am. Bd. Family Practice. Resident in family medicine Duke U. Med. Ctr., Durham, NC, 1978-81, Kellogg fellow, 1981-82, prof. dept. cmty. and family medicine, 1994—, chmn. dept. cmty. and family medicine, 1994—; dir. Duke Ctr. Cmty. Rsch., 2006—. V.p. Durham Health Care, Inc., 1985-86; project reviewer Ctrs. Disease Control and Prevention, 2002-; vis. prof. work group pub. health and med. edn. Ctrs. Disease Control, Atlanta, 2005. Co-author: Nutrition in Practice, 1990, 2d edit., 1992; contbr. numerous articles to med. pubs. including Academic Medicine, The Jour. of Family Practice, Medical Care, others; mem. editl. bd. Rx Nutrition, 1989-91; presenter in field. Bd. dirs. N.C. Med. Soc. Found., 1995—2004; STFM rep. resource com. on nutrition edn. Am. Acad. Family Practice Found., 1987-91. Grantee The Fullerton Found., Inc., The Josiah Macy, Jr. Found., U.S. Dept. Health and Human Svcs., Kate B. Reynolds Charitable Trust, N.C. Health and Wellness Trust. Mem. AMA, NIH (co chair com. engagement com., NCRR, 2007-, Fogarty/Ellison fellowship selection com. 2005-), Assn. Am. Med. Colls. (exec. com. 2005-06, exec. coun. 2001-07, bd. dirs. 2008-), Assn. Tchrs. Preventive Medicine (chmn. coun. acad. units 2002-, pres. 2008-), Am. Acad. Family Physicians Found., N.C. Acad. Family Physicians, Assn. Dept. Family Medicine (bd. dir. 1997—, sec. 1998—2005), Coun. Acad. Socs. (adminstrn. bd. 2000-07, chair 2005-06), World Orgn. Nat. Colls., Acads. and Academic Assn. Gen. Practitioners and Family Physicians, Am. Austrian Founds. Internat. Health Forum (mem. steering com.), Nat. Patient Safety Found. (bd. govs. 2009). Home: 4011 Duck Pond Trail Chapel Hill NC 27514-9758 Office: Duke U Med Ctr PO Box 2914 Durham NC 27710-0001 Business E-Mail: miche001@mc.duke.edu.

MICHL, JOSEF, physician scientist educator; b. Oberstaufen, Bavaria, Germany, June 5, 1941; BA, Humanistisches Gymnasium St. Stephan, Augsburg, Germany, 1962; MD magna cum laude, Johannes Gutenberg U., Mainz, Germany, 1970. Resident, internal medicine & allergology U. Clinic and Policlinic, Inselspital U. Bern, Switzerland, 1970—72; fellow, asst. prof., Inst. Med. Microbiology and Immunology Johannes Gutenberg U., Mainz, Germany, 1972—74, Ruhr U., Bochum, Germany, 1972—74; guest investigator, fellow Lab. Cellular Physiology and Immunology, Rockefeller U., NY, 1974—77, asst. prof., 1977—82; assoc. prof. pathology, cell & molecular biology, microbiology & immunology Downstate Med. Ctr., SUNY, 1982—. Editl. bd. mem. Cell and Molecular Biology Rsch., 1993—96; mem. sci. adv. bd. Immunitaet und Infektion, 1997—2000; adj. prof., dir. immunology program divsn. basic med. scis. NY Coll. Podiatric Medicine, 2000—; sci. advisor Hoffmann-La Roche, Inc., 2000—02. Rsch. Tng. fellowship, Deutsche Forschungsgemeinschaft, 1973—74, Postdoc. fellowship, Heiser Program Rsch. in Leprosy and Tb, NY Cmty. Trust, 1976—77. Mem.: AAAS, Harvey Soc. (sci. coun. mem. 2002—05), AACR. Avocations: theater, classical music, swimming, travel, hiking. Office: Downstate Med Ctr SUNY Brooklyn NY 11203 Office Fax: 718-270-3313. Business E-Mail: jmichl@downstate.edu.

MICHNICH, MARIE E., health policy analyst, consultant, educator; BS in Nursing, U. Conn.; M in Health Svs. Adminstrn., UCLA, DrPH in Health Svs. Rsch. Legis. asst., health policy Medicare, Medicaid, maternal and child health; legis. asst. U.S. Senate Majority Leader Robert Dole; asst. prof. health services U. Washington; sr. exec. v.p. Health Policy and Clin. Practice and Sci. Services Divisions, Am. Coll. Cardiology; dir., Health Policy Ednl. Programs and Fellowships Bd. Inst. of Medicine-Nat. Academies, 2002—; exec. dir. President's Commn. on Care America's Returning Wounded Warriors, 2007. Cons. & spkr. in field; mem. several nat. health policy groups; bd. mem. then chair Health Care Quality Alliance, 1994—2001. Recipient Disting. Alumni Leadership award, U. Conn., Outstanding Achievement award, Sec. Def.; Robert Wood Johnson Health Policy fellow. Mem.: Am. Pharm. Assn. Found. (1st pub. mem. bd. dirs. 2002—), Robert Wood Johnson Health Policy Fellows Program (mem. adv. bd., dir.), Health Care Quality Alliance (former chmn.). Office: Institute of Medicine 500 5th St NW Washington DC 20001 Office Phone: 202-334-1296. Business E-Mail: mmichnich@nas.edu.

MICKE, OLIVER D., radiation oncologist; b. Hamm, Westfalia, Germany, Mar. 5, 1967; s. Rolf D. and Christel C. Micke. MD, U. Münster, Germany, 1992, PhD, 2006. Cert. Med. Bd. of Radiation Oncologist. Med. trainee Münster U. Med. Ctr., 1992—98, cons. physician, 1998—2005; dept. head radiotherapy Franziskus Hosp., Bielefeld, Germany, 2006—. Spl. tchg. faculty Med. Sch., U. Bishkek, 2001—; pub. Diplodocus-Pubs., Altenberge, Germany, 1999—. Author: Radiotherapy of Esophageal Cancer, 1998, Ottoman Lyrics, 1999; editor: Selenium in Tumor Treatment, 2001; mng. editor (periodical) BenigNews, 2000. Recipient G.v. Pannewitz award, DEGRO, 2005, Trace award, AUTE, 2005. Mem.: Cooperative German Group on Benign Diseases (sec. 1999), German Working Group on Trace Elements and Electrolytes (chmn. 2000, Trace Medal in Gold 2001). Office: Franziskus Hosp Dept Radiotherapy Kiskerstr 20 33615 Bielefeld Germany Office Phone: 49-521-589-1801. Business E-Mail: strahlenklinik@web.de.

MICONG, JIN, medical educator; b. Wenlin, Feb. 10, 1969; D, Zhejiang U., 2007. Prof. NBCDC, 2006—. Office: 237 Yongfeng Road Zhejiang Ningbo 315010 China Business E-Mail: jmcjc@163.com.

MICZEK, KLAUS ALEXANDER, psychology professor; came to U.S., 1967; s. Erich and Irene (Wirthl) M.; m. Christiane Baerwaldt, Aug. 8, 1970; 1 child, Nikolai A. Tchrs. cert., Paedagogische Hochschule, Berlin, 1966; PhD, U. Chgo., 1972. Asst. prof. Carnegie-Mellon U., Pitts., 1972-74, assoc. prof., 1974-79, Tufts U., Medford, Mass., 1979-83, prof., 1983-93, Moses Hunt prof. psychiatry, psychology, pharmacology and neuroscience, 1993—2009; dir. Neurosci. Rsch. Ctr., 2009—. Cons. Solvay-Pharma v.b., Weesp, The Netherlands, 1984-99, NIH, Rockville, Md., 1984—, Forest Labs., N.Y.C., 2003-; Boehringer Ingelheim, Germany, 2003-; Boerhaave prof. U. Leiden, The Netherlands, 1987; mem. panel on violence, NAS, 1989-92. Editor: Ethopharmacology, 1983, Ethopharmacological Aggression Research, 1984; field editor, coord. editor Behavioral Pharmacology, Jour. Psychopharmacology; contbr. articles on psychopharmacology, 1973—. Rsch. grantee Nat. Inst. Drug Abuse, 1973—, Nat. Inst. Alcoholism and Alcohol Abuse, 1981—; recipient Solvay-Duphar award APA, 1993, Bundesverdienstkreuz Cross of Merit, Fed. Republic of Germany, 1996, Gold medal Charles U., Prague, 2004; named disting. scholar Tufts U., 2006, recipeint disting. achievement award European Behavioural Pharmacol Soc., 2007. Fellow AAAS, APA (program chmn. 1981, pres. div. psychopharmacology 1990-91, master lectr. 1999), Behavioral Pharmacol. Soc. (pres. 1992-94), Internat. Soc. for Rsch. on Aggression (councilor 1987); mem. Soc. Neurosci., N.Y. Acad. Scis., Internat. Primatol. Soc. Office: Tufts U Dept Psychology 530 Boston Ave Medford MA 02155-5532 Business E-Mail: klaus.miczek@tufts.edu.

MIDDELKAMP, JOHN NEAL, pediatrician, educator; b. Kansas City, Mo., Sept. 29, 1925; s. George H. and Clara M. (Ordelheide) M.; m. Roberta Gill, Oct. 3, 1949 (div. 1970); children— Sharon Ann, Steven Neal, Susan Jean, Scott Alan; m. Lois Harper, Mar. 1, 1974 BS, U. Mo., 1946; MD, Washington U., St. Louis, 1948. Diplomate Am. Bd. Pediatrics. Intern D.C. Gen. Hosp., Washington, 1948-49; resident St. Louis Children's Hosp., 1949-50, 52-53; instr. pediatrics Washington U., 1953-57, asst. prof. pediatrics, 1957-64, assoc. prof., 1964-70, prof., 1970-98, prof. emeritus, 1998—; dir. ambulatory pediatrics St. Louis Children's Hosp., 1974-91. Author: Camp Health Manual, 1984; contbr. articles, chpts. to profl. publs. Served to comdr. M.C., USNR, 1943-66. NIH postdoctoral fellow, 1961-62 Mem. Am. Acad. Pediatrics, Am. Soc. Microbiology, Infectious Diseases Soc. Am., Am. Pediatric Soc., Acad. Pediatric Assn., Sigma Xi, Alpha Omega Alpha Home: 8845 Paragon Cir Saint Louis MO 63123-1114 Office: Office Assoc Dean for Grad Med Edn Washington Univ Sch Medicine 660 S Euclid Box 8033 Saint Louis MO 63110 Office Phone: 314-747-4479.

MIDDLEBROOKS, DELORIS JEANETTE, retired nursing educator; b. Cedar Rapids, Iowa, Apr. 9, 1931; d. Harland R. and Rosa V. (Anderson) Hickey; m. Johnnie L. Middlebrooks, Apr. 25, 1962 (dec.); children: James, Kathleen. Diploma, Evang. Hosp. Sch. Nursing, 1956; BSN, State U. Iowa, 1958; MS in Nursing, U. Calif., San Francisco, 1960; EdD, U. Nev., Las Vegas, 1985. Instr., coord. Nev. State Hosp. Sch. Practical Nursing, Sparks, 1963-66; staff nurse St. Mary's Hosp., Reno, 1968; instr., coord. Reno VA Sch. Practical Nursing, 1968-72; instr. coord. health occupations Wooster High Sch., 1972-73; nursing faculty Truckee Meadows C.C., 1973-94, ret., 1994; intermittent staff nurse VA Hosp., 1984-86; instr., review course Stanley Kaplan Ednl. Ctr., 1987-89; clin. nursing faculty Western Nev. C.C., Carson City, 1987, Northern Nev. C.C., Elko, 1979-93; guest assoc. prof. nursing Lewis-Clark State Coll., Lewiston, Idaho, 1989. Cons. Irish Bd. Nursing, Dublin, Ireland, 1985. Nominated Nev. Voc. Tchr. of Yr., 1975, 79, 88, 89; Recipient March of Dimes Community Leadership award, 1990. Mem.: ANA, Am. Assn. for the History of Nursing, Nev. Nurses Assn., Phi Kappa Phi, Sigma Theta Tau. Home: 1385 Ebbetts Dr Reno NV 89503-1918

MIDDLESWORTH, WILLIAM, pediatric surgeon; b. Atlantic City, May 30, 1961; BA, Dartmouth Coll., Hanover, NH, 1983; MD, U. Medicine and Dentistry NJ Robert Wood Johnson Med. Sch., Camden, 1989. Cert. Am. Bd. Surgery, 2007, in pediatric surgery Am. Bd. Surgery, 2007. Rsch. fellowship Children's Hosp., Harvard Med. Sch., Boston, 1983—85, The John Radcliffe Hosp., Oxford U., England, 1985, U. Pa., Phila., 1986; internship in gen. surgery U. Md. Med. Sys., Balt., 1989—91, residency in gen. surgery, 1992—95; rsch. fellowship Royal Children's Hosp., U. Melbourne, Australia, 1991—92; pediatric surgery resident Morgan Stanley Children's Hosp. NY Presbyn., NYC, 1995—97, attending surgeon, 1997—, dir., regional pediatric trauma program, 2005—; asst. prof. surgery & pediatric surgery Columbia U. Coll. Physicians & Surgeons, NYC, 1997—; chief, divsn. pediatric surgery Bronx-Lebanon Hosp. Ctr., Bronx, NY, 1997—, St. Barnabas Hosp., Bronx, 1999—. Chair, quality assurance com., dept. surgery NY Presbyn. Hosp. Columbia U. Med. Ctr., quality and patient safety com.; quality assurance com. Morgan Stanley Children's Hosp. NY Presbyn., operating rm. com.; faculty coun. Columbia U. Coll. Physicians & Surgeons, Faculty Medicine. Contbr. articles to profl. jours. Mem.: ACS, Assn. Academic Surgery, Children's Oncology Group, Am. Pediatric Surg. Assn., Internat. Pediatric Endosurgery Group, Am. Acad. Pediat. Surg. Sect. Office: Morgan Stanley Children's Hosp NY-Presbyn Babies & Children's Hosp N Rm 3959 Broadway New York NY 10032 Office Phone: 212-305-5804. Office Fax: 212-305-5971.

MIDDLETON, ANTHONY WAYNE, JR., urologist, educator; b. May 6, 1939; s. Anthony Wayne and Dolores Caravena (Lowry) M.; m. Carol Samuelson, Oct. 23, 1970; children: Anthony Wayne, Suzanne, Kathryn, Jane, Michelle. BS, U. Utah, 1963; MD, Cornell U., 1966. Intern U. Utah Hosps., Salt Lake City, 1966-67; resident in urology Mass. Gen. Hosp., Boston, 1970-74; practice urology Middleton Urol. Assocs., Salt Lake City, 1974—2005; physician cons. LDS Ch., 2008—. Mem. staff LDS Hosp., chmn. divsn. urology, 1995—2004, Salt Lake Regional Med. Ctr., 1977—79, 1984—86; assoc. clin. prof. surgery U. Utah Med. Coll., 1977—2005, staff mem., divsn. urology, 2009—, mem. admissions com., 2009—; vice-chmn. bd. govs. Utah Med. Self-Ins. Assn., 1980—81, 1996—2005, chmn., 1985—87; chmn. med. adv. bd. Uroquest Co., 1996—99; med. dir. Uromed, prostate microwave co., 1999—2000, Utah divsn. Rocky Mountain Prostate, 2001—04, Utah-Idaho Lithotripsy, 2001—03; staff Mission Med., LDS Ch., 2008—. Editor: AACU-FAX, 1992-2005; assoc. editor Millenial Star Brit. LDS mag., 1960-61; contbr. articles to profl. jours. Mem. U. Utah Coll. Medicine Dean's Search Com., 1983—84; bd. dirs. Utah Symphony, 1985—2005, Primary Children's Found., 1989—96; mem. Utah Crime Reparations Bd., 2000—05, chmn., 2002—05; staff pres. Primary Children's Med. Ctr., 1982; pres. elect Collegium Aesculapium LDS Nat. Physicians Org., 2010—11, pres., 2011—; high priest group leader, 2011—; vice chmn. Utah Med. Polit. Action Com., 1978—81, chmn., 1981—83, Utah Physicians for Reagan, 1983—84; del. Utah State Rep. Conv., 2000—01; bishop, later stake presidency Ch. Jesus Christ Latter-day Saints; mission pres. Canada Vancouver Mission, 2005—08; bd. dirs. Utah chpt. Am. Cancer Soc., 1978—86, Timpanogos Club, 1978—, 2d asst. to pres., 2002—03, 1st asst. to pres., 2003—04, pres., 2004—05, 2011—; tng. dir. Red Butte Coun., Boy Scouts America, 2009—11. Capt. USAF, 1968—70. Mem.: AMA (del. to Ho. of Dels. 1998—2005, chmn. ref. com. I 2001, mem. governing coun. SSS 2002—05, alt. del. to Ho. of Dels., 1987-88, 89-92, 94, 96-98), ACS, Am. Assn. Clin. Urologists (bd. dirs. 1989—90, nat. pres.-elect 1990—91, pres. 1991—92, nat. bd. chmn. urologic polit. action com. UROPAC 1992—98, Disting. Svc. award 2000), Salt Lake Surg. Soc. (treas. 1977—78), Utah Urol. Assn. (treas. 1977—78, pres.

1978—79), Salt Lake County Med. Assn. (sec. 1965—67, pres. liaison com. 1980—81, pres.-elect 1981—83, pres. 1984), Am. Urologic Assn. (socioecons. com. 1987—90, chmn., Western Sect. Socioecons. Com. 1989—90, chmn., Western Sect. Health Policy Com. 1990—2002, pres.-elect western sect. 1999—2000, pres. 2000—01, Outstanding Svc. award 2005, Disting. Svc. Nat. award 2011), Utah Med. Assn. (pres. 1987—88, bd. dirs. 1998—2005, Disting. Svc. award 1993), Beta Theta Pi (chpt. pres. Gamma Beta 1962, mem., Beta Rising Reorganization Com. 2010—), Alpha Omega Alpha, Phi Beta Kappa. Republican. Home: 2798 Chancellor Pl Salt Lake City UT 84108-2835 Office: 1060 East 1st South Salt Lake City UT 84102-1520 Office Phone: 801-707-5482. Personal E-mail: awmiddleton@msn.com.

MIDDLETON, DONALD B., pediatrician, internist; MD, U. Rochester, NY, 1972. Diplomate Am. Bd. Pediatrics, Am. Bd. Internal Medicine, cert. Geriatrics. Intern Univ. NC Sch. Medicine, Chapel Hill, 1973, resident, 1975; hosp. affiliation Univ. Pitts. Med. Ctr. St. Margaret. Bd. dirs. St. Margaret Found. Mem.: Soc. Tchrs. Family Medicine, Am. Acad. Family Physicians. Avocation: French. Office: University of Pittsburg Medical Center Renaissance Family Practice 200 Delafield Ave Ste 2030 Pittsburgh PA 15215 Office Phone: 412-782-2101.

MIDELFART, ANNA, ophthalmologist, educator; b. Strakonice, Czechoslovakia, 1947; arrived in Norway, 1969; d. Josef and Anna Hyka; m. Erik Midelfart; children: Jana, Sven. MS, Norges Tekniske Högskole, Norway, 1971; MD, U. Trondheim, Norway, 1978, PhD, 1988. Cert. ophthalmologist, Norway. Prof. dept. ophthalmology Univ. Hosp., Trondheim, 1996—. Contbr. articles to profl. jours. Mem. Assn. Physicians in Sci. (chmn. 1990-94, 2005—09), Norwegian Med. Assn., Am. Acad. Ophthalmology, Norwegian Ophthalmol. Soc. (pres. 2004-05).

MIDTURI, JOHN KIRAN, physician, educator; b. India, Sept. 21, 1972; DO, U. North Tex. HSC, 1999; MPH, Tex. A&M SRPH, 2006. Jr. staff Scott & White Hosp., 2005—06; physician Baylor Internat. Pediatric AIDS Initiative, Baylor Coll. Medicine, 2006—08; staff physician, asst. prof. Scott & White Hosp., Tex. A&M U. HSC, 2008—. Office: 2401 S 31st St Temple TX 76508 Office Fax: 254-724-2061. Business E-Mail: jmidturi@swmail.sw.org.

MIDTVEDT, KARSTEN, nephrologist, consultant; b. Norway, Apr. 6, 1957; MD, Oslo U., 1986, PhD, 1998. Cons. in nephrology OUS, 1993—. Cons. Oslo U. Hosp., 1993. Recipient Norwegian Rsch. award, Norwagian Rsch. Assn. Internal Medicine. Mem.: Am. Thoracic Soc. Avocation: skiing. Office: Rikshospitalet Oslo 0027 Norway Business E-Mail: karsten.midtvedt@ous-hf.no.

MIELE, EVELINA, medical researcher; b. Benevento, Italy, Aug. 7, 1980; MD, U. Rome, Sapienza, 2005, PhD student, 2009—. Rsch. fellow U. Rome, Sapienza, 2009—. Mem.: AACR. Avocations: cooking, reading, dance. Office: Viale Regina Elena 324 Rome 00161 Italy Business E-Mail: evelina.miele@uniroma1.it.

MIELKE, CLARENCE HAROLD, JR., hematologist; b. Spokane, Wash., June 18, 1936; s. Clarence Harold and Marie Katherine (Gillespie) M.; m. Marcia Rae, July 3, 1964; children: Elisa, John, Kristina. BS, Wash. State U., 1959; MD, U. Louisville, 1963. Intern San Francisco Gen. Hosp., 1963-64; resident in medicine Portland VA Hosp., 1964-65, San Francisco Gen. Hosp., 1965-67; fellow in hematology U. So. Calif., 1967-68; tchg. fellow, asst. physician, instr. Tufts-New Eng. Med. Ctr. Hosps., Boston, 1968-71; sr. scientist Med. Rsch. Inst., San Francisco, 1971-90; chief hematology Presbyn. Hosp., San Francisco, 1971-82, asst. prof. clin. medicine U. Calif. Sch. Medicine, San Francisco, 1971-80, assoc. clin. prof., 1979-90, bd. dirs. Inst. Cancer Rsch., 1992—; founder, owner Arbor Crest Winery, 1982—; with Regent Gonzaga U., 2009. Trustee, bd. dirs. Med. Rsch. Inst. San Francisco, Sacred Heart Hosp. Found., 1997-2000, Rockwood Clinic Found., 1994—; dir. emeritus Inst. Cancer Rsch.; trustee emeritus, bd. dirs. Med. Rsch. Inst., 1988—; dir. Health Rsch. and Edn. Ctr., Wash. State U., 1989-2005, prof. pharmacology, 1989—, prof. vet. medicine, 1989—, assoc. dean rsch., 1992-2004; dir. Spokane (Wash.) Heart Study, 1994-2006. Editor emeritus Jour. Clin. Aphesis, 1981; contbr. chpts. to books, articles to med. jours. Named Nat. Disting. Eagle Scout, 1998; NIH grantee, 1973-88. Fellow ACP, Am. Heart Assn.; mem. AAAS, AMA, Am. Heart Assn., Internat. Acad. Clin. and Applied Thrombosis and Hemostasis, Internat. Soc. Hematology, Am. Coll. Angiology; mem. Am. Soc. Internal. Medicine, Internat. Soc. Thrombosis and Hemostasis, N.Y. Acad. Scis., Spokane Med. Soc., Internat. Soc. Angiology. Office: 25415 E Misson Ave Liberty Lake WA 99019 Business E-Mail: harry@arborcrest.com.

MIELKE, SUSAN KAY, denials management specialist; b. Saginaw, Mich., Apr. 4, 1963; d. Walter John Jr. and Sally Jane (Spiekerman) Hetzner; m. Gary Alan Mielke, Aug. 16, 1986; children: Caroline, Elizabeth, Trevor, Julia. BSN, Mich. State U., 1985. Staff nurse Weight Loss Clinic, Saginaw, 1987, St. Mary's Hosp., Saginaw, 1985-88; nurse mgr. 13 supr. psychiat. nursing Caro (Mich.) Ctr., 1987—2002; co-dir., co-owner CM Med.-Legal Cons. Inc, Saginaw, 1990—; agy. nurse Catalyst Healthcare, 2001—, Nurses Stat, 2002—, Home Health Care: TLC, 2002—; denials mgmt. specialist Covenant Health Care, Saginaw, Mich., 2005. Mem. Mich. State U. Nursing Alumni Assn. Lutheran. Avocations: travel, reading. Office: Covenant Health Care 1447 Harrison 3rd Fl Andersen Ctr Saginaw MI 48602 Personal E-mail: gsmielke@gmail.com. Business E-Mail: smielk@chs-mi.com.

MIES, SERGIO, surgeon, educator; b. Sao Paulo, Brazil, Dec. 25, 1942; MD, Sao Paulo Med. Sch., U. Sao Paulo, 1968, PhD, 1973. Physician in surgery Sao Paulo Med. Sch., U. Sao Paulo, 1972—, assoc. prof. surgery, 1992—2011. Recipient Oswaldo Cruz award, Sao Paulo Med. Sch., 2002, V Einstein prize, Albert Einstein's Hosp., 2004; named Hon. Citizen, Legis. Chamber of Mex., Alagoas, Legis. Chamber of Sorocaba, Sao Paulo; named one of Best Dr. in Brazil, Oswaldo Cruz Found. Mem.: Internat. Liver Transplantation Soc. Avocations: aquariums, skydiving. Home: Rua Capepuxis 215 Alto de Pinheiros Sao Paulo SP 05452-030 Brazil Home Fax: 55-11-3032-9944. Personal E-mail: smies@usp.br.

MIGEON, BARBARA RUBEN, pediatrician, geneticist, educator; b. Rochester, NY, July 31, 1931; d. William Saul and Sara (Gitin) Ruben; m. Claude Jean Migeon, Apr. 2, 1960; children: Jacques Claude, Jean-Paul, Nicole. BA, Smith Coll., Northampton, Mass., 1952; MD, SUNY, Buffalo, 1956. Diplomate Am. Bd. Pediatrics; cert. in med. genetics. Pediatric residency The Johns Hopkins U., Balt., 1956-59; fellow in endocrinology Harvard U. Med. Sch., Boston, 1959-60; fellow in genetics The Johns Hopkins Sch. Medicine, Balt., 1960-62, asso. prof. pediatrics, 1970-79, joint appointment in biology, 1978—, prof., 1979—, founding dir. PhD program in human genetics and molecular biology, 1979-89; Exch. prof. Guys Hosp., 1986. Mem. Genetics Study Sect., NIH, Bethesda, Md., 1975-77, Mammalian Genetics Study Sect., NIH, Bethesda, 1977-79, Human Genome Study Sect., NIH, Bethesda, 1991-93; vis. investigator Carnegie Instn. Washington, 1975. Contbr. more than 100 rsch. papers to profl. publs. Recipient Outstanding Woman Physician award Med. Coll. Pa. Mem. Am. Soc. Human Genetics. Office Phone: 410-955-3049. Business E-Mail: bmigeon@jhmi.edu.

MIGEON, CLAUDE JEAN, pediatrics educator; b. Lievin, Pas-De-Calais, France, Dec. 22, 1923; came to U.S., 1950, naturalized, 1967; s. André and Pauline (Descamps) M.; m. Barbara Lou Ruben, Apr. 2, 1960; children: Jacques, Jean-Paul, Nicole. MD, Sch. Medicine, U. Paris, 1950. Fellow dept. pediatrics Sch. Medicine, Johns Hopkins U., 1950-52, asst. prof., 1954-60, asso. prof., 1960-71, prof. pediatrics, 1971—; instr. biochemistry U. Utah, 1952-54; pediatrician Johns Hopkins Hosp., 1954—. Mem. diabetes metabolism tng. grants com. NIH, 1963-67, gen. clin. rsch. ctrs. com., 1968-71, mem. endocrinology study sect., 1974-78; cons. Med. Rsch. Coun. Can., 1969-85, mem. Nat. Ctr. for Rsch. Resources data and safety monitoring bd. NIH, 2006-, others; vis. prof. Maadi Armed Forces Hosp., Cairo, 1985, Guy's Hosp., London, 1986. Co-editor: (textbook) The Diagnosis and Treatment of Endocrine Disorders in Childhood and Adolescence, 4th edit., 1994; mem. editl. bd.: Johns Hopkins Med. Jour., 1970-72, Jour. Clin. Endocrinology and Metabolism, 1971-77, Hormone Rsch., 1979—; contbr. articles to profl. jours. Fulbright fellow, 1950; Am. Field Svc. fellow, 1950-51; Andre and Bella Meyer fellow, 1951-52; recipient rsch. career award NIH, 1964-85. Fellow AAAS; mem. Endocrine Soc. (coun. 1971-74, chmn. pub. affairs com. 1974-91, Ayerst award, Williams award), Soc. Pediatric Rsch. (emeritus), Am. Pediatric Soc., Lawson Wilkins Pediatric Endocrine Soc. (founding pres. 1972, Van Wyk prize, 2009), Am. Soc. Clin. Investigation (emeritus), Am. Physiol. Soc., Japanese Pediatric Endocrine Soc. (hon.), Found. Am. Meml. Hosp. (bd. dirs. 1985—, v.p. 2001-), Soc. Francaise d'Endocrinologie (fgn. corr. mem.). Home: 502 Somerset Rd Baltimore MD 21210-2720 Office: Johns Hopkins Hosp Harriet Ln Children Ctr 200 N Wolfe St Baltimore MD 21287-2520 Office Phone: 410 502 8326. Business E-Mail: cmigeon1@jhmi.edu.

MIGHTY, HUGH E., gynecologist, educator; b. Kingston, Jamaica, Sept. 13, 1956; MD, U. Md. Sch. Medicine, 1982; MBA, Loyola Coll., 2000. Clin. asst. prof. U. Md. Sch. Medicine, 1995—99; assoc. prof., interim chair Dept. Ob-Gyn. & Reproductive Scis., U. Md. Sch. Medicine, 2001—02, assoc. prof. chair, 2002—10; prof., dept. ob-gyn. LSU Health, 2010, vice chancellor clin. affairs, 2010—. Trustee Endowment Fund, U. Md. Fellow: ACOG (vice chair CREOG Edn. Com.); mem.: Soc. Perinatal Obstetrician, Soc. Critical Care Medicine, Soc. Maternal Fetal Medicine Specialists, Am. Diabetes Assn. Office: 1501 Kings Hwy Shreveport LA 71103 Office Fax: 318-675-4170. Business E-Mail: hmighty@lsuhsc.edu.

MIGLIORE, ALBERTO, rheumatologist; b. Rome, Jan. 19, 1960; MD, U. Sapienza, 1984. Chief rheumatology unit St. Peter Hosp., 2002—. Mem.: Italian Soc. Rheumatology (bd. mem.). Office: Via Cassia 600 Rome 00189 Italy Office Phone: 390633585802. Business E-Mail. albertomigliore@terra.es.

MIGLIORE, MARCELLO, thoracic surgeon, educator; b. Siracusa, Aug. 10, 1961; MD, U. Catania, 1985. Sr. resident thoracic surgery Cath. U. Leuven, 1996—97; cons. thoracic surgeon Papworth Hosp., Cambridge, 2004—06, Royal Devon Hosp., Exeter, England, 2009, Papworth Hosp., Cambridge, 2009—10; assoc. prof. to prof. thoracic surgery U. Catania, 2010—. Recipient Best Rschr., EACTS; Rsch. grant, ESOT. Mem.: SICU, STS, ESTS, SCTS, ISDE. Avocations: sailing, swimming, golf. Home: Trav S Agostino 7a Siracusa Sicily 96100 Italy Personal E-mail: mmiglior@hotmail.com.

MIGLIORI, CLAUDIO, neonatologist; b. Voghera, Italy, July 23, 1962; s. Paolo Migliori and Carla Malaspina; m. Elena Garzoli, Dec. 1, 2001. Degree, U. Pavia, Italy, 1989, cert. in pediat., 1993. Fellow neonatal S. Matteo Hosp., Pavia, 1993—95; asst. pediat. divsn. Hosp. Lodi, Italy, 1995—97; chief NICU Hosp. Novara, Italy, 1997—97; exec. doc. intensive care beds neonatology Spedali Civili, Brescia, Italy, 1999—. Prof. U. Novara, 1998—99. Mem.: European Soc. Pediat. & Neonatology Intensive Care, Italian Soc. Neonatology (councillor (lombard sect.) 2002—06, sec. (lombard sect.) 2005—), Italian Soc. Pediat. Office: Neonatal Intensive Care Unit Piazzale Spedali Civili 1 25123 Brescia BS Italy Home Phone: 0039-030-2807031; Office Phone: 0039-030-3996295-6. Personal E-mail: claudio.migliori@libero.it.

MIGLIORI, FRANCO CARLO, plastic surgeon, hospital unit director; b. Genova, Italy, Jan. 13, 1956; s. Ennio Silvio Migliori and Paola Maria Tedde; life ptnr. Grazia Zaccaini; 1 child, Martina. Medicine, U. Genoa, Italy, 1980. Trainer San Martino Gen. Hosp., Genova, Italy, 1981—85; resident U. Pavia, 1986—91; asst. San Martino Gen. Hosp., Genova, 1992—93, sr. asst., 1993—2000, plastic surgery unit dir., 2001—. With Alpini Army, 1982—83. Mem.: European Assn. Plastic Surgeons, Internat. Soc. Aesthetic Plastic Surgery, Società Italiana di Chirurgia Plastica, Ricostruttiva ed Estetica, Am. Soc. Plastic Surgeons (corr.), Glia Soc., One-In-A-Thousand-Soc., Internat. Soc. Philos. Enquiry, Triple Nine Soc., Mensa Internat. Roman Catholic. Avocations: golf, tennis, soccer. Office: San Martino General Hospital Mon 8 Lev largo Rosanna Benzi 10 Genoa 16132 Italy Office Fax: +39-010-5556735; Home Fax: +39-178-2206427. Personal E-mail: franco.migliori@fastwebnet.it. Business E-Mail: franco.migliori@hsanmartino.it.

MIGLIORI, MASSIMILIANO, nephrologist, researcher; b. Viareggio, Italy, Apr. 1, 1968; s. Otello Migliori and Maria Rosaria Romboni; m. Gianna Letizia Musetti, Apr. 14, 1996; children: Jonathan, Maria. MD, U. Pisa, 1994, degree in Nephrology, 1998. Rschr. U. Pisa, Italy, 1998—2004; nephrology Ospedale Versilia, Camaiore, Italy, 2004—. Contbr. articles to profl. jours. Mem. com. Italian Socialist Dem. Party, Viareggio, Italy, 2003. Mem.: European Dialysis and Transplantation Assn., European Renal Assn. (award 2001). Socialist Labor. Roman Catholic. Avocations: game, tennis, reading. Office: Ospedale Versilia Via Aurelia 335 Lu Camaiore 55043 Italy Home: Via Gianni Schicchi 56/B 55049 Lu Torre dek Lago Puccini LU Italy Office Fax: +05846059600. Personal E-mail: maxmigliori@yahoo.it.

MIGOWA, ANGELA NYANGORE, physician; b. Nairobi, Kenya, July 12, 1983; MBChB, U. Nairobi, 2007. Resident Aga Khan U. Hosp. Nairobi Dept. Pedit. and Child Health, 2010—. Home: Gogo Falls Rd Nairobi 00200 Kenya Personal E-mail: angela.migowa@yahoo.com.

MIGUEL, RAFAEL, anesthesiologist; b. Havana, Cuba; MD, U. Cadiz. Diplomate Am. Bd. Anesthesiology-pain medicine, 2007, Am. Bd. Anesthesiology, 2009. Resident anesthesiology Tulane Univ. Med. Ctr., 1982—84; prof. anesthesiology Univ. of S. Fla. Coll. of Medicine. Mem.: Fla. Soc. of Anesthesiologist (pres.). Office: H. Lee Moffitt Cancer Center & Research Institute 12902 Magnolia Drive Tampa FL 33612 Office Phone: 888-663-3488.

MIHAELA, STOIA, occupational medicine specialist; b. Sibiu, Oct. 26, 1964; PhD, Lucian Blaga U. Sibiu, 2007. Physician U. Medicine and Pharmacy Cluj-Napoca, 1991; sr. physician, occupl. health expert Pub. Health Directorate Sibiu, 1996—; lectr. ULBS, Faculty Medicine, 2004. Cons., occupl. health com. Ministry of Health, 2003. Recipient Letter Appreciation award, Astra Libr. Sibiu. Mem.: Romanian Soc. Occupl. Medicine, Romanian Coll. Physicians. Home: NEGOI 71 Sibiu Central Region 550275 Romania Office Phone: 0040269210071. Personal E-mail: mihaelas_mm@yahoo.com, medmuncii@dspsibiu.ro.

MIHALTZ, KATA, ophthalmologist; b. Budapest, Hungary, Oct. 26, 1974; MD, 2000. Physician, dept. ophthalmology Hietzing Hosp., Vienna, 2011—. Home: Lessinggasse 19/7 Vienna 1020 Austria Personal E-mail: mihaltzkata@yahoo.com.

MIHAN, RICHARD, retired dermatologist; b. Dec. 20, 1925; s. Arnold and Virginia Catherine (O'Reilly) M. MD, St. Louis U., 1949. Diplomate Am. Bd. Dermatology. Intern L.A. County Gen. Hosp., 1949-51, resident in dermatology, 1954-57; pvt. practice in dermatology LA, 1957-95; prof. emeritus U. So. Calif., 1989—. Lt. Comdr. USNR, 1951-53. Fellow ACP; mem. AMA, Pacific Dermatol. Assn. (exec. bd. 1971-74), Am. Acad. Dermatol., Calif. Med. Assn. (chmn. dermatol. sect. 1973-74), L.A. Met. Dermatology Soc. (pres. 1975-76), L.A. Acad. Medicine (pres. 1988-89), Order of St. John of Jerusalem, of Rhodes, and of Malta, Order of St. Lazarus (comdr.), Calif. Club. Roman Cath. Home: 3278 Wilshire Blvd Apt 503 Los Angeles CA 90010-1431

MIHM, MARTIN CHARLES, JR., pathologist, educator; s. Martin Charles and Cecilia Matilda (Hepp) M. AB, Duquesne U., 1955; MD, U. Pitts., 1961; MA (hon.), Harvard U., Cambridge, Mass., 1990. Diplomate Am. Bd. Dermatology, Am. Bd. Pathology. Intern Mt. Sinai Hosp., NYC, 1961-62, resident in medicine, 1963-64; resident in dermatology Mass. Gen. Hosp., Boston, 1964-67, resident in Pathology, 1968-72, chief dermatopathology, 1973-94; asst. prof. pathology Harvard U. Med. Sch., Boston, 1972-75, assoc. prof., 1975-79, chief dermatopathology, 1982-93; prof. pathology Mass. Gen. Hosp., Harvard U., Boston, 1980-93; prof., chief dermatopathology, dermatology Albany (N.Y.) Med. Coll., 1993—. Pathologist Malignant Melanoma Coop. Group, 1972—77; chmn. pathology com. Intergroup Melanoma Study, 1983—88; chief sr. adminstr. Wellman Labs., Mass. Gen. Hosp., 1985—93, cons. WHO, 1985—; adj. prof. pathology Vanderbilt U., 1989—; chmn. pathology standing com., 1991—; clin. prof. pathology Harvard Med. Sch., 1996—; sr. dermatopathologist and pathologist Mass. Gen. Hosp., 1996—; adj. prof. Thomas Jefferson Med. Sch., 2000—; prof. otolaryngology U. of Ark. Sch. of Med. Scis., 2002—. Author: Primer of Dermatopathology, 1984, 2d edit., 1992, Problematic Pigmented Lesions, 1990; co-author: Melanoma and Nevi, 1997, The Melanocytic Proliterations, 2001; editor: Lymphoproliferative Disorders of the Skin, 1986, Pathbiology and Recognition Malignant Melanoma, 1988, Dermatologia Practica, 2005; contbr. articles to med. jours.; overseer Boston Symphonic Orch., 2001—. Bd. overseers Boston (Mass.) Symphony Orch., 2001—. Served to comdr. USPHS, 1967-69. Recipient Gold Humanism award, Harvard Med. Sch., 2004. Fellow: ACP, Am. Soc. Dermatopathology, Am. Acad. Dermatology; mem.: AMA (Harvard Med. Sch. rep. to med. sch. sect. 1991), Annenberg Cir. of Dermatologic Found., Italian Assn. Ambulatory Dermatologists (hon.), Soc. of Dermatology, Mexico (hon.), Italian Soc. of Anatomic Pathology (hon.), Austrian Dermatology Soc. (hon.), Harvard Dermatology House Officer's Assn. (pres. 1982), Fort Orange Club, Albany, Harvard Club (Boston, N.Y.C.), Pi Gamma Mu, Alpha Omega Alpha. Independent. Roman Catholic. Home: 27 Chilton St Brookline MA 02446 Office: Brigham and Womens Hosp Alumnae Hall Room #317 Boston MA 02115 Office Phone: 617-724-1350. Business E-Mail: mmihm@partners.org.

MI JUNG, CHI, ophthalmologist, educator; b. Gwangju, Republic of Korea, June 9, 1976; d. Dae Yoon and Yang Hee; m. Jin Sung Moon; children: Yubin, Jiyu. MS, Grad. Sch., Gachon U. Medicine and Sci., 2008; PhD, Gachon U. Medicine & Sci., 2010. Diplomate HHS. Fellow Korea U. Coll. Medicine, Ansan, Republic of Korea, 2005—06; instr. Gachon U., Gil Hosp., 2006—08, asst. prof. Republic of Korea, 2008—. Contbr. articles to profl. jours. Avocations: golf, snowboarding, travel, yoga. Office: Gachon University Gil Hosp Dept Ophthalmology Guwol-Dong Namdong-Gu # 1198 405-760 Incheon Incheon Republic of Korea Office Phone: 82-10-9434-3452. Office Fax: 82-32-460-3358. Business E-Mail: cmj@gilhospital.com.

MIKHAILOV, ALEXANDER TROFIMOVICH, biologist, researcher; b. Moscow, Aug. 31, 1945; s. Trofim Vasilevich M. and Taissia Ivanovna Khodorevskaya; m. Irina Avelinovna Rey-Carro, Sept. 13, 1966; 1 child, Marina Alexandrovna. MD, 2nd Moscow Med. Inst., 1968; PhD, Inst. Human Morphology, Moscow, 1973; DSc in Biology, Inst. Devel. Biology, Moscow, 1985. Diploma in medicine, embryology. Intern, rsch. student Inst. Human Morphology USSR Acad. Med. Scis., Moscow, 1968-70, pre, postdoct. Inst. Human Morphology, 1970-75, rsch. officer Koltzov Inst. Devel. Biology, 1975-80, sr. rsch. officer, group leader Koltzov Inst. Devel. Biology, 1980-87, chief Lab. Organogenesis Koltzov Inst. Devel. Biology, 1987-98; prof. embryology, histology and cytology Russian Acd. Scis., 1992; rsch. dir. Inst. Health Scis. U. La Coruña, Spain, 1995—. Vis. prof. dept. cell and molecular biology U. La Coruña, 1992-93; grant-aided rschr. Ministry of Edn. and Sci., Spain, 1993-94; participant med. projects, Finland and Germany; dep. chmn. Sci. Coun. on Developmental Biology USSR/Russian Acad. Scis., 1986-

98; mem. Coun. Biol. Scis. Superior Certifying Commn. Coun. Mins. USSR, 1987-93, Sci. Coun. Embryology, Histology and Cytology Moscow U., 1986-95; mem. organizing com. Soviet-Finnish Symposia on Developmental Biology, Inductive Processes and Cell Interactions, Tallinn, Estonia, 1981, membrane and cell interactions during devel., Tbilisi, Georgia, 1984, cell differentiation and gene expression, Tashkent, Uzbekistan, 1988, signal molecules and cell differentiation, Suzdal, Russia, 1991, Soviet/Russian Symposia on Developmental Biology, Moscow, 1982, 87, 90, Pushchino-on-Oka, 1988, Spanish Symposium, La Coruña, Spain, 1995; lectr., rschr., presenter in field. Author: (in Russian) Embryonic Inducers, 1988, Immunochemical Methods in Developmental Biology, 1991, (in Spanish) Immunochemical Analysis: Bases and Protocols, 1994, (in Russian) Introduction in Neurogenetics, 2000; editor: Immunological Aspects of Developmental Biology, 1984, Hemopoetic Stem Cells, 1988; Developmental Biology in Russia, 1997 (in English), Shaping the Heart in Development & Disease, 2010; editor-in-chief: Soviet/Russian Jour. Developmental Biology (Ontogenez), 1988-95; mem. editl. bd. Russian Jour. Developmental Biology (Ontogenez), 1995—; mem. adv. bd. Internat. Jour. Developmental Biology, 1994-2002; patent for diagnostic method for early stages of ascarid infection, 1980; contbr. over 100 articles to profl. jours. Grantee Deutsche Forschungsgemeinschaft, 1993-95, Internat. Sci. Found., 1993-95, Spanish Ministry of Sci. and Tech., 2001-04, 04-07, 08-11, French Nat. Rsch. Agy., 2009-. Mem.: AAAS, Nature Reader Panel, Spanish Nat. Agy. Evaluation & Prospective, European Soc. Cardiology (working group devel. anatomy and pathology 2006—), Internat. Soc. for Heart Rsch., Sci. Adv. Bd., Frontiers in Biosci. Soc. Scientists, Alexander Kowalevsky Award Com., Russian Acad. Natural Scis., NY Acad. Scis., Spanish Soc. Devel. Biology (founder 1995, bd. dirs. 2001—10, expert 2009—), Domus Human House (mem. internat. com. 1993—), Internat. Cytoskeleton Club, Internat. Soc. Devel. Biologists (bd. dirs. 1989—98), St. Petersburg Soc. Naturalists (hon.; Alexander Kowalevsky award com. 2001—), Med. Surg. Acad. of Lugo, Spain (assoc.). Avocations: jazz, car travel, playing with dogs. E-mail: margot@udc.es.

MIKHAILOV, THERESA ANN, pediatrician, educator; b. Chgo., Nov. 29, 1962; MD, Northwestern U., 1986; PhD, U. Ill. Chgo., 2011. Asst. prof. pediat. Rush Med. Coll., 1992—99, Med. Coll. Wis., 1999—2010, assoc. prof. pediat., 2010—. Staff physician Rush-Presbyn. St. Luke's Med. Ctr., 1992—99, Cook County Children's Hosp., 1992—99, Children's Hosp. Wis., 1999—2011. Fellow: Am. Acad. Pediat.; mem.: Soc. Critical Care Medicine. Avocation: puzzles. Office: 9000 W Wisconsin Ave M/S #681 Milwaukee WI 53201 Office Fax: 414-266-3563. Business E-Mail: tmikhail@mcw.edu.

MIKHAILOV, VICTOR SERGEEVICH, biologist, educator; b. Moscow, Soviet Union, Jan. 12, 1948; Degree in Engring. Physics, Moscow Phys. Engring. Inst., 1971; PhD in Biol. Scis., Inst. Devel. Biology, SSSR Acad. Scis., 1974. Head biochem. lab. N. K. Koltzov Inst. Devel. Biology, RAS, 1989—2006, chief scientist, prof., 2006—. Vis. prof. Oreg. State U., United States, 2001—08. Recipient Eminent Scientist award, RIKEN, Japan. Avocation: travelling. Office: 26 Vavilova Str Moscow 119991 Russia Office Fax: 7-4991358012. Business E-Mail: mikhailov48@mail.ru.

MIKI, YOSHIHARU, university executive, administrator, educator; b. Kobe, Japan, Feb. 23, 1932; m. Miya Miki, May 13, 1961. MD, Osaka U., Japan, 1955; MSc, Colo. U., 1959; PhD, Osaka U., 1963. Asst. prof. dermatology Osaka U. Med. Sch., 1963-75, assoc. prof., 1975-76; prof., chmn. dept. dermatology Ehime (Japan) U. Med. Sch., 1976-94, dir. hosp., 1989-91, dean, 1991-93, pres., 1994-97, prof. emeritus, 1997—. Author: Dermatopathology, 1976, Color Atlas of Dermatology, 1977, Modern Dermatology, 1981, Dermatology, Case Study, 1983. Recipient Gold and Silver Star, The Order of the Sacred Treasure, Japan, 2008.

MIKI, YOSHITSUGU, oncologist; b. Neyagawa, Japan, Jan. 1, 1954; s. Atsushi Setsuko (Nagata) M.; m. Machiko Tsuchiya, Nov. 26, 1989. MD, Osaka U., 1984. Pres. Miki Clinic, Neyagawa, 1985—. Mem. Japanese Soc. Immunology, Japanese Cancer Assn. Avocation: fine arts. Office: Miki Clinic 2-2-1 Kuzuhara 572-0075 Neyagawa Osaka Japan Fax: 81-72-838-6568. E-mail: mikiy@po.aianet.ne.jp.

MIKI, YUKIO, medical educator, department chairman; b. Osaka, Japan, June 15, 1960; MD, Kyoto U., 1986, PhD, 1994. Assoc. prof. Kyoto U. Grad. Sch. Medicine, 2007—09; prof., chmn. Osaka City U. Grad. Sch. Medicine, 2009—. Mem.: Japanese Soc. Magnetic Resonance Medicine (Pres. prize), Japan Radiol. Soc., Japanese Soc. Neuroradiology (Kato prize), Radiol. Soc. N.Am., Internat. Soc. Magnetic Resonance Medicine. Avocation: photography. Office: 1-4-3 Asahi-machi Abeno-ku Osaka 545-8585 Japan Office Fax: 81-6-6646-6655. Business E-Mail: yukio.miki@med.osaka-cu.ac.jp.

MIKNEVICH, MARY ANN, physical medicine and rehabilitation physician; MD, U. of Pitts. Sch. of Medicine, 1980. Diplomate Am. Bd. Physical Medicine and Rehab., Am. Bd. Electrodiagnostic Medicine. Intern Mercy Hosp., 1981; resident St. Francis Hosp., 1983; asst. clin. prof. Univ. of Pitts. Sch. of Medicine; pres. Pa. Acad. of Physical Medicine and Rehab., 1996—97; chair dept. of physical medicine Mercy Hosp. of Pitts. Mem.: Am. Acad. of Pain Medicine. Office: Medical Rehabilitation Incorporated 1350 Locust St Ste 409 Pittsburgh PA 15219 Office Phone: 412-232-7608.

MIKOV, ALEXANDER, engineer; b. Perm, Mar. 14, 1959; Degree, MPTI, 1982. Engr. POLYUS R & D Inst., 1982—. Avocations: football, music. Office: Wwedenskogo 3 Moscow 117342 Russia Business E-Mail: alex.micow@mtu-net.ru.

MILADI, NAJOUA BEN KHALED, neurologist, educator; b. Tunis, Tunisia, Feb. 19, 1953; d. Tahar Khaled and Naima Bellagha; m. Mongi Miladi, July 9, 1977; children: Hager, Mehdi. MD, Faculty of Medicine, Tunisia, 1980; Specialization in Neurology, Faculty of Medicine, 1983; Specialization in Child Neurology, UCL, Belgium, 1985. Chief of neurol. dept. Faculty of Medicine, 1993-99; chief pediatric neurology svc. Nat. Inst. Neurology, 2002—05; sec. State Pub. Health, Tunisia, 2007—. Pres. Tunisian Assn. Neurology, 1995-2001; gen. sec. Tunisian Assn. Against Epilepsy, 1995-2000, v.p., 2000—09, sec., State Pub. Health, 2007-10. Mem. editl. bd. Jour. Child Neurology, 2000. Mem. Internat. Child Neurology Assn. (edit. bd. 1991-, Stobo Prichard award 1994), Child Neurology Soc. U.S.A (Bernie D'Souza award 1990), European Child Neurology Soc., Nat. Union Women of Tunisia. Islamic. Avocations: tennis, swimming, scuba diving, dance. Home: 35 Rue des Sciences Riadh Ennasr II 2037 Ariana Tunisia Office: Ministere de la Sante Pub Bab Saadoun 1030 Tunisia Home Phone: 0021671828166. Business E-Mail: najoua.miladi@rns.tn.

MILAM, JOHN DANIEL, pathologist, educator; b. Kilgore, Tex., May 22, 1933; s. Ott G. and Effie (White) Milam; m. Carol Jones, Aug. 1, 1959; children: Kay, Beth, John Daniel, Julie. BS, La. State U., 1955, MS, 1957, MD, 1960. Attending pathologist St. Luke's Episcopal Hosp., Houston, 1967—89, chief of staff, 1981—83; emeritus Tex. Children's Hosp., Houston, 2000—; adj. prof. lab. medicine M.D. Anderson Cancer Ctr., U. Tex., Houston, 1990—2001; prof. pathology and lab. medicine U. Tex. Med. Sch., Houston, 1989—2001, prof. emeritus, 2001—; active med. staff Hermann Hosp., Houston, 1988—, med. dir. lab. svcs., 1990—95; chief pathology Lyndon B. Johnson Gen. Hosp., Houston, 1995—2001. Trustee Am. Bd. Pathology, 1985—96, pres., 1995, life trustee, 1996—; cons. in field. Contbr. articles and abstracts to profl. jours., chapters to books. Bd. dirs. Greater Houston area chpt. ARC, 1978—. Recipient Disting. Physician award, Hermann Hosp., 1996. Mem.: Coll. Am. Pathologist (bd. govs., vice spkr. house of dels. 2005—), Houston Soc. Clin. Pathologists (pres. 1975, Harlan J. Spjut award 2003), Am. Soc. Clin. Pathologists (Commn. on Continuing Edn. Disting. Svc. award 1993, Israel Davidsohn Disting. Svc. award 2001), Tex. Soc. Pathologists (pres. 1978, George T. Caldwell award 1981), Am. Assn. Blood Banks (pres. 1984, Disting. Svc. award 1988). Republican. Baptist. Home: 11927 Arbordale Ln Houston TX 77024-5001 Office: U Tex Houston Med Sch Rm 2-022 Dept Pathology 6431 Fannin St Houston TX 77030-1501 Office Phone: 713-500-5336. Business E-Mail: john.d.milam@uth.tmc.edu.

MILANDRI, GIAN LUIGI, physician, gastroenterologist, medical statistician and epidemiologist; b. Cesena, Italy, June 21, 1952; s. Arturo and Norina (Maroni) M.; m. Diletta Burioli, Oct. 26, 1980; children: Paolo, Agnese. MD, U. Bologna, Italy, 1979. Cert. gastroenterology U. Bologna, 1985, health stats. 2003. Asst. physician L. Cappelli Hosp, Mercato Saraceno, Italy, 1984-89; gastroenterologist Bellaria Hosp., Bologna, 1989-99; asst. prof. stats. and epidemiology Toxicology Sch. U., Bologna, 1989-2000; cons. gastroenterology and gastrointestinal endoscopy unit M. Bufalini Hosp., Cesena, Italy, 1997—. Cons. gastroenterologist local health unit, Cesena, 1990-94; gastroenterologist Eastbourne Dist. Gen. Hosp., UK, 2009. Mem.: Am. Gastroentology Assn., Am. Coll. Gastroenterology, Soc. Italiana Endoscopia Digestiva, Assn. Italiana Studio Fegato, Assn. Italiana Gastroenterologi Ospedalieri, Am. Soc. Gastrointestinal Endoscopy, N.Y. Acad. Sci., Nat. Geog. Soc. Avocations: skiing, sailing, photography, surfing. Home: Via Iris Versari 75 47023 Cesena Italy Office: M Bufalini Hosp Viale Ghirotti 286 Cesena Italy E-mail: glm1@interfree.it, glm@ausl-cesena.emr.it.

MILANI, RICHARD VIRGIL, cardiologist; b. Washington, Aug. 24, 1955; MD, U. Fla., 1979. Vice-chmn., dept. cardiovasc. disease Ochsner Health Sys., 1991—. Prof., medicine U. Queensland, 2011. Fellow: Am. Heart Assn., Am. Coll. Cardiology. Office: 1514 Jefferson Hwy New Orleans LA 70121 Office Fax: 504-842-5875. Business E-Mail: rmilani@ochsner.org.

MILDER, DAN GEORGE, neurologist; b. Kosice, Czechoslovakia, July 28, 1947; s. Emil and Frida Milder; m. Karen Ruth Strauss, Dec. 18, 1983; children: Sarah Emily, Tamara Yael, David Aladar. MBBS, U. Sydney, 1970. Conjoint sr. lectr. U. NSW, Sydney, 2000—. Author: (book) Combination Therapy In Multiple Sclerosis (Eureka Sci. award, 2003). Fellow: Royal Australasian Coll. Physicians. Achievements include discovery of combination therapy in mutliple sclerosis. Office: Inst Neurol Scis 3 Waverley St Bondi Junction NSW 2022 Australia Personal E-mail: dmilder@ozemail.com.au.

MILDVAN, DONNA, infectious diseases physician; b. Phila., June 20, 1942; d. Carl David and Gertrude M.; m. Rolf Dirk Hamann; 1 child, Gabriella Kay. AB magna cum laude, Bryn Mawr Coll., 1963; MD, Johns Hopkins U., 1967. Diplomate Am. Bd. Internal Medicine and Infectious Diseases. Intern, resident Mt. Sinai Hosp., NYC, 1967-70, fellow, infectious diseases, 1970-72; asst., assoc. prof. clin. medicine Mt. Sinai Sch. Medicine, NYC, 1972-87; prof. clinical medicine Dept. Medicine, Mt. Sinai Sch. Medicine, NYC, 1987-88, prof. medicine, 1988-94; physician-in-charge infectious diseases Beth Israel Med. Ctr., NYC, 1972-79, chief, div. infectious diseases, 1980—; prof. medicine Albert Einstein Coll. of Medicine, NYC, 1994—. Mem. AIDS charter rev. com., NIH/Nat. Inst. Allergy and Infectious Diseases, Bethesda, 1987—; cons. FDA, Rockville, 1987—, Ctrs. for Disease Control, Atlanta, 1985-86; among first to describe AIDS, "Pre-AIDS", AIDS Dementia, 1982, among first to study AZT, 1986; Keynote speaker, II Internat. Conf. on AIDS, Paris, 1986 and other achievements in field; Sophie Jones Meml. lectr. in infectious diseases U. Mich. Hosps., 1984. Contbr. numerous articles to profl. jours; co-editor two books, many book chpts. and abstracts on infectious diseases and AIDS; editor: Atlas of AIDS, edits. 1-4. Recepient Alumna of the Yr. award, Johns Hopkins U., Sch. Medicine, 2011; Grantee N.Y. State AIDS Inst., 1986-87; Henry Strong Denison scholar Johns Hopkins U. Sch. Medicine, 1967; recipient Woman of Achievement award AAUW, 1987, Hero in Medicine award Internat. Assn. Physicians in AIDS Care, 2000; contract for antiviral therapy in AIDS, Nat. Cancer Inst./Nat. Inst. Allergy and Infectious Diseases, 1985-86, subcontract Nat. Inst. Allergy and Infectious Diseases, ACTU, 1987-99, prin. investigator, 2000-09. Fellow Infectious Diseases Soc. Am.; mem. Am. Soc. Microbiology, AAAS, Harvey Soc., Internat. AIDS Soc. Democrat. Jewish. Avocation: old movies. Office: Beth Israel Med Ctr 1st Ave New York NY 10003-7903

MILES, BRIAN JOHN, urologist; b. Belfast, No. Ireland, Nov. 8, 1946; s. William Livingston and Kathleen (Jamison) M.; m. Renee' Gig DeBlaise, Sept. 15, 1990. BS, Mich. State U., 1967; MS in Engring., U. Mich., 1968, MD, 1974. Diplomate Am. Bd. Urology. Surg. intern Georgetown U., Washington, 1974-75; resident in urology Walter Reed Army Med. Ctr., Washington, 1978-82; instr. dept. urology Army Med. Ctr., Tacoma, 1982-84; instr. dept. surgery U. Wash., Seattle, 1982-84; staff physician dept surgery Henry Ford Hosp., Detroit, 1984-91; assoc. prof. U. Mich., Ann Arbor, 1984-93; dir. resident edn. Henry Ford Hosp., Detroit, 1987-93, dir. urologic oncology, 1988—91; assoc. prof. Scott Dept. Urology, Houston, 1993-2000, prof., 2000—08, disting. Cullen chair in Urology, 2003—08; chief of urology VA Med. Ctr., Houston, 1993-98, St. Luke's Episcopal Hosp., Houston, 1993—; med. dir. Tex. Cancer Inst., 1999—2008; assoc. dir. for clin. affairs Baylor Comprehensive Cancer Ctr., Houston, 2006—08; clin. prof. urology, 2008—. Assoc. editor: Comprehensive Textbook of Genitourinary Oncology, 1995. Lt. col M.C., U.S. Army, 1975-84. Mem. ACS, Am. Urologic Assn. (Prostate Cancer Outcomes Analysis Grant 1995, 96), Soc. Urologic Oncology, Soc. Univ. Urologists, Internat. Soc. Urology. Avocations: history, sports, reading. Home: 3781 Farbar St Houston TX 77005-3713 Office Phone: 713-441-8110. Business E-Mail: bmiles@drbrianmiles.com.

MILES, JENNIFER MICHELE, dental hygienist; b. Lynnwood, Calif., Nov. 26, 1962; d. Jack and Janet Kirbo; m. Michael Paul Miles, Apr. 16, 1994. BA in Psychology, Ark. Tech U., Russellville, 1987; AS, DeKalb Coll., Dunwoody, Ga., 1998. Registered dental hygienist Ga. Bd. Dentistry, 1998. Psychol. case mgr. Friendship Mental Retardation Svcs., Russellville, Ark., 1987—89; psychosocial case mgr. Region Ten Cmty. Svcs., Louisa, Va., 1990—92; registered dental hygienist North Point Dental Assocs., P.C., Alpharetta, Ga., 1999—. Dental hygiene adv. com. chair Ga. Perimeter Coll., Dunwoody, Ga., 2001—. Creator (exhibition) Body Dysmorphic Disorder (First Pl. Table Clinic Presentations, 1998). Mem.: Ga. Dental Hygienists' Soc., Atlanta Dental Hygienists' Soc. (pres. 1999—2000), Am. Dental Hygienist Assn., Sigma Phi Alpha, Phi Theta Kappa. Avocations: music, reading, exercise, travel, continuing education. Home: 2620 Little John Circle Cumming GA 30040 Office: North Point Dental Assocs PC 3005 Royal Blvd S Suite 150 Alpharetta GA 30022 Personal E-mail: jammiles@bellsouth.net. E-mail: jennifer@northpointdental.com.

MILESTONE, BARTON N., diagnostic radiologist; MD, Yale U. Sch. of Medicine, 1981. Diplomate Am. Bd. of Radiology-diagnostic radiology. Resident diagnostic radiology Temple Univ. Hosp., 1986, fellow diagnostic radiology, 1988, Hosp. of the Univ. of Pa.; vice chmn. dept. of radiology Fox Chase Cancer Ctr., dir. MRI. Named top dr., Phila. Mag., 2010. Mem.: Radiol. Soc. of N. Am., Internat. Soc. for Magnetic Resonance in Medicine, Am. Coll. of Radiology. Office: Fox Chase Cancer Center 333 Cottman Ave Philadelphia PA 19111-2497 Office Phone: 215-728-3024.

MILETICH, ROBERT S., nuclear medicine physician, educator; b. Ill., Aug. 24, 1954; MD, U. Ill., 1981, PhD, 1985. Assoc. prof. SUNY, Buffalo, 2005—, interim chair, dept. nuc. medicine, 2010—. Fellow: AAAS; mem.: Alpha Omega Alpha. Avocation: sports. Office: 105 Parker Hall 3435 Main St Buffalo NY 14214-3007 Office Fax: 716-838-4918. Business E-Mail: miletich@buffalo.edu.

MILETTI, LUIZ CLAUDIO, biology professor; b. São Paulo, Brazil, Sept. 8, 1970; BS in Pharmacy, U. São Paulo, 1993, PhD in Biochemistry, 2001. Prof. State U. Snata Catarina, 2005—. Mem.: Brazilian Soc. Protozoology, Brazilian Soc. Biochemistry and Molecular Biology, Rotary Club. Office: Av Luis de Camões 2090 Lages Santa Catarina 88520-000 Brazil E-mail: lcmilett@yahoo.com.br.

MILEUSNIC, RADMILA, neurobiologist, educator; b. Pancevo, Serbia and Montenegro, Dec. 17, 1947; d. Milan and Desa Mileusnic; m. Miroslav Simic, Nov. 7, 1992 (dec.); 1 child, Miroslava Simic. BSc in Biology, U. Belgrade, MSc in Molecular Biology, MD, DrSc in Neuroradiology, U. Belgrade. Rsch. fellow Inst. Biol. Rsch., Belgrade, Serbia and Montenegro, 1971—79; asst. prof. Sch. Medicine, Belgrade, 1979—86, assoc. prof., 1986—91, prof. biochemistry, 1991—93; lectr. The Open U., Milton Keynes, England, 1995—2001, sr. lectr. Milron Keynes, 2001—04, reader in neurobiology Milton Keynes, 2004—. Vis. prof. medicine U. Belgrade, 2005—. Mem. Dem. Initiative for United Yugoslavia, Belgarde, 1989—2003; bd. dirs. The Brit. Scholarship Trust, London, 2001—05; mem. The Open Soc. Inst. Bd., Sect. Edn., London, 1993—2001. Recipient Med. Innovations award, 2003;, Alexander von Humboldt fellow, 1984, 1995. Achievements include patents for the use of APP-related peptides in treatment of neurodegenerative disease. Office: The Open U Walton Hall MK7 6AA Milton Keynes England

MILFELD, DOUGLAS J., surgeon; b. Saint Charles, Mo., Mar. 31, 1945; s. Dwight Joseph Milfeld and Nellie Eleanor Pillar; m. Nual Bussarangsee, Feb. 1, 1975; children: Tyler Dwight, Nelissa Danelle. BA, Baylor U., Waco, Tex., 1968; MD, Baylor U., Houston, 1972. Ptnr. Wichita Surg. Specialists, Kans., 1979—, also bd. dirs. Mem. mgmt. bd. Kans. Heart Hosp., Wichita, 2001—; pres. Wichita Surg. Soc., 1996—97. Mem. exec. com. Midwest Winefest for Gladalude Clinic, Wichita, 1996—. Fellow: ACS (gov. Kans. chpt. 1977—2003); mem.: Denton Cooley Surg. Soc., Soc. Thoracic Surgeons. Republican. Roman Catholic. Avocations: wine collecting, golf, gardening. Home: 7340 Elm Ct Wichita KS 67206 Office: Wichita Surg Specialists 9350 E 35th St N Ste 103 Wichita KS 67226 Office Phone: 316-858-5000.

MILHORAT, THOMAS HERRICK, neurosurgeon; b. NYC, Apr. 5, 1936; s. Ade Thomas and Edith Caulkins (Herrick) M.; m. Edith Mostile, 1961; children: John Thomas, Robert Herrick. BA, Cornell U., 1957, MD, 1961. Intern, asst. resident in gen. surgery N.Y. Hosp.-Cornell Med. Ctr., 1961—63, asst. resident, chief resident in neurosurgery, 1965—68, asst. neurosurgeon NIH, 1968—71; clin. assoc., dept. surg. neurology Nat. Inst. Neurol. Diseases and Blindness, Bethesda, 1963—65; assoc. prof. neurol. surgery, assoc. prof. child health and devel. George Washington U. Sch. Medicine, Washington, 1971—74, prof. neurol. surgery, prof. child health and devel., 1974—81; chmn. dept. neurosurgery Children's Hosp. Nat. Med. Ctr., Washington, 1971—81; prof. neurol. surgery, dept. chmn. SUNY Health Sci. Ctr., Bklyn., 1982—2001; chmn. dept. neurosurgery North Shore/L.I. Jewish Health System, 2002—09; founder, dir. Chiari Inst. North Shore Univ. Hosp., 2002—09; founder dir. Harvey Cushing Insts. Neurosci., Northshore-LI Jewish Health System, 2006—09, emeritus chmn. dept. neurosurgery, 2009—; prof. neurol. surgery NYU Sch. Medicine, 2002—07; neurosci. scholar in resident Feinstein Inst. Med. Rsch., 2009—; fellow Am. Assn. Neurological Surgery, 2010—. Neurosurgeon-in-chief Kings County Hosp. Ctr., 1982—2001; regional chmn. neurol. surgery LI Coll. Hosp., 1986—2001; program dir. Neurosurgery Rsch. Tng. Program, 1982—2001; mem. Nat. Coun. Scientists NIH, 1969—82; dir. Harvey Cushing Inst. Neurosci. North Shore LI Jewish Health Sys., NY, 2006—. Author: Hydrocephalus and Cerebrospinal Fluid, 1972, Pediatric Neurosurgery, 1978, Cerebrospinal Fluid and the Brain Edemas, 1987; (with M.K. Hammock) Cranial Computed Tomography in Infancy and Childhood, 1981; mem. editl. bd. Neurosurgery, 1997—, Neurosurg Focus: Syringomyelia, 2000—; contbr. more than 340 articles to profl. jours. Lt. comdr. USPHS, 1963—65. Recipient 1st prize in pathology, Cornell U. Med. Sch. Dept. Ob-Gyn., 1960,

Charles L. Horn prize Cornell Med. Sch., 1961, Best Paper award ann. combined meeting NY Acad. Medicine/NY Neurosurg. Soc., 1965, Pudenz award for Excellence in CSF Physiology, 1994, E. Jefferson Browder award for excellence in Neurosurgery, 1996, Arthur A. Kaplan award for excellence in neurosurgery, 1999, White House Recognition Lifetime Achievement award 2008. Fellow Am. Assn. Neurol. Surgery; mem. AAAS, Internat. Soc. Pediat. Neurosurgery, Am. Syringomyelia Alliance Project (chmn. med. adv. bd. 1996-2007, bd. dirs. 1996-2007), Am. Acad. Pediat. (surg. sect.), Soc. Pediat. Rsch., NY Acad. Medicine, NY Soc. Neurosurgery (pres. 1988-90), Bklyn. Neurologic Soc. (pres. 1988-95), Soc. Neurosci., Internat. Soc. Neurosci., Soc. Neurol. Surgeons, Sigma Xi. Avocations: golf, billiards, gardening. Office: North Shore Univ Hosp Dept Neurosurgery Manhasset NY 11030 Office Phone: 516-570-4419. Business E-Mail: milhorat@nshs.edu.

MILIC-EMILI, JOSEPH, physiologist, educator; b. Sezana, Slovenia, May 27, 1931; arrived in Can., 1963; s. Joseph Milic-Emili and Giovanna Milic-Emili Perhavec; m. Ann Harding, Nov. 2, 1957; children: Claire, Anne-Marie, Alice, Andrew. MD, U. Milan, 1955; Dr. honoris causa, U. Louvain, Belgium, 1987, Kunming Med. Coll., China, 1987, U. Montpellier, France, 1994, U. Ferrara, Italy, 1996, U. Athens, Greece, 1998, U. Ljubljana, Slovenia. Asst. prof. physiology and exptl. medicine McGill U., Montreal, Que., Canada, 1963-65, assoc. prof., 1965-69, prof., 1970-97, prof. emeritus, 1998—, dir. Meakins-Christie Labs., 1979-94. Vis. prof. Lab. de Physiologie Faculte de Medecine Saint-Antoine, Paris, Svc. de Pneumologie Hosp. Beaujon, Paris, 1978-79, 94-95, chmn. dept. physiology, 1973-78; vis. cons. medicine Royal Postgrad. Med. Sch., London, 1969-70; vis. cons. Aeronautics Imperial Coll. Tech., London, 1969-70; asst. prof. physiology U. Liege, Belgium, 1958-60; asst. prof. U. Milan, 1956-58. Mem. editl. bd. Jour. Applied Physiology, 1970-76, Rev. Française des Maladies Respiratoires, 1979-96, Rivista de Biologia, 1979-86, Am. Rev. Respiratory Disease, 1982-89, Reanimation, Soins Intensifs, Medicine d'Urgence, 1984-95. Mem. applied physiology and bioengring. study sect. NIH, 1975-78. Decorated Order of Can.; recipient Gold medal C. Forlanini U. Pavia, Italy, 1982, Am. Coll. Chest Physicians medal, 1984, 98, Harry Wunderly medal Thoracic Soc. Australia, 1988, medal Italian Sch. Mil. Medicine, 1990, medal Med. Sch. Brest, 1997, medal Med. Sch. Ferrara, 1997, medal Med. Sch. Bologna, 2006, Trudeau medal Am. Thoracic Soc., 2006; author of one of 100 most cited articles in clin. rsch. of 1960s; named one of 1,000 most-cited contemporary scientists, 1965-78, 1998 Presdl. award European Respiratory Soc., 1998 Disting. Lectr. in Physiology Am. Coll. Chest Physicians. Fellow Royal Soc. Can., Slovenian Acad. Sci. (fgn. corr.), Soc. Med. Clin. Bononiensis Sci.; mem. Am. Physiol. Soc., Am. Thorasic Soc. (hon.), Can. Physiol. Soc., Can. Thoracic Soc., Med. Rsch. Coun. (mem. grants com. 1980), Soc. Pneumologie Belge (hon.), Brazilian Physiol. Soc. (hon.), Hellenic Thoracic Soc. (hon.), Polish Pneumological Soc. (hon.), Chilean Resp. Soc. (hon.), European Respiratory Soc. (hon.). Home: 4394 Circle Rd Montreal PQ Canada H3W 1Y5 Office: McGill U Meakins-Christie Labs 3626 Rue Saint-Urbain Montreal PQ Canada H2X 2P2 Business E-Mail: joseph.milic-emili@mcgill.ca.

MILKEN, MICHAEL R., think tank executive, philanthropist; b. Calif., July 4, 1946; m. Lori Milken, Aug. 11, 1968; 3 children. Grad. summa cum laude, U. Calif., Berkeley; MBA, U. Pa. Securities trader Drexel Burnham Lambert, until 1990; chmn. The Milken Inst., 1991—; founder Prostate Cancer Found. (formerly CaPCure), 1993—; chair Knowledge Universe, 1996—; chmn. FasterCures/Ctr. for Accelerating Med. Solutions, 2003—. Author: Taste for Living Series cookbooks. Chair Assn. Cure of Cancer of the Prostate; co-founder Milken Family Found., 1982. Named one of Forbes 400: Richest Americans, 2006—. Office: Milken Inst 1250 Fourth St Ste 200 Santa Monica CA 90401

MILLAR, JOHN DONALD, physician, occupational & environmental health services consultant, musician; b. Newport News, Va., Feb. 27, 1934; s. John and Dorothea Virginia (Smith) M.; m. Joan M. Phillips, Aug. 17, 1957; children: John Stuart, Alison Gordon, Virginia Taylor. BS, U. Richmond, 1956; MD, Med. Coll. Va., 1959; DTPH, London Sch. Hygiene and Tropical Medicine, 1966; D of Pub. Svc. (hon.), Greenville Coll., Ill., 1994. Cert. specialist in Gen. Preventive Medicine 1969. Intern U. Utah Affiliated Hosps., Salt Lake City, 1959-60, asst. resident in medicine, 1960-61; chief Epidemic Intelligence Svc., Ctr. for Disease Control, USPHS, HEW, Atlanta, 1961-63, dep. chief surveillance sect. epidemiology br., 1962-63, chief smallpox unit, 1963-65, dir. smallpox eradication program, 1966-70, dir. Bur. State Svcs., 1970-78, asst. dir. Ctr. for Disease Control for Pub. Health Practice, 1979-80; dir. Nat. Ctr. Environ. Health, Atlanta, 1980-81, Nat. Inst. for Occupation Safety and Health, Atlanta, 1981-93, chmn. exec. com. Nat. Toxicology Program, 1989-93; pres. Don Millar & Assocs., Inc., Atlanta, 1993—. Adj. prof. occupl. and environ. health Sch. Pub. Health Emory U., Atlanta, 1988-98; cons. on smallpox, smallpox eradication, immunization programs and occupl. and environ. health WHO; mem. WHO expert adv. panel on occupl. health; bd. dirs. Farm Safety 4 Just Kids, 1993-98; tech. adv. bd. Ctr. Protect Workers' Rights, 1993; disting. fellow, vice chmn. Pub. Health Policy Adv. Bd., Inc., Washington, 1998-2007; mem. bd. dirs. Coll. Pub. Health, U. Ga., 2007-08, mem. Dean's Practice Com., 2008-; mem. string bass sect. DeKalb Symphony Orch., 1982-06, Gainesville (Ga.) Symphony Orch., 2000-04, N.E. Ga. Mountain Chamber Orch., 2001-05, Truett-Macconnell Coll. Wind Symphony, 2002-10, Toccoa Falls Coll. Orch., 2005—, Toccoa Symphony Orch., 2005—11, Piedmont Coll. diameber Orchestra, 2011-. Mem. editl. bd. Am. Jour. Indsl. Medicine, 1985-05, Am. Jour. Occupl. Psychology, 1993-00, Am. Jour. Preventive Medicine, 1993-00; contbr. articles to profl. jours. Recipient Surgeon Gen's. Commendation medal, 1965, Okeke prize London Sch. Hygiene and Tropical Medicine, 1966, Presdl. award for mgmt. improvement, 1972, W.C. Gorgas medal Assn. Mil. Surgeons U.S., 1987, Lucas lectr. Faculty Occupational Medicine Royal Coll. Physicians, London, 1987, Outstanding Med. Alumnus award Med. Coll. Va., 1988; also recipient Equal Employment Opportunity award, 1975, Medal of Excellence, 1977, Joseph W. Mountin lectr. award, 1986, Alexander D. Langmuir MD Meml. lectr. award, 2001, all from Ctrs. for Disease Control, Disting. Svc. medal USPHS, 1983, 88, Exemplary Svc. medal Surgeon Gen. U.S., 1988, Giants in Occupational Medicine lectr. U. Utah, 1989, William S. Knudsen award Am. Coll. Occupational Medicine, 1991, presdl. citation APA, 1991, William Steiger Meml. award Am. Conf. Govtl. Indsl. Hygienists, 1993, Health Watch award for outstanding contbns. toward improving health of minority populations, 1992, Award of Merit Minerva Edn. Inst., 1993, Alumni Disting. Svc. award U. Richmond, 1993, Jeff Lee Mem. Lectr. Am. Indusl. Hygiene Assoc. San Diego, Calif., 2002; named to Order Bifurcated Needle, World Health Orgn., 1978, Faculty Occupational Medicine, Royal Coll. Physicians, London, 1990; elected Safety and Health Hall of Fame Internat., Nat. Safety Coun., 1997. Mem. Am. Indsl. Hygiene Assn. (hon.), Am. Coll. Occupl. and Environ. Medicine, Am. Epidemiol. Soc., Collegium Ramazzini, Am. Assn. Pub. Health Physicians., Assn. Mil. Surgeons U.S., Pub. Health Svc. Commissioned Officers Assn., Alpha Omega Alpha.

MILLENSON, MICHAEL M., hematologist, oncologist; MD, Temple U., 1984. Lic. Pa. Prin. investigator; intern Temple Univ. Hosp., Phila., 1985, resident, 1987; fellow Beth Israel Hosp., Boston, 1991; hematologist- oncologist Fox Chase Cancer Ctr., 1994, dir. hematology svc. Office: Fox Chase Cancer Center 333 Cottman Ave Philadelphia PA 19111 Office Phone: 888-369-2427.

MILLER, ALAN B., health facility administrator, real estate company executive; b. NYC, Aug. 17, 1937; s. Daniel and Mary (Blumenthal) M.; m. Jill K. Stein, Oct. 5, 1968; children: Marc Daniel, Marni Elizabeth, Abby Danielle. BA, Coll. of William and Mary, 1958; MBA, U. Pa., 1960; PhD (hon.), U. SC. V.p. Young & Rubicam, Inc., NYC, 1964-69; sr. v.p. Am. Medicorp., Inc., LA, 1970, pres., CEO Phila., 1973-77, chmn., 1977, Hosp. Underwriting Group, 1977-78; founder, chmn., pres., CEO Universal Health Services, Inc., King of Prussia, Pa., 1978—; chmn., founder UHT-Real Estate Trust, King of Prussia, Pa., 1986—. Health care adviser Fed. Mediation and Conciliation Svc.; N.Y. Stock Exch., 1986—, bd. dirs. CDI Corp., Broadlane, Penn Mut. Life Ins. Co., Genesis Health Ventures, N.Y. Stock Exch.; Wharton Sch., U. Pa., 1996-2004, overseers, 2005-. Former chmn. Opera Co. of Phila.; dir. Regional Performing Arts Ctr. Capt. 77th Inf. Divsn. US Army. Recipient Ellis Island Medal of Honor, 1998, William and Mary medallion, George Washington U. Pres.'s medal. Office: Universal Health Services Inc 367 S Gulph Rd King Of Prussia PA 19406-0958 Office Phone: 610-265-0688. Office Fax: 610-768-3336. E-mail: alan.miller@uhrit.com. *

MILLER, ALBERT J., cardiologist, internist; b. Chgo., 1922; MD, Northwestern U., 1946. Diplomate Am. Bd. Internal Medicine, Am. Bd. Cardiovascular Diseases. Intern Michael Reese Hosp., Chgo., 1945-46, resident in medicine, 1950, fellow in cardiology rsch. Cardiovascular Inst., 1948-50; resident in medicine VA Hosp., Hines, Ill., 1950-51; attending physician Northwestern Meml. Hosp., Chgo.; prof. clin. medicine, cardiology Northwestern U. Med. Sch. Author: The Lymphatics of the Heart, 1982, Diagnosis of Chest Pain, 1988, Chest Pain, When and When Not to Worry, 2005; has done basic rsch. on lymphatics of the heart. Fellow ACP, Am. Coll. Cardiology, Am. Fedn. for Clin. Rsch., Ctrl. Soc. for Clin. Rsch. Office: Clin Cardiol Group Ltd 33 Lakeside Pl Highland Park IL 60035 Personal E-mail: ajmiller22@sbcglobal.net. *

MILLER, ALEC L., psychologist, educator; BA with honors, U. Mich., Ann Arbor, 1988; MA, Yeshiva U., Ferkauf Grad. Sch. Psychology, 1991; Psy.D, Yeshiva U., Ferkauf Grad. Sch. (Clin. Psychology), 1993. Lic. NY. Intern, clin psychology Albert Einstein Coll. Medicine/Montefiore Med. Ctr., Bronx, NY, 1992—93, co-dir., adolescent depression and suicide program, dept. psychiatry, 1995—96, assoc. dir., psychology internship tng. program, 1995—, dir., adolescent depression and suicide program, dept. psychiatry and behavioral scis., 1997—, dir., dialectical behavior therapy (DBT) clin. rsch. svcs., HIV mental health rsch. group, dept. psychiatry and behavioral scis., 1998—2004, chief, child and adolescent psychology, dept. psychiatry and behavioral scis., 2000—, assoc. prof., dept. psychiatry and behavioral scis., 2000—, dir. mental health svcs., P.S. 8 Sch.-Based Health Program, Dept. Pediatrics and Dept. Psychiatry and Behavioral Scis., 2001—; clin. instr. psychiatry Four Winds Hosp./Albert Einstein Coll. Medicine, Bronx, NY, 1993—95; staff/supervising psychologist, acute adolescent inpatient unit Four Winds Hosp., Katonah, NY, 1993—95; attending psychologist, adult outpatient psychiatry dept., dept. psychiatry and behavioral scis. Montefiore Med. Ctr., Bronx, NY, 1995—96; asst. prof., dept. psychiatry and behavioral scis. Albert Einstein Coll. Medicine, Bronx, NY, 1995—2000; dialectical behavior therapy trainer Behavioral Tech, Seattle, 1997—; private practice White Plains, NY. Invited spkr. in field; invited panelist in field; cons. in field; adj. tng. faculty Cognitive Therapy Ctr., NY, 1996—99; adj. clin. supr. Ferkauf Grad. Sch. Psychology, Yeshiva U., Bronx, NY, 1997—; invited grant reviewer Nat. Inst. for Health Rsch. United Kingdom, 2006—; mem. evaluation bd., psychiatry faculty Faculty of 1000 Medicine. Reviewer Cognitive and Behavioral Practice, 2001—, assoc. editor-elect, 2004—05, assoc. editor, 2005—08, reviewer Jour. Clin. Psychology, 2001—, Am. Jour. Psychotherapy, 2001—, Jour. Soc. Sci. and Medicine, 2002—, Jour. Consulting and Clin. Psychology, 2004—, Clin. Psychology: Sci. and Practice, 2004—, Behaviour Rsch. and Therapy, 2005—, Archives of Suicide Rsch., 2007—, editl. bd. Cognitive and Behavioral Practice, 2003—; co-author: Childhood Maltreatment, In Series, Advances in Psychotherapy-Evidence-Based Practice, 2006, Dialectical Behavior Therapy with Suicidal Adolescents, 2007; contbr. several articles to profl. jours.; media highlights include CNN, CBS TV, Teen People Mag., Redbook, NY Daily News, HealthyDay News, MSNBC, AP, Ladies' Home Jour., Trenton Times, NY Sun, Hartford Courant, Clin. Psychiatry News, Physicians Mag., Daily Freeman and News Talk TV.; contbr. chapters to books. Nominee Emmy award, Channel 13, PBS, Keeping Kids Healthy, guest interview about suicidal adolescents, 2004. Fellow: Am. Psychol. Assn. (mem., divsn. 12, Soc. Clin. Psychology 1992—, mem., divsn. 53, Soc. Clin. Child and Adolescent Psychology 2000—); mem.: Westchester County Group Psychotherapy Assn., Westchester County Psychological Soc., New Eng. Personality Disorder Assn., Soc. for the Exploration Psychotherapy Integration, Nat. Edn. Alliance for Borderline Personality Disorder, Am. Assn. Suicidology, Anxiety Disorders Assn. Am., NY State Psychol. Assn., Assn. for Behavioral and Cognitive Therapies, Internat. Soc. for the Improvement and Tng. of Dialectical Behavior Therapy (Svc. award 2002). Office: Montefiore Med Ctr Albert Einstein Coll Medicine Dept Psychiatry and Behavioral Scis 111 E 210th St Bronx NY 10467 Office Phone: 718-920-7666. Office Fax: 718-405-5953. Business E-Mail: aleclmiller@msn.com.

MILLER, ANTHONY BERNARD, physician, researcher; b. Woodford, Eng., Apr. 17, 1931; married, 1952; 5 children. BA, U. Cambridge, 1952, MB, BChir, 1955; MA, 2004, MD, 2006. House officer Oldchurch Hosp., Romford, Eng., 1955-57; med. registrar Luton and Dunstable Hosp., Eng., 1959-62; mem. sci. staff Med. Research Council Tb and Chest Disease Unit, London, 1962-71; assoc. prof. preventive medicine and biostats. U. Toronto, 1972-76, prof., 1976-96, chmn. dept., 1992-96, dir. grad. program in epidemiology, 1986-91; dir. epidemiology unit Nat. Cancer Inst. Can., Toronto, 1971-86; dir. Nat. Breast Screening Study, 1980—, WHO Collaborating Ctr. on Evaluation of Screening for Cancer, 1991-2000; prof. emeritus pub. health scis., 1997—; head divsn. of clin. Epidemology German Cancer Rsch. Ctr., Heidelberg, 1999—2003; assoc. dir. rsch. Dalla Lana Sch. Pub. Health, 2009—10. Nat. Health scientist, 1988-93; mem. working cadre Bladder Cancer Project, U.S., 1973-75; mem. epidemology com. Breast Cancer Task Force, U.S., 1973-77, chmn., 1975-77; mem. Fed. Task Force Cervical Cytol. Screening, Can., 1974-76, 80-81, Union Internat. Contre le Cancer com., controlled therapeutic trials, 1978-82, Multidisciplinary project breast cancer, 1978-82, chmn. project on screening, 1982-93; mem. sci. council Internat. Agy. Research Cancer, Lyon, 1981-85, chmn., 1985; mem. com. on diet, nutrition and cancer NRC of U.S., 1980-83, mem. oversight com. radioepidemiologic tables, 1983-84, com. on diet and health, 1986-89, com. on dietary guidelines implementation, 1988-91, chmn. com. on environmental epidemiology, 1990-94; chmn. Ont. Task Force on Primary Prevention of Cancer, 1994-95; mem. Coun. Can. Strategy Cancer Control, 2000-06; mem. adv. coun. Can. Partnership Against Cancer, 2007—09, act coun. 2009-. Served with RAF, 1957-59. Mem. Can. Oncology Soc. (sec.-treas. 1975-79, pres. 1980-81), Soc. Epidemiology Research, Internat. Epidemiology Assn., Am. Soc. Preventive Oncology (pres. 1983-85), Am. Coll. Epidemiology (bd. dirs. 1987-89). Home: 3800 Yonge St # 406 Toronto ON M4N 3P7 Canada Personal E-mail: ab.miller@sympatico.ca. Business E-Mail: ab.miller@utoronto.ca.

MILLER, BRUCE LAWRENCE, neurologist, educator; b. Indpls., Aug. 24, 1949; s. Milton Howard and Harriet Bernice Miller; m. Deborah Scofield Heintz, May 7, 1977; children: Hannah Amanda, Elliott Clemens. BS, Butler U., Indpls., 1974; MD, U. B.C., 1978. Diplomate Am. Bd. Neurology 1985. Resident, internal medicine Vancouver Gen. Hosp., 1980; fellow, neurology U. Western Ont., 1981; asst. to prof. UCLA, LA, 1985—98; prof. neurology & psychiatry, A.W. and Mary Margarfet Clausen disting. chair U. Calif., San Francisco, 1998—. Med. dir. John Douglas French Found. for Alzheimer's Disease Rsch., LA, 1984—; dir. Memory and Aging Ctr., U. Calif., San Francisco. Author: (textbook) The Human Frontal Lobes, editions 1 and 2; contbr. several articles to profl. jours. Jewish. Office: UCSF Memory and Aging Center 350 Parnassus Avenue Ste 905 San Francisco CA 94143-1207 Office Fax: 415-476-4800. E-mail: bmiller@memory.ucsf.edu.

MILLER, C. ARDEN, physician, educator; b. Shelby, Ohio, Sept. 19, 1924; s. Harley H. and Mary (Thuma) Miller; m. Helen Meihack, June 26, 1948; children: John Lewis, Thomas Meihack, Helen Lewis, Benjamin Lewis. Student, Oberlin Coll., Ohio, 1942—44; MD cum laude, Yale U., New Haven, Conn., 1948. Intern, then asst. resident pediatrics Grace-New Haven Community Hosp., 1948—51; faculty U. Kans. Med. Center, 1951—66, dir. childrens rehab. unit, 1957—60, dean Med. Sch., dir., 1960—66; prof. pediatrics and maternal and child health U. N.C., Chapel Hill, 1966—98, emeritus, 1998—, vice chancellor health scis., 1966—71, chmn. dept. maternal and child health, 1977—87. Chmn. exec. com. Citizens Bd. Inquiry into Health Svcs. for Am., 1968—71. Mem. editl. bd.: Jour. Med. Edn., 1960—66; contbr. articles to profl. jours. Trustee Appalachian Regional Hosps., 1974—84, Planned Parenthood Fedn.; chmn. Alan Guttmacher Inst., 1978—84, 1986—. Recipient Robert H. Felix Disting. Svc. award, St. Louis U., 1977, Martha Mae Eliot award in pub. health, 1984, O. Max Gardner award, U. N.C., 1987; scholar Am. Markle scholar in med. scis., 1955—60. Fellow: Royal Soc. Health (hon.), Clare Hall Cambridge (Eng.) U. (life); mem.: APHA (chmn. action bd. 1972—75, pres. 1974—75, Sedgewick Meml. medal 1986), Inst. of Medicine NAS, Assn. Am. Med. Colls. (v.p. 1965—66), Soc. Pediat. Rsch., Delta Omega, Alpha Omega Alpha, Sigma Xi. Home: 350 Carolina Meadows Villa Chapel Hill NC 27517-7549

MILLER, CAROL A., pediatrician, educator; b. Kansas City, Kans., Oct. 28, 1948; MD, Stanford U., 1975. Intern pediat. Mt. Zion Hosp. and Med. Ctr., San Francisco, 1975—76, resident, 1976—77, fellowship neonatology, 1977—79; attending physician U. Calif. Med. Ctr., San Francisco, dir. Well-Baby Nursery; faculty mem. U. Calif. San Francisco Sch. Medicine, 1989—, clin. prof. pediat. Adv. coll. mentor Sinkler Miller Med. Assn., exec. bd. mem.; com. mem. Shaken Baby Syndrome Prevention; physician edn. com. San Francisco Immunization Coalition. Named one of Top Docs-the Top 425 Doctors in the Bay Area, San Francisco Mag., 2001, 2002; named to Acad. Med. Educators, U. Calif. San Francisco Sch. Medicine, 2002. Office: UCSF Sch Medicine AC - 01, Box 0374 400 Parnassus Ave San Francisco CA 94143 Office Phone: 415-353-2000. Office Fax: 415-353-2822. E-mail: millerc@peds.ucsf.edu.

MILLER, D. CRAIG, cardiovascular surgeon; b. Dec. 3, 1946; Student in Chemistry and Math., Dartmouth Coll., 1965-68; BS in Basic Med. Scis., Stanford U. Sch. Medicine, 1969, MD, 1972. Lic. Calif., cert. Am. Bd. Surgery, Am. Bd. Thoracic Surgery, Am. Bd. Surgery (spl. qualifications gen. vascular surgery). Resident, gen. surgery Stanford U. Med. Ctr. and Affiliated Hosps., Calif., 1972—75; chief resident, peripheral vascular surgery Stanford U. Med. Ctr., Calif., 1975—76, chief resident, cardiovasc. surgery Calif., 1976—77, chief resident, thoracic surgery Calif., 1977, program dir., vascular surgery residency Calif., 1985—93; chief, cardiac surgery sect. VA Med. Ctr., Palo Alto, Calif., 1978—86, staff surgeon, cardiac surgery sect., 1978—96; clin. asst. prof., cardiovasc. surgery Stanford U. Sch. Medicine, Calif., 1978, assoc. prof., cardiovasc. surgery Calif., 1983—89, prof., cardiovasc. surgery Calif., 1989—; Thelma and Henry Doelger Prof., Cardiovasc. Surgery Stanford U., 1998—. Invited lectr. in field. Guest editor, circulation supplement Cardiovasc. Surgery, 1990—92, mem. editl. bd. Jour. Thoracic and Cardiovasc. Surgery, 1984—91, assoc. editor (acquired heart disease), 1998—2007, mem. editl. bd. Jour. Cardiac Surgery, 1985—95, Cardiac Chronicle, 1985—93, Jour. Surgical Rsch., 1990—94, Circulation, 1991—93, Jour. Heart Valve Disease, 1992—, Heart and Vessels, 1998—, ad hoc referee for several peer-reviewed publications; contbr. several articles to peer-reviewed jours. Lt. med. corps. USNR, 1970—82. Recipient Stanford U. Med. Sch. Disting. Alumni award, 1997, Wilfred Bigelow award, Canadian Cardiovasc. Soc., 2000, Antoine Marfan award, Nat. Marfan Found., 2001. Mem.: Santa Clara County Med. Soc. (mem. ethics com. 1980—82, Outstanding Achievement in Medicine award 2004), AMA, Calif. Med. Assn., San Francisco Surgical Soc., Am. Fedn. for Clin. Rsch., Pan-Pacific

Surgical Assn., Sociedad de Cardiocirujanos (Spain) (pres. 1987—88), Soc. Thoracic Surgical Edn., Soc. for Clin. Vascular Surgery, Bay Area Soc. Thoracic Surgeons, Northern Calif. Vascular Soc., Am. Coll. Chest Physicians, Am. Coll. Cardiology (scientific abstract review com. 1986, 1990, peripheral vascular disease com. 1994—98), ACS (cardiovasc. surgery com. 1986—88, exec. com. 1987—88), Soc. Heart Valve Disease, Am. Heart Assn. (bd. dirs., Santa Clara County Chpt. 1980—82, mem. rsch. com., Santa Clara County Chpt. 1981—83, optimal resources for vascular surgery com. 1985—89, program com., cardiovasc. surgery coun. 1988—92, chmn. 1989—92, vice-chmn., cardiothoracic-vascular surgery coun. 1993—95, chmn., cardiothoracic and vascular surgery coun. 1995—97, chmn., cardiothoracic-vascular surgery coun. 1995—97, Disting. Scientist 2003), Western Vascular Soc. (co-chmn., com. scientific sessions 1992—93), Soc. for Thoracic Surgeons, Western Thoracic Surgical Assn. (prog. com. 1983—88, sec. 1989—93, v.p. 1993—94, pres. 1994—95), Soc. for Vascular Surgery (chmn. 1986—88), Soc. Univ. Surgeons, Am. Assn. for Thoracic Surgery (coun. 2003—07, pres. 2007—08), Am. Surgical Assn., Soc. Clin. Surgery, Cardiac Soc. Australia and New Zealand (corr.) (hon.), Sociedad Chilena de Cardiologia y Cirugia Cardiovasc. (Chile) (hon.), Sociedad Colombiana de Cirugia (Columbia) (hon.), Sociedad Espanola de Cirugia Cardiovasc. (Spain) (hon.), European Assn. for Cardio-Thoracic Surgery (hon.), Cardiac Surgery Biology Club. Office: Dept Cardiothoracic Surgery Falk Cardiovasc Rsch Ctr Stanford U Sch Medicine 300 Pasteur Dr Stanford CA 94305-5407 Office Phone: 650-723-5771, 650-725-3826. Office Fax: 650-725-3846. Business E-Mail: dcm@stanford.edu.

MILLER, DAVID G., medical association administrator; b. Lorain, Ohio, Dec. 29, 1966; BS, Ohio State U., 1989; MD, U. Cin., 1993. Pres. Retina Assocs. Cleve., Inc., 1998—. Med. dir. Cleve. Eye & Laser Surgery Ctr., 2007. Mem.: Cleve. Ophthal. Soc. Office: 3401 Enterprise Pky Ste 300 Beachwood OH 44122 Office Fax: 216-831-1959. Business E-Mail: dmiller@retina-assoc.com.

MILLER, DENNIS EDWARD, health medical executive; b. Detroit, Dec. 21, 1951; m. Deborah Ann Keith, Feb. 12, 1977. BS, Austin Peay State U., 1973; MBA, U. South Fla., 1981. CPA. Chief exec. officer Hosp. Corp. of Am., Bennettsville, SC, 1976-84; div. v.p. Westworld Community Healthcare, Waco, Tex., 1984-86; group v.p. Nat. Healthcare, Inc., Dothan, Ala., 1986-87; COO Healthcare Connections, Brentwood, Tenn., 1988; cons. VHA Physician Svcs., Inc., Dallas, 1988-90; asst. adminstr., CFO Clarksville (Tenn.) Meml. Hosp., 1990; Franklin, Tenn., 1990; sr. v.p., COO Eastside Ventures, Inc., Birmingham, Ala., 1990-93; sr. v.p. Ea. Health System, Inc., Birmingham, 1993—2002; CEO Williamson Med. Ctr., Franklin, 2002—. Chmn. Minority Leadership Task Force, Ea. Health System, Inc., 1994-95. Sec. Ala. Health Svcs. Bd.; mem. Literacy Coun. Ala., Ala. Hosp. Assn. State Legis. Com., future directions com.; chmn. Birmingham Regional Healthcare Exec. Forum; chmn. friends of scouting campaign Boy Scouts Am., 1996; mem. Franklin Land Use Steering Com. subcom., Leadership Franklin, 2002, Franklin Tomorrow, Williamson 25, 2004, 05, Franklin Bus. Leadership Coun., 2006, Hosp. Alliance Tenn., 2006, Tenn. Hosp. Ass., 2006; chmn. Healthcare Exec. Forum Mid. Tenn., 2006; mem. coun. Boy Scouts Mid. Tenn., 2006; mem. archives and mus. com. Williamson County, 2006; adv. com. mem. Tenn. Pub. Health Emergency, 2006-08., with Hosp. Alliance TN Exec. Com., 2011, MIddleton Coun., BSA, 2011 Recipient ACHE Svc. award, Miiddle TN, 2008; named one of Top 25 Hop. Operators, 2009—11. Fellow Am. Coll. Healthcare Execs. (chmn diplomate credentials com., pres. mid. Tenn. chpt. 2006, Ala. Regent's award for exec. excellence 1995), Hosp. Fin. Mgmt. Assn. (Follmer Bronze Merit award for outstanding svc.); mem. AICPA, Tenn. Soc. CPAs, Ala. Soc. CPAs (chmn. state legis. com.), Ala. Hosp. Assn. (future directions com.), Birmingham C. of C. (chmn. memberhsip com.), Birmingham East Rotary Club (pres., chmn. membership com.), Leadership Franklin Class 2003, Franklin Noon Rotary Club, Mensa, Shriners, Masons, Birmingham Touchdown Club, Sigma Chi. Avocations: hunting, fishing, gardening, antiques. Office: Williamson Med Ctr 2021 Carothers Rd Franklin TN 37067 Home Phone: 615-599-0325; Office Phone: 615-435-5151.

MILLER, DOROTHY ANNE SMITH (SANDY), retired cytogenetics educator; b. NYC, Oct. 20, 1931; d. John Philip and Anna Elizabeth (Hellberg) Smith; m. Orlando Jack Miller, July 10, 1954; children: Richard L., Cynthia K., Karen A. BA in Chemistry magna cum laude, Wilson Coll., Chambersburg, Pa., 1952; PhD in Biochemistry, Yale U., 1957. Rsch. assoc. dept. ob-gyn Columbia U., NYC, 1964-72, from rsch. assoc. to asst. prof. dept. human genetics-devel., 1973-85; prof. dept. molecular biology and genetics Wayne State U., Detroit, 1985-94, prof. dept. pathology, 1985-96, prof. Ctr. for Molecular Medicine and Genetics, 1994-96. Vis. scientist clin. and population cytogenetics unit Med. Rsch. Coun., Edinburgh, Scotland, 1983-84; vis. prof. dept. genetics and molecular biology U. la Sapienza, Rome, 1988; vis. disting. fellow La Trobe U., Melbourne, Australia, 1992. Contbr. numerous articles to sci. jours. Grantee March of Dimes Birth Defects Found., 1974-93, NSF, 1983-84; recipient Disting. Cytogeneticist award Am. Cytogenetics Conf., 2008. Mem. Am. Soc. Human Genetics, Genetics Soc. Am., Genetics Soc. Australia, Phi Beta Kappa. Presbyterian. Home: 19365 Cypress Ridge Terr #817 Lansdowne VA 20176 Personal E-mail: damiller@smartneighborhood.net.

MILLER, EDWARD DORING, anesthesiologist, hospital administrator, dean; b. Rochester, NY, Feb. 1, 1943; s. Edward D. and Natalie (Sidam) Miller; m. Leslie Coombs, June 15, 1968 (dec. Apr. 1987); children: Sara Davenport, Katherine Coombs; m. Lynne Root, Apr. 30, 1988; children: Lawrence Root, Elizabeth Root Fusco. AB, Ohio Wesleyan U., 1964; MD, U. Rochester, 1968. Diplomate Am. Bd. Anesthesiology, Am. Coll. Anesthesiology; cert. critical care medicine. Surg. intern Univ. Hosp., Boston, 1968-69; anesthesia resident Peter Bent Brigham Hosp., Boston, 1969-71; fellow in physiology Harvard Med. Sch., Boston, 1971-73; dir. anesthesia research Brooke Army Med. Ctr., Ft. Sam Houston, Tex., 1973-75; asst. prof. anesthesiology U. Va. Med. Ctr., Charlottesville, 1975-79, assoc. prof. anesthesiology, 1979-82, prof. anesthesiology, 1982-83, prof. anesthesiology, surgery, 1983-86; E.M. Papper prof. anesthesiology, chmn. dept. Columbia U. Coll. Physicians and Surgeons, NYC, 1986-94; Mark C. Rogers prof., chmn. dept. anesthesiology Johns Hopkins U., Balt., 1994—; interim dean med. faculty, v.p. medicine Johns Hopkins U. Sch. Medicine, Balt., 1996-97, dean, CEO, 1997—; vice chmn. Johns Hopkins Health Sys. Corp., Balt., 1997—. Sr. scientist physiology, pharmacology Hosp. Necker, Paris, 1981-82; examiner Am. Bd. Anesthesiology; v.p. clin. faculty U. Va., 1983-85, pres. 1985-86. Editor Anesthesia and Analgesia, 1982-92; contbr. numerous articles to profl. jours. Pres. Barracks-Rugby-Preston Neighborhoods, Va., 1977-79; vestry Christ Episc. Ch., Va., 1985-86. Served to maj. M.C., U.S. Army, 1973-75. Recipient Rsch. Career Devel. award Nat. Inst. Gen. Med. Scis., 1978-83; NIH grantee, 1977-87, Inst. Nat. de la Sante et de la Recherche Medicale grantee, 1981-82. Mem. Assn. U. Anesthetists (sec. 1984-87), Am. Soc. Anesthesiologists, Am. Physiol. Soc., Internat. Anesthesia Research Soc. (trustee 1988—), Soc. Critical Care Medicine, Soc. Cardiovascular Anesthesiologists, Assn. Univ. Anesthesiologists (pres. 1990-92), Found. for Anesthesia Edn. and Rsch. (bd. dirs. 1986—), Up Med. Bd. Presbyn. Hosp. Office: Johns Hopkins U Sch Med Adminstrn 733 N Broadway Ste 100 Baltimore MD 21205-2196 Office Phone: 410-955-3180. Business E-Mail: emiller@jhmi.edu. *

MILLER, FREDERICK, pathologist; b. NYC, Apr. 5, 1937; s. Alex and Sarah Miller; m. Emilie J Kronish, June 2, 1962; children: David, Allison. BS, U. Wis., 1956; MD, N.Y. U., 1961. Diplomate Am Bd Pathology. Intern Bellevue Hosp., NYC, 1961-62, resident, 1962-63; practice medicine specializing in pathology, 1965—; clin. assoc., attending physician Nat. Inst. Arthritis and Metabolic Diseases, 1963-65; resident chief pathology dept. NYU Med. Ctr., 1965-67; attending pathologist Bellevue and Univ. Hosps., NYC, 1967; asst. prof. pathology NYU, 1967-70, assoc. prof., 1970, SUNY, Stony Brook, 1970-75, prof., 1975—, chmn. dept. pathology, 1973-2000, emeritus prof. pathology, 2011, Marvin Kuschner prof. pathology Stony Brook, 1991—2009, dir. lab. for arthritis and related diseases, 1976—2009; dir. labs. U. Hosp., Stony Brook, 1978—2003, assoc. dir. labs., 2003—10, pathologist-in-chief, 1979—2003. Mem. Nat. Bd. Med. Examiners in Pathology, 1996—98. Contbr. articles to profl jours. With USPHS, 1963—65. Recipient Bausch and Lomb Medal for Research, 1961, Pres's Award, SUNY, Stony Brook, 1990, Chancellor's Award, 1990, Aesculapius Award, 1993, Golden Apple Award, ASMA, 1995; grantee NIH, 1963—87. Mem.: AAAS, Am. Orchid Soc, Am. Assn. Immunologists, N.Y. Acad. Sci., Internat. Acad. Pathology, Am. Soc. Clin. Pathologists (award 1961), Harvey Soc., Alpha Omega Alpha (counselor 2000—03), Sigma Xi. Home: 46 Manchester Ln Stony Brook NY 11790-2826 Office: Univ Hosp USB L2-743B Stony Brook NY 11794-7025 Office Phone: 631-444-2222.

MILLER, GARY EVAN, psychiatrist, mental health services professional; b. Cleve., Aug. 19, 1935; s. Henry M. and Mollie (Price) M.; m. Karen Ann Marie Barrett, Sept. 16, 1972; children: Anna Charis, Rebecca Elizabeth. MD, U. Tex., Galveston, 1960. Diplomate in psychiatry, addiction psychiatry, and geriatric psychiatry Am. Bd. Psychiatry and Neurology. Intern Montefiore Hosp., NYC, 1960-61; resident in psychiatry U. Hosp. Cleve., 1961-62, Austin State Hosp., Tex., 1963-65; dep. commr. mental health services Dept. Mental Health and Mental Retardation, Tex., 1967-70; dir. Rio Grande State Ctr. for Mental Health and Mental Retardation, Dept. Mental Health, Harlingen, Tex., 1966-67; asst. commr., dir. Rochester regional office State Dept. Mental Hygiene, NY, 1970-72; clin. asst. prof. psychiatry U. Rochester Sch. Medicine and Dentistry, 1970-72; asst. clin. prof. psychiatry SUNY, Buffalo, 1970-72; cons. mental health Ga. Dept. Human Resources, Atlanta, 1972, dir. div. mental health, 1972-74; clin. prof. psychiatry Emory U. Sch. Medicine, Atlanta, 1972-74; vice chmn. Ga. State Planning and Adv. Coun. for Devel. Disabilities Services and Constrn., 1972-73; cons. mental health services orgn. and adminstrn., 1974-76; dir. mental health and devel. services State of NH Concord, 1976-82; commr. Tex. Dept. Mental Health and Mental Retardation Austin, 1982-88; clin. prof. psychiatry U. Tex. Health Sci. Ctr., Houston, adj. assoc. prof. psychiatry San Antonio, 1984-95; dir. profl. svcs. HCA Gulf Pines Hosp., Houston, 1988-94, chief of staff, 1993; clin. dir. adult psychiatry Cypress Creek Hosp., Houston, 1994-2000, med. dir., 2000—03, pres. med. staff, 1996; assoc. clin. psychiatry Post Oak Psychiatry Assoc., Houston, 1988-90; pres. Alternative Svc. Network, Houston, 1990—; chief of staff Kingwood (Tex.) Pines Hosp., 2003—04, dir. Psychiatric Svcs., 2004—08, med. dir., 2008—11. Dir. state alcoholism program in South Tex. region, 1966—67; dir. state alcoholism program in Ga., 1972—74; mem. faculty U. SC Sch. Alcohol and Drug Studies, 1975; mem. quality assurance com. Aetna US Healthcare Pharmacy, 1999—2001. Contbr. articles to profl. jours. Served as capt. M.C., US Army, 1962-63. Recipient Cert. Recognition, Ga. Psychol. Assn., 1973, Resolution Commendation, Assn. Retarded Citizens Tex., 1990, Helen Farabee Cmty. Leadership award, Mental Health Assn. Greater Houston, 1993, Pres.'s award, 1990, Elected Top Docs Houston, H Tex. Mag., 2004. Fellow Am. Psychiat. Assn. (disting. life; cert. in adminstrv. psychiatry, com. on psychiat. adminstrn. and mgmt. 1999-2002); mem. AMA, Am. Soc. Clin. Psychopharmacology (cert.), Am. Soc. Addiction Medicine (cert. alcoholism and other drug dependencies), Am. Acad. Addiction Psychiatry, NH Psychiat. Soc. (pres. 1981-82), Nat. Assn. State Mental Health Program Dir. (bd. dir. 1984-88, sec. 1986-88), NH Med. Soc., Am. Acad. Psychiatry and the Law, Am. Assn. Psychiat. Adminstr. (pres. Tex. chpt. 1986), Tex. Med. Assn., Tex. Soc. Psychiat. Physicians (chair socioecons. com. 2006—), Mental Health Assn. Greater Houston (bd. dir. 1989-95, v.p. advocacy 1990-95, adv. coun. 1999—), Alpha Omega Alpha. Home: 5314 Westminster Ct Houston TX 77069-3338 Office: 530 Wells Fargo Dr Ste 110 Houston TX 77090-4026 Office Phone: 281-440-6899. Personal E-mail: gemhou@yahoo.com.

MILLER, GEOFFREY, child neurologist; b. Manchester, Eng., Feb. 1, 1947; came to U.S., 1988; s. Erwin and Cynthia Sarah Miller; m. Patricia Sarah Craigie, June 21, 1985; children: Joanne, Sally, Alethea. BA, MB, ChB, BAO, Trinity Coll., Dublin, Ireland, 1972, MA, 1982; MD, U. Western Australia, 1985; MPhil, U. Glasgow, Scotland, 2002. Diplomate Am. Bd. Psychiatry and Neurology, Am. Bd. Child Neurology, Am. Bd. Neurodevelopmental Disabilities. Fellow Royal Postgrad. Med. Sch., London, 1982-83; devel. pediatrician Princess Margaret Hosp. for Children, Perth, Australia, 1983-85; med. dir. Sir David Brand Ctr. for Cerebral Palsy, Perth, Australia, 1983-84; assoc. prof. pediat. Pa. State U., Hershey, 1988-92; co-dir. Muscular Dystrophy Assn. Clinic, Hershey, 1988-92, clinic physician Houston, 1998—; prof. pediat. & neurology Baylor Coll. Medicine, Houston, 1992—2004, chief devel. pediat. sect., 2000—02; dir. Meyer Ctr. Devel. Pediat., Tex. Childrens Hosp., 2000—02; prof. pediat. & neurology Yale U., 2004—. Vis. specialist West Australian Soc. for Crippled Children, Perth, 1983; investigator Neuromuscular Rsch. Inst., Perth, 1984-87; clin. dir. Child Neurology Svc. Yale U. Sch. Medicine, 2004—; mem. Yale Bioethics Ctr., 2004. Author: Extreme Prematurity, 2007. Practices, Bioethics, and Law, 2007; editor: Static Encephalopathies, 1992, Cerebral Palsies, 1998, Pediatric Bioethics, 2009; contbr. articles to jours. in field. Capt. Royal Army Med. Corps, 1970-78. Elected and inducted into Am. Neurol. Assn., 1996. Fellow Royal Coll. Physicians, Royal Coll. Australasian Physicians; mem. Royal Coll. Physicians (London), Royal College of Paediatrics and Child Health, Child Neurology Soc. (membership com. 1996-97, internat. affairs com. 1997—, chmn. 2002-05, ethics com. 2005-), Internat. Child Neurology Soc., Soc. for Devel. Pediat., Am. Acad. Cerebral Palsy and Devel. Medicine (outcomes com. 2001—06, sci. selection com. 2006), March of Dimes (rsch. adv. com. 2008-). Avocations: rugby, soccer. Office: Yale Univ Sch Medicine Dept Pediat New Haven CT 06510 Office Phone: 203-785-5708. Business E-Mail: geoffrey.miller@yale.edu.

MILLER, GEORGE ARMITAGE, psychologist, educator; b. Charleston, W.Va., Feb. 3, 1920; s. George E. and Florence (Armitage) M.; m. Katherine James, Nov. 29, 1939 (dec. Jan. 1996); children: Nancy, Donnally James. BA, U. Ala., 1940, MA, 1941; AM, Harvard U., 1944, PhD, 1946; PhD (hon.), U. Louvain, 1976; D Social Sci. (hon.), Yale U., 1979; DSc (hon.), Columbia U., 1980, U. Sussex, 1984, New Sch. Social Rsch., 1993; LittD (hon.), Charleston U., 1992; DSc (hon.), DSc (hon.), New Sch. Social Rsch., 1993, Princeton U., 1996, Williams Coll., 2000; DSc (hon.), Carnegie Mellon U., 2003. Instr. psych. U. Ala., 1941-43; rsch. fellow Harvard Psycho-Acoustic Lab., 1944-48; asst. prof. psych. Harvard U., 1948-51, assoc. prof., 1955-58, prof., 1958-68, chmn. dept. psych., 1964-67, co-dir. Ctr. for Cognitive Studies, 1960-67; prof. Rockefeller U., NYC, 1968-79, adj. prof., 1979-82; prof. psych. Princeton U., 1979-90, James S. McDonnell Disting. prof. psych., 1982-90, James S. McDonnell Disting. prof. psych. emeritus, 1990—, prog. dir. McDonnell-Pew Prog. in Cognitive Neurosci., 1989-94; assoc. prof. MIT, 1951-55. Vis. Inst. for Advanced Study, Princeton, 1972-76, 82-83, mem., 1950, 70-72; vis. prof. Rockefeller U., 1967-68, MIT, 1976-79, grp. leader Lincoln Lab., 1953-55; fellow Ctr. Advanced Study in Behavioral Scis., Stanford U., 1958-59; Fulbright rsch. prof. Oxford (Eng.) U., 1963-64; Sesquicentennial prof. U. Ala., 1981. Author: Language and Communication, 1951, (with Galanter and Pribram) Plans and the Structure of Behavior, 1960, Psychology, 1962, (with Johnson-Laird) Language and Perception, 1976, Spontaneous Apprentices, 1977, Language and Speech, 1981, The Science of Words, 1991; editor: Psychol. Bulletin, 1981-82. Recipient Disting. Service award Am. Speech and Hearing Assn., 1976, award in behavioral scis. N.Y. Acad. Scis., 1982, Hermann von Helmholtz award Cognitive Neurosci. Inst., 1989, Nat. Medal Sci. NSF, 1991, Gold Medal Am. Psychol.Found. 1990, Nat. Medal of Sci. 1991, Louis E. Levy medal Franklin Inst., 1991, John P. Govern award, Am. Assn. for Advancement of Sci., 2000; Guggenheim fellow, 1986, William James fellow Am. Psychol. Soc., 1989; Fondation Fyssen Priz Internat. for cognitive sci., 1992. Fellow Brit. Psychol. Assn. (hon.); mem. NAS, AAAS (chmn. sect. J 1981, John P. McGovern award 2000), APA (pres. 1968-69, Disting. Sci. Contbn. award 1963, William James Book award divsn. gen. psych. 1993, Outstanding Lifetime Contbn. to Psych. award 2003), Eastern Psychol. Assn. (pres. 1961-62), Acoustical Soc. Am., Linguistic Soc. Am., Am. Statis. Assn., Am. Philos. Soc., Am. Physiol. Soc., Psychometric Soc., Soc. Exptl. Psychologists (Warren medal 1972), Am. Acad. Arts and Scis., Psychonomic Soc., Royal Netherlands Acad. Arts and Scis. (fgn.), Sigma Xi. Office: Princeton Univ Dept Psychology Green Hall Princeton NJ 08544 Home: PO Box 228 Spring Lake NJ 07762-0228

MILLER, I. GEORGE, physician, educator, researcher; b. Chgo., Apr. 18, 1937; s. Irving George and Florence (Levy) M.; m. Arlette Goldmuntz, Mar. 25, 1962; children: Lisa, John, David. AB, Harvard U., 1958, MD, 1962. Intern Univ. Hosp., Western Res, U., Cleve., 1962-63; resident Univ. Hosp., Western Res., U., Cleve., 1963-64; epidemiology intelligence officer Communicable Disease Ctr. USPHS, Atlanta, 1964-66; rsch. fellow in medicine Harvard U. Med. Sch., Boston, 1966-69; asst. prof. pediat., epidemiology, biophysics and biochemistry Yale Sch. Medicine, New Haven, 1969-72, J.F. Enders prof., 1979—. Mem. exptl. virology study sect. NIH, 1974-77; mem. sci. adv. com. Damon Runyon Fund, 1979-85, dir., 1985-94; Leukemia Soc. Am., 1976-81. Contbr. numerous articles, chpts. to profl. publs.; editl. bd. Jour. Virology, 1981-87, Virology, 1982-86. Recipient epidemic Intelligence Svc. Alumni Assn. prize, 1967; Macy faculty scholar, 1977, Am. Cancer Soc. scholar, 1990; Howard Hughes Med. Inst. investigatorship, 1972-80 Fellow Infectious Diseases Soc. (Squibb award 1982, Enders award 1989), AAAS, Am. Acad. Microbiology.; mem. Am. soc. Clin. Investigation, Am. Pediatric Soc., Am. Soc. Virology, Assn. Am. Physicians, Inst. Medicine. Jewish. Office: Yale U Sch Medicine Pediatrics Infectious Diseases PO Box 208064 New Haven CT 06520-8064 Home Phone: 203-389-6621; Office Phone: 203-785-4758. Business E-Mail: george.miller@yale.edu.

MILLER, IRENE M., physician assistant; b. Berlin; arrived in U.S., 1955; d. Siegfried and Anneliese Mueller; m. Harold E. Miller (div.); children: Deborah, Duane, Kirstie. Student, Phila. Coll. Performing Arts, 1956—58, Musikakademie, Berlin, 1958, West Chester U., 1977—79; BS Physician Asst., Hahnemann U., 1981. Lic. physician asst. Mass., Maine, NH, NC, NY, cert. ACLS, ATLS. Resident in surgery Norwalk Hosp./Yale U. Sch. Medicine, New Haven, 1981—82; physician asst. dept. neurosurgery U. Pitts., 1982—83; physician asst. Family Medicine and Bariatrics, Fairfield, Conn., 1984—86; physician asst. dept. medicine Hall-Brooke Hosp., Westport, Conn., 1987—89; physician asst. occupl. medicine Bankers Trust Co., NYC, 1989—90; physician asst. Okemo Mountain Ski Clinic, Emergency Svcs. of New England, Springfield, Vt., 1990—91; physician asst. Jaffrey (NH) Family Medicine, 1991—95, CompHealth, Salt Lake City, 1995—98; fgn. svc. med. officer Am. Embassy U.S. State Dept., Kampala, Uganda, 1998—2000; pvt. practice internal medicine/holistic medicine Keene, NH, 2000—. Lectr., spkr., presenter in field; cellist symphony orchs. U.S. and Europe. Author: Love Letters from Uganda, 2003. Mem. med. mission, China, 1994. Grantee, London Grove Quaker Meeting, 1979; scholar, Phila. Music Acad., 1956—58. Fellow: Am. Acad. Physician Assts.; mem.: NH Soc. Physician Assts. (pres. 1993—94). Avocations: hiking, dance, painting. Home: 105 Lampman Rd Harrisville NH 03450

MILLER, JAMES MCCALMONT, pediatrician; b. Springfield, Mass., Sept. 25, 1938; s. John Haynes and Josephine (Darrah) M.; m. Jane Rose, July 7, 1975; children: John, Charlotte, Willard. AB, Hamilton Coll., 1960; MD, Cornell U., 1964. Resident U. Colo. Med. Ctr., Denver, 1964-67; staff pediatrician Kaiser Permanente Med. Ctr., Walnut Creek, Calif., 1969-87, chief pediatrician, 1971-82, Pleasanton, Calif., 1982-87; staff pediatrician Appalachian Regional Health, Hazard, Ky., 1987-92, N.W. Pediat. Ctr., Centralia, Wash., 1992—. Clin. assoc. U. N.Mex., Albuquerque, 1967-69; instr. U. Calif., San Francisco, 1969-87, U. Ky., Lexington, 1988-92. With U.S. Army, 1967-69. Fellow Am. Acad. Pediat.; mem. Wash. State Med. Assn. Office: Northwest Pediatric Ctr 1911 Cooks Hill Rd Centralia WA 98531-9027 Office Phone: 360-736-6778. E-mail: jmiller@localaccess.com.

MILLER, JANEL HOWELL, psychologist; b. Boone, NC, May 18, 1947; d. John Estle and Grace Louise (Hemberger) Howell; m. C. Rick Miller, Nov. 24, 1968; children: Kimberly, Brian, Audrey, Rachel. BA, DePauw U., 1969; postgrad., Rice U., 1969; MA, U. Houston, 1972; PhD, Tex. A&M U., 1979. Lic. clin. psychologist, sch. psychologist Tex. Assoc. sch. psychologist Houston Ind. Sch. Dist., 1971-74; rsch. psychologist VA Hosp., Houston, 1972; assoc. sch. psychologist Clear Creek (Tex.) Ind. Sch. Dist., 1974-76; instr. psychology, counseling psychology intern Tex. A&M U., 1976-77; clin. psychology intern VA Hosp., Houston, 1977-78; coord. psychol. svcs. Clear Creek Ind. Sch. Dist., 1978-81, assoc. dir. psychol. svcs., 1981-82; pvt. practice Houston, 1982—. Faculty U. Houston-Clear Lake, 1984—; adolescent suicide cons., 1984—; mem. DePaww U. Alumni Bd. Dirs., 2008-. DePauw U. Alumni scholar, 1965-69; NIMH fellow U. Houston, 1970-71. Mem. APA, Am. Assn. Marriage and Family Therapists, Soc. for Personality Assessment, Am. Coll. Forensic Examiners, Internat. Rorschach Soc., Tex. Psychol. Assn., Tex. Assn. Marriage and Family Therapists, Houston Psychol. Assn. (media rep. 1984-85), Houston Assn. Marriage and Family Therapists. Home: 806 Walbrook Dr Houston TX 77062-4030 Office: 16854 Royal Crest Dr Houston TX 77058-2529 Office Phone: 281-461-4098. Business E-Mail: shrinkskate@sbcglobal.net.

MILLER, JO CAROLYN DENDY, family and marriage counselor, educator; b. Gorman, Tex., Sept. 16, 1942; d. Leonard Lee and Vera Vertie (Robison) Dendy; m. Douglas Terry Barnes, June 1, 1963 (div. June 1975); children: Douglas Alan, Bradley Jason; m. Walton Sansom Miller, Sept. 19, 1982. BA, Tarleton State U., Stephenville, Tex., 1964; MEd, U. North Tex., Denton, 1977; PhD, Tex. Woman's U., Denton, 1993. Tchr. Mineral Wells H.S., Tex., 1964-65, Weatherford Mid. Sch., Tex., 1969-74; counselor, instr. psychology Tarrant County Jr. Coll., Hurst, Tex., 1977-82; pvt. practice Dallas, 1982—. Author: (with Velma Baker, Jeannene Ward) Becoming: A Human Relations Workbook, 1981. Mem. ACA, Tex. State Bd. Examiners Profl. Counselors, Tex. State Bd. Marriage and Family Therapists, Tex. Counseling Assn., North Ctrl. Tex. Counseling Assn., Dallas Symphony Orch. League, Nat. Coun. Family Rels., Tex. Mental Health Counselors Assn., Internat. Assn. for Marriage and Family Counselors. Methodist. Office: 8222 Douglas Ave Ste 777 Dallas TX 75225-5938 Office Phone: 214-691-0400. Personal E-mail: jcdmphd@sbcglobal.net.

MILLER, JON MICHAEL, microbiologist, director; b. Winnfield, La., Mar. 30, 1945; MS, Northwestern State U. La., 1970; PhD, U. Tex. Health Sci. Ctr., San Antonio, 1977. Assoc. dir., lab. sci. Nat. Ctr. Emerging and Zoonotic Infectious Diseases Ctrs. Disease Control and Prevention, 1976—, Cons., dir. Microbiology Tech. Svcs. LLC, 1978—2011. Named to Long Purple Line Alumni Hall of Fame, Northwestern State U. La. Fellow: Am. Acad. Microbiology; mem.: South Eastern Assn. Clin. Microbiology, Am. Soc. Microbiology (BioMerieux-Sonnenwirth award, Gen Probe Joseph Pub. Health award, ASM Founders Disting. Svc. award). Avocations: camping, golf, gardening. Office: Damon Ct Dunwoody GA 30338 Office Fax: 770-396-0955. Personal E-mail: jmm8@comcast.net.

MILLER, JOSEPH MORTON, internist, former state legislator; b. Boston, Nov. 9, 1921; s. Benjamin and Esther (Sugar) M.; m. Betty Jean Harris, Sept. 17, 1976; children: Beth, Keith, Eric, Gregory, Coralia. AB, Harvard Coll., 1942; MD, Harvard Med. Sch., 1945; MPH, Harvard Sch. Pub. Health, 1960. Diplomate American Bd. Internal Medicine, Preventive Medicine. Intern Mt. Sinai Hosp., NYC, 1945-46; resident Cushing VA Hosp., Framingham, Mass., 1949-50; mem. Dist. 72 NH House of Reps., 2002—04. Cons. environ. and toxicology. Capt. U.S. Army, 1946-48. Mem. APHA, American Coll. Environ. and Occupl. Medicine. fellow American Coll. Phys. Democrat. *

MILLER, LEE TODD, pediatrician, educator; b. NYC, Aug. 1, 1957; BA, Bowdoin Coll.; MD, U. Va., 1982. Cert. Pediat., 1987. Intern pediat. U. Va. Med. Ctr., Charlottesville, 1982—83, resident, 1983—86, chief resident pediat.; vice chair edn., dept. pediat. Cedars-Sinai Med. Ctr., LA; prof. pediat. David Geffen Sch. Med., UCLA. Recipient Golden Apple Tchg. Award. Mem.: Assn. Pediat. Program Dirs., Ambulatory Pediat. Assn., Am. Acad. Pediat. Office: Cedars-Sinai Med Ctr 8700 Beverly Blvd Los Angeles CA 90048 Office Phone: 310-423-4467. Office Fax: 310-423-0145. E-mail: lee.miller@cshs.org.

MILLER, LEWIS AMES, medical educator, consultant; b. Bklyn., Aug. 4, 1928; s. Joseph Burke and Charlotte Keller Miller; m. Jean Chandler Miller, Dec. 28, 1949; children: David Chandler, Kathryn Ann. BA, Princeton U., NJ, 1949; MS, Columbia U. Bus. Sch., NYC, 1976. Cert. CCMEP Nat. Commn. Cert. CME Profls., 2008. Reporter, editor Schenectady Union-Star, NY, 1949—50; editor-in-chief Glastonbury Citizen, Conn., 1950—52; copy editor Newark Star Ledger, 1952—53; copy editor, asst. mng. editor NY World-Telegram & Sun, NYC, 1953—59; exec.editor Med. Economics, Oradell, NJ, 1960—66; pres., editor Miller & Fink Corp., Darien, Conn., 1966—78; pres. Miller Comm., Inc., Norwalk, Conn., 1978—86, Life Options, Norwalk, Conn., 1986—2008; corp. editl. dir. Dowden Health Media, Montvale, NJ, 1996—2008; prin. WentzMiller & Assocs., Darien, Conn., 2004—; chmn., CEO BestPractice CPD, LLC, Darien, Conn., 2008—. Dir. Manisses Comm., Inc., Providence, 1987—2006; founder, dir. Project Globe Consortium CPD, Caracas, Venezuela, 2004—07. Author: (book) The Life You Save; contbr. articles to profl. jour. Dir. Nat. Assn. Pvt. Industry Couns., Washington, 1992—97; founder, chmn. Darien Cmty. Homes, Inc., Darien, 1975—85; chmn. Pvt. Industry Coun. Southern Conn., Bridgeport, 1987—93; dir. Conn. State Employment & Tng. Comm., Hartford, 1999—2007; moderator Darien Congl. Ch., Conn., 1966—70; founder, chmn. United Ch. Christ Residences, Inc., Stamford, Conn.; chair Princeton U. Alumni Studies Comm., 1997—2004. Recipient Founder's Cert. Appreciation, Pilgrim Tower Housing Elderly, 1966—86, Founder's award, Alliance Continuing Med. Edn., 1975—95, Bus. Leader Appreciation award, Workplace, Inc., 1985—97, PIC Leadership award, Pvt. Industry Coun. Southern Conn., 1988—90, Crain award, Am. Bus. Media, 2004; named Med. Advt. Hall Fame, Med. Advt. Orgn., 2007. Fellow: Alliance Continuing Med. Edn. (founder, dir. 1975—88); mem.: Beta Gamma Sigma, Roton Point Club, Can. Assn. Continuing Health Edn., Global Alliance Med. Edn. (founder, dir. 1995—), Am. Assn. Individual Investors, City Clubs Am., Princeton Club NY. Home: 90 Goodwives River Rd Darien CT 06820 Office: WentzMiller & Assocs 90 Goodwives River Rd Darien CT 06820 Office Phone: 203-662-9690. Office Fax: 203-655-2904. Business E-Mail: lew@wentzmiller.org.

MILLER, LILLIE M., nursing educator; b. Atlanta, Nov. 16, 1937; d. George W. and Lillie M. (Reese) McDaniel; m. Harold G. Miller, June 30, 1962; children: Daren K., Lisa K. Diploma in nursing, Jewish Hosp. of Cin., 1959; BSN, U. Cin., 1961; MEd, Temple U., 1970; MSN, Villanova U., 1987. RN, Pa.; cert. sch. nurse, cert. clin. specialist in med.-surg. nursing ANCC. Instr. sch. nursing Jewish Hosp. Cin., 1959-62; instr. Phila. Gen. Hosp. Sch. Nursing, 1962-67; sch. nurse Norristown (Pa.) Area Sch. Dist., 1967-70; nursing instr. Villanova U., Villanova, Pa., 1988; asst. prof. Montgomery County C.C., Blue Bell, Pa., 1983-93, assoc. prof, 1993-98, prof., 1998—. Advisor Student Nurses Assn. Pa. Pi Tau Delta scholar, Chapel of Four Chaplains. Mem.: ANA, Pa. State Nurses Assn., Pa. Med. Soc. (patient adv. bd. 2001—), Villanova U. Alumni Assn., Temple U. Alumni Assn., Jewish Hosp. Alumni Assn., Pa. League for Nursing, Nat. League for Nursing, Phi Theta Kappa, Sigma Theta Tau. Office Phone: 215-641-6471. Personal E-mail: profmill@aol.com. Business E-Mail: lmiller@mc3.edu.

MILLER, LINDA B., foundation administrator; Pres. Vol. Trustees Found., Washington. Mem.: Inst. Medicine ((in conjunction w/NRC) mem. adv. com. Human Embryonic Stem Cell Rsch. 2006—). Office: Vol Trustees Found 818 18th St NW Ste 410 Washington DC 20006 Office Phone: 202-659-0338, 202-659-0116.

MILLER, LORI L., environmental health scientist, life scientist; b. Miami, Fla., Dec. 9, 1963; BS in Biology, Tuskegee U., 1985; PhD in Nursing Sci., U. Wash., 2010. Agrl. commodity grader US Dept. Agr., 1985—88; emergency substitute tchr. Miami-Dade Sch. Bd., 1988—91; scientist US EPA, 1991—96; environ. health scientist CDC/Agy. Toxic Substances and Disease Registry, 1996—2003; rsch. ethics course devel. & instr. U. Wash., 2003—10, rsch. engr., scientist, 2011—. Mem.: Sigma Theta Tau Internat. Avocations: reading, travel, dance. Office: Box 352180 301 Loew Hall Seattle WA 98195 Business E-Mail: lorimill@uw.edu.

MILLER, MARCIA, physician; b. Cedar Rapids, Iowa, Sept. 26, 1959; BS, Iowa State U., 1982, MD, U Iowa, 1985. Physician Family Practice Assoc., 1996—2002; clin. asst. prof. U Fla. Coll. Medicine, 2002—11, adj. prof., 2011; primary care physician Va., 2011—. Recipient Faculty Employment Opportunity, U. Fla.; grant, U. Fla. Coll. Medicine. Fellow: Soc. Family Medicine, Am. Acad. Family Physicians. Avocations: hiking, music. Office: Va Med Ctr 619 6 Marion Ave Lake City FL 32025 Personal E-mail: marcia.miller@shands.ufl.edu.

MILLER, MARGERY, psychologist, educator, speech pathology/audiology and mental health services professional, university administrator, professor, academic administrator, coach; m. Donald F. Moores; children: Kip Lee, Tige Justice. BA, Elmira Coll., 1971; MA, NYU, 1972; EdS, MS, SUNY, Albany, 1975; MA, Towson State U., 1987; PhD, Georgetown U., 1991. Lic. life coach speech pathologist Md., psychologist Md., diplomate sch. neuropsychologist, sch. neuro-psychologist; cert. tchr. nursery-6th grades, spl. edn. NY, nationally cert. sch. psychologist. Speech and lang. pathologist Mental Retardation Inst. Flower and Fifth Ave. Hosp., NYC, 1971—72; cmty. speech/lang. pathologist, dir. speech and hearing svc. NY State Dept. Mental Hygiene, Troy, 1972—74; instr. comm. disorders dept. Coll. St. Rose, Albany, NY, 1975—77; clin. supr. U. Md., College Park, 1978; speech/lang. pathologist Md. Sch. for Deaf, Frederick, 1978—84; auditory devel. specialist Montgomery County Pub. Schs., Rockville, Md., 1984—87; coord. Family Life program Nat. Acad. Gallaudet U., Washington, 1987—88, interim dir., 1988—89; dir. Counseling and Devel. Ctr. N.W. Campus, Washington, 1989—93; prof. psychology, coord. psychology internship program, dir. undergrad. psychology program Gallaudet U., Washington, 1993—2007, dean enrollment, mgmt., 2007—11; lic. practicing psychologist Bethesda, Md., 1998—; higher ed. cons. life exec. coach writer, 2011—. Instr. sign-lang. program Frederick CC; dance instr. for deaf adolescents; diagnostic cons. psychology and speech pathology; presenter at confs.; profl. coaching, Md., Fla., 2002—. Author: It's O.K. to be Angry, 1976; co-author: Cognition, Education and Deafness: Directions for Research and Instruction, 1985, Deaf People Around the World: Educational and Cultural Perspectives, 2009; mem. editl. rev. com. Gov.'s Devel. Disabilities Coun., Md.; contbr. articles to profl. jours. Vol., choreographer Miss Deaf Am. Pageant, 1984. Office Edn. Children's Bur. fellow, 1971. Mem.: APA, Montgomery County Md. Mental Health Assn., Am. Assn. Higher Edn., Nat. Assn. Sch. Psychologists, Nat. Assn. Deaf, Am. Speech, Lang. and Hearing Assn. (cert. clin. competence in speech/lang. pathology). Office: Gallaudet U 800 Florida Ave NE Washington DC 20002-3660 Personal E-mail: margeryrose@aol.com.

MILLER, MARILYN T., ophthalmologist, educator; b. Chgo., Apr. 15, 1933; MS, U. Ill. Coll. Medicine, 1966, MD, 1959; PhD (hon.), U. Goethenborg. Prof. ophthal. U. Ill. Dept. Ophthal., 1961—. Mem. Internat. Region Ophthalmologyanizations Pan American, 1989—, Bd. Am. Acad. Ophthal., 2009—. Recipient Humanitarian award, Am. Acad. Ophthal., Howe medal, Am. Ophthal. Soc., Pks. Silver medal, Am. Assn. Pediat. Ophthal., Alumni of Yr., U. Ill. Coll. Medicine. Fellow: Am. Bd. Ophthal.; mem.: Am. Assn. Pediat. Ophthal., Am. Ophthal. Soc. Office: University Ill Eya & Ear Infirmary 1 Chicago IL 60612

MILLER, MARK C., waste management executive; BS in Computer Sci., Purdue U. Mgr. Abbott Laboratory, Inc., 1976—89, v.p., Internat. Divsn., 1989—92; chmn., pres. & CEO Stericycle, Inc., Lake Forest, Ill., 1992—. Bd. dirs. Ventana Med. Sys., Inc., Lake Forest Hosp. Mem.: Phi Beta Kappa. Office: Stericycle Inc 28161 N Keith Dr Lake Forest IL 60045 Office Phone: 847-367-5910. Office Fax: 847-367-9493. Business E-Mail: mmark@stericycle.com. *

MILLER, MICHAEL, physician, educator; b. Queens, NY, June 19, 1957; s. Irving Maltz and Lenore (Goldstein) Miller; m. Lisa L. Miller; children: Avery Lauren, Ilana Frieda, Myles Solomon. BA, Rutgers U., 1979; MD, Robert Wood Johnson Med. Sch., 1983. Diplomate Am. Bd. Internal Medicine, Am. Bd. Cardiovascular Disease, Nat. Bd. Med. Examiners. Intern dept. medicine Med. Ctr. U. Cin., 1983-84, resident internal medicine, 1984-86; lipoprotein metabolism fellow Sch. Medicine Johns Hopkins U., Balt., 1986-89, cardiovascular disease fellow, 1988-91; dir. ctr. preventive cardiology U. Md. Med. Sys., Balt., 1991—; assoc. prof. medicine divsn. cardiology Sch. Medicine U. Md., Balt., 1991—; asst. prof. medicine divsn. cardiology Sch. Medicine Johns Hopkins U., Balt., 1997—2009, prof. medicine epidemiology & preventive medicine, 2009—; adj. asst. prof. dept. medicine Baylor Coll. Medicine, Houston, 1992—. Tchr. Sch. Medicine U. Md., 1994—, Johns Hopkins U., 1993—, Balt. Pub. Sch. Sys., 1991—; lectr. in field, chair, AHA Sci. Statement Trislyarides & Cardiovascular Disease, 2011. Author: The Practice of Coronary Disease Prevention, 1996, The Cholesterol Planner, 3d edit., 2004, 5th edit., 2006; contbr. chpts. to books and articles to profl. jours.; reviewer numerous jours.; featured in ednl. recordings, 1990—; co-author: The AMA Guide to Preventing and Treating Heart Disease, 2008. Mem. Gov.'s Task Force Cardiovasc. Disease Prevention; mem. Food Policy Workshop, State Md., 2010. Grantee NIH/Am. Heart Assn., 1989—, Bristol-Myers Squibb, 1991-93, Sandoz, 1992-93, Pfizer, 1992—, Merck, 1997—; recipient Robert Galbraith award, 1979, William F. Grupe award, 1983, Samuel Kaslev award, 1994, Named Most Influencial Drs., USA, 2009, USA Today, 2009, Americas Best Doctors, US News & World Report Castle Connelly Ltd., 2011. Fellow Am. Coll. Cardiology (co-author Preventive Cardiology, 1998—), Am. Heart Assn. (chair 2011, mem. coun. arteriosclerosis); mem. AAAS, Am. Soc. Preventive Cardiology (past pres. 2007), Am. Heart Assn. Coun. Epidemiology, Phi Beta Kappa. Jewish. Avocations: skiing, tennis, hiking. Home: 5 Green Heather Ct Baltimore MD 21208 Office: U Md Divsn Cardiology 22 S Greene St Baltimore MD 21201-1544 Office Phone: 410-328-6299. E-mail: mmiller@medicine.maryland.edu.

MILLER, MICHAEL J., plastic surgeon, educator; b. Tenn., Oct. 23, 1955; MD, U. Mass., 1982; degree in Reconstructive Microsurgery, Tulane U., 1990. Prof., chair, dept. plastic surgery Ohio State U. Med. Ctr., 2010—. Historian Am. Soc. Reconstructive Microsurgery, 2011. Recipient award, Am. Soc. Reconstructive Microsurgery, 2010. Mem.: Am. Soc. Plastic Surgeons. Avocation: bicycling. Office: 915 Olentangy River Rd Ste 2100 Columbus OH 43212 Office Fax: 614-293-9024. Business E-Mail: michael.miller@osumc.edu.

MILLER, ORLANDO JACK, obstetrician, gynecologist, educator, geneticist; b. Okla. City, May 11, 1927; s. Arthur Leroy and Iduma Dorris (Berry) M.; m. Dorothy Anne Smith, July 10, 1954; children: Richard Lawrence, Cynthia Kathleen, Karen Ann. BS, Yale U., 1946, MD, 1950. Intern St. Anthony Hosp., Okla. City, 1950-51; asst. resident in obstetrics and gynecology Yale-New Haven Med. Center, 1954-57, resident, instr., 1957-58; vis. fellow dept. obstetrics and gynecology Tulane U. Service, Charity Hosp., New Orleans, 1958; hon. research asst. Galton Lab., Univ. Coll., London, 1958-60; instr. Coll. Physicians and Surgeons Columbia U., NYC, 1960, asso. dept. obstetrics and gynecology, 1960-61, asst. prof., 1961-65, asso. prof., 1965-69, prof. dept. human genetics and devel., dept. obstetrics and gynecology, 1969-85; asst. attending obstetrician, gynecologist Presbyn. Hosp., NYC, 1964-65, assoc., 1965-70, attending obstetrician and gynecologist, 1970-85; prof. molecular biology, genetics and ob-gyn. Wayne State U. Sch. Medicine, Detroit, 1985-94, prof. Ctr. for Molecular Medicine and Genetics, 1994-96, prof. emeritus, 1996—, chmn. dept. molecular biology and genetics, 1985-93, dir. Ctr. for Molecular Biology, 1987-90. Bd. dirs. Am. Bd. Med. Genetics, 1983-85, v.p., 1983, pres., 1984, 85. Author: (with E. Therman) Human Chromosomes, 2000; editor Cytogenetics, 1970-72; assoc. editor: Birth Defects Compendium, 1971-74, Cytogenetics and Cell Genetics, 1972-97; mem. editl. bd. Cytogenetics, 1961-69, Am. Jour. Human Genetics, 1969-74, 79-83, Gynecologic Investigation, 1970-77, Teratology, 1972-74, Cancer Genetics and Cytogenetics, 1979-84, Jour. Exptl. Zoology, 1989-92, Chromosome Rsch., 1994-99; mem. editl. bd. com. Genomics, 1987-93, assoc. editor, 1993-96; mem. adv. bd. Human Genetics, 1978-98; cons. Jour. Med. Primatology, 1977-94; consulting editor McGraw-Hill Yearbook of Sci. and Tech., 1995-2007, Encyclopedia of Science and Technology, 1997-2007; contbr. chpts. to textbooks and articles to med. and sci. jours. Mem. sci. adv. com. on rsch. Nat. Found. March of Dimes, 1967-96, mem. sci. com., 1996—; mem. sci. rec. com. Basil O'Connor starter grants, 1973-77, 86-94; mem. human embryology and devel. study sect. NIH, 1970-74, chmn., 1972-74; mem. com. for study of inborn errors of metabolism NRC, 1972-74; mem. sci. adv. com. virology and cell biology Am. Cancer Soc., 1974-78, mem. sci. adv. com. cell and devel. biology, 1986-90; mem. human genome study sect. NIH, 1991-94; U.S. rep. permanent com. Internat. Congress of Human Genetics, 1986-91. With AUS, 1951-53. James Hudson Brown Jr. fellow Yale U., 1947-48; NRC fellow, 1953-54; Population Council fellow, 1958-59; Josiah Macy Jr. fellow, 1960-61; NSF sr. postdoctoral fellow U. Oxford, 1968-69; vis. scientist U. Edinburgh, 1983-84; Disting. vis. fellow, Fogarty Internat. fellow LaTrobe U., Melbourne, Australia, 1992; recipient Pres. Disting. Scientist award Soc. for Gynecol. Investigation, 1999, Disting. Cytogeneticist award Am. Cytogeneticist Conf., 2008. Fellow AAAS; mem. AAAS, Am. Soc. Human Genetics (bd. dirs. 1970-73, 86-90), Genetics Soc. Am., Acad. Scholars, Wayne State U. (life, pres. 1996-97), Sigma Xi. Home: 19365 Cypress Ridge Terr # 817 Lansdowne VA 20176 Office: 540 E Canfield St Detroit MI 48201-1928 E-mail: ojmiller@smartneighborhood.net.

MILLER, R. WARBURTON, psychologist, farmer; b. Bellefonte, Pa., Nov. 23, 1921; s. Joseph Frederick and Mary (Warburton) Miller; m. Joyce Larayne Miller; children: Pamela Joyce, Page Layne. AB, Pa. State U., State College, 1942; MA, U. Redlands, Calif., 1951; PhD, U. So. Calif., LA, 1957; postgrad., San Bernardino Valley Coll., Calif., Columbia U., NYC, U. Mich., Ann Arbor, U. Minn., Mpls., LA State Coll., U. Internat., Saltillo, Coah, Mex., Inst. Mex. Cultura Internat., Guadalahara; JD, Loma Linda Coll. Law, 1985. Lic. clin. psychologist, marriage, family and child counselor, clin. speech pathologist. Capt. USN, 1942—44, 1951—53; officer USNR, 1942—74; staff psychologist San Bernardino County Med. Ctr., 1968—74; forensic psychologist/clin. psychologist; pvt. practice with Dr. Joyce Miller. Mem. psychology examining com. State Bd. Med. Examiners, 1970—74; dir. Mojave Valley Coordinating Coun. Family Mental Health, 1971—72; lectr. U. So. Calif., U. Redlands, Loma Linda U.; bd. dirs., v.p. E. Pioneer Mut. Water Co.; expert witness in forensic psychology; chmn. bd. dirs. AVORA Corp. Author (with Joyce Miller): Dealing with the Behavioral Problems in the Elementary School, 1968, A Layman's Handbook for Aphasic Rehabilitation, 1973; contbr. articles to profl. jours. Bd. dirs. State of Calif. Psychologists Polit Action Com.; past pres. Carriage Club, Civic Light Opera Assn., San Bernardino chpt. City of Hope Hosp. # 434, San Bernardino County Navy League; bd. dirs., past pres. Goodwill Industries Inland Counties; pres. San Bernardino Libr. Found., 1995—. Recipient George Washington medal, Freedoms Found. Valley Forge, 1970, 1972, 1973, honor cert., 1974, Disting. citizens Lifetime Achievement award, Calif. Inland Empire Coun., Boy Scouts Am., 2000. Fellow: Am. Assn. Marriage Counselors; mem.: SAR (nat. trustee 1970—74, chmn. nat. soc. Ind. Day com. 1971—73, v.p. gen. nat. soc. we. dist. 1972—74, nat. exec. com. 1973—74, sec. gen. nat. soc. 1974—76, past pres. So. Calif. chpt. Riverside, past pres. State of Calif.), Inland So. Calif. Soc. Clin. Psychologists, Calif. Sate Psychol. Assn., San Bernardino Area C. of C. (bd. dirs., pres. 1999), Naval Res. Assn., Rotary (Paul Harris award), Hon. Order Ky. Cols., Masons, Kappa Sigma, Pi Delta Sigma, Tau Kappa Alpha. Avocation: travel. Home and Office: 6836 Palm Ave Highland CA 92346-2513 Office Phone: 909-881-2786.

MILLER, RICHARD A., pathologist, educator; BS, Haverford Coll., Pa., 1971; PhD in Human Genetics, Yale U., New Haven, 1976, MD, 1977. Postdoc. training Meml. Sloan—Kettering Cancer Ctr., NYC, Harvard U., Cambridge, Mass.; faculty pathology dept. Boston U., 1982—90; prof. pathology U. Mich. Sch. Medicine, Ann Arbor, 1990—, assoc. rsch. dir. Geriatrics Ctr. Rsch. scientist Ann Arbor VA Healthcare Sys. Contbr. articles to profl. jours. Recipient Nathan Shock award, Nat. Inst. Aging, 1994, AlliedSignal award, Alliance Aging Rsch., 1994. Mem.: Am. Fedn. Aging Rsch., Gerontological Soc. America (Robert W. Kleemeier award for rsch. in aging 1997). Achievements include research in genetics, cell biology and immunology of aging. Office: U Mich Sch Medicine Rm 3001 BSRB Box 2200 109 Zina Pitcher Pl Ann Arbor MI 48109 Office Phone: 734-936-2122. Office Fax: 734-647-9749. E-mail: millerr@umich.edu. *

MILLER, RICHARD LYNN, retired pharmaceutical researcher; b. Stevens Point, Wis., Sept. 27, 1945; s. Gordon L. and Jean Ellen (Leary) M.; divorced; remarried; children: Analiese, Colin, Autumn. BS, U. Wis., Stevens Point, 1968; PhD, U. Minn., 1974. Med. lab. technician US Army, 1968—70; post-doctoral fellow Penn State Med. Sch., Hershey, Pa., 1975—77; corp. scientist 3M Pharmaceuticals, 3M Co., 1977—2007. Cons. Graceway Pharmaceuticals, 2008—10. Contbr. articles and abstracts to profl. jours. With US Army, 1968-70. Recipient Skin Sense award, Skin Cancer Found., NYC, Minn. TEKNE Award for Life Sci. Rsch., Minn. Tech., Inc; named Hero of Chemistry, Am. Chem. Soc. Mem. AAAS, NY Acad. Sci., Internat. Soc. Antiviral Rsch., Inflammation Rsch. Assn. Avocations: bird watching, fishing, hiking. Home: 2643 Promontory Pl East Maplewood MN 55119-5896 Home Phone: 612-859-2150. Personal E-mail: rlmiller2643@comcast.net.

MILLER, ROBERT HAROLD, medical association administrator, otolaryngologist, educator; b. Columbia, Mo., July 2, 1947; s. Harold Oswald and Ruth Nadine (Ballew) M.; m. Nancy Eaves, Aug. 19, 2007; children: Morgan Guillory, Reed Thurston. BS in Biology, Tulane U., 1969, MD, 1973, MBA, 1996. Diplomate Am. Bd. Otolaryngology. Resident otolaryngology, head/neck surgery UCLA, 1978; from asst. prof. to assoc. prof. otolaryngology-head and neck surgery Baylor Coll. Medicine, Houston, 1978—87; prof., chmn. otolaryngology-head and neck surgery Tulane Sch. Medicine, New Orleans, 1987—98, vice-chancellor for clin. affairs, 1997—99; dean U. Nev. Sch. Medicine, 1999—2001, prof., 1999—2002; prof. otolaryngology-head and neck surgery Tulane Sch. Medicine, New Orleans, 2002—03; exec. dir. Am. Bd. Otolaryngology, Houston, 2004—. Bd. dirs. Am. Bd. Otolaryngology; chief of staff Tulane Hosp., 1995-96; vis. prof. otolaryngology Baylor Coll. Medicine, Houston, Tex., 2004—. Mem. editl. bd. Archives of Otolaryngology, 1986-05, Head & Neck Surgery, 1987-03, Laryngoscope, 1996-, ENToday, chmn., 2006-. Named Outstanding Young Man, Houston C. of C., 1980; Robert Wood Johnson Health Policy fellow, 1996-97. Fellow ACS, Am. Soc. Head & Neck Surgery, Am. Acad. Oto-Head & Neck Surgery (Disting. Svc. award 1994, Honor award 1991), Triological Soc. (exec. sec. 1992-97, treas. 1997-2004). Avocations: tennis, computers. Home: 2616 Wroxton Rd Houston TX 77005 Office: Am Bd Otolaryngology 5615 Kirby Dr 600 Houston TX 77005 Office Phone: 713-850-0399. Business E-Mail: rmiller@aboto.org. *

MILLER, ROBERT SCOTT, clinical social worker, psychotherapist; b. Seattle, Dec. 12, 1947; s. Bert Lester and Carol Theresa (Gustafson) M.; m. Karen Ann Staake, Nov. 12, 1977; children: Sarah, Megan, Emily. BA in Sociology cum laude, Seattle Pacific U., 1970; AM in Social Work, U. Chgo., 1972; MA in Human Resources Mgmt., Pepperdine U., Malibu, Calif., 1977; diploma in life skills coaching, Stonebridge Associated Colls., UK, 2002; DBA, Calif. Pacific U., Escondido, 2006; cert. in Aging, Inst. for Geriatric Social Work, Boston U., 2009. LCSW, cert. in aging Inst. Geriat. Social Work, Boston U., 2009. Br. supr. Wash. State Dept. Social and Health Svcs., Oak Harbor and Anacortes, 1975—78, supr. casework Everett, 1973—75; lectr., coord. rural cmty. mental health project U. Wash., Seattle, 1978—83; exec. dir. Armed Svcs. YMCA, Oak Harbor, 1984—86; area dir. United Way of Island County, 1986—88, exec. dir., 1988—92, Saratoga Cmty. Mental Health, Coupeville, 1992—93; outpatient therapist, attention-deficit/hyperactivity disorder mental health specialist Cath. Cmty. Svcs. Northwest, Oak Harbor, 1993—96; dir. Cath. Cmty. Svcs. NW, 1996—2001, Mount Vernon, 1996—99, clin. dir. Everett, 1998—2004; privacy officer Health Ins. Portability and Accountability Act, 2001—04; pvt. practice counselor, 2001—07, 2009—; psychiat. hosp. surveyor, quality control reviewer Ascellon Corp., Landover, Md., 2004—07, project mgr. psychiatric hosp. fed. monitoring oversight & HIPAA privacy officer, 2008—09; supr., mgr. skill cert. Rutgers U., 2007, project mgr. skill cert., 2007; pvt. practice psychotherapist, 2009—. Internship supr. counseling program, Seattle U., 1998-99, Bastyr U., 2000-01; instr. sociology and psychol. Chapman U. Naval Air Sta. Whidbey Island, Orange, Calif., 1988-95, 2004; practicum instr. sch. social work Ea. Wash. U., 2003, site visitor US Dept. Vets. Affairs Mental Health Residential Rehab. Quality Review Project, Mathmatica Policy rsch. Inc., 2010-11. Contbr. articles to profl. jours. Pres. Wash. Assn. Social Welfare, 1975-76; bd. dir. Puget Sound chpt. Huntington's Disease Soc. Am., 1989-93, pres., 1991, fundraising chmn., 1989-91, v.p., 1990; adv. bd. United Ways Wash., 1991-92; chmn. Island County bd. emergency food and shelter program Fed. Emergency Mgmt. Agy.; vice chmn. Cmty. Resource Network, Oak Harbor, 1991; steering com. Greater Oak Harbor Econ. Summit, 1991; strategic planning com. Whidbey Gen. Hosp., Coupeville, 1992-93; exec. com. Mt. Baker coun. Boy Scouts Am., 1993; bd. dir. Opportunity Coun., Bellingham, 1993-94, Concerts on the Cove, Coupeville, 1993-96, v.p., 1994-95; active Oak Harbor Citizen's Comprehensive Plan Task Force, 1994, Readiness to Learn Coupeville Cmty. Team, 1996; risk mgmt. subcom. chair Assoc. Provider Network, 1997-98; child study team Island County, 1996-99, child protective team, 1997-99; health adv. bd. Head Start, Mt. Vernon, Wash., 1999-2002. Recipient outstanding svc. award Armed Svcs. YMCA of US, Dallas, 1985, two program merit awards McDonald's Corp., Oak Harbor, 1986; named Alumni of a Growing Vision, Seattle Pacific U., 1991, Diplomat of Yr. Greater Oak Harbor C. of C., 1991, Celebrating Excellence award, Ascellon Corp., 2005. Mem. NASW (bd. dirs. Wash. chpt. 1982-85, mem. nominations leadership identification com.), Acad. Cert. Social Workers, Greater Oak Harbor C. of C., Soc. Mayflower Descendants. Democrat. Roman Catholic. Avocations: kayaking, genealogy, fishing. Home: 2450 Rocky Way Coupeville WA 98239-9610 Office: Ste B206 275 SE Cabot Dr Oak Harbor WA 98277 Office Phone: 866-885-5921, 360-632-5267. Business E-Mail: robertmiller@onebox.com.

MILLER, ROSS HAYS, retired neurosurgeon; b. Ada, Okla., Jan. 30, 1923; s. Harry and Helen (Rice) M.; m. Catherine Railey, May 2, 1943; children— Terry Hays, Helen Stacy. BS, East Central State Coll., Ada, 1943; MD, U. Okla., 1946; MS in Neurosurgery, U. Minn., 1952. Diplomate: Am. Bd. Neurol. Surgery (chmn. exam. com. 1978-84). Intern St. Luke's Hosp., Cleve., 1946-47; fellow in neurosurgery Mayo Clinic, Rochester, Minn., 1950-54; instr. in neurosurgery Mayo Med. Sch., 1954-63, asst. prof. neurosurgery, 1963-73, asso. prof., 1973-75, prof., chmn. dept. neurosurgery, from 1975, now ret. Vis. prof. neurol. surgery Med. Coll. Ga., Augusta Contbr. articles to profl. jours. Trustee East Central State U. Found. Served as capt., M.C. U.S. Army, 1947-49, Korea. Named to Okla. Hall of Fame, 1977, Athletic Hall of Fame, East Central U. Okla., 1977; recipient Disting. Alumnus award East Central U. Okla., 1974, Mayo Found. Disting. Alumnus award, 1992. Mem. AMA, ACS, Am. Assn. Neurol. Surgeons (chmn. com. profl. practice 1976-79, dir. 1976-79, v.p. 1979, rep. to Council Med. Splty. Socs. 1980-84), Congress Neurol. Surgeons (exec. com. 1963-65), Minn. Soc. Neurol. Scis., Neurosurg. Soc. Am. (v.p. 1975), Soc. Neurol. Surgeons (v.p. 1983), Sigma Xi.

MILLER, SCOTT T., pediatrician, hematologist, oncologist; Studied, Yeshiva U., 1976. Diplomate Am. Bd. of Pediatrics, cert. pediatric hematology-oncology. Resident Montefiore Hosp. Med. Ctr., 1977—79; fellow Cornell Med. Ctr., 1979—81, Meml. Sloan Kettering Cancer Ctr.; with Kings County Hosp. Ctr.; physician Univ. Physicians of Bklyn. Inc. Office: University Physicians of Brooklyn Incorporated 450 Clarkson Ave Brooklyn NY 11203 Office Phone: 718-270-4741. Office Fax: 718-270-1692.

MILLER, STEPHEN HERSCHEL, surgeon, educator; b. NYC, Jan. 12, 1941; s. Morris Louis and Mildred Lily (Beller) M.; children: Mark, David. MD, UCLA, 1964; MPH, San Diego State, 1996. Diplomate Am. Bd. Surgery, Am. Bd. Plastic Surgery (mem. exec. com. 1985—, chmn. written examination sect. 1985—, bd. dirs. 1984—, chmn. 1989-90). Asst. prof. surgery U. Calif., San Francisco, 1973-74; from assoc. prof. to prof. surgery Milton S. Hershey Med. Ctr., Hershey, Pa., 1974—78; chief div. plastic surgery Oreg. Health Scis. U., Portland, 1979-88, Staff Scripps Clinic, La Jolla, Calif., 1988—98; clin. prof. surgery U. Calif., San Diego, 1989—98; adj. prof. surgery Northwestern U., Evanston, Ill., 1998—; pres., CEO Am. Bd. Med. Specialities, Evanston, Ill., 2004—07. Bd. dirs. Edn. Commn. for Foreign Med. Grads. Editor-in-chief Yearbook of Plastic, Reconstructive and Aesthetic Surgery, 1988-95, 2007. Physician advisor Boy Scouts Am., dist. chmn. scoutmaster exec. coun., 1983-84; bd. dirs. Temple Beth Israel, Portland, 1984-86. Recipient Physician Recognition award, 1976; grantee Med. Rsch. Found. of Oreg., 1980, Oreg. Health Scis. U., 1980. Mem. ACS (chmn. program com. 1983-87), Am. Soc. Plastic and Reconstructive Surgery (bd. dirs. 1980-89, v.p. 1985-86, pres.-elect 1986-87, pres. 1987-88, grantee 1976), Am. Assn. Plastic Surgeons (chmn. rsch. com. 1983-84, trustee 1988-91, sec. 1990-93, pres. 1994-95), Assn. Acad. Chmn. Plastic Surgery (sec./treas. 1985—); Am. Bd. Med. Specialites (sect., exec. v.p., 1998). Avocations: reading, golf. Office: 39289 Beringer Dr Murrieta CA 92563

MILLER, TIMOTHY ALDEN, plastic and reconstructive surgeon; b. Inglewood, Calif., Dec. 11, 1938; s. Henry Bernard and Florence Algena (Maddock) M.; 1 child, Matthew Christopher. Student, U. Calif., Berkeley; MD, UCLA, 1963. Diplomate Am. Bd. Surgery, Am. Bd. Plastic Surgery (dir. 1991-97). Intern Vanderbilt U. Hosp., Nashville, 1963-64; resident in surgery, dept. surg. pathology UCLA, 1966-67, resident, then chief resident gen. and thoracic surgery, 1967-69, acting asst. prof., 1969-70, prof. surgery, 1981—, Timothy D. Miller chair, plastic and reconstructive surgery, Med. Ctr. LA, prof., chief plastic and reconstructive surgery, Sch. Medicine, 2002—, exec. dir., chief surgeon, Ops. Mend; asst. surg. resident John Hopkins Hosp., 1967; fellow plastic and reconstructive surgery U. Pitts., 1970-72; chief plastic surgery West Wadsworth VA Med. Ctr., 1973—. Author: (novel) Practice to Deceive, 1991; assoc. editor Jour. Plastic & Reconstructive Surgery, 1987-93, co-editor, 1994-99. Trustee Children's Inst. Internat., 1995-2000. Capt. U.S. Army, 1964-66, Vietnam (Bronze Star, 1966, Vietnam Spl. Forces Parachute award, 1966). Recipient Thomas Symington award Pitts. Acad. Medicine, 1971, Ralph Goldman Rsch. award, 1996, 1999; named Hero of Yr., People Mag., 2010. Mem. Am. Soc. for Plastic Surgery (co-editor Jour. Plastic and Reconstructive Surgery), Am. Soc. for Aesthetic Plastic Surgery (bd. dirs. 1990-95), Am. Soc. Surgery of Hand, Am. Soc. Maxillofacial Surgeons, Plastic Surgery Ednl. Found. (bd. dirs. 1991-95), Plastic Surgery Rsch. Coun.; Phi Beta Kappa. Office: UCLA Med Ctr 200 UCLA Med Plz Ste 465 Los Angeles CA 90095-8344 Office Phone: 310-825-5644, 310-794-7180. Business E-Mail: tmiller@mednet.ucla.edu.

MILLER, WAENARD LIVINGSTON, cardiologist; b. Greenville, SC, Mar. 1, 1947; s. Waenard Livingston and Margaret Evelyn (Burns) M.; m. Sheila McLawhorn, Dec. 20, 1969; children: Waenard Livingston III, Bernyrd Carlysle. BS in Physics, Clemson U., 1969; MS in Nuclear Physics, U. Tenn., 1970; MS in Biology, Wright State U., 1974; MD, Med. U. S.C., 1978; MS in Med. Mgmt., U. Tex., 2000. Diplomate Am. Bd. Internal Medicine, subspecialty of cardiovascular disease. Intern in internal medicine Southwestern Med. Sch., Dallas, 1978-79, resident in internal medicine, 1979-81, fellow in cardiology, 1981-83; pvt. practice cardiology Plano, Tex., 1983—; lab. dir. Cardiac Catheterization HCA Med. Ctr., Plano, 1994; co-founder Legacy Heart Ctr. Trustee Baylor Healthcare Sys., 2004. 1st lt. USAF, 1971-74. Fellow Am. Coll. Cardiology, Am. Coll. Cardiology (councilor Tex. divsn., 2004-05), Am. Heart Assn. Avocations: travel, golf. Office: Legacy Heart Ctr 6601 Preston Rd Plano TX 75024 Personal E-mail: wmiller095@yahoo.com.

MILLER, WALTER LUTHER, scientist, pediatrician, educator; b. Alexandria, Va., Feb. 21, 1944; s. Luther Samuel and Beryl (Rinderle) M. SB, MIT, 1965; MD, Duke U., 1970. Diplomate Am. Bd. Pediatrics. Intern, then resident Mass. Gen. Hosp., Boston, 1970-72; staff assoc. NIH, Bethesda, Md., 1972-74; sr. resident U. Calif., San Francisco, 1974-75, rsch. fellow, 1975-78, asst. prof. pediatrics, 1978-83, assoc. prof., 1983-87, prof., 1987—2005, disting. prof., 2005—, dir. Child Health Rsch. Ctr. San Francisco, 1992—2003, faculty biomed. scis. grad. program, 1982—, faculty genetics grad. program, 1998—, dir. pediat. endocrinology tng. program, 1994—, chief divsn. endocrinology, 2000—, assoc. prof. metabolic rsch. unit, 1983-87, disting. prof., 2005—. Bd. scientific counselors Nat. Inst. of Child Health & Human Devel., 2004—09. Editor DNA and Cell Biology Jour., 1983-2006; mem. editl. bds. numerous sci. jours.; contbr. articles to profl. jours., chpts. to books. Del. Dem. Nat. Conv., NYC, 1976. Served with USPHS, 1972-74. Recipient Nat. Rsch. Svc. award NIH, 1975, Clin. Investigator award, 1978, Albion O Bernstein award NY Med. Soc., 1993, Clin. Endocrinology Trust medal Brit. Endocrine Soc., 1993, Henning Andersen prize European Soc. Pediatric Endocrinology, 1993, Samuel Rosenthal Found. prize for excellence in acad. pediatrics, 1999, Disting. Clin. Rsch. Lectr. award U. Calif., San Francisco, 2009, Disting. Alumnus award Duke U. Sch. Medicine, 2010. Fellow: AAAS, Molecular Medicine Soc.; mem.: Androgen Excess Soc. (founding mem., bd. dirs. 2002—05), Am. Soc. Biochem. Molecular Biology, Lawson Wilkins Pediat. Endocrine Soc. (edn. com. 1992—96, coun. 1995—96, corp. adv. bd. 1998—2002, program dirs. com. 2004—), Am. Soc. Clin. Investigation, Am. Soc. Human Genetics, Endocrine Soc. (fin. com. 1999—2002, annual meeting steering com. 2005—07, Edwin B. Astwood lecture award 1988, Clin. Investigator Lectr. award 2006), European Soc. for Paediatric Endocrinology (hon.), Japanese Soc. for Pediat. Endocrinology (hon.), We. Soc. Pediat. Rsch. (Ross Rsch. award 1982), Soc. Pediat. Rsch., Am. Pediat. Soc., Am. Acad. Pediats., Assn. Am. Physicians, Am. Soc. for Microbiology, Theta Delta Chi. Achievements include patents in field; published in over 370 publs. Office: U Calif Med Ctr Dept Pediat Rm 672 S San Francisco CA 94143-0978

MILLER, YORK E., oncologist; b. New Haven, May 6, 1950; AB, Harvard Coll., 1972; MD, Duke U., Durham, 1976. Leader, lung, head and neck cancer program U. Colo. Cancer Ctr., 1998—. SPORE Lung Cancer grant, Nat. Cancer Inst., Early Detection Rsch. grant, LUNGevity Found. Mem.: Am. Soc. Clin. Investigation. Office: Pulmonary 111A DVAMC 1055 Clermont St Denver CO 80220 Office Fax: 303-393-4639. Business E-Mail: york.miller@ucdenver.edu.

MILLER-BRESLOW, ANNE J., orthopedist, surgeon; Attended, Harvard U., 1983. Diplomate Am. Bd. of Orthopaedic Surgery, Am. Bd. of Orthopaedic Surgery-hand surgery. Intern Deaconess Hosp.; resident Albert Einstein Coll. of Medicine; resident orthopaedic surgery Montefiore Med. Ctr., 1984—88; fellow hand surgery New England Med. Ctr., 1988—89; with Orthopedic Assoc. of Englewood, Holy Name Med. Ctr., Englewood Hosp. & Med. Ctr. Office: Englewood Hospital & Medical Center 3rd Fl 401 S Van Brunt St Englewood NJ 07631 Office Phone: 201-569-2770, 201-569-1774.

MILLER-HANCE, WANDA C., anesthesiologist; b. NYC, July 11, 1956; d. Juan R. Miller and Julia Hance. Student, U. P.R., 1974-77; MD, U. Wis., 1981. Diplomate in pediat. and pediatric cardiology Am. Bd. Pediatrics; diplomate Am. Bd. Anesthesiology. Intern, resident in pediats. U. Tex. SW Med. Ctr., Dallas, 1981-84, rsch. fellow, 1985-87; fellow in pediat. cardiology Baylor Coll. Medicine, Houston, 1987-90; asst. prof. U. Calif., San Diego, 1991-93; resident in anesthesia Mass. Gen. Hosp., Boston, 1993-96; asst. prof. U. Calif., San Francisco, 1996-99; assoc. prof. Baylor Coll. Medicine, Houston, 2002—. Author: Critical Care Secrets, 2003, Cardiology Clinics, 2000; contbg. author: Anesthesia for Congenital Heart Disease, 2005; contbr. articles to profl. jours. Bugher Found. fellow Am. Heart Assn., 1991, grantee, 1992; recipient investigator award NIH, San Diego, 1991, Found. for Anesthesia Edn. and Rsch., San Francisco, 1999. Fellow Am. Coll. Cardiology; mem. Am. Coll. Cardiology, Am. Soc. Anesthesiologists, Am. Soc. Echocardiography, Internat. Anesthesia Rsch. Soc., Soc. Cardiovasc. Anesthesiologists, Soc. for Pediatric Anesthesia, Soc. Pediatric Echocardiography. Office: Tex Children's Hosp Div Pediat Cardiovasc Anes 6621 Fannin St 19345H Houston TX 77030 Office Phone: 832-826-5824.

MILLER-MEEKS, MARIANNETTE JANE, public health service officer, ophthalmologist; b. Herlong, Calif., Sept. 6, 1955; d. Fred and Annette Miller; m. Curt Miller-Meeks; children: Jonathan, Taylor. BS in Nursing, Tex. Christian U., 1976; MS in Sci & Edn., U. Southern Calif., 1980; MD, U. Tex. Health Sci. Ctr., 1986. Asst. prof. opthalmology U. Mich., Ann Arbor, 1991—94, U. Iowa, 1994—97; pvt. practice Ottumwa, Iowa, 1997—2008; dir. Iowa Dept. Pub. Health, Des Moines, 2011—. Served in USAR, 1983—2000. Recipient Charles Phelps Award, 1995. Mem.: Iowa Med. Soc. (pres. 2006), American Bd. Ophthalmology (examiner), American Acad. Ophthalmology (AAO) (councilor for Iowa), Wapello County Medical Soc. (former pres.), Alpha Omega Alpha. Republican. Roman Catholic. Office: Iowa Department Public Health 321 E 12th St Des Moines IA 50319 Office Phone: 515-281-7689. *

MILLET, JOHN BRADFORD, retired surgeon; b. Buffalo, Aug. 8, 1916; s. John Alfred Parsons and Alice Jeannette (Murrell) Millet; m. Constance Hopkins Dallas, Nov. 1974; children: John Bradford Jr., David Francis, Polly Watson. BS, Harvard U., 1938, MD, 1942. Diplomate Am. Bd. Surgery. Surg. intern Mass. Gen. Hosp., Boston, 1942-43, surg. resident, 1946-49; chief thoracic surgery, partner Slocum Dickson Clinic, Utica, NY, 1949-55; pvt. practice medicine specializing in surgery Utica, 1955—; sr. attending surgeon St. Luke's Meml. Hosp. Ctr., Utica, 1955-81, chief dept. surgery, 1969-70; sr. attending surgeon St. Elizabeth's Hosp., 1955—, 1963—64, Faxton Hosp., 1979-86; ret., 1985; asst. to pres. Mohawk Metal Products Inc., 1989-91; pres. Miltel divsn. Millwheel, Inc., 1992-94. Former cons. surgeon Herkimer Meml. Hosp., Rose Hosp., Rome, Marcy State Hosp., NY; former med. adv. Vis. Nurse Assn.; former dir. Health Sys. Agy. Ctrl. NY, Med. Securities Fund, 1964—65, Med. Funds Mgmt. Corp., 1964—65, Digimetrics Inc., M. V. Hockey Inc., Millwheel Inc.,

IEX Inc., JDC Resources, Inc., B.F.I Telcom. Co. Inc., Utica Disposables Inc., Input Specialists Inc., LJB Ventures Inc.; pres. White Birch Home Utica, Inc.; adminstrv. asst. US Bur. Census, 2000, H&R Block, 2001. Former med. adv. com. Planned Parenthood Mohawk Valley; pres. Midstate Com. Area Wide Health Planning, 1966—72; co-chmn. citizens com. devel. med. sch. Utica area; co-developer Brookside Racquet Club, Wedgewood Apts., Treadway Resort, Meadows. Maj. M.C. US Army, 1943—46. Fellow: ACS, Am. Coll. Chest Physicians; mem.: AMA, Med. Soc. NY State, Utica Med. Club, Pan Pacific Surg. Assn., Pan-Am. Med. Assn., NY State Med. Soc. (mem. com. homeless), NY State Soc. Surgeons (bd. dirs. 1970—85), Ctrl. NY Acad. Medicine, Oneida County (chmn. edn. com. 1968—69), Mohawk Valley Surg. Soc. (pres. 1968—69), Ctrl. NY Surg. Soc., Coll. Angiology, Am. Thoracic Soc., Harvard Coll. Alumni Club (fund area chmn.), Harvard Club Mohawk Valley (pres. 1951—66), Night Stick Club (chief 1965—66), Shriners (potentate 1981—82), Masons, Rotary. Republican. Episcopalian. Home: Acacia Village # 223 2160 Bleecker St Utica NY 13501-1734 Personal E-mail: bmillet111@peoplepc.com.

MILLICHAP, JOSEPH GORDON, neurologist, educator; b. Wellington, Eng., Dec. 18, 1918; came to U.S., 1956, naturalized, 1965; s. Joseph P. and Alice (Flello) M.; m. Mary Irene Fortey, Feb. 25, 1946 (dec. Oct. 1969); children: Martin Gordon, Paul Anthony; m. Nancy Melanie Kluczynski, Nov. 7, 1970 (dec. Apr. 1995); children: Gordon Thomas, John Joseph. MB Surgery honors, St. Bartholomew's Med. Coll., U. London, 1946, MD Internal Medicine, 1951, diploma child health, 1948. Diplomate Am. Bd. Pediat., Am. Bd. Neurology and Child Neurology, Am. Bd. Electroencephalography. Intern, resident St. Bartholomew's Hosp., 1946—49, Hosp. Sick Children, London, 1951—53, Mass. Gen. Hosp., Boston, 1958—60; pediat. neurologist NIH, 1955—56; USPHS fellow neurology Mass. Gen. Hosp., Boston, 1958—60; cons. pediat. neurology Mayo Clinic, 1960—63; pediat. neurologist Children's Meml. Hosp., Northwestern Med. Ctr., Chgo., 1963—; prof. neurology and pediat. Northwestern U. Med. Sch., 1963—. Cons. surgeon gen. USPHS; mem. med. adv. bds. Ill. Epilepsy League, Muscular Dystrophy Found., Cerebral Palsy Found., 1963—; vis. prof. Gt. Ormond St. Hosp., U. London, 1986-87 Author: Febrile Convulsions, 1967, Pediatric Neurology, 1967, Learning Disabilities, 1974, The Hyperactive Child with MBD, 1975, Nutrition, Diet and Behavior, 1985, Dyslexia, 1986, Progress in Pediatric Neurology, 1991, Vol. II, 1994, Vol. III, 1997, Environmental Poisons in Our Food, 1993, A Guide to Drinking Water, Hazards and Health Risks, 1995, Attention Deficit Hyperactivity and Learning Disorders, 1998, (with G.T. Millichap) The School in a Garden, 2000; editor Jour. Pediatric Neurology Briefs; contbr. articles to profl. jours., chpts. to books Chmn. rsch. com. med. adv. bd. Epilepsy Found., 1965—. Served with RAF, 1949-51 Named New Citizen of Year in Met. Chgo., 1965; recipient Americanism Medal DAR, 1972, Brennemann award Chgo. Pediat. Soc., 1998; USPHS rsch. grantee, 1957 Fellow Royal Coll. Physicians; mem. AMA, Am. Neurol. Assn., Am. Pediat. Soc., Am. Soc. Pediat. Rsch., Am. Acad. Neurology, Am. Soc. Pharmacology and Exptl. Therapeautics, Soc. Exptl. Biology and Medicine, Am. Bd. Psychiatry and Neurology (asst. examiner 1961—) Episcopalian. Office: Children's Meml Hosp Box 51 2300 N Childrens Plz Chicago IL 60614-3394 Office Phone: 773-880-4352.

MILLIKAN, LARRY EDWARD, dermatologist; b. Sterling, Ill., May 12, 1936; s. Daniel Franklin and Harriet Adeline (Parmenter) M.; m. Jeanine Dorothy Johnson, Aug. 27, 1960; children: Marshall, Rebecca. BA, Monmouth Coll., 1958; MD, U. Mo., 1962. Intern Great Lakes Naval Hosp., Ill., 1962-63; housestaff in tng. U. Mich., Ann Arbor, 1967-69, chief resident, 1969-70; asst. prof. dermatology U. Mo., Columbia, 1970-74, assoc. prof., 1974-81; chmn. dept. dermatology Tulane U., New Orleans, 1981—, chair/prof. emeritus, 2006—. Cons. physician Charity Hosp., New Orleans, Tulane U. Hosp., New Orleans, Riley Hosp., Anderson Hosp., Rush Hosp., all Meridian, Miss.; mem. bd. trustees Sulzberger Inst. for Dermatological Edn., 1995-99; chmn. cont. med. edn. com. La. State Med. Soc., 1994-97. Assoc. editor Internat. Jour. Dermatology, 1980-99, Clinics in Dermatology, 1999—; mem. editl. bd. Current Concepts in Skin Disorders, Am. Jour. Med. Scis.; mem. editl. bd. Clinics in Dermatology, 1985—, assoc. editor, 1999—; contbr. articles to med. jours. Bd. dirs. Women's Dermatol. Assn., 1994-99. With USN, 1960-67. Recipient Andres Bello awrd Govt. of Venezuela, 1989, citation of merit Sch. Medicine, U. Mo., 1993, Faculty Alumnus award U. Mo., 1997; named Disting. Alumnus, Monmouth Coll., 1990; Nat. Cancer Inst. grantee, 1976-84. Fellow ACP; mem. AAAS, AMA, Am. Acad. Dermatology (bd. dirs. 1986-90), Am. Dermatol. Assn., Am. Dermatol. Soc. for Allergy and Immunology (pres., bd. dirs.), Soc. for Investigative Dermatology (past pres. South sect.), So. Med. Assn. (vice chmn. dermatology sect. 1984, chmn. 1994), Coll. Physicians Phila., Assn. Profs. Dermatology (bd. dirs. 1984-86), Orleans Parish Med. Soc., La. Med. Soc., Pan Am. Med. Assn., Internat. Soc. Dermatology (dep. sec. gen. 1989-99), Mo. Allergy Assn. (past pres.), Am. Coll. Cryosurgery, Assn. Acad. Dermatol. Surgeons, Internat. Soc. Dermatol. Surgery, Internat. Acad. Cosmetic Dermatology (sec. gen. 1996-), Dermatol. Found. Leaders Soc. (state chmn. 1993-97). Office: Tulane Univ Sch Medicine Dept of Dermatology 1430 Tulane Ave TB36 New Orleans LA 70112-2699

MILLINER, DAWN SCHMAUTZ, pediatrician; b. Missoula, Mont., July 6, 1949; MD, Temple U., 1976. Chair, divsn. pediat. nephrology Mayo Clinic, 1993—2002, chief med. info. officer, 2009—; med. dir. Mayo Eugenio Litta Children's Hosp., 1995—99. Prof., medicine and pediat. Mayo Med. Sch., 2002. Office: Mayo Clinic Rochester MN 55905 Business E-Mail: milliner.dawn@mayo.edu.

MILLIS, JAMES MICHAEL, surgeon; b. Nashville, Tenn., Feb. 22, 1959; MD, U. Tenn. Ctr. Health Scis., Memphis, 1985. Diplomate Am. Bd. Surgery, Am. Bd. Surg. Critical Care. Intern UCLA Med. Ctr., LA, 1985-86, resident in gen. surgery, 1986-92, fellow organ transplants, 1992-94; asst. prof. surgery U. Chgo., 1994-97, assoc. prof. to prof. surgery, 1997—; chief, sect. transplantation U. Chgo. Med. Ctr., med. dir., transplantation svcs. Mem. ACS, Am. Soc. Transplant Surgeons, Am. Soc. Transplant Physicians, Assn. Acad. Surgery, Am. Assn. Study of Liver Disease, Internat. Pediatric Transplant Assn., Soc. U. Surgeons. Achievements include performing more liver transplants than any other surgeon in the Chicago region; has pioneered new techniques of operating on the liver, and these innovations have helped the University of Chicago perform more liver transplants than any other program in the region over the past 15 years; performed a liver cell infusion on a 3-pound premature infant with liver failure. The baby is the youngest and smallest person to receive this innovative form of liver "transplant". Office: U Chgo Med Ctr Transplant Sect MC 5027 5841 S Maryland Ave Chicago IL 60637 Address: Center for Advanced Medicine 5758 S Maryland Ave Chicago IL 60637 Office Fax: 773-702-7511, 773-702-6319. Business E-Mail: mmillis@surgery.bsd.uchicago.edu.

MILLOT, JEAN-LOUIS, epidemiologist; b. Noisy-le-sec, France, Aug. 21, 1947; s. Louis Marie Millot and Helene Gilberte Juillerat; m. Marie-Odile Pruvost, Mar. 14, 1970 (dec. Mar. 27, 2005). MD, Faculty Medicine, Lyon, France, 1975; MS in Biomath. and Stats., Faculty Medicine, Kremlin-Bicetre, France, 1985. Pvt. practitioner, Cluses, France, 1976—80; med. advisor EDF Gas de France, Annecy, 1980—. Contbr. articles to profl. jours. Avocations: mountain climbing, climbing. Home: 5 rue des Fondeurs Paccard 74940 Annecy-le-Vieux France Office: EDF GDF Svcs Annecy Leman 5 Blvd Decouz BP 2334 74011 Annecy France Office Phone: 033-0450653685. Office Fax: 033-0450653696. Business E-Mail: jean-louis.millot@erdf-grdf.fr.

MILLS, CHARLES N., healthcare supplies and products company executive; b. Sept. 30, 1961; BS, MBA, Cornell U. With IBM; joined Medline Industries, Mundelein, Ill., 1986, pres. textile divsn., 1991—97, CEO, 1997—. Trustee Lake Forest Hosp. Office: Medline Industries One Medline Pl Mundelein IL 60060 *

MILLS, DORA ANNE, public health service officer; BA, Bowdoin Coll.; MD, Univ. Vt. Coll. Med. Residency Children's Hosp., LA; dir. & chief med. officer Maine Bur. Health, Augusta, 1996—; dir. Maine Ctr. Disease Control and Prevention. Recipient Lightship award, Maine Public Rels. Council. Office: Health & Human Svc Dept 11 State House Sta Augusta ME 04333

MILLS, RICHARD PENCE, ophthalmologist; b. Evanston, Ill., Sept. 13, 1943; s. Glen Earl and Ruth Arlene (Pence) M.; m. Catherine Louise Baily, June 1, 1966 (div. Sept. 1975); 1 child, Lianne Louise; m. Karen Elisabeth, Aug. 1, 1976; children: Elisabeth Ruth, Emily Carole. BA magna cum laude, Yale U., 1964, MD cum laude, 1968. Clin. instr. dept. ophthalmology U. Wash., Seattle, 1972-75, clin. asst. prof., 1975-80, clin. assoc. prof. depts. ophthalmology, medicine, 1980-84, assoc. prof. dept. ophthalmology, 1984-87, prof., vice chmn. dept. ophthalmology, 1987-97, acting chmn. dept. ophthalmology, 1997—99; prof. U. Ky., 1999—2003, chmn., 1999—2003; pvt. practice Glaucoma Cons. NW, Seattle, 2003—. Adj. prof. depts. medicine and neurol. surgery, U. Wash., 1987-99, pres. St. Peter Hosp. Med. Staff, Olympia, Wash., 1982; trustee Bishop Found., Seattle, 1996-99; trustee Prevent Blindness Am., 1998-2000. Author: (books) Glaucoma Surgical Techniques, 1991, Perimetry Update: 1990-91, 1991, Perimetry Update: 1992-93, 1993, 94-95, 95. Surgeon USPHS, 1969-73. Recipient Optic Neuritis Treatment Trial award Nat. Eye Inst., Washington, 1988-91, Collaborative Initial Glaucoma Treatment Study, 1993-97, Collaborative Normal Tension Glaucoma Study award Glaucoma Rsch. Found., San Francisco, 1988-97. Fellow AMA (del. 1996-2001), Am. Acad. Ophthalmology (pres. 1995, chief med. editor EyeNet Mag. 2002-; Honor award 1989, Sr. Honor award 1996, Lifetime Honor award 2007), Found. Am. Acad. Ophthalmology (adv. bd. 2007-10, chief eye Care America, 2007-), Am. Bd. Ophthalmology (bd. dirs. 1998-2005), Wash. Acad. Eye Physicians and Surgeons (pres. 1983, Spl. Honor 1993), Wash. State Med. Assn. (trustee 1996), Am. Glaucoma Soc. (dir. 1993-94, sec. 2006-09), No. Am. Neuro Ophth. Soc., Internat. Perimetric Soc. (sec. 1988-94, treas. 1997-2005). Avocations: piano, hiking. Office: Glaucoma Cons NW 1221 Madison St Ste 1124 Seattle WA 98104 Personal E-mail: rmillswa@comcast.net. *

MILLS-WISNESKI, SHARON MARIE, critical care nurse, educator; b. Phila., June 22, 1952; d. Charles Edward and Hilda Marie (Riley) Ashley. Degree in Nursing, Wesley Coll., 1979, BSN, 1985; MSN, Widener U., 1991, PhD, 2003. ACLS. Charge nurse, med.-surg. ICU Milford (Del.) Meml. Hosp.; clin. instr. Wesley Coll., Dover, Del., Del. Tech. and CC, Dover; critical care per-diem nurse Med. Ctr. Del., Newark; instr. nursing Del. State U., Dover, 1991-95, asst. prof., 1995—2004; postdoc. rsch. fellow U. Mich., Ann Arbor, 2004—07; postdoc. rsch. fellow in women's health U. Mich. Sch. Nursing, Ann Arbor, 2007—; asst. prof. nursing U. Mass., Amherst, 2010—, Oakland U., 2007—; nurse rschr. Kans. Cancer Inst., Detroit, 2007—08. Nurse rschr. women's health disparities Sch. Nursing, U. Mich.; apptd. rev. bd. Del. Medicaid Drug Utilization Rev. Bd., 1993-2004; mem. Del. Bd. Nursing Practice Adv. Com., 1994-2004. Contbr. chapters to books. Recipient Young Publisher of Yr. award Assn. of Black Nursing Faculty, Inc., 1999, Dissertation award Assoc. of Black Nursing Faculty, Inc., 2001; named Faculty Mem. of Yr., Del. Student Nurse Assn., 1999, Young Pub. of Yr., Assn. Black Nursing Faculty, 1999. Mem.: AAUW, AACCN, ANA (nurse strategic action team 1993—, rev. panelist ANA continuing edn. ind. study 1995—97), Quality Life Com., Oncology Nurse Soc., Ann Arbor chpt., Interdisciplinary Rsch. Consortium Health Disparities, Midwest Nurses Rsch. Soc., Am. Lung Assn. (bd. dirs. Del. chpt. 2003—04), Nat. Assn. Black Nurses Inc., Inst. Constituent Mems. in Nursing Practice, Ea. Nurses Rsch. Soc., Del. Nurses Assn. (chmn. nursing practice com. 1992, mng. editor 4 issues The Reporter newspaper 2003—04, pres.-elect 2004—, co-chair, nurse practice com. 2003, Del. Nurse of Yr. 1993), Assn. Black Nursing Faculty, Inc (bd. dirs., state coord., Young Pub. of Yr. 1999, Pres. award 2000, Dissertation award), Wesley Coll. Hon. Soc. Nursing (treas.), Chi Eta Phi, Sigma Theta Tau. Home: 336 Pine Valley Rd Dover DE 19904-7113 Office Phone: 413-545-5089. Personal E-mail: pinevalley2@earthlink.net. Business E-Mail: millswis@nursing.umich.edu.

MILNER, BRENDA ATKINSON LANGFORD, neuropsychologist; b. Manchester, Eng., July 15, 1918; arrived in Can., 1944; d. Samuel and Leslie (Doig) Langford. BA, Cambridge U., Eng., 1939, MA, 1949, DSc, 1972; DSc (hon.), McGill U., 1991, U. Man., 1982; PhD, McGill U., 1952; DSc (hon.), Wesleyan U., 1991, Acadia U., 1991, U. St. Andrews, 1992, U. Hartford, 1997, McMaster U., 1999, Meml. U., 2002; LLD (hon.), Queen's U., 1980, U. Lethbridge, 1986, Mt. Holyoke Coll., 1986, U. Laval, 1987, U. Toronto, 1987, Cambridge U., 2000; LHD (hon.), Mt. St. Vincent U., 1988; Doctorate (hon.), U. Montrèal, 1988, U. Ottawa, 2004; ScD (hon.), Columbia U., 2002, U. Naples II, 2002; ScD, Ryerson U., 2004; DSc (hon.), U. Quebec, Montreal, 2010; DSc, U. Quibec, Bataouais, 2010. Exptl. officer U.K. Ministry of Supply, 1941-44; prof. agrégé Inst. Psychology U. Montreal, 1944-52; rsch. assoc. psychology dept. McGill U., Montreal, 1952—53, lectr. dept. neurology and neurosurgery, 1953-60, from asst. prof. to assoc. prof. psychology, 1960-93, prof. Dept. Neurology and Neurosurgery; Dorothy J. Killam prof. Montreal Neurol. Inst., 1993—. Head neuropsychology rsch. unit Montreal Neurol. Inst., 1953-90; Clothworkers fellow Girton Coll., Cambridge, 1972-73; hon. fellow Newnham Coll., Cambridge, 1989—. Mem. editl. bd. Neuropsychologia, 1973-93, Behavioral Brain Rsch., 1980-88, Hippocampus, 1990-96. Decorated Officer Order of Can., officer Nat. Order of Que., 1985; Career investigator Med. Rsch. Coun. Can., 1964-99; recipient Kathleen Stott prize Newnham Coll., 1971, Karl Spencer Lashley award Am. Philos. Soc., 1979, Izaak Walton Killam Meml. prize Can. Coun., 1983, Hermann Von Helmholtz prize Cognitive Neurosci. Inst., 1984, Penfield award Can. League Against Epilepsy, 1984, Wilder Penfield prize Province of Que., 1993, Neural Plasticity prize Found. IPSEN, Paris, Met. Life Found. award, 1996; named Gt. Montrealer, 1987; named to Can. Med. Hall of Fame, 1997; Hon. mem., European Brain and Behavior Soc., 1999; John P. McGovern award in the Behavioral Sci., Ammerican Assn. to the Advancement of Sci., 2001; D.O. Hebb award, Canadian Soc. for Brain Brain Behaviour and Cognitive Sci., 2001; Micheal Sarrazin award, Club de rechereches cliniques du Québec, 2002; Golden Jubilee Medal Her Majesty Queen Elizabeth II, 2002; Gairdner Found. Internat. award, 2005, Pearl Meister Greengard prize Rockefeller U., 2011; William James fellow American Psychol. Soc., 1989; promoted to Companion of Order of Can., 2004. Fellow APA (Disting. Contbn. award 1973), AAAS, Royal Soc. London, Royal Soc. Can. (McLaughlin medal 1995), Can. Psychol. Assn.; mem. NAS (fgn. assoc., 1976, Award in Neurosciences, 2004), American Epilepsy Soc. (William G. Lennox award 1974, 95), American Neurol. Assn., Association de Psychologie Scientifique de Langue Française, Brit. Soc. Exptl. Psychology, Exptl. Psychol. Soc., Psychonomic Soc., Ea. Psychol. Assn., Internat. Neuropsychology Symposium, Internat. Brain Rsch. Orgn. (exec. sec. 1993-97), Soc. Neurosci. (Ralph W. Gerard prize 1987), American Acad. Neurology (assoc.), Assn. Rsch. in Nervous and Mental Diseases (assoc.), Royal Soc. Medicine (affiliate), European Brain and Behavior Soc. (hon.), American Acad. Arts & Scis. (fgn. mem.), Sigma Xi. Office: Montreal Neurol Inst 3801 University St Montreal PQ Canada H3A 2B4 Office Phone: 514-398-8503. Business E-Mail: brenda.milner@mcgill.ca.

MILNER, ROSS, surgeon, educator; b. Phila., Apr. 18, 1968; s. Martin Sheldon and Janie Lynn Milner; m. Dara Leigh Jacobsohn, Aug. 10, 1996; children: Jake Michael, Callie Grace. BA in Biology, U. Pa., Phila., 1990; MD, U. Pa., 1994. Resident in surgery U. Pa., 1994—2001, fellow in vascular surgery, 2001—02; Marco Polo fellow Utrecht, Netherlands, 2002—03; asst. prof. surgeon Emory U. Sch. Medicine, Atlanta, 2003—. Grantee Wallace Coulter award, Ga. Inst. Tech., 2007. Office: Emory Univ Sch Medicine 1364 Clifton Rd NE Ste H-122 Atlanta GA 30322 Office Fax: 404-727-3316. Business E-Mail: ross.milner@emoryhealthcare.org.

MILOSAVLJEVIC, ALEKSANDAR, medical geneticist, educator; MS, Santa Clara U., 1986; PhD, U. Calif., Santa Cruz, 1990. Assoc. prof. dept. molecular & human genetics Baylor Coll. Medicine. Office: Human Genome Sequencing Center Baylor College of Medicine One Baylor Plaza MS BCM226 Houston TX 77030 Office Phone: 713-798-8719. Office Fax: 713-798-4373. E-mail: amilosav@bcm.edu.

MILOSESCU, PANTELIMON, sports medicine physician, researcher; b. Bala Mehedinti, Oltenia, Romania, July 26, 1928; s. Ion and Eleonora (Petrescu) Milosescu; m. Carmela Munteanu, Dec. 30, 1964; 1 child, Daniela Josefina. MD with honors, Inst. Medicine Carol Davila, Bucharest, Romania, 1953. Chief physician Calafat Hosp., Oltenia, Romania, 1953—59; lectr. Inst. Medicine Carol Davila, Bucharest, 1959—67; chief physician Coutscufino Hosp., 1967—90, Cobentina Hosp., 1990—96; pvt. practice Santa Maria Surgery, Romania, 1995—2006. Author: Olfactia, Gustal, Vertijele- Patologia si terapeutica sistemuli ventibular, Micofele Câ lor aero-digestive si auriculerte, Zgonistele auriculerte, Ozena, Drn tracutal spitalulu Colentina, Retete magistrate diu practica medicata a secolului XX, Drn trecutal Spritalului clinic central de Copu Srigore Alexandrescu Primal spital de cofii; author: (with C.I Bercus) Drn trecutal ore in Romania; contbr. chapters to books, scientific papers, articles to profl. jours. Recipient medicine awards, Romanian Ministry of Health, 1953—2005. Orthodox. Avocations: literature, music. Home: Dr Lister Nr 44A, Apt 1 50544 Bucharest Romania

MILSOM, JEFFREY, colon and rectal surgeon, educator; Grad. summa cum laude, U. Pa., Phia.; MD, U. Pitts., Pa., 1979. Diplomate Am. Bd. Colon and Rectal Surgery, 1986. Resident surgery St. Luke's Roosevelt Hosp., NYC, 1980—81, Univ. Va. Med. Ctr., Charlottesville, 1981—84, chief resident; fellow colon & rectal surgery Ferguson Hosp., Grand Rapids, Mich., 1984—85; prof. surgery Weill Med. Coll. Cornell Univ.; chief colon and rectal surgery NY Presbyn. Hosp. Weill Cornell Med. Ctr., program dir. residency tng. laparoscopic & conventional and rectal surgery; asst. prof. Mich. State Univ., Eat Lansing, 1986—89; dir. dept. surgical rsch. Ferguson Clinic, 1986—89; dir. rsch. minimally invasive surgery ctr. Cleveland Clinic, 1997—98; prof. surgery Mt. Sinai Med. Ctr., NYC, 1998, chief. divsn. colorectal surgery, co-dir. minimally invasive surgery. Mem. oper. room new tech, com. Mt. Sinai Med. Ctr., mem. minimal access surgical com.; participated laparoendoscopic surgical edn. Com. Assn. Program Dirs. Colon & Rectal Surgery; sr. examiner Am. Bd. Colon and Rectal Surgeons; reviewer Surgical Endoscopy, Diseases of the Colon & Rectum, Annals of Surgery. Sr. editor WebSurg. Dir. rsch. dept. colorectal surgery CLeveland Clinic Found., 1990—98. Fellow: Soc. Surgical Oncology, Am. Coll. Surgeons, Am. Soc. Colon & Rectal Surgeons (emerging technologies com.); mem.: Soc. Am. Gastrointestinal Endoscopic Surgeons, 14 prestigious profl. socs. Office: New York Presbyterian Hospital Weill Cornell Medical Center 1315 York Ave 2nd Fl New York NY 10021 Office Phone: 212-746-6030. Office Fax: 212-746-6370.

MILTIADOUS, GEORGE ANDREAS, internist, researcher; b. Nicosia, Cyprus, Sept. 13, 1971; s. Andreas George Miltiadous and Agathi Andreas Miltiadou; m. Agni Theodoros Procopiou, Jan. 9, 1978. MD, U. Ioannina, Greece, 1997—2007, PhD (hon.), 2003. Ho. officer, internal medicine clinic U. Hosp. Ioannina, 2001—. Rsch. fellow U. Ioannina, Dept. Internal Medicine, 2001—. Achievements include research in novel LDL receptor mutation causing familial hypercholesterolaemia in Greek patients. Office: Univ Hosp Ioannina Douroudi Ioannina 45110 Greece Home: Komninis Annas 4 452 21 Ioannina Greece Personal E-mail: me00521@cc.uoi.gr.

MILUNSKY, AUBREY, geneticist, pediatrician, educator; b. Johannesburg, Nov. 3, 1936; came to U.S., 1969; 1 child, Jeffrey M. MB, BCh, U. Witwatersand, Johannesburg, 1960, DSc, 1982; postgrad., Gt. Ormond St. Hosp., London, 1965. Diplomate Am. Bd. Pediatrics, Am. Bd. Med. Genetics. Intern Johannesburg Gen. Hosp./Baragwanath Hosp., Johannesburg, 1961; resident in internal medicine and pediat. Baragwanath Hosp., 1961-64; pediat. registrar Queen Mary's Hosp. for Children, Surrey, Eng., 1965-66; asst. pediatrician New England Med. Ctr. Tufts U., Boston, 1966-70, from instr. to asst. prof. pediat. Sch. Medicine, 1966-70; rsch. fellow and assoc. in neurology Mass. Gen. Hosp./Harvard Med. Sch., Boston, 1969-70; dir. Birth Defects and Genetics Clinic Mass. Gen. Hosp., Boston, 1971-73, asst. pediatrician, 1971-82, assoc. dir. Cystic Fibrosis Clinic, 1975-79; asst. prof. pediatrics Harvard Med. Sch., Boston, 1971-81; prof. pediatrics and ob-gyn. Sch. Medicine, dir. Ctr. for Human Genetics, assoc. physician Univ. Hosp. Boston U., 1981—, prof. pathology, 1985—, Endowed chair human genetics, 1991—; pediatrician Boston City Hosp., 1981—. Mem. Mass. State Genetics Adv. Bd., 1983-84; profl. adv. bd. Nat. Tuberous Sclerosis Assn., 1990-93; quality assurance com. New England Regional Genetics Group, 1990-96. Author: The Prenatal Diagnosis of Hereditary Disorders, 1973, Know Your Genes, 1977, How to Have the Healthiest Baby You Can., 1987, Choices, Not Chances: An Essential Guide to your Heredity and Health, 1989, Heredity and Your Family's Health, 1992, Your Genetic Destiny: Know Your Genes, Secure Your Health, Save Your Life, 2001, Your Genes, Your Health: A Critical Family Guide That Could Save Your Life, 2011; editor: Clinics in Perinatology, Vol. II, 1974, The Prevention of Genetic Disease and Mental Retardation, 1975, Genetic Disorders and the Fetus: Diagnosis, Prevention and Treatment, 6th edit., 2010, Coping with Crisis and Handicap, 1981, (with G.J. Annas) Genetics and the Law 1, 1976, Genetics and the Law II, 1980, Genetics and the Law III, 1986, (with E.A. Friedman and L. Gluck) Advances in Perinatal Medicine, 1981, Vol. II, 1982, Vol. III, 1983, Vol. IV, 1985, Vol. V, 1986; mem. editl. bd. Am. Jour. Law and Medicine, 1974-93, Am. Jour. Med. Genetics, 1977-94, Bioethics Digest, 1977-78, Prenatal Diagnosis, 1980-90, 92—, Intelligence Reports in Ob-Gyn., 1982-88, Fetal Therapy, 1986—; peer reviewer New England Jour. Medicine, Pediatrics, Am. Jour. Med. Genetics, Am. Jour. Ob-Gyn., Am. Jour. Law and Medicine, Am. Jour. Pub. Health, Prenatal Diagnosis, Fetal Therapy, Ob-Gyn., Epidemiology, Jour. Pediatrics; contbr. over 300 articles to profl. jours. Recipient First Place Film award Nat. Coun. Family Rels. Media Awards Co., 1990, Tinsley Harrison award So. Soc. for Clin. Investigation, 1991; Aubrey Milunsky Endowed Chair in Human Genetics named in his honor Boston U., 1991. Fellow Am. Coll. Med. Genetics (founding), Royal Coll. Physicians (diploma in child health 1965); mem. Am. Pediat. Soc., Am. Soc. Human Genetics (social issues com. 1983-87), Am. Soc. Law and Medicine (v.p. 1982-83, pres.-elect 1983-85, pres. 1985-86, bd. dirs. 1986-88, 90-93), Soc. for Pediat. Rsch., Mass. Med. Soc. Office: Boston U Sch Medicine Ctr for Human Genetics 715 Albany St Boston MA 02118-2307

MIMICA, MARKO, gynecologist, researcher; b. Split, Croatia, Oct. 29, 1960; s. Ivan and Ruth (Fischbach) M.; m. Radojka Ulić, May 14, 1994; children: Dorotea, Bianka, Ivan. MD, U. Zagreb, Croatia, 1985; MSc, U. Rijeka, Croatia, 1996; specialist in ob-gyn., U. Zagreb, 1996; PhD, U. Split, Crotia, 2010. Rsch. fellow Clin. Hosp., Split, 1988-92, ob-gyn. staff, 1992-96, gynecologist, 1996—. Contbr. articles to profl. med. jours. Mem. Croatian Med. Assn. Avocations: photography, sports. Home: Šime Ljubica 14 21000 Split Croatia Office: Gynenova Polyclinic Istarska 21 21000 Split Croatia Business E-Mail: marko.mimica1@st.t-com.hr.

MIMICA, NINOSLAV, psychiatrist; b. Zagreb, Croatia, June 20, 1959; s. Milorad-Miro and Nikica-Nine (Majstorović) Mimica; m. Nevenka-Nena Vajdić, May 8, 1982; children: Nina, Mislav. MD, U. Zagreb, Croatia, 1987; postgrad., Inter U. Ctr., Dubrovnik, Croatia, 1987; MSc, U. Zagreb, 1994, DSc, 2002. Primarius Min. Health, Republic of Croatia, 2005, subspecialist in biol. psychiatry Min. Health, Republic of Croatia, 2007, subspecialist in forensic psychiatry Min. Health, Republic of Croatia, 2007. Physician Clin. Hosp. (now Sestre Milosrdnice), Zagreb, Croatia, 1988—89, Clin. Psychiat. Hosp. Vrapče, Zagreb, Croatia, 1989—94; cons. psychiatrist Psychiat. Hosp. Vrapče, Zagreb, Croatia, 1994—. Guest investigator Psychiat. Inst. Columbia U., NYC, 1991; cons. psychiatrist Gen. Hosp. Knin, Croatia, 1996; cons. rschr. Croatian Inst. Brain Rsch., Zagreb, 1994—, Dept. Psychiat. Rsch., Zagreb, 1994—; asst. prof. psychiatry Sch. Medicine U. Zagreb, 2007—; lectr. in field. Contbr. articles to profl. jours. Recipient Young Scientist award, Biennial European Workshop Schizophrenia, Switzerland, 1994, 1996, Sr. Scientist award, 2002, 2004; Roche Edn. grantee, Budapest, Hungary, 1993. Mem.: Alzheimer Europe, World Fedn. Socs. Biol. Psychiatry, Alzheimer's Disease Internat., Croatian Assn. Med. Anthropology, Croatian Assn. Biol. Psychiatry and Psychopharmacology, Croatian Psychiat. Soc., European Assn. Psychiatry. Avocations: conchology, movies, gardening, walking, fishing. Home: Bolnička cesta 29 HR 10090 Zagreb Croatia Office: U Dept Psy/Psy Hosp Vrapče Bolnička cesta 32 HR 10090 Zagreb Croatia Office Phone: 385 1 3780 678. Business E-Mail: ninoslav.mimica@bolnica-vrapce.hr.

MIMURA, HIROSHI, orthodontist; b. Nagano, Japan, Feb. 23, 1960; DDS, Nihon U. Sch. Dentistry, 1985; PhD, Tokyo Med. and Dental U., 1989. Assoc. prof. Matsumoto Dental U., 1991—95; dir. Mimura Orthodontic Office, 1995—. Exec. dir. Japanese Assn. Orthodontists, 2011. Mem.: MOrth RCSEd, European Bd. Orthodontists. Office: Takano Bldg 6F 2-15-11 Nishi-Tokyo Tokyo 188-0001 Japan Office Fax: 81-424-3983. Business E-Mail: mimura@m-ortho.com.

MIMURA, TOSHIKI, gastroenterologist, educator; b. Japan, May 3, 1963; MD, Tokyo U., PhD, 1988. Prof., dir., Pelvic Fl. Ctr. Kochi Med. Sch. Hosp., 2008—. Fellow: Japan Soc. Coloproctology, Japanese Soc. Gastroent. Surgery, Japan Surg. Soc.; mem.: Am. Gastroenterology Assn. Avocations: running, tennis, ping pong/table tennis. Office: 185-1 Kohasu Oko-cho Nankoku Kochi 783-8505 Japan Office Fax: 81-(0)88-880-2574. E-mail: mimura0523@aol.com.

MIN, BALSHIK, pathologist; b. Seoul, Republic of Korea, Jan. 15, 1942; arrived in USA, 1971, naturalized, 2007; s. Young-Ock and Yang-Hee (Kim) Min; m. Jungsoon Ahn, Apr. 25, 1970; children: James, Susan. MD, Seoul Nat. U., 1966. Pathologist Faxton-St. Luke's Healthcare, Utica, NY, 1978—, dir. labs., 1984—2005; pathologist Centrex Clin. Labs., New Hartford, NY, 1978—, dir. labs., 1990—96; pathologist Rome Meml. Hosp., NY, 2005—, dir. labs., 2005—07. Capt. Republic of Korea Army, 1966—70. Fellow: Coll. Am. Pathologists; mem.: AMA, Ctrl. NY Acad. Medicine, Nat. Soc. Histotechnology, Am. Soc. Clin. Pathology. Republican. Avocations: reading, classical music, gardening, golf. Office: Centrex Clinical Lab 1656 Champlin Ave Utica NY 13502 Home Phone: 315-793-3238.

MIN, BYUNG-WOO, orthopaedic surgeon, educator; b. Daegu, Republic of Korea, Dec. 26, 1959; s. Won-Sik Min and Yil-Sang Lee; m. Hee-Jung Lee, July 27, 1987; children: Eun-Gee, Yoon-Gee. MD, Kyungbook Nat. U., Daegu, 1984, PhD, 1995. Lic. MD Ministry of Health and Welfare, Korea, 1984, diplomate Korean Bd. Orthopaedic Surgeon 1989, cert. Ednl. Commn. Fgn. Med. Grads., 1996. Intern Keimyung U., Daegu, Republic of Korea, 1984—85, resident, 1985—89, instr., 1992—94, asst. prof., 1995—98, assoc. prof., 1999—; chief orthop. surgery Yechon Mil. Hosp., Republic of Korea, 1989—92; clin. fellow U. So. Calif., Arthritis Ctr., LA, 1996—98. Staff, orthopaedic surgery Dongsan Med. Ctr., Daegu, 1992—. Contbr. articles to profl. jours. Lt. comdr. Air Force, 1989—92, Yechon. Mem.: Korean Fracture Soc. (licentiate Acad. award 1996), Soc. Internat. Chirurgie Orthopedique Traumatologic (licentiate), Western Pacific Orthopaedic Assn. (licentiate), Korean Hip Soc. (licentiate Acad. award 2001), Korean Orthopaedic Assn. (licentiate Poster award 2000), Korean Med. Assn. (licentiate). Home: 102/1006 Hoban Apt Jisandong Soosungu 706-090 Daegu Daegu Republic of Korea Home Phone: 82-53-250-7204. Office Fax: +82-53-250-7205; Home Fax: +82-53-250-7205. Business E-Mail: min@dsmc.or.kr.

MIN, GYESIK, cellular physiology professor; b. Jinju, Gyeongsangnam-Do, Republic of Korea, Aug. 18, 1960; s. Youngbu Min and Sookae Kwon; m. Sungju Hong; children: David Hong, Duun Justin Hong. BAS, Konkuk U., Seoul, 1986; MS in Physiology, U. Ill., Urbana-Champaign, 1994, PhD in Physiology, 1997. Postdoctoral fellow Stanford U., Calif., 1997—99; sr. post-doctoral rsch. fellow U. Ill. at Urbana-Champaign, 1999—2001, instr. endocrinology, 2001; asst. prof. Jinju Nat. U., Gyeongsangnam-Do, Republic of Korea, 2001—. Tchg. asst. human physiology, endocrinology and immunocytochemistry U. Ill.-Urbana-Champaign, 1992—96; reviewer abstracts for 30th ann. meeting Soc. Reprodn., 1997; mem. health tech. planning and evaluation bd. for health genomic project Korea Health Industry Devel. Inst., 2004—05. Contbr. articles to profl. jours.; author: Human Physiology, 2006, The Cell: Molecular Approach, 2006. Vol. Korean Red Cross. Grantee, Korean Sci. and Engring. Found., 2002—05, Korean Agrl. R&D Promotion Ctr., 2004—07; Dean's Fellowship, Stanford U. Med. Sch., 1998, Rsch. Grants Fellowship, Lalor Found., 1998. Mem.: Korean Soc. Molecular and Cellular Biology (assoc.). Roman Catholic. Achievements include discovery of relaxin-binding sites in pig and human tissues; research in the role of growth differntiation factor-9 in promoting growth and differentiation of ovarian follicles; mechanism of nuclear translocation and activation of constitutive androstane receptor; identification of cross-talk between estrogen receptor and constitutively activated androstane receptor; mechanism of CAR/RXR-mediated activation of the CYP2B1 phenobarbital-responsive unit; Relaxin's effects on cellular proliferation. Avocations: reading, hiking, travel, violin. Office: Jinju Nat Univ Chilam-Dong 150 660-758 Jinju Gyeongsangnam-do Republic of Korea Office Fax: 055-751-3399. Business E-Mail: g-min@jinju.ac.kr.

MIN, JUN-HONG, neurosurgeon; b. Seoul, Republic of Korea, Sept. 26, 1971; s. Min Kyoung-Chil and Bong-Hee Park; m. Joo-Yeon Ryu, Oct. 3, 2002; children: Ra-Hee, Ra-Eun. MD, Korea U., Seoul, 1996, MS in Neurosurgery, 2001, PhD in Neurosurgery, 2006. Intern Korea U. Med. Ctr., 1996—97, resident, 1997—2001, asst. prof. dept. neurosurgery, 2005—; chief, dept. neurosurgery Capital Armed Forces Hosp., Gyeonggi-do, 2002—04, Seoul Wooridal Hosp., Seoul, 2007—. Contbr. articles to profl. jours. Fellow, Korea U. Med. Ctr., 2004—05, Seoul Wooridul Hosp., 2005—06. Mem.: Korean Spinal Neurosurgery Soc., Korean Neurosurg. Soc. Office: Seoul Wooridul Hosp Dept Neurosurgery 676 GuaHae-dong Gangseo-gu Seoul 157-822 Republic of Korea Office Fax: 82 2 2660 7599. Business E-Mail: apuzo@rivav.com.

MIN, TAESUN, program director; Postgrad., Seoul Nat. U., 2003. Cert. valuation analyst KVA, Seoul, 2005; postdoctoral rschr. U. Calif., Davis. Sr. advisor Assn. Korea-China Cooperation. Office: KOSEF 180-1 Kaneong-Dong 305-350 Daejeon Daejeon Republic of Korea

MINAKAMI, KOREBUMI, medical school educator; b. Kumamoto, Japan, Apr. 17, 1944; s. Masatoshi and Kinu (Ishibashi) M.; m. Michiko Tanoue, Mar. 25, 1970; children: Kanae, Yoshie. BF, Kagoshima U., Japan, 1967, DF, 1968, PhD, 1994; MSc, Kumamoto U., Japan, 1970. Asst. prof. Kagoshima (Japan) U., 1970-86, assoc. prof., 1986-93, prof., 1993—. JICA expert U. Ghana, Accra, 1980-81; vis. prof. Aston U., Birmingham, Eng., 1995. Contbr. articles to profl. jours. Grantee Ministry of Edn., 1995. Mem. Zool. Soc. Japan, Japanese Pharmacological Soc., Japanese Soc. Parasitology, Herpetological Soc. Japan, Japanese Assn. Lab. Animal Sci., Brit. Assn. Psychopharmacology. Avocations: reading, music, painting, mountain climbing, sightseeing. Office: Kagoshima U Sch Health Sci Pub Health Nursing Nurse Informatics and Biology 8-35-1 Sakuragaoka Kagoshima 890-8506 Japan Home Phone: 099-258-1296; Office Phone: +099-275-6742. Personal E-mail: biomina@health.nop.kagoshima-u.ac.jp. Business E-Mail: minakami@health.nop.kagoshima-u.ac.jp.

MINAMI, KATSUHIRO, dentist, educator; b. Japan, July 19, 1960; PhD, Osaka U. Grad. Sch., 1991. Assoc. prof. faculty dentistry Aichi Gakuin U., 2005—. Office: 2-11 Suemori Chikusa Nagoya Aichi 464-8651 Japan Business E-Mail: k-minami@dpc.agu.ac.jp.

MINAMIDE, SEIKI, biomedical educator, researcher; b. Yoichi Town, Hokkaido, Japan, July 8, 1942; s. Masatoshi and Shima (Abe) M.; m. Hiroko Hagiwara, Apr. 10, 1971; children: Rena, Remi. BSc in Vet. Medicine, Hokkaido U., 1969. Sect. leader Kisseipharm. Co. Ltd., Matsumoto, 1969-78; asst. prof. Teikyo U., Tokyo, 1978-82; dir. Nihon Kayaku, Tokyo, 1982-86, Japan Immuno Rsch. Lab., Takasaki, Japan, 1987-96; rsch. fellow Biomembrane Inst., Seattle, 1986-87; lectr. dept. lab. sci. Gunma U., Maebashi, Japan, 1996—2003. Contbr. articles to sci. jours. Mem. Democratic Party. Achievements include elucidation of mechanism of human epidermal renewal. Home: Yamana machi 1671-109 Takasaki 370-1213 Japan Office: Hills Internat Yamana machi 1671-108 Takasaki 370-1213 Japan Office Phone: 027-346-4894.

MINAS, IRAKLIS HARRY, psychiatrist, educator, science association director; s. Matheos and Zoi Minas; m. Christine Tangas, Jan. 7, 1979; children: Stephen Matthew, James Alexander. BMedSc, Med. Sch. U. Melbourne, Victoria, Australia, 1972, MBBS, 1975, DPM, 1986. Cons. psychiatrist Royal Pk. Hosp., Melbourne, 1986—89, St. Vincent's Hosp., Melbourne, 1988—89; dir. Victorian Transcultural Psychiatry Unit, Melbourne, 1989—, Ctr. Cultural Studies Health, Melbourne, 1996—2000, Ctr. Internat. Mental Health, Melbourne, 2000—; co-dir. WHO Collaborating Ctr. Rsch. and Tng. Mental Health and Substance Abuse, Melbourne, 2000—; mem., ministerial adv. group immigration detention Dept. Immigration and Citizenship, Canberra, Act, Australia, 2001—, chmn., detention health adv. group, 2006—; hon. lectr. Harvard Med. Sch., Cambridge, Mass., 2002—; vis. prof. Taipei Med. U., Taiwan, 2008—. Cons. WHO, Internat. Orgn. Migration, Australian AID. Contbg. editor numerous profl. jours. Fellow: Royal Australian and New Zealand Coll. Psychiatrists; mem.: World Assn. Social Psychiatry, Australian Pub. Health Assn., Australian Med. Assn., Pacific Rim Coll. Psychiatrists. Office: Univ Melbourne 207 Bouverie St Parkville Victoria 3010 Australia Office Fax: 61393482794. Business E-Mail: h.minas@unimelb.edu.au.

MINAS, TOM, surgeon, educator; b. Can., Feb. 27, 1958; MD, U. Toronto, 1982, Harvard Sch. Pub. Health, 1991. Physician Brigham and Women's Hosp., 1989—, asst. prof., 2000—. Mem.: Am. Bd. Orthop. Surgery. Office: 850 Boylston St Ste 112 Chestnut Hill MA 02467 Office Fax: 617-732-9272. Business E-Mail: tminas@partners.org.

MINASIAN-BATMANIAN, LAURA CORINNE, education educator, researcher; b. Bucharest, Romania, May 1, 1950; d. Agop and Elisabeta Minasian; m. Vahan Batmanian, May 30, 1975; children: Julia Jasmine Batmanian, Andrew Vahan Batmanian. BSc Hons, U. Melbourne, Australia, 1971, PhD, 1976. Tutor St Hilda's Coll./Women's Coll., Parkville, Victoria, Australia, 1972—74, Cumberland Coll. of Health Scs./St John's Coll., Lidcombe/Camperdown, Nsw, Australia, 1976—77; lectr. iii Cumberland Coll. of Health Scis., Lidcombe, Nsw, Australia, 1977—79, lectr. ii, 1979—84; lectr. Cumberland Coll. of Health Scis./U. Sydney, Lidcombe, Nsw, Australia, 1984—2000; sr. lectr. U. Sydney, Lidcombe, Nsw, Australia, 2000—03. Contbr. chapters to books, articles to profl. jour. Recipient Vice-Chancellor's Award for Outstanding Tchg., U. Sydney, 2003, Pearson Edn. U. Sci. Tchg. award, 2003, Tchg. award, Sch. Biomedical Sci., 2002—03; finalist Innovation Challenge, U. Sydney, 2005; grantee, 1995—2006; fellow Tchg. Fellowship, Ctr. for Tchg. and Learning, 1996, Centre for Tchg. and Learning, 1996; Tchg. grants, 2000—09. Mem.: Rsch. Inst. for Asia and the Pacific, Australian Cancer Soc. Achievements include development of A novel online problem-based ultrasonography subject; design of Adaptation of WebCT as a pedagogical infrastructure to enhance interactive problem-based learning in oncology at undergraduate level; development of A novel case study presentation of pathophysiology; design of Research-led teaching at undergraduate level; first to Student-centred perspectives, especially in online teaching and learning; development of A technique for isolating pure, viable parenchymal cells and their nuclei from rat mammary gland; research in Progesterone, dimethylbenzanthracene and carcinogenesis. Avocations: music, reading, chess, bushwalking, gardening. Office: U Sydney East St Nsw Lidcombe 2141 Australia Office Fax: +61 2 93519520. Business E-Mail: laurabatmanian@sydney.edu.au.

MINCHUL, KANG, medical researcher; b. Republic of Korea, June 22, 1970; PhD, U. Minn., 2005. Rsch. fellow Vanderbilt Sch. Medicine, 2005—. Mem.: Biophys. Soc. Office: Vanderbilt University Sch Medicine Goodlettsville TN 37072 Business E-Mail: minchul.kang@vanderbilt.edu.

MINCKLER, DON SAIER, ophthalmologist, educator; b. Mpls., July 12, 1939; m. Ann Marie Welling, 1981; 3 children. BA, Reed Coll., 1962; MD, U. Oreg., Portland, 1964. Commd. ensign USN, 1963, advanced through grades to lt. comdr., 1967, resigned, 1971; intern US Naval Hosp., San Diego, 1964-65; resident in gen. pathology and ophthalmology U. Wash., Seattle, 1968-73; fellow in ophthalmic pathology Armed Forces Inst. of Pathology, Washington, 1973-75; chief of ophthalmology VA Hosp., Seattle, 1975-76; in-svc. tng. resident U. So. Calif., LA, 1976-78, asst. prof. ophthalmology, asst. prof. pathology, 1976-79, assoc. prof. pathology, 1979-84, prof. ophthalmology, 1984—, dir. glaucoma svcs., 1988—. Dir. glaucoma svcs. Estelle Doheny Eye Found., LA, 1982-87; adj. assoc. mem. dept. basic and clin. rsch. Scripps Clinic and Rsch. Found., La Jolla, Calif., 1988; cons. VA Hosp., San Francisco, 1981-82, US Naval Hosp., San Diego, 1988-89; vis. prof. various schs. including U. Calif., Davis, 1994, U. Ill., Chgo., 1995, U. Fla., Gainesville, 1996. Editor-in-chief Ophthalmology, 1995—; contbr. more than 100 articles to profl. jours. Fellow Glaucoma Shalter Assn., U. Calif. San Francisco. Mem. Am. Bd. Opthalmology (current chair, dir.), Am. Acad. Ophthalmology, Am. Assn. Ophthalmic Pathologists, Am. Glaucoma Soc., Am. Ophthal. Soc., Assn. of Ophthalmic Alumni of the Armed Forces Inst. Pathology, Assn. for Rsch. in Vision and Ophthalmology, Glaucoma Soc. So. Calif., LA County Ophthalmology Soc., Michael Hogan Eye Pathology Soc., Glaucoma Rsch. Soc. Internat. Congress of Ophthalmology (organizing com. 1986—), Profl. Staff Assn. U. So. Calif., Shaffer Soc., West Coast Glaucoma Study Club. Office: U Calif Irvine Dept Ophthalmology 118 Med Surgical Irvine CA 92697 Home Phone: 760-942-5250; Office Phone: 949-824-8089. Business E-Mail: minckler@uci.edu.

MINDE, JAN KARE, surgeon, consultant; b. Gellivare, Sweden, Feb. 27, 1954; s. Gun Minde; m. Anita Gunvor Stockel, June 26; children: Peder, Jenny Redinger, Robert. MD, PhD, Umea U., 2006. Cert. in orthop. surgery Sweden, 1989. Lt. Field Hosp., Sweden, 1983—96; sr. cons. Gellivare Hosp., Sweden, 1989—, chief surgeon, 2001—; sr. cons. orthop. surgery Harstad Hosp., Norway, 2000—06. Sec. Luth. Ch., 1990—. Lutheran. Achievements include discovery and research of hereditar sensory autonomic neuropathy, Norrbottnian insensitivity to pain (HSAN type V); genetic mutation patent. Avocations: fishing, book binding, old books. Home: Skogssnavav 7 Gellivare 982 35 Sweden Office: Gellivare hosp NLL Kallg 14 Gellivare 982 32 Sweden Home Phone: 4697014461; Office Phone: 4697019000. Office Fax: 4697019259. Personal E-mail: janminde@gmail.com. Business E-Mail: jan.minde@nll.se.

MINDELL, EUGENE ROBERT, surgeon, educator; b. Chgo., Feb. 24, 1922; s. Leon and Tillie (Rosenthal) M.; m. June A. Abrams, Sept. 19, 1945; children: Barbara, Ruth, David, Douglas. BS, U. Chgo.,

1943, MD, 1945. Diplomate Am. Bd. Orthopaedic Surgery (bd. dir. 1977-84, pres. 1983-84). Resident in orthopaedic surgery U. Chgo. Clinics, 1948-52; instr. U. Chgo., 1952; mem. faculty dept. orthopaedic surgery Sch. Medicine SUNY, Buffalo, 1953—, prof. Sch. Medicine, 1964—; chmn. dept. SUNY Sch. Medicine, Buffalo, 1964-88, dir. orthopaedic oncology Sch. Medicine, 1988—. Mem. bd. mgrs. Erie County Med. Ctr., 1990-96. Assoc. editor Jour. Bone and Joint Surgery, 1984-88, trustee, 1991—; dep. editor Clin. Orthopaedics and Related Rsch. representing Musculoskeletal Tumor Soc., 1997—; contbr. articles to profl. jours. Lt. (j.g.) M.C. USNR, 1946-48. Eugene R. Mindell Endowed Chair of Orthopaedic Surgery established in his honor SUNY, Buffalo, 1996, chair fully funded, 2008; recipient Disting. Svc. award Alumni U. Chgo. Sch. Medicine, 1990, award for achievement in health care D'Youville Coll., 2002, Lifetime Acheivement Excellence in Tchg. award, SUNY Buffalo Dept. Orthop. Surgery, 2002; NRC fellow, 1949-50. Fellow ACS; mem. Am. Acad. Orthopaedic Surgeons (bd. dirs. 1991-92), Am. Orthopaedic Assn. (v.p. 1990-91), Assn. Orthopaedic Chmn., Am. Assn. Surgery of Trauma, Am. Orthopaedic Rsch. Soc. (pres. 1972-73, residency rev. com. 1985-91), Musculoskeletal Tumor Soc. (pres. 1989-90), Coun. Musculoskeletal Specialty Socs. (chmn. elect 1991, chmn. 1992). Jewish. Office: 100 High St Buffalo NY 14203-1126 Home: 705 Renaissance Dr Apt T218 Williamsville NY 14221-8030 Home Phone: 716-929-5726; Office Phone: 716-859-1293. Business E-Mail: emindell@kaleidehealth.org.

MINEMATSU, KAZUO, neurologist, director; b. Ohmuta, Dec. 19, 1952; MD, Kyushu U., 1977. Staff physician stroke care unit Nat. Cardiovasc. Ctr., 1982—87, chief cerebrovascular lab., Rsch. Inst., 1987—95, dir. cerebrovascular divsn., dept. medicine, 1995—2010; dep. dir. gen. hosp. Nat. Cerebral and Cardiovasc. Ctr., 2010—. Bd. dirs. Japan Stroke Soc., 2006, World Stroke Orgn., 2008, Japan Stroke Assn., 2008, Japanese Soc. Cerebral Blood Flow and Metabolism, 2010; pres. Japan Acad. Neurosonology, 2010. Recipient Mihara award, Charitable Trust Mihara Cerebrovascular Disorder Rsch. Promotion Fund. Mem.: Am. Heart Assn., Internat. Soc. Cerebral Blood Flow and Metabolism, Am. Stroke Assn. Avocations: research of ancient history of japan, walking. Office: 5-7-1 Fujishirodai Suita Osaka 565-8565 Japan Office Fax: 81-6-6835-5267. Business E-Mail: kminemat@hsp.ncvc.go.jp.

MINEUR, LAURENT, oncologist; b. Luzy, France, Aug. 15, 1967; MD, 1999. Head clin. rsch. dept. Sainte Catherine Inst., 2008—11, oncologist and radiotherapy, 1999—2011. Tchg. Nurse Sch. Avignon, 2007—11, AFCOR, 2005—11. Decorated médaille de la défense nationale France; grant, Chef De Clinique Des Universités. Master: Provence Stomy Contact; mem.: Chevaliers Du Tastevin, EORTC, SFRO, ASCO. Avocations: winemaking, archaeology, tennis. Home: Chemin De La Fougasse La Calade Le Thor Vaucluse 840250 France Business E-Mail: l.mineur@isc84.org.

MINFORD, EUNICE JANE, surgeon, holistic consultant, esoteric healer; b. Antrim, Northern Ireland, Oct. 21, 1965; d. James Owen Baird and Martha Joyce Minford. MBChB, Aberdeen U., 1989; MA, Nat. U. Ireland, Dublin, 2007—09. Cert. in surgical tng. RCS Edinburgh, 2001; interfaith minister Interfaith Sem., London, 2006; in esoteric healing 2007, in med. edn. 2011. Resident HO. officer Aberdeen Royal Infirmary, Grampian, Scotland, 1989—90, sr. HO. officer surgery, 1990—94; registrar gen. surgery & transplantation U. Newcastle & Freeman Hosp., Northumberland, England, 1994—2000; specialist registrar hepatobiliary & liver transplant Queen Elizabeth Hosp., Brimingham, 2000—01; locum cons. gen., vascular & trauma surgery Royal London Hosp., 2001—02; transplant fellow recanti-miller transplant inst. Mt. Sinai Hosp., NYC, 2002—03; cons. gen. surgeon No. Health & Social Care trust, Antrim, Northern Ireland, 2004—; holistic cons., esoteric healer, 2009. Author: The Soulful Doctor, 2011; contbr. articles to profl. jours. Fellow: RCS. Avocations: travel, reading, walking, gardening, swimming. Office: Antrim Area Hosp Bush Rd Antrim Co Antrim BT 41 2RL Northern Ireland Office Phone: 00442894424000, 07770414758. Personal E-mail: eunice@thesoulfuldoctor.co.uk. E-mail: eunice.minford@northerntrust.hscni.net.

MING, GUAN, molecular pathologist, researcher; b. Nanchang, Jiangxi, China, Oct. 29, 1970; PhD, Fudan U., Shanghai, 2003. Rsch. assoc. Hua Shan Hosp., Fudan U., Shanghai, 1998—2001, assoc. prof., 2002—. Vis. scholar Chinese Univ. of Hong Kong, 2001—02; vis. prof. Kantonsspital Aarau, Switzerland, 2003. Contbr. articles to profl. jours. Grantee Nat. Natural Sci. Found. of China, Inspection Com. of the Nat. Natural Sci. Found. of China, 2003. Achievements include patents pending for Tree Analysis of Mass Spectral Urine Profiles Discriminates Transitional Cell Carcinoma of the Bladder from Non-cancer Patient. Office: Hua Shan Hosp Fudan Univ 12 Central Urumqi Rd Shanghai 200040 China E-mail: guanming88@yahoo.com.

MING, MICHAEL EUDENE, dermatologist, educator; s. Si-Chun and Pen-Ming Lee Ming. AB, Harvard Coll., Cambridge, Mass., 1987; MD, Harvard Med. Sch., Boston, Mass., 1993; MS in Clin. Epidemiology, U. Pa., Phila., 2003. Diplomate Am. Bd. of Dermatology, 1997, in dermatopathology 1999. Intern medicine Mass. Gen. Hosp., Boston, 1993—94; resident dermatology Harvard Med. Sch. Dermatology Residency Tng. Program, Boston, 1994—97; fellow dermatopathology U. Calif., San Francisco, 1997—99; fellow San Francisco Veterans Affairs Med. Ctr., 1999—2000; instr. dermatology U. Pa. Sch. Medicine, Phila., 2000—02; dir., pigmented lesion clinic Hosp. U. Pa., Phila., 2000—; asst. prof. dermatology U. Pa. Sch. Medicine, 2002—. Sect. editor editl. bd. mem. Archives Dermatology, Chgo., 1999—2009; bd. dirs. Womens Dermatologic Soc., San Francisco, 2004—08; pres. Am. Dermatoepidemiology Network, Phila., 2009—11. Contbr. articles to profl. jours. Recipient Young Investigators award, Am. Acad. Dermatology, 2000, Outstanding Abstract award, Internat. Melanoma Rsch. Congress, 2006; scholarship, Nat. Merit Scholarship Corp., 1983, Grad. fellowship, NSF, 1987—88, Co-investigator grant, NIH, 2000—. Mem.: Phi Beta Kappa, Am. Dermatoepidemiology Network, Mass. Med. Soc., AMA, Womens Dermatologic Soc., Soc. Investigative Dermatology. Office: University Pa Sch Med 3600 Spruce St 2 Maloney Bldg Philadelphia PA 19104

MING, PEN-MING LEE, retired physician, educator; b. Beijing, Nov. 9, 1927; MD, Nat. Ctrl. U. Sch. Medicine, China, 1952. Resident ob-gyn. Taiwan Provincial Women's Hosp., 1952—55, New Eng. Hosp., Boston, 1955—57; resident pathology Peter Bent Brigham Hosp., Boston, 1960—64, assoc. pathologist, 1965—67; fellow genetics Karolinska Hosp., Stockholm, 1964—65; asst. prof. pathology U. Md. Sch. Medicine, 1967—71; asst, assoc prof. pathology Temple U. Sch. Medicine, 1971—82, dir. cytogenetics lab., 1972—98, prof. pathology, 1982—98, prof. ob-gyn., 1985—98. Vis. prof. Tianjin Med. Coll., China, 1982—, Shandong Med. Coll., Jinan, China, 1984—, Fourth Mil. Med. Sch., Xi'an, China, 1984—94, Nat. Def. Med. Coll., Taipei, Taiwan, 1986—89, Shanghai Second Med. U., 1988—94. Recipient Excellence Fund award, Temple U. Sch. Medicine, Golden Apple awards, Christian R and Mary F Lindback Found. award, Temple U., Am. Bd. Pathology, 1964, Am. Bd. Med. Genetics, 1984. Home: 655 Heatherwood Rd Bryn Mawr PA 19010 Personal E-mail: mmingmd@yahoo.com.

MING, SI-CHUN, pathologist, educator; b. Shanghai, Nov. 10, 1922; arrived in US, 1949, naturalized, 1964; s. Sian-Fan and Jan-Teh (Kuo) M.; m. Pen-Ming Lee, Aug. 17, 1957; children: Carol, Ruby, Stephanie, Michael, Jeffrey, Eileen. MD, Nat. Ctrl. U. Coll. Medicine, China, 1947. Resident in pathology Mass. Gen. Hosp., Boston, 1952-56; assoc. pathologist Beth Israel Hosp., Boston, 1956-67; asst. prof. pathology Harvard U. Med. Sch., 1965-67; assoc. prof. U. Md., 1967-71; prof. Temple U., Phila., 1971-93, prof. emeritus, 1993—, acting chmn. dept. pathology, 1978-80, dep. chmn. dept. path., 1980-86. US rep. WHO Collaborating Ctr. for Primary Prevention, Diagnosis and Treatment of Gastric Cancer, 1984-98; hon. prof. Tianjin Med. Coll., Shanghai Second Med. U., Fourth Mil. Med. U., China, 1988—. Author: Tumors of the Esophagus and Stomach, 1973, supplement, 1985, Precursors of Gastric Cancer, 1984, Pathology of the Gastrointestinal Tract, 1992, 2d edit., 1998; mem. editl. bd. World Jour. Gastroenterology, 1998-05, Gastric Cancer, 1998-05. Nat. Cancer Inst. sr. fellow Karolinska Inst. Stockholm, 1964-65. Mem. AAAS, US Canadian Acad. Pathology, Am. Soc. Investigative Pathology, Am. Gastroenterol. Assn., NY Acad. Scis. Achievements include development of classification method for stomach carcinoma based on the growth pattern of the cancer; establishment of pathological criteria for the diagnosis of premalignant lesions of the digestive tract. Office: 3401 N Broad St Philadelphia PA 19140-5104 Business E-Mail: ming@temple.edu.

MING, XUE, pediatrician, pediatric neurologist, neuroscientist, pharmacologist; b. Wenzhou, Zhejiang, China; MD, Shanghai Med. U., 1984; PhD, U. Medicine and Dentistry NJ Med. Sch., 1991. Pediatrics resident SUNY-Upstate Med. Ctr.; fellow, pediatric neurology John Hopkins Med. Inst., Balt., 1994—97; pediatric neurologist, neuroscientist, dept. neuroscience U. Medicine and Dentistry NJ, Univ. Hosp., Newark, 1997—; assoc. prof., dept. neurology & neuroscience U. Medicine and Dentistry NJ-NJ Med. Sch. Contbr. articles to profl. jours. Office: Dept Neurology & Neurosciences 90 Bergen St DOC 8100 Newark NJ 07101 Address: UMDNJ NJ Med Sch Behavioral Health Sciences Bldg F-Level 183 South Orange Ave Newark NJ 07103 Office Phone: 973-972-5204. Office Fax: 973-972-2369. Business E-Mail: mingxu@umdnj.edu.

MING, ZHONG, neurosurgeon, department chairman; b. Nanjing, China, Mar. 27, 1959; B, Wenzhou Med. Coll., 1982. Vice chmn., neurosurgery dept. 1st Affiliated Hosp. Wenzhou Med. Coll., 2004—. Prof. Wenzhou Med. Coll., 2004. Recipient Primary Investigator award, Sci. and Tech. Advancement Wenzhou. Fellow: World Fedn. Interventional and Therapeutic Neuroradiology, Soc. Neurosurgery (China). Avocation: swimming. Office: 2 Fu Xue Ln Wenzhou Zhejiang 325000 China Personal E-mail: zhongming158@sohu.com.

MING-HUA, ZHENG, medical educator; b. Rui'an, People's Republic of China, Apr. 13, 1980; MD, Wenzhou Med. Coll., 2003. Assoc. prof. Dept. Infection and Liver Diseases, Liver Rsch. Ctr., First Affiliated Hosp. Wenzhou Med. Coll., 2009—. Recipient AGD prize, Fourth Ditan Internat. Conf. Infectious Diseases, Second Ditan Internat. Conf. Infectious Diseases, Young Scientist award, Internat. Liver Congress, 2008; Travel grant, Fourth Ditan Internat. Conf. Infectious Diseases. Mem.: Asian Pacific Assn. Study Liver, European Assn. Study Liver (Young Investigators Bursaries award). Office: 2 Fuxue Ln Wenzhou Zhejiang 325000 China Office Fax: 86-577 8807 8262. Business E-Mail: blueman1320@163.com.

MINIATI, MASSIMO, clinician and physiologist, educator; b. Pisa, July 5, 1950; MD, U. Pisa, 1976; PhD, U. Rome, 1988. Rschr. Nat. Rsch. Coun. Italy, Inst. Clin. Physiology, Pisa, 1983—, adj. prof., 2006—; assoc. prof., internal medicine U. Florence, Sch. Medicine, 2005. Fogarty fellowship, dept. physiology U. South Ala., Mobile, 1985—86; vis. prof., dept. clin. physiology U. Lund, Sweden, 2004—. Mem.: European Assn. Nuc. Medicine, Am. Physiol. Soc. (JF Perkins Meml. award). Avocations: literature, history, painting. Home: Via Berlinghieri 8 Pisa Tuscany 56127 Italy Personal E-mail: massimo.miniati@unifi.it.

MINIER, TÜNDE, rheumatologist; b. Gheorgheni, Romania, May 23, 1982; MD, U. Medicine and Pharmacy, Tg-Mures, Romania, 2006; PhD, U. Pécs, 2011. Rheumatology resident dept. rheumatology and immunology U. Pécs, Hungary, 2009—. Mem.: EUSTAR Young Investigators Group, Emerging EULAR Network, Hungarian Assn. Immunology, Hungarian Assn. Rheumatologists. Office: Akác u 1 Pécs 7632 Hungary Office Phone: 3672536802. Business E-Mail: tunde.minier@aok.pte.hu.

MINIKES, NEIL IRA, pediatrician, allergist, immunologist; b. NYC, 1951; MD, Columbia U. Coll. Physicians & Surgeons, 1980. Diplomate Am. Bd. Pediat., 1986, Am. Bd. Allergy & Immunology. Resident in pediat. Columbia Presbyn. Med. Ctr., NYC, 1980—83; fellow in allergy & immunology LI Jewish Med. Ctr., New Hyde Park, NY, 1986—90; pvt. practice Pediat. and Adult Allergy Immunology, NJ, pediat. and adult allergy immunology, Closter, NJ. Asst. clin. prof. pediat. Columbia U. Coll. Physicians & Surgeons. Recipient Best Drs., NY Mag., 2002, 2009, NJ Monthly Mag., 2006—11, Best Allergists, NJ Savvy Mag., 2010; named one of America's Top Doctors, Castle Connolly Med. Ltd., 2000—10. Mem.: NJ Allergy Soc., Am. Coll. Allergy & Immunology, Am. Acad. Pediat., Am. Acad. Allergy & Immunology. Office: Allergy and Asthma Ctr Northern NJ 500 Piermont Rd Ste 304 Closter NJ 07624

MINNERS, HOWARD ALYN, federal agency administrator, researcher, preventive medicine physician; b. Rockville Center, NY, Sept. 1, 1931; s. Howard A. and Marie Henriette (Soberski) M.; m. Gretchen Paffenbarger, Oct. 25, 1958; children: Todd, Bradford. AB, Princeton U., 1953; MD, Yale U., 1957; MPH, Harvard U., 1960. Diplomate Am. Bd. Preventive Medicine, Nat. Bd. Med. Examiners. 2d. lt. USAF, 1956; intern Wilford Hall USAF Hosp., San Antonio, 1957-58; resident Sch. of Aerospace Medicine, USAF, Brooks AFB, Tex., 1960-62; advanced through grades to maj. USAF, 1966; advanced through grades to rear adm. USPHS, ret., 1987; dir. office rsch. promotion and devel. WHO, Geneva, Switzerland, 1977-80; dir. Office of Sci. Advisor Agy. Internat. Devel., Washington, 1981-91; dep. dir. Office Internat. Health USPHS and Asst. Surgeon Gen., 1980-81. Assoc. dir. NIH NIAID, 1966-77; astronaut flight surgeon NASA, Houston, 1962-66; mem. Dean's Coun. Yale Med. Sch., 2007-. Pres. Model A Ford Found., 1994-2000. Fellow World Acad. Art and Sci., Am. Coll. Preventive Medicine; mem. AAAS, Internat. Found. Sci. Stockholm (pres., chmn. bd. trustees 1991-97), Yale Med. Alumni Fund (chmn. bd. trustees 2003-06). Avocations: Model A Ford restoration, history.

MINNI, ANTONIO, otolaryngologist, educator; b. Rome, Nov. 2, 1961; s. Bartolo Minni and Maria Bracco; m. Ornella Iannone, Oct. 12, 1994; 1 child, Luca. Degree in Medicine, U. La Sapienza, Rome, 1986. Cert. in otolaryngology U. La Sapienza, 1990. ENT rschr. & prof. U. La Sapienza, 1989—; pvt. practice Vatican City, 1996—. Aviere Air Force, 1987—88, Rome. Fellow, U. La Sapienza, 1986. Mem.: Europena Laryngol. Soc., Italian Otolaryngologist Assn., Rotary Club. Roman Catholic. Home: Via Monti Di Creta 30 Rome 00100 Italy Office: Univ La Sapienza Viale Del Policlinico 155 Roma 00100 Italy Business E-Mail: antonio.minni@uniroma1.it.

MINOR, GEORGE GILMER, III, drug and hospital supply company executive; b. 1940; married. BA, Va. Mil. Inst., 1963; MBA, U. Va., 1966. With Owens & Minor, Inc., Richmond, Va., 1963—, mgr. sales Acme Candy Co. div., 1966-68, mgr. retail mktg., 1968-73, div. mgr. wholesale drug br., 1973-77, v.p., 1977-80, exec. v.p., 1980-81, pres., 1981—99, CEO, 1984—2005, chmn., 1994—. Bd. dir. SunTrust Banks Inc. Bd. dir. Va. Biotechnology Rsch. Park Authority, Richmond Renaissance; v.p. bd. vis. Va. Mil. Inst.; chmn. bd. trustees Va. Health Care Found.; mem. adv. bd. Univ. Va. Sch. Nursing. Named Va. Industrialist of the Year, 2001; named to Greater Richmond Bus. Hall of Fame, 2003. Office: Owens & Minor Inc 9120 Lockwood Blvd Mechanicsville VA 23116 *

MINSHEW, NANCY J., neurologist, educator; MD, Wash. U. Sch. Medicine, 1974. Prof. psychiatry & neurology U. Pitts. Office: 811 O'Hara St Webster Hall Ste 300 Pittsburgh PA 15213 Office Phone: 412-246-5485. Office Fax: 412-246-5470. E-mail: minshewnj@upmc.edu.

MINTZ, DANIEL HARVEY, endocrinologist, educator, academic administrator; b. NYC, Sept. 16, 1930; s. Jacob A. and Fanny Mintz; m. Dawn E. Hynes, Jan. 15, 1961 (dec.); children: David, Denise, Debra; m. Marge Kleiman, Nov. 30, 1996. BS cum laude, St. Bonaventure Coll., 1951; MD, N.Y. Med. Coll., 1956. Diplomate Am. Bd. Internal Medicine. Intern Henry Ford Hosp., Detroit, 1956-57; resident Georgetown med. div. D.C. Gen. Hosp., Washington, 1957-59, Georgetown U. Hosp., Washington, 1958-59; fellow medicine Nat. Inst. Arthritis and Metabolic Diseases, 1959-60, Am. Diabetes Assn., 1960-61; practice medicine, specializing in diabetes and endocrinology U. Miami. (Fla.) Sch. Medicine, prof. medicine, 1969—2011, Mary Lou Held prof. medicine, 1981-96, chief div. endocrinology and metabolism, dept. medicine, 1969-80, Sci. dir. Diabetes Research Inst., 1980-96, sci. dir. emeritus, 1996—, asst. prof. medicine Georgetown U. Sch. Medicine, 1963-64; assoc. prof. medicine U. Pitts. Sch. Medicine, 1964-69, chief svc. Georgetown U. Med. div. D.C. Gen. Hosp., Washington, 1963-64; chief medicine Magee-Women's Hosp., Pitts., 1964-69, emeritus prof. medicine, 2011—. Guest prof. U. Geneva, 1976—77. Contbr. articles to profl. jours. Fellow: ACP; mem.: Am. Assn. Physicians, So. Soc. Clin. Investigation, Ctrl. Soc. Clin. Investigation, Am. Soc. Clin. Investigation, Am. Fedn. Clin. Rsch., Am. Diabetes Assn., Endocrine Soc. Office: U Miami Diabetes Rsch Inst PO Box 016960 R-77 Miami FL 33101-6960

MINTZ, DOUGLAS N., radiologist; b. NYC, Sept. 6, 1962; s. Norman N. and Marcia Belford Mintz. AB, Columbia U., NY, 1984, MD, 1988. Cert. radiologist Am. Bd. Radiology, 1997, lic. NY, Fla. Resident surgery U. Minn. Hosp. and Clinics, Mpls., 1988—90; attending physician Kaiser Permanente Med. Group, San Diego, 1990—92; rsch. assoc. Scripps Rsch. Inst., La Jolla, Calif., 1990—92; resident radiology Lenox Hill Hosp., 1993—97; attending radiologist Hosp. for Spl. Surgery, NYC, 1998—2010, fellow musculoskeletal radiology, 1997—98; attending radiologist NY Presbyn. Hosp., 1998—2010; asst. prof. radiology Weill Med. Coll., Cornell U., 1998—2004, assoc. prof. clin. radiology, 2004—10; radiologist Assocs. South Fla., Bapt. Health South Fla., 2010—; assoc. prof. clin. radiology Fla. Internat. U., 2010—. Author: (scientific exhibit) Load Dependence of the Thumb and Carpal Bone Configuration during Static Pinch; contbr. scientific papers to profl. pubs. and confs., chapters to books; co-author: Orthopedic Pathology. Grantee, NYPH Inst. of Aging, 2002—05, NIH, 2002—05, Bayer Found., 2005—07. Mem.: Alumni Assn., Hosp. Spl. Surgery (sec., treas.), Coconut Grove Sailing Club, Soc. Skeletal Radiology, Argentina Assn. Orthops. and Trauma (hon.), Oxford/ Cambridge Club. Jewish. Achievements include patents for methods of identifying inhibitors of LPS-mediated LBP binding. Home: 720 NE 69th St Apt 17S Miami FL 33138-5758 Office: 8900 N Kendall Dr Miami FL 33176 Business E-Mail: dmintz@baptisthealth.net.

MINTZ-HITTNER, HELEN ANN, physician, researcher; b. Houston, Aug. 12, 1944; d. Bert and Jeanette (Haydis) Mintz; m. David Hittner, Sept. 8, 1968 (div. May 11, 1989); children: Miriam Annette Hittner Tondera, Susan Michelle Hittner, George Jacob Hittner. BA, Rice U., 1965; MD, Baylor Coll. Medicine, 1969. Lic. Tex. Bd. of Med. Examiners, 1969. Intern pediat. Baylor Affiliated Hosps., Houston, 1969—70, resident ophthalmology, 1970—73; fellow pediat. ophthalmology Tex. Children's Hosp., Houston, 1973—74; pediat. ophthalmologist Houston, 1974—95; Alfred W. Lasher III prof. pediat. ophthalmology U. Tex. Health Sci. Ctr. Houston Med. Sch., 1995—. Prin. investigator clin. trial Bevacizumab Eliminates the Angiogenic Threat of Retinopathy of Prematurity (Beat-Rop). Author: several rsch. reports and jour. articles. Fellow: Am. Acad. Ophthalmology (Honor award 1986, Sr. Honor award 2005); mem.: N.Y. Acad. Med., N.Y. Acad. Sci., Ciba Found., Soc. Heed Fellows (life), Assn. Rsch. in Vision and Ophthalmology, Am. Assn. Pediat. Ophthalmology and Strabismus, Phi Beta Kappa (life), Alpha Omega Alpha (life). Independent. Jewish. Achievements include discovery of Primary etiology of retinopathy of prematurity; research in Genetic linkage of aniridia to chromosome 11p13 (PAX6); Genetic identification of anterior segment dysgenesis on chromosomes 10q25 (PITX3), 1p32 (FOXE3), 20p11.2 (VSX1); Genetic linkage of Exudative Vitreo Retinopathy AR to chromosome 7q31.31 (TSPAN12). Home: 1500 A California St Houston TX 77006-2605 Office: University Tex Health Sci Ctr Houston Med Sch 6400 Fannin St #1800 Houston TX 77030 Office Phone: 713-559-5277. Business E-Mail: helen.a.mintz-hittner@uth.tmc.edu.

MINZTER, DAVID M., oncologist, educator; MD, Thomas Jefferson U. Diplomate Am. Bd. Internal Medicine, 1980, Am. Bd. Internal Medicine-hematology, 1982, Am. Bd. Internal Medicine-med. oncology, 1983, Am. Bd. Anesthesiology-hospice and palliative care medicine, 2005. Intern Pa. Hosp., resident, chief, sect. hematology-oncology, dir., palliative care, assoc. dir., cancer risk evaluation program (CREP) Univ. Pa.; clin. assoc. prof. medicine Univ. Pa.; fellow Meml. Sloan Kettering-Thomas Jefferson Univ. Hosp. Named one of Best Doctors in America, 2003—04, 2005—06, 2007—08, 2009—10, Top Docs, Phila. Mag., 2004—11, America's Top Doctors, 2008, 2010, Top Physicians, Suburban Life Mag., 2010. Mem.: Am. Soc. of Clin. Oncology, Am. Soc. of Hematology, ACP. Office: Pennsylvania Hospital Farm Journal Bldg, 2nd Fl 230 W Washington Sq Philadelphia PA 19106 Office Phone: 800-789-7366.

MIODOVNIK, AMIR, pediatrician; b. Israel, May 14, 1974; BA, U. Va., 1996; MD, Ohio State U., 2000. Attending pediatrician USN, 2004—06, Children's Hosp. LA, 2005—06; physician Drs. Without Borders, 2006—07; pediatrician Mt. Sinai Sch. Medicine, 2008—. Fellow: AAP. Office: Mount Sinai Sch Medicine One Gustave L Levy Pl New York NY 10029 Business E-Mail: amir.miodovnik@mssm.edu.

MIOTTO, KAREN ANN, psychiatrist, educator; MD, U. Colo., Denver, 1989. Lic. Calif., 1990, diplomate Am. Bd. Psychiatry and Neurology-psychiatry, 1995, Am. Bd. Psychiatry and Neurology-psychiatry, 2005, Am. Bd. Psychiatry and Neurology-addiction psychiatry, 1996, Am. Bd. Psychiatry and Neurology-addiction psychiatry, 2006. Intern medicine Reading Hosp. and Med. Ctr., 1989—90; resident psychiatry UCLA Neuropsychiatric Hosp., 1990—93, fellow psychiatry, 1993—94; asst. clin. prof. UCLA, 1994—2002, dir. alcoholism and addiction medicine svcs., 1997—2000, med. dir. addiction medicine program, 2006—, clin. prof., 2009—; physician psychiatry and behavioral sciences, adult psychiatry Ronald Reagan UCLA Med. Ctr., hosp. affiliations include, Stewart and Lynda Resnick Neuropsychiat. Hosp. Office: Ronald Reagan UCLA Medical Center 760 Westwood Bld Los Angeles CA 90024 Office Phone: 310-206-2782.

MIRACLE, DORIS JEAN, retired medical/surgical nurse; b. Louisville, July 23, 1931; d. Bernard Louis and Catherine Federle; m. Earl Miracle, Aug. 31, 1951; 1 child, David. Surg. nurse Norton Hosp., Louisville, 1951, Norton-Children's Hosp., Louisville, 1969—86; ret., 1986. Poetry (albums) Sounds of Poetry, 2003; author: (poetry) Silver Music Box, 2009, Springtime in the City, 2009, Shark, 2009, The Sunshine Cart, 2009, numerous poems; contbr. articles to profl. jours.:, author poetry to anthology, (poetry) The Wishing Well, 2010 (award), Sunflowers and Seashells. Recipient Editors Choice award, Internat. Libr., 2003, 2006, 2007; named Best Poets of 2010, EBER & WEIN Publising Co. Mem.: Wilderness Rd. Writers, Gaslight Writers, Internat. Soc. of Poets, Soc. Children's Book Writers and Illustrators, Louisville Astronomical Soc. Avocations: reading, poetry, astronomy, art, music. Personal E-mail: doriskitm@aol.com.

MIRACLE-LOPEZ, SIGFRIDO, endocrinologist, researcher; b. Mex. City, Mex., Feb. 27, 1972; s. Sigfrido Miracle-Feliu and Matilde Lopez-Rivero; m. Paloma De Leon, July 20, 1996. MD, Universidad Anahuac Sch. of Medicine, Mex. City, 1990—95; Clin. Endocrinologist, Universidad Nacional Autonoma de Mex., Mex. City, 1998—2002; Cert. Thyroid Ultrasonografist, Am. Assn. of Clin. Endocrinologist, West Palm Beach, 2003—03. Bd. cert. Consejo Mexicano de Endocrinología (Mex.), 2002, cert. Thyroid Ultrasonografist Am. Assn. of Clin. Endocrinologists, W. Palm Beach, 2003. Class pres. Universidad Anahuac Sch. of Medicine, Huixquilucan, Estado de Mex., Mexico, 1990—92; intern Hosp. Español de Mex., Mex. City, Mex. City, Mexico, 1994—95; internal medicine resident Instituto Mexicano del Seguro Social (Centro Medico Nacional Siglo XXI), Mex. City, Mex. City, Mexico, 1998—2000; chief resident of internal medicine Instituto Mexicano del Seguro Social (Hosp. Gabriel Mancera), Mex. City, Mex. City, Mexico, 1998—99; fellow of endocrinology Instituto Mexicano del Seguro Social (Centro Medico Nacional Siglo XXI), Mex. City, Mex. City, Mexico, 2000—02; attending internal medicine/endocrinology Am. Brit. Cowdray Med. Ctr., Mex. City, Mexico, 2002—; attending ICU Instituto Mexicano del Seguro Social (Hosp. Los Venados), Mex. City, Mex. City, Mexico, 2002—02; chief of external consult of endocrinology Hosp. Obregon, Mex. City, Mex., Mexico, 2002—02; attending transplant unit Hosp. Angeles de las Lomas, Huixquilucan, Estado de Mex., Mexico, 2002—, attending endocrinology, 2002—; cert. thyroid ultrasonografist Am. Assn. of Clin. Endocrinologist, West Palm Beach, Fla., 2003—. Mem. coun. of associates (representing Latin Am.) ACP, Phila., 2000—03; mem. internat. com. Am. Assn. of Clin. Endocrinologist, Jacksonville, Fla., 2002—; members tchg. com. Sociedad Mexicana de Nutricion y Endocrinologia, Mex. City, Mex., Mexico, 2002—; ofcl. amb. Am. Assn. of Clin. Endocrinologist, Jacksonville, Fla., 2002—; mem. internat. com. ACP, Phila., 2003—. Recipient 3rd Pl. Young Investigator, Am. Assn. of Clin. Endocrinologists, 2002, Hon. mention, Internat. Poster Competition, ACP, 2002, Outstanding Achievement as a Resident, Instituto Mexicano del Seguro Social, 1998—99, Hon. Mention, 1999. Fellow: Am. Coll. Endocrinology, Sociedad Mexicana de Nutricion y Endocrinologia; mem.: ACP, Endocrine Soc., Am. Assn. of Clin. Endocrinologists. Roman Catholic. Avocations: role playing games, chess, Karate. Office: Hosp Angeles de las Lomas Vialidad de la Barranca S/N con 830 Huixquilucan 52763 Mexico Office Fax: (0115255)52-54-18-45. E-mail: smiracle911@msn.com.

MIRAND, EDWIN ALBERT, medical researcher, educator; b. Buffalo, July 18, 1926; s. Thomas and Lucy (Papier) M. BA, U. Buffalo, 1947, MA, 1949; PhD, Syracuse U., NY, 1951; DSc (hon.), Niagara U., NY, 1970, D'Youville Coll., Buffalo, 1974. Successively undergrad. asst., grad. asst., instr. U. Buffalo, 1946-48; teaching fellow Syracuse U., 1948-51; instr. Utica (N.Y.) Coll., 1950; mem. staff Roswell Park Meml. Inst., Buffalo, 1951—; head W. Seneca labs., 1961—, assoc. inst. dir., head dept. edn., 1967—, dir. cancer rsch., 1968-73, head dept. viral oncology, 1970-73, head dept. biol. recources, 1973—. Rsch. prof. biology Grad. Sch., prof. biochem. pharmacology Sch. Pharmacy, SUNY, Buffalo, 1955-97, dean emeritus, 1997—, dean Roswell Park grad. divn. SUNY, 1967—; rsch. prof. biology Grad. Sch.; human cancer virus task force, clin. cancer edn. com. NIH; sr. advisor to pres. and CEO, Roswell Park Cancer Inst., 1997—, dir. alumni, 1997—; bd. adv. Niagara U., 1985—. Mem. editl. bd. Jour. Surg. Oncology, Cancer Rsch., Jour. Cancer Edn., Cancer jour.; contbr. articles to profl. jours. U.S. nat. com. Union Internat. Contra Cancer NAS; profl. edn. com. cancer control Nat. Cancer inst.; liaison mem. Pres.'s Nat. Cancer Adv. Bd.; sec. N.Y. State Cancer Programs, Inc., 1984—; bd. dirs. Network in Aging of We. N.Y., Inc., 1986—; mem. N.Y. State Health Rsch. Coun., Gov.'s AIDS adv. coun., 1982—; trustee D'Youville Coll., 1998—. Recipient Billings Silver medal AMA, 1963, Sci. Rsch. Mammalian Tumor Viruses award Med. Soc. State N.Y., 1963, Citation award in sci. coll. arts and scis.SUNY, Buffalo, 1964, Margaret Hays Edwards award in Edn., 1993, Life Time Achievement award Bus. First, Buffalo, 2005, D'Youville Coll., 2008, Buffalo Bus. 1st Lifetime Achievement award, 2005, Roswell Pk. Cancer Inst., 2010. Fellow: AAAS (life), N.Y. Acad. Sci. (life); mem.: Am. Soc. Preventive Oncology (founding mem.), Internat. Union Against Cancer (chmn. U.S. nat. com. 1979-2001, sec.-gen. 13th Internat. Cancer Congress), Pub. Health Cancer Assn. Am., Internat. Soc. Hematology, Am. Soc. Hematology, Buffalo Acad. Medicine, Am. Assn. for Cancer Edn., Soc. Exptl. Biology and medicine, Am. Soc. Zoologists, Radiation Rsch. Soc., Am. Assn. Cancer Rsch., Assn. Am. Cancer Insts. (sec.-treas. 1968-99), Internat. Assn. for Gnotobiology (pres. 1981-84), Assn. Gnotobiotics (pres. 1968-69, dir. 1975-78), Am. Cancer Soc. (state pub. edn. com. 1982-, nat. adv. com. on rsch. personnel 1985-), Buffalo Fine Arts Acad. (life), Buffalo Hist. Soc. (life), Sigma Xi (life). Home: 925 Delaware Ave Buffalo NY 14209 Office: Roswell Park Meml Inst Elm and Carlton Streets Buffalo NY 14263-0002 Office Phone: 716-845-3028. Business E-Mail: edwinmirand@roswellpark.org.

MIRANDA, ANGELICA ESPINOSA, physician, educator; b. Brazil, Mar. 20, 1965; MD, Escola Medicina da Santa Casa de Misericordia de Vitoria, 1987; PhD, Escola Nacional Saúde Pública-FIOCRUZ, 2003. Assoc. prof. U. Fed. do Espirito Santo, 2002—. Physician Health Dept. in Vitória Municipality, 1992—2002, Santa Casa de Misericórdia de Vitória, 1988—95. Master: Brazilian Soc. Sexually Transmitted Diseases; mem.: Brazilian Soc. Tropical Medicine, Internat. Union Against Sexually Transmitted Infections. Office: Universidade Federal do Espirito Santo Vitoria Espirito Santo 29040-091 Brazil Office Fax: 5527 33357504. Business E-Mail: espinosa@ndi.ufes.br.

MIRKIN, GABE BARON, retired physician, medical educator, writer, radio personality; b. Brookline, Mass., June 18, 1935; s. Mitchell and Vera (Baron) M.; children: Gene, Jan, Jill, Geoffrey, Kenny; m. Diana Purdie Rich, 1998. BA, Harvard U., 1957; MD, Baylor U., 1961. Diplomate Am. Bd. Pediatrics, Sub Bd. Allergy, Am. Bd. Allergy and Immunology, Am. Bd. Sports Medicine. Resident in pediatrics Mass. Gen. Hosp., Boston, 1961-63; fellow allergy, immunology, dermatology Johns Hopkins Hosp., Balt., 1963-65; allergy, immunology, dermatology, sports medicine pvt. practice, Silver Spring, Md., 1966—. Tchg. fellow pediat. Harvard Med. Sch., 1962-63; tchg. fellow allergy and immunology Johns Hopkins Med. Sch., 1963-65; asst. prof. dept. phys. edn. U. Md., College Park, 1976-83; assoc. clin. prof. dept. pediat. Georgetown U. Sch. of Medicine, 1984—. Author: The Sportsmedicine Book, 1978, Getting Thin, 1983, Dr. Gabe Mirkin's Fitness Clinic, 1986, The Complete Sportsmedicine Book for Women, 1985, 2d rev. edit. 1991; (with Shangold) Women and Exercise, 1988, Dr. Gabe Mirkin's Fatfree, Flavorfull Book, 1995; (with Diana Mirkin) The 20 Gram Diet, 1995, The 20/30 Fat and Fiber Diet Plan, Dr. Gabe Mirkins Pocket Guide to Fitness & Sports; (with Rich) The Whole Grains Cookbook, 1997, The Good Food Book, 2001, Healthy Heart Miracle, 2004; author (newsletter) The Mirkin Report, 1990—; columnist: N.Y. Times, 1978-89, United Features, 1989-94, Washington Post, 1976, Singer Media Corp., 1994-99; appearances on P.M. Mag. WDVM-TV, Washington, 1979, House Party, NBC TV, 1990, The Learning Channel; host internationally syndicated radio talk show, 1996-2003; daily radio spots on fitness and nutrition, CBS Radio Stations News Svc., 1979—; host talk show on health fitness and nutrition, KMOX Radio, St. Louis, 1982-98; nightly talk show host NBC Washington, WRC, 1982-84, 87—, WNTR, 1984-86; weekly spots for Physicians Radio Network, 1984-85; daily talk show syndicated by Sun Radio Network, 1992; weekly talk show WEEI, Boston, 1993-94, others; columnist and contbg. editor to health and fitness mags.; contbr. articles to profl. jours., chpts. to books. Major USAF, 1968-70. Fellow Am. Coll. Allergists, Am. Assn. Cert. Allergists, Am. Assn. for Clin. Immunology and Allergy, Am. Acad. Pediatrics, Am. Acad. Allergy and Immunology. Avocation: bicycle tandem racing. Home: 2001 Hartford Path The Villages FL 32162 Personal E-mail: gabe@drmirkin.com.

MIRONIDOU-TZOUVELEKI, MARIA, pharmacologist, educator; b. Thessaloniki, Greece, Feb. 12, 1951; MD, Aristotle U., Thessaloniki, 1975, PhD in Pharmacology, 1985. Sci. co-worker Dept. Pharmacology, Med. Sch., Aristotle U., Thessaloniki, 1982—87, lectr. pharmacology, 1987—91, asst. prof. in pharmacology, 1991—99, assoc. prof. pharmacology, 1999—2011, prof. pharmacology, 2011—. Mem.: Greek Soc. Study Dependence Drugs, Hellenic Soc. History Medicine, NY Acad. Scis., Greek Pharmacological Soc., Greek Anaesthesiological Soc. Office: Aristotle University Dept Pharmacology Thessaloniki 541 24 Greece Business E-Mail: mmyronid@auth.gr.

MIRRA, SUZANNE SAMUELS, pathologist; BA, Hunter Coll., 1962; MD, SUNY, Bklyn., 1967. Instr. pathology Yale U. Sch. Medicine, New Haven, 1971-73; staff pathologist Atlanta VA Med. Ctr., Decatur, Ga., 1973-97; asst. prof. pathology Emory U. Sch. Medicine, Atlanta, 1973-80, assoc. prof. pathology, 1981-93, prof. pathology, 1993-97; prof., chair dept. pathology SUNY Health Sci. Ctr., Bklyn., 1997—; disting. svc. prof. SUNY, 2010—. Dir., prin. investor Emry Alzheimer's Disease Ctr., Atlanta, 1991—97. Mem. editl. bd. Arch Pathol. Lab. Med., 1988-2000, Jour. Neuropathology Exptl. Neurology, 1991-95, Brain Pathology, 1995-99. Recipient Albert E. Levy Sci. Faculty Rsch. award Emory U., 1987, Disting. Alumnus Achievement award SUNY, 1992; named to Hunter Coll. Hall of Fame, 1996. Fellow Coll. Am. Pathologists (Presdl. award 1987,89, Herbert Lansky award 1990, chair neuropathology commn. 1992-95); mem. Am. Assn. Neuropathologists (v.p. profl. affairs 1992-97, pres. 1999-2000, Meritorious Contributions to Neuropathology award, 2005), Alzheimer's Assn. (bd. dir. Atlanta chpt. 1987-97, nat. bd. dir. 1997-05), Alpha Omega Alpha. Office: SUNY Health Sci Ctr 450 Clarkson Ave Brooklyn NY 11203-2056 Office Phone: 718-270-4599. Business E-Mail: suzanne.mirra@downstate.edu.

MIRZA, SOHAIL K., orthopedist, educator; MD, U. Colo. Sch. Medicine, 1989; MPH, U. Wash. Sch. Pub. Health, 2005. Cert. orthopaedic surgery 1994. Intern U. Wash. Hosp., 1989—90, resident, 1990—94; fellow Beth Israel Deaconess Med. Ctr., 1994—95; vice chmn. dept. orthopaedics Dartmouth-Hitchcock Med. Ctr. Office: Dartmouth-Hitchcock Medical Center Orthopaedic Surgery One Medical Center Dr Lebanon NH 03756 Office Phone: 603-650-2225. Office Fax: 603-650-6322.

MISAWA, SONOKO, neurologist; b. Okaya, Nagano, Japan, Oct. 17, 1974; d. Kyoko Misawa; m. Sonoko Misawa, July 19, 2004. PhD, MD, Chiba U., Japan, 1999. Resident in neurology Chiba U. Sch. Medicine, Chiba, Japan, 1999—2003; rsch. assoc. dept. neurology Chiba U. Sch. of Medicine, 2003—. Grantee, Japanese Ministry of Edn., Culture, Sports, Sci., and Tech., 2005. Mem.: Japanese Soc. Neurology (sr.). Avocations: travel, music, interior decorating. Office: Chiba Univ Sch Medicine Inohana 1-8-1 Chuo-ku Chiba 260-8670 Japan Office Fax: +81-43-226-2160. Business E-Mail: sonoko.m@mb.infoweb.ne.jp.

MISERY, LAURENT, dermatologist, scientist; b. St. Etienne, Loire, France, July 23, 1963; s. Laurent and Yvette (Bougault) Misery. MD, U. Lyon I, France, 1992, PhD in Human Biology, 1995. Physician Hosps. of Lyon, 1992-97, Hosps. of St. Etienne, 1998—2001, Hosps. of Brest, 2001—; prof. dermatology U. Hosp., Brest, 2003—. Author: Neuronal Skin, 2000. Nat secy Movement Young Reps, Paris, France, 1989—92; pres research comn Parti Rep, Paris, France, 1991—97, fed secy Loire, France, 1995—98. Recipient L'Oreal prize, 1996, Noviderm prize, 2000, Coloplast prize, 2001. Mem.: French Soc. of Human Scis. on Skin (founder, pres. 2006—), InterSyndicat Nat des Chefs de Clinique-Assts (v.p. 1995—96). Avocations: history, music, sea. Home: Leur ar Marc'h 29470 Plougastel-Daoulas France Office: Morvan Hosp 29609 Brest France Office Phone: +33 298 22 33 15. E-mail: laurent.misery@chu-brest.fr.

MISHKIN, MORTIMER, neuropsychologist; b. Fitchburg, Mass., Dec. 13, 1926; AB, Dartmouth Coll., 1946; MA, McGill U., Montreal, Can., 1949, PhD, 1951; DSc (hon.), McGill U., 2004. Asst. in research and physiology and psychiatry Yale U. Med. Sch., New Haven, 1949-51; research assoc. Inst. of Living, Hartford-Conn. and NYU Bellevue Med. Ctr., NYC, 1951-55; research psychologist, sect. on neuropsychology NIMH, Bethesda, Md., 1955-75, research physiologist, lab. of Neuropsychology, 1976-78, chief sect. cerebral mechanisms Lab. of Neuropsychology, 1979-80, chief Lab. of Neuropsychology, 1980-97, assoc. dir. basic rsch. DIRP, 1994-97, chief sect. cognitive neuroscience, 1997—, acting chief, lab neuropsychology, 2005—, sr. investigator. Part-time instr. psychology Howard U., 1956-58; vis. scientist Nencki Inst. Exptl. Biology, Warsaw, Poland, winter 1958, 68, Tokyo Met. Inst. Neuroscis., summer 1978, Oxford U. Dept. Exptl. Psychology, summer 1979, Inst. Child Health U. Coll. London, 1993, vis. prof., 2000-; mem. psychol. scis. panel NIH, 1959-61, exptl. psychology study sect., 1965-69; mem. NIMH Assembly of Scientists Council, 1962-64, 72-74; mem. NIMH Scientist Promotion Rev. Com., 1984-86; mem. adv. com. Cognitive Neurosci. Inst., 1982-86; mem. NIH Fogart Internat. Scholars-in-Residence Adv. Panel, 1985-89, McDonnell Found. Study panel, 1987-89; adv. bd. McDonnell-Pew Program Cognitive Neurosci., 1989-94; cons. Developmental Cognitive Neurosci. Unit, Inst. Child Health, U. Coll. London, 1990—, vis. prof., 2000—; active Human Frontier Sci. Program, 1992-94, chmn. 1993; adv. bd. Ctr. for the Neural Basis of Cognition, U. Pitts. and Carnegie Mellon U., 1994-96, chair, 1999, 2004; adv. bd. La. State U. Neurosci. Ctr., 1994-96, Frontier Rsch. Program, RIKEN, Japan, 1994-96, Zanvyl Krieger Mind-Brain Inst., Johns Hopkins U., 1994-2000, Cognitive and Behavioral Neurosci. Panel, SUNY, Stony Brook, 1996, Mental Health and Neurosci. Clin. Rsch. Ctr., U. N.C., Chapel Hill, 1996-98, Krasnow Inst., George Mason U., Fellow Mentor Program, 1997-2002. Cons. editor Jour. Comparative and Physiol. Psychology, 1963-73, Exptl. Brain Rsch., 1965—, Brain Rsch., 1974-78, Neuropsychologia, 1963-92, Human Neurobiology, 1981-87, Jour. Cognitive Neurosci., 1989—, Jour. NIH Rsch., 1989-97, Cerebral Cortex, 1990-95, Advances in Neurobiology, 1990—, Handbook Behavioral Neurology, 1991—, Current Opinion in Neurobiology, 1991—, Neurobiology of Learning and Memory, 1992—, Learning and Memory, 1993—, Jour. Internat. Neuropsychol. Soc., 1995-99, Internat. Encyclopedia of the Social and Behavioral Scis., 1998-2002; reviewing editors Sci., 1985-93; assoc. editor Neuroreport, 1990-2000; contbr. numerous articles to profl. jours., also abstracts and book revs. Served to lt. (j.g.) USNR. Recipient U.S. Presdl. Disting. Rank award, 1992, Karl Spencer Lashley prize Am. Philos. Soc., 1996, Found. Ipsen Neuronal Plasticity prize, 1995, Med. Rsch. award Met. Life Found., 2000, Nat. Medal Sci. The White House, 2010. Fellow AAAS (chair-elect 1990-91, chair 1991-92, past chair 1992-93), APA Assn. (officer, divsn. 6 mem. at large 1964-66, coun. rep. 1967-69, pres. 1968-69, Disting. Scientific Contribution award, 1985); mem. NAS (officer, sect. 52 chmn. 1989-92), Ea. Psychol. Assn., Internat. Brain Research Orgn. (officer, rep.-at-large governing coun. 1993-98), Internat. Neuropsychol. Soc., Internat. Neuropsychol. Symposium, Internat. Primatological Soc., Internat. Soc. Neuroethology, Cognitive Neuroscience Soc. (Hermann von Helmholtz award, 1989) Soc. Exptl. Psychologists (Howard Crosby Warren medal 1998), Soc. Neurosci. (officer, pres.-elect 1985-86, pres. 1986-87, past pres. 1987-88), Inst. Medicine, Brazilian Acad. Sci., Sigma Xi, Phi Beta Kappa. Achievements includes research in behavioral and cognitive neuroscience in primates. Office: NIMH Lab Neuropsychology 49 Convent Dr Msc 4415 Bldg 49 Bethesda MD 20892-0001 Business E-Mail: mishkinm@mail.nih.gov. *

MISHLER, JOHN MILTON (YOCHANAN MENASHSHEH BEN SHAUL), science educator, artist; b. Cairo, Ill., Sept. 25, 1946; s. John Milton and Mary Jane (Woodbury) Mishler; m. Mary Therese Stember, Apr. 15, 1972 (div. Nov. 1981); m. Sigrid Ruth Elizabeth Fischer, Dec. 15, 1981; 1 child, Joshua Evan. AA with honors, Orange Coast Coll., Costa Mesa, Calif., 1966; AB in Molecular Biology, U. Calif., San Diego, 1969, ScM in Engring. Scis., 1971; DPhil in Immunohematology, St. John's Coll., Oxford U., 1978. Cert. cmty. coll. instr. Calif. Clin. coord. McGaw Labs., Costa Mesa, 1972-78; rsch. fellow Royal Postgrad. Med. Sch., Eng., 1977-78, Med. U.,

Cologne, Fed. Republic Germany, 1978-80; br. chief Nat. Heart, Lung and Blood Inst. NIH, Bethesda, Md., 1980-82; prof. med., basic life scis. and pharmacol. U. Mo., Kansas City, 1983-89, asst. vice chancellor, 1983-85, dir. div. basic med. scis., 1985-86, assoc. vice chancellor, 1985-89; prof. nat. scis. U. Md. Ea. Shore, Princess Anne, 1989-94, dean grad. studies and rsch., 1989-91; prof. biology Delaware Valley Coll. Sci. and Agrl., Doylestown, Pa., 1994—, dean of Coll., 1994-95. Frequent nat. and internat. lectr.; chmn. 13 nat. and internat. meeting sects. Author: Pharmacology of Hydroxyethyl Starch. Use in Therapy and Blood Banking, 1982; mem. editl. bd. Jour. Soc. Rsch. Adminstrs., 1987-91; book rev. editor Grants Mag., 1987-89; contbr. over 100 articles to profl. jours. Bd. dirs. Ctr. for Bus. Innovation, Inc., 1987, Bucks Assn. for Retarded Citizens, 1995-96; v.p. Artsbridge, 1999-2000. Recipient Outstanding Adminstrn. Svc. award U. Mo., Kansas City, 1987, Excellence award Soc. Rsch. Adminstrn., 1989, Cert. Appreciation, 1991, Silver and Bronze awards Artist Guild of Delaware Valley, 1998, Second prize Chester County Art Assn., 1998, Bd. Dirs. award Gtr. Norristown Art League, 1998, Award of Merit Westmoreland Art Nats., 1998, Perkins Ctr. for Arts, 2000, Robert Ransley Outstanding Talent award, 1999, 2d prize drawing Ctr. for the Creative Arts, 1999, 1st prize graphics Perkiomen Valley Art Ctr., 1999, 2d prize, 2002, Wayne Art Supply award Wayne Art Ctr., 2002, Pres.'s award Salmagundi Club, 2002, Honorable Mention, 2008; Best of Show/1st Pl. award Louisville Art Assn., 2003, Jerry's Artarama award Montana Watercolor Soc., 2003, honorable mention Associated Artists Southport, 2004, Franklin Square Gallery, 2004, hon. mention Taos Nat. Watercolor Soc., 2004, Winston Churchill award Mo. Watercolor Soc., 2005, Ursus Abstract award Tubac Ctr. of Arts, 2006, 3rd prize Conneaut Cmty. Ctr. for Arts, 2006, Art student League NY award, Audubon Artists Inc., 2007, Arches Paper award, Oklahama watercolor Assn., 2007; Sr. rsch. fellow Alexander von Humboldt Foun.,Germany, 1978-80. Fellow Internat. Soc. Haematology, Royal Coll. Pathologists; mem. Am. Soc. Hematology, German Soc. Hematology, Nat. Coun. Univ. Rsch. Adminstrn., Nat. Assn. State Univs. and Land-Grant Colls. (mem. exec. com. coun. on rsch. policy and grad. edn. 1990-91), Coun. Grad. Schs., N.Y. Acad. Scis., Sigma Xi. Jewish. Avocations: reading, abstract art painting, writing, music. Home: 475 North St Apt 6F Doylestown PA 18901-3863 Office: Delaware Valley Coll 700 E Butler Ave Doylestown PA 18901-2607 Office Phone: 215-489-2351. Business E-Mail: mishlerj@devalcol.edu.

MISHRA, D. K., orthopedist; s. D. and S. Mishra; m. N. Mishra, June 9, 2003. MBBS, JIPMER, Pondicherry, India, 1996; MSc in Orthopaedics, Pondicherry U., 2000; MCh, U. Dundee, 2008. House officer JIPMER, 1995—96, demonstrator, anatomy, 1996—97, jr. resident, trauma & orthopaedics rotation, 1997—2000, sr. resident, trauma & orthopaedics, 2000; observer, limb reconstrn. and complex trauma Royal Liverpool U. Hosp., England, 2003; sr. house officer, hip & knee unit South Tyneside NHS trust, South Shields, England, 2004—05, clin. fellow, emergency medicine and critical care, 2007; sr. house officer, hip & knee unit Chase Farm Hosp., Enfield, England, 2005—06; clin. fellow, lower limb & spinal unit Sunderland Royal Hosp., England, 2004, registrar, hip & knee unit and spine unit, 2006 North East Surgery Ctr., Gateshead, England, 2008—. Master: RCS; mem.: RCS (Edinburgh), Gen. Med. Coun., Med. Coun. India. Achievements include research in the evaluation of in-shoe & barefoot plantar pressure measurement between gender and ethnicity. Personal E-mail: drdeepakmishra@yahoo.com.

MISHRA, R.K., hospital administrator; MS in Minimal Access Surgery, UK. With Indraprastha Apollo Hosp., New Delhi; chmn. Delhi Laparoscopy Hosp. Pvt. Ltd., India; chief laparoscopic surgeon World Laparoscopy Hosp., Nat. Capital Region Delhi, Gurgaon, India, dir. Prof. minimal access surgery The Global Open Univ., India, head minimal access surgery, India. Author: Text Book of Practical Laparoscopic Surgery, Essentials of Laparoscopy, Mastering the technique of Laparoscopic suturing and knotting, 2007; editor-in-chief World Journal of Laparoscopic Surgery; prodr.: Jaypee's Video Atlas of Laparoscopic Surgery. Recipient Global Laparoscopic Trainer award, Global Med. Edn. award. Mem.: All India Specially Abled Assn. (pres.), Indian Med. Assn., Assn. of Surgeons of India, Soc. of Am. Gastrointestinal and Endoscopic Surgeons, Indian Assn. of Gastrointestinal Endosurgeons, European Assn. for Transluminal Surgery, European Assn. for Endoscopic Surgery, World Assn. of Laparoscopic Surgeon. Avocation: software programming. Office: World Laparoscopy Hospital Cyber City DLF Phase II Gurgaon NCR Delhi India Office Phone: 9101242351555. *

MISHRA, SHRI KANT, neurologist, educator, neuroscientist; s. Jai Gopal and Dil Raji Mishra; m. Ann Mishra, Mar. 3, 1968; children: Alok Kumar, Arvind Kumar. ABMS, Ims BHU, Varanasi, India, 1964; MD, U. Toronto, Canada, 1971; MS, U. Wis., Maddison, 1990. Cert. neurologist ABPN, 1976, in neuromuscular medicine ABPN, 2008. Prof. neurology Keck Sch. Medicine, U. Southern Calif., Los Angeles, 1987—; dir. neuromuscular Va Gla, Los Angeles, 1998. Prof. neurology UCLA, 2007. Bd. dir. Health World on Line, Los Angeles, 2004. Colonel Army Med. Core Res. US Army, 2000—04, Los Angeles. Recipient Best tchr. award, David Geffen Sch. Medicine UCAL, 2004, Lifetime achievement award, AINA, 2009. Office: Univ Southern Calif 1100 N State st 4th fl Clinic Tower Neurology Los Angeles CA 90033 Office Phone: 818-895-9473. Home Fax: 818-895-5801. Business E-Mail: smishra@usc.edu.

MISK, NABIL AHMED, medical educator, researcher; b. Assiut, Egypt, Aug. 8, 1945; s. Ahmed Ali Misk and Hayat Abd El-All Ahmed; m. Samia Ali Ismail, Dec. 4, 1976; children: Tarik Nabil, Ehab Nabil, Noura Nabil. PhD, Moscow Vet. Acad., 1975. Lectr. vet. surgery Assiut U., 1975—79, asst. prof., 1979—83, prof., head dept., 1983—90, prin. investigator, project supplied ministry of internat. cooperation, 1994—, prof., head dept., 2000—05, prof. emeritus, 2005—, dir., project entitled continuous improvement and qualifying accreditation, 2008—; vice dean students affairs Faculty Vet. Medicine, Assiut, 1990—96, dean, 1996—99. Mem. sci. bd. Jour. Camel Practice and Rsch., India, 1995—2011. Sci. dir. Egyptian Vet. Syndicate, Cairo, 1993—2011. Soldier Vet. Svc. Egyptian Army, 1975—76, Cairo. Recipient State Vet. Sci. award, Acad. Sci. Rsch., 1992, Honor of Excellency, Pres. Hosny Moubarak, 1995, Vet. Sci Excellent award, Assiut U., 1998, Best Sci. Rsch. award, 2002. Avocations: swimming, tennis, photography, travel. Home: West Campus Univ Assiut 71526 Egypt Office: Assiut Univ Assiut University St Assiut 71526 Egypt Home Phone: 20882349696; Office Phone: 20882331595. Personal E-mail: nabil.misk@gmail.com.

MISKIMEN, THERESA MARIE, psychiatrist, educator; b. Mayaguez, P.R., Sept. 5, 1964; d. George William and Carmen M. (Rivera) M.; m. Juan Carlos Ortiz. BS in Biology magna cum laude, U. P.R., 1986, MD, 1990. Diplomate Am. Bd. Psychiatry and Neurology. Instr. psychiatry U. Medicine and Dentistry N.J., Newark, 1994-97, asst. prof. psychiatry, 1997—2002; assoc. prof. psychiatry Robert Wood Johnson Med. Sch., Piscataway, 2002—11, prof. psychiatry, 2011—. Med. dir., acute inpatient unit, U. Behavioral Health Care, 2004-, v.p., med. svcs., 2006-. Am. Assn. Med. Colls. fellow, 1997, Disting. fellow. Mem. Am. Psychiat. Assn. (disting. & fellow-chairperson early career psychiatry com. 1997-98); mem. N.J. Psychiat. Assn. (treas. 2004-06, v.p. 2006-08, pres. 2009-10), Beta Beta Beta. Business E-Mail: miskimtm@umdnj.edu.

MISRA, KSHIPRA, research scientist; d. Indu Prabha and Shanti Prakash Atreya; m. Anil Kumar Misra. PhD, MLK Coll., Balrampur, 1982. Scientist E Def. Rsch. & Devel. Orgn., Ambernath, Maharashtra, India, 2001—05; rschr., dir. Dept. Sci. & Tech., New Delhi, 2005—. Recipient Anveshan award, IIM, 2004, Ahmedabad and Bhartiya Stree Shakti award, 2004. Achievements include development of tech. for the removal of arsenic poison from water.

MISRA, RAGHUNATH PRASAD, physician, educator; b. Kolkata, West. Bengal, India, Feb. 1, 1928; came to U.S., 1964; s. Guru Prasad and Anandi M.; m. Therese Rettenmund, Sept. 13, 1963; children: Sima, Joya, Maya, Tara. BSc honors, Calcutta U., 1948; MBBS, Med. Coll., Calcutta, 1953; PhD, McGill U., Montreal, Que., 1965. Diplomate Am. Bd. Anat. and Clin. Pathology. Asst. prof., dir. kidney lab. U. Louisville Sch. Medicine, 1964—68; assoc. investigator and dir. kidney lab Mt. Sinai Hosp., Cleve., 1968—73; asst. prof. Case We. Res. Med. Sch., Cleve., 1973—76; asst. prof., dir. kidney lab. Sch. Medicine La. State U., Shreveport, 1976—80, assoc. prof. Sch. Medicine, 1980—86, prof. Sch. Medicine, 1986—98, emeritus prof. Sch. Medicine, 1998—. Cons. VA Med. Ctr., Shreveport, 1977-98, EA Conway Meml. Hosp., Monroe, La., 1980-98; clin. prof. ophthalmology & dir. Ocular Pathology Sch. Medicine La. State U., Shreveport, 1988— Author: Atlas of Skin Biopsy, 1983 Pres. India Assn. of Shreveport, 1979, 81 Tallisman fellow Mt. Sinai Hosp., 1970-73. Fellow Am. Coll. Pathologists, Am. Soc. Clin. Pathologists, Am. Coll. Internat. Physicians, U. Calcutta Med. Alumni Assn. Am. (pres. 1992-93), Sigma Xi (pres. 1987-89) Democrat. Hindu. Avocations: photography, travel. Office: La State U Health Scis Ctr 1501 Kings Hwy Shreveport LA 71103-4228 Office Phone: 318-675-5012. Business E-Mail: rmisra@lsuhsc.edu. *

MISRA, SATYAJEET, anesthesiologist, educator; b. Cuttack, Orissa, India, May 9, 1974; MD, DNB, MKCG Med. Coll. and Hosp., Berhampur, Orissa, MBBS, 1997, MD, 2003. Diplomate Nat. Bd. Exams, New Delhi. Cons. Sree Chitra Tirunal Inst. Med. Scis. and Tech., Trivandrum, Kerala, India, 2007, asst. prof., anesthesiology, 2010—. Cons. Max Heart Inst., New Delhi, 2006—07. Mem.: Indian Soc. Anesthesia (P.K. Tripathy Meml. award 2002, Kops award 2010), Indian Soc. Cardiothoracic and Vascular Anesthesiologists. Avocations: music, reading, ping pong/table tennis. Home: Flat B-6 NFH SCTIMST Quarters Poonthi Trivandrum Kerala 695011 India Personal E-mail: satyajeetmisra@rediffmail.com.

MISSONI, EDUARDO, global health expert; b. Rome, July 31, 1954; Degree in Medicine and Surgery, U. Roma La Sapienza, 1979. Prof. global health and devel. U. Commerciale Luigi Bocconi, 2002—. Office: Bocconi University CERGAS via Roentgen 1 Milan 20136 Italy Business E-Mail: mail@eduardomissoni.net, eduardo.missoni@unibocconi.it.

MITA, SHUJI, neurologist, researcher; b. Kumamoto, Japan, Sept. 9, 1955; s. Yasuyoshi and Asami Mita; m. Hiroko Nagashima, Dec. 19, 1956; children: Shuichiro, Yuko, Shuhei, Reiko. MD, Kumamoto U. Sch. of Medicine, Japan, 1980, PhD, 1987. Cert. Neurology Japanese Soc. Neurology, 1986. Asst. prof. Kumamoto U. Sch. of Medicine, Japan, 1990—2002; sect. chief neurology Nat. Hosp. Orgn., Kumamoto Saishunso Hosp., Kikuchi-gun, Kumamoto, Japan, 2002—03. Achievements include research in establishment of DNA diagnosis of Familial amyloidotic polyneuropathy; relationship between mitochondrial DNA mutations and muscle pathology; gene therapy of amyotrophic lateral sclerosis using SOD1 mice, adenoviral vectors and human Bcl-2. Home: Hirata 1009 Mashiki-Machi Kamimashiki Kumamoto 861-2212 Japan Office: Nat Hosp Orgn Kumamoto Saishunso Hosp 2659 Suya Nishigoshi-machi Kikuchi Kumamoto 861-1102 Japan Office Fax: +81-96-242-2619; Home Fax: +81-96-286-4435. Personal E-mail: ccn15610@syd.odn.ne.jp. E-mail: mita@saisyunsou.hosp.go.jp.

MITAKA, CHIEKO, anesthesiologist, intensivist; b. Kofu, Japan, June 6, 1949; d. Masahiko and Yachiko (Aikawa) Shimizu; m. Shoun Mitaka, Dec. 21, 1975; 2 children. MB, Tokyo Med. and Dental U., 1975, MD, 1986. Cert. Prof. Bd. Intensive Care Medicine. Resident Tokyo Med. and Dental U., 1975-77, fellow, 1977-80; staff Hiroo Hosp., Tokyo, 1980-82; asst. Tokyo Med. and Dental U., 1982-94, instr., 1994-99, assoc. prof., 1999—. Contbr. articles to profl. jours. Recipient Grant-in-aid for sci. rsch. Ministry of Edn., Sci. and Culture, Japan, 1993-95, 97-99, 2002-05, 06—. Mem. Soc. Anesthesiology, Soc. Intensive Care Medicine, Soc. Critical Care Medicine, Soc. Emergency Medicine. Avocation: playing piano. Office: Tokyo Med and Dental U Grad Sch 1-5-45 Yushima Bunkyo-ku Tokyo 113-8519 Japan Office Phone: +81-3-5803-5650. Business E-Mail: c.mitaka.icu@tmd.ac.jp.

MITANI, AKIO, dental educator; b. Osaka, Japan, July 21, 1971; PhD, Aichi Gakuin U., Nagoya, Japan, 2000. Lectr. dept. periodontology Aichi Gakuin U., 2000—. Mem.: Japan Acad. Esthetic Dentistry, Japanese Soc. Oral Implantology, Japanese Soc. Periodontology, Japanese Soc. Immunology, Internat. and Am. Assn. Dental Rsch. Avocation: movies. Office: Aichi Gakuin University Dept Periodontology Sch Dentistry 2-11 Suemori-dori Chikusa-ku Nagoya Aichi 464-8651 Japan

MITCH, WILLIAM EVANS, nephrologist; b. Birmingham, Ala., July 22, 1941; s. William Evans and Mary Elizabeth (Ackerman) Mitch; m. Frances Alexandra Fisher, Aug. 21, 1965; children: Eleanor Baylor, William Armistead. BA, Harvard Coll., Cambridge, Mass., 1963; MD, Harvard Med. Sch., 1967. Cert. internal medicine and nephrology Am. Bd. Internal Medicine. Intern Brigham & Women's Hosp., Boston, 1967-68, resident, 1968-69, 1973—74, Johns Hopkins Hosp., Balt., 1972-73; clin. assoc. NIH, Bethesda, Md., 1969-72; from asst. prof. to assoc. prof. dept. pharmacology Johns Hopkins U., Balt., 1974-78; assoc. prof. medicine Harvard Med. Sch., Boston, 1978-87; prof. Emory U. Sch. Medicine, Atlanta, 1987—2002; disting. prof. U. Tex., Galveston, 2002—04; prof. Baylor Coll. Medicine, Houston, 2004—. Mem. study sect. NIH, 1988—92, mem. nat. adv. com., Nat. Inst. Diabetes, Digestive and Kidney Diseases, 2007—. Editor: The Progressive Nature of Renal Disease, 1986, 2d edit., 1992, Nutrition and the Kidney, 1988, 6th edit., 2010. Pres. region II Nat. Kidney Found., 1990—92, chmn. sci. adv. bd., 1996—98; chmn. exec. coun. kidney Am. Heart Assn. Recipient John Peters award, Am. Soc. Nephrology; grantee, NIH, 1979—, Merit award, 2004—. Mem.: Internat. Soc. Nephrology (treas. 1997—2003), Am. Soc. Nephrology (pres. 2004), Am. Clin. and Climatol. Assn., Assn. Am. Physicians, Am. Soc. Clin. Investigation. Office: Baylor Coll Nephrology Divsn MS Alkek N-520 1 Baylor Plz Houston TX 77030 Office Phone: 713-798-8350. Business E-Mail: mitch@bcm.edu.

MITCHARD, HELEN MARGARET, cognitive scientist; d. John Charles Mitchard and Beverley Margaret Friling; m. Conn Valentine Copas. BA in Performing Arts, U. Adelaide, 1989; diploma in Arts Adminstrn., U. South Australia, 1990, BSc in Computing and Info. Sci., 1999; BSc in Social Scis., Flinders U., 1997. Tchr. Dept. Edn. South Australia, 1985—93; artist in residence Gladstone and Dists. Cmty. Dance, Gladstone, South Australia, Australia, 1989; computer operator Adelaide (Australia) Casino, 1996; cognitive scientist Def. Sci. and Tech. Orgn., Edinburgh, South Australia, Australia, 1997—. Arts coord. Come Out '91 Festival, 1991; choreographer stage and tour mgr. Vitalstatistix Theatre Co., 1992; treas. Adelaide (Australia) Festival Fringe, 1992. Home: 58 Diamantina Cres 2617 Kaleen ACT Australia Office Phone: 61 2 61286415. Personal E-mail: helen.mitchard@dsto.defence.gov.au.

MITCHELL, ANN MARGARET, psychiatric nurse practitioner, educator; b. Pitts. d. John G. and Joan M. RN diploma, Pa. State U., 1974, BS, 1976, MS, 1979; PhD, U. Pitts., 1987. Clin. nurse specialist Western Psychiat. Inst. and Clinic, Pitts., 1985-89; pvt. practice, traveling nurse, cons. Pa., Calif, 1989-91; rsch. asst. prof. U. Pitts. Sch. Nursing, Pitts., 1991-95, asst. prof. nursing & psychiatry, 1995—. Bd. trustees Mayview State Hosp., 2001—. Collaborator: Interpersonal Relationship Skills Tng. Program, 1978, Rels. Tng., 1984. Mem. Exec. Women's Coun., Greater Pitts., Inc., 1992. Recipient traineeship Pa. State U., University Park, 1976-78, scholarship U. Pit ts., Pa., 1980-82; grantee faculty scholar Uppsala U., Sweden, 1996, Keio U., Tokyo, 1998. Mem. ANA, Am. Assn. Suicidology, Am. Found. Suicide Prevention (bd. dirs. Pitts. chpt.), Psychiat. Nurse Mgrs. Pa., Inc. (hon.), Assn. Clin. Nurse Specialists, Sigma Theta Tau, Kappa Delta Pi. Home: 5826 Nicholson St Pittsburgh PA 15217-2341 Office: Univ Pitts Sch Nursing # 415 Victoria Bldg 3500 Victoria St Pittsburgh PA 15261 Business E-Mail: ammi@pitt.edu.

MITCHELL, BEVERLY SHRIVER, hematologist, oncologist, educator; b. Balt., May 14, 1944; m. John Robert Pringle; children: Robert Mitchell, Elizabeth Greene. AB summa cum laude in Biochemistry, Smith Coll., 1965; MD, Harvard U., 1969. Hematology fellow U. Mich., Ann Arbor, 1975-77, from instr. to asst. prof. internal medicine, 1977-81, assoc. prof., 1981-87, prof. internal medicine and pharmacology, 1987-91, U. N.C., Chapel Hill, 1991—, divsn. chief hematology/oncology, 1994—2003; assoc. dir. Lineberger Cancer Ctr., Chapel Hill, 1994—2005; deputy dir. Stanford Cancer Ctr., Stanford U., 2005—. Mem. bd. sci. counselors Cancer Treatment divsn. Nat. Cancer Inst. Vice chair med. and sci. affairs Leukemia and Lymphoma Soc., 2003—05. Recipient Stohlman award Leukemia Soc., 1988. Mem. Am. Soc. Hematology (treas. 1991-96, v.p. 1998, pres. 2000), Phi Beta, Inst. Medicine. Achievements include research in nucleotide metabolism and the development of novel therapies for hematologic malignancies. Office: Stanford Blood Center 3373 Hillview Ave Palo Alto CA 94304-1204 Office Phone: 650 736 7716. Business E-Mail: bmitchell@stanford.edu.

MITCHELL, CAROL ANN, nursing educator; b. Portsmouth, Va., Aug. 31, 1942; d. William Howell and Eleanor Bertha (Wesarg) M.; m. David Alan Friedman, June 17, 1971 (div. 1988). Diploma, NYU, 1963; BS, Columbia U., 1968, MA, 1971, EdM, 1974, EdD, 1980; MS, SUNY, Stony Brook, 1990. Charge nurse Nassau County Med. Ctr., East Meadow, N.Y., 1963-65; staff nurse Meml. Hosp., NYC, 1965-68; head nurse, supr. Cmty. at Glen Cove (N.Y.), 1969-71; assoc. prof. dept. nursing Queensborough C.C. CUNY, Bayside, 1971-80; assoc. prof. Marion A. Buckley Sch. Nursing Adelphi U., Garden City, N.Y., 1981-88; ednl. cons. Nat. League for Nursing, NYC, 1980-81; prof. sch. nursing SUNY, Stony Brook, 1988-92, chmn. adult nursing, 1988-92; prof. chair Coll. Nursing East Tenn. State U., 1992-95, mem faculty, 1995-96; geriat. nurse practitioner, dir. geriat. evaluation unit Vet. Affairs Med. Ctr., Mountain Home, Tenn., 1997—2004; tchr. Therapeutic Yoga & Taichi. Mem. faculty Regents Coll. degrees in nursing program USNY, Albany, 1978-91, cons., 1978—; faculty cons. geriats. Montefiore Med. Ctr., 1991-93. Editor emeritus: Scholarly Inquiry in Nursing Practice, 1983—; contbr. articles to profl. jours. Robert Wood Johnson clin. nurse scholar postdoctoral fellow U. Rochester (N.Y.), 1983-85. Mem.: Am. Geriatrics Soc., Am. Nurses Assn. Avocations: reading, gardening, bicycling, travel, cooking.

MITCHELL, JAMES B., medical researcher; PhD in cellular radiation biology, Colo. State U., 1978. Joined Radiation Br. Nat. Cancer Inst., NIH, 1979, ind. investigator, 1984—, past chief radiobiology sect., past dep. chief Radiation Oncology Br., chief Radiation Biology Br. Ctr. Cancer Rsch., 1993—, head tumor biology sect. Office: Ctr Cancer Rsch 10 Center Dr Bldg 10 Rm B3B69 9000 Rockville Pike Bethesda MD 20892 Office Phone: 301-496-7511. Office Fax: 301-480-2238. E-mail: jbm@helix.nih.gov. *

MITCHELL, JASON WAYNE, interventional radiologist; b. Passaic, NJ, Dec. 29, 1976; s. William Steven and Diane Lee (Brum) Mitchell; m. Amy Michelle Morin, July 10, 1999; 1 child, Caoilfhionn Lynn. BS, Boston Coll., Chestnut Hill, 1994—98; MD, UMDNJ-NJMS, Newark, 2000—04. Intern transitional program St. Barnabas Med. Ctr., Livingston, NJ, 2004—05; resident diagnostic radiology UMDNJ, 2005—09; fellow interventional radiology Northwestern Meml. Hosp., Chgo., 2009—. Mem.: Soc. Interventional Radiology, Radiologic Soc. N.Am., Am. Coll. Radiology, Am. Mensa. Conservative. Roman Catholic. Achievements include research in diagnostic and interventional radiology with a focus in hepatic pathology and the treatment of hepatocellular carcinoma. Office: UMDNJ 150 Bergen St C-320 Newark NJ 07103 Home: 2355 Eckert Rd Mansfield OH 44904-8729 Office Phone: 973-972-5188. Personal E-mail: mitchejn@gmail.com.

MITCHELL, JO KATHRYN, retired hospital technical supervisor; b. Clarksville, Ark., Dec. 1, 1934; d. Vintris Franklin and Melissa Lucile (Edwards) Clark; m. James M. Mitchell, June 4, 1955 (dec. Feb. 1973); children: James, Karen Ann, Leslie Kay, Vicki Lynn. Student, U. Ark., Fayetteville, 1952-53; student, Coll. Ozarks, 1953-54, U. Ark., 1954-55, Little Rock U., 1958. Technologist clin. chemistry U. Hosp., Little Rock, 1956-57, asst. supr., 1957-59, rsch. technologist, 1960-62, asst. supr. clin. chemistry, 1979-82, supr. clin. chemistry, 1982—2003; technologist Conway County Hosp., Morrilton, Ark., 1959; office mgr., co-owner Medic Pharmacy, Little Rock, 1962-71; owner The Cheese Shop, Little Rock, 1977-80, Pharmacy Tech., 2009—. Adult advisor Order Rainbow Girls local, Little Rock, 1970-84, state, Ark., 1977-84. Mem. Pharmacy Aux. (pres. 1967-69). Methodist. Avocations: reading, needlecrafts, genealogy, travel. Home: 6908 Lucerne Dr Little Rock AR 72205-5029 Personal E-mail: jkmitch@sbcglobal.net.

MITCHELL, KENNETH DAVID, physiologist, educator; b. Musselburgh, Scotland, Mar. 5, 1959; children: Elaine J., Fraser K., Keith J. BSc with upper 2d class honors, U. Edinburgh, Scotland, 1981, PhD in Physiology, 1986. Physiology tutor Univ. Med. Sch., Edinburgh, 1981-84; rsch. assoc. dept. physiology and biophysics Nephrology Rsch. and Tng. Ctr. U. Ala., Birmingham, 1984-86, postdoctoral rsch. fellow, 1986-87, rsch. instr., 1987-88, scientist I, 1987-88; asst. prof. dept. physiology Tulane U. Sch. Medicine, New Orleans, 1988-95, assoc. prof., 1995—. Contbr. articles to profl. jours. Fellow Am. Heart Assn. (fellow Coun. High Blood Pressure Rsch. 1993—, Established Investigator award 1995-2000), Am. Soc. Nephrology; mem. Am. Physiol. Soc., Internat. Soc. Nephrology. Office: Tulane U Sch Medicine Dept Physiology SL39 1430 Tulane Ave New Orleans LA 70112-2699 Office Phone: 504-988-2593. Business E-Mail: kdmitch@tulane.edu.

MITCHELL, MADELEINE ENID, retired nutritionist; b. Jamaica, West Indies, Dec. 14, 1941; came to U.S., 1963, naturalized, 1974. d. William Keith and Doris Christine (Levey) M. BSc in Home Econs., McGill U., Montreal, Que., Can., 1963; MS, Cornell U., 1965, PhD, 1968. Asst. prof. Wash. State U., Pullman, 1969-77, assoc. prof., 1978—2004, acting. chmn. home econs. rsch. ctr., 1981-83; ret., 2004. Nutrition scientist U.S. Dept. Agr., Washington, 1980-81. Author: Jamaican Ancestry: How to Find Out More, 2009. Episcopalian. Avocations: genealogy, music. Personal E-mail: mitchelm@pullman.com.

MITCHELL, MARY JENKINS, public health service officer; b. Rochester, NY; d. Hudson and Clara May Jenkins; m. Floyd Mitchell, Aug. 24, 1991; 1 child, Derek Scot. B Cmty. Health, St. Joseph's Coll., Bklyn., 1984; MPA, LI U., Bklyn., 1999. Cert. non-profit mgmt. Columbia U., 1986. Asst. to pres. Bklyn. Borough Pres.' Office, 1987—95; dir., health careers inst. LI U., 1995—2000; regional v.p. Am. Cancer Soc., Bklyn., 2000—03; exec. dir. MSI Area Health Edn. Ctr., NYC, 2004—. Adj. prof. LI U., Brooklyn, NY, 1998—2000; student cons. Pub. Svc. Commn., Pretoria, South Africa, 1998. V.p. Justice Works Cmty., Inc., Bklyn., 1995—2000; deaconess Flatbush Tompkins Congl. Ch., Bklyn., 1997—2004; bd. dirs. NY Women's Found., NYC, 1993—95. Recipient Ability, Accomplishment and Cmty. Svc. award, Outstanding Young Women Am., 1986, Cmty. Leadership award, Bklyn Exec. Bus. Women's Assoc., 2004. Mem.: Pi Alpha Alpha (life). Office: Manhattan-State Area Health Educ Ctr 43 Central Park North New York NY 10026 Personal E-mail: mljm1@excite.com. Business E-Mail: mary@msiahec.org.

MITCHELL, PAULA RAE, nursing educator, dean; b. Independence, Mo., Jan. 10, 1951; d. Millard Henry and E. Lorene (Denton) Gates; m. Ralph William Mitchell, May 24, 1975. BS in Nursing, Graceland U., Lamoni, Iowa, 1973; MS in Nursing, U. Tex., 1976; EdD in Ednl. Adminstrn., N.Mex. State U., 1996. RN, Tex., Mo. Instr. nursing El Paso C.C., Tex., 1979-85, dir. nursing Tex., 1985—2003, acting divsn. chmn. health occupations Tex., 1985-86, divsn. dean Tex., 1998-99, dean health occupations Tex., 1999-2000, curriculum facilitator Tex., 1984—85, dean health occupations, math and sci., campus dean Rio Grande, 2000—08, dean health career tech. edn. Math and sci. campus dean Rio Grade, 2008—. Ob-gyn. nurse practitioner Planned Parenthood, El Paso, 1981-86, med. com., 1986-98; cons. in field, army med. dept. officer Acad. Health Scis.Ft. Author: (with Grippando) Nursing Perspectives and Issues, 1989, 93; contbr. articles to profl. jours. Founder, bd. dirs. Health-CREST, El Paso, 1981—85; mem. pub. edn. com. Am. Cancer Soc., El Paso, 1983—84, mem. profl. activities com., 1992—93; mem. El-Paso City-County Bd. Health, 1989—91; mem. Govt. Applications Rev. Com. Rio Grande Coun. Govts., 1989—91; mem. collaborative coun. El Paso Magnet H.S. for Health Care Professions, 1992—94; co-chair health and human svcs. task force Unite El Paso Health, 1996—98, mem. steering com., 1999—2000; co-chair health taskforce El Paso Cmty. Legis. Agenda, 1997—99; mem. adv. com. Ctr. for Border Health Rsch., Paso del Norte Health Found., 1998—2004; mem. Leadership El Paso, 1999; mem. health profl. shortage task force Greater El Paso C. of C., 2001—, mem. health care coun., 2002—; mem. star adv. com. Canutillo Tex. Ind. Sch. Dist., 2003—05; mem. El Paso County Civil Svc. Commn., 2006—10, chair, 2009—10; coord. West Tex. Med. Res. Corps, 2006—; vice chair El Paso VOAD, 2011—; bd. dirs. Border Health Inst., El Paso, 2001—08, sec.-treas., 2003—08; mem. cmty. adv. bd. Victory Warriors Drill and Dance Acad., El Paso, 2001—11; mem. governing bd. Mesa Hills Specialty Hosp., 2002—09. Capt. US Army, 1972—78, capt. USAR, 1978—98, ret. USAR, 1998. Decorated Army Commendation medal, Meritorious Svc. medal; named to Women's Hall Fame, El Paso Commn., 1999; named Outstanding Alumni, N.Mex. State U. Dept. Edn. Mgmt. and Devel., 2002-03; recipient Unite El Paso Legacy award 1997, Merit and Svc. cert. Victory Warriors Drill and Dance Acad., 2003, Outstanding Cmty. Svc. award, 2003, Appreciation and Cmty. Responsibility cert., 2005, Appreciation cert., 2006. Mem. Nat. League Nursing (resolutions com. Assocs. Degree coun. 1987-89, accreditation site visitor, AD coun. 1990—2010, Tex. edn. com. 1991-92, Tex. 3d v.p. 1992-93, Tex. 1st v.p. 1997-99, nominating com. 1999-2000), Am. Soc. Psychoprophylaxis Obstetrics (cert. childbirth educator 1978), Nurses Assn. Am. Coll. Ob-Gyn. (cert. in ambulatory women's healthcare, 1983, chpt. coord. 1979-83, nat. program rev. com. 1984-86, corr. 1987-89), Advanced Nurse Practitioner Group El Paso (coord. 1980-83, legis. com. 1984), Am. Phys. Therapist Assn. (commn. on accreditation, site visitor for phys. therapist asst. programs 1991-), Orgn. Assoc. Degree Nursing (Tex. membership chmn. 1985-89, chmn. goals com. 1989-2004, nat. bylaws com. 1990-95), Am. Vocat. Assn., Am. Assn. Women Cmty. and Jr. Colls., Tex. Orgn. Nurse Execs., Nat. Coun. Workforce Edn. (articulation task force 1986-89, program standards task force 1991-93), Nat. Coun. Instrnl. Adminstrs., Tex. Soc. Allied Health Profls. (sec. 2004-2007, elect pres. 2007-08, pres. 2008-09, past pres. 2009-10), Tex. Nurses Assn. (pres. elect dist. one 2002-03, pres. 2003-05, past pres. 2005-06, bd. mem., 2008-09, nomination com. mem. 2009-), Am. Soc. Allied Health Profls. (edn. com. 1993-96), El Paso C. of C. (healthcare coun. 2001-05), El Paso Commn. for Women (treas. 2007—), Am. Legion, Mil. Order World Wars (El Paso chpt. staff officer 2007-08, jr. vice comdr., 2008-10, sr. vice comdr., 2010-, chair Phoenician Award Com. 2009-, Dept. Rio Grande jr. vice comdr., 2010-11, svc. cmdr. 2010-11, sr. vice comdr., dept. Rio Grande 2011-, Merit award, 2008, Silver Patrick Henry, 2009, Otstanding Chpt. Companion, 2010, Outstanding Svc. medal, 2011), Sigma Theta Tau, Phi Kappa Phi. Mem. Christian Ch. (Disciples Of Christ). Home: 4616 Cupid Dr El Paso TX 79924-1726 Office: El Paso C C PO Box 20500 El Paso TX 79998-0500 Office Phone: 915-831-4030. Business E-Mail: pmitche8@epcc.edu.

MITCHELL, PETER WILLIAM, alcohol and drug abuse services professional; b. Queens, NY, Sept. 2, 1950; s. James Francis and Margaret (Tiernan); children: Bryan Scott, Shannon Marie, Kevin James, Michael Ryan; m. Kathryn Ann (Comune), Dec. 5, 2008; step children: Tracey Ann, Russell William. BS in Mktg., Fordham U., 1972; MBA, Calif. Coast U., 1984; PhD in Chem. Dependency magna cum laude, La Salle U., 1997. Cert. criminal justice specialist, master addictions counselor, bd. cert., clin. supr., Internationally Cert. Alcoholic & Drug Coun., lin. Clin. Alcohol & Drug Coun., Compulsive Gambling Counselor. Spl. agt. FBI, Washington, 1972-77; store co-mgr. First Nat. Stores, Inc., Somerville, Mass., 1977-78; area sales mgr. H.J. Heinz Co., Indpls., 1978-83; exec. sales rep. Sandoz Nutrition Corp., Mpls., 1983-91; regional sales mgr. Fresenius Pharma USA, Inc., New Brunswick, N.J., 1991-92; sales cons. Cardinal Health/Marmac Div., East Windsor, Conn., 1992-93; primary counselor, case mgr. Sunrise House Found., Lafayette, NJ, 1993-98; clin. dir. Turning Point, Inc., Secaucus, NJ, 1998-00; sr. clinician St. Clare's Hosp., Boonton Twp., NJ, 2000—01; pres. Mitchell Addiction Cons. Svcs., NJ, 1992—; clinician Overlook Hosp., Summit, NJ, 2002—. Apptd. mem. behavioral health tech. adv. panel substance use disorders Nat. Quality Forum, Washington, 2006—. Bd. mem. Vernon (N.J.) Twp. Little League, 1985-89, Vernon (N.J.) Bd. Ethics, 1991—. Recipient Capitol award Nat. Leadership Coun., Washington, 1991. Mem. Nat. Assn. Alcoholism and Drug Abuse Counselors, Am. Assn. Compulsive Gambling Counselors, Nat. Assn. Forensic Counselors. Republican. Episcopalian. Avocations: softball, basketball, volleyball, Karate. Office: Overlook Hosp 99 Beauvoir Ave Summit NJ 07902 Home: 24 Ben Franklin Dr Franklin NJ 07416 Office Phone: 908-522-4875. Personal E-mail: drpwm125@aol.com.

MITCHELL, PHILIP BOWDEN, psychiatrist; b. Sydney, Jan. 19, 1953; s. Kenneth Shorter and Shirley Lorraine Mitchell; m. Margaret Susan Denny, Nov. 15, 1977; children: Katherine Ellen Gambell, Stuart James Denny, Amelia Elizabeth. MBBS, U. Sydney, 1976; MD, U. NSW, Sydney, 1990. Registrar Bethlem Royal and Maudsley Hosps., London, 1982—83; guest rschr. psychopharmacology NIMH, Bethesda, Md., 1993; prof. U. NSW, 1999—, head sch., 2002—, convenor, brain scis., 2005—, scientia prof., 2008—; guest prof. Shanghai Jiaotong U., 2006—. Samuel Novey psychol. medicine lectr. Johns Hopkins U., 2008. Contbr. articles to numerous rsch. jours. Dir. Anika Found., Sydney, 2006—08. Recipient Founders medal, Australasian Soc. Psychiat. Rsch., 2004, Vocat. Excellence award, Rotary Internat., 2008. Fellow: Royal Coll. Psychiatrists, Royal Australian and New Zealand Coll. Psychiatrists (Sr. Rsch. award 2002). Achievements include patents for bipolar disorder gene. Office: Univ NSW 2052 Sydney Australia Office Fax: 61-2-93828151. Business E-Mail: phil.mitchell@unsw.edu.au.

MITCHELL, STEPHEN RAY, dean, rheumatologist; MD, U. NC, 1976. Cert. in internal medicine 1981, in pediat. 1983, in rheumatology 1986, in pediatric rheumatology 1999. Internship and residency NC Meml. Hosp.; practicing adult and pediatric rheumatologist; faculty mem. Georgetown U. Sch. Medicine, Washington, 1988—, program dir. Internal Medicine Residency Program, 1992—99, assoc. dean clinical curriculum, 1998—2000, sr. assoc. dean undergrad. acad. affairs, 2000, Joseph J. Butenas prof. med. edn., dir. medicine/pediatric program, assoc. program dir. medicine/pediatrics, dean med. edn. Recipient Upjohn Young Investigator award. Office: Georgetown Univ Sch Med Box 570417 Medical & Dental Bldg Rm 106 Washington DC 20057-0417 Office Phone: 202-687-3922. Office Fax: 202-687-2792. E-mail: mitchelr@georgetown.edu. *

MITCHELL, STUART, observing physician, medical entomologist; m. Martha Mitchell. BS in Physics, Iowa State U., Ames, 1981, BS in Forensic Psychology, 2007; PhD in Entomology, Trinity Coll., 2000, PhD in Zoology, 2002, PhD in Biology, 2003, PhD in Naturopathy, 2005, D of Naturopathy; PhD in Complimentary and Alternative Care (hon.), Breyer State U., 2006; DSc in Osteo. Medicine, Des Moines U., 2005, MPH, 2007. Cert. in traditional naturopathy, bd. cert. family practice, bd. cert. fellow integrative medicine, diplomate Am. bd. forensic examiners; bd. cert. entomologist, cert. in homeland security, trainer in food safety Nat. Environ. Health Assn., med. investigator. Tech. dir. Springer Svcs., Des Moines, 1996—2010; prin. tech. specialist PestWest LLC, Sarasota, Fla., 1996—. Tchr., food mgr. NSF Internat., Des Moines, 2002—, tchr. HACCP, 2002—; cons. Whitmire Micro-Gen Labs., 2003. Author PestWest tng. manual; contbr. columns to Pest Mgmt. Mag. Developer Quality Pro Inst.; mem. Des Moines Parks Bd., 2002—03; bd. dirs. Blank Pk. Zoo, Des Moines, 2002—03, Des Moines Bot. Ctr., 2002—03. Fellowship, Am. Assn. Integrative Medicine. Mem.: Am. Acad. Family Physicians, Entomol. Soc. Am., Am. Inst. Baking, Phi Chi Omega (BCE dir. 2009). Democrat. Lutheran. Avocations: science, walking, lecturing. Office: PestWest LLC 1705 45th St Des Moines IA 50310 Home Phone: 515-333-8923. Personal E-mail: docmitchell@me.com.

MITCHELL, SUSAN LISA, geriatrician; b. Montreal, Canada; BS, McGill U., 1984; MD cum laude, U. Ottawa, 1988; MPH, Harvard U., 1996. Lic. Buffalo, NY, 1988, Commonwealth of Mass., 1992, cert. Coll. Physicians and Surgeons Ont., 1989, Med. Coun. Can., 1989, Royal Coll. Physicians and Surgeons of Canada, 1994, diplomate Am. Bd. Internal Med. Intern in internal medicine Ottawa Civic Hosp., 1988—89; resident in internal medicine Ottawa Civic and Gen. Hospitals, 1989—91, staff physician, 1997—98; clin. fellow in medicine, aging divsn. Harvard Med. Sch., 1992—94, rsch. fellow in medicine, aging divsn., 1994—95; staff geriatrician Hebrew Rehab. Ctr. Aged, Boston, 1994—97, med. dir. Agewell Sr. Services Outpatient Clinic, 1995—96, staff physician, 2000—, assoc. scientist, 2002—05; asst. prof. medicine U. Ottawa, 1997—2000, asst. prof. epidemiology and cmty. medicine, 1999—2000; dir. rsch., geriatrics divsn. Ottawa Hosp., 1997—2000; instr. medicine Harvard Med. Sch., 2000—01, assoc. dir. fellowship in geriatric medicine, 2000—, asst. prof. medicine, 2001—05, assoc. prof. medicine, 2005—; assoc. dir. Harvard Geriatric Medicine Fellowship Prog., Boston, 2000—05, assoc. dir. rsch. training, 2005—; assoc. scientist Hebrew Sr. Life Inst. Aging Rsch., Boston, 2001—05, sr. scientist, 2006—. Affiliate mem., clin. epidemiology unit Loeb Health Rsch. Inst., Ottawa, 1997—2000. Recipient Career Scientist award, Ont. Ministry Health, 1998—2000, NIH-NIA K23 Mentored Clin. Scientist award, 2001—04; fellow Charles A. King Trust, 1995—97. Fellow: Royal Coll. Physicians and Surgeons of Canada; mem.: Nat. Alzheimer's Assn. (grant reviewer 2005—, abstract review com. 2006—), Gerontological Soc. America, Physicians for Human Rights, Am. Geriatrics Soc. (ethics com. 2004—07, Best Paper in Biol. Sciences 2003, Best Paper in Health Services Rsch. 2006), Am. Coll. Physicians, Coll. Physicians and Surgeons Ont. Office: Hebrew Senior Life 1200 Centre St Boston MA 02131 Office Phone: 617-363-8626. Office Fax: 617-363-8936. E-mail: smitchell@hrca.harvard.edu.

MITCHELL, TEDDY LEE, physician; b. Columbia, La., Feb. 24, 1962; s. Oliver Clayton nad Mary Elizabeth (Johnston) M.; m. Janet Luisa Tornelli, Apr. 9, 1988; children: Mary Katherine, Oliver Charles, Christopher Tornelli. BS in Biology, Stephen F. Austin State U., 1983; MD, U. Tex. Med. Br., 1987. Diplomate Am. Bd. Internal Medicine, Cert. of Added Qualification-Sports Medicine. Intern U. Tex. Med. Br., Galveston, 1987-88, resident, 1988-90, 90-91; med. dir. wellness program Cooper Aerobics Ctr., Dallas, 1991—2006, pres., med. dir., 2006—, pres. & CEO, 2008—. Mem. Rep. Sen. Inner Cir., Washington, 1993, Heritage Found., Washington, 1993. Capt. U.S. Army Res. Med. Corps, 1988-96. Fellow ACP (cert. Merit 1990), Am. Coll. Sports Medicine; mem. AMA, Tex. Med. Assn., Dallas County Med. Soc. Methodist. Avocations: exercise, travel, music. Home: 3224 Lovers Ln Dallas TX 75225-7626 Home Phone: 214-750-1278.

MITCHELL, WAYNE LEE, retired health administrator; b. Mar. 25, 1937; s. Albert C. and Elizabeth Isabelle (Nagel) M.; m. Marie Galletti. BA, U. Redlands, Calif., 1959; MSW, Ariz. State U., 1970, EdD, 1979. Social worker various county, state, and fed. agys., 1962-70; social worker Bur. Indian Affairs, Phoenix, 1970-77, USPHS, 1977-79; asst. prof. Ariz. State U., 1979-84; with USPHS, Phoenix, 1984—2003, ret., 2003; pvt. practice cons. Phoenix, 2003—. Lectr. in field. Contbr. articles to profl. jours. Bd. dirs. Phoenix Indian Cmty. Sch., 1973-75, ATLATL, 1994-98, Partnership for Cmty. Devel. Ariz. State U.-West, 1996-99, Cen. Ariz. Health Sys. Agy., 1982-85; mem. Phoenix Area Health Adv. Bd., 1975, Cmty. Behavioral Mental Health Bd., 1976-80, Fgn. Rels. Com., Phoenix; trustee Heard Mus. Anthropology, Phoenix, 1996; apptd. Ariz. State Bd. Behavioral Health Examiners, 2000-2002. With USCG, 1960-62. Recipient Comty. Svc. award, Ariz. Temple of Islam, 1980, Ariz. State U., 1996, Dir. Excellence award, Phoenix Area IHS Dir., 1992, 1993, Nat. IHS Dir.'s award for outstanding svc., 2001, NARD Lifetime Achievement award, 2005; named in Voices and Faces, 2003. Mem. NASW (Lifetime Achievement award 2003), Fgn. Rels. Coun., U.S.-China Assn., Kappa Delta Pi, Phi Delta Kappa, Chi Sigma Chi. Democrat. Congregationalist. Home: PO Box 9592 Phoenix AZ 85068-9592 Personal E-mail: drwlmitch@cox.net.

MITCHISON, TIMOTHY JOHN, cell biologist, pharmacology educator; b. Edinburgh, July 20, 1958; came to US, 1980; s. Avrion and Lorna (Martin) M. BA in Biochemistry, Oxford U., Eng., 1980; PhD in Biochemistry, U. Calif., San Francisco, 1984. Asst. prof. U. Calif., San Francisco, 1987-92, assoc. prof., 1992—97; co-dir. Harvard Med Sch. Inst. Chem. and Cell Biology, Boston, 1997—2005; prof. cell biology Harvard Med Sch., Boston, 1997—2003, Hasib Sabbagh prof., 1999—, prof. systems biology, 2003—. Contbr. numerous sci. articles to profl. publs. Rsch. grantee NIH, 1987; fellow Packard Found., Searle Found. Fellow Am. Acad. Arts and Sciences, Royal Soc.; mem. Am. Soc. Cell Biology. Avocations: dog-walking, fishing. Office: Harvard Med Sch Dept Systems Biology Alpert 536 200 Longwood Ave Boston MA 02115 Office Phone: 617-432-3805. Office Fax: 617-432-5012. E-mail: timothy_mitchison@hms.harvard.edu.

MITEVA, MARIYA, dermatologist, researcher; b. Sofia, Bulgaria, Apr. 18, 1978; MD, Med. U. Sofia, 2002. Resident, dermatology Med. U. Sofia, 2003—07; postdoc. rsch. fellow Skin Physiology Lab. Dept. Dermatology and Allergology Friederich Schiller U., Jena, Germany, 2005—07; assoc. scientist U. Miami Miller Sch. Medicine, Fla., 2008—. Reviewer, Dermatology Jours., 2010—. Recipient Rsch. award, Women's Dermatology Soc., 2011, Nail Coun. Rsch. award, 2011, NAHRS Mentorship award, 2011. Mem.: Internat. Soc. Dermoscopy, Internat. Soc. Dermatology, Internat. Soc. Dermatopathology. Achievements include research in hair pathology. Avocations: travel, hiking. Office: 1600 NW 10th Ave Dept Dermatology Miami FL 33136 Business E-Mail: mmiteva@med.maimi.edu.

MITRE, EDSON IBRAHIM, otolaryngologist, educator; b. São Paulo, Brazil, Feb. 6, 1968; s. Ibrahim and Samyra Cahali Mitre; m. Rita de Cássia Pari, June 24, 1998; children: Pedro Pari, Lucas Pari. MS in Otolaryngology, Santa Casa de São Paulo, 1998, PhD, 2001. Cert. otolaryngology specialist Assn. Brasileira de Otorrinolaringologia Cirurgia Cérvico-Facial, 2001, Ministério da Educação e Cultura, 1995. Otolaryngology head neck surgeon Hosp. Paulista de Otorrinolaringologia, São Paulo, 1994—98, Hosp. Santa Catarina, São Paulo, 1997—2002; grad. prof. Centro U. São Camilo, São Paulo, 2000—05; postgrad. prof. Ctr. Especialização em Fonoaudiologia Clínica, São Paulo, 1999—, Faculdade de Ciências Médicas da Santa Casa de São Paulo, 2005—, instr., prof.; second asst. physician Irmandade da Santa Casa de Misericórdia de São Paulo, 2006—. Mem. editl. bd. Brazilian Jour. Otolaryngology, 2002—; chief, resident physicians Ambulatório de Especialidades Geraldo Bourroul, 2006—. Mem. Assn. Beneficente 2 de Julho, São Paulo, 1999—2008. Recipient Bronze Worth medal, Augusta e Respeitável Loja Simbólica Força, Lealdade e Perseverança, 2006. Fellow: Internat. Fedn. Facial Plastic Surgery Socs., Assn. Brasileira de Otorrinolaringologia e Cirurgia Cérvico-Facial; mem.: Academia Brasileira de Cirurgia Plástica da Face. Roman Catholic. Achievements include research in peripheral facial palsy and middle ear diseases. Avocations: travel, literature, music, basketball. Office: RUA Carcov Sampaio 10 304 CJ 92 Sao Paro Sao Paulo 0133- 020 Brazil Office Phone: 55 11 3287-1666, 55 11 3262 3825. Office Fax: 55 11 3251-1954, 55-11-3541-2314.

MITROPOULOS, FOTIOS A., surgeon; b. Bad Scwalbach, Germany, July 24, 1968; s. Anastasios Mitropoulos and Kiriaki Mitropoulou; m. Maria K Angelopoulou, June 7, 1996; children: Kiriaki-Alkistis Mitropoulou, Milta Mitropoulou. MD, U. Athens, 1992. Chief resident Yale New Haven Hosp., 2000—01; vis. asst. prof. UCLA, David Geffen Sch. Medicine, 2003—04. Lectr. cardiac surgery U. Athens Sch. Medicine, 2004—. With Greek Mil., 1993—94. Recipient Young investigator's award, Am. Transplant Soc., 2003. Fellow: ACS (assoc.), Soc. Thoracic Surgeons; mem.: Am. Coll. Cardiology, Am. Heart Assn., Internat. Soc. Minimally Invasive Cardiac Surgery. Greek Orthodox. Home: Monastiriou 8 Thracomacedones Athens 13676 Greece Office: Attikon U Hosp Rimini 1 Haidari Athens 12462 Greece E-mail: fotiosmitropoulos@yahoo.com.

MITSUAKI, KIMURA, allergist; b. Yamaguchi, Japan, Oct. 7, 1953; MD, Kyoto U., 1980, PhD, 1990. Chief Dept. Allergy and Clin. Immunology, Shizuoka Children's Hosp., 2003—. Dir. Shizuoka Office Vaccination Ctr., Japan, 2005—; chmn., Shizuoka Workshop Infectious Diseases Children, 2005—, Treatment Kawasaki Disease, 2005—, Food Allergy and Atopic Dermatitis Children, 2006—. Fellow: Japanese Soc. Allergology. Avocation: golf. Office: Shizuoka Childrens Hosp Urushiyama 860 Shizuoka City Shizuoka Prefecture 420-0953 Japan Business E-Mail: kimurami@sch.pref.shizuoka.jp.

MITSUHATA, HIROMASA, anesthesiologist, educator; b. Okayama, Japan, Feb. 27, 1952; s. Kiyoji and Asako (Doih) Mitsuhata; m. Ruriko Aratame, Sept. 30, 1979. MD, Akita U., Japan, 1976, PhD, 1983. Asst. Akita U. Hosp., 1976—83; rsch. assoc. Baylor Coll. Medicine, Houston, 1983—84; lectr. Akita U. Sch. Medicine, 1985—89; chief anesthesiologist Hiraka Gen. Hosp., Yokote, Japan, 1989—91; lectr. Juchi Med. Sch., Minamikawachi, Japan, 1991—2001; lectr. anesthesiology Juntendo U. Sch. Medicine, Tokyo, 1997—2001, dir. pain clinic and anesthesiology Juntendo Tokyo Koto Geriat. Med. Ctr., prof. dept. anesthesiology and pain medicine, 2001—. Contbr. articles to profl. jours. Sci. Rsch. grantee, Ministry of Sci., Edn. and Culture Japan, 1979, 1985—87, 1993—95, 1997—2000. Mem.: Shock Soc., Soc. Critical Care Medicine, Am. Soc. Anesthesiologists. Buddhist. Avocations: collecting oriental arts, making nomen (traditional japanese mask). Home: 2-24-26-203 Nishiazabu Minatoku 106-0031 Japan Office: Juntendo Tokyo Koto Geriatric Med Ctr Dept Pain Medicine & Anesthesiology 3-3-20 Shinsuna Koto 136-0075 Japan Office Phone: 81 3 5632 3111. Business E-Mail: h-hmituhata@lares.dti.ne.jp.

MITSUI, IWANE, ophthalmologist, educator, neurosurgeon, journalist; b. Numazu, Shizuoka, Japan, Dec. 10, 1959; s. Takashi and Tomoko Mitsui. MD, U. Tsukuba, 1989. Diplomate. Resident U. Tsukuba Hosp., Japan, 1989—92; med. officer Internat. Med. Ctr. Japan, Tokyo, 1992—95; sr. rsch. assoc. Ames Rsch. Ctr. NASA, Moffet AFB, Calif., 1995—98; dir. hosp. Mitsui Med. Clinic, Tokyo, 1999—. Vis. scientist MIT, Boston, 1997—98; lectr. Osaka U. Med. Sch., 1998—2002, Toho U. Med. Sch., 2006—; dir. med. dept. Skymark Airlines, Tokyo, 1998—2003; pres. DNA Future, Tokyo, 2004—; mem. adv. bd. Henry Taube Inst., San Francisco, 2003—. Author: Human Evolution in Space, 1999, Orthokeratology: Myopia Reduction During Sleep, 2000; editor (textbook). Orthokeratology Handbook, 2002. Recipient Tech. award, NASA, 1997; grantee, Nat. Rsch. Coun., 1995, Japan Space Forum and Japan Space Agy., 1998. Mem.: Am Acad. Japan OSEIRT/Ortho-K Assn., Japan Orthokeratology Assn. (pres. 2001—04), Orthokeratology, Aviation Med. Dept., Aerospace Med. Assn. (life). Achievements include research in Aerospace medicine, Neurosurgery, Myopia Reduction; development of lens design to effect high myopia, severe astigmatism, hyperopia. Avocations: scuba diving, skiing, camping, helicopters, horseback riding. Office: Mitsui Med Clinic 5-4-11-3F Akasaka Minato 107-0052 Japan Home: 6-15-14 Shirogane Minato 108-0072 Japan Office Phone: 81 3 5570 2321. Business E-Mail: mitsui@ortho-k.co.jp.

MITSUMORI, LEE M., medical educator; b. Sept. 5, 1966; MS in Bio-engring., U. Wash., 1988; MD, U. Hawaii, 1996. Assoc. prof. U. Wash., 2002—. Office: University Wash Med Ctr Seattle WA 98195 Business E-Mail: lmits@u.washington.edu.

MITSUOKA, TAKAO, cardiac electrophysiologist; b. Isahaya, Nagasaki, Japan, Nov. 4, 1948; s. Mitsuji and Rise (Itho) M.; m. Takako Gotho, Mar. 10, 1974; children: Yoshiki, Kotoba, Naoki. MD, Hokkaido U., 1974; PhD, Nagasaki U., Japan, 1991. Intern Nagasaki U. Hosp., 1974-76, resident cardiac dept., 1976-81, asst. in cardiology 3d dept. internal medicine, 1982-91; dir. of hosp. Taiki Town Hosp., Hiroo, Japan, 1991-97; dir. The Sasaki Clinic, Obihiro, Japan, 1998-99, The Mitsuoka Clinic, Obihiro, 1999—. Clin. rsch. fellow in cardiology Westminster Hosp. Med. Sch., London U., 1983-84; cardiovascular rsch. assoc. The Lankenau Hosp., an affiliate Thomas Jefferson Med. Coll., Phila., 1984-86; lectr. Nagasaki U. Sch. of Medicine, 1988-91; cons. cardiologist for cardiac arrhythmias Obihiro Nat. Hosp., 1998—. Contbr. articles to profl. jours. Grantee Scientific Rsch. for the Ministry of Edn., 1991, Pollution-related Health Damage Compensation and Prevention Assn., 1996-97, Award for Med. Contbns. to Rural Areas in Japan Japanese Mcpl. Hosp. Assn., 1997. Fellow Am. Coll. Cardiology, European Soc. Cardiology, Japanese Coll. Cardiology. Avocations: golf, tea ceremony, japanese dance. Home: 22-19 Minami-5 Chome Nishi-19-Jo Obihiro 080-2469 Japan Office: The Mitsuoka Clinic 3-14 Ozora-cho Obihiro 080-0838 Japan

MITSUYASU, HIROMICHI, orthopedist; b. Japan, Mar. 17, 1968; MD, Kagoshima U., PhD, 1993, Kyushu U., 1998—98. Pres. Mitsuyasu Orthop. Clinic, 2011. Mem.: Japanese Soc. Surgery Hand. Office: 2-3-26 Arato Chuou-ku Fukuoka 810-0062 Japan Business E-Mail: hiro@ortho.med.kyushu-u.ac.jp.

MITTEMEYER, BERNHARD THEODORE, urology and surgery educator; arrived in U.S., 1944, naturalized; BS in Biology, Moravian Coll., 1952, LLD (hon.), 1982; MD, Temple U., 1956; DSc, William Jewell Coll., 1985. Diplomate Am. Bd. Urology, Am. Bd. Quality Assurance and Utilization Rev. Physicians. Rotation intern Santa Barbara (Calif.) Cottage and County Hosps., 1956—57; advanced through grades from capt. to lt. gen. U.S. Army, 1957—81; resident in gen. surgery Fitzsimons Army Med. Ctr., Denver, 1959—61; resident in urol. surgery Tripler Army Med. Ctr., Honolulu, 1962—65; asst. chief urol. surgery svc. urol. residency tng. program Walter Reed Army Med. Ctr., Washington, 1965—68, 1971—74, chief urol. surgery svc. and urol. residency tng. program, 1974—77, chief dept. surgery, 1976—77, comdg. gen., 1980—81; surgeon gen. Dept Army, Washington, 1981—85; ret., 1985—86; sr. v.p., corp. med. dir. Whittaker Health Svcs., LA, 1985—2002; prof. urology and surgery Tex. Tech U. Sch. Medicine, Lubbock, 1986—, exec. v.p., provost Health Scis. Ctr., 1986—96, interim dean, 1988—90, 1995—96, 2005—06, interim pres. Health Scis. Ctr., 2006—07, spl. asst. veterans affairs. Clin. assoc. prof. urology George Washington U. Sch. Medicine, Washington, 1974—85; clin. prof. surgery Uniformed Svcs. U. Health Scis., Bethesda, Md., 1976—; vis. prof., guest lectr. urology U. Mo., U. Pitts., Korea U., Pa. State U., U. Mass., U. Va., Wake Forest U., Armed Forces Inst. Pathology, Walter Reed Army Inst. Rsch., 1975—; ctrl. com. of pub.-acad. liaison Tex. Dept. Mental Health and Mental Retardation, 1990—; managed health care adv. com. ex. Dept. Criminal Justice, 1993—96; presenter in field. Contbr. articles to profl. jours. Trustee Moravian Coll., 1982—86; bd. dirs. Sci. Spectrum, Lubbock, 1988—, Lubbock Symphony Orch., 1989—92, Lubbock Conv. and Visitors Bur., 1991—93. Decorated D.S.M., Legion of Merit with oak leaf cluster, DFC, Bronze Star with V device, Air medal with oak leaf cluster; recipient Comenius award, Moravian Coll., 1978, Founders medal, Assn. Mil. Surgeons, 1978, Alumni Achievement award in health policy, Temple U. Sch. Medicine, 1988. Fellow: ACS, Am. Coll. Quality Assurance and Utilization Rev. Physicians, Am. Coll. Physician Execs.; mem.: AMA (ho. of dels. 1981—85), South Ctrl. Sect. Am. Urol. Assn., Lubbock-Crosby-Garza County Med. Soc. (armed svcs. com. 1988—96), Tex. Med. Assn. (cons. coun. on med. edn. 1987—96), Assn. U.S. Army, Soc. Med. Cons. to Armed Forces, Am. Acad. Med. Dirs., Uniformed Svcs. U. Surg. Assocs., Soc. U. Urologists, Soc. Govt. Svc. Urologists, Am. Urol. Assn., Lubbock C. of C. Office: Tex Tech University Health Sci Ctr Urology Dept Lubbock Gen 3601 4th St Stop 7260 Lubbock TX 79430-7260 Office Phone: 806-743-1810. Business E-Mail: bernhard.mittemeyer@ttuhsc.edu. *

MITTEN, MATTHEW JOHN, law educator; b. Tiffin, Ohio, Apr. 26, 1959; BA in Economics, Ohio State U., 1981; JD magna cum laude, U. Toledo Coll. Law, 1984. Bar: Ga. 1984; cert. in mediation A.A. White Dispute Resolution Inst., Houston, 1992. Assoc. Kilpatrick Stockton LLP, Atlanta, 1984—89; asst. prof. South Tex. Coll. Law, Houston, 1990—92, assoc. prof., 1992—94, prof., 1994—99; prof. law, dir. Nat. Sports Law Inst., Marquette U. Law Sch., Milw., 1999—, assoc. dean academic affairs, 2002—04, dir. LLM Sports Law program for fgn. lawyers, 2007—. Vis. asst. prof. U. Toledo Coll. Law, 1992; vis. lectr. sports medicine U. Tenn. Grad. Sch. Medicine, Knoxville, 1994; vis. faculty comparative sports law U. Queensland Sch. Law, Brisbane, Australia, 2002; vis. faculty internat. sports law U. Barcelona Sch. Law, 2006; sr. fellow US sports law U. Melbourne Law Sch., Australia, 2006, 08, 10; mem. Ct. Arbitration for Sport, Lausanne, Switzerland, 2007—. Co-author: (textbook) Sports Law and Regulation: Cases, Materials, and Problems, 2009; articles editor Tex. Entertainment & Sports Law Jour., 1995—99, mem. editl. bd. Jour. Intercollegiate Sport, 2007—, Sports Medicine Digest, Sports Law Reporter; contbr. articles to profl. jours. Mem. NCAA Com. Competitive Safeguards & Med. Aspects of Sports, 1999—2005, chair, 2002—05; mem. USADA Doping Arbitration Panel, 2007—, LPGA Drug Testing Arbitration Panel, 2008—. Mem.: ABA, Ga. Bar, St. Thomas More Lawyers Soc. Wis. (bd. govs. 2004—07), American Arbitration Assn. (mem. comml. arbitration panel 2009—), Internat. Acad. Sports Law Practitioners & Execs. (exec. mem. 2006—), American Assn. Law Schools (chair sect. Law & Sports 2000—01), Sports Lawyers Assn. (bd. dirs. 2003—), Phi Kappa Phi, Order of the Coif. Office: Marquette Univ Law School National Sports Law Inst 1215 W Michigan St Milwaukee WI 53233-1881 Office Phone: 414-288-7494. Business E-Mail: matt.mitten@marquette.edu.

MITTENDORF, ROBERT LEE, physician, epidemiologist; b. Ironton, Ohio, Ironton, Ohio, Aug. 6, 1943; s. Robert William and Martha Jane (Whitley) M.; m. Marguerite Jean Herschel, Nov. 10, 1979; children: Jeffrey David, Robert William II, Inga. BS, Ohio State U., 1966; MD, U. Ky., 1974; MPH, Harvard U., 1987, D Pub. Health, 1991. Diplomate Am. Bd. Ob-Gyn. Attending physician St. Margaret's Hosp., Boston, 1977-87; chief of surgery Winthrop (Mass.) Hosp., 1986-88; project dir., collaborative breast cancer study Harvard U., Boston, 1989-91; dir. Office Clin. Rsch. Tufts Sch. Medicine, Boston, 1991-92; dir. health studies, dept. ob-gyn. U. Chgo., 1992-99; prof. Loyola U. Med. Ctr., Maywood, Ill., dir. divsn. gen. ob-gyn, 2000—. Mem. sci. adv. com. anti-epileptic drugs in pregnancy registry Mass. Gen. Hosp., Boston, 1997—; cons. Nat. Ctrs. for Disease Control and Prevention, Atlanta, 1994; bd. dirs. U. Chgo. Health Plan, Chgo., Quadrangle Faculty Club, U. Chgo.; manuscript reviewer The Lancet, 1998. Author: Control of Transmissible Diseases in Health Care, 1995; contbr. articles to profl. jours. Med. dir. Cambridge Econ. Opportunity Com., 1977-78. Capt. USAF, 1966-70. Recipient Magnesium Rsch. Prize, Ctrl. Assn. of Obstetricians and Gynecologists. Mem. AMA, Soc. Maternal Fetal Medicine, Soc. Epidemiol. Rsch. Democrat. Achievements include devel. of a linear regression model that permits the more precise determination of the estimated date of confinement in pregnant women (Mittendorf-Williams Rule); discovery that strenuous phys. activity is associated with a reduced risk of breast cancer, using a multivariable logistic regression model. Prin. investigator of the MAGnet Trial (magnesium and neurologic endpoints randomized control trial) to determine if using antenatal magnesium sulfate is associated with the prevention of severe cerebral palsy. Through statis. meta-analysis, discovered that certain prophylactic antibiotics are highly efficacious in preventing the serious infections associated with total abdominal hysterectomy. Office: Loyola U Med Ctr 2160 S 1st Ave Maywood IL 60153-3304 Home: 4800 S Chicago Beach Dr Chicago IL 60615 Office Phone: 708-216-2465, 773-502-1491. Business E-Mail: rmitten@lumc.edu.

MITTEREGGER, DIETER, microbiologist, educator; b. Neunkirchen, Austria, May 19, 1972; MD, U. Vienna, 2003. Asst. prof. Med. U. Vienna, 2008—. Mem.: ESCMID Study Group Clin. Parasitology, European Soc. Clin. Microbiology and Infectious Diseases. Office: Währinger Gürtel 18-20 Vienna 1090 Austria Business E-Mail: dieter.mitteregger@meduniwien.ac.at.

MITTERHAUSER, MARKUS ALEXANDER, radiopharmacist; b. Vienna, May 19, 1970; s. Josef and Ingeborg Mitterhauser; m. Eva Sabine Biermeier, June 6, 1998; children: Moritz Jakob, Lena Ida. D, U. Vienna, Vienna, 2004. Lic. Radiopharmacist ETH Zürich, 2001. Rschr. Karolinska Hosp., Stockholm, 1994, Chinese U. Hong Kong, Hong Kong, 1994—95, svc. Hospitalier frederic joliot, Orsay, France, 1996; chief radiopharmacist AKH Vienna, Vienna, 1998—. Author: (research article) Bioevaluation of FETO (THP Price for Nature Scientists, 2004). Fellow Austrian Chamber of Pharmacists, 1996. Mem.: Working Group for Radiopharmacy. Home: Schulweg 8 Austria Mödling 2340 Austria Office: AKH Wien Währinger Gürtel 18-20 Vienna 1090 Austria Office Fax: +431404001559. Personal E-mail: markus.mitterhauser@meduniwien.or.at.

MITTLER, MARK A., neurosurgeon; b. NYC, May 24, 1965; MD, U. Rochester, NY, 1991. Diplomate Am. Bd. Neurol. Surgery, Am. Bd. Pediatric Neurol. Surgery. Intern neurol. surgery Brown U./RI Hosp., Providence, 1991—92, resident pediatric neurology; chief resident Hasbro Children's Hosp., RI; fellow pediatric neurol. surgery Children's Hosp. LA, 1998—99; staff LI Neurosurgical Assoc., New Hyde Park, NY, 1999—; co-chief divsn. pediatric neurosurgery LI Jewish Health Sys./Schneider Children's Hosp., Manhasset, NY, 2002—. Clin. asst. prof. NYU. Contbr. articles to profl. jours., chapters to books. Mem.: AMA, Nassau County Med. Soc., NY State Med. Soc., Am. Soc. Pediatric Neurosurgeons, Congress Neurol. Surgeons, Am. Assn. Neurol. Surgeons. Office: LI Neurosurgical Assoc 410 Lakeville Rd Ste 204 New Hyde Park NY 11042 Office Phone: 516-354-3401. Office Fax: 516-354-8597.

MITTMAN, NEAL, nephrologist, medical educator; b. NYC, Jan. 24, 1953; s. Arnold and Tess (Blumenthal) M.; m. Candace Clark (Martin), Sept. 21, 1980; children: Alexander Clark and Zachary Wade. BA, Queens Coll., CUNY, 1973; MD, N.Y. Med. Coll., 1977. Diplomate Am. Bd. Internal Medicine and Am. Bd. Nephrology. Intern N.Y. Med. Coll., Met. Hosp. Ctr., 1977-78, resident, 1978-80; resident nephrologist Albert Einstein Coll. Medicine, Bronx, NY, 1980-82; asst. prof. medicine Mt. Sinai Sch. Medicine, 1982-86; assoc. chief nephrology Beth Israel Med. Ctr., NYC, 1982-86, L.I. Coll. Hosp., Bklyn., 1986—2011, State U. NY Dawnstate Med. Ctr. LI Coll. Hosp., 2011—; program dir. nephrology fellowship L.I. Coll. Hosp., 2005—; assoc. prof. clin. medicine State Univ. of N.Y. Health Sci. Ctr., Bklyn., 1993—; med. dir. Atlantic Hemodialysis, 2000—. Med. adv. bd. Nat. Kidney Found. NY, NJ, and N.Y.C., 1994-2002; grants and fellowship rev. com., 1995-2002; sec. med. adv. bd., chmn. corp. partnerships com. Med. Adv. Bd. Kidney and Urology Found. Am., 2002-; Bd. of trustees, Kidney and Urology Found. Am., 2003-. Co-editor: Ambulatory Peritoneal Dialysis, 1990; contbg. articles to med. jour. Recipient Clin. Rsch. Award NIH, 1980-82; named NY Met. Best Dr., Castle, Connolly Med., Ltd., 1997-; named one of NY Times Super Drs., 2008-11. Fellow ACP, Am. Soc. Nephrology, Royal Coll. Medicine (London); mem. Am. Soc. Artificial Internal Organs, Am. Soc. Hypertension, Internat. Soc. Nephrology, Nat. Kidney Found., NY Soc. Nephrology (sec. treas. 1996-97, v.p. 1997-98, pres. 1998-99), Met. Renal Care Network (bd. dir., sec.). Avocations: opera, gourmet cooking. Office: State University NY Dawn State Med Ctr LI Coll Hosp 339 Hicks St Brooklyn NY 11201-5509 Office Phone: 718-780-1248. Personal E-mail: nmittman@aol.com. Business E-Mail: ncal.mittman@downstate.edu.

MIURA, KATSUYUKI, pharmacologist, educator; b. Osaka, Aug. 15, 1953; MD, Osaka City U. Med. Sch., 1979, PhD, 1983. Prof. Osaka City U. Med. Sch., 2001—. Mem.: Internat. Soc. Nephrology, Japanese Soc. Toxicology, Japanese Soc. Nephrology, Japanese Soc. Pharmacology, Am. Soc. Nephrology. Office: Osaka City University Med Sch Pharmacol Therapy 1-4-3 Asahimachi Abeno Osaka 545-8585 Japan Office Fax: 81-6-6646-3048. Business E-Mail: miura-pha@med.osaka-cu.ac.jp.

MIURA, KENJI, cell biologist, biochemist; b. Tokyo, 1961; m. Hiromi Miura, 1993; 1 child, Wakuya. BS, U. Tsukuba, 1984, MS, 1986, MS in Med. Scis., 1988, PhD, 1992. Postdoc. fellow, Inst. Med. Sci. U. Tokyo, 1992—95; asst. Nat. Def. Med. Coll., Tokorozawa, Saitama, Japan, 1995—97, lectr., 1997—. Editl. bd. mem. Global Jour. Biochemistry, 2010—, World Jour. Methodology, 2011—. Contbr. articles to med. jours. Bd. dirs. local, parenting, gender equality, town revitalization Sch. Child Club Assn., Tokorozawa, Saitama, Japan, 2009—11. Mem.: Japanese Assn. Anatomists, Japan Soc. Biomed. Gerontology, Molecular Biology Soc. Japan, Japanese Biochem. Soc. Achievements include discovery of novel ERK2-binding protein, EBITEINI; first to proposal of phosphor-protein atlases, systematized representations of the localizations of phosphorylated proteins; research in protein-protein interactions, structural and functional analysis of proteins, in situ detection of phosphorylated proteins, intercellular signal transduction, cellular response. Avocations: photography, travel, skiing, music. Office: 3-2 Namiki Tokorozawa Saitama 359-8513 Japan E-mail: ken_miura_yh@yahoo.co.jp.

MIXON, AARON MALACHI, III, medical products executive; b. May 22, 1940; m. Barbara Weber; 2 children. BA, Harvard U., 1962, MBA, 1968. Pres. Invacare Corp., Elyria, Ohio, CEO, 1979—2010, chmn., 1983—. Bd. dirs. The Sherwin-Williams Co., 1993—, Park-Ohio Holdings Corp., 2008—. Chmn. bd. trustees Cleve. Clinic Found., Cleve. Inst. Music. Recipient Alumni Achievement award, Harvard Bus. Sch., 2007. Office: Invacare Corp 1 Invacare Way Elyria OH 44036 Office Phone: 440-329-6000. Office Fax: 440-366-9008. Business E-Mail: mmixon@invacare.com. *

MIYAHIRA, SUSANA, hospital administrator; b. Suzano, Brazil, Sept. 5, 1961; Grad, FCM-UNICAMP, 1987, postgrad, 1991. Coord. Hosp. Mcpl. Dr. José Carvalho Florence, 1992—. Mem.: Soc. Brasileira Anestesiologia, Internat. Assn. Study Pain. Avocations: Karate, running. Home: Rua Alvaro Pereira 200 Taubaté São Paulo 12093500 Brazil Home Fax: 551236335386. Business E-Mail: susana_miyahira@uol.com.br.

MIYAISHI, SATORU, forensic pathologist; b. Nagoya, Japan, Apr. 3, 1960; BA, MD, Okayama U., Japan, 1986, PhD, 1991. Resident Okayama U. Hosp., Japan, 1986-87, rsch. assoc. dept. legal medicine, 1991-92, asst. prof. dept. legal medicine, 1992-96, assoc. prof., 1996—2007, prof., 2007—. Guest prof. U. Hamburg, Germany, 1997-2003. Author: Encyclopedia of Analytical Science, 1995; contbr. articles to profl. jours., contbns. to Ency. Analytical Sci., 2d edit., 2005, Ency. Forensic and Legal Medicine, 2005. Office: Okayama U Grad Sch Med Dentistry and Pharm Scis 2-5-1 Shikata-cho Kita Ward Okayama 700-8558 Japan Fax: 81-86-235-7201. E-mail: miyaishi@md.okayama-u.ac.jp.

MIYAKE, KENSAKU, ophthalmologist; b. Nagoya, Japan, Nov. 24, 1940; s. Torazo and Chiyo Miyake; m. Yumi Miyake, Dec. 24, 2002; children: Minami, Goichiro, Minori Kashima. MD, Nagoya U., 1972. Dir., head Shohzankai Med. Found., Miyake Eye Hosp., Nagoya, Japan, 1975—. Past pres. Intra-Ocular Implant Club, 1988—92.

Recipient Ridley medal, 1986, Binkhorst medal, 100th Ann. Am. Acad. of Ophthalmology Meeting, 1996, award, Alcon Rsch. Inst., 2001, Binkhorst medal, 2002, C. Kelman Innovation's award, 2006. Mem.: Internat. Intra-Ocular Implant Club, Academia Ophthalmologica Internationalis, Japanese Ophthalmic Surg. Soc. (pres. 2001—06), Japanese Soc. Cataract and Refractive Surgery, Japan Ophthalmologist Assn. (pres. 2004—10), Japanese Soc. Ophthalmology (hon.). Achievements include research in Surgical Biology and Pharmacology. Office: Miyake Eye Hospital 3-15-68 Ozone Kita-ku Nagoya 462-0825 Japan Office Phone: 81-52-915-8001. Office Fax: 81-52-915-8525. E-mail: miyake@spice.or.jp.

MIYAKE, YOSHIHIRO, medical educator, researcher; b. Osaka, Japan, Feb. 11, 1968; MD, Nat. Def. Med. Coll., 1993; PhD, Kyushu U. Grad. Sch. Med. Scis., 2000. Rsch. assoc. Kinki U. Sch. Medicine, 2000—02; asst. prof. Faculty Medicine, Fukuoka U., 2002—04, assoc. prof., 2004—11. Office: 7-45-1 Nanakuma Jonan-ku Fukuoka 814-0180 Japan Office Fax: 81 92 863 8892. Business E-Mail: miyake-y@fukuoka-u.ac.jp.

MIYAKOSHI, NAOHISA, surgeon, educator; b. Akita, Japan, Apr. 22, 1965; s. Noboru and Yoko Miyakoshi; m. Miwako Yoshida Miyakoshi, Feb. 4, 1995; children: Kent, Marie. MD, Akita U., 1990, PhD, 1996. Resident Akita U. Med. Ctr., Japan, 1990—91, rsch. fellow, 1993—97, rsch. assoc., 1998—2005, asst. prof., 2005—07, assoc. prof., 2007—; clin. fellow Taihei Children's Hosp., Akita, Japan, 1991—92, Akita Rosai Hosp., Odate, Japan, 1992—93. Postdoctoral fellow Loma Linda U., Calif., 1998—2000. Contbr. articles to profl. jours. Recipient Travel award, Am. Soc. for Bone and Mineral Rsch., 2000, Outstanding Poster award, Japanese Soc. for Bone and Mineral Rsch., 2001. Office: Akita Univ Dept Orthopedic Surg 1-1-1 Hondo Akita 010-8543 Japan

MIYAMOTO, HIROSHI, orthopedist; b. Wakayama, Japan, June 17, 1965; s. Takao and Midori Miyamoto; m. Miki Fujimoto. MD, Kobe U. Sch. Medicine, Japan, 1991. Cert. spine surgeon Bd. Tokyo, 2007, spine endscopic surgeon 2008. Clin. asst. prof. Kobe U. Hosp., 2004—; chief, dept. rehab. Kobe Med. Ctr., 2004—. Reviewer European Spine Jour., Bern, Switzerland, 2008—. Recipient Best Paper award, Japanese Soc. Lumbar Spine Disorders, 1998, Japanese Br. Internat. Soc. Study of Lumbar Spine, 2003; Traveling fellowship, Internat. Soc. Study of Lumbar Spine, 2001, Japanese Soc. Spinal Surgery and Related Rsch., 2006. Office: Kobe Med Ctr 3-1-1 Nishiochiai Suma-ku Kobe 654-0155 Japan

MIYAMOTO, HIZURU, oral surgeon, researcher; b. Kanazawa, Ishikawa, Japan, Aug. 31, 1965; s. Noboru and Mitsuko Tamura Miyamoto; m. Kaoru Toyama, Apr. 25, 1966; children: Hidehiro, Hiyori, Anley. DDS, Aichi Gakuin U., Nagoya, 1990, PhD, 2000. Staff dept. dentistry and oral surgery Ishikawa Prefecture Ctrl. Hosp., Kanazawa, Ishikawa, Japan, 1990—96; rsch. fellow oral and maxillofacial surgery unit Adelaide U., Australia, 1996—99; instr., rschr. oral and maxillofacial surgery unit Meikai U. Sch. Dentistry, Sakado, Japan, 2000—07; chair Temporomandibular Joint Diseases Ctr. Meikai U. Hosp., 2003—07; chief dir. dentistry & oral surgery Happy Town Shiki, Saitama, Japan, 2007—; assoc. prof. Oral & Maxillofacial Surgery Unit Meikai U. Sch. Dentistry Sakado, Saitama, 2008—. Contbr. articles to profl. jours. (Merit award 13th Ann. Meeting of Japanese Soc. Temporomandibular Joint, 2001). Achievements include research in genesis and the effects of various factors on ankylosis of the temporomandibular joint. Home: 1-2-18 Shin-machi Tsurugashima 350-2227 Japan Office: Dentistry & Oral Surgery Happy Town 1 12 16 Saiwaicho Shiki 353 0005 Japan Office Phone: 81 48 456 7500. Office Fax: +81 49 285 6036; Home Fax: +81 49 285 0092. Personal E-mail: unley-road@tcat.ne.jp. Business E-Mail: hezlu@dent.meikai.ac.jp, hezlu@mbe.nifty.com.

MIYAMOTO, RICHARD TAKASHI, otolaryngologist; b. Feb. 2, 1944; s. Dave Norio and Haruko (Okano) Miyamoto; m. Cynthia VanderBurgh, June 17, 1967; children: Richard Christopher, Geoffrey Takashi. BS cum laude, Wheaton Coll., 1966; MD, U. Mich., 1970; MS in Otology, U. So. Calif., 1978; D Engring. (hon.), Rose Hulman Inst. Tech., 2001. Diplomate Am. Bd. Otolaryngology. Intern Butterworth Hosp., Grand Rapids, Mich., 1970—71, resident in surgery, 1971—72; resident in otolaryngology Ind. U. Sch. Medicine, Indpls., 1972—75; fellow in otology and neurotology St. Vincent Hosp. and Otologic Med. Group, LA, 1977—78; asst. prof. Ind. U. Sch. Medicine, Indpls., 1978—83, assoc. prof., 1983—88, prof., 1988—, chmn., 1987—, chief otology and neurotology dept. otology, head and neck surgery, 1982—, chmn. dept. otolaryngology, 1987—, Arilla DeVault prof. otolaryngology, 1991; chief otolaryngology, head and neck surgery Wishard Meml. Hosp., 1979—2002. Mem. editl. bd.: Laryngoscope, Am. Jour. Otology, Otolaryngology - Head and Neck Surgery, European Archives of Oto-Rhino-Laryngology, Anales de Otorrinolaringologia Mexicana; contbr. articles tto profl. jours. Mem. adv. coun. Nat. Inst. Deafness and other Commication Disorders, 1989—94, 2002—; mem. adv. bd. Alexander Graham Bell Assn. for the Deaf, The Ear Found., St. Joseph Inst. Deaf, chmn., 2004—. Maj. USAF, 1975—77. Fellow: ACS, Am. Auditory Soc. (mem. exec. com. 1985—2003), Am. Otological, Rhinological and Laryngological Soc. (v.p. mid. sect. 2002—03), Am. Acad. Otolaryngology (gov. 1982—); mem.: Assn. Acad. Depts. in Otolaryngology-Head and Neck Surgery (sec.-treas. 2002—04, pres.-elect 2004—06), Deafness Rsch. Inst. (bd. dirs., pres. Centurion group, comm. com.), Inst. of Medicine of NAS, Am. Neurotology Soc. (pres.-elect 1999—2000, pres. 2000—01), Collegium Oto-Larytologicum Amecitiae Sacrum, Royal Soc. Medicine London, Assn. Rsch. Otol. (pres.-elect 2000—01, pres. 2001—), Am. Otol. Soc. (coun. 1992—), Otosclerosis Study Group (coun. 1993—), NY Acad. Scis., Am. Acad. Pediats., Marines Meml. Assn., Cosmos Club of Washington, Alpha Omega Alpha (pres. Ind. chpt. 2003—), Wheaton Coll. Scholastic Honor Soc., Psi Iota Xi. Office: Ind U Sch Med 702 Barnhill Dr Indianapolis IN 46202-5128

MIYATA, HIROTO, pharmaceutical executive; b. Tokyo, July 17, 1963; DVM, Rakuno Gakuen U., 1990, PhD, 1994. Veterinarian Royal Pet Clinic, 1990—91; rsch. specialist Zeria Pharm. Co. Ltd., 1994—96; dep. gen. mgr. Taisho Pharm. Co. Ltd., 1996—. Recipient Incentive award, Japanese Assn. Vet. Anatomists. Master: Japanese Soc. Vet. Sci.; mem.: Japanese Soc. Toxicologic Pathology. Avocation: reading. Office: 24-1 Takada 3-chome Toshima Tokyo 170-8633 Japan Office Fax: 81-3-3989-0779.

MIYAUCHI, AKIRA, surgeon, endocrine surgeon, thyroid, parathyroid; b. Matsuyama, Ehime, Japan, Nov. 10, 1945; m. Mitsuyo Magemura; children: Masahisa, Takako Ogawa, Miwa. MD, Osaka U. Med. Sch., 1970. Cert. med. dr. Japanese Govt., 1970. Pres. dir. Kuma Hosp., Kobe, Hyogo, Japan, 2001—. Vis. prof. Nippon Med. Sch., Tokyo, 2006—, U. Belgrade, Sch. Medicine, Serbia. Recipient Hichijo prize, 1985, Miyake prize, Japan Thyroid Assn., 2007, Best Endocrine Surgeon of the Yr., Japan Endocrine Soc., 2008. Office: Kuma Hosp 8-2-35 Shimoyamate-dori Chuo-ku Kobe Hyogo 650-0011 Japan Office Phone: 81-78-371-3721. Office Fax: 81-78-371-3645. Business E-Mail: miyauchi@kuma-h.or.jp.

MIYAZAKI, NAOYUKI, research scientist; b. Kurashiki, Japan, June 4, 1977; MS in Chemistry, 2002, PhD in Chemistry, 2005. Postdoc. fellow Nat. Agrl. Rsch. Ctr., Japan, 2005, Karolinska Inst., Sweden, 2005—07, U. Calif., Davis, 2007, Inst. Protein Rsch., Osaka U., 2007—. Mem.: Molecular Biology Soc. Japan, Japanese Soc. Microscopy, Protein Sci. Soc. Japan, Crystallographic Soc. Japan. Office: 3-2 Yamadaoka Suita Osaka 565-0871 Japan Business E-Mail: naomiyazaki@protein.osaka-u.ac.jp.

MIYAZAKI, SHUNICHI, academic administrator, medical educator; b. Kochi, Japan, Jan. 31, 1955; s. Takao and Chie Miyazaki; m. Chika Ogura; children: Hiroko, Yoko, Wakako. MD, Kyoto U., Japan, 1979, PhD, 1987. Resident Kyoto U.; internist Shimada Mcpl. Hosp., Japan; rsch. physiologist U. Calif., San Diego; cardiologist Nat. Cardiovasc. Ctr., Osaka, Japan, 1989—2006; prof. Kinki U. Sch. Medicine, Osaka; pres. Tokyo Women's Med. U., 2007—. Avocation: golf. Office: Tokyo Womens Medical Univ 8-1 Kawada-cho Shinjuku-ku Tokyo 162-8666 Japan *

MIYOSHI, ISAO, former medical professor; b. Yoshinocho, Tokushimaken, Japan, July 15, 1932; s. Shoichi and Sakae (Matsuka) Miyoshi; m. Shigeko Kagawa, Apr. 1964; children: Ken, Ko, Tetsu. MD, Okayama U., Japan, 1957, PhD, 1965. Intern U.S. Army Hosp., Tokyo, 1957—58; resident Ohio State U., Columbus, 1958—59; mem. staff Okayama U. Hosp., Japan, 1966—81; assoc. prof. Kochi Med. Sch., Japan, 1981—82, prof. medicine, 1982—98, prof. emeritus, 1998—. Recipient Hideyo Noguchi prize, Hideyo Noguchi Meml. Assn., 1983, Princess Takamatsu Cancer prize, Princess Takamatsu Cancer Rsch. Fund, 1984, Hammer prize, Occidental Petroleum, 1985, Asahi prize, Asahi Shinbun Pub. Co., 1987, medal with purple ribbon, Japanese Prime Min.'s Office Decoration Bur., 1996, The Order of Sacred Treasure, Gold Rays with Neck Ribbon, 2007. Mem.: Japanese Cancer Assn. Avocation: tennis. Office: Kochi Med Sch Kochi 783-8505 Japan Office Phone: 088 880 2345.

MIYOUNG, CHEONG, pharmacist; b. Republic of Korea, Apr. 12, 1973; PharmD, U. Buffalo, 2003. Head pharmacist Rite Aid, 2004. Office: 485 Tennessee 76 White House TN 37188-9202 E-mail: realblue412@yahoo.com.

MIZGALA, HENRY F., physician, consultant, retired medical educator; b. Montreal, Can., Nov. 28, 1932; s. Louis and Mary (Ropeleski) M.; m. Pauline Barbara Delaney, Oct. 26, 1957; children: Paul Stephen, Cynthia Louise, Liane Mary Mizgala Sizemore, Melanie Frances Mizgala Dressler, Nancy Elizabeth Mizgala Lewis. BA magna cum laude, Loyola Coll., Montreal, 1953; MD, CM, McGill U., 1957. Rotating intern, then resident in medicine St. Mary's Hosp., Montreal, 1957—59, asst. physician, 1963—66; resident in medicine Royal Victoria Hosp., Montreal, 1959—60; Dazian fellow cardiology Mt. Sinai Hosp., NYC, 1960—61, USPHS fellow cardiology, 1961—62; resident in cardiology Montreal Gen. Hosp., 1962—63, assoc. physician, 1966—74; asst. physician, cons. cardiology Lachine Gen. Hosp., Que., 1964—80; mem. faculty McGill U. Med. Sch., Montreal, 1968—74, assoc. prof. medicine, 1973—74; assoc. prof., then prof. Montreal U. Med. Sch., 1974—81; cardiologist Montreal Heart Inst., also dir. CCU, 1974—80; prof. medicine U. B.C., 1980—87, prof. medicine, head divsn. cardiology, 1980—87, prof. medicine emeritus, 1998—; hon. attending med. staff, cardiologist Vancouver Hosp. and Health Scis. Ctr. Cons. Centre Hosp. Baie des Chaleurs, Gaspe, Que., 1975—80, B.C. Cancer Agy., Vancouver, 1981—; cons. staff Univ. Hosp., U. B.C. site, 1981—94; hon. cons. Montreal Heart Inst., 1980—2009. Mem. editl. bd. Can. Jour. Cardiology, 1988-99, Jour. Am. Coll. Cardiology, 1992-95; contbr. articles to profl. jours. Fellow Royal Coll. Physicians and Surgeons Can., Am. Coll. Cardiology, Am. Heart Assn. (coun. clin. cardiology); mem. Can. Med. Assn., Can. Cardiovasc. Soc. (treas. 1974-90), Que. Med. Assn., B.C. Med. Assn., B.C. and Yukon Heart and Stroke Found. (bd. dirs., sr. bd. dirs.), Alpha Omega Alpha. Office: UBC Hosp Dept Cardiology Rm S110 UBC Hosp 2211 Wesbrook Mall Vancouver BC V6T 2B5 Canada Office Phone: 604-822-1747. Business E-Mail: mhenry@interchange.ubc.ca.

MIZRAHI, ABRAHAM MORDECHAY, retired health products executive, pediatrician; b. Jerusalem, Apr. 16, 1929; came to U.S., 1952, naturalized, 1960; s. Solomon R. and Rachel (Haliwa) M.; m. Suzanne Eve Glasser, Mar. 15, 1956; children: Debra, Judith, Karen. BS, Manchester Coll., 1955; MD, Albert Einstein Coll. Medicine, 1960. Diplomate: Am. Bd. Pediatrics, Nat. Bd. Med. Examiners. Intern U. N.C., 1960-61; pediatric resident Columbia-Presbyn. Med. Center, NYC, 1961-63, NIH fellow in neonatology, 1963-65; assoc. dir. Newborn Service Mt. Sinai Hosp., NYC; also dir. Newborn Service Elmhurst Med. Center, 1965-67; staff physician Geigy Pharm. Corp., NYC, 1967-69, head cardio-pulmonary sect., 1969-71; sr. v.p. corp. med. affairs USV Pharm. Corp., Tuckahoe, NY, 1971-76; v.p. health and safety Revlon, Inc., NYC, 1976-89, sr. v.p. human resources, 1989-94; ret., 1994. Assoc. in pediatrics Columbia U., 1963-67; cons. in neonatology Misericordia-Fordham Med. Ctr., 1967-89; clin. affiliate N.Y. Hosp.; clin. asst. prof. Cornell U. Med. Coll., 1982—. Contbr. articles to profl. jours. Trustee Westchester (N.Y.) Jewish Center. Mem. AMA, N.Y. State and County Med. Soc., Am., N.Y. acads. medicine, Am. Soc. Clin. Pharmacology and Therapeutics, Am. Pub. Health Assn., Am. Occupational Med. Assn. Home: 7 Jason Ln Mamaroneck NY 10543-2108

MIZUGUCHI, HIROYUKI, biology professor; b. Osaka, June 27, 1968; PhD, Osaka U., 1996. Prof. Osaka U., 2008. Office: Yamadaoka 1-6 Suita Osaka 565-0871 Japan Business E-Mail: mizuguch@phs.osaka-u.ac.jp.

MIZUGUCHI, NANA N., plastic surgeon; BA, UCLA, 1986—91; MD, Tulane U., 1992—96. Diplomate American Bd. Surgery, 2001, Am. Bd. Plastic Surgery, 2005. Fellow plastic surgery, divsn. plastic and reconstructive surgery Univ. of NC, 2001—03; intern dept. surgery Univ. of Louisville, Ky., 1996—97, resident dept. surgery Ky., 1997—2001, chief resident dept. surgery Ky., 2000—01, asst. prof. dept. surgery Ky., 2003—06, dir., microsurgery program Ky., 2005—06, dir., student tchg. program Ky., 2005—06, clin. faculty, dept. surgery Ky., 2006—, hosp. affiliations include, Jewish Hosp., Norton Hosp., Dupont Surgery Ctr., Calobrace Plastic Surgery Ctr. Recipient Conf. Attendance award, Univ. of Louisville, 2001, Better Care award, Norton Hosp., 2004; fellow Acad. of Surgeons, 2006. Mem.: Facial Action Coding System, Hirum C. Polk Surg. Soc., Am. Soc. of Plastic Surgeons, Ky. Soc. of Plastic Surgeons. Office: Calobrace Plastic Surgery Center 2341 Lime Kiln Lane Louisville KY 40207 Office Phone: 502-899-9979.

MIZUKAMI, TAKESHI, physician; b. Japan; MD, Keio U., Tokyo, PhD, 1990. Head dr. Endoscopy Ctr., Yokohama Mcpl. Citizen's Hosp., Kanagawa, Japan, 2007—. Office: Yokohama Mcpl Citizen's Hosp 56 Okazawa-cho Hodogaya-ku Yokohama city Kanagawa 240-8555 Japan

MIZUMORI, SHERI J.Y., psychology professor, department chairman; BS in Psychology, U. Wash., Seattle, 1977; MA in Psychology, U. Calif., Berkeley, 1983, PhD in Psychology, 1985. Postdoctoral fellow U. Colo., 1985—89; asst. prof. U. Utah, 1989—92, assoc. prof., 1992—2000, acting chair psychology dept., 1995; assoc. prof. U. Wash., 2000—03, prof. psychology, 2003—, chair psychology dept., 2005—, co-dir. grad. program in neurobiology and behavior, 2007—. Contbr. articles to profl. jours. Office: Univ Wash Psychology Dept Box 351525 Seattle WA 98195-1525 Office Phone: 206-543-2699. Business E-Mail: mizumori@u.washington.edu.

MIZUNO, SHUGO, hepatobiliary-pancreas and transplant surgeon; b. Numazu, Shizuoka, Japan, July 19, 1969; MD, Mie U., 1995, PhD, 2001. Asst. prof. Dept. Hepatobiliary Pancreas and Transplant Surgery, 2008; vice dir. Organ Transplantation Ctr., Mie U., 2010—. Recipient Young Investigator Travel award, Am. Pancreatic Assn., Japan Pancreas Soc., 2009; grant, 2003—05, YASUDA Med. Fund, 2006, 2009—. Mem.: Japanese Soc. Hepato-Biliary-Pancreatic Surgery (Presdl. award 2010), Japanese Soc. Gastroenterology, Japanese Soc. Gastroent. Surgery, Japan Surg. Soc., Am. Soc. Transplantation. Avocation: tennis. Office: 2-174 Edobashi Tsu Mie 5140001 Japan Office Fax: 81-59-2328095. Business E-Mail: mizunos@clin.medic.mie-u.ac.jp.

MIŠKIC, BLAZENKA, endocrinologist, educator; b. Slavonski Brod, Croatia, July 2, 1960; d. Tomo and Milica Galovic; m. Djuro Miškic; children: Karla, Luka. MD, PhD, Med. U., Zagreb, 1983. Cert. in edn. bone densitometry, in ultrasound thyroid gland, in genetic polimorphism. Head, densitometric unit internal dept. Gen. Hosp., Slav.Brod, Croatia, 1998—, main endocrynologist, 2007—; prof., docent Internal Medicine Med. U. Osijek, head endocrinology, metabolic disease. Pres., local soc. osteoporosis Orgn. Osteoporosis Edn. and Prevention, Slav.Brod, 2006—, dir., 2007—. Mem.: Lions Club. Roman Catholic. Avocations: sports, travel, literature, painting, music. Office: Gen Hosp Dr Josip Bencvi A Štampara 42 Slavonski Brod 35 000 Croatia Office Fax: 00385 35 446 121. Personal E-mail: mickicblazenka@gmail.com.

MJORUD, JAN, orthopedist; b. Norway, Aug. 25, 1946; MD, U. Oslo, 1976. Physician Diakonhjemmet Hosp., Oslo, 1982—. Home: Grimelundshaugen 5 Oslo N-0374 Norway Personal E-mail: jan.m@mailbox.as.

M. KIRSZTAJN, GIANNA, nephrologist, educator; b. Brazil, May 10; Superior, UFPE, 1983; PhD, UNIFESP, 1990. Prof. UNIFESP, 1990—. Nephrologist Fed. U. Sao Paulo, 2003. Mem.: Brazilian Soc. Nephrology. Office: Rua Borges Lagoa 1080 CJ 1206 Sao Paulo 04038-002 Brazil Business E-Mail: gianna@nefro.epm.br.

MLADICK, RICHARD ANTHONY, plastic surgeon; b. Melrose Park, Ill., May 28, 1934; s. Edward Anthony and Gladys Jane (Castens) M.; m. Elly Dalgas Jensen, Aug. 13, 1966; children: Kristen, Richard. BA, Northwestern U., 1955, MD, 1959. Diplomate Am. Bd. Plastic Surgery, Am. Bd. Surgery. Intern Cook County Hosp., 1959—60, resident in gen. surgery, 1960—64; resident in plastic and reconstructive surgery Duke U. Med. Ctr., 1965—68; asst. prof. plastic surgery Duke U. Med. Sch., Durham, N.C., 1968-69; prof. plastic surgery Eastern Va. Med. Sch., Norfolk, 1969-75; dir. Ctr. for Cosmetic Plastic Surgery, Virginia Beach, Va., 1975—. Guest editor: Clinics in Plastic Surgery, 1989; contbr. articles, chpts. to profl. publs. Bd. dirs. Va. Orchestral Assn., Virginia Beach; mem. Orgn. Pub. Safety. Fellow Am. Coll. Surgeons; Mem. AMA, Am. Assn. Plastic Surgeons, Am. Soc. Aesthetic Plastic Surgery, Lipoplasty Soc. N.Am. (bd. dirs., past pres.), Med. Soc. Va., Seaboard Med. Assn., Am. Soc. Plastic and Reconstructive Surgeons, Va. Soc. Plastic and Reconstructive Plastic Surgeons (pres. 1973-74), Southeastern Soc. Plastic Surgeons, So. Med. Assn., Va. Beach Med. Soc. Virginia Beach Rotary Club. Presbyterian. Avocations: running, tennis, gardening, biking. Office Phone: 757-481-5151.

MLINARIC-GALINOVIC, GORDANA, microbiologist, researcher; b. Fužine, Croatia, Feb. 15, 1950; d. Ivan and Ana (Subotić) Mlinarić; m. Mili Galinović, Feb. 23, 1974; children: Ivana, Andro. MD, U. Zagreb, Croatia, 1973, MSc, 1978, DSc, 1985. Gen. practitioner Clin. Hosp. Ctr., Zagreb, 1974—75; from asst. lectr. to assoc. prof. U. Zagreb Med. Sch., 1975—2002, prof., 2002—; assoc. dept. virology microbiology svc. Croatian Nat. Inst. Pub. Health, Zagreb, 2001—04, head microbiology svc., 2004—; head microbiology Med. Sch. U. Zagreb, 2009—, NMFP ECDC, 2008. Prin. investigator on respiratory syncytial virus infections Ministry of Sci., Zagreb, 1986—; chief WHO Virus Collaborating Ctr., Zagreb, 1988—. Contbr. articles to profl. jours. British Coun. fellow RVI, New Castle Upon Tyne, 1985; P.L. Ogra grant U. Tex., Galveston, 1991-92. Mem. European Soc. Clin. Virology, Croatian Acad. Med. Sci., Croatian Med. Soc., Croatian Soc. Med. Microbiology. Roman Catholic. Office: Croatian Nat Inst Pub Health Dept Virology Rockefellerova 12 10 000 Zagreb Croatia Home: Bartolici 5 10-000 Zagreb Croatia Office Phone: 385-1-4863-210. Business E-Mail: gordana.galinovic@hzjz.hr.

MLYNARSKI, RAFAL, cardiologist, arrhythmia specialist; b. Sosnowiec, Poland, Oct. 6, 1975; m. Agnieszka Mlynarska. MD, PhD, Med. U. Silesia, Katowice, Poland. Asst. Upper-Silesian Cardiology Ctr., Katowice, 2003—. Contbr. articles to sci. publs. Active mem. Klub 30, Warsaw, 2008. Recipient Best Regional Abstracts winner, European Soc. Cardiology, ICNC8; Sci. grants. Office: Upper-Silesian

Cardiology Ctr Ziolowa 45 Katowice 40-635 Poland Home: Ul. Wielka Skotnica 38/58 Myslowice 41-400 Poland Business E-Mail: rafal_mlynarski@mp.pl.

MO, LOAR KA-KEUNG, geriatrician, consultant, educator; b. Hong Kong, Sept. 11, 1962; s. Kam Wah Mo and Sau Fong Wong; m. Yee Man Chan; children: Cheuk Yan, Cheuk Hei. MBChB, Chinese U. Hong Kong, 1986, MBA, 1996. Reg. med. practitioner. Intern Med. & Health Dept., Hong Kong, 1986-87; med. officer Hosp. Svcs. Dept., Hong Kong, 1987-92; sr. med. officer Hosp. Svcs. Dept./Hosp. Authority, Hong Kong, 1992-96; cons. Hosp. Authority, Hong Kong, 1996—. Hon. clin. tutor, hon. lectr. Faculty of Medicine The Chinese U., Hong Kong, 1988—89, 1995—96, hon. assoc. prof., 1996—97, adj. assoc. prof., 1997—; hon. clin. assoc. prof. Faculty of Medicine, U. Hong Kong, 2002—09; part-time lectr. Hong Kong Bapt. U., 1998—2006; part-time instr. The Open U. of Hong Kong, 1997—2001; hon. adv. elderly svcs. Internat. Buddhist Progress Soc. (Hong Kong) Ltd., 1997—2003; profl. adv. Cmty. Rehab. Network Hong Kong Soc. Rehab., 1996—; honorable advisor Hong Kong Neuromuscular Disease Assn., 1999—, Hong Kong Stroke Assn., 1997—98, 1999—; hon. med. advisor Yan Chai Nursing Home, 1998—2003; hon. clin. supr. Hong Kong Coll. Family Physicians, 1997—; advisor Stroke Adv. Bd., Medicmedia (HK) Ltd., 2003—05; hon. advisor Social Svc. Dept., Yan Chai Hosp. Bd., 2010—; mem. geriat. medicine specialty bd. Hong Kong Coll. Physicians, 2009—. Reviewer Hong Kong Jour. Gerontology, 1993, Hong Kong Med. Jour., 2004. Mem. coun. Ch. of Mt. Carmel, 1995-97, Windshield Charitable Found., 2004—06, The Yan Chai Hosp. Chaplaincy Com., 2004—06. Fellow: Royal Coll. Physicians Glasgow, Royal Coll. Physicians Edinburgh, Hong Kong Coll. Physicians, Hong Kong Acad. Medicine; mem.: Hong Kong Mgmt. Assn., Hong Kong Geriatrics Soc. (coun. 2000—04, 2008—), Hong Kong Assn. Gerontology (coun. 1991—92), Hong Kong Alzheimers Disease and Brain Failure Assn. (coun. 1996—97). Avocations: badminton, bowling, swimming, stamp collecting/philately. Office: Yan Chai Hosp 7-11 Yan Chai St Tsuen Wan Hong Kong Hong Kong Home: Kam Sing Mansion 19H Taikoo Shing Hong Kong

MOCK, BEVERLY A., geneticist, researcher; children: Alex, Chris; m. Douglas Lowy. MS, U. Md., 1980, PhD in zoology, 1983. Studies on the genetics of susceptibility to parasitic diseases Dept. Immunology Walter Reed Army Inst. Rsch.; assoc. dir. sci. programs Ctr. Cancer Rsch., Nat. Cancer Inst., NIH, 1999—2007, chief Lab. Genetics, 2004—06, dep. chief Lab. Cancer Biology and Genetics. Office: Lab Cancer Biology and Genetics 37 Convent Dr Bldg 37 Rm 3146 Bethesda MD 20892-4258 Office Phone: 301-496-2360. Office Fax: 301-402-1031. E-mail: bev@helix.nih.gov. *

MOCKFORD, EDWARD LEE, biologist, educator; b. Indpls., June 16, 1930; s. Harry Grover and Helen (Lewis) Mockford. AB, Ind. U., 1952; MS, U. Fla., 1954; PhD, U. Ill.-Urbana, 1960. Grad. asst. biology U. Fla., Gainesville, 1952—54; rsch. asst. Ill. Natural Hist. Survey, Champaign, 1956—60; asst. prof. to prof. biol. scis. Ill. State U., Normal, 1960—86; rsch. assoc. Fla. Dept. Agr., Gainesville, 1959—; coop. scientist US Dept. Agr., Washington, 1960—; vis. prof. Inst. Technologico, Monterrey, 1963—64. Contbr. articles to profl. jours. With US Army, 1954—56. Recipient Disting. Prof. award, Ill. State U., 1984; grant, Am. Mus. Natural History Travel, 1959, Rsch. grant, NSF, 1961, 1963, 1965, 1967, 1983. Mem.: Soc. Tropical Biology, Soc. Systematic Zoology, Sociedad Mex. de Entomologia, Entomol. Soc. Am., Ill. Acad. Sci. Democrat. Avocations: hiking, birdwatching, swimming, fishing, reading. Office: Ill State U Dept Biol Scis Normal IL 61790 Home: 505 Bowles St Normal IL 61761-1519 Office Phone: 309-438-2666. Business E-Mail: elmockf@ilstu.edu.

MOCKIENE, VIDA, healthcare educator; b. Klaipeda, Lithuania, Oct. 6, 1961; MSW, Klaipeda U., 2006; D in Health Scis., Tampete U., Finland, 2010. Faculty health scis. Klaipeda U., 2006—, adj. prof., 2011. Office: Herkaus Manto St 84 Klaipeda LT-92294 Lithuania Office Fax: 37046398552. E-mail: mockienevida@gmail.com.

MOCKINĖ, ASTA, medical educator; b. Jurbarkas, Oct. 21, 1965; MS, Kauno Radvilenu vidurine mokykla, 1983; EdD in Biomedicine, Lithuanian Acad. Phys. Edn., 2010. Educator Vytautas Magnus U., 1990—. Home: Savanoriu pr Kaunas 50186 Lithuania Business E-Mail: a.mockiene@spc.vdu.lt.

MOCUMBI, PASCOAL MANUEL, international organization administrator, former prime minister of Mozambique; b. Maputo, Mozambique, Apr. 10, 1941; m. Adelina Mocumbi; 4 children. Grad. in medicine, U. Lausanne, Switzerland. Founding mem., head info. and propaganda dept. FRELIMO, 1963; elected to Mozambique People's Assembly, mem. ctrl. com., 1983; provincial health dir., prin. physician Sofala Province, 1976-80; min. health Govt. of Mozambique, Maputo, 1980-87, min. for fgn. affairs, 1987-94, prime min., 1994—2004; high rep. European & Developing Countries Clin. Trials Partnership, The Hague, Netherlands, 2004—. Mem. bd. Internat. Women's Health Coalition, Medicines for Malaria Venture, African Med. & Rsch. Found.; mem. WHO, Commn. on Social Determinants of Health. Mem.: Inst. Medicine (assoc.). Office: EDCTP Postbus 93015 2509 AA The Hague Netherlands *

MODAN-MOSES, DALIT, endocrinologist, educator; b. Balt., June 27, 1961; MD, Sackler Sch. Medicine, 1988. Resident, pediat. Sheba Med. Ctr., Tel-Hashomer, Israel, 1989—94, pediat. endocrinologist, 1997; postdoc. fellow, pediat. endocrinology Johns Hopkins Hosp., Balt., 1994—97; lectr. Tel-Aviv U., 1997—. Mem.: Israel Soc. Clin. Pediat., Israel Pediat. Endocrine Soc., Israel Endocrine Soc. Office: Pediat Endocrinology Unit Sheba Med Ctr Ramat Gan 52653 Israel Office Fax: 972-3-5305055. Business E-Mail: dmodan@sheba.health.gov.il.

MODIC, MICHAEL, radiologist, educator; MD, Case Western Reserve U. Sch. Medicine, 1975. Resident in radiology Cleveland Clinic, fellow in neuroradiology, neuroradiologist, 1980—82, head magnetic resonance, 1982—85, chmn. radiology, 1989—2000, bd. govs., 2000; asst. prof. radiology Cleveland U. Hosp., 1979—80; dir. magnetic resonance & neuroradiology Case Western U. Reserve Sch. Medicine, 1985—89; prof. radiology Ohio State U., 1993—, Cleveland Clinic Lerner Coll. Medicine, 2004—07; chmn. Neurological Inst., 2007—. Editorial bd. Radiology, Am. Jour. Neuroradiology, Neurology, Magnetic Resonance in Medicine, Magnetic Resonance Imaging. Fellow: Am. Coll. Radiology; mem.: Am. Stroke Assn., Am. Heart Assn., Am. Soc. Spine Radiology, Am. Soc. Neuroradiology, Radiological Soc. North America, Soc. Magnetic Resonance Imaging (bd. dirs.), Soc. Magnetic Resonance in Medicine (pres. 1992—93, former bd. trustees, Gold Medal in Clinical Sci. 1991). Office: Cleveland Clinic Main Campus 9500 Euclid Ave MC-T13 Cleveland OH 44195 Office Phone: 216-444-9308.

MODIN, SONJA AGDA ELEONORA, physician, researcher; b. Stockholm, July 13, 1947; d. Sten Olof and Helfrid Anna Maria Modin; m. Anders Kjell Hjalmar Sandell; children: Jesper Olof Rolandh Sandell, Staffan Olof Hjalmar Sandell, Lisa Maria Helena Sandell. MD, Ctr. Family Medicine, 1998—, Karolinska Inst., Stockholm, 2010. Cert. family physician Nat. Bd. Health and Wellfare, Sweden, 1973. Family physician Årsta Healthcare Centre, Stockholm, 1983—99; head of primary care in Enskede/Årsta Stockholm County Coun., 1987—94, med. adviser to polit. bd. on primary care matters, so. part, 1992—94, med. adviser to health care purchaser orgn., 1994—95, med. adviser info. tech. dept., 1995—2005; family physician Fammi, 2005—06, Stuvsta Health Ctr., 2007—. Avocations: painting, photography. Business E-Mail: sonja.modin@sll.se.

MODINE, THOMAS, cardiologist; b. Beyrouth, Lebanon, June 20, 1970; MD, U. Lille, PhD, 1999. Cons. CHRU de Lille, 1996—. Office: Hopital Cardiologique Bd J Leclerc Lille Nord 59037 France Business E-Mail: thomas.modine@chru-lille.fr.

MODISHER, MELVIN WAYNE, obstetrician, gynecologist, educator; b. Sharpsville, Pa., May 9, 1916; MD, Temple U., Phila., 1943. Diplomate Am. Bd. Ob-Gyn. Intern Abington Meml. Hosp., 1944; resident in ob-gyn. Bethesda Hosp., Cin., 1946-49; mem. staff U. Hosp. Vol., San Diego. Assoc. clin. prof. reproductive medicine Med. Sch. U. Calif. San Diego. Fellow ACS. Personal E-mail: melandcorla@san.rr.com. *

MODRALL, J. GREGORY, surgeon, educator; b. Okla. City, June 15, 1962; BS, Colo. State U., 1984; MD, U. Colo., 1989. Prof., surgery U. Tex. Southwestern Med. Ctr., 1998—. Home: 7400 Ivanhoe Dr Plano TX 75024 E-mail: greg.modrall@utsouthwestern.edu.

MODY, KETAN RAJENDRA, sports medicine physician; b. Hinsdale, Ill., Oct. 5, 1977; BS, Ill. Inst. Tech., 1998; MD, Chgo. Med. Sch., 2003. Family medicine resident UPMC Shadyside Hosp., 2003—06; sports medicine physician U. Conn., St. Francis Hosp., 2006—07, Hinsdale Orthop. Assocs., 2007—09, Elite Sports Medicine Inst. Ltd., 2009—, founder, owner, 2009—11. Mem.: Am. Med. Soc. Sports Medicine, Am. Acad. Family Practice. Avocations: sports, travel. Office: 908 N Elm St Ste 109 Hinsdale IL 60521 Office Fax: 630-794-9998. E-mail: ketansportsmed@yahoo.com.

MOELLEKEN, BRENT RODERICK WILFRED, plastic surgeon; b. Vancouver, BC, Can., Apr. 19, 1960; m. Dayna Devon; 2 children. BA, Purdue U., 1979; MD, Yale U., 1985; postgrad., Harvard U., 1980-81. Diplomate Am. Bd. Surgery, Am. Bd. Plastic Surgery. Intern U. Calif., San Francisco, 1985-86, resident in gen. surgery, 1986-92, rsch. fellow in plastic surgery, 1988-90, resident in plastic surgery, 1992-94; fellow in aesthetic surgery UCLA, 1994-95, pvt. practice Beverly Hills, Calif., 1995—, Santa Barbara, Calif., 1995—. Attending surgeon UCLA Hosp., Cedars-Sinai Hosp., LA, instr. U. Calif. Sch. Medicine, San Francisco, 1992-94, clin. instr. UCLA, 1994-99, assoc. clin. prof., 1999-2007; surgeon ABC-TV Extreme Makeover, Oprah, Discovery Channel, E!, CNN, NBC. Plastic surgery before and after lead surgeon: (TV series) Discovery Health Channel; contbr. several articles to profl. jours.; appeared in: over 60 TV shows. Founder About Face surg. found. Fellow ACS; mem. AMA, AAAS, Am. Soc. Plastic Surgeons, Am. Soc. Aesthetic Plastic Surgery, Calif. Med. Assn., Calif. Soc. Plastic Surgeons, Santa Barbara County Med. Soc., LA County Med. Assn., LA Soc. Plastic Surgeons, LA Surg. Soc., Wound Healing Soc. (founding mem.), Lipoplasty Soc. N.Am. Achievements include invention of Livefill graft; superficial check lift operation; hybrid abdominoplasty 360 facelift. Office: 120 S Spalding Dr Ste 340 Beverly Hills CA 90212 Office Phone: 310-273-1001. Office Fax: 310-205-4881. Personal E-mail: drbrent@drbrent.com. Business E-Mail: info@drbrent.com.

MOELLER, CHRISTOPH, child and adolescent psychiatrist, professor, psychotherapist; b. Germany, Dec. 27, 1969; s. Jürgen and Irmela Möller; 2 children. MD, U. Witten/Herdecke, 1997. Pediatric physician, Herdecke, 1997—98; child and adolescent psychiatrist Osnabrück, Hannover, Germany, 1999—2002; cons., head dept. child and adolescent psychiatry Hannover, 2010—. Tchr. in group therapy and Balint groups; spkr. in field. Author, editor: Addiction and Drug Abuse in Adolescence, 2001, 2009; author: Seeking Adolescence, 2009; contbr. articles to profl. jours., newspapers; author: Computer And Internet Addictions, 2011. Office: Kinderkrankenaus Auf der Bult Abt Kinder-Und Jugendpsychiatrie Janusz-Korczak-Allee 12 30173 Hannover Germany

MOELLER, HARALD E., chemist, researcher; b. Pelkum, Germany, Sept. 17, 1960; s. Wilhelm Moeller and Lotte Vogel; m. Carola E.I. Prigge, Dec. 21, 1992. PhD, U. Munster, Germany, 1988. Rsch. assoc. U. Munster Inst. Phys. Chemistry, 1991—93, sci. asst., 1993—2001; head magnetic resonance physics Max Planck Inst. Human Cognitive and Brain Sci., Leipzig, Germany, 2001—04, 2006—; lectr. dept. chemistry U. Leipzig, 2002—04, hon. prof., exptl. physics, 2007—; prof. exptl. magnetic resonance dept. radiology U. Hosp. Munster, Germany, 2004—06. Vis. scientist Duke U. Med. Ctr., Ctr. for In Vivo Microscopy, Durham, NC, 1996—97, Durham, 2000, Durham, 06, Durham, 08, 10, rsch. assoc., NC, 1997—98. Contbr. articles to profl. jours. Recipient Bennigsen-Foerder prize, Dept. Sci., State of N. Rhine-Westphalia, Germany, 1992, Bundesministerium Bildung und Forschung award for Innovative Projects in Med. Tech., Fed. Ministry Edn. and Rsch., 2004. Mem.: German Chem. Soc., Internat. Soc. for Magnetic Resonance in Medicine. Office Phone: 49 341 9940 2212. Business E-Mail: moeller@cbs.mpg.de.

MOELLERING, ROBERT CHARLES, JR., internist, educator; b. Lafayette, Ind., June 9, 1936; s. Robert Charles and Irene Pauline (Nolde) M.; children: Anne Elizabeth, Robert Charles, Catherine Irene; m. Mary Jane Ferraro, July 11, 1987. BA, Valparaiso U., 1958, DSc (hon.), 1980; MD cum laude, Harvard U., 1962; DPH (hon.), St. Elizabeth U., 2005. Diplomate: Am. Bd. Internal Medicine. Intern Mass. Gen. Hosp., Boston, 1962-63, resident, 1963-64, postdoctoral fellow in infectious diseases, 1967-70, resident, 1966-67, mem. infectious disease unit and asst. physician, 1970-76, assoc. physician, 1976-83, hon. physician, 1983—, cons. bacteriology, 1972-87; instr. medicine Harvard U. Med. Sch., Boston, 1970-72, asst. prof., 1972-76, assoc. prof., 1976-80, prof., 1980—; chmn. dept. medicine, physician-in-chief New Eng. Deaconess Hosp., 1981-96; pres., CEO Deaconess Profl. Practice Group, 1995-98; Shields Warren-Mallinckrodt prof. rsch. Harvard U. Med. Sch., Boston, 1981-89, Shields Warren-Mallinckrodt prof. med. rsch., 1989-99, 2005—, Herrman Blumgart prof. medicine, 1999—2005; assoc. physician-in-chief Beth Israel Deaconess Med. Ctr., 1996—98, physician-in-chief, 1998—2005, pres., CEO, Harvard Med. Faculty physician, 1998—2003, chmn. bd. dirs., pres., trustee, 2003—05; vis. prof. infectious diseases Catholic U. Rome, 2003—. Mem. subcom. on susceptibility testing Nat. Com. for Clin. Lab. Standards, 1976-88; mem. subcom. on antimicrobial agts. and chemotherapy, 1978-80; subcom. on antimicrobiol disc. diffusion suceptibility testing, 1980-88; chmn. data safety monitoring bd. Nat. Inst. Allergy and Infections Disease, NIH, 1997—2002; trustee Caregroup, 1998-2005, BIDMC, 1998-2005; bd. dirs. NanoBio Corp., Nabriva Therapeutics Forschungs GmbH, editor European J Clin. Invest, 2009-. Mem. editl. bd. Antimicrobial Agts. and Chemotherapy, 1977-81, editor, 1981-85, editor-in-chief, 1985-95; editor European Jour. Clin. Microbial Infectious Diseases, 1990-2007; consulting. editor Infectious Disease Clinics N.Am., 1986—; editor Les Infections, 1983; editl. bd. New Eng. Jour. Medicine, 1977-81, European Jour.Clin. Microbiology, 1981—, Jour. Infectious Diseases, 1981-85, 89-93, Infectious Disease Alert, 1981-92, Pharmacotherapy, 1982—, Antimicrobial Agts. Ann., 1984-87, Zentralblatt Fur Bacteriologie, Microbiologie and Hygience, 1984—, Jour. of Infection, 1986—, Innovations, 1986-90, Residents Forum in Internal Medicine, 1988-90, Diagnostic Microbiology and Infectious Disease, 1989-90, Internat. Jour. Antimicrobial Agts., 1990—, Infectious Diseases in Clin. Practice, 1991-92, Jour. Infection and Chemotherapy, 1995—, Clin. Infectious Disease, 1999-2004, jour. Inf.Public Health, 2008-. Served with USPHS, 1964-66. Grantee USPHS, NIH. Master ACP, Am. Acad. Microbiology, Infectious Diseases Soc. Am. (v.p. 1988-89, pres. elect 1989-90, pres. 1990-91, past pres. 1991-92); fellow Royal Coll. Physicians (hon.); mem. Am. Soc. Microbiology, Am. Clin. and Climatol. Assn., Internat. Soc. Chemotherapy, Am. Soc. Clin. Investigation, Assn. Am. Physicians, European Soc. Clin. Microbiology, Am. Fedn. Clin. Rsch., Assn. Profs. Medicine, Roxbury Clin. Records Club, Mass. Med. Soc. (councilor), Brit. Soc. Antimicrobial Chemotherapy, Coun. Biology Editors, Alpha Omega Alpha, Phi Kappa Psi. Home: 49 Longfellow Rd Wellesley MA 02481-5220 Office: Beth Israel Deaconess Med Ctr Dept Medicine 110 Francis St Boston MA 02215-5501 E-mail: rmoeller@bidmc.harvard.edu.

MOEMEN, MOHAMED EZZAT, anesthesiologist, educator; b. Cairo, May 18, 1938; s. Ahmed Ali Moemen and Naeama Zein El-Marsafi; m. Laila Fathi Hassan; children: Amr Ezzat, Noha Ezzat, Dalia Ezzat, Hazem Ezzat. MB, BcH, Cairo U., 1960, diploma in Medicine, 1963, diploma in anesthesia, 1965, PhD in Anesthesia, 1971, D in Med. Scis. (hon.), Yorker Internat. U., Florence, Italy, 2007. Ho. officer faculty of medicine Cairo U., 1960—62; specialist of anesthesia MOPH Hosps., Cairo, 1966—70; lectr. of anesthesia Faculty of Medicine, Zagazig U., Zagazig, Egypt, 1971—75, asst prof. of anesthesia, 1976—80, prof. of anesthesia, 1981—98, emeritus prof. of anesthesia, 1999—. Founder, dir. anesthesia and ICU dept. Zagazig U., 1971—98, cons. anesthesia ICU, 1993—; head sci. com. Egyptian Health Orgn. Ins. Hosps., spkr. in field. Author: Monitoring and Patient Safety; sr. editor: Egypt Jour. Anesthesia, Egyptian Jour. Intensive Care. Recipient prize of clin. med. scis., Zagazig U., 2004, Gold Medal in Edn., World Forum, 2007; named to Outstanding Intellectuals of the 21st Century, 2000. Mem.: Egyptian Crisis Mgmt. Assn., Internat. Assn. for Study of Pain, Soc. Egyptian Anesthesia, El-Shams Sporting Club. Muslim. Achievements include first to create the first congress of anesthesia in the history of Egypt; create the Egypt Resuscitation Council; create a new classification of liver disease. Avocations: reading, travel, sports, music. Home: 2 Gamal el-Din wassel Cairo 11371 Egypt Office: Zagazig U Faculty of Medicine Zagazig Egypt Business E-Mail: ezzatmoemen@yahoo.com.

MOFFITT, CAROLYN MULLINS, program director; b. Victoria, Ark. d. Jefferson Forrest and Mabel Mullins: children: James S. Crone, Jr., Jefferson Edward Crone, Laurie Kittrell. BBA, U. Memphis, 1994. Supr. Medicare billing City of Memphis Hosp., 1968-71; dir. budget and reimbursement Regional Med. Ctr., Memphis, 1971-90, bus. mgr. ambulatory svcs., 1990-91; patient accounts mgr. radiology dept. U. Tenn. Med. Group, Memphis, 1992-99; mgmt. analyst, compliance officer U. Tenn. Health Sci. Ctr., Memphis, 1999—. Cons. Meth. Healthcare, Memphis, 1982-84, Brannon McCullough, Primary Health Care Ctr., Memphis, 1990-92; mem. adv. bd. Porter Leath Children's Home, Memphis, 1989-92. Mem. Healthcare Fin. Mgmt. Assn. (cert., fellow, bd. dirs. 1995-96, v.p. 1996-98, pres. 1999-2000, bd. chmn. 2000-2001, compliance officers forum adv. coun. 2001-2004; Frederick C. Morgan award 2010). Avocations: stained glass creations, collectibles, reading. Office: U Tenn Health Sci Ctr Ste 807 920 Madison Ave Memphis TN 38163 E-mail: cmoffitt@utmem.edu.

MOFFITT, CHRISTINE M., biologist, educator; PhD, U. Mass., 1978; BA, U. Calif., Santa Cruz, 1969; AM, Smith Coll., 1973. Instr. Smith Coll., Northampton, Mass., 1978—80; postdoctoral assoc. U. Mass., Amherst, 1980—81; asst. prof. U. Idaho, Moscow, 1982—88, assoc. prof., 1989—98, prof., 1999—. Asst. unit leader Idaho Coop. Fish and Wildlife Rsch. unit U.S. Geol. Survey. Contbr. articles to profl. jours.; author (with Cassinelli J.): Growth and Physiology of Selected Desert and Montane Adapted Populations of Redband Trout (Oncorhynchus mykiss gairdneri). Transactions of the American Fisheries Society; author: (with Williams C. J.) Estimation of Fish and Wildlife Disease Prevalence from Imperfect Diagnostic Tests on Pooled Samples With Varying Pool Sizes Ecological Informatics, 2010; author: (with Anlauf, K. A.) Modelling of Landscape Variables at Multiple Extents to Predict Fine Sediments and Suitable Habitat for Tubifex Tubifex in a Stream System. Freshwater Biology, 2010; author: (with Bruce, R. L.) Quantifying Risks of Volitional Consumption of New Zealand; author: (with G. Whelan, and R. Jackson) History of Inland Fisheries Management. American Fisheries Society. Bethesda, Maryland, 2010. Recipient Emmeline Moore prize, Am. Fisheries Soc. Pitts., Alumni award, U. Idaho, 2009, USGS Headquarters Diversity award, 2009; named Outstanding Alumna, U. Mass. Natural Resources Coll., 1999. Mem.: Am. Fisheries Soc. (pres, pres.

elect, 1st vp and 2 vp 1996—2000, Meritorious Svc. award 1994). Office: Dept Fish and Wildlife Resource USGS Coop Rsch Unit Univ Idaho PO Box 441141 Moscow ID 83844-1141 Business E-Mail: cmoffitt@uidaho.edu.

MOFFLIN, LIONEL HUGH (HARRY MOFFLIN), biomedical engineer, physician; b. Fremantle, Australia, Dec. 20, 1923; arrived in US, 1974; s. Horace Elgar and Ida Beatrice (Moseley) Mofflin. MB, BS, U. Adelaide, Australia, 1948; MSc in Biomed. Engring., Case Western Res. U., 1980; cardiac tech. cert. of proficiency, Cuyahoga C.C. Engr. Cleve. Hearing & Speech Ctr., 1981—83; engr. Electronics Design Ctr. Case Western Res. U., Cleve., 1983—86; circuit designer, 1986—92; project engr. Mofflin Enterprises, Cleve., 1992—. Electronic circuit designer, 1986—98. Fellow: ACP, Royal Coll. Physicians (Edinburgh). Avocations: preventive medicine, art, music.

MOHAIDEEN, A. HASSAN, surgeon, consultant, health products executive; b. Ramanathapuram, India, Aug. 14, 1940; s. Abdul and Mariam (Pitchai) Kader; m. Zarina M. Meera, May 30, 1965 (dec. July 1986); children: Ahamed, Mariam, Najeeba, Azeema; m. Laurie J. Kucich, June 23, 1989; children: Yasmin Sara, Leila Jahan. MD, U. Madras, India, 1965; MBA, Wagner Coll., 1996. Diplomate Am. Bd. Surgery, Am. Bd. Quality Assurance and Utilization; cert. physician exec. Am. Coll. Physician Execs. Intern Govt. Stanley Hosp., Madras, 1965-66, Good Samaritan Hosp., West Islip, NY, 1967-68; resident in gen. and vascular surgery L.I. Coll. Hosp., Bklyn., 1968-73, asst. attending surgeon, 1973-76, assoc. attending surgeon, 1976-78, attending surgeon, 1978—, chief divsn. vascular surgery, 1980-93, dir. vascular lab., 1981-93; v.p. Bklyn.-Caledonian Hosp. Ctr. (affiliate of NYU), 1994-95; sr. v.p., managed care and exec. vice-chmn. dept. surgery The Bklyn.-Caledonian Hosp. Ctr. (affiliate of NYU), 1995-96; pres., CEO, Health Plan Systems, Inc., Rochelle Park, NJ, 2001—. Asst. surgeon G.H.Q. Hosp., Ramnad, India, 1966-67; assoc. attending surgeon Meth. Hosp., Bklyn., 1982-90, attending surgeon, 1991-97; asst. attending surgeon Bklyn. Caledonian Med. Ctr., 1973-85, mem. courtesy staff, 1985-94, 97—, attending surgeon, 1994-96; attending surgeon Victory Meml. Hosp., Bklyn., 1982—; vis. physician Kings County Hosp. Ctr., Bklyn., 1973-94; clin. instr. in surgery Downstate Med. Ctr., SUNY, Bklyn., 1973-78, clin. asst. prof. surgery, 1978—; mem. exec. com. of med. staff L.I. Coll. Hosp., Bklyn., 1979-93, treas. med. staff, 1982-85, pres., 1985-87, med. chmn. Guild Ball com., 1981, mem. quality assurance com. dept. surgery, 1988-94, chmn. credentials com., 1990-93, quality assurance and risk mgmt. com., 1990-93; bd. dirs. Aetna Health Plans of N.Y., AIDS adv. com., 1987-93, stds. com., 1986-94, quality assurance com.; bd. dirs. Aetna-U.S. Healthcare, 1997; mem. credentials com. Prucare, 1988-92; sr. v.p. managed care Bklyn. Hosp., 1995-96; mem. quality mgmt. com. Oxford Health Plans, 1995-2002; mem. quality improvement com. Chubb Health, N.Y., 1994-96, Cigna (HealthSource), 1997-2003; mem. credentials com. United Healthcare, 1997—; exec. dir. Mayan Health, PPO, Atlantic Med. Assocs. IPA; pres. Health Plan Sys., Inc. Contbr. articles to med. jours. Fellow ACS (com. on Long Island dist. applicants, 1988-99, bd. dirs. Bklyn.-L.I. chpt.), Royal Coll. Physicians and Surgeons Can. (cert.), Internat. Coll. Surgeons; mem. AMA (Physician's Recognition award), AAAS, Am. Coll. Physician Execs., Med. Soc. of State of N.Y., N.Y. State Soc. of Surgeons, N.Y. Acad. of Scis., Med. Soc. of County of Kings (mediation com., 1979-85), Bklyn. Surg. Soc., Soc. for Non-Invasive Vascular Technicians, Kings Physicians I.P.A. (pres./med. dir., 1985-95), Bklyn. Physicians I.P.A. (v.p., 1985-96, pres.). Avocations: photography, walking, computers. Home Phone: 718-816-8866. E-mail: hassan@mohaideen.com.

MOHAMADI, MASOUD, retired surgeon; b. Tehran, Iran, June 8, 1937; arrived in U.S., 1962; children: Hooman, Michele, Robert; m. Soheila Emami, 1990. MD, U. Tehran, 1961. Diplomate Am. Bd. Surgery. Intern Coney Island Hosp., NYC, 1962-63; resident in gen. surgery Maimonides Med. Ctr., Bklyn., 1963-67; fellow in vasc. surgery SUNY, Bklyn., 1967-68. Mem. AMA. Personal E-mail: mmohamadi@tampabay.rr.com. *

MOHAMMAD, ESHRAT HALIM, medical researcher; arrived in Canada, 2010, permanent resident, 2010; PhD in Medical Chemistry, U. Pune, Marathwada, India, 2003. Postdoc. rsch. assoc. Ottawa Hosp. Rsch. Assoc. and Zemin Yao; postdoc. dept. endocrinology All India Inst. Medical Scis., New Delhi, 2004—08, postdoc. dept. dermatology, virology, 2010—. Reviewer Jour. Medicine and Medical Scis., 2008—, Internat. Jour. Dermatology, 2009—. Contbr. diabetes complication (Post doct, but it is terminated by team of iranian poeple, 2004), chapters to books; author: Preservation or Reversal of Diabetic Nephropathy, 2011. Vol. work in villages India on nutritional treatment, care of patients. Recipient Am. Order Merit award, 2011; named to Women of Yr. award, 2011; fellow, U. Grants Commn., India, 2003—04. Mem.: Soc. Medicinal Plant & Natural Produst Rsch. Germany, Indian Gen. Clin. Biochemistry Assn., Canadian Diabetes Assn. Ottawa, Canadian Diabetes Assn. Toronto, Indian Science Congress, Diabetes Complication Club (assoc.). Muslim. Achievements include discovery of reversal of diabetic retinopathy in India; retinal changes by new treatment with herbal plants to remove hemorrages and exudates related to diabetic retinopathy. Avocations: swimming, poetry, gardening, music, dance, singing. Home: 154 Osgoode St Apt 6 Ottawa ON K1N 6S6 Canada Office: All India Inst Medical Scis Dept Derrmatology Ansure Nager New Delhi India Home Phone: 011-9999202695; Office Phone: 613-218-8416. Personal E-mail: halim222003@yahoo.co.in.

MOHAMMADI, NOOREDIN, nursing educator; b. Tehran, Aug. 21, 1963; PhD in Nursing, 2008. Asst. prof. Tehran U. Med. Scis., 1998—. Cons., rschr. Ctr. Nursing Rsch., 2008—. Mem.: ICN, Iranian Cardiac Nurses Assn. Avocations: travel, sports, music. Home: 1/643 Greenhill Rd Burnside Adelaide South Australia 5066 Australia Personal E-mail: mohammadi_no@tums.ac.ir.

MOHAMMED, HALIM ESHRAT, medical researcher; b. Firoza, Iran, Nov. 11, 1964; arrived in India, 1984; d. Mohammed Ali and Parveen Halim. MBBS, Tehran, Iran, 1984; BSc in Biochemistry, Dr. B.A. Marathwada U., Aurangabad, India, 1986, MSc in Biochemistry, 1989, diploma in Med. Pathology, 1991; PhD in Medical Chemistry, U. Pune, India, 1999. Cert. Med. Coun. Iran. Cons. dietician Grant Med. Coll., Mumbai, 2003—04; rsch. assoc. Dr. Shashank R. Joshi Lilavati Hosp., Mumbai, 2004—05; cons. diabetologist Nizam Hosp., Hyderabad, India, 2005—06; rsch. assoc., lab. medicine AIMS, New Delhi, 2006—07, rsch. assoc., dept. dermatology, 2008—09, Hamdard U., New Delhi, 2007—08. Mem. Indian Sci. Congress, Kolkata, 2004—07. Contbr. articles to profl. jours. Fellowship, Dhaka Med. U., Bangladesh, 2002, U. Grant Commn., New Delhi, 2003. Mem.: Diabetes Assn. (Can.), India Jour. Clin. Biochemistry (New Delhi) (life). Achievements include discovery of structure of neem, abroma augusta and curcumine plants. Avocations: gardening, swimming, singing, writing. Home: C-17 Datt Colony Kerbala Safdarjung Airport New Delhi Delhi India Office: Dept Dermatology Rm 402 Ansari Nagar New Delhi Delhi 110018 India Personal E-mail: halim222003@yahoo.co.in.

MOHAN, ANANT, internist, pulmonologist, educator, researcher; b. Varanasi, India, Apr. 14, 1970; MBBS, Mahatma Gandhi Inst. Med. Scis., 1992, MD, 1998. Assoc. prof. pulmonary medicine & sleep disorders All India Inst. Med. Scis., New Delhi, 2003—, cons. Tertiary Level Hosp., 2003—11. UK Commonwealth fellowships, UK Scholarship Divsn. Mem.: Nat. Coll. Chest Physicians (India), Assn. Physicians India, Nat. Acad. Med. Scis., European Respiratory Soc. Avocations: reading, sports. Office: 3rd Fl All India Inst Med Scis New Delhi 110029 India Office Phone: 91-11-26593006. Personal E-mail: anantmohan@yahoo.com.

MOHAN, CHANDRA, research biochemistry educator; b. Lucknow, India, Aug. 3, 1950; came to U.S., 1977; s. Prithivi Nath and Tara Rani (Sharma) Shastri; m. Nirmala Devi Sharma, July 23, 1978; children: Deepak, Naveen. BS, Bangalore U., India, 1970, MS, 1972, PhD, 1976. Research assoc. U. So. Calif. Med. Sch., L.A., 1977-83, asst. prof., 1983-93; sr. dir. tech. svc., sr. tech. writer EMD Bioscis., San Diego, 1993—. Assoc. editor Biochem. Medicine, 1986-93; contbr. articles to profl. jours. Recipient BRSG award U. So. Calif., 1983. Mem. AAAS, Am. Diabetes Assn., Am. Soc. for Biochemistry and Molecular Biology, N.Y. Acad. Scis., Am. Inst. Nutrition. Hindu. Avocations: photography, coin collecting/numismatics. Office: EMD Bioscis Inc 10394 Pacific Center Ct San Diego CA 92121-4340 Office Phone: 858-450-5554. Personal E-mail: csharma4@aol.com. Business E-Mail: chandra.mohan@merckgroup.com.

MOHAN, PARVATHI, physician; b. Washington, Sept. 2, 1948; MBBS, Calicut Med. Sch., India, 1972, MD, North Shore U. Hosp., NY, 1985. Attending physician, pediat. gastroenterology Children's Nat. Med. Ctr., 1988—, dir., hepatology, 2000—, assoc., intestinal rehab. and liver transplant svcs., 2007—. Assoc. prof., pediat. Kottayam Med. Sch., India, 1980—83, George Wash. U. Sch. Medicine, 2003—, asst. prof., pediat., 1988—2003. Recipient Silver medal, Pres. India, Ann. Simon Komarov Rsch. award, Phila. Gastrointestinal Rsch. Forum, 1988, New Investigator award, Advances Pediat. Sci. Forum, CNMC, 1989; named one of Top Drs. Gastroenterology, Washingtonian Mag., 1999, 2001, 2005, 2008, 2010. Mem.: Hepatitis Found. Internat. (bd. dirs. 2004—09), Am. Assn. Physicians Indian Origin, Assn. Kerala Med. Grads. (pres. 2004—05), North Am. Soc. Pediat. Gastroenterology, Hepatology and Nutrition, Am. Assn. Study Liver Diseases. Avocations: music, painting, travel. Office: Childrens Nat Med Ctr 11 Washington DC 20010 Office Fax: 202-476-4156. Business E-Mail: pmohan@cnmc.org.

MOHAN, PAVITRA, physician; b. Jaipur, Rajasthan, India, Oct. 23, 1967; s. Bharat Bhooshan and Satya Prabha; m. Sanjana Brahmawar, Nov. 29, 1993; 1 child, Madhav. MBBS, Delhi U., India, 1990, MD, 1994; MPH, Sch. Pub. Health, U. NC, Chapel Hill, 1999. Registered physician Med. Coun. India, 1990. Asst. prof. RNT Med. Coll., Udaipur, Rajasthan, 1996—2001; bd. mem. Action Rsch. & Tng. Health, Udaipur, 2000—08, coord. child health, 2001—03; health specialist UNICEF, New Delhi, 2003—. Contbr. articles to profl. publ. on pub. health. Office: United Nations Children's Fund 73 Lodi Estate New Delhi 110003 India Home: A 596 Sarita Vihar New Delhi 110076 India Office: United Nations Children's Fund 73 110 003 New Delhi India Home: L 141 Sarita Vihar New Delhi 110076 India Personal E-mail: mohan.pavitra@rediffmail.com. Business E-Mail: pmohan@unicef.org.

MOHANARUBAN, KANTHAYA, physician; b. Colombo, Sri Lanka, June 27, 1951; arrived in U.K., 1978; d. Appakudtti and Navamalar Kanthaya; m. Savithri Kumarakulasingam, May 15, 1981; 2 children. MB, BChir, Colom Med. Coll., Colomb, 1975. Registrar U. Wales Hosp., Cardiff, 1982—84, sr. registrar, 1984—89; cons. physician Pembrokeshire NHS Trust, Haverfordwest, 1989—. Contbr. articles to profl. jours. Fellow: Royal Coll. Physicians London (licentiate); mem.: Welsh Physians, Brit. Geriatric Soc., Brit. Med. Assn., Royal Coll. Surgeons London. Hindu. Avocations: travel, photography. Home Phone: 0044-1437-760967; Office Phone: 0044-1437-773328.

MOHAN RAO, MANCHALA, surgeon, educator; arrived in Australia, 1976; s. Manchala Ratnam and Manchala Soubhagyam; m. Dora Hemalatha, June 7, 1962; children: Albert Rajeev, Shirley, Sheena. BSc, Andhra U., 1955; MB, BChir, U. Madras, India, 1959; MS in Gen. Surgery, U. Madras, 1965, MChir in Urology, 1967. Ho. surgeon Christian Med. Coll., Vellore, India, 1960—62, sr. ho. surgeon, 1962—63, registrar in gen. surgery, 1963—65, jr. lectr. in gen. surgery, 1965—67, lectr. urology, 1967—69, reader in urology, 1969—72, assoc. prof. urology, 1972—74, prof. urology, 1974—78, head dept. urology, 1975—78, gen. hosp. supt., 1975—77; sr. surg. registrar transplant unit Queen Elizabeth Hosp., Woodville, Australia, 1968—71, transplant surgeon renal unit, 1976—85; tutor in surgery U. Adelaide, Australia, 1970—71, sr. staff cons. transplant surgeon, 1985—, assoc. prof. surgery, 2005—. Sr. clin. lectr. surgery U. Adelaide, 1985—2004; cons. surgeon Alice Springs (Australia) Hosp., 1994—2006, Royal Darwin (Australia) Hosp., 1994—2006; vis. cons. surgeon Royal Adelaide Hosp., Flinders Med. Ctr., Women and Children's Hosp. Fellow: ACS, Royal Australasian Coll. Surgeons. Achievements include first to perform successful renal transplant in India and establishment of transplant units in India; introduction of laparoscopic live donor nephrectomy to Australia. Office: Dept Surgey Queen Elizabeth Hosp Woodville SA 5011 Australia Office Phone: 618822265. Business E-Mail: mohan.rao@health.sa.gov.au, mohanrao@health.sa.gov.al.

MOHANTY, KAILASH CHANDRA, physician; b. Gandibed, India, Apr. 4, 1948; s. Arjun Charan and Kamala (Raul) Mohanty; m. Suravi Naik, July 11, 1974; children: Anurag, Lucyann. MBBS, SCB Med. Coll., 1972; MD, Delhi U., 1977. Med. registrar Nat. Health Svc., England, 1978, sr. registrar, 1979, cons. physician, 1982—. Mem. indsl. tribunal Dept. Employment, Leeds, 1991-2003; employment appeal tribunal London High Ct., 2003; mem. ct. U. Bradford; former chmn. KCM Textiles. Author: Sexual Behavior and Sexual Dysfunction in Men, 1997, 2d edit., 2001; editor: Jour. OSUK, 2001—04; mem. editl. bd.: Jour. of Sexual Health, 1990—; contbr. articles to profl. jours. Justice of the Peace Bradford City Cts., 1987. Recipient Merit award C Nat. Health Svc., 1995. Fellow: RCP (London) (mem. examiner); mem.: Brit. Med. Assn. (Bradford divsn. sec. 1990, pres. Yorkshire Regional Coun. 1995—97, hon. sec., fellowship 2008). Achievements include invention of inosine pranobex in warts; discovery of physiological phenomenon dyslymphocytosis in patients with warts. Avocations: jogging, exercise. Office: Darlington Meml Hosp Hollyhurst Rd Darlington DL3 6HX England Home: 136 Bradford Road LS29 6ED Ilkley England Office Phone: 01325-743203. Personal E-mail: kmohanty@hotmail.co.uk. Business E-Mail: kailash.mohanty@cddft.nhs.uk.

MOHANTY, RAMESH CHANDRA, pathologist; b. Cuttack, Feb. 20, 1956; MBBS, VSS Med. Coll., 1978, MD in Pathology, 1992. Asst. surgeon Govt Of Orissa, 1983—92; asst. prof., pathology Dmet, Govt.of Orissa, 1992—2008; sr. cons. pathologist Adk Hosp., 2008—. Faculty pathology Govt. Orissa, 1983—92. Mem.: IAPM Orissa Chpt (Dr. B. K. Rath award). Avocations: reading, travel. Home: Justice Chhak Mahanadivihar Cuttack Orissa 753004 India Personal E-mail: drrcmohanty56@gmail.com.

MOHANTY, SANJIB, medical association administrator; b. Puri, Orissa, India, Aug. 23, 1954; MD in Internal Medicine, SCB Med. Coll., Cuttack, 1978. Cons., medicine & critical care Ispat Gen. Hosp., Rourkela, India, 1983, joint dir., head, medicine & critical care, 1983—. Contbr. articles to profl. jours. Recipient Jawahar award, Steel Authority of India. Mem.: Assn. Physicians India. Avocations: reading, travel, movies. Office: F-140 Sector 19 Rourkela Orissa 769005 India Personal E-mail: sanjibmalaria@rediffmail.com.

MOHAPATRA, SARITA, nuclear medicine physician; b. Paralakhemundi, Orissa, India, July 20, 1976; MBBS, VSS Med. Coll., Orissa, 2001; MD, MKCG Med. Coll., Orissa, 2008. Sr. resident All India Inst. Med. Scis., New Delhi, 2008—11, pool officer, microbiology, 2011—. Mem.: India Soc. Med. Microbiologists. Avocation: reading. Home: F 21 Ansari Nagar West New Delhi 110029 India Personal E-mail: saritarath2005@yahoo.co.in.

MOHAPATRA, SURYA N., laboratory executive; PhD in Med. Physics, U. London; MSEE, Sambalpur Univ., India. Sr. v.p. Picker Internat., 1981—99; sr. v.p., COO Quest Diagnostics, Inc. (formerly Corning Life Sciences, Inc.), Teterboro, NJ, 1999, pres., COO, 1999—2004, chmn., pres., CEO, 2004—. Bd. dirs. Vasogen Inc., 1999—. Contbr. articles to profl. jours. Mem.: Royal Coll. Surgeons Eng. (hon.). Achievements include patents in field. Office: Quest Diagnostics One Malcolm Ave Teterboro NJ 07608 *

MOHAPATRA, TRIBHUBAN MOHAN, medical educator, director; b. Orissa, Nov. 21, 1947; MBBS, MKCG Med. Coll., 1971; MD, Inst. Med. Scis.-Banaras Hindu U., 1976. Med. tchr., patient care, rsch. & adminstrn. Inst. Med. Scis., Banaras Hindu U., 1973—, dir., 2009—. Contbr. articles to profl. publs. Recipient Commonwealth Med. awards, UK, Excellence award, NACO & Nat. Instn. Biol., Glory of India Gold medal, Internat. Inst. Success Awareness, Vijay Rattan award, India Internat. Friendship Soc., Prof. Bikram Dash Oration & Gold medal, Indian Assn. Med. Microbiologist (Orissa br.). Fellow: Royal Soc. Tropical Medicine & Hygiene; mem.: Citizen Amb. Programme (Wash.), Nat. Bd. Directory Malaria Rsch. New Delhi, NY Acad. Scis., Nat. Acad. Med. Scis. Avocations: music, acting. Office: Inst Med Scis Varanasi Uttar Pradesh 221005 India Office Fax: 91-542-2367568. E-mail: tmmohapatra2000@yahoo.com.

MOHD-ALI, BARIAH, medical educator; b. Perak, Malaysia, June 1, 1967; B in Optometry with honors, U. Kebangsaan Malaysia, 1992; PhD, U. NSW, 2001. Assoc. prof. U. Kebangsaan Malaysia, 2009—. Curriculum design cons. Internat. Islamic U., Malaysia, 2003, U. Teknologi Mara, 2004; cons. Malaysia Optical Coun., Ministry of Health, Malaysia, 2007—09; auditor instl. audit Malaysia Qualification Agy., 2008. Rsch. award, Australia Contact Lens Soc., Rsch. Travel grant, Asia Pacific Optometry Coun., Rsch. grant, Menicon, Japan, Ministry Sci., Tech. and Innovation, Malaysia. Fellow: Assn. Malaysian Optometrist; mem.: UKM Alumni, Internat. Assn. Contact Lens Educators. Avocations: reading, cooking. Office: Dept Optometry UKM Jalan Raja Muda Kuala Lumpur 50300 Malaysia Office Fax: 603-26910488. Business E-Mail: bariah@medic.ukm.my.

MOHGAZY, AMR, plastic surgeon, educator; b. Alexandria, Egypt, May 4, 1964; BS in Medicine & Gen. Surgery, Alexandria U., 1987; PhD in Surgery, Suez Canal U., Ismailia, Egypt, 2004. Cons. plastic surgery and emergency medicine Faculty Medicine, Suez Canal U., 2004—, lectr. plastic surgery, 2005—10, assoc. prof. plastic surgery, 2010—. Founding mgr. Cmty. Svc. Ctr. Burns and Disasters, 2007—. Grant, Higher Edn. Enhancing Project FundS, Ministry Higher Edn., Egypt. Mem.: Egyptian Med. Syndicate. Achievements include goodwill ambassador for networking and development. Office: Ismailia Ring Rd Ismailia 42121 Egypt

MOHIUDDIN, SYED MAQDOOM, cardiologist, educator; b. Hyderabad, India, Nov. 14, 1934; came to US, 1961, naturalized, 1976; s. syed Nizamuddin Mohiuddin and Amat-Ul-Butool Mahmoodi; m. Ayesha Sultana Mahmoodi, July 16, 1961; children: Sameena J., Syed R., Kulsoom S. MB, BS, Osmania U., 1960; MS, Creighton U., Omaha, 1967; DSc, Laval U., Que., Can., 1970. Diplomate in internal medicine and cardiovasc. disease Am. Bd. Internal Medicine. Intern Altoona Gen. Hosp., Pa., 1961-62; resident in cardiology Creighton Meml. Hosp., also St. Joseph Hosp., Omaha, 1963-65, mem. staff, 1965—; prof. adjoint Laval U. Med. Sch., 1970; practice medicine specializing in cardiology Omaha, 1970—; prof. Creighton U. Med. Sch., 1977—, assoc. dir. div. cardiology, 1983-96; prof. pharmacy practice Creighton U. Sch. Pharmacy, 1986—, dir. divsn. cardiology, 1996—2007, assoc. chair for acad. affairs dept. medicine, 1998—2007, Richard W. Booth MD prof. cardiology, 2005—, chair dept. medicine, 2007—. Cons. Omaha VA Hosp. Rsch. fellow Med. Rsch. Coun. Can., 1968; grantee Med. Rsch. Coun. Can., 1970, NIH, 1973, 2000-03. Fellow ACP, Am. Coll. Cardiology (gov. for Nebr. 1987-90), Am. Coll. Clin. Pharmacology, Am. Coll. Chest Physicians; mem. AAAS, Am. Heart Assn. (fellow coun. clin. cardiology, bd. dirs. 1973-75), Am. Fedn. Clin. Rsch., Nebr. Heart Assn. (chmn. rsch. com. 1974-76, dir. 1973—), Gt. Plains Heart Com. (Nebr. rep. 1976-84, pres. 1977-78), N.Y. Acad. Scis., Nebr. Cardiovasc. Soc. (pres. 1980-81), Creighton Med. Assn. (v.p. 2005-07), Am. Inst. Islamic Study & Culture(pres. 2007-), Tri-Faith Initiative Omaha (bd. mem. 2007-). Democrat. Muslim. Home: 12531 Shamrock Rd Omaha NE

68154-3529 Office: Cardiac Ctr Creighton U 3006 Webster St Omaha NE 68131-2027 Office Phone: 402-280-4570. Personal E-mail: smm12521@yahoo.com. Business E-Mail: smm@cardiac.creighton.edu.

MOHL, NORMAN DAVID, dental educator; b. Paterson, NJ, May 15, 1931; s. Irving and Fannie (Weiss) M.; m. Eldene Jaffe, Dec. 27, 1953; children: Ilana, Lawrence, Daniel, Steven. DDS, U. Buffalo, 1956; MA, SUNY, Buffalo, 1968, PhD in Anatomy, 1971. Dentist, pvt. practice, Buffalo, 1958-67; from prof. to disting. svc. prof. SUNY, 1971—2005, emeritus, 2005—, assoc. dean acad. affairs, 1972-87, dir. oral sci. grad. program, 1977-94. Coun. mem. on dental materials, instruments and equipment ADA, Chgo., 1987-92; cons. NIH, Washington, 1988-92, FDA, Washington, 1989-97; chmn. dept. oral diagnostic scis., SUNY, Buffalo, 1994-2004. Author, editor: A Textbook of Occlusion, 1988, TMJ and Masticatory Muscle Disorders, 1995; contbr. articles to profl. jours. Lt. USNR, 1956-58. Serv. USN, 1956—58. Named Disting. Svc. Prof., SUNY, 1971—2005. Mem. Internat. Assn. for Dental Rsch., Neuroscis. TMJ-Orofacial Pain Programs (pres. 1991-92), Am. Coun. on Edn. (fellow Acad. Adminstrn., spl. asst. v.p. for health scis. 1975-76). Avocations: bicycling, reading, hiking. Home: 7631 Uliva Way Sarasota FL 34238-4797 Home Phone: 941-929-9507. Personal E-mail: ndmohl@comcast.net.

MOHR, JAY PRESTON, neurologist, educator; b. Mar. 5, 1937; s. John G. and Marguerite F. Mohr; m. Joan L. Seal, Mar. 10, 1962; children: Thea, Gregory. AB, Haverford Coll., 1958; MS, MD, U. Va., 1963. Diplomate Am. Bd. Neurology and Psychiatry. Intern then asst. resident Mary Imogene Bassett Hosp., Cooperstown, NY, 1963-65; asst. resident N.Y. Neurol. Inst., Columbia-Presbyn. Med. Ctr., NYC, 1965-66; instr. neurology Johns Hopkins U. Med. Sch., U. Md. Med. Sch., 1969-71; assoc. neurologist Mass. Gen. Hosp., Boston, 1972-78; asst. prof. Harvard U. Med. Sch., 1972-78; prof. neurologi, chmn. dept. U. South Ala. Med. Sch., Mobile, 1978-83; Sciarra prof. clin. neurology Columbia U. Coll. Physicians & Surgeons, NYC, 1983—. Dir. cerebrovascular research N.Y. Neurol. Inst., N.Y.C., 1983—; dir. Doris and Stanley Tananbaum Stroke Ctr., 2003—. Contbr. articles to med. jours. Mag. M.C., U.S. Army, 1969-72. Recipient Johan Josef Wepfer award European Stroke Soc., 2009; Neurology fellow Mass. Gen. Hosp., 1966-69. Fellow Am. Acad. Neurology; mem. Am. Neurol. Assn., Am. Heart Assn. (Stroke coun., named Disting. Scientist 2006), Sigma Xi. Democrat. Mem. Soc. Of Friends. Office: Doris & Stanley Tananbaum Stroke Ctr NY Neurol Inst 710 W 168th St New York NY 10032-2603 also: Presbyn Hosp Columbia-Presbyn Med Ctr New York NY 10032-3784 Office Phone: 212-305-8033. Business E-Mail: jpm10@columbia.edu.

MOHR, LAWRENCE CHARLES, physician; b. S.I., NY, July 8, 1947; s. Lawrence Charles Sr. and Mary Estelle (Dawsey) M.; m. Linda Johnson, June 14, 1970; 1 child, Andrea Marie. AB with highest honors, U. N.C., 1975, MD, 1979. Diplomate Am. Bd. Internal Medicine. Commd. 2d lt. U.S. Army, 1967, advanced through grades to col., 1989; med. intern Walter Reed Army Med. Ctr., Washington, 1979-80, resident in medicine, 1980-82, chief resident, 1982-83, attending physician, 1984-86, pulmonary fellow, 1986-87; command surgeon 9th Inf. Div., Ft. Lewis, Wash., 1983-84; med. cons. Madigan Army Med. Ctr., Tacoma, 1983-84; White House physician Washington, 1987-93; asst. prof. medicine Uniformed Svcs. U. of the Health Scis., Bethesda, Md., 1984-91; assoc. prof. medicine Uniformed Svcs. U. Health Scis., Bethesda, Md., 1991-94; assoc. clin. prof. medicine George Washington U., Washington, 1990-94; prof. medicine Med. U. S.C., Charleston, 1994—, dir. environ. bioscis. program, 1995—. Attending physician Med. U. Hosp., Charleston, 1994—, Charleston Meml. Hosp., 1994—; mem. Working Group on Disability in U.S. Presidents, 1995—. Editor: International Case Studies in Risk Assessment and Magagement, 1997, Biomarkers, Medical and Workplace Applications, 1998; contbr. articles to profl. jours. and books. Bd. dirs. Internat. Lung Found., Washington; mem. adv. bd. Nat. Mus. Health and Medicine, Washington; mem. sci. adv. bd. Consortium in Environ. Risk Evaluation; prin. investigator Consortium in Molecular Epidemiology and Biomarker Rsch. Decorated Silver Star, Bronze Star with 2 V devices and 3 oak leaf clusters, Purple Heart, Meritorious Svc. medal with oak leaf cluster, Air medal, Army Commendation medal with oak leaf cluster, D.S.M.; recipient Erskine award Walter Reed Army Med. Ctr., 1982; named Outstanding Med. Resident, 1982. Fellow ACP, Am. Coll. Chest Physicians; mem. AMA, Army and Navy Club, Order Mil. Med. Merit, Harbour Club, Phi Beta Kappa. Episcopalian. Avocations: mountain climbing, skiing. Home: 673 Lake Francis Dr Charleston SC 29412-4345 Office: Med U S C Environ Bioscis Program 171 Ashley Ave Charleston SC 29425-0001

MOHSIN, MOHAMMED, medical educator; b. Hyderabad, Andhra Pradesh, India, Jan. 8, 1955; MBBS, Gandhi Med. Coll., MD, 1980, Nizam's Inst. Med. Scis., 2000. With Darrus Salam Ednl. Trust, 1994—98, Al Ameen Ednl. Trust, Bijapur, 2006—08, Al Fateh Med. U., Tripoli, Libya, 2008—09, Chalmeda Anandrao Inst. Med. Scis., Arihant Ednl. Soc., 2005—06, prof., head pharmacology dept., 2010—. Mem.: Indian Med. Assn. Home: New Malakpet Hyderabad Andhra Pradesh 500036 India Personal E-mail: mohammeddrmohsin@rediffmail.com.

MOHTA, MEDHA, anesthesiologist, consultant; b. Delhi, India, June 10, 1966; d. Chandra Prakash and Bimla Sharma; m. Anup Mohta, June 1, 1990; children: Nishita, Kavya. MBBS, Lady Hardinge Med. Coll., New Delhi, 1988; MD in Anesthesiology, Lady Hardinge Med. Coll., 1992. Sr. resident Lady Hardinge Med. Coll. and SK Hosp., Delhi, India, 1992—95; sr. rsch. assoc. Safdarjang Hosp., Delhi, 1995—97; asst. prof. All India Inst. of Med. Sciences, 1997; lectr. U. Coll. of Med. Sciences and GTB Hosp., Delhi, 1997—98, sr. lectr., 1998—2001, reader, 2001—. Cons. anesthesiologist Guru Teg Bahadur Hosp., Delhi, 1997—. Contbr. chapters to books, articles to profl.jours. Recipient Commonwealth award, 2007; grant, U. Grants Commn., 2004, Indian Nat. Sci. Acad., Dept. of Sci. and Tech., India, Nat. Talent Search scholarship, Nat. Coun. of Ednl. Rsch. and Tng., India, 1983. Mem.: Indian Med. Assn., Nat. Acad. Med. Scis., Indian Soc. of Anaesthesiologists, Resorts Consortium Internat. Hindu. Achievements include invited as an expert in 'Trauma' in World Congress of Anaesthesiologists 2004 at Paris; showed that mephentermine(used in some Asian countries) is as good as ephedrine(used all over the developed world) for management of hypotension during spinal anaesthesia for caesarean section. Avocations: travel, music, poetry, swimming, exercise. Home: 28-B Pkt-C SFS Flats Mayur Vihar III Delhi 110096 India Office: Univ Coll of Med Sci Dilshad Garden Shahdara Delhi 110095 India Personal E-mail: medhamohta@hotmail.com.

MOIRANGTHEM, GULAMJAT SINGH, gastroenterologist, surgeon; b. Ningthoukhong, Manipur, India, Mar. 1, 1954; s. Mohon Singh and Ibeton Devi Moirangthem; m. Hema Devi Moirangthem, Jan. 15, 1976; 1 child, Pooja. Student, D.M.Coll., Imphal, India, 1969—70, Salipur Coll., Cuttuck, India, 1970—71; B Medicine B Surgery, Gauhati U., 1978; M Surgery, Postgrad. Med. Inst., Chandigarh, India, 1985. Registrar in surgery Regional Med. Coll., Imphal, Manipur, India, 1980—83, 1985—93, asst. prof. surgery, 1993—96; jr. resident Post Grad. Med. Inst., Chandigarh, India, 1983—85; WHO fellow in laproscopic surgery Western Gen. Hosp., Edinburgh, Scotland; asst. prof. gastrointestinal surgery Regional Inst. Med. Scis., Imphal, assoc. prof. surgery, assoc. prof., head, 2001—. Cons. surgeon Regional Inst. Med. Scis., 1996—; examiner Calcutta (India) U., 2002—, Manipur U., Imphal, 2001—. Contbr. articles to profl. jours. Recipient Best Paper award All Manipur Med. Conf., Manipur chpt. Indian Med. Assn., 1990; trainee fellow, Soc. Gastrointestinal Endoscopy India, 1987. Fellow: Royal Coll. Surgeons Edinburgh, Assn. Indian Surgeons, Internat. Coll. Surgeons; mem.: Assn. Surgeons of India (state sec. Manipur chpt. 1995—2001), Manipur Ostomy Assn. (life; chmn. 2000), Internat. Assn. Hepatobiliary Surgeons (life), Indian Med. Assn. (life), Indian Assn. Surg. Gastroentrology (life), Soc. Gastrointestinal Endoscopy India (life). Shri Sathya Sai. Achievements include research in Ggstrointestinal related diseases. Avocations: travel, gardening. Office: Regional Inst Medicine Surg Gastroenterology Sect Manipur Imphal 795004 India Home: Chingmeirong West 795 001 Imphal 795001 India Office Fax: 0385-2310625; Home Fax: 0385-2310625. Personal E-mail: drmoirangthem@yahoo.co.in.

MOISEEVA, ELISABETHA BORISOVNA, biologist, researcher; d. Boris Markovich Moiseev and Sima Israilevna Nodelman; life ptnr. Levon Michaylovich Chailakhyan; 1 child, Konstantin Moiseev. MSc, Kharkov State U., 1962; PhD, Leningrad State U., 1973. Acad. worker Azov-Black Sea Sci. Rsch. Inst. of Marine Fisheries and Oceanography, Kerch, Ukraine, 1963—66, sr. acad. worker, 1967—92; leading acad. worker So. Sci. Rsch. Inst. of Marine Fisheries and Oceanography, Kerch, 1993—96; rsch. scientist Israel Oceanog. and Limnol. Rsch., Lab. Genetic Engring., Haifa, 1997—2000, Israel Oceanog. and Limnol. Rsch., Minerva Ctr. for Marine Invertebrate Immunology and Devel. Biology, Haifa, 2000 , Aquaculture Rsch. Sta., Dor, Israel, 1998—2000. Sci. reviewer All-Union Inst. Sci. and Tech. Info., Moscow, 1973—96; hon. vis. lectr. biology high schs., Kerch, 1994—96. Contbr. articles to profl. jours. Grantee, Ministry of Environment, 2000—02. Mem.: Internat. Group Specialists for Conservation of Nature and Natural Resources, European Ichthyol. Union, USSR Hydrobiol. Soc. Avocations: archaeology, reading, travel. Office: Israel Oceanog and Limnol Rsch Tel Shikmona Haifa 31080 Israel Office Fax: 04-8511911. Personal E-mail: liliamois@yahoo.com. Business E-Mail: mois@ocean.org.il.

MOISES, HANS WERNER, psychiatrist, molecular geneticist; b. Celle, Germany, July 3, 1948; s. Hans Ludwig and Sophia Aloisia (Schorler) M.; m. Qiong Wang, June 8, 1999; children: Miriam, Maurice. Student, U. Louvain, Belgium, 1973; MD, U. Heidelberg, 1980. Diplomate in medicine; lic. psychiatrist. Rsch. asst. in psychiatry Ctrl. Inst. Mental Health, Mannheim, Germany, 1978-86; fellow in genetics/molecular genetics with Prof. Luca L Cavalli-Storza Stanford U. Sch. Medicine, 1987-89, attending dept. psychiatry Univ. Hosp., Kiel, Germany, 1989—2003; lectr. U. Kiel, 1994—2001, dir. Molecular Genetics Lab. dept. psychiatry, 1989—2003, prof. psychiatry, 2002—. Contbr. articles to profl. jours., books, and Encyclopedia of the Human Genome. Schizophrenia Theory Rsch. Career Devel. awardee, 1980. Mem. German Soc. Biol. Psychiatry, Soc. Biol. Psychiatry. E-mail: moises@psychiatry.uni-kiel.de.

MOIZESZOWICZ, JULIO, psychiatrist; b. Buenos Aires, May 25, 1943; s. Pascual Moizeszowicz and Elisa Raijelson; m. Noemi Gueler, Jan. 4, 1982; children: Karin, Eric, Alejandro, Laura. MD, Sch. Medicine Buenos Aires, 1966, psychiatrist, 1978, assoc. prof., 1994; psychoanalyst, Psychoanalytical Assn., Buenos Aires, 1983; prof. (hon.), Sch. Medicine Cordoba, 1983. Lic. psychiatrist. Resident in internal medicine Sch. Medicine, 1965—68; fellow in pharmacology Hoechst Pharms., Frankfurt, Germany, 1970—73; mem. psychiat. faculty Sch. Medicine, Borda Hosp., Buenos Aires, 1973—78, Sch. Medicine, Ezrah Hosp., Buenos Aires, 1978—89, assoc. prof., 1983—94, cons. psychopharmacology, 1978—89; faculty dir. Fundacion Docencia Investigacion Psicofarmocologica, Buenos Aires, 1990—2010. Cons. Hoechst Pharms., Buenos Aires, 1970—78. Author: (book) Psicofarmacologia Psicodinanica IV, 1998, Psicofarmacologia y Territorio Freudiano, 2000, Psicofarmacologia Geriatrica, 2001; contbr. articles to profl. jours. Mem.: Assn. de Psiquiatras Argentinos (cons.), Am. Psychiat. Assn. Achievements include research in relation between psychopharmacology and psychotherapies and neuroscience. Avocation: tennis. Office: Coronel Diaz 2277 App 24B 1425 Buenos Aires Argentina Business E-Mail: jmoizeszowicz@fibertel.com.ar.

MOJARRA-ESTRADA, JOSE M., obstetrician, gynecologist, endocrinologist; MD, Universidad Anahuac, Mexico City, 1989. Ast. dir. reproduction unit Hosp. CIMA Hermosillo, Sonora, Mexico, 1999—, chief obstetrics and gynecology, 2002—05; edn. chief Hosp. Infantil Estado, 1999—2001, chief infertility dept. Pres. Federacion Mexicana Endoscopia, Hermosillo, 2002—04. Contbr. articles to profl. jours. Fellow: Asrm; mem.: Acog, Aagl. Office: Hospital CIMA Hermosillo Paseo Rio San Miguel 35-230 Hermosillo 83280 Mexico

MOJUMDER, DEB KUMAR, physician; b. Kolkata, Jan. 30, 1969; MS in Health Rsch., Tex. State U.; MD, Inst. Post Grad. Med. Edn. and Rsch., 1997; PhD, U. Houston, 2006. Ophthalmologist Union Pub. Svc. Commn. India, 1997—2000; rsch. asst. microbiology Tex. Sate U., 2000—01; predoctoral rsch. asst. retinal electrophysiology U. Houston, 2002—06; postdoctoral fellow, dept. ophthalmology Baylor Coll. Medicine, 2007—11; physician Nassau U. Med. Ctr., 2011—. Jour. reviewer Vision Rsch., 2008—; inventor Zapper Baylor Coll. Medicine, 2008—; mem. bd. grant reviewers Inst. Space Sys. Ops., NASA-Johnson Space Ctr., Houston, 2011. Fellowship, Baylor Coll. Medicine, Sid Richardson Found., Dept. Ophthalmology, Baylor Coll. Medicine, 2010. Mem.: Soc. Neurosci., Internat. Soc. Clin. Electrophysiology Vision, Assn. Rsch. Vision and Ophthalmology. Achievements include discovery of 2 novel animal models of human disease-maturity onset obese mice mutant and mouse model of congenital stationary night blindness. Avocations: writing, art, photography. Home: 2750 Holly Hall Houston TX 77054 Personal E-mail: dkmj7@yahoo.com.

MOK, CHING-MAN CYCBIE, occupational therapist; d. Chung-man Mok and Yuk-king Lee; m. Wing-cheong Fung, Apr. 5, 2004; 1 child, Chi-fan Fung. Diploma in Occupl. Therapy, Hong Kong Poly. U., 1987, MSc in Health Care, 2002. Occupl. therapist II Hosp. Authority, Hong Kong, 1988—93, occupl. therapist I, 1994—2008, sr. occupl. therapist, 2008—. Hon. mem. Hong Kong Alzheimer's Disease Assn., 1998—. Recipient Pfizers Rsch. award, Hong Kong Psycho Geriatric Assn., 2002. Achievements include research in validation of functional assessment for people with dementia, efficacy of computerized cognitive training. Personal E-mail: cycbie@hgcbroadband.com. Business E-Mail: mokcm@ha.org.hk.

MOK, NGAI-SHING, cardiologist; b. Hong Kong, July 6, 1962; s. Mau-Hong Mok and Lai-Chun Tai; m. Sin-Seung Chan, Dec. 18, 1994; children: Chun-Hin, Hiu-Ching, Chun-Ho. MBBS, U. Hong Kong, 1987. Cert. specialist in cardiology China, specialist in internal medicine China. Ho. officer Princess Margaret Hosp., Hong Kong, 1987—88, med. officer, 1989—93, sr. med. officer, 1993—. Vis. cardiology fellow Royal Prince Alfred Hosp., Sydney, 1995; mem. adv. com. ICD Hosp. Authority, Hong Kong, 2003; hon. treas. Hong Kong Inter-Hosp. Network Pacing and Cardiac Electrophysiology, 1998—, editor-in-chief, 1999—, v.p., 2004—06, pres., 2006—; dir. adult arrythymia svc. Princess Margaret Hosp., Hong Kong, 1996—; med. officer Queen Elizabeth Hosp., Hong Kong, 1988—89. Contbr. articles to profl. jours.; editor: Cardiology Jour., 1998—. Recipient Best Paper award, 11th Ann. Sci. Congress, Hong Kong Coll. Cardiology, 2003; named Badminton Competition champion, Hong Kong Med. Assn., 1991. Fellow: Hong Kong Acad. Medicine, Royal Coll. Physicians Edinburgh; mem.: Heart Rhythm Soc. Avocations: tennis, bridge, golf, Scrabble, astronomy. Office: Princess Margaret Hosp 2-10 Princess Margaret Hospital Rd Hong Kong China Home Phone: (852) 25579367; Office Phone: (852) 73829626. E-mail: isaacmok@netvigator.com.

MOKADDAS, EIMAN MOHAMED, medical educator, department chairman; b. Kuwait, Jan. 10, 1962; MBBCH, Kuwait U., 1986. Assoc. prof. Faculty Medicine, 2003—09, prof., clin. microbiology, 2009—. Chmn., microbiology dept., dir., labs. and Tb labs. Ibn Sina Hosp., 1993—. Fellow: Royal Coll. Pathologist; mem.: European Soc. Clin. Microbiology and Infectious Disease, Am. Soc. Microbiology. Avocations: reading, sports, travel. Office: PO Box 11238 Dasma 35153 Kuwait Office Fax: 00965-25332719. Business E-Mail: e.mokaddas@hsc.edu.kw.

MOKBEL, THARWAT HASSANEN, medical educator; b. Jan. 13, 1951; Degree in medicine, 1986. Prof. medicine Mansoura U., 2009—. Prof. & head, dept. ophthalmology, 2009. Mem.: ESG, EOS, ICO, SOE. Office: Mansoura Ophthalmic Ctr Mansoura Un Mansoura Dekahliy 35516 Egypt Office Fax: 0200502239414. Personal E-mail: tharwatmokbel@yahoo.com.

MOKHTAR, SABARUL AFIAN, orthopedist, researcher; b. Malaysia, Aug. 12, 1968; MD, U. Kebangsaan Malaysia, 1996. Registrar physician dept. orthopedics & traumatology, faculty medicine U. Kebangsaan Malaysia, 2001—03; orthopedics surgeon, lectr. Spine Surgery Unit, Dept. Orthopedics and Traumatology, Faculty Medicine, U. Kebangsaan Malaysia, 2003—05, spine surgeon, sr. lectr., head, 2006—09, assoc. prof., 2010—11; fellow spine surgery Tohoku U., Japan, 2004; spine surgeon, postdoc. rsch. fellow Australian Sch. Advanced Medicine, Sydney, 2008—. Sr. fellow Tun Dr. Ismail Coll., 1998—2002; med. team mem. Commonwealth Game, 1998, Japan GT Motor Race, 2004; cons. adv. bd. Ministry of Health, Malaysia, 2006—10; pub. forum spkr. PERKIM, 2006. Recipient Skipper award, Skipper Jacob Found., HDR Showcase award, Macquarie U., award, Invention and New Product Expn., World Intellectual Property Orgn., Young Spine Surgeon award, Japanese Spine Rsch. Soc. Fellow: Malaysia Spine Soc., Malaysian Orthopaedics Assn.; mem.: Asian Acad. of Minimally Invasive Spinal Surgery, AO Spine Internat., N.Am. Spine Soc. Avocations: football, basketball, tennis, cooking, travel. Office: Dept Orthopedics PPUKM Jalan Kuala Lumpur Wilayah Persekutuan 56000 Malaysia Personal E-mail: drsam2020@yahoo.com.

MOKOS, IVICA, urologist; b. Zagreb, Sept. 10, 1967; MD, U. Zagreb, 1998, PhD, 2006. Cert. urologist U. Hosp. Ctr. Zagreb, Dept. Urology, 2002. Urologist U. Hosp. Ctr. Zagreb, Dept. Urology, 2002—. Sci. assoc. U. Zagreb, Sch. Medicine, 2007—10, sr. sci. assoc., 2011. Recipient Best Poster Presentation award, EUA Meeting Birmingham, 2002. Mem.: Croatian Med. Chamber, Croatian Urol. Assn., European Urol. Assn. Avocations: basketball, tennis. Office: Kispaticeva 12 Zagreb 10000 Croatia Business E-Mail: ivica.mokos@zg.htnet.hr.

MOKRUSHIN, ANATOLY ALEXANDROVICH, neurophysiologist; b. Votkinsk, Udmurtia, Russia, Oct. 16, 1948; s. Alexandr Grigor'evich and Maria Pavlovna Mokrushin; m. Yafia Yosiff Hana; 1 child, Amalia. M in Mechanics, Tech. U., Votkinsk, 1968; MS, U. Leningrad, Russia, 1974; DSc, Pavlov Inst. Physiology, Leningrad, 1978, PhD, 1997. Lic. neurophysiologist. Technician-mechanic Machine Bldg. Plant, Votkinsk, 1968-69; jr. rsch. worker Pavlov Inst. Physiology, Russian Acad. Sci., Leningrad, 1977-90, sr. rsch. worker, 1990-97, leading rsch. worker, 1997—. Author: (book) Habituation in Visceral Systems, 1979, Surviving Slice of Brain as the Object for Neurophysiol. and Neurochem. Investigation, 1986; (contbr.) articles to profl. jours. With Russian Army, 1964—. Grantee, Soros Fund, 1993, ASGL Firm, 1998—99, Russian Pres., 2000—03. Achievements include patents in field; research on isolation and identification of endogenous peptides regulators (nootrops) for learning and memory; investigation molecular mechanisms of the hemorrhagic stroke. Avocations: gardening, woodcarving. Office: Pavlov Inst Physiology Nab Makarova 6 199034 Saint Petersburg Russia Home: App 9 Bykova Str 25a 188680 Saint Petersburg S Pavlovo Russia Office Phone: 813 70 72501. Office Fax: 328-05-01. Business E-Mail: mok@inbox.ru.

MOLD, JAMES WILLIAM, geriatrician, preventive medicine physician, educator; b. Detroit, Oct. 29, 1948; MD, Duke U., 1974; MPH in biostatistics, U. Okla. Coll. Medicine, 1999. Cert. Family Medicine, 1978, Geriatric Medicine, 1988. Resident in family medicine U.

Rochester, NY, 1974—77; fellow in geriatrics U. NC, Chapel Hill, 1986—87; asst. prof. family and preventive medicine U. Okla. Health Sciences Ctr., Oklahoma City, 1984—90, assoc. prof. family and preventive medicine, 1990—96, prof. and dir. rsch. family and preventive medicine, 1996—, adj. prof. geriatric medicine, 1997—; Smock endowed chair U. Louisville, Ky., 1992—93. Mem.: Inst. Medicine. Office: Family Medicine Ctr 900 NE 10th St Oklahoma City OK 73104-5420

MOLDEN, STEPHANIE MARIE, gynecologist; b. Falls Ch., Va., Mar. 5, 1976; BS in Chemistry, U. Va., 1998, MD, 2002. Med. dir. Female Pelvic Health Ctr., 2009—. Recipient Rsch. award, Soc. Gynecologic Surgeons. Mem.: ACOG, Internat. Soc. Urogynecology, Am. Urogynecology Soc. Office: 760 Newtown Yardley Rd Suite 115 Newtown PA 18940 Business E-Mail: smolden@fphcenter.com.

MOLDOVER, JONATHAN R., physiatrist, educator; MD, Columbia U., 1974. Diplomate Am. Bd. Physical Medicine and Rehab., 1979, Am. Bd. Physical Medicine and Rehab.-pain medicine. Resident internal medicine Strong Meml. Hosp. Univ. of Rochester Med. Ctr., NY, 1975—76; resident rehab. medicine Columbia-Presbyn. Med. Ctr., NYC, 1976—78; fellow rehab. medicine Columbia Univ., NYC; clin. assoc. prof. physical medicine and rehab. Albert Einstein Coll. of Medicine Yeshiva Univ., Bronx, NY; attending physician Milton & Carol Petrie divsn. Beth Israel Med. Ctr. Office: New York Back Pain Ste 608 200 W 57th St New York NY 10019 Office Phone: 212-581-4488. Office Fax: 212-581-4141.

MOLENDIJK, LEENDERT WILLEMMINUS, obstetrician, gynecologist; b. Deventer, Overijssel, The Netherlands, Oct. 23, 1957; arrived in Belgium, 1982; s. Willemminus Johannes Molendijk and Digna Elisabeth Van Santen; m. Mireille Lucy Louise Fifi, Mar. 3, 1979; children: Sebastien, Rebecca, Laura. MD, Erasmus U., Rotterdam, The Netherlands, 1982. Cert. med. specialist in ob-gyn. Med. officer Nikolas Hosp., Eupen, Belgium, 1983-85; registrar Siegburg Hosp., Cologne, Germany, 1985-89; cons., head dept. ob-gyn. Knappschafts Hosp., Wurselen, Germany, 1989—, head cytology lab., 1989-96. Dir. dept. gynecol. pharmacology Chemist Commn., Bochum, Germany, 1993—; cons. Regional Cancer Ctr., Aachen, Germany, 1993—; clin. rsch. scientist Cancer Inst., Aachen, 1993—. Author: Effect of Plasma Expanders in Toxemia in Pregnancy, 1996; translator Rodzynek edits. med. books, 1992-95; corr. editor Netherlands Jour. Medicine, 1993—; contbg. author Belgian Med. Jour., 1993—. 1st lt. NATO Armed Forces, The Netherlands, 1982-83. Mem. German Doppler Soc. (founder, New Techniques award 1992), German-Namibien Friendship Assn., Theol. Philosophy Assn., European Orgn. for Rsch. and Treatment of Cancer. Christian-Democrat. Mem. Dutch Reformed Ch. Achievements include development of clinical Hemorheology in pregnancy, new methods surgical therapy of ovarian cancer. Home: 10 Rue Mathysart B-4053 Embourg Liège Belgium Office: Knappschafts Hosp CMB rue Selys 2 B 4000 Liège Belgium E-mail: lmolendijk@excite.com.

MOLERO, TERESA, physician; b. Madrid, Jan. 17, 1955; MD, 1972. Physician, medicine Complutense U. Madrid, 1972—77. Mem.: ISLH. Office: Barranco de la Ballena Las Palmas de Gran Canaria Las Palmas 35010 Spain Business E-Mail: tmollab@gobiernodecanarias.org.

MOLINA, JOSEPH MARIO (MARIO MOLINA), medical administrator; b. Long Beach, Calif., May 16, 1958; s. C. David and Mary R. (Salandini) Molina; m. Therese Ann Flynn; children: Carley, Colleen, David, Mary Clare. BA, Calif. State U., Long Beach, 1980; MD, U. So. Calif., 1984. Diplomate Am. Bd. Internal Medicine. Intern and residency Johns Hopkins University, 1984—87; assoc. investigator VA, San Diego, 1988—90; asst. clin. prof. U. So. Calif., LA, 1990-91; med. dir. Molina Healthcare, Inc., Long Beach, 1991-94, v.p. HMO, 1994—96, chmn., pres., CEO, 1996—. Bd. dirs. New Am. Alliance. Nat. trustee Boys and Girls Club Am. Recipient Ernst & Young Gr. L.A. Entrepreneur of Yr. award, 2002; named one of Top 10 Latinos in Healthcare, LatinoLeaders mag., 2004, 25 Most Influential Hispanics, Time Mag., 2005; named to Hall of Fame, Long Beach Cmty. Coll., 2002. Mem.: ACP, Calif. Med. Assn., Am. Diabetes Assn. Avocation: collecting antique medical books. Office: Molina Health Care 200 Oceangate Ste 100 Long Beach CA 90802-4317 Office Phone: 562-435-3666. Business E-Mail: mario.molina@molinahealthcare.com.

MOLINA, MARIO JOSE, physical chemist, educator; b. Mexico City, Mar. 19, 1943; arrived in U.S., 1968; s. Roberto Molina-Pasquel and Leonor Henríquez; m. Guadalupe Alvarez, Feb. 11, 2006; 1 child, Felipe. BS in Chem. Engring., Nat. Autonomous U. Mex., 1965; MS, U. Freiburg, Germany, 1967; PhD in Chemistry, U. Calif., Berkeley, 1972. Asst. prof. Nat. Autonomous U., 1967—68; rsch. assoc. U. Calif., Berkeley, 1972—73, U. Calif., Irvine, 1973—75, asst. prof. phys. chemistry, 1975—79, assoc. prof., 1979—82; sr. rsch. scientist Jet Propulsion Lab., Calif. Inst. Tech., 1983—89; prof. earth, atmospheric & planet sci. MIT, Cambridge, Mass., 1989—96, Martin prof. atmospheric chemistry, 1997—2004; prof. chemistry & biochemistry U. Calif., San Diego, 2004—; faculty Ctr. Atmospheric Sci., Scripps Instn. Oceanography, La Jolla, Calif., 2004—. Mem. Pres.'s Coun. of Advisors on Sci. and Tech. (PCAST), 2009—. Bd. dirs. MacArthur Found. Recipient Tyler prize for Environ. achievement, 1983, Esselen award for chemistry in pub. interest, 1987, NASA Exceptional Sci. Achievement Medal, 1989, Nobel prize in chemistry, 1995, Sasakawa prize, UN Environment Programme, 1999, Heinz award in environment, Heinz Family Found., 2003; named a Trailblazer in Sci., Sci. Spectrum Mag., 2005; named one of 50 Most Important Hispanics in Govt. & Edn., Hispanic Engineer & Info. Tech. mag., 2005. Mem.: NAS, Pontifical Acad. Sci., Inst. Medicine, Am. Geophys. Union (Pres.'s com. advisors sci. & tech. 1994—2000, Pres.'s Com. on Advisors on Sci. and Tech. 2009—), Am. Phys. Soc., Am. Chem. Soc. Achievements include discovery of the theory that fluorocarbons deplete ozone layer of stratosphere. Office: U Calif Dept Chem & Biochem UHA 3050E 9500 Gilman Dr La Jolla CA 92093-0356 Office Phone: 858-534-1696. Business E-Mail: mjmolina@ucsd.edu.

MOLINARO, JOSEPH DANIEL, dentist, director; b. Phila., May 4, 1969; s. Daniel Joseph and Antoinette Marie (Napolio) Molinaro; m. Ellen Catherine Frank, June 14, 2003. BS in Biology, Villanova U., Pa., 1991; DMD, Temple U., Phila., 1995; MS in Oral Biology, George Washington U., Washington, 2001. Diplomate Fed. Svcs. Bd. Gen. Dentistry, 2002, Am. Bd. Gen. Dentistry 2002. Gen. dentist U.S. Naval Dental Ctr. USN, Agana, Guam, 1995—97, dental clinic divsn. officer, 1996—97, gen. dentist USS George Washington CVN 73 Norfolk, Va., 1997—99, dental clinic divsn. officer, 1998—99, resident, comprehensive dentistry Nat. Naval Dental Ctr. Bethesda, Md., 1999—2001, comprehensive dentist, dental clinic dept. head dental annex br. Indian Head, Md., 2001—04, dep. sr. dental surgeon pers. exch. program Portsmouth, England, 2004—06; operative dentistry dept. head Dental Clinic MC Recruit Depot, 2006—07; dir. advanced edn. gen. dentistry program Branch Dental Clinic, San Diego, 2007—. Contbr. articles to profl. jours. Comdr. Dental Corps USN, 1995—, Dental Corps. Decorated Navy and Marine Corps Commendation medal, Navy and Marine Corps Achievement medal, Humanitarian Svc. medal USN; recipient Martin I. Munin award, Temple U. Sch. Dentistry, 1995, Comdg. Officer's award for excellence, Nat. Naval Dental Ctr., 2000, Chief of the Dental Corps award, 2001; Health Profls. scholar, USN, 1994—95. Fellow: Acad. Gen. Dentistry; mem.: ADA, Acad. Operative Dentistry, Edward C. Penick Endodontic Study Club. Roman Catholic. Achievements include completed a study comparing the influence of various dental restorative materials on tooth cusp stiffness. Avocations: travel, reading, sports. Personal E-mail: joeandellen@molinaro.us.

MOLINE, JACQUELINE, occupational physician; b. Buffalo, Nov. 10, 1962; d. Sheldon Walter and Gloria Bettina Moline; m. Antoine Drye, Nov. 17, 2001. BA, U. Chgo., 1984, MD, 1988; MsC, Mt. Sinai Sch. Medicine, 1993. Diplomate Nat. Bd. Med. Examiners, Am. Bd. Internal Medicine, Am. Bd. Preventive Medicine. Resident in internal medicine Yale U./New Haven Hosp., 1988—91; resident in occupl. medicine Mt. Sinai Sch. Medicine, 1991—93, residency dir. occupl. medicine NYC, 1998—2006, vice chmn. dept. cmty. and preventive medicine, 2002—, assoc. prof. community and preventative medicine, assoc. prof. gen. internal medicine; dir. NY NJ Edn. & Rsch. Ctr., 2006—. Cons. United Fedn. Tchrs., NYC, 1992—; med. core dir. WTC Worker and Vol. Screening Program, NYC, 2002—06; dir. WTC Med. Monitoring & Treatment Program Clin. Ctr., Mt. Sinai, 2006—. Bd. dirs. JazzReach, NYC, 2002—. Recipient fellowship award, Found. for Occupl. Medicine, 1993, Laborer's award, NY-NJ Laborers, 1999. Mem.: ACP, Am. Coll. Occupl. and Environ. Medicine (bd. dirs. NY 2001—). Office: Mt Sinai Sch Medicine 1 Gustave Levy Pl New York NY 10029 E-mail: jacqueline.moline@mssm.edu.

MOLITERNO, DAVID J., cardiologist, educator; b. Flint, Mich., Oct. 29, 1960; m. Judith Ann Delp; children: Nathaniel, Benjamin. BS with honors, U. Mich., 1982; MD, Med. Coll. Va., 1987. Diplomate Am. Bd. Internal Medicine, Am. Bd. Cardiovascular Medicine, Am. Bd. Interventional Cardiology. Intern Vanderbilt U. Hosps., Vanderbilt U. Med. Ctr., Nashville, 1987—88; resident Vanderbilt U. Hosps. and Nashville VA Med. Ctr., 1988—90; fellow Parkland Meml. Hosp. and Dallas VA Med. Ctr., U. Tex. Southwestern Med. Ctr., 1990—93; fellow in interventional cardiology The Cleve. Clinic Found., 1993—94, staff physician sect. interventional cardiology dept. cardiovascular medicine, 1994—2003; vice chmn., internal medicine, chief, divsn. cardiology, Jefferson M. Gill prof. cardiology Univ. Ky., 2003—. Contbr. numerous articles to profl. jours.; reviewer: jours. in field, sect. editor: Jour. Thrombosis and Thrombolysis, mem. editl. bd.: Jour. Am. Coll. Cardiology. Named one of Best Doctors in Am., 2007. Fellow: ACP, European Soc. Cardiology, Am. Coll. Cardiology; mem.: AMA, Am. Heart Assn. Office: Gill Heart Inst U Ky Health-Care 800 Rose St Lexington KY 40536 Address: U Ky Divsn Cardiovascular Medicine Wethington Bldg Rm 317 900 S Limestone St Lexington KY 40536-0200 Office Phone: 859-323-5843. Office Fax: 859-257-3537. Business E-Mail: moliterno@uky.edu.

MOLITOR, RICHARD EDWARD, pharmacist; b. Seattle, Nov. 24, 1958; BS in Pharmacy, U. Wash., 1982. Pharmacy mgr. Evergreen Healthcare, 2002—. Clin. asst. prof. U. Wash., 1986—. Recipient Recognition Innovation award, Am. Coll. Physician Execs., 1992, Website of Week award, Am. Pharmacist Mag., 1997. Avocations: tennis, astronomy, languages. Office: 12303 NE 130th Ln #210 Kirkland WA 98034 Office Fax: 425-899-2795. Business E-Mail: remolitor@evergreenhealthcare.org.

MOLL, GEORGE WILLIAM, pediatrician, educator; b. Milw., Nov. 23, 1947; s. George William, Sr. and Laverne Delores (Klein) M.; m. Susana Valdez Ramos, June 24, 1978; children: Christina, Teresa. BA in Chemistry cum laude, Carleton Coll., 1969; PhD in Biochemistry, U. Chgo., 1975, MD, 1977. Diplomate Nat. Bd. Med. Examiners; diplomate in pediatrics and pediat. endocrinology Am. Bd. Pediatrics; cert. PALS, CPR. Pediatric resident Mott Children's Hosp., U. Mich., Ann Arbor, 1977-79; pediatric endocrinology fellowship Wyler Children's Hosp., U. Chgo., 1979-81; asst. prof. pediatrics U. Chgo., 1981-85, Emory U. Sch. Medicine, Atlanta, 1985-87; assoc. prof. pediatrics U. Miss. Med. Ctr., Jackson, 1987-93, prof. pediatrics, 1993—; assoc. staff pediatric endocrinology Little Co. of Mary Hosp., Evergreen Park, Ill., 1981-85, The Meth. Hosps., Gary and Merrillville, Ind., 1981-85; staff pediatric endocrinologist The Emory Clinic, Atlanta, 1985-87, Henrietta Egleston Hosp. for Children, Atlanta, 1985-87, Grady Meml. Hosp., Atlanta, 1985-87; staff Emory Univ. Hosp., 1987, dir. pediatric endocrinology; staff U. Miss. Med. Ctr., Jackson, 1987—. Contbr. articles to profl. jours. Active Diabetes Found. of Miss., Inc., 1998, Juv. Diabetes Found. Internat., 1998, Filipino-Am. Assn. of Miss., 1990—, Chronic Disease Coalition of Miss., 1996—. Recipient med. scientist NIH scholarship/grant U. Chgo., 1970-77, Andrew Mellon Found. fellowship, 1981-82, Med. Excellence award So. Med. Assn., 1995; grantee Am. Lung Assn., 1987-89, Eli Lilly Co., Mobil Oil Co., 1991, Diabetes Rsch. and Edn. Found., Inct., 1992, Pharmacia & Upjohn, 1998, others. Fellow Am. Acad. Pediatrics, Am. Coll. Endocrinology; mem. AAAS, Nat. Bd. Med. Examiners (comprehensive task force for reprodn./endocrinology 1989-90), Chgo. Endocrine Club (sec. 1984-85), N.Y. Acad. of Sci., Am. Fedn. for Med. Rsch., Lawson Wilkins Soc. for Pediat. Endocrinology, Midwest and So. Soc. for Pediatric Rsch., Miss. State Med. Assn., Cen. Miss. Med. and Pediatric Soc., The Endocrine Soc. (regional rep. U.S. Pharmacopeia Quinquennial), Am. Diabetes Assn., Juv. Diabetes Found., Sigma Xi, others. Achievements include isolation of a bovine brain protein kinase and establishment of a protein kinase assay employing a novel PEI-cellulose thin-layer system as part of a PhD Biochemistry; established a novel modified flow-dialysis system for steady state hormone action studies; assisted the delineation of a LH-receptor defect related to precocious puberty and a novel genetic mutation in thyroid binding globulin in males; novel genetic mutation in succinate dehydrogenase subunit B gene for malignant paraganglioma. Avocations: carpentry, general handicrafts, electronics, computer repair work. Office: Univ Miss Med Ctr 2500 N State St Jackson MS 39216-4500 Business E-Mail: gmoll@ped.umsmed.edu.

MOLL, STEPHAN, medical educator; b. Wuppertal, German, Sept. 22, 1959; married; 4 children. Cert. in internal medicine 2002, Germany, Norway, 1998, in hematology, lic. NC. Fellow and head clin. lab. Dept. Cardiology Humboldt U. Charite, Berlin, 1997—99; assoc. prof. Dept. Medicine, Divsn. Hematology-Oncology, U. NC. Bd. mem. Anticoagulation Forum, 2006—; bd. dir., chmn. med. and sci. adv. bd. Nat. Allaince Throntbosis and Thrombophilia, 2007—. Contbr. articles to jours., chapters to books. Recipient Recognisation award, UNC Dept. Medicine, 2006; grant, Bldg. Interdisciplinary Rsch. Ctr. Mem.: Am. Soc. Hematology (bd. mem. 2008—), Internat. Soc. Thrombosis and Haemostasis. Avocations: hiking, bicycling, travel. Office: Univ NC Sch Medicine Dept Medicine Divsn Hematology Oncology CB 7035 Chapel Hill NC 27599 Office Fax: 919-966-7369. Business E-Mail: smoll@med.unc.edu.

MOLL, VOLKER KARL-GEORG, urologist, educator; m. Petra Waltraud Weinzierl-Moll, June 8, 1990; children: Maximilian Korbinian, Florian Sebastian, Tobias Alexander. MD, U. Saarland, Homburg, Germany, 1984. Asst. dr. Urol. Clinic, Med. Sch., Homburg, Germany, 1984—90, cons., 1990—94; specialist in urology Augsburg, Germany, 1994—. Tchr. Sch. Nursery Diaconese Inst., Augsburg, 1994—; cons. urology dept. Diaconese Hosp., Augsburg, 1994—, lectr., urology, 1996—. V.p. Verbund Interdisziplinaere Ambulant Stationaere Versorgung, Augsburg, 2002—08. Roman Catholic. Achievements include research in urological oncology, urinary bladder dysfunction, erectile dysfunction, kidney stone disease. Office: Uro Aktiv Froelichstrasse 13 Augsburg 86150 Germany Business E-Mail: v.moll@uro-aktiv.de.

MOLLA, AHMED ABDIN, surgeon; b. Al Madinah, Saudi Arabia, Oct. 15, 1929; s. Abdin Amin Molla and Azeeza Mustafa Khalil; m. Fayza Niazi, 1956 (div. 1961); 1 child, Nadia; m. Roberta Jean Sadowski, June 1962 (div. 1981); children: Nezar, Dina, Nora, Sara; m. Sarah Hamed Al Abbadi, Feb. 8, 1983; children: Amr, Asem, Adnan, Azeez, Ola. MB, BChir, Cairo U., 1954; diploma, Coll. Med. Evangelist, LA, 1960. Diplomate Am. Bd. Surgery. Dir. Sch. Health, Madinah, Saudi Arabia, 1956-59; head sch. health Almadina, 1960—61; resident St. Francis Gen. Hosp., Pitts., 1961—66; chief surgery King's Hosp., Madinah, 1966-74, Mil. Hosp., Jeddah, Saudi Arabia, 1975-87; vol. free cons. to the poor Al Madina, 1987—. Contbr. articles to newspapers. Recipient Al Istihkak medal Syrian Pres., Damascus, 1973. Fellow ACS, Internat. Coll. Surgeons. Muslim. Avocations: reading, travel. Office Phone: 96648481675. Home Fax: 96648485096.

MOLLAH, KABIRUL AHSAN, research scientist; b. Dhaka, Sept. 21, 1971; MS, Asian Inst. Tech., 2006; PhD, U. Yamanash, 2009. Rsch. assoc. Asian Inst. Tech., 2006; rsch. asst. U. Yamanshi, 2006—09, tech. asst., 2009—10; cons. Enviro Care, 2010—. Rsch. grant, U. Yamanashi, JICA grant, Asian Inst. Tech.-Govt. Japan, fellow, Govt. of Japan. Avocations: swimming, reading. Home: 34 Frontier Pathway Toronto ON Canada M1B 4G4 Personal E-mail: kabirulmolla@yahoo.com.

MOLLE, VIRGINIE, research scientist; b. Rouen, France, Apr. 2, 1974; PhD, U. East Anglia, 2000. Rsch. scientist CNRS, 2004—. Recipient Bronze medal, CNRS, 2010. Office: University Montpellier 2-CNRS UMR 5235 Montpellier Languedoc-Roussillon 34095 France Business E-Mail: virginie.molle@univ-montp2.fr.

MOLLER, JAMES HERMAN, pediatrician, educator; b. Fresno, Calif., Aug. 12, 1933; s. Leonard Hansen and Eloise Jean (Hunter) M.; m. Carol Suzanne Eymann, Sept. 8, 1957; children: James, Elizabeth. AB, Stanford U., 1954, MD, 1958. Instr. pediat. U. Minn., Mpls., 1965-66, asst. prof., 1966-70, assoc. prof., 1970-73, prof., 1973—, Dwan prof., 1975—2005, interim head pediat., 1976-78, 97-99, chief pediat., 1976-78, head pediat., 1999—2003; chief of staff U. Minn. Hosp., Mpls., 1984-89. Vis. prof. Nat. Heart & Lung Inst., London, 1989-90, Inst. Child Health, London, 1989-90. Contbr. over 200 sci. articles to profl. jours. Bd. dirs. U. Minn. Hosp., 1984-89, Mpls. Children's Health Ctr., 1975-78, Children's Hosp., St. Paul, 1975-78, Minn. Assn. Pub. tchg. Hosps., Mpls., 1984-89, Variety Club Heart Assn., Mpls., 1980-83. Capt. U.S. Army, 1961-63. Fellow Am. Acad. Pediat. (exec. bd. 1991-92, dist. chmn. 1991-92, alternate dist. chmn. 1985-91, Ross Edn. award 1989), Am. Coll. Cardiology; mem. Am. Heart Assn. (pres. 1993-94, v.p. 1986-91, bd. dirs. 1986-95, award of Merit 1989), Am. Fedn. Clin. Rsch., Am. Pediatric Soc., Am. Bd. Pediat. Nat. Bd. Med. Examiners, Midwest Soc. Pediatric Cardiology Soc., Minn. Med. Assn. (intersplty. coun. 1979-82, resource group child health 1980-82), Minn. Acad. Medicine, Mpls. Met. Pediatric Soc, No. Pediatric Cardiology Soc. (pres. 1978-79), Midwest Soc. Pediatric Rsch. Soc. Pediatric Rsch., Hennepin County Med. Soc. (bd. dirs. 1986-89), Irish Am. Paediatric Soc., British Paediatric Cardiac Assn., Coun. Med. Splty. Socs. (bd. dirs., 1991—), Sub-bd. Pediatric Cardiology (chmn. 1992-94), Internam. Heart Found. (pres. 1997-98), World Heart Fedn. (bd. dirs. 1999). Independent. Congregationalist. Avocations: gardening, travel, oriental carpets, reading. Home: 4816 Sheridan Ave S Minneapolis MN 55410-1917 Office: U Minn 420 Delaware St SE Minneapolis MN 55455-0374 Office Phone: 612-626-2790. Business E-Mail: molle002@umn.edu.

MØLLER, SØREN, chief physician, associate professor, researcher; b. Killerup, Odense, Denmark, Feb. 5, 1959; s. Erik and Ester M.; m. Bjørka Skriver, Sept. 10, 1988; children: Anne-Cathrine, Anders Christian, Alexander. MD, U. Copenhagen, 1987, DMS, 1997. Registrar dept. hepatology, gastroenterology and cardiology Hvidovre (Denmark) Hosp., 1987-90, registrar dept. clin. physiology, 1990-92, rsch. fellow, 1992-95, sr. registrar, 1996-97, sr. registrar dept. clin. physiology, 1997-99, chief physician dept. clin. physiology, 1999—. Clin. lectr., assoc. prof. dept. clin. physiology and nuclear medicine U. Copenhagen; pres. Danish Soc. Clin. Physiology and Nuc. Medicine, 2006-. Reviewer in field; contbr. articles to profl. jours. Mem. European Assn. for the Study of the Liver (sci. com. 1999—), Danish Assn. for the Study of Liver (pres. 2003-06), Internat. Club Ascites (mem. sci. com. 2006-). Achievements include research in systemic haemodynamics in cirrhosis and portal hypertension with focus on vasoactive substances and prognosis. Home: Kajerødvej 36 DK-3460 Birkerød Denmark Office: Hvidovre Hospital Dept ClinicalPhysio &

Nuclear Med 239 Kettegaard Alle 30 DK-2650 Hvidovre Denmark Fax: 45 3862 3750. Business E-Mail: soeren.moeller@hvh.regionh.dk. E-mail: moeller@dadlnet.dk.

MØLLERLØKKEN, ANDREAS, medical researcher; b. Trondheim, Norway, May 15, 1974; PhD, Norwegian U. Sci. & Tech., 2008. Rsch. scientist Norwegian U. Sci. & Tech., 2008—09, postdoc. rschr., 2009—. Exec. com. mem. European Underwater & Baromed. Soc., 2009. Mem.: NAUI, European Underwater & Baromed. Soc. (Zetterstrom award 2005). Avocation: diving. Office: Olav Kyrres gt 9 Trondheim 7489 Norway Business E-Mail: andreas.mollerlokken@ntnu.no.

MOLNÁR, PÉTER PÁL, pathologist, educator; b. Pécs, Baranya, Hungary, Mar. 2, 1951; s. László F. and Maria M. (Pump) Molnár. MD summa cum laude, U. Med. Sch., Debrecen, Hungary, 1975, Habilitation, 1995; PhD, Acad. Sci., Budapest, Hungary, 1987, DMS, 1999. Cert. pathologist, neuropathologist. Resident in pathology U. Med. Sch., Debrecen, 1975-79, assoc. prof., 1982-95, prof. pathology, 1995—; vis. fellow Lab. Chem. Pharmacology, Divsn. Cancer Treatment, Nat. Cancer Inst., NIH, Bethesda, Md., 1979-82; head, dir. Hungarian-Japanese Electron Microscopic Ctr., Debrecen, 1994—2002. Vis. prof. Northwestern U., Chgo., 1986—2003; prof. dept. pathology Ross U. Med. Sch., Dominica, West Indies, 2003—04. Mem. editl. bd.: Jour. Neuro-Oncology; contbr. articles to profl. jours. 2d lt. Hungarian Army, 1976—82. Recipient Univ. Ednl. award, Ministry of Health, Budapest, 1976. Mem.: AAAS, Am. Assn. Cancer Rsch., European Cell Biology Orgn., Soc. Neuro-Oncology, London Diplomatic Acad., Hungarian Soc. Pathology (bd. dirs. 1995), Soc. Ultrastructural Pathology, N.Y. Acad. Scis., Brit. Giloma Group, Internat. Brain Rsch. Orgn. (Travel award to Am. Assn. Neuropathologists' ann. meeting 2001), Internat. Acad. Pathology, Internat. Soc. Neuropathology (councilor Hungarian sect. 1995, bd. dirs. Hungarian divsn. 1996), European Assn. Neuro-Oncology, European Soc. Pathology, Hungarian Soc. Neurology and Psychiatry (neuropathology sect.), Hungarian Soc. Microscopy, Hungarian Soc. Biology, Am. Assn. Neuropathology. Office: OEC Dept Pathology Nagyerdei Krt 98 Debrecen H 4032 Hungary Personal E-mail: molnarp@dote.hu.

MOLNAR, VIOLET, mental health nurse; b. Budapest, Hungary; arrived in U.S., 1960; d. Janos Molnar and Erzsebeth Krekacs. ADN, Atlantic Union Coll., 1967; BSN, Walla Walla Coll., Wash., 1973. RN Mass., Calif. Staff nurse New Eng. Meml. Hosp., Stoneham, Mass., 1968—70; IV therapist Loma Linda U. Med. Hosp., Calif., 1970—72; psychiat. nurse St. Bernardines Med. Ctr., San Bernardino, Calif., 1974—89, Corona Regional Med. Ctr., San Bernardino, 1990—. Pub. spkr. Pres. Lady's Club Friendly Cir., Loma Linda, 1997—99, pres., 2006—, elder, deaconess, greeter Seventh Day Adventist Ch. Loma Linda U., 1975—. Mem.: Rotary Club San Bernardino/Highland (Paul Harris fellow 2001). Avocations: travel, reading, church activities. Home: 11422 Benton St Loma Linda CA 92354 Personal E-mail: imolnar@juno.com, vmolnar129@gmail.com.

MOLODAVKIN, GENNADY MATVEEVITCH, pharmacologist; b. Dalny, Russia, Aug. 4, 1950; s. Matvey Vasilievitch Molodavkin and Valentina Dievna (Ignatova) Molodavkina; m. Olga Ivanovna Podobulkina, Oct. 22, 1977; children: Elena Molodavkina, Ilia. PhD, Moscow State U., Russia. Diplomate biology Moscow State U. Jr. lab. asst. Inst. Pharm., Moscow, 1972—73, jr. rschr., 1973—81, sr. rschr., 1981—91, leading rschr., 1991—, dr. biol. sci., 1998—. Sci. coun. mem. Inst. Pharm., 2006—09, Med. Acad., Smolensk, 2004—09. Contbr. articles various profl. jours. Avocations: electronics, computers. Office: Zakusov Inst Pharm RAMS ul. Baltiyskaya 8 125315 Moscow Moskva Russia Office Phone: 8 495 601-24-14. Business E-Mail: molod@istel.ru.

MOLOFF, ALAN LAWRENCE, retired military officer, physician; s. Louis and Muriel Moloff. BS, U. Vt., 1976, DO in Medicine, U. Medicine and Dentistry NJ, 1983; MPH, Harvard U., 1988. Fellow Am. Bd. Preventive Medicine, bd. cert. aerospace medicine, bd. cert. in undersea medicine & disaster medicine. Commd. platoon leader U.S. Army, 1976, advanced through grades to col., 1999; intern Fitzsimons Army Med. Ctr., Aurora, Colo., 1983—84; med. officer lst Battalion 10th Spl. Forces Group, Bad Tolz, Germany, 1984—87; resident in aerospace medicine Harvard U., Boston, 1987—89; chief spl. ops. forces divsn. Acad. Health Scis., San Antonio, 1989—92; command surgeon Spl. Forces Command, Ft. Bragg, NC, 1992—93; dep. surgeon U.S. Army Spl. Ops. Command, Ft. Bragg, 1993—94; with command and gen. staff coll. U.S. Army, 1994—95; dep. surgeon 30th Med. Brigade, Heidelberg, Germany, 1995—96; SETAF surgeon, 1995—97; dep. U.S. Army Europe Fwd Surgeon, Hungary, 1995—96; surgeon V Corps, Germany, 1996—97; comdr. 212th M.A.S.H., Wiesbaden, Germany, 1997—99; fellow environ. policy inst. Army War Coll., 1999—2000; comdr. U.S. Army Aeromed. Ctr., 2000—02, Def. Med. Readiness Tng. Inst., 2002—06; ret., 2006; assoc. dean Internat. Ctr. Prehosp. & Disaster Medicine; med. dir., mem. bd. dirs. Pyng Med. Corp., Richmond, Canada; assoc. med. dir. Regional Emergency Med. Svcs. Authority, Reno. Founding mem. Bd. Disaster Medicine; prof. emergency medicine Med. Coll. Ga.; faculty Ctr. for Disaster Medicine and Humanitarian Assistance, U. South Fla.; cons. in disaster medicine and preparedness; lectr. in field; instr. Advanced Trauma Life Support; instr. Disaster Life Support; internat. spkr. media comm. during complex disasters. Contbr. articles to profl. jours. Active in civic activities. Decorated Def. Superior Svc. medal, Legion of Merit, Meritorious Svc. medal with 4 oak leaf clusters, Joint Svc. Commendation medal, S.W. Asian Svc. medal, Army Commendation medal with oak leaf cluster, Joint Army Achievement medal, Armed Forces Svc. medal, Armed Forces Expeditionary medal, NATO medal, Kuwait Liberation medal, Kosovo Campaign medal, German Paratrooper badge, Pathfinder badge, Expert Field Med. badge, Order of Mil. Med. Merit, Master Parachutist award, Ranger, Spl. Forces Qualified Master Flight Surgeon badge, Navy Dive Med. Officer badge, Order of Aeromed. Merit. Fellow: Aerospace Med. Assn., Am. Coll. Preventive Medicine; mem.: Assn. Mil. Osteo. Physicians and Surgeons, Spl. Ops. Med. Assn. (life; past pres. 2003—06), Soc. US Army Flight Surgeons (life). Avocations: skiing, scuba diving, weightlifting, military history, rock climbing. Personal E-mail: moloffa@hotmail.com.

MOLOFSKY, WALTER J., pediatrician, neurologist; Attended, NYU, 1976. Diplomate Am. Bd. of Pediatrics, 1982, Am. Bd. of Psychiatry and Neurology-child neurology, 1986. Resident pediat. Columbia Presbyn. Med. Ctr., 1977—78, fellow, 1978—81, Am. Acad. of Neurology, The Child Neurology Soc.; assoc. prof. neurology and pediat. Albert Einstein Coll. of Medicine; assoc. chmn. neurology Beth Israel Med. Ctr., St. Luke's-Roosevelt Hosp. Ctr. Pres. Tri-State Child Neurology Soc. Named one of Top Doctors-New York Metro Area, Castle Connolly, 2009. Mem.: Am. Assn. for the study of Headaches. Office: Beth Israel Medical Center 1st Ave 16th St New York NY 10003 Office Phone: 212-420-2000. Business E-Mail: wmolofsky@chpnet.org.

MOLON, GIULIO, cardiologist, director; b. Verona, Italy, Aug. 15, 1960; s. Attilio Molon and Maria Zenoni; m. Claudia Castelli; children: Nicola, Luca, Giulia. MD, Verona U., 1986. Cert. Cardiology Inst., Verona U., 1990. Fellow Cardiology Inst., Verona, 1987—91; cardiology dept. staff Sacro Cuore Hosp., Negrar, Verona, 1992—, electrophysiology and cardiostimulation dir., 2008—. Fellow: Am. Coll. Cardiology, European Soc. Cardiology. Office: Cardiology Dept Sacro Cuore Hosp Via Sempreboni 5 Negrar Verona 37024 Italy Office Fax: 390457500480. Business E-Mail: giulio.molon@sacrocuore.it.

MOLTENI, AGOSTINO, pathology educator; b. Como, Lombardy, Italy, Nov. 12, 1933; came to U.S., 1963; s. Enrico and Antonia (Signorini) M.; m. Loredana Brizio, Sept. 5, 1963; children: Claudio Enrico, Ronald Stephen. MD, U. Milan, Italy, 1957; PhD in Pathology, SUNY, Buffalo, 1970. Lic. Italian Bd. Internal Medicine, 1963. Intern and resident in internal medicine U. Milan (Italy), 1957-62; asst. prof. U. Milan, 1957-63; chief rsch. sect. Farmitalia Drug Co., Milan, 1963-65; rsch. assoc. SUNY, Buffalo, 1965-69, asst. prof., 1969-71; assoc. prof. U. Kans., Kansas City, 1971-76; prof. pathology Northwestern U., Chgo., 1976-96, prof. emeritus, 1996—; prof. pathology and pharmacology U. Mo., Kansas City, 1996—, adj. prof. basic med. scis. Vis. prof. Harvard U., 1983-84; dir. med. students rsch. program U. Mo. Kansas City, 2004-; adj. prof. anesthesia, U. Mo., Kansas City, 2007-. Editor, author: Endocrinology and Thermal Trauma, 1990, Menopause Update, 1992; exec. editor Current Pharmaceutical Design, 2000—, Nutrition Rsch., 2003, PPAR Rsch., 2005; contbr. articles to profl. jours., chpts. to books. Recipient Sharer in Lasker award Lasker Found., N.Y.C., 1983, Rsch. Career Devel. award NIH, Washington, 1970, award Am. Heart Assn., Chgo., 1982. Fellow Am. Acad. Clin. Biochemistry; mem. Am. Acad. Pathology, Am. Soc. Investigative Pathology, Clin. Chemistry Soc., Endocrine Soc. (emeritus), Am. Assn. Clin. Chemistry (emeritus). Achievements include patent for captopril as a cancer chemo-preventive agent; research on hypertension and hormonal regulation of cancer. Office: U Mo Truman Med Ctr 2301 Holmes St Kansas City MO 64108-2640 Business E-Mail: moltenia@umkc.edu.

MOMAH, ETHEL CHUKWUEKWE, retired women's health nurse; b. Iyi-Enu, Ogidi, Nigeria, May 28, 1934; arrived in US, 1978; d. Zaccheus C. and Victoria U. (Orizu) Obi; m. Christian Chike Momah, Nov. 21, 1959; children: Chukwudi, Adaora, Azuka. SRN, Harrow Hosp., Middlesex, UK, 1956; SCM, Mothers Hosp., London, 1957; MTD, Midwife Tchrs. Coll., Surrey, UK, 1964; BS, Upsala Coll., 1988. Cert. inpatient obstetric nurse Nat. Cert. Corp. Nurse-midwife Guy's Hosp., London, 1959; nursing sister, head nurse labor/delivery Univ. Coll. Hosp., Ibadan, Nigeria, 1960-62; midwife tutor Lagos Island Maternity Hosp., Nigeria, 1963-66, nurse-midwife Brit. Hosp., Paris, 1966, Hosp. Cantonal, Geneva, 1967-78; staff nurse St. Peters Med. Ctr., New Brunswick, NJ, 1980—85, patient care coord., 1985-90, antenatal testing nurse, 1990—2005; ret., 2005; substitute sch. nurse Arlington Ind. Sch. Dist., Tex., 2006—. Recipient Disting. Svc. award, NNEWI Union NY Tri-State Inc., 2000, Cultural Performance award, Anambra Enugu States Assn. N.J., 2001, Disting. Svc. award, Anambia Enugu States Assn., 2002, Cmty Leadership award, Assocs. Mental Health Devel. Disabilities, NJ, 2004, Legion of Honor award, Chapel of Four Chaplains, 2005, Courageous Leadership award, Anambra State Assn. N.J., 2006, Invaluable and Devoted Svc. award, Nnewi N.Y. Tri-State, 2006. Mem.: Nrewi Union Dallas Fortworth Tex. (pres. 2010—), Nnewi USA, Inc. (v.p. 2003—08), NUSA (DFW chpt. 2008—10), Anambra State Assn., Umunne Women's Assocs. Dallas, Anambra Enugu States Assn., Nne-Egwu (dance mother 1990—2006). Personal E-mail: nnanne@sbcglobal.net.

MOMENI, REZA, plastic surgeon; BA, Haverford Coll., 1990—94; MD, Med. Coll. of Pa., 1994—98. Diplomate Am. Bd. Plastic Surgery. Resident in gen. surgery Yale U., New Haven, 1998—2001, resident in plastic surgery, 2001—04, chief resident in plastic surgery, 2003—04; plastic, reconstructive, & hand surgeon Summit Med. Group, Summit, NJ, 2004—; chmn. plastic surgery Overlook Hosp., 2010—. Cons. MedSN.com, Santa Monica, Calif., 1998—2000; med. illustration J/B Woolsey, Conshohocken, Pa., 1998—99. Nat. spkty. rep. Am. Assn. of Med. Colleges - Orgn. of Resident Representatives, Washington, 2003—. Recipient Phi Beta Kappa, Haverford Coll., 1994, 1st Pl., US Pharmacopaeia Competition, 1996, Nat. Pathology Honor Soc., Med. Coll. of Pa., 1996, Alpha Omega Alpha, 1998, Ellis Island medal, 2009; named Top Dr., NJ Monthly, 2007, 2009—10, America's Top Plastic Surgeons, 2008, 2010; named to NJ Monthly Top Drs. List, 2011; scholar Class of 1934 scholarship, Haverford Coll., 1992; Howard Hughes Med. Inst. Rsch. scholarship, Howard Hughes Inst., 1993, Med. Coll. of Pa., Haverford Coll., 1995, Class of 1910 scholarship, Med. Coll. of Pa., 1995, Huldah Kerner scholarship, 1996, Ruth Weil Meml. scholarship, 1997, Weston Ellsworth scholarship, 1997, William Goldman scholarship, William Goldman Found., 1996—98, Yale Plastic Surgery Scholastic award, Yale Univ., 2002. Fellow: ACS; mem.: AMA, Summit Med. Group (mem. bd. dirs. 2011—), Am. Soc. Aesthetic Plastic Surgery, NJ Soc. Plastic Surgeons, NY Regional Soc. Plastic Surgery, Am. Soc. Plastic Surgeons (amb. surgeon 2007—), Union County Med. Soc., NJ Med. Soc., Phi Beta Kappa, Alpha Omega Alpha, Yale Surg. Soc. Achievements include research in cranial reconstruction after dural complications; pulse oximetry in melanoma sentinel node dissection may be false; frontal sinus fractures: an institutional review. Avocations: travel, sailing, skiing, snowboarding. Office: Summit Plastic Surgery 1 Diamond Hill Rd Berkeley Heights NJ 07922 Office Phone: 908-277-8759.

MONACO, ANTHONY P., academic administrator, medical geneticist, educator; b. Wilmington, Del. m. Zoia Monaco; 3 children. AB, Princeton U., 1981; MD, PhD, Harvard U. Postdoctoral fellow Imperial Cancer Rsch. Fund (ICRF) (now Cancer Rsch. UK), London, sr. scientist; head Human Genetics Lab. Inst. Molecular Medicine, Oxford, England; joined Wellcome Trust Centre for Human Genetics (WTCHG), Oxford, England, 1995, dir., 1998—2007; pro-vice chancellor planning and resources U. Oxford, 2007—11; pres. Tufts U., 2011—. Instr. European Sch. Med. Genetics, Sestri Levante, Italy, 1988—92, Sestri Levante, 1995. Contbr. articles to profl. jours. Recipient Gaetano Conte Prize for Basic Rsch. on Muscular Diseases, 1993, Jacob's Ladder Lectureship and Award, Canadian Found. for Control of Neurodegenerative Disorders, 2002, Outstanding Physician Scientist Award in Neurological Rsch., European Genomics & Neurodegenerative Diseases, 2010. Fellow: Royal Soc. Medicine, Acad. Med. Scis., Molecular Medicine Soc.; mem.: European Molecular Biology Orgn., Nat. Autistic Soc., Autism Soc. of America, German Soc. Neurogenetics, Human Genome Orgn., European Soc. Human Genetics, American Soc. Human Genetics (Travel Award for Internat. Congress of Human Genetics 1986), Phi Beta Kappa Soc., Sigma Xi Rsch. Soc. Office: Tufts University Office of President Ballou Hall, 2nd Floor Medford MA 02155 Office Phone: 617-627-3300. *

MONACO, ROBERT ANTHONY, radiologist; b. NYC, July 5, 1945; s. Edmond V. and Jean M.; m. Susan Margaret Thompson; children: Kevin, Robert, Christopher, Sarah. BS, Siena Coll., 1967; MD, N.J. Coll. Medicine, 1971. Diplomate Am. Bd. Radiology, Am. Bd. Nuclear Medicine. Radiology resident NJ Coll. Medicine, Newark, 1971-75; fellow in nuclear medicine med. ctr. NYU, NYC, 1975-76; attending radiologist Med. Ctr. Ocean County, Point Pleasant, NJ, 1976-87, dir. dept. radiology, 1987—, sec. med. staff, 1998-2000. Gen. ptnr Point Pleasant Radiology Group, 1987—; sec. bd. dirs. Found. Med. Ctr. Ocean County, Mid-Coastal IPA, 1997; mng. ptnr. Open MRI of Wall, 1999—. Capt. USAR, 1972-76. Mem. Am. Coll. Radiology, Am. Coll. Nuc. Medicine, Radiol. Soc. NJ (exec. com. 2005-). Roman Catholic. Avocations: tennis, fishing, swimming. Home: 13 Bretwood Dr Colts Neck NJ 07722 Office: Open MRI of Wall Rt 34 Wall NJ 07719 Office Phone: 732-974-8060. Personal E-mail: rammdo1@aol.com.

MONAGHAN, W(ILLIAM) PATRICK, immunohematologist, medical educator, consultant, retired military officer; b. Ashtabula, Ohio, June 24, 1944; s. Paul E. and June E. (Sober) M. m. Mary Lou Gustafson, Mar. 15, 1976; children: Ian Patrick, Erin Kelly. BS, Old Dominion U., Va., 1968; MS in Biology, Bowling Green State U., 1972, PhD, 1975. Cert. clin. lab. specialist, med. technologist, blood bank specialist. Enlisted U.S. Navy, 1961, commd. ensign Med. Service Corps, 1969, advanced through grades to comdr., 1983; staff med. technologist officer Nat. Naval Med. Ctr., Bethesda, Md., 1969; clin. lab. and blood bank officer USS Sanctuary (AH-17), S. Vietnam, 1969-70; clin. lab. officer Naval Med. Ctr., Charleston, S.C., 1970-72; blood bank fellow U.S. Army Med. Rsch. Lab., Ft. Knox, Ky., 1972-73; head blood bank Nat. Naval Med. Ctr., 1975-85, faculty and course dir. for immunohematology med. tech., 1976-84, dir. blood bank, 1976-84; asst. prof. pathology George Washington U. Sch. Medicine, Washington, 1976-83, assoc. prof., 1983-88; mem. faculty Walter Reed Army Med. Ctr., Washington, 1976-88; asst. dean grad. and continuing edn. Uniformed Svcs. U. of Health Sci., Washington, 1984-88, ret., 1988; prof. Grad. Sch. Nursing Uniformed Svcs. U. of Health Sci., 1994-2000; prof. Coll. Health, Fla. Internat. U., North Miami, Fla., 2002—05, U. North Fla., Coll. Health, U. Fla., Coll. Medicine, 2005—. V.p. Met. Washington Blood Banks, 1976-81, ex officio mem. bd. dirs. 1981-87; cons. D.C. chpt. Hemophilias Found., 1977-78; spl. USN rep. Am. Soc. Med. Tech., 1976-88; dir. N.E. area blood system Navy Blood Program, 1978-88, mem. tri-service blood bank com. Dept. Def. Blood Program, 1978-88; faculty and program adv. com. ARC, Washington, 1978-84, Johns Hopkins Med. Sch., Balt., 1978-85; faculty U. Tenn. Center for Health Scis., Memphis, 1978, U. Ill. Sch. Medicine, Peoria, 1978-79, Grad. Sch. Nursing Uniformed Svcs. U. of Health Scis., Bethesda, Md.; guest lectr. NIH Blood Bank, 1978-90; adj. assoc. prof. Bowling Green State U., Ohio, 1981-89; bd. dirs. Exam, Inc., Rockville, Md. Navy editor Procs. Armed Forces Med. Lab. Scientists, 1976, 79, 80, editor-in-chief, 1982-85; assoc. editor Am. Jour. Med. Tech., 1978-88, Jour. Allied Health; Navy editor History of the Blood Program of the U.S. Mil. Svcs. in Vietnam and S.E. Asisa, 1976; contbr. articles to profl. jours. Decorated numerous combat and svc. medals; USN grantee, 1977-89, 95; recipient Lifetime Achievement award Armed Svcs. Blood Program, 2010. Mem. Am. Soc. Med. Technologists (chmn. immunohematology task group 1976), Am. Blood Commn. (task force 1976, regionalization), Am. Assn. Blood Banks (sci. assembly 1976—, adminstrv. sect. 1976—, blood component therapy com. 1977-79, edn. com. 1976-83), AAAS, Am. Soc. Clin. Pathologists, Soc. Mil. Surgeons, Naval Inst., Sigma Xi, others Avocations: reading, boating, golf. Home: 86193 Meadowfield Bluffs Rd Yulee FL 32097 Office: University Fla Dept Anesthesiology Coll Medicine Health Sci Ctr Jacksonville FL 32209 Office Phone: 904-244-3402. Personal E-mail: wpatrickmonaghan@aol.com. Business E-Mail: patrick.monaghan@jax.ufl.edu.

MONAHAN, BRIAN PATRICK, internist, federal official; b. Bridgeport, Conn, Dec. 13, 1960; m. Mary E. Monahan. BS, Fairfield U.; MD, Georgetown U., DC, 1986. Diplomate Am. Bd. Internal Medicine, 2006. Resident internal medicine Nat. Naval Med. Ctr., 1991—93; fellow med. oncology and hematology Nat. Cancer Inst., 1993—96; asst. prof. medicine Uniformed Svcs. U., Bethesda, Md., 1991—99, assoc. prof. medicine, 1999—2006, prof., 2006—, chmn. medicine, 2005—; dep. attending physician US Congress, attending physician, 2009—. Dir. hematology and med. oncology Nat. Naval Med. Ctr. Recipient Clin. Investigation Program award, 2003; named Outstanding Teacher of Yr., Nat. Cancer Inst., 2000. Fellow: ACP. Home: 9905 Old Spring Rd Kensington MD 20895 Office: Uniformed Svcs Univ 4301 Jones Bridge Rd Bethesda MD 20814 also: US Congress Attending Physician The Capitol H-166 Washington DC 20515-6907 Office Phone: 202-225-5421. Office Fax: 301-295-0981; Home Fax: 301-295-0981. Personal E-mail: brian_monahan@nih.gov. *

MONAHAN, DANIELLE JOAN, renal nutritionist; b. Tacoma, Feb. 22, 1952; d. Daniel Gustav and Bernice Elizabeth (Nordlund) Anderson; m. Jay Mitchell Littlefield, Nov. 13, 1976 (dec. 1997); children: David, Rachel, Paul; m. Aldrich B. Monahan, Jr., Oct. 30, 1999. BS, Va. Poly. Inst., 1974; MS, U. Md., 1975. Registered dietitian, Va. Therapeutic dietitian Samaritan Hosp., Troy, NY, 1976; renal dietitian BMA/Fresenius Med. Care (formerly Nat. Med. Care), Washington, 1977-85, Fairfax Dialysis (formerly BMA of Arlington), 1985—. Cons. Fairfax, 1985—; rep. network coordinating coun. Nat. Kidney Found., Chevy Chase, Md., 1980-84; chmn. BMA Dietitians Group, Washington, 1980-93. Contbr. articles to profl. jours., mags. Del. Va. Rep. Party, Vienna, 1982. Mem. Am. Dietetic Assn., No. Va. Dietetic

Assn. Republican. Avocation: cooking. Office: Fairfax Dialysis 8316 Arlington Blvd #108 Fairfax VA 22031-5216 Home Phone: 703-698-0104; Office Phone: 703-698-8070. Personal E-mail: amonahan3@cox.com.

MONAHAN, PAUL EDWARD, pediatrician; b. Winchester, Va., July 3, 1963; AB, Princeton U., 1986; MD, U. Va., 1990. Assoc. prof. pediat. U. NC at Chapel Hill Sch. Medicine, 1998—, dir. pediat. hemostasis, 1998. Regional dir. region IV-N US Hemophilia Treatment Ctr. Network, 2005. Grants, NIH, numerous grants. Office: Physicians Office Bldg CB#7326 1185 1st Fl Chapel Hill NC 27599-7236 Office Fax: 919-966-0907. Business E-Mail: paul_monahan@med.unc.edu.

MONCURE, ASHBY CARTER, surgeon, educator; b. Richmond, Va., Dec. 27, 1934; s. Powhatan and Maude Leah (Carley) M.; m. Patricia Juanita Leighton, June 21, 1960 (dec. Oct. 2001); children: Diana, Ann Marie, Ashby, Elizabeth; m. Margot Graham Lord, June 19, 2004 (dec. Feb. 2009). MD, U. Va., 1960. Diplomate Am. Bd. Surgery, Am. Bd. Thoracic Surgery, Am. Bd. Vascular Surgery. Intern Mass. Gen. Hosp., Boston, 1960-61, resident, 1961-62, 64-68; practice medicine specializing in surgery Boston, 1969—. Instr. surgery Harvard Med. Sch., Boston, 1969-71, asst. prof. surgery, 1971-77, asst. clin. prof. surgery, 1977-86, assoc. clin. prof. surgery, 1986—2000, clin. prof. surgery, 2000-03, clin. prof. surgery emeritus, 2003; assoc. vis. surgeon Mass. Gen. Hosp., Boston, 1973-79, vis. surgeon, 1980—2003, sr. surgeon, 2003—, med. dir. surg. clinic, 2003-. Editor: MGH Textbook of Emergency Medicine, 1978, 2d edit., 1983, 3d edit., 1989, Complex Operations at the Mass. Gen. Hospital, 1983. Capt. U.S. Army, 1962-64. Fellow ACS; mem. New Eng. Surg. Soc. (pres. 2000), Ea. Surg. Soc. (pres. 2004), Am. Surg. Assn., Soc. Thoracic Surgeons, Internat. Cardiovascular Soc., Am. Assn. Thoracic Surgery, Soc. Vascular Surgery, Boston Surg. Soc. (pres. 1995). Clubs: Union Boat, Weston Golf. Episcopalian. Home: 3 Glen Oak Dr Wayland MA 01778 Office Phone: 617-724-3760.

MONDAL, ANUPAM, research scientist; b. Kolkata, Apr. 4, 1956; DRM, INMAS, 1981, DNB, 1992, MD. Head pet imaging & nuc. medicine Inst. Nuc. Medicine & Allied Scis., 2005—. Head dept., sr. cons. INMAS, 2000—05. Mem.: Soc. Nuc. Medicine. Home: D Rdo Complex Timarpur New Delhi 110054 India Personal E-mail: anupam88@rediffmail.com.

MONDAL, NEELIMA, research scientist; b. Ledarson, West Bengal, India, July 21, 1971; MSc, Sch. Life Scis., Jawaharlal Nehru U., India, 1992, PhD, 1999. Postdoc. fellow Brigham & Women's Hosp., Harvard Med. Sch., Boston, 1999—; asst. prof. Jawaharlal Nehru U., New Delhi, 2003, prof. & rschr., 2003, advisor, 2011. Fellowship, DAAD, Germany. Avocations: reading, music. Home: 1442 Type IV Poorvanchal Complex Jawa New Delhi 110067 India Personal E-mail: nmondal@hotmail.com.

MONDEN, MORITO, surgeon, educator; b. Fukuyama, Japan, Aug. 8, 1945; s. Kazuo and Ayako Monden; m. Yasuko Matsumoto, Apr. 12, 1975; children: Masayuki, Kazuyuki. MD, Osaka U., Japan, 1970, PhD, 1979. Mem. surg. staff Osaka U. Hosp., 1973-79, lectr., 1979-87, asst. prof., 1987-90, assoc. prof., vice chmn. dept. surgery, 1990-94, prof., chmn. dept. surgery, 1994—2009; v.p. Osaka U., 2007—11. Vis. fellow Meml. Sloan-Kettering, NYC, 1979—81. Contbr. articles to profl. jours. Mem. Am. Gastroenterol. Assn., Am. Soc. Clin. Oncology, Am. Assn. Study Liver Disease, Internat. Soc. Surgery, NY Acad. Scis., Transplantation Soc., Am. Assn. Cancer Rsch., Japanese Cancer Assn. (v.p. 2010), Japanese Liver Transplantation Soc. (pres. 1999-2011), Japan Soc. Clin. Oncology (pres. 2005-09), Japan Surg. Soc. (pres. 2006-07), Liver Cancer Study Group Japan (pres. 2007—08), Japanese Assn. Med. Scis. (v.p. 2010-), Cancer Control Promotion Coun. (chmn. 2011-). Avocations: opera, classical music, golf. Home: 4-3-4 Midoricho Ashiya Hyogo 659-0042 Japan Office: Osaka Univ 1-1 Yamadaoka Suita Osaka 565-0871 Japan

MONDINO, BARTLY J., ophthalmologist; b. Sacramento, May 24, 1945; married; children: Kara, Kristen. BA in Med. Scis., Stanford U., 1967, MD, 1971. Diplomate Am. Bd. Ophthalmology. Intern Stanford (Calif.) U. Hosp., 1971-72; ophthalmology resident N.Y. Hosp., Cornell U., NYC, 1972-75; fellow in cornea, external disease U. Pitts. Sch. Medicine - Eye and Ear Hosp., Pitts., 1975-76, asst. prof. ophthalmology, 1976-79, assoc. prof. ophthalmology, 1979-82; dir. Charles T. Campbell Microbiology Lab. Eye and Ear Hosp., Pitts., 1978-82; assoc. prof. ophthalmology UCLA - Jules Stein Eye Inst., LA, 1982-83, prof. ophthalmology, 1983—, Wasserman Endowed chair dept. ophthalmology, 1988—; chief cornea-external disease divsn. UCLA, 1991-99, chmn. dept. ophthalmology, 1994—; dir. UCLA - Jules Stein Eye Inst., 1994—; with exec. program for acad. healthcare mgmt. The John E. Anderson Grad. Sch. Mgmt./UCLA, 1992. Bd. dirs. Charles R. Drew U. of Medicine and Sci., L.A., Braille Inst., L.A.; mem. adv. com. Rsch. Study Club, Murrieta, Calif., 1994—, scientific adv. panel on ophthalmology Calif. Med. Assn., San Francisco, 1994—. Editl. bd.: Am. Jour. Ophthalmology, Chgo., 1992—, ophthalmic Surgery and Lasers, 1995—, Ophthalmology Times, 1996—, Ophthalmic Practice (Can.), 1996—; editor-in-chief: EYE Newsletter, 1994—; co-chair corneal diseases program planning panel of Nat. Eye Inst.'s Vision Rsch. Program Planning Subcom., Bethesda, md., 1997—, others. Recipient scholarship Stanford U. Sch. Medicine, Rsch. to Prevent Blindness Manpower award 1983-84, Rsch. to Prevent Blindness Sr. Scientific Investigator's award 1994, various lectureships, others. Mem. AMA, Assn. for Rsch. in Vision and Ophthalmology, Assn. Univ. Profs. of Ophthalmology, Am. Acad. Ophthalmology, Calif. Assn. Ophthalmology, Calif. Cornea Club, Calif. Med. Assn., Contact Lens Assn. of Ophthalmologists, Eye Bank Assn. of Am., L.A. County Med. Assn., L.A. Soc. Ophthalmology, Ophthalmology Rsch. Found., Ophthalmic Surgery and Laser Therapy, Rsch. Study Club. Office: 100 Stein Plz # 2-142 Los Angeles CA 90095-7000 Business E-Mail: mondino@jsei.ucla.edu.

MONDOVÍ, BRUNO, biochemist, educator; b. Verona, Italy, Dec. 27, 1927; s. Arturo and Rosita (Bianchini) M.; m. Anna Maria Vincenti, Dec. 22, 1957; children: Gian Giacomo, Maria Teresa, Stefano Arturo, Debora. Asst. prof. U. Rome, 1951-60, assoc. prof., 1961-69, prof., 1970—2003, prof. emeritus, 2004—. Assoc. prof. U. Camerino, Italy, 1968-69; vis. prof. Yeshiva U., N.Y.C., 1986, U. Quebec, 1995, Polish Acad. Sci., Lodz, Poland, 1996; pres. Copper in Biol. Symposia, 1971-95; co-pres. PQQ-B6 Symposium, Capri, Italy, 1994. Editor: Applied Biochemistry, 1972, Structure and Function of Amine Oxidases, 1985, Selective Heat Sensitivity of Cancer Cells, 1977, Copper Amineoxidases Structure Catalitic Mechanisms and Role in Pathophysiology, 2009; co-patentee Amine Oxidases Inhibitors, Single Step Purification of Ceruloplasmin, a plant histaminase in the treatment of allergic and septic shock and in allergic asthma; contbr. over 397 papers to sci. publs. Recipient Roentgen award Accademia Lincei, 1987, Feltrinelli award, 1989. Mem. Inst. Applied Biochemistry (bd. dirs. 1970-86), Italian Biochemistry and Molecular Biology Soc. (bd. dirs. 1983-86), N.Y. Acad. Scis. (emeritus mem.), Am. Chem. Soc(emeritus mem.), Polish Histamine Rsch. Soc. (hon.), European Histamine Rsch. Soc. (hon.). Office: U Rome Dept Biochem Scis Univ La Sapienza P Le Aldo Moro 5 00185 Rome Italy Home: Via Giovanni Severano 1 161 Rome RM Italy Office Phone: 390649910449. Business E-Mail: bruno.mondovi@uniroma1.it.

MONEGRO, FRANCISCO, alternative medicine consultant, psychology professor; b. La Vega, Dominican Republic, Apr. 20, 1949; s. Francisco Monegro-Fdez and Ana A. (Pena) Monegro. Grad. cum laude, Pontifical U., Santiago, Dominican Republic, 1973; grad. psychology, Autonomous U. Santo Domingo, 1978, MD, 1986; MA in Ednl. Psychology, Tech. Inst. Santo Domingo, 1981; PhD in Nutrition, LaSalle U., Mandeville, La., 1993. Cert. natural health profl., hypnotherapist, profl. biofeedback profl.; diplomate in behavioral medicine, diplomate in pain mgmt.; lic. in psychology Autonomous U. Santo Domingo, 1978. Tchr. Peace H.S., Santo Domingo, Dominican Republic, 1975-76; dir. dept. psychology Holy Trinity Ednl. Ctr., Santo Domingo, 1978-80; prof. Sch. Medicine Tech. Inst. Santo Domingo, 1986-87; dir. dept. psychology Interam. U., Santo Domingo, 1988-89; prof. psychology and medicine Autonomous U. Santo Domingo, 1978-89, psychologist, counseling dept., 1979-84; staff mem. spl. edn. Bd. Edn. Dist. X, Bronx, NY, 1991-93; founder, chmn. N.Y. Inst. for Holistic Life, NYC, 1991—; prof. psychology CUNY at HCC, Bronx, 1990—. Founder, pioneer in behavioral medicine Behavioral Medicine Clinic, Santo Domingo, 1987-94. Author: Biofeedback-Bio-retroalimentacion, 1988, Holistic Behavioral Medicine, 1993, Biomagnetic Medicine: Secrets and Power of Magnetic Energy, 1996, Psychology and Life Mind, Body and Society, 1997, Commonly Prescribed Psychiatric Drugs. A Guide for Clinicians and Care Takers, 2003, A Guidebook for Behavioral Evaluators, 2003, (interactive CD-ROMs) Psychology and Life, 2000, Developmental Aphasia, 2002, Commonly Prescribed Psychiatric Drugs. A Guide for Clinicians and Care Takers, 2003, A Guide for Behavioral Evaluators, 2003; editor, pub.: BOEST, 1978, Dominican Bull. Behavioral Medicine, 1987, Holistic Life/Vida Holistica, 1991, others. Mem. Dominican Psychol. Assn. (treas. 1978-79), Soc. Behavioral Medicine, Assn. for Advancement of Behavior Therapy, Am. Acad. Pain Mgmt., Assn. for Applied Psychophysiology and Biofeedback. Democrat. Roman Catholic. Avocations: golf, basketball, swimming, travel, computers. Home: PO Box 302 Bronx NY 10458-0302 Office: NY Inst for Holistic Life 976 Mclean Ave Ste 370 Yonkers NY 10704-4105 Office Phone: 917-783-2431. Personal E-mail: holisticlife@msn.com.

MONGIN, ALEXANDER ANATOLIEVICH, neuroscientist, educator; b. Minsk, Belarus, Mar. 9, 1965; arrived in U.S., 1997; s. Anatoli I. and Tamara N. Mongin; m. Alena Rudkouskaya, July 22, 1987; children: Feodor, Anton, Katrine. MS, Belarussian State U., 1989; PhD, Acad. Scis. Belarus, 1995. Rsch. fellow Acad. Scis. Belarus, Minsk, 1995-97, sr. scientist, 1997; Fogarty fellow Albany (N.Y.) Med. Coll., 1997-99, asst. prof., 1999—2009, assoc. prof., 2009—. Contbr. chpts. to books, articles to profl. jours. Recipient award Fedn. European Societies Biochemistry, 1995, 1st prize European Soc. Neurochemistry, 1997, prize and medal European Acad., 1997, Career Devel. award APS, 2008; Fogarty fellowship NIH, 1997, Wiggers fellowship, 2005. Mem.: Am. Heart Assn., Am. Soc. Neurochemistry, N.Y. Acad. Scis., Soc. Neuroscience, Am. Physio. Soc. Office: Albany Med Coll MC136 47 New Scotland Ave Albany NY 12208 Business E-Mail: MonginA@mail.amc.edu.

MONHEIT, ALAN GOODMAN, obstetrician, gynecologist; b. Phila., Apr. 5, 1949; s. Richard S. and Jane G. Monheit; children: Robin, Jeffrey, Daniel. BSc, Muhlenberg Coll., 1971; MD, U. Pa., 1975. Intern U. Calif., San Diego, 1975-76, resident physician dept. ob-gyn., 1975-79, fellow, maternal/fetal medicine, 1979-81; attending physician U. Hosp., Stony Brook, 1981—; clin. assoc. prof. SUNY, Stony Brook, 1981—. Tchr. medicine, specialist in high risk pregnancy SUNY, Stony Brook, 1981—. Contbr. articles to profl. jours. Recipient Tchg. award Coun. on Resident Edn. in Ob-gyn., 1997. Mem. ACOG, Assn. Profs. Ob-Gyn., Soc. Perinatal Obstetricians (poster prize 1987), Suffolk County Ob-Gyn. Soc., Phi Beta Kappa. Avocations: bicycling, hiking, space exploration, meteorology. Office: SUNY Dept Obstetrics Gynecology HSC T-9 Stony Brook NY 11794 Office Phone: 631-444-7650.

MONJAN, ANDREW ARTHUR, retired neuroscientist; b. NYC, Feb. 9, 1938; s. Victor Momjian and Sonia (Sherinian) Dardarian; m. Susan Vollenweider, July 1961 (div. Nov. 1965); m. Usha Bose, Aug. 14, 1969; children: Matthew, Vanessa. BSc, Rensselaer Poly. Inst., 1960; PhD, U. Rochester, 1965; MPH, Johns Hopkins U., 1970. Rsch. asst. Sterling-Winthrop Rsch. Inst., Rensselaer, NY, 1960; USPHS rsch. fellow Ctr. for Brain Rsch. U. Rochester, NY, 1964-66; asst. prof. depts. psychology and physiology U. Western Ont., London, Canada, 1966-69; from asst. prof. to assoc. prof. dept. epidemiology Sch. Hygiene and Pub. Health Johns Hopkins U., Balt., 1971-83; expert epidemiology extramural programs br. NIH, Bethesda, Md., 1983-85, chief neurobiology/immunology programs physiology aging br., 1985-87, acting assoc. dir., 1987, chief neurobiology, 1987—2009; exec. sec. Nat. Commn. on Sleep Disorders Rsch., 1990-92. Presenter in field. Contbr. articles to profl. jours. N.Y. State Regents scholar, 1955-59; N.Y. State Regents Grad. Tchg. fellow, 1960-62, USPHS rsch. fellow, 1962-64, 69-70. Personal E-mail: amonjan@verizon.net.

MONK, SUSAN MARIE, pediatrician, educator; d. John Spotz and Mary Elizabeth (Shelly) M.; m. Jaime Pacheco, June 5, 1971; children: Benjamin Joaquin, Maria Cristina. AB, Colby Coll., Waterville, Maine, 1967; MD, Jefferson Med. Coll., Phila., 1971. Diplomate Am. Bd. Pediatrics. Pediatrician Children's Med. Ctr., Dayton, Ohio, 1975—; asst. clin. prof. pediat. Wright State U., Dayton, 1976—83, assoc. clin. prof. pediat., 1983—2000, asst. prof. pediat., 2000—08, assoc. proff. pediat., 2008—. Mem. bd. dirs. Children's Med. Ctr., Dayton, 1991-96, chief-of-staff, 1992-94. Mem. Am. Acad. Pediatrics, We. Ohio Pediatric Soc., Pediatric Ambulatory Care Soc., Academic Pediat. Assn. Avocations: reading, gardening, travel, movies, theater. Office: Childrens Health Clinic 730 C Valley St Dayton OH 45404-1845 Office Phone: 937-641-5355.

MÖNKÄRE, SINIKKA, physician; b. Sippola, Finland, Mar. 6, 1947; m. Juha Laisaari, 1996; 2 children. MD in Medicine and Surgery, U. Turku, 1973. Asst. physician Salo Regl. Hosp., Finland, 1973-74; health ctr. physician City of Turku, 1974-75; ward physician Imatra Regl. Hosp., 1975-77; asst. sr. physician Tiuru Hosp., 1977-85; specialist occupl. lung disease, 1985-91; mem. Finnish Parliament Govt. of Finland, Helsinki, 1987—91, 1995—2005; asst. sr. physician Imatra Health Ctr., Kymi, 1991—95; min. Ministry Environ. (housing and bldg.), 1995—99; min. social affairs and health Govt. of Finland, 1995-99, min. of labour, 1999-2000, min. trade, industry, 2000—03, min. social affairs and health, 2003—05; mng. dir. Raha-automaattiyhdistys. Mem. Imatra City bd., 1981—95, 2005—06, chmn., 1985—86, 1994—95, 2005—06. Democrat. Office: Raha-automaattiyhdistys PL 32 2601 Espoo Finland

MONLLAU, JOAN CARLES, surgeon, educator; b. Tortosa, Tarragona, Oct. 1, 1960; MD, U. Barcelona, 1983, PhD, 1999. Sect. head Hosp. del Mar, 1997—2004, knee unit head, 2004—09, Hosp. de Sant Pau, Inst. U. Dexeus, 2009—. Assoc. prof. U. Barcelona, 1997—2011, prof., 2011—. Grant, Tissue Engring., Macro-porous Synthetic Scaffolds, 8th EFFORT Congress Florence, 2007. Mem.: SLARD, ICRS, ISAKOS, ESSKA, AEA, SECOT. Avocations: skiing, mountain climbing, sailing. Office: St Antoni M Claret 167 Barcelona 08025 Spain Office Fax: 34 93 553 70 33. Business E-Mail: jmonllau@santpau.cat.

MONNET, XAVIER, medical educator; b. Baden-Baden, Germany, June 13, 1971; MD, Paris-6 U., 2000; PhD, Paris-11 U., 2004. Prof. Med. ICU - Bicêtre Hosp., 2002—. Mem.: European Soc. Intensive Care Medicine, Société de réanimation de langue française. Office: Bicêtre Hosp 78 rue du Général Lec Le Kremlin-Bicêtre IdF F-94270 France E-mail: xavier.monnet@bct.aphp.fr.

MONNEUSE, OLIVIER JY, surgeon; b. Besancon, Franche Comte, France, Oct. 13, 1971; s. Jean Yves and Marie Jose Monneuse; m. Isabelle Bourgeois, July 22, 2000; children: Agathe children; Charlotte. Degree in Medicine, U. Besancon, France, 1996; MD, Lyon Faculty Medicine, France, 2003; PhD, U. Lyon I, France, 2005. Asst. chief Faculty de Medecine Laennec - Hospices Civils de Lyon, Lyon, France, 2003—06; hosp. practitioner Hospices Civils de Lyon, 2006—; clin. fellow gen. surgery Trauma Program Gen. Surgery, Toronto, Ontario, 2006—; prof. gen. surgery, 2009. Assoc. chief French Union Young Hosp. Surgeons, Paris, 2004—05. Antonin Poncet prize fellowship, 2003. Fellow: Trauma Assn. Can. (assoc.). Office Phone: 33472110102. Business E-Mail: olivier.monneuse@chu-lyon.fr.

MONNO, SATOSHI, physician; b. Toyama, Japan, May 19, 1955; s. Shou-ichi and Satoko Monno; m. Kikuko Matsumoto Monno, May 4, 1984; children: Koyuru, Itaru, Yutaka. MD, Shinshu U. Sch. Medicine, 1980, DMSc, 1984. Instr. medicine Shinshu U. Sch. Medicine, Matsumoto, Japan, 1984; staff Iiyama Red Cross Hosp., 1984—91; instr. medicine Toyama Med. & Pharm. U., Toyama, 1991—93; resident JEfferson Med. Coll., Phila., 1994—96; fellow Northwestern U., Chgo., 1996—98; asst. prof. medicine Juntendo U. Urayasu Hosp., Japan, 1998—2000; clin. rsch. physician Chiba Nishi Gen. Hosp., Matsudo, 2001—. Avocations: travel, fishing. Office: Chiba Nishi Gen Hosp 107-1 Kanegasaku Matsudo 270-2251 Japan E-mail: monno-satoshi@lilly.com.

MONROCHE, ANDRÉ VICTOR JACQUES, physician; b. Saumur, France, May 31, 1941; s. Maurice and Thérèse (Chevreau-Rocheron) M.; m. Bodet-Pasquier, July 8, 1966(dec. Nov. 3, 1998); children: Benoît, Sabine, Hélène, Matthieu; m. Gouarin Christiane, July 30, 2004. MD, Faculté de Médecine, Angers, France, 1970; Degree in Rheumatology, Faculté de Médecine, Paris, 1972. Practice spa medicine Villa Forestier, Aix-les-Bains, France, 1970-72; practice rheumatology and sports medicine Cabinet Med., Angers, 1973—. Author: Eléments de Rhumatologie, 1975, Eau et Sport pour votre Santé, 1988, L'eau et la Forme, 1995, Eloge du Verre d'eau, 1998; co-author: Droit de la Santé ed Masson, 2003; editor Chiron-Paris, 1998; editor-in-chief Cinésiologie, 1980, Internat. Sport Médecine Rev. Mem. Soc. Française de Médecine du Sport (pres. 2001-05), Panathlon Internat.Club d'Angers (founder, pres. 1990), Club of Paris (v.p. 1986, 89, gov. XVII dist. 2006-08), Med. Nat. Savate French Boxing (pres., coun. med. interfiderale sport de combert de confed, 2011, midaille d'or genuene sport). Office: Cabinet Medical 1 rue d'Alsace 49100 Angers France Office Phone: 0033 (0) 241 883535. Business E-Mail: monroche@sport-medical.org.

MONROE, JUDITH ANN, public health service officer; b. Dayton, Ohio, Apr. 4, 1953; m. Robert Lubitz; 3 children. BS, Eastern Ky. Univ., 1975; MD, U. Md., 1983. Residency U. Cin., 1983—86; physician Nat. Health Svc. Corps, Morgan County, Tenn., 1986—90; dir. clinics Ind. U. Dept. Family Med., Indpls., 1990—92; dir. primary care ctr. & family med. residency prog. St. Vincent Hosp. & Health Svc., Indpls., 1992—2005; commr. Ind. Dept. Health, Indpls., 2005—10; dep. dir. Centers for Disease Control & Prevention (CDC), Atlanta, 2010—, dir. state, tribal, local & territorial support, 2010—. Chairwoman Tobacco Prevention and Cessation Exec. Bd.; mem. Ind. Health Info. Exch. Bd.; pres. Assn. State and Territorial Health Officials. Recipient Merit Award, Ind. Hosp. Assn., 2009, McGovern award, 2010, MVP Award, Peyton Manning Children's Hosp., 2011, Governor's Disting. Svc. Medal, State of Ind., 2011; named a Woman of Influence, Indpls. Bus. Journal, 2009; fellow, Eastern Tenn. State U., 1990, U. Wis., 1993. Office: Centers for Disease Control (CDC) 1600 Clifton Rd Atlanta GA 30333 *

MONSAN, PIERRE FRÉDÉRIC, engineering educator; b. Prades, France, June 25, 1948; s. Dominique Jean Monsan and Odile Perez; m. Dominique Augusta Picard, July 1, 1969; children: Elise, Max. Degree in engring, Nat. Inst. Applied Scis., Toulouse, France, 1969, DEng, 1971; DSc, U. Sabatier, Toulouse, 1977. Lectr. Nat. Inst. Applied Scis., Toulouse, 1969—73, asst. prof., 1973—81, prof., 1981—; founder, CSO BioEurope, Toulouse, 1984—89, CEO, 1989—93; prof. Ecole des Mines, Paris, 1993—, French U. Inst., Paris, 2003—. Cons., mem. sci. adv. bds. pharm. and food cos., 1993—; chmn. sci. adv. bd. Region Midi-Pyrenees, France, French Inst. for Brewing and Malting, 2006—. Author: (books) Immobilized Enzymes, 1975, Use of Enzymes in Food Industries, 1982; contbr. articles to profl. jours., chapters to books. Recipient Innovation award, ADERMIP, Toulouse, 1996, Chaptal award, Nat. Soc. Promotion Industry, Paris, 1999, Acad. Palms award, Ministry of Edn., Paris, 2002. Mem.: French Biochemistry Soc., French Microbiology Soc.,

Club Crin Biotech. (chmn. 1993—2003). Achievements include patents in field; development of dermocosmetic products, product for prevention of Type II diabetes. Avocations: horseback riding, downhill skiing, guitar. Home: 22 Chemin de la Gravette 31700 Mondonville France Office: DGBA-INSA 135 Ave de Rangueil 31077 Toulouse France Office Phone: 33 561 559415. Office Fax: 33 569 559400. Business E-Mail: pierre.monsan@insa-toulouse.fr.

MONSANTO, HOMERO ANTONIO, pharmacist; b. San Juan, July 30, 1959; B in Pharmacy, U. PR, 1982; PhD, Purdue U., 1987. Prof. Sch. Pharmacy, U. PR, 1987—2004; outcomes rsch. mgr. Merck, 2004—10, market access leader, 2010—. Bd. dirs. Colegio de Farmaceuticos de PR, 1999—2001; mem. PR Health Care Coun., 2008—. Recipient Abigail Robles award, Colegio de Farmaceuticos de PR, Disting. Young Pharmacist award, Excellence award, Sch. Pharmacy Student Coun. Mem.: Internat. Soc. Pharmacoeconomics & Outcomes Rsch., Am. Pharmacists Assn. Personal E-mail: hmonsanto@cogui.net.

MONSEN, ELAINE RANKER, nutritionist, educator, editor; b. Oakland, Calif., June 6, 1935; d. Emery R. and Irene Stewart (Thorley) Ranker; m. Raymond Joseph Monsen, Jr., Jan. 21, 1959; 1 dau., Maren Ranker Grainger-Monsen. BA, U. Utah, 1956; MS (Mead Johnson grad. scholar), U. Calif., Berkeley, 1959, PhD (NSF fellow), 1961; postgrad. NSF sci. faculty fellow, Harvard U., 1968-69. Dietetic intern Mass. Gen. Hosp., Boston, 1956-57; asst. prof. nutrition, lectr. biochemistry Brigham Young U., Provo, Utah, 1960-63; mem. faculty U. Wash., 1963—, prof. nutrition, adj. prof. medicine, 1976-84, prof. nutrition and medicine, 1984—2004, prof. emeritus, 2004—, chmn. div. human nutrition, dietetics and foods, 1977-82, dir. grad. nutritional scis. program, 1994-99, mem. Council of Coll. Arts and Scis., 1974-78; chmn. Nutrition Studies Commn., 1969-83; bd. dirs. U. Wash. Found., 2007—. Vis. scholar Stanford U., 1971-72; mem. sci. adv. com. food fortification Pan-Am. Health Orgn., São Paulo, Brazil, 1972; tng. grant coordinator NIH, 1976-97. Editor-in-chief Jour. Am. Dietetic Assn., 1983-2003; Editor Emeritus, Jour. Am. Dietetic Assn., 2003—; mem. editorial bd. Coun. Biology Editors, 1992-96; author rsch. papers on lipid metabolism, iron absorption, Research: Successful Approaches, 3rd edit., 2008. Bd. dirs. A Contemporary Theatre, Seattle, 1969-72; trustee, bd. dirs. Seattle Found., 1978-95, vice chmn., 1987-91, chmn., 1991-93; pres. Seattle bd. Santa Fe Chamber Music Festival, 1984-85; mem. Puget Sound Blood Ctr. Bd., 1996-99. Grantee Nutrition Found., 1965-68, Agrl. Rsch. Svc., 1969-84; recipient Disting. Alumnus award U. Utah, F. Fischer Meml. Nutrition Lectr. award, 1988, L.F. Cooper Meml. Lectr. award, 1991, L. Hatch Meml. Lectr. award, 1992, Goble Lectr. award Purdue U., 1997. Fellow: Am. Soc. Clin. Nutrition (sec. 1987—90), Am. Inst. Nutrition; mem.: Wash. Heart Assn. (nutrition coun. 1973—76), Am. Soc. Parenteral and Enteral Nutrition, Soc. Nutriton Edn., Am. Dietetic Assn.

MONTAGNIER, LUC ANTOINE, virologist, researcher; b. Chabris, Indre, France, Aug. 18, 1932; BS, U. Poitiers, France, 1955; MD, U. Paris, 1960. Rsch. asst. Faculty Scis., U. Paris, 1955-60; rsch. officer Nat. Ctr. Sci. Rsch. (CNRS), Paris, 1960-63, rsch. fellow, 1963-67, master rschr., 1967-72, dir. rsch., 1974—98, emeritus dir. rsch.; co-founder, dir. viral oncology unit Inst. Pasteur, Paris, 1972—2000, prof., 1974—2000, head dept. AIDS and Retroviruses, 1990-96, emeritus prof. Staff virus rsch. unit Med. Rsch. Coun., London, 1960—63; rschr. Inst. Virology, Glasgow, Scotland, 1963—64, Inst. Curie, Paris, 1965—72; disting. prof., dir. Ctr. Molecular & Cellular Biology Queens Coll., CUNY, 1997—2001. Co-founder, pres. World Found. AIDS Rsch. & Prevention, 1993—. Decorated Comdr., Legion of Honor France; recipient Albert Lasker award for basic med. rsch., 1986, Gairdner Found. Internat. award, 1987, Papan prize, 1988, King Faisal Found. Internat. prize, Saudi Arabia, 1993, Warrent Alpert prize, Harvard U., 1998, Prince of Asturias award, 2000, Nobel prize in physiology/medicine, 2008. Mem.: Nat. Acad. Medicine, French Acad. Scis. Achievements include co-discovery of the Human Immunodeficiency Virus (HIV). Office: World Found AIDS Rsch and Prevention 1 rue Miollis F 75015 Paris France Office Phone: 33(0)145684545. Business E-Mail: c.resvif@unesco.org. *

MONTAGUE, DROGO K., urologist; b. Alpena, Mich., Dec. 11, 1942; s. Frank Wright and Susan Alice (Kidder) M.; children: Mark Andrew, Lisa Joy. Student, U. Mich., 1960—63, MD cum laude, 1968. Diplomate Am. Bd. Urology. Intern Cleve. Clinic Hosp., 1968-69, resident in gen. surgery, 1969-70, resident in urology, 1970-73; assoc. staff urologist Cleve. Clinic Found., 1973-75, staff urologist, 1975—, head sect. prosthetic surgery, 1981—, urology residence program dir., 1985—2006, dir. Ctr. for Sexual Function, 1987—; prof. surgery Cleve. Clinic Lerner Coll. Medicine Case Western Res. U., 2004—. Trainee cardiovascular rsch. tng. program NIH, 1962-68; trustee Am. Bd. Urology, 1989-95, mem. examination com., 1975-80, examiner cert. exam., 1980-88, rep. to Am. Bd. Med. Specialties, 1989-95. Reviewer various publs. in field; contbr. numerous articles to profl. publs., chpts. to books; editor: Disorders of Male Sexual Function, 1988, Surgical Treatment of Erectile Dysfunction, 1993, Textbook Reconstructive Urologic Surgery, 2008; author audio-visual tapes in field; mem. editl. bd. Jour. Urology. James B. Angell scholar, 1961, 62, Nat. Found. scholar, 1963-68; recipient Russell and Mary Hugh Scott Edn. award, 1989, Iowa Rsch. award, 1967, Parker J. Palmer Courage to Teach award ACGME, 2009, F. Brantley Scott Excellence award, 2011 Fellow ACS; mem. Am. Urolog. Assn. (chmn. sci. exhibits com. North Cen. sect. 1977, mem. residency edn. com. 1979-83, vice chmn. audio visual com. 1989-95, mem. various coms., editor Am. Urolog. Assn. Video Libr. 1995-2000, chmn. audio visual com. 1996-2002, chmn. erectile dysfunction guidelines panel 1999—), Am. Assn. Genitourinary Surgeons, Cleve. Urolog. Soc. (sec.-treas. 1978-80, v.p. 1980-81, pres. 1981-82, 94-95), Soc. for Study of Impotence (pres. 1995), Soc. Urological Prosthetic Surgeons (pres. 2010-2011). Office: Cleve Clinic Glickman Urol & Kidney Inst A/100 9500 Euclid Ave Q10-1 Cleveland OH 44195-0001 Home Phone: 216-831-9937; Office Phone: 216-444-5590. Business E-Mail: montagd@ccf.org.

MONTELLA, JOSEPH M., gynecologist; MD, Jefferson Med. Coll., 1984. Resident, ob-gyn Thomas Jefferson Univ. Hosp., Phila., 1988; fellowship, urogynecology, pelvic reconstructive surgery Univ. Calif., 1989; assoc. prof., dept. Ob-Gyn Jefferson Med. Coll., Phila., dir., divsn. urogynecology, 1989—, med. dir., women's med. specialties, 2003—. Mem.: Am. Urologic Soc. (pres. 2006). Office: Jefferson Med Coll OB/GYN #400 834 Chestnut St Philadelphia PA 19107 Office Phone: 215-955-5577. Office Fax: 215-955-5041. Business E-Mail: joseph.montella@jefferson.edu.

MONTENEGRO, MARY LOURDES, physical therapist; b. Amazonas, Brazil, Dec. 29, 1981; PhD, U. Sao Paulo, 2011. Phys. therapist U. Sao Paulo, 2005—. Mem.: Sexuality Group U. Sao Paulo, Chronic Pelvic Pain Group U. Sao Paulo. Avocation: travel. Office: Bandeirantes 3900 Monte Alegre Ribeirao Preto Sao Paulo 14049-900 Brazil

MONTERO, JOAQUIN LABBE, physician, educator; b. Santiago, Chile, June 16, 1944; MD, Escuela Medicina, Pontificia U. Católica Chile, 1969; MPH, U. NC, Chapel Hill, 1990. Prof. Pontificia U. Católica Chile, 1981—. Recipient Career Excellence award, Facultad Medicina, Pontificia U. Católica Chile, 2008. Fellow: ACP. Avocations: mountain climbing, bonsai. Office: Lira 63 1200 Santiago 99999 Chile Business E-Mail: jmontero@med.puc.cl.

MONTES, LEOPOLDO FELICIANO, dermatologist, educator; b. Buenos Aires, Nov. 22, 1929; came to U.S., 1955, naturalized, 1974; s. Leopoldo A. and Celia (Gaztambide) M.; m. Maria Mercedes Pfeiffer, Nov. 25, 1961; children: Carolina, Mercedes, Ana, Leopoldo, Teresa, William. MD, U. Buenos Aires, 1954; MS, U. Mich., 1959. Intern City of Buenos Aires Hosps., 1954-55; resident in dermatology Pa. Hosp., Phila., 1955-56; resident in dermatology, then instr. U. Mich. Med. Center, Ann Arbor, 1956-60; practice medicine specializing in dermatology Buenos Aires, 1960-63, 82—, Houston, 1963-66, Birmingham, Ala., 1966-81; dermatologist U. Ala., Eye Found.; asst. prof. Baylor U. Coll. Medicine, Houston, 1963—66; mem. faculty U. Ala. Med. Ctr. and Med. Coll. Ala., Birmingham, 1966—, prof. dermatology, 1969—81, assoc. prof. microbiology, 1968—91, prof. emeritus, 1982—; dermatologist Birmingham Dermatology Ctr., 1985—; clin. prof. dermatology U. South Ala., 2002—03; dermatologist Inst. Argentino de Diagnostico & Tratamiento, 1995—. Adj. prof. anatomy Coll. Medicine, U. South Ala., Mobile, 1981-89; adj. prof. large animal surgery and medicine Auburn U. Sch. Veterinary Medicine, 1977—; dir. Dermatology Rsch. Structural Rsch. Ctr., Mobile, 1990—, Vitiligo Unit, 1990; cons. Johnson & Johnson, Del-Ray Lab., Procter & Gamble, Upjohn Co., Delbay Co., Bayer, Warner, Lambert, Westwood Pharms., Tex. Pharm., Alcon, Owen Lab., Hoffman-La Roche, 1963—; CEO Westhoven Press. Author: Atlas of Skin Diseases of the Horse, 1983, Vitiligo-Nutritional Therapy, 1999, Scanning Electron Microscopy of Normal and Abnormal Skin, 1985, Vitiligo-Current Knowledge and Nutritional Therapy, 2006; founding editor Jour. Cutaneous Pathology, 1973-83. Mem. internat. adv. bd. Nat. Vitiligo Found., 2002—. Recipient Rsch. Career Devel. award USPHS, 1965-70; grantee USPHS, NSF, Kresge Found., John A. Hartford Found., NASA. Fellow Am. Acad. Dermatology, Am. Acad. Microbiology, Royal Coll. Physicians and Surgeons Can. (life); mem. AAAS, Am. Soc. Microbiology, Soc. Investigative Dermatology, Histochem. Soc., Am. Soc. Cell Biology, Am. Fedn. Clin. Rsch., Electron Microscope Soc. Am., Internat. Soc. Tropical Dermatology (Asst. sec. gen. 1969-74), Am. Dermatol. Assn., Am. Soc. Dermatopathology, Nat. Acad. Medicine Buenos Aires (life), Jockey Club Argentina (life), Sigma Xi. Achievements include patents in field. Home: Suipacha 1308 1011 Buenos Aires Argentina Office: Paraguay 2302 1121 Buenos Aires Argentina also: Structural Rsch Ctr 120 Novatan Rd Mobile AL 36608 Home Phone: 54149624289; Office Phone: 011-5411-4962-4684. Fax: 011-5411-4314-4328. Personal E-mail: leopoldo.montes@hotmail.com.

MONTESERÍN, ROSA, physician; b. Lleida, Spain, May 11, 1960; MD, U. Zaragoza, 1983; PhD, U. Autónoma Barcelona, 2010. Family phisician Inst. Català de La Salut, 1992—2001, bd. dir. 1996—2001; family phisician EAP Sardenya. Servei Català de La Salut, 2001—. Cons. tuor Ud- Aceba, 2004—. Recipient Rsch. award, Catalan Soc. Family Medicine & Cmty., Spanish Soc. Family Medicine & Cmty., Profl. Excellence award, Med. Assn. Barcelona. Mem.: Spanish Soc. Geriatry & Gerontology, Spanish Soc. Family Medicine & Cmty., Catalan Soc. Family Medicine & Cmty. Avocations: reading, swimming, travel. Office: Sardenya 466 Barcelona 08025 Spain Office Fax: 34 93 567 43 81. Business E-Mail: rmonteserin@eapsardenya.cat.

MONTETE, PHILIPPE, urologist; b. Neuilly sur seine, France, Nov. 20, 1953; s. Pierre and Claude Montete; m. Joëlle Lorans, May 8, 1982; children: Laurent, Claire, Pauline. BS, U. Paris, 1970, PhD, 1985, degree in Anatomy, 1986, PhD, 2002. Tchr. anatomy U. Paris, 1980—88; surgeon French Hosps., Pontoise, Val d'Oise, France, 1989—; intern Paris Hosps., 1979—85. Head clinicals Paris Hosps., 1985—89. Roman Catholic. Achievements include research in treatment of genito-urinary prolapses using synthetic prothesis. Avocations: flying, bridge, piano. Office: Centre Hosp Rene Dubos 6 ave L'ile France 95201 Pontoise France Office Fax: + 33 1 30 75 53 84; Home Fax: + 33 1 47 50 91 97. Personal E-mail: ph.montete@wanadoo.fr.

MONTGOMERY, DENISE KAREN, nurse; b. NYC, Dec. 23, 1951; d. Thomas Cornell and Dorothy Marie (Castine) Simons; m. Timothy Bruce Montgomery, July 19, 1974 (div. Feb. 1981); m. Joseph Samuel Montgomery, Aug. 20, 1983. A in Nursing, San Jacinto Coll., 1971. RN, Tex. Charge nurse Aarons Womens Clinic, Houston, 1977; rsch. asst. dept. ob-gyn. Baylor Coll. Medicine, Houston, 1977-81, nursing supr., 1979-81, program coord. population control program, 1979-81; nurse Dr. Eric J. Haufrect, Houston, 1982-83; office mgr., supr. Dr. Samuel Law, Houston, 1983-84, Dr. J.S. Montgomery III, 1987—. Contbr. articles to profl. jours. Recipient Disting. Pub. Svc. award Am. Heart Assn., 1976; numerous rsch. grants. Mem. Nat. Assn. Coll. Ob-Gyn. Republican. Mem. Christian Ch. Home: 8202 N Tahoe Dr Houston TX 77040-1256 Office Phone: 281-955-5330. E-mail: denmnt@hotmail.com.

MONTGOMERY, JOHN RICHARD, pediatrician, educator; b. Burnsville, Miss., Oct. 24, 1934; s. Guy Austin and Harriet Pauline (Owens) M.; m. Dottye Ann Newell, June 26, 1965; children: John Newell, Michelle Elizabeth. BS, U. Ala., 1955, MD, 1958. Cert. Am. Bd. Pediat. Intern U. Miss., Jackson, 1958-59, resident in pediat., 1959-60, Baylor Coll. Medicine, Houston, 1960-61, fellow in pediat. infectious diseases and immunology, 1964-66, asst. prof. pediat., 1966-70, assoc. prof., 1970-75; chief pediat. programs U. Ala. Sch. Medicine, Huntsville, 1975-95, prof., 1975-97, prof. emeritus, 1997—. Bd. dirs. State Bd. Health, Ala. Bd. Med. Examiners; adv. com. Ala. EMS for Children. Contbr. articles to books and profl. jours. With AUS, 1961—62, Korea, ret. col. USAR, 1999. Mem. Soc. Pediat. Rsch., Am. Assn. Immunologists, Infectious Diseases Soc., N.Y. Acad. Scis., Am. Acad. Pediats. (pres. Ala. chpt. 1991-93), Sigma Xi, Phi Beta Kappa. Achievements include assisting in development of germ-free invironmental bubble to protect patient with no natural immunity (patient later subject of movie The Boy in the Plastic Bubble, 1976 and PBS documentary on American Experience, 2006). Home Phone: 256-883-9029; Office Phone: 256-551-4600. Personal E-mail: dnjrmont@bellsouth.net.

MONTGOMERY, OWEN C., obstetrician, gynecologist, educator; m. Kimberly Montgomery; 6 children. BA, Yale U.; MD, Hahnemann U., 1981. Diplomate Am. Bd. Ob-Gyn., 1987, Am. Bd. Ob-Gyn.-urogynecology, Am. Bd. Ob-Gyn.-gynecology. Pres. Phila. Obstetrical Soc.; mem. exec. bd. ACOG; chief resident in ob-gyn. Jefferson Med. Coll., Phila., fellow in ob-gyn.; dir. spl. projects for clin. care assocs. Univ. Pa. Hosp.; asst. prof. SUNY, Allegheny Univ. of Health Sciences; clin. asst. prof. Thomas Jefferson Univ. Hosp., Pa. Univ., 1998; chmn. dept. ob-gyn. Drexel Univ. Co-author: (papers) Maternal Varicella History as a Factor in Maternal Varicella Antibody Status, Massive Fetal Maternal Hemorrhage Treated by Percutaneous Umbilical Blood Transfusion, CO2 Response in Pregnant Women after Intrathecal Narcotics. Recipient Lang award for Academic Excellence, J. Marion Sims award, 1985, Franklin award, 1990; named one of Top Doctors, Phila. mag., 2011. Mem.: North Am. Soc. for Pediat. and Adolescent Gynecology, Phila. Obstetrical Soc., Am. Urogynecology Soc., ACOG. Office: Hahnemann University Hospital Broad and Vine Philadelphia PA 19102 Office Phone: 215-762-7000. Office Fax: 215-762-8109.

MONTGOMERY, PAUL G., sports association administrator; b. Sydney, Mar. 24, 1966; PhD, Griffith U., 2010. Sport sci. coord. St Kilda Football Club, 2007—. Office: East Rd Seaford Melbourne Victoria 3198 Australia Business E-Mail: paulm@saints.com.au.

MONTGOMERY, ROBERT AVERY, transplant surgeon; b. Buffalo, Jan. 22, 1960; MD, U. Rochester, 1987; PhD, Oxford U., Eng.; DSc honoris causa, St. Lawrence U. Intern John Hopkins Hosp., Balt., 1987—88, resident, 1988—89, fellow, 1997, asst. surgeon, 1995—97; assoc. prof. surgery John Hopkins Univ. and Hosp., Balt., dir., Incompatible Kidney Transplant Program, chief, divsn. transplantation, dir., Comprehensive Transplant Ctr., 2003—. Pres., med. advisor Montgomery Heart Found. for Cardiomyopathy. Fulbright Scholar, Thomas J. Watson Fellow. Mem.: Alpha Omega Alpha, Phi Beta Kappa. Achievements include being part of the team that performed the world's first live donor kidney removal using minimally invasive techniques; led the team that performed the first triple domino kidney transplant in 2005; being part of the team the performed historic domino donor quintuple kidney transplant in 2006; led the team that performed the first 6-way kidney transplant in 2008; considered a world's expert on kidney transplantation for highly-sensitized and ABO incompatible patients; led the team that removed a donor kidney through the vagina for the first time in 2009; orchestrated nation's first multi-center six-way kidney transplant involving 12 patients at three different hospitals, nine surgeons and a team of nearly 100 people in 2009. Office: Johns Hopkins Comprehensive Transplant Ctr Incompatible Kidney Transplant Program 720 Rutland Ave Turner 76 Baltimore MD 21205

MONTGOMERY, THEODORE ASHTON, physician; b. LA, Oct. 27, 1923; s. Wayne A. and Hazel (Osmer) M. MD, U. So. Calif., 1947; MPH cum laude, Harvard U., 1955. Diplomate: Am. Bd. Preventive Medicine, Am. Bd. Pediatrics. Intern Los Angeles County Gen. Hosp., 1946-48; intern L.A. Children's Hosp., 1948, resident, 1950-51, St. Louis Children's Hosp., 1951-52; asst. in pediatrics Washington U., St. Louis, 1951-52; instr. pediatrics U. So. Calif., 1952-55, practice medicine specializing in pediatrics, LA, 1952-54; lectr. pub. health U. Calif., Berkeley, 1960-83. Cons. child health Calif. Dept. Pub. Health, 1954-60, chief maternal and perinatal health, 1960-61, acting chief bur. maternal and child health, 1961-63, asst. chief div. preventive med. services, 1963-66, chief, 1966-68, chief preventive medicine program, 1968-69, dep. dir. of Dept., 1969-73; mem. mental retardation projects rev. com. USPHS, 1965-66, charter mem. surgeon gen.'s adv. com. on immunization practices, 1964-66; mem. task force on alcoholism, drug and narcotic abuse Calif. Commn. on Criminal Justice, 1968-70; chief div. disease control Alameda County Health Care Svcs. Agy., 1973-74; cons. maternal and child health Calif. Dept. Health, Berkeley, 1974-78; chief maternal and child health br. No. Calif. Regional Office, Calif. Dept. Health Svcs., 1978-83; WHO fellow med. care adminstrn., Europe, 1966; co-chmn. Calif. Inter-agy. Council on Tb, 1966-72; vice chmn. Calif. Drug Rsch. Adv. Panel, 1969-70; participant White House Conf. Mental Retardation, 1963, White House Conf. on Mental Retardation Cmty. Ctrs., 1965; Gov's. chmn. Calif. Regional Hemodialysis Rev. Com., 1968-73; exec. sec. Gov.'s Population Study Commn., 1966; mem. com. on Tb, Calif. Lung Assn., 1973-74 Author: (with others) Standards and Recommendations for Public Prenatal Care, 1960, Guide to Hearing Testing of School Children, 1961; contbr. articles to med. jours. Bd. dirs. Calif. Interagy. Coun. on Family Planning, 1970-73; chmn. Calif. State Interdepartmental Com. on Food and Nutrition, 1977-79, pres. Clan Montgomery Soc. Internat., 1981-84, regional commr., 1985-91. With M.C. AUS, 1948-50. Fellow Am. Acad. Pediatrics (chmn. Calif. com. Indian health 1973-76, mem. nat. com. on Indian health 1963-79, vice chmn. 1977-79), Am. Pub. Health Assn. (chmn. task force on population policy 1971-72); mem. Alpha Epsilon Delta, Delta Omega. Home: 85 Wildwood Gdns Piedmont CA 94611-3831

MONTGOMERY, THOM MATHEW, health program administrator, counselor; b. Delaware, Okla., Dec. 30, 1942; s. Francis Thomas and Ellen Grace (Whelan) M.; m. Dinah Lee Hicks, Feb. 4, 1961 (div. 1964); 1 child, Laura Diane; m. A.N.D. Miller (dec. 2006); 1 child, Raymond Hunter. Degree, Highlands U., 1966; student, Tulsa U., 1961-64, U. Calif., Irvine, 1980-81, Glenn U., Dublin, Ireland, 1993—2002. Brokerage mgr. John Hancock Life Ins. Co., Boston, 1964-70; mng. editor Renown Publs., Reseda, Calif., 1970-77; publs. dir. Am. Pub. Health Found., Corona Del Mar, Calif., 1977-79; program adminstr. Life Plus Martin Luther Hosp., Anaheim, Calif., 1979-92; dir. rsch. Brookside Inst., Irvine, Calif., 2001—09. Pres. Montgomery Counseling Assocs., Tustin, 1986—. Author: Ennobled Blood: The Heiresses of Monkstown Castle, 2002, Naltrexone: Pulling Back the Curtain, 2004; contbr. articles to profl. jours. Founding mem. Task Force on Alcohol & Drug Abuse for Disabled, Orange County, 1981, bd. dirs. Mid Valley Cmty. Police Coun. Fellow Am. Pub. Health Found.; mem. Nat. Assn. Alcohol and Drug Abuse Counselors, Internat. Assn. Alcohol and Drug Abuse Counselors, Calif. Assn. Alcohol and Drug Abuse Counselors. Republican. Presbyn. Avocations: chess, hiking, swimming, poetry. Office: 16587 Brookhurst St Fountain Valley CA 92708 Home: 31656 Chaparral Way Lake Elsinore CA 92532 Office Phone: 310-413-4672. Business E-Mail: thom@thommont.com.

MONTGOMERY RICE, VALERIE, dean, reproductive endocrinologist, infertility specialist, medical educator; BS in Chemistry, Ga. Inst. Tech., 1983; MD, Harvard U., 1987. Intern Dept. Gynecology and Obstetrics Emory U. Sch. Medicine and Affiliated Hospitals, Atlanta, 1987—88, resident, 1988—91; fellowship reproductive endocrinology and infertility Hutzel Hosp., Detroit, 1991—93; clin. instr. Wayne State U., 1991—93; asst. prof. U. Kans. Sch. Medicine, Kansas City, 1993—97, vice chmn. Dept. Obstetrics and Gynecology, 1996—97, med. dir. Clin. Trials Divsn., Clin. Rsch. Inst., 1996—97, divsn. head reproductive endocrinology and infertility, 1998—2003; sr. staff physician Divsn. Reproductive Endocrinology Henry Ford Med. Ctr., Troy, Mich., 1997—98; assoc. prof., dir. Divsn. Reproductive Endocrinology and Infertility U. Kans. Med. Ctr., 1998—2003; prof., chair Dept. Obstetrics and Gynecology Meharry Med. Coll., Nashville, 2003—06, program dir. OB-GYN Residency Training Program, 2004—06, Joy McCann prof., 2004—06, exec. dir. Ctr. for Women's Health Rsch., 2005—, prof., 2006—, sr. v.p. health affairs, dean Sch. Medicine, 2006—09; prof. radiology, clin. prof. obstetrics and gynecology Vanderbilt U. Med. Ctr., Nashville, 2006—11; dean, exec. v.p. Morehouse Sch. Medicine, Atlanta, 2011—. Chair Wal-Mart Healthcare Insights Panel, 2007—; mem. Nat. Aids Fund Bd. Trustees, 2007—, chair Every Life Matters, Every Dollar Counts Campaign, 2009—; mem. FDA Panel for Reproductive and Urological Drugs; spkr. in field. Contbr. articles to med. jours. Recipient John D. Thompson Resident Rsch. Day First Place Award, Emory U., 1989, 1991, Michelle Marrs Vision Award, Matthew Walker Comprehensive Health, 2005, Bridge of Honor Award, Women in NAACP, 2006, YM Acad. for Women of Achievement Award, 2007, Disting. Svc. Award, NAACP, 2007, Tenn. Ladies of Distinction Svc. Award, 2007, Dr. Dorothy Brown Humanitarian Award, Minerva Found., Delta Sigma Theta Sorority, 2008, Freedom's Sister Awardee, Ford Found., 2010, Nat. Nefertiti Award, Nat. Societas Docta, Inc., 2010, Multicultural Women's Legacy award, Working Mother Media, 2011; Commonwealth Fund Med. Fellowship, 1986—87, Nat. Med. Fellowship, 1986—87. Fellow: American Coll. of Obstetrics and Gynecology; mem.: AMA, Internat. Women's Forum, Ctrl. Assn. Obstetricians and Gynecologists, North American Menopause Soc., Nat. Med. Assn., Clay-Platte County Med. Soc., Kansas City Med. Soc., Kansas City Gynecological Soc., American Med. Women's Assn. (Elizabeth Blackwell Award 2011), Soc. Reproductive Endocrinology and Infertility, Soc. Gynecological Investigation, American Soc. Reproductive Medicine, Aesculapian Club of Harvard Med. Sch., Omicron Delta Kappa. Office: Morehouse School of Medicine 720 Westview Dr SW Atlanta GA 30310 Office Phone: 404-752-1720. Office Fax: 404-752-1594. *

MONTI, LOUIS, pediatrician, educator; MD, Mt. Sinai Sch. Medicine, 1980. Diplomate Am. Bd. Pediatrics. Resident in pediat. Mt. Sinai Hosp., NY, 1980—83; fellow in infectious disease Childrens Hosp., Los Angeles, Calif., 1983—84; asst. clin. prof. pediat. Mt. Sinai Sch. Medicine; pediatrician Mt. Sinai Med. Ctr. Office: Mount Sinai Medical Center 55 E 87th St Ste 1G New York NY 10128 Office Phone: 212-722-0707. Office Fax: 212-987-1949.

MONTICONE, MARCO, physiatrist; b. Asti, Italy, Nov. 8, 1973; s. Lorenzo Monticone and Lilia Barbero; m. Barbara Rocca, Apr. 23, 2005; children: Lorenzo, Martina. Degree in Medicine, Medicine Sch., Pavia, 1998; degree in Phys. Medicine and Rehab. Specialization, Phys. Medicine and Rehab. Sch., Pavia, 2002. Physiatrist Salvatore Maugeri Found., Milan, 2007—08, head rehabilitative operative unit, 2008—. V.p. Lions Club Regisole Internat., Pavia, 1998—. Office: Salvatore Maugeri Found Monsignor Bernasconi 16 Milan 20035 Italy Business E-Mail: marco.monticone@fsm.it.

MONTO, ARNOLD SIMON, epidemiology educator; b. Bklyn., Mar. 22, 1933; s. Jacob and Mildred (Kaplan) M.; m. Ellyne Gay Polsky, June 15, 1958; children: Sarah D. Monto Maniaci, Jane E., Richard L., Stephen A. BA in Zoology, Cornell U., Ithaca, NY, 1954; MD, Cornell U., NYC, 1958. Diplomate Am. Coll. Epidemiology. Intern, asst. resident in medicine Vanderbilt U. Hosp., Nashville, 1958—60; USPHS postdoctoral fellow in infectious disease Stanford U. Med. Ctr., Palo Alto, Calif., 1960—62; mem. staff virus diseases sect. mid. Am. rsch. unit Nat. Inst. Allergy and Infectious Disease, Panama, 1962—65; assoc. prof. U. Mich. Sch. Pub. Health, Ann Arbor, 1965—76, prof., 1976—, chmn. dept. population planning and internat. health, 1993—97, dir. Ctr. for Population Planning, 1993—97, dir. U. Mich. Bioterrorism Preparedness Initiative, 2002—04. Vis. scientist Clin. Rsch. Ctr., Northwick Park Hosp., Harrow, Eng., 1976; scholar-in-residence bd. on sci. and tech. for internat. devel. NAS and Inst. Medicine, Washington, 1983-84; vis. scientist div. communicable diseases WHO, Geneva, 1986-87; mem. pulmonary diseases adv. com. Nat. Heart, Lung and Blood Inst., Bethesda, Md., 1979-83; mem. nat. adv. coun. Nat. Inst. Allergy and Infectious Diseases, Bethesda, 1989-93; mem. WHO Influenza Pandemic Task Force, 2006—. Contbr. articles to med. jours. Recipient career devel. award NIH. Fellow Am. Coll. Epidemiology, Infectious Diseases Soc. Am.; mem. APHA (governing coun. 1978-80), Am. Epidemiol. Soc. (pres. 2004-05). Achievements include research on respiratory viral infections in the community; demonstration of effectiveness of influenza vaccine in severe disease in the elderly; prevention of spread of influenza virus and treatment of illness, occurrence, causes and treatment of common cold. Office: U Mich Sch Pub Health I 109 Observatory St Ann Arbor MI 48109-2029 Office Phone: 734-764-5453. Business E-Mail: asmonto@umich.edu. *

MONTONEY, MARK R., medical officer; BA in Psychology magna cum laude, Case Western Res. U., Cleve.; MBA, Regent U., Virginia Beach, VA; MD, U. Cin. Cert. in internal medicine and geriatric medicine. Practiced, internal medicine & geriatric medicine, 1986—98; med. dir., primary care Riverside Meth. Hosp., chief resident, internal medicine, v.p., quality & clin. support, 2000—05; v.p., physician consulting OhioHealth Corp., system v.p. & chief med. officer, 2005—08; exec. v.p., chief med. officer Vanguard Health Sys., Inc., 2008—. Past chmn. Ohio Partnership for Excellence; examiner Malcolm Baldrige Nat. Quality award; bd. mem. Tenn. Ctr. for Performance Excellence Recipient Malcolm Baldrige Quality award. Mem.: Am. Coll. Physician Execs., Phi Beta Kappa Honor Soc. (elected mem. 1978). Office: Vanguard Health System Inc Ste 100 20 Burton Hills Blvd Nashville TN 37215 Office Phone: 615-665-6000. Office Fax: 615-665-6099. Business E-Mail: mmontoney@vanguardhealth.com. *

MONTORSI, MARCO, surgeon, educator; b. Milan, Jan. 14, 1954; s. Walter Montorsi and Leopoldina Ferrari; m. Antonella Ferro, Apr. 23, 1983; children: Alberto, Ilaria. Degree in Medicine, U. Milan, 1978. Prof., surgery U. Milan, 2001—. Head dept., surgery Inst. Clinico Humanitas, Rozzano, Italy, 2004—. Fellow: European Surg. Assn. Office: Inst Clinico Humanitas Manzoni 56 Rozzano 20089 Italy Home: Via Carlo Goldoni 39 20129 Milan MI Italy Office Fax: 02 8224 4590. Personal E-mail: marco.montorsi@unimi.it. Business E-Mail: marco.montorsi@humanitas.it.

MONTRESOR, ANTONIO, epidemiologist; b. Milano, Italy, June 10, 1961; s. Gianfranco Montresor and Mariateresa Prometti; m. Maria Terzano, Aug. 3, 1991; children: Francesco, Leonardo, Riccardo, Rocco. MD, U. Milan, 1986; student in Med. Statistic and Epidemiology, U. of Milan, 1997; M in Infectious Diseases, London Sch. Hygiene and Tropical Medicine, 2008; MD. Head pub. health dept. Ngo Cuamm-Italy/Moh Tanzania, 1988—90; assoc. profl. officer World Health Orgn., Geneva, 1994—97, scientist, 2008—; med. officer World Health Org., Switzerland, 1997—2004, pub. health specialist Hanoi, Vietnam, 2004—08, scientist Geneva, 2009—. Author: (book) Helminth Control in School-Age Children, 2002; contbr. over 80 articles to profl. jours. Office: World Health Orgn Appia 20Av Geneva Switzerland Business E-Mail: montresorA@who.int.

MONZON, CARLOS MANUEL, physician; s. Carlos Manuel and Amparo (Letona) Monzon; children: Carlos Rodolfo, Juan Pablo. MD, U. San Carlos, Guatemala, 1976; MSc, U. Minn. Campus, 1982. Diplomate Am. Bd. Pediat., Am. Bd. Pediat. Hematology and Oncology. Resident in pediat. U. San Carlos, 1976-77, U. Mo., Columbia, 1977-80; fellow in pediat. hematology and oncology Mayo Grad. Sch. Medicine, Rochester, Minn., 1980-82; instr. pediat. U. Mo., Columbia, 1982-83, asst. prof. child health, 1983-89; clin. asst. prof. in pediatrics Kansas U. Sch. Medicine, Kans. City, 1992—2003. Contbr. articles to med. jours. Recipient Fritz Kenny Meml. award in pediat. rsch. Midwest Soc. Pediat. Rsch., 1981. Fellow Am. Acad. Pediat. Home: 14201 Melrose St Overland Park KS 66221 Office: 20375 W 151st St Olathe KS 66061-7218

MOOCHHALA, SHABBIR M., pharmacologist, educator, toxicologist, director; b. Mumbai, Dec. 21, 1957; s. Mohammed Y. and Kheroon M. Moochhala; m. Kausar S. Kajiji; 1 child, Zahabia S. BSc with honors, U. Aberdeen, Scotland, 1982; PhD, Dalhousie U., Nova Scotia, Canada, 1986. Assoc. prof. Nat. U. Singapore, 1999—; disting. mem. tech. staff DSO Nat. Labs., Singapore, 2005—. Program dir. DSO Nat. Labs., 2005—. Contbr. articles to profl. jours. Recipient Sandoz award, Basle, Switzerland; grantee Singapore Joint Rsch. grant, European Commn., several conf. fellowships. Achievements include patents for drug delivery system; discovery of role of gases in pathology; development of novel resuscitative fluids. Home: 31 Jalan Baiduri 428402 Singapore Office: DSO Nat Labs 27 Medical Drive 117510 Singapore Singapore Office Fax: 65 64857226; Home Fax: 65 3449723. Personal E-mail: moochhalashabbir@gmail.com. Business E-Mail: mshabbir@dso.org.sg.

MOODY, DIXON MCGUIRE, radiologist; b. Tyler, Tex., Jan. 12, 1937; s. Dwight Lyman Moody and Helen Blaine McGuire; m. Lucinda L. Blitz, Aug. 15, 1964; children: Abigail Ann (Moody) Sinwell, Susan Eloise (Moody) Prieto, Sarah Katherine (Moody) Bialas. MD, U. of Tex. Southwestern, Dallas, 1963. Diplomate Diagnostic Radiology Am. Bd. of Radiology, 1971, Neuroradiology Am. Bd. of Radiology, 1995. Resident physician Stanford U. Sch of Medicine, Palo Alto, Calif., 1963—70; asst. physician Cornell U. Sch of Medicine, NYC, 1970—71; asst. prof. U. of N.Mex Sch Medicine, Albuquerque, 1971—73; prof. and chief of neuroradiology Wake Forest U. Sch. Medicine, Winston-Salem, NC. Mem. Nat. Adv. Coun. NINDS, NIH, Bethesda, Md., 1994—97, Ctr. for Sci. Rev., NIH, Bethesda, Md., 1998—2004; mem., sci. program com. Radiol. Soc. of N.Am., Oak Brook, Ill. Capt. US Army, 1966—67. Decorated Bronze Star Medal US Army; recipient Established Investigator, Clin. Sci. Award, Wake Forest U. Sch. of Medicine, 2002; grantee Jacob K Javits Neurosci. Investigator, NIH, 1984—2008, Clin. Hypotheses in Neuroscience Imaging Rsch., Charles A Dana Found., 1996-1999. Fellow: Am. Coll. of Radiology; mem.: Am. Soc. of Neuroradiology (Outstanding Contributions in Rsch. award 2005), Soc. for Neurosci., Radiol. Soc. of N.Am. (Outstanding Rschr. award 2005), Forsyth Country Club, Cornell Club NY, Hillsboro Club, Alpha Omega Alpha. Achievements include research in Brain injury during heart surgery due to fat emboli; brain hemorrhage in neonates due to rupture of veins; dementia due to obstruction of veins and loss of capillaries; significant vascular disease in Alzheimer's brains; cause and prevention of brain injury during cardiopulmonary bypass. Avocation: tennis. Office: Wake Forest University School Medicine Medical Center Blvd Winston Salem NC 27157-1088 Office Phone: 336-716-2463. Business E-Mail: dmmoody@wfubmc.edu.

MOODY, FRANK G., surgeon; b. Franklin, NH, May 3, 1928; BA, Dartmouth Coll., 1953; attended, Dartmouth Med. Sch., 1952—54; MD, Cornell Univ., 1956. Cert. FACS, 1967, Am. Bd. Surgery, 1980. Asst. prof. Univ. Calif. Med Sch., San Francisco, 1965—66; assoc. prof. through prof. Univ. Ala. Med. Sch., 1966—71; prof., chmn. dept. surgery Univ. Utah Sch. Med., 1971—82; staff surgeon Vet. Adminstrn. Hosp., Salt Lake City, 1971—82; chmn. dept. surgery Univ. Tex. Med. Sch., Houston, 1982—94, Denton A. Cooley prof. surgery, 1982—. Recipient Sci. Achievement award AMA, 1995. Mem.: AMA, Am. Gastroenterological Assn., Am. Pancreatic Assn. (pres. 1979), Am. Physiological Soc., Am. Surgical Assn., Phi Beta Kappa, Alpha Omega Alpha. Office: U Tex Med Sch Dept Surgery 6431 Fannin St Houston TX 77030-1501 Home Phone: 713-664-3047; Office Phone: 713-500-7241. Business E-Mail: frank.g.moody@uth.tmc.edu.

MOODY, JONES OLANREWAJU, pharmacist, educator; b. Egbe, Nigeria, Sept. 3, 1953; PharmB, U. Ife, Nigeria, 1977; PhD, U. London, 1990. Postdoc. fellow Xenova Ltd, 1990—91; sub-dean U. Ibadan, 1992—96, head dept., 2007—09, prof. pharmacognosyand dean, faculty pharmacy, 2009—. Traditiional medicine cons. West African Health Orgn., 2009; coun. mem. Pharmacists Coun. Nigeria, 2009. Fellowship, Japanese Govt. Mem.: Pharm. Soc. Nigeria. Avocations: basketball, reading, travel. Office: Dept Pharmacognosy Ibadan Oyo 200005 Nigeria Personal E-mail: lanmoody@yahoo.com.

MOODY, PATRICIA ANN, psychiatric nurse, small business owner, artist; b. Oceana County, Mich., Dec. 16, 1939; d. Herbert Ernest and Dorothy Marie (Allen) Baesch; m. Robert Edward Murray, Sept. 3, 1960 (div. Jan. 1992); children: Deanna Lee Cañas, Adam James Murray, Tara Michelle Murray, Danielle Marie Murray; m. Frank Alan Moody, Sept. 26, 1992. BSN, U. Mich., 1961; MSN, Washington U., St. Louis, 1966; student, Acad. of Art, San Francisco, 1975-78. RN; lic. coast guard, ocean operator. Psychiat. staff nurse U. Mich., Ann Arbor, 1961-62, Langley-Porter Neuro-Psychiat. Inst., San Francisco, 1962-63; instr. nursing Barnes Hosp. Sch. Nursing, St. Louis, 1963; psychiat. nursing instr. Washington U., St. Louis, 1966-68; psychiat. nurse instr. St. Francis Sch. Nursing, San Francisco, 1970-71; psychiat. staff nurse Calif. Pacific Med. Ctr., San Francisco, 1991-97. Psychiat. staff nurse Charter Heights Behavioral Health Sys., Albuquerque, 1996-97, Nurse Finders, 2002-04; owner, cruise cons. Good Mood Cruises, 1995—. Oil and watercolors included in various group exhbns., 1982-93. V.p. Belles-Fundraising Orgn., St. Mary's Hosp., San Francisco, 1974; pres. PTO, Commodore Sloat Sch., 1982; docent Albuquerque Mus. Art and History, 1998—. Recipient Honor award Danforth Found., 1954, Freshman award Oreon Scott Found., 1958; merit scholar U. Mich., 1957. Mem. Nat. Alliance for Mental Illness (sec. bd. dirs. 2000), San Francisco Women Artists (Merit award for oil painting 1989), Artist's Equity (bd. dirs. No. Calif. chpt. 1987-89, pres. No. Calif. chpt. 1990), Met. Club. Republican. Lutheran. Avocations: hiking, photography, piano, travel, swimming. Home: 219 Spring Creek Ln NE Albuquerque NM 87122-2013 Office: Good Mood Cruises Inc 12231 Acad Rd NE 301-305 Albuquerque NM 87111-3962 Home Phone: 505-856-7419; Office Phone: 800-803-5288, 505-296-6255. Business E-Mail: patmoody@goodmoodcruises.com, cruises@goodmoodcruises.com.

MOODY, ROBERT ADAMS, neurosurgeon; b. Swampscott, Mass., Oct. 1, 1934; s. George F. and Florence P. M.; m. Claudia; children: Robert Adams, II, Cathy, Paul, Lisa, Sherri. BA, U. Chgo., 1955, BS, 1956, MD, 1960. Intern Royal Victoria Hosp., Montreal, Que., Canada, 1960-61; resident in neurosurgery U. Vt. Affiliated Hosps., 1961-66; fellow Lahey Clinic, Boston, 1963-64; asst. prof. neurol. surgery U. Chgo. Med. Sch., 1966-71; sr. clin. instr., then asst. clin. prof. Tufts U. Med. Sch., 1972-74; prof. neurosurgery Abraham Lincoln Med. Sch., U. Ill., Chgo., 1975-81; chmn. div. neurosurgery Cook County Hosp., Chgo., 1974-81, assoc. chmn. dept. surgery, 1976-81; clin. prof. neurosurgery SUNY-Binghamton, 1983—2005; chmn. neurosurgery Guthrie Clinic, Sayre, Pa., 1981-95; ret., 1995. Contbr. articles med. jours. USPHS fellow, 1957-58 Mem. ACS, Am. Assn. Neurol. Surgeons, Pa. Neurosurg. Soc. (councillor 1986-87, pres.-elect 1988, pres. 1989), Mid-Atlantic Neurosurg. Soc., Ctrl. Neurosurg. Soc. (pres. 1978-79), Alumni Assn. Lahey Clinic Found., Sigma Xi. Office: Guthrie Clinic Guthrie Sq Sayre PA 18840 Business E-Mail: rcmoody1@gmail.com.

MOON, CHEOL-HYUN, medical educator; b. Seoul, Republic of Korea, Mar. 14, 1960; s. Sun-Gil Moon and Yeun-Gu Yang; m. Jung-Yeun Kim; children: Jae-Woong, Jae-Duck. PhD, KyungHee U., Seoul, 1996. Cert. DDS Seoul, 1984. Chair person, dept. orthodontics Gachon Med. Sch., Dental Hosp., Namdong-Gu, Inchon, Republic of Korea, 1990—, prof., 1999—. Contbr. articles to numerous med. jours. Office: Gachon Medical Sch Dental Hosp 1198 Guwol-Dong Namdong-Gu Inchon 405-760 Republic of Korea Office Phone: 82-32-460-3881.

MOON, DONG-EON, medical educator; b. Kyeongsangbukdo, Republic of Korea, Dec. 11, 1956; s. Yangsoo Moon; m. Mi Hee Son; children: Youngkwan, Jaewon. Degree, Cath. U. Grad. Sch., Seoul, 1987, PhD, 1988—90. Md Cath. U. Med. Coll., 1984, fellow interventional pain practice World Inst. Pain, 2007. Intern Kangnam St.Mary's Hosp., Seoul, Republic of Korea, 1984—85, resident, 1985—88; clin. fellow Pain Inst., Robertwood Johnson Med. Sch., NJ, 1998—98; assoc. prof. Cath. U. Korea, Seoul, 1999—2004, prof., 2004—, instr., 1988—95, asst. prof., 1995—99; clin. fellow Dept. Pain Clinic, Kantoteishin Hosp., Tokyo, 1993—93; vis. scientist Marine Biomedical Inst., U. Tex. Med. br., Galbeston, 1995—96. Contbr. articles to numerous profl. jours. Recipient Scientic paper, Korean Soc. Aneathesiology, 1996, The Best Staff, Kangnam St. Mary,s Hosp., 2003, Sci. paper, Korean pain Soc., 2005. Fellow: World Inst. Pain, Korean Spine Rsch. Soc. (2001), Korean Pain Rsch. Soc., Korean pain Soc.; mem.: Internat. Assn. Study Pain. Office: Seoul St Mary's Hosp Seochogu Banpodong 505 Seoul 137-040 Republic of Korea Office Phone: 82-2-2258-6150. Office Fax: 82-2-537-1951. Business E-Mail: demoon@catholic.ac.kr.

MOON, HYUN-JOON, urologist; s. Nam-Sik Moon and Jeong-Soon Kim; m. Myoung-Ran Choi; children: Young-Min, Ji-Young. PhD, Chosun U., Gwangju, Republic Of Korea, 1987. Diplomate in urology 1992. Chmn. SCLINIC, Gwangju, 2002—06; chief exec. dir. CR Microsurgery Ctr., Gwangju, 2006—. Chmn. UROVISION, Gwangju, 2003—08. Contbr. articles to profl. jours. Cons. physician Korean Med. Assn., Gwangju, 1998—2008. Capt. Cheongpyung Mil. Hosp., 1993—95. Recipient award, Korea Rep. Med. Technique Korean Ministry Health, Korea Health Industry Devel. Inst., Convenient Real No Scalpel Vasectomy & Minimally Invasive Supermicrosurg. Vasectomy Reversal, Overseas Paper Acad. award, Korean Assn. Urol. Practitioners Pvt. Clinic Fall Acad. Competition, 2010; named one of Great Minds of 21st Century, Am. Biog. Inst., 2008. Mem.: Am. Urol. Assn. Achievements include patents for medical instrument - double ringed clamp for new no-scalpel vasectomy; Korea's Outstanding and Representative Medical procedure- vasectomy sevseral and CRNSV. Home Phone: 821046407585; Office Phone: 82-62-375-6699. Business E-Mail: doctormedi@medimail.co.kr.

MOON, IK-SANG, dentist, educator; b. Kwang-Ju, Republic of Korea, Feb. 26, 1958; s. Jae-Sool Moon and Gooy-Rae Sim; m. Jin-Myo Kim, Sept. 10, 1988; children: Hyun-Ji, Hye-Eun, Hyung-Woo. DDS, Yonsei U. Sch. Dentistry, Seoul, 1984, MS, 1987, PhD, 1993. Registered Korean Dental Assn., 1984. Rsch. instr. Yonsei U. Sch. Dentistry, Seoul, 1990—92, instr., 1992—93, asst. prof., 1993—98, assoc. prof., 1999—2003, prof., 2004—. Dir. dept. periodontology Yongdong Severance Dental Hosp. Yonsei U. Sch. Dentistry, Seoul, 2005—. Office: Yonsei U Sch Dentistry Yongdong Severance Dental Hosp Gangnam-Gu Dogog-Dong Seoul 135-270

Republic of Korea Home: Family Apt 211-504 Songpa-Gu Moonjung-Dong Seoul 138-769 Republic of Korea Office Fax: 822-3463-4052. Business E-Mail: ismoon@yumc.yonsei.ac.kr.

MOON, JAE GON, medical educator, consultant; b. Jinju, Republic of Korea, Nov. 7, 1959; m. Min Young Park; children: Jee Sun, Hee Kyung. MD, Ministry Health & Social, Republic of Korea, 1985; PhD, Gyeongsang Nat. U., Jinju, 2001; attending, Kangnam Sacred Heart Hosp., Republic of Korea, 1999—. Cert. neurosurgeon Ministry of Health and Social, 1990. Prof. Hallym U., Choonchun, Republic of Korea, 2005—. Neurosurg. consulting dr. Korea Pub. Corp. Labor Welfare, Seoul, Republic of Korea, 2006—; mem. spl. trial com. Supreme Ct. Korea, Seoul, 2009—10. Capt., 1991—93, Capital Armed Forces Gen. Hosp., Seoul. Home: Banghwa 5 Danji Apt 501-206 Banghwa-3 Dong Kangseo-gu Seoul 157-785 Republic of Korea Office: Kangnam Sacred Heart Hosp 948-1 Daerim-1-dong Youngdeungpo-gu Seoul 150-951 Republic of Korea Office Fax: 82-2-833-0219. Business E-Mail: moonnsun@chollian.net.

MOON, MARILYN LEE, economist; b. El Dorado, Kans., July 7, 1947; d. Jesse Morris and Shirley Lois M.; m. Douglas Gomery, Jan. 13, 1973. BA in Econs., Colo. Coll., 1969; MS in Econs., U. Wis., 1972, PhD in Econs., 1974. Rsch. assoc. Inst. for Rsch. on Poverty U. Wis., Madison, 1973-74; asst. prof. econs. U. Wis., Milw., 1974-80, assoc. prof. econs., 1980-81; sr. analyst human resources and cmty. devel. divsn. The Congl. Budget Office, Washington, 1981-83; sr. rsch. assoc. Health Policy Ctr. The Urban Inst., Washington, 1983-86; dir. pub. policy inst. AARP, 1986-89; sr. rsch. assoc. The Urban Inst., 1989-94, sr. fellow, 1994—2003; v.p. Am. Insts. for Rsch., 2003—, dir. health program. Cons. The Pepper Commn., 1989. Author: The Meaurement of Economic Welfare: Its Application to the Aged, 1977, Medicare Now and in the Future, 1993, 2d edit., 1996, Medicare: A Policy Primer, 2006; co-author: Balancing Access, Cost and Politics: The American Context for Health System Reform, 1991, Entitlements and the Elderly: Protecting Promises, Recognizing Realities, 1995; editor: Economic Transfers in the United States, vol. 49, 1984; co-editor: Improving Measures of Economic Well-Being, 1977; columnist The Washington Post, 1993-00; contbr. articles to profl. jours. Pub. trustee social security and Medicare trust funds, 1995-00. Ford Found. fellow, 1971-73. Mem. Nat. Acad. Social Ins. (bd. dirs. 1993-00, pres. 2005-), Medicare Rights Ctr. (bd. dirs. 1998, pres. 2005-), Inst. Medicine, Phi Beta Kappa. Avocations: photography, hiking, reading. Office: Am Insts for Rsch 10720 Columbia Pike Silver Spring MD 20901 Home Phone: 301-951-4385; Office Phone: 301-592-2101. E-mail: mmoon@air.org.

MOON, SHIN-YONG, gynecologist, medical educator; b. Kong Ju, Korea, Apr. 1, 1948; MD, Seoul Nat. U. Coll. Medicine, 1977; PhD, Seoul Nat. U. Med. Sch., 1987. Prof. obstetrics & gynecology Seoul Nat. U. Coll. Medicine, 1983—, dir. Inst. Reproductive Medicine & Population, 1999—. Contbr. articles to jour. on human cloning, to profl. jours. Recipient Best Scientist award, South Korean Govt., 2004. Mem.: Korean Soc. Med. Ultrasound (v.p. 1998). Achievements include recognition as member of a team that first cloned human embryos and extracted their stem cells. Office: Seoul Nat U Coll Medicine Dept Obstetrics & Gynecology 28 Yeongeon dong Jongno gu Seoul 110 799 Republic of Korea Office Phone: 760 2384. Office Fax: 765 7082. E-mail: shmoon@plaza.snu.ac.kr. *

MOON, SUNGWOO, medical educator; b. Seoul, Republic of Korea, Jan. 13, 1971; MD, Korea U., PhD, 1996. Assoc. prof. Korea U. Med. Sch., 2009—; chief, emergency dept. Korea U. Ansan Hosp., 2010. Office: Emergency Dept Korea University Ansan City Gyunggido 425-707 Republic of Korea Office Fax: 82-31-412-5315. Business E-Mail: yg9912@korea.ac.kr.

MOON, SURK-SIK, chemistry professor; b. Hapchun, Kyoungnam, Republic of Korea, May 15, 1958; m. Joungrae Ryu, Jan. 27, 1985; children: Cindy Nahae, Jason Hansol. PhD in Chemistry, U. Calif., San Diego, Calif., 1989. Postdoc. U. Hawaii, Manoa, Honolulu, 1989—91; prof. Kongju Nat. U., Chungnam, Republic of Korea, 1992—. Vis. scholar, U. Calif., Davis, 2000—01. Achievements include patents for hanultarin as an anticancer agent. Home: Shinkwandong 5 Gomnaru Apt #101-1505 Kongju Chungnam 314-802 Republic of Korea Office: Kongju Nat Univ Shinkwandong 182 314-701 Kongju Chungcheongnam-do Republic of Korea Office Fax: 82-41-850-8479. Business E-Mail: ssmoon@kongju.ac.kr.

MOON, WON, internist, educator; b. Gunsan, Julabuk-do, Republic of Korea, Aug. 6, 1970; MD, Kosin U. Coll. Medicine, 1996. Med. profl. Samsung Seoul Hosp., Sungkyunkwan U. Sch. Medicine, 1996—2001, foreign prof., 2006—11, med. instr., 2004—05; med. specialist Korean Assn. Pub. Health, 2001—04; prof. internal medicine Kosin U. Coll. Medicine, Kosin U. Gospel Hosp., 2005—. Recipient prize, Gyeongsangnam-do Govt. Mem.: Fedn. Busan Sci. and Tech., Korean Assn. Study Intestinal Diseases, Korean Assn. Gastrointestinal Endoscopy, Korean Assn. Internal Medicine, Korean Soc. Gastroenterology. Avocations: music, running. Office: Amnamdong 34 Seo-gu Busan 602-702 Republic of Korea Office Fax: 82-51-990-5055.

MOONEY, ROBERT THURSTON, healthcare educator; b. Bryan, Tex., Jan. 5, 1935; s. Archie T. and Eda Belle (Arrington) M.; m. Jean Russell, June 24, 1955; children: Cynthia Mooney Conyers, Sandra Mooney Cook. BS, Tex. A&M U., College Station, 1958, MEd, 1963. Cert. trainer. Tchr. Navasota (Tex.) Ind. Sch. Dist., 1958-61, Bay City (Tex.) Ind. Sch. Dist., 1961-65, dir. audio-visual instrn., 1965-66; ednl. media specialist Ednl. Media Labs., Austin, Tex., 1967-68; dir. edn. and tng. Bexar County Hosp. Dist., San Antonio, 1968-75; asst. prof. Southwest Tex. State U., San Marcos, 1974-80, assoc. prof., 1980—, chmn. allied health scis., 1976-81, dir. health svcs. mgmt., 1988-90, dir. Health Resource Ctr., 1981-82; mayor pro tem City of San Marcos, San Marcos, 1995-96; dir. undergraduate studies Tex. State U., San Marcos, 2003—. Dir. Sch. Paramed. Tng., Bexar County Hosp. Dist., San Antonio, 1970-72; cons. pvt. contractor, San Marcos, 1975—; mem. community/environ. task force Cen. Tex. Health Systems Agy., 1977; mem. health occupations edn. adv. com. Tex. Edn. Agy., 1989-91; mem. summer games organizing com. Tex. Spl. Olympics, 1990-91, security chmn., 1990; mem. health occupations projects adv. com. U. Tex., Austin, 1990-91. Author: Overhead Projection, 1968; (with Sister Rene Fisher and Beth Knox) Guidelines for the Development of a Hospital-Wide Education Service, 1979; contbr. articles to profl. jours. Chmn. disaster svc. Hays County Red Cross, San Marcos, 1988-89, bd. dirs., 1986-89; res. comdr. San Marcos Police Res., 1984-85; treas. Hays/Caldwell Counties Alcohol and Drug Abuse Coun., 1984-85, exec. bd. mem., 1984-85; res. dep. Hays County Sheriffs Dept., 1985-86, San Marcos Police Dept., 1986-87; zoning commr. City of San Marcos, 1991-93, city councilman, 1993-96; bd. dirs. Hays County Ctrl. Appraiser Dist., 1994-97; bd. pres. San Marcos/Hays County EMS; planning and zoning commr. City of San Marcos, 1997-2001; v.p. Hays County Appraisal Dist. Bd., 1996-98; chair Planning and Zoning Commn., City San Marcos, 1998-2000; pres. San Marcos Coun. Neighborhood Assns., 2001-02; pres.-elect Heritage Assn. San Marcos, 2002-03. Mem. ASTD, Am. Coll. Healthcare Execs., Soc. Human Resource Mgmt., Am. Soc. Healthcare Edn. and Tng. (bd. mem. 1971-72), Am. Hosp. Assn., Tex. Soc. Healthcare Educators (pres. 1971-72, pres. 1991-92, disting. svc. and achievement award 1989), Bay City Classroom Tchrs. Assn. (pres.), Navasota Classroom Tchrs. Assn. (pres.), Alamo Tng. and Insvc. Coun. Hosp. and Allied Health Educators (pres. 1969-71), Internat. Personnel Mgmt. Assn. (publs. adv. bd. 1988), Tex. Hosp. Assn., Assn. of Univ. Programs in Health Adminstrn., Soc. for Human Resource Mgmt. (reviewer HR magazine 1990-96), Heritage Assn. San Marcos (pres.-elect 2002-03), Kiwanis, Hays County A&M Club (pres. 2002-03). Avocations: hunting, fishing. Office Phone: 512-245-3511. Business E-Mail: rm02@txstate.edu.

MOONGKARNDI, PRIMCHANIEN, pharmacist, researcher; b. Bangkok, Thailand, Sept. 14, 1951; d. Chanien and Boosabong Moongkarndi. Cert. of Secondary Sch. Pharmacy (hon.), Rajini Sch., Bangkok, 1969; BSc in Pharmacology, Chulalongkorn U., Bangkok, 1974—74; MSc in Microbiology, Mahidol U., Bangkok, 1977; D in Immunology, Heidelberg U., 1984. Licenced Pharmacist Pharm. Assn. of Thailand, 1974. Lectr. and staff Dept. of Microbiology, Faculty of Pharmacy, Mahidol U., Bangkok, 1977—85, asst. prof., 1985—92, assoc. prof., 1992—. Head dept. Dept. of Microbiology, Faculty of Pharmacy, Mahidol U., 1995—99; acting assoc. dean Faculty of Pharmacy, Mahidol U., Bangkok, 2004. Editor: (book) Development and Application of Vaccines. Scholarship, Faculty of Sciences, Mahidol U., 1974—77, Faculty of Pharmacy, Heidelberg U., Germany, 1980—84, grant, Tng. in Japan, 1987, fellowship, Duke Comprehensive Cancer Ctr., Duke U., NC, USA, 1992—94. Mem.: Allergy and Immunology Soc. of Thailand (life), Pharm. Assn. of Thailand (life), Mahidol U. Alumni (life). Avocations: travel, music, shopping, movies, reading. Home: 226/1 Arunamarin Rd Bangkok 10700 Thailand Office: Faculty of Pharmacy Mahidol Univ Sri Ayudthaya Rd 447 10400 Bangkok Bangkok Thailand Office Fax: 66-2-6448692; Home Fax: 66-2-4124034. Personal E-mail: moongkarndi@yahoo.com. E-mail: pypmk@mahidol.ac.th.

MOONIS, MAJAZ, neurologist, educator; m. Mariyam Moonis. Diplomate ABSM, cert. FAAN, ABCN, diplomate in vascular neurology Am. Bd. Psychiatry & Neurology. Prof. neurology, dir., stroke svcs. & fellowship program U. Mass Med. Ctr., Worcester, 2009—. Pres., bd. trustees, Ctrl. Mass. Am. Heart Assn., Worcester, 2005—; dir. Sleep Ctr., Day Kimball Hosp. Contbr. scientific papers to 130 profl. publs. (Best Presentation award, 2004). Recipient Cmty. Consci. award. Master: RCP; fellow: AHA, RCP; mem.: ABPN (Vascular Neurology), ABCN, ABSN. Achievements include research in outcome prevention in stroke. Home: 47 Camelot Dr Shrewsbury MA 01545 Office: University Mass Med Sch 55 Lake Ave N Worcester MA 01655 Business E-Mail: moonism@ummhc.org.

MOORADIAN, ARSHAG DERTAD, internist, educator; b. Aleppo, Syria, Aug. 20, 1953; arrived in U.S., 1981; s. Dertad and Araxi (Halajian) Mooradian; m. Deborah Lynn Miles, June 25, 1985; children: Arshag Dertad, Jr., Ariana Araxie. BS, Am. U., Beirut, 1976, MD, 1980. Diplomate Am. Bd. Internal Medicine. Asst. prof. medicine UCLA, 1985-88; assoc. prof. U. Ariz., Tucson, 1988-91; prof. St. Louis U., 1991—2006; prof. medicine, chmn. dept. medicine U. Fla., 2006—. Contbr. articles to profl. jours. Grantee VA, 1985—97. Mem.: Am. Diabetes Assn. (chmn. task force micronutrients 1990—91, chmn. coun. nutrition and metabolism 2000—02), Endocrine Soc., Gerontol. Soc. Am., Am. Fedn. Clin. Rsch., Phi Kappa Phi, Alpha Omega Alpha. Mem. Armenian Orthodox Ch. Achievements include identification of a potential biomarker of aging; research in on age-related changes in the blood-brain barrier; on age-related changes in thyroid hormone action; on diabetes related changes in the central nervous system. Office: U Fla Coll Medicine Dept Medicine 653-1 West Eighth St Jacksonville FL 32209 Business E-Mail: arshag.mooradian@jax.ufl.edu.

MOORCROFT, WILLIAM HERBERT, retired bio-psychologist, educator, researcher; b. Detroit, Feb. 1, 1944; s. Leonard and Elsie Moorcroft; m. Christina Louise Perrin, Nov. 27, 1971; children: Marcile Louise Cappel, Partick Richard, Andrew William. PhD, Princeton U., 1970. Prof. psychobiology Luther Coll., Decorah, Iowa, 1971—2002; adj. prof. psychology Colo. State U., Ft. Collins, Colo., 2001—04. Cons. Northern Colo. Sleep Consultants, Ft. Collins, 2002—. Author: (textbook) Understanding Sleep and Dreaming. Mem.: APA, Am. Acad. Sleep Medicine, Phi Beta Kappa. Democrat. Episcopalian. Avocations: hiking, internationaltravel. Home: 4443 Vista Dr Fort Collins CO 80526 Office: 662 Grant St Denver CO E-mail: bill@sleeplessincolorado.com. *

MOORE, ALISOUN, information technology executive; BA in Polit. Sci. and Biology, U. Albany, 1978—82; MPA in Info. Tech., U. Balt., 1988—91; MBA in Healthcare Mgmt. and Bus., Johns Hopkins U. With State of Maryland, 1999—2001, Montgomery County, 2001—06; dir. health and human svcs. state and local Northrop Grumman, 2007—09; dir. healthcare sys. mgmt. Northrop Grumman Info. Sys., 2007—11; v.p. health svcs. divsn. Computer Sciences Corp., 2011—, gen. mgr. health svcs. divsn., 2011—. Office: Computer Sciences Corporation 3170 Fairview Park Drive Falls Church VA 22042 Office Phone: 703-876-1000.

MOORE, ANNE, physician; b. NYC, Apr. 28, 1944; d. John D.J. and Mary Foote Moore; m. Arnold L. Lisio, Sept. 6, 1969; children: Philip Moore, Mary Foote. BA, Smith Coll., 1965; MD, Columbia U., 1969. Diplomate Am. Bd. Internal Medicine, Am. Bd. Hematology (chmn. 1996), Am. Bd. Oncology. Intern dept. medicine N.Y. Hosp., NYC, 1969-73, assoc. attending physician, 1981-95, attending physician, 1996—; postdoctoral fellow Rockefeller U., 1972-73, hematology-oncology fellow, 1973-75; asst. prof. medicine Cornell U. Med. Coll., NYC, 1975-91, assoc. prof. clin. medicine, 1981-95, prof. clin. medicine, 1996—. Cons. Strang Cancer Prevention Ctr.; lectr., cons., in field. Author: Patient's Guide to Breast Cancer Treatment, 1992, rev. edit., 1997; ad hoc reviewer Am. Jour. Clin. Oncology, 1994, New Eng. Jour. Medicine, 1994, 96, 97; contbr. articles to profl. jours., chpts. to books. Trustee St. David's Sch., 1983-89, HealthCare Chaplaincy, Inc., 1991—; bd. dirs. Camilli Found., 1990—, Cure Myeloma Fund, 1988-98, N.Y. Community Trust. Recipient award SHARE, 1992, Wholeness of Life award Hosp. Chaplaincy, 1992, Alumnae award Oak Knoll Sch., 1994, Eileen Dreyer Meml. Lectureship award Sass Found. for Med. Rsch., 1996, Commendation award Office of Exec. Nassau County, 1996, award Artists for Breast Cancer Survival, Inc., 2000. Mem. Am. Bd. Internal Medicine (bd. dirs. 1996—), Am. Soc. Hematology, Am. Soc. Clin. Oncology, N.Y. Acad. Scis., Soc. for Study of Blood (membership chmn. 1979-80), N.Y. Met. Breast Cancer Group (membership chmn. 1992-93, sec.-treas. 1993-95, v.p. 1995-96, pres. 1997-99), Soc. for Study of Breast Disease, N.Y. Cancer Soc., N.Y. Acad. Medicine (trustee 1998-2006). Office: Weill Cornell Breast Ctr 425 E 61st St 8th Fl New York NY 10065

MOORE, BRIAN CECIL JOSEPH, auditory researcher; b. London, Feb. 10, 1946; s. Cecil George and Maria Anna Moore. BA, Cambridge U., Eng., 1968, PhD, 1971. Lectr. U. Reading, England, 1971-73, 1974-77, U. Cambridge, England, 1977-89, reader, 1989-95, prof., 1995—. Vis. prof. Bklyn. Coll., 1973-74, U. Calif. Berkeley, 1990, U. Ulster North Ireland, 1991-94; sci. adv. bd. Resound Corp., Redwood City, Calif., 1988-2000. Author: An Introduction to the Psychology of Hearing, 1977, 83, 89, 97, 2003 (Littler prize 1983), Perceptual Consequences of Cochlear Damage, 1995, Cochlear Hearing Loss, 1998, 2007; contbr. articles to profl. jours. Recipient Internat. award in Hearing, Am. Acad. Audiology, 2004, Merit award, Assn. Rsch. in Otolaryngology, 2008, Hugh Knowles prize, 2008. Fellow Acoustical Soc. Am. (Silver medal 2003), Belgian Soc. Audiology (hon.), Brit. Soc. Hearing Aid Audiologists (hon.), Acad. Med. Sci., Royal Soc. Avocations: music, playing jazz, collecting musical instruments. Office: U Cambridge Dept Exptl Psychology Downing St Cambridge CB2 3EB England Office Phone: 441223333574. E-mail: bcjm@cam.ac.uk.

MOORE, DANIEL CHARLES, retired anesthesiologist; b. Cin., Sept. 9, 1918; s. Daniel Clark and May (Strebel) M.; m. Betty Maxine Tobias, Aug. 5, 1945 (div. 1988); children: Barbara, Nancy, Daniel, Susan. Grad., Amherst Coll., Mass., 1940; MD, Northwestern U., 1944. Diplomate Am. Bd. Anesthesiologists. Intern Wesley Meml. Hosp., Chgo., 1944, resident, 1945; dir. anesthesia Va. Mason Hosp., Seattle, 1947-72; anesthesiologist (Mason Clinic), 1947-72, sr. cons. in anesthesia, 1972-83. Clin. prof. U. Wash. Sch. Medicine, 1963—89. Author: Regional Block, 1953, Stellate Ganglion Block, 1954, Complications of Regional Anesthesia, 1955, Anesthetic Techniques for Obstetrical Anesthesia and Analgesia, 1964, also papers. Served as capt. M.C. AUS, 1945-47. Recipient Ralph M. Waters award Ill. Soc. Anesthesiologists, Carl Koller Gold medal European Soc. Regional Anaesthesia, 1995, Eagle Scout, 1930. Mem. Am. Soc. Anesthesiologists (1st v.p. 1953-54, 2d v.p. 1954-55, pres. 1958-59, distinguished service award 1976), AMA (sec. anesthesiology sect. 1956-58), Am. Acad. Anesthesiology, Am. Soc. Regional Anesthesia (adv. bd., Gaston Labat award 1977), Wash. Soc. Anesthesiologists (pres. 1949-50), Wash. Med. Soc., King County Med. Soc., Faculty Anaesthetists Royal Coll. Surgeons (hon.), Northwest Forum, Beta Theta Pi, Nu Sigma Nu. Home: Madison Park Pl # 103 2000 43rd Ave E Seattle WA 98112-2704 Office: PO Box 900 Seattle WA 98111-0900 Office Phone: 206-223-6980. Fax: 206-223-6982. E-mail: daniel.moore@vmmc.org.

MOORE, DANIEL EDMUND, psychologist, educator, retired educational administrator; b. Pitts., Dec. 31, 1926; s. John Daniel and Alma Helen (Goehring) M.; m. Rose Marie Blunkosky, Nov. 11, 1949; children: Catherine Chiodo, Claire Marie Moore Caveney, Mary Moore Brilmyer, Suzanne Moore Gray, Elizabeth Moore Sullivan. BSEd, Duquesne U., 1949, MEd, 1952; postgrad., California State Coll., Pa., 1954-56, U. Pitts., 1958-59, Mt. Mercy Coll., 1959-60, Cath. U. Am., 1966, W.Va. U., 1970-72. Lic. psychologist; cert. sch. psychologist. Tchr. math. Cecil Twp. Sch. Dist., McDonald, Pa., 1949-52, Pitts. Public Schs., 1952-53; with Mt. Lebanon Twp. (Pa.) Sch. Dist., 1953-88, psychologist, 1954-71, dir. pupil personnel svcs., 1988; psychol cons. Peters Twp. Sch. Dist., McMurray, Pa., 1961-88; psychol. cons. Blackhawk Sch. Dist., Beaver, Pa., 1989—98; psychol cons. Quaker Valley Sch. Dist., Sewickley, Pa., 1989-90; lectr., supr. Grad. and Undergrad. Sch. Edn. Duquesne U.; psychologist DePaul Inst., Pitts., 1992—98. Lectr. ednl. psychology Grad. Sch. Edn., Duquesne U., 1957-92, supr. student tchrs., 1989-92; ednl. cons. St. Francis Schs. Nursing, New Castle and Pitts., 1959-91; mem. test adv. bd. Ednl. Records Bur., 1976-86; hearing officer Right to Edn. Office, Dept. Edn., Harrisburg, Pa., 1975—; in-svc. adv. bd. Pa. Dept. Edn. Hearing Officers; clients assessment Pa. Bur. Disability(BDD), 1988-, Attys. Law, 1990-. Mem. Chartiers Valley Sch. Dist. Bd., 1963-94, pres., 1971, v.p., 1991; mem. Pkwy. West Tech. Sch. Bd. 1965-67; bd. dirs. secondary sch. rsch. program Ednl. Testing Svc., Princeton, 1971-85; bd. dirs. Robert E. Ward Home for Children, 1975-87, St. Agatha Parish Coun., 1988—, Pathfinder Sch., 1989, v.p., 1990-94, pres. sch. bd., 1991-92; vol. Bridgeville Area Food Bank, 1988—; chairperson Parish 100 Jubilee Ceremony, Goodwill Villa Bd., Goodwill Plaza, Inc., Goodwill Villa Bd. of Incorporators, 1992—; pres. bd. dirs. Goodwill Plaza, 1992—; active assessment Psychol. Corp. Harcourt Assessment, 2002-; jubilee chairperson St. Agatha's, Bridgeville, Pa. With USNR, 1945-48. Henry C. Frick grantee, 1970, 73; named Jaycee Educator of Yr. for South Hills Area, Ward Home Outstanding Community Leader, 1984, Outstanding Cmty. Leader, Chartiers Valley Human Rels. Coun., 1998; recipient Human Rels. award Chartiers Valley Inter-relationships Soc., 1998, Key award Harcourt-Brace Psyschol. Testing Svc., Outstanding Achievement Pearson Testing Program award, 2008. Mem. Am., Pa. psychol. assns., Coun. Exceptional Children (pres. 1957), Phi Delta Kappa (pres. chpt. 1974-75, chmn. lay awards com. 1979-2001, Svc. Key award 1985). Roman Catholic. Home: 213 Station St Bridgeville PA 15017-1806 Office Phone: 412-221-5217.

MOORE, DANIEL JENSEN, pediatrician, endocrinologist; b. Memphis, Tenn., Jan. 13, 1974; AB, Harvard U., 1996; MD, U. Pa., PhD, 2004. Resident pediat. Vanderbilt U., 2004—07, fellow pediatric endocrinology, 2007—10, instr. pediat., 2010—. Dir., penn mentoring program U. Pa., 2002—03; reviewer Jour. Immunology, 2006, Am. Jour. Transplantation, Annals NY Acad. Sci., 2006—. Recipient House Officer Rsch. award, Soc. Pediatric Rsch.; Ruth Kirschstein Rsch. Svc. grant, NIH, Career Devel. grant. Fellow: Am. Acad.

Pediat.; mem.: Soc. Biomedical Diabetes Rsch., Am. Soc. Transplantation, Endocrine Soc., Pediatric Endocrine Soc. Avocation: golf. Office: Divsn Endocrinology and Diabetes 2200 Children's Way 11136 DOT Nashville TN 37232

MOORE, DONNICA LAUREN, physician, medical writer; b. Queens, NY, May 14, 1961; d. Dennis Brian and Toby (Lapkin) M.; m. Stanley Bernard Jr. BA cum laude, Princeton U., 1981; MD, SUNY, Buffalo, 1986. Diplomate Am. Bd. Med. Examiners. Resident in ob-gyn Temple U. Hosp., Phila., 1986-88; resident in family medicine Meml. Hosp., Mount Holly, NJ, 1988-89; assoc. dir. med. ops. Sandoz Pharmaceuticals, Hanover, NJ, 1989-90, dir. med. edn. ctr., 1990-93, assoc. dir. profl. rels., med. edn. ctr., 1993; founder, pres. Sapphire Women's Health Group LLC, DrDonnica.com, 2000—. Freelance med. writer, 1986-90; adj. clin. prof. dept. physiology U. Medicine and Dentistry NJ, 1990-92; attending physician Planned Parenthood NJ, 1991; editl. bd. Jour. Women's Health; columnist First for Women mag. Co-auth: (with Sarah Jarvis) Women's Health for Life, 2009; women's health contbr.: NBC's Weekend Today Show, NBC's Later Today, 1999-2000; guest contbr.: The Oprah Winfrey Show, ABC's The View, Good Morning America, CNN-Internat., others; radio host: Dr. Donnica's Women's Health Report, 2000-2002. Named one of The Most Influential Forces in Healthcare Info. Tech., Advance for Healthcare Tech. Mag., 2000; recipient Alumnae Leadership award, Princeton U. Women's Ctr., Connie Woodruff award, NJ Commn. on the Status of Women's Health, 1999; Rotary scholar U. Coll., Dublin, Ireland, 1981-82. Mem. AMA, Am. Med. Women's Assn. (v.p., bd. dirs.), NJ Med. Soc., Am. Med. Writers Assn., Soc. for Advancement of Women's Health Rsch. (past pres. corp. adv. coun.), Coalition for Women's Health, Nat. Coun. Women's Health (bd. dirs.), Research! America (bd. dirs.), Nat. Acad. Women's Health Med. Edn. (bd. dirs.), Am. Coll. Physician Execs. Jewish. Avocations: swimming, writing.

MOORE, DORSEY JEROME, dentistry educator, maxillofacial prosthetist; b. Boonville, Mo., Feb. 8, 1935; s. Lloyd Elliott Moore and Mary Elizabeth (Day) Katemann; m. Mary Louise Foote, May 2, 1959; children: Elizabeth L., David J. DDS, U. Mo., Kansas City, 1959. Diplomate Am. Bd. Prosthodontics. Commd. ensign USN, 1955, advanced through grades to capt., 1973; gen. practice dentistry various naval stas., 1959-63; practice in prosthodontics USS Proteus AS-19, 1963-66; resident in prosthodontics and maxillofacial prosthetics Naval Dental Sch., Bethesda, Md., 1966-69, chief maxillofacial prosthetics divsn., 1969-70; sr. dental advisor Naval Adv. Group, Comdr. Naval Forces, Saigon, Vietnam, 1970-71; chief maxillofacial prosthetics div. Nat. Naval Dental Ctr., 1971-76; chief maxillofacial prosthetics br. Naval Regional Med. Ctr., Great Lakes, Ill., 1976-79, ret., 1979; vis. lectr. U. Mo. Sch. Dentistry, Kansas City, 1976-79, H.G.B. Robinson prof., chmn. dept. removable prosthodontics, 1979-2000, Hamilton G.B. Robinson emeritus prof. dentistry, 2000, ret., 2000; chief maxillofacial prosthetics Truman Med. Ctr., Kansas City, Mo., 2000—. Assoc. prof. U. Saigon Sch. Dentistry, 1970-71; advisor to Min. of Health, Saigon, 1970-71; profl. lectr. George Washington U., Washington, 1971-76; clin. assoc. prof. surgery U. Kans. City Sch. Medicine, 1987—; cons. maxillofacial prosthetics NIH Treatment Ctr., 1973—, Nat. Cancer Inst., 1973—, VA Hosp., North Chicago, Ill., 1976—, ADA Couns. Dental Edn., Hosp. Dental Svc. and Commn. on Accredition, 1978—; vice chancellor Devel. Adv. Com., 1983—; examiner Mo. Specialty Bd. Prosthodontics, 1982—; internat. cir. course lectr. Am. Prosthetics Soc., Indonesia, 1974, Guatelmala, 1975, N.Z., 1976, S.Africa, 1981, Japan, Taiwan, 1989, Mexico City, 1994, Beijing and Chengdu, China, 1998; nat. cons. U.S. Naval Dental Sch., Bethesda, 1991—; chief maxillofacial prosthetics Truman Med. Ctr., 2000-. Author: Practical Oral Rehabilitation of the Edentulous Patient, 8th edit., 1995; mem. editl. bd. Cancer of the Head and Neck: A Comprehensive Review of the Literature, 1982—; contbr. articles to profl. jours. Mem. adminstrv. ch. bd. Cen. Methodist Ch., 1981-88, pres. offcl. ch. bd., 1983-85; bd. dir. Ednl. Rsch. Found. Prosthodontics, 1982—, chmn. 1988—; bd. dir. Penn Valley Fitness Trail Assn. Decorated Legion of Merit with combat V, other awards; Navy Cross of Gallantry with palm (Republic of Vietnam); recipient Ackerman Meml. award outstanding contbns. to maxillofacial prosthetics, 1999, Disting. Svc. award, Mo. Dental Assn., 2000. Fellow Am. Acad. Maxillofacial Prosthetics (bd. dir. 1972-75, mem. exec. com. 1973-76, pres. 1978-79, mem. exec. coun. 1979-82), Am. Coll. Prosthodontics (charter), Am. Coll. Dentists, Acad. Prosthodontics, Internat. Coll. Dentist, Midwest Acad. Prosthodontics; mem. ADA, Greater Kansas City Dental Soc., Mo. Dental Assn. (award). Avocations: jazz musician, string bassist. Office: Truman Med Ctrs Hospital Hill 2301 Holmes Kansas City MO 64108 Office Phone: 816-404-0500. Business E-Mail: mooredj@umkc.edu.

MOORE, DUNCAN THOMAS, optics scientist, educator; b. Biddeford, Maine, Dec. 7, 1946; s. Thomas Fogg Moore and Virginia Robinson Wing; m. Gunta Liders, July 1995. BA in Physics, U. Maine, 1969, DSc (hon.), 1995; MS in Optics, Rochester U., NY, 1970, PhD in Optics, 1974. Asst. prof. U. Rochester, 1974-78, assoc. prof., 1978-86, prof., 1986—, Kingslake prof., 1993—, dean engring. and applied sci., 1995-97, prof. biomed. engring., 2001—, prof. bus. adminstrn., 2005—, vice provost entrepreneurship, 2007—; pres. and founder Gradient Lens Corp., Rochester, 1980—97; dir. N.Y. State Ctr. Advanced Optical Tech., Rochester, 1987—94; assoc. dir. technology White House Office Sci. & Technology Policy, Washington, 1997—2000; CEO Infotonics Tech. Ctr. Inc., 2002—04. Vis. scientist Nippon Schlumberger, Tokyo, 1983; Congl. fellow Am. Phys. Soc., Washington, 1993—94; sci. advisor Sen. John D. Rockefeller IV, W.Va., 1993—94; exec. dir. Univ. Industry and Govt. Partnership Advanced Photonics, 2001—02; mem. environ. and energy svc. rev. com. Idaho Nat. Engring. and Environ. Lab., 2001—02; mem. bd. assessment for Nat. Inst. Stds. and Tech. programs NRC, 2001—05, mem. panel for physics, 2001—05, chmn. panel for physics, 2002—05, chmn., 2002—05, mem. adv. coun. US commn. optics, 2006—, mem. com. sci., tech. and law, 2006—; mem. engring. vis. com. NASA-Goddard Space Flight Ctr., 2002—06, chair applied engring. and tech. directorate vis. com., 2002—06, mem. James Webb Space Telescope product integrity team, 2002—; mem. nat. innovation initiative Coun. on Competitiveness, 2004; v.p. Internat. Commn. Optics, 2008—; lectr. in field. Contbr. articles to profl. jours. Chmn. Hubble Ind. Rev. Panel, 1990—91. Recipient Disting. Inventor of Yr. award, Rochester Intellectual Property Law Assn., 1993, Grin Optics award, Japanese Applied Physics Soc., 1993, Sci. and Tech. award, Greater Rochester C. of C., 1992, Gold medal, Internat. Soc. Optical Engring., 2006, Edwin H. Land medal, Soc. Imaging Sci. and Tech. and, 2009; named Engr. of the Yr., Rochester Engring. Soc., 1999. Mem.: AAAS (mem. com. sci. engring. and pub. policy 2005—, fellow 2004), NAE, IEEE Lasers and Electro-Optics Soc. (govt. fellows selection com. 2005—), Am. Inst. Physics (state dept. fellowship selection com. 2001—02), Coalition Photonics and Optics (chair 1996—97), Forum Physics and Soc. (exec. com. 1996—97), Coun. Sci. Soc. (co-chair govt. affairs com. 1996—97), Materials Rsch. Soc., Am. Assn. Engring. Soc. (bd. govs. 1995—97, Nat. Engring. award 1999), Optical Soc. Am. (bd. dirs. 1987—89, editor Applied Optics 1990—92, bd. dirs. 1992—97, v.p. 1994, pres. 1996, adv. coun. homeland security 2004—, Leadership award 2001), Am. Soc. Precision Engring., Am. Ceramic Soc. (Edward Orton, Jr. Meml. lectr 2002). Achievements include patents in field. Home: 4 Claret Dr Fairport NY 14450-4610 Office: The Inst Optics U Rochester Rochester NY 14627-0186 Office Phone: 585-275-5248. Business E-Mail: moore@optics.rochester.edu.

MOORE, ERNEST EUGENE, JR., surgeon, educator; b. Pitts., June 18, 1946; s. Ernest Eugene Sr. and Mary Ann (Burroughs) M.; m. Sarah Van Duzer, Sept. 2, 1978; children: Hunter Burroughs, Peter Kitrick. BS in Chemistry, Allegheny Coll., 1968; MD, U. Pitts., 1972. Surg. resident U. Vt., Burlington, 1972-76; chief of trauma Denver Health Med. Ctr., 1976—, chief dept. surgery, 1984—. Prof. surgery, vice chmn. dept. U. Colo., 1984—; dir. facilities Colo. Trauma Inst., 1984-95. Editor: Critical Decisions in Trauma, 1987, Trauma, 1988, rev. edits., 1991, 96, 00, 05, 07, Early Care of the Injured, 1989, Surgical Secrets, 1996, rev. edit., 2002, 05, Trauma Manual, 2003, Medicine for Mountaineering, rev. edit., 2010, World Jour. Emergency Surgery; assoc. editor Jour. Trauma, Am. Jour. Surgery, World Jour. Surgery, Surgery-Problem Solving Approach, 2d edit., 1994, others; patentee retrohepatic vena cava shunt. Fellow ACS (com. on trauma, vice chair 1990), Soc. Univ. Surgeons (pres. 1989), Am. Assn. Surgery of Trauma (pres. 1993), Internat. Assn. Surgery of Trauma and Surg. Intensive Care (pres. 1998-99), Pan Am. Trauma Assn. (pres. 1991), Southwestern Surg. Congress (pres. 1998), Western Trauma Assn. (pres. 1989), World Soc. Emergency Surgery (pres. 2008). Republican. Avocations: skiing, mountaineering, hunting, ultramarathons, fishing, triathlons. Home: 2909 E 7th Avenue Pky Denver CO 80206-3839 Office: Denver Health Med Ctr Dept Surgery Denver CO 80204 Office Phone: 303-436-6558. Business E-Mail: ernest.moore@dhha.org. *

MOORE, FREDERICK ALAN, surgeon, educator; b. Butler, Pa., Mar. 14, 1953; BS, Alegheny Coll., 1975; MD, U. Pitts., 1979. Med. dir. surg. ICU Denver Gen. Hosp., 1986—96; chief gen. surgery, prof. U. Tex. Houston Med. Sch., 1996—2006; head acute care surgery Meth. Hosp., 2006—. Asst. prof. surgery U. Colo., 1986—91, assoc. prof. surgery, 1991—96; prof. surgery Weill Cornell Med. Coll., 2007. Recipient 14th Asmund S. Laerdal Meml. Lecture award, Soc. Critical Care Medicine, 2004, Moran Found. Publ. award, Meth. Hosp. Rsch. Inst., 2009; Trauma Ctr. grant, NIH, Tng. grant. Fellow: ACS, Coll. Critical Care Medicine; mem.: Soc. Clin. Surgery, Am. Assn. Surgery Trauma, Am. Surg. Assn. Avocations: skiing, skeet shooting, bicycling. Home: 8106 Bois D Arc Ln Fulshear TX 77441 Home Phone: 281-346-2376. Personal E-mail: famoore@tmhs.org.

MOORE, HUBERT, JR., retired addictions counselor, consultant; b. Oklahoma City, Jan. 2, 1932; s. Hubert and Goldie Edith Moore; m. Mary Alene Jarnet, Dec. 9, 1958 (div. Oct. 1959); 1 child, LeAnne; m. Shirley M. Mumchuck, Apr. 1978 (dec. Nov. 8, 1985); children: Peggy, JoAnn, Lisa, Sharon. AA in Counseling, U. Alaska, 1986, BA in Human Svcs., 1992, BA in Psychology, 1992, BA in Sociology, 1996; MA in Anthropology, U. Mindanao, Philippines, 1998. Cert. addictions counselor II Alaska, Nat. Assn. Alcohol and Drug Abuse Counselors, master forensic counselor and criminal justice specialist Nat. Assn. Forensic Counselors, Nat. Register Addiction Counselors, Calif. Registry Addiction Specialists. Health and safety insp. Alaska Offshore Drilling, 1968—77; substance abuse counselor II No. Regional Ctr. for Addictions, Fairbanks, Alaska, 1977—85; forensic counselor Fairbanks Correction Facility, 1995—96; addictions cons. Soldotna, Alaska, 1991—2005; owner, operator (daycare ctr.) Papa's Playhouse, Soldotna, 1998—2006; ret., 2006. Campaign vol. Rep. Caucus, Soldotna, 1991—. Mem.: Phi Theta Kappa (bd. mem., Aurora Borealis Charter Sch.). Republican. Muslim. Avocations: writing, motorcycling, philosophy, mountain climbing. Home: PO Box 1057 Soldotna AK 99669 Business E-Mail: altcounselingconsult@lycos.com.

MOORE, HUGH LESLIE, retired pediatrician; b. Dallas, Jan. 6, 1939; s. Robert Leslie and Maybeth (Thompson) Moore; m. LeAnn Kridelbaugh, May 25, 1996; children: Gwen Moore Holliday, Carolyn Moore Becker, Hugh Samuel. BA, U. Colo., 1960; MD, U. Tex.Southwestern Med. Sch., 1964. Diplomate Am. Bd. Pediat., Am. Bd. Pediat. Nephrology. Resident in pediat. Cin. Children's Hosp., Cin., 1964—67; fellow in pediat. nephrology U. Minn. Hosp., Mpls., 1969—71; pediatrician Clin. Pediat. Assoc., Dallas, 1971—; clin. prof. pediat. U. Tex. Southwestern Med. Sch., Dallas, 1982—2005; ret. Pediat. tchr. Childrens Med. Ctr., Dallas, 1971—, bd. trustees, 1984—. Lt. comdr. USN, 1967—69. Recipient Outstanding Tchr. award, Children's Med. Ctr., Mead Johnson Pediat. Lifetime Achievement award, 2006; named one of Top Doctors, D Mag., 1992, 1996, 1999, 2002, Best Doctor's in Am., 2000—01, 2001—02, 2003—04, 2004—05. Mem.: Tex. Pediat. Soc., Am. Soc. Pediat. Nephrology, Am. Soc. Nephrology, Dallas County Med. Soc., Tex. Med. Assn. Avocations: travel, photography, birdwatching, motorcycling. Office: 7547 Greenbrier Dr Dallas TX 75225 *

MOORE, JEAN E., social worker, academic administrator, educator, radio personality; d. Hugh Huriel and Theodora H. Buchanan Campbell; m. Robert M. Moore, Jr.; children: Robert M. III, Doreen R. Moore Closson. BA, Hunter Coll., 1947; M of Social Svc., Bryn Mawr Coll., 1949; EdD, Temple U., 1978. Cert. social worker Acad. Cert. Social Workers, LSW Pa., 1989. Social worker Children's Svc., Inc., Phila., 1949—52; asst. chief clin. social work svcs. Med. and Mental Hygiene Clinic Region 10 U.S. VA, Phila., 1952—60; social work specialist Ctrl. Relocation Bur., Phila. Redevel. Authority, 1962—67; social work/human svcs. adviser for Model Cities Region III U.S. Dept. Housing and Urban devel. for 6 states and D.C., 1967—69; assoc. prof., grad. faculty, dir. new career ladders Temple U., Phila., dir. program devel. Office of Rsch. and Program Devel., 1969—89, assoc. prof. emerita, 1989—; exec. asst. to pres. Cheyney U. of Pa., 1985—91; v.p. instnl. advancement U. Md. Ea. Shore, Princess Anne, Md., 1991—97; host, Univ. Forum WESM, 1994—97; host, exec. prodr. Univ. Forum Temple U. Pub. Radio, Phila., 1997—. Mem. internat. bd. advisors Radio for Peace Internat.; bd. dirs., club dir. Gundaker Found., Inc.; cons., spkr., presenter, lectr. Contbr. articles to profl. publs. Past bd. trustees Lackawanna Jr. Coll., C.C. of Phila.; past pres. Fair Housing Coun. Suburban Phila.; chair vis. accreditation teams Mid. States Assn. Colls. and Schs. Commn. on Higher Edn.; past bd. pres. Spectrum Health Svcs., Inc.; chair State Bd. Pvt. Corresp. Schs.; elder Lansdowne First Presbyn. Ch.; bd. dirs. Children's Svc., Inc. Recipient Documentary Gold award, Internat. Assn. Audio Visual Commns., 1999, Crystal awards of Excellence, The Communicator Awards, 1999, 2000, 2002, 2003, 2004, 2005, 2006, 2008, 1st pl. radio/ednl., Broadcast Edn. Assn., 2000, Documentary award, 2000, Achievement in Radio award, March of Dimes, 2000—04, Gold Cindy award, Internat. Assn. Audio Visual Communicators, 2000, 2002, 2003, Undoing Racism Unity award, Radnor Twp., 2002, Media award, Kelly Anne Dolan Meml. Fund, 2003, Martin Luther King Jr. Humanitarian award, Upper Merion, 2004, Mayor's Fire Prevention medal, City of N.Y., Outstanding Contbn. in Edn. award, Theta Nu Sigma, Image award, Black Women in Sport Found., Radio Program awards, Best Coverage Maternal Health Issues/Problems Risk Pregnancies, numerous academic awards, Alumni Lifetime Achievement award, Bryn Mawr Coll. Grad. Sch. Social Work and Social Rsch., 2008; named Paul Harris fellow, Rotary Found., 2005, Guy Gundaker fellow, Gundaker Found. Rotary Internat. Dist. 7450, 2006; named to Hall of Fame, Hunter Coll., 1999. Mem.: NASW (charter mem. 1955, Golden Membership Disting. Svc. award 2005), Broadcast Pioneers of Phila., Inc., Pa. Abolition Soc. (bd. mgrs.), Darby Lansdowne Club, Rotary Club Upper Darby-Lansdown (bd. dirs. 2001—05), Phi Delta Kappa, Alpha Chi Alpha, Phi Beta Kappa, Delta Sigma Theta. Avocations: international travel, writing, poetry. Office Phone: 215-204-4376.

MOORE, LOIS JEAN, health science facility administrator; married; 1 child. Grad., Prairie View Sch. Nursing, Tex., 1957; BS in Nursing, Tex. Woman's U., 1970; MS in Edn., Tex. So. U., 1974. Nurse Harris County (Tex.) Hosp. Dist., 1957—; pres., chief exec. officer Harris County Hosp.; adminstr. Jefferson Davis Hosp., Houston, 1977-88, exec. v.p., chief ops. officer, 1988—2001; chief adminstr. U. Tex. Harris County Psychiat. Hosp., Houston, 2001—. Mem. adv. bd. Tex. Pub. Hosp. Assn. Contbr. articles to profl. jours. Mem. Mental Health Needs Council Houston and Harris County, Congressman Mickey Leland's Infant Mortality Task Force, Houston Crackdown Com., Gov.'s task force on health care policy, 1991; chairperson Tex. Assn. Pub. and Nonprofit Hosps., 1991, subcom. of Gov.'s task force to identify essential health care svc., 1992; bd. dirs. ARC, 1991—, Greater Houston Hosp. Coun., March of Dimes, United Way. Recipient Pacesetter award North-East C. of C., 1991; named Nurse of Yr. Houston Area League Nursing, 1976-77, Outstanding Black Achiever YMCA Century Club, 1974, Outstanding Women in Medicine YWCA, 1989. Mem. Am. Coll. Hosp. Adminstrs., Tex. Hosp. Assn. (chmn. pub. hosp. com.), Young Hosp. Adminstrs., Nat. Assn. Pub. Hosps. (bd. dirs., mem. exec. com. Tex. assn.), License Vocat. Nurses Assn., sigma Theta Tau. Home: 3730 S Macgregor Way Houston TX 77021-1506 Office: Univ Texas Harris County Psychiatric Ctr 2800 S Macbryor Way Houston TX 77021 Office Phone: 713-741-7803.

MOORE, LOUISE HILL, surgical technologist; b. Knoxville, Tenn., July 9, 1950; d. Mary Elizabeth Hill; m. David Oscar Moore; children: Kimberly Hill, Daveisha. Cert. surg. technologist; cosmetologist, aesthetician. Cosmetologist Millers Dept. Store, Knoxville, 1968—70, Austinian Beauty Shop, Knoxville, 1970—74, Hair Fashions E., Knoxville, 1974—78; gen. laborer Alcoa, Alcoa, Tenn., 1978—94; cert. surg. technologist St. Mary's Med. Ctr., Knoxville, 1995, Ft. Sanders Hosp., Knoxville, U. Tenn. Med. Ctr., Knoxville, 1997, safety, slip/pack/utility mem., 1997—. Mem.: Knoxville Writers Guild, Assn. Surg. Technologists. Home: 225 Grata Rd Knoxville TN 37914 Personal E-mail: elvenia@aol.com.

MOORE, MARTHA MAY, toxicologist; b. Feb. 17; BA, Western Md. Coll., 1971; PhD, U. NC, Chapel Hill, 1980. Dir., divsn. genetic, molecular toxicology Nat. Ctr. Toxicological Rsch., FDA, 2000—. Recipient Tech. Achievement award, EPA. Mem.: Environ. Mutagen Soc., Soc. Toxicology. Office: 3900 NCTR Rd Jefferson AR 72079 Business E-Mail: martha.moore@fda.hhs.gov.

MOORE, MARY JOHNSON, retired community health nurse; b. West Point, NY, Feb. 8, 1940; d. Robert Phillip and Edith Virginia (Carr) Johnson; m. Prentis Monroe Moore, Dec. 28, 1960 (dec. Jan. 1990); children: Carol Edith, Tracey Marie. Diploma, Boston City Hosp. Sch. Nursing, 1960. RN. Clinic nurse in pediat. and obstetrics Harris County Health Dept./Lyons Clinic, Houston, 1982—85; clinic nurse Tex. Sch. for Deaf, Austin, 1986—87; staff nurse pediat. Ben Taub Hosp., Houston, 1989—92; telephone triage nurse, ob-gyn. McGregor Clinic, Houston, 1992—93; staff nurse pediat. Grant Hosp., Chgo., 1994—96; clinic nurse Columbus-Maryville Hosp., Chgo., 1996—2002; travel nurse Star-Med Profl. Staffing, 2002—03; case mgr. Brockton Neighborhood Health Ctr., Mass., 2003—04; ret., 2004. Active Sr. Chorus Massasoit C.C., 2006—; bd. dirs. Boston City Hosp., Sch. Nursing Alumnus, 2008; mem. Sullivan & Cogliano Tng. Sch., 2010; mem. vol. choir St. Chrysostoms Episcopal Ch., 1997—2002; lay reader Trinity Episcopal Ch., Brockton, 2006—; mem. Brockton Area Med. Res. Corp., 2008—. George Monks Meml. scholar, 1960. Democrat. Avocations: art, music, poetry, collecting unicorns, angels and lighthouses. Home: 72 Pine St Brockton MA 02302 Personal E-mail: mryjrn@yahoo.com.

MOORE, PAUL E., physician, director; b. Nashville, Sept. 20, 1966; BA, Vanderbilt U., 1988; MD, Harvard U., 1992. Dir. pediat. allergy, immunology, and pulmonary medicine Vanderbilt U. Sch. Medicine, 2009—. Office: 2200 Children's Way DOT 11215 Nashville TN 37232-9500 Office Fax: 615-343-7727. Business E-Mail: paul.moore@vanderbilt.edu.

MOORE, PEARL B., retired nursing educator; b. Pitts., Aug. 25, 1936; d. Hyman and Ethel (Antis) Friedman; 1 child, Cheryl. BS in Nursing, U. Pitts., 1968, M in Nursing, 1974. Staff nurse Allegheny Gen. Hosp., Pitts., 1957-60; instr. Liliane S. Kaufman Sch. Nursing, Pitts., 1960-70, asst. dir., 1970, dir., 1970-72; cancer nurse specialist Montefiore Hosp., Pitts., 1974-75; coord. Brain Tumor Study Group, Pitts., 1975-83; adj. asst. prof. U. Pitts., 1983—. Contbr. articles in field to profl. publs. Fellow Am. Acad. Nursing; mem. ANA, Oncology Nursing Soc. (exec. dir. 1983—, CEO 1999-2007, Disting. Svc. award 1995), Nurses Alumnae U. Pitts., Sigma Theta Tau. Home: 5701 Centre Ave Pittsburgh PA 15206

MOORE, ROGER ADDISON, pediatrician, anesthesiologist; b. Portsmouth, Va., 1948; MD, U. Va. Sch. Medicine, Charlottesville, 1973. Diplomate Am. Bd. Pediat., Am. Bd. Anesthesiology. Intern pediat. U. Colo., Denver, 1974—75, resident anesthesia, 1975—77; resident pediatric anesthesia/critical care mgmt. U. Pa. Hosp., Phila., 1977-79; fellow pediatric anesthesia/intensive care Children's Hosp., Phila., 1979; chmn. anesthesiology dept. Deborah Heart & Lung Ctr., Browns Mills, NJ, 1993—2005, chair emeritus, 2005—; clin. assoc. prof. anesthesiology U. Medicine & Dentistry NJ, Newark, 1998—. Exam. question writer Am. Bd. Anesthesiology, 1986—2002, assoc. oral bd. sr. examiner, 1996—2002. Named a Top Doc, South Jersey Mag., 2006—08. Mem.: AMA, Med. Soc. NJ (sec. anesthesia sect. 1983—84, chair anesthesia sect. 1984—85), NJ State Soc. Anesthesiologists (v.p. 1987—89, pres. 1989—91, treas. 1999—, treas. polit. action com. 1999—), Soc. Cardiovasc. Anesthesiologists (v.p. 1999—2001, pres. 2001—03), Am. Soc. Anesthesiologists (NJ dir. 1995—96, sec.-treas. 1996—99, asst. treas. 1999—2003, treas. 2004—06, v.p. 2007, pres. 2008—09, pres. elect 2008), Alpha Omega Alpha. Office: Deborah Heart & Lung Ctr 200 Trenton Rd Browns Mills NJ 08015 Office Phone: 609-893-6611. Personal E-mail: rogermoore435@yahoo.com. *

MOORE, TERRY LYNN, physician, researcher; s. Kenneth Clyde and Mary Elizabeth Moore; m. Carol Louise Miller, July 9, 1971; children: Heather Elizabeth Baldanza, Tara Ellen Medlock, Misti Louise Benson, Kendra Lauren McNichols. AB, U. Mo., Columbia, 1968; MD, St. Louis U., 1972. Diplomate in rheumatology Am. Bd. Internal Medicine, 1976. Prof. internal medicine, pediat., molecular biology and immunology St. Louis U. Med. Ctr., 1976—, dir. adult and pediatric rheumatology, 1976—, 1983—. Contbr. articles to over 180 med. publs. Recipient Rsch. Juvenile Arthritis award, NIH, Am. Coll. Rheumatology, Campbell-Avery Trust Found. Fellow: ACP, Am. Coll. Rheumatology, Am. Acad. Pediat. Achievements include research in juvenile arthritis; systemic lupus erythematosus; other immunological topics. Avocations: softball, soccer. Office: Saint Louis Univ Medical Ctr 1402 S Grand Blvd Saint Louis MO 63104 Office Phone: 314-977-8838. Office Fax: 314-977-8818. Business E-Mail: mooretl@slu.edu. *

MOORE, THOMAS, psychotherapist, spiritual writer; b. Detroit, Oct. 8, 1940; s. Thomas Benjamin and Mary Virginia (Owens) Moore; m. Joan Hanley; 2 children. BA, DePaul U., Chgo., 1967; MA in Musicology, U. Mich., 1969; MA in Theology, U. Windsor, Ontario, Can., 1972; PhD in Religion, Syracuse U., NY, 1975. Asst. prof. Glassboro State Coll., NJ, 1975-76, Southern Meth. U., Dallas, 1976-81; psychotherapist pvt. practice, Amherst, Mass., 1985-91; prof. Lesley Coll., Cambridge, Mass., 1987-91; columnist Beliefnet.com, Spirituality & Health mag. Author: The Planets Within: The Astrological Psychology of Marsilio Ficino, 1982, Rituals of The Imagination, 1983, Dark Eros: The Imagination of Sadism, 1990, Care of the Soul: A Guide for Cultivating Depth and Sacredness in Everyday Life, 1992 (NY Times bestseller), Soul Mates: Honoring the Mysteries of Love and Relationship, 1994, The Re-Enchantment of Everyday Life, 1996, The Education of The Heart, 1996, The Soul of Sex: Cultivating Life as an Act of Love, 1998, Original Self: Living With Paradox and Originality, 2000, The Soul's Religion: Cultivating a Profoundly Spiritual Way of Life, 2002, Dark Nights of the Soul: A Guide to Finding Your Way Through Life's Ordeals, 2004, A Life At Work: The Joy of Discovering What You Were Born To Do, 2008, Writing in the Sand: Jesus and the Soul of the Gospels, 2009 (Books foe a Better Life award, Nat. Multiple Sclerosis Soc., 2010). Avocations: piano, photography, wood working. *

MOORE, THOMAS JOSEPH, endocrinologist, educator; b. Cin., Dec. 17, 1945; AB with honors, Xavier U., 1967; MD, U. Cin., 1971. Prof., medicine, endocrinology, diabetes, and metabolism Boston U., 2001—, provost ad interim, med. campus, 2004—05, chmn., dept. medicine ad interim, Sch. Medicine, 2005—06; assoc. provost, clin. rsch. Boston U. Med. Ctr., 2001—05, assoc. provost, 2006—. Faculty Harvard Med. Sch., 1977—2000; physician Brigham and Women's Hosp., 1977—2000. Recipient Career Devel. award, NIH. Fellow: Am. Heart Assn. (high blood pressure coun., Established Investigator award); mem.: AMA, Mass. Med. Soc., Endocrine Soc. Office: Boston University Med Ctr 72 East Concord St Boston MA 02118 Business E-Mail: tmoore@bu.edu.

MOORE, WARD WILFRED, medical educator; b. Cowden, Ill., Feb. 12, 1924; s. Cecil Leverett and Velma Leona (Frye) M.; m. Frances Laura Campbell, Jan. 29, 1949; children— Scott Thomas, Ann Gail, Brian Dean, Kevin Lee. AB, U. Ill., 1948, MS, 1951, PhD, 1952; DSc (hon.), Mahidol U., Bangkok, 2001. Instr., rsch. assoc. U. Ill., 1952-54; asst. prof. Okla. State U., Stillwater, 1954-55, Ind. U., Bloomington, 1955-59, assoc. prof., 1959-66, prof. physiology, 1966-89, prof. physiology and biophysics emeritus, 1989—, acting chmn. dept. anatomy, 1971-73, assoc. dean basic med. scis., 1971-89, assoc. dean, dir. med. scis. program, 1976-89. Vis. prof. Postgrad. Med. Center, Karachi, Pakistan, 1963-64; staff mem. Rockefeller Found., 1968-71; vis. prof., chmn. dept. physiology, faculty sci. Mahidol U., Bangkok, Thailand, 1968-71 Served with U.S. Army, 1943-46. Mem. Am. Physiol. Soc., Endocrine Soc., Am. Soc. Nephrology, Soc. Study Reproduction, Am. Assn. Anatomists, Soc. Exptl. Biology and Medicine, Am. Assn. Med. Colls., AAAS, Am. Inst. Biol. Scis., AAUP, Ind. Acad. Sci., Ind. Hist. Soc., Shelby County (Ill.) Hist. Soc., Monroe County (Ind.) Hist. Soc., Soc. Sons of Am. Revolution, Sigma Xi, Phi Sigma. Home: 3500 E Bradley St Bloomington IN 47401-4201 Office: Indiana U Jordan Hall # 105 Bloomington IN 47405 Business E-Mail: moorew@indiana.edu. *

MOORE, WESLEY SANFORD, vascular surgeon; b. San Bernardino, Calif., Aug. 1, 1935; s. Louis and Anna M.; m. Patricia Lorenz, Oct. 25, 1960; children: Edward Lorenz, Michael Robertson. BS, U. So. Calif., 1955; MD, U. Calif., 1959. Diplomate: Am. Bd. Surgery (examiner 1980). Intern U. Calif., San Francisco, 1959-60; asst. resident gen. surgery U. Calif. Hosps., San Francisco, 1960-63, chief resident, 1963-64; chief vascular surgery VA Hosp., 1966-77, asst. chief surgery service, 1975-77; asst. prof., surgery U. Calif. Sch. Medicine, San Francisco, 1968—73, assoc. prof., 1973—77; practice medicine specializing in vascular surgery San Francisco, 1966-77; chief, vascular surgery sect. Ariz. Health Scis., 1977—80, VA Hosp., 1977—80; prof. surgery U. Ariz. Coll. Medicine, Tuscon, 1977—80; chief vascular surgery section UCLA Sch. Medicine, 1980—96, chief emeritus, div. vascular surgery, 1996—2004, prof. surgery, 1980—2004; prof., chief emeritus David Geffen Sch. Medicine UCLA, divsn. vascular surgeon, 2004—. Cons. Blue Cross of Calif., Med. Policy Com., 1987—96. Mem. editorial bd. Stroke, 1981—, Jour. Vascular Surgery, 1983—, Annals of Vascular Surgery, 1985—; assoc. editor Vascular Surgery; contbr. over 290 articles on vascular surgery to profl. jours., 195 chpts. to med. texts; editor or co-editor: Vascular Surgery, 1977, 3d edit. 1989, Vascular Surgery: A Comprehensive Review, 1983, 2d edit., 1986, 3rd edit, 1991, 4th edit. 1993, 5th edit. 1998, 6th edit. 2001,Surgery for Cerebrovascular Disease, 1987, 2d edit., 1996, Lower Extremity Amputation, 1989, Endovascular Surgery, 1989, 2d edit., 1992, Cerebrovascular Iscnaemia: Investigation and Management, 1992, Vascular and endovascular Surgery, A Comprehensive Review, 7th edit., 2006 Served to capt., M.C. U.S. Army, 1964-66. Capt. Army Med. Corps, 1964—66, Germany. NIH grantee, 1973-76 Fellow A.C.S. (sec. treas. No. Calif. chpt. 1971-77), Am. Heart Assn. (council on cerebrovascular disease), Am. Surg. Assn.; mem. Internat. Cardiovascular Soc. (membership com. 1977—), Soc. for Vascular Surgery (sec. 1980, pres. 1986-87), Assn. Acad. Surgery, Western Vascular Soc. (founder 1985, pres. 1991-92), San Francisco Surg. Soc., Los Angeles Surg. Soc., Soc. of Univ. Surgeons, Assn. VA Surgeons, Pacific Coast Surg. Assn., Bay Area Vascular Soc. (sec. 1967-77), Rocky Mountain Vascular Soc. (founding mem. 1979, pres. 1979-80), Phi Beta Kappa. Office: David Geffen Sch Medicine at UCLA 200 Medical Plaza Rm 510-6 Los Angeles CA 90095 *

MOORE, WILLIAM HENRY, radiologist; b. Pompton, NJ, Dec. 6, 1973; m. Rebecca Anne Case, May 30, 1999; children: Charlotte Catherine, Matthew John Hartey. MD, Albany Med. Coll., NY, 1999. Diplomate Am. Bd. Radiology. Intern Albany Med. Ctr., 1999—2000; resident in radiology U. Hosp., Stony Brook, NY, 2000—04, chief thoracic imaging, 2004—; vis. fellow thoracic imaging NYU, NYC, 2003—04; dir. med. student edn., dept. radiology Stony Brook U. Med. Ctr., 2005—, med. dir., dept. radiology, 2007—, radiology program dir., residency tng. radiology. Contbr. articles to profl. jours. Recipient Roentgen Rsch. award, 2003, Outstanding Tchr., Stony Brook Med. Sch., 2008; named Tchr. of Yr., 2005, Outstanding Tchr., Stony Brook Med. Sch., 2006. Mem.: Soc. Thoracic Radiologist (sr.), Alpha Omega Alpha, A3CR2 (assoc.; vice chair problem solving 2002—03). Office Fax: 631-444-7538. Business E-Mail: william.moore@stonybrook.edu.

MOORE, WISTAR, cardiovascular surgeon; b. Feb. 16, 1959; BA, U. N.C., 1981, MD, 1985. Bd. cert. gen. surgery, thoracic surgery. Gen. surgery resident Mass. Gen. Hosp., 1985-90; cardiothoracic resident The Emory Clinic, 1990-93; cardiovasc. surgeon Watson Clinic, Lakeland, Fla., 1993-2000; chief divsn. cardiovasc. thoracic surgery Lakeland Regional Med. Ctr., 1996-2000; cardiovasc. surgeon Cardiovasc. Surgeons, Orlando, Fla., 2000—04, Leesburg-Ocala Heart Inst., 2001—. Fellow ACS, Am. Coll. Chest Physicians; mem. Fla. Soc. Thoracic and Cardiovasc. Surgeons, So. Thoracic Surg. Assn., Soc. Thoracic Surgeons. Office: 700 Doctors Ct Leesburg FL 34748

MOORE SIMAS, TIFFANY ANNE, medical educator; b. Woonsocket, RI, May 17, 1974; BA, Clark U., 1996; MD, MPH, U. Mass., Boston, MEd, 2000. Asst. prof., ob-gyn. and pediat. U. Mass. Med. Sch., 2004—, dir., ob-gyn. rsch. divsn., 2009. Fellow: Am. Coll. Obstetrician Gynecologists; mem.: AMA, Worcester Dist. Med. Soc., Mass. Med. Soc., Assn. Profs. Gynecology and Obstetrics Office: University Mass Med Sch Meml Ctr Worcester MA 01605 Office Fax: 508-334-9844. Business E-Mail: tiffanya.mooresimas@umassmemorial.org.

MOOS, WALTER HAMILTON, pharmaceutical company executive; AB in Chemistry cum laude, Harvard U., 1976; PhD in Chemistry, U. Calif., Berkeley, 1982. Scientist Parke-Davis Rsch. Divsn. Warner Lambert Co., Ann Arbor, Mich., 1982-83, sr. scientist, 1984, rsch. assoc., 1984-86, sr. rsch. assoc., 1986-87, sect. dir. chemistry, 1987-89, dir. chemistry, 1989, sr. dir. chemistry, 1990, v.p. neurosci. and biol. chemistry, 1990-91; v.p. rsch. devel. Chiron Corp., Emeryville, Calif., 1991-97, chmn., CEO MitoKor, San Diego, 1997—2004; v.p. bioscience div. SRI Internat., Menlo Park, Calif., 2005—. Adj. asst. prof. dept. medicinal chemistry Coll. Pharmacy, U. Mich., 1990, adj. assoc. prof., 1990-91; adj. prof. dept. pharm. chemistry U. Calif., San Francisco, 1992—, adj. prof. integrated sci. & tech., James Madison U., Harrisonburg, Va.; bd. dirs. Migenix, Rigel Pharm., Biotech. Industry Orgn., Alnis, Anterion, Axiom, Keystone Symposia, Mimotopes, Oncologic, Onyx, Critical Path Inst.; presenter to numerous sci. confs. Co-editor: Drug Discovery Technologies, 1990, Cognitive Disorders: Pathophysiology and Treatment, 1991, Drug Developement Research, 1992-, Strategy & Drug Research, 2007; editor-at-large Medicinal Chemistry, 1988-2004; cons. editor Bio-Organic and Medicinal Chemistry Letters. Mem. Am. Peptide Soc. (charter mem.), U. Mich. Enzyme Discussion Group (co-founder), ACS Divsn. Medicinal Chemistry (chmn. membership com. 1989, councilor 1990), Am. Chem. Soc. Office: SRI Internat 333 Ravenswood Ave Menlo Park CA 94025

MOOSSA, A. R., surgeon, educator; b. Port Louis, Mauritius, Oct. 10, 1939; s. Yacoob and Maude (Rochecoute) M.; m. Denise Willoughby, Dec. 28, 1973; children: Pierre, Noel, Claude, Valentine. BS, U. Liverpool, Eng., 1962, MD (hon.), 1965; postgrad., Johns Hopkins U., 1972—73, U. Chgo., 1973—74. Intern Liverpool Royal Infirmary, 1965—66; resident United Liverpool Hosps. and Alder Hey Children's Hosp., 1966—72; from asst. prof. surgery to assoc. prof. U. Chgo., 1975-77, prof., dir. surg. rsch., chief gen. surgery svc., vice chmn. dept., 1977-83; chmn. dept. surgery U. Calif.-San Diego Med. Ctr., 1983—2004, disting. prof., surgery, emeritus chmn., assoc. dean, spl. counsel clin. affairs, 2004—. Litchfield lectr. U., Oxford, Eng., 1978; praelector in surgery U. Dundee, Scotland, 1979; Hampson Trust vis. prof. U. Liverpool, 1992, G.B. Ong. vis. prof. U. Hong Kong, 1993, Philip Sandblon vis. prof. U. Lund, Sweden. Editor: Tumors of the Pancreas, 1982, Essential Surgical Practice, 1983, 4th edit., 2000, Comprehensive Textbook of Oncology, 1985, 2d edit., 1991, Gastrointestinal Emergencies, 1985, Problems in General Surgery, 1989, Operative Colorectal Surgery, 1993. Fellow Royal Coll. Surgeons (Hunterian prof. 1977); mem. ACS, Am. Surg. Assn., Soc. Univ. Surgeons, Am. Soc. Clin. Oncology, European Surg. Assn. Office: U Calif San Diego Thornton Hosp 9300 Campus Point Dr 7212 La Jolla CA 92037 Office Phone: 858-657-6112. Personal E-mail: armoossa@gmail.com. Business E-Mail: amoossa@ucsd.edu.

MOOSSY, JOHN, neurologist, consultant, pathologist; b. Shreveport, La., Aug. 24, 1925; s. John Yazbeck and Rose (Ferris) M.; m. Yvonne Reese, Mar. 15, 1951; children: John Jefferson, Joan Marie. MD, Tulane U., 1950. Intern Charity Hosp. of New Orleans, 1950-51, neurology resident, 1951-53; neuropathology fellow Columbia U. Coll. of Physicians and Surgeons, NYC, 1953-54; assoc., lectr. in neuropathology Tulane U. Sch. Medicine, New Orleans, 1954-57; asst. to prof. in pathology, neurology La. State U., New Orleans, 1957-65; prof. pathology, grad. faculty U. Pitts., 1965-67; prof. pathology neuropathology Bowman Gray Sch. of Medicine, Winston-Salem, NC, 1967-72; prof. pathology and neurology, dir. div. neuropathology U. Pitts., 1972-93, emeritus prof., 1993—. Dir. Cerebrovascular Disease Study, World Fedn. of Neurology, Antwerp, Belgium, 1960-61; cons. Armed Forces Inst. of Pathology, Washington, 1977—, mem. sci. adv. bd., Washington, 1984-86. Editor: Cerebral Vascular Disease Seventh Conference, 1970, Cerebrovascular Diseases 12th Research Conference, 1981; editor-in-chief Jour. Neuropathology and Exptl. Neurology, 1981-91; mem. editorial bd. Archives Neurology, 1982-92. Recipient Excellence in Teaching award U. Pitts. Sch. of Medicine, 1987-88; named Commencement Speaker U. Pitts. Sch. of Medicine, 1989. Mem. Am. Acad. Neurology (sec.-treas. 1963-655), Am. Neurol. Assn. (v.p. 1977-78), Am. Assn. Neuropathologists (pres. 1974-75, Neuropathology award 1992), Internat. Soc. Neuropathology, Coun. Biology Editors.

MOOTHA, ADITYA KRISHNA, physician; b. Kakinada, Andhra Pradesh, India, Dec. 16, 1982; MBBS, Banaras Hinu U., 2005; MS, Post Grad. Inst. Med. Edn. and Rsch., 2008. Physician Sunshine Hosps., 2010—, cons., 2010. Recipient Gold medal, Pres. of India, Banaras Hinu U. Home: 15-8-5 Venkataratna puram Kakinada Andhra Pradesh 533001 India Personal E-mail: akmootha2005@yahoo.com.

MOR, GIL, immunologist, educator; b. Quito, Ecuador, Dec. 23, 1960; m. Anette Mor; children: Jechiel, Adaja. MD, Hebrew U., Med. Sch., Jerusalem, Israel, 1987; MSc in Neuroendocrinology, Hebrew U., Jerusalem, Israel, 1988; PhD in Immunoendocrinology, Weizmann Inst. Sci., Rehovot, Israel, 1993. Clin. tng. reproductive endocrinology, dept. ob-gyn. Kaplan Hosp., Rehovot, Israel, 1990—93; fellow, reproductive endocrinology Max-Planck Inst. for Exptl. Endocrinology, Hanover, Germany, 1991; postdoctoral fellow, lab. immunobiology Ctr. for Biologics Evaluation and Rsch., FDA, NIH, Bethesda, Md., 1994—96; assoc. rsch. scientist, dept. ob-gyn. Yale U. Sch. Medicine, New Haven, 1997—98, asst. prof., dept. ob-gyn., 1998—2002, assoc. prof., dept. ob-gyn., 2003—, tenure ob-gyn., 2008. Adj. lectr. U. New Haven, Conn., 1997—; webmaster, dept. ob-gyn., 2001—03; mem. CME task force Yale U. Sch. Medicine, 2003, Yale CME adv. com. mem., 04; dir., Tranlational Rsch, in Gynecologic Oncology: Discovery to Cure: Ovarian Cancer Detection and Treatment Program, Dept. Ob-gyn. Yale U., 2004—; organizer, dir. Discovery to Cure HS Internship; editor-in-chief Am. Jour. Reproductive Immunology; invited spkr. and presenter in the field. Author: Immunology of Implantation, 2006; contbr. several articles to profl. jours.; mem. editl. bd. Jour. Soc. for Gynecologic Investigation, 2004—, Eureka Bioscience, 2005—, reviewer for several peer-reviewed jours. Recipient Israel Endocrine Soc. award in Basic Endocrine Sci., 1991—92, Minerva Tng. Fellowship award, 1991, Guerchenson Scholarship award, 1991—93, Soc. for Maternal-Fetal Medicine: Rsch. Excellence award (mentor), ann. meeting, 2002, Placental Assn. Americas: Rsch. award (mentor), 2004; grantee, NIH (several different studies), 2000—06; ORISE Fellowship award, 1995—96. Mem.: AAAS, Soc. for Gynecologic Investigation (Oustanding Presentation award 2000), Am. Assn. for Cancer Rsch., Am. Soc. Reproductive Immunology (councilor 2001—, sec. 2005—, program chmn. for 2003 ann. mtg., Mentor award, ann. meeting 1999, 2000, New Investigator award (mentor), ann. meeting 2001), Climacteric Soc.-Paraguay (hon.), Menopause Soc.-Argentina (hon.), Menopause Soc. Chile (hon.), Climacteric Soc.-Ecuador (hon.). Achievements include development of new test for early detection of ovarian cancer; new treatment for ovarian cancer; discovery of action of estrogens on the immune system; role of apoptosis in ovarian cancer; patents in field, discovery of isolation and characterisation of ovarian cancer stem cells. Office: Yale U Sch Medicine Dept Ob-Gyn & Reproductive Sciences 333 Cedar St FMB 302 New Haven CT 06520-8063 Office Fax: 203-785-4883. Business E-Mail: gil.mor@yale.edu.

MORA, CHRISTINA THERESA, medical educator, director; b. Trenton, NJ, May 26, 1953; MD, Rutgers U., 1979. Asst. prof. Jefferson Med. Coll., 1985—89, Emory U., 1989—94; prof. Stanford U., 1995—, dir., divsn. cardiovasc. anesthesiology, 2003—. Pres. Soc. Cardiovasc. Anesthesiologists, 2007—09; editor Jour. Thoracic and Cardiovasc. Surgery, 2009—. Fellow: Am. Heart Assn. Office: 300 Pasteur Dr Stanford CA 94305 Personal E-mail: ctmora@comcast.net.

MORA, RENZO, otolaryngologist, educator; b. Savona, Italy, July 6, 1970; s. Enzo and Anna (Fenoglio) Mora; m. Barbara Crippa, May 5, 1999; children: Martina, Mattia. MD, Genoa U., Italy, 1994; Specialization Otolaryngology, Ear, Nose, Throat Clin. U. Genoa, 1998. Diplomate in Otolaryngology ENT Clin., U. of Genoa, Italy, 1998. Specialist in otolaryngology San Giovanni Bosco Hosp., Torino, Italy, 1999—2000; physician San Martino Hosp.l-U. of Genoa, Genoa, Italy, 2000—; asst. prof. otolarynology U. Genoa Hosp., Italy, 2005—. Chmn, Otolaryngology Dept. U. Genoa, 2001—. Achievements include treatment of tinnitus and hearing loss using sodium enoxaparin and use of electronystagmography in the diagnosis of peripheral and central vertigo, in particular the visuo-vestibul interaction test; development of a new bony scalpel (piezosurgery). introducted for the first time in the world by his chairman proof, a salami and on analysis of speech and voice; a new piezosurgery, introduced for the first time in the world. Office: Univ Genoa ENT Dept Largo R Benzi 10 Genoa 16132 Italy Home: 9 Via Dei Mille 11 16147 Genoa GE Italy Office Phone: 390103537631, 393421213242, 0333285304828. Office Fax: 390103537684. Business E-Mail: renzomora@libero.it.

MORABITO, ANTONINO, pediatric surgeon; b. Terni, Italy, Oct. 15, 1965; s. Nicola Morabito and Paola Bartoli. MD, U. Perugia, Italy, 1990. Cons. paediatric and neonatal surgeon Manchester Children's Hosp., NHS, England, 2003—. Hon. lectr. U. Manchester, Sch. Medicine, 2003. With Italian Air Force, 1993—94. Fellow, Manchester Children's Hosp., NHS, 2000—02. Fellow: RCS (Edinburgh), RCS (Eng.), ICS; mem.: Nat. Assn. Asst. Surg. Practice, Italian Med. Assn. Roman Catholic. Achievements include interests in the management of children with congenital anomelies, endocrine surgery, the management of neurologically impaired children with severe gastroesophageal reflux; the surgical treatment of short bowel state. Avocations: mountain biking, photography, reading. Office: Manchester Children's

Hospital Hospital Rd Manchester M27 4HA England Home: 5 Hendon Close Regents Pk Wilmslow Cheshire SK9 2G2 England Office Phone: 004401617012194. Office Fax: 004401612766854; Home Fax: 004401612766854. Personal E-mail: antonino.morabito@cmmc.nhs.uk. E-mail: antonino.morabito@manchester.ac.uk.

MORABITO, ROCCO ANTHONY, urologist; b. Huntington, W.Va., Nov. 23, 1950; s. Nicola F. and Theresa M. (Lobaldo) M.; m. Deborah Gayle Hall, 1973 (div. 1986); m. Brenda Kay Lyons, June 14, 1991; children: Shawn, Chris, Rocco Jr., Justin. BA, W.Va. U., 1972, MD, 1976. Diplomate Am. Bd. Urology, Nat. Bd. Med. Examiners. Surg. residency W.Va. U. Hosp., Morgantown, 1976-78, urol. residency, 1978-81; pres. Huntington (W.Va.) Urol. Assn., 1981—, Midwest Mobile Lithotripsy, Huntington, 1989-96, Tri-State Health Ptnrs., Huntington, 1994-96; pres. med. staff Cabell Huntington Hosp., Huntington, 1991-93, St. Mary's Hosp., 1997-99. Clin. prof. urology, W.Va. U. Sch. Medicine, 1981—, Marshall U. Sch. Medicine, Huntington, 1981—. Fellow ACS; mem. AMA, Am. Urol. Assn., So. Med. Assn., W.Va. State Med. Assn., Cabell County Med. Soc., W.Va. U. Sch. Medicine Alumni Assn. (chmn. 1989-94). Republican. Roman Catholic. Avocations: tennis, boating, skiing, music, cooking, golf. Home: 20 Kensington Ln Huntington WV 25705-3860 Office: Huntington Urological Assn 2860 3rd Ave Ste 230 Huntington WV 25702-1453 Office Phone: 304-525-3711. Business E-Mail: huairam@frontier.com.

MORACA-SAWICKI, ANNE MARIE, oncology nurse; b. Niagara Falls, NY, Sept. 28, 1952; d. Joseph R. and Joan (Forgione) Moraca; m. Richard L. Sawicki, Sept. 15, 1979. BSN, D'Youville Coll., 1974; MS in Nursing, SUNY at Buffalo, 1977. Asst. prof. nursing D'Youville Coll., Buffalo, 1977-81; clin. editor Springhouse (Pa.) Corp., 1981-82; charge nurse Mt. St. Mary's Hosp., Lewiston, N.Y., 1982-84; surg. coord., adminstrv. asst. Dr. Richard L. Sawicki, Niagara Falls, N.Y., 1983—. Clin. cons., externship site supr. Niagara County C.C., Sanborn, N.Y.; bd. dirs. Health Assn. Niagara County, Inc., adult day care program Health Assn. Niagara County Inc. Contbr.: Nurses Legal Handbook, 1985, Pharmacotherapeutics: A Nursing Process Approach, 1986, 2d edit., 1990, 3rd edit., 1994, 4th edit., 1998; clin. editor, contbr. Nurses Ref. Libr. Series Vols. on Drugs, Definitions, Procedures and Practices; clin. reviewer Manual of Med./Sug. Nursing, 1995, contbr., 1996; clin. reviewer Critical Care Handbook and IV Drug Handbook, 1995; clin. cons. Critical Care Plans, 1987, Taber's Cyclopedic Med. Dictionary, 16th edit., 1989; grant writer LaSalle Bus. and Profl. Assn. Mem. Niagara Falls Cmty. Devel. Bd.; bd. dirs. Barbara Zimmer Holiday Wish Show, Barbara Zimmer Holiday Wish Breast Cancer Fund Raiser; co-chairperson LaSalle Bus. and Profl. Cmty. Devel. Fund Raising Com.; com. mem., The Premier Fundraiser 4 yrs. Niagara Falls Meml. Med. Ctr., 2011, co-chair, 2011; premier fundraiser Stroke Ctr. for Hosp.; bd. mem. Niagara County Med. Res. Corps.; mem. Niagara Falls Devel. Corp.; founder, chairperson Our Lady of Fatima Shrine Festival of Lights Banquet & Auction; pres. St. Peter's Altar Rosary Guild, Lewiston, NY, Program of All-Inclusive Care of Elderly Bd., Niagara Falls, Bd. PACE; mem. bd. Found. Lifelong Health; mem. devel. com. 1st PACE Program in Niagara County. Recipient Cert. of Appreciation Niagara County C.C., 1988, 91, 92, Cmty. Svc. award Am. Cancer Soc., 1978, Miss Hope award, 1977, Am. Cancer Soc. Nursing Fellowship Grant, 1977, Good Neighbor award Niagara Falls Meml. Med. Ctr., 2003, LaSalle Bus. and Profl. Assn. Cmty. Svc. award, 2003, Pres.'s award, Health Assn. Niagra County Inc., 2004, named Small Bus. Person of Yr., 2006; Grad. fellow SUNY, Buffalo, 1976-77; grantee mulitple grants for cmty. devel., beautification and health and safety, LaSalle. Mem. AAUP, NY State Nurse's Assn., Health Assn. Niagara County (chairperson 1995—, bd. dirs. adult day care program), LaSalle Bus. and Prof. Assn. (publicity chairperson, v.p.), Am. Bus. Women's Assn. (Woman of Yr., 2008), Sigma Theta Tau. Home: 4658 Vrooman Dr Lewiston NY 14092-1049 Home Phone: 716-754-4413; Office Phone: 716-283-3338. E-mail: ams928@webtv.net.

MORADY, FRED, cardiac electrophysiologist, educator; MD, U. Calif., San Francisco, 1975. Diplomate Am. Bd. Internal Medicine, 1978, cert. Am. Bd. Internal Medicine-cardiovasc. disease, 1982, diplomate Am. Bd. Internal Medicine-clin. cardiac electrophysiology. Resident internal medicine Univ. Calif.-San Francisco Med. Ctr., 1976—78, fellow cardiovasc. disease, 1978—80; prof. medicine Univ. of Mich., McKay prof. cardiovasc. disease. Office: University of Michigan Health System Cardiovascular System 1500 E Medical Center Drive Ann Arbor MI 48109 Office Phone: 734-763-7392, 734-936-7026.

MORAES, MIGUEL RICARDO BARBOSA, sports medicine physician; b. Fortaleza, Brazil, July 3, 1961; s. João and Antoinette Barbosa Moraes; m. Jacqueline Leão Moraes, Mar. 25, 1986; children: Juliana Leão, Emanuel Ricardo Leão. MS, Fed. U. Ceara, Fortaleza, Bazil, 2006, PhD, 2008. Medicine grad. U. Ceara, 1979—; specialist, orthopedia Dr. Jose Frota Inst., Fortaleza, 1986—; sport medicine physician Brazilian Soc. Sport Medicine, Sao Paulo, Brazil, 2007—. Dir. Clinic Traumatology Rehab., Brazil; specialist, orthopedia Brazilian Soc. Orthop. Traumatology, Sao Paulo, 2001—. Athlete runner, Fortaleza, 1980—2008. Lt. second med. Brazilian Army, 1989—91, Fortaleza. Master: Brazilian Soc. Sports Medicine; mem.: Brazilian Soc. Orthop. and Traumatology. Office: Fed Univ Ceara 1608 Costa Mendes Professor St 3rd Fl Fortaleza 60530-140 Brazil Personal E-mail: luzete6@hotmail.com, miguelbm@secrel.com.br. Business E-Mail: luciene@ufc.br.

MORAHAN-MARTIN, JANET MAY, psychologist, educator; b. NYC, Jan. 13, 1944; d. William Timothy and May Rosalind (Tarangelo) Morahan; m. Curtis Harmon Martin, June 2, 1979; 1 child, Gwendolyn May. AB, Rosemont Coll., Pa., 1965; MEd, Tufts U., 1968; PhD, Boston Coll., 1978. Asst. mkt. rsch. analyst Compton Advt. Co., NYC, 1965-67; mkt. rsch. analyst Ogilvy & Mather Advt., NYC, 1967; ednl. rsch. asst. Tufts U., Medford, Mass., 1968-69; counselor Psychol. Inst. Bentley Coll., Waltham, Mass., 1971-72; dir. counseling svcs. Bryant U., Smithfield, RI, 1972-75, psychology instr., 1972—76, asst. prof. psychology, 1976—81, assoc. prof. psychology, 1981—91, prof. psychology, 1991—, chair dept. applied psychology, 2007—. Bd. dirs. Multi-Svc. Ctr., Newton, Mass., 1980-82. Contbr. articles to profl. jours., chpts. to books; reviewer APA Conv., 1985—, Teaching of Psychology Jour., 1988—, Collegiate Micro-Computer Jour., 1991, 93, Nat. Soc. Sci. Jour., 1991; mem. editl. bd., spl. edit. editor Cyber Psychology and Behavior. Bd. dirs. Wellesley (Mass.) Community Children's Ctr., 1986-90, Coun. for Children, Newton, Mass., 1984-86. NIMH fellow, 1967-68; NSF grantee, 1974-76, U.S. Office Edn. grantee, 1980. Mem. APA, Mass. Audubon Soc., Internat. Soc. for Online Mental Health (founding mem.), Soc. for Tchg. of Psychology, Soc. Computers in Psychology. Avocations: photography, antiques, gardening, literature. Home: 17 Fuller Brook Rd Wellesley MA 02482-7108 Office: Bryant U 1150 Douglas Pike Smithfield RI 02917-1291 Business E-Mail: jmorahan@bryant.edu.

MORALES, RAUL E., urologist; b. Santiago, Chile, Dec. 23, 1947; s. Raul J. and Julia G. (Iturrizagastegui) Morales; m. Marianella R. Olivi; children: Fernanda, Ignacio, Josefa. MD, U. Chile, 1973. Gen. surgeon Melipilla Hosp., Chile, 1973—76; urology trainer Hosp. U. Chile, Santiago, 1976—79; urologist Hosp. San Juan de Dios, 1979—92; mem. urology staff Clinica Las Condes, 1992—2003; urologist Assoc. Clinica Las Condes, 2003—08; mem. urology staff Clinica Indisa, 2008—. Med. counselor Mormon Ch., Santiago, 1995—2009; physician Little Sisters of the Poor, Santiago, 1979—2009. Fellow: ACS; mem.: Chilean Urol. Soc., Chilean Transplant Soc. (pres. 1998—2000), Soc. Internat. Urology, Am. Urol. Soc. (corr.). Avocation: reading. Office: Av 11 de Sepnembre 1363 OF307 Santiago Chile Home: Camino Del Cerro Alto Casa D Lo Barneche 10056 Santiago Chile Office Phone: (56)2 2352083. Business E-Mail: raulmoralesi@mi.cl.

MORALES-GALARRETA, JULIO, psychiatrist, child psychoanalyst; b. Trujillo, Peru, Dec. 1, 1936; came to U.S., 1973; s. Julio Morales-Fernandez and Lidia (Galarreta) Morales; (div.); children: Lourdes Lydia, Julio Fernando. MD, U. Trujillo, 1966; grad., St. Louis Psychoanalytic Inst., 1984, grad. in child psychoanalysis, 1985. Diplomate Am. Bd. Psychiatry and Neurology; cert. psychoanalyst.; cert. child psychoanalyst. Resident in psychiatry Ministry of Pub. Health, Peru, 1965-68; supr. psychiat. tng. program Ministry Pub. Health, Peru, 1970-72; physician and surgeon U. Trujillo, 1966; instr. psychaitry St. Marcos U., Peru, 1968-72; resident in psychiatry Fairfield Hills Hosp., Newtown, Conn., 1972-74; fellow in child psychiatry Washington U., St. Louis, 1974-76, instr. child psychiatry, 1976-82; dir. child devel. project St. Louis Psychoanalytic Inst., 1982-94, dir. child and adolescent psychotherapy program, 1993—2008, dir. child psychoanalysis, 1996—2008; assoc. clin. prof. psychiatry and pediatrics St. Louis U., 1983-96, clin. prof. psychiatry and pediatrics, 1996—. Faculty psychoanalysis and child analysis St. Louis Psychoanalytic Inst., 1984—, supervising analyst in child analyst, 1988, tng. and supervising analyst in adult and child psychoanalysis, 1991—. Fellow Peruvian Psychiat. Assn., Am. Psychiat. Assn. (mem. cert. com. bd. on profl. stds. 1996—), Am. Psychol. Assn.; mem. St. Louis Met. Med. Soc., Am. Acad. Child Psychiatry, Am. Psychoanalytic Assn. (mem. of cert. com. in psychoanalysis 1996—), Am. Soc. Adolescent Psychiatry, Assn. Child Psychoanalysis, St. Louis Psychiat. Soc. (pres. 1997-99). Avocations: classical music, biking, tennis, golf. Office: St Louis U 8820 Ladue Rd Saint Louis MO 63124-2079 Home Phone: 314-727-2617; Office Phone: 314-754-3254.

MORAN, CHRISTOPHER JOHN, radiologist, educator; b. Detroit, Apr. 2, 1948; s. Frank William and Susan T. Moran; m. Eleanor M. Maldeon, Sept. 5, 1969; children: Christopher John Jr., William Joseph, Mary Catherine. BS, U. Notre Dame, South Bend, Ind., 1970; MD, St. Louis U., 1974. Diplomate Am. Bd. Radiology in diagnostic radiology, 1978, cert. neuroradiology Am. Bd. Radiology, 95. Resident Mallinckrodt Inst. Radiology, 1974—78; prof. radiology, neurol. surgery Washington U., St. Louis, 2003—09. Mem. sci. adv. bd. Stereotaxis Inc., St. Louis, 1999—. Assoc. editor: Radiology, 2002—05, cons. to editor:, 2005—06. Bd. dirs. St. Louis Fiends Injured Marine Semper Fi Fund, Injured Marine Semper Fi Fund, 2005—. Fellow: Am. Coll. Radiology; mem.: Am. Soc. Interventional and Therapeutic Neuroradiology (sr.), Am. Soc. Neuroradiology (sr.). Achievements include patents in field. Home: 12559 Amersham Ct Saint Louis MO 63141 Office: Washington U 510 S Kingshighway Saint Louis MO 63110 Office Phone: 314-362-5949.

MORAN, DANIEL THOMAS, dentist, poet, educator, humanist celebrant; b. NYC, Mar. 9, 1957; s. Thomas Daniel and Jean Elizabeth Moran; m. Karen Kay; children: Lindsay Alison, Ashley Zurl, Gregory Riordan. AS, Nassau Coll., 1977; BS, SUNY, Stony Brook, 1979; D in Dental Surgery, Howard U., 1983. Staff assoc. Southhampton (N.Y.) Hosp., 1988-94; host L.I. Radio mag., Southampton, NY, 1994—99; literary corr. L.I. Pub. Radio, Southampton, NY, 1994—2001; pvt. practice Shelter Island, NY, 1987—2009; v.p. Ludwig Vogelstein Found., 2007—; clin. asst. prof. Boston U. Sch. Dental Medicine, 2008—. Author: Dancing for Victoria, 1991, Gone to Innisfree, 1993, Sheltered by Islands, 1995, In Praise of August, 1999, From Hilo to Willow Pond, 2002, Looking for the Uncertain Past, 2006, The Light of City and Sea, 2006; contbr. poetry to profl. publs. Trustee Shelter Island chpt. ARC; dir. Gardiner's Bay Country Club, 1993-98, historian 1993—, tournament chmn., 1993-96); v.p. Walt Whitman Birthplace Assn., Huntington, N.Y., 1997-2005, v.p., 2001-05; hon. dir. Wildlife Rescue Ctr. of the Hamptons. Grantee Poets and Writers, Inc., 1996-2007; named Poet Laureate Suffolk County Legislature, NY, 2005-07, Humanist Celebrant Am. Humanist Assn; named to Dean's Coun., Melville Libr., Stonybrook U., 2005, Named to Hall Of Fame Massapequa, NY, 2007; nominee Pushcart prize. Mem. Irish Am. Writers Assn., Assn. Literary Scholars, Critics and Writers, PEN Am. Ctr., New England Poetry Club, Am. Dental Edn. Assn., Password Project, Am. Humanist Assn. (Humanist Celebrant). Avocations: harmonica, drums, piano. Address: 515 Shawmut Ave Boston MA 02118 Home: 141 Dustin Rd Webster NH 03303 Home Phone: 857-350-3338; Office Phone: 857-350-3338. Personal E-mail: dan@danielthomasmoran.net.

MORAN, JOHN FRANCIS, cardiologist; b. Chgo., Sept. 5, 1938; MD, Loyola U., Stritch Sch. Medicine, 1964. Cert. cardio. disease 1973. Office: Loyola U Med Ctr 2160 S 1st Ave Maywood IL 60153 Office Phone: 708-327-2784.

MORANA, GIOVANNI, radiologist, director; b. Vittoria, Ragusa, Italy, Nov. 4, 1961; MD, U. Catania, 1986; degree in Radiology, U. Verona, 1992. Radiologist Gen. Hosp. Verona, 1988—97; asst. prof. U. Verona, 1997—2004; dir. radiol. dept. Gen. Hosp. Treviso, 2004—. Fellow: Internat. Cancer Imaging Soc., European Soc. Gastrointestinal and Abdominal Radiology; mem.: Internat. Soc. Magnetic Resonance Medicine, Radiol. Soc. N.Am., Italian Soc. Med. Radiology. Avocations: reading, theater, sailing. Office: General Hosp Ca' Foncello Radiological Dept Treviso 31100 Italy Office Fax: 390422322202. Business E-Mail: gmorana@ulss.tv.it.

MORASSO, GABRIELLA GIOVANNA, psychologist; b. Savona, Italy, Aug. 23, 1951; d. Cesare and Paola (Gaggino) M. MSc in Psychology, U. Genoa, Italy, 1974, PhD in Psychology, 1978. Cert. Italian Order Psychologists, Italian Order Psychotherapists. Rsch. fellow Nat. Cancer Inst., Genoa, 1979-81, asst. psychologist, 1982-87, 1st asst. psychologist, 1988-90, head psychol. svc., 1991—. Prof. Sch. Social Workers, Genoa, 1992—; sci. coord. Stop Smoking Program, Italian League Against Cancer, 1985—, Cancer Info. Helpline, Ministry of Health, 1995—, Psychol. Assistance for Dying Patients program Ministry of Health, 1993—. Mme. Italian Psychosocial Oncology Soc. (pres.). Office: Nat Cancer Inst Pzle Rosanna Benzi 10 16132 Genoa Italy

MORAVEK, JIRI, pediatrician, surgeon, medical educator, consultant; b. Teplice, Bohemia, Czech Republic, Apr. 21, 1948; s. Jan Moravek and Eliska Moravkova; m. Hana Petruvova, May 26, 2001; children: Tereza, David, Jakub. Diploma in English, State Linguistic Sch., Prague, 1969; diploma in German, State Linguistic Sch., Pilsen, Czech Republic, 1976; MD, Charles U., Prague, 1976, postgrad., 1999. Bd. cert. gen. surgeon Charles U., Prague, 1979, bd. cert. pediat. surgeon Charles U., Prague, 1986, bd. cert. pediat. urology Charles U., Prague, 1991. Mechanic, machinist Tesla Elec. Co., Prague, Czech Republic, 1966—69; tech. asst. dept. paleontology Charles U., Prague, 1969—70, gen. surgeon country hosp., 1976—81, pediat. surgeon tchg. hosp., 1981—95, univ. tchr., 1995—. Lectr. Inst. Postgrad. Edn. Medicine and Pharmacology, Prague, 1995—2008. Mem.: Czech Transplant Soc., European Assn. Urology, Czech Assn. Pediat. Surgeons. Avocations: classical music, bicycling, crafts. Office Phone: 2 2443 2401.

MORBECK, DEAN, lab administrator, consultant; b. West Allis, Wis., Feb. 15, 1964; BS, U. Wis., 1986; PhD, NC State U., 1992. Cons. Mayo Clinic, 2006—. Office: 200 1st St SW Charlton 3A Rochester MN 55905 Business E-Mail: morbeck.dean@mayo.edu.

MORE, BALAJI, pharmacologist; b. Latur, India, Nov. 25, 1973; MD, Govt. Med. Coll., Miraj, India, 1996; DM, Seth GS Med. Coll. & KEM Hosp., Mumbai, 2004. Mgr., med. svcs. Merck Ltd., India, 2010—. Cons. Mem.: Am. Coll. Clin. Pharmacology. Home: 902 Kasturi Tower Plot 24 Sector 8 Airoli Mumbai Maharashtra 400708 India Personal E-mail: bdmdcp@yahoo.com.

MOREAU, DONNA L., psychiatrist, educator; MD, SUNY, 1980. Diplomate Am. Bd. Psychiatry and Neurology, Am. Bd. Psychiatry and Neurology-child and adolescent psychiatry. Resident in psychiatry NY Hosp., 1984—86, fellow in child and adolescent psychiatry, 1984—86; assoc. clin. prof. psychiatry Columbia P&S; child and adolescent psychiatry NewYork-Presbyn. Hosp. Recipient Castle Connolly Top Doctors: NY Metro Area, 1999—2010, 2011. Office: NewYork-Presbyterian Hospital 525 E. 68th St. New York NY 10021 Office Phone: 212-746-5454.

MOREAU, PATRICK MARCEL, thoracic and vascular surgeon; b. Perpignan, France, Sept. 5, 1948; s. Marcel Jules and Yvonne Henriette (Delaunay) M.; children: Dominique, Magali, Eric, Charles; Sylvie Puel, Feb. 15, 2003. MD, U. Montpellier, France, 1972. Intern Hosp. of Montpellier, 1974-79; resident in gen. surgery Paris, 1981; resident in vascular surgery, 1982; resident in thoracic surgery, 1982; pvt. practice thoracic and vascular surgery Béziers, France, 1982—. Contbr. articles to med. jours. Capt. French Navy, 1975-76. Recipient Lauréat de la Faculté de Médecine de Montpellier, 1982. Mem. Internat. Soc. for Cardiovascular Surgery, Soc. Chirurgie Thoracique et Cardiovasculaire, soc. Chirurgie Vasculaire. Republican. Roman Catholic. Avocations: hiking, bicycling. Office: Ctr Med du Trencavel 16 avenue Jean Moulin 34500 Béziers France Office Phone: 33 (4) 67-31-75-85. E-mail: vasculairemoreau@free.fr.

MOREIRA, CÍCERO DA SILVA, pharmacist; b. Mar de Espanha, Minas Gerais, Brazil, June 1, 1983; Pharmacist Faculty Pharmacy and Biochemistry, Fed. U. Juiz de Fora, 2005, adminstr., 2011; tech. mgr., Pharmacy Svc. Hosp. Santa Casa Misericórdia Juiz de Fora, 2007—, adj. prof., Nursing Sch., 2008. Decorated Royal Dragon Mines medal Brazil. Avocations: Judo, boxing. Home: St Doutor Maurício Guerra 24/401 Juiz de Fora Minas Gerais 36062-057 Brazil Personal E-mail: cicerosmoreira@hotmail.com.

MOREIRA-ALMEIDA, ALEXANDER, psychiatrist, researcher; b. Tres Rios, Rio de Janeiro, Brazil, Mar. 28, 1974; s. Helio de Almeida and Elizabeth C. M. Almeida; m. Angelica A. S. Silva, Nov. 6, 1999; children: Laura Silva de children: Caio Silva de Almeida. MD, Fed. U. Juiz de Fora Sch. Medicine, Brazil, 1997; PhD, U. Sao Paulo, 2005. Cert. cognitive behavioral therapist Inst. Psychiatry U. Sao Paulo, 1999. Resident Inst. Psychiatry, U. Sao Paulo, 1998—2000, coord. grand rounds, 1999, co-founder, dir. neper, 1999—2005; mem. PhD dissertation com. Inst. Transpersonal Psychology, Palo Alto, Calif., 2005—06; dir. evidence based medicine clin. meetings Hosp. Joao Evangelista, Sao Paulo, 2004—05; prof. Fed. U. Juiz de Fora Sch. Medicine, Brazil, 2006—; dir. Svc. Psychiatry and Psychol. Medicine of U. Hosp. Fed. U. Suiz Fora, 2009—. Clin. dir. Joao Evangelista Psychiat. Hosp., Sao Paulo, 2002—05, Revista De Psiquiatria Clinica; founder & dir. Nupes Spirituality and Health Rsch. Ctr. Sci. reviewer: Brazilian Jour. Cognitive Therapy, 2004—, European Psychiatry, 2006—, Social, Sci. and Medicine, 2007—. Vol. physician Grupo Espirita Batuira, Sao Paulo, 2000—05. Recipient Darci Corazza, Brazilian Soc. of Cognitive Therapy, 2001, IV UFJF Sci. Initiation Quiral Award, Fed. U. of Juiz de Fora, 1997, Best poster, Fed. U. of Juiz de Fora Sch. of Medicine, 1997; scholar, Duke U. Med. Ctr., Ctr. Spirituality, Theology and Health, 2005—06; fellowship, João Evangelista Hosp. Hose. Mem.: Brazilian Soc. Nephrology (com. mental health and nephrology 2002—05), Brazilian Psychiat. Assn. Achievements include research in the first comprehensive scientific research about the Profile and Psychopathology of Spiritualist Mediums using rigorous methodology; guest editor of the first issue of a Brazilian Scientific Journal entirely devoted to Spirituality and Health, Rvista Psiquiatria Clinica, vol.34, 2007; development of a wide process of modernization and humanization of a mental health inst. Office: Fed U Juiz de Fora Sch Medicine Juiz de Fora Brazil Business E-Mail: alex.ma@ufjf.edu.br.

MOREL, KENNETH R., psychologist; b. Hartford, Conn., Sept. 21, 1958; BA, Our Lady Lake U., 1988; MS, U. Utah, 1993. Psychologist

NIMH, 1997—99, Army Med. Command, 1999—2002; psychometrist Dept. Ves. Affairs Med. Ctr., 2002—09; psychologist Dept. Navy, 2009. Reviewer Archives Clin. Neuropsychology Jour., 2001—11, Clin. Neuropsychologist Jour., 2001—11, Jour. Forensic Psychiatry and Psychology, 2001—11, Jour. Traumatic Stress, 2001—11. Decorated Superior Civilian Svc. medal US Army Med. Command; recipient Recognition Cert., USN, Performance award, Dept. Vets. Affairs Med. Ctr., Excellence Rsch. award, citation, Dept. Health and Human Svcs. Achievements include development of morel emotional numbing test for posttraumatic stress disorder. Office: 6433 Rock Forest Dr 401 Bethesda MD 20817 Personal E-mail: k_morel@yahoo.com.

MORELLI, LUCA, pathologist, educator; b. Trento, Italy, June 24, 1969; s. Manlio Morelli and Maria Eccel. MD, U. Verona, Italy, 1994. Specialization in anatomic pathology U. Verona, 1998. Asst. dept. anatomic pathology Hosp., Rovereto, Trento, Italy, 2000—. Home: via Belenzani 47 38100 Trento Italy Office: UO di Anatomia e Istologia Patologica Piazzale Santa Maria 6 38068 Rovereto TN Italy Office Fax: 00390464453029. Personal E-mail: morellarius@hotmail.com. Business E-Mail: morelli@rov.apss.tn.it.

MORELLO, CANDIS MARGUERITE, pharmacist, educator; b. Lynwood, Calif., May 5, 1969; d. Albert James and Darcy Lovgren Pavich (Stepmother), Keith R. (Stepfather) and Claire Barragan Kerr; m. Christopher Salvatore Morello; children: Joseph Salvatore, Lucas Sebastian. BA, U. Calif., Davis, 1991; PharmD, U. Calif., San Francisco, 1996. Cert. Diabetic educator Nat. Cert. Bd. Diabetes Educators, 1999. Ambulatory care pharmacist specialist Vets. Affairs San Diego Healthcare Sys., 1997—99; ambulatory care pharmacist specialist Spectrum Healthcare Resources Naval Med. Ctr. San Diego Ambulatory Care Clinics, 1999—2002; affiliate faculty mem. dept. pharmacy Idaho State U., Pocatella, 1999—2002; clin. asst. prof. Sch. Pharmacy Western U. Health Scis., Calif., 1999—2002; asst. clin. prof. Sch. Pharmacy U. Calif., San Francisco, 2000—08, asst. prof., clin. pharmacy Skaggs Sch. Pharmacy and Pharm. Scis. San Diego, 2002—08, assoc. prof. clin. pharmacy Skaggs Sch. Pharmacy and Pharm. Scis., 2008—; ambulatory care pharmacist specialist, vets. affairs San Diego Healthcare Sys., 2008—. Co-author: A Process Guide for Pharmacists, 3rd ed.; contbr. articles to profl. jours. Clin. pharmacist vol. Various Cmty. Outreach Projects, San Diego, 1996—, Taking Control of Your Diabetes, San Diego, 1996; clin. pharmacist vol. Free Med. Clinic Project U. Calif, San Diego, 2000—; co-chair and coord., Ask a Pharmacist session Taking Control of Your Diabetes Conf., San Diego, 2002—; clin. pharmacist vol., Project Stand Down Vetrans Village, San Diego, 2002—03. Recipient Faculty Excellence award, U. Calif., San Diego, 2003, Excellence in Tchg. award, 2005, 2006. Fellow: Calif. Soc. Health-Sys. Pharmacists (assoc.; del. 1997, co-chair continuing edn. com. 1998—99, faculty student liason 2003—, Practitioner Recognition Program award 2003); mem.: Am. Pharm. Assn. (assoc.), Am. Soc. Health-Sys. Pharmacists (assoc.; student faculty liason 2003—05), San Diego Soc. Health-Sys. Pharmacists (assoc.; sec., mem. cmty. outreach com. 1998—2001, del. seminar meetings 1999—2005, bd. dirs. 2002—05, Pharmacist of the Yr. 2002, Dena L. Barker Meml. award 2002), Am. Coll. Clin. Pharmacy (assoc.), Am. Assn. Colls. Pharmacy (assoc.), Phi Lambda Sigma (assoc.), Rho Chi (assoc.), Phi Delta Chi (assoc.; v.p. 1993—94). Office: U Calif San Diego Skaggs Sch Pharmacy, Pharm-Sci 9500 Gilman # 0719 La Jolla CA 92093-0719 Office Fax: 858-822-5624. Business E-Mail: candismorello@ucsd.edu.

MORELLO, DANIEL CONWAY, plastic surgeon; b. Vineland, NJ, Nov. 12, 1943; s. John B. and Mina M. (Conway) M.; m. Mona L. Comras; children: Amy, Elise, Kate. BS, U. Notre Dame, 1965; MD, Georgetown U., 1969. Diplomate Am. Bd. Plastic Surgery, Am. Bd. Surgery, Nat. Bd. Med. Examiners. Intern Hahnemann Med. Coll. Hosp., Phila., 1969-70, surgery resident to chief resident, 1970-74; plastic surgery resident to chief resident NYU Med. Ctr. Inst. for Reconstructive Plastic Surgery, NYC, 1974-76; attending surgeon White Plains (N.Y.) Hosp. Med. Ctr., 1976—, chief of plastic surgery, 1992-98; pvt. practice in plastic surgery White Plains, 1976—; emeritus chief, 1999—; attending surgeon Mank Eye, Ear and Throat Hosp., 1999—. Asst. attending surgeon Bellevue Hosp., Manhattan VA Hosp., Manhattan Eye, Ear and Throat Hosp., N.Y.C., 1976-85; attending surgeon No. Westchester (N.Y.) Hosp. Ctr., 1976—; cons. Burke Rehab. Ctr., 1977-81; asst. instr. surgery, Hahnemann Med. Coll., 1973-74, clin. instr. plastic surgery, NYU Sch. Medicine, 1974-78, clin. asst. prof. plastic surgery, 1978-86. Contbr. numerous articles to profl. jours., chpts. to books; presenter in field, including co-chair symposia 1993, 95. Bd. dirs., golf chmn. Whippoorwill Club, 1989-95, extensive com. work 1988-95. Fellow: ACS; mem.: Nat. Endowment for Plastic Surgery (bd. govs. 2005—08), Westchester County Med. Soc. (bd. dirs. 1986—88, med.-legal rels. com. 1988—98, numerous other coms.), Med. Soc. State of NY, NY Regional Soc. Plastic Surgery (membership com. 1978—80, chair program com. 1987—88, sec. 1988—90, bd. dirs. 1988—91), Am. Assn. for Accreditation of Ambulatory Surgery Facilities (bd. dirs. 1989—98, strategic planning com. 1991—2004, pres. 1994—98, trustee 1998—, other offices, coms.), Am. Soc. Plastic and Reconstructive Surgeons (ofcl. spokesperson 1992—, pub. edn. com. and sci. program subcom. 1994—99, other coms.), Am. Soc. Aesthetic Plastic Surgery (ofcl. spokesperson 1988—, bd. dirs. 1990—2010, chair pub. edn. com. and internat. task force 1994—97, treas. 1995—98, v.p. 1998—99, 1999—2000, pres. 2000—01, chair bd. trustees 2001—02, trustee 2001—04, chair nominating com. 2009—10, trustee 2005—08, other offices and coms.). Avocations: golf, travel, reading. Office: 10 Chester Ave White Plains NY 10601-5112 also: 531 E 88th St New York NY 10128 Home: 18525 SE Village Cir Tequesta FL 33469 Office: 641 University Blvd Ste 103 Jupiter FL 33458 Office Phone: 914-761-8667. Business E-Mail: info@drmorello.com.

MORENO, MIGUEL FRANCIS, obstetrician, gynecologist, perinatologist; b. Villaflores, Chiapas, Mex., Apr. 16, 1962; naturalized, USA, 1999; s. Ildefonso Moreno and Elizabeth Gloggner; m. Maria de Lourdes Martinez (div.); children: Miguel Gerardo, Ana Lourdes; m. Gloria Juarez Ramirez, Feb. 15, 2004; 1 child, Rodrigo Sebastian. Grad. in medicine, U. Autonoma de Chiapas, Mex., 1985; grad. in ob-gyn., U. Nacional Autonoma de Mex., 1990; grad. in perinatology, Inst. Nat. Perinatology, Mexico, 1991. Pvt. practice, Tuxtia Gutierrez, Chiapas, 1991—2006. Founder State of Chiapas Perinatology and Neonatology Soc., 2001. Fellow: ACOG; mem.: Am. Soc. Reproductive Medicine. Partido Accion Nacional. Roman Catholic. Avocations: soccer, jogging. Home: Alpes 294 Cumbres 29100 Tuxtla Gutierrez Mexico Office Phone: (961)6028140. Office Fax: (961)6028140. Personal E-mail: mimogle62@hotmail.com.

MORENO, NIBERTO L., cardiologist; MD, Am. U., Plymouth, Monserratt, 1979. Fellowship Loyola U. Med. Ctr., Maywood, Ill., The Children's Meml. Hosp.; residency tng. Met. Group Hosps., U. Ill.; med. staff Baptist and South Miami Hosps., 1987; chief, cardiothoracic surgery, Cardiac & Thoracic Chirurg. Group Baptist Health, 2009—. Named A Physician Who Cares award, Fla. Med. Assn., 2007. Office: Baptist Health 9601 Interstate 630 Exit 7 Little Rock AR 72205-7299 Office Phone: 501-202-2000. Office Fax: 501-202-1115. Business E-Mail: niberto.moreno@baptisthospital.com. *

MORENO, RAUL, cardiologist, researcher, educator; b. Salamanca, Spain, Aug. 21, 1969; s. Porfirio Moreno and Felipa Gómez. MD, Faculty of Medicine, Valladolid, Spain, 1993; cardiologist, Gregorio Marañon Hosp., Madrid, 1998. Prof. cardiology CTO Medicina, Madrid, 1994—; cardiologist Gregorio Marañon Hosp., 1994—. Med. dir. Primary Med. Care Course CGM, Madrid, 1998. Contbr. articles to profl. jours. Recipient Cardiovasc. Rsch. MAPFRE Medicine award, 1997. Mem. Spanish Cardiology Soc., Castellon Cardiology Soc. (Cardiovasc. Rsch. award 1997). Home: Jose-Luis Arrese 26 1-C E-47014 Valladolid Spain Office: Hosp Gregorio Maranon Dr Esquerdo 46 E-28007 Madrid Spain

MORENO, TAMARA LYNN, physical therapist; b. Sept. 23, 1977; DPT, Temple, UCSF-SFSU, 2003, MS. Phys. therapist, athletic trainer Stanford U., 2007. Mem.: NATA, APTA. Office: 341 Galvez St Stanford CA 94305 Personal E-mail: tamarajohann@hotmail.com.

MORENO, ZERKA TOEMAN, psychodrama educator; b. Amsterdam, June 13, 1917; d. Joseph and Rosalia (Gutwirth) Toeman; m. Jacob L. Moreno, Dec.1949; 1 child, Jonathan D.; 1 stepchild, Regina. Student, Willesden Tech. Coll., 1937-38, NYU, 1948-49. Cert. trainer, educator, practitioner of psychodrama and group psychotherapy Am. Bd. Examiners. Rsch. asst. Psychodramatic and Sociometric Insts., NYC, 1942-51; pres. Moreno Inst., NYC and Beacon, N.Y., 1951-82; trainer in psychodrama Studiefrämjandet, Stockholm, 1976-83, Finnish Psychodrama Assn., Lahti, Finland, 1976-83. Lectr., trainer, Gt. Britain, Australia, China, New Zealand, Norway, Sweden, Italy, Germany, Japan, 1976-96, Argentina, Brazil, Greece, The Netherlands, Denmark, Belgium, Spain, Israel, Korea and Taiwan, 1977—; hon. pres. Internat. Zerka Moreno Inst., Nanjing, China; acad. advisor mental health Nanjing Brain Hosp., China, 1997. Co-author: Psychodrama, Surplus Reality, and the Art of Healing, 2000, Psychodrama, Vol. II, 1967, Vol. III, 1969, The First Psychodramatic Family, 1964; author: (poetry) Love Songs to Life, 1971, 2d edit., 1993, Psychodrama, Surplus Reality and the Art of Healing, 2000, The Quintessential Zerka, 2006. Named hon. citizen Comune di Roma, Assessorato Alla Cultura, 1983, Municipalidad de la Ciudad de Buenos Aires, 1984, Hon. Mem. Federacao Brasiliero de Psicodrama, Sao Paulo, 1996; first recipient of prize from Astrid Badina Stiftung (Baden-Baden, Germany), 1999 Fellow Am. Soc. Group Psychotherapy and Psychodrama (pres. 1967-69, hon. pres. 1988—, sec.-treas. 1955-66); hon. mem. Internat. Assn. Group Psychotherapy (treas. 1974-76, bd. dirs. 1976-80), Soc. Psicodrama Sao Paulo (hon.), Sociedad Argentina Psicodrama (hon.). Home: The Colonnades C24 2600 Barracks Rd Charlottesville VA 22901-2198

MORENO-ASPITIA, ALVARO, physician, researcher; s. Ricardo Moreno-Azorero and Susana Aspitia; m. Maga; children: Sebastian, Camila, Pablo. MD, U. Nacional de Asuncion, Paraguay, 1991. Diplomate Internal Medicine Am. Bd. of Internal Medicine, PA, 1997, Medical Oncology Am. Bd. of Internal Medicine, 2000, Hematology Am. Bd. of Internal Medicine, 2000, Pediatrics Am. Bd. of Pediat., 1997, Am. Bd. of Pediat., 2004. Resident internal medicine/pediat. Scott and White Hosp. Tex. A&M Coll. of Medicine, Temple, Tex., 1993—97, chief resident, 1996—97; fellow Mayo Clinic Grad. Sch. Medicine, Jacksonville, Fla., 1997—2000; cons., asst. prof. medicine Mayo Clinic and Mayo Grad. Sch. of Medicine, Jacksonville, Fla., 2000—. Assoc. dir. clin. studies unit Mayo Clinic, Jacksonville, Fla., 2001—, assoc. dir. multidisciplinary breast clinic, 2005—; assoc. program dir. hematology & oncology fellowship Mayo Grad. Sch. of Medicine, Jacksonville, Fla., 2005—. Contbr. scientific papers. Recipient, Alpha Omega Alpha Honor Med. Soc., 1997, Sr. yr. gold medal, Coll. Internat., 1985, 2000 Shahin Award for Rsch., DCMS, 2000, Tchr. of the Yr. (Hematology/Oncology), Dept. of Internal Medicine, 2004; scholar Oncology Fellow Scholarship Methods in Clin. Cancer Rsch., AACR-ASCO, 1998. Fellow: ACP, Am. Acad. of Pediat.; mem.: Am. Assn. for Cancer Rsch., Am. Soc. of Hematology, Am. Soc. of Clin. Oncology, Alpha Omega Alpha Honor Med. Soc. Achievements include research in Clinical trials in the treatment of hematologic and solid malignancies. Office: Mayo Clinic 4500 San Pablo Rd Jacksonville FL 32224

MORENO-CABRAL, CARLOS EDUARDO, cardiac surgeon; b. Zacatecas, Mex., Nov. 4, 1951; s. Manuel Julio Moreno and Dominga Cabral; m. Elaine Nakamura; children: Rodrigo, Iza, Daniel. MD, Nat. U. Mex., 1976. Diplomate Am. Bd. Thoracic Surgery. Resident in gen. surgery U. Hawaii, 1977-80, Mich. State U., 1980-82; fellow in cardiac surgery Stanford (Calif.) U., 1982-84, 86-88; tng. in thoracic surgery SUNY, Bklyn., 1984-86; dir. cardiac transplant program St. Francis Hosp., Honolulu, 1989—. Author: Postoperative Management in Adult Cardiac Surgery, 1988. Fellow ACS; mem. Soc. Thoracic Surgeons, European Assn. Cardio-Thoracic Surgery. Avocation: photography. Office: 1380 Lusitana St Ste 912 Honolulu HI 96813-2448 E-mail: cemoreno@aol.com.

MORENO-JIMENEZ, SERGIO, neurosurgeon, educator; b. Mex. City, Sept. 4, 1971; MD, U. Anahuac, 1996; MSc, U. Nat. Autonoma Mex., 2006. Chmn. radio surgery unit Nat. Inst. Neurology and Neurosurgery, 2006—, adj. prof., radio surgery, 2006—11, adj. prof., neuro-imaging surgery, 2006—11, adj. prof., epilepsy surgery, 2007—11, adj. prof., skull base surgery, 2009—11. Adj. prof. neurology Inst. Poly. Nat., 2006—11. Master: Seccion Radiocirugia de la SMCN; mem.: Internat. Stereotactic Radiosurgery Soc., Soc. Mexicana de Cirugia Neurologica. Avocations: tennis, piano. Office: Insurgentes Sur 3877 Col la Fama Mexico City 14269 Mexico Personal E-mail: radioneurocirugia@gmail.com.

MORENO MONTOYA, JOSÉ, research scientist; b. Bogotá, Colombia, Jan. 3, 1980; Degree in Stats., Nat. U. Colombia, 2004, MSc in Epidemiology; DSc in Epidemiology, Nat. Inst. Pub. Health Mex., 2008. Rschr. Found. FES Social, 2003—11; rschr., epidemiologic surveillance Nat. Inst. Pub. Health Colombia, 2006—08; tchr. Pontificia U. Javeriana, 2007—09; rschr., dept. pub. health Nat. U. Colombia, 2007—. Reviewer PAHO Peruvian Jour. Pub. Health, Bull. of WHO, Jour. Affective Disorders, Colombian Jour. Pub. Health, 2006—11. Recipient Young Investigator award, Colombian Coun. Scis. COLCIENCIAS; fellow, Nat. Coun. Sci. and Tech. Mex. CONACYT. Avocations: reading, movies, music. Home: Calle 53A 28-73 Sur Bogotá Cundinamarca 110611 Colombia Personal E-mail: josemorenomontoya@gmail.com.

MORENO VÁZQUEZ, JUAN MANUEL, physiologist, educator; b. Badajoz, Spain, Nov. 19, 1959; m. M. Dolores Rubio Pérez, May 20, 1994. Med. dr. Extremadura U. Spain, 1983. Vis. rsch. fellow UK Med. Rsch. Coun., London, 1989—91; associated prof. Extremadura U., Badajoz, Spain, 1985—89, prof. physiology, 1992—, vice dean faculty medicine, 2008. Consulting Spanish Air Force (Talavera Air Base), Badajoz, 1985—98, Neofacial Inst., Badajoz, 2005—. Recipient Spanish Air Force Aeromed. Rsch. award, 1994. Mem.: Aerospace Med. Assn. (U:S:). Achievements include research in aerospace medicine. Home: Paseo de San Francisco 9 6° Badajoz Badajoz 06001 Spain Office: UEx Sch Medicine Avda de Elvas S/N Badajoz Badajoz 06071 Spain Personal E-mail: jmmoreno@clindiab.e.telefonica.net. E-mail: jmmoreno@unex.es.

MOREYRA, ABEL E., medical educator; b. Mar del Plata, Argentina, Dec. 2, 1941; came to U.S., 1972; s. Genaro and Emilia (Basso) M.; m. Maria Elena Moreyra; children: Maria Eugenia, Maria Evelina, Fernando Abel. MD, U. Nacional de La Plata, Argentina, 1967. Fellow Cleve. Clinic Found., 1972-75; asst. prof. medicine UMDNJ-Robert Wood Johnson Med. Sch., New Brunswick, NJ, 1975-83, assoc. prof., 1983-95, prof., 1995—. Fellow ACP, Am. Coll. Cardiology; mem. Am. Coll. Angiology. Office: UMDNJ-RW Johnson Med Sch CN-19 Rm 582A New Brunswick NJ 08903 Office Phone: 732-235-7851. E-mail: moreyrae@umdnj.edu.

MORFORD, CRAIG S., health products executive, former prosecutor; b. Schenectady, NY, Feb. 10, 1959; married; 4 children. BA in Econ., Hope Coll., 1981; JD, Valparaiso U. Sch. Law, 1984. Trial atty. Office Chief Counsel IRS, 1984—87; spl. trial atty. Cleve. Organized Crime Taskforce US Dept. Justice, 1986—89, asst. US atty. (no. dist.) OH, 1989—2002, interim US atty. (ea. dist.) Mich., 2004—05, spl. atty. to US atty. gen. heading investigation into first major US post Sept. 11th trial, 2004, 1st. US atty. (no. dist.) Ohio, 2005—06, interim US atty. (mid. dist.) Tenn., 2006—07, acting dep. atty. gen., 2007—08; chief compliance officer Cardinal Health, Inc., Dublin, 2008—, chief legal officer, 2009—. Recipient Dir. award for Superior Performance, US Dept. Justice, 1996, 2000, Atty. Gen. Disting Svc. award, 2003, 2005; named Outstanding Asst. US Atty., Nat. Assn. Former US Attorneys, 2005. Fellow: Am. Coll. Trial Lawyers. Office: Cardinal Health Inc 7000 Cardinal Pl Dublin OH 43017 *

MORGAN, ALAN E., lobbyist, health association executive; b. Holton, Kans., May 22, 1968; m. Kathy Lee Morgan, Nov. 20, 1993; children: Robert, Chandler. BS, U. Kans., 1990; MPA, George Mason U., 1998. Asst. press sec. Office of the Gov., Kans., 1990-91; legis. asst. Congressman Dick Nichols, Washington, 1991-92; mgr. govt. rels. am. Soc. of Clin. Pathologists, Washington, 1992-95, Washington rep. N.Am. Soc. of Pacing Electrophysiology, Washington, 1995-98; mgr. govt. rels. VHA, Inc., Washington, 1998—; joined Nat. Rural Health Assn., Washington, 2001, CEO. Serves as policy resource for the nat. media; presenter at both nat. and state health conferences. Republican. Baptist. Office: National Rural Health Assn 1108 K St NW 2nd Fl Washington DC 20005-4094 Office Phone: 202-639-0550. Business E-Mail: morgan@NRHArural.org. *

MORGAN, ANDREW LANE, urologist, educator; b. May 13, 1920; s. James Albert and Elsie Edna (Johnson) M.; m. Miriam Cleary, June 9, 1951; children: Andrew Lane, Christine, Martha, James. Exch. fellowship, St. John's U., Shanghai, China, 1939—40; BA, Dartmouth Coll., 1942; MD, Cornell U., 1945. Diplomate Am. Bd. Urology. Intern Lenox Hill Hosp., NYC, 1945—46; resident Queen's Med. Ctr., Honolulu, 1948—50, Yale U., 1950—52; practice medicine, specializing in urology Honolulu, 1952—87; ret., 1987. Chmn. dept. surgery Queen's Med. Ctr., 1979; clin. prof. urology John Burns Sch. Medicine, U. Hawaii; mem. renal transplant team St. Francis Med. Ctr.; past pres. Hawaii Med. Libr., 1957-58 Served to capt., AUS, 1946-48 Fellow ACS; mem. AMA, Am. Urol. Assn. (past pres. We. sect.), Hawaii Med. Assn., Societe Internationale d'Urologie, Honolulu County Med. Soc. (bd. govs. 1970-76, treas. 1978-79), Pacific Club Honolulu Episcopalian. Home: 69-1716 Puako Beach Dr Kamuela HI 96743-8700

MORGAN, BEVERLY CARVER, pediatrician, educator; b. NYC, May 29, 1927; d. Jay and Florence (Newkamp) Carver; children: Nancy, Thomas E. III, John E. MD cum laude, Duke U., 1955. Diplomate Am. Bd. Pediat. (oral examiner 1984-90, mem. written examination com. 1990—), Nat. Bd. Med. Examiners. Intern, asst. resident Stanford U. Hosp., San Francisco, 1955-56; clin. fellow pediat., trainee pediatric cardiology Babies Hosp.-Columbia Presbyn. Med. Ctr., NYC, 1956-59; rsch. fellow cardiovasc. diagnostic lab. Columbia-Presbyn. Med. Ctr., NYC, 1959-60; instr. pediat. Coll. Physicians and Surgeons, Columbia U., NYC, 1960; dir. heart sta. Robert B. Green Meml. Hosp., San Antonio, 1960-62; lectr. pediat. U. Tex., 1960-62; spl. rsch. fellow in pediatric cardiology Sch. Medicine, U. Wash., Seattle, 1962-64, from instr. to prof. pediat., 1962-73, chmn. dept. pediat., 1973-80; mem. staff U. Wash. Hosp., chief of staff, 1975-77; mem. staff Harborview Med. Ctr., Children's Orthop. Hosp. and Med. Ctr., dir. dept. medicine, 1974-80; prof., chmn. dept. pediat. U. Calif., Irvine, 1980-88, prof. pediat. and pediatric cardiology, 1980—; pediatrician in chief Children's Hosp. Orange County, 1988. Mem. pulmonary acad. awards panel Nat. Heart and Lung Inst., 1972-75; mem. grad. med. edn. nat. adv. com. to sec. HEW, 1977-80; mem. Coun. on Pediatric Practice; chmn. Task Force on Opportunities for Women in Pediat., 1982; mem. nursing rev. com. NIH, 1987-88. Contbr. articles to profl. jours.; mem. editl. bd. Clin. Pediat., Am. Jour. Diseases of Children, Jour. of Orange County Pediatric Soc., Jour. Am. Acad. Pediat., LA Pediatric Soc. Recipient Women of Achievement award Matrix Table, Seattle, 1974; Disting. Alumnus award Duke U. Med. Sch., 1974; Ann. award Nat. Bd. Med. Coll. Pa., 1977; Career Devel. award USPHS, 1966-71; Moseby scholar, 1955. Mem. Am. Acad. Pediat. (chmn. com. on pediat. manpower 1984-86), Am. Coll. Cardiology, Soc. for Pediat. Rsch., Am. Fedn. Clin. Rsch., Am. Pediat. Soc., Assn. Med. Sch. Pediat. Dept. Chmn. (sec.-treas.

1981-87), Western Soc. for Pediat. Rsch., Alpha Omega Alpha. Office: U Calif Irvine Med Ctr Dept Pediatrics 101 The City Dr S Orange CA 92868-3201 Business E-Mail: bcmorgan@uci.edu.

MORGAN, C.A. (MANDY MORGAN), psychology professor, researcher; BA, PhD, DipEd. Assoc. prof. Massey U. Sch. Psychology, New Zealand, prin. rschr. domestic violence interventions and services rsch. program. Editor chapters to books; contbr. articles to profl. jours. Mem.: Internat. Soc. Theoretical Psychology (pres. 2011—). Office: Massey University Sch Psychology Rm P2 21 Turitea Palmerston North 4442 New Zealand Office Phone: 64 6 3569-099 ext. 2063. Office Fax: 64 6 350-5673. Business E-Mail: c.a.morgan@massey.ac.nz. *

MORGAN, CATHERINE MARIE, psychologist, writer; b. Duluth, Minn., Mar. 27, 1947; m. Ralph Morgan, 1967; 1 child, Andrew. BS, U. Nebr., 1968; MEd, U. Okla., 1973; PhD, Okla. State U., 1987; postgrad. Menninger Found., Psychotherapy Tng. Program, 1987-89. Child devel. specialist Southwest Guidance Ctr., Wheatland, Okla., 1973-74; pvt. practice Family Counseling Assocs., San Antonio, 1974-75; psychol. asst. Edmond Guidance Ctr., Okla., 1975-82; psychol. asst. supr. Southeast Guidance Ctr., Del City, Okla., 1982-86; psychol. intern Cleve. County Health Dept., Moore, Okla., 1986-87; psychologist Cen. State Hosp., Norman, Okla., 1987-89; pvt. practice assocs. in psychology Edmond, Okla.; vice chair bd. mgrs. Integris Mental Health; pres. Assocs. in Psychology, 1988—. Mem. AAUW, APA, Okla. Psychol. Assn., Am. Bus. Women's Assn., P.E.O., Kappa Delta Pi. Avocations: writing, reading, knitting, racquetball. Office: 11212 N May Ste 302 Oklahoma City OK 73120 Office Phone: 405-753-9009.

MORGAN, CLYDE NATHANIEL, dermatologist; b. Bell County, Tex., Nov. 2, 1923; s. Xenophen William and Rhoda Ella (Deck) M.; m. Birdie Joyce Rich, Mar. 3, 1951 (dec. Feb. 19, 2009); children: Clyde Nathaniel Jr., Reinette Jean, Nancy Elaine. BS, Abilene Christian Coll., 1948; MD, U. Tex., Galveston, 1953. Cert. Bd. of Am. Acad. Cryosurgery, 1978. Assoc. prof. biology Abilene (Tex.) Christian Coll., 1954-56; pvt. practice Abilene, 1954-67; dermatologist, 1969—. Author 2766th Provisional Headquarters Flight WWII, 2010; contbr. articles to profl. jours. Chmn. Taylor County Republican Party, 1965—70; delegate Republican Nat. Convention, 1968, 1980, alt. delegate, 1976. 1st lt. air corps US Army, 1943—46. Recipient Med. Econs. award, 1963; named Disting. Pres., Greater Abilene Kiwanis Club, 1979. Fellow Am. Acad. Family Practice; mem. AMA, SAR (chpt. pres. 1997-99, past pres. Big Country chpt., award 1995), Am. Coll. Cryosurgery, Internat. Soc. Cryosurgery, Tex. Med. Assn., So. Med. Assn., Tex. Dermatologic Soc., Taylor-Jones-Haskell County Med. Soc., Indian Coun. on Cryogenics (hon. fellow). Republican. Mem. Ch. Of Christ. Avocations: golf, fishing, hunting, cryogenics research. Home: 1718 Cedar Crest Dr Abilene TX 79601-3228 Office: 1166 Merchant St Abilene TX 79603-5014 Office Phone: 325-673-4242. Personal E-mail: clybird@juno.com.

MORGAN, DANIEL J., orthopedist, surgeon; MD, U. Md., 1985. Diplomate Am. Bd. of Orthopedic Surgery. Resident surgery Wash. Hosp. Ctr., 1985—86; resident orthopaedic surgery Kingsbrook Jewish Med. Ctr., 1993—97; with Beth Israel Med. Ctr. Named one of Best Doctors, NY Mag., 2011, Top Doctors NY Metro Area, Castle Connolly, 2011. Office: Beth Israel Medical Center Ste C11 3131 Kings Hwy Brooklyn NY 11234 Office Phone: 718-258-2588. Office Fax: 718-258-4138. E-mail: morgan.daniel@worldnet.att.net.

MORGAN, DONNA JEAN, psychotherapist; b. Edgerton, Wis., Nov. 16, 1955; d. Donald Edward and Pearl Elizabeth (Robinson) Garey. BS, U. Wis., Whitewater, 1983, MS, 1985. Cert. lic. psychotherapist, Wis.; lic. mental health and alcohol and drug counselor, Wis.; nat. cert. alcohol and drug abuse counselor; lic. marriage and family therapist, Wis.; lic. ind. social worker; lic. clin. ind. social worker; nat. cert. counselor; lic. profl. counselor; lic. advanced practice social worker; lic. mediator, Wis., 2008-; profl. christian counselor. Clin. supr. Stoughton (Wis.) Hosp., 1985-88; pvt. practice Janesville, Wis., 1988-91; prin. Morgan and Assocs., Janesville, Wis., 1991-96; pvt. practice New Focus, Waukesha and Mukwonago, Wis., 1996-97, William N. Watson & Assocs., MD, S.C., Oconomowoc, Waukesha, Wis., 1997—, Morgan Counseling, LLC, Janesville, Wis., 1998—. Ptnr. Humane Soc. US, 2008—. Mem. underaged drinking violation alternative program Rock County, 1986—96; co-chmn. task force on child sexual abuse, 1989—91; mem. Rock County Multidisciplinary Team on Child Abuse, 1990—96; mem. spkrs. bur. Rock County C.A.R.E. House, 1990—; adv. bd. Parents Place, Waukesha County, Wis., 1997—99; active ARC, 2001—; vol. Red Cross, 2001—. Mem. APA, ACA, ASPCA, Am. Profl. Soc. on Abuse of Children, Wis. Profl. Soc. on Abuse of Children (bd. dirs. 1994-98, v.p. 1997-98), Am. Assn. Mental Health Counselors, Wis. Assn. Mental Health Counselors, Am. Assn. Marriage and Family Therapy (clin. mem.), Am. Assn. Christian Counselors, Wis. Counseling Assn., Am. Psycotherapy Assn., So. Wis. Ducks Unltd. (mem. com. 1980—), Wis. Assn. Mediators, WI Vest-A-Dog Inc. (pres. & founder), Future Farmers Am. (PALS trainer). Office Phone: 608-757-1994.

MORGAN, ELIZABETH K., retired critical care nurse; b. Lansdowne, Pa., Feb. 18, 1951; d. Charles Knight and Marian Swope (Wing) Morgan; m. James Tracy Grey III, Dec. 27, 1980 (div. 2002); children: Michael Grey, James Tracy IV Grey, Joshua S. Grey. AA, Elmira Coll., NY, 1976; grad. in practical nursing, Upper Bucks Voc-Tech, Perkasie, Pa., 1979; AA in Nursing, Bucks County Community Coll., Newtown, Pa., 1989; student, LaSalle U., 1992—96. Cert. health profl. paramedic, Pa.; cert. CPR, ACLS, TNCC. Paramedic Warminster Ambulance, Pa., 1986; staff practical nurse Warminster Gen. Hosp., 1986—89; ICU/CCU staff nurse Nazareth Hosp., Phila., 1989—96, coord. cardiac rehab., 2001—02, staff to charge nurse telemetry stroke fl., part-time nurse IV team, 2002—. Mem. Warrington Ambulance Corps. Mem. AACN. Home: 4345 Teesdale St Philadelphia PA 19136

MORGAN, FRANKLIN BAXTER DOWNS, neurosurgeon, director; b. Corn Island, Zelaya, Nicaragua, Jan. 9, 1946; s. Fernando Garcia and Cassilda Evereth Downs; m. Vera Luccia Oliveira, Dec. 31, 1990; children: William Downs, Franklin Downs. MD, Faculdade de Medicina-U. Fed. da Bahia, Salvador, Brazil, 1964—69. Cert. md Conselho Fed. De Medicina Do Brasil, 1975. Dir PRONEURO, Salvador, Bahia, Brazil, 1975—; prof. neurosurgery Hosp. das Clinicas, U. Fed. da Bahia, 1972—74, U. Fluminense, Niteroi, Rio de Janeiro, 1973—78. Dir. PRONEURO, Salvador, 1975—. Recipient Hon. award, Camara de Deputados da Bahia, 2001. Mem.: Conselho Fed. de Medicina. Baptist. Achievements include invention of a technique for ventriculoscopy. Avocations: sailing, fishing, yoga, music, movies. Home: Rua Antonio Augusto Machado Quadra 12 Salvador Bahia 41600090 Brazil Office: Proneuro Rua Humberto de Campos 40150-130 Salvador BA Brazil Office Fax: 55-071-33366769; Home Fax: 55-071-33743010. Business E-Mail: fmorgan@atarde.com.br.

MORGAN, JACOB RICHARD, cardiologist; b. East St. Louis, Ill., Oct. 10, 1925; s. Clyde Adolphus and Jennie Ella Henrietta (Van Ramshorst) M.; m. Alta Eloise Ruthruff, Aug. 1, 1953 (dec. 2000); children: Elaine, Stephen Richard; m. Linda S. Azuar, May 22, 2005. BS in Pharmacy, U. Tex., 1953; MD, U. Tex., Galveston, 1957. Diplomate Am. Bd. Internal Medicine, Am. Bd. Cardiology. Ensign USN, 1944, advanced through grades to capt., 1969; intern U.S. Naval Hosp., Oakland, Calif., 1957-58, chief medicine Taipei, Republic of China, 1962-64; internal medicine staff San Diego, 1964-67, chief cardiology, 1969-73; ret., 1973; dir. medicine R.E. Thomas Gen. Hosp., El Paso, Tex., 1973-75; asst. clin. prof. medicine U. Calif., San Diego, 1970-73; prof. medicine, assoc. chmn. dep. Tex. Tech U. Sch. Medicine, Lubbock and El Paso, 1973-75; pvt. practice National City, Calif., 1976—; dir. cardiology Paradise Valley Hosp., National City, 1976-88. Presenter in field. Contbr. articles on cardiology to sci. jours. Recipient Casmir Funk award, l972. Fellow ACP, Am. Coll. Cardiology, Am. Coll. Chest Physicians, Am. Heart Assn. (coun. on clin. cardiology). Avocation: golf. Home and Office: 4998 Lamia Way Oceanside CA 92056

MORGAN, JAMES PHILIP, pharmacology and cardiology educator; b. Cin., Jan. 13, 1948; s. James Weldon and Dorcas Adele (Meyer) M.; m. Kathleen Greive, Dec. 22, 1973; children: James Patrick, Jonathan Michael. BS, U. Cin., 1970, PhD, 1974, MD, 1976. Diplomate Am. Bd. Internal Medicine, Am. Bd. Cardiovascular Disease. Fellow internal medicine Mayo Clinic, Rochester, Minn., 1976—79, fellow cardiovascular disease, 1979—83; asst. medicine Beth Israel Hosp., Boston, 1983—. Instr. pharmacology U. Cin., 1975—76; asst. prof. pharmacology, instr. medicine Mayo Clinic, 1981—83; asst. prof. medicine Harvard U., Boston, 1983, assoc. prof., 1988—96, Herman Dana prof. medicine, 1996—2005; affiliate faculty, dept. pharmacology Harvard Med. Sch., 1986—2000; chief and program dir. cardiovascular divsn. Beth Israel Hosp., 1994—2001, vice chmn. medicine, 2000—05; chief cardiovasc. medicine St. Elizabeth's Med. Ctr., Boston, 2005—08, dir. Caritas Christi Cardiovasc. Ctr., 2006—08, 2011—; chief cardiovasc. medicine Caritas Carney Hosp.; med. dir. cardiovasc. svcs. Carney Hosp., 2008—. Contbr. articles to profl. jours. Recipient Young Investigators award Am. Coll. Cardiology, 1982, Balfour award Mayo Clinic, 1983, Advanced Cardiac Life Support Spl. Recognition award Mayo Clinic, 1983, Rsch. Career Devel. award NIH, 1985-90. Mem. AMA, Am. Heart Assn., Biophys. Soc. Am. Soc. Pharmacology and Exptl. Therapeutics, Masons. Avocation: philatelics. Office: Caritas St Elizabeth's Med Ctr 736 Cambridge St Boston MA 02135-2997 Office Phone: 617-789-2226. Business E-Mail: james.morgan@caritachristi.org.

MORGAN, JEAN ELIZABETH, plastic surgeon; b. Washington, July 9, 1947; d. William James and Antonia (Bell) Morgan; 1 child, Elena. BA magna cum laude, Harvard U., 1967; postgrad. (fellow), Oxford U., 1967, postgrad. (fellow), 1970; MD, Yale U., 1971; PhD in Psychology, U. Canterbury, Christchurch, New Zealand, 1995; MPH in Health Scis., UCLA, 2009. Cert. Am. Bd. Plastic Surgery, Am. Bd. Surgery, 1988. Intern Yale-New Haven Hosp., 1971-72, resident, 1972-73, 76-77, Tufts-New Eng. Med. Center, Boston, 1973-76, Harvard-Cambridge Hosp., Mass., 1977-78; columnist Cosmopolitan mag., 1973-80; pvt. practice specializing in cosmetic plastic surgery Washington, 1978-87, McLean, Va., 1998—2006, Chevy Chase, Md., 1998—2006; chief plastic surgery Beverly Hills Physicians, Calif., 2006—07; asst. clin. prof. dept. plastic surgery UCLA, 2006—09; clin. chief surgery U. Medicine & Health Scis., 2010. Faculty dept. psychology U. Md., 1995; assoc. faculty dept. law, justice and soc. Am. U., 1998. Author: The Making of A Woman Surgeon, 1980, Solo Practice, 1982, Custody, A True Story, 1986, The Complete Book of Cosmetic Surgery for Men, Women and Teens, 1988. Fellow: ACS, Am. Soc. Plastic Surgeons; mem.: APA, APA, Am. Pub. Health Soc., Am. Soc. Aesthetic Plastic Surgery. Avocations: ballet, opera, exercise, writing, travel. Home: 2210 Fairhaven Cir NE Atlanta GA 30305 Office: 2045 Peachtree St #412 Atlanta GA 30305 Business E-Mail: drmorgan@drelizabethmorgan.com.

MORGAN, JOHN W., epidemiologist, educator; b. Bermuda, Jan. 23, 1951; BS, Pacific Union Coll., 1978; DPH, Loma Linda U., 1987. Prof. Loma Linda U., 1982—; epidemiologist Calif. Cancer Registry, 1995. Mem. bd. sci. & policy advisors Am. Coun. Sci. and Health, 1995; mem. cancer & environment team Am. Cancer Soc., Calif., 2004, chair cancer evaluations team, 11. Office: Loma Linda University Dept Epidemiology & Biostatistics Loma Linda CA 92350 Office Fax: 909-558-6178. Business E-Mail: jmorgan@llu.edu.

MORGAN, LYLE WARNER, II, medical educator; b. Fremont, Nebr., Apr. 5, 1947; s. Lyle W. and Ione E. Morgan. AB, Doane Coll., 1969; MEd, Fla. Christian U., 1970; MA, Wayne State Coll., Nebr., 1973, MS in Edn., 1976; PhD, U. Nebr., 1980; D in Homeopathic Medicine, Internat. U., Brussels, Belgium, 1984. Prof. Pittsburg State U., Kans., 1984—, chmn. pre-medicine & health scis. program, 2000—04. Dir. composition Pittsburg State U., 1984—, dir. English edn., 1984—; sachem Tribe of Mic-O-Say, 1980; chieftain Tribe of Lone Bear, Mo., 2005. Author: Homeopathic Treatment of Sports Injuries, 1988, Homeopathic Medicine: First-Aid & Emergency Care, 1989, Treating Sports Injuries the Natural Way, 1990, Homeopathy and Your Child, 1992. Mem. Ozark Trails Coun. Boy Scouts of Am., Springfield, Mo., 1984—, exec. bd. mem., v.p., 1994—. Recipient Vigil Honor award, Order of the Arrow, 1979, Silver Beaver award, Boy Scouts Am., 1983, Distinguished Eagle Scout award, 1995, Silver Antelope award, 1997; fellow, Coll. Preceptors, UK, 1993. Mem.: SAR, Rockefeller Family and Assocs. Republican. Office: Pitts State U 1701 S Broadway Pittsburg KS 66762-7515

MORGAN, MARK A., gynecologic oncologist; Attended, Rutgers U.; MD, SUNY, 1982. Diplomate Am. Bd. Ob-Gyn, Am. Bd. Ob-Gyn-gynecologic oncology. Resident ob-gyn Hosp. of the Univ. Pa., fellow gynecologic oncology; prof. gynecologic oncology Univ. Pa. Health System, founder & dir. divsn. of urogynecology and female reconstructive pelvic surgery; chief sect. of gynecologic oncology Fox Chase Cancer Ctr., prof. dept. of surg. oncology. Recipient Merck Co. award for Gen. Excellence. Mem.: ACS (with bd. of govs., with com. on young surgeons, with com. on ethics), Internat. Gynecologic Cancer Soc., Gynecologic Oncology Group, Am. Soc. of Clin. Oncology. Office: Fox Chase Cancer Center 333 Cottman Ave Philadelphia PA 19111-2497 Office Phone: 215-728-6900.

MORGAN, TIMOTHY MATTHIAS, pharmacist; b. Geelong, Victoria, Australia, July 13, 1970; s. Sidney Matthias Morgan and Pamela Dawn Coxall; m. Angela Jayne Little, Apr. 5, 2008; 1 child, Alexander Patrick. Bachelor in Pharmacy, Victorian Coll. Pharmacy, Melbourne, Australia, 1991; B in Pharmacy with honors, Monash U., Melbourne, 1994, PhD in Pharmaceutics, 1998. Registered pharmacist Pharmacy Bd. Victoria, 1992, cert. project mgmt. profl. Project Mgmt. Inst., 2001. Product devel. scientist Glaxo, Melbourne, 1992, med. rep., 1993; co-founder Acrux Ltd., West Melbourne, 1998—, project mgr., 1999—2002, dir. market devel., 2003—, dir. bus. devel., 2004—05; co-founder Lachesis Biosci. Pty. Ltd., Melbourne, 2005—, exec. dir., 2005—. Recipient Mollie Holman medal, Monash U., 1999, Grad. Symposia prize, Am. Assn. Pharm. Scientists, 1997. Mem.: Royal Australian Chem. Inst. (corr.; treas. pharm. sci. group 2001—11). Achievements include patents in field. Office: 24 Mickle Crescent Warrnambool VIC 3280 Australia Business E-Mail: tim.morgan@lachesisbio.com.au.

MORGENSTERN, DIANA M., internist, director; BA, Yale U., New Haven, 1984; MD, Med. Coll. Pa., 1988. Diplomate Am. Bd. Internal Med., 2001. Asst. prof. Temple U. Sch. Medicine, 1991—98; clin. asst. prof. U. Pa., 1998—2001; med. dir. MedCases, Inc., 2001—04; clin. asst. prof. Drexel U. Coll. Med., 2001—; assoc. dir. GI & Metabolism Global Medical Affairs Wyeth Pharm., 2004—07, dir., 2007—09; dir., vaccines Pfizer, Inc., Collegeville, Pa., 2009—. Contbr. articles to profl. jours. Named one of Best Drs. in America, 1996—99, 2009—11. Fellow: Am. Coll. Physicians, Coll. Physician Phila. Office: Pfizer Inc 500 Arcola Rd Collegeville PA 19426 Business E-Mail: diana.morgenstern@pfizer.com.

MORGENSTERN, KENNETH E., plastic surgeon; 3 children. BS, Emory U., Atlanta, Ga., 1991; MD, Hahnemann U., Phila., 1995. Ophthalmology Am. Bd. of Ophthalmology, 2005, Orbital and Plastic Surgery Am. Soc. of Ophthalmic Plastic and Reconstructive Surgery, 2005. Categorical gen. surgery resident Med. Coll. of Pa., Hahnemann U., 1995—99; ophthalmology resident W.Va. U., Morgantown, 1999—2002, chief resident, 2001—02; asst/ clin. prof Ohio State U., Columbus, 2002—04; pediatric orbital and reconstructive surgery Children's Hosp. of Columbus, Ohio, 2002—04; facial cosmetic surgery Ctr. for Facial Rejuvination, Columbus, Ohio, 2003—04; asst. clin. prof Va. Commonwealth U., 2004—05, U. Pa., Phila., 2005—06; pres. Morgenstern Ctr. for Orbital and Facial Plastic Surgery, Phila., 2006—; dir. of orbital and facial plastic surgery Veterans Adminstrn. Med. Ctr., Phila., 2006—. Rsch. Morgenstern Ctr. for Orbital and Facial Plastic Surgery, Phila., 2002—; assoc. fellowship preceptor U. Pa., Phila., 2006—, Childrens Hosp. of Pa., Phila., 2006—; editl. com. BioMed Ctrl., Opthalmic Plastic and Reconstructive Surgery; resident rev. com. Am. Coll. of Gen. Med. Edn.; bd. mem. Resident Coun. of ACGME; pres. Honor Ct. of Med. Coll. of Pa. Dir.: (educational course) Ophthalmology for the Internist; contbr. educational course; dir.: (educational program) Talking with Patients in Difficult Situations; contbr. scientific papers, chapters to books. Recipient W.Va. U. Resident Rsch. award, Dept of Opthalmology, W.Va. U., 2002, Resident Rsch. Aaward, W.Va. Acad. of Opthalmology, 2002, Physician Humanitarian award, County Med. Soc. of Phila., 1998, Intern of Yr., Med. Coll. of Pa. and Hahnemann U., 1995—96, Cheif Resident, W.Va. U., 2002; grant, Nat. Inst. of Health, 1997—99, Am. Thyroid Cancer Assn. Rsch. grant, Am. thyroid Cancer Assn., 2002—04, Departmental grant, Dept Ophthalmolgy, W.Va. U., 2000—02, Rsch. Devel. grant, W.Va. U., 2000—01. Fellow: Am. Soc. of Ophthalmic Plastic and Reconstructive Surgery, Am. Bd. of Ophthalmology; mem.: AMA, Assn. Rsch. in Vision and Ophthalmology, Pa. Med. Soc., ARVO, W.Va. Acad. of Ophthalmology, Va. Acad. of Ophthalmology. Achievements include patents for blocking agent for I131 induced lacrimal injury. E-mail: kmorgenstern@pol.net.

MORGENSTERN, LEON, surgeon; b. Pitts., July 14, 1919; s. Max Samuel and Sarah (Master) M.; m. Laurie Mattlin, Nov. 27, 1967; 1 son, David Ethan. Attended, CCNY, 1936—37; BA magna cum laude, Bklyn. Coll., 1940; MD, NYU, 1943. Diplomate: Am. Bd. Surgery. Intern Queens Gen. Hosp., Jamaica, NY, 1943—44, fellow, asst. resident in pathology, 1947—48, resident in surgery, 1948—52; practice medicine, specializing in surgery LA, 1953—, Bronx, NY, 1959—60; dir. surgery Cedars of Lebanon Hosp., LA, 1960—73, Cedars-Sinai Med. Ctr., LA, 1973—88, emeritus dir. surgery, 1989—, dir. bioethics program, 1995—; prof. surgery UCLA Sch. Medicine, 1973-90, prof. surgery emeritus, 1990—. Asst. prof. surgery Albert Einstein Coll. Medicine, NYC, 1959-60; adj. prof. bioethics U. Judaism, LA, 1996—; dir. Ctr. Health Care Ethics Cedars-Sinai Med. Ctr., 1998-2004, emeritus dir. 2004-, sr. advisor 2008-. Assoc. editor Mount Sinai Jour. Medicine, 1984-88, Surg. Innovation, 2004-; contbr. articles to profl. publs. Served to capt. MC US Army, 1944-46. Mem. Soc. for Surgery Alimentary Tract, Soc. Am. Gastrointestinal Endoscopic Surgeons (hon.), Am. Gastroent. Assn., LA Surg. Soc. (pres. 1977), ACS (sec.-treas. 1976-77, pres. 1978, bd. dirs. So. Calif. chpt. 1976-84, gov.-at-large), Internat. Soc. Surgery, Western Surg. Assn., Pacific Coast Surg. Assn., AMA, Calif. Med. Assn., LA County Med. Assn., Am. Surg. Assn., others. Home: 5694 Calpine Dr Malibu CA 90265-3812 Office Phone: 310-423-1630. Personal E-mail: lmorgenstern@verizon.net. Business E-Mail: morgenstern@cshs.org.

MORGENSTERN, LEWIS B., medical educator; BA in Psychology, Pomona Coll., Claremont, Calif., 1984; MD, U. Mich. Med. Sch., Ann Arbor, 1990; postgrad., U. Tex. Sch. Pub. Health, Houston, 1996. Resident in neurology Johns Hopkins Hosp., Balt.; assoc. prof. neurology U. Tex. Med. Sch., Houston, 1994—2002; dir. stroke program U. Mich. Sch. Pub. Health, 2002—, prof. epidemiology, neurology emergency medicine, neurosurgery, 2005—. Recipient Clinician Scientist award, Am. Heart Assn., 1996. Mem.: Alpha Omega Alpha. Office: U Mich Sch Pub Health 1920 Taubman Ctr Ann Arbor MI 48109

MORGENSTERN, NORA, cytologist, educator; b. Argentina, 1965; MD, U. Buenos Aires, 1990. Chemistry technologist ORT, 1983; dir., FNA clinic Integrated Pathology Svcs. North Shore LIJ Health Sys., assoc. dir., cytopathology, rsch. coord., cytopathology, 2007—. Asst. prof. Albert Einstein Coll. Medicine and Hofstra U. Med. Sch.,

2000—. Recipient Travel award, UT MD Anderson Cancer Ctr., 1997; named one of Ams. Top Pathologists, Consumer Rsch. Coun. America, 2010—11. Fellow: Am. Soc. Cytopathology, Coll. Am. Pathologists. Avocations: travel, skiing, swimming. Office: 6 Ohio Dr Ste 202 New Hyde Park NY 11042 Business E-Mail: nmorgens@nshs.edu.

MORHOUSE, SANFORD W., lawyer; b. Keene Valley, NY, Dec. 13, 1944; BA, Williams Coll., 1966; JD, Columbia Univ., 1969. Bar: N.Y. 1969, US Dist. Ct. so. N.Y. Assoc. to ptnr. to of counsel Dewey & LeBoeuf (formerly Dewey Ballantine LLP), NYC, 1969—, co-chmn. mgmt. com., mem. exec. com. & chmn. pvt. equity group. Dir. Damon Runyon Cancer Rsch. Found., Broad Hollow Estates Inc. Mem.: ABA, N.Y. State Bar Assn., Assn. of the Bar City of N.Y., Am. Coll. Real Estate Lawyers. Office: Dewey & LeBoeuf 1301 Ave of the Americas New York NY 10019-6092 Office Phone: 212-259-8400. Office Fax: 212-259-8499. Business E-Mail: smorhouse@dl.com. *

MORI, AKIKO, nursing educator; b. Japan, Feb. 27, 1958; MSN, St. Luke's Coll. Nursing, 1986, PhD in Nursing, 2006. Prof. St. Luke's Coll. Nursing, 2006—. Bd. dirs. Japanese Soc. Fertility Nursing, 2002. Mem.: Japan Soc. Reproductive Medicine, Japan Acad. Midwifery, Japan Acad. Nursing Sci. Office: Akashi-cho 10-1 Chuo-ku Tokyo 104-0044 Japan Office Fax: 81-3-5565-1626. Business E-Mail: akiko-mori@slcn.ac.jp.

MORI, ISSEI, electrical engineer, medical physicist, educator; b. Yamada-shi, Fukuoka-ken, Japan, Dec. 23, 1948; s. Shigeo and Senko Mori; m. Yoshiko Kashimura, Nov. 11, 1955; children: Emiko, Toshihiro. D in Med Sci., Tohoku U., Sendai, Japan, 1971. Sr. specialist Toshiba, Minato-ku, Tokyo, 1971—95, chief specialist, 1996—2001, Toshiba Med. Sys. Engring., Akabane, Tokyo, 2002—04. Lectr. Tohoku U., 1995—, prof. Recipient Ichimura prize, New Tech. Devel. Found., 1998, Cert. of Commendation, Japan Inst. Invention and Innovation, 1999, DSM, Sci. and Tech. Agy., Japan, 2000, Shiju-Hosho medal, Decoration Bur. Japan, 2001. Mem.: Am. Assn. Physicists in Medicine, Japanese Soc. Radiol. Tech., Japanese Soc. Med. Imaging. Achievements include invention of helical CT; development of slipring CT. Home: Kamisugi 3-9-40-302 Aoba ku Sendai 980 0011 Japan Office: Faculty of Medicine Tohoku Univ Seiryo-machi 2-1 Aoba-ku Sendai Japan Personal E-mail: imori@med.tohoku.ac.jp, imori@aa.cyberhome.ne.jp.

MORI, KAZUTOSHI, biophysicist, educator; b. July 7, 1958; PhD, Kyoto U., Japan, 1987. Prof. dept. biophysics Kyoto U., Japan. Mem. Global COE Project. Recipient Gairdner Found. Internat. award, 2009; co-recipient Wiley prize in Biomedical Sciences, Wiley Found., 2005. Office: Dept Biophysics Grad Sch Sci Kyoto U Kitashirakawa-Oiwake Sakyo-ku Kyoto 606-8502 Japan Office Phone: 81-75-753-4067. Office Fax: 81-75-753-3718. Business E-Mail: mori@upr.biophys.kyoto-u.ac.jp. *

MORI, KENJI, chemistry professor; b. Seoul, Mar. 21, 1935; s. Sakuichi and Yoshi (Ayukawa) Mori; m. Keiko Suzuki, Nov. 4, 1962; 1 child, Nobuko. BSc, U. Tokyo, 1957, MSc, 1959, PhD, 1962. From asst. to prof. U. Tokyo, 1962-95, prof. emeritus, 1995; prof. Sci. U. Tokyo, 1995—2001; tech. cons. Fuji Flavor Co. Ltd., 2002—06; rsch. cons. Riken Inst. Phys. Chem. Rsch., 2003—; tech. cons. Toyo Gosei Co. Ltd., 2006—. Mem. Sci. Coun. Japan, 1988-91. Author: Total Synthesis of Natural Products, 1992. Pres. Internat. Soc. Chem. Ecology, 1992-93. Recipient Japan Acad. award, 1981, Agrl. Soc. prize Fedn. Agrl. Soc., 1992, silver medal Internat. Soc. Chem. Ecology, 1996, Ernest Guenther award Am. Chem. Soc., 1999, Šorm medal Acad. Sci. Czech Republic, 2003, Chirality medal, Italian Chem. Soc., 2010, Order of Sacred Treas. award, Emperor & Japanese Govt., 2010. Mem. Soc. Synthetic Organic Chemistry (pres. 1993-95, Spl. prize 2003), Japan Soc. Biosci., Biotech. and Agrochemistry (pres. 2001-03). Mem. Christian Ch. Avocation: collecting fossils. Home: 1-20-6-1309 Mukogaoka Bunkyo Tokyo 113-0023 Japan

MORI, KOJI, biologist; b. Japan, Apr. 3, 1972; PhD, GIfu U., 2000. Postdoc. fellow Nat. Inst. Advanced Indsl. Sci. and Tech., 2000—03; chief Biol. Resource Ctr., Nat. Inst. Tech. and Evaluation, 2003—. Office: 2-5-8 Kazusakamatari Kisarazu Chiba 292-0818 Japan Business E-Mail: mori@nbrc.nite.go.jp.

MORI, NORIO, medical educator; b. Japan, July 7, 1950; PhD, Fukushima Med. U., 1983, MD, 1997. Lic. in med 1983. Prof. dept. psychiatry, chmn. Hamamatsu Med. U., Sch. Medicine, 1996—. Roman Catholic. Office: 1-20-1 Handayama Hamamatsu-shi 431-3192 Japan Business E-Mail: morin@hama-med.ac.jp.

MORI, YOSHIKI, medical association administrator; b. Japan, June 9, 1954; MD, Asahikawa Med. Coll., 1980; PhD, TokyoWomen' Med. U., 1999. Asst. prof., dept. pediatric cardiology Tokyo Women's Med. U., 2003—09; dir., divsn. pediatric cardiology Seirei Hamamatsu Gen. Hosp., 2009—. Mem.: Japanese Coll. Cardiology, Japanese Circulation Soc., Japan Pediatric Soc., Japanese Soc. Pediatric Cardiology and Cardiac Surgery. Office: 3-12-12 Sumiyoshi Naka-ku Hamamatsu Shizuoka 430-8558 Japan Office Fax: 81-53-475-7596. Business E-Mail: y.mori@sis.seirei.or.jp.

MORI, YOSHIMASA, neurosurgeon; b. Ichinomiya, Japan, Dec. 18, 1960; s. Shizumi and Hiroko Mori; m. Junko Mano, Sept. 15, 1987; children: Akira, Haruka. MD, Nagoya U., Japan, 1985, DMS, 1995. Lic. Japanese Med. Bd., 1985, cert. Japan Acute Medicine Assn., 1991, Japan Neurosurg. Assn., 1991. Resident Nagoya (Japan) Ekisaikai Hosp., Nagoya, Japan, 1985—87, staff neurosurgeon, 1987—89, Komaki (Japan) City Hosp., 1990—92, dir. Gamma Knife Ctr., 1998—2002; resident Sch. Medicine Nagoya (Japan) U., 1992—95; dir. Dept. Neurosurgery Handa (Japan) City Hosp., 1995—96; vis. rsch. asst. prof. Med. Ctr. U. Pitts., 1996—98; dir. Nagoya Radiosurgery Ctr. Nagoya Kyoritsu (Japan) Hosp., 2002—03, v.p., 2003—. Contbr. articles to profl. jours. Mem.: Am. Assn. Neurol. Surgeons. Office: Nagoya Kyoritsu Hospital 1-172 Hokke Nakagawa Aichi 454-0933 Japan Office Fax: 81-52-353-9126. Business E-Mail: ymori@kaikou.or.jp.

MORI, YUKIO, retired healthcare educator; m. Hisako Mori, Mar. 29, 1969; children: Mizuki, Yukihito. BA, Tokyo Coll. Pharmacy, 1968, MS, 1970; PhD, Tokyo Pharm. Coll., Tokyo, 1971. Cert. Pharmacist Ministry of Health, Labor and Welfare, 1968; Radiation Protection Officer Ministry of Edn., Culture, Sports, Sci. and Tech., 1970. Radiation protection officer Gifu Pharm. U., Gifu, Gifu-ken, Japan, 1973—2009, chief radioisotope rsch. lab., 1989—2009. Recipient Ministry of Edn., Culture, Sports, Sci. and Tech. award, 1992. Personal E-mail: yuhimor@ccn5.aitai.ne.jp.

MORICE, RODOLFO C., pulmonologist, educator; b. Costa Rica, Jan. 9, 1949; MD, U. Costa Rica, 1973. Prof. medicine U. Tex., MD Anderson Cancer Ctr., 1984—, chief, sect. interventional pulmonology, 1996—2011, dep. chair, dept. pulmonary medicine, 2002—11, chair, sedations and procedures com., 2008—11. Fellow: Am. Coll. Chest Physicians; mem.: Am. Thoracic Soc. Office: 1515 Holcombe Blvd Unit # 1462 Houston TX 77030 Office Fax: 713-794-4922. Business E-Mail: rmorice@mdanderson.org.

MORIGUCHI, TAKASHI, medical educator; b. Yokohama, Mar. 9, 1970; MD, PhD, Tsukuba U., 2001. Asst. prof. Tohoku U., 2007—. Recipient Sakisaka award, Tohoku U. Office: 2-1 Seiryo-Aoba Sendai Miyagi 980-8575 Japan Office Fax: 81-22-717-8090. E-mail: 5thgatasymposium@gmail.com.

MORIHIKO, KIMURA, breast surgeon, consultant; b. Ota, Gunma, Japan; MD, Gunma Med. Sch., Japan, 1965, PhD, 1970. Lic. Health and Welfare, Japan, 1966. Reader dept. surgery Gunma Med. Sch., Maebashi, 1970—73; dir. dept. surgery Gunma Cancer Ctr., Ota, 1973—2005; spl. adv. Gen. Ota Hosp., 2005—, super adv., 2005—, health check, 2005. Achievements include research in neoadjuvant paclitaxel for operable breast cancer. Home: Toriyama Shimochou 665 Ota Gunma 3730063 Japan

MORIKAWA, AKIHIRO, medical educator; s. Kikuo and Kimiko Morikawa; m. Morikawa Kazuko; children: Hisahisro, Kyoko Mashio, Masahiro. MD, Gunma U., Japan, PhD, 2008. Cert. md. Welfare Ministry, Japan, 1969. Rsch. fellow Gothenberg U., Sweden, 1988—89; prof. Gunma U. Grad. Sch. Medicine, Maebashi, 1994—2008, prof. emeritus, 2008—; head Kitakanto Allergy Inst., 2008—. Pres. Asia Pacific Assn. Pediat. Allergy, Respirology, and Immunology, 2009—. Grant, Welfare Ministry and Ministry Edn. and Tech., 1993, 1999, 2002, 2003—05, 2007—11. Buddhist. Achievements include research in patients of airway hypersensitivity with bronchial asthma. Avocations: travel, reading, swimming. Office: Kitakanto Allergy Inst Ohmanamachi 22-4 Midorishi Gunma 376-0101 Japan Office Phone: 81-27-732-6022.

MORIMOTO, CHIKAO, physician; b. Mie, Japan, Mar. 12, 1948; MD, PhD, Keio U. Sch. Medicine, 1973. Assoc. prof. medicine Dana-Farber Cancer Inst., Harvard Med. Sch., 1988—; prof., chmn. clin. immunology Inst. Med. Sci., U. Tokyo, 1995, dir. advanced clin rsch. ctr., 2008. Recipient Austria Rheumatology award, Austria Govt. Mem.: Am. Soc. Clin. Investigation. Avocations: reading, gardening. Home: 5-25-16 Matsubara Setagaya-ku Tokyo 156-0043 Japan Business E-Mail: morimoto@ims.u-tokyo.ac.jp.

MORIMOTO, KIYOSHI, medical researcher; b. Japan, June 10, 1968; PhD, U. Tokyo, 1994. Sr. rschr. Daiichi-Sankyo Co., Ltd, 1994—. Office: 1-16-13 Kitakasai Edogawa-ku Tokyo 134-8630 Japan Business E-Mail: morimoto.kiyoshi.f4@daiichisankyo.co.jp.

MORIMOTO, MIE, medical educator, researcher; b. Sapporo, Hokkaido, Japan, Apr. 19, 1964; d. Akinobu and Reiko Morimoto; m. Hidekatsu Yanai, Oct. 2, 2001; 1 child, Daiki Yanai. BS, Hokkaido U., Sapporo, 1986; BA, Hokkai-Gakuen U., Sapporo, 1990. Cert. medical technologist Japan Ministry of Welfare. Asst. prof. Coll. of Med. Tech., Hokkaido U., Sapporo, 1987—. Contbr. articles to profl. jours. Dir. Citizens Health Improving Campaign, Sapporo, 2000—03. Grantee, Ministry Edn., Sci. and Culture, 2002—03, Coll. of Med. Tech., Hokkaido U., 2000. Mem.: Hokkaido Soc. Lab. Hematology (bd. dirs. 2000—), Hokkaido Assn. Med. Tech. (bd. dirs. 1989—, grand prize 2003), Japanese Soc. Lab. Medicine (tokyo/japan 1998—2003), Japanese Soc. Lab. Hematology (tokyo/japan 2000—03), Japanese Assn. Med. Tech. (tokyo/japan 1998—2003). Buddhist. Achievements include research in investigation and development of urinalysis. Avocations: travel, shopping, reading. Office Fax: +81-11-706-4916. E-mail: mie@cme.hokudai.ac.jp.

MORIMOTO, SHINJI, medical educator, researcher; s. Shinpei and Reiko Morimoto; m. Kaori Ikeda, Oct. 12, 1995; children: Mao, Tarou. Degree, Juntend U. Sch. Medicine, Tokyo, 1989. Diplomate Juntendo U. Sch. Medicine, 1997. Staff Juntendo U. Sch. Medicine, Hongo, Bunkyo-Ku, Tokyo, 1997—2003, asst. prof., 2003—05, assoc. prof., 2005—. Contbr. articles to profl. jours. Fellow: Japan Coll. Rheumatology (councilor 2007—). Office: Juntendo Univ Sch Medicine 2-1-1 Hongo Bunkyo-Ku Tokyo 113-8421 Japan

MORIMOTO, TADAOKI, surgeon, educator; b. Kochi, Japan, Jan. 1, 1942; s. Toyoo and Hanako Morimoto; m. Yasuko Morimoto, Mar. 14, 1968; children: Yuka, Rie, Masafumi. MD, U. Tokushima, Japan, 1967, PhD, 1977. Asst. prof. to assoc. prof. U. Tokushima, 1985—90, prof., 1990—. Translator (assoc. editor): Breast Cancer Jour., 1994—; contbr. articles to profl. jours. Avocations: reading, travel, swimming. Home: 2-1-21-1 Minamiyaso-cho Tokushima 770-0005 Japan Office: Univ Tokushima Sch Health Sci 3-18-15 Kuramoto-cho Tokushima 770-8509 Japan Office Phone: 81-88-633-9031.

MORIMOTO, TAKESHI, epidemiologist, clinician, educator; b. Takamatsu, Japan, Nov. 5, 1970; MD, Kyoto U. Sch. Medicine, Japan, 1989—95; PhD, Kyoto U. Grad. Sch. Medicine, 2000—04; MPH, Harvard Sch. Pub. Health, Boston, Mass., 2001—02. Diplomate Japan, 1995. Instr. Kyoto U. Grad. Sch. Medicine, 2004—05, asst. prof., 2005—11; dir., clin. rsch. support unit Kyoto U., 2005—; staff physician Kyoto U. Hosp., 2004—; CEO Inst. Clin. Effectiveness, Kyoto, 2010—; prof. medicine Kinki U. Sch. Medicine, 2011—. Dir., clin. epidemiology unit Internat. Clin. Epidemiology Network, Kyoto, 2005—; cons. Patient Safety Programme, WHO, Geneva, 2006—. Recipient Excellence award for Atherosclerosis, Japan Heart Found., 2005, Young Investigators award, Japanese Soc. Internal Medicine, 2008; grantee, Pfizer Health Svc. Rsch. Found., 2001, St. Lukes Life Sci. Inst., 2001, Patient Safety Rsch., Health Care Sci. Inst., 2003. Fellow: ACP (licentiate). Office: Med Edn Kyoto Univ Konoe-cho Yoshida Sakyo-ku Kyoto 606-8501 Japan Office Fax: 81-75-751-4250.

MORIN, CHRISTOPHER JOSEPH, vascular surgeon; s. Louis Peter and Rosamond Agatha Morin; m. Christine Sotorp, Feb. 17, 1996; children: Colleen Campbell, Kelly Anne, Christopher Jr. BA, Coll. the Holy Cross, Worcester, Mass.; MD, Brown U., Providence, RI; MBA, U.RI, Kingston. Lic. Vascular Surgery Am. Bd. Surgery, Clincial Instr. Surgery Harvard Med. Sch., cert. Vascular Surgery Bd., Am. Bd. Surgery, 2008. Chmn. dept. surgery St. Luke's Hosp. and Health Network, Bethlehem, Pa., 1997—2002; clin. asst. prof. surgery Brown U., 1982—97, U. Pa., 1998—2005; chmn. cardiovasc. ops. St. Francis Cardiac and Vascular Care Ctr., Indpls., 2002—06; vascular surgeon Brantigan and Morin, Denver, 2006—; cons. Heart Works Advisors, Indpls., 2006—; endovascular surgery cons. Internat. Hosp., Cairo, 2006—; chmn. dept. surgery PSL Med. Ctr. Denver, 2009—, Health One Network Rocky Vista U., 2009—; clin. prof. DeSales U., 1998—. Cons. DeSales U. Ctr. for Faith and Culture, Center Valley, Pa.; dir. Brown U. Med. Alumni Assn., Providence, 1980—97, pres., 1986—88; chair dept. surgery, PSL Presbyterian St. Lukes Med. Ctr., 2008—; chair dept. surgery St. Lukes Hosp. & Health Network, Bethlehem, Pa. Comdr. USNR, 1984—91. Named one of Top Surgeon in the US, Consumer Rsch. Concil. Fellow: ACS; mem.: Am. Coll. Physician Execs., Internat. Soc. for Vascular Surgery, European Soc. for Vascular Surgery, Soc. for Vascular Surgery. Office: Brantigan & Morin 2253 Downing St Denver CO 80205 Business E-Mail: vascsurg@aol.com.

MORIN, FREDERICK C., dean, pediatrician, educator; BS in Biology, U. Notre Dame; MD, Yale U. Asst. prof. pediat. U. Buffalo, 1986, assoc. prof. pediat. and physiology, 1989, prof. pediat., vice chmn. rsch. Pediat. Dept., 1994, chair Pediat. Dept., 1997, interim v.p. health affairs, 2005; chief neonatology divsn. Women and Children's Hosp. of Buffalo, 1989, pediatrician-in-chief, 1997; chief pediat. svc. Women and Children's Hops. of Buffalo and Kaleida Health; A. Conger Goodyear prof., chmn. Dept. Pediat. U. Buffalo Sch. Medicine and Biomedical Scis., interim dean, 2005; dean U. Vt. Coll. Medicine, 2007—. Contbr. articles to med. jours. Mem.: Nitric Oxide Soc., Am. Soc. Pediat. Dept. Chairs, Am. Physiological Assn., Am. Acad. Pediat., Am. Thoracic Soc., Am. Pediat. Soc., Soc. Pediat. Rsch. Office: U Vt Coll Medicine Office of Dean Given E Rm 126 Burlington VT 05405 Office Phone: 802-656-2156. E-mail: Frederick.Morin@uvm.edu.

MORINGLANE, ARISTIDE JEAN RICHARD, neurosurgeon, educator; b. Pétionville, Haiti, Feb. 16, 1944; s. Robert Aristide Gravier and Marie Augustine (Duhamel) M.; m. Maria-Cecilia Margarita Toro La Roche, May 19, 1978; children: Denise M. Charlotte, René Bernard, Philipp Georges, Alice Esther. Bachelor's, Coll. St. Martial, Port-Au-Prince, Haiti, 1963; MD, Freiburg U., Germany, 1971. Trainee, rsch. fellow dept. neurosurgery U. Freiburg, 1971-78; asst. dept. neurosurgery Nordstadt City Hosp., Hannover, Germany, 1978-81; neurosurgeon Hosp. Ste Anne, Paris, 1982; asst. med. dir. Nordstadt City Neurosurgery, Hannover, 1983-84; asst. med. dir. dept. stereotaxic neurosurgery U. Saarland, Homburg/Saar, Germany, 1984—, with neuro-oncol. outpatient unit, 1990—. Mem. New Rsch. Group on Proliferation and Oncogenese. Contbr. articles to profl. jours. Mem. Saarland Med. Assn., German Neurosurg. Soc., French Speaking Neurosurg. Assn., European Soc. for Stereotactic and Functional Neurosurgery, World Soc. Functional and Stereotactic Neurosurgery, German Cancer Soc., German Assn. for Parkinson's Disease, Assn. of Friends and Supporters Music Acad. Avocations: literature, history, music, tennis. Home: Sperlingweg 4 D-66459 Kirkel Germany Office: Dept Neurosurg U Saarland Kirrbergerstrasse 1 D-66421 Homburg Saar Germany E-mail: ncjrmo@uniklinik-saarland.de.

MORINO, YOSHIHIRO, medical educator; b. Atami, Shizuoka, Japan, Aug. 21, 1967; s. Tomoharu and Setsuko Morino; m. Junko Kondo; children: Yuka, Madoka. MD, Gifu U., 1993. Assoc. prof. Tokai U. Sch. Medicine, Isehara, Kanagawa, Japan, 2005—. Fellow: Japanese Soc. Internal Medicine. Office: Tokai Univ Sch Medicine 143 Shimokasuya Isehara Kanagawa 2591193 Japan Office Fax: 81463936679. Business E-Mail: ymorino@is.icc.u-tokai.ac.jp.

MORIOKA-DOUGLAS, NANCY, physician, educator; b. Honolulu, Hawaii, Aug. 2, 1954; MD, U. Hawaii, 1981, MPH, 1985. Clin. prof. Stanford U. Sch. Medicine, 1993—. Clinic chief Stanford Family Medicine, Stanford Hosp. and Clinics, 1998—. Office: Stanford Family Medicine 300 Pasteur Dr Stanford CA 94305 Business E-Mail: nmd@stanford.edu.

MORISHITA, RYUICHI, medical educator; b. Sojya, Okayama, Japan, May 12, 1962; s. Morishita Kazuo and Morishita Kayoko; m. Mayumi Shinoda; children: Keira children: Shota. PhD, Osaka U. Grad. Sch., Japan, 1991. Diplomate Osaka U. Grad. Sch., 1987. Dir. AnGes Inc., Ibaraki, Osaka, 1999—. Contbr. scientific papers. Recipient Clin. Pharmacology award, Japan Rsch. Found., 1991, Young Investigator award, Internat. Soc. Hypertension, 1994, Vascular Disease Rsch. Found., Japan, 1994, Japanese Circulation Soc., 1996, Japanese Atherosclerosis Soc., 1996, 11th Internat. Symposium Atherosclerosis, 1997, Soc. Cardiovasc. & Endocrinology, 1997, Soc. Endocrinology, 1998, Soc. Pharmacology, 1999, Japanese Soc. Hypertension, 2001, Japan Heart Found., 1991—92, Am. Fedn. Clin. Rsch., 1993, Upjohn Cardiology Young Investigator award, Stanford U., 1993, Am. Fedn. Clin. Rsch., 1994, Harry Goldbratt award, Am. Heart Assn., 1996, Japan Med. Soc., 1999, Takamine Jokichi award, Soc. Cardiovasc. & Endocrinology, 2001, Sato award, Japanese Circulation Soc., 2002, Japan Innovator award, Nikkei BP, 2003, Invitrogen Nature Biotechnology award, 2005; Postdoc. fellowship grant, Am. Heart Assn. Calif., 1992—94. Fellow: Coun. Circulation. Office: Osaka Univ Yamada-oka2-2 Suita Osaka 565-0871 Japan Office Fax: 81-6-6879-3409. Business E-Mail: morishit@cgt.med.osaka-u.ac.jp.

MORITA, HIROYUKI, nephrologist; b. Toyohashi, Aichi, Japan, 1956; s. Masao and Yaeko Morita; m. Takako Matsuyama, 1994; children: Kentaro, Kotaro. MD, Nagoya U., Japan, 1984. Fellow The Branch Hosp. Nagoya U., 1985—87, 1988—95, Nagoya Meml. Hosp., 1987—88; rsch. resident Japan Found. for Aging and Health, 1995—96; postdoctoral fellow Karolinksa Inst., Sweden, 1996—98; assoc. prof. Fujigaoka Hosp. Showa U., Yokohama, Japan, 1998—. Grantee, Japanese Ministry Edn., Sci., Sports and Culture, 1999, 2000, 2002, 2003, 2006, 2007. Fellow: Japanese Soc. Dialysis Therapy (bd. cert. sr. mem.), Japanese Soc. Nephrology (assoc. councilor), Japanese Soc. Internal Medicine; mem.: Am. Soc. Nephrology (corr.). Office: Showa Univ Fujigaoka Hosp 1-30 Fujigaoka Aoba-ku Kanagawa 227-8501 Japan Yokohama Office Fax: +81-45-973-3010; Home Fax: +81-45-974-2302. Business E-Mail: morita@showa-university-fujigaoka.gr.jp.

MORITA, MASARU, surgeon; b. Nagasaki, Japan, Mar. 30, 1962; MD, Kyushu U., 1987. Assoc. prof. Kyushu U., 2005—11; chief surgeon Nat. Kyushu Cancer Ctr., 2011—. Fellow: ACS. Office: 3-1-1 Notame Minami-ku Fukuoka 811-1395 Japan Business E-Mail: masarum@surg2.med.kyushu-u.ac.jp.

MORITA, MITSUHIRO, orthopedist, surgeon, researcher; s. Tsuneo and Hisako Morita; m. Asako Watanabe, Aug. 4, 2001; children: Sayaka children: Shogo Galen, Rei. MD, Nat. Defense Med. Coll., Tokorozawa, Japan, 1992; PhD, Nat. Def. Med. Coll., Tokorozawa, Saitama, 2003. Diplomate Bd. Orthop. Surgery, Rheumatology and Geriatrics, cert. infection control dr. Resident Nat. Def. Med. Coll. Hosp., Tokorozawa, Saitama, Japan, 1992—98; army divsn. surgeon 7th divsn. Hdq., Chitose, 2003—05; mem. staff med. planning group Ground Staff Office, Ministry Def., Tokyo, 2005—06; sr. lectr. Self Def. Forces Ctrl. Hosp., Setagaya, Tokyo, 2006—07; sr. asst. prof. dept. orthopaedic surgery Fujita Health U., 2007—. Mil. exch. physician Walter-Reed Army Med. Ctr., Washington, 1995—96. Staff Second Iraqi-Reconstruction Support Group, Samawa, Muthanna, 2004; chief med. doctors Disaster Relief Indonesia, Banda Aceh, Aceh, 2005. Lt. col. Japanese Mil., 2006. Decorated Order of Def. (Grade 3) Ministry of Def.; recipient Honors of Med. Resque, 7th Divsn., 2004, Mil. Person of the yr., 2005, Fuji Sankei Newspaper, 2005, Prize of Rsch., Japanese Orthopaedic and Traumatology Found., 2008; fellow, Nat. Def. Med. Coll. Grad. Sch. Medicine, 1999—2003, NIH, Bethesda, Md., 2002—03. Mem.: Internat. Soc. Tech. in Arthroplasty, Internat. Soc. Orthop. Surgery and Traumatology, Am. Acad. Orthop. Surgeons (internat. affiliate), Japanese Orthopaedic Assn. Avocations: travel, languages, volleyball. Office: Fujita Health Univ 1-98 Dengakugakubo Kutsukake Toyoake Aichi 470-1192 Japan Office Fax: 0562-93-9252. Business E-Mail: mimorita@fujita-hu.ac.jp.

MORITA, TAKASHI, urologist; b. Toyama, Japan, July 22, 1967; married; 3 children. Attended, Toyama U. Elem. Sch., 1980, Toyama U. Jr. High Sch., 1983; grad., Toyama U. High Sch., 1986; attended, U. Tsukaba, 1986, grad., 1992. Cert. Occupational Physician Japan. Med. Assn., 2000. Jr. resident dept. of urology Univ. of Tsukaba Univ. Hosp., 1992, chief resident dept. of urology, 1997; hosp. med. staff of comm. dept. of urology Tokyo, 1998; med. dir. med. lab. Sumitomo Life Ins. Co., 1999; urologist Dean Healthcare Hosp., 2004; mem. fiscal and fin. com. Upper House Budget Com., 2007; dep. sec. health care reform faction teams Govt. of Japan, 2007, dep. sec. project team pandemic influenza faction, 2007, internal affairs vice min., 2010; joined Nat. New Party, 2008, dep. sec. nat. economy com. of councilors, 2008. Med. dir. Jin Shin Inst. of Med. Veritas Assn., 2004. Recipient Assn. Chmn. award, Med. Assn. Japan, 2004. Mem.: Japan Soc., Japan Med. Assn., Japanese Urological Assn. (Med. Advisor 2002). Office: Takashi Morita 2 2 17 Takara Cho Toyama Japan Mailing: c/o The House of Representatives 1 7 1 Chiyoda-ku Tokyo Japan Office Phone: 0764455775. Office Fax: 0764455785. *

MORITANI, TOSHIO, radiologist, educator; b. Okayama, Japan, Jan. 21, 1961; arrived in U.S., 1999; s. Hideo and Tomoko Moritani; m. Yumiko Moritani, June 8, 2003. MD, Showa U., Tokyo, 1987; PhD, Showa U., 1991. Lic. Am. Bd. Radiology, Japanese Bd. Radiology; cert. Edn. Commn. Fgn. Med. Grads. Head physician Saitama Children's Med. Ctr., Japan, 1993—99; asst. rsch. prof. U. Rochester, NY, 1999—2004; clin. assoc. U. Iowa, Iowa City, 2004—05, asst. prof., 2005—10, assoc. prof., 2010—. Asst. prof. Showa U. Sch. Medicine, 1991—97, 1997—99, adj. assoc. prof., 2004—; vis. prof. U. Iowa, Iowa City, 2003; adj. asst. prof. U. Rochester, 2004—10, adj. assoc. prof., 2010—. Author: Diffusion-Weighted Imaging of the Brain, 2003, Japanese transl., 2005, 2nd edit., 2009; contbr. articles to profl. jours. Mem.: Am. Coll. Radiology, Japanese Coll. Radiology, Am. Soc. Neuroradiology (several citations 1999—2006), Radiol. Soc. N.Am. (several citations 1997—2005). Avocations: golf, tennis, travel, reading, shorinji. Office: U Iowa Dept Radiology 200 Hawkins Dr Iowa City IA 52242 Home: 221 E Coll St 1207 Iowa City IA 52240 Office Phone: 319-356-1177, 319-356-3767, 319-356-3676. Personal E-mail: moritani2001@yahoo.com.

MORITOKI, EGI, physician; b. Japan, Dec. 12, 1973; MD, Okayama U., 1999. Physician Okayama U. Hosp., 2005—. Office: 2-5-1 Shikata-cho Okayama 700-8558 Japan Office Fax: 812356984. Business E-Mail: moriori@tg8.so-net.ne.jp.

MORITSUGU, KENNETH PAUL, medical association administrator, retired military officer; b. Honolulu, Mar. 5, 1945; s. Richard Yutaka and Hisayo Joan (Nishikawa) M.; m. Donna Lee Jones (dec. 1992); children: Erika Lizabeth, Vikki Lianne (deceased), Emily Renee; m. Lisa Kory. Student, Chaminade Coll. Honolulu, 1963-65; BA in Classical Langs. with honors, U. Hawaii, 1967; MD, George Washington U. Sch. Medicine, 1971; MPH in Health Adminstrn. and Planning, U. Calif., Berkeley, 1975; DSc (hon.), Coll. Osteopathic Medicine, U. New Eng., 1988; DSc, U. New England; DSc (hon.), Midwestern U. Chgo., 1993, Des Moines U., Iowa, 2005; DSC (hon.), Still U., 2005; D Pub. Svc. (hon.), U. North Tex., 1994; DHL (hon.), Western U. Health Scis., 2002, Alliant Internat. U., 2002; DDL (hon.), Phila. Coll. Osteo. Medicine; DHL (hon.), Campbell U., 2003, Nova Southeastern U., 2004. Diplomate Am. Bd. Preventive Medicine (fellow); cert. correctional health profl. Intern USPHS Hosp., San Francisco, 1971-72, resident, 1972-75; commd. USPHS, 1968, advanced through grades to med. dir., 1979; promoted to rank of rear adm., asst. surgeon gen., 1988; staff med. officer USPHS Hosp., San Francisco, 1972-73; regional cons. med. manpower planning and devel. US Dept. Health, Edn. & Welfare, San Francisco, 1976-78, chief internat. edn. programs br. Washington, 1978, dep. dir. divsn. medicine, 1978; asst. bur. dir., med. dir. Fed. Bur. Prisons US Dept. Justice, Washington, 1987-98; dir. Bur. Health Professions, div. medicine US Dept. Health & Human Services, Rockville, Md., 1978-83, dir. Nat. Health Service Corps, 1983-87, dep. dir. Bur. Health Professions, 1987, asst. surgeon gen., 1988, dep. surgeon gen., 1998—2006, acting surgeon gen., 2006—07; chmn. Johnson & Johnson Diabetes Inst., LLC, Milpitas, Calif., 2007—. Adj. assoc. prof. pub. health Uniformed Svcs. U. Health Scis.; invited spkr. in field. Bd. dir. United Network for Organ Sharing; founding chair bd. trustees Certified Correctional Health Professions Program; chair Am. Correctional Assn. Com. on Health Care in Corrections; dedicated advocate for tissue and organ donation; active participant Donor Family Recognition Programs, Washington; sec., treas., bd. dir. Washington Regional Transplant Consortium; mem. nat. adv. bd. Minority Organ and Tissue Transplant Edn. Program; active vol. Transplant Recipients Internat. Orgn.; former bd. trustee Nat. Kidney Found.; former mem. exec. com. Nat. Donor Family Coun.; former past mem. pub. affairs com. and minority affairs com. Washington Regional Transport Consortium Donor Family Coun.; trustee, treas. Physician Assistants Found., Am. Acad. Physician Assistants; chmn. bd. Anchor and Caduceus Soc. U.S. Pub. Health Svc.; bd. dir. Royal Soc. Medicine Found.; corp. trustee American Acad. Family Physicians Found. Decorated D.S.M., knight grand cross Mil. and Hospitaller Order St. Lazarus of Jerusalem; recipient Commendation medal, U.S. Pub. Health Svc., Meritorious Svc. medal, Outstanding Svc. medal, Disting. Svc., Surgeon Gen.'s medallion, Surgeon Gen.'s medal for Exemplary Svc., Army Achievement medal, Coast Guard Arctic Svc. medal, Dirs. Spl. Achievement award, U.S. Marshal's Svcs., John D. Chase award, Assn. Mil. Surgeons US, Nathan Davis award, AMA, Disting. Svc. award, Am. Correctional Health Svcs. Assn., Disting. Svc. medal, U.S. Dept. Justice, Fed. Bur. Prisons, Meritorious Svc. medal, Health Leader of Yr., Commd. Officers Assn., William B. Miller award, Assn. Colls. Osteopathic Medicine, Spl. Achievement award, Nat. Comm. on Correctional Health Care, Phillips medal Pub. Svc., Ohio U.; named Disting. Alumnus, George Washington U., 2002. Fellow Am. Coll. Preventive Medicine, Royal Soc. Health (past chair US chpt.), Royal Soc. Medicine; mem. APHA, Assn. Tchrs. Preventive Medicine, Assn. Mil. Surgeons U.S., Res. Officers Assn., Mensa, Am. Guild Organists, Am. Acad. Physicians Assts. (hon. life mem.)(President's award), Delta Omega, Omicron Delta Kappa. Office: Johnson & Johnson Diabetes Inst 1001 S Milpitas Blvd Milpitas CA 95035 *

MORITZ, CHAD HENRY, retired research scientist; Grad. magna cum laude, U. Wis., 1977. Diagnostic radiographer Aurora Health Care, Milw., 1991—93, Covenant Health Care, Milw., 1993—94; MRI rsch. technologist Med. Coll. Wis., Milw., 1994—96; rsch. assoc. Dartmouth Coll., Hanover, NH, 1996—98; rsch. program mgr. radiology dept. U. Wis. Med. Sch., Madison, 1999—2010. Presenter in field. Contbr. chapters to books, articles to profl. jours. Recipient award for Excellence, St. Luke's Sch. Radiol. Tech., 1993; Profl. devel. grantee, U. Wis., 2003, 2010. Avocations: bicycling, accordion.

MORITZ, MICHAEL LAREDO, nephrologist, director; b. Oct. 2, 1965; AB, U. Miami, 1987; MD, U. Chgo., Pritzker Sch. Medicine, 1991. Clin. dir., divsn. nephrology, med. dir., pediat. dialysis Children's Hosp. Pitts. UPMC, 2009—. Assoc. prof. pediat. U. Pitts. Sch. Medicine, 2006; editor-in-chief Internat. Jour. Clin. Medicine, 2010. Contbr. articles to profl. jours., chapters to books. Recipient ACES award, U. Pitts., UPMC. Mem.: Internat. Pediat. Nephrology Assn., Am. Soc. Pediat. Nephrology, Am. Soc. Nephrology. Home: 5515 Darlington Rd Pittsburgh PA 15217 Office Phone: 412-692-5182. Business E-Mail: michael.moritz@chp.edu.

MORIYA, FUMIO, forensic toxicologist; b. Mabi-cho, Okayama, Japan, Oct. 3, 1959; s. Hakuo and Sachiko (Takemasa) M.; m. Etsuko Yoshii, Feb. 16, 1986; children: Manami, Hikari, Yuto. B in Pharmacy, Okayama U., 1982, PharmM, 1984, PhD, 1991. Pharmacist Okayama Rosai Hosp., 1984-85; instr. Okayama U. Med. Sch., 1985-94, lectr., 1994; assoc. prof. Kochi Med. Sch., Kochi U., 1994—2008; prof. Kawasaki U. Med. Welfare, Kurashiki, Japan, 2008—. Vis. scholar U. So. Calif. Sch. Medicine, L.A., 1992-93. Inventor in field. Grantee aid for sci. rsch., Ministry Edn., Sci. and Culture, Japan, 1991, 1994—2002, 2004—08;, 2011—. Fellow The Medico-Legal Soc. Japan, Japanese Assn. Forensic Toxicology; mem. Am. Acad. Forensic Scis. Avocations: sprinting, reading, music, photography, fishing. Office: Kawasaki Univ Med Welfare Dept Nursing Faculty Health Welfare 288 Matsushima Kurashiki Okayama 701-0193 Japan Home: 2-9-20-701 Daiku 7000913 Japan Office Phone: 81 86 462 1111 ext. 54981. Business E-Mail: moriyaf@mw.kawasaki-m.ac.jp.

MORIYAMA, NARIAKIRA, psychiatrist, writer; b. Ogori, Fukuoka, Japan, Jan. 22, 1947; BA, Tokyo U., 1969; MD, Kyushu U., Fukuoka, Japan, 1978, PhD, 1988. Fgn. asst. St. Marguerite Hosp., Marseilles, France, 1979—80; fgn. resident St. Anne Hosp., Paris, 1980—81; asst. prof. Kyushu U., Fukuoka, 1982—88; chief psychiatrist Yahata Kosei Hosp., Kitakyushu, Japan, 1988—90, vice dir., 1990—. Recipient Yoshikawa Eiji beginner prize, Kodansha, Tokyo, 1993, Yamamoto Shugoro prize, Shinchosha, 1995, Shibata Renzaburo prize, Shueisha, 1997. Fellow: Japanese Assn. Morita Therapy; mem.: Japanese Impotence Assn. Home: 2-7-21 Toritani Nakama 809-0018 Japan Office: Toritani Mental Clinic 1-8 Nabeyama Nakamashi 809 0022 Japan Home Phone: +81-93-244-9484; Office Phone: +81-93-243-5569.

MORJARIA, JAYMIN BHAGWANJI, pulmonologist; s. Bhagwanji Dayalal and Pushpa Bhagwanji Morjaria; m. Rishma Jaymin Morjaria, July 10, 2004. MBBS, St. Bartholomew's & Royal London Sch. Medicine & Dentistry, 2000; MD, U. London, 2009. Clin. rsch. fellow U. Southampton, 2003—06; specialist registrar East Eng. Deanery, Cambridge, Cambridgeshire, England, 2006—, Addenbrooks NHS Hosp. Trust, Cambridgeshire, 2009—; cons. Castle Hill Hosp. Mem. European Respiratory Jour. Contbr. articles to profl. jours. Mem.: Gen. Med. Coun., British Med. Assn. Thorax, Royal Coll. Physicians, (London). Office: NHS 49 Swanland Rd Hessle East Yorkshire HU13 0NN England Business E-Mail: jbm@soton.ac.uk.

MORK-KNUTSEN, BJØRN B., dentist, consultant; b. Halden, Norway, July 8, 1955; m. Ellen Cathrine Mork-Knutsen, June 3, 1995; children: Ingeborg Aase, Peer Olaf, Paal Harald, Astrid Ellensdatter. DDS, U. Oslo, 1983. Gen. practitioner Tannlegene på Wiels Plass, Halden, Norway, 1985—, specialist maxillofacial radiology, 2002—. Asst. prof. Dept. Maxillofacial Radiology U. Oslo, 2004—; cons. in field. Chmn. Østfold Tannlægeforening, Norway, 1994—97. Recipient Best Poster Presentation award, VII European Congress Dept. Maxillofacial Radiology, 1999. Home: Wiels Plass 2 Halden N 1768 Norway Office: U Oslo Inst Clin Dentistry Dept Maxillofacial Radiology 317 Oslo Norway Home Fax: +4769211061. Personal E-mail: bjmork@odont.uio.no.

MORLEY, JOHN EDWARD, physician; b. Eshowe, Zululand, South Africa, June 13, 1946; came to U.S., 1977; s. Peter and Vera Rose (Phipson) M.; m. Patricia Morley, Apr. 4, 1970; children: Robert, Susan, Jacqueline. MB, BCh, U. Witwatersrand, Johannesburg, South Africa, 1972. Diplomate Am. Bd. Internal Medicine, subspecialty cert. endocrinology and geriatrics. Asst. prof. Mpls. VA Med. Ctr. and U. Minn., 1979-81; assoc. prof. U. Minn., Mpls., 1981-84; prof. UCLA San Fernando Valley, 1985-89; dir. GRECC Sepulveda (Calif.) VA Med. Ctr., 1985-89; Dammert prof. gerontology, dir. div. geriatric medicine St. Louis U. Med. Ctr., 1989—; dir. geriatric rsch., edn. and clin. ctr. St. Louis VA Med. Ctr., 1989—2011. Author: (with others) Nutritional Modulation of Neuronal Function, 1988, Neuropeptides and Stress, 1988, Geriatric Nutrition, 1990, 2d edit., 1995, Medical Care in the Nursing Home, 1991, 2d edit., 1997, Endocrinology and Metabolism in the Elderly, 1992, Memory Function and Aging Related Disorders, 1992, Aging and Musculoskeletal Disorders, 1993, Aging, Immunity and Infection, 1994, Sleep Disorders and Insomnia in the Elderly, 1993, Quality Improvement in Geriatric Care, 1995, Focus on Nutrition, 1995, Applying Health Services Research to Long-Term Care, 1996, Cardiovascular Disease in Older People, 1997, Hydration and Aging, 1997, Advances in Care of Older People with Diabetes, 1999, Endocrinology of Aging, 1999, Science of Geriatrics, 2000, Subacute Care, 2000, Anti-Aging, 2004, Principles and Practices of Geriatric Medicine, 4th edit., 2006; The Sci. Staying Young, 2007; mem. editl. bd. Peptides, 1983—, Internat. Jour. Obesity, 1986-89, Jour. Nutritional Medicine, 1990—, Clinics in Applied Nutrition, 1990-92; editor geriatrics sect. Yearbook of Endocrinology, 1987-2001, Nursing Home Medicine, 1992-97, Clin. Geriatrics, 1992-97, Sandwich Generation, 1997, others; editor Jour. Gerontology: Med. Scis., 2000-06, Jour. Am. Med. Dirs. Assn., 2006—. Mem. adv. bd. Alzheimer's Assn., St. Louis, 1990-92; mem. adv. com. for physicians Mo. Divsn. Aging, Jefferson City, 1990-2001; bd. dirs. Mo. Assn. Long Term Care Physicians, 1991—, Long Term Care Ombudsman Program, St. Louis, 1992, Fund for Psychoneuroimmunology, 1990-2001, Hamilton Hts. Health Resource Ctr., 1992—. Recipient Mead Johnson award, Am. Inst. Nutrition, 1985, Cmty. Svc. award, BREM, 1997, Robert H. Bollinger Disting. Acad. award, U. Kans., 1997, Longevity prize, Ispen Found., 1999, Circle award, Am. Dietetics Assn., 2001, Marsha Goodwin-Beck Interdisciplinary award for excellence in geriatric leadership, Dept. Vets. Affairs, 2005, AMDAs Pattee Ednl. Excellence award, 2011. Mem. ACP (geriatrics subcom. 1991-92), Am. Geriatric Soc. (Nasher/Manning award 2002), Internat. Soc. Study-Aging Male, Am. Soc. Clin. Investigation, Endocrine Soc., Am. Fedn. Clin. Rsch., Am. Acad. Behavioral Sci., Gerontology Soc. Am. (Freeman award, 2004), Am. Diabetes Assn., Am. Soc. Pharmacy and Therapeutics, Soc. for Neurosci., La Asociacion de Gerontologica y Geriatrica, A.C. (hon.), Assn. Dirs. Geriatric Acad. Programs, Internat. Soc. Study Male Aging, Phi Beta Kappa. Office: Saint Louis U Sch Medicine 1402 S Grand Blvd Rm M238 Saint Louis MO 63104-1004 Office Phone: 314-977-8462. Business E-Mail: morley@slu.edu.

MORO, STEFANO, chemistry professor; b. Treviso, Italy, Feb. 5, 1965; m. Marta Ziggiotto, Dec. 14, 1996; children: Greta, Emma. PhD in Phys. Organic Chemistry, U. Padova, 1996. Post-doc computational medicinal chemistry NIH, Bethesda, Md., 1997—98; prof. medicinal chemistry U. Padova, Italy, 1999—. Vis. prof. Dept. Applied Bio-Sciences Inst. Pharm. Chemistry ETH Zurich, Switzerland, 2002. Recipient Nat. Rsch. Excellence award, IBM Italian Found., 1993, Rsch. Excellence in Chemistry award, U. Padova, 2000, Italian Nat. Rsch. Excellence in Medicinal Chemistry award, Federchimica, 2000, Farmindustria, 2002; fellow, NIH, 1998. Achievements include research in mecidinal chemsitry and drug discovery. Office: University of Padova Via Francesco Marzolo 5 35131 Padova PD Italy Office Fax: +39 049 8275366. Business E-Mail: stefano.moro@unipd.it.

MORONT, MATTHEW LEONARD, pediatric surgeon; MD, Georgetown U., 1990. Diplomate Am. Bd. Surgery, Am. Bd. Surgery-pediatric surgery, lic. Pa., 1999, NJ, 2001. Intern Univ. Mass. Meml. Med. Ctr., 1991, resident, 1993; fellow Children's Meml. Hosp., 1999; asst. prof. of pediat. and surgery Drexel Univ. Coll. of Medicine; hosp. affiliations include Capital Health System, Faxton St. Luke's Healthcare, Hahnemann Univ. Hosp., Univ. Mass. Meml. Med. Ctr.; attending surgeon St. Christopher's Hosp. for Children, med. dir. trauma program. Named one of Top Doctors, Phila. Mag., 2011. Fellow: ACS. Office: Saint Christopher's Hospital for Children 3601 A St Philadelphia PA 19134 Office Fax: 215-427-5000, 215-427-5555.

MOROOKA, HIROSHI, neurosurgeon; b. Kurashiki, Okayama, Japan, Aug. 28, 1946; s. Shigeru and Akiko (Kobayashi) M.; m. Michiko Ninomiya, June 6, 1976; children: Takatoshi, Hanako, Teruko. MD, U. Okayama, 1971, PhD, 1978. Diplomate Japanese Bd. Neurol. Surgery. Clin. asst. neurosurgery U. Okayama Med. Sch., 1972—77, instr. neurosurgery, 1980-83, asst. prof. neurosurgery, 1984-86; rsch. assoc. neurology U. Miami Med. Sch., Fla., 1977-79; chief neurosurgery Okayama Rousai Hosp., 1987-92, Bizen City Hosp., 1993-95, Okayama Saidaiji Hosp., 1996—2007, Morooka Neurosurg. and Pediat. Clinic, Okayama, 2008—. Author: Cytoprotection & Cytobiology, 1995-97, Medical Biochemical & Chemical Aspects of Free Radicals, 1989, Intracranial Pressure VII, 1989, Brain Edema IX, 1993. Recipient Disting. Prof. award, BWW Soc., Inst. Advancement of Positive Global Solutions, Calif., 2003, Legion of Honor award, United Cultural Conv., NC, 2005; Nat. Rsch. grantee, 1981. Mem. AAAS, Japan Neurol. Soc., Societas Neurologica Japonica, NY Acad. Scis., Am. Heart Assn., Am. Chem. Soc. Liberal Dem. Christian. Avocation: golf. Home: 880-165 Minato 703 8266 Okayama Japan Office: Morooka Neurosurgical & Pediatric Clinic 492-1 Kitajima Okucho Setouchi City Okayama 701-4232 Japan Office Phone: 086-943-1222. Business E-Mail: morooka@okym.enjoy.ne.jp.

MORRA, MARION E., medical writer; BA in Journalism, U. Bridgeport; MA in Comms., Fairfield U.; DSc, Albertus Magnus Coll. From program mgr. to assoc. dir. Yale Cancer Ctr. Yale U. Sch. Medicine, New Haven, 1975-97. Assoc. rsch. scientist Yale U. Sch. Medicine; assoc. clin. prof. Yale U. Sch. Nursing. Co-author: Choices: A Sourcebook for Cancer Education, 1980, 87, 94, 2003, The Prostate Cancer Answer Book, 1996, Triumph: Getting Back to Normal When You Have Cancer, 1990, Understanding Your Immune System, 1986; contbr. articles to profl. jours.; editl. bd. Cancer Practice, Jour. Cancer Edn., Seminars in Oncology Nursing. Bd. dirs. Nat. Am. Cancer Soc., chair tobacco com., vice chair detection and treatment com., prevention com.; nat. adv. bd. Look Good...Feel Better Program; scientific adv. com. Nat. Cancer Inst., evaluation task force; active vice chair, Bd. Conn. Cancer Partnership. Recipient disting. svc. award Am. Cancer Soc., 1996. Home and Office: 1 Platt St Milford CT 06460-7640 *

MORREIM, E. HAAVI, medical ethics educator; b. 1950; d. Paul and Florence Morreim. BA in Philosophy, St. Olaf Coll., 1972; PhD, U. Va., 1980; JD, U. Memphis, 2009. Med. philosopher program in human biology and soc. U. Va. Sch. Medicine, Charlottesville, 1980-82, asst. prof. philosophy in medicine, 1982-84; from asst. to assoc. prof. dept. human values and ethics U. Tenn. Coll. Medicine,

Memphis, 1988—93, prof. dept. human values and ethics, 1993—2009, prof. dept. internal medicine, Health Sci. Ctr., 2009—. Adj. prof. philosophy Va. Commonwealth U., Richmond, 1980; vis. prof. philosophy St. Olaf Coll., Northfield, Minn., 1982; Andrew Mellon vis. asst. prof. humanities and medicine Georgetown U. Sch. Medicine, Washington, 1983; sr. vis. rsch. scholar Kennedy Inst. Ethics, Georgetown U., 1983; manuscript reviewer; presenter and lectr. in field. Author: Balancing Act: The New Medical Ethics of Medicine's New Economics, 1991, Holding Health Care Accountable: Law and the New Medical Marketplace, 2001; bd. editors: Jour. Law, Medicine and Ethics, IRB: Ethics and Human Research, Accountability in Research; contbr. articles to profl. jours. Active Hastings Ctr. Mem. Am. Health Lawyers Assn., Am. Soc. Law, Medicine, and Ethics, Am. Soc. for Bioethics and Humanities, Phi Beta Kappa. Avocations: running, high-performance automobile driving, photography, skiing. Office: University Tenn Coll Medicine 956 Ct G 212 Memphis TN 38163-2814 Office Phone: 901-448-5725. Business E-Mail: hmorreim@uthsc.edu.

MORRELL, DEAN SCOTT, pediatric dermatologist; b. Norwich, NY, May 11, 1965; s. Edward Arthur and Clarissa (Hyuck) M.; m. Karen Anne Hendrix, Sept. 12, 1989. BS magna cum laude, Wake Forest U., Winston-Salem, NC, 1987; M Phys. Therapy, Hahnemann U., Phila., 1989; MD, U. NC Sch. Medicine, Chapel Hill, 1997. Lic. phys. therapist Md., cert. in dermatology 2001, in pediatric dermatology 2006. Staff phys. therapist Burch, Rhoads, Loomis, P.A., Balt.; internship in pediat. U. NC Hosps., Chapel Hill, 1997—98, residency in dermatology, 1998—2000; fellow in pediatric dermatology Children's Hosp. Wis., Med. Coll. Wis., Milw., 2000—01; asst. prof. dermatology U. NC Sch. Medicine, 2001—06, assoc. prof., program dir., dir. pediatric and adolescent dermatology, dept. dermatology, 2006—. Contbr. articles to profl. jours., chapters to books. Coach YMCA Ladies Baseball Team, Towson, Md., 1990. Mem. Am. Phys. Therapy Assn. Democrat. Methodist. Avocations: running, basketball, volleyball. Office: U NC Sch Medicine Dept Dermatology 3100 Thurston-Bowles Bldg CB 7287 Chapel Hill NC 27599-7287 Office Phone: 919-966-0785. Office Fax: 919-966-3898.

MORRIELLO, GREGORI J., chemist; b. Newark, Mar. 21, 1970; BS, Stevens Inst. Tech., 1992; PhD, Rutgers U., 2001. Project team leader Merck, 1992—. Recipient Excellence award, Merck and Co., UPTAM Rsch. award, Stevens Inst. Tech. Mem.: North NJ Bergan Am. Chemistry Soc. (Most Outstanding award). Avocation: golf. Home: 16 Arrowgate Dr Randolph NJ 07869 Office Phone: 732-594-3867. Home Fax: 732-594-5350. Personal E-mail: greg_morriello@merck.com.

MORRIS, ALVIN LEONARD, retired dentist, academic administrator; b. Detroit, July 2, 1927; s. Frank and Lulu (Cornett) M.; m. Arlene Teschler, Feb. 1, 1947 (dec. Apr. 1974); children: Jeffry, Gregg, Beth; m. Beverly Hackman, 1975. Student, U. Ill., 1944-45; D.D.S., U. Mich., 1951; PhD, U. Rochester, 1957; D.Sc. (hon.), U. Md., 1983. Intern Letterman Army Hosp., San Francisco, 1951-52; postdoctoral research fellow NIH, 1954-57; head dept. oral diagnosis U. Pa. Sch. Dentistry, 1957-61; dean U. Ky. Coll. Dentistry, Lexington, 1961-68; asst. v.p. U. Ky. Coll. Dentistry (Med. Center), 1968-69, v.p. adminstrn. univ., 1970-75; exec. dir. Assn. for Acad. Health Centers, Washington, 1975-79; prof. dental care systems Sch. Dental Medicine, asso. v.p. health affairs U. Pa., 1979-87, sr. assoc. Leonard Davis Inst. Health Econs., Wharton Grad. Sch., 1980-87, prof. emeritus, 1987-89; research prof. Health Services Research Ctr./Sch. of Dentistry, U. N.C., Chapel Hill, 1987-89. Cons. Dental Corps, U.S. Army, 1960-70, VA, 1962-73, U.S. Dept. Def., 1969-72; pub. health service cons. dental study sect. USPHS, 1963-67, also chmn.; cons., lectr. USN Dental Sch.; cons. Army Med. Service Adv. Com. Preventive Dentistry, 1967-71; mem. Nat. Adv. Council Edn. Health Professions, 1968-72; bd. dirs. Nat. Center Health Edn., 1977-84; adv. com. Ednl. Testing Service, 1977-82; chmn. adv. com. Nat. Preventive Dental Demonstration Program, 1976-83 Dir. W. K. Kellogg Project Evaluating Quality Pvt., 1982-86; cons. Metlife Quality Initiative Program, 1989-99. Served with inf. AUS, 1944-46; to 1st lt. Dental Corps 1951-54. Recipient Pierre Fauchard medal, 1974, Henry Spenadel medal, 1982, Callahan medal, 1991. Fellow Internat., Am. colls. dentists; mem. ADA (Disting. Svc. award 1985), Inst. Medicine of NAS, AAAS, Internat. Assn. Dental Rsch., So. Conf. Dental Deans and Examiners (pres. 1964-65), Sigma Xi. Presbyterian (deacon, trustee). Home: 3051 Rio Dosa Dr Apt 334 Lexington KY 40509-1546

MORRIS, COLLEEN ANNETTE, clinical geneticist, educator; MD, Loyola U. Chgo., 1981. Diplomate Am. Bd. Pediatrics, 1986, cert. Am. Bd. Clin. genetics-Med. Genetics, 1987. Resident pediat. Phoenix Hosp., 1981—84; fellow clin. genetics Univ. Utah, 1984—86; prof. pediat. Univ. Nev.; hosp. affiliation include Univ. Med. Ctr., Nev. Office: University Medical Center Ste 401 2040 W Charleston Blvd Las Vegas NV 89102 Office Phone: 702-671-2200.

MORRIS, DOUGLAS CLAUDE, cardiologist, educator; b. Marietta, Ga., Apr. 18, 1942; BA in Chemistry, Duke U.; MD, Baylor Coll. Medicine, Houston, 1968. Cert. Internal Medicine, Cardiovascular Disease, Interventional Cardiology. Intern, internal medicine Vanderbilt U. Hosp., Nashville, 1968—69, resident, cardiology, 1969—70, 1972—73; fellow Emory U. Hosp., 1973—75; faculty staff mem., dept. medicine, divsn. cardiology Emory U. Sch. Medicine, 1973—, J. Willis Hurst prof. medicine, 1996—; dir., Carlyle Fraser Heart Ctr. Crawford Long Hosp., 1986; dir. Emory Heart Ctr., 1993; vice-chair, dept. medicine Emory U., 1999. Named one of Ten Best Doctors in Cardiovascular Disease, Atlanta Mag., 1999—. Mem.: Soc. Cardiac Angiography, Am. Coll. Cardiology (co-chair scientific sessions 1996—2000), ACP. Avocation: running. Office: Emory U Rm A2205 Emory Clinic 1365A Clifton Rd NE Atlanta GA 30322 Office Phone: 404-778-5310. Office Fax: 404-778-5320. Business E-Mail: douglas.morris@emoryhealthcare.org.

MORRIS, JAMES BRUCE, internist; b. Rochester, NY, May 13, 1943; s. Max G. and Beatrice Ruth (Becker) M.; m. Susan Carol Shencup, July 31, 1966; children: Carrie, Douglas, Deborah, Rebecca. BA, U. Rochester, 1964; MD, Yale U., 1968. Diplomate Am. Bd. Internal Medicine, Am. Bd. Infectious Diseases. Intern SUNY, Buffalo, 1968-69, resident, 1969-70, 72-73, chief resident, 1973; pvt. practice medicine & infectious diseases Plantation, Fla., 1974—. Chmn. infection control com. Lauderdale Lakes Gen. Hosp., 1974-76; chmn. infection control com. Plantation Gen. Hosp., 1976-80, 83-85, chmn. pharmacy com., 1980-81, chmn. tissue com., 1982; sec., program chmn. dept. medicine Bennett Community Hosp., 1978-80, chmn. dept. medicine, 1980-81, vice chief staff, 1981-83; chmn. infection control com. Fla. Med. Center, 1980-82; chief staff Humana Hosp. Bennett, 1983-85, trustee, 1983-88, chmn. infection control com., 1985-87; bd. trustees Westside Regional Med. Ctr., 2008-. With USAR, 1970-72. Recipient Recognition, Town & Country Guide to Primary Care Physicians; named one of Top Docs in South Fla., Miami Metro; fellow, U. Miami, 1974. Fellow ACP; mem. AMA, Am. Soc. Microbiology, Infectious Diseases Soc. Am., Am. Soc. Internal Medicine, Fla. Med. Assn., Broward County Med. Assn. Office: Morris Sklaver Mestre & Perez MD PA 7353 NW 4th St Plantation FL 33317-2202 Office Phone: 954-584-9111.

MORRIS, JOHN CARL, neurologist, educator, researcher; b. Cleve., Feb. 13, 1948; s. Edward Francis and Eleanor Caroline (Pongratz) M.; m. Lucy Laub Babcox, Apr. 14, 1979; children: Carrie Laub, Edward Babcox, Mary Pongratz. BA, Ohio Wesleyan U., 1970; MD, U. Rochester Sch. Medicine and Dentistry, 1974. Diplomate Am. Bd. Internal Medicine, Am. Bd. Psychiatry and Neurology; cert. Nat. Bd. Med. Examiners. Intern San Francisco Gen. Hosp., 1974-75; pvt. practice Fairbanks (Alaska) Clinic, 1975-76, Carlsbad (N.Mex.) Regional Med. Ctr., 1976-77; asst. resident and sr. resident in medicine Akron (Ohio) Gen. Med. Ctr., 1977-79; asst. resident and sr. resident in neurology Cleve. Met. Gen. Hosp., 1979-81, resident in neuropathology, 1981-82; fellow in neuropharmacology Washington Univ. Sch. Medicine, St. Louis, 1982-85, rsch. instr. pharmacology, 1982-84, instr. neurology, 1983-85, asst. and assoc. prof. neurology and neuropathology, 1985-98, asst. prof. pathology and immunology, 1989-2000; Friedman prof. neurology Alzheimers Disease Rsch. Ctr., 2001—, prof. pathology and immunology, 2001—; dir. Alzheimer's disease rsch. ctr. Barnes-Jewish Hosp. St. Louis, 1989—, dir. ctr. aging., 1995—. Bd. dirs. Alzheimer Assn., Chgo., 1998—, Jewish Ctr. for the Aged, St. Louis, 2001—; sci. adv. bd. Inst. for the Study of Aging, Inc., 2000—, Leeza Gibbons Memory Found., 2005—; adv. bd. mem. St. Louis chpt. Alzheimer's Assn., Alzheimer Rsch. Forum, 2002—; lectr. in field. Editl. bd. mem. The Neurologist, 1992—; editor-in-chief: Alzheimer's Disease and Associated Disorders: An International Jour., 2001—; ad hoc reviewer and contbr. articles, chaps. to numerous profl. jours. Recipient Disting. Achievement Citation Ohio Wesleyan U., 2000, MetLife Found. award for rsch. in Alzheimer's Disease, 2004, Physician-Scientist Lifetime Achievement award, Barnes-Jewish Hosp. Found., 2005, Dr. Neville Grant award, 2006, Academic Women's Network Mentor award, Washington U., 2008. Fellow ACP, Am. Acad. Neurology (chair geriatric neurology section, Potamkin prize 2005); mem. Soc. for Neuroscience, Am. Neurol. Soc., Am. Geriatrics Soc., Ctrl. Soc. Neurological Rsch. (pres., 1995-96), Soc. Exptl. Neuropathology, Mo. State Neurological Assn., Am. Soc. Exptl. NeuroTherapeutics, Internat. Coll. Geriatric Psychoneuropharmacology, Rsch. Group on Dementia (exec. com., 2001—), World Fedn. Neurology, Asia-Pacific Internat. Working Group on Harmonization of Dementia Drug Guidelines (exec. com., 2001—) Office: Wash U Sch Medicine Dept Neurol Campus Box 8111-ADRC 660 S Euclid Ave Saint Louis MO 63110-1010 E-mail: morrisj@abraxas.wustl.edu.

MORRIS, JONATHAN, obstetrician, educator; b. Stockport, Eng., Mar. 8, 1962; MBBCh, Edinburgh U., 1985; PhD, Sydney U., 1998. Ob-gyn. prof. U. Sydney, 2006, head, 2011—. Office: Level 7 Kolling Bldg Reserve Rd Sydney NSW 2065 Australia Business E-Mail: jonathan.morris@sydney.edu.au.

MORRIS, JOSEPH ANTHONY, retired health science association administrator; b. Marboro, Md., Sept. 6, 1918; s. Charles Lafayette and Essie (Stokes) M.; m. Ruth Savoy, Nov. 1, 1942; children: Carol Ann, Marilyn T., Joseph A., Larry A. BS, Cath. U. Am., 1940, MS, 1942, PhD, 1947. Asst. scientist Josiah Macy, Jr. Found., NYC, 1943-44; virologist Depts. Agr., Interior, Laurel, Md., 1944-47; virologist, chief hepatitis virus rsch. Walter Reed Army Inst. Rsch., Washington, 1947-56; virologist, asst. chief, dept. virus and rickettsial dis. U.S. Army Med. Command, Japan, 1956-59; virologist chief sect. respiratory diseases divsn. biologics stds. NIH, Bethesda, Md., 1959—2003; ret. Dir. slow, latent and temperate virus br. FDA, Bethesda, 1972-76; lectr. dept. microbiology U. Md., College Park, 1977-79; vice-chmn. Bell of Atri, Inc., College Park, 1979-82, chmn., 1983; cons. Commn. on Influenza, Armed Forces Epidemiologic Bd., 1960—, Nat. Inst. Neurol. Diseases and Blindness, 1962—. Mem. Soc. Tropical Medicine and Hygiene, Soc. Am. Microbiologists, Soc. Exptl. Biology and Medicine, Am. Assn. Immunologists, N.Y. Acad. Scis. Achievements include discovery of respiratory sycytial virus; research on infectious hepatitis, respiratory diseases of virus etiology and zoonosis. Home: 23E Ridge Rd Greenbelt MD 20770-0714

MORRIS, JOSEPH WESLEY, physician assistant; b. Kansas City, Mo., Feb. 17, 1958; s. Glenn Wesley and Julia Ann (Witt) M.; m. Sharon Kennedy, Oct. 2, 1982 (div. Aug. 1989). A Engring.; AAS, Penn Valley CC, Kans. City, Mo., 1980; BS, Physician Assoc. with distinction, U. Okla., Oklahoma City, 1989; MS in Med. Sci. emphasis in Emergency Medicine, Alderson-Broaddus Coll., Philippi, W.Va., 1995. Nat. cert. physician asst. in primary care and surgery. Firefighter/paramedic North Kansas City (Mo.) Fire Dept., 1981-89; residency for physician assts. in surgery St. Vincent's Med. Ctr., SI, NY, 1989-90, physician asst. in surgery, 1990-91, physician asst. in ob-gyn., 1991-93; NY physician asst. in emergency medicine St. Joseph's Hosp., Parkersburg, W.Va., 1993-95; acad. coord., asst. prof. clin. medicine PA program Coll. W.Va., Beckley, 1995—96; physician asst. in emergency medicine Emergency & Acute Care Svcs., Inc., Gastonia, NC, 1996—2007, Carolina Urgent Care, Gastonia, 2007—08; active US Pub. Health Svc., 2008—. Emergency medicine svcs. instr., Kansas City, Mo., 1980-86; emergency medicine svcs. coord., Kansas City, 1981-86; bd. dirs. CPR Now!, Kansas City, 1981-86; asst. med. dir. emergency medicine svcs. St. Joseph's Hosp., Parkersburg, W.Va., 1993-95. Mem. dist. com. Boy scouts Am., Kans. City, Mo., 1979-86; mem. agrl. com. of Rep. Thomas Coleman, Kansas City, 1980-82; mem. planning com. W.Va. Managed Care Conf., Flatwoods, W.Va., 1996; mem. citizen issue com. of Rep. Sue Myrick, Gastonia, NC, 1997-2000. USMCR, 1977-81; with US Army NG, 1986-2008, US Pub. Svc., 2008-, Ops. Iraqi Freedom, 2003-05, Operation Enduring Freedom, 2005-07. Fellow: Am. Acad. Physician Assts. (disting. fellow), Am. Acad. Experts in Traumatic Stress; mem.: AAPA (mem. Vets Caucus), USPHS Soc. of PAS, Hawaii Acad. PAS, Internat. Soc. Travel Medicine, Nat. Assn. Search and Rescue, Wilderness Med. Soc., Am. Heart Assn., Am. Trauma Soc., Undersea and Hyperbaric Medicine Soc., Soc. Emergency Medicine Physician Assts., Soc. Army Physician Assts., NOAA Dive Med. Officer, Nat. Field Archery Assn. (life), Nat. Archery Assn. (life; level 3 coach), Nat. Eagle Scout Assn. (life). Avocations: archery, astronomy, painting, reading, scuba diving. Home: 1897 Ranger Loop 184 Honolulu HI 96818-5072

MORRIS, LEIGH EDWARD, retired health facility administrator, former mayor; b. Hartford, Ind., Dec. 26, 1934; s. Fredus Orlando and Martha (Malott) M.; m. Marcia Renee Meredith, Oct. 7, 1967; children: Meredith Anne, Curtis Paul. BS in Commerce, Internat. Coll., 1954; BSBA, Ball State U., 1958; M in Health Adminstrn., U. Minn., 1972. Mem. labor relations staff Borg-Warner Corp., Muncie, Ind., 1961-64; various positions then personnel mgr. Internat. Harvester Co., Ft. Wayne, Ind., 1964-70; pres. Huntington (Ind.) Meml. Hosp., 1972-78, La Porte (Ind.) Hosp., 1978-2000; ret., 2004—07; mayor City of LaPorte; dep. commr. Ind. Dept. Transp.; exec. dir. Ind. Toll Rd.; chmn. Northern Ind. Regional Devel. Authority; dir., bus. recruitment NW Ind., Ind. Econ. Devel. Corp.; dir. Meml. Health Found., South Bend. Bd. dirs. First of Am. Bank of Ind., Am. Hosp. Svcs., Inc., Health Forum, Inc.; chmn., bd. dirs. Am. Hosp. Pub. Co.; chmn. La Porte Devel. Corp., 1980-81; exec. dir. Ind. Toll Rd.; chmn. Northwest Ind. Regional Devel. Authority. Chmn. LaPorte chpt. ARC, 1984-86; bd. dirs., vice chmn. John G. Blank Ctr. for the Arts, Lubeznik Ctr. for the Arts; chmn. LaPorte County Symphony Orch. With U.S. Army, 1958-60. Recipient Disting. Alumni award Ball State U., Muncie, Ind., 1968, James A. Hamilton award U. Minn., Mpls., 1972, Trustees award Am. Hosp. Assn., 1996. Fellow Am. Coll. Healthcare Adminstrn. (life), Health Care Fin. Mgmt. Assn.; mem. APHA, Am. Hosp. Assn. (trustee, regional chmn. 1985-89), Soc. for Healthcare Planning and Mktg. (bd. dirs.), Soc. Ind. Pioneers (bd. dirs., pres.), Ind. Hosp. Assn. (chmn. 1980-81), La Porte C. of C. (chmn. 1981-82), Union League Club Chgo. Republican. Presbyterian. Avocations: classic cars, civic affairs. Home: 424 Upper Lake Shore Dr La Porte IN 46350-2917 Office Phone: 219-325-7511. Personal E-mail: lmorris@csinet.net. Business E-Mail: lmorris2@indot.in.gov, lemorris@iedc.in.gov.

MORRIS, LINZETTE DEIDRÉ, psychotherapist, researcher; b. Bellville, Western Cape, South Africa, Aug. 29, 1981; BSc in Physiotherapy, U. Western Cape, 2005; MSc in Physiotherapy, Stellenbosch U., 2009. Cmty. svc. physiotherapist Pholosong Hosp., 2005—06; clin. physiotherapist Quinette Louw Physiotherapists, 2006—07; rschr. Stellenbosch U., 2006—10, postgrad. com. student rep., 2008—11, cons., virtual reality projects, 2010—11, co-supr., master degree students, 2010—11, Ad Hoc lectr., 2011—. Recipient Stellenbosch U. Merit Bursary award; grant, Nat. Rsch. Fund. Mem.: Health Profls. Coun. South Africa, South African Soc. Physiotherapy. Home: 140 Spencer St Goodwood Western Cape 7460 South Africa Personal E-mail: ldmorris@sun.ac.za.

MORRIS, MICHAEL JAMES, internist, director; b. Mt. Pleasant, Mich., Oct. 4, 1961; BA, U. Dallas, 1983; MD, Eastern Va. Med. Sch., 1987. Pulmonary, critical care physician Brooke Army Med. Ctr., 1995—2006, asst. chief, dept. clin. investigation, 2002—04, dir., med. edn., 2004—06, assoc. program dir., internal medicine, 2008—. Clin. asst. prof. U. Tex. Health Sci. Ctr. San Antonio, 1995—2004; asst. prof. Uniformed Svcs. Health Scis. U., 2009—11. Decorated Bronze Star US Army. Fellow: ACP (Army Chpt. Laureate award), Am. Coll. Chest Physicians; mem.: AMSUS. Avocations: genealogy, basketball. Home: 1518 Belclaire San Antonio TX 78258 Office Fax: 210-916-4721. Business E-Mail: michael.morris@amedd.army.mil.

MORRIS, PAUL, psychologist, educator; PhD, U. Southampton. Prin. lectr. dept. psychology U. Portsmouth. Office: University of Portsmouth Dept of Psychology King Henry Building King Henry I Street PO1 2DY Hampshire England E-mail: paul.morris@port.ac.uk.

MORRIS, PETER E., internist, educator; MD, Cornell U. Med. Coll., 1985. Resident Vanderbilt U., 1988, fellow, 1988—91; assoc. prof., dir. critical care clin. trials group, med. dir. intermediate care unit Wake Forest U. Baptist Med. Ctr. Fellow: College of Chest Physicians, ACP. Office: Wake Forest Univ Sch Medicine Dept Pulmonary Critical Care Allergy and Medical Center Boulevard Winston Salem NC 27157 Office Phone: 336-716-8898. Office Fax: 336-716-7277.

MORRIS, ROHINTON J., thoracic surgeon; Attended, Juniata Coll., Huntingdon, Pa.; MD, MCP Hahnemann U., Phila., 1984. Diplomate Am. Bd. Thoracic Surgery, lic. Pa., 1986. Resident gen. surgery Hahnemann Univ. Hosp., 1984—89, resident cardiothoracic surgery, 1989—92, attending physician cardiothoracic surgery, 1992—98, surg. dir. cardiac transplantation, 1992—98; with Med. Coll. Pa., 1997—98, Presbyn. Med. Ctr., 1999—2010; mem. divsn. cardiothoracic surgery Hosp. Univ. Pa., 1999—2010, surg. dir. heart transplantation and mech. assist programs, 1999—2010, site coord thoracic surgery program, 1999—2010; chief divsn. cardiothoracic surgery Pilla heart ctr. Abington Meml. Hosp., 2010—, surg. dir. Porter inst. for valvular heart disease, 2010—. Pres. Pa. Assn. for Thoracic Surgery; vice chmn. Gift of Life Med. Adv. and Policy Bd. Named one of America's Top Doctors, 2008, 2010, Top Doctors, Phila. Mag., 2008—, America's Top Surgeons, Castle-Connolly, 2008. Fellow: ACS; mem.: AMA, Phila. Acad. of Surgeons, Soc. of Critical Care Medicine, Soc. of Cardiothoracic Surgeons, Internat. Soc. for Heart and Lung Transplantation. Office: Abington Memorial Hospital 1200 Old York Rd Abington PA 19001 Office Phone: 215-481-4200. Office Fax: 215-881-9587.

MORRIS, SHARON LOUISE STEWART, emergency medical technician, paramedic; b. Washington, Feb. 9, 1956; d. George Arthur Jr. and Shirley Ann (Dickinson) S. (dec.); m. Brian Stanley Morris, Feb. 9, 1979 (div.); children: Jessica Kristin, Krystle Maria. BS, Atlantic Christian Coll., Wilson, NC, 1978; student, Wilson County Tech. Coll., 1998; paramedic stud., Nash C.C. Cert. tchr. elem. edn. and math., N.C., EMT paramedic, ACLS, Pediatric Advanced Life Support, pediat. edn. prehosp. profls., AHA CPR/BLS instr.; cert. pre-hosp. trauma life support Prehosp. Edn. for Prehosp. Profls.; automatic external defibrilator (AED) instr.; basic trauma life support (BTLS); farm medic. Cashier Safeway Fin., Wilson, 1980-81, Provident Fin., Wilson, 1981-85; mktg. svc. mgr. Beneficial of NC Inc., Wilson, 1985-91; ind. carrier Wilson Daily Times, 1991-94; child care provider Crestview Day Sch., Wilson, 1994-95; EMT vol. Elm City, NC, 1996—; EMT paramedic Wilson County Emergency Med. Svcs., 1998—2004, training office, 2003—04, shift asst. supr., 2004—. Agt. Cen. Nat. Life Ins., Wilson, 1988-91, Olde Republic, 1990; EMT Elm City Emergency Svcs., 1996, attendant, driver Am. Med. Response,

1997; Avon rep., 2005-; paramedic Sch. Nash Tech. CC, Wayne County EMS, 2006-. Notary pub. State of NC, 1986—2006; bd. dirs. Elm City, 1997, 99; full time paramedic for Johnston Ambulance Svc., 2002-07, 1st responder instr. EMT, 2003; paramedic Wayne County EMS, 2006-11. Democrat. Methodist. Avocations: crocheting, cross-stitch, needlepoint, plants, baking. Home: PO Box 9053 Wilson NC 27895 Personal E-mail: emsbabygirl120@peoplepc.com.

MORRIS, STEVEN, gastroenterologist, educator; b. Atlanta, Ga. MD, SUNY, Buffalo, 1973; JD, Georgia State U. Coll. Law. Cert. Internal Medicine, Gastroenterology. Intern, gastroenterology Emory U. Affiliated Hosps., Atlanta, 1973—74, resident, 1974—76; fellow, digestive diseases U. Miami, 1976—78; clin. assoc. prof. Emory U. Sch. Med., Atlanta; former chief of staff Emory Crawford Long Hosp.; CEO Atlanta Gastroenterology Assocs., Ga. Fellow: Am. Coll. Gastroenterology, ACP; mem.: Ga. Gastrointestinal Soc. (past pres.), Med. Assn. Ga., Med. Assn. Atlanta, Am. Gastroenterology Assn., AMA, Phi Beta Kappa. Office: Atlanta Gastroenterology Assocs Emory Crawford Long Med Office Tower 550 Peachtree St NE Ste 1600 Atlanta GA 30308 Office Phone: 404-881-1094. Office Fax: 404-874-1249.

MORRISON, DEBORAH K., medical researcher; PhD, Vanderbilt U. Postdoctoral fellow Harvard Med. Sch., Mass., U. Calif., San Francisco, rschr. Berkeley, 1996—97; joined ABL-Basic Rsch. Program Nat. Cancer Inst., NIH, Frederick, Md., 1990, head cellular growth mechanisms sect., 1995—; joined Ctr. Cancer Rsch., Nat. Cancer Inst., NIH, Frederick, 1999, chief Lab. Cell and Developmental Signaling, 2006—. Office: Nat Cancer Inst, NIH Bldg 560 Rm 22-103 NCI-Frederick Frederick MD 21702 Office Phone: 301-846-1733. Office Fax: 301-846-1666. E-mail: dmorrison@ncifcrf.gov. *

MORRISON, GLENN LESLIE, minister; b. Cortez, Colo., Feb. 26, 1929; s. Ward Carl Morrison and Alma Irene (Butler) Anderson; m. Beverely Joanne Buck, Aug. 26, 1949; children: David Mark, Betty Jo Morrison Mullen, Gary Alan, Judith Lynn Morrison Oltmann, Stephen Scott. Student, San Diego State U., 1948-49, Chabot Coll., 1968-69. Ordained ministry Evang. Ch. Alliance, 1961. Dir. counseling follow-up Oakland (Calif.) Youth Christ, 1954-56; pres. Follow Up Ministries, Inc., Castro Valley, Calif., 1956—. Assoc. pastor 1st Covenant Ch., Oakland, 1956-58; exec. dir. East Bay Youth Christ, Oakland, 1960-66; supervising chaplain Alameda County (Calif.) Probation Dept., 1971-90; vol. chaplain Alameda County Sheriff's Dept., 1971—; founder, dir. God Squad Vol. Program Prison Workers, 1972—; seminar leader Calif. Dept. Corrections, Sacramento, 1978—, mem. chaplains coordinating com., 1988—. Author: Scripture Investigation Course, 1956, Tired of the Same Ol' Same Ol'? There is a Better Way, 1978. Mem. Am. Correctional Assn. (coord. prayer & meditation rm. 1990-2009), Am. Protestant Correctional Chaplains Assn. (regional pres., sec. 1980-86, nat. sec. 1986-88, nat. 2nd v.p. 1996-98). Office: Follow Up Ministries Inc PO Box 2514 Castro Valley CA 94546-2514 Personal E-mail: fumi2000@cox.net.

MORRISON, SHIRLEY MARIE, retired nursing educator; b. Stuttgart, Ark., June 13, 1927; d. Jack Vade Wimberly and Mabel Claire (Dennison) George; m. Dana Jennings, Mar. 12, 1951 (dec. Dec. 1995); children: Stephen Leslie, Dana Randall, William Lee, Martha Ann Morrison Comardo. Diploma, Bapt. Hosp. Sch. Nursing, Nashville, 1949; BSN, Calif. U., Fullerton, 1977; MSN, Calif. U., LA, 1980; EdD, Nova Southeastern U., 1987. RN, Tex., Calif.; cert. pub. health nurse, Calif.; cert. secondary tchr., Calif. Staff nurse perinatal svcs. Martin Luther Hosp., Anaheim, Calif., 1960-77, relief 11-7 house supr., 1960-77; dir. vocat. nursing program Inst. Med. Studies, 1978-81; mem. faculty BSN program Abilene (Tex.) Intercollegiate Sch. Nursing, 1981-92, dir. ADN program, 1992-97; nursing educator Cisco Jr. Coll., Abilene, Tex., 1997—2008. Mem. profl. adv. bd. Nurse Care, Inc., Abilene, 1988-2003, bd. dirs. West Tarpas Rehab Ctr., 2000-. Mem. adv. bd. parent edn. program Abilene Ind. Sch. Dist., 1985-2000; active Mar. Dimes, Abilene, 1990—, Ednl. Coalition for Bob Hunter, Abilene, 1994; bd. dirs. Hospice Big Country, Abilene, 1987—, The House That Kerry Built, 2000—. Grantee NIH, 1992; recipient Nat. Humor Project award Jour. Nursing Jocularity, 1996. Mem. Nat. Orgn. Assn. Degree Nurses (mem. program com. 10th anniversary nat. conv.), Tex. Orgn. Assoc. Degree Nurses, So. Nursing Rsch. Soc. (rsch. presenter), Health Edn. Resource Network Abilene (founding mem., pres. elect, pres. 1995-96), Sigma Theta Tau (bd. dirs. 1999-2004, bd. dirs. Omicron Zeta chpt. 1999-2001), West Tex. Rehab. Ctr. (bd. dir. 2003-). Democrat. Methodist. Avocations: travel, reading. Home: 3149 ELM #27 Abilene TX 79602

MORRISON, SUSAN H., pediatrician, allergist, immunologist, educator; MD, U. of Medicine & Dentistry of NJ, 1981. Diplomate Am. Bd. Pediatrics, Am. Bd. Pediatrics-pediatric infectious disease, Am. Bd. Allergy & Immunology. Intern Univ. of Medicine & Dentistry of NJ Med. Sch., 1982, resident, 1985, fellow, 1987, prof. pediat.; affiliation Clara Maass Med. Ctr. Office: Clara Maass Medical Center Ste 322 36 Newark Ave Belleville NJ 07109 Office Phone: 973-450-0100. Office Fax: 973-450-8088.

MORRISS, FRANK HOWARD, JR., pediatrics educator; b. Birmingham, Ala., Apr. 20, 1940; s. Frank Howard Sr. and Rochelle (Snow) M.; m. Mary J. Hagan, June 29, 1968; children: John Hagan, Matthew Snow. BA, U. Va., 1962; MD, Duke U., 1966; MPH, Harvard U., 2006. Diplomate Am. Bd. Pediatrics, Am. Bd. Perinatal and Neonatal Medicine. Intern Duke U. Med. Ctr., Durham, NC, 1966-67, resident in pediatrics, 1967-68, fellow in neonatology, 1970-71, U. Colo., Denver, 1971-73; asst. prof. to prof. U. Tex. Med. Sch., Houston, 1973-86; prof. U. Iowa Coll. Medicine, Iowa City, 1987—, chmn. dept., 1987—2004. Editor: Role of Human Milk in Infant Nutrition and Health, 1986; contbr. numerous articles to profl. jours, chpts. to books. Lt. comdr. USN, 1968-70. Grantee, NIH, 1977—87, 1990—2004. Mem. Am. Pediatric Soc., Soc. Pediatric Rsch., Am. Acad. Pediatrics, Midwest Soc. Pediatric Rsch. Office: U Iowa Hosps & Clinics Dept Pediatrics Iowa City IA 52242 Office Phone: 319-384-6530.

MORRISSEY, PATRICIA A., federal agency administrator; AA in Liberal Arts, Hartford CC, 1964; BA in Psychology, Stetson U., 1966; M.Ed. in Spl. Edn., Pa. State U., 1971, PhD in Spl. Edn., 1974. Positions with US Ho. of Reps. Com. on Edn. and Labor, Senate Com. on Health, Edn., Labor, and Pensions; sr. assoc. Booz Allen Hamilton, McLean, Va.; commr. Adminstrn. Devel. Disabilities Adminstrn. Children and Families, HHS, 2001—. Republican. Office: Adminstrn Children and Families Adminstrn Devel Disabilities 370 L'Enfant Promenade SW Washington DC 20447 Office Phone: 202-690-6590. Business E-Mail: pmorrissey@acf.hhs.gov.

MORROW, BRENDA, physiotherapist; d. Jasper and Ethel Stupart; m. Carl Dylan Morrow, Oct. 23, 1999. BS in Physiotherapy, U. Cape Town, South Africa, 1995; PhD in Pediat., 2005. Cert. paediatric neurodevelopmental therapist Neurodevelopmental Therapy Assn. Chief physiotherapist Red Cross Children's Hosp., Cape Town, South Africa, 1996—; head Associated Pediat. Disciplines divsn. Sch. Child and Adolescent Health, U. Cape Town, 2000—. Ad hoc paediatric lectr. U. Western Cape, South Africa, 2000—03; ad hoc lectr. U. Cape Town, South Africa, 2000—. Recipient Full Provincial Colours for Fencing, Fencing Assn. of Western Cape, 1993, 1994, 1995, Full U. Cape Town Colours for Fencing, U. Cape Town, 1995, Merit Award for excellent svc. at RCCH., Provinvial Adminstrn., Western Cape, 2003; scholar Cape Provincial Adminstrn. Bursary, Cape Provincial Adminstrn., 1993-1995, Cuthbert Meml. Entrance Scholarship, U. of Cape Town, 1992. 1993. Mem.: South African Soc. Physiotherapy, Critical Care Soc. So. Africa (Runner- up award for best rsch. presentation by an Allied Health Profl. Critical Care Congress (Sun City). 2001, Bristol- Myers Squibb Award for best rsch. presentation at a meeting of the Western Cape Br. of the Critical Care Soc. of So. Africa. 2001, 2002, Award for best presentation of original rsch. by an Allied Health Profl. COPICON Critical Care Congress, Sun City. 2002, Best Publication award 2005), Western Cape Cardiopulmonary Rehab. Group (sec. 2000—05), Internat. Physiotherapy Group for Cystic Fibrosis (South African contact person 2002—06). Achievements include research in the effects of nonbronchoscopic bronchoalveolar lavage and endotracheal suctioning in critically ill. Avocations: pottery, yoga, travel, hiking. Office: Red Cross Children's Hosp Klipfontein RdRondebosch Cape Town 7700 South Africa E-mail: bmorrow@ich.uct.ac.za.

MORROW, MONICA, medical educator; b. Abington, Pa., Sept. 16, 1953; d. James Robert and Maxine Cooper Morrow; m. Virgil Craig Jordan, OBE, PhD, DSc. BS magna cum laude, Pa. State U., 1974; MD, Jefferson Med. Coll., 1976. Diplomate Am. Bd. of Surgery. Fellow in surg. oncology Meml. Sloan Kettering Cancer Ctr., New York, NY, 1981—83; asst. prof. surgery SUNY Health Sci. Ctr., Bklyn., 1983—88; assoc. prof. surgery U. Chgo., 1988—93, Northwestern U., Chgo., 1993—97, prof. surgery, 1997—2004; chmn. dept. surgical oncology and G. Willing Pepper chair cancer rsch. Fox Chase Cancer Ctr., Phila., 2004—08; chief breast surg. svc. Meml. Sloan Kettering Cancer Ctr.; prof. surgery Weill Cornell Med. Coll. Dir., cancer dept. ACS, Chgo., 1999—2001; exec. dir. Am. Joint Com. on Cancer, Chgo., 1999—2001; mem. Nat. Cancer Policy Bd., Inst. of Medicine, Washington, 1999—2002; co-chair Joint Com. of the ACS, Am. Coll. of Radiology, and Coll. of Am. Pathologists on Standards for Breast Conservation, 2000—02, 2005. Editor: (book) Managing Breast Cancer Risk, American Joint Committee on Cancer Staging Manual, sixth edition, Diseases of the Breast, Breast Diseases: A Problem Based Approach. Recipient Alumni Achievement award, Jefferson Med. Coll., 2006; named Distinguished Alumni, Pa, State U., 2002; Co-Principal Investigator, Specialized Program Rsch. Excellence in Breast Cancer grantee, Nat. Cancer Inst., 2000—05, Avon Found. Ctr. Excellence grantee prin. investigator, 2000—06. Fellow: Am. Coll. Surgeons, Royal Coll. Physicians and Surgeons Glasgow (hon.); mem.: Am. Surg. Assn., Am. Soc. Clin. Oncology (bd. dirs. 1998—2001), Soc. Surg. Oncology (exec. com. 1993—96, 2003—06, sec. 2007—). Avocations: travel, history, wine. Office: Meml Sloan Kettering Cancer Ctr MRI 1026 1275 York Ave New York NY 10021 Business E-Mail: morrowm@mskcc.org.

MORROW, PHUONG KHANH HUYNH, oncologist, educator; BS, U. Houston, 1994; MD, U. Tex., Houston, 2003. Diplomate Am. Bd. Internal Medicine, 2003, in med. oncology 2006. Asst. prof. U. Tex. M.D. Anderson Cancer Ctr., Houston, 2006—. Faculty adv. M.D. Anderson Physician's Network, Houston, 2006—; med. dir. Beth Sanders Moore Young Survivors' Program, Houston, 2009—. Contbr. articles to profl. jours. Recipient Clifton D. Howe award, ASCO Young Investigator award. Mem.: Am. Soc. Clin. Oncology. Office: University Tex MD Anderson Cancer Ctr 1515 Holcombe Blvd PO Box 1354 Houston TX 77030

MORROW, STEPHEN ERIC, medical educator, director; b. Milton, Fla., Apr. 25, 1959; BA, Vanderbilt U., 1981; MD, Uniformed Svcs. U., 1985. Asst. prof., surgery, dir., trauma Vanderbilt U. Children's Hosp., 2005—. Fellow: ACS, Am. Acad. Pediat.; mem.: Eastern Assn. Surgery Trauma, Am. Pediatric Surg. Assn. Office: 2200 Children's Way Ste 7100 Nashville TN 37234 Office Fax: 615-936-1047. Business E-Mail: stephen.morrow@vanderbilt.edu.

MORSE, LEONARD J., epidemiologist, public health service officer; MD, U. Md., 1955. Intern and resident in internal medicine, fellow in infectious diseases U. Md. Med. Sys.; resident in internal medicine New Eng. Med. Ctr. Hosp.; pvt. practice Worcester, Mass.; ret., 1996; med. dir. New Bedford Cmty. Health Ctr., 1996—2001; prof. clin. medicine, family medicine, cmty. health U. Mass. Med. Sch., Worcester; pub. health commr. Worcester, 2001—. Mem.: AMA (past chair coun. ethical and jud. affairs, Pride in Profession award 2004), Am. Soc. History Medicine, Am. Soc. Microbiology, Infectious Diseases Soc. Am., Mass. Med. Soc. (pres. 1993—94, past chmn. com. ethics and discipline, Lifetime Achievement award 1997, Grant V. Rodkey award 1997), Am. Coll. Physicians (Named Internist of Yr. Mass. chpt. 1998). Office: Worcester Pub Health 25 Meade St Worcester MA 01610 Office Phone: 508-799-8531. Business E-Mail: morsel@worcesterma.gov, lmorsemd@massmed.org.

MORSE, STEPHEN SCOTT, virologist, epidemiologist, immunologist, educator; b. NYC, Nov. 22, 1951; s. Murray H. and Phyllis Morse; m. Marilyn Gewirtz, Feb. 1991. BS, CCNY, 1971; MS, U. Wis., 1974, PhD, 1977. NSF trainee dept. bacteriology U. Wis., Madison, 1971-72, rsch. asst., 1972-77; Nat. Cancer Inst. rsch. fellow Med. Coll. Va./Va. Commonwealth U., Richmond, 1977-80, instr. microbiology, 1980-81; asst. prof. microbiology Rutgers U., New Brunswick, NJ, 1981-85; rsch. assoc. Rockefeller U., NYC, 1985-88, asst. prof., 1988-96, adj. faculty, 1996—; program mgr. Def. Advanced Rsch. Projects Agy., 1996-2000; asst. prof. to prof. epidemiology, Mailman Sch. Pub. Health, Columbia U., 1996—2008, prof., Mailman Sch. Pub. Health, 2008—, dir. Ctr. Pub. Health Preparedness, Mailman Sch. Pub. Health, 2000—05; dir. USAID Predict Project, 2009—. Cons. US Congress Office Tech. Assessment, Washington, 1989; chair conf. on emerging viruses NIH, 1989; mem. com. microbial threats to health, chair subcom. on viruses Inst. Medicine-NAS, 1990—92, steering com. forum on emerging infections, 1996—2010, com. future biothreats, 2003—05; chair program for monitoring emerging diseases (ProMED) Fedn. Am. Scientists, 1993—99; mem. com. on biodef. analysis and countermeasures NAS-NRC, 2005—08. Author: Emerging Viruses, 1993, Evolutionary Biology of Viruses, 1994; editor-in-chief Pasteur Inst. Virology Jour., 1996—99; sect. editor: Ctr. for Disease Control and Prevention Jour., Emerging Infectious Diseases, 1995—2002, mem. editl. bd.: Emerging Infectious Diseases, 2003—06, EcoHealth, 2003—10, Biosecurity and Bioterrorism, 2003—. Fellow: AAAS, NY Acad. Medicine, Am. Coll. Epidemiology, NY Acad. Scis. (vice chair microbiology sect. 1994—96, chair 1996—98), Am. Acad. Microbiology; mem.: Marine Biology Lab., Am. Assn. Immunologists, Am. Soc. Microbiology, Coun. on Fgn. Rels., Cosmos Club, Sigma Xi. Office: Columbia U Mailman Sch Pub Health 722 W 168th St New York NY 10032-3722 Office Phone: 212-305-8054. Business E-Mail: ssm20@columbia.edu.

MORSELLI, PAOLO LUCIO, psychiatrist, clinical pharmacologist; b. Bergamo, Italy, Apr. 2, 1937; arrived in France, 1976; s. Libero and Clelia (Moretti) M.; m. Rosetta Franco, Sept. 16, 1976; children: Lisalinda, Lorenzo. MD with full honors, U. Milan, 1961. Asst. dept. psychiatry U. Milan Med. Sch., 1962-65; clin. assoc. Pharm. Rsch. Inst. Mario Negri, Milan, 1965; rsch. fellow in pharmacology Med. Coll. Va., Richmond, 1965-67; head Lab. Clin. Pharmacology Inst. Mario Negri, 1968-76; dir. dept. clin. rsch. Synthelabo Recherche L.E.R.S., Paris, 1976—90; v.p. Synthelabo-Pharmacie, 1991—94. Chmn. 3d Commn. on Epileptic Drugs, Internat. League Against Epilepsy, 1978-81, mem. IV Commn. on Antiepileptic Drugs, 1981-84; mem. Clin. Pharmacology Surveillance Commn., French Ministry Health, 1985-88; speaker numerous workshops, meetings, symposia, congresses and confs. Author, editor or co-editor 19 books and monographs; mem. editorial bd. various internat. sci. jours.; contbr. over 480 articles to med. jours. V.p. Fondazione Inst. for Rsch. and Prevention of Depression and Anxiety, Milan, 1996—; sec. gen. GAMIAN-Europe, 1996—; v.p. ISSBD, 2000—. Lt. Italian Air Force, 1963. Recipient Amgrogino d'Oro award Comunt of Milan, 1973, Internat. League Against Epilepsy rsch. award Am. Soc. Pharm. Explt. Therapeutics, 1964-65, Fulbright-Hayes scholar, 1965; Coun. for Tobacco Rsch. fellow, 1966. Achievements include research in social and therapeutic aspects of depression and other mood disorders and anxiety disorders; stigma and prejudices associated with mental illnesses. Home: 1067 rue Louis Blériot 78530 Buc France

MORSHED, SYED A., research scientist; b. Dhaka, Bangladesh, July 28, 1961; MD, Mymensingh Med. Sch., 1984; PhD, Kagawa Med. U., 1993. Rsch. scientist James J. Peters Bronx VA Med. Ctr., 2006—. Adj. instr. Mt. Sinai Sch. Medicine, 2007. Named Young Clinician, Soc. Gastroenterology. Avocation: travel. Office: 130 W Kingsbridge Rd Bronx NY 10468 Business E-Mail: syed.morshed@mssm.edu.

MORSI, YOSRY SADEIK, mechanical engineering educator, researcher; b. Alexandria, Egypt, Sept. 16, 1948; arrived in Australia, 1986; s. Sadeik Mohammed and Khadiga Mohammed (Ibrahim) M.; divorced; children: Yassir, Sarah. BSc (hons.), U. Tech., Cairo, 1972; diploma in ednl. tech., Huddersfield Poly., Eng., 1975, BSc, 1978; MSc, DIC, London U., 1979, PhD in Mech. Engring., 1983. Trainee engr. Ford, Alexandria, 1969, 70, 71; cadet engr. Petro-Chem. Engring., 1972-74; design dngr. Kenward Specialist Engring., 1976-80; rsch. assoc., fellow U. Coll., London, 1980-84; lectr. Loughborough U., 1984-86; from sr. lectr. to assoc. prof. Swinburne U., Australia, 1990—; dir., leader Energey Sys. Engring. Ctr. (now Modelling & Process Analysis, 1994—. Cons. engr. Loughborough Consultants, 1984-86; rsch. engr., cons., group mgr. UniSearch, NSW, 1986-88; R & D engr. Power Victoria, 1986-90; dir. Rsch. Testing Pty. Ltd., Victoria, 1991—; acad. rsch. assoc. Melbourne U., Victoria, 1990—. Editor, author: Experimental Diagnostics Techniques, 1991; contbr. nomerous articles to profl. jours.; inventor of several fluids and thermal devices. Grantee England and Australia; Brit. Coun. scholar, 1975. Fellow Instn. Engrs. Avocations: reading, travel. Office: Swinburne U Tech John St Hawthorn VIC Australia

MORSY, MOHAMED A., pharmacologist, educator; b. Beni-Suef, Egypt, May 16, 1967; PhD in Pharmacy, Kumamoto U., Japan, 2004. Diploma in clin. pharmacy El-Minia U. Lectr. Faculty Medicine, El-Minia U., Egypt, 2004—10, coord. in quality assurance and accreditation com., 2008—11, assoc. prof., 2011—. Contbr. articles to profl. jours. Joint Rsch. scholarship, Egyptian Govt., 2007. Mem.: Egyptian Soc. Basic Med. Scis., Egyptian Soc. Pharmacy, Egyptian Soc. Natural Toxins, Egyptian Soc. Toxicology, Egyptian Soc. Pharmacology and Exptl. Therapeutics. Avocations: photography, fishing. Office: El-Minia University St El-Minia 61511 Egypt Personal E-mail: mamm222@hotmail.com.

MORSY, MOHAMED DARWESH, physiologist, educator; b. Egypt, Aug. 19, 1964; MD in physiology, Coll. Medicine Menoufyia U., Egypt, 1999. Assoc. prof. Coll. Medicine Menoufyia U., 2005, assoc. prof. physiology, King Kaled U., Saudi Arabia, 1999—. Reviewer bd. mem. various jours. Mem. Mem.: Eithical Com. Rsch. Coll. Medicines. Avocations: reading, swimming. Office: King Kaled University Coll Medicine Abha Saudi Arabia Personal E-mail: morsydarwesh@yahoo.com.

MORSY, MOHAMED SAAD, medical educator; b. Alexandria, Egypt, Oct. 22, 1953; M in Ophthalmology, Faculty Medicine Alexandria, 1982, D in Ophthalmology, 1988. Prof. Alexandria U., 1988—2006, King Faisal U., 2006—11. Home: 178 Omar Lotfi St Sporting Alexandria 400 Egypt Personal E-mail: morsy4@gmail.com.

MORT, JANE R., medical educator; b. Pawnee, Nebr., Dec. 30, 1960; PharmD, U. Nebr., 1985. Pharmacy resident U. Iowa Hosps. and Clinics, 1985—86; prof., assoc. dean, academic programs Coll. Pharmacy SD State U., 1986—. Cons. Nusring Homes Brookview Manor and United Retirement Ctr., 1986—96, SD Drug Edn. and Evaluation Program, 1991—2011, Rapid City Regional Hosps. Geriatric Assessment Team, 1998—2003, SD Found. Med. Care, 2004—11. Recipient Pharmacy Rsch. award, Upjohn, 1991, Recognition award, Coll. Pharmacy SD State U., 1993, 1996, Faculty Recognition award, 2000, 2002; grant, Nat. Inst. Health Agy. Health Care Policy and Rsch. Fellow: Am. Soc. Cons. Pharmacists; mem.:

Am. Assn. Colls. Pharmacy, Alpha Lambda Delta, Phi Eta Sigma, Rho Chi Soc. Office: Coll Pharmacy SDSU Box 2202C Brookings SD 57007 Office Fax: 605-688-6232. Business E-Mail: jane.mort@sdstate.edu.

MORTIZ, JACQUES, obstetrician, gynecologist, educator; BS, U. Miami, 1981; MS in Biology, Barry U., 1983; MD, U. Miami Sch. Medicine, 1988. Cert. obstetrics & gynecology. Resident Columbia-Presbyterian Med. Ctr., 1988—92; asst. clinical prof. obstetrics & gynecology Columbia U. Coll. Physicians & Surgeons; dir. endoscopy section & divsn. gynecology St. Luke's-Roosevelet Hosp. Office: 315 W 57th St Ste 204 New York NY 10019 Office Phone: 212-603-4160.

MORTON, JOHN M., surgeon, consultant; b. Montgomery, Ala. BS in Biology & English, Tulane U., 1988, MPH, MD, Tulane U., 1993; MHA, U. Wash., Seattle, 1997. Cert. Am. Bd. Surgery, 2002, lic. Calif. Resident Tulane Sch. Medicine, 1993—95, 1997—99, Swedish Med. Ctr., 1999—2001; fellow U. NC, 2001—03; assoc. prof. dept. surgery Stanford U. Sch. Medicine, 2003—, dir. bariatric surgery, 2003—, med. dir. surgical sub-specialties clinic, 2005—, dir. minimally invasive surgery fellowship, 2005—, dir. Surgery Ctr. for Outcomes Rsch. & Evaluation, 2006—, dir. quality, surgery & surgical subspecialties, 2007—; co dir. Digestive Health Ctr.; sect. chief Minimally Invasive Surgery; exec. coun. mem. Am. Soc. Metabolic & Bariatric Surgeon; adv. bd. mem. Am. Coll. Surgeon Bariatric Surgery, Ctr. Eruelaro Network. Assoc. editor SOARD Jour. of Am. Soc. for Bariatric Surgery, 2004—; reviewer for various industry jours.; editl. bd. mem. World JOurs. Gastroentology Obesity Soc. Recipient Outstanding Resident award, Soc. Laparoscopic Surgeons, 2001, Excellence in Teaching award, Stanford Sch. Medicine, 2005, 2007, 2009, Golden Laparoscope award, SAGES, Henry J. Kaiser Tchg. award, 2011. Fellow: Am. Coll. Surgeons; mem.: SAGES, AMA, Western Surgical Assn., Pacific Coast Surgical Assn., Assn. for Surgical Edn., Assn. for Acad. Surgery, Am. Soc. Bariatric Surgeons. Office: Stanford University School of Medicine 300 Pasteur Dr Rm H 3680 Stanford CA 94305-5655 Home: 735 Valparaiso Ave Menlo Park CA 94025-4244 Office Phone: 650-725-5247. Office Fax: 650-725-0791. E-mail: morton@stanford.edu.

MORTON, NEWTON ENNIS, human geneticist; b. Camden, NJ, Dec. 21, 1929; arrived in U.K., 1988; s. Newton and Laura Rebecca (Jones) M.; m. Nancy Okazaki, Feb. 11, 1949 (div. Jan. 1972); children: Teru, Peter, Amy, John, Robert; m. Patricia Ann Jacobs, May 15, 1972. BA, U. Hawaii, 1951, MA, 1952; PhD, U. Wis., 1955; MD, Umea U., Sweden, 1976. Geneticist Atomic Bomb Casualty Commn., Japan, 1952-53; postdoc. fellow U. Wis., 1955-56, asst. to assoc. prof., 1956-62; prof. U. Hawaii, 1962-85; dept. head Sloan Kettering Cancer Ctr., 1985-87; prof. U. Southampton, 1988—2011, prof. emeritus, 2011. Pres. 9th Internat. Congress Human Genetics, 1997. Mem. adv. bd. Jour. of Human Genetics, 1997—; author: Genetics of Interracial Crosses in Hawaii, 1967, Genetic Structure of Populations, 1973, Outline of Genetic Epidemiology, 1982; editor: Genetic Epidemiology, 1978; mem. editl. bd. Proc. NAS. Recipient Lederle Med. Faculty award, 1951, Allan award Am. Soc. of Human Genetics, 1963, Hon. Symposium award, Am. Soc. Human Genetics, 2009. Fellow: Royal Coll. Physicians, mem.: Brazilian Acad. Scis., US Nat. Acad. Sci. Avocations: tennis, walking, gardening. Office: Human Genetics U Southamptn Duthic Bldg Southampton SO16 6YD England Home Phone: 44-1722-710393; Office Phone: 44-23-8079-6536. Business E-Mail: nem@soton.ac.uk.

MOSCA, LORI JEAN, internist, educator; b. Syracuse, NY, July 9, 1958; married; 2 children. MD, SUNY, Syracuse, 1984; MPh, Columbia U., 1992, PhD, 1996. Intern, cardiology SUNY-HSC, Syracuse, NY, 1984—85, resident, epidemiology, 1985—87; fellow, medicine Columbia U., NYC, 1990—91, fellow, 1991—92; asst. prof., edpidemiology U. Mich., Ann Arbor; with Columbia U. Med. Ctr., NY, 2000—, assoc. prof. medicine NY; dir. preventative cardiology NY-Presbyn. Hosp./Columbia U. Med. Ctr., NY; founder, dir. Columbia Ctr. for Heart Disease Prevention, NY. Prin. investigator NIH funded study to test the effectiveness of a family heart health screening and ednl. intervention; mem. exec. com. Raloxifene Use for the Heart (RUTH) Internat. Prevention Trial in women; expert panel chair Am. Heart Assn. Evidence-Based Guidelines for Cardiovascular Disease Prevention in Women, and Hormone Replacement Therapy, 2004, 07; chair Am. Heart Assn. Nat. Women's Heart Disease and Stroke Campaign; invited lecturer at many nat. and internat. scientific programs. Reviewer for several journals including New England Journal of Medicine, Circulation, Jour. AMA; author: of several scientific publications; participated in several nat. news programs and documentaries, sr. editor Preventive Cardiology; author: Heart to Heart: A Personal Plan for Creating a Heart-Healthy Family, 2005. Chief med. advisor Sister to Sister Everyone Has a Heart Found. Recipient Upstate Med. U. Outstanding Young Alumni award, 2004, Women's Day Red Dress award, 2004, Women in Sci. award, Am. Med. Women Assn., 2007, NIH Mid-Career Investigator Develop. award in Applied Preventative Cardiology Rsch.; named a Top Doctor in the NY Metropolitan Area. Mem.: Am. Soc. Preventive Cardiology (immediate past pres.), Am. Heart Assn. (immediate past chair, Coun. on Epidemiology and Prevention, mem. nat. bd. dirs., chair, Nat. Women's Heart Disease and Stroke Campaign). Avocation: competitive triathlete and Hawaii Ironman finisher. Address: Columbia U Dept Medicine PH Room 10-203D 622 W 168th St New York NY 10032 Mailing: Preventive Cardiology Columbia U Med Ctr 601 W 168th St Ste 43 New York NY 10032 Office Phone: 212-305-4866. Office Fax: 212-342-5238. Business E-Mail: ljm10@columbia.edu.

MOSCATELLO, AUGUSTINE, otolaryngologist, educator; MD, Mt. Sinai Sch. of Medicine. Diplomate Am. Bd. Otolaryngology. Resident in surgery Mt. Sinai Hosp., 1982—87, resident in otolaryngology, 1987; assoc. prof. otolaryngology NY Med. Coll.; dir. of otolaryngology Westchester Med. Ctr. Mem.: ACS, NY Head and Neck Soc., American Acad. of Facial Plastic and Reconstructive Surgery, American Acad. of Otolaryngology, Alpha Omega Alpha Med. Honor Soc. Office: Westchester Medical Center 100 Woods rd. Valhalla NY 10595 Office Phone: 914-493-7000. Office Fax: 914-493-2925.

MOSEL, KRISTA, nursing researcher; b. Adelaide, Jan. 5, 1973; BNg with honors, Flinders U., 2008, PhD student. Peer tutor U. South Australia, 2004—09; rsch. asst. Flinders U., 2005—, lectr., 2010; RN Modbury Hosp., 2006—08, NASANSB - Critical Care, 2007—08. Reviewer Jour. Psychiat. and Mental Health Nursing, 2009—, Internat. Jour. Mental Health Nursing, 2009—; rater McMaster U., Health Info. Rsch. Unit, Ont., Canada, 2010—. Recipient Chancellor's Letter Commendation award, Flinders U., Merit award, U. South Australia; award, Australian Govt. Mem.: Australian Coll. Mental Health Nurses, Royal Coll. Nurses, Golden Key Internat. Honour Soc. Avocations: motorcycling, painting. Office: GPO Box 2100 Adelaide South Australia 5001 Australia

MOSER, JAMES MICHAEL, medical educator; b. Cincinnati; s. James L. and Bettie Moser; m. Joanna M. Mack; 1 child. BS, U. Dayton, Ohio; MD, U. Ky., Lexington; MPH, U. NC, Chapel Hill. Diplomate in general preventive medicine and public health Am. Bd. Preventive Medicine, in internal medicine Am. Bd. Internal Medicine. Asst. prof. Ohio State U., Columbus, 1983—87; dir. epidemiology divsn. Ky. Dept. Health Svcs., Frankfort, 1987—89; asst. chief preventive medicine bur. Ohio dept. health Columbus, 1990—93; assoc. prof. U. Kans., 1993—95; dir. epidemiology divsn. NC Dept. HHS, 1995—97; dir. health Kans. Dept. Health and Environment, Topeka, 1999—2003; dir. Akron Health Dist., 2003—09; prof. NE Ohio Med. U., Rootstown, 2003—11, Kent State U., 2011—. Adj. asst. prof. U. NC, 1981—83, adj. assoc. prof., 1995—99; res. dir. Ohio State U. Coll. Medicine, 1985—87; MPH dir. U. Kans., 1993—95; dir. Kans. Turning Point Project, 1999—2003, Office Pub. Health Practice, Northeastern Ohio Univs. Coll. Medicine, 2006—10; asst. clin. prof. U. Ky., 1987—89; adj. prof. Consortium Eastern Ohio MPH Program, 2004—; site visitor Coun. Edn. Pub. Health, 1988—92. Contbr. chapters to books, articles to profl. jours. Mem. Kans. Commn. Emergency Planning and Response, 1999—2003; chmn. Kans. Bioterrorism Coordinating Coun., 2002—03; mem. Summit County Domestic Preparedness Task Force, 2003—09; bd. dirs. Planned Parenthood Summit, Portage, and Medina Counties, Akron, Ohio, 2003—07; bd. trustees Summit/Akron Solid Waste Mgmt. Authority, Ohio, 2003—09; chmn. Emergency Med. Svcs. Bd., Akron, Ohio, 2003—09; pres. Summit-Portage Area Health Edn. Ctr., Akron, Ohio, 2006—10; vice chmn. Summit County Family and Children First Coun., 2007—09; bd. dirs. Ohio Assn. Health Commn., 2006—09; co-chair Cmty. Health Adv. Com., Summa Health Sys., Akron, Ohio, 2007—09; chmn. academic adv. bd. Pfizer Fellowship Pub. Health, 2009—11; mem. Coun. Linkages Between Academia and Pub. Health Practice, 2003—04; co-chair, MPH epidemiology core competencies panel Assn. Schs. Pub. Health, 2004—05, mem., applied epidemiology competencies task force, 2006—08; mem. Comm. & Informatics MPH Core Competencies Panel, 2005—06. Fulbright Scholarship, Coun. Internat. Exchange Scholars, 2011, Specialist scholar, Bur. Ednl. and Cultural Affairs, US Dept. State. Fellow: Am. Coll. Preventive Medicine, mem.: APHA, Internat. Soc. Infectious Diseases, Assn. State and Territorial Health Officials, Fulbright Assn., Alpha Omega Alpha Honor Med. Soc. Office: Coll Pub Health Kent State University PO Box 5190 Kent OH 44242

MOSER, MARVIN, physician, educator, author; b. Newark, Jan. 24, 1924; s. Sol and Sophia (Markowitz) M.; m. Joy Diane Lipez, July 1, 1954; children: Jill, Stephen, John. AB, Cornell U., 1943; MD, Suny Downstate Coll. Medicine, NYC, 1947. Diplomate in internal medicine and cardiovasc. disease Am. Bd. Internal Medicine; cert. specialist in hypertension Am. Soc. Hypertension. Intern univ. div. Kings County Hosp., NYC, 1947-48, resident in medicine, 1948-49, Montefiore Hosp., NYC, 1949-50; Nat. Heart Assn. fellow Mt. Sinai Hosp., NYC, 1950-51, charge vascular service Walter Reed Army Hosp. Med. Centre, Washington, 1951-53; practice medicine specializing in cardiology White Plains, NY, 1953-95; assoc. physician cardiology Montefiore Hosp., 1953-75, in charge hypertension sect., 1960—74. Attending physician cardiology White Plains Hosp., 1968-95, chief cardiology, 1969-78, adj. physician in cardiology Grasslands Hosp., Valhalla, NY, 1953-60, attending physician in medicine in charge Hypertension Clinic, Westchester County Med. Center, Valhalla, 1974-84; asst. clin. prof. medicine Albert Einstein Coll. Medicine, 1965-75; clin. prof. medicine NY Med. Coll., 1974-84, Yale U. Sch. Medicine, 1984—; sr. med. cons. nat. high blood pressure program NIH, 1975-2002, mem. nat. high blood pressure coordinating com., 1976-2005; chmn. Joint Nat. Com. Hypertension, 1977, vice-chmn., 1979, mem., 1984-88, 92, 96, 2003; exec. com. Nat. Citizens for Treatment High Blood Pressure, 1976-78, vice-chmn., 1978-88; mem. NY State Adv. Com. on Hypertension, 1977-84; chmn. Nat. Conf. on High Blood Pressure Control, 1979; mem. select panel on hypertension in Am. Congl. Subcom. on Aging, 1978-79; cons. cardiology NY State Dept. Health, Gen. Hosp., Saranac Lake, NY, 1980-90; med. dir. Westchester County Hypertension Program, NY, 1979-88, editor-chief The Med. Roundtable, 2009- Author: (with A.M. Master, M. Moser. H. Jaffee) Cardiac Emergencies and Heart Failure, 2d edit., 1955; (with A. Goldman) Hypertensive Vascular Disease, 1967, Hypertension, A Practical Approach, 1975, Lower Your Blood Pressure and Live Longer, 1988; co-editor, contbr. Yale University School of Medicine Heart Book, 1992, Week by Week to a Strong Heart, 1992, Heart Healthy Cooking for all Seasons, 1996, Clinical Management of Hypertension, 1996, 7th edit., 2004, 8th edit., 2008, Myths, Misconceptions and Heroics, the Story of the Treatment of Hypertension, 1997, 2002, (with J. Sowers) Management of Cardiovascular Risk Factors in Diabetes, 2001, 2d edit., 2005, 3rd edit., 2007, 4th edit., 2010; mem. editl. bd. Preventive Cardiology, 1998—2009, Jour. Medicine and Sports, 1999-2004; assoc. editor Angiology, 1976-85; bd. editors Primary Cardiology, 1975-78, assoc. editor-in-chief, 1978-96; editor-in-chief Jour. Clin. Hypertension, 1999—2009, emeritus, 2009-; sr. editor Jour. of Cardio Metabolic Syndrome, 2006—09; contbr. 500 sci. papers., chapters to 35 books. Chmn. Narcotics Guidance Coun., Scarsdale, 1968-72; trustee Scarsdale Bd. Edn., 1970-73, Trudeau Inst., 1990-2004, Nat. Hypertension Found., 1992-2001, Nutrition 21, 1997-2001, Comprehensive Neuroscience; bd. dirs. Third Ave. Value and Small Cap Funds, 1994—; pres. Hypertension Edn. Found., 1977—. Served U.S. Army, 1941-46; capt. M.C. USAF, 1951-53. Recipient Achievement awards Nat. Heart lung and Blood Inst., 1985, 95, 97, award Internat. Soc. Hypertension, 2004, 06, award Am. Soc. Hypertension, 2006, award Suny Down State Coll. Medicine, 2007; grantee NIH, 1958-62. Fellow: ACP, Am. Soc. Hypertension, Am. Heart Assn. ((various offices: pres. coun. geriatric cardiology 1996-97, others)), Am. Coll. Cardiology, Royal Coll. Physicians and Surgeons (hon.); mem.: Century Country Club. Home and Office: 13 Murray Hill Rd Scarsdale NY 10583 Personal E-mail: moserbp@aol.com.

MOSER, ROBERT HARLAN, internist, educator, writer; b. Trenton, NJ, June 16, 1923; s. Simon and Helena (Silvers) Moser; m. Linda Mae Salsinger, Mar. 18, 1989; children from previous marriage: Steven Michael, Jonathan Evan. BS, Loyola U., Balt., 1944; MD, Georgetown U., Washington, DC, 1948. Diplomate Am. Bd. Internal Medicine. Commd. 1st lt. U.S. Army, 1948, advanced through grades to col., 1966, intern D.C. Gen. Hosp., 1948—49, fellow pulmonary disease D.C. Gen. Hosp., 1949—50, bn. surgeon Republic of Korea, 1950—51; asst. resident Georgetown U. Hosp., 1951—52; chief resident Georgetown U. Hosp. U.S. Army, 1952—53, chief med. service U.S. Army Hosp. Salzburg, Austria, 1953—55, Wurzburg, Germany, 1955—56, resident in cardiology Brooke Gen. Hosp., 1956—57, asst. chief dept. medicine Brooke Gen. Hosp., 1957—59, chief Brooke Gen. Hosp., 1967—68, fellow hematology U. Utah Coll. Medicine, 1959—60, asst. chief U.S. Army Tripler Gen. Hosp., 1960—64, chief William Beaumont Gen. Hosp., 1965—67, chief Walter Reed Gen. Hosp., 1968—69, ret., 1969; chief of staff Maui (Hawaii) Meml. Hosp., 1969—73, chief dept. medicine, 1975—77; exec. v.p. Am. Coll. Physicians, Phila., 1976—86; v.p. med. affairs The NutraSweet Co., Deerfield, Ill., 1986—91. Assoc. prof. medicine Baylor U., 1958—59; clin. prof. medicine Hawaii U., 1969—77, Washington U., 1970—77, Abraham Lincoln Sch. Medicine, 1974—75; adj. prof. medicine U. Pa., 1977—86, Northwestern U., 1987—91; adj. prof. Uniformed Svcs. U. Health Scis., 1979—97; clin. prof. medicine U. N.Mex. Coll. Medicine, 1992—96, emeritus, 1996—; flight contr. Project Mercury, 1959—62; cons. mem. med. evaluation team Project Gemini, 1962—66; cons. Project Apollo, 1967—73; Tripler Gen. Hosp., 1970—77, Walter Reed Army Med. Ctr., 1974—86; sr. med. cons. Canyon Cons. Corp., 1991—2004; mem. cardiovascular and renal adv. com. FDA, 1978—82; chmn. life scis. adv. com. NASA, 1984—87, mem. adv. coun., 1983—88; chmn. gen. med. panel Hosp. Satellite Network, 1984—86; mem. adv. com. NASA Space Sta., 1988—93; mem. Dept. Def. Com. on Grad. Med. Edn., 1986—87, Life Scis. Strategic Planning Study Group, 1986—88; mem. space studies bd. NRC, 1988—93, space exploration initiation study, 1990; mem. NASA Space Sta. Commn., 1992—93, mem. com. adv. tech. human supp. space, 1996—97; mem. med. adv. bd. the patient channel GE Healthcare, 2001—. Editor, chief divsn. sci. publs. Jour. AMA, Chgo., 1973—75, contbg. editor Med. Opinion and Rev., 1966—75, chmn. editorial bd. Diagnosis mag., 1986—89, mem. editorial bd. Hawaii Med. Jour., Family Physicians, Archives of Internal Medicine, 1967—73, Western Jour. Medicine, 1975—87, Chest, 1975—80, Med. Times, 1977—84, Quality Rev. Bull., 1979—91, The Pharos, 1991—, book rev. editor, 2000—05, mem. editorial bd. Travel Medicine, 1994—96, contbr. over 200 articles to med. sci. jours. and med. books; author: Diseases of Medical Progress, 1955, 1969, House Officer Training, 1970, Decade of Decision, 1992, Past Imperfect A Personal History of Life In and Around Medicine, 2003; co-author Adventures in Medical Writing, 1970, editor chief divsn. sci. publs. Jour. AMA, Chgo., 1973—75, contbg. editor Med. Opinion and Rev., 1966—75, chmn. editl. bd. Diagnosis mag., 1986—89; contbr. articles to med. sci. jours. and med. books. Master: ACP (exec. v.p. 1977—86); fellow: Am. Clin. and Climatol. Assn., Am. Coll. Cardiology, Royal Coll. Physicians and Surgeons Can. (hon.); mem.: AMA (adv. panel registry of adverse drug reactions 1960—67, coun. on drugs 1967—73), Soc. Med. Cons. to Armed Forces, Coll. Physicians Phila., Chgo. Soc. Internal Medicine, Nat. Assn. Physician Broadcasters, Inst. Medicine-NAS, Am. Osler Soc., Am. Therapeutic Soc., Am. Med. Writers Assn., Alpha Omega Alpha, Alpha Sigma Nu. Democrat. Jewish. Avocations: hiking, travel, writing. Home and Office: 943 E Sawmill Canyon Pl Green Valley AZ 85614 Office Phone: 520-399-2526. Personal E-mail: rhmoser@earthlink.net.

MOSER, ROBERT PAUL, JR., public health service officer, state official; b. Denver, June 18, 1958; BS in Pharmacy, U. Kans., 1981, MD, 1985. Diplomate American Bd. Family Practice. Resident family medicine Smoky Hill Family Practice Residency, Salina, Kans., 1988; with Greeley County Health Sys.; vol. asst. clin. prof. sch. medicine dept. family and cmty. medicine Univ. Kans., clin. assoc. prof., 2010, dir. rural health and outreach, 2010, spl. asst. to the exec. vice chancellor sch. medicine; dir. divsn. health Kans. Dept. Health and Environment. Pres. Kans. Acad. of Family Physicians, 2001; exec. bd. dirs. Kans. Practice-based Rsch. Network, 2000—05; served rural health com. Am. Acad. of Family Physicians; chmn. coordinating com. Kans. Primary Care Collaborative. Fellow: Am. Acad. of Family Physicians; mem.: Kans. Acad. of Family Physicians. Office: Kansas Department of Health and Environment Curtis State Office Bldg 1000 SW Jackson Topeka KS 66612 Office Phone: 785-296-1086. Office Fax: 785-368-6368. *

MOSER, ROYCE, JR., preventive medicine physician, educator; b. Versailles, Mo., Aug. 21, 1935; s. Royce and Russie Frances (Stringer) M.; m. Lois Anne Hunter, June 14, 1958; children: Beth Anne Moser McLean, Donald Royce. BA, Harvard U., Cambridge, Mass., 1957, MD, 1961; MPH, Harvard Sch. Pub. Health, Boston, 1965. Diplomate Am. Bd. Preventive Medicine (trustee 1989-98). Commd. officer USAF, 1962, advanced through grades to col., 1974; resident in aerospace medicine USAF Sch. Aerospace Medicine, Brooks AFB, Tex., 1965-67; chief aerospace medicine Aerospace Def. Command, Colorado Springs, Colo., 1967-70; comdr. 35th USAF Dispensary Phan Rang, Vietnam, 1970-71; chief aerospace medicine br. USAF Sch. Aerospace Medicine, Brooks AFB, 1971-77; comdr. USAF Hosp., Tyndall AFB, Fla., 1977-79; chief clin. scis. divsn. USAF Sch. Aerospace Medicine, Brooks AFB, 1979-81, chief edn. divsn., 1981-83, sch. comdr., 1983-85, ret., 1985; prof. dept. family and preventive medicine U. Utah Sch. Medicine, Salt Lake City, 1985—2011, vice chmn. dept., 1985-95; dir. Rocky Mountain Ctr. for Occupl. and Environ. Health, Salt Lake City, 1987—2003. Cons. in occupl., environ. and aerospace medicine, Salt Lake City, 1985—; presenter in field. Author: Effective Management of Health and Safety Programs, 1992, 3d. edit. 2008; contbr. chpts. to books, articles to profl. jours. Past pres. 1st Bapt. Ch. Found., Salt Lake City, 1987-89, moderator, 2006; chmn. numerous univ. coms., Salt Lake City, 1985—; bd. dirs. Hanford Environ. Health Found., 1990-92; preventive medicine residency rev. com. Accreditation Coun. Grad. Med. Edn., 1991-97; ednl. adv. bd. USAF Human Sys. Ctr., 1991-96; chmn. long-range planning com. Am. Bd. Preventive Medicine, 1992-95; mem. alumni coun. Harvard Sch. Pub. Health, 2003-06, chair alumni award of merit com., 2005-09, chair, Harvard Sch. Pub. Health Alumni Coun. 2009—11; pres. Harvard Sch. Pub. Health Alumni Assoc., 2009-11. Decorated Legion of Merit (2); recipient Harriet Hardy award New Eng. Coll. Occupl. and Environ. Medicine, 1998, Rutherford T. Johnstone award Western Occupl. and Environ. Med. Assn., 2002. Fellow Aerospace Med. Assn. (pres. 1989-90, chair fellows group 1994-97, Harry G. Mosely award 1981, Theodore C. Lyster award 1988, Eric Liljencrantz award 2001, Pres.'s citation, 2006), Am. Coll. Preventive Medicine (regent 1981-82), Am. Coll. Occupl. and Environ. Medicine (v.p. med. affairs 1995-97, Robert A. Kehoe award

1996); mem. Internat. Acad. Aviation and Space Medicine (selector 1989-94, chancellor 1994-98), Soc. of USAF Flight Surgeons (pres. 1978-79, George E. Schafer award 1982), Phi Beta Kappa, Delta Omega. Avocations: photography, fishing. Home: 664 Aloha Rd Salt Lake City UT 84103-3329 Office: Rocky Mountain Ctr Occupl & Environ Health 391 Chipeta Way Ste C Salt Lake City UT 84108 Office Phone: 801-581-4800. Business E-Mail: Royce.Moser@hsc.utah.edu.

MOSES, HAMILTON, III, neurologist, hospital administrator, consultant, author; s. Hamilton Jr. and Betty Anne Moses; m. Elizabeth Hormel, 1977 (dec. 1988); m. Alexandra McCullough Gibson, 1992. BA in Psychology, U. Pa., 1972; MD, Rush Med. Coll., Chgo., 1975. Clk. Nat. Hosp. for Nervous Diseases, London, 1974; intern in medicine Johns Hopkins Hosp., Balt., 1976-77, resident in neurology, 1977-79, chief resident, 1979-80, assoc. prof. neurology, 1986-94, vice chmn. neurology and neurosurgery, 1980-88, v.p., 1988-94, dir. Parkinson's Ctr., 1984-94; dir. neurol. inst., prof. neurology and neurosurgery and mgmt. U. Va., Charlottesville, 1994-97; sr. advisor Boston Cons. Group, 1995—; prof. Darden Sch. Bus. U. Va., Charlottesville, 1994-98; cons. neurologist Mass. Gen. Hosp., Boston, 1997—; vis. prof. neurology and psychiatry Harvard U. Sch. Medicine, Boston, 1997-99; chmn. The Alerion Inst., 2002—; hon. prof. neurology Johns Hopkins U. Sch. Medicine, 2009—. Sr. advisor Ptnrs. Healthcare, Boston; spl. advisor Nat. Health Svc., Eng., 1988-91; dir. various tech. companies. Co- editor, major author: Hopkins' Principles and Practice of Medicine, 1985-96; editor newsletter Johns Hopkins Health, 1988-94; contbr. articles to profl. jours. Com. on med. ministries Episcopal Diocese Md., Balt., 1987; bd. dirs. Valleys Planning Ct.; trustee McLean Hosp., Belmont, Mass., 1997—; commr. Land Preservation Trust, Albemarle County, Va. Recipient Hon. col., Nat. Pk. Svc. Fellow Am. Acad. Neurology (sec. 1989-91), Royal Soc. Medicine (UK); mem. Am. Neurol. Assn., Md. Neurol. Soc. (pres. 1984-86), Movement Disorders Soc. Episcopalian. Avocations: photography, sailing. Office: PO Box 150 North Garden VA 22959-0150 Business E-Mail: hm3@alerion.us.

MOSES, JAMES ANTHONY, JR., neuropsychologist; b. San Francisco, Feb. 25, 1947; m. Maureen M. Panganiban. BA magna cum laude, San Francisco State U., 1968; MS, San Jose State U., 1970; MA, U. Colo., 1971, PhD, 1974. Diplomate Am. Bd. Profl. Psychology. From clin. instr. psychiatry to clin. assoc. prof. Stanford (Calif.) U. Med. Sch., 1975-94, clin. prof., 1994—; rsch. psychologist Palo Alto (Calif.) VA Med. Ctr., 1977—, clin. neuropsychologist, 1974—; jujitsu instr. Stanford U. Athletic Dept., Palo Alto, 1981—; chief neuropsychology program VA Med. Ctr., 1999—; prof. clin. psychology Pacific Grad. Sch. Psychology, Palo Alto U., 2002—; adj. clin. prof. emeritus Stanford U. Sch. Medicine, 2005—. Assoc. editor Internat. Jour. of Clin. Neuropsychology, Madison, Wis., 1985-91; mem. editorial adv. bd. Archives of Clin. Neuropsychology, 1986—2010; bd. dirs. Am. Bd. Profl. Neuropsychology, 1989-91; head instr. Stanford U. Jujitsu Club, 1981-; master prof., 9th degree black belt Aiki Jujitsu Zen Budokai Martial Arts Soc., 2005, 4th degree black belt Master Sensei instr. Karate-Do, 1980. Author: Interpretation of the Luria-Nebraska Neuropsychological Test Batter, 1983; co-author: Interpretation of the Halstead-Reitan Neuropsychological Battery, 1982; co-editor: Clinical Neuropsychology: Theoretical Foundations for Practitioners, 1997; contbr. articles to numerous profl. publs. Named Nat. Acad. Neuropsychology fellow, 1984. Fellow Am. Psychol. Soc., Am. Acad. Clin. Psychology; mem. APA, Internat. Neuropsychol. Soc., Soc. Personality Assessment, Masons, Shriners, PsycCRITIQUES.-APA Review of Books (editl. bd. mem. 2006-). Independent. Achievements include co-validation of Luria-Nebraska Neuropsychological Battery with American and foreign populations; extension of clinical neuropsychological research findings to psychiatric patient populations; research in neuropsychology of schizophrenia with identification of specific deficit pattern for cognitive deficit in the disorder. Office: VA Med Ctr 3801 Miranda Ave Palo Alto CA 94304-1207 Home: 3337 Ross Rd Palo Alto CA 94303-4157 Office Phone: 650-562-1111, 650-493-5000. Business E-Mail: jmoses@PabAltoU.edu.

MOSES, JEFFREY WARREN, cardiologist, educator; b. Bklyn., May 12, 1948; s. Julian and Mildred Moses; m. Laurie Levinberg, Nov. 4, 1983 (div. 2008); children: Ariel, Jarret, Chandler, Harrison. BA, Yale U., New Haven, Conn., 1970; MD, U. Pa., Phila., 1974. Intern Presbyn.-U. Pa., Phila., 1974—75, resident in medicine, 1975—77, fellow in cardiology, 1978—80; asst. instr. U. Pa., Phila., 1975—77; med. adv. staff Blue Cross/Blue Shield Greater N.Y., 1977—78; asst. med. dir. Equitable Life Soc., NYC, 1977—78; asst. attending physician NY Hosp., NYC, 1980—87, asst. dir. Adult Cardiac Catheterization Lab., 1980—83, dir. clin. electrophysiology, 1981—87, assoc. dir. Adult Cardiac Catheterization Lab., 1983—87, assoc. attending physician, 1987; instr. medicine Cornell U. Med. Coll., NYC, 1980—81, asst. prof., 1981—87, assoc. prof. clin. medicine, 1987; chief interventional cardiology Lenox Hill Hosp., NYC, 1987—2004, assoc. attending physician, 1987—88, sr. attending physician, 1988—2004; clin. assoc. prof. medicine NYU Sch. Medicine, NYC, 1993—96, clin. prof. medicine, 1996—2004; prof. medicine, dir. Ctr. Interventional Vascular Therapy, dir. Cardiac Catheterization Lab. NY Presbyn. Hosp./Columbia U. Med. Ctr., NYC, 2004—, interventional cardiologist, 2005—. Fellow: ACP, Soc. Cardiac Angiography and Intervention, Am. Coll. Cardiology. Office: NY Presbyn Hosp Columbia U Med Ctr 161 Fort Washington Ave New York NY 10032 Office Phone: 212-305-7060. Office Fax: 212-305-4825, 212-342-3660. Business E-Mail: jm2456@columbia.edu.

MOSES, LOUIS J., psychology professor, department chairman; BA in Psychology, U. Western Australia, 1983; PhD in Psychology, Stanford U., Calif., 1991. Tutor, dept. psychology U. Western Australia, 1984—85; lectr., dept. psychology U. BC, Canada, 1991—92, Simon Fraser U., 1992; asst. prof., dept. psychology U. Oreg., Eugene, 1992—99, assoc. prof., dept. psychology, 1999—, prin. investigator, developing mind lab, associated faculty, inst. cognitive and decision sciences, chmn., dept. psychology. Co-editor (with B.F. Malle and D.A. Baldwin): Intentions and Intentionality: Foundations of Social Cognition, 2001; contbr. articles to profl. jours. Vis. scholar, Stanford U. Dept. Psychology, 1999—2000; Izaak Walton Killam Meml. Postdoctoral Rsch. fellow, U. BC, 1990—92. Mem.: Am. Psychol. Soc., Cognitive Devel. Soc., Soc. Rsch. in Child Devel. Office: Dept Psychology 1227 Univ Oreg Eugene OR 97403-1227 Office Phone: 541-346-4918. Office Fax: 541-346-4911. Business E-Mail: moses@uoregon.edu.

MOSES, MARSHA ANNE, biochemist, researcher; b. New Bedford, Mass., July 21, 1953; d. George Francis and Matilda Theresa (Thomas) M. BS, Stonehill Coll., 1975; PhD, Boston U., 1986. Postdoctoral rsch. assoc., rsch. fellow Children's Hosp. Med. Ctr., Boston, 1986—; rsch. fellow Harvard Med. Sch., Boston, 1986-90, instr. dept. surgery, 1991-92, asst. prof. surgery, assoc. prof. surgery, 1992—2006, prof. surgery, 2006—; interim dir. vascular biology prog. Children's Hosp. Boston. Author: (with others) Microcirculation and Cancer Metastasis, 1991, Clinical Applications of Cytokines, 1991; contbr. articles to various sci. jours. Recipient Cancer Rsch. Found. award, Am. Cancer Soc. Rsch. award, CaPCURE Rsch. award, A. Clifford Barger Mentoring award, Harvard Med. Sch., 2003; Gordon Conf. postdoctoral scholar, 1986; NIH postdoctoral rsch. fellow, 1987-89, Mary Ingraham Bunting Inst. Biomed. Rsch. fellow. Mem. AAAS, Am. Soc. Biochemistry and Molecular Biology (Young Investigator Travel award 1991), Am. Soc. Cell Biology, Am. Women in Sci., Assn. Rsch. in Vision and Ophthalmology, Inst. Medicine. Achievements include patents pending in field; rsch. in vascular growth control via endogenous inhibitors, the role of metalloproteinases and their inhibitors in the control of neovascularization. Office: Childrens Hosp Karp 12-214 300 Longwood Ave Boston MA 02115 Office Phone: 617-919-2207. Office Fax: 617-730-0231. E-mail: marsha.moses@childrens.harvard.edu.

MOSES, PRABHAKAR DEVARAJAN, pediatrician, educator; b. Tuticorin, Tamil Nadu, India, May 9, 1952; s. Henry Daniel and Grace (Leelavathy) Moses; m. Grace Manorama, Oct. 16, 1993; 1 child, Immanuel Henry. MBBS, Christian Med. Coll., Vellore, India, 1974, MD in Pediat., 1981. Diplomate MRCP Royal Coll. Physicians, 1986, FRCP Royal Coll. Of Physicians, Edinburgh, Scotland, 2000, FCAMS Christian Acad. Of Med. Sciences, Newdelhi, 2002. Registrar in pediat. Victoria Hosp., Kirkcaldy, Scotland, 1985—89; reader in child health Christian Med. Coll., Vellore, 1990—93, assoc. prof. in child health, 1993—95, prof. in child health, 1995, registrar, 2008, protem registar, 2008, coun. exec. com. mem., 2008—09, head OPD svcs., 2010—, assoc. med. supt., 2010, mem. adminstrv. com., 2010; mem. rsch. com. Inst. Review Bd., 2010. Dep. med. supt. Christian Med. Coll., Vellore, 1998—2002, head of child health unit III, 2001—; exec. bd. mem. Bapt. Hosp., Bangalore, Karnataka, India, 2001—03, Asha Kiran Hosp., Lamtaput, Orissa, India, 2003—05; mem. med. adv. com. Missionary Upholders Trust, 2006. Recipient Nat. Merit Scheme, Indian Govt., 1968, TCF Gold Medal In Paediatrics, Christian Med. Coll., Vellore, India, 1974, Somerwell Gold Medal In Surgery, Christian Med. Coll., Vellore, 1974. Mem.: Christian Acad. Med. Scis., Royal Coll. Physicians (diplomate 1986), Royal Coll. Physicians, Edinburgh (hon.), Indian Acad. Paediat. (life; pres. North Arcot br. 2003—06), Christian Med. Assn. India (life), Evang. Grad. Fellowship (life; treas. local br. 2000—03). Avocation: travel. Office: Child Health Dept CMC Ida Scudder Rd Tamil Nadu Vellore 632 004 India Home: 714B CMC Campus 632 002 Vellore TN India Office Fax: 0416-2232035/2232103. Personal E-mail: pdmoses@cmcvellore.ac.in. E-mail: child3@cmcvellore.ac.in. *

MOSESSO, VINCENT NICHOLAS, JR., emergency physician; b. Pitts., Pa., Sept. 28, 1957; s. Vincent Nicholas and Jean Lois Mosesso; m. Janet L. Mosesso, June 17, 1983; children: Jennifer Moss, Chadwick. BA, Duquesne U., Pitts., 1979; MD, U. of Pitts., 1988. Lic. emergency medicine Am. Bd. of Emergency Medicine. Assoc. prof. of emergency medicine U. of Pitts. Sch. of Medicine, 1991—. Asst. med. dir. dept. of pub. safety City of Pitts., 1993—; med. dir. prehospital care U. of Pitts. Med. Ctr., 1996—; mem. nat. BLS subcom. Am. Heart Assn., Emergency Cardiac Care Com., Dallas, 2001—08; med. dir. advanced med. life support Nat. Assn. of Emergency Med. Technicians, Clinton, Miss., 2002—. Mem. editl. bd.: med. jours. Prehospital Emergency Care, Reservation. Mem. Allegheny divsn. Am. Heart Assn., Pitts., 1998—2008; bd. dirs., med. dir. Sudden Cardiac Arrest Assn., Washington, 2005—. Named Emergency Physician of the Yr., Pa. Emergency Health Svcs. Coun., 1998; grantee, Medtrionic Found., 2000—02. Fellow: Am. Coll. of Emergency Medicine; mem.: Nat. Assn. of EMS Physicians (bd. dirs. 2003—05). Avocations: golf, travel, sports, exercise. Office: U Pitt Ste 911 230 McKee Pl Pittsburgh PA 15213 E-mail: mosessovn@upmc.edu.

MOSIER, HARRY DAVID, JR., physician, educator; b. Topeka, May 22, 1925; s. Harry David and Josephine Morrow (Johnson) M.; m. Nadine Oclea Merilatt, Aug. 24, 1949; children: Carolyn Josephine Mosier Pohlmeyer, William David, Daniel Thomas, Christine Elizabeth Mosier Mahoney; m. Marjorie Knight Armstrong, Sept. 26, 1963. BS magna cum laude, U. Notre Dame, 1948; MD, Johns Hopkins U., 1952. Diplomate Am. Bd. Pediatrics, Am. Bd. Pediatric Endocrinology. Intern Johns Hopkins Hosp., Balt., 1952-53; resident in pediat. Los Angeles Children's Hosp., 1953-54, resident pediatric pathology, 1954-55; fellow pediatric endocrinology Johns Hopkins U., 1955-57; asst. prof. pediat. UCLA, 1957-61, assoc. prof., 1961-63; dir. rsch. Ill. State Pediatric Inst., Chgo., 1963-67; assoc. prof. U. Ill., 1963-67; prof. pediat. U. Calif.-Irvine, 1967—2002, emeritus, 2002—, head divsn. pediat. endocrinology, 1967-2000; staff Children's Hosp. Med. Ctr., Long Beach, Calif., 1970—2005, U. Calif. Irvine Med. Ctr., Orange, 1979—; dist. cons. Med. Bd. Calif., 1995—2008. Contbr. articles to med. jours. With AUS, 1943-46, col. U.S. Army Med. Corps, 1990-91, Persian Gulf War. USAR Med. Corps. 1952-62, 83-93 (ret.).

MOSIER, WILLIAM ARTHUR, psychiatrist, psychotherapist, director, medical educator, researcher; b. Richmond, Calif., Oct. 21, 1946; s. William Nathaniel and Violet Olga (Luzum) M.; m. Virginia Rondero (div. Apr. 1992); children: Robert Carlos, Cristina Dominique; m. Gloria Sifuentes (div. 1998); 1 child, William Nathaniel; m. Gabriela Pickett; children: Gabriela, Diana. BA, Webster U., 1971, MA in Tchg., 1973; MD, U. Ctrl. del Este, Dominican Republic, 1986; EdD, U. So. Calif., 1987; BS with distinction, U. Okla., 1991; MPAS in Psychiatry, U. Nebr., 1997. Diplomate Am. Bd. Forensic Medicine, Am. Bd. Med. Psychotherapists, Am. Bd. Psychol. Specialties, lic. physician asst. Tex., Fla., N.Y., Va.; marraige and family therapist, chem. dependency counselor Tex.; marriage and family therapist Ohio. Tchr. St. Louis Pub. Schs., 1971—74; tchr., ctr. dir. Project Head Start, Vallejo, Calif., 1975—77; dir. rsch. Ctr. for Study of Child Devel., Sacramento, 1977—95; physician asst. U.S. Army, Ft. Hood/Ft. Sam Houston, Tex., 1989—91; assoc. prof. U. Mary Hardin-Baylor, Belton, Tex., 1991—92; psychotherapist pvt. practice, Tex., 1993—95; mem. adj. faculty dept. psychiatry Barry U., Miami Shores, Fla., 1997—2000; med. dir. Fla. Inst. Neuro Devel., Vero Beach, Fla., 1995—2000; clin. assoc. prof. psychiatry Nova Southeastern U., Ft. Lauderdale, Fla., 1997—99; asst. prof. medicine, assoc. dir. acad. curriculum George Washington U., 2000—01; assoc. prof. psychiatry Kettering Coll. med. Arts Kettering (Ohio) Med. Ctr., 2001—02, dir. physicians asst. program; child devel. cons., marriage and family therapist, 2001—; asst. prof., child devel. Wright State U., Dayton, Ohio, 2002—. Mem. test writing com. Nat. Assn. Cert. Physicians Assts., 1995—, Nat. Bd. Med. Examiners; bd. dir. Ohio State Counselor, Social Worker and Marriage and Family Therapist Regulatory Bd. Newspaper columnist:, mem. editl. adv. bd.: Advance for PAs; contbr. articles to profl. jours., chapters to books. Lt. col. USAF, 1967-68, Vietnam, maj. USAFR, 1987—. Decorated Bronze Star, Air medal. Fellow: APA (mem. adv. bd. 1997—, editl. adv. bd. Annals of Am. Psychotherapy Assn.), Am. Assn. Surg. PAS, Am. Acad. Physician Assts., Assn. Mil. Surgeons U.S. (life), Aerospace Med. Assn. (life), Am. Coll. Forensic Examners (life); mem.: Ohio Assn. Marriage and Family Therapy (bd. dir.), Am. Assn. Marriage and Family Therapy (del. regulatory bd. Ohio), Assn. of Psychiat. PAs (founding mem., pres.), Soc. PAs in the Addiction Medicine (exec. bd., pres.). Democrat. Mem. Soc. Of Friends. Avocations: musical composition, piano, guitar, swimming, yoga. E-mail: drwillmosier@yahoo.com.

MOSKOVICH, RONALD, surgeon; b. South Africa, Feb. 9, 1955; MD, U. Witwatersrand, Johannesburg, 1978. Assoc. chief, spine surgery NYU Hosp. Joint Diseases, 1990—. Fellow: Royal Coll. Surgeons; mem.: AMA, Assn. Bone and Joint Surgeons, North Am. Spine Soc., Cervical Spine Rsch. Soc., Scoliosis Rsch. Soc. Office: 301 East 17th St New York NY 10003 Office Fax: 212-598-6291. Business E-Mail: rmoskovich@nyumc.org.

MOSKOWITZ, CHAYA, research scientist; b. Feb. 31; BS, Rutgers U., 1994; PhD, U. Wash., 2002. Asst. mem. Meml. Sloan-Kettering Cancer Ctr., 2002—. Mem.: Soc. Clin. Trials, Am. Statis. Assn. Office: 307 E 63rd St New York NY 10065 Business E-Mail: moskowc1@mskcc.org.

MOSKOWITZ, JAY, health science association administrator, educator, dean; b. NYC, Jan. 9, 1943; s. Murray and Helene Moskowitz; m. Joanne Cathy Schindelheim, Dec. 27, 1970; children: Michael Bradley, Andrew Cory. BS, Queens Coll., 1964; postgrad., CUNY, 1965; PhD, Brown U., 1969. From research assoc. in pharmacology to dep. dir. NIH, Bethesda, Md., 1969—93, dep. dir. sci. policy and tech. transfer, prin. dep. dir., 1993; with Nat. Heart, Lung and Blood Inst., Bethesda, 1976—86; acting dir. Nat. Inst. Deafness and Other Comm. Disorders, Bethesda, 1988—90, dep. dir., 1993—95; sr. assoc. dean rsch. devel., prof. pub. health scis. Wake Forest U. Sch. Medicine, Winston-Salem, NC, 1995—2001, sr. assoc. dean, 1997—2001; assoc. v.p. health sci. rsch. Pa. State U., University Park, 2002—, vice dean rsch. coll. medicine, 2002—07, prof. medicine, 2002—07; chief sci. officer Milton Hershey Med. Ctr., Pa., 2004—07; pres., CEO Health Scis. SC, Columbia, 2007—; prof. medicine Med. U. SC, 2007—; prof. pub. health U. SC, 2007—; adj. prof. Clemson U. Contbr. articles to profl. jours. Served to lt. comdr. USPHS. Recipient Meritorious award William A. Jump Meml. Found., 1977, Dir.'s award NIH, 1978, Superior Svc. award USPHS, 1980, performance awards Sr. Exec. Svc., Presdl. Meritorious Exch. Rank award 1989, Disting. Svc. award HHS, 1991, Disting. Svc. award Nat. Inst. on Deafness and Other Comm. Disorders, 1994. Mem. AAAS, Soc. Exptl. Biology and Medicine, N.C. Inst. Medicine. Jewish. Home: 1760 Adeline Dr Mechanicsburg PA 17050 Office: 1320 Main St Ste 625 Columbia SC 29201 Office Phone: 803-576-5902. Business E-Mail: jmoskowitz@healthsciencesc.org, jmoskowitz@sc.edu.

MOSKOWITZ, RANDI ZUCKER, nurse; b. NYC, Oct. 19, 1948; d. Seymour and Gertrude (Levy) Zucker; m. Marc N. Moskowitz, July 11, 1976. RN, Jewish Hosp. and Med. Ctr., 1969; BA, Marymount Manhattan Coll., 1975; MS, Hunter Coll., 1979; MBA, Columbia U., 1990. Gen. staff nurse neurosurgery unit N.Y. Hosp., NYC, 1969—71, sr. staff nurse recovery rm., 1971—76, nurse coord. utilization rev., 1976—79; health educator Office of Cancer Commn. Meml. Sloan-Kettering Cancer Ctr., NYC, 1979—81; adminstrv. nurse oncologist Bklyn. Cmty. Hosp. and Meth. Hosp., 1981—83, grants coord. radiotherapy dept., 1983—86; adminstr. Ambulatory Oncology Ctr. Columbia-Presbyn. Med. Ctr., NYC, 1986—89; adminstr. Surg. Day Hosp., 1990—98; mgr. Oncology Svcs., St. Vincent Cath. Med. Ctrs., Jamaica, NY, 1999—2006; adminstr. pediat. oncology & rheumatology Columbia U. Med. Ctr., NYC, 2006—. Masters prof. oncology Columbia U. Sch. Nursing. Co-editor Oncology Nursing: Advances, Treatments and Trends into the Twenty-first Century; contbr. articles to profl. jours. Mem. N.Y. Assn. Ambulatory Care, Oncology Nursing Soc. (sec. N.Y.C. chpt. 1983-87, pres. 1988-89). Home: 446 E 86th St Apt 5F New York NY 10028-6474 Office: Columbia Univ Med Ctr 161 Ft Washington Ave New York NY 10032 Office Phone: 212-342-3455. Personal E-mail: rm2505@columbia.edu. *

MOSKOWITZ, ROLAND WALLACE, internist; b. Shamokin, Pa., Nov. 3, 1929; MD, Temple U., 1953. Intern Temple U. Hosp., Phila., 1953-54; fellow in internal medicine Mayo Clinic, Rochester, Minn., 1954-55, 57-60; mem. staff U. Hosps. Cleve.; prof. medicine Case Western Res. U. Sch. Medicine, Cleve. Mem.: ACR, Alpha Omega Alpha.

MOSKOWITZ, WILLIAM B., cardiologist; b. Bronx, NY, Feb. 23, 1954; s. Arthur and Helen R. Moskowitz; m. Gail Shookoff, May 30, 1993; children: Michael J., Holly M., Andrea D., Juliana R. BS, U. Ctrl. Fla., 1975; MD, U. South Fla., Tampa, 1978. Diplomate Am. Bd. Pediat., 1985, Am. Bd. Pediatric Cardiology. Prof. pediat. and internal medicine, vice chiar, dept pediat., dir. pediatric catheterization lab. Va. Commonwealth U. Health Scis., Richmond, Va., 1984—. Pediat. residency fellow Childrens Hosp. Phila., 1981—84. Fellow: Soc. Cardiac Angiography and Intervention, Am. Acad. Pediat. (pres. elect. Va. chpt. 2008—, pres. 2010—); mem.: Am. Coll. Cardiology. Office: Virginia Commonwealth U Health Scis PO Box 980543 Richmond VA 23298-0543 Office Fax: 804-828-8517. E-mail: wmoskowitz@mcvh-vcu.edu. *

MOSOW, JULIE WILEY, psychologist; b. Oct. 14, 1951; BA, U. Miss., Oxford, 1972; MEdn, Delta State U., Cleveland, Miss., 1973. Guidance counselor Trinity Episc. Sch., Natchez, Miss., 1973—76; Title IV coord. Forrest County Sch., Hattiesburg, Miss., 1976—83; sch. psychologist Hollandale Schs., Miss., 1987—2010, spl. edn. dir., 1987—2010; sch. psychometrist Greenville Pub. Schs., Miss., 2010—. Mem.: Miss. Assn. Psychology in Sch., Jr. Greenville Garden Club.

MOSS, ARTHUR JAY, physician; b. White Plains, NY, June 21, 1931; s. Abraham Loeb and Ida (Bank) M.; m. Joy Folkman, June 23, 1957; children: Katherine, Deborah, David. BA, Yale U., 1953; MD, Harvard U., 1957. Resident Mass. Gen. Hosp., 1957-58, 60-61; fellow in cardiology med. ctr. U. Rochester, NY, 1961-65, from asst. to assoc. prof. sch. medicine and dentistry, 1966-71, clin. assoc. prof., 1971-82, clin. prof., 1982-91, prof. medicine, 1991—, dir. heart rsch. follow-up program med. ctr., 1971—. Mem. cardiology adv. com. Nat. Heart, Lung, and Blood Inst., NIH, 1980-82, chmn., 1982-84, mem. epidemiology and disease control study sect., 1998—2008. Author: Antiarrhythmic Agents, 1973; editor: Clinical Aspects of Life-threatening Arrhythmias, 1984, QT Prolongation and Ventricular Arrhythmias, 1992, Noninvasive Electrocardiology, 1995; editor-in-chief Ann. Noninvasive Electrocardiology, 1996—; mem. editl. bd. Am. Jour. Cardiology, 1988—, Jour. Am. Coll. Cardiology, 1997-2001, 2005— Lt. USNR, 1958—60. Mem.: Assn. Am. Physicians, Alpha Omega Alpha. Home: 581 Claybourne Rd Rochester NY 14618-1224 Office: Univ Rochester Med Ctr PO Box 653 Rochester NY 14642-8653 Office Phone: 585-275-5391. Business E-Mail: heartajm@heart.rochester.edu.

MOSS, MARGARET, nutritionist, researcher; d. Charles and Joan Moss. BA with honors, Cambridge U., 1967, MA, 1971; diploma, Inst. for Optimum Nutrition, 1992. Cert. tchr. of the deaf Manchester U., 1979. Tchr., headmistress Govt. of Kenya, 1967—78; tchr., dep. headmistress Zimbabwe, 1982—90; dir. Nutrition and Allergy Clinic, Stockport, Cheshire, England, 1992—. Lectr. in field. Contbr. articles to profl. jours. Mem.: Soc. Biology (chartered biologist), Brit. Soc. for Ecol. Medicine, Brit. Assn. Applied Nutrition and Nutritional Therapy. Home: 11 Mauldeth Close Stockport Cheshire SK4 3NP England Office: Nutrition and Allergy Clinic 11 Mauldeth Close Stockport Cheshire SK4 3NP England Business E-Mail: margaret@nutritionandallergyclinic.co.uk.

MOSSAD, EMAD B., anesthesiologist, director; b. Egypt, Sept. 15, 1960; MBBCh, MD, Cairo U., 1984. Dir. pediat. cardiac anesthesia Baylor Coll. Medicine, 2008—. Sec. treas. Congenitla Cardiac Anesthesia Soc., 2005. Mem.: Soc. Pediat. Anesthesia. Office: 6621 Fannin St W17417 Houston TX 77030 Office Fax: 832-825-1903. Business E-Mail: ebmossad@texaschildrens.org.

MOSSERI, MORRIS, cardiologist, educator; b. Cairo, Dec. 3, 1951; s. Raymond Nissim and Nelli Mosseri; m. Sarah Flaks; children: Aviram, Elinor Briskin, Lilac. MD, Hebrew U. Hadassah Med. Sch., Jerusalem, 1975. Lic. Bd. Registration Medicine, Israel, 1976, in practice cardiology Bd. Cert. Cardiology, Israel, 1987, cert. asst. prof. medicine Tufts U. Med. Sch., Boston, 1990, lic. in practice medicine Bd. Registration Medicine, Boston, 1991, diplomate cCardiologist European Soc. Cardiology, 2006. Co-dir. catheterization and cardiology inpatient units Hadassah Med. Ctr., Jerusalem, 1987—2006; rsch. assoc. St. Elizabeth's Hosp., Boston, 1989—91, Wash. Hosp. Ctr., Washington, 1998—98; sr. lectr. internal medicine, cardiology Hebrew U. Hadassah Med. Sch., Jerusalem, 1992, assoc. prof., 1999, head internal medicine sect., 2000—03; assoc. prof. cardiology Tel-Aviv U., 2009; dir. interventional cardiology Hadassah Hebrew U. Med. Ctr., Jerusalem, 2000—06, dir. excellence ctr. vascular diseases, 2006—06; head cardiology divsn. Meir Med. Ctr., Kfar-Sava, Israel, 2006—. Jour. editor Israel Heart Soc., 1997—2003, chmn. israeli working group, 2005—09; coun. mem. Nat. Coun. Diabetes Mellitus, Israel, 2003—. Contbr. articles to profl. jours. Maj. Israeli Def. Forces, 1977—81, Israel. Recipient Rsch. award, Israel Heart Soc., 1989, Elizabeth Greibach Cardiology Rsch. award, Keren Kayemet Le-Israel, 1993, Faculty award, Hebrew U. Hadassah Med. Sch., 2002, Internat. Anesthesia Rsch. award, 2006—08; grantee, Chief Scientist, Ministry Health in Israel, 1995—99. Fellow: European Assn. Percutaneous Cardiovasc. Interventions, European Soc. Cardiology; mem.: Israel Heart Soc. Achievements include patents for stereotactic radiotreatment and prevention of restenosis; patents pending for a novel method for navigating in the coronary arteries during diagnostic and therapeutic heart catheterization. Home: 1 Streichman St Tel-Aviv 69671 Israel Office: Meir Med Ctr Cardiology Divsn 59 Tshernichovsky St Kfar-Sava 44281 Israel Office Fax: (972) -9-7410704. Personal E-mail: mosseri@cc.huji.ac.il. Business E-Mail: morris.mosseri@clalit.org.il.

MÖSSNER, JOACHIM, internist, gastroenterologist; b. Würzburg, Bavaria, Federal Republic of Germany, Nov. 17, 1950; s. Franz Emil and Ursula Amalie (Gunder) M.; children: Lone Dorothea, Flora Eleonore. Student, U. Würzburg, Fed. Republic Germany, 1970-76, MD, 1978, Habilitation, 1987. Intern Dept. of Surgery, Tauberbischofsheim, Fed. Republic Germany, 1977, Medizinische Poliklinik, U. Würburg, 1978; resident Med. Poliklinik U. Würburg, 1978—82, 1985—93, chief gastroenterology unit Med. Poliklinik, 1983—85; chief dept. internal medicine, gastroenterology U. Leipzig, 1993—, dean med. faculty, 1997—2002. Prof. medicine U. Wurzburg, 1989—; rsch. assoc. Dept. Physiology U. Calif., San Francisco, 1993—. Mem. editl. bd. Pancreatology, German Jour. Gastroenterology, Med. Klinik, Chir. Gastroent. Grantee Deutsche Forschungsgemeinschaft, 1982—. Mem. German Soc. Internal Medicine, Am. Soc. Gastroenterology, German Soc. Gastroenterology, Internat. Soc. Pancreatology, Deutsche Akademic der Naturforscher/Leopoldina, European Pancreatic Club. Office: Univ Leipzig Medizinische Klinik Dept Gastroenterology & Rheumatology Liebig Str 18 04103 Leipzig Germany Office Phone: 0049 341 9712200. Office Fax: 9712209. Business E-Mail: moej@medizin.uni-leipzig.de.

MOSS-SALENTIJN, LETTY (ALEIDA), anatomist, educator; b. Amsterdam, The Netherlands, Apr. 14, 1943; arrived in U.S., 1968; d. Ewoud and Johanna Maria (Schoonhoven) Salentijn; m. Melvin Lionel Moss, Apr. 17, 1970. DDS, State U. Utrecht, Netherlands, 1967, PhD, 1976. Asst. prof. histology State U. Utrecht, 1967-68; asst. prof. Columbia U., NYC, 1968-74, assoc. prof., 1974-86, prof., 1986—, Edwin S. Robinson prof., 1999—, dir. dental radiology, 1980-86, dir. grad. program dental sci., 1986—, dir. postdoctoral affairs, 1987-90, asst. dean postdoctoral programs, 1990-94, assoc. dean acad. affairs, 1994—2005, sr. assoc. dean, acad. affairs, 2005—10, vice dean, acad. affairs, 2010—. Author: Orofacial Histology & Embryology, 1972; Dental and Oral Tissues, 1980, 2d edit., 1984, 3d edit., 1990; contbr. chpts. to books, articles to profl. jours. Fellow Royal Microscopical Soc., Am. Coll. Dentists, NY Acad. Dentistry; mem. Am. Assn. Anatomists, Internat. Assn. Dental Rsch., Am. Soc. Biomechs., Sigma Xi (chpt. sec. 1980-87, pres. 1987-89, 98-99), Omicron Kappa Upsilon (pres. local chpt. 1987, 2009). Avocation: stained glass art. Home: 560 Riverside Dr Apt 20K New York NY 10027-3239 Office: Columbia University Coll Dental Medicine Vice Dean Acad Affairs 630 W 168th St New York NY 10032-3702 Office Phone: 212-305-8334. Business E-Mail: lm23@columbia.edu.

MOSTAFA, MOSTAFA IBRAHIM, dental educator; b. Giza, Egypt, July 3, 1966; B in Dental Sci., Cairo U., 1988, DDS, 1995. Prof. oro-dental genetics Nat. Rsch. Ctr., 2011—. Cons. oral medicine and oral radiology Nat. Rsch. Ctr., 1995. Recipient Encouragement award, Nat. Rsch. Ctr. Mem.: Nat. Soc. Human Genetics, Internat. Assn. Dental Rsch., European Soc. Human Genetics. Avocations: football, swimming, photography, poetry. Office: 33 Tahreer Cairo 12311 Egypt Personal E-mail: mostafanrc@yahoo.com.

MOSTAFAVI ABDOLMALEKY, HAMID, psychiatrist, researcher; b. Behshahr, Mazandaran, Iran, Apr. 9, 1956; arrived in US, 2001, arrived in Canada, 2005; s. Hossein Mostafavi Abdolmaleky and Massomeh Motamedi Nassab; m. Batol Aleali, Sept. 14, 1984; children: Sahar, Saba, Siavash. MD, Iran Nat. U., Tehran, 1982; specialist in Psychiatry, Iran U. Med. Sci., Tehran, 1988. Asst. prof. psychiatry Kermanshah U. Med. Scis., Kermanshah, Bakhtaran, Iran, 1988—92, Iran U. Med. Scis., Tehran, 1992—; postdoctoral rsch. fellowship Harvard Med. Sch., Boston, 2001—07. Dir. Farabi Mental Hosp., Kermanshah, Bakhtaran, Iran, 1989—92; dir. edn. Esmaeli Mental Hosp., Tehran, 1994—2000. Contbr. articles to profl. jours. Fellow, Harvard U., 2001—07, Harvard Med. Sch., Boston, 2001—07. Mem.: Collegium Internationale Neuro-Psycho-Pharmacologicum, Epigenetics Soc., Internat. Soc. Psychiat. Genetics, Iranian Med. Coun. Achievements include patents pending for treatment of psychiatric disorders using entacapone, tolcapone and other COMT inhibitor drugs. Office: Harvard Med Sch Lab Nutrition 330 Brookline Ave BIDMC Dana Bldg Rm 838 Boston MA 02215 Personal E-mail: hamostafavi@yahoo.com, hamostafavi@gmail.com.

MOSTASHARI, FARZAD, federal official; b. Sept. 27, 1968; AB in Biochemistry, Harvard U., 1989; MS in Population Health, Harvard U. Sch. Pub. Health, 1991; MD, Yale U. Sch. Medicine, 1996. Diplomate American Bd. Internal Medicine. Resident internal medicine Mass. Gen. Hosp., Boston, 1996—98; officer Epidemic Intelligence Svc., Centers Disease Control & Prevention, 1998—2000; founder Bur. Epidemiology Services, chair Primary Care Info. Task Force, asst. commr. NYC Dept. Health & Mental Hygiene; dep. nat. coord. for programs & policy US Dept. Health & Human Services, Washington, 2009—11, nat. coord. for health info. tech., 2011—. Office: US Department of Health and Human Services 200 Independence Ave SW Washington DC 20201 Office Phone: 202-690-7151. *

MOSTILLO, RALPH, medical association administrator; s. Joseph and Antoinette Mostillo. BA in Chemistry magna cum laude, Rutgers U., Newark, 1972; MA in Biochemistry, Princeton U., NJ, 1974, PhD in Biochemistry, 1978. Rsch. fellow Princeton U., 1972-78; sr. scientist drug regulatory affairs Hoffmann-La Roche, Inc., Nutley, NJ, 1979-85; founder, chmn., CEO Am. Cancer Assn., Nutley, 1986—. With USN, 1962—66, Vietnam. Fellow, NIH, 1972—78. Mem.. NY Acad. Scis., Am. Mktg. Assn., Am. Mgmt. Assn., Am. Chem. Soc., Vietnam Vets. Am., Am. Legion, Phi Beta Kappa, Sigma Xi. Achievements include research in molecular transport systems in E. coli as general models for drug delivery into cells. Home: PO Box 505 Nutley NJ 07110-0505 Office: Am Cancer Assn PO Box 87 Nutley NJ 07110-0087

MOSZCZYNSKI, PAULIN, hematologist; b. Janów Lubelski, Lublin, Poland, Jan. 3, 1936; s. Paulin and Bronislawa (Malawska) M.; m. Maria Leokadia Otto, Feb. 11, 1961; children: Paulin, Anna. Degree, U. Med. Sch., Cracow, Poland, 1960, MD, 1968; postgrad., Med. Postgrad. Ctr., Warsaw, Poland, 1975; degree (hon.), State Med. U., Odessa, Ukraine, 1997. Asst. dept. med. physics U. Med. Sch., Cracow, 1960—63; registrar dept. medicine L. Rydygier Hosp., Brzesko, Poland, 1963—76, cons. hematology, 1975—, chief med. outpatient clinic, 1975—, head dept. medicine, 1976—2008; lectr. Open Tech. U., Cracow, 1995—. Vice dir. Health Care Complex, Brzesko, 1975-78; head Province Immunol. Lab., Brzesko, 1978—2008; cons. immunologist L. Rydygier Hosp., 1978—2008; pres. Internat. Inst. Universalistic Medicine, Tarnów, Poland, 1996-03, lectr., Malopolska U., Brzesko, Poland, 2008-. Co-author: (textbook) Industrial Hematology; contbr. over 900 articles to profl. jours. and over 800 popular sci. articles to various mags. Chmn. Internat. Fair of Health Life and Food, Tarnów, 1992-95. Recipient 2d prize Ministry of Health and Social Welfare, Poland, 1989, Chivalry and Officer Cross of Order of Rebirth of Poland, 1992, 99, Individual prize Ministry of Health and Social Welfare, 1995, Golden medal Albert Schweitzer World Acad. Medicine, 1996, 99. Mem.: Internal Medicine Hematology Soc. (internal medicine/hematology 2001—03), N.Y. Acad. Scis., Polish Acad. Medicine (Golden medal 1996), Polish Soc. of Health Life and Food Promotion (physicians' coun. 1992—, Golden medal 1995), Polish Med. Assn. (Gloria Medicinae medal 1994). Roman Catholic. Achievements include research in immunohematology; influence of mercury and organic solvents on human immune systems, influence of nutrition and eatables on population health. Avocations: theater, tennis, travel. Office: Malopolska University Brzesko Krolowej Jadwigi 18 Brzesko 32-800 Poland Home: Ul. Wyzwolenia 7 32-800 Brzesko Poland Office: Malopolska University Krolowej Jaolwigi 18 Brzesko 32 800 Poland Office Phone: 48146210556, 48146633135. Business E-Mail: paauulin@wp.pl.

MOSZKOWSKI, NEAL, investment company executive; BA in Economics & History magna cum laude with honors, Amherst Coll., 1988; MBA, Stanford U., 1993. V.p., exec. dir., prin. investment Goldman Sachs & Co., 1993—98; co-head, mng. dir. Soros Fund Mgmt., LLC, 1998, Soros Pvt. Equity Ptnrs., LLC, 1998—2002; chmn. Soros Pvt.e Equity Ptnrs., LLC, 2002—05; co-CEO TowerBrook Capital Partners LP, 2005—; chmn. WellCare Health Plans Inc., 2002—06; bd. dirs. WellCare Health Plans, Inc., 2006—. Bd. dirs. Bluefly, Inc., Day Internat Group, Inc., Jet Blue Airways Corp., Integra LifeSciences Holding Corp., 1999—2005, 2006—. Office: TowerBrook Capital Partners LP 430 Park Ave New York NY 10022 Office Phone: 212-699-2290. Office Fax: 718-398-2649. *

MOTA, LUIZ ALBERTO ALVES, otolaryngologist, educator; b. João Pessoa, Paraíba, Brazil, Nov. 10, 1959; MD, U. Fed. Pernambuco, 1984, MS, 2003. Prof. otorhinolaryngology U. Pernambuco, 1989—2011, regent otorhinolaryngology, 2011; head otorhinolaryngology svc. Hosp. Oswaldo Cruz U. Hosp., 2011—. Reviewer Jour. Associação Médica Brasileira, 2010—. Mem.: Brazilian Assn. Otorhinolaryngology and Cervico-Facial Surgery. Avocations: exercise, movies, travel. Office: Venezuela 182 Espinheiro Recife Pernambuco 52020170 Brazil Office Fax: 558132227060. E-mail: luizmota10@hotmail.com.

MOTAMED, THOMAS FIROUZ, insurance company executive; BA in Biology, Adelphi U., Garden City, NY, 1971; JD, Widener U., 1975. Sci. faculty Malvern Prep. Sch., Pa., 1975-76; field underwriter NY Life, Carle Place, NY, 1976-77; claims trainee The Chubb Corp., LI, 1977—78, claims unit mgr., 1978—80, NY br. office mgr., 1980—81, litig. mgr. claims dept. Short Hills, NJ, 1981—83, nat. claim audit mgr. Warren, NJ, 1983—84, nat. claim adminstr., 1984—86, claim mgr. NYC, 1986—88, adminstrv. mgr., 1988—89, LI mktg. mgr., 1989—90, br. mgr. Westchester, NY, 1990—93, midtown NY br. mgr., 1993—96, western zone officer, 1996—97, exec. v.p., COO Warren, NJ, 1997—2002, vice chmn., COO, 2002—08; pres., COO, mng. dir. Chubb & Son Inc. divsn. of Fed. Ins. Co., Warren, NJ; chmn., CEO CNA Fin. Corp., Chgo., 2009—. Office: CNA Fin Corp 333 S Wabash Chicago IL 60604 *

MOTCHAN, DENNIS GLENN, physician; b. St. Louis, Apr. 6, 1950; s. Harold Lloyd and Radine (Goldman) Motchan; m. Nancy Helene Shulman, Jan. 26, 1975; children: Randall Kenneth, Katherine Rae. BS, Northwestern U., Evanston, Ill., 1972, MD, 1974. Diplomate Am. Bd. Internal Medicine. Intern St. John's Mercy Med. Ctr., Creve Coeur, Mo., 1974-75, resident in internal medicine, 1975-77, chief resident in internal medicine, 1977-78, attending physician, instr. internal medicine, 1978—; practice medicine specializing in internal medicine Northway Internists, Inc., Bridgeton, Mo., 1978—2005; pvt. practice specializing in occupl. medicine, 2006—. Mem. AMA. Office: Concentra Med Ctr 8340 N Broadway Saint Louis MO 63147 Office Phone: 314-385-9563. Business E-Mail: dennis_motchan@concentra.com. *

MOTHKUR, SRIDHAR RAO, radiologist; b. Mothkur, India, Oct. 5, 1950; arrived in U.S., 1975, naturalized; s. Venkat Rao and Laxmi Bai (Gundepally) Mothkur; m. Sheila Rama Rao Paga, Nov. 30, 1973; children: Swathi, Preethi, Venkat Krishna. Student, Coll. Arts and Sci. Osmania U., Hyderabad, India, 1966; MB, BS, Osmania U., Hyderabad, India, 1972, DPH, 1974; MPA, Ind. U. N.W., 2000. Diplomate Am. Bd. Radiology. Rotating intern Osmania Gen. Hosp., Hyderabad, 1972-73, internal medicine intern, 1973, resident in surgery, 1974-75; resident Resurrection Hosp., Chgo., 1975-76; resident in radiology Luth. Gen. Hosp., Park Ridge, Ill., 1976-79, chief resident radiology, 1978-79; with rotations in nuclear medicine, angiography and neuroradiology Rush-Presbyn. St. Luke's Med. Ctr., Chgo., 1978; chmn. and med. dir. dept. radiology Louise Burg Hosp., Chgo., 1979-85, Shriner's Hosp., Chgo., 1986-88; fellow in ultrasound and computered tomography U. Ill., Chgo., 1988-89, fellow in magnetic resonance imaging, 1988-89; staff radiologist St. Anthony Hosp., Michigan City, Ind., 1989—, med. dir. MRI Ctr., 1989—; pvt. practice, Michigan City, 1989—; staff radiologist Kingwood Hosp., Michigan City, 1989-94, Charter Hosp., Behavioral Health Sys. Ind., Michigan City, 1994-96; pres. Michigan City Radiologists, Inc., Michigan City, 1998—2003; med. dir. dept. diagnostic imaging St. Anthony Meml. Med. Ctr., Michigan City, 2004—. Cons., radiologist Med. Group Michigan City, 1989—98, Franklin Clin. and Med. Watch, Michigan City, 1989—; spl. staff radiologist Christ hosp. Med. Ctr., Oak Lawn, Ill., 1988—89, Jasper County Meml. Hosp., Rensselaer, Ind., 1994—, United Diagnostic Svcs., Westchester, Ill., 1979—2000; dir. MRI Ctr. Meml. Hosp., 1989—97; med. dir. interventional radiology St. Anthony and Meml. Hosp., Michigan City, 1989—93; clin. asst. prof. radiology U. Ill., Chgo., 1990—2004; cons. radiologist Health Partners Medical Group, St. Francis, 2004—; others in field. Mem. Chinmaya Mission, Vishva Hindu Parishad. Fellow: Internat. Coll. Angiology, Am. Coll. Angiology, Am. Coll. Internat. Physicians; mem.: AMA, AmAm. Assn. Therapeutic and Interventional Neuroradiology, La Porte County Med. Soc., Telugu Assn. Greater Chgo., Chgo. Med. Soc., Ind. Med. Soc., Ill. Med. Soc., Ind. Assn. Physicians Indian Origin, India Med. Assn. N.W. Ind. (bd. dirs. 1999—2001), Am. Assn. Radiologists Indian Origins, Ind. Interventional Radiol. Assn., Tristate Telugu Assn., Indian Radiol. and Imaging Assn., Ind. Assn. Physicians from India, Soc. Magnetic Resonance in Medicine, Soc. Cardiovascular and Interventional Radiology, Soc. Magnetic Resonance Imaging, Am. Coll. Healthcare Execs., Am. Telugu Assn., Am. Soc. Head and Neck Radiology, Am. Coll. Emergency Physicians, Am. Diabetes Assn., Am. Assn. Physicians of Indian Origin, Am. Roentgen Ray Soc., Telugu Assn., Radiol. Soc. N.Am., Am. Assn. Andhra Brahmins, Internat. Soc. Krishna Consciousness, Pi Alpha Alpha. Republican. Home: 1481 Nelson Dr Chesterton IN 46304-3393 Office: Michigan City Radiologists Inc 8865 W 400 N Ste 115 Michigan City IN 46360-9223 Office Phone: 219-872-7268.

MOTOHIRO, KIYOSAWA, ophthalmologist, educator; b. Nagano, Nov. 28, 1953; MD, Tohoku U., 1978, PhD in Med. Sci., 1984. Assoc. prof. Tokyo Med. and Dental U., 1992—2006, clin. prof., 2006; chief Kiyosawa Eye Clinic, 2006. Rsch. fellow CEA, France, 1984—85; clin. fellow Wills Eye Hosp., Jefferson U., Phila., 1985—86. Master: Japanese Assn. Neuroophthalmology; mem.: Asian Soc. Neuroophthalmology, Am. Acad. Ophthalmology, Japanese Ophthalmology Soc. Avocation: writing. Office: Shinsuna 3 Tyoume 3-53 Koto Tokyo 136-0075 Japan Office Fax: 81-3-5677-3929. E-mail: nra12337@nifty.com.

MOTOHIRO, SAWATSUBASHI, otolaryngologist, educator; b. Miyazaki, Japan, Dec. 10, 1968; MD, Saga Med. Sch., 1993, PhD, 1998. Asst. prof. Saga Med. Sch., 1999—2003, Kyushu U., 2009—; vis. fellow Sahlgrenska U. Hosp., 2002—03; head, otolaryngology ENT Surgery Ctr., Oda Hosp., 2003—09. Mem.: Japanese Broncho-Esophagological Soc., Oto-Rhino-Laryngological Soc. Japan. Office: Dept Otolaryngology Kyushu University Fukuoka 812-8582 Japan Office Fax: 81-92-642-5685. Business E-Mail: motohiro@qent.med.kyushu-u.ac.jp.

MOTSITSI, NKOSANA SILAS, orthopedist; children: Puleng Nokwanda, Nkosana Silas Jr. MB ChB, Med. U. South Africa, Pretoria, Gauteng, 1988, MMed in Orthop. Surgery, 1994. Diploma in med. tech. HPCSA, 1983, cert. assoc. surgeon Coll. Surgeons East, Ctrl. and Southern Africa, 2005. Cons. orthop. trauma Med. U. South Africa, 1995, fellow spine surgery, 1995; cons. orthop. surgeon Sebokeng Hosp., Vereeniging, Gauteng, 1996—2002; prin. specialist

U. Pretoria, 2002—03, head dept., 2004—. Contbr. articles to profl. publs. Fellow, Coll. Surgeon Assn. East Africa, 2005. Mem.: Ao Alumni, Ao Spine. Office Fax: +2712 373 9031. Business E-Mail: silas.motsitsi@up.ac.za.

MOTSWALEDI, MOJAKGOMO HENDRICK, dermatologist, department chairman; b. Polokwane, Limpopo, South Africa, June 23, 1966; MBChB, 1992, M Medicine in Dermatology, 2001. Cert. med. specialist Health Professions Coun. South Africa, 2001. Fellow Coll. Medicine South Africa, South Africa, 2002; jr. specialist, lectr. U. Limpopo Medunsa Campus, Pretoria, Gauteng, South Africa, 2001—02, sr. specialist, lectr., 2002—04, prin. specialist, acting head dept. dermatology, 2004—. Editl. bd. mem. Internat. Jour. Dermatology. Contbr. articles to profl. jours. Home: 27 Ancrohof Orange St Orchards Pretoria 0001 South Africa Office: U Limpopo Medunsa Campus PO Box 1911 Medunsa 0204 South Africa Home Phone: 0824644703; Office Phone: 0125214001. Office Fax: 27125213266. Business E-Mail: motswaledi1@webmail.co.za.

MOTTER, BRAD, medical researcher; b. Ohio, 1950; BA, Wittenberg U., 1972; PhD, UCLA, 1977. Rsch. health scientist Veterans Affairs Med. Ctr., Syracuse, NY, 1986—. Bd. dirs. Ctrl. NY Rsch. Corp., 2001. Mem.: Soc. Neurosci. Office: Veterans Affairs Med Ctr 800 Irving Ave Syracuse NY 13210 Business E-Mail: brad.motter@va.gov.

MOTTO, JEROME ARTHUR, psychiatrist, educator; b. Kansas City, Mo., Oct. 16, 1921; MD, U. Calif., San Francisco, 1951. Diplomate Am. Bd. Neurology and Psychiatry. Intern San Francisco Gen. Hosp., 1951-52; resident Johns Hopkins Hosp., Balt., 1952-55; sr. resident U. Calif., San Francisco, 1955-56; from instr. to prof. U. Calif. Sch. Medicine, San Francisco, 1956—91, prof. emeritus, 1991—. Pres. Am. Assn. Suicidology, 1972—73; sec. gen. Internat. Assn. Suicide Prevention, 1973—77. Contbr. articles to profl. jours. With AUS, 1942-46, ETO. Recipient Outstanding Achievement award, Northern Calif. Psychiatric Soc., 2009, Marcia Linehan award, Am. Assn. Suicidology, 2009. Fellow: Am. Psychiatric Assn. (life; disting. fellow).

MOTULSKY, ARNO GUNTHER, internist, geneticist, educator; b. Fischhausen, Germany, July 5, 1923; arrived in U.S., 1941; s. Herman and Rena (Sass) Molton; m. Gretel C. Stern, Mar. 22, 1945; children: Judy, Harvey, Arlene. Student, Cen. YMCA Coll., Chgo., 1941—43, Yale U., 1943—44; BS, U. Ill., 1945, MD, 1947, DSc (hon.), 1982, MD (hon.), 1991. Diplomate Am. Bd. Internal Medicine, Am. Bd. Med. Genetics. Intern, fellow, resident Michael Reese Hosp., Chgo., 1947—51; staff mem. charge clin. investigation dept. hematology Army Med. Service Grad. Sch., Walter Reed Army Med. Ctr., Washington, 1952—53; research assoc. internal medicine George Washington U. Sch. Medicine, 1952—53; from instr. to assoc. prof. dept. medicine U. Wash. Sch. Medicine, Seattle, 1953—61, prof. medicine, prof. genetics, 1961—; head div. med. genetics, dir. genetics clinic Univ. Hosp., Seattle, 1959—89; dir. Ctr. for Inherited Diseases, Seattle, 1972—90. Attending physician Univ. Hosp., Seattle; cons. Pres.'s Commn. for Study of Ethical Problems in Medicine and Biomed. and Behavioral Rsch., 1979—83; cons. various coms. NRC, NIH, WHO, and others. Editor: Am. Jour. Human Genetics, 1969—75, Human Genetics, 1969—97. Fellow Commonwealth Fund in human genetics, Univ. Coll., London, 1957—58, Ctr. Advanced Study in Behavioral Scis., Stanford U., 1976—77, Inst. Advanced Study, Berlin, 1984; scholar John and Mary Markle in med. sci., 1957—62. Fellow: AAAS, ACP; mem.: NAS, Am. Philos. Soc., Am. Acad. Arts and Scis., Inst. of Medicine, Am. Assn. Physicians, Am. Soc. Clin. Investigation, Am. Soc. Human Genetics, Western Soc. Clin. Rsch., Genetics Soc. Am., Am. Fedn. Clin. Rsch., Internat. Soc. Hematology. Office: Univ Wash Medicine and Genome Scis PO Box 355065 Seattle WA 98195-5065 Business E-Mail: agmot@u.washington.edu.

MOU, THOMAS WILLIAM, retired physician, medical educator, consultant; b. Phila., May 17, 1920; s. Thomas Simonsen and Ellen Marie (Mathiesen) Mou; m. Marie Elizabeth Hartmann, Dec. 29, 1945 (div. Oct. 1976); m. Delma Jane Schreiber, Nov. 11, 1976. BSc in Bacteriology, Phila. Coll. Pharm & Sci., 1941; MD, U. Rochester, 1950. Diplomate Nat. Bd. Med. Examiners. Instr. medicine and bacteriology Sch. Medicine U. Rochester, NY, 1954-56; from asst. prof. preventive medicine to prof. cmty. medicine SUNY, Syracuse, 1956-70, from exec. dean to assoc chancellor health sci. Ctrl. Adminstrn. Albany, 1970-77; dean clin. campus W. Va. U., Charleston, 1977-85, dean emeritus Med. Ctr. Morgantown, 1986—; pres. Ednl. Commn. Fgn. Med. Grads., Phila., 1986-88; geriatric practice Adult Medicine Specialists, Pueblo, Colo., 1990-2000, ret. Cons. Carnegie Commn. Advancement Tchg., Princeton, NJ, 1987—88, Charles A. Dana Found., NYC, 1988, Geriatric Pharmacy Inst., Phila. Coll. Pharmacy and Sci., 1988. Contbr. articles to profl. jours. Trustee Phila. Coll. Pharmacy and Sci., 1972—81. Capt. Sanitary Corps US Army, 1941—45. Recipient Alumnus award, Phila. Coll. Pharmacy and Sci., 1975, award of distinction and honor, Ben Franklin Soc. SUNY, 1975, Koch medal, Am. Optometric Soc., 1976; named T. W. Mou Endowment Lectureship in his honor, W.Va. U., 1985—. Fellow: ACP, Infectious Diseases Soc. Am. (founding fellow), Phila. Coll. Physicians, Am. Coll. Preventive Medicine. Avocations: violin, travel. Home: 3050 Valleybrook Ln Colorado Springs CO 80904-1154 Personal E-mail: moutw@comcast.net.

MOUGHAN, PAUL J., nutritionist, educator; s. Frank John and Kathleen Morva Moughan; m. Meredith Ann Harvey, May 15, 1982; children: Michael Francis, Stella Jane, Jane Esme. B in Agrl. Sci. with honors, Massey U., 1978, PhD, 1984, DSc, 1996. Acad. faculty Massey U., Palmerston North, New Zealand, 1985—90, prof., dir., 1990—, Disting. prof., 2005—. Dir. Gardiner Found., Melbourne, Australia, 2001—. Contbr. scientific papers. Fellowship, Royal Soc. of New Zealand, Wellington, 1997, Royal Soc. Chemistry, Cambridge, 2011. Office: Massey University Riddet Inst Palmerston North New Zealand E-mail: p.j.moughan@massey.ac.nz.

MOULANA, ABDULRAHEEM, nephrologist; b. Hyderabad, India, Oct. 2, 1946; arrived in Saudi Arabia, 1975; s. Mohammed Bhikku and Kulsum Mohammed Moulana; m. Arifunnisa Abdulaleem Hyder, Apr. 1972; children: Arjumand, Ashraf, Amena, Hanan. MB BS, Osmania Med. Coll., Hyderabad, 1972, MS in Gen. Surgery, 1976; DM in Nephrology, U. Vienna, Austria, 1986. Registered med. practitioner Gen. Med. Coun.-U.K., Indian Med. Coun. Resident nephrology King Abdul Aziz Hosp., Makkah, Saudi Arabia, 1975-85, nephrologist, 1986-90, head nephrology, 1990—2009, cons. nephrologist, 1990—; resident nephrology 1st U. Med. Clinic, Vienna, 1985-86. Head Kidney Ctr., Makkah, 1990—2009, consulting nephrologist Al-Birr Charitable Soc. Makkah, 2010, Al-Birr Charitable Dialysis Ctrs., Makkah, 2011-. Translator: Divya Quran Sandesham, Into Telugu Hadees Translated, (in Telegu) Mishkat al-Masabih; contbr. articles to profl. jours. Mem.: Saudi Soc. Nephrology, Arab Soc. Dialysis and Transplant, Internat. Soc. Nephrology, European Dialysis and Transplant Soc. (assoc.). Achievements include development of database patient management programs; writing of Arabic-Telugu Dictionary, first of its kind in the market. Avocation: computers. Office: Al-Birr Charitable Soc Zahir Makkah Saudi Arabia Home: Po Box 2043 Makkah Saudi Arabia Office Phone: 966503529194. Personal E-mail: telquran_1@yahoo.com.

MOUNT, GRAHAM JAUNAY, retired dentist, researcher; b. Adelaide, Australia, Dec. 19, 1924; s. Horace Stanley Mount and Gladys Hilda Jaunay; m. Margaret Wilson Jones, Nov. 11, 1949; children: Jeffrey Douglas, Nicholas John, Alexander James, Marianne Elizabeth. B in Dental Surgery, U. Sydney, 1945; D in Dental sci., U. Adelaide, South Australia, 2003. Lectr. crown and bridge Dental Sch., U. of Adelaide (Australia), 1960—80, vis. rsch. fellow, 1980—. Regent Acad. of Dentistry Internat., Adelaide, Australia, 1988—2003. Author: (textbook) An Atlas of Glass-ionomer Cements, Preservation and Restoration of Tooth Structure. Recipient Mem. of the Order of Australia, Queen of Eng., 1988, Hillenbrand award, Acad. of Dentistry Internat., 1994, Medaille de la Ville de Paris, 2000. Mem.: Australian Dental Assn. (life Disting. Svc. award 1984, Meritorius Svc. award 1988). Achievements include research in Development of glass-ionomer cements. Avocations: reading, gardening, travel, caravaning. Home: 13 MacKinnon Parade South Australia North Adelaide 5006 Australia Personal E-mail: gjmount@ozemail.com.au.

MOUNTAIN, DEIDRA JILL HOPKINS, medical educator, researcher; b. Morristown, Tenn., Sept. 10, 1979; BA, Carson-Newman Coll., 2001; PhD, Quillen Coll. Medicine, 2006. Postdoc. rsch. assoc. Vascular Rsch. Lab., U. Tenn. Grad. Sch. Medicine, Knoxville, 2007—08, asst. sci. dir., 2010—; asst. prof., dept. surgery U. Tenn. Grad. Sch. Medicine, 2008—. Nat. Scientist Devel. grant, Am. Heart Assn., Seed grant, Physicians Med. Edn. and Rsch. Found. Mem.: AAAS, Am. Heart Assn. Avocations: travel, cooking. Office: University Tenn Grad Sch Medicine 1924 Alcoa Hwy Box U-11 Knoxville TN 37920 Business E-Mail: dmountain@utmck.edu.

MOUNTCASTLE, VERNON BENJAMIN, retired neuroscientist; b. Shelbyville, Ky., July 15, 1918; s. Vernon and Anne-Francis Marguerite (Waugh) Mountcastle; m. Nancy Clayton Pierpont, Sept. 6, 1945; children: Vernon Benjamin III, Anne Clayton, George Earle Pierpont. BS in Chemistry, Roanoke Coll., Salem, Va., 1938, DSc (hon.), 1968; MD, Johns Hopkins U., 1942; DSc (hon.), U. Pa., 1976, Northwestern U., 1985, U. Minn., 1995; MD (hon.), U. Zurich, 1983, U. Siena, 1984, U. Santiago, Spain, 1990. House officer surgery Johns Hopkins Hosp., 1942—43; mem. faculty Johns Hopkins Sch. Medicine, 1946—, prof. physiology, 1959, dir. dept., 1964—80, prof. neurosci., 1980—92, prof. emeritus, 1992—; dir. Bard Labs. Neurophysiology Johns Hopkins U., Balt., 1981—91. Spl. rsch. physiology brain; chmn. physiology study sect., mem. physiology tng. com. NIH, 1958—61; adv. coun. Nat. Eye Inst., 1971—74; vis. prof. Coll. de France, Paris, 1980. Author: Perciptual Neuroscience: The Cerebrel Cortex, 1996, The Sensory Hand: Neural Mechanisms in Somatic Sensation, 2005; editor-in-chief: Jour. Neurophysiology, 1961—64, editor, contbr.: Med. Physiology, 12th edit., 1968, Med. Physiology, 13th edit., 1974, Med. Physiology, 14th edit., 1980; contbr. articles to profl. jours. Lt. (s.g.) M.C. USNR, 1943—46. Recipient Lashley prize, Am. Philos. Soc., 1974, F.O. Schmitt prize and medal, MIT, 1975, Sherrington prize and Gold medal, Royal Acad. Medicine, London, 1977, Horowitz prize, Columbia U., 1978, Helmholtz prize, 1982, Fyssen Internat. prize, Paris, 1983, Lasker award, 1983, Nat. Medal Sci., 1986, Zotterman prize and medal, Swedish Physiol. Soc., 1989, award in neurosci., Fidia Fedn., 1990, Australia prize, 1993. Mem.: AAAS (McGovern prize and medal 1990), NAS (chmn. sect. on physiology 1971—74, award in neurosci. 1998), Acad. Sci. (Finland, fgn.), Royal Soc. London (fgn.), Acad. Scis. (France, fgn.), Nat. Inst. Medicine, Am. Philos. Soc. (councillor 1979—82), Soc. Neurosci. (pres. 1970—72, Gerard prize 1980), Harvey Cushing Soc., Am. Acad. Arts and Scis., Am. Physiol. Soc., Physiol. Soc. London (hon.), Am. Neurol. Assn. (hon. Bennett lectr. 1978), Sigma Xi, Phi Chi, Alpha Omega Alpha, Phi Beta Kappa. Home: 6605 Walnutwood Cir Baltimore MD 21212 Business E-Mail: mountcastle@mbi.mb.jhu.edu.

MOUNTZ, JAMES MICHAEL, radiologist, educator, biomedical researcher; b. Dayton, Ohio, Nov. 15, 1947; s. Taulbeel Preston and Mary (Sawyer) M.; m. Kathy Ann Mountz, Dec. 17, 1988; children: Jammie Michelle, Kristina Ann, Jennifer Mary, Victorial Natalie, Elizabeth Joan BS in Physics magna cum laude, Wright State U., 1969; MS in Physics, Mich. State U., 1971, PhD in Physics, 1974; MD, Case Western Res. U., 1981. Diplomate Am. Bd. Radiology, Am. Bd. Nuclear Medicine. Intern, resident and fellow U. Mich. Med. Ctr., Ann Arbor, 1981-86; asst. chief VA Med. Ctr., Ann Arbor, 1986-90; asst. prof. U. Mich. Med. Ctr., Ann Arbor, 1986-90; scientist U. Ala., Birmingham, 1994—, dir. molecular imaging devel. lab., 1994—, dir. neuro-nuclear medicine, 1990—, prof. radiology, 1990—; dir. neuronuclear medicine U. Pitts. Med. Ctr, 2003—, chief, divsn. nuclear medicine, med. dir. pet imaging, 2005—. Lectr., presenter in field. Patentee in field; contbr. articles to profl. jours. Mem. AMA, AAAS, Soc. Nuclear Medicine (bd. dirs. 1994-96, com. organizer brain imaging coun. 1996), Radiol. Soc. N.Am., Am. Coll. Radiology, Ala. Soc. Nuclear Medicine (pres. 1996-97), Sigma Pi Sigma, Phi Eta Tau. Avocations: flying, trumpet playing, amateur radio, photography, astronomy. Office: Univ Pitts Med Ctr 200 Lothrop St B-938 Pet Facility Pittsburgh PA 15215 Office Phone: 412-647-0104. Business E-Mail: mountzjm@upmc.edu.

MOUNTZ, WADE, retired healthcare executive; b. Winona, Ohio, Nov. 19, 1924; s. Lowell J. and Ethel M. (Coppock) M.; m. Betty G. Wilson, June 3, 1946; children: David John, Timothy Wilson. BA, Baldwin-Wallace Coll., Berea, Ohio, 1948; MHA, U. Minn., Mpls., 1951; LHD (hon.), Ky. Wesleyan Coll., Owensboro, 1991. With Norton Meml. Infirmary, Louisville, 1951—58, asst. adminstrn., 1958—69, adminstr., 1969—81; pres. Norton-Children's Hosps., Inc., Louisville, 1981—87, NKC, Inc., Louisville, 1981-85, vice chmn., 1985-87; pres. emeritus Norton Healthcare, 1987—. Vice chmn. Comprehensive Health Planning Council Ky., 1968-73, chmn., 1973-79; bd. dirs. Louisville chpt. ARC, 1961-74; trustee Blue Cross Hosp. Plan, 1959-72; trustee Am. Hosp. Assn., 1971-76, chmn. bd., 1975. Served with A.C., USNR, 1943-45. Recipient Disting. Service award Ky. Hosp. Assn.; Disting. Layman award Ky. Med. Assn. Fellow Am. Coll. Hosp. Healthcare Execs. (life, gold medal), Modern Health Hall of Fame 2008, Masons. Home and Office: Betty & Wade Mountz 8021 Christian Ct # 401 Louisville KY 40222-9023 Home Phone: 502-426-5478; Office Phone: 502-412-9210. Personal E-mail: wmountz@insightbb.com.

MOURGELA, SOFIA, neurosurgeon, consultant; d. Dimitrios Mourgelas and Vasiliki Siourounis; m. Antonios Sakellaropoulos, Sept. 22, 1967. MD, U. Athens, 1993. Asst. neurosurgery Paracelsus Clinic, Zwickau, Germany, 1995—96; cons. neurosurgeon level b Agios Savvas Anticancer Inst., Athens, 2003—09. Cons. neurosurgeon b Med. Ctr. Athens Hosp., 2001—03. Bd. dirs. Panarcadian Soc., Athens, 1997—2001. Scholar, Bakala Inst., 1987—93. Mem.: Soc. Promotion Rsch. Microsurgical & Endoscopic Anatomy, Internat. Study Group Thecaloscopy (corr.). Greek Orthodox. Achievements include research in endoscopy of thecal sac; corpus callosuiy dimentions and morphology. Avocation: travel. Office: Agios Savvas Anticancer Institute Leoforos Alexandras 171 Athens 11524 Greece Home: Vikatu 12 115 24 Athens Greece Office Fax: 0030-210-6409515; Home Fax: 0030-210-6925520. Personal E-mail: sofiamou@otenet.gr.

MOUSALI, YAHYA MAHMOUD, neurologist; b. Makkah, Saudi Arabia, Mar. 27, 1952; MD, King Abud Aziz U., 1983. Physician King Abud Aziz Med. City, 1986—; fellow epilepsy U. Alberta Can., 2006. Avocation: football. Home: Po Box 40923 Jeddah Western Region 21511 Saudi Arabia Home Fax: 96626981392. Personal E-mail: ymousali@hotmail.com.

MOUSSOUTTAS, MICHAEL M., medical clinician educator; b. NYC, Sept. 7, 1968; s. Constantine and Christina Moussouttas; m. Maria Iuanow, Nov. 5, 2000. BA, NYU, 1990; MD, SUNY Syracuse, 1994. Lic. NY, 1995, diplomate Am. Bd. Neurology 1999, Neurosonology 2001, Am. Bd. Vascular Neurology, 2006, Am. Bd. Neurocritical Care, 2008. Intern North Shore U. Hosp., Manhasset, NY, 1994—95; resident Mt. Sinai Hosp., NYC, 1995—98; cerebrovascular fellow Yale-New Haven Hosp., 1998—2000; asst. prof. NY Med. Coll., Valhalla, 2000—03, Seton Hall U. Neurosci. Inst., Edison, NJ, 2003—06; neurocritical care fellow Columbia Presbyn. Hosp., NYC, 2006—07; asst. prof. Thomas Jefferson Med. Ctr., Phila., 2007—. Neurovascular program dir. NY Med. Coll., 2000—03. Contbr. articles to profl. jours. Mem.: AMA, Neurocritical Care Soc., Am. Heart Assn., Am. Acad. Neurology. Greek Orthodox. Avocations: sports, chess, travel, guitar. Office: Dept Neurology 900 Walnut St Ste 200 Philadelphia PA 19107 Personal E-mail: arista1@pol.net.

MOUTON, CHARLES PETER, dean, physician, educator; b. New Orleans, Jan. 9, 1960; m. Yvette Mouton. BS, Howard U., 1981, MD, 1986; MS, Harvard U., 1997. Diplomate Am. Bd. Family Practice. Resident Prince George's Hosp. Ctr., Cheverly, Md., 1987-90; fellow George Washington U. Med. Ctr., D.C., 1990-92; asst. prof. Sch. Medicine U. Medicine and Dentistry N.J., Newark, 1992-97; asst. prof. Health and Sci. Ctr. U. Tex., San Antonio, 1997—2004; prof. cmty. and family medicine Howard U., Washington, 2004—10; prof. family medicine Mehary Med. Coll., 2010—, dean Sch. Medicine, 2010—, sr. v.p. health Affairs, 2010—. Adv. bd. Guardianship Svcs., San Antonio, 1997-2001. Contbr. articles to profl. jours., chpts. to books. Fellow Am. Acad. Family Physicians, Assn. Am. Med. Colls.; mem. AMA, Am. Geriatrics Soc., Nat. Med. Assn., Gerontol. Soc. Am., Soc. Tchrs. Family Medicine, Knights Peter Claver. Avocations: reading, sports, Judo, music. Office: Meharry Med Coll 1005 Dr DB Todd Jr Blvd Nashville TN 37208 Home: 9101 Rouen Ln Potomac MD 20854-3133 Office Phone: 615-327-6204. Business E-Mail: cmouton@mmc.edu. *

MOVSHON, J. ANTHONY (JOSEPH ANTHONY MOVSHON), neuroscience educator; b. NYC, Dec. 10, 1950; s. George and Irene (Dann) M.; m. Margaret Elizabeth Beardsley, Aug. 30, 1975; children: Nicholas Anthony, Clare Elizabeth. BA, Cambridge U., 1972, PhD, 1975, MA, 1976. Asst. prof. psychology NYU, NYC, 1975-78, assoc. prof., 1978-84, prof. psychology, 1984—, prof. neural sci., 1987—, dir. Ctr. for Neural Sci., 1987-91, 1993—98, 2004—, Presdl. prof., 1999—2002, Silver prof., 2002—; investigator Howard Hughes Med. Inst., NYC, 1991—2003. Mem. visual scis. study sect. NIH, Bethesda, Md., 1982-87; adj. prof. physiology and neurosci. NYU Sch. Medicine, 1990-. Mem. editorial bd. Ann. Rev. Neurosci., 1983-87, Visual Neurosci., 1987-90, Jour. Cognitive Neurosci., 1988—; contbr. numerous articles to sci. jours., chpts. to books. Recipient rsch. career devel. award Nat. Eye Inst., 1980-85, Vision award Champalimaud Found., 2010; NIH grantee, 1976—, NSF grantee, 1976—; Alfred P. Sloan Found. fellow, 1977-81. Fellow AAAS, Am. Psychol. Soc.; mem. NAS, Assn. Rsch. in Vision and Ophthalmology, Soc. Neurosci. (program com. 1987-91, chmn. 1991, Young Investigator award 1985), Am. Physiol. Soc., Cognitive Neurosci. Soc., Vision Sciences Soc. (bd. dirs. 2007-, pres. 2009-)Am. Acad. Arts & Sciences. Democrat. Avocations: music, opera. Office: NYU Ctr for Neural Sci 4 Washington Pl New York NY 10003-6621 Office Phone: 212-998-7880. Office Fax: 212-995-4183. Business E-Mail: movshon@nyu.edu.

MOW, VAN C., engineering educator, researcher; b. Chengdu, China, Jan. 10, 1939; B. Aero. Engring., Rensselaer Poly. Inst., 1962, PhD, 1966. Mem. tech. staff Bell Telephone Labs., Whippany, NJ, 1968-69; assoc. prof. mechanics Rensselaer Poly. Inst., Troy, NY, 1969-76, prof. mechanics and biomed. engring., 1976-82, John A. Clark and Edward T. Crossan prof. engring., 1982-86; prof. mech. engring. and orthopedic bioengring. Columbia U., NYC, 1986—98, chmn. dept. biomed. engring. Fu Found. Sch. Engring. and Applied Sci., 1998—; dir. Orthopedic Rsch. Lab., Columbia-Presbyn. Med. Ctr., NYC, 1986—, Stanley Dicker prof. biomed. engring., 1998—. Vis. mem. Courant Inst. Math. Sci., NYU, 1967-68; vis. prof. Harvard U., Boston, 1976-77; chmn. orthopaedics and musculoskeletal study sect. NIH, Bethesda, Md., 1982-84; hon. prof. Sichuan U., 1981, Shanghai Jiao Tong U., 1987, Shanghai U., 1983, Hong Kong Poly. U., 2003, Zhejiang U., 2004, Beihang U., 2004; chmn. grants rev. bd. Orthopaedic Rsch. Edn. Found., 1992-96; bd. dirs. Hoar Rsch. Found., 1993—; chmn. adv. com. divsn. Med. Engring. Rsch. Nat. Health Rsch. Inst., Taiwan, 1999—; cons. in field. Assoc. editor Jour. Biomechanics, 1981—, Jour. Biomech. Engring., 1979-86; chmn. editorial adv. bd. Jour. Orthopedic Rsch., 1983-90; adv. editor Clin.

Orthopedic Rel. Rsch., 1993—; assoc./co-editor Osteo-arthritis & Cartilage; contbr. numerous articles to profl. jours. Founder Gordon Research Conf. on Bioengring. and Orthopedic Sci., 1980, chair, editl. adv. bd.Cellular and Molecular Biology. NATO sr. fellow, 1978; recipient William H. Wiley Disting. Faculty award Rensselaer Poly. Inst., 1981, ASME Van C. Mow medal for bioengring., 2004; Japan Soc. for Promotion Sci. Fellow, 1986, Fogarty Sr. Internat. fellow, 1987; Alza disting. lectr. Biomed. Engring. Soc., 1987; H.R. Lissner award ASME, 1987, Kappa Delta award AAOS, 1980, Giovani Borelli award, 1991, Outstanding Basuc Sci. award, OARSI, 2008. Fellow ASME (chmn. biomechanics divsn. 1984-85, Melville medal 1982, R.H. Thurston lectr.), Am. Inst. Med. Biol. Engring.; mem. Orthopaedic Rsch. Soc. (pres. 1982-83), Am. Soc. Biomechanics (founding), Internat. Soc. Biorheology, U.S. Nat. Com. on Biomechanics (sec.-treas. 1985-90, chmn. 1991-94), Nat. Acad. Engring., Inst. of Medicine, Nat. Acad. Sci., Academia Sinica, Acad. Sci. Developing World. Business E-Mail: vcm1@columbia.edu.

MOWER, MORTON MAIMON, cardiologist; b. Balt., Jan. 31, 1933; MD, U. Md. Sch. Medicine, 1959. Diplomate Am. Bd. Internal Medicine, Am. Bd. Cardiovac. Disease. Intern U. Md. Hosp., Balt., 1959-60; resident Sinai Hosp., Balt., 1960-63, fellow in cardiology, 1965-66; v.p. med. scis. Guidant Corp., St. Paul, 1989—96; assoc. prof. medicine Johns Hopkins U. Sch. Medicine, Balt.; prof. physiology and biophysics Howard U. Sch. Medicine; chmn., CEO Mower Rsch. Assocs., Balt., 1996—2006; chmn. MR3 Med., Balt., 2006—. Named to Nat. Inventors Hall of Fame, 2002. Fellow: ACP, Am. Coll. Chest Physicians, Am. Coll. Cardiology; mem.: Am. Soc. Internal Medicine, Am. Fedn. Clin. Rsch. E-mail: mmower@aol.com.

MOXLEY, JOHN HOWARD, III, internist; b. Elizabeth, NJ, Jan. 10, 1935; s. John Howard Jr. and Cleopatra (Mundy) Moxley; m. Doris Banchik; children: John Howard IV, Brook, Mark. BA, Williams Coll., 1957; MD, U. Colo., 1961; DSc (hon.), Sch. Medicine Hannemann U. Diplomate Am. Bd. Internal Medicine. Intern Peter Bent Brigham Hosp., Boston, 1961—62, resident in internal medicine, 1962—66; with Nat. Cancer Inst., USPHS, 1963—65; asst. to dean, instr. medicine Harvard Med. Sch., Boston, 1966—69; dean Sch. Medicine, U. Md., 1969—73; vice chancellor health scis., dean Med. Sch., U. Calif.-San Diego, 1973—79, asst. sec. for health affairs Dept. Def., Washington, 1979—81; sr. v.p. Am. Med. Internat., Beverly Hills, Calif., 1981—87; pres. MetaMed. Inc., Playa Del Rey, Calif., 1987—89; mgr. dir. Korn/Ferry Internat., LA, 1989—. Cons. FDA, NIH; dir. Nat. Fund for Med. Edn., 1986—94, chmn., 1993—94; dir. Henry M. Jackson Found. for Adv. Mil. Medicine. Contbr. articles to profl. jours. Dir. Polyclinic Health Svcs. Games of XXIII Olympiad. Recipient Gold and Silver award, U. Colo. Med. Sch., 1974, commr.'s citation for outstanding svc. to over the counter drug study, FDA, 1977, spl. achievement citation, Am. Hosp. Assn., 1983, Sec. of Def. medal for disting. pub. svc., 1981. Fellow: ACP, Am. Coll. Physician Execs. (disting.); mem.: AMA (chmn. coun. sci. affairs 1985), Am. Hosp. Assn. (trustee 1979—81), Soc. Med. Adminstrs., Calif. Med. Assn. (chmn. sci. bd. 1978—83, councilor), Inst. Medicine NAS, San Diego C. of C., Rotary, Alpha Omega Alpha. Office: Korn Ferry Internat 1900 Ave of the Stars Ste 2600 Los Angeles CA 90067 1512 Office Phone: 310-200-1296. E-mail: moxleyj@kornferry.com.

MOY, ALAN BRENT, biotechnologist, director, pulmonologist; 4 children. MD, Creighton U., Omaha, Nebr., 1985. Asst. prof. medicine, biomed. engring. U. Iowa, Iowa City, 1995—2000, assoc. prof. medicine, biomed. engring., 2000—05; CEO Cellular Engring. Techs. Inc., Coralville, Iowa, 2000—; pvt. practice pulmonologist Pulmonary Associates Iowa city, 2005—, physician; dir. John Paul II Stem Cell Rsch. Inst., Iowa City, 2006—. Fellow: Am. Coll. Chest Physician. Achievements include research in regenerative medicine.

MOYERS, SYLVIA DEAN, retired medical librarian; b. Independence, W.Va., Oct. 22, 1936; d. Wilkie Russell and Ina Laura (Watkins) Collins; m. Paul Franklin Moyers, June 29, 1957; children: Tammy Jeanne, Thomas Paul, Tara Sue. Student, Am. Med. Record Assn., 1977—79. Sec. Teets Lumber Co., Terra Alta, W.Va., 1954-58, Preston County News, 1958-60; med. record clk. med. record dept. Hopemont (W.Va.) Hosp., W.Va., 1960-75, dir., 1975-88; sec. The Terra Alta Bank, 1990-95; ret., 1995. Charter mem., past mother advisor Order of Rainbow Girls (Terra Alta Assembly No. 26), past grand editor Mountain Echoes; vol. Preston Meml. Hosp., ARC, Salvation Army, Am. Cancer Soc., Boy Scouts Am.; active Kingwood Fire Dept. Aux. Named Kingwood Citizen of Yr., 2005; named one of 100 Most Influential Persons, 2004. Mem.: Preston County Hist. Soc., Kingwood Red Hat Mamas (charter), Preston Meml. Hosp. Aux., Kingwood Women's Civic Club. Republican. Methodist. Home: 120 Miller Rd Kingwood WV 26537-1321

MOZENA, JOHN DANIEL, podiatrist; b. Salem, Oreg., June 9, 1956; s. Joseph Iner and Mary Teresa (Delaney) M.; m. Elizabeth Ann Hintz, June 2, 1979; children: Christine Hintz, Michelle Delaney. Student, U. Oreg., 1974-79; B in Basic Med. Scis., Calif. Coll. Podiatric Medicine, D in Podiatric Medicine, 1983. Diplomate Am. Bd. Podiatric Surgery. Resident in surg. podiatry Hillside Hosp., San Diego, 1983-84; pvt. practice podiatry Portland, Oreg., 1984—; dir. residency Med. Ctr. Hosp., Portland, 1985-91; clin. assoc. pediat. prof. medicine surgery Western U. Health Scis., 2010—. Lectr. Nat. Podiatric Assn. Seminar, 1990, Am. Coll. Gen. Practitioners, 1991, Am. Coll. Family Physician, 1995; adj. faculty health profl. sect. Portland CC, 1999; legis. chmn. OPMA, 2002-. Cons. editor Podiatry Today Mag., 1999—, Podiatry Today, 1999—; contbr. articles to profl. jours.; patentee sports shoe cleat design, 1985. Podiatric adv. coun. Oreg. Bd. Med. Examiners, 1994-97. Named Clinician of the Yr., Eastmoreland Hosp., 2000-01. Fellow Am Coll. Ambulatory Foot Surgeons, Am. Coll. Foot Surgeons, Oregon Podiatric Med. Assn. (legis. chmn.) Republican. Roman Catholic. Avocations: softball, basketball, piano, electric bass guitar, running, ironman triathlon. Office: Town Ctr Foot Clinic 8305 SE Monterey Ave Ste 101 Portland OR 97086-7728 Office Phone: 503-652-1121.

MÓZSIK, GYULA, internist, gastroenterologist, clinical pharmacologist, educator; b. Dancsháza, Hungary, June 7, 1938; s. Károly Mózsik and Mária Pozsár; m. Ilona Vizi; 1 child, Andrea. MD, U. Debrecen, Hungary, 1962. Asst. to 2d dept. medicine Med. U., Debrecen, 1962-67, asst. prof. medicine, 1967—; assoc. prof. medicine U. Pécs, Hungary, 1975, prof. medicine, 1989—, head 1st dept. medicine, 1993, vice-dean clin. matters, 1996—. Vis. scientist Dept. Pharmacology, Oslo, Norway, 1968-69; vis. scientist chem. pathology lab. Harvard Med. Sch., Boston, 1985. Contbr. over 180 chpts. to books, over 350 articles to profl. jours.; editor numerous textbooks. Mem. Am. Gastroenterol. Assn., Internat. Soc. Internal Medicine, Nat. Inst. Dietetics (adv. bd.), Hungarian Ministry of Health (adv. bd.), European Soc. Clin. Investigation, Hungarian Soc. Physiology, Hungarian Soc. Pharmacology, Hungarian Soc. Nutrition (medal József SOS 1984), Hungarian Soc. Gastroenterology (Pro Optimo Merito medal 1989), Internat. Brain-Gut Soc. (diplome, winner Széchenyi scolarship for prof. 1999—), Internat. Soc. Internal Medicine, Internat. Soc. Metabolic Therapy, N.Y. Acad. Scis., Internat. Union Pharmacology (gastrointestinal sect.). Office: U Med Sch First Dept Medicine 7643 Pécs Hungary Office Phone: 3672 536494. Personal E-mail: gyula.mozsik@gmail.com. Business E-Mail: gyula.mozsik@aok.pte.hu.

MOZSIK, GYULA, retired physician; b. Dancshaza, June 7, 1938; MD, Med. U. Debrecen, Hungary, 1962; PhD, Med. U. Pécs, Hungary, 1970, ScD in Medicine, 1970. Prof., head medicine first dept. medicine Med. and Health Ctr., U. Pécs, Hungary, 1993—2003. Prof. emeritus first dept. medicine Med. U. Sch., Pécs, 1989—2011. Contbr. articles to profl. jours. Mem.: European Soc. Clin. Rsch., Am. Gastroent. Assn., Am. Dietical Assn., Am. Chem. Soc. Office: Ifjuság Street 13 Pécs Baranya H-7624 Hungary Office Phone: 36 -72-536 494. Office Fax: 36-72-536 495. Personal E-mail: gyula.mozsik@gmail.com. Business E-Mail: gyula.mozsik@aok.pte.hu.

MOZZI, ENRICO, surgeon, educator; b. Milan, Oct. 6, 1951; MD, Sch. Medicine U. Milan, 1976; degree in Gen. & Vascular Surgery, Specialization Sch. Surgery U. Milan, 1982. Diploma in piano Milan Conservatory. Rschr. U. Milan, 1980—2006, aggregate prof. surgery, 2006—. Fellow: Soc. Italiana per la Chirurgia dell Obesitâ, Internat. Fedn. Surgery Obesity. Avocation: music. Office: Via Francesco Sforza 35 Milan 20124 Italy Office Fax: 390255033218. Business E-Mail: enrico.mozzi@unimi.it.

MRAZEK, DAVID ALLEN, child and adolescent psychiatrist; b. Ft. Riley, Kans., Oct. 1, 1947; s. Rudolph George and Hazel Ruth (Schayes) M.; m. Patricia Jean, Sept. 2, 1978; children: Nicola, Matthew, Michael, Alissa. AB in Genetics, Cornell U., 1969; MD, Wake Forest U., 1973. Lic. psychiatrist, child psychiatrist, N.C., Ohio, Colo., D.C., Va., Md., Minn., Ariz., Fla. Lectr. child psychiatry Inst. of Psychiatry, London, 1977-79; dir. pediatric psychiatry Nat. Jewish Ctr. for Immunology and Respiratory Medicine, Denver, 1979-91; chmn. psychiatry Children's Nat. Med. Ctr., Washington, 1991-98; chair psychiatry and behavioral scis. George Washington U. Sch. Medicine, 1996-2000; dir. Children's Rsch. Inst. Neurosci., 1995-98; chair psychiatry and psychology Mayo Clinic, Rochester, Minn., 2000—10; prof. psychiatry and pediatrics Mayo Sch. Medicine, Rochester, 2000—; dir. Mayo Clinic S.C. Johnson Genomics of Addictions Program, 2004—. Asst. prof. psychiatry U. Colo. Sch. Medicine, 1979-83, assoc. prof. psychiatry and pediatrics, 1984-89, prof., 1990-91; prof. psychiatry and pediatrics George Washington U. Sch. Medicine, 1991-2000, Leon Yochelson prof. psychiatry and behavioral scis.; dir. Am. Bd. Psychiatry and Neurology, 2003-10, bd. chair, 2010; mem. ACGME Residency Rev. Com. in Psychiatry, 2003-2009. Contbr. chapters to books, articles to profl. jours. Recipient Rsch. Scientist Devel. awards NIMH, 1983-88, 88-91, Irving Phillips Meml. award for outstanding rsch. in prevention Acad. Child and Adolescent Psychiatry, 2000, Simon Wile award Am. Acad. Child and Adolescent Psychiatry, 2005, Agnes Purcell McGavin award for Lifetime Achievement in Child and Adolescent Psychiatry, Am. Psychiatric Assn., 2008, Pyschiat. Edn. award Am. Coll., 2005, Provider of Yr., NAMI, SE Minn., 2010, Adelaid M. Johnson award, Mayo Clinic, 2010. Fellow Am. Acad. Child and Adolescent Psychiatry (Simon Wile award 2005), Am. Psychiat. Assn. (life, disting. fellow, 2009, chmn. coun. children, adolescents and families 2006 08, Blanche F. Ittleson award 1996, Agnes Purcell McGavin award 1999, 2008), Royal Coll. Psychiatrists, Am. Coll. Psychiatrists; mem. Benjamin Rush Soc. Office: Mayo Clinic Dept Psychiatry/Pschology 200 1st St SW Rochester MN 55905 Home Phone: 507-285-5656; Office Phone: 507-284-8891. Office Fax: 507-255-9416. Business E-Mail: mrazek.david@mayo.edu.

MRUK, CHRISTOPHER J., psychologist, educator; b. Mt. Clemens, Mich., May 21, 1949; s. Joseph and Veronica (Harris) M; m. Marsha Jean Oliver, Dec. 24, 1983. BS, Mich. State U., East Lansing, 1971; MA, Duquesne U., Pitts., 1974, PhD, 1981. Lic. clin. psychologist, Ohio, Pa. Staff psychologist Mon Valley Mental Health Ctr., Monessen, Pa., 1981-82; dir. counseling St. Francis Coll., Loretto, Pa., 1982-83; prof. Firelands Coll., Bowling Green State U., Huron, Ohio, 1984—. Cons. psychologist Firelands Cmty. Hosp., Sandusky, Ohio, 1988—. Author: Self-Esteem: Research, Theory and Practice, 1995, 2d edit., 1999, 3rd edit, 2006; co-author: Zen and Psychotherapy: Integrating Traditional and Non-Traditional Approaches, 2003; contbr. chpts. in books and articles to profl. jours. Bd. dirs. Safe Harbour Domestic Violence Ctr., Sandusky, 1992. Mem. Am. Psychol. Assn. Avocations: computers, writing, working out. Business E-Mail: cmruk@bgsu.edu.

MU, YIMING, endocrinologist, educator; b. China, Jan. 30, 1962; MD, 2nd Mil. Med. U., PhD, 1984. Cert. physician Chinese Med. Soc., 2004. Dir., prof., dept. endocrinology Chinese PLA Gen. Hosp., 2010—. Mem.: Chinese Endocrine Soc. (vice chmn. 2008—). Office: Chinese PLA Gen Hosp Dept Endocrinology Beijing 100853 China Office Fax: 86-10-6816-8917. Business E-Mail: muyiming@301hospital.com.cn.

MUANGPAISAN, WEERASAK, geriatrician, neurologist, consultant; s. Kimsoom and Yenjit Saejoo. MD with honors, Mahidol U., 1995; diploma in Geriatric Medicine, RCP, 2008; MPhil in Epidemiology, Cambridge, 2008. Diplomate Internal Medicine Med. Coun. of Thailand, 2001, Neurology Med. Coun. of Thailand, 2003, cert. in stats. for healthcare rsch. Oxford, 2007. Gen. practitioner Takuapa dist. Hosp., Phanga, Thailand, 1995—98; resident, fellow in internal medicine and neurology faculty medicine Siriraj Hosp., Bangkok, 1998—2003, cons. geriat. medicine dept. preventive and social medicine, 2003—, asst. prof. geriat. medicine dept. preventive and social medicine, 2005—; fellow acute stroke program, geratology John Radcliffe Hosp., Oxford, England, 2006—07. Vis. fellow Harris Manchester Coll., U. Oxford, 2006—; mem. Med. Coun. Thailand. Scholar, U. Oxford; Shell Centenary scholar, Cambridge U. Mem.: Internat. Psychogeriatrics Assn., Am. Geriatrics Soc., Dementia Soc. Thailand, Royal Coll. Physicians Thailand, Neurol. Soc. Thailand. Personal E-mail: drweerasak@gmail.com.

MUCHNICK, RICHARD STUART, ophthalmologist, educator; b. Bklyn., June 21, 1942; s. Max and Rae (Kozinsky) Muchnick; m. Felice Dee Greenberg, Oct. 29, 1978; 1 child, Amanda Michelle. BA with honors, Cornell U., 1963, MD, 1967. Diplomate Am. Bd. Ophthalmology, Nat. Bd. Med. Examiners. Intern in medicine NY Hosp., NYC, 1967—68, resident in ophthalmology, 1970—73, practice medicine, specializing in ophthalmology, notably strabismus & ophthalmic plastic surgery, 1974—. Clin. prof. ophthalmology Cornell U., NYC, 2009—; clin. rschr. strabismus, ophthalmic plastic surgery, 1973—; attending med. staff Lenox Hill Hosp., NYC; attending ophthalmologist NY-Presbyn. Hosp, NYC. With USPHS, 1968—70. Recipient Coryell Prize Surgery, Cornell U. Med. Coll., 1967, McLean Medal in Ophthalmology, Weill Med. Coll. of Cornell U., 2006. Fellow: ACS, Am. Acad. Ophthalmology; mem.: AMA, Manhattan Ophthal. Soc., Greater N.Y. Soc. Pediat. Ophthalmology and Strabismus (pres.), N.Y. Acad. Medicine, N.Y. Soc. Clin. Ophthalmology, Internat. Strabismological Assn., Am. Assn. Pediatric Ophthalmology and Strabismus, Am. Soc. Ophthalmic Plastic and Reconstructive Surgery, 7th Regt. Tennis, Lotos, Alpha Epsilon Delta, Alpha Omega Alpha. Office: 69 E 71st St New York NY 10021-4213 Office Phone: 212-744-1726.

MUCKLE, DAVID SUTHERLAND, surgeon, educator; b. Weardale, Durham, Eng., Aug. 30, 1939; s. John L. and Ruth J. (Sutherland) M.; m. Christine Haymonds; children: Carolyn Jane, Deborah Christine. BMed, BSurgery, U. Durham, 1963, MD, 1981, MSurgery, 1971, DSc, 2010; diploma in sports medicine (hon.), Scottish Royal Colls. Surgeon Oxford, 1970-77, South Cleveland Hosp., 1977—95. Cons. orthopedic surgeon, 1977—; med. advisor Fédération Internationale de Football Assn., Switzerland, 1977—; surgeon, dep. chmn. med. com. Football Assn., 1983-98; surgeon Nuffield Hosp., Cleveland, 1981-98; med. com. Union Des Assns. Européennes de Football, 1990-98, Switzerland; vis. prof. U. Teesside, 1994-95. Author: Femoral Neck Fracture, 1977; Injuries in Sport, 1982, An Outline of Fractures, 1985, An Outline of Orthopedic Practice, 1986, (3 vols.) A Country Doctor, 2003, A Sower Went Forth Sowing, 2003, A Highland Story, 2008, Dickens by charles Dickens, 2010, (poems) Such Happiness is Life, 2003, Endangered Species, 2004—. Recipient Championship medal European Nations Cup Final, 1992, 96. Fellow Brit. Orthopedic Assn. (rsch. scholarship com. 1990—), Brit. Orthopedic Rsch. (com. mem. 1979, Pres. Orthopedic Rsch. prize 1973), Royal Coll. Surgeons (Eng. and Edinburg), Royal Geog. Soc. Office: Parkview Med Clinic Middlesbrough TS4 2NS England

MUDER, ROBERT RICHARD, physician, epidemiologist; b. Pitts., June 11, 1951; s. Richard Edward and Gemma (Lombardi) M.; m. Janet D. Vlha, June 4, 1977 (div. 1993); children: Jane Elizabeth, Michael Richard. BA, Oberlin Coll., Ohio, 1973; MD, U. Pitts. Sch. Medicine, 1977. Diplomate Am. Bd. Internal Medicine; subspecialty of infectious diseases. Intern then resident internal medicine Mercy Hosp., Pitts., 1977—80, chief med. resident, 1980—81, asst. coord. med. edn., 1983-84, coord. med. edn., 1984-86, assoc. program dir., 1986-89, fellow in infectious disease, 1981-83; asst. prof. medicine U. Pitts., 1989-94, assoc. prof., 1994—2001, prof. medicine, divsn. infectious diseases; chief infection control VA Pitts. Healthcare Sys., 1986—2006, chief infectious disease sect., 2007—. Sect. editor Infectious Disease Alert; contbr. articles to profl. jours. Mem. Infectious Diseases Soc. Am., Soc. for Healthcare Epidemiology Am. Office: VA Pitts Healthcare Sys 2A135 University Dr C ID Section Pittsburgh PA 15240 Office Phone: 412-360-6179. Office Fax: 412-360-6950. Business E-Mail: robert.muder@va.gov. *

MUDGE, GILBERT H., JR., cardiologist; b. Cooperstown, NY; MD, Columbia U. Coll. Physicians & Surgeons, 1970. Cert. Internal Medicine, 1973, Cardiovasc. Disease, 1979. Intern Presbyn. Hosp., NYC, 1970—71, resident in internal medicine, 1971—73; fellow in cardiology Peter Bent Brigham Hosp., 1977; sr. cardiologist Brigham & Women's Hosp., Boston, dir. Brigham Cardiovasc. Cons.; assoc. prof. Harvard Med. Sch., Boston. Sr. med. advisor Partners Internat. Med. Services, Boston. Office: Brigham & Womens Hosp Cardiovasc Divsn 75 Francis St PBB-1 Boston MA 02115 Office Phone: 617-732-7140. Office Fax: 617-278-6931. E-mail: gmudge@partners.org.

MUDRY, ALBERT, ear surgeon, historian; b. Sion, Switzerland, Mar. 7, 1958; s. Gérard Mudry and Thérèse Pralong; m. Florence Secrétan, Sept. 16, 1989; children: Yoan, Ludovic, Raphael, Aude. MD, U. Lausanne, Switzerland, 1990. Chief-resident U. Hosp., Lausanne, 1992—95; pvt. practice Lausanne, 1995—. Collaborator Inst. for History Medicine, Lausanne, 2001. Contbr. articles to profl. jours. Grantee, Switzerland, 2001. Mem.: Politzer Soc., European Acad. Otology and Neuro-Otology. Office: Avenue de la Gare 6 Lausanne 1003 Switzerland Office Fax: 0041213238325.

MUELLER, ALEXANDER, endocrinologist, consultant, nephrologist; b. Baden-Baden, Germany, Nov. 19, 1963; s. Hermann and Ermelinde Mueller; m. Britta Hensel; children: Marisa, Saskia, Charlotte. MD, Phillipps-U., Marburg, Germany, 1994. Cert. internal medicine, nephrologist, endocrinologist. Cons. nephrologist, endocrinologist U. Heidelberg-Mannheim, Germany, 1999—.

MUELLER, ARTHUR JOSEPH, ophthalmologist; b. Schramberg, Germany, Aug. 21, 1962; s. Artur Friedrich and Gertrud (Wahl) M.; m. Cornelia Maria Trottler, Oct. 3, 1992; children: Kilian, Severin, Benedikt. MD, Ludwig-Maximilians U., Munich, 1988, PhD, 2000. Bd. cert. diplomate ophthalmology. Resident Univ. Eye Hosp., Munich, 1990-93; attending physician Univ. Eye Clinic, Munich, 1993—94; clin. rsch. fellow U. Calif.- San Diego Shiley Eye Ctr., 1995-96; attending physician Univ. Eye Clinic, Munich, 1997—2002, prof. ophthalmology, 2003—, head dept. ophthalmology, 2004—. Grantee Fed. Ministry Rsch. and Tech., Bonn, 1989, 95. Fellow Am. Acad. Ophthalmology; mem. Deutsche Ophthalmologische Gesellschaft, Assn. Rsch. in Vision and Ophthalmology. Roman Catholic. Office: U Eye Hosp Stenglinstr 2 86156 Augsburg Germany Office Phone: 49 (0) 821-400-2551. Office Fax: 49 (0) 821-400-2140.

MUELLER, CHARLES FREDERICK, radiologist, educator; b. Dayton, Ohio, May 26, 1936; s. Susan Elizabeth (Wine) W.; m. Kathe Louise Lutterbei, May 28, 1966; children: Charles Jeffrey, Theodore Martin, Kathryn Suzanne. BA in English, U. Cin., 1958, MD, 1962. Diplomate Am. Bd. Radiology, Am. Bd. Nuclear Medicine. Asst. prof. radiology U. N.Mex., Albuquerque, 1968-72, assoc. prof. radiology, 1972-74, Ohio State U., Columbus, 1974-79, acting chmn. dept. radiology, 1975, prof. radiology, 1979—2002, prof. radiology, dir.

post grad. program radiology, 1980-2000, acting chmn. dept. radiology, 1990—93, prof. emeritus, 2002—. Bd. dirs. Univ. Radiologists, Inc., Columbus, v.p., 1980—86; pres., founder Ambulatory Imaging, Inc., Columbus, 1985—2002. Author: Emergency Radiology, 1982; contbr. numerous articles to profl. jours.; editl. bd. Emergency radiology, 1995-2002; editor Internat. Trauma, Am. Jour. Roentgenology, 1997-2004. Com. chmn. Boy Scouts Am., Columbus, 1980—84; vol. Columbus Free Clinic, 2003—, Franklin Park Conservatory, 2003—. Capt. USAF, 1966—68. Research grantee Ohio State U. 1975, Gen. Electric Co., 1986-88; Gold medalist ASER, 2001. Fellow Am. Coll. Radiologists; mem. AMA, Assn. Univ. Radiologists, Am. Roentgen Ray Soc., Am. Soc. Emergency Radiology (founder 1988, pres. 1993-94, Gold medal 2001), Radiol. Soc. N.Am., N.Mex. Soc. Radiologists (pres. 1973-74), Ohio State Radiol. Soc. (pres. 1986-87). Republican. Presbyterian. Avocations: fly fishing, hiking, model railroading. Office: Ohio State Univ Hosps Dept Radiology 410 W 10th Ave Columbus OH 43210-1240 E-mail: cmueller@columbus.rr.com.

MUELLER, CHRISTA, radiologist; b. Sonthofen, Germany, June 5, 1962; d. Joachim Friedrich and Waltraud Mueller. MD, Ludwig-Maximilians U., Munich, Germany, 1994; PhD, Ludwig-Maximilians U., 1995. Physician Technic U., Munich, 1992—93, Ludwig-Maximilians U., Munich, 1994—96, Katharinen Hosp., Stuttgart, Germany, 1996—98; physician, rschr. Georg-August U., Goettingen, Germany, 1998—2002, sr. radiologist, rschr., 2002—04; radiologist Paracelsus U., Salzburg, Austria, 2004—. Contbr. articles to profl. jours. Mem.: German Roentgen Soc. Office: Paracelsus Univ Hinterreit 478 A 5084 Grossgmain Austria Home Phone: 0043-6247-7369; Office Phone: 0043-662-4482-57769. Personal E-mail: christamueller@yahoo.de. Business E-Mail: ch.mueller@salk.at.

MUELLER, MARKUS M., medical researcher, transfusion medicine and hemostaseology, assistant medical director, consultant, blood donation department head; b. Ravensburg, Germany, July 15, 1965; 1 child, Katharina F. Diploma, Bildungszentrum St. Konrad, Ravensburg, Germany, 1984; MD magna cum laude, U. Ulm Med. Sch., Germany, 1992. Intern St. Elisabeth Ctrl. Hosp., Ravensburg, Germany, 1993—94; resident hematology and hemostaseology U. Hosp. Ulm, 1995—96; sr. clin. team leader Novartis Pharma, Nuernberg, Bayern, Germany, 1996—2001; registrar transfusion medicine and immunohematology German Red Cross Blood Donor Svc., Frankfurt, Germany, 2001—07, cons. in transfusion medicine, 2008—, asst. med. dir., 2010, head, dept. blood donation, 2011. Cons. Novartis Oncology, 2005—; cons. in transfusion medicine, 2008. Mem. editl. bd.: Hemotherapy Jour. With med. dept. German Air Force, 1985—86. Mem.: Internat. Soc. Blood Transfusion, Soc. Thrombosis and Hemostasis Rsch., German Soc. Transfusion Medicine and Immunohematology. Roman Catholic. Avocation: running. Office: German Red Cross Blood Donor Service Sandhofstrasse 1 Frankfurt 60528 Germany Office Phone: 49 69 6782 233. Business E-Mail: m.mueller@blutspende.de.

MUELLER, NICOLAS JOHANNES, infectious disease specialist, researcher; s. Johannes and Jacqueline Mueller; m. Catherine Burkhard, Aug. 14, 1998; children: Jules Camille, Rémy Vincent, Florine Sylvie. BA in Gen. Edn. and Langs., Literargymnasium Ramibuhl; MD, U. Zurich Sch. Medicine, 1990. Bd. Cert. Internal Medicine Swiss Med. Assn., 1998, Swiss Med. Assn., 2004. Rsch. fellow in medicine Harvard Med. Sch., Infectious Diseases Divsn., Mass. Gen. Hosp., Boston, 1998—2003; Privatdozent Faculty of Medicine, U. Zurich, Switzerland, 2005—. Recipient Nat. Rsch. Svc. award, Tng. in Transplantation Biology, Pub. Health Services grant, NIH, 2000—03, Rsch. Project, Swiss Soc. for Infectious Disease, 2004; Post Doctoral grant, Swiss NSF, 1998—2000. Mem.: Swiss Transplantation Soc., Internat. Immunocompromised Host Soc., Am. Soc. Transplantation, Swiss Soc. for Infectious Diseases, Swiss Soc. Internal Medicine. Roman Catholic. Achievements include research in infectious disease related to Xenotransplantation (Laboratory of Prof. Jay Fishman, Dir., Transplant Infectious Disease and Compromised Host Program, Infectious Disease Divsn., Mass.). Avocation: winemaking. Office: U Hosp Zurich Ramistrasse 100 Zurich 8091 Switzerland Office Fax: +41 44 255 32 91. E-mail: nicolas.mueller@usz.ch.

MUELLER, PETER STERLING, psychiatrist, educator; b. NYC, Dec. 28, 1930; s. Reginald Sterling and Edith Louise (Welleck) M.; m. Ruth Antonia Shipman, Aug. 9, 1958; children: Anne Louise, Peter Sterling, Paul Shipman, Elizabeth Ruth. AB, Princeton U., 1952; MD, U. Rochester, 1956. Am. Cancer Soc. student fellow Francis Delafield Hosp., NYC, summer 1955; intern Bellevue Hosp., Columbia U., NYC, 1956-57; asst. resident in psychiatry Henry Phipps Psychiat. Clinic, Johns Hopkins Hosp., Balt., 1963-66; asst. prof. psychiatry Sch. Medicine, Yale U., New Haven, 1966-72; asso. prof. psychiatry Coll. Medicine and Dentistry of N.J., Rutgers Med. Sch., Piscataway, 1972-76, clin. prof. psychiatry, 1976-82; cons. for Rehab. Unit and Center for Indsl. Human Resources, Community Mental Health Center, 1973—; mem. courtesy staff dept. psychiatry Princeton Med. Center, 1976—. Cons. in psychotherapy Conn. Valley Hosp., Middletown, 1966-72; cons. in psychiatry Carrier Clinic, Belle Mead, N.J., 1973-82, VA Hosp., Lyons, N.J., 1975-78 Contbr. writings in field to profl. publs. U.S. and Brit., papers to profl. confs. on the use patents in U.S. and fgn. countries for direct dopamine agonists in the treatment of tobacco addiction. Served with USPHS, 1957-63. Recipient Exemplary Psychiatrist award Nat. Alliance for the Mentally Ill, 1994. Mem. Am. Psychosomatic Soc., Am. Psychiat. Assn., AAAS, Amyotrophic Lateral Sclerosis Found. (adv. bd.), Sigma Xi. Episcopalian. Achievements include patents for treatment of disorders secondary to organic impairment with sibutramine; method of treatment of Irritable Bowel Syndrome with a fibric acid. Home: 182 Snowden Ln Princeton NJ 08540-3915 Office: 601 Ewing St Ste B-3 Princeton NJ 08540-2757 Office Phone: 609-924-4061.

MUELLER, STEFAN CAJETAN, urologist, educator; m. Romy Behrmann; children: Matthias, Claudia, Franziska. Abitur, Gymnasium, Kronach, 1971; MD, Bavaria, Germany, 1977. Rsch. fellow and vis. asst. prof. Dept. Urology UCSF, 1986—87; asst. prof. Dept. Urology, Mainz, Germany, 1987—90, assoc. prof., 1990—94, prof. urology chmn. Bonn, Germany, 1994—. Dept. dir. U. Hosp., Bonn, Germany, 1994—. Recipient Maximilian Nitze prize, German Soc. Urology, 1999. Office: Dept Urology Sigmund-Freud St 25 Bonn 53105 Germany Office Fax: 49 228 287 14185. Business E-Mail: stefan.mueller@ukb.uni-bonn.de.

MUELLERBUCHHOF, RALF, psychologist; b. Dresden, Saxony, Germany, Nov. 23, 1971; s. Günter Kurt Robert and Dietrun Pauline Marie Muellerbuchhof; m. Franziska Charlotte Seyfferth, June 27, 2003; children: Theo Ludwig, Till Emil. MSc in Psychology, Tech. U. Dresden, Germany, Dr. rer. nat., 2006. Rsch. asst. Tech. U. Dresden, Saxony, 2000—; postdoc. rsch. fellow Leipzig U., Saxony, 2007—. Achievements include research in comparison of competence assessment by self and supervisory ratings vs. situational judgment tests on technically skilled personnel. Office: Univ Leipzig Karl-Heine-Str 22b Leipzig 04229 Germany Office Phone: 49-341-9731572. Office Fax: 49-341-9731499. Business E-Mail: muellerbuchhof@uni-leipzig.de.

MUELLER-HEUBACH, EBERHARD, medical educator; b. Berlin, Feb. 24, 1942; came to U.S., 1968; s. Heinrich Gustav and Elisabeth (Heubach) M.; m. Cornelia Rosemarie Uffmann, Sept. 6, 1941; 1 child, Oliver Maximilian. MD, U. Koeln, 1966. Intern U. Koeln (Germany) Women's Hosp., 1967-68, Middlesex Gen. Hosp., New Brunswick, NJ, 1968-69; rsch. fellow Columbia U., 1969-71; resident Columbia-Presbyn. Med. Ctr., NYC, 1971-74, chief resident, 1974-75; asst. prof. Magee-Women's Hosp. U. Pitts., 1975-81, assoc. prof. Magee-Women's Hosp., 1981-89; prof., chmn. ob-gyn. Sch. Medicine Wake Forest U., Winston-Salem, 1989—2002, prof. ob-gyn., 2002—07, prof. emeritus, 2007—. Mem. editl. bd.: Ob-Gyn, 1999—2002. Mem. Am. Gyn.-Ob. Soc. (asst. sec. 1999-2001, sec. 2002-04, pres.-elect 2004-05, pres. 2005-06), Soc. Gynecol. Investigation, The Perinatal Rsch. Soc., Coun. Univ. Chairs Ob-Gyn. (pres. 1998-2000). Avocations: travel, art. E-mail: emueller@wfubmc.edu.

MUENCH, KARL HUGO, clinical geneticist; b. St. Louis, May 3, 1934; MD, Washington U., St. Louis, 1960. Diplomate Am. Bd. Med. Genetics. Intern Barnes Hosp., St. Louis, 1960-61; fellow in biological chemistry Stanford U. Sch. Medicine, 1961-65; staff mem. Jackson Meml. Hosp., Miami, Fla.; prof. medicine U. Miami Sch. Medicine. Mem. AMA, ACP, Am. Coll. Med. Genetics. Office: U Miami Sch Med Divsn Endocrinology Diabetes and Metabol PO Box 16960 Miami FL 33101-6960 Office Phone: 305-243-5950. Business E-Mail: kmuench@med.miami.edu.

MUFSON, MAURICE ALBERT, infectious diseases physician, educator; b. NYC, July 7, 1932; s. Max and Faye M.; m. Diane Cecile Weiss, Apr. 1, 1962; children: Michael Jeffrey, Karen Andrea, Pamela Beth. AB, Bucknell U., 1953; MD, NYU, 1957. Intern Bellevue Hosp., NYC, 1957-58, resident, 1958-59; chief resident Cook County Hosp., Chgo., 1965-66; sr. surgeon USPHS Lab. Infectious Diseases, NIH, 1961-65; from asst. prof. medicine to prof. U. Ill., 1965-76; prof. Marshall U., 1976—2002, prof. emeritus, 2002—, chmn. dept. medicine, 1976—2000, chmn. emeritus, 2000—. Vis. scientist Karolinska Inst., 1984-85. Contbr. articles to profl. jours. Served with U.S. Navy, 1959-61. WHO grantee, 1967; recipient Meet-the-Scholar award Marshall U., 1986, Rschr. of Yr. award Sigma Xi, Marshall U., 1989, Solomon A. Berson Alumni Achievement award in health sci. NYU Sch Medicine, 1997; co-recipient Louis Weinstein award Jour. Clin. Infectious Diseases, 1994; named to Greater Huntington Wall of Fame, 2002. Master ACP (traveling scholar 1987, Laureate award W.Va. chpt.), Infectious Diseases Soc. Am.; mem. AMA, Soc. Exptl. Biology and Medicine, Ctrl. Soc. Clin. Rsch., So. Soc. Clin. Investigation, W.Va. State Med. Assn., Assn. Profs. Medicine (counselor 1992-95, pres.-elect 1995-96, pres. 1996-97, past pres. 1997-98), Marshall U. Joan C. Edwards Sch. Medicine Alumni Assn. (hon.), Alpha Omega Alpha. Office: Marshall U Sch Medicine 1249 15th St 2nd Fl Huntington WV 25701 Home Phone: 304-522-9357; Office Phone: 304-691-1050. Personal E-mail: maurymufson@comcast.net. Business E-Mail: mufson@marshall.edu.

MUFSON, ROBERT ALLAN, cell biologist; b. NYC, June 10, 1946; s. Morton and Anne T. (Stein) M.; m. Doris Ettlinger, May 14, 1973 (div. Dec. 30, 1980); m. Dolores V. Espinoza; children: Jeffrey, Laura. BA, CUNY, 1968; PhD, Brown U., 1974. Postdoctoral fellow Nat. Cancer Inst. U. Wis., Madison, 1974-77; staff fellow Inst. Cancer Rsch. Columbia U., NYC, 1977-80; asst. prof. Inst. Environ. Medicine NYU, 1980-83; sr. sci. Genetics Inst. Inc., Cambridge, Mass., 1983-88; sr. sci. dept. immunology Holland Lab./ARC, Rockville, Md., 1988-98; program dir. cancer immunology and hematology br. Nat. Cancer Inst., NIH, Bethesda, Md., 1998—, br. chief Cancer Immunology and Hematology br., 2000—. Cons. Genetics INst., Cambridge, Mass., 1988-89, Otsuka Pharm., Rockville, 1989; ad hoc study sect. mem. NIH, Bethesda, 1989-95. NIH fellow, 1974; grantee NIH, 1981, 82, 91. Mem. Internat. Soc. for Exptl. Hematology, Am. Assn. Cancer Rsch., Am. Soc. Hematology, Am. Soc. for Biochemistry & Molecular Biology. Office: Nat Cancer Inst Cancer Immunol Hematology 6130 Executive Blvd Bethesda MD 20892-0001 Office Phone: 301-496-7815. Business E-Mail: rm401g@nih.gov, am214t@nih.gov.

MUGABURE, BORJA, anesthesiologist; b. Donostia- San Sebastián, Spain, Oct. 5, 1965; Degree in Medicine, Basque Country U., 1982; degree in Anesthesiology, U. Donostia Hosp., 1987. Mgr. in chief acute pain svc. dept. anesthesiology U. Donostia Hosp., 1988—. Avocation: mountain climbing. Home: Paseo de Berio n° 22 3° B Donostia-San Sebastián Guipuzcoa 20018 Spain Personal E-mail: mugabure@yahoo.es.

MUGNAINI, ENRICO, neuroscience educator; b. Colle Val d'Elsa, Italy, Dec. 10, 1937; came to U.S., 1969. children: Karin E., Emiliano N.G. MD cum laude, U. Pisa, Italy, 1962; degree (hon.), U. Torino, 2005, U. Pisa, 2005, U. Salamanca, 2006. Microscopy lab. rsch. fellow dept. anatomy U. Oslo Med. Sch., 1963, asst. prof., head of electron microscopy lab., 1964-66, assoc. prof., 1967-69; prof. biobehavioral scis. and psychology, head lab. of neuromorphology U. Conn., Storrs, 1969-95; E.C. Stuntz prof. cell biology, dir. Inst. for Neurosci., Northwestern U., Chgo., 1995—2006. Vis. prof. dept. anatomy Harvard U., Boston, 1969-70; traveling lectr. Grass Found., 1986, 1990. Mng. editor USA Anatomy and Embryology Jour., 1989—; contbr. more than 200 articles to books and jours. Recipient Decennial Camillo Golgi award Acad. Nat. dei Lincei, 1981, Campano d'Oro award, 2005; Sen. Javits Neurosci. Rsch. Investigator grantee NIH, 1985-92, Fernandez-Lindsay Lectureship grantee U. Chgo., 2003. Mem. AAAS, Am. Assn. Anatomists, Am. Soc. Cell Biology, Internat. Brain Rsch. Orgn., Internat. Soc. Developmental Neurosci., Norwegian Nat. Acad. Scis. and Letters, Soc. Neurosci., Inst. Lombardo, Acad. Sci. Lettere (corr. 2005-), Cajal Club (pres. 1987-88). Office: U Northwestern Feinberg Sch Medicine 5-474 Searle Bldg 320 E Superior St Chicago IL 60611-3010 Business E-Mail: e-mugnaini@northwestern.edu.

MUHN, JUDY ANN, psychologist, genealogist, trainer; b. Detroit, Dec. 29, 1952; d. Wilbur William and Dolores Eleanor (Sutinen) Nimer; m. Dennis James Muhn, June 6, 1975. BS, Mich. State U., East Lansing, 1975; MEd, Boston U., Mass., 1992; MA in Counseling, U. San Francisco, Calif., 1997. Lic. psychologist Mich. Legis. aide press sec. to Calif. state senator, 1982—84; dir. pub. rels. Tierra del Oro coun. Girl Scouts U.S., 1984—86, mgr. mem. devel. San Antonio area coun., 1986—90; adj. faculty U. Md. Germany, 1992—94; ind. cons. Capital Enquiry, Sacramento, 1994—96; counselor Yuba City Indian Health Ctr., 1997; intervention counselor Sutter-Yuba Mental Health, 1997—98; counselor, intern White Ho. Cmty. Counseling Ctr., 1998; pvt. practice Wixom, Mich., 1998—; dep. exec. dir. U. Santo Tomas Alumni Assn., 1998—2000; therapist Brighton Hosp., 2000—01, Advanced Counseling Svcs., Brighton, 2001—03; dir. adult devel. and vol. svcs. Girl Scouts Metro Detroit, 2002—08; Area Mngr. Oakland County United Way, Southeastern, Mich., 2008—. Adj. faculty Henry Ford CC, 1998—2001, Oakland CC, 1998—2001; spkr. in field. Columnist: Press-Republican, 1995—98. Bd. dirs., chmn. pub. affairs com. Planned Parenthood Clinton County, NY, 1980—81; bd. dirs. Family Planning Advs., Albany, 1981, Planned Parenthood San Antonio, 1987—89; founder Women's Roundtable, Plattsburgh, 1981; pres. Planned Parenthood Assn. Sacramento Valley, 1982—84; sec. San Antonio Coun. Native Ams., 1986—89; co-founder Womanspirit Rising, 1987—89; mem. Metis Cmty. Ea. Can. Recipient Human Rights award, Sacramento Fair Housing Commn., 1983, Woman of Yr. award-Nonprofit, YWCA, Sacramento, 1984, Diversity Champien award, Birmingham Race Rels. U. Task Force, 2009; named Bd. Mem. of Yr., Planned Parenthood Sacramento Valley, 1982. Mem.: ASTD, Nat. Geneal. Soc., Assn. Prof. Genealogists, Metis Cmty. Ea. Can., Assn. Vol. Adminstrs., Met. Detroit Vol. Adminstrs., Assn. Univ. Women, Amnesty Internat., Greenpeace, San Antonio Women's C. of C. (bd. dirs. 1989), Assn. Girl Scout Exec. Staff. Personal E-mail: jmuhn@aol.com. Business E-Mail: judy.muhn@uwsem.org.

MUHR, WILLIAM, diagnostic radiologist; MD, MCP Hahnemann U., 1983. Diplomate Am. Bd. of Radiology-diagnostic radiology. Fellow Hahnemman Univ. Hosp., intern, 1984, resident, 1987. Mem.: AMA, Soci. for Cardiovasc. Magnetic Resonance, N. Am. Soc. for Cardiac Imaging, Internat. Soc. for Magnetic Resonance in Medicine, Am. Roentgen Ray Soc., Radiol. Soc. of N. Am., Am. Coll. of Radiology, West Jersey Med. Soc., Camden County Med. Soc. Office: South Jersey Radiology Associates PO Box 23355 Newark NJ 07189 Office Phone: 856-770-0300. Office Fax: 856-770-0395.

MUIR, RUTH BROOKS, alcohol and drug abuse services professional, consultant; b. Washington, Nov. 27, 1924; d. Charles and Adelaide Chenery (Masters) B.; m. Robert Mathew Muir, Nov. 26, 1947 (dec. Feb. 20, 1996); children: Robert Brooks, Martha Louise, Heather Sue. BA in Art, Rollins Coll., Winter Park, Fla., 1947; MA in Rehab. Counseling, U. Iowa, 1979. Cert. substance abuse counselor, Iowa. Program advisor Iowa Meml. Union, Iowa City, 1959-66; counselor, coord. Mid Eastern Coun. on Chem. Abuse, Iowa City, 1976-81; patient rep. Univ. Hosp., Iowa City, 1982-85; rsch. project interviewer dept. psychiatry U. Iowa Coll. Medicine, 1985-88; pvt. practice family counselor, 1984—. Artist: exhibitions include Iowa City Sr. Ctr., 1987, 92, Iowa City Art Ctr., 1989, U. Iowa Hosp., 1991, Great Midwestern Ice Cream Co., 1991, Summit St. Gallery, 1995, Iowa City C. of C., 2001, Iowa City's First Art Walk March, 2003; creator, coord. therapeutic series Taking Control, Iowa City Sr. Ctr., 1986-87, Art Walk Lorenz Boot Shop, 2003; one woman shows include Pastels, Paintings and Prints Englert Theatre, Iowa City, 2006. Vol. coord. art exhibits Sr. Ctr., Iowa City, 1992-94, Iowa City Arts Exhbn. Com., 1996, Arrowmont Sch. Art, 1996—, Arrowmont Amb., 1996-98; treas. bd. dirs. Crisis Ctr., Iowa City, 1976-77; sec. coun. elders Sr. Citizens Ctr., Iowa City, 1976-78; pres. Unitarian-Universalist Iowa City Women's Fedn., 1985, mem. pastoral com., 2006; friend U. Iowa Mus. Art, docent, 1999-2006; active Opera Supers, Iowa City Unitarian U.N. Envoy; fgn. rels. coun., bd. dirs. annual changing family conf. U. Iowa, 1986-92; non-govtl. rep. Earth Summit Global Forum, 1992; care review bd. Mental Health Homes, 1997-99; bd. dirs., exhbn. chair Arts Iowa City, 2002—; coord. art exhbns. Melrose Meadows, 2004—; UU pastoral care com. 2005-07. Mem.: AAUW (state cultural rep. 1990—92, Iowa City chpt. co-chair for programs 1998—99, rep. Earth S), Health Care: Health Svcs., Nat. League Am. PEN Women (membership chair 2002—04, v.p. 2004—, 2007—, program chair 2008—), Iowa City Unitarian Soc. (adult program com. 1993—94, unitarian care com. 1993—, membership com.), Nat. Soc. Colonial Dames, U. Iowa Retirees Assn. (bd. mem. 2004—, chair membership 2005—), U. Iowa Print and Drawing Study Club (bd. dirs. 2003—04, pres. elect 2005), Pi Beta Phi (pres. alumnae club 1995—97). Home and Office: 6 Glendale Ct Iowa City IA 52245-4430 Office Phone: 319-337-7287. Business E-Mail: ruthmuir@q.com.

MUIR-TAYLOR, DOUGLAS JAMES, ophthalmologist; b. Edinburgh, May 4, 1932; s. Thomas William and Jane Craig Muir-Taylor; m. Lesley Elizabeth Muir-Taylor; children: Victoria Grace, Elizabeth Laura. Grad., Heriot-Watt U., Edinburgh, 1954; MB BChir, U. London, 1960. House surgeon ophthalmology Kings Coll. Hosp., London, 1960—60, house physician medicine, 1960—61; sr. house surgeon A&E Lewisham Hosp., London, 1961—62; gen. practice prin. London Redbridge, 1962; clin. assoc. ophthalmology Moorfields Hosp., London, 1962—66, Royal London Hosp., 1978—85, assoc. specialist ophthalmology, 1978—85, clin. dir. contact lens and prosthetic dept., 1991—. Clin. dir. Telephone Cables GEC, London, 1963—90, Electric Windings Ltd., London, 1970—94, F.J. Cipa Panel Craft PT Ltd., London, 1996—. Fellow: Rpyal Soc. Medicine, Brit. Optical Assn., Brit. Coll. Optometry; mem.: Contact Lens Assn. Ophthalmologists, Royal Coll. Physicians (licentiate), Am. Soc. Cataract and Refractive Surgery, Royal Coll. Ophthalmologists, Royal Coll. Surgeons. Achievements include research in photorefractive keratectomy in high myopia; photorefractive keratectomy after corneal surgery; photorefractive keratectomy in pregnancy and menopause; correction of aphakia with extended wear gas permeable contact lenses, serum markers in germ cell tumours. Avocations: fishing, winter sports, shooting, fine wines, golf.

MUKAI, AI, physiatrist; b. Tokyo, Oct. 13, 1977; arrived in U.S., 1989; d. Kazuko Mukai. Studied piano, Manhattan Sch. of Music, 1993—95; BA in Psychology, Columbia U., NYC, 1999; MD, Pa. State U., 2004. Lic. Ill., 2005, cert. in advanced cardiac life support 2004, in pediat. advanced life support 2004; in advanced cardiac. life support & basic life support 2004, lic. Calif. State Med., 2008, Tex.

State Med., 2009. Intern Pa. State U. Coll. Medicine, Hershey Med. Ctr., 2004—05; resident phys. medicine and rehab. Northwestern U., Rehab. Inst. Chgo., 2005—; with Tex. Orthop., Sports & Rehab., 2009—. Preceptor phys. diagnosis curriculum Pa. State Coll. Medicine, 2004—05; co-moderator Phys. Medicine and Rehab. Forum, Studentdoctor.net & painrounds.com, 2005—; mem. various coms. Rehab. Inst. Chgo., 2005—, mem. ethics com., 2005—06, mem. continuous quality improvement, 2005—, mem. labs. and x-rays com., 2006—, super-user, Cerner Project Mercury, 2006—; presenter, lectr., rschr. in field. Contbg. editor, coord.: Rehab in Review, 2006—, book reviewer: Lippincott Williams and Wilkins, 2001—; contbr. articles to profl. jours., chapters to books; jour. reviewer: Archives of Phys. Medicine and Rehab., 2005—, Jour. Gen. Internal Medicine, 2005. Recipient 1st pl., NYC Dept. Health, Health Rsch. Tng. Program Competition, 1998, Med. Student Rsch. award, Pa. State Coll. Medicine, 2004, 2nd pl., Pa. Med. Soc. Poster Competition, 2004, Sarah Baskin award, 2008, Scholl Recognition award, 2008; named Intern of Yr., Hershey Med. Ctr., Dept. Gastroenterology and Hepatology, 2005, Hershey Med. Ctr., Dept. Hematology and Oncology, 2005; grantee, William Randolph Hearst Found., 2006—08; scholar, Internat. Starr Found., 1995, Japanese-Am. Assn., 1995; Roslyn S. Silver '27 scholar, 1999, Gen. Clin. Rsch. Ctr. scholar, Pa. State Coll. Medicine, 2000, Mohler scholar, 2000, Hammersla scholar, 2001, 2002, Hershey Foods scholar, 2003. Mem.: AMA, Asian and Pacific Islander Am. Health Forum, Student Nat. Med. Assn. (chpt. co-pres. Penn State Coll. Medicine 2000—01, nat. liaison to Am. Med. Student Assn. 2001—02), Asian and Pacific Am. Med. Student Assn., Am. Med. Student Assn. (chpt. co-pres. Penn State Coll. Medicine 2000—01, assoc. trustee region III 2001—02), Am. Acad. Phys. Medicine and Rehab. (chair bylaws/ops. and strategic planning com. resident physician coun. 2004—05, sec. 2005—06, mentor med. student mentoring program 2005—, pres. resident physician coun. 2006—07, chair membership com. bd. gov. 2009—), Am. Congress Rehab. Medicine (mem. membership com. and info. tech. com. 2005—06, 2005—), Physiatric Assn. for Spine Sports and Occupl. Rehab., Assn. Acad. Physiatrists, Ill. State Phys. Medicine and Rehab. Soc. Avocations: piano, drawing, photography, languages. Office: Tex Orthop, Sports & Rehab 4700 Seton Ctr Pky Austin TX 78757 Home: 421 W 3RD ST APT 1008 Austin TX 78701-4168

MUKAI, HIDEFUMI, research scientist; b. Osaka, Japan, Mar. 22, 1981; PhD, Kyoto U., 2009. Rsch. fellow Kyoto U., 2009; rsch. scientist RIKEN Ctr. Molecular Imaging Sci., 2009—. Recipient prize, Kinki br., Pharm. Soc. Japan. Mem.: Japan Soc. Drug Delivery Sys., Japanese Soc. Molecular Imaging, Pharm. Soc. Japan. Avocation: violin. Office: 6-7-3 Minatojima-minamimachi Chuo-ku Kobe Hyogo 650-0047 Japan Business E-Mail: hmukai@riken.jp.

MUKAI, MINORU, oncologist; b. Ryugasaki, Japan, July 28, 1947; s. Masu Makai and Jun Sakurai; m. Takako Mukai; children: Tomomi, Manami. MD, Chiba U., Japan, 1972, PhD, 1985. Resident Chiba U., 1972-77; chief surgeon Shioya Hosp., Tochigi, Japan, 1970-79, Naruto Hosp., Chiba, 1980-83; asst. prof., surg. oncologist 2d dept. surgry Chiba U., 1984-86; chief oncologist Nat. Inst. Radiol. Sci., Chiba, 1987-97, dir. Kamogawa City Hosp., Chiba, 1997-99, Shioya Gen. Hosp., Tochigi, 2000—02; med. scientist Kumamoto City, Japan, 2002—04, Wakayama City, Japan, 2005—06, Ryugasaki City, 2007—. Mem. Japan Soc. Clin. Oncology, Order Internat. Fellowship. Avocations: hiking, monochrome painting. Home: 3993 Kome-machi Ryugasaki City 309-0018 Japan Business E-Mail: xa48728@cg7.so-net.ne.jp.

MUKAIYAMA, TERUAKI, chemist, educator; b. Ina, Japan, Jan. 5, 1927; s. Mikio and Akiko (Osada) M.; m. Hiroko Hoshino, Mar. 30, 1953; 1 child, Taketo. BSc, Tokyo Inst. Tech., 1948; PhD, Tokyo U., 1957; degree (hon.), Tech. U. Munich, 1976. Asst. prof. Gakushuin U., Tokyo, 1953-58; from asst. prof. to prof. Tokyo Inst. Tech., 1958-73, prof. U. Tokyo, 1973-87, prof. emeritus chemistry; prof. Sci. U. Tokyo, 1987—2002; prof. Ctr. Basic Rsch. Kitasato Inst., Tokyo, 2002—. Disting. prof. Sci. U. Tokyo, 1992—; pres. Rsch. Inst. Sci. & Tech., Noda, Japan, 1991-02; advisor basic rsch. ctr. Mitsui Petrochem. Industries, Ltd., Chiba, Japan, 1987-90; cons. Syntex, Palo Alto, Calif., 1976-94. Author: Challenges in Synthetic Organic Chemistry, 1990. Decorated Chevalier de l'ordre Nat. du Mérite, France, Order of Culture, Japan, 1997; recipient Imperial and Acad. prize, Japan, 1983, Copernicus medal, Poland, 1985, Sir Derek Barton Gold medal, Eng., 2006; named Person of Cultural Merit, Japan, 1992. Mem. Polish Acad. Scis., French Acad. Scis., Pharm. Soc. Japan, Chem. Soc. Japan, NAS (fgn. assoc.). Office: Basic Rsch TCI 6-15-9 Toshima Tokyo 114-0003 Japan Office Phone: 81-3-3911-3111. E-mail: mukaiyam@abeam.ocn.ne.jp.

MUKAMAL, KENNETH J., internist; b. Oct. 20, 1966; MD, U. Calif., San Francisco, 1990. Cert. Internal Medicine, 1993. Intern and resident in internal medicine Yale-New Haven Hosp., 1993; fellow in internal medicine Beth Israel Deaconess Med. Ctr., Boston, 1998, physician; assoc. prof. medicine Harvard Med. Sch., Boston. Office: Healthcare Associates Beth Israel Deaconess Med Ctr E 330 Brookline Ave E/CC-6 Boston MA 02215 Office Phone: 617-667-9600. Office Fax: 617-667-8665.

MUKHERJEE, DIPANKAR, surgeon; b. New Delhi, Feb. 9, 1953; arrived in US, 1976; BS, U. New Delhi, 1970; MD, All-India Inst. Med. Sci., New Delhi, 1975. Cert. Am. Bd. Surgery, Am. Registry Diagnostic Med. Sonographers. Sr. house officer surgery Auckland Hosp. Bd., New Zealand, 1976—77; intern gen. surgery St. Mary's Hosp., Rochester, NY, 1977—78; resident gen. surgery Genesee, Highland and Rochester Gen. Hosps., 1978—79, 1981—82, Genesee, Rochester Gen. and Strong Meml. Hosps., 1979—82, Rochester Gen. and Strong Meml. Hosps., 1980—81; fellow peripheral vascular surgery St. Vincent Hosp., Portland, Oreg., 1982—83; pvt. practice, 1983—87; chief divsn. vascular surgery Madigan Army Med. Ctr., Tacoma, 1988—90, surg. dir. ICU, 1988—90, active staff Inova Fairfax Hosp., Falls Church, Va., 1990—, apptd. chief sect. vascular surgery, 2008—; active staff Va. Hosp. Ctr., Arlington, 1990—, Columbia Reston Hosp., Va., 1990—, chief dept. surgery, 1998—99; clin. asst. prof. surgery Uniformed Svs. U. Health Scis., F. Edward Herbert Sch. Medicine, Bethesda, Md., 1990—, Georgetown U. Hosp., Washington, 1998—; pvt. practice Cardiac, Vascular and Thoracic Surgery Assocs., P.C., Annandale, Va., 2003—; clin. assoc. prof. surgery and neurol. surgery George Washington U. Sch. Medicine and Health Scis., 2006—. Clin. asst. prof. surgery divsn. vascular surgery Oreg. Health Scis. U. Sch. Medicine, Portland, 1983—88; program co-chmn. Pacific NW Vascular Soc., 1988; pres. India Physicians No. Va., 1995—96; spkr. in field. Contbr. articles to profl. jours. Decorated Army Commendation medal Dept. of the Army; named Outstanding Tchr. of Yr., Georgetown U. Med. Ctr., 1999; named one of Top Doctors, Washingtonian Mag., 1993, 1995, 1999, 2001, 2003, 2005, 2008, Area's Outstanding Physician Specialists, Washington Consumers Checkbook, 1996, 1998, 2000, 2002, 2004, 2006, Best Doctors in Am., 1998. Fellow: ACS, Soc. for Vascular Surgery (disting.); mem.: Faifax County Med. Soc., Portland Surg. Soc. (program chmn. 1986), Portland Vascular Soc. (program chmn. 1985), NW Vascular Soc., North Pacific Surg. Assn., Internat. Soc. for Endovascular Surgery, Internat. Soc. for Cardiovasc. Surgery, Chesapeake Vascular Soc. (pres.-elect 2004—05). Achievements include patents for catheter introducer for antegrade and retrograde medical procedures. Office: Vascular Surg Assoc Inc 3022 Williams Dr Ste 100 Fairfax VA 22031 *

MUKHERJEE, SAMUDRA, pediatrician; b. Kolkata, West Bengal, India, June 12, 1967; MBBS, Calcutta Med. Coll., 1991; MD, Royal Coll. Paediat. and Child Health, DCH, 2000. Paediat. cons. Basildon and Thurrock U. Hosp. Nhs Found. Trust, 2007—. Master: Royal Coll. Paediatrics And Child Health. Avocation: gardening. Home: 174 Priests Ln Brentwood Essex CM15 8HT England Personal E-mail: samudra@doctors.org.uk.

MUKHERJEE, SIDDHARTHA, oncologist, educator; b. New Delhi, July 21, 1970; m. Sarah Sze. Grad., Stanford U., Calif.; PhD in Immunology, Magdalen Coll., Oxford U.; MD, Harvard Med Sch., 2000. Diplomate American Bd. Internal Medicine, cert. in med. oncology. Internist, oncology fellow Mass. Gen. Hosp.; former faculty Harvard Med. Sch., Boston; asst. prof. medicine Columbia U., NYC, 2009—. Staff cancer physician Columbia U. Med. Ctr., 2009—. Author: The Emperor of All Maladies: A Biography of Cancer, 2010 (one of Top 10 Books of 2010, NY Times, O-The Oprah mag., Pulitzer prize for gen. nonfiction, 2011); contbr. articles to profl. jours. Rhodes Scholar, 1993—95. Office: Columbia U Herbert Irving Comprehensive Cancer Ctr 1130 St Nicholas Ave Rm 603 New York NY 10032 Office Phone: 212-851-4617. E-mail: sm3252@columbia.edu. *

MUKHERJEE, SWARUPANANDA, medical educator; b. Burdwan, India, Apr. 2, 1981; PharmM, Rajiv Gandhi U. Health Scis., Bangalore, India, 2004; degree in Intellectual Property Rights, Indian Inst. Sci., Bangalore, 2008. Lectr., rsch. scientist Krupanidhi Coll. Pharmacy, Bangalore, 2007—10; asst. prof. NSHM Coll. Pharm. Tech., Kolkata, 2010—. Rsch. grant, Rajiv Gandhi U. Health Scis. Mem.: Indian Pharm. Assn. Avocations: writing, cricket. Office: NSHM Knowledge Campus Dept Pharmacy Kolkata Westbengal 700053 India Personal E-mail: swarup_mukherjee@rediffmail.com.

MUKHOPADHYAY, SAIKAT, medical researcher; b. Murshidabad, India, Nov. 28, 1973; MBBS, MD, Brandeis U., PhD, 2008. Postdoc. fellow Genentech., 2008—. Mem.: Am. Soc. Cell Biology. Office: Genentech MS231B 1 DNA Way South San Francisco CA 94080 Office Phone: 650-225-7181. E-mail: saikat.mukhopadhyay1@gmail.com.

MUKHTAR, MUHAMMED, dermatologist, researcher; b. Patna, Bihar, India, Jan. 20, 1968; s. Muhammed Matin and Rabia Khatoon; m. Safia Akhtar, Feb. 8, 1994; children: Sofia, Nadia, Maria. MBBS, Hindu U., Varanasi, India, 1991; MD in Skin, Banaras Hindu U., Varanasi, India, 1995. Cons. dermatologist Sofia Skin Ctr., Patna, Bihar, India, 1996—2008; asst. prof. dept. dermatology Katihar Med. Coll. And Hosp., Katihar, Bihar, 1998; lectr. dept. skin Jawaharlal Nehru Med. Coll. And Hosp., Aligarh Muslim U., Aligarh, Uttar Pradesh, India, 1998; cons. dermatologist Al-quwaiyah Gen. Hosp., Ministry Health, Riyadh, Saudi Arabia, 1998—2004; cons. dermatologist and dermatosurgeon Nadia Dermatosurgery Ctr., Binodpur Rd., Katihar, 1999—. Author (innovator): (innovative techniques in skin diseases) Suction Syringes Of Epidermal Grafting And Its Transfer. With Indian Navy, 1979—82. Scholar, Islamic Devel. Bank, Jeddah, Saudi Arabia, 1986—90; Nat. Merit scholar, Govt. of India, 1976—90. Mem.: IADVL, Nadia Dermatosurgery Ctr. (corr.). Islam. Achievements include research in new techniques in the treatment of vitiligo, skin tags, comedo, prolabial mucoceles, acne, recurrent furunculosis, uses of levamisole in chronic infections, nasal ala stabilization. Home: 13/289 Wazidpur Barh Patna 803213 India Office: Nadia Dermatosurgery Center Binodpur Road Katihar 854105 India Personal E-mail: muhammedmukhtar@hotmail.com, muhammedmukhtar20@gmail.com.

MUKWEGE, DENIS, obstetrician, gynecologist, surgeon; b. Mar. 1, 1955; m. Kaboyi Mapendo Madeleine; children: Alain, Patricia, Sylvie, Lisa, Denise. Bachelor's degree; med. degree, Burundi; med. degree in gynecology and obstetrics, CHU d'Angers, France. Podiatry specialist The Christian Hosp., Lemara, Democratic Republic of Congo; gynecologist, obstetrician Hosp. of Lemera, 1989—96; founder, dir., chief surgeon Panzi Hosp. of Bukavu, 1999—. Recipient UN Prize in the Field of Human Rights, 2008, Olof Palme prize, 2008; named African of Yr., Nigerian Daily Trust, 2009. Office: Panzi Hosp Bukavu CEPAC Med Dept B.P. 266 Bukavu Democratic Republic of Congo

MULA, MARCO, neuropsychiatrist; b. Novara, Italy, Dec. 16, 1974; MD cum laude, Amedeo Avogadro U., Novara, 1999; PhD in Psychiatry, U. Pisa, Italy, 2007. Resident Divsn. Neurology, Maggiore Hosp., Amedeo Avogadro U., Novara, Italy, 1999—2004; clin. rsch. fellow dept. clin. & exptl. epilepsy UCL Inst. Neurology, London, 2001—03; clin. rsch. fellow dept. neurology Amedeo Avogadro U., 2005—. Editor: Brain & Mind Matters-The Newsletter of the International Neuropsychiatry Association. Recipient Epilepsy award, Italian League Against Epilepsy, 2003; scholar, European Concerted Action Against Epilepsy, 2001. Mem.: European Fedn. Neuropsychiatry (internat. sci. com. 2004), Internat. Neuropsychiatry Assn. (internat. sci. com. 2003—04), Internat. Neuropsychiatry Assn. (exec. com. 2006), Internat. League Against Epilepsy (subcommn. affective disorder, psychobiology commn. 2002—05), Italian League Against Epilepsy (assoc.), Italian Soc. Neurosci. (assoc.), Fedn. European Neurosci. Socs. (assoc.), Italian Soc. Neurology (assoc.). Avocations: opera, poetry. Office: Dept Neurology A Avogadro University Cso Mazzini 18 Novara 28100 Italy Office Fax: 3903213733298. Personal E-mail: marcomula@yahoo.it.

MULCAHY, GABRIEL M., pathologist; b. Jersey City, Feb. 16, 1929; s. Joseph Alphonsus and Anna Elizabeth Mulcahy; m. Vesna Maria Mulcahy, May 24, 1958; children: Mary, Michael, Robert, Richard, Thomas, John, Gabriel Jr. AB, St. Peter's Coll., Jersey City, 1950; MD, Georgetown U., 1954. Diplomate Nat. Bd. Med. Examiners, Am. Bd. Pathology. Intern St. Michaels Hosp., Newark, 1954-55; med. officer U.S. Pub. Health Svc., Crownpoint, N.Mex., 1955-57, resident in pathology Seattle, 1957-59, Staten Island, NY, 1959-61, chief pathology svc. Detroit, 1961-62; with pathology faculty Creighton U., Omaha, 1962-69; dir. pathology Jersey City Med. Ctr., 1969-78; mem. pathology faculty Univ. Medicine and Dentistry N.J., Newark, 1978-2001; chief lab. med. Univ. Hosp., Newark, 1978-2001. Mem. editl bd.: Annals of Clin. and Lab. Sci., 2000—; contbr. articles to profl. jours. Mem. adv. bd. St. Ann's Home for the Aged, Jersey City, 1973-89, sec., 1973-83; pres. bd. edn. St. Paul's Parish Sch., Jersey City, 1973-78. Mem. AAAS, Am. Soc. Human Genetics, Am. Assn. Blood Banks, Assn. Clin. Scientists (sci. coun. 1999—), Coll. Am. Pathologists, Soc. Med. Decision Making. Roman Catholic. Avocations: history, philosophy, philology, photography. Home Phone: 201-434-1897. Personal E-mail: mulcahy21@comcast.net.

MULCH, ROBERT F., JR., physician; b. Quincy, Ill., June 21, 1951; s. Robert Franklin and Martha Jo (Nisi) M.; m. Barbara Ann Best, Apr. 5, 1975; children: Matthew, Luke. BS, U. Ill., 1973; MD, Rush Med. Coll., Chgo., 1977. Diplomate Am. Bd. Family Practice. Intern Riverside Meth. Hosp., Columbus, Ohio, 1977-78, resident in family practice, 1978-80; family physician Hillsboro (Ill.) Med. Ctr., 1980—; ptnr., med. dir. Springfield Clin., 1998—. Asst. clin. prof. family medicine So. Ill. U., Springfield, 1981—90; reviewer Ctrl. Ill. Peer Rev. Orgn.; mem. Hillsboro Planning Commn., Montgomery County Economic Devel. Corp. Fellow Am. Acad. Family Practice; mem. Am. Coll. Physician Execs. Lutheran. Avocations: swimming, computers. Office: Springfield Clinic Hillsboro 1250 E Tremont St Hillsboro IL 62049-1912 Office Phone: 217-532-6911. E-mail: rmulch@consolidated.net, rmulch@springfieldclinic.com.

MULDER, DAVID S., cardiovascular surgeon; b. Eston, Sask., Can., July 28, 1938; s. Peter and Laura (Lovie) M.; m. Norma D. Johnston, Aug. 19, 1961; children— Scott D., Lizabeth J., John C. MD, U. Sask., 1962; M.Sc., McGill U., 1964. Intern, resident in surgery Montreal Gen. Hosp., McGill U., 1963-67; resident in cardiac surgery U. Iowa, 1967-69; surgeon-in-chief Montreal Gen. Hosp., 1977-98; prof. surgery McGill U., 1979—; chmn. dept. surgery, 1993-98. Contbr. articles to med. jours. Fellow: ACS, Royal Coll. Surgeons Can.; mem.: Soc. Thoracic Surgeons (named Order Can. 1997), Am. Assn Thoracic Surgery, Am. Assn. Trauma, Nat. Hockey League Team Physicians Assn., Soc. Univ. Surgeons. Conservative. Office: Montreal Gen Hosp Room L-512 Montreal PQ Canada H3G 1A4 Home: 76 Sunnyside Ave Westmount PQ Canada H3Y 1C2 Home Phone: 514-482-4620; Office Phone: 514-935-4888. Personal E-mail: dsmulder@sympatico.ca. Business E-Mail: david.mulder@muhc.mcgill.ca.

MULERT, CHRISTOPH, psychiatrist, researcher, professor; b. Frankfurt am Main, Hessen, Germany, June 9, 1971; m. Monika Mulert; children: Maximilian, Sebastian. Abitur, Franz-Marc Gymnasium, 1990; MD, Free U., Berlin, 1998. Elective student Nat. Hosp. of Neurology, London, 1998; rsch. asst. Free U., Berlin, 1998—99; rsch. fellow Charite, dept. neurology, Berlin, 1999—2000; rschr. Lab. Clin. Neurophysiol., Munich, Bavaria, 2000—09, head sect. functional brain imaging, 2006—09; vis. assoc. prof., dept. psychiatry Harvard Med. Sch., 2008; prof. psychiatry U. Clinic Hamburg, 2009; head psychiatry neuroimaging branch U. Klinikum. Travel grant, World Fedn. Socs. Biol. Psychiatry, 2009. Mem.: Deutsche Gesellschaft für Biologische Psychiatrie (Sponsorship award 2006), Rsch. Group Combination EEG & FMRT, Internat. Soc. Neuroimaging Psychiatry (award), EEG & Clin. Neurosci. Soc. (award), German Soc. Psychiatry, Psychotherapy & Neurology (Rsch. grant), Orgn. Human Brain Mapping (Travel award 2007). Office: University Hosp Hamburg-Eppendorf Clinic & Outpatiens' Clinic Psychiatry&Psychotherapy Martinistr. 52 Hamburg 20246 Germany Office Phone: 49-40-7410-59520, 49-40-7410 59521. Business E-Mail: c.mulert@uke.uni-hamburg.de.

MULHEM, ELIE, physician, educator; b. Damascus, Syria, July 30, 1965; MD, U. Damascus, 1988. Family medicine resident U. Minn., 1995; assoc. prof. Oakland U. William Beaumont Sch. Medicine, 1998—. Dir. women's health Beaumont Family Medicine Residency, 2002—11. Recipient Best Rsch., Am. Soc. Colposcopy and Cervical Pathology; named Tchr. of Yr., Beaumont Family Medicine Residency. Mem.: Am. Acad. Family Physician, Soc. Tchrs. in Family Medicine. Avocations: fishing, hunting. Office: 44250 Dequindre St Sterling Heights MI 48314 Office Fax: 248-964-0402. Business E-Mail: emulhem@beaumont.edu.

MULJACIC, ANTE, surgeon; b. Dubrovnik, Croatia, Nov. 17, 1951; s. Zarko Muljacic and Ita Koncina Muljacic; m. Ljudmila Dezelic. MD, Med. Sch., Zagreb, Croatia, 1975; PhD in Med Sci., Med. Sch., Zagreb, 2006. Cert.: Croatian Ct. (med. ct. expert) 1989; specialist in Gen. surgery German Med. Chamber, 1983, specialist in trauma surgery Croatian Med. Chamber, 2006. Ward surgeon Zagreb U. Hosp. Traumatology, 1984—98, trauma ward chief, 1998—2007, head, 2007—10; quality mgr. Sestre Milosrdnice U. Hosp. Ctr., 2010—, head, clin. dept. traumatology, 2010—. Pres. Croatian Trauma Soc., 2007—. Contbr. scientific papers to profl. jours. Mem.: EFORT, SICOT, AO Internat. Home: Marulicev trg 10 Zagreb 10000 Croatia Office: Sestre Milosrdnice University Hosp Ctr Clin Dept Traumatology Draskoviceva Ulica 19 Zagreb 10000 Croatia Office Fax: 38514610365. Business E-Mail: ante.muljacic@kbcsm.hr.

MULKEY, SHARON RENEE, gerontology nurse; b. Miles City, Mont., Apr. 14, 1954; d. Otto and Elvera Marie (Haglof) Neuhardt; m. Monty W. Mulkey, Oct. 9, 1976; children: Levi, Candice, Shane. BS in Nursing, Mont. State U., 1976. RN, Calif.; nat. cert. gerontol. nursing. Staff nurse, charge nurse VA Hosp., Miles City, Mont., 1976-77; staff nurse obstetrics labor and delivery Munster (Ind.) Cmty. Hosp., 1982-83; nurse mgr. Thousand Oaks Health Care, 1986-88; unit mgr. rehab. Semi Valley (Calif.) Adventist Hosp., 1988-89, DON TCU, 1989-91; DON Pleasant Valley Hosp. Extended Care Vacility and Neuro Ctr., 1991-93, Victoria Care Ctr., Ventura, Calif., 1993—; clin. supr. Procare Home Health, Oxnard, Calif., 1996-97; staff nurse acute rehab. Los Roboles East Campus Rehab. Unit, Westlake, Calif., 1998, clin. coord., 1998—2004; founder, CEO Internat. Womens Conf. Spkr. for Spiritual Growth and Devel., 2000—, Women of Destiny. Internat. conf. spkr. WCCD, 1991—; amb. World Forum in Cambridge, England, 2010; spkr. in field. Author: You Can Love Again, The Alcoholic Syndrome, Grief, the

Gateway to Genuine Love. Del. AAUW, 2011. Recipient Amb., World Forum in London, 2010, ABI, 2010; named Profl. Woman of Yr., Nat. Assn. Profl. Woman, 2011—; named one of 500 Great Leaders, ABI, 2011. Mem. ANA, Nat. Gerontol. Nursing Assn., Internat. Platform Assn., Alpha Tau Delta (pres. 1973-75), Phi Kappa Phi, Am. Justice League, Am. Univ. Women Home: 3461 Pembridge St Thousand Oaks CA 91360-4565 Personal E-mail: smulkey1@aol.com.

MULKEY, TAYLOR BENOIT, dermatologist; b. Louisville, May 18, 1980; BS, Vanderbilt U., 2002; MD, U. Louisville, 2007. Resident physician Med. U. SC, 2007—11; assoc. dermatologist Dermatology Assocs., 2011—. Mem.: Am. Acad. Dermatology. Home: 2544 Dell Rd Louisville KY 40205 Personal E-mail: taylor.benoit@gmail.com.

MULLAN, FITZHUGH, public health physician; b. Tampa, Fla., July 22, 1942; s. Hugh and Mariquita (MacManus) Mullan; children: Meghan Elizabeth, Jason Michael, Caitlin Patricia. BA, Harvard U., 1964; MD, U. Chgo., 1968; DSc, U. Osteo. Medicine, 1993; LHD, Coll. Osteo. Medicine Pacific, 1993. Intern Jacobi Hosp., Bronx, 1968—70; resident Lincoln Hosp., Bronx, 1970—72; physician Nat. Health Svc. Corps., Santa Fe, 1972—75; dir. Nat. Health Svc. Corps, Rockville, Md., 1977—81; scholar-in-residence Inst. Medicine, Washington, 1981—82; dir. pub. health history project Office of Surgeon Gen., Rockville, 1988—90; sr. med. officer NIH, Bethesda, Md., 1982—84; sec. for health and environment State of N.Mex., Santa Fe, 1984—85; assoc. prof. Johns Hopkins Sch. Hygiene and Pub. Health, Balt., 1986—88; dir. bur. health professions USPHS, Rockville, 1990—96; contbr. editor Health Affairs, Bethesda, 1996—; clin. prof. pediats. and pub. health George Washington U., 1996—; staff physician Upper Cardozo Cmty. Health Ctr., 1996—; Asst. Atty. Gen. US Pub. Health Svc. Author: White Coat, Clenched Fist: The Political Education of an American Physician, 1976, Vital Signs: A Young Doctor's Struggle With Cancer, 1983, Plagues and Politics: The Story of the United States Public Health Service, 1989; contbr. articles to profl. jours.; contbg. editor: Health Affairs, narrative matters section. Fellow: Am. Acad. Pediats.; mem.: Inst. of Medicine of NAS, Am. Assn. for History of Medicine, APHA, AMA. Office: Health Affairs 7500 Old Georgetown Rd Ste 600 Bethesda MD 20814-6133 *

MULLAN, JOHN FRANCIS (SEAN MULLAN), neurosurgeon, educator; b. County Derry, Northern Ireland, May 17, 1925; came to U.S., 1955; naturalized, 1962; s. John and Catharine Ann (Gilmartin) M.; m. Vivian C. Dunn, June 3, 1959; children: Joan Claire, John Charles, Brian Francis. MB, BCh, BAO, Queen's U., Belfast, Northern Ireland, 1947, DSc (hon.), 1976; postgrad., McGill U., 1953-55. Diplomate Am. Bd. Neurol. Surgery. Trainee gen. surgery Royal Victoria Hosp., Belfast, 1947-50, trainee in neurosurgery, 1951-53; trainee gen. surgery Guy's Hosp. and Middlesex Hosp., London, 1950-51, Montreal Neurosurg. Inst., Que., Canada, 1953—55; asst. prof. neurol. surgery U. Chgo., 1955-61, assoc. prof., 1961-63, prof., 1963—2009, John Harper Seeley prof., 1967—95, chmn. dept., 1967—93, emeritus, 1995—, dir. Brain Rsch. Inst., 1970-84. Author: Neurosurgery for Students, 1961; contbr. over 150 articles to profl. jours.; mem. editorial bd. Jour. Neurosurgery, 1974-84, Archives of Neurology, 1976-87. Recipient Olivecrona medal Karolinska Inst., 1976, Wilder Penfield medal Can. Neurosurg. Soc., 1979, Jamieson medal Australian and New Zealand Neurosurg. Soc., 1980. Fellow ACS, Royal Coll. Surgeons; mem. Soc. Neurol. Surgeons (past pres.), Acad. Neurol. Surgery, Am. Assn. Neurol. Surgeons, Am. Neurol. Assn., Cen. Neurosurg. Soc., Chgo. Neurol. Soc., World Fedn. of Neurosurg. Socs. (sec. 1989-93, hon. pres. 1993—). Roman Catholic. Achievements include conducting research on vascular diseases of the brain, pain, head injury. Home Phone: 773-241-6546.

MULLANE, JOHN FRANCIS, pharmaceutical executive; b. NYC, Mar. 10, 1937; s. John Gerard and Rita Ann (Hoben) Mullane; m. Ruth Ann Cecka, Nov. 17, 1962; children: Rosemarie, Michael, Kathleen, Therese, Thomas. MD, SUNY Med. Ctr., 1963; PhD, SUNY, 1968; JD, Fordham U., 1977. Bar: NY 1978, DC 1979. Assoc. med. dir. Ayerst Labs. div. Am. Home Products Corp., NYC, 1973-75, dir. clin. research, 1975-76, v.p. clin., 1977, v.p. sci., 1978-82, sr. v.p., 1982, exec. v.p., 1983-88; pres. Mullane Health Care Cons., NYC and Sarasota, Fla., 1989—; dir. drug devel. DuPont Med. Products, Wilmington, Del., 1990; sr. v.p. DuPont-Merck, Wilmington, 1991-94; exec. v.p. Amylin Pharms., 1994-96. Contbr. articles to profl. jours. Served to lt. col. US Army, 1970-73 Recipient Upjohn Achievement award, 1970; NY Heart Assn. Crawford-Maynard fellow, 1966-68 Fellow Am. Coll. Clin. Pharmacology; mem. ABA, Am. Soc. Clin. Pharmacology and Therapeutics, Am. Assn. Study of Liver Diseases, Misty Creek Country Club (pres. 2004-2005). Roman Catholic. Achievements include development of major drugs including Inderal, Premarin, Lodine, Coumadin, Cozaar. Avocation: golf. Home and Office: 9047 Misty Creek Dr Sarasota FL 34241-9542 E-mail: johnmullane9047@comcast.net.

MULLEN, JEWEL MARIE, public health service officer, state official; b. New Rochelle, NY, Apr. 26, 1955; BS in Pub. Health, Yale U., New Haven, 1981, MPH, 1996; MD, Mt. Sinai Sch. Medicine. Diplomate American Bd. Internal Medicine. Resident Hospital of the Univ. Pa.; mem. nat. health svc. corps Bellevue Hosp., NY; med. faculty U. Va.; med. staff Hosp. St. Raphael, Yale Univ. Health Services, Yale New Haven Hosp.; dir. bur. cmty. health & prevention Mass. Dept. Pub. Health; med. dir. Baystate Mason Sq. Neighborhood Health Ctr., Springfield, Mass.; commr. Conn. Dept. Pub. Health, Hartford, 2010—. Office: Connecticut Department of Public Health 410 Capitol Ave Hartford Hartford CT 06134 Office Phone: 860-509-8000. *

MULLEN, ROD, nonprofit organization executive; b. Puyallup, Wash., Aug. 2, 1943; s. Charles Rodney and Grace Violet (Fritsch) M.; m. Lois Fern Tobiska, May 3, 1963 (div. Jan. 1977); children: Cristina, Charles, Moneka; m. Naya Arbiter, Oct. 17, 1977; 1 child: Angelo. Student, U. Idaho, Moscow, 1961—63; AB in Polit. Sci., U. Calif., Berkeley, 1966; postgrad., San Francisco Art Inst., 1968. Dir. Oakland (Calif.) facility Synanon Found., Inc., 1971-72, dir. San Francisco facility, 1972-73, dir. Tomales Bay (Calif.) facility, 1976-78, dir. Synanon edn. programs, 1973-76; treatment dir. nat. programs Vision Quest, Inc., Tucson, 1981-82; dir. resources and devel. Amity, Inc., Tucson, 1982-84, exec. dir., 1984-95; founder, pres., CEO, Amity Found., Porterville, Calif., 1995—. Mem. Nat. Adv. Com. Substance Abuse Prevention, 1990-96; adv. bd. Ctr. Therapeutic Cmty. Rsch., Nat. Devel. and Rsch. Insts., NYC, 1991-2002; cons. Calif. Office Criminal Justice Planning, Sacramento, 1993; prin. investigator program Nat. Inst. on Drug Abuse, 1990-93; pres. Calif. Therapeutic Com., 2004-06; editl. adv. bd. Offender Substance Abuse Report, 2000-2004; bd. dirs. Amity Found., Calif., 1995-, Amity Works Found.-Dragonfly Village, Ariz., 2006-11. Dir.: (documentaries) Prodigal Daughters, 2002, TC Pioneers, 2003, Essential Elements of the Therapeutic Community, 2005, Improving TC Encounter Groups, 2006, History of Therapeutic Communities in Corrections, 2006, Tell Me About It, 2008; contbr. chapters to books, articles to profl. jours. Mem.: Calif. Therapetic C. (pres. 2004—06), Therapeutic Coms. of Am. (treas. 2006—08), Am. Correctional Assn. Achievements include development of in-prison therapeutic community programs for addicted offenders and violent offenders which demonstrated significant reductions in recidivism to drug abuse, violence and other criminal activities; implementation of a comprehensive holistic curriculum for therapeutic communities, adaptation of mindfulness based cognitive therapy for Residential Treatment Programs; research in holistic addiction treatment. Avocations: hiking, photography, videography. Office: Amity Found 120 S Houghton Rd Ste 138-321 Tucson AZ 85748-2155 Office Phone: 520-749-7178. Business E-Mail: rmullen@amityfdn.org.

MULLER, ELMI, surgeon; b. Kempton Pk., South Africa, June 17, 1971; MBChB, U. Pretoria, 1995; M in Medicine, U. Cape Town, 2006. Registrar U. Cape Town, 2001—05, specialist surgeon, 2006—. Councilor Transplantation Soc., 2010—. Recipient Young Rsch. award, U. Cape Town Fellows. Fellow: Coll. Medicine South Africa; mem.: RCS (Edinburgh). Avocations: music, cooking. Office: Groote Schuur Hosp Observatory Cape Town Western Cape 7925 South Africa Business E-Mail: elmi.muller@uct.ac.za.

MÜLLER, HANS EMIL, bacteriologist; b. Zweibrücken, Palatinate, Germany, Mar. 26, 1930; s. Emil and Erna Müller; m. Ilse von Voigt, Apr. 12, 1966; children: Ulrike, Sibylle. Diploma in chemistry, U. Mainz, Germany, 1959, Dr.rer.nat., 1961, MD, 1964. Asst. U. Mainz, 1961—65, Med. Clinic, Bochum, Germany, 1965—66, U. Göttigen, Germany, 1966—67, U. Bonn, Germany, 1967—74; head Pub. Health Lab., Braunschweig, Germany, 1975—95; cons. Braunschweig, 1995—. Co-author: (book) Symposiun on Neuramindase, March 10-12, 1974, Liver Transplantation, 1974, Arthritis. Models and Mechanisms, 1981, Abwasserlandbehandlung. Organisatorische, ökologische und hygienische Probleme, 1979, Workshop Conference on Legionnaires' Disease, 1983, Legionella. Proceedings of the 2nd International Symposium, 1984, Recycling International, 1984, Umweltschäden! Gesundheitsschäden? Was ist wirklich dran?, 1985, Mikrobiologische Diagnostik, 1992, Why Risk? ESEF Science, Politics & Public Health, 1997, Zeckenborreliose Lyme-Krankheit bei Mensch und Tier, 4, 2003, Environment and Health-Myths and Realities, 2004; author, editor: book Infektionserreger in Praxis und Krankenhaus, 1981; author: Hygien-Untersuchungen bei der biologischen Abwasservorbehandlung und Verregnung, 1986, Die Infektionserreger des Menschen, 1989, Lebensmittelinfektionen und Vergiftungen, 2002; co-author, co-editor: book Legionellen - ein aktuelles Problem der Sanitärhygiene, 1992, Innenraum-Luftverunreinigungen, Chemie, Physiologie, Hygiene, Medizin und Toxikologie, 2001; contbr. articles to profl. jours. Home and Office: Alter Rautheimer Weg 16 D-38126 Braunschweig Germany

MULLER, HANS KONRAD, pathology educator, university dean; b. Broken Hill, NSW, Australia, July 16, 1937; s. Hans and Margaret (Daley) M.; m. M. Jill Brady, Apr. 23, 1962; seven children. B in Med. Sci. with honors, U. Adelaide, Australia, 1961, MB, BChir, 1963; PhD, U. NSW, Sydney, Australia, 1970. Cert. univ. med. prof. in pathology and immunology. Rsch. fellow pathology U. NSW, Sydney, 1965-68; lectr. pathology Monash U., Melbourne, Australia, 1968-69, sr. lectr., 1970-74, assoc. prof. pathology and immunology, 1975-83; prof., head pathology U. Tasmania, Hobart, Australia, 1983—2002, acad. dean Faculty Medicine, 1994-97, assoc. dean rsch. Faculty Health Sci., prof. emeritus, 2003; faculty sci. Royal Coll. Pathologists, Australia, 2010. Sr. fellow St. John Fisher Coll., U. Tasmania, Hobart, 1990—; vis. prof. M.D. Anderson Cancer Ctr., Houston, 1991-92, 97-98; vis. prof. med. scis. U. Calif., Riverside, 2002; pres. Internat. Acad. Pathology-Australasian Divsn., 1991-93, Royal Coll. Pathologists Australasia, Sydney, 1993-95. Contbr. chpts. to books and articles to profl. jours. Commonwealth Med. fellow Govt., U.K., 1972-73, Inaugural Dick Buttfield Meml. fellow Govt. Tasmania, Hobart, 1997—. Fellow Royal Coll. Pathologists Australasia, Royal Coll. Pathologists, Hong Kong Coll. Pathologists (hon. 1993), Acad. Medicine Singapore; mem. Internat. Acad. Pathology (internat. v.p. 1998, internat. pres. 2006-08), Queensland Health Pathology Svc., Brisbane.(acting dir. Anat. Pathology, 2004-09) Avocations: archaeology, history, Australian football, cricket. Home: 9 Pillinger St Dynnyrne Hobart TAS 7005 Australia Office: U Tasmania Clin Sch Gpo Box 34 7001 Hobart TAS Australia Home Phone: 61-3-6223-2493; Office Phone: 61-3-6226-4806. E-mail: konrad.muller@utas.edu.au.

MÜLLER, HANS-WILHELM, medical educator, director; b. Duisburg, Germany, June 22, 1954; s. Wilhelm and Margot Müller; m. Gabriele Heuveldop-Müller; children: Juliane Heuveldop, Phuong Duy Nguyen. MD, U. Duesseldorf, 1980; Habil, U. Hamburg, Eppendorf, 1989; attending, Open U., Milton Keynes, 1998—. Cert. in med. approbation State of Germany, NRW, 1980, Am. Clin. Med. Eam., ECFMG, Phila., 1981, Am. Pre-Clin. Med. Exam., ECFMG, Phila., 1982, lic. nuc. medicine physician Ärztekammer Hamburg, Germany, 1986. Med. asst. internal medicine St. Vincenz Hosp. Duisburg, NRW, 1981—82; med. asst. nuc. medicine U. Hosp. Hamburg-Eppendorf, Germany, 1983—89, dep. dir. dept. nuc. medicine, 1985—89; clin. fellow Johns Hopkins Med. Inst., Balt., 1989—93; Européan chair Coll. France, Paris, 1999—2000; prof. & dir. dept. nuc. medicine Heinrich Heine-U., Rsch. Ctr. Juelich, Duesseldorf, NRW, 1993—. Contbr. articles to sci. publs. Achievements include discovery of neural correlates of conscious letter processing, widely distributed cortical processing of sensory information. Avocations: hiking, philosophy. Home: Leo-Statz-Str 13 Düsseldorf NRW 40474 Germany Office: Heinrich Heine University Rsch Ctr Jülich Moorenstr 2 Düsseldorf 40225 Germany Office Fax: 49 211 811 7041; Home Fax: 49 211 303 2442. Business E-Mail: nuk@uni-duesseldorf.de.

MULLER, JENNY HELEN, physician, psychiatrist; b. Johannesburg, Dec. 21, 1953; d. Eric and Lily Muller; 1 child, Jonathan Meshekow. MD, U. Witwatersrand, South Africa, 1977. Diplomate Am. Bd. Psychiatry and Neurology. Intern in internal medicine, surgery, orthop., Johannesburg, 1978; intern in internal medicine and psychiatry Va. Med. Ctr., Sepulveda, Calif., 1986—87, resident in psychiatry, 1987—90, VA and Olive View Hosp. Child and Adolescent Rotation UCLA, 1987—90; pvt. practice LA, 1990—. Mem.: APA, So. Calif. Psychiat. Assn. Avocation: horseback riding. Office: 3760 Motor Ave # 210 Los Angeles CA 90034-6404 Office Phone: 310-204-1053. Office Fax: 310-204-1006.

MULLER, PATRICIA ANN, nursing administrator, educator; b. NYC, July 22, 1943; d. Joseph H. and Rosanne (Bautz) Felter; m. David G. Smith, Mar. 19, 1988; children: Frank M. Muller III, Kimberly M. Muller. BSN, Georgetown U., 1965; MA, U. Tulsa, 1978, EdD, 1983. RN. Coord. staff devel. St. Francis Hosp., Tulsa, 1978—79, asst. dir. for nursing svc., nursing edn., 1979—82, dir. dept. edn., 1982—98, St. Francis Health Sys., 1998—2002, cons., 2002—; CEO Smith Assocs. LLC, 2002—. Mem. faculty Okla. U., Northeastern U., Tulsa U.; presenter at confs. and convs. Contbg. editor JOPAN, 1992-2001; contbr. articles to profl. jours. Mem. Leadership Tulsa, 1991; bd. dirs. Am. Heart Assn., Ronald McDonald House. Mem. ANA, Nat. League for Nursing, Am. Soc. for Nursing Svc. Adminstrs., Am. Soc. for Health Manpower Edn. and Tng., Okla. Nurses Assn., Okla. Orgn. of Nurse Execs. (pres. 1992-93), Sigma Theta Tau. Home and Office: 6203 W Utica Ct Broken Arrow OK 74011 Office Phone: 918-671-7767. E-mail: mullsmi@aol.com.

MULLER, RALPH W., hospital administrator; b. Oct. 26, 1945; married. BA in economics, Syracuse U., NY, 1966; MA in govt., Harvard U., Cambridge, Mass., 1968. Asst. to commr. Nicholas Johnson FCC, Washington, 1967; assoc., health care consulting Orgn. for Social and Tech. Innovation, Cambridge, Mass., 1969-70; rsch. asst. to Prof. Samuel H. Beer Harvard U., 1967—68, teaching fellow, govt., and resident tutor, 1969—72; govt. instr. Suffolk U., Boston, 1972—74; budget dir., dept. of public welfare Commonwealth of Mass., Boston, 1975—78, dep. commr., dept. public welfare, 1978—80; dir. fin. planning and budget U. Chgo., 1980—83, assoc. v.p. budget, computing and info. sys., 1984, v.p., hospitals and clinics and dep. dean, divsn. biological sciences, 1985—86; pres., CEO U. Chgo. Hospitals and Health Sys., 1986—2003; CEO U. Pa. Health Sys., 2003—. Fellow: AAAS; mem.: Inst. Medicine, Coun. of Tchg. Hospitals (chmn. 1997—98), Am. Assoc. of Med. Colleges (AAMC) (chmn. 1999—2000). Office: Univ Pa Health Sys 3900 Civic Ctr Blvd Philadelphia PA 19104

MÜLLER, SUZANA, nurse; b. Canoas, Aug. 1, 1962; Degree in Nursing, Nursing Sch. U. Fed. do Rio Grande do Sul, 1985; PhD in Gastroenterology, Medicine Sch. U. Fed. do Rio Grande do Sul, 2008. RN Clínica Solar do Tempo -Elder Assistance, 1985—86, Ctr. Neurologic Assistance, 1987—89; RN, clin assitance Hosp. Clínicas Porto Alegre, Rio Grande do Sul, Brazil, 1987—96, RN- endoscopist nurse, 1996—2009, chief clin. rsch. ctr., 2009—, mem. Ethics Com. Pres. Soc. Gastrointestinal Endoscopy Nursing Rio Grande do Sul, 1998—2003, Brazilian Soc. Gastrointestinal Endoscopy Nursing, 2004—08; mem. at large Soc. Internat. Gastroenterology and Endoscopy Nurses, 2004—08; treas. Soc. Internat. Gastroenterology and Endoscopy Nurses and Assocs., 2008—. Contbr. articles to profl. publs. Avocations: travel, photography, bicycling. Home: Ave Guaiba 4400/01 Assunção Porto Alegre Rio Grande do Sul 91900-420 Brazil Home Fax: 51 33598001. Personal E-mail: sumuller@unl.com.br.

MÜLLER, THOMAS, neurologist; b. Clauthal-Zellerfeld, Germany, Dec. 13, 1960; s. Karl-Herman and Ottilie Müller; life ptnr. Katharina Möhr; children: Jan-Dominique Möhr, Nicholas Möhr. Abitur, Gymnasium, Marktredwitz, 1967—80; PhD, 1996. Specialist in neurology & psychiatry 1995. Fellow, dept. psychiatry U. Würzburg, Germany, 1987—90; fellow, dept. neurology U. Marburg, 1992—2007; sr. physician, dept. neurology U. Bochum, Germany, 1996, lectr., sr. physician specialist & cons. in neurology, psychiatry, psychotherapy, 2001; mem. faculty neurosci. Ruhr U. Bochum, 2002, prof., 2007; head dept. neurology Berlin Weissensee, 2008; cons. neurology, psychiatry St. Joseph Berlin Tempelhof, 2009, Ctr. Multiple Sclerosis, 2009. Editl. bd. Jour. Neural Transmission, Clin. Neuropharmacology, Psycho Neuro, Current Signal Transduction Therapy, Neurology Internat., The Open Toxicology Jour., Multiple Sclerosis; editor in chief The Open Clin. Trials Jour., Neuroscience & Medicine, The Open Psychology Jour. Contbr. 296 peer reviewed papers to scientific jous., chapters to books. Mem.: IGSN. Achievements include research in GCP trials in mild cognitive impairment, Parkinson's disease, dementia, vascular dementia, RLS, Alzheimer's disease, somatoform disorders, epilepsy. Avocations: travel, sports, skiing, music, literature. Office: Dept Neurology St Joseph Hosp Berlin Weibensee Gartenstr 1 Berlin 13088 Germany also: Ihnestr. 23 14195 Berlin Germany Home Phone: 49 177 2819454; Office Phone: ++493092710223. Business E-Mail: thomas.mueller@ruhr-uni-bochum.de, th.mueller@alexius.de.

MULLETTE, JULIENNE PATRICIA, health facility administrator; b. Sydney, Nov. 19, 1940; came to U.S., 1953; d. Ronald Stanley Lewis and Sheila Rosalind Blunden (Phillips) M.; m. Fred Gillette Sturm, Nov. 24, 1964 (div. Dec. 1969); m. Kenneth Walter Gillman, Dec. 28, 1971 (div. Dec. 1978); children: Noah Khristoff Mullette-Gillman, O'Dhaniel Alexander Mullette-Gillman. BA, Western Coll. for Women, Oxford, Ohio, 1961; postgrad., Harvard U., 1964, U. Sao Paulo, Brazil, 1965, Inst. Philosophy, Sao Paulo, 1965, Miami U., Oxford, 1967—69. Tchr. English, High Mowing Sch., Wilton, N.H., 1962-64, Stoneleigh-Prospect Hill Sch., Greenfield, Mass., 1964; seminar dir. Western Coll. for Women, 1967-69; pres. Family Tree, Home U., Montclair, NJ, 1978—88; dir. Pleroma Holistic Health Ctr., Montclair, 1980—. Dir. Astrological Rsch. Ctr., Sydney, 1983; founder Spiritual Devel. Rsch. Group, 1986—; pvt. counselor, 1962—; guest on radio & TV shows, 1962—; lectr. worldwide, 1963—; founder Pleroma Found. for Astrological Rsch. & Studies, 1990; breeder, trainer exotic animals; mem. Woodstock Pub. Access Com., 1993—. Author: The Moon-Understanding the Subconscious, 1973; contbg. columnist: mags; contbr. articles to profl. jours.; editor (founding): KOSMOS Mag., 1968—78, Jour. Astrological Studies, 1970—; hostess (radio talk shows) The Julienne Mullette Show, 1985—, You and the Cosmos, Binghamton, N.Y., others, (TV series) You and the Cosmos, Woodstock, NY, 1992—, The Julienne Mullette Show Connections TV, Newark, NJ, 1985—, (radio) You and The Cosmos, WHRW, Binghamton, NY, 2006—. Founder local chpt. La Leche League, Montclair, 1974; founding pres. The Internat. Astrology Forum, 2000. Mem. AAUW (chmn. cultural affairs Montclair chpt. 1987—), NAFE, Spiritual Devel. Group (founder), Internat. Soc. Astrological Rsch. (founding pres. 1968-78), Cosmos Hyperspace Astrological Origins and Supergravity Studies (founder), Am. Fedn. Astrologers (cert.), Belgian Soc. Astrology, Am. Assn. Humanistic

Psychology, Internat. Llamas Assn., Internat. Soc. Astrological Studies and Rsch. (founder 2002). Avocations: tennis, local theatre, singing. E-mail: julienne@nep.net.

MULLICK, FLORABEL GARCIA, pathologist, director; b. Spain; MD, U. PR, 1964; DSc (hon.), Met. U., PR. Diplomate Am. Bd. Pathology, lic. Md., Washington, PR. Internship pediatric pathology U. Hosp. PR, Rio Piedras, 1964—65, residency, 1965—66, Children's Hosp. DC, 1966—67, fellow, 1967—68; residency Georgetown U. Hosp., Washington, 1968—69; assoc. dir. Armed Forced Inst. Pathology, Washington, prin. dep. dir., 1999—2007, dir., 2007—. Dir. Ctr. for Advanced Pathology Armed Forces Inst. Pathology, 1994—, chair dept. environ. and infectious disease scis., 1996—; prof. pathology U. PR, Uniformed Svcs. U. of Health Scis., Bethesda, Md.; adj. prof. pathology Georgetown U. Hosp. Med. Sch.; disting. physician exec. med. adv. bd. FindCancerExperts.com; bd. dirs. Ana G. Mendez U. Sys.; cons. in field. Cons. editor: Annals of Diagnostic Pathology, mem. editl. bd.: Modern Pathology, Toxicology Pathology, Electronic Jour. Pathology and Histology; contbr. chapters to books, scientific papers to profl. jours. Recipient Disting. Exec. Svc. award, Sr. Execs. Assn. Profl. Devel. League, 1994, Excellence in Edn. award, Ana G. Mendez U. Sys. Fellow: Coll. Am. Pathologists; mem.: History of Pathology Soc. (founding trustee), US Fed. Sr. Exec. Svc. (Meritorious Exec. 1992, Disting. Exec. 1993), Spanish Soc. Pathology (hon.), Internat. Acad. Pathology (sec. 1995—2006, mem. fin. com. 2006—, pres.-elect 2006—). Achievements include development of the International Database on Toxic Lesions in Animals and Humans (INTOX); research in human health effects of toxic drugs and toxic trace metals with emphasis on liver diseases and pediatric pathology cases. Office: Armed Forces Inst Pathology 6825 16th St NW Washington DC 20306-6000 Business E-Mail: mullick@afip.osd.mil.

MULLIGAN, DAVID COBOURN, medical educator; b. Louisville, Mar. 30, 1959; s. Robert Cobourn and Marguerite Stevens Mulligan; m. Pamela Christine Argue, Apr. 2, 1999; children: Madeline Rose, Benjamin Cobourn, Grace Anne. BA in Chemistry and Biology, Bellarmine Coll., 1981; MD, U. Louisville, 1986. Diplomate Nat. Bd. Med. Examiners, 1987, lic. in multi-organ transplant surgery Am. Soc. Transplant Surgeons, 1995, diplomate Am. Bd. Surgery, 2003. Internship in gen. surgery U. Louisville, 1986—87, residency in gen. surgery, 1987—88, residency in urol. surgery, 1988—91; residency in gen. surgery Case We. Reserve U., 1991—93, asst. prof. surgery Cleve., 1995—2008; fellowship in multi-organ transplantation Baylor U. Med. Ctr., 1993—95; prof. surgery Mayo Clinic Med. Sch., Phoenix, 2006—. Chair transplant, hepatobiliary and pancreatic surgery Mayo Clinic Ariz., Phoenix, 1998—; surg. dir., divsn. transplant surgery, dept. surgeryA Mayo Clinic, Scottsdale. Region 5 councilor United Network Organ Sharing, Richmond, Va., 2005—08; bd. dirs. Donor Network Ariz., Phoenix, 1999—2008. Named Outstanding Clinician for Mayo Clinic, Mayo Clinic Ariz., 2006. Fellow: ACS (licentiate). Avocations: running, swimming, rock climbing, travel. Office: Mayo Clinic Hosp 5777 E Mayo Blvd Phoenix AZ 85054 Office Fax: 480-342-2324. Business E-Mail: mulligan.david@mayo.edu. *

MULLINS, CHARLES BROWN, physician, academic administrator; b. Rochester, Ind., July 29, 1934; s. Charles E. and Mary Ruth B. (Bamberger) Mullins; m. Stella Churchill Mullins, Dec. 27, 1955; children: Holly, David. BA, North Tex. State U., 1954; MD, U. Tex., 1958. Diplomate Am. Bd. Internal Medicine. Intern. U. Colo. Med. Ctr., Denver, 1958—59; resident internal medicine Parkland Meml. Hosp., Dallas, 1962—64; USPHS rsch. fellow Tex. Southwestern Med. Sch., Dallas, 1964—65; chief resident medicine Parkland Meml. Hosp., 1965—66; USPHS spl. rsch. fellow cardiology br. Nat. Heart Inst., Bethesda, Md., 1967—68; practice medicine specializing cardiology Dallas, 1966—81; sr. attending staff Parkland Meml. Hosp., dir. med. affairs, 1977—79, asst. prof. medicine U. Tex. Southwestern Med. Sch., Dallas, 1968—71, assoc. prof., 1968—71, 1971—75, dir. clin. cardiology, 1971—77, prof., 1975—79, clin. prof. medicine, 1979—81; prof. medicine U. Tex. Health Sci. Ctr., Dallas, 1981—; exec. vice-chancellor health affairs U. Tex. Sys., 1981—2001, spl. projects dir., 2001—02; CEO Dallas County Hosp. Dist., 1979—81. Contbr. articles to profl. jours. With M.C. USAF, 1959—62. Mem.: AMA, ACP, Laennec Soc., Assn. Univ. Cardiologists, Assn. Acad. Health Ctrs., Am. Fedn. Clin. Rsch., Am. Heart Assn. Coun. Clin. Cardiology, Am. Coll. Cardiology (Tex. gov. 1974—77, chmn. bd. govs. 1976), Alpha Omega Alpha.

MULLINS, JACK ALLEN, cardiologist, educator; b. Oklahoma City, 1952; MD, U. Okla., 1982. Diplomate in internal medicine, cardiovasc. disease, interventional cardiology Am. Bd. Internal Medicine. Intern U. Tex., Houston, 1982-83, resident in internal medicine, 1983-85; fellow in cardiology U. Okla., Oklahoma City, 1985-88; clin. instr. cardiology Baylor Coll. Medicine, 1988—, U. Tex. Med. Sch., Houston, 1988—. Mem. Am. Coll. Cardiology, Am. Heart Assn. Office: Cardiovasc Ctr PA 3337 Plainview St Ste 8 Pasadena TX 77504-1924 Office Phone: 713-941-6083.

MULLINS BERG, RUTH GLADYS, nurse; b. Westville, NS, Can., Aug. 25, 1943; came to U.S., 1949, naturalized, 1955; d. William G. and Gladys H.; m. Leonard E. Mullins, Aug. 27, 1963 (dec.); children: Deborah R. Jenkins, Catherine M., Leonard III; m. Bernard J. Berg, June 19, 2004 BS in Nursing, Calif. State U., Long Beach, 1966; MSN, UCLA, 1973; PhD, Columbia Pacific U. Cert. pediatric nurse practitioner. Pub. health nurse Los Angeles County Health Dept., 1967-68; nure Meml. Hosp. Med. Ctr., Long Beach, 1968-72; dir. pediatric nurse practitioner program Calif. State U., Long Beach, 1973-97, asst. prof., 1975-80, assoc. prof., 1980-85, prof., 1985—2010, coord. accelerated BSN program, 2003—04, prof. emeritus, 2010—; v.p., CFO Mutual 8, Seal Beach Leisure World, 2010—. Health svc. credential coord. Sch. Nursing Calif. State U., Long Beach, chmn., 1979-81, coord. grad. programs, 1985-92; mem. Calif. Maternal, Child and Adolescent Health Bd., 1977-84; vice chair Long Beach/Orange County Health Consortium, 1984-85, chair 1985-86. Author: (with B. Nelms) Growth and Development: A Primary Health Care Approach; contbg. author: Quick Reference to Pediatric Nursing, 1984; assoc. editor Jour. Pediatric Health Care, 1985-2008. Tng. grantee HHS, Divsn. Nursing Calif. Dept. Health. Fellow Nat. Assn. Pediatric Nurse Assocs. and Practitioners (exec. bd., pres. 1990-91), Nat. Fedn. Nursing Splty. Orgns. (sec. 1991-93); mem. APHA, Nat. Alliance Nurse Practitioners (governing body 1990-92), Assn. Faculties Pediatric Nurse Practitioner Programs. L.A. and Orange County Assn. Pediatric Nurse Practitioners and Assocs. (treas. 1998—05), Am. Assn. Univ. Faculty. Republican. Methodist. Home: 13240 Eldorado Dr #187A Seal Beach CA 90740 Office: Calif State U Dept Nursing 1250 N Bellflower Blvd Long Beach CA 90840-0001 Office Phone: 562-985-4476. Personal E-mail: rgmullins@sprintmail.com. Business E-Mail: rmullins@csulb.edu.

MULLIS, KARY BANKS, biochemist; b. Lenoir, NC, Dec. 28, 1944; s. Cecil Banks Mullis and Bernice Alberta (Barker) Fredericks; m. Richards Mullis (div.); 1 child, Louise; m. Cynthia Mullis (div.); children: Christopher, Jeremy; m. Nancy Lier Cosgrove, 1998. BS in Chemistry, Ga. Inst. Tech, 1966; PhD in Biochemistry, U. Calif., Berkeley, 1973; DSc (hon.), U. S.C., 1994. Lectr. biochemistry U. Calif., Berkeley, 1962; postdoc. fellow U. Kans. Med. Sch., Kansas City, 1973—76, U. Calif., San Francisco, 1977—79; scientist Cetus Corp., Emeryville, Calif., 1979—86; dir. molecular biology Xytronyx, Inc., San Diego, 1986—88; pvt. cons. nucleic acid chemistry Calif., 1987—2002; v.p. rsch. Atomic Tags, Inc., La Jolla, Calif., 1992—93; v.p. molecular biology Vyrex Inc., La Jolla, 1997—98, Burstein Technologies, Irvine, Calif., 1999—2003; v.p. Histotec, Inc., Cedar Rapids, Iowa; disting. rschr. Children's Hosp., Oakland Rsch. Inst., Calif., 2003—; founder, chief scientific officer Altermune LLC, Newport Beach, Calif., 2003—. Disting. vis. prof. U. SC Coll. Sci. & Math., 1994—. Author: (autobiography) Dancing Naked in the Mind Field, 1998; contbr. articles to profl. jours. Bd. dirs. Nat. Orgn. Reform Marijuana Laws, 2000—. Recipient Preis Biochemische Analytik award, German Soc. Clin. Chemistry, 1990, Allan award, 1990, Gairdner Found. Internat. award, 1991, Nat. Biotech. award, 1991, Robert Koch award, 1992, Chiron Corp. Biotechnology Rsch. award, Am. Soc. Microbiology, 1992, Japan prize, Japan Sci. & Tech. Found., 1993, Nobel prize in chemistry, 1993; named Scientist of Yr., R&D Mag., 1991, Calif. Scientist of Yr., 1992; named to National Inventors Hall of Fame, 1998. Mem.: Am. Acad. Achievement, Am. Chem. Soc. Achievements include patents in field. Avocations: astrology, surfing.

MULROW, CYNTHIA DIANE, internist, editor; b. May 23, 1953; MD, Baylor U., 1978; MS. Cert. Internal Medicine, 1981. Dir. VA Cochrane Ctr., San Antonio; prof. medicine U. Tex. Health Sci. Ctr., San Antonio; dir. generalist physician faculty scholars prog. Robert Wood Johnson Found.; dep. editor Annals of Internal Medicine. Fellow: ACP, Coun. for High Blood Pressure Rsch., Am. Heart Assn.; mem.: Inst. Medicine. Mailing: 11711 Elmscourt San Antonio TX 78230

MULROW, PATRICK JOSEPH, medical educator; s. Patrick J. and Delia M.; m. Jacquelyn Pinover, Aug. 8, 1953; children: Deborah, Nancy, Robert, Catherine. AB, Colgate U., 1947; MD, Cornell U., 1951; MSc (hon.), Yale U., 1969; DSc (hon.), Med. Coll. Ohio, 2005. Intern N.Y. Hosp., 1951-52, resident, 1952-54; instr. physiology Med. Coll. Cornell U., 1954-55; research fellow Stanford U., 1955-57; instr medicine Yale U., 1957-60, asst. prof., 1960-66, assoc. prof., 1966-69, prof. medicine, 1969-75; chmn. dept. medicine Med. Coll. Ohio, Toledo, 1975—95, prof. medicine, 1975—97, prof. emeritus, 1997—. Chmn. ednl. com. Council for high blood pressure rsch. Am. Heart Assn., 1968-70, mem. exec. com., 1986-96, vice-chmn. of coun., 1990-92, chmn. 1992-94, past chmn., 1995-96; mem. study sect. NIH, 1970-74. Editorial bd. Jour. Clin. Endocrinology and Metabolism, 1966-70, 75-79, Endocrine Rsch., 1974—, Jour. Exptl. Biology and Medicine, Hypertension, 1994-98; contbr. articles to profl. jours. With USNR, 1944-46. Mem. ACP, Am. Soc. Clin. Investigation, Assn. Am. Physicians, Am. Physiol. Soc., Endocrine Soc., Am. Fedn. Clin. Rsch., Am. Clin. and Climatol. Assn., Am. Heart Assn. (nat. rsch. com., chmn. cardiovasc. regulation rsch. study com. 1986-91), Assn. Profs. Medicine, Assn. Program Dirs. in Internal Medicine, Cen. Soc. Clin. Rsch. (pres. 1988-89), Internat. Soc. Hypertension, World Hypertension League (sec. gen. 1995-2005), Inter-Am. Soc. Hypertension, Sigma Xi (pres. Yale chpt. 1965-66), Alpha Omega Alpha. Home: 9526 Carnoustie Rd Perrysburg OH 43551-3501 Office: Univ Toledo Dept Medicine 3000 Arlington Ave Toledo OH 43614-5809 Office Phone: 419-383-6016.

MULTON, OLIVIER JEAN-LOUIS, obstetrician, gynecologist; b. Paris, Mar. 16, 1966; s. Jean-Louis and Eve-Marie Multon; m. Isabelle Multon; children: Charlotte, Robin, Justine. B, Lycée Jules Verne, Nantes, 1983; MS in Biol. Sci., 1993; MD, Faculté Cochin-Port Royal. Obstetrician gynecologist surgeon Poly. De L'atlantique, Saint Herblain, France, 2000—; hospitalier CHU, Nantes, 1999—2000. Chef clin. asst. Hôsp. Paris, 1996—99. Recipient Silver medal, Prix Thèse, 1996. Fellow: Network Security Birth (bur. mem.). Home: Nantes France Office: Polyclinique de l'Atlantique Rue Bernard Palissy 44819 Saint Herblain 44819 France Office Fax: +33(0)240958411. Personal E-mail: omulton@gmail.com. E-mail: drmulton@polyclinique-atlantique.fr.

MULVIHILL, JAMES EDWARD, periodontist, educator, health center administrator; b. Cleve., Sept. 24, 1940; s. John F. and Teresa J. (Carlos) M.; m. May Jane Forino, 1963; children— Karen, Kristen, Jason BA, Coll. of Holy Cross, 1962; DMD, Harvard U., 1966. Asst. dean for student affairs, coordinator Harvard-VA continuing edn. program Harvard Sch. Dental Medicine, Boston, 1970-71; dean clin. campus L.I. Jewish-Hillside Med. Ctr., Queens Hosp. Ctr. Affiliation, Jewish Inst. for Geriatric Care, Health Scis. Ctr. SUNY-Stony Brook, 1971-80; v.p. for edn. and research L.I. Jewish-Hillside Med. Ctr., New Hyde Park, NY, 1975-80; v.p., provost for health affairs, exec. dir. Health Ctr., prof. periodontics U. Conn., Farmington, 1980-92; attending periodontist John Dempsey Hosp., U. Conn. Health Ctr., Farmington, 1982-92; pres. John Dempsey Fin. Corp., Farmington, 1988-92; sr. v.p. for health policy The Travelers Corp., Hartford, Conn., 1992-94; chmn. bd. The Travelers Health Co., Hartford, 1992-93; sr. fellow in health policy Assn. of Acad. Health Ctrs., 1994; pres., CEO Managed Health, Inc., 1994, Comty. Health Plan of Queens/Nassau, New Hyde Park, NY, 1994-95, Forsyth Dental Ctr., Boston, 1995-96, Juvenile Diabetes Found. Internat., 1996-99; dir. instnl. advancement and corp. rels. Am. Dental Edn. Assn., 2000—08; asst. to pres. So. Maine Med. Ctr., 2000—01; chief dept. dentistry Harvard U. Health Svcs., 2003—07; resource devel. mgr. The First Tee. Adv. bd. mem. TBS Techs., Inc; cons. in field. Author: (with others) Guide to Foreign Medical Schools, 1975, Editorial Instructions for Dental Authors, 1979-80, 1979, Human Subjects Research: The Operational Handbook for IRB's, 1982, 2d edit., 1984, Japanese edit., 1987; also articles, chpt. in book With Nat. Fund for Med. Edn.; overseer Joslin Diabetes Ctr. Recipient Disting. Alumnus award Harvard Sch. Dental Medicine, 1982, Disting. Alumnus award Holy Cross Coll., 1991, Disting. Svc. award Am. Dental Edn. Assn., 2008. Fellow AAAS, Am. Coll. Dentistry, Internat. Coll. Dentistry; mem. ADA, Am. Acad. Periodontology, Conn. State Dental Assn. (Fones award 2004), Alpha Sigma Nu, Sigma Psi. Avocations: golf, gardening, photography. Address: 117 Kings Hwy Kennebunkport ME 04046-5606 Personal E-mail: mulvi@roadrunner.com.

MUMENTHALER, MARCO, neurologist, educator; b. Bern, Switzerland, July 23, 1925; s. Giovanni Jakob Mumenthaler and Lydia Giannina Piccoli; m. Livia Maria Morandini, Nov. 19,1949 (div. 1991); children: Maia, Manuela, Isabel; m. Regula Christine Dejung Hausammann, Feb. 4, 1992 (div. 2002); 1 child, Sofia Rebecca. Degree in medicine, U. Basle, Switzerland, 1950; MD, U. Zurich, Switzerland, 1951. Intern various clinics, Switzerland, 1951-60; asst. étranger Hôp. Paris, 1952; vis. assoc. NIH, Bethesda, Md., 1961; asst. prof. neurology Berne U., Switzerland, 1962-66, prof. neurology, head dept., 1966-90, univ. pres., 1989-91; pvt. practice specialized in neurology Zürich. Author: Ulnarislahmungen, 1961, Klinische Neurologie ein Lernbuch, 1973, Der Schulter-Arm-Schmerz, 3rd edit., 2011, Synkopen, 1984, Atlas der Klinischen Neurologie, 2d edit., 1987, Der Kopfschmerz, 1990, Neuromuskuläre Erkrankungen, 1992, Pratique de Neurologie Clinique, 2d edit., 1995, Basiswissen Neurologie, Läsionen peripherer Nerven, 9th edit., 2007, Neurologie, 12th edit., 2008, Kompendium der Läsionen des peripheren Nervensystems, 2003, Neurology, 4th edit., 2004, Neurologische Differenzialdiagnostik, 5th edit., 2004; author: (CD Roms) Neurologie Interaktiv, 1998, Kopfschmerz interaktiv, 2000, Headache, 2001, maux de tête, 2001, Fallgruben der Neurologie, 2001, Grundkurs Neurologie, 2002, Kurzlehrbuch Neurologie, 3rd edit., 2011. Mem. Internat. Com. Red Cross, Geneva, 1990-94. Maj. Med. Corps Swiss Army. Mem. Swiss Neurol. Soc. (former pres., hon. pres.), German Neurol. Soc. (hon.), French Neurol. Soc. (hon.), Italian Neurol. Soc. (hon.), Belgian Neurol. Soc. (hon.), Polish Neurol. Soc. (hon.), Austrian Neurol. Soc. (hon.), European Neurol. Soc. (hon.), Am. Neurol. Assn. (hon.), Acad. Scis. Leopoldina Halle (ancient senator), Royal Brit. Soc. Medicine (affiliate). Avocations: literature, photography. Office Phone: 00 41/44/ 381 76 85. Personal E-mail: mumenthaler33@bluewin.ch.

MUMMERY, CHRISTINE, developmental biologist, educator; Studied Physics, U. Nottingham; PhD in Biophysics, Guy's Hospital Med. Sch., London. Postdoctoral rsch. to group leader Hubrecht Lab., Netherlands Inst. for Develop. Biology, Netherlands; ICIN prof. develop. biology of the heart Leiden U. Med. Ctr., Netherlands, 2002—. Harvard Stem Cell Inst. Radcliffe Fellow, Molecular and Cellular Biology, Hubrecht Lab., Netherlands, 2007—08, Royal Soc. Fellow (2), multiple EU and Netherlands Heart Found. grants. Mem.: Netherlands Ministry Health (mem. ethical councils), Royal Netherlands Acad. Sci. (mem. ethical councils). Achievements include being a leading stem cell expert specializing in the conversion of embryonic stem cells into cardiac and vascular cells. Office: Leids Univy Medical Ctr Postbus 9600 2300 RC Leiden Netherlands Office Phone: 31 71 5269300. E-mail: c.l.mummery@lumc.nl.

MUMOLI, NICOLA, emergency physician; b. Gioia Tauro, Italy, Sept. 18, 1963; s. Raul Mumoli and Emma De Masi. Cert. in Maturita Classica, 1982; MD, U. Siena, Italy, 1989. Cert. specialist in internal medicine U. Siena, 1994, specialist in cardiology U. Siena, 2005, specialist in diving medicine U. Chieti, Italy, 2000. Physician Dept. Internal Medicine, Morbegno, Italy, 1995—97, Livorno, Italy, 1997—2001, Dept. Emergency Medicine, Livorno, 2001—. Dir. Clin. Ultrasound Emergency Medicine Dept., Livorno, Italy, 2002—05. Contbr. articles to profl. jours. Tenent Marina Militare Italiana, 1990—91, Accademia Navale di Livorno, Italy. Mem.: Società Italiana di Medicina Subacquea (assoc.), Società Italiana Medicina Interna (assoc.), Società Italiana di Cardiologia (assoc.), Am. Diabetes Assn. (assoc.). Achievements include research in deep venous thrombosis; heart Failure; emergency Medicine. Avocations: travel, diving. Office: Dept Emergency Medicine viale Alfieri 36 Livorno 57100 Italy Home: Borgo Dei Cappuccini 277 57126 Livorno LI Italy Office Fax: +390586223285; Home Fax: 390586223285. Personal E-mail: nimumoli@tiscali.it. E-mail: n.mumoli@nord.usl6.toscana.it.

MUN, GOO-HYUN, surgeon; b. Seoul, Republic of Korea, Oct. 2, 1967; s. Chae-Sik Mun and Shin-Ja Yoon; m. Yoon-Jeong Park, July 13, 1998; children: Ye-Jin, Ye-Eun. MD, Seoul Nat. U., 1993. Lic. Ministry of Health and Welfare. Asst. prof. dept. plastic surgery Chungbuk Nat. U. Hosp., Cheongju, Republic of Korea, 1998—2001, Samsung Med. Ctr., Seoul, Republic of Korea, 2002—. Contbr. articles to profl. jours. Mem.: World Soc. Reconstructive Microsurgery, Am. Soc. Plastic Surgeons, Korean Soc. of Plastic and Reconstructive Surgery. Office: Samsung Med Ctr Plastic Surgery Ilwon-Dong 50 Kangnam-Gu Seoul 135-710 Republic of Korea Office Fax: 82-2-3410-0036. E-mail: supramicro@gmail.com.

MUN, SEOG KYUN, otolaryngologist, educator; b. Seoul, Apr. 12, 1971; MD, Chung-Ang U., 2000, PhD, 2006. Assoc. prof. Dept. Otolaryngology-Head and Neck Surgery, Chung-Ang U. Coll. Medicine, 2001—. Office: Chung-Ang University Coll Medicine Seoul 156-755 Republic of Korea Business E-Mail: entdoctor@cau.ac.kr.

MUNARRIZ, RICARDO, medical educator; b. Caracas, Venezuela, June 13, 1966; MD, U. Ctrl. de Venezuela, 1991; degree in Urology, Boston U. Sch. Medicine, 2000. Asst. prof. urology Boston Med. Ctr., 2002—05, assoc. prof. urology, 2005—. Contbr. articles to profl. sci. jours., chapters to books. Recipient Urology award, Pfizer. Fellow: Sexual Medicine Soc. N.Am.; mem.: New Eng. Sect. AUA, Am. Urol. Assn. Avocations: running, skiing. Office: 725 Albany St Ste 3B Boston MA 02118 Office Fax: 617-638-8960. Business E-Mail: munarriz@bu.edu.

MUNAS, FALIES A., psychiatric physician; b. Colombo, Sri Lanka, Aug. 30, 1946; came to U.S., 1972; s. M.H.M. and C.P. M. MBBS, MD, Christian Med. Coll., Vellore, India, 1971. Diplomate Am. Bd. Psychiatry and Neurology. Dir. geropsychiatry Trinity Meml. Hosp., Cudahy, Wis., 1991-95; dir. clin. svcs./chief of staff De Paul Hosp., Milw., 1996-97; dir. behavioral medicine VA Med. Ctr., Marion, Ill., 1998-2000; assoc. clinical prof. psychiatry S.I.U. Sch. Medicine, Springfield, Ill., 1999—2004. Pres. Extended Family Svc, Pitts., 1989—; assoc. clin. prof. psychiatry So. Ill. U. Sch. Medicine, Springfield, 1999—2004. Home: 23107 Galatia Post Rd Pittsburg IL 62974-1832 Office: Extended Family Svc PO Box 753 Marion IL 62959 Business E-Mail: famunasmd@gmail.com.

MUNAVALLI, GIRISH S. (GILLY MUNAVALLI), dermatologist; BS in Biology minor in Chemistry, 1987—92; M in Health and Sciences, Immunology and Infectious Disease, Johns Hopkins U., Balt., 1993—94; MD, Morehouse Coll., Atlanta, 1994—98. Diplomate Am. Bd. Dermatology, 2002, lic. Ga., cert. Calif., Md., NC.

Transitional year internship Mayo Clinic Mayo Grad. Sch. of Medicine, Scottsdale, Ariz., 1998—99; dermatology residency tng. Emory Univ. Sch. of Medicine, Atlanta, 1999—2002; fellowship mohs micrographic surgery and cosmetic dermatologic surgery San Francisco Sch. of Medicine Univ. of Calif., San Francisco, 2002—03; fellowship advanced lasers and vein surgery Maryland Laser, Skin and Vein Inst. LLC, Hunt Valley, Md., 2003—04; clin. faculty dermatology dept. Johns Hopkins Sch. of Medicine, Balt., 2004—; clin. faculty dermatology dept. Balt. Sch. of Medicine Univ. of Md., 2004—06; part-time faculty Veterans Adminstrn. Md. Health Care System, Balt., 2004—06; med. dir. The Goslen Aesthetic and Skin Ctr.; assoc. Md. Laser, Skin, and Vein Inst. Co-author: (textbooks chpts.) Presentations of Venous Disease, 2005, Sclerotherapy and Lasers for the Treatment of Leg Veins, 2004, Intense Pulsed Light, 2004, Computers in Mohs Surgery, 2004, Laser Treatment of Leg Veins, Ambulatory Phlebectomy, (sci. jours.) Advances in Techniques for Endovenous Ablation of Truncal Veins, Our Approach to Non-ablative Treatment of Photoaging, Photoaging and Nonablative Photorejuvenation in Ethnic Skin, and numerous others. Fellow: Am. Acad. of Dermatology (bd. dirs. 2003—); mem.: Md. Dermatology Soc., Johns Hopkins Univ. Sch. of Hygiene and Pub. Health Alumni Assn., Mayo Alumni Assn., Am. Pathology Imaging, Informatics, and the Internet, Internat. Soc. of Dermatologic Surgery, Internat. Transplant Skin Cancer Collaborative, Am. Coll. of Mohs Micrographic Surgery and Cutaneous Oncology (website and CME com. 2005—), Am. Soc. for Dermatologic Surgery (online CME com. 2003—, website com. mem. 2003—), Am. Soc. for Lasers and Surgery in Medicine (website com. 2005—, CME com. 2005—), Alpha Omega Alpha Nat. Med. Honor Society (Gamma chpt.). Office: Midtown Medical Plaza Ste 550 1918 Randolph Rd Charlotte NC 28207 Office Phone: 704-375-6766. Office Fax: 704-332-6552.

MUNCIE, HERBERT LEE, physician, educator; b. Oklahoma City, Oct. 7, 1946; MD, Med. Coll. Ga., 1971. Dir. student edn., dept. family medicine LSU Sch. Medicine, 2005—, prof. family medicine. Mem.: La. Acad. Family Physicians. Avocation: woodcarving. Office: 1542 Tulane Ave Rm 123 New Orleans LA 70112 Office Fax: 504-568-6793. Business E-Mail: hmunci@lsuhsc.edu.

MUNCK, ALLAN ULF, physiologist, educator; b. Buenos Aires, July 4, 1925; came to U.S., 1945, naturalized, 1959; s. Carl and Elisabeth (Schmidt) M.; m. Claire Brosi, Oct. 5, 1957; children: Alexander Charles, Ingrid Claire, Kirsten Tanya. BS in Chem. Engring, MIT, 1948, MS, 1949, PhD in Biophysics, 1956. Chem. engr., Ducilo, Buenos Aires, 1949-50; mem. staff Huntington Lab. Mass. Gen. Hosp., Boston, 1956-57, Worcester Found. Exptl. Biology, Shrewsbury, Mass., 1957-59; mem. med. sch. faculty Dartmouth Coll., 1959—; prof. physiology Dartmouth Med. Sch., 1967—2001, prof. physiology emeritus, 2001—. Marius Tausk prof. Leiden U., The Netherlands, 1998. Served with Argentine Army, 1949. Office: Dartmouth Med Sch Dept Physiology Lebanon NH 03756 Home: 80 Lyme Rd Apt 422 Hanover NH 03755 Business E-Mail: allan.u.munck@dartmouth.edu.

MUNDEE, YUTTANA, medical researcher, educator; b. Ubonratchathani, Thailand, Sept. 23, 1957; s. Pichai Mundee and Radchanee Srimanard. BS in Med. Tech., Chiang Mai U., Thailand, 1981; MS in Clin. Pathology, Mahidol U., Bangkok, 1988; PhD, U. Coll. London, 2001. Med. scientist Faculty of Medicine, Chiang Mai U., Chiangmai, Thailand, 1981—95, lectr. Dept. Clin. Microscopy, Faculty of Assoc. Med. Scis., 1995—2004, asst. dean grad. studies Dept. Clin. Microscopy, Faculty of Assoc. Med. Scis., 2003—04, asst. prof., 2004—06, assoc. dean rsch. and grad. studies, 2004—06; head assoc. med. scis. Clin. Svc. Ctr., 2006—10; dep. dir. Biomed. Engring. Ctr., 2006—10; mem. Directory Bd. Forensic Sci. Ctr., 2007—10. Cons. Chang Puek Hosp., Chiangmai, Thailand, 1991—96. Contbr. articles to profl. jours. Vol. Thai Red Cross Soc., Chiangmai, Thailand, 1981—96. Recipient Travel award, Am. Soc. Hematology, 1999; grantee Travel grantee, Brit. Jour. Haematology, 1999. Mem.: Med. Tech. Coun. Thailand (com. mem. 2005—), The Thai Soc. of Hematology, The Med. Technologist Assn. of Thailand. Home: 209/176 M10 T Padad A Muang Chiang Mai 50100 Thailand Office: Faculty Associated Med Scis Dept Med Tech Chiang Mai U 50200 Chiang Mai Thailand Home Phone: 66-53-272826; Office Phone: 66-53-949288. Office Fax: 66-53-216424. Personal E-mail: myuttana@hotmail.com. Business E-Mail: yuttana@chiangmai.ac.th.

MUNDORFF SHRESTHA, SHEILA ANN, dental educator; b. Rochester, NY, Dec. 14, 1945; d. Karl Mundorff and Elizabeth Mary (Braun) Ross; m. Buddhi Man Shrestha, June 18, 1988. BS in Biology, Nazareth Coll., Rochester, 1967; MS in Microbiology, U. Rochester, 1984. Lab. technician Eastman Dental Ctr. U. Rochester, 1967-69; rsch. asst. Eastman Dental Ctr., 1969-71, rsch. assoc., 1971-92, small animal expt. coord., 1984-92, sect. head animal/microbiol. rsch., 1987—, chmn. Instl. Animal Care and Use Com., 1990-97, vivarium dir., 1990-97, med. emergency program dir., 1991-92, asst. prof., 1992-97; assoc. prof. U. Rochester Eastman Dept. Dentistry, 1997—. Mem. univ. com. on animal resources U. Rochester, 1997-2003; mem. animal resource group ADA Health Found., Chgo., 1981-83; cons. working group Sci. Consensus Conf.-Assessment Cariogenic Potential of Foods, San Antonio, 1985; participant, reactor, co-chair animal caries models working groups Conf. on Clin. Aspects of Demineralization of Teeth, Rochester, N.Y., 1994; invited session chair symposium 2000, Univ. Leeds, 2000. Patentee in field. CPR instr. ARC, Rochester, 1978-94, cert. 1st responder, N.Y.S., 1992-95, co-pres. Publicity Irondegquoit Art Ch., 2006-08. NIH, Nat. Inst. Dental Rsch. grantee, 1986, 87, 88. Mem. Am. Assn. Dental Rsch. (sec.-treas. Rochester sect. 1977-92). Roman Catholic. Avocations: dance, sewing, swimming, flower arranging, painting on silk. Personal E-mail: bshrestha@rochester.rr.com.

MUNERA, PEDRO ANTONIO, child and adolescent psychiatrist; b. Granollers, Spain, May 16, 1970; s. Pedro Munera and Dolores Cordoba; m. Sherry Lynn Rowlett, Mar. 7, 2003. MD, U. Autonoma de Barcelona, Spain, 1994. Diplomate in psychiatry and in child and adolescent psychiatry Am. Bd. Psychiatry and Neurology. Child and adolescent psychiatrist Weems Cmty. Mental Health Ctr., Meridian, Miss., 2003—; clin. asst. prof. dept. psychiatry U. Miss., Jackson, 2003—; owner, operator Children's Clinic Meridian, 2009—. Author book reviews and case reports. Mem.: Miss. Psychiat. Assn. (assoc.; chair early career psychiatrist com., exec.coun. 2006—), Am. Acad. Child and Adolescent Psychiatry (assoc.; residents and early career psychiatrists com. 2002—03), Am. Psychiat. Assn. (assoc.). Roman Catholic. Avocations: travel, reading. Office: Univ Miss Med Ctr 2500 N State St Jackson MS 39216 Address: 1430 Highway 19 N Meridian MS 39307 Office Phone: 601-282-5346. Personal E-mail: pedromunera@comcast.net, ccom@comcast.net.

MUNEY, ALAN MARC, investment company executive; b. NYC, Aug. 20, 1953; m. Karen Lorene Phillips, May 5, 1984; children: Sara, Rachel, Michael, Matthew. BS in Biology, Brown U., Providence, 1975, MD, 1978; M in Health Adminstrn., U. LaVerne, Calif., 1992. CEO Equity Healthcare; regional med. dir., Greater LA Mullikin Med. Ctr., 1988—95; chief med. officer, sr. v.p., med. affairs Avanti Health Sys., 1995—98; exec. v.p., chief med. officer Oxford Health Plans Inc., Trumbull, Conn., 1998—2007; chief med. officer, Northeast Region United Healthcare, 1998—2007; exec. dir., Pvt. Equity Group The Blackstone Group, L.P., 2007—. Bd. dirs. Vanguard Health System, Team Health. Office: The Blackstone Group 345 Park Ave New York NY 10154 Office Phone: 212-583-5000. Office Fax: 212-583-5749. Business E-Mail: muney@blackstone.com. *

MUNIER, WILLIAM BOSS, medical service executive; b. Corning, NY, Dec. 8, 1942; s. John Hammond and Marguerite (Boss) M.; m. Sandra Lorraine Koerber, 1965 (div. 1976); m. Ann Elizabeth Wessel, 1980 (div. 2005); children: Michael, Andrew, Laura. BA, U. Pa., 1964; MD, Columbia U., 1968; MBA, Harvard U., 1973. Diplomate Nat. Bd. Med. Examiners. Surg. intern Roosevelt Hosp., NYC, 1968-69; profl. staff HEW, Washington, 1969-71, 73-75, dir. Office Quality Standards, 1975-77, dir. Office Health Practice Assessment, 1977-79; exec. v.p. Mass. Med. Soc., Boston, 1979-84; prin. Ernst & Whinney, Boston, 1984-85; pvt. practice mgmt. cons. Wellesley, Mass., 1985-86; dir. program for civilian peer rev. Commn. on Profl. and Hosp. Activities/Dept. Def., 1986-87; pres. Quality Standards in Medicine, Inc., Boston, 1986-99; chief med. officer Health Mgmt. Sys., Inc., Waltham, Mass., 1996-99; pres., CEO Wang Healthcare Info. Sys., Inc., Billerica, Mass., 1999—2004; sr. advisor for IT and quality Agy. for Healthcare Rsch. and Quality, 2004—05; dir. Ctr. for Quality Improvement and Patient Safety, 2005—. Vis. prof. Harvard Sch. Pub. Health, Boston, 1980-90. Contbr. articles to profl. jours. Mem. human services com. Town of Wellesley, 1984-85. Served with USPHS, 1969-79. Mem. AMA, Mass. Med. Soc., St. Botolph Club. Episcopalian. Avocations: golf, skiing, music.

MUNIR, IQBAL, medical researcher, research scientist, physician; s. Monir Uddin Ahmed and Hazera Khatun; m. Salma Khan, Feb. 11, 1994; children: Tazrean, Tarannum. MD, Mymensingh Med. Coll., 1984—90; PhD, Kumamoto U. Sch. of Medicine, 1995—2000. Rsch. fellow Internat. Ctr. for Diarrhoeal Disease Rsch. Bangladesh (ICDDR, B), Dhaka, Bangladesh, 1992; med. officer Bangladesh Inst. of Rsch. and Rehab. in Diabetes, Endocrine & Metabolic disorders (BIRDEM), Dhaka, Bangladesh, 1992—93, Ministry of Health and Family Welfare, Bangladesh, 1993—94; PhD student Kumamoto U. Sch. of Medicine, Japan, 1995—99, vis. scientist, 1999—2000; postdoctoral scientist/ rschr. Cedars-Sinai Med. Ctr., Los Angeles, 2000—. Reviewer Jour. of Molecular Endocrinology, United Kingdom, 2003—. Contbr. articles to profl. jours. Kumamoto U. fellowship, Kumamoto U., 1996—99, Talent Pool scholarship, Dhaka Bd., 1983—84. Mem.: Endocrine Soc., Soc. of the Study of Reproduction. Achievements include discovery of involvement of a novel protein in PCOS and mechanism of insulin action in androgen production. Office: Cedars-Sinai Med Ctr 8700 Beverly Blvd Davis 2058 Los Angeles CA 90048 Personal E-mail: iqbal.munir@cshs.org.

MUNK, ZEV MOSHE, physician, researcher; b. Stockholm, July 14, 1950; m. Susan Deitcher; 4 children. BS, McGill U., 1972; MD, C.M., 1974. Licentiate Med. Coun. Can.; diplomate Am. Bd. Internal Medicine, Am. Bd. Allergy and Clin. Immunology. Intern Royal Victoria Hosp., Montreal, 1974-75, resident, 1975-76; resident in clin. immunology and allergy Montreal Gen. Hosp., 1976-78; practice medicine specializing in allergy/clin. immunology Houston, 1978—; founder, CEO Pharm-Olam Internat. Contbr. articles to med. jours. Pres. Young Israel Synagogue of Houston, 1994-96; founder Allergy Ctr., P.A., Houston, Breco Rsch., Houston; founder, past pres. Torah and Outreach Resource Ctr. of Houston. McGill U. scholar, 1968-74. Fellow ACP, Am. Acad. Allergy Asthma and Immunology, Am. Coll. Allergy and Immunogy, Royal Coll. Physicians (Can.); mem. Tex. Med. Assn., Que. Med. Assn., Tex. Allergy Soc., Harris County Med. Soc., Houston Allergy Soc. Office: 450 N Sam Houston Pwky Ste 250 Houston TX 77060

MUNLEY, PATRICK H., psychologist, educator; b. Somerville, NJ, July 9, 1947; s. Edward Francis Munley and Elizabeth Mildred Toolan; m. Mary Anne Collins, June 5, 1971; children: Elizabeth Anne (Munley) Peot, Thomas Edward, John Patrick, Katherine Claire, Michael Patrick. BS in Math., Seton Hall U., South Orange, NJ, 1969; MA in Psychology, U. Md., Coll. Pk., 1972, PhD in Counseling Psychology, 1973. Lic. Nat. Register Health Svc. Providers Psychology, 1977, diplomate in counseling psychology Am. Bd. Profl. Psychology, 1984, lic. psychologist Mich., 1989, profl. counselor Mich., 2005. Psychologist VA Med. Ctr., Lyons, NJ, 1973—80, East Orange, NJ, 1980—84, chief, psychology svc. Battle Creek, Mich., 1984—99; adj. faculty Western Mich. U., Kalamazoo, 1987—98, assoc. prof. tng. dir. counseling psychology doctoral program, 1999—2005, prof., chair dept. counselor edn. counseling psychology, 2005—. Editl. bd. Jour. Counseling Psychology, 1981—87, Counseling Psychologist, 2003—05. Contbr. articles numerous prof. jours. (W.James Cosse Disting. Svc. award, 2006). Fellow: Am. Psychol. Assn., Am. Acad. Counseling Psychology (pres. 2004—05, past pres. 2006—07, sec. 2004—06). Office: Western Michigan Univ 1903 West Michigan Ave Kalamazoo MI 49008-5226 Office Fax: 269-387-5090. Business E-Mail: patrick.munley@wmich.edu.

MUNLEY, WILLIAM EDWARD, health services administrator; b. Scranton, Pa., Apr. 8, 1958; s. William Edward and Ann J. (McLaughlin) M.; m. Catherine Mary, Sept. 10, 1988; children: William E. III, Patrick S. BS in Gen. Sci., U. Rochester, 1981; M in Health Svcs. Adminstrn., George Washington U., 1984. cert. rehab. adminstr. Team leader-emergency Strong Meml. Hosp., Rochester, N.Y., 1979-81; adminstrv. resident Muhlenburg Med. Ctr., Bethlehem, Pa., 1983; from dir. ops. to outpatient mgr. Good Shepherd Rehab. Hosp., Allentown, Pa., 1983-86; from dir. vitality ctr. to adminstr. rehab. svcs. St. Francis Hosp., Greenville, S.C., 1988—. Home: 303 Clevington Way Simpsonville SC 29681-4641

MUNOZ, JOSE, epidemiologist, educator; Grad., Yale U., 1978. Cert. pediatric infectious disease. Resident pediatrician Yale New Haven Hosp., NY, NY, 1979—81; fellowship pediatric infectious disease Univ. Rochester, Rochester, NY, 1981—84; assoc. prof. pediat. NY Med. Coll.; with Westchester Med. Ctr., Children's & Women's Physicians of Westchester, LLP. Mem.: Pediatric Infectious Diseases Soc., Am. Soc. for Microbiology. Mailing: Children's & Women's Physicians of Westchester LLP Munger Pavilion rm 123 Valhalla NY 10595 Office: Westchester Medical Center Ste 1400 19 Bradhurst Ave Hawthorne NY 10532 Office Phone: 914-493-8333.

MUNOZ, SANTIAGO J., gastroenterologist, educator; MD, U. Chile, 1978. Diplomate transplant hepatology Am Bd. Internal Medicine, Am Bd. Internal Medicine, gastroenterology Am Bd. Internal Medicine, lic. Pa. Intern Thomas Jefferson Univ. Hosp., Phila., resident, 1985, fellow, 1987, Johns Hopkins Sch. Medicine, Baltimore, Md., 1983; prof. medicine dept. Temple Univ., med. dir. liver transplantation dept., dir. clin. hepatology dept.; physician Temple Univ. Hosp. Co-author: Hemodynamics in Acute Porcine Heterotopic Liver Transplantation: Effects of Graft Reduction, 1993, Regeneration of the Native Liver After Heterotopic Liver Transplantation For Fulminant Hepatic Failure, 1993, Factors Associated With Severe Intracranial Hypertension In Candidates for Emergency Liver Transplantation, 1993, Chemosensory Function, Food Preferences And Appetite In Human Liver Disease, 1993, Clinicopathologic Features of Late Hepatic Dysfunction In Orthotopic Liver Transplants, 1993, various publs. Mem.: Am. Assn. for the Study of Liver Diseases, An. Gastroent. Assn., Am. Coll. of Gastroenterology, ACP. Office: Temple University Hospital 3401 N Broad St Philadelphia PA 19140 Office Phone: 215-707-5067. Office Fax: 215-707-5126.

MUÑOZ-CUEVAS, J. HEBERTO, anesthesiologist, educator; b. Méx. City, Sept. 11, 1958; MD, Nat. Autonomous U. Mex., 1982. Anesthesiologist Nat. Autonomous U. Méx., 1988. Anesthesia resident Hosp. Gen. Mex. SS, 1984—88, anesthesiologist, 1988—, prof., 1994—, chief, dept. anesthesiology, 1998—2009. Mem.: Mexican Coll. Anesthesiology. Avocations: softball, reading, jogging. Home: Salaverri 910 Col Lindavista GA Madero México 07300 Mexico Home Fax: (55) 85 03 42 77. Personal E-mail: toheber@prodigy.net.mx.

MUÑOZ-FERNANDEZ, M ANGELES, biomedical researcher; PhD in Biology and Medicine, U Automona, Madrid, 1985. Asst. Hosp. Gregorio Marañon, Madrid, 1992—2008. Office: Gregorio Marañon Hosp Dr ESQUERDO 46 Madrid 28007 Spain Business E-Mail: mmunoz.hgugm@salud.madrid.org.

MUÑOZ-GUERRA, MARIO FERNANDO, maxillofacial surgeon; b. Madrid, Jan. 19, 1967; s. Jose Luis Muñoz and Maria Guerra; m. Angeles Gomez, Sept. 21, 1997; children: Sergio Muñoz, Rebeca Muñoz. MD, Complutense U., Madrid, 1991; PhD, Autonoma U., Madrid, 2001. With dept. Maxillofacial Surgery La Princesa Hosp., Madrid, 1994-98, staff surgeon, 1998—. Assoc. prof. San Pablo CEU U., Dept. Dentistry Contbr. articles to profl. jours. Recipient Ernesto Seco award, Royal Acd. Medicine (Spain), 2003; grantee Basic Rsch., Spanish Soc. of Maxillofacial Surgery, 2003. Office: U Hosp La Princesa Diego de Leon 62 Madrid 28006 Spain Office Phone: 34 91 5202429. Office Fax: 34 91 4013582. Personal E-mail: maxmferm@excite.com.

MUÑOZ ROBLES, JORGE ANDRÉS, immunologist, researcher; b. Popayán, Cauca, Colombia, Oct. 25, 1966; s. Alfonso Muñoz Bravo and Ayda Nelly Robles Sarria; life ptnr. Ainhoa Centeno Muñoz (div. Jan. 16, 1999); children: Christian Andrés Muñoz Orozco, Nathalia Muñoz Orozco. BS in Biology, U. Cauca, Colombia, 1988; MD, U. Cauca Med. Sch., Colombia, 1994. Physician San José Hosp., Popayán, Cauca, Colombia, 1993—94, Piloto Jamundí Hosp., Cali, Valle del Cauca, 1995—96, Terrón Colo. Health Ctr., 1996—98, Seguros Sociales Inst., 1997—98, Saludcoop, Popayán, 1998—98, Santa Margarita Hosp., La Cumbre, Valle del Cauca, 1999—2001, Aquarium Soc., Madrid, 2001—02; immunologist 12 de Octubre U. Tchg. Hosp., 2003—. Dist. health sec. Major's Office, 2001. Mem.: Coll. Physicians Popayán (assoc.), Spanish Soc. Immunology (assoc.), Royal Coll. Physicians Madrid (assoc.). Roman Catholic. Avocations: travel, guitar, scuba diving, weightlifting, tennis. Office: Hospital 12 de Octubre Av Andalucía s/n 28041 Madrid Spain Home: Calle Oca 92 2-C 28025 Madrid Spain Office Fax: (0034)913908315. E-mail: jmunozr.hdoc@salud.madrid.org.

MUNRO, BARBARA HAZARD, retired nursing educator, dean, researcher; b. Wakefield, RI, Nov. 28, 1938; d. Robert J. and Honore (Egan) Hazard; children: Karen Aimee, Craig Michael, Stephanie Anne. BS, MS, U. RI, Kingston; PhD, U. Conn. RN, Conn. Asst. prof. U. RI Coll. Nursing, Kingston; assoc. prof., chmn. program in nursing rsch. Yale U., New Haven; assoc. prof., asst. dir. Ctr. for Nursing Rsch. U. Pa., Phila.; dean, prof. Boston Coll. Sch. Nursing, 1991—2008. Presenter and workshop leader various nursing confs. and seminars in U.S. Contbr. articles and rsch. to profl. pubs. Trustee St. Elizabeth's Med. Ctr. Boston, 1994—2007. Recipient Nat. Rsch. Svc. award. Fellow Am. Acad. Nursing; mem. ANA, Golden Key, Sigma Theta Tau, Pi Lambda Theta, Phi Kappa Phi. Personal E-mail: barbara.hazard.1@verizon.net. Business E-Mail: barbara.hazard.1@bc.edu.

MUNSON, DAVID A., pediatrician; MD, U. Pa. Diplomate Am. Bd. Pediatrics-hospice and palliative medicine, Am. Bd. Pediatrics-neonatal-perinatal medicine. Intern Children's Hosp. of Phila., Pa., resident, fellow, attending neonatologist, assoc. med. dir. newborn/infant intensive care unit, assoc. med. dir. pediat. advanced care team. Author: (papers) Framing permission for halting or continuing life-extending therapies, 2008, Supporting bereaved parents: practical steps in providing compassionate perinatal and neonatal end-of-life care - A North American perspective, 2008, (books) Chapter 10-Delivery Room. Now what?, 2009, The ethics of perinatal palliative care, 2009. Office: Children Hospital of Philadelphia 34th St and Civic Blvd Philadelphia PA 19104-4399 Office Phone: 215-590-1000.

MUNSON, EDWARD HARRY, JR., medical investigator; b. Birmingham, Ala., Apr. 3, 1948; s. Edward H. Sr. and Elizabeth (W.) M.; married, Dec. 6, 1968 (div. Dec. 1985); children: Laura Davis, Kathleen DeLacy Munson, Matthew Edward; m. Patricia Beth Wool, July 29, 1989. BA in Biology, Huntingdon Coll., 1971; student, U. Mo. Law Enforcemnt Tng. Nat. cert. investigator. Investigator Montgomery (Ala.) Police Dept., 1970-81; instr. Ala. Advanced Criminal Justice Acad., 1974-80; med. investigator Ala. Bd. Med. Examiners, Montgomery, 1981—. Cons. State Bd. of Health-Controlled Substance Adv. Panel, Montgomery, 1989—, Stae Methadone Authority, Fedn. of State Med. Bds., Ft. Worth, 1990—; mem. Med. Investigator

Tng. Com., chair, 1994, 97; mem. work com. prescription monitoring programs Nat. Alliance for Model State Drug Laws. Recipient Silver Star, Am. Fedn. Police, Miami, Fla., 1975, Ronald K. Williamson Meml. award Nat. Adminstrs. in Medicine, 2004; named Firearms Expert, NRA, 1978. Mem. Internat. Narcotic Officers Assn., Nat. Assn. Drug Diversion Investigators, Nat. Criminal Justice Assn., Nat. Assn. State Controlled Substance Authorities. Jewish. Avocations: travel, cooking, shooting. Office: Ala Bd Med Examiners PO Box 946 Montgomery AL 36101-0946

MUNSON, JOHN LAWRENCE, surgeon; b. Quincy, Mass., Nov. 14, 1950; BA, U. Pa., 1973; MD, U. Mass., 1979. Sr. surgeon Lahey Clinic Med. Ctr., 1984—. Asst. prof., surgery Tufts U. Sch. Medicine, 1991. Decorated Nat. Def. medal USN; named one of Top Surgeons in America, Consumer's Rsch. Coun. America, America's Top Drs., Castle Connolly Med. Ltd. US News & World Report, Top Dr., Boston Consumers Checkbook, Boston Super Drs., Key Profl. Media. Fellow: ACS; mem.: Mass Chpt. ACS, New Eng. Surg. Soc., Boston Surg. Soc. Avocations: hiking, swimming, gardening. Office: 41 Mall Rd Burlington MA 01805 Office Fax: 781-744-5636. Personal E-mail: jayellem@comcast.net.

MUNTER, GABRIEL, endocrinologist; b. Santiago, Chile, Mar. 22, 1966; MD, Cath. U. Chile, 1990; degree in Internal Medicine and Endocrinology, Hebrew U., Jerusalem, 2002. Internal medicine sr. cons. Shaare Zedek Med. Ctr., 1997—2010, dir. endocrine unit, 2010—. Lectr. Faculty Medicine, Hebrew U., 2010. Recipient Faculty prize, Faculty Medicine, Hebrew U. Mem.: Israel Diabetes Assn., Israel Soc. Endocrinology, European Soc. Endocrinology. Avocation: photography. Home: Karl Netter 129/5 Jerusalem 97762 Israel Personal E-mail: gabriel_munter2000@yahoo.com.

MUNTZ, JAMES EDWIN, medical educator; b. July 7, 1950; BS in Economics & Zoology, Ind. U., Bloomington, Houston, Tex., 1972; MD in Internal Medicine, Baylor Coll. Medicine, 1975. Straight medicine internship St. Luke's Episcopal Hosp. Program, Houston, 1976—77; med. residency Baylor Coll. Medicine, Houston, 1977—78, clin. assoc. prof., dept. orthop. surgery, 1996—, clin. assoc. prof., thrombosis rsch. sect. dept. medicine, 2003—, clin. prof., internal medicine, 2006—; pvt. practise Houston, 1979—; clin. assoc. prof., internal medicine U. Tex. Health Sci. Ctr., 2001—; clin. prof. medicine Weill Cornell Med. Sch., 2009—. Med. dir. Ctrl. United Insurance, Houston, 1991—2004; anticoagulation cons. total hip/total knee clin. pathways, Methodist Hosp., Houston, 1993—, chmn. clinical pathways for DVT prophylaxis and treatment, 1996—, cons. antithrombosis orthop. svc, critical pathways total hip/knee replacement St. Luke's Episcopal Hosp., Houston, 1995—; med. cons. initiation outpatient treatment program DVT Kelsey-Seybold Clinic, Houston, 1996—; anticoagulation cons. Arthritis Clinic, Houston, 1997—; with epidural catheters and anticoagulants Nat. Adv. Panel, 1997. Contbr. articles to numerous jours. Team physician USFL Houston Gamblers, 1984—85, Houston Oilers, 1986—97, Houston Comets, 1993—95, Houston Rockets, 1994—; team internist U. Houston, 1994—95, internal medicine cons., 1996—; team physician WNBA, 1997—99, Houston Thunderbears, 1996—98, Houston Marshals, 2000—01, Houston Texans, 2001—, Houston Astros, 2002—; med. cons. NBA China Games, 2004; team internist Houston Dynamo, 2006. Named Outstanding Internist, Dept. Orthopedic Surgery, Baylor Coll. Medicine, 1995. Fellow: ACP; mem.: The Athletics Congress, Tex. Soc. Sports Medicine, Tex. Med. Assn., Nat. Football League Physicians Soc., Nat. Basketball Assn. Physicians Soc., Houston Soc. Internal Medicine (Sec. 1997), Harris County Med. Soc., Am. Soc. Internal Medicine, Am Med. Soc. Sports Medicine, Am. Med. Joggers Assn., Am. Med. Assn., Am. Coll. Sports Medicine. Office: 6550 Fannin #2339 Houston TX 77030

MUNZNER, ROBERT FREDERICK, biomedical engineer; s. Robert F. Munzner and Catherine E. (Appel) Gay; m. Jo Ann Goettee, Sept. 2, 1960 (dec.); children: Elizabeth Mae, Robert Victor, Ann Catherine; m. Karen E. Winstedt, Oct. 1, 1988. BS in Physics, Loyola Coll., Balt., 1963; PhD in Biomed. Engring., U. Va., 1976. Aerospace engr. Westinghouse Def. and Space, Balt., 1963-69; rsch. assoc. Johns Hopkins U., Balt., 1975-77; chief, neurol. devices br. U.S. FDA, Rockville, Md., 1977-97, expert sci. reviewer, 1998-99; regulatory affairs cons. Schuyler, Va., 1999—. Exec. sec. neurol. device adv. panel. U.S. FDA, Rockville, Md.; bd. standards IEEE, 1999-2001; mem. biomed. engring. adv. bd. UNC, Chapel Hill, 2004—08. Co-author: Cerebellar Stimulation for Spasticity, 1984, The Physicians Perspective on Medical Law, 1997, Wiley Encyclopedia of Biomedical Engineering, 2006; contbr. articles to profl. jours. Fellow Johns Hopkins U., Balt., 1975, U. Va. fellow, Charlottesville, 1972-73, Thornton fellow, 1971. Mem. IEEE (sr., Millennium medal 2000), Biomed. Engring. Soc., Engring. in Medicine and Biology Soc. (chmn. stds. com., ad com. 1999-2005), Sigma Xi. Achievements include research in atrial mechanical stimulation producing vasomotor reflex. Home Phone: 434-263-8862; Office Phone: 434-263-8862. Business E-Mail: robert@doctordevice.com.

MURA, ANTONIO, retired anesthesiologist, hyperbaric medicine specialist, director; b. Ozieri, Italy, Sept. 5, 1931; s. Francesco Mura and Luisa Cattina; m. Rosa Maria Virgara, Oct. 27, 1958; children: Ester, Marcello, Paola. Degree in medicine, U., 1951—57. Specialization in Anesthesiology U. of Rome, 1959. Asst. dept. anesthesia S. Francesco Hosp., Nuoro, Italy, 1957—62, Gen. Hosp., Foggia, Italy, 1962—67, dir. dept. anesthesia FOGGIA, 1967—69, dir. dept. anesthesia Palmi, 1969—97; dir. hyperbaric medicine ctr. S. Anna Hosp., Catanzaro, Italy, 1999—; prof. specialization sch. anesthesiology Faculty Medicine - U., Catanzaro, Italy, 1992—97. Mem. directive com. Syndicate Italian Hosp. Physicians (A.N.A.A.O.), Rome, 1964—66, Italian Soc. Anesthesiology (S.I.A.A.R.T.I.), Rome, 1987—89. Pres. Lions Club, Palmi, Calabria, Italy, 1989—90. Recipient Commendatore Republic Italy, Pres. Republic, 2000. Mem.: Lions Club (assoc.). Office: S Anna Hosp Viale Pio X 111 Cz Catanzaro 88100 Italy Home: Via Papa Giovanni Xxiii 33 89015 Palmi RC Italy Office Fax: 0039-0961-701509; Home Fax: 0039-0966-23060. Personal E-mail: iperb@i-2000net.it.

MURAD, FERID, pharmacologist, physician; b. Whiting, Ind., Sept. 14, 1936; s. John and Josephine Murad; m. Carol Ann Leopold, June 21, 1958; children: Christine, Marianne, Carrie, Julie, Joseph. BA, DePauw U., Greencastle, Ind., 1958; MD, PhD, Case Western Res. U., Cleve., 1965, DSc (hon.), 2000, Thomas Jefferson U., 2000, State U. Ceara, Brazil, 2000, Chinese U., Hong Kong, 2002, DePauw U., 2004, Charles U., Prague, 2005, Southeastern U., 2006; degree (hon.), Tirana U., Albania, 1999. Diplomate Nat. Bd. Med. Examiners, Am. Bd. Internal Medicine. Intern, resident internal medicine Mass. Gen. Hosp., Boston, 1965—67; clin. assoc. molecular disease br. Nat. Heart & Lung Inst., NIH, Bethesda, Md., 1967—70; assoc. prof. dept. internal medicine and pharmacology U. Va. Sch. Medicine, Charlottesville, 1970—75, prof., 1975—81, dir. Clin. Rsch. Ctr., 1971—81, dir. divsn. clin. pharmacology, 1973—81; prof. dept. internal medicine and pharmacology Stanford U., Calif., 1981—89, acting chmn. dept. medicine, 1986—88; divsn. v.p. pharm. discovery Abbott Labs., Ill., 1988—90, v.p. pharm. rsch. & devel., corp. officer, 1990—92; pres., CEO Molecular Geriatrics Corp., Lake Bluff, Ill., 1993—95; prof., dir. divsn. clin. pharmacology U. Tex. Health Sci. Ctr., Houston, 1997—99, chmn. dept. integrative biology and pharmacology, 1997—2005, prof. dept. medicine, John S. Dunn disting. chair physiology and medicine, regental prof., 1998—2011, dir. Inst. Molecular Medicine, 1999—2011; univ. prof. dept. biochemistry and molecular biology George Wash. U. Sch. Medicine and Health Sciences, Washington, 2011—. Chief of medicine Palo Alto VA Med. Ctr., Calif., 1981—86; adj. prof. dept. pharmacology Northwestern U. Med. Sch., Chgo., 1988—96; adj. prof. dept. biochemistry Ohio State U., Columbus, 1999—. Co-editor: The Pharmacological Basis of Therapeutics, 1985; assoc. editor Jour. Applied Cardiology, 1986—92, Jour. Clin. Investigation, 1987—88, mem. editl. bd. Jour. Cyclic Nucleotide Rsch., 1974—88, Jour. Biol. Chemistry, 1979—84, Analytical Biochemistry, 1980—83, Endothelium, 1992—, Cell Biology Internat., 2005—; contbr. articles to profl. jours. Bd. dirs. Albanian Internat. Scholarship Found., 1999—, Kosova Found. Med. Devel., 2001—. Recipient Ciba award, Am. Heart Assn., 1988, Albert Lasker award for basic med. rsch., 1996, Nobel prize in physiology/medicine, 1998, Honor of Nation award, Albania, 1999, Sagamore Wabash award, Ind., 1999, Golden Plate award, Am. Acad. Achievement, 1999, Disting. Alumnus award, Case Western Res. U., 1999, Macedonian Medal of St. Apostle Paul, 2000, Baxter award for disting. rsch. in biomed. scis., Assn. Am. Med. Colleges, 2000, Santiago Grisolia award, Spain, 2005; named an Hon. Citizen, City of Gostivar, Macedonia, 1999. Fellow: ACP, European Acad. Scis.; mem.: AAAS, NAS, Albanian Acad. Scis. (fgn.), Macedonian Acad. Scis. & Arts (fgn.), Am. Physiol. Soc., NY Acad. Scis., Am. Coll. Clin. Pharmacology, Southern Soc. Clin. Investigation, Endocrine Soc., Albemarle Med. Soc., Am. Fedn. Clin. Rsch., Inst. Medicine, Western Assn. Physicians, Assn. Am. Physicians, Am. Soc. Clin. Investigation, Am. Soc. Physiology, Am. Soc. Biol. Chemists, Am. Soc. Pharmacology & Exptl. Therapeutics, Am. Acad. Arts & Scis., Islamic Acad. Scis. (hon.), Kosovo Acad. Arts & Scis. (hon.), World Innovation Found. (hon.), Phi Beta Kappa, Alpha Omega Alpha. Achievements include patents in field. Avocations: golf, carpentry. Office: Dept Biochemistry and Molecular Biology Sch Medicine and Health Sciences 2300 Eye St NW Ste 530 Washington DC 20037 Office Phone: 202-994-5040. Business E-Mail: bcmfxm@gwumc.edu. *

MURAD, HOWARD, dermatologist, educator; Grad., The Arnold and Marie Schwartz Coll. of Pharmacy and Health Sciences; MD, U. Calif., Irvine. Diplomate Am. Bd. Dermatology. Rotating intern Queen's Hosp., NY; resident dermatology Veteran's Adminstrn. Hosp., 1969—72; pharmacist; founder and CEO Murad Inc.; assoc. clin. prof. UCLA. Author: (books) Wrinkle-Free Forever, 2004, The Cellulite Solution. Gen. med. officer USAR, battalion surgeon, Vietnam. Decorated Bronze Star. Fellow: Am. Acad. of Dermatology. Office: Murad Incorporated 5th Fl 2121 Rosecrans Ave El Segundo CA 90245 Office Phone: 310-726-0600.

MURADIAN, KHACHIK KAZAROVICH, physiologist; b. Yerevan, Armenia, July 19, 1944; PhD, Inst. Physiology NAS Ukraine, 1976, D in Biol. Scis., Inst. Gerontology Nat. Acad. Med. Scis. Ukraine, 1993. Sr. scientist Inst. Gerontology Nat. Acad. Med. Scis. Ukraine, 1973—, head rsch. group, chief rschr., 1996—. Recipient Mechnikov award, NAS Ukraine, Sandoz award. Mem.: Physiol. Soc. Ukraine, Biochem. Soc. Ukraine, Gerontol. Soc. Ukraine. Office: Vyshgorodskaya St 67 Kiev 04114 Ukraine Office Fax: (38044) 43 9956. Business E-Mail: kkm1@ukr.net.

MURAI, HIROYUKI, neurologist, director; b. Fukuoka, Japan, Jan. 30, 1963; MD, Kyushu U., PhD, 1988. Rsch. fellow Roswell Pk. Cancer Inst., 1995—98; assoc. dir., dept. neurology Kyushu Kosei Nenkin Hosp., 1998—2000; asst. prof., dept. neurology Kyushu U., 2000—07, clin. prof., 2007; dir., dept. neurology Iizuka Hosp., 2007—. Mem. Creutzfeldt-Jakob Disease Surveillance Com., 2000; assoc. editor BMC Neurology, 2010. Recipient Kuroiwa-Goto award, Kyushu U.; grant, Ministry of Health, Labour and Welfare, Japan. Master: Japanese Headache Soc., Japan Soc. Dementia Rsch., Japan Stroke Soc., Japanese Soc. Neurology; mem.: Am. Acad. Neurology. Avocation: music. Office: 3-83 Yoshio-machi Iizuka Fukuoka 820-8505 Japan Office Fax: 81-948-29-5744.

MURAI, NORIMOTO, plant molecular biologist, educator; b. Sapporo, Japan, Mar. 4, 1944; came to U.S., 1968; s. Nobuo and Hideko (Odagiri) M.; m. Andreana Lisca, Nov. 14, 1977; 1 child, Naoki. BS, Hokkaido U., 1966, MS, 1968; PhD, U. Wis., 1973. Rsch. assoc. dept. botany U. Wis., Madison, 1974-78, project assoc. dept. bacteriology, 1979, postdoctoral fellow dept. plant pathology, 1980-82; lab. head dept. molecular biology Nat. Inst. Agrobiol. Resources, Tsukuba, Japan, 1983-84; assoc. prof. plant pathology and crop physiology La. State U., Baton Rouge, 1985-92, prof., 1992—. Adj. prof. biochemistry, full mem. grad. faculty and interdept. studies in plant physiology and genetics La. State U.; mem. study sect. on minority biomed. rsch. support program NIH, 1993; grant reviewer USDA, NSF, NIH. Reviewer manuscripts Genome, Protein Engring., Plant Cell, Plant Physiol., Planta, Plant Molecular Biology, Plant Cell Report, Australia Jour. Plant Physiol. Named Honors Rschr., Phi Delta Kappa, 1989; grantee Fulbright Found., 1968, Sci. and Tech. Agy., Tokyo, 1984, La. Edn. Quality Support Fund, 1988, 89, 91, 94, 95, 97, 98, Monsanto Co. Fund, 1992, 93, U.S. Dept. Agr., 1995, Rockefeller Found., 1995-96; Fulbright scholar. Mem. AAAS, Am. Soc. Plant Biologists, Internat. Soc. Plant Molecular Biology, Japan Molecular Biology Assn., Crop Sci. Soc. Am., Fulbright Assn., Sigma Xi, Gamma Sigma Delta, Phi Delta Kappa. Avocations: running, skiing, gardening, golf, tennis. Office: La State Univ Dept Plant Pathology & Crop Physiology Baton Rouge LA 70803-1720 Office Phone: 225-578-1380. Business E-Mail: nmurai@lsu.edu.

MURAKAMI, HARUO, internist; b. Sapporo, Japan, June 16, 1930; s. Teikichi and Shizue Kuranami; m. Hiroko Murakami, May 27, 1959; children: Keiko, Tomoko, Chiharu. MD, Tokyo Med. and Dental U., 1957. Fellow 1st Clinic Internal Medicine Tokyo Med. and Dental U., 1957—67; chief Ichikawa Daiichi Hosp., Tokyo, 1967—77; dir. Murakami Clinic, Tokyo, 1977—. Contbr. articles to med. jours. Mem.: Den-en-Chofu Med. Assn. (dir. 1980—84, com. mem. 1984—), Japan Med. Assn., Japanese Soc. Internal Medicine. Democrat. Bhuddist. Home and Office: Murakami Clinic 5-11-7 Minami-Yukigaya Ohta Ku Tokyo 145-0066 Japan

MURAKAMI, MASAAKI, medical educator; b. Otaru, Japan, July 13, 1963; DVM, Hokkaido U.; PhD, Osaka U., 1993. Assoc. prof. Osaka U., 2002. Mem.: Am. Assn. Immunologists, Japanse Soc. Immunology. Office: 2-2 Yamadaoka Suita Osaka 565-0871 Japan

MURAKAMI, SHIO, herbal medicine researcher; b. Kofu, Yamanashi, Japan, Apr. 18, 1963; MS, Waseda U., 1988; PhD, Toho U., 2009; BS, Waseda U., 1986. Prin. rschr. Green Flask Lab., 2000; rep. Totolab Sch. Herbal Medicine, 2009—. Mem.: Japanese Soc. Pharmacognosy, Japan Med. Herb Assn. Avocation: mountain climbing. Home: 204 2-14-4 Saginuma Miyamae-ku Kawasaki Kanagawa 216-0004 Japan Home Fax: 81-44-856-4278. Business E-Mail: shio@totolab.com.

MURAKAMI, TERUO, pharmaceutical educator; b. Fukui, Japan, Jan. 24, 1949; s. Kiyoshi and Masae Murakami; m. Norie Murakami; children: Masahiko, Tatsuhiko. BS, Osaka U., Pharm. Scis., Japan, 1972; MS, Grad. Sch. Pharm. Scis., Osaka U., Japan, 1976, PhD, 1979. Asst. prof. Osaka U. Pharm. Scis., 1972—74, Faculty of Pharm. Scis., Hiroshima U., Japan, 1980—88, assoc. prof., 1988—2004, Grad. Sch. Biomed. Scis. Hiroshima U., 2004—05; prof. Faculty of Pharm. Scis., Hiroshima Internat. U., Kure, Japan, 2005—. Recipient Meritorious Manuscript award, AAPS, 1992. Mem.: Acad. Pharm. Sci. & Tech. Japan, Pharm. Soc. Japan, Japan Soc. Drug Delivery Sys., Japanese Soc. Study of Xenobiotics. Home: 3-42-22 Aita Asaminami-ku Hiroshima 731-0141 Japan Office: Hiroshima Internat Univ 5-1-1 Hiro-koshingai Kure 737-0112 Japan Office Phone: 81-823-73-8994. Business E-Mail: t-muraka@ps.hirokoku-u.ac.jp.

MURAKAWA, MUSAHIRO, hospital administrator; b. Jan. 1955; Grad., Kyoto U., 1980. Vice dir. sch. of medicine, dept. of anesthesiology Fukushima Med. Univ., Japan, dir. sch. of medicine, dept. of anesthesiology, pres. sch. of medicine, dept. of anesthesiology. Office: Fukushima Medical University Hospital 1-Hikariga-oka Fukushima Japan Office Phone: 810245471342. *

MURAKI, MICHIRO, medical researcher; b. Osaka, Japan, Aug. 16, 1957; s. Muraki Saburo and Muraki Misako; m. Muraki Keiko, Nov. 17, 1985. Dr., Osaka City U., 1982. Sr. rschr. Nat. Inst. Adv. Ind. Sci. Tech., Tsukuba, Ibaraki, Japan, 1982—. Contbr. scientific papers to sci. jours. Achievements include development of genetic engineering methods to produce a large amount of biomedically important proteins. Office: Nat Inst Adv Ind Sci Tech Japan 1-1-1 Higashi Tsukuba Central 6 Tsukuba Ibaraki 305-8566 Japan Business E-Mail: m-muraki@aist.go.jp.

MURAKI, YASUSHI, medical educator; b. Japan, Oct. 16, 1962; MD, Yamagata U., 1987. Prof. Kanazawa Med. U., 2009—. Office: Uchinada Kahoku Ishikawa 9200293 Japan Business E-Mail: ymuraki@kanazawa-med.ac.jp.

MURALI, RAJ, neurosurgeon, educator; m. Lakshmi Murali; 2 children. Postgrad, U. of Edinburgh, MD, Madras U., 1968. Diplomate Am. Bd. Neurol. Surgery. Intern Madras Univ., 1967—68; resident Royal Infirm Univ., 1968—74, NYU Med. Ctr., 1974—79; sr. house officer and registrar in gen. surgery Edinburgh Univ., fellow; sr. registrar neurosurgery Western Gen. Hosp., Edinburgh, 1968—71; chief resident Bellevue Hosp. Med. Ctr., 1979; chmn. neurosurgery dept. St.Vincent's Hosp. and Med. Ctr., 1996—2002; prof. and chmn. of neurosurgery NY Med. Coll., 2002; dir. neurosurgical svcs Westchester Med. Ctr. Mem.: Am. Assn. of Neurol. Surgeons, ACS. Office: Westchester Medical Center Ste 329 Munger Pavilion Valhalla NY 10595 Office Phone: 914-493-8392.

MURALI, RAJMOHAN, pathologist; b. Pandalam, Kerala, India, May 25, 1972; s. Murali Mahadevan and Usha Murali; m. Marianne O'Reilly, May 8, 1999. MBBS, U. Sydney, Australia, 1995. Intern Westmead Hosp., Westmead, Sydney, 1996—97, resident med. officer Sydney, 1997—98; registrar in hematology Liverpool Hosp., Sydney, 1998—99, Wollongong Hosp., Sydney, 1999; registrar in forensic pathology Dept. Forensic Pathology, Westmead, Sydney, 1999—2000; registrar in tissue pathology ICPMR, Westmead Hosp., Sydney, 2000—05; pathologist Nepean Hosp., Penrith, Australia, 2005—06; pathologist Sydney Melanoma Unit and dept. anat. pathology Royal Prince Alfred Hosp., Camperdown, Sydney, 2006—. Mentor, jr. med. officer mentorship program Australian Med. Assn., Sydney, 2003—04. Contbr. articles to profl. jours. Child sponsor World Vision, Sydney, 2001—06; supporter Amnesty Internat., Greenpeace, Oxfam Internat. Recipient prize, Royal Australian Chem. Inst., 1988; grantee, Cancer Inst. NSW, 2005—; scholar, U. Sydney, 1989. Fellow: Royal Coll. Pathologists Australasia; mem.: Internat. Acad. Cytology, Australian Soc. Cytology, US and Can. Acad. Pathology. Achievements include research in the molecular pathology of malignant melanoma. Avocations: music, reading, motorcycles, travel. Office: Royal Prince Alfred Hosp Missenden Rd Camperdown Sydney NSW 2050 Australia Office Fax: 612 9515 8405. Personal E-mail: glossus@yahoo.com.

MURALI, SRINIVAS, internist, educator; MD, Jawaharlal Inst. of Med. Edn. and Rsch. Diplomate Am. Bd. Internal Medicine-cardiovascular disease. Intern Jewsih Hosp. and Med. Ctr., resident; fellow Univ. Pitts. Med. Ctr., Interfaith Med. Hosp.; practice Gerald McGinnis Cardiovascular Inst.; prof. medicine Drexel Univ.; dir. divsn. cardiology Allegheny Gen. Hosp. Named one of Top Doctors, Pitts. mag., 2011. Office: Allegheny General Hospital 320 E N Ave Pittsburgh PA 15212 Office Phone: 412-359-3131. Office Fax: 412-359-4108.

MURAMATSU, HIKARU, physician, researcher, director; b. Misaka, Yamanashi, Japan, June 25, 1957; s. Hisawo and Chieko Muramatsu; m. Hiroko Odagiri, Aug. 6, 1959; children: Takumi, Satoru, Kanoko. MD, Nippon Med. Sch., Tokyo, 1984, DMS, 1990; PhD, Tex. Tech U. Health Scis. Ctr., 1993. Diplomate 1984, Bd. Am. Acad. Phys. Medicine and Rehab., 2002, bd. cert. Japan Gen. Physicians, 2006. Internship and residency in cardiology Nippon Med. Sch., Tokyo, 1984—86; postgrad. rsch. course Oita Med. U. Physiology, Japan, 1988—89; clin. asst. prof. Nippon Med. Sch. Cardiology, Tokyo, 1989—90; rsch. assoc. Tex. Tech U. HSC Physiology,

Lubbock, 1990—93; exec. dir. med. Kasugai Rehab. Hosp., Yamanashi, Japan, 1993—, v.p., 1998—; assoc. prof. Nippon Med. Sch. Internal Medicine Cardiology, Tokyo, 2009—. Vis. rschr. U. Yamanashi Interdisciplinary Grad. Sch. Medicine and Engring., 1997—, Bd. Heart Rhythm Soc., 2004, Japan Bd. Indsl. Medicine, 2005, Japan Bd. Sports Medicine, 2005, Japan Bd. Gen. Physician, 2006, Japan Bd. Antimicrobial Chemotherapy Physician, 2009, Japan Bd. Diabetes Edn. & Care, 2011; ICLS, ACLS instr., Japan, 04; instr. cardiac rehab., 05. Author: (novels) Molecular physiology and pharmacology of cardiac ion channels and transporters, 1996; translator Textbook of Medical Physiology, 1999, Essential Cardiac Electrophysiology with Self-Assessment, 2011; contbr. articles to profl. jours. Mem.: Japanese Soc. Chemotherapy, Japan Bd. Gen. Physiology, Internat. Brain Injury Assn., Japanese Soc. Internal Medicine, Japan Physicians Assn., Japanese Soc. Electrocardiology, Cardiac Electrophysiol. Soc., Japanese Soc. Clin. Physiology, World Fedn. Neuro. Rehab., Japanese Soc. Rehab. Network Rsch., Japanese Assn. Cardiac Rehab., Heart Rhythm Soc., Am. Stroke Assn., Am. Coll. Chest Physicians, Am. Acad. Phys. Medicine and Rehab. (bd. mem. 2002), Assn. Acad. Physiatrists, Internat. Soc. Electrocardiology, Japanese Circulation Soc., Japanese Assn. Rehab. Med., Internat. Soc. Heart Rsch., Internat. Soc. Phys. Med. and Rehab., Am. Congress of Rehab. Med., Am. Heart Assn., Japan Med. Assn. Home: 7-3 Daiwa Koufu Yamanashi 400-0072 Japan Office: Kasugai Rehab Hosp Cardiology 436 Kokufu Kasugai Fuefuki Yamanashi 406-0014 Japan Home Phone: 81 55 251 4828; Office Phone: 81 55 326 4126 ext. 223. Office Fax: 81 55 326 4366; Home Fax: 81 55 251 4828. Personal E-mail: m-hikaru@rainbow.plala.or.jp. Business E-Mail: m-hikaru@nms.ac.jp.

MURARIU, DUMITRU TOADER, biologist, zoologist, researcher; b. Ungureni-Botosani, Romania, Sept. 21, 1940; s. Toader A. and Elena D. (Amortitoaie) M.; m. Angela Al. Vasiliu, July 28, 1966; children: Mihail, Magdalena. Grad., Faculty of Biology, Iasi, Romania, 1966; PhD, Faculty of Biology, Bucharest, Romania, 1975. Tchr. Gymnasium, Ungureni-Botosani, Romania, 1957-58; biologist Tuberculozis Hosp., Bucharest, 1966-69; museologist Mus. Natural History, Bucharest, 1969-76, head sect., 1976-88, sr. rschr., 1991—. Dir. Mus. Natural History, 1988-2011; tchr. museology Ministry of Culture, Bucharest, 1982-94; sr. rschr. Faculty of Biology, Bucharest, 1995; mem. adv. com. EUROBATS, 1998—2008. Author: On the Life of Mammals, vol. I, 1989, vol. II, 1993, vol. III, 1998, vol. IV, 2010, Animals from Africa, 2003, Romanian Fauna and Mammals, vol. 16 (part 1) 2000, (part 2) 2001, (part 4) 2004, (part 5) 2005; editor-in-chief Travaux du Museum HN, 1991-2011. With Romanian mil., 1958-61. Recipient Fulbright grant Am. Coun. Edn., 1975-76; expdn. grant to Indonesia, 1991, Brazil, 1994, Tunisia, 2006, Morocco, 2008, Turkey, 2009, Romanian Ministry of Edn. Mem. Am. Soc. Mammalogists (life), Romanian Soc. Biology, Romanian Assn. Museologists, Romanian Assn. Scientists, Soc. for Conservation of Bats in Europe, Romanian Acad. (corr.). Avocations: gardening, music, reading, trips. Office: Grigore Antipa Mus Natural History Sos Kiseleff No 1 011341 Bucharest Romania Home: Strada Amman 20A Bucharest 11613 Romania Office Phone: 4021 3128855. Business E-Mail: dmurariu@antipa.ro.

MURASAWA, SATOSHI, cardiologist, researcher; b. Osaka, Japan; MD, Kansai Med. U., 1989, PhD, 1996. Lic. internal medicine specialist Japanese Internal Medicine Soc., 1997. Rsch. fellow dept. medicine II Kansai Med. U., Moriguchi, Japan, 1989—97; postdoctoral fellow Japan Soc. for Promotion of Sci., 1997—2000; rsch. fellow in cardiovasc. rsch. St. Elizabeth's Med. Ctr., Boston, 2000—03; sr. rsch. scientist Inst. Biomedical Rsch. and Innovation, Kobe, Japan, 2002—. Recipient Molecular Cardiology Rsch. awards, Japan Heart Found., 1996, Hypertension and Vascular Metabolism Rsch. awards, Pfizer Pharm., Japan, 1997; grantee, Cardiovasc. Endocrine Metabolism Soc., Japan, 1998, Internat. Stem Cell Conf., Singapore, 2003. Mem.: Japanese Coll. Angiology Soc. (45th Ann. Conf. Basic Sci. Category award 2004, 45th Ann. Conf. grantee 2004), Am. Heart Assn. (Louis N and Arnold M. Katz Rsch. prize 2001, grantee 2001, 2005, New Investigator Travel award 2005). Achievements include research in molecular and functional analyses of renin-angiotensin system; clinical application of endothelial progenitor cells transplantation for vascular regeneration; analyses of regenerative properties in endothelial progenitor cells. Office: Inst of Biomed Research and Innovation 2-2 Minatojima-Minamimachi Chuo-ku Hyogo 650-0047 Japan Kobe Office Fax: +81-78-304-5263. Business E-Mail: s-murasawa@cdb.riken.go.jp.

MURASE, YOSHIRO, medical researcher; b. Aichi, Japan, June 29, 1976; PhD, U. Tokyo, 2005. Rschr. Rsch. Inst. Tuberculosis, Japan Anti-Tuberculosis Assn., 2005—. Office: 3-4-15 Matsuyama Kiyose Tokyo 204-8533 Japan E-mail: yoshiromurase@gmail.com.

MURASHIMA, YOSHIYA LUCA, psychiatrist, neuroscientist; b. Osaka, Japan, Dec. 30, 1954; s. Zensaku Petro and Nobuko Maria (Sugimoto) Murashima; m. Ryoko Noeala Maeda, July 1986; children: Yoshiko Angerica, Eiko Maria del Fiore, Koya Marco del Aurelio, Naoya Tomaso del Aquino. MD, Tokyo U., 1980, PhD, 1984. Med. diplomate and sci. rsch. Intern Murakami Mental Hosp., Tokyo, 1980-82, resident, 1982-84; chief Tokyo Inst. Psychiatry, 1984-91, dir., 1991—2006, vis. sr. rsch. scientist, 2007—. Vis. prof. Tokyo Met. U. Grad. Sch., 2007—, Orgn. Frontier Sci. Innovation Ctr., Gumma U., Tenjin-cho Kinyu-shi, 2007—. Avocations: classical music and arts, european travel, scuba diving. Home: 5-12-2-202 Kamikitazawa Setagaya-Ku Tokyo MZ 156-0057 Japan Office: 5-12-2-202 2-1-8 Kamikitazawa, Setagaya-ku Tokyo MZ 156 Japan E-mail: murasima-epi@umin.ac.jp.

MURASUGI, AKIRA, biochemist; b. Tokyo, Sept. 20, 1948; s. Hideo and Yaeko Murasugi; m. Hisako Takanashi; 1 child. BS, Saitama U., 1971; MS, Nagoya U., 1973, DSc, 1982. Asst. Nagoya U., Japan, 1976—78; rschr. Inst. for Devel. Rsch., Aichi, Japan, 1979—86; post doctoral fellow City of Hope Nat. Med. Ctr., Duarte, Calif., 1983—85; rschr. Meiji Inst. Health Sci., Odawana, Japan, 1986—90, head, 1990—2000; mgr. Meiji Dairies Corp., Tokyo, 2000—08, sr. advisor, 2008—. Contbr. articles to profl. jours. Office: Meiji Corp Tech Dept 1-2-10 Shinsuna Koto ku Tokyo 136 8908 Japan Business E-Mail: akira.murasugi@meiji.com.

MURAT, YUSEF J., plastic surgeon; b. Oaxaca, Mex., Sept. 2, 1964; arrived in U.S., 2003; s. Mateo Jiménez and Zandra Luz Murat; m. Ireri Salazar Urquiza, Nov. 29, 1997; children: Valentina, Miranda. MD, UNAM, Mexico City, 1989. Cert. plastic surgeon UNAM, 1996, Bd., 1997. Fellowship hand surgeon UNAM, Mexico City, 1997; fellowship microsurgery Hosp. Gen. Manuel Gea Gonzalez, UNAM, Mexico City, 1998, prof. plastic surgery, hand surgery, microsurgery, 1997—. Contbr. scientific papers in plastic surgery, hand surgery and microsurgery. Mem.: Assn. Dr. Ortiz-Monasterio. Avocations: tennis, golf. Office Phone: 956-544-7197. E-mail: yusmd@prodigy.net.mx.

MURATA, ATSUHIKO, physician; b. Yukuhashi, Mar. 17, 1975; MD, Kagoshima U., 2001. Clinician, rschr. U. Occupl. & Environ. Health, 2009—. Master: Japanese Soc. Internal Medicine, Japan Gastroent. Endoscopy Soc., Japanese Soc. Gastroenterology. Achievements include development of Japanese case-mix system project called DPC. Avocation: football. Office: 1-1 Iseigaoka Yahatanishi-ku Kitakyushu Fukuoka 807-8555 Japan Office Fax: 81-93-603-4307. Business E-Mail: amurata@med.uoeh-u.ac.jp.

MURATA, KOICHIRO, radiologist; b. Tokyo, Dec. 24, 1954; s. Takeshi and Teruko Murata; m. Kinuko Tethuka; children: Akio, Toshiaki. MD, Kitasato U., Sagamihara, Japan, 1980. Resident Kitasato U. Hosp., 1980-86, mem. staff, 1986, Kitasato U. East Hosp., Sagamihara, 1987-88; dir. radiology Kitasato Inst. Med. Ctr. Hosp., Saitama, Japan, 1989-94, Kitasato Inst. Hosp., Tokyo, 1995—2003, Kitasato U. Hosp., 2003—. Lectr. Kitasato U. Sch. Medicine, 1989—. Contbr. articles to med. jours. Fellow Am. Roentgen Ray Soc.; mem. Japan Radiol. Soc. Office: Kitasato U Hosp Kitasato 1-15-1 Sagamihara Kanagawa 228-8555 Japan

MURATA, MIHO, neurologist, director; b. Yamanashi, Japan, June 15, 1958; MD, Tsukuba U., 1984, PhD, 1992. Assoc. prof., dept. neurology U. Tokyo, 1996—2003; dir., dept. neurology Nat. Ctr. Neurology & Psychiatry, 2004—. Mem.: Movement Disorder Soc., Japanese Soc. Neurology (Narabayashi award). Office: 4-4-1 Ogawa-higashi Kodaira Tokyo 187-8551 Japan Office Fax: 81-42-346-1735. Business E-Mail: mihom@ncnp.go.jp.

MURAYAMA, SADAYUKI, radiologist, educator; b. Nichinan, Japan, July 1, 1955; MD, Kyushu U., PhD, 1981. Prof. dept. radiology Grad. Sch. Med. Sci., U. Ryukyus, 1999—. Pres. U. Ryukyus Hosp., 2011. Mem.: Japan Radiol. Soc. Avocation: birdwatching. Office: 207 Uehara Nishihara Okinawa 903-0215 Japan Office Fax: 81-98-895-1420. Business E-Mail: sadayuki@med.u-ryukyu.ac.jp.

MURAYAMA, YOKO, internist; b. Kurume, Japan, Aug. 16, 1962; d. Tsunenori and Junko Murayama. MD, Shimane Med. Sch., Izumo, Japan, 1988; PhD, Osaka U., Japan, 1997. Resident Toyonaka (Japan) Mcpl. Hosp., 1988—90; rschr., gastroenterologist Osaka U. Hosp., Suita, Japan, 1990—98, postdoctoral fellow dept. internal medicine and molecular sci. Grad. Sch. Medicine, 1999—2002; gastroenterologist Ikeda (Japan) Mcpl. Hosp., 1998—99; asst. prof. dept. internal medicine and molecular sci. Grad. Sch. Medicine Osaka U., 2003—05; directorate of gastroenterology Itami City Hosp., Japan, 2005—. Presenter in field. Contbr. articles to profl. jours. Mem.: Japan Gastroenterol. Endoscopy Soc., Japanese Soc. Gastroenterology, Japanese Soc. Internal Medicine. Avocations: tennis, golf, skiing. Office: Itami City Hosp 1-100 Koyaike Itami 664 8540 Japan Home Phone: +81-6-6834-3707; Office Phone: +81-72-777-3773. Business E-Mail: murayama@hosp.itami.hyogo.jp.

MURDEN, ROBERT A., medical administrator, physician; b. Radford, Va., May 5, 1951; s. William P. and Mabel S. Murden; m. Linda L. Murden; children: Rob, Nick, Chelsea. BS, U. Mich., 1972; MD, U. Mo., Columbia, 1977. Diplomate Am. Bd. Internal Medicine; cert. added qualifications in geriatrics. Resident in internal medicine U. Tex., Galveston, 1977-80; fellow in geriatrics Mt. Sinai Sch. Medicine, NYC, 1983-85; faculty medicine and geriatrics SUNY, Stony Brook, 1985-86, Bklyn., 1986-89, U. Kans. Med. Ctr., Kansas City, 1990-91; faculty medicine Ohio State U., Columbus, 1991—, divsn. dir. gen. medicine, 1994—2006, fellowship dir. geriatrics, 2006—. Co-dir. Alzheimer's Disease Assistance Ctr., SUNY, Bklyn., 1988-89. Contbr. articles to profl. jours. Fellow ACP; mem. Soc. Gen. Internal Medicine, Am. Geriatrics Soc. Office: Ohio State Univ 2050 Kenny Rd Ste 2400 Columbus OH 43221 Office Phone: 614-293-4953. Business E-Mail: robert.murden@osumc.edu.

MURDJEVA, MARIANNA ATANASSOVA, microbiologist, educator; b. Plovdiv, Bulgaria, July 28, 1960; d. Atanas Nikolov Murdjev and Lilliana Dimitrova Murdjeva; 1 child, Lubomir Dimitrov Paounov. MD Med. U. Plovdiv, 1985. Diplomate in microbiology Med. Academy, Sofia, 1991, in clin. immunology Med. U. Plovdiv, 2002, in health mgmt. Med. U. Plovdiv, 2006. Microbiologist Regional Ctr. Disease Control, Karlovo, Bulgaria, 1985—88; cons. microbiology and immunology U. Hosp., Plovdiv, 1988—, German-Bulgarian Med. Lab, Plovdiv, 2003—, Info. Ctr. Rare Diseases Orphan Drugs, Plovdiv, 2005. Biomedical rsch. scientist Nat. Inst. Med. Rsch., Lab. Molecular Immunology, London, 1992—95; assoc. prof. Med. U., Plovdiv, Bulgaria, 2001—. Grant, Leukaemia Rsch. Fund, 1992—94. Mem.: Union Scientists Bulgaria, Bulgarian Assn. Clin. Immunology, Bulgarian Assn. Clin. Microbiology. Office: Med Univ Dept Microbiology 15A Vassil Aprilov Plovdiv 4000 Bulgaria Personal E-mail: mmurdjeva@yahoo.com.

MURLIMANJU, B. V., medical educator; b. Mayakonda, May 22, 1980; MD, KMC, Manipal, 2009. Asst. prof. Manipal U., 2009—. Office: CBS Kasturba Med Coll Dept Anatomy Mangalore Karnataka 575004 India E-mail: flutesnowmm@gmail.com.

MURO AMADOR, MANUEL, immunologist, consultant; b. Almeria, Spain, Nov. 9, 1965; s. Francisco Muro Soriano and Concesa Amador Santoyo; m. Maria Jose Perez Lopez, July 5, 1992; children: Manuel Muro Perez, Javier Muro Perez. Grad., U. Granada, Spain, 1984—89; D, U. Murcia, Spain, 2002. Cert. immunologist Health and Edn. Ministeries, Spain, 1994. Internal resident immunology U. Hosp., Murcia, 1991—94, fellow health min., 1995, cons., 1995—; cons., rsch. immunology svc. U. Hosp. Virgen Arrixaca, Murcia, 1995—2008, co-directorship histocompatibility regional lab., 1997—2008, tutor residents immunology, 2008. Contbr. 54 articles to profl. jours., chptr. to books. Mem.: Found. Study and Devel. Immunology Murcia, Transplant Commn. Hosp., European Fedn. Immunogenetics, Spanish Soc. Immunology. Independent. Roman Catholic. Achievements include research in antibody screening, transplant immunology and immunogenetics markers. Office: Univ Hosp Virgen Arrixaca Ctra Madrid-Cartagena S/N 30120 El Palmar Spain Office Fax: 34 968 369029. Business E-Mail: manuel.muro@carm.es.

MUROFF, LAWRENCE ROSS, nuclear medicine physician, educator; b. Phila., Dec. 26, 1942; s. John M. and Carolyn (Kramer) M.; m. Carol R. Savoy, July 12, 1969; children: Michael Bruce, Julie Anne. AB cum laude, Dartmouth Coll., Hanover, NH, 1964, B of Med. Sci., 1965; MD cum laude, Harvard U., Cambridge, Mass., 1967. Diplomate Am. Bd. Radiology, Am. Bd. Nuclear Medicine. Intern Boston City Hosp., Harvard, 1968; resident in radiology Columbia-Presbyn. Med. Ctr., NYC, 1970-73, chief resident, 1973; instr. dept. radiology, asst. radiologist Columbia U. Med. Ctr., NYC, 1973-74; dir. dept. nuc. medicine, computed tomography and MRI Univ. Cmty. Hosp., Tampa, Fla., 1974-94, H. Lee Moffitt Cancer Hosp., Tampa, 1994—; pres. Edn. Symposia Inc., Tampa, 1975-2001; pres., CEO Imaging Cons. Inc., Tampa, 1994—; chmn. bd. Am. Phys. Ptnrs. Inc. (Radiologix), Dallas, 1996—98. Clin. asst. prof. radiology U. South Fla., 1974-78, clin. assoc. prof., 1978-82, clin. prof., 1982—; clin. prof. U. Fla., 1988—. Contbr. articles to profl. jours. Lt. comdr. USPHS, 1968-70. Fellow Am. Coll. Nuclear Medicine (disting. fellow., Fla. del.), Am. Coll. Nuclear Physicians (regents 1976-78, pres.-elect 1978, pres. 1979), Am. Coll. Radiology (councilor 1979-80, 91-96, 2001-06, 08-, chancellor 1981-87, chmn. commn. on nuclear medicine 1981-87, bd. dirs. Radiology Leadership Inst., 2011-); mem. Am. Assn. Acad. Chief Residents Radiology (chmn. 1973), AMA, Boylston Soc., Fla. Assn. Nuclear Physician (pres. 1976), Fla. Med. Assn., Hillsborough County Med. Assn., Radiol. Soc. N.Am., Soc. Nuclear Medicine (coun. 1975-90, trustee 1980-84, 86-89, pres. Southeastern chpt. 1983, vice chmn. correlative imaging coun. 1983), Fla. Radiol. Soc. (exec. com. 1976-91, treas. 1984, sec. 1985, v.p. 1986, pres. elect 1987, pres. 1988, gold medal 1995), West Coast Radiol. Soc., Soc. Magnetic Resonance Imaging (bd. dirs. 1988-91, chmn. ednl. program 1989, chmn. membership com. 1989-93), Clin. Magnetic Resonance Soc. (pres.-elect 1995-98, pres. 1998-2000, bd. dirs. 1995—2011), Am. Coll. Radiology Leadership Inst.(bd. dirs. 2011-). Office: 16804 Avila Blvd Tampa FL 33613-5220 Personal E-mail: lrmuroff@hotmail.com.

MURPHEY, SHEILA ANN, infectious diseases physician, educator, researcher; b. Phila., July 10, 1943; d. William Joseph and Sara Esther (Mallon) M. AB, Chestnut Hill Coll., 1965; MD, Women's Med. Coll. of Pa., 1969. Diplomate Am. Bd. Internal Medicine, Am. Bd. Infectious Diseases. Intern in internal medicine Mt. Sinai Hosp. of NY, 1969—70, resident in internal medicine, 1970—72, instr. internal medicine, 1971—72; fellow infectious diseases U. Pa. Sch. Medicine, Phila., 1972—74, instr. dept. medicine, 1974—75, asst. prof. dept. medicine, 1975—77; chief infectious diseases sect. Phila. Gen. Hosp., 1974—77; attending physician Hosp. U. Pa., Phila. Gen. Hosp., 1974—77; dir. divsn. infectious diseases, asst. prof. medicine Jefferson Med. Coll., Phila., 1977—80, clin. assoc. prof. medicine, 1980—2003; dir. divsn. infectious diseases Thomas Jefferson U., Phila., 1977—88; infection control officer, attending physician Thomas Jefferson U. Hosp., Phila., 1977—2003; br. chief infection control devices br., Office Device Evaluation Ctr. for Devices and Radiologic Health, FDA, Rockville, Md., 2005—. Contbr. articles to profl. jours. Fellow Coll. Physicians Phila.; mem. ACP, Am. Soc. Microbiology, Soc. Healthcare Epidemiology of Am., Infectious Diseases Soc. Am., Alpha Omega Alpha. Democrat. Roman Catholic.

MURPHY, ALLISON ANN, pediatrician, educator; d. Charles Westbrook and Cynthia Smith Murphy; m. Keith Victor Johnson, June 26, 1999; 1 child, Nathaniel Prescott Johnson. BS, Yale U., 1991; MD, U. Calif., Irvine, 1998. Diplomate Am. Bd. Pediat., cert. Controlled Substance Registration US Drug Enforcement Agy., 1999, Pediatric Advanced Life Support Am. Heart Assn./Am. Acad. of Pediat., 1998, Neonatal Resuscitation Program Am. Heart Assn./Am. Acad. of Pediat., 1998. Chemistry and physics tchr. Cate Sch., Carpinteria, Calif., 1991—94; gross anatomy tutor U. of Calif., Irvine Coll. of Medicine, Irvine, Calif., 1995—96; pediatric intern and resident Lucile Salter Packard Children's Hosp. at Stanford, Palo Alto, Calif., 1998—2001; rsch. asst./study coord. Stanford U., Palo Alto, 2001—03; preceptor, physicians and patients class Stanford U. Sch. of Medicine, Palo Alto, Calif., 2002—03; fellow in neonatal-perinatal medicine Stanford U., Palo Alto, 2003—06; instr. Ctr. for Advanced Pediatric Edn., Palo Alto, 1998—; staff physician Santa Clara Valley Med. Ctr., San Jose, Calif., 2001—. Contbr. chapters to books, articles to profl. jours. Recipient Evangeline N. Percival award, U. of Calif., Irvine Coll. of Medicine, 1998, Janet M. Glasgow Meml. Achievement award, Am. Med. Women's Assn., 1998, Physician's Recognition award, AMA, 2001—, Cert. of Spl. Congl. Recognition, 2003; grantee, Katherine McCormick Fund for Women, 2003—. Fellow: Am. Acad. of Pediat.; mem.: Western Soc. for Pediat. Rsch., Soc. for Med. Simulation, Alpha Omega Alpha. Democrat. Roman Catholic. Achievements include research in Working with virtual reality technologies to teach medical techniques and procedures. Avocations: soccer, sailing. Office: Stanford U 750 Welch Rd Suite # 315 Palo Alto CA 94304

MURPHY, DENNIS L., neuroscientist, researcher; BS, Marquette U., Milw., 1958; MS in Physiology, U. Wis., 1963, MD, 1963. Diplomate Am. Bd. Psychiatry and Neurology, lic. Md. Rsch. fellow dept. physiology Med. Coll. Wis., Milw., 1958—62; intern U. Minn. Hosp., Mpls., 1963—64; resident Johns Hopkins U. Sch. Medicine, Balt., 1964—66; clin. assoc. adult psychiatry br. Nat. Inst. Mental Health, NIH, Bethesda, Md., 1966—83, chief Lab. Clin. Sci., 1983—. Adj. faculty Johns Hopkins U. Sch. Medicine, 1977—86; faculty Washington Sch. Psychiatry, Washington, 1983—97. Mem. editl. bd.: Progress in Neuropsychopharmacology, 1977—87, Psychopharmacology Comms., 1978—81, Psychiatry Rsch., 1980—, Anxiety and Depression, 1993—, Internat. Jour. Neuropsychopharmacology, 1998—, mem. editl. adv. bd.: Jour. Neurotransmission, 1982—, Dementia, 1991—, Human Psychopharmacology, 1996—, CNS Spectrums: The Internat. Jour. Neuropsychiat. Medicine, 1996—, assoc. editor: Neuropsychopharmacology, 1986—96. Recipient A.E. Bennett award, Soc. Biol. Psychiatry, 1970, Psychopharmacology Rsch. award, Am. Psychol. Assn., 1970, Internat. Anna-Monika Found. award, 1971, Hofheimer prize for rsch., Am. Psychiat. Assn., 1971, Meritorious Svc. award, Alcohol, Drug Abuse & Mental Health Adminstrn., 1977, Superior Svc. award, USPHS, 1980, Disting. Svc. award, US Dept. Health & Human Svcs., 1984, Presdl. Meritorious Exec. Rank award, 1985, 1991. Mem.: Soc. Neurosci., Psychiat. Rsch. Soc., Internat. Soc. Neurochemistry, Found. Advanced Edn. in Scis., Collegium Internat. Neuropsychopharmacologium, Am. Coll. Neuropsychopharmacology, Latchkeyers, Alpha Sigma Nu, Alpha Omega Alpha. Achievements include research in neurobiology of neuropsychiatric disorders using molecular, neurochemical and genetic techniques. Office: NIMH Lab Clinical Sci Nat Inst Health 10 Center Dr MSC 1264 Bldg 10 Rm 3D 41 Bethesda MD 20892-1264 Fax: 301-402-0188. E-mail: dm30h@nih.gov. *

MURPHY, DOUGLAS A., cardiothoracic surgeon; b. Mpls., Minn., Oct. 14, 1949; BS, Middlebury Coll., Middlebury. Vt., 1971; MD, U. Pa., 1975. Cert. Am. Bd. Thoracic Surgeons, Am. Bd. Surgery. Intern, internal medicine Mass. Gen. Hosp., Boston, 1975—76, resident, internal medicine, 1976—77, intern, gen. surgery, 1977—78, resident, gen. surgery, 1978—81; resident, cardiothoracic surgery Emory U. Affliated Hosps., Atlanta, 1981—83; with Peachtree Cardiothoracic and Thoracic Surgeons, PA, Atlanta, 1983—; chief, cardiothoracic surgery St. Joseph's Hosp., Atlanta; chair St. Joseph's Heart and Vascular Inst., Ga., 2007—. Hosp. appointment St. Joseph's Hosp., Atlanta, 1987—, Piedmont Hosp., Atlanta. Address: Peachtree Cardiovascular and Thoracic Surgeons PA 5665 Peachtree Dunwoody Rd Ste 150 Atlanta GA 30342 Office Phone: 404-847-9683, 404-252-6104. Office Fax: 404-257-1808. E-mail: dmurphy407@aol.com.

MURPHY, EDRIE LEE, laboratory administrator; b. Redwood Falls, Minn., Dec. 4, 1953; d. Melvin Arthur and Betty Lou (Wenholz) Timm; m. David Joseph Murphy, July 28, 1984; children: Michael David, Scott Christopher. BS in Med. Tech. summa cum laude, Mankato State U., 1976; MBA, U. St. Thomas, 1984. Registered med. technologist. Med. technologist Children's Hosps. and Clinics, St. Paul, 1976-81, chemistry supr., 1981-85, lab. mgr., 1985-95, dir. lab. sys. Mpls., St. Paul's Campus, 1995-99; lab. mgr. Fairview Health Svcs., Mpls., 2000—07, lab. dir., 2007—. Contbr. articles to profl. jours. Charles H. Cooper scholar, 1975. Mem.: Minn. Soc. Clin. Lab. Mgmt. Assn. (sec.-treas. Minn. chpt. 1994—96, bd. dirs. 1996—98, pres.-elect 1998—2000, pres. 2000—02), Am. Soc. Clin. Lab. Scis. (bd. mem. 2006—08), Elan Vital Ski Club (v.p. membership 1981—82), Phi Kappa Phi. Avocations: photography, sailing, skiing, tennis, travel. Office: 2450 Riverside Ave S F-180 Minneapolis MN 55454 Office Phone: 612-672-4185. E-mail: emurphy2@fairview.org.

MURPHY, FRANCES M., federal agency administrator; MD with honors, Georgetown U., Washington, 1979; MPH, Uniformed Svcs. U. of the Health Scis., 1993. Diplomate Am. Coll. Psychiatry and Neurology. Resident in neurology Georgetown U., Washington; staff neurologist Andrews AFB, Md., 1983—87; chief cons. occupl. and environ. medicine US Dept. Veterans Affairs, Washington, dep. under sec. for health, 1999—2002, acting under sec. for health, 2002, dep. under sec. for health policy coordination, 2002—. Adj. assoc. prof. neurology Uniformed Svcs. U. of the Health Scis. Contbr. articles to profl. jours. With USAF.

MURPHY, FREDERICK AUGUSTUS, virologist, researcher; b. NYC, June 14, 1934; s. Frederick A. and Louise A. (Knizak) Murphy; m. Irene M. Warwas, July 2, 1960 (dec.); children: Frederick A., W. Timothy, John G., Terence D. BS in Microbiology, Cornell U., 1956, DVM, 1959; PhD in Comparative Pathology, U. Calif., Davis, 1964; MD (hon.), U. Turku, Finland, 1987; DSc (hon.), U. Guelph, Can., 2000. Chief viral pathology br. Ctrs. for Disease Control, Atlanta, 1964-78; assoc. dean Coll. Vet. Medicine Colo. State U., Ft. Collins, 1978-83; dir. divsn. viral & rickettsial diseases Ctrs. for Disease Control, Atlanta, 1983-87, dir. Nat. Ctr. for Infectious Diseases, 1987-91; dean Sch. Vet. Medicine U. Calif., Davis, 1991-96, disting. prof. Sch. Vet. Medicine, 1996—2005, disting. prof and dean emeritus, 2006—; prof. dept. pathology U. Tex. Med. Br., Galveston, 2006—. Program chair virology divsn. Internat. Union Microbiology Socs., 1978—87, chair virology divsn., 1981—84; adv. bds. Lawrence Livermore Nat. Lab., 1996—; v.p. Found. Human Rabies Edn. & Eradication, 1999—; com. mem. on Future Contributions to Public Health, Agr., Basic Rsch. Counterterrorism, Non-Proliferation Activities in Russia US Nat. Acad. Scis., 2001—03, co-chair Comm. on Occupational Health and Safety in Care of Non-Human primates, 2001—03, com. mem. on Food Safety and Nutrition, 2001—02; com. mem. on Emerging Microbial Threats to Health in 21st Century Inst. Medicine and US Nat. Acad. Scis., 2001—03, com. mem. on Transmissible Spongiform Encephalopathies, 2002—04. Editor: (book series) Advances in Virus Research, 1983—, (book) Virus Taxonomy, 1995; editor in chief: jour. Archives of Virology, 1984—2000, sr. author: book Veterinary Virology III, 1999; contbr. over 450 articles to profl. jours., reports, reviews, monographs, books, and chapters to books. Mem. Pew Trusts Nat. Vet. Edn. Program: Future Directions in Vet. Medicine, 1986—89; mem. Internat. Advisory Group Royal Vet. Coll., London, 2004—; mem. Secretary's Coun. Public Health Preparedness US Dept HHS, 2002—. Capt. US Army, 1959—62, cmdr. USPHS, 1964—68. Recipient K.F. Meyers Gold Headed Cane, Am. Vet. Epidemiology Soc., 1986, Davis medal, U. Calif., 1998, Pres. Rank award, US Govt., 1992, Richard Moreland Taylor award, Am. Com. Arthropod-Borne Viruses, Am. Soc. Tropical Medicine & Hygeine, 2003; named elected mem., German Acad. Nat. Scis., 1985, Inst. Medicine, US Nat. Acad. Scis., 1999, Acad. Medicine Engrng. Sci. Tex., 2006. Fellow: Infectious Diseases Soc. Am., John Curtin Sch. Med. Rsch., Australian Nat. U. (hon.); mem.: Am. Soc. Virology (founding coun. mem.), Internat. Com. on Taxonomy of Viruses (life; pres. 1990—96), Am. Soc. Microbiology (com. public health 2006—, public and scientific affairs bd.). Democrat. Roman Catholic. Office: U Tex Med Br Dept Pathology 3 145 A Keiller Bldg 301 Univ Blvd Galveston TX 77555-0609 Office Phone: 409-747-2430. Business E-Mail: famurphy@utmb.edu.

MURPHY, HEDWIG SESKI, pathologist, educator; b. Chgo., Jan. 30, 1949; MD, Wayne State U., 1990, PhD, 1979. Assoc. prof. U. Mich., 1994—; staff pathologist Vets. Affairs Ann Arbor Health Sys., 1997—. Office: Veterans Affairs Ann Arbor Health Sys Ann Arbor MI 48105 Business E-Mail: hsmurphy@umich.edu.

MURPHY, JANE M., epidemiologist, educator; b. Denver, Oct. 9, 1929; d. Rex Leo Murphy and Marie Aurelia Stevens; m. Alexander Hamilton Leighton, July 30, 1966 (dec. Aug. 2007). BA, Phillips U., Enid, Okla., 1951; PhD, Cornell U., Ithaca, NY, 1960; MA (hon.), Harvard U., Cambridge, Mass., 1994. Asst. prof., psychiatry Cornell Med. U., NY, 1963—66; assoc. prof., behavioral scis. Harvard Pub. Health, Boston, 1969—79, prof., epidemiology, 1995; assoc. prof., psychiatry Harvard Med., 1985—94, prof., 1994, Dalhousie Med., Halifax, Canada, 1995. Dir., stirling county study, psychiatric epidemiology, 1975; chief, psychiatric epidemiology Mass. Gen. Hosp., 1985. Author: Cross Cultural Concepts Mental Illness, 1976; contbr. articles to med. jours. Co-chair Libr. Com. Local History, Canada, 1997. Recipient Rema Lapouse award, Am. Pub. Health, 1993, Paul Hoch Disting. Svc. award, Psychopathological Assn., 2005; grant, Nat. Inst. Mental Health, 1984—. Fellow: Am. Psycho Pathological Assn.; mem.: Canadian Acad. Psychiatric Epidemiology (award), Internat. Fed. Psychiatric Epidemiology (hon.). Avocations: camping, hiking, history, languages, music. Office: Psychiatry Mass Gen Hosp Rm 215 5 Longfellow Pl Boston MA 02114

MURPHY, JOHN D., pediatric cardiologist, educator; MD, U. Vt., 1975. Diplomate Am. Bd. Pediatrics, Am. Bd. Pediatrics-pediatric cardiology, lic. Pa., 1976, Fla., 2000, NJ, 2003. Resident pediat. Children's Hosp. of Pitts., 1977; fellow pediat. Children's Hosp. Med. Ctr., Boston, 1980; prof. pediat. coll. medicine Drexel Univ., Phila.; attending cardiologist St. Christopher's Hosp. for Children; hosp. affiliations include Albert Einstein Med. Ctr., Bryn Mawr Hosp., Main Line Hosp. Bryn Mawr Campus, Main Line Hosp. Paoli, Paoli Hosp., Riddle Meml. Hosp. Named one of Top Doctors, Phila. Mag., 2010—. Office: St Christopher's Hospital for Children 3601 A St Philadelphia PA 19134 Office Phone: 215-427-5000. Office Fax: 215-427-5555.

MURPHY, JOSEPH JAMES, chiropractic physician; b. Newark, July 30, 1956; s. Joseph P. and Roberta (Nittolo) Murphy; children: Joseph Raymond, Alexandra Renee; m. Maria Elena Sileo, Feb. 17, 2002; children: Sean Alfred, Mia Carmen. BA in Biology, Rider Coll., Lawrenceville, NJ, 1978; D in Chiropractic Medicine, Palmer Coll., Davenport, Iowa, 1984. Diplomate Nat. Bd. Chiropractic Examiners; cert. NJ State Bd. Med. Examiners. Rsch. chemist Mallinkrodt, Inc., Englewood, NJ, 1979-81; staff physician Mid-Island Chiropractic, Levittown, NY, 1984; dir., chief exec. officer Suburban Chiropractic Ctr., Chatham, NJ, 1984—. Apptd. mem. NJ Bd. Chiropractic Examiners, 2000—, sec., 2003, pres., 2006. Mem. editl. bd. Am. Chiropractor Mag., 2000—; editor-in-chief newsletter The Column. Advisor Chatham High Sch. Key Club, 1986-87; chmn. Bd. Trustees, 2008; trustee Early Childhood Learning Ctr., Chatham, 1999—, sec. 2002, chmn. bd., 2008-; mem. spkrs. bur. Am. Heart Assn. D. D. Palmer scholar, 1981, 82, 83. Mem.: AAAS, APHA, Chatham Mayors Wellness Commn., Morris County Chiropractic Soc. (pres. 1987—, bd. pres. 2006), Bd. Chiropractic Examiners (apptd. mem. State of N.J.), Internat. Soc. Food Technologists, NY Acad. Sci., NJ Chiropractic Soc. (editor-in-chief Jersey Jour. 1986—, bd. dirs. 1987—, chmn. inter profl. rels. com. 1989—, 1st v.p. 1992—95, pres. 1995—, Meritorious Svc. award 1986, Disting. Svc. award 1987—97), Am. Chiropractic Assn., Am. Assn. Cereal Chemists, Chatham C. of C. (chmn. profl. rels. com. 1988—92, pres. 1989—92, Dist. Mem. Svc. award 1996), Chatham Hist. Preservation Commn. (mayor apptd. mem.), Kiwanis (bd. dirs. Chatham club 1986—89, Disting. Svc. award 1995), Tri Beta. Republican. Presbyn. Avocations: skiing, photography, model building, automobiles, bicycling. Home: 20 Squire Ct Basking Ridge NJ 07920 Office: Suburban Chiropractic Ctr 301 Main St Chatham NJ 07928-2410 Office Phone: 973-635-0036. Business E-Mail: drmurphy@drmurphy.com.

MURPHY, KEVIN R., psychology professor; BA in Psychology, Siena Coll., Loudonville, NY, 1974; MS in Indsl./Orgnl. Psychology, Rennsselaer Poly. Inst., 1976; PhD in Indsl./Orgnl. Psychology, Pa. State U., 1979. Asst. prof. psychology Rice U., Tex., 1979—81, NYU, NYC, 1981—84, Colo. State U., 1984—86, assoc. prof. psychology, 1986—88, prof. psychology, 1988—2000, Pa. State U., 2000—06, head dept. psychology, 2003—06, dir., Internat. Ctr. the Study Terrorism, 2006—, prof. psychology and info. sciences and tech., 2006—. Editor: Jour. Applied Psychology; editl. bd. Human Performance, Human Resource Mgmt. Rev., Jour. Indsl. Psychology, Internat. Jour. Mgmt. Rev., Internat. Jour. Selection and Assessment. Fellow: APA (coun. editors 1996—, mem. conf. rev. com., sci. directorate 2004—06, mem. com. on sci. awards 2006—08), Assn. Psychol. Sci., Soc. Indsl. and Orgnl. Psychology (pres. 1997, Disting. Sci. Contbn. award 2004); mem.: Internat. Assn. Applied Psychology Office: Dept Psychology Pa State Univ 415 Moore Bldg & 431 Beam Bldg University Park PA 16802-3106 Office Phone: 814-863-3373, 814-865-4818. Office Fax: 814-863-7002. E-mail: krmurphy@psu.edu.

MURPHY, MARGARET A., nursing educator, adult nurse practitioner; b. NYC, Apr. 4, 1934; d. William J. and Margaret (Burchill) Allen; m. Raymond L.H. Murphy, Jr., July 12, 1958; children: Raymond L.H. III, Michael W., Ann Murphy Postell, Maureen D. Murphy Olsen, Alice M., Matthew D. BSN, St. Joseph Coll., West Hartford, Conn., 1955; MS, NYU, 1957; PhD, Boston Coll., Chestnut Hill, Mass., 1987. RN Mass., cert. adult nurse practitioner. Instr. Boston U. Sch. Nursing, 1971-72; pulmonary clin. nurse specialist Pulmonary Assocs., Boston, 1972-73; pulmonary nurse clinician Tufts U., Medford, Mass., 1973-76; from instr. prof. nursing to assoc. prof. nursing Boston Coll., 1976—2001, assoc. prof. emeritus, 2001, chmn. adult health nursing, 1988-92, dir. adult nurse practitioner program, 1987—2001, dir. Kennedy Audio Visual Resource Ctr., 1991-95, coord. MBA-MSN program, 1993-99. Rschr. in lung sound patterns in health and disease, women's attitudes toward menopause. Co-editor: Pharmacotherapeutics and Advanced Nursing Practice, 1998; co-author: (CD) Learning Lung Sounds, 2002, (CD) Learning Heart and Lung Sounds, 2005-08; contbr. articles to profl. jours. Grantee, Uniformed Svcs. U. Health Scis., 1995—96; fellow, USPHS, 1957—58. Fellow: Am. Coll. Nurse Practitioners; mem.: ANA, Mass. Thoracic Soc. (chmn. com. on nursing practice, counselor 1989—91), Am. Thoracic Soc., Mass. Nurses Assn. (co-chmn. cabinet on legis. 1985—88), Sigma Theta Tau (chmn. awards and scholarships com. Alpha Chi chpt. 1994—96, pres. 1996—98, newsletter editl. bd. 1998—2004, Alpha Chi chpt. Mentor award 2001).

MURPHY, MARK R., plastic surgeon; BA in English Lit., Tulane U., 1989—93, MD, 1994—98. With gen. surgery Columbia Univ., 1998—99; fellow in facial plastic surgery Tulane Univ., New Orleans, 2003—04; with med. missions for children Antigua, Guatemala, 2002; with NY Presbyn. Hosp., The Univ. Hosps. of Columbia & Cornell, Meml. Sloan Kettering Cancer Ctr. Contbr. (book) Masters of Facial Rejuvenation, 2006, (publs.) "Balanced" orbital decompression for severe Graves orbitopathy: Technique with treatment algorithm, Cost Effective Diagnosis of Acoustic Neuromas: A Philosophical, Macroeconomic, and Technological Decision, The Extended Columellar Strut-Tip Graft, Hypopharyngeal perforation "near misses" during traditional (blind) transesophageal echocardiography superior safety of optically-guided transesophageal echocardiography, Laparoscopic incisional hernia repair after transverse rectus abdominis myocutaneous flap reconstruction, Breast cancer in reduction mammoplasty: case reports and a survey of plastic surgeons. Mem.: AMA, Am. Acad. of Otolaryngology, Am. Acad. of Facial Plastic & Reconstructive Surgery. Office: Palm Beach Facial Plastic Surgery Suite 310 4280 Professional Center Dr Palm Beach Gardens FL 33410 Office Phone: 561-659-9766. Office Fax: 561-799-4090.

MURPHY, MICHAEL FURBER, hematologist; b. Liverpool, Eng., May 2, 1951; s. Arthur Furber and Jean Marjorie (Frazer) M.; m. Sarah Elizabeth Green, Sept. 1, 1984; children: James, Anna. MB BChir, St. Bartholomew's Hosp. Med. Coll., London, 1973; MD, U. London, 1988. Sr. lectr. in hematology St. Bartholomew's Hosp. Med. Coll., London, 1985-96; cons. hematologist Nat. Blood Svc. and Oxford Radcliffe Hosps., 1996—. Prof. blood transfusion medicine U. Oxford, 2004—; mem. blood transfusion task force Brit. Com. Stds. in Hematology, 1995-01. Contbr. numerous papers, rev. articles and book chpts. on clin. aspects of transfusion medicine and platelet immunology to profl. publs. Sec. Nat. Blood Transfusion com., 2001—. Recipient Kenneth Goldsmith award Brit. Blood Transfusion Soc., 1994. Govt. Computing award John Redcliffe Hosp., 2007, Govt. Pub. Svc. award, 2008. Fellow Royal Coll. Physicians, Royal Coll. Pathologists (mem. coun. 2005—08), Am. Assn. Blood Banks (bd. mem. 2010-). Office: Nat Blood Svc John Radcliffe Hosp Oxford OX3 9BQ England

MURPHY, MICHAEL JOHN, dermatologist, educator; b. London, Aug. 30, 1969; MB, BCh, U. Coll. Dublin, BAO, 1992, M in Med. Sci., 1994. Assoc. prof., dermatopathologist U. Conn. Health Ctr., 2000—. Office: 21 South Rd Farmington CT 06030 Personal E-mail: drmichaelmurphy@netscape.net.

MURPHY, RAMON J.C. (RAMON JEREMIAH CASTROVIEJO MURPHY), pediatrician, physician, educator; b. NYC, Feb. 12, 1944; s. William J. and Angelines (Castroviejo) M.; m. Lila, Sept. 12, 1971; children: Jessica, David. BA, U. Notre Dame, 1965; MD, Northwestern U., 1969; MPH, Columbia U., 1974. Diplomate Am. Bd. Pediats. Intern medicine Cook County Hosp., Chgo., 1969—70; resident in pediats. Children's Meml. Hosp., Chgo., 1970—71, Babies Hosp.-Columbia-Presbyn. Med. Ctr., NYC, 1971—73; resident in cmty. medicine Mt. Sinai Hosp., NYC, 1973—74, clin. asst. pediatrician, 1974—75, asst. attending pediatrician, 1975—83, assoc. attending pediatrician, 1983—, assoc. instr. cmty. medicine, 1974—75, asst. prof. clin. pediats., asst. prof. cmty. medicine, 1975—83, assoc. prof. clin. pediats., 1983—2006, clin. prof. pediat., clin. prof. preventive and cmty. medicine, 2006—07; pediatrician Uptown Pediat., P.C., NYC, 1976—, pres., 1990—. Co-dir. Mt. Sinai Children's Cmty. Health, 1999—, Mt. Sinai Global Health Ctr., 2005-; dir. Mt. Sinai Off-Site Pediat. Residency Tng. Program, 1999—, Mt. Sinai Pediat. Global Health Tng. Program, 2004—; vis. clin. fellow pediat. Columbia U., Coll. Physicians and Surgeons, NYC, 1971-73; pediat. cons. Oxford Health Plan, 1990-94, Children's Aid Soc., 2000—, Commonwealth Fund, 1995—. Contbr. articles to profl. jours. Co-med. dir. Benito Juarez People's Health Ctr., Chgo., 1970-71; dep. co-dir. Wagner Child Health Project, NYC, 1973-75; sch. physician The Day Sch., 1984—, The Trinity Sch., 1992—, trustee, 1993-99. Named one of Top Doctors in NY, NY Mag. Fellow Am. Acad. Pediat.; mem. NY Pediat. Soc. (program chmn. 1986-89, pres. 1989-90), Soc. for Adolescent Medicine, Mt. Sinai Alumni Assn. Avocations: golf, fishing. Office: 1245 Park Ave New York NY 10128-1211 Office Phone: 212-427-0540. Office Fax: 212-534-1086. E-mail: ramon.murphy@mssm.edu.

MURPHY, SEAMUS JOSEPH, gastroenterologist, consultant; s. James Anthony Murphy and Kathleen Murray; m. Grainne Marie McManus, July 17, 1996; children: Megan, Niamh, Niall, Aoife, Ronan. BSc, Queen's U. Belfast, 1994, MB, BCh, BAO, Queen's U. Belfast, 1996, PhD, 2005. Inflammatory bowel disease fellow Mt. Sinai Med. Ctr., New York, 2006—07; cons. physician Southern Trust, Newry, Co. Down, Ireland, 2007—. Contbr. scientific papers. Grant, Am. Gastroent. Assn., 2006—07. Mem.: Royal Coll. Physicians, Am. Coll. of Gastroenterology, Am. Gastroent. Assn. Office: Daisy Hill Hosp 5 Hosp Rd Newry County Down BT35 8DR Ireland Home Phone: 00442830889629; Office Phone: 00442830835000. Personal E-mail: s.murphy@qub.ac.uk.

MURPHY, TRACY DOUGLAS, public health service officer; b. Bloomfield, Iowa, Apr. 23, 1965; MD, Kans. U. Sch. Medicine, 1993. Hosp.-based anatomic and clin. pathologist; state epidemiologist Wyo. Dept. Health, 2005—, dep. state health officer, acting state health officer, 2011—. Office: Wyoming Department of Health 401 Hathaway Bldg Cheyenne WY 82002 Office Phone: 307-777-7656. Office Fax: 307-777-7439. *

MURPHY, WILLIAM ALEXANDER, JR., diagnostic radiologist, educator; b. Pitts., Apr. 26, 1945; s. William Alexander and LaRue (Eshbaugh); m. Judy Marie Lang, June 18, 1977; children: Abigail Norris, William Lawrence, Joseph Ryan. BS, U. Pitts., 1967; MD, Pa. State U., 1971. Diplomate Am. Bd. Radiology. Intern Barnes Hosp., St. Louis, 1971-72, staff radiologist, 1975-93; radiology resident Washington U., St. Louis, 1972-75, prof. radiology, 1983-93; sec. chief Mallinckrodt Inst. Radiology, St. Louis, 1975-93; cons. Office Med. Examiner City and County St. Louis, 1993—. Radiologist, prof. radiology, John S. Dunn Sr. prof., disting. chair MD Anderson Cancer Ctr. U. Tex., 1993—, v.p. hosp. and clinics, 1996-97, COO, 1997; chmn. bd. dirs. MD Anderson Physicians Network Corp., 2001—. Fellow Am. Acad. Forensic Scis., Am. Coll. Radiology; mem. Radiol. Soc. N.Am. (1st. v.p. 1997-98), Am. Roentgen Ray Soc., Am. Soc. Bone and Mineral Rsch., Internat. Skeletal Soc., Assn. Univ. Radiologists. Methodist. Home: 4808 Bellview St Bellaire TX 77401-5306 Office: University Tex Anderson Cancer Ctr Divsn Dx Imaging 1475 1515 Holcombe Blvd Houston TX 77030-4009 Office Phone: 713-792-4916. Business E-Mail: wmurphy@mdanderson.org.

MURRAY, CHRISTOPHER J.L., medical educator; BA in biology, summa cum laude, Harvard U., 1984; DPhil in internat. health economics, Oxford U., 1987; MD magna cum laude, Harvard Med. Sch., 1991. Asst. prof. internat. health economics Harvard Sch. Pub. Health, 1991—94, assoc. prof. internat. health economics, 1994—98, prof. internat. health economics, 1998—2001, adj. prof. internat. health economics, 2001—03, Richard Saltonsall prof. pub. policy, 2003—07; dir. burden of disease unit Harvard Ctr. Pop. and Devel. Studies, 1994—2007, dir., 2005—07, Harvard Initiative for Global Health, 2003—07; prof. social medicine Harvard Med. Sch., 2003—07; dir. global prog. on evidence of health policy, evidence and info. for policy cluster WHO, 1998—2000, exec. dir. evidence and info. for policy cluster, 2001—03; dir. Inst. Health Metrics and Evaluation U. Wash. Sch. Medicine, Seattle, 2007—, prof. global health, 2007—. Editor-in-chief Pop. Health Metrics. Recipient Elias Bengtsson medal, 2000; MacArthur fellow, Ctr. Pop. and Devel. Studies, 1990—92. Mem.: Inst. Medicine. Office: Inst Health Metrics and Evaluation Ste 600 2301 5th Ave Seattle WA 98121 E-mail: cjlm@u.washington.edu.

MURRAY, ELLEN GLONINGER, federal agency administrator; b. 1948; BA in Economics, Trinity Coll., Washington, 1970; JD, George Mason U. Sch. Law, Fairfax, Va., 1990. Economist Social Security Adminstrn., Washington, 1970—77; real estate developer, 1977—87; gen. counsel US Dept. Health & Human Services, 1990—92, budget dir. Adminstrn. Children & Families, 1992—99, asst. sec. for fin. resources, 2010—; staff dir. US Senate Appropriations Subcom. Labor, Heath and Human Services, Edn. & Related Agencies, 1999—2009. Office: US Department Health & Human Services 200 Independence Ave SW Washington DC 20201 Office Phone: 202-690-6396. E-mail: ellen.murray@hhs.gov. *

MURRAY, JAMES E., managed health care company executive; Ptnr. Coopers & Lybrand, Louisville; joined Humana, Inc., Louisville, 1989, interim CFO, until 1997, CFO, 1997-2000, COO Health Plan Div., 2000—01, COO svc. ops., 2001—02, COO Market and Bus. Segments Ops., 2002—06, COO 2006—. Office: Humana Inc 500 West Main St Louisville KY 40202 *

MURRAY, JOHN FRANCIS, psychologist; b. Ft. Lauderdale, Fla., Nov. 30, 1961; s. John Richard and Joan Pfluger Murray; m. Charlotte Greenman, June 14, 1997; 1 child, Caroline. BA, Loyola U., La., 1983; M of Exercise/Sport Scis., U. Fla., 1992, MS in Psychology, 1995, PhD in Psychology, 1998. Lic. Psychologist Fla., 1999. Pvt. practice clin. and sport performance psychologist John F. Murray, PhD, Palm Beach, Fla., 1999—. Author: Smart Tennis: How to Play and Win the Mental Game, The Mental Performance Index: Ranking the Best Teams in Super Bowl History; creator (performance index for football teams) Mental Performance Index (MPI); prodr.(radio talk show host): (sport psychology radio program) Mental Equipment Radio. Post-Doctoral fellow, Fla. Internat. U., 1998—99. Mem.: APA (assoc.), Fla. Psychol. Assn. Palm Beach County Chpt. (assoc.; pres. 2002—02), Alpha Delta Gamma Epsilon Chpt. (life; treas. 1981—81, Most Valuable Athlete Epsilon Chpt. 1982). Avocations: travel, tennis, reading, writing, pub. speaking. Office: 139 N County Rd Ste 18C Palm Beach FL 33480 Office Fax: 561-828-6234; Home Fax: 561-805-8662. Personal E-mail: johnfmurray@mindspring.com.

MURRAY, JOHN FREDERIC, pulmonologist, educator; b. Mineola, NY, June 8, 1927; s. Frederic S. and Dorothy Murray; m. Diane Lain, Nov. 30, 1968; children— James R., Douglas S., Elizabeth. AB, Stanford, 1949, MD, 1953; D.Sc. (hon.), U. Paris, 1983, U. Athens, 2000. From instr. to asso. prof. medicine U. Calif. at Los Angeles, 1957-66; mem. sr. staff Cardiovascular Research Inst., U. Calif., San Francisco, 1966-94; asso. prof. medicine Cardiovascular Research Inst., U. Calif. (Sch. Medicine), 1966-69, prof., 1969-94; chief chest service San Francisco Gen. Hosp., 1966-89. Vis. prof. Brompton Inst. for Diseases of the Chest, London, 1972-73; Macy faculty scholar Inst. Nat. de la Santé et de la Recherche Medicale, Paris, 1979-80; mem. adv. council and pulmonary disease adv. com. Nat. Heart, Lung and Blood Inst.; mem. clin. studies panel NRC.; bd. govs. Am. Bd. Internal Medicine, Am. Bd. Emergency Medicine. Author: The Normal Lung, 1976, 2d edit., 1986; co-author: Diseases of the Chest, 5th edit., 1980; co-editor: Textbook of Respiratory Medicine, 1988, 2d edit., 1994, 3rd edit., 2000, 4th edit., 2005; editor: Am. Rev. Respiratory Disease, 1973-79; contbr. articles to profl. jours. Chmn. Internat. Union Against Tb and Lung Disease. Served with USNR, 1945-46. Sr. Internat. fellow Fogarty Inst.; recipient Pres.'s award European Respiratory Soc., 1996. Fellow Royal Coll. Physicians; mem. Assn. Am. Physicians, Am. Soc. Clin. Investigation, Am. Physiol. Soc., Western Soc. Clin. Research, Western Assn. Physicians, Am. Thoracic Soc. (pres. 1981-82, Trudeau medal 1994), Académie Nationale de Médecine Francaise. Office: U Calif PO Box 0841 San Francisco CA 94143-0841 Home: PO Box 542 Bolinas CA 94924-0542 Personal E-mail: johnfmurr4@aol.com.

MURRAY, JOHN PATRICK, psychologist, educator, researcher; b. Cleve., Sept. 14, 1943; s. John Augustine and Helen Marie (Lynch) M.; m. Ann Coke Dennison, Apr. 17, 1971; children: Jonathan Coke, Ian Patrick. PhD, Cath. U. Am., 1970. Rsch. dir. Office U.S. Surgeon Gen. NIMH, Bethesda, Md., 1969-72; asst. to assoc. prof. psychology Macquarie U., Sydney, 1973-79; vis. assoc. prof. U. Mich., Ann Arbor, 1979-80; dir. youth and family policy Boys Town Ctr., Boys Town, Nebr., 1980-85; prof., dir. Sch. Family Studies and Human Svcs. Kans. State U., Manhattan, 1985-98, interim assoc. vice provost rsch., 1998—2000; Scholar-in-residence Mind Sci. Found., San Antonio, 1996—97; mem. children's TV com. CBS, 1996—99; emeritus prof. devel. psychology Kans. State U., 2008—; vis. scholar Ctr. on Media and Child Health Harvard U. Med. Sch., 2004—; rsch. fellow dept. psychology Wash. Coll., 2009—. Author: Television and Youth: 25 Years of Research and Controversy, 1980, The Future of Children's TV, 1984, (with H.T. Rubin) Status Offenders: A Sourcebook, 1983, (with E.A. Rubenstein, G.A. Comstock) Television and Social Behavior, 3 vols., 1972, (with A. Huston and others) Big World, Small Screen: The Role of Television in American Society, 1992, (with C. Fisher and others) Applied Developmental Science, 1996, Children and Television: Fifty Years of Research (with N. Pecora and E. Wartella), 2007; contbr. numerous articles to profl. jours. Mem. Nebr. Foster Care Rev. Bd., 1982-84; mem. Advocacy Office for Children and Youth, 1980-85; mem. Nat. Coun. Children and TV, 1982-87; trustee The Villages Children's Homes, 1986—, Menninger Found., 1996—; mem. children's TV adv. bd. CBS-TV, 1996-99. Fellow Am. Psychol. Assn. (pres. div. child youth and family svcs. 1990); mem. Internat. Comm. Assn., Soc. Rsch. in Child Devel., Royal Commonwealth Soc. (London), Chester River Yacht and Country Club. Home: 312 Landing Ln Chestertown MD 21620 Home Phone: 443-282-0593. Personal E-mail: johnpatrickmurray@hotmail.com.

MURRAY, JOSEPH EDWARD, retired plastic surgeon; b. Milford, Mass., Apr. 1, 1919; s. William Andrew and Mary (DePasquale) Murray; m. Virginia Link, June 2, 1945; children: Virginia, Margaret, Joseph, Katharine, Thomas, Richard. AB, Coll. Holy Cross, Worcester, Mass., 1940; MD, Harvard Med Sch., 1943; DSc (hon.), Rockford Coll., 1966, Roger Williams Coll., 1986; PhD (hon.), Anna Marie Coll., 1993, SUNY, Albany, 1993, U. Suffolk, 1993, Magill U., Montreal, 1996. Diplomate Am. Bd. Surgery, Am. Bd. Plastic Surgery. Chief plastic surgeon Peter Bent Brigham Hosp., Boston, 1951—86; prof. surgery Harvard Med. Sch., 1970—86; chief plastic surgeon

Children's Hosp. Med. Center, Boston, 1972—85; ret., 1986. Chmn. Am. Bd. Plastic Surgery, 1969. Author: (autobiography) Surgery Of The Soul: Reflections on a Curious Career, 2001. Maj. US Army Med. Corps, 1944—47. Recipient Gold medal, Internat. Soc. Surgeons, 1963, Lifetime Achievement award, Mass. Med. Soc., 1988, Nobel prize for medicine/physiology, 1990, Sabin award, 1994. Fellow: AMA, AAAS (hon.), Royal Coll. Surgeons Edinburgh, Royal Coll. Surgeons Ireland, Royal Coll. Surgeons Eng., Royal Australasian Coll. Surgeons; mem.: NAS, ACS (regent 1970—79, v.p. 1983), Am. Acad. Arts & Scis. (Hon. award 1962), Am. Assn. Plastic Surgeons (pres. 1964—65, Hon. award 1969), Soc. Univ. Surgeons, Boston Surg. Soc. (pres. 1975), New Eng. Surg. Assn. (pres. 1986—87), Am. Surg. Assn. (v.p. 1979), Tavern Club, Wellesley Country Club, Alpha Omega Alpha. Achievements include performing the world's first successful human kidney transplant from an adult to his identical twin in 1954. *

MURRAY, JULIA KAORU (MRS. JOSEPH E. MURRAY), retired occupational therapist; b. Wahiawa, Oahu, Hawaii, 1934; d. Gijun and Edna Tsuruko (Taba) Funakoshi; m. Joseph Edward Murray, 1961; children: Michael, Susan, Leslie. BA, U. Hawaii, 1956; cert. occupl. therapy, U. Puget Sound, 1958. Therapist Inst. Logopedics, Wichita, Kans., 1958; sr. therapist Hawaii State Hosp., Kaneohe, 1959; part-time therapist Centre County Ctr. for Crippled Children and Adults, State College, Pa., 1963; vice chmn. adv. bd. Hosp. Improvement Program East Oreg. State Hosp., Pendleton, 1974; v.p. Ind. Living, Inc., 1976—79; instr. job search; mem. adv. com. Oreg. Ednl. Coordinating Commn., 1979—82; mem. Oreg. Bd. Engring. Examiners, 1979—87; supr., occupl. therapist Fairview Tng. Ctr., Salem, Oreg., 1984—94; occupl. therapist U.S. Naval Hosp., Okinawa, Japan, 1994—99; occupl. therapist, Yokota A B divsn. Yokosuka, Japan, 1999—2005, occupl. therapist Misawa AB divsn., 2005—09; ret., 2010. Rep. from Umatilla County Commrs. to Blue Mountain Econ. Devel. Council, 1976-78; mem. Ashland Park and Recreation Bd., 1972-73; vice chmn. adv. bd. LINC, 1978; mem. exec. bd. Liberty-Boone Neighborhood Assn., 1979-83. Decorated Meritorious Civilian Svc. medal USN. Mem. Am. Occupational Therapy Assn., Oreg. Occupational Therapy Assn., Hawaii Occupational Therapy Assn. (sec. 1960, LWV (bd. dirs. Pendleton 1974, 77-78, pres. 1975-77; bd. dirs. Oreg. 1979-81, Ashland, Wis., 1967-71, Wis. v.p. 1970). Home Phone: 503-363-6558. Personal E-mail: jkfmurray@hotmail.com.

MURRAY, KEVIN DENNIS, surgeon; b. Paterson, NJ, June 22, 1953; s. Robert Emmet and Florence Sophie (Nordman) M. BS in Chemistry, Mt. St. Mary's Coll., 1974; MD, U. Md., 1978. Cert. Am. Bd. of Surgery, 1995, Am. Bd. of Thoracic Surgery, 1997. Intern U. Chgo.-Pritzker Med. Sch., 1978-79; resident in surgery U. Chgo.-Pritzker Med. Sch. Hosps. and Clinics, 1979-82; Cardiothor resident Yale-New Haven (Conn.) Hosp.-Yale U. Sch. Medicine, 1984-86; fellow in bioengring. U. Utah, 1982-84; asst. prof. Ohio State U. 1986-93; staff Arthur James Cancer Inst., Columbus, Ohio, 1990-93; staff cardiothoracic surgery Barnes-Jewish Hosp., St. Louis, 1996-97; faculty cardiothoracic surgery Washington U., St. Louis, 1996-97; assoc. prof., chief cardiothoracic surgery U. Nev. Sch. of Medicine, Las Vegas, 1997—2002; chief thoracic surgery So. Nev. VA Sys., 1998—2002; cardiothoracic surgeon Kaiser Permanenti Moanalua Hosp., Honolulu, 2003—06; faculty cardiothoracic surgery U. Mo., assoc. prof. Divsn. Cardiothoracic Surgery, 2009—. Med. dir. dept. circulation tech. Sch. Allied Health, Ohio State U., 1988-93; cons. Inst. Bioengring., Salt Lake City, 1995—; dir. The Heart and Lung Inst., U. Nev. Sch. Medicine, 1999-2002. Fellow Am. Coll. Surgery, Am. Coll. Cardiology, Am. Coll. Chest Physicians, Internat. Soc. Heart and Lung Transplantation, Soc. Thoracic Surgeons; mem. Am. Soc. Artificial Internal Organs, Assn. Thoracic Surgeons, Alpha Omega Alpha. Home: 2206 Saddlebrook Lake Rd Lohman MO 65053-9839 Office: 181A 312 One Hospital Dr Columbia MO 65212 Personal E-mail: kdmurray622@aol.com.

MURRAY, LIZ, legislative staff member; b. Rochester, NY; BA, Yale U., New Haven; MPP, Harvard U. Kennedy Sch. Govt. Sr. policy advisor, Rep. Steny Hoyer US House of Reps., Washington. Democrat. Office: 1705 Longworth House Office Bldg Washington DC 20515 Office Phone: 202-225-4131. Office Fax: 202-225-4300.

MURRAY, MARTHA MEANEY, medical educator; b. Boston, Jan. 12, 1966; BS, U. Del., 1987; MD, U. Pa., 1994. Assoc. prof., orthop. surgery Children's Hosp. Boston, 2003—. Exec. com. mem. ACL Study Group, 2006—11; standing study sect. mem. NIH, 2009—11. Recipient Cabaud award, AOSSM. Mem.: Am. Acad. Orthop. Surgery. Office: Dept Orthop Surgery Hunnewell 2 300 Boston MA 02115 Business E-Mail: martha.murray@childrens.harvard.edu.

MURRAY, PAMELA J., pediatrician, educator; Spl. tng. in Biophysics, Pa. State U., 1972; spl. tng. in Nutrition, Columbia Univ., NYC, 1974; spl. tng. in Health Planning, U. NSW, Australia, 1986; MD, Drexel U., Phila., 1978. Diplomate Am. Bd. Pediatrics, 1983, Am. Bd. Pediatrics-adolescent medicine, 2009. Resident pediat. Children's Hosp., Phila., 1979—81; fellow pub. health Univ. NSW, Sydney, 1986—87; chief adolescent medicine W.Va Univ., co-chief divsn. of gen. pediat. and adolescent medicine, vice chmn. dept. of pediat., prof. pediat. Office: West Virginia University Department Pediatrics PO Box 9214 Morgantown WV 26506-9214 Office Phone: 304-293-1225. Office Fax: 412-692-6677.

MURRAY, ROBERT FULTON, JR., physician; b. Newburgh, NY, Oct. 19, 1931; s. Robert Fulton and Henrietta Frances (Judd) Murray; m. Isobel Ann Parks, Aug. 26, 1956; children: Colin Charles(dec.), Robert Fulton III, Suzanne Frances, Dianne Akwe. BS, Union Coll., Schenectady, 1953; MD, U. Rochester, NYC, 1958; MS, U. Wash., Seattle, 1968. Diplomate Am. Bd. Internal Medicine, Am. Bd. Med. Genetics. Intern Denver Gen. Hosp., 1958—59; resident in internal medicine U. Colo. Med. Ctr., 1959—62; staff investigator (service with USPHS) Nat. Inst. Arthritis and Metabolic Diseases, NIH, Bethesda, Md., 1962—65; NIH spl. fellow med. genetics U. Wash., 1965—67; faculty Howard U. Coll. Medicine, Washington, 1967—74, prof. pediatrics and medicine, 1974—, grad. prof., 1976, prof. oncology, 1976, chief divsn. med. genetics, 1968—; chmn. dept. genetics and human genetics Howard U. Coll. Medicine Grad. Sch., 1976—. Nat. adv. gen. med. scis. coun. NIH, 1971—75, recombinant DNA adv. com., 1988—92; ethics adv. bd. to sec. HEW, 1978—80; chmn. Washington Mayor's Adv. Com. on Metabolic Disorders, 1980—89; mem. Med. Com. Human Rights. Co-author: Genetic Variation and Disorders in Peoples of African Origin, 1990; co-editor:

Genetic, Metabolic and Developmental Aspects of Mental Retardation, 1972, Genetic Counseling: Facts, Values and Norms, 1979, The Human Genome Project and the Future of Health Care, 1996; mem. editl. bd.: Am. Jour. Clin. Genetics, 1977—93, Ency. Bioethics, 1975—77, 1993—95, Jour. Clin. Ethics, 1990. Sci. adv. bd. Nat. Sickle Cell Anemia Found.; trustee Union Coll., 1972—80. Grantee Rsch. grantee, NIH, 1969—75; fellow Rotary Found. fellow, 1955—56. Fellow: AAAS, ACP, Am. Coll. Med. Genetics, Inst. Soc., Ethics and Life Scis., Inst. Medicine; mem.: Acad. Medicine Washington, Genetics Soc. Am., Am. Soc. Human Genetics, Assn. Acad. Minority Physicians, AAUP, Neighbors Inc. D.C., Alpha Omega Alpha, Sigma Xi. Unitarian Universalist. Home: 510 Aspen St NW Washington DC 20012-2740 Office Phone: 202-806-6382. Personal E-mail: murrayjrf31@rcn.com.

MURRAY, ROBIN MACGREGOR, psychiatrist, educator, consultant; b. Glasgow, Scotland, Jan. 31, 1944; s. James Alistair and Helen MacGregor Murray; m. Shelagh Harris Murray, Jan. 17, 1970; children: Graham Keith, Clare Alison. MB BChir, U. Glasgow, 1968, MD, 1974; MPhil, U. London, 1976, DSc, 1988. Sr. house officer, registrar U. Glasgow, 1969—72, Maudsley, Inst. Psychiatry, London, 1972—75; traveling fellow NIMH, Bethesda, Md., 1976—77; sr. lectr. Bethlehem, Inst. Psychiatry, London, 1978—82; dean Inst. Psychiatry, London, 1982—89, prof., head psychol. medicine, 1989—99; chair divsn. psychol. medicine GKT Sch. Medicine, London, 1998—2009; prof. psychiatric rsch. Inst. Psychiatry, Kings Coll., London, 1999—. Pres. European Assn. of Psychiatrists, 1995; cons. psychiatrist Maudsley Hosp., London. Editor: (book) Essentials of Postgraduate Psychiatry, 3d edit., 1997, The New Genetics of Mental Illness, 1991, Epidemiology of Schizophrenia, 2002. Recipient Adolf Meyer award, Am. Psychiat. Assn., 1997, Paul Hoch award, Am. Psychopathol. Assn., 1998, Dean award, Am. Coll. Psychiatrists, 1999, Robert Sommer award, 2000, Fifth Castilla del Pino award for achievement in psychiatry, 2002, Lieber prize for Schizophrenia Rsch., Nat. Alliance for Rsch. on Schizophrenia and Depression, 2003. Fellow: Royal Soc. London, Royal Coll. Physicians Glasgow, Royal Coll. Physicians UK; mem.: (fgn.) US Inst. of Med. (elected 2003), Royal Coll. Psychiatrists. Office: Inst Psychiatry Kings Coll De Crespigny Park 63 Box SE5 8AF London England Office Phone: 44 207 848 0100. Fax: 44 0 20 7701 9044. E-mail: robin.murray@kcl.ac.uk.

MURRAY, THOMAS JOHN (JOCK MURRAY), physician, neurologist, educator; b. Halifax, NS, Can., May 30, 1938; m. Janet Kathleen Pottie; children: Shannon, Bruce, Suellen, Brian. Grad. pre-med., St. Francis Xavier U., 1958, LLD (hon.), 1989; MD, Dalhousie U., 1963; DSc (hon.), Acadia U., 1991; DLitt (hon.), St. Thomas U., 2004. Family physician, Nashwaaksis, N.S., 1963-65; chief medicine Camp Hill Hosp., Halifax, N.S., 1974-79; chief neurology Dalhousie U., Halifax, 1979-85, dir. multiple sclerosis rsch. unit, 1980—2003, dean medicine, 1985-92, prof. med. humanities, 1992—2003, prof. emeritus, 2003—. Mem. working group on Diability in U.S. Pres., 1994—96. Co-author: (textbook) Essential Neurology, Quotable Osler, Medicine in Quotations, Treatment and Management of MS, History of MS; author over 200 pub. works, including 7 books and contbns. to 24 textbooks. Bd. dirs. St. Francis Xavier U., Pictou Acad. Found., Robert Pope Found., Nat. Coun. on Bioethics and Health Rsch., Mus. Healthcare. Decorated officer Order Can., order of Nova Scotia; recipient Neilson award Hannah Inst. for Med. History, Disting. Profl. award Discovery Ctr., 2005; named Dalhousie Alumnus of Yr., Dalhousie U., 2003; grantee 91 rsch. grants. Fellow Royal Coll. Physicians (Can. and London, Mentor of Yr. award 2002), ACP (master; gov. 1985-90, chmn. bd. govs. 1990-91, chair bd. regents 1995-97, emeritus chair; Dr. Nicholas Davies award, Laureate award, Stengel award); mem. Can. Neurol. Soc. (pres. 1982-84), Am. Acad. Neurology (v.p. 1981-83, Dr. A.B. Baker award, Lawrence McHenry award); Am. Osler Soc. (pres. 2006-07), London Osler Club (hon. mem.), Royal Soc. Med., Can. Med. Assn., N.S. Med. Soc., Assn. Can. Med. Colls. (pres. 1991-92), Can. Med. Forum (chmn. 1992-95), Multiple Sclerosis Soc. Can. (chmn. med. adv. bd., Perkins award), Consortium of Multiple Sclerosis Ctrs. (pres. 1997-99), Can. Soc. for History of Medicine (pres. 1997-99, Scheinberg award), Canadian Acad Hlth. Scis. (fellow), FRCP (London), Rotary Internat. (Paul Harris fellow). Avocations: medical history, piano, windsurfing. Home: 16 Bobolink St Halifax NS Canada B3M 1W3 Office: Dalhousie Med Sch Clin Rsch Ctr Halifax NS Canada B3H 4H7 Home Phone: 902-443-1074; Office Phone: 902-494-1533. Business E-Mail: jock.murray@dal.ca.

MURRELL, DEIRDRE FRANCES (DEDEE MURRELL), dermatologist, researcher; b. Bradford, Yorkshire, Eng., Mar. 1, 1963; d. Anthony Paul Blackburn and Sarah Deirdre Langtry-Langton; m. George Anthony Calvert Murrell; children: Oliver, Alexander, Isabella Langtry. MA, Cambridge U., Cambridge, Eng., 1984; BMBCh, Oxford U., Eng., 1987; MD, U. NSW, Sydney, 2007. Diplomate Am. Bd. of Dermatology 1993. Intern, medicine & surgery Oxford Tchg. Hospitals, Oxford, Oxon, England, 1987—88; resident, medicine Addenbrooke's Hosp., Cambridge, England, 1988—89; med. resident Duke Univ Med Ctr., Durham, NC, 1989—90; resident dermatology Univ of NC Hospitals, Chapel Hill, NC, 1990—92, chief resident, 1992—93; instructor-assistant prof. NY Univ Med Ctr Derm Dpt, New York, NY, 1993—94; clin. scholar Rockefeller U., New York, NY, 1995—96; sr. lectr. U. of NSW, Sydney, Nsw, 1996—2002, assoc. prof., 2003—, prof., 2008—; staff specialist dermatologist St George Hosp. Campus, Sydney, Nsw, 1996—2002, sr. staff specialist, 2002—, chair dermatology dept., 2004—. Med. adv. bd. mem. Nat. Pemphigus Found., 1996—; epidermolysis bullosa clinic Sydney Children's Hosp., Sydney, 1996—; med. adv. bd. Photocure (Norway), Melbourne, VIC, Australia, 2001—; Elidel adv. bd. Novartis, Sydney, 2002—; dermatologist MIMS, Australia, 2003—. Editor: skin diseases group Cochrane Collaboration, 1997—; mem. editl. bd.: Jour. Am. Acad. Dermatology, 2008—; contbr. articles to profl. jours. Recipient Postdoctoral award, Howard Hughes Med. Inst., 1993, Physician-Scientist award, NIH, 1994, award, Dystrophic EB Rsch. Assn., 2001, Career Devel. award, Internat. Women's Dermatologic Soc., 2003. Fellow: Australasian Coll. Dermatologists, Brit. Assn. Dermatology, European Acad. Dermatology (internat. adv. bd. mem., Australasia 2009—), Am. Acad. Dermatology (Everett C. Fox award 1995); mem.: World Congress Task Fund (chair 2011—), Internat. Soc. Dermatology (Maria Duran com. 2005—, Maria Duran lectr. 2008, vice chair 2009—, chair 2009—, v.p. 2009—, exec. v.p. 2011—), Am. Dermatological Assn. (hon.), Philippine Dermatological Soc. (hon.), Am. Acad. Skin Cancer (adv. bd. 2004—), Soc. Pediatric Dermatology (Sidney Hurwitz lectr. 2009), Women's Dermatol. Soc.

(internat. affairs com. 2006—, chair, internat. affairs com. 2009—, Mentorship award 2002, Career Devel. award 2003), Soc. Investigative Dermatology. Office: St George Hosp Dept Dermatology Gray St 2217 Sydney NSW Australia Office Phone: 61-2-9113-2543. Office Fax: 61-2-9113-2906.

MURRY, J. WARREN, surgeon, educator; b. Kansas City, Mo., Mar. 28, 1925; BS in Medicine, U. Ark., 1946; MD, U. Ark., Little Rock, 1947. Diplomate Am. Bd. Surgery. Intern Charity Hosp., New Orleans, 1947-48; resident in surgery Univ. Hosp., Little Rock, 1948-53; instr. family medicine dept. U. Ark. for Med. Sci., Little Rock, 1993—2002, instr. N.W. Ark. A.H.E.C. Family Med. Ctr. Fayeteville; pvt. practice Fayetteville, Ark., 1957—89, Heber Springs, Ark., 1989—92; ret., 2002. Fellow ACS; mem. AMA, So. Med. Assn. Personal E-mail: jwmurry@cox.net. *

MURTAGH, RYAN D., radiologist, educator; s. F. Reed and Carol D. Murtagh; m. Paige A. Murtagh, Apr. 1, 2000; children: Owen, Cannon. BS, U. Fla., Gainesville, 1996; MD, MBA, U. South Fla., Tampa, 2001. Diplomate Am. Bd. Radiology, Ariz., 2006, cert. neuroradiologist 2008. Radiologist U. Diagnostic Inst., Tampa, 2007—; asst. prof. radiology U. South Fla., 2008—; asst. mem. Moffitt Cancer Ctr., Tampa, 2008—; mem. Am. Bd. Radiol., 2006—. Sr. mem. Am. Soc. Neuroradiology, 2008—10; mem. Am. Soc. Spine Radiology, 2008—10, Am. Bd. Radiology, 2006—10. Contbr. articles to profl. jours., chapters to books. Exec. mem. Hillsborough County Med. Assoc., Tampa, Fla., 2009—11. Recipient Blue Key Leadership Frat., U. Fla., 1995; Outstanding fellow, U. Miami Sch. Medicine, 2007. Mem.: Alpha Omega Alpha, Beta Gamma Sigma. Independent. Avocations: fishing, skiing, travel.

MURTHA, AMY, gynecologist; b. Bronx, NY, Apr. 27, 1963; MD, Med. Coll. Pa., 1992. Asst. prof. Duke U. Med. Ctr., 1998—2007, program dir., 2007—, assoc. prof., 2007—09, 2009—, rsch. med. dir. ob-gyn., 2009—, adj. assoc. prof., dept. pediat., 2010—. Adj. prof. UNC Sch. Dentistry, 2007—; vice chair rsch. Dept. Ob-gyn., 2010—. Fellow: Am. Coll. Obstetricians & Gynecologists, Soc. Maternal Fetal Medicine (Best Oral Presentation); mem.: Bayard Carter Soc., Infectious Disease Soc. Ob-gyn., Soc. Gynecologic Investigations. Avocation: cooking. Office: PO Box 3967 Divsn MFM DUMC Erwin R Durham NC 27705 Office Fax: 919-681-7861. Business E-Mail: murth002@mc.duke.edu.

MURTHY, P. KALPANA, research scientist; b. Raibarely, India, Dec. 17, 1951; d. Ganesh Chandra and Monimala Karmaker; m. PSR Murthy, Aug. 10, 1975; 1 child, Deepika Madhusudhan. PhD, Kanpur U., India. Scientist Ctrl. Drug Rsch. Inst., Lucknow, India, 1981—91, asst. dir., 1991—2002, dep. dir., 2002—07, sr. dep. dir., 2007—. Contbr. articles to profl. jours. Rsch. fellowships, CSIR, New Delhi, 1973—78, vis. scientist fellow, CNRS, France, 1988, numerous rsch. grants, Rsch. Rsch. Associateship, DBT, New Delhi, 1998. Mem.: Soc. Indian Sci. Congress, Lab. Animal Sci. Assn. India, Indian Soc. Parasitology, Indian Immunology Soc., India. Achievements include research in identifiaction of inflammation modulating molecules of human filarial parasite; development of collaboration with TDR/WHO on new antifilarials; management of an interinstitutional network project; development of potential antifilarials of plant origin and humans. Office: Ctrl Drug Rsch Inst MG Marg Lucknow 226 001 India Personal E-mail: drpkmurthy@yahoo.com, drpkmurthy@gmail.com.

MURTHY, TATAVARTI VENKAT, physician; b. Visakhapatnam, Sept. 15, 1956; Degree, AFMC, 1980—80; MD, Ramakrishna Mission, 1980, DNB, 1985. Brig Army Forces, 2010—. Prof. AFMC, 2010. Decorated Army Chief Decorations Min of Def, Govt. of India. Fellow: Inst. Liver Studies, Kings Coll. (London). Avocations: travel, reading. Office: Golibar Maidan Nr Kondwah Pune Maharashtra 411040 India Office Fax: 020-2606160. E-mail: tvspmurthy@yahoo.com.

MURTOMÄKI, LASSE, research scientist; b. Jyväskylä, Finland, July 2, 1961; DSc, Helsinki U. Tech., 1992. Sr. rschr. Aalto U., 1996—. Group leader phys. pharmacy U. Helsinki, 2008. Office: Kemistintie 1 PO Box 16100 Espoo 00076 Aalto Finland Business E-Mail: lasse.murtomaki@aalto.fi.

MUSACCHIA, X(AVIER) J(OSEPH), physiology and biophysics educator; b. Bklyn., Feb. 11, 1923; s. Castrense and Orsolina (Mazzola) M.; m. Betty Cook, Nov. 23, 1950; children: Joseph, Mary, Thomas, Laura Ann. BS, St. Francis Coll., Bklyn., 1944; MS, Fordham U., 1947, PhD, 1949. Instr. biology Marymount (N.Y.) Coll., 1948-49; from instr. to prof. biology St. Louis U., 1949-65; prof. physiology U. Mo., Columbia, 1965-78; prof. physiology and biophysics U. Louisville, 1978-91, prof. emeritus, 1991—, dean Grad. Sch., 1978-89, assoc. provost for rsch., 1985-89. Bd. dirs. Coun. Grad. Schs., 1986-89. Author: Depressed Metabolism, 1969, Regulation of Depressed Metabolism and Thermogenesis, 1976, Survival in Cold, 1981; also articles. Bd. govs. J. Graham Brown Cancer Ctr., Louisville, 1978-83; bd. dirs. Oak Ridge Associated Univs. Served with AUS, 1943-45. Research grantee NIH; Research grantee NASA. Fellow AAAS; mem. Am. Physiol. Soc., Am. Soc. Zoologists, Am. Soc. for Space and Gravitational Biology (v.p. 1988-89, pres. 1989-90), Soc. Exptl. Biology and Medicine, Corp. Marine Biol. Lab., Sigma Xi. (past chpt. pres.) Home: 1770 East Overland Dr Fayetteville AR 72703-5202

MUSACCHIO, MARILYN JEAN, nurse midwife, administrator, educator; b. Louisville, Dec. 7, 1938; d. Robert William and Loretta C. (Liebert) Poulter; m. David Edward Musacchio, May 13, 1961; children: Richard Peter, Michelle Marie. BSN cum laude, Spalding Coll., 1968; MSN, U. Ky., 1972, cert. in nurse-midwifery, 1976; PhD, Case Western Res U., 1993; diploma, St Joseph Infirmary Sch, 1959. RN; cert. nurse-midwife; advanced registered nurse practitioner. Staff nurse gynecol. unit St. Joseph Infirmary, Louisville, 1959-60, staff nurse male gen. surgery unit, 1960; instr. St. Joseph Infirmary Sch. Nursing, Louisville, 1960-71; from asst. prof. to assoc. prof., dir. dept. nursing edn. Ky. State U., Frankfort, 1972-75; asst. prof. U. Ky. Coll. Nursing, Lexington, 1976-79, assoc. prof., coord., 1979-92, acting coordinator nurse-midwifery, 1982-84, coordinator for nurse-midwifery, 1987-92; assoc. prof., dir. nurse-midwifery U. Ala., Birmingham, 1992-96, assoc. prof., 1997-98; dean, prof. Tenn. Technol. U., Cookeville, 1998—2005; prof. Spalding U., Louisville, 2005—09, chmn.; dir. RN to BSN Program Aquinas Coll., Nashville, 2008—09; dean & prof. nursing edn. Sullivan U. Spencerian Coll., Louisville, 2009—. Cons. in field, dean nursing edn. Sullivan U. Mem. editorial bd. Jour. Obstet., Gynecol. and Neonatal Nursing, 1976-82; author pamphlet; contbr. articles to profl. jours. Mem.Louisville Safety Coun., 1973-80. Brig. Gen. Army Nurse Corps, USAR, 1992-95. Recipient Disting. Citizen award City of Louisville, 1977, Jefferson Cup award Jefferson County, Ky., 1991; named Outstanding Alumna, Mercy Acad., 1993; named to Hall of Disting. Alumni, U. Ky., 1995; recipient scholarships and fellowships, other awards. Fellow Am. Acad. Nursing; mem. AWHONN, ANA, Nurse Assn. Am. Coll. Ob-Gyn. (charter; nat. sec. 1970-72, chmn. dist. V 1969), Am. Coll. Nurse-Midwives, Res. Officers Assn., Assn. Mil. Surgeons U.S., Sr. Army Res. Comdr. Assn., Assn. U.S. Army, Army Nurse Corps. Assn., Army War Coll. Alumni Assn. (life). Roman Catholic. Avocations: reading, candy making, cake decorating, cooking, sewing. Home: PO Box 4907 Louisville KY 40204-4907 Personal E-mail: mjmusacchio@gmail.com.

MUSAYEV, SURKHAY NOVRUZ, pediatrician, department chairman; b. Khanlar, Azerbaijan, Feb. 1, 1951; s. Novruz Bayram Musayev and Mafilya Binnat Musayeva; m. Balakhatin Behbud Tagiyeva, Nov. 21, 1976; children: Matanet Surkhay Musayeva, Jeyhun Surkhay. MD, Azerbaijan Med. U., 1974; PhD in Pediat., Moscow U., 1992. Cert. pediatrician Ministry of Health, Azerbaijan, 1974. Asst. Azerbaijan Med. U., Baku, 1974—86, asst. prof., 1986—92, prof., 1992—. Author: (sci. book) Children Rheumatism, 1996; co-editor: Children Disease of Digestive Apparatus, 1996. Head trade union Azerbaijan Med. U., Baku, 1994—2005. Lt. Med. Svcs., 1974. Recipient Medal for Distinction in Labour, Pres. of USSR, 1981; named Honored Physician, Pres. of the Republic of Azerbaijan, 2000. Mem.: Internat. Pediatric Assn. (sec. gen. Azerbaijan divsn. 1996—2005, Hon. Cert. 1997). Avocations: poetry, hunting. Office: Azerbaijan Med U Bakikhanov str 23 Baku AZ1022 Azerbaijan Office Fax: (99412) 495 3870. Personal E-mail: surkhay_musayev@yahoo.com.

MUSCHAWECK, ULRIKE, surgeon; b. Herford, Germany, Mar. 5, 1948; m. Leonhard Muschaweck. MD, U. Göttingen, Germany, 1974. Lic. abdominal surgeon Germany. Chief attending surgery dept. U. Hosp. Rechts der Isar, Munich, 1986—93; surg. chief Munich Hernia Ctr., Munich, 1993—. Co-founder Suvretta, Switzerland, 1994—. Contbr. articles to profl. jours.;, author books in field. Mem.: European Hernia Soc. (mem. internat. adv. bd. 1994—98), German Hernia Soc. (founding mem.), Am. Hernia Soc. Achievements include development of Minimal-Repair-Technique in hernia surgery, especially for athletes. Office: Arabellastrasse 17 Munchen 81925 Germany Office Fax: 0049 89 92090120. E-mail: info@hernien.de.

MUSCHENHEIM, FREDERICK, retired pathologist; b. NYC, July 9, 1932; s. Carl and Haroldine (Humphreys) M.; m. Linda Alexander, Mar. 29, 1958; children: Alexandra Lydia, Carl William, David Henry. AB, Harvard U., 1953; MDCM, McGill U., Montreal, Can., 1963. Intern Santa Clara County Hosp., San Jose, Calif., 1963—64; resident pathology U. Colo. Med. Ctr., Denver, 1964—68, chief resident clin. pathology, 1968—69; pathologist Freeman, Hanske, Munkittrick & Foley PA, Mpls., 1969—77; clin. pathologist Union-Truesdale Hosp., Fall River, Mass., 1977—78; chief pathologist St. Clare's Hosp., Denville, NJ, 1978—83, Oneida Healthcare Ctr., 1984—99, ret., 1999; cons. pathologist St. Jude Hosp., Vieux Fort, St. Lucia, West Indies, 1999—2002. Clin. asst. prof. SUNY Health Sci. Ctr., Syracuse, 1984-90, clin. assoc. prof., 1990-97, clin. prof., 1998-99, clin. prof. emeritus, 1999-2001; chief med. staff Oneida City Hosps., 1991; pres. Sunderman Fund, Bermuda Biol. Sta. for Rsch., v.p. Madison County (NY) bd. health, 1993-96, pres., 1997-2000. Choir 1st Presbyn. Ch. of Cazenovia, NY, 1984-2000, trustee, 1985-89, choir Wayzata (Minn.) Cmty. Ch., 2001—. Mem.: Minn. Acad. Medicine (v.p. 2009—10, pres. 2010—11), Syracuse ARC Blood Svcs. (chmn. med. adv. coun. 1995—99), Minn. Soc. Pathologists (sec. 2002—05), N.Y. State Soc. Pathologists (councilor 2d dist. 1991—2000, chmn. legis. com. 1991—2000, del. to MSSNY 1998—99), N.Y. State Assn. Pub. Health Labs. (v.p. 1992—93, pres. 1993—94, edn. chmn. 1994—95), Med. Soc. Madison County (v.p. 1990—91, pres. 1991—93), Med. Soc. State N.Y. (legis. com. 1991—2000), Coll. Am. Pathologists (govt. affairs com. 1994—97, nominating com. 1995, steering com. ho. dels. 1999—2002), Assn. Clin. Scientists (v.p. 1989, pres. 1990, rec. sec. 1995—, del. Intersoc. Pathology Coun. 2004—05, interim sec., treas. 2011, Diploma of Honor 1991), Ausable Club (NY) (co-chair lawn bowl's com. 2009—). Home: 1159 Hollybrook Dr Wayzata MN 55391-1364

MUSCI, MICHAEL N., JR., pediatrician, healthcare company executive; DO, Mich. State U., 1975; MBA, St. Joseph U., 1994. Cert. neonatal/perinatal medicine, pediatrics. Med. dir. Virtua Health, 1993—96; chief med. officer Paradigm Health, 1998—2002; nat. med. dir. Amerigroup Corp., 2002—05; chief med. officer CarePlus Health Plan, 2005—06, UnitedHealth Group, Inc., 2006—07; CEO, Amerigroup Cmty. Care SC Amerigroup Corp., 2007—09, CEO, SC, 2009—. Office: Amerigroup Corp Ste 100 4425 Corporation Ln Virginia Beach VA 23462 Office Phone: 757-490-6900. Office Fax: 757-518-3600. Business E-Mail: mmusci@amerigroupcorp.com. *

MUSHLIN, STUART BRUCE, physician; b. DC, Mar. 23, 1947; BA with honors, U. Rochester, 1969; MD, Cornell U., 1973. Physician Partners Health Care, 1998—; dir. primary care Brigham and Women's Hosp., 2007—09, master clinician, 2011. Asst. prof. medicine Harvard Med. Sch., 2005—11. Recipient Robert Glaser Vis. Prof., Barnes Jewish Hosp. Fellow: ACP, Am. Coll. Rheumatology; mem.: Phi Beta Kappa, Alpha Omega Alpha. Avocations: jazz, saxophone, photography, aviation. Home: 511 Boylston St Brookline MA 02445 Personal E-mail: smushlin@partners.org.

MUSIAL, JACEK ZDZISLAW, physician; b. Ruda Ślaska, Upper Silesia, Poland, Feb. 11, 1956; s. Michal and Malgorzata Agata Gwóźdź; m. Alicja Elżbieta Grzyb, Sept. 7, 1996; children: Michal, Karol. Grad., Mil. Tech. Acad., Warsaw, Poland, 1975-79; MME, U. Kraków, 1981; MD, Med. Acad., Kraków, 1987, grad. in anesthesiology, 1991; grad. in Internal Diseases I, 2001, grad. in Internal Diseases II, 2006. Cert. Gastroscopy Jagiellonian U., Kraków, Poland; cert. colonoscopy Silesian Med. Acad., Katowice. Jr. asst. Cardiovascular Clinic, Kraków, Poland, 1987-88, Ob/Gyn Ward, Kraków, Poland, 1988; anesthesiology asst. St. Anna hosp., Miechów, Poland, 1989-93, asst. resuscitation ambulance emergency dept., 1993-95; pvt. gen. practitioner Miechów, Poland, 1993—2008; gastroscopist, colonoscopist St. Anna Hosp., Miechów, Poland, 1997-99; gen. practitioner Village Health Ctr., Nasiechowice, Poland, 1997—2007; sr. asst. internal diseases ward Silesian Hosp., Cieszyn, Poland, 2007—08; head pub. health ctr. Charsznica, Poland, 2009—. Tchr. Nursing H.S., Miechów, Poland, 1995-96; mgr. med. equipment team, mem. med. coun. St. Anna Hosp., 1995-97. Contbr. articles to profl. jours. Recipient 4 Young Inventors hon. patents Mlody Technik, Poland, 1973, 74. Roman Catholic. Home: ul Powstańców 23/27/21 32-200 Miechow Poland Office: PZOZ Charsznica ul Mie-chówska 51 Charsznica 32-250 Poland Personal E-mail: jacekmusial@gmail.com. E-mail: jacek.2123177@pharmanet.com.pl.

MUSIALIK, JOANNA, gastroenterologist, educator; b. Bielsko-Biala, Sept. 14, 1966; MD, Med. U. Silesia, 1992, PhD, 2000. Asst. prof., dept. basic med. sci. Med. U. Silesia, 2008—. Sr. asst. Dept. Gastroenterology and Hepatology, 2007. Mem.: European Assn. Study Liver. Avocation: history. Office: Medyków 14 Katowice Silesia 40-752 Poland Business E-Mail: joanna@sla.com.pl.

MUSK, ARTHUR WILLIAM, physician, researcher; b. Kalgoorlie, W. Australia, Aug. 12, 1943; s. Arthur Thomas and Jean Mary (Scott) M.; children: Gabrielle, Michael. MB, BS, U. W. Australia, 1967; MSc, Harvard Sch. Pub. Health, Boston, 1977; MD, U. New S. Wales, Sydney, 1987. Resident med. officer Royal Perth Hosp., Perth, W. Australia, 1966-67, Sir Charles Gairdner Hosp., Perth, W. Australia, 1967, med. registrar, 1968, Royal Perth Hosp., Perth, W. Australia, 1969, Sir Charles Gairdner, Perth, W. Australia, 1970-71; rsch. fellow Prince Henry Hosp., Sydney, 1972-74, Harvard Sch. Pub. Health, Boston, 1975-77, Med. Rsch. Coun. Pneumoconiosis Rsch. Unit, Penarth, Wales, 1977-78; physician, clin. prof. medicine and population health U. W. Australia, Perth, 1978—, head dept. respiratory medicine, 1978-93. Sec., pres. Thoracic Soc. Australia (Western Australia Br.), Perth, West Australia, 1981-96; pres. Australian Coun. on Smoking and Health, 1991-2001; chmn. Busselton Population Rsch. Found., 1998—. Contbr. articles to profl. jours. Pres. TCC Emergency Welfare Found., Perth, W. Australia, 1981-84, U. Camp for Children, 1965-66. Decorated Order of Australia; recipient Wunderly Medal, Thoracic Soc. Australia and New Zealand, 1991, Rsch. medal, 2011; named gov. Am. Coll. Chest Physicians, 1996-2000, Elphick medal Australian Coun. on Smoking and Health, 2009. Fellow Royal Australasian Coll. Physicians, Australasian Faculty of Occupl. and Environ. Medicine, Am. Coll. Chest Physicians (gov. West Australia 1996-2000), mem. Faculty of Occupl. Medicine Royal Coll. Physicians. Office: Sir Charles Gairdner Hosp Verdun St Nedlands 6009 Australia Office Phone: 61-8-93463252. Business E-Mail: bill.musk@health.wa.gov.au.

MUSS, HYMAN BERNARD, oncologist, educator; b. Bklyn., Apr. 18, 1943; m. Loretta Anne Lassam; children: Sarah, Jonathan, Daniel. BA in Chemistry cum laude, Lafayette Coll., 1964; MD summa cum laude, SUNY, 1968. Diplomate Am. Bd. Internal Medicine, sub-splty. med. oncology, Am. Bd. Hematology, Am. Bd. Oncology. Intern Peter Bent Brigham Hosp., Boston, 1969-69, jr. asst. resident, 1969-70, rsch. fellow in medicine, 1972-73, rsch. fellow in hematology, 1973-74, Children's Hosp. Med. Ctr., Boston, 1972-73; fellow in oncology Dana Farber Cancer Inst., Boston, 1973-74; asst. prof. medicine, hematology/oncology Wake Forest U., Winston-Salem, N.C., 1974-78, assoc. prof., 1978-85, assoc. dir. clin. rsch. Comprehensive Cancer Ctr., 1979-96, prof. medicine, 1985-96, U. Vt., 1996—2009; assoc. dir. U. Vt. Cancer Ctr., 1996—2009; prof. medicine, breast cancer & geriatric oncology Lineberger Comprehensive Cancer Ctr., U. NC Sch. Medicine, Chapel Hill, 2009—. Peer review com. Health Scis. Consortium, Inc., 1978-80; sci. adv. com. black/white survival study, 1985-96; com.consulting staff Forsyth Meml. Hosp., Winston-Salem, N.C., N.C. Bapt. Hosp., Winston Salem. Mem. edtl. bd. Am. Jour. Med. Sci., 1986—, Jour. Clin. Oncology, 1994, Nat. Cancer Insts. Computerized, 1986-91, Contemporary Oncology, 1990—; reviewer New Eng. Jour. Medicine, Jour. Clin. Oncology, Archives of Internal Medicine, Breast Cancer Rsch. & Treatment, Cancer, Gynecologic Oncology, Surg. Neurology, Jour. Nat. Cancer Inst., Jour. Immunotherapy, Clin. Chemistry; contbr. articles, abstracts to profl. jours., chpts. to books. Active Am. Cancer Soc., 1978—, bd. dirs., 1985-87; trustee Blumenthal Jewish Home, 1992-93, chair med. ethics com., chair HIV/infectious disease com. Maj. U.S. Army, 1970-72, Vietnam. Decorated Bronze Star U.S. Army; recipient Cooper Meml. award Wake County, 1979; Jr. Faculty fellow Am. Cancer Soc., 1975-79. Fellow ACP; mem. AMA, Am. Coll. Obstetricians and Gynecologists (com. human rsch.), Internal Soc. Geriatric Oncology, Vt. State Med. Soc., New England Cancer Soc., Am. Bd. Internal Medicine, Internat. Soc. Breast Disease, Am. Soc. Hematology, Am. Fedn. Clin. Rsch., Am. Soc. Clin. Oncology, Am. Assn. Cancer Rsch., Internat. Gynecologic Cancer Soc., Internat. Assn. Breast Cancer Rsch., So. Assn. Oncology (edn. com. 1988—), So. Med. Assn., So. Soc. Clin. Rsch., N.C. Med. Soc. (cancer com.), Forsyth County Med. Soc. (chmn. cancer com. 1977-80, med. adv. com. 1977-79), Cancer and Acute Leukemia Group B, Gynecologic Oncology Group (sarcoma com. 1977-79, endometrial com. 1978-90, quality control com. 1978-90, chemotherapy com. 1977—, chmn., 1980—, protocol com. 1980-90, new drug liaison com. 1980—, exec. comb. 1991—, quality of life com. 1993—, cervix com. 1993—), Piedmont Oncology Assn. (chmn. 1991—), Phi Beta Kappa, Alpha Omega Alpha. Office: University of North Carolina Chapel Hill 170 Manning Dr CB #7305 Chapel Hill NC 27599 Office Phone: 919-966-3856. E-mail: muss@email.unc.edu.

MUSTACCHI, PIERO, preventive medicine physician, educator; b. Cairo, May 29, 1920; came to U.S., 1947; naturalized, 1962; s. Gino and Gilda (Rieti) M.; m. Dora Lisa Ancona, Sept. 26, 1948; children: Roberto, Michael. BS in Humanities, U. Florence, Italy, 1938; postgrad. in anatomy, U. Lausanne, Switzerland, 1938-39; MB, ChB, Fouad I U., Cairo, Egypt, 1944, grad. in Arabic lang. and lit., 1946; D Medicine and Surgery, U. Pisa, 1986; Degree (hon.), U. Aix-Marseille, France, 1988, U. Alexandria, Egypt, 1985. Qualified med. examiner, Calif. Indsl. Accident Commn., 1994. House officer English Hosp., Ch. Missionary Soc., Cairo, 1945-47; clin. affiliate U. Calif., San Francisco, 1947-48; intern Franklin Hosp., San Francisco, 1948-49; resident in pathology U. Calif., San Francisco, 1949-51; resident in medicine Meml. Ctr. Cancer and Allied Diseases, NYC, 1951-53; rsch. epidemiologist Dept. HEW, Nat. Cancer Inst., Bethesda, Md., 1955-57; cons. allergy clinic U. Calif., San Francisco, 1957-70, clin. prof. medicine and preventive medicine, 1970-90, clin. prof. medicine and epidemiology, 1990-96, head occupl. epidemiology, 1975-90, head divsn. internat. health edn. dept. epidemiology and internat. health, 1985-90; médecin agréé, official physician Consulate Gen. of France, San Francisco, 1995—2007; sr. cons. internat. health care U. Calif., San Francisco. Med. cons., vis. prof. numerous edn1. & profl. instns., U. Marseilles, 1981—82, U. Pisa, Italy, 1983, U. Gabon, 1984,

U. Siena, Italy, 1985; cons. U. Calif., 1975—, U. El Azhar, 1986; sr. cons. internat. med. care U. Calif., San Francisco, 2000—06. Contbr. chpts. to books, articles to profl. jours. Editorial bd. Medecine d'Afrique Noire, Ospedali d'Italia. With USPHS USN, 1955—57. Decorated comdr. Order of Merit (Italy), officer Ordre de la Legion d'Honneur (France), Medal of St. John of Jerusalem, Sovereign Order of Malta, Order of the Republic (Egypt); Scroll, Leonardo da Vinci Soc., San Francisco, 1965; award Internat. Inst. Oakland, 1964; Hon. Vice Consul. Italy, 1971-90. Fellow ACP, Am. Soc. Environ. and Occupational Health; mem. AAAS, Am. Assn. Cancer Rsch., Calif. Soc. Allergy and Immunology, Calif. Med. Assn., San Francisco Med. Soc., West Coast Allergy Soc. (founding), Mex. Congress on Hypertension (corr.), Internat. Assn. Med. Rsch. and Continuing Edn. (U.S. rep.), Acad. Italiana della Cucina, Acta Medico Historica Adriatica, 2007. Democrat. Avocations: music, math, languages. also: 3838 California St San Francisco CA 94118-1522 Office Phone: 415-668-2626.

MUSTION, ALAN LEE, pharmacist; b. Oklahoma City, Feb. 6, 1947; s. Granville E. and Iris E. (Graham) Mustion; m. Mary Jane Bozek, Dec. 4, 1982; children from previous marriage: Jeffrey Alan, Jennifer Chere. BS in Pharmacy, Southwestern Okla. State U., 1970. Staff pharmacist VA Med. Ctr., Oklahoma City, 1970—74, dir. pharmacy Richmond, Va., 1976—77, Iowa City, 1977—90; dir. pharmacy svcs. VA Hosp., Houston, 1990—2002; pharmacy mgr. Integris Bapt. Med. Ctr., Oklahoma City, 2002—. Clin. instr. clin./hosp. divsn. U. Iowa, 1977—90; adj. asst. prof. pharmacy practice U. Houston, 1990—2002. Contbr. articles to profl. jours. Served to lt. col. USAR. Grantee Rsch., Travenol Labs., 1980—87, VA HSR&D, 1984, 1988. Mem.: Okla. Soc. Health Sys. Pharmacists, Am. Soc. Health Sys. Pharmacists, Kappa Psi. Methodist. Office: 3300 NW Expressway Oklahoma City OK 73112 Home: 513 Winding Creek Rd Yukon OK 73099-4471 E-mail: alan.mustion@integris-health.com.

MUSTOE, THOMAS ANTHONY, physician, plastic surgeon; s. Robert and Carolyn M.; m. Kathryn Claire Stallcup, 1977; children: Anthony, Lisa. BA cum laude in biology, Harvard Coll., 1973, MD cum laude, 1978. Diplomate Am. Bd. Otolaryngology, Am. Bd. Plastic Surgery, Ill. 1991. Rsch. assoc. dept. microbiology Harvard Med. Sch., Cambridge, Mass., 1976-77; intern in medicine Mass. Gen. Hosp., Boston, 1978-79; resident in surgery Peter Bent Brigham Hosp., Boston, 1979-80; resident in otolaryngology Mass. Eye and Ear Infirmary, Boston, 1980-82, chief resident, 1982-83; resident in plastic surgery Brigham and Women's Hosp., Children's Hosp., Boston, 1983-84, chief resident, 1984-85; asst. prof. in surgery Wash. U. Sch. Medicine, St. Louis, 1985-89, assoc. prof., 1989-91; prof., chief divsn. plastic surgery Northwestern U. Med. Sch., Chgo., 1991—; plastic surgeon Northwestern Meml. Hosp., 1991—, Evanston Hosp., 1991—, Children's Meml. Hosp., 1992—, Shriner's Hosp. Chgo., 1994—. Co-chmn. Gorden Rsch. Conf., 1995; spl. cons. FDA, 1994—98; mem. sci. adv. panel Biologies, 1997, NCI, 1998; lectr. seminars, 2001. Editl. bd. Archives of Surgery, 1992-2004, Plastic and Reconstructive Surgery, 1993-2001, Wound Repair and Regeneration, 1992—, Jour. Surg. Rsch., 1997-2006; contbr. articles to profl. jours., more than 200 publs., book chpts.; book reviewer. Named one of Top Chgo. Doctors, Chgo. Mag., 1998, 2001, 2004, 2006-08, America's Top Physicians, Consumers Rsch. Coun. America, 2003-07; Harvard Nat. scholar, 1969-73. Fellow: ACS (adv. coun. plastic surgery 1999—2002, surg. forum com. 1999—2002, editl. bd. jour. 2003—, surg. biology club III); mem.: AMA, Am. Soc. Plastic Surgery (sci. program chair 2005—), Am. Bd. Plastic Surgery (bd. dirs. 2006—12), Coun. Plastic Surger Org., Double Boarded Soc. (pres. 1995—98), Chgo. Surg. Soc., Chgo. Plastic Surg. Soc. (sec. 1996—97), Wound Healing Soc. (program com. 1990, audit com. 1992, program com. 1992, bd. dir. 1993—96, program com. 1994, fin. com. 1994—96, program com. 1997, pres. 1997—99, v.p. 1999—2001, bd. mem. 2000—05, bd. dirs. 2006—09, Lifetime Achievement award 2004), Assn. Acad. Chmn. Plastic Surgery (matching program and ctrl. application svc. com. 1994), Soc. U. Surgeons, Soc. Head and Neck Surgeons (membership com. 1993—95), Plastic Surgery Rsch. Coun. (rep. coun. acad. surgeons 1991—94, com. indsl. rels. 1992, program com. 1992—94, 1995, Judge Snyder & Crikelair awards 1991), Midwest Assn. Plastic Surgeons, Lipoplasty Soc. N.Am. (lipoplasty ednl. rsch. found. 1998—2000), Am. Assn. Plastic Surgery (rsch. and edn. com. 1994—96, chmn. 1996, mem. com. 1998—, co-chmn.ASPRS-ASAPS task force on emerging trends 1999—2000, chmn. instl. coun. com. 1999—), Am. Soc. Plastic and Reconstructive Surgery (rsch. fund proposal com. 1987—92, plastic surgery device com. 1989—93, resource book for plastic surgery residents com. 1991—93, socioecon. 1992—94, sci. program com. 1993—95, chmn. device and tecyhnique assessment com. 1994—96, co-chmn. gen. reconstruction subcom. 1995, ultrasonic lipectomy task force 1995—96, task force for outcomes and guidelines 1995—98, devices and tech. com. 1995—98, chmn. instrnl. com. 1999—2002, chmn. edn. com. 1999—, chmn. resource book com.), Aesculapian Club, Sigma Xi. Business E-Mail: tmustoe@nmh.org.

MUTALIPASSI, LOUIS RICHARD, psychologist, educator; b. Kansas City, Kans., Jan. 23, 1937; s. Louie R. Mutalipassi and Cleda E. (Miller) Wolverton; m. Edalee Kenworthy, July 14, 1962 (div. 1970); 1 child, Annemarie; m. Laura Ruth Posner, July 17, 1976; 2 children: Michael and Anthony. BA in Psychology, U. Calif., Santa Barbara, 1962; MA in Psychology, UCLA, 1965, PhD in Psychology, 1969. Lic. psychologist Calif. Staff psychologist VA Med. Ctr., LA, 1969—76, chief psychology svc. Albany, NY, 1976—80; clin. assoc. prof. psychology UCLA and U. So. Calif., LA, 1980—; chief psychology svc. VA Med. Ctr., Long Beach, 1980—97; ret., 1997; clin. psychologist in pvt. practice Cypress, Calif., 1982—. Oral commr. State Bd. Med. Examiners, Calif., 1996—. Contbr. articles to profl. jour.; presenter in field. With USAF, 1954—58. Mem.: APA, Mission Lakes Country Club. Avocations: golf, photography. Home and Office: PO Box 1109 Desert Hot Springs CA 92240 Office Phone: 760-880-1711. Personal E-mail: loum@roadrunner.com.

MUTISYA, ELIZABETH M., pharmaceutical executive; B in Neurobiology, Cornell U., Ithaca, NY; med. degree, Harvard Med. Sch.; MBA, U. Pa. Intern gen. surgery U. Calif. San Francisco, resident neurological surgery; positions of increasing responsibility in med. and sci. affairs Pfizer, Inc.; sr. dir., clinical leader Johnson & Johnson; v.p. med. affairs Cephalon, Inc., 2004—08; v.p. US med. affairs, chief med. officer Solvay Pharmaceuticals, Inc., 2008—. Office: Solvay Pharmaceuticals Inc 901 Sawyer Rd Marietta GA 30062 *

MUTO, CARMINE, cardiologist; b. Casamarciano, Naples, Italy, Aug. 8, 1958; Degree in Medicine and Surgery, 2nd U. Naples, 1991. Physician Loreto Nuovo Hosp., 1999—2011. Mem.: Assn. Italian Arrhythmology. Office: via Amerigo Vespucci Naples 80100 Italy Office Fax: 00390812542839. Business E-Mail: carminemuto@libero.it.

MUTO, CRESCENZO, surgeon; b. Legnano, Milano, Italy, July 27, 1964; s. Pasquale Crescenzo Muto and Cetara Alba; m. Marchesiello, July 20, 1991; 1 child, Alba Alossandro. Degree in Medicine, Naples U., 1989. Cert. specialist in gen. surgery U. Naples, 1994. Asst. Anatomy Inst., Naples, Italy, 1984—86, Surgery Inst., Naples, 1986—94; resident S. Anna Clinic, Caserta, 1990—95; chief surgery. laparoscopic divsn. Pineta Grande Clinic, Castel Volturno, Caserta, 1996—; chief gen., laparoscopic, oncologic surgery divsn. S. Maria della Salute Clinic, S. Maria Capua Vetere, Caserta, 2006—. Sec. Liberal Politic, Caserta, Italy, 1990—94. Recipient prize, Irving U., 1990. Master: Italian Soc. Pvt. Health Surgeon, Caserta Surgery Soc. (hon.); mem.: Lap Club, Italian Soc. Obesity Surgery, Italian Soc. Endoscopic Surgeon, European Soc. Endoscopic Surgery, Lions Club Caserta Terra Di Lavoro (charter mem. 2002, pres. 2004—06). Liberal. Achievements include research in new tecniques for surgical operations; appendectomy using mini-laparoscopic instruments; endoscopic retroperitoneal approach for surgical treatment of chronic pain after hernia repair; a new prosthesis for surgical laparoscopic treatment of inguinal hernia suture less and tension free. Avocations: travel, books, modellism. Office: S Maria della Salute Clinic - Surgery Avezzana St Caserta 81040 Italy Home: Via Mohandas Karamchand Gandhi 81100 Caserta CE Italy Home Fax: +39 0823 810832. Personal E-mail: pglaparomuto@virgilio.it.

MUTOH, MICHIHIRO, oncologist; b. Tokyo, Feb. 24, 1969; s. Hiroshi and Miwako Mutoh; m. Tomoko Koshiba, May 20, 2001; m. Rintaro Mutoh; 1 child, Rihito. MD, Yamaguchi U., Japan, 1995; PhD, U. Tsukuba, Ibaragi, Japan, 2001. Intern U. Hosp., U. Tsukuba, Japan, 1995—97; rsch. resident fellow Nat. Cancer Ctr. Rsch. Inst., Tokyo, 1997—2001, staff scientist, 2004—05, sect. head., 2005—; vis. assoc. prof. faculty pharm. scis. Tokyo U. Sci., 2009—. Vis. fellow NIH, Nat. Cancer Inst., 2001—03; sec.-gen. Internat. Symposium Princess Tahamatsu Cancer Rsch. Fund, Tokyo, 2007—08; with Ministry Health, Labour & Welfare, Japan, 2010—. Author: Food Factors in Health Promotion and Disease Prevention, 2003. Recipient IU Yr. Strategy award, Ministry of Health, Labour & Welfare Japan, 2010—; grantee, Pub. Trust Nishi Cancer Rsch. Fund, 2004, Yukult Bio-Sci. Found., 2007—09; rsch. fellow, Japan Soc. for the Promotion Sci., 2001—03, travel grantee, Found. for Promotion Cancer Rsch., 2004, 2005, 2007, 2009. Mem.: The Japanese Cancer Assn., Japanese Soc. Internal Medicine, Japanese Soc. Gastroenterology, Japanese Assn. Cancer Rsch. (sec.-gen. ann. meeting 2007). Avocations: skiing, scuba diving. Office: Nat Cancer Ctr Rsch Inst 1-1 Tsukiji 5-Chome Chuo-ku Tokyo 104-0045 Japan Home: Apt 1516 1-1 Tsukiji 5-Chome Chuo-ku Tokyo 104-0045 Japan Business E-Mail: mimutoh@ncc.go.jp.

MUTTAMARA, SUPHAVIT, obstetrician, gynecologist, consultant; b. Bangkok, Thailand, Oct. 25, 1946; s. Kosol and Charam Muttamara; m. Sirimas Asasu; children: Supasiri, Siriwit. MD, Siriraj Med. Sch., Bangkok, 1970. Cert. Am. Coll. Ob-gyn., 1978, ob-gyn. Thai Med. Coun., 1993, maternal and fetal medicine Royal Thai Coll. Ob-gyn., 1997, Thai Med. Coun., 2005. Clin. assoc. prof. dept. ob-gyn. U. Medicine and Dentistry NJ, Newark, 1978—81; ob-gyn. Phramongkutklao Med. Coll., Dept. Ob-gyn., Bangkok, 1982—99, chmn., 1999—2001; dir. dept. ob-gyn. Phramongkutklao Hosp., Bangkok, 2002—05, cons., 2005—. Med. dir. Maternal and Infant Care project, Newark, 1977—81; chmn. sub-com. tng. and exam. for splty. in ob-gyn. Thai Med. Coun., Bangkok, 2004—06; v.p. Royal Thai Coll. Ob-Gyn. Author: (medical textbook) Operative Obstetrics, 1982; contbr. articles to profl. jours. Lt. gen. Med. Corp ob-gyn., 2006—, Thailand. Fellow: Am. Coll. Ob-gyn.; mem.: Thai Perinatal Soc. (mem. exec. bd. 2007—09), Royal Thai Coll. Ob-gyn. (v.p. 2010—). Buddist. Avocation: travel. Home: 16-87 Soi Vipavadee17 Vipavadee Rangsid Bangkok 10900 Thailand Office: Phramongkutklao Hosp Dept Obgyn 315 Rajvithi Rd Bangkok 10400 Thailand Office Fax: 66-2-3547630. Personal E-mail: suphavitmu@yahoo.com. Business E-Mail: suphavim@pmk.ac.th.

MUTTERPERL, MITCHELL, internist; MD, U. Rome, Italy, 1981. Diplomate Am. Bd. Internal Medicine. Resident internal medicine Univ. of Medicine and Dentistry of NJ-Med. Ctr., 1982—85; hospital affiliations include Bayonne Med. Ctr., Jersey City Med. Ctr., St. Barnabas Med. Ctr. Office: Bayonne Medical Center 29 St Ave E Bayonne NJ 07002 Home: 19 W 33rd St Bayonne NJ 07002 Office Phone: 201-858-5000.

MUUSS, ROLF EDUARD, retired psychologist, author; b. Tating, Germany, Sept. 26, 1924; came to U.S., 1953, naturalized, 1992. s. Rudolf A. and Else M.; m. Gertrude Louise Kremser, Dec. 22, 1953 (dec. April 1999); children: Michael John (dec.), Gretchen Elise. Diploma, Tchr. Coll., Flensburg, Germany, 1951; student, U. Hamburg, Germany, 1951, Ctrl. Mo. State Coll., 1951—52, Columbia Tchrs. Coll., 1952; MEd, Western Md. Coll., 1954; PhD, U. Ill., 1957; Masters Degree (hon.), U. Ambrosiana, Milan, 2004. Tchr. pub. sch., Germany, 1945-46, 51, 52-53; substitute prin., 1952-53; tchr. trainee U.S. Office Edn., 1951-52; houseparent Child Study Ctr., Balt., 1953; grad. asst. U. Ill., 1954-57; rsch. assoc. prof. Iowa Child Welfare Rsch. Sta., State U. Iowa, 1957-59; rsch. cons., 1960, 61; mem. faculty Goucher Coll., 1959-95, prof. edn., 1964-95, chmn. dept., 1972-75, dir. spl. edn., 1977-92, Elizabeth C. Todd disting. prof., 1980-85, chmn. dept. sociology and anthropology, 1983-85, prof. emeritus, 1995—. Rsch. assoc. edn. Johns Hopkins, 1962-63; tchr. U. B.C., 1962, Johns Hopkins U., 1962, 65, U. Del., 1965, Towson U., 1967, U. Ill., 1967; tchg. assoc. Sheppard and Enoch Pratt Hosp., 1969-80; guest lectr. Tchrs. Coll., Kiel, Fed. Republic Germany, 1977-78; hearing officer spl. edn. cases State of Md., 1980-96. Author: First-Aid for Classroom Discipline Problems, 1962, Theories of Adolescence, 1962, 6th edit., 1996, Grundlagen der Jugendpsychologie, 1982; editor: Adolescent Behavior and Society: A Book of Readings, 1971, 5th edit., 1998; contbr. articles to profl. jours. Served with German Air Force, 1942-45. Recipient award for disting. scholarship Goucher Coll., 1979; grantee Andrew W. Mellon Found., 1976-77. Fellow Am. Psychol. Soc., Am. Psychol. Assn., Md. Psychol. Assn. (treas. 1971-73); mem. Balt. Psychol. Assn. (chmn. membership com. 1966, v.p. 1970-71), Soc. Rsch. Child Devel., Soc. Rsch. on Adolescence, Kappa Delta Pi (v.p. Alpha chpt. 1956-57), Phi Delta Kappa. Home: Edenwald # 304 800 Southerly Rd Towson MD 21286-8400

MUZAFFAR, ARSHAD R., plastic surgeon, educator; b. London, Eng., Oct. 15, 1969; arrived in U.S., 1979; BS, Stanford U., 1991; MD, Yale U., 1995. Bd. cert. Am. Bd. Plastic Surgery, cert. added qualification in hand surgery. Intern, resident U. Tex. Southwestern; hand/micro fellow U. Tex. Southwestern and Tex. Scottish Rite Hosp.; craniofacial fellow Children's Hosp., U. Wash.; asst. prof. plastic surgery U. Wash., Seattle, 2001—05; assoc. prof. plastic surgery U. Mo., Columbia, 2005—. Editor-in-chief Cleft Palate Craniofacial Jour., 2008—. Assoc. editor: Selected Readings in Plastic Surgery, 2000—, sect. editor: craniofacial surgery Cleft Palate-Craniofacial Jour., 2005—; contbr. chapters to books, articles to profl. jours. Traveling scholar/fellow, Am. Soc. Maxillofacial Surgeons, 2004. Mem.: Am. Assn. Plastic Surgeons, Am. Soc. for Surgery of the Hand, Am. Cleft Palate Craniofacial Soc., Am. Soc. Plastic Surgeons. Office: Univ Mo Plastic Surgery One Hospital Dr Columbia MO 65212 Office Phone: 573-882-2275. Business E-Mail: muzaffara@health.missouri.edu.

MUZEVIC, DARIO, neurosurgeon; b. Osijek, Feb. 4, 1978; MD, Zagreb U. Sch. Medicine, 1996. Neurosurgeon Osijek U. Hosp. Ctr., 2010—. Recipient U. Rector's award, Josip Juraj Strossmayer U. Osijek. Mem.: Croatian Neurosurg. Soc. Office: Josipa Huttlera 4 Osijek 31000 Croatia Office Fax: 385 31 512 183. Business E-Mail: muzevic.dario@kbo.hr.

MUZUR, AMIR, medical historian, neuroscientist; b. Rijeka, Croatia, Jan. 12, 1969; s. Mehmed and Smiljka (Jačić) M. MD, U. Rijeka, Croatia, 1993; MA, Ctrl. European U., Budapest, Hungary, 1996; PhD, Internat. Sch. Advanced Studies, Trieste, Italy, 2000. Intern Dom zdravlja, Opatija Rijeka, Croatia, 1993-95; fellow, rschr. CEU, Budapest, 1995-96, SISSA/ISAS, Trieste, 1996—2000; post-doctoral rsch. fellow lab. neurophysiology dept. psychiatry Med. Sch. Mass. Mental Health Ctr. Harvard U., 2001—02; asst. prof. dept. family medicine U. Rijeka, Croatia, 2003—05, assoc. prof., head dept. social scis. and med. humanities, 2008—; mayor of Opatija Croatia, 2005—09. Author: Synaesthesеon Libri, 1995, Opatija-Promotor of Health Tourism, 1996, The Zora of Opatija, 1997, How Opatija was Created, 1998, FK Zora Opatija, 1998, Immersions, 2000 (Literary 1st prize, 1999), Opatija-Abbazia: A Stroll Through Space and Time, 2000, Lovran: A Guide, 2000, Miraculous Healings, 2001, Opatija: Itineraries for Researchers and the Inquisitive, 2001, Medical History for Practioners, 2003, American Diary, 2003, A Chronicle of the Tomašić-Červar Family, 2003, The Golden Book of the Guests of Opatija, 2004, The Microcosm of Liburnia, 2004, Ars Speculandi, 2004, The Mysteries of the Brain, 2011. Recipient Commendatore della Stella della solidarieta, Pres. of Italian Republic, 2008; named Mayor of Yr., Croatian Nat. TV and Croatian Chamber of Economy, 2006, Hon. Consul, Republic of Poland, 2011. Avocations: local history, coin collecting/numismatics. Home: Popovicev put 33a Matulji 51211 Croatia Office Phone: 385 51 651-213. Personal E-mail: amirmuzur@yahoo.com.

MWANG'OMBE, NIMROD JUNIAHS, neurosurgeon, consultant; b. Mombasa, Kenya, Aug. 25, 1951; s. Peter Mwakota Mwang'ombe and Maryamu Majala Mwazo; m. Agnes Wakesho Kirangu, Aug. 13, 1983; 1 child, Majala Zawadi. MB, ChB, U. of Nairobi Med. Sch., Kenya, 1976; PhD in Neuro-Oncology, U. London, 1990. Physician, Neurosurgeon Med. Practitioners and Dentists Bd. of Kenya, 1988. Rsch. registrar dept. neurosurgery The Nat. Hosp. for Neurology and Neurosurgery, Inst. of Neurology, London, 1984—88; prof. neurosurgery Coll. of Health Scis., U. of Nairobi., Kenya, 1988—. Cons. neurosurgeon, program dir. and divsn. head. Kenyatta Nat. Referral and Tchg. Hosp., Nairobi, Kenya, 1988—; program dir. neurosurgery tng. program East Africa Found. of Internat. Edn. in Neurosurgery. Fundraiser Taita-Taveta Diocess, Anglican Ch. of Kenya, Voi, 2000—03. Internat. Fellow at McMaster U., Congress of Neurol. Surgeons of USA, 2002. Fellow: Coll. of Surgeons of East and Ctrl. Africa. Mem. Anglican Ch. Achievements include research in Tropical Neurosurgery; tuberculomas, brain abscess, frontal encephaloceles, craniovertebral anomalies; Induction of tumor differentation as a tool in chemotherapy of gliomas. Avocations: jogging, squash, gardening, music, reading. Office: Coll Health Sci Univ Nairobi Kenyatta Nat Hosp Ngong Rd Nairobi Kenya Office Fax: 254-020-226673. Personal E-mail: juniahs@yahoo.com. Business E-Mail: juniahs@insightkenya.com.

MYEROWITZ, P(AUL) DAVID, cardiac surgeon, educator, writer; b. Balt., Jan. 18, 1947; s. Joseph Robert and Merry (Brown) M.; m. Susan Karen Macks, June 28, 1967 (div.); children: Morris Brown, Elissa Suzanne, Ian Matthew; m. Kathleen Mary Murphy, Aug. 10, 2001. BS, U. Md., 1966; MD, 1970; MS, U. Minn., 1977. Intern in surgery U. Minn., Mpls., 1970-71, resident in surgery, 1971-72, 74-77; resident in cardiothoracic surgery U. Chgo., 1977-79; practice medicine specializing in cardiovascular surgery Madison, Wis., 1979—; asst. prof. thoracic and cardiovascular surgery U. Wis., Madison, 1979-85; assoc. prof., 1985; chief sect. cardiac transplantation, 1984-85; Karl P. Klassen prof., 1985-97; chief thoracic and cardiovascular surgery Ohio State U. and Hosps., Columbus, 1985-97. Author: (book) Heart Transplantation, 1987, Heartland for Profit, 2004; contbr. articles to profl. jours. Served with USPHS, 1972-74. Mem.: ACS, Am. Assn. Thoracic Surgeons, Am. Coll. Cardiology. Jewish. E-mail: drpdmmd@gmail.com.

MYERS, ALLEN RICHARD, rheumatologist; b. Balt., Jan. 14, 1935; s. Ellis Benjamin and Rosina (Blumberg) M.; m. Ellen Patz, Nov. 26, 1960; children: David Joseph, Robert Todd, Scott Patz. BA, U. Pa., Phila., 1956; MD, U. Md., 1960. Diplomate Am. Bd. Internal Medicine, Am. Bd. Rheumatology. Intern Univ. Hosp., Balt., 1960-61, resident in medicine Ann Arbor, Mich., 1961-64; fellow in rheumatology Mass. Gen. Hosp. and Harvard Med. Sch., Boston, 1966-69; dir. clin. tng. rheumatology U. Pa. Sch. Medicine, Phila., 1969-72, chief rheumatology sect., 1972-78; dep. chair medicine Temple U. Sch. Medicine, Phila., 1978-84, acting chmn. medicine, 1984-86, dean, 1991-95, prof. medicine, 1978—, assoc. v.p. Health Scis. Ctr., 1988-95. Vis. prof. Cardiothoracic Inst., U. London, 1988; mem. med. adv. bd. Scleroderma Rsch. Found., Santa Barbara, Calif., 1986. Mem. editl. bd. Arthritis & Rheumatism, 1985—90, Brit. Jour. Rheumatology, 1989—94; editor: Systemic Sclerosis, 1985, Medicine, 1986, 1993, 1996, 2000, 2004. Pres. Phila. Health Care Congress, 1994—; adv. com. Pa. Lupus Found., 1976—; bd. dirs. Phila. Conv. and

Visitors Bur., 1994—. With USPHS, 1964-66. Recipient Margaret Whitaker prize U. Md. Sch. Medicine, 1960, Lindback Found. award Temple, 1981; named Physician of Yr. Temple U. Hosp., 1986. Master: Am. Coll. Rheumatology; fellow: ACP, Phila. Coll. Physicians (pres. 2000); mem.: Am. Fedn. Clin. Rsch. Avocations: walking, classical music, reading. Office Phone: 215-707-5127.

MYERS, EDDIE EARL, psychologist; b. Ardmore, Okla., Nov. 24, 1937; s. Finis Weldon and Fern Durrell (Johnson) M.; m. Ineta June Moore, July 2, 1955 (div. Mar. 1988); children: Richard Weldon, Ronald Leland, Marilyn June, Rebecca Jean; m. Ann Clymer Taylor, July 15, 1988 (div. May 1996); Clark Clymer Taylor, Katy Ann Taylor; m. Katherine Call Emch, Dec. 28, 1996. BSEd, Tex. Christian U., 1958; MEd, U. N. Tex., 1967, EdD, 1969. Lic. psychologist Ohio, Nat. Drug Edn. Leadership Tng. Adelphi U., 1970. Machinist Chance Vaught Aircraft, Grand Prairie, Tex., 1957-58; 5th grade tchr., jr. high coach Ft. Worth Christian Schs., 1958-59; 6th grade tchr., jr. high coach Corpus Christi (Tex.) Ind. Sch. Dist., 1959-60; youth, music, edni. min. Norton St. Ch. Christ, Corpus Christi, 1960-61, Procter St. Ch. Christ, Port Arthur, Tex., 1963-65; min. Cameron (Tex.) Ch. Christ, 1961-63; high sch. English tchr. Christian Schs., Inc., Dallas, 1965-66; psychology instr. Tex. Women's U., Denton, 1968-69; sr. rsch. assoc., dir. psychology dept. Ednl. Rsch. Coun. Am., Cleve., 1969-78; clin. psychologist pvt. practice Cleve., 1978—. Faculty dept. guidance anc counseling U. Oreg. Workshop, Frankfurt, German, 1972; Ea. U.S. drug abuse task force Am. Soc. Health Assn., N.Y.C., 1971-73; chmn. drug abuse and alcoholism task force Fedn. Cmty. Planning, Cleve., 1970-71; adv. bd. Freedom House Rehab. Ctr., Cleve., 1993—; adj. assoc. prof. ednl. specialists Cleve. State U., 1970-74; mem. med. staff St. John Westshore Hosp., West Lake, Ohio, Fairview Hosp., Cleve. Author: Social Isolation and Personality, 1973, Handy Asks the Psychologist, 1974, (tchr. manual) Human Persons and Use of Psychoactive Agents, 1974; co-author: (tchr. manual) New Model Me: Operator's Guide to Coping with Aggression, 1974; contbr. articles to profl. jours. R & D grantee NIMH, Washington, 1974-78, Nat. Def. Edn. Rsch. Tng. grantee U.S. Dept. Edn., Washington, 1965-69. Mem. APA, Cleve. Psychol. Assn. (bd. trustees 1981-85), Cleve. Acad. Consulting Psychologists (pres. 1984-86), Ohio Psychol. Assn. (bd. trustees 1978—), Phi Delta Kappa. Avocations: computers, golf, jet boating. Office: 3865 Rocky River Dr Ste 2 Cleveland OH 44111-4114 Office Phone: 216-251-5161. Personal E-mail: emyersbvoh@aol.com.

MYERS, HECTOR, psychology professor, department chairman; AA in Behavioral Sci., Canal Zone Coll., Panama, 1966; BA in Psychology cum laude, Claremont Men's Coll., 1969, MA in Psychology, UCLA, 1971, PhD in Clin. Psychology, 1974. Dir. children's early identification program Ctrl. City Cmty. Mental Health Ctr., 1973—76; asst. prof. psychology UCLA, 1974—81, assoc. prof. psychology, 1981—92, dir. minority health tng. program, 1983—93, prof. psychology, 1993—, chmn. clin. psychology; dir. rsch. & scholar-in-residence, Fanon R&D Ctr. Charles R. Drew Postgraduate Med. Sch., 1975—85; dir. behavioral lab., dept. psychology Charles R. Drew U. Medicine and Sci., 1985—93, prof. psychiatry, 1993—, dir. rsch., ctr. on ethnicity, health and behavior, 1993—. Contbr. articles to profl. jours. Grantee, NIH Nat. Inst. Mental Health. Fellow. APA. Office: UCLA Dept Psychology 1285 Franz Hall Box 951563 Los Angeles CA 90095-1563 Office Phone: 310-825-1813. Business E-Mail: myers@psych.ucla.edu.

MYERS, JEFF L., surgeon; b. Lawton, Okla., Nov. 11, 1964; s. Lawrence Joseph and Rita Joyce Myers; m. Dahri Anna Zenker, Sept. 3, 1989; children: Connor Joseph, Cameron Marie, Tyler Gustave. MD with distinction, U. Okla., Okla. City, 1991; PhD, Georgetown U., DC, 2006. Diplomate Am. Bd. Surgery, 2002, Am. Bd. Thoracic Surgery, 2003. Chief pediatric cardiac surgery Tulane U., New Orleans, 2003—05, Lebonheur Children's Med. Ctr., Memphis, 2005—07, Mass. Gen. Hosp., 2007—10; assoc. prof. surgery Harvard Med. Sch., 2007—10; assoc. residency dir., cardiac surgery Mass. Gen. Hosp.; med. dir. Genzyme Corp., 2009—11; sr. dir. Giead Sciences, 2011—. Dir. cardiac surg. rsch. Tulane U., 2003—05; vis. prof. surgery UCLA, 2006. Editor: (web-based textbook) E-medicine, Textbook of Pediatrics, 2005; author: articles, book chpts. Bd. govs. Operation Mend-a-Heart, New Orleans, 2004—05; mem. Children's Heartlink, Rochester, Minn., 2005. Recipient Pfizer Prize, Wash. Soc. History of Medicine, 1999. Fellow: ACS (Zehner Travelling fellowship 1999); mem.: Am. Physiol. Soc., Am. Coll. Cardiology, Internat. Soc. for Heart and Lung Transplantation, Soc. Thoracic Surgeons, Kappa Sigma (chpt. pres. 1986). Office: Mass Gen Hosp 55 Fruit St Cox 662 Boston MA 02114 Personal E-mail: myersjeff@yahoo.com.

MYERS, JONATHAN, ophthalmologist; BA in Chemistry magna cum laude, Princeton U., 1984—88; MD, U. Pa., 1988—92. Diplomate Am. Bd. Ophthalmology, 1997. Intern Kaiser Permanente Med. Ctr., Oakland, Calif., 1992—93; fellow glaucoma Duke Univ. Eye Ctr., Durham, NC, 1996—97; resident ophthalmology Wills Eye Hosp., Phila., 1993—96, co-chief resident, 1995—96, med. dir. 1st ann. cares conf., 2007; dir. 28th ann. glaucoma conf. Wills Eye Inst., 2007, dir. 29th ann. glaucoma conf., 2008. Mem. residency selection com. Wills Eye Hosp., 1995, mem. resident edn. com., 1995—96, 1999—, mem. new facility com., 1999—2002; mem. Wills Exec. Coun., 1995—96, Wills Med. Records Com., 1997—98; mem. ethics com. N. Penn Hosp., 1998—99; mem. shipman awards com. Wills Eye Hosp. Ann. Conf., 1999—2002; mem. basic and clin. sci. curriculum com. glaucoma sect. Am. Acad. of Ophthalmology, 2000—05, mem. online edn. com., 2000—05; assoc. examiner Am. Bd. of Ophthalmology, 2001, 2003—07, mentor examiner, 2006, mem. port panel, 2006—07. Co-author of numerous abstracts, of numerous publications. Grantee Pharmacia Research Fellowship grant, 2000. Mem.: AMA, Am. Glaucoma Soc. (mem. ann. meeting com. 2007—), Greater Phila. Ophthalmic Soc. (sec. treas. 2007—), Phila. Ophthalmic Club (sec. treas. 2006—), Assn. for Rsch. in Vision and Ophthalmology, Pa. Acad. of Ophthalmology, Am. Acad. of Ophthalmology (Achievement award 2004). Office: Wills Eye Institute 840 Walnut St Ste 1110 Philadelphia PA 19107 Office Phone: 215-928-3197.

MYERS, LAWRENCE STANLEY, JR., retired radiation biologist; b. Memphis, Apr. 29, 1919; s. Lawrence Stanley and Jane Myers; m. Janet Vanderwalker, June 13, 1942; children: David Lee, Frederick Lawrence, Lee Scott. BS, U. Chgo., 1941, PhD, 1949. Jr. chemist Metall. Lab. of Manhattan Engring. Dist. U. Chgo., 1942—44; asst. chemist Clinton Labs. Manhattan Engring. Dist., Oak Ridge, Tenn., 1944—46; chemist Inst. Nuc. Studies U. Chgo., 1947—48; assoc. chemist Argonne Nat. Lab., Lemont, Ill., 1948—52; assoc. rsch. phys. chemist Atomic Energy project UCLA, 1952—59, asst. prof. radiology, 1953—70, lectr. in radiol. scis., 1970—76, adj. prof. radiol. scis., 1976—82; rsch. radiobiologist, chief radiobiology div. UCLA Lab. Nuclear Medicine and Radiation Biology, 1959—76; prof. radiology and nuclear medicine Uniformed Svcs. U. Health Scis., Bethesda, Md., 1982—88; sci. advisor Armed Forces Radiobiology Rsch. Inst., Bethesda, 1982—87; cons. Oak Ridge Assoc. Univs., 1987—94; adj. biophysicist radiation biology br. Nat. Cancer Inst. NIH, Bethesda, 1993—2007; ret., 2007. Vis. scientist AFRRI, 1987-93; co-organizer UCLA Internat. Conf. on Radiation Biology, 1957, 59; participant in three major Fed. Govt. planning exercises related to energy rsch. and devel. in U.S., 1973-74; mem. adv. com. Ctr. Fast Kinetic Rsch. U. Tex., Austin, 1975-81, chmn., 1977-81; mem. adv. bd. Radiation Chemistry Data Ctr., U. Notre Dame, 1976-84, sec. 1979-81, chmn. 1981-83; chmn. Long Range Planning Com., Radiation Rsch. Soc., 1976-78; dir. Issues and Requirements Workshop Analysis of 1976 Inventory of Fed. Energy Related Environ. and Safety Rsch., 1977. Contbr. more than 100 sci. articles and abstracts to profl. jours. Com. mem. Boy Scouts of Am., Pacific Palisades and Malibu, Calif., 1956-67. Fellow AAAS; mem. Radiation Rsch. Soc., N.Y. Acad. Sci., Soc. for Free Radical Biology and Medicine, Sigma Xi. Home: 11810 Coldstream Dr Potomac MD 20854-3612 E-mail: larrymyers@earthlink.net.

MYERS, MARILYN GLADYS, pediatric hematologist, oncologist; b. Lyons, Nebr., July 17, 1930; d. Leonard Clarence and Marian N. (Manning) M.; m. Paul Frederick Motzkus, July 24, 1957 (dec. Aug. 1982). BA cum laude, U. Omaha, 1954; MD, U. Nebr., 1959. Diplomate Am. Bd. Pediat. Intern Orange County Gen. Hosp., Orange, Calif., 1959-60, resident, 1960-62; fellow in hematology/oncology Orange County Gen. Hosp./Children's Hosp. L.A., 1962-64; assoc. in rsch., chief dept. hematology/oncology Children's Hosp., Orange, 1964-80, dir. outpatient dept., 1964-73, assoc. dir. leukapheresis unit, 1971-80; clin. practice hematology, oncology, rheumatology Orange, 1964-80; instr. Coll. Medicine U. Calif., Irvine, 1968-71, asst. clin. prof. pediatrics, 1971—; pvt. practice hematology, oncology, rheumatology Santa Ana, Calif., 1980—. Clin. rschr. exptl. drugs. Contbr. articles to med. jours. Med. adv. com. Orange County Blood Bank Hemophiliac Found. Grantee Am. Leukemia Soc., 1963, Am. Heart Assn., 1964. Fellow Am. Acad. Pediat.; mem. AMA, Calif. Med. Assn., LA County Med. Assn., Orange County Med. Assn., Orange County Pediat. Soc., Southwestern Pediat. Soc., LA Pediat. Soc., Internat. Coll. Pediat., Orange County Oncologic Soc., Am. Heart Assn. (Cardiopulmonary Coun.). Republican. Methodist. Avocation: reading. Office: 2220 E Fruit St Ste 217 Santa Ana CA 92701-4459 Office Phone: 714-541-3393, 714-541-3343, 714-541-8830.

MYERS, NEELY ANNE LAURENZO, anthropologist, educator; b. Piqua, Ohio, Nov. 28, 1979, BA, U. Va., 2001; PhD, U. Chgo., 2009. Rsch. assoc. U. Va., 2009; adj. prof. clin. rsch. Georgetown U., 2011—. Rsch. asst. Harvard U., 2002; lectr. U. Chgo., 2005; postdoc. fellow Nat. Ctr. Complementary & Alternative Medicine, 2009. Recipient Luhrmann award, Stanford U. Mem.: Soc. Psychol. Anthropology, Soc. Med. Anthropology, Am. Anthrop. Assn. Avocation: cooking. Office: 2215 Wis Ave NW Washington DC 20007 Personal E-mail: neelymyers@gmail.com.

MYERS, PHILLIP WARD, retired otolaryngologist; b. Evanston, Ill., Nov. 11, 1939; s. R. Maurice and Vivian (Ward) M.; m. Lynetta Sargent, Dec. 22, 1963; children: Andrea, Ward, Alycia, Amanda, Andrew. BS, Western Ill. U., 1961; MD, U. Ill., 1965. Diplomate: Am. Bd. Otolaryngology. Intern St. Paul-Ramsey Hosp., 1965-66; resident in otolaryngology U. Louisville, 1966-68; resident Northwestern U., 1968-70, fellow, 1970-71; practice medicine specializing in otolaryngology Springfield, Ill., 1973—; clin. prof. otolaryngology Southern Ill. U., Springfield, 1973—2008. Served to maj. M.C. AUS, 1971-73. Fellow Am. Soc. for Head and Neck Surgery, Am. Acad. Facial Plastic and Reconstructive Surgery; ACS, Am. Acad. Otolaryngology-Head and Neck Surgery. Achievements include research in perilymphatic fistulas. Home: 3423 N Oak Hill Rd Rochester IL 62563-9273 *

MYERSON, ROBERT J., radiologist, educator; b. Boston, May 12, 1947; s. Richard Louis and Rosemarie M.; m. Carla Wheatley, Aug. 8, 1970; 1 child, Jacob Wheatley. BA, Princeton U., 1969; PhD, U. Calif., Berkeley, 1974; MD, U. Miami, 1980. Diplomate Am. Bd. Radiology. Asst. prof. dept. physics Pa. State U., State Coll., 1974-76; fellow Inst. Advanced Studies, Princeton, NJ, 1976-78; resident U. Pa. Hosp., Phila., 1981-84; assoc. prof. radiology Washington U. Sch. Medicine, St. Louis, 1984-97; prof. radiation oncology Wash. U. Sch. Medicine, St. Louis, 1997—. Contbr. articles to profl. jours. Recipient Career Devel. award Am. Cancer Soc., 1985. Fellow Am. Coll. Radiology; mem. Am. Coll. Radiation, Am. Soc. Therapeutic Radiologists, Am. Phys. Soc. Democrat. Jewish. Avocation: bicycling. Office: Washington U Radiation Oncology Ctr Box 8224 4921 Parkview Pl Saint Louis MO 63110-1001 Office Phone: 314-362-8516. Business E-Mail: rmyerson@radonc.wustl.edu.

MYHREN, HILDE, physician; b. Bærum, Norway, Mar. 31, 1971; Degree in Medicine, U. Oslo, 1997, PhD, 2010. Physician Oslo U. Hosp., 2002—. Mem.: Den norske legeforening. Office: Kirkeveien 166 Oslo 0477 Norway Business E-Mail: himy@uus.no.

MYINT, AYE MU, neuroscientist, physician; d. Ohn and Aye Myint. MBBS, Myanmar Med. Coun., 1987; MD, U. Maastricht, Netherlands, PhD, 2007. Rsch. scientist Advanced Practical Diagnostics n.v., Turnhout, Belgium, 2006—, Ludwig-Maximilians U., Munich, 2007—. Sec. Sect. Immunology and Psychiatry, WPA, 2009—. Mem.: ASPET, ISTRY, PNIRS, CINP. Achievements include patents for psychiatric biomarkers; first to propose neurodegeneration hypothesis of depression and emphasize the role of tryptophan metabolism in depression. Office Phone: 498951603433. Business E-Mail: ayemu.myint@med.uni-muenchen.de, ayemu.myint@apdia.be.

MYLLYLÄ, VALTTERI, physician; b. Oulu, Finland, Sept. 17, 1936; s. Leevi Benjamin and Siiri Ellen (Toivonen) M.; m. Marjatta Keskuoja, May 25, 1948; children: Karoliina, Ulriika, Hannele, Juliaana, Birgitta, Henriika, Charlotta, Angelika. Lic. in medicine, U. Helsinki, Finland, 1963; specialist in radiology, U. Oulu, Finland, 1974, D Med. Science and Surgery, 1980, Docent in Radiology, 1984; competant as prof., U. Kuopio, Finland, 1989, U. Tampere, 1991. Mcpl., city physician Haapajärvi, Lahti, Kuhmalahti, Finland, 1963-67; gen. practitioner Oulu, 1968-70; house officer U. Cen. Hosp., Oulu, 1970-73, specialist, 1974-90, asst. sr. physician, 1990-95, sr. physician, 1995-99. Cons. radiologist Pub. Health Care, Hyrynsalmi, Finland, 1977-2005, Finland, 1983-2000, Dr. Centrum Plasma, Raahe, Finland, 1990-2004, Dr. Centrum Kirurgi-paivelu, Tampere, Finland, 1990-2003, Västa Nylands Sjukhus, 2004. Author: (textbook) Radiologia, 1991, Vastra Nylands Sjukhus, 2004; contbr. articles to profl. jours. Elected employees' rep. Oulu U. Cen. Hosp., 1986-99; city councilman City of Oulu, 1969-72; mem. parish coun. Evangelical Lutheran Ch., Oulu-Karjasilta, 1995-2001. Med. sr. lt. Army of Finland, 1975. Mem. Evangelical Lutheran Ch. Avocations: fishing, history. Home: Taipaleentie 6 33900 Tampere Finland

MYSLINSKI, NORBERT RAYMOND, medical educator; b. Buffalo, Apr. 14, 1947; s. Bernard and Amelia Joan (Lesniak) M.; m. Patricia Ann Byrne, June 19, 1970 (dec. 1980); m. René Carter, Nov. 21, 1993; children: Matthew Ryan, Kelly Lynn. BS in Biology, Canisius Coll., Buffalo, NY, 1969; PhD in Pharmacology, U. Ill., Chgo., 1973. Rsch. assoc. Tufts U., Boston, 1973—75; asst. prof. U. Md., Balt., 1975—80, assoc. prof. physiology, 1980—, co-dir. Facial Pain Clinic, 1980—84, instr. nursing, 1982—84; rsch. fellow U. Bristol, England, 1984—85; adj. assoc. prof. U. Md. Sch. Nursing, 1997—; adj. prof., psychology dept. Stevenson U., 2008—; content cons. Walden U., 2008—. Instr. C.C. Balt., 1980—82; dir. grad. program dept. physiology U. Md., 1981—97, mem. faculty Marine-Estuarine Environ. Scis. grad. program, 1988—97, dir. HS biomedical rsch. program, 2000—; founder, dir. Patricia Byrne Nursing Scholarship Fund Trocaire Coll., Buffalo, 1985; dir. NIH Minority Rsch. Apprentice Program Balt. Coll. Dental Surgery, 1988—; mem. grant rev. com. Nat. Inst. Nursing Rsch., 1993—94; grant reviewer Dept. Health and Human Svcs., 1993—94; cons. in field; founder, dir. Internat. Brain Bee, 1999—; chmn. Neuroscience Edn. Workshop, Prague, Czech Republic, 2003. Editor newsletters Med. Soc. Md. Rsch., 1977-82, Brain Storm, 1999-2005; mem. editl. bd. Jour. Environ. Neurosci. and Biomedicine; author book chpts., revs. and numerous abstracts on pharmacology and neurosci.; reviewer 7 jours; appeared on more than 20 live TV and radio programs Rep. task force on aging U. Md., 1979—84; instr. Am. Heart Assn., Balt., 1978, ARC, Balt., 1977—83; Internat. Co. Md. chpt. ARC, 2003—; com. mem. Md. Higher Edn. Edn. Commn., 2003—07; mem. Pres. Bush's Sec. of Edn. Summit on Sci., Washington, 2004; eucharistic min., pastoral visitor Cath. Ch., 1983—93; bd. dirs. Md. Brain Awareness Week, Md., 1996—, Balt. Brains Rule!, 2002—04, Md. Brain Lit. Competition, 2000—, Md. Brain Art Competition, 2000—; mem. ethics com. Govs. K-20 Edn. Council. Capt. US Army, 1969—77. Grantee NIH, others; USPHS fellow, 1969-73; recipient Alumni of Yr. award St. Mary's HS, Lancaster, NY, 1996, Disting. Alumni award outstanding career Canisius Coll., Buffalo, 1997, Time to Care Cmty. Svc. award U. Md., 1998, Founders Day Pub. Svc. award U. Md., 2000. Mem.: HS Neuroscience (founder 2003), Am. Soc. Pharmacology Exptl. Therapeutics, Soc. Neurosci. (pres. Balt. chpt. 2010—11, editor newsletter 1990—97, neuroscience literacy com. 1997—2001, treas. Balt. charter 2007—, Educator award 2007), Am. Physiol. Soc., Internat. Assn. Dental Rsch. (adv. 1980—81, brain awareness com. 2008—), Md. Soc. Med. Rsch. (exec. com. 1978—86, bd. dir. 1978—86), Internat. Brain Rsch. Orgn. (sch. bd. 2007—08), European Brain Behavior Soc. (hon.). Republican. Achievements include inventor in field; represented Maryland state in the USA National Senior Olympics in 2005 and 2007, 2009; competed in track and field. Home: 9395 Carric Way Ellicott City MD 21042-1701 Office: U Md Sch Dentistry Dept Neurosci 650 W Baltimore St Baltimore MD 21201-1510 Office Phone: 410-706-7258. Office Fax: 410-706-0193. Business E-Mail: nmyslinski@umaryland.edu.

NA, DONG HEE, pharmacist, educator; b. Seoul, Republic of Korea, Dec. 29, 1972; m. Eun Ji Park; 1 child, Yun Sung. BS, SungKyunKwan U., Suwon, Korea, 1996, MS, 1998, PhD, 2001. Registered pharmacist Ministry Health and Welfare, 1996. Postdoctoral rschr. coll. pharmacy SungKyunKwan U., 2001—02, U. Ky., Lexington, 2003—05; assoc. prof. coll. pharmacy Kyungsung U., Busan, Republic of Korea, 2005—. Assoc. editor Archives Pharmacal Rsch., 2010—. Contbr. articles to profl. jours. Mem.: Korean Soc. Pharm. Sci. and Tech., Pharm. Soc. Korea, Controlled Release Soc., Am. Assn. Pharm. Scientists. Achievements include development of peptide and protein delivery systems; PEGylation technology, microparticle delivery, and bioanalytical methods. Office: Kyungsung Univ Coll Pharmacy 314-79 Daeyeon-Dong Nam-Ku 608-736 Busan Republic of Korea Office Fax: 82-51-663-4809. Business E-Mail: dhna2@ks.ac.kr.

NABARRO, DAVID, public health service officer, infectious diseases physician; b. Aug. 26, 1949; m. Gillian Frances Holmes, 2002; 5 children. BA, Oxford U., MA in Animal Physiology and Biochemistry, 1970, MSc in Medicine, 1974, BM, BCh, 1974; MSc in Pub. Health, London U., 1979. Med. officer Relief Expedition Save the Children, Iraq, 1974—75, dist. child health officer Dhankuta Dist. Nepal, 1976—78; house officer to sr. house officer Nat. Health Svc., Hillingdon, Northampton, Oxford, England, 1975—77; lectr. nutrition and pub. health London U., 1980—82; regional mgr. Save the Children Fund, South Asia, 1982—85; sr. lectr. Internat. Cmty. Health Liverpool Sch. of Medicine, 1985—89; strategic adviser Health and Population in East Africa Overseas Devel. Adminstrn., UK Govt., Nairobi, 1989—90, chief health and population advisor, head Health and Population Div., 1990—97, co-coord. UK Govt. Relief for No. Iraq, 1991, dir. human devel., 1996—97; dir. human devel., chief heath and population advisor, head Health and Population Div. Dept. Internat. Devel., UK Govt., 1997—99; project mgr. Roll Back Malaria WHO, Geneva, 1999—2000, exec. dir. Office of Dir. Gen., 2000—02, exec. dir. sustainable devel., sr. policy advisor to dir. gen., 2002—03, rep. of dir. gen. for Health Action in Crises, 2003—05; asst. sec.-gen., sr. sys. coord. Avian and Human Influenza UN Devel. Group, NYC, 2005—; spl. rep. of sec. gen. on food security and nutrition UN, 2009—. Hon. cons. Mersey Regional Health Authority, 1985—89. Fellow: Royal Coll. of Physicians of London; mem.: Royal Coll. of Physicians, Faculty of Pub. Health Medicine. Office: UN Devel Group Devel Ops Coordination Office One UN Plaza DC1-1600 New York NY 10017 E-mail: david.nabarro@undp.org.

NABATIAN, SEPIDEH, physician; b. Tehran, Iran, July 9, 1971; MA, CUNY Queens Coll., 1995; MD, St. George's, 1999. Assoc. NY Med. Health Care P.C., 2006—. Fellow: ACC. Home: 155 Overlook Ave Great Neck NY 11021 Home Fax: 516-487-4352. Personal E-mail: snabatian@yahoo.com.

NABAVIZADEH, FATEMEH, cardiologist; b. Ghom, Iran, Sept. 14, 1973; PhD in Medicine, Iran Med. Scis., 1998. Prof., Iran, 1991; cardiologist Med. Care Hosp., 2006—. Fellow: Am. Coll. Cardiology. Office: Jumeirah 1 Dubai 2330 United Arab Emirates Personal E-mail: fatemenabavizadeh@yahoo.com.

NABEL, ELIZABETH GUENTHNER, hospital administrator, former federal agency administrator; b. 1952; BA summa cum laude, St. Olaf Coll., Northfield, Minn., 1974; student, Union Theol. Sem., NYC, Columbia U.; MD, Cornell U., Ithaca, NY, 1981; DSc (hon.), U. Leuven, Belgium, 2001, Mt. Sinai Sch. Medicine, NY, 2006, U. Glasgow, Scotland, 2008. Diplomate Am. Bd. Internal Medicine & Cardiovasc. Diseases. Intern/resident internal medicine Brigham & Women's Hosp.-Harvard Med. Sch., Boston, 1981—84, clin. rsch. fellow cardiovasc. divsn., 1984-87; asst. prof. internal medicine U. Mich., Ann Arbor, 1987-91, assoc. prof. internal medicine, 1991-94, dir. Cardiovasc. Rsch. Ctr., 1992—99, prof. internal medicine & physiology, 1994—99, dir. divsn. cardiology, 1997-99; sci. dir. clin. rsch. Nat. Heart, Lung & Blood Inst. (NHLBI), NIH, Bethesda, Md., 1999—2005, dir. NHLBI, 2005—09; pres. Brigham and Women's Hosp., Boston, 2010—. Mem. sci. adv. bd. Vical Inc., San Diego, 1992—96, Keystone Symposia, Silverthorne, Colo.; pres. N.Am. Vascular Biology Orgn., 1996—97; disting. vis. prof. Molecular Cardiology Rsch. Inst., Tufts-New Eng. Med. Ctr., 2004; physician-in-chief pro tempore, dept. internal medicine Brigham & Women's Hosp., 2006; Sampson vis. prof. U. Calif., LA, 2007; Bulfinch vis. prof. Mass. Gen. Hosp., Boston, 2008. Assoc. editor Jour. Clin. Investigation, 1997—2002, mem. editl. bd., 2002—05, New Eng. Jour. Medicine, 2001—, mem. bd. reviewing editors Science, 1998—2005; editor: Trends in Cardiovasc. Medicine, 2001; cons. editor Circulation, Circulation Rsch., Atherial Thrombosis & Vascular Biology, 2000—05; contbr. articles to profl. jours. Recipient Leadership award, Personalized Medicine Coalition, 2006, Vision & Advocacy award, Nat. Alliance Hispanic Health, 2007, Spl. Recognition award, Nat. Human Genome Rsch. Inst., 2008, WomenHeart's Wenger award for disting. leadership, 2008, Sci. Leadership award, Nat. Marfan Found., 2008; named one of The 100 Most Powerful Women in DC, Washingtonian mag., 2009. Fellow: Am. Coll. Cardiology, Am. Heart Assn. (bd. dirs. 1996—97, Russell Ross Meml. Lectureship in vascular biology 2005, Disting. Achievement award 2005, Eugene Braunwald Academic Mentorship award 2008); mem.: ACP, AAAS, Inst. Medicine (coun. mem.), Am. Acad. Arts & Sciences, Am. Soc. Gene Therapy (bd. dirs. 1996), Am. Soc. Investigative Pathology, Am. Fedn. Clin. Rsch., Am. Soc. Biochemistry & Molecular Biology (Amgen-Sci. Achievement award 1996), Assn. Am. Physicians, Am. Soc. Clin. Investigation, Alpha Omega Alpha, Phi Beta Kappa. Office: Brigham and Women's Hospital 75 Francis St Boston MA 02115 *

NABEL, GARY JAN, virologist; b. July 2, 1953; BA in Biochemistry magna cum laude, Harvard Coll., 1975; PhD in Cell and Devel. Biology, Harvard U., 1980, MD, 1982. Instr. biology Harvard U., Boston, 1980-81, resident tutor in biology, 1980-83, clin. fellow medicine, 1983-85; intern and resident in internal medicine Brigham and Women's Hosp., Boston, 1983-85; instr. Harvard Med. Sch., Boston, 1984-87; assoc. Howard Hughes Med. Inst., Whitehead Inst., MIT, Lab. David Baltimore, 1985-87; assoc. physician Brigham and Women's Hosp., 1985-87; asst. prof. internal medicine and biol. chemistry U. Mich., Ann Arbor, 1987-90, asst. investigator Howard Hughes Med. Inst., 1987-91, assoc. prof. internal medicine and biol. chemistry, 1990-93, assoc. investigator Howard Hughes Med. Inst., 1991-94, prof. internal medicine and biol. chemistry, 1993—, investigator Howard Hughes Med. Inst., 1994—, Henry Sewall prof., 1995—99; dir. Vaccine Rsch. Ctr. NIH, 1999—. Mem. AIDS rsch. adv. com. Nat. Inst. Allergy and Infectious Diseases, NIH. Contbr. articles to profl. jours. Fellow Dana-Farber Cancer Inst., Harvard U., 1980-84; Harvard Nat. scholar, 1971-75, Harvard Grad. Nat. scholar, 1976-82; recipient Mallinkrodt Book prize, 1975, James Tolbert Shipley prize for rsch. Harvard Med. Sch., 1982, Ofcl. citation Conn. State Gen. Assembly for Contbns. to Human Gene Therapy, 1992, Young Investigator award Midwest Am. Fedn. for Clin. Rsch., 1992, Amgen award Am. Soc. Biochemistry and Molecular Biology, 1996. Mem. Am. Soc. Clin. Investigation, Assn. Am. Physicians. Office: Vaccine Rsch Ctr 40 Convent Dr Bldg 40 Rm 4502 Bethesda MD 20892 E-mail: gnabel@nih.gov.

NACE, MORTON OLIVER, JR., human services manager; b. Tampa, Fla., June 30, 1937; s. Morton Oliver and Penelope Adele (Holland) N.; m. Eleanor Hart Moslow, June 27, 1964; children: Morton Oliver III, Jennifer Ann. BS, Boston U., 1964; MS, Syracuse U., 1974. Cert. literacy tutor Laubach Literacy Internat., Syracuse, NY, proliteracy tutor Rochester, NY. Exec. dir. Episcopal Diocese Chgo., 1964-70; dir. comm. Laubach Literacy Internat., Syracuse, N.Y., 1970-80; tng. and devel. specialist Rochester (N.Y.) Inst. Tech., 1980-96; adminstrv. asst., cons. City of Rochester, 1997—. Cons. tng. and orgn. devel., Rochester, 1982-98; facilitator retreats/tng. for new parish model The Apostle, 1990—; designer/presenter formats on discernment and daily ministry, 2000; asst. prof. Rochester Inst. Tech., Henrietta, N.Y., 1994; sales and consulting staff Human Resource Svcs., Rochester, 1995-97. Facilitator planning retreat City Coun. of Rochester, 1993; regional planning cons. Mayor-elect City Coun., Rochester, 1997, performance cons. and trainer, 1998—. With USAF, 1957-61. Mem. ASTD (Genesee Valley chpt., conf. presenter 1981-96), Profl. and Orgn. Devel. in Higher Edn. (nat. presenter on faculty/staff devel. 1993-96). Episcopalian. Avocations: photography, piano, physical exercise, history, travel. Home and Office: 2271 Westfall Rd Rochester NY 14618-3126

NACHAMKIN, IRVING, microbiologist, educator; b. NYC, Oct. 18, 1953; s. Gerald and Sandra (Reisman) Nachamkin; m. Diance C. Church, May 28, 1983. BSc, U. Bridgeport, 1975; MPH, U. NC, 1978, DPH, 1980. Cert. Am. Bd. Med. Microbiology. Postdoc. fellow in clin. microbiology Med. Coll. Va., Richmond, 1980—82; asst. prof. pathology and lab. medicine and microbiology Hosp. U. Pa., Phila., 1982—88, assoc. prof. pathology and lab. medicine, 1988—; assoc. dir. Clin. Microbiology Lab. Contbr. articles to profl. jours. Recipient Hon. Prof. award, Hebei Med. Sch., People's Republic of China. Mem.: Infectious Disease Soc. Am., Am. Soc. Microbiology. Office: Hosp U Pa Dept Pathology 3400 Spruce St # 4283 Philadelphia PA 19104-4206 E-mail: inachamkin@gmail.com.

NACHMAN, JAMES BURT, pediatric hematologist-oncologist; b. Chgo., 1948; MD, Johns Hopkins U., Balt., 1974. Cert. in pediat. 1979, in pediatric hematology-oncology 1980. Internship in pediat. Children's Meml. Hosp., Chgo., 1974—75, residency in pediat., 1975—77, fellowship, 1977—79; residency in pediatric hematol. oncology Wylers Children's Hosp., Chgo., 1979—80, hosp. appointment; prof. pediat., dir. clin. programs, hematology/oncology U. Chgo. Comer Children's Hosp. Contbr. articles to profl. jours. including the New Eng. Jour. Medicine. Mem.: Am. Soc. Hematology, Am. Soc. Pediatric Hematology Oncology, Children's Oncology Group (mem. acute lymphoblastic leukemia and Hodgkin's disease study com.), Internat. Ponte de Legno (co-founder internat. acute lymphoblastic leukemia study com.), Nat. Cancer Inst. (mem. PDQ bd. pediatric cancer). Office: Univ Chgo Comer Children's Hosp 5841 S Maryland Ave MC 4060 Chicago IL 60637 Office Phone: 773-702-6808. Office Fax: 773-702-9881. Business E-Mail: jnachman@peds.bsd.uchicago.edu.

NACKEL, JOHN GEORGE, health venture capital executive; b. Medford, Mass., Nov. 4, 1951; s. Michael and Josephine (Maria) N.; m. Gail Helen Becker, Oct. 30, 1976; children: Melissa Anne, Allison Elizabeth. BS, Tufts U., 1973; MS in Pub. Health and Indsl. Engring., U. Mo., 1975, PhD, 1977. Sr. mgr. Ernst & Young, Chgo., 1977—83; nat. dir. health care cons. Cleve., 1983—87; regional dir. health industry svcs., 1987—91; mng. dir. health care Ernst & Young, Cleve., 1991—93; mng. dir. Health Consulting, LA, 1993—99, New Ventures, 1999—2000; CEO, Sogeti USA, LLC, 2000—01; chmn., CEO, Sértan Corp., Santa Fe Springs, Calif., 2002—03; exec. v.p. US Tech., Beverly Hills, Calif., 2003—05; pres., COO Salick Cardiovascular Ctrs., 2006—07; CEO Three Sixty Group, 2007—09, Ingenix Cons., 2009—. Author: Cost Management for Hospitals, 1987 (Am. Hosp. Assn. book award 1988); mem. editl bd. Jour. Med. Systems, 1983-; contbr. articles to profl. jours Grantee Dept. Health Edn. Welfare, Washington, 1973-76. Fellow Am. Coll. Healthcare Execs., Healthcare Info. and Mgmt. Systems Soc. (articles award); mem. Inst. Indsl. Engrs. (sr.), U. Mo. Health Svcs. Mgmt. Alumni Assn. (pres.), L.A. Country Club, Annandale Golf Club. Republican. Avocations: golf, tennis, squash, paddle, photography. Home: 666 Linda Vista Ave Pasadena CA 91105-1145 Office Phone: 818-484-9063. Personal E-mail: jnackel@360ag.com.

NADAS, JOHN ADALBERT, psychiatrist, educator; b. Innsbruck, Austria, Mar. 14, 1949; arrived in U.S., 1950; s. Julius Zoltan and Ibolya Erzsebet (Szöllösy) Nadas; m. Gabriella Ilona Ormay, Apr. 11, 1981; children: János, Miklós, István. BA, Case We. Res. U., 1970; MD, Duke U., 1974. Resident in psychiatry U. Chgo., 1974—77; pvt. practice Munster, Ind., 1977—84, Canton, Ohio, 1984—; instr. psychiatry Northeastern Ohio U. Coll. Medicine, Rootstown, 1985—86, asst. prof., 1986; coord. psychiat. edn. Mercy Med. Ctr., Canton, 1985—87, clin. dir. psychiat. svcs., 1990-91. Cons. Crisis Ctr., Canton, 1985—92. Author: Philosophical Basis of Depth Psychotherapy, 1983, Journey Toward Energy, 1995, Transformation, 1999, (book) Sweet Nonexistence, 2006. Trustee Sisters of Charity Found., Canton, 1996—2003. Named NCAA nat. collegiate epee champion, 1970; named to All-Am. Fencing Team, 1969, 1970. Mem.: AMA, Am. Psychiat. Assn., Hungarian Assn. (pres. 2000—). Roman Catholic. Avocations: basketball, computer programming. Office: 1330 Mercy Dr NW Ste 320 Canton OH 44708-2624 Office Phone: 330-489-1495.

NADELSON, CAROL COOPERMAN, psychiatrist, educator; b. Bklyn., Oct. 13, 1936; children: Robert, Jennifer. BA magna cum laude, Bklyn. Coll., 1957; MD with honors, U. Rochester, NYC, 1961. Dir. med. student edn. Beth Israel Hosp., Boston, 1974-79, psychiatrist, 1977; assoc. prof. psychiatry Harvard U. Med. Sch., Boston, 1976-79; rsch. scholar Radcliffe Coll., Cambridge, Mass., 1979-80; prof. psychiatry Tufts Med. Sch., Boston, 1979-95; vice-chmn., dir. tng. and edn. dept. psychiatry Tufts-New Eng. Med. Ctr., Boston, 1979-93; prof. psychiatry Harvard Med. Sch., Boston; psychiatrist Brigham and Women's Hosp., Boston, dir., office for women's careers, 1998. Cons. Peace Corps, 2000. Editor: The Woman Patient, Vols. 1, 2 and 3, 1978, 82; Treatment Interventions in Human Sexuality, 1983; Marriage and Divorce: A Contemporary Perspective, 1984, Women Physicians in Leadership Roles, 1986, Training Psychiatrists for the '90s, 1987, Treating Chronically Mentally Ill Women, 1988, Family Violence, 1988, Women and Men: New Perspectives on Gender Differences, 1990, International Review of Psychiatry Vols. 1 & 2, 1993, 96, Major Psychiatric Disorders, 1982, The Challenge of Change: Perspectives on Family, Work and Education, 1983; editor-in-270 articles to profl. jours.; chpts. to books. Trustee Menninger Found., 1988—. Recipient Gold Medal award Mt. Airy Psychiat. Ctr., 1981, award Case Western Res. U., 1983, Elizabeth Blackwell award Am. Med. Women's Assn., 1985, Women in Medicine Leadership Devel. award Am. Assn. Med. Colls., 1999, Alexandra Symonds award 2002; Picker Found. grant, 1982-83. Fellow: Am. Acad. Arts & Scis. (Renaissance Woman award 2009), Am. Psychiat. Assn. (pres. 1985—86, Seymour D. Vestermark award 1992, Disting. Svc. award 1995), Ctr. Advanced Study Behavioral Scos.; mem.: AMA (impaired physicians com. 1984, Sidney Cohen award 1988), Group for Advancement of Psychiatry (bd. dirs. 1984, pres. 2002—04), Am. Coll. Psychiatrists (bd. regents 1991—94, Disting. Svc. award 1989), Phi Beta Kappa, Alpha Omega Alpha. Avocation: travel. Office: Brigham and Women's Hosp 75 Francis St Boston MA 02119 Home: 50 Longwood Ave 1114 Brookline MA 02446 Business E-Mail: carol_nadelson@hms.harvard.edu.

NADELSON, SANDRA G., nursing educator, student services director; m. Louis Nadelson. MSN, MEd, Calif. State U., LA, 1990; PhD, U. Nev., Las Vegas, 2007. RN Calif., 1984. Faculty mem. CC of S. Nev., Las Vegas, 2002—04, U. Nev. Las Vegas, 2005—07, Boise State U., 2008—. Mem.: MENSA, Sigma Theta Tau (assoc.; sec. 2005—06). Office: 1910 University Dr Boise ID 83725 Home: 2915 N 32nd St Boise ID 83703 Business E-Mail: sandranadelson@boisestate.edu.

NADERI, SHERVIN, plastic surgeon; B in Psychology, minor in Chemistry, Boston U., M in Med. Sciences; MD, Drexel U.(formerly Med. Coll. Pa - Hahneman U. Sch. of Medicine). Diplomate Am. Bd. Facial Plastic and Reconstructive Surgery (ABFPRS), Am. Bd. Otolaryngology, Am. Bd. Medical Specialties. Intern gen. surgery Ind. Univ. Sch. of Medicine, resident otolaryngology - head and neck surgery, clin. assoc. prof. facial plastic surgery; fellow facial plastics and reconstructive surgery under Dr. Stephen Perkins Meridian Plastic Surgery Ctr.; pvt. practice The Naderi Ctr. For Cosmetic Surgery and Skin Care. Med. bd. examiner ABFPRS; guest lectr. dept. of surgery Sch. of Medicine George Washington Univ. Author multiple chpts. in major facial plastic surgery and head and neck surgery textbooks on nose surgery and facelift surgery techniques, multiple med. papers. Fellow: ACS; mem.: Am. Acad. of Facial and Reconstructive Surgery (past pres., officer). Office: The Naderi Center Rhinoplasty and Cosmetic Surgery 297 Herndon Pky Ste 101 Herndon VA 20170 also: 5454 Wisconsin Ave Ste 1655 Chevy Chase MD 20815 Office Phone: 703-481-0002, 301-222-2020. *

NADLER, HENRY LOUIS, pediatrician, educator, geneticist; b. NYC, Apr. 15, 1936; s. Herbert and Mary (Kartiganer) N.; m. Benita Weinhard, June 16, 1957; children: Karen, Gary, Debra, Amy. AB, Colgate U., 1957; MD, Northwestern U., 1961; MS, U. Wis., 1965. Diplomate Am. Bd. Pediatrics, Am. Bd. Med. Genetics. Intern NYU Med. Ctr., 1961-62, sr. resident pediatrics, 1962-63, chief resident, 1963-64; teaching asst. NYU Sch. Medicine, 1962-63, clin. instr., 1963-64, U. Wis. Sch. Medicine, 1964-65; practice medicine specializing in pediatrics Chgo., 1965—; fellow Children's Meml. Hosp. dept. pediatrics Northwestern U., 1964-65; assoc. in pediatrics Northwestern U. Med. Sch., 1965-66, asst. prof., 1967-68, assoc. prof., 1968-70, prof., 1970-81, chmn. dept. pediatrics, 1970-81; prof. Northwestern U. Med. Sch. (Grad. Sch.), 1971-80; mem. staff Children's Meml. Hosp., 1965-81, head div. genetics, 1969-81, chief of staff, 1970-81; dean, prof. pediatrics, ob-gyn Wayne State U. Med. Sch., Detroit, 1981-88; prof. U. Chgo., 1988-89, U. Ill., 1989—; pres. Michael Reese Hosp. and Med. Ctr., Chgo., 1988-91; market med. dir. Aetna Health Plans, Phoenix, 1993-94, mktg. v.p., CEO, 1994-95; v.p. managed care/physician integration, med. dir. Am. Healthcare Sys., San Diego, 1995. Mem. vis. staff, div. medicine Northwestern Meml. Hosp., 1972-81; staff Children's Hosp. of Mich., 1981-88. Mem. editl. bd. Comprehensive Therapy, 1973-84, Am. Jour. Human Genetics, 1979-83, Pediatrics in Rev., 1980-83, Am. Jour. Diseases of Children, 1983-91; contbr. articles to profl. jours. Recipient E. Mead Johnson award for pediatric rsch., 1973, Meyer O. Cantor award for Disting. Svc. Internat. Coll. Surgeons, 1987; Irene Heinz Given and John La Porte Given rsch. prof. pediatrics, 1970-81. Fellow Am. Acad. Pediatrics; mem. Am. Soc. for Clin. Investigation, Am. Soc. Human Genetics, Am. Pediatric Soc., Soc. for Pediatric Rsch., Midwest Soc. for Pediatric Rsch., Pan Am. Med. Assn., Alpha Omega Alpha. Home and Office: 17720 Camino de La Mitra PO Box 3665 Rancho Santa Fe CA 92067-3665 Personal E-mail: hlnadler@aol.com.

NADTOCHIY, ANDREY G., radiologist, researcher; b. Moscow, Oct. 30, 1956; s. Guennadi and Alla Nadtochiy; m. Irina Chapochnik; 1 child, Guennadi Nadtotchi. MD, Moscow Med. Stomatological Inst., 1979, PhD, 1985, Moscow State Medico-Stomatological U., 1995. Asst. prof. Moscow Med. Stomatological Inst., 1982—95; prof. Moscow State Medico-Stomatological U., 1996—2001; professor, leading scientist dept. child cranio-facial surgery Ctrl. Sci. Rsch. Inst. Stomatology, Moscow, 2002—07, diagnostic chief, 2007—09; chief radiol. dept Clin. Hosp. No 85, Moscow. Cons. Moscow State Medico-Stomatological U., 1992—. Co-author: Ultrasound Diagnostics in Children Surgery, 1997, Ultrasound Diagnostics in Pediatrics, 2001, Ultrasound Diagnostics Guidebook, 2003, Ultrasound Normal and Variant Anatomy in Children, 2007, Ultrasound Anatomy of Healthy Child, 2009, Radiological Diagnostics in Stomatology, 2010; mem. editl. bd.: Ultrasound and Functional Diagnostics. Pres. Charity Fund Healthy Child, Moscow, 1999. Avocations: sports, fishing, travel. Personal E-mail: naggan@mail.ru.

NAES, JENNIFER LE, medical technologist; d. Jackie Mare. BS in Clin. Lab. Sci., SUNY, Stonybrook, 2002; M in Forensic Scis., Nat. U., San Diego, 2004. Cert. med. technologist Am. Soc. Clin. Pathology, 2003, lic. Fla., 2005. Med. technologist Boca Raton Cmty. Hosp., Fla., 2006—, point of care coord., 2006—. Mem.: Pi Delta Chi (assoc.).

NAFE, REINHOLD, neuropathologist; b. Mainz, Germany, July 14, 1959; s. Reinhold and Elfriede (Henrici) N. MD, Gutenberg U., 1985; PhD, U. Clinics, Frankfurt, 2001. Cert. in professorship U. Clinics, Frankfurt. Mil. physician NATO, Tongeren, Belgium, 1986—87; rschr. dept. urology Duren Hosp., Germany, 1987—88; rschr. dept. pathology U. Hannover Med. Sch., Germany, 1989—96, rschr. dept. neuropathology, 1996—97, U. Clinics, Frankfurt, Germany, 1997—. Mem. German Soc. Cytology, European Soc. Pathology, German Soc. Pathology, German Soc. Neuropathology. Office: Univ Clinics Dept Neuroradiology Schleusenweg 2-16 60528 Frankfurt Main Germany Business E-Mail: r.nafe@em.uni-frankfurt.de.

NAFOURI, NASHAT, quality assurance professional; Post Grad. Diploma in biotechnology, BC Inst. Tech., 1996—98; BSc in med. tech., King Abdulaziz U., 1987—91; PhD in Bus. Adminstrn., WIU, 2005. Clinical Laboratory Scientist The Nat. Credentialing Agy., USA, 1994. Lab. services qi mgr. King AbdulAziz Med. City, Jeddah, Saudi Arabia, 2002—; mktg. mgr. Viridae Clin. Sciences, Inc., Vancouver, Canada, 2000—01, clin. lab. rschr., 1998—2000; liason lab. safety officer King Abdulaziz Med. City, Jeddah, Saudi Arabia, 2002—; safety officer Viridae Clin. Sciences, Inc., Vancouver, Canada, 1998—2002; med. lab. technologist King Abdulaziz U. Hosp., Jeddah, Saudi Arabia, 1992—95. Cons. Nafouri Intellectual Property, Jeddah, Saudi Arabia, 2002—, Healthcare Interest group, Saudi Arabian Quality Coun., Jeddah, Saudi Arabia, 2002—; registered cap insp. Coll. of Am. Pathologist, Middle East and Asia, 2002—; trainee quality sys. assessor Am. Assn. of Blood Bank (AABB), 2003—; coord. safety com. King Abdulaziz Med. City-WR, Jeddah, Western Region, Saudi Arabia; owner and pres. MediLogic, Vancouver, Canada; spkr. in field. Contbr. articles to profl. jours. First job in Sci., NRC, 1998. Mem.: Bus. Intelligence Forum, Drug Info. Assn., Internat. Soc. for Antiviral Rsch., Am. Soc. of Clin. Lab. Sciences, BC for Lab. Sciences, BC Biotech, Am. Soc. for Microbiology, Saudi Arabian Coun. for Quality. Achievements include development of type specific Western Blot Assay for detecting herpes 1&2 in human serum; participated with Viridae team in many multination clinical trails for herpes, hepatitis B & C and HIV; passed with Viridae team many Good Laboratory Practices and Good Clinical Practices audits; design of many standard operating procedures (SOPs) in molecular assays, safety and quality. Avocations: travel, photography, fishing, skiing. Office: King Abdulaziz Med City Mekkah-Jeddah Hwy Exit 23 PO Box 9515 Jeddah 21423 Saudi Arabia Personal E-mail: nafourin@ngha.med.sa, n_nafouri@yahoo.com.

NAFTOLIN, FREDERICK, gynecologist, scientist, educator; b. Bronx, NY, Apr. 7, 1936; s. Nathan and Jean (Pesacov) N.; children: Michael Eugene, Joshua Joseph; m. Marcie Myerson, Nov. 1, 1987. AA, UCLA, 1957; BA with honors, U. Calif., Berkeley, 1958; MD with honors, U. Calif., San Francisco, 1961; DPhil, U. Oxford, 1970. Intern King County Hosp., Seattle, 1961-62; resident in ob-gyn

UCLA, 1962-66; asst. chief gynecology, reproductive endocrine fellow USPHS, Seattle, 1966-68; NIH fellow Oxford U., England, 1968-70; asst. prof. ob-gyn U. Calif., San Diego Sch. Medicine, 1970-73; assoc. prof. ob-gyn Harvard Med. Sch., 1973-75; prof., chmn. dept. ob-gyn McGill Faculty Medicine, Montreal, 1975-78, Yale Med. Sch., New Haven, 1978-2000, prof. debt. ob-gyn., 1978—2005, prof. dept. biology, 1983—2005; dir. Yale U. Ctr. for Rsch. in Reproductive Biology, 1986—2005, head reproductive neurosci. unit, 2000—03; rsch. prof. dept. ob-gyn. NYU, 2006—, dir. rsch. in reproductive biology, 2006—, adj. assoc. prof., Coll. Dentistry. Co-dir., Inter-disciplinary Prog., Menopausal Medicine, 2007; med. dir. PEARL Network NYU Coll. Dentistry, 2009-; vis. prof. U. Geneva, 1982-83, Weizmann Inst., 1991-92; med. dir. PEARL Dental PBRN Network, 2009-, adj. prof., NYU Coll. Dentistry, 2010-, vis. prof. Complutense U., Spain, 1999, prof extraordinaire, 1999. Author: 15 books including: Subcellular Mechanisms in Reproductive Neuroendocrinology, 1976, Abnormal Fetal Growth, 1978, Clinical Neuroendocrinology, 1979, Dilation of the Uterine Cervix, 1980, 2-vol. series Basic Reproductive Medicine, Vol. I, Basis of Normal Reproduction, Vol. II, 1981, Male Reproduction, Vol. III, Metabolism of Steroids by Neuroendocrine Tissues, Follicle Stimulation and Ovulation Induction, 1986; mem. editl. bd.: Jour. Soc. Gynecologic Investigation, Menopause, Gynecol. Endocrinology, African Jour. Reproductive Medicine, sect. editor: Reproductive Biology, jour. Exptl. Zoology, 2002—; editor: Reproductive Divsn. Am. Jour. Zoology; contbr. more than 600 articles to med. jours. Recipient Arnaldo Bruno prize, Acad. Di Lincei, Italy, 2002; named Fogarty Internat. fellow, 1982, John Simon Guggenheim fellow, 1983, Berlex Internat. scholar, 1991; fellow ad enundem, Royal Coll. Ob-Gyn. Mem. Am. Gynecol. and Obstet. Soc., Soc. Gynecol. Investigation (pres. 1991-92, Disting. Scientist award 2003), Endocrine Soc., Internat. Soc. Neuroendocrinology, New Haven Ob-Gyn. Soc., Can. Fertility Soc., Soc. for Neurosci., N.Am. Menopause Soc. (pres. 1998-99), Internat. Menopause Soc. (exec. com. 2000-08), Soc. Exptl. Biology and Medicine (coun. 2000-06), Pan Am. Health and Edn. Found. (bd. trustees 2005-10). Office: NYU Sch Med Dept Ob-Gyn 550 1st Ave TH528 New York NY 10016 Business E-Mail: frederick.naftolin@nyumc.org.

NAGAI, NOBUTAKA, gynecologist, obstetrician; MD, PhD, Hiroshima U., Japan, 2006. Cert. gynecological oncologist Japan Soc. Gynecologic Cancer, 2006. Assoc. prof. Hiroshima U., 1995—2006. Office: Hiroshima Ladies Clinic 1-20 Mikawa-cho Naka-ku Hiroshima 730 0029 Japan Office Phone: 81-82-815-5211. Office Fax: 81-82-814-1791. Personal E-mail: n-nagai@asa-hosp.city.hiroshima.jp.

NAGAKAWA, YUICHI, medical educator; b. Ishikawa, Japan, Mar. 26, 1969; MD, Tokyo Med. U., PhD, 1994. Assoc. prof. Tokyo Med. U., 2011—. Office: 6-7-1 Nishi-shinjuku Shinjuku-ku Tokyo 160-0023 Japan Office Fax: 81-3-3340-4575. Business E-Mail: nagn@tokyo-med.ac.jp.

NAGAMINE, MASARU, epidemiologist, educator; b. Okinawa, Japan, July 18, 1949; MD, Nagasaki U., 1980; PhD, Tokyo U., 1992. Assoc. prof. Tropical Biosphere Rsch. Ctr. U. Ryukyus, 2000—. Office: University Ryukyus 1-Senbaru Nishihar Okinawa 903-0213 Japan Office Fax: 81-98-895-8944. Business E-Mail: mnagamin@comb.u ryukyu.ac.jp.

NAGAOKA, HIROYUKI, food scientist, researcher; b. Sawae, Yamaguchi, Japan, June 2, 1969; s. Sinetu and Mituko Nagaoka; m. Kyoko Wakabayashi, May 7, 2000. BS, Okayama U., Japan, 1994; MS, Shinshu U., Nagano, Japan, 1996; PhD, Gifu U., Japan, 2000. Main rschr. Sanyo Foods Co., Ltd., Maebashi, Japan, 1996—. Patentee in field; contbr. articles to profl. jours. Recipient Internat. Health Profl. of the Yr., IBC, 2003. Fellow: AAAS; mem.: Chem. Soc. Japan, Japan Soc. Biosci., Biotech. and Agrochemistry. Office: Sanyo Foods Co Ltd 555-4, Asakuramachi Gumma Maebashi 371-0811 Japan Home Phone: +81-27-255-2031; Office Phone: +81-27-220-3471. Office Fax: +81-27-220-3477; Home Fax: +81-27-255-2031. Business E-Mail: hnagaoka@sanyofoods.co.jp.

NAGARAJ, VINAY SWARNALATHA, research scientist; b. Mysore, India, Oct. 15, 1978; PhD, U. Mysore, 2009. Rsch. scientist audiology Norwegian U. Sci. and Tech., 2009—. Home: Bugges Vei 11 Trondheim Sør Trondelag 7051 Norway Business E-Mail: vinaysn@lycos.com.

NAGARAJAN, BALASUBRAMANYAM, oncologist; b. Madras, India, July 13, 1937; s. Balasubramanyam and Parvati B.; m. Thirunagavalli Nagarajan, July 1959; children: Ramesh, Satya. BS with honors, Annamalai U., 1958; MS, Madras U., 1960; PhD, Vanderbilt U., 1970. Biochemist Cancer Inst., Madras, 1960-64, head of lab., 1970-80, prof., chmn., 1980—; rsch. asst. Vanderbilt Med. Sch., Nashville, 1964-69, rsch. assoc., 1969-70. Guest scientist Fed. Govt. of Germany, 1992-97; fellow Internat. Union Against Cancer, 1993; mem. expert com. Union pub. Svc. Com., Govt. India, med. rsch. com. CSIR, Govt. India, bd. rsch. Madras U.; vis. scientist Govt. of France, 1999—; vis. prof. Anna Annamalai and Madras U.; guest faculty Fedn. Govt. Germany, 2004. Prin. investigator numerous refereed jours.; contbr. 200 sci. articles to profl. jours. Recipient B.C. Roy Nat. award Med. Coun. of India, 1996; doctoral fellow U.S. Pub. Health Svc., 1964-70; merit scholar Annamalai U., 1953-58; Indira Gandhi Nat. award, 2003, Disting Prof. award, Med. U. Adj. Prof. Vanderbilt U. Fellow Nat. Acad. Med. Scis. (India); mem. Environ. Mutagen Soc./India (life), Soc. Biology Chemists (life). Office: Cancer Inst Chennai 600 020 India Home: 17 12th Cross St Indiranagar Chennai 600 020 India Home Phone: 91-44-24421131; Office Phone: 91-44-24910754. Personal E-mail: bnaga20000@yahoo.com.

NAGASAKA, KENJI, hospital administrator; b. Japan, Nov. 29, 1970; MD, Tokyo Med. & Dental U., 1996; PhD, Grad. Sch., Tokyo Med. & Dental U., 2002. Asst. dir. Ome Mcpl. Gen. Hosp., 2003—. Mem.: Japan Coll. Rheumatology. Office: 4-16-5 Higashi-Ome Ome Tokyo 198-0042 Japan E-mail: nagasaka-k@mghp.ome.tokyo.jp.

NAGASAKI, AKITOSHI, physician; b. s. Mitsuru and Tamami Nagasaki; m. Yuriko Moriuchi, Feb. 23, 2000; children: Satoshi, Kohki. MD, Kumamoto U., Japan, 1990, PhD, 1997. Bd. cert. Japanese Soc. of Internal Medicine, 2003. Rschr. Kumamoto U. Sch. of Medicine, Japan, 1997—99; staff physician Kumamoto U. Hosp., Japan, 1999—2000; part-time lectr. faculty of medicine U. of The Ryukyus, Nishihara, Nakagami-gun, Okinawa, Japan, 2000—; part-time lectr. Okinawa Prefectural Urase Nursing Sch., Urasoe, Okinawa, Japan, 2001—; physician Pub. Clinic of Okianwa Juvenile Tng. Sch., Japan, 2001—. Author: (journal) Jour. Biological Chemistry, Internal Medicine, Platelet, Medical Pediatric Oncology, Am. Jour. Physiology, Leukemia, Nitric Oxide, Acta Haematologica, Circulation, Internat. Jour. Hematology, British Jour. Hematology, Blood, Histochemical Jour., (jour.) FEBS Letters. Grantee, Tokyo Biochem. Rsch. Found., 1998. Mem.: Japanese Soc. Med. Oncology, Japanese Assn. for Correctional Medicine, Japanese Med. and Dental Practitioners for the Improvement Med. Care, Molecular Biology Soc. Japan, Japanese Biochem. Soc., Japanese Soc. Clin. Hematology, Japanese Soc. Hematology, Japanese Soc. Internal Medicine.

NAGASE, SOHJI, medical educator; b. Mitsukaido, Ibaraki, Japan, May 23, 1954; s. Senpei and Kikue (Iizumi) N.; m. Etsuko Ishitsuka, Apr. 2, 1978; children: Chihiro, Rei, Yui. MD, Yamagata U., Japan, 1979; PhD, U. Tsukuba, Ibaraki, Japan, 1985. Resident internal medicine U. Tsukuba, Japan, 1979-85, asst. prof., 1986-97, assoc. prof., 1997—2006; clin. fellow Tsukuba Gakuen Hosp., Japan, 1985-86; prof., Ctr. Clin. Medicine Rsch. Internat. U. Health and Welfare, Japan, 2006—07; pres. Nagase Med. Clinic, 2007—. Rsch. fellow Albert Einstein Med. Coll., N.Y., 1989-90. Contbr. articles to profl. jours. Mem. Am. Soc. Nephrology, European Dialysis and Transplant Assn. Avocations: car, audio, Japanese soba making. Office: 1580 Matsunami Moriya Ibaraki 302-0108 Japan Personal E-mail: nazo_otoko@ybb.ne.jp. Business E-Mail: info@nagase-md.com.

NAGASHIMA, HIDEKI, orthopedist, educator, surgeon; b. Matsue, Japan, Nov. 28, 1963; s. Mizuo and Minee Nagashima; m. Kiyoe Takeuchi; children: Toshiki, Masato, Takashi. MD, Tottori U., Yonago, Tottori, Japan, 1988, PhD, 1994. Diplomate med. lic. Ministry of Health and Welfare, Tokyo, Japan, 1988, cert. Japanese Orthopaedic Assn., Tokyo, Japan, 1995, infection control doctor Com. ICD, Tokyo, Japan, 2002, bd. cert. spine surgeon Japanese Soc. Spine Surgery and Related Rsch. Resident dept. orthopedic surgery, faculty medicine Tottori U., Yonago, Japan, 1988—94, asst. prof. dept. orthopedic surgery faculty medicine, 1994—2003, jr. assoc. prof. orthpedic surgery faculty medicine, 2003—. Vis. prof. dept. neurol. surgery and The Miami Project to Cure Paralysis U. Miami (Fla.) Sch. Medicine, 1998. Mem.: Japanese Spine Rsch. Soc. Office: Tottori Univ Faculty Medicine Nishi-machi 36-1 Tottori Yonago 683-8504 Japan Home: 322-22 Kawasaki Yonago Tottori 6830852 Japan Home Phone: 81-859-21-2144; Office Phone: 81-859-38-6587. Office Fax: 81-859-38-6589. Business E-Mail: hidekin@med.tottori-u.ac.jp.

NAGATA, KAZUMA, physician; b. Hyogo, Nov. 1, 1982; MD, Kyoto U., 2007. Physician Kobe City Med. Ctr. Gen. Hosp., 2009—. Office: 4-6 Minatojima-nakamachi Chuo-ku Kobe Hyogo 650-0046 Japan Personal E-mail: kazuma_n1101@yahoo.co.jp.

NAGATA, KOJI, biology professor; b. Nagasaki, Japan, June 18, 1967; BSA, U. Tokyo, 1990, PhD, 1995. Rsch. assoc. Biotech. Rsch. Ctr., U. Tokyo, 1997—2002, Grad. Sch. Agrl. and Life Scis., U. Tokyo, 2002—05, assoc. prof., 2005—. Recipient Rsch. award, Inoue Found. Sci., Japan, 1997; Rsch. fellowship, Japan Soc. Promotion Sci., 1993—95, Postdoc. fellowship, 2000—02. Mem.: Crystallographic Soc. Japan, Molecular Biology Soc. Japan, Japanese Peptide Soc. (Young Scientists award 1999), Protein Soc. Japan, Japan Soc. Biosci., Biotech. & Agrochemistry (Young Scientists award 2007). Office: 1-1-1 Yayoi Bunkyo Tokyo 113-8657 Japan Business E-Mail: aknagata@mail.ecc.u-tokyo.ac.jp.

NAGATA, SATORU, plastic surgeon, educator, medical director; b. Nagasaki, Japan, Aug. 28, 1950; s. Fukujyuro and Tomoko Nagata; m. Nobuko Nagata, Aug. 10, 1977; children: Makoto, Maki, Shingo. MD, Tottori Nat. U., Japan, 1978; PhD, Kyorin U., Tokyo, 2000. Resident surgeon Tokyo U., 1979—84; staff surgeon Tokyo Senbai Hosp., 1986—87, Tokyo Mcpl. Bokuto Hosp., 1987—89; chief surgeon Tokyo Senbai Hosp., 1989—91, dept. dir., 1991—96, Chiba Tokushukai Hosp., Funabashi City, Chiba, Japan, 1996—2001, Akiba Hosp., Saitama City, Shitama, Japan, 2001; med. dir. Nagata Microtia and Reconstructive Plastic Surgery Clinic, Toda City, Japan, 2005—. Vis. prof. U. Calif., Irvine, U. Alberta, U. Rotterdam; vis. prof. Internat. Cranifacial Inst. Cleft Lip and Palate Ctr. Mex. Gen. Hosp.; vis. prof. Milan U., Hosp. for Sick Children St. Joseph Health Ctr.; sci. adv. com. mem. Internat. Conf. Advanced Digital Tech. Head and Neck Reconstruction, Canada. Mem. (editl. bd.) British Jour. Plastic Surgery. Mem.: European Assn. Plastic Surgery, Am. Soc. Plastic, Reconstructive and Asthetic Surgery, French Soc. Plastic Surgeons (fgn. mem.), Japan Soc. Plastic Reconstructive Surgery. Home: 1-7-3 Soya Chiba Ichikawa 272-0832 Japan Office: Nagata Microtia and Reoconstructive Plastic Surgery Clinic 22-1 Sasame Minami-Cho Toda City Saitama 335-0035 Japan E-mail: nagatas7133@aol.com.

NAGATA, TETSUJI, anatomist, medical educator; b. Suwa, Nagano, Japan, Feb. 5, 1931; s. Kamashige and Haruko (Takeuchi) N.; m. Kyoko Nakamura, Mar. 15, 1962; children: Seiji, Hiroko. BSc, Shinshu U., Matsumoto, Japan, 1951, MD, 1955, PhD, 1962. From instr. to prof. emeritus anatomy Shinshu U., Matsumoto, 1956—96, prof. emeritus, 1996—, dean Sch. Medicine, 1990—92; rsch. assoc. in physiology U. Ill., 1962-64; prof. emeritus Hebei Med. U., China, 1987—, pres. emeritus, 1991—; prof. anatomy and physiology Nagano Women's Jr. Coll., 1997—2002; prof. anatomy Shinshu Inst. Alternative Medicine Welfare, 2005—, dean, 2008—. Pres. 4th Japan-U.S. Joint Congress Histochemistry and Cytochemistry, 1994, 4th Internat. Symposium Radioautography, 1993; vis. prof. Nat. U. Singapore, Singapore, 1995—, U. Sao Paulo, Brazil, 1989—, U. Campinas, Brazil, 1995—; prof. emeritus ChangDe Med. U., ChengDe, China, 1999—. Assoc. editor Cellular and Molecular Biology, 1989—. Hon. pres. 5th Internat. Symposium Radioautography, 1997. Mem. Japanese Assn. Anatomists (bd. dirs. 1988-95, hon. dir. 1996—), Japan Soc. Histochemistry and Cytochemistry (bd. dirs. 1989-96, hon. dir. 1999—, pres. 1994, 4th Japan-U.S. congress 1994), Clin. Electron Microscopy Soc. Japan (pres. 1992-93, bd. dirs. 1988-99, hon. dir. 2000-), World Soc. Cellular and Molecular Biology (v.p. 1991-96, pres. 1996-2000, hon. pres. 2000—), NY Acad. Sci., Sigma Xi. Home: 1361 Matsuoka Okada Matumoto 390-0313 Japan Office: Dept Anatomy Cell Biology Shinshu U Sch Med 3-1-1 Asahi Matumoto 390-8621 Japan Office Phone: 81-26-233-0555. Office Fax: 81 26 233 0560. Business E-Mail: nagatas@po.cnet.ne.jp, nagata@kowagakuen.ac.jp.

NAGATSU, MASAYOSHI, cardiothoracic surgeon, researcher; b. Tokyo, Apr. 15, 1957; s. Hiroshi and Reiko (Komatsu) N.; m. Yuko Komatsu, Dec. 18, 1988; children: Kazuki, Naoki, Koki. MD, Tsukuba U., 1983. Intern, resident Heart Inst. Japan, Tokyo Women's Med. Coll., 1983-91; fellow, rsch. fellow Gazes Cardiac Rsch. Inst. Med. U. S.C., 1991-93; asst. in pediat. cardiovasc. surgery Heart Inst. Japan Tokyo Women's Med. U., 1993-97, assoc. prof. cardiovasc. surgery Heart Inst. Japan, 2002—05; chief in pediat. cardiac surgery Gifu Prefecture Hosp., Japan, 1997—2002; dir. Imamura Clinic, Japan, 2006—. Mem. Japan Surg. Soc., Japan Assn. for Thoracic Surgery (surg. instr. 1996—), Am. Heart Assn., Internat. Soc. for Cardiovasc. Surgery, Soc. Thoracic Surgery. Avocations: guitar synthesizer, medical multimedia. Office: Imamura Clinic 1 16 17 Popolo Bldg 5F Higashi Kunitachi shi Tokyo 186 0002 Japan Office Phone: 81 42 573 3321. Home Fax: 81 3 5346 2056. Business E-Mail: snagatu@hij.twmu.ac.jp.

NAGATSUKA, YUKA, research scientist; b. Japan, June 25, 1974; PhD, Osaka U., 2006. Rsch. scientist, tech. dept. NCIMB group TechnoSuruga Lab. Co., Ltd., 2006—. Office: 330 Nagasaki Shimizu-ku Shizuoka City 424-0065 Japan Business E-Mail: ynagatsuka@tecsrg.co.jp.

NAGEGOWDA, DINESH A., botanist; b. Addihalli, India, Mar. 21, 1974; PhD, U. Hong Kong, 2004. Scientist Ctrl. Inst. Medicinal and Aromatic Plants, 2008—. Ramalingaswami fellowship, Govt. of India. Mem.: Am. Soc. Plant Biologists. Office: Plant Biotech Dept CIMAP Lucknow Uttar Pradesh 226015 India Personal E-mail: dinu33@yahoo.com.

NAGEL, EDGAR, ophthalmologist, consultant; MD, U. Greifswald, Germany, 1990. Diplomate Pub. Health Office Dist. Rostock, 1989. Asst. Eye Hosp. U. Jena, Germany, 1990—94; cons. Ophthalmic Outpatient Dept., Rudolstadt, Germany, 1994—. Cons. in field. Mem.: German Soc. Ophthalmology. Office: Ophthalmic Outpatient Dept Schwarzburger Chaussee 76 Rudolstaclt Germany

NAGEL, JEFFREY A., pharmaceutical executive; BS in Mech. Engring., Carnegie Mellon U., 1987, MBA. Mgr. bus. devel. GE Lighting, 1997—98; pres. GE Home Electric Products, 1998—2000; gen. mgr., bus. devel. General Electric Aviation, 2001—03; pres. GE Inspection Technologies, 2003—06; v.p., global services General Electric Oil & Gas, 2006—10; CEO NBTY, Inc., Ronkonkoma, NY, 2010—. Office: NBTY Inc 2100 Smithtown Ave Ronkonkoma NY 11779 Office Phone: 631-200-2000. *

NAGELBERG, STEVEN B., endocrinologist, educator; b. 1953; Attended, Bucknell U.; MD, Columbia U., 1974. Diplomate Am. Bd. Internal Medicine, 1981, Am. Bd. Internal Medicine-endocrinology, diabetese and metabolism, 1985. Resident internal medicine U. Calif., San Francico; med. staff fellow clin. endocrinology br. NIH, Bethesda, Md.; med. staff fellow divsn. of endocrinology and metabolism Thomas Jeffferson Univ., Pa., 1985; joined Endocrine Metabolic Assocs., 1987, sr. mem.; clin. prof. medicine Drexel Univ., sect. head. Named a Top Doc, Phila. Mag.; named one of America's Top Physicians, Consumer's Rsch. Coun. of America. Fellow: ACP, Am. Coll. of Endocrinologists; mem.: Endocrinology, Diabetes and Metabolism SEP Com., Am. Bd. Internal Medicine (physician sec. Endocrinology, Diabetes and Metabolism Bd.). Office: Endocrine Metabolic Associates 555 City Line Avenue Bala Cynwyd PA 19004 Office Phone: 215-969-9511.

NAGERA, HUMBERTO, psychiatrist, psychoanalyst, educator, writer; b. Havana, Cuba, May 23, 1927; m. Gloria Maria Hernandez, Sept. 8, 1952; children: Lisette Maria, Humberto Felipe, Daniel. B.Sc., U. Havana, 1945; MD, Havana Med. Sch., 1952. Intern, resident in psychiatry Havana U. Hosp., 1950-55; sr. staff, chmn. research Anna Freud's Clinic, London, 1958-68; prof. psychiatry U. Mich., Ann Arbor, 1968-87, chief youth services, 1973-79, prof. emeritus, 1987; prof. psychiatry U. South Fla., 1987—2010, prof. emeritus, 2010, dir. adolescent inpatient unit and children's inpatient unit, 1987-97, dir. Carter Jenkin Ctr., 2002—. Lectr. in field. Author: Early Childhood Disturbances, Problems of Developmental Psychoanalytic Psychology, 1966, Vincent Van Gogh, 1966, Basic Psychoanalytic Concepts on the Libido Theory, 1969, Basic Psychoanalytic Concepts on the Theory of Instincts, 1970, Basic Psychoanalytic Concepts of Metapsychology Conflicts, Anxiety, and Other Subjects, 1970, Female Sexuality and the Oedipus Complex, 1975, Obsessional Neurosis: Developmental Psychopathology, 1977, 2nd edit., 1993, The Developmental Approach in Child Psychopathology, 1981; Contbr. articles to profl. jours. Mem. Am. Psychiat. Assn., Internat. Psychoanalytic Assn., Mich. Psychoanalytic Inst. (pres. 1975-77), Am. Assn. Child Psychoanalysis, Cuba Med. Assn. in Exile, South Fla. Tampa Bay Psychoanalytic Soc. (pres. 1992-93). Home: 5202 Dwire Ct Tampa FL 33647-1016 Office: 1325 W Fletcher Ave Tampa FL 33612 Office Phone: 813-908-8686.

NAGESWARA RAO, RAMISETTI, research scientist; b. Machilipatnam, Jan. 15, 1955; MSc, Osmania U., 1983, PhD, 1990. Scientist Indian Inst. Chem. Tech., 1978—. Contbr. articles to profl. publs. Recipient Rsch. award, Indian Drug Manufacture Assn., Outstanding Pharm. Analyst award, Publ. awards, IICT. Mem.: Oil Tech. Assn. India, AMIC Assn., Indian Soc. Analytical Scientists (Hyderabad chpt.) (Dr. Husain Zaheer Meml. award). Office: D-215 Discoevry Lab IICT Tarnaka Hyderabad Andhra Pradesh 500007 India Office Fax: 91-40-27160387. E-mail: rnrao55@yahoo.com.

NAGLER, HARRIS M., urologic surgeon; b. Bklyn., Dec. 23, 1949; s. Simon H. and Thelma N.; m. Freema Gluck, May 25, 1978; children: Arielle Rachel, Gabrielle Marin. BS, Union Coll., 1971; MD, Temple U., 1975. Diplomate Nat. Bd. Med. Examiners, 1975, Am. Bd. Urology, 1982; lic. physician N.Y., 1976, N.J., 1993. Intern in gen. surgery Columbia-Presbyn. Med. Ctr., NYC, 1975-76, resident in urology, 1976—79, fellow in reproductive medicine, 1979—80; instr. urology Columbia U. Coll. Physicians and Surgeons, NYC, 1980—81, asst. prof. urology, 1982-87, assoc. prof. urology, 1987-89; dir. dept. urology Beth Israel Med. Ctr., NYC, 1989-94, chmn. dept. urology, 1995—, lab. dir., 1996—, chief grad. med. edn. and acad. affairs, 1999—2010; interim pres. Beth Isreal Med. Ctr., 2009—, pres., 2010. Co-dir. N.Y. Male Reproductive Ctr., 1981-84, dir., 1984-89; chief Vanderbilt Urology Clinic, 1982-87; asst. attending urologist Presbyn. Hosp., N.Y.C., 1982-87, assoc. attending urologist, 1987-89; chmn. dept. urology Beth Israel Med. Ctr., N.Y.C., 1989—, com. of surgery, 1989—, med. bd. com., 1989—, adminstrv. adv. com., 1989—, faculty practice plan adv. coun., 1989-92, chmn.

faculty practice plan adv. coun., 1992—; mem. devel. com., Beth Israel Med. Ctr., 1995-, Cancer Com., 1997-, Dept. of Surgery Chmn. Search Com., 1998-99, Surgical Svcs. Oversight Com., 1998-, Faculty Practice Plan Com. (chmn.), 1998-, chief of acad. affairs, 1998-2010, chair, Philips Ambulatory Care Mgmt. Com., 2002-10; prof. urology Mt. Sinai Sch. Medicine, 1989-94, Albert Einstein Coll. Medicine, 1995—. Editl bd. Molecular Andrology, 1989, Investigative Urology, 1989-93, Gynecologic and Obstetric Investigation, 1992, Fertility and Sterility, 1993-2001, Assisted Reproductive Reviews, 1991; reviewer Fertility and Sterility, 1986-93, Investigative Urology, 1986-89, Nature Urology. Bd. dirs. Coalition to Save City & Suburban Housing, N.Y.C., 1993-94. Ferdinand C. Valentine fellow, 1981; Recipient Kidney and Urology Found., 2008 Fellow ACS, N.Y. Acad. Medicine (pres. sect. urology); mem. AMA, Am. Assn. Med. Colls. (task force inegrating edn. and patient care 1999—), Am. Kidney and Urology Found. (bd. mem., John Kingsley Lattimer award, 2008), 2002-, Am. Urol. Assn. (1st prize in clin. rsch. 1982), Am. Soc. Andrology, Soc. Productive Surgeons (sec. 1993, treas. 1993-94, v.p. 1995, pres. 1996), Soc. for Study of Male Reprodn. (pres. 1993, bd. dirs. 2005—), N.Y. County Med. Soc., Harvey Soc., Am. Fertility Soc. (Pacific Coast chpt., urology com. 1984, urology-andrology com. 1985, movies com. 1987-2005, co-chmn. male reproduction/urology com. 1986-88, award selection com. 1987-88, program com. 1988-90, co-chmn. male reproduction/urology com. 1988-90, program chair N.Y. sect. annual meeting 1991, exec. com. N.Y. chpt., 2000—, urology prize 1985), Am. Cystoscope Makers Inc. (urology prize 1982), Alpha Omega Alpha, NY Sect. AUA (treas. 2006-08, elect pres., Russell Lavengood award 2008), AUA Judicial Com. (chair 2007-08), AUA Investment & Fin. Com., AUA Bylaws Com. (co-chair, 2010, Disting. Svc. award 2011). Office: Beth Israel Med Ctr 1st Ave at 16th St New York NY 10003

NAGUIB, IBRAHIM AHMED, chemistry professor; b. Beni-Suef, Egypt, Nov. 9, 1979; PhD in Pharmacy, 2001. Asst. prof. analytical chemistry Faculty Pharmacy, Beni-Suef U., 2001—. Recipient Silver medal, Syndicate Pharmacists. Mem.: Gen. Syndicate Pharmacists (Egypt). Home: 26 Karam St Beni-Suef 62111 Egypt Business E-Mail: inaguieb@bsu.edu.eg.

NAGUMO, MICHIHIKO, retired materials science and engineering educator; b. Hokkaido, Japan, Apr. 2, 1932; s. Junji and Ryoko (Yamaguchi) N.; m. Yasuko Tamama, Oct. 3, 1959. BS, U. Tokyo, 1955, MS, 1957, DrSci, 1960. Rschr. Nippon Steel Corp., Tokyo, 1960-88, dir. R&D Lab. 1, 1985-87, exec. councillor, 1987-88; prof. materials sci. and engring. Waseda U., Tokyo, 1988—2002, lab. dir. materials sci. tech., 2000—02, prof. emeritus, 2003—. Contbr. articles to profl. jours. Recipient Allan Dove award Wire Assn. Internat., 1983, Honorable Mention award, 1984. Mem. Japan Inst. Metals, Iron and Steel Inst. Japan (hon., Nishiyama Meml. prize 1983), Phys. Soc. Japan, TMS.

NAGY, ANDRAS, cardiologist; b. Szeged, Hungary, Aug. 9, 1963; s. Sandor Nagy and Gizella Karacsony; m. Marta Nagy; children: Orsolya, Viktoria, Andras. MD, Szeged U., PhD, 1987. Cert. in internal medicine BC Postgrad. U., 1991, in cardiology BC 1994, cardiologist Union Europeenne des Medicins Specialistes, 2000. Head, cardiology Bacs-Kiskun County Hosp., Kecskemet, Hungary, 2002—. Chmn. bd. Hungarian Nat. Heart Found., Budapest, 2003—. Mem.: Hungarian Soc. Cardiology. Office: Bacs-Kiskun County Hosp 38 Nyiri Kecskemet 6000 Hungary Business E-Mail: nagya@kmk.hu.

NAGY, CHRISTA FIEDLER, biochemist; b. Marienbad, Czech Republic, July 8, 1943; d. Herbert A. Fiedler and Anna C. (Gluth) Rathmann; m. Bela Imre Nagy, Aug. 22, 1969; 1 child, Byron. BS in Biology, Fairleigh Dickinson U., Teaneck, NJ, 1967, MS in Biochemistry, 1974; PhD in Biochemistry, Rutgers U., 1981. Sr. scientist Hoffmann-La Roche Inc., Nutley, NJ, 1981-88, assoc. rsch. investigator, 1988-95; asst. dir. preclin. rsch. Eisai Inc., Teaneck, 1997-98; assoc. dir. clin. pharmacology Eisai Med. Rsch., Inc., Ridgefield Park, NJ, 1998—2005, dir. clin. pharmacology, 2005—. Mem.: Am. Soc. Clin. Pharmacology and Therapeutics, Drug Info. Assn., Am. Soc. Biol. Chemists. Roman Catholic. Avocations: travel, skiing, tennis, hiking. Office: Eisai Med Rsch Inc 55 Challenger Rd Ridgefield Park NJ 07660 Office Phone: 201-287-2174. Business E-Mail: christa_nagy@eisai.com.

NAGY, STEPHEN MEARS, JR., physician, allergist; b. Yonkers, NY, Apr. 1, 1939; s. Stephen Mears and Olga (Zahoruiko) N.; m. Brenda Yu Nagy, 1966; children: Catherine, Stephen III. BA, Princeton U., 1960; MD, Tufts U., 1964. Diplomate Am. Bd. Internal Medicine, Am. Bd. Allergy and Immunology. Pvt. practice, Sacramento, Calif., 1971-2000; prof. Sch. Medicine U. Calif., Davis, 1974—. Author, editor Evaluation & Management of Allergic and Asthmatic Diseases, 1981; mem. editl. bd. Clinical Reviews in Allergy; creator Famous Teachings in Modern Medicine-Allergy Series slide collection. Capt. U.S. Army, 1966-68, Vietnam. Fellow Am. Acad. Allergy, Am. Coll. Allergy; mem. CMA, Sacramento-El Dorado Med. Soc. (bd. dirs. 1971-95, 1989-95). Avocations: bicycling, book collecting, opera, fencing. Office: 4801 J St Ste A Sacramento CA 95819-3746 Office Phone: 916-456-4782.

NAHABEDIAN, MAURICE Y., plastic surgeon; MD, U. Calif., Irvine, 1983—87. Diplomate Am. Bd. Plastic Surgery, 1997. Intern in surgery U. Calif., Irvine, 1987—88, resident in plastic surgery, 1988—92; resident in surgery John Hopkins U., Balt., 1992—95, attending in plastic surgery, 1996; assoc. prof. plastic surgery Johns Hopkins U., Balt., 1996—. Achievements include research in breast reconstruction with autologous tissue. Office: Georgetown University Hosp 3800 Reservoir Rd NW Washington DC 20007 Office Fax: 202-444-7180. E-mail: DrNahabedian@aol.com.

NAHAI, FOAD, plastic surgeon, educator; b. Teheran, Iran, Sept. 23, 1943; came to U.S., 1970; m. Shahnaz Mossanen, Aug. 4, 1969; children: Farzad, Fariba BSc with honors, U. Bristol, Eng., 1966, MB ChB, 1969. Diplomate Am. Bd. Surgery, Am. Bd. Plastic Surgery (dir. 2001-2007); lic. Eng., Ga. Med. and surg. intern United Bristol Hosps., Bristol, England, 1969-70; intern in surgery Balt. City Hosps., 1970-71; resident in surgery Johns Hopkins Hosp., Balt., 1971-72; resident in gen. surgery Emory U. Affiliated Hosps., Atlanta, 1972-74, chief resident, gen. surgery, 1974-75, fellow in hand surgery and microsurgery, 1975-76, resident in plastic surgery, 1976-77; instr. in surgery Emory U., Atlanta, 1975—76, 1978, asst. prof. surgery (plastic surgery), 1978—83, assoc. prof. surgery (plastic surgery), 1983—91, prof. plastic surgery, 1991—97; pvt. practice Paces Plastic Surgery, Atlanta, 1998—. Invited spkr. in field; vis. prof. at various universities, colleges and institutions, domestically and internationally. Co-author (with S.J. Mathes) Clinical Atlas of Muscle and Musculocutaneous Flaps, 1979, Clinical Applications for Muscle and Musculocutaneous Flaps, 1982, Reconstructive Surgery: Principles Anatomy and Technique, 1996, (with others) Microvascular Surgery in Reconstruction of the Head and Neck, 1989, Plastic and Reconstructive Breast Surgery, 1990, Grabb's Encyclopedia of Flaps, 1990, Chirurgie Due Cancer Due Sein Diagnostique, 1997, (with Bostwick and Eaves) Endoscopic Plastic Surgery, 1995; mem. editl. bd. Annals Plastic Surgery, 1984-88, Outlook Plastic Surgery, 1988-97, Perspectives in Plastic Surgery 1994-97, Plastic and Reconstructive Surgery 1998, Aesthetic Plastic Surgery, 1999, Aesthetic Surgery Jour., 2000, Roundtables in Plastic Surgery, 2003; author Art of Aesthetic Surgery Principles and Techniques, 2005; co-editor Vertical Scar Mammoplasty, 2005; contbr. articles to profl. jours.; co-prodr. (movies) Breast Reconstruction After a Radical Mastectomy with Latissimus Dorsi Musculocutaneous Flap, 1978, The Tensor Fascia Lata Free Flap, 1979; prodr. (videotapes) TFL Neurosensory Flap for Coverage of Greater Trochanteric and Ischium, Rectus Abdominis Flap for Sternal Coverage, Gastrocnemius Muscle Flap for Coverage of Tibia, others; contbr. chpts. to books. Recipient Russell Cooper prize, U. Bristol, Eng., 1968, Gold Medal Paper Presentation Southeastern Surg. Conf., 1976, Best Paper award Atlanta Clin. Soc., 1980, award Am. Med. Writers Assn., 1983; named one of Best Doctors in Am., Best Doctors in the US, Top Plastic Surgeon Good Housekeeping, More Mag., Atlanta Mag., Top Plastic Surgeon in the World, W Mag. Fellow ACS (3d Ann. Residents Competition award Ga. chpt. 1977); mem. Am. Soc. Plastic Surgeons (President's award, 2005), Am. Assn. Plastic Surgeons (James Barrett Brown award 1982), Am. Soc. for Aesthetic Plastic Surgery (jud. coun. 1997, bd. dirs. 1999-, tchg. course subcommittee chmn., 1999-2002, sec. 2002-04, edn. commn. co-chair, 2002-05 chair 2005, v.p. 2005, pres.elect 2006, pres. 2007-2008), Am. Soc. Plastic and Reconstructive Surgeons (rsch. grantee ednl. found.), Ga. Soc. Plastic Surgeons, Med. Assn. Ga., Ga. Surg. Soc., Med. Assn. Atlanta, Southeastern Soc. Plastic and Reconstructive Surgeons (Outstanding Resident award 1977), Internat. Assn. Univ. Plastic Surgeons, Plastic Surgery Rsch. Coun. (program chmn. 1988, chmn. 1989), Soc. Residents and Ex Residents of Inst. Reconstructive Surgery (hon.), Sociedad Jaime Planas de Cirurgia Plastica (hon.), Internat. Soc. Aesthetic Plastic Surgery (1st term course dir. 1999, sec. gen. 2000-2004, 2d v.p. 2004-06, 1st v.p. 2006-07, pres.-elect 2007, pres. 2008), Am. Soc. for Laser Medicine and Surgery, Plastic Surgery Ednl. Found. (bd. dirs. 2003-05), Internat. Plastic & Reconstructive Surgery Found. (v.p. 1999), Am. Soc. for Reconstructive Microsurgery (sec. 1986-89); corr. mem. Brazilian Coll. Surgeons, Brazilian Soc. Plastic Surgeons, Italian Soc. Plastic, Reconstructive and Aesthetic Surgery, Fla. Soc. Plastic and Reconstructive Surgeons, Israeli Assn. Plastic and Cosmetic Surgeons, Japanese Soc. Plastic and Reconstructive Surgery, Assn. Plastic and Reconstructive Surgeons So. Africa (also hon.), Lebanese Soc. Plastic, Reconstructive, and Aesthetic Surgery (hon.), New Eng. Soc. Plastic Surgeons (hon.). Office: Paces Plastic Surgery 3200 Downwood Cir NW Ste 640 Atlanta GA 30327-1624 Office Phone: 404-351-0051. Office Fax: 404-351-0632. Business E-Mail: nahaimd@aol.com. E-mail: pacesplasticsurgery@aol.com.

NAHAS, GABRIEL GEORGES, pharmacologist, educator, writer; b. Alexandria, Egypt, Mar. 4, 1920; came to U.S., 1947, naturalized, 1962; s. Bishara and Gabrielle (Wolff) N.; m. Marilyn Cashman, Feb. 13, 1954; children: Michele, Anthony, Christiane. BA, U. Toulouse, France, 1937, MD, 1944; MS, U. Rochester, 1949; PhD, U. Minn., 1953; DSc (hon.), U. Uppsala, 1988. Rockefeller Found. fellow U. Rochester, 1947-48; Mayo Found. fellow Mayo Clinic, 1949-50; rsch. fellow U. Minn., 1950-53, mem. faculty, 1955-57; mem. staff Walter Reed Army Inst. Rsch., 1957-59; faculty George Washington U. Med. Sch., 1957-59; mem. faculty Columbia U. Coll. Physicians and Surgeons, NYC, 1959-92, prof. anesthesiology, 1962-92; prof. emeritus, 1992; rsch. prof. anesthesiology NYU Med. Sch., NYC, 1992—. Disting. vis. scientist Addiction Rsch. Ctr., NIDA, 1987; adj. rsch. prof. anesthesiology U. Paris, 1968-71; fellow Coun. Circulation and Basic Sci., Am. Heart Assn., 1961—; mem. com. on trauma NRC, 1964-66; mem. adv. bd. Cousteau Soc.; cons. commn. on narcotics, drug control program UN. Author 700 sci. publs. and 40 books and monographs in English and French. Decorated Presdl. Medal of Freedom with gold palm Govt. of U.S.; comdr. Legion of Honor, Croix de Guerre with 3 palms (France), Order Brit. Empire, Order Orange Nassau Netherlands, Silver medal City of Paris; recipient Medal of Honor, Statue of Liberty Centennial, 1986; Fulbright scholar, 1966. Fellow AAAS, N.Y. Acad. Sci.; mem. Am. Physiol. Soc., Harvey Soc., Am. Soc. Pharmacology and Exptl. Therapeutics, Soc. Physiol. Langue Française, French Acad. Medicine (laureate 1995, 96), Brit. Pharm. Soc., Sigma Xi. Achievements include research on med. instrumentation, pharmacology Tham, acid-base regulation, pharmacology of cannabis and cocaine, drug dependence, consciousness, college problem on drug dependence. Home: 40 E 74th St New York NY 10021-2732

NAHATA, MILAP CHAND, pharmacy educator; b. Sardar Shahr, Rajasthan, India, Oct. 20, 1950; came to U.S., 1974; s. Bachh Rajji and Ratani Devi (Anchalia) N.; m. Suchitra Kothari, June 22, 1978; 1 child, Leena. BS, U. Jodhpur, India, 1970; BS in Pharmacy, U. Bombay, India, 1973; MS in Pharmaceutics, Duquesne U., 1975, PharmD, 1977. Asst. prof. pharmacy Ohio State U., Columbus, 1977-83, asst. prof. pediatrics, 1979-83, assoc. prof. pharmacy, pediatrics, 1983-88, prof. pharmacy, pediatrics, 1988—. Dir. infectious disease rsch. lab. Children's Hosp., Columbus, 1980—; cons. Hoechst Roussel Pharms., N.J., 1989—, Adria Labs., Columbus, 1990; presenter in field. Author: Pediatric Drug Formulations, 1990, 92; sr. editor: Annals of Pharmacotherapy; column editor; Jour. Clin. Pharmacy and Therapeutics; guest editor: Jour. Pharmacy Practice, 1990; mem. editl. bd. pharmacy-related jours., 1980—; referee 20 pharmacy and med. jours., 1980—; contbr. over 300 articles to profl. publs. Named Pharmacist of Yr., Ohio Soc. Hosp. Pharmacists, 1987, Outstanding Tchr. of Yr., Student Nat. Pharm. Assn., 1993; recipient Award for Sustained Contbns. to Lit., Am. Soc. Hosp. Pharmacists, 1987, R.G. Leonard award U. Tex., 1989, Edn. Award for Sustained and Outstanding Contbns. to Clin. Pharmacy Edn., Am. Coll. Clin. Pharmacy, 1990, Alumni award for disting. teaching Ohio State U., 1991, Disting. Pharmacy Educator award Am. Assn. Coll. Pharmacy, 1993. Fellow AAAS, Am. Coll. Clin. Pharmacy (pres. 1990-93, regent 1986-89, Edn. award 1990), Am. Acad. Microbiology; mem. Inst. Medicine. Avocation: singing. Office: Childrens Hosp 700 Childrens Dr Columbus OH 43205-2696 also: Ohio State U A206 Parks Hall 500 W 12th Ave Columbus OH 43210-1291 E-mail: nahata.1@osu.edu.

NAHLOVSKY, JIRI, neurosurgeon, educator; b. Prague, Dec. 15, 1943; MD, Charles U., 1968. Head, dept. neurosurgery Tchg. Hosp., Hradec Kralove, 1994—2009, neurosurgeon, dept. neurosurgery, 1972—; mem. World Fedn. Neurosurgical Socs., Exec. Com., 1998—2010; pres. Czech Neurosurgical Soc., 1995—98, v.p., 1999—2010; asst. prof. Charles U., Prague, 1989—. Mem.: European Assn. Neurosurgical Socs., World Fedn. Neurosurgical Socs. Avocation: sports. Home: Prazska tr 754 Hradec Kralove 500 04 Czech Republic Office Phone: 420- 495 832 550. Personal E-mail: nahlovsky@fnhk.cz.

NAHM, DONG-SEOK, dentist, educator; b. Kunsan, Chunbook, Republic of Korea, Aug. 20, 1941; s. Myoung-Ju and Deok-Soon Lee Nahm; m. Man-Ja Lee, Jan. 10, 1972; children: Eun-Young, Kyoung-Soo. DDS, Seoul Nat. U., 1965, MS in Orthodontics, 1971, PhD, 1976. Cert. orthodontist Korean Assn. Orthodontists, 1995. Prof. Seoul Nat. U., Republic of Korea, 1976—2006; pres. Korean Assn. Orthodontists, Seoul, 1984—86, Korean Divsn. IADR, Seoul, 1999—2001, Korean Assn. Cleft Lip & Palate, Seoul, 1999—2001; assoc. dean Seoul Nat. U., 1985—87; v.p. Korean Dental Assn., Seoul, 1993—94; dir. Inst. Dental Rsch., Seoul Nat. U., 1999—2001. Advisor editl. bd. Orthodontic Waves, Tokyo, 2006—; prof. emeritus Seoul Nat. U., 2006—. Author: (med. book) New Paradigm of Maxillofacial Distraction Osteogenesis (Outstanding Book in Field of Scis., NAS, 2007); contbr. articles to profl. jours. Capt. Navy, 1966—70, Pohang, Korea. Recipient Grand prix of Sci. Affairs, Korean Dental Assn., 2004. Mem.: Nat. Acad. Medicine Korea. Avocations: travel, photography. Office: Seoul Barum Dental Clinic #1318-2 Seocho-dong Seoul Seocho-ku 137-856 Republic of Korea Office Phone: 82-2-534-2755. Office Fax: 02-534-2721. Business E-Mail: dsnahm@snu.ac.kr.

NAHM, WALTER K., dermatologist, researcher; s. James J. and Hyun S. Nahm; m. Lauren Y. Nahm; 1 child, William J. BA, U. Tex., Austin, 1993; PhD, Baylor Coll., 1996; MD, Baylor Med. Sch., 1998. Diplomate Am. Bd. Dermatology. Intern St. Joseph Hosp., Houston, 1999; chief resident Boston U. Sch. Medicine, 2002; Mohs Micrographic Surgery fellow Conn U. Calif., LA Sch. Medicine, 2003, cosmetic surgery fellow, 2003; staff physician Scripps Mercy Hosp., San Diego, 2003—, VA San Diego Healtcare Sys., 2003—, West LA VA Med. Ctr., 2003—04, Kindred Hosp., San Diego, 2004—05; dir. Mohs Micrographic Surgery U. Calif., San Diego, 2005—. Asst. clin. prof. U. Calif., 2003—. Editor: PCI Jour. Recipient Excellence in Scholarly Activities award, Boston U. Sch. Medicine, 2002, Citizen's award, 2002; named Young Investigator of Yr., Tex. Neurol. Soc. Tex. Med., 1997; grantee, Soc. Investigative Dermatology, 2002; fellow Albert M. Kligman fellow, Soc. for Investigative Dermatology, 2002. Fellow: AMA (Physician's Recognition award 2005), Am. Soc. Dermatologic Surgery (Young Investigator's Writing Competition award 2003), Am. Acad. Cosmetic Surgery (membership com. 2005—, Excellence award 2005), Am. Acad. Dermatology (Continuing Med. Edn. award 2005), Am. Coll. Mohs Micrographic Surgery and Cutaneous Oncology, Am. Soc. for Laser Medicine and Surgery; mem.: San Diego Dermatology Soc. (pres. 2008), Internat. Hyperhidrosis Soc., San Diego County Med. Soc., Calif. Med. Assn., Am. Soc. for Lipo-Sucton Surgery, San Diego Soc. Dermatologic Surgery (pres. 2007), Soc. for Investigative Dermatology, Am. Soc. Cosmetic Dermatology and Aesthetic Surgery, Phi Beta Kappa. Office: 7695 Cardinal Ct Ste 200 San Diego CA 92123 Office Phone: 858-278-8835. Office Fax: 858-386-4776. Personal E-mail: tire99@yahoo.com.

NAHMAD, MICHEL HENRY, thoracic surgeon; b. Nov. 7, 1938; married; 4 children. BSc in Biology, U. NM, Albuquerque, 1960; MD, Tulane U. Med. Sch., New Orleans, 1964. Diplomate Am. Bd. Surgery, 1971, Am. Bd. Thoracic and Cardiac Surgery, 1971, cert. spl. competence pediatric surgery 2005. Internship in mixed medicine Charity Hosp. La., Tulane Svc., New Orleans, 1964—65, residency in gen. surgery, 1965—66; residency in gen. surgery, assoc. resident in surgery Bronx Mcpl. Hosp., the Albert Einstein Coll. Medicine, NY, 1966—67, clin. instr., surgery, 1966—70, surg. rsch. fellow, 1967—68, residency in surgery, 1968—69, chief resident in surgery, 1969—70; clin. instr., surgery Ohio State U. Coll. Medicine, Columbus, 1967—70, thoracic surgery specialist, U. Hosp., 1970—71, instr. surgery, 1970—72, pediatric surgery specialist, gen., thoracic and urologic surg. tng., Children's Hosp., 1971—72; attending pediatric surgeon, chief thoracic surgery Miami Children's Hosp. Pediatric and Thoracic Surgery, Fla., 1972—; pvt. practice in pediatric and thoracic surgery Dade and Broward Counties, Fla. Active Bapt. Hosp., Miami, 1972—; cons. Mt. Sinai Hosp., Miami, 1972—. Contbr. articles to profl. jours. Former med. bd. mem., treas. Miami Children's Hosp., vice chmn. bd. trustees; mem. Soc. Hosp. Founders. Grantee Gen. Rsch. Support, CHRF NIH, 1972. Fellow: ACS, Am. Acad. Pediat.; mem.: AMA, Greater Miami Pediatric Soc., Fla. Assn. Pediatric Surgeons, Dade County Med. Assn., Fla. Med. Assn. Office: Miami Children's Hosp 3200 SW 60th Ct Ste 201 Miami FL 33155 Office Phone: 305-662-8320. Office Fax: 305-665-2467.

NAHO, YOSHIZAWA, physician; b. Osaka, Japan, Sept. 3, 1976; MD, Keio U. Medicine, 2001. Physician dermatology dept. Keio U. Sch. Medicine, 2001—06. Home: 1-21-10-1205 Ichikawa Chiba 272-0034 Japan Personal E-mail: naho@suite.plala.or.jp.

NAHRWOLD, DAVID LANGE, surgeon, educator; b. St. Louis, Dec. 21, 1935; s. Elmer William and Magdalen Louise (Lange) Nahrwold; m. Carolyn Louise Hoffman, June 14, 1958; children: Stephen Michael, Susan Alane, Thomas James, Anne Elizabeth. AB, Ind. U., Bloomington, 1957; MD, Ind. U., Indpls., 1960. Diplomate Am. Bd. Surgery, Am. Bd. Thoracic Surgery. Postdoctoral scholar in gastrointestinal physiology VA Ctr., UCLA, 1965; asst. prof. surgery Ind. U. Med. Sch., 1968-70; assoc. prof. Coll. Medicine Pa. State U., 1970-73; vice-chmn. dept. surgery Pa. State U., 1971-82, assoc. provost, dean health affairs, 1981-82, prof., chief divsn. gen. surgery, 1974-82; Loyal and Edith Davis prof., chmn. dept. surgery Northwestern U. Med. Sch., Chgo., 1982-97; surgeon-in-chief Northwestern Meml. Hosp., Chgo., 1982-97; intern, then resident in surgery Ind. U. Med. Ctr., Indpls., 1960-65; pres., CEO Northwestern Med. Faculty Found., Inc., 1996-99; prof. surgery, exec. assoc. dean clin. affairs Northwestern U. Med. Sch., 1997-99, prof. emeritus, 1999—.

Mem. Nat. Digestive Disease Adv. Bd., 1985—89; bd. dirs. Am. Bd. Surgery, vice chmn., 1994—95, chmn., 1995—96; bd. dirs. Am. Bd. Med. Specialties, 1997—2005, pres., 2002—04; bd. dirs. Northwestern Healthcare Network; mem. exec. com. Accreditation Coun. for Grad. Med. Edn., 1999—2000; bd. commrs. Joint Commn. Accreditation Healthcare Orgns., 2002—08, vice chmn. bd. commrs., 2005—06, chmn. bd. commrs., 2007—08; bd. dirs. Joint Commn. Resources, 2004—08, vice chmn. bd. dirs., 2005—06; bd. dirs. Luth. Social Svcs., Ill., 2008—11, Holy Family Ministries, 2006—09. Editor emeritus Jour. Laparoendoscopic Surgery, 1997-2004; mem. editl. bd. Surgery, 1981-94, Archives of Surgery, 1983-93, Digestive Surgery, 1986-99, Am. Jour. Surgery, 1994-2000, Jour. Gastrointestinal Surgery, 1996-2000, Current Opinion in Gen. Surgery, Jour. Lithotripsy and Stone Disease, 1988-92; contbr. articles to profl. jours. With MC US Army, 1966—68. Recipient John P. Hubbard award, Nat. Bd. Med. Examiners, 2003, Derrick Vail award, Am. Bd. Med. Specialties, 2007. Fellow: ACS (bd. govs. 1992—98, vice chmn. 1994—96, chmn. bd. govs. exec. com. 1996—98, interim dir. 1999—2000, 1st v.p. elect 2005—06, 1st v.p. 2006—07, bd. regents, Disting. Svc. award 2001), Philippine Coll. Surgeons (hon.); mem.: AMA, Chgo. Surg. Soc. (pres. 1993—94), Chgo. Med. Soc., We. Surg. Assn., Soc. Univ. Surgeons, Soc. Surgery Alimentary Tract (pres. 1989—90, trustee), Soc. Clin. Surgery (sec. 1984—88), Internat. Biliary Assn., Ill. Surg. Soc., Ill. State Med. Soc., Internat. Fedn. Surg. Colls. (hon.; treas. 1999—2002), Gastroenterology Rsch. Group, Collegium Internat. Chirurgiae Digestive (pres. U.S. chpt. 1988—90), Ctrl. Surg. Assn. (sec. 1994—97, pres.-elect 1997—98, pres. 1998—99, pres. Found. 2002—03), Assn. Surg. Edn., Assn. Acad. Surgery, Am. Surg. Assn. (2d v.p. 1993—94), Am. Phys. Soc., Alpha Omega Alpha, Sigma Xi. Home Phone: 847-714-1143.

NAIDICH, THOMAS PAUL, neuroradiologist, educator; b. Bklyn., Apr. 8, 1944; s. James and Rose (Bitko) N.; m. Rochele Miriam Pudlowksi, Feb. 2, 1975 (div. Nov. 1981); children: 1 child, Sandra Rebecca; m. Michele W. Levin, Dec. 29, 1990. BA, Cornell U., 1965; MD, NYU, NY, 1969. Diplomate in radiology and in neuroradiology Am. Bd. Radiology. Intern Bronx Mcpl. Hosp. Ctr., NY, 1969-70; resident in radiology Montefiore Hosp., Bronx, NY, 1970-73; fellow in neuroradiology NYU Sch. Medicine, NY, 1973-75; prof. radiology and neurosurgery Mt. Sinai Med. Ctr. NYU, NY, 1998—, dir. neuroradiology NY, 1998—, vice chmn. radiology for acad. affairs, 2001—, Irving and Dorothy Regenstreif Rsch. prof. of neurosci., 2002—; asst. prof. Albert Einstein Coll. Medicine, Bronx, NY, 1975-77; from asst. prof. to assoc. prof. Mallinckrodt Inst. Radiology, St. Louis, 1978-80; from assoc. prof. to prof. Northwestern U. Sch. Medicine, Chgo., 1980-88; clin. prof. neuroradiology U. Miami Sch. Med., Fla., 1988-98; dir. neuroradiology Bapt. Hosp. Miami, Fla., 1988-98; dir Clin. Imaging Rsch. Core, Mt. Sinai Med. Ctr., Mt. Sinai, NY, 2001—05. Hon. prof. Inst. Neurology, London, 2008—. Author: (with R. M. Quencer) Clinical Neurosonography, 1987; (with Valavanis, Schubiger) Clinical Imaging of the Cerebello-Pontine Angle, 1987; (with Daniels, Haughton) Cranial and Spinal Magnetic Ressonance Imaging, 1987, (with Duvernoy, Cattin, Fatterpeker, Raybaud, Risold, Salvolini, Scarabino) The Human Hippocampus, Anatomy, Vascularization and Serial Sections with MRAI, 3d edit., 2005, (with Naidich, TP, Duvernoy HM, Delman BN, Sorensen AG, Kollias SS, Haacke EM) Duvernoy's Atlas of the Human Brain Stem and Cerebellum, Springer Verlag, Wein, New York, 2009, Imaging of the Spine, 2010; editor-in-chief Neuroradiology, 1980-91, chmn. editl. bd., 1991-93; assoc. editor Surg. and Radiol. Anatomy, 1991-97; founding editor Internat. Jour. Neuroradiology, 1994-00; contbr. articles to profl. jours. Recipient John Caffey award Soc. Pediatric Radiology, 1983. Mem. Am. Soc. Neuroradiology (treas. 1991-93, Cornelius Dyke award 1975), Am. Soc. Pediatric Neuroradiology (pres. 1994-95, Gold medal), Sociedad Ibero-latino Americana de Neurorradiologia (SILAN, Gold medal), European Soc. Neuroradiology (hon.), Brit. Soc. Neuroradiologists (hon.), Swiss Soc. Neuroradiology (hon.). Avocation: antique furniture. Office: Mt Sinai Med Ctr Dept Radiology Box 1234 1 Gustave Levy Pl New York NY 10029 Business E-Mail: thomas.naidich@mountsinai.org.

NAIK, SALEEM, surgeon, consultant; b. Jammu & Kashmir, Dec. 15, 1974; MS, JLNMC, Raipur, 2002; DNB in Surg. Gastroenterology, BMHRC, Bhopal, 2008. Sr. cons. Global Hosp., 2010—. Recipient Best Paper award, IHPBA. Mem.: Nat. Acad. Med. Scis. Avocations: mountain climbing, sports, fishing. Home: Gagribal Srinagar Jammu and Kashmir 190001 India Personal E-mail: saleemnaik@gmail.com.

NAIMI, TIMOTHY S., epidemiologist, researcher; b. Feb. 6, 1964; MD, U. Mass. Sch. Medicine, 1991; MPH, Harvard Sch. Pub. Health, 1995. Diplomate Am. Bd. Pediat., Am. Bd. Internal Medicine, Am. Bd. Preventive Medicine. Resident internal medicine & pediat. Mass. Gen. Hosp., Boston, 1991—95; staff Zuni Pub. Health Svc. Indian Hosp., N.Mex., 1995—98; Epidemic Intelligence Svc. fellowship Minn. Dept. Pub. Health, 1998—2000; med. epidemiologist, divsn. adult & cmty. health Centers Disease Control & Prevention (CDC), Atlanta, 2000—. Clin. faculty Emory U. Med. Sch., Atlanta; staff Emory Dunwoody Med. Ctr., Zuni Pub. Health Svc. Indian Hosp. Contbr. articles to profl. jours. Office: CDC 1600 Clifton Rd Atlanta GA 30333 Business E-Mail: timothy.naimi@cdc.hhs.gov, tbn7@cdc.gov. *

NAIR, GANESH KUMAR VENUGOPALAN, endocrinologist, internist; arrived in U.S., 1995; s. Venugopalan and Sreekumari Nair; m. Usha Kartha, Jan. 21, 1996; 1 child, Nikhil. Student, U. Kerala, 1981—83, MBBS, 1989. Diplomate in endocrimology, diabetes and metabolism Am. Bd. Internal Medicine, 2008, cert. in thyroid ultrasound and guided biopsy, clin. densitometrist, lic. Jamaican Med. Coun. Intern Kerala U., Trivandrum, Kerala State, India, 1990—91; sr. ho. surgeon Gastroenterology Med. Coll. Trivandrum, 1991, rsch. asst. Gastroenterology, 1991—92; intern Ministry Health, Kingston, Jamaica, 1992; jr. resident Kingston Pub. Hosp., 1993—95; resident internal medicine Conemaugh Valley Meml. Hosp. Program Temple U., Johnstown, Pa., 1995—98, chief resident, internal medicine Conemaugh Valley Meml. Hosp. Program, 1998—99; fellow endocrinology, diabetes and metabolism U. Ark., 1999—2001, asst. prof. medicine, 2002—05; staff physician Ctrl. Ark. Vets. Healthcare Sys., Little Rock, 2002—05; attending endocrinologist Little Rock Diagnostic Clinic, 2005—. Assoc. program dir. endocrinology, diabetes and metabolism fellowship program U. Ark., Little Rock, 2003—05. Contbr. articles to profl. jours. Recipient Cert. of Merit, Sahodara Samajam Nair Sanodara Samajam. Karayogam, 1981, 1983, Clin. award, Internal Medicine Residency, Temple U., 1998, Chief Resident Award, 1999, Excellence award, U. Ark. Med. Sci., 1999—2001, Outstanding Svc. award, Appreciation Cert., Dept. Vets. Affairs, Ctrl. Ark. Vets. Healthcare System, Little Rock, 2005; named Best Doctors in America, 2011—. Fellow: ACP, Am. Coll. Physicians, Am. Coll. Endocrinology; mem.: Am. Diabetes Assn., Internat. Soc. Clin. Densitometry, The Endocrine Soc., Am. Assn. Clin. Endocrinologists. Office: 10001 Life Dr Little Rock AR 72205 Office Phone: 501-227-8000.

NAIR, VELAYUDHAN, pharmacologist, academic administrator, medical educator; arrived in U.S., 1956, naturalized, 1963; m. Jo Ann Burke, Nov. 30, 1957; children: David, Larry, Sharon. PhD in Medicine, U. London, 1956, DSc, 1976, LHD (hon.) h.c., 2003. Rsch. assoc. U. Ill. Coll. Medicine, 1956-58; asst. prof. U. Chgo. Sch. Medicine, 1958-63; dir. lab. neuropharmacology and biochemistry Michael Reese Hosp. and Med. Ctr., Chgo., 1963-68, dir. therapeutic rsch., 1968-71; prof. pharmacology FUHS/Chgo. Med. Sch., 1971—, disting. prof., 2001, vice chmn. dept. pharmacology and therapeutics, 1971—76, dean Sch. Grad. and Postdoctoral Studies, 1976—2003, v.p. rsch., 1999—2003, v.p., dean emeritus, 2003—, disting. prof., 2001. Vis. assoc. prof. pharmacology FUHS/Chgo. Med. Sch., 1963—68, vis. prof., 1968—71, Harvard U., 1994, Johns Hopkins Sch. Medicine, 1995. Contbr. articles to profl. jours. Recipient Morris Parker award, U. Health Scis./Chgo. Med. Sch., 1972. Fellow: AAAS, Am. Coll. Clin. Pharmacology, NY Acad. Scis.; mem.: AAUP, Internat. Soc. Devel. Neurosci., Am. Coll. Toxicology, Internat. Soc. Chronobiology, Soc. Neurosci., Soc. Exptl. Biology & Medicine, Pan Am. Med. Assn. (coun. on toxicology), Royal Inst. Chemistry (London), Brit. Chem. Soc., Am. Chem. Soc., Soc. Toxicology, Radiation Rsch. Soc., Am. Soc. Clin. Pharmacology & Therapeutics, Am. Soc. Pharmacology & Exptl. Therapeutics, Internat. Soc. Biochem. Pharmacology, Internat. Brain Rsch. Orgn., Cosmos Club (Washington), Alpha Omega Alpha, Sigma Xi. Office: Rosalind Franklin Univ Medicine and Sci 3333 Green Bay Rd North Chicago IL 60064-3037 Personal E-mail: velnair@comcast.net.

NAITO, AKIRA, otolaryngologist; s. Takeshi and Yasuko Naito; m. Yuki Hosako; 1 child, Sato. MD, Kochi Med. Sch., 1988; PhD, Tokyo U., 2001. Neuro-otolaryngologist Tokyo Neurol. Hosp., 1991—93; faculty med. sch. Tokyo U., 1993—94; sr. rschr. Haskins Labs., Yale U., New Haven, 1994—96; faculty Tokyo U., 1996—98; sr. head and neck surgeon NTT Kanto Hosp., 1998—2000; dir. Naito Otolaryngology Clinic, 2001—. Avocation: sailboat racing.

NAITO, HARUHIKO, surgeon; b. Nirasaki, Japan, Mar. 18, 1946; m. Kayoko Imai, May 11, 1974, children: Miyuki, Satsuki, Kanna. MD, Hokkaido U., 1971, PhD, 1986. Clin. resident Hosp. Hokkaido U. Sch. Medicine, Sapporo, 1971—74; lab. resident dept. pathology Sapporo Nat. Hosp., 1974—76; surgeon dept. surgery Obihiro Kyokai, 1976—78; rsch. fellow dept. surgery Hokkaido U. Sch. Medicine, Sapporo, 1978—81, asst. first dept. surgery, 1984—85; surg. rsch. fellow Children's Hosp. Phila., 1981—83, surgeon dept. surgery Hokkaido Cancer Ctr., 1986—95, surgeon-in-chief, 1995—, dir., 2003—04, v.p., 2005—08. Fellow: Japanese Soc. Stoma Rehab. (trustee), Japanese Assn. Pediat. Cancer (dir.), Japanese Soc. Pediat. Surgeons; mem.: Japanese Assn. Clin. Oncology, Japanese Soc. Gastrointestinal Surgery, Japanese Soc. Surgeons. Home: 12-8 Nishino Nishi-ku Sapporo 063 0042 Japan Office: Hokkaido Cancer Ctr 4-2 Kikusui Shiroishi-ku Sapporo 003-0804 Japan Office Phone: 011-811-9111. *

NAITO, MICHITAKA, medical educator, department chairman; b. Gifu, Japan, July 13, 1953; s. Sachiko Naito, m. Michiko Kokuryu; children: Michitaro, Kojiro. MD, Nagoya U., Japan, PhD, 1978. Assoc. prof. Nagoya U., 1998—2002; prof. Sugiyama Jogakuen U., 2002—, dean, 2008—. Recipient award, Japan Geriatric Soc., 1997. Mem.: Japan Atherosclerosis Soc. Office: Sugiyama Jogakuen Univ 17-3 Hoshigaoka Motomachi Chikusa-ku Nagoya 464-8662 Japan Business E-Mail: naito@sugiyama-u.ac.jp.

NAITO, MIKA, psychologist, educator; d. Tomimitsu Naito and Hiroko Hamazaki. MEd, Yokohama Nat. U., 1986; PhD in Lit., Tokyo Met. U., 1991. Japan Soc. Promotion Sci. rsch. fellow Tokyo Met. U., 1989—91, rsch. assoc., 1991—95; lectr. Joetsu U. Edn., Japan, 1995—97, assoc. prof., 1997—2009, prof., 2009—. Office: Joetsu U Edn 1 Yamayashiki-machi Joetsu 943 8512 Japan

NAITO, YOSHIRO, cardiologist, educator; b. Japan, Dec. 16, 1972; MD, Hyogo Coll. Medicine, 1997. Assoc. prof. Hyogo Coll. Medicine, 2011—. Fellowship, Am. Heart Assn. Office: 1-1 Mukogawa cho Nishinomiya Hyogo 663-8501 Japan Office Fax: 81-798-45-6551. Business E-Mail: ynaito@hyo-med.ac.jp.

NAJARIAN, JOHN SARKIS, surgeon, educator; b. Oakland, Calif., Dec. 22, 1927; s. Garabed L. and Siranoush T. (Demirjian) N.; m. Arlys Viola Mignette Anderson, Apr. 27, 1952; children: Jon, David, Paul, Peter. AB with honors, U. Calif., Berkeley, 1948; MD, U. Calif., San Francisco, 1952; LHD (hon.), U. Athens, 1980; DSc (hon.), Gustavus Adolphus Coll., 1981; LHD (hon.), Calif. Luth. Coll., 1983. Diplomate Am. Bd. Surgery. Surg. intern U. Calif., San Francisco, 1952-53, surg. resident, 1955-60, asst. prof. surgery, dir. surg. research labs., chief transplant service dept. surgery, 1963-66, prof., vice chmn., 1966-67; spl. research fellow in immunopathology U. Pitts. Med. Sch., 1960-61; NIH sr. fellow and assoc. in tissue transplantation immunology Scripps Clinic and Research Found., La Jolla, Calif., 1961-63; Markle scholar Acad. Medicine, 1964-69; prof., chmn. dept. surgery U. Minn. Hosp., Mpls., 1967-93; med. dir. Transplant Ctr., clin. chief surgery Univ. Hosp., 1967-94; chief hosp. staff U. Minn. Hosp., Mpls., 1970-71, Regents' prof., 1985-95, Jay Phillips Disting. Chair in Surgery, 1986-95, prof. emeritus, prof. surgery, 1995—. Spl. cons. USPHS, NIH Clin. Rsch. Tng. Com., Inst. Gen. Med. Scis., 1965-69; cons. U.S. Bur. Budget, 1966-68; mem. sci. adv. bd. Nat. Kidney Found., 1968; mem. surg. study sect. A div. rsch. grants NIH, 1970; chmn. renal transplant adv. group VA Hosps., 1971; mem. bd. sci. cons. Sloan-Kettering Inst. Cancer Rsch., 1971-78; mem. screening com. Dernham Postdoctoral Fellowships in Oncology, Calif. div. Am. Cancer Soc. Editor: (with Richard L. Simmons) Transplantation, 1972; co-editor: Manual of Vascular Access, Organ Donation, and Transplantation, 1984; mem. editorial bd. Jour. Surg. Rsch., 1968—, Minn. Medicine, 1968—, Jour. Surg. Oncology, 1968—, Am. Jour. Surgery, 1967—, assoc. editor, 1982—; mem. editorial bd. Year Book of Surgery, 1970-85, Transplantation, 1970—, Transplantation Procs, 1970—, Bd. Clin. Editors, 1981-84, Annals of Surgery, 1972—, World Jour. Surgery, 1976—, Hippocrates, 1986—, Jour. Transplant Coordination, 1990—; assoc. editor: Surgery, 1971; editor-in-chief: Clin. Transplantation, 1986—. Bd. dirs., v.p. Variety Club Heart Hosp., U. Minn.; trustee, v.p. Minn. Med. Found. Served with USAF, 1953-55. Hon. fellow Royal Coll. Surgeons of Eng., 1987; hon. prof. U. Madrid, 1990; named Alumnus of Yr., U. Calif. Med. Sch., San Francisco, 1977; recipient award Calif. Trudeau Soc., 1962, Ann. Brotherhood award NCCJ, 1978, Disting. Achievement award Modern Medicine, 1978, Internat. Gt. Am. award B'nai B'rith Found., 1982, Uncommon Citizen award, 1985, Sir James Carreras award Variety Clubs Internat., 1987, Silver medal IXth Centenary, U. Bologna, 1988, Humanitarian of Yr. award, U. Minn., 1992, Najarian Festschrift award Am. Jour. Surgery, 1993, Jubilee medal Swedish Soc. Medicine, 1994. Fellow ACS; mem. AAAS, AMA, Internat. Pediat. Transplantation Assn. (pres. 1998-2000), Soc. Univ. Surgeons, Soc. Exptl. Biology and Medicine, Am. Soc. Exptl. Pathology, Am. Surg. Assn. (pres. 1988-89), Am. Assn. Immunologists, Transplantation Soc. (v.p. western hemisphere 1984-86, pres. 1994-96, Medawar prize 2004, Ellis Island medal of Hon, 2005), Am. Soc. Nephrology, Internat. Soc. Nephrology, Am. Assn. Lab. Animal Sci., Assn. Acad. Surgery (pres. 1969), Internat Soc. Surgery, Soc. Surg. Chairmen, Soc. Clin. Surgery, Ctrl. Surg. Assn., Minn. Med. Soc., Hennepin County Med. Socs., Minn. Surg. Soc., Mpls. Surg Soc, St. Paul Surg. Soc. Howard C. Nafziger Surg. Soc., Portland Surg Soc., Halsted Surg. Soc., Am. Heart Assn., Am. Soc. Transplant Surgeons (pres. 1977-78), Coun on Kidney in Cardiovasc. Disease, Hagfish Soc., Italian Rsch. Soc., Minn. Acad. Medicine, Minn. Med. Assn., Minn. Med. Found., Surg. Biology Club, Sigma Xi, Alpha Omega Alpha, others. Office: U Minn Surgery Dept Mayo Mail Code 195 420 Delaware St SE Minneapolis MN 55455-0374 Home Phone: 612-823-0051; Office Phone: 612-625-8444. Business E-Mail: najar001@umn.edu.

NAJDOWSKI, ADEL C., medical association administrator; b. Calif., June 13, 1976; BA, U. Nev., Reno, 1998, PhD, 2004. Dir., co-creator skills Ctr. Autism & Related Disorders, Inc., 2005—. Mem.: Internat. Soc. Autism Rsch., Calif. Assn. Behavior Analysis. Office: 19019 Ventura Blvd Tarzana CA 91356 Business E-Mail: a.najdowski@centerforautism.com.

NAJERA, RAFAEL, virologist; b. Córdoba, Spain, Feb. 19, 1938; s. Luis and María (Morrondo) Najera; m. Margarita de Parga Vazquez, July 1, 1965; children: Isabel, Gonzalo. MB, Madrid U., 1962, MD, 1967; MSc, Birmingham Med. Sch., Eng., 1967; postgrad., Birmingham Med. Sch., 1968; DPH, Sch. Pub. Health Madrid, 1965. Assoc. chief, svc. respiratory and exanthematic viruses Nat. Ctr. Virology, Majadahonda, Madrid, 1963—72, chief svc., 1972—80; med. officer virus diseases unit WHO, Geneva, 1980—81; assoc. prof. virology Madrid Faculty Medicine, 1970—73; dir. Nat. Ctr. Microbiology, 1982—86; dir. gen. NIH, Min. Health, Madrid, 1986—92; dir. Dept. Retrovirus Rsch., Dept. Viral Pathogenesis Inst. Salud Carlos III, Madrid, 1992—. Contbr. articles to profl. jours. Dir. WHO Collaborating Ctr. AIDS; pres. Spanish Soc. AIDS, 1989—. Decorated Knight Comdr., Civil Order Sanidad; recipient Great Cross Gold medal, Galicia Health Svcs. Mem.: Am. Pub. Health Assn., Internat. Epidemiol. Assn., European Teratology Soc., Internat. Assn. Biol. Standardization, Am. Soc. Microbiology, Soc. Gen. Microbiology, Spanish Soc. Virology (pres. 1988—90), Spanish Soc. Microbiology (sec., pres. virology group 1970—). Office: Instituto de Salud Carlos III Majadahonda 28220 Madrid Spain E-mail: rafael.najera@isciii.es.

NAJJAR, SOUHEL, neurologist, educator; MD, Damascus U., 1977—83. Diplomate Am. Bd. Neurology. Resident in pathology Albany Med. Ctr., NY, 1985—88, resident in neurology, 1989—92, intern NY Downtown Hosp., 1988—89; assoc. clin. prof. neurology NYU; joined Comprehensive Epilepsy Ctr. NYU Med. Ctr., 1998, dir. EEG Lab.; dir. Neuroscience Ctr. Staten island univ. Hosp. Author: (journ.) Clinical features of patients with unilateral mesial temporal sclerosis (MTS) with persistent seizures following antero-mesial temporal resection, 2004, Adult-onset epilepsy in focal cortical dysplasia of Taylor type, 2005, Race/ethnicity, sex, and socioeconomic status as predictors of outcome after surgery for temporal lobe epilepsy, 2006, Pediatric language mapping: sensitivity of neurostimulation and Wada testing in epilepsy surgery, 2007, Immunology and epilepsy, 2008, Phenotypic Heterogeneity and Type-1/2 PrPSc Co-Occurrence in Creutzfeldt-Jakob Disease Associated With a new Mutation of PRNP, 2010, Paraneoplastic myelitis related to diffuse large B-cell lymphoma and Hodgkin's lymphoma: Two case reports and literature review, 2010, Cardiac care for older adults time for a new paradigm, 2011, Extralimbic autoimmune encephalitis associated with glutamic acid decarboxylase antibodies: An underdiagnosed entity?, 2011, Spontaneously resolving seronegative autoimmune limbic encephalitis, 2011, numerous journs. in publs. Office: Staten Island University Hospital 475 Seaview Ave Staten Island NY 10305 Office Phone: 718-226-9000. Office Fax: 718-226-2734.

NAKABEPPU, YUSAKU, medical educator; b. Miyazaki, Japan, Jan. 2, 1957; DVM, Miyazaki U., 1979; DSc, Kyushu U., 1984. Postdoc. fellow Johns Hopkins U., 1987—90; rsch. assoc. Kyushu U., 1985—87, 1990—97, prof., 1997—2010, disting. prof., 2010—. Editor Genes to Cells, 2010, Genes and Genetic Sys., 2010; editl. bd. DNA Repair, 2002. Recipient Incitement award, Japanese Cancer Assn.; Gen. Rsch. award, Showa Shell Sekiyu Found. Promotion Environ. Rsch.; Rsch. fellow, Japan Soc. Promotion Sci. Mem.: Japan Neuroscience Soc., Molecular Biology Soc. Japan, Am. Soc. Microbiology, Am. Soc. Biochemisry and Molecular Biology, Soc. Neuroscience. Avocations: photography, classical music, history. Office: 3-1-1 Maidashi Higashi-ku Fukuoka 812-8582 Japan Office Fax: 81-92-642-6791. Business E-Mail: yusaku@bioreg.kyushu-u.ac.jp.

NAKAE, KIMIHIRO, epidemiologist, researcher, educator; b. Kumamoto, Japan, Feb. 6, 1937; s. Sadajiro and Chiyoko (Yakabe) N.; m. Yukiko Kakihara, March 31, 1967; 1 child, Nakae Yuko. PhD, Tokyo University, 1974. Assoc. prof. Dokkyo U. Sch. Medicine, Tochigi, Japan, 1978—92, prof., 1992—2002, dir. med. info. and media ctr., 1998—2000; prof. South Kyushu U., Miyazaki, Japan, 2004—07; chief rschr. WHO Coraborating Ctr. for Prevention and Control Chronic Resperatory Disease, Tochigi, 2006—; prof. Yamaguchi U. Welfare and Culture, Japan, 2008—. Author: Lancet, 1971, 2nd edit, 1973, Oxford Textbook of Medicine, 1987. Avocation: classic music. Home: 1872-6 Kuniya Mibu Shimotsuga-gun 321-0211 Japan Office: Dokkyo Univ School Medicine Mibu Shimotsuga-Gun Tochigi 321-0293 Japan Home Phone: 81-282-82-1202; Office Phone: 81-358-19-7521.

NAKAGAMI, HIRONORI, physician, educator; b. Gifu, Japan, June 30, 1968; MD, PhD, Nara Med. U., 1994. Prof. divsn. vascular medicine and epigenetics Osaka U. United Grad. Sch. Child Devel., 2010—. Office: 2-1 Yamadaoka Suita Osaka 565-0871 Japan Business E-Mail: nakagami@gts.med.osaka-u.ac.jp.

NAKAGAWA, TAKUMI, medical educator; b. Sapporo, Hokkaido, Japan, June 3, 1966; m. Hisa Yoshimaru, Dec. 2, 1995. PhD, Grad. Sch. Medicine, U. Tokyo, 2000. Cert. med. dr. Japan, 1992. Staff surgeon Tokyo met. geriatric Hosp., Itabashi-ku, Tokyo, Japan, 1994—96, Saitama red-cross Hosp., Japan, 2000—01; asst. prof. Juntendo U. Hosp., Bunkyo-ku, 2001—03, U. Tokyo Hosp., Bunkyo-ku, 2003—. Rsch. fellow U. Pitts. Med. Ctr., Dept. Orthopaedic Surgery, 2005—06. Home: 5-12-24-607 Minami-Aoyama Minato-ku Tokyo 107-0062 Japan Office: Univ Tokyo Hosp 7-3-1 Hongo Bunkyo-ku Tokyo 113-8655 Japan Office Fax: +81-3-3818-4082; Home Fax: +81-3-6425-7204. Business E-Mail: takumintky@umin.ac.jp.

NAKAGAWA, TANEAKI, dental educator; b. Osaka, Japan, Jan. 4, 1961; PhD, Tokyo Dental Coll., DDS, 1985. Prof. Keio U. Sch. Medicine, 2002—. Office: 35 Shinanomachi Shinjuku-ku Tokyo 160-8582 Japan Business E-Mail: tane@z6.keio.jp.

NAKAI, TOSHIHIRO, biologist, educator; b. Japan, May 11, 1951; MAgr, Hiroshima U., 1979; DAgr, U. Tokyo, 1986. Prof. Grad. Sch. Bioshere Sci., Hiroshima U., 2002—. Reference lab. Office Internat. Des Epizooties, 1997—; editor-in-chief Japanese Soc. Fish Pathology, 2007—10. Mem.: European Assn. Fish Pathologist. Avocation: golf. Office: Kagamiyama Higashi-Hiroshima 739-8528 Japan Office Fax: 81 82 424 4380. Business E-Mail: nakaitt@hiroshima-u.ac.jp.

NAKAJIMA, AKIRA, ophthalmologist, educator; b. Kumamoto, Japan, July 14, 1923; s. Minoru and Chitose Nakajima; m. Michiko Kuno, Nov. 10, 1953; children: Izumi Miyazaki, Kaoru. MD, U. Tokyo, 1945, D in Med. Sci., 1953. Lic. physician Tokyo. With dept. ophthalmology Univ. Hosp., U. Tokyo, 1945-49; Akita prof. eye clinic Hanaoka Mine Hosp., 1949-54; asst. prof. ophthalmology Juntendo U., Tokyo, 1954-60, prof., 1960-89, prof. emeritus, 1989—. Chief WHO Collaborating Ctr., Tokyo, 1979—89. Recipient Gonin medal, Lausanne U., 1986, Jose Rizal medal, Asia Pacific Acad. Ophthalmology, Kuala Lumpur, 1987, 3d order middle rising sun, Japanese Emperor, 2000. Mem.: Academia Ophthalmologica Internationalis, Internat. Coun. Ophthalmology (pres. 1990—98, hon. life pres. 1998—). Home: 1-41-12 Miyasaka Setagayaku Tokyo 156-0051 Japan Office: Juntendo U Sch Medicine Dept Opthalmology 3-1-3 Hongo Bunkyoku Tokyo 113-8431 Japan 113 Home Phone: 813-3429-6918. Home Fax: 813-5477-7168. Personal E-mail: a-nakjma@yb3.so-net.ne.jp.

NAKAJIMA, HIDEO, immunologist, educator; b. Gunma, Japan, Nov. 18, 1963; MD, Tokyo Med. and Dental U., PhD, 1988. Sect. chief immunology Nat. Inst. Longevity Scis., Japan, 2000—04; assoc. prof. Kanazawa Med. U., 2005—. Mem.: Japanese Soc. Med. Oncology. Avocation: swimming. Office: Daigaku 1-1 Uchinada Ishikawa 920-0293 Japan Office Fax: 81-76-218-8283. Business E-Mail: hideonak@kanazawa-med.ac.jp.

NAKAJIMA, MASATO, surgeon; b. Tsukuba, Ibaraki, Japan, Sept. 11, 1969; s. Masayuki and Sadako Nakajima; m. Hiromi Nishikawa, Sept. 13, 1974; 1 child, Masaharu. MD, Tsukuba U., Ibaraki, Japan, 1994. Diplomate Japanese Assn. for Thoracic Surgery, 2002. Resident Tokyo women's Med. U., The Heart Inst. of Japan, Shinjuku, 1994—2001; dir. dept. cardiovasc. surgery Yamanashi Ctrl. Hosp., Kofu, Japan, 2001—03. Author: (orginal report) Long-term Result Of Aortic Root Replacement, (brief report) aortic valve anomaly, The Journal of Thoracic and Cardiovascular Surgery, myocardial protection in redo aortic arch repair, The Journal of Thoracic and Cardiovascular Surgery, Modified Dagget technique, Annals of Thoracic Surgery, (original report) Reoperation of mitral valve repair, The Japanese journal of Thoracic and Cardiovascular Surgery, (brief report) Biventricular pacing and cardiac surgery, The Journal of Thoracic and Cardiovascular Surgery, Subdural hemorrhage after cardiac surgery, Annals of Thoracic Surgery. Mem.: Japanese Surg. Soc., Japanese Assn. of Thoracic and Cardiovasc. Surgery. Office: Yamanashi Ctrl Hosp 1-1-1 Fujimi Yamanashi Kofu 400-0027 Japan Office Fax: 81-55-253-8011; Home Fax: 81-55-237-7617. E-mail: m-nakajima2a@ych.pref.yamanashi.jp.

NAKAJIMA, YUSUKE, dental educator; b. Tokyo, June 22, 1968; DDS, Tokyo Med. and Dental U., 1994, PhD, 1998. Assoc. prof. Tokyo Med. and Dental U., 2007—. Mem.: Japanese Soc. Oral and Maxillofacial Surgeons. Office: 1-5-45 Yushima Bunkyo Tokyo 113-8549 Japan Office Fax: 03-5803-0199. Business E-Mail: nakaji.osur@tmd.ac.jp.

NAKAKI, TOSHIO, pharmacologist, educator; b. Nagoya, Aichi, Japan, July 1, 1952; s. Hisao and Eiko (Yamashita) N.; m. Hiroko Yoshizawa, May 17, 1981; children: Fumio, Michio. MD, Keio U., Japan, 1979, PhD, 1983. Diplomate in medicine. Asst. Keio U., 1983-89, asst. prof. pharmacology, 1989-96; assoc. prof. Teikyo U., 1996-2000, prof. and chmn., 2000—. Postdoctoral fellow NIH, Bethesda, Md., 1983-85. Contbr. articles to profl. jours. Recipient Sanshikai award, 1988, Kitsasato award, 1992, Mitsukoshi Med. award, 1992. Mem. Japanese Pharmacol. Soc., Am. Soc. Pharmacology and Exptl. Therapeutics, NY Acad. Scis. Avocations: ancient oriental literature, skiing. Office: Teikyo U Sch Medicine Dept Pharmacology 2-11-1 Kaga Itabashi-ku 173-8605 Tokyo Japan Office Phone: +81-3-3964-3793. E-mail: nakaki@med.teikyo-u.ac.jp.

NAKAMOTO, BEAU, physician; b. Hawaii, Nov. 25, 1971; MD, U. Hawaii, 1999. Physician Straub Clinics and Hosp., 2004—. Office: 888 S King St Honolulu HI 96813 Personal E-mail: beau_nakamoto@yahoo.com.

NAKAMOTO, HIDETOMO, physician, educator; b. Chiba, Japan, Sept. 22, 1957; MD, Keio U., Sch. Medicine, 1983. Assoc. prof. dept. nephrology Saitama Med. U., 1999—2007, prof. dept. gen. internal medicine, 2007—. Fellow: ACP, JSH. Home: 1-22-8 Hayamiya Nerima-ku Tokyo 1790085 Japan Home Fax: 81-1-33993-4512. Personal E-mail: nakamo_h@saitama-med.ac.jp.

NAKAMURA, HIDEAKI, biotechnologist; b. Arakawa, Tokyo, 1969; s. Isamu and Tomoko Nakamura. Deng, U. Tokyo, 1998. Rsch. fellow Japan Soc. Promotion Sci., Tokyo, 1999—2001; asst. prof. Tokyo U. Tech., Hachioji, 2001—. Vis. rschr. Nat. Inst. Advanced Indsl. Sci. and Tech., Japan, 2002—. Contbr. scientific papers. Mem.: Soc. Biology, Am. Chem. Soc. Achievements include patents for glucose biosensor chips. Office: Tokyo University Tech Sch Biosci & Biotech Grad Sch Bionics Computer & Media Scis 1404-1 Katakura Hachioji Tokyo 192-0982 Japan

NAKAMURA, HIROSHI, urology educator; b. Tokyo, Mar. 22, 1933; s. Yataroh and Hideko (Tanaka) N.; m. Miyoko Kodachi, Aug. 13, 1966. MD, Keio U., Tokyo, 1960, PhD, 1966. Med. diplomate. Asst. resident Mt. Sinai Hosp., NYC, 1962—63; rsch. fellow Cornell U. Med. Coll., NYC, 1966—68; asst. Sch. Medicine Keio U., Tokyo, 1968—70; chmn. urology dept. Tokyo Elec. Power Hosp., Tokyo, 1970—73; vis. asst. prof. surgery Cornell U. Med. Coll., NYC, 1973; chmn. urology Kitasato Inst. Hosp., Tokyo, 1973—77; chmn. dept., prof. urology Nat. Def. Med. Coll., Tokorozawa, Saitama, Japan, 1977—98, dir. dept. acad. affairs, 1994—96, prof. emeritus, 1999—; emeritus dir. Tokorozawa Ishikawa Clinic, 1998—. Author: Bedside Urology, 1983, Modern Clinical Point-Urology, 1993; editor: Up-to-Date Urology, 1983, Caveats & Pitfalls in Clinical Urology, 1999, Medical Ethics Q&A, 2002. Recipient Tamura award, Keio U. Sch. Medicine, 1967, All-around Med. award, Igaku-Shoin, Ltd., Tokyo, 1967, The Order of the Sacred Treasure, Emperor of Japan, 2003, Proclamation of Thanks, New Orleans City Coun., 2008. Buddhist. Avocations: jazz, audiophile, travel. Home: 11-1-1204 Higashicho Tokorozawa Saitama 359-1116 Japan Office: Tokorozawa Ishikawa Clin Iseki Bldg 4F 9-22 Hiyoshicho Tokorozawa 359-1123 Japan Office Phone: 81 4 2925 7355. Business E-Mail: hiroshin@xd5.so-net.ne.jp.

NAKAMURA, HIROSHIGE, thoracic surgeon, educator; b. Tottori, Japan, Mar. 10, 1959; MD, Tottori U., 1984, PhD, 1988. Assoc. prof. Tottori U. Hosp., 2005—. Mem.: IASLC. Achievements include research in thoracoscopic surgery, robotic surgery, surgical treatment for lung cancer. Office: Nishicho 36 1 Yonago Tottori 6838504 Japan Office Fax: 81-859-38-6730. Business E-Mail: hnaka@med.tottori-u.ac.jp.

NAKAMURA, ISAO, acoustician, researcher; b. Ookuwa, Nagano, Japan, Sept. 19, 1925; m. Yuriko Taniyama, Apr. 3, 1952 (dec. Sept. 2000). BS, Tohoku U., Sendai, Japan, 1950, D Engring., 1981. Tech. ofcl. Meteorol. Agy., Japan, 1950-61; assoc. prof. Shizuoka U., Hamamatsu, Japan, 1962-81, prof., 1981—84, U. Electro-Communications, Chofu, Japan, 1984-91, Teikyo U. Tech., Ichihara, Japan, 1991-95, Teikyo Heisei U., Ichihara, 1995-98; dir. Athena Co., Tokyo, 1998—2007, adviser, 2007—. Chmn. organizing com. Internat. Symposium on Mus. Acoustics, Tokyo, 1992, mem. sci. com., Dourdan, France, 95, Edinburgh, 97; mem. Internat. Sci. Adv. Bd., Leavenworth, Wash., 1998, Perugia, Italy, 2001, chmn. adv. com., Nara, Japan, 04; chmn. (Japan side) organizing com. Japan-China Joint Meeting on Mus. Acoustics, Beijing, 1994; chmn. adv. com. Chofu, Tokyo, 1997. Author: Computer and Electronics Terms Dictionary, 1977; co-author: Acoustical Measurement of Musical Instruments Performance and Emotion, 2007; contbr. articles to profl. jours. Mem. Inst. Electronics Info. and Comm. (life), Acoustical Soc. Japan (life, chmn. tech. com. on mus. acoustics 1982-86, advisor 2009-; Sato prize for outstanding papers 1982, prize for disting. achievement in acoustics 1996), Catgut Acoustical Soc. (internat. v.p. 1995-2003). Avocation: travel. Home: 1-33-25 Kokuryo Chofu 182-0022 Japan E-mail: nakamura@ga2.so-net.ne.jp.

NAKAMURA, JUN, research scientist; b. Matsuda-machi, Kanagawa, Japan, Nov. 23, 1942; s. Seiichi and Yukie Nakamura; m. Yuriko Sasaki, Jan. 5, 1973; children: Ryo, Izuru. BS, Tohoku U., Sendai, Japan, 1966, MS, 1968, DSc, 1971. Postdoctoral fellow Tohoku U., Sendai, 1972—72, rsch. asst., 1972—76, rsch. assoc., 1976—95, assoc. prof., 1995—2006; vis. rschr. Nat. Inst. Advanced Indsl. Sci. and Tech., Tsukuba, Japan, 2006—. Vis. asst. prof. U. Cin., 1981—83. Contbr. articles to profl. jours. Mem.: Am. Chem. Soc., Am. Soc. for Biochemistry and Molecular Biology, Biophys. Soc. Japan, Japanese Biochem. Soc. Achievements include research in findings of the existence of two conformational variants of chemically equivalent, ATP-driven calcium-pump molecules in rabbit sarcoplasmic reticulum and of their oligomeric behaviors. Avocations: kitchen gardening, skiing, swimming. Home: Moniwa-dai 2-3-21 Miyagi Sendai 982-0252 Japan Office: AIST Umezono Central 6 1-1-4 Tsukuba 305-8568 Japan Ibaraki Office Phone: 81298615562. Personal E-mail: jun-n@fm2.seikyou.ne.jp.

NAKAMURA, KATSUNORI, pharmacist; b. Japan, July 18, 1969; PhD, Hokkaidou U., 1999. Assoc. prof., vice dir. Shinshu U. Hosp., 2009—. Mem.: Pharm. Soc. Japan. Office: 3-1-1 Asahi Mtasumoto Nagano 390-8621 Japan Business E-Mail: nkatsu777@gmail.com.

NAKAMURA, KAZUHIKO, medical educator; b. Iizuka, Fukuoka, Japan, Oct. 21, 1962; s. Akihiko and Shigeko Nakamura; m. Magu Masuyama, Aug. 25, 1978; children: Rino, Kazuaki. MD, PhD, Kyushu U., Fukuoka, 1993. Cert. gastroenterologist Bd. Japanese Soc. Gastroenterology, Tokyo, 1998. Asst. prof. Kyushu U., 2002—. Vis. fellow NIH, Bethesda, Md., 1998—2002. Contbr. scientific papers to profl. jours. (Postdoc. Fellow award, 2001). Fellow: Japan Gastroent. Endoscopy Soc.; mem.: Japanese Soc. Internal Medicine. Office: Kyushu Univ 3-1-1 Maidashi Higashi-ku Fukuoka 812-8582 Japan Office Fax: 81-92-642-5287. Business E-Mail: knakamur@intmed3.med.kyushu-u.ac.jp.

NAKAMURA, KAZUHIKO, medical educator; b. Japan, Dec. 25, 1961; MD, Kagawa Med. Sch., PhD, 1990. Assoc. prof., dept. psychiatry and neurology Hamamatsu U. Sch. Medicine, 2009—. Office: 1-20-1 Handayama Higashi-ku Hamamatsu Shizuoka 431-3192 Japan Office Fax: 81-53-435-3621. Business E-Mail: nakamura@hama-med.ac.jp.

NAKAMURA, KEN, immunologist; b. Toyotama-cho, Nagasaki, Japan, Sept. 20, 1957; s. Hisato and Sachiko Nakamura; m. Kaori Hirotani, May 31, 1987; children: Aya, Mai, Taku, Kei. Student, Med. Coll. Kagoshima U., 1983; PhD, Fukuoka U., Japan, 1996. Diplomate Japan Govt., 1983. Resident 2nd dept. surgery Kagoshima (Japan) U. Sch. Medicine, 1983—87; med. officer Pub. Health Office Fukuoka Prefecture, 1987—91; clin. fellow 1st Dept. Internal Medicine, Fukuoka, 1991—97; asst. prof. 1st Dept. Biochemistry, Fukuoka, 1997—2000; rsch. fellow Dept. Cell Biology, NYC, 2000—02; asst. prof. Dept. Biochemistry, Fukuoka, 2002—03; vice dir. Med. Corp., Aishin-Kai, Japan, 2004—; dir. dept. clin. lab. Fukuoka Tokushukai Med. Ctr., 2003—. Mem.: Am. Assn. Immunologists. Achievements include discovery of immunosuppressive effect of apoptotic cells upon T cell proliferation. This has led to the expansive investigations of immunosuppression by apoptosis. Office: Fukuoka Tokushukai Med Ctr 4-5 Suku-kita Fukuoka Kasuga 816-0864 Japan Office Phone: 81-92-5736622. Office Fax: 81-92-502-3460.

NAKAMURA, MASAHARU, chemistry professor; b. Tokyo, July 13, 1967; DSc, Tokyo Inst. Tech., 1996. Prof. Kyoto U., 2006—. Office: Gokasho Uji Kyoto 611-0011 Japan Business E-Mail: masaharu@scl.kyoto-u.ac.jp.

NAKAMURA, ROBERT MOTOHARU, pathologist; b. Montebello, Calif., June 10, 1927; s. Mosaburo and Haru (Suematsu) N.; m. Shigeyo Jane Hayashi, July 29, 1957; children: Mary, Nancy. AB, Whittier Coll., 1949; MD, Temple U., 1954. Cert. of spl. qualification in pathologic anatomy, clin pathology, immunopathology, Am. Bd. Pathology. Prof. pathology U. Calif., Irvine, 1971-74, adj. prof. pathology, 1974-75; chmn. dept. pathology Scripps Clinic and Rsch. Found., La Jolla, Calif., 1974-92; sr. cons., 1992—; pres. Scripps Clinic Med. Group, La Jolla, 1981-91; prof. dept. immunology and exptl. and molecular medicine Scripps Rsch. Inst., 1997—; chmn. pathology Scripps Clinic, 1998-99, chmn. emeritus pathology, 1999—. Adj. prof. pathology U. Calif., San Diego, 1975-93. Co-editor: Jr. Clin. Lab. Analysis, 1989—; contbr. articles to profl. jours. Fellow: Coll. Am. Pathologists, Am. Soc. Clin. Pathologists, Assn. Clin. Scientists, Am. Coll. Nutrition; mem. Internat. Acad. Pathology. Avocation: reading. Home: 8841 Nottingham Pl La Jolla CA 92037-2131 Office Phone: 858-554-8166, 858-410-2804. Personal E-mail: rnakamura@pol.net.

NAKAMURA, TAKEHIRO, neurosurgeon, educator; MD, Kagawa Med. Sch., Japan, 1989; PhD, Kagawa Med. Sch., 1999. Asst. prof. Kagawa U. Faculty Medicine, Miki, Japan, 2006—07, assoc. prof., 2007—. Office: Kagawa Univ Faculty Medicine 1750-1 Ikenobe Miki Kagawa 761-0793 Japan Office Fax: 81-87-891-2208. Business E-Mail: tanakamu@kms.ac.jp.

NAKAMURA, TOMOHIKO, medical association administrator; b. Japan, Feb. 18, 1959; MD, Shinshu U., 1984. V.p. Nagano Children's Hosp., 2011. Office: 3100 Toyoshina Azumino Nagano 399-8288 Japan

NAKAMURA, TOSHIYASU, orthopedist, educator; b. Hamamatsu, Japan, Oct. 20, 1963; MD, Sch. Medicine, Keio U., 1988; PhD, Grad. Sch. Medicine, Keio U., 1994. Asst. prof. dept. orthop. surgery Fujita Health U. Sch. Medicine, 1995—98; rsch. fellow Biomechanics Lab., Mayo Clinic, 1998—99, Hand Ctr. Western NY, SUNY, Buffalo, 1999—2000; instr. Dept. Orthop. Surgery, Sch. Medicine, Keio U., 2000—04, asst. prof., 2004—. V.p. European Wrist Arthroscopy Soc., 2010—11. Mem.: Internat. Soc. Magnetic Resonance in Medicine, Am. Assn. Hand Surgery, Am. Soc. Surgery Hand. Avocations: golf, travel. Office: 35 Shinanomachi Shinjuku-ku Tokyo 1608582 Japan Business E-Mail: tosiyasu@sc.itc.keio.ac.jp.

NAKAMURA, YASUHIDE, community health educator; b. Tanabe City, Japan, Feb. 18, 1952; s. Hiroshi and Yoko (Yamakawa) N.; m. Mariko Morii, Aug. 21, 1986; children: Fumi, Yuto. MD, U. Tokyo, 1977, PhD, 1993. Med. diplomate. Med. staff Metro. Fuchu (Japan) Hosp., 1978-85; expert of JICA North Sumatra Health Project, Medan, Indonesia, 1986-89; health officer UNHCR, Islamabad, Pakistan, 1990-91; asst. prof. U. Tokyo, 1992-95, assoc. prof., 1997-99; prof. Osaka U., 1999—. Author: The Handicapped Baby, 1986; co-editor: Textbook of Maternal and Child Health Community Care, 1994; editor: International Health for High School Children, 1995. Pres. Shishinoko Camp, Fuchu, Japan, 1982-86; pres. HANDS, 2000—. Fellow Harvard Sch. Pub. Health; mem. Japan Assn. Internat. Health, Japan Child Health Assn., Japan Primary Care Assn. Avocations: travel, music, noh play. Home: # 404 4-37-12 Nishiogi-kita Suginami-ku Tokyo 167 Japan Office: Faculty Human Scis Osaka U 1-2 Yamadaoka Suita City Osaka 565-0871 Japan Office Phone: 81 6 6879 8064. Personal E-mail: yastisch@aol.com.

NAKAMURA, YASUHIKO, physician, researcher; b. Kitakyusyu, Japan, Dec. 3, 1957; s. Yoshio and Tomeko Nakamura; m. Kyoko Nakamura, June 7, 1986; children: Yukari, Toshiki, Koichi. MD, Yamaguchi U. Sch. Medicine, Ube, 1976—82; PhD, Yamaguchi U., 1984—90. Cert. physician Ministry of Health and Welfare, 1982. Rsch. assoc. Yamaguchi U. Sch. Medicine, Ube, Japan, 1990—95, asst. prof., 1995—98, assoc. prof., 1998—2003, assoc. clin. prof., 2005—, chmn. dept. gynecology, 2004—; dir. reproductive unit Yamaguchi Grand Med. Ctr., 2005—. Vice dir. Perinatal Care Ctr. in Yamaguchi U. Hosp., Ube, Japan, 1998—2003; chmn. dept. gynecology, dir. reproductive unit Grand Med. Ctr., Hofu, Japan, 2004—. Chmn. Adminstrv. Com. of Fertility and Sterility in Yamaguchi Prefecture, Japan, 1998. Mem.: Soc. for Endocrinology (assoc.), Am. Soc. for Reproductive Medicine (assoc.), Soc. for the Study of Reproduction (assoc.), Japanese Soc. Fertility and Sterility (assoc.), Japan Endocrine Soc. (assoc.), Japan Soc. Obstetrics and Gynecology (assoc.). Achievements include research in the roles of local factors in the ovarian follicle. Office: Yamaguchi Grand Med Ctr 77 Ohsaki Hofu Yamaguchi 747-8511 Japan E-mail: yasu-ygc@umin.ac.jp.

NAKAMURA, YASUKA, medical educator; b. Japan, Jan. 7, 1973; PhD, Chiba U. Grad. Sch. Nursing, 2007. Asst. prof. Tohoku U. Grad. Sch. Medicine, 2007—. Recipient Excellent Record award, Chiba U., 2006. Office: 2-1 Seiryo-Machi Aoba-ku Sendai Miyagi 980-8575 Japan E-mail: nyasuka@gmail.com.

NAKANISHI, ALAN, state legislator; m. Sue Nakanishi Nakanishi; children: Pamela, Jennifer, Jon. Mayor Livermore, Calif.; state assemblyman, Dist. 10 Calif., 2003—; pres. Delta Eye Med. Group, 1971—, Dameron IPA. Fellow: ACS, Am. Med. Assn.; mem.: Lodi Rotary Svc. Club, San Joaquin Med. Soc., Calif. Med. Assoc. Mailing: State Capitol PO Box 942849 Rm 5175 Sacramento CA 94249 Fax: 209-333-6807.

NAKANISHI, SHIGETADA, molecular neuroscientist; b. Ogaki, Gifu, Japan, Jan. 7, 1942; s. Tadayoshi and Ayako (Inagaki) N.; m. Chieko Ikeda, Oct. 15, 1970 (dec. Dec. 1981); children: Atsuko, Jun-ichi; m. Masako Kinoshita, Mar. 30, 1985; 1 child, Hiroto. MD, Kyoto U., Japan, 1966, PhD of Med. Scis., 1974. Vis. assoc. Lab. Molecular Biology Nat. Cancer Inst./NIH, 1971-74; assoc. prof. dept. med. chemistry Kyoto U. Faculty Medicine, Japan, 1974-81, prof. dept. biol. sci., 1981—2005, dean, 2000—02; dir. Osaka Biosci. Inst., Suita Osaka, Japan, 2005—. Contbr. articles to sci. jours. Recipient

Asahi award Asahi Shimbun, 1982, Takeda Med. award Takeda Sci. Found., 1987, Erwin von Baelz prize Boehringer Ingelheim, 1991, Uehara award Uehara Meml. Found., 1992, Bristol-Myers Squibb award for disting. achievement in neurosci. rsch., 1995, Toray Scis. and Tech. Prize, 1996, Keio award, 1996, Imperial award, Japan Acad. award, 1997, Peter and Patricia Gruber Found. Neuroscience prize, Soc. for Neuroscience, 2007; named fgn. hon. mem. AAAS, 1995; named Person of Cultural Merit, 2006. Mem. NAS (fgn. assoc.). Avocations: tennis, classical music. Office: Osaka Biosci Inst 6-2-4 Furuedai Osaka 565 Japan Office Phone: 81-6-6872-4810. Business E-Mail: snakanis@obi.or.jp.

NAKANO, ATUSHI, research scientist; b. Japan, July 25, 1963; PhD, KEIO, 1986. Rsch. scientist Nat. Cerebral and Cardiovasc. Ctr., 1989—. Office: 5-7-1 Fujishiro-dai Suita Osaka 565-8565 Japan Office Phone: 816-6833-5004-2518. Business E-Mail: nakano@ri.ncvc.go.jp.

NAKANO, JIRO, medical educator; b. Toyooka City, Hyogo, Japan, Jan. 21, 1925; s. Kijiro and Kame (Kashiwara) Nakano; m. Hisako Shibutani, Sept. 30, 1987; 1 child, Serene Keiko. MD, Hyogo Prefectural Med. Coll., Kobe, Japan, 1949; PhD in Physiology, Kobe U., 1959. Resident, chief resident Jersey City Med. Ctr., 1952—55; cardiology rsch. fellow Columbia U. Coll. P&S, NYC, 1956—58; asst. prof. medicine St. Louis U. Sch. Medicine, 1958—60; assoc. prof. medicine and pharmacology U. Okla. Coll. Medicine, Oklahoma City, 1961—68, prof. pharmacology, 1969—74; vis. prof. Karolinska Inst., Stockholm, 1968—69; assoc. clin. prof. medicine U. Hawaii Sch. Medicine, Honolulu, 1976—85; practice in cardiology Hilo, Hawaii, 1986—91; internist Kobe Kaisei Hosp., 1992—95, Kobe U. Sch. Medicine, Japan, 1996—, lectr., 1996—. Spkr. in field; lectr. Osaka Furitsu U., 1992—95. Contbr. 135 med. essays, 21 med. books. Recipient Jersey City Med. Ctr. Resident Rsch. award, 1955, Ford Found. citation excellence in tchg., 1967, The 1985 Before Columbus Found. Book award, 1985; grantee, Am. Heart Assn., 1956—57, NIH, 1963—75, alcohol study, Bennet Found., 1967, US Dept. Def., 1969—74; Japanese Govt. scholar univ. edn., 1944—49, Rsch. grantee, AMA, 1965—66, Rsch. grantee rsch. Japanese Immigrants in Hawaii, Japanese Soc. Hawaii, 1991—93. Fellow: AAAS, ACP, Japan Ednl. Clin. Cardiology Soc., Am. Coll. Clin. Pharmacology, Am. Coll. Cardiology; mem.: Am. Soc. Pharmacology and Exptl. Therapeutics, Am. Physiol. Soc., Assn. Life Ins. Med. Dirs. Am.

NAKANO, TOSHIAKI, nephrologist, educator; b. Fukuoka, Sept. 29, 1972; MD, Kumamoto U., 1998; PhD, Kyushu U., 2006. Asst. prof. Kyushu U. Hosp., 2010—. Mem.: Internat. Soc. Nephrology, Japanese Soc. Dialysis Therapy, Japanese Soc. Nephrology. Office: 3-1-1 Maidashi Higashi-ku Fukuoka 812-8582 Japan Office Fax: 81-92-642-5846. Business E-Mail: toshink@med.kyushu-u.ac.jp.

NAKASE, TAKANOBU, surgeon, educator; b. Osaka, Japan, Sept. 5, 1962; MD, Osaka U. Grad. Sch. Medicine, 1988, PhD, 1995. Asst. prof., dept. orthop. surgery Osaka U. Med. Sch., 1996—2002; dir., dept. orthop. surgery Hoshigaokakouseinenkin Hosp., 2005—. Recipient Best Scientific Paper award, 4th Conf. Internat. Soc. Fracture Repair, Orthobiology award, Spine Soc. Europe, 2001, Young Investigator award, Japanese Orthop. Assn., Sci. award, Japanese Soc. Bone and Mineral Rsch. Mem.: Internat. Soc. Fracture Repair, Orthop. Rsch. Soc., Am. Acad. Orthopaedic Surgery. Office: 4-8-1 Hoshigaoka Hirakata Osaka 573-8511 Japan Office Fax: 81-72-840-2266. Business E-Mail: tnakase@ff.iij4u.or.jp.

NAKASUJJA, NOELINE, psychiatrist, educator; b. Namirembe, Uganda, Dec. 3, 1973, MBChB, Makerere U., 1999, PhD, 2011. Sr. lectr. Coll. Health Scis., Makerere U., 2008—. Cons. psychiatrist Internat. Hosp. Kampala, 2002—11. Recipient Outstanding Mentor award, Am. Acad. Child and Adolescent Psychiatry. Mem.: Namagunga Old Girls Assn., Uganda Psychiat. Assn. and Uganda Medical Assn., Uganda Soc. Health Scientists, Internat. Psychogeriatric Assn., Karolinska Inst. Alumni. Avocations: travel, reading, swimming. Office: Dept Psychiatry 7072 Mulago Hill Kampala 256 Uganda Office Fax: 256 414 532204. Personal E-mail: drnoeline@yahoo.com.

NAKATA, YOSHINORI, anesthesiologist, educator; b. Osaka, Japan, Nov. 20, 1965; MD, U. Tokyo, 1990; MBA, Yale U., 1996; BA in Econs., U. Tokyo, 1999, PhD, 1999. Resident Mass. Gen. Hosp., Boston, 1991-94; from asst. prof. to assoc. prof. Teikyo U., Tokyo, 1996—2002, prof., 2002—. Cons. in field. Yale-New Haven Hosp. fellow, 1995—96. Office: Teikyo University Sch Medicine 2-11-1 Kaga Itabashi-ku Tokyo 173-8605 Japan Office Phone: 81-33964-1211. Business E-Mail: ynakata@med.teikyo-u.ac.jp.

NAKATA, YOSHIO, medical educator, researcher; b. Japan, Feb. 19, 1976; PhD, U. Tsukuba, 2004. Rsch. assoc. U. Tsukuba, 2004—07, asst. prof., 2007—, Nara Sangyo U., 2007. Mem.: Obesity Soc., Am. Coll. Sports Medicine. Office: 1-1-1 Tennodai Tsukuba Ibaraki 305-8575 Japan Office Fax: 81298533076. Business E-Mail: nakata@md.tsukuba.ac.jp.

NAKATANI, HIROKI, international organization administrator; b. Japan; MD, Keio U. Sch. Medicine, 1977; MHPEd, U. New South Wales, 1980; PhD, Keio U. Dept. Hygiene and Pub. Health, 2001. Pub. health official with sr. level positions in adminstrn., mgmt., orgn. and legis. devel. Ministry Health, Labor and Welfare, Japan, dir. gen., dept. health and welfare of disabled persons; scientist, divsn. devel. human resources and health WHO, Geneva, 1988—93, asst. dir. gen. HIV/AIDS, tuberculosis, malaria and neglected tropical diseases, 2007—. Mem. G8-Mexico Global Health Security Group; chmn. Chem. Events Working Group; sr. rsch. fellow Keio U. Security Rsch. Inst. Office: WHO avenue Appia 20 1211 Geneva Switzerland *

NAKATANI, KAZUKI, medical researcher; b. Osaka, Japan, Nov. 17, 1965; s. Kazuya and Setsuko N.; m. Junko Tatsuke, Feb. 19, 2000; children: Minori, Kazuma. MD, Osaka City U., 1997. Lectr. Osaka City U. Grad. Sch. of Medicine, 1997—. Buddhist. Avocation: reading. Office: Osaka City U Grad Sch Medicine 1-4-3 Asahimachi, Abeno-ku Osaka 545-8585 Japan Home Phone: 81-6-7892-7868. Business E-Mail: kazuki@med.osaka-cu.ac.jp.

NAKATSUJI, TADAKO, medical researcher, educator; b. Kochiken, Takaoka-gun, Nakatosa-cho, Kaminokae, Japan, Mar. 30, 1947; s. Kanoo and Yoshiko Nakatsuji. MD, Yamaguchi U., Japan, 1974; DSc, Yamaguchi U., 1980. Clin. tng. Yamaguchi U. Hosp., 1974-75, 76, Osaka (Japan) U. Hosp., 1975-76; asst. Sch. Medicine Yamaguchi U., 1976-79; asst. U. Tokyo, 1979-81; asst. prof. Med. Coll. Ga., 1981-85; asst. prof., assoc. dir. dept. transfusion Hamamatsu (Japan) U. Sch. Medicine, 1986—. Contbr. articles to profl. jours. Mem. Japanese Soc. Transfusion (councilor 1992, qualifying doctor 1993). Avocation: drawing. Office: Hamamatsu U Sch Medicine 1-20-1 Handayama Hamamatsu 431-3192 Japan Home Phone: (0)53-435-3339. E-mail: nh80415@hama-med.ac.jp.

NAKATSUKA, MIKIYA, healthcare educator; b. Japan, Aug. 28, 1961; MD, Okayama U. Med. Sch., 1986; PhD, Okayama U. Grad. Sch. Medicine, 1994. Prof. Grad. Sch. Health Scis., Okayama U., 2006—. Chairperson bd. dirs. Japanese Soc. Gender Identity Disorder, 2010—11. Office: 2-5-1 Shikata Kita Ward Okayama 700-8558 Japan Office Fax: 81862356895. Business E-Mail: mikiya@cc.okayama-u.ac.jp.

NAKAYA, RINTARO, microbiologist, consultant; b. Ohno, Japan, Nov. 10, 1924; s. Rinzaemon and Tomi (Kurota) N.; m. Yukie Tanaka, Nov. 22, 1951; children: Saeko Nakaya Fujino, Mizuhov Nakaya. MD, U. Tokyo, 1947, DMS, 1958. Cert. med. practitioner Min. of Health and Welfare, Japanese Govt. Chief labs. NIH, Tokyo, 1948-68; dir. dept. Nat. Inst. Pub. Health, Tokyo, 1968-73; prof. microbiology Tokyo Med. and Dental U., 1973-90, prof. emeritus, 1990—; prof. Sch. Home Econs. Japan Women's U., Tokyo, 1990-93. Adviser Japan Bifidus Found., Tokyo, 1999—; dir. Kurozumi Med. Found., Tokyo, 1999—. Author: Drug Resistance, 1976; author, editor: Infectious Enteritis in Japan, 1986; editor Infectious Enteritis in Japan II, 1997. Rsch. fellow Rockefeller Found. Yale U. Sch. Medicine, 1957-58; vis. prof. U. Wis., 1967-68. Mem. AAAS, Am. Soc. Microbiology (emeritus), Japanese Soc. Bacteriology (hon.), Japanese Assn. for Infectious Diseases (hon.). Buddhist. Avocations: kendo, swimming, fishing, reading. Home: 1-23-3 Chuo Nakano-Ku Tokyo 164-0011 Japan

NAKAYAMA, HARUHIKO, thoracic surgeon; MD, Gunma U., 1982. Cert. Japanese Bd. Gen. Thoracic Surgery, 2004. Chair, dept. thoracic surgery Kanagwa Cancer Ctr., Yokohama, Japan, 1999—. Attending surgeon, divsn. thoracic surgery Nat. Cancer Ctr., Tokyo, 1993—99. Mem.: Soc. Thoracic Surgeons, Japanese Assn. Chest Surgery, Japanese Assn. Thoracic Surgery, Internat. Assn. Study Lung Cancer, Japan Surg. Soc. Office. Kanagawa Cancer Ctr Nakao 1-1-2 Asahi-ku Yokohama 241-0815 Japan

NAKAYAMA, KEN-ICHI, research scientist; b. Koga, Japan, Apr. 20, 1961; MSc, Hokkaido U., 1987; PhD, U. Tsukuba, 1999. Sr. rschr. Nat. Inst. Advanced Indsl. Sci. and Tech., 1993—. Avocation: mountain climbing. Office: 2-17-2-1 Tsukisamu-Higashi Toyohiraku Sapporo Hokkaido 062-8517 Japan Business E-Mail: k-nakayama@aist.go.jp.

NAKAYAMA, MASASHI, engineering educator, researcher; b. Yamaguchi, Yamaguchi, Japan, Dec. 31, 1982; PhD, Hiroshima City U., 2010. Invited rsch. scientist Nat. Inst. Advanced Indsl. Sci. and Tech., 2008—; asst. prof. Kagawa Nat. Coll. Tech., 2008—. Mem.: IEEE. Achievements include research in body-conducted speech, spoken language processing, noise robust speech recognition and embedded technology. Office: 355 Chokushi Takamatsu Kagawa 7618058 Japan Office Fax: 81-87-869-3905. Business E-Mail: m-nakayama@t.kagawa-nct.ac.jp.

NAKAYAMA, TOSHIYUKI, pathologist, physiologist, cell biologist; MD, Nagasaki U., Japan. Assoc. prof. Nagasaki U., 2001—. Achievements include research in pathology and cell biology. Office: Nagasaki U 1-12-4 Sakamoto Nagasaki 852-8523 Japan Office Fax: 81-958197056. Business E-Mail: toshi-n@net.nagasaki-u.ac.jp.

NAKAZAWA, MITSURU, ophthalmologist, educator; b. Hakodate, Japan, Jan. 20, 1956; s. Mitsutake and Chie (Kanazawa) N.; m. Junko Oizumi, Apr. 8, 1980; 1 child, Yuki. MD, Tohoku U., Sendai, Japan, 1980, PhD, 1989. Diplomate Japanese Bd. Ophthalmology. Resident in ophthalmology Tohoku Univ. Hosp., Sendai, 1980-82, fellow in ophthalmology, 1982-85, mem. ophthalmology staff, 1985, 88-89, asst. prof. ophthalmology, 1989-95, assoc. prof. ophthalmology, 1995-98; postdoctoral asst. ophthalmology U. Cin., 1985-88; prof., chmn. ophthalmology Hirosaki U. Sch. of Medicine, 1998—2007; prof., chmn. dept. ophthalmology Hirosaki U. Grad. Sch. Medicine, Japan, 2007—. Bd. dirs. Japanese Soc. Ophthalmic Diabetology; mem. Rsch. Com. on Chorioretinal Degenerations and Optic Atrophy, Ministry Health and Welfare, 1996—2008; chmn. bd. dirs. Hirosaki U. Eye Bank, 1998—. Editor: Japanese Jour. Ophthalmology, 1997—, Japanese Jour. Clin. Ophthalmology, 2005—; contbr. articles to profl. jours. Grantee Ministry Edn., 1989, 91, 93, 97, 99-00, 02, 04, 06, 09, Japan Eye Bank Assn., 1989, Japan Soc. Prevention of Blindness, 1993, Nanbyo Igaku Kenkyu Zaidan, 1996, Rohto award, 1996, 18th Karouji Meml. Med. Rsch. Fund, 2000. Mem. Japanese Soc. Ophthalmology (councilor 1999-, Acad. award 1996), Japan Ophthalmologists Assn., Assn. Rsch. in Vision and Ophthalmology, Japanese Soc. Ophthalmic Surgeons, Japanese Soc. Clin. Vision and Electrophysilogy, Vitreoretina Soc. Japan (bd. dirs. 2001-09), Japanese Soc. Ocular Circulation (bd. dirs. 2003-), Japanese Soc. Gene and Clinical Practice, Japanese Soc. Low Vision. Avocations: travel, ballroom dance, karaoke. Office: Dept Ophthal Hirosaki U Sch Medicine Sch Med/5 Zaifu-cho Hirosaki Aomori 036-8562 Japan Office Phone: 81 172 39 5094. Business E-Mail: mitsuru@cc.hirosaki-u.ac.jp.

NAKAZAWA, TAKAHIDE, medical educator, researcher; b. Tokyo, Mar. 8, 1963; MD, Kitasato U., Sch. Medicine, PhD, 1988. Assoc. prof. Kitasato U., Sch. Medicine, 2006—. Avocations: skiing, travel. Office: Asamizodai 2-1-1 Sagamihara Kanagawa 252-0380 Japan Office Fax: 81-42-740-1881. Business E-Mail: tnakazaw@kitasato-u.ac.jp.

NAKEEB, ATTILA, surgeon, educator; b. Ames, Iowa, Apr. 28, 1965; BS, Cornell U., 1987; MD, SUNY, Buffalo, 1991. Prof. surgery Ind. U. Sch. Medicine, 2003—. Fellow: ACS. Office: 535 Barnhill Dr RT 130 Indianapolis IN 46202 Office Fax: 317-274-4554. Business E-Mail: anakeeb@iupui.edu.

NAKHLA, TONY N., dermatologist; DO with honors, Nova Southeastern U., 1998—2005. Chief intern St. Vincent's Midtown Hosp., 2005—06; chief resident dermatology Western Univ. of Health Sciences/ Pacific Hosp., 2006—09; med. dir. OC Skin Inst. Recipient President's Endowment award, 2003; named one of Best Resident Abstract, 2007. Mem.: Osteopathic Physicians and Surgeons Med. Bd. of Calif., Am. Osteopathic Assn., Am. Soc. for Dermatologic Surgery, Am. Osteopathic Coll. of Dermatology, Am. Acad. of Dermatology. Office: OC Skin Institute 800 N Tustin Ave Suite G Santa Ana CA 92705 Office Phone: 714-547-6111. Office Fax: 714-547-0833.

NAKSHABANDI, ZIAD M., pediatric urologist; s. Mohammad A. Nakshabandi and Maryam H. Ahmad; m. Liza F. Badr; children: Abdulrahman Z., Ayah Z., Ahmad Z. MBBS, King Saud U., MD, 1993. Cert. urology Arab Bd. Health Specialization, Saudi Arabia, 2000, Saudi Coun. Health Speciality, Saudi Arabia, 2000, USMLE 2000. Clin. asst. prof. Tufts U. Sch. Medicine, Boston, 2002—03, clin. fellow, urology, 2003; head, pediat. urology Riyadh Mil. Hosp., Ctrl., Saudi Arabia, 2007—, cons., pediat. urology, 2003—; chmn. Saudi Pediat. Urology Fellowship Program SCFHS, 2011; mem. sci. bd. Saudi Bd. Urology; mem. Ctrl. Tng. Com. Sauoi Bd. Urology SCFHS; chmn. Saudi Ped Urology Fellowship Program SCFHS, 2011; mem. sci. bd. Ctrl. Tng. Com. Saudi Bd. Urology SCFHS. Dir. RMH Saudi Pediat. Urology Fellowship. Recipient Appreciation award, Tufts New Eng. Med. Ctr., Boston, 2003. Fellow: Saudi Commn. Health Splty.; mem.: Internat. Childrens Continence Soc., Aua Am. Urol. Assn. Personal E-mail: drziad@hotmail.com. Business E-Mail: drziad@rmh.med.sa.

NALACHANDRAN, SANJAY, surgeon; Grad., Royal Coll. Surgeons, Ireland, 1997; MMed in Gen. Surgery, Nat. U., Singapore, 2002. Basic surg. tng., Ireland; fellowship Royal Coll. Surgeons, Edinburgh, Ireland; advanced vascular surgery tng. Freeman Hosp., Newcastle upon Tyne, England; advanced tng. gen. and vascular surgery Tan Tock Seng Hosp. (TTSH), 2001, cons. gen. srug. dept. Recipient Manpower Devel. Plan Scholarship, Singapore Health Ministry, 2005. Fellow: Internat. Coll. Surgeons, USA, Acad. Medicine Singapore, Royal Coll. Surgeons (Edinburgh 2005). Office: Tan Tock Seng Hospital 11 Jalan Tan Tock Seng 308433 Singapore Office Phone: 6562566011. Office Fax: 6562527282. *

NALAMADA, SUMA, microbiologist; b. Mancherial, Andhra Pradesh, India, Nov. 30, 1970; MBBS, Osmania med. coll., 1997; MD, Gandhi Med. coll., 2002. Microbiologist LV Prasad Eye Inst., 2009—. Office: LV Prasad Marg banjara Hills Hyderabad Andhra Pradesh 500034 India

NALDINI, GABRIELE, gastroenterologist; b. Milan, Jan. 27, 1965; Degree in Medicine, Milan U., 1992, degree in Gastroenterologic Surgery, 1997. Proctological and perineal surgery dir. Azienda Ospedaliero U. Pisa, 2010—. Home: Via Matteotti 140 Orzignano Pisa 56017 Italy Home Fax: 0039050997818. Personal E-mail: g.naldini@ao-pisa.toscana.it.

NALE, JULIA ANN, nursing educator; b. Chgo., Oct. 27, 1948; d. Anthony John and Mary Elizabeth (Magrady) Doheny; m. Robert Douglas Nale, Feb. 27, 1971; children: Daniel, Kerry. Diploma, St. Francis Sch. Nursing, Evanston, Ill., 1969; BS, U. S.C. Coastal Carolina Coll., Conway, 1989. Staff nurse St. Francis Hosp., 1969-71; charge nurse McDonough Dist. Hosp., Macomb, ill., 1971-72; supr. surg. ICU Victory Meml. Hosp., Waukegan, ill., 1973-78, charge nurse St. Mary's Hosp., Galesburg, ill., 1978-79; assoc. dir. nursing Community Meml. Hosp., Monmouth, Ill., 1979-85; staff nurse Loris (S.C.) Community Hosp., 1987-91; instr. health occupations Horry County Sch. Dist., Conway, SC, 1985-89, 2002instr. LPNs, 1989; staff nurse Conway Hosp., 1992—, patient edn. coord., 2002—. Mem. S.C. Textbook Selection Com., 1988-90. Lectr., tchr. Tommy Trauma Program for Pub. Sch. Children, Monmouth, 1982-84; charter mem. Com. to Combat Alcohol/Drug Abuse, Monmouth, 1985. Named Tchr. of the Yr. Finklea (S.C.) Career Ctr., 1989, Aynor-Conway Career Ctr., 1991, other awards. Mem. AACN, NEA, S.C. Ednl. Assn., Horry County Vocat. Assn., S.C. Vocat. Assn. (pres. health occupations div. 1990-91), Am. Vocat. Assn. Roman Catholic. Avocations: swimming, reading, cross stitch. Office: Conway Hosp 300 Singleton Ridge Rd Conway SC 29528 Business E-Mail: jnale@cmc-sc.com.

NALINI, ATCHAYARAM, neurologist, educator; b. Bangalore, India, Feb. 7, 1964; MBBS, Bangalore Med. coll., 1989; degree in Neurology, NIMH and Neuroscis., 1994. Clinician, tchr. NIMH and Neuroscis., 1999, additional prof., 2008—. Recipient Sir C.V. Raman Young Scientists award, Karnataka State Coun. Sci. and Tech. Office: Hosur Rd Bangalore Karnataka 560029 India Office Fax: 91-80-26564830. Personal E-mail: atchayaramnalini@yahoo.co.in.

NAM, HAE JEONG, medical educator; b. Seoul, Republic of Korea, Dec. 9, 1970; PhD, Kyung Hee U., 2006. Lectr. Kyungwon U., 2003—05; asst. prof. Kyung Hee U., 2007—. Chief dept. opthalmology and otolaryngology Oriental Med. Hosp. Kyung Hee U., 2006—11. Office: Hoegi-dong Korea Kyung Hee University Oriental Medicine Hosp Seoul Dongdaemun 130-702 Republic of Korea Office Phone: 82-2-958-9244. Office Fax: 82-2-958-9180. Business E-Mail: ophthrl@khu.ac.kr.

NAM, KUNG-WOO, pharmacologist; b. Chungnam, Republic of Korea, Oct. 17, 1968; PhD, Seoul Nat. U., 2004. Rschr. Natural Products Rsch. Inst., Seoul Nat. U., 1995—98; postdoc. rsch. fellow BWH, Harvard Med. Sch., Boston, 2005—06; with Jung San Biotech. Co., Osan City, 2007—09; rsch. prof. Korea U., Seoul, 2010. Mem.: Korean Soc. Toxicology, Korean Soc. Applied Pharmacology, Pharm. Soc. Korea. Avocation: hiking. Home: 126-1 5-Ga Anam-Dong Seongbuk-Gu Seoul 136-705 Republic of Korea Home Fax: 82-2-953-6095. Business E-Mail: kwnam1@snu.ac.kr.

NAM, KWANG IL, medical educator; b. Gwangju, Republic of Korea, Sept. 1, 1967; MB, Chonnam Nat. U., 1993, MD, 1998. Asst. prof., dept. anatomy Chonnam Nat. U. Med. Sch., 2002—06. Vis. scientist Ctr. Anatomy & Cell Biology, Med. U. Vienna, Austria, 2007—09. Recipient Acad. prize, Han Kok Med. Sci. Found. Mem.: Anatomische Gesellschaft, Assn. Med. Edn. Europe, Korean Assn. Anatomists. Avocation: mountain climbing. Office: Hak-dong 5 Gwangju 501-746 Republic of Korea Office Fax: 82-62-228-5834. Business E-Mail: atlas@jnu.ac.kr.

NAM, KYE-HYUN, educational association administrator, director; b. Daejeon, Nov. 5, 1957; PhD, Busan Nat. U., 1982. Dir. Soonchunhyang U., Bucheon, Gyeonggi, Republic of Korea, 2001—11. Office: Soonchunhyang University Hosp #1174 Bucheon Gyeonggi 420-767 Republic of Korea Office Fax: 82-32-621-5018. Personal E-mail: khnambc@yahoo.co.kr.

NAM, SEON YOUNG, research scientist; b. Masan, Republic of Korea, June 23, 1967; d. Duk Hee Nam and Sang Keum Lee; m. Kyoung Min You, Dec. 3, 1994; 1 child, Yejin You. BS, Duksung Women's U., 1991, MS, 1995, PhD, 1998. Lic. pharmacist Republic of Korea, 1991. Pharmacist HANIL Pharm. Co., Seoul, 1991—93; tchg. asst. Duksung Women's U., Seoul, 1993—95; postdoctoral fellow Korea Inst. Radiol. and Med. Sci., Seoul, 1998—99, U. Pitts., 2000—01, Seoul Nat. U., 2001—02, asst. prof., 2002—04; sr. rschr. Radiation Health Rsch. Inst., Korea Hydro and Nuc. Power Co., Seoul, 2004—. Lectr. Dankook U., Seoul, 2002—03, Duksung Women's U., Seoul, 2004—05. Contbr. articles to profl. jours. Recipient Young Investigators' award, Internat. Fedn. Assn. Anatomists, 2004; grantee, Korea Rsch. Found., 2003. Mem.: Am. Assn. for Cancer Rsch. (assoc.). Achievements include patents in field. Avocations: travel, movies, skiing.

NAM, SOON YUHL, otolaryngologist, medical educator, consultant; b. Dae Gu City, Republic of Korea, Dec. 13, 1957; s. Yong Jin Nam and Oak Hae Jeon; m. Eun Sok Suh, June 7, 1983; children: Jee Min, Yoo Min. PhD, Kyungpook Nat. U., Dae Gu City, 1991. MD Republic of Korea, 1983. Staff Vanderbilt U., Nashville, 1994—95. Cons. Asan Med. Ctr., Seoul, 1995—, assoc. prof., 1995—2004, prof., 2004—. Author: J of Voice, 2001, Laryngoscope, 2002, Oral Oncology, 2005. Capt. 3rd Mil. Sch. Korean Army, 1987—90. Grantee, Asan Inst. For Life Scis., 1998, 1999. Mem.: Korean Soc. Logopedics and Phoniatronics, Korean Soc. Head and Neck Surgery (corr.). Freedom Party. Buddism. Avocations: golf, travel, music, tennis, book reading. Office: Asan Med Ctr 388-1 Pungnap-Dong Songpa Gu Seoul 138-736 Republic of Korea Office Fax: 82-2-489-2773. E-mail: synam@www.amc.seoul.kr.

NAM, TAEK-JEONG, food scientist, educator; b. Masan, Kyungnam, Republic of Korea, Apr. 20, 1954; s. Li-Yong Nam and Young-Lim Sung; m. Mee-Young Kim, Dec. 17, 1981; 1 child, On-You. BS, Pukyong Nat. Univ., Pusan, 1979; PhD, Tokyo U., 1989. Chief divsn. food and life sci. Pukyong Nat. U., Pusan, Republic of Korea, 2002—; dir. Seafood & Marine Bioresources Development Cent, Pusan, 2002—03. Elder Seo-Moon Presbyn. Ch., Pusan, Korea (South), 2000. Office: Pukyong Nat U 599-1 Daeyeon-dong Nam-gu Pusan 608-737 Republic of Korea Office Fax: +82-51-620-6330. Business E-Mail: namtj@pknu.ac.kr.

NAMDARI, BAHRAM, surgeon; b. Oct. 26, 1939; s. Rostam and Sarvar Namdari; m. Kathleen Wilmore, Jan. 5, 1976; children; Mondona, Mietra, Ariana. MD, 1966. Diplomate Am. Bd. Surgery. Resident in gen. surgery St. John's Mercy Med. Ctr., St. Louis, 1969-73; practice medicine specializing in gen. and vascular surgery Milw., 1976—. Mem. staff St. Mary's Hosp., Milw., St. Luke's Hosp., Milw.; founder, pres. Famous Mealwaukee Foods Enterprises. Contbr. articles to med. jours.; patentee med. instruments and other devices. Cardiovascular Surgery fellow with Michael DeBakey, Baylor Coll. Medicine, Houston, 1974-75. Fellow ACS, Internat. Surgeons; mem. AMA, Med. Soc. Milwaukee County, Milw. Acad. Surgery, Wis. Med. Soc., Wis. Surg. Soc., Royal Soc. Medicine Eng. (affiliate), Am. Soc. Bariatric Surgery, World Med. Assn., Internat. Acad. Bariatric Medicine (founding mem.), Am. Acad. Cosmetic Surgery, Michael DeBakey Internat. Cardiovascular Soc. Office: Great Lakes Med and Surg Ctr 6000 S 27th St Milwaukee WI 53221-4805

NAMEROW, DAVID MARK, pediatrician; b. NYC, Dec. 12, 1947; s. Nathan and Claire (Goodstein) N.; m. Pearila Brickner, June 14, 1981; children: Jordan Ilana, Evan Gabrielle, Zoe Alexandra. BS, CCNY, 1968; MD, U. Louisville, 1972. Pediatric intern Children's Hosp. Med. Ctr., Cin., 1972-73, resident in pediatrics, 1973-75; fellow in adolescent medicine U. Md. Hosps., Balt., 1975-77; pediatrician Plaza Med. Assocs., Flanders, NJ, 1977-79; dir. adolescent medicine St. Joseph's Hosp. Med. Ctr., Paterson, NJ, 1977-81; founder, pediatrician PediatriCare Assocs., Fair Lawn, NJ, 1979—. Attending pediatrician, assoc. dir. dept. pediatrics Valley Hosp., Ridgewood, N.J., 1979—; adj. asst. clin. prof. pediatrics N.Y. Hosp.-Cornell Med. Ctr., N.Y.C., 1979—; dir. dept. pediatrics Valley Hosp., 2001-05. Fellow Am. Acad. Pediatrics; mem. Soc. for Adolescent Medicine, Ambulatory Pediatric Assn. Office: PediatriCare Assocs 20-20 Fair Lawn Ave Fair Lawn NJ 07410-2319 also: 400 Franklin Tpke Mahwah NJ 07430-3516 also: 901 Rte 23 S Pompton Plains NJ 07444 Office Phone: 201-791-4545. Personal E-mail: dnamerow@optonline.net, dnamerow@gmail.com.

NAMI, RENATO, cardiologist; b. Montefiascone, Italy, Dec. 18, 1946; MB BChir, U. Siena, Italy, 1971. Ordinay asst. internal medicine U. Siena, 1973—86, assoc. prof. cardiology, 1986—. Dir. ipertension ctr. Azienda Ospedaliera U., Siena, 1983—2011. Contbr. articles to profl. publs. Mem.: ANCE-Cardiologia del Territorio, Soc. Italiana Medicina Interna, Soc. Italiana Cardiologia, Soc. Italiana dell' Ipertensione Arteriosa, European Clin. Hypertension Soc. Office: Viale Bracci 12 Siena 53100 Italy Office Fax: 00390577585362. Business E-Mail: nami@unisi.it.

NAMIAS, NICHOLAS, surgeon, educator; b. NYC, Feb. 17, 1964; BA, State U. NJ, Rutgers, 1985; MD, Robert Wood Johnson Med. Sch., 1989. Asst. prof. surgery Emory U. Sch. Medicine, 1996—98; promotion and tenure com., Dewitt Daughtry family dept. surgery U. Miami Miller Sch. Medicine, 1999—2011, assoc. prof. surgery and anesthesiology, dir., burn ICU and surg. infectious diseases, 1998—2004, assoc. prof. surgery and anesthesiology, chief, divsn. burns, 2004—08, prof. surgery and anesthesiology, chief, divsn. burns, 2008—10, prof. surgery and anesthesiology, chief, divsn. trauma, 2010—, bd. dirs., 2006—, chmn., clin. practice and profl. standards com., 2007—, infection control com., 2004—. Med. exec. com. Jackson Health Sys., 2008—11. Recipient Outstanding and Tireless Dedication award, Jackson Health Sys., Ellen Whiteside McDonnell Edn. award, U. Miami Miller Sch. Medicine. Fellow: ACS, Am. Coll. Critical Care Medicine; mem.: Surg. Infection Soc., Fla. Com. Trauma, Am. Burn Assn., Phi Beta Kappa. Office: PO Box 016960 (D-40) Miami FL 33101 Office Fax: 305-326-7065. Business E-Mail: nnamias@med.miami.edu.

NAMIKAWA, TSUTOMU, surgeon, educator; b. Kochi, Japan, Feb. 23, 1967; MD, Kochi Med. Sch., 1991, PhD, 1998. Assoc. prof. Kochi Med. Sch., 2006—. Grant, Japan Soc. Promotion Sci. Mem.: Japanese Gastric Cancer Assn., Japanese Soc. Gastroenterology, Japanese Soc. Gastroent. Surgery, Japan Surg. Soc., Internat. Gastric Cancer Assn. Avocation: tennis. Office: Kohasu Oko-cho Nankoku Kochi 783-8505 Japan Office Fax: 81-88-880-2371.

NAMISATO, MASAKO, dermatologist; b. Kuwana, Japan, June 12, 1947; s. Kendo and Toshiko Hirata; m. Tsugio Namisato, July 8, 1990; 1 child from previous marriage, Takushi Shirai. M of Medicine, Mie U., 1972, MD, 1972; PhD in Medicine, Juntendo U., 1995. Asst. dermatology Mie U. Sch. Medicine, Tsu-City, Japan, 1972—74; sub-dir. pub. health Mie Profectural Govt., 1975—80; mem. dept. dermatology Juntendo U. Sch. Medicine, Tokyo, 1980—89; dir. dermatology Okinawa Prefectural Hosp., Naha-City, 1989—91, Nat. Tama-Zenshoen Sanatorium, Tokyo, 1992—2001; depty dir. gen. Nat. Kuryu-Rakusenen Sanatorium, Gunma-pref., 2001—. Recipient Shioda award, Min. Health, Labor and Welfare, Tokyo, 2003. Mem.: Internat. Leprosy Assn., Japanese Soc. Leprosy, Japanese Soc. Dermatology, Internat. Soc. Dermatology and Tropical Medicine. Home: 5-22-5 Shaku-jiidai Tokyo 177-0045 Japan Office: Nat Kuryu-Rakusenen Sanatorium 647 Kusatsumachi Agatsuma 377-1711 Japan Office Fax: +81 279-88-5473. E-mail: fukenc@dan.wind.ne.jp.

NAM JU, MOON, ophthalmologist, department chairman; b. Seoul, Republic of Korea, July 10, 1961; B in Med. Sci., Chung-Ang U., 1985, PhD in Ophthalmology, 1991. Chmn., ophthalmology dept. Sung-Ae Gen. Hosp., 1989—94, Nat. Med. Ctr., 1995—2002, Chung-Ang U. Hosp., 2006—; prof. Coll. Medicine Chung-Ang U., 2003—11. WHO fellow Pediat. Ophthalmology and Low Vision Clinic Juntendo U., Japan, 1993, Low Vision Clinic Melbourne U., Australia, 1999; vis. assoc. prof. Pediat. Ophthalmology and Low Vision Clinic Karolynska U., Sweden, 1998, Yale Eye Ctr. Med. Coll. Yale U., 2006—07. Master: Korean Found. Prevention of Blindness, Korean Low Vision Study Group; mem.: Korean Soc. Ophthalmic Plastic and Reconstructive Surgery, Korean Strabismus & Pediat. Ophthal. Soc., Korean Ophthal. Soc. Avocations: languages, running, skiing, golf. Office: Chung-Ang University Hosp Dept Ophthalmology 224-1 Heukseok-Dong Dongjak-Ku Seoul 156-755 Republic of Korea Office Fax: 82-2-825-1666. Business E-Mail: njmoon@chollian.net, njmoon@chol.net.

NAMMOUR, SAMIR, dentist, educator; b. Ezzeh, Nabatieh, Lebanon, Feb. 10, 1957; s. Youssef Hanna Nammour and Hanné Maroun Haddad; m. Edmée Langohr, Aug. 30, 1986; children: Amaury Joe, Mélanie. DDS, Free U. Brussels, Brussels, 1983, PhD, 1988, Habilitation Thesis, 1991, MS in Oral Laser Therapy, 1994; DU in Occlusodontics and Gnathology, U. Nice, France, 1998. Dental diplomate U. Brussels. Asst. prof. Free U. Brussels, 1984—92, assoc. prof., 1992—96; prof. of faculty U. Liège, Belgium, 2004—. Dir. European master CUS oral lasers applications, dept. dental scis. Faculty of Medicine, U. Liège, 2004; bd. mem. Many Internat. Sci. Jours. Author: (book) Atlas of Oral Laser Surgery. Recipient Lauréate of G.I.R.S.O. award, Groupement Internat. pour la Recherche Scientifique en Stomatologie et en Odontologie., 1990, Bronze award, UE Lifelong Learning, 2007. Achievements include patents for Method and laser apparatus for preventing tooth decay; Method and apparatus for preventing tooth decay. Office: Univ Liege Dept Dental Scis Se Rue Paul Spaak 3 Brussels B 1000 Belgium Personal E-mail: s@nammour.be. Business E-Mail: s.namour@ulg.ac.be.

NAMNOUM, ANNE BRAWNER, obstetrician, gynecologist; b. Balt., Apr. 26, 1960; m. James Daniel Namnoum; children: Timothy Spencer, Anne Addison, Reed Daniel, Hannah Paine, Eliza Stewart, Isabelle Austin. MD, Johns Hopkins U., Balt., 1987. Diplomate Am. Bd. Ob-Gyn., cert. in Reproductive Endocrinology/Infertility. Ob-gyn. intern Johns Hopkins U., 1987-88, residnet in ob-gyn., 1988-91, fellow in reproductive endocrinology, 1991-93, asst. prof., 1993-95, Emory U. Sch. Medicine, Atlanta, 1995—. Contbr. articles to profl. jours. Mem.: Am. Coll. Ob-Gyn. Office: 2001 Peachtree Rd NE Ste 545 Savannah GA 30309

NAMNOUM, JAMES DANIEL, plastic surgeon; b. Hartford, Conn. m. Anne Brawner Namnoum; 6 children. MD, John Hopkins Sch. Medicine, 1987. Cert. Am. Bd. Plastic Surgery. Resident, surgery John Hopkins Hosp., Baltimore, Md., 1987—93, resident, plastic surgery, 1993—95; fellow, plastic surgery Reconstructive Surgery Found., Atlanta, 1996; co-dir. Atlanta Breast Symposium; chief, plastic surgery St. Joseph's Hosp.; med. dir. AYA Med. Spa; private practice Atlanta Plastic Surgery. Lectr. in field; cons. to companies specializing in products for cosmetic surgery. Mem.: Med. Assn. Ga., Med. Assn. Atlanta, Ga. Soc. Plastic Surgery, Southeastern Soc. Plastic Surgery, Am. Soc. Aesthetic Plastic Surgery, Am. Soc. Plastic Surgeons. Avocations: cooking, reading, fitness tng., wine enthusiast. Office: Atlanta Plastyic Surgery PC STE 100 975 Johnson Ferry RD NE Atlanta GA 30342-1618 Office Phone: 404-256-1311. Office Fax: 404-256-5487. Business E-Mail: aps@atlplastic.com.

NAMPERUMALSAMY, PERUMALSAMY, ophthalmologist, educator; MBBS, Madras U., 1963, DO, 1966, MS in Ophthalmology, 1970. Fellowship diabetic retinopathy U. Ill., 1972—73; fellowship retinal retachment and vitreous surgery Retina Assocs., Boston, 1977—78; fellowship Mass. Eye and Ear Infirmary, Harvard Med. Sch., 1977—78; asst. prof. ophthalmology Madurai Med. Coll., 1973—77, asst. prof., 1970—72; prof. ophthalmology, chief med. officer Aravind Eye Hosps. & Postgraduate Inst. Ophthalmology, 1979—97, dir., prof., 1997—; adj. assoc. prof. Abraham Lincoln Sch. Medicine. Contbr. articles to med. jours. Recipient Conrad N. Hilton Humanitarian Prize, 2010; named one of The 100 Most Influential People in the World, TIME mag., 2010. Mem.: Indian Medical Assn., All India Ophthalmological Soc., Tamilnadu State Ophthalmic Assn., Am. Acad. of Ophthalmology, Vitreo-Retinal Soc. of India, Diabetic Assn. of India (life), Vijayawada Ophthalmological Soc. (life). Office: Aravind Eye Hospital 1, Anna Nagar, Madurai - 625 020 Tamilnadu India Office Phone: 91-452-5356100. Office Fax: 91-452-2530984. E-mail: dr.nam@aravind.org. *

NAMPIAPARAMPIL, DEVI ELIZABETH, physician; b. NYC, May 13, 1977; d. Joseph Xavier and Mary Joseph Nampiaparampil; MD, Northwestern U. Feinberg Sch. Medicine, Chgo., 2002. Diplomate Am. Bd. Phys. Medicine & Rehab., 2007. Intern Beth Israel Deaconess Med. Ctr., Harvard Med. Sch., 2002—03; resident Spaulding Rehab. Hosp., 2003—06; clin. fellow Brigham & Women's Hosp., Boston, 2006—07; attending physician VA Puget Sound Healthcare Sys., Lakewood, Wash., 2008; dir. chief pain medicine VA Hudson Valley Healthcare Sys., Castle Point, NY, 2008—; dir. brain injury clinic VA Castle Pt. NY Ctrl. Calif. Healthcare Sys., Fresno, 2008—09; chief interventional pain mgmt. VA NY Harbor Healthcare Sys., 2009—. Contbr. articles to profl. jours. Recipient award, Northwestern U., 1998, Northwestern U. Feinberg Sch. Medicine, 2002, Clin. Rsch award, Harvard Med. Sch., 2006. Mem.: AMA, North Am. Spine Soc., Am. Pain Soc. Office: VA NY Harbor Healthcare Sys 423 E 23rd St New York NY 10010 Personal E-mail: devichechi@gmail.com.

NAMPOOTHIRI, K MADHAVAN, research scientist; b. Thevanoor, Kerala, India, May 30, 1969; s. M. Kesavan Nampoothiri and N. Gouri Antherjanam; m. Subhadra K. Nampoothiri, Apr. 26, 2001; children: Abhilash, Amrutha. BSc in Zoology, U. Kerala, 1989, MSc in Zoology, 1991, BEd in Natural Scis., 1992; PhD in Biotechnology, Cochin U. Sci. Tech., Kerala, 1997. Rsch. fellow Regional Rsch. Lab., Coun. Sci. and Indsl. Rsch., Trivandrum, Kerala, 1992—97, scientist, 2001—; rsch. assoc. Indian Inst. Sci., Bangalore, India, 1997—98; Humboldt rsch. fellow Inst. for Biotechnology 1, Forschungzentrum, Germany, 1998—2000; postdoctoral fellow U. Newcastle upon Tyne, Newcastle, England, 2000—01. Contbr. chapters to books, articles to profl. jours. Alexander von Humboldt fellow, Humboldt Found., Germany, 1998. Mem.: All India Biotech Rsch. Assn., Biotech Rsch. Soc. India (Young Scientist award 2003). Achievements include patents in field. Home: H 14 Chandramana Sreevalsom Vishnu Nagar Trivandrum 695018 India Office: Regional Rsch Lab CSIR Industrial Estate 695 019 Trivandrum India Office Phone: 91-471-2515366. Personal E-mail: madhavan85@hotmail.com.

NAM YEOL, YIM, radiologist, educator; b. Gwangju, Jeollanam-do, Republic of Korea, Sept. 1, 1976; MD, Chonnam Nat. U. Hosp., 2001. Rsch. fellow Chonnam Nat. U. Hosp., 2008—09, asst. prof., 2011—; physician, dir. chief Armed Forces Yangju Hosp. Korea, 2009—11. Mem.: Korea Soc. Interventional Radiology, Korean Soc. Radiology (Grand Prix award 2004, Hon. award 2009). Home: Global Apt 101-602 Woonrim-Dong Gwangju Jeollanam 501-200 Republic of Korea Office Phone: 82 62 220 5746. Personal E-mail: radiologistyim@me.com. Business E-Mail: apleseed@chol.com.

NAN, LI, physician; b. Hangzhou, China, Apr. 28, 1964; MSc in Medicine, Zhejiang Med. U., 1990; PhD in Medicine, U. Hong Kong, 2004. Asst. prof., hon. prof., clin. nutrition, internat. coll. clin. nutrition, Nutrition Ctr. Zhejiang U. Med. Sch., 1990—96, asst. prof., dept. clin. pharmacology, Sir Run Run Shaw Hosp., 2000—10; postdoc. fellow, clin. pharmacology Dept. Medicine, Queen Mary Hosp., U. Hong Kong, 1996—2000, hon. clin. rsch. assoc., 2010—; pres. Shanghai Sunshiny Health Consulting Co., Ltd., 2010—. Recipient First prize, Gt. Wall Internat. Congress Cardiology. Fellow: Internat. Coll. Clin. Nutrition (life); mem.: Med. Tourism Assn. Avocations: tennis, travel, art. Office: Rm 2208 Unit2 Internat Med Zone Hangzhou Shanghai Zhejiang 310012 China Office Fax: 0086-571-87216575. E-mail: nli_hz@hotmail.com.

NAN, ZHONGREN, engineering educator; b. Weinan, China, Nov. 7, 1962; PhD, Lanzhou U., 2000. Prof. Lanzhou U., 2003—. Office: 222 Tianshui Rd Lanzhou Gansu 730000 China Office Fax: 86-931-8912574. Business E-Mail: submitpaper@163.com.

NANCE, MICHAEL L., pediatric surgeon; BS in Biology, Rhodes Coll., 1980—84; MD, La. State U., 1984—88. Diplomate Am. Bd. Surgery, Am. Bd. Surgery-pediatric surgery, Am. Bd. Surgery-surg. critical care. Intern surgery Hosp. of the Univ. of Pa., 1988—89, resident surgery, 1989—91, 1993—95, fellow surg. critical care, 1995—96, consulting surgeon, 1998—; surgery rsch. fellow Harrison dept. of surg. rsch. Univ. of Pa., 1988—91, instr. in surgery dept. of surgery, 1994—95, instr. trauma and critical care surgery dept., 1996—98, asst. prof. surgery, 1998—2004, assoc. prof. surgery, 2004—10, prof. surgery, 2010—; asst. chief resident pediatric surgery Children's Hosp. of Phila., 1996—97, Louise Schnaufer sr. fellow pediatric surgery, 1997—98, attending physician divsn. of pediatric gen. and thoracic surgery, 1997—98, attending surgeon divsn. of pediatric gen. and thoracic surgery, 1998—2004, assoc. dir. of trauma, 1998—2003, dir. resident edn. gen. surgery, 1999—2003, dir. pediatric trauma program, 2003—, sr. surgeon divsn. of pediatric gen. and thoracic surgery, 2004—, jr. chair in pediatric trauma surgery dept., 2004—; consulting surgeon Pa. Hosp., 1998—, Abington Meml. Hosp., 1999—. Co-author: (publs.) Neuro-cognitive evaluation of mild traumatic brain injury in the hospitalized pediatric population, 2007, Vehicle crash characteristics and anatomic injuries in airbag exposed child decedents, 2007, Utilization of laparoscopic cholecystec-tomy for biliary dyskinesia in the child, 2007, and other numerous publications. Pediatric stds. com. Pa. Trauma Sys. Found., 2003—, mem. rsch. com., 2009—. Named one of Top Doctors, Phila. Mag., 2010—11. Fellow: Coll. of Physicians of Phila., Am. Acad. of Pediat. (surg. sect. mem. 2000—, sect. on injury & poison prevention mem. 2001—, sect. on child abuse & neglect mem. 2001—); mem.: Phila. Trauma Dirs. Group, Phila. Med. Soc., Pa. Med. Soc., Soc. of Critical Care Medicine, Assn. for the Advancement of Automotive Medicine, Am. Assn. for the Surgery of Trauma (pediatric trauma com. mem. 2010—), APHA, AMA, Am. Pediatric Surgery Assn. (trauma com. mem. 2006—, vice chmn. trauma com.), ACS (mem. trauma com. 2008—11), Physicians for Social Responsibility, Eastern Assn. for the Surgery of Trauma (bd. dirs. 2003—05, mem. careers in trauma com. 2003—05, chmn. mentoring com. 2003—05, mem. nominations com. 2006—07, mem. pediatric trauma com. 2010—), Am. Trauma Soc. Mailing: Children's Hospital of Philadelphia 34th St and Civic Center Blvd Philadelphia PA 19104 Office Phone: 215-590-1000.

NAND, SUCHA, medical educator; b. Thiriewal, Punjab, India, Feb. 3, 1948; d. Narsingh Dass and Swaran Devi; m. Surinder S. Nand, June 15, 1973; children: Ranveer, Rahul. Pre-med. student, Dayanand Ayur Vedic Coll., Amritsar, India, 1966; MB, BS, Med. Coll., Amritsar, India, 1971. Diplomate Am. Bd. Internal Medicine, Am. Bd. Hemotology, Am. Bd. Med. Oncology. Asst. prof. Stritch Sch. Medicine Loyola U., Maywood, Ill., 1981-88, assoc. prof. Stritch Sch. Medicine, 1989-95; prof. medicine, 1996—. Editor Jour. of Med. Coll., 1969-71; contbr. articles to profl. jours. Clin. fellow Am. Cancer Soc., 1981; Brilliant Student scholarships, 1962-71. Mem. Am. Soc. Hematology, Am. Soc. Clin. Oncology, S.W. Oncology Group (mem. leukemia com. 1988—). Avocations: chess, reading, running. Office: Loyola Univ Med Ctr 2160 S 1st Ave Maywood IL 60153-3304

NANDA, NAVIN CHANDAR, cardiologist, educator; b. Kabarnet, Kenya, July 6, 1937; came to U.S., 1971; s. Balwantrai and Maya (Vati) N.; m. Kanta Kumari Markan, Sept. 13, 1967; children: Nitin, Anil, Anita. Inter Sci. cert., Bombay U., 1956, MD, 1962. Resident house officer King George IV Hosp., Nairobi, Kenya, 1962; med. registrar King Edward Meml. Hosp., Bombay, 1963-64, sr. med.

registrar, 1964-67; fellow Inst. Cardiology and Nat. Heart Hosp., London, 1967-68; sr. house physician, registrar Rotherham (Eng.) Hosp., 1968-71; instr., trainee in cardiology U. Rochester (N.Y.) Sch. Medicine, 1971-73; asst. prof. medicine and radiology, assoc. physician U. Rochester Sch. Medicine and Strong Meml. Hosp., Rochester, 1971-73, assoc. prof. medicine, dir. noninvasive cardiology labs.; cons. cardiology Genesee Hosp., Rochester Gen. Hosp., 1979—84; prof. of medicine div. cardiovascular disease U. Ala., Birmingham, 1984—2011, disting. prof. medicine and cardiovascular disease, 2011—. Dir. heart sta. and echocardiography labs. U. Ala.-Birmingham Hosp., 1984—, past pres. soc. geriat. cardiology, 2008-09; hon. vis. dean Dr. Navin C. Nanda Nat. Inst. Echocardiography and Cardiac Rsch., Mool Chand K.R. Hosp., New Delhi, 1988—; hon. vis. cons. dept. cardiology Bombay Hosp. Inst. of Med. Scis., 1988—; overseas vis. coms. P.D. Hinduja Hosp. and Med. Rsch. Ctr., Bombay, 1989—. Author: (with R. Gramiak) Clinical Echocardiography, 1978; editor: Doppler Echocardiography, 1985, 2d edit., 1993, Atlas of Color Doppler Echocardiography, 1989, Textbook of Color Doppler Echocardiography, 1989; (videotapes) Videotextbook of Two-Dimensional and Doppler Echocardiography, 1982-88; Case Studies in Doppler Echocardiography, 1985, Case Studies in Color Doppler Echocardiography; mem. editorial bd. numerous jours.; contbr. numerous articles, abstracts, revs. to profl. publs. Recipient Ellis Island medal of honor, Nat. Ethnic Coalition of Orgns., 2006. Fellow Am. Coll. Angiology, Am. Coll. Cardiology (mem. com., Internat. Svc. award 2010), Am. Heart Assn. (coun. on clin. cardiology), Internat. Coll. Angiology, Soc. Geriatric Cardiology, Rochester Acad. Medicine, N.Y. Cardiol. Soc., Soc. Geriat. Cardiology (past pres.); mem. AAAS, AMA, Am. Inst. Ultrasound Medicine, Am. Soc. Echocardiography (bd. dirs. 1978-80), Assn. Acad. Minority Physicians, Inc., Ala. Acad. Sci., Internat. Soc. Cardiovasc. Ultrasound (pres.), Am. Assn. Cardiologists Indian Origin (founding pres.), Am. Assn. Physicians Indian Origin (past pres.), numerous others. Achievements include pioneering use of new innovative technique of color Doppler flow mapping. Office: U Ala Birmingham Heart Sta Swb S 102 Birmingham AL 35249 Office Phone: 205-934-8256. Business E-Mail: nanda@uab.edu. E-mail: navinnanda@bellsouth.net.

NANDI, ASOKE KUMAR, engineering educator; b. Haripal, West Bengal, India, Jan. 1, 1954; arrived in Eng., 1971; s. Satish Chandra and Laksmi (Das) N.; m. Marion McLauchlan, June 25, 1983; children: Robin James, David Anil, Anita Katharine. PhD, U. Cambridge, 1979. Chartered engr., Eng.; chartered mathematician, Eng.; chartered physicist, Eng.; chartered elec. engr., Eng. chartered information tech prof, Eng; chartered scientist, Eng. Solartron lectr. Imperial Coll. London, 1987—91; sr. lectr. U. Strathclyde, 1991—95, reader, 1995—98, prof., 1998—99; David Jardine chair of signal processing U. Liverpool, 1999—. Session chmn. numerous confs. and workshops; co-discoverer of W+, W- and Z particles (1983). Finland disting. prof. 2010-, adj. prof. U. Calgary, 2009-, disting. Internat. Rsch. Fellow U. Calgary Guest co-editor spl. issue in IEE Proceedings Part F, 1993, Jour. Franklin Inst., 1996; assoc. editor Jour. Franklin Inst., 1995—; contbr. articles to profl. jours. Mem. Resident's Assn., Castlehill, 1992—, pres., 1996—; mem. PTA, Castlehill, 1993-94, Nat. Assn. Gifted Children in Scotland, 1995—. Recipient scholarship Trinity Coll., Cambridge U., 1975; advanced fellow Sci. and Engring. Rsch. Coun., 1984, Glory of Bengal award, 2010. Fellow IEEE (USA), Cambridge Philos. Soc., Instn. Elec. Engrs., Inst. Math. and Its Applications, Inst. Physics; Inst. Mech. Engrs., British Computer Soc., Royal Soc. Arts. Achievements include over 450 publications including more than 180 journal papers; h-index of publications is 37 (according to Web of Science). Avocations: problem solving, photography, sport. Home: 33 Brimstage Rd Wirral Heswall CH60 1XE England Office Phone: +44 151 794 4525. Personal E-mail: a.nandi@liverpool.ac.uk.

NANDY, RANJAN KUMAR, bacteriologist, director; b. Berhampore, Nov. 30, 1965; PhD, Hooghly Collegiate Sch., 1987; MSc in Biochemistry, U. Calcutta, PhD in Biochemistry, 1997. Asst. dir., scientist D, divsn. bacteriology Nat. Inst. Cholera and Enteric Diseases, Kolkata, 2008—. Mem.: Indian Sci. Congress. Office: Nat Inst Cholera and Enteric Diseases P33 CIT Rd Scheme XM Kolkata West Bengal 700010 India E-mail: nandy_rk@hotmail.com.

NANGIA, AJAY, urologist, educator; BSc, London U., 1987, MBBS, MD, London U., 1990. Assoc. prof. surgery urology Dartmouth-Hitchcock Med. Ctr., Lebanon, NH, 2001—07; assoc. prof. urology Kans. U. Med. Ctr., 2007—. Past pres. Soc. Study Male Reproduction, 2010—. Office: Dept Urology Kans University Med Ctr 3901 Rainbow Blvd Kansas City KS 66160 Office Phone: 913-588-0799. Office Fax: 913-588-7625. Business E-Mail: anangia@kumc.edu.

NANJAPPA, RAJESH, chemistry professor; b. Mysore, India, July 3, 1978; MSc in Biochemistry, 2003, PhD in Biopolymers, 2011. Lectr. GopalaGowda Hosp., 2003—06; asst. prof. CSI Holds Worth Meml. Hosp. & Coll., Mysore, Karnataka, India, 2006—. Named Young Rsch. Scientist, Amal Jothi Coll. Engring., Kerala, India. Fellow: Indian Soc. Biochemist & Polymer Sci. Home: 3481 / 1- L - 44 Behind Church Rd V Mysore Karnataka 570 001 India Personal E-mail: rajeshnayakmysore@rediffmail.com.

NANJO, KISHIO, medical educator; b. Wakayama, Japan, Aug. 16, 1945; s. Kimio and Teruko Nanjo; m. Tomoko Tsutsumi; children: Shigeki, Sakiko. MD, PhD, Wakayama Med. U., Japan, 1970. Asst. prof. Wakayama Med. U., 1973—82, assoc. prof., 1982—89, prof., chmn. dept. medicine, 1989—2005, v.p. U. Hosp., 1998—2000, pres., 2005—10, Wakayama Rosai Hosp., 2011—, Rsch Ctr. Nachi-Katsuura Spa Hosp., 2010—11. Rsch. assoc. U. Chgo., 1984—86. Editor: Jour. Diab. Invest, 2010—. Recipient Lilly award, Japan Diabetes Soc., 1988, Hagedorn award, 2003. Mem.: Japanese Constl. Medicine (pres. 2001). Office: Wakayama Rosai Hosp 93-1 Kinomoto Wakayama 640-8505 Japan Office Fax: 81-73-452-7171. Business E-Mail: k-nanjo@wakayama-med.ac.jp.

NANJUNDA SWAMY, SHIVANANJU, engineering educator; b. Mysore, Karnataka, India, Nov. 14, 1977; PhD in Chemistry, U. Mysore, 2007, MSc in Biochemistry, 2001. Asst. prof. Sri Jayachamarajendra Coll. Engring., Mysore, 2007—, rschr., 2007; rsch. fellow dept. pharmacology Yong Loo Lin Sch. Medicine, Nat. U. Singapore, 2010. Sr. Rsch. fellowship, CSIR, Govt of India, 2006. Mem.: Indian Coun. Chemists. Office: Sri Jayachamarajendra Coll Engineering Dept Biotechnology JSS Mysore Karnataka 570006 India Office Phone: 919743921122. Office Fax: 918212515770. Personal E-mail: nanju_chem@yahoo.com.

NANKO, RAYMOND S., physician; b. Inglewood, Calif., Feb. 13, 1962; s. John and Veronica Marie (Thunder) N. DC, Cleve. Chiropractic Coll., 1985; MD, Ross U., 1994. Diplomate Am. Bd. Disability Analysts, Am. Bd. Family Practice, Am. Bd. Chiropractic Orthopedics, Am. Bd. Pain Mgmt. With ActiveCare Med. Spine & Pain Ctr., Muncie, Ind. Fellow Am. Back Soc., Am. Bd. Chiropractic Orthopedics; mem. AMA, Am. Acad. Spine Physicians, Ind. State Med. Assn., Ind. State Chiropractic Assn., Am. Chiropractic Assn., Am. Acad. Orthop. Medicine, Nat. Found., Ind. State Med. Assn., Ind. State Chiropractic Assn., Coun. Orthop., Acad. Chiropractic Orthopedics, Arthritis Found., Internat. Spinal Injection Soc., Am. Assn. Orthopedic Medicine. Office: Active Care Med Spine & Pain Ctr 919 W Jackson St Muncie IN 47305-1554

NANNEY, DAVID LEDBETTER, geneticist, educator; b. Abingdon, Va., Oct. 10, 1925; s. Thomas Grady and Pearl (Ledbetter) Nanney; m. Jean Kelley, June 15, 1951; children: Douglas Paul, Ruth Elizabeth Beshears. AB, Okla. Bapt. U., 1946; PhD, Ind. U., 1951; Laurea honoris causa, U. Pisa, Italy, 1994. Asst. prof. zoology U. Mich., Ann Arbor, 1951-56, assoc. prof., 1956-58; prof. U. Ill., Urbana-Champaign, 1959-76, prof. genetics and devel., 1976-86, prof. ecology, ethology and evolution, 1987-91, prof. emeritus, 1991—. NIH sr. predoctoral fellow Ind. U., 1949—51; NIH sr. postdoc. fellow Calif. Inst. Tech., 1958—99. Author (with Herbert Stern): The Biology of Cells, 1965, Experimental Ciliatology, 1980. Recipient Disting. Alumnus award, Okla. Bapt. U., 1972, Preisträger, Alexander von Humboldt Stiftung, Germany, 1984; named Disting. Lectr., Sch. Life Scis., U. Ill., 1981. Fellow: AAAS, Am. Acad. Arts and Scis.; mem.: Soc. Protozoologists, Am. Genetic Assn. (pres. 1982), Genetics Soc. Am. Home: 703 W Indiana Ave Urbana IL 61801-4835 Office: U Ill Dept Animal Biology 505 S Gregory St Urbana IL 61801 Business E-Mail: d-nanney@life.uiuc.edu.

NANSHAN, ZHONG, medical researcher; b. Nanjing, Jiangsu Province, China, Oct. 1939; Grad., Beijing U., 1960; studied fellow scholar, Edinburgh U., Eng., 1979—81, London U., 1979—81. Vice-dir. dept. medicine and healthcare Chinese Acad. of Engring.; works in the fields of clin. practices, tchg. and sci. rsch. of respiroloy; head Guangzhou Inst. of Respiratory Diseases, China; vice chmn. Guangdong Soc. of Sci. Tech., China; chmn. Guangzhou Soc. of Sci. Tech., China. Prof. Chinese Acad. of Engring., doctorate tutor, academician; med. tutor Smoking and Health WHO. Recipient Nat. Labor medal. Mem.: 15th Chinese Communist Party Com. (rep.), 8th and 9th Chinese People's Polit. Consultative Congress. Achievements include research in SARS Prevention and Management, of which he was one of the main professionals in the institution, was accepted as a blueprint for Guidelines of SARS Prevention and Management issued by Health Ministry of China. Office: c/o The Holeung Ho Lee Foundation 15-B Fuxing Rd Beijing 100862 China Office Phone: 008610685155441534. E-mail: hlhl@public.sti.ac.cn. *

NAOMI, UEMURA, gastroenterologist; b. Japan, Mar. 26, 1951; MD, PhD, Hiroshima U. Pres. Kohnodai Hosp., Nat. Ctr. Global Health and Medicine, 2010—. Home: Shinden 1-16-27 Ichikawa Chiba Prefecture 272-0035 Japan Home Fax: 81-47-321-6550. Personal E-mail: n uemura@mua.biglobe.ne.jp.

NAONOBU, TAKAHIRA, orthopedist, educator; b. Tokyo, Dec. 18, 1964; MD, Kitasato U., Sch. Medicine, 1989, PhD, 1998. Prof., dept. rehab. Sch. Kitasato U. Allied Health Scis.; prof. Kitasato U. Grad. Sch. Med.; head, dept. orthop. surgery Treatment Ctr. Neurol. and Locomotion Disease, Kitasato U. East Hosp., 2007—. Councilor Japanese Hip Soc., 2007, Japanese Soc. Tech. Arthroplasty, 2007, Eastern Japan Assn. Orthops. and Traumatology, 2007. Recipient Pres. award, 15th Asia Pacific Orthop. Soc., Young Scientist award, 54th Eastern Japan Assn. Orthop. and Traumatology. Mem.: SICOT, Deutsch-Japanische Tagung Fur Orthopadie, Japanese Orthop. Assn. Avocation: tennis. Office: 1-15-1 Kitasato Sagamihara Kanagawa 2520374 Japan Business E-Mail: takahira@med.kitasato-u.ac.jp.

NAOTO, FUKUYAMA, physician, educator; b. Osaka, Jan. 5, 1964; MD, Tokai U. Sch. Medicine, 1991, PhD, 1998. Assoc. prof. Tokai U. Sch. Medicine, 2007—; editor Hindawi Pub. Corp., 2011. Recipient award, Japan Health Scis. Found., St. Lukes Internat. Hosp. Mem.: Japanese Circulation Soc., Japanese Soc. Parenteral and Enteral Nutrition (mem. academic com. 2009), Japanese Soc. Internal Medicine, Japan Geriat. Soc. Avocation: fishing. Office: Shimokasuya 143 Isekara Kanagawa 259-1193 Japan Business E-Mail: nfpres@ezweb.ne.jp.

NAOUM, JOSEPH J., vascular surgeon educator; b. Ecuador, June 19, 1972; BS in Engring., Vanderbilt U., 1994, MD summa cum laude, 1998. Instr. surgery U. Tex. Med. Br., Galveston, 2003—05; asst. prof., cardiovasc. surgery assocs. Meth. Hosp., 2007—. Asst. prof. Weill-Cornell Med. Coll., 2007; expert in vascular and endovascular, aortic surgery, limb salvage procedures, carotid surgery and stenting, dialysis access placement. Recipient Molecular Surgeon Young Investigator award, Baylor Coll. Medicine, Sch. Engring. Dean's award, Vanderbilt U., Outstanding Surg. PGY-1 House Officer award, U. Tex. Med. Br. Fellow: ACS; mem.: Assn. Academic Surgery, Peripheral Vascular Surgery Soc., Soc. Clin. Vascular Surgery, Soc. Vascular Surgery, Tau Beta Pi Honor Soc. Office: 6550 Fannin St Ste 1401 Houston TX 77030 Office Phone: 713-441-5200. Personal E-mail: jjnaoum@tmhs.org.

NAOYUKI, YAMADA, research scientist; b. Tokyo, Jan. 7, 1965; MS, Chiba U., 1990; PhD, U. Tokyo. Vis. assoc. prof. Yokohama City U., 2009; prin. rschr. Inst. Innovation, Ajinomoto Co., Inc., 2009—. Com. mem. Mass Spectrometry Soc. Japan, 2009. Recipient JMSSJ award, Mass Spectrometry Soc. Japan. Avocation: travel. Office: 1-1 Suzuki-Cho Kawasaki-Ku Kawasaki Kanagawa 210-8681 Japan Business E-Mail: naoyuki_yamada@ajinomoto.com.

NAPOLITANO, GIULIO, medical researcher; b. Naples, Italy, Feb. 10, 1969; Degree in Philosophy, U. Sapienza, Rome, 1997; degree in Bioinformatics, Manchester U., 2010. Freelance analyst, developer, 1997—99; sr. developer Bit Media, 1999—2000; sr. analyst, developer S.M.S. Italia - Siemens Group Med. Sys., 2000—01; ICT officer, rschr., med. informatics Queen's U. Belfast, 2001—. Recipient Innovation Oncology award, NI Med. Rev., 2007, 1st prize, All Ireland Cancer Conf.; grant, Northern Ireland Svc. Delivery Unit. Mem.: BCS Health Northern Ireland. Avocations: astronomy, cello, photography. Office: Queen's University Belfast Mulhouse Bldg Belfast BT12 6BJ Northern Ireland Business E-Mail: g.napolitano@qub.ac.uk.

NAPOLITANO, LENA MARIE, surgeon, educator; b. Waterbury, Conn., Oct. 31, 1957; d. Carmine and Mary (Dell'Anno) N. BA, Boston U., 1979; MD, George Washington U., 1984. Diplomate Nat. Bd. Med. Examiners, Am. Bd. Surgery. Rsch. asst. dept. surgery Yale U. Med. Ctr., New Haven, 1979-80; resident in gen. surgery George Washington U. Med. Ctr., Washington, 1984-87, sr. resident in gen. surgery, asst. in surgery, 1988-89, chief resident in gen. surgery, clin. instr. in surgery, 1989-90; clin. and rsch. fellow dept. anesthesia and surgery Mass. Gen. Hosp./Harvard Med. Sch., Boston, 1987-88; instr., fellow in surg. critical care and trauma U. NC Hosp., Chapel Hill, 1990-91; trauma rsch. fellow dept. surgery U. NC, Chapel Hill, 1991-92, attending in surgery, trauma and critical care, 1991-92; asst. prof. surgery and anesthesia U. Mass. Med. Ctr., Boston, 1992-95, dir. surg. critical care, co-dir. surg. ICU, trauma svcs., 1992-95; asst. prof. surgery U. Md. Med. Ctr. and Balt. VA Med. Ctr., 1995-97, assoc. prof., 1997—2000, prof. surgery, 2000—05, dir. surg. critical care, nutrition support svcs., 1995—2005; divsn. chief surg. critical care U. Md. Med. Systems; prof. surgery, chief surgical critical care, assoc. chair surgery U. Mich., Ann Arbor, Mich., 2005—. Program dir., surg. critical care fellow U. Md. Med. Sys.; mem. disaster med. assistance team Internat. Inst. for Disaster and Emergency Medicine, U. Mass. Med. Ctr., 1993—; rschr., lectr. in field. Contbr. chpts. to books and articles to profl. publs.; reviewer Critical Care Medicine, Jour. Intensive Care Medicine, Chest. Conn. State scholar, 1975-79, Davis & Geck scholar, 1991; recipient Outstanding Resident award Holy Cross Hosp., 1988, Surg. Resident award Alpha Omega Alpha, 1989; grantee U. Mass. Med. Ctr., 1993, Burroughs Wellcome, Sterling Winthrop Inc., Soc. Critical Care Medicine, Cetus Corp., Alpha-Beta Tech., Inc., Healthcare Innovation. Fellow ACS (Harry Zehner Jr. Meml. Travelling Fellowship award Wash. chpt. 1989), Am. Coll. Chest Physicians; mem. AMA, Assn. for Acad. Surgery (mem. exec. coun. 1993—, mem. nominations com. 1994—), Surg. Infection Soc. (mem. edn. and fellowship com. 1995—), Assn. Women Surgeons (specialty rep. for trauma and critical care), Nathan Womack Surg. Soc., Soc. Critical Care Medicine, Worcester Med. Soc., Am. Med. Women's Assn., Ea. Assn. for Surgery of Trauma, Am. Soc. Parenteral and Enteral Nutrition, Am. Burn Assn., Shock Soc., Assn. VA Surgeons, Phi Beta Kappa. Office: Univ Mich Sch Medicine 1C421 UH SPC 5033 1500 East Medical Center Dr Room IC421 Ann Arbor MI 48109-0033 Business E-Mail: lenan@umich.edu.

NARAHASHI, TOSHIO, pharmacology educator; b. Fukuoka, Japan, Jan. 30, 1927; arrived in U.S., 1961; s. Asahachi and Itoko (Yamasaki) Ishii; m. Kyoko Narahashi, Apr. 21, 1956; children: Keiko, Taro. BS, U. Tokyo, 1948, PhD, 1960. Instr. U. Tokyo, 1951-65; research assoc. U. Chgo., 1961, asst. prof., 1962, Duke U., Durham, NC, 1962-63, 65-67, assoc. prof., 1967-69, prof., 1969-77, head pharmacology div., 1970-73, vice chmn. dept. physiology and pharmacology, 1973-75; prof., chmn. dept. pharmacology Northwestern U. Med. Sch., Chgo., 1977-94, Alfred Newton Richards prof., 1982—2005; John Evans prof. Northwestern U., Evanston, Ill., 1986—. Mem. pharmacology study sect. NIH, 1976-80; rsch. rev. com. Chgo. Heart Assn., 1977-82, vice chmn. rsch. coun., 1986-87, chmn., 1988-90; mem. Nat. Environ. Health Scis. Coun., 1982-86; rev. com. Nat. Inst. Environ. Health Scis., 1991-93. Editor: Cellular Pharmacology of Insecticides and Pheromones, 1979, Cellular and Molecular Neurotoxicology, 1984, Insecticide Action: From Molecule to Organism, 1989, Ion Channels, 1988—; specific field editor Jour. Pharmacology and Exptl. Therapeutics, 1972-97, assoc. editor Neurotoxicology, 1994—; contbr. articles to profl. jours. Recipient Javits Neurosci. Investigator award, NIH, 1986. Fellow AAAS, Acad. Toxicol. Scis.; mem. Am. Soc. for Pharmacology and Exptl. Therapeutics (Otto Krayer award 2000), Am. Physiol. Soc., Soc. for Neurosci., Biophys. Soc. (Cole award 1981), Soc. Toxicology (DuBois award 1988, Merit award 1991, Disting. Investigator Lifetime Achievement award 2001, Disting. Lifetime Toxicology Scholar award 2008), Agrochem. Divsn. Am. Chem. Soc. (Burdick L. Jackson Internat. award 1989). Home: 175 E Delaware Pl Apt 7911 Chicago IL 60611 7745 Office: Northwestern U Med Sch Dept Mol Pharmaco Biol Chem 303 E Chicago Ave Chicago IL 60611-3008 Office Phone: 312-503-8284. Business E-Mail: narahashi@northwestern.edu.

NARAIN, RALPH B., biologist; b. Wakenaam, Guyana, Feb. 22, 1968; s. Aaron and Rose Narain. AS, Suffolk County CC, Riverhead, NY, 2001; BS, SUNY, Oneonta, 2003; MS in entomology, U. Nebr., Lincoln, 2010. Lab. tech. Aroaima Mining Co., Berbice, Guyana, 1992—96; machine operator NY Twist Drills Inc., Bohemia, NY, 1997—2000; biologist Suffolk County Dept. Health Services, Arthropod-Borne Diseases Lab., Yaphank, 2003—07; grad. asst. U. Nebr., Lincoln, 2006—. Field evaluator dept. entomology U. Nebr., Lincoln, Nebr. Contbr. articles to profl. jours. Vol. Shiv Uma Ganesh Temple, Central Islip, NY, 2000—06. Scholar, Proctor & Gamble, 2002—03; John J. New scholar, SUNY Coll., Oneonta, 2002—03. Mem.: Entomology Soc. America, Nat. Scholar Honor Soc., Phi Theta Kappa. Avocations: travel, coin collecting/numismatics, photography. Home: 745 S 45 St Lincoln NE 68510 Office: U Nebr Lincoln 201A Entomology Hall Lincoln NE 68583-0816 Business E-Mail: ralph@huskers.unl.edu.

NARASIMHAN, PADMA MANDYAM, physician; b. Bangalore, India; came to U.S., 1976; d. Alasingracher Mandyam and Alamela Mandyam Narasimhan; 1 child, Ravi. MD, Maulana Azad Med. Coll., New Delhi, 1970. Diplomate Am. Bd. Internal Medicine, Am. Bd. Med. Oncology. Intern in internal medicine Flushing Hosp., NYC, 1976-77; resident in internal medicine Luth. Med. Ctr., NYC, 1977-79; fellow hematology, oncology Beth-Israel Med. Ctr., NYC, 1979-81; asst. prof. King Drew Med. Ctr., LA, 1983-87, Harbor UCLA, Torrance, 1987—2000, USC, 2003—07, Lomalinda, Va., 2007—09. Mem. editorial bd. Jour. Internal Medicine, 1986—. Mem. ACP, AAPI, Am. Soc. Clin. Oncology, So. Calif. Acad. Clin. Oncology. Hindu. Avocations: travel, reading, music, walking. Home: 6604 Madeline Cove Dr Palos Verdes Peninsula CA 90275-4608 Office Phone: 310-377-9555. Personal E-mail: padmanarasim@yahoo.com. *

NARAYAN, ROGER JAGDISH, engineering educator; b. Knoxville, Oct. 27, 1976; s. Jagdish and Ratna Narayan; m. Pallavi Katiyar; children: Roger, Andrew, Gregory. MD, Wake Forest U., Winston-Salem, NC, 2001; PhD in Materials Sci. & Engring., N Carolina State U., Raleigh, NC, 2002. Asst. prof. Ga. Inst. Tech., Atlanta, 2002—05; assoc. prof. U. NC/NCSU, Chapel Hill, 2005—09, prof., 2009—. Young leader Minerals, Metals & Materials Soc., Warrendale, Pa., 2004; editl. bd. mem. Jour. Nanotech. in Engring. and Medicine. Editor-in-chief Materials Sci. and Engring. C: Materials for Biological

Applications, key reader Metall. & Materials Transactions A. Recipient Young Investigator award, Office Naval Rsch., 2005, Early Career Devel. award, Nat. Sci. Found., 2006, Faculty Devel. award, U. NC, 2007, Sigma Xi Fac. Rsch. award, NCSU, 2008, Alcoa Found. Engrng. Rsch. Achievement award, 2010, Global Star award, ACerS, 2010, Vis. Lectureship award, ASM/IIM, 2010; Jefferson Pilot fellowship, U. NC, 2007, AAAS fellowship, 2007, ASM Internat. fellowship, 2009. Mem.: ACerS, TMS, ASM Internat. Home: 8210 Stonetown Ave Raleigh NC 27612 Office: UNC/NCSU Joint Dept Biomed Engineering Campus Box 7575 Chapel Hill NC 27599 Personal E-mail: roger_narayan@msn.com. Business E-Mail: roger_narayan@unc.edu.

NARAYANAN, SAREESH NADUVIL, physiologist, educator; b. Vallissery, Kerala, India, May 31, 1984; BSc in Zoology, St. Thomas Coll., Thrissur, 2004; MSc in Med. Physiology, Kasturba Med. Coll., Manipal U., 2007. Physiology coord. Melaka Manipal Med. Coll., Manipal U., 2009, curriculum devel. com. mem., 2010, libr. in charge, 2010, lectr., 2007—. Recipient Best Audio-Visual Tchg. Material, Manipal U., 2010, Young Scientist award, Jawaharlal Nehru U. New Delhi, India, 2011. Mem.: Internat. Brain Rsch. Orgn., Indian Acad. Neurosci. Avocations: listening to music, cricket, badminton. Office: Manipal University Melaka Manipal Med Coll Madhav Nagar Manipal Karnataka 576 104 India Office Phone: 08202922637o. Office Fax: 918202571905. Personal E-mail: sareeshnn@yahoo.co.in.

NARCISI, CALVERN E., psychiatrist, educator; b. Bklyn., May 1, 1947; BA, NYU, 1969; MD, SUNY Downstate, 1973. Child, adolescent & adult psychiatrist, psychoanalyst, 1978—. Clin. prof. psychiatry U. Colo. Sch. Medicine, 2002—. Fellow: Am. Psycoanalytic Assn., Am. Psychiat. Assn. (named Disting. Fellow). Avocations: golf, tennis, skiing. Office: 4900 Cherry Creek South Dr Ste 10 Denver CO 80246 Office Fax: 303-698-2817. Personal E-mail: cnarcisi@aol.com.

NARDO, BRUNO, surgeon, educator, researcher; b. Vibo Valentia, Italy, Feb. 19, 1961; s. Giuseppe Nardo and Mariarosa Arena; m. Monica Pastina, Apr. 23, 1994; 1 child, Giuseppe. MD, PhD, Italy, 1985. Surgeon specialist U. Bologna, Italy, 1990—2005, assoc. prof., 2001—. Cons. surgery and transplantations Hosp. SS Annunziata, Cosenza, Italy, 2004—05. Capt. Italian Health Svc., 1986—87. Recipient Social Activity award, Govt. Achievements include patents for liver extracorporeal oxygenation system to induce liver regeneration for the treatment of acute hepatic failure. Home: Misa 49 40138 Bologna Italy Office: Univ Bologna Italy 40138 Bologna Italy Office Fax: +051397661. Business E-Mail: nardo@aosp.bo.it.

NARDO, LUCIANO GIOVANNI, obstetrician, gynecologist; b. Catania, Sicily, Italy, Nov. 4, 1975; s. Filadelfo Nardo and Grazia Bottino; m. Carina Harriet-Anderson Nardo. MD with 1st class honors, U. Catania, Italy, 1999; Diploma, Faculty of Planning and Reproductive Health Care, 2002. Diplomate Italy, 2000, cert. specialist registrar modular tng. program U. of Catania, 2001. Clin. rsch. fellow Dept. of Reproductive Medicine and Sci., ICSM, St Mary's Hosp., London, 2000—01, hon. clin. rsch. fellow, 2001—02; registrar dept. ob-gyn. Wexham Pk. Hosp., Slough, Berkshire, England, 2001—02; specialist registrar dept. ob-gyn. Northampton Gen. Hosp. NHS Trust, Northampton, England, 2002—02, Frimley Pk. Hosp., Camberley, Surrey, England, 2002—03, Kingston Hosp., Surrey, 2003—. Peer-review sci. jour. referee Human Reproduction Jour., Cambridge, 2001—, Elsevier Sci., European Jour. of Obstetrics Gynecology and Reproductive Biology, 2001—, Reproductive Biomedicine Online, 2003; rsch. coord. Ctr. for Reproductive Medicine and Infertility, U. Catania, Sicily, Italy, 2000—; internat. sci. sec. Mediterranean Soc. for Reproductive Medicine. Editor (co-editor): (medical illustration of endometrium) Creative interactive CD-rom. U. Catania Rsch. grantee, 2000, Italian Ministry of Sci. Rsch. and U., 2001. Mem.: Mediterranean Soc. for Reproductive Medicine (founder), European Soc. of Gynaecological Endoscopy (assoc.), Internat. Working Group on PGD (assoc.), European Soc. of Human Reproduction and Embryology (assoc.), Am. Soc. for Reproductive Medicine (assoc.). Catholic. Achievements include first to Luteinizing hormone and testosterone are not correlated with pregnancy outcome in women with recurrent miscarriage; 3D assessment of ultrasound features in PCOS; research in insulin-like growth factor system modifies the oocyte maturation pattern during ovarian hyperstimulation; diagnosis of pulmonary metastasizing leiomyomatosis in pregnant women undergoing caesarean section. A prompt diagnosis of this life-threatening condition may contribute to reduce maternal death; design of multicentric research project looking at the expression of integrins into the endometrium during the implantation phase. Avocations: reading, music, tennis, skiing, theater. Office: St Mary's Hosp Dept Reprod Medicine Praed St W2 1PG London England Office Fax: +44 0207 886 6054; Home Fax: +44 0207 886 6054. Personal E-mail: lnardogyn@hotmail.com.

NARISETY, SATYA DEVI, medical researcher; b. India, May 29, 1978; BS, Tufts U., 1999; MD, UMDNJ-NJMS, 2004. Postdoc. fellow, allergy and immunology Johns Hopkins U., 2008—. Office: 600 N Wolfe St CMSC 1102 Baltimore MD 21287 Business E-Mail: snarise1@jhmi.edu.

NARITA, MITSUO, pediatrician, microbiologist; b. Otaru, Japan, Apr. 12, 1957; s. Tomio and Masuho (Takaoka) N.; m. Yuko Fukao, Sept. 23, 1984; children: Rina, Kenji. MD, Hokkaido U., Sapporo, Japan, 1982, PhD, 1993. Physician Hokkaido U., 1982-86, 88-96, Tetsudo Hosp., Sapporo, 1997—; cons. ING Corp., 2004—. Rschr. Sapporo Med. Coll., 1987; cons. Japan Soc. Mycoplasmology, 1996—, Japan Soc. CNS Infection, 1997-, Asian Org. Mywplasmol, 2004—. Contbr. articles to profl. jours. Grantee, Ministry of Health, Labor and Welfare of Japan, 2003. Mem. Am. Soc. Microbiology, Internat. Orgn. Mycoplasmology, Japan Soc. Mycoplasmology (pres. 29th ann. meeting 2002). Avocation: running marathons. Home: Chuo-ku Odori W-26 3-5-601 Hokkaido Sapporo 064-0820 Japan Office Phone: 81-11-8511110.

NARSAVAGE, GEORGIA ROBERTS, nursing educator, researcher; b. Pittston, Pa., Jan. 1, 1948; d. George H. Roberts and Betty (Smith) Brown; m. Peter P. Narsavage, Oct. 26, 1968; children: Peter A., Paul J., Marea L. BSN, U. Md., Washington DC, 1969; MSN, Misericordia U., 1984; PhD in Nursing, U. Pa., Phila., 1990. RN, W.Va.; cert. adult nurse practitioner, Ohio, Ga., W.Va. Staff nurse Mercy Hosp., Scranton, Pa., 1970-72; pvt. duty nursing Pa., 1972-79; clinical instr. Lackawanna County Vo-Tech Practical Nursing Program, Dunmore, Pa., 1979-82; clinical and theoretical instr. Mercy Hosp. Sch. of Nursing, Scranton, Pa., 1982-84; asst. prof. nursing dept. U. Scranton, Pa., 1984-93, assoc. prof., 1993—99, chmn. dept., 1991-94, dir. RN program dept. nursing, 1990-92, assoc. dean Panuska Coll. Profl. Studies, 1998—99; assoc. prof. Case Western Res. U., Cleve., 1999—2005, dir. MSN program Sch. Nursing, 1999—2004, assoc. dean Academic Programs, 2003—05; prof. and assoc. dean academic affairs Med. Coll. Ga., 2005—07; dean, prof. W.Va. U., Sch. Nursing, Morgantown, 2007—. Postdoctoral fellow U. Pa., Phila., 1995-97, mem. bd. dirs., W.Va. U Hosp., mem. W.Va. Rural Health Adv. Bd.; cons. in field. Contbr. articles to profl. jours. Gifted program mentor Scranton Sch. Dist.; active in ch. and civic choirs. Grantee U. Scranton, 1989, 91, 94-98, NIH NRSA, 1995-97, Health Resources and Svcs. Adminstrn. Divsn. Nursing, 2004—, NIH, NCI, 2010-; recipient Rsch. award European Respiratory Soc., 2002, Ednl. Rsch. award Midwest Nursing Rsch. Soc., 2004; Alumni award Nursing Edn. Coll. Misericordia, 2005. Fellow Am. Acad. Nursing(expert panel global health mem.), Nat. Acad. Practice, Nursing (disting. fellow 2000); mem. ANA, APHA, AAUW (W. Va. chair coll. u. commn., 09-, Morgantown br. pres., 2010-)Am. Thoracic Soc./Am. Lung Assn. (chmn. nursing assembly 2004—06, edn. commn., 08-10, bd. dirs., Abstract award 2002), Pa. Nurses Assn. (bd. dirs., chmn. com., conv. del., Excellence award 1996), Lackawanna Nurses Assn. (bd. dirs., com. chmn., dist. pres.), Nat. League for Nursing, Coun. Nursing Informatics (chair nominating com. 1993-95), Pa. League for Nursing (chair nominating com.), Ohio Nurses Assn. (chmn. practice com.), Midwest Nursing Rsch. Soc. (chmn. membership com., vice chmn. conf. com.), U. Md. Nurses Alumnae Assn., Ea. Nursing Rsch. Soc. (mem.-at-large bd. dirs., interim treas., rsch. grantee 1994), Southern Nursing Rsch. Soc. (co-chair rsch. com., mem. legis. Com.), Am. Assn. Colls. Nursing (elect Nominating com. mem. 2011-), Theta Phi, Sigma Theta Tau (Rsch. award 1994), Iota Omega (Mentor award 2002). Office: W Va Univ Sch Nursing HSS 6700 PO Box 9600 Morgantown WV 26506-9600 Office Phone: 304-293-6521. Personal E-mail: narsavageg1@hotmail.com. Business E-Mail: gnarsavage@hsc.wvu.edu.

NARULA, PRAMOD, pediatrician, pulmonologist; Attended, Maulana Azad Med. Coll., 1976. Diplomate Am. Bd. of Pediatrics, pediatric pulmonology. Resident Winthrop Univ. Hosp., 1989, Columbia Univ., 1992; with Cornell Weill Med. Coll., NY Methodist Hosp., chmn. dept. of pediat. Office: New York Methodist Hospital 506 6th St Brooklyn NY 11215 Office Phone: 718-780-3000.

NARULA, PREETA KAUR, physician; b. New Delhi, Feb. 1, 1982; MBBS, J.N. Med. Coll., Aligarh Muslim U., 2005; MD, Lady Hardinge Med. Coll., Delhi U., 2009. Sr. resident Maulana Azad Med. Coll. and Associated Hosps., 2009. Home: Greater Kailash New Delhi 110048 India Personal E-mail: docpreeta@yahoo.com.

NARURKAR, VIC, dermatologist; Grad., Brown U., Stanford U. Diplomate Am. Bd. of Dermatology. Dermatology dir. UC Davis Laser Ctr., asst. prof., asst. clin. prof. dermatology; dermatology chmn. Calif. Pacific Med. Ctr.; founder Bay Area Laser Inst. Pres. Am. Soc. Of Cosmetic Dermatology And Aesthetic Surgery; mem. editl. bd. Am. Acad. of Dermatology and Cosmetic Dermatology. Recipient Alan Scott award; named one of Best Doctors In America. Office: Bay Area Laser Institute 2100 Webster St No 505 San Francisco CA 94110 Office Phone: 415-923-3377.

NASCA, THOMAS JOSEPH, medical association administrator, former dean; b. Bklyn., June 1, 1949; m. Jean S. Styslinger; children: Patrick T., Brian J. children: Thomas J, Andrew J. BS, U. of Notre Dame, Ind., 1971; MD, Jefferson Med. Coll., Philla., 1975. Diplomate Am. Bd. Internal Medicine 1978, Am. Bd. Nephrology 1982. Intern Mercy Hosp. of Pitts., 1975—76, resident in internal medicine, 1976—79; fellow in nephrology RI Hosp.-Brown U., Providence, 1979—81; coord. of clin. services, dept. of medicine Mercy Hosp. of Pitts., 1981—85, chmn. and residency program dir., dept. of medicine, 1985—92; vice chmn., dept. of medicine Jefferson Med. Coll., Phila., 1992—97, assoc. dean for edn. and rsch., 1997—2000, acting dean, 2000—01, dean, 2001—07; sr. v.p. Thomas Jefferson U., Phila., 2001—; pres. Jefferson U. Physicians, Phila., 2001—; CEO Accreditation Coun. Grad. Med. Edn., Chgo., 2007—. Chmn. Residency Rev. Com. for Internal Medicine, Chgo., 2001—. Contbr. over 40 articles to profl. jours. Recipient Caduceus Award for Exemplary Leadership, Mercy Hosp. of Pitts., 1986, W.W.G. Mclauchlan Award for Exemplary Contbns. in Edn., 1993, The Christian R. and Mary F. Lindback Award for Disting. Tchg., Jefferson Med. Coll., 1994, Presentation of Portrait to Thomas Jefferson U., Class of 2000, Jefferson Med. Coll., 2000, Sister M. Ferdinand Clark Outstanding Alumnus Achievement Award, Mercy Hosp. of Pitts., 2001; named White Plains H.S. Citizen of the Yr., Nat. Exch. Club, 1967. Fellow: ACP, Coll. of Physicians of Phila.; mem.: Myasthena Gravis Assn. Western Pa. (bd. dirs. 1990—92), Assn. of Program Dirs. in Internal Medicine (mem. coun. 1990—2001, sec.-treas. 1995—99, pres. 2000—01), Chester Valley Golf Club, Pyramid Club, Alpha Omega Alpha. Avocations: golf, photography, basketball, marine aquarist, rugby. Office: Accreditation Coun Grad Med Edn Ste 2000 515 N State St Chicago IL 60654 Office Phone: 312-755-5000. *

NÄSE, LEENA MARJATTA, retired dentist; d. Toimi August Villikko and Bertta Katri Villikko; m. Martti Kalervo Näse, Dec. 5, 1970; 1 child, Mari Katriina Siekkinen. MS, U. Helsinki, 1971; DDS, U. Kuopio, 1978. Asst. tchr. applied microbiology U. Helsinki, 1971—72, tchr. clin. dentistry, 1995—2001; assoc. tchr. med. microbiology U. Kuopio, 1972—75, spezializing dentist, 1991—94; dentist, specialist clin. dentistry Kuopio City Health Dept., 1977—95; cons. specialist clin. dentistry Tampere City Health Dept., 2001—04; ret., 2004. Mem.: Guild Microbiologists (assoc.), Finlands Dentist Soc. (assoc.), Finlands Dentist Fedn. (assoc.). Avocations: study and scientific letters, literature, gardening, botany, studying geology.

NASH, DAVID REINTHAL, pediatrician; b. Dec. 25, 1960; MD, U. Cin. Coll. Medicine, 1989. Cert. Am. Bd. Pediat., 2007, Am. Bd. Allergy and Immunology, 2005. Residency Northwestern U. Sch. Medicine, Chgo.; fellowship Duke U. Med. Ctr., Durham, NC; chief and clin. services dir., allergy and immunology sect., asthma ctr. U. Pitts. Sch. Medicine, asst. prof. pediat., divsn. allergy, immunology, and infectious diseases. Contbr. articles to profl. jours. Mem.: Am. Acad. Allergy and Immunology, Am. Bd. Pediat. Office: Divsn Pediatric Allergy and Immunology Children's Hosp Pitts UPMC 3705 Fifth Ave Ste 32 Pittsburgh PA 15213 Office Phone: 412-692-7885. Office Fax: 412-692-8499. Business E-Mail: david.nash@chp.edu.

NASH, DENIS, healthcare educator; b. May 1, 1968; PhD, U. Md., 1999; MPH, Johns Hopkins U., 1995. Dir., monitoring, evaluation, and rsch. unit Internat. Ctr. AIDS Care and Treatment Programs, Columbia U. Mailman Sch. Pub. Health, 2004—10; assoc. prof. epidemiology Columbia U. Mailman Sch. Pub. Health, 2004—10; assoc. prof. CUNY Sch. Pub. Health, Hunter Coll., 2010—. Office: CUNY Sch Public Health 425 E 25t New York NY 10010 Business E-Mail: dn2145@columbia.edu.

NASH, ROSS W., dentist, educator; Attended, NC State U.; DDS, U. NC, 1978. Faculty mem. sch. dentistry The Med. Coll. Ga.; dir. contemporary dentistry The Inst. for Advanced Studies, Charlotte, NC. Named one of World's Finest Cosmetic Dentists. Fellow: Am. Acad. of Cosmetic Dentistry; mem.: Am. Acad. of Cosmetic Dentistry, The Charlotte Dental Soc., Acad. of Gen. Dentistry, NC Dental Soc., ADA. Office: The Nash Institute for Dental Learning 6302 Fairview Rd Ste 102 Charlotte NC 28210 Office Phone: 888-442-0242.

NASKA, ANDRONIKI, nutritionist, epidemiologist educator; b. Athens, Feb. 8, 1972; MSc, King's Coll., U. London, 1997; PhD, Sch. Medicine, U. Athens, 2002. Rsch. asst., dept. nutrition & biochemistry Greek Nat. Sch. Pub. Health, 1996—; asst. prof., dept. hygiene, epidemiology & med. stats. Sch. Medicine, U. Athens, 1999. Recipient Rsch. award, Com. II World Congress Pub. Health Nutrition. Mem.: European Assn. Cancer Rsch., European Fedn. Sci. & Tech. Lipids. Office: 75 Mikras Asias Str Athens Goudi 11527 Greece Office Fax: 30 210 746 2079. E-mail: anaska@nut.uoa.gr.

NASLUND, THOMAS C, surgeon, educator; b. Amarillo, Aug. 31, 1958; BA, Trinity U., 1980; MD, Vanderbilt U., 1984. Prof. surgery Vanderbilt U. Med. Ctr., chief vascular surgery, 1994—. Fellow: ACS. Office: 1215 21st Ave S Ste 5209 MCE Nashville TN 37232 Office Fax: 615-343-4251. Business E-Mail: thomas.naslund@vanderbilt.edu.

NASMYTH, KIM, science association director; b. London, 1952; PhD in Zoology, U. Edinburgh, 1977. Postdoctoral rsch., Seattle, 1978—80; Robertson rsch. fellow at Cold Spring, molecular biology Cambridge U., 1982—87; sr. scientist Rsch. Inst. Molecular Pathology, Vienna, 1988—97, dir., 1997—2006; Whitley Chair, Biochemistry, Dept. Biochemistry, head, dept. biochemistry U. Oxford, 2006—. Invited lectr. in field. Recipient FEBS Silver medal, 1995, Max Perutz prize, Unilever Sci. prize, 1996, Louis Jeantet prize for medicine, 1997, Austrian Wittgenstein prize, 1999, Boveri award for Molecular Cancer Genetics, 2003, Gairdner Found. Internat. award, 2007. Fellow: Royal Soc. (Croonian lecture/medal 2002); mem.: European Molecular Biology Orgn., Am. Acad. Arts and Scis. (fgn.) (hon.), Austrian Acad. Scis. Achievements include being the co-discover of cohesin, a protein complex crucial for faithful chromosome segregation during cell division. Office: Dept Biochemistry U Oxford South Parks Road Oxford OX1 3QU England *

NASON, DOLORES IRENE, computer company executive, social services administrator, minister; b. Seattle; d. William Joseph and Ruby Irene Lockinger; m. George Malcolm Nason, Jr.; children: George Malcolm III, Scott James, Lance William, Natalie Joan. Student, Long Beach City Coll., Calif.; cert. in Religious Edn. for elem tchrs., Immaculate Heart Coll., cert. teaching, cert. secondary teaching; attended, Salesian Sem. Buyer J. C. Penney Co., Barstow, Calif.; prin. St. Cyprian Confraternity of Christian Doctrine Elem. Sch., Long Beach; prin. summer sch. St. Cyprian Confraternity of Christian Doctrine Elem. Sch., Long Beach; pres. St. Cyprian Confraternity Orgn., Long Beach; dist. co-chmn. LA Diocese; v.p. Nason & Assocs., Inc., Long Beach, 1978—; pres. LA County Commn. on Obscenity & Pornography, 1984—; eucharistic minister St. Cyprian Ch., Long Beach, 1985—; bd. dirs. LA County Children's Svcs., 1988—; exec. dir. social svcs. Disabled Resources Ctr., Inc., Long Beach, 1992—. Scholarship com. Long Beach City Coll., 1984—90, Calif. State U., Long Beach, 1984—90; chmn. bd. dirs. LA County Access Para Transit Svcs. Inc., 2004—; chairman Long Beach Transit Paratransit Coms., 2007—. Mem. Nat. Com. Am. Disabilities Act; active Long Beach Civic Light Opera, 1973—96, Assistance League Long Beach, 1976—; vol. Meml. Children's Hosp., Long Beach, 1977—92; founding mem. Theater West Footlighters; pres. St. Cyprian's Parish Coun., 1962—; adv. com. mem. Long beach City Coll. DSPS, 2007—. Mem.: KC (Family of Month award 1988). Roman Catholic. Avocations: physical fitness, theater, choir, travel.

NASON, KATIE S., thoracic surgeon, educator; b. Portland, Oreg., June 27, 1970; MPH, U. Wash., 2005; MD, Oreg. Health & Scis. U., 1997. Acting instr. U. Wash., 2004—05; asst. prof., divsn. thoracic and foregut surgery U. Pitts., 2008—. Assoc. program dir., thoracic surgery residency program edn. com., dept. cardiothoracic surgery U. Pitts., 2008, com. mem., spl. instl. edn. programs com., 09, com. mem., grad. med. edn. com., 09; com. mem., peer rev. com. U. Pitts. Cancer Inst., 2010; com. mem., clin. sci. rev. com. ACS Oncology Group, 2010. Recipient Shadyside Hosp. Found. Quality award, UPMC Shadyside Hosp., 2010, award, Behavioral & Population Scis. Career Devel., 2011; grant, Assn. Women Surgeons Found. and Ethicon Endo-Surgery, Shadyside Hosp. Found., U. Pitts. Med. Ctr., KO7 Cancer Prevention Control. Mem.: ACS, Assn. Women Surgeons, Am. Gastroent. Assn., Am. Soc. Clin. Oncology, Soc. Thoracic Surgeons. Avocations: running, bicycling, skiing. Office: 5200 Centre Ave Ste 715 Shadyside Pittsburgh PA 15232 Office Fax: 412-623-0329. Business E-Mail: nasonks@upmc.edu.

NASS, SHARYL JEANNE, health science policy study director, medical educator; d. Wiliam Nass and Jeanne Goeglein; m. Eric John Costello, May 13, 2000; children: Elisa Costello, Kenna Costello, Mia Costello. BS, U. Wis.-Madison, 1989, MS, 1991; PhD, Georgetown U., Washington, 1996. Postdoc. fellow Johns Hopkins U., Sch. Medicine, 1997—99; health sci. policy study dir. Nat. Acads. Inst. Medicine, Washington. Guest lectr. U. Md. Sch. Nursing, Balt., 2001—, clin. instr., 2010—. Contbr. scientific papers. Recipient Cecil award, 2007, Disting. Svc. award, NAS, 2011; Heinrich-Hertz-Stiftung fellowship, 1992—93. Mem.: AAAS, Am. Assn. Cancer Rsch. Office: Nat Acads Inst Medicine 500 5th St NW Washington DC 20001

NASSAB, REZA, surgeon; b. Tehran, Iran, June 6, 1977; CM, U. of Birmingham, 2000. Sr. ho. officer in plastic surgery Nottingham City Hosp., 2005—; clin. fellow in plastic surgery U. Hosp. Birmingham, 2004—05. Contbr. articles to profl.jours. Recipient Pub. Health and Epidemiology Project prize, U. of Birmingham, 1998, Midland Gastroent. Soc. Poster prize, Midland Gastroent. Soc., 2001; Onnesley

Bursary grant, U. Birmingham, 1998. Mem.: Royal Coll. Surgeons of Edinburgh, Royal Coll. Surgeons of Eng. Personal E-mail: rsnassab@doctors.net.uk.

NAST, CYNTHIA C., pathologist, educator; b. NY, Dec. 1, 1953; MD, NY Med. Coll., 1979. Prof. pathology Cedars-Sinai Med. Ctr., 1992—. Prof. pathology UCLA, 1985. Recipient Jacob Churg award, Renal Pathology Soc. Mem.: ASN, USCAP. Office: Cedars-Sinai Med Ctr 8700 Beverly Blvd Los Angeles CA 90048 Office Fax: 310-423-5881. Business E-Mail: nast@cshs.org.

NAST, EDWARD PAUL, cardiothoracic and vascular surgeon; b. Balt., Dec. 13, 1958; s. Richard Cecil and Lenora (Heilig) N.; m. Lauren Jean Nast; children: Bennett Ross, Jaclyn Rose, Jacob Martin. BS, Emory U., 1979; MD, U. Md., 1984. Diplomate Am. Bd. Thoracic Surgery, Am. Bd. Surgery. Intern Georgetown U. Med. Ctr., Washington, 1984-85, resident in gen. surgery, 1985-86, 88-91; fellow in cardiac surgery NIH, Bethesda, Md., 1986-88; resident in thoracic and cardiovascular surgery U. Md. Med. Sys., Balt., 1991-93; attending cardiothoracic surgeon St. Joseph's Hosp. Health Ctr., Syracuse, NY, 1993—2002; cardiothoracic and vascular surgeon Arnot Ogden Med. Ctr., Elmira, NY, 2001—, med. dir. cardiothoracic surgery, 2006—. Asst. attending cardiothoracic surgeon NY Presbyn. Hosp., Columbia U. Med. Ctr., NYC, 2002—; asst. clin. prof. cardiothoracic surgery Columbia U., NYC, 2002—. Contbr. articles to profl. jours. Named one of Outstanding Young Men of Am., 1996, 98. Fellow ACS, Am. Coll. Cardiology, Am. Coll. Chest Physicians; mem. Soc. Thoracic Surgeons, Phi Beta Kappa. Office: 600 Ivy St Ste 201 Elmira NY 14905 Home: 14 Prospect Ridge Horseheads NY 14845 Office Phone: 607-737-7780. Personal E-mail: enast@stny.rr.com. Business E-Mail: enast@aomc.org.

NATANI, KIRMACH, forensic psychologist; b. Milw., June 5, 1935; s. Whit Baer Naabane and Natasha Rucoss Nabona. MSc in Clin. Psychology, Okla. U., 1970; PhD in Biopsychology, Okla. U. Health Sci. Ctr., 1977; postgrad., USAF Sch. Aerospace Medicine, San Antonio, 1977—79. Lic. clin. psychologist, health svc. provider, cert. forensic neuropsychologist, sr. disability analyst, divorce mediator. Physics tech./profl. Lawrence Berkeley Lab., Berkeley, Calif., 1958—63; vol. Peace Corps, Thailand, 1963—65; clin. rschr. Okla. City VA Hosp., 1966—77; human factors engr. McDonnell-Douglas, St. Louis, 1980—92; postodoctoral resident/cons. St. Mary's Hosp., East St. Louis, Ill., 1992—97; pvt. practice clin. neuropsychologist, cons. Bi-State Neurometric Svcs., various cities, 1998—. Clin. mgr. Mo. Dept. Corrections, Farmington, Mo., 1999—2001; sr. care mgr. Magellan Behavior Health, St. Louis, 2001—02; ad hoc peer reviewer profl. psychology, rsch., practice, 2001—; mem. adv. com. NRC, 1978—83; assoc. Social Security Disability Attorney, Clayton. Contbr. numerous articles to profl. jours., chpts. to books. With USAF, 1955—63. Recipient, Roche Labs. awards, 1973; grantee, Divsn. Polar Programs, NSF, 1966—75, Nature Publishing Group, 2006. Fellow: Am. Coll. Forensic Examiners; mem.: AAAS, APA, NY Acad. Sci., Mo. Am. Psychol. Assn., Am. Bd. Disability Analysts, Am. Bd. Psychol. Specialities, Internat. Soc. Neurofeedback and Rsch. Avocations: computer graphics, digital photographic restoration. Office Phone: 314-426-1875, 314-727-3445. Personal E-mail: knat3@juno.com.

NATARAJAN, GIRIJA, medical educator, director; b. New Delhi, Mar. 25, 1969; MBBS, Maulana Azad Med. Coll., 1993. Med. dir. NICU; asst. prof. Children's Hosp. Mich. & Wayne State U., 2006— Office: 3901 Beaubien Blvd Detroit MI 48201 Business E-Mail: gnatara@med.wayne.edu.

NATARAJAN, S., surgeon; b. Madurai, Tamil Nadu, India, Sept. 4, 1957; s. N. S. and Kamla N. Sundaram; children: Aditya S., Aditi S. MBBS, DO, Madras U., TamilNadu. Vitreo retinal surgeon Sankara Nethralaya, Chennai, Tamil Nadu, India, 1985—88; vitreo retinal surgeon Taparia Inst. Ophthalmology; Bombay Hosp. & Rsch. Ctr., Mumbai, Maharashtra, 1988—90; hon. vitreo retinal surgeon PD Hinduja Nat. Hosp. & Rsch. Ctr.; med. dir. Aditya Jyot Eye Hosp., 1990—2004; eye surgeon, vitreo retinal specialist, chmn., med. dir. Aditya Jyot Eye Hosp. Pvt Ltd, 2004; chmn., med. dir. Aditya Jyot Inst. Optometry. Chmn. sci. com. All India Ophthal. Soc., 2003—; hon. dir. Indian Eye Injury Registry; chmn. Aditya Joyt Found. Twinkling Little Eyes, Mumbai; v.p. Vitreo Retinal Soc. India; chmn. sci. com. Maharashtra Ophthal. Soc., 2005—; sci. convenor Bombay Ophthalmologist Assn., Mumbai, 2005—; gen. sec. Ocular Trauma Soc. India; pres. Nat. Soc. Prevention Blindness, Mumbai; sec. Aditya Jyot Rsch. Inst.; mng. trustee Aditya Jyot Rsch. Found.; exec. com. mem. Internat. Soc. Ocular Trauma. Author: (book: clinical practice in ophthalmology) Ocular Trauma, (book) 25-Gauge Transconjunctival Sutureless Vitrectomy, Management of Postoperative Endophthalmitis, Retinopathy of Prematurity, Diagnostics in Macular Disorders, Management of Ocular Trauma.; Update onn Photodynamic Therapy (Verterporfin) in ARMD, Indocyanine Green Angiography, (text book) Photodynamic Therapy, (textbook) Indocyanine Green Angiography, (book) Management of Anterior segment Complications, Posterior Seg Complications in SICS Mgnt, Recent Advances in Surgical Management of ARMD, Wide Angle Viewing Systems in Vitreous Surgeries. Recipient Dr. Joseph Gnandickam Gold Medal Oration award, Tamil Nadu Ophthalmic Assn., Vasantrao Naik Krushisanshodhan & Gramin Vikas Pratishthan Puraskar, Gov. of Maharashtra, Parasnath Gold medal, Bihar Ophthal. Soc., Dr. E. Balakrishnan Meml. award, Indian Assn. Biomed. Scis., DS Mathias prize, Madras Christian Coll., Innovation award, Maharashtra Ophthal. Soc., Indira Gandhi Sadbhavna award, Global Econ. Coun., Sr. Honour award, Vitreous Soc. USA, CN Shroff award, All India Ophthal. Soc., Best Rsch. award, Andhra Pradesh Acad. Sci., Disting. award, Asia Pacific Acad. Ophthalmology, 2006. Mem.: Asian-Pacific Assn. Laser Medicine and Surgery, Care & Share Inc, Vitreous Soc., Internat. soc. Ocular Trauma, Indo-Japanese Ophthal. Found. (life), Nepal Ophthal. Soc. (life), Youth Hostels Assn. India (life), Fedn. Ob-gyn. Socs. India (life), Indian Acad. Paediatrics (life), Indian Assn. Preventive and Social Medicine (life), Madras Ophthalmologists Assn. (life), Oberoi Plus Programme (life), Young Men Christian Assn. (life), Bharatiya Vidya Bhavan (life), Bombay Tamil Sangham (life), Rajpath Club Ltd (life), Nellai Saiva Vellalar Sangam (life), Bombay Mgmt. Assn. (life), Nat. Soc. Prevention Blindness (life), Nat. Sports Club India (life), Delhi Ophthal. Soc. (life), A.P. State Ophthal. Soc. (life), All India Ophthal. Soc. (life), Indian Assn. Occupl. Health Bombay Br. (life), Ophthal. Soc. West Bengal (life), Maharashtra Soc. Donation Eyes (life), Fedn. Ophthalmic Rsch. & Edn. Ctr. (life), Ophthalmic Digest (life), Indian Intraocular Implant Soc. (life), Kerala State Ophthal. Soc. (life), Ophthalmic Laser Soc. (life), Tamilnadu Ophthalmologists Assn. (life), Gujarat Ophthal. Soc. (life), Ophthalmic Photographers Cir. India (life), All India Ophthal. Soc. (life), Maharashtra Ophthal. Soc. (life), Bombay Ophthalmologists Assn. (life), Rajasthan Ophthalmology Soc. (life), Bihar Ophthal. Soc. (life), M.P. State Ophthalmic Soc. (life), Eye Care Centre (life), Strabismological Soc. of India (life), Nat. Integrated Med. Assn. (life), All India Medicos Soc. (life), Indian Soc. Human Genetics (life), Vitreo Retinal Soc. India (life), I.M.A. Acad. Med. Specialities (life), Dadar Medicos Brotherhood (life), Madras Inst. Magnetobiology (life), Assn. Med. Cons. (life), Indian Assn. Biomed. Scientists (life), Internat. Soc. Ocular Trauma (life), Soc. Med. Learning Resources Transfer (life), Indian Med. Assn. (life), World Wide Fund Nature-India (life), Pan Arab Coun. Ophthalmology (life), Retina Soc. (life), Internat. Acad. Sports Vision (life), Ophthalmic Photographers' Soc., Inc (life), Internat. Union Health Edn. South East Asia Regional Bur. (life), Schepens Internat. Soc. (life), Am. Acad. Ophthalmology (life), Assn. Rsch. Vision & Ophthalmology (life). Avocations: travel, teaching, stamp collecting/philately, dance, swimming. Home: 2B/11 Lloyds Garden Appasaheb Marathe Mumbai 400025 India Office: Aditya Jyot Eye Hosp Pvt Ltd Opp Siws Coll Gate No3 Road No9 400 031 Mumbai India Office Fax: +912224177630. Business E-Mail: ajeh@vsnl.com.

NATER-MEWES, RICARDA, psychologist, researcher; b. Essen, Germany, 1979; Diploma, Theodor-Heuss-Gymnasium, Ratingen, Germany, 1999; MS, Heinrich-Heine-U., Düsseldorf, Germany, 2005; PhD, Philipps U. Marburg, Germany, 2009. Sci. officer Dept. Psychosomatic Medicine, U. Duisburg-Essen, 2005—07, Clin. Psychology, Philipps-U. Marburg, Germany, 2007—. Psychol. psychotherapist Inst. Psychotherapy, U. Marburg, 2007—. Office: Philipps-Univ Marburg Gutenbergstr. 18 35037 Marburg Germany Business E-Mail: mewesr@staff.uni-marburg.de, mewesr@uni-marburg.de.

NATHAN, CARL FRANCIS, medical educator; b. NYC, 1946; BA, Harvard U., 1967, MD, 1972. Intern Mass. Gen. Hosp., Boston, 1972-73, resident, 1973-74; clin. assoc. Nat. Cancer Inst., Washington, 1974-76; fellow in med. oncology Yale U., New Haven, 1976-77; attending physician N.Y. Hosp., 1985—; asst. prof. Rockefeller U., NYC, 1977-83, assoc. prof., 1983-85, adj. prof., 1986—; prof. medicine Weill Cornell Med. Coll., NYC, 1986—, prof. microbiology and immunology, R.A. Rees Pritchett prof. microbiology, chmn. microbiology and immunology. Mem.: NAS. Office: Weill Cornell Med Coll Mailbox 62 1300 York Ave New York NY 10021-4805 Office Phone: 212-746-2985. Office Fax: 212-746-8536. Business E-Mail: cnathan@med.cornell.edu. *

NATHAN, GERALD DALE, retired psychologist, researcher, writer; b. Norfolk, Nebr., Oct. 1, 1938; s. Raymond John and Esther Marie (Neuwerk) N.; m. Jo Anne Williams, Aug. 19, 1993; 1 child, Jerald John; stepchildren: Rodney Wade, Erica Wren. Student, Wayne State Coll., Nebr., 1956—57, Yale U., 1959—60; BA, U. Nebr., 1966, MA, 1968, PhD (NDEA fellow), 1970. Diplomate Am. Bd. Sexology; lic. marriage counselor, Calif., lic. marital therapist, Oreg.; cert. sex educator, sex therapist; lic. psychologist, Oreg. Cons. psychologist Calavaras County Edn. Dept., San Andreas, Calif., 1970—72; pvt. practice sex and marital therapy, lifestyle stress mgmt. Salem, Oreg., 1972—2000; ret., 2000. Cons. psychologist Cmty. Counseling Center, Salem, 1972-73, William Temple House, Portland, Oreg., 1974-77; sex educator Oreg. Dept. Continuing Edn., Salem, 1972-74; vis. prof. Willamette U., Salem, 1981; bd. dirs. Morrison Charter H.S., Dallas, Oreg.; adj. instr. Chemeketa C.C., Salem, 2001-04 Active Salem Cmty. Chorus, 1978-84, pres., 1980-81; active Festival Chorale Oreg., 1986, 96, 2001-05; adv. bd. Friends Oreg. Area, 1997-98. With USAF, 1959-63 Fellow Am. Bd. Sexology; mem. APA, Am. Assn. Marriage and Family Therapy, Am. Assn. Sex Educators, Counselors and Therapists, Oreg. Assn. Marriage and Family Therapists (dir. 1976-77), Soc. Sci. Study Sex, Salem Psychol. Soc. (co-chmn. 1981-82), Nature Conservancy, Union Concerned Scientists, Am. Farmland Trust, Am. Minor Breeds Conservancy, World Wildlife Fund Personal E-mail: j_nathan1977@hotmail.com.

NATHAN, MATTHEW LINCOLN, career military officer, physician; b. Feb. 10, 1955; Grad., Ga. Inst. Tech., Atlanta, 1977; MD, Med. Coll. Ga., 1981; M, Indsl. Coll. Armed Forces, Washington, 1999. Intern, spl. residency internal medicine U. South Fla. Affiliated Hosps., 1981—84; internal medicine specialist Naval Hosp., Guantanamo Bay, Cuba, 1984; practicing internist, leader Med. Mobilization Amphibious Readiness Team, Naval Hosp., Groton, Conn., 1985—87; head divsn. internal medicine Naval Med. Ctr., San Diego, 1987—90; acting dept. head Naval Hosp., Beaufort, SC; various positions Naval Clinics Command, London; med. specialist assignment officer Bur. Naval Pers.; fleet surgeon to comdr. US 7th Fleet, USS Blue Ridge, Yokosuka, Japan, 1999—2001; dep. comdr. Naval Med. Ctr., Portsmouth, Va.; command tour Naval Hosp., Pensacola, Fla.; fleet surgeon to comdr. US Fleet Forces Command, 2006—07; comdr. Navy Medicine East & Naval Med. Ctr., Portsmouth, 2007—08, Navy Medicine Nat. Capitol Area & Walter Reed Nat. Mil. Med. Ctr., Bethesda, Md., 2008—; chief Navy Med. Corps. Decorated Legion of Merit (5), Meritorious Svc. Medal (2), Navy Achievement Medal (2), Navy Commendation Medal; recipient Excellence in Leadership award, Am. Hosp. Assn., 2005. Office: Walter Reed Nat Mil Med Ctr 8901 Rockville Pike Bethesda MD 20889 Office Phone: 301-295-4611. *

NATHANSON, IAN THOMAS, pediatric pulmonologist; b. NYC, Nov. 22, 1948; BA, SUNY Buffalo, MD, 1974. Cert. Am. Bd. Pediat., 1979, in pediatric pulmonology Am. Bd. Pediat., 2003, in sleep medicine Am. Bd. Pediat., 2007. Internship in pediat. Buffalo Gen. Hosp., 1974; residency in pediatric pulmonology Children's Hosp., Buffalo, 1976—77, fellowship in pediatric pulmonology, 1977—79; rsch. fellowship U. Calif. Med. Sch., San Farancisco; pediat. staff Arnold Palmer Hosp. Women & Children, Jacksonville, Fla.; assoc. prof. Mayo Med. Sch., Fla.; med. dir. Nemours Children's Clinic, Orlando, Fla. Contbr. articles to profl. jours. Office: Nemours Childrens Clinic 496 Delaney Ave Ste 408 Orlando FL 32801-3851 Office Phone: 407-650-7000. Office Fax: 407-650-7124.

NATHANSON, KATHERINE L., medical geneticist, educator; BA in Biology, Haverford Coll., 1987; MD, U. Pa. Sch. Medicine, 1993. Diplomate Am. Bd. Internal Medicine, Am. Bd. Med. Genetics. Resident Beth Israel Hosp.; chief resident West Roxbury VA Hosp.; fellow in med. genetics Phila. Children's Hosp.; asst. prof. divsn. med. genetics U. Pa. Sch. Medicine. Office: University of Pennsylvania Division of Medical Genetics 421 Curie Blvd 513 BRB2/3 Philadelphia PA 19104 Office Phone: 215-573-9840. Office Fax: 215-573-2486.

NATHANSON, LARRY, medical educator; b. Boston, Dec. 23, 1928; s. Robert Bernard and Leah (Rabin) N.; m. Anna Bloch, May 27, 1962; children: Andrew, Aran, Nicholas. AB, Harvard Coll., 1950; MD, U. Chgo., 1955. Diplomate Am. Bd. Internal Medicine, Am. Bd. Med. Oncology. Instr. medicine Harvard Med. Sch., Boston, 1966-68; from asst. to prof. Tufts U. Sch. Medicine, Boston, 1968-79; prof. medicine SUNY Stony Brook Sch. of Medicine, 1980-96, prof. emeritus, 1996—. Pres., CEO Oncology Cons., Cambridge, Mass., 1996—; IACUC mem. Amgen Inc., 2010-; advisor Cambridge Hist. Soc.; bd. dirs. Mass. Soc. for Med. Rsch. Editl. bd. Cancer, 1977—, Jour. Clin. Oncology, 1995-98, Seminars in Oncology, 1979-83, Med. & Pediat. Oncology, 1977-96, Jour. Cancer Edn., 1986-92; editor 6 books; contbr. 148 articles to profl. jours. Trustee Cold Spring Harbor Lab., 1990-94, Soc. Preservation L.I. Antiquities, Setauket, N.Y., 1982-92, Cambridge Sch. of Weston, 1997—, Mass. Soc. Med. Rsch., 2002—; active Herreshoff Marine Mus., Bristol, R.I., 2000—, Reliance Soc. Capt. U.S. Army Med. Corps., 1956-58, mem. Harvard Inst. For Learning in Retirement, 2006-. Recipient Disting Svc. award Cancer Rsch., Vet. Affairs Rev. Bd., 1974—78, Disting Svc. award, Winthrop U. Hosp., 1993, Disting Alumni award, Cambridge Sch. Weston, 2006, Hist. Preservation award, Cambridge Hist. Commn., 2011; grantee, Nat. Cancer Inst., 1964—80. Fellow ACP; mem. Mass. Soc. Med. Rsch. (trustee 2002—), Harvard Club (N.Y.), Seawanhaka Corinthian Yacht Club (race com. 1990-96), Harvard Faculty Club (chair 60th reunion com., Harvard Coll. Class of 1950), Sigma Xi. Achievements include advances in biology and chemoprevention of melanoma, combination chemotherapy and immunotherapy of cancer, clinical trials design. Avocations: sailing, astrophysics, tennis, history. Office: Oncology Cons 3 Gray Gdns E Cambridge MA 02138-1401 Personal E-mail: larrymd1@comcast.net.

NATHANSON, NEAL, virologist, epidemiologist, educator; b. Boston, Sept. 1, 1927; s. Robert B. and Leah (Rabinowitch) N.; m. Constance Allen, June 8, 1954; children: Katherine L., John A., Daniel R.; m. Phoebe Starfield, Oct. 7, 1984. BA, Harvard U., 1949, MD, 1953. Chief polio surveillance unit USPHS, 1955-57; rsch. assoc., asst. prof. anatomy Johns Hopkins U., Balt., 1957-63, assoc. prof. epidemiology, 1963-68, prof., 1968-79; chmn. dept. microbiology U. Pa., Phila., 1979-93, vice dean rsch., 1993-95, dir. Office of AIDS Rsch., 1998-2000, vice provost rsch., 2000—03; assoc. dean Global Health Programs, 2003—. Editor-in-chief: Am. Jour. Epidemiology, 1964-79, Microbial Pathogenesis, 1985-88. Achievements include research in pathogenesis, immunology, and epidemiology of viral infections. Home: 1600 Hagys Ford Rd Apt 9W Narberth PA 19072-1049 Office Phone: 215-898-0848. E-mail: nathansn@mail.med.upenn.edu.

NATHANSON, SAUL DAVID, oncologist, surgeon, educator; b. Johannesburg, Dec. 12, 1943; came to U.S., 1975; s. Hymie Barnett and Freda Charlotte (Weinberg) N., m. Maxine Elaine Zacks, Nov. 29, 1966 (div. Sept. 1978); children: Laurence Cecil, Joshua Russel; m. Jerrilyn Marie Burke, Feb. 18, 1979; children: Abigail Mary, Alison Megan. MD, U. Witwatersrand, Johannesburg, 1966. Diplomate Am. Bd. Surgery. Resident in surgery U. Witwatersrand, 1967-74, fellow in immunology UCLA, 1975-77, fellow in surg. oncology, 1977-80; chief resident in surgery U. Calif.-Davis, Sacramento, 1980-82; surg. oncologist Henry Ford Health Sys., Detroit, 1982—, dir. breast cancer ctr., 1995—; prof. surgery Case Western Res. U., Cleve., 1993—2005, Wayne State U. Sch. Medicine, 2008—; dir. Breast Ctr. Henry Ford Hosp., West Bloomfield, Mich. Assoc. clin. prof. surgery U. Mich., Ann Arbor, 1985—2000; adj. assoc. prof. med. physics Oakland U., Rochester, Mich., 1993—; cancer liaison physician, 1988-2011, Commn. on Cancer; prin. investigator for HFHS, ACS Oncology Group; endowed chair Breast Cancer Rsch., 2001. Author: Ordinary Miracles, 2006; contbr. over 200 articles and abstracts to sci. jours., chpts. to books. Recipient Outstanding Tchr. awards U. Mich., 1982-2000, Humanitarian Cancer award, 2006; named Resident Tchr. of Yr., Henry Ford Health Sys. Dept. Surgery, 2006; NIH grantee Nat. Cancer Inst., 1989, Whitehouse Disting. Career award 2007. Fellow ACS, Soc. Surg. Oncology, Royal Coll. Surgeons; mem. Am. Soc. Clin. Oncology, Western Surg. Assn., Am. Assn. Cancer Rsch., Wayne County Med. Soc. (alt. del. 1994—96). Office: Henry Ford Health Sys 2799 W Grand Blvd Detroit MI 48202-2608 Office Phone: 248-661-6592, 313-916-2917. Business E-Mail: dnathan1@hfhs.org.

NATOCHIN, YURI VICTOROVICH, physiologist, researcher; b. Charcov, Charc Reg., USSR, Dec. 6, 1932; s. Victor Mironovich and Frida Eremeevna (Kogan) N.; m. Tatjana Michailovna Sobstel, Jan. 4, 1957; children: Michail, Natalja. MD, High Med. Sch., Novosibirsk, Russia, 1956; Cand. of Sci., Inst. Evolutionary Morphology, Moscow, 1961; DSc, Inst. Physiology, Leningrad, Russia, 1968. Sci. worker Inst. of Evol. Physiology, Leningrad, 1959-64, head of lab. St. Petersburg, 1964—. Mem. Renal Commn. IUPS, Freiburg, Germany, 1977-97; chmn. coun. physiol. sci. Russian Acad. of Sci., St. Petersburg, 1993—, chmn. Dept. Physiology, 1996-2002, counselor of presidium of Russian Acad. Sci., 2002—; dean med. faculty, 1995-2002, prof. physiology St. Petersburg State U., 1995—. Author: The Kidney: Regulation of Ion Balance, 1976 (Orbeli prize 1980), Renal Physiology, 1982; co-author: Water and Electrolyte Balance and Space Flight, 1986, Fluid and Electrolyte Regulation in Spaceflight, 1998 (Internat. Acad. Astronautics prize 1999), Introduction to Nephrology, 2007; editor: Handbook of Water and Salt Balance, 1993; editor-in-chief Russian Jour. Physiology, 1996—; mem. editl. bd. Renal Failure, 1990—, Kidney Internat., 1991-97, Comparative Biochemistry and Physiology, 1999—, Trends in Comparative Physiology, 2005—. Recipient J. Purkinje Gold medal, Czechoslovakian Acad. Sci., Praha, 1982, S. Rucz medal, Hungarian Physiol. Soc., Budapest, 1984, Moleucular Medicine, 2003- Mem. Internat. Acad. Astronautica (Paris, trustee, 2000—07), Acad. Europaea, Russian Acad. Sci.(I. Pavlov Gold medal 2002), Physiol. Soc. Russia (pres. 2004—07, I. Pavlov medal 1992), Presdl. Nephrol. Soc. Russia. Avocations: art, photography, poetry, travel. Office: Inst Evol Physiol & Biochem Toryeza Pr-Kt 44 194223 Saint Petersburg Sankt-Pyetyerburg Russia Office Phone: 7 (812) 5523086. Business E-Mail: natochin@iephb.ru.

NATTEL, STANLEY, cardiologist, research scientist; b. Haifa, Israel, Jan. 28, 1951; arrived in Can., 1952; s. William and Julie (Zwirek) N.; m. Celia Anne Reich, Sept. 25, 1973; children: Jonathan,

Ilana, Daniel, Sarah. BSc magna cum laude, McGill U., 1972, MD, 1974. Diplomate Am. Bd. Internal Medicine, Am. Bd. Cardiology. Intern in medicine Royal Victoria Hosp., 1974-75, resident in internal medicine, 1975-76; resident in clin. pharmacology Montreal Gen. Hosp., Que., Canada, 1976-78, cardiologist, clin. pharmacologist, 1981-87, dir. coronary care unit, 1983-87; fellow in cardiology Ind. U., 1978-80; fellow in physiology U. Pa., 1980-81; asst. prof. pharmacology, medicine McGill U., Montreal, 1981-87, assoc. prof., 1987—; cardiologist Montreal Heart Inst., 1987—, dir. rsch. ctr., 1990—2004; prof. dept. medicine U. Montreal, 1995—, Paul-David chair in cardiovasc. electrophysiology, 2003—. External reviewer Med. Rsch. Coun., 1981—, Ont. Health Ministry, 1983-84, NSF, 1992, others; chmn. libr. com. dept. pharmacology McGill U., 1982-86, mem. grad. com., 1984-89, chmn. grad. tng. com., 1986-89, departmental rep. grad. faculty coun., 1989-91, coord. grad. tchg. pharmacology, 1989-91; mem. oper. grants com. Can. Heart Found., 1983-86; chmn. clin. trials com. Montreal Gen. Hosp., 1983-87, chmn. pharmacy and therapeutics com., 1984-87, sec. clin. chemistry rev. com., 1984, course dir. drug therapy, 1984-87, acting dir. divsn. clin. pharmacology, 1984-85, mem. various coms., 1985-87; mem. fellowship awards com. FRSQ, 1988-90, mem. ctr. grants pharmacology/pharmacy com., 1989-90; chmn. pharmacology com. Montreal Heart Inst., 1988-90, mem. search com. pharmacist-in-chief, 1989-90, mem. ethics com., 1991-2004, chmn. internal rsch. com., 1991-2004, mem. consultative com. exec. dir., 1991-2004, chmn. consultative com. rsch. ctr., 1991-2004; cons. coun. pharmacology Province of Quebec, 1989-90; mem. safety monitoring com. CAMIAT Study, 1990-95; assoc. prof. medicine U. Montreal, 1991-95, prof. 1995—, chmn. search com. dir. rsch. Sacré-Coeur Hosp., 1991, mem. rsch. com. Cormes faculty medicine, 1991—2002, mem. rsch. com. dept. medicine, 1991-2004; chmn. search com., dir. rsch. Maisonneuve Rosemont Hosp., 1996; mem. site visit team program project grant NIH, 1991, cons. program project grant, 1993, spl. reviewer cardiovascular study sect., 1993, 95, 97, 98; mem. oper. grants com. Med. Rsch. Coun. Can., 1988-93, chmn., 2002-05; mem. sr. pers. awards com. Can. Heart Found., 1994-96; lectr. in field. Assoc. editor Can. Jour. Physiology and Pharmacology, 1990-95, Br. Jour. Pharmacology, 2000-2005; mem. editl. bd. Jour. Cardiovasc. Electrophysiology, 1991—, Drugs, 1993—, Cardiovasc. Drugs and Therapy, 1993-2001, Circulation Rsch., 1995—, JACC, 1995-2000, Cardiovascular Rsch., 1999-2002, J Physiol, 2007, JMCC, 2007, others; manuscript reviewer Am. Jour. Cardiology, Nature, Nature Medicine, Nature Genetics, New Eng. Jour. Medicine, PNAS, Science, others; contbr. chpts. to books and articles to profl. jours. Chmn. edn. com. Hebrew Acad. Sch., Montreal, 1991-92. Grantee Que. Heart Found., 1981—, Nordic Pharms., 1985-87, Knoll Pharms., 1991-93, others; fellow Med. Rsch. Coun. Can., 1979-81; McGill U. scholar, 1967-74, Sir Edward Beatty scholar McGill U., 1967-70, Rsch. scholar Med. Rsch. Coun., 1982-87, Sr. Rsch. scholar Fonds de la Recherche en Santé du Quebec, 1990-93; recipient Career Rsch. Achievement award Can. Cardiovasc. Soc., 2001. Fellow Am. Coll. Cardiology, Royal Coll. Physicians Can. (cert. medicine, cardiology), Acad. Scis. Royal Soc. Can.; mem. Am. Heart Assn. (coun. basic sci., leadership com. 2003-05), Royal Soc. Can., Heart Rhythm Soc., Am. Soc. Pharmacology and Exptl. Therapeutics, Can. Cardiovasc. Soc. (councilor 1992-95), Can. Soc. Clin. Pharmacology (Kenneth M. Piafsky Young Investigator award 1985), Pharm. Soc. Can. Biophys. Soc., Am. Heart Assn. (leadership com.). Avocations: studying jewish religious works, sports. Home: 5609 Alpine Ave Côte Saint Luc PQ Canada H4V 2X6 Office: Montreal Heart Inst 5000 Belanger St E Montreal PQ Canada H1T 1C8 Home Phone: 514-482-0715; Office Phone: 514-376-3330. Personal E-mail: stanleynattel@aol.com. Business E-Mail: stanley.nattel@icm-mhi.org.

NAU, ROLAND, neurologist; b. Kassel, Germany, Dec. 12, 1958; s. Heinz and Marianne (Huhn) N.; m. Jutta Gietz, June 19, 1992; children: Inga, Cora. MD, Georg August U., Göttingen, Germany, 1984, Habilitation, 1994. Rsch. asst. Max-Planck Soc., Göttingen, 1984-85; asst. physician dept. neurology U. Göttingen, 1986-93, attending physician, 1994—2007, assoc. prof., 1998—. Vis. asst. rschr. U. Calif., San Francisco, 1993; chief, dept. geriat. Evangelisches Krankenhaus Göttingen Weende, Germany, 2008-. Contbr. chpts. to books and articles to profl. jours. Fellow Walter Marget Soc. for Promotion of Infectiology; mem. Internat. Soc. Neurochemistry, German Neurologic Soc., German Soc. Clin. Neurophysiology, Am. Soc. Microbiology. Achievements include research in degradation of neuropeptides; drug transport into the cerebrospinal fluid; antibiotics, cytokines and neuronal damage in experimental meningitis. Office: Univ Göttingen Dept Neuropathology Evangelisches Krankenhaus Göttingen Weende An der Lutter 24 37075 Göttingen Germany Office Phone: 49-551-5034-1560. Business E-Mail: rnau@gwdg.de.

NAUDIN, MICHEL GEORGES, urologist, department chairman; b. Ottignies, Belgium, Mar. 13, 1959; s. Roger Naudin and Maria Delloye; m. Katty Lebrun; children: Loick, Caroline. Baccalaureat, Lycee Francais, Brussels, 1977; MD, U. Brussels, 1984. Specialist in urology Erasme Hosp., Brussels, 1991; chief dept. urology Ambroise Paré Hosp., Mons, Belgium, 1999—. Prof. Gerontology Assn., Mons, 1996, Lic. Urophysiotherapy, Brussels, 1991; presenter in field. Contbr. articles to med. jours. Lt. French armed forces, 1988—89. Recipient award, European Bd. Urology, 1992. Mem.: Am. Urol. Assn., Belgian Laparoscopy Urol. Assn. Avocations: sports, tennis, skiing. Office: Hosp Ambroise Pare 2 Kennedy Blvd 7000 Mons Belgium Home: Rue des Canadiens 168 7022 Hyon Mons Belgium Personal E-mail: michel.naudin@skynet.be.

NAUGHTON, GAIL K., academic administrator; 3 children. BS, St. Francis Coll., NYC, 1976; MS, NYU, 1978, PhD in Med. Sci., 1981, postdoc. in Dermatology, 1982; MBA, UCLA, 2001. Asst. rsch. prof. NYU Med. Ctr., 1983—85; asst. prof. biology Queensborough Cmty. Coll., NYC, 1985—87; co-founder, bd. dirs. Advanced Tissue Sciences Inc., 1987—2002, prin., scientist, 1987—89, sr. v.p., chief sci. officer, 1989—91, exec. v.p., COO, 1991—95, pres., COO, 1995—2000, vice chmn., 2000—02; dean, Coll. Bus. Adminstrn. San Diego State University, 2002—. Bd. dirs. Calif. Health Inst., San Diego World Trade Ctr., San Diego Corp. Governance Inst.; bd. advisor Johns Hopkins U., Ga. Inst. Tech., U. Calif., San Diego, U. Wash., MIT; bd. dirs. Celera Corp., C. R. Bard, 2004—. Mem. San Diego Sci. & Tech. Council, UCSD Connect Leadership Council. Named Inventor of the Yr., Intellectual Property Owners Assn., 2000. Mem.: Rotary Internat. Achievements include holding over 75 U.S. & fgn. patents in tissue engring. Office: San Diego State University 5500 Campanile Dr San Diego CA 92182-8230 also: C R Bard Inc Bd Directors 730 Central Ave Murray Hill NJ 07974 Office Phone: 908-277-8000. Office Fax: 908-277-8412. E-mail: gail.naughton@crbard.com. *

NAUGHTON, JOHN PATRICK, cardiologist, educator; b. West Nanticoke, Pa., May 20, 1933; s. John Patrick and Anne Frances (McCormick) N.; children: Bruce, Marcia, Lisa, George, Michael, Thomas. AA, Cameron State U., Lawton, Okla., 1952; BS, St. Louis U., 1954; MD, Okla. U., 1958; MD (hon.), Kosin U., 1995. Intern George Washington U. Hosp., Washington, 1958-59; resident U. Okla. Med. Center, 1959-64; asst. prof. medicine U. Okla., 1966-68; assoc. prof. medicine U. Ill., 1968-70; prof. medicine George Washington U., 1970-75, dean acad. affairs, 1973-75, dir. div. rehab. medicine and Regional Rehab. Research and Tng. Center, 1970-75; dean Sch. Medicine SUNY, Buffalo, 1975-96, prof. medicine, physiology, social, preventive and rehab. medicine Sch. Medicine, 1975—, acting v.p. for health scis., 1983-84, v.p. clin. affairs, 1984-96, interim chmn. rehab. medicine, 2003—. Dir. Nat. Exercise and Heart Disease Project, 1972-83; chmn. policy adv. bd. Beta-blocker Heart Attack Trial Nat. Heart, Lung and Blood Inst., 1977-82; pres. Western N.Y. chpt. Am. Heart Assn., 1983-85, v.p. N.Y. State affiliate, 1985, pres. N.Y. State affiliate, 1988-90; chmn. clin. applications and preventions adv. com. Nat. Heart, Lung and Blood Inst., 1984; mem. Fed. COGME working group on consortia, 1996-97, N.Y. Gov.'s Commn. on Grad. Med. Edn., 1985, N.Y. State Coun. on Grad. Med. Edn., 1988-90, chmn. 1996—; pres. Assoc. Med. Schs. N.Y., 1982-84, mem. adminstrv. com. Coun. of Deans, 1983-89; mem. N.Y. State Dept. of Health Adv. Com. on Physician Recredentialing; mem. exec. coun. Nat. Inst. on Disability and Rehab. Rsch. 1991-92; v.p. James H. Cummings Found. Author: Exercise Testing and Exercise Training in Coronary Heart Disease, 1973, Exercise Testing: Physiological, Biomechanical, and Clinical Principles, 1988 Career devel. awardee Nat. Heart Inst., 1966-71; recipient Brotherhood-Sisterhood award in medicine NCCJ, N.E. Minority Educators award, 1990, Acad. Alumnus of Yr. award Okla. U., 1990, award for svc. to minorities in med. edn., 1991, Frank Sindelar award N.Y. State Am. Heart Assn., 1995, James Platt White Soc. award, 1995, Outstanding Contbns. in the field of Health Care award Sheehan Meml. Hosp., 1995, Chancellor Charles P. Norton medal, SUNY, Buffalo, 1997, AMS Disting. Svc. award, 2001. Fellow ACP, Am. Coll. Cardiology, Am. Coll. Sports Medicine (pres. 1970-71, Citation award 2000), Am. Coll. Chest Physicians; Am. Coll. Preventive Medicine, Am. Heart Assn. (epidemiology coun. 2000—, coun. on nutrition, phys. activity and metabolism), Acad. Health Profls. Ins. Assn. (hon.).

NAUL, L. GILL, radiologist; b. Rockdale, Tex., Mar. 15, 1956; BS, MD, Tex. A&M U., 1981. Staff radiologist Scott and White Healthcare, 1985—95, chmn., dept. radiology, 1995—, bd. dir., 2005. Mem.: Am. Coll. Radiology (fellowship). Office: 2401 S 31st St Temple TX 76508 Business E-Mail: lgnaul@swmail.sw.org.

NAUMANN, GOTTFRIED OTTO HELMUT, ophthalmology educator; b. Wiesbaden, Hessen, Germany, Apr. 25, 1935; s. Otto and Margarete (Fuerer) N.; m. Lieselotte Regine Mueller, Nov. 27, 1964; children: Uta-Rike, Maike-Liesel, Doerte-Iris, Frauke-Elke. MD, U. Leipzig, 1957; D (hon.), Semmelweis U., 2000, Lublin U., 2002. Diplomate Am. Bd. Ophthalmology. Intern Ventnor Found., Atlantic City, 1959—60; resident dept. ophthalmology U. Hamburg, Germany, 1961—64, instr. dept. ophthalmology, 1967, assoc. prof. ophthalmology, 1968—74; fellow Armed Forces Inst. Pathology, Washington, 1965—66; internat. vis. prof. Assoc. U. Profl. Ophthalmology, Balt., 1972; prof., chmn. dept. ophthalmology U. Tübingen, Germany, 1975—80, U. Erlangen, Germany, 1980—2004. Co-founder European Bd. Ophthalmology, London, 1992, pres., 1996-98; 7th Harvard lectr. ophthalmology, Boston, 1994; 30th Bjerrum lectr. Danish Ophthal. Soc., 1995; 11th European guest lectr. Oxford intern Congress, 1996; spl. lectr. Internat. Acad. Ophthalmology, Chgo., 1996; Zimmerman lectr. Am. Acad. Ophthamology, 2003. Prin. author: Pathology of the Eye, German edit., 1980, 97 (2 vols.), English edit., 1986, Japanese edits., 1987, 2003; co-editor: Wound Healing of the Eye, 1979, Applied Pathology Ophthalmic Microsurgeons, 2008, Klin. Monatsblätter Augenheilkunde, 1980-2000; co-founder Jour. Ophthal. Rsch., 1970; mem. editl. bd. Am. Jour. Ophthalmology, Chinese Jour. Ophthalmology, Japanese Jour. Ophthalmology, others. Mem. Founding Coun. Univ., Dresden, Germany, 1992-94; reviewer WHO, Geneva, 1972-95; co-founder German-Speaking Ophthal. Pathologists, Hamburg, 1972, European Univ. Prof. Ophthalmology, Nijmegen, The Netherlands, 1986. Recipient William Mackenzie medal, U. Glasgow, 1991, T. Krwawicz Gold medal, Polish Ophthal. Soc., 1993, 56 Bowman medal, Royal Coll. Ophthalmology, 1994, Alcon Rsch. Inst. award, 1996, German Fed. Order of Merit, 1st class, 1996, Dr. Frank Claffy medal, 2000, Jules Gonin Gold medal, 2002, Jose Rizal Gold medal, Asia-Pacific Acad. Ophthalmology, 2004, Bernardo Streiff Gold medal, Acad. Ophthalmology Internat., 2005, Albrecht v. Graefe gold medal, German Ophthal. Soc., 2006, award, Am. Acad. Ophth., 2007; fellow Hon. Royal Coll. Ophthalmology Thailand, 2004. Fellow: Am. Acad. Ophthalmology (Honor award 1992, Sr. Achievement award 2001, Lorenz E. Zimmerman medal 2003, Co recipient Internat. Blindness Prevention award 2007), German Ophthal. Soc. (councillor 1970—75, 1978—85, hon. mem., Bavarian Order of Merit 2001), Royal Coll. Ophthalmology (UK) (hon.); mem.: European Ophthal. Path. Soc. (pres. 1990—93), German Univ. Profs. Ophthalmology (pres. 1985—88), European Ophthalmology Soc. (gen. sec. 1976, 6th Charamis medal 1995), Hungarian Ophthal. Soc. (hon.), Assn. Rsch. in Vision and Ophthalmology (life), Italian Ophthal. Soc. (hon.), Polish Ophthal. Soc. (hon.), Internat. Agy. Prevention Blindness (v.p. 1998—2006), Internat. Coun. Ophthalmology (pres. 1998—2006), Acad. Ophthalmology Internat (spl. lectr. Chgo.), Rotary. Lutheran. Office: Univ-Augenklinik Schwabachanlage 6 91054 Erlangen Germany Office Phone: 49 9131 8534363. Business E-Mail: gottfried.naumann@uk-elangen.de, gottfried.naumann@netsurf.de.

NAVAR, LUIS GABRIEL, physiology educator, director, researcher; b. El Paso, Tex., Mar. 24, 1941; s. Luis and Concepcion (Najera) N.; m. Randa Ann Bumgarner, Oct. 15, 1965; children: Tonia, Tess, Gabriel, Daniel. BS, Tex. A&M U., 1962; PhD, U. Miss., 1966, postdoctoral study, 1966-69. Instr. dept. physiology/biophysics U. Miss., Jackson, 1966-67, asst. prof., 1967-71, assoc. prof., 1971-74, U. Ala., Birmingham, 1974-76, prof., 1976-88, assoc. prof. Nephrology Rsch. and Tng. Ctr., 1979-83, prof., 1983-88; prof., chmn. dept. physiology Tulane U. Med. Sch., New Orleans, 1988—, co-dir. Hypertension and Renal Ctr. of Excellence, 2001—. Vis. scientist Duke U. Med. Ctr., Durham, N.C., 1972-73; adv. bd. NIH Ctr. Sci. Rev., 1998-99; bd. dirs. Fedn. Am. Socs. Exptl. Biology, 1997-01. Assoc. editor News in Physiol. Scis., 1994-2000, Am. Jour. Physiology, 1983-89, mem. editl. bd., 1982-83, 97—; mem. editl. bd. Kidney Internat., 1976-87, Kidney, 1992—, Clin. Sci., 1994-99, Jour. Am. Soc. Nephrology, 1996-2001, Jour. Am. Soc. Nephrology, 1996-2001, Am. Jour. Kidney Disease, 1997-2001, Am. Jour. Hypertension, 1999—, Hypertension, 1980-83, 2002-04, assoc. editor, 1993-2000, cons. editor, 2006—; contbr. chpts. to books, articles to profl. jours. Cardiovascular and renal study sects. NIH, 1998—2000, chmn., 2000—02; bd. dirs. Consortium for Southeastern Hypertension Control, 1998—2000. Recipient Rsch. Career Devel. award, Nat. Heart, Lung and Blood Inst., 1974—79, Merit award, 1988—97, Bodil M. Schmidt Nielson Disting. Mentor and Scientist award, 2006, Lifetime Achievement award, COSEHC, 2006, Robert W. Berliner award for excellence in renal physiology, 2007, Daggs award, 2008; vis. scholar Pfizer/ACCF, 2002. Fellow: AAAS; mem.: High Blood Pressure Rsch. Am. Heart Assn., Assn. of Am. Med. Coll. (administrv. bd. of coun. of academic soc. 2004—), Assn. Chmn. Depts. Physiology (councillor 1993—95, pres.-elect 1995—96, pres. 1996—97, Disting. Svc. award 2003), Interam. Soc. Hypertension (chair awards com. 2003—), Am. Soc. Hypertension (coun. 1992—94, chmn. basic. sci. com. 1997, treas. 1997—2001, Richard Bright award 2001), Internat. Soc. Nephrology, Am. Soc. Nephrology, Am. Heart Assn. (chmn. cardiorenal rsch. study com. 1994—95, nat. rsch. com. 1994—99, Lewis K. Dahl Lectr. 1997, profl. and pub. edn. com. 1999—, chmn. coun. high blood pressure rsch. 2006—, kidney, high blood pressure couns., vice chmn. leadership com. coun. high blood pressure rsch., Sci. Coun. Disting. Achievement award 1999, Corcoran Lectr. award 2001), Am. Physiol. Soc. (coun. 1991—94, Gottschalk Disting. Lectr. Renal Physiology 1997, pres.-elect 1997—98, pres. 1998—99, Bodil M. Schmidt-Nielson Disting. Mentor and Sci. award 2006, Robert W. Berliner award 2007, Ray G. Daggs award 2008). Democrat. Roman Catholic. Home: 10020 Hyde Pl New Orleans LA 70123-1522 Office: Tulane U Med Sch Dept Physiology 1430 Tulane Ave New Orleans LA 70112-2699 Home Phone: 504-738-5547; Office Phone: 504-988-5251. Business E-Mail: navar@tulane.edu.

NAVARRO, JEAN, pediatrician, educator; b. Paris, Apr. 30, 1937; s. Emile and Frida Navarro; children: Vincent, Julie, Alice. MD, U. Paris. Prof. pediatrics Faculté Bichat, Paris, 1976—; pres. health technologic innovations assistance pub. Assistance Publique de Paris, 2005—; dir. med. policy Pub. Hosps. of Paris, 2005—07. V.p. V L M, Paris; pres. Internat. Congress Cystic Fibrosis, France Canceropole, 2008. Pres. commn. particular alimentation Interministerial Com., Paris, 1989—95. Lt. French Navy, 1964—65. Decorated Légion d'honneur. Mem.: European Cystic Fibrosis Assn. Roman Catholic. Achievements include research in pediatric gastroenterology and nutrition and cystic fibrosis. Avocations: art, history. Office Fax: 33140273853. Personal E-mail: jean.navarro@canceropole_idf.fr.

NAVARRO, PAULA A., obstetrician, gynecologist, educator; b. São José do Rio Preto, São Paulo, Brazil, May 17, 1972; MS, Ribeirão Preto Med. Sch., 1995; PhD, Ribeirão Preto Med. Sch., Brown U., 2003. Adj. prof., Ribeirão Preto Med. Sch. São Paulo U., 2008—11, adj. prof., IVR dir., Ribeirão Preto Clin. Hosp., 2008, prof., divsn. human reprodn., dept. ob-gyn., 2008—. Rsch. fellow in human reprodn. and infertility Women and Infant's Hosp., Brown U., Lab. Reproductive Medicine, Providence. Recipient Best Rsch. award, Brazilian Soc. Human Reprodn.'s Congress. Mem.: Brazilian Soc. Human Reprodn. Avocations: reading, movies. Home: Ave Caramuru 1280 Apt 132 Ribeirão Preto São Paulo 14030-000 Brazil Home Fax: 55-16-36331038. Personal E-mail: pnavarro@fmrp.usp.br.

NAVARRO, VICTOR J., gastroenterologist, physician; MD, Pa. State U., Hershey, 1988. Diplomate Am. Bd. Internal Medicine, Am. Bd. Internal Medicine-gastroenterology, Am. Bd. Internal Medicine-transplant hepatology. Intern Temple Univ. Hosp., resident; fellow Yale-New Haven Hosp., Conn.; physician Thomas Jefferson Univ., med. dir. Liver Transplant Program; hospital affiliations include Thomas Jefferson Univ. Hosp., Meth. Hosp. Named recognized dr., HealthGrades; named one of the Top Doctors, Phila. Mag., 2010. Office: Thomas Jefferson University Hospital Main Bldg Ste 480 132 S 10th St Philadelphia PA 19107 Office Phone: 215-955-8900. Office Fax: 215-503-2527.

NAVARRO COSTA, PAULO ALEXANDRE, embryologist, educator; b. Lisbon, Portugal, Oct. 2, 1980; PhD in Biomed. Scis., U. Lisbon, 2010. Clin. embryologist CEMEARE-Assisted Reprodn. Ctr., Lisbon, 2009—; aux. tchr. faculty medicine U. Lisbon, 2010—. Sci. referee Oxford U. Press, England, 2010, Springer, Germany, 2010, Wiley-Blackwell, NJ, 2011, Nature Pub. Group, 2011; sci. expert Agence Nat. de la Recherche, France, 2011. Recipient Best Clin. Rsch. Presentation award, Portuguese Soc. Medicine of Reprodn., 2005, Portuguese Soc. Human Genetics, 2006. Mem.: European Soc. Human Reprodn. and Embryology. Avocations: writing, art. Office: University Lisbon Inst Histology and Devel Biology Faculty Medicine Lisbon 1649-028 Portugal Business E-Mail: navarro-costa@fm.ul.pt.

NAVEA, AMPARO, ophthalmologist; b. Valencia, Apr. 2, 1959; MD in Medicine, 1982, PhD in Medicine, 1985. Med. dir. Fundacion Oftalmológica Del Mediterráneo, 2005—. Assoc. prof. Valencia U., 1994—2005. Mem.: ARVO, Soc. Española Retina Vitreo, Soc. Española Oftalmologia, AAO. Avocations: diving, skiing, golf. Office: Bifurcacion Pio Baroja General Aviles Valencia 46015 Spain Business E-Mail: navea_amp@gva.es.

NAY, RHONDA MAREE, nursing educator, researcher; b. Lismore, NSW, Australia, Mar. 6, 1952; d. William Robert and Annie Ellen (Arandale) Nay; life ptnr. John Ross McLennan; children: Larissa Nay-Brock children: Darrel John, Sherin Anne(dec.), Stewart Andrew McLennan, Rebecca Emily McLennan. BA, U. New England, NSW, 1983, MLitt, 1985; PhD, U. NSW, Sydney, Australia, 1993. RN NSW. Head dept. of nursing U. New England, Armidale, 1988—91; prof. gerontic nursing La Trobe U., Melbourne, Victoria, Australia, 1996—2010, head Sch. Nursing, 1998—2001, prof. interdisciplinary aged care, 2010—; dir. Australian Ctr. for Evidence Based Aged Care, Melbourne, 2001—. Expert adviser Internat. Coun. Nurses; dir. Aged Care Stds. and Accreditation Agy. Bd., Sydney, 2002—, Dementia Tng. Studies Ctr., 2006—, Inst. Social Participation, 2009—, Aust Inst. Primary Care and Aging, 2009—, DCRC Victoria Lab, 2011—; mem. adv. com. dementia Min. Ageing & Mental Health. Co-editor: Nursing Older People (Named Best Publ. in the field of aging

Australasian Jour. on Aging, 2004). Recipient Chair Min.'s awards for excellence in aged care, Australian Govt. Dept. of Health and Aging, 1999, 2001, 2003. Fellow: Coll. of Nursing (hon.), Royal Coll. Nursing Australia (hon.), Australian Assn. Gerontology (hon.; pres. Victorian divsn. 2002—05); mem.: Australia Pain Soc. (assoc.). Office: La Trobe University Melbourne Campus Bundoora Victoria 3086 Australia Office Fax: 03 9479 5977. E-mail: r.nay@latrobe.edu.au.

NAYAK, BIBEKANANDA, physicist; b. Jagatsinghpur, June 24, 1984; MS, Utkal U., 2006, PhD student. Rsch. scholar PG Dept. Physics, Utkal U., 2007—. Mem.: Odisha Phys. Soc. Avocations: reading, writing. Office: Utkal University PG Dept Physics Bhubaneswar Odisha 751004 India Business E-Mail: bibeka@iopb.res.in.

NAYAK, NABEEN C., pathologist, department chairman; b. Puri, India, Jan. 31, 1931; MBBS, S.C.B. Med. Coll., 1952; MD in Pathology, K.G. Med. Coll., 1956. Asst. prof. pathology All India Inst. Med. Scis., 1960—72, prof. pathology, chmn. dept., 1972—89, chief Cancer Ctr., 1980—88; prof. pathology, chmn. dept. Faculty Medicine, Kuwait U., 1990—2000; chmn. dept. pathology & chmn., rsch. com. Sir Ganga Ram Hosp., New Delhi, 2000—. Dir. labs. Mubarak Al Kabir Hosp. Ministry Health, Kuwait, 1990—2000, chmn., MRC-Path. tng. program, 1992—2000; vis. scientist Japanese Soc. Promotion Sci. Recipient awards, Indian Coun. Med. Rsch., Univs. & Sci. Orgns. Abroad & India, plaque, Fedn. Indian C. of C. and Industry. Fellow: Internat. Assn. Study Liver, Nat. Acad. Med. Scis. (New Delhi), Indian Acad. Scis. (Bangalore), Indian Nat. Sci. Acad. (New Delhi), Royal Coll. Pathologists. Avocations: music, bridge, badminton, ping pong/table tennis, reading. Home: X-29 Hauz Khas New Delhi Delhi 110016 India Personal E-mail: dr_ncnayak@yahoo.com.

NAYLOR, ANDREW ROSS, vascular surgeon, educator; b. Chester, Eng., Mar. 22, 1958; s. Robert Charles and Patricia Mary Naylor; m. May Bruce MacPherson, Apr. 24, 1982; children: Sarah May, Iain Bruce. MB, BChir, Aberdeen U., Scotland, 1981, MD, 1990. Preregistration ho. officer Aberdeen Tchg. Hosps., 1981—82, sr. ho. officer in surgery, 1982—85, registrar in surgery, 1985—91; lectr. in surgery, sr. registrar U. Leicester, England, 1991—93; cons. vascular surgeon Aberdeen Royal Infirmary, 1993—95; prof. vascular surgery, cons. vascular surgeon Univ. Hosps. of Leicester, 1995—. Hon. reader in surgery Leicester U., 2000—, hon. prof. surgery; assoc. editor European Jour. Vascular and Endovascular Surgery, 2008—, sr. editor, 2011—. Author: (textbook) Carotid Artery Disease: A Problem Based Approach, 2000. Fellow: Royal Coll. Surgeons Edinburgh, Royal Coll. Surgeons Eng. (Hunterian Prof. 2002), Vascular Soc. Gt. Britain and Ireland (life; coun. 2006—, pres. elect). Office: Dept Surgery Leicester Royal Infirmary Leicester LE27LX England Home: 9 Dalby Ave LE7 9RE Leicester England Office Fax: 44 116 2523179. Personal E-mail: arnaylor@hotmail.com. Business E-Mail: ross.naylor@uhl-tr.nhs.uk.

NAYLOR, C. DAVID, academic administrator; b. Woodstock, Ont., Canada, 1954; s. Thomas and Edna Naylor; m. Ilse Naylor; 4 children. MD (hon.), U. Toronto, 1978; Rhodes Scholar, Oxford U., 1979; DPhil, 1983. Fellow Royal Coll. Physicians & Surgeons, 1986; trainee in gen. internal medicine U. Western Ontario, 1983—86; fellow in clin. epidemiology Med. Rsch. Coun. Can., Toronto, 1986—87; asst. prof. dept. medicine U. Toronto, 1988—92, assoc. prof., 1992—96, prof., 1996—, dean of medicine, 1999—2005, vice provost, Relations with Health Care Institutions, 1999—2005, pres., 2005—. Head rsch. program Sunnybrook Health Sci. Ctr., Toronto, 1990—96; CEO Inst. Clin. Evaluative Sciences, 1991—98; sr. scientist Med. Rsch. Coun. Can., 1999; editorial bd. Jour. Am. Med. Assn., Brit. Med. Jour., 1996—98, Can. Med. Assn. Jour., 1996—2000. Co-author approximately 300 scholarly publications. Chair Nat. Adv. Com. on SARS & Pub. Health, Canada, 2003. Decorated officer Order of Can.; recipient John Dinham Cottrell medal, Royal Australasian Coll. Physicians, 1996, Malcolm Brown award, Royal Coll. Physicians & Surgeons, 1996, Michael Smith award, Med. Rsch. Coun., 1999, Rsch. Achievement award, Can. Cardiovascular Soc., 2002, Defries award, Can. Pub. Health Assn., 2005. Fellow: Royal Soc. Can.; mem.: Inst. Medicine (fgn. assoc.). Office: UToronto Office of the President 27 King's College Circle Toronto ON Canada M5S 1A1 Home Phone: 416-929-3800. Business E-Mail: president@utoronto.ca.

NAYLOR, ILLANA, pediatrics nurse; b. Denver, May 13, 1954; d. Kurtis Friend and Gladys Shank Naylor; m. Richard David Barrett, June 27, 1981; children: Rianna, Benjamin, Alisa. BA in Theology, Colo. Coll., Colo. Springs, 1976; LPN, 1979; BSN, George Mason U., Fairfax, Va., 1985, MSN, 2005. RN Va., cert. pediat. nurse, 2006. Pediat. nurse Prince William (Va.) Health Sys., 1980—. PALS/BLS instr. Inova Health Sys., 1985—; infant CPR instr. Prince William (Va.) Health Sys., 1995—, mem. nurse devel. coun., 1998—99, mem. ednl. com., 2003—; presenter in field; chair pediat. clin. practise coun., 2007—; vice chair clin. practise coun.; coord coun. mem.; chair maternal child health edn. com., 2003—07, 2009; mem. symposium com., 08, 2010—11; rsch. fellow Prince William Hosp., 2009—; facilitator Adapt A Sport Program. Contbr.: book Outcry: American Voices of Conscience Post-9/11, 2005; contbr. articles to jours. Vol. literacy program Baldwin Elem. Sch., 1999—2009; founder Unity in Cmty., 1995—, treas., 1996—2006; beautification chmn. Baldwin Elem. Sch. PTA, 1992—99; Mid-Atlantic dist. rep. Decade to Overcome Violence; peace advocate with Cindy Sheehan White House, 2005; founder mem. Prince William Peacemakers; chair Mid Atlantic Dist. Peace Justice Com., 2009—, Nat. Coun. Chs., 2008—11; vol. with med. missionaries; active Virginians Alternative to Death Penalty, 1993—; mem. manassas pk. dem. com., 2009; mem. peace com. Manassas (Va.) Ch. Brethren, 1976—2008; organisor Internat. Day of Prayer for Peace, 2007—; citizens adv. com. Solid Waste Man, Manassas, Va., 1991—. Recipient Cmty. Svc. award, Prince William County Human Rights Commn., 1997, award, Baldwin Elem. Sch., 1999, Golden Rule award, J.C. Penney, 2000, D. Riley award, Gainesville Dem. Com., 2004; named one of Ten People of Yr., Manassas Jour. Messenger, 2001. Mem.: Sigma Theta Tau, Golden Key, Alpha Lambda Delta. Avocations: reading, singing, dance, hiking, gardening. Home: 10294 Grant Ave Manassas VA 20110-6135 Office: Prince William Health Sys 8700 Sudley Rd Manassas VA 20110 Office Phone: 703-369-8408. Personal E-mail: naylorbarrett5@gmail.com.

NAYLOR, JAMES CHARLES, psychologist, educator; b. Chgo., Feb. 8, 1932; s. Joseph Sewell and Berniece (Berg) N.; m. Georgia Lou Mason, Feb. 14, 1953; children— Mary Denise, Diana Darice, Shari Dalice. BS, Purdue U., 1957, MS, 1958, PhD, 1960. Asst. prof. Ohio State U., 1960-63, asso. prof., 1963-67, prof. vice chmn. dept. psychology, 1967-68; prof. Purdue U., Lafayette, Ind., 1968-86, head dept. psychol. scis., 1968-79; prof., chmn. dept. psychology Ohio State U., Columbus, 1986-98, prof. emeritus, 1999—. Fulbright rsch. scholar, Umea, Sweden, 1976; Disting. scholar, vis. scientist Flinders U., South Australia, 1982-83, UNESCO ednl. cons. to Hangzhou U., Peoples Republic of China, 1984; chmn. Coun. Grad. Depts. Psychology, 1993-94; lead reviewer Psychology Program Rev., State U. Sys. Fla., 1996. Author: Industrial Psychology, 1968, A Theory of Behavior in Organizations, 1980; founder, editor: Organizational Behavior and Human Decision Processes; mem. editorial bd.: Prof. Psychology; Contbr. articles to profl. jours. Served with USN, 1950-54. Fellow AAAS, Am. Psychol. Soc., Am. Psychol. Assn.; mem. Psychonomic Soc., Psychmetric Soc., Internat. Assn. Applied Psychology, Soc. Organizational Behavior (founder), Midwestern Psychol. Assn. (coun. 1994-97), Phi Beta Kappa, Sigma Xi. Home: 176 Tucker Dr Columbus OH 43085-3064 Office: Ohio State U Dept Psychology Columbus OH 43210 E-mail: naylor.2@osu.edu.

NAYLOR, MAGDALENA RACZKOWSKA, psychiatrist, educator; b. Warsaw, Aug. 4, 1950; arrived in U.S., 1981; d. Wlodzimierz Raczkowski and Urszula Raczkowska-Cieslik; m. Thomas Herbert Naylor, Dec. 14, 1985; 1 child, Alexander Watkins. MD, Warsaw Med. U., Poland, 1976, PhD, 1987. Diplomate psychiatry and neurology Nat. Bd. Certification in Psychiatry and Neurology, 1994. Asst. prof. Warsaw Med. U., 1977—83; rsch. assoc. Med. Coll. Va., Richmond, 1981—82; resident psychiatry Duke U., Durham, NC, 1984—88; pvt. practice psychiatry Richmond, Va., 1988—93; attending physician psychiatry Fletcher Allen Health Care, Burlington, Vt.; asst. prof. U. Vt., Burlington, 1993—99, assoc. prof., 1999—2008, prof. psychiatry, 2008—. Rsch. assoc. Med. Coll. Va., Richmond, Va., 1981—82; med. dir. women's program Psychiat. Inst. Richmond, Va., 1991—92; med. dir. partial hospitalization program Charter Westbrook Hosp., 1992—93; med. dir. psychiat. unit Flecher Allen Health Care, Burlington, Vt., 1994—97; dir. mindbody medicine clinic U. Vt. Med./Flecher Allen Health Care, 1998—; assoc. dir. clin. neuroscience rsch. unit U. Vt. Med.; spkr. on search for meaning and integration of mind, body and spirit into med. practice. Author (with Thomas Naylor and William Willimon): The Search for Meaning, 1994, The Search for Meaning Workbook, 1994; contbr. articles to profl. jours. Com. mem. Vt. Pain & Symptom Mgmt. Com.; mem. Gailer Sch., Shelburn, Vt., 2001—03. Recipient Best Tchr. of Yr. Dept. of Psychiatry, U. Vt. Med. Sch., 1996, 1998; grantee, NIH, 2002, 2004—05, 2008, 2010, U. Vt. Med. Sch., 2004. Mem.: Am. Pain Soc., Vt. Med. Assn. Achievements include research in coping skills training for patients in chronic pain, neuroimaging. Home: 202 Stockbridge Rd Charlotte VT 05445 Office: U Vt UHC 1 S Prospect St Burlington VT 05401 Business E-Mail: magdalena.naylor@uvm.edu.

NAYLOR, PAUL, psychologist, researcher; b. Wakefield, England, Jan. 14, 1947; BEd in Edn. and Geography, U. Birmingham, England, 1970; BA in Psychology with 1st class honors, Open U., Milton Keynes, England, 1983; MA in Psychology of Edn., Loughborough U., England, 1985, PhD in Social Psychology, 1996. Secondary sch. tchr. geography and social and human scis., Nottingham, Barnsley, East Yorkshire and Worley, England, 1970—96, rsch. fellow Roehampton U., London, 1997—2002, U. Nottingham, England, 2002—04; rsch. fellow conflict and reconciliation U. Sheffield, England, 2004—, dir. Sheffield Bullying Obs., 2004—. Part time assoc. lectr. psychology Open U., 1985—. Contbr. articles to profl. jours., chapters to books. Grantee, Pvt. Patients Plan Healthcare Trust Fund, 1999—2001, Nat. Coll. Sch. Leadership, Nat. Assn. Head Tchrs., Secondary Heads Assn., 2002—03, Edn. Subject Ctr. Advanced Learning and Tchg. in Edn., 2002—03, Rsch. Autism, 2007—. Fellow: Higher Edn. Acad. (chartered scientist 2007, chartered psychologist), Brit. Psychol. Soc. (assoc.); mem.: European Soc. Devel. Psychology, Assn. for Psychol. Sci., Brit. Psychol. Soc. Business E-Mail: p.b.naylor@sheffield.ac.uk.

NAYYAR, GEETA, communications executive, medical educator; b. Apr. 8, 1978; BS in Biology, U. Miami, MD, 2003; MBA, George Washington U., 2009. Resident internal medicine George Washington U., fellow rheumatology, asst. clin. prof. medicine Dept. Rheumatology, 2008—11; chief med. officer APCO Worldwide Inc., 2008—10; prin. med. officer Vangent Inc., 2010—11; chief med. info. officer AT&T ForHealth AT&T Inc., 2011—. Clin. adv. bd. Provide Health Solutions, 2010—; spkr. in field. Office: AT&T Inc ForHealth One AT&T Way Bedminster NJ 07921 *

NAZAIRE, MICHEL HARRY, physician; b. Jérémie, Haiti, Sept. 29, 1939; s. Joseph and Hermance Nazaire; m. Nicole Lamarque, Dec. 28, 1968 (div.); children: Hanick, Carline. BS, DOE, Port-Au-Prince, Haiti, 1959; MD Faculty of Medicine and Pharmacology, State U. Haiti, 1966. Intern State U. Hosp., Port-Au-Prince, Haiti, 1965-66; resident physician Sanitarium, Port-Au-Prince, Haiti, 1966-68; physician pneumology, 1966-68; physician pneumo-phtisiology Port-Au-Prince, 1966—; fellow Klinik Havelhohe and Heckeshorn, Berlin, 1969-70, 89-91; attending physician Sanitarium, Port-Au-Prince, 1976-91. Dep. mem. Internat. Parliament for Safety and Peace, envoy-at-large Internat. State Parliament, mem. global environ. technol. network WHO. Contbr. articles to profl. jours. Recipient Physician's Recognition award, Am. Med. Assn., 2002, AMA, 2002, 2005. Fellow Internat. Soc. for Respiratory Protection, Am. Coll. Chest Physicians (recognition award, 2006); mem. AMA (Physician's Recognition award 2002-2005), APHA, Am. Conf. Govtl. Indsl. Hygienists, Internat. Union Against Tb, Internat. Platform Assn., Physicians for Social Responsibility, European Respiratory Soc. Home: 1495 Fulton St Brooklyn NY 11216 Personal E-mail: nazaire.michelharry@yahoo.com.

NAZARI, STEFANO GIACINTO, thoracic and vascular surgeon; b. Venice, Italy, Jan. 2, 1949; s. Giovanni and Maria (Gambardella) N. Med. Diploma, U. Med. Sch., Pavia, Italy, 1973; Diploma Postgrad. Specialization Surgery, U. Pavia, 1979; Diploma Specialization in Thoracic Surg., U. Turin, Italy, 1983; Fellowship Inst. Internat. Med. Edn., SUNY, Rome, 1974. Intern-resident Patologia Chirurgica I San Matteo Hosp., Pavia, Italy, 1973-78; staff surgeon Patologia Chirurgica I IRCCS San Matteo, Pavia, Italy, 1978—2005; lectr. U. Pavia, Italy, 1974-82, prof. exptl. surgery, 1991—2005. Stage at divsn. Organ Transplantation, U. Cin., 1974, Stage at Klinik fur Hertz, Thorax un Gefasschirurgie, Hannover U., 1987, Stage at Divsn. Thoracic Surgery, U. Toronto, Can., 1988, Stage at Divsn. Cardiovasc. Surgery, Hosp. Broussai, Paris, 1997; founder, pres., Fondazione Alexis Carrel, 1997 Contbr. numerous articles, sci. papers to profl. jours. and chpts. to books. Grantee Italian Ministry of Health, 1989, 90, 92, for Lung Transplantation; expandable prothesis for sutureless anastomosis in thoracic aorta, 1995, Intraluminal Net prothesis for aortic anurisms care, 1995. Mem. European Soc. for Surg. Rschs., European Assn. for Cardiothoracic Surgery, Soc. of Thoracic Surgery, N.Y. Acad. Sci. Avocations: hunting, fishing, flying.

NAZARIAN, LAWRENCE FRED, pediatrician; b. NYC, May 17, 1940; s. Samuel George and Winifred Lucia (Zotian) N.; m. Sharon Louise Carlson, June 22, 1963; children: Douglas, Stephen, Sarah. BA, Yale U., 1960; MD, U. Rochester, 1964. Cert. Am. Bd. Pediatrics 1970. Pediatrician Panorama Pediatric Group, Rochester, NY, 1969—2004; clin. prof. pediatrics U. Rochester Sch. Medicine and Dentistry, 1969—. Bd. dirs. James P. Wilmot Found., Rochester. Assoc. editor Pediatrics in Rev. Jour., 1990-2004, editor-in-chief, 2005-; contbr. articles to profl. jours. Mem. troop com. Boy Scouts Am., Penfield, N.Y., 1978-88; mem. coun. com. Luth. Ch. of Reformation, Rochester, 1969—. Maj. USAR, 1967-69. Recipient Nat. Pediatric Tchg. award, Ambulatory Pediatric Assn., 2002. Fellow Am. Acad. Pediatrics; mem. Med. Soc. State of N.Y., Ctrl. N.Y. Pediatric Club, Monroe County Med. Soc., Rochester Acad. Medicine, Rochester Pediatric Soc. Avocations: hiking, camping, canoeing, gardening, cross country skiing. Office: U Rochester Med Ctr 601 Elmwood Ave Box 777 Rochester NY 14642 Office Phone: 585-275-0225.

NAZIK, EVSEN, nursing researcher; b. Trabzon, Turkey, June 22, 1981; PhD, Atatürk U. Nursing Sch., 2009. With Erzurum Health Sch., Atatürk U., 2003—09; rschr., nursing dept. Çukurova U., Adana Health Sch., 2009—. Office: Çukurova Üniversitesi Adana Saglik Adana 011000 Turkey Personal E-mail: eceevsen_61@hotmail.com.

NAZMETDINOVA, DANIYA, psychiatrist; b. Russia, June 11, 1977; MD, Bashcirskiy Med. U., PhD, 2000. Sr. rschr. Moscow Rsch. Inst. Psychiatry, 2011—. Office: 3 Poteshnaya Str Moscow 107076 Russia Business E-Mail: d.nazmetdinova@mail.ru.

NDEBIA, EUGENE JAMOT, physical education educator; b. Ayos, Cameroon, Mar. 17, 1975; MSc in Physiol. Scis., U. Yaounde, Cameroon, 2003; PhD student in Health Scis., Walter Sisulu U., South Africa. Lectr. Walter Sisulu U., 2008—. Mem.: Physiol. Soc. Southern Africa. Office: Nelson Mandela Dr Mthatha Eastern Cape 5117 South Africa Office Fax: 0475022758. Business E-Mail: endebia@wsu.ac.za.

NEAGU, STEFAN ILIE, surgeon, educator; b. Bucharest, Romania, Sept. 13, 1949; s. Valentin and Natalia (Stoenescu) N.; m. Eugenia Cristina Marin, Oct. 15, 1972; 1 child, Manuela Stefana. MD, Faculty Medicine Bucharest, 1974, PhD, 1984; dipl. cancer surgery, Cancer Inst. Bucharest, 1982; dipl. transplantation surgery, Strasbourg U., 1992, dipl. visceral surgery, 1994. Asst. prof. surgery Faculty Medicine Bucharest, 1976-79, asst. prof. titular, 1980-93, assoc. prof. surgery, 1993—; head 2nd. dept. surgery U. Hosp., Bucharest, 1998—; prof European Sch. Surg. Oncology, 2007. Pres. "Alexis Carrel" Found. Med. Rsch., 2000; prof. European Sch. Surg. Oncology. Author: Renal Preservation by Cold Storage, 1990, Surgery, 2 vols., 1992, 94; inventor in field. Fellow Serbian Soc. Surgery (hon.), Internat. Assn. Surgeons and Gastroenterologists, European Hernia Soc., Roman Soc. Surgery, French Assn. Surgery, Internat. Assn. Pancreatology, Jockey Club Romania, European Digestive Surgery; mem. NY Acad. Scis., Nat. Geog. Soc. Avocations: fencing, gardening, history. Office: Univ Hosp Dept Surgery Splaiul Independentei 169 Bucharest Romania Home: Strada Viitorului 22 20612 Bucharest Romania Office Phone: 4021-318-0538. Personal E-mail: stephanneagu@gmail.com. Business E-Mail: msneagu@cmb.ro.

NEAL, DAVID EDGAR, surgery educator; b. Otley, Yorkshire, England, Mar. 9, 1951; s. Norman and Beth N.; m. Deborah Mary Heyworth; children: Rebecca, Emily, Miriam. MB BS, MS, U. Coll., London, 1975. FRCS (Engl) Royal Coll. of Surgeons of Eng., 1980, F Med Sci Acad. of Med. Sciences, 1998, FRCS (Edin) Royal Coll. of Surgeons of Edinburgh, 1994. Sr. lectr. urology U. Newcastle upon Tyne, England, 1988-92, prof. surgery, 1992—2002; prof. surg. oncology U. Cambridge, Cambridge, England, 2002—. Non-exec. dir. Newcastle upon tyne Hosps. NHS Trust, 1992—; coun. mem. Royal Coll. Surgeons, Eng., 2002—, Acad. Med. Scis., 2007—. Author: Scientific Basis of Urology, 1999 (Brit. Med. Jour. award 2000). Mgmt. com. King's Fund, London, 1996-2001. Recipient St Peter's Medal, Brit. Assn. of Urol. Surgeons, 2000. Fellow Royal Coll. Surgeons Edinburgh; mem. Am. Assn. Genito-Urinary Surgeons, MMC Programme Bd., Acad. Med. Sci. (coun. mem.) Office: Addenbrooke's Hosp Surg Oncology Ctr Hills Rd Po Box 279 CB2 0QQ Cambridge England Office Phone: 44 1223 331940. Business E-Mail: den22@cam.ac.uk.

NEAL, GAIL FALLON, physical therapist, educator; b. New Haven, May 6, 1938; d. Edward Francis and Ruth Alexina (Hutchinson) Fallon; m. Marcus Pinson Neal Jr., (dec. Dec. 23, 2009); children: Sandra Neal Dawson, Marcus Pinson III, Ruth-Catherine Neal Perkins. Student, Mary Washington Coll., 1955-57; BS in Phys. Therapy, Med. Coll. Va., 1959. Lic. phys. therapist. Staff phys. therpist Univ. Hosps., U. Wis., Madison, 1959-61; chief phys. therapy Stoughton (Wis.) Cmty. Hosp., 1961-63; vol. phys. therapy Cerebral Palsy Ctr., Richmond, Va., 1963-64; pvt. practice Richmond, 1965—68; interim dir. Stuart Cir. Hosp., Richmond, 1968-69; phys. therpist on call St. Mary's Hosp., Richmond, 1968-74; pres., owner Capital Phys. Therapy Assocs., Richmond, 1989—. Phys. therapist St. Mary's Hosp., Richmond, 1975-88; lectr. Med. Coll. Va., Richmond, 1992-93, John Tyler C.C., Richmond, 1992-94; adv. bd. phys. therapy Va. State Bd. Medicine, 1990-96, vice chmn., 1992-93, chmn. 1995-96, Gov. Com. Cmty. Work. Adv. bd. Va. Opera, 1979—2010; bd. visitors Mary Washington Coll., Fredericksburg, Va., 1980-82, rector bd. visitors, 1982-84; pres. Richmond Symphony Orch. League, 1986-88. Named Clubwoman of Yr., Richmond Newsleader, 1972. Mem. Am. Phys. Therapy Assn., Richmond Acad. Medicine Aux. (pres. 1967-68), Med. Soc. Va. Alliance (pres. 1980-81), Med. Coll. Va. Hosps. Aux. (pres. 1973-75), Va. Cultural Laureate Soc. Avocations: reading, music, indian folklore. Home: Pony Bluffs 7301 Riverside Dr Richmond VA 23225-1066 Office: Capital Phys Therapy Assocs Pony Bluffs Richmond VA 23225 Office Phone: 804-330-2440. Personal E-mail: gfncpta@verizon.net.

NEALIS, JAMES GARRY THOMAS, III, pediatric neurologist, educator, author; b. NYC, Mar. 7, 1945; s. James and Catherine N.; m.

Arlene Dee Kramer, Feb. 6, 1981; children: Peyton Colleen, Douglas Andrew, Gregory Haynes, James Garry Thomas IV, Patrick Ryan. BA, Fordham U., 1966; MD, U. Miami, 1971. Diplomate Am. Bd. Psychiatry and Neurology, Am. Bd. Electroencephalography. Intern in pediatrics Babies Hosp., Columbia Presbyn. Med. Ctr., Columbia U. Sch. Medicine, NYC, 1971—72, resident, 1972—73; resident neurology Boston U. Sch. Medicine, 1973—76, Harvard U. Sch. Medicine, Boston, 1975—76, instr. pediatric neurology, 1976—78; chief resident Boston City Hosp., 1975—76; asst. neurophysiology Boston Children's Hosp., 1976—78; founder Neuro-Ednl. Evaluation Clinic, 1977—78; asst. prof. clin. neurology U. Fla., Jacksonville; chief pediatric neurology Jacksonville Children's Hosp., 1979—; lectr. U. N. Fla.; clin. instr. neurology cons. Naval Regional Med. Ctr., Jacksonville, 1979—. Adviser Pres.'s Com. Med. Ethics, Washington, 1980; sec. Fla. Neurol. Inst., 1985; lectr. in field; host radio talk show. Author: Physical Disabilities and Health Impairments; contbr. chapters to books, articles to med. jours. Founder, bd. dirs. Northeast Fla. League Against Reye's Syndrome; bd. dirs. Speech and Hearing Clinic; trustee Epilepsy Found.; active Jacksonville Police Coun., 1981—; founder Jacksonville Alzheimer's Ctr.; profl. adviser Parents Action Against Drugs and Substance Abuse, 1983—; with To Your Health, WJXT, 1983, The Brain, WJXT, 1985, Drugs and Your Brain, 1986, Alzheimers Disease, 1984, The 700 Club, CBN, 1985. Named Outstanding Young Man of Yr., Bold City Jr. C of C, 1980. Mem.: Jacksonville C of C, Coun. Exceptional Children, Fla. Med. Assn., Fla. Soc. Neurology, Child Neurology Soc. (mem. nat. com. med. ethics 1984—85, adv. 1985—86, nat. adv. pediatric brain death 1985, practice com.), Duval County Med. Soc. (trustee), Am. Epilepsy Soc., Jacksonville Assn. Children Learning Disabilities (bd. advisers), Am. Med. Electroencephalographic Assn. (pres. 1984), Eastern Assn. EEG, Am. Acad. Neurology.

NEAL-PARKER, SHIRLEY ANITA, obstetrician, gynecologist; b. Washington, Aug. 28, 1949; d. Leon Walker and Pearl Anita (Shelton) Neal; m. Andre Cowan Dasent, June 21, 1971 (div. Feb. 1978); 1 child, Erika Michelle Dasent; m. James Carl Parker, Feb. 11, 1979; 1 child, Amirah Nabeehah. BS in Biology, Am. U., 1971; MD, Hahnemann U., 1979. Lic. Md., Calif., Wash., Oreg. Intern Howard U. Hosp., 1979-80, resident, 1980-84; physician Nat. Health Svc. Corp., Charleston, W. Va., 1984-86; clin. instr. W.Va. U., Charleston, 1985-86; pvt. practice ob./gyn. Sacramento, 1986-95; pvt. practice Chehalis, Wash., 1995—2004; chair dept. perinatology Providence Centralia Hosp., 1999-2000; group practice Tulare County Health and Human Svcs., 2004—05, Grand Med. Group, 2005—06; with St. Rita Med. Clinic, Montclair, Calif., 2006—07, Michael Women's Med. Group, 2008—. Bd. dirs. Ruth Rosenberg Dance Ensemble, Sacramento, 1992-95, Human Response Network, Chehalis, 1995-97. Mem.: Calif. Med. Assn., Tulare County Med. Soc., Wash. State Med. Assn., Am. Med. Women's Assn. (comty. svc. award Mother Hale br. 1994), Nat. Med. Assn., Am. Reproductive Health Profls., Am. Assn. Gynecologic Laparoscopists. Avocations: travel, reading, crocheting. Home: 1949 Santa Maria Ave Porterville CA 93257-8863 Office: Family Healthcare Network 1107 W Poplar Ave Porterville CA 93257 Office Phone: 554-781-7242 ext. 3189. Home Fax: 559-791-1897. Personal E-mail: drsanp@earthlink.net.

NEAMAN, MARK ROBERT, hospital administrator; b. Buffalo, Oct. 22, 1950; married. B, Ohio State U., 1972, MHA, 1974. Adminstrv. asst. Evanston Hosp., Ill., 1974-76, asst. to v.p., 1976-78, asst. v.p., 1978-80, v.p., 1980-84, sr. v.p., 1984-85, pres., exec. v.p., 1985-90, pres., 1990-92, pres., CEO, 1992—. Bd. trustees Healthcare Leadership Coun. Fellow Am. Coll. Healthcare Execs. (chmn., RS Hudgens award 1988). Office: Evanston Hosp 2650 Ridge Ave Evanston IL 60201 Office Phone: 847-570-2000. *

NEAS, RALPH GRAHAM, JR., pharmaceutical association administrator; b. Brookline, Mass., May 17, 1946; s. Ralph Graham Sr. and Elsie Marie (Barone) N. AB cum laude, U. Notre Dame, 1968; JD, U. Chgo., 1971. Legis. atty. American law divsn. Library of Congress, Washington, 1971-73; chief legis. asst. to Senator Edward W. Brooke US Senate, Washington, 1973-79, chief legis. asst. to Senator David Durenberger, 1979-80; exec. dir. Leadership Conf. on Civil Rights, Washington, 1981—95; pres. Neas Group, Washington, 1995—99; pres., CEO People for the American Way, Washington, 2000—07, Nat. Coalition on Healthcare (NCHC), Washington, 2007—11, Generic Pharmaceutical Assn. (GphA), 2011—. Instr. Univ. Chgo. Law Sch., Georgetown Univ. Law Ctr., Harvard Univ. John F. Kennedy Sch. Govt. Democratic candidate for US House of Reps., 8th dist. Md., 1998; served as 1st lt. U.S. Army, 1972. Recipient Hubert H. Humphrey Civil Rights award, Leadership Conf. on Civil Rights, Benjamin Hooks Keeper of the Flame award, NAACP, Isaiah award for Pursuit of Justice, American Jewish Com., Flag Bearer award, Parents Families & Friends of Lesbians & Gays, Kennedy Lifetime Achievement award, Disability Rights Edn. & Def. Fund, Edison Uno Meml. Civil Rights award, Japanese-American Citizens League, Citizen of the Year award, Guillian-Barre Syndrome Found. Internat., Nat. Good Guy award, Nat. Women's Political Caucus; named Person of the Week, ABC News, 1987. Mem. ABA, D.C. Bar Assn. Democrat. Roman Catholic. Office: Generic Pharmaceutical Assn (GphA) 777 Sixth Street NW Ste 510 Washington DC 20001 Office Phone: 202-249-7100. *

NEAVES, WILLIAM BARLOW, cell biologist, educator; b. Spur, Tex., Dec. 25, 1943; s. William Fred and Revvie Lee (Hefner) Neaves; m. Priscilla Wood, Jan. 28, 1965; children: William Barlow, Clarissa D'laine. AB magna cum laude, Harvard U., 1966; postgrad., Med. Sch., 1966-67, PhD, 1969. Lectr. vet. anatomy U. Nairobi, 1970-71, vis. prof., 1978; lectr. anatomy Harvard U., 1972; asst. prof. cell biology U. Tex. Health Sci. Ctr., Dallas, 1972-74, assoc. prof., 1974-77, prof., 1977—, Doris and Brian Wildenthal Prof. of Biomed. Sci., 1993—, dean Grad. Sch. Biomed. Scis., 1980-88, interim dean Southwestern Med. Sch., 1986-88, dean Southwestern Med. Sch., 1989-98, exec. v.p. acad. affairs, 1998—2000; prof. medicine U. Mo., Kansas City, 1998—2000; pres., CEO Stowers Inst. Med. Rsch., Kansas City, 2000—09, CEO, 2009—10, pres. emeritus, 2010—. Dir. Cerner Corp., Midwest Rsch. Inst., Kansas City Area Life Scis. Inst.; trustee Wash. U.; mem. nat. coun. Wash. U. Sch. Medicine; rsch. assoc. herpetology Los Angeles County Mus., 1970—73; vis. lectr. U. Chgo., 1976—77. Assoc. editor Anat. Record, 1975—87, mem. editl. bd. Biology of Reproduction, 1983—86, Jour. Andrology, 1987—89; contbr. articles to profl. jours. Bd. dirs. Dallas Zool. Soc., 1989—94, Dallas Mus. Natural History, 1993—95, Damon Runyan-Walter Winchell Cancer Fund, 1986—92, v.p., 1990—92; bd. dirs. Sarnoff Endowment, 1998—. Rockefeller Found. fellow, 1970—71, Milton Fund grantee, 1970—71, Population Coun. grantee, 1973—75, NIH grantee, 1973—89, Ford Found. grantee, 1976—78. Fellow: AAAS; mem.: Liaison Com. on Med. Edn. (joint com. of AMA and Assn. Am. Med. Colls.), Soc. Study of Reproduction, NY Acad. Scis., Dallas Assembly, Am. Soc. Andrology (Young Andrologist award 1986), Am. Assn. Anatomists, Alpha Omega Alpha, Sigma Xi. Methodist. Office: Stowers Institute for Medical Research 1000 East 50th St Kansas City MO 64110 Office Phone: 816-926-4040. Business E-Mail: wbn@stowers-institute.org. *

NEBERT, DANIEL WALTER, molecular geneticist, research administrator; b. Portland, Oreg., Sept. 26, 1938; s. Walter Francis Nebert and Marie Sophie (Schick) Kirk; m. Myrna Sisk, Mar. 12, 1960 (div. 1975); children: Douglas Daniel, Dietrich Andrew; m. Kathleen Dixon, Aug. 15, 1981 (div. 1997); children: Rosemarie Dixon, Rebecca Frances, David Porter, Lucas Daniel; m. Lucia Fung Jorge, Mar. 6, 2000. BA, Wesleyan U., 1959; BS and MS in Biochemistry, U. Oreg., 1964, MD, 1964. Lic. physician, Ohio; bd. qualified in pediats. and human genetics; Am. Bd. Pediat. and Human Genetics. Pediat. intern UCLA Hosps., 1964—65, resident pediat., 1965—66; postdoctoral fellow Nat. Cancer Inst., NIH, Bethesda, Md., 1966—68; sr. investigator Nat. Inst. Child Health and Human Devel., Bethesda, 1968—71, sect. head, 1971—74, lab. chief, 1974—89; prof. dept. environ. health U. Cin. Med. Ctr., 1989—, prof. dept. pediat. and molecular devel. biology, 1991—, Cin. Children's Hosp. Faculty bd. cert. in human genetics NIH, 1981-89; coord. med. genetics program US-China Coop. Med. Health Protocol, 1982-89; Pfizer lectr. U. Vt., Burlington, 1978, Stanford U., 1979; Wellcome vis. prof. biochemistry and molecular biology U. SD, Vermillion, 1991; assoc. dir. physician scientist tng. program MD/PhD, U. Cin. Med. Ctr., 1994-98; nat. adv. Environ. Health Scis. Coun., 2000-04; external adv. bd. Howard U. Cancer Ctr., Wash., 1998-2002, U. Lisbon, 1998-2002, Inst. DNA and Human Genomics U. Panama, 1999-2004; dir. Ctr. Environ. Genetics, 1992-97, assoc. dir. Ctr. Environ. Genetics, 1997-. Mem. editl. bd. Molecular Pharmacology, 1972-1984, Biochem. Pharmacology, 1972-2008, Archives of Biochemistry and Biophysics, 1973-76, Archieves Internationales de Pharmacodynamie et de Therapie, 1975-81, Jour. Environ. Scis. and Health, 1976-81, Chemico-Biol. Interactions, 1977-83, Teratogenesis, Carcinogenesis and Mutagenesis, 1978-82, Devel. Pharmacology and Therapeutics, 1980-86, Anticancer Rsch., 1981-83, DNA and Cell Biology, 1986—2003, Jour. Exptl. Pathology, 1986-1994, Molecular Endocrinology, 1988-1992, Endocrinology, 1989-2002, Molecular Toxicology, 1990-92, Pharmacogenetics Genomics, 1991—, Mutation Rsch., 1996-2001, European Jour. Pharmacology, 2002-, Human Genomics, 2003—; assoc. editor DNA and Cell Biology, 1987-2003, commn. edit. Biochem. Pharmacology (N.Am.), 1994-2001, Environ. Health Perspectives, 1997—; commn. edit. Human Mutation, 2005-; contbr. more than 610 articles to profl. jours. Capt. USPHS, 1966-89 Recipient Meritorious Svc. medal USPHS, 1978, Frank Ayrey fellow award in clin. pharmacology, U.K., 1984, Bernard B. Brodie award, 1986, Ernst A. Sommer Meml. award, 1988; GM scholar, 1956-59, Lawrence Selling scholar, 1961, 63, Disting. Rsch. Professorship award, U. Cin., 1998, George Rieveschl Jr. award for disting. sci. rsch., U. Cin., 1999 Fellow: AAAS; mem. Am. Soc. Human Genetics, Am. Soc. Pharmacology and Exptl. Therapeutics, Am. Soc. Biochemistry and Molecular Biology, Am. Soc. Clin. Investigation (emeritus 1984-), Soc. Toxicology (Disting. Lifetime Toxicology Scholar award, 2005), Human Genome Variation Soc. (founder), Sigma Xi. Independent. Episcopalian. Avocations: gardening, golf, piano, skiing, art. Home: 20 Oliver Rd Cincinnati OH 45215-2631 Office: Univ Cin Med Ctr Dept Environ Health PO Box 670056 Cincinnati OH 45267-0056 Office Phone: 513-821-4664.

NEBGEN, DENISE R., physician, researcher; b. San Antonio, Feb. 23, 1964; d. Marvin Carl and Marlene Marie Nebgen; m. Jason Edward Johnson, Mar. 11, 2000; children: Christopher, Sean. DDS, U. Tex. Health Sci. Ctr., San Antonio, 1988; PhD, Northwestern U., Chgo., 1995, MD, 1997. Resident ob-gyn. Baylor Coll. Medicine, Houston, 2001; physician ob-gyn. Methodits Hosp., Houston, 2001—; nat. med. dir. Sightline, 2009. Mem. Meth. Ctr. Performing Arts Medicine, Houston, 2003—, Meth. Ctr. Pelvic Medicine, 2005—. Membership care Shepperd Heart United Meth. Ch., Pearland, 2007, mem. Fellow: ACOG; mem.: Houston Gynecol. Obstet. Soc. Methodist. Avocation: running. Office: MD Anderson Cancer Ctr Dept Gynecologic Oncology & Reproductive Medicine Unit 1362 PO Box 301439 Houston TX 77230-1439 Office Fax: 713-797-0661.

NECCHI, ANDREA, oncologist; b. Vimercate, May 9, 1979; Student, Found. IRCCS Inst. Nat. dei Tumori, 2002—04; MD, U. Milan, 2004, degree in Med. Oncology, 2008. Postdoc. tng. fellow Found. IRCCS Inst. Nat. dei Tumori, 2005—08, rsch. fellow, 2009—, staff physician, 2011—. Recipient Young Oncologist prize, Found. IRCCS Inst. Nat. dei Tumori. Mem.: Ctr. Studi Silvia Santagata-Ebla (sci. bd. mem.), European Urol. Assn., Am. Soc. Hematology, European Orgn. Rsch. and Treatment Cancer, European Soc. Med. Oncology, Am. Soc. Clin. Oncology, Rotary Club. Office: Via G Venezian 1 Milan 20133 Italy Business E-Mail: andrea.necchi@istitutotumori.mi.it.

NEDOMA, JIRÍ, mathematician, physicist; b. Prague, Czechoslovakia, Mar. 11, 1934; s. Josef Nedoma and Jirina Nedomova; m. Bronislava Kantorova, Feb. 9, 1963 (div. 1965); 1 child, Jana Nedomova; m. Anna Vavrova, Feb. 2, 1984 (div. Mar. 9, 1988). MSc, Transp.Tech. U., Prague, 1959; PhD, Czechoslovak Acad. Scis., 1991. Rsch. worker Phys. Inst. Slovak Acad. Sci., High Tatras, Czech Republic, 1961—63; rsch. worker Inst. Computer Sci. Czech Acad. Sci., Prague, 1963—69, rsch. worker Geophys. Inst., 1969—82, sr. rsch. fellow, 1982—94; assoc. prof. U. West Bohemia, 1994—. Dir. dept. math. Chem. Tech. U., Prague, 1964—65; rsch. worker United Nuc. Rsch. Inst., Dubna, Russia, 1965; lectr. Bergakademie, Freiberg, Germany; coord. internat. rsch. project Commn. German Acad. Scis. for Planetary and Geophysical Rsch., Moscow, 1970—80; vis. prof.; mem. program and orgn. com. Internat. Confs. on Math. Modeling and Computing Methods in Mech., Phys., Biomech. others, 1994, 98, 2001, 05. Author: Numerical Modelling in Applied Geodynamics, 1998, (textbook) Finite Element Technique in Geophysics, 1978; co-author: Biomechanics of Human Skeleton and Replacements of It's Parts, 2006; co-editor: Computational Methods in Geophysics, 1971; reviewer: Math. Rev., 1971—, sr. editor: Jour. Math. and Computers in Simulation (MATCOM); contbr. articles to profl. jours.; author: Mathematical and Computational Methods in Biomechanics of Human Skeletal Systems, 2011. Programme and orgn. com. Internat. Confs. Com. Crimes, 1991, 1992; ctrl. coun. Club Engaged Non-Party People, Prague, Czech Republic, 1968, 1990—94. With Czechoslovak Army, 1959—61. Recipient medal, KAPG, 1976, Fund prize, Czech Lit., 1987, Zable Excellent Tech. medal, US, 2003; named to Hall of Fame, Engring. Sci. and Tech. US European Level, 2003, Engring. Sci. and Tech. US World Level, 2007; grantee Rsch. grant, Czech Republic, Ministry Edn., Youth and Sports, Czech Republic, 1995—2001, European Grant Commn., 1995—2001, Ministry Industry and Trade, Czech Republic, 2004—07;, Mgmt. Strategy TMJ Dir., 2009—. Mem.: Internat. Tech. Inst., Internat. Assn. Math. and Computers Simulation (bd. dirs.), Am. Math. Soc. Avocations: classical music, painting and sculpting. Office: Acad Sci Czech Republic Inst Computer Sci Pod Vodárenskou Vezí 2 18207 Prague 8 Czech Republic Office Phone: 420 26605 3280. Business E-Mail: nedoma@cs.cas.cz.

NEEDHAM, GLEN RAY, entomology and acarology educator, researcher; b. Lamar, Colo., Dec. 25, 1951; s. Robert Lee and Evor Elaine (Kern) N.; m. Karla Marie Lohr, May 28, 1983; children: Kathleen Marie, John Harrison, Elizabeth Anne. BS, S.W. Okla. State U., 1973; MS, Okla. State U., 1975, PhD, 1978. Grad. rsch. asst. Okla. State U., Stillwater, 1974-78; asst. prof. Ohio State U., Columbus, 1978-84, assoc. prof., 1984—, co-organizer and coord. acarology summer program. Co-editor: Africanized Honey Bees and Bee Mites, 1988, Acarology IX: Proceedings and Symposia. Donor ARC, Columbus. Recipient Dist. Alumnus award Okla. State U., 1992; fellowship Christian Faculty and Staff Ohio State U. Mem. Acarology Soc. Am. (pres. 1994), Ohio Asthma Coalition (past chair), Ctrl. Ohio Asthma Coalition, Gamma Sigma Delta. Methodist. Achievements include research in tick, dust mite, flea, bedbug biology and control. Office: Ohio State U 318 W 12th Ave Columbus OH 43210 Office Phone: 614-688-3026. Business E-Mail: needham.1@osu.edu.

NEEDLEMAN, PHILIP, museum administrator, cardiologist, pharmacologist; b. Bklyn., Feb. 10, 1939; m. Sima Needleman. BS in Pharmacology, Phila. Coll. Pharm. & Sci., 1960, MS in Pharmacology, 1962; PhD in Pharmacology, U. Md. Med. Sch., 1964. Fellow Sch. Medicine Washington U., St. Louis, 1965—67, from asst. prof. to prof. Sch. Medicine, 1967—75, prof. Sch. Medicine, 1975—89, adj. prof., 1976—89, chmn., dept. pharmacology, 1989, chief scientist, 1991, assoc. dean, spl. projects, 2004; sr. v.p., chief scientist Monsanto, 1989—93; pres. Searle Pharma. Co., 1993—2000; sr. exec. v.p., chief scientist, chmn. R&D Pharmacia (fomerly Monsanto/Searle), 2000—03; former ptnr. Prospect Ventures Ptnrs., Palo Alto, Calif.; interim pres., CEO Donald Danforth Plant Sci. Ctr., 2010—11, St. Louis Sci. Ctr., 2011—. Served on com. NIH study sects.; adv. com. FDA, NIH, Nat. Coun. Washington Univ. Med. Sch. Contbr. numerous articles to profl. jours. Bd. trustee Washington U.; bd. dir. Barnes-Jewish Hosp., St. Louis Plant and Biotechnology consortium, St. Louis Sci. Ctr.; sci. advisor to pres. for R&D Ben Gurion U., 2002—, bd. trustee; mem. adv. com. for the creation of Nat. Inst. for Biotechnology in the Negev; bd. trustee Donald Danforth Plant Sci. Ctr. Recipient John Jacob Abel award, Am. Pharmacology Soc., 1974, Rsch. Career Devel. award, NIH, 1974, 1976, Wellcome Creesy award in clin. pharmacology, 1977, 1978, 1980, 1987, Cochems Thrombosis Rsch. prize, 1980, Rsch. Achievement award, Am. Heart Assn., 1988, Second Century award, 1994, C. Chester Stock award Lectureship, Meml. Sloan Kettering Cancer Ctr., 2001, Indsl. Rsch. Inst. medal, 2001, Am. Soc. Exptl. Therapeutics award, Dart/NYU Biotechnology Achievement awards, Biotechnology Study Ctr. NYU Sch. Medicine, 2005. Mem.: IOM, NAS (chair phamacology-physiology sect. 2001—04, bd. trustee NAS Coun. 2004, award for Indsl. Application of Sci. 2005). Achievements include pioneering studies on the role of Cox 1 and Cox 2 enzymes in inflammation, cardiovascular and renal disease, and in tumor progression; developing the first angiotensin receptor antagonist, the first thromboxane synthetase inhibitor; discovering atriopeptin, the atrial natriuretic factor, a novel endocrine peptide that allows the heart to communicate with the kidneys and blood vessels. Office: St Louis Science Ctr 5050 Oakland Ave Saint Louis MO 63110 *

NEEL, HARRY BRYAN, III, surgeon, scientist, educator; b. Rochester, Minn., Oct. 28, 1939; s. Harry Bryan and May Birgitta (Bjornsson) N.; m. Ingrid Helene Vaga, Aug. 29, 1964; children: Carlton Bryan, Harry Bryan IV, Roger Clifton. BS, Cornell U., 1962; MD, SUNY-Bklyn., 1966; PhD, U. Minn., 1976. Diplomate Am. Bd. Otolaryngology. Intern Kings County Hosp., Bklyn., 1966-67; resident in gen. surgery U. Minn. Hosps., Mpls., 1967-68; clin. assoc. NCI/NIH, 1968—70; resident in otolaryngology Mayo Grad. Sch. Medicine Mayo Clinic, Rochester, Minn., 1970-74, cons. in otorhinolaryngology, 1974—2005, cons. in cell biology, 1981—2005, assoc. prof. otolaryngology and microbiology Med. Sch., 1979-84, prof., 1984—, also chmn. dept. otolaryngology. Mem. sci. adv. com. Pitts. Eye and Ear Found.; lifetime vis. prof. Hunan U., China, 2003—. Author: Cryosurgery for Cancer, 1976; contbr. chpts. to books, articles to profl. jours. V.p. bd. dirs. Minn. Orch. in Rochester, Inc., 1982, pres., chmn., 1983—84; mem. devel. com. Minn. Orchestral Assn., 1983, Mayo Found., 1983—86, mem. acad. appointments and promotion com., 2005—07; bd. dirs. Mayo Health Plan, 1986—92, chmn., 1990—92; mem. bd. Mayo Mgmt. Svcs., Inc., 1992—94; mem. bd. regents U. Minn., 1991—2003, chair faculty staff, student affairs com., 1993—95, 1999, vice chmn. bd., 1995—97, chmn. fin. and ops. com., 1999, mem. audit com., 1995—2000, chair litigation review com., 2001—03, chair facilities com., 2001—03, chmn. investment adv. com., 1999—2003, mem. conflict interest com., 2006—, founder Neel Scholarship Endowment Fund Health Scis. Rochester, 2003; bd. dirs. Greater Rochester Area Univ. Ctr., 1993—2003; trustee U. Minn. Found., 1996—2005, mem. fin. com., 1999—2005; mem. State Commn. on U. Minn. Excellence, 2002. With USPHS, 1968—70. Recipient travel award Soc. Acad. Chmn. Otolaryngology, 1974, Ira J. Tresley rsch. award Am. Acad. Facial Plastic and Reconstructive Surgery, 1982, Master Tchr. award in surgery Alumni Assn. Coll. Medicine, SUNY, Health Sci. Ctr., Bklyn., 1991, Notable award Nat. Assn. Collegiate Women Athletic Adminstrs., 1992; name one of Best Drs. in Am., Good Housekeeping, 1991, Best Drs. in Am., Woodward/White, 1992—, Best Drs. in Minn., Minn. Monthly, 2003, Cmty. Leaders of World, Am.'s Top Physicians, Consumers' Rsch. Coun., Neel lectrship Otolaryn. Head Neck Surgery Mayo Found. Endowment Fund Mem. ACS (bd. govs. 1985-90, devel. bd. 1988-04, treas. 1990-98, sec.-treas. Minn. chpt. 1983-85, pres. 1988-89), Am. Acad. Otolaryngology-Head and Neck Surgery (prize for basic rsch. in otolaryngology 1972, bd. dirs. 1988-91, established Neel Disting. Rsch. Lectureship Endowment Fund 1994, audit com. 1998-2000, chair investment adv. com. 1995—2000, chmn. audit com. 1999-2000), Minn. Med. Assn. (com. on adminstrn. and fin. 2003—05, Cmty. Svc. award for outstanding cmty. svc. 2003, Pub.

Svc. Achievement award 2003), Zumbro Valley Med. Soc., Am. Broncho-Esophagological Assn. (pres. 1989-90), Am. Laryngological, Rhinological and Oto. Soc. (Mosher award 1980, pres.-elect 1995-96, centennial pres. 1996-97, investment com. 1994—, historian, 2001—), Am. Laryngological Assn. (Casselberry award 1985, sec. 1988-93, v.p. 1994, pres. 1994—, Newcomb award 1996, Baker lectr. 1998, presdl. citation 2009), Assn. for Rsch. in Otolaryngology, Assn. Acad. Depts. in Otolaryngology (sec.-treas. 1984-86, pres.-elect 1986, pres. 1988-9), Alumni Assn. Cornell U. (Outstanding Alumni award 1985), Collegium ORL Amicitiae Sacrum (bd. dirs., 2d sec. 2000-08, Svc. medal, 2008), Am. Bd. Otolaryngology (bd. dirs. 1986-2005, treas. 1998-2004), Am Laryngol. Voice Rsch. and Edn. Found. (charter bd. dirs. 1996-2003), Rochester Golf and Country Club. Republican. Presbyterian. Home: 828 8th St SW Rochester MN 55902-6310 Office: Mayo Clinic 200 1st St SW Rochester MN 55905-0002 Home Phone: 507-282-0035. Office Fax: 507-284-5036. Personal E-mail: ivyneel@aol.com.

NEEL, JUDY MURPHY, management consultant; b. Rhome, Tex. d. James W. and Linna B. (Vess) Neel; m. Ellis F. Murphy, Jr., Dec. 30, 1975; children from previous marriage: Mary B. Schmidt, Janet E. Hollingsworth, Susan E. Salinas. BS, Northwestern U., 1977; MBA, Roosevelt U., 1983. V.p. Murphy, Tashjian & Assocs., Chgo., 1960-73; exec. dir. Automotive Affiliated Rep. Assn., Chgo., 1973-78; mgr. Automotive Svc. Ind. Assn., Chgo., 1978-80; exec. dir. Am. Soc. Safety Engrs., Des Plaines, Ill., 1980-98, Am. Assn. Diabetes Educators, 1999—2003; dir. Borgess-Lee Meml. Hosp. Found., 1997—; mgmt. cons., 2003—. Recipient Assn. Leadership Award Bus. Women's Network/Assn. Trends Mag., 1998. Mem. Chgo. Soc. Assn. Execs. (bd. dirs. 1979—, pres. 1985—, Shapiro award 1991), Am. Soc. Assn. Execs. (sec.-treas. 1994, found. dir. 1986-90, bd. dirs. 1990-95, Key award 1986). Republican. Personal E-mail: jneelcae@aol.com.

NEELY, JOHN GAIL, otolaryngologist; b. Oklahoma City, Dec. 10, 1939; MD, U. Okla., 1965. Intern U. Oreg. Med. Ctr., Portland, 1965-66; resident in surgery Baylor Hosp., Houston, 1968-69, resident in otolaryngology, 1969-72; fellow Otologic Med. Group, LA, 1972-73; staff Barnes Hosp., St. Louis, 1992—, Jewish Hosp., St. Louis, 1992—; prof., dir. rsch. Washington U., St. Louis, 1992—. Mem. ACS, Am. Neurotology Soc., Am. Otol. Soc., Am. Acad. Otolaryngology, Head and Neck Surgery, Soc. Univ. Otolaryngologists, Triologic Soc. Office: Washington U Sch Medicine Dept Oto Head-Neck Surgery 660 S Euclid Ave Box 8115 Saint Louis MO 63110-1010 Office Phone: 314-362-7344. Business E-Mail: neelyg@ent.wustl.edu.

NEER, CHARLES SUMNER, II, orthopedic surgeon, educator; b. Vinita, Okla., Nov. 10, 1917; s. Charles Sumner and Pearl Victoria (Brooke) N.; m. Eileen Meyer; children: Charlotte Marguerite, Sydney Victoria, Charles Henry. BA, Dartmouth Coll., 1939; MD, U. Pa., 1942. Diplomate Am. Bd. Orthopaedic Surgery (bd. dirs. 1970-75). Intern U. Pa. Hosp., Phila., 1942-43; asso. in surgery N.Y. Orthopedic-Columbia-Presbyn. Med. Center, NYC, 1943-44; instr. in surgery Coll. Physicians and Surgeons, Columbia U., NYC, 1946-47, instr. orthopaedic surgery, 1947-57, asst. prof. clin. orthopaedic surgery, 1957-64, asso. prof., 1964-68, prof. clin. orthopaedic surgery, 1968-90, prof. clin. orthopaedic surgery emeritus, spl. lectr. orthopaedic surgery, 1990—. Attending orthopaedic surgeon Columbia-Presbyn. Med. Ctr., N.Y.C.; chief adult reconstructive svc. N.Y. Orthopaedic Hosp.; chief shoulder and elbow clinic Presbyn. Hosp.; cons. orthopaedic surgeon emeritus N.Y. Orthopaedic-Columbia-Presbyn. Med. Ctr., 1991—; chmn. 4th Internat. Congress Shoulder Surgeons; chmn. Internat. Bd. Shoulder Surgery, 1992—. Founder, chmn. bd. trustees Jour. Shoulder and Elbow Surgery, 1990—; contbr. articles to books, tech. films, sound slides. Served with U.S. Army, 1944-46. Recipient Disting. Svc. award Am. Bd. Orthopaedic Surgeons 1975. Fellow ACS (sr. mem. nat. com. on trauma), Am. Acad. Orthop. Surgeons (com. on upper extremity, shoulder com.); mem. AMA, ACS (mem. com. trauma), Am. Bd. Orthop. Surgeons (bd. dirs. 1970-75, Disting. Svc. award 1975), Am. Shoulder and Elbow Surgeons (inaugural pres.), Am. Assn. Surgery Trauma, Am. Orthop. Assn., Mid-Am. Orthop. Assn. (hon.), N.Y. Acad. Medicine, Allen O. Whipple Surg. Soc., N.Y. State Med. Soc., N.Y. County Med. Soc., Pan Am. Med. Assn., Am. Trauma Soc., Soc. Latino Am. Orthop. y Traumatology, Internat. Soc. Orthop. Surgery and Traumatology, Va. Orthop. Soc. (hon.), Carolina Orthop. Alumni Assn. (hon.), Conn. Orthop. Club (hon.), Houston Orthop. Assn. (hon.), Soc. Française de Chirurgie Orthop. et Traumatology (hon.), Soc. Italiana Orthop. Etravmatologia e Traumatologia; patron, Shoulder and Elbow Soc. Australia, South African Shoulder Soc., Giraffe Club, Internat. Bd. Shoulder Surgery (chmn. 1992—), Alpha Omega Alpha, Phi Chi. Home and Office: PO Box 555 Vinita OK 74301 Office Phone: 918-256-6673. E-mail: elmcreekacres@junct.com. *

NEESON, FRANCIS J., cardiologist; Attended, NYU Sch. Medicine, 1985. Diplomate Am. Bd. Cardiology-cardiovascular disease, Am. Bd. Internal Medicine. Intern Bronx Mcpl. Hosp., NY, resident in internal medicine, 1986—88; fellow in cardiovascular disease Montefiore Med. Ctr., Bronx, NY, 1988—91; fellow Albert Einstein Coll. Medicine; cardiologist Greenwich Hosp. Office: Greenwich Hospital 75 Holly Hill Ln Greenwich CT 06830 Office Phone: 203-869-6960. Office Fax: 203-869-5103.

NEFF, BRIAN A., otolaryngologist; b. Ind., June 7, 1971; MD, Ind. U. Sch. Medicine, 1997. Cons., dept. otolaryngology, head & neck surgery Mayo Clinic, Rochester, Minn., 2005—11. Office: 200 First St SW Rochester MN 55905 Business E-Mail: brianalanneff@msn.com.

NEGRI, GIOVANNI, pathologist, consultant; b. Livorno, Italy, Oct. 11, 1961; s. Lionello Negri and Martha Mueller; m. Christiane Robl; 2 children. MD, Pisa Med. Sch., Pisa, Italy, 1981—90; PhD, U. Innsbruck Austria, 2007. Lic. Pathologist Germany, Italy, 1999. Trainee Dept. Pathology U. Ulm, Germany, 1991—96, U. Freiburg, Germany, 1996—98; cons. Gen. Hosp. Dept. Pathology, Bolzano, Italy, 1998—. Mem.: Internat. Acad. Cytology. Roman Catholic. Avocation: reading. Office: Gen Hosp Bolzano Dept Pathology Via Lorenz Boehler 5 39100 Bolzano BZ Italy Personal E-mail: ginegri@gmail.com.

NEGURA, LUCIAN, medical educator; b. Piatra Neamt, Romania, Dec. 30, 1975; M, U. Louis Pasteur, Strasbourg, France, 2001; PhD, Alexandru Ioan Cuza U., Iasi, 2009. Asst. lectr., immunology U. Medicine and Pharmacy Grigore T. Popa, Iasi, 2007—. Sr. rschr., forensic Inst. Legal Medicine, 2011. Postdoc. Rsch. grant, CNCSIS Romania, fellowship, European Soc. Human Genetics, 2008, 2010, Found. European Biochemisry Socs., 2011. Mem.: Romanian Soc. Biochemistry and Molecular Biology, European Soc. Human Genetics. Office: Board Independentei Nr 1 Iasi 700111 Romania Personal E-mail: luciannegura@yahoo.fr.

NEHER, ERWIN, biophysicist, research scientist; b. Landsberg, Bavaria, Germany, Mar. 20, 1944; s. Franz Xaver and Elisabeth (Pfeiffer) N.; m. Eva-Maria Ruhr, Dec. 26, 1978; children: Richard, Benjamin, Carola, Sigmund, Margret. MS, U. Wis., 1967; PhD, Tech. U., Munich, 1970. Rsch. assoc. Max Planck Inst. for Psychiatry, Munich, 1970-72, Max Planck Inst. for Biophys. Chemistry, Göttingen, 1972-75, 1976-83, rsch. dir., 1983—; rsch. assoc. Yale U., 1975—76. Fairchild Scholar, Calif. Inst. of Tech., 1988-89. Author: Elektronische Messtechnik, 1974; editor: Single Channel Recording, 1983; contbr. articles to profl. jours. Co-recipient Nobel prize physiology or medicine, 1991; recipient Louisa Gross-Horwitz award Columbia U., N.Y.C., 1986, Leibniz award Deutsche Forschungsgemeinschaft, Bonn, 1986, Gairdner Found. award, 1989. Mem. NAS (fgn. assoc.), Royal Soc. (fgn. mem.), Bavarian Acad. Scis. (corr.), Academia Europea, Acad. d. Wissensch. zu Goettingen, Ukrainian Acad. Sci. (fgn.), Leopoldina Halle. Roman Catholic. Office: Max Planck Inst Biophys Chemistry Am Fassberg 11 37070 Göttingen Germany *

NEHER, ROBERT TROSTLE, biology professor; b. Mt. Morris, Ill., Nov. 1, 1930; s. Oscar Warner and Etha Mae (Trostle) N.; m. Mary Rebecca Timmons, June 12, 1954; children: Kenneth, Jon, Daniel. BA in Sci., Manchester Coll., Ind., 1953; MAT in Biology, Ind. U., 1955, PhD in Botany, 1963; MRE in Counseling, Bethany Sem., Chgo., 1957. Assoc. Christian edn. Ch. of Brethren, Elgin, Ill., 1956; asst. prof., then assoc. prof. biology U. LaVerne, Calif., 1958-62, prof. biology Calif., 1966—, chmn. nat. sci. divsn. Calif., 1978—, provost, v.p. acad. affairs Calif., 2000-01, 2005—07; dir. U. LaVerne Field Sta. Magpie Ranch, Drummond, Mont., 1994—. Dep. dir. Nat. Energy Rsch. and Info. Inst., 1982-88, chair pre-health sci. com., program dir., academic coun., 1985—; aquaculture cons. Bolsa Aquaculture Consortium, 1973-76, AM China Corp., 1981; cons. devel. of in-svc. tchg. tng. in environ. edn. L.A. Pub. Schs.; dir. coll. level curriculum program Montclair High Sch., Van Nuys, Calif. Co-editor: Energy from Biomass, 1979; contbr. articles to profl. jours. City councilman LaVerne City Coun., 1976-84, mayor pro tem, 1980-84; commr. L.A. County Watershed Commn., 1976-91; bd. dirs. Pomona Valley Youth Svcs.; juvenile divsn. chmn. 1978-79; chmn. San Gabriel Valley Get-About Transp. Bd., 1980-84; mem. L.A. County Solid Waste Curbside Recycling Task Force, 1980-82; chmn. La Verne City Commn. on Environ. Quality, 1972-75; mem. La Verne City Planning Commn., 1966-72; moderator La Verne Ch. of Brethren, 1966-75, chmn. bd. 1977-80, mem. ch. bd. dirs., 1966-84; trustee, officer San Gabriel Valley Mosquito and Vector Control Dist., 1991—. Recipient Els Johnson Cmty. Svc. award, U. La Verne, 2003, Disting. Prof. award, U. LaVerne, 2005, 50 Yr. Svc. Recognition, 2008; named Outstanding Tchr. of Yr., La Verne Coll., 1969—70;, NSF grantee, 1960—61, NSF faculty fellow, Ind. U., Bloomington, 1961—62. Mem. AAAS (life mem), Am. Soc. Plant Taxonomists, Calif. Bot. Soc., San Bernardino County Mus. Assn., Audubon Soc., Sierra Club, Nat. Geog. Soc., Sigma Xi. Office: U La Verne Natural Science Divsn 1950 3rd St La Verne CA 91750 4401 Office Phone: 909-593-3511 ext. 4601. Business E-Mail: rneher@laverne.edu.

NEHLIL, JACQUES, neurologist, educator; b. May 7, 1917; MD, Paris, 1946. Cert. tchr. neurology. Clin. head infectious disease, Paris, 1946—47; clin. head nervous diseases, 1947—49; dept. head hospitable Faculty Medicine, Paris, 1960; intern Hosps. Paris, 1940; clin. tchg. dir. Paris, 1972; head Dr. neurology Psychiatry Svc. Hosp. Ctr. Argentina, 1960. Author: (book) The Streptomycin, 1948. Recipient Neurology award, Med. Boarding Sch., 1970. Mem.: Am. Acad. Neurology, Psychol. Soc. (elder treas.), French Soc. Neurosurgery (partner member 1959—). Home: 8 Sq Alboni Paris 75016 France

NEIBART, RICHARD MICHAEL, cardiovascular and thoracic surgeon; b. NYC, Nov. 15, 1956; s. Emil and Sheila (Sperber) N.; m. Denise Foley, Sept. 24, 1988; 1 child, Samantha Rose. BA, U. Pa., 1978; MD, Mt. Sinai Sch. Medicine, 1982. Diplomate Am. Bd. Surgery, Am. Bd. Thoracic Surgery. Intern, resident St. Vincent's Hosp., NYC, 1982-87; fellow U. Miami-Jackson Meml. Hosp., Miami, 1987-89; cardiovascular and thoracic surgeon Morristown (N.J.) Meml. Hosp., 1989—, Overlook Hosp., Summit, N.J., 1989—. Fellow ACS, Am. Coll. Cardiology, Am. Coll. Chest Physicians, Soc. Thoracic Surgeons; mem. AMA. Office: Mid Atlantic Surg Assn 100 Madison Ave Morristown NJ 07960-6136 *

NEIBERGER, RICHARD EUGENE, pediatrician, nephrologist, educator; b. Onaga, Kans., Nov. 16, 1947; s. Earl Edward and Margaret Bell (Grim) N.; m. Mary June Chamberlin, Oct. 31, 1971; children: Ami, Eric, Chris, Robert. BS in Physics, U. Ctrl. Fla., 1971; PhD, U. Louisville, 1979, MD, 1982. Diplomate Am. Bd. Pediat., Nat. Bd. Med. Examiners. Intern, then resident in pediat. Albert Einstein Coll. Med., Bronx, N.Y., 1982-85, fellow in pediat. nephrology, 1985-88; asst. prof. U. Fla. Coll. Med., Gainesville, 1988-93, assoc. prof., 1993—; med. dir. pediatrics Renal Stone Disease Clinic, 1996—. Assoc. med. dir. Children's Kidney Ctr., Gainesville, 1989—; co-investigator on 7 rsch. studies, dir. Pediatric Rsch. Stone Disease Clin. U. Fla., rsch. peer rev. com. Am. Heart Assn., 1997-99; physician advisor Fla. Med. Quality Assurance, Tampa, 1994-2002; pres. Coll. Medicine Faculty Coun., 2008-09; vice chair, UF IRB, 2001. Contbr. articles to profl. jours. Pres. U. Fla. Coll. Med. Faculty Coun., 2008; mem., vice chairman Organ Transplant Adv. Com., Fla.; active Children's Home Soc., Gainesville, 1994—2002, Ronald McDonald House, 1996—2007. Named one of Best Drs. in Am., Best Drs. in Fla., Best Pediatricians in Am.; grantee, Colnvest, Bethesda, Md., 1995—2004. Mem. AMA, Fla. Med. Assn., So. Med. Assn., Am. Soc. Nephrology, Internat. Pediat. Nephrology Assn., Am. Soc. Pediat. Nephrology, Fla. Soc. Pediat. Nephrology (pres. 1998). Republican. Methodist. Avocations: camping, skiing, travel. Office: HD 216 Univ Fla Coll Med Pediats 1300 Archer Rd Gainesville FL 32610-0296 Personal E-mail: rienne@aol.com. Business E-Mail: neibere@peds.ufl.edu.

NEIFELD, JAMES PAUL, surgical oncologist; b. Paterson, NJ, June 5, 1948; s. Herbert S. and Elinor (Charney) N.; m. Ramona S. Simmons, Apr. 27, 1985; children: Emily Claire, Jillian Rose. Student, Lafayette Coll., 1965-68; MD, Med. Coll. Va., 1972. Intern Med. Coll. Va., Richmond, 1972-73, resident in surgery, 1973-74, 76-78, asst. prof. surgery, 1978-82, assoc. prof., 1982-86, prof., 1986—, vice-chair dept. surgery, 2002—03, Stuart McGuire prof. and chair, dept. surgery, 2003—. Lt. comdr. USPHS, 1974-76. Office: PO Box 980645 Richmond VA 23298-0645 Office Phone: 804-827-1033.

NEIL, JEFFREY JOSEPH, medical educator; b. Cleve., Oct. 16, 1955; MD, PhD, Wash. U. Sch. Medicine, 1984. Prof., neurology, pediat. and radiology Wash. U. Sch. Medicine, 1989—. Fellow: Internat. Soc. Magnetic Resonance Medicine; mem.: Soc. Neurosci., Child Neurology Soc. Office: Washington University Sch Medicine Saint Louis MO 63105 Office Fax: 314-454-2523. Business E-Mail: neil@wustl.edu.

NEIL, SANDRA EILLEEN SILVERBERG, clinical and family psychologist; b. NYC, Sept. 30, 1945; d. Marcus and Pearl (Bloom) Glickfeld; m. Robert Silverberg; children: Gerard David, Simonne Elizabeth, Julien Richard, Shari Beth Silverberg. BA, LaTrobe U., Melbourne, Australia, 1974, BEd in Counseling, 1976; MA in Clin. Psychology, U. Melbourne, 1986, PhD in Medicine, 1993. Registered clin. and forensic psychologist 1979, cert. family therapist The Virginia Satir Global Network (formerly AVANTA), 1987. Rsch. asst. dept. ednl. psychology U. Melbourne, 1965—68; clin. psychologist Janefield Hosp., Melbourne, 1975—77, Prince Henry Hosp., Melbourne, 1977—79, Cairnmillar Inst., Melbourne, 1979—83; pvt. practice Melbourne, 1983—; clin. psychologist St. Vincent's Hosp., Melbourne, 1986—93; clin. psychologist and family therapist, founding dir. Satir Centre Australia, Armadale, Victoria, Australia, 1993—. Forensic psychologist Civil County & Supreme Ct., Melbourne, 1976—87; media psychologist, 1977—; sworn marriage counsellor Atty. Gen.'s Dept., Melbourne, 1978—. Author: The Persistence of Obesity, 1986, The Psychodynamics of Obesity, 1993, The Family Chessboard, 1995; editor: A Matter Of Life: Psychological Theory, Research And Practice, 1999; author: A Journey Through Three Continents And Four Generations: A Family Reconstruction, 2001. Active Pres.'s Club Arts Australia. Fellow: Australian Psychol. Soc. (chmn. pub. and media rels. Victorian br. 1983—2004); mem.: ACP, APA, Pres. Club Art Ctr. (Melbourne), Internat. Assn. Applied Psychology, Internat. Coun. Psychologists (chair, Internat. Rels. and Human Rights Interest Group 1990—, pres. 1997—2000, World Area chair coord. 2000—07, 2009—), Internat. Acad. Family Psychology (Australian nat. rep. 1997—), Ptron Melbroune Theatre Co., Patron Opera Australia. Office: Satir Centre of Australia Suite 2 1051-A/B High St Armadale VIC 3143 Australia Office Phone: 61398247755. Office Fax: 61398247865. Personal E-mail: office@satiraustralia.com. Business E-Mail: drneil@satiraustralia.com.

NEILAN, AIDAN JOSEPH, radiologist; b. Galway, Ireland, Sept. 30, 1923; arrived in U.S., 1950; s. John and Honoria Killeen Neilan; m. Nuala Mary McCarthy, June 1, 1959; children: Katherine Honoria, Rosemary Collette, David Aidan. MD, Nat. U. Ireland, 1948. Diplomate Am. Bd. Radiology. Intern New Rochelle Gen. Hosp., 1950—51; resident Wadsworth VA Hosp., 1970—74; chief orthop. radiology Wadsworth Hosp., LA; prof. radiology UCLA, LA, 1979, prof. emeritus. Pres., CEO AJNCO, Inc., LA, 1958. Capt. US Army, 1953—55, France. Mem.: AMA, Irish Med. Assn., Brit. Med. Assn. Republican. Roman Cath. Avocations: piano, swimming, reading. Home: 30639 Rue Langlois Rancho Palos Verdes CA 90275 Personal E-mail: aneilan@verizon.net.

NEILSON, ERIC GRANT, physician, educator, health facility administrator; b. Bklyn., Sept. 14, 1949; s. Jack Drew and Lynette Elsie (Lundquist) N.; m. Linda Roe Apolzon, May 27, 1972; children: Tinsley, Sigrid. BS magna cum laude, Denison U., 1971; MD magna cum laude, U. Ala., 1975; MA (hon.), U. Pa., 1987. Asst. prof. U. Pa., Phila., 1980-87, assoc. prof., 1987-91, prof., 1991-98, C. Mahlon Kline prof., 1993-98, chief renal-electrolyte & hypertension divsn. dept. medicine, 1988-98; Hugh Jackson Morgan prof., chmn. dept. medicine Vanderbilt U. Med. Ctr., Nashville, 1998—2010, sr. prof. medicine Thomas Fearn Frist. Attending physician Hosp. of U. Pa., 1980-98; physician-in-chief Vanderbilt U. Hosp., 1998—; cons. in field. Med. editl. bds. on sci. jours.; assoc. editor Kidney Internat., 1997-2006; editor-in-chief Jour. Am. Soc. Nephrology, 2007-; contbr. numerous articles to profl. jours. Chmn. med. adv. bd. Lupus Found. of Phila., 1985-95; chmn. pathology A study sect. NIH, Bethesda, Md., 1990-92; chmn. grant rev. com. Nat. Kidney Found. of Delaware Valley; mem. adv. coun. NIDDK, NIH; mem. bd. sci. advisors Polycystic Kidney Found., 1997-2000; mem. postdoctoral fellowship com. Howard Hughes Med. Inst., 1997-2000. Recipient Clin. Scientist award Am. Heart Assn., 1980, Young Investigator award Am. Soc. Nephrology/Am. Heart Assn., 1985, Established Investigator award Am. Heart Assn., 1985-90, President's medal Am. Soc. Nephrology, 1994, AN Richard Disting. Achievement award U. Pa., 1998, John P. Peters award, Am. Soc. Nephrology, 2005; named Disting. Alumnus, U. Ala., Birmingham, 2006. Fellow: ACP; mem.: Internat. Soc. Nephrology (treas. 2003—), Assn. Prof. Medicine (chmn. rsch. com. 2000—02, named Robert H. Williams Disting. Chmn. 2010), Assn. Subsplty. Profs. (pres. 1994—96, Disting. Prof. award 2003), Am. Assn. Immunologists, Am. Clin. Climatol. Assn., Am. Soc. Nephrology (John P. Peters award 2005), Assn. Am. Physicians, Am. Soc. Clin. investigation. Mem. Soc. Of Friends. Office: Vanderbilt U Med Ctr Dept Medicine D3100 Med Ctr N Nashville TN 37232-0001 Office Phone: 615-322-3146. Business E-Mail: eric.neilson@vanderbilt.edu.

NEIMAN, JOSEPH BRUCE, dermatologist, hair transplant surgeon, educator; b. NYC, July 28, 1947; s. Nathan and Sarah Neiman; m. Karen Marcia Simon, Aug. 31, 1975. BA, NYU, 1968; MD, U. Tenn., 1972. Intern Brown U., Providence, 1973—74; resident SUNY, Buffalo, 1974—78, chief resident, 1977; dir. adult health svcs., head cmty. health screening Erie County Health Dept., Buffalo, 1975—76; pvt. practice, 1978—79, Williamsville, NY, 1980—. Mem. staffs Buffalo Gen. Hosp., Millard Fillmore Hosp., Buffalo,, Sisters of Charity Hosp., Buffalo; clin. asst. prof. dept. dermatology SUNY, Buffalo, 1980—; cons. USPHS, Buffalo, 1979—81. Fellow: Am. Acad. Dermatology; mem.: AMA, NY State Med. Soc., Erie County Med. Soc., Buffalo-Rochester Dermatol. Soc., NY State Soc. Dermatology, N.AM. Soc. Phlebology, Am. Soc. Dermatologic Surgery, Internat. Soc. Hair Restoration Surgery, Internat. Soc. Dermatologic Surgery. Office: Neiman Ctr for Dermatology & Hair Transplantation 1140 Youngs Rd Williamsville NY 14221-3625 Home: 134 Cape Hatteras Walk East Amherst NY 14051 Office Phone: 716-688-0011, 716-688-0020. Personal E-mail: jneimanmd@aol.com, neimanstaf@aol.com.

NEIMS, ALLEN HOWARD, pediatrician, educator, dean, researcher; b. Chgo., Oct. 24, 1938; s. Irving Morris and Ruth (Geller) N.; m. Myrna Gay Robins, June 18, 1961; children: Daniel Mark, Susan Roberta, Nancy Elizabeth. BA, BS, U. Chgo., 1957; MD, Johns Hopkins U., 1961, PhD, 1966. Intern, resident in pediatrics Johns Hopkins Hosp., 1961-62, 66-68; research asso. Lab. Neurochemistry, NIH, 1968-70; asst. prof. physiol. chemistry and pediatrics Johns Hopkins Med. Sch., 70-72; assoc. prof. McGill U., 1972-77, prof. pharmacology and pediatrics, 1977-78; dir. Roche developmental pharmacology unit, 1972-78; prof., chmn. dept. pharmacology and therapeutics, prof. pediatrics U. Fla., Gainesville, 1978-89, dean Coll. Medicine, 1989-96, prof. pharmcology, pediat., 1996—2007; dir. Ctr. for Spirituality and Health, 2002—07, prof. emeritus, 2007—. Dir. Ctr. Spirituality and Health; Fulton Bequest prof. U. Melbourne, Australia, 1974; mem. human embryology and devel. study sect. NIH, 1979-83; sci. cons. Can. Found. for Study of Sudden Infant Death, 1974-77, Nat. Soft Drink Assn., 1976-78, Internat. Life Scis. Inst., 1978-89; bd. sci. counsellors Nat. Inst. Child Health and Human Devel., 1984-89. Contbr. chpts. to books, articles to med. jours. Served to comdr. USPHS, 1968-70. NIH, Can. Med. Research Council grantee. Mem. Can. Assn. Research in Toxicology (pres. 1976-78), Am. Soc. Pharmacology and Exptl. Therapeutics (past mem. exec. coms. clin. pharmacology and drug metabolism), Am. Pediatric Soc., Am. Acad. Pediatrs. Democrat. Jewish. Office: U Fla Coll Medicine PO Box 100267 Gainesville FL 32610-0267 Office Phone: 352-392-0687. Personal E-mail: ahneims@aol.com. Business E-Mail: ahneims@ufl.edu.

NEIS, ARTHUR VERAL, construction material company executive; b. Lawrence, Kans., May 30, 1940; s. Veral Herbert and Louise (Schlegel) N.; m. Fleeta Weigel, Apr. 12, 1969 (dec. 1999); children: Frederich Arthur, Benjamin Jason, Sarah Louise. BS in Bus., U. Kans., 1962, MS in Acctg., 1963. CPA, Kans., Iowa. Mgmt. cons. Arthur Andersen & Co., Kansas City, Mo. and Mpls., 1963-74; chief corp. acctg. Carlson Co., Mpls., 1974-76; contr. The Fullerton Cos., Mpls., 1976-78; asst. treas. Fru-Con Corp., St. Louis, 1978-80, asst. contr., 1981, contr., 1982-86; corp. contr. LCS Holdings, Inc. (Weitz Corp. and Subs.), Des Moines, 1986-87, v.p., treas., CFO, 1987—2007, v.p., treas., CFO, mem. exec. com., 1995—2007, also bd. dirs., trustee retirement plan; treas., CFO Weitz Co., Des Moines, 1987-93, Life Care Svcs. LLC, Des Moines, 1987—2007; pres. Alliance Minerals N.Am., LLC, 2007—. Adv. group Nat. Assn. Ins. Com., 1990—93; treas., exec. com. bd. Villa de Maria Montessori Sch., St. Louis, 1984—86; trustee Fin. Execs. Rsch. Found., 1994—2000, chair audit com., 1997—98, vice chair rsch., 1998—2000, chmn., 2000—01; mem. internat. acctg. stads. bd. working group Internat. Fin. Reporting Stads., 2005—08; trustee Plymouth Congl. Ch., 1997—97, found. trustee, 1998—2001, chair, 2000—01; active Des Moines Poetry Festival, 2000—04, treas. bd. dirs., 2003—04; bd. dirs. Inst. Humane Studies, George Mason U., Fairfax, Va., 1971—2006, exec. com., 1975—83, chmn., 1978—83; bd. dirs. Lake Country Sch., Mpls., 1973—78, Alliance for Arts and Understanding, co-chair, 1993—96, bd. trustees, 1993—2002, chair, 1996—2002. Recipient Amb. award, Iowa Asian Alliance, 2004; named to Bus. and Industry Hall Fame, AICPA, 2007. Mem. AICPA (pvt. co. fin. pvt. task force 2004, mem. task force pvt. co. reporting generally accepted acctg. practices 2004, mem. nominating com. 2006—07), Kans. Soc. CPAs, Iowa Soc. CPAs, Fin. Execs. Inst. (bd. dirs. Iowa chpt. 1986, 88-94, sec. 1988-90, v.p. 1990-91, pres. 1991-92, com. on pvt. co. reporting stds. 2004—), U. Kansas Mus. Art(Adv bd., 2008-) Avocations: history, Asian art. E-mail: veral01@att.net.

NEL, LEONORA, occupational therapist; b. Port Elizabeth, June 6, 1974; BS in Occupl. Therapy, U. Pretoria, 1997. Head dept. occupl. therapy Pretoria Sch. Learners with Cerebral Palsy, 2001—, rschr., 2006. Avocations: music, dance. Office: 2 Dr Savage Rd Gezina Pretoria Gauteng 0031 South Africa Office Fax: 012-323 0347. Business E-Mail: buildingtomorrow@workmail.co.za.

NELDAM, STEEN, physician; b. Copenhagen, Mar. 13, 1949; MD, U. Copenhagen, 1975, DMS, 1984. Physician, gen. practice, 1984—. Asst. prof., 1994. Contbr. articles to profl. publs. Mem.: Danish Soc. GCP. Avocation: boating. Office: Rødovre Centrum 294 Rødovre Copenhagen 2610 Denmark Office Fax: 4536702069. Business E-Mail: neldam@dadlnet.dk.

NELIGAN, PETER C., plastic surgeon, educator; b. July 20, 1952; married; 2 children. BA, U. Dublin, Trinity Coll., 1973, MBBCh, 1975. Cert. Ont., 1985. Clin. fellow, plastic surgery The Hosp. for Sick Children, Toronto, Canada, 1983—84, rsch. fellow, plastic surgery, 1984—85, assoc. staff surgeon, 1995, rsch. project dir., rsch. inst., 1995; clin. fellow, microvascular surgery Toronto Gen. Hosp., Canada, 1985; clin. burn fellow The Ross Tilley Burn Ctr., Wellesley Hosp., Toronto, Canada, 1986; dir. The Ross Tilley Burn Ctr., The Wellesley Hosp., Toronto, Canada, 1992—93; attending plastic surgeon Laurentian Hosp., Sudbury, Canada, 1987—91, Sudbury Gen. Hosp., Canada, 1987—91, Sudbury Meml. Hosp., Canada, 1987—91, The Wellesley Hosp., Toronto, Canada, 1991—93, assoc. staff, 1993—2000; asst. prof., dept. surgery U. Toronto, Canada, 1991—97, chair, divsn. plastic surgery, 1996, assoc. prof., dept. surgery, 1997—2002, prof., dept. surgery, 2002—07; attending plastic surgeon The Toronto Hosp., Canada, 1993—2007, dep. head, divsn. plastic surgery, 1994—96; assoc. staff surgeon Mt. Sinai Hosp., Toronto, Canada, 1993; cons., dept. surg. oncology Princess Margaret Hosp., Toronto, Canada, 1995, Wharton chair in reconstructive plastic surgery, 1999; prof. surgery U. Wash., 2007—. Mem. editl. bd. Can. Jour. of Plastic Surgery, 1996—, Annals of Plastic Surgery, 2002—, Jour. of Reconstructive Microsurgery, 2002—, Brit. Jour. of Plastic Surgery, 2003—, editor-in-chief Jour. of Reconstructive Microsurgery, —. Fellow: Royal Coll. Physicians and Surgeons of Can., Am. Coll. Surgeons (mem., adv. com. on plastic and maxillofacial surgery 2000—03), Royal Coll. Surgeons Ireland; mem.: Plastic Surgery Ednl. Found. (nominating com. mem. 2002—, joint outcomes com. mem. 2002—, pres.), Ontario Soc. Plastic Surgery, Am. Burn Assn., Can. Med. Protective Assn., Irish Assn. Plastic Surgeons, Internat. Soc. for Burn Injuries, Can. Med. Assn., World Soc. Reconstructive Microsurgery (adv. coun. mem. 2001—), Plastic Surgery Rsch. Coun. (Snyder Award 1998, Hardesty Award 2000), Internat. Confederation for Plastic Reconstructive and Aesthetic Surgery, Internat. Microsurg. Soc., Ontario Med. Assn., N.Am. Skull Base Soc. (program com. mem. 2003—, v.p. 2007—08, pres.-elect), Can. Soc. Plastic Surgeons, Am. Soc. Plastic and Reconstructive Surgeons (mktg. com. mem. 1999—2002, scientific program com. mem. 1999—, bd. dirs. 2001—, ethics com. mem. 2003—, Certificate of Merit, Investigator award 1984), Am. Soc. for Reconstructive Microsurgery (nominating com. mem. 1999—2001, membership com. mem. 1999—, program com. mem. 2001—, pres.-elect), Am. Assn. Plastic Surgeons (comm. com. mem. 1999—), Inst. Med. Sci. Office: U Wash Med Ctr / Dept Surgery 1959 NE Pacific St Box 356410 Seattle WA 98195-6410 Office Phone: 206-543-5516. Office Fax: 206-543-8136. E-mail: pneligan@u.washington.edu.

NELKEN, NICOLAS ANTHONY, surgeon; b. LA, Apr. 8, 1955; MD, U. Calif., San Francisco, 1982. Pvt. practice, 1995—2003; asst. prof. surgery U. Calif., San Francisco, 1992—95, clin. asst. prof. surgery, 1995; vascular surgeon Kaiser Permanent Hawaii, 2003—, chief endovascular, 2005. Named one of Best Drs. in Am., Best Doctors Inc. Fellow: ACS; mem.: Western Vascular Soc., Internat. Soc. Endovascular Specialists, Alpha Omega Alpha. Avocations: painting, music. Office: Vascular Therapy 2B Kaiser Hosp 32 Honolulu HI 96819 Business E-Mail: nicolas.a.nelken@kp.org.

NELKIN, BARRY DAVID, oncology researcher and educator; b. New Orleans, Dec. 12, 1951; s. Joseph William and Bertha (Washastrom) N.; m. Deborah Ann Medetsky, June 4, 1975; children: Moshe, Aryeh, Yehuda, Esther, Yisroel, Rivka, Bina, Yaakov, Miriam, Shira. BS, Johns Hopkins U., 1972; PhD, George Washington U., 1979. Postdoctoral fellow Johns Hopkins U. Sch. Medicine, Balt., 1979—82, instr. oncology, 1982—84, asst. prof., 1984—90, assoc. prof., 1990—2004, prof., 2004—. Mem. ad hoc study sect. U.S. Nat. Cancer Inst., Bethesda, 1989-; grant reviewer Dutch Cancer Soc., 1990, VA, 1990; co-founder Internat. Thyroid Oncology Group. Author: (with others) Tumor Cell Heterogeneity, vol. 4, 1982, Progress in Nonhistone Protein Research, 1985; editor: Genetic Mechanisms in Multiple Endocrine Neoplasia Type 2, 1996; mem. editl. bd. oncology rep., 1997-98; contbr. articles to profl. jours. Nat. Cancer Inst. grantee, 1988-. Mem. Am. Assn. Cancer Rsch., Am. Soc. Microbiology. Achievements include the cloning of human calcitonin gene; demonstration of oncogene mediated differentiation of medullary thyroid carcinoma cells; isolation of ras oncogene responsive transcriptional element in human calcitonin gene; cloning of human BARX2 and RREB transcription factor genes. Home: 3831 Labyrinth Rd Baltimore MD 21215-1505 Office: Johns Hopkins Sch Medicine 1650 Orleans St Baltimore MD 21231 Home Phone: 410-358-4975; Office Phone: 410-955-8506. Business E-Mail: bnelkin@jhmi.edu. *

NELLIGAN, MAURICE JOHN, psychologist; b. Phila., Dec. 11, 1926; arrived in Mex., 1960; s. Maurice and Helen Louise (Provost) Nelligan; m. Ramona Angelica Loza-Medina, June 5, 1964; 1 child, Maurice. BA, Boston Coll., 1950; MA, Boston U., 1957; D Psychology, Nat. U. Mex., Mexico City, 1965. Diplomate psychology, lic. Prof., coord. psychology dept. Monterrey (Mex.) Inst. Tech., 1965-70; owner, dir. Human Devel. Ctr., Mexico City, 1971-82; program dir. Yalentay, Cuernavaca, Mexico, 1983-89; chief counselor Pizarro Clinic, LA, 1990-92; owner, dir. Stress Mgmt., Mexico City, 1993-97; prof., tech., cons. Cisle, Mexico City, 1996—; pres., owner Inst. of Motivation and Leadership, Mexico City, 1999—. Cons. Productivity Ctr., Monterrey, 1965—70, Channel-13 TV, Mexico City, 1971—82, Inst. Latin Am. Integration, Mexico City, 1973—76, Radio Centro, Mexico City, 1975—82; cons. to pres. Radio Mex., 2002—05, Banobras, 2007—09, Conduset, 2010—11. Author: The Art of Reading, 1976, The Other Side of Machismo, 1982, A Guide to Good Living, 1995 (Gold medal, 1996), The Funny Mexican, 1996, How to Catch a Husband, 1999, Authentic Leadership, 2001, Changing Bad Habits, 2005, Visions of Glory, 2007, How to Kick Drugs, 2008, Leadership in a Few Words, 2010, others. Bd. dirs. Juvenile Ctrs., Mexico City, 1978—82, Inst. Latin Am. Integration, Mexico City, 1994—96; active Families Against Drugs, Mexico City, 1993—97. Lt. USCG, 1952—54. Recipient Gold medal, Assn. Authors and Composers, Mexico City, 1985, diploma, Mexican Psychol. Assn., Mexico City, 1981. Mem.: APA, Univ. Club Mex. Democrat. Avocations: music, organ, piano. Home: Col Malinche Norte 92 # 4229 07899 Mexico City Mexico Home Phone: (5255) 5186-4372; Office Phone: (5255) 5551-0186. Personal E-mail: mxnelligan@yahoo.com.

NELSON, AUDREY MAY, physician; b. Austin, Minn., Apr. 1, 1940; d. Glen Stanley and Clara May (Torgerson) N. BA, U. Minn., Mpls., 1962, BS, 1963, MD, 1965. Diplomate in internal medicine and rheumatology Am. Bd. Internal Medicine. Assoc. cons. Mayo Clinic, Rochester, Minn., 1972, cons. in internal medicine and rheumatology, 1972—2002; instr. medicine Mayo Med. Sch., Rochester, 1973—76, from asst. prof. to assoc. prof. medicine, 1976—2000, prof., 2000—02, prof. emeritus, 2002—, chair pediat. rheumatology, 1993—2001; cons. staff Shriners Hosp. for Children, Mpls., 1985—2006. Bd. govs. Mayo Clinic, 1982-89; trustee Mayo Found., 1982-93, v.p., 1989-92. Trustee Christ United Meth. Ch., Rochester, 1995—2002, vice chair, 1999—2001, chair, 2001—02. Recipient Woman of Achievement award YWCA, Alumni Recognition award U. Minn. Alumni Med. Soc., 2002; named Woman Physician of Yr., Alpha Epsilon Iota. Master: Am. Coll. Rheumatology; fellow: ACP, Am. Coll. Pediat., Am. Coll. Rheumatology (bd. dirs. 1995—99, master 2006, Disting. Svc. award 2002); mem.: AMA (del. 1984—2002), Am. Group Practice Assn. (trustee 1991—96, v.p. 1995, pres.-elect 1996), Am. Med. Group Assn. (chair elect 1996—97, bd. dirs. 1996—99, chair bd. dirs. 1997—98), Minn. Med. Assn. (trustee 1985—2002, Disting. Svc. award 1999), Phi Beta Kappa, Alpha Omega Alpha. Avocation: sailing. Office: Mayo Clinic 200 1st St SW Rochester MN 55905-0002 Home: 3471A Sunset Key Cir Punta Gorda FL 33955-1973

NELSON, CHRISTOPHER GRANT, dermatologist; b. Peoria, Ill., Feb. 11, 1946; s. Grant Leonard and Shirlee Ann (Brunnenmeyer) N.; m. Mary Jo Donnelly, June 30, 1972; children: Christopher Jr., Andrew Anthony. BS, U. Iowa, 1968, MD, 1971. Diplomate Am. Bd. Dermatology; cert. clin. trial investigator. Intern Ball Meml. Hosp., Muncie, Ind., 1971-72; resident in dermatology U. Tex. Med. Br., Galveston, 1974-77; staff Bayfront Med. Ctr., St. Petersburg, 1977—, St. Anthony's Hosp., St. Petersburg, 1977—; tchr. Bayfront Med. Ctr., 1977—; affiliate assoc. prof. U. South Fla. Coll. Medicine, 1977—; staff Tampa Gen. Hosp., 2001—. Contbr. articles to profl. jours. Vol. Am. Cancer Soc. Mem. ACP, So. Med. Assn., Fla. Med. Assn., Am. Acad. Dermatology (fellow), Am. Soc. Dermatologic Surgery, Soc. Investigative Dermatology, Pinellas County Med. Soc., Fla. West Coast Soc. Dermatology (sec.-treas. 1982-84, pres. 1984-87), Fla. Soc. Dermatologic Surgery, St. Petersburg Yacht Club (bd. dirs. 1989-95, entertainment chmn. 1989-92, house and grounds com. 1987-95), Dragon Club, Masons, Royal Order of Jesters. Presbyterian. Avocations: sailing, scuba diving, photography, amateur ham radio. Office Phone: 727-895-8131.

NELSON, DAVID LOREN, geneticist, educator; b. Washington, June 25, 1956; s. Erling Walter and Marlys Joan (Jorgenson) N.; m. Claudia Jane Hackbarth, July 31, 1982; children: Jorgen William, Erik Alexander. BA, U. Va., 1978; PhD, MIT, 1984. Staff fellow NIH, Bethesda, Md., 1985-86; sr. assoc. Baylor Coll. Medicine, Houston, 1986-89, instr., 1989-90, asst. prof., 1990-94, assoc. prof., 1994-99, prof., 1999—. Dir. Human Genome Ctr., 1995-96. Editor: Genome Data Base, 1992-2000; assoc. editor Genomics, 1994-2002. Mem.: Am. Soc. Human Genetics (sec. 2002—). Achievements include development of Alu PCR; discovery of fragile X syndrome gene (FMR-1), new form of genetic mutation (simple repeat expansion); identification of gene defects in Lowe Syndrome and Incontinentia Pigmenti. Office: Baylor Coll Dept Medicine Molecular & Human Genetics 1 Baylor Plz Houston TX 77030-3411 Personal E-mail: nelson@bcm.edu.

NELSON, FRED RITCHIE TREW, surgeon; b. Washington, Apr. 19, 1941; s. Donald P. and Marjorie Ann (Trew) N.; children: Eric, Geoffrey, Christian; m. Colleen Collins, Sept. 23, 2006. BA, Johns Hopkins U., 1963; MD, U. Md., 1967. Diplomate Am. Bd. Orthopaedic Surgery. Commd. ensign USN, 1966, advanced through grades to comdr.; intern Bethesda Naval Hosp., 1967-68, resident, 1968-72; pvt. practice Rockville, Bethesda, Md., 1975-92; vis. asst. prof. McGill U., Montreal, 1992-94; sr. staff orthopedist Henry Ford Hosp., Detroit, 1994-97, dir. edn. and rsch. dept. orthopaedics, 2003—, dir. Osteoarthritis Ctr., 2005—; fellow joint reconstruction U. Calif., San Diego, 1997—98; major joint surgeon Naval Med. Ctr., 1998—2003. Assoc. prof. health sci. George Washington U., 1984-92; vis. assoc. prof. USUHS, Bethesda, 1985-87; mem. adv. bd. Nat. Exercise and Fitness for Life Ins., Mpls., 1989-95. Author: A Manual of Orthopaedic Terminology, 1977, 7th edit., 2007. Mem. planning bd. Montgomery County Health System Agy., Md., 1980-83. Recipient Founders medal honorable mention Canadian Orthopaedic Rsch. Soc., 1994, New Investigation award Combined Orthopaedic Rsch. Soc., 1995. Fellow Am. Acad. Orthopaedic Surgeons; mem. Soc. for Phys. Regulation Biol. Medicine (pres. 1996-98). Methodist. Business E-Mail: nelson@bjc.hth.edu.

NELSON, GLEN DAVID, health products executive, physician; b. Mpls., Mar. 28, 1937; s. Ralph and Edna S. Nelson; m. Marilyn Carlson, June 30, 1961; children: Diana, Curtis, Wendy. BA, Harvard U., Cambridge, Mass., 1959; MD, U. Minn., 1963. Diplomate Am. Bd. Surgery, also sub-bd. bariatric and peripheral vascular surgery; cert. Am. Bd. Surgery, 1970. Intern Hennepin County Gen. Hosp., Mpls., 1963—64, resident in gen. surgery, 1964—69; staff surgeon Park Nicollet Med. Ctr. (formerly St. Louis Park Med. Ctr.), Mpls.; practiced surgery, 1969—86; chmn., pres. and CEO Park Nicollet Med. Ctr., 1975—86; chmn. and CEO Am. MedCenters, Inc., 1984—86; dir. Medtronic, Inc., 1980—2002, exec. v.p., 1986—88, vice chmn., 1988—2002; chmn., prin. owner GDN Holdings, LLC, Minnetonka, Minn., 2002—. Bd. dirs. Arstasis, Inc., Goji Ltd., Harvard U. Com. on U. Resources, Cardiovascular Systems, Inc., chmn.; Carlson Holdings, Inc., Carlson, Impulse Dynamics, Guided Delivery Sys., Inc., MetaCure, Motorika, Spectrum Dynamics, Johns Hopkins Medicine Bd. of Advisors, Inspire Med. Sys., LLC, chmn.; bd. dirs., trustee Am. Pub. Media/Minn. Pub. Radio; RedBrick Health, RF Dynamics; emeritus clin. prof. surgery, U. Minn, bd. dirs., Inter Valve, Nxthera.

NELSON, JAMES ALONZO, radiologist, educator; b. Cherokee, Iowa, Oct. 20, 1938; s. Joe George and Ruth Geraldine (Jones) N.; m. Katherine Metcalf, July 16, 1966; children: John Metcalf, Julie Heaps. AB, Harvard U., 1961, MD, 1965. Asst. prof. radiology U. Calif., San Francisco, 1972-74; assoc. prof. U. Utah, Salt Lake City, 1974-79, prof., 1979-86, U. Wash., Seattle, 1986-2000, prof. emeritus, 2000—04; ptnr. Integra Ventures, Seattle, 2004. Dir. radiol. rsch. U. Calif./Ft. Miley VA Hosp., 1973—74, U. Utah, 1974—85, U. Wash., 1986—98; mem. bd. sci. advisors NeoVision, 1995—96, Oreg. Life Scis., 1995—; co-founder Circulation, Inc., 1996; mem. adv. panel on non-radioactive diagnostic agts. USP, 1984—96; mem. NIH RSN study sect., 1998—; RSN study sect., 1998—2004. Contbr. chpts. to books, articles to Am. Jour. Roentgenology, Radiology, Investigative Radiology, others. Capt. USAF, 1967-69. John Harvard scholar, 1957-61, James Picker Found. scholar, 1973-77; recipient Mallinkrodt prize Soc. Body Computerized Tomography, 1990, Roscoe Miller award Soc. Gastrointestinal Radiology, 1991. Fellow Am. Coll. Radiology (diplomate); mem. Radiol. Soc. N.Am., Assn. Univ. Radiology. Achievements include patents (with others) for Non-Surgical Peritoneal Lavage, Recursive Band-Pass Filter for Digital Angiography, for Unsharp Masking for Chest Films, Oral Hepatobiliary MRI Contrast Agent, non-surgical myocardial revascularization, magnetic gut motility monitor, k-edge brachy therapy enhancement, self-debriding catheter. Office: Integra Ventures 300 E Pine Seattle WA 98122 Home Phone: 206-523-4546; Office Phone: 206-832-1995. Business E-Mail: jalonzonel@comcast.net, nelson@integraventures.net.

NELSON, JAMES HAROLD, health sciences administrator; b. Gosnell, Ark., Apr. 26, 1936; s. J.D. and Louise (Gann) N.; m. Betty Sue Leonard, Sept. 21, 1974; children: Amelia Rebecca, Rachel Louise. BS, Ark. State U., 1961, MS, 1969; PhD, Okla. State U., 1972. Br. chief US Army Environ. Hygiene Agy., Edgewood, Md., 1972-76; from rsch. area mgr. to div. chief US Army Biomed. R & D Lab., Ft. Detrick, Md., 1976-92; project mgr. applied med. systems US Army Med. Materiel Devel. Activity, Ft. Detrick, Md., 1992-96, dir. & program mgr., combat med. sys., 1996—2000; chief liaison office US Army Med. Rsch. & Materiel Command US Army Med. Dept. Ctr. and Sch., Ft. Sam Houston, Tex., 2000—06, sr. med. cons., dir. combat and doctrine devel., 2006—07; sr. rsch. scientist Battelle Meml. Inst. San Antonio Battelle Ops., 2007—09. Mem. Fed. Work Group Pest Mgmt., Washington, 1977-81; chmn. equipment com. Armed Forces Pest Mgmt. Bd., Washington, 1979-83; cons. dir. engrs. Ft. Detrick, 1976-2000; guest lectr. Acad. Health Scis., U.S. Army, Ft. Sam Houston, Tex., 1986-88. Contbr. articles to profl. jours.; assoc. editor: Jour. Am. Mosquito Control Assn., 1982-88; chmn. editorial bd.: Equipment & Insecticides-Mosquito Control, 1989. With USN, 1954-58. Recipient numerous commendations U.S. Army, Ft. Detrick, 1981-2000, R&D Achievement award Asst. Sec. of the Army, 1988, Order of Mil. Med. Merit, 1992. Mem. AAAS, AMVETS, Am. Pub.

Health Assn., Assn. Mil. Surgeons U.S., Am. Legion, N.Y. Acad. Scis., Sigma Xi (pres. 1987-88). Achievements include patent for far-forward surgical table. Home: 1315 Brook Bluff San Antonio TX 78248-2632 Home Phone: 210-408-0990. Personal E-mail: nelsonjh@sbcglobal.net.

NELSON, JANIE RISH, health facility administrator; b. Mar. 1, 1941; d. William Hubert and Essie Dell (Davis) Rish; m. John Preston Nelson, Aug. 19, 1984. Student, S.W. Miss. Jr. Coll., 1959—61, Stephens Coll., 1981—. Accredited record tech. Admissions clk. Field Hosp., Centreville, Miss., 1963—68, asst. dir. med. records, 1968—73; dir. med. records West Feliciana Parish Hosp., St. Francisville, La., 1976—2000; ret., 2000. Med. records cons. Beverly Enterprises & Centreville Health Care, 1983—84. Mem. U.S. Congl. Adv. Bd. for La., 1985; fund raiser Rep. Com., 1984; mem. nat. adv. bd. Am. Security Coun., 1984—85. Mem.: NAFE, Tumor Registration Assn. La., La. Med. Records Assn., Am. Med. Records Assn., Miss. Sheriffs Assn. (hon.), Civic Club. Republican. Presbyterian. Avocations: reading, public speaking, gardening. Home: PO Box 374 Centreville MS 39631-0374

NELSON, JOHN C., obstetrician, gynecologist; b. 1944; m. Linda Nelson; 8 children. MPH, U. Utah, 1993, MD. Diplomate Am. Bd. Ob-Gyn. Intern Providence Hosp., Portland, Oreg.; resident U. Utah Sch. of Medicine. Charter mem. Prospective Payment Assessment Commn.; dep. dir. Utah's Dept. of Health; leader govs. task force on child abuse and neglect, teenage pregnancy prevention. Com. mem. Utah Domestic Violence adv. com.; former bd. mem. Salt Lake City Boys and Girls Club. Served in US Army. Recipient Light of Learning award Utah State Office of Edn. Fellow Am. Coll. of Ob-Gyn.; mem. AMA (bd. trustees 1994-2006, sec-treas. 2002-04, pres-elect 2004, pres. 2004-05, immediate past pres. 2005-06), Utah Med. Assn. (former pres.), Salt Lake County Med. Soc. (past pres.), Motion Picture Assn. Am. TV Parental Guidelines Monitoring Bd. Office: AMA 515 N State St Chicago IL 60610-4325 Home: 330 Paradiso Ln Centerville UT 84014-2826

NELSON, JOHN WOOLARD, neurology educator, physician; b. Hagerstown, Ind., Mar. 9, 1928; s. John Hans and Marvel May (Woolard) N.; m. Nancy Louise Elam, July 21, 1966; 1 son, John Hancock. AB, Earlham Coll., 1950, MD, Ind. U., 1953. Diplomate Am. Bd. Psychiatry and Neurology. Instr. neurology U. Tenn. Coll. Medicine, 1959-61; asst. prof. neurology W. Va. U. Sch. Medicine, 1961-63; assoc. prof. neurology U. Tenn., 1963-66; assoc. prof. to prof. Med. Coll. Wis., Milw., 1966-72; clin. prof. neurology U. Minn., Duluth, 1972-73; prof., head dept. neurology U. Okla. Coll. of Medicine, Oklahoma City, 1973-88, prof. emeritus neurology, 1989—. Served with M.C. U.S. Army, 1955-56. Mem. Okla. County Med. Soc., Okla. Med. Soc., AMA, Am. Acad. Neurology, Am. Clin. Neurophysiology Soc.

NELSON, JOYCE M., medical association administrator; d. Wesley and Margaret N.; m. John Hansell. BA in English, Secondary Edn., North Park U., Chgo., 1972. Devel. mgr., No. Calif. Chpt. Nat. Multiple Sclerosis Soc., exec. dir., Mid-Am. Chpt. Kansas City, 1985—91, nat. dir. campaign devel. Denver, 1991—94, v.p. chpt. programs, 1994—2000, v.p. field ops., 2000—05, pres., CEO, 2005—. Office: Nat Multiple Sclerosis Soc 900 S Broadway Ste 200 Denver CO 80209 *

NELSON, KAREN, legislative staff member; b. Elgin, Ill. BA, Cornell U., Ithaca, NY; grad. student, Harvard U., Cambridge, Mass. Staff mem. US Commn. on Civil Rights, Fed. Programs Divsn., 1965-66, Office Mgmt. and Budget, 1966-70; chief of office, program planning and evaluation Dept. Health, Edn. and Welfare, 1970-74; profl. staff mem., interstate and fgn. commerce com. US House of Reps., Washington, 1974-75, staff dir., energy & commerce com. subcom. on health & the environment, 1980—, spl. asst., Rep. Henry Waxman, health policy dir., govt. reform com. Democrat. Office: 2204 Rayburn House Office Bldg Washington DC 20515

NELSON, KRISTIN SCHAD, otolaryngology and facial plastic surgeon; b. Ashland, Wis., Jan. 3, 1968; d. John Edward Schad and Lynda Jean Zeise; m. Brent David Nelson, June 23, 2002; children: Lake Mattias, Meadow Monet. BS in Engring. Mechanics, U. Wis., 1990; MS in Engring., U. Ala., 1992; DO, Kirksville Coll. Osteo. Medicine, 1999. Alumni diplomate Kirksville Coll. Osteo. Medicine, 2000. Resident Northeast Regional Med. Ctr., Kirksville, Mo., 1999—2004; clin. asst. prof., divsn. clin. edn. Midwestern U., Ariz. Coll. Osteopathic Medicine, 2008—; otolaryngologist Phoenix, 2007—; cosmetic surgeon Scottsdale, Ariz., 2005—06; cosmetic surgeon, pres. Zen Surgical Aesthetics, Boise, 2006—07; adj. asst. prof. At Still U. Sch. Osteopathine Medicine Ariz., 2010—. Supv. physician free health clinic Golden Gate Cmty. Ctr., Phoenix, 2004—05; vol. physician Kirksville Coll. Osteo. Medicine, Belize, 2000, 2003. Fellow, The Body Sculpting Ctr., Scottsdale, 2004—05. Mem.: Ariz. Soc. Otolaryngology, Am. Osteo. Assn., Am. Acad. Otolaryngology, Am. Osteo. Coll. Ophthalmology and Otolaryngology, Ariz. Osteopathic Med. Assn. (del. bd. trustees, pres. dist. five 2009—11). Avocations: travel, yoga, hiking, running.

NELSON, LEONARD B., ophthalmologist; BA, Columbia Univ., 1968—72; MD, Harvard Med. Sch., 1972—76; MBA, St. Joseph's U., 1995—2000. Diplomate Am. Bd. Ophthalmology. Intern gen. surgery New England Deaconess Hosp., Boston, 1976—77; resident ophthalmology NY Univ., 1977—80; fellow pediatric ophthalmology Children's Hosp. Nat. Med. Ctr. of George Wash. Univ. Med. Ctr., 1980—81; fellow ocular genetics Wilmer Eye Inst. of Johns Hopkins Univ., 1981—82; hops. affliation include/s Children's Hosp. of Phila., Main Line Hosp. Lankenau, Methodist Hosp., St. Christopher's Hosp. for Children, Thomas Jefferson Univ. Hosp., Wills Eye Inst. Named one of America's Top Doctors, Castle Connolly, 2009, Top Doc, Phila. Mag., 2010. Mem.: Am. Acad. of Ophthalmology. Office: Wills Eye Institute Ste 1210 840 Walnut St Philadelphia PA 19107 Office Phone: 215-928-3240. Office Fax: 215-928-3983.

NELSON, LIONEL M., otolaryngologist; BA in Physics, CUNY Queens, 1965; MD, Yale U., 1969. Diplomate Am. Bd. Otolaryngology, 1974. Pvt. practice, otolaryngology-head and neck surgery Lionel M. Nelson, MD, San Jose, Calif., 1974—; clin. faculty Stanford U. Sch. Medicine, Calif., 1986—; co-founder and med. officer Apneon, Inc., Cupertino, Calif., 2003—08; med. advisor Gyrus ENT, Bartlett, Tenn., 2001—05; med. dir. Somnus Med. Technologies, Inc, Sunnyvale, Calif., 1998—2001. Guest lectr. sleep apnea treatments, surg. instrumentation, airway implants. Contbr. articles to profl. jours. Capt. USAFR, 1971—77, col. USAR, 1984—2009, brigade surgeon US Army, 2008—09, Iraq. Recipient Outstanding Tchr. Recognition Award, Am. Acad. Family Practice, 1987—91; Jonas Salk Med. Rsch. Scholar, City of NY, 1965. Fellow: ACS, Am. Acad. Otolaryngology-Head and Neck Surgery; mem.: Soc. U.S. Flight Surgeons, Am. Acad. Sleep Medicine, Alpha Omega Alpha, Phi Beta Kappa. Achievements include patents for Airway Implants for Sleep Apnea Treatment; Radiofrequency surgical instrumentation; invention of Airway implants for sleep apnea; development of Surgical and radiofrequency devices. Office: 2505 Samaritan Dr Ste 510 San Jose CA 95124

NELSON, MARVIN DALE, JR., radiologist, educator; b. Hastings, Nebr., June 16, 1954; s. Marvin Dale Sr. and Patricia J. (Pingenot) N.; m. Mary C. Baron, Sep. 30, 1990; children: Kevin James, Andrew John. BS, MD, Loma Linda U., 1978; MBA, U. So. Calif., 1999. Diplomate Am. Bd. Radiology, Am. Bd. Daignostic Radiology, Am. Bd. Pediat. Radiology, Am. Bd. Neuroradiology. Intern, resident in radiology Loma Linda U. Med. Ctr., 1978-82; fellow in neuroradiology Nat. Hosp. for Nervous Disease, London, 1985-86, Rothschild Founds., Paris, 1986; fellow in pediat. neuroradiology Children's Mem. Hosp., Chgo., 1986-87; asst. prof. radiology Children's Hosp.-USC Sch. Med., 1987-93, assoc. prof., 1993-2001; chmn. dept. radiology Children' Hosp., LA, 1998—, prof., 2001—, John L. Gwinn prof. pediat. radiology, 2002—. Maj. USAF, 1982-85 Recipient Cornelius Dyke award for original rsch. Am. Soc. Radiology, 1990, Gabriel Wilson award for best paper Western Neuroradiol. Soc., 1994, Gold medal, Am. Soc. Pediat. Neuroradiology Fellow Am. Coll. Radiology; mem. Am. Soc. Neurol. Radiology, Am. Soc. Pediat. Neuroradiology (pres. 2004-05), Western Neuroradiog. Soc. (pres. 2001). Office: Children's Hosp 4650 W Sunset Blvd Los Angeles CA 90027-6062 Office Phone: 323-361-4572. E-mail: mdnelson@chla.usc.edu.

NELSON, PAUL D., podiatrist; Attended, Scholl Coll. Podiatric Medicine. Cert. Am. Bd. Podiatric Surgery Examiners. Resident Genesys Regional Med. Ctr., Grand Blanc, Mich.; podiatrist Sacred Heart Hosp., Hosp. Plz. Foot and Ankle Inst. Mem.: Am. Podiatric Med. Assn. Office: Hosp Plz Foot and Ankle Inst Ste 102 3800 Highland Ave Downers Grove IL 60515

NELSON, RICHARD LAWRENCE, JR., surgeon, educator; b. Evanston, Ill., Oct. 11, 1946; s. Richard Lawrence and Mary Jane Nelson; m. Susan Jane Berryman, June 17, 1972; children: Cicely Adams, Jospeh Lawrence, Moira Louise, Eric James, Patrick Matthew. BA, Stanford U., 1968; MD, U. Chgo., 1972. Diplomate Am. Bd. Surgery, Am. Bd. Colon and Rectal Surgery. Prof. surgery U. Ill., Chgo., 1980—2005; asst. prof., epidemiology and biometry U. Ill. Sch. Pub. Health, Chgo., 1987—2005; consult. surgeon Northern General Hospital, Sheffield, South Yorkshire, England, 2005—. Cons. NIH, Bethesda, Md., 1991—2004; cons. consultation on incontinence WHO, 2001, 04; invited lectr. NAS, 1999. Author: (book) Surgery of the Samll Intestine, 1998, 2d edit., 2000; musician: (albums) Championship Brass, 1998, Shaken Not Stirred, 2000; mem.: Champion Brass Band (Champions, NABBA, 1996, 1997, 1998, 2000, 2001, 2002). Past pres. Am. Bd. Colon & Rectal Surgery, past chair, Residency Rev. Com.; co-coordinating editor, colorectal cancer collaborative rev. group mem. Cochrane Collaboration, 2008—, public arbiter, 2009—. Recipient Order of Brass Band World - New Years Honors List, Brass Band World, 2000; named one of Top 25 Cancer Rschrs. in U.S., Am. Cancer Soc., 1996. Fellow: Am. Coll. Surgeons, Assn. Coloproctology of Great Britain & Ireland, Am. Soc. Colon and Rectal Surgery; mem.: European Soc. Coloproctology. Roman Catholic. Achievements include patents for intestinal tubes. Avocations: music, bicycling, skiing, hiking, brass banding. Home: 2651 Hillside Ln Evanston IL 60201-4933 Home Fax: 011441142266986. Personal E-mail: rick.nelson@sth.nhs.uk *

NELSON, RUSSELL MARION, surgeon, educator; b. Salt Lake City, Sept. 9, 1924; s. Marion C. and Edna (Anderson) N.; m. Dantzel White, Aug. 31, 1945 (dec.); children: Marsha Nelson Workman, Wendy Nelson Maxfield, Gloria Nelson Irion, Brenda Nelson Miles, Sylvia Nelson Webster, Emily Nelson Wittwer (dec.), Laurie Nelson Marsh, Rosalie Nelson Ringwood, Marjorie Nelson Helsten, Russell Marion Jr.; m. Wendy Lee Watson, April 6, 2006. BA, U. Utah, 1945, MD, 1947; PhD in Surgery, U. Minn., 1954; ScD (hon.), Brigham Young U., 1970; DMS (hon.), Utah State U., 1989; LHD (hon.), Snow Coll., 1994. Diplomate: Am. Bd. Surgery, Am. Bd. Thoracic Surgery (dir. 1972-78). Intern U. Minn. Hosps., Mpls., 1947, asst. resident surgery, 1948-51; first asst. resident surgery Mass. Gen. Hosp., Boston, 1953-54; sr. resident surgery U. Minn. Hosps., Mpls., 1954-55; practice medicine (specializing in cardiovascular and thoracic surgery), Salt Lake City, 1959-84; staff surgeon LDS Hosp., Salt Lake City, 1959-84, dir. surg. research lab., 1959-72, chief cardiovascular-thoracic surg. div., 1967-72, also bd. govs., 1970-90, vice chmn., 1979-89; staff surgeon Primary Children's Hosp., Salt Lake City, 1960; attending in surgery VA Hosp., Salt Lake City, 1955-84, Univ. Hosp., Salt Lake City, 1955-84; asst. prof. surgery Med. Sch. U. Utah, Salt Lake City, 1955-59, asst. clin. prof. surgery, 1959-66, asso. clin. prof. surgery, clin. prof., 1966-69, research prof. surgery, 1970-84, clin. prof. emeritus, 1984—; staff services Utah Biomed. Test Lab., 1970-84. Dir. tng. program cardiovascular and thoracic surgery at Univ. Utah affiliated hosps., 1967-84; mem. policyholders adv. com. New Eng. Mut. Life Ins. Co., Boston, 1976-80 Contbr. articles to profl. jours. Mem. White House Conf. on Youth and Children, 1960; bd. dirs. Internat. Cardiol. Found.; bd. govs. LDS Hosp., 1970-90, Deseret Gymnasium, 1971-75, Promised Valley Playhouse, 1970-79; mem. adv. com. U.S. Sec. of State on Religious Freedom Abroad, 1996-99. lst lt. to capt. M.C., AUS, 1951-53. Markle scholar in med. scis., 1957-59; Fellowship of Medici Publici U. Utah Coll., 1967; Gold Medal of Merit, Argentina, 1974; named Hon. Prof. Shandong Med. U., Jinan, People's Republic of China, 1985; Old People's U., Jinan, 1986; Xi-an (People's Republic of China) Med. Coll., 1986, Legacy of Life award, 1993. Fellow A.C.S. (chmn. adv. council on thoracic surgery 1973-75), Am. Coll. Cardiology, Am. Coll. Chest Physicians; mem. Am. Assn. Thoracic Surgery, Am. Soc. Artificial Internal Organs, AMA, Dirs. Thoracic Residencies (pres. 1971-72), Utah Med. Assn. (pres. 1970-71), Salt Lake County Med. Soc., Am. Heart Assn. (exec. com. cardiovascular surgery 1972, dir. 1976-78, chmn. council cardiovascular surgery 1976-78), Utah Heart Assn. (pres. 1964-65), Soc. Thoracic Surgeons, Soc. Vascular Surgery (sec. 1968-72, pres. 1974), Utah Thoracic Soc., Salt Lake Surg. Soc., Samson Thoracic Surg. Soc., Western Soc. for Clin. Research, Soc. U. Surgeons, Am., Western, Pan-Pacific surg. assns., Inter. Am. Soc. Cardiology (bd. mgrs.), Phi Beta Kappa, Sigma Xi, Alpha Omega Alpha, Phi Kappa Phi, Sigma Chi. Mem. Ch. of Jesus Christ of Latter-day Saints (pres. Bonneville Stake 1964-71, gen. pres. Sunday sch. 1971-79, regional rep. 1979-84, Quorum of the Twelve Apostles 1984—). Office: 47 E South Temple Salt Lake City UT 84150-1200

NELSON, SYDNEY WALTER (PIP NELSON), geneticist, researcher; b. Harare, Zimbabwe, Apr. 10, 1938; s. Walter Robert and Beatrice Flora Nelson; m. Lynette Nelson, Dec. 9, 1961; children: Lloyd Robert, Grant Lee. BSc in Agr., Natal U., South Africa, 1960; MS, N.C. State U., Raleigh, 1967, PhD, 1968. Maize breeder Fed. Govt. Rhodesia and Nyasaland, Salisbury, 1960—62, Rhodesian Govt., 1962—72, Rhodesian Seed Maize Assn., 1972—76; head plant breeding rsch. CIBA Geigy (SA) Ltd., Isando, South Africa, 1976—88; gen. mgr. summer crops rsch. Sensako Coop Ltd., Delmas, 1988—99; gen. mgr. Nelson Genetics CC, Bryanston, 1999—. Cons. Southeast Asia Maize Breeding Programme CIBA Geigy, Basel, Switzerland, 1985—88; mgmt. bd. mem. Sensako Coop Ltd., Brits, South Africa, 1988—99. Vol. Zimbabwe Air Force Res., 1973—76. Scholar, Rockefeller Found., 1964—66. Mem.: Southern African Plant Breeders Assn. (pres. 1996—98, Roll of Honor 2000), Crop Sci. Soc. Am. (hon.). Achievements include discovery of gene HtN which carries single dominant gene resistance to Northern Leaf Blight; original African breeder of very large volume commercial maize hybrids with sales exceeding 400,000 metric tons; development of a high yielding disease resistant single cross recombinant hybrid, incorporation the human monoclonal antibody 2G12 with potential properties for the prevention of HIV 1 Transmission. Office: Nelson Genetics CC 18 Hunt Rd Bryanston 2021 South Africa Office Phone: 27 82 575 2798. E-mail: pnelson@mweb.co.za.

NELSON, W. JAMES, biology professor, researcher; Prof. biology Stanford U., Calif., prof. molecular & cellular physiology; prin. investigator, Nelson Lab Molecular and Cellular Physiology Stanford U. Sch. Medicine. Contbr. articles to profl. jours. Mem.: Am. Acad. Arts & Sciences. Office: c/o Dept Biology Gilbert Hall Stanford Univ Stanford CA 94305-5020 Business E-Mail: wjnelson@stanford.edu.

NELSON, WILLIAM MYLES, radiologist, consultant; b. Belfast, No. Ireland, Jan. 3, 1968; s. William McClure and Margaret Elizabeth Daphane (Bloomfield) Nelson; m. Jacqueline Louise Small, July 8, 1993; children: Sophie May, Joshua James McClure, Emily Jane. BSc in BioChemistry, Queen's U., Belfast, 1989, MB, BChir, 1992. Houseman Royal Victoria Hosp., Belfast, 1992—93; surgical sr. houseman Antrim Hosp., Northern Ireland, 1993—94, surgical sr. houseman (rotation), 1994—96; specialist registrar radiology Hull and East Yorkshire Tng. Schemce, 1996—2001; cons. radiologist Antrim Hosp., 2001—; clinical dir. radiology, 2004—; chmn. rsch. devel. com., 2005—. Treas. Soc. Radiologists in Tng., 1998—2001; mem. No. Ireland Radiology Tng. Com., 2001—06. Fellow: Royal Coll. Radiologists (clin. tutor 2002—). Home: Downhillybegs House 137 Whitesides Rd Ballymena BT42 2JG Northern Ireland Office: Antrim Area Hospital Services Yard 45 Bush Road BT41 2RL Antrim Northern Ireland E-mail: myles_nelson@yahoo.co.uk.

NELZÉN, OLLE PER, vascular surgeon; b. Stockholm, Apr. 2, 1952; s. Karl-Vilhelm Per and Margit Elsa (Norell) N.; m. Yvonne Margareta Wester, July 9, 1983; children: Oskar, Elias, Sofia. MD, Karolinska Inst., Stockholm, 1978; D of Med. Sci., 1997. Lic. med. doctor; qualified gen. surgeon. Gen. surgeon Ctrl. Hosp., Skövde, Sweden, 1985-91, cons. vascular surgeon, 1992—; vascular surgeon U. Hosp., Malmö, Sweden, 1991-92; dir. Uppsala U. Wound Ctr., 1998-99; dir. leg ulcer rsch. Skaraborg Leg Ulcer Ctr., 1999—; head Skaraborg Vascular Surgery Unit, 2006; assoc. prof., vascular surgery Uppsala U., 2008—, apptd. lectr. vascular surgery, 2009—. Mem. Internat. Com. on Wound Mgmt., 1992—, European Panel on Endoscopic Vein Surgery, 1995—. Author: Patients with Chronic Leg Ulcer, 1997; contbr. articles to profl. jours. Mem. Swedish Med. Assn., Swedish Soc. Surgery and Vascular Surgery (Swedish Vascular award 1992), Soc. Phlebologica Scandinavica (bd. dirs. 1996-2000, chmn. 2000—08, Gunnar Bauer prize 1994), Scandinavian Veuous Forum (pres., 2008-) Avocations: cross-country running, downhill skiing. Home: Vårvägen 25 S-541 33 Skövde Sweden Office: Skaraborg Hosp Leg Ulcer Ctr 541 85 Skövde Sweden Home Phone: 46 500 480732; Office Phone: 46 500 431000. Personal E-mail: olle.nelzen@vgregion.se.

NEMAZIE, SIAMACK, nephrologist, consultant; s. Farrokh and Fazileh Nemazie; m. Ammu Joyce James Gopalan, Nov. 3, 2000. MBBS, Kasturba Med. Coll., Manipal, India, 1998. Diplomate Am. Bd. Internal Medicine, 2004. House officer Rainy Hosp., Madras, 1998—99; resident house officer Apollo Specialty Hosp., Madras, 1999—2000, Harvey Heart Hosp., Madras, 2000—01, 2000—01; resident Brookdale Hosp. and Med. Ctr., Bklyn., 2001—04, chief resident internal medicine, 2003—04, nephrology fellow, 2004—. Hosp. del. Com. Interns and Residents, Bklyn., 2004—05. Named Best First Yr. Resident, Alumni Assn., 2002. Mem.: AMA, ACP, Am. Soc. Hypertension (cert. specialist in clin. hypertension 2005), Am. Soc. Nephrology (assoc.). Achievements include research in platelet dysfunction in hemodialysis patients. Avocation: travel. Office: Brookdale Hosp and Med Ctr Divsn Nephrology 1 Brookdale Plz Brooklyn NY 11236 E-mail: snemazie@hotmail.com.

NEMEC, JOSEF, retired organic chemist, researcher; b. Ostresany, Czechoslovakia, Sept. 7, 1929; came to U.S., 1969; s. Josef Nemec and Marie (Joskova) Nemcova; m. Anna Pastush, Aug. 29, 1975; 1 child, Marketa. MS, Inst. Chem. Tech., Prague, Czechoslovakia, 1954; PhD, Czechoslovak Acad. Scis., Prague, 1958. Organic chemist Inst. Chem. Tech., Prague, 1954-61; sr. rsch. chemist Czechoslovak Acad. Scis., Prague, 1961-69; rsch. fellow in organic chemistry Wayne State U., Detroit, 1969-70; sr. rsch. scientist Squibb Inst. Med. Rsch., New Brunswick, NJ, 1970-75; staff mem. St. Jude Children's Rsch. Hosp., Memphis, 1975-84; sr. scientist Nat. Cancer Inst.-Program Resources, Inc. Cancer R&D Ctr., Frederick, Md., 1984-95; ret., 1995. Adj. prof. med. chemistry U. Tenn., Memphis, 1979-91; external examiner U. Zimbabwe, Harare, 1994—; cons. in field. Contbr. articles to scholarly and profl. jours. Grantee Nat. Cancer Inst., 1975-85. Mem. AAAS, Am. Chem. Soc., Royal Soc. Chemistry, Czechoslovak Soc. Arts and Scis. Achievements include patents in fields of anticancer agents, organic chemicals, semimicroequipment in organic chemistry; research in natural products, synthetic anticancer agents, monosaccharides, experimental semimicrotechniques in organic chemistry.

NEMEC, PAVEL, physician, researcher; b. Nove Mesto na Morave, Czech Republic, Feb. 9, 1971; s. Vladimir Nemec and Miroslava Nemcova; m. Jarmila Hupakova, July 12, 1997; children: Matyas, Anna Sara Nemcova. MD, Charles U., 1995. Sr. physician Eye Clinic, Ctrl. Mil. Hosp., Prague, 1996—; don 1st Sch. Medicine, Charles U., 2004—. Cons. Gen. Health Clinic, Prague, 1998—. Grantee, Elekta AB, 2003—; scholar, Moorfields Eye Hosp., London, 2004. Mem.: Czech Vitreoretinal Soc., Czech Ophthalmology Soc., European Vitreoretinal Soc. Achievements include research in Applications of Leksell Gama Knife in ARMD. Avocations: literature, movies, sports, travel. Office: Eye Clinic Ctrl Mil Hosp U Vojenske Nemocnice Street 1200 169 02 Prague Czech Republic E-mail: pavel.nemec@uvn.cz.

NEMEC, PETR, rheumatologist, consultant; b. Boskovice, Czech Republic, Dec. 4, 1972; s. Maria Nemcova and Alexandr Nemec; m. Vera Cipkova, June 6, 1998; children: Ondrej, Krystof. MD, Faculty Medicine Masaryk U., Brno, Czech Republic, 1997, PhD, 2006. Cert. in Internal Medicine Inst. Health Postgrad. Edn., 2000, in Rheumatology 2004. Fellow internal medicine Hosp. Brno, Novy Liskovec, 1997—99; jr. dr. internal medicine St. Anna's U. Hosp., Brno, 2000—04, cons. rheumatology, 2004—; asst. prof. faculty medicine Masaryk U., 2005—. Mem. accreditation com. Ministry Health Czech Republic, Prague, 2006—. Grant, Grant Agy. Ministry Health, Czech Republic, 2004—06. Mem.: Czech Rheumatology Soc. (life). Avocations: travel, biking. Office: Saint Anna's Univ Hosp Pekarska 53 Brno 65691 Czech Republic Business E-Mail: petr.nemec@fnusa.cz.

NEMEROFF, CHARLES BARNET, neurobiology and psychiatry educator; b. Bronx, NY, Sept. 7, 1949; s. Philip Peace and Sarah (Greenberg) N.; m. Melissa Ann Pilkington, May 24, 1980 (div.); children: Matthew P. (dec. 1997), Amanda P., Sarah-Frances P.; m. Gayle Applegate, June 11, 2001. BS, CCNY, 1970; MS, Northeastern U., 1973; PhD, U. N.C., 1976, MD, 1981. Diplomate Am. Bd. Psychiatry and Neurology; lic. physician, N.C., Ga. Rsch. asst. ichthyology Am. Mus. Natural History, NYC, 1968-71; neurochemistry lab. McLean Hosp., Belmont, Mass., 1971-72; rsch. assoc. surgery Beth Israel Hosp., Boston, 1972-73; tchg. asst. biology Northeastern U., 1972-73; postdoctoral fellow Biol. Scis. Rsch. Ctr., U. N.C., Chapell Hill, 1976-77, rsch. fellow, 1977-83, clin. instr. psychiatry, 1983; resident psychiatry N.C. Meml. Hosp., Chapel Hill, 1981-83; asst. prof. dept. psychiatry and pharmacology Duke U., Durham, NC, 1983-85, assoc. prof. psychiatry, 1985-89, assoc. prof. pharmacology, 1986-89, prof. depts. psychiatry and pharmacology, 1989-91, chief divsn. biol. psychiatry, 1988-91; prof., chmn. dept. psychiatry and behavioral scis. Emory U. Sch. Medicine, Atlanta, 1991—2008, Reunette W. Harris prof. psychiatry and behavioral scis., 1994—2009; leonard M. Miller prof. chmn. dept. psychiatry & behavioral scis. U. Miami, Fla., 2009—; dir. Ctr, Aging U. Miami, 2011—. Vis. prof. physiology Cath. U., Santiago, Chile, 1978; sci. coun. Nat. Alliance for Rsch. Schizophrenia and Depression, 1997—; mem. coun. NIMH, 1999-2002; mem. biomed. rsch. coun. NASA, 2000-03; bd. dirs. George West Mental Health Found., 1999—2009, Cypress Bioscis. Inc., 2001—05, NovaDel Pharma, 2005—. Editor: (with A.J. Prange Jr.) Neurotensin, a Brain and Gastrointestinal Peptide, 1982, (with A.J. Dunn) Peptides, Hormones and Behavior, 1984, (with P.T. Loosen) Handbook of Clinical Psychoneuroendocrinology, Neuropeptides in Psychiatric and Neurological Disorders, 1987, Neuropeptides in Psychiatric Disorders, 1991, Neuroendocrinology, 1992, (with P. Kitabgi) The Neurobiology of Neurotensin, 1992, (with A.F. Schatzberg) Textbook of Psychopharmacology, 1995, 4th edit., 2009, (with A. F. Schatzberg) Recognition and Treatment of Psychiatric Disorders, 1999, The Corsini Encyclopedia of Psychology and Behavioral Science, 3d edit., vols. 1-4, 2001, (with W.E. Craighead) concise edit. 2004, (with Dennis S. Charney) The Peace of Mind Prescription, 2004 (Ken award Nat. Alliance of The Mentally Ill), (with David Purselle and Arthur Jongsmia) The Psychopharmacology Treatment Planner, 2003, (with Jeffrey Kelsey and D. Jeffrey Newport) Principles of Psychopharmacology for Mental Health Professionals 2006; editor-in-chief: Depression, 1993-00, Psychopharmacology Bull., 2001-02, Neuropsychopharmacology, 2001-06; co-editor-in-chief: Critical Revs. in Neurobiology, 1992-01; contbr. chpts. to books and articles and abstracts to profl. jours. Recipient Michiko Kuno award U. N.C., 1978, 79, Merck award for acad. excellence, 1981, Merck award for young investigators Am. Geriatrics Soc., 1985, 2nd prize Anna Monica Found. for Rsch. in Endogenous Depression, 1987, Merit award NIMH, 1987, rsch. prize World Fedn. Socs. Biol. Psychiatry, 1991, Edward J. Sachar award Columbia U., 1993, Edward A. Strecker prize Instnl. Pa. Hosp., 1993, Outstanding Alumni award in health scis. Northeastern U., 1995, Disting. Alumni award U. NC Sch. Medicine, 1999, George Ham Alumni award dept. psychiatry U. NC, 2000, Charles Burlingame prize Inst. Living, 2002, Alumni award U. NC, 2006; grantee Nat. Inst. Aging, 1982-83, NIMH, 1983—, NIDA, 1996-98; predoctoral fellow Schizophrenia Rsch. Found., Soc. Scottish Rite, Lexington, Mass., 1975-76, postdoctoral fellow Nat. Inst. Neurol., Communicative Disorders and Stroke, 1977, Nanaline Duke fellow Duke U. Med. Ctr., 1985-87. Fellow Am. Coll. Neuropsychopharmacology (Mead Johnson Travel award 1982, Efron award 1987, coun. 1993—99, pres. 1997), Am. Coll. Psychiatrists (chmn. contbns. com. 1991-93, 95—, edn. com. 1993-96, 96—, bd. regents 1994-97, 1st v.p. 1999, pres.-elect 2000, pres. 2001, chair sci. program com. 2005-07, 2009, Mood Disorders Rsch. award 1998, Bowis award 1999, Dean award 2004); mem. AAAS, AMA, Soc. Neurosci. (program com. 1993-95), Internat. Soc. Psychoneuroendocrinology (pres. 1993-96, Curt P. Richter award 1985), Internat. Soc. Neuroendocrinology, Internat. Soc. Neurochemistry, Am. Soc. Neurochemistry (Jordi-Folch-Pi award 1987), Endocrine Soc., Soc. Neuroendocrinology, Soc. Biol. Psychiatry (A.E. Bennett award 1979, Gold medal award 1996), Am. Fedn. Clin. Rsch., Am. Pain Soc., Am. Psychiat. Assn. (coun. rsch. 1993-98, 02-04, chmn. 1994-95, bd. dirs. rsch. inst. 1999—2007, chair coun. rsch. subcom. on psychiat. treatments 1999-2003, chair, subcom. rsch. tng. 2006-, Kempf award 1989, Samuel Hibbs award 1991, Rsch. prize 1996, Judson Marmor award, 2008, Vestermark award 2006, Disting. Psychiatrist lectr. Ann. Meeting 1999, 2003, Rsch. Mentoring award 2008), Am. Coll. Physicians (William C. Menninger award 2000), Argentine Assn. Psychoneuroendocrinology (sci. coun.), Nat. Depressive and Manic Depressive Disorders Assn. (vice chair 1996-98, bd. dirs. 1999—2002, chair 1999-2000, Gerald L. Klerman Lifetime Achievement award 1997), Anxiety Disorder Assn. Am. (chmn. sci. adv. bd. 2001-2003), NY Acad. Scis., Am. Found. for Suicide Prevention (sci. adv. bd. 1997—, bd. dirs. 1998—, v.p. 2006, pres. Sci. Coun. 2007—, pres. 2008-,Rsch. prize 2001), Inst. Medicine, Sigma Xi, Alpha Omega Alpha. Democrat. Jewish. Office: University Miami Sch Medicine Dept. Psychaitry & Behavioral Scis 1120 NW 14th St Miami FL 33136 Office Phone: 305-243-6400. Business E-Mail: cnemero@emory.edu, cnemero@med.miami.edu.

NEMOTO, HIROSHI, medical educator; b. Yokosuka, Japan, Mar. 3, 1960; MD, Toho U., 1984, PhD, 1988. Asst. prof. Toho U. Ohashi Med. Ctr., 1988—. Office: 2-17-6 Ohashi Meguro Tokyo 1538515 Japan

NENASHEV, ALEXANDER ANDREEVICH, physiologist, educator, researcher; b. Kuibyshev, Russia, June 12, 1932; s. Andrew Petrovich Nenashev and Maria Ivanovna Nenasheva; m. Tamara Petrovna Marinina, Mar. 18, 1959. Grad. student, Medicine U. Kuibyshev, 1962—65, MD, 1966. Head dept. hyperbolic oxygenation Medicine U. Kuibyshev, 1965—73, dr. medicine, 1973; head dept. normal and pathologic physiology medicine dept. Kabardino-Balkaria's U., Russia, 1973—93; prof. dept. med. diagnostic sys. Samara (Russia) State Aerospace U., 1994—. Cons. Diagnostic Ctr., Samara, 1994—; rschr. in field. Author: Remove the cause of disease, 1998, (monograph) Key to Health, 1997, Functional features and characteristics of erythrocytes of patients with hemorrhagic hemostasiapathies, 2003, Method of decrease of chronicle hypoxia of tissues (Bronze medal Brussels Eureka, 1999). Recipient Golden medal, Brussels, Eureka, 1999, Moscow, 2001, Silver medal, Paris, 2000. Mem.: Russian Acad. Med. and Tech. Sci., Sci. Soc. Path. Physiology, Sci. Soc. Clin. Physiology. Russian Orthodox. Achievements include patents for method of investigation of erythrocytes' mechanical resistance; device for investigation of erythrocytes' mechanical resistance; method of decrease of chronicle hypoxia of tissues; TDI-02 (individual breathing trainer). Avocation: radioamateur. Office: Samara State Aerospace U Moskovskoe shosse 34 Samara 443086 Russia Home: Karla Marksa Pr-Kt 404-5 443091 Samara Samarskaya obl. Russia Personal E-mail: bundov@mail.radiant.ru.

NEOGI, DEVDATTA SUHAS, surgeon, educator; b. Mumbai, Feb. 6, 1976; MBBS, Karnatak Inst. Med. Scis., 2000; MS in Orthop., Bangalore Med. Coll. and Rsch. Inst., DNB, 2005. Sr. resident Goa Med. Coll., 2005—06, All India Inst. Med. Scis., New Delhi, 2006—08; fellow, adult oint reconstruction Nat. U. Hosp., Singapore, 2009; asst. prof. ESI Post Grad. Inst. Med. Scis., Mumbai, 2009—10, K. J. Somaiya Hosp. and Rsch. Ctr., Mumbai, 2011—. Fellow, sports medicine and arthroscopy Korea U. Guro Hosp., Seoul, 2009; fellow, trauma Columbia U. Presbyn. Hosp., 2009. Recipient Lester Lowe SICOT award, Internat. Soc. Orthopaedic Surgery and Traumatology. Master: RCP (Glasgow), RCS (Edinburgh); mem.: Soc. Internationalle de Chirurgie Orthopedique et de Traumatology, Indian Arthroscopy Soc., Indian Fedn. Sports Medicine, Indian Orthopaedic Assn. Avocations: cricket, travel, reading. Home: 1/26 Ambekar Nagar Near ChunaBhatti Mumbai Maharastra 400022 India Personal E-mail: drdevdatt@gmail.com.

NEPPE, VERNON MICHAEL, neuropsychiatrist, behavioral neurologist, psychopharmacologist, writer, phenomenologist, consciousness researcher, forensic specialist, philosopher; b. Johannesburg, Transvaal, Rep. South Africa, Apr. 16, 1951; came to U.S., 1986; s. Solly Louis and Molly (Hesselson) N.; m. Elisabeth Selima Schachter, May 29, 1977; children: Jonathan, Shari. BA, U. South Africa, 1976; MB, BCh, U. Witwatersrand, Johannesburg, 1973, diploma in psychol. medicine, 1976, M in Medicine, 1979, PhD in Medicine, 1981; MD, U.S., 1982. Diplomate Am. Bd. Psychiatry and Neurology, 1994, specialties in psychiatry 1988, geriatric psychiatry 1991, 2001, forensic psychiatry 1994, Am. Bd. Psychol. Specialties in Psychopharmacology, 1991; registered psychiatry specialist U.S., Republic of South Africa, Can.; bd. cert. behavioral neurologist/neuropsychiatrist, 2006. Specialist in tng. dept. psychiatry U. Witwatersrand, Johannesburg, 1974-80; sr. cons. U. Witwatersrand Med. Sch., Johannesburg, 1980-82, 83-85; neuropsychiatry, behavioral neurology, psychopharmacology fellow Cornell U., NYC, 1982—83; divsn. neuropsychology dir. U. Wash. Med. Sch., Seattle, 1986—92; dir. Pacific Neuropsychiat. Inst., Seattle, 1992—; neuropsychiatrist, behavioral neurologist N.W. Hosp., 1992—. Adj. prof. dept. neurology and psychiatry St. Louis U. Sch. of Medicine, dept. psychiatry and human behavior, 1994—; attending physician Overlake Hosp., 1993—; mem. clin. faculty dept. psychiatry and behavioral scis. U. Wash. Med. Sch., 1992-2001; neuropsychiatry cons. South African Brain Rsch. Inst., Johannesburg, 1985—; chief rsch. cons. Epilepsy Inst., N.Y.C., 1989; mem. faculty lectr. Epilepsy: Refining Med. Treatment, 1993-94. Author: The Psychology of Déjà Vu: Have I Been Here Before?, 1983, Innovative Psychopharmacotherapy, 1990, Cry the Beloved Mind: A Voyage of Hope, 1999, How Attorneys Can Best Utilize Their Medical Expert Consultant: A Medical Expert's Perspective, 2006, 2nd edit., 2009, BROCAS SCAN, 1992; (plays) Quakes, 2002, Tomorrow the Earthquake, 2001; Deja Vu: A Second Look, 2006, Deja Vu Revisited, 2006, Deja Vu: Glossary and Library, 2006; contbr. (with others) 64 book chpts.; editor 14 jours. issues; 300 other contbn., contbr. articles to profl. jours. Recipient Rupert Sheldrake prize for rsch. design award New Scientist, 1983, Marius Valkhoff medal South African Soc. for Psychical Rsch., 1982, George Elkin Bequest for Med. Rsch., U. Witwatersrand, 1980; named Overseas Travelling fellow, 1982-83. Fellow Am. Psychiat. Assn. (disting. fellow 2008, US transcultural collaborator diagnostic and statis. manual 1985-86, cons. organic brain disorders 1988-92), Exceptional Creative Achievement Orgn. (exec. dir., disting. prof. 2010), Psychiatry Coll. South Africa (faculty), Royal Soc. South Africa, Royal Coll. Physicians of Can., North Pacific Soc. for Neurology, Neurosurgery and Psychiatry, Coll. Internat. Neuropharmacologicum, Am. Coll. Forensic Examiners; mem. AMA, Parapsychologic Assn., Am. Epilepsy Soc., Soc. Biol. Psychiatry, Can. Psychiat. Assn., Soc. Sci. Exploration, Am. Soc. Clin. Psychopharmacology, Am. Neuropsychiat. Assn. (People to People del. leader for U.S. plus internat. del. in psychopharmacology and neuropsychiatry to China 2006), Internat. Soc. Philos. Enquiry (diplomate 2009, sr. rsch. fellow 2008). Jewish. Avocations: chess, tennis, Scrabble, computers. Office: Pacific Neuropsychiat Inst 6300 Ninth Ave NE Ste 353 Seattle WA 98115 Office Phone: 206-527-6289.

NEREM, ROBERT MICHAEL, engineering educator, consultant; b. Chgo., July 20, 1937; s. Robert and Borghild Guneva (Bakken) Nerem; m. Jill Ann Thomson, Dec. 21, 1958 (div. 1977); children: Robert Steven, Nancy Ann; m. Marilyn Reed, Oct. 7, 1978; stepchildren: Christina Lynn Maser, Carol Marie Maser. BS, U. Okla., 1959; MS, Ohio State U., 1961, PhD in Aero. and Astronautical Engring., 1964; D (hon.), U. Paris, 1990, Imperial Coll. London, 2010, Ill. Inst. Tech., 2010. Asst. prof. Ohio State U., Columbus, 1964-68, assoc. prof., 1968-72, prof., 1972-79, assoc. dean Grad. Sch., 1975-79; prof. mech. engring., chmn. dept. U. Houston, 1979-86; Parker H. Petit prof. Ga. Inst. Tech., Atlanta, 1987—2010, Inst. prof., 1991—, dir. Parker H. Petit Inst. for Bioengring. and Biosci., 1995—2009; dir. Ga. Tech/Emory Ctr. pregenetive medicine NSF Engring. Rsch. Ctr., Atlanta, 1998—, inst. prof. emeritus, 2010—. Mem. Ga. Gov.'s Adv. Coun. on Sci. and Tech. Devel., Atlanta, 1992—95; Alza disting. lectr. Biomed. Engring. Soc., 1991; ASME Thurston lectr., 94; mem. sci. bd. FDA, 2000—03; sr. adv. for bioengring. Nat. Inst. Biomed. Imaging and Bioengring., 2003—06. Contbr. articles to profl. jours. Fellow: AAAS, ASME, Instn. Mech. Engrs. UK (hon.), Am. Inst. Med. and Biol. Engring. (founding pres. 1992—94); mem.: NAE (Founders award 2008), Royal Swedish Acad. Engring. Scis., Polish Acad. Scis., US Nat. Com. on Biomechanics (chmn. 1988—91), Japanese Soc. for Med. & Biol. Engring. (hon.), Internat. Fedn. for Med. and Biol. Engring. (pres. 1988—91), Internat. Union for Phys. and Engring. Scis. in Medicine (pres. 1991—94), Inst. Medicine, Biomed. Engring. Soc., Am. Acad. Arts and Scis. Home: Park Springs 9435 Creekside Trail Stone Mountain GA 30087 Office Phone: 404-894-2768. Business E-Mail: robert.nerem@ibb.gatech.edu.

NERHOOD, ROBERT CLARKE, dean, obstetrician, gynecologist; b. Altoona, Pa., Aug. 27, 1944; s. Albert and Jeanne (VanOrmer) N.; m. Carolyn Haught, Aug. 27, 1965; children: Robert, Timothy; m. Deborah Brooks, Nov. 30, 1984. Student, W.Va. U., 1962-65, MD, 1969. Diplomate Am. Bd. Ob-Gyn. Intern Polyclinic Hosp., Harrisburg, Pa., 1969-70; resident in ob-gyn. W.Va. Hosp., Morgantown, 1970-73, Kessler Air Force Med. Ctr., 1973-75; clin. assoc. prof. Sch. Medicine Marshall U., Huntington, 1977-87; dir. resident edn. Allegheny Gen. Hosp./Med. Coll. Pa.; assoc. prof. ob-gyn. Med. Coll. Pa., 1989-92; chief ob-gyn. Berkshire Health Sys.; assoc. prof. Med. Sch. U. Mass.; with Mass. Bd. Perinatal Medicine; chmn. bd. Cabell Huntington Hosp., 2002—; prof. chmn. ob-gyn. divsn. Sch. Medicine Marshall U., Huntington, W.Va., 1992—2010, emeritus faculty mem., 2010—, interim dean Joan C. Edwards Sch. Medicine, 2011—. Mem. W.Va. Bd. Perinatal Medicine, 1977-87. Ob-gyn. editor Postgraduate Medicine, 1997—. Maj. USAF, 1973-75. Mem. Am. Coll. Ob-Gyn. (vice chair W.Va. sect. 1992-95, chair W.Va. sect. 1995-98, 2001-, mem. adv. coun. dist. IV 1992-98, 2001-). Office: Marshall University Joan C Edwards Sch Medicine 1600 Medical Center Dr Huntington WV 25701-3655 Office Phone: 304-691-1400. Office Fax: 304-691-1453. *

NERKAR, AMIT GAJANAN, pharmacist, educator; b. Akola, July 9, 1981; PhD, Sch. Pharmacy and Tech. Mgmt., Mumbai, 2010; PharmM in Medicinal Chemistry, Coll. Pharm. Scis., Bput, Roukela Orissa, 2005. Sr. rsch. fellow SPTM, SVKM's NMIMS U., Mumbai, 2008—10; sr. lectr. SGSPS Inst. Pharmacy, 2005—06; assoc. prof. STES Smt. Kashibai Navale Coll. Pharmacy, Pune, 2009, physician, 2009—. Sr. Rsch. fellowship, Indian Coun. Med. Rsch., New Delhi. Mem.: Indian Pharm. Assn. Avocation: cricket. Home: Jaswandi Aadarsh Colony Sambhaji Nag Akola Maharshtra 444001 India Personal E-mail: dragnerkar@gmail.com.

NERSESYAN, HRACHYA, neurologist; b. Yerevan, Armenia, May 25, 1968; MD, Yerevan State Med. U., 1993; PhD, Burdenko Neurosurgery Inst., Moscow, 1998. Dir. headache program Ill. Neurol. Inst., 2009—. Clin. asst. prof. neurology U. Ill. Coll. Medicine, Peoria, 2009. Postdoc. Rsch. fellowship, Epilepsy Found. America, Milken Family Found. Mem.: Am. Headache Soc., Am. Acad. Neurology. Office: 100 N Randolph St Peoria IL 61606 E-mail: hrachyan@msn.com.

NESBIT, ROBERT RAYMOND, JR., surgeon; b. New Haven, Apr. 1, 1939; BA, Harvard U., 1961; MD, U. Rochester, 1965. Diplomate Am. Bd. Surgery. Intern Strong Meml. Hosp., Rochester, 1965-66, resident in surgery, 1966-67, 69-74; chief vascular surgery Med. Coll. Ga. Hosps., Augusta, 1994-2000; prof. surgery Med. Coll. Ga., 1994-2000, prof. surgery emeritus, 2000—, dir. med. student edn. dept. surgery, 2002—. Fellow ACS; mem. Am. Assn. for Vascular Surgery, So. Surg. Assn., Assn. VA Surgeons, So. Assn. Vascular Surgery, Augusta-Richmond County Hist. Soc. (pres. 2003-05), Am. Osler Soc., Atlanta Vascular Soc., (pres. 2004-06), So. Assn. History Medicine and Sci. (pres. 2006-08, sec. treas., 2009-), Assn. Surg. Edn. (chair surgery clerkship dirs. com. 2006-08), Phi Beta Kappa, Alpha Omega Alpha. Office: Med Coll Ga Dept Surgery Augusta GA 30912 Home Phone: 706-733-8861; Office Phone: 706-721-1967. Business E-Mail: rnesbit@mail.mcg.edu. *

NESCOLARDE SELVA, LEXA, electronics engineer, educator; b. Baracoa, Cuba, Mar. 27, 1970; Dr. Eng., U. Poly. De Catalunya, 2006. Assoc. prof. electronic dept. U. Poly. De Catalunya, 2006. Office: Jordi Girona 1-3 Edifici C4 Barcelona 08034 Spain Business E-Mail: lexa.nescolarde@upc.edu.

NESTLE, MARION, nutritionist, educator; BA in Bacteriology, U. Calif., Berkeley, 1959, PhD in Molecular Biology, 1968, MPH in Pub. Health Nutirition, 1986. Lab. technician, rsch. asst., Encephalitis Rsch. Lab. Sch. Pub. Health, U. Calif. Berkeley, 1959—61; postdoctoral trainee, dept. molecular biology U. Calif., Berkeley, 1963—68; postdoctoral fellow, dept. biology, biochemistry Brandeis U., 1968—70, postdoctoral fellow, dept. biology, develop. biology, 1970—71, lectr., biology Waltham, Mass., 1971—73, asst. prof. biology, 1974—76; lectr. biochemistry and biophysics U. Calif., Sch. Medicine, San Francisco, 1976—84, lectr. medicine, 1979—84, associated faculty, Inst. for Health Policy Studies and Inst. for Aging Health Policy, 1983—86, lectr. family medicine and cmty. medicine, 1984—85, adj. assoc. prof., family and cmty. medicine, 1985—86, assoc. dean, human biology programs, adminstrv. dir., med. scientist tng. program, acting dir., 1983—84, dir., John Tung/Am. Cancer Soc. Clin. Nutrition Edn. Ctr., 1984—86; sr. nutrition policy advisor, staff dir. for nutrition policy Office of Disease Prevention and Health Promotion, Dept. Health and Human Services, Washington, 1986—88, mng. editor, Surgeon General's Report on Nutrition and Health, 1988; prof., chair NYU, Steinhardt Sch. Edn., Dept. Nutrition, Food Studies & Pub. Health, 1988—2003, prof., dir., pub. health initiatives, 2003—04, Paulette Goddard prof., 2004—. Former bd. dir. Ctr. for Sci. in the Pub. Interest; mem. Calif. nutrition coun. State of Calif., Interdepartmental Coun. on Food and Nutrition, 1976—86; William Evans vis. fellow, physiology dept. U. Otago Sch. Medicine, 1983; faculty, US-Nicaragua Health Colloquium Health Ministry of Nicaragua and the Com. for Health Rights in Ctrl. Am., 1984; faculty, Sino-US workshop on edn. and culture Shanghai Mcpl. Health Dept., People's Republic of China, 1986; staff dir., nutrition policy bd. US

Dept. Health and Human Services, 1986—88, staff liason Task Force on the 1990 Nutrition Objectives, 1986—88, mem. Task Force on the Homeless, 1986—88, staff liason NIH Nutrition, 1986—88, liason, USDA Dietary Guidance Working Group, 1986—88; dietetic intern Veterans Adminstrn. Med. Ctr., Bronx, NY, 1988—95; mem. Project LEAN NYC Health Dept., 1989—94; mem. external peer reviewed com. Univ. Medicine and Dentistry NJ, 1992—93; mem. expert advisory panel on changing the Am. diet Assn. of State and Territorial Health Officers, 1993; mem. external advisory com., WHELS trial U. Calif. San Diego Cancer Ctr., 1994—2000, mem. data mgmt. com., WHELS trial, 2000—; mem. vis. com., nutrition dept. Lehman Coll., 1996, Hunter Coll., 1996; ad hoc reviewer USDA grant awards, 1996; judge, final examinations French Culinary Inst., 1996—97; mem. com. on nutrition and food habits Internat. Union Nutritional Sci., 1997; mem. internat. jury Grande Covian award (Barcelona), 1997—2002; mem. Research!America! Nat. Advisory Com. on Prevention Rsch., 2000—; ad hoc grant reviewr NSF, 2001; mem. exec. com. World Health Policy Forum, Lausanne, 2002; mem. external advisory bd. Hunter Coll. Urban Pub. Health Program, 2002—; mem. internat. jury Slow Food award for Def. Biodiversity, 2002; chair NY State Health Dept. Heart Prevention Plan, 2002; mem. selection com. USDA Helios award for Communication Excellence, 2005; mem. Pediatric Pulmonary Ctr., Mt. Sinai Med. Ctr., 1990—92, Nat. Cancer Inst. Ethnic and Law Literacy Materials Project, 1991—93, Vis. Com., Nutrition Dept., NY Med. Coll., 1991, HRSA/NIH Resource Com. on Nutrition Edn. for Physicians, 1992, FDA Food Adv. Com., 1992—95, NY State Commn. on Dietetics and Nutrition, 1993—97, US Dept. Health and Human Services/USDA Dietary Guidelines Adv. Com., 1994—95, Private and Pub., Scientific, Academic and Consumer Food Policy Com., Harvard Bus. Sch., 1995—, Dept. Health and Human Services/PHS editl. adv. bd. for the Surgeon General;s Report on Dietary Fats and Health, 1998—99, Nat. Cancer Inst. Nutrition Implementation Com., 1998—2000, FDA Sci. Adv. Bd., 1998—2001, Expert Panel on Dietary Supplementation for Food Stamp Recipients, Life Sciences Rsch. Office, 1998; cons. US Agy. for Internat. Develop., Bangkok and Jakarta, 1986, Fed. Trade Commn., 1988—91, 1996—97, Nutrition Counseling Sect., US Preventative Services Task Force, 1988—89, Hungarian Ministry of Health and Social Welfare, Budapest, 1989, N.Am.-Cuban Scientific Exchange, Ministry of Health, Havana, 1990, NYC Human Resources Adminstrn., 1990—91, NYC Dept. Health, 1990—91, Iowa State Atty. General's Office, 1990—91, Nat. Cancer Inst., Multi-Ethnic Nutrition Project, 1991—93, WHO Regional Office for Europe, Health Ministry of Mauritus, 1991, Consumer Reports, Zillions TV Project, 1992, U. Calif. San Diego, Cancer Rsch. inst., 1992, Scribner's/Simon & Schuster, The Joy of Cooking, 1996, WHO Regional Office for Europe, Copenhagen, 1995, Hunter Coll. Sch. Health Sciences, 1996, World Bank, 2002, WHO, Geneva, 2002—; invited presenter in field; conference spkr. Pub. Health Advocacy Inst.; mem. adv. com., Wagner Sch. Pub. Svc., Advanced Mgmt. Program for Clinicians NYU, 1988—92, mem., faculty resource network planning com., 1991—92, mem. curriculum challenge grant review com., 1991—98, mem., middle state organizational profile com.: internat. edn. and rsch., 1993, mem. adv. com., biology core curriculum, 1996—97, mem. review com., Whitehead faculty fellowship, 1995—98, mem., com. on promotion and tenure, sch. edn., 1996—98, chair, com. on promotion and tenure, sch. edn., 1998, mem. steering com., Internat. MPH program develop., 2003—, mem. adv. com., faculty collections, Bobst Libr., 2004—, mem. com. on promotion and tenure, Steinhardt Sch. Edn., 2004—; chair to all the following committees at U. Calif. San Francisco, Sch. Medicine: Women's Faculty Assn., Med. Scientist Tng. Program Coun., Human Biology adv. coun., curriculum subcommittee on nutrition, Chancellor's Task Force on the Child Care/Study Ctr., Chancellor's Com. on the Status of Women, Biochemistry med./pharmacy course com., admissions com. med. scientist panel, 1976—86; mem. of the following committees at Brandeis U. Adv. Com. to the Health and Mental Health Services, adv. com. minority spl. services bd. of premedical advisors, com. on admissions and financial aid, & program planning com., women's studies, 1971—76. Contbr. articles to profl. jours., chapters to books, to editorials, commentaries, encyclopedias, proceedings and reports; author: Nutrition in Clinical Practice, 1985, Food Politics: How the Food Industry Influences Nutrition and Health, 2002 (World Hunger Year Harry Chapin Media award, 2003, Assn. of American Publishers, Outstanding Profl. and Scholarly Titles of 2002 (Category: Nursing and Allied Health), 2003, James Beard Found. Book award (category: Literary), 2003), 2004, 2005, Safe Food: Bacteria, Biotechnology, and Bioterrorism, 2003 (San Francisco Chronicle Best Books of 2003, Daniel E. Griffiths Rsch. award, NYU Steinhardt Sch. Edn., 2004), What to Eat, 2006; co-editor: Taking Sides: Clashing Views on Controversial Issues in Food and Nutrition, 2004, Pet Food Politics, 2008, Feed Your Pet Right, 2010, Safe Food: The Politics of Food Safety, 2010; mem. adv. bd. Botany of Desire (PBS), 2002—, mem. editl. adv. bd. Nutrition Week, Gastronomica, and Jour. of Pub. Health Policy, Pub. Health Nutrition (UK), Jour. Culinary Sci. & Tech. (Dublin), Food and Foodways (UK) and European Jour. Pub. Health, editl. cons. The Lancet, former mem. editl. bd. Nutrition Reviews, Jour. Nutrition Edn., Eating Well, Cambridge World History of Food and Nutrition, Longevity Mag., Am. Health Mag., Nutrition Action Healthletter, frequent guest appearances and interviews ABC News, Boston Globe, British Medical Journal, Business Week, CNN, CBS News, Der Spiegel, Die Zeit, Financial Times, Fortune, Lancet, London Times, LA Times, Newsday, Newsweek, NY Observer, NY Times, People, Phila. Inquirer, Portland Oregonian, San Francisco Chronicle, TIME, USA Today, US News & World Report, Wall Street Journal, Washington Post, and others. Bd. dir. Ctr. for Cuban Studies, 1995—2002; mem. Commonwealth Policy Adv. Com., 1976—86, Episcopal Sanctuary Adv. Bd., 1976—86, East Harlem Healthy Heart Program, 1988—93; bd. dir. Ctr. for Sci. in Pub. Interest, 1988—93, mem. Citizens' Commn. on Sch. Nutrition, 1989—91; mem., Task Force on Nutrition Edn. Am. Heart Assn., NY, 1990—91; mem., Coun. on Sports Medicine and Sci., Nutrition Subcommittee US Olympic Com., 1990—91; chair, expert panel on children's food guidelines Ctr. for Sci. in Pub. Interest, 1990—92; mem. adv. bd. World Food Mus., 1992—98; mem., food adv. bd. Food and Hunger Hotline, 1993—94; grant reviewer Am. Cancer Soc., 1992—93, chair, prevention subcommittee on nutrition; dietary guidelines com., 1995—96, mem. nutrition and physical activity adv. com., 1995—2002; mem. adv. bd. NY Restaurant Sch., 1998—2002; disting. sci. sponsor NY Hall of Sci., 1998—; mem. scientific adv. com. Union of Concerned Scientists, 2001—; mem. scientific advisor Calif. Ctr. for Pub. Health Advocacy, 2002—; bd. dir. Slow Food, U.S.A., 2003—04; mem. adv. bd. Chez Panisse Found., 2005—. Recipient Health Quality award, Nat. Com. for Quality Assurance, 2005; named Nutrition Educator of Yr., Eating Well Mag., 1997, Food Influential, Self Mag., 1999, Pacesetter Educator of Yr., Roundtable for Women in Food Service, 1999, Women Who Change the Way We Eat, Health Mag., 2001, The Saveur 100 Favorites, Saveur Mag., 2004, Alumni of Yr., U. Calif. Berkeley, Sch. Pub. health, 2004, Obesity Warrior, Time Mag., 2004; named one of 100 Women Who Shape Our City, NY Daily News, 2004, Organic Style Environ. Power 50 List -Guardian of Good Eating, 2004; UCLA Ctr. for Soc., the Individual, and Genetics Fellow, 2004. Fellow: Soc. for Nutrition Edn. (mem. jour. policy advisory com. 1986—88), AAAS; mem.: Am. Dietetic Assn. (mem. com. on legislation and pub. policy 1986—88), Soc. for Epidemiological Rsch., NY Acad. Pub. Edn., NY Acad. Sciences, NY Acad. Medicne (mem. com. on pub. health 1988—94, mem. NY-NJ Regional Ctr. for Clin. Nutrition 1989—92, chair, subcommittee on nutrition edn. 1992—93), Pub. Health Assn. NYC, Nat. Assn. for Pub. Health Policy (vice-chair, coun. on food policy 1991—93), James Beard Found. (judge, journalism awards 1993—96, judge, book awards 1996—2002, Lifetime Achievement, Who's Who in Food and Beverage in America 2003), Internat. Assn. of Culinary Profls., Ctr. for Sci. in the Pub. Interest, Assn. for the Study of Food and Soc., Am. Soc. for Nutrition Sci., Am. Soc. for Clin. Nutrition (mem. awards com. 2000—02), Am. Pub. Health Assn. (mem. food and nutrition sect. coun. 1997—98, Food and Nutrition Sect., Excellence in Dietary Guidance award 1994, David P. Rall award for Advocacy in Pub. Health 2004), Les Amis D'Escoffier, Am.Inst. Wine and Food, Women Chefs and Restaurateurs, Les Dames d'Escffier. Office: Dept Nutrition Food Studies & Pub Health NYU 35 W 4th St 12th Fl New York NY 10012-1172 Office Phone: 212-998-5595. Office Fax: 212-995-4192. Business E-Mail: marion.nestle@nyu.edu.

NESTLER, ERIC JONATHAN, neuroscientist, medical educator; b. NYC, July 7, 1954; s. Herbert A. and Mildred D. Nestler; m. Susan DeRenzo, Mar. 6, 1980; children: David I., Matthew E., Jane D. BA, Yale U., 1976, MD, PhD, 1983; PhD (hon.), Uppsala U., Sweden, 2011. Diplomate American Bd. Psychiatry & Neurology. Resident psychiatry McLean Hosp., Mass.; prof., dir. Divsn. Molecular Psychiatry Yale U. Sch. Medicine, New Haven, 1987—2000; disting. prof., chmn. Dept. Psychiatry U. Tex. Southwestern Med. Ctr., Dallas, 2000—08; Nash Family prof. neuroscience, chmn. Dept. Neuroscience, dir. Friedman Brain Inst. Mt. Sinai Med. Ctr., NYC, 2008—. Co-author (with Dennis S. Charney): Neurobiology of Mental Illness; co-author: (with Steven E. Hyman and Robert C. Malenka) Molecular Neuropharmacology; contbr. articles to med. jours. Recipient Pfizer Scholars Award, 1987, McKnight Scholar Award, 1989, Jordi-Folch-Pi Meml. Award, American Soc. Neurochemistry, 1990, Bristol-Myers Squibb Freedom to Discover Neuroscience Rsch. Grant, 2004, Patricia S. Goldman-Rakic Award, 2008, Falcone Prize, 2009; Sloan Rsch. Fellowship, 1987. Fellow: AAAS; mem.: Inst. of Medicine (Rhonda and Bernard Sarnat Internat. Prize in Mental Health 2010). Achievements include discovery of how drugs of abuse change nerve cells in the brain to cause addiction. Office: Mount Sinai Medical Center Icahn Medical Institute Fl 10 Rm 10-23 1425 Madison Ave New York NY 10029 Office Phone: 212-659-5656. Office Fax: 212-659-8510. E-mail: eric.nestler@mssm.edu. *

NESTOR, MICHAEL LAWRENCE, medical technology specialist; b. Bklyn., Mar. 12, 1964; s. Mitchell Nestor; m. Elvia Gabriela Hansen, Mar. 27, 2002. BS, Northridge State U., Calif., 1988. ISD, MSE. Pres. MMA Worldwide Group Inc., Miami, Fla., 1994—; v.p. tech. Advanced Dermatology Mgmt., Miami, 1995—. Dir. Dermnetwork Orgn., Plantation, Fla., 1995—. Contbr. Blue Jour. Dermatology, 2001. Mem.: Am. Acad. Dermatology (hon.; tech. cons. 2002—, Merit award 2000, 2001, 2002). Democrat. Avocations: swimming, travel. Office: Advanced Dermatology Mgmt 1111 Park Center Blvd Ste 300 Miami FL 33169 E-mail: m.nestor@admcorp.com.

NETO, SALVADOR GULLO, gastroenterologist; b. Porto Alegre, Aug. 28, 1974; MD, PUCRS, 1996, MS, 2005. Surgeon Gen. and Gastrointestinal Surgery Dept., 1998—. Bd. dirs., Hosp. Sao Lucas PUCRS, 2008, adj. prof., Med. Sch., 11; v.p. Porto Alegre Health Care Cluster, 2010. Mem.: Assn. Brasileira Transplantes Orgaos. Avocations: music, running. Office: Av Ipiranga 6690 607 Porto Alegre Rio Grande do Sul 90610-000 Brazil Office Fax: 51 3320-5015. E-mail: sgulloneto@yahoo.com.

NETSIRI, CHAIYAPOJ NUANGNIYOM (POJ NETSIRI), research scientist, engineer, consultant; b. Bangkok, May 29, 1964; arrived in US, 2001, naturalized, 2010; s. Chote and Patcharin Netsiri. BSEE, King Mongkut's Inst. Tech., Bangkok, Thailand, 1986; MS in Computer Sci., Chiba U., Japan, 1996; PhD in Elec. Engring., U. Tokyo, 1999. Prodn. engr. Kang Yang Electric MFG Co., Ltd., Samutprakarn, Thailand, 1987—89; elec. engr. Tom Tech Co., Ltd., Bangkok, 1990—92; R&D engr. Yamada Kikai Kogyo Co., Ltd., Chiba, Japan, 1992—94; rsch. assoc. U. Cambridge, England, 1999—2001, Albert Einstein Coll. Medicine, Bronx, NY, 2001—03; sr. staff assoc. Columbia U., NYC, 2003—04; rsch. scientist Rice U., Houston, 2004—05; sr. applications engr. MicroMRI, Inc., Phila., 2005—06; rsch. scientist NexTech Solutions Inc., Austin, Tex., 2006—07, Bench Tree Group LLC, Georgetown, Tex., 2007—08; cons. DacQuest LLC, Wash., Mo., 2008—09, Nitto Denko Technical Corp., Oceanside, Calif., 2009, CTO SVP Talk222 LLC, Nev., 2010—, St. Jude Med. Inc., Irvine, Calif., 2010, Western Digital Corp., Lake Forest, Calif., 2010, Mikasa Sports LLC, Irvine, Calif., 2010—. Grantee, Royal Soc., 2000—01; fellow, U. Cambridge, 1999—2001; scholar, Nagai Found., 1994—95, Japanese Govt., 1995—99. Mem.: Soc. Neurosci. (assoc.), IEEE (assoc.). Buddhist. Avocation: tennis. Office: Mikasa Sports 1821 Kettering St Irvine CA 92614

NETTER, KARL JOACHIM, pharmacology educator; b. Kiel, Germany, Feb. 8, 1929; s. Hans and Margarethe (Jürgens) N.; m. Petra S. (Munkelt), Aug. 23, 1965. MD, U. Hamburg, Germany, 1953. lic. physician, Kiel, Germany. Intern Atlantic City Hosp., 1953—54; biochemist Max Planck Inst. for Cell Chemistry, Munich, 1954—57; pharmacologist dept. pharmacology U. Hamburg, Germany, 1957—66; head sect. on toxicology U. Mainz Med. Sch., Germany, 1966—76; prof. pharmacology and toxicology, chmn. dept. U. Marburg, Germany, 1976—97. Vis. scientist NIH, Bethesda, MD., 1959-60; mem. sci. com. on food European Cmty., Brussels, 1981-92; bd. mem. Internat. Life Sci. Inst. Europe, 1986-96. Editor: Toxicology, 1981-99; editl. bd. Naunyn-Schmiedebergs Arch. Pharmacol., European Jour. Clin. Pharmacology, Xenobiotica, Biochemical Pharmacology, Toxicol. Appl. Pharmacology, 1978-82, European Jour. Clin. Investigation; contbr. articles to profl. journals. Mem. European Soc. Biochem. Pharmacology (charter mem., pres. 1992-94, hon. mem. 1996—), German Soc. Biol. Chemistry, German Pharmacol. Soc. (pres., exec. com. 1970-74), Brit. Pharmacol. Soc., Brit. Toxicology Soc., Am. Soc. Pharmacol. Exptl. Therapeutics, Soc. Toxicology, Internat. Soc. Study Xenobiotics (charter mem.), German Assn. Chemistry, Deutsche Forschungsgemeinschaft (chmn. food safety commn. 1968-94, spl. grant rev. 1988-95), Internat. Union Pharmacology (treas. 1987-94), German Pharmacology Soc.(hon.) Office: Univ Marburg Dep Pharm Sch Med Karl von Frisch Strasse 1 Marburg D35032 Germany Business E-Mail: netter@staff.uni-marburg.de.

NETTLES, JOHN BARNWELL, obstetrics and gynecology educator; b. Dover, NC, May 19, 1922; s. Stephen A. and Estelle (Hendrix) N.; m. Eunice Anita Saugstad, Apr. 28, 1956; children: Eric, Robert, John Barnwell; m. 2d, Sandra Williams, Sept. 14, 1991; stepchildren: Steven Williams, Clayton Williams. BS, U. S.C., 1941; MD, Med. Coll. S.C., 1944. Diplomate: Am. Bd. Obstetrics and Gynecology. Intern Garfield Meml. Hosp., Washington, 1944-45; research fellow in pathology Med. Coll. Ga., Augusta, 1946-47; resident in ob-gyn. U. Ill. Rsch. and Ednl. Hosps., Chgo., 1947-51; instr. to asst. prof. ob-gyn. U. Ill. Coll. Medicine, Chgo., 1951-57; asst. prof., assoc. prof., prof. ob-gyn. U. Ark. Med. Ctr., Little Rock, 1957-69; dir. grad. edn. Hillcrest Med. Ctr., Tulsa, 1969-73; prof. ob-gyn Coll. Medicine, U. Okla., Oklahoma City, 1969-78; chmn. dept. ob-gyn. U. Okla.-Tulsa Med. Coll., 1975-80, prof., 1980—, mem. coun. on residency edn. in ob-gyn., 1974-79. Dir. Tulsa Obstet. and Gynecol. Edn. Found., 1969-80; Coordinator med. edn. Nat. Def., Ark., 1961-69; mem. S.W. regional med. adv. com. Planned Parenthood Fedn. Am., 1974-78; mem. adv. com. Health Policy Agenda Am. People, 1982-85, rev. com. Accrediation Coun. for Continuing Med. Edn., 1987-92. Contbr. articles on uterine malignancy, kidney biopsy in pregnancy, perinatal morbidity and mortality, human sexuality sch. age pregnancy to profl. jours. Served as lt. (j.g.) M.C. USNR, 1945-46; as lt. 1953-54. Recipient Nat. Faculty award. Fellow Am. Coll. Ob-Gyn. (dist. sec.-treas. 1964-70, dist. chmn. exec. bd. 1970-73, v.p. 1977-78, Disting. Svc. award 1998, Dist. VII Outstanding Clin. Prof. award 1989, Nat. Tchr. award 1992), ACS (bd. govs. 1969-71, program com. 1970-71, Surg. forum 1977-84, adv. com. gyn/ob 1985-92), Royal Soc. Health, Royal Soc. Medicine; mem. Ark. Obstet. and Gynecol. Soc. (exec. sec. 1959-69), Ctrl. Assn. Obstetrics and Gynecology (exec. com. 1966-69, pres. 1978-79), Internat. Soc. Advancement Humanistic Studies in Gynecology, Assn. Mil. Surgeons U.S., AMA (sect. coun. on obstetrics and gynecology 1975-96, chmn. 1982-96, del. from Am. Coll. Obstetricians and Gynecologists 1987-96, governing coun. sr. physicians group 2003 , Young at Heart award Young Physicians sect. 1994), Nurses Assn. So. Med. Assn. (chmn. obstetrics 1973-74), Okla. Med. Soc. (Ed L. Calhoun Leadership in Organized Medicine award, 2004), Tulsa County Med. Soc., Chgo. Med. Soc., Am. Assn. for Maternal and Infant Health, Assn. Am. Med. Colls., APHA, Am. Assn. Sex Edn. Counselors and Therapists (S.W. regional bd. 1976-79), Soc. for Gynecol. Investigation, AAAS, Am. Soc. for Study Fertility and Sterility, Internat. Soc. Gen. Semantics, So. Gynecol. and Obstet. Soc. (pres. 1981-82), Am. Cancer Soc. (pres. Okla. div. 1979-83, St. George's medal 1991), Com. on In-Tng. Exam. in Ob-Gyn, Am. Coll. Nurse Midwives (governing bd. examiners 1979-83), Sigma Xi (pres. Tulsa chpt. 1992-93), Phi Rho Sigma. Lutheran. Office: 4502 E 41ST ST Tulsa OK 74135-9923

NEU, ALICIA MALLARE, pediatric nephrologist; married. MD, U. of Va., Charlottesville, 1988. Diplomate Am. Bd. Pediatric Nephrology. Intern in pediat. Johns Hopkins Hosp., Balt., 1988—89, resident in pediat., 1989—91, clin. and rsch. fellow pediat. nephrology, 1991—94; instr. pediat. nephrology Johns Hopkins U. Sch. Medicine, Balt., 1991—95; pediatric nephrologist Johns Hopkins Sch. of Medicine, Balt., 1994—; assoc. prof. pediat. nephrology Johns Hopkins U. Sch. Medicine, Balt., 2002—, clin. dir., med. dir. pediat. dialysis and renal transplantation, 2002—. Office: Johns Hopkins Hosp 200 N Wolfe St Rm 3065 Baltimore MD 21287

NEUBERGER, MANFRED ARTHUR, medical educator, researcher; b. Vienna, Sept. 14, 1946; s. Arthur and Erika (Grimm) N.; m. Marion Binderberger, May 26, 1975; 1 child, Danja. MD, U. Vienna, 1971. Assoc. prof. Med. Sch. U. Vienna, 1971-80, prof. Inst. Environ. Health, 1980-2000, dep. dir. Inst. Environ. Hygiene, 1980—, dep. dir. Inst. Environ. Medicine, 1989—, head dept. preventive medicine, 1992—. Cons. Workers Compensation Bd., Vienna, 1980-2000, WHO-Internat. Program Chem. Safety, Geneva, 1992-93, 95-96, WHO-Europe, Copenhagen, 1979-84, UN Devel. Program, N.Y.C., 1986-87, ILO Delegation, Geneva, 1985-86. Author: New Approaches to Risk Estimation of Air Pollution, 1979 (U. Vienna award 1980), Prevention of Noise Induced Hearing Loss, 1989 (Austrian Soc. Occpl. Medicine award 1983); contbr. articles to profl. jours. Mem. planning commn. City of Vienna, 1986—2002. With Austrian Army, 1974. Grantee U. Vienna, 1982, 95, 91. Mem. Austrian Soc. Occpl. Medicine (bd. dirs. 1997—), Austrian Soc. Lung Diseases (bd. dirs. 1997—2000, chair working group 1997—2000), European Network for Smoking Prevention, Austrian Acad. Sci. (clean air com. 1993—), Austrian Soc. Ecology (sci. adv. bd. 1997—), Australian Soc. Toxicology (bd. dirs. 2000), Australian Soc. Hygiene Preventive Medicine (bd. dirs. 1999-), Internat. Soc. Environ. Medicine (bd. dirs. 2000—). Avocations: music, bicycling, hiking, gardening. Office: U Vienna Dept Prev Medicine Kinderspitalgasse 15 A-1095 Vienna Austria Office Phone: 4314016034920. E-mail: manfred.neuberger@meduniwien.ac.at.

NEUBURG, EWALD MANFRED, pain medicine physician; s. Hermann Josef and Hedwig (Sparmann) Neuburg; children from previous marriage: Patrick, Jan Hendrik. MD, U. Essen, Essen, Germany, 1972. Pvt. practice treatment of pain and diseases of movement, Marl, North-Rhine Westphalia, Germany, 1979—96, Schortens, Lower Saxony, 1996—. Asst. med. dir. U. Bochum, Germany, 1972—; lead physician Clinik of Rehabilitation, Horumersiel, 2005. Author: Enclosure, 1992. Achievements include invention of enclosure; research in system of acupuncture and points of pain. Avocations: philosophy, golf. Office: Facharzt fur Orthopaedie Menkestr 3 26419 Schortens Germany Office Phone: 04461 80508. Business E-Mail: info@orthopaedie-spezielle-schmerztherapie.de.

NEUBURGER, MICHAEL, anesthesiologist, consultant, department head; b. Germany, Mar. 5, 1969; MS, PhD, U. Freiburg, 1996. Cert. in emergency medicine Germany, 2001, diplomate in anaesthesiologist European Diploma Anesthesiology, 2005. Cons. anaesthesiology Trauma Ctr. Murnau, 2004—, cons. emergency medicine,

2004—, cons. intensive care medicine, 2005—. Specialist pathology rsch., 1997; cons. pain medicine, 2006—. Recipient Nat. award, Regional Anaesthesia, 2007. Mem.: Alliance of German Anesthetists, German Soc. Anesthesiology and Intensive Care Medicine (August-Bier award 2007). Office: Dept Anesthesia & Intensive Care Ortenau Klinikum Achern 77855 Germany Office Phone: 004978417000. Office Fax: 498841482114.

NEUDERT, UDO WILHELM, internist; b. Eger, Germany, Jan. 5, 1941; s. Wilhelm Richard and Marianne (Kohl) Neudert; m. Edda Olschowka, Aug. 4, 1978. degree, MD, Frankfurt U., Germany, 1971. Cert. internal medicine, prevention and rehab. in cardiology. Intern several hosps., Frankfurt and Flensburg, Germany, 1968—70; resident Kerckhoff Clinic, Bad Nauheim, Germany, 1970—72, Konitzky Stift Hosp., Bad Nauheim, 1972—75; fellow in internal medicine Bd. Internal Medicine, Frankfurt, Germany, 1975; med. dir. Klinik Roemerwall, Bad Salzhausen, Germany, 1975—82, Taunusklinic BFA, Bad Nauheim, Germany, 1982—. Spokesperson for med. dirs. Bundesversicherungs-Anstalt for Angestellte BFA, Berlin, 1992—2002. Capt. German Air Force, 1972. Mem.: German Heart Found., German Soc. Cardiology, German Soc. Internal Medicine. Roman Catholic. Avocations: history, literature, photography, travel. Home: Wilhelm-Leuschner Strasse 41 D61231 Bad Nauheim Germany Office: Taunus Rehaklinic BFA LIndenstr 6 D61231 Bad Hauheim Germany Fax: 06032 1230.

NEUFANG, KARL FRIEDRICH RUDOLF, radiologist, educator; b. Cologne, Germany, Nov. 21, 1953; s. Karl Friedrich and Hedwig Johanna (Kopp) N.; m. Ursula Anna Mueller Neufang, Oct. 18, 1985; 1 child, Benedikt Johannes Cornelius. MD, U. Sch. Medicine, Cologne, Germany, 1978. Resident U. Hosp. Radiology, Cologne, Germany, 1979, 81-85; med. capt. Ctrl. Army Hosp. Koblenz, Germany, 1979-80; sr. officer, 1985-90; first sr. officer, 1990-92; asst. prof. U. Cologne, 1988-94, assoc. prof., 1994—; pvt. practice Inst. for Diagnostic Radiology and Nuclear Medicine, Euskirchen, Germany, 1992—. Co-author: Digital Subtraction Angiography, 1988, Degenerative Vascular Disease, 1992; co-editor: Vascular Stenting/Magnetic Resonance Angiography, 1991; assoc. editor: Aktuelle Radiologie, 1991-93; contbr. articles to profl. jours. Mem.: German Rontgengesellschaft, Am. Roentgen Ray Soc., Radiol. Soc. N.Am., Internat. Soc. Magnetic Resonance in Medicine. Roman Catholic. Avocations: architecture, paintings, history, photography, model building. Office: Praxis Radiologie Berliner St 2 Euskirchen D-53879 Germany Business E-Mail: neufang.kfr@uni-koeln.de.

NEUFELD, ELIZABETH FONDAL, biochemist, educator; b. Paris, Sept. 27, 1928; BSc, Queens Coll., NYC, 1948; PhD, U. Calif., Berkeley, 1956; DSc (hon.), U. Rene Descartes, Paris, 1978, Russell Sage Coll., Troy, NY, 1981, Hahnemann U. Sch. Medicine, Phila., 1984, Queens Coll., 1996. Rsch. asst. Jackson Lab., Bar Harbor, Maine; asst. rsch. biochemist U. Calif., Berkeley, 1957—63; rsch. biochemist Nat. Inst. Arthritis, Metabolism & Digestive Diseases, NIH, Bethesda, Md., 1963—73, chief sect. human biochem. genetics, 1973—79, chief genetics and biochem. br., 1979—84; prof. dept. biol. chemistry UCLA Sch. Medicine, 1984—, chmn. dept. biol. chemistry, 1984—2004. Contbr. articles to profl. jours. Recipient Dickson prize, U. Pitts., 1974, Hillenbrand award, 1975, Gairdner Found. Internat. award, 1981, Albert Lasker award for clin. med. rsch., 1982, William Allan award, 1982, Elliott Cresson medal, 1984, Wolf Found. prize in medicine, Israel, 1988, Christopher Columbus Discovery award for biomed. rsch., 1992, Nat. Medal of Sci., 1994; named Passano Found. sr. laureate, 1982, Calif. Scientist of Yr., 1990. Fellow: AAAS; mem.: NAS, Am. Soc. Gene Therapy, Am. Soc. Clin. Investigation, Am. Soc. Cell Biology, Am. Soc. Biochemistry & Molecular Biology (pres. 1992—93), Am. Chem. Soc., Am. Soc. Human Genetics, Am. Philos. Soc., Am. Acad. Arts & Scis, Inst. Medicine. Office: UCLA David Geffen Sch Medicine Dept Biol Chemistry BSRB 350B 615 Charles E Young Dr Los Angeles CA 90095-1737 Business E-Mail: eneufeld@mednet.ucla.edu. *

NEUFELD, NAOMI DAS, endocrinologist; b. Butte, Mont., June 13, 1947; d. Dilip Kumar and Maya (Chaliha) Das; m. Timothy Lee Neufeld, Nov. 27, 1971 (div. 2009); children: Pamela Anne, Katherine Louise. AB, Pembroke Coll., 1969; M. in Med. Sci., Brown U., 1971; MD, Tufts U., 1973. Diplomate Am. Bd. Pediatrics, Am. Bd. Endocrinology. Intern R.I. Hosp., Providence, 1973-74, resident in pediatrics, 1974-75; fellow in pediatric endocrinology UCLA, 1975-78; staff endocrinologist Cedars-Sinai Med. Ctr., Los Angeles, 1978-79, chief pediatric endocrinology sect., 1979-85, dir. pediatric endocrinology, 1985—95. Asst. research pediatrician UCLA, 1978-79, asst. prof.-in-residence pediatrics, 1979-85, assoc. prof.-in-residence, 1985—, founder and med. dir., CEO, Kidshape Found., 2008-; med. dir. Kidshape Program Children's Weight Control, 1986—, pres., Kidshape, 2008-; pres. Neufeld Med. Group, Inc., 1996—; consulting physician Ventura County Med. Ctr., 1989—; attending physician Cedars Sinai Med. Ctr., 1995—; clin. prof. pediatrics Sch. Med. UCLA, 1995—; med. dir., owner, founder Kidshape, 1986—; cons. physician Pasadena Diabetes & Endoscopy Med. Group, 1998-2002 Contbr. articles to profl. jours., author. Kidshape: A Practical Prescription for Raising Healthy Fit Children, 2003, Kidshape Cafe, A Cook Book, 2004, Candidate for Surgeon General, 2006. Named Clin. Investigator, NIH, 1978; grantee United Cerebral Palsy Soc., 1979, March of Dimes, 1981, NIH, 1983-88. Fellow Am. Coll. Endocrinology; mem. Am. Diabetes Assn., Soc. Pediatric Research, Endocrine Soc., Juvenile Diabetes Found. (research grantee 1980). Presbyterian. Avocations: running, reading, knitting, cooking. Home: 16821 Charmel Ln Pacific Palisades CA 90272-2218 Office: 8733 Beverly Blvd Ste 202 Los Angeles CA 90048-2218

NEUHAUSER, DUNCAN VONBRIESEN, medical educator; b. Phila., June 20, 1939; s. Edward Blaine Duncan and Gernda (vonBriesen) Neuhauser; m. Elinor Toaz, Mar. 6, 1965; children: Steven, Ann. BA, Harvard U., 1961; MHA, U. Mich., 1963; MBA, U. Chgo., 1966, PhD, 1971. Rsch. assoc. U. Chgo., 1965—70; asst. prof. Sch. Pub. Health, Harvard U., Boston, 1970—74, assoc. prof., 1974—79; cons. in medicine Mass. Gen. Hosp., Boston, 1975—80; assoc. dir. Health Systems Mgmt. Ctr. Case Western Res. U., Cleve., 1979—85, prof. epidemiology, biostats., orgnl. behavior, 1979—, prof. medicine, 1981—, prof. family medicine, 1990—, Charles Elton Blanchard prof. health mgmt., 1995—, co-dir. Health Systems Mgmt. Ctr., 1985—. Mem. biomed. staff Metrohealth Med. Ctr., 1981—; adj. mem. med. staff Cleve. Clinic Found., 1984—99; vis. prof. Vanderbilt U. Sch. Nursing, 1998—, Karolinska Med. Sch., Stockholm, 2002—. Author: numerous books, sci. papers; editor (jours.): Health Matrix, 1982—90, Med. Care, 1983—97. Vice chmn. bd. dirs. Vis. Nurse Assn. Greater Cleve., 1983—84, chmn., 1984—85; bd. dirs. New Eng. Grenfell Assn., Boston, 1972—, Braintree Hosp., Mass., 1975—86; trustee Internat. Grenfell Assn., St. Anthony, Nfld., Canada, 1975—83, Blue Hill Hosp., Maine, 1983—94, Hough Norwood Health Ctr., 1983—94, chmn., 1993—94; mem. vis. com. Columbia U. Sch. Nursing, 2000—; founding bd. dirs. Acad. for Healthcare Improvement, 2004—. Recipient E.F. Meyers Trustee award, Cleve. Hosp. Assn., 1987, Hope award, Nat. Multiple Sclerosis Soc., 1992, Neuhauser lectr., Soc. Pediatric Radiology, 1982, Freedlander lectr., Ohio Permanente Med. Group, 1986, Univ. medal, Tohoku Med. U., Sendai, Japan, 2001, Arthur Shapiro Best Book of Yr. Hypnosis award, 2003, McAuley lectr., Georgetown U., 2007, Duncan Neuhauser Curricular Innovation award, Acad. Health Care Improvement, 2009—; scholar Keck Found., 1982—; Duncan Neuhauser Endowed chair in cmty. health improvement at Case Western Res. U. and MetroHealth Med. Ctr., 2003, Kellogg fellow, U. Chgo., 1963—65. Mem.: Inst. Medicine NAS, Cleve. Skating Club, Kollegewidgwok Yacht Club (Blue Hill) (commodore 1991—93), St. Botolph Club (Boston), Beta Gamma Sigma. Home (Summer): PO Box 932 Blue Hill ME 04614-0932 Office: Case Western Reserve U Med Sch 10900 Euclid Ave Cleveland OH 44106-4945 Home (Winter): 2641 Idlewood Rd 1st Fl Cleveland Heights OH 44118-4249 Office Fax: 216-368-3970. Business E-Mail: dvn@case.edu.

NEUHOUSER, MARIAN L., nutritionist, researcher; BS in Nutrition, U. Calif., Davis, 1980; PhD in Nutritional Sciences, U. Wash., 1996. Nutritionist Fred Hutchinson Cancer Rsch. Ctr. Recipient JACN Best Scientific Paper award, Am. Coll. Nutrition, Folate & Neural Tube Defects, 1999. Mem.: Am. Soc. Preventive Oncology, Am. Soc. Nutrition, Am. Dietetic Assn., Am. Assn. Cancer Rsch. Office: Fred Hutchinson Cancer Research Center 1100 Fairview Ave N PO Box 19024 Seattle WA 98109 Office Phone: 206-667-4797. Office Fax: 206-667-7850. E-mail: mneuhous@fhcrc.org.

NEUMANN, FORREST KARL, retired public health service officer; b. St. Louis, Oct. 7, 1930; s. Metz Earl and Ruth (McGhee) N.; m. Erika Stefanie Turkl, Feb. 11, 1955; children: Tracey Neumann Liberson, Karen Neumann Kruger, Scott, Lisa. BS, Roosevelt U., 1953; MS in Hosp. Adminstrn., Northwestern U., 1955. Adminstrv. resident Louis A. Weiss Hosp., Chgo., 1954-55; mem. staff Sparrow Hosp., Lansing, Mich., 1958-90; CEO, pres., dir. Edward W. Sparrow Hosp., Lansing, 1962-90; pres., chief exec. officer, dir. Mason Gen. Hosp., Mich., 1973-85; chmn. bd. Caymich Ins. Co. Ltd., Cayman Islands, 1979-91, emeritus dir. Cayman Islands, 1991—; chmn. bd. Caymich Ins. Co. (Barbados) Ltd., 1986-91; pres., CEO, Mich. Hosp. Assn. Ins. Co., 1990-96; dir. Mich. Hosp. Assocs. Ins. Co., 1976-98; pres., CEO, Sparrow, Inc., 1984-90. Chmn. bd. Mich. Hosp. Assn. Ins. Co., 1979-90; dir. First of Am. Bank Corp., 1980-95, Auto Owners Ins. Co., 1980-90. Chmn. hosp. div. United Community Chest, 1965-68, chmn. budget steering com., 1970-71, bd. dirs., mem. exec. com., 1969-75; mem. adv. com. Capitol Area Comprehensive Health Planning Assn., 1969, bd. dirs., 1971-75, treas., 1974-75; mem., vice chmn. Mich. Arbitration Adv. Com., 1975-80; bd. dirs. Grad. Med. Edn., Inc., 1971-80, pres., 1972-73, treas. 1973. 1st lt. Med. Svcs. Corps USAF, 1955—58. Fellow Am. Coll. Hosp. Adminstrs. (life); mem. Southwestern Mich. Hosp. Council (trustee 1968-73, pres. 1970-71), Am. Hosp. Assn. (del. 1979-87), Mich. Hosp. Assn. (1st v.p. 1972-73, bd. dirs., exec. com., treas. 1974-75, chmn. 1976-77, Meritorious Key award 1979), Rotary. Personal E-mail: forrest.neumann@gmail.com.

NEUMANN, PAUL G., insurance company executive, lawyer; B, Haverford Coll., Pa., 1981; JD, U. Va., Charlottesville, 1987. Cert.: Calif. (admitted to practice) 1987. Ptnr. Foley and Lardner (merged with Weissburg and Aronson in 1996), Weissburg and Aronson, San Francisco; sr. v.p. legal svcs., gen. counsel Cath. Health Initiatives, Denver; sr. v.p., gen. counsel Trinity Health, 2009. Served on hosp. and med. staff coms., including instl. rev. bds. and bioethics coms. of numerous northern Calif. hosps. Office: Trinity Health 27870 Cabot Dr Novi MI 48377 Office Phone: 248-489-6000.

NEUMANN, SERINA ANN LOUISE, psychologist, researcher; b. Fitchburg, Mass., Dec. 29, 1970; d. James Martin Neumann and Annette Marie Rooney; m. Mark Cardiff, Feb. 19, 1973. BS in Psychology and Bus. cum laude, U. Pitts., 1992; MA in Clin. Psychology and Behavioral Medicine, U. Md., Balt., 1999, PhD in Clin. Psychology and Behavioral Medicine, 2001. Lic. psychologist Bur. Profl. Occupl. Affairs, Pa., 2003, Va., 2006. Postdoctoral scholar, cardiovasc. behavioral medicine rsch. tng. program U. Pitts., 2001—04, rsch. asst. prof., 2004—05; assoc. prof. psychiatry and behavioral scis. Eastern Va. Med. Sch., 2006—. Author articles and papers in field. Fellow Ruth L. Kirschstein Nat. Rsch. Svc. award, NIH, Nat. Heart, Lung, and Blood Inst., 2001-2004; Loan Repayment Program grant, NIH, 2002—, Grant (NIMH) Kiosk award, 2005—. Mem.: APA (mem. Health Psychology Divsn. 38), Internat. Soc. Behavioral Medicine, Soc. Behavioral Medicine, Am. Psychosomatic Soc., Phi Kappa Phi. Achievements include discovery of preliminary evidence of an association between genetic variation in the choline transporter gene and parasympathetic-cardiac function, depressive symptomatology; corticolimbic reactivity and subclinical measures of atherosclerosis. Office: Eastern Va Med Sch Dept Psychiatry 825 Fairfax Ave Norfolk VA 23501 Business E-Mail: neumansa@evms.edu.

NEUMILLER, STEVEN ROBERT, career planning administrator; b. Kenosha, Wis., Sept. 27, 1949; BA, U. Wis., 1971; MA, U. West Fla., 1976. Dir. Casper Coll., Career Planning and Placement Ctr., 1985—90; pres., cons. Inland NW Proposal Devel., 1990—. Apptd. State Bd. Vocat. Edn. by Gov. Wyo., Citizens Adv. Coun. Alcohol and Substance Abuse, by Dir. Dept. Social and Health Svcs. Mem.: Nat. Bd. Cert. Counselors, Am. Evaluation Assn. Avocations: running, gardening, history. Office: 1204 W 10th Ave PO Box 1801 Spokane WA 99210-1801 E-mail: neumillers@aol.com.

NEUNDOERFER, BERNHARD, neurologist; b. Worms/Rhein, Germany, July 20, 1937; s. Carl and Leonie (Geiger) N.; m. Gerta Zirngibl, Jan. 7, 1966; children: Gabriele, Andreas. MD, U. Heidelberg, Germany, 1963, Dr.med.habil, 1972. Med. asst. Univ. Hosp., Heidelberg, 1966-69, cons. Mannheim, Germany, 1969-78; chmn. neurol. dept. U. Lübeck, Germany, 1978-84, U. Erlangen, Germany, 1984—2005. Prof. U. Heidelberg, 1974; prof. U. Lübeck, 1978, U. Erlangen, 1984. Author: Polyneuritiden und Polyneuropathien, 1987, EEG-Fibel, 5th edit., 2002; editor: Praxis der amyotrophen Lateralsklerose, 2002, RRN: Polyneuropathien, 2008; editor jour. Fortschritte Neurologie Psychiatrien. With res. Germany armed forces. Mem. Am. Acad. Neurology, European Neurol. Soc., Rotary. Home: Platenstr 56 91054 Erlangen Germany Office: Clin Parcside Am Stadtpark 2 90409 Nûrnberg Germany Home Phone: 49 9131 26885; Office Phone: 49 911 241221. Fax: 49/9131/897601. Personal E-mail: gerta.neundoerfer@gmx.de. Business E-Mail: bernhard.neundoerfer@dgm.org.

NEUNTEUFL, THOMAS NEUNTEUFL, cardiologist; b. Gmünd, Feb. 19, 1966; Matura, Piaristengymnasium Krems, U. Entrance, 1984; MD, U. Vienna Med. Sch., 1992. Dir., cardiac catheterization lab., divsn. cardiology Dept. Internal Medicine II Vienna Gen. Hosp., 2009—. Prof. Med. U. Vienna, 2002. Mem.: Austrian Soc. Cardiology (prize 1998). Avocations: skiing, bicycling, swimming. Office: Währinger Gürtel 18-20 Wien A-1090 Austria E-mail: thomas.neunteufl@meduniwien.ac.at.

NEUPERT, WALTER, chemistry professor; PhD in BioChemistry, U. Munich, 1968, MD, 1970. Asst. prof., Inst. Physiological Chemistry U. Munich, 1969—72, privatdozent, Inst. Physiological Chemistry Germany, 1972—77, prof. biochemistry & cell biology, 1983—, prof., Inst. Physiological Chemistry, Physical Biochemistry and Cell Biology, 1983—; assoc. prof., Inst. Biochemistry U. Göttingen, Germany, 1977—79, prof., Inst. Biochemistry, 1979—89. Former mem. ed. bd. Cell, Jour. of Biological Chemistry, European Molecular Biology Orgn. Jour., now chmn. Editl. bd. Biological Chemistry, 1987—93, Cell, 1988—90, Seminars in Cell Biology, 1989—92, Protein Science, 1990—93, Journal Biological Chemistry, 1998—2000, European Journal Cell Biology, 1995—, Cell Stress and Chaperones, 1995—, monitoring editor Journal of Cell Biology, 1989—95, mng. editor European Journal of Biochemistry, 1988—91. Recipient Heinrich-Wieland prize, 1993, Academia Europaea award, 1993, Feldberg Found. prize, 1996, Gairdner Found. Internat. award, 1998. Mem. European Molecular Biology Orgn.(EMBO)(coun. mem., 1996-, coun. chmn. 1997-2000, editor-in-chief, EMBO Reports, 1999-2000, adv. bd. of EMBO jour. 1986-89, 1998-2000, 2001-), Cell Stress Soc. Internat., Protein Soc., Am. Soc. for Cell Biology(E.B. Wilson award, 2000), German Soc. of Cell Biology, German Soc. Chemistry, German Soc. Biochemistry and Molecular Biology (pres. 1995-97, v.p., 1997-99, Otto Warburg medal, 2000), Bavarian Acad. Sciences, German Acad. Sciences Leopoldina (Schleiden medal, 1999), Nordrhein-Westfalische Acad. Sciences (corr. mem.), Royal Netherlands Acad. Arts and Sciences (fgn. mem.), German Rsch. Soc. (mem. Senate and coun.); chmn. nominating com., Internat. Union of Biochemistry and Molecular Biology, 1997-. Office: Adolf-Butenandt Institut Physiological Chemistry U Munich Butenandtstr 5 Gebäude B Rm B2 024 81377 Munich Germany Office Phone: 49 89 2180 77095. Business E-Mail: Neupert@med.uni-muenchen.de. *

NEURATH, A. ROBERT, retired virologist, consultant; b. Bratislava, Czechoslovakia, Slovak Republic, May 8, 1933; arrived in U.S., 1964; s. Ernest Neurath and Lenka Weinberger; m. Paula F Krauss, Nov. 19, 2003. Ing., Inst. of Tech., Bratislava, Czechoslovakia, 1957; PhD, Inst. of Tech., Vienna, Austria, 1968. Investigator Slovak Acad. of Sciences, Bratislava, 1957—59; lab. head Bioveta Nitra, Nitra, 1959—61; rsch. scientist Acad. of Sciences, Bratislava, 1961—64, Wistar Inst., Philadelphia, Pa., 1964—65; lab. head Wyeth Laboratories, Radnor, Pa., 1965—72; mem. NY Blood Ctr., New York, NY, 1972—2006. Contbr. articles to profl. jours.; co-author: (book) Viral Structural Components as Immunogens of Prophylactic Value, vol. 4, 1971; co-editor: Immunochemistry of Viruses, 1985, Immunochemistry of Viruses II, 1990. Grantee, NIH, 1972—2006. Achievements include patents for; research in virology, immunology; Influenza, Rabies, Hepatitis B, HIV. Home Phone: 212-529-4584.

NEUSTADT, DAVID HAROLD, physician; b. Evansville, Ind., Dec. 2, 1925; s. Mose and Leah (Epstein) N.; m. Carolyn Jacobson, June 15, 1952; children: Susan Miriam, Jeffrey Bruce, Robert Alan. Student, DePauw U., 1943-44, 46-47; MD, U. Louisville, 1950. Intern Morrisania City Hosp., NYC, 1950-51; resident in internal medicine Lenox Hill Hosp., NYC, 1951-52, NIH trainee in rheumatic diseases, 1952-53, resident in gastroenterology, 1953-54; practice medicine specializing in rheumatic diseases Louisville, 1954—; chief arthritis clinic Louisville Gen. Hosp., 1960-76; asst. prof. medicine Sch. Medicine, U. Louisville, 1963-67, asso. prof. clin. medicine, 1967-75, clin. prof. medicine, 1974—, head sect. rheumatic diseases, 1960-76; chief dept. medicine Jewish Hosp., Louisville, 1965-67, pres. med. staff, 1967-69; cons. in rheumatology VA, 1970—. Advisor Network for Continuing Med. Edn., 1983—. Author: The Chemistry and Therapy of Collagen Diseases, 1963, (with other) Aspiration and Injection Therapy in Arthritis and Musculoskeletal Disorders, 1972; editor: (with other) Arthritis Abstracts, References Indexes, 1970-75; contbr. articles to profl. jours. Former pres., chmn. bd. med. sci. com. Ky. chpt. Arthritis Found. Served with AUS, 1944-46. Master Am. Coll. Rheumatology (formerly Am. Rheumatism Assn.; mem. editl. bd. 1989-94, exec. com., pres. ctrl. region 1982-84, Disting. Rheumatologist award 1997); fellow Am. Med. Writers Assn., ACP; mem. AMA, N.Y. Acad. Sci., N.Y. Rheumatism Soc., Ky. Rheumatism Assn. (pres. 1956-57), Internat. Soc. Internal Medicine, So. Med. Assn. (edn. com., sect. rheumatology), Am. Physicians Fellowship (nat. trustee 1984—), Spondylitis Assn. (adv. bd. 1986—, contbg. editor 1989—, mem. editl. bd. Arthritis Care and Rsch. Newsletter 1989—), Mason, Shriner. Jewish. Home: 216 Smithfields Rd Louisville KY 40207-1267 Office: Med Towers Louisville KY 40202 Office Phone: 502-585-4163. E-mail: MD@DavidHNeustadt.com.

NEUWIRTH, MICHAEL G., orthopedist, surgeon, educator; b. NYC, Oct. 9, 1948; BA with distinction, Cornell U.; MD cum laude, SUNY Downstate Med. Sch., 1974. Cert. Am. Bd. Orthopaedic Surgery, 1980, lic. NY. Intern, dept. surgery Kings County Hosp., Bklyn., 1973—74; resident orthopaedics Hosp. For Joint Diseases Orthopaedic Inst., NYC, 1974—78, attending, orthopaedics, 1979, chief scoliosis svc., 1988, chief spine svc., 1991; fellow spinal surgery rsch. Rush-Presbyn.-St. Luke's Med. Ctr., Chgo., 1978—79; spinal cons. City Hosp. Ctr., Elmhurst, NY, 1979—83; attending, orthopaedics Beth Israel Med. Ctr., NY, 1979; assoc. attending NYU/Tisch, NYC, 1995; dir. Spine Inst. of NY, Beth Israel Med. Ctr., NYC, 1996—. Asst. clin. prof. orthopaedics Mount Sinai Sch. Medicine, 1979; assoc. clin. prof. orthopaedics NYU Sch. Medicine, 1995—. Author: The Scoliosis Sourcebook; contbr. articles to med. jours. Fellow: ACS, Am. Acad. Orthop. Surgeons, Scoliosis Rsch. Soc. (bd. mem. 1996, chmn., instrumentation com. 1990, sect. leader, core curriculum 1999); mem.: Scoliosis Assn., NY State Soc. Orthop.

Surgeons, NY State Med. Soc., NY County Med. Soc., NY Acad. Medicine, Alpha Omega Alpha. Office: Spine Inst of NY Beth Israel Med Ctr 10 Union Square E Ste 5P New York NY 10003 Office Phone: 212-844-8680. Office Fax: 212-844-8681.

NEUWIRTH, ROBERT SAMUEL, obstetrician, gynecologist, educator; b. NYC, July 11, 1933; s. Abraham Alexander and Phyllis Neuwirth; children from previous marriage: Susan, Jessica, Laura, Michael, Alexander. BS, Yale U., 1955, MD, 1958. Intern Presbyn. Hosp., NYC, 1958-59, resident, 1959-64; asst. prof. ob-gyn. Columbia U., NYC, 1964-68, assoc. prof., 1968-71, prof., 1972-2001, Babcock prof., 1977-2001, Babcock prof. emeritus, 2001—. Dir. ob-gyn. Bronx Lebanon Hosp., NYC, 1967-72, Woman's Hosp., NYC, St. Luke's Hosp. Ctr., 1974—, St. Luke's Roosevelt Hosp., 1981-91; prof. Albert Einstein Coll. Medicine, 1971-72; cons. WHO, NIH, AID, FDA; interim dir. St. Luke's Roosevelt Hosp., 1998-2000. Author: Hysteroscopy, 1975; contbr. articles to profl. jours. Mem.: ACOG, Assn. Vol. Sterilization (chmn. biomed. com. 1971—), Am. Assn. Profs. Ob-Gyn., NY Obstet. Soc., Soc. Gynecol. Investigation, Am. Gynecol. and Obstet. Soc. Office: St Lukes Roosevelt Hosp 1000 10th Ave Dept Ob New York NY 10019-1147 Office Phone: 212-523-8368.

NEUZIL, PETR, cardiologist, researcher; b. Prague, Feb. 1, 1962; s. Josef Neuzil and Marie Neuzilova; m. Ivana Boturova, Apr. 14, 1989; children: Ondra, Kamila Neuzilova. MD, Charles U., Prague, 1987, PhD, 2001. Residency in internal medicine Gen. Hosp. Charles U., Prague, Czech Republic, 1989—91; fellowship in cardiology Heart Centrum, Bad Krozingen, 1991—93; with Beth Israel Deaconnes Med. Ctr., 1997, 1998, Mass. Gen. Hosp., 1998—2000; dir. cardiac arrhythmia svc. Na Homolce Hosp., Prague, 2004—, head cardiology, 2009; dir. animal lab. Charles U., Prague, 2006—, assoc. prof., 2007. Dir. Cardiac Arrhythmias Found., Prague, 2005—07; cons. Tech. Sch., Prague, 2005—. Editor: (jour.) Practicioner. Grantee, NIH, 2003, 2006. Fellow: European Soc. Cardiology (assoc.); mem.: European Heart Rhythm Assn., Heart Rhythm Soc. Achievements include development of Esophageal temperature probe; research in robotic cardiac catheterization; electromechanical robotic catheterization system Sensei and electromagnetic navigation Niobe; balloon technology in catheter ablation technology, mainly laser energy. Office: Na Homolce Hosp Roentgenova 2 150 30 Prague Czech Republic Personal E-mail: petr.neuzil@gmail.com. Business E-Mail: pneuzil@seznam.cz.

NEVA, MARKO HENRIK, surgeon, consultant; b. Pori, Finland, Sept. 29, 1968; s. Lasse Olavi and Kerttu Maria Neva; m. Pia Johanna Isomaki, May 15, 2003; children: Joonatan Rudolf, Aurora Emilia, Minea Maria. MD, Turku U., 1993; PhD, Tampere U., Finland, 2002. Cert. specialist in orthop. and trauma surgery Finland, 2002. Cons. orthop. and trauma surgeon, rschr. Tampere U. Hosp., 2002—, head orthop. spine surgery. Contbr. scientific papers, articles to profl. med. internat. jours. Med. capt. Finnish Army. Mem.: Finnish Soc. Spine Surgery (chmn. 2008—09), Finnish Soc. Rheumatology, Finnish Surg. Soc., AO-Spine, Spine Soc. Europe. Office: Tampere Univ Hosp PO Box 2000 Tampere FIN-33521 Finland Office Fax: 358 3 31169370. Business E-Mail: marko.neva@pshp.fi.

NEVILL, DAVID SCOTT, health facility administrator; s. Gailyn Richard and Velda Lee Nevill; m. Neoma David Patel, Dec. 28, 1990; children: Nisha, Nina. BA, Graceland Coll., 1983; MSc in Healthcare Adminstrn., U. Mo., 1989, MSc in Bus. Adminstrn., 1992. Asst. exec. dir. San Leondro (Calif.) Hosp., 1991—93; assoc. exec. dir. Overland Pk. (Kans.) Regional Med. Ctr., 1993—94; v.p. profl. svcs. Independence (Mo.) Regional Health Ctr., 1994—95; v.p., COO Mt. Oread Med. Arts Ctr., Lawrence, Kans., 1995—96; CEO Halstead (Kans.) Hosp., 1996—98; COO Wesley Med. Ctr., Wichita, Kans., 1998—2001, CEO, 2001—. Cons. Witt, Kieffer, Ford, Hadelman and Lloyd, Oak Brook, Ill., 1989—90. Bd. trustees Ctrl. Pains Regulation Health Found., Wichita, 2002—, United Way, Wichita, 2004. Mem.: Coalition Advancement Crners in Healthcare (bd. dir.), Rotary. Avocations: sailing, photography, reading, rebuilding cars. Office: Wesley Medical Ctr 550 N Hillside Wichita KS 67214

NEVO, EVIATAR, biology educator; b. Tel Aviv, Feb. 2, 1929; s. David and Lea (Goldis) Levitas; m. Sarah Schneider, July 1951 (div.); children: Tal (dec.), Orit. MS in Biology with spl. distinction, Hebrew U., Jerusalem, 1958; PhD in Biology summa cum laude, Hebrew U., 1964. Lectr. biology Oranim Tchrs. state Coll., Israel, 1956-63; fellow in biology Harvard U., 1965-66; rsch. assoc. dept. genetics Hebrew U., Jerusalem, 1967-68, lectr. genetics, 1968-70, sr. lectr., 1970-71; rsch. assoc. Mus. Vertebrate Zoology U. Calif., Berkeley, 1972-73, U. Chgo., Berkeley, 1972—73; assoc. prof. biology U. Haifa, Israel, 1973—75, prof. biology, 1975—, dir. Inst. Evolution, 1977—2008, incumbent chair evolutionary biology, 1984—2008; dir. Internat. Grad. Ctr. Evolution, 2004—. Editl. bd. mem. Open Sys. Biology Jour., 2008, Bentham Open Sys. Biology Jour., 2009, Ecology & Noospherology, 1995; adj. prof. Wuhan Bot. Gardens, Chinese Acad. Scis., 2010—. Editor: (with S. Karlin) Population Genetics and Ecology, 1976, The Evolutionary Significance of Genetic Diversity: Ecological, Demographic And Life History Correlates, 1984, Cosmic, Biological and Human Evolution, 1989, Evolutionary Processes and Theory, 1986, Evolution of Subterranean Mammals at the Organismal & Molecular Levels, 1990, (with O.A. Reig) Evolution of Subterranean Mammals at the Organismal and Molecular Levels, 1990, Medicinal Mushrooms Ganoderma Lucidum, 1997, Evolution Canyon, 1999, Mosaic Evolution of Subterranean Mammals: Regression, Progression and global Conversion, 1999, Biodiversity of Cyanoprocaryotes, Algae and Fungi of Israel: Cyanoprocaryotes and Algae & Fungi of Israel: Soil Microfungi of Israel, 2001, (with E. Ivanitskaya and A. Beiles) Adaptive Radiation of Blind Subterranean Mole Rats: Naming & Revisiting the Four Sibling Species of the Spalax Ehrenbergi Superspecies in Israel, 2001, Evolution of Wild Emmer And Wheat Improvement, 2002, Coleoptera of Evolution Canyon II Lower Nahal Keziv, 2002, Biodiversity of Cyanoprocaryotes algae & fungi of Israel, 2002, Fungal Life in the Dead Sea, 2003, Late Cretaceous Turonian of Southern Negev, Israel, 2005, author: Mosaic Evolution of Subterranean Mammals: Regression, Progression, and Global Convergence, 1999, Microstructures of Vegetative Mycelium of Macromycetes in Pure Cultures, 2009, Microscopic Algae in the Yarqon, 2010; mem. editorial bd.: Theoretical Population Biology, 1975, Evolutionary Theory, 1978-2011, Israel Jour. Zoology, 1981, Genetique, Selection, Evolution, 1985, The First Checklist of Lichen Forming and Lichenicolous Fungi of Israel, 1996, Bolletino Zoologico, 1985, Internat. Jour. Glirology, 1991, Evolutionary Ecology, 1991-2002, Ecology and Noospherology, 1995; contbr. over 1200 articles to profl. sci. publs., profl. jours. in Natural Sci. Recipient Foremost Scientists of World, IBC, Cambridge, 2009, Man of Yr., ABI, Israel, 2009, Iconic Achievement & Internat. Einstein award, IBC, 2009, 2011, Internat. Peace prize, United Cultural Conv., 2010, Am. Order of Merit, ABI, 2010, Intellectual of Yr., 2010, Gold medal, ABI, Israel, 2011, Top 100 Educators, IBC, 2011, Albert Einsein award, 2011, Internat. Peace prize, 2010, award, Seat Wisdom ABI, 2010, medal, IBC Cambridge, 2008; named Man of Yr., ABI, Israel, 1997, 2003, 2005—11, Internat. Scientist of Yr., IBC, 2008; named one of Leading Scientist of World, IBC, Cambridge, 2009, Man of Yr., IBC, 2011, 2000 Outstanding Intellectuals of 21st Century, 2011; named to Hall of Fame, ABI, Israel, 2009, 2011, Gt. Minds of 21st Century Hall of Fame, 2011. Fellow AAAS (fgn. mem.), N.Y. Acad. Sci. (Charles Darwin Assocs.); mem. Nat. Acad. Sci. US (fgn. assoc.), Soc. for Study Evolution (v.p. 1978), Am. Soc. Naturalists, Genetics Soc. Am., Genetics Soc. Israel, Zool. Soc. Israel, Geol. Soc. Israel, Ukrainian Bot. Soc. (hon.), Assn. Iberoamericana Biology Evolution (directing coun. 1993), Human Genome Orgn., Ukraine NAS (fgn.), World Univ. Roundtable (hon. cultural doctorate), Linnean Soc. London (fgn. mem.), Internat. Soc. Molecular Evolution. Avocations: music, theater, art. Home: 3 Hazaz St Haifa 34996 Israel Office: Haifa U Inst Evolution Mount Carmel 31999 Haifa Israel Office Phone: 972 4 8240448. Fax: 972 04.8246554. Business E-Mail: nevo@research.haifa.ac.il.

NEVRLY, MARTIN, neurologist; b. Olomouc, Mar. 7, 1978; MD, Palacky U. Olomouc, 2003. Physician Dept. Neurology, U. Hosp. Olomouc, 2004—. Mem.: Ceská Lékarská Spolecnost J.E.Purkyne, Movement Disorders Soc. Office: IPPavlova 6 Olomouc Haná 77520 Czech Republic Business E-Mail: nevrly.martin@post.cz.

NEW, MARIA IANDOLO, pediatrician, educator; b. NYC; d. Loris J. and Esther B. (Giglio) Iandolo; m. Bertrand L. New, 1949 (dec. 1990); children: Erica, Daniel, Antonia. BA, Cornell U., 1950; MD, U. Pa., 1954; degree in medicine (hon.), U. degli Studi di Roma, Rome, 1999, U. di Parma, Italy, 2000. Diplomate Am. Bd. Pediat. Med. intern Bellevue Hosp., NYC, 1954-55; resident in pediat. N.Y. Hosp., 1955-57; fellow NIH, 1957-58, 61-64; practice medicine specializing in pediat. NYC, 1955—; mem. staff N.Y. Hosp., dir. Pediatric Endocrine and Metabolism Clinic, 1964—2004, attending pediatrician, 1971-80; pediatrician-in-chief N.Y.-Presbyn. Hosp., 1980—2002, dir. pediatric endocrinology, 1964—2004; prof. pediat. and human genetics Mt. Sinai Sch. Medicine, NYC. Asst. prof. dept. pediat. Joan and Sanford Weill Med. Coll. of Cornell U., N.Y.C., 1963-68, assoc. prof., 1968-71, prof., 1971-2004, Harold and Percy Uris prof. pediatric endocrinology, 1978-2004, prof., 1980-2004, chmn. dept. pediat., 1980-2002; program dir. Childrens Clin. Rsch. Ctr., 1996-2002; assoc. dir. Pediatric Clin. Rsch. Ctr., 1980-88; adj. faculty prof. Rockefeller U., 1981—; career scientist N.Y.C. Health Rsch. Coun., 1966-75; adj. attending pedatrician dept. pediat. Meml. Sloan-Kettering Cancer Ctr., 1979-93; cons. United Hosp., Port Chester, N.Y., 1977—, North Shore Univ. Hosp., 1982-97, dept. pediat. Cath. Med. Ctr. Bklyn. and Queens, N.Y., 1987—; vis. physician Rockefeller U. Hosp., N.Y.C., 1973-87; mem. endocrine study sect. NIH, 1977-80, Gen. Clin. Rsch. Ctrs. Adv. Com.; chmn. Divsn. Rsch. Resources Gen. Clin. Rsch. Ctrs. Com. NIH, 1987-88; bd. dirs. Robert Wood Johnson Clin. Scholars Program; mem. N.Y. State Gov.'s Task Force on Life and Law, 1985-2008; mem. NIH Reviewers Res.; mem. FDA endocrinology and metabolism drug adv. com., 1994—; panelist ACGME bd. appeals, 1994—, cons. Meml. Sloan-Kettering Cancer Ctr., 1993-2007, Meml. Hosp. for the Cancer and Allied Diseases, 1993—; hon. mem. pediat. dept. Blythedale Children's Hosp., Valhalla, N.Y., 1992—; mem. rsch. adv. com. Population Coun. Ctr. for Biomed. Rsch., 1991-97. Editor-in-chief Jour. Clin. Endocrinology and Metabolism, 1994-99; mem. editl. adv. coun. Jour. Endocrinological Investigation, 1995—; mem. editl. bd. Jour. Women's Health, 1993, Endotext; corr. editor Jour. Steroid Biochemistry, 1985; mem. adv. bd. pediatric anns., assoc. editor Metabolism. Trustee Irma T. Hirschl Trust. Recipient Mary Jane Kugel award Juvenile Diabetes Found., 1977, Katharine D. McCormick Disting. Lectureship, 1981, Robert H. Williams Disting. Leadership award, 1988, Albion O. Bernstein award Med. Soc. State N.Y., 1988, medal N.Y. Acad. Medicine, 1991, Disting. Grad. award U. Pa. Sch. Medicine, 1991, Optimate Recognition award Assn. Student-Profl. Italian-Ams., 1991, Outstanding Woman Scientist award N.Y. chpt. Am. Women in Sci., 1986, Maurice R. Greenberg Disting. Svc. award, 1994, Humanitarian award Juvenile Diabetes Found., 1994, Rhône Poulenc Rorer Clin. Investigator Lecture award, 1994, Dale medal Brit. Endocrine Soc., 1996, MERIT award USPHS, NIHCHD, 1998, 11th Ann. award for excellence in clin. rsch. USPHS, NIH, 1998, Judson J. Van Wyk prize Lawson Wilkins Pediat. Endocrine Soc., 2010, Pioneer award CARES Found., Inc., 2010; grantee; named to Hall of Honor, NICHD, 2003. Fellow AAAS, Italian Soc. Endocrinology (hon.); mem. NAS (sr. mem. Inst. Medicine), AAAS, APHA, Am. Soc. Human Genetics, Am. Acad. Pediat., Soc. for Pediatric Rsch., Harvey Soc., Endocrine Soc. (mem. coun. 1981-84, pres. 1991-92, Fred Conrad Koch award 2003), Lawson Wilkins Pediatric Endocrine Soc. (pres. 1985-86), Am. Soc. Nephrology, Am. Soc. Pediatric Nephrology, Am. Pediatric Soc., Am. Fedn. Clin. Rsch., Am. Diabetes Assn., European Soc. Pediatric Endocrinology, Soc. for the Advancement of Women's Health Rsch. (basic sci. award 1996), Am. Coll. Clin. Pharmacology, Am. Clin. and Climatol. Assn., N.Y. Acad. Scis., Pan Am. Med. Assn., Assn. Am. Physicians, Am. Fertility Soc., U.S. Pharmacopeial Conv. (elected), Am. Acad. of Arts and Scis. (elected 1992), Alpha Omega Alpha. Office: Mt Sinai Sch Medicine Box 1198 1 Gustave L Levy Pl New York NY 10029 Office Phone: 212-241-7847. E-mail: maria.new@mssm.edu.

NEWBRUN, ERNEST, oral biology and periodontology educator; b. Vienna, Dec. 1, 1932; came to U.S., 1955; s. Victor and Elizabeth (Reichl) N; m. Eva Miriam, June 17, 1956; children: Deborah Anne, Daniel Eric, Karen Ruth. BDS, Sydney U., Australia, 1954; MS, U. Rochester, 1957; DMD, U. Ala., 1959; PhD, U. Calif., San Francisco, 1965; Odont. Dr. (hon.), U. Lund, Sweden, 1988; DDSc (hon.), U. Sydney, 1997. Cert. periodontology, 1983; hon. diplomate, Am. Bd. Dental Pub. Health, 2009. Rsch. assoc. Eastman Dental Ctr., Rochester, NY, 1955-57, U. Ala. Med. Ctr., Birmingham, 1957-59; rsch. fellow Inst. Dental Rsch., Sydney, 1960-61; rsch. tchr. trainee U. Calif., San Francisco, 1961-63, postdoctoral fellow, 1963-65, assoc. prof., 1965-70, prof. oral biology, 1970-83, prof. oral biology and periodontology, 1983-94, prof. emeritus, 1994—; prof. Fromm Inst. Lifelong Learning U. San Francisco, 2000—. Cons. FDA, 1983—. Author: Cariology, 1989, Pharmacology and Therapeutics for Dentistry, 2004, (with others) Pediatrics, 1991; editor: Fluorides and Dental Caries, 1986; mem. editl. bd. Jour. Periodontal Rsch., 1985-90, Jour. Periodontology, 1990-2005. Bd. dirs. Raoul Wallenberg Dem. Club, San Francisco, 1987-92. Fellow AAAS (chmn. dental section, 1988-89), Internat. Assn. Dental Rsch. (pres. 1989-90) Jewish. Avocations: gardening, hiking, opera, theater. Personal E-mail: enewbrun@gmail.com.

NEWBURGER, HOWARD MARTIN, psychoanalyst; b. NYC, May 16, 1924; s. Bernhard and Bertha (Travers) N.; m. Doris Schekter, July 3, 1949; children: Amy, Barry, Cary. BA, NYU, 1948, MA, 1950, PhD, 1952; tng. in Jungian, Neo-Freudian and Horneyian psychoanalysis. Cert. in group psychotherapy and psychodrama. Rotating intern N.J. Dept. Instns. and Agys., 1948-49; chief psychologist N.J. State Instn., Annandale, 1949-52; dir. psychoanalysis Div. Social Def. UN, 1952; pvt. practice in psychoanalysis and group psychotherapy, 1952—; dir. rsch. HEW, 1958; rsch. assoc. Beth Israel Hosp., 1958-69. Staff mem. St. Agnes Hosp., White Plains, 1991-93; lectr., adj. assoc. prof. NYU, 1951-60, chmn. dept. exceptional child and youth, 1954-62; chmn. faculty and supr. treatment Inst. Applied Human Dynamics, 1960-99; prelect prof. psychology John Jay Coll. Criminal Justice, 1969-72; chmn. bd. dirs. Inst. Applied Human Dynamics, N.Y.C. and Westchester, N.Y., 1960-81, exec. v.p., 1983-85; dean faculty IAHD, 1999-2002; forensic examiner N.Y.S. Supreme Ct., 2005-06; lectr., cons. in field. Co-author: Winners and Losers. Assoc. editor: Excerpta Medica, 1951-62. Contbr. articles and papers to tech. jours. Trustee Acad. Jewish Religion, 1991-96. Served with AUS, World War II, ETO; with AUS, MTO. Recipient Outstanding Service to Humanity award Inst. Applied Human Dynamics for Handicapped, 1970 Mem. Am. Psychol. Assn., Am. Soc. Group Psychotherapy and Psychodrama (sec.-treas. 1954-55). Office: 4 Timber Trl Rye NY 10580-1935 Office Phone: 914-967-4011. Business E-Mail: howardornew@optonline.net.

NEWBURGER, JANE WIMPFHEIMER, pediatric cardiologist; b. NYC, 1949; AB summa cum laude, Bryn Mawr Coll., Pa., 1971; MD, Harvard U. Med. Sch., Boston, 1974; MPH, Harvard U. Sch. Pub. Health, 1980. Cert. Nat. Bd. Med. Examiners, 1975, Am. Bd. Pediat., 1979, in pediatric cardiology 1983, lic. Mass., 1979, registered in controlled substance US, 2002, Mass., 2003. Internship in medicine Children's Hosp. Med. Ctr., Boston, 1974—75, jr. asst. residency in medicine, 1975—76, fellowship in cardiology, 1976—79, attending physician, cardiology svc., 1979—, asst. in cardiology, 1979—80, assoc. in cardiology, 1980—90, sr. assoc. cardiology, 1990—, assoc. cardiologist-in-chief, dept. cardiology, 1995—2006, assoc. chief academic affairs, dept. cardiology, 2006—; clin. fellowship in pediat. Harvard U. Med. Sch., 1974—79, instr. pediat., 1979—84, asst. prof. pediat., assoc. prof. pediat., 1989—98, prof. pediat., 1998—. Dir. Friday cardiology clinic Children's Hosp. Med. Ctr., 1979—88, dir. preventive cardiology clinic, 1987—, dir. outpatient cardiology, 1990—94, assoc. dir. tng. program in pediatric cardiology and cardiovascular rsch., 1990—, dir. clin. rsch. svc., dept. cardiology, 1993—, mem. numerous adminstrv. and academic committees and boards, 1985—, Harvard U. Med. Sch., 1997—. Co-editor: Brain Injury and Pediatric Cardiac Surgery, 1995, ad hoc reviewer: New Eng. Jour. Medicine, Jour. Pediat., Pediat., Am. Jour. Cardiology, Jour. Thoracic and Cardiovascular Surgery, assoc. editor, ad hoc reviewer: Circulation, 2004—, mem. editl. bd.: Harvard Heart Letter, 1992—, theheart.org, 2000—, Cardiology in the Young, 2006—, contbr. articles to numerous profl. med. jours., chapters to books. Active on various committees Nat. Heart, Lung and Blood Inst. Recipient Scholastic Achievement award, Am. Women's Med. Assn., 1974, Nat. Rsch. Svc. award, Nat. Heart, Lung and Blood Inst., 1978—80, New Investigator award, 1982—85, Spirit award, Children's Hosp., 1991; named to Best Doctor's in America, 1992—, Best Doctor's in Boston, Boston Mag., 1997, 2003, Best Doctor's in Women's Health, 2001, America's Top Doctor's, Castle Connolly, 2002—, Boston Area's Top Doctors, Boston Consumer Checkbook, 2004—; grantee, NIH. Fellow: Am. Coll. Cardiology (program com., pediatric chair 1997—, pediatric cardiology fellowship subcom. 1997—, writing com., Bethesda conf. 2004—05, Disting. Scientist award, clin. 2007), Am. Heart Assn. (com. on tng. in pediatric cardiology 1993—95, membership com., Coun. on Cardiovascular Disease in the Young 1993—95, exec. com., Coun. on Cardiovascular Disease in the Young 1993—, rheumatic fever, endocarditis, Kawasaki disease com. 1994—97, assoc. chair, com. on RF, endocarditis, KD 1999, chair, com. on RF, ednocarditis, KD 2000—04, mem. writing group 2004—05, chair, comm. com., Quality of Care and Outcomes IWG 2004—), Am. Acad. Pediat. (exec. com., cardiology sect. 1999—, chair nominations com., pediatric cardiology sect. 2005—); mem.: Mass. Med. Soc., Soc. Pediatric Rsch. Office: Children's Hosp Boston Dept Cardiology 300 Longwood Ave Boston MA 02115 Office Phone: 617-355-5427. Office Fax: 617-739-3784. Business E-Mail: jane.newburger@cardio.chboston.org.

NEWCOMER, JOHN WHITNEY, psychiatrist, researcher, educator; b. Subic Bay Naval Base, Philippines; s. John L. and Barbara L. Newcomer; children: Leah Eliza, Adam Samuel. AB, Brown U., 1981; postgrad., U. Calif., San Francisco, 1984, Yale U., 1984; MD, Wayne State U., 1985. Diplomate Nat. Bd. Med. Examiners, Am. Bd. Psychiatry and Neurology. Intern in internal medicine Sinai Hosp., Detroit, 1985—86; resident in psychiatry Stanford U. Sch. Medicine, Calif., 1986—89, rsch. fellow in psychiatry Dept. Vets. Affairs Med. Ctr. Palo Alto, Calif., 1988—90; instr. dept. psychiatry Washington U. Sch. Medicine, St. Louis, 1990—92, asst. prof. psychiatry, 1992—2000, adj. asst. prof. psychology, 1997—2001, assoc. prof. psychiatry, 2000—, med. dir. Ctr. for Clin. Studies, 2006—; assoc. prof. psychology rsch. Malcolm Bliss Mental Health Ctr., St. Louis, 1990—95, prof. psychology rsch., 2005—08, Gregory B. Couch prof., 2008—; co-dir. Regulatory Support Ctr., Washington U., 2007, dir. clin. trials unit, 2007—. Chmn. drug utilization rev. bd. Mo. Dept. Social Svcs., Divsn. Med. Svc., 1997—; mem. study sect., spl. emphasis panels, ad hoc mem. treatment assessment sect. NIMH, 1998—; rsch. med. safety officer Gen. Clin. Rsch. Ctr., 2001—04; lectr. in field.; mem. med. staff Barnes Hosp., St. Louis, 1990—94, Jewish Hosp., St. Louis, 1990—94, Barnes/Jewish Hosps., St. Louis, 1994—; cons. in field; adhoc reviewer for numerous jours., 1990—; editl. bd. mem. neuropsychopharmacology, 2002—07; editl. bd. mem. Jour. Psychotic Disorders, 2003—, Clin. Schizophrenia & Related Psychoses, 2006—, Current Psychiatry, 2007—09, Obesity Jour., 2007—, Neuropsychiatry Reviews, 2008—, Schizophrenia Bulletin, 2009—. Contbr. numerous articles, abstracts to profl. publs. Recipient Scientist Devel. award, NIMH, 1992—97, Ind. Scientist award, 1997—2002. Mem.: AMA, AAAS, NIMH IRC, ITVA Commn., Am.

Diabetes Assn., Am. Coll. Psychiatrists, Internat. Soc. Psychoneuroendocrinology, Soc. for Neurosci., Am. Pschopathol. Assn., Ea. Mo. Psychiat. Soc., Am. Psychiat. Assn., Am. Coll. Neuropsychopharmacology, Alpha Omega Alpha, Sigma Xi, Phi Beta Kappa. Office: Washington U Sch Medicine Dept Psychiatry 660 S Euclid Ave Campus Box 8134 Saint Louis MO 63110 Office Phone: 314-362-5939. E-mail: newcomerj@wustl.edu.

NEWGARD, CHRISTOPHER B., medical educator; B in Botany and Zoology, Duke U.; PhD, U. Tex., 1984. Prof. dept. biochemistry, dept. internal medicine U. Tex. Southwestern Med. Ctr., Dallas, Gifford O. Touchstone and Randolph G. Touchstone Disting. chair, prof., 1994—2002, co-dir., Touchstone Ctr. for Diabetes Rsch.; dir., Sarah W. Stedman Nutrition and Metabolism Ctr. Duke U. Sch. Medicine, 2002—, W. David and Sarah W. Stedman Disting. Prof., 2002—, prof. pharmacology and cancer biology, 2002—, prof. medicine, 2002—. Contbr. several articles to profl. jours. Trustee Insulin-Free World Found. Mem.: NIH (mem. metabolism study sect.), Am. Diabetes Assn. (mem. grant rev. bd., Outstanding Sci. Achievement award 2001). Office: Duke U Med Ctr Duke Independence Park Facility 4321 Medical Park Dr Durham NC 27704 Office Phone: 919-668-6059. Business E-Mail: christopher.newgard@utsouthwestern.edu, newga002@mc.duke.edu.

NEWGENT, REBECCA ANN, counselor, educator; b. Ohio; BA in Psychology, Kent State U., Ohio, 1986, MEd in Cmty. Counseling, 1993; PhD in Guidance and Counseling, U. Akron, Ohio, 2001. Cert. family and divorce mediator. Case mgr. II/counselor trainee Cmty. Support Svcs., Inc., Akron, Ohio, 1988—93; counselor, family life edn. coord., vol. coord., divorce mediator Jewish Family Svc., Akron, 1993—95; counselor Cath. Svc. League, Akron, 1995—96; divorce mediator Domestic Rels. Divsn. Summit County Ct. Common Pleas, Akron, 1995—99; pvt. practice counselor, divorce mediator Akron Psychol. Assocs., 1995—98; counselor, sch.-based counselor, divorce mediator Cath. Social Svcs. of Summit County, Inc., Akron, 1997—99; emergency clinician Portage Path Behavioral Health-Psychiat. Emergency Svcs., Akron, 1997—2000; grad. asst. dept. counseling and spl. edn. U. Akron, 1998—2000, mem. adj. faculty dept. ednl. founds. and leadership, 2000, mem. ad hoc temporary grad. faculty, doctoral intern dept. counseling and spl. edn., 2000—01; asst. prof. counselor edn. U. Ark., Fayetteville, 2001—06, assoc. prof., 2006—10; prof., chairperson Western Ill. U.-Quad Cities, 2011—. Bd. advisors The Clinic for Child Study and Family Therapy U. Akron, 1998—2001. Mem. mental health trauma action team Summit County Red Cross Disaster Svcs., Akron, 1998—2000. Recipient Southern Assn. Coun. Edn. & Supervision award, 2008; named Rschr. of Yr., Ark. Counseling Assn., 2008, COEHS Faculty scholar, Assn. Child & Adolescent Counseling, 2011. Mem.: ACA, Am. Ednl. Rsch. Assn., Assn. Assessment in Counseling & Devel., Assn. Counselor Edn. and Supervision, Chi Sigma Iota (Outstanding Doctoral Student award 2001). Office: Western Ill University-Quad Cities 3561 60th St Moline IL 61265 Office Fax: 309-762-6989. Business E-Mail: ra-newgent@wiu.edu.

NEWHOUSE, JOSEPH PAUL, economist, educator; b. Waterloo, Iowa, Feb. 24, 1942; s. Joseph Alexander and Ruth Linnea (Johnson) Newhouse; m. Margaret Louise Locke, June 22, 1968; children: Eric Joseph, David Locke. BA, Harvard U., 1963, PhD, 1969; postgrad (Fulbright scholar), Goethe U., Frankfort, Germany, 1963—64. Staff economist Rand Corp., Santa Monica, Calif., 1968—72, dep. program mgr., health and biosci. rsch., 1971—88, sr. staff economist, 1972—81, head econs. dept., 1981—85, sr. corp. fellow, 1985—2001; John D. MacArthur prof. health policy and mgmt., dir. div. Health Policy Rsch. and Edn., Harvard University, 1988—. Lectr. UCLA, 1970—83, adj. prof., 1983—88; mem. faculty Rand Grad. Sch., 1972—88; dir. Rand-UCLA Ctr. for Study Health Care Fin. Policy, 1984—88, co-dir., 1988—92; prin. investigator health ins. study grant HHS, 1971—86; chmn. health svcs. rsch. study sect. HHS-Agy. for Health Care Policy and Rsch., 1989—93; mem. Nat. Commn. Cost Med. Care, 1976—77; mem. health svcs. devel. grants study sect. HEW, 1978—82, Inst. Medicine of NAS, 1978—, mem. coun., 1991—97; mem. Physician Payment Rev. Commn., 1993—96; chmn. Prospective Payment Assessment Com., 1996—97; vice chair Medicare Payment Assessment Commn., 1997—2001, mem., 2001—; bd. regents Nat. Libr. Medicine, 1999—; bd. dirs. Aetna, ABT Assocs., Nat. Com. Quality Assurance. Author: The Economics of Medical Care, 1978, The Cost of Poor Health Habits, 1991, A Measure of Malpractice, 1993, Free for All?, 1993, Pricing the Priceless, 2002; editor: Jour. Health Econs., 1981—; assoc. editor: Jour. Econ. Perspectives, 1992—98, mem. editl. bd.: New Eng. Jour. Medicine, 2003—; contbr. articles to profl. jours. Recipient David Kershaw award and prize, Assn. Pub. Policy and Mgmt., 1983, Baxter Am. Found. prize, 1988, Adminstr.'s citation, Health Care Fin. Adminstrn., 1988, Hans Sigrist Found. prize, 1995, Elizur Wright award, 1995, Zvi Griliches award, 2000, Kenneth Arrow award, 2001, Paul A. Samuelson Excellence cert., TIAA CREF, 2003, Adam Yarmolinsky medal, Inst. of Medicine, 2009. Fellow: AAAS, Am. Acad. Arts and Scis.; mem.: Am. Soc. Health Economists (pres. 2005—), Internat. Health Econs. Assn. (pres. 1996—98, bd. dirs. 1996—2002), Econometric Soc., Royal Econ. Soc., Am. Econ. Assn., Assn. for Health Svcs. Rsch. (bd. dirs. 1991—, pres. 1993—94, Article of Yr. award 1989). Office: Harvard U Health Policy Rsch and Edn 180 Longwood Ave Boston MA 02115-5821

NEWLON, CHRISTINE M., research scientist; b. Richland, Wash., Jan. 22, 1954; BS in Microbiology, Mont. State U., 1976; MS in Informatics, Ind. U., Indpls., 2008; PhD in Human-Computer Interaction. Rsch. asst. to assoc. Purdue U., 1980—83; mgr., analyst State of Ind. Utility Regulatory Commn., 1983—94, State of Ind. Divsn. Info. Tech., 1994—2005; contractor Ind. U., 2005—06, usability cons. for med. interfaces, Sch. Nursing, 2007—11; rsch. asst. to assoc. Ind. U., Sch. Informatics, 2007—, faculty instr., 2009—11, database devel. cons. for med. interfaces, 2009—11. Mem.: IEEE, Assn. Computing Machinery. Office: Walker Plaza Bldg 719 Indiana Ave Indianapolis IN 46202 Business E-Mail: cnewlon@iupui.edu.

NEWMAN, BARBARA MILLER, psychologist, educator; b. Chgo., Sept. 6, 1944; d. Irving George and Florence (Levy) Miller; m. Philip R. Newman, June 12, 1966; children: Samuel Asher, Abraham Levy, Rachel Florence. Student, Bryn Mawr Coll.; AB with honors in Psychology, U. Mich., 1966, PhD in Devel. Psychology, 1971. Undergrad. research asst. in psychology U. Mich., 1963-64, research asst. in psychology, 1964-69, teaching fellow, 1965-71, asst. project dir. Inst. for Social Research, 1971-72, univ. lectr. in psychology and research assoc., 1971-72; asst. prof. psychology Russell Sage Coll., 1972-76, assoc. prof., 1977-78; assoc. prof. and chair dept. family rels. and human devel. Ohio State U., 1978-83, prof. and chair, 1983-86, assoc. provost for faculty recruitment and devel., 1987-92, prof., 1992-2000; prof., chair dept. human devel. and family studies U. R.I., 2000—06, prof., 2006—. Author: Living: The Process of Adjustment, 1981, Development Through Life, 1975, 11th edit., 2011, Adolescent Development, 1986, When Kids Go to College, 1992, Childhood and Adolescence, 1997; author: (with P. Newman) Understanding Adulthood, 1983; author: (with P. Newman, L. Landry-Meyer and B. Lohman) Life Span Development: A Case Book, 2003; author: (with P. Newman) Theories of Human Development, 2007; contbr. articles to profl. jours. Vis. scholar, UCLA, 2006—07. Mem.: AAAS, APA, Soc. Rsch. in Child Devel., Am. Psychol. Soc., Groves Conf. on Marriage and Family, Soc. for Rsch. on Adolescence. Office: U RI Human Devel and Family Studies Transition Ctr Kingston RI 02881 Home Phone: 401-559-1243; Office Phone: 401-874-7135. Business E-Mail: bnewman@uri.edu.

NEWMAN, BARRY MARC, pediatric surgeon; b. NYC, Dec. 13, 1951; s. Sheldon and Miriam Newman; m. Jane Post, July 2, 1989; children: Alex, Sara. BA in Psychology, Biology, Anthropology, U. Pa., 1973; MD, SUNY, Stony Brook, 1976. Diplomate Nat. Bd. Med. Examiners, Am. Bd. Surgery, Am. Bd. Pediatric Surgery. Resident in surgery N.Y. Med. Coll., NYC, 1976-78; sr. resident in surgery SUNY, Stony Brook, 1978-81; chief resident pediatric surgery Childrens Hosp. of Buffalo, 1981-83, fellow pediatric surgery and gastroenterology, 1983-84; asst. prof. surgery U. Va., Charlottesville, 1984-88, U. Ill., Chgo., 1988-93; dir. pediatric surgery Luth. Gen. Children's Hosp., Park Ridge, Ill., 1991-96; clin. assoc. prof. surgery U. Chgo., 1993-95; dir. pediatric surg. svcs. Loyola U. Med. Ctr., Maywood, Ill., 1996—2008, co-dir. surg. laparoscopy lab., 1996-97, assoc. prof. surgery and pediatrics, 1996—2004, prof. surgery and pediatrics, 2004—08; med. dir., pediat. surgery Providence Med. Group, Portland, Oreg., 2008—. Instr. Adv. Trauma and Life Support, ACS, Chgo., 1984—. Contbr. articles to profl. jours., chapters to books. Grantee, NIH, 1982—83, 1987—88. Fellow ACS, Am. Coll. Chest Physicians, Am. Acad. Pediatrics; mem. Am. Pediatric Surg. Assn. Democrat. Avocations: wine collecting, scuba diving, underwater photography, personal computing. Office: Providence Med Group Dept Pediatric Specialties 9427 SW Barnes Rd Ste 598 Portland OR 97225 Home Phone: 503-477-6794; Office Phone: 503-216-8654. Business E-Mail: barry.newman@providence.org.

NEWMAN, BEVERLEY, radiologist, educator; b. Johannesburg, Oct. 8, 1952; BSc, U. Witwatersrand, 1973, MBBCh, 1976. Prof. radiology Stanford U., 2006—. Fellow: Am. Coll. Radiology. Office: 725 Welch Rd Stanford CA 94305 Business E-Mail: bev.newman@stanford.edu.

NEWMAN, DONALD LYNN, psychologist, consultant; b. Jeffersonville, Ind., Jan. 5, 1951; s. Mason Lynn and Rita Scott Newman; m. Kathy Jean Hopkins, July 28, 1993; children: Higgens McPheaters, Isabella Catalina, Fannie Jean. BA in Sociology, U. Ariz., 1974; MSW, Ariz. State U., 1976; M in Sch. Psychology, No. Ariz. U., 1996. LCSW Ariz.; cert. sch. psychologist Ariz. Dept. Edn. Founder, CEO Family Preservationists: Counseling Assocs., Phoenix, 1991—94, AmeriPsych, Inc., Phoenix, 1994—2005; exec. dir. Gen. Health Corp. ResCare Inc. (formerly AmeriPsych, Inc.), Phoenix, 2005—07. With Retail Food Preserving Jam & Jellyman Dot Com. Author: PREP-R: Parenting and Resource Education Program-Revised. Exec. dir. Cmtys. in Need, Phoenix, 1991—2005; pres. Children with Challenges, Phoenix, 1995—2005. Grantee State of Ariz., 1995—2005. Mem.: Nat. Assn. Sch. Psychologists (life). Democrat. Buddhist. Avocations: running, travel, fly fishing, gardening, food preserving. Office: D&K Diversified Investments Inc 3101 N Manor Dr E Phoenix AZ 85014 Personal E-mail: sirdonaldnewman@gmail.com.

NEWMAN, GARY A., gastroenterologist, educator, physician; Attended summa cum laude, Tufts Coll., 1975; MD, U. Pa., 1979. Diplomate Am. Bd. Internal Medicine, 1982, Am. Bd. Internal Medicine-gastroenterology, 1985. Intern Hosp. Univ. Pa., Pa., 1980, resident internal medicine Pa., 1980—82; fellow gastroenterology and hepatology Yale-New Haven Hosp., Conn., 1983—85; clin. assoc. prof. Gastroenterology Jefferson Med. Coll.; hosp. affiliations include Lankenau Hosp., Bryn Mawr Hosp.; physician Main Line Endoscopy Ctr., Main Line Gastroenterology Assocs. Gastroenterology editor Internal Medicine Bull., W. B. Saunders; author: (textbook) Medicine. Recipient Biology and Chemistry prizes, recognized dr., Health-Grades. Mem.: AMA, Am. Coll. of Gastroenterology, Phi Beta Kappa, Alpha Omega Alpha. Office: Main Line Gastroenterology Associates Medical Office Bldg Ste 252 100 E Lancaster Ave Wynnewood PA 19096 Office Phone: 610-896-7360.

NEWMAN, HUBERT NEIL, periodontist, educator, ecologist, poet; b. Dublin, Sept. 13, 1943; s. Victor J.P.C. and Nettie (Jackson) Newman. BA, U. Dublin, 1964, BDentSc, 1967, MA, 1968, ScD, 1980; PhD, U. Bristol, 1973, MDS, 1976. House surgeon Dublin Dental Hosp., 1967—68, registrar in oral surgery, 1968-69; sci. asst. Med. Rsch. Coun. U.K., Bristol, Eng., 1969-76; lectr. in dental medicine U. Bristol, 1973-76; from sr. lectr. to reader periodontology Eastman Dental Inst., London, 1977—85, head dept. periodontology, 1993-99, vice dean, 1984-87, vice dean for tchg., 1990-93, head electron microscopy unit, 1989—94; dir. Eastman Dental Inst. Clin. Rsch. Ctr., London, 1999—2000; prof. periodontology and preventive dentistry personal chair U. London, 1985-99, emeritus prof. periodontology and preventive dentistry, 1999—, emeritus prof., 1999—. Hon. cons. Eastman Dental Hosp., 1980—99; hon. dir. Oral Health Rsch. Ctr., NW London Cmty. Dental Svc., 2001—05; guest prof. Semmelweis U., Hungary, 2008; vis. prof. U. Seville, Spain, 2009, Hebrew U. Jerusalem, 1989, U. Witwatersrand, Pretoria, Stellenbosch & Western Cape, South Africa, 1990. Author: more than 270 chpts. to books; contbr. articles to profl. jours. Recipient medal, Paris Assn. Odontology, 1990, U. Athens, 1991, City of Paris, 1991. Fellow: RCS (Eng.) (hon.), Faculty Gen. Dental Practice (Eng.), Royal Coll. Physicians & Surgeons (Glasgow), Internat. Coll. Dentistry, FICD, Royal Coll. Pathologists; mem.: CBiol, FSB, Brit. Soc. Periodontology (hon.; pres. 2000—01), Internat. Assn. Dental Rsch. (life; chmn. periodontal rsch. group Brit. divsn. 1982—84), Internat. Acad. Periodontology (chmn. sci. com. 1996—98, pres. 1999—2001, counsellor 2003—). Avocations: thinking, travel, gardening, music, poetry. Office Phone: 011 44 7973 111351. Office Fax: 011 44 208 3499900.

NEWMAN, KURT DOUGLAS, pediatric surgeon; b. Chgo., Aug. 10, 1951; s. Slater Edmund Newman and Corrine Lois (Silfen) Brickell; m. Alison Nichols Grisemer, May 9, 1992; children: Robert Adams, Jackson Slater. BA, U. N.C., 1973; MD, Duke U., 1978. Diplomate Am. Bd. Surgery, Am. Bd. Pediatric Surgery. Resident in surgery Brigham and Women's Hosp., Harvard U., Boston, 1978-83; fellow in surgery Harvard U. Med. Sch., Boston, 1983-84; fellow in pediatric surgery Children's Nat. Med. Ctr., Washington, 1984-86, pres., CEO, 2011—; asst. prof. surgery George Washington Sch. Medicine, Washington, 1992-96, prof. surgery and pediat., 1997—; surgeon-in-chief, sr. v.p. Joseph E. Robert, Jr. Ctr. Surg. Care, Washington; acting v.p. Sheikh Zayed Inst. Pediatric Surg. Innovation, Washington. Bd. dirs. Children's Nat. Health Network, Washington; mem. physicians adv. bd. Nat. Com. Quality Assurance, Washington; med. dir. clin. resource mgmt. Children's Hosp.; vice chmn. bd. govs. Orgn. Children's Hospitals' Surgeons in Chief, 2010—. Contbr. chpt. to books and numerous articles to profl. jours.; reviewer several scientific jours., including Jour. Pediatric Surgery, and Pediat. Fellow ACS (pres. Met. Washington chpt. 1998-99, sec./treas. 1996); mem. AMA, Am. Acad. Pediat. (chmn. surgery sect. 2007-09), Am. Pediatric Surgery Assn., Soc. Univ. Surgeons, Pediatric Surgery Biology Club (pres. 1993-94), Am. Surg. Assn., Southern Surg. Assn. Office: Childrens Nat Med Ctr Ctr Cancer & Immunology Rsch 111 Michigan Ave NW Washington DC 20010-2970 Office Phone: 202-476-2151. Business E-Mail: knewman@childrensnational.org. *

NEWMAN, PHILIP ROBERT, psychologist; b. Dec. 17, 1942; s. Samuel M. and Sara Rose (Dumain) N.; m. Barbara Miller, June 12, 1966; children: Samuel Asher, Abraham Levy, Rachel Florence. AB with high distinction, U. Mich., 1964, PhD, 1971. Asst. prof. psychology U. Mich., Ann Arbor, 1971-72, Union Coll., Schenectady, NY, 1972-76; dir. human behavior curriculum project APA, Washington, 1977-81; pvt. practice psychology Columbus, Ohio, 1978-2000, South Kingston, RI, 2000—. Adj. prof., sr. rschr. young scholars program Ohio State U., 1990-98; adj. prof. human devel. and family studies U. R.I., 2000—; cons. Agy. Instrnl. TV, 1979; vis. scholar psychology, UCLA, 2006-07. Author: (with B. Newman) Development through Life: A Psychosocial Approach, 1975, 11th edit., 2011; Infancy and Childhood Development and Its Context, 1978, An Introduction to the Psychology of Adolescence, 1979, Personality Development through the Life Span, 1980, Living: The Process of Adjustment, 1981, Understanding Adulthood, 1983, Principles of Psychology, 1983, Adolescent Development, 1986, When Kids Go to College: A Parents Guide to Changing Relationships, 1992, Childhood and Adolescence, 1997, Theories of Human Development, 2007, (with B. Newman, L. Landry-Meyer, B. Lohman) Life Span Development: A Case Book, 2003; editor: (with B. Newman) Development Through Life: A Case Study Approach, 1976. Woodrow Wilson fellow U. Mich., 1964, Univ. fellow, 1964-66, Horace H. Rackham Rsch. scholar, 1969-71. Mem. APA, APHA, Internat. Assn. Applied Psychology, Internat. Sociol. Assn., Soc. Psychol. Study Social Issues, Am. Sociol. Assn., Nat. Coun. Family Rels., Groves Conf. Marriage and Family, Ea. Psychol. Assn., N.Y. Acad. Sci., Gerontol. Soc. Am., Am. Orthopsychiat. Assn., Am. Statis. Assn., Soc. for Rsch. on Child Devel., Soc. for Rsch. on Adolescence, Soc. Study Human Devel., Phi Beta Kappa, Sigma Xi, Phi Kappa Phi. Personal E-mail: prn10@yahoo.com.

NEWMAN, PHYLLIS, retired counselor, therapist, hypnotist; b. NYC, Aug. 20, 1933; m. Milton Newman, Dec. 28, 1952; children: Renee Holly, Eileen Sharon, Jeffrey Mark. BS, Mercy Coll., 1977; MS, LIU, 1979. With Local Radio; pvt. practice hypnosis & therapy Peekskill, NY; lectr. Pepsico Fitness Ctr., Purchase, 1984, Purdue U., 1986, 1988, Girl Scouts' Coun.; dir. counseling Hypnosis Group, 1979—89, featured local TV, 2004, 60 Minutes 2, 2004, Ivanhoe Broadcasting Co., 2005, Purdue Alumnus Mag., 2005, Tampa Tribune, 2010. Contbr. articles to profl. jours. Lectr. Ahwautukee Cancer Assn., 2002; soc. act. chair, bd. dirs. Cong Beth Shalom, Brardon, Fla., 2009—; bd. dirs. Cong. Beth. Shalom, Fla., 2010—, social action chair, 2010—; leader meditation JCC, 1994—2001; liaison Union Reform Judaism, SW Coun. Jewish Family Concerns; mem. parents exec. bd. Purdue U., 1978—83, mem. pres.' coun., 1982—89; bd. dirs. Hand Mouth Players, Garrison, NY, Yorktown Cmty. Players, NY, 1988—89; v.p., prodr. Tempe Little Theatre, 1990—95; pres. Tempe Welcome Wagon Social Club, 1990—91; v.p. bd. dirs. Temple Emanuel Tempe, Ariz., 1996—2009; chair Beit Am. (Ho. of People), 2000—09, healing svc., 2005—08; active mem. Normal Pressure Hydrocephalus Support. Mem.: Am. Assn. Profl. Hypnotherapists, NY Soc. Ericksonian Hypnosis, Am. Mental Health Counselors Assn., Am. Assn. Counseling & Devel. Personal E-mail: phylnew@verizon.net.

NEWMAN, RICHARD AUGUST, psychiatrist, educator; b. Oak Park, Ill., May 27, 1931; s. Henry Adolph and Mildred Kathyn (Haaker) N.; m. Nancy Jane Werdelin, Aug. 28, 1954; children: John Henry, Kurt Alan, Richard Steven, Scott David. BS, U. Ill., 1953, MD, 1956. Diplomate Am. Bd. Psychiatry and Neurology. Intern Swedish-Am. Hosp., Rockford, Ill., 1956-57; resident in psychiatry Walter Reed Gen. Hosp., Washington, 1958-61; rschr. Walter Reed Army Inst., 1961; chief psychiat. svc. Valley Forge Gen. Hosp., Phoenixville, Pa., 1962-64, also asst. chief dept. psychiatry and neurology, 1962-64; practice medicine, specializing in psychiatry Paoli, 1962-96; dir. milieu therapy Phila. Gen. Hosp., 1968-69; dir. residency tng., dept. mental health scis. Hahnemann Med. Coll., 1969-73, assoc. prof., 1970-79; prof. psychiatry Med. Coll. Pa., 1979—. Dir. continuing mental health edn., 1983—87, 1983—87; dir. continuing med. edn., 1985—87; regional med. dir. for mental health Intracorp/Cigna, 1989—93; assoc. med. dir. for mental health U.S. Healthcare, 1993—95; vis. prof. psychiatry U. Alta., 1975; chief cons. psychotherapy Chester County Cmty. Mental Health Clinic, 1967—68; psychiatrist Chester County Commr.'s Bd. for Mental Health/Mental Retardation, 1971—77; instr. Phila. Psychoanalytic Soc. Extension Sch., 1972—90; mem. faculty Inst. of Phila. Psychoanalytic Soc.; chmn. psychiatric sect. Paoli Meml. Hosp., 1974—83, med. dir. psychiatry svc., 1977—83; psychiat. cons. St. Judes Hosp., St. Lucia, West Indies, 1983—89, St. Jones Ctr. for Behavioral Health, 1999, Kent Gen. Hosp., Dover, Del., 1999, Fairbanks (Alaska) Health Ctr., Alaska, 1999—2000; interim med. dir. Connections CSP, Wilmington, Del., 1995—96; staff psychiatrist Philhaven Hosp., Mt. Gretna, Pa., 1996—97; cons. St. Joseph's Hosp., Reading, Pa., 2000—04, The Reading Hosp. Med. Ctr., Dept. Mental Health, Pa., 2005—06; assoc. dept. psychiat. Geisiugers Health Sys., 2007—. Contbr. articles to profl. jours. Maj. M.C., AUS, 1958-64. Fellow APA (disting. life fellow) Pa. Psychiat. Assn. (chmn. ethics com.); mem. AMA, Phila.

Psychoanlaytic Soc., Am. Psychoanalytic Assn. (cert. psychoanalyst), Christian Med. Soc., Soc. Med. Coll. Dirs. Continuing Med. Edn., Pa., Chester County Med. Socs., Dirs. of Residency Tng. in Psychiatry of Del. Valley (past pres.). Lutheran. Home: 600 Nancy Jane Ln Downingtown PA 19335-1670 Office Phone: 610-988-8012.

NEWMAN, SARA BETH, epidemiologist, director; b. Cleve., Oct. 15, 1965; MCP, MIT, 1993; PhD, Uniformed Svcs. U. Health Scis., 2002. Tech. cons. World Bank, 1993—95; assoc. John Snow, Inc., 1995—98; sr. epidemiologist Divsn. Immigration Health Svcs., 2003—05; project advisor asst. sec. HHS, 2005—06; program dir. Nat. Pk. Svc., 2006—. Bd. dirs. Commd. Officers Assn., 2009—11. Active duty officer US Pub. Health Svc. Decorated Outstanding Svc. medal USPHS, Commendation medal, Achievement medal, Spl. Assignment award. Mem.: APHA (Injury Control and Emergency Health Svcs. Com. award). Avocations: sports, singing, pottery. Office: 1201 Eye St NW Washington DC 20005 Office Fax: 202-371-2226. Business E-Mail: sara_newman@nps.gov.

NEWMAN, SLATER EDMUND, psychologist, educator; b. Boston, Sept. 8, 1924; s. Max and Gertrude (Raphael) N.; m. Corrine Lois Silfen, June 18, 1950 (div. 1968); children: Kurt Douglas, Jonathan Mark, Eric Bruce; m. Patricia Ellen Christopher Thomas, July 2, 1969; 1 stepchild, Arthur C. Thomas III. BS, U. Pa., 1947; MA, Boston U., 1948; PhD, Northwestern U., 1951. Research psychologist U.S. Air Force, 1951-57; mem. faculty N.C. State U., Raleigh, 1957—2003, prof. emeritus psychology, 2003—. Vis. fgn. mem. Exptl. Psychology Soc. U.K., 1973-74, 82-83, 90. Contbr. chpts. to books, articles to profl. publs. Bd. dirs. ACLU, 1992—97, mem. biennial conf. com., 1994—97, mem. task force internat. human rights, 1994—2005, mem. spl. nominating com., 1996, mem. constn. com., 1996—97, mem. youth affairs com., 1997, mem. nat. adv. coun., 1998—; organizing com. NC Civil Liberties Union, 1965, pres., 1980—82, exec. com., 1986—87, bd. dirs., 1969—73, 1976—82, 1984—90, 1992—97; chair Com. on Internat. Human Rights, 1988—; chair founding com. Wake County chpt. ACLU, 1969, pres., 1969—72, 1984—86, bd. dirs., 1969—73, 1976—82, 1984—90, life mem., 2002—; founding mem. North Carolinians Against the Death Penalty, 1967, bd. govs., 1967—73; mem. Mayor's Com. UN Week, Raleigh, 1986—95; active Amnesty Internat., 1984—; co-founder, mem. steering com. North Carolinians Against Apartheid, 1985—87; mem. Wake County Com. Bicentennial US Constn., 1987—89; co-founder, co-chair NC Com. for Celebration of Human Rights, 1989—97; mem. Human Rights Week Com., NC State U., 1993—99, founder, 1993, chair, 1993—96; co-founder Human Rights Coalition NC, 1997—, co-chair, 1997—; co-prodr. North Carolinians for Ratification, Convention on Elimination, Com. on Elimination of All Forms of Discrimination Against Women, 1997; chair North Carolinians for Ratification, 1998—2009; mem. bd. adv. Womens NC, 2009—; mem. civil rights adv. bd. NC Mus. History, 2001—05, adv. bd. mem., Women NC, 2009—; coun. adv. bd., 2010—. Served with USAAC, 1943—46, 2d lt. USAF, 1952—53. USPHS spl. rsch. fellow U. Calif.-Berkeley, 1965-66; U. London hon. rsch. fellow, 1973-74, 82-83, 90; recipient W.W. Finlator award ACLU of Wake County, 1997, Norman Smith award ACLU of NC, 1998; recipient Frank Porter Graham Award, ACLU of NC, 2001, Human Rights award, Wake County and West Triangle Chpts., UN Assn., 2007; Slater Newman annual debate established by Wake County ACLU, 2006, Peacemaker award NC Peace Action, 2010. Fellow: APA, AAAS, Assn. for Psychol. Sci.; mem.: AAUP (pres. N.C. State U. chpt. 1968—69), Carolinas Conf. for Undergrad. Rsch. in Psychology (co founder 1976), Ea. Psychol. Assn., N.C. Cognition Group (founder 1972), S.E. Psychol. Assn. (exec. com. 2001—07, sec.-treas. 2004—07), S.E. Workers in Memory (founder 1969), So. Soc. Philosophy and Psychology, Psychonomic Soc., UN Assn. (bd. dirs. Wake County chpt. 1991—95), Psi Chi (v.p. southea. region 1990—94, nat. coun. 1990—94, nat. pres.-elect 1996—97, nat. coun. 1996—99, nat. pres. 1997—98, nat. past pres. 1998—99), Sigma Xi. Home: 315 Shepherd St Raleigh NC 27607-4031 E-mail: slaterpat@mindspring.com.

NEWMARK, EMANUEL, ophthalmologist; b. Newark, May 25, 1936; s. Charles Meyer and Bella (Yoskowitz) Newmark; m. Tina Steinberg, Aug. 25, 1957; children: Karen Beth, Heidi Ellen, Stuart Jeffrey. BS in Pharmacy, Rutgers U., Newark, 1959; postgrad., U. Amsterdam, The Netherlands, 1960-63, Armed Forces Inst. Pathology, Washington, 1971; MD, Duke U., Durham, NC, 1966; postgrad., Harvard U., Cambridge, Mass., 1967. Diplomate Am. Bd. Ophthalmology. Intern George Washington U. Hosp., Washington, 1966; trainee NIH rsch. U. Fla., Gainesville, 1967—70; resident ophthalmology U. Fla. Hosp., 1967—70; instr. dept. ophthalmology U. Fla., 1970; cons. ophthalmology Gainesville VA Hosp., 1970; clin. instr. ophthalmology U. Tex. Med. Sch., San Antonio, 1971—72; cons. ophthalmology Kerrville VA Hosp., Tex., 1971—72; asst. chief ophthalmology svc. Brooke Army Gen. Hosp., Fort Sam, Tex., 1971—72. Clin. asst. prof. ophthalmology Bexar County Hosp. and Clinics, San Antonio, 1971—72; tchg. faculty Joint Commn. Allied Health Pers. in Ophthalmology, commr., 2004—09; sec., treas. Palm Beach Eye Assocs., Atlantis, Fla., 1973—98; pharm. adv. com. Agy. Health Care Adminstrn. Bd. Optometry, 1991—; chief ophthalmology JFK Med. Ctr., 1984, chmn. CME and edn. com., 2004—07; staff ophthalmologist West Palm Beach VA Hosp., 2005—, Regional Eye Inst., 1998—2006. Exec. editor Ophthalmic Medical Assisting: An Independent Study Course, 2006, Cert. Ophthalmic Asst. Exam Study Guide, 2010; contbr. chapters to books, articles to profl. jours. & publs. Alumni assoc. Rutgers Coll. Pharmacy, 1990—, chmn. reunion, 1986, 2001, Duke U. Med. Alumni Assn., NC, 1967—; centurian Davison Club-Duke U. Med. Sch., NC, 1982—; campaign chmn., nat. vice chmn. Israel Bonds, Palm Beach County, Fla., 1988—90; participant charitable orgns.; v.p. Palm Beach Liturgical Culture Found., 1994—2000, pres., 2000—01. Jt. Commn. Allied Health Personal Opthal. Statesmanship Award, 2010. Decorated Lion of Judea State of Israel; recipient Gates of Jerusalem medal, 1991, Jerusalem medal, 1996, Recognition award, Joint Commn. Allied Health Personnel in Ophthalmology, 2001, 2006, US Army Commendation medal, Joint Commn. Fellow: ACS, Am. Acad. Ophthalmology (del. to coun. 1996—2001, allied health edn. com. 1997—2002, editor Refinements 1998—2000, rep. to joint com. allied health pers. in ophthalmology 2004—09, Fla. state chmn. ednl. trust, Achievement award 2001, Councillors award 2001, Secretariat award 2005, 2010); mem.: AMA, Fla. Soc. Ophthalmology (ethics chmn. 1985—90, pres. 1990—91, James W. Clower Jr. Cmty. Svc. award 1995, Shalar Richardson, MD Svc. to Medicine award 2007), Palm Beach County Ophthal. Soc. (pres. 1984—85, Ophthalmologist of Yr. 2004), Palm Beach County Med. Soc. (chair ethics com. 1997—2000, vice chair ethics com. 2002, bd. dirs. 2003, bd. dirs. mem.-at-large 2003—06, svcs. bd. mem. 2004—10, coun. on ethical and jud. affairs 2004—, trustee 2005, v.p. svcs. bd. 2008—09, Heroes in Medicine award 2009, Svc. award 2011), Fla. Med. Assn. (ho. dels. 1993—95, 2001—06, 2008—), Am. Orgn. for Rehab. Through Tng. Fedn. (nat. exec. com.-campaign cabinet 1987, pres. 1987—90, hon. del. 1993—95, 2001—03, Palm Beach Men's Achievement award 1988, Pres. award 1989), Founder's Soc. Duke U. Jewish. Avocation: travel. Home: 180 Palm Cir Atlantis FL 33462-6627 Office: West Palm Beach Vets Med Ctr 7305 Military Trail West Palm Beach FL 33410 Personal E-mail: mannynewmark@msn.com. *

NEWMARK, THOMAS S., psychiatrist, educator; MD, Hahnemann Univ. Cert. psychiatry, geriatrics, psychosomatic medicine. Intern Albert Einstein Med. Ctr.; resident Med. Univ. of SC, Germantown Hosp. and Dispensary, Hahnemann Univ. Hosp.; physician Cooper Univ., chief dept. of psychiatry. Office: Cooper University Hospital One Cooper Plaza Camden NJ 08103 Office Phone: 800-826-6737.

NEWPORT, D. JEFFREY, psychiatrist, researcher; MD, U. SC; MS in Clinical Rsch., Emory U. Resident Emory U. Sch. Medicine, assoc. prof. psychiatry & behavioral sciences, assoc. dir. Emory Women's Mental Health Program. Contbr. chapters to books. Recipient Young Faculty award, Am. Psychiatric Inst. for Rsch. & End., Young Investigator award, Nat. Alliance for Rsch. on Schizophrenia & Depression, Hoechst Marion Roussel award, Am. Soc. Clinical Psychopharmacology, Psychiatry Resident of Yr. award, Pfizer. Fellow: Am. Psychiatric Assn., Am. Coll. Psychiatrists, Soc. Biological Psychiatry. Office: Emory University School of Medicine Emory Clinic Bldg B 1365 Clifton Rd NE Ste 6100 Atlanta GA 30322 Office Phone: 404-778-2524. Office Fax: 404-778-2535. E-mail: wmhp@emory.edu.

NEWPORT, L. JOAN, retired social worker; b. Newkirk, Okla., July 5, 1932; d. Crawford Earl and Lillian Pearl (Peden) Irvine; m. Don E. Newport, July 9, 1954 (div. 1971, dec. 1999); children: Alan Keith, Lili Kim. BA cum laude, Wichita State U., Kans., 1955; MSW, U. Okla., Norman, 1977. Diplomate Acad. Cert. Social Workers; lic. clin. social worker, Okla. Dir. children's work Wesley United Meth. Ch., Oklahoma City, 1969-71; social worker Dept. Human Svcs., Newkirk, Okla., 1972-77; in-sch. suspension counselor Kay County Youth Svcs., Ponca City, Okla., 1977; med. social worker St. Joseph Med. Ctr., Ponca City, 1977-78, dir. social work, 1978-83; pvt. practice, Ponca City, 1979-97; med. social worker Healthcare Svcs., Ponca City, 1983-84; pvt. practice Newkirk, 1997—2005; ret., 2005. Sponsor, organizer Kay County Parents Anonymous, Ponca City, 1976-83; vice chair Okla. State Bd. Lic. Social Workers, Oklahoma City, 1988-90; supr. students Okla. U. Sch. Social Work, Okla. State U., No. Okla. Coll., Okla. Christian Coll., 1977-85; supr. for clin. social workers working toward lic. in Okla., 1985-2005; cons., presenter, lectr. in field Mem. Okla. Women's Network, 1989-96; adv. bd. Displaced Homemakers, Ponca City, 1985-89; adv. bd. Kay County Home Health, 1979-83, chair, 1979-81; Sunday sch. tchr. Newkirk United Meth. Ch.; mem. Newkirk Main St., 1999-2000. Named Hon. State Life Mem. Burbank PTA, Oklahoma City, 1971, scholar Wichita Press and Radio Women, Kans., 1953, Conoco, Inc., Houston, 1951-54. Mem. NASW (Okla. del. Del. Assembly Washington 1987, chmn. vendorship com. 1985-87, pres. Okla. chpt. 1988-90, Social Worker of Yr. 1987), Child Abuse Prevention Task Force (pres. dist. 17 1986-88, mem. grant evaluation com. 1986-96), Zeta Phi Eta. Democrat. Methodist.

NEWSCHAFFER, CRAIG J., epidemiologist, educator; BA in Pub. Rels., Boston U., 1984, BS in Biology, 1984; SM in Health Policy & Mgmt., Harvard Sch. Pub. Health, 1987; PhD in Chronic Disease Epidemiology, Johns Hopkins U., 1996. Policy analyst Project HOPE Ctr. for Health Affairs, 1987—89, sr. rsch. assoc., 1991—93; rsch. asst. Johns Hopkins Bloomberg Sch. Pub. Health, 1989—93, asst. prof., 1999—2002, dir. Ctr. for Autism & Devel. Disabilities, 2001—06, dir. gen. epidemiology, 2002—06, assoc. prof. dept. epidemiology, 2002—06; asst. prof. cmty. health-epidemiology St. Louis U. Sch. Pub. Health, 1993—96, dir. divsn. epidemiology, 1996, rsch. assoc., 1996—2006, adj. asst. prof. cmty. health-epidemiology, 1996—2006; rsch. assoc. epidemiologist Thomas Jefferson U. Med. Coll., 1996—99, rsch. asst. prof., 1996—99; adj. scholar U. Pa. Med. Ctr., 1997—99; prof. & chmn. dept. epidemiology & biostatistics Drexel U. Sch. Pub. Health, 2006—. Assoc. editor Am. Jour. Epidemiology; editorial bd. mem. Developmental Epidemiology. Mem.: Soc. Gen. Internal Medicine, Gerontological Soc. America, Am. Pub. Health Assn. (epidemiology section coun. mem. 1991—2002, gov. coun. mem. 2002—04), Soc. for Epidemiologic Rsch. Office: Drexel University School of Publich Health 245 N 15th St Mail Stop 660 Philadelphia PA 19102-1192 Office Phone: 215-762-7152. Office Fax: 215-762-4088. E-mail: cnewscha@drexel.edu.

NEWSOME, FREDERICK V., medical educator; b. Charleston, W.Va., July 7, 1946; s. Moses and Ruth (Bass) N.; m. Osila Chindo, Mar. 23, 1974, (dec. Aug. 31, 2008); children: Akasemi, Imhotep, Nubia, Hatshepsut. BA in Chemistry, Harvard U., 1968; MD, W.Va. U., 1972; MSc in Tropical Medicine, London Sch. Hygiene & Tropical Medicine, 1981. Diplomate Am. Bd. Internal Medicine. Instr. in medicine Coll. of Physicians and Surgeons Columbia U., NYC, 1975-78; instr. in medicine Albert Einstein Med. Sch., Bronx, 1979-80; sr. lectr. in medicine U. Jos, Nigeria, 1981-88; clin. prof., head dept. of medicine Coll. of Health Scis. Usmanu Danfodio U., Sokoto, Nigeria, 1988-90; chief ambulatory medicine The Meth. Hosp., Bklyn., 1991-92; assoc. attending physician Harlem Hosp. Ctr.; asst. prof. medicine Columbia U. Coll. Physicians & Surgeons, NYC, 1992—. Author: An African American Philosophy of Medicine, 2005; contbr. articles to profl. jours. Fellow ACP, West African Coll. Physicians, Royal Soc. Tropical Medicine and Hygiene; mem. Nat. Med. Assn., Assn. for Study Afro-Am. Life and History. Office: 506 Malcolm X Blvd New York NY 10037 Office Phone: 212-939-1000 ext 8089.

NEWSOME, GARY D., hospital operations company executive; BS, Bluefield State Coll., W.Va.; MBA, Butler U., Indpls.; advanced studies, U. Mich. Sch. Bus. Hosp. ops. Humana, Inc.; divisional v.p. group ops., asst. v.p. group ops., hosp. CEO Health Mgmt. Associates, Inc., 1993—98; v.p. group ops. Cmty. Health Systems, Inc., divsn. pres. hosp. ops.; pres., CEO Health Management Associates, Inc., 2008—. Bd. dirs. Health Mgmt. Associates, Inc., 2008—. Office: Health Mgmt Associates Inc 5811 Pelican Bay Blvd Ste 500 Naples FL 34108 Office Phone: 239-598-3131. *

NEWSTEAD, CHARLES GEORGE, renal physician; b. London, Apr. 8, 1956; s. Charles Arthur and Clara Amelia (Forrest) N.; m. Catherine Lucy McEwen, Apr. 19, 1980; children: David, Douglas, George, Heather. BSc 1st class, U. London, 1978, M.B.BS, 1981, MD, 1991. Accreditation in gen., internal and renal medicine. Sr. house officer/registrar London Hosp., 1982-86; lectr. renal medicine Royal London Hosp. Med. Coll., 1986-90; clin. lectr. medicine U. Manchester, 1990-93; cons. renal physician St. James's U. Hosp., Leeds, 1993—. Mem. nat. com. on renal medicine and transplantation. Contbr. numerous articles to profl. jours. Grantee Med. Rsch. Coun., Nat. Kidney Rsch. Fund. Fellow Royal Coll. Physicians London; mem. Physiol. Soc., Internat. Soc. Nephrology, Transplantation Soc. Labour Party. Avocations: bicycling, scottish hill walking. Office: St James's Univ Hosp Beckett Street LS9 7TF Leeds England Business E-Mail: chas.newstead@leedsth.nhs.uk.

NEWTON, EDWARD R., obstetrician, educator; Grad., Northwestern U., 1974; MD, Loyola U., 1977. Cert. Ob-Gyn., Maternal-Fetal Medicine, 1984. Intern Chgo. Stritch Sch. Medicine, Loyola U., 1977—78; fellow Tufts U. Sch. Medicine, 1981—83, resident, 1978—81; with dept. ob-gyn. Brody Sch. Medicine, East Carolina U., Greenville, 1998—, prof., chmn. ob-gyn. Office: E Carolina U Brody Sch Medicine Dept Ob-Gyn PCMH Tchg Annex Greenville NC 27834 Office Phone: 252-744-5695. Office Fax: 252-744-2988. E-mail: newtoned@ecu.edu.

NEWTON, JOHN MILTON, academic administrator, psychologist, educator; b. Schenectady, Feb. 25, 1929; s. Harry Hazleton and Bertha A. (Lehmann) N.; m. Elizabeth Ann Slattery, Sept. 11, 1954; children: Patricia, Peter, Christopher. BS, Union Coll., Schenectady, 1951; MA, Ohio State U., 1952, PhD, 1955. Lic. psychologist, Nebr. Rsch. psychologist Electric Boat divsn. Gen. Dynamics Corp., Groton, Conn., 1957-60; mem. faculty U. Nebr., Omaha, 1960—, prof. psychology, 1966-99, chmn. dept., 1967-74, acting vice chancellor acad. affairs, 1994-95, prof. emeritus, 1999—, dean Coll. Arts and Scis., 1974-94, dean emeritus, 1999—. Cons. in field, 1960-72 Author research papers in field. Served to 1st lt. Med. Service Corps, AUS, 1955-57. Mem. Am. Psychol. Assn., Psychonomic Soc., Midwestern Psychol. Assn. Home: 5611 Jones St Omaha NE 68106-1232 Office: Univ of Nebr-Omaha Dept Psychology Omaha NE 68182-0274 Business E-Mail: jnewton@mail.unomaha.edu.

NEWTON, TERRY FERNANDO, health facility specialist, writer; b. Miami, Fla., Dec. 10, 1956; s. Julius Lee Newton and Frances Louise Cason; children: Torrence Levine, Patrick Fernando. Student, Fla. Montanari, 1976—78; BATh, 2007; Theology, Prog. Universal Life Ch. Specialist child care Montanari Clin. Sch., Hialeah, Fla., 1976—79; technician mental health Miami Variety Children's Hosp., Coral Gables, Fla., 1979—80; psychiat. nurse technician Cedars of Lebanon Hosp., Miami, Fla., 1980—82; from office asst. dir. of safety to health info. specialist II Jackson Hosp., Miami, 1982—83, health info. specialist II, 1983—. 1st v.p. Lip Tongue & Ear Prodn., Miami, 1999—. Author: A Composition in Verse, 1996, A Cascade of Memories, 1998, America at the Millenium, 2000, Earthbeat, 2002, Theatre of the Mind, 2003, The Dream of Time, 2007. Active media rep. Concern & Committed Bros. Inc., Miami, 2002; bd. dir. BMS Movement, 2001—. Recipient Accomplishment award, Gov. Lawton Chiles, 1997, Renaissance award, Macedonia Ch., 2006, Unsung Hero award, Coconut Grove Negro Women Club, 2006, Coconut Grove Wall Walk of Fame, Land Trust, Inc., 2009; named African Am. Achiever, JM Family Enterprise, Inc., 1998—2003, Cmty. Achiever, Macedonia Ch., 1999; named to Internat. Poetry Hall of Fame, 1997, Miami Dade Office of Mayor, Bd. County Commrs., Hall Walk of Fame, Coconut Grove, 2009. Mem.: Fla. State Poetry Hosts Coalition (promotor 2003), Concern Bros. Inc. Poetry Club (dir. 2001, Mentor award 1997). Avocations: reading, performing, basketball, birdwatching. Home: 2529 NW 92nd St Miami FL 33147 Home Phone: 786-267-3314; Office Phone: 786-436-6543. E-mail: renee@jazzandpoetry.net.

NEWTON, THOMAS (TOM NEWTON), public health service officer; BA in Environ. Planning & Polit. Sci., U. Northern Iowa, Cedar Falls, MA in Pub. Policy. Sanitarian Washington County, Iowa, 1996—97; pub. health officer Black Hawk County Health Dept., Iowa, 1997—2000; cmty. health cons. Iowa Dept. Pub. Health (IDPH), 2000—02, dir. divsn. environ. health, 2002—07, pub. health dir., 2007—11; dir. network engagement Wellmark Blue Cross & Blue Shield, 2011—. Named Gov. Golden Dome Leader of Yr., Iowa Dept. Pub. Health, 2004. Mem.: APHA, Iowa Pub. Health Assn., Nat. Environ. Health Assn. Office: Wellmark Blue Cross & Blue Shield 1331 Grand Ave PO Box 9232 Des Moines IA 50306 *

NEWTON, WILLIAM ALLEN, JR., pediatrician, pathologist; b. Traverse City, Mich., May 19, 1923; s. William Allen and Florence Emma (Brown) N.; m. Helen Patricia Goodrich, Apr. 21, 1945; children: Katherine Germaine, Elizabeth Gale, William Allen, Nancy Anne. BSc cum laude, Alma Coll., Mich., 1943; MD, U. Mich., 1946. Diplomate: Am. Bd. Pathology, Am. Bd. Pediatrics. Intern Wayne County Gen. Hosp., Detroit, 1947; resident in pediatric pathology/oncology/hematology Children's Hosp. Mich., Detroit, 1948-50; resident in pediat. Children's Hosp. Phila., 1950; dir. labs. Children's Hosp. Columbus, Ohio, 1952-88, rsch. pathologist Ohio, 1989—93; mem. faculty Coll. Medicine, Ohio State U., 1952—, prof., 1965—, chief pediatric pathology, 1952-89, chief divsn. pediatric hematology, 1952—82, prof. emeritus, 1989—. Chmn. pathology com. Children's Cancer Study Group, 1965-91; chmn. Pathology Com. Intergroup Rhabdomyosarcoma Study Group; chmn. pathology com. Late Effects Study Group. Contbr. articles to med. jours. Trustee, exec. com. Ohio divsn. Am. Cancer Soc., 1972-86; adv. com. on childhood cancer Am. Cancer Soc.; chmn. exec. com. Consortium for Cancer Control Ohio, 1982-86; sci. adv. com. Armed Forces Inst. Pathology; pres. Cure of Childhood Cancer in China, 2000—. Served to capt. M.C. U.S. Army, 1950-52, brig. gen. Res. ret. Mem. Am. Assn. Cancer Rsch., Ohio State Med. Assn. (com. on cancer), Midwest Soc. Pediatric Research (mem. council 1960-63, pres. 1964-65), Soc. Pediatric Research, Am. Pediatric Soc., Pediatric Pathology Club (pres. 1968-69), Am. Soc. Clin. Oncology, Internat. Soc. Pediatric Oncology, Sigma Xi, Phi Sigma Pi. Republican. Baptist. Home: 2500 Harrison Rd Johnstown OH 43031-9540 Office: 700 Childrens Dr Columbus OH 43205 Home Phone: 740-817-0272. Business E-Mail: wnewton@chi.osu.edu.

NEYLAN, THOMAS COOGAN, psychiatrist; b. Chgo., Ill., Jan. 31, 1957; s. John Francis and Mary Alice Neylan; m. Mary Genevieve De May, Sept. 20, 1986; children: Michael De May, Matthew De May, Kyra De May. MD, Rush U., Chgo., Ill., 1984. Cert. Am. Bd. of Psychiatry and Neurology, 1989. Assoc. prof. psychiatry U. Calif., San Francisco, 2003—; med. dir., PTSD program San Francisco Dept. of VA Med. Ctr. Contbr. scientific papers pub. to profl. jour. Grantee Rsch. Grants, NIH, 1998-present. Achievements include research in Multiple grants from the Nat. Inst. of Health. Office: Univ Calif San Francisco VAMC-116P 4150 Clement St San Francisco CA 94121 E-mail: thomas.neylan@ucsf.edu.

NG, CALVIN SZE HANG, thoracic surgeon, consultant; b. Kowloon, Hong Kong, China, May 31, 1975; s. Chiu Lap and Monica Shiu Mai (Lam) Ng. BSc with Hons., U. London, 1998, MBBS with hon., 1999. Cert. Mem. Royal Coll. Surgeons, Edinburgh Eng., 2003. Rsch. fellow, Chinese U. div. cardiothoracic surgery, Shatin, Hong Kong, China, 2000—01, med. officer, 2001—, hon. adj. tutor, 2002—03, hon. clin. tutor, 2003—, clin. asst. prof., 2010. Fellow: RCS (Edinburg), Coll. Chest Physician. Office: Chinese University Hong Kong Dept Surgery Prince of Wales Hosp Shatin Hong Kong Office Fax: (852) 2637 7974. Personal E-mail: cshng@netvigator.com.

NG, JOSEPH KIM-FAI, physiotherapist, educator; b. Hong Kong, July 22, 1962; s. Sik Keung Ng, Wai Chun Wong; m. Karin Hil-Wan Yeung, Apr. 25, 1998; children: Felix Ching-Chi, Kayley Ching-Hang. Profl. Diploma in physiotherapy, Hong Kong Poly., 1986, Post-registration Cert. in spinal manipulative therapy, 1990; M of Physiotherapy Studies, U. Queensland, Brisbane, Australia, 1993, PhD in Physiotherapy, 2001. Registered physiotherapist. Physiotherapist Hosp. Svcs. Dept. Hong Kong Govt., 1986—89; physiotherapist in-charge South Kwai Chung Geriatric Day Hosp., Hong Kong, 1990—91, Tang Shiu Kin Hosp., Hong Kong, 1991—92; tutor dept. physiotherapy U. Queensland, Brisbane, Australia, 1994—97; asst. prof. dept. rehab. scis. Hong Kong Poly. U., 1997—2005, assoc. prof., 2005—. Assoc. editor: Hong Kong Physiotherapy Jour., 2002—05, mem. internat. adv. bd.: Manual Therapy, 2004—, mem. editl. rev. bd.: Hong Kong Physiotherapy Jour., 2006—; contbr. articles to profl. jours. Recipient Dorothy Hopkins award for clin. study, Australian Physiotherapy Assn. (Queensland Br.), 1994, 1995. Mem.: Hong Kong Physiotherapy Assn. Avocations: swimming, jogging. Office: Dept Rehab Scis The Hong Kong Poly Univ Hung Hom Hong Kong Office Phone: 852 2766 6765. Office Fax: 852 2330 8656. Business E-Mail: joseph.ng@polyu.edu.hk.

NG, KOCK CHAI, pediatric consultant, medical educator; s. Shieh Eng Ng and Boon Eng Quek; m. Cindy Mui Ee Yeo, Dec. 25, 1980; children: Aaron Thye Wang, Ernest Thye Sern, Isaac Thye Yuan. MBBS, U. Malaya, Kuala Lumpur, 1973—78; Diploma Child Health, Royal Coll. Physicians, London, 1982. Mem. Royal Coll. Physicians, Ireland, 1983, fellow Royal Coll. Physicians, Ireland, 1991. Med. officer Malaysian Armed Forces, Sibu, Malaysia, 1979—80, Armed Forces Hosp., Terendak, Malaysia, 1980—81; sr. ho. officer Gt. Ormond St. Hosp., London, 1981; neonatal sr. ho. officer Barking & King George Hosp., Ilford, Essex, United Kingdom, 1982; lectr. U. Hosp., Kuala Lumpur, Malaysia, 1983; pediatrician Armed Forces Hosp., Terendak, Malaysia, 1983—90; cons. pediatrician Pvt. Practice, Malacca, Malaysia, 1990—95, The So. Hosp., Malacca, Malaysia, 1995—. Lectr. Melaka-Manipal Med. Coll., Malacca, Malaysia, 2001—; vis. cons. pediatrician Armed Forces Hosp., Malacca, 2003—; com. mem. Med. Adv. Com., Malacca, Malaysia, 2000—; chmn. Continuing Med. Edn. Com., Malacca, Malaysia, 1995—2000; founder/mem. The Southern Hosp. Dep. pres. Suspected Child Abuse and Neglect (SCAN) Com., 1983—86, pres., 1987—90; dir. Mediquest Pte Ltd, 1995, Ng Child Specialist Clinic, Malacca, Malaysia, 1995. Lt. col. M.C., 1979—90, Terendak. Decorated Gen. Svc. Medal (PPA) Malaysian Armed Forces; recipient Excellent Svc. Medal (BKT), Malacca State Govt., 2000; Armed Forces scholar. Fellow: Royal Coll. Physicians Ireland; mem.: Malaysian Pediatric Assn. (life), Malaysian Med. Assn. (life). Buddhist. Avocation: golf. Office: Southern Hosp Jalan Bendahara 169 75100 Melaka Malaysia Business E-Mail: kchaing@streamyx.com.

NG, KONG WAH, endocrinologist, director; s. Tong Lam Ng and Woon Loy Ho; m. Yim Mooi Lye, Aug. 20, 1971; children: Ashley Peng Chee, Jason Peng Soon, Natasha May Yoke. MBBS with honors, Monash U., Australia, 1972; MD, U. Melbourne, Australia, 1982. Dep. head, dept. medicine, U. Melbourne St. Vincent's Hosp., Fitzroy, Victoria, 1999—2002, dir., dept. endocrinology & diabetes, 2002—. Fellow: RCP (Edinburgh), Royal Australasian Coll. Physicians; mem.: Endocrine Soc. America, Australian-New Zealand Bone and Mineral Soc., Am. Soc. Bone and Mineral Rsch., Endocrine Soc. Australia. Achievements include discovery of membrane protein inhibiting osteoclast differentiation. Office: Saint Vincent's Hosp 35 Victoria Parade 3065 Fitzroy VIC Australia

NG, YUEN-YEE JENNY, physiotherapist; d. Chung Shum Ng and Siu Ling Yum; children: Yi Ting Lily Tam, Yi Ling Tam. Profl. diploma in Physiotherapy, Hong Kong Poly. U., 1981; MS in Tng., Leicester U., Eng., 1995. Registered physiotherapist Hong Kong, cert. in peripheral manipulative therapy Hong Kong, 1991, clin. exercise specialist Am. Coll. Sports Medicine, 2003. Physiotherapist Grantham Hosp., Hong Kong, 1981—, mem. cardiac rehab. program, 1994—, training officer allied health Hosp. Authority (part-time secondment), 2006—08. Hon. lectr. Hong Kong Poly U., 1996—97, 1999—2003; vis. lectr. Hong Kong Poly. U., 2011. Contbr. articles to profl. jours. Chairperson PTA Canossa Coll., Hong Kong, 2003—05, 2006—07, 2010—11; chair organising com. Am. Coll. Sports Medicine Exercise Specialist Workshops, Hong Kong, 2005—07, workshop dir., 2009—; physio corresponding reference group The Joanna Briggs Inst., 2008—09. Recipient Best Hosp. Program awards, Grantham Hosp., 1998, 2000, 1 Yr. Healthy Staff award, 2004—09. Mem.: Asian Assn. Social Psychology, Internat. Soc. Quality Life Rsch., Am. Coll. Sports Medicine (site coord. 2004—07), Hong Kong Physiotherapy Assn. (chair cardiopulmonary specialty group 2004—08), Orthop. Assn. (assoc.), Assn. Critical Care Assn. (assoc.). Office: Grantham Hosp Physiotherapy Dept Grantham Hospital 125 Wong Chuk Hang Rd Aberdeen Hong Kong Island Hong Kong Business E-Mail: ngyy4@ha.org.hk.

NGAI, YIU HING WILLIAM, surgeon; b. China, Apr. 22, 1972; MBChB, Chinese U. Hong Kong, 1997. Orthop. specialist St. Paul's Hosp., 2010—. Fellow Vis. fellow, Japanese Orthop. Assn. Fellow: RCS(Edinburg), RCOS, HKAM; mem.: HKSHS. Avocations: tennis, photography. Office: 2 Eastern Hospital Rd Causeway Bay Hong Kong 852 Hong Kong Personal E-mail: dr.williamngai@gmail.com.

NGEH, JOSEPH, geriatrician; b. Sibu, Sarawak, Malaysia, Aug. 23, 1967; s. David Ngeh and Mildred Tang; m. Vivien Toh, June 26, 1999; children: Jacinta, Justina, Joshua. MB in Medicine, Surgery and Obstetrics with honors, Nat. U. Ireland, Dublin, 1993; diploma in Geriatric Medicine, Royal Coll. Physicians, 1999; MS in Geriatric Medicine with distinction, U. Keele, Eng., 2000. Cert. of completion of specialist tng. Specialist Tng. Authority, 2004, diploma in medicine of the elderly Royal Colleges Physicians and Surgeons, Ireland, 1997. Specialist registrar in geriatric and gen. internal medicine Oxford (Eng.)/London Deaneries, 1999—2004; cons. physician and geriatrician, lead for stroke services Warwick (Eng.) Hosp., 2004—. Rsch. manuscript peer reviewer Stroke, 2004—, Internat. Immunopharmacology. Contbr. articles to profl. jours. Fellow: Royal Coll. Physicians Edinburgh; mem.: Brit. Assn. Stroke Physicians, Brit. Geriat. Soc. (Ferguson Anderson Best Poster prize 2001, Specialist Registrar Rsch. grant 1999, 2002, 2004), Royal Coll. Physicians London. Roman Catholic. Office: Warwick Hospital Lakin Road Warwick CV34 5BW England Office Fax: 01926 600049. Personal E-mail: jngeh@aol.com. Business E-Mail: joseph.ngeh@swh.nhs.uk.

NGEOW, JEFFREY Y.F., pain medicine physician, educator; MD., U. London Hosp. Med. Sch., UK, 1971. Diplomate Am. Bd. Anesthesiology, Am. Bd. Pain Medicine, lic. NY, Conn. Resident anesthesiology Peter Brent Brigham Hosp., Mass., 1975—77; fellow pain medicine Tufts New England Med. Ctr., Mass., 1975—78; assoc. clin. prof. anesthesiology Weill Cornell Med. Coll.; assoc. attending anesthesiologist Hosp. for Spl. Surgery. Named one of Best Doctors in NY, NY Mag., 1998—2011. Mem.: Chinese Am. Med. Soc., Am. Coll. of Acupuncture, Eastern Pain Assoc., Internat. Assoc. of the Study of Pain, Am. Soc. of Anesthesiologists. Office: Hospital for Special Surgery 535 East 70th St New York NY 10021 Office Phone: 212-606-1059. Office Fax: 212-535-3354.

NGHIEM, HANH, radiologist, educator; b. Saigon, Vietnam, Dec. 8, 1957; MD, Wayne State U., 1987. Prof. radiology U. Mich. Med. Ctr., 1999—2005, Oakland U. William Beaumont Sch. Medicine Med. Ctr., 2005—. Body Imaging fellowship, Stanford U. Med. Ctr., 1992. Fellow: Soc. Radiologists Ultrasound, Soc. Computed Body Tomography and MRI. Avocations: walking, reading, tennis. Home: 30270 Rosemond Dr Franklin MI 48025 Business E-Mail: hnghiem@beaumont.edu.

NGHIEM, PAUL T., dermatologist, educator; AB in Biological Sciences, Harvard U., 1986; MD, Stanford U. Sch. Medicine, 1994, PhD in Cancer Biology, 1994. Assoc. prof. divsn. dermatology U. Wash., assoc. prof. dept. pathology; affiliate investigator clinical rsch. divsn. Fred Hutchinson Cancer Rsch. Ctr. Office: UW Medical Center 815 Mercer St Box 358050 Seattle WA 98195-8050 Office Phone: 206-221-4364.

NGUMAH, QUINTUS CHUKWUEMEKA, optometrist, researcher; arrived in U.S., 1974; s. Festus Ekpewerechi and Pauline Osita Ngumah; m. Ijechi Ndidi Onuoha, July 1, 2000; children: Primadoris Chinonso, Anthony Chimaoge. OD, Abia State U., Nigeria, 1990; postgrad., U. Ala., 2001—. Sr. lectr. Imo State U., Sch. Optometry, Owerri, Nigeria, 1994—; mem. Ministry of Health's Com. for the Prevention of Blindness, Owerri, Nigeria, 1994—2001; zonal rep. Exam Ethics Bd., Optometrists and Dispensing Opticians Bd. Nigeria, 1998—2001; external examiner U. Benin (Nigeria), Sch. Optometry, 2000—01. Contbr. articles toprofl. jours. Mem., vol. Ala. chpt. Optometric Svc. to Humanity; mem. Cooper Green Hosp. Vol. Svcs. Scholar, Arthur Nzeribe Found., 1988, 1989, 1990; Rsch. grantee, Eyesight Found. Ala., 2003—04, Nat. Glaucoma Found., 2003—04, Travel grantee, Internat. Assn. Contact Lens Educators, 1997, World Coun. Optometry, 1998, Vision'99/Lighthouse Internat., 1999, PhD fellow in vision sci., U. Ala. Birmingham, 1. Mem.: Nigerian Optometric Assn. (state chmn. 1996—98), Phi Beta Delta. Achievements include founded and published the first private journal for vision research in Nigeria, 'Eye and Vision'.

NGUMBI, PHILIP MUTINDA, entomologist; b. Machakos Dist., Dec. 20, 1950; BSc in Biology, Ramapo Coll. NJ, 1984; MSc in Med. Entomology, U. Nairobi, Kenya, 1995; PhD in Zoology, U. Nairobi, 2011. Asst. rsch. officer Walter Reed Project, USAMRU-Kenya, 1985—95; sr. rsch. officer Kenya Med. Rsch. Inst., 1995—. Chmn., bd. govs. Miangeni Secondary Sch., 2005—. Recipient Recognition award, USAMRU. Mem.: Entomol. Soc. Africa chpt. Avocations: sports, volleyball, movies, soccer. Office: PO Box 54840-00200 Nairobi Kenya Office Fax: (254) (020) 2715105. Business E-Mail: pngumbi@kemri.org.

NGUYEN, DUC MINH, pharmacist, educator; b. Nha Trang, Khanh Hoa, Vietnam, Mar. 1, 1955; s. Tuat Nguyen and To Nhung Thi Le; m. Luong Ha Thi Nguyen; children: Nhat Minh, Huy Truong, Nhan Tri. BSc, Sch. Pharmacy, U. Med. & Pharm., Ho Chi Minh City, Vietnam, 1979, MSc, 1982; PhD in Pharm. Scis., Sch. Medicine, Hiroshima U., Japan, 1994. Lectr. dept. pharmacognosy Sch. Pharmacy, U. Med. & Pharm., 1979—2002, assoc. prof. dept. pharmacognosy, 2002—06, full prof. dept. pharmacognosy, 2006—, head divsn. pharm. scis. & tech., dep. dir. ctr. edn. & devel. natural medicines. Sr. r & d cons. ICA Biotechnol. & Pharm. JSC, Binh Duong, Vietnam, 1999—; sr. cons. FT- Pharma, Ho Chi Minh City, 2001—; GMP cons. Korea United Pharma, Binh Duong, 2003—04, Phil Interpharma, Binh Duong, 2005—06, ADC Pharma, Can Tho, Vietnam, 2006—08. Contbr. articles to pharmacol. jour. Recipient VIFOTEC award, Ministry of Scis. & Tech., Vietnam, 2002. Mem.: Pharm. Assn. Ho Chi Minh City, Ho Chi Minh City Assn. Chemistry. Buddhist. Avocations: travel, music, sports. Office: Univ Medicine and Pharmacy HCMC 41 Dinh Tien Hoang Dist 1 70000 Ho Chi Minh Vietnam Office Phone: 84 8 8395641 ext. 224. Office Fax: 84 8 38225435. Business E-Mail: ducng@hcm.vnn.vn.

NGUYEN, KHANH GIA, medical educator; b. Hanoi, Vietnam, Dec. 17, 1940; arrived in Can., 1972; s. Lien Bich and Lan Chi Nguyen; m. Nga Thi Ho, Dec. 30, 1940; children: Van Thanh Nguyen-Ho, Phong Nguyen-Ho. Cert. of physics, chemistry and biology, Saigon U., 1961, MD, 1969. Diplomate Am. Bd. Pathology, Am. Bd. Pathology in Cytopathology, cert. pathologist Royal Coll. Physicians and Surgeons, Can. Asst. prof. pathology U. Sask., Saskatoon, Canada, 1978—82; pathologist Plains Health Ctr., Regina, Canada, 1978—80; pathologist, head provincial cytology lab. Pasqua Hosp., Regina, Canada, 1980—82; asst. prof. pathology U. Alta., Edmonton, Alberta, Canada, 1982—84, assoc. prof. pathology, 1984—92, prof. lab. medicine and pathology, 1992—2006, prof. emeritus lab. medicine and pathology, 2006—; pathologist U. Alta. Hosp., Edmonton, Alberta, Canada, 1982—2006, pathologist and head of electron microscopy, 1987—2000, pathologist and head of cytology, 1997—2004; pathologist BC Cancer Agy., Vancouver, Canada, 2006—. Cons. pathologist Can. Tumor Reference Ctr., Ottawa, Ontario, Canada, 1982—87. Author: Essentials of Aspiration Biopsy Cytology, 1991, Essentials of Exfoliative Cytology, 1992, Essentials of Cytology: An Atlas, 1993, Critical Issues in Cytopathology, 1996, Essentials of Lung Tumor Cytology, 2008, Essentials of Abdominal Fine-Needle Aspiration Cytology, 2008, Essentials of Head and Neck Cytology, 2009, Essentials of Fluid Cytology, 2010, Essentials of Gynecologic Cytology, 2011; mem. editl. bd.: Acta Cytologica Jour., 1985—2006, Vietnamese Med. Jour., 2001—06; contbr. articles to profl. jours. Accreditation com. for Can. sch. cytotechnology Can. Med. Assn., Ottawa, Ont., Canada, 1992—2000. Recipient Med. Excellency award, Vietnamese Am. Rsch. Found., Westminster, CA, USA, 2004. Fellow: Internat. Acad. Cytology (assoc.; membership com. 1989—92, editl. com. 1992—95, exam. bd. 1995—2002); mem.: European Acad. Scis., Royal Coll. Physicians and Surgeons of Can., Can. Soc. Cytology (hon.; chmn. 1984—85, sec.-treas. 1985—89), Papanicolaou Soc. Cytopathology (assoc.; member-at-large 1991—99). Achievements include research in cytopathology, pathology, patient care. Personal E-mail: khanhnguyen1730@hotmail.com.

NGUYEN, KHUE VU, molecular biologist, researcher; b. Ha Noi, Vietnam, Sept. 24, 1952; arrived in France, 1974; s. Cang Van Nguyen and Dy Thi Vu; m. Martine Françoise Juilleret, Sept. 18, 1979; 3 children. BS in Biochemistry, U. Louis Pasteur, Strasbourg, France, 1979, MS in Molecular Biology, 1980, PhD in Macromolecular Phys. Chemistry, 1983, PhD (D d'Etat) in Phys. Scis., 1986. Postdoctoral rschr. Faculty Medicine, Strasbourg, 1986-87; rsch. scientist Anda Biols. Co., Strasbourg, 1987-97, Neurofit Co., Strasbourg, 1998-99, U. Calif. San Diego Sch. Medicine, 1999—2001, 2008—, Vista Biols. Corp., Carlsbad, Calif., 2001—08. Contbr. articles to profl. jours.; patentee in field. Mem. AAAS, Am. Soc. Microbiology, Am. Chem. Soc., NY Acad. Scis. Address: 4079 Front St Apt # 403 San Diego CA 92103 Home Phone: 760-481-4520; Office Phone: 619-543-2105. Personal E-mail: kv52nguyen@yahoo.com.

NGUYEN, LAN THI HOANG, physician, educator; b. Hai-Duong, Vietnam, July 18, 1950; came to U.S., 1975; d. Thua Nang and Niem Thi (Do) N.; m. Khanh Vinh Quoc, Oct. 15, 1981. MD, U. Kans., 1983. Intern St. Mary Med. Ctr./UCLA, Long Beach, Calif., 1983-84; resident City of Faith Med. Rsch. Ctr.-Oral Roberts Sch. Medicine, Tulsa, 1986-88; fellow VA Med. Ctr.-Wadsworth-UCLA, 1988-90; physician Santa Ana (Calif.) Med. Ctr., Doctors Hosp. Santa Ana, Fountain Valley (Calif.) Regional Med. Ctr. Clin. assoc. prof. family medicine Keck Sch. Medicine U. So. Calif., LA, 2002—. Contbr. articles to profl. jours. V.p. Vietnamese Am. Med. Rsch. Found. Kans. Med. scholar, 1979-81. Fellow: ACP, Am. Coll. Endocrinology, Am. Coll. Nutrition; mem.: Am. Assn. Clin. Endocrinologists (charter). Office: 14971 Brookhurst St Westminster CA 92683-5556 Office Phone: 714-839-5898.

NGUYEN, THACH NGOC, cardiologist; b. Feb. 2, 1953; s. Sau Ngoc Nguyen and Hanh Hong Tran. Diploma, Hue Med. Sch., 1978. Diplomate Am. Bd. Internal Medicine, Am. Bd. Cardiovasc. Diseases and Interventional Cardiology. Resident internal medicine Bklyn. Hosp., 1982-85, fellow cardiology, 1985-87; clin. asst. prof. medicine Ind. U. Sch. Medicine, 1992—; dir. cardiovascular rsch. St. Mary Med. Ctr., Hobart, Ind., 1997—, dir. cardiology, 2001—, pres. med. staff, 2002—04, 2006—. Editl. cons. Jour. of Interventional Cardiology, 1998, Vietnamese Med. Jour., 2001; sect. editor Mgmt. of Patients, Lesion & Complication; hon. prof. Inst. Geriatric Cardiology, Chinese PLA Ctrl. Hosp., Beijng, 2004—, Chao Yang Red Cross Hosp., 1998—, Beijing Friendship Hosp., Nanjing U. Hosp., 2006, Hanoi Med. Coll., 2007. Editor: Cardiology Today, 1995, Advances and Challenges in Today's Cardiology, 1997, Management of Complex Cardiovascular Problems: The Consultant's Approach, 2002, Spanish edit., 2002, Vietnamese edit., 2002, Practical Handbook of Advanced Interventional Cardiology, 2000;: 3d edit., 2007, Management of Complex Cardiovascular Problems: The Evidence-Based Medicine Approach, 2007, Cardiology of the 21st Century, 2009; co-editor: Jour. Geriatric Cardiology, 2003. Fellow: ACP, Soc. Cardiovasc. Angiography and Intervention; mem.: Am. Coll. Cardiology (internat. com. 2006—09, internat. membership task force 2007, strategic adv. 2009—). Roman Catholic. Address: 200 E 86th Pl Merrillville IN 46410-6258 Home Phone: 219-872-7275; Office Phone: 219-756-1400. E-mail: thachnguyen2000@yahoo.com.

NGUYEN, TUNG T., medical educator; b. Vietnam, Dec. 6, 1964; MD, Stanford U., 1991. Prof. medicine UCSF, 1997—. Office: 1545 Divisadero UCSF Box 0320 San Francisco CA 94143 Business E-Mail: tung.nguyen@ucsf.edu.

NGUYEN-TRONG, HOANG, physician, consultant; b. Hue, Republic of Vietnam, Sept. 4, 1936; s. Nguyen-Trong Hiep and Nguyen-Phuoc Ton-nu-Thi Sung. B in Math., Lycée d'Etat Michel Montaigne, Bordeaux, 1956; state diploma of medicine, Sch. Medicine, Paris, 1966, cert. in Health and Sanitation, 1965, diploma Health and Smoking, 1993; diploma post traumatic stress disorder, crises and disasters, The Am. U. and Centre Internat. de Scis. Criminelles de Paris, Washington, 1995. Resident surgeon Compiegne State Hosp., 1963-64, Meaux State Hosp., 1964-66, Lagny State Hosp., 1966; specialist in health and sanitation Paris Sch. Medicine, 1965—; specialist in family planning French Action of Family Planning, Paris, 1968—; practice medicine, Nanterre, France, 1969—. Cons. physician various pharm. labs., Paris, 1987; investigator physician WHO regional office for Europe, 1991. Contbr. articles to profl. jours. Active mem. task force on tobacco dependency Biomed. Saints Péres Rsch. Unit, Paris, 1993, AIDS treatment assn. Le Val de Seine, 1993. Recipient World Decoration of Excellence, 1990, Commemorative Medal of Honor, 1990, Internat. Order of Merit, 1990. Mem. French Soc. Aviation and Space Physiology and Medicine (titulary, specialist in aviation medicine), Assn. Nanterre Physicians, Assn. Vietnamese Practitioners in France, Assn. Le Val de Seine, Chambre Syndicale des Medecins des Hauts de Seine, Assn. Les Transmetteurs Paris, Ordre des Medecins de Paris, Les Ex du XIV Shooting Club, European Soc. of Victimology. Avocations: painting, poetry, classical and modern jazz music, riflery, martial arts. Office: 3 Rue Gazan 75014 Paris France

NIAGOLOVA, SVETLANA IORDANOVA, medical association administrator; b. Gorna Orqhovitza, Veliko Turnovo, Bulgaria, Sept. 21, 1961; d. Iordan Iordanov Markov and Maria Ivanova Markova; m. Georgi Niagolov Niagolov, Sept. 13, 1980; children: Zornitza Georgieva, Svetlin Georgiev Niagolov. MD, Med. U., Pleven, 1985. Diplomate radiologist Med. Acad., 1990. Head x-ray dept, & MRI unit U. Hosp., Pleven; med. dir. Euromedic Bulgaria Mdl Eood Pleven, Bulgaria, 2009—. Mem.: RSNA. Home: 4 Stoian Zaimov St Pleven 5800 Bulgaria Office: Euromedic Bulgaria Mdl Eood-Pleven 91 Gen Vladimir Vazov Pleven 5800 Bulgaria Office Fax: 0035964820208; Home Fax: 0035964824508. Personal E-mail: drsvet@yahoo.com. Business E-Mail: drsvet@abv.bg.

NICCHI, VINCENT, JR., cardiologist; b. Bklyn., Nov. 16, 1955; s. Vincent Sr. and Rosalie (Martino) N.; m. Kathleen Mary Healy, May 26, 1985; children: Kristina Rose, Lisa Marie, Michelle Kathleen, Vincent Michael. BS in Chemistry, Bklyn. Coll., 1977; MD, U. Noreste, Tampico Tamps, Mex., 1981. Diplomate Am. Bd. Internal Medicine, Am. Bd. Cardiovasc. Diseases, Am. Bd. Nuc. Cardiology. Intern Maimonides Med. Ctr., Bklyn., 1982-83, resident, 1983-85; fellow in cardiology Deborah Heart Lung Ctr., Browns Mills, NJ, 1985-87; invasive/interventional cardiologist Ariz. Heart Inst., 1987-96; founder Cardiac Care Consultants, Sun City, Ariz., 1996—; chmn. cardiology divsn. Boswell Hosp., Sun City, 2007—, mem. staff. Past chmn. credential com. Del Webb Hosp., Sun City West, Ariz., past mem. med. exec. com. Fellow: Am. Coll. Cardiology; mem.: AMA. Roman Catholic. Office: Cardiac Care Consultants 13634 North 93rd Ave Ste 30 Peoria AZ 85381

NICHOLAS, LYNN B., medical association administrator; b. Tenn. BS in Med. Tech., Tenn. Wesleyan Coll.; M in Mgmt., Cent. Mich. U., 1983. Cert. in healthcare mgmt. Various positions including med. technologist, lab mgr., head lab svcs., sr. v.p. clin./ambulatory svc. Morristown Meml. Hosp., NJ, 1976—95; exec. v.p., COO NJ Hosp. Assn., 1995—2000; pres., CEO La. Hosp. Assn., 2000—04; CEO Am. Diabetes Assn., Alexandria, Va., 2004—06, Mass. Hosp. Assn., 2007—. Former chair La. Health Works Commn. Fellow: Am. Coll. Healthcare Execs. (bd. govs. 2003—06). Office: Mass Hosp Assn 5 New Eng Exec Pk Burlington MA 01803 Office Phone: 703-549-1500, 800-342-2383, 781-262-6000. Office Fax: 703-739-9346.

NICHOLAS, PETER M., medical products executive; married; 3 children BS, Duke U.; MS, U. Pa. Former corp. dir. mktg., gen. mgr. med. products divsn. Millipore Corp.; various sales, mktg., and gen. mgmt. positions Eli Lily and Co.; co-chmn. bd. Boston Sci., Natick, Mass., 1979—95, CEO, 1979—99; chmn. bd. Boston Scientific Corp., Natick, Mass., 1995—. Chmn. bd. trustees, mem. bd. exec. com. Duke U.; mem. Mass. Bus. Roundtable, Mass. Bus. High Tech. Coun., CEOs for Fundamental Change in Edn., Boys and Girls Club Boston. Named one of World's Richest People, Forbes Mag., 2001—04. Fellow: Nat. Acad. Arts and Scis. (trustee); mem.: Boys and Girls Club, Boston, CEOs Fundamental Change Edn., Mass. Bus. High Tech. Coun., Mass. Bus. Roundtable. Office: Boston Sci 1 Boston Sci Pl Natick MA 01760-1537 *

NICHOLAS, STEPHEN J., orthopedic surgeon, sports medicine physician; BA in Biology, Harvard U., Cambridge, Mass., 1982; MD, NY Med. Coll., Valhalla, NY, 1986. Dir. Nicholas Inst. Sports Medicine and Athletic Trama, Lenox Hill Hosp., NYC, 2001—; chief, bioskills lab. Lenox Hill Hosp., NYC. With Lenox Hill Hosp.; worked extensively with profl. and collegiate athletes; orthopaedist NY Jets, NY Islanders, Hofstra U., & NJ Galdiators. Mem. NYC Sports Commn.; mem. alumni adv. bd. NY Med. Coll. Mem.: AMA, Surgicare Manhattan (mng. dir.), Arthroscopy Assn. North America, AANA, Am. Orthopaedic Assn., Quigley Orthopedic Soc., Med. Soc. State NY, Am. Orthopedic Soc. for Sports Medicine (mem. publs. com.), Am. Acad. Orthopedic Surgeons. Office: 130 E 77th St New York NY 10075 Office Phone: 212-737-3301.

NICHOLLS, ANTHONY, biophysicist, software company executive; b. Plymouth, England; BS in Physics, Oxford U.; PhD, Inst. for Molecular Biophysics, Fla. State U., 1988. Rschr. Columbia U., NYC, 1989—97; founder, pres. & CEO OpenEye Scientific Software, Santa Fe, 1997—. Achievements include re-writing the electrostatics program DelPhi and writing widely-used graphics software GRASP that displays electric potentials around macromolecules. Office: Openeye Scientific Software 9D Bisbee Ct Santa Fe NM 87508-1338 *

NICHOLS, BUFORD LEE, JR., pediatrician, nutritionist; b. Ft. Worth, Dec. 12, 1931; married; 3 children. BA, Baylor U., 1954, MS, 1958; MD, Yale U., 1960. Diplomate Am. Bd. Pediatrics, Am. Bd. Nutrition. Instr. pediatrics Baylor U. Coll. Medicine, Houston, 1956-57, instr. physiology and pediatrics, 1964-66, from asst. prof. to assoc. prof. pediatrics, 1966-67, instr. physiology, 1967-74, chief sect. nutrition and gastroenterology, dept. Pediatrics, 1970-78, assoc. prof. community medicine, 1975—, prof. physiology and pediatrics, 1977—, head sect. nutrition and physiology, 1979-92; intern in pediatrics Yale-New Haven Med. Ctr., 1960-61, chief resident in pediatrics, 1963-64; resident in pediatrics Johns Hopkins Hosp., 1961-63; instr. pediatrics Yale U. Sch. Medicine, 1963-64; dir. USDA Children's Nutritional Rsch. Ctr., Houston, 1979-92, emeritus dir., 1992—2010, emeritus prof., 2010. Recipient award Bristol-Myers, 1984, Nutrition award, Am. Acad. Pediats., 1998, Shwachman award, N.Am. Soc. for Pediat. Gastroenterology, Hepatology and Nutrition, 2002. Mem. Am. Acad. Pediatrics, Am. Soc. Clin. Nutrition, Am. Coll. Nutrition (v.p. 1975-76, pres. 1977-79). Baptist. Achievements include research in environmental effects upon growth and development in the infant especially alterations in body composition and muscle physiology in malnutrition, chronic diarrhea and malnutrition; cloned, sequenced and expressed recombinant intestinal maltase-glucoamylase gene, knocked out the maltase-glucoamylase gene in mice to determine its role in digestion and glucose homeostasis. Office: Baylor Coll Medicine Childrens Nutrition Rsch Ctr 1100 Bates Ave Houston TX 77030-2600 Office Phone: 713-798-7018. Personal E-mail: blnjr@sbcglobal.net. Business E-Mail: bnichols@bcm.tmc.edu. *

NICHOLS, CLYDE RICHARD, minister, consumer products company executive; b. NYC, Apr. 15, 1945; s. William and Novella Nichols; m. Marsha A. Wade, Oct. 11, 1986; children: Forest, Marvin, Anthony, Gerald. BS, Met. State Coll., Denver, 1985; ThD, Berean Bible Coll., Dallas, 1994. Ordained pastor and bishop Fellowship of Deliverance Chs., Inc. Correction officer City and County Denver, 1981-92; sr. pastor, founder Redeeming Love Ch., Denver; sr. dir. M&C Enterprises, Inc., Denver; exec. dir. Josie M. Bedford Found. Dir. membership Greater Metro Denver Ministers Alliance Orgn., Denver, 1997-99. Bd. dirs. Denver Opportunities for Outreach and Reflection 2000—. Recipient award for outstanding cmty. work Cheyenne br. NAACP, Wyo., 1982, award for outstanding cmty. activities 24th Syl Morgan Acad. Arts, Denver, 1992, Juanita Gray award. Avocations: travel, reading, computers. Home and Office: PO Box 31092 Aurora CO 80041-0092 Business E-Mail: mcenterpr31092@aol.com. E-mail: rev98crn@aol.com.

NICHOLS, DAVID EARL, pharmacy educator, researcher, consultant; b. Covington, Ky., Dec. 23, 1944; s. Earl and Edythe Lee (Brooker) N.; m. Cibele Ruas Nichols; children: Charles D., Daniel P. BS, U. Cin., 1969; PhD, U. Iowa, 1973. Asst. prof. medicinal chemistry Purdue U., West Lafayette, Ind., 1974-79, assoc. prof., 1979-85, prof., 1985—, Robert C & Charlotte P Anderson chair pharm., 2007. Founder, pres. Heffter Rsch. Inst., Santa Fe, 1993—. Contbr. articles to profl. jours. Recipient Provost's Outstanding Grad. Mentor award, 2006; grantee Nat. Inst. on Drug Abuse, 1978—, NIMH, 1978—. Fellow: Am. Assn. Pharm. Scientists, Am. Pharm. Assn. (Irwin H. Page lectr. 2004); mem.: Am. Coll. Neuropsychopharmacology. Achievements include patents in field. Office: Purdue U Sch Pharmacy West Lafayette IN 47907 Business E-Mail: drdave@purdue.edu.

NICHOLS, DAVID GREGORY, anesthesiologist, pediatrician, educator; b. Hampton, Va., Oct. 1, 1951; MD, Mt. Sinai Sch. Medicine, 1977. Diplomate Am. Bd. Anesthesiology, Am. Bd. Pediatrics, Am. Bd. Critical Care Medicine. Intern Children's Hosp., Phila., 1977-78, resident in pediatrics, 1978-80; resident in anesthesiology U. Pa. Hosp., Phila., 1981-83; fellow in anesthesiology Critical Care Children's Hosp., Phila., 1983; assoc. prof. anesthesiology, critical care & pediatric medicine Johns Hopkins U. Sch. Medicine, Balt., 1991—98, prof. anesthesiology, critical care & pediatric medicine, 1998—, vice dean edn., 2000—. Dir. Pediat. ICU, Johns Hopkins U. Hosp., Balt., 1991-97, Pediat. Anesthesiology and Critical Care Medicine, 1997—. Mem. Am. Soc. Anesthesiology, Soc. for Pediat. Rsch., Soc. Critical Care Medicine Office: Johns Hopkins Sch Medicine 733 N Broadway Ste 115 Baltimore MD 21205

NICHOLS, KAREN J., dean; b. Ind. m. Jim Nichols. DO, U. Health Scis., Coll. Osteo. Medicine, Kansas City. Intern and resident in internal medicine Okla. Osteo. Hosp., Tulsa; asst. dean grad. med. edn. Ariz. Coll. Osteo. Medicine; dean Chgo. Coll. Osteo. Medicine, 2002—, prof. medicine. Contbr. articles to profl. jours. Bd. trustees Mut. Ins. Co. of Ariz.; with Mesa Symphony, Mesa United Way, Central Christian Ch. Recipient Physician of Yr., Ariz. Osteo. Med. Assn., 1996, Educator of Yr., Mesa Gen. Hosp. Mem.: Am. Osteo. Assn. (chair bur. state and govt. affairs, mem. health related and fed. health policies coms., chair adv. com. of end of life care). Office: Chgo Coll Osteo Medicine Midwestern U 555 31st St Downers Grove IL 60515 *

NICHOLS, RONALD LEE, surgeon, educator; b. Chgo., June 25, 1941; s. Peter Raymond and Jane Eleanor (Johnson) N.; m. Elsa Elaine Johnson, Dec. 4, 1964; children: Kimberly Jane, Matthew Bennett. MD, U. Ill., 1966, MS, 1970. Diplomate Am. Bd. Surgery (assoc. cert. examiner, New Orleans, 1991), Nat. Bd. Med. Examiners. Intern U. Ill. Hosp., Chgo., 1966-67, resident in surgery, 1967-72, instr. surgery, 1970-72, asst. prof. surgery, 1972-74; assoc. prof. surgery U. Health Scis. Chgo. Med. Sch., 1975-77, dir. surg. edn., 1975-77; William Henderson prof. surgery Tulane U. Sch. Medicine, New Orleans, 1977—2002, vice chmn. dept. surgery, 1982-91, staff surgeon, 1977—2002, prof. microbiology, immunology, 1979—, William Henderson prof. surgery emeritus, 2003—; sr. vis. surgeon Med. Ctr. La., New Orleans, 1988—2009, hon med. staff, 2009—. Cons. surgeon VA Hosp., Alexandria, La., 1978-93, Huey P. Long Hosp., Pineville, La., 1978-2002, Lallie Kemp Charity Hosp., Independence, La., 1977-85, Touro Infirmary, New Orleans, Monmouth Med. Ctr., Long Branch, NJ, 1979-88; sr. vis. surgeon Med. Ctr. La., New Orleans, 1988—; mem. VA Coop. Study Rev. Bd., 1978-81, VA Merit Rev. Bd. in Surgery, 1979-82; sci. program com. 3d Internat. Conf. Nosocomial Infections, Ctr. Disease Control, sci. program and fundraising com. 4th Internat. Conf.; bd. dirs. Nat. Found. Infectious Diseases, 1988-2003, v.p., 1994-97, pres.-elect, 1997-99, pres., 1999-2001, trustee, 2003-2008, bd. dirs., 2008-; hon. fellow faculty Kasr El Aini Cairo U. Sch. Medicine, 1989; adv. com. on infection control Ctrs. for Disease Control, 1991-97; disting. guest, vis. prof. Royal Coll. Surgeons Thailand, 1989, 1992; infectious diseases adv. bd. Roche Labs., 1988-95, Abbott Labs., 1990-92, Kimberly Clark Corp., 1990-99, SmithKline Beecham Labs., 1990-95, Fujisawa Pharm., chmn., 1990-99, Bayer Pharm., 1994-2001, Merck Sharpe Dohme, 1996, Depotech, 1996, Zeneca Pharm., 1997-2000, Rhone-Poulenc Rorer, 1997-99, Wyeth-Ayrest Labs., 1998-2003, Pfizer Pharm., 1999, Searle Pharm., 1999-2001, GlaxoWellcome, 1999, Aventis, 1999-2000, Cubist Pharm., 2000—05, Regent Med., 2003—06, others; study group Prophylaxis Antibiotic Project La. Health Care Rev., Inc., 1995-2000, Nat. Com. Study Blood Borne Disease Transmission make Nat. Policy, Rockefeller Brothers Fund, 2001-03; apptd. by gov. La. commn. HIV and AIDS, 1999-2007; lectr. Royal Coll. Physicians and Surgeons, Can., 1998, Internat. Infectious Disease Soc. Ob-gyn., 1998, 20th NY State Surg. Symposium, 1998, Dept. Surgery, U. Ark., 1998; nat. policy com. study innovative surgery reg. Greenwall Found., 2003—06; lectr. in field. Author: (with Gorbach, Bartlett and Nichols) Manual of Surgical Infection, 1984; author, guest editor: (with Nichols, Hyslop Jr. and Bartlett) Decision Mking in Surgical Sepsis, 1991; guest editor, author: Surgical Sepsis and Beyond, 1993; mem. editl. bd. Current Surgery, 1977-2006, Hosp. Physician, 1980—2006, Infection Control, 1980-86, Guidelines to Antibiotic Therapy, 1976-81, Am. Jour. Infection Control, 1981-99, Internat. Medicine, 1983—, Confronting Infection, 1983-86, Current Concepts in Clin. Surgery, 1984—, Fact Line, 1984-91, Host/Pathogen News, 1984—, Infectious Diseases in Clin. Practice, 1991—2005, surg. sect. editor, 1992-2005, Surg. Infections: Index and Revs., 1991—, So. Med. Jour., 1992-97, ANAEROBE, 1994—, Surg. Infections, 1998—, Clin. Infectious Diseases, 1999—; editl. adv. bd. MD Consult Infectious Diseases, 2002-04; mem. adv. bd. Physician News Network, 1991-95; patentee (with S.G. schoenberger and W.R. Rank) Helical-Tipped Lesion Localization Needle Device; patentee in field. Elected faculty sponsor graduating class Tulane Med. Sch., 1979-80, 83, 85, 87, 88, 91-92; apptd. La. Commn. HIV and AIDS, 1999-2007. Maj. USAR, 1972-75. Recipient House Staff tchg. award U. Ill. Coll. Medicine, 1973, rsch. award bd. trustees U. Health Scis., Chgo. Med. Ctr., 1977, Clin. Prof. of Year U. Health Sci., 1977, Tchg. award Owl Club, 1980-86, 90, Douglas Stubbs Lectr. award Nat. Med. Assn. Surg. Sect., 1987, Prix d'Elegance award Men of Fashion, New Orleans, 1993; named Prof. of Yr. U. Health Sci., Chgo. Med. Sch., 1977, Clin. Prof. of Yr. Tulane U. Sch. Medicine, 1979, Brit. Jour. Surgery Lectr., 1997, 1st Ann. Warren Cole Lectr., 2001; elected to Wall of Fame, Lakeview HS, Chgo., 2006. Fellow Infectious Disease Soc. Am. (mem. FDA subcom. to develop guidelines in surg. prophylaxis 1989-93, co-recipient Joseph Susman Meml. award 1990), Am. Acad. Microbiology, Internat. Soc. Univ. Colon and Rectal Surgeons, ACS (mem. oper. rm. environ. com. 1978-80, vice chair oper. rm. environ. com. 1980-81, chmn. oper. rm. environ. com. 1981-83, sr. mem. oper. rm. environ. com. 1983-87, mem. internat. rels. com. 1987-93, sr. mem. internat. rels. com. 1993-97); mem. AMA, Joint Commn. on Accreditation of Health Care Orgn. (Infection Control adv. group, 1988-98, sci. program com. 3d internat. conf. nosocomial infections CDC/Nat. Found. Infectious Diseases 1990, FDA Subcom. to Develop Guidelines in Surg. Prophylaxis, 1989-93; prophylactic antibiotic study group La. Health Care Rev. Inc. 1996-2000, clin. advisor, mem., 2001-08, AIDS commr. State of La. 1992-94, mem. 1999-2007), 5th Nat. Forum on AIDS (sci. program com.), US Pharmacopeial Convention Inc. (adv. panel surg. drugs and devices 1995-2000, nominating com. The Heinz Awards 1995-96), Assn. Practitioners in Infection Control (physician adv. coun. 1991-98), Internat. Soc. Anaerobic Bacteria, So. Med. Assn. (vice chmn. sect. surgery 1980-81, chmn. 1982-83), Assn. Acad. Surgery, NY Acad. Sci., Warren H. Cole Soc. (pres.-elect 1988, pres. 1989-90), Assn. VA Surgeons, Soc. Surgery Alimentary Tract, Inst. Medicine Chgo., Midwest Surg. Assn., Ctrl. Surg. Assn., Ill. Surg. Soc., European Soc. Surg. Rsch., Collegium Internationale Chirugiae Digestivae, Chgo. Surg. Soc. (hon.), New Orleans Surg. Soc. (bd. dirs. 1983-87), Soc. Univ. Surgeons, Surg. Soc. La., Southeastern Surg. Soc., Phoenix Surg. Soc. (hon.), Hellenic Surg. Soc. (hon.), Ctrl. NY Surg. Soc. (hon.), Tulane Surg. Soc., Alton Ochsner Surg. Soc., Am. Soc. Microbiology, Soc. Internat. de Chirugie, Surg. Infection Soc. (sci. study com. 1982 83, fellowship com. 1985-87, ad hoc sci. liaison com. 1986-89, program com. 1986-87, chmn. ad hoc com. rels. with industry 1990-93, mem. sci. liaison com. 1995-96), Soc. for Intestinal Microbial Ecology and Disease, Soc. Critical Care Medicine, Am. Surg. Assn., Kansas City Surg. Soc., Bay Surg. Soc. (hon.), Cuban Surg. Soc. (hon.), Panhellenic Surg. Soc. (hon.), Tacoma Surg. Club (hon.), Sigma Xi, Alpha Omega Alpha. Episcopalian. Home: 1521 7th St New Orleans LA 70115 2322 Office: 1430 Tulane Ave New Orleans LA 70112-2699 Office Phone: 504-988-5168. Personal E-mail: rlnmd@yahoo.com. Business E-Mail: ronald.nichols@tulane.edu.

NICHOLS, WILLIAM CURTIS, clinical psychologist, educator, marriage and family therapist, consultant; b. Fayette, Ala., Apr. 16, 1929; s. William Curtis and Eva (Hargett) N.; m. Alice Louise Mancill, May 29, 1954 (dec. 1990); children: Alice Camille, William Mancill, David Paul; m. Mary Anne Pace, Feb. 29, 1992. AB, U. Ala., 1953; EdD, Columbia U., 1960. Diplomate Am. Bd. Profl. Psychology. Asst. prof. sociology U. Ala., Birmingham, 1960-63; postdoctoral fellow Merrill-Palmer Inst., 1963-64, mem. psychotherapy faculty, 1965-69; prof. sociology Samford U., Birmingham, Ala., 1963-65; pvt. practice clin. psychology and marital and family therapy Grosse Pointe, Mich., 1969-73, 76-87, pvt. practice psychology, marital and family therapy Birmingham, Mich., 1976 87; prof. home and family life, dir. marriage and family counseling Fla. State U., 1973-76; exec. dir. Gov.'s Constituency Children, Fla., 1987-89; pvt. practice marital and family therapy S.E. Family Inst., 1989-90; pres. William Nichols Assocs., Organizational Cons., 1990-91; cons., marital and family therapist Atlanta, 1992—97; cons. in field, 1997-98; with The Nichols Group, Inc., 1998. Adj. prof. clin. psychology U. Detroit, 1976-83; adj. prof. family therapy Fla. State U., 1990-91; adj. prof., grad. faculty child and family devel. dept. U. Ga., 1992-05, founder, chair adv. com. Family Therapy Archives, 1993—, The Nichols Group, Inc., 1998-99. Author: Treating People in Families: An Integrative Framework, 1996, Marital Therapy: An Integrative Approach, 1988, Treating Adult Survivors of Childhood Sexual Abuse, 1992, The AAMFT: Fifty Years of Marital and Family Therapy, 1992, Family Therapy Around the World: A Festschrif to Florence Kaslow, 2004; co-author: Systematic Family Therapy, 1986; editor: (with others) Handbook of Family Development and Intervention, 2000; editor The Family Coord., 1970-75, Jour. Marriage and Family Counseling, 1974-76, Contemporary Family Therapy: An Internat. Jour., 1986-2006, Family Therapy News, 1986-91, The Internat. Connection, 1996-99; mem. editl. bd. Internat. Jour. Family Therapy, 1977-85, Jour. Divorce and Remarriage, 1976-83, 85—, Sage Family Studies Abstracts, 1977-99, Family Systems Medicine, 1982-96, Jour. Marital and Family Therapy, 1984—, Jour. Family Psychotherapy, 1990—, Jour. Family Psychology, 1986-90. Mem. mental health and health coms. Detroit Mayor's Commn. on Children and Youth, 1966-69; bd. dir. Family and Children's Svc., Oakland, Mich., 1977-87, chmn., 1984-86, dir. emeritus, 1987—. With C.E., U.S. Army, 1948-49. Recipient Svc. award Ala. Assn. for Mental Health, 1962, Spl. award for Outstanding Contbns. Fla. Assn. Marriage and Family Therapy, 1977, 82, 90; NSF fellow U. Colo., 1963, Disting. Svc. Families award Southeastern Coun. on Family Rels., 1996. Fellow: Am. Assn. Marriage and Family Therapy (dir. 1969—72, founding editor Jour. Marital and Family Therapy 1974—76, chmn. accreditation com. 1976—77, pres.-elect 1979—80, dir. 1979—83, pres. 1981—82, Spl. awards 1976, 1978, Disting. Leadership awards 1982, 1983, Disting. Leadership award 1991, Orgnl. Contbns. award 1992), Am. Psychol. Soc.; mem.: APA, Soc. for Family Psychology (Disting. Contbn. award 2010), Am. Family Therapy Acad., Internat. Family Therapy Assn. (bd. dirs. 1996—98, editor Internat. Connections 1996—99, pres. 1999—2001, 2009—11), Ga. Assn. for Marriage and Family Therapy (pres.-elect 1994—95, pres. 1996), Mich. Bd. Marriage Counselors (chmn. 1980—87), Nat. Coun. on Family Rels. (bd. dir., exec. com. 1969—78, pres. 1976—77), Mich. Assn. Marriage Counselors (pres. 1969—71, chmn. profl. liaison com. 1972—73), Mich. Inter-Profl. Assn. on Marriage, Divorce and Family (com. chmn. 1968—71, 1976—86, trustee 1977—80, Orgnl. Contbn. award 1992), Assn. Marital and Family therapy Regulation Bds. (MFT examination adv. bd. 1989—92), Am. Assn. Marriage and Family Therapy Edn. and Rsch. Found. (trustee 1992—94). Home: 755 W Lake Dr Athens GA 30606 Personal E-mail: nicholsw@aol.com.

NICHOLS, WILLIAM FORD, JR., health science association administrator, educator; b. Palo Alto, Calif., July 4, 1934; s. William Ford and Elizabeth (Woodyatt) N.; m. Rosemary Peterson, 1988; children: Deborah, John, Andrew. AB, Stanford U., 1956, MBA, 1958. CPA, Calif. With Price Waterhouse, San Francisco, 1958-69, Price Waterhouse & Co., Sydney, Australia, 1966; asst. contr. Saga Corp., Menlo Park, Calif., 1969-72, contr., 1972—, asst. treas., 1981-83; assoc. prof. San Jose State U., 1983-88; treas. William and Flora Hewlett Found., Menlo Park, 1985-2000. Trustee Investment Fund for Founds., 1991-2001. Bd. dirs. Lucile Packard Found. for Children's Health, Palo Alto, Calif., 1999—2006; trustee Oreg. Shakespeare Festival Endowment Fund, 2005-, pres. 2009-. Mem. AICPA, Calif. Soc. CPA's, Inst. Mgmt. Accts. (nat. v.p. 1974-75, bd. dirs.), Fin. Execs. Inst. (pres. Santa Clara Valley chpt. 1979-80), Palo Alto Club, Alpha Omega Alpha (asst. treas. 1985—). Home: 620 Sand Hill Rd Apt 220-D Palo Alto CA 94304-2098 *

NICHOLSON, GREG POWELL, orthopedist; b. Columbus, Ind., Dec. 22, 1959; m. Margaret Nicholson, May 21, 1988; children: Benjamin, Madeline, Samuel, Isabel. BA with highest distinction in Bio., Ind. Univ., Bloomington, 1982; MD, Ind. Univ. Sch. Med., Indianapolis, 1986. Diplomate Nat. Bd. Med. Examiners. Orthopedist Orthopaedic Specialists Ind., Indianapolis, 1992—95, Orhtopaedics Indianapolis, PC, 1995—2001, Rush Univ. Hosp. Supervisor, resident edn. orthopedic dept. St. Vincent Hosp. for Ind. Univ., 1991—95; physician Ind. Indians AAA Baseball Team, 1992—2001; clin. asst. prof. orthopaedics Ind. Univ.; vice-chmn., dept. orthopaedics St. Vincent Hosp., 1997—2001; prof., dept. orthopaedic surgery Rush Univ. Mem.: Indpls. Orthopaedic Club, Ind. Orthopaedic Soc., Marion County Med. Soc., AMA, Mid Am. Orthopaedic Assn., Assn. Bone and Joint Surgeons, Am. Shoulder and Elbow Surgeons, Am. Acad. Orthopaedic Surgeons. Office: Midwest Orthopaedics Ste 1063 1725 W Harrison St Chicago IL 60612 Office Phone: 312-432-2332.

NICHOLSON, HENRY HALE, JR., retired surgeon; b. Statesville, NC, June 22, 1922; s. Henry Hale and Martha Haseltine (Miller) N.; m. Freda Hyams, Sept. 24, 1956; children: Henry Hale III, Thomas Dalton Miller, John Christie, Michael Witherspoon, Freda Amanda, W. Stuart Cooper. BA in Chemistry, Duke U., 1944, MD, 1947; grad., USAF Sch. Aviation Medicine, 1952. Diplomate Am. Bd. Gen. Surgery, Am. Bd. Colon and Rectal Surgery. Rotating intern U. Wis. Gen. Hosp., Madison, 1947-48; resident in gen. surgery Med. Coll. Va., Richmond, 1948-49, Alton Ochsner Hosp. and Clinic, New Orleans, 1949-51, 53-55, inaugeral resident in colon and rectal surgery, 1955-56; resident in gen. surgery Tulane U., La. Charity Hosp., New Orleans, 1949-51, 53-55; pvt. practice gen., colon and rectal surgery, aerospace medicine Charlotte, NC, 1956—2002; sr. surg. staff mem. Carolinas Med. Ctr. and Mercy Hosp., Charlotte; ret., 2002. Sr. surg. staff Presbyn. Hosp., Charlotte, 1956-2002; sr. active teaching staff Carolinas Med. Ctr., 1956-85, cons. staff, 1985—; surg. cons. Surgeon Gen. USAF, 1971-82. Mem. Airport Authority Charlotte/Douglas Internat. Airport, 1992-2009, chmn., 2008-09; mem. Mayor's Com. of 100 to study regional transp. and make appropriate recommendations, 1993-94; sr. examiner FAA, 1952-2007, active pilot; mem. athletic-med. bd. N.C. Shrine Bowl, 1980-2003. With U.S. Army, 1943-46. Maj. flight surgeon USAF, 1951-53, Korea; col. USAFR, 1961-82, NCANG, command air surgeon 1961-1982. Decorated Legion of Merit, Disting. Svc. medal USAF NC; named Flight Surgeon of Yr., USA N.G., 1981, 1st Alternate Flight Surgeon of Yr. award USAF, 1982. Fellow ACS, Am. Soc. Colon and Rectal Surgeons; mem. Mecklenburg County Med. Soc. (pres. 1972), Charlotte Surg. Soc. (pres. 1987), Shriners, Masons (32 degree), Jesters, Alton Ochsner Surg. Soc., Hazel Creek Trout Club, Rotary Internat., Robert Burns Soc. (pres. 1963-64), St. Andrews Soc. of Carolina, Air Force Assn., Hound Ears Club (Blowing Rock, N.C.), Charlotte Country Club, Alpha Tau Omega, Phi Chi, Omicron Delta Kappa. Methodist. Avocations: golf, skiing, fly fishing, travel, painting.

NICHOLSON, WILLIAM NOEL, clinical neuropsychologist; b. Detroit, Dec. 24, 1936; s. James Eardly and Hazel A. (Wagner) N.; m. Nancy Ann Marshall, June 15, 1957; children: Anne Marie, Kristin, Scott. AB, Wittenberg U., 1959; MDiv, Luth. Theol. Sem., Phila., 1962; PhD, Mich. State U., 1972. Diplomate Am. Bd. Forensic Examiners, Am. Bd. Med. Psychotherapists; lic. clin. psychologist, Mich.; ordained to ministry Luth. Ch., 1962; cert. Nat. Register Health Care Providers in Psychology, Assn. of State and Provincial Psychology Bds. Parish pastor Our Saviour Luth. Ch., Saginaw, Mich., 1962-69; intern in psychology Ingham Mental Health Bd., 1971-72; resident in psychology Bay-Arenac Mental Health Bd., 1972-74; dir., psychologist Riverside Ctr., Bay City, Mich., 1974-75; pastor, psychologist Psych Studies and Clergy Consultation of Mich., 1989—2003. Pres. Bay Psychol. Assocs., P.C., Bay City, 1975—2002; cons. Gov.'s Office of Drug Abuse, 1972-74. Author: A Guttman Facet Analysis of Attitude-Behaviors Toward Drug Users by Heroin Addicts and Mental Health Therapists, 1972, An Episcopalian Guide to the Augsburg Confession, 1997; contbr. articles to profl. jours. Mem. APA (life), Mich. Psychol. Assn. (life), Nat. Acad. Neuropsychology. Office: Burns Profl Bldg 560 W Mitchell Ste 208 Petoskey MI 49770 Office Phone: 231-347-4700, 231-347-0117.

NICKEL, JANET MARLENE MILTON, retired geriatrics nurse; b. Manitowoc, Wis., June 9, 1940; d. Ashley and Pearl Milton; m. Curtis A. Nickel, July 29, 1961; children: Cassie, Debra, Susan. Diploma, Milw. Inst., 1961; ADN, N.D. State U., 1988. Nurse Milw. VA, Wood, Wis., 1961-62; supervising nurse Park Lawn Convalescent Hosp., Manitowoc, 1964-65; newsletter editor Fargo Model Cities Program, ND, 1970—73; supervising night nurse Rosewood on Broadway, Luth. Hosps. and Homes, Fargo, 1973-92; assoc. dir. nursing Elim Care Ctr., Fargo, 1992-94, night nurse, 1994—2005, 2007—08; ret., 2007. Night nurse Elim Care Ctr., 2007—. Vol. Elim Garden Angels; past pres. Neighborhood Toast Mistress. Mem. Phi Eta Sigma.

NICKEL, MARIUS KONRAD, psychotherapist, educator; b. Saybusch, Poland, Sept. 16, 1961; s. Eugeniusz Wilhelm and Ricarda Nickel; m. Cerstin Schirrmacher, Dec. 30, 2002. MD, Jagiellonian U., Cracow, Poland, 1986; post doctoral in Psychiatry, Paracelsus Medizinische Privatuniversität; post doctoral in Psychosomatic Medicine, U. Regensburg, Germany. Asst. dr., head dept. misc. clin., Germany, 1986—2000; chief physician Clin. for Psychiatry and Psychosomatics, Simbach am Inn, Germany, 2002—; rschr. 1 U. Clin. for Psychiatry, Salzburg, Austria, 2003—; prof. psychosomatics and psychotherapy Medizinische U. Graz, Austria, 2006—. Cons. and tchg. U. Dept. Psychosomatics, Regensburg, 2000—. Contbr. articles

numerous pub. to profl. jour., chapters to books. Mem.: Academic Soc. Physicians in Styria, Austrian Soc. for Neuropsychopharmacology and Biol. Psychiatry, German Profl. Soc. for Depth Psychology-Based Psychotherapy, German Soc. Therapeutic Medicine, German Soc. for Psychoanalysis, Psychotherapy, Psychosomatics and Depth Psychology, Austrian Assn. Psychiatry and Psychotherapy. Roman Cath. Avocations: classical music, jogging. Office: Inntalklinik Jakob-W St 1 84359 Simbach am Inn Germany Personal E-mail: marius.nickel@meduni-graz.at.

NICKELL, PATTON VANMETER, psychiatrist, educator; MD, W.Va. U. Diplomate Am. Bd. Internal Medicine, Am. Bd. Psychiatry and Neurology, cert. electroconvulsive therapy. Intern W.Va. Univ. Med. Ctr., resident; fellow Nat. Inst. of Mental Health; asst. prof. psychiatry Coll. of Medicine Drexel Univ.; system chair dept. of psychiatry West Penn Allegheny Health System; program dir. ECT svcs. Allegheny Gen. Hosp., hosp. affiliations include, Forbes Regional Hosp. Office: Allegheny General Hospital East Commons Professional Bldg Eighth Fl Pittsburgh PA 15212 Office Phone: 412-330-4000. Office Fax: 412-330-4377.

NICKENS, CATHERINE ARLENE, retired nurse, freelance writer; b. Litchfield, Ill., Oct. 30, 1932; d. Harley Lloyd Moore and Ida Mae Reynolds; m. Carl Roland Nickens, Sept. 4, 1954 (div. Apr. 1975); children: Linda Dianne, Carl Roland Jr., Karen Patricia, Eric Moore. Nursing diploma, St. Joseph's Hosp., 1954. RN, Calif. Staff nurse St. Joseph's Hosp., Alton, Ill., 1954-55, St. Mary's Hosp., Streator, Ill., 1962-68, supr., acting dir., 1968-70; nursing supr. Illini Hosp., Silvis, Ill., 1970-74; office nurse pediatrician's office Silvis, 1974-75; staff nurse telemetry/drug abuse North Miami Gen. Hosp., Miami, Fla., 1975-80; staff nurse, relief supr. Petaluma (Calif.) Valley Hosp., 1981-97. Participant women's health study Brigham and Women's Hosp., Boston, 1994-2004. Author: (hist. fiction) The Thoroughly Compromised Bride, 1991 (award 1992), The Highwayman, 1993 (award 1994). Mem. ACLU, N.Y.C., 1995, Parents, Families and Friends of Lesbians and Gays, Washington, 1994-99, Nat. Mus. of Am. Indian/Smithsonian Instn., Washington, 1996-97; friend of the quilt NAMES Project Meml. Quilt, San Francisco, 1992-99; mem. friendship cir. Am. Found. for AIDS Rsch., Washington, 1994—; vol. Santa Rosa Police Dept., 1997-2000. Mem. Romance Writers of Am. (mentor to unpublished writers 1995-99). Avocations: reading, travel, needlecrafts, doll-making. Home and Office: 105 Olive St Santa Rosa CA 95401-6241

NICKLIN, DAVID E., physician, educator; BS, Haverford Coll., 1976; MD, U. Pa., 1981. Diplomate Am. Bd. Emergency Medicine, 2000, Am. Bd. Family Practice, 1984, Am. Bd. Family Practice, 2004. Intern Thomas Jefferson Univ. Hosp., resident family medicine, 1981—84; assoc. dir. family medicine residency program Univ. Pa.; assoc. prof. clin. family medicine and cmty. health Univ. Pa. Health Sys.; med. dir. penn family care Penn Presbyn. Med. Ctr. Author: (publs.) GI Bleeding, Chest Pain, 2003, Medicine and religion, 2000; co-author: Characteristics of primary care practices affect patients' emergency department use, 2003, Primary Care Practices May Lack the Capacity To Adequately Treat Asthma, Has managed care improved accessibility of urgent care for Medicaid patients, 2004, Association between primary care practice characteristics and emergency department use in a medicaid managed care organization, 2005. Named Top Docs, Phila. Mag., 2005—11; named one of Best Doctors in America, 2003—04, 2005—06, 2007—08, 2009—10. Office: Penn Family Care Penn Presbyterian Medical Center Mutch Bldg 7th Fl 51 N 39th St Philadelphia PA 19104 Office Phone: 215-662-8777.

NICKSON, JACK, physician; b. London, Eng., Jan. 31, 1926; s. Clifford and Violet Lily Nickson; m. Elly Ingegärd Ivarsson, July 14, 1979; children: Annika Christine, Steven Erik; m. Betty Helena Kift, Sept. 15, 1954 (div. 1978); children: Martin Christopher, Jacqueline. MB BS, Kings Coll. Hosp., London, 1953, D in obstetrics Rcog, 1955. Casualty house surgeon King's Coll. Hosp., London, 1953—54; house physician Sutton & Cheam Hosp., Surrey, England, 1954—55; obstetric house surgeon Luton Maternity Hosp., Luton, England, 1955; prin. gen. practice Chieveley practice, Newbury, England, 1957—86; cons. Manual Therapy Clin., Newbury, England, 1976—. Contbr. articles to profl. jour. Achievements include patents for load supporting pelvic belt; development of mobile surgery for rural practice; advocate of iliolumbar ligaments as the main source of mechanical low back pain. Avocations: gardening, archaeology, ornithology. Home: Warren Down Peasemore Newbury RG20 7JL England Office Phone: 44 (0) 1635 248331.

NICOL, EDWARD DAVID, cardiologist, researcher; b. Ely, Cambridgeshire, Eng., Dec. 16, 1973; s. David and Linda Nicol; m. Emily Charlotte Leonard, Oct. 5, 2002; children: William, Chloe, Toby. MB, Nottingham U., Eng., 1998; MD, Imperial Coll., London, 2008; MBA, 2010. Squadron leader Various Med. Br., 1995—; cardiology SpR Chelsea and Westminster Hosp., London, Greater London, 2003—05, Royal Brompton Hosp., London, 2005, cardiac CT fellow, 2005—; med. advisor Healthcare Commn., London, 2005—; cardiology specialist registrar John Radcliffe Hosp., Oxford, England, 2008—09. Chmn. Haywood Club Tri-Svc. Med. Soc., London, 2003—07; chief med. officers, venous-thromboembolism expert working group Dept. Health, London, 2005—07, chief med. officers, venous thromboe embolism implementation working group, 2007—, clin. advisor, 2008—. Contbr. articles to profl. jour. Recipient Chadwick medal and prize, London Sch. Hygeine and Tropical Medicine, 2005. Fellow: Royal Geog. Soc.; mem.: Chartered Mgmt. Inst. (mgr. 2006), Royal Coll.Physicians. Achievements include research in clinical validation and application of cardiac CT. Office: John Radcliffe Hosp Headley Way Headington Oxford Oxfordshire OX3 9DU England Home Fax: 442073518555. Personal E-mail: cyprusdoc@doctors.org.uk. Business E-mail: e.nicol@orh.nhs.uk.

NICOLA, OANA, chemical engineer; b. Bucharest, Romania, Mar. 26, 1969; Degree in Chem. Engring., U. Poly. Bucharest, 2004, M, 2005. Engr. Pacard Co. Impex SRL, 2004—08; chem. engr. U. Poly. Bucharest, 2008—; mins. asst. Ministry of Edn. and Rsch., 2009. Mem.: Romanian Soc. Ceramics, Romanian Soc. Chemistry. Avocations: travel, reading. Office: 313 Splaiul Independentei St Bucharest 060042 Romania Office Fax: 4021-402-9257. Personal E-mail: oana_ncl@yahoo.com.

NICOLAOU, NICOS, radiation oncologist educator; MD, U. Cape Town. Diplomate Am. Bd. Radiology-radiation oncology, cert. radiation oncology Royal Coll. of Physicians and Surgeons of Canada.

Resident radiation oncology BC cancer agency Univ. BC; fellow radiation oncology Fox Chase Cancer Ctr., assoc. prof., attending physician; affiliated Phila. Cancer Treatment's Radiation Oncology Ctr. Named Top Doctor for Radiation Oncology, Phila. Mag., 2009—10; named one of America's Top Doctors, Castle Connolly's, 2009—10. Office: Phila Cancer Treatment Center Radiation Oncology Center 1 Presidential Blvd Ste 100 Bala Cynwyd PA 19004 Office Phone: 610-513-2027.

NICOLELIS, MIGUEL A. L., neuroscientist, educator; MD, U. Sao Paulo Med. Sch., 1984; PhD, U. Sao Paulo, 1988. Intern U. Sao Paulo, 1983—84, rsch. assoc. dept. pathology, 1985—86, rsch. instr. dept. pathology, 1986—88, asst. prof. dept. pathology, 1988—92; rsch. instr. dept. physiology & biophysics Hahnemann U., 1989—94; asst. prof. dept. neurobiology Duke U. Med. Ctr., 1994—97, assoc. prof. dept. neurobiology, 1998—2001, assoc. prof. biomedical engineering, 1999—2001, assoc. prof. experimental psychology, 1991—2001, prof. nuerobiology biomedical engring & psychological & brain sciences, 2001—, co-dir Ctr. for Neuroengineering, 2001—. Editorial bd. mem. Neuroinformatics, Jour. Neuroscience Methods; editor-in-chief Frontiers in Neuroscience. Mem.: Brazilian Soc. Animal Physiology, Am. Assn. Advance Sci., Internat. Soc. Neuroscience, Soc. Neuroscience. Office: Duke University Medical Center Dept Neurobiology 327 E Bryan Research Bldg Box 3209 Durham NC 27708 Office Phone: 919-684-4580. Office Fax: 919-668-2248. E-mail: nicoleli@neuro.duke.edu.

NICOLINI, PHILIPPE HUGUES, vascular surgeon, consultant; b. Metz, France (incl. Monaco), Mar. 14, 1959; s. Antoine and Georgette Nicolini; m. Pascale Monique Tabaka; children: Edouard Alexis, Charles Arthur, Berenice Hortense. B, Jean XXIII Coll., 1978. Diplomate U. of Medicine, Strasbourg, France, 1992, in Vascular Surgery U. of Medicine, Strasbourg, France, 1992. Internship Hosp., Strasbourg, France, 1986—, resident, 1992—; vascular surgeon Clinique du Grand Large, Decines Charpieu (Lyon), France, 1996. Rschr. INSERM, Strasbourg, France (incl. Monaco), 1988—90; chief dept., vascular suergery unit Clinique Mutualiste, Lyon, 2004—; directorship European Group of Rsch., Strasbourg, 1994—; adminstr. French Soc. of Vascular Surgery, Lyon, France (incl. Monaco), 2003—; directorship French Coll. of Vascular Surgery, Paris, 2000—04. Contbr. scientific papers. Gen. sec. French Soc. of Vascular Surgeon, Lyon, 2003. Officer Med., 1988—89, German. Mem.: French Coll. of Vascular Surgery, French Soc. of Phlebology, European Venous Forum, Internat. Soc. for Endovascular Surgery, European Soc. of vascular surgery, French Soc. Vascular Surgery (assoc.). Liberal. Catholic. Avocation: squash. Home: 25 rue Franklin Roosevelt Ecully 69130 France Office: Clinique du Grand Large 2 avenue Léon Blum Decines Charpieu 69150 France Personal E-mail: phnicolini@wanadoo.fr.

NICOLLS, MARK ROBERT, pulmonologist, educator; b. Los Gatos, Calif., Sept. 5, 1964; BS, U. Portland, 1987; MD, Stanford U., 1993. Assoc. prof. medicine Stanford U. Med. Ctr., 2007—, chief, divsn. pulmonary and critical care medicine, 2010—. Rsch. grant, NIH. Mem.: Am. Assn. Immunology, Am. Soc. Transplantation, Internat. Soc. Heart and Lung Transplantation, Am. Thoracic Soc. Avocation: running, music. Office: Stanford University Med Ctr 300 Pasteur Dr Stanford CA 94305 Business E-Mail: mnicolls@stanford.edu.

NICOLODI, MARIA, neuropharmacologist, medical researcher; b. Florence, Italy, June 2, 1955; d. Beniamino and Giovanna (Zicari) N. B in Medicine, U. Florence, 1984, PhD, 1992; specialist in neurology, U. Pavia, Italy, 1994. Asst. prof. U. Catania, Italy, 1997-99; fellow U. Florence, 1990-93. Internat. cons. Med. Inst. Treatment of Pain, Santiago, Chile, 1997—; gen. sec. Interuniv. Ctr. Neurochemistry and Clin. Pharmacology of Primary Headaches, Italy; asst. rschr. U. Florence, 1999—; asst. prof. U. Siena, Italy, 2000—; pres. Found. Prevention Primary Pain, 2003—; head physician Ctr. Headache and Pain Medicine Villanova Hosp., Oncologic Ctr., Florence, 2008. Contbr. over 295 articles to profl. jours.; editor 2 Congress Procs. books; inventor in fields of therapy for chronic headache, primary fibromyalgia and prevention of primary pain in children; patentee in field; referee Jour. Internat. Headache Soc., 1993—, Jour. Am. Assn. Headache, Sci. Cooperator Italian Soc. Study of Headache. Rsch. grantee Glaxo Solvay-Pharma and Florence U., 1994, Nat. Coun. Rsch., Rome, 1995 recipient Internat. Greppi Jr. prize, 1990, Sr. prize, 1995, Migraine Trust prize, 2006. Mem. Internat. Headache Soc., Internat. Club Functional Organic and Non-Organic Nociceptive Diseases (founder, mem. scientific bd. 1991), Found. Prevention and Therapy of Primary Pain and Headache (pres.), World Neurol. Fedn. Avocations: gardening, painting. Office: Via Costa de' Magnoli 28 I-50125 Florence Italy Office Phone: 390552466010, 390552480716. Business E-Mail: info@fondazionesicuterinicolodi.it.

NICOUCAR, KEYVAN GÉRARD, otolaryngologist, educator; b. Geneva, Jan. 14, 1973; s. Gholam-Reza and Kochnoud Nicoucar; m. Elvira Ivanova, June 4, 2005. MD, U. Geneva, 1999. Diplomate Bd. Otolaryngology Swiss Soc. Otolaryngology- Head and Neck Surgery. Rsch. fellow in otolaryngology Univ. Hosp. Geneva, 1998—99, intern in neurosurgery, 2000—01, resident in otolaryngology-head and neck surgery, 2002—05, chief resident in otolaryngology-head and neck surgery, instr. otolaryngology-head and neck surgery, 2005—; intern in gen. surgery Riviera Hosp., Montreux, Switzerland, 1999—2000. Mem.: Swiss Med. Assn., Assn. Residents and Chief Residents in Tng. (treas. 2004—). Achievements include research in Neuropeptide Y. Avocations: skiing, swimming, travel.

NIDECKER, ANDREAS CORNELIS, radiologist, educator; b. Tiel, The Netherlands, Oct. 1, 1947; s. Hans Jakob and Rosemarie (Huggenberg) Nidecker; children from previous marriage: Florian, Maja, Eva. MD, Med. Sch. U. Basel, Switzerland, 1973. Diplomate Am. Bd. Radiology. Internship Lawrence Gen. Hosp., Toronto, Canada, 1973—74, 1976—79; asst. prof. radiology U. Basel, 1985-99, prof., 1999—; pvt. practice Basel, 1982—. Mem. Arbeitsgruppe Knochentumoren, Deutsches Krebforschungsfentrur; co-owner IMAMED Radiologie Nordwest, Basel. Mem. exec. com., past pres. Internat. Physicians Prevention Nuc. War, 1982—; mem. constl. coun. Basel Canton. Mem.: Swiss Soc. Radiology, Radiol. Soc. N.Am., Internat. Soc. Skeletal Radiology. Avocations: hiking, skiing, travel, music. Office: IMAMED Radiologie Nordwest Untere Rebgasse 18 4058 Basel Switzerland E-mail: anidecker@bluewin.ch, andreas.nidecker@imamed.ch.

NIEBYL, JENNIFER ROBINSON, obstetrician, gynecologist, educator; BSc, McGill U., Mont., 1963; MD, Yale U., 1967. Diplomate Am. Bd. Ob-Gyn., Am. Bd. Maternal and Fetal Medicine. Intern in Internal Medicine N.Y. Hosp.-Cornell Med. Ctr., 1967-68, resident in ob-gyn., 1968-70, Johns Hopkins Hosp., Balt., 1970-73, fellow in maternal and fetal medicine, 1976-78, mem. staff, 1973—88, U. Iowa Hosps. and Clinics, Iowa City, 1988—; prof., head ob-gyn. dept. U. Iowa Sch. Medicine, Iowa City, 1988—2009, prof. ob-gyn. dept., 2009—. Mem. ACOG, Am. Gynecol. and Obstetrical Soc., Soc. Gynecol. Investigation, Soc. Maternal Fetal Medicine, Inst. Medicine of NAS. Office: U Iowa Hosps & Clinics 200 Hawkins Dr Iowa City IA 52242 Office Phone: 319-356-1976, 319-384-9247.

NIEDERHUBER, JOHN EDWARD, medical researcher, surgeon, former federal agency administrator; b. Steubenville, Ohio, June 21, 1938; s. William Henry and Helen (Smittle) Niederhuber; m. Tracey J. Williamson (dec. Dec. 2001); children: Elizabeth Ann, Matthew John. BS, Bethany Coll., W.Va., 1960; MD, Ohio State U. Coll. Medicine, 1964. Diplomate Am. Bd. Surgery. Intern surgery Ohio State U. Hosp., Columbus, 1964-65; vis. fellow divsn. immunology Karolinska Inst., Stockholm, 1970—71; resident surgery U. Mich. Med. Ctr., Ann Arbor, 1971—73, faculty, 1973—87, prof. surgery, prof. microbiolog/immunology, 1980-87, assoc. dean rsch., 1982—85, sr. assoc. dean med. sch., 1983—85, chief divsn. surg. oncology, 1983—86; vis. prof. molecular biology & genetics Johns Hopkins U. Sch. Med., Balt., 1986—87, prof. surgery, oncology, molecular biology & genetics, 1987-91; chief surgery Stanford U. Hosp., Calif., 1991-95; Emile Holman prof. surgery, chair dept. surgery, head sect. surg. scis. Stanford U. Sch. Medicine., 1991-95, prof. microbiology/immunology, 1991-97; asst. dean oncology, dir. Comprehensive Cancer Ctr. U. Wis. Sch. Medicine, Madison, 1997—2002, prof. surgery/oncology, 1997—2005; dep. dir. translational & clin. scis., COO Nat. Cancer. Inst. (NCI), NIH, Bethesda, Md., 2005—06; acting dir. Nat. Cancer Inst., NIH, 2006, dir., 2006—10; exec. v.p., CEO Inova Inst. Translational Rsch. and Personalized Medicine Inova Health Sys., Falls Church, Va., 2010—. Cons. Wayne County Gen. Hosp., Mich., 1973—84, Ann Arbor VA Hosp., 1973—87; vis. prof. Howard Hughes Med. Inst., Chevy Chase, Md.; bd. dirs. Emergent BioSolutions Inc., 2010—. Mem. editl. bd. Jour. Immunology, 1981—85, Current Opinion in Oncology, 1989—95, Annals of Surgery, 1991—97, Surg. Oncology, 1991—, Jour. Clin. Oncology, 1993—95, Annals of Surg. Oncology, 1993—, The Oncologist, 1995—, Surgery, 1999—2004; contbr. articles to profl. jours., chapters to books. Mem. awards assembly GM Cancer Rsch. Found., 1988—92, 1998—2003; mem. rsch. adv. com. Burroughs-Wellcome Found., 1999—2006. Capt. US Army, 1965—67. Recipient Disting. Faculty Svc. award, U. Mich., 1978, Alumni Achievement award, Ohio State U. Coll. Medicine, 1989, Disting. Alumni award in medicine, Bethany Coll., 1989, Career Devel. award, USPHS. Fellow: ACS; mem.: Soc. Clin. Surgery, Am. Soc. Clin. Oncology, Am. Assn. Cancer Rsch., Soc. Surg. Oncology (v.p. 1999—2001, pres. 2001—02, 2001—03), Assn. Acad. Surgeons, Soc. Univ. Surgeons, Coller Surg. Soc., Am. Assn. Cancer Insts. (v.p. 1999—2001), Am. Soc. Transplant Surgeons, Am. Assn. Immunologists, Am. Surg. Assn., Transplantation Soc., Inst. Medicine. Avocations: golf, gardening. Office: Inova Health System 8110 Gatehouse Rd Falls Church VA 22042 *

NIEDERLAND, TAMAS, pediatrician; b. Gyor, Gyor-Sopron-Moson, Hungary, July 13, 1955; s. Vilmos and Vilmosne Niederland; m. Eva Firczi, Sept. 19, 1987; children: Zsofia, Akos. Degree, Semmelweis Med. U., Budapest, 1981. Cert. pediatrician Semmelweis U. Budapest, 1985, diabetologist Hungarian Diabetes Assn., 1996. Leading cons. Petz Aladar County Tchg. Hosp., Gyor, Gyor-Sopron-Moson, Hungary, 1997—, head outpatient clinic of pediatric diabetology and pediatric endocrinology, 1997—, head dept. pediat., 1998—, head West Hungarian Pediat. Insulin Pump Ctr., 2004—. Leadership mem. Hungarian Pediat. Diabetes Assn. Hungarian Diabetes Assn., Budapest, Pest, 1996—; mem. diabetes group Hungarian Pediat. Bd., 2005—. Contbr. articles to profl. jours. Leadership mem. Help the Diabetic Children, Gyor, 1985—2006. Recipient Best Poster prize, Internat. Symposium GH and Growth Factors, 2006, 2007. Mem.: Mid. European Pediatric Endocrine Assn. (assoc.), European Assn. Study for Diabetes (assoc.), Endocrine Soc. (assoc.). Avocations: travel, diving, skiing. Office: Petz Aladar County Tchg Hosp Vasvari Pal u 2 Gyor-Sopron-Moson Gyor 9024 Hungary Personal E-mail: tnieder@axelero.hu. Business E-Mail: niederlandt@petz.gyor.hu.

NIEDERLE, PETR MILOSLAV, retired cardiologist; b. Hradec Kralove, Bohemia, Czech Republic, May 9, 1944; s. Miloslav and Anna (Hanusova) N.; m. Milena Kozelska, Sept. 27, 1968; children: Cenkerova Katerina, Niederlova Klara. MD, Charles U., 1968; PhD I, Inst. Clin. and Exptl., Medicine, Prague, 1977; PhD II, Czech Acad. Scis., 1992. Bd. cert. in internal medicine and cardiology. Physician County Hosp., Havlickuv Brod, Czech Republic, 1968-72; jr. rschr. Inst. Clin. Exptl. Medicine, Prague, 1972-82, sr. rschr., 1982-85, Inst. Physiol. Regul. CSAV, Prague, 1985-92; head cardiology dept. Hosp. Na Homolce, Prague, 1992—; prof. medicine Charles U., 2004—. Mem. nucleus of the working group on echocardiography European Soc. Cardiology, 1987-90; bd. dirs. Czech Soc. Cardiology. Author: Doppler Echocardiography, 1996, Transesophageal Echocardiography, 2000, Echocardiography, 2002, Echocardiography, 2d edit, 2005; co-author: Echocardiography, 1984, 2nd edit., 1991, Hypertension, 1987, Chronic Ischemic Heart Disease, 1991, Trends in Cardiology Today, 1999 Mem.: Czech Soc. Cardiology (bd. dirs. 1995—99), European Soc. Cardiology. Avocations: music, fishing, literature. Home: Terronska 12 160 00 Prague Czech Republic Office: Hosp Na Homolce Roentgenova 2 150 00 Prague Czech Republic E-mail: petr.niederle@homolka.cz.

NIEDERMAN, JAMES CORSON, retired internist, educator; b. Hamilton, Ohio, Nov. 27, 1924; s. Clifford Frederick and Henrietta (Corson) N.; m. Miriam Camp, Dec. 12, 1951; children— Timothy Porter, Derrick Corson, Eliza Orton, Caroline Noble. Student, Kenyon Coll., 1942—45, DSc (hon.), 1981; MD, Johns Hopkins U., 1949. Intern Osler Svc. Johns Hopkins Hosp., Balt., 1949-50; asst. resident in medicine Yale-New Haven Med. Center, 1950-51, assoc. resident, 1953-55; med. ctr. practice specializing in internal medicine, infectious disease and clin. epidemiology New Haven, 1955-97; instr. Yale U., 1955-58, asst. prof., 1958-66, assoc. prof., 1966-76, clin. prof. medicine and epidemiology, 1976-97, emeritus clin. prof. medicine and epidemiology, 1997—, clin. prof. emeritus epidemiology and pub. health, 1998; mem. Nat. Coun. for Johns Hopkins Medicine. Trustee Kenyon Coll., 1974-97, trustee emeritus, 1997—; bd. counselors Smith Coll., 1970-77. Served to 1st lt. M.C. U.S. Army, 1951-53. Fellow Silliman Coll., Yale U. Fellow Am. Coll. Epidemiology; mem. Infectious Diseases Soc. Am., Am. Epidemiol. Soc., Johns Hopkins Med. and Surg. Assn.; mem. The Kenyon Rev. Bd. Trustees, Conn. Soc. Arts and Scis. Clubs: Yale (N.Y.C.); New Haven Lawn. Democrat. Episcopalian. Achievements include research in clin. epidemiology of Epstein Barr virus infections and demonstration of its causal relationship of infectious mononucleosis. Home: 429 Sperry Rd Bethany CT 06524-3544 Home Fax: 203-393-1902. E-mail: jcniederman@sbcglobal.net.

NIEDERMAN, MICHAEL STEVEN, physician, educator; b. NYC, Mar. 30, 1953; s. L. Louis and Betty Doris N.; m. Ronna Diane Kay, Aug. 15, 1976; children: Alex, Eric. AB, Boston U., 1974, MD, 1977. Intern Northwestern U. Med. Sch., Chgo., 1977-78, resident, 1978—80; pulmonary medicine fellow Yale U. Sch. Med., New Haven, 1980—83; dir. Med. ICU Winthrop U. Hosp., Mineola, NY, 1983—97, chief pulmonary and critical care medicine, 1997—99, chmn. dept. medicine, 1999—; assoc. prof., then prof. medicine SUNY, Stony Brook, 1990—. Dir. Microbiology Assembly, Am. Thoracic Soc., NYC, 1990—91. Editor: Respiratory Infections (textbook), 1994; editor-in-chief Clin. Pulmonary Medicine, 1994—; mem. editl. bd. Am. Jour. Respiratory and Cridical Care Medicine, 1994—2002, Chest, 1994—, Critical Care Medicine; contbr. numerous articles to profl. jours. Fellow ACP, Am. Coll. Chest Physicians (credentials com. 1991—), Coll. Critical Care Medicine; mem. Phi Beta Kappa, Alpha Omega Alpha. Avocations: skiing, tennis, golf, jazz music. Office: Winthrop Univ Hosp 222 Station Plz N Ste 509 Mineola NY 11501-3893 Office Phone: 516-663-2381. Business E-Mail: mniederman@winthrop.org. *

NIEDERMEIER, MARY B., retired nutritionist; b. Webster Groves, Mo., Oct. 20, 1914; d. Albertus and Daisey May (Christman) Wickersham; m. Walter H. Niedermeier, Sept. 9, 1939; children: Gail Santarelli, Bart. BS, Mich. State U., 1937; MA, Columbia U., 1958, diploma, 1959. Cert. in dietetic internship Miami Valley Hosp., Dayton, Ohio, 1938. Dist. nutritionist N.J. State Dept. of Health, Newark; instr. nutrition edn. Sch. of Dentistry Fairleigh Dickinson U., Teaneck, NJ, instr. nutrition edn. Sch. of Nursing St. Louis U. Pres. Oradell (N.J.) Pub. Sch. PTA, 1954—57; bd. dirs. Rancho Bernardo (Calif.) Oaks N. Cmty. Ctr., 1974—76; treas. PEO-TV chpt., Rancho Bernardo, 1990; bd. deacons Rancho Bernardo Presbyn. Ch., 1975—76. Mem.: AAUP, AAUW, N.J. Dietetic Assn., Calif. Dietetic Assn., Am. Dietetic Assn., Alpha Omicron Pi. Republican. Avocations: electronic organ music, painting, golf, lawn and indoor bowling. Home: 16925 Hierba Dr # 430 San Diego CA 92128-2223 Home Phone: 858-487-6481.

NIEHM, BERNARD FRANK, retired health facility administrator; b. Sandusky, Ohio, Feb. 7, 1923; s. Bernard Frank and Hedwick (Panzer) N.; m. Eunice M. Patterson, Oct. 4, 1924; children: Julie, Patti, Bernie. BA, Ohio State U., 1951, MA, 1955, PhD in Ednl. Exceptional Children, Guidance and Couseling, Psychology, 1968. Tchr. pub. schs., Sandusky, 1951-57; chief ednl., vocat. and occupational therapy svcs. Vineland Tng. Sch., NJ, 1957-61; exec. dir. Franklin County Coun. Retarded Children, Columbus, Ohio, 1962-64; dir. Ohio Sheltered Workshop Planning Project Mental Retardation, 1964-66, coordinator mental retardation planning, 1966-68; project dir. Ohio Gov.'s Citizen Com. on Mental Retardation Planning, 1966-68; adminstr. Franklin County Program for Mentally Retarded, 1968-70; supt. Gallipolis State Inst., Ohio, 1970-76; tchr. spl. edn. Ohio U., Columbus, 1975-77, dir. consultation and edn., 1977-79, dir., 1978-95; exec. dir. Woodland Ctrs. Inc., Gallipolis, 1995; ret. Woodland Farm, Gallipolis, 1995. Pres. Gallco, 1989-90. Contbr. articles to profl. jours. Active Foster Grandparents Adv. Coun., Gallia County, 1974-76, Gallipolis State Inst. Parent Vol. Assn., 1970-76, Franklin County Bd. Mental Retardation, 1967-68; chmn. MGM dist. Tri-State Boy Scout Coun.; chmn. Meigs, Gallia, Mason Counties Boy Scout Dist., 1972-94; pres. Gallipolis Girls Athletic Assn. Booster Club, 1976—, Gallia County Arthritis Unit, 1986-96, Galleo Industries Bd. to Serve Handicapped Adults, 1987-94; pres. bd. dirs. Outreach Ctr. Gallia County, 1997-99; mem. Ch. Coun., St. Paul Luth. Ch., 1994-99, pres.; bd. dirs. United Cerebral Palsy, Columbus, 1968-70, Gallco Sheltered Workshop for Mentally Handicapped, Outreach Inc., Tri-State coun. Boy Scouts of Am.; mem. gov. bd. Gallia County Coun. on Aging; bd. alcohol, drug addiction and mental health svcs. Gallia-Jackson, Meigs; pres. Gallia County Pub. Employment Retiree Inc.; mem. United Way Gallia County. With U.S. Army, 1943-46. Mem. Am. Assn. Mental Deficiency (past chmn. Ohio chpt., chmn. Great Lakes region), Am. Mental Health Adminstrs. (nat., Ohio chpts.), Nat. Rehab. Assn., Ohio Rehab. Assn., Ohio Assn. Retarded Children (2d v.p. 1974-76, dir.), Vocat. Rehab. Assn., Ohio Coun. Community Mental Health Ctrs., Gallia County Arthritis Assn. (pres. 1991—), Gallipolis Area C. of C., Gallipolis Rotary. Lutheran. Office: Woodland Ctr Inc 3086 State Route 160 Gallipolis OH 45631-8418 Home: 907 Jones St Hollidaysburg PA 16648-2223 Home Phone: 814-695-5648.

NIELSEN, HENRIK, medical educator; b. Nykøbing Falster, Denmark, Aug. 25, 1956; MD, U. Copenhagen, 1983. Prof. Aalborg Hosp., Aarhus U. Hosp., 1996—. Office: Aalborg Hosp Århus University 18 Hobrovej Aalborg North Jutland Region DK9000 Denmark Business E-Mail: henrik.nielsen@rn.dk.

NIELSEN, HILDE GRINDVIK, exercise physiologist, researcher; PhD, Rsch. Coun. Norway, Oslo, 2006. Rschr. Ullevaal U. Hosp., 2000—07. Cons. exercise physiology Norwegian Sport Med. Ctr., Oslo, 1999—2000; advisor Directorate Health and Social Affairs, 2004—06, Rsch. Coun. Norway, 2006—. Mem.: Internat. Soc. Exercise and Immunology. Office: Rsch Coun of Norway Divsn Soc and Health Stensbergg 26 0131 Oslo Norway Home: Rådyrveien 10F 1413 Tårnåsen Oslo Norway Personal E-mail: hdgn@c2i.net.

NIELSEN, NANCY H., medical educator; b. Elkins, W.Va., 1942; m. Don Nielsen; 5 children. BA, W.Va. U., 1964; MS in Microbiology, Cath. U., 1967, PhD in Microbiology, 1969; MD, SUNY Medicine and Biomedical Scis., Buffalo, 1976. Past chief med. officer NY State Dept. Health Western Region; former pres. med. staff Buffalo Gen. Hosp.; asst. dean med. edn., clin. prof. medicine U. Buffalo Sch. Medicine and Biomed. Sci., Buffalo; apptd. to serve US Dept. Health and Human Svcs. Adv. Com. on Regulatory Reform, 2002; assoc. med. dir. for quality, interim chief med. officer Independent Health Assn., NY, chief med. officer NY; clin. prof. medicine, sr. assoc. dean med. edn. Sch. Medicine and Biomedical Scis., U. Buffalo. Bd. dir. Med. Liability Mut. Ins. Co., Kaleida Health, Nat. Patient Safety Found.; former trustee SUNY; former mem. Commn. for the Prevention of Youth Violence, Task Force on Quality and Patient Safety. Bd. dirs. Nat. Patient Safety Found. Recipient Samuel P. Capen award, U. Buffalo Alumni Assn., 1996. Fellow: ACP; mem.: AMA (vice spkr. Ho. of Dels. 2000—03, spkr. Ho. of Dels. 2003—07, pres.-elect 2007—08, pres. 2008—09, immediate past chair 2009—10, former mem. bd. trustees, former mem. Coun. on Sci. Affairs, del. med. sch. sect., liaison to the Coun. on Med. Edn.), Inst. Medicine (Consumer Empowerment Com. of America's Health Information Cmty., Roundtable on Evidence Based Medicine), NY State Soc. Internal Medicine (bd. dir.), Med. Soc. State of NY (spkr. ho. dels. 1995—2000), Erie County Med. Soc. (former pres.). Office: University Buffalo Sch Medicine And Biomedical Scis 40 Biomedical Education Bldg Buffalo NY 14214 Business E-Mail: nielse@buffalo.edu. *

NIELSEN, PETER FAST, cardiologist, educator; b. Ikast-Brande, Denmark, Oct. 27, 1959; ECCP, Scandinavian Sch. Cardiovasc. Tech., 1999, M in Cardiovasc. Tech., 2008. Perfusionist, sr. lectr. Aarhus U. Hosp., 1997—. Ednl. bd. Scandinavian Sch. Cardiovasc. Tech., 2005; sci. com. Scansect, 2009. Mem.: Scansect. Avocation: kayaking. Office: Brendstrupsgaardsvej 1 Aarhus 8200 Denmark Business E-Mail: peterfast@city.dk.

NIELSEN, SOREN U., research scientist; b. Grindsted, Denmark, Oct. 3, 1961; s. Erik and Gerda M. Nielsen; m. Julie Greensill, Sept. 23, 2000; 1 child, Daniel J. PhD, U. Muenster, Germany, 1993. Postdoctoral asst. U. Minn., Mpls./St. Paul, 1993—96, Tex. A & M, Coll. Sta., Tex., 1996—97, Univ. Newcastle, Newcastle uponTyne, England, 1998—. Contbr. articles to profl. jours. Fellow, Danish Med. Rsch. Coun., 1988-1993;, Wellcome Trust rsch. fellow, 2000—08. Fellow: Brit. Assn. for the Study of the Liver; mem.: AAAS, EASL, AASLD, Soc. Gen. Microbiology. Achievements include research in Hepatitis C virus association with very low density lipoprotein, antibody binding to hepatitis C virus circulating in blood. Office: University Newcastle Richardson Rd Newcastle upon Tyne NE2 4AX England Home: 288 Stanton St Newcastle Upon Tyne NE4 1LJ England Office Phone: 0191 208 3226. Office Fax: 0191 208 0723. Personal E-mail: s.u.nielsen@ncl.ac.uk.

NIEMCZYK, MARIUSZ, medical educator; b. Warsaw, Nov. 2, 1974; MD, Med. U. Warsaw, 1999, PhD, 2007. Postgrad. tng. Ctrl. Clin. Hosp., Warsaw, 1999—2001; asst. Jesus Child Clin. Hosp., Warsaw, 2001; lectr. Med. U. Warsaw, 2008. Recipient Sci. award, Rector Med. U. Warsaw. Office: Nowogrodzka 59 Warsaw Mazowieckie 02-006 Poland

NIEMINEN-VON WENDT, TAINA SOLVEIG, pediatrician, neurologist, researcher; b. Lappajärvi, Finland, Nov. 21, 1960; d. Pertti and Anne-Cathrine Nieminen; life ptnr. Lennart Olof Willehad von Wendt, Aug. 3, 2001 (dec.); 1 child, Alexandra Cicilia Cathrine von Wendt. MD with honors, U. Oulu, Finland, 1994; PhD (hon.), U. Ctrl. Hosp. Helsinki, Finland, 2005. Locum physician Ctrl. Hosp Vaasa, Finland, 1900—90, asst. physician Oulu U. Ctrl. Hosp., 1991—94, physician child neurology U. Ctrl. Hosp. Helsinki, 1994—2005, postgrad. rschr., 2005; leading physician NeuroMental, Neuropsychiatric Clinic, Helsinki, 1999—; Locum adolescent psychiatry Hosp. Jorvi, Espoo, Finland, 2005—07. Contbr. articles to med. jours. Bd. mem. Finnish Autism and Asperger Soc., Helsinki, 2000—04; chmn. Finnish ADHD-Ctr., Helsinki, 2004—08. Achievements include research in neuropsychiatric disorders especially in Asperger syndrome. Home: Rakuunanpiha 14 b Espoo 02620 Finland Office: NeuroMental Kaupintie 11 a Helsinki 00440 Finland Office Phone: 358 400 750 810. Personal E-mail: taina.nieminen@kolumbus.fi.

NIESEL, ACHIM, gynecologist, obstetrician; b. Wiefelstede, Germany, Mar. 7, 1954; s. Oskar and Ursel Niesel; m. Elisabeth Jander; children: Stefan, Miriam, Jonathan, Sarah. MD, U. Luebeck, 1979. Cert. floor surgery specialist. House officer Hosp. of Luth. Ch., Rotenburg /Wuemme, Germany, 1979—83; sr. cons. Hosp. Peine, Germany, 1983—; head dept. ob-gyn. Preetz Specialist Pelvic Surgery, 2004—. Registrar U. Goettingen, Germany, 1989; missionary doctor Luth. Ch. Germany, Ramotswa, Botswana, 1989—91; cons. U. Alexandroupolis, Greece, 1995; lectr. in field. Contbr. articles to profl. jours. Bd. dirs. Hospice Assn., Peine, 1996—. Mem.: Assn. Drs. Pro Life, North German Assn. Obstetricians and Gynecologists. Lutheran. Office: Klinik Preetz Am Krankenhaus 5 24211 Preetz Germany Business E-Mail: info@klinik-preetz.de. E-mail: a.niesel@klinik-preetz.de.

NIETO, JUAN MANUEL, emergency medicine physician; b. Alpine, Tex., Sept. 24, 1949; s. Edmundo Miguel and Socorro; children: Ana Raquel, Cristina Marie. BS, U. Notre Dame, 1970; MD, U. Colo., 1974. Intern LA County, U. So. Calif. Med. Ctr., 1974-75; physician Cmty. Health Found., LA, 1975-77; physician emergency dept. Physicians Med. Group, Marina Del Ray, Calif., 1977-78; resident in emergency medicine Denver Gen.-St. Anthony Hosp. Sys., 1978-80; mem. staff North Colo. Med. Ctr., Greeley, 1980-83; emergency physician, med. dir. emergency dept. Brackenridge Hosp., Austin, Tex., 1984-85; practice medicine Austin, 1983—. Emergency physician Emergency Physicians Affiliates, 1986-89; assoc. prof. U. Tex. Health Sci. Ctr., San Antonio, 1994—; mem. planning com. Starflight Helicopter Air Transport, 1985; instr. advanced cardiac life support, 1977; bd. dirs. Nat. Chicano Health Orgn., 1971-74; advisor East Los Angeles Hypertension Screening Program, 1978; med. advisor Weld County Ambulance Service, 1980-83; med. dir. Air Life, 1980-83; med. dir. Alamo Heights Emergency Med. Svc., 1988-90, med. dir. AMR Ambulance, 1991-98; amb. Nat. Health Svc. Corps, 2003—. Del. Colo. Med. Soc., 1983. Fellow: Nat. Hispanic Med. Assn., Am. Acad. Emergency Medicine, Am. Coll. Emergency Physicians, NYU Wagner Sch. (leadership fellow 2001); mem.: APHA, Nat. Hispanic Medicine Assn., Soc. Academic Emergency Medicine, Physicians for a Nat. Healthcare Program, Nat. Hispanic Med. Assn., Travis County Med. Soc., Tex. Med. Assn., Nat. Hispanic Med. Assn. (leadership fellow, advisor, board mem. 2001—, mem. adv. bd. 2003—, Leadership award 2006), Amnesty Internat. Personal E-mail: jnietomd@sbcglobal.net, juan-nieto@msn.com.

NIETO ENRIQUEZ, JOSE, plastic surgeon; b. Barcelona, Mar. 5, 1979; MD, U. De Barcelona, 2003; degree in Ophthalmology, U. Autonoma De Barcelona, 2008. Dir. Consultores En Cirugia Oculoplastica, 2009—. Cons. oculoplastic surgeon Hosp. Moisses Broggi, 2009—. Fellow: Am. Soc. Ophthalmic Plastic & Reconstructive

Surgery; mem.: Inst. Barraquer, European Soc. Ophthalmic Plastic & Reconstructive Surgery. Office: Clinica Corachan Plz Manuel Corachan Barcelona 08021 Spain Business E-Mail: pepenieto@telefonica.net.

NIETO-ZERMEÑO, JAIME, pediatric surgeon; m. Virginia Eguiarte, June 12, 1971 (div. June 5, 2000); children: Monica Nieto Eguiarte, Jaime Gabriel Nieto Eguiarte, Pablo Nieto Eguiarte. MD, Nat. U. of Mex., 1967—72, Pediatrician, 1974—76, Pediatric Surgery, 1977—79. Lic. surgeon Mexican Bd. of Pediat.; Mexican Bd. of Pediatric Surgery, 1979. Asst. prof. histology Nat. U. Mex., 1968—71, asst. prof. anatomy, 1971—72; assoc. prof. pediatric surgery postdoctoral Children's Hosp. Mex., Nat. U. of Mex., 1979—2003, prof. pediatric surgery postdoctoral, 1993—2003, attending pediatric surgery, 1979—89, dept. chmn., pediatric surgery, 1989—92; head divsn. surgery Children's Hosp. Mex., Nat. U. Mex., 1993—2003, asst. prof. pediatrics, 1979—2003. Head Bd. Dirs., Pediatric Surgery Nat. U. Mex., 2003—; pres. Med. Soc. Children's Hosp. Mex., 1995—97. Author: (book) Pediatric Surgery for the Pediatrician, 2001; contbr. chapters to books, articles to profl. jours. Chmn. comition academy Nat. U. of Mex., 2003—. Recipient Soc. Venezuela of Pediatric Surgery, 2001. Mem.: Mexican Soc. Pediatric Surgery (pres. 1989—91). Home: Dr Marquez numero162 Colonia Doctores Distrito Federal 06720 Mexico Office: Mexican National Hospital Institute Dr Marquez número 162 Colonia Doctores Distrito Federal 06720 Mexico Office Fax: (52) 5555781701.

NIEWIADOMSKI, WIKTOR JERZY, medical researcher; b. Lódz, Mar. 19, 1954; MSc, Warsaw Tech. U., 1978. Rsch. scientist Mossakowski Med. Rsch. Ctr. Polish Acad. Scis., 1979—. Achievements include research in noninvasive methods of circulatory and autonomic nervous system examination, circulatory and autonomic nervous system response to exercise, combating interaction between respiratory and cardiovascular systems. Office: Pawinski Warsaw Mazovia 02-106 Poland Business E-Mail: wiktorn@cmdik.pan.pl.

NIGAM, PRANESH, medical educator; b. Banda, India, June 18, 1943; s. Sri Chhail Behari and Guru Kishori Nigam; m. Laxmi K. Nigam, May 31, 1969; children: Pratima, Anupama, Aparna. BSc, Lko Christian Coll., Lucknow, India, 1959; MB BS, K.G. Med. Coll., Lucknow, India, 1965, MD in Medicine, 1969. Physician Dist. Hosp., 1970—72; lectr. in medicine MLB Med. Coll., Jhansi, 1973—81; assoc. prof. medicine BRD Med. Coll., 1986—96, prof. medicine Gorakhpur, 1996—2003; prof. medicine, dept. head UFHT Med. Coll., Haldwani, 2003—08; Hony vis. cons. physician Shivanand Charitable Hosp., Rishikesh, India; prof. medicine SRMS Inst. Med. Scis., Bareilly, UP, India, 2011—. Cons. physician MLB Med. Coll., 1970—81, BRD Med. Coll., 1981—2003, UFHT Med. Coll., 2003—08. Contbr. articles to profl. jours. Fellow: Am. Coll. Angiology, Am. Coll. Chest Physicians, Indian Acad. Clin. Medicine, Indian Coll. Physicians; mem.: Nat. Acad. Med. Sci. Home: C-14 Rapti Nagar Phase II Chargawan Gorakhpur Uttar Pradesh 273009 India Office: SRMS Inst Med Scis Bareilly Uttar Pradesh 243202 India Home Phone: 05512506124; Office Phone: 05512500180.

NIGG, JOEL THOMAS, psychologist, educator; b. Dubuque, Iowa, Oct. 17, 1957; AB, Harvard Coll., 1980; PhD, U. Calif., Berkeley, 1996. Asst. to prof. Mich. State U., 1996—2008; prof. Oreg. Health & Sci. U., 2008—. Office: Oregon Health & Sci University 3181 SW Sam Jackson Park Rd Portland OR 97239 Business E-Mail: niggj@ohsu.edu.

NIGHTINGALE, EDMUND JOSEPH, clinical psychologist, educator, consultant; b. St. Paul, Jan. 10, 1941; s. Edmund Anthony and Lauretta Alexandria (Horejs) N.; m. Marie Arcara, Apr. 9, 1978 (dec. April 1992); 1 child, Edmund Bernard. Student, Nazarath Hall Prep. Sem., 1959—61; AB, St. Paul Sem., 1963; AB magna cum laude, Cath. U. Louvain, Belgium, 1965, MA, 1967, STB cum laude, 1967; postgrad., U. Minn., 1971; MA, Loyola U., Chgo., 1973, PhD of Clin. Psychology, 1975. Lic. clin. psychologist, Minn., cert. Nat. Registry Health Svc. Providers in Psychology; diplomate clin. psychology Am. Bd. Profl. Psychology. With Cath. Archdiocese St. Paul and Mpls., 1967—73; intern clin. psychology Michael Reese Hosp. and Med. Ctr., Chgo., 1973—74; with West Side VA Hosp., Chgo., 1974—75; staff psychologist Student Counseling Ctr., Loyola U., Chgo., 1975; staff psychologist, clin. coord. inpatient unit Drug Dependency Treatment Ctr., 1975—80; chief psychology VA Med. Ctr., Danville, Ill., 1980—86, VA Med. Ctr. Mpls., 1986—2006; ret., 2006; cons., 2006—. Mem. pers. bd. Archdiocese St. Paul and Mpls., 1968-70; lectr. psychology, Loyola U., Chgo., 1975; asst. professorial lectr. psychology, St. Paul Xavier Coll., Chgo., 1975-78; adj. asst. prof. psychology in psychology, Abraham Lincoln Sch. Medicine, Med. Ctr. U. Ill., Chgo., 1977-82; adj. prof. psychology Purdue U., 1981-87; asst. prof. psychology Med. Sch., U. Minn., 1987—, clin. assoc. prof. psychology Coll. Liberal Arts, 1986-90; adj. asst. prof., 1990—; clin. asst. prof. U. Ill. Sch. Medicine, Urbana/Champaign, 1982-87; mem. grad. faculty counseling psychology Ind. State U., Terre Haute, 1983-86 Founding editor: Louvain Studies, 1966; editor: VA Dir. Psychology Staffing and Svcs., 1982, 83, 84, 85, 87; ad hoc reviewer, editl. bd. 2008-, Psychol. Svcs., 2006-. Bd. dirs. Inst. Postgrad. Studies, Ill. Psychol. Assn Recipient Exemplary Career award, US Dept. VA, 2006. Fellow APA (clin. psychology, psychotherapy, pub. svc., psychol. hypnosis, fellow Trauma Psychology, sec. treas. pub. svc. 1990-91, coun. reps. 1999-2004, pres. elect pub. svc. 2006, pres. pub. svc. 2007-08, past pres., 2008-09, mem. com. on accreditation, 2006-07, fellowship com. 2008-09, Karl F. Heiser Presdl. award for Adv. 2002, divsn. Psychologists Pub. Svc. Disting. Contbns. award 2002); mem. AAAS, Am. Psychol. Sci., Assn. Advancement Psychology, Ill. Psychol. Assn. (clin. psychology and acad. sects., sec. 1982-83, pres.-elect 1983-84, pres. 1984-85), Am. Group Psychotherapy Assn., Am. Soc. Clin. Hypnosis, Minn. Psychol. Assn. (pub. svc.- pres. 1997-99), Eagle Scout, Assn. VA Chief Psychologists (sec., treas. 1987-90, pres.-elect 1990-91, pres. 1991-92, past pres. 1992-93, Outstanding Leadership award 1992), Minn. Soc. Clin. Hypnosis (bd. dirs. 1999-2001), ULLR Found. (bd. dirs. 2004-11, pres. 2006-08), Nat. MS Soc. (bd. trustees, Minn. chpt., 2005-). Home: 28 W Marie Ave West Saint Paul MN 55118 Business E-Mail: night002@umn.edu.

NIGHTINGALE, ELENA OTTOLENGHI, pediatric geneticist, academic administrator, educator; b. Livorno, Italy, Nov. 1, 1932; arrived in U.S., 1939, naturalized; d. Mario Lazzaro and Elisa Vittoria (Levi) Ottolenghi; m. Suart L. Nightingale, July 1, 1965; children: Elizabeth, Marisa. AB summa cum laude, Barnard Coll., 1954; PhD, Rockefeller U., 1961; MD, NYU, 1964. Asst. prof. Cornell U. Med. Coll., NYC, 1965—70, Johns Hopkins U., Balt., 1970—73; fellow in clin. genetics and pediat. Georgetown U. Hosp., Washington, 1973—74; sr. staff officer NAS, Washington, 1975—77, sr. program officer Inst. Medicine, 1977—82, sr. scholar-in-residence, 1982—83; spl. advisor to pres. Carnegie Corp. N.Y., NYC, 1983—94, sr. program officer, 1989—94; scholar-in-residence Inst. of Medicine, NAS, Washington, 1995—. Vis. assoc. prof. Harvard Med. Sch., Boston, 1980—84, vis. lectr., 1984—95; adj. prof. pediat. Georgetown U. Med. Ctr., 1984—, George Washington U. Med. Ctr., 1994—; mem. recombinant DNA adv. com. NIH, Bethesda, Md., 1979—83. Editor: The Breaking of Bodies and Minds: Torture, Psychiatric Abuses and the Health Professions, 1985, Prenatal Screening, Policies and Values: The Example of Neural Tube Defects, 1987, Promoting the Health of Adolescents: New Directions for the 21st Century, 1993, Adolescent Risk and Vulnerability: Concepts and Measurement, 2001; co-author: Before Birth: Prenatal Screening for Genetic Disease, 1990; contbr. numerous sci. articles to profl. publs. Bd. dirs. Amnesty Internat., U.S.A., Washington, 1989—91, Ctr. for Youth Svcs., Washington, 1980—84, Sci. Svc., Inc., Washington, 1985—96. Recipient Walsh McDermott medal, Inst. Medicine, 2006. Fellow: AAAS (chmn. com. on sci. freedom and responsibility 1985—88), N.Y. Acad. Scis.; mem.: Inst. Medicine of NAS (chmn. com. on health and human rights 1987—90), Genetics Soc. Am., Am. Soc. Human Genetics (social issues com. 1982—85), Am. Soc. Microbiology, Sigma Xi, Phi Beta Kappa. Office: NAS 500 5th St NW Washington DC 20001 Business E-Mail: enightin@nas.edu.

NIGHTINGALE, STUART LESTER, public health consultant; b. NYC, Jan. 26, 1938; s. Lester M. Nightingale and Beatrice L. N. Helpern; m. Elena Ottolenghi, July 1, 1965; children: Elizabeth S., Marisa O. BA, Yale U., 1959; MD, NYU, 1964. Diplomate Am. Bd. Internal Medicine. Intern in medicine and surgery Montefiore Hosp. and Med. Ctr., Bronx, 1964—65, resident in internal medicine, fellow in adolescent medicine, 1965—66, 1967—69, asst. attending physician, 1969—70; resident in anatomical pathology NYU Sch. Medicine, 1966—67; med. dir. drug abuse adminstrn. Dept. Health and Mental Hygiene State of Md., Balt., 1971—72; chief treatment and rehab., office of programs, spl. action office for drug abuse prevention Exec. Office of Pres., Washington, 1972—74, chief office treatment and rehab., spl. action office for drug abuse prevention, 1974—75; dir. divsn. resource devel. Nat. Inst. on Drug Abuse, Rockville, Md., 1974—76; asst. to dir. Bur. Drugs, FDA, Rockville, 1976—79; dep. assoc. commr. for health affairs FDA, Rockville, 1979—82, acting assoc. commr. for health affairs, 1979—82, assoc. commr. for health affairs, 1982—2000; sr. med. adv. to dir. global health affairs Dept. HHS, Washington, 2000—07, chief med. officer Office of the Asst. Sec. for Planning and Evaluation, 2000—03, chief med. officer Office Pub. Health Emergency Preparedness, 2004—07, dep. asst. sec. Office Pub. Health Emergency Preparedness, 2005—07; cons. NIH, Office of Sci. Policy, Office of Dirs., HHS, 2007—. Vis. physician Balt. City Hosps., 1970-72; clin. instr. dept. medicine Coll. Medicine SUNY, Bklyn., 1970; asst. physician out-patient dept., instr. dept. medicine Johns Hopkins U. Sch. Medicine, Balt., 1970-72, med. dir. drug abuse ctr., 1970-71, instr. dept. med. care and hosps. Sch. Hygiene and Pub. Health, 1971-74, rsch. program mgr. health svcs. rsch. and devel. ctr., 1970-71; chmn. rsch. involving human subjects com. FDA, 1979-84; liaison mem. Commn. on Fed. Drug Approval Process, U.S. Congress, 1980-81; mem.-at-large U.S. Pharmacopeial Conv., Inc., 1985-95; bd. trustees The Milton Helpern Libr. of Legal Medicine, N.Y.C., 1982-2005; bd. dirs. Nat. Coun. on Patient Info. and Edn., Washington, 1982-2000; mem. forum on drug devel. and regulation Inst. Medicine, NAS, Washington, 1986-2000. Contbg. author Jour. AMA, 1985-99, Am. Family Physician, 1986-99. Capt. M.C., USAR, 1966-72; with USPHS. Recipient Disting. Svc. Spl. Action Office for Drug Abuse Prevention award Exec. Office of Pres., 1975, Pub. Health Superior Svc. award, 1983, Disting. Contbn. award Nat. Coun. Patient Info. and Edn., 1987, Achievement award Am. Assn. Physicians for Human Rights, 1990, Presdl. Meritorious Exec. Rank award, 1990, 2005, Pub. Health Svc. Spl. Recognition award, 1993, Sec.'s Recognition award Dept. HHS, 1999, Surgeon Gen. Exemplary award, 2007. Fellow ACP; mem. AMA, Sr. Execs. Assn., Cosmos Club., Acad. Medicine Wash., FDA Alumni Assn., Med. Adminstrs. Conf. Office: OBA NIH 6705 Rockledge Dr Bethesda MD 20892 Office Phone: 301-496-9838. Business E-Mail: nightins@od.nih.gov.

NIGRIN, DANIEL J., hospital administrator, endocrinologist, medical educator; BA in Biophysics, Johns Hopkins U., 1987, MD, 1991; MS in Med. Informatics, Mass. Inst. Tech., 1999. Asst. prof. pediatrics Harvard Medical School; pediatric internship Johns Hopkins University, 1992—94, pediatric residency, 1994—96; asst. in endocrinology Children's Hospital Boston, fellowships in pediatric endocrinology and informatics, 1996—98, chief info. officer, sr. v.p., info. svcs., 2001—. Named one of Premier 100 IT Leaders, Computerworld, 2005. Office: Children's Hospital Boston Wolbach Bldg Rm 115 300 Longwood Ave Boston MA 02115 Office Phone: 617-355-5067. Office Fax: 617-730-0019. E-mail: daniel.nigrin@childrens.harvard.edu.

NIHOUL-FEKETE, CLAIRE, pediatrician, educator; arrived in France, 1949; d. Rene Nihoul and Ellen Fox; m. François Fékété, Apr. 16, 1963 (div. July 2005); children: Thomas, Rémy. Baccalauréat, Lycée Jean De La Fontaine, Paris, 1956; MD, Paris U., 1966. Cons. pediatric surgery Necker Hosp., Paris, 1990, chief dept., 2007; full prof. U. Paris Descartes, 1983. Gen. sec. French Soc. Pediatric Surgery, 1975—83; mem. Nat. Coun. French U., 1991—98. Mem. Nat. Bd. Dr., Paris, 1976—2008, Nat. Ethical Com. Med. Scis., Paris, 1994—99, Coun. INSERM, Paris, 2003—04. Decorated Chevalier Ordre Nat. du Mérite République Française, Officer Ordre Nat. de la Legion d' Honneur. Mem.: ACS (hon. mem. 2006), Brit. Assn. Pediatric Surgery (oversea's mem. 1980), Am. Acad. Pediat. (hon. mem. 1989). Achievements include humanitary surgery in west Africa 1988-2005; surgery congenital malformations chain of hope. Avocations: music, sailing. Office: Hosp Necker 149 Rue de Sèvres Paris 75015 France Home Phone: 33 142248041; Office Phone: 33 144494152. Office Fax: 33 144494160. Personal E-mail: fekete.claire@wanadoo.fr. Business E-Mail: claire.fekete@nck.aphp.fr.

NII, SHIRO, director, virologist, educator; b. Naruto, Tokushima, Japan, Jan. 12, 1932; parents Atsushi and Toyoo (Toyota) N.; m. Etsuko Tada, Mar. 29, 1960; children: Satoshi, Keiko Maeda, Yoshiko Fujita. MD, Osaka U., 1956, PhD, 1961. Lic. physician. Rsch. assoc. Rsch. Inst. for Microbial Diseases Osaka U., Japan, 1961—66, assoc. prof. Rsch. Inst. for Microbial Diseases, 1966—78; prof. Okayama U. Med. Sch., Japan, 1978—97, dean, 1993—95; prof. emeritus Okayama U., 1997—; prof. Kawasaki Coll. Allied Health Professions, Kurashiki, Japan, 1997—98; pres. Niimi Coll., Japan, 1998—2002; academic adminstr. CAC Rehab. Coll., Hiroshima, 2002—03, dir., 2003—06, dir. emeritus, 2006—. Councilor Okayama U., 1990-92; hon. prof. Jiangxi Med. Coll., China, 1993; guest prof. Dalian Med. Coll., China, 1994; expert adviser Sci. and Tech. Com., 1994; pres. Univ. and Coll. Assn. Okayama Prefecture, 1995, 43d Ann. Meeting of Japanese Virologists, 1995. Co-author: (book) Virology, 1997; editor, co-author: (book) Essentials of Microbiology, 1983, 98; contbr. articles to sci. jours. Mem.: Japanese Assn. Infectious Diseases (auditor 1995—98), Japanese Soc. Virology (hon.). Avocations: reading, baseball, walking. Home: 372-1-206 Hama Okayama 703-8256 Japan E-mail: snii@po12.oninet.ne.jp.

NIIT, TOOMAS, psychologist, educator; b. Tartu, Estonia, June 7, 1953; s. Heldur and Ellen (Hiob) N.; m. Helle Kalliver, Dec. 15, 1973 (div. 1991); children: Kaisa-Kitri, Eeva-Liisa, Madli-Maria, Hanna-Maarja; m. Kadi Liik, Aug. 1, 1991; 1 child, Öösike. Diploma in psychology, Tartu U., Estonia, 1976; MSc in Psychology, Tallinn U., Estonia, 1993. Rsch. psychologist Inst. History Estonian Acad. Scis., Tallinn, 1976-88, rsch. psychologist Inst. Philosophy Sociology and Law, 1989-93; assoc. to prof. dept. psychology Tallinn U. Ednl. Scis., 1993—2001, assoc. dean, fac. of social scis., 1993—99, chmn. dept. psychology, 1994—99, rsch. psychologist and head of psychology BSc and MSc curriculum, 2001—; assoc. prof. U. Tartu, 1994-98. Project coord. European Commn. PHARE (Tempus), 1999-2001; exchange prof. social psychology dept., U. Helsinki, 2003-07. Author: (edn.handbook) Handbook of Enviromental Psychology, 1987, (encyclopedia) Encyclopedia of Psychology, 2000; author: (editor) (book) Environmental Conditions for Community Development, 1989; editor: (sci. conf. proceedings) Identity, Freedom, Values and Memory: Proceedings of the 2d Internat. Baltic Psychology Conf., 1996; editor: (author) (Edn.book) Quality Assurance in Higher Education, 2001; editor: (book) Environment and Social Development, 1991; mem.editl. bd.: jour. Jour. Environ. Psychology, 1981—, mem. editorial bd.: jour. European Psychologist, 1996—2004. Named Nordic Coun. of Ministers scholar, Danish Bldg. Rsch. Inst., 1991—92, U. Oslo, 1993, U. Tampere, Finland, 1993, U. Iceland, Reykjavik, 1995, European Coun. scholar, U. Kent, Canterbury, Eng., 1994, Galician Govt. (Spain) scholar, U. Coruna, 2000. Mem. APA (affiliate), Union Estonian Psychologists (v.p. 1990-94, 97—; pres. 1995-97), Internat. Assn. Applied Psychology, Internat. Assoc. for People - Environment Studies (bd. mem. 1994-96), Internat. Assn. for Cross-Cultural Psychology, Soc. for Personality and Social Psychology, European Network for Housing Rsch. Avocation: collecting beer cans and labels. Office: Univ Tallinn Narva Mnt 25 10120 Tallinn Estonia Home Phone: 372 6623 274; Office Phone: 372 6409 476. Business E-Mail: tniit@tlu.ee.

NIJEVITCH, ALEXANDER ALBERTOVICH, pediatrician, researcher; b. Ufa, Bashkortostan, USSR, Sept. 15, 1962; s. Albert Vasiljevich and Zakhida Mullajarovna (Sufijarova) N.; m. Valentina Vladimirovna Loguinovskaja; 1 child, Natalia. Student, Bashkir State Med. Inst., Ufa, 1986, MD, 1996, PhD in Medicine, 1996. Physician Children's Rep. Hosp., Ufa, 1987. Cons. Ufa Emergency Hosp., 1994—98; chief of outpatient dept. Children's Rep. Hosp., 2001; asst. prof. Bashkir State Med. U., 2004; reviewer in fields. Co-author (with A. Khavkin, S. Belmer, P. Scherbakov): (textbook) Pediatric Gastroenterology, 2010; contbr. scientific papers. Mem. Russian Helicobacter Pylori Study Group. Achievements include patents in field. Avocation: classical and jazz music. Home: A/Ya 4894 450057 Ufa Bashkortostan Ryesp. Russia

NIKAIDO, HIROSHI, microbiologist; b. Tokyo, Mar. 26, 1932; arrived in U.S., 1962; s. Tatsuya and Ryo Nikaido; m. Kishiko Jokura, Mar. 11, 1963; children: Michio, George. MD, Keio U., Tokyo, 1955, D in Med. Sci., 1961. Assoc. bacteriology Harvard Med. Sch., Boston, 1963-64, asst. prof., 1965-69; assoc. prof. U. Calif., Berkeley, 1969-71, prof., 1971—. Sci. adv. Essential Therapeutics, Mountain View, Calif., 1992—2002. Co-author: Microbial Biotechnology, 1995, 2nd edit., 2007; contbr. articles to profl. jours. Recipient Paul Ehrlich award, Paul Ehrlich Found., 1969, Freedom to Discover Achievement award, Bristol-Myers Squibb, 2004. Fellow: Am. Acad. Microbiology; mem.: Natl. Acad. Sci., Am. Acad. Arts and Scis., Am. Soc. Biochemistry and Molecular Biology, Am. Soc. Microbiology (editor Jour. Bacteriology 1998—2002, Hoechst-Roussel award 1984).

NIKAM, SHIVPRASAD, vascular and endovascular surgeon; b. India; MBBS, B.J. Med. Coll., Pune, India, 1993, MS, 1998; MD, Ednl. Commn. Fgn. Med. Grads., 1999. Diplomate Nat. Bd. Med. Exams. New Delhi, 1998, cert. in gen. surgery Am. Bd. Surgery, 2006, in vascular surgery Am. Bd. Surgery, 2008. Intern Sassoon Gen. Hosps., Pune, Maharashtra, 1993—94, resident surgery, 1995—98, lectr. surgery, 1998—99; clin. observer Meml. Sloan Kettering Cancer Ctr., NYC, 1999; registrar surgery Royal Albert Edward Infirmary, Wigan, England, 2000; resident, surgery Bronx Lebanon Hosp. Ctr., NY, 2001—05, chief resident, 2004—05; fellow, vascular and endovascular surgery Geisinger Med. Ctr., Danville, Pa., 2005—07; vascular and endovascular surgeon Geisinger Wyo. Valley Med. Ctr., Wilkes Barre, Pa., 2007—. Contbr. articles to profl. jours. Recipient Late Minu Mehta Meml. award, 1998, Late Dr. Balawant Narayan Ranade Meml. award, 1998, All India Maratha Samaaj award, 2000. Fellow: ACS, Royal Coll. Surgeons; mem.: Soc. Vascular Surgery. Office: Geisinger Wyoming Valley Medical Ctr 1000 E Mountain Blvd Wilkes Barre PA 18711

NIKAS, SPYROS P., biology professor; b. Souli, Korinth, Greece, Apr. 10, 1966; PhD, Aristotle U., 1996. Rsch. assoc. prof. Northeastern University, 2010—. Mem.: Am. Assn. U. Profs. Home: 272 LaGrange St Newton MA 02467 Business E-Mail: s.nikas@neu.edu.

NIKBERG, ILLYA ISAY, preventive medicine physician, medical columnist, educator; b. Kiev, Ukraine, Nov. 19, 1929; arrived in Australia, 2000; s. Isay Moisey Nikberg and Berta Aron Harshan; m. Svitlana David Tsodikova, June 6, 1969; children: Elvira, Vadim. Diploma, Kiev Med. Inst., 1952. Doctoral specialist San.-Epidemiol. Sta., Makeevka, Ukraine, 1952—56; sci. staff, head dept. hygiene Inst. Epidemiology, Microbiology and Hygiene, Kishinev, Moldova, 1956—64; lectr. Nat. Med. U., Kiev, 1964—96; prof., head dept. preventive medicine Kiev Med. Inst., 1996—2000. Leader group Inst. Project Hosp., Kiev, 1965—69; leader dept., cons. Inst. Endocrinology, Kiev, 1995—99; chief specialist Ctr. Med. Edn., Kiev, 1996—99;

med. columnist mass media, 2000—. Author: Helio - Meteorol. Reactions of Human Being, 1986, Atomic Radiation and Health, 1989, Hygiene of Hospitals, 1993, Hygiene Gen., 1995 (Winner of Ukrainian State prize, 1997), Diabetes-Adv. Diseases, 1996, Hygiene Radiation, 1999, Hygiene Gen. and Human Ecology, 2001, Conversations About Health and Healthy Lifestyle, 2009, Hygiene & Health, 2009, Environmental Factors and Diabetes, 2011. Mem.: Internat. Fedn. Journalists, Ukrainian Diabetic Fedn. (v.p. 1996—2000), Ukrainian Diabetes Assn. (organizer and head 1988—92), N.Y. Acad. Sci., Russian Acad. Natural Scis. (corr.), Diabetes Australia Assn. (hon.). Avocations: photography, ballet, crossword puzzles, literature. Home: 2/2 a Edmund Str Waverley 2024 Sydney PO NSW Australia Personal E-mail: inikberg@hotmail.com.

NIKICA, DRUZIJANIC, surgeon, educator; b. Ploce, Jan. 23, 1950; Prof. Med. Sch. U. Split, 2005—. Cons. Clin. Hosp. Split, 2002. Avocations: sports, hunting, swimming. Home: AB imica 5 Split Dalmacija 21000 Croatia Home Fax: 38521 556 691. Business E-Mail: ndruzija@kbsplit.hr.

NIKISCH, GEORG PETER, psychiatrist, psychologist; b. Oppeln, Poland, Apr. 8, 1959; s. Ewald and Apolonia Nikisch; m. Anette Gutberlet, May 30, 1998; children: Niklas, Sophia. MD, Johann-Wolfgang-Goethe U., 1997, diploma in Psychology, 1988. Asst. med. dir. Klinikum Fulda, Fulda, Germany, 1997. Contbr. articles to profl. jours. Grant, Bayer Pharmaceutical, Germany, 1997—2004, Astra-Zeneca, Germany, 2005. Office: Klinikum Fulda Pacelliallee 4 Fulda 36043 Germany Office Fax: +49 661 84 5722. Personal E-mail: dr.georg.nikisch@web.de. E-mail: georg.nikisch@klinikum-fulda.de.

NIKITENKO, LEONID L., endocrinologist, researcher; b. Irkutsk, Russia, Apr. 19, 1972; s. Leonid A and Lidia I Nikitenko. BSc (hon.), U. Irkutsk, Russia, 1993; MSc in Physiology, U. Irkutsk, 1994; PhD in Embryology & Cell Biology, Russian Acad. Med. Scis., 1997; MA, Linacre Coll., Oxford, Eng., 2002; DSc in Pathology & Physiology, Russian Acad. Med. Sci., 2007. Rsch. asst. The Babraham Inst., Cambridge, England, 1996—97; postdoctoral sr. rsch. asst U. Liverpool, England, 1997—98; postdoctoral rsch. fellow U. Oxford, England, 1999—2002, postdoctoral rsch. fellow of the Welcome Trust, 2002—06; sr. rsch. fellow Wolfson Inst. Biomed. Rsch. U. Coll. London, 2006—07, UCL Cancer Inst., 2007—. Tutorship U. Oxford, Keble Coll., 2003—. Contbr. articles to profl. jours., chapters to books; author: Adrenomedullin and It's Role in Endothelial Cell Biology. Lt. Russian Mil. Recipient E.P.A. Cephalosporin Rsch. fellow, Linacre Coll., Oxford, 2002—04, Merit award, U. Oxford, 2003. Mem.: Mansfield Rd. Football Club (mgr. 2002—03). Orthodox. Achievements include invention of isolation and culture of primary human microvascular endothelial cells from uterus; discovery of peptide Adrenomedullin is angiogenic for human endothelial cells; promoter of a CALCRL (adrenomedullin and CGRP receptor) gene; variants of CALCRL (adrenomedullin and CGRP receptor) gene; the mechanism underlying desensitization of the endogenous CL receptor in human endothelial cells; patents for transcriptional regulation of a CRLR gene and CALCRL gene structure and DNA conformation and fingerprinting. Avocations: building, soccer, swimming, reading, languages. Office: Univ Coll London Cancer Inst 72 Paul O'Garman Bldg 46 Huntley Street WC1E 6DD London England Business E-Mail: l.nikitenko@ucl.ac.uk.

NIKITIN, ALEXANDER YU., pathologist; b. St. Petersburg, Russia, Sept. 28, 1960; s. Yurii V. Nikitin and Valentina D. Nikitina; m. Andrea Flesken-Nikitin, Feb. 24, 1995; children: Dmitrii Yu., Maria Yu. Nikitina. MD (hon.), Acad. Pavlov First Med. Inst., St. Petersburg, Russia, 1983; PhD, Prof. Petrov Rsch. Inst. Oncology, St. Petersburg, Russia, 1988. Asst. prof. rsch. dept. molecular medicine Univ. Tex. Health Sci. Ctr., San Antonio, 1999—2000; asst. prof. pathology Cornell U., Ithaca, NY, 2000—06, assoc. prof. pathology, 2007—. Contbr. articles to profl. jours. Vice chair pathology and lab. medicine standing com. Mouse Models of Human Cancers Consortium, Bethesda, Md., 1999—2004; organizer Ann. Practical Workshop on Pathology of Mouse Models for Human Disease, Bar Harbor, Maine, 2002—. Recipient Midcareer award in Mouse Pathobiology, NIH, 2002—06; grantee, 2002—, Dept. of Def., 2001—04, 2000—03. Mem.: AAAS, Soc. Toxicologic Pathology, Am. Assn. Cancer Rsch. Achievements include first to develop a novel genetic model of human ovarian cancer; development of new classification of mouse proliferative pulmonary lesions; discovery of syndrome of multiple endocrine neoplasia in Rb +/- mice. p53 dependent micro RNAs. Office: Cornell Univ T2014AVRT Ithaca NY 14850

NIKOLAEV, ANDREY VLADIMIR, research scientist; b. Kiev, Ukraine, Aug. 16, 1973; MS, MIPT, 1997; PhD, 2010. Rsch. scientist N.N. Semenov Inst. Chem. Physics Russian Acad. Scis., 2005—. Lab. chief, tchg. asst. chair informatics MIPT, 2001—. Avocations: tai chi, reading. Office: Inst Chemical Kosygina St 4 Moscow 119991 Russia E-mail: gentoorion@gmail.com.

NIKOLAUS, SUSANNE, psychologist, researcher; b. Hinsbeck, Germany, Apr. 30, 1965; d. Ferdinand and Mathilde Nikolaus. BS, Heinrich-Heine U., Düsseldorf, Germany, 1993, PhD, 1997. Rsch. assoc. Inst. Physiol. Psychology, Düsseldorf, 1993—98, Clinic Nuc. Medicine, Düsseldorf, 1998—, postdoc. lectr., 2007; 0. Contbr. articles to profl. jours. Roman Catholic. Achievements include research in tachykinin NK-1 receptor mediation of reinforcement and anxiety; assessment of dopamine transporter and receptor binding with small animal tomography; neurotransmitter regulation in movement, mental and affective disorders. Avocations: classical music, literature, soccer. Office: Clinic Nuc Medicine Moorenstr 5 40225 Düsseldorf Germany Office Phone: (0211) 8117048. Office Fax: (0211) 8117041. Business E-Mail: susanne.nikolaus@uni-duesseldorf.de.

NIKOLOPOULOS, DIMITRIOS D., orthopedist; b. Athens, Dec. 5, 1976; MD, U. Athens Med. Sch., 2002. Orthopedist Asklepeion Voulas Gen. Hosp., 2007—. Mem.: Hellenic Soc. Orthopaedic Surgery and Traumatology. Avocations: poetry, politics. Home: Latheas 81 St Axarnai Attiki 13674 Greece Personal E-mail: drdnikol@hotmail.com.

NIKU, SOHEIL DANIEL, urologist; b. Tehran, Iran, Nov. 20, 1963; s. Saleh and Sara Niku; m. Doris Aghaei Niku. BS, UCLA, 1985, MD, 1989. Diplomate Am. Bd. Urology, 1997. Urologist resident U. Calif., San Diego, 1989—95. Mem.: Am. Coll. Surgeons, Am. Urol. Assn. Office: 14901 Rinaldi St #205 Mission Hills CA 91345 Office Phone: 818-365-0259.

NIKUS, KJELL CHRISTER, cardiologist; b. Vörå, Finland, July 24, 1954; s. Gunnar Ingemar and Elin Gunhild Nikus; life ptnr. Maarit Hannele Jääskeläinen, Sept. 5, 1998; children: Tomas Kristian, Anna Maria. MD, Oulu U., Finland, 1978. Lic. in medicine Oulu U., 1978, cert. physician Helsinki Nat. Bd. Health, 1978, specialist in internal medicine Tampere U., 1989, specialist in cardiology Tampere U., 1998. Gen. practitioner Nykarleby, 1978—82, Korsholm, 1983—86; resident in internal medicine Vasa Ctrl. Hosp., 1987—88, chief physician in clin. physiology, 1989; assoc. chief physician Jakobstad Hosp., 1990—96; internship in cardiology Vasa Ctrl. Hosp., 1997, Tampere U. Hosp., 1998, cardiologist. Grantee, Finnish Culture Found., 2005. Home: Sorkkalantie 220 Pirkkala 33980 Finland Office: Heart Center Pirkanmaa Hosp Dist Biokatu 6 Tampere 33520 Finland Office Fax: 358 3 3116 4157. Business E-Mail: kjell.nikus@pshp.fi.

NILES, BARBARA ELLIOTT, psychoanalyst; b. Boston, Jan. 31, 1939; d. Byron Kauffman and Helen Alice (Heissler) Elliott; m. John Denison, June 25, 1960 (div. 1981); children: Catherine Elliott, Andrew Elliott. AA, Briarcliff Coll., 1958; BA, SUNY, 1984; MSW, Hunter Coll. Sch. Social Work, 1986. Cert. psychotherapy and psychoanalysis Inst. Contemporary Psychotherapy, 1990. Exec. com. Legal Aid Soc. Women's Aux., NYC, 1965-67; sec. Scientists' Com. for Pub. Info. Water Quality Task Force, NYC, 1973-74; founding dir., sec. Consumer Action Now Inc., NYC, 1970-77; dir. devel. Consumer Action Now's Council Environ., NYC, 1976-77; dir. 170 Tenants Corp., NYC, 1979-81; mem. pub. interest com. Cosmopolitan Club, NYC, 1979-82; dir. INFORM Inc., NYC, 1978-84; pvt. practice psychotherapy and psychoanalysis NYC, 1986—2005. Mem. adj. faculty metro ctr. Empire State Coll., NYC, 1987—96. Editor: (biography) Off the Beaten Track, 1984. Bd. trustees Salisbury Assn., 2001—11; active Land Trust Bd., 2001—09; bd. dirs. Salisbury Vis. Nurse Assn., 2000—06, Salisbury Housing Trust, 2001—07. Mem.: NASW, St Botolph Club (Boston), Vincent Club (Boston), Cosmopolitan Club (NYC). Avocations: travel, literature, camping.

NILES, DANA E., medical researcher; b. Orange, NJ, Jan. 1, 1964; MS, Northeastern U., 1990. Clin. rsch. program mgr. Children's Hosp. Phila., 2006—. Mem.: Am. Heart Assn. Office: 8NW100 3400 Civic Ctr Blvd Philadelphia PA 19104 Business E-Mail: niles@email.chop.edu.

NILLIUS, PETER, research scientist; b. Sweden, Dec. 25, 1969; MSc, Linkoping U., Case Western Res. U., 1995; PhD, Royal Inst. Tech., 2004. Software developer Sectra Imtech., 1994—96, 2004, rsch. engr., 2005; rschr. Found. Rsch. & Tech., 2005—06; rsch. scientist Royal Inst. Tech., 2006—. Office: Albanova University Ctr Stockholm SE 10691 Sweden Office Fax: nillius@mi.physics.kth.se.

NILOFF, PAUL HYMAN, surgeon, educator; b. Sherbrooke, Quebec, Can., July 1, 1921; arrived in US, 1978; s. Solomon and Mindel Niloff; m. Madelaine Harriet Fromson, Nov. 12, 1952; children: Jonathan, Donna Hirschfeld, Susan Weisz. BA in Biology & Chemistry with honors, Bishop's U., Lennoxville, Quebec, 1940; MD, MCGill U., Montreal, Quebec, CM, 1943, MSc in Exptl. Surgery, 1950, Diploma in Surgery, 1951. Diplomate ACS, 1952, cert. surg. specialist Royal Coll. Surgeons, Can., 1952, Coll. Physicians & Surgeons, Quebec, 1952, diplomate Am. Bd. Surgery, 1952, Am. Bd. Quality Assurance & Utilization Review Physicians, Inc., 1995. Sr. surgeon pvt. practice Sir Mortimer Davis Jewish Gen. Hosp., Montreal, 1951—78; surgeon-in-chief Reddy Meml. Hosp., Montreal, 1971—76; assoc. prof. surgery MCGill U., 1971—78; pvt. practice Palm Beach Regional, JFK Hosp., Lake Worth, Fla., 1978—2002; physician advisor, surg. svcs. JFK Hosp., Atlantis, 2002—06; assoc. dir. postgrad. surg. edn. Palms West Hosp., Wellington, 2006—08; clin. assoc. prof. NOVA Southeastern U., 2006—08. Pres. Montreal Clin. Soc., 1962. Contbr. articles to profl. jours. Chmn. med. div. Combined Jewish Appeal, Montreal, 1961, Red Feather Campaign, 1962. Capt. Royal Canadian Army Med. Corp., 1942—46, Can. Fellow: ACS, Royal Coll. Surgeons (Can.); mem.: Montreal Clin. Soc. (past pres.), Palm Beach County Med. Soc., Fla. Med. Assn., Am. Hernia Soc. (charter), Canadian Med. Assn., Am. Bd. Surgery. Personal E-mail: niloffpaul@gmail.com.

NILSEN, DENNIS WINSTON T., physician, cardiologist, educator; b. Florø, Norway, Sept. 1, 1950; s. Trygve Karl Nilsen and Grace Olive Vaughan; m. Klazien Annie Dekker, Apr. 16, 1981; children: Gøran Jan, Bengt Ove, Derek Hein. MD (hon.), U. Bergen, 1976; PhD in Medicine, U. Oslo, Norway, 1986, prof., 2000, U. Bergen, 2000; DHC (hon.), Cath. U. Salta, Argentina, 2005. Lic. physician. Intern Lillehammer Hosp., Norway, 1976—77; intern gen. practice Stryn, Norway, 1977—78; jr. doctor Ullevål U. Hosp., Oslo, 1978—82, u. lectr., 1982—85; sr. doctor cons. Aker U. Hosp., Oslo, 1985—87; sr. resident U. Hosp. Tromsø, Tromsø, Norway, 1987—89; chief physician Ctrl. Hosp. in Rogaland, Stavanger, Rogaland, Norway, 1989—95, chief physician, dir. invasive cardiology unit, 1997—; chief physician Haukeland U. Hosp., Bergen, Hordaland, Norway, 1995—97; dir. invasive cardiology Ctrl. Hosp. Rogaland (now Stavanger U. Hosp.), Stavanger, Norway, 1997—. Adv. cons. Pharmaceutics (A/S Farmasøytisk Industri), Oslo, 1982—86. Contbr. more than 80 articles in internat. med. jours. Fellow: Am. Coll. Cardiology, Coun. Arteriosclerosis Thrombosis and Vascular Biology, Am. Heart Assn., European Soc. Cardiology, Coun. Epidemiology and Prevention; mem.: Norwegian Soc. Health Administrn., Norwegian Med. Assn., Norwegian Soc. Cardiology (co-editor), Internat. Soc. Thrombosis and Haemostasis. Avocations: mountain climbing, swimming, gardening. Office Phone: (47)51519455. Personal E-mail: dnilsen@getmai.no.

NILSON, PATRICIA, clinical psychologist; b. Boulder, Colo., Oct. 22, 1929; d. James William and Vera Maude (Peacock) Broxon; m. Eric Walter Nilson, Dec. 23, 1950; children: Stephen Daniel, Eric Jon, Christopher Lawrence. Registered Phys. Therapist, Med. Coll. Va., 1951; MA in Clin. Psychology, L.I. U., 1972, PhD, 1973. Cert. psychologist N.Y. Clin. psychologist Court Cons. Unit, Hauppauge, NY, 1972-92, Three Village Counseling Svc., Setauket, NY, 1974-75, Farmingville (N.Y.) Mental Health Ctr., NY, 1992-95; pvt. practice Commack, NY, 1975—. Adj. asst. prof. C.W. Post Coll., Brookdale, 1974-80; cons., supr. psychologist Wayside Sch. for Girls, Valley Stream, 1975-85; cons. L.I. Lighting Co., 1980; lectr. in field. Author children's therapeutic stories; author therapeutic games: The Road to Problem Mastery; contbr. articles to profl. jours. Mem.: APA (life), Soc. for Clin. and Exptl. Hypnosis (life). Office: 11 Montrose Dr Commack NY 11725-1312 Home Phone: 631-670-7199. Personal E-mail: drpat11@optonline.net.

NILSSON, BERNT OVE, human anatomy educator; b. Falun, Sweden, Jan. 8, 1929; s. Johan Bernhard and Gurli Elisabet (Hogman) N.; m. Irene Brann, Dec. 16, 1956; children: Sven Ludvig, Karin Elisabet, Ebba Agneta. MB, Karolinska Inst., Stockholm, 1953, DMS, 1959, MD, 1960. Instr. Karolinska Inst., 1951-60, lectr., 1961-62; assoc. prof. Uppsala (Sweden) U., 1963-68, prof. anatomy, 1969-93, chmn., 1969-93, vice dean med. faculty, 1975-77. Active Swedish Med. Rsch. Coun. Stockholm, 1973-79. Author: Ljusmikroskopisk teknik, 1968, Elektronmikroskopisk teknik, 1972, Immunocontraception, 1995, Prostasomes, 2002; mem. editl. bd. several jours.; contbr. articles to profl. jours. Decorated knight Royal Order Pole Star (Sweden). Fellow Royal Soc. Scis., Swedish Soc. Medicine; mem. Soc. for Study Reprodn., Am. Soc. for Reproductive Immunology, Internat. Com. on Morphological Scis., Scandinavian Soc. for Electron Microscopy. Home: Götgatan 12A S-753 15 Uppsala Sweden Office: U Uppsala Dept Anatomy Box 571 Biomedical Ctr S-751 23 Uppsala Sweden

NILSSON, GUNNAR HENRIK, physician, educator; b. Stockholm, Jan. 28, 1955; MD, Karolinska Inst., 1980, PhD, 2002. Dean med. edn. Karolinska Inst., 2008, prof., 2009—. Avocations: ping pong/table tennis, badminton, squash, tennis. Office: Alfred Nobels allé 12 Huddinge 13334 Sweden Business E-Mail: gunnar.nilsson@sll.se.

NILSSON, STEFAN, nurse; b. Värnamo, Nov. 22, 1972; PhD, Sch. Health Scis., 2010. Pain mgmt. nurse Queen Silvia Children's Hosp., 2005. Office: Queen Silvia Childrens Hosp Gothenburg 43833 Sweden Business E-Mail: stefan.r.nilsson@vgregion.se.

NIMER, STEPHEN DAVID, physician, leukemia researcher; b. Chgo., May 20, 1954; m. Georgia Takigawa, Oct. 18, 1987. BS, MIT, 1975; MD, U. Chgo. Sch. Medicine, 1979. Diplomate Am. Bd. Internal Medicine, Am. Bd. Hematology, Am. Bd. Med. Oncology. Intern, internal medicine UCLA Sch. Medicine, 1979—80, resident, hematologic oncology, 1980—82, fellow, 1983—86, asst. prof. medicine, 1987-92; dir. transplantation biology Jonsson Compr. Cancer Ctr., LA, 1991-92; assoc. mem. Sloan-Kettering Inst., NYC, 1993-99, mem., 1999—; chief hematology svc. Meml. Hosp., NYC, 1993—2010; head, divsn. hematologic oncology Meml. Sloan-Kettering Cancer Ctr., NYC, 1996—2008, vice chair faculty devel., 2008—; prof. medicine Weill Medical Coll., 2000—; chair Alfred P. Sloan, 2008—. Funded investigator NIH, 1990—. Mem. editl. bd.: Blood, 1997—2002; co-editor: Hematologic Complications of Cancer, 1996, contbr. over 200 sci. articles to profl. jours. Chmn. med. adv. bd. Gabrielle's Angel Found. for Cancer Rsch., 1998-; bd. dirs. Bone Marrow Found., Aplastic Anemia, Myelodysplastic Syndrome Internat. Found., Inc.; chmn. Myelodysplastic Syndrome (MDS) Found., 2010-. Recipient Irma T. Hirschl Career Scientist award Cornell U. Med. Sch., 1995. Fellow ACP; mem. Am. Soc. for Clin. Investigation, Am. Soc. for Hematology, Am. Soc. Clin. Oncology, Am. Assn. for Cancer Rsch., Leukemia Soc. Am. (bd. trustees NY chpt. 1998-2004), Alpha Omega Alpha. Office: Meml Sloan Kettering Cancer Ctr Box 575 1275 York Ave New York NY 10065 Office Phone: 646-888-3040. Business E-Mail: nimers@mskcc.org.

NIMKARN, SAROJ, endocrinologist, researcher; MD (hon.), Mahidol U., Bangkok, 1991. Lic. Am. Bd. of Pediats, and Subboard Pediat. Endocrinology. Clin. instr. pediats. dept. pediats. Siriraj Hosp., Mahidol U., Bangkok, 2001—03, asst. prof. pediats. dept. pediats. faculty medicine, 2003—04; asst. prof. pediats. Med. Coll. of Wis., Milw., 2004—05, Mt. Sinai Sch. of Medicine of NYU, NYC, 2005—09, Weill Cornell Med. Coll., 2009—. Recipient Recognition Winning Poster award, Nat. Coop. Growth Study, 1999, Fellowship Rsch. Tng. grant, Lilly Rsch. Labs., Divsn. of Eli Lilly & Co., 1999, Endocrine Soc. Endocrinology award, Endocrine Soc. of Thailand, 2003, Investigator award, 11th Asian Congress of Pediat. and 1st Asian Congress of Pediat. Nursing, 2003, Free Paper award, 44th Siriraj Sci. Ann. Meeting, Faculty of Medicine, Siriraj Hosp., 2004, grant for rsch. devel., Faculty of Medicine, Siriraj Hosp., 2001. Mem.: Pediat. Endocrine Soc. of Thailand, Asia Pacific Pediat. Endocrine Soc., Lawson Wilkins Pediat. Endocrine Soc., Med. Coun. of Thailand, The Endocrine Soc. Office: Well Cornell Med Coll Box 103 525 E 68th St New York NY 10065 Office Phone: 212-746-3462. Business E-Mail: san2002@med.cornell.edu. *

NIMMON, CYRIL CARSON, retired medical physicist; b. Belfast, Northern Ireland, Oct. 15, 1940; BSc in Physics, Queens U. Belfast, 1962. Rsch. asst., physics dept. U. Coll. London, 1965—68; physicist Nuc. Medicine Dept., St. Bartholomew's Hosp., London EC1, 1969—95, cons. physicist, 1995—98. Contbr. articles to profl. jours. Recipient Long Svc. award, Royal Hosps. Trust, London, 1994. Mem.: IEEE Engring. in Medicine and Biology Soc., European Assn. Nuc. Medicine. Avocations: classical music, violin. Home: PO Box 12 Bor Sang Sankampaeng Chiang Mai 50131 Thailand Home Fax: 6653386977. Personal E-mail: c.c.nimmon@ieee.org.

NINA, ZHERNAKOVA, medical educator; b. Belgorod, June 23, 1960; Assoc. prof. Belgorod State U., 1990—. Office: Pobedyu Belgorod 308000 Russia Business E-Mail: zhernakova@bsu.edu.ru.

NING, RUIPENG, engineer; b. Heilongjia, China, June 1, 1979; PhD, East China Normal U., 2011. Engr. East China Normal U., 2006—. Office: 3663 N Zhongshan Rd Shanghai 200062 China Business E-Mail: rpning@phy.ecnu.edu.cn.

NING, XUE-HAN (HSUEH-HAN NING), physiologist, researcher; b. Peng-Lai, Shandong, People's Republic of China, Apr. 15, 1936; came to U.S., 1984; s. Yi-Xing and Liu Ning; m. Jian-Xin Fan, May 28, 1967. MD, Shanghai 1st Med. Coll., People's Republic of China, 1960; post grad., Chinese Traditional Medicine Coll. for Advanced Study, 1960—61; postgrad. in Physiology, U. Mich., 1984—87. Rsch. fellow, rsch. assoc., leader cardiovasc. rsch. group Shanghai Inst. Physiology, Acad. Sinica, 1960—87, head, assoc. prof. cardiovasc. rsch. unit, prof., chair hypoxia dept., 1988-90, vice chairperson academic com., 1988-90; NIH internat. rsch. fellow U. Mich., Ann Arbor, 1984-87; prof. and dir. Key Lab of Hypoxia Physiology Academia Sinica, Shanghai, 1989-90. Acting leader, High Altitude Physiology Group, Chinese mountaineering and sci. expdn. team to Mt. Everest, 1975; leader High Altitude Physiology Group, Dept. Metall. Industry of China and Ry. Engring. Corps, 1979; vis. prof. dept. physiology Mich. State U., East Lansing, U. Mich., U. Wash. Med. Sch., 1989-97; affiliate prof., U. Wash., 1997—; rsch. scientist Children's Hosp. and Regional Med. Ctr., Seattle, 1997—. Author: High Altitude Physiology and Medicine, 1981, Reports on Scientific

Expedition to Mt. Qomolungma, High Altitude Physiology, 1980, Environment and Ecology of Qinghai-Xizang (Tibet) Plateau, 1982, Self-Health Care at High Altitude, 2006; mem. editl. bd. Chinese Jour. Applied Physiology, 1984-1992, Acta Physiologica, 1988-90, Chinese Jour. Physiology (Taiwan) 2004-; contbr. articles to profl. jours. Recipient Merit award Shanghai Sci. Congress, 1977, All-China Sci. Congress, Beijing, 1978, Super Class award Academia Sinica, Beijing, 1986, 1st Class award Nat. Natural Scis., Beijing, 1987, 2d Class award Acad. Sinica Sci. and Technol. Achievements, Beijing, 1992, # 1 Best Article award Tzu-Chi Med. Jour., Taiwan, 1995, Shanghai 2006 Excellent Popular Sci. Reading award, 2007. Mem. Am. Physiol. Soc., Am. Heart Assn., Internat. Soc. Heart Rsch., Royal Soc. Medicine, Internat. Soc. for Mountain Medicine. Achievements include first to electrocardiographly record at summit of Mt. Everest; research in predictive evaluation of mountaineering performance; characteristics for high altitude adaptation and acclimatization; effect of medicinal herbs on cardiac performance; cardiovascular adaptation and resistance to hypoxia and ischemia; injury threshold of short-cycle-intermittent hypoxia and gene expression in heat; the critical temperature 30 degrees celsius "temperature protectine threshold" for modulating myocardial energy, metabolic pathways, and gene expression to resist ischemia and hypoxia; the 28 degrees celsius "temperature injury threshold" for cardiac contractility in the beating heart in vivo; hypothermic cross adaptation protects heart from subsequent ischema and hypoxia by preserving signaling for mitochondrial biogenesis, activateing stress pathways and inactivating apoptosis to maintain myocardial stability and improve functional recovery during reperfusion and reoxygenation; the hypothermia protection has also been proved in human by treated with a hypothermia rescue (32 degrees C Central catheter then 33-35 degrees C for 24 hrs) after his own heart stopped more than 6 mins in 2009. Home: 7033 43rd Ave NE Seattle WA 98115-6015 Office: Wash Dept Pediats CHRMC 4800 Sand Point Way NE Box G0035 Seattle WA 98105-0371 Business E-Mail: xh@u.washington.edu.

NINO, GUSTAVO, physician; b. Colombia, Mar. 27, 1977; MD, U. Nat. Colombia Sch. Medicine, 1999; degree in Pediatric Pulmonology, U. Pa. Childrens Hosp. Phila., 2006. Asst. prof. pediatric pulmonary & sleep medicine Pa. State U., 2009—. Rschr. U. Pa. Childrens Hosp. Phila., 2006; pediatric sleep medicine cons. Pa. State Sleep Rsch. & Treatment Ctr., 2010. Recipient Excellence in Rsch., Residency award, Dept. Pediat., Maimonides Infants & Childrens Hosp. Bklyn, NY, 2006, Best Academic Performance, Residency award, 2006, Young Investigator award, Am. Coll. Chest Physicians & CHEST Found., 2008, Ann. Faculty Tchg. award, Dept. Pediat., Pa. State U., 2010; finalist Lung & Childhood Young Investigator award, Internat. Congress Pediatric Pulmonology, 2006—08. Mem.: Am. Acad. Sleep Medicine, Am. Coll. Chest Physicians, Am. Thoracic Soc. Office: 500 University Dr Hershey PA 17033-0850 Business E-Mail: gninobarrera@hmc.psu.edu.

NIR, ELKA, specialty medical device company executive; BS, U. Haifa, Israel; BSc in Computer Sci., Technion-Israel Inst. of Tech., Haifa. With Johnson & Johnson; head life sciences sector Giza Venture Capital; bd. dirs. VisionCare Ophthalmic Technologies Inc., Calif., 2011—. Office: VisionCare Ophthalmic Technologies Incorporated 14395 Saratoga Ave Ste 150 Saratoga CA 95070 Office Phone: 408-872-9393. Office Fax: 408-872-9395.

NIRENBERG, SHEILA, medical educator, researcher; b. NYC, 1961; d. Jesse and Edna Fontek Nirenberg. PhD, Harvard Medical Sch., 1993. Asst. assoc. prof. UCLA, LA, 1997—2005; assoc prof. physiology and biophysics Weill Med. Coll. Cornell U., NYC, 2005—, assoc prof. computational neuroscience in computational biomedicine. Contbr. articles to profl. jours. Recipient Lovenheim Short Story award, SUNY Albany, Coll. Math & Sci. award, Beckman Young Investigator award, Beckman Found., Frontiers Sci. award, UCLA, Stein-Oppenheimer award, NYC Investment Fund Bioaccelerate NYC award, 2011; Fellowship, Klingenstein Fund, Dupont/Harvard. Mem.: Soc. Neurosci. Office: Weill Medical College Cornell University 1300 York Ave New York NY 10065 Office Phone: 212-746-6372. Office Fax: 212-746-8690. Business E-Mail: shn2010@med.cornell.edu. *

NIRSCHL, ROBERT PHILLIP, orthopedic surgeon; b. South Milwaukee, Wis., Aug. 28, 1933; s. Boyd A. and Helen (Wozny) N.; m. Mary Ann Oleniczak, June 21, 1958; children: Suzanne, Robert C., Julie. Student, Coll. Holy Cross, 1951-53, Marquette U., 1953-54; MD, Med. Coll. Wis./Marquette U., 1958; MS, U. Minn., 1965. Diplomate Am. Bd. Orthop. Surgery. Intern St. Mary's Hosp., Duluth, Minn., 1958-59; resident in orthop. Mayo Clinic, Rochester, Minn., 1959-63; lt. comdr. USN, Washington, 1963-65; pvt. practice Arlington, Va., 1965—. Attending orthop. surgeon Va. Hosp. Ctr., Arlington, dir. Hand Surgery Svc., 1975—85, v.p. med. staff, 1980—83, mem. hosp. med. exec. com., 2006—; chief orthop. surgery No. Va. Cmty. Hosp., 1971—82; founding dir. Nirschl Orthop. Ctr. for Sports Medicine and Joint Reconstrn., 1974—, Nirschl Orthop. Sport Med. Ctr. Orthop. Sports Medicine Fellowship Program Va. Hosp. Ctr., Arlington, 1987—; mem. clin. faculty Georgetown U. Med. Ctr., 1965—; orthop. cons. Pres.'s Coun. Phys. Fitness, Washington, 1981—87; mem. sports sci. com. USTA, NYC, 1987—94; chief orthopedic sports med. cons. Athletic Dept. Marymount U., 2006—; course dir. numerous symposia in field. Author: Arm Care, 1981, rev. edit., 1996, Isoflex Exercise System, 1983; chief med. editor Orthop. Today, 1983-93; mem. editl. bd. The Physician and Sportsmedicine, 1992-2005, The Med. Sentinel, 1996-02, Orthopedics Today, 2003-; creator 10 video programs; contbr. 45 chpts. to books and over 125 articles to profl. publs.; patentee in field. Chmn. Jeffersonian Health Policy Found., Williamsburg, Va., 1994—97; mem. Va. Bd. Medicine, 2000—04; trustee Marymount U., Arlington, 2005—. Grantee Pfizer Inc., 1992-93, Sano Corp, 1993-94, Iomed Corp., 1999-2000, Travanti Pharma Inc, 2008-09. Mem.: AMA, Am. Orthop. Assn., VA Orthop. Soc. (Lifetime Career award 2005), Arlington County Med. Soc. (pres. 1977, chmn. legis. com. 1987—2004, Welburn award 1995), Med. Soc. Va. (chmn. sports medicine com. 1973—84, trustee polit. action com. 1990—2002, legis. com. 1995, liability com. 2005—, trustee polit. action com. 2006—), Va. Orthop. Soc. (pres. 1998—99, career award 2005), Washington Orthop. Soc., Ea. Orthop. Assn., Soc. Tennis Medicine and Sci. (exec. com.), Am. Orthop. Soc. Sports Medicine (ethics com. 1992—97, bd. dels. 2002—), Am. Acad. Orthop. Surgery (health fin. com. 1994—2000, comm. and state soc. coms. bd. of counselors 2000—03, bd. counselors 2000—06), Washington Golf and Country Club. Republican. Roman Catholic. Avocation: fitness activities. Office: Nirschl Orthop Ctr Sports Medicine & Joint Reconstrn 1715 N George Mason Dr Ste 504 Arlington VA 22205-3670 Home Phone: 703-237-8706; Office Phone: 703-525-2200. Personal E-mail: nirschlorthopaedics@comcast.net.

NISENBAUM, HARVEY LEONARD, radiologist; b. Boston, Sept. 2, 1943; s. Jack and Anne Nisenbaum; m. Sylvia T Tymowczak; 1 child, Eric. BSEE cum laude, Tufts U., Medford, Mass., 1965; MD, Tufts U., 1970. Diplomate Am. Bd. Radiology with subspecialty in diagnostic radiology 1975. Intern in surgery Mt. Sinai Hosp., NYC, 1970—71; resident in diagnostic radiology Montefiore Hosp. and Med. Ctr., Bronx, 1971—74; head ultrasound sect. Albert Einstein Med. Ctr., Phila., 1976—92, assoc. chmn. dept. radiology, 1986—91, chmn. divsn. diagnostic radiology, 1991—92, acting chmn. dept. radiology, 1991—92; chmn. dept. radiology Phila. Geriatric Ctr., 1983—93; staff radiologist U. Pa. Med. Ctr., Phila., 1993—, chmn. dept. med. imaging, 2001—. Lt. comdr. USN, 1974—76. Fellow, Coll. of Physicians of Phila., 1979. Fellow: Soc. of Radiologists in Ultrasound (chmn. external affairs com. 2000—03), Am. Inst. of Ultrasound in Medicine (chmn. membership com. 2000—03, pres. 2009—11), Am. Coll. of Radiology (councilor 1992—98); mem.: AMA, Radiology Alliance for Health Svcs. Rsch. in Radiology, Radiol. Soc. N.Am., Am. Roentgen Ray Soc., Phila. Roentgen Ray Soc. (pres. 2001—02), Pa. Radiol. Soc. (pres. 1999—2000), Greater Delaware Valley Ultrasound Soc. (pres. 1979—80). Avocation: Travel. Office: Penn Presbyterian Medical Ctr 39th & Market Sts Philadelphia PA 19104 Office Phone: 215-662-9206. Office Fax: 215-662-9871. Business E-Mail: harvey.nisenbaum@uphs.upenn.edu. *

NISENBAUM, LAYNE D., dermatologist, educator; Attended, U. Fla., 1976—80; DO, Southeastern U. of Health Sciences. Diplomate Nat. Bd. of Examiners for Osteo. Physician and Suregeons of the USA, 1986, Am. Osteopathic Bd. of Dermatology, 1992. Intern Doctors Green Hosp., 1985; resident dermatology Dr. Edwin H. Cohen (preceptor/dir.), 1987—90; dir. and dermatologist Cocoanut Creek Dermatology Ctr., 1990—98; with Good Samaritan Hosp.; med. dir. of dermatology Island Dermatology and Laser Inst., 1998—. Clin. assoc. prof. dermatology Southeastern Univ. of Health Sciences. Fellow: Am. Soc. of Laser Medicine and Surgery; mem.: Am. Soc. of Anti-Aging Medicine, North Am. Soc. of Phlebology, Fla. Osteo. Medicine Assn., Am. Osteo. Assn., Am. Osteo. Coll. of Dermatology, Fla. Soc. of Dermatology, Am. Acad. of Dermatology. Office: Island Dermatology and Laser Institute 50 Cocoanut Row 120 Palm Beach FL 33480 Office Phone: 561-832-1950.

NISHI, GREGG K., surgeon, educator; BS, U. Calif., Irvine; MD, George Washington U. Sch. Medicine. Intern North Shore U. Hosp., Manhasset, NY; resident Cedars-Sinai Med. Ctr., surgeon Ctr. for Weight Loss, surgeon Surgical Intensive Care Unit & Trauma Surgery Svcs.; asst. clinical prof. surgery UCLA David Geffen Sch. Medicine. Recipient Leo G. Rigler MD award, Cedars-Sinai Med. Ctr., Paul Rubenstein MD Prize for Excellence. Fellow: Am. Coll. Surgeons; mem.: AMA, Soc. Laparoendoscopic Surgeons (Resident Achievement award), Soc. Am. Gastrointestinal Endoscopic Surgeons.

NISHI, HIROTAKA, medical educator; b. Kumamoto, Japan, Jan. 7, 1968; s. Yukihiro and Keiho Nishi. MD, Tokyo Med. U., Japan, 1994; PhD, Tokyo Med. U. Grad. Sch., Japan, 1998. Vis. fellow Nat. Cancer Inst., NIH, Bethesda, Md., 1999—2001; instr. Tokyo Med. U., 2001—02, asst. prof., 2002—. Directorship Tokyo Med. U., 2003—. Councilor, sec. Japan Placenta Assn., Tokyo, 2001—, Japan Soc. of Gynecologic Oncology, Tokyo, 2004—. Recipient New Investigator's award, Internat. Fedn. Placental Assns., 1998, Hippocrates award, Tokyo Med. U., 1999, Academic award, 2003, Sasa award, Sasa Meml. Found., 2004; scholar Proposal, Japan Soc. for the Promotion of Sci., 2003; Rsch. grant, Tokyo Med. U. Cancer Ctr., 2001, grant, Haraguchi Meml. Found. Cancer Rsch., 2002, Grants-in-Aid for Sci. Rsch., Japan Soc. for the Promotion of Sci., 2002—05. Mem.: Japan Soc. Ob-Gyn., Am. Assn. for Cancer Rsch. Achievements include research in tissue and cell hypoxia. Avocations: golf, gourmet cooking. Office: Tokyo Med U 6-7-1 Nishishinjuku Shinjuku-ku Tokyo 1600023 Japan Office Phone: 81333426111 Ext. 5869, 81353393758. Office Fax: 81333485918. Business E-Mail: nishih@tokyo-med.ac.jp.

NISHIDA, HIROMI, biologist, researcher, educator; b. Osaka, Japan, Feb. 9, 1966; s. Koukichi and Hiroko Nishida. BS, U. Tokyo, 1990, M in Agr., 1992, PhD, 1995. Rsch. fellow Japan Soc. Promotion of Sci., Tokyo, 1994-96; postdoctoral rsch. fellow RIKEN Inst., Wako, Japan, 1996-97, rschr. Yokohama, Japan, 2003—05; asst. prof. U. Tokyo, 1997—2003, assoc. prof., 2005—. Mem. Japan Soc. Biosci., Biotech., and Agrochemistry, Soc. Genome Microbiology Japan. Office: U Tokyo Grad Sch Agr and Life Scis Agrl Bioinformatics Rsch Unit 1-1-1 Yayoi Bunkyo-ku Tokyo 113-8657 Japan

NISHIDA, MASATO, obstetrician, gynecologist; b. Tokyo, July 15, 1946; MD, Keio U., PhD, 1972. Resident Kitasato U. Hosp., 1972—79; assoc. prof. Tsukuba U., 1979—2001; pres. Kasumigaura Med. Ctr., 2001—. Mem.: Japan Soc. Ob-Gyn., Am. Soc. Clin. Oncology. Avocation: jogging. Office: 2-7-14 Shimotakatsu Tsuchiura Ibaraki 300-8585 Japan Office Fax: 029-824-0494. Business E-Mail: nishidamasato@mac.com, mnishida@kasumi.hosp.go.jp.

NISHIDA, YUICHIRO, medical educator; b. Soka, Japan, May 27, 1974; PhD, Nagoya U., 2002. Asst. prof. Dept. Preventive Medicine, Faculty Medicine, Saga U., 2008—. Office: 5-1-1 Nabeshima Saga 849-8501 Japan Business E-Mail: ynishida@cc.saga-u.ac.jp.

NISHIHARA, HIROFUMI, microbiologist; BA, Tohoku U., Miyagi, 1986; PhD, Tokyo U., 1993. Rschr. Tokyo Gas Co. Ltd., Minato-Ku, Tokyo, 1986—91; asst. prof. Ibaraki U., Mito, Japan, 1993—97, assoc. prof., 1997—. Vis. rschr. Nat. Inst. Environ. Studies, Tsukuba, Ibaraki, 1994—2000; assoc. prof. Tokyo U. Agr. and Tech., Fuchu, Tokyo, 1998—. R&D mem. nat. rsch. project New Energy and Indsl. Tech. Devel. Orgn., Japan, 1995—98, 2001—11, overseas dispatched rschr., 1998—98. Achievements include discovery of genus Hydrogenovibrio in prokaryotes.

NISHIHARA, KEN, physical therapist, educator; m. Yayoi Tabushi; 1 child, Yuki. MS, Waseda U., Tokyo, 1988; PhD, Kitasato U., Kanagawa, Japan, 2004. Phys. therapist Nat. Ctr. Neurology and Psychiatry, Kodaira, Japan, 1999—2001; instr. Saitama Prefectural U., Japan, 2001—. Achievements include research and development of a new surface electromyogram analysis technique to estimate muscle activities. Office: Saitama Prefectural U 820 Sannomiya Koshigaya 343-8540 Japan Office Fax: 81-48-973-4315. E-mail: nishihara-ken@spu.ac.jp.

NISHIHARA, MINORU, surgeon; b. Naha, Okinawa, Japan, July 24, 1962; s. Shigeru and Takako Nishihara; m. Yasuko Ishibashi, July 30, 1967; children: Katsumi, Shiori. MD, Nagasaki U., Japan, 1988, PhD, 1999. Physician Nagasaki U. Sch. Medicine, 1988-93, Nishi-Isahaya Hosp., Nagasaki, 1997-98; chief surgery Nat. Tsushima Hosp., Nagasaki, 1998-99, Heart-Life Hosp., Okinawa, 1999—2003, sub-mgr. surgery, 2003—07, mgr. surgery, 2007—, dir., 2009—. Mem.: Japan Surg. Assn., Japanese Soc. Gastroent. Surgery, Japan Surg. Soc. Achievements include research in parathyroid hormone-related protein; digestive surgery; hepato-biliary-pancreatic surgery. Avocations: kendo player, computers. Office: Heart Life Hosp 208 Iju Nakagusuku-son Nakagami-gun Okinawa 901-2492 Japan Office Phone: 098-895-3255. Office Fax: 098-895-3066. Personal E-mail: minorunish@aol.jp. Business E-Mail: m.nishihara@heartlife.or.jp.

NISHIIKE, SUETAKA, otolaryngologist, researcher; b. Oita, Japan, July 21, 1965; MD, Osaka U., 1990, PhD, 1996. Resident Osaka U. Hosp., Suita, Japan, 1990—91; otolaryngologist Pub. health Kinan Gen. Hosp., Tanabe, 1991—92; asst. prof. Osaka U., Suita, 1996—98, 2000—01; chief Osaka Prefectural Habikino Hosp., Habikino, 1998—2000, Suita Mcpl. Hosp., 2001—05; asst. prof. Kawaski Med. Sch., Kurashiki, 2005—08; assoc. prof. Osaka U., Suita, 2008—. Lectr. U. Tokushima, 2003—. Contbr. articles to profl. jours. Grantee, Ministry Edn., Sci., Sports, Culture and Tech. Japan, 1999—2000, 2001—02, Japanese Space Forum, 2001—03; fellow, German Academic Exch. Svc., 1996—98. Fellow: Japan Soc. Equilibrium Rsch., Oto-Rhino-Laryngological Soc. Japan; mem.: Barany Soc. Office: Osaka Univ Dept Otolaryngology 2-2 Yamadaoka Suita Osaka 565-0871 Japan Office Fax: 81 6 6879 3959. Business E-Mail: snishiike@ent.med.osaka-u.ac.jp.

NISHIKAWA, YASUO, psychologist, educator; b. Chiba-shi Chiba-ken, Japan, July 30, 1939; s. Kenro and Fujiko (Oguchi) N.; m. Nobuko Nagatsuka, Dec. 11, 1970; 1 child, Yuichi. BA, Keio U., 1964, M, 1966, PhD, 1978. Asst. Sophia U., Tokyo, 1969—70, asst. prof., 1970—74, assoc. prof., 1974—81, prof., 1981—98, prof. emeritus, 1998—; prof. Hokkaido U., Sapporo, 1998—2002, Open U. Japan, 2002—10, vis. prof., 2010—. Vis. rsch. fellow Pa. State U., State College, 1974, 1990—91; specialist mem. Ctrl. Coun. for Edn., 1989—91. Author: What is the Mind?, 1975, Behavior Analysis, 1978, Human Being Viewed as a Black Box, 1979, Behavior Medicine, 1981, Pattern of Cognition, 1988, Experimental Science of Behavior, 1988, Frontiers of Mental Science, 1994, Cognitive-Behavioral Science, 2002, 2006, Mental Engineering, 2003, History of Psychology, 2010; author, editor: Invitation to Modern Psychology, 1989, Cognitive Science, 1997, Life Style Related Diseases, 1998, Introduction to Cognitive Science, 2000, Science of Mind, 2004, History of Psychology in Japan, 2005, Psychometrics, 2006, Progress in Cognitive Science, 2008; co-author: An Introduction to Linguistic Research, 1999, Engineering of Impression, 2000, What is the Mind?, 2001, The 75 Year History of Japanese Psychological Association, 2002, Psychology as the Science, 2004; co-translator: An Illustrated History of American Psychology, 2001. Mem. Internat. Soc. History Behavioral and Social Scis., Am. Soc. Psychol. Sci., N.Y. Acad. Scis., Japanese Psychol. Assn., Japanese Cognitive Sci. Soc. (editor in chief, 1987-90), Japanese Psychonomic Soc., Japanese Assn. Philosophy Sci. (editl. bd.), Japanese Soc. Theoretical Psychology (bd. trustees). Avocation: classical music. Home: 13-2 Inage 3-chome Inage-ku Chiba-Shi Chiba 263-0034 Japan Personal E-mail: nishikawa-yasuo@cuc.jp.

NISHIKAWA, YOSHIYUKI, gastroenterologist, director; b. Okayama, Japan, July 25, 1958; s. Syounosuke and Miyako Nishikawa; m. Kozue Ishihara, June 30, 1985; children: Megumi, Naoki. MD, Okayama U., 1983. Cert. in endoscopist Japan Gstroenterological Endoscopy Soc. Dir. Nishikawa Gastrointestinal Clinic, Matsuyama, Ehime, Japan, 1999—, Matsuyama Med. Assn., 2006—. Councilor Japan Gastroenterological Endoscopy Soc., Tokyo, 2005—; internat. mem. Am. Soc. Gastrointestinal Endoscopy, Oak Brook, Ill. Contbr. articles to profl. med. jours. Achievements include research in simultaneous combination of endoscopic sclerotherapy and endoscopic ligation (EISL) for esophageal varices. Office: Nishikawa Gastrointestinal Clinic 2-72 Katsuyama-cho Matsuyama Ehime 790-0878 Japan Office Fax: 81899151508; Home Fax: 81899475091. Business E-Mail: yonishik@ehime.med.or.jp.

NISHIMOTO, SOH, plastic surgeon; b. Osaka, Japan, Oct. 28, 1964; s. Nobushige and Itsuyo Nishimoto; m. Chie Nishimoto, Feb. 11, 1995; children: Ryoka, Keitatsu. MD, PhD, Osaka U., 1989. Asst. prof. Osaka U., Suita, 1995—97; chief plastic surgeon Osaka Cancer Ctr., 1997—99; rsch. fellow Pitts. U., 1999—2001; dir. plastic surgery Kobe Children's Hosp., Japan, 2001—06; assoc. prof. dept. plastic surgery Hyogo Coll. Medicine, Japan, 2006—. Grantee, Sasagawa Clin. and Med. Found., 1999; fellow, Pitts. Tissue Engring. Initiative, 2000—01; Seed grant, Pitts. Children's Hosp., 2000. Avocations: skiing, scuba diving, meteorology. Office: Hyogo Coll Medicine 1-1 Mukogawa Cho Nishinomiya Hyogo 663 8131 Japan Business E-Mail: nishimoto_kch@hp.pref.hyogo.jp.

NISHIMURA, AKINOBU, physician; b. Japan, Sept. 3, 1976; MD, Mie U., 2001. Physician dept. orthop. and sports medicine Mie U. Grad. Sch. Medicine, 2009—. Office: Edobashi 2-174 Tsu City Mie 514-8507 Japan Business E-Mail: meiten@clin.medic.mie-u.ac.jp.

NISHIMURA, MASATO, internist, researcher; b. Kyoto, Kyoto, Japan, July 15, 1957; s. Kouzou and Masako Nishimura; m. Misako Uragami, Nov. 4, 1984; children: Kazuma, Yuka. MD, Kyoto Prefectural U. Medicine, 1983, PhD, 1990. Diplomate The Ministry of Health and Welfare, Japan, 1983. Resident dept. internal medicine Kyoto Prefectural U. Medicine, 1983—85; staff dept. internal medicine Matsushita Meml. Hosp., Moriguchi, Osaka, 1985—86, Yohkaichi Nat. Hosp., Shiga, 1986—87; asst. prof. dept. clin. and lab. medicine Kyoto Prefectural U. Medicine, 1989—90, 1992—95; staff dept. internal medicine Nishijin Hosp., 1995—96; assoc. prof. dept. clin. and lab. medicine Kyoto Prefectural U. Medicine, 1996—2000; chief dir. cardiovasc. divsn. Toujinkai Hosp., 2000—. Rschr. in field. Recipient Young Investigator award, The Kimura Meml. Heart Found., 1996, Pfizer Circulatory Disease Found., 1998, Excellent Investigator award, The Japanese Soc. of Lab. Medicine, 1998, Best

Abstract award, XLII ERA-EDTA Congress, 2005; grantee, The Salt Sci. Rsch. Found., 1998, The Charitable Trust Clin. Pathology Rsch. Support, 1999; fellow, Kyoto Prefectural U. Medicine, Dept. Internal Medicine, 1987—89, Cleve. Clinic Found., 1990—92. Mem.: The Japan Endocrine Soc., Soc. for Spontaneously Hypertensive Rat, Soc. Cardiovasc. Endocrinology and Metabolism, Japanese Soc. Hypertension. Avocations: mountain climbing, travel, music. Office: Toujinkai Hosp 83-1 Iga Momoyama-cho Fushimi-ku Kyoto 612-8026 Japan Office Fax: +81-75-623-0226. Business E-Mail: mnishimura@tea.ocn.ne.jp.

NISHIMURA, MIKIO, biologist; b. Nagoya, Aichi, Japan, Mar. 15, 1949; s. Kazuhiko and Shizu (Sato) N.; m. Ikuko Hara, Apr. 20, 1980; children: Kohei, Naoko. B Agr., Nagoya U., 1971, M Agr., 1973, D Agr., 1977. Rsch. assoc. faculty agr. Nagoya U., 1975-87; postdoctoral fellow U. Calif., Santa Cruz, 1977-79; assoc. prof. faculty sci. Kobe (Hyogo) U., 1987-89; prof. dept. cell biology Nat. Inst. Basic Biology, Okazaki, Aichi, 1989—, chmn. dept. cell biology, 1996—. Author: Nature, 1979, Plant Physiology, 1986, Plant Cell, 1993, Science, 2004. Sci. grantee Natsunaga Sci. Found., Tokyo, 1976, Ishida Sci. Found., Nagoya, Japan, 1982, Naito Sci. Found., Tokyo, 1991, Nissan Sci. Found., Tokyo, 1994, Mitsubishi Sci. Found., Tokyo, 2004; recipient Young Scientist award Agrl. Chem. Soc. Japan, Tokyo, 1984, Chunichi Cultural prize, 2006. Mem. Japanesse Soc. Plant Physiologists, Bot. Soc. Japan. Home: Tatsumi-Asahi 6-16 Okazaki 444 0877 Japan Office: Nat Inst Basic Biology Myodaiji Okazaki 444 8585 Japan Office Phone: 81 564 55 7500. Business E-Mail: mikosome@nibb.ac.jp.

NISHIMURA, MOTOKO, pharmacist, researcher; b. Tokyo, Oct. 12, 1954; M in Pharmacology, Tokyo U., 1979, PhD, 1984. Rschr. Japanese Red Cross Blood Ctr., Tokyo, 1981—. Mem.: Japanese Transfusion Soc. Achievements include research in transfusion related acute lung injury; graft virus host disease. Office: Tokyo Met Red Cross Blood Ctr 4-1-31 Hiro-o Shibuya-ku Tokyo Japan Office Phone: (81)3-3406-1211. Office Fax: (81)3-3406-7892. Business E-Mail: mo-nishimura@tokyo.bc.jrc.or.jp.

NISHIMURA, NOBUHIRO, medical educator; b. Fukuoka, Japan, Jan. 20, 1966; BS, Fukuoka U., 1989, PhD, 2001. Assoc. prof. Shimane U. Faculty Medicine, 2008—. Mem.: JSSX. Office: Enya-cho 89-1 Izumo Shimane 693 8501 Japan Office Fax: 81-853-20-2593. Business E-Mail: nnishi@med.shimane-u.ac.jp.

NISHIMURA, PETE HIDEO, oral surgeon; b. Hilo, Hawaii, Aug. 7, 1922; s. Hideichi and Satsuki N.; m. Tomoe Nishimura, June, 1949; children— Dennis Dean, Grant Neil, Dawn Naomi. Student, U. Hawaii, 1940-44; D.D.S., U. Mo., 1947; MSD., Northwestern U., 1949. Practice dentistry specializing in oral surgery, Honolulu, 1952—; pres. Oral Surgery Group, 1978—. Mem. coun. Nat. Bd. Dental Examination; dir. Hawaii Dental Svc., 1962-85, pres., 1970-72, 76-78; pres. State Bd. Dental Examiners, Delta Sigma Delta, Fedn. Dentaire Internat. Served with U.S. Army, 1952-54. Recipient Citation for outstanding pub. svc. toward the devel. of state plan for emergency mgmt. resources, Dir. Emergency Planning, Exec. Office of Pres. of U.S., 1968, Lifetime Achievement award, Hawaii Dental Assn.; named Disting. Alumni, U. Mo. Hawaii, 2004. Fellow Am. Coll. Dentists, Internat. Coll. Dentists; mem. ADA, Hawaii Dental Assn. (past pres., Lifetime Achievement award 2006), Delta Dental Plans Assn. (dir.), Honolulu County Dental Soc., Hawaii Soc. Oral Surgeons, Am. Assn. Oral and Maxillofacial Surgeons, Western Soc. Oral and Maxillofacial Surgeons, Am. Assn. Dental Examiners, Pierre Fauchard Acad. (citation for oustanding contbn. to arts and sci. of dentistry 1987). Democrat. Home: Apt 606 4389 Malia St Honolulu HI 96821 Office: 848 S Beretania St Honolulu HI 96813-2551 Personal E-mail: hilopete@aol.com.

NISHIMURA, YOSHIKI, botanist, educator; b. Tokyo, Mar. 6, 1974; PhD, U. Tokyo, 2001. Postdoc. fellow Boyce Thompson Inst., Cornell U., 2003—06; asst. prof. U. Tokyo, 2006—08, Kyoto U., 2008—. Recipient Incentive award, Bot. Soc. Japan. Office: Oiwake-cho Kita-Shirakawa Sakyo-ku Kyoto 606-8502 Japan Business E-Mail: yoshiki@pmg.bot.kyoto-u.ac.jp.

NISHIMURA, YUKIO, pharmacist, educator, cell biologist; b. Kagoshima, Japan, Sept. 4, 1951; s. Harusumi and Fukumi Nishimura. BS, Kyushu U., Fukuoka, Japan, 1974, MS, 1976, PhD, 1979. Cert. pharmacist Ministry Health and Welfare, Japan, 1975. Rsch. assoc. NY U., Sch. Medicine, 1981—84, Kyushu U., Fukuoka, Japan, 1984—92, assoc. prof., 1992—. Contbr. articles to profl. jours. Rsch. grant, Kyushu U. Found., Fukuoka, 2007. Mem.: Japanese Cancer Assn.(Tokyo), Japanese Assn. Metastasis Rsch., (Osaka) (trustee 2005—, Outstanding Presentation award 2004). Home: 6 15 3 406 Yoshizuka Hakata-ku Fukuoka 812 0041 Japan Office: Kyushu Univ Chemo-Pharm Sci Grad Sch Pharm Sci Maidashi 3-1-1 Fukuoka Higashi 8128582 Japan Personal E-mail: ynkio443@yahoo.co.jp. Business E-Mail: nishimur@bioc.phar.kyushu-ac.jp.

NISHINA, TOMOHIRO, oncologist; b. Japan, May 25, 1971; MD, Okayama U., 1996, PhD, 2004. Staff physician Nat. Hosp. Orgn. Shikoku Cancer Ctr., 2001—. Mem.: ASCO. Avocation: tennis. Office: Nat Shikoku Cancer Ctr Dept Med Oncology 160 Kou Minamiumemotomachi Matsuyama Ehime 791-0280 Japan Business E-Mail: tnishina@shikoku-cc.go.jp.

NISHIO, KAZUAKI, medical educator; b. Tajimi-shi, Gifu, Japan, Apr. 26, 1965; m. Shiho Nishio; children: Takakazu, Masakazu. MD, PhD, Showa U., Tokyo, 1992. Lectr. Showa U., Shinagawa-ku, Tokyo, 2005—. Contbr. articles to profl. med. jours. Mem.: Japanese Soc. Internal Medicine, Japanese Circulation Soc. Office: Showa Univ 1-5-8 Hatanodai Shinagawa-ku Tokyo 142-8666 Japan Home: 2-7-10 Ikegami Ota-Ku Tokyo 146-0082 Japan Office Phone: 81-555-72-2222, 81-3-3784-8000, 81 3 3752 1111. Business E-Mail: kazukun@jg7.so-net.ne.jp.

NISHIYAMA, MISUZU, anesthesiologist; b. Sapporo, Japan, Dec. 15, 1951; d. Taro and Yoshiko (Kuroda) Hikita; m. Hiroaki Nishiyama, July 2, 1978 (dec. Jan 1986); 1 child, Rumina. BM, Hokkaido U., 1976. Resident Hokkaido U., Sapporo, Japan, 1976-77; staff anesthesiologist St. Luke's Internat. Hosp., Tokyo, 1986-95, Tokyo Jikeikai U. Sch. of Medicine, 1996-2000, Asahi Ctrl. Hosp., Chibaken, 2001—04, Ito Mcpl. Hosp., 2005—09, Shizuoka Kosei Hosp., 2010—. Author & editor: Anesthesiology Resident Manual, 1994, 2d edit., 2000, 3rd edit., 2008. Home: 1317 4982 Futo Ito Shizuoka-Ken 413-0231 Japan Office: Shizuoka Kosei Hosp 23 Kitabancho Shizuokashi Japan Personal E-mail: n5548@abox5.so-net.ne.jp.

NISHIYAMA, OSAMU, physician; b. Nishinomiya, Hyogo, Japan, Aug. 30, 1968; s. Takashi and Fumiko Nishiyama; m. Makiko Torii, Sept. 15, 1966; children: Shohei, Tomoki. PhD, Nagoya U., Nagoya, Aichi, Japan. Asst. dir. Dept. Respiratory Medicine and Allergy Tosei Gen. Hosp., Seto, Aichi, Japan, 2003—. Contbr. medical journals. Office: Tosei General Hosp 160 Nishioiwake-cho Aichi Seto 489-8642 Japan Office Fax: +81-561-82-9139.

NISHIYAMA, SUSUMU, rheumatologist; MD, PhD, Kagawa U., Japan, 2005. Contbr. articles to profl. jours. including Clin. Rheumatology, Internat. Immunopharmacology, Jour. Rheumatology. Office: Kurashiki Med Ctr 250 Bakuro-cho Kurashiki 710-0824 Japan Business E-Mail: newcity@mtd.biglobe.ne.jp.

NISHIYAMA, TOMOKI, anesthesiologist, researcher; b. Okayama, Japan, Nov. 8, 1960; came to U.S., 1996; s. Kiyoshi and Kyoko (Nakatsuka) N.; m. Rie Hirao, June 6, 1988; children: Yurika, Yasutaka, Yoshitaka. MD, Okayama U., 1985, PhD, 1989. Diplomate Japanese Bd. Anesthesiology. Anesthesiologist Kagawa Prefectural Ctrl. Hosp., Takamatsu/Kagawa, Japan, 1989-92, chief anesthesiologist, 1992-93, JR Tokyo Gen. Hosp., Shibuya/Tokyo, 1993—95; instr. U. Tokyo, 1995-96; rsch. fellow U. Calif., San Diego, 1996-97; rsch. assoc. UCLA, 1997-1999; inst. U. Tokyo, 1999-2000; assoc. prof. Inst. Med. Sci., 2000—02, U. Tokyo, 2002—04; dir. anesthesiology and critical care Kamagara Gen. Hosp., 2008—10, Higashi Omiya Gen. Hosp. Contbr. articles to profl. jours. Avocations: photography, travel, tennis. Home: 4-7-3-2015 Minamisenju Arakawa-ku Tokyo Japan Office: 5 18 Higaski Oumiya Mimumer-ku Satiama 337 0051 Japan Home Phone: 81 33806 75 98; Office Phone: 81474988111. Business E-Mail: nishit-tky@umin.ac.jp.

NISHIZAWA, HIROTOSHI, hospital administrator; MD. Pres. Japan Hosp. Assn. Office: Japan Hospital Association Office of the President Chiyoda-ku Misaki-cho 3712 7Fl Tokyo Japan Office Phone: 0332345165. *

NISHTAR, SANIA, healthcare executive; d. Syed and Tahira Hamid; m. Ghalib Nishtar, July 11, 1986; children: Kassim, Leena. MBBS, Khyber Med. Coll., 1986; PhD, Kings Coll., 2002. Pres. & exec. dir. Heartfile, Islamabad, Pakistan, 1998. Mem., exec. bd. World Heart Fedn., Geneva, 2003—, chairperson, foundations adv. bd., 2003—; mem., exec. bd. Internat. Non-Governmental Coalition Against Tobacco, Geneva, 2004—, chair, world heart day steering com. World Heart Fedn., Geneva, 2003—; mem., steering com., mega country network on health promotion. WHO, Geneva, 2003—04. Author: (book) National Action Plan for Prevention and Control of Non-Communicable Diseases and Health Promotion in Pakistan, Nishtar S. Prevention of Coronary Heart Disease in South Asia. Temp. advisor WHO, 2005. Recipient Sitara-i-Imtiaz civil award, Govt. of Pakistan, 2005, Population Sci. award and Silver medal, European Soc. of Cardiology, 2005; scholar All Pakistan Quaid-e-Azam Merit scholarship, 1989. Mem.: Internat. Heart Health Declarations (assoc.). Home: 1 - Park road Chak Shahzad Federal Capital Islamabad 44000 Pakistan Office: Heartfile 1 - Park road Chak Shahzad Fedral Capital Islamabad 44000 Pakistan Office Fax: 0092512240773. Business E-Mail: sania@heartfile.org.

NISSAPATORN, VEERANOOT, medical educator; b. Nakhon Si Thammarat, Thailand, May 25, 1965; d. Longheing Sae Oui and Kesorn Nissapatorn. BSc in Biology, Ramkhamhaeng U., Thailand, 1986; MBBS, Lady Hardinge Med. Coll., New Delhi, 1994; diploma in Tropical Medicine and Hygiene, Mahidol U., Bangkok, 1997; M in Clin. Tropical Medicine, Mahidol U., 1998; diploma in STD & AIDS, Prince of Songkla U., Thailand, 1998. Lectr. U. Malaya, Lemabah, Kuala Lumpur, Malaysia, 1999—. Contbr. articles reviewer, editl. bd. to profl. jours. Recipient award of excellence, U. Malaya, 2004; grantee, 2000, 2001; scholar, Indian Coun. Cultural Relationship, 1989—94, Hosp. Tropical Diseases, Faculty Tropical Medicine, Mahidol U., 1997—98. Mem.: Internat. AIDS Soc. (corr.), Internat. Union Against Sexually Transmitted Infections (corr.), Malaysian Soc. Parasitology and Tropical Medicine (corr.). Buddhist. Avocations: travel, reading, music. Home: Phet-Kasem 94 Rd Bangkok 10600 Thailand Office: U Malaya Lembah Pantai 50603 Kuala Lumpur Malaysia Office Fax: 6-03-79674754. E-mail: nissapat@hotmail.com.

NISSEN, STEVEN EVAN, cardiologist, researcher; b. Toledo, Sept. 1, 1948; m. Linda Butler. BS, U. Mich., Ann Arbor; MD, U. Mich. Sch. Medicine, Ann Arbor, 1978. Intern internal medicine Univ. Calif. Davis, Sacramento, resident internal medicine; fellowship in cardiology Chandler Med. Ctr. Univ. Ky., Lexington; cardiologist Cleveland Clinic, 1992—, dir. coronary ICU, 1992—97, sect. head clinical cardiology, 1992—2002, vice chmn. dept. cardiology, 1993—2002, interim chmn., dept. cardiovascular med., 2006, chmn., dept. cardiovascular med., 2006—, dir., Joseph J. Jacobs Ctr. for Thrombosis and Vascular Biology; prof. medicine Cleve. Clinic Lerner Sch. Medicine. Mem. and chmn. CardioRenal adv. panel US FDA; spl. govt. employee US FDA Committees; mem. med. & sci. adv. bd. Forbes Medi-Tech Inc.; vis. prof. at med. colleges and universities internationally and nationally. Contbr. articles to profl. jours., chapters to books; mem. editl. bd. Internat. Jour. Cardiac Imaging, Cardiology Today, Clinical Cardiology; editor: Current Cardiology Reports, 2006—; sr. consulting editor Journal of American College of Cardiology, 2002—. Recipient Award for Outstanding Rsch. in Cardiovascular Rsch., Gill Heart Inst., U. Ky., 2004; named one of The World's Most Influential People, TIME mag., 2007. Mem.: Am. Coll. Cardiology (pres., chmn. bd. trustees 2006—, ednl. products com., info. tech. com.). Achievements include development of intravascular ultrasound imaging; published rsch. on cardiovascular problems caused by Cox-2 inhibitor drugs, such as Vioxx & Celebrex. Avocation: bicycling. Office: Cleveland Clinic Mail Code F 15 9500 Euclid Ave Cleveland OH 44195 Office Phone: 216-445-6852. Business E-Mail: nissens@ccf.org. *

NISSENBLATT, MICHAEL JEFFREY, medical oncologist; b. Bronx, NY, June 4, 1948; m. Marlene Nissenblatt; 1 child, Doree; 1 child, Paulina. MD, Columbia P&S, 1973. Diplomate Am. Bd. Internal Medicine. Intern Johns Hopkins, Balt., 1973-74, resident, 1974-75, 75-76, fellow, 1976-78; assoc. dir. med. oncology RW Johnson U. Hosp., New Brunswick, 1996—; staff St. Peter's Med. Ctr., New Brunswick; clin. prof. medicine RW Johnson U. Sch. Medicine, 1996—. Dir. Ctrl. NJ Oncology Ctr., 1981—. Recipient Chamber of Commerce award, 2003, Partners in Caring award, Am. Cancer Soc., 2004, Pres. Excellence award, Robert Wood Johnson U. Hosp., 0208; named Best Doctor NY Mag., 1998—2010. Fellow ACP; mem. AMA, AAAS, Am. Radiol. Soc., Am. Soc. Clin. Oncology, Cancer Chemotherapy Found., Johns Hopkins Med. Surgeons Soc., Maimonides Soc., Middlesex County Med. Soc., N.J. Breast Cancer Coalition, others. Jewish. Avocations: running, astronomy, anthropology, motivational speaking. Office: Ctrl Jersey Oncology Ctr PA 205 Easton Ave New Brunswick NJ 08901-1722 Office Phone: 732-828-9570. Personal E-mail: mjnmotor@aol.com. *

NISSENSON, ALLEN RICHARD, physician, educator; b. Chgo., Dec. 10, 1946; s. Harry and Sylvia Lillian (Chapnitsky) N.; m. Charna H. Karp, May 28, 1978; 1 child, Ariel Rose. BS in Medicine, Northwestern U., 1967, MD, 1971. Diplomate Am. Bd. Internal Medicine, bd. cert. internal medicine and nephrology. Intern in medicine Michael Reese Hosp. and Med. Ctr., Chgo., 1971-72, resident in internal medicine, 1972-74; fellowship in nephrology Northwestern U., Chgo., 1974-76; assoc. medicine Northwestern U. Med. Sch., Chgo., 1976-77; asst. prof. medicine UCLA Sch. Medicine, 1977-82, assoc. prof. medicine, 1982-88, prof. medicine, 1988—; dir. dialysis program UCLA Ctr. for the Health Scis., 1977—, med. dir. renal mgmt. strategies, assoc. dean David Geffen Sch. Medicine, 2006—. Adj. attending physician Northwestern Meml. Hosp., Chgo., 1976-77; asst. attending physician UCLA Ctr. for Health Scis., 1977-82, assoc. attending physician, 1988—; attending physician nephrology Wadsworth VA Hosp., 1978—; cons. on peritoneal dialysis Baxter-Travenol Labs., 1981—; mem. nephrology adv. com. Nephrology Nursing Edn. Grant, Calif. State U., 1983-90; vice chmn. Forum of End Stage Renal Disease Networks, 1988-91; mem. sci. adv. bd. Nat. Kidney Found., 1989-91, chmn. coun. on clin. nephrology, dialysis and transplantation, 1989-91; cons. on End Stage Renal Disease reimbursement Rand Corp., 1990—, others. Editor-in-chief Advances in Renal Replacement Therapy, 1993—, Hemodialysis Internat., 2004—, Medscape Nephrology, 2006; mem. editl. bd. Dialysis and Transplantation, 1978—, UCLA Health Insights, 1981-89, Perspectives in Peritoneal Dialysis, 1983—, Internat. Jour. Artificial Organs, 1984—, Seminars in Dialysis, 1987—, Am. Jour. Nephrology, 1989—, Am. Jour. Kidney Diseases, 1989—, Geriat. Nephrology and Urology Jour., 1989—; mem. editl. adv. bd. Contemporary Dialysis, 1983—, Nephrology Practice Today, 1989—, Hematopoietic Therapy Index and Revs., 1993—, Primary Care Reports, 1994—; editl. cons. Am. Jour. Nephrology, 1981-88; contbr. chpts. to books, abstracts and articles to profl. publs. Recipient Nat. Kidney Found. So. Calif. Cmty. Svc. award, 1981, Pres.'s award Nat. Kidney Found., 1998, Lifetime Achievement award in hemodialysis U. Mo., 2007; Robert Wood Johnson policy fellow Office of Sen. Paul Wellstone, 1994-95. Fellow ACP; mem. Am. Soc. for Artifical Internal Organs, Am. Fedn. for Clin. Rsch., Am. Soc. Nephrology, Internat. Soc. Nephrology, Internat. Soc. Artificial Organs, Western Soc. for Clin. Investigation, European Dialysis and Transplant Assn., N.Am. Soc. for Dialysis and Transplantation, Renal Physicians' Assn. (bd. dirs. 1993—, sec. bd. dirs. 1994—, pres. 1999-2001), Calif. Renal Physicians (bd. dirs. 1987—). Office: 601 Hawaii St El Segundo CA 90245 Office Phone: 310-536-2549. E-mail: anissenson@mednet.ucla.edu.

NITOWSKY, HAROLD MARTIN, physician, educator; b. Bklyn., Feb. 12, 1925; s. Max and Fannie (Gershowitz) N.; m. Myra Heller, Nov. 28, 1954; children— Fran Ellen, Daniel Howard. AB, N.Y. U., 1944, MD, 1947; MS, U. Colo., 1952. Intern Mt. Sinai Hosp., NYC, 1947-48; resident pediats. U. Colo. Med. Center, 1948-50; USPHS postdoctoral fellow U. Colo., 1950-51; staff Sinai Hosp., Balt., 1953-67, dir. pediat. rsch., 1960-67; faculty Johns Hopkins Sch. Medicine, 1953-67, assoc. prof. ob-gyn., pediats., molecular genetics, 1962-67; prof. pediats. and genetics Albert Einstein Coll. Medicine, 1967—. Cons. Nat. Inst. Child Health and Human Devel., 1966—; Sr. surgeon USPHS, 1951-53 Contbr. articles on nutrition, metabolism, genetics to profl. jours. Mem. Am. Pediat. Soc., Soc. Pediat. Rsch., Am. Soc. Human Genetics. Home: 25 Devonshire Rd New Rochelle NY 10804-3925 Office: 122 Palmer Hill Rd Apt 3334 Stamford CT 06902 Personal E-mail: nidoc@aol.com.

NITSCHKE, JACK B., psychology professor; b. Freiburg, Germany, Feb. 24, 1967; PhD, U. Ill., Urbana-Champaign, 1998. Assoc. prof. psychiatry and psychology U. Wis., Madison, 2003—. Office: 6001 Research Pk Blvd Madison WI 53719 Business E-Mail: jnitschke@wisc.edu.

NITTI, VICTOR, urologist; BA, U. of Rochester, 1981; MD, U. of Medicine and Dentistry New Jersey, 1985. Diplomate Am. Bd. Urology. Intern surgery SUNY Health Sciences Ctr., Bklyn., 1985—86; resident urology SUNY, Bklyn., 1987—91, resident surgery, 1986—87; clin. fellow female urology UCLA, 1991—92; v.p. Soc. for Urodynamics and Female Urology. Prof. SUNY, Bklyn.; with NYU, 1995; assoc. editor Neurourology and Urodynamics, Journal of Pelvic Medicine and Surgery, Internat. Urogynecology Journal, Reviews in Urology. Editor: (textbook) Practical Urodynamics; author: (articles) The role of urodynamics in the evaluation of voiding dysfunction in men after cerebrovascular accident, The role of clinical research in the diagnosis and treatment of urinary incontinence, and other sevaral articles. Named one of Best Doctors in NY, NY Mag., 2010. Fellow: Am. Bd. of Urology, Am. Coll. of Surgeons; mem.: Internat. Continence Soc., Soc. for Urodynamics and Female Urology, Am. Urological Assn. Office: 150 East 32nd St 2nd Fl New York NY 10016 Office Phone: 646-825-6324. Office Fax: 646-825-6399.

NITZKI-GEORGE, DIANE M., pharmacist, medical writer; d. Rosemary F. and Edward H. Nitzki, Raymond F. Nitzki (Stepfather); m. Gerald J. George, May 22, 1982; 1 child, Michael L. George. B in Chemistry, No. Ill. U., 1976; B in Pharmacy, Creighton U., 1980; MBA, Keller Grad. Sch., 1992. Registered pharmacist Nebr., 1980, Ill., 1982. Staff pharmacist Bishop Clarkson Meml. Hosp., Omaha, 1980—82, Luth. Gen. Hosp., Park Ridge, Ill., 1982—87; inpatient pharmacy mgr. U.S. Naval Hosp., Great Lakes, Ill., 1987—89; pharmacy mgr. Parkside Luth. Hosp., Park Ridge, Ill., 1989; clin. info. mgr. Baxter Healthcare Corp., Deerfield, Ill., 1990—2002; med. writer DNG Consulting, Deerfield, Ill., 2002—; clin. pharmacist Evanston Hosp. Home Infusion Svc., Evanston, Ill., 2003—. Author: Generic Alternatives to Prescription Drugs, Extended Stability for Parenteral Drugs, 3d edit. Vol. webmaster Holy Cross Sch. & Ch., Deerfield, Ill., 1999—; vol. middle sch. sci. fair judge, 1999—2003, 2005—; active Highland Park Music Club, 2003—. Recipient Achievement award, Baxter Healthcare Corp., 1991—97, Svc. award,

Rho Chi Honor Soc., 1980, Pres.'s award for Sci. Achievement, Arnar-Stone Labs., 1978, others. Mem.: Am. Soc. Health-Sys. Pharmacist, Am. Med. Writers Assn. Achievements include worked closely with FDA to import an injectable multivitamin drug to the U.S. during a period of national shortage in which patients were at risk of injury (1997). Avocation: singing. Office: DNG Consulting 401 Locust Place Deerfield IL 60015 E-mail: dngconsulting@comcast.net.

NIVARTHI, RAJU NAGA, anesthesiology educator; b. Nandyal, India, June 16, 1964; came to U.S., 1993; s. Kameswara Sarma and Suseelamma Nivarthi; m. Aparna Nagaraju Nivarthi; children: Nidhi, Aditya. BSc with Chemistry, Zoology and Botany, Sri Venkateswara U., Tirupati, India, 1984; MSc in Biochemistry, Sri Kirshnadevaraya U., Anantapur, India, 1986; PhD, U. Hyderabad, 1996. Fellow Sch. Life Scis., U. Hyderabad, India, 1987-93; rsch. asst. prof. dept. anesthesiology NYU Med. Ctr., NYC, 1993—96, scientist, 1996-99, Wyeth-Ayerst Rsch., Pearl River, NY, 1999-2001; sr. scientist, mgr. analytical biochemistry Bristol-Myers Squibb, Syracuse, NY, 2001—05, mgr. immunology and molecular biology, biologics quality control, 2005—08; sr. scientist quality control tech. svc. Genzyme, Framingham, Mass., 2008—. Contbr. articles to profl. jours. Jr. Rsch. fellow Coun. Sci. and Indsl. Rsch., India, 1987, Sr. Rsch. fellow Coun. Sci. and Indsl. Rsch., 1990, Postdoc. fellowship NIH, 1998; recipient cert. of merit Pharmacia & Biotech Prize for Young Scientists, 1997, named 2000 Outstanding Scientist of 20th Century, 1998, Internat. Biographical Ctr. Mem. AAAS, Acad. Med. Cmty., Am. Chem. Soc., Am. Soc. Anesthesiologists, Am. Soc. Biochemistry and Molecular Biology, Internat. Anesthesia Rsch. Soc., Internat. Soc. for Study of Xenobiotics, Nat. Geographic Soc., N.Y. Acad. Scis. Home: 2 Copley Dr Northborough MA 01532-3603 Office: Genzyme 45 New York Ave Framingham MA 01701 Office Phone: 315-432-9612. Personal E-mail: rnivarthi@yahoo.com.

NIVOCHE, YVES, anesthesiologist, educator; b. Paris, Sept. 20, 1950; MD, U. Denis Diderot, 1977. Prof. anesthesiology U. Denis Diderot, 1989—. Head anesthesia, 2000—06. Mem.: European Malignant Hyperthermia Group, Soc. Française d'anesthésie Réanimation. Avocation: yachting. Office: Blvd Sérurier Hôpital Robert Debré Paris Ile de France 75935 France Office Fax: 33140032236. Business E-Mail: ynivoche.debre@invivo.edu.

NIWAS, RAM, neonatologist; s. Ram Swaroop and Ram Bati Sharma; m. Anita Sharma, May 17, 1991; children: Aman Sharma, Shubhi Sharma. MBBS, MD, S.N Med. Coll., Agra, India, 1990. Diplomate Am. Bd. Pediat., 2004, Am. Bd. Neonatal-Perinatal Medicine, 2008. House staff, pediat. Monklands and Bellshill Hosp., Airdrie, 1997—2000; fellow, neonatal-perinatal medicine SUNY, Stony Brook, NY, 2000—02, John H Stroger Hosp. Cook County, Chgo., 2004—06; pediatric resident NY Meth. Hosp., Bklyn., 2002—04; pediatrician, neonatologist Cmty. Health Care Inc., Davenport, Iowa, 2006—09; clin. asst.-prof. U. Iowa Children's Hosp., 2009—. Fellow: Am. Acad. Pediat.; mem.: Royal Coll. Physicians. Achievements include research in neonatal-perinatal medicine. Home: 1408 Chateau Knoll Bettendorf IA 52722 Office: Genesis Med Ctr 1227 E Rusholme St Davenport IA 52803 Office Phone: 563-421-7740. Personal E-mail: ram_niwas@yahoo.com. Business E-Mail: ram-niwas@uiowa.edu.

NIX, CHASTITY, nursing administrator; b. Demorest, Ga., Aug. 3, 1973; BSN, Brenau U., 1996; MBA, U. Ga., 2011. RN. Practice adminstr. Longstreet Clinic, P.C., 2001—. Bd. vice chmn. Glory, Hope and Life, 2009—. Mem.: Kiwanis Club. Office: 725 Jesse Jewell Pky Gainesville GA 30501 Office Fax: 770-718-1877. Business E-Mail: chastity.nix@longstreetclinic.com.

NIX, J. ELMER, retired orthopedist, surgeon; b. Ellisville, Miss., Oct. 24, 1931; s. Robert Leroy and Gladys Jane (Strahan) Nix; m. Rosemary Jane Cochrane, Nov. 16, 1956; children: Georgia Miller, Susan Hill, James Elmer Jr., Robert L. II. MD, Jefferson Med. Coll., Phila., 1956. Diplomate Am. Bd. Orthop. Surgery, 1965. Intern Hermann Hosp., Houston, 1956—57, resident, 1959—63; orthop. surgeon Am. Acad. Orthop. Surgeons, Chgo., 1965—2007; ret., 1995. Asst. prof. orthop. surgery U. Miss. Sch. Medicine, 1963—. Pres. N.Am. Spine Soc., Chgo., 1986—87; AMA del. Miss. Spine Soc., 1987—99, N.Am. Spine Soc., 1987—99; pres. Clinical Orthop. Soc., 1995—96, Miss. State Med. Soc., Jackson, 1990—91. Capt. USAF, 1957—59. Recipient Clinical Surgery award, Jefferson Med. Coll., 1956, David Selby award, N.Am. Spine Soc., 1997; named Intern of Yr., Hermann Hosp., Houston, 1957, Violet Keller Outstanding Resident, 1963; named one of Am. Top Surgeons, Consumer Rsch. Coun. Am., 2002. Fellow: Am. Bd. Orthop. Surgery, Am. Acad. Orthop. Surgery; mem.: N.Am. Spine Soc. (founder), Walter Scott Club. Republican. Presbyterian. Avocations: golf, reading, poetry, football. Home: 420 St Andrews Dr Jackson MS 39211

NIXON, DANIEL WALKER, oncologist, researcher; b. Brunswick, Ga., Sept. 8, 1943; s. Marvin Elesberry and Mildred Anita (Whitehead) N.; m. Sandra Gayle Brakefield, July 18, 1970; children: William B., Marvin A. BS, U. Ga., 1965, MD, 1969. Diplomate Am. Bd. Internal Medicine, Am. Bd. Med. Oncology; lic. physician S.C. Asst. prof. Med. Coll. Ga., Augusta, 1973-75; from assoc. prof. to prof. Emory U., Atlanta, 1975-87; assoc. dir. divsn. cancer prevention and control, Nat. Cancer Inst. NIH, Bethesda, Md., 1987-89; v.p., prof. edn. Am. Cancer Soc., Atlanta, 1989-94; Folk prof., assoc. dir. prevention and control Hollings Cancer Ctr., Med. U. S.C., Charleston, 1994—99; pres. Inst. Cancer Prevention, NYC, 1999—2004; rsch. prof. dept. biol. scis. Clemson U., 2008—09. Mem. sci. bd. Cancer Treatment Rsch. Found., chmn. bd. sci. counselors, 1999-2008. Author: Cancer Recovery Eating Plan, 1994; editor: Cancer Chemoprevention, 1994; editor-in-chief Preventive Medicine, 1999—2004; contbr. more than 100 articles to med. jours. Capt. USNR. Recipient several found. awards; grantee NIH, 1975—2004. Mem. Army and Navy Club, Fripp Island Golf Club. Achievements include research in cancer prevention and nutrition; chemoprevention and cancer metabolism. Office: Cancer Treatment Ctr America 14200 W Fillmore St Goodyear AZ 85338 Home: 10235 S Santa Fe Ln Goodyear AZ 85338 Personal E-mail: dnixonun@aol.com.

NIXON, PETER FRANK, medical educator; b. Sydney, Jan. 31, 1937; BSc in Medicine, U. Sydney, 1958, MBBS, 1961, MD, 1975; PhD, Australian Nat. U., 1968. Rsch. fellow Yale U. Sch. Medicine Dept. Pharmacology & Internal Medicine, 1967—69, asst. prof., 1969—70; sr. rsch. fellow Australian Nat. U., 1970—75; reader U. Queensland, 1975—2002, hon. reader, 2002—. Reviewer, numerous sci. jours. and rsch. grant bodies, 1973—2009; cons. Working Party NH & MRC, 1974—76; vis. scientist Yale U. Sch. Medicine, 1982—83, USDA Human Nutrition Rsch. Ctr. Aging Tufts U., 1993; mem. to chairperson Med. Rsch. Ethics Com. U. Queensland, 1992—2004. Eleanor Roosevelt fellowship, Am. Cancer Soc., Merck Sharp & Dohme Internat. fellowship, Merck Found., Rsch. scholarship, Commonwealth of Australia and Australian Nat. U. Fellow: Royal Australasian Coll. Physicians; mem.: Assn. UICC Fellows, Internat. Soc. Biomed. Rsch. Alcoholism, Australian Soc. Med. Rsch., Australian Soc. Biochemistry & Molecular Biology. Avocations: music, photography. Home: PO Box 4203 St Lucia South Queensland 4067 Australia Business E-Mail: p.nixon@uq.edu.au.

NIXON, ROSEMARY LOUISE, dermatologist; b. Bristol, Eng., Nov. 26, 1955; d. John Cramond and Barbara Dorothy Nixon; m. Stephen Cameron Ashton, Nov. 23, 1985; children: Louisa Clare Ashton, Katrina Ann Ashton. BS with honors, Monash U., Melbourne, Australia, 1977, B Medicine and Surgery, 1981, MPH, 1995. With Prince Henry Hosp., Melbourne, 1982—83, registrar, 1986—87, Royal Melbourne Hosp., Melbourne, 1985; dermatologist, unit head Monash Med. Ctr., Melbourne, 1991—2001; dir. Occupl. Dermatology Rsch. and Edn. Ctr., Melbourne, 2001—; mem. Internat. Contract Dermatits Record Group, 2009—; adj. clin. assoc. prof. Monash U., 2010—. Dermatologist in charge occupl. dermatology clinic Skin and Cancer Found. Victoria, Melbourne, 2001—. Scout leader Scouts Australia, Melbourne, 2003—. Fellow: Australasian Coll. Dermatologists (mem. Victorian faculty exec. 1994—, councillor 1997—2000, bd. censors 2006—). Achievements include research in occupational dermatology. Office: Occupl Dermatology 1/80 Drummond St Carlton South Victoria 3053 Australia Business E-Mail: rnixon@occderm.asn.au.

NIZZE, HORST KARL GERHARD, pathologist, educator; b. Schwerin, Germany, Apr. 14, 1942; s. Franz Ludwig Martin and Elisabeth Johanna Christa Nizze; m. Bärbel Renate Lange, Jan. 18, 1963; 1 child, Susanne. MD, U. Rostock, 1967, Habilitation, 1976. Postgrad. asst. Inst. Pathology Dist. Hosp., Schwerin, 1967-72; pathologist U. Rostock, 1973-78, reader in pathology, 1979-88, extraordinary prof. pathology, 1989-91, prof. pathology, 1992, head Inst. Pathology, 1993—2010, ednl. dean med. faculty, 1990-98. Mem. editl. bd. Der Pathologe, 1993-2010; contbg. author numerous pathology textbooks; contbr. more than 200 articles to profl. jours. Mem. Deutsche Gesellschaft für Pathologie (vice sec. 1993-99, pres. 2000-2001), Gesellschaft Deutscher Naturforscher und Ärzte, Gesellschaft für Nephrologie Goethe-Gesellschaft, Internat. Acad. Pathology. Evang. Lutheran. Avocation: literature. Office: U Rostock Inst Path Strempelstrasse 14 Pob 100888 18051 Rostock Germany Business E-Mail: horst.nizze@med.uni-rostock.de.

NJAA, BRADLEY L., pathologist; b. Edmonton, Alta., Can., Nov. 13, 1964; DVM, Western Coll. Vet. Medicine, U. Sask., 1991; MVSc, U. Sask., 1999. Anatomic vet. pathologist Purdue U., 1999—2001; asst. prof. pathology Cornell U., 2001—07; assoc. prof. pathology Okla. State U., 2007—. Mem.: Am. Assn. Vet. Lab. Diagnosticians, Am. Coll. Vet. Pathologists (exam com. mem. 2010). Avocation: bicycling. Office: 226 McElroy Hall Stillwater OK 74078 Business E-Mail: brad.njaa@okstate.edu.

NMOR, JEPHTHA CHRISTOPHER, research scientist, educator; b. Delta State, Nigeria, Dec. 28, 1976; BSc in Zoology, Delta State U., 2001, MSc in Zoology, 2006. Lectr. Delta State U., 2004—08; rschr. Nagasaki U., Japan, 2008—. Rsch. fellowship, Japanese Govt., Ministry of Edn. Mem.: Nigeria Soc. Parasitology, Internat. Soc. Infectious Diseases (corr.). Avocation: reading. Office: Nagasaki University 1-12-4 Sakamoto Nagasaki 852-8523 Japan Office Fax: 81958197812. E-mail: jcnmor@yahoo.com.

NOBACK, RICHARDSON KILBOURNE, medical educator; b. Richmond, Va., Nov. 7, 1923; s. Gustav Joseph and Hazel (Kilborn) N.; m. Nan Jean Gates, Apr. 5, 1947; children: Carl R., Robert K., Catherine E. MD, Cornell U., 1947; BA, Columbia U., 1993. Diplomate Am. Bd. Internal Medicine. Intern N.Y. Hosp., 1947-48; asst. resident Cornell Med. div. Bellevue Hosp., NYC, 1958-50, chief resident, 1950-52; instr. medicine Cornell U., NYC, 1950-53; asst. prof. medicine SUNY Upstate Med. Ctr., Syracuse, 1955-56; assoc. prof. medicine U. Ky. Med. Ctr., Lexington, 1956-64; exec. dir. Kansas City (Mo.) Gen. Hosp. and Med. Ctr., 1964-69; assoc. dean, prof. medicine U. Mo. Sch. Medicine, Columbia, 1964-69, founding dean Kansas City, 1969-78, prof. medicine, 1969-90, prof. and dean emeritus, 1990—. Cons. U. Tenn., U. Mich., U. Del., Northeastern Ohio Group, U. Mo., Eastern Va. Med. Sch., Tex. Tech. U. Author Realism, Standards, and Performances: Three Essentials in Assessment, Planning, and Action, 2005; contbr. numerous articles to profl. jours. Bd. dirs. Kansas City Gen. Hosp., Truman Med. Ctr., Wayne Miner Health Ctr., Jackson County Med. Soc., The Shepherd's Ctr., Am. Fedn. Aging Rsch., Mo. Gerontol. Inst., The Shepherd's Ctrs. of Am.; dir. Mo. Geriatric Edn. Ctr., 1985-88. With US Army, 1943—46, with USAF, 1953—55. Recipient medal of honor Avila Coll., Kansas City, 1968, merit award Met. Med. Soc., 1991, recognition award Mo. Soc. Internal Medicine, 1993. Mem. AMA, Mo. Med. Assn. (former mem. ho. of dels., v.p. 1992), Am. Geriatric Soc., Alpha Omega Alpha, Phi Kappa Phi. Avocations: photography, writing, travel. Home: 2912 Abercorn Dr Las Vegas NV 89134-7440 Personal E-mail: nanori@embarqmail.com, rkn628@hotmail.com.

NOBEL, JOEL J., biomedical researcher; b. Phila., Dec. 8, 1934; s. Bernard D. and Golda R. (Nobel) Judovich; m. Bonnie Sue Goldberg, June 19, 1960 (div.); children: Erika, Joshua; m. Loretta Schwartz, Oct. 28, 1979 (div.); 1 child, Adam; m. Qingqing Lu, Aug. 28, 2010. AB, Haverford Coll., 1956; MA, U. Pa., 1958; MD, Thomas Jefferson Med. Coll., Phila., 1963. Intern Presbyn. Hosp., Phila., 1963-64; resident in surgery Pa. Hosp., Phila., 1964-65; resident in neurosurgery U. Pa. Hosp., 1965-66; practice medicine specializing in biomed. engrng. rsch. and healthcare tech. assessment, hosp. planning and mgmt., Phila., 1968—; dir. research Emergency Care Research Inst., Plymouth Meeting, Pa., 1968-71, dir., pres., 1971—2001; bd. dirs. Consumers Union, 1976—79, 1980—2005, Conflict Interest Com., 2008—; pres. Plymouth Inst., 1979—; founder and pres. emeritus ECRI, 2001—; founder, pres. ECRI Bhd, Malaysia, 2001—; CEO The Nobel Group, 2002—, chmn. Arab Health award, 2004—; mng. dir. IMD, 2006—10. Chmn. tech. policy com., exec. bd., chmn. strategic planning com. Consumers Union; cons. in field. Publisher Health Devices, 1971-2001, Health Devices Alerts, 1977-2001; contbr. articles to profl. jours. With submarine force USN, 1966—68. Smith, Kline & French fgn. fellow, 1962; grantee HEW, 1968-72; grantee Am. Heart Assn., 1965-66 Mem. AMA, APHA, Assn. Advancement Med. Instrumentation, Critical Care Med. Soc., Pa. Med. Assn., Navy League, US Naval Inst., Brit. Officers Club Phila. Office: ECRI 5200 Butler Pike Plymouth Meeting PA 19462-1298 Home: 361 Righters Mill Rd Gladwyne PA 19035

NOBLE, ERNEST PASCAL, pharmacologist, biochemist, educator, psychiatrist; b. Baghdad, Iraq, Apr. 2, 1929; came to U.S., 1946; s. Noble Babik and Barkev Grace (Kasparian) Babikian; m. Inga Birgitta Kilstromer, May 19, 1956; children: Lorna, Katharine, Erik BS in Chemistry, U. Calif.-Berkeley, 1951; PhD in Biochemistry, Oreg. State U., 1955; MD, Case Western Res. U., 1962. Diplomate Nat. Bd. Med. Examiners. Sr. instr. biochemistry Western Res. U., Cleve., 1957-62; intern Stanford Med. Ctr., Calif., 1962-63, resident in psychiatry Calif., 1963-66, research assoc., asst. prof. Calif., 1965-69; assoc. prof. psychiatry, psychobiology and pharmacology U. Calif.-Irvine, 1969-71, prof., chief neurochemistry, 1971-76, 79-81; dir. Nat. Inst. Alcohol Abuse and Alcoholism HEW, 1976-78, assoc. adminstr. sci., alcohol, drug abuse and mental health, 1978-79; Pike prof. alcohol studies, dir. Alcohol Research Ctr. UCLA Sch. of Medicine, 1981—. Mem. various med./sci. jour. editorial bds.; contbr. numerous articles to profl. jours., chpts. to books V.p. Nat. Coun. on Alcoholism 1981-84; pres. Internat. Commn. for the Prevention of Alcoholism and Drug Dependency, 1988. Fulbright scholar, 1955-56; Guggenheim fellow, 1974-75; Sr. Fulbright scholar, 1984-85; recipient Career Devel. award NIMH, HEW, 1966-69 Fellow Am. Coll. Neuropsychopharmacology; mem. Internat. Soc. Neurochemistry, Am. Soc. Pharmacology and Exptl. Therapeutics, Research Soc. on Alcoholism. Office: UCLA 760 Westwood Plz Los Angeles CA 90095-8353

NOBOA, ABDIN I., psychologist, educator; arrived in US, 1947; s. Israel and Carmen L. Noboa; m. Migdalia Rivera de Noboa, July 28, 1985; children: Rafael, Maria; m. Patricia L. Hakes; children: Aric, Rene. BA, U. Ill., Urbana, 1969; EdM, Harvard U., Cambridge, 1970; MA, CPhil, U. Calif., Berkeley, 1974, PhD, 1981. Dep. dir. Aspira, Inc. Ill., Chgo., 1970—71; staff psychologist Boston U. Mental Health Ctr., 1971—72; rsch. assoc. Nat. Inst. Edn., Dept. Health, Edn. and Welfare, Washington, 1974—77; dir. rsch. Latino Inst., Reston, Va., 1980—85; dir. rsch., evaluation and planning New Haven Pub. Schs., 1985—87; v.p. rsch. and evaluation Quest Internat., Granville, Ohio, 1987—93; program dir. Ohio Dept. Mental Health, Columbus, 1997—99; rsch. assoc. Cosmos Corp., Bethesda, 2000—01; dir. rsch. and evaluation IQ Solutions, Inc., Rockville, Md., 2002—03; pres. Innovative Consultants Internat., Inc., Washington, 2004—. Mem. Com. Racial and Ethnic Definitions, Washington, 1975; IRB scientific review bd. Danya, Inc., Silver Spring, Md., 2006. Author: (book) Segregation Trends Among Hispanics in the Nation, 1982; editor: Language Policy in the United States, 1982. Rsch. Grant, U. Boricua, 1978, U. Tex., 1980. Independent. Avocations: violin, chess, racquetball. Office: Innovative Consultants Internat 10419 Rodney Rd Silver Spring MD 20903-1133

NÓBREGA, AGLAÊR ALVES DA, public health service officer; b. Mauriti, Ceará, Brazil, July 10, 1973; BS in Biol. Sci., Fed. U. Pernambuco, 1995; MPH in Pub. Health and Epidemiology, Fed. U. State Ceará, 2005. Supr., field epidemiology tng. program Secretariat Health Surveillance, Ministry of Health, Brasília, 2008—. Recipient Clin. Group Student Book award, Am. Soc. Tropical Medicine and Hygiene. Avocations: travel, dance. Home: SQN 411 bloco D Apt 110 Asa Nor Brasilia 70866040 Brazil Personal E-mail: aglaeran@hotmail.com.

NOBUHIRO, KITO, physical therapist, educator; b. Japan, Mar. 7, 1968; D, Hiroshima U., 2009. Assoc. prof. Hiroshima Internat. U., 2006—. Spl. adviser Kawashima Orthop. Hosp., 2006—11. Mem.: Japanese Phys. Therapy Assn. Avocation: football. Office: 555-36 Kurose-Gakuendai Higashi Hiroshima 739-2695 Japan Office Fax: 81-823-70-4542. Business E-Mail: n-kito@hs.hirokoku-u.ac.jp.

NOBUYOSHI, MASAKIYO, surgeon; Grad., Kyoto U. Head Kokura Meml. Hosp. Co-author: (publs.) Long-term clinical outcome after endovascular treatment in patients with intermittent claudication due to iliofemoral artery disease, Safety of early exercise training after elective coronary stenting in patients with stable coronary artery disease, Percutaneous balloon mitral valvuloplasty: a review. Achievements include as the best surgeon of cardiac catheterization in Japan; patents for Method of implanting a stent within a tubular organ of a living body and of removing; Catheter equipped with expansible member and production method; Catheter; Blood perfusion system and tube used therein; Blood vessel dilator. Office: Kokura Memorial Hospital 1-1 Kufuna Town Kokura Kita Kyusu Fukuoka 8028555 Japan Office Phone: 810939212231. *

NOBUYUKI, OHIKE, medical educator; b. Komoro-shi, Nagano, Japan, Dec. 17, 1969; MD, Showa U. Sch. Medicine, 1995. Assoc. prof., dept. pathology Showa U. Sch. Medicine, 1995—. Office: 1-5-8 Hatanodai Shinagawa-ku Tokyo 142-8555 Japan Office Fax: 813-3784-8249. Business E-Mail: ohike@med.showa-u.ac.jp.

NOBUYUKI, SAKAI, neurosurgeon; b. Kyoto, May 17, 1956; MD, Kansai Med. U., 1984, DSc, 1993. Chief, neurosurgery Nat. Cardiovasc. Ctr., 1998—2001; asst., neurosurgery Kyoto U., 1996—97, clin. prof., 2011; dir., neurosurgery Kobe City Med. Ctr. Gen. Hosp., 2001—. Fellow: Japanese Soc. Neuroendovascular Soc., Japan Stroke Soc., Japan Neurosurgical Soc. Office: 2-1-1 Minatojima Minamimachi Chuo-ku Kobe Hyogo 650-0046 Japan

NOCE, WALTER WILLIAM, JR., hospital administrator; b. Neptune, NJ, Sept. 27, 1945; s. Walter William and Louise Marie (Jenkins) N.; m. Susan Harris, Nov. 6, 2005; children: Krista Suzanne, David Michael. BA, LaSalle Coll., Phila., 1967; M.P.H., UCLA, 1969. Regional coordinator USPHS, Rockville, Md., 1969-71; v.p. Hollywood Presbyn. Hosp., LA, 1971-75; sr. v.p. Hollywood Presbyn. Med. ctr., 1975-77; v.p. adminstrn. Huntington Meml. Hosp, Pasadena, Calif., 1977-83; pres., CEO St. Joseph Hosp., Orange, Calif., 1983-90, Children's Hosp., LA, 1995—2006, vice chmn., 2006—; pres. so. Calif. region St. Joseph Health Sys., 1987-90, exec. v.p., 1990-94. Preceptor UCLA Health Svcs. Mgmt. Program, 1977—; chmn. bd. Health Plan of Am., 1985-91; chmn. Hosp. Coun. So. Calif., 1989. Exec. v.p. Mental Health Assn. in LA County, 1979-82; regional v.p. Calif. Mental Health Assn., 1982-83; vice chmn., bd. trustees Childresn's Hosp. LA, 2006-07. W. Glenn Ebersole finalist Assn. Western Hosp., 1969; recipient USPHS letter commendation, 1971, leadership in health affairs award Healthcare Assn. So. Calif., 1997. Mem. Am.

Coll. Hosp. Adminstrs., Am. Hosp. Assn. (ho. of dels. 1994—), Nat. Assn. Children's Hosps. (bd. dirs. 1995—), Calif. Assn. Cath. Hosps. (chmn. 1990-91), Calif. Assn. Hosps. and Health Sys. (chmn. 1992), UCLA Hosp. Adminstrn. Alumni Assn. (pres. 1979-80), Pasadena C. of C. (v.p. 1980-82). Home: 1012 Glen Oaks Blvd Pasadena CA 91105-1108 Office: Childrens Hosp LA 4650 Sunset Blvd Los Angeles CA 90027 Home Phone: 626-796-3809; Office Phone: 323-671-1779. Business E-Mail: wnoce@chla.usc.edu.

NOCERINO, GIOVANNI, pediatrician, consultant; b. Naples, Italy, Apr. 21, 1952; s. Ciro Nocerino and Maria Campana; m. Adele Tomeo, Aug. 6, 1981; children: Ciro, Rosaria, Emanuele. MD, Second U. Sch. Medicine, Naples, 1977; postgrad., 1986. Diplomate Italy, 1977. Fellowship in Infectivology, 1976—77; fellowship in pediat., 1978—83; asst. pediatrician SS. Annunziata Hosp., Naples, 1983—97, sr. asst. pediatrician, 1997—98, head Allergology, Respiratory Physiology and Respiratory Diseases Unit, 1998—; prof. Infectivology Second U. Sch. Medicine, Naples. Contbr. articles to profl. jours. Mem.: Italian Soc. Infant Respiratory Medicine, Italian Soc. Pediat. Allergy and Immunology, Italian Soc. Pediat. Office: Unit Pediat Pulmonary Medicine Hosp SS Via Egiziaca a Forcella 18 80139 Naples NA Italy Office Fax: +39-081-254-2515. E-mail: pneumologiannunziata@hotmail.it, pneumologiannunziata@libero.it.

NOCK, BRUCE, medical educator; b. Columbia, Pa., Feb. 16, 1947; s. Bennie and Doris Nock; m. Jean Nock. BS, Elizabethtown Coll., Pa., 1969; MS, Bucknell U., Lewisburg, Pa., 1975; PhD, Rutgers U., Newark, NJ, 1980. Postdoc. fellow Rutgers U., 1980—82, Rockefeller U., NYC, 1982—84, rsch. assoc., 1984—85; faculty Wash. U. Sch. Medicine, St. Louis, 1985—. Author: (book) Ten Golden Rules of Horse Training, Ride For Tomorrow: Dressage Today; contbr. articles to profl. publs. Staff sgt. USAF, 1969—73, Guam, Viet Nam. Grantee, NIH. Achievements include liberated horsemanship founder. Office: Washington University Sch Medicine 660 S Euclid Ave Saint Louis MO 63110

NOCK, MATTHEW KELLEY, psychology professor, researcher; b. 1973; BA, Boston U., 1995; MS, Yale U., 2000, M in Philosophy, 2001, PhD, 2003. Asst. prof. Dept. of Psychology Harvard U., Cambridge, Mass., 2003—07, John L. Loeb assoc. prof., 2007—10, affiliated faculty/steering com. Ctr. on Developing Child, 2009—, prof., 2010—; rsch. scientist Judge Baker Children's Ctr. Harvard Med. Sch., Boston, 2007—. Crisis intervention & intake clinician Covenant House, NYC, 1996—97; clin. rsch. asst. Payne Whitney Clinic, Cornell U. Med. Ctr., NYC, 1996—98; patient care coord. Corp. Health Systems, NYC, 1997; clinician Yale Psychological Services Clinic, New Haven, 1998—2002, Yale Child Study Ctr., New Haven, 1998—2002; psychology intern NYU Child Study Ctr. & Bellevue Hosp. Ctr., 2002—03; clin. rsch. fellow Two Brattle Ctr., Cambridge, Mass., 2003—05. Author: Understanding nonsuicidal self-injury: Origins, assessments, and treatment, 2009; co-author: Single-case experimental designs: Strategies for studying behavior change, 2009; contbr. articles to profl. jours. Named a MacArthur Fellow, John D. & Catherine T. MacArthur Found., 2011. Mem.: World Psychiatric Assn., American Assn. of Suicidology (Edwin S. Shneidman Award 2010), Assn. for Psychological Sci., Assn. for Behavioral and Cognitive Therapies, American Found. for Suicide Prevention, Internat. Soc. for Study of Self-Injury, American Psychological Assn. (David Shakow Early Career Award 2009, Disting. Sci. Award 2010). Office: Harvard University Department of Psychology William James Hall, 1220 33 Kirkland St Cambridge MA 02138 Office Phone: 617-496-4484. Office Fax: 617-493-9462. E-mail: nock@wjh.harvard.edu. *

NODA, MITSUHIKO, endocrinologist, diabetologist, medical researcher; b. Seki, Gifu, Japan, Mar. 10, 1954; s. Goichi and Shigeko (Nishida) Noda; m. Yasuko Hasemura, Nov. 3, 1986; 1 child, Shoko. BS in Electronic Engring., U. Tokyo, 1976, MSEE, 1978, MD, 1984, PhD, 2009. Bd. cert. Japanese Soc. Internal Medicine, Japan Endocrine Soc., cert. diabetologist Japan Diabetes Soc. Internist Toshiba Ctrl. Hosp., Tokyo, 1985-86, Tokyo Women's Med. Coll. Hosp., 1986-87; asst. prof. Jichi Med. Sch., Omiya, Japan, 1989—95; vis. prof. dept. pharmacology Cornell U., Ithaca, NY, 1995—97; asst. prof. dept. metabolic diseases U. Tokyo/Tokyo U. Hosp., 2000—01, assoc. prof., 2002—10; dir. dept. endocrinology & metabolism Toranomon Hosp., Tokyo, 2004—05, dir. diabetes & metabolism info. ctr., 2008—10; dir. dept. endocrinology & metabolism, dir. clin. lab. dept. Internat. Med. Ctr. Japan, Tokyo, 2005—07, dir. dept. diabetes & metabolic medicine, 2007—10; dir. dept. diabetes & metabolic medicine, dir. dept. diabetes rsch. Nat. Ctr. Global Health & Medicine, Tokyo, 2010—. Chief investigator Inst. Diabetes Care & Rsch., Asahi Life Found., Tokyo, 2001—03; vis. fellow Nat. Inst. Health & Nutrition, Tokyo, 2004—; assoc. prof. Nat. Coll. Nursing, Tokyo, 2006—10; dir. dept. strategic outcomes rsch. programs Japan Found. Internat. Med. Rsch. Cooperation, Tokyo, 2006—; assoc. prof. Yokohama City U. Sch. Medicine, Kanagawa, Japan, 2007—. Contbr. articles to profl. jours. Fellow: Japanese Soc. Internal Medicine; mem.: Am. Diabetes Assn., Japan Endocrine Soc., Japan Diabetes Soc., European Assn. Study of Diabetes. Avocations: golf, singing. Mailing: National Center Global Health & Medicine 1-21-1 Toyama Shinjuku-ku Tokyo 162-8655 Japan Address: 1-2-10-302 Yushima Shinjuku Tokyo 113-0034 Japan Office Phone: 81-3-3202-7181. Business E-Mail: noda-3im@io.ocn.ne.jp.

NODA, MITSURU, psychologist, educator; b. Osaka, Japan, Sept. 3, 1956; m. Mika Takeshima, Dec. 25, 1996. B in Lit., Waseda U., Tokyo, 1983, M in Lit., 1985. Cert. clin. psychologist Japan, 1997. Clin. psychologist Itsukaichi Pub. Health Svc. Ctr., Tokyo, 1984—92, Akikawa Pub. Health Svc. Ctr., Tokyo, 1985—93; lectr. Edogawa U. Health and Welfare Tech. Coll., Nagareyama, Chiba, 1992—, dept. head psychology, 2000—04, dean depts. psychology, mental health, health welfare, 2004—07, provost, 2007—09; head child-care, 2010—. Lectr. Rissho U., Tokyo, 1996—. Co-author: (textbook) Kukan ni ikiru, 1995, Imeji no Sekai, 2001, Kodomo to Hoiku no Shinrigaku, 2003, Jikken de manabu Hattatsu shinrigaku, 2004, Human Science, 2004, Human Development, 2007; contbr. articles to profl. jours. Mem.: APA, European Soc. Devel. Psychology, Soc. for Rsch. in Child Devel., Japanese Psychol. Assn. Avocations: outdoor activities, travel. Home: Yachiyo TY Plz A-206 Kayada 1057 Yachiyo Chiba 276-0043 Japan Office: Edogawa Univ Health and Welfare Tech Coll Komaki 474 Nagareyama Chiba 270-0198 Japan

NODA, YUTAKA, otolaryngologist, physician; b. Toyonaka, Osaka, Japan, Sept. 22, 1937; s. Masayuki and Yukiko (Yuasa) N.; m. Hiroko Tamura, Nov. 19, 1963; children: Maki, Miki. BA, Med. Faculty Keio U., Tokyo, 1962; MD, Nihon U., Tokyo, 1972. Intern Keio U. Hosp., Tokyo, 1962-63; resident Nihon U. Hosp., Tokyo, 1963-65, asst. Tokyo, 1965-68, asst. lectr. Tokyo, 1972-73; asst. Hamburg (Fed. Republic of Germany) U. Hosp., 1968-72; assoc. prof. Ryukyu U. Hosp., Naha-Shi, Okinawa, Japan, 1973-81, prof., 1981-83; prof. medicine Ryukyu U., Nishihara, 1983—2003, prof. emeritus, 2003. Dir. Med. Sci. Rsch. Found., Okinawa, chmn. bd., 2007—. Mem. Otorhinolaryngology Soc. Japan, German Soc. Throat, Nose and Ear Medicine, Soc. Head and Neck Surgery (hon.), Soc. Welfare of Hearing Impaired Okinawa (hon. pres. 2003—). Avocations: japanese archery, travel. Office: Uchima 1-2-6 Uraso-sh Okinawa 901-2103 Japan Office Phone: 098-879-3952.

NOEL, JOHN GREGORY, research scientist; b. Frankfort, Nov. 1, 1955; BS, Mich. State U., 1977; MS, Ind. U., 1980. Rsch. specialist III Shriners Hosp. Children, 1982—. Mem.: Shock Soc. Home: 3229 Burnet Ave Cincinnati OH 45229 Business E-Mail: gnoel@shrinenet.org.

NOGGLE, SCOTT ALLEN, research scientist; b. 1973; BS, MS, U. Ark.; PhD, Med. Coll. of Ga. Adjunct assoc. rsch. scientist pediatrics and molecular genetics Columbia U.; dir. NY Stem Cell Found. Lab., 2009—. Postdoc. fellow Rockefeller Univ. Named one of The 40 Under 40, Crain's NY Bus., 2011. Office: New York Stem Cell Foundation 163 Amsterdam Ave Box 309 New York NY 10023 Office Phone: 212-787-4111. E-mail: snoggle@nyscf.org. *

NOGIMORI, MASAFUMI, pharmaceutical executive; With Fujisawa Pharm. Co., Ltd.; v.p. Astellas Pharma Inc., pres., CEO, rep. dir., 2006—11, rep. dir., chmn., 2011—. Office: Astellas Pharma Inc 2-3-11 Nihonbashi-Honcho Chuo-Ku Tokyo 103-8411 Japan *

NOGUCHI, HIDEO, orthopedist, director; b. Himeji, Hyogo, Japan, Aug. 28, 1965; MD, Gunma U., 1992. Dir. Ishii Orthop. and Rehab. Clinic, 2004—. Councilor Japanese Soc. Surgery Foot, 2010. Mem.: Am. Orthop. Foot and Ankle Soc. Avocations: running, basketball. Office: 1089-1 Shimo-Oshi Gyoda Saitama 361-0037 Japan Office Fax: 81-48-555-3520. Business E-Mail: hid_166super@mac.com.

NOGUCHI, HIROFUMI, surgeon; b. Fukuyama, Japan, June 23, 1971; s. Yasufumi and Setsuko Noguchi. MD, Okayama U., Japan, 1996, PhD in Medicine and Dentistry, 2002. Diplomate Okayama, Japan, 1996. Clin. fellow grad. sch. medicine and dentistry Okayama U., 1996—2002; post doctoral fellow med. sch. Harvard U., Boston, 2002—03; clin. fellow grad. sch. medicine Kyoto U., 2003—05; assoc. dir. Diabetes Rsch. Inst. Kyoto, 2005—06, Diabetes Rsch. Inst. Japan, Toyoake, Japan, 2006—07. Vis. assoc. prof. Fujita Health U., Toyoake, Japan, 2006—07; asst. prof. Nagoya U., Japan, 2006—; lectr. in field; assoc. investigator Baylor Rsch. Inst., 2007—09, dir., 2009—. Grantee, Ministry Edn., Culture, Sports, 2005, Pub. Welfare Trust, 2006, Nagoya U., 2006. Mem.: Japanese Soc. Hepato-Biliary-Pancreatic Surgery (Pres. award 2005, 2006), Japanese Soc. Regenerative Medicine (Excellent Lectr. award 2004), Okayama Med. Soc. (Yuki award 2005), Japan Soc. Promotion of Sci. (2 grants 2005, fellowship 2005—06). Achievements include first to perform islet transplantation from non heart beating donor pancreata in Japan; perform successful Islet transplantation from living donor pancreas in worldwide. Office: Baylor Research Institute 3434 Live Oak St Dallas TX 75204 Office Phone: 214-820-9016. Office Fax: 214-820-4932. Business E-Mail: noguchih@med.nagoya-u.ac.jp, hirofumn@baylorhealth.edu.

NOGUEIRA, JOAO FLAVIO, medical association administrator; b. Fortaleza, Brazil, Aug. 30, 1978; MD, Fed. U. Ceara, 2004. Dir. Sinus Ctr. de Excelencia em Otorrinolaringologia, 2009—. Mem.: Am. Acad. Otolaryngology, Head and Neck Surgery (Pres.'s award). Avocations: computers, football. Office: Avenida Pontes Vieira 2531 Fortaleza Ceara 60130-241 Brazil Personal E-mail: joaoflavioce@hotmail.com.

NOH, JUNW WOO, medical educator, director; b. Seoul, Republic Of Korea, May 1, 1954; s. Hee Yop Noh and Dongsook Lee; m. Mi-Kyung Shin, Mar. 30, 1982; children: Ji Hee, Ka Young, Ji Young. MD, Korea U., Seoul, 1988, PhD. Cert. med. dr. Korean Med. Assn., 1979. Prof. internal medicine Coll. Medicine, Hallym U., Choon Chun, Kangwon-do, 1995—, v.p. Seoul; dir. Hallym U. Kidney Rsch. Inst., Seoul, 2003—. V.p. Kangnam Sacred Heart Hosp., Seoul, 2006—08. Contbr. articles to profl.jours. Chairperson com. ethical issues Korean Soc. Nephrology, Seoul, 2004—06. Capt. US Army, 1983—86, Korea. Mem.: Korean Soc. Nephrology (life). Christian. Achievements include research in renal fibrosis, oxLDL. Avocations: music, travel. Office: Dept Inst Med Kangnam Scred Heart H 948-1 Daelim-1-dong Youngdeungpo-ku Seoul 150-950 Republic of Korea Office Phone: 82228295108. Office Fax: 82-2-846-4669. Business E-Mail: jwn86nl@unitel.co.kr.

NOH, SEUNG-MOO, surgeon, educator; b. Daejeon, Korea, Aug. 28, 1949; s. Kyu-Ho Noh and Keyng-Im Park; m. Won-Joong Im, Nov. 4, 1980; children: Jae-Ryung, Hyung-Rae. MD, PhD, Chungnam Nat. U., Daejeon, South Korea, 1976. Prof. medicine Chungnam Nat. U., Daejeon, Republic of Korea, 1990—, dean Med. Sch., 2002—04, dean Grad. Sch., 2006—07. Dir. The Korea Cancer Assn., Daejeon, 2000—. Capt. Med. Corps Korean Army, 1981—84. Grantee, Korea Rsch. Inst. Biosci. and Biotech., 2001—. Mem.: The Korea Gastric Cancer Assn. (life; bd. dirs. 1992). Achievements include patents for abdominal wall retractors; development of Noh's operation in stomach; improvement of uncut roux limb; measurement of normal peritoneal fluid pH. Avocations: travel, reading. Home: Keyngnam Honor's Vil Apt 209-403 Yongsan-dong Yuseong-gu Daejeon 305-500 Republic of Korea Office: Chungnam Nat Univ Hosp Daesa-Dong Joong-Gu 640 301-721 Daejeon Daejeon Republic of Korea Office Phone: 82-42-280-7181. Office Fax: 82-42-257-8024. E-mail: seungnoh@cnu.ac.kr.

NOHIRA, TOMOYOSHI, obstetrician, researcher; b. Tokyo, Dec. 5, 1963; s. Tomoo and Tsuneko Nohira; m. Kaori Ando, Jan. 25, 1996; 1 child, Yuri. MD, Tokyo Med. U., 1994. Asst. dept. ob-gyn. Tokyo Med U., 1994—2000, lectr. dept. ob-gyn., 2000—, chief mgr. dept. ob-gyn., 2003—. Mem.: Japan Soc. Diabetes and Pregnancy (councilor 2000—), Japan Soc. Ob-Gyn. Naonatal Hematology (councilor 2001—). Office: Hachioji Med Ctr Tokyo Med Univ Tate-machi 1163 Hachioji Tokyo 193-0998 Japan Office Fax: +81-426-65-1796. E-mail: tnohira@mac.com.

NOIREAUD, JACQUES MICHEL RENE, physiologist; b. Bressuire, France, May 18, 1952; s. Rene and Suzanne (Raymond) N.; m. Dominique Bodin Louisot, June 21, 1973 (div. 1979); 1 child, Nadege; m. Christine Malburet, June 20, 1986; children: Sandy, Yann. BS, U. Poitiers, 1974, MD, 1977; DSc, U. Nantes, 1985. Asst. prof. U. Calgary, Canada, 1978-79; rsch. asst. U. Homburg, Germany, 1980-81; med. attache U. Nantes, 1982-84; fellow U. Edinburgh, Scotland, 1985-86; rsch. asst. INSERM, Nantes, France, 1987-91, dir. rsch., 1992—. Mem. Fedn. Cardiology, Rsch. Def. Soc., Physiol. Soc., French Pharmacology Soc. Home: 6 Rue de la Cedraie 44240 La Chapelle Erdre France Office: INSERM U694 Angers 49100 France Home Phone: 33 2 40 71 81 54; Office Phone: 33 2 40 68 85 81. Office Fax: 33 2 40 68 85 85. Business E-Mail: jacques.noireaud@inserm.fr.

NOLAN, JAMES PAUL, internist, educator, researcher; b. Buffalo, June 21, 1929; s. James Paul and Isabel (Curry) N.; m. Christa Paul, July 23, 1956; children— Lisa, James, Christopher, Thomas. BA, Yale U., 1951, MD cum laude, 1955. Diplomate Am. Bd. Internal Medicine. Instr. in medicine Yale U., New Haven, 1961-63; intern Grace-New Haven Hosp., 1955-56, resident, 1958-60, chief med. resident, 1961-62, asso. physician, 1962-63; asst. prof. medicine SUNY, Buffalo, 1963-67, asso. prof., 1967-69, prof., 1969—, vice-chmn. dept. medicine, 1973-77, acting chmn. dept., 1978-79, chmn. dept., 1979-95, disting. svc. prof., 1996—; chief of medicine Buffalo Gen. Hosp., 1969-80, attending, 1969—; asso. attending Edward J. Meyer Meml. Hosp., Buffalo, 1963-68, attending, 1968-71, cons., 1971—; cons. physician Millard Fillmore Hosp., 1981—, Deaconess Hosp., 1973—. Attending Buffalo VA Hosp., Children's Hosp. Buffalo; cons. Roswell Park Meml. Inst., 1970—; acting dir. dept. medicine Erie County Med. Center, 1978-80, dir. dept., 1980—; trustee Buffalo Gen. Hosp., 1974—; bd. dirs. Kaleid Health, ACP Found. Editl. adv. bd. Jour. Medicine Exptl. and Clin, 1971—; reviewer: Gastroenterology, 1973—; contbr. numerous articles to med. and sci. jours. Served to lt. comdr., M.C. USN, 1956-58. NIH grantee, 1979-86; Hartford Found. grantee, 1981 Mem. ACP (master, chair bd. regents 1994-95), Am. Fedn. Clin. Rsch., AAAS, Am. Gastroent. Assn. (procedures com.), Am. Assn. Study of Liver Disease, Reticuloendothelial Soc., N.Y. Acad. Sci., Am. Clin. and Climatol. Assn., Interurban Club, Ctrl. Soc. Clin. Rsch., Internat. Assn. Study of Liver, Assn. Am. Physicians, Assn. Profs. Medicine (pres. 1993-94), Phi Beta Kappa, Alpha Omega Alpha. Office: 462 Grider St Buffalo NY 14215-3021 Address: 213 Burbank Dr Snyder NY 14226-3938 E-mail: jpnolanmd@yahoo.com.

NOLAN, JANIECE SIMMONS, retired health system administrator, consultant; b. Ft. Worth; d. James Coleman and Berenice Johnson Simmons; m. Robert L. Nolan; children: Douglas, Patricia, Nancy, Margaret, Sheffield, Gemini Janiece. BA, U. Tex., 1961, MA, 1963; PhD, Tulane U., 1968; MPH, U. Calif., Berkeley, 1975. Diplomate Am. Coll. Healthcare Execs. Rsch. scientist Tex. Nuc. (Nuc. Chgo.), Austin, 1963-65; head cell biology Gulf South Rsch. Inst., New Orleans, 1968-70; postdoctoral fellow dept. physiology/anatomy U. Calif., Berkeley, 1970-72; rsch. physiologist, acting assoc. chief of staff for rsch. VA Hosp., Martinez, Calif., 1970-75; COO, v.p. adminstrn. John Muir Med. Ctr., Walnut Creek, Calif., 1977-97; pres. & CEO John Muir Physician Network, Walnut Creek, 1997—2008. Commr. State Commn. Emergency Svcs., Sacramento, 1997—2000; mem. corp. adv. bd. for grad. program in health mgmt. rsch. U. Calif., Berkeley, 2003—08; mem. industry adv. bd. Ctr. Health Mgmt. Rsch., 2004—08, health care cons., 2008—. Capt. USNR, (ret.). Woodrow Wilson fellow, 1960; named Woman of Yr., Women Health Care Execs., San Francisco, 1989, Women's Hall of Fame for leadership, Contra Costa County Commn. for Women, 2008; recipient Navy Commendation medals (3), Humanitarian Svc. medal, Armed Forces Res. medals (2), Disting. Leadership award, Grad. Program Health Mgmt., Alumni Assn., U. Calif., Berkeley, 2009. Mem.: Berkeley Writers Workshop, Southern Calif. Geneal. Soc., Internat. Berkeley Soc. Genetic Genealogy, Calif. Geneal. Soc., Naval Res. Assn. (life), U. Sect. Club, U. Calif., Rotary (Paul Harris fellow), Phi Beta Kappa (Northern Calif. Assn. bd. dirs. 2005—11, Northern Calif. Assn. pres. 2010—11). Avocations: international travel, genealogy, writing, tap dancing. Office: PO Box 1137 Lafayette CA 94549-1137 Personal E-mail: jn1137@aol.com.

NOLAN, MARILYN ANN, health facility administrator; b. Brighton, Mass., July 17, 1935; d. Anthony Henry and Anne Claire Nikiel; m. George Francis Nolan; 2 children. BA, Trinity Coll., Washington, 1957; MSS in Social Wk., Boston U., 1959. Diplomate Am. Inst. Hypnotherapy; lic. ind. clin. social worker. Med. social worker Peter Bent Brigham Hosp., Boston, 1959—60; geriatric and psychiat. social worker Modesto State Hosp., Calif., 1960—63; psychiat. social worker, geriatric med. substance abuse therapist, visual impairment svc. coord. VA Med. Ctr., Bedford, Mass., 1966—87, psychiat. social worker, substance abuse therapist, 1989—91, visual impairment svc. team coord. Long Beach, Calif., 1987—89, St. Petersburg, Fla., 1991—2004; pvt. practice guided imagery, visualization and stress mgmt. Largo, Fla., Wareham, Mass., 2004—. Chmn. disabled people's program Bay Pines VA Med. Ctr., St. Petersburg, 1991—94; field work instr. Boston Coll., 1972—86, Boston U., 1972—86. Recipient Outstanding Contbn. award, Am. Legion, 1990, Tampa Bay Fed. Equal Employment Opportunity, 1993, Blinded Vets. Assn., 2002. Mem.: NASW (bd. cert. diplomate), Nat. Guild Hypnotists (cert.), Acad. Cert. Social Workers. Roman Catholic. Avocations: reading, piano, accordion. Studio: 63 Edgewater Dr Wareham MA 02571 Home Phone: 727-399-0258; Office Phone: 508-291-0507. Personal E-mail: magenol@aol.com.

NOLAN, RICHARD THOMAS, clergyman, educator; b. Waltham, Mass., May 30, 1937; s. Thomas Michael and Elizabeth Louise (Leishman) N.; m. Robert C. Pingpank, June 4, 2009. BA, Trinity Coll., 1960; Diploma in Theol. Studies, Berkeley Div. Sch., 1960; MDiv. in Theol. Studies, Hartford Sem. Found., 1963; postgrad. in Religious Edn., Union Theol. Sem., 1963; MA in Religion, Yale U., 1967; PhD in Religion, NYU, 1973; postgrad. in Career Assessment, Ctr. Career Devel. and Ministry, 1987; postgrad. in Biomed. Ethics, Harvard U., 1991. Ordained deacon Episcopal Ch., 1963, priest, 1965; cert. in clinical pastoral edn. Conn. Valley Hosp., 1962, in death, dying and bereavement Waterbury Hosp. Health Ctr., Conn., 1977. Instr. Latin and English Watkinson Sch., Conn., 1961-62; instr. math.

Choir Sch. of Cathedral of St. John the Divine, NYC, 1962-64; instr. math. and religion, assoc. chaplain Cheshire Acad., Conn., 1965-67; instr. philosophy Hartford Sem. Found., Conn., 1967-68, asst. acad. dean, lectr. philosophy and edn., 1968-70; instr. Mattatuck C.C., Waterbury, Conn., 1969-70, asst. prof. philosophy and history, 1970-74, assoc. prof., 1974-78, prof. philosophy and social sci., 1978-92, prof. emeritus, 1992—; vicar St. Paul's Parish, Bantam, Conn., 1974-88, pastor emeritus, 1988—; pres. Litchfield Inst., Conn. and Fla., 1984-96; adj. lectr. in philosophy Palm Beach C. C., Fla., 2000—02. Ethics com. Waterbury Hosp. Health Ctr., 1984—88; vis. and adj. prof. philosophy, theology and religious studies Trinity Coll., Conn., L.I. U., U. Miami, St, Joseph Coll., Conn., Pace U., Teikyo Post U., U. Conn., Hartford Grad. Ctr., Ctrl. Conn. State U., 1964—95, Broward C.C., Fla.; lectr. philosophy and theology Barry U., Fla., 1973, 1989—92, 1997—98; adj. assoc. in continuing edn. Berkeley Div. Sch. Yale U., 1987—89; Rabbi Harry Halpern Meml. lectr., Southbury, Conn., 1987; adj. prof. philosophy Fla. Atlantic U., 1998—99; adj. prof. The Union Inst., Fla., 1999; faculty of cons. examiners Charter Oak State Coll., Conn., 1990—93; assoc. for edn. Christ Ch. Cathedral, Hartford, Conn., 1988—94, hon. canon, 1991—; cons. Dept. Def. Activity Non-Traditional Ednl. Support, Ednl. Testing Svc., Princeton, NJ, 1990; vis. scholar Coll. Preachers, Washington Nat. Cathedral, 1994; supply priest Episcopal Diocese of S.E. Fla., 1994—2002; ret. priest-in-residence St. Andrew's Ch., Lake Worth, Fla., 2002—; soc. regents Cathedral Ch. St. John the Divine, 2002—; rsch. fellow med. ethics Yale U., 1978; mem. Norton Mus. Art, West Palm Beach; guest spkr. Trinity Coll. Chapel, 2011. Author (with H. Titus and M. Smith): Living Issues in Philosophy, 7th edit., 1979, Indonesian edit., 1984, 8th edit., 1986, 9th edit., 1995; author: (with F. Kirkpatrick) Living Issues in Ethics, 1982, 2d edit., 2000, Chinese edit., 1988 (Honored Author for Books Exceeding 100,000 Copies award Wadsworth Pub. Co., 1986); editor, contbr. Diaconate Now, 1968, host Conversations With..., 1987—89; author (with Robert C. Pingpank): Soul Mates: More Than Partners (online), 2004. Notary pub., Fla. Recipient Founder's Day award, NYU, 1973; co-recipient award with Robert C. Pingpank, Cathedral St. John Divine, 2005, award Exceptional Leadership and Cmty. Svc., ACLU Palm Beach Chpt., 2008. Mem. Am. Acad. Religion, Am. Philos. Assn., Authors Guild, Hemlock Soc. Fla. (adv. bd. 1998-), Interfaith Alliance, Integrity, 1635 Soc. Boston Latin Sch. Alumni Assn., Elizabeth S. Taber Soc. Tabor Acad. Alumni Assn., ELMS Soc. Trinity Coll., Yale Legacy Partners, Harwood Soc. Cheshire Acad., Society of The Torch of NYU, Founders Soc. of the Wash. Nat. Cathedral, Planned Parenthood, Lambda Legal, Compass Lake Worth Fla., Compassion & Choices, Conn. Episcopal Clergy Assn., SAGE(NYC), Ft. Lauderdale, PFLAG, People Am. Way, ACLU, GLAAD, Planned Parenthood, Pride Ctr, Ft. Lauderdale, Friends of St. Patrick's Cathedral (Dublin), Phi Delta Kappa. Independent. Episcopalian. Home: John Knox Village 451 Heritage Dr Apt 1014 Pompano Beach FL 33060-7777 Personal E-mail: canon@rtnolan.com.

NOLAN, STANTON PEELLE, surgeon, educator; b. Washington, May 29, 1933; s. James Parker and Ellen Dubose (Peelle) N.; m. Marion Faro, June 16, 1955; children: Stanton Peelle Jr., Tiphanie Ravenel Clarke. BA, Princeton U., NJ, 1955; MD, U. Va., Charlottesville, 1959, MS, 1962. Diplomate Am. Bd. Surgery, Am. Bd. Thoracic Surgery. Intern U. Va. Med. Ctr., Charlottesville, 1959-60, asst. resident gen. surgery, 1960-61, research fellow surgery, 1961-62, sr. asst. resident gen. surgery, 1962-64, chief resident gen surgery, 1964-65, chief resident thoracic cardiovascular surgery, 1965-66; sr. rsch. assoc. Clinic of Surgery Nat. Heart Inst., NIH, Bethesda, Md., 1966-68; asst. prof. surgery U. Va. Med. Ctr., Charlottesville, 1968-70, assoc. prof. surgery, 1970-74, surgeon in charge div. thoracic cardiovascular surgery, 1970-93, prof. surgery, 1974-81, Claude A. Jessup prof. surgery, 1981-98, clin. prof. surgery, 1998—2004, prof. surgery, 2004—06, med. dir. Thoracic Cardiovascular post-operative unit, 1989-93, prof. emeritus of surgery, 2006—. Established Investigator Am. Heart Assn., 1969-74; mem. surgery A study sect. NIH, Washington, 1972-76, surgery and bioengring. study sect. 1984-87, chmn. 1985-87; cons. thoracic cardiovascular surgery VA Hosp., Salem, Va., 1968-98, Am. Bd. Surgery cons. to qualifying examination com., 1988-91; surg. cons. Bur. Crippled Children, Charlottesville, 1968-93; vis. cons. cardiothoracic surgery Aga Khan U., Karachi, Pakistan, 1995, vis cons. Vol. Health Svcs., Madras, India, 1997, cons. So. Petrochem. Industries Corp. SPIC, Chennai, India 2000; vis. prof. U. Hanover, Germany, 1990; vis. prof. Cardiac Surgerey, U. Wis. 1992; keynote spkr., assoc. surg. physician asst., 2000. Mem. editl. bd. Jour. Surg. Rsch., 1973-79, Annals of Thoracic Surgery, 1979-88; mem. sci. adv. bd. Jour. for Heart Valve Disease, 1993—2006; mem. editl. adv. bd. ECRI Operating Rm. Risk Mgmt., 1992-2006; co-editor: Comprehensive Thoracic Surgery Curriculum, TSDA, 1995; contbr. articles to profl. jours., chpts. to books. Bd. mgrs. Ctrl. Va. Health Network, 2000—05, Westminster Canterbury Blue Ridge, chmn. Residents' Assn., 2004—06, Westminster Canterbury Found. bd., 2007—, chmn. found. bd., 2010—; bd. dirs. Piedmont Liability Trust, 1989—2005, emeritus mem., 2006—, chmn. claims com., 1989—2006, chmn. bd., 1991—2004, emeritus mem., 2007—. Recipient John Horsley Meml. prize U. Va. Med. Sch., 1962, Merit award Rsch. Forum of Am. Coll. Chest Physicians, 1968, Clyde Watson Disting. Svc. award Pastoral Care and Edn., 2006, Stanton P. Nolan Professorship Thoracic and Cardiovascular Surgery, U. Va. Bd. Visitors, 2006; Rsch. fellow Va. Heart Assn., 1961-62, Am. Cancer Soc., 1963-64; grantee NIH, 1968-84, Am. Heart Assn., 1970-73, Medtronic Corp., 1975-81. Fellow ACS (com. allied health pers. 1996—2004, exec. com. 1997-2000, vice chair), Am. Coll. Cardiology, Am. Surg. Assn., Am. Assn. Thoracic Surgery; mem. Am. Heart Assn. (coun. on cardiovasc. surgery 1969-99, anesthesiology, radiology and surgery study com. 1991-94), Andrew G. Morrow Soc., Assn. Acad. Surgery, Assn. Advancement of Med. Instrumentation (chair 1998-2000, co-chmn. cardiac valve prostheses stds. com. 1974-2005, internat. stds. strategy com. com. 1989—2005, bd. dirs. 1990-2000, stds. bd. 1991—2005, edn. com. 1992-93, nominating com. 1996-2000, chair 1998-2000, exec. com. 1996-2000, govt. rels. com. 1996-2000), Internat. Stds. Orgn. (chmn. subcom. on cardiovascular surg. implants 1982-2004), Assn. Clin. Cardiac Surgeons, Halsted Soc. (exec. com. 1985-89), Coord. Com. on Perfusion Affairs (chmn. 1990-2000), Internat. Assn. Cardiac Biol. Implants (sci. com. 1994), Am. Assn. for Vascular Surgery, Muller-Jones Surg. Soc. (pres. 1979), Soc. Internat. de Cirurgie, Soc. Vascular Surgery, Soc. Thoracic Surgeons (ad hoc com. on industry rels. 1992-97, stds. and ethics com. 1993-95, 98-2001, edn. and resources com. 1996-97), Soc. Univ. Surgeons, Southeastern Surg. Congress, So. Surg. Assn. (2d v.p. 1982), Thoracic Surgery Found. Rsch. and Edn. (chair New Century Soc. com. 1997-2000), Va. Surg. Soc. (v.p. 1980-83, pres. 1984), Va. Vascular Soc. (exec. coun. 1985-86), Soc. Critical Care Medicine, Raven Soc., Assn. Am. Med. Colls. (rep. coun. acad. socs. 1992-01), Chevy Chase Club, Alpha Omega Alpha, Omicron Delta Kappa, Commn. on Accreditation Allied Health Education Programs (Award for Exceptional Svc. 2007). Home: #5204 250 Pantops Mountain Rd Charlottesville VA 22911-8702 Office: U Va TCV Surgery PO Box 800679 Charlottesville VA 22908-0679 Business E-Mail: snolan@virginia.edu.

NOLAND, THOMAS TURLEY, JR., managed healthcare company executive; b. Norwalk, Conn., July 16, 1953; s. Thomas Turley and Judy (Kwis) N.; m. Vivian Ruth Sawyer, July 17, 1982; children: Andrew Montgomery, Sidney Victoria. Student, Duke U., 1971-73; BA magna cum laude, Yale U., 1975. Staff writer Anniston Star newspaper, Anniston, Ala., 1976-79; spl. correspondent Atlanta Constitution newspaper, Paris, 1979-84; instr. English and journalism Am. Coll. in Paris, 1979-81; inst. English Centre de Perfectionnement Linguistique, Paris, 1981-84, co-dir. Am. dept., 1982-84; mgr. pub. affairs Humana Inc., Louisville, 1984-85, sr. mgr. pub. affairs, 1985-87, dir. communications, 1987-91, v.p. communications, 1991-93; pub. Health Care Industry Group, The Cobb Group, Louisville, 1993-95, Profl. Pub. Course, Stanford U., 1993; pub. Vertical Mkts. Group The Cobb Group, Louisville, 1995-97; v.p. corp. comms. Humana Inc., Louisville, 1997-99, sr. v.p. corp. comms., 1999—. Author: The Permissive Will of God, 1979, The Celestine Travesty, 1996; co-author (play) Columbia Preserved, 1983, (play) The Neglected Few, 2000; editor (book) September 11 2001: Stories from 55 Broad Street, 2002; co-editor Remembering Wendell Cherry, 2003, The Dacian Chronicles, 2006. Chmn. bd. Ky. chpt. Nat. Multiple Sclerosis Soc., Louisville, 1987-88, bd. dirs., 1985-90; bd. dirs. Ky. Shakespeare Festival, 1986-91, U.S.A. Harvest, Louisville, 1989-94; bd. dirs., Filson Club Hist. Soc., Louisville, 1991—, treas., 1994-96. v.p., 1997, pres., 1998-03; bd. dirs., Cabbage Patch Settlement House, Louisville, 1994-97, Ky. Ctr. African-Am. Heritage, 1999-2005, Yale in Ky., 2000-, Ky. Opera, 2002-05; mem. Leadership Louisville Class, 1989-90; vestry Calvary Episc. Ch., 1990-92, jr. warden, 1995, sr. warden, 1996-97, vestry St. Francis in Fields Episc. Ch., 2004-2007; bd. dirs., Louisville Orch., 2006-, chmn. bd., 2008-, Partnership for Creative Economies, 2006-08; bd. dirs., Greater Louisville Fund For Arts, 2006-. Recipient 1st place award feature writing Ala. AP Assn., 1978, Silver Anvil award Pub. Rels. Soc. Am., 1985, 2009. Mem. Health Ins. Assn. Am. (pub. rels. policy com. 1989-93), America's Health Ins. Plans (strategic Commns. com. 1997-2004), Arthur W. Page Soc., Americas Health Insurance Plans(strategic com., 2004-) Republican. Anglican. Avocations: history, travel, French language and literature, running, racquetball. Office: Humana Inc 500 W Main St Louisville KY 40202-4268 Home Phone: 502-895-9635; Office Phone: 502-580-3674. Business E-Mail: tnoland@humana.com.

NOLL, RICHARD DEAN, JR., psychologist, educator, historian; b. Detroit, Oct. 27, 1959; s. Richard Dean and Betty Ann (Adamczak) Noll. BA, U. Ariz., 1979; MA, New Sch. for Social Rsch., 1982; PhD, New Sch. for Rsch., 1992. Lic. clin. psychologist, Pa. Staff clin. psychologist Ancora Psychiat. Hosp., Hammonton, NJ, 1985-88; clin. psychologist in pvt. practice Phila., 1988-92; instr. dept. psychology West Chester U., Pa., 1992-94; postdoctoral fellow Harvard U., Cambridge, Mass., 1994-96, Lectr. in History of Sci., 1997-98; resident fellow Dibner Inst. History of Sci. and Tech. MIT, 1995-96; assoc. prof. psychology De Sales U., 2000—. Lectr. in field. Author: The Encyclopedia of Schizophrenia and the Psychotic Disorders, 1992, 3d rev. edit., 2006, Vampires, Werewolves and Demons: Twentieth Century Case Reports in the Psychiatric Literature, 1992, The Jung Cult, 1994 (Best Book in Psychology Assn. Am. Publishers 1994), The Aryan Christ, 1997, American Madness: The Rise & Fall of Dementia Praecox, 2011; contbr. articles to profl. jours. Rsch. grant Wenner-Gren Found. for Anthropol. Rsch., 1993, vis. scholar MIT, 1995-96. Office Phone: 610-282-1100 ext. 1268. Business E-Mail: richard.noll@desales.edu.

NOLLER, HARRY FRANCIS, JR., biochemist, educator; b. Oakland, Calif., June 10, 1939; s. Harry Francis and Charlotte Frances (Silva) N.; m. Betty Lucille Parnow, Nov. 25, 1964 (div. 1969); 1 child, Maria Irene; m. Sharon Ann Sussman; 1 child, Eric Francis; stepchildren: Django Sussman, Seb Sussman; m. Laura Lancaster, 2008. AB, U. Calif., Berkeley, 1960; PhD, U. Oreg., 1965. NIH postdoctoral fellow MRC Lab. of Molecular Biology, Cambridge, 1965—66, Inst. Molecular Biology, Univ. Geneva, Switzerland, 1966—68; asst. prof. biology U. Calif., Santa Cruz, 1968-73, assoc. prof., 1973-79, prof. biology, 1979—, Robert Louis Sinsheimer prof. molecular biology, 1987—. Dir. Ctr. Molecular Biology of RNA, 1992-; lectr. in field. Contbr. articles to profl. jours. Recipient Newcomb-Cleve. Prize, 2001, Rosenstiel award in Basic Biomed. Sci., 2002, Judd award, Sloan Kettering, 2003, Massry prize, 2004, Paul Ehrlich and Ludwig Darmstaedter prize, Paul Ehrlich Found., 2007, Gairdner Found. Internat. award, 2007; named Spkr. of Yr., Netherlands Soc. for Biochemistry and Molecular Biology, 2002; Sherman Fairchild Disting. Scholar, Divsn Biology, Calif. Inst. Tech., 1989—90. Fellow Am. Acad. Arts and Scis.; mem. NAS, The RNA Soc. (pres.-elect 1997, pres. 1998, Lifetime Achievement award, 2003), Russian Acad. Scis., Am. Acad. Microbiology, AAAS (Newcomb Cleveland prize, 2002). Office: U Calif Santa Cruz 225 Sinsheimer Laboratories Santa Cruz CA 95064 Office Phone: 831-459-3703. Office Fax: 831-459-3737. Business E-Mail: noller@biology.ucsc.edu. *

NOLLY, ROBERT J., pharmacist, educator, health facility administrator; married; 3 children. BS in Pharmacy, Albany Coll. Pharmacy, NY, 1970; MS in Hosp. Pharmacy, Ohio State U., Columbus, 1979. Pharmacist Park Row Drugs, Canajoharie, NY, 1970—71, asst. mgr., 1971—72; staff pharmacist Mary Imogene Bassett Hosp., Cooperstown, NY, 1972—74, 1975—77; med. svc. rep. Dista Products Co., Eli Lilly and Co., Indpls., 1974-75; resident hosp. pharmacy Grant Hosp., Columbus, Ohio, 1977-79; asst. dir. pharmacy svcs. City of Memphis Hosp., 1979-81, U. Tenn. Bowld Hosp., Memphis, 1982, dir. pharmacy svcs. and materials mgmt., 1982-85, asst. adminstr. pharmacy svcs. and materials mgmt., 1985—90, adminstr., 1991—92, adminstr. ops., 1992—98, exec. dir., 1999—2002. Asst. prof. Coll. Pharmacy U. Tenn., Memphis, 1979-92, assoc. prof. 1992-2005; prof. 2005; bd. dir. Tenn. Hosp. Assn. Solution Group, 1997-2000; trustee, Diversified Svcs., Inc., Tenn. Hosp. Assn., 1990-94, mem. pharmacy adv. com., 1990; bd. dirs. Ava Marie Nursing Home, chmn. nom. com., 1988, 89, mem. long-range planning com., 1989, 90, mem. constn. and by-laws com., 1990, mem. govtl. rels. com., 1991-93; presenter in field. Editor U. Tenn. Bowld Hosp. Pharmacy Newsletter, 1987-91; mem. editl. bd. Drug and Therapeutics Newsletter, U. Tenn. Coll. Pharmacy, 1989, 90. Mem. adv. bd. Trinity Home Care and Hospice, Memphis Managed Care Formulary, Memphis and Shelby County Pub. Libr.; mem. cmty. adv. bd. Hope Health Care. Recipient Med. Staff Disting. Svc. award, U. Tenn. Bolwd Hosp. Mem. Parenteral Drug Assn., Am. Assn. Pharmaceutical Scientists, Tenn. Soc. Health Sys. Pharmacists (mem. com. 1980, constn. and by-laws com. 1985, 88, 89, 90, chmn. nominating com. 1989, orgn. and goals com. 1991, strategic planning com. 1992, 98, 2005, pharmacy tech. task force 1988, 89, 90, chmn. tech. curriculum com. 1991, tech. edn. accreditation com. 1994, 95, Technician Edn. Com. 1991, 92, 93), Memphis Area Soc. Hosp. Pharmacists (pres.-elect 1984, pres. 1985, past pres. 1986, chmn. nominating com. 1991), Memphis Area Pharmacists Society, Tenn. Hosp. Assn. (liaison Tenn. Med. Assn. com. 1993), Kappa Psi, Rho Chi. Office Phone: 901-448-1144. Business E-Mail: rnolly@utmem.edu.

NOLPH, GEORGIA BOWER, physician; b. Appleton, Minn., Jan. 26, 1938; d. Clarence Walter and Gladys Mae (Hanson) Bower; m. Karl David Nolph, July 26, 1961; children: Erika Lynn, Kristoper Karl. BA, St. Olaf Coll., 1960; MD, Woman's Med. Coll. Pa., 1964. Pvt. practice with G.H. Ferguson MD, Bala-Cynwyd, Pa., 1965-67; civil service Walter Reed Army Med. Ctr., Washington, 1967-69; instr. community health and med. practice U. Mo., Columbia, 1969-70; asst. prof. U. Mo. Med. Sch., Columbia, 1970-77, assoc. prof. family and community medicine, 1977—. Acting med. dir. Family Med. Care Ctr., U. Mo. Hosp. and Clinics, Columbia, 1980—87; med. dir. NBA Lenoir Retirement Cmty., 1987—99, Lenoir bd. dirs., 2000—05, v.p., 2001—03, pres., 2003—05. Assoc. editor. (profl. jour.) Continuing Education for the Family Physician, 1972-73. V.p. Parents for Drug Free Youth, Columbia, Mo., 1985-86, 86-87, pres. 1987-88, 88-89; bd. dir. Columbia Civic Orch., choir-dir. Lenoir Retirement Village, 2008-, reader bd., Columbia, Mo., 2009-, Bratton-Cunningham Cir. United Meth. Woman, 2005-, pres. 2006-. Mem.: Boone County Med. Soc., Mo. State Med. Assn., Am. Bus. Women's Assn. (pres. Boone Belles chpt. 2004—06), Am. Med. Women's Assn. (state dir. 1975—2003, region VII gov. 1996—2003), Boone Belles Social Club (pres. 2006—), Am. Legion Aux. Republican. Methodist. Avocations: music, reading, travel, needlecrafts. Home: 908 Hickory Hill Dr Columbia MO 65203-2320 Office: U Mo Med Sch Dept Family and Cmty Medicine 1 Hospital Dr Columbia MO 65201-5276

NOLST TRENITE, GILBERT JAN, surgeon; b. Amsterdam, The Netherlands, Mar. 10, 1944; s. Jan G. and Alida J. Nolst Trenité; m. Bregtje F. Everts, Oct. 17, 1970; children: Sanne W., Tessa L., Gilean A. MD, U. Leiden, 1969; ENT specialist, U. Amsterdam, 1980; PhD, U. Rotterdam, 1984. Rsch. fellow clin. and exptl. cochleography U. Amsterdam, The Netherlands, 1973-76, assoc. prof., vice-chmn. ENT dept. acad. med. ctr., 1993—; resident ENT dept. U. Hosp. of Amsterdam, The Netherlands, 1976-80; head ENT dept. Bergweg Hosp., Rotterdam, The Netherlands, 1980-93; guest prof. ENT Dept., U. Pécs, Hungary, 1997—, ENT Dept., U. Ghent, Belgium, 2001—. Pres. bd. Rotterdam Cleft Palate Ctr., 1994—; dir. internat. course in rhinoplasty, 1994—. Editor: Rhinoplasty, a practical guide to functional and aesthetic surgery of the nose, 1992, 2nd enlarged edit. with interactive CD ROM, 1998; editor in chief Facial Plastic Surgery: Internat. Quar. Monographs, 2001—, Facial Aesthetic Communications in Europe, 1995; mem. editl. bd. Archives Facial Plastic Surgery, 2002—; contbr. articles to profl. jours. Mem. Rotterdam Med. Specialists Soc. (pres. 1985-88), Dutch ENT Soc. (v.p. 1988-94, pres. com. plastic and reconstructive facial surgery 1990-95, rep. for Union European Medicine Specialities 1995—, pres., co-founder 1985), Internat. Fedn. Facial Plastic Socs. (bd. dirs.), South African ENT Soc. (hon.), Hungarian ENT Soc. (hon.), Internat. Lazarus Leprosy Soc. (pres.), Internat. Fedn. Facial Plastic Surgery Soc., (exec. bd., sec. 2002—), European Acad. of Facial Plastic Surgery (pres. 1997—, pres. ednl. bd. 1992—), Am. Acad. of Facial Plastic and Reconstructive Surgery, Am. Cleft Palate Craniofacial Assn., Archives Facial Plastic Surgery (mem. internat. adv. com. 1998—, editor 2002--). Avocations: tennis, golf, fly fishing, wine hobby, poetry. Home: 84 Vijverlaan 3062 HM Rotterdam Netherlands Office: Acad Med Ctr U Amsterdam Meibergdreef 9 1105 AZ Amsterdam Netherlands Office Phone: 00 31 20 566 8586. E-mail: g.j.nolsttrente@amc.uva.nl.

NOMELINI, ROSEKEILA SIMOES, medical educator; b. Uberaba, Brazil, Oct. 13, 1977; MD, Fed. U. Triângulo Mineiro, PhD, 2000. Rschr. Oncological Rsch. Inst., 2004; adj. prof. Fed. U. Triângulo Mineiro, 2004—. Home: Palmeiras Ave 215 Uberaba Minas Gerais 38066-110 Brazil Home Fax: 5534-33185326. Personal E-mail: rosekeila@terra.com.br.

NOMIYA, TAKUMA, physician; b. Japan; MD, Tohoku U., 1998, PhD, 2003. Lic. Japan. Med. staff Tohoku U. Hosp., Sendai, Japan, 2003—04; head dept. Hiraka Gen. Hosp., Yokote, 2004—06; asst. prof. Yamagata U. Sch. Medicine, 2006—. Office: Yamagata Univ Sch Medicine 2-2-2 Iida-nishi Yamagata 990-9585 Japan Business E-Mail: t.nomiya@med.id.yamagata-u.ac.jp. E-mail: nomiya@rad.med.tohoku.ac.jp.

NOMOTO, HIROYUKI, physician, educator; b. Japan, Apr. 20, 1972; MD, Okayama U., 1997, PhD, 2003. Asst. prof. Kagawa U., 2004—. Recipient 8th Akagi Young Investigator award, Okayama U.; fellow, Japanese Ministry of Edn., Sci. and Culture. Mem.: Japanese Ophthal. Soc., Am. Acad. Ophthalmology. Office: 1750-1 Ikenobe Miki-Cho Kita-Gun Kagawa 761-0793 Japan Business E-Mail: nomoto@med.kagawa-u.ac.jp.

NOMURA, ROSELI M. Y., obstetrician, educator; b. Sao Paulo, Mar. 12, 1965; married. PhD, U. Sao Paulo, Brazil. Cert.: OAB (lawyer) 2007; ob-gyn. specialist AMB, 1990. Prof. U. Sao Paulo, 2002—. Office: University São Paulo Ave Dr Eneas Carvalho Aguiar 255 Sao Paulo 05403000 Brazil Office Fax: 551130696209.

NOMURA, SETSUZO, microbiologist, researcher; b. Sannan, Tanba, Hyogo, Japan, Feb. 11, 1934; s. Uichi and Fuyuko (Fujimoto) N.; m. Miho Haruna, Apr. 20, 1965; children: Yasushi, Tadashi. BS, Tokyo Coll. Sci., 1957; DSc, Nagoya U., Japan, 1972. Mem. staff Kitasato Inst., Tokyo, 1957-76; lectr. Sch. Hygiene Kitasato U., Tokyo, 1966-70, lectr. Sch. Pharm. Sci., 1970-74; rsch. fellow dept. chemistry Harvard U., Cambridge, Mass., 1974-75; assoc. prof. Sch. Fisheries Scis. Kitasato U., Ofunato, Japan, 1976-80, prof., 1980-99, prof. emeritus, 1999—, chief Lab. Aquatic Microbiology, 1980-99, curatory Libr. Fisheries Sci., 1990-92, head prof. dept. sea food chemistry, 1994-96. Councilor Kitasato Ednl. Instn., Tokyo, 1994-97,

1999—; internat. tech. cons. UN, 1999—; chmn. Sanriku Bd. Edn., 2000-01; vice chmn. Sanriku Adminstrv. Coun., 2002—06. Author: Ozone Annual, 1992, New techniques of ozone utilization, 1993, others; contbr. articles to profl. jours. Mem. Japanese Soc. Bacteriology, Japanese Soc. Fish Pathology, Intelligent Cosmos Rsch. Inst., Japanese Soc. Symposium on Toxins. Avocation: photography. Home: 67-5 Sugishita, Okirai Ofunato Iwate 022-0101 Japan Office: Nomura Lab Environ Microbiology 67-5 Sugishita Okirai Ofunato Iwate 022-0101 Japan

NOMURA, TETSUYA, cardiologist; b. Kyoto, Aug. 21, 1973; MD, Kyoto Prefectural U. Medicine, 1999. Chief, dept. cardiovasc. medicine Nantan Gen. Hosp., 2007—. Fellow: Japanese Assn. Cardiovasc. Intervention & Therapeutics; mem.: Japanese Soc. Internal Medicine, Japanese Circulation Soc. Office: 25 Yagi-Ueno Yagi-cho Nantan Kyoto 629-0197 Japan Office Fax: 81(0771)42-2096. Business E-Mail: t2-ya@nike.eonet.ne.jp.

NOMURA, WATARU, medical educator; b. Fukui, Japan, May 10, 1977; PhD, Kyoto U., 2005. Rsch. assoc. Scripps Rsch. Inst., 2005—07; asst. prof. Tokyo Med. & Dental U., 2007—. Mem.: Am. Chem. Soc. Office: 2-3-10 Kandasurugadai Chiyoda-ku Tokyo 1010062 Japan Office Fax: 81352808039. Business E-Mail: nomura.mr@tmd.ac.jp.

NOONAN, JACQUELINE ANNE, pediatrician, educator; b. Burlington, Vt., Oct. 28, 1928; BA (hon.), Albertus Magnus Coll., New Haven, Conn., 1950; MD, U. Vt., Burlington, 1954, DSc (hon.), 1980. Diplomate Am. Bd. Pediatrics, Am. Bd. Pediatric Cardiology. Intern N.C. Meml. Hosp., Chapel Hill, 1954-55; resident in pediatrics Children's Hosp., Cin., 1955-57; rsch. fellow Children's Med. Ctr., Boston, 1957-59; asst. prof. pediatrics State U. Iowa Sch. Medicine, 1959-61; asst. prof. pediatrics cardiology U. Ky. Coll. Medicine, Lexington, 1961-64, assoc. prof., 1964-69, prof., 1969-99, chmn. dept. pediatrics, 1974-92, emeritus prof., 1999—. Mem. embryology and human devel. study sect. NIH, 1973-78; mem. US-USSR Symposium on Congenital Heart Disease, 1975; mem. sub. bd. pediatric cardiology Am. Bd. Pediatrics, 1977-82; examiner, mem. test. com. Nat. Bd. Med. Examiners, 1984-90, exec. com., 1991-95; participant various confs. in field, vis. prof. Vanderbilt U., Nashville, 1987-; spkr. in field. Contbr. articles, revs. to med. publs.; mem. editl. bd. Am. Jour. Diseases Children, 1970-80, Am. Jour. Med. Edn., 1975-78, Pediatric Cardiology, 1978-90, Am. Heart Jour., 1994-96, Clin. Pediatrics, 1990-99. Recipient Lifetime Achievement award, Castle Connolly, 2008, Bradley Soule award, 2009. Fellow: Royal Coll. Irish Physicians (hon.); mem.: AMA, So. Soc. Pediat. Rsch. (pres. 1972), Soc. Pediat. Rsch., NIH Alumni Assn., Ky. State Med. Assn., Irish Am. Pediat. Soc. (pres. 1999—2001), Fayette County Pediat. Soc., Am. Pediat. Soc., Assn. Med. Sch. Pediatrics (dept. chmn. exec. com. 1978—81), Am. Coll. Cardiology (gov. Ky. chpt. 1989—92), Am. Acad. Pediatrics (chmn. cardiol. sect. 1972—74). Business E-Mail: jnoonan@uky.edu.

NOONAN, JOHN DANIEL, plastic surgeon; b. Bklyn., Aug. 2, 1947; s. William Jerome and Eleanor F. (Kells) Noonan; m. Barbara Shea Noonan, June 11, 1972; children: Kristen, John, Brendan, William, Kathleen. BA, Marist Coll., 1969; MD, SUNY Bklyn., 1973. Diplomate Am. Bd. Plastic Surgery, Am. Soc. Aesthetic Plastic Surgeons, Nat. Bd. Med. Examiners, Am. Bd. Surgery, Am. Bd. Plastic Surgery. Resident Albany Med. Ctr., NY, 1973—77, Ea. Va. Med. Ctr., Norfolk, 1977—80; practice medicine specializing in plastic surgery Albany, 1981—. Co.-dir. Albany Med. Burn Unit, 1980—81; cons. Albany VA Hosp., Sunnyview Rehab. Ctr., Schenectady, Regional Emergency Med. Orgn., Albany; assoc. prof. clin. surgery Albany Med. Coll., 1984—; dir. Cranio-Facial Ctr., St. Peter's Hosp. Contbr. articles to med. jours. Fellow: ACS; mem.: Operation Smile, Med. Soc. State of NY, Soc. Plastic Surgeons Upstate NY, Am. Soc. Plastic Surgeons, Albany County Med. Soc., Rotary. Office: Plastic Surgery Group Ste 200 1365 Washington Ave Albany NY 12206-1098 Office Phone: 518-438-0505.

NOONE, ROBERT BARRETT, plastic surgeon; b. Scranton, Pa., Oct. 30, 1939; s. Robert Patrick and Margaret Ann (Barrett) N.; m. Barbara Ellen Atkins, May 29, 1965; children: Robert B. Jr., Megan J., Genevieve C., Rebecca B., Theresa Ann. BS, U. Scranton, 1961; MD, U. Pa., 1965. Diplomate Am. Bd. Surgery, Am. Bd. Plastic Surgery. Rotating intern Hosp. of U. Pa., Phila., 1965-66, resident in surgery, 1966-71, resident in plastic surgery, 1971-73; asst. prof. surgery Sch. Medicine, U. Pa., Phila., 1974-83, clin. assoc. prof. surgery, 1983-89, clin. prof. surgery, 1989—; head sect. on plastic surgery Pa. Hosp., Phila., 1974-80; chief svc. plastic surgery Bryn Mawr (Pa.) Hosp., 1977—2005, chmn. dept. surgery, 1991—2001; chief svc. plastic surgery Lankenau Hosp., Phila., 1980-91; exec. dir. Am. Bd. Plastic Surgery, 1997—. Bd. dirs. Am. Bd. Plastic Surgery, Phila., 1987-94, vice chmn. 1993-94; bd. dirs. Plastic Surgery Ednl. Found., Chgo., 1981-91, pres. 1989-90. Contbr. articles to profl. jours. Bd. dirs., trustee Rosemont Sch. of the Holy Child, Pa., 1983-87, U. Scranton, 1998—2004, vice-chair, 2002-04. Capt. USAF, 1967-69. Recipient Frank J. O'Hara Disting. Alumnus award U. Scranton, 1986, Magee-Woodruff award Bryn Mawr Hosp., 2005. Fellow ACS (bd. govs. 1994-98); mem. AMA (del. plastic surgery 1986-88), Am. Soc. Plastic and Reconstructive Surgery (bd. dirs. 1989-90, 92-95, chmn. bd. trustees 1994-95), Am. Assn. Plastic Surgeons (sec. 1995-98, v.p. 1998-99, pres.-elect 1999-2000, pres. 2000-01, disting. fellow 2006), Northeastern Soc. Plastic Surgeons (pres. 1985-86), Robert H. Ivy Soc. (pres. 1982-83), Merion Cricket Club, Phila. Country Club, Eagles Mere Country Club. Republican. Roman Catholic. Avocations: golf, tennis, photography, swimming, travel, reading. Office: Plastic & Reconstructive Surg Assocs 888 Glenbrook Ave Bryn Mawr PA 19010-2506 also: Am Bd Plastic Surgery Seven Penn Ctr Ste 400 Philadelphia PA 19103-2204 Office Phone: 610-527-4833. *

NOPPENEY, THOMAS, surgeon, consultant; s. Arnold and Helene Noppeney; m. Jeanette Dix; 1 child, Samantha Sabine. Student, Friedrich-Alexander U., Erlangen, 1973—80, U. Vienna, 1979; MD, Med. U. Erlangen, 1980; PhD, Friedrich-Alexander U., Erlangen, 1982. Resident in surgery First Surg. Hosp., Nuremberg, Germany, 1982—83; chief resident in gen. surgery Surg. U. Hosp., Erlangen, 1983—85, resident dept. cardiac surgery, 1989—92; resident dept. vascular surgery Gen. Hosp. Nuremberg, 1985—89; cons. vascular surgeon dept. vascular surgery Hosp. Hallerwiese, 1993—; chief dept. vascular surgery Hosp. Martha-Maria, 2005—; pvt. practice, 1993—2003; dir. Ctr. for Vascular Diseases, 2003—. Pres. Ann. German Congress Phlebology, Nuernberg, 2003; lectr. in field; mem. sci. panel Getaesschirargie, 2004—, Phlebologie, 2005—; mem. internat. adv. bd. Endovascology Congress, Shanghai, 2003, 2003—, UIP World Congress, 2005. Author: Quality Management System for Physicians, 2003, 2006; co-author (with T. Noppeney, H. Nüllen): Primary Varicosis, 1998; mem. bd. contbg. editors Venous Digest, 2004—, internat. editl bd. Med. Sci. Monitor, 2004—, mem. editl. bd. Gefässchirurgie, 2004—; contbr. over 70 articles to profl. jours. and mags. including Vascular Surgery mag.; co-author (with H. Nuellen): Lehosand Qualistish management des antigen, 2007; editor (with H. Nucken): Lehelude Varilose-Jyajnoshh Therapie Begutaditung, 2010. Named one of Top 10 German Phebologists, Focus News Mag., 2000, Top 50 Vascular Surgeon in Germany, 2010. Fellow: Am. Coll. Angiology; mem.: Soc. for Vascular Surgery, Internat. Soc. Endovascular Specialists, Internat. Soc. Vascular Surgery, European Soc. Vascular Surgery, Am. Venous Forum, German Soc. Gen. Surgery, German and Internat. Soc. Angiology, German Soc. Phlebology (bd. dirs. 2001—), Internat. Soc. Cardio-Vascular Surgery, German Soc. Vascular Surgery (bd. dirs. 1998—2008). Avocations: golf, skiing. Office: Dres Noppeney & Assoc Obere Turnstrasse 8-10 Nuremberg Germany Home Phone: ++49 9131 56017; Office Phone: ++49 911 2706130.

NORA, AUDREY HART, physician; b. Picayune, Miss., Dec. 5, 1936; d. Allen Joshua and Vera Lee (Ballard) H.; m. James Jackson Nora, Apr. 9, 1966; children: James Jackson Jr., Elizabeth Hart. BS, U. Miss., 1958, MD, 1961; MPH, U. Calif., 1978. Diplomate Am. Bd. Pediat., Am. Bd. Hematology and Oncology. Resident in pediat. U. Wis. Hosp., Madison, 1961-64; fellow in hematology/oncology Baylor U., Tex. Childrens Hosp., Houston, 1964-66, asst. prof. pediat., 1966-70; assoc. clin. prof. pediat. U. Colo. Sch. Medicine, Denver, 1970—; dir. genetics Denver Childrens Hosp., 1970-78; commd. med. officer USPHS, 1978, advanced through grades to asst. surgeon gen., 1983, cons. maternal and child health Denver, 1978-83, asst. surgeon gen. regional health adminstr., 1983-92, dir. maternal & child health bur., health resources and svc. adminstrn., 1992-99. Mem. adv. com. NIH, Bethesda, 1975-77; mem. adv. bd. Metronet Health, Inc., Denver, 1986-92; mem. adv. bd. Colo. Assn. Commerce and Industry, Denver, 1985-92, WIC Adu Bd. USDA, 1989-99; mem. adv. coun. NICHD, 1992 99; bd. mem. RMC for Health Promotion and Edn., pres., 2004-05. Author: (with J.J. Nora) Genetics and Counseling in Cardiovascular Diseases, 1978, (with others) Blakiston's Medical Dictionary, 1980, Birth Defects Encyclopedia, 1990, (with J.J. Nora and K. Berg) Cardiovascular Diseases: Genetics, Epidemiology and Prevention, 1991; contbr. articles to profl. jours. Recipient Virginia Apgar award Nat. Found., 1976. Fellow Am. Acad. Pediat.; mem. Am. Pub. Health Assn. (governing coun. 1990-92, coun. mem. maternal and child health 1990-93), Commd. Officers Assn., Am. Soc. Human Genetics, Teratology Soc., Western Soc. Pediatric Rsch. Presbyterian. Avocations: cooking, hiking, quilting. Office: 1973 S Kenton Ct Aurora CO 80014-4709

NORA, JAMES JACKSON, physician, writer, educator; b. Chgo., June 26, 1928; s. Joseph James and Mae Henrietta (Jackson) N.; m. Barbara June Fluhrer, Sept. 7, 1949 (div. 1963); children: Wendy Alison, Penelope Welbon, Marianne Leslie; m. Audrey Faye Hart, Apr. 9, 1966; children: James Jackson Jr., Elizabeth Hart Nora. AB, Harvard U., 1950; MD, Yale U., 1954; MPH, U. Calif., Berkeley, 1978. Diplomate Am. Bd. Pediat., Am. Bd. Cardiology, Am. Bd. Med. Genetics. Intern Detroit Receiving Hosp., 1954-55; resident in pediat. U. Wis. Hosps., Madison, 1959-61, fellow in cardiology, 1962-64; fellow in genetics McGill U. Children's Hosp., Montreal, Canada, 1964-65; assoc. prof. pediat. Baylor Coll. Medicine, Houston, 1965-71; prof. genetics, preventive medicine and pediat. U. Colo. Med. Sch., Denver, 1971—, prof. emeritus, 1986. Dir. pediatric cardiology and cardiovasc. tng. U. Colo. Sch. Medicine, 1971-78; mem. task force Nat. Heart and Lung Program, Bethesda, Md., 1973; cons. WHO, Geneva, 1983—; mem. U.S.-U.S.S.R. Exch. Program on Heart Disease, Moscow and Leningrad, 1975. Author: The Whole Heart Book, 1980, 2d rev. edit., 1989; author: (with F.C. Fraser) Medical Genetics, 4th Rev. edit., 1994; author: Genetics of Man, 2d rev. edit., 1986, Cardiovascular Diseases: Genetics, Epidemiology and Prevention, 1991, The Upstart Spring, 1989, The Psi Delegation, 1989, The Hemingway Sabbatical, 1996, Songs from a Brazen Bull, 2001, Panacea, 2002, What Every Senior Needs to Know About Health Care, 2004, Half-Open Windows, 2005, Progress Notes, 2005, The 9/11 Dialogues, 2006, Rules of the Game, 2008, Climate, 2008, War Crimes, 2009, By a Truthful Storyteller, 2009, Homeless, 2010, Later, 2011. 2nd lt. USAAC, 1945—47. Grantee Nat. Heart, Lung and Blood Inst., Nat. Inst. Child Health and Human Devel., Am. Heart Assn., NIH; recipient Virginia Apgar Meml. award. Fellow: Am. Coll. Med. Genetics, Am. Coll. Cardiology; mem.: Poets and Writers, Acad. Am. Poets, Mystery Writers Am., Authors League Am., Authors Guild. Democrat. Presbyterian. Avocations: writing fiction, poetry.

NORA, LOIS MARGARET, dean, academic administrator, neurologist, educator; BS in Biology with honors, U. Ill., 1976; MD, Rush Med. Coll., Chgo., 1979; JD, U. Chgo., 1987; MBA, U. Ky., 2002. Fellow Am. Bd. Neurology, Am. Bd. Electrodiagnostic Medicine; bar: Ill. 1988, D.C. 1988. Intern in family medicine Cmty. Meml. Gen. Hosp., LaGrange, Ill., 1980; resident in neurology Rush-Presbyn.-St. Luke's Med. Ctr., Chgo., 1981-84, chief resident in neurology, 1983-84, fellow electromyography and neuromuscular disease, 1984-85; asst. prof. dept. neurology, asst. dean clin. curriculum Rush Med. Coll., Chgo., 1987-94, assoc. prof. dept. neurology, 1994-95; fellow Ctr. for Clin. Med. Ethics U. Chgo., 1993-95; assoc. dean acad. affairs, assoc. prof. dept. neurology U. Ky. Coll. Medicine, 1995—2002; prof. neurology U. Ky. Coll. Law, 1996—2002; pres., dean Northeastern Ohio Univ. Coll. of Med., 2002—10, prof. internal medicine and behavioral and cmty. health sciences, 2002—10; pres. & dean emeritus Northeastern Ohio Med. Univ., 2010; interim pres. & dean The Commonwealth Med. Coll., Scranton, Pa., 2011—. Spkr. in field. Contbr. articles to profl. jours., chpts. to books. Vice chair Epilepsy Found. of Greater Chgo., 1988-90, chair, 1991, chair strategic planning com. 1990-91, bd. dirs., 1987-94; bd. dirs. Epilepsy Found. of Am., 1992-95, co-chair quality standards com. 1992-94; mem. needs assessment com. United Way of Chgo., 1989-90; camp physician children's summer camp program Muscular Dystrophy Assn., 1984-86; vol. tchr. Christ the King Elem. Sch., 1996—2002. Mem. AMA (mem. dean's com. on family violence curriculum 1993, mem. report and resolutions subcom. for reference com. C 1997), Am. Acad. Neurology (mem. ethics com. 1997—2002), Am. Assn. Electrodiagnostic Medicine (chair profl. practice com. 1991—97, sec., treas., 1999-2002, pres.-elect, 2002-03, pres. 2003-04), Soc. Clin. Neurologists. Office: The Commonwealth Med Coll Office of Dean 525 Pine St Scranton PA 18509 *

NORBECK, JANE S., retired nursing educator; b. Redfield, SD, Feb. 20, 1942; d. Sterling M. and Helen L. (Williamson) N.; m. Paul J. Gorman, June 28, 1970. BA in Psychology, U. Minn., 1965, BSN, 1965; MS, U. Calif., San Francisco, 1971, DSN, 1975. Psychiat. nurse Colo. Psychiat. Hosp., Denver, 1965-66, Langley Porter Hosp., San Francisco, 1966-67; pub. health nurse San Francisco Health Dept., 1968-69; prof. U. Calif. Sch. of Nursing, San Francisco, 1975—2003, dean, 1989-99, dept. chair, 1984-89, prof. and dean emeritus, 2003. Chair study sect. Nat. Inst. of Nursing Rsch., 1990-93, mem. editl. bd. Archives of Psychiat. Nursing, 1985-95, Rsch. in Nursing and Health, 1987-2003. Co-editor: Annual Review of Nursing Research, 1996-97; contbr. articles to profl. jours. Mem. ANA, Am. Acad. Nursing, Inst. of Medicine, Sigma Theta Tau.

NORDEN, ANTHONY G.W., pathologist, consultant; b. London, Jan. 6, 1951; s. William and Sasha Alexandra Norden; m. Lorraine Ella Gardener, May 14, 1994. BSc with 1st class honors, U. Coll., London, 1971, MBBS, 1979; PhD, U. Calif., San Diego, 1974. Sr. registrar U. Coll. Hosp., London, 1980—88; cons. chem. pathologist Chase Farm Hosp., Enfield, Middlesex, England, 1988—2000, Cambridge U. Hosps., Cambridgeshire, England, 2000—10. Sci. adv. bd. Lowe Syndrome Trust, London, 2004—10. Fellow: Royal Coll. Pathologists. Achievements include research in renal tubular disease. Office Fax: 01223 216862. Business E-Mail: agwnorden@aol.com.

NORDENSTAM, GUNNAR ROLAND, physician; b. Stockholm, Oct. 17, 1938; s. Bengt Torgny and Greta Hulda Sofia (Lundh) N.; m. Natalia Korzhinskaya (div.); m. Elisabet Litsmark, Apr. 9, 1985; children: Maria, Olof, Jakob. MD, Med. Faculty U. Göteborg, Sweden, 1976, PhD, 1989. Med. diplomate in geriat., clin. immunology. Tchr. dept. polit. sci. U. Göteborg, 1963-68; physician Göteborg, 1976-77, Bissau, 1978, Vasa Hosp., Göteborg, 1979-88, Primary Care Bd., 1989-92; pvt. practice Profytema AB, Lerum, Sweden, 1993—. Chmn. Future Party Sustainable Devel., 2010—. Avocations: gardening, music, poetry. Office: Profytema Ltd Bråta Gärdesväg 14 S-44351 Lerum Sweden Home: Sanatoriegatan 62 Göteborg S-41657 Sweden Office Phone: 0046 302 12243. Business E-Mail: gunnarnordenstam@telia.com.

NORDENSTRÖM, ERIK, surgeon, educator; b. Kristianstad, July 28, 1973; MD, Lund U., 1999, PhD, 2003. Cons. surgeon, assoc. prof. Lund U. Hosp., 2010—. Sec. South Swedish Network Diseases Thyroid, Parathyroid, Adrenals and Neuroendocrine Tumours, 2009; chmn. Working Group, Guidelines Neuroendocrine Tumours Southern Sweden, 2009—; med. advisor, South Sweden, 2009—. Recipient Honor award, Lund U. Mem.: Swedish Assn. Endocrine Surgeons (exec. coun. 2009), Swedish Med. Assn., Swedish Surg. Soc. Avocation: walking. Office: Lund University Hosp Lund Skåne 221 85 Sweden Business E-Mail: erik.nordenstrom@skane.se.

NORDGREN, MATS OLAV, otolaryngologist, surgeon, consultant; b. Malmö, Sweden, May 9, 1959; s. Kurt Edvin and Berit Kolvereid Nordgren; m. Margareta Anna Pettersson, Dec. 3, 1999; children: Harald, Egil. MD, Lund U., Sweden, 1989, PhD, 2005. Diplomate bd. cert. otorhinolaryngology and phoniatrics Swedish Bd., 1997. Resident Thoracic Surgery, Lund, Sweden, 1990—91, Urologic Surgery, Lund, Sweden, 1991—92, Gen. Practice, Malmö, Sweden, 1992—93, ENT-Surgery, Malmö, Sweden, 1994—2010; cons. Phoniatrics, ENT Surgery, Malmö, Sweden, 1997—2010, pvt. practice Helsingborg, Sweden, 2010—. Panel mem. quality of life in head and neck cancer Internat. Fedn. of Otorhinolaryngol Soc., Rome, 2005. Named one of Outstanding Intellectuals of 21st Century, Internat. Biog. Ctr., Cambridge, Eng., 2008. Fellow: Swedish Assn. Otorhinolaryngology, Swedish Coll. Surgeons; mem.: European Laryngological Soc., Am. Head and Neck Soc. (corr.), Am. Acad. Otolaryngology Head and Neck Surgery. Democrat. Avocations: golf, interior decorating, skiing, travel, violin. Home: Ehrensvardsgatan 15A 212 13 Malmö Sweden

NORDLI, DOUGLAS R., neurologist; m. Jo-Anne Tierney. BA, Haverford Coll., Pa.; MD, Columbia U. Coll. Physicians and Surgeons, NYC, 1984. Cert. in pediat. Am. bd. Pediactrics, 1990, in neurology with spl. qualifications in child neurology Am. bd. Neurology Psychiatry, 1990, in neurology with spl. qualifications in clin. neurophysiology Am. bd. Clinical Neurophysiology, 1997. Residency in pediat. Columbia-Presbyn. Med. Ctr., 1986, residency in child neurology, 1988, fellowship in clin. neurophysiology and epilepsy, 1990; asst. prof. child neurology Columbia U., NYC, 1994—99; Lorna S. and James P. Langdon chmn. pediat. epilepsy, dir., attending physician neurology, epilepsy ctr. Children's Meml. Hosp., Chgo., 1999—; assoc. prof. neurology and pediat. Northwestern U. Feinberg Sch. Medicine, Ill.; fellowship program dir. epilepsy Northwestern U. McGaw Med. Ctr., Ill. Asst. bd. examiner Am. Bd. Clin. Neurophysiology; profl. adv. bd. Epilepsy Found., Greater Chgo., Epilepsy Services Northeastern Ill. Editor: Pediatric Neurology; contbr. articles to profl. jours., chapters to books. Mem.: Child Neurology Soc., Am. Epilepsy Soc., Am. Acad. Neurology, Alpha Omega Alpha. Office: Childrens Meml Hosp 2300 Childrens Plz Chicago IL 60614

NORFLEET, LEONTINE SANDRA, retired biologist; d. James Edward and Dorothy Calloway Norfleet. BS, CUNY, NYC, 1957; MA in Biol. and Physiol. Scis., Hunter Coll., NYC, 1964; MBA in Human Resources Mgmt., Adelphi U., Garden City, NY, 1994. Clin. microbiologist Bklyn. Jewish Hosp., 1957—63; asst. bacteriologist Byrd S. Coler Hosp., Roosevelt Island, NY, 1963—64; med. rschr. LI Jewish Hosp., Ney Hyde Pk., NY, 1964—67; biochemistry assoc. Endo Labs./Dupont-Merck/Bristol Meyers Squibb, Garden City, 1967—2004, quality assurance specialist, scientist, auditor, quality engr. Author: (poem) Speaking for Myself (Editor's Choice award, 2008), A Friend, 2010. Vol. NYC Ballet, 2004—; vol. math tutor, HS Learning Leaders program, NYC, 2007. Mem.: Internat. Soc. Poets, Met. Opera Guild, Am. Ballet Theater Guild, NYC Ballet Guild. Democrat. Roman Catholic. Avocations: exercise, ballet, reading, movies. Home: 111-39 201 St Saint Albans NY 11412

NØRGAARD, JENS PETER, research and development company executive, consultant; b. Holstebro, Denmark, Aug. 6, 1952; s. Axel and Inga Nørgaard; m. Dagny Ørts Nørgaard; children: Christian Fibiger, Anders Fibiger. MD, Aarhus U., Denmark, DMSc, 1981. Cert. urologist, pediatric surgeon Danish And Swedish Health Authorities, 1995. Sr. registrar urology dept. U. Aarhus, 1981—95; vis. prof. U.

Mich. dept. urology and pediatric urology, Ann Arbor, 1992—92; cons. U. Copenhagen dept. Pediatric Surgery, Denmark, 1994—97; cheif sci. officer Ferring Pharma. A7S, Copenhagen, 1997—. Prof. Dept. Urology, Lund, Sweden, 2004—. Achievements include discovery of nighttime voiding dysfunctions most often can be explained by a lack of hormone production and regulation of urine productionation and important mechanisms in bedwetting and nocturia. Office: Ferring Pharmaceuticals A/S Kay Fiskers Plads 11 2300 Copenhagen Denmark Business E-Mail: jenspeter.norgaard@ferring.com.

NORI, KATHERINE E., physician; b. Mich., Aug. 21, 1971; MD, WSU, 1997. Physician William Beaumont Hosp., 2002—. Office: 4949 Coolidge Hwy Royal Oak MI 48073 Business E-Mail: knori@beaumont.edu.

NORINS, ARTHUR LEONARD, dermatologist, educator; b. Chgo., Dec. 2, 1928; s. Russell Joseph and Elsie (Lindemann) N.; m. Mona Lisa Wetzer, Sept. 12, 1954; children: Catherine, Nan, Jane, Arthur. BS in Chem. Engring, Northwestern U., 1951, MS in Physiology, 1953, MD, 1955. Diplomate: Am. Bd. Dermatology; subcert. in dermatopathology. Intern U. Mich., Ann Arbor, 1955-56; resident in dermatology Northwestern U., Chgo., 1956-59; asst. prof. Stanford U., 1961-64; prof., chmn. dept. dermatology, prof. pathology Ind. U. Sch. Medicine, Indpls., 1964-93, prof. emeritus, 1993—. Mem. staff Riley Children's Hosp., Univ. Hosp., Wishard Hosp.; cons. VA Hosp. Contbr. articles to profl. jours. Capt. M.C. U.S. Army, 1959-61. Recipient Pres.' award Ind. U., 1979 Fellow ACP; mem. Am. Acad. Dermatology (bd. dirs.), Am. Dermatol. Assn., Soc. Pediatric Dermatology (founder, past pres.), Am. Soc. Dermatopathology, Am. Soc. Photobiology (founder), Soc. Investigative Dermatology, Am. Acad. Dermatology (hon.), 2008 Home: 10100 Torre Ave Apt 211 Cupertino CA 95014-2168 Office: 550 University Blvd Ste 3240 Indianapolis IN 46202-5149 Personal E-mail: norinssr@sbcglobal.net.

NORKIN, CYNTHIA CLAIR, retired physical therapist; b. Boston, May 6, 1932; d. Miles Nelson and Carolyn (Green) Clair; m. Stanislav A Norkin, Feb. 19, 1955 (dec. 1970); 1 child, Alexandra. BS in Edn., Tufts U., 1954; cert. phys. therapist, Bouve Boston Coll., 1954; MS, Boston U., 1973, EdD, 1984. Instr. Bouve Boston Coll., 1954—55; staff phys. therapist New Eng. Med. Ctr., Boston, 1954—55, Abington (Pa.) Meml. Hosp., 1965—70, Ea. Montgomery Country Vis. Nurse Assn., 1970—72; asst. prof. phys. therapy Sargent Coll./Boston U., 1973—84; assoc. prof. phys. therapy, dir., founder Ohio U. Sch. Phys. Therapy, Athens, 1984—95, ret., 1995. Consult Boston Ctr Independent Living, Cambridge Vis Nurse Asn, Mass Medicaid Cost Effectiveness Project, 1978; secy Health Planning Coun Greater Boston, 1976—78; book, manuscript reviewer F A Davis Co, 1986—; arthritis adv comt Ohio Dept Health. Author (with P Levangie and C Norkin): Joint Structure and Function: A Comprehensive Analysis, 1983, 4th edit., 2005, 5th edit., 2011; author: (with D J White) Joint Measurement: A Guide to Goniometry, 1985; author: 4th edit., 2009. Trustee Brimmer and May Sch, 1980. Mem.: APHA, AAAS, Athens County Vis Nurse Asn (secy adv coun 1984—95), Mass Asn Mental health, Mass Physical Therapy Asn (chair quality assurance comt 1980—83), Am Physical Therapy Asn (on site evaluator comn on accreditation 1986—95). Episcopalian.

NORMAN, LISA, healthcare educator; b. Glasgow, Ky., Feb. 13, 1964; PhD, Emory U., 2000; PhD student, Walden U. Assoc. prof. Ponce Sch. Medicine and Health Scis., 2005—. Bd. mem. Caribbean Drug Abuse Rsch. Inst., 2007, Internat. Hard Reduction Assn., 2011; chair, academic group Internat. Network People Who Use Drugs, 2010. Grant, NIH, 2009—. Mem.: NIH/OAR Initiative, Behavioral and Social Scis. Group, Nat. Hispanic Med. Assn., Trans-Caribbean HIV/AIDS Rsch. Initiative, Am. Sociol. Assn., Internat. AIDS Soc. Avocations: reading, ceramics, movies. Home: Estancias Del Golf Club #532 Calle Luis Ponce PR 00730 Office Phone: 787-840-2575. Business E-Mail: lnorman@psm.edu.

NORMAN, MARK H, chemist, director; b. Kittery Maine, Jan. 12, 1960; BS in Chemistry, U. New Hampsire, 1982; PhD in Organic Chemistry, U. Calif., Berkeley, 1987. Rsch. scientist Burroughs Wellcome Co., 1987—95; sr. rsch. investigator Glaxo Wellcome, Inc, 1995—96; rsch. scientist to assoc. dir. rsch. Amgen, Inc., 1996—2006, dir. rsch., 2006—11, sci. exec. dir., 2011—. Assoc. editor Jour. Pharmacognosy, 2011; editl. adv. bd. mem. Pharm., Medicinal Chemistry Reviews, Medicinal Chemistry-Online, Current Topics Medicinal Chemistry, 2000—06. Recipient Bruce H. Mahan Meml. Tchg. award, U. Calif., Berkeley, Sophomore award, U. NH, Valedictorian award, Sanborn Regional HS, Kingston NH, Bailey prize, Richard M. Ford Meml. award, Bioorg. Med. Chem. Lett. award, 2004—07; Heman C. Fogg fellowship. Mem.: Am. Chem. Soc., Phi Kappa Phi Honor Soc., Phi Beta Kappa Honor Soc., Phi Lambda Upsilon Honor Soc., Sigma Xi Sci. Rsch. Soc. Office: One Amgen Ctr Dr MS B29 M 2 Thousand Oaks CA 91320 Business E-Mail: markn@amgen.com.

NORMAN, MIKAEL, medical educator, director; b. Stockholm, Sept. 5, 1957; MD, Karolinska Inst., Stockholm, 1982. Med. dir. Karolinska U. Hosp., Stockholm, 2004—; prof. Karolinska Inst., 2008—. Office: Neonatal Intensive Care Unit K78 Karolinska Inst & University Hosp Stockholm S-14186 Sweden Office Phone: 46-736 204 596.

NORMAN, PHILIP SIDNEY, physician; b. Pittsburg, Kans., Aug. 4, 1924; s. P. Sidney and Mildred A. (Lawyer) Norman; m. Marion Birmingham, Apr. 15, 1955 (dec.); children: Margaret Reynolds, Meredith Andrew, Helen Elizabeth. AB, Kans. State Coll., 1947; MD cum laude, Washington U., St. Louis, 1951. Intern Barnes Hosp., St. Louis, 1951-52; resident Vanderbilt U. Hosp., Nashville, 1952-54; fellow Rockefeller Inst., 1954-56; instr. medicine Johns Hopkins U. Sch. Medicine, Balt., 1956-59, asst. prof., 1959-64, assoc. prof., 1964-75, prof., 1975—, chief allergy and immunology div., 1971-91. Editor Jour. of Allergy and Clin. Immunology, 1993-98; contbr. chpt. to books, articles to profl. jours. Served with USAAF, 1943-46; Served with USPHS, 1954-56. Fellow Am. Acad. Allergy (pres. 1975); mem. Am. Fedn. Clin. Research, Am. Assn. Immunologists, Am. Soc. Clin. Investigation, Am. Assn. Physicians, N.Y. Acad. Scis., Soc. Exptl. Biology and Medicine, Am. Thoracic Soc., Am. Clin. and Climatol. Assn., Johns Hopkins Med. Soc., Alpha Omega Alpha. Episcopalian. Office: Johns Hopkins U Asthma and Allergy Ctr 5501 Hopkins Bayview Cir Baltimore MD 21224-6821 Office Phone: 410-550-2300. Business E-Mail: pnorman@jhmi.edu.

NORMAN, REID LYNN, physiology educator, researcher; b. Scott City, Kans., Feb. 26, 1944; s. Everett Eugene and Edith Rose (Brooks) Norman; children: Lara Anne, Douglas Everett. BS, Kans. State U., 1966, MS, 1969; PhD, U. Kans., 1971. Asst. scientist to scientist Oreg. Primate Ctr., Beaverton, 1972—83; asst. prof. to prof. anatomy Oreg. Health Scis. U., Portland, 1973—83; prof., assoc. chmn. cell biology & anatomy Health Sci. Ctr. Tex. Tech U., Lubbock, 1983—99, chair pharmacology & neurosci., 1999—; cons. Wis. Regional Primate Ctr., Madison, 1983. Editor: Neuroendocrine Aspects of Reproduction, 1983, The Active Female: Health Issues Throughout the Life Span, 2008; contbr. articles articles to profl. jours. Postdoc. fellow, Nat. Inst. Gen. Med. Scis., 1971—72, grantee, Nat. Inst. Child Health & Human Devel., 1974—. Mem.: AAAS, Soc. Study Reprodn., Am. Physiol. Soc., Soc. Neurosci., Endocrine Soc., Am. Assn. Anatomists (REB study sect. 1990—94). Democrat. Mem. Christian Ch. (Disciples Of Christ). Office: Tex Tech U Health Sci Ctr Dept Pharmacology and Neurosci Lubbock TX 79430-0001 Office Phone: 806-743-2425. Business E-Mail: reid.norman@ttuhsc.edu.

NORMAN, ROBERT JOHN, obstetrics and gynecology educator; b. Woking, U.K., June 19, 1949; arrived in Australia, 1988; s. John P. and Mary N.; m. Susan Gay Tracey, June 24, 1972; children: Michael, David, Rachel. BSc with honors, U. Birmingham, Eng., 1972, MB ChB with honors, 1974. Intern Harare Hosp., Zimbabwe, 1974, resident Rhodesia, 1978-79, 1975-79, U. Natal, South Africa, 1979-83, sr. lectr., 1983-86, assoc. prof., 1986-88; sr. lectr., assoc. prof. U. Adelaide, Australia, 1988-98, prof. ob-gyn., 1998—2009, dir., Robinson Inst., 2009—. Dir. Reproductive Endocrine Labs., 1988—2009, Repromed, Adelaide, 1993—. dir. Robinson Inst., U. Adelaide; specialist reproductive medicine Fertility SA. Contbr. articles to profl. publs. Parish councillor Trinity Ch., Adelaide, 1994. ICI clin. scholar, South Africa, 1984. Mem. Austrailian Soc. Reproductive Biology, Australian Menopause Soc. (sec. 1995-99). Mem. Anglican Ch. Avocations: sports, religion, current affairs, cooking, fishing. Home: 39 Brookside Ave Tranmere 5073 Australia Office: U Adelaide Adelaide 5005 Australia Home Phone: 61883329116; Office Phone: 61883038166. Business E-Mail: robert.norman@adelaide.edu.au.

NORMAN, THENA MONTS DURHAM, microbiologist, researcher, health facility administrator; b. Bradenton, Fla., July 10, 1945; d. Turner and Silverrene (Taylor) M.; m. Millard Durham, Aug. 30, 1969 (div. 2001); children: Bryce Vincent-Barnard, Brittanie Yvonne; m. Herman H. Norman, August 6, 2005. BS, Fisk U., 1966; MS, Purdue U., 1968. Rsch. microbiologist Ctrs. for Disease Control, Atlanta, 1968-86, assoc. dir. for programs Nat. Ctr. for Prevention Svcs., 1988-95; program analyst Office Dir. Ctr. for Health Promotion and Edn., 1986-88; dir. exec. secretariat Ctrs. for Dis. Control and Prevention, Atlanta, 1995—2001; dep. dir. for policy Nat. Ctr. for HIV, STD, and TB Prevention for CDC, Atlanta, 2001—05; ret., 2005. Cons. FDA; mem. alumnae adv. com., pres. coun. dept. biol. scis. Purdue U.; bd. dirs. Balm in Gilead, Inc. Contbr. articles to profl. jours. Mem. NAACP, Neighborhood Planning Unit, SCLC/Women Adv. Coun., So. Christian Leadership Council/Women, Atlanta, 2005; bd. dirs. Cmty. Advanced Practices Nurses, Atlanta, 2004, Three Star Fitness Inc. Recipient Sec.'s award for Disting. Svc. Dept. HHS, 2001. Mem. AAAS, Sci. Rsch. Soc., Am. Soc. Microbiologists, CDC Assn. Exec. Women (founder, co-chmn.), Women in Sci. and Engring., Alumni Adv. Com., Nat. Assn. Broaden and Enchance Images (bd. dirs.), Three-Star Youth Fitness, Inc. (bd. dirs.). Democrat. Office Phone: 404-753-1322, 678-613-6265. Personal E-mail: thena1@bellsouth.net.

NORONHA, MARIA GLÍCIA, nurse; b. Teresina, Brazil, Nov. 11, 1959; Degree in Nursing, Fed. U. Piauí, 1988; M, UTFPR, 2007. Pub. servant Curitiba's Mcpl. Prefecture, 1999—. Home: Rua Antônio Sanzovo 211 Curitiba Paraná 82400490 Brazil Personal E-mail: mglicia@hotmail.com.

NORREFALK, JAN-RICKARD ARNE, physiatrist, consultant; b. Stockholm, Oct. 8, 1952; s. Arne Sjutti Johan and Lilian Barbro Norrefalk; m. Gun Kerstin Marianne Alvinger; children: Ola Arne, Emma Katarina. Degree in Physiotherapy, U. Tübingen, Germany, 1975, MD, 1981; PhD, Karolinska Inst., Stockholm, 2006. Cert. specialist in rehab. medicine Swedish Nat. Bd. Health and Welfare, 1988, specialist occupl. health Swedish Nat. Bd. Health and Welfare, 1992, gen. practitioner Swedish Nat. Bd. Health and Welfare, 1994, specialist in pain mgmt. Swedish Nat. Bd. Health and Welfare, 1998, med. practitioner Belgium, 1994, specialist phys. medicine and rehab. Belgium, 1994, qualified doctor sports medicine Swedish Soc. Sports Medicine, 1996, cert. European specialist in phys. medicine and rehab. European Bd. Phys. Medicine and Rehab., 1998, med. practitioner Gen. Med. Coun., UK, 2002. Physician rehab. medicine Swedish Red Cross Hosp., Stockholm, 1984—85, 1987, cons. physician rehab. medicine, 1991; physician rehab. medicine Södersjukhuset Hosp., Stockholm, 1985—86, physician internal medicine, 1987; physician psychiatry Beckomberga Hosp., Stockholm, 1988; geriartic physician Rosenlunds Hosp., Stockholm, 1988; physician occupl. health State Assn. for Occupl. Health, Stockholm, 1988—96; pvt. practice Waterloo, Brussels, Belgium, 1994—96; cons. physician rehab. medicine, head pain unit Huddinge U. Hosp., Stockholm, 1997—2003; cons. physician Painkiller Ltd., London, 2003—06, Sophiahemmet Rehab. Ctr., Stockholm, 2007—; cons. physician dept. rehab. medicine Karolinska U. Hosp., Stockholm, 2004—05, Danderyd U. Hosp., Stockholm, 2005—. Acct. Swedish Assn. Med. Students Abroad, Stockholm, 1978—79; med. cons. Confarm, Royal Inst. Tech. Sweden, Electron Microscope Unit U. Adelaide, Australia, 1983—84; sec. Stockholm County Coun. for the Health Care Investigation of Mastectomy Patients, Stockholm, 1985; translator Tra Medica, Brussels, 1994—97; head sports medicine team Stockholm Half Marathon, 1997; lecturer, responsible trainer Karolinska Inst., Stockholm, 1999—; chmn. 1st World Congrsss, Internat. Soc. Phys. and Rehab. Medicine, Amsterdam, 2001; adv. bd. Swedish Med. Products Agy., Stockholm, 2001; cons. Altea Therapeutic's Pain Cons. Meeting, Miami, Fla., 2004; coord. poster session 3rd World Congress. Internat. Soc. Phys. and Rehab. Medicine, Sao Paulo, Brazil, 2005—05; examiner Inst. for Profl. Devel. and Edn. for Swedish Physicians, Stockholm, 2007—. Named IBC Foremost Internat. Scientists, Best Poster Presentation, KICPR, 2000. Mem.: Swedish Soc. Ins. Medicine, Swedish Doctors Assn. for the Pain Mgmt., Internat. Assn. for the Study of Pain, Swedish Med. Soc., Swedish Med. Assn. Achievements include development of functional barometer, an instrument to guide physicians with patients suffering from persistent pain. Avocations: tennis, horses, music, writing, singing. Home: Nyodlingsvägen 25 167 66 Stockholm Sweden Office: Danderyds Univ Hospital Divsn Rehabilitation Medicine 182 88 Stockholm Sweden Office Fax: + 46 8 655 77 54. Personal E-mail: norrefalk@hotmail.com.

NORRID, HENRY GAIL, osteopathic physician and surgeon, researcher, educator, healthcare facility administrator; b. Amarillo, Tex., June 4, 1940; s. Henry Horatio and Johnnie Belle (Combs, Cummins) N.; m. Andreia Maybeth Hudson, Jan. 29, 1966 (dec. 1988); children: Joshua Andrew, Noah Adam; m. Cheryll Diane Payne, Mar. 19, 1989 (div. Aug. 2000); stepchildren: Kim Sheri Payne, Matthew Dominic Payne; m. Carolyn A. Layton, June 8, 2002; stepchildren: Crissey Ann Elizabeth Bruce, David Randall Marshall Bruce. AA, Amarillo Coll., 1963; BA, U. Tex., 1966; MS, W. Tex. State U., 1967; DO, Kirksville Coll., 1973. Diplomate Bd. Osteo. Physicians and Surgeons, Nat. Bd. Examiners Osteo. Physicians and Surgeons; cert. basic sci. tchr. Iowa, Tex., Colo. Intern Interboro Gen. Hosp., Bklyn., 1973-74; attending physician dept. gen. practice Osteo. Hosp. and Clinic NY, NYC, 1974-77; gen. practice medicine specializing in osteo. Amarillo, Tex., 1978—; emergency care physician Amarillo Emergency Receiving Ctr. Amarillo Hosp. Dist., 1978-79, Ready Care Emergency Ctr., Arlington and Bedford, Tex., 1990-92, St. Anthony Hosp., Amarillo, 1992; history cons. Tex. Panhandle Heritage Found., 2004—. Emeritus mem. consulting staff physician dept. family practice Northwest Tex. Hosp., Amarillo, 1995; emergency/trauma physician Tex. EM Care, 1995—; mem. mass casualty nat. disaster response team ARC, 1995; contract staff physician Tex. Tech. Univ. Sch. Medicine and Health Scis. Ctr., med. dept. and infirmary Tex. Dept. Corrections, Tex. Dept. Criminal Justice, 1992-94; med. cons. rehab. medicine vocat rehab. divsn. Tex. Rehab. Commn., Plano, 1992-94; cattleman, ranch owner, Van Zandt County, Tex.; lectr. osteo. prins. and practice, The Osteo. Hosp. and Clinic NY, 1974-77, mem. credentials com., 1975-76; mem. exec. com. Southwest Osteo. Hosp., Amarillo, 1983-84, chief of staff, 1984-85; sec. dept. family practice Northwest Tex. Hosp., Amarillo, 1981-82, mem. credentials com., 1984-85, joint practice com. dept. family practice, 1986-87; mem. orgnl. com. for devel. of dept. osteo. prins. and practices, chmn. NYC group NY Coll. Osteo. Med., 1977; mem. founding com. NY Coll. Osteo. Medicine, NY Inst. Tech., Old Westbury LI, 1976-77; mem. North Tex. Support Group, Dallas; instr. human anatomy and physiology dept. biol. scis. Amarillo Coll., 1998-2001, fall 2003. Contbr. articles to Tex. Jour. Sci., other publs. Scout physician Llano Estecato coun. Boy Scouts Am., Tex., 1978-85; vol. physician Hurricane Katrina, 2005; active Polk St. Meth. Ch., Amarillo. Served to E-4 U.S. Army, 1956-63. Recipient William M. Giltner Meml. Fund award 1972, Humanitarian award Am. Cath. Conf., 1979, Century award Boy Scouts Am., 1982, Pfizer Sr. Med. Student award, 1973; Maxwell D. Warmer Meml. scholar 1973; scholar Kirksville Coll. Osteo. Medicine, 1970; Tex. Legislature scholar, 1969-73; named to Eminent Soc. Border Legionaires, 11th Armored Cavalry Regiment, Germany, 1958. Mem. Am. Coll. Gen. Practitioners, Tex. Osteo. Med. Assn. (life) (pres. dist. I, mem. ho. of dels. 1981-82, 95), Tex. C.C. Tchrs. Assn., SAR, The Sons of Republic of Tex., Am. Osteo. Assn., World Future Soc. (profl.), Gen. Soc. War of 1812, NY Acad. Scis., Ex-Student's Assn. of The U. Tex. (life), 11th Armored Cavalry Regiment Assn., 36th (Tex.) Inf. Divsn. Assn. (life), Baron of the Magna Charta (Somerset chpt. Magna Charta Barrons 1994—), Masons, Am. Legion, Beta Beta Beta, Sigma Sigma Phi (pres. 1972), Alpha Phi Omega, Psi Sigma Alpha, Theta Psi, Theta Psi Clowns (1969-73). Avocations: astronomy, short wave listening, camping, fishing, history.

NORRIS, CHARLES RICHARD, JR., physician, psychiatrist; b. Danville, Ill., Jan. 6, 1949; s. Charles Richard and Elenor Joy (Bailey) Norris; m. Francesca Emanuele Norris, May 18, 1979; children: Charles III, Jacqueline L. BS in Chemistry, Bates Coll., Lewiston, Maine; MD, U. Vt., Burlington. Internship Albany Med. Sch., NY, 1975—76; residency Inst. of Living, Hartford, Conn., 1976—79; dir., alcohol & substance abuse svc. Horizon Hosp., Clearwater, Fla., 1981—82; dir. outpatient svcs. Inst. of Living, Hartford, Conn., 1983—85, dir. ambulatory svcs., 1985—86; dir. addiction treatment Fair Oaks Hosp., Delray Beach, Fla., 1986—91; dir. MetLife Health Care, Miami, Fla., 1991—95; pvt. practice Boca Raton, Fla., 1996—; vol. asst. prof. clin. biomed. sci. Charles E. Schmidt Coll. Medicine. Cons. in field. Author: Family Addictions, 1990; contbr. articles pub. to profl. jour., chapters to books. Fellow: APA; mem.: AMA, Fla. Psychiat. Soc. Office: 7301a W Palmetto Pk Rd, Ste 106C Boca Raton FL 33433 Office Phone: 561-482-7850.

NORRIS, LONNIE HAROLD, dean; b. Houston, Nov. 22, 1942; m. Donna M. Farmer, June 18, 1966; children: Marlaina M., Michael A. BA in Chemistry, Fisk U., 1964; DMD, Harvard U., 1976, MPH, 1977. Cert. diplomate Am. Bd. of Oral/Maxillofacial Surgeons. Asst. prof. oral & maxillofacial surgery Tufts U. Sch. Dental Medicine, Boston, 1981-88, assoc. prof., 1988-95, prof., 1995—, interim dean, 1995-96, dean, 1996—. Mem. com. dental accreditation, 1994—2003; chmn. coun. deans Am. Dental Edn. Assn., 2005—06. Named Disting. Practitioner, Nat. Acads. Practice, Dentist of the Yr., New Eng. chpt. Pierre Fauchard Acad. Fellow: Pierre Fauchard Acad., Internat. Coll. Dentists, Am. Bd. Oral/Maxillofacial Surgery, Am. Assn. Oral/Maxillofacial Surgeons, Am. Coll. Dentists, Am. Acad. Dental Sci., Phi Beta Kappa, Omicron Kappa Upsilon. Avocation: travel. Office: Tufts U Sch Dental Medicine 1 Kneeland St Boston MA 02111-1527 Office Phone: 617-636-6636. Business E-Mail: lonnie.norris@tufts.edu.

NORTH, A. FREDERICK, physician; b. Milw., July 3, 1931; s. Alexander F. and Florence (Reineking) N.; m. Jane Whittlesey, Dec. 18, 1954; children: Lindsay Elizabeth, Robert Whittlesey, Katherine North Creel. Student, Yale Coll., 1944—52; MD, Yale U., 1956. Intern Strong Meml. Hosp., Rochester, N.Y., 1956-58, resident pediatrics, 1960-62; instr. pediatrics U. Rochester, 1962-66; sr. pediatrician Project Head Start, Washington, 1966-68; assoc. prof. pediatrics George Washington U., Washington, 1968-72; assoc. med. dir. Children's Hosp. of D.C., Washington, 1968-72; vis. prof. pediatrics, pub. health U. Pitts., 1972-79; physician for retarded persons Govt. of D.C., Washington, 1978-88; pvt. practice in pediat. Rockville, Md., 1988—2008. Cons. various locations, 1966-88. Author: Infant Care, 1980; contbr. articles to publs. Lt. USNR, 1958-60. Fellow Acad. of Pediatrics, Am. Pub. Health Assn.; mem. Am. Pediatric Soc., Ambulatory Pediatric Assn. (pres. 1966-67), Chevy Chase Club. Democrat. Episcopalian. Home: 4982 Sentinel Dr #504 Bethesda MD 20816-3578 Office Phone: 301-229-2159. Personal E-mail: afnorth@msn.com.

NORTH, STEVEN EDWARD, lawyer, educator; b. Oct. 16, 1941; s. Irving J. and Barbara (Grubman) N.; m. Sue J. Buznitsky, Dec. 24, 1966; children: Jennifer, Samantha. BA, CCNY, 1963; JD, Bklyn. Law Sch., 1966; LLM, NYU, 1967. Bar: NY 1967, US Dist. Ct. (so. and ea. dists.) NY 1970, US Supreme Ct. 1971. Asst. dist. atty. homicide bur. NY County Dist. Atty. Office, NYC, 1967-71; spl. asst. atty. gen., bur. chief NY State Atty. Gen.'s Office, NYC, 1972-75; pvt. practice NYC, 1975. Mem. adv. com. Ann. Civil Litigation Inst., Practicing Law Inst., 1996; chmn. Assn. Bar Subcom. on Investigation into Imposition of Legis. Limits on Awards for Non-Econ. Damages, 1995; mediator US Dist. Ct. (so. dist.) NY, 1994—, apptd. jud. screening program; mem. adv. coms. solo law practice Practicing Law Inst., 1991, adv. bd. tort litigation, 1989—; vis. faculty Sch. Law, NYU, faculty workshop Cardozo Sch. Law, judge appellate argument, alumni advisor; faculty advisor Trial of Breast Cancer Case, Law Jour. Seminars, 2000, faculty Annual Intensive Trial Program, 1997-; guest lectr. Advanced Medium Malpractice Cases, 2007, Grand Rounds Jacobi Hosp., Bronx, NY, 2001, Mt. Sinai Sch. Medicine, 2006; faculty chmn. Contuining Legal Edn. Programs, commentator, Court TV, Eyewitness News, Talk News TV; lectr. and spkr. in field. Author: Prevention and Detection of Fraud in Industry, 1973, Controlling the Deposition: Winning Your Case Before Trial, 1978, Deposition Strategy, Law and Forms, vol. 1 (Introduction and Law), vol. 5 (Medical Malpractice), vol. 8 (Personal Injury), 1981, (course handbooks) Trial Mechanics, Personal Injury Desbook, 1983, Trial Mechanics and Discovery, 1985, 86, Medical Malpractice Litigation, 1988, Managing the Multi-Million Dollar Case, 1990, Objectifying Brain Damage in Closed Head Injury, 1990, Fundamentals of Medical Malpractice Litigation, 1991, Damage Update, 1992, 93, 94, 95, 96, 97—, Proving & Defending Damages, 1993, Conducting & Defending Depositions, 1993; contbr. chpts. to books; editor: Cancer Litigation Bull., 1994—, Fear of Developing Cancer; contbg. editor: Law and Order mag.; med.-legal editor Perinatology, 1983; 2009, Medical Malpractice Chapter NYS Bar Assoc., 2009; contbr. articles to legal jour., Chapter to Books; commentator Eyewitness News, 1994, Court TV, 1994-98, Talk News TV, 1996. Mem. leadership coun. So. Poverty Law Ctr. Recipient Ten Highest Verdicts award, NY State, Eight Highest Verdicts award, NY Law Jour., 2005, 2008; named NY Times Super Lawyer, 2009, 2010; named one of Top 100 Attorneys, NY Times Super Lawyer, 2008, Top NY Lawyers, 2006, NY Super Lawyers, 2008, 2009, Leading Plaintiff Lawyers, 2007, Best Lawyers in NY, 2005—10, Best Lawyers in America, 2010, Best Lawyers, NY, 2005—, NY Area's Top Attys., NY Mag., 2011. Mem. ATLA, NCCJ (lawyers divsn., ann. dinner com.), NOW (benefits com.), US Holocaust Mus. (charter mem.), Am. Bd. Trial Adv., Soc. Med. Jurisprudence, NY State Bar Assn. (faculty), NY State Trial Lawyers Assn. (bd. dir. 1990—, faculty chmn. Depositions in Action 2000, North's Ninety-Nine Pointers on Advanced Deposition Practices 1999), Lotos Club, Nat. Eagle Scout Assn., State Trial Lawyers Assn. (bd. dir. 1990—, seminar faculty chmn. 1993, faculty decisions program 1991—, Law Day dinner com.), NY County Lawyers Assn. (exec. com. med. malpractice sect., exec. com. gen. tort law sect.), Assn. Bar of City of NY (civil ct. com. 1980-83, legal and continuing edn. com. 1983—, legal referral svc. com., med. malpractice mediator 1994—, chmn. subcom. on imposition of legis. limits to awards for non-econ. damages), Vol. Lawyers for the Arts, Million Dollar Adv. Forum, Vol. Lawyers for the Arts, NY County Supreme Ct. Com. Med. Malpractice Litigation, NY Soc. Anesthesiologist (speaker), NY State Bar Assn. Office: 148 E 74th St New York NY 10021 Office Phone: 212-861-5000. Business E-Mail: north@north-law.com.

NORTHEY, WILLIAM THOMAS, microbiologist, educator; b. Duluth, Minn., Aug. 10, 1928; s. William Thomas Northey and Mary Ellen Riley; m. Margaret Esparza, July 1, 1972; m. Elizabeth L. Van Laeke, Aug. 12, 1950 (div. June 15, 1970); children: Kathleen, William Northey III, Bruce, Brian, Barry, Brett, Suzanne. BA, U. of Minn., 1950; MA, U. of Kans., 1957, PhD, 1959. Rsch. asst. Abbott Labs., Chgo., 1950—51, Naval Med Rsch. Unit #4, Gt. Lakes, Ill., 1951—55; tchg. and rsch. U. of Kans., Lawrence, Kans., 1955—59; from asst. prof. to prof. emeritus Ariz. State U., Tempe, Ariz., 1959—85, prof. emeritus, 1985—. Cons. Unidynamics Corp., Goodyear, Ariz., 1960—63, AiResearch Corp., Phoenix, 1963—65; pres., dir. Iatric Corp., Tempe, 1960—92. Contbr. articles to profl. jours. Vol. United Fund, Phoenix; grant reviewer Ariz. Heart Assn., Phoenix; bd. dir. Ariz. Br. of Allergy Found. of Ariz., Phoenix. Seaman second USNR, 1946—51. Grantee, NIH, 1960—85, USAF, 1963—68. Fellow: Am. Acad. of Microbiology; mem.: Am. Soc. of Immunology, Am. Soc. of Microbiology (pres. Ariz. chpt. 1963). Achievements include development of scorpion anti-venom; research in aeroallergens in Arizona. Avocations: skiing, swimming, reading. Home: 4818 N 72nd Way Scottsdale AZ 85251-1302

NORTHOVER, BASIL JOHN, pharmacologist, educator; b. Northampton, Eng., July 7, 1936; s. Eric and Winifred (Mead) N.; m. Ann Howden, aug. 30, 1958; 3 children. B in Pharmacology, London U., 1958, M in Pharmacology, 1959, PhD, 1965; DSc, Coun. Acad. Awards, 1988. Lectr. pharmacology Christian Med. Coll., Vellore, South India, 1959-64; sr. lectr. pharmacology De Montfort U., Leicester, Eng., 1965-88, prof. pharmacology, 1989—. Cons., external examiner, Eng. Author: The Electrical Activity of Mammalian Tissues, 1992; mem. editl. bd. rsch. jours.; contbr. articles to profl. publs. Mem. British Pharmacol. Soc., British Microcirculation Soc. Home: 12 Newport Terr Barnstaple Devon EX32 9BB England Office Phone: 01271 346995. Personal E-mail: anorthover@postmaster.co.uk.

NORTHRUP, CHRISTIANE, obstetrician, gynecologist; b. Buffalo, Oct. 4, 1949; BA, Case Western Res., 1971; MD, Dartmouth Coll., 1975. Diplomate Am. Bd. Ob-Gyn. Intern Tufts New Eng. Med. Ctr. Affiliated Hosps., Boston, 1975; intern then resident Tufts New Eng. Med. Ctr., Boston, 1976-79; assoc. clin. prof. ob-gyn Tufts U. Sch. Medicine, Boston, 1979-80; clin. instr. ob-gyn U. Vt. Coll. Med., Portland, Maine, 1980—82, asst. clin. prof. ob-gyn, 1982—2001; practice medicine specializing in ob-gyn Gynecol. Assocs., South Portland, 1979-85, Women's Health Care Orgn. Women to Women, Yarmouth, Maine, 1985—96; private practice ob-gyn, Yarmouth, Maine, 1979—. Mem. high risk perinatal group Maine Med. Ctr., Portland, 1981-83. Author: Mother-Daughter Wisdom, 2005, The Wisdom of Menopause, 2006, Women's Bodies, Women's Wisdom, 2006; contbr. various articles on women's health to profl. jours. Fellow Am. Coll. Ob-Gyn; mem. Am. Holistic Med. Assn. (sec. 1986-88, pres. 1988-90), Am. Holistic Med. Found. (pres. 1986-88). Avocations: music, harpist, skiing, movies, pilates. Office: PO Box 199 Yarmouth ME 04096

NORTHRUP, HOPE A., clinical geneticist, pediatrician; MD, Med. U. SC, 1983. Lic. Tex., 1988, cert. Am. Bd. Clin. Genetics-Med. Genetics, Am. Bd. Clin. Biochemical/Molecular Genetics-Med. Genetics, diplomate Am. Bd. Pediatrics. Resident Children's Med. Ctr., 1984, Dallas, 1986; fellow Inst. Molecgene, Baylor, 1989; hosp. affiliation includes Shriners Hosp., Lyndon B. Johnson Gen. Hosp., Meml. Hermann Hosp. System. Office: Memorial Hermann Hospital 6410 Fannin St Ste 500 Houston TX 77030 Office Phone: 713-500-5760. Office Fax: 713-500-5760.

NORTON, LARRY, oncologist, researcher; b. Bronx, NY, 1947; MD, Columbia U. Coll. Physicians and Surgeons, 1972. Diplomate Am. Bd. Internal Medicine, Am. Bd. Oncology. Intern Bronx Mcpl. Hosp.-Einstein, NYC, 1972-73, resident, 1973-74; mem. staff Meml. Sloan-Kettering Cancer Ctr., NYC, dep. physician-in-chief breast cancer programs, dir. Specialized Program of Rsch. Excellence in Breast Cancer, med. dir. Evelyn H. Lauder Breast Ctr. and Iris Cantor Diagnostic Ctr., Norna S. Sarofim chair clin. oncology, 1995—. Former chair breast com. Cancer and Leukemia Group B, Nat. Cancer Inst.; mem. cancer clin. investigations review com. NCI, mem., consensus develop. conf. on treatment of early stage breast cancer, 1990, mem, cooperative breast cancer tissue resource registry; prin. investigator Program Project Grant, Nat. Cancer Inst.; Presdl. appointee National Cancer Adv. Bd., NCI, 1998—2004. Contbr. articles to profl. jours.; mem. several editl. bd. Recipient Sci. Achievement Award, Susan G. Komen Found., 1997; co-recipient NYC Award for Advancement of Cancer Medicine, Gilda's Club, 2006. Mem.: Nat. Alliance of Breast Cancer Organs. (pres.), Am. Soc. Clin. Oncology (pres. 2001—02, past found. chair, David A. Karnofsky Meml. award 2004), Alpha Omega Alpha. Achievements include being the co-developer of the Norton-Simon Hypothesis; co-developer of an approach to therapy called dose density. Office: Meml Sloan-Kettering Cancer Ctr 1275 York Ave New York NY 10021-6094 Office Phone: 212-639-5325.

NORVELL, JOHN EDMONDSON, III, retired neuroscientist, educator; b. Charleston, W.Va., Nov. 18, 1929; s. John Edmondson Jr., and Mathilde (Wood) N.; m. Rosemary Justice, June 2, 1962; children: John Edmondson IV, Scott Justice. BS, U. Charleston, W.Va., 1953; MS, W.Va. U., Morgantown, 1956; PhD, Ohio State U., Columbus, 1966. From asst. to assoc. prof. Med. Coll. Va., Richmond, 1966-76; prof., chmn. Oral Roberts U., Tulsa, 1976-87, prof., 1987-89; prof., chmn. Universidad Central del Caribe, Bayamon, P.R., 1990-91; prof. Oral Roberts U., Tulsa, 1992—98, prof. emeritus, 1998. Lectr. dept. surgery US Naval Hosp., Portsmouth, Va., 1968-1971; invited sci. editor New Eng. Jour. Medicine, 1970; vis. lectr. dept. anatomy U. Va., Hebrew U., Hadassah Med. Sch., Jerusalem, 1974, U. Va., Dept. Anatomy; chmn. Okla. State Anatomical Bd., Tulsa, 1978-89; gov.'s mini-cabinet on health and human resources, Okla., 1980-90; vis. prof. Sch. Medicine U. Nairobi, Kenya, 1982, Sch. Med. Scis., U. Benin, Nigeria, 1989; seminar speaker Zhongshan Med. Coll., Guangzhou, People's Republic of China, 1983; presenter in field. Author: Atlas of Neuroanatomy, 1976, Atlas of Cross Sections of Human Body, 1982; contbr. articles to profl. jours. Mem. Am. Assn. Anatomists, Soc. Neurosci., Transplantation Soc. Sigma Xi. Achievements include research in degeneration and regeneration of the intrinsic nerve fibers of hearts and kidneys after transplantation, aorticorenal ganglion. Home: 7018 E 100th St Tulsa OK 74133-6235 Office: Oral Roberts U Dept Biology 7777 S Lewis Ave Tulsa OK 74171-0003 Personal E-mail: jnorvell9@cox.net.

NORWOOD, FELICIA F., insurance company executive; b. Camilla, Ga. m. Garry Karch. BA in Polit. Sci., magna cum laude, Valdosta State U., Ga.; MA in Polit. Sci., U. Wis., Madison; JD, Yale U., New Haven, 1989. Atty. Hopkins and Sutter, Chgo.; sr. policy advisor health and human services to Jim Edgar Office of Gov., Ill., 1991—94; various sr. mgmt. positions Aetna, Inc., 1994—2006, pres. mid-America region, 2010—; pres., COO Active Health Mgmt., Inc., 2006—10. Patron Boys and Girls Club, Camilla; vestry Ch. of Transfiguration, NYC. Recipient American Enterprise award, Prairie Inst., 1999; named one of 40 Under 40, Crain's Chgo. Bus., 1999, 25 Influential Black Women in Bus., The Network Jour., 2008, 100 Most Powerful Executives Corp. America, Black Enterprise, 2009, 75 Most Powerful Women in Bus., 2010. Mem.: Exec. Leadership Coun., Milbank Soc. Office: Aetna Inc 1 S Wacker Dr 12th Fl Chicago IL 60606 *

NOSÉ, YUKIHIKO, surgeon, educator; b. Iwamisawa, Hokkaido, Japan, May 7, 1932; came to U.S., 1962; s. Minoru and Haru (Murakami) N.; m. Bonnie Jean MacDonald, Mar. 15, 1965 (div. 1987); children: Kimi Willhelmina, Ken Willem, Kevin Scott; m. Ako Funakoshi, May 5, 1990. MD, U. Hokkaido, Sapporo, Japan, 1957, PhD, 1962. Surgeon in charge sect. artificial organs U. Hokkaido Sch. Medicine, 1961-62; rsch. assoc. Maimonides Hosp., Bklyn., 1962-64; postgrad. fellow dept. artificial organs Cleve. Clinic Found., 1964-66; mem. staff dept. artificial organs Cleve. Clinic, 1966—89, chmn. dept. artificial organs, 1970—90, chmn. emeritus, 1990—; prof. surgery Baylor Coll. Medicine, Houston, 1991—. V.p. Internat. Ctr. Artificial Organs and Transplantation, Cleve., 1979—; cons., mem. surgery and bioengring. study sect. NIH, 1981-87; assoc. dean Asian region Internat. Faculty Artificial Organs, 1992—; prof. Bologna (Italy) U. Sch. Medicine, 1994—. Author: Manual on Artificial Organs: Volume I-The Artificial Kidney, 1969, Volume II-The Oxygenator, 1973, Cardiac Engineering, 1970, Die Kunstliche Niere, 1974, Plasmapheresis, Historical Perspective, Therapeutic Applications and New Frontiers (with Kambic), 1983, Future Perspective for the Development of Artificial Organs (with Kolff), 1988; contbr. to numerous profl. publs. Fellow Am. Inst. Med. and Biol. Engring., N.Y. Acad. Sci.; mem. AMA, AAAS, Internat. Soc. Artificial Organs (trustee, past pres.), Am. Soc. Artificial Internal Organs (past pres., trustee), World Apheresis Assn. (congress pres. 1994), Am. Soc. Testing Materials (chair subcom. on cardiovascular prosthesis in med. and surg. materials and devices, Moses award 1979), Am. Heart Assn., Am. Soc. Apheresis, Am. Soc. Artificial Internal Organs (pres. 1992, congress pres. 1994), Am. Soc. Biomaterials, Assn. Advancement Med. Instrumentation. Achievements include development of various types of artificial organs including cardiac prosthesis, artificial kidney, hepatic assist, respiratory assist, plasmapheresis, biomaterials. Home Fax: 713-522-2960. Personal E-mail: noseyuki@gmail.com.

NOSEWORTHY, JOHN H., hospital administrator, neurologist, educator; b. Melrose, Mass., Nov. 9, 1951; s. Donald Wilbur and Natalie Hawthorn (Jones) N.; m. Patricia Ann Miller, May 31, 1974; children: Peter Alexander, Mark Douglas. MD, Dalhousie U., Halifax, Nova Scotia, 1975; FRCPC, U. Western Ont., 1981. Diplomate Nat. Bd. Med. Examiners, Med. Coun. Can. Rotating intern Royal Columbian Hosp., New Westminster, B.C., Can., 1975-76; resident in internal medicine Dalhousie U., Halifax, 1976-78; resident in neurology U. Western Ont., 1978-79, 79-91; Centennial fellow Med. Rsch. Coun. Can., rsch. fellow dept. pathology Harvard U., Boston, 1981-83; rsch. fellow dept. pathology Harvard Med. Sch., Boston, 1981-83; asst. prof. clin. neurology scis. U. Western Ont., London, 1983-88, assoc. prof. dept. clin. neurology scis., 1989-90; assoc. prof. dept. neurology Mayo Clinic, Rochester, Minn., 1990—92, prof. dept. neurology, 1992—, chmn. dept. neurology, 1997—2006, vice chmn. exec. bd., 2006—09, med. dir. devel., 2006—09, pres., CEO, mem. bd. trustees, 2009—. Adv. com. clin. trials, Nat. Multiple Sclerosis Soc., 1989-92; med. adv. bd. Internat. Fedn. Multiple Sclerosis Socs., 1989-93; mem. Clin. Trial Monitoring Com., Bethesda, Md., 1990-94. Editor-in-chief Neurology, 2007—09; contbr. articles to profl. jours. Recipient Career Devel. award Mustiple Sclerosis Soc. Can., 1986-91, operating grants, 1986-91; Centennial fellow Med. Rsch. Coun. Can., 1981-83, operating grants, 1985-91. Fellow Am. Acad. Neurology; mem. Am. Neurol. Assn., Cen. Soc. Neurol. Rsch., Soc. Magnetic Resonance in Medicine, Royal Coll. Physicians and Surgeons of Can. Home: 821 8th Ave SW Rochester MN 55902-6374 Office: Mayo Clinic 200 1st St SW Rochester MN 55905-0002 *

NOSKO, MICHAEL GERRIK, neurosurgeon, educator; b. Montreal, Feb. 24, 1957; came to U.S., 1991; s. Joseph John and June Elizabeth (Salter) N.; m. Deborah Anne Branciere, May 23, 1981; children: Douglas Joseph, Denise Elizabeth, Keith Michael. BS, McMaster U., 1978; MD, U. Toronto, 1982; PhD, U. Alberta, 1986. Intern U. Toronto Gen. Hosp., Ont., Canada, 1982—83; resident U. Alberta Hosps., Edmonton, Canada, 1986—91; assoc. prof. neurosurgery Robert Wood Johnson Med. Sch., New Brunswick, NJ, 1991—, chief, neurosurgery divsn., 1991—. Cons. and presenter in field. Contbr. articles to profl. jours., chpts. to books. Rsch. fellow Alberta Heritage Found., 1983-86; Chancellor' scholar McMaster U., 1975, Univ. scholar, 1976, Edwin Marwin Dalley Meml. scholar, 1977; recipient Acad. award Am. Acad. Neurol. Surgery, 1986. Fellow Am. Coll. Surgeons (Resident Rsch. award 1986), Royal Coll. Surgeons Can., Acad. Medicine N.J., mem. AMA, Am. Assn. Neurol. Surgeons, Can. Neurosurg. Soc., N.J. Neurosurg. Soc., N.Y. Acad. Scis., Middlesex County Med. Soc., Soc. Critical Care Medicine, Congress Neurol. Surgeons, Alpha Omega Alpha. Anglican. Avocations: instructing/flying aircraft and helicopters, fishing. Office: Divsn Neurosurgery 125 Paterson St Ste 2100 New Brunswick NJ 08901-1962 Office Phone: 732-235-7756. Business E Mail: nosko@umdnj.edu.

NOTTER, ROBERT H., biomedical researcher, educator; s. Dr. Harley A. and Margaret T. Notter; m. Barbara B. Notter; m. Mary Frances Dolsky Notter (dec. 1991); children: Becket A., Tracy M., Kelley C., Sarah A., Emily Blake. BS, Stanford U., 1964, MS, 1965; PhD, U. Wash., 1969; MD, U. Rochester, 1980. Prof. pediat., environ. medicine, and chem. engring. U. Rochester, NY, 1989—2001, prof. pediat. and environ. medicine, 2001—. Dir., biomedical engring. program U. Rochester, 1984—95; dir. neonatology rsch. U. Rochester, 1989—2000; dir. NIH Spl. Ctr. Rsch. in Lung Biology and Disease in Infants and Children, U. Rochester, 1989—97. Author: Lung Surfactants: Basic Science and Clinical Applications, 2000; editor: Lung Surfactant Replacement Therapy, 1989, Lung Injury: Mechanisms, Pathophysiology and Therapy, 2005; contbr. over 250 articles and abstracts to profl. jours. Recipient Rsch. Career Devel. award, NIH, 1981, Health Leadership award, March of Dimes, 2003; grantee multiple grants, NIH, 1975—. Mem.: Soc. for Pediatric Rsch. Achievements include research and development of surfactant-based therapies for lung disease and injury. Office: U Rochester Sch of Med 601 Elmwood Ave Rochester NY 14642

NOTTERMAN, DANIEL A., pediatrician, educator; BA, Cornell U., 1973; MA in Philosophy, Tufts U., 1977; MD, NYU, 1978. Diplomate Am. Bd. Pediatrics. Intern, resident NYU Med. Ctr., NYC, 1978—81, chief resident in pediat., 1981—82; rsch. fellow clin. pharmacology Cornell Med. Ctr., NYC, 1983—84; dir. divsn. pediatric critical care medicine N.Y. Hosp. Cornell Med. Ctr., NYC, 1985—97; postdoc. rschr., prof. Princeton U., NJ, 1992—2001, prof., dept. molecular biology, 2007—09, chair, com. health professions, 2007—; chair, dept. pediats. Robert Wood Johnson Med. Sch., 2001—07, chief pediat. svc., 2001—07; vice dean rsch. Penn State Coll. Medicine, 2009—, prof. pediat. biochemistry, molecular biology, 2009—. Home: 7 Symmes Ct Cranbury NJ 08512 Office: Penn State Coll Medicine 500 University Dr Hershey PA 17033 Office Phone: 609-258-7185. Business E-Mail: dan1@princeton.edu.

NOUR, NAWAL M., obstetrician, gynecologist, health facility administrator; arrived in US, 1980; BA, Brown U, 1984; MD, Harvard U., 1994; MPH, Harvard U, 1999. Chief residency Brigham and Women's Hosp., Boston, 1998; instr. dept of Obstetrics, Gynecology and Reproductive Biology Harvard Sch. of Medicine; dir. obstetric resident practice Brigham and Women's Hosp., Boston; founder African Women's Health Practice, 1999—. Recipient Commonwealth Fund Harvard U., 1999; fellow H. Rchard Nesson Fellowship, Brigham and Women's Hosp., 1999, MacArthur Found., 2003. Office: Brigham and Women's Hosp 75 Francis St Boston MA 02115 *

NOURI, SHAHIN, neurologist; MD, Erlangen-Nuremberg U., Germany, 1994. Diplomate Am. Bd. Psychiatry and Neurology, Am. Bd. Clin. Neurophysiology. Resident in internal medicine Staten Island Univ. Hosp., NY, 1997—98; resident in neurology Georgetown Univ. Med. Ctr., Washington, 1998—2001; fellow clin. neurophysiology NYU Med. Ctr., 2001—01; founder comprehensive epilepsy ctr. NY Meth. Hosp., dir. comprehensive epilepsy ctr. Office: New York Methodist Hospital 263 7th Ave Ste 5C Brooklyn NY 11215 Office Phone: 718-246-8614.

NOVACK, ALVIN JOHN, physician; b. Red Lodge, Mont., Mar. 11, 1925; s. John and Anna Geraldine (Maddio) N.; m. Betty P. Novack, Jan. 10, 1952; children— Vance, Deborah, Michelle, Mitchel, Craig, Brad, Mary Ellen, Garth. MD, U. Wash., 1952. Intern Harper Hosp., Detroit, 1952, resident in surgery, 1953; resident in otolaryngology Johns Hopkins U., 1954-57; resident in surgery Columbia-Presbyn. Med. Center, NYC, 1957-60, fellow head and neck surgery, 1957-60; dir. head and neck surgery Swedish Hosp., Seattle, 1960-91; dir. otolaryngology Children's Orthopedic Hosp., Seattle, 1965-78; ret., 1991. Contbr. articles to med. jours. Served to lt. AUS, 1940-43. Nat.

Cancer Inst. fellow, 1957-60 Fellow A.C.S.; mem. AMA, Am. Acad. Otolaryngology and Head and Neck Surgery, Soc. Head and Neck Surgeons, North Pacific Surg. Assn., Pacific Coast Surg. Assn., Seattle Surg. Soc.

NOVAES, ARTHUR B., JR., dental educator; b. Pontal, Sao Paulo, Brazil, Apr. 6, 1955; s. Arthur Belem Novaes and Maria Aparecida S. Novaes; m. Maria Beatriz Moreira Bezerra, Sept. 6, 1977 (div. 1985); 1 child, Bianka B.; m. Cristiana Fernandes da Silva Evangelista, Apr. 12, 1990; 1 child, Laura Fernandes da S. Novaes. DDS, Pontifical U. Campinas, 1976; CAGS in Periodontology, Boston U., 1978, MScD, 1980; DSc, Inst. Microbiology, UFRJ, Boston, 1996. Chmn. grad. periodontology Sch. Dentistry, Fed. U. Rio de Janeiro, 1983—97; chmn. periodontology Sch. Dentistry Ribeirao Preto, U. Sao Paulo, Brazil, 1997—. Cons. Nat. Found. Rsch., Brazil, 1995—; rschr. Nat. Coun. Rsch., 1995—. Mem. editl. bd. Sao Paulo U. Dental Jour., 1990—, Brazilian Dental Jour., 1999—, Jour. Periodontology.; co-editor in chief Jour. Osseointegiation. Fellow Acad. Osseointegration; mem. Am. Acad. Periodontology, Acad. Osseointegration (internat. rels. com. 1996—), Brazilian Soc. Periodontology (v.p. 1983-85, Jose Cassio M. Carvalho medal 1995), Internat. Acad. Periodontonlogy (bd. mem. 2003—). Avocations: swimming, travel. Office: Sch Dentistry Ribeirao Preto USP Avenida do Cafe s/n Ribeirão Preto 14040-904 Brazil Office Fax: 5516 3602-4788. Business E-Mail: novaesjr@forp.usp.br.

NOVAK, DENNIS E., physician; BA, Bklyn. Coll., 1966; MD, U. Medicine & Dentistry NJ, 1974. Lic. in med. sci. U. Brussels, 1972, diplomate Am. Bd. Family Medicine, Nat. Bd. Med. Examiners; cert. Nat. Com. Quality Assurance, Level 3 Patient Centered Med. Home. Resident in family practice Monmouth Med. Ctr., Long Branch, NJ, 1974-77; clin. asst. prof. UMDNJ-Robert Wood Johnson Med. Sch., 1977—; chmn. dept. family medicine Cmty. Med. Ctr., 1984—; pvt. practice, 1978—. Physician reviewer, quality assurance HealthSouth Rehab. Hosp. Mem. exec. adv. bd. Ocean County Boy Scouts America; asst. scoutmaster Ocean Coun., 1997-2010, com. chair Troop 165, 2000—10; chair dept. Family Medicine Cmty. Med. Ctr., St. Barnabas Healthcare Sys., 1989-2010; former trustee United Way Ocean County., Area VII Physician Rev. Org., 1983-86; bd. dir. Interfaith Hospitality Network Ocean County Homeless Program, 2002-04. Named one of Top Docs in NJ, Castle-Connolly NJ Monthly, 2001, 2003, 2005, Best of Southern Ocean County, 2009, Inside Jersey Best Drs. in NJ, 2010—11. Fellow Am. Acad. Family Medicine; mem. Ocean County Acad. Family Medicine (v.p. 1983), Ocean County Med. Soc. (bd. trustees 1983-87), NCQA Patient Centered Med. Home. Jewish. Avocations: photography, guitar. Address: PO Box 780 1001 Lacey Rd Forked River NJ 08731-0780 Office Phone: 609-693-8900. Personal E-mail: dennisnovakmd@expressfind.com.

NOVAK, ERNEST J., JR., hospital administrator; b. 1944; BA, John Carroll U., Univ. Heights, Ohio; MS in Acctg., Bowling Green State U., Ohio; grad. advanced mgmt. program, Northwestern U., Ill. Various positions including coordinating ptnr. and area industry leader Ernst & Young LLP, 1969—2003, ptnr., 1980—2003, mng. ptnr. Akron, Canton, Ohio, 1986—98, 1998—2003; chmn. University Hospitals Case Medical Center, 2004—. Bd. dirs. A. Schulman, Inc., 2003—, BorgWarner Inc., 2003—, FirstEnergy Corp., 2004—, U. Hosps. Health Sys., 2007—. Former bd. dirs. Cleve. Botanical Garden, Cleve. Conv. and Visitors Bur.; trustee Greater Cleve. Growth Assn. Office Phone: 216-844-1000. *

NOVAK, RAYMOND FRANCIS, environmental services administrator, pharmacology educator; s. Joseph Raymond and Margaret A. (Cerutti) N.; m. Frances C. Holy, Apr. 12, 1969; children: Jennifer, Jessica, Janelle, Joanna. BS in Chemistry, U. Mo., St. Louis, 1968; PhD in Phys. Chemistry, Case Western Res. U., 1973. Assoc. in pharmacology Northwestern U. Med. Sch., Chgo., 1976-77, asst. prof. pharmacology, 1977-81, assoc. prof., 1981-86, prof., 1986-88; prof. pediat., dir. clin. pharmacology Wayne State U. Sch. Medicine, Children's Hosp. Mich., Detroit, 1988—; dir. Inst. Environ. Health Scis. Wayne State U., Detroit, 1988—2008, dir. EHS Ctr. in Molecular and Cellular Toxicology with Human Application, 1994—2009, dir. interdisciplinary grad. program in Molecular and Cellular Toxicology, 1994—2008; bd. sci. counselors Nat. Toxicology Program, NIH Nat. Inst. Environ. Sci., 2008—; chair Bd. Sci. Counselors NTP NIEHS, 2010; corporate dir. rsch. Shriners Hosps. Children, 2010—. Mem. toxicology study sect. NIH, Bethesda, Md., 1984-88, mem. and chair numerous grant review com.; adj. sci. Inhalation Toxicology Rsch. Inst., Lovelace Biomed. and Environ. Rsch. Inst., 1991-98; program leader Epidemiology and Environ. Carcinogenesis, Karmanos Cancer Inst. and Comprehensive Cancer Ctr., 1996-98. Assoc. editor Toxicol. Applied Pharmacology, 1992-96, Toxicol. Scis., 2004—09; editor Drug Metabolism and Disposition, 1994-2000; mem. editorial bd. Jour. Toxicology and Environ. Health, 19 87-92, In Vivo, 1986—, Toxic Substances Jour., 1993-98; mem. bd. pub. trustees Am. Soc. Pharmacology and Experimental Therapeutics, 1994-2000; publr. over 140 sci. manuscripts, review articles and book chpt. in profl. jour. and books. Co. comdr., field grade officer (Major) USAR, 1968—99. Recipient Disting. Alumni award U. Mo., St. Louis, 1988; grantee Nat. Inst. Environ. Health Sci., 1979—2010, Gen. Medicine sect. NIH, 1979-82, 89-94. Mem. Am. Soc. for Biochem. and Molecular Biology, Soc. Toxicology (councilor 1996-98, chmn. cont. edn. com. 1995-96), Am. Assn. for Cancer Rsch., Am. Soc. for Pharmacology and Exptl. Therapeutics (bd. publ. trustees 1994-99), Am. Soc. Hematology, Internat. Soc. for Study Xenobiotics. Achievements include patents in field. Office: Shriners Int Hqdrs 2900 Rocky Point Dr Tampa FL 33607 Office Phone: 313-745-5767. Business E-Mail: R.Novak@wayne.edu.

NOVAK, ZOLTAN, pediatrician; b. Baja, Hungary, Nov. 21, 1949; MD, U. Szeged, 1975; PhD, Hungarian Acad., 1991. Prof. U. Szeged, 1991—. Mem.: Hungarian Soc. Pediat. Pulmonology (pres. 2009—), Hungarian Soc. Pediat. Allergology (pres. 2000—). Avocations: sports, art. Office: Koranyi Szeged Csongrad 6720 Hungary Office Fax: 3662544580. Business E-Mail: novakzol@pedia.szote.u-szeged.hu.

NOVAS, ANABELA MARIA PEREIRA CASAS, research scientist; b. Lisbon, Portugal, June 22, 1967; d. Francisco and Maria Novas; life ptnr. Richard Trevorrow; children: Sydney Pereira Novas-Trevorrow, Steffi Pereira Novas-Trevorrow, George Pereira Novas-Trevorrow. B Phys. Edn. and Sport Sci., Tech. U. of Lisbon, 1991, M Exercise and Health, 1997; PhD, Queensland U. of Tech., Brisbane, Australia, 2003. Sports cons. Portuguese Tennis Fedn., Lisbon, 1991—96; health ctr. mgr. Triangulo da Saude - Carnaxide, Lisbon, 1991—98; lectr. in sports sci. Instituto Superior Matematicas Aplicadas e Gestao, Lisbon, 1992—93; health and fitness assessor Queensland U. Tech., 2003—. Personal trainer Davis Cup Team athlete, Nat. Tennis Champion (males), Olympic athlete, Lisbon, Portugal, 1992—98; profl. tennis player Portuguese Tennis Fedn., 1985—96. Contbr. articles to profl. jours. Mem.: U. Queensland Club. Achievements include research in specific method of quantifying tennis in terms of energy expenditure, effects of phtsical activity / training on the immune system and incidence of respiratory infections in elite tennis players. Avocations: tennis, swimming. Home: 56/1060 Waterworks road The Gap Queensland Brisbane 4061 Australia Office: QUT Sch Human Movement Studies Victoria Park Rd Kelvin Grove Campus Queensland Brisbane 4059 Australia Office Fax: 61-7-38643980. Personal E-mail: anovas2002@yahoo.com.au.

NOVE, PATRICIA ANN, public health service officer; d. Frederick Martin Uren and Margaret Helen Fraser; children: Felicity Catherine, Susan Caroline, Jeannie Frances, Ananda Zoe. BA, Sydney U., 1958; diploma in Edn., U. New Eng., Armidale, NSW, 1972; MA, Macquarie U., Ryde, NSW. Guidance counselor NSW Dept. Edn., Sydney, 1958—60; social group worker YWCA, West Toronto, Ontario, Canada, 1960—61; child welfare officer Children's Office London County, 1961—63, 1972—74; tchr. Cath. Edn. Sys., Sydney, 1972—74, U. NSW, Sydney, 1979—89; health edn. officer Health Media & Edn. Ctr., Sydney, 1979—89; mgr., WD Ctr. Population Health SWAHS, Parramatta, NSW, 1989—; mgr. statewide network, WD coord. health promotion NSW Health, Australia. Tng. cons. Health Media & Edn. centre, Sydney, 1983—85; internat. health cons. to Singapore, 1985—88. Contbr. articles to jours. Recipient, Ctr. Aboriginal Health, NSW Health; grantee, Australian Training Guarantee Act, NSW Health. Master: Inst. Group Leaders (founding mem. 1983—2008, chairperson 2000—08); mem.: Health Promotion Assn. (dir. 2000—09). Avocations: sailing, skiing, opera, ballet, theater. Office: Ctr Population Health SWAHS Locked bag 7119 Parramatta BC NSW 2066 Australia

NOVELLI, WILLIAM DOMINIC (BILL NOVELLI), former retirement association executive; b. Pitts., May 21, 1941; s. Dominic M. and Celeste J. (DeFife) Novelli; m. Frances D. Bickell, Aug. 1, 1964; children: Peter M., Alexander G., Sarah J. BA, U. Pa., 1963, MA, 1964. Mktg. mgr. Lever Bros. Co., NYC, 1964—69; account supr. Wells, Rich, Greene, NYC, 1969—70; dir. advt./creative svcs. Peace Corps & Action, Washington, 1970—72; pres., co-founder Porter Novelli, 1972—90; exec. v.p. CARE; pres. Campaign Tobacco-Free Kids; assoc. exec. dir. Am. Assn. Retired Persons (AARP), Washington, 2000—01, CEO, 2001—09. Instr. mktg. mgmt., health comm. & mass media U. Md. Author: 50+: Give Meaning and Purpose to the Best Time of Your Life, 2007; mem. editl. rev. bd. Jour. Health Care Mktg. Mem. adv. coun. population comm. svcs. prog. Johns Hopkins U.; mem. adv. panel US AID; vol. cons. United Way America; vice chmn. task force profl. comm. Nat. Coun. Patient Info. & Edn.; bd. dirs. Ctr. Consumer Health Edn., Reston, Va. Named one of The 50 Most Powerful People in DC, GQ mag., 2007, The 100 Most Influential Pub. Rels. Profls. of 20th Century. Mem.: Am. Mktg. Assn. (chmn. attitude rsch. conf. 1985).

NOVELLO, ANTONIA COELLO, pediatric nephrologist, former state health commissioner, former United States Surgeon General; b. Fajardo, PR, Aug. 23, 1944; d. Antonio and Ana D. (Flores) Coello; m. Joseph R. Novello, May 30, 1970. BS, U. P.R., Rio Piedras, 1965; MD, U. P.R., San Juan, 1970; MPH, Johns Hopkins Sch. Hygiene, 1982; DrPh, Johns Hopkins U., 2000; DSc (hon.), Med. Coll. Ohio, 1990, U. Ctrl. Caribe, Cayey, PR, 1990, Lehigh U., 1992, Hood Coll., 1992, U. Notre Dame, Ind., 1991, N.Y. Med. Coll., 1992, U. Mass., 1992, Fla. Internat. U., 1992, Cath. U., 1993, Washington Coll., 1993, St. Mary's Coll., 1993, Ea. Va. Med. Sch., 1993, Ctrl. Conn. State U., 1993, Georgetown U., 1993, U. Mich., 1994, Mt. Sinai Sch. Medicine, 1995; LHD (hon.), Alvernia Coll., 1996; HHD (hon.), Kings Coll., 1996; D in Health Sci. (hon.), Ponce Sch. of Medicine, 1996; D in Law (hon.), Gannon U., 1997; LHD (hon.), Loyola U., 1997; DSc (hon.), U. North Tex., Ft. Worth, 2002, Howard U., 2003, NYU, 2003, Pace U., 2003, Coll. New Rochelle, NY, 2003, Chatham Coll., Pitts., 2005; LHD (hon.), Coll. St. Rose, NY, 2004, Setton Hall U., 2006, Nova Southeastern U., 2007. Diplomate Am. Bd. Pediatrics. Intern in pediatrics U. Mich. Med. Ctr., Ann Arbor, 1970-71, resident in pediatrics, 1971-73, pediatric nephrology fellow, 1973-74, Georgetown U. Hosp., Washington, 1974-75; project officer Nat. Inst. Arthritis, Metabolism and Digestive Diseases NIH, Bethesda, Md., 1978-79, staff physician, 1979-80; exec. sec. gen. medicine B study sect., div. of rsch. grants NIH, Bethesda, 1981-86; dep. dir. Nat. Inst. Child Health & Human Devel., NIH, Bethesda, 1986-90; surgeon gen. US Dept. Health & Human Services, Washington, 1990-93; spl. rep. for health and nutrition UNICEF, NYC, 1993—96; vis. prof. health policy and mgmt. Johns Hopkins U. Sch. of Hygiene and Pub. Health, 1996—99; commr. of health State of NY, 1999—2007; v.p. Women and Children's Health and Policy Affairs, Fla. Children's Hosp., 2008—; exec. Disney Children's Hosp., Orlando, Fla., 2009—; exec. dir. Pub. Health Policy Fla. Hosp., 2010. Clin. prof. pediatrics Georgetown U. Hosp., Washington, 1986, 89, Uniformed Svcs. U. of Health Scis., 1989; adj. prof. pediatrics and communicable diseases U. Mich. Med. Sch., 1993; adj. prof. internat. health Sch. Hygiene and Pub. Health, Johns Hopkins U., Balt.; prof. dept. health policy mgmt. and behavior SUNY, 1999—; clin. prof. pediats. U. Rochester, N.Y., 1999—; mem. Georgetown Med. Ctr. Interdepartmental Rsch. Group; legis. fellow U.S. Senate Com. on Labor and Human Resources, Washington, 1982-83; mem. Com. on Rsch. in Pediatric Nephrology, Washington; participant grants assoc. program seminars Nat. Inst. Arthritis, Diabetes and Digestive and Kidney Diseases, NIH, Bethesda, 1980-81; pediatric cons. Adolescent Medicine Svc., Psychiat. Inst., Washington, 1979-83; nephrology cons. Met. Washington Renal Dialysis Ctr. affiliate Georgetown U. Hosp., Washington, 1975-78; phys. diagnosis class instr. U. Mich. Med. Ctr., Ann Arbor, 1973-74; chair Sec.'s Work Group on Pediatric HIV Infection and Diseases, DHHS, 1988; cons. WHO, Geneva, 1989; mem. Johns Hopkins Soc. Scholars, 1991. Contbr. numerous articles to profl. jours. and chpts. to books in field; mem. editorial bd. Internat. Jour Artificial Organs, Jour. Mexican Nephrology. Served in USPHS, 1978-99. Recipient Intern of Yr. award U. Mich. Dept. Pediatrics, 1971, Woman of Yr. award Disting. Grads. Pub. Sch. Systems, San Juan, 1980, PHS Commendation medal HHS, 1983, PHS Citation award HHS, 1984, Cert. of Recognition, Divsn. Rsch. Grants, NIH, 1985, PHS Outstanding medal HHS, 1988, PHS Unit Commendation, 1988, PHS Surgeon Gen.'s Exemplary Svc. medal, 1989, PHS Outstanding Unit citation, 1989, DHHS Asst. Sec. for Health Cert. of Commendation, 1989, Surgeon Gen. Medallion award, 1990, Alumni award U. Mich. Med. Ctr., 1991, Elizabeth Blackwell award, 1991, Woodrow Wilson award for disting. govt. svc., 1991, Congl. Hispanic Caucus medal, 1991, Order of Mil. Med. Merit, 1992, Washington Times Freedom award, 1992, Charles C. Shepard Sci. award, 1992, Golden Plate award, 1992, Elizabeth Ann Seton award, 1992, Ellis Island Congl. Medal of Honor, 1993, Legion of Merit medal, 1993, Athena award Alumnae Coun., 1993, Nat. Citation award Mortar Bd., 1993, Disting. Pub. Svc. award, 1993, Healthy Am. Fitness Leaders award, 1994, Pub. Leadership Edn. Network Mentor award, 1994, Disting. Svc. award Nat. Coun. Cath. Women, 1995, James E. Van Zandt Citizenship award, 1995, Ronald McDonald Children's Charities Excellence award, 1995, Hispanic Heritage Leadership award, 1998, Disting. Alumnus award Am. Assn. of State Colls. and Univs., 1997, Humanitarian award Am. Cancer Soc., 2001, James Smithson Bicentenial medal Smithsonian Inst., 2002; named Health Leader of Yr., COA, 1992; inductee Nat. Women's Hall of Fame, 1994, Internat. Pediatric Hall of Fame Miami Children's Hosp., 1996, Am. Med. Women Assn. Hall of Fame, 2002. Fellow Am. Acad. Pediatrics (Excellence Pub. Svc. award 1993); mem. AMA (Nathan Davis award 1993, Meritorious Svc. award 1993, Luther L. Terry award, 2000), Inst. Medicine Nat. Acad. Scis., Internat. Soc. Nephrology, Am. Soc. Nephrology, Latin Am. Soc. Nephrology, Soc. for Pediatric Rsch., Am. Pediatric Soc., Assn. Mil. Surgeons U.S., Am. Soc. Pediatric Nephrology, Pan Am. Med. and Dental Soc. (pres.-elect, sec. 1984), D.C. Med. Soc. (assoc.), Johns Hopkins U. Soc. Scholars, State Govt. Nat. Govs. Assn. (Disting. Svc. award, 2005), Scis. Smithsonian Latino Ctr. (Legacy award, 2008), Alpha Omega Alpha. Achievements include being the first woman and first Hispanic to serve as surgeon general. Avocation: collecting antique furniture. Office Phone: 407-303-1760. Business E-Mail: antonia.novello.md@flhosp.org.

NOVICK, LEONARD, foundation administrator; Exec. dir. Nat. Found. Infectious Diseases. Office: Nat Found Infectious Diseases 4733 Bethesda Ave Ste 750 Bethesda MD 20814 Office Phone: 301-656-0003. Office Fax: 301-907-0878. *

NOVICK, NELSON LEE, dermatologist, internist, consultant, cosmetic dermasurgeon, writer; b. Bklyn., June 27, 1949; s. Benjamin and Vivian (Meltzer) N.; m. Meryl Sohnis, June 20, 1971; children: Yonatan, Yoel, Ariel, Daniel, Avraham, Shmuel, Yehudah. BA in Biology magna cum laude, Bklyn. Coll., 1971; MD, Mt. Sinai Sch. Medicine, 1975. Diplomate Am. Bd. Internal Medicine, Am. Bd. Dermatology, Am. Bd. Med. Examiners. Resident internal medicine Mt. Sinai Med. Ctr., NYC, 1975—78, postgrad. preceptee, 1980—83, outpatient dept. clinic chief, dermatology svc., 1983—2003, attending, 2004—; resident Skin and Cancer Unit NYU Med. Ctr., NYC, 1978—80; clin. prof. Mt. Sinai Sch. Medicine, NYC, 2004—. Cons. Westwood-Squibb Skin Care Info. Ctr., Vaseline Intensive Care Rsch., Bausch & Lomb, Schering-Plough, Sandoz Internat., Procter & Gamble, Lever-2000, Novartis, Bradley Pharms., Merz Pharms., Inst. for Med. Info., Collagenesis Corp., PediFix, Biocell Tech. Network, others; skin health and beauty expert, Runner's World Mag., 2000-02; expert cons. Dermatology, Guidelines Expert, Nitron Advisors Healthcare Circle of Experts, 2003-, various med. websites; mem. MSSM spkrs. bureau, 2003-. Author: Saving Face, Skin Care for Teens, Super Skin, Baby Skin, You Can Do Something About Your Allergies, You Can Look Younger at Any Age, Diseases of the Mucus Membranes, (novel) In the Path of the Wolf, (audiotape series) Keeping That Baby Skin Look, Healthier and Younger-Looking Skin, Lunchtime Beauty Fixes for a Prettier Face, Breathing Easier, Fido, Food and Fumes; co-author: The External Ear; reviewer Annals Internal Medicine, Jour. Am. Acad. Dermatology, Jour. Dermatol. Surgery, Internat. Jour. Dermatology; editl. advisor Exec. Health's Good Health Report, Snyder Comm., Your Baby Wallboard Program; former med. editor Current Podiatric Medicine, Jour. Am. Analgesia Soc., Consumer Rsch. Coun. America's Guide to America's Top Physicians, 2003, Consumer Research Council of America's Guide to America's Top Dermatologists, 2007-08; contbr. articles to profl. jours. Regent's Coll. scholar, 1971, Max and Leah Strauss Fund scholar, 1971, Grand St. Found. scholar, 1971; recipient Dept. Dermatology award for contbg. to edn. of residents, 2000-01, Dept. Dermatology award for exceptional svc. in patient care, 2001-02; Dept. Dermatology award for two decades of outstanding svc., 2003, Dermatology award for Excellence, 2006-07. Fellow ACP (direct election), Am. Acad. Dermatology (Leadership Cir. 2006-08), Am. Soc. Dermatol. Surgery, Am. Acad. Cosmetic Surgery, Skin Cancer Found. (hon.); mem. AMA, AAAS, Soc. Investigative Dermatology, Skin Phototrauma Found., Internat. Soc. for Androgenic Disorders, Skin Cancer Found. (charter), N.Y. Acad. Scis., N.Y. County Med. Soc., Am. Soc. Dermatologic Surgery, Am. Analgesia Soc. (past bd. dirs.), Am. Soc. Cosmetic Dermatology & Aesthetic Surgery (charter), Nature Conservancy, Audubon Soc., Nat. Geog. Found., N.Y. Zool. Soc., Am. Mus. Natural History, Smithsonian Instn., Nat. Wildlife Fedn., The Wilderness Soc., Author's Guild, Author's League Am., Phi Beta Kappa. Jewish. Office: CosMediSpa 49 Hahayil St Raanana 077-2100818 Israel also: 500 E 85th St Apt P1 New York NY 10028-7409 Office Phone: 212-772-9300. Personal E-mail: nnovickmd@aol.com. E-mail: CosMediSpa@gmail.com.

NOVICK, STEPHEN ALAN, cardiologist; b. Hackensack, NJ, July 25, 1938; m. Rita Lynn Schneider; children: David, Michael, Jonathan. BA in Chemistry magna cum laude, Bklyn. Coll., 1959; MD with honors, SUNY, 1963. Intern L.I. Coll. Hosp., Bklyn., 1963—64, resident, chief resident in internal medicine, 1965—67; fellow cardiology Mt. Sinai Med. Ctr., NYC, 1967—69; dir. prenatal cardiology clinic Mt. Sinai Hosp., NYC, 1969—2008. Dir. cardiac clinic Mt. Sinai Hosp., NYC, 1970—2000; dir. cardiology, dir. ICU Yonkers (N.Y.) Profl. Hosp., 1972—79; cons. cardiologist St. John's Riverside Hosp., Yonkers, NY; cons., presenter in field. Contbr. articles to profl. jours. Founder, dir. Little TOR Homeowners Assn., New City, NY, 1973—75, Bklyn. Coll. Soc. for Free Discussion of Politics, 1955—59. Recipient cardiology fellowship, NIH, 1967—69. Fellow: N.Y. Cardiol. Soc.; mem.: Phi Beta Kappa. Avocations: history, violin, singing, writing. Office: 984 N Broadway Ste L08A Yonkers NY 10701 also: 1160 5th Ave Ste 105 New York NY 10029 Office Phone: 914-423-7267.

NOVIK, BENGT A., surgeon; b. Linköping, Oct. 17, 1956; MD, Karolinska Inst., 1987. Cons. surgeon, dept. surgery Skaraborg Hosp., 1998—. Mem.: European Hernia Soc. Office: Södra Trängallén 7A Skövde Vgr 54146 Sweden E-mail: bengt.novik@ki.se.

NOVIK, YELENA, oncologist; b. June 29, 1959; MD, Sch. Medicine and Dentistry, Moscow, 1988. Attending physician, asst. prof. medicine MOntefiore/ Einstein Cancer Ctr., Albert Einstein Coll. Medicine, NYC, 1996—98; attending physician Comprehensive Cancer Ctr. Our Lady of Mercy/ Montefiire North Divsn., NYC, 1998—2000, Beth Israel Cancer Ctr., NYC, 2001—03; asst. prof. medicine, med. dir. clin. trials office NYU Cancer Inst., 2003—, med. dir. Clin. Trials Office, 2008—. Contbr. articles to med. jours. Fellow ACP; mem. Am. Soc. Clin. Oncology, Am. Breast Disease Soc., NSABP, ECOG Office: NYU Cancer Inst 160 East 34th St New York NY 10016 Office Phone: 212-731-5350. Business E-Mail: yelena.novik@med.nyu.edu, yelena.novik@nyumc.org.

NOVIKOV, VADIM VICTOROVICH, biophysicist; b. Rostov-on-Don, Mar. 16, 1963; PhD, Med. U. Rostov-on-Don, 1990; DSc, Inst. Cell Biophysics, RAS. Leading rschr. Inst. Cell Biophysics, RAS, 2005—. Home: Microregion G-22 14 Pushchino Moscow 142290 Russia Personal E-mail: dogmag@mail.ru.

NOVIKOVA, NATALIYA DMITRIEVNA, microbiologist; b. Moscow, June 20, 1948; PhD, Moscow U., 1971; D in Biol. Scis., State Sci. Ctr. Russian Fedn.--Inst. Biomed. Problems Russian Academia Sci., 2002. Head, lab. environ. microbiology State Sci. Ctr. Russian Fedn., Inst. Biomed. Problems Russian Academia Sci., 1971—. Mem.: Environ. Health Working Group, Russian Acad. Scis., IAA. Office: 76-A Khoroshevskoye shosse Moscow 123007 Russia Office Fax: 7 (499) 195-22-53. Business E-Mail: novikova@imbp.ru.

NOVOGRODER, MICHAEL, pediatric endocrinologist; b. NYC, Dec. 22, 1943; MD, SUNY Health Sci. Ctr., Coll. Medicine, Syracuse, 1969. Cert. in pediat. 1974, in pediatric endocrinology 1980. Internship in pediat. Bronx Mcpl. Hosp. Ctr., NY, 1969—70, residency in pediat., 1970—72, residency in pediatric endocrinology, 1972—73; fellowship NY Presbyn. Hosp. Weill Cornell Med. Ctr., NYC, 1975—76; staff physician Columbia Presbyn. Med. Ctr., NYC; clin. prof. pediat. Morgan Stanley Children's Hosp. NY Presbyn. Babies & Children's Hosp., NYC; endocrinologist Met. Pediat. Group, Teaneck, NJ. Contbr. articles to profl. jours. Fellow: Am. Acad. Pediat., Endocrine Soc., Lawson Wilkins Pediatric Endocrine Soc. Office: Met Pediat Group 704 Palisade Ave Teaneck NJ 07666 Office Phone: 201-836-4301. Office Fax: 201-836-5110.

NOVOTNA, BRONISLAVA, allergist, researcher; b. Brno, Czech Republic, Jan. 19, 1954; d. Oldrich Jansa and Kvetena (Hurwicz) Jansova; m. Jan Novotny, June 1, 1979; children: Daniel Novotny, Nora. MD, Masaryk U., Brno, 1979; PhD, Masaryk U., 2006, degree in Pediat., 1988; degree in Allergology and Immunology, Charles U., Prague, Czech Republic, 1991. Microbiologist St. Anna U. Hosp., Brno, 1979—85, allergologist, clin. immunologist, 1989—93; pediatrician Children's U. Hosp., Brno, 1986—89; allergologist U. Hosp. Brno, 1993—. Supr. of immunol. lab. VIAMEDA, Brno, 1994—. Co-author: (textbook) Gastroenterology, Internal medicine, Allergology; contbr. articles to profl. jours; mem. adv. bd. Allergy. Lectr. Czech Initiative for Asthma, Prague, 1996. Mem.: World Allergy Orgn. (assoc.), European Respiratory Soc. (assoc.; gold mem.), European Acad. Allergology and Clin. Immunology (assoc.), Czech Assn. Allergology and Clin. Immunology (assoc.; com. 1989, Vladimir Zavazal award 2004). Achievements include research in asthma in pregnancy, aspirin sensitivity. Home: Straznicka 3 62700 Brno Czech Republic Office: University Hosp Jihlavska 20 62500 Brno Czech Republic Office Fax: 420532233733. Business E-Mail: bnovotna@fnbrno.cz.

NOVOTNY, LADISLAV, medical educator; b. Hradec Kralove, Czech Republic, Aug. 6, 1976; DVM, U. Vet. and Pharm. Scis., 2001, PhD, 2004. Assoc. prof. U. Vet. and Pharm. Scis., 2010—. Adj. prof. Faculty Mil. Health Sics. U. Def., 2007—10; assoc. prof., histology Med. Faculty Charles U., Hradec Kralove, 2008—11. Mem.: Royal Coll. Vet. Surgeons UK, European Coll. Vet. Pathologists. Office: Palackeho 1-3 Brno 61242 Czech Republic Business E-Mail: novotnyl@pmfhk.cz.

NOVOTNY, THOMAS EDWARD, healthcare educator, consultant; b. Omaha, May 3, 1947; s. Anton Joseph and Anne Prazan Novotny; m. Andrea Borges Sereno, July 9, 2004. BS, U. Nebr., Lincoln, 1969; MD, U. Nebr. Med. Ctr., Omaha, 1973; MPH, Johns Hopkins Bloomberg Sch. Pub. Health, Balt., 1991. Diplomate Calif., 1974. Adm. US Pub. Health Svc., Washington, 1979—2002; family physician Nat. Health Svc. Corps, Guerneville, Calif., 1979—84; med. epidemiologist Ctr. Disease Control Prevention, Atlanta, 1984—91; asst. dean, pub. health practice U. Calif., Berkeley, Calif., 1992—97, prof., epidemiology and biostatistics San Francisco, 2002—08; cdc liaison World Bank, Washington, 1997—99, cons., 2002—; dep. asst. sec. internat. refugee health USDHHS, Washington, 1999—2002. Mem. Coun. Fgn. Rels. Author: (book) Global Health Diplomacy; contbr. articles to med. & sci. jours. Decorated Surgeon Gens. Exemplary Svc. medal US Pub. Health Svc. Fellow: Am. Coll. Preventive Medicine; mem.: Commioned Officers Assn., Am. Pub. Health Assn., Coun. Fgn. Rels. Liberal. Avocations: saxophone, sailing, kayaking, scuba diving, travel. Office: San Diego State Univ Hardy Tower 119 5500 Campanile Dr San Diego CA 92182-4162 Office Phone: 619-594-3109. Office Fax: 619-594-6112. Business E-Mail: tnovotny@mail.sdsu.edu.

NOWAK, JACEK, clinical pathologist, transplantation immunologist; b. Wloszczowa, Poland, Dec. 1, 1959; s. Zygmunt and Zenobia Nowak; m. Elzbieta Anna Bielecka, Sept. 26, 1981; children: Piotr, Agnieszka, Stanislaw. PharmM in Clin. Analysis, Med. U., Warsaw, 1983; PhD, Ctrl. Clin. Hosp. Mil. Med. U., Warsaw, 1992. Cert. lab. diagnostics Ministry Def., 1986, in clin. analysis 1988, European specialist clin. chemistry and lab. medicine EC4, 2006, in lab. hematology Med. U., 2007. Head, tissue typing lab. Ctrl. Clin. Hosp. Mil. Med. U., 1984—96; head, lab. of immunogenetics Inst. Haematology and Transfusion Medicine, Warsaw, 1999—2008, head dept., immunogenetics, 2008—, prof., 2010—. Reviewer, accreditation World Marrow Donor Assn., Leiden, Netherlands, 2003—; vice-chmn., blood transfusion divsn. Polish Soc. Hematology and Transfusion Medicine, Gdansk, Poland, 2007—; v.p. Polish Soc. Immunogenetics, Wroclaw, Poland, 2008—; mem. European Fedn. Immunogenetics, Leiden, 2008—; sect. editor Jour. Hematologia. Contbr. scientific papers to profl. publs. (Rector Sci. award, 1989, Rector award, 1997, Sci. award, 2002, 2007, Individual Sci. award, 2008). Rsch. grant, Ministry Health, 2003—04, KBN grant, Ministry Scis., 2004—06, 2010—. Achievements include design of IWO v.1.0 computer program; ML-EM-HW v.5.2 and PHASE_KEY v.1.0 computer programs. Office: Inst Haematology and Transfusion Medicine 14 Indira Gandhi Warsaw 02-776 Poland Office Phone: 48 22 3436605. Office Fax: 48 22 3496607. Business E-Mail: szpik@ihit.waw.pl.

NOWAK, PETER GEORG, internist; b. Katowice, Poland, Oct. 25, 1978; s. Andreas and Maria-Magdalena Nowak; m. Susanne Henckels, Dec. 1, 2007; children: Jan Felix, Jule Marie. Dr. med., Heinrich-Heine-U. Düsseldorf, Germany, 2006. Resident, internal medicine St. Lukas Klinik, Solingen, NRW, Germany, 2006—08, Krankenhaus Wermelskirchen, NRW, 2008—. Docent anatomy AKH Viersen, NRW, 2001—04. Office: Krankenhaus Wermelskirchen GmbH Königstr 100 Wermelskirchen NRW 42929 Germany Home: Hermann-Milde-Str. 1 51379 Leverkusen Germany Home Phone: 0049 2171 46201; Office Phone: 02126-98 0. Home Fax: 0049 2171 365610. Personal E-mail: dr.nowak@netcologne.de.

NOWELL, PETER CAREY, pathologist, educator; b. Phila., Feb. 8, 1928; s. Foster and Margaret (Matlack) Nowell; m. Helen Worst, Sept. 9, 1950; children: Sharon, Timothy, Karen, Kristin, Michael. BA, Wesleyan U., Middletown, Conn., 1948; MD, U. Pa., 1952. Intern Phila. Gen. Hosp., 1952—53; resident pathology Presbyn. Hosp., Phila., 1953—54; lt. working as pathologist US Naval Radiological Def. Lab, 1954—56; from instr. to prof. pathology Sch. Medicine U. Pa., 1956—2006, chmn. dept. pathology, 1967—73, dir., Cancer Ctr., 1973—75, prof. emeritus, 2006—. Lt. M.C. USNR, 1954—56. Recipient Rsch. Career award, USPHS, 1964—67, Parke-Davis award, 1965, Phila. Pathological Soc. Gerhardt medal, Am. Cancer Soc. (Phila.) Scientific award, Lindback Disting. Tchg. award, 1967, Passano award, 1984, Rous-Whipple award, Am. Assn. Pathology, 1986, Robert de Villers award, Leukemia Soc. Am., 1987, Mott prize, GM Cancer Rsch. Found., 1989, 3M award, FASEB, 1993, Lasker-DeBakey Clin. Med. Rsch. award, Lasker Found., 1998, Meml. Sloan Kettering Cancer Ctr. Fred W. Stewart award, Leukemia and Lymphoma Soc. of Am. (Eastern Pa. Chapter) Lifetime Achievement award, Benjamin Franklin medal in Life Sci., Franklin Inst., 2010. Mem.: Am. Acad. Arts & Sciences. Office: U Pa Sch Medicine Dept Pathology & Lab Medicine Philadelphia PA 19104-6082 Office Phone: 215-898-8066. Business E-Mail: nowell@mail.med.upenn.edu. *

NOYES, RUSSELL, JR., psychiatrist; b. Indpls., Dec. 25, 1934; s. Russell and Margaret (Greenleaf) N.; m. Martha H. Carl, Nov. 13, 1960; children: Marjorie Noyes-Aamot, Nancy Heifner, James R. BS, DePauw U., 1956; MD, Ind. U., 1959. Diplomate Am. Bd. Psychiatry and Neurology. Intern Phila. Gen. Hosp., 1959-60; residency U. Iowa, Iowa City, 1961-63, asst. prof. psychiatry, 1966-71, assoc. prof., 1971-78, prof., 1978—2002, prof. emeritus, 2002—. Co-author: The Anxiety Disorders, 1998; editor: Handbook of Anxiety, 1988-91; contbr. 250 articles to profl. jours. With USN, 1963-65. Fellow Am. Psychiat. Assn., Acad. Psychosomatic Medicine (pres. 1990-91); mem. Iowa Psychiat. Soc. (pres. 1986-87). Republican. Lutheran. Avocation: gardening. Home: 326 MacBride Rd Iowa City IA 52246 1716 Office: Psychiatry Rsch Med Edn Bldg Iowa City IA 52242-1009

NOZOHOOR, SHAHAB, surgeon; b. Tehran, Iran, May 25, 1977; MD, Karolinska Inst., 2002; PhD, Lund Med. U., 2009. Cardiothoracic surgeon, 2005—. Office: Getingevägen 4 Lund Skane 22185 Sweden Business E-Mail: shahab.nozohoor@med.lu.se.

NOZZA, SILVIA, epidemiologist; b. Bergamo, Italy, July 13, 1973; Laurea, U. Studies Milan, 1998. Cert. in infectious diseases Vita Salute San Raffaele Sci. Inst., 2004. Physician San Raffaele Sci. Inst., 1998—, co-investigator, 25 clin. trials, 2000. Mem.: Clin. Trials Unit, Immunotherapy and Vaccine, San Raffaele Sci. Inst. (Best Young MD award). Avocations: reading, bicycling, volleyball. Office: Via Stamira DAncona 20 Milan 20127 Italy Office Fax: 390226437903. Business E-Mail: silvia.nozza@hsr.it.

NUCKOLS, FRANK JOSEPH, psychiatrist; b. Akron, Ohio, Apr. 7, 1926; s. William Alexander, Jr. and Jean (Harrison) Nuckols; m. Jane Fleetwood McIntosh, June 16, 1948; children: Claud Alexander, John Andrew. BA, U. Louisville, Ky., 1946; MD, U. Ala., Birmingham, 1951. Diplomate Am. Bd. Psychiatry and Neurology, 1959, cert. med. profl. Nat. Assn. Disability Examiners, 2005. Intern Holy Name Jesus Hosp., Gadsden, Ala., 1951; ward physician Ala. State Hosp., Tuscaloosa, 1951-52; resident U. Louisville, USPHS Hosp., Lexington, Ky., 1953-56; mem. faculty dept. psychiatry U. Ala. Med. Ctr., Birmingham, 1958-68, dir. tng. psychiat. residents, 1964-68, head div. community psychiatry, 1964-68, head continuing psychiat. edn. for physicians, 1964-68; chief psychiat. staff in-patient svc. U. Hosp., Birmingham, 1966-68; dir. tng. Hill Crest Hosp., Birmingham, 1975-79; pvt. practice Birmingham, 1968-93; cons. Ala. Div. Disability Determinations, Birmingham, 1993—. Staff Med. Ctr. East Hosp., Birmingham, Bapt. Med. Ctr. Montclair, Birmingham; cons. staff St. Vincent's Hosp., Birmingham, Lloyd Noland Hosp., Birmingham, South Highland Hosp., Birmingham; vis. faculty, mem. interuniv. forum cmty. psychiatry Harvard U., Boston, 1963—66; vis. faculty Baylor U. Med. Sch., Houston, 1967—71. Sr. surgeon USPHS, 1956—. Ensign USNR, 1943—45. Fellow: So. Psychiat. Assn., Am. Psychiat. Assn. (life; disting.); mem.: Nat. Assn. Disability Examiners (cert. med. prof. 2005, State Ala. Med. Cons. of Yr. 2005, Commr.'s citation 2005), Mental Health Assn. State Ala. (chmn. profl. adv. com. 1961), Jefferson County Med. Soc., Jefferson County Mental Health Assn. (v.p. 1960), So. Med. Assn., Med. Assn. Ala., Tau Kappa Epsilon, Phi Beta Pi. Home and Office: 300 Royal Towers Dr Apt 720 Vestavia AL 35209

NUEBLER-MORITZ, MICHAEL, oral and maxillofacial surgeon; b. Oberhausen, Rheinland, Germany, Oct. 2, 1962; s. Heinz Joachim and Ursula Maria (Sippli) M.; m. Gundula Nuebler, Oct. 1, 1994; 1 child, Sarah Ann-Kathrin. DMD, U. Mainz, Germany, 1988, MD, 1991. Oral and maxillofacial surgeon U. Regensburg, Germany, 1991—96; cranio-maxillofacial surgeon U. Zurich, Switzerland, 1996-98; mem. staff OMF Clinic Applied Laser Dentistry, Tafers, Switzerland, 1998—2000, OMF Clinic, Amberg, Germany, 2000—01, OMF Clinic Applied Laser Medicine and Dentistry, Alzey, Germany, 2001—07, OMF Surgery, Wiesbaden, Germany, 2007—08, Bad Soden, Germany, 2008—10, Zies, Frankfurt, Germany, 2010—. Vis. prof. Inst. for Laser Medicine U. Duesseldorf, 1996—98. Mem. editl. bd: Internat. Jour. Oral and Maxillofacial Surgery, 1998—99; contbr. articles to profl. jours. Mem. Internat. Soc. Lasers in Dentistry (country rep. Switzerland 1997-2000), German Soc. for Laser-Zahnheilkunde, German Soc. for Mund-Kiefer-Gesichts-Chirurgie, Swiss Study Group for Laser Surgery, Schweizerische Soc. for Oro-Faziale Lasermedizin (sec. 1998-2000). Roman Catholic. Achievements include research in applications of fibers and lasers in the field of cranio-maxillofacial surgery. Office: ZIES An der Hauptwache 7 D-60313 Frankfurt Germany Business E-Mail: info@zies-frankfurt.de.

NUGENT, GEORGE ROBERT, neurosurgeon; b. Yonkers, NY, Feb. 6, 1921; s. George Fitzsimmons and Alberta Belle (Wolven) N.; m. Virginia Ellen Hayes, July 3, 1947; children: Dana A., Robert W., Leslie Ellen, Barnes L., Courtney A. BA, Kenyon Coll., 1950; MD, U. Cinn., 1953. Diplomate Am. Bd. Neurol. Surgery. Resident Duke U. Med. Ctr., Durham, 1958, instr. of neurosurgery, 1957-58; asst. dir. Divsn. Neurosurgery U. Cinn. Coll. Medicine, 1958-61; asst. prof. neurosurgery to prof. neurosurgery W. Va. U. Med. Ctr., Morgantown, 1961—, chmn. dept. neurosurgery, 1970-85, prof. neurosurgery, 1985—. Cons. VA Hosp., Clarksburg, W.Va., 1961-93, Pa. Trauma Found., Pittsburgh, 1991-92; participant seminars in field; guest prof. various univs. Exhibitor various sci. exhibits, 1973-79; contbr. articles to profl. jours. and publs. Team physician W. Va. U. Mountaineers, Morgantown, 1966—. Lt. (j.g.) U.S. Maritime Svc., 1943-45. Fellow Am. Bd. Neurol. Surgery; mem. Am. Assn. Neurol. Surgeons, Congress Neurol. Surgeons, So. Neurosurg. Soc. (v.p. 1970-96), Soc. Neurol. Surgeons. Democrat. Avocations: tennis, woodworking, travel, cooking, reading. Office: Robert Byrd Health Scis Ctr Morgantown WV 26506 Office Phone: 304-293-5041. Fax: 304-292-4944. *

NUGENT, WILLIAM C., cardiothoracic surgeon; b. Oct. 17, 1949; BS, Franklin & Marshall Coll., Lancaster, Pa., 1971; MD in Medicine, cum laude, Albany Med. Sch., NY, 1975. Diplomate Am. Bd. Thoracic Surgery, Am. Bd. Surgery, lic. NH. Intern internal medicine Boston U., 1975—76; resident gen. surgery Beth Israel Hosp., Boston, 1976—79, chief resident gen. surgery, 1979—80, emergency unit staff surgeon, 1980—81; surgical rsch. fellow cardiothoracic surgery Mass. Gen. Hosp., Boston, 1980—81; resident thoracic surgery U. Mich., Ann Arbor, 1981—83; chief cardiothoracic surgery Dartmouth-Hitchcock Med. Ctr., Lebanon, NH, 1983—. Surg. rsch. cons. AVCO Med. Rsch. Lab., Everett, Mass., 1980—81; staff surgeon Mary Hitchcock Meml. Hosp., Hanover, NH, 1983—; cons. VA Hosp., White River, Vt., 1983—; asst. prof. surgery Dartmouth Med. Sch., Hanover, NH, 1983—92, assoc. prof. surgery, 1992—98, prof. surgery, 1998—, prof. cmty. family medicine, 2001—; assoc., Ctr. Evaluative Clin. Sci. Dartmouth Hitchcock Med. Ctr., 1994—; clinical oncology affiliate, Norris Cotton Cancer Ctr. Dartmouth Hitchcock Med. Ctr., 2004—. Contbr. articles to profl. jours. Recipient Daggett Trust prize for Profl. Conduct, 1975, Frederick D. McAndless prize for Psychiatry, 1975, Chmn. award, Dartmouth Hitchcock Med. Ctr., 1997; Sheridan-Alley Scholar, Thoracic Surgery Found. Rsch. Edn., 1998. Mem.: Soc. Thoracic Surgeons, Gen. Thoracic Surg. Club, Cardiothoracic Surgery Network, Am. Assn. Thoracic Surgery, Alpha Omega Alpha. Avocations: fly fishing, flying, computers. Office: Dartmouth-Hitchcock Med Ctr Dept Cardiothoracic Surgery One Medical Ctr Dr Lebanon NH 03756 Office Phone: 603-650-8572. Office Fax: 603-650-6346. Business E-Mail: william.c.nugent@hitchcock.org.

NUMATA, SANAE, medical technician; b. Yatsushiro, Kumamoto, Japan, June 29, 1967; d. Takeo and Toshiko Numata. B in Med. Tech., Kumamoto U., 1989; MSc in Med. Sci., Kurume U., 2006. Cert. med. technologist HHS, 1989. Med. technologist clin. lab. St. Mary's Hosp., Kurume, Fukuoka, Japan, 1989—. Contbr. articles to profl. jours. Recipient Sci. Encourgement prize, Japanese Assn. Med. Technologists, 1999. Mem.: Japanese Assn. Med. Technologists (assoc. Sci. Encouragement prize 2002). Avocations: golf, tennis, painting, travel, flower arranging. Office: St Mary's Hosp Tsubukuhon-machi Fukuoka Kurume 830-8543 Japan Office Fax: 81-942-34-3299. E-mail: s-numa@st-mary-med.or.jp.

NUNES, ADRIANA BEZERRA, endocrinologist, researcher; MD in Genetics, Fed. U. Paraiba; PhD in Endocrinology, U. Sao Paulo. Prof. U. Fed. da Paraiba, Joao Pessoa, Brazil, 1992—. Coord. endocrinology, Brazil; tchr., rschr. Fed. U. Paraiba. Mem.: Endocrine Soc., Brazilian Soc. Endocrinology and Metabolism. Personal E-mail: adr001@uol.com.br.

NUNES, GILBERTO LAHORGUE, cardiologist; b. Porto Alegre, Rio Grande do Sul, Brazil, July 1, 1961; MD, U. Fed. do Rio Grande do Sul, 1984, PhD, 2004. Rsch. fellow Andreas Gruentiz Cardiovasc. Ctr., Emory U., 1991—93; staff interventional cardiology Dante Pazzanese Cardiology Inst., 1993—97; dir., interventional cardiology and cardiac cath. lab. Hosp. São Francisco, Santa Casa Porto Alegre, 1997—2010; dir., interventional cardiology Hosp. Divina Providencia, 2011—. Master: Brazilian Soc. Interventional Cardiology (sec. 1996—98), Latin Am. Soc. Interventional Cardiology (sec. 1996—98, del. 2010—); mem.: Rio Grande do Sul State Soc. Cardiology (pres. 2010—), Clin. Cardiology Coun., Am. Heart Assn. Avocation: tennis. Home: Av Cel Lucas Oliveira 1133 Ap 501 Porto Alegre Rio Grande do Sul 90440-011 Brazil Home Fax: 55-51-32860066. Personal E-mail: gilberto.nunes@terra.com.br.

NUNEZ, DESMOND ANTONIO, otolaryngologist; b. Port of Spain, Trinidad, June 13, 1959; arrived in U.K., 1983; s. Vernon Lennox and Naomi Ann (Roberts) N.; m. Geraldine McCahill, 2000; 2 children. MB, BS, U. W.I., Kingston, Jamaica, 1982; MD, Leicester U., Eng., 1998. Registrar Greater Glasgow (Scotland) Health Bd., 1987-89; rsch. registrar North Riding Infirmary, Middlesborough, Eng., 1989-90; tutor U. Leeds, Eng., 1990-92; sr. registrar Leicester (Eng.) Royal Infirmary, 1992-94, U. Hosp., Nottingham, England, 1994—95; cons. otolaryngologist Royal Infirmary, Aberdeen, Scotland, 1995—2002, North Bristol NHS Trust, Bristol, England, 2002—, ENT dir., 2006—; cons. otolaryngologist Nuffield Hosp., Bristol, 2002—09, Spire Hosp., Bristol, 2002—, Bristol Royal Children's Hosp., 2007—. Cons. Royal Aberdeen Children's Hosp., 1995-2002, Albyn Hosp., Aberdeen, 1995-2002; sr. lectr. U. Aberdeen, 1995-2002; clin. sr. lectr. U. Bristol, 2002-09, reader, 2009-; mem. acad. senate Aberdeen U., 1998-2002. Contbr. articles to profl. jours. Recipient Aaron Matalon prize U. W.I., 1982, Intern's Rsch. prize Princess Margaret Hosp., Bahamas, 1983; TWJ Found. Travel grantee, 1995. Fellow: Royal Coll. Surgeons Edinburgh (examiner 2001—), Royal Coll. Surgeons Eng. (examiner 1999—2008); mem.: Brit. Soc. Acad. Otolaryngol (sec. 2008—10), S.W. Laryngological Assn. (hon. sec. 2003—08), Royal Soc. Medicine (coun. sect. otology 2000—01), Otolaryngology Rsch. Soc. (coun. 1997—2004), North of Scotland Otolaryngology Tng. Com. (chmn. 1996—99), Brit. Assn. Pediat. Otolaryngologists, Brit. Skull Base Soc. (sec. 2000—02), Brit. Med. Assn. (hon. divsnl. sec. 1994—95, divsn. com. 1997—98). Avocations: chess, sailing, skiing, scuba diving. Office: Southmead Hosp Dept Otolaryngology BS10 5NB Bristol England Office Phone: 44 (0) 117 323 6222. Personal E-mail: dnunez1orl@aol.com.

NUÑEZ-DELICADO, ESTRELLA, dietician, nutritionist, educator; b. Bonete, Albacete, Spain, Apr. 14, 1969; d. Emilio Nuñez-Munera and Maria Delicado-Cebrian; m. Manuel Manjon-Gejo, Apr. 23, 1959; children: Maria Manjon-Nuñez, Estrella Manjon-Nuñez. BS in Biology, U. Murcia, Spain, 1992, PhD (hon.) in Biology, 1997. Rsch. grant Edn. and Sci. Ministry, Murcia, Murcia, Spain, 1993—96, Caja Murcia, 1996—2000; phd rsch. grant Murcia U., 2000—02; prof. at the sch. of dietetics and human nutrition Cath. U., Guadalupe, Murcia, Spain, 2002—03, prof. of sci. and food tech., 2003—. Sub-dir. of sci. and food tech. Cath. U. of Murcia, Guadalupe, Murcia, 2003—. Contbr. chapters to books, articles to sci. and profl. jours. Mem.: Spanish Soc. of Biochemical and Molecular Biology. Office: Cath Univ of Murcia Avenida de los Jeronimos s/n Murcia Guadalupe 30107 Spain E-mail: enunez@pdi.ucam.edu.

NURSE, SIR PAUL MAXIME, geneticist, cell biologist, former academic administrator; m. Anne Nurse; children: Sarah, Emily. BS, U. Birmingham, 1970; PhD, U. East Anglia, 1973. Chair microbiology U. Oxford, 1988—93; dir. rsch. Imperial Cancer Rsch. Fund, London, 1993—96, dir. gen., 1996—2002; chief exec. London Rsch. Inst., 2002—03; pres. Rockefeller U., NYC, 2003—11, prof., head Lab. of Yeast Genetics and Cell Biology, 2003—11; dir., chief exec. UK Centre for Med. Rsch. and Innovation, 2011—. Recipient Gairdner Found. Internat. award, 1992, H. P. Heineken prize, Royal Netherlands Acad. Arts & Scis., 1996, Dr. Josef Steiner prize, Cancer Found., Bern, Switzerland, 1996, Alfred P. Sloan Jr. prize, GM Cancer Rsch. Found., 1997, Albert Lasker award for basic med. rsch., 1998, Katharine Berkan Judd award, Meml. Sloan-Kettering Cancer Ctr., NYC, 1998, Nobel Prize in physiology/medicine, 2001; named one of 25 Leaders Reshaping NY, Crain's NY mag., 2008. Fellow: Am. Acad. Arts & Scis. (fgn. hon.), The Royal Soc. (pres. 2010—, Copley medal 2005); mem.: NAS (fgn. assoc.). Avocations: hiking, flying. Office: UKCMRI Ltd Francis Crick Inst 215 Euston Rd London NW1 2BE England also: The Royal Society 6-9 Carlton House Terrace London SW1Y 5AG England *

NUSBAUM, MURRAY L., obstetrician, gynecologist; b. Utica, NY, Feb. 22, 1922; s. Morris and Anna Gertrude Nusbaum; m. Bridgetta A. Nusbaum, July 31, 1949; children: Devra L., Korrine P. AB, Antioch Coll., 1946; MD, Case We. Res. U., 1947. Diplomate Am. Bd. Ob-Gyn. Rotating intern No. Permanente Hosp., Vancouver, Wash., 1947—48; resident in ob-gyn. and pathology Dr.'s Hosp., Cleve., 1948—50; surg. resident Woman's Hosp., Detroit, 1950, 1953; sr. resident in ob-gyn. Florence Crittenden Hosp., Detroit, 1953—54; clin. asst. prof. SUNY, Syracuse, 1974—80, assoc. prof., 1980—83, prof., 1983—94; pvt. practice Utica, 1954—94; ret., 1994. Med. dir. Ferre Inst., Utica, 1975—, Planned Parenthood of Mohawk Valley, Utica, 1966-83; hon. staff Faxton Hosp., utica, St. Elizabeth Hosp., Utica, St. Luke's Meml. Hosp. Ctr., Utica; cons. Masonic Home, Utica; mem. adj. staff State Univ. Hosp., Syracuse. Contbr. articles to profl. jours. Bd. dirs. Utica Coll. of Syracuse U., 1972-81, mem. emeritus, 1982—; bd. dirs. Temple Emanuel, Utica, Family Svcs. of Greater Utica, 1962-64; past pres., bd. dirs. Jewish Social Svcs., Utica. With USN, 1942-45, 50-52. Fellow Am. Coll. Ob-Gyn (life, med. advisor, exec. com. local dist. 1988—, grievance com. 1996—, internat. affairs com., nominations com., Pres.'s Cmty. Svc. award 1995, Outstanding Dist. Svc. award 1988); mem. AMA, Med. Soc. N.Y. (com. on state legislation 1988—), Am. Acad. Medicine and Sci. (bd. dirs.), Am. Soc. Reproductive Medicine (life), Ctrl. N.Y. Acad. Medicine (past pres., Scroll award 1984, 97), Ctrl. N.Y. Assn. Gynecologists and Obstetricians (past pres.), Fertility Soc. Upstate N.Y., Am. Assn. Gynecol. Laparoscopists, Soc. Reproductive Surgeons, Fallopius Internat. Soc. Avocations: skiing, gardening. Office Phone: 315-724-4348. Personal E-mail: mlnusbaum@aol.com.

NUSS, WAYNE JOHN, medical association administrator; b. Toowoomba, Australia, July 23, 1948; Diploma in Applied Sci., Queensland U. Tech., 1981; grad. in Pub. Mgmt., Ctrl. Queensland U., 1986. Dir. Prince Charles Hosp., 1985—97; dir., med. imaging Princess Alexandra Hosp., 1997—. Chmn. Queensland Br. Australian Inst. Radiography, 1985—91, Med. Radiation Technologists Bd., 2002—10; nat. councillor Australian Inst. Radiography, 1994—2000, nat. pres., 1997—98; nat. chmn. Med. Radiation Practitioners Nat. Registration and Accreditation Steering Com., 2008—11. Fellow: Australian Inst. Radiography; mem.: Assn. Med. Radiation Dirs. Queensland Hosps., Med. Radiation Technologists Registration Bd. Avocations: reading, gardening, rugby. Office: Radiology Dept PA Hosp Ipswic Brisbane Queensland 4102 Australia Business E-Mail: wayne_nuss@health.qld.gov.au.

NUSSBAUM, MICHAEL SCOT, physician, medical educator; b. Cleve., Nov. 4, 1956; s. Fritz S. and Elaine (Sukenik) N.; m. Sue Ellen Weinstein, Aug. 6, 1983; children: Jaclyn, Rachel. BA, Northwestern U., 1977; MD, U. Pa., 1981. Intern dept. surgery U. Cin., 1981-82, resident dept. surgery, 1982-86, chief resident dept. surgery, 1985-86; dir. surg. edn. Jewish Hosp., Cin., 1986-90; asst. prof. surgery U. Cin., 1986-96, assoc. prof. surgery, 1996—, asst. prof. molecular and cellular physiology, 1991—, prof. surgery, 2006—; attending physician dept. parenteral and enteral nutrition U. Cin. Hosp., 1989—, dir. surg. endoscopy and laparoscopy, 1993—2000, chief sect. gen. surgery, 1999—2003, chief of staff, 2000—08, vice chmn. clin. affairs, 2003—08, asst. dean for hosp. affairs, 2003—06, interm chair dept. surgery, 2006—07; prof. U. Fla. Coll. Med. Jacksonville Dept. Surgery, 2008—, chair, 2008—. Med. records com. Jewish Hosp. Cin., 1986-88, med. incident rev. com., 1986-92, intensive care com., 1986-2000, CPR com., 1986-92, course dir. ACLS, 1987-92, chmn. nutrition support com., 1988-2000; chmn. adverse drug reaction com. U. Cin. Hosp., 1988-92, edn. coordinating com., 1990-93, oper. rm. adv. com. 1992-2000, patient care rev. com., 1992-2000, chmn. pharmacy and therapeutics com., 1992-2000, med. co-dir. collaborative care unit, 1993—, clin., tech. and support design team, 1994—, others; ACLS subcom. Am. Heart Assn.-Southwestern Ohio Chpt., 1988-95, affiliate faculty ACLS, 1988-95; assoc. examiner The Am. Bd. Surgery, 1990, 94, 96; trauma adv. com. Ohio Emergency Med. Svcs. Bd., 1993-2000; intern chair dept. surgery, U. Cin., 2006-. Editor-in-chief: The Mont Reid Handbook, The University of Cincinnati Surgical Manual, 1987; editl. bd. mem. Current Summaries in the Jour. Parenteral and Enteral Nutrition, 1991-97; contbr. chpts. to books and articles to profl. jours. Bd. mem. Yavneh Day Sch., Cin., 1992-95. Fellow ACS (com. on trauma, instr. advanced trauma life support 1987—, Ohio chpt. chmn. resident essay contest 1994—, sec. Ohio chpt. 1997-2000, chair local arrangements 1996 annual meeting); mem. Am. Soc. for Parenteral and Enteral Nutrition (liaison com. 1993-95), Am. Trauma Soc., Assn. for Acad. Surgery (com. on edn. 1989-91, nominating com. 1992, com. on issues 1992-94, councilor 1994-96), Assn. for Surg. Edn., Ctrl. Surg. Assn. (sec. 2006-2009, pres. elec. 2009-10, pres. 2010-11), Cin. Acad. Medicine, Cin. Surg. Soc. (treas. 1990-92), Collegium Interatn. Chirurgia Digestivae, Mont Reid Surg. Soc. U. Cin., Ohio Soc. for Parenteral and Enteral Nutrition (dir.-at-large 1990, pres.-elect 1991, pres. 1991-92), Ohio State Med. Assn., Pancreas Club, Inc., Soc. Am. Gastrointestinal Endoscopic Surgeons (resident edn. com. 1998-2006, rsch. com. 1998-2005, 2001-2006, membership com. 2001--), Am. Bd. Surgery, 2000-2006, Soc. Critical Care Medicine, Soc. for Parenteral Alimentation, Soc. for Surgery of the Alimentary Tract, Surg. Infection Soc., Soc. Univ. Surgeons (com. on surg. edn. 1998-2002, chair 1999-2002), Am. Surg. Assn., Halsted Soc., Alpha Omega Alpha, Southern Surg. Assn. Office: University Fla Coll Medicine Jacksonville Dept Surgery 653 W 8th St 3rd Fl Faculty Clinic Jacksonville FL 32209 Office Phone: 904-244-5502. Business E-Mail: michael.nussbaun@jax.ufl.edu. *

NUSSBAUM, MICHEL ERNEST, physician; b. LA, Nov. 7, 1947; s. Schymen and Jeannette Eleanor (Pequignot) N.; m. Joyce Wendy Laudon, Nov. 1, 1981; children: Eleanor, Anna. BA, Cornell U., 1969; MD, Free U. Brussels, 1977. Intern internal medicine NY Hosp. Queens, Flushing, 1977-78, resident, 1978-80, fellow gastroenterology, 1980-82, attending physician, 1982—; physician pvt. practice, Flushing, NY, 1982—; clin. instr. medicine Weill Med. Coll. Cornell U., NYC, 1994-98, clin. asst. prof. medicine, 1998—, clin. assoc. prof. medicine, 2009—; med. dir. Franklin Ctr. for Nursing and Rehab., Flushing, 1995-99. Dir. endoscopy NY Hosp. Queens, 1990—, asst. dir. gastroenterology, 1998-2004, assoc. dir. gastroenterology, 2004—, pres. med. staff soc., 1992-96, chmn. med. bd., 1997-2003, trustee, 1998-2003 Fellow: ACP, Am. Gastroent. Assn., Am. Coll. Gastroenterology. Office: 142-43 Booth Memorial Ave Flushing NY 11355-5343 Office Phone: 718-886-1919.

NUSSENZWEIG, MICHEL CLAUDIO, immunologist, educator; b. Brazil, Feb. 10, 1955; BA, NYU, 1975; PhD, Rockefeller U., NYC, 1981; MD, NYU Sch. Medicine, 1982. Diplomate American Bd. Internal Medicine. Intern, resident internal medicine Mass. Gen. Hosp., Boston, 1982—85, clin. fellow infectious diseases, 1984—85; postdoc. rschr. genetics Harvard Med. Sch., 1986—90; asst. prof. Rockefeller U., 1990—94, assoc. prod., 1994—96, prof., sr. physician, 1996—, Sherman Fairchild prof. immunology, 2000—. Investigator Lab. Molecular Immunology, Howard Hughes Med. Inst., 1990—. Recipient Solomon A. Berson Alumni Achievement award for basic sci., NYU, 2003, Meritorious Career award, American Assn. Immunologists-Huang Found., 2004, Lee C. Howley Sr. prize for arthritis rsch., Arthritis Found., 2008. Fellow: Am. Acad. Arts & Scis.; mem.: NAS, American Soc. Clin. Investigation, Inst. Medicine. Office: Rockefeller Univ 1230 York Ave New York NY 10021 Office Phone: 212-327-8000. Business E-Mail: Michel.Nussenzweig@rockefeller.edu. *

NÜSSLEIN-VOLHARD, CHRISTIANE, biologist, medical researcher; b. Magdeburg, Germany, Oct. 20, 1942; d. Rolf and Brigitte (Haas) Volhard. Diploma in Biochemistry, Eberhard Karls U., Tübingen, Germany, 1968; PhD in Biology, U. Tübingen, 1973; DSc (hon.), Oxford U., 2005, Yale U. Rsch. assoc. Max-Planck Inst. Virus Rsch., Tübingen, 1972-74; postdoc. fellow Biozentrum, U. Basel, Switzerland, 1975-76, U. Freiburg, Germany, 1977; head rsch. group European Molecular Biology Lab., Heidelberg, Germany, 1978-80; rsch. group leader Friedrich-Miescher Lab., Tübingen, 1981-85; dir. genetics divsn. Max-Planck Inst. Devel. Biology, 1985—. Author: Of Fish, Fly, Worm, and Man: Lessons from Developmental Biology for Human Gene Function and Disease, 2000, Zebrafish: A Practical Approach, 2002, Coming to Life: How Genes Drive Development, 2006; contbr. articles to profl. jours. Founder, dir. Christiane Nüsslein-Volhard Found., 2004—; mem. Nat. Ethics Coun. Germany, 2001—; head curatorium Internat. HugoWolf Acad., Stuttgart, Germany, 2010—; vice chancellor Order Pour Le Mérite, 2010—. Recipient Albert Lasker award for basic med. rsch., 1991, Louisa Gross Horowitz prize, Columbia U., 1992, Gottfried Wilhelm Leibniz prize, German Rsch. Found., 1986, Franz Vogt prize, U. Giessen, 1986, Carus medal, German Acad. Leopoldine, 1989, Schering prize, Berlin, 1993, Nobel prize in physiology/medicine, 1995. Mem.: NAS, Am. Philos. Soc., European Molecular Biology Orgn., Royal Soc. Achievements include creation of a detailed database of fruit fly mutations, research that has helped explain how a single-celled embryo, whether fruit fly or human, grows into a complex living animal. Office: Max Planck Inst Devel Biology Spemannstr 35 72076 Tübingen Germany *

NUTAN, MOHAMMAD TAWHIDUL HAQUE, pharmacy educator, researcher; s. Enamul and Fatema Haque; m. Manna Salowa, 2000; 1 child, Mohammad Muhitul Haque (Arnob). B of Pharmacy, U. Dhaka, Bangladesh, 1994, PharmM, 1997; PhD, Tex. Tech U. Health Scis. Ctr., Amarillo, 2004. Cert. FPGE Nat. Assn. of Bds. of Pharmacy, 2004. Lectr. dept. pharmacy U. Asia Pacific, Dhaka, Bangladesh, 1997; lectr. pharmacy discipline Khulna U., Bangladesh, 1997—2000; tchr, rsch. asst. sch. pharmacy Tex. Tech U. Health Scis. Ctr., Amarillo, 2000—04; grad. pharmacy intern Walgreen Co., Miami, Fla., 2004—06; asst. prof. Tex. A&M U. Health Scis. Ctr., Irma Lerma Rangel Coll. Pharmacy, Kingsville, Tex., 2006—. Chair, pharms. faculty search com. Tex. A&M U. Health Scis. Ctr. Coll. Pharmacy, Kingsville, 2006—, mem., acad. credentialing com., 2006—, mem., curriculum affair com., 2006—, advisor PharmD students, 2006—. Contbr. articles to scientific jours. Named Tchr. Of Year, Tex. A&M Coll. Pharmacy, 2007—08. Mem.: Am. Assn. Coll. Pharmacy, Am. Assn. Pharm. Scientists, Bangladesh Pharm. Soc., Pharmacy Grad. Assn. Bangladesh, Sigma Xi. Achievements include research in developed a controlled release multi-particulate formulation coated with starch acetate; developed a limonene-based coenzyme Q-10 self-nanoemulsified dosage form; developed an enteric dual-controlled gastrointestinal therapeutic system of salmon calcitonin; developed a cellulose acetate butyrate dispersion for controlled release coating; discovery of isolated a new alkaloid, Bismurrayafoline E, from plant source. Avocations: astronomy, geography, reading, travel, movies. Office: Texas A&M Coll Pharmacy 1010 West Ave B MSC 131 Kingsville TX 78363

NUTT, RONALD, electrical engineer; b. Apr. 24, 1938; BSEE, U. Tenn., Knoxville, 1961, MSEE, 1962, PhD in Elec. Engring., 1969; MD (hon.), U. Essen, Germany, 2008. Rschr. Oak Ridge Nat. Lab., Tenn.; elec. engring. instr. U. Tenn.; v.p. EG&G Ortec, 1969—79; co-founder Tech. for Energy Corp., Radio Systems Corp., Delta M Corp.; co-founder, v.p. R&D, tech. dir. CTI Molecular Imaging Inc., Knoxville, 1983—98, pres., CEO, 2002—05, CTI PET Systems, Inc. (joint venture between CTI, Inc. & Siemens Med. Systems), Knoxville, 1998—2003; founder, chmn., CEO ABT Molecular Imaging, Inc., Louisville, Tenn., 2006—09, chmn., 2009—. Recipient Nathan Dougherty award, U. Tenn. Coll. Engring., 1997; named Disting. Scientist of Yr., Inst. Clin. PET, 1999. Fellow: IEEE (Outstanding Engr. award 1999, Medal for Innovations in Healthcare Tech. 2010); mem.: Acad. Molecular Imaging (Disting. Scientist of Yr. 1999). Achievements include with physicist David Townsend, implementing design, commercial development and clinical implementation of hybrid PET/CT scanners, named TIME Magazine's Invention of the Year in 2000; patents in field. Mailing: ABT Molecular Imaging Inc 3024 Topside Business Pk Louisville TN 37777 *

NUUTILA, PIRJO RIITTA, medical educator; b. Finland, June 19, 1959; m.; 1 child, Kristian. MD, U. Turku, 1984, PhD, 1992. Prof. medicine U. Turku, 2005—, vice-rector, 2010—; prof. metabolic rsch. Turku Pet Ctr., 1998—. Contbr. articles to Jour. of Clin. Investigation, Am. Jour. Physiology, Diabetes, Circulation, New Eng. Jour. Medicine and others. Mem. Finnish Med. Assn., Finnish Diabetes Rsch. Soc., Scandinavian Soc. for Study of Diabetes, European Assn. for Study of Diabetes. Business E-Mail: pirjo.nuutila@utu.fi.

NWANGBURUKA, OKECHUKWU NKEM, psychiatrist; b. Aba, Nigeria, Mar. 9, 1965; arrived in US, 1994; s. Joseph and Festa Nwangburuka; m. Iheoma B. Nwangburuka. MD, U. Maiduguri, Nigeria, 1988. Resident physician MCP/Hahnemann U. Hosps., Phila., 1995—98; clin. instr. Ohio State U., Columbus, 1998—2000; sr. psychiatrist Shasta County Mental Health, Redding, Calif., 2000—. Named Physician of the Yr., NRCC, 2005. Mem.: Nigeria Nat. Assn. USA, Central Calif. Acad. Child and Adolescent Psychiatry, Central Calif. Psychiatry Soc., North Valley Med. Assoc., Nigerian Med. Assn., Shasta Psychiat. Soc., Am. Acad. Child and Adolescent Psychiatry, Am. Psychiat. Assn. Office: Shasta County Mental Health 2640 Breslauer Way Redding CA 96001 Home: PO Box 581086 Elk Grove CA 95758-0019 Home Phone: 530-355-0655; Office Phone: 530-225-5200. Business E-Mail: onwangburuka@co.shasta.ca.us.

NWARU, BRIGHT IBEABUGHICHI, medical researcher; b. Lagos, Nigeria, Feb. 8, 1978; MPhil, U. Oslo, Norway, 2005; MSc in Health Scis., U. Tampere, Finland, PhD in Epidemiology, 2007. Rschr. Sch. Health Scis., U. Tampere, Finland, 2007—. Recipient Avellan Found. prize, Sch. Health Scis., U. Tampere, Finland., 2008, award, U. Tampare Finland, 2009—11; Rsch. grant, U. Tampere Found., Finland, 2008, Juho Vainio Found., Finland, 2008—09, Yrjo Johnson Found., Finland, 2009. Office: Sch Health Scis University Tampe Tampere 33014 Finland Office Fax: 358 3 3551 6057. Business E-Mail: bright.nwaru@uta.fi.

NWOSU, EZECHI CALLY, obstetrician; s. Nwazaoku Benedict and Uwaemenchehe Veronica Nwosu; m. Ijeoma Beverley Egereonu; children: Amara Callistus, Ugonna Simpson, Nneka Ijeoma Nicola. BMChB, U. Nigeria, Enugu, 1978; MS in Ob-Gyn., U. Liverpool, England, 1994. Specialist tng. GMC, 1996. Sr. registrar Mersey Deanery Hosp., Liverpool, 1993—95; cons. obstetrician & gynecologist Whiston Hosp., St Helens & Knowsley, Prescot, Merseyside, 1995—. Clin. dir. ob-gyn. Whiston Hosp., STHK, Prescot, 2002—07. Contbr. articles to profl. jours. Found. gov. St Edward's Roman Cath. Coll., Liverpool; found. sec. Med. Assn. Nigerian Specialist & GP's, Liverpool, 1997—2004. Fellow: RCOG; mem.: British Assn. Med. Mgrs., Med. Defence Union. Office: Whiston Hosp STHK NHS Warrington Rd Prescot L35 5DR England Office Phone: 0150 430 1054. Office Fax: 441514301335. Personal E-mail: ezechinwosu@hotmail.com. Business E-Mail: cally.nwosu@sthk.nhs.uk.

NWOSU, VERONICA C., microbiologist, science educator, medical researcher; d. Peter E. and Elizabeth E. Dike; m. Basil Derrick Nwosu, Apr. 23, 1983; children: Ijeoma Yvonne, Arinze Clement, Nkem Derrick, Jr., Chiedu Victor. BS in biol. sciences, U. of Ill., 1972—76; MS in microbiology, Roosevelt U., 1976—78; PhD in microbiology, Wayne State U., 1986—92. Quality control scientist Fearn Food Inc., Franklin Pk., Ill., 1978—81; sr. lectr. in microbiology Anambra State U. of Tech., Enugu and Awka, Nigeria, 1981—86; rsch. scientist Apex Bioscis., Inc., Research Triangle Park, NC, 1992—94; assoc. prof. NC Ctrl. U., Durham, NC, 1994—. Vis. rsch. fellow Nat. Inst. of Environ. Health Scis., Research Triangle Park, NC, 1998—; cons. DNA Scis., Morrisville, NC, 2000—01. Contbr. articles to profl. jours. Eucharistic min. St. Raphael Cath. Ch., Raleigh, NC, 1994—2003; sch. bd. mem. St. Raphael Cath. Sch., Raleigh, NC, 2003—; dir. of biology grad. program NC Ctrl. U., Durham, NC, 1998—2003, chairperson, biology faculty evaluation com., 2001—03. Recipient Best Biology Tchr. award, Kano State, Nigeria, 1978—79; Academic Merit scholarship, U. of Ill., 1974—76, B. Haley fellowship, Wayne State U., 1991, Faculty fellowship, Am. Soc. for Microbiology, 1997, Rsch. Grant award, Nat. Inst. of Gen. Med. Sciences, 2002—, Provost's Enhancement Rsch. fellowship, Wayne State U., 1990—91, Travel grant, NRC/NAS in conjunction with IUMS, 1999, HMU Ednl. Grant award, NC Biotechnology Ctr., 1994—96, Student Traineeship award, EPA, 2001—. Mem.: NC Acad. of Sci., Inst. of food Tech., Am. Soc. for Microbiology. Achievements include research in antibiotic resistance mechanisms; mechanism of benzene induction of leukemia in bone marrow cells; prevalence of e. coli in meats; characterization of recombinant hemoglobin; isolation, purification, and characterization of D-3-phosphoglycerate mutase enzyme. Avocations: travel, reading, writing, music, dance. Home: 1409 Shadyside Dr Raleigh NC 27612 Office: NC Central Univ 1801 Fayetteville St Durham NC 27707 Business E-Mail: vcnwosu@nccu.edu.

NYBORG, VANESSA MARIE, psychologist, researcher, educator; b. San Francisco, Mar. 1, 1972; d. Milton and Beatrice Nyborg. BA, UCLA, 1995; PhD, Duke U., 2001. Postdoctoral rsch. fellow Brown Med. Sch., Providence, 2001—03; rschr. Ctr. for Sch. Based Youth

Devel., U. Calif., Santa Barbara, 2003, asst. rschr., adj. prof. Gevirtz Sch. Edn., 2003—. Grantee, NIH, 2003—. Mem.: APA, Psi Chi. Office: U Calif Gevirtz Grad Sch Edn Santa Barbara CA 93106 Business E-Mail: vnyborg@education.ucsb.edu.

NYHAN, WILLIAM LEO, pediatrician, educator; b. Boston, Mar. 13, 1926; s. W. Leo and Mary N.; m. Christine Murphy, Nov. 20, 1948; children: Christopher, Abigail. Student, Harvard U., 1943-45; MD, Columbia U., 1949; MS, U. Ill., 1956, PhD, 1958; doctorate (hon.), Tokushima U., Japan, 1981. Intern Yale U.-Grace-New Haven Hosp., 1949-50, resident, 1950-51, 53-55; asst. prof. pediatrics Johns Hopkins U., 1958-61, assoc. prof., 1961-63; prof. pediatrics, biochemistry U. Miami, 1963-69, chmn. dept. pediatrics, 1963-69; prof. U. Calif., San Diego, 1969—, chmn. dept. pediatrics, 1969-86. Mem. FDA adv. com. on Teratogenic Effects of Certain Drugs, 1964-70; mem. pediatric panel AMA Council on Drugs, 1964-70; mem. Nat. Adv. Child Health and Human Devel. Council, 1967-71; mem. research adv. com. Calif. Dept. Mental Hygiene, 1969-72; mem. med. and sci. adv. com. Leukemia Soc. Am., Inc., 1968-72; mem. basic adv. com. Nat. Found. March of Dimes, 1973-81; mem. Basil O'Connor Starter grants com., 1973-93; mem. clin. cancer program project rev. com. Nat. Cancer Inst., 1977-81; vis. prof. extraordinario U. del Salvador (Argentina), 1982. Author (with E. Edelson): The Heredity Factor, Genes, Chromosomes and You, 1976; author: Genetic & Malformation Syndromes in Clinical Medicine, 1976, Abnormalities in Amino Acid Metabolism in Clinical Medicine, 1984, Diagnostic Recognition of Genetic Diseases, 1987; author: (with P. Ozand) Atlas of Metabolic Diseases, 1998; author: (with B. Barshop and P. Ozand) 2d edit., 2005; author: (with G. Hoffmann, J. Zschocke, S.G. Kahler and E. Mayatepek) Inherited Metabolic Diseases, 2001; editor: Amino Acid Metabolism and Genetic Variation, 1967, Heritable Disorders of Amino Acid Metabolism, 1974; mem. editl. bd.: Jour. Pediat., 1964—78, Western Jour. Medicine, 1974—86, King Faisal Hosp. Med. Jour., 1981—85, Annals of Saudi Medicine, 1985—87, mem. editl. com.: Ann. Rev. Nutrition, 1982—86, mem. editl. staff: Med. and Pediat. Oncology, 1975—83. Served with U.S. Navy, 1944-46; U.S. Army, 1951-53. Nat. Found. Infantile Paralysis fellow, 1955-58; recipient Commemorative medallion Columbia U. Coll. Physicians and Surgeons, 1967, Guthrie award Am. Assn. Mental Retardation, 1998, Pool of Bethesda award Bethesda Luth. Homes and Svcs., 1999. Fellow: Inst. Medicine of Nat. Acad. Scis., Am. Acad. Pediat. (Borden award 1980, Lifetime Achievement award 1999, Leonard Tow Humanism Medicine award Arnold P. Gold Found. 2008); mem.: AAAS, Biochem. Soc., Am. Coll. Med. Genetics, Am. Assn. Clin. Chemists, Am. Soc. Human Genetics (dir. 1978—81), Am. Soc. Clin. Investigation, Soc. Exptl. Biology and Medicine, Am. Inst. Biol. Scis., South African Human Genetics (hon.), Nat. Acad. Scis. Inst. Medicine (hon.), Inst. Investigaciones Citologicas (Spain) (corr.), Soc. Francaise de Pediatrie (corr.), Am. Pediatric Soc., Western Soc. Pediatric Rsch. (pres. 1976—77), Am. Soc. Pharmacology and Exptl. Therapeutics, Am. Assn. Cancer Rsch., Soc. Pediatric Rsch. (pres. 1970—71), Am. Chem. Soc., Am. Fedn. Clin. Rsch., Alpha Omega Alpha, Sigma Xi. Office: U Calif San Diego Dept Pediatrics # 0830 9500 Gilman Dr La Jolla CA 92093-0830 Office Phone: 619-543-3237. Business E-Mail: wnyhan@ucsd.edu.

NYIRI, PETER, orthopedist; b. Budapest, Hungary, Jan. 21, 1964; Grad., Semmelweis Med. Sch., 1988. Asst. prof. Orthop. Clinic Semmelweis Med. Sch., 1988—2004; cons. dept. trauma & orthop. St. John Hosp., Budapest, 2004. Mem.: Hungarian Trauma Assn., Hungarian Orthop. Assn. Office: Diós árok 1 3 Budapest Post 1125 Hungary Business E-Mail: nyirpet@vipmail.hu

NYIRJESY, ISTVAN, retired obstetrician, gynecologist; b. Budapest, Hungary, Nov. 14, 1929; came to U.S., 1954, naturalized, 1960; s. Sandor D. and Margit (Bertalan) N.; m. Michelle Shoepp, June 16, 1956; children: Francis, Paul, Christine. MD, Catholic U. Louvain, Belgium, 1955. Diplomate: Am. Bd. Ob-Gyn. Intern Cath. U. Louvain and Little Co. Mary Hosp., Evergeen Park, Ill., 1954-55; resident in gynecology obstetrics, 1960-63; chief obstetrical research Nat. Naval Med. Center, Bethesda, Md., 1966-68; ret., 1968; practice medicine specializing in Ob-Gyn Bethesda, 1968—2008; tchr. Georgetown Med. Sch. Clin. prof. Ob-Gyn Georgetown U., 1968—; cons. NIH, 1974—, FDA, 1977-88. Lit. editor Breast Disease: contbr. articles to med. jours.; author: Prevention and Detection of Gynecologic and Breast Cancer, 1994. Pres., Internat. Found. for Gynecol. Cancer Detection and Prevention, 1993—. Officer M.C. USN, 1956-68; advanced through grades to comdr. Recipient Sword of Hope pin Am. Cancer Soc., 1973, Vicennial medal Georgetown U., 1988. Fellow ACOG (Host award 1964), Hungarian Gynecologic Soc. (hon.), Internat. Coll. Surgeons; mem. Montgomery County (Md.) Med. Soc. (chmn. profl. edn. com. 1971-72), Am. Soc. of Breast Disease (past pres.), Assn. Profs. Ob-Gyn., Am. Soc. Reproductive Medicine, Washington Gynecol. Soc. (v.p. 1993-94, 1st v.p. 1994-95, pres. 1996-97). Office Phone: 301-229-3387. Personal E-mail: stnyir@aol.com.

NYMADAWA, PAGBAJABYN, physician, public health administrator; b. Barunburen, Selenghe, Mongolia, Jan. 11, 1947; s. Makhbolyn Pagbajab and Serenengyin Chimid; m. Tumur-ochiryn Oyunbat; children: Naranbaatar, Naranbat, Naranbold. Dr., Med. U., Ulaanbaatar, Mongolia, 1971; MD, Humboldt U., Berlin, 1977; DSc, Acad. Med. Scis., Moscow, 1989; MD (hon.), Rangsit U., Thailand, 1994. Lectr., chair physiology Med. U., 1971-74; postgrad. fellow Inst. Applied Virology, Berlin, 1974-77; head dept. virology Nat. Inst. Hyg. Epid. Microbiology, Ulaanbaatar, 1978-85; WHO fellow Med. Rsch. Inst., Eng., 1980; dep. dir. rsch. and devel. Nat. Inst. Hyg. Epid. Microbiology, Ulaanbaatar, 1985-87; dep. min. Ministry of Health, Ulaanbaatar, 1987-90; min. health Govt. of Mongolia, Ulaanbaatar, 1990—96, 2000—04; social policy advisor Pres. of Mongolia, 1998—2000; M.P. Mongolia. V.p. 43d World Health Assembly, Geneva, 1990; pres. 44th World Health Assembly, Geneva, 1991; chmn. Subassembly Med. Scis., Mongolian Acad. Sci., 1997—. Author 20 books. Recipient medal for 70th and 80th Jubilee of People's Revolution in Mongolia, Pres. of Mongolia, 1991, Order of the Polar Star, 1996. Mem. WHO (mem. exec. bd. 1992-95), Acad. Scis. Mongolia, Mongolian Med. Scis. (mem. editorial bd. jour. 1987-90, editor-in-chief 1990-2000), N.Y. Acad. Scis. Home: Central Post PO Box 596 Ulaanbaatar 13 Mongolia Office: Mongolian Acad Scis PO Box 596 Central Post Ulaanbaatar 13 Mongolia Home Phone: 976-11-345599; Office Phone: 976-11-450267. Personal E-mail: nymadawa@gmail.com.

OAKES, ELLEN RUTH, psychotherapist, health facility administrator; b. Bartlesville, Okla., Aug. 19, 1919; d. John Isaac and Eva Ruth (Engle) Harboldt; m. Paul Otis Oakes Sr., June 12, 1937 (div. April 1974); children: Paul Otis Jr., Deborah Ellen, Nancy Elaine Masters; m. Siegmar Johann Knopp, Nov. 24, 1975 (div. Feb. 1998). BA in Sociology, Psychology summa cum laude, Oklahoma City U., 1961; MS in Clin. Psychology, U. Okla., 1963, PhD, 1967. Lic. clin. psychologist, Okla. Chief psychometrist Okla. U. Guidance Ctr., Norman, 1962; psychology trainee VA Hosp., Oklahoma City, 1962-64, Cerebral Palsy Ctr., Norman, Okla., 1964-65; psychology intern Guidance Service, Norman, 1965-66, staff psychologist, 1966-67; asst. prof. psychology Okla. U. Med. Sch., Oklahoma City, 1967-70; supr. psychology interns Okla. Univ. Health Scis. Ctr., 1967-80; founder, dir. Timberridge Inst., Oklahoma City, 1970-90, pres., 1980-90; pvt. practice clin. psychologist Oklahoma City, 1970-92. Instr. Okla. U. extension course, Tinker AFB, Oklahoma City, 1963, U. Okla., 1965-66; discussion leader Inst. for Tchrs. of Disadvantaged Child Oklahoma City Sch. System, 1966; leader group therapy sessions Asbury Meth. and Westminster Presbyn. Chs., Oklahoma City, 1966; mem. psychology team confs. for hearing disorders, Okla. U. Med. Sch., 1967-70; cons. Oklahoma City Pub. Schs., 1970-72; cons., group leader halfway house, 1972; mem. Okla. State Bd. Examiners Psychologist, 1974, 75; lectr. chs., PTAs, hosps.; reviewer Am. Psychol. Assn. Civilian Health and Med. Program of the Uniformed Svcs., 1978-89. Workshop conductor on Shame & Sexuality, Zurick Jungian Inst. winter seminar, 1992; attended Européen Congrés de Gestalt Thérapie in Paris, 1992; contbr. articles to profl. jours. Speaker Okla. County Mental Health Assn. Annual Worry Clinic, St. Luke's Ch., Oklahoma City, 1968-92, psychology dept. Sorosis Club, St. Luke's Ch.; charter mem. English spkg. Christian Congregation mission outreach Pauluskirche, Bochum, Germany, 1993-97, exec. coun., 1996-97. Mem. APA (peer rev. project with CHAMPUS, 1978-89), Okla. Psychol. Assn. (life, pres. 1975-76, named Pioneer Psychologist of Okla. by exec. com. 1998). Avocations: art, travel, poetry, photography, walking.

OAKES, WALTER JERRY, pediatric neurosurgeon; b. De Soto, Mo., July 10, 1946; s. Marvin Melton and Mildred Florene (Link) O.; m. Linda Helen Maas (div. Jan. 1985); 1 child, Kathleen Suzanne; m. Jean Evans, Dec. 1988; children: Matthew Marvin, Peter Clifford. BA in Chemistry, U. Mo., 1968; MD, Duke U., 1972. Diplomate Am. Bd. Neurol. Surgeons. Neurosurgery resident Duke U., Durham, NC, 1972-78, asst. prof. neurosurgery, 1979-90, assoc. prof. neurosurgery, 1991—, asst. prof. pediatrics, 1981-92, assoc. prof. pediatrics, 1992; pediatric neurosurgery resident U. Toronto Hosp. for Sick Children, Ont., Canada, July-Dec., 1975; registrar pediatric neurosurgery U. London Hosp. for Sick Children, England, Sept., 1978-Feb., 1979; prof. neurosurgery and pediat. U. Ala., Birmingham, 1992—, Dan Hendley chair pediatric neurosurgery, 2002—. Fellow: ACS. Office: Children's Hosp Ala 1600 7th Ave S Ste 400 Birmingham AL 35233-1785 Office Phone: 205-879-7754. Business E-Mail: wjomd@uab.edu.

OAKLEY, AMANDA MARGARET MEREDITH, dermatologist; d. Michael Meredith Brown and Margaret Brown; m. David John Oakley, Oct. 2, 1982; children: Emily Margaret, Rebecca Lynette. MB, ChB, U. Bristol, Eng., 1979; diploma in health informatics, Otago U., New Zealand, 2000. Specialist dermatologist Tristram Clinic, Hamilton, New Zealand, 1986—, Health Waikato, Hamilton, 1987—, clin. dir. dept. dermatology, 1998—2010. Mem. med. adv. com. Waikato & Bay of Plenty Br., Cancer Soc. New Zealand, Hamilton, 1994—2010, clin. assoc. prof. Waikato Clin. Sch. faculty med. and health scis. U. Auckland, Hamilton, 2002—; website mgr., author. Co-editor: textbook Teledermatology, 2002; author: (numerous online pages) NZ DermNet; contbr. articles to profl. jours. Fellow: Royal Australasian Coll. Physicians (chairperson, specialist adv. com. 1994—99); mem.: Waikato Postgraduate Medicine Inc. (pres. 1999—2004), New Zealand Dermatol. Soc. (website mgr. 1996—, exec. com. mem. 1998—2001, pres. 2011—). Achievements include research in teledermatology. Office: Tristram Clinic 6 Knox Street 3204 Hamilton New Zealand Office Fax: +64 7 838-2032. Personal E-mail: oakley@wave.co.nz.

OAKLEY, DEBORAH JANE, educator; b. Jan. 31, 1937; d. George F. and Kathryn (Willson) Hacker; m. Bruce Oakley, June 16, 1958; children: Ingrid Andrea, Brian Benjamin. BA, Swarthmore Coll., 1958; MA, Brown U., 1960; MPH, U. Mich., 1969, PhD, 1977. Dir. teenage and adult programs YWCA, Providence, 1959-63; editl. asst. Stockholm U., 1963-64; rsch. investigator, lectr. dept. population planning U. Mich., 1971-77, asst. prof. cmty. health programs Ann Arbor, 1977-79, asst. prof. nursing rsch., 1979-81, assoc. prof., 1981-89, prof., 1989—2002, interim dir. Ctr. Nursing Rsch., 1988-90, acting dir. Ctr. Nursing Rsch., 1998, prof. emeritus, 2002—, interim dir. Health Asian Ams. program, 2005. Vis. prof. Beijing Med. U., 1996-2002; prin. investigator NIH, CDC and pvt. found. funded rsch. grants and contracts on family planning, women's health and health care in China, nat. adv. com. nursing rsch., 1993-97; adv. workshop on Nat. Survey on Family Growth, 1994-97; co-chair Mich. Initiative for Women's Health, 1993-95. Author: (with Leslie Corsa) Population Planning, 1979; contbr. articles to profl. jours. Bd. dirs. Planned Parenthood Fedn. Am., 1975-80; bd. mem. Friends of Hekab Be Biblioteca de Akumal, 2010-. Recipient Margaret Sanger award Washtenaw County Planned Parenthood, 1975, Outstanding Young Woman of Ann Arbor award Jaycees, 1970, Dist. Faculty award Mich. Assn. Gov. Bds., 1992, Blue Cross Blue Shield Found. of Mich. award for Excellence in Health Policy, 1996. Mem. APHA (chmn. population sect. coun.), Internat. Union Sci. Study Population, Midwest Nursing Rsch. Soc., Population Assn. Am., Delta Omega, Sigma Theta Tau (hon.). Democrat. Home: 5200 S Lake Dr Chelsea MI 48118-9481 Office: U Mich Sch Nursing Ann Arbor MI 48109-5482 E-mail: doakley@umich.edu.

OATES, JOHN ALEXANDER, III, medical educator and biomedical scientist; b. Fayetteville, NC, Apr. 23, 1932; s. John Alexander and Isabelle (Crowder) O.; m. Meredith Stringfield, June 12, 1956; children: David Alexander, Christine Larkin, James Caldwell. BS magna cum laude, Wake Forest Coll., 1953; MD, Bowman Gray Sch. Medicine, 1956. Intern, asst. resident medicine N.Y. Hosp.-Cornell U. Med. Center, NYC, 1956-58, 61-62; from clin. assoc. to sr. investigator Nat. Heart Inst., 1958-63; faculty Vanderbilt U. Sch. Medicine, Nashville, 1963—, prof. medicine and pharmacology, 1969—, Werthan prof. investigative medicine, 1974-84, chmn. dept. medicine, 1983-97, Thomas F. Frist Sr. prof. medicine, 1984—. Drug rsch. bd. Nat. Acad. Scis.-NRC, 1967-71; chmn. pharmacology and toxicology tng. com. Nat. Inst. Gen. Med. Scis., 1969-70; adv. coun. Nat. Heart, Lung and Blood Inst., 1985-89. Master ACP; fellow Am. Acad. Arts and Scis., Am. Assn. Advancement Sci.; mem. Am. Fedn. Clin. Rsch. (pres. 1970-71), Am. Soc. Clin. Investigation (v.p. 1976-77), Assn. Am. Physicians (pres. 1981-82), Am. Soc. Pharmacology and Exptl. Therapeutics (chmn. exec. com. divsn. clin. pharmacology 1967-69), Inst. of Medicine. Achievements include co-discovery of antihypertensive effect of methyldopa, elucidation of a number of interactions between drugs in humans; research in biochemistry and pathophysiology of eicosanoids. Home: 2032 Sunset Hills Terr Nashville TN 37215 Office: Vanderbilt Med Ctr 536 RRB Nashville TN 37232-6602 Home Phone: 615-665-1976; Office Phone: 615-343-4845. Business E-Mail: john.oates@vanderbilt.edu.

OATES, THOMAS W., JR., periodontist, researcher; s. Thomas Sr. and Jean Oates; m. Joan Oates, Aug. 20, 1980; children: Brian Jr., Kevin, Tyler. BA, Wash. and Jefferson Coll., 1979; DMD, U. Pa., 1983; PhD, Va. Commonwealth U., 1994. Diplomate Am. Bd. Periodontology. Prof. U. Tex. Health Sci. Ctr., San Antonio, 1994—, asst. dean clin. rsch. Fellow: Internat. Team for Implantology. Office Fax: 210-567-6858. Business E-Mail: oates@uthscsa.edu.

OBAGI, ZEIN E., dermatologist; Diplomate Am. Bd. of Dermatology. Chief med. cons. Obagi Med. Products (OMP), Calif., 1984—2006; chmn. dermatology dept. Obagi Dermatology and Plastic Surgery Hosp., Saudi Arabia, 1994—; chief cons. Obagi Laser and Skin Health Ctr., 1996—, Obagi Dermatology and Cosmetic Ctr., United Arab Emirates, 1997—. Author: (book) Obagi Skin Health-Restoration and Rejuvenation, 1999. Fellow: Am. Acad. of Dermatology; mem.: AMA, Am. Acad. of Aesthetic and Restorative Surgery, Soc. of Investigative Dermatology, Internat. Soc. of Dermatology, Am. Soc. of Dermatologic Surgery, Am. Acad. of Cosmetic Surgery. Office: Obagi Skin Health Institute 270 N Canon Drive Suite 100 Beverly Hills CA 90210 Office Phone: 310-275-3030.

OBAMOGIE, MERCY A., physician; b. Lagos, Nigeria, Jan. 18, 1954; d. Godwin I and Janet E. (Amiolemen) O.; m. Abiodun O. Odunmbaku, June 20, 1980 (div. 1995); children: Abisola, Adenike, Abiodun. BS, Columbia U., 1980; MD, U. Medicine and Dentistry N.J., Piscataway, 1984; MPH, Johns Hopkins U., 1987; MBA, U. Calif., Irvine, 2000; JD, Thomas Cooley Law Sch., Lansing, MI, 2006. Diplomate Am. Bd. Family Practice, Nat. Bd. Med. Examiners. Intern in internal medicine Muhlenberg Hosp., Plainfield, NJ, 1984-85; resident in gen. preventive medicine Johns Hopkins U., Balt., 1985-86; resident in family practice Georgetown U./Providence Hosp., Washington, 1986-89; pvt. practice Washington, Greenbelt, Md., 1989—; med. dir. Doctors Slim and Fitness Ctr., Greenbelt, 1996-98. Med. adv. bd. Metra Health Ins. Co., 1992-94; utilization com. Aetna Ins. Co., 1993-95, credentialing com., 1996; med. adv. com. United HealthCare, 1997; mem. planning com. Providence Hosp., Washington, 1996-98; with Prince George's Hosp. Ctr., Cheverly, Md., Howard U. Hosp., Washington, Doctors Cmty. Hosp., Lanham, Md., Providence Hosp., Washington; pres., med. dir. Mercy Med. Ctr., Benin City, Nigeria, 1996—; pres., CEO ASAKI Corp., Greenbelt, Md., 2000—. Contbr. articles to profl. jours. Office: 7323 Hanover Pkwy Ste A Greenbelt MD 20770-3017 Home: 12810 Willow Marsh Ln Bowie MD 20720-4651 Office Phone: 301-345-5900. Business E-Mail: obamogie.mercy@gmail.com.

OBANA, WILLIAM G., neurosurgeon; BS, Stanford U., Calif., 1983; MD, U. Calif., San Francisco, 1987. Clin. prof. chief neurosurgery dept. surgery U. Hawaii John A. Burns Sch. Medicine, Honolulu, 1994—. Mem.: Congress Neurol. Surgeons, Am. Assn. Neurol. Surgeons. Office: William G Obana MD Inc 1380 Lusitana St Ste 410 Honolulu HI 96813

OBANDO, IGNACIO, pediatrician, educator; b. Baena, Cordoba, Spain, Aug. 13, 1955; MD, U. Seville, PhD in Medicine, 1978. Attending physician Servicio Andaluz Salud, 1984—. Asst. prof. pediat. U. Seville, Sch. Medicine, 2006—11. Avocations: photography, mountain climbing. Home: Londres 98 Sevilla 41012 Spain Personal E-mail: iobando@us.es.

OBEIDAT, WASFY MOHAMMED, pharmacist, educator; b. Irbid, Jordan, Dec. 3, 1972; BSc in Pharmacy, Jordan U. Sci. and Tech., 1995; PhD in Pharmaceutics, U. Ga., 2002. Assoc. prof. pharmaceutics Jordan U. Sci. and Tech., 2003—. Recipient Best Invention award, Phila. U., Jordan, Best Rsch. award, Hisham Hijjawee Establishment. Mem.: Jordanian Pharmacist Assn. Avocations: reading, sports, travel. Home: Petra St Irbid 2438 Jordan

OBERFIELD, RICHARD ALAN, oncologist; b. NYC, July 29, 1932; s. George B. and Frances Oberfield; m. Valerie I. Oberfield, Feb. 14, 1954 (dec. Jan. 1980); children: Elizabeth A., Alice A.; m. Keren G. Oberfield, July 28, 1988. BA cum laude, Alfred U., 1953; MD, NYU, 1957. Lic. physician, Mass., N.Y.; diplomate Am. Bd. Internal Medicine. Intern Greenwich (Conn.) Hosp., 1957-58; USPHS sr. asst. surgeon venereal disease br. Detroit Receiving Hosp., 1958-60; tng. fellow pathology NYU Med. Ctr., NYC, 1960-61; resident in medicine Dartmouth Med. Ctr. Affiliated Hosps., Hanover, NH, 1961-63, fellow in hematology and cancer chemotherapy, 1963-65; staff physician sect. med. oncology dept. internal medicine Lahey Clinic Med. Ctr., Burlington, Mass., 1965—, head sect. med. oncology dept. internal medicine, 1969-85. Hosp. appts. include New Eng. Bapt. Hosp., Boston, 1965—80, New Eng. Deaconess Hosp., Boston, 1965—97, Mary and Arthur R. Clapham Hosp., Lahey Clinic Med. Ctr., Burlington, 1980—97; chmn. emeritus sect. med. oncology dept. internal medicine Lahey Clinic Med. Ctr., Burlington, 1997—; clin. rsch. cons. dept. rsch., 1997—; clin. instr. medicine Harvard Med. Sch., Boston, 1972—; asst. prof. dept. medicine Tufts U. Sch. Medicine, 2000—. Contbr. numerous articles to profl. publs. Fellow ACP (Meade Johnson postgrad. scholar 1962-63); mem. AMA (Cert. Merit 1966), Internat. Assn. for Study of Lung Cancer (founding mem.), Nat. Bd. Med. Examiners (diplomate), Am. Assn. for Cancer Rsch., Inc., Am. Soc. Clin. Oncology, Am. Assn. for Cancer Edn., Mass. Med. Soc., Mass. Soc. Internal Medicine, New Eng. Cancer Soc., Mass. Soc. Clin. Oncologists. Avocations: piano, writing, running, reading. Office: Lahey Clinic Med Ctr 41 Mall Rd Burlington MA 01805

OBERFIELD, SHARON ELEFANT, pediatric endocrinologist; b. NYC, Aug. 14, 1950; d. Nicholas and Anna (Weiss) Elefant; m. Richard A. Oberfield; 2 children. AB in Biology, Cornell U., 1970, MD, 1974. Diplomate in pediat. and pediatric endocrinology Am. Bd. Pediat. Intern in pediat. The NY Hosp., 1974-75, resident in pediat.,

1975-76, fellow in pediatric endocrinology, 1976-79, asst. attending pediatrician, 1979-84; asst. attending pediatrician endocrinology Meml. Sloan Kettering Cancer Ctr., NYC, 1986—2001. Provisional pediatrician to outpatient dept. NY Hosp., 1976-79; assoc. attending pediatrician St. Luke's-Roosevelt Hosp. Ctr., NYC, 1984-91, Presbyn. Hosp., NYC, 1991, Tisch Hosp., Bellevue Hosp., NYC, 1992—; attending pediatrician Children's Hosp. of NY-Presbyn. Hosp., 1998—; asst. attending pediatrician Meml. Sloan Kettering Cancer Ctr., 1979-84; asst. prof. pediat. Cornell U. Med. Coll., NYC, 1979-84, Columbia U. Coll. Physicians & Surgeons, NYC, 1984-91, assoc. prof. clin. pediat., 1991, prof., 1998—, dir. pediat. endocrinology, 2004—. Grantee NIH, 1978-84, 2005-, Hoffman-LaRoche, 1985-89, Eli Lilly, 1986-92. Children's Brain Tumor Found., 1995-98; recipient Mitchell Spivak Meml. prize in pediatrics, 1974. Mem. Am. Med. Women's Assn. (citation 1974), NY Acad. Scis., NY Pediatric Soc., Soc. Pediatric Rsch., Endocrine Soc., Lawson Wilkins Soc., Pediatric Endocrinology, Alpha Omega Alpha. Office: Divsn Pediat Endocrinology Columbia Univ 630 W 168th St PH-5E-522 New York NY 10032 Office Phone: 212-305-6559. Business E-Mail: seo8@columbia.edu.

OBERG, LYLE, physician, academic administrator; b. Forestburg, Alberta, Can. m. Evelyn Oberg; children: Jillian, Scott. Pre-med studies, Red Deer Coll.; MD, U. Alberta, Can. Physician Gen. Practice, Alberta; elected to legis. assembly Alberta Parliament, Edmonton, 1993—, appointed minister of learning, 1999—2004, appointed minister infrastructure and transp., 2005—06, minister fin., 2006—. Chmn. standing policy com. on health restructuring Alberta Legis. Assembly, Edmonton, Canada, 1995—97, minister of family and social svcs., 1997—99; Alberta rep. Ministerial Coun. on Social Policy Renewal; mem. treasury bd, and standing com. on learning and employment Alberta Legislative Assembly, 1999—. Avocations: golf, hunting, sailing.

OBERHELMAN, HARRY ALVIN, JR., surgeon, educator; b. Chgo., Nov. 15, 1923; s. Harry Alvin and Beatrice (Babel) O.; m. Betty Jane Porter, June 12, 1946; children: Harry Alvin III, James I., Robert P., Thomas L., Nancy L. Student, Yale U., 1942-43; BS, U. Chgo., 1946, MD, 1947. Diplomate: Am. Bd. Surgery. Intern U. Chgo. Clinics, 1947—48, resident surgery, 1948—51, 1952—57; asst. prof., assoc. prof. surgery U. Chgo. Sch. Medicine, 1957—60; mem. faculty Stanford Sch. Medicine, Calif., 1960—, prof. surgery, 1964—95, emeritus prof. surgery, 1995—; med. dir. Stanford Internat. Med. Svc., 2006—. Mem. div. licensing Calif. Bd. Med. Quality Assurance, 1970-82 Author papers in field. Served with USAF, 1951-53. Mem. AMA, Calif. Med. Assn., Soc. Univ. Surgeons, Am., Western, Pacific Coast surg. assns., Soc. Alimentary Tract, Halsted Soc., Fedn. State Med. Bds. U.S. (bd. dirs. 1979-82) Home: 668 Cabrillo St Stanford CA 94305-8404 Office Phone: 650-736-7964. Personal E-mail: hoberhelman@hotmail.com. E-mail: hoberhelman@stanfordmed.org.

OBERHOLTZER, J. CARL, pathologist, researcher; BA in Biochemistry, PhD in Biochemistry, U. Pa., Phila.; MD, Jefferson Med. Coll., Phila. Postdoctoral tng., residency in anatomic pathology, fellowship in neuropathology U. Pa.; faculty mem. dept. pathology and lab. medicine U. Pa. Sch. Medicine, chief divsn. neuropathology, vice chmn. dept. pathology and lab. medicine; assoc. dir. tng. Ctr. Cancer Rsch., Nat. Cancer Inst., NIH, Bethesda, Md., 2006—08, sr. clinician, chief Lab. Pathology, 2008—. Mem.: American Soc. Clin. Investigation, American Assn. Univ. Pathologists (Pluto Club), Coll. Physicians, Phila. Office: Nat Cancer Ctr Bldg 10, Rm 2N208 10 Center Dr Bethesda MD 20892 Office Phone: 301-594-1884. Office Fax: 301-402-0043. E-mail: oberholtzerc@mail.nih.gov. *

OBIMBO, MOSES MADADI, medical educator; b. Kenya, June 20, 1981; MBBCh, U. Nairobi, 2006, MS, 2009. Med. officer P.C.E.A Kikuyu Mission Hosp., 2007—08; tutorial fellow U. Nairobi, 2008—10, lectr., sch. medicine, 2011—. Sec. Cmty. Medicare Africa, 2008. Mem.: Med. Students Against Aids. Avocations: singing, writing, travel. Office: Riverside Dr Nairobi 00100 Kenya Personal E-mail: obimbo24@yahoo.com.

OBINATA, GORO, mechanical engineer, educator; b. Miyagi, Japan, Nov. 30, 1949; MS in Engring., Tohoku U., 1974, Deng, 1977. Prof. dept. mech. engring. Mining Coll., Akita U., 1990—2001; prof. dept. mech. engring. Grad. Sch. Engring. Nagoya U., 2001—03, prof. Intelligent Sys. Divsn., Ctr. Coop. Rsch. Advanced Sci. and Tech., 2003—06; prof. divsn. integrated rsch. projects EcoTopia Sci. Inst., Nagoya U., 2006, dep. dir., 2010—. Vis. prof. Rsch. Sch. Phys. Scis. Dept. Sys. Engring., Australian Nat. U., 1986—87, vis. prof. Rsch. Sch. Info. Sci. and Engring., 1995; vis. prof. Dept. Aero. Tech., Purdue U., 1995—96, Faculty Mech. Engring. & Marine Tech., Delft U. Tech., 1995. Fellow: Japan Soc. Mech. Engrs. (Achievement award, Best Paper award), Japanese Soc. Automobile Engrs.; mem.: Soc. Instrument and Control Engrs., Inst. Elec. and Electronic Engrs., Robotics Soc. Japan. Office: Nagoya University Foro-cho Chikusa-ku Nagoya 464-8603 Japan Office Fax: 81-52-789-5589. Business E-Mail: obinata@mech.nagoya-u.ac.jp.

OBINATA, TAKASHI, retired biology professor; b. Nagano, Japan, Jan. 2, 1940; BSc, U. Tokyo, 1963, DSc, 1969. Prof. faculty sci. Chiba U., 1981—2005, dean Grad. Sch. Sci. & Tech., 2000—04, emeritus prof., 2005—. Adj. prof. Grad. Sch. Sci., U. Tokyo, 1993—2000. Recipient Zool. Sci. award, Japan. Mem.: Zool. Soc. Japan, Am. Soc. Cell Biology. Avocation: running. Home: Makuhari-hongo 3-31-14 Hanamigawa-ku Chiba 262-0033 Japan Business E-Mail: tobinata@faculty.chiba-u.jp.

OBOT, ISIDORE SILAS, public health scholar; s. Silas and Jane Obot; m. Theresa Isidore Adadiaha, Dec. 1, 1984; children: Ifiok Isidore, Aniekan Isidore, Ubong Isidore, Tete Isidore. BA, Loyola Coll., Balt., 1976, MA, 1978; PhD, Howard U., Washington, 1982; MPH, Harvard U., 1984. From lectr. to sr. lectr. psychology U. Jos, Nigeria, 1985—2001; rsch. fellow Johns Hopkins U. Sch. Pub. Health, Balt., 1998—2000; scientist substance abuse WHO, Geneva, 2002—06; prof. sch. pub. health and policy Morgan State U., Balt., 2006—, chmn. dept. behavioral health scis., 2006—. Bd. dirs. Centre for Rsch. and Info. on Substance Abuse, Jos, 1990—2002. Editor: African Jour. Drug and Alcohol Studies. Rsch. and Writing grant, John D. and Catherine T. McArthur Found., 2000—01. Mem.: Internat. Soc. Addiction Jour. Editors (bd. dirs. 2004—), Kettil Bruun Soc. for Alcohol Rsch. (steering com. 2003—), Coll. on Problems of Drug Dependence, Beta Kappa Chi, Psi Chi. Roman Catholic. Avocations: travel, reading, music, walking. Office Fax: 443-885-8309. Personal E-mail: obotis@gmail.com.

OBRAMS, GUNTA IRIS, clinical research administrator; b. Düsseldorf, Germany, Sept. 2, 1953; came to U.S., 1961; d. Robert and Olga (Baltins) O.; m. Malcolm DeWitt Patterson, Dec. 22, 1975; 1 child, Andrew McDougal Patterson. BS in Biology cum laude, Rensselaer Poly. Inst., 1977; MD, Union U., Albany, NY, 1977; MPH, Johns Hopkins U., 1982, PhD, 1988. Resident in obstetrics and gynecology Ea. Va. Grad. Sch. Medicine, Norfolk, 1977-78; community physician Southampton Meml. Hosp., Franklin, Va., 1978-81; resident in gen. preventive medicine sch. hygiene and pub. health Johns Hopkins U., Balt., 1981-84, project dir., 1983-85, med. dir., 1985-86; med. officer divsn. cancer etiology Nat. Cancer Inst., Bethesda, Md., 1986-89, dep. chief, 1989-90, chief, 1990-96, dir. extramural epidemiology & genetics program, 1996-2001; mgmt. US Coast Guard Health Svcs., 2001—05; med. officer divsn. clin. resources NIH, Bethesda, 2005—08, dep. divsn. dir. clin. resources, 2008—. Editor: (with M. Potter): The Epidemiology and Biology of Multiple Myeloma, 1991; contbr. articles to profl. jours. With USPHS, 1987—. Recipient Nat. Cancer Inst. Nat. Rsch. Svc. award, 1981, Rsch. Career award Nat. Inst. Occupational Safety & Health; scholar Am. Med. Women's Assn., 1977. Mem. Phi Beta Kappa, Delta Omega, Alpha Omega Alpha. Office: DCRR NCRR NIH 6701 Democracy Blvd MSC-4874 Bethesda MD 20892 Office Phone: 301-435-0768. Personal E-mail: go4wellness@comcast.net.

O'BRIEN, JAMES EDWARD, JR., surgeon; b. Hartford, Conn., June 15, 1963; s. James Edward and Joan O'Brien; m. Lina Maheswata Pattanayak, Jan. 10, 1998; children: Lauren Maya, Connor Rajan, Christine Mira. BS, Rensselaer Polytechnic Inst., Troy, NY, 1985; MD, U. Conn., Farmington, 1989. Resident Thomas Jefferson U. Hosp., 1989—99, Children's Hosp. Phila., 1999—2001; pediatric cardiothoracic surgeon Children's Mercy Hosp., Kans. City, Mo., 2001—. Contbr. articles to profl. jours. Fellow: ACS; mem.: AMA, So. Thoracic Surg. Assn., Am. Heart Assn., Soc. Thoracic Surgeons. Avocations: swimming, golf, travel. Office: Children's Mercy Hosp 2401 Gillham Rd Kansas City MO 64108 Office Fax: 816-802-1245. Business E-Mail: jobrien@cmh.edu.

O'BRIEN, JENNIFER CARROLL, medical researcher, consultant; b. Dec. 1, 1984; AB in Neurosci., Harvard Coll., 2007; MPhil in Pub. Health, U. Cambridge, 2010. Rsch. asst. Harvard Sch. Pub. Health, 2007—09, rsch. cons., 2009—. Cons. Economist Intelligence Unit, 2009; tech. advisor Longitudinal Aging Study in India, 2010; bd. advisors WaterWalla, Inc., 2011. Contbr. articles to profl. jours., chapters to books. Homerton Coll. Rsch. grant, U. Cambridge. Mem.: Cambridge U. Pub. Health and Epidemiology Soc., Global Health Coun. Avocations: cooking, travel, reading. Office: 80 Broad St Ste 395 Boston MA 02110 Personal E-mail: jeniaifercarroll.obrien2@gmail.com.

O'BRIEN, JOSEPH R., surgeon, educator; b. Washington, May 24, 1974; BA, Vanderbilt U., Nashville, 1996; MD, George Wash. U., 2001. Spine fellow Johns Hopkins U., 2006—07; asst. prof., orthop. and neurol. surgery George Wash. U., 2007—. Assoc. dir., spine surgery George Wash. U. Hosp., 2007. Fellow: Am. Acad. Orthop. Surgeons; mem.: Soc. Lateral Access Surgery, Scoliosis Rsch. Soc., Cervical Spine Rsch. Soc., Alpha Omega Alpha. Avocation: golf. Office: 2150 Pa Ave NW Dept Washington DC 20037 Business E-Mail: jobrien@mfa.gwu.edu.

O'BRIEN, KEVIN D., medical educator; BS summa cum laude, U. Idaho, 1980; MD honors, U. Wash., 1984. Diplomate Am. Bd. Internal Medicine, Cardiovascular Diseases Am. Bd. Internal Medicine. Intern, resident U. Wash., Seattle, 1984—87, chief med. resident, 1987—88, prof., medicine, 2008—; atteding physician U. Wash. Med. Ctr., Seattle, 1988—. Med. student rsch. fellow Fred Hutchinson Cancer rsch. Ctr., Seattle, 1981. Contbr. articles to profl. jours. Recipient Sheard-Sanford award, Am. Soc. Clin. Pathologists, 1983. Fellow: Am. Heart Assn.; mem.: Western Soc. Clin. Investigation (pres. 2007—, councilor 2003—06, Outstanding Investigator award 2003), Am. Fedn. Med. Rsch. (pres. 2001—02, found. pres. 2002—03). Office: Univ Wash Med Ctr Campus Box 356422 1959 NE Pacific St Seattle WA 98195-6422 Office Phone: 206-685-3930. Business E-Mail: cardiac@u.washington.edu.

O'BRIEN, KYLIE ANN, associate dean; b. Victoria, Australia, 1965; MPH, Monash U., 1997, PhD, 2006. Program head, masters traditional Chinese medicine & acupuncture U. Western Sydney, 2003—05; course coord. Chinese medicine Victoria U., 2006—09, assoc. dean, tchg. & learning, 2009—. V.p. Victorian Br. Fedn. Chinese Medicine & Acupuncture Socs., Australia, 2011; external mem. academic bd. Think Edn., 2010—11. Mem.: Fedn. Chinese Medicine & Acupuncture Societies (Australia). Avocation: dance. Office: PO Box 14428 Melbourne Victoria 8001 Australia Business E-Mail: kylie.obrien@vu.edu.au.

O'BRIEN, MARK STEPHEN, pediatric neurosurgeon; b. West New York, NJ, Jan. 2, 1933; s. Mark Peter and Hannah (Dempsey) O'B.; m. Mary Morris Johnson, June 3, 1961 (div.); children: David, Derek, Marcia; m. Karen-Marie Sampson, June 1, 1984; children: Blythe, Blake, Lauren-Blair, Connor. AB cum laude, Seton Hall U., 1955; MD, St. Louis U., 1959. Diplomate Am. Bd. Neurol. Surgery, Am. Bd. Pediat. Neurol. Surgery. Intern St. John's Hosp., St. Louis, 1959-60, resident in surgery, 1960; resident in neurology Charity Hosp., New Orleans, 1962-63; resident in neurosurgery St. Vincent's Hosp., NYC, 1963-64, resident in surgery, 1965; sr. resident, chief resident Cin. Children's Hosp., U. Cin., 1965-68, research fellow in neurosurgery, 1966-67, 67-68; NIH spl. fellow in neuroradiology Albert Einstein Coll. Medicine, NYC, 1968-69; mem. faculty dept. surgery Emory U. Sch. Medicine, Atlanta, 1969—2003, prof. surgery, assoc. prof. pediatrics, 1979—2003; chief neurosurgery Henrietta Egleston Hosp. for Children, Atlanta, 1971—2003; prof. neurosurgery U. Ark. for Med. Scis., Little Rock, 2005—. Trustee Elaine Clark Center for Exceptional Children; mem. med. adv. bd. Nat. Found., March of Dimes; trustee Henrietta Egleston Hosp. for Children; mem. profl. adv. panel Spina Bifida Assn. Am. Editorial bd. Pediatric Neurosurgery; contbr. chpts. to books, articles to med. jours. Served with USNR, 1960-62. Mem. Am. Assn. Neurol. Surgeons, Soc. Neurol. Surgeons, Congress Neurol. Surgeons, Internat. Soc. Pediatric Neurosurgery, Greater Atlanta Pediatric Soc., Med. Soc. Atlanta, AMA, ACS, Ga. Neurosurg. Soc., Am. Acad. Pediatrics, Am. Soc. Pediatric Neurosurgery, Pediatric Oncology Group, Am. Bd. Pediatric Neurol. Surgery (sec.), Acad. Pediatric Neurosurgeons. Home: 5720 Hawthorne Rd Little Rock AR 72207 Office: Ark Childrens Hosp 800 Marshall St Slot 838 Little Rock AR 72202 Office Phone: 501-364-1448. Personal E-mail: mobrien33@aol.com. Business E-Mail: obrienmark@uams.edu.

O'BRIEN, RICHARD L(EE), physician, educator, academic administrator; b. Shenandoah, Iowa, Aug. 30, 1934; s. Thomas Lee O'B. and Grace Ellen (Sims) Parish; m. Joan Frances Gurney, June 29, 1957; children: Sheila Marie, Kathleen Therese, Michael James, Patrick Kevin. MS in Physiology, Creighton U., 1958, MD, 1960. Diplomate Nat. Bd. Med. Examiners. Intern and resident Columbia med. divsn. Bellevue Hosp., NYC, 1960-62; postdoctoral fellow in biochemistry Inst. for Enzyme Rsch., U. Wis., 1962-64; asst. prof. to prof. pathology Sch. Medicine, U. So. Calif., LA, 1966-82, dep. dir. Cancer Ctr., 1975-80, dir. rsch. and edn. Cancer Ctr., 1980-81, dir. Cancer Ctr., 1981-82; dean Sch. Medicine Creighton U., Omaha, 1982-92, acting v.p. health scis., 1984-85, v.p. health scis., 1985-99, prof. health policy and ethics, univ. prof., 2002—11, dir. office of interprofl. edn., 2002—05, prof. emeritus, 2011—. Vis. prof. molecular biology U. Geneva, 1973-74; mem. cancer control rsch. grants rev. com. NIH, Nat. Cancer Inst.; mem. Cancer Ctr. Support grant rev. com. Nat. Cancer Inst., 1984-88, chmn. 1987-88; co-chmn. United Way/CHAD Pacesetter campaign, 1988, 94; bd. dirs. Health Future Found., 2003-09; cons. in field. Contbr. articles to profl. jours.; editor various profl. jours. Bd. dirs. Opera Omaha, 1994-2001, 04-10, pres., 1998-2000, Opera Omaha Found., 2000—06, chmn., 2004—06; co-chair, Building Bright Futures Adolescent Behavioral Health Task Force, 2007-09, NE Medical Assn. Health Care Reform Task Force, 2007-10. Capt. US Army, 1964-66. Recipient Disting. Svc. award Met. Omaha Med. Soc., 1987, 2010, Silver Rose Opera Omaha, 2000; Spl. fellow Nat. Cancer Inst., 1967-69; named Citizen of Yr. Combined Health Agys. Drive-Health, 1986. Mem. ACP, Am. Assn. Pathologists, Am. Assn. Cancer Rsch., Am. Assn. Cancer Edn., AAAS, Am. Assn. Cancer Insts. (dir. 1982-83), Assn. Am. Med. Colls. (chmn. MCAT evaluation panel 1987-88, liaison com. on med. edn., 1988-93, co-chmn, 1989-93, adv. panel Strategic Planning Health Care Reform 1992-96), Assn. Acad. Health Ctrs. (long-range planning com. 1986, 2000, nominating com. 1987, 96, Task Force Health Care Delivery 1992, mem. task force on leadership and instl. values 1993-99, bd. dirs. 1998-99), Am. Cancer Soc. (adv. com. Inst. Rsch. Grants 1977-80, Outstanding Leadership award 1981, dir. Calif. divsn. 1980-82, dir. Nebr. divsn. 1992-96), Am. Hosp. Assn. (com. on med. edn. 1986-89), Alpha Omega Alpha. Home: 9927 Essex Dr Omaha NE 68114-3873 Office: Creighton Univ California At 24th Omaha NE 68178-0001 Home Phone: 402-392-0331; Office Phone: 402-280-2017. Business E-Mail: rlo@creighton.edu.

O'BRIEN, STEPHEN JAMES, geneticist, researcher; b. Rochester, NY, Sept. 30, 1944; s. Bernard Carroll and Kathryn Marie O'Brien; m. Diane Louise Rockhill, Nov. 28, 1968; children: Mary, Meghan. BS, St. Francis Coll., Loretto, Pa., 1966; PhD, Cornell U., 1971. Postdoctoral fellow genetics-biochemistry Gerontology Rsch. Ctr., Balt., 1971-72; NIH postdoctoral fellow Nat. Cancer Inst., NIH, Bethesda, Md., 1972-73, staff fellow Lab. Viral Carcinogenesis, 1973-78, rsch. geneticist Lab. Viral Carcinogenesis Frederick, Md., 1978-80, chief genetics sect., 1980—, acting chief Lab. Viral Carcinogenesis, 1983-85, chief Lab. Genomic Diversity, Ctr. Cancer Rsch., 1986—. Zoology and botany tchg. asst. St. Francis Coll., 1965-66; gen. genetics lab. instr. and lectr. Cornell U., 1966-71, biology and soc. tchg. asst., 1969-71, human genetics discussion leader, 1970-71; adj. prof. genetics George Washington U., 1974—; adj. grad. advisor dept. biology Am. U., 1979—, Hood Coll., 1982—; adj. prof. dept. zoology U. Md., 1982—, dept. biology Johns Hopkins U., 1982—; faculty affiliate dept. pathology Colo. State U., 1994—; affiliate prof. dept. biology George Mason U., 1994—; apptd. rsch. fellow Smithsonian Instn., Washington, 1982—; bd. trustees Am. Type Culture Assn., Rockville, Md., 1983—; apptd. exec. bd. Am. Type Culture Collection, Rockville, 1984—, sec.-treas. bd. trustees, 1987—; founder, co-dir. New Opportunities in Animal Health Scis., Ctr. for Wildlife Scis., Smithsonian Instn., 1985—; mem. cat specialist group Internat. Union for Conservation of Nature, Geneva, 1985—, mem. captive breeding specialist group species survival commn., 1986—; lectr. in field. Editor Isozyme Bulletin, 1975-78, Genetic Maps, 1980—; exec. editor Jour. Heredity, Am. Genetics Assn., 1987—; assoc. editor Genomics, 1987-91, Mammalian Genome, 1990—, Molecular Phylogenetics and Evolution, 1990—; guest editor Current Biology, 1993; jour. adv. bd. Cosmos, 1994; contbr. numerous articles to profl. jours. Mem. AAAS, Genetics Soc. Am., Am. Soc. Naturalists, Tissue Culture Assn., Am. Genetics Assn. (bd. dirs. 1984—, chmn. long range planning com. 1985—), Am. Assn. Zool. Pks. and Aquariums (advisor spl. survival plan-cheetah 1986—), N.Y. Acad. Sci., Cosmos Club. Achievements include research in molecular genetics, developmental and cell biology, genetics of oncology, viral oncology, immunology and reproductive physiology, molecular evolution, paleontology, cytology, populations genetics. Office: Nat Cancer Inst Lab Genomic Diversity Bldg 560 Rm 21-105 PO Box B Frederick MD 21702-1201 Office Phone: 301-846-1296. Office Fax: 301-846-1686. Business E-Mail: steveobrien@mail.nih.gov. *

O'BROCHTA, DAVID A., molecular biologist, researcher; b. Manhassett, NY, Apr. 26, 1955; married. BSc in Biology (Entomology), U. Kans., Lawrence, 1977; PhD in Devel. & Cell Biology, U. Calif., Irvine, 1984. Rsch. and tchg. asst. dept. develop. and cell biology U. Calif., Irvine, 1979—84, NSF postdoctoral rsch. fellow in microbial molecular genetics & plant biology San Diego, 1985—86; postdoctoral rsch. fellow in insect molecular genetics USDA-ARS, Gainesvile, Fla., 1986—89; asst. prof. Ctr for Agricultural Biotechnology U. Md. Biotechnology Inst., 1989—95, assoc. prof. Ctr for Agricultural Biotechnology, 1995—2004, prof. Ctr. for Biosystems Rsch., 2004—. Hon. prof. Bangalore U., India, 1998. Assoc. editor Insect Molecular Biology, 1992—, mem. editl. bd., 1995—; contbr. of several articles to profl. journsls, chapters to books. Mem.: Am. Soc. of Tropical Medicine and Hygiene, Entomological Soc. America, Genetic Soc. of America. Achievements include patents in field. Office: University of Maryland Biotechnology Institute 5115 Plant Sciences Bldg College Park MD 20742-4450 Home: Center for Biosystems Research Univ Maryland Biotechnology Inst 5141 Plant Sciences Bldg College Park MD 20742 Office Phone: 301-405-7680. Office Fax: 301-314-9075. Business E-Mail: obrochta@umbi.umd.edu.

O'CALLAGHAN, CLARE CECILIA, music therapist, educator; b. Melbourne, Victoria, Australia, Jan. 6, 1961; d. Vincent Clarence and Eileen Rosalie O'Callaghan; m. Richard John Hiscock, Mar. 22, 1986; children: Nathaniel John Hiscock, Hilary Brigid Hiscock, Joshua Richard Hiscock. BSW, U. of Melbourne, 1982, BMus, 1987, MMus, 1994, PhD, 2001. Registered music therapist Australian Music Therapy Assn., 1985. Social worker Bethlehem Hosp., Melbourne, Victoria, Australia, 1982—86, music therapist, 1985—91; music therapist sr. clinician Caritas Christi Hospice, Melbourne, 1992—94, Peter MacCallum Cancer Ctr., Melbourne, 1998—; clin. assoc. prof. Dept. Medicine, U. Melbourne. Hon. rsch. fellow U. Melbourne; lectr. in field; editl. bd. mem. Jour. Music & Medicine, 2009—, Jour. Nursing & Health Scis., 2009—, Jour. Music Therapy, 2011; editl. adv. bd. mem. Nordic Jour. Music Therapy. Editor: Australian Jour. Music Therapy, 2002—05; editl. bd. mem.:, 1993—2000, 2008—; editl. bd. mem. Music Therapy Perspectives, 2001—06. Recipient Postgrad. Rsch. award, Australia, 1998—2000; grantee, Dept. of Edn., Tng. and Youth Affairs, Australia, 1998—2001; fellow Queen Elizabeth Silver Jubilee fellowship for young Australians, The Brit. Coun., Australia, 1985; postdoc. fellowship, Nat. Health and Med. Rsch. Coun., 2008—10. Mem.: Internat. Assn. Music & Medicine (exec. bd. mem. 2009—), World Fedn. of Music Therapy (mem. rsch. and ethics com. 1997—2003, 2008—10, chair 2011), Australian Music Therapy Assn. (Ruth Bright Excellence award 1995, 2008, 2010). Avocations: time with family, hiking, cross country skiing, attending concerts. Office: Peter MacCallum Cancer Ctr Locked Bag 1 8006 Victoria VIC Australia Office Fax: 61 3 9656 1410. Business E-Mail: clare.ocallaghan@petermac.org.

O'CALLAGHAN, NATHAN JAMES, research scientist; b. Australia, Oct. 21, 1977; BSc, U. Adelaide, 1998; PhD, ANU, 2007. Postdoc. fellow CSIRO-Food and Nutritional Scis., 2007—10, rsch. scientist, 2010—. Office: PO Box 10041 Adelaide 5000 Australia Office Fax: 61883038899. Business E-Mail: oca018@csiro.au.

OCEAN, ALLYSON JOY, oncologist, educator; b. Jan. 27, 1972; MD with honors, Tufts U. Sch. Medicine, 1998. Cert. Internal Medicine, Hematology, Med. Oncology. Intern NY Presbyn.-Cornell Campus, resident, fellow, hematology and med. oncology; med. oncologist, attending physician gastrointestinal oncology NY Presbyn. Hosp.-Columbia U. Coll. Physicians & Surgeons & Weill Med. Coll. Cornell U.; asst. prof. medicine Weill Med. Coll. Cornell U.; med. oncologist Jay Monahan Ctr. for Gastrointestinal Health. Mem. bd. advisors OralChemo. Contbr. articles to profl. publications. Mem.: Am. Assn. for Cancer Rsch., Am. Soc. Hematology, Am. Soc. Clin. Oncology. Office: 525 E 68th St Payson 3 New York NY 10021 Office Phone: 212-746-2844. Office Fax: 212-746-0416.

OCHS, SIDNEY, neurophysiology researcher, educator; b. Fall River, Mass., June 30, 1924; s. Nathan and Rose (Kniaz) O.; m. Bess Rutner; children: Rachel F., Raymond S. Susan B. PhD in Physiology, U. Chgo., 1952. Rsch. assoc. Ill. Neuropsychiat. Inst., Chgo., 1952-54; rsch. fellow Calif. Inst. Tech., Pasadena, 1954-56; asst. prof. dept. physiology U. Tex. Med. Br., Galveston, 1956-58; assoc. prof. dept. physiology Ind. U., Indpls., 1958-61, prof., 1961-94, prof. emeritus, 1994—. Author: Elements of Neurophysiology, 1965, Axoplasmic Transport and Its Relation to Other Nerve Functions, 1982, A History of Nerve Functions: From Animal Spirits to Molecular Mechanisms, 2004; founding editor, editor-in-chief: Devel. Neurobiology (formerly Jour. Neurobiology), 1969-76, assoc. editor, 1977-86. With US Army, 1943-45. Mem. Internat. Brain Rsch. Orgn., Internat. Soc. Neurochemistry, Internat. Soc. Hist. Neurosciences, Am. Physiol. Soc., Soc. Neurosci., Am. Soc. Neurochemistry, Peripheral Nerve Soc., Hist. Sci. Soc. Democrat. Jewish. Avocations: amateur radio, history. Office: Ind U Med Ctr Dept Cellular & Integ Physiology 635 Barnhill Dr Indianapolis IN 46202-5126 Office Phone: 317-274-7940. Business E-Mail: sochs@iupui.edu.

OCHSNER, JOHN LOCKWOOD, thoracic-cardiovascular surgeon; b. Madison, Wis., Feb. 10, 1927; s. Edward William Alton and Isabel (Lockwood) O.; m. Mary Lou Hannon, Mar. 20, 1954; children: John L., Joby Hannon, Katherine Lockwood, Frank Hannon. MD, Tulane U., 1952; hon. diploma (hon.), U. Delgado, San Salvador, El Salvador, 1999. Diplomate Am. Bd. Thoracic Surgery (chmn. 1993-95), Am. Bd. Surgery, Am. Bd. Vascular Surgery. Intern Univ. Mich. Hosp., Ann Arbor, 1952-53, resident, 1953-54, Baylor U. Affiliated Hosp., Houston, 1956-58, 1958-59; chief surg. resident Tex. Children's Hosp., 1959-60; instr. Baylor U., Houston, 1960-61; mem. staff Ochsner Clinic, New Orleans, 1961—, chmn. dept. surgery, 1966-87, chmn. emeritus dept surgery, 1987—; clin. asst. prof. Tulane U., New Orleans, 1961-65, clin. assoc. prof., 1965-70, clin. prof. surgery, 1970—. Vis. prof. to more then 40 univs. and colls. Author: (with others) Coronary Artery Surgery, 1978. Pres. Tennis Patrons Assn. New Orleans, 1972; image amb. City of New Orleans, 1982; bd. dirs. Internat. Trade Mart, New Orleans, 1983. Capt. USAF, 1954-56. Recipient award, Life Mag., 1961, Golden Plate Acad. Achievement award, 1962, award of distinction, Am. Heart Assn. La., 1976, Svc. award, Cystic Fibrosis Rsch. Found., 1977—78, medal of honor, Ecuador, 1981, Crystal Achievement award, Child's Wish of Greater New Orleans, 1987, Young Leadership Coun. award, 1987, medal of honor, Czechoslovakian Surg. Soc., 1996, Honor of Achievement, Am. Heart Assn., 1997, Internat. Recognition award, Denton A. Cooley Cardiovasc. Surg. Soc., 1998, Outstanding Alumnus award, Tulane Sch. Medicine, 1998, Spirit of Love award, Ronald McDonald House Charities, 1999, DeBakey award, DeBakey Internat. Surg. Soc., 2000, Outstanding Physician award, Orleans Parish Med. Soc., 2002, Weiss Brotherhood award, New Orleans chpt. Nat. Conf. for Cmty. and Justice, 2002, Outstanding Person award, Family Svc. Greater New Orleans, 2004, DeBakey medal, Covenant Heart Inst., 2007, Order of the Plimsoll Mark, World Trade Ctr.; named Rex, King of Carnival, Mardi Gras, New Orleans, 1990, Grand Marshall, Oktoberfest, 1990, 1992. Mem. Am. Assn. Thoracic Surgery (sec. 1979-83, pres. 1992-93), New Orleans Surg. Soc. (pres. 1977-78), So. Surg. Assn. (pres. 1991), So. Assn. for Vascular Surgery (pres. 1983), Boston Club, La. Club, New Orleans Country Club, City Club, Alpha Omega Alpha. Republican. Office: Ochsner Clinic Found 1514 Jefferson Hwy BH 231 New Orleans LA 70121-2483 Home: 170 Walnut St 9-H New Orleans LA 70118

OCHSNER, MIMS GAGE, surgeon; b. New Orleans, La., May 10, 1953; BA in Chemistry, Southern Meth. U., 1975; MD, Tulane U. Sch. Medicine, 1979. Chief trauma svcs. and surg. critical care Meml. U. Med. Ctr., Savannah, Ga., 1994—. Prof. surgery Mercer U. Sch. Medicine, 1998—2011; pres. Ga. Surg. Soc., 2007—08, Western Trauma Assn., 2010—11; trauma com. ACS, 2010—11; 2nd v.p. Southeastern Surg. Congress, 2011—. Decorated Def. Meritorious Svc. medal USN, Navy Commendation medal; recipient Barry Goldwater Svc. award, Uniformed Svcs. U., Ann. Outstanding Faculty award, Mercer U. Sch. Medicine Sr. Class. Fellow: Am. Assn. Surgery Trauma; mem.: Ea. Assn. Surgery Trauma, Western Trauma Assn., Southeastern Surg. Congress, Alpha Omega Alpha. Avocations: hunting, fishing, skiing. Office: 4700 Waters Ave Savannah GA 31404 Business E-Mail: ochsnmg1@memorialhealth.com.

O'CONNELL, DANIEL CRAIG, retired psychologist, educator; b. Sand Springs, Okla., May 20, 1928; s. John Albert and Letitia Rutherford (McGinnis) O'C. BA, St. Louis U., 1951, Ph.L., 1952, MA, 1953, S.T.L., 1960; PhD, U. Ill., 1963. Joined Soc. of Jesus, 1945; asst. prof. psychology St. Louis U., 1964-66, asso. prof., 1966-72, prof., 1972-80, trustee, 1973-78, pres., 1974-78; prof. psychology Loyola U., Chgo., 1980-89, Georgetown U., Washington, 1990-98, emeritus, 1998—, chmn., 1991-96. Vis. prof. U. Melbourne, Australia, 1972, U. Kans., 1978-79, Georgetown U., 1986, Loyola U., Chgo., 1998-2003; Humboldt fellow Psychol. Inst. Free U. Berlin, 1968; sr. Fulbright lectr. Kassel U., W. Ger., 1979-80. Author: Critical Essays on Language Use and Psychology, 1988, Communicating with One Another, 2008; contbr. articles to profl. jours. Recipient Nancy McNeir Ring award for outstanding teaching St. Louis U., 1969; NSF fellow, 1961, 63, 65, 68; Humboldt Found. grantee, 1973; Humboldt fellow Tech. U. of Berlin, 1987. Fellow: APA, Mo. Psychol. Assn.; mem.: AAAS, AAUP, Mo. Acad. Sci., N.Y. Acad. Sci., Psychonomic Soc., Eastern Psychol. Assn., Southwestern Psychol. Assn., Midwestern Psychol. Assn., Soc. Scientific Study of Religion, Psychologists Interested in Religious Issues, Phi Beta Kappa. Home and Office: 4517 W Pine Blvd Saint Louis MO 63108-2109 Office Phone: 314-758-7143. Business E-Mail: doconnell@jesuits-mis.org.

O'CONNELL, EDWARD JAMES, JR., psychologist, educator, systems administrator, consultant; b. Sterling, Ill., Aug. 15, 1932; s. Edward James and Elizabeth E. (Clapham) O.; m. Pamelia Canon Floyd, Aug. 21, 1959; children— Edward James III, John Matthew BS in Psychology, Ill. Inst. Tech., 1958; MA in Psychology, Northwestern U., 1961, PhD in Psychology, 1962. NSF postdoctoral fellow Carnegie Inst. Tech., Pitts., 1962-63, asst. prof. psychology, 1963-65; psychology faculty Syracuse (N.Y.) U., NY, 1965-93, prof., 1975-93, prof. emeritus, 1993—. Cons. Rand Corp., Santa Monica, Calif., 1962-64, Abt Assocs., Boston, 1970-73, Marcy Psychiat. Hosp., N.Y., 1979-82 Served to cpl. U.S. Army, 1952-54 NSF predoctoral fellow, 1959-62: NSF postdoctoral fellow, 1962-63; Northwestern U. predoctoral fellow, 1958-59 Mem. Sigma Xi. Democrat. Avocations: billiards, computer programming. Address: PO Box 570 Cashiers NC 28717-0570 Office Phone: 828-743-3257. Personal E-mail: ejoconn@dnet.net.

O'CONNELL, JOHN BERNARD, JR., medical educator, department chairman; b. Chgo., July 27, 1949; s. John B. O'Connell; m. Mary Owens, Jan. 12, 1980; children: Jessica, Moira, Claire, Sheila, John. BS, U. Ill., Chgo., 1971; MD magna cum laude, Loyola U., Maywood, Ill., 1974. Diplomate Nat. Bd. Med. Examiners, Am. Bd. Internal Medicine, Am. Bd. Cardiovascular Disease. Intern Loyola U. Med. Ctr., Maywood, 1975-76, resident in internal medicine, 1976-78, chief resident in internal medicine, 1977-78, fellow in cardiology, 1978-80, staff physician emergency dept., 1979-81, attending cardiologist, 1980-86, med. dir. Cardiac Transplantation Program, 1984-86; clin. instr. in medicine Loyola U., Stritch Sch. Medicine, Maywood, 1977-80, asst. prof. medicine, 1980-85, assoc. prof. medicine, 1985-86; asst. chief med. svc. Hines VA Hosp., Maywood, 1981-83; attending cardiologist LDS Hosp., Salt Lake City, 1986-91, U. Utah Med. Ctr., Salt Lake City, 1986-91; assoc. prof. medicine Sch. Medicine, U. Utah, Salt Lake City, 1986-91, prof., 1991; attending physician Univ. Hosp., U. Miss. Med. Ctr., Jackson, 1991—97; prof. medicine U. Miss. Med. Sch., Jackson, 1991—97, chmn. dept. medicine, 1991—97; prof., chair dept. internal medicine Wayne State U., Detroit, 1997—2005; prof. cardiology Feinberg Sch. Medicine, Northwestern U., Chgo., 2005—; assoc. dir., dir. network devel. Bluhm Cardiovasc. Inst., Northwestern Meml. Hosp., Chgo., dir. Ctr. Heart Failure, 2005—. Cons. Salt Lake VA Med. Ctr., Salt Lake City, 1988-91, Primary Children's Med. Ctr., Salt Lake City, 1988-91; med. dir., chmn. exec. com. UTAH Cardiac Transplant Program, Salt Lake City, 1986-91; chmn. adv. bd. Exptl. Organ Transplantation Procedures, apptd. by Gov. of Ill., 1985-86; mem. working group on myocarditis Nat. Heart, Lung and Blood Inst., 1985; com. mem. Internat. Symposium Inflammatory Heart Disease, Snowmass, Colo., July, 1988; mem. sci. coun. Internat. Soc. and Fedn. Cardiology, 1990—; mem. spl. study sect. NIH, 1990; mem. sci. bd. Internat. Congress of Cardiology on Cardiovascular Pharmacotherapy and Cardiomyopathies, Greece, 1990; mem. adv. com. Miss. Health Scis. Info. Network, 1992-94; med. dir. Miss. Organ Procurement Agy., 1992-93; mem. sci. com. Internat. Workshop on the Cardiomyopathies, LaCoruna, Spain, 1993. Co-editor (monographs): Myocarditis: Precursor of Cardiomyopathy, 1983, Drug Therapy of Dilated Cardiomyopahty and Myocarditis, 1988, Intrathoracic Transplantation 2000, 1993; mem. editorial bd. Jour. Heart and Lung Transplantation, 1986—, Internat. Jour. Cardiology, 1992—, Transplantation, 1993—; manuscript cons. numerous publs.; contbr. articles to profl. jours. Recipient Norris L. Brookens Outstanding Resident award Ill. Soc. Internal Medicine, 1978, Robert Kark, M.D. Rsch. award Chgo. Soc. Internal Medicine, 1981, Outstanding Young Citizen award Chgo. Jr. Assocs. Commerce and Industry, 1985, Shinshu U. medal Matsumoto City, Nagano, Japan, 1992; grantee Earl M. Bane Charitable Trust, 1979-83, Fraternal Order Eagles, 1983-86, BRSG, 1983-84, NHLBI, 1986-91, Deseret Found., 1987-91, Bristol Myers Squibb, 1988-91, Burroughs Wellcome, 1992—, Otsuka Pharm., 1993—, Smith Kline Beecham Pharm., 1993—. Fellow ACP, Am. Coll. Chest Physicians, Am. Coll. Cardiology (cardiac transplantation com. 1991—, conf. steering com. 1991-92), Am. Coll. Angiology; mem. AMA, AAAS, Assn. of Profs. of Medicine (bd. dirs. 1997—, treas. 1998-2001, pres.-elect 2001-02, pres. 2002-03), Am. Soc. Transplant Physicians (mem. tng. and manpower com. 1990—, mem. pub. policy com. 1993—, numerous others), N.Y. Acad. Scis., Internat. Soc. Heart and Lung Transplant (mem. sci. program com. 1987, 89, 90, councilor 1989-91, pres.-elect 1991-92, pres. 1993-94, past pres. 1993-94, others), Transplantation Soc., Assn. Profs. Medicine, Rsch., Miss. (bd. dirs.), Jackson Acad. Medicine, So. Soc. Clin. Investigation, Am. Fedn. Clin. Rsch. (sen. midwest sect. 1983-86), So. Soc. Clin. Rsch., Ctrl. Soc. Clin. Rsch., Miss. State Med. Assn., Ctrl. Med. Soc., Am. Heart Assn. (bd. dirs. West Cook County 1982-86, v.p. 1985-86, chmn. 1990-92, numerous others), United Network for Organ Sharing (mem. coalition on organ doning 1991-92, mem. thoracic com. 1992—, mem. sci. adv. com. 1993—), Alpha Omega Alpha.

O'CONNELL, MARY ITA, psychotherapist; b. Balt., July 3, 1929; d. Richard Charles and Ona (Buchness) O'C.; m. Leon Jack Greenbaum, Dec. 28, 1962 (div. Jan. 1986); children: Jessie A., Elizabeth K. BA, U. Md., 1956; postgrad., Am. U., Washington, DC, 1960—; M in Creative Arts in Therapy, Hahnemann Med. Coll., Phila., 1978. Registered Acad. Dance Therapists. Tchr. Robert Cohan Sch. Dance, Boston, 1958-61; instr., choreographer Wheaton Coll., Norton, Mass., 1959-60, Harvard/Radcliffe Colls., Boston, 1960-62; tchr., performer, choreographer Profl. Studios, Washington, 1962-69; asst. prof., adminstr. Fed. City Coll., Washington, 1969-74; movement psychotherapist Woodburn Ctr. for Cmty. Mental Health, Fairfax, Va., 1975-76, Gundry Hosp., Balt., 1976-77, Prince Georges' Community Mental Health Dept., Capitol Heights, Md., 1978-80; lectr. George Washington U., DC, 1981-85; pvt. practice psychotherapy specializing in stress mgmt., anger mgmt. and internal energy, Silver Spring, Md., 1987—. Sr. movement psychotherapist Regional Inst. for Children and Adolescents, Rockville, Md., 1980-82; movement cons. Ctr. for Youth Svcs., Washington, 1981-83; movement psychotherapist DC Mental Health Ctrs., Washington, 1985-87, 90-99, Community for Creative Non-Violence Women's Shelter, Washington, 1986, LICSW, Washington, 1989. Choreographer, soloist (dance performance) The Artist: A Theatre Happening, 1963; choreographer, co-dir. (outdoor dance event) Tree Sculpting, 1974; choreographer (dance performance) Excitations, 1967, A Dance Event, 1974; soloist, New England Opera, 1961; performer, choreographer WGBM TV/Laboratory Concert Series, 1961; performer, CBS-TV/Erika Thimey Dance Theatre, 1965; guest artist, Harford Coll. Art Festival, 1967. U. Md. scholar, 1955-56. Mem. Dance Circle of Boston (life, pres. 1959-61), Modern Dance Council of Washington (exec. bd dirs., editor 1965-69), Am. Dance Therapy Assn. (treas. metro chpt. 1977-81), Assn. Humanistic Psychology, Family Therapy Network, Am. Dance Guild, NIH (movement specialist 1978-79). Democrat. Avocations: sailing, lacrosse, stone collecting, collage making. Home and Office: 1617 Mass Ave #23 Cambridge MA 02138

O'CONNELL, MICHAEL JOHN, medical association administrator; b. Mpls., Sept. 23, 1944; BA cum laude, U. Minn., 1965, MD, 1969. Prof. oncology Mayo Clinic, 1974—2001; chmn. North Ctrl. Cancer Treatment Group, 1994—2001; chmn. gi cancer steering com. Nat. Cancer Inst., 2000—05; cancer ctr. dir. Allegeheny Gen. Hosp., 2002—07; assoc. chmn. Nat. Surg. Adjuvant Breast and Bowel Project, 2002—. Clin. assoc. Balt. Cancer Rsch. Ctr., 1971—74; hematology com. chmn. Ea. Coop. Oncology Group, 1980—84; bd. dirs. Coalition Cancer Coop. Groups, 1994—2001; dep. dir. Mayo Clinic Comprehensive Cancer Ctr., 1994—2001; mem. Nat. Dialogue Cancer, 1994—2003. Named one of Best Drs. in America. Mem.: Am. Soc. Clin. Oncology, Phi Beta Kappa, Alpha Omega Honor Med. Soc. Avocations: fishing, boating, photography, reading. Home: 812 Paxton Rd SW Rochester MN 55902 Personal E-mail: mikeoc812@hotmail.com.

O'CONNELL, RALPH ANTHONY, dean, psychiatrist, educator; b. NYC, Jan. 26, 1938; s. Ralph E. and Agnes H. (O'Connell) O'C.; m. Jane Burke, June 15, 1963; children: Ralph E. III, Ellen C., John B. AB cum laude, Coll. of Holy Cross, Worcester, Mass., 1959; MD, Cornell U., 1963. Diplomate Am. Bd. Psychiatry and Neurology. Intern St. Vincent's Hosp. and Med. Ctr. N.Y., NYC, 1963-64, resident, 1964, 67-69, rsch. psychiatrist, 1969-71, chief inpatient dept. psychiatry, 1971-76, clin. dir. and vice chmn. psychiatry, 1974-95; prof. psychiatry N.Y. Med. Coll., Valhalla, 1984—, dean and provost, 1996—. Editor-in-chief Comprehensive Psychiatry, 1983-96. Served to capt. U.S. Army, 1965-66. Fellow Am. Psychiat. Assn., N.Y. Acad. Medicine (trustee 1989—). Clubs: Univ. (N.Y.C.). Roman Catholic. Office: NY Med Coll Valhalla NY 10595 Office Phone: 914-594-4900. *

O'CONNELL, RICK, insurance company executive; Pres., CEO Penrose-St. Francis Health Services, Colorado Springs; CEO Lucerne Med. Ctr., Orlando, Fla., Columbia Med. Ctr., Daytona Beach, Fla., Pembroke Pines Hosp., Fla.; COO, CFO Miami Heart Inst., Miami Beach Cmty. Hosp., Doctors Hosp., Tulsa, Okla.; exec. v.p., COO hosp. networks Trinity Health. Named Bus. Citizen of the Yr., Colo. Springs C. of C. Office: Trinity Health 27870 Cabot Dr Novi MI 48377-2820 *

O'CONNELL, ZELDA M., medical association administrator; b. LA, Sept. 18, 1975; AA in Health Adminstrn., Axia Coll., 2008; BS in Health Adminstrn., Health Info., U. Phoenix. Supr. dental claim, supr. clerical team Continental Gen. Ins. Co., 1995—99; biller, workers compensation specialist Scripps Clinic Health Orgn., 2000—02; biller, coder Boise Minor Emergency Ctr., PA, 2002—05; office mgr., health adminstr. Idaho Minor Emergency & Family Practice, 2005—. Mem.: AAPC. Avocation: drawing. Office: 3041 E Copper Point Dr Meridian ID 83642 Office Fax: 208-514-4404. E-mail: zoconnell@idahominoremergency.com.

O'CONNOR, CHRISTOPHER M., cardiologist; b. Dec. 8, 1957; MD, U. Md., 1983. Cert. Internal Medicine, 1988, Cardiovasc. Disease, 1989. Resident in internal medicine/cardiology Duke U. Med. Ctr., Durham, NC, 1983—86, 1986—87, 1988—89, exec. dir. cardiology, dir. Heart Ctr. Office: Duke Sch Medicine 129 Davison Bldg DUMC 3356 Durham NC 27710 Office Phone: 919-681-5816, 919-681-3447. Office Fax: 919-681-7755.

O'CONNOR, EDWARD JOSEPH, neurologist; b. LA, Jan. 12, 1944; s. Edward Joseph and Claire Smith O'Connor; m. Laura Davidson Folks, Mar. 6, 1982; children: Charles, Kevin, Andrew. BS, U. Notre Dame, Ind., 1966; MD, UCLA, 1970. Diplomate Am. Bd. Neurology and Psychiatry, Am. Bd. Electrodiagnostic Medicine. Intern U. Calif. Affiliate Hosps., 1970—71; resident internal medicine Wadsworth VA Hosp., LA, 1971—72; resident neurology U. N.Mex., 1974—76; chief resident UCLA, 1976—77; registrar Inst. Neurology, London, 1977—78; chief section neurology White Meml. Hosp., LA, 1979—86; owner Nerol. Assocs. West LA, Santa Monica, Calif., 1986—. Assoc. prof. neurology USC & UCLA. Bd. dirs. UCLA Rugby. Recipient UCLA Rugby Hall of Fame, 2008; named to Santa Monica Rugby Club Hall of Fame, 2009, Hall of Fame, Albuquerque Rugby Club, 2011. Fellow: Am. Acad. Neurology. Democrat. Roman Catholic. Office: Neurol Assocs West LA 2811 Wilshire Blvd # 790 Santa Monica CA 90403

O'CONNOR, FRANCIS G., physician; b. Syracuse, NY, June 20, 1959; BS, US Mil. Acad., 1981; MD, SUNY Syracuse Health Sci. Ctr., 1985. Med. dir., consortium health and mil. performance US Mil., 2007—. Immediate past pres. Am. Med. Soc. Sports Medicine, 2011; prof. Uniformed Svcs. U. Fellow: Am. Coll. Sports Medicine. Avocation: running. Home: 7305 Scarlet Oak Ct Fairfax Station VA 22039 Business E-Mail: foconnor@usuhs.mil.

O'CONNOR, R. D., retired healthcare executive; BS in Psychology and Sociology, U. So. Miss., 1960, MS Adminstrv. Pers., 1961, PhD Mgmt. and Orgnl. Comm., 1983. Asst. dean student affairs Holmes Jr. Coll., Goodman, Miss., 1961-64, Dept. Edn., Jackson, Miss., 1964-65; asst. adminstr. Hinds Gen. Hosp., Jackson, Miss., 1965-68; adminstr. Rankin Gen. Hosp., Brandon, Miss., 1968-76; v.p. Human Resources/ Mktg. Delta Mgmt. Systems, Metairie, La., 1976-79; asst. to pres. Bapt. Med. Ctr., Jacksonville, Fla., 1979-82; pres. RiverGroup Riverside Hosp., Rivercorp Inc., Riverside Found., Jacksonville, Fla., 1982-87; owner O'Connor & Assocs., Jacksonville, Fla., 1987-91; pres. Fla. 1st: Managed Health Care, Winter Haven, Orlando & Tampa, Fla., 1991-94; dir. orgn. devel. Mid Florida Med. Svcs. Inc., Winter Haven, Fla., 1994-97. Instr. U. So. Miss., Hattiesburg, Ms.; tchr., lectr. various univs., C.C.s, military acads.; grad. faculty coord. Webster U.; online instr. for univs; pres. All Things Med., 2009-. Contbr. articles to profl. jours. and books. Commr. Cleary Heights Sewer Dist., 1978-79; pres'. selective task force Induction Procedures, 1969; chmn. personnel com. San Jose Baptist Ch., 1981-86, strategic planning com., 1986-87; gov's. com. Statewide Planning Vocat. Rehab., 1968; bd. dirs. Rankin County C. of C., 1970-73, exec. com., chmn. health affairs com., 1970-72, chmn. highway com. 1970-74, fin. com. 1971-73), Family Blood Assurance Program, 1972-77, v.p. 1977, Vol. Action Coun., 1973-76, United Givers Fund, 1973-76. With Army Security Agy., Air Nat. Guard, Med. Svc. Corps., ret. Fellow Am. Coll. Healthcare Execs. (life); mem. Fla. Hosp. Assn. (com. chmn. 1984), Greater Jacksonville Area Hosp. Coun. (chmn. 1985), Jackson-Vicksburg Hosp. Coun. (chmn. 1974), Nat. Assn. Mental Health (bd. dirs. 1973-74), Miss. Assn. Mental Health (pres. 1972-74), Miss. Hosp. Assn. (bd. dirs.1973-76, exec. devel. com. 1972-75, mgmt. engring. adminstrv. bd. 1973, fin. com. 1972-74, chmn. nominating com. 1971, coord. divsn. profl. practice 1970). Office Phone: 904-268-4560.

O'CONNOR, RAYMOND FRANCIS, general practitioner; b. Cork City, Ireland, Jan. 23, 1959; s. John and Kathleen (Harrington) O'C.; m. Margaret Mary Doherty, June 1, 1991; children: John, Cornelius, Siobhan. MB BCh, U. Coll. Cork, 1982. Intern Mid West Health Bd., Limerick, Ireland, 1982-83; sr. house officer in pediats. So. Health Bd., Cork, 1983-84, sr. house officer obstetrics Tralee, 1984-85, med. sr. house officer, 1985-86; psychiatry sr. house officer S. Health Bd., Killarney, 1986-87; trainee gen. physician NHS, Preston, Eng., 1987-88, accident and emergency sr. house officer, 1988; asst. gen. physician So. Health Bd., Boherbue, 1988-90; prin. gen. practitioner Mid West Health Bd., Limerick, 1990—; asst. programme dir. Mid Western Health Bd. Vocat. Tng. Scheme in Gen. Practice, Limerick, 2000—; chmn. Med. West Regional Diabetes Steering Com., 2006—; mem. Duably Com. ICGP, 2008—. Mem. distance learning courses assessment bd. Irish Coll. Gen. Practice, 2002—05, examiner for diploma in therapeutics and diploma in prevention, 2002—04. Author: (guideline booklets) Guideline on Management of Epilepsy in General Practice, 1992, 1999, 2002, Guideline on Immunization in General Practice, 1993, 2000; contbr. articles to profl. jours. Recipient Charles Gold medal Nat. Univ. Ireland, 1979; Cert. in Med. Edn., ICGP and QUB, 2005. Master: Med. Edn. ICGP & QUB; fellow: Royal Coll. Gen. Practitioners; mem.: Am. Acad. Family Physicians, Irish Coll. Gen. Practitioners (coun. rep. 1989—90, faculty sec. 1991—94, chmn. clin. stds. com. 1993—98, rep. nat. immunization com. 1993—95), Royal Coll. Physicians (diploma in obstetrics, Ireland), Royal Coll. Surgeons (diploma in child health). Roman Catholic. Avocations: reading, hillwalking, Irish set dancing, music. Home: Sliabh Luachra Stonepark Meelick County Clare Ireland Office: 19 Cregan Ave Kileely Limerick Ireland Office Phone: 353 61 327797. Fax: 353 61 328229. E-mail: rocthedoc@eircom.net.

ODA, JUN, surgeon, researcher; s. Kuniyoshi and Kumiko Oda; m. Kaori Oda, Jan. 20, 2010. MD, Osaka U., Japan, 1993, PhD, 1999. Diplomate Osaka, Japan, 1993. Resident physician med. sch. hosp. Osaka U., Suita, Japan, 1993—94, clin. rschr. dept. traumatology sch. medicine, 1995—99; resident surgeon Nat. Tohsei Hosp., Numadu, Japan, 1994—95; rsch. fellow dept. surgery med. coll. Va. Va. Commonwealth U., Richmond, Va., 1999—2001; chief physician dept. critical care mgmt. and burn ctr. Chukyo Hosp., Nagoya, Japan, 2002—07; asst. prof. dept. emergency and critical care mgmt. Tokyo Med. U., Shinjuku, Japan, 2007—, assoc. prof. dept. emergency and critical care mgmt., dir. Japan, 2009—. Contbr. articles to profl. jours. Instr. Japan Advanced Trauma Evaluation and Care, Tokyo, 2001—07. Recipient, Gen. Ins. Assn. Japan, 2006, Mitsui Sumitomo Ins. Welfare Found., 2006; grantee, Japanese Ministry Edn., 1999—2002, Marumo Rsch. Found. Emergency Medicine, 2005, Osaka U. Sch. Medicine, 2006; fellow, Japan Soc. Promotion Sci., 1999—2002. Mem.: Japanese Soc. Burn Injuries (councilor 2006—), Am. Assn. Surgery Trauma, Japanese Assn. Acute Medicine (councilor 2007—). Office: Emergency CCM Tokyo Med Univ 6-7-1 Nishishinjuku Shinjuku Tokyo 160-0023 Japan Office Fax: 81 3 3342 5687. Business E-Mail: junoda@v001.vaio.ne.jp.

ODA, TAKASHI, medical educator; s. Noriharu and Kumiko Oda. MD, Nat. Def. Med. Coll., Saitama, 1987; PhD, Tohoku U., 1996. Resident Nat. Def. Med. Coll. Hosp., 1987—89, chief resident nephrology, 1991—93; mem. med. staff Nerima Sta., 1989—91; head physician Dept. Internal Medicine Sendai Hosp., Japan, 1993—97; rsch. scholar Sch. Medicine Wash. U., 1997—99; dir. Dept. Urology Kumamoto Hosp., Japan, 1999—2002; asst. Dept. Pub. Health Nat. Def. Med. Coll., 2002—06, asst. dept. medicine, 2006—10, asst. prof. dept. medicine, 2010—. Councilor Japanese Soc. Nephrology, 1996—. Contbr. articles to profl. jours. Lt. col. Army, 1987—2002, Nerima, Sendai, Kumamoto. Decorated 5th grade mil. decoration Japanese Army, 4th grade mil. decoration, 3rd grade mil. decoration, 4th grade mil. decoration; grantee, Kawano Found. For promotion of Pediat., 2004. Achievements include research in mechanism of progression in progressive renal disease. Office: Nat Def Med Coll Dept Medicine 3-2 Namiki Saitama Tokorozawa 359-8513 Japan

ODAGIRI, KEIICHI, physician; b. Japan, May 16, 1972; MD, Hamamatsu U. Sch. Medicine, PhD, 1998. Physician Yamaha Health Care Ctr., Yamaha Corp., 2009—. Office: 10-1 Nakazawa-cho Naka-Ku Hamamatsu Shizuoka 430-8650 Japan Business E-Mail: k-altair@nifty.com.

O'DAY, DENIS MICHAEL, ophthalmologist, educator; b. Melbourne, Victoria, Australia, Dec. 10, 1935; came to U.S., 1967; s. Kevin John and Bernadette John (Hay) O'D.; m. Ann Georgina Despard, May 28, 1966; children: Luke Gerard, Simon Patrick, Edward Daniel. Diploma, Xavier Coll., 1953; MBBS, Melbourne U., 1960. Diplomate Am. Bd. Ophthalmology. Intern St. Vincent's Hosp./U. Melbourne, 1961; resident in internal medicine St. Vincent's Hosp., 1962-64, chief resident dept. medicine, 1964, clin. asst. medicine, 1965-66; 3d asst., mem. asst. Royal Victoria Eye & Ear Hosp., Melbourne, 1967-70; resident in ophthalmology U. Calif., San Francisco, 1970; Wellcome rsch. fellow in corneal disease Inst. Opthalmology, London, 1970-72; asst. prof. ophthalmology Vanderbilt U. Sch. Medicine, Nashville, 1972-74, assoc. prof. ophthalmology, 1974-77, prof. ophthalmology, now chmn., 1977-92, chmn. ophthalmology dept., 1992—; exec. dir. Am. Bd. Ophthalmology, Bala Cynwyd. Cons. ophthalmologist Royal Commonwealth Soc. of Blind, Nigeria, 1972; cons. VA Hosp., 1973-74, active staff, 74; mem. active staff Nashville Gen. Hosp., 1974, Park View Hosp., 1980, Vanderbilt Hosp., 1972; mem. cons. staff St. Thomas Hosp.; bd. dirs. Am. Bd. Ophthalmology, Phila., 1988-, current exec. dir.; proctor lectr. U. Calif., San Francisco, 1993; co-med. dir. Lions Eye Bank and Sight Svc., 1973-86, med. dir. 1986—; bd. dirs. Lions Eye Bank Mid. Tenn., 1987—; ad-hoc mem. NIH Visual Sci. Study Sect., 1977. Author: Management of Functional Impairment due to Cataract, 1993; contbr. numerous articles, abstracts to profl. publs., chpts. to books. Chair ethics com. Cath. Pub. Policy Commn., Nashville, 1991—. Joyn Hayden rsch. fellow, 1965; recipent Felton Bequest and Potter Found. awards, 1967, recognition award Alcon Rsch. Inst., 1983, Sr. Sci. Investigator award Rsch. to Prevent Blindness, 1987, Health Profl. of Yr. award Tenn. chpt. Assn. for Edn. and Rehab. of Blind and Visually Impaired, 1990. Fellow ACS, Royal Australia Coll. Physicians, Royal Soc. Medicine, Am. Acad. Ophthalmology (sec. quality of care com. 1993—, Honor award for Ednl. Contbns. 1981-85, dir. clin. alert program, pub. health com. 1985-88); mem. AMA, AAUP, Am. Ophthalmol. Soc., Assn. for Rsch. in Vision and Ophthalmology, Nashville Acad. Medicine, Nashville Acad. Ophthalmology (v.p. 1980-81), Oxford Ophthalmol. Soc., Royal Australasian Coll. Physicians, Tenn. Acad. Medicine, Tenn. Acad. Ophthalmology. Roman Catholic. Avocation: sailing. Office: Vanderbilt U Med Ctr East Dept Ophthalmology Med Ctr Fl 8 Nashville TN 37232-0001

O'DAY, STEVEN J., oncologist; b. San Mateo, Calif., Dec. 20, 1960; MD, Johns Hopkins U. Sch. Medicine, Balt., 1988. Diplomate Am. Bd. Internal Medicine, cert. med. oncology. Intern intern medicine Johns Hopkins Hosp., 1988—91; fellow med. oncology Dana Farber Cancer Inst./Harvard Med. Sch., Boston; founding mem., chief clin. rsch., dir. melanoma program Angeles Clinic & Rsch. Inst., LA; clin. assoc. prof. medicine U. So. Calf. Keck Sch. Medicine. Contbr. articles to profl. jours. Mem.: Am. Soc. Hematology, Am. Soc. Clin. Oncology. Achievements include research in novel immunotherapy treatments for patients with advanced melanoma. Office: Angeles Clinic & Rsch Inst 2001 Santa Monica Blvd Ste 560W Santa Monica CA 90404 also: Angeles Clinic & Rsch Inst 11818 Wilshire Blvd Los Angeles CA 90025 *

ODDIS, JOSEPH ANTHONY, health associations executive; b. Greensburg, Pa., Nov. 5, 1928; s. Giacinto and Felicetta (D'Amico) O.; m. Jeanne Trevena, July 10, 1954; children: Joseph Michael, Marie Theresa/ BS, Duquesne U., 1950; DSc (hon.), Mass. Coll. Pharmacy, 1975, Phila. Coll. Pharmacy and Sci., 1975, Albany Coll. Pharmacy, Union U., 1976, Duquesne U., 1989, Mercer U., 1995; LHD (hon.), L.I. U., 1991. Staff pharmacist Mercy Hosp., Pitts., 1950-51, asst. chief pharmacist, 1953-54; chief pharmacist Western Pa. Hosp., Pitts., 1954-56; staff rep. hosp. pharmacy Am. Hosp. Assn., Chgo., 1956-60; dir. div. hosp. pharmacy Am. Pharm., Washington, 1960-62; exec. v.p. Am. Soc. Health-System Pharmacists, Washington, 1960-98. Pres. Am. Soc. Hosp. Pharmacists Research and Edn. Found., 1986-98. Active Boy Scouts Am., Camp Fire Girls; Sec. Am. Soc. Health-System Pharmacists Research and Edn. Found., 1970-86. Served with AUS, 1951-53. Recipient 1st cert. Honor award Duquesne U. Sch. Pharmacy, 1969, named Outstanding Alumnus, 1978; recipient Harvey A.K. Whitney award Am. Soc. Hosp. Pharmacists, 1970, Julius Sturmer Meml. Lecture award Rho Chi soc. Phila., 1971, Howard C. Newton Lecture award 1977, Samuel Melendy Lecture award, 1978, Hugo H. Schaefer award, 1983, Reed and Alice Henninger Lecture award, 1984, Donald E. Francke medal, 1986, Remington medal award, 1990. Fellow AAAS; mem. Am. Pharm. Assn., Am. Soc. Hosp. Pharmacists, Am. Inst. History Pharmacy, Internat. Pharm. Fedn. (pres. hosp. pharmacy sect. 1977-81, v.p. 1984-86, pres. 1986-90), Drug Info. Assn., Am. Soc. Assn. Execs., Can. Soc. Hosp. Pharmacists (hon.), Soc. Hosp. Pharmacists Australia (hon.), Pharm. Soc. Gt. Britain (hon.), Pharm. Soc. Nigeria (hon.), Nat. Coun. Patient Info. and Edn. (sec. 1982-85), Israel Pharm. Soc. (hon.), Rho Chi, Kappa Psi (hon.), Duquesne U. Century Club (charter). Home: 6509 Rockhurst Rd Bethesda MD 20817-1661 Office: Am Soc Health-System Pharmacists 7272 Wisconsin Ave Bethesda MD 20814-4836 Personal E-mail: jao@ashp.org.

ODELL, ANTHONY MICHAEL, chiropractor; b. NY, July 14, 1980; DC, UBCC, 2005. Owner, chiropractor, ptnr. Odell Chiropractic, Health 1st Chiropractic & Wellness, 2009—. Office: Odell Chiropractic 3227 Perkiomen Ave Reading PA 19606 Office Fax: 610-743-8550. Personal E-mail: chiro_tony@yahoo.com.

ODEN, GREGG, psychology professor; b. Dec. 27, 1947; BA in Psychology and Sociology, U. SD, 1969; PhD in Psychology, U. Calif., San Diego, 1974. Asst. prof. psychology U. Wis., Madison, 1973—79, 1979—85, assoc. prof. computer sci., 1983—85, prof. psychology and computer sci., 1985—90, U. Iowa, Iowa City, 1990—, chmn. dept. psychology, 2000—06. Co-editor-in-chief Cognitive Systems Rsch.; contbr. articles to profl. jours. Mem.: Soc. Mathematical Psychology, Am. Psychol. Soc., Assn. Computing Machinery, Cognitive Sci. Soc., Psychonomic Soc. Office: Dept Psychology Univ Iowa 11 Seashore Hall E Iowa City IA 52243-1407 Office Phone: 319-335-2405. Office Fax: 319-335-0191. E-mail: gregg-oden@uiowa.edu.

ODENDAAL, HEIN J., medical educator; b. Vrede, South Africa, July 17, 1942; MBChB, U. Pretoria, 1965; MD, Stellenbosch U., 1976. Prof., head, dept. ob-gyn. Stellenbosch U., 1983—2003, prof., 2003—. Office: PO Box 19083 Tygerberg Western Cape 7505 South Africa Office Fax: 27-21-938-9718. Business E-Mail: hjo@sun.ac.za.

ODLAND, RICK, surgeon; b. SD, 1954; MD, Creighton U., 1981; PhD, U. Minn., 1990. Staff surgeon Hennepin County Med. Ctr., 1995—. Assoc. prof. U. Minn., 1995—; med. dir. Twin Star Med., 1998—. Mem.: Am. Acad. Otolaryngology. Office: 701 Park Ave Minneapolis MN 55415 Office Fax: 612-630-8320. Business E-Mail: odlan007@umn.edu.

O'DONNELL, JAMES FRANCIS, retired health scientist administrator; b. Cleve., July 22, 1928; s. John Michael and Mary Louise (Hayes) O'D.; m. Winifred Locke, Sept. 10, 1955; children— Anne Catherine, Patrick John, Mary Elizabeth BS in Biology, St. Louis U., 1949; PhD in Biochemistry, U. Chgo., 1957. Asst., then. assoc. prof. biol. chemistry and exptl. medicine Coll. Medicine, U. Cin., 1957—68; grants assoc., divsn. rsch. grants NIH, Bethesda, Md., 1968—69; program dir. population and reprodn. grants br. Ctr. for Population Research, Nat. Inst. Child Health and Human Devel., NIH, 1969—71; asst. dir. divsn. rsch. resources NIH, Bethesda, 1971—76, dep. dir. divsn. rsch. resources, 1976—90, acting dir. divsn. rsch. resources, 1981—82, dir. Office of Extramural Programs, Office of the Dir., 1990-99; ret., 1999. Sci. cons. Commonwealth Health Rsch. Bd., Richmond, Va., 1999—. Served with U.S. Army, 1950-52 Home: 11601 Bunnell Ct S Rockville MD 20854-3603 Home Phone: 301-299-9378. Personal E-mail: jfwlodonnell@erols.com.

O'DONOGHUE, J. MORGAN, dermatologist; b. Washington, June 1, 1969; MD, Georgetown U., 1996. Owner O'donoghue Dermatology, 2000—. Named one of Americas Top Physicians, Consumer Rsch. Coun., 2003—10. Office: 195 Field Rd Sarasota FL 34231-2316 E-mail: hoyaderm@yahoo.com.

O'DONOVAN, PATRICK G., hospital administrator; b. Lansing, Mich., Jan. 14, 1959; BA, Mich. State U., 1981; MS in Health Svcs. Adminstrn., U. Mich., 1984. Diplomate in healthcare adminstrn. Am. Acad. Med. Adminstrs. Dir., planning Beaumont Health Sys., 2002—10, v.p., planning, 2010—. Fellow: Am. Acad. Med. Adminstrs. (named State Dir. of Yr., Disting. Svc. award). Avocation: sports. Home: 3809 Estates Dr Troy MI 48084 Business E-Mail: podonovan@beaumont.edu.

ODOR, RICHARD LANE, mental health administrator, psychologist; b. Oberlin, Ohio, Aug. 11, 1954; s. Frank and Marjorie O. Student, Moody Bible Inst., 1972-74; BA, Ohio State U., 1977, MA, 1978, PhD, 1986. Counselor children's groups Gladden Community House, Columbus, Ohio, 1978-79; partial hospitalization counselor Columbus Area Cmty. Mental Health Ctr., 1979-81, residential counselor, 1978-82; grad. rsch. assoc. dept. family rels. and human devel. Ohio State U., 1983-85; emergency svcs. counselor S.E. Cmty. Mental Health Ctr., Columbus, 1983-86, dir. emergency svcs., 1986-87; program dir., psychologist Southeast Counseling Svcs., Columbus, 1987-92; psychologist Psychol. and Counseling Svcs., Reynoldsburg, Ohio, 1989-98, Richard L. Odor, PhD, Inc., Reynoldsburg, Ohio, 1998—; pres. Achieve Performance Cons., Inc., Reynoldsburg, 2002—; sr. cons. The Global Cons. Partnership, Inc., Wayne, Pa., 2003—. Psychologist, clin. supr. New Source Counseling Ctrs., Twinsburg, Ohio, 1990-97; psychologist, owner Psychol. and Recovery Svcs., Columbus, 1991-94; employee assistance program affiliate McDonnell Douglas Corp., Columbus, 1992-95; staff Grant Med. Ctr., Columbus, 1995—; profl. adv. com. Mt. Carmel Behavioral Healthcare, 1998-99. Profl. adv. bd. Ctrl. Ohio chpt. Nat. Multiple Sclerosis Soc., 1995-97; cert. nat. referee USA Weightlifting, Inc., 1997-. Recipient Silver medal IWF Pan Am. Master's Weightlifting Championships, 1999, Bronze medal, 2000, Gold medal, 2003, 04, Gold medal Nat. Masters Championships, 2005, Bronze medal, World Masters Championships, 2007, 09. Mem. Interact Behavioral Healthcare (credentialling com. 1996-98), Ohio Psychol. Assn., U.S.A. Weightlifting, Ohio State U. Weightlifting Club (coach 1982-85, faculty advisor 1984-85), Rotary (bd. dirs. Reynoldsburg-Pickerington chpt. 1992-94, Paul Harris fellow), Phi Kappa Phi, Omicron Nu, Phi Upsilon Omicron. Republican. Avocations: competitive weightlifting, internat. travel. Office: 7664 Slate Ridge Blvd Reynoldsburg OH 43068-8158

O'DOWD, MARY E., state official, public health service officer; b. NJ, 1977; d. Anthony and Maureen Marchetta; m. Kevin O'Dowd; 1 child, Patrick Edward. BA, Rutgers U., 1999; MPH, Columbia U. Fellow hosp. finance NYU Med. Ctr., mgr. emergency dept.; legis. aid NJ Gen. Assembly; chief of staff NJ Dept. Health & Sr. Services, Trenton, 2008—10, dep. commr., 2010—11, commr., 2011—. Asst. v.p. legis. and policy NJ Hosp. Assn.; serve Rutgers Inst. for Women's Leadership Bd.; chmn. Inst. for Women's Leadership Scholar's Program Alumnae Bd. Named Number 8, 50 Most Powerful People in NJ Health Care. Office: New Jersey Department of Health and Senior Services PO Box 360 Trenton NJ 08625-0360 Office Phone: 609-292-7837. *

ODZE, ROBERT D., pathologist; s. Walter Karl Odze and Helen Natasha Menkes. BSc, McGill U., Montreal, 1980, MDCM, 1984. Cert. anatomic pathology. Staff pathologist Mount Sinai Hosp., Toronto, Canada; instr. pathology U. Toronto Med. Sch., Canada, 1991—93; cons. GI pathology New Eng. Deaconess Med. Ctr., Boston, 1994—99, Beth Israel Deaconess Med. Ctr., Boston, 1996—99; dir. GI pathology svc. Brigham and Women's Hosp., Boston, 1997—; assoc. prof. pathology Harvard Med. Sch., Boston, 1999—; cons. pathologist Dana Farber Cancer Inst., Boston, 2004—. Author, editor: Surgical Pathology GI Tract, Liver, Bilary Tract and Pancreas, 2003, assoc. editor: Am. Jour. Gastroenterology, 2003—, mem. editl. bd.: Human Pathology, 2001—, Gastrointestinal Endoscopy, 2001. Recipient MRC award, McGill U. Dept. Sci., 1980, CIBA prize for anatomy, McGill U. Med. Sch., 1981, MRC award, 1981, Joseph Morley Drake prize for pathology, 1982, Outstanding Surgery Student award, ACP and McGill U. Med. Sch., 1983, Pathology Finlayson Rsch. award, McGill U., 1988; grantee, Am. Coll. Gastroenterology, 1994—95, 1998—99, Stanley Robbins Rsch. Award, 1996—97; Univ. scholar, McGill U. Dept. Sci., 1981, Faculty scholar, McGill U. Med. Sch., 1982. Mem.: Arthur Purdy Stout Soc. Surg. Pathologists, U.S. and Can. Acad. Pathology Gastrointestinal Pathology Soc., U.S. and Can. Acad. Pathology, Am. Gastroenterol. Assn.,

Am. Coll. Gastroenterology, Crohn's Colitis Found. Am. Home: 1175 Chestnut St Unit 3 Newton MA 02464 Office: Brigham & Womens Hosp 75 Francis St Boston MA 02115

OEHLERT, WILLIAM HERBERT, JR., cardiologist, administrator, educator; b. Murphysboro, Ill., Sept. 11, 1942; s. William Herbert Sr. and Geneva Mae (Roberts) O.; m. L. Keith Brown, Mar. 14, 1976; children: Emily Jane, Amanda Elizabeth. BA, So. Ill. U., 1967; MD, Washington U., St. Louis, 1967; M in Med. Mgmt., Tulane U., 1998. Diplomate Nat. Bd. Med. Examiners, Am. Bd. Internal Medicine, Am. Bd. Cardiovascular Disease, North Am. Soc. Pacing and Electrophysiology, Am. Coll. Physician Execs. Med. intern Union Meml. Hosp., Balt., 1967-68, resident, 1968-69, U. Iowa, Iowa City, 1969-70, cardiology fellow, 1970-72; asst. prof. medicine, dir. coronary care units U. Okla. Health Sci. Ctr., Oklahoma City, 1972-74, asst. clin. prof. medicine, 1974-82, assoc. clin. prof. medicine, 1982-88, clin. prof. medicine, 1988—; chmn. dept. cardiology Bapt. Med. Ctr., 1992-95; pvt. practice Oklahoma City, 1974—. Med. dir. cardiovasc. svcs. Integris Bapt. Med. Ctr., 1993-98; pres. Cardiovasc. Clinic, Oklahoma City, 1987-91, chmn. exec. com., 1987-91; med. dir. Cardiovasc. Imaging Svcs. Corp., Oklahoma City, 1987-92; v.p. Plaza Med. Group, 1992-93; CEO W.H. Oehlert, MD, P.C., 1993—; prin. clin. coord Okla. Found. Med. Quality, 1998-2002, med. clin. coord., 2002-06. Author: Arrhythmias, 1973, Cardiovascular Drugs, 1976; contbr. articles to profl. jours. Fellow ACP, Am. Heart Assn. (nat. program com. 1979-82, pres. Okla. affiliate 1985-86, bd. dirs. 1974-88, ACLS nat. affiliate faculty 1987-90, bd. dirs. Oklahoma City 1999-2005), Am. Coll. Cardiology; mem. AMA (del. 2007—), ACP-Am. Soc. Internal Medicine, Nat. Assn. Residents and Interns, Am. Coll. Physician Execs. (cert.), Am. Diabetes Assn. (western coun. 2000-03, ea. coun. 2000-01), Okla. State Med. Assn. (pres., 2007—08, trustee 2001—, chmn. Physicians Campaign for Healthier Okla., 2003-04, chmn. CME accreditation rev. com. 2003—04, chmn. CME planning com. 2004-07), Okla. City Clin. Soc., Okla. Cardiac Soc. (pres. 1978-79), Osler Soc., Soc. Nuc. Medicine, Okla. Found. for Med. Quality (bd. dirs. 1995-98), Okla. County Med. Soc. (chmn. quality of care com. 1990-91, pres. 2006), Wilderness Med. Soc., Stewart Wolf Soc., Sportman's Club (bd. dirs. 2003-09), Okla. Blood Inst. (bd. dirs. 2007-), Phi Eta Sigma, Phi Kappa Phi. Home: 3017 Rock Ridge Pl Oklahoma City OK 73120-5713 Personal E mail: woehlert@cox.net.

OEHMICHEN, MANFRED, academic administrator; b. Görlitz, Germany, May 18, 1939; s. Heinz and Margarethe Oehmichen; m. Brigitta, May 24, 1968; children: Holger, Kim, Anna. Student, U. Göttingen, Germany, 1960-66; MD, U. Homburg, Saar, Germany, 1967; Habilitation, U. Tubingen, Germany, 1977. Prof. medicine U. Cologne, Germany, 1981-90; dir. forensic medicine U. Lübeck, Germany, 1990—2000, U. Kiel, Germany, 2000—06. Author: Cerebrospinal Fluid Cytology, 1976, Mononuclear Phagocytes in the CNS, 1978, Wundheilung, 1990; editor: Rechtsmedizin in Deutschland Ost und West, 1991, Drogenabhängigkeit, 1992, Der Tauchunfall, 1994, Biomechanik-Rekonstruktion, 1994, The Wound Healing Process-Forensic Pathological Aspects, 1996, Lebensverkürzung, Tötung und Serientötung-eine interdisziplinare Analyse der Euthanasie, 1996, Neurotraumatology: Biomechanic Aspects, Cytologic and Molecular Mechanisms, 1997, Maltreatment and Torture, 1998, Hyperthermie, Brand und Kohlenmonoxid, 2000, Brain Hypoxia and Ischemia, 2000, Osteogene Identification, 2000, Aging: Morphological, Biochemical, Molecular and Soc. Aspects, 2002, Praktische Ethik in der Medizin, 2003, Hypothermia, 2004, Gewalt gegen Frauen und Kinder, 2004, Schuld und Sühne, Verbrechen und Strafe, 2005, Terrorism, 2006, Forensic Neuropathology and Associated Neurology, 2006—09; co-editor: (book) Kindesmisshandlung und sexueller Missbrauch, 1993; editor: (book series) Rechtsmedizinische Forschungsergebnisse (Research in Legal Medicine), 1990; co-editor: Plötzlicher Säuglingstod, 1993, Vergiftungen im Kindesalter, 1994, Rechsfragen in der Kinderheilkunde, 1995, Das behinderte Kind, 1996, Drogen bei Kindern und Jugendlichen, 1997, Ethik in der Kinderhellkunde, 1999, Der "Mord", 2007. Personal E-mail: moehmichen@gmx.de.

OEIRIA, DAVID SUDARTO, dermatologist, plastic surgeon, educator; b. Medan, Indonesia, May 15, 1956; s. Darmawan Oei Lian Goan and Sulasmi Geok Sie O.; m. Ratna Maitri Dewi Gondowardojo, Sept. 25, 1983; children: Christopher Toshihiro, Stephen Akihiro, Andrew Yoshihiro. Drs. Med., Airlangga U., 1979, MD, 1982; dermatologist, dermatologic surgeon, Kanazawa Med. U., 1990. Bd. cert. dermatologist and venereologist, Indonesia, 1991. Dermatologist U. Indonesia, Jakarta, 1991; dir. Dermatology and Skin Laser Ctr., Surabaya, 1991—; plastic and reconstructive surgeon Kanazawa Med. U. Sch. Medicine, 1997; plastic surgery bd., 1997; dir. Klinik Dr. Ratna, Surabaya, Indonesia; v.p. supr. bd. Indonesian Chinese Businessman Assn. Chmn. dept. dermatology U. Wijaya, Kusuma Sch. Medicine, Surabaya, Indonesia; dir. Indonesian Internat. Med. Coop., Surabaya, 1996—, Indonesia-Japan Med. Assn., Surabaya, 1996—, Indonesia-China Med. Assn., Surabaya; chmn. Surabaya Dermatologic Surgery Tchg. Program; educator, cons. cosmetic dermatol. surgeon dept. dermato-venereology, Airlangga U. Sch. Medicine, Dr Soetomo Tchg. Hosp., Indonesia; nat. trainer in cosmetic surgery; hon. prof. Southeast Asia Coll. Cosmetic Surgery; internat. spkr. in cosmetic surgery. Contbr. articles to profl. jours. Clin. rsch. fellow in plastic surgery Kanazawa (Japan) Med. U., 1995—. Fellow Internat. Coll. Cosmetic Surgery; mem. Am. Acad. Dermatology, European Acad. Dermato-Venereology, Indonesian Soc. Dermato-Venereology (vice nat. chmn. dermatologic surgery study group 2000—, chief editor Indonesian Dermatol. Surgery Jour.), Japan Soc. Plastic and Reconstructive Surgery, Internat. Soc. for Dermatologic Surgery, Am. Soc. Dermatologic Surgery, Indonesian Soc. Medicine, Asian Coll. Cosmetic Surgery (co-chmn.), Am. Soc. Laser Medicine & Surgery. Avocations: reading, art, music, sports, swimming. Office: Klinik Dr Ratna Jl Raya Kertajaya Indah 121 Surabaya 60117 Indonesia

OELBERG, DAVID GEORGE, neonatologist educator, researcher; b. Waukon, Iowa, May 26, 1952; s. George Robert and Elizabeth Abigail (Kepler) O.; m. Debra Penuel, Aug. 4, 1979; children: Anna Elizabeth, Benjamin George. BS with highest honors, Coll. William and Mary, 1974; MD, U. Md., 1978. Diplomate in pediat. and in neonatal-perinatal medicine Am. Bd. Pediat. Intern U. Tex. Med. Br., Galveston, 1978-79, resident, 1979-81, house pediat. staff, 1978-81; postdoctoral fellow in neonatal medicine U. Tex. Med. Sch., Houston, 1981-84, asst. prof. dept. pediat., 1984-90, assoc. prof., 1990-93; assoc. prof. pediat., head perinatal rsch. Ctr. Pediat. Rsch. Ea. Va. Med. Sch., 1993-2001, prof., interim chmn. dept. pediat. Ctr. Pediat. Rsch., 2001—, dir. divsn. neonatal-perinatal medicine. Mem. hosp. staff Hermann Hosp., Houston, 1983-93; physician Crippled Children's Svcs. Program, Houston, 1985-93; mem. hosp. staff Lyndon B. Johnson County Hosp., 1990-93; vis. prof. Wyeth-Ayerst Labs., 1992; med. dir. Office Rsch., Children's Hosp. of King's Daus., 1993—, v.p. for acad. devel., 2001—; med. dirs. Office of Rsch., Sentara-Norfolk Gen. Hosp., 1993—, pres. med. staff. Mem. editl. adv. bd. jour. Neonatal Intensive Care; contbr. articles to profl. jours.; ad hoc reviewer profl. jours.; patentee in field. Physician cons. Parents of Victims of Sudden Infant Death Syndrome, Houston, 1984; chmn. Instl. Animal Care and Use Com., bd. mem. Fund for William Mary Recipient award in analytical chemistry Am. Chem. Soc., 1974, NIH Clin. Investigator award NHLBI, 1989-94; rsch. grantee Am. Lung Assn., 1989-90, NIH, 1989-94. Fellow Am. Acad. Pediat. NY Acad. Scis.; mem. AMA, NAS, Soc. Exptl. Biology and Medicine, So. Soc. Pediatric Rsch. (councilor, pres., sec.-treas.), Soc. Pediatric Rsch. Achievements include development of a method for optical measurement of bilirubin in tissue and ion channel proteins in pulmonary surfactant. Home: 1624 W Little Neck Rd Virginia Beach VA 23452-4720 Office: Ea Va Med Sch Ctr Pediatric Rsch 855 W Brambleton Ave Norfolk VA 23510-1005 also: Neonatal Medicines CHKD 601 Childrens Lane Norfolk VA 23507 Office Phone: 757-668-7456. Business E-Mail: doelberg@chkd.org.

OEPEN, GODEHARD, psychiatrist; b. Freiburg, Germany, Oct. 15, 1950; s. Heinrich and Irmgard Oepen; m. Gulnaz Soomro; 3 children. MD, Philipps U., Marburg, Germany, 1974; PhD, Albert-Ludwigs-U., Freiburg, 1982. Diplomate Am. Bd. Psychiatry and Neurology, Am. Bd. Forensic Medicine. Asst. prof. neurology Univ. Clinic, Freiburg, 1982—89, assoc. prof. neurology, 1989—, med. dir. outpatient dept. psychiatry, 1985—89; assoc. prof. psychiatry Boston U., 1994—99; med. dir. acute psychiatry VA Hosp., Bedford, Mass., 1994—98; med. dir. geriatric psychiatry Salem Hosp./Harvard Med. Sch., Boston, 1998—99; clin. prof. psychiatry U. Ala., Birmingham, 1999—. Lectr. in psychiatry Harvard Med. Sch., 1994—99; rsch. affiliate McLean Hosp./Harvard U., 1999—; asst. med. dir. Ala. Psychiat. Svcs. Editor: Psychiatry of the Right and Left Brain, Huntington's Disease, Philosophy and Psychopathology; musical recs.: Germany and U.S. Concert master, 1st violinist Majic City Cmty. Orch., 2000—. Maj. Bundeswehr, 1976—78, Germany. Named one of Am.'s Top Psychiatrists, Consumers Rsch. Coun. Am., 2003. Mem.: Am. Assn. Geriatric Psychiatry, Am. Psychiat. Assn. (Karl Jaspers prize 1993). Office: Ala Psychiat Svcs 2868 Acton Rd Birmingham AL 35243

OERTEL, MATTHIAS FRIEDRICH, neurosurgeon, educator; b. Hof, Saale, Germany, Jan. 15, 1967; s. Friedrich Klaus and Irmgard Elisabeth Oertel; m. Susanne Hümmer; children: Maximilian, Sebastian. MD, U. Erlangen, Germany, 1993. Cert. Ednl. Commn. FFgn. Med. Grads., Phila., 1997, neurol.surgery Landesärztekammer Hessen, 2004, neurosurg. intensive care Landesärztekammer Hessen, 2007. Neurosurgical resident U. Erlangen, 1993—99; clin. rsch. fellow, divsn. neurosurgery UCLA Med. Ctr., 1999—2001; neurosurg. resident U. Hosp. Giessen Marburg, Germany, 2001—04, asst. prof. neurosurgery, 2004—07, assoc. prof. neurosurgery, 2007—. Mem. editl. review bd. Jour. Neurology, Neurosurgery & Psychiatry, London, 2003—; contbr. articles to profl. jours. Mem. CSU, München, Germany, 2007—. Mem.: Mountain and Expdn. Medicine, Internat. Soc. Cerebral Blood Flow & Metabolism, German Soc. Neurol. Surgery (Spine Fellowship award 2006), Congress Neurol. Surgeons. Conservative. Lutheran Protestant. Achievements include invention of Xenon-133 crusher. Avocations: rock climbing, swimming, running, skiing. Home: Am Vogelsang 14 Staufenberg 35460 Germany Office: Univ Hosp Giessen-Marburg Klinikstr. 29 35392 Giessen Germany Office Fax: 49 641 9945509. Personal E-mail: mfoertel@yahoo.com. Business E-Mail: matthias.oertel@neuro.med.uni-giessen.de.

OERTEL, YOLANDA CASTILLO, pathologist, educator; b. Lima, Peru, Dec. 14, 1938; came to U.S., 1966; d. Leonardo A. and Dalila (Ramirez) C.; m. James E. Oertel, Sept. 24, 1969. MD, Cayetano Heredia, Lima, 1964; Dr. honoris causa, U. Peruana Cayetano Heredia, 1999. Diplomate Am. Bd. Pathology (mem. test com. for cytopathology 1988-94). Internat. postdoctoral fellowship NIH, Bethesda, Md., 1966-68; asst. prof. pathology Sch. Medicine George Washington U., Washington, 1975-78, assoc. prof., 1978-84, prof., 1984-98, prof. emerita, 1998—. Adj. prof. pathology and lab. medicine MCP Hahnemann U. Sch. Medicine; cons. Registry Cytology Armed Forces Inst. Pathology, Washington, 1981—. Author: Fine Needle Aspiration of the Breast, 1987; contbr. chpts. to books, articles to profl. jours. Decorated comendador de la Orden Cayetano Heredia, 1999; recipient Francisco A. Camino prize Peruvian Med. Assn., 1965, cert. Meritorious Svc. Armed Forces Inst. Pathology, 1974; named Disting. Alumna Cayetano Heredia Med. Sch., 1989. Mem. Assn. Mil. Surgeons (hon.), Colombian Soc. Pathology (hon.), Argentinian Soc. Pathology (hon.), Peruvian Soc. Pathologists (hon.), Argentinian Soc. Cytopathology, (hon.), Am. Soc. Cytopathology, Internat. Acad. Pathology, Soc. Latinoamericana Patologia, Am. Soc. Clin. Pathologists (coun. on cytopathology 1982-88), Coll. Am. Pathologists, Arthur Purdy Stout Soc. Surg. Pathologists, Am. Thyroid Assn., L.Am. Thyroid Soc. Avocations: reading, opera. Office: Washington Hosp Ctr Pathology Dept Washington Cancer Inst 1340 Old Chain Bridge Rd Ste 202 Mc Lean VA 22101-3943 Home Phone: 703-836-0639; Office Phone: 202-877-2740. Office Fax: 202-877-0197. Business E-Mail: Yolanda.C.Oertel@medstar.net.

OERTER, CYNTHIA LYNN, medical technologist; b. Waupaca, Wis., Mar. 8, 1948; d. Lavern Charles and Geraldine Mae (Huffcutt) Trinrud; m. Gregory Van Oerter, June 8, 1968; children: Nathan, Justin. BS, U. Wis., Oshkosh, 1971; MS, Cardinal Stritch Coll., 1993. Cert. Am. Soc. Clin. Pathologists. Med. technologist Mercy Med. Ctr., Oshkosh, Wis., 1970-76, Iola (Wis.) Hosp., 1978-86, wellness cons., 1985-86, Riverside Med. Ctr., Waupaca, Wis., 1986—95, med. technologist, hematology supr., insvc. coord., 1987-95; pres. Pro Health Consul, Inc., Waupaca, Wis., 1994—; bus. ptnr., adminstr. Garden Park House, 1994—2000, owner, adminstr., 2000—; owner Back Door Bakery, 2003—, Secret Garden Cafe, 2003—. Tchr. Fox Valley Coll., Appleton, Wis., 1986, 87; organizer Overeaters Anonymous, Iola, 1985-89; owner Green Fountain Inn, 1995—; com. mem. Cmty Clinic, 2008-09; bd. dirs. Bethany Nursing Home, 2010-. Mem. parent's com. gifted and talented Waupaca Sch. Sys., 1984, charter mem. edn. employment coun., 1989-92, mem. adv. com. guidance program K-12, 1992; vol. Nat. Wellness Inst., 1986-97, Am. Lung Assn., 1986-87; tchr. smokeless program Am. Inst. Preventative Medicine, 1988-93; com. mem. Main St. Design, 1999-01. Mem. NAFE, Nat. Platform Assn., Am. Sch. Health Assn. (com. mem.), Waupaca C. of C. (tourism com. 2002—, Athena award 2003), Rotary (sec. 1996-98, bd. dirs. 1995-04, 2006—, pres. 2000-01), Bethany (bd. dirs. 2010-). Republican. Lutheran. Avocations: gardening, gourmet cooking, sailing, Bible study.

OESCH, FRANZ, medical educator; s. Josef and Clara Oesch; m. Barbara Bartlomowicz. PhD, U. Fribourg, Switzerland, 1969; habil., U. Basel, Switzerland, 1973. Postdoc. fellow NIH, Bethesda, Md., 1969—71; sr. rsch. assoc., dept. pharmacology, biozentrum, U. Basel, 1972—74; prof., pharmacology and toxicology U. Mainz, Germany, 1974—2004, dir., Inst. Toxicology, 1983—2004, emeritus prof., pharmacology and toxicology, 2004—; cons., toxicology Oesch-Tox Toxicological Consulting & Expert Opinions, Wackernheim, Germany, 1999—. Contbr. articles to sci. profl. publs. Recipient Prof. Max Cloetta prize, 1977, Robert Koch prize, 1982, GUM prize, 1985, Rheinisch-Westfalische Acad. Scis. prize, 1989, Sci. Innovation prize, State Rheinland-Pfalz, 1999, German Cancer prize, 1990; named Most Quoted Scientists, 1981. Master: Internat. Union Pharmacology (chmn. sect. toxicology), Internat. Soc. Study Xenobiotics (pres.), German Cancer Soc. (chmn. sect. exptl. cancer rsch.), German Soc. Pharmacology & Toxicology (sect toxicology chmn.). Home: Rheinblick 21 Wackernheim D-55263 Germany Office: Oesch-Tox Toxicological Consulting & Expert Opinions Rheinblick 21 Wackernheim D-55263 Germany Office Fax: 49-6132-577 59. Business E-Mail: oesch@uni-mainz.de.

OESTERLE, STEPHEN N., medical products executive, cardiologist, educator; b. LaGrande, Oreg., Mar. 3, 1951; BA summa cum laude, Harvard Univ., 1973; MD, Yale Univ., 1977. Intern & resident Mass. Gen. Hosp., 1977—80; fellowship in cardiology Stanford Univ., 1981—83; cardiologist Good Samaritan Hosp., LA, 1986—91; cardiologist, med. educator Georgetown Univ., 1991—92; assoc. prof. med. & dir. cardiac catheterization & coronary intervention labs Stanford Univ. Med. Ctr., 1992—98; assoc. prof. med. Harvard Medical School, 1998—2002; dir. invasive cardiology svc. Mass. Gen. Hosp., 1998—2002; sr. v.p. medicine & tech. Medtronic, Inc., Mpls., 2002—. Office: Medtronic Inc 710 Medtronic Pkwy Minneapolis MN 55432-5604

OETTGEN, HERBERT FRIEDRICH, physician; b. Cologne, Germany, Nov. 22, 1923; came to U.S., 1958; s. Peter and Minna (Kaul) O.; m. Trudi Hesberg, Feb. 16, 1957; children: Hans Christoph, Joerg Peter, Anne Barbara. MD, U. Cologne, 1951. Diplomate Bd. Internal Medicine, Fed. Republic of Germany. Resident in pathology City Hosp., Cologne, 1952-54, resident in medicine, 1955-58; fellow Meml. Sloan-Kettering Cancer Ctr., NYC, 1958-62, assoc. to assoc. mem., 1963-69, mem., 1972—, attending physician, 1971—; prof. medicine Cornell U. Med. Coll., NYC, 1972—. Assoc. dir. Cancer Rsch. Inst., N.Y.C., 1985—. Author over 350 publs. in hematology, cancer rsch., immunology and clin. oncology. Recipient award for cancer rsch. Wilhelm Warner Found., Hamburg, Fed. Republic Germany, 1970, Lisec-Artz award Friedrich Wilhelm U., Bonn, Fed. Republic of Germany, 1982. Presbyterian. Avocations: violin, wood working. Home: 48 Overlook Dr New Canaan CT 06840-6825 Office: Meml Sloan-Kettering Cancer Ctr 1275 York Ave New York NY 10021-6094 Home Phone: 203-966-5709; Office Phone: 212-639-7505. Business E-Mail: oettgenh@mskcc.org, hoettgen@licr.org.

OFFIT, PAUL ALLAN, pediatrician; b. Balt., 1951; BS in Psychology, Tufts U., 1973; MD, U. Md. Sch. Medicine, 1977. Cert. Pediat. Resident, pediat. Children's Hosp., Pitts., 1977—80, chief, divsn. infectious diseases Phila., 1982—, dir., Vaccine Edn. Ctr., prof. pediat. U. Pa. Sch. Medicine, Maurice R. Hilleman Prof. Vaccinology. Mem. adv. com. on immunization practices Ctr. for Disease Control. Contbr. several articles to profl. jours.; co-author: Breaking the Antibiotic Habit: A Parent's Guide to Coughs, Colds, Ear Infections, and Sore Throats, 1999, Vaccines: What Every Parent Should Know, 1999, Vaccine Handbook: A Practical Guide for Clinicians, 2003, Vaccines: What You Should Know, 3rd edit., 2003; author: Cutter Incident: How America's First Polio Vaccine Led to Today's Growing Vaccine Crisis, 2005, Vaccinated: One Man's Quest to Defeat the World's Deadliest Diseases, 2007, Autism's False Prophets: Bad Science, Risky Medicine, and the Search for a Cure, 2008. Recipient J. Edmund Bradley prize for Excellence in Pediat., U. Md. Med. Sch., Young Investigator award in Vaccine Develop., Infectious Diseases Soc. Am., Rsch. Career Develop. award, NIH. Achievements include being co-inventor of a rotavirus vaccine, RotaTeq. Office: Divsn Infectious Diseases Abramson Rsch Bldg Rm 1202D 34th St and Civic Center Blvd Philadelphia PA 19104 Office Phone: 215-590-2020. Office Fax: 215-590-2025. Business E-Mail: offit@email.chop.edu.

OFMAN, JOSHUA J., biotechnology company executive; b. Apr. 13, 1964; BA in History and Philosophy of Sci., U. Calif., Berkeley, 1986; MD, U. Calif., Irvine, 1991; MS in Health Services, UCLA Sch. Pub. Health, 1997. Intern, resident internal medicine UCLA Med. Ctr., 1991—94, VA/UCLA/RAND fellowship in ambulatory care and health services rsch., 1994—97, fellowship in digestive diseases, 1994—97; asst. prof. dept. medicine and health services rsch., divsn. gastroenterology UCLA Sch. Medicine/Cedars-Sinai Med. Ctr., 1997—2003; sr. v.p. Zynx Health Inc., LA, 1997—2003; dir. US med. affairs, head US health economics & outcomes rsch. Amgen, Inc., Thousand Oaks, Calif., 2003—04, v.p. global coverage & reimbursement, global govt. affairs, global health economics and global devel., 2004—. Contbr. articles to med. jours. Office: Amgen Inc 1 Amgen Center Dr Newbury Park CA 91320-1799 Office Phone: 805-447-1000. Office Fax: 805-447-1010. Personal E-mail: jofman@amgen.com. *

O'GARA, PATRICK THOMAS, internist, cardiovascular physician; b. Chgo., Apr. 17, 1952; s. Thomas E. and Eileen L. (Lamb) O.; m. Laura A. Daniel, Oct. 10, 1981, children: Brian, Grady, Katherine. BA, Yale U., 1974; MD, Northwestern U., 1978. Diplomate Am. Bd. Internal Medicine, Am. Bd. Cardiovascular Medicine. Intern in med. Mass. Gen. Hosp., Boston, 1978—79, resident in internal med., 1979—81, fellow in cardiology, 1981-83, chief resident internal medicine, 1984; rsch. fellow Nat. Heart Lung and Blood Inst./NIH, 1985-86; assoc. prof. medicine Harvard Med. Sch., Boston; dir. clinical cardiology Brigham & Womens Hosp., Boston, vice-chmn. clinical affairs dept. medicine. Co-editor Cardiology in Review; mem. editl. bd. Chest. Fellow: AHA (mem. sci. advance com.), Am. Coll.

Cardiology (bd. trustees). Office: Brigham & Womens Hosp Cardiovasc Divsn 75 Francis St Boston MA 02115 Office Phone: 857-307-1990. Office Fax: 857-307-1955. Business E-Mail: pogara@partners.org.

OGATA, HIROMARU, anesthesiologist, educator; b. Tokyo, Jan. 17, 1931; s. Otomaru and Kouko Ogata; married May 28, 1961; children: Saeko, Hiroyuki. D of Medicine, Kumamoto U., Kumamoto City, Japan, 1957; DMS, U. Tokyo, 1964, postgrad., 1964. Diplomate Japan Soc. Anesthesiology. Intern Nat. Tokyo 2d Hosp., 1957-58; resident in anesthesia U. Tokyo, 1958-63; lectr. Sch. Med. Nihon U., Tokyo, 1964-65, assoc. prof., 1970-72; rsch. fellow Albert Einstein Coll. Med., Bronx, N.Y., 1966-67; prof. Sch. Medicine Juntendo U., Tokyo, 1975-78; prof. Dokkyo U., Tochigi, Japan, 1979-96, prof. emeritus, 1996—; prof. Toukai U. Oiso Hosp., 1996; dir. Dept. Anesthesia, Yamato Tokushukai Hosp., 2001—07; chair Yumegaoka Nursing Home, 2007—08; pres. Meguro Med. Clinic, 2008—, Shonan Tobu Gen. Hosp., 2009—10, Kokubunji Hosp., 2010—, Hodogaya Hosp., 2011—. Author: Anesthesia and Resuscitation, 1978, Emergency Drugs ABC, 1983; co-author: Anesthesia Handbook, 1970, How to Manage Anesthesia, 1989. Recipient Research fellow Dept. Anaesthesiology Albert Einstein Coll. Medicine. Mem. Japan Soc. Anesthesiologists (hon., bd. dirs. 1979), Japan Resuscitation Soc. (hon., bd. dirs. 1982), Japan Shock Soc. (hon. auditor, bd. dirs. 1986, pres. 1992), Am. Shock Soc., Internat. Fedn. Shock Socs. (sec. 1998-2002, rep. Japan 1993, sec. 1999). Avocation: tennis. Office: 7-11-1 Shirane Asahi-ku Yokohama Japan 241-0005

OGATA, MASANA, retired industrial medicine scientist; b. Okayama, Japan, Feb. 13, 1926; s. Masuo and Fuku Ogata; m. Sachiko (Noda) Ogata Mar. 23, 1958; children: Munetomo Reiko, Ogata Masatoshi. MD, Okayama Med. Sch., Japan, 1949, PhD, 1956. Prof. Okayama U. Med. Sch., 1962-91, dean, 1983-85, ret., 1991, prof. emeritus, 1991—; prof. Kawasaki U. Med. Welfare, Okayama, 1991-99; dean Okayama Coll. Med. Tech. Scis., 1999—2005, dean emeritus, 2005. Trustee Nat. Coun. Pvt. Schs. Rehab., 2002—04. Author: Biological Monitoring Theory and Practice, 1991; editor: Biological Monitoring of Exposure to Industrial Chemicals, 1990, Biological Monitoring and Industrial Medicine in Asia, 1990; contr. articles to profl. jours. Chmn. Coun. for Anti-Pollution Measures, Okayama Prefectural Govt., 1989-93, mem. Ministry of Labor, Govt. of Japan Comm. for Workers Health Check, 1989. Decorated Order of the Sacred Treasure, The Emperor Japan, 2004; recipient ofcl. commendation Ministry Environ. Protection, 1989, Cert. of honor Beijing Soc. Preventive Medicine, 1996. Mem. Assn. Med. Drs. in Asia, NGO (hon., exec. adviser 2005), Japan Soc. Occupl. Health, Am. Conf. Govtl. Indsl. Hygienists (biol. expos indices Cin. chpt. 1987-95, Outstanding Contbn. award 1990). Achievements include patents for flicker test apparatus or fatigue examination using diode as light source. Home: 1-3-8 Kounancho Kita-ku 700-0866 Okayama Japan Fax: 81-86-222-6158. Personal E-mail: mo.26213@cameo.plala.or.jp.

OGATA, MOTOI, psychiatrist, educator; b. Obihiro, Hokkaido, Japan, Aug. 15, 1930; s. Shichirou and Shigee (Nishioka) O.; m. Makiko Watanabe, Oct. 7, 1958; children: Kakuya, Noriko, Hiroko. MD, Sapporo Med. Coll., Japan, 1956, D in Med. Sci., 1964. Med. diplomate. Internship Sapporo Medical Coll. Hosp., 1956-57, residency dept. psychiatry, 1957-60; chief psychiatrist Red Cross Hosp., Kushiro, Japan, 1961-65; asst. prof. Sapporo (Japan) Med. Coll., 1965-69, assoc. prof., 1969-78; chief scientist Hokkaido Mental Health Ctr., Sapporo, 1978-83; prof. Sch. Health Allied Profession, Sapporo, 1983-93, Sch. Health Scis., Sapporo, 1993-96; prof. emeritus Sapporo Med. U., 1996—. Rsch. fellow Harvard Med. Sch., Boston, 1965; vis. scientist NIMH, Bethesda, Md., 1967; mem. working group WHO, Geneva, 1975; mem. membership com. Internat. Soc. Biomedical Rsch. on Alcoholism, 1985-96; prin. investigator WHO & ISBRA, 1990-96; chief dirs. Med. Soc. Alcohol, Kyoto, Japan, 1991-93; rschr. in field. Contbr. articles to profl. jours. Recipient Hokkaido Med. prize Hokaido Prefecture, Sapporo, 1987, prize Hokkaido Med. Assn., 1987. Mem. Japenese Medical Soc. Alcohol Studies (dir. 1995—). Home: 4-7 Oasa Harumichou Ebetsu 069-0866 Japan Home Phone: 011-386-4453; Office Phone: 0126-22-3731. Personal E-mail: motoi815@aol.com.

OGAWA, KATSUTOSHI, pharmacist, researcher; b. Chosei-Gun, Chiba Prefecture, Japan, Jan. 7, 1963; s. Shoji and Tomiko Sase, adopted s. Kazue Ogawa; m. Akemi Ogawa, Aug. 7, 1960; children: Mizuka, Takafumi. B in Pharm. Sci., Hoshi U., 1987; PhD in Pharmacology, Showa U., 2004. Advisor Sekino Rsch. Inst., Toshima-ku, Tokyo, 2004—; chmn. bd. dirs. Iruma Nursery Sch. Welfare Corp., Sayama, Saitama Prefecture, 2002—; rsch. sect. chief Sekino Rsch. Inst., 1994—2004, Tsukuba Clin. Pharmacology Ctr., Tukuba, Ibaragi Prefecture, 1993—94; rschr. Tokyo Rsch. Ctr. Clin. Pharmacology, Shinjuku-ku, Tokyo, 1991—93; pharmacist Saitama Med. Ctr., Kawagoe, Saitama Prefecture, 1988—90. Libr. assn. com. Sayama City Libr., Saitama Prefecture, Japan, 2005—; mcpl. sch. councilor Irumano Elem. Sch., Saitama Prefecture, 2005—. Pres. Parents and Tchrs. Assn. of Irumano Elem. Sch., Saitama Prefecture, 2004—05. Mem.: Japanese Soc. Clin. Pharm. and Therapeutics. Office: Sekino Rsch inst 3-28-3 Ikebukuro Toshima-ku Tokyo 171-0014 Japan Personal E-mail: pxm00676@nifty.com. E-mail: ogawa_katsutoshi@seri.co.jp, jihei@p1.s-cat.ne.jp.

OGAWA, KAZUHARU, agriculturist, educator; b. Ibigawa, Gifu, Japan, June 28, 1958; PhD, Grad. Sch. Agr., Nagoya U., 1989. Guest rschr. Swedish U. Agrl. Scis., 1989—90; asst. prof. Grad. Sch. Bioagrl. Scis., Nagoya U., 1990—. Mem.: Japan Soc. Tropical Ecology, Bot. Soc. Japan, Japanese Forest Soc., Ecol. Soc. Japan, Internat. Union Forest Rsch. Orgns. Avocations: tennis, swimming, skiing. Office: Furo-cho Chikusa-ku Nagoya Aichi 464-8601 Japan Office Fax: 81 52 789 5014. Business E-Mail: kazogawa@agr.nagoya-u.ac.jp.

OGAWA, SEIJI, research scientist, biophysicist; b. Tokyo, Jan. 19, 1934; came to U.S., 1962; s. Shimpei and Mitsu O.; m. Kazuko, Mar. 10, 1962; 1 child, Miwako. BS, U. Tokyo, 1957; PhD, Stanford U., 1967. Rsch. assoc. Mellon Inst., Pitts., 1962-64; postdoctoral Stanford U., Calif., 1967-68; disting. mem. tech. staff Bell Labs., Murray Hill, NJ, 1968—2001; dir. Ogawa Laboratories for Brain Function Rsch., Hamano Life Science Research Found., Tokyo, 2001—; visiting prof. Dept. Biophysics and Physiology, Albert Einstein Coll. Medicine, Yeshiva U., Bronx, NY, 2001; disting. vis. prof., dir. fMRI rschr., neurosci. rsch. inst. Gachon U. Medicine & Sci., Republic of Korea, 2008—. Elected mem. Inst. of Medicine, 2000. Contbr. articles in numerous sci. journals. Recipient Eastman Kodak award in Chem., 1967, Nakayama prize, Nakayama Found. Human Sci., 1998, Asahi prize, Asahi-Shinbun Cultural Found., 1999, Japan Internat. prize, Japan Found. for Sci. and Tech., 2003, Gairdner Internat. award, Gairdner Found., 2003. Fellow: Internat. Soc. Magnetic Resonance (Gold medal 1995, ISMAR prize 2007); mem.: NAS, Soc. Neuroscience, Am. Phys. Soc. (Biol. Physics prize 1996), Nat. Magnetic Resonance Soc. India (hon.), Japanese Soc. Magnetic Resonance in Medicine (hon.), Japanese Soc. Nuc. Magnetic Resonance (hon.), Soc. for Neuroscience, Inst. of Medicine. Achievements include research in devel. nuclear magnetic resonance (NMR) and functional magnetic resonance imaging (fMRI) of the brain. Office: Neuroscience Rsch Institute 2F 1198 Guwol-dong Namdong-gu Incheon 405-760 Republic of Korea Office Phone: 82 32 460 2082. Office Fax: 82 32 460 2081. Business E-Mail: s.ogawa33@nifty.com. *

OGAWARA, HIROSHI, biochemist, educator; b. Tokyo, Sept. 11, 1935; m. Hiroko Ogawara, Feb. 27, 1961; children: Yuki, Reiko. BS, U. Tokyo, 1958, MS, 1960, Dr.Pharm.Sci., 1968. Rschr. Nat. Inst. Health Japan, Tokyo, 1960-75; prof. biochemistry Meiji Pharm. U., Tokyo, 1975-2001, prof. emeritus, 2001—. Mem.: Asian Pharm. Soc. (Ishidate award 2002), Antibiotic Soc. Japan (councilor), Pharm. Soc. Japan (Sci. Contbn. award 2001), Biochemistry Soc. Japan (councilor), Soc. Actinomycetes Japan (hon.; hon. mem., Actinomycetes award 1996). Office: HO Bio Inst 33-9, Yushima-2 Bunkyo-ku Tokyo 113-0034 Japan E-mail: hogawara@my-pharm.ac.jp.

OGBUANU, CHINELO AMARACHUKWU, medical epidemiologist; b. Akokwa, Nigeria, Jan. 10, 1975; MD, U. Nigeria, Nsukka, 1998; PhD in Pub. Health, U. SC, Columbia, 2009. House officer, intern U. Benin Tchg. Hosp., Benin City, Nigeria, 1999—2000; corps. physician Imaobong Missionary Outreach Med. Ctr., Uyo, Nigeria, 2001—02; med. officer St. Luke's Hosp., Uyo, 2002—04; grad. rsch. asst. U. SC, Columbia, 2006—09; sr. maternal and child health epidemiologist Ga. Dept. Pub. Health, Material & Child Health Program, 2009—. Recipient Cert. of Appreciation, Ga. Dept. Cmty. Health, Divsn. Pub. Health, Maternal and Child Health Program, Emily Thompson award, U. SC., Women's and Gender Studies Program; Arnold fellowship, U. SC., Arnold Sch. Pub. Health. Mem.: Ga. Pub. Health Assn., Golden Key Internat. Honor Soc., Delta Omega Hon. Soc. Avocations: cooking, music, dance. Home: 3086 Willow Leaf Dr Suwanee GA 30024 Home Phone: 678-548-5736; Office Phone: 404-657-2559. Personal E-mail: chilo_ezeh@yahoo.com, chogbuanu@dhr.state.sa.us.

OGBUANU, IKECHUKWU UDO, physician; b. Arochukwu, Abia, Nigeria, Feb. 28, 1974; s. Sebastian Njoku and Veronica Chinyere Ogbuanu; m. Chinelo Amarachukwu Ezeh; children: Joseph Chiedozie, Hannah Chinyere. MD, U. Nigeria, Nsukka, 1998; MPH, U. SC, Columbia, 2006, PhD, 2009. House officer, intern Nigerian Army Reference Hosp., Kaduna, Nigeria, 1999—2000; med. officer, corp. physician Imaobong Missionary Outreach Med. Ctr., Uyo, Akwa-Ibom, Nigeria, 2000—02; med. officer St. Luke's Hosp. Dept. Surgery, Anua, Akwa-Ibom, 2002—03; med. dir. Faith Med. Ctr., Uyo, 2003—04; rsch.-grad. asst. Arnold Sch. Pub. Health, Columbia, SC, 2006—09, Dept. Internal Medicine, U. SC., Sch. Medicine, Columbia, 2006—09; epidemic intelligence svc. officer Ctrs. Disease Control & Prevention, Atlanta, 2009—11, med. epidemiologist, 2011—. Contbr. chapters to books, articles to profl. jours. Deacon Winners Chapel Internat., Atlanta, 2004—. Program Excellence Sci. fellow, Am. Assn. Advancement Sci., 2010. Mem.: SAS Users Group, Nigerian Med. Assn., APHA, Delta Omega Honors Soc., Nat. Scholars Honor Soc., Golden Key Internat. Honor Soc. Office: Ctrs Disease Control & Prevention 1600 Clifton Rd MS A-04 Atlanta GA 30333 Business E-Mail: ige2@cdc.gov. E-mail: dr_iyke@yahoo.com.

OGDEN, ALFRED T., medical educator; b. NYC, Apr. 19, 1970; BS in Biology, Yale U., 1993; MD, Columbia U., 2000. Asst. prof. Columbia U., 2008—. Office: Neurological Inst 710 W 168th St New York NY 10032 Business E-Mail: ato2@columbia.edu.

OGIHARA, MASAHIKO, medical educator; b. Hokkaido, Japan, Dec. 4, 1951; BS, Hokkaido U., 1975, PhD, 1980. Prof. faculty pharm. scis. Josai U., 1984—. Mem.: Japanese Pharmacol. Soc. Avocation: golf. Office: 1-1 Keyakidai Sakado Saitama 350-0295 Japan Office Phone: 81-492-71-7316. Office Fax: 81-492-71-7316. Business E-Mail: clin-p@josai.ac.jp, ogiharam@josdi.ac.jp.

OGIHARA, SHIGEKI, periodontist; b. Tokyo, Jan. 23, 1955; s. Kanji and Yukiko Ogihara; m. Naoyo Ogihara. DDS, PhD, Nihon U. Sch. Dentistry & Medicine, Tokyo, 1989. Cert. periodontics Japan Periodontal Soc., Tokyo, 1998. Pvt. practice Ogihara Dental Clinic, Tokyo, 1981—. Contbr. scientific papers to profl. jours. Mem.: Am. Acad. Periodontilogy. Achievements include research in tissue engineering. Office: Ogihara Dental Clinic 7-16 Adachi 3chome Adachi-ku Tokyo 1200015 Japan Office Phone: 81338498483. E-mail: oshigeki@fantasy.plala.or.jp.

OGILVIE, RICHARD IAN, clinical pharmacologist; b. Sudbury, Ont., Can., Oct. 9, 1936; s. Patrick Ian and Gena Hilda (Olson) O.; m. Ernestine Tahedl, Oct. 9, 1965; children— Degen Elisabeth, Lars Ian. MD, U. Toronto, 1960. Intern Toronto (Ont.) Gen. Hosp., 1960-61; resident Montreal Gen. and Univ. Alta. hosps., 1962-66; fellow in clin. pharmacology McGill U., Montreal, 1966-68, asst. prof. medicine, pharmacology and therapeutics, 1968-73, assoc. prof., 1973-78, prof., 1978-83, chmn. dept. pharmacology and therapeutics, 1978-83. Prof. emeritus, U. Toronto, 2002-, clin. pharmacologist Montreal Gen. Hosp., 1968-83, dir. div. clin. pharmacology, 1976-83; prof. medicine and pharmacology U. Toronto, 1983—2002; dir. div. cardiology Toronto Western Hosp., 1983-88, div. clin. pharmacology, 1983-91; mem. pharm. grants com. Med. Research Coun. Can., 1977-82, chmn. 1980-82; mem. med. adv. com. Que. Heart Found., 1976-82, chmn. 1977-81. Editor Hypertension Canada, 1989-2008. Bd. dirs. PMAC Health Care Found., 1986-92; hon. sec.-treas. Banting Research Found., 1984-87, chmn. grant rev. com., 1985-86 Decorated knight comdr. Sovereign Mil. Order St. John of Jerusalem, Knights of Malta, 1987, nat. chmn., recipient prize in med. ethics, 1988-98, sci. advisor to the prior, 1987—, Knight Grand Cross, 1990; jury mem. Can. Prix Galien, 1994-99; grantee Can. Kidney Found., J.C. Edwards Found., Med. Rsch. Coun., Que. Heart Found., Can. Found. Advancement Therapeutics, Conseil de la recherche en sante du Que. Fellow ACP, Royal Coll. Physicians of Can.; mem. Can. Soc. Clin. Investigation (coun. 1977-80), Can. Hypertension Soc. (bd. dirs. 1979-81, 89-94, 96—2006, v.p. 1991-92, pres. 1992-93, Disting. Svc. award, 2002), Can. Found. Advancement Clin. Pharmacology (dir. 1978-86), Canadian Soc. for Clin. Pharmacology (pres. 1979-82, Sr. Investigator award 1993), Internat. Union Pharmacology (coun. mem. clin. pharmacology sect. 1981-84, chmn. 1984-87), Can. Soc. Pharmacology & Therapeutics (Disting. Lectr. award 2011), Can. Cardiovascular Soc., Am. Soc. Pharmacology and Exptl. Therapeutics, Am. Soc. Clin. Pharm., Toronto Hypertension Soc. (pres. 1988-98). Home: 79 Collard Dr King City ON Canada L7B 1E4 Office: Toronto Western Hosp 399 Bathurst St Toronto ON Canada M5T 2S8 Office Phone: 416-603-5176.

OGIYA, AKIKO, oncologist; b. Japan, Feb. 20, 1974; MD, Yokohama City U., 1998; PhD in Med. Sci., Tokyo Med. & Dental U., 2009. Attending physician Japanese Red Cross Med. Ctr., 1998—2005; resident Cancer Inst. Hosp., 2005—08; primary physician Shizuoka Cancer Ctr. Hosp., 2009—. Mem.: Japan Assn. Breast Cancer Screening, Japan Surg. Soc., Japanese Breast Cancer Soc. Avocations: movies, travel, music. Office: 1007 Shimonagakubo Nagaizumi-cho Shizuoka Suntou-gun 4118777 Japan E-mail: a.ogiya@scchr.jp.

OGNIBENE, ANDRE JOHN, retired military officer, internist, educator; b. NYC, Nov. 18, 1931; s. Morris S. and Josephine C. (Macaluso) O.; m. Margaret A. Haug, Apr. 21, 1957; children: Judy, Andrea, Adrienne, Marc, Eric. BA cum laude, Columbia U., 1952; MD, NYU, 1956. Diplomate Am. Bd. Internal Medicine, Am. Bd. Geriatrics, Am. Bd. Med. Mgmt. Intern in medicine Bellevue Hosp., NYC, 1956-57, resident in medicine, 1957-59; commd. capt. US Army M.C., 1957, advanced through grades to brig. gen., 1978; resident in medicine Manhattan VA Hosp., NYC and chief resident in medicine, 1959-60; chief med. service US Army Hosp., Nurnburg, Germany, 1961-62, chief dept. medicine, 1962-64; fellow in cardiology Walter Reed Gen. Hosp., Washington, 1964-65, asst. in cardiology, 1965-66, asst. chief dept. medicine, 1969-72; chief dept. medicine, chief profl. services US Army Hosp., Ft. Meade, Md., 1966-68; cons. in medicine Hdqrs. US Army, Vietnam, 1969; asst. chief dept. medicine Walter Reed Army Med. Ctr., 1970-72; from chief dept. medicine to dir. med. edn. Brooke Army Med. Ctr., Ft. Sam Houston, Tex., 1972-78, dir. med. edn., 1976-78, dep. comdr. and chief profl. services, 1976-78, comdr., commanding gen., 1978-81; hosp. dir. San Antonio State Chest Hosp., 1981-85; program dir. internal medicine Canton, Ohio, 1985-95; prof. medicine NE Ohio U., Rootstown, 1985-98, prof. emeritus, 1998—, chmn. dept. medicine, 1989-98, assoc. dean for med. edn., 1989—98; med. dir. Mercy Med. Ctr., 1995—98; v.p., treas. Majomed Corp., San Antonio, 1999—2008. Instr. medicine NYU, 1960; assoc. clin. prof. Georgetown U., 1970-72; clin. prof. U. Tex. Health Sci. Ctr., San Antonio, 1973-85, mem. postgrad. adv. com., 1977-78; mem. Instl. Rev. Bd., 1981-85; pres. Bexar Met. unit Am. Cancer Soc., 1984; dir. Eisenhower Nat. Bank; bd. dirs. Cancer Therapy and Rsch. Ctr.; chmn. South Tex. Epilepsy Found., 1985. Contbr. articles to med. publs. and chpts. to books; editor, prin. author Internal Medicine in Vietnam, Vol. II, 1982; editor-in-chief: Internal Medicine in Vietnam, vol. I, 1977. Trustee Regina Health Ctr., 1992-97; mem. med. adv. bd. Access Health Inc., 1998-2000. Decorated DSM, Legion of Merit; named among Am. Top Physicians, Consumer Rsch. Coun., 2003-05. Master ACP (laureate, master tchr.); fellow Am. Coll. Physician Execs. (cert.), Am. Coll. Angiology; mem. NY Acad. Scis., Am. Fedn. Clin. Rsch., Bexar County Med. Soc., Stark County Med. Soc., Assn. Profs. Medicine, Tex. Med. Found., Alpha Omega Alpha. Home and Office: 193 Shores Point Canyon Lake TX 78133 Business E-Mail: aognibene@clear.net.

OGNIBENE, FREDERICK PETER, internist; b. Jamestown, NY, Aug. 30, 1953; s. Vincent Larry and Alma Linda (Martinelli) O. BA, U. Rochester, 1975; MD, Cornell U., 1979. Diplomate Am. Bd. Internal Medicine, Am. Bd. Internal Medicine-Critical Care. From intern to resident NY Hosp./Cornell Med. Ctr., 1979-82; from med. to sr. staff fellow Critical Care Medicine Dept. NIH, Bethesda, Md., 1982-87, sr. investigator, 1987—, fellowship dir., 1998—2003. Assoc. clin. prof. George Washington U., Washington, 1996—; adj. assoc. prof. U. Md., 2000—; dir. clin. rsch. tng. program NIH, 2000—, dir. office clin. rsch. tng. and med. edn., 2003—, dep. dir. ednl. affairs and strategic partnerships Clin. Ctr., 2009-. Manuscript reviewer; contbr. articles to profl. jours., chpts. to books. Mem. bd. dirs. Washington Project Arts, 2007-; bd. dirs. Cultural Devel. Corp. D.C., 2003—06, Curator's Cir. Hirshhorn Mus. and Sculpture Garden, 2004-. Capt. USPHS, 1985-2007. Fellow ACP, Am. Coll. Critical Care Medicine (chair credentials com. 1992-94, bd. regents 1994-2000); mem. Cornell U. Med. Coll. Alumni Assn. (bd. dirs.), Am. Fedn. Clin. Rschs. (nat. coun. 1987-95, sec.-treas. ea. sect. 1987-91, chair-elect 1991-92, chair 1992-93), Am. Fedn. Clin. Rsch. Found. (trustee), Assn. Am. Physicians, Soc. Critical Care Medicine (co-chair symposium 1998, governing coun. 2000-04, sec. 2004-05, pres. 2007), Alpha Omega Alpha. Democrat. Roman Catholic. Avocations: travel, studying Italian language, collecting contemporary American art. Home: 1661 Crescent Pl NW Apt 308 Washington DC 20009 Office: NIH Rm BIL 403 9000 Rockville Pike Bldg 10 Bethesda MD 20892 Office Phone: 301-496-9425, 301-402-0563. Business E-Mail: fognibene@cc.nih.gov.

OGODESCU, ALEXANDRU SIMION, orthodontist, educator; b. Timisoara, Feb. 2, 1975; DMD in Orthodontics and Dentofacial Orthop., U. Medicine & Pharmacy Victor Babes Timisoara Romania, 1999, PhD in Orthodontics, Interdisciplinary Orthodontics, 2006. Ass. prof. dept. orthodontics & paedodontics U. Medicine & Pharmacy Victor Babes Timisoara, 2000—. Dir. owner Orthodontic Pvt. Clinic, 2001—. Recipient First prize, Romanian Nat. Assn. Orthodontics, Romanian Assn. Straight-Wire, Best Oral Presentations award, Timisoara Dental Students Assn. Mem.: ADA, Romanian Nat. Assn. Orthodontics, Romanian Assn. Straight-Wire, World Fedn. Orthodontists, European Orthodontic Soc. Avocations: travel, sports. Office: StrMartir Dumitru Juganaru Albac Nr9 Timisoara Timis 300765 Romania Business E-Mail: ogodescu@yahoo.com.

OGONDA, LUKE, orthopedist, surgeon; No. Ireland, 1998; s. Ogonda Agingu and Peres Ogonda; m. Sylvia Sitati, Nov. 18, 1994; children: Susan, Florence. MB, BChir, U. Nairobi, 1992; MPhil, Queen's U., Belfast, No. Ireland, 2005. Basic surg. tng. Royal Group of Hosps., Belfast, 1998—2002, higher specialist tng. orthopaedics, 2003—05; specialist registrar Southwest Eng. Orthopaedic tng. program, 2005—06, North Ireland Orthopaedic program, 2007—; cons. orthop. surgeon Ulster Hosp., Belfast, 2010—. Contbr. articles to profl. jours. Vol. med. profl. No. Ireland Schools Work Placement

Program, Belfast, Northern Ireland, 2003—05. Recipient Norman Martin medal, No. Ireland Regional Orthop. and Trauma Com., 2005; BART Arthroplasty Rsch. fellow, Belfast Arthroplasty Rsch. Trust, 2003—05, Smith & Nephew Limb Reconstruction fellowship, Royal Liverpool Hosp., 2010. Fellow: Royal Coll. Surgeons (Edinburgh). Achievements include research in first large scale prospective randomised controlled trial on minimal incision total hip arthroplasty. Avocations: travel, swimming, bicycling. Office: Musgrave Pk Hosp Stockmans Ln Belfast BT9 7BA Ireland Business E-Mail: jokogonda@doctors.org.uk.

OGRA, PEARAY L., pediatrician, educator; b. Srinagar, Kashmir, India, Mar. 19, 1937; came to U.S., 1961, naturalized, 1969; s. Govinda Kaul and Gunvati (Daftari) O.; children: Sanjay, Monica. MB, Christian Med. Coll., Ludhiana, India, 1961. Intern Binghamton Gen. Hosp., NY, 1962-63; resident U. Chgo., 1963-64, NYU.-Bellevue Med Center, 1964-66, fellow in infectious diseases, 1966-68; asst. prof. pediatrics SUNY, Buffalo, 1968-71, assoc. prof. pediatrics and microbiology, 1972-74, prof., 1974-91; John Sealy disting. chair, prof. U. Tex. Med. Br., Galveston, 1991-2000, chmn. dept. pediatrics, 1991-99; prof. pediatrics Children's Hosp., Buffalo, 2000—09; prof. emeritus SUNY, 2010—. Dir. divsn. virology Children's Hosp. Buffalo, 1969-81, chief dept. infectious diseases, 1970-91; dir. Clin. Labs. Children's Hosp., 1985-90; mem. study sect. NIH, 1979-85, maternal child health com., 1987-91; mem., chmn. bd. Internat. Pediat. Rsch. Found., Inc., 1984-89; mem. com. on vaccines for 21st century Inst. of Medicine NAS, 1997-2000, com. in infant formula, 2002; adv. bd. Internat. Vaccine Inst., Seoul, Rep. Korea, 2003—, Merck scholar-in-residence, 2006—10, commencement spkr., guest honor Christian Med. Coll., Ludhiana, India; chmn. external rev. group Program on Mucosal Vaccines, European Commn., 2005—10. Contbr. articles to profl. jours.:, editor 18 books on mucose immunology and infections, and childhood vaccination. Recipient E. Mead Johnson award for Pediatric Research Am. Acad. Pediatrics, 1978; Kalhana award Kashmir Sci. Culture and Soc., 1984; Stockton Kimball award SUNY, 1985, Outstanding Sci. Contribution award Am. Asian Phys. Assn.; Buswell fellow, 1968-71. Fellow Royal Soc. Medicine, Assn. Am. Physicians, Am. Acad. Pediatrics, Am. Acad. Microbiology; mem. Am. Soc. Clin. Investigation, Soc. Pediatric Rsch., Infectious Disease Soc. Am., Soc. Exptl. Biology and Medicine, Am. Assn. Immunologists, Am. Soc. Microbiology, AAAS, Am. Fedn. Clin. Rsch., Am. Soc. Virology, Pediatric Infectious Disease Soc. (chmn. com. internatl health 2006—). Home: 163 Troy Del Way Williamsville NY 14221-4505 Office Phone: 716-878-7407. Business E-Mail: pogra@upa.chob.edu. E-mail: plogra@buffalo.edu.

O'GRADY, BARBARA VINSON, retired community health nurse, administrator; b. Alhambra, Calif., July 6, 1928; d. Weston Wright and Merdith Alyda (Noble) Vinson; m. Joseph Putnam O'Grady, Oct. 24, 1952; children: Joseph Jr., Jeffrey, Kent, Kimberly, Kathryn; m. John Mark Prebish, June 28, 1997. BS, UCLA, 1951; MS, U. Minn., 1972. Staff public health nurse San Diego Co. Health Dept., 1952; staff nurse U. Minn. Hosp., 1954-56; staff public health nurse Family Nursing Svc., St. Paul, 1972; asst. prof. Gustavus Adolphus Coll., St. Peter, Minn., 1972-77; dir. Ramsey County Public Health Nursing Svc., St. Paul, 1977-88, health staff Senator Dave Durenberger, Mpls., 1988; cons. pvt. practice, Waterville, Minn., 1989-97, ret., 1998. Mem. bd. govs. U. Minn. Hosp. and Clinic, Mpls., 1983-91, chair, 1985-87; clin. faculty Sch. Pub. Health, 1984-88. Author: (with others) Computer Applications in Medical Care, 1982, Nursing and Computers, 1989, NCNIP: Models for the Future of Nursing, 1989, Procs. of Impact of DRG's on Nursing Conf., 1988; mem. edtl. bd. Jour. Cmty. Health Nursing, 1984-94. Mem. Mpls. Charter Commn., 1967-72; co-chair Minn. GOP Issues Devel., 1968, Minn. GOP Constn. Com., 1966-70; chair Dick Erdall Campaign Com., 1965-71; bd. dirs. Presbyn. Homes of Minn., St. Paul, 1982-88; bd. dirs. Living at Home/Block Nurse Program, 1986-98, chair external rels. com., 1988-98, Women's Environ. Watch, Santa Ynez Valley, Calif., 2001-; adminstrv. asst. to coord., Valley Mentoring Program, 2003-. Recipient Outstanding Contbn. Midwest Alliance in Nursing, 1984, Outstanding Achievement award Bd, of Ramsey County Commrs., 1987; Annie Yates scholar L.A. County General Hosp. Alumni Assn., 1948, named One of One Hundred Disting. Nursing Alumni awards U. Minn., Nursing Alumni Soc., 2009; Living At Home grantee The Commonwealth Fund, 1986. Fellow Am. Acad. of Nursing; mem. ANA, APHA, Nat. League for Nursing, Minn. Public Health Assn., Sigma Theta Tau. Presbyterian. Avocations: swimming, reading, travel. Home: PO Box 624 Santa Ynez CA 93460-0624 Personal E-mail: barbandjohn624@gmail.com.

OGREY, CAROLYN J., health facility administrator; b. Davenport, Iowa, Nov. 28, 1961; Degree in Resource Mgmt., Iowa State U., 1984. Mgmt. cons. Coopers & Lybrand, 1987—89; sr. ops., fin. analyst Calif. Pacific Med. Ctr., 1990—93; assoc. HFS Cons., 1994—2000; with, bus. devel. Christiana Care Health Sys., 2006—. Mem.: Del. Med. Group Mgmt. Assn. Avocations: tennis, piano. Office: 200 Hygeia Dr Newark DE 19713 Personal E-mail: cogrey@verizon.net.

OGSBURY, JAMES STANLEY, III, neurosurgeon, educator; s. James Stanley and Lucile (Becker) Ogsbury; m. Kathleen McBride Ogsbury. BS, Denison U., 1965; MD, Cornell U. Med. Coll., 1969. Diplomate Am. Bd. Neurosurgery. Intern, resident N.Y. Hosp., NYC, 1969—71; resident U. Colo. Health Sci. Ctr., Denver, 1973—77, clin. asst. prof. neurosurgery, 1977—; clin. neurosurgeon Luth. Med. Ctr., Wheat Ridge, Colo., 1977—, St. Anthony's Hosp., Denver, 1977—. Med. dir. Colo. Low Back Colaborative, 2009—. Maj. USAF, 1971—73. Mem.: Colo. Neurosurg. Soc. Avocations: skiing, bicycling. Office: Rocky Mountain Neurosurgical Consultants LLC 2460 W 26th Ave Bldg C Ste 220-C Denver CO 80211 Office Phone: 303-431-6678. Business E-Mail: rmns@guest.net.

OGUNKOYA, YETUNDE OLUFUNMILAYO, biology professor; b. Nigeria, June 12, 1957; DVM, Ahmadu Bello U., Nigeria, 1982; PhD, Murdoch U., West Australia, 1997. Adj. prof. Morehouse Coll., 2000—03; rsch. assoc. Morehouse Sch. Medicine, 2000—03; assoc. prof. So. U., New Orleans, 2003—06, So. U. & A & M Coll., 2006—. Coord. LS-LAMP, 2006—10. Rsch. grant, NSF, INBRE. Mem.: AVMA, HAPS, ASM, ASCB. Avocations: reading, travel. Office: 244 James Hall Baton Rouge LA 70813 Office Fax: 225-771-4877. Business E-Mail: yetunde_ogunkoya@subr.edu.

OGURO, HIROAKI, neurologist, educator; b. Tokyo, Oct. 10, 1965; MD, Shimane Med. U., PhD, 1992. Assoc. prof., dept. neurology Faculty Medicine, Shimane U., 2006—. Office: 89-1 Enya Cho Izumo City Shimane 6938501 Japan Office Fax: 81853202194. Business E-Mail: oguro@med.shimane-u.ac.jp.

OGURTAN, ZEKI, veterinarian, researcher; b. Mugla, Turkey, Sept. 14, 1958; married, May 10, 1998; children: Ahmet, Aysenur. Assoc. prof dept. surgery Selçuk U., Turkey, 2004—. Achievements include patents for intramedullary compression and antirotational device; anti overflow cup. Office: Selcuk Univ Veteriner Fakultesi Cerrahi Abd 42100 Selçuklu Konya Turkey Office Fax: 332-241-0063. Personal E-mail: ogurtan@hotmail.com, zogurtan@hotmail.com, agurtan@gmail.com. Business E-Mail: zogurtan@selcuk.edu.tr.

OGUS, NOYAN TEMUCIN, cardiovascular surgeon, consultant; b. Ankara, Turkey, Mar. 30, 1963; s. Hikmet and Melahat Ogus; m. Halide Yener, Dec. 9, 1994; children: Damla, Yagmur. Lic., D of Medicine, Istanbul U., Turkey, 1988. Specialist, asst. prof. Maltepe U. Med. Faculty, Istanbul, 1996—2001; asst. prof. Yeditepe U. Med. Faculty, Istanbul, 2001—02; assoc. prof., cons. physician Pvt. Medicana Hosp., Istanbul, 2002—. Dept. chief cardiovasc. surgery Goztepe Pvt. Safak Hosp., Istanbul, 2005—. Avocations: bicycling, travel. Office: Private Goztepe Safak Hosp Fahrettin Kerim Gokay C 192 Goztepe 81300 Istanbul Turkey Office Fax: 902165658585. E-mail: togus@superonline.com.

OH, AH-YOUNG, anesthesiologist, educator; b. Seoul, Republic of Korea, Aug. 16, 1970; d. Sang Hyun Oh and Chong Hyun Paik; m. Jin-Ho Kim, Jan. 18, 1997; children: So-Hyeong Kim, Sang-Mok Kim. PhD, Seoul Nat. U., Republic of Korea, 1996, M in Anesthesiology and Pain Medicine, 2001, D in Anesthesiology and Pain Medicine, 2003. Diplomate Ministry Health and Welfare, Republic of Korea, 2001. Intern, resident, fellow Seoul Nat. U., 1996—2002; asst. prof. Seoul Nat. U. Hosp., 2002—05, Seoul Nat. U. Bundang Hosp., 2005—. Contbr. articles to profl. jours. Mem.: The Korean Soc. Anesthesiologists. Achievements include research in hypoxic pulmonary vasoconstriction using isolated rat lung model, pediatric anesthesia, neuromuscular physiology and pharmacology. Office: Seoul Nat University Bundang Hosp Gumi Ro Bundang Gu 166 Gyeonggi Seongnam 463-707 Republic of Korea Office Fax: 82-31-787-4063. Personal E-mail: ohahyoung@hanmail.net. Business E-Mail: oay1@snubh.org.

OH, CHANG-KEUN, dermatologist, dermatologic surgeon; b. Busan, Republic of Korea, Sept. 27, 1964; s. Man-Yong Oh and Yang-Ja Kim; m. Gwi-Young Chung, May 11, 1991; children: Hyeon-Seok, Hyeon-Ho. Pre-med., Pusan Nat. U., Busan, 1985, MD, 1989, PhD, 2000. MD Ministry Health and Welfare, Korea, 1989. Chair dept. dermatology Pusan Nat. U., Busan, 2005—, asst. prof. dept. dermatology, 2006—; intern Pusan Nat. U. Hosp., Busan, Republic of Korea, 1989—90, resident, 1990—94, dematologic surgery fellow, 1997—99; staff dr. Chuncheon and Pusan Armed Forces Hos., 1994—97; postdoctoral fellow, divsn. dermatology UCLA, 2003—05; asst. prof. dermatology Pusan Nat. U., Busan, Republic of Korea, 1999—2006, assoc. prof. dematology, 2006—07. Author: (CD) eBook of Dermatology, 2003, (textbook) Textbook of Aesthetic and Dermatologic Surgery, 2006, Phlebology, 2007, Aesthetics and Cosmetic Surgery for Darker Skin Types, 2007, Textbook of Dermatology, 2008; contbr. articles to profl. jours. Com. mem. of supporters Suyoung-gu Vol. Ctr., Busan, 2001. Capt. Korean Mil., 1994—96. Recipient Travel award, 12th Korea-Japan Joint Meeting Dermatology, 2001, 3rd Janssen award, Korean Soc. for Med. Mycology, 2002, Inbong Academic award, 2008. Mem.: Soc. Investigative Dermatology, Korean Soc. for Investigative Dermatology (Poster award 2007), Korean Soc. Phlebology, Am. Soc. Dermatologic Surgery, Korean Soc. for Aesthetic and Surg. Dermatology, Korean Dermatol. Assn. (Amore Pacific scholar 2003, Poster award 1992, 1993, 2001, 2003, 2005), Korean Med. Assn. Home: LG Metrocity 124-202 Yonghodong Nam-gu Busan 608-890 Republic of Korea Office Fax: 82-51-746-3017. Business E-Mail: ckoh@pusan.ac.kr.

OH, CHANG-KWON, surgeon, educator; b. Seoul, Republic Of Korea, Aug. 15, 1961; s. Key Sun Oh and Jung Sup Choi; m. Hyeon Woo Suh, May 27, 1988; children: Sung Eun, Sung Hyeon. MD, Yonsei U. Coll. Medicine, Seoul, 1985; MS, Yonsei U. Grad. sch., Seoul, 1995, PhD, 1998. Lic. Korean Med. Ministry of Health, 1985, cert. general surgery Ministry of Health, 1990, ECFMG Ednl. Commn. Fgn. Med. Grad., 1997, lic. Commonwealth of Va., Dept. Health Professions, 1998. Intern Yonsei U. Severance Hosp., Seoul, 1985—86, resident Dept. Surgery, 1986—90, clin. fellow Dept. Transplant Surgery, 1990—93; instr. Ajou U. Sch. Medicine, Suwon, Republic of Korea, 1995—95, asst. prof., 1998—2003, assoc. prof., 2003—08, prof., 2008—; clin. transplant fellow Dept. Surgery U. Va. Health Sys., Charlottesville, 1998—2000. Contbr. scientific papers to numerous profl. jours. Mem.: Am. Soc. Transplant Surgeons (fellowship). Office: Ajou Univ Sch of Medicine 5 Wonchon-Dong Yeongtong-Gu Suwon Kyonggi-443-749 Republic of Korea Office Fax: 82-31-219-5755. Business E-Mail: ohck@ajou.ac.kr.

OH, CHEE WON, dermatologist, educator; b. Seoul, Republic of Korea, Aug. 23, 1964; d. Chang Kwon Oh and Hei Ok Choi; m. Eun Sang Kim, Sept. 16, 1958; children: Dae Jin Kim, Kwang Hyun Kim. MD, Ewha Womans U., Seoul, Korea, 1988; PhD, Ewha Womans U., 1994. Lic. Doctoral Ministry of Health & Welfare, Korea, 1988, cert. Nat. Bd. on Dermatology Ministry of Health & Welfare, Korea, 1992. Internship Ewha Womans U. Hosp., Seoul, Republic of Korea, 1988—89, dermatology residency, 1989—92; prof. Gyeongsang Nat. U., Chinju, Republic of Korea, 1992—. Vis. clinician Mayo Clinic, Rochester, Minn., 1995; fellow Thomas Jefferson U. Hosp., Philadelphia, 1996; vis. clinician Cutaneous Pathology, Saint Louis, 1998; fellow St. Louis U. Hosp., 1998—99. Recipient 1st Internat. Publ. award, Korean Med. Women's Assn., 1997, 3rd Internat. Publ. award, 1999, 9th Internat. Publ. award, 2005. Mem.: Am. Soc. Of Dermatopathology (assoc.), Korean Dermatol. Assn. (life Donga Academic award 1996, Tae Pyoung Yang Scholarship 1997, Best Poster award 2000). Office: Kangwon Nat University Hosp Derm 17-1 Hyoja 3 200-722 Chuncheon Gangwon-do Republic of Korea Personal E-mail: cheewon@hotmail.com. Business E-Mail: deroh@kargnon.ac.kr.

OH, CHIL-HWAN, education educator, dermatologist; b. Seoul, Korea, June 28, 1953; s. Han-Kwoen and Sook-Ja Oh; m. Song-Sil Chang Oh; children: Ji-Yeon, Beum-Hyuk. MD, Korea Univ., Seoul, 1972, MSc, 1982, PhD, 1985. Lic. bd. Dermatologist, Korea. Prof. Korea Univ., 1990—, chmn., 1999—2001; rsch. assoc. Boston Univ., Mass., 2001—04. Dir. Rsch. Inst. Skin Imaging, Seoul, 2001—, mem. academic com., 2001—. Contbr. articles to profl. jour. (first prize, 2001, sec. prize, 2003, pres. prize Korean patent award, Korean govt., 2003). Achievements include 5 patents in Korea. Office: Dept Dermatology Korea Univ 97 Gurodong Seoul 155705 Republic of Korea

OH, DOYEUN, medical educator; b. Busan, Republic of Korea, Sept. 20, 1955; s. Deok-Moon Oh and Jeong-Ja Cho; m. Anna Yoon, Nov. 19, 1955; children: Eun-Joo, Jin-Seok, Eun-Seok. MD, Yonsei U., 1980, MS, 1984, MD, 1987, PhD, 1990. Lectr. Coll. Medicine, Soonchunhyang U., Chunan, Chungnam, Republic of Korea, 1987—89, asst. prof., 1990—94; assoc. prof. Coll. Medicine, Kyunghee U., Seoul, 1995—96, Coll. Medicine, Pochon CHA U., Sungnam, Kyunggido, 1996—2000, prof., 2000—. Dir. med. staffs Bundang CHA Gen. Hosp., 2003—; dir. Inst. Clin. Rsch., Coll. Medicine, Pochon CHA U. Contbr. articles to profl. jours. Mem.: Internat. Soc. Thrombosis and Hemostasis (Travel award 2003), Korean Soc. Thrombosis and Hemostasis, Korean Soc. Hematology, Korean Soc. Internal Medicine. Roman Catholic. Achievements include patents for MTHFR 677TT genotype for prediction or prevention of an ischemic stroke(PCT/KR02/00684) since Apr 15, 2002. Avocation: swimming. Office: Pochon CHA Univ Yatap-Dong Bundang-Gu 351 462-712 Seongnam Gyeonggi-do Republic of Korea Office Fax: 82-31-780-5219. E-mail: doh@cha.ac.kr.

OH, HEUNGBUM, pathologist, educator; b. Pyoseon, Jeju, S. Korea, May 5, 1963; s. Boosik Oh and Soonja Song; m. Nayoung Hwang, Oct. 10, 1963; children: Suhyun, Suhee. PhD, Seoul Nat. U., Republic of Korea, 1999. Diplomate Ministry of Health and Welfare, 1996. Dir. transfusion rsch. inst. Korean Nat. Red Cross, Seoul, 1996—98; prof. Coll. Medicine and Asan Med. Ctr. U. Ulsan, Seoul, 1998—. Com. mem. transfusion safety Ministry of Health and Welfare, Seoul, 2005—; tech. counselor LG Life Sci., Inc., Seoul, 2005—. Dir. med. aid to the needy Christian Fellowship of Asan Med. Ctr., Seoul, 2005—06. Recipient Abbott Academic Award, Korean Assn. of Lab. Medicine, 1998, 2001. Mem.: Korean Assn. Transfusion Medicine, Korean Assn. Lab. Medicine (chmn. com. diagnostic immunology). Achievements include research in histocompatibility antigens in Koreans. Office: University of Ulsan College of Medicine 388-1 Poongnap-dong Songpa-gu Seoul 138-736 Republic of Korea Office Fax: 82-2-478-0884. Business E-Mail: hboh@amc.seoul.kr.

OH, HONG KEUN, medical educator, physician; b. Suncheon, Korea (South), June 4, 1950; s. Gil Yeon Oh and Deuk Up Huh; m. Soon Hwa Choi, Sept. 19, 1980; children: Dong Hoon, Yoon Ju. MB, Kyung Hee U., Seoul, Republic of Korea, 1975; M in Medicine, Kyung Hee U., 1978, PhD, 1984; Naturopathic Dr., Can. Coll. Naturopathic Medicine, Toronto, Can., 1991; M in Healing Ministry, United Theol. U., Seoul, 1999. Cert. Dr. Ministry of Health and Welfare, 1975, Naturopathic Dr. Assn. Naturopathic Medicine, 1991. Prof. Sch. of Medicine, U. Toronto, 1986—88; mem. Physician and Surgeon of Ont., 1986—88; pres. Korea Soc. Comprehensive and Alternative Medicine, Seoul, 1997—; dean, prof. Jeonju U., Republic of Korea, 2005—. Pres. Korea Aromatherapy Assn., Seoul, Cheonra Buk Do, 1997—, Korea Soc. Stress Sci., Seoul, 1999—2001; chmn. World Orgn. Aromatherapy, Tokyo, 2002—04; pres. Dr. Oh's Neuropsychiatric Hosp., Seoul, 1997—2000. Author: (medical textbook) Dr. Oh's Naturopathic Medicine, (health book) Handbook of aromatherapy, (book) Dr. Oh's Aromatherapy textbook; contbr. scientific papers. Dir. Korean Mental Health Ctr., Toronto, 1986—89. Maj. 57 Mil. Army Hosp., 1980—83, Euijungbu, Korea. Presbyterian. Achievements include patents for effective composition of essential oils. Avocations: travel, bicycling, swimming, skiing, hiking. Office: Jeonju U Hyoja Dong Wansan Gu 1200 560-757 Jeonju Chonra Buk do Republic of Korea Office Fax: 82 63 220 2054.

OH, HYOUNG-CHUL, gastroenterologist, educator; b. Seoul, Oct. 8, 1971; MD, Kyung-Hee U., 1997, PhD, 2007. Clin. instr. Asan Med. Ctr., U. Ulsan Coll. Medicine, 2007—08; asst. prof. Chung-Ang U. Coll. Medicine, 2008—. Recipient Young Investigator award, Asia-Pacific Digestive Week, Korean Soc. Gastrointestinal Endoscopy. Mem.: Korean Pancreatobiliary Assn., Korean Soc. Gastroenterology, Am. Soc. Gastrointestinal Endoscopy. Office: 102 Heukseokro Dongjak-gu Seoul 156-755 Republic of Korea E-mail: ohcgi@cau.ac.kr.

OH, IN-SUK, medical educator; b. Seoul, Republic of Korea, Nov. 12, 1945; s. Se Jin Oh and Yang Ok Lee; m. Hyun-Jung Park, Oct. 19, 1975; children: Sang-Yup, Sang-Yoon. MD, Seoul Nat. U., 1971, MS, 1979; PhD, Korea U., Seoul, 1985. Lic. dr. 1971, orthop. surgeon 1980, cert. in sports medicine Korean Soc. Sports Medicine, 2005. Prof. Inje U. Paik Hosp., Seoul, 1981—86; chmn. Gachon U. Gill Hosp., Inchon, Republic of Korea, 1987—95; prof. Inha U. Sch. Medicine, Inchon, 1996—; orthop. surgeon Inha U. Hosp., Inchon, 1996—. Capt. Korean Mil., 1972—75. Mem.: Korean Orthopaedic Assn., Inchon-gyunggi Knee Soc. (pres. 2005—), Internat. Cartilage Repair Soc. (assoc.), Internat. Soc. Arthroscopy, Knee Surgery and Orthropaedic Sports Medicine (assoc.). Achievements include research in early detection of degenerative arthritis of the knee joint; regeneration of hyaline cartilage with irradiated transforming growth factor B1-producing fibroblasts; new modified technique of osteotomy for hallux valgus; continuous transforming growth factor B1 secretion by cell-mediated gene therapy maintains chondrocyte redifferentiation; hyaline cartilage regeneration using mixed human chondrocytes and transforming factor B1 producing chondrocytes; clinical and radiological results after distal metatorsal osteotony hallux valgus. Home: 8-306 Banpo Apt Banpo-dong Secho-gu Seoul Republic of Korea Office: Inha University Hospital 7-206 3-Ga Shinheung-Dong Jung-Gu 400-711 Incheon Incheon Republic of Korea Office Fax: 82-32-890-3099. Business E-Mail: orthooh@inha.ac.kr.

OH, MICHAEL Y., neurosurgeon; b. June 20, 1967; BA in Math., U. Calif., Santa Cruz, 1990; MD, U. So. Calif., 1996. Registered Ont. Coll. Physicians and Surgeons. Intern in gen. surgery Allegheny Gen. Hosp., Pitts., 1997—2001, resident in neurosurgery, 2001, chief resident dept. neurosurgery, 2002; clin., rsch. fellow in stereotactic and functional neurosurgery U. Toronto, Canada, 2000; asst. prof., dir. stereotactic and functional neurosurgery U. Mo., Columbia, 2002—. Mem.: World Soc. for Stereotactic and Functional Neurosurgery, Movement Disorder Soc., Internat. Assn. for the Study of Pain, Am. Soc. for Stereotactic and Functional Neurosurgery, Am. Pain Soc.,

Congress Neurol. Surgeons, Am. Assn. Neurol. Surgeons. Office: Univ Mo N521 One Hospital Dr Columbia MO 65212-0001 Office Phone: 573-882-4908. E-mail: ohm@health.missouri.edu.

OH, MOON-YOU, retired dean; s. Jung-Hung Oh and Yun-Hong Kim; m. Jung-Ja Moon, May 18, 1969; children: Ju-Hyung, Tae-Hyung, Seung-Ju. BS, Cheju Nat. U., Jeju, Republic of Korea, 1964; MS, Seoul Nat. U., Republic of Korea, 1969, PhD, 1986. Diplomate VMD Ministry Agr. & Forestry, 1965. Dean Coll. Natural Sci. Cheju Nat. U., 1989—91, dean planning & rsch. affairs, 1992—94, dir. Info. Telecommunication Ctr., 2000—01, dean ctrl. libr., 2000—02, emritus prof. Roman Catholic. Avocations: running, travel, golf. Home: 310-18 Yeon-Dong 690-815 Jeju Jeju-do Republic of Korea Office Fax: +82-64-756-3541. Business E-Mail: mike@cheju.ac.kr.

OH, PHIL SOO, pediatrician, educator; b. Seoul, Republic Of Korea, July 2, 1962; m. Kyung Hwa Kim. MD, Hanyang U., 1987, PhD, 2000. Cert. pediat. Korean Ministry of Health & Welfare, 1996. Pediat. endocrinologist, prof. Hallym U. Med. Ctr., 1997—; dir., dept. pediats. Hangang Sacred Heart Hosp., Hallym U. Med. Ctr., 2007—09. Pediatric endocrinology fellowship Samsung Med. Ctr., 1996—97; fellow, dept. pediatric endocrinology U. Mich., 2005—06. Mem.: Korean Soc. Pediats., Korean Soc. Pediat. Endocrinology, Asia-Pacific Pediat. Endocrine Soc. Achievements include development of the EMR (electronic medical record) growth chart program for Hallym University Medical Center with a programmer, Tae Hoon Kim. Office: Hallym University Medical Center Gyo-Dong 153 200-704 Chuncheon Gangwon-do Republic of Korea Office Phone: 82-33-240-5167, 82-33-240-5169. Personal E-mail: ohphilia@unitel.co.kr. Business E-Mail: ohphilia@hallym.or.kr.

OH, POK-JA, nursing educator; b. Seoul, Republic of Korea, Feb. 7, 1960; m. Dae Sik Ha Oh; children: Yo Han Ha, Yo Sub Ha. BSN, Sahmyook U., Seoul, 1982; MSN, Yonsei U., Seoul, 1984; PhD, Seoul Nat. U., Republic of Korea, 1994. RN Seoul, 1984, NY, 1999, registered sch. nurse, 1984, cert. nurse, 2001, Korean advanced oncology cert. nurse, 2008. Nurse Seoul Nat. U. Hosp., 1982—84; postdoc. rsch. fellow George Mason U., Coll. Nursing &. Health Sci., 1998; assoc. prof. Dept, Nursing, Sahmyook U., 1985—99, prof., dir., 2000—. Peer reviewer Jour. Korean Acad. Adult Nursing, 1995—. Contbr. to profl. publs.; author: (book) Leukemia: Hope and Self-care, 1996, Introduction to Oncology Nursing Care, 2005, Introduction to Health & Social Welfare, 2006, Essentials of Physical Examination and Health Assessment, 2008. Qualification exam. bd. mem. Korean Accreditation Bd. Nursing, 2003—06; invited mem. Nat. Cancer Control Planning Bd. Ministry Health & Welfare, 2004; organizing com. mem. Global Breast Cancer Conf., 2009, 2011. Recipient Outstanding Rschr. award, Korean Fedn. Sci. and Tech. Soc., 1997, Outstanding Academic Advisor award, Ministry Edn. Sci. and Tech., Republic of Korea, 2008; grants, Korean Rsch. Found., 1996—97, 2006—07, Korean Nurses Assn. Rsch. Fund, 2001, Korea Sci. and Engring. Found., 2002—04, Ministry Edn. Sci. and Tech., 2005. Mem.: Korean Oncology Nursing Soc. (exec. com. mem. 2000—08, pres. 2009—10, advisor 2011—), Am. Oncology Nursing Soc., Korean Academic Soc. Nursing Edn. (exec. com. mem. 2005—08), Am. Oncology Nursing Soc., Korean Nurses' Assn., Korean Assn. Coll. Nursing (exec. com. mem. 2011—), Sigma Theta Tau Alpha. Adventist. Office: Sahmyook University Dept Nursing Hwarangro-815 Seoul Nowon 139-742 Republic of Korea Home: Junggyebon-dong 101-1203 Daerimbyeoksan Apt Seoul Nowon 139-229 Republic of Korea Office Phone: 82-2-3399-1589, 011-9117-9199. Office Fax: 82-2-3399-1594. Business E-Mail: ohpi@syu.ac.kr.

OH, SANG CHEUL, medical educator, researcher; b. Jeju, Jeju-do, Sept. 24, 1968; s. Jung Seung Oh and Sin Ja Hur; m. Hyung Joo Sohn; 1 child, Jin Won. PhD, Korea U., Seoul, Republic Of Korea, 2002. Cert. Hematology-Oncology Bd. Assn. Internal Medicine, Seoul, 2003, in internal medicine Assn. Internal Medicine, 1998, Ministry of Health and Welfare, Republic Of Korea, 1993. Chief Icheon Province Hosp., Republic of Korea, 2000—01; clin. fellow Korea U. Anam Hosp., Seoul, 2001—03; clin. prof. Korea U. Guro Hosp., Seoul, Republic of Korea, 2003—04, asst. prof., 2005—08; postdoc. fellow MD Anderson Cancer Ctr., U. Tex., Houston, 2004—05; vice-dir. Premed. Sch. Korea U., 2006—, assoc. prof., 2008—. Sec. academic com. Korean Assn. Clin. Oncology, Seoul, 2008—. Contbr. articles to profl. jours. Mem. rescue Korea U. Med. Ctr., Seoul, 2006. Capt. Land Force, 1998—2001, Gyunggi-Do. Recipient Excellence of Yr., Gyunggi Province Govt., 2001; Rsch. fellowship, MD Anderson Cancer Ctr., U. Tex., 2004. Mem.: Korean Cancer Soc., Korean Cancer Study Group (hepato-biliary cancer com. 2005—, colorectal cancer com. 2006—), Korean Assoc. Internal Medicine, Alumni Assn. MD Anderson Cancer Ctr. Home: 7-602 G-W Apt Daechi-dong Gangnam-gu Seoul 135-828 Republic of Korea Office: Korea Univ Guro Hosp 80 Guro-dong Guro-gu Seoul 152-703 Republic of Korea Office Fax: 82-2-862-4453; Home Fax: 82-2-577-8276. Business E-Mail: sachoh@korea.ac.kr.

OH, SEIKWAN, pharmacologist, educator; b. Jinchon, Chungbuk, South Korea, Oct. 2, 1960; s. Jeonghwan Oh, Jaesoon Park; m. Soonhee Ahn; children: Sugene, Sukyong, Yunseok. PhD, U. Miss., 1995. Lic. pharmacist 1983. Rsch. assoc. U. Miss. Med. Ctr., Jackson, 1995—98; sr. rsch. scientist Korea Rsch. Inst. of Biosci. and Biotech., Yusong, Daejon, Republic of Korea, 1998—99; asst. prof. Ewha Med. Coll., Yangchon, Seoul, Republic of Korea, 1999—. Author: (book) CNS Neurotransmitters and Neuromodulators: Glutamate, 1995. Korean tchr. Jackson Korean Sch., 1995—98. Sgt. Korean Mil. Acad., 1983—85. Basic Sci. Fund grantee, Korea Rsch. Found., 2001. Mem.: Soc. for Neurosci. Office: Ewha Univ Coll Medicine Mok-dong Yangchon-ku Seoul 158-710 Republic of Korea Office Phone: 82-2-2650-5749. Office Fax: 82-2-2653-8891. Business E-Mail: skoh@mm.ewha.ac.kr.

OH, SUK JOON, plastic surgeon; b. Seoul, Republic of Korea, Aug. 15, 1946; s. Soo Bog Oh and Gum Soon Kang; m. Hea Ja Paek; children: Jae Won, Soyoung, Jae Min. MD, Yonsei U., Coll. Medicine, Seoul, 1970; PhD, Yonsei U., Postgrad. Sch., Seoul, 1979. Cert. gen. surgeon Health & Welfare Ministry of Korean Govt., 1975, plastic surgeon 1976. Internship Yonsei Med. Ctr., Seoul, 1970—71, residency, gen. surgery, 1971—74, residency, plastic surgery, 1974—75, tchg. fellow, surgery; staff surgeon Nat. Med. Ctr., Seoul, 1979—86; craniomaxilofacial fellow Brigham, Women's and Children's Hosp., Boston, 1983—84; assoc. prof. Hallym U., Coll. Medicine, Seoul, 1986—92, prof., 1992—. Pres. Korean Soc. Microsurgery, Seoul, 1998—2000, Korean Soc. Hand Surgery, Seoul, 1999—2000, Asian Pacific Fedn. Socs. Surgery of Hand, Seoul, 2001—02, Korean Soc. Plastic & Reconstructive Surgery, Seoul, 2002—04, Korean Soc. Head & Neck Oncology, Seoul, 2002—04, Korean Burn Found., Seoul, 2003—06; dir. Hangang Sacred Heart Hosp., Seoul, 2000—04; dir. standardization and tng. com. Korean Hosp. Assn., Seoul, 2003—04; v.p. Hallym U. Med. Ctr., Seoul, 2005—06. Maj. army surgeon, 1976—79, Korean Army, Seoul, cons. 121st Gen. Hosp. US Army. Recipient Peony medal, Pres. Korean Govt., 2004. Home: 7-903 Asia Apt 86 Jamsil7dong Songpagu Seoul 138-797 Republic of Korea Office: Hallym Univ Sacred Heart Hosp Pyeungandong Dongangu 896 431-796 Anyangsi Gyeounggido Republic of Korea Home Phone: 82-2202-2186; Office Phone: 82-31-380-3780. Office Fax: 82-31-380-5980. Personal E-mail: sjoh46@hotmail.com. Business E-Mail: sjoh@hallym.or.kr.

OH, SUNG-TACK, medical educator; b. Gwangju, Republic of Korea, May 4, 1954; s. Oh Jae-Dong and Jin-Sim Park; m. Sung-Hee Hur, Sept. 23, 1984; 1 child, Oh Kyung-Rok. MD, Korean Med. Assn., 1979, Chonnam U., Gwangju; PhD in Biochemistry, Honam U., Gwangju, 1988, PhD in Computer Engring., 2008. Cert. Korean Soc. Ob-gyn., 1983. Prof. Chonnam U. Med. Sch., Gwangju, 1985—; dir. ob-gyn. Red Cross Hosp., Gwangju, 1983—85; vis. assoc. prof. Osaka City U. Med. Sch., Japan, 1983; with edn. & caring patients Chonnam U. Hosp., 1985, prof., 1985—; rsch. fellow U. NC, Chapel Hill, 1990—91. Mem.: N.Am. Menopause Soc. (corr.), Soc. Laparoscopic Surgeons (corr. Sci. Poster award 2010), Am. Soc. Reproductive Medicine (corr.), Am. Assn. Gynecologic Laparoscopists (corr. Sci. Poster award 1997, 2005). Home: 290-31 Hwajungdong Seoku Gwangju 502-240 Republic of Korea Office: Chonnam University Med Sch Hakdong Dong-gu 5 501-190 Gwangju Republic of Korea Office Phone: 82-62-220-6374. Office Fax: 82-62-227-1637; Home Fax: 82-62-366-9797. Business E-Mail: ohst@chonnam.ac.kr.

OH, TAE HEE, urologist, educator; b. DaeGu, Republic of Korea, Feb. 3, 1962; s. Sang O Oh and Ki Soon Kwon; m. Myeong Sook Park, Dec. 23, 1989; children: Chung Jae, Ji Hyun. MD, Yeungnam U., Daegu, Republic of Korea, 1986; PhD, Yeungnam U., Tae Gu, Republic of Korea, 2003. Diplomate Korean Bd. Urology, 1991. Intern Yeungnam U. Hosp., Dae Gu, Republic of Korea, 1986—87, resident urology, 1987—91; chmn. Masan Samsung Hosp., Republic of Korea, 1994—, prof., 2003; asst. prof. Sungkyunkwan U., Seoul, Republic of Korea, 1997—2003, assoc. prof., 2003—08, prof., 2009—. Capt. Korean Navy, 1991—94. Mem.: Korean Urologic Soc., Korean Endourologic Soc. (dir., Wolf prize 2003). Office: Masan Samsung Hosp Sungkyunkwan Univ Hapsung 2-Dong 50 631-052 Kyungsangnam Gyeongsangnam-do Republic of Korea Office Fax: 82-55-290-6278. Business E-Mail: natissururo@yahoo.co.kr.

OH, WILLIAM KYU, oncologist; b. Inchon, Korea (South), Aug. 14, 1965; s. Daniel K and Esther A Oh; m. Easter Chiu, Oct. 18, 1997; children: Christopher J, Andrew M. BS, Yale U., 1983—87; MD, NY U., 1988—92. Diplomate Internal Medicine and Medical Oncology Am. Bd. of Internal Medicine, 1997, lic. Medical Doctor Mass., 1992. Intern Brigham and Women's Hosp., Boston, 1992—93, resident, 1993—95, assoc. physician; fellow Harvard Med. Sch., Boston, 1992—97, instr. medicine, 1997—2000, asst. prof. medicine, 2000—07, assoc. prof. medicine, 2007—; fellow Dana-Farber Cancer Inst., Boston, 1995—98, clin. dir., Lank Ctr. Oncology, 2002—09. Mem.: Cancer and Leukemia Group B, Am. Soc. Clin. Oncology (mem., cancer edn. com. 2004—). Office: Dana-Farber Cancer Inst Mailstop D1230 44 Binney St Boston MA 02215 also: Mount Sinai Sch Medicine One Gustave L Levy Pl Box 1079 New York NY 10029 Business E-Mail: william.oh@mssm.edu.

OH, YU-KYOUNG, medical educator; b. Changwon, Korea, Jan. 22, 1965; d. Wan-Jei Oh and Shin-Ja Jeong; m. Won-Ki Kim, Jan. 9, 1991; 1 child, Ye-Jin Kim. B, Seoul Nat. U., Korea, 1986, M, 1988; PhD, SUNY, Buffalo, 1994. Adv. mem. KFDA, Seoul, 2003—. Contbr. articles to profl. jours. Recipient Young Investigator's award, Soc. Biomed. Rsch., 1995. Mem.: Am. Assn. Pharm. Scientists, Korean Soc. Pharmaceutics. Office: Korea U Sch Life Scis and Biotech 5-Ga Anam-dong Seungbuk-gu Seoul 136-713 Republic of Korea Office Phone: 82-2-3290-3413. Fax: 82-031 543-2818. E-mail: ohyk@cha.ac.kr.

OH, YUN KYU, medical educator; b. Jinju, Republic of Korea, Mar. 27, 1967; MD, Seoul Nat. U., PhD, 2006. Clin. prof., dept. internal medicine Seoul Nat. U., Boramae Med. Ctr., 2005. Office: 425 Shindaebang2-dong Dongjak-gu Seoul 156-707 Republic of Korea E-mail: yoonkyuoh@gmail.com.

OHAMA, GARY LOUIS, dental ceramist; b. Abington, Pa., Dec. 9, 1948; s. Benjamin Saburo and Kuniko Hirokawa Ohama; m. Susanne Louise Clinton; stepchildren: Philip, Holly, Hana; 1 child from previous marriage, Jennifer Suzanne. BS, Pa. State U., 1971. Owner, ceramist Ohama Dental Studio, Inc., Abington, 1973—91; finisher Nakashima Woodworkers, New Hope, Pa., 2000—02; dental ceramist Ft. Washington (Pa.) Dental Lab., 2002—11, Am. Dental Designs Inc., Montgomeryville, Pa., 2011—. Cons., lectr. on dental ceramics N.Y. Dental Lab. Congress, Dentsply Internat., Ney Co., Sterngold, Colo., others. Aikido instr. Served with USAR, 1971—77. Recipient Outstanding Alumni award, Pa. State U., 1982, Eagle Scout award. Mem.: Am. Dental Design (Mont., Pa.). Lutheran. Achievements include development of internal translucency and effects of refractive index in dental ceramics; of special oil, and oil/polyurethane wood finishing processes; research in breath dynamics and biomechanical movements and body functions; effects of breathing and spinal cord alignment on bio-mechanical performance. Avocation: Aikido instructor. Home: 402 Fretz Rd Perkasie PA 18944 Home Phone: 215-249-1614; Office Phone: 215-393-8330. Personal E-mail: gary.ohama@gmail.com.

OHANJANIAN, RUZANNA, clinical psychologist; d. Vladimir and Nina Ohanjanian; 1 child, Irene Gyulnazarian. BA in Linguistics & Lit. with honors, Leninakan Ednl. Inst., 1977; MA in Psychology, Yerevan P. State U., 1981; PhD, Moscow Acad. Scis., 1985; postdoctoral, U. San Francisco Med. Ctr., 1996. Cert. trauma specialist, Traumatic Incident Reduction Calif., 1991, lic. clin. psychologist Bd. Psychology, Calif., 1999. Clin. psychologist Dept. Pub. Health, San Francisco, 1998—2002, Family Svcs., Palo Alto, Calif., 1998—2002, Multilingual Psychology Cons., Mountain View, Calif., 1996—98, UCSF Med. Ctr., Mt. Zion Hosp., San Francisco. Nat. disaster team mem. Min. Health, Armenia, 1989—91; assoc. prof. Yerevan State U., Armenia, 1990—92, vis. prof., 1992; presenter State of World Forum, San Francisco, 1997; crisis mgmt. team mem. Family Enterprise Internat. Behavioral Health, 1999—. Contbr. over 30 publs. and presentations in field. Chmn. Irene Gyulnazarian Ednl. Fund for Armenia, Los Gatos, Calif., 2003—. Recipient Appreciation award, FEI Behavioral Health, 2000, Alaska Airlines, 2000, Make a Difference award, Total Employee Assistance and Mgmt. Inc., 2002, Employee Assistance Program Appreciation award, Pacific Care Behavioral Health; named Hon. Dr., Yerevay State U., 2005. Mem.: APA, Armenian Profl. Soc. Avocations: painting, piano. Office: Ohanjanian Ruzanna POBox 320652 Los Gatos CA 95032 Personal E-mail: irachka2@hotmail.com.

OHAR, JILL A., physician, director; b. Coatesville, Pa., July 5, 1951; MD, Med. Coll. Pa., Phila., 1977. Dir. clin. ops. Wake Forest Sch. Medicine, 2002—. Office: Wake Forest Sch Medicine Medical Center Blvd Winston Salem NC 27157 Office Fax: 336-716-7277. Business E-Mail: johar@wfubmc.edu.

O'HARA, JOHN PAUL, III, orthopedic surgeon; b. Detroit, June 10, 1946; m. Randy Baird, Mar. 11, 1987; children: Riley Anne, Nolan Baird, Evan John. BA, U. Mich., Ann Arbor, 1968, MD, 1972. Resident U. Va. Med. Ctr., Charlottesville, 1973-77; fellow Nuffield Orthopaedic Ctr., Oxford, Eng., 1977; practice medicine specializing in orthopaedic surgery Southfield, 1978—; staff Providence Hosp., Southfield, Mich., 1978—, pres. elect med. staff, 1990, pres. med. staff, 1991; past sect. chief orthopedics; pres. Porretta Orthopedic Ctr., 1996—, med. dir., 2001—; pres. Providence Med. Group, 2005—07. Pres. Providence Hosp. Med. Staff Research Found., 1984-85, bd. dirs., 1982—85; bd. dirs. Mich. Master Health Plan, Southfield, 1982. Contbr. articles to profl. jours. Past pres. Birmingham (Mich.) Little League Baseball. Recipient Disting. Alumni award Brother Rice High Sch., 1986. Fellow Am. Acad. Orthopaedic Surgery, Mid Am. Orthopaedic Soc.; mem. Detroit Orthopaedic Soc., Mich. Orthopaedic Soc., Detroit Acad. Orthopaedic Surgeons (past pres.), Oakland Hills Country Club (Birmingham, Mich.), Beverly Hills (Mich.) Club. Avocations: travel, sports. Home: 627 Waddington St Bloomfield Hills MI 48301-2346 Office Phone: 248-349-7015.

O'HARA, SARA MARIE, radiologist; d. John Francis and Claire Annastasia O'Hara; m. Jeffrey Brian Betts, Sept. 6, 1997; children: Sailor Delaney Betts, Sanibel Star Betts. BS in Chemistry and Physics, Georgetown U., Washington, 1984, MD, 1988. Diplomate Am. Bd. Radiology, 1993, CAQ pediat. radiology Am. Bd. Radiology, cert. spl. competence in nuc. medicine Am. Bd. Radiology. Intern Riverside Meth. Hosp., Columbus, 1989; resident Georgetown U. Med. Sch., 1990; resident in diagnostic radiology U. Cin. Med. Ctr., 1990—93; fellow in pediatric radiology Cin. Children's Hosp., 1993—94; tng. in nuc. medicine DC Children's Hosp.; head pediatric nuc. medicine Duke U. Med. Ctr.; chief ultrasound divsn. Cin. Children's Hosp., 2000—. Recipient Outstanding Contribution to Dept. Morale, Cin. Children's Hosp., 2003—04, Radiology Editor's Recognition award, 2004. Mem.: Soc. Uroradiology, Soc. Nuc. Medicine, Radiol. Soc. North America, Soc. Pediatric Radiology, Soc. Radiologists in Ultrasound, Ohio Med. Soc., NC Med. Soc., Assn. U. Radiologists, Am. Roentgen Ray Soc., Am. Coll. Radiology, Am. Inst. Ultrasound in Medicine, Alpha Omega Alpha. Avocation: travel. Office: Cincinnati Childrens Hosp Radiology 3333 Burnet Ave MLC 5031 Cincinnati OH 45229 Business E-Mail: sara.ohara@cchmc.org.

OHAYON, MAURICE M., research center administrator, psychiatrist; b. Casablanca, Morocco, June 22, 1948; arrived in Can., 1990; MD, U. Aix Marseille II, France, 1979, Cert. d'Etudes Spéciales Psychiatry, 1980, D in Computer Scis., 1992; PhD in Human Biology, U. Calude Bernard, Lyon, France, 1997. Resident in psychiatry and neurology C.H.U. Marseille, 1975-77; hosp. psychiatrist France, 1980-90; sci. dir. Rsch. Ctr. Fernand Seguin, Montreal, Que., Can., 1990-92; dir. rsch. ctr. Inst. Philippe Pinel, Montreal, 1992—; rsch. coord. U. Montreal, 1992-96; pres. Ctr. Evaluation and Statistics, Montreal, 1998—; project dir. Ctr. for Human Sleep Rsch. Stanford (Calif.) U. Med. Ctr. Assoc. prof. U. Que. Trois-Rivières, 1993—; sci. conseiller Ctr. Hos. Vinatier, France, 1994—; vis. clin. scientist St. Mary's Hosp., London, 1995—; cons. prof. psychiatry Stanford U., 1995—; adj. prof. psychiatry NYU, 1998—. Author: Intelligence Artificielle et Psychiatrie, 1989, Apprentissage, Adaptation et Réadaptation: Etat de la Recherche, 1995; Dis-moi comment tu dors, 1997. Mem. APHA, Can. Psychol. Assn., N.Y. Acad. Scis. Office: Ctr Rsch Philippe Pinel 10905 Henri Bourassa E Montreal PQ Canada H1C 1H1 *

O'HERN, JANE SUSAN, psychologist, educator; b. Winthrop, Mass., Mar. 21, 1933; d. Joseph Francis and Mona (Garvey) O'H. BS, Boston U., 1954, EdD, 1962; MA, Mich. State U., 1956. Instr. Mercyhurst Coll., 1954-55, Hofstra Coll., 1956-57, State Coll., Salem and Boston, 1957-60; asst. prof. Boston U., 1962-67, assoc. prof., 1967-75, prof. edn. and psychiat. (psychology), 1975-95, prof. emeritus, 1995—, chmn. dept. counseling psychology, 1972-75, 88-89, dir. mental health edn. program, 1975-81, dir. internat. edn., 1978-81, asst. v.p. internat. edn., 1981; prof. emeritus mental health and behavioral medicine program Boston U. Sch. Medicine, 2001—. Pres. ASSIST Internat., Inc., 1989—98; adv. bd, Internat. Study Cons., 1994—98; founder BettyBoston LLC, 2002—. Contbr. articles to profl. jours. Trustee Boston Ctr. Modern Psychoanalytic Studies, 1980-92. Recipient grants U.S. Office Edn., NIMH, Dept. of Def. Mem. Assn. Counselor Edn. and Suprs., Am. Counseling Assn., North Atlantic Assn. Counselor Edn. and Supervision (past pres.), Mass. Psychol. Assn., Am. Psychol. Assn., Mortar Bd., Pi Lamda Theta, Sigma Kappa, Phi Delta Kappa, Phi Beta Delta. Home: 111 Perkins St Apt 287 Boston MA 02130-4324 Office Phone: 617-414-2325. Personal E-mail: janeohern@gmail.com. Business E-Mail: johern@bu.edu.

OHGAMI, TATSUHIRO, physician; b. Fukuoka, Japan, June 19, 1973; MD, Kyushu U., 2000, PhD, 2010. Head physician Miyazaki Prefectural Miyazaki Hosp., 2010—. Home: 2-31-A103 Nishiike-cho Miyazaki 880-0027 Japan Office Phone: 81 985 24 4181. Personal E-mail: gamitatu@kyudai.jp.

OHHASHI, TOSHIO, physiology educator, researcher, academic administrator; b. Mito, Japan, Mar. 27, 1949; s. Takeo and Masa (Ono) O.; m. Yumiko Ichimura, Sept. 15, 1974; children: Tsukasa, Aya MD, Shinshu U., Matsumoto, Japan, 1974; PhD, Shinshu U., 1979. Temp. lectr. physiology Queen's U. Belfast, Northern Ireland, 1979—81; instr. physiology Shinshu U. Sch. Medicine, 1974—77, asst. prof., 1977—79, assoc. prof., 1981—84, prof., chmn. dept., 1985—. Dir. Inst. Animal Rsch. Shinshu U. Sch, Medicine, 1987-89, 1991-93, 1995-97, 1999-2001, mem. coun., 2001—, prof. Inst. Organ Transplant Reconstruction Med. Tissue Engring., 2000-04, dean, 2003—08; chmn. Assn. Japanese Med. Colls., 2006—08; honors guest rschr. in clin. scis. NIMH, Bethesda, Md., 1983, 85, 87; bd. dirs. Skinos Co. Ltd Author: Handbook of Physiological Sciences, Vol. 16 Cardiovascular Physiology, 1991, Textbook of Human Physiology by Studying Experiments and Experiences in Daily Life, 1996; author, editor: Emotional Perspiration and Its Clinical Application, 1993; contbr. Pharmacol. Therapy, 2005; mem. editl. bd. Microvascular Rsch., 1985-88, Internat. Jour. Angiology, 1992—, Am. Jour. Physiology (Heart and Circulatory Physiology), 1994-98, Japan Jour. Physiology, 2002-2005, Jour. Phys. Sci., 2006—10, Lymphatic Res. Biology, 2007-; patentee device for continuously measuring local sweating rate in human beings (Japan, Am., Europe), device for self-evaluating character and condition of ego in human beings by means of measuring emotional perspiration (Japan), cell line of human lymphatic endothelial cells Dir. Nagano Prefecture Com. for Health Sci. in Human Beings and Its Bus. Application, 1993—2009. Recipient Disting. Rschr. award Japanese Heart Assn., 1983, Young Investigator award European Soc. Microcirculation, 1984; rsch. grantee Japanese Ministry Edn., Sci. and Culture, 1975, 77-78, 84-88, 92-2000, 03-05, 05-06 Mem. Japanese Coll. Angiology (councillor 1994—, v.p. 2003—), Japanese Soc. Microcirculation (councillor 1985—), Japanese Soc. Lymphology (councillor 1985-2001, pres. 2001—), Japanese Soc. Perspiration Rsch. (bd. dirs., pres. 2002—), Assn. Japanese Med. Colls. (chmn. 2006-08) Avocations: golf, baseball. Office: Shinshu U Dept Physiol 3-1-1 Asahi Nagano Matsumoto 390-8621 Japan Office Phone: 81-263-37-2595. Business E-Mail: ohhashi@sch.md.shinshu-u.ac.jp, ohhashi@shinshu-u.ac.jp.

OHHIRA, IICHIROH, microbiologist, educator; b. Osaka, Japan, Feb. 6, 1936; s. Yutaka and Akiko (Tsubaki) Fujita; m. Masumi Ohhira. B in Agr., Okayama U., Japan, 1960, M in Agr., 1973, PhD in Natural Sci. (NSD), 1990, student in grad. sch. nat. sci. tech., 2002—; student in lab. microbiology, Kagawa Med. U., Japan, 1992—2001; DSc in Health Sci. (SD), Adam Smith U. Am., 2000; PhD in Vet. Med. Sci. (VMD), Azabu U., Japan, 2000. Dealer Shinko Securities Co., Ltd., Okayama, Japan, 1960-71; rep. dir. Ohhira Gardens & Parks Designing Office, Okayama, 1973—85, Ohhira Plant Pathology Rsch. Ctr., Okayama, 1973—85, Bio Activity R & D Inst., Okayama, 1974—2000; founder Biobank Co., Ltd., Okayama, 2000—. Prof. Pusan (Republic of Korea) Fisheries Coll., tech. adviser Office Tech. Adviser Agrl. Environ. Issue, Chengdu, Suchuan, China; lectr. Chugoku Jr. Coll., Okayama, Japan. Contbr. scientific papers. Recipient Meritorious Svcs. prize, Kota Kinabalu Town Bd. and Sandakan Town Bd., Malaysia, 1980, Ari Daja Kinabalu (ADK), Sabah, Malaysia, 1981, Okayama Daily Newspaper award, 1981, Japanese Dairy Scis. Assn. award, 1991, Presdl. citation, Philippine Med. Assn., Philippines, 2002, Internat. Coll. Surgeons, Philippine sect., Philippines, 2004, Gusi Peace prize, Manilla, Philippines, 2004. Mem.: Japanese Soc. Food Microbiology, Japan Health Food and Nutrition Food Assn., Soc. Antibacterial and Antifungal Agts., Japan, Japanese Soc. Virology, Japanese Soc. Vet. Scis., Japanese Soc. Food Scis. and Tech., Japan Soc. Lactic Acid Bacteria, Japanese Soc. Bacteriology, Japanese Soc. Soil Scis. and Plant Nutrition, Brewing Soc. Japan, Japan Dairy Scis. Assn., Japan Soc. Biosci., Biotech. and Agrochemistry, NY Acad. Scis. (prize 1991). Achievements include discovery of and research on Enterococcus faecalis TH10, a highly active and useful lactic acid bacterium isolated and identified from Tempeh, a fermented food in S.E. Asia; developed and manufactured a wide range of unique health and organic products using lactic acid bacteria, the most well known product among them is Ohhira's Probiotics OM-X; US version. Dr. Ohhira's Probiotics 12+; an all natural probiotic dietary supplement containing Enterococcus faecalis TH10; development of other Ohhira's Probiotics-related products include Ohhira's Probiotics BTO, an agricultural organic fertilizer with antifungal activity, Ohhira's Probiotics Amintohru; a wastewater deodorizer and dissolver, and Ohhira's Probiotics Amintohru-M, a deodorizer for livestock and accelerator for compost fermentation; research on fish farms and preventative measures for human dermatologic diseases underway for further development of probiotic products. Avocations: Kendo, reading, travel, antiques. Office: Biobank Co Ltd Hirata 388-1 Okayama 700-0952 Japan Office Fax: 81-86-222-0622. Business E-Mail: biobank@omx.co.jp.

OHIGASHI, SEIJI, surgeon; b. Okayama, June 18, 1956; MD, Hiroshima U., 1982. Staff surgeon St. Luke's Internat. Hosp., 1993—. Office: 9-1 Akashi-cho Chuo-ku Tokyo 104-8560 Japan Business E-Mail: ohsei@luke.or.jp.

OHIRA, AKIHIRO, ophthalmologist, educator; b. Kumamoto, Oct. 6, 1958; MD, Fukuoka U., 1978, PhD, 1984. Asst. prof. Fukuoka U. Sch. Medicine, 1984—87, Kyoto U. Faculty Medicine, 1991—93; rschr. Duke U. Eye Ctr., 1987—90; assoc. prof., vice-chmn. Nagasaki U. Sch. Medicine, 1993—98; prof., chmn. Shimane U. Sch. Medicine, 1998—, vice dean, 2007. Bd. dirs. Japanese Soc. Photomedicine and Photobiology, 1998—. Mem.: Japanese Ophthal. Soc. (councilor 1998—2011). Office: 89-1 Enya Izumo Shimane 693-8501 Japan Office Fax: 81-853-20-2278. Business E-Mail: aohira@med.shimane-u.ac.jp.

OHISHI, KOHSHI, medical educator, director; b. Shingu, Wakayama, Japan, May 12, 1961; MD, Kanazawa U., 1988; PhD, Mie U., 1996. Dir., assoc. prof. Blood Transfusion Svc., Mie U. Hosp., 2007—. Fellow: Leukemia and Lymphoma Soc. Ameria; mem.: Am. Soc. Hematology. Avocation: Climbing. Office: 2-174 Edobashi Tsu Mie 514-8507 Japan Office Fax: 81-1-59-231-5200. Business E-Mail: koishi@clin.medic.mie-u.ac.jp.

OHK, SEUNG-HO, microbiologist, educator; b. Seoul, Republic of Korea, Oct. 4, 1965; married. BS, Yonsei U., Seoul, 1991, MS, 1993, PhD, 1997. Postdoc. assoc. SUNY Buffalo, 1997—2000; instr. Yonsei U., 2000—03; prof. Chonnam Nat. U., Gwangju, Republic of Korea, 2003—. Pres. Korean Bio-Venture Bus. Assn., Seoul, 1997. Contbr. articles to profl. jours. Sgt. Korean Army, 1984—88. Grant, Korea Rsch. Found., 2003, Small & Medium Bus. Adminstrn., Korea, 2005, Korea Sci. & Engring. Found., 2007. Mem.: Korean Acad. Oral Biology, Korean Soc. Microbiology & Biotech. Achievements include patents for UV-A skin care product, osteoporosis control agent, enzyme for treatment of dental caries, bacterial cell wall hydrolase. Office: Sch Dentistry Chonnam Nat Univ 300 Yongbong-dong Buk-gu Gwangju 500-757 Republic of Korea Office Fax: 82 62 530 4855. Business E-Mail: shohk@chonnam.ac.kr.

OHKUCHI, AKIHIDE, obstetrician; b. Himi City, Toyama Prefecture, Japan, Dec. 12, 1962; s. Akio and Eiko Ohkuchi; m. Satomi Ohkuchi; 1 child, Yukie. MD, Jichi Med. Sch., Tochigi, Japan, 1987, PhD, 2001. Lic. MD. Resident Toyama Prefectural Ctrl. Hosp., 1987—89, obstetrician and gynecologist, 1987, obstetrican-gynecol. physician, 1993—98; obstetrician-gynecol. physician Himi Mcpl. Hosp., 1989—90, Himi Health Ctr., 1991—92, Takoaka Health Ctr., 1991—92; gen. physician Nishiakao Clinic, 1992—93; asst., dept. obstetrician-gynecol. Jichi Med. U., Shimotsuke-shi, Tochigi-ken, Japan, 1998—2001, asst. prof. obstetrician-gynecol., 2002—07, assoc. prof. obstets.-gyn., 2007—. Contbr. articles to profl. jours. Avocation: reading. Office: Jichi Med Univ Sch Medicine Dept Ob-Gyn Yakushiji 3311-1 Tochigi Shimotsuke 329-0498 Japan Office Phone: 81 285 58 7376. Office Fax: 81 285 44 8505; Home Fax: 81 285 40 8452. Business E-Mail: okuchi@jichi.ac.jp.

OHL, JOAN ESCHENBACH, former federal agency administrator; b. Harrisburg, Pa. m. Ronald E. Ohl. BA in Edn., U. Del., 1967; EdM, SUNY, Buffalo, 1969; post grad., Pa. State U. Dir. women's housing Colo. Coll., Colo. Springs, 1969; positions at U. Ark., Pa. State U.; asst. to v.p. Fairleigh Dickinson U., Rutherford, NJ, 1975—82; v.p. Independent Coll. Fund of NJ; cons. to C.E. "Jim" Compton of FIVE-J Energy Inc. & Grafton Coal Co., 1984—93; sec. Dept. Health and Human Resources State of W.Va., 1997—2001; commr. Adminstrn. Children, Youth & Families US Dept. Health & Human Services, Washington, 2002—09. Bd. mem. W.Va. Health Care Cost Rev. Authority, 1993—97. Recipient Disting. West Virginian award, 2000, Joan E. Ohl Rural Health Leadership award, W.Va. Rural Health Assn., 2000, Leadership award, Multi-CAP, Inc., 2000, Bateman award, W.Va. Hosp. Assn., 2000, Leadership award, W.Va. Pub. Health Assn., 2000, James Hansen Humanitarian award, U. Buffalo, 2004.

OH-LEE, JUSTIN DOHOON, psychology professor; b. Seoul, Republic of Korea, May 23, 1963; arrived in US, 1979; s. Myung Suck and Bong Sun Oh; m. Connie Chong Lee, Mar. 31, 1996; 1 child, Grace Nara. Degree in chemistry with distinction, Colo. Coll., 1986; PhD in Psychology, UCLA, 1995. Postdoctoral fellow Nat. Inst. Neurol. Disorders and Stroke, NIH, Bethesda, Md., 1995—99, rsch. fellow clin. pharmacology, 1999—2001; faculty psychiatry and psychology Found. for Advanced Edn. in the Scis., NIH, Bethesda, 1999—2001; assoc. prof. psychology Ctrl. Mich. U., Mount Pleasant, 2001—. Spl. vol., cons. Nat. Inst. Neurol. Disorders and Stroke, NIH, Bethesda, Md., 2001—03. Contbr. chapters to books, articles to profl. jours. Faculty advisor Adventist Students for Christ, Mount Pleasant, 2003—05; sci. advisor Parkinson's Support Group, Mount Pleasant, 2002—05. Recipient Outstanding Rsch. award, Assn. Korean Neuroscientist Assn., Grad. Divsn. award, UCLA, Grad. Divsn. Travel Grant Rsch. award, 1990—91, Pres. AA Fellowship award, 1993, Coll. Letters and Sci. Grad. Student award, 1993, Disting. Svc. award, NINDS ACUC, NIH, 1999, Spl. Act/Svc. award, U.S. Dept. Health and HUman Svcs., 2000, Rsch. Professorship award, Ctrl. Mich. U., 2003; named Hon. Recognition for Outstanding Rsch., Nat. Inst. Neurol. Disorders and Stroke; grantee, NIH, 2001, 2005, Pres. Rsch. Investment Fund grantee, Ctrl. Mich. U., 2002; fellow, Nat. Parkinson Found. Ctr. Excellence, 2003; Rsch. Enhancement Award grantee, NIH, NINDS, Summer Faculty scholar, CHSBS, Ctrl. Mich. U., 2003. Mem.: APA, NIH, Asian and Pacific Islanders Am. Orgn., Soc. for Neuroscience, Am. Psychol. Soc. (faculty advisor Student Caucus, Ctrl. Mich. U. 2002—05). Home: 1412 Abbey Ln Mount Pleasant MI 48858 Office: Central Michigan Univ Psychology 1280 E Campus Dr HP 2181 Mount Pleasant MI 48859 Office Fax: 989-774-2553; Home Fax: 989-774-2253. Business E-Mail: oh1jd@cmich.edu.

OHMAN, E. MAGNUS, cardiologist, educator; s. Karl-Erik Ohman and Maj-Britt Borjeson; m. Elspeth O'Reilly-Hyland, June 12, 1987; children: Edward, Elsa-Maria, Henry. MB, BCh, MD, Royal Coll. of Surgeons in Ireland, Dublin, 1981. Resident gen. internal med. St. Laurence's Hosp., St. Vincent's Hosp., Dublin, 1981—84; rsch. fellow in cardiology St. Laurence's Hosp., Dublin, 1984—87; fellow in cardiology Duke U. Med. Ctr., Durham, NC, 1987—91, asst. prof. medicine, 1991—96, assoc. prof. medicine, 1996—2001; prof. medicine U. NC, Chapel Hill, NC, 2001—05, Duke U. Med. Ctr., Durham, NC, 2005—. Dir. Heart Ctr. U. of N.C., Chapel Hill, 2001—05. Contbr. articles to profl. jours.; editor (assoc.): Am. Heart Jour. Recipient Edith Walsh award, Brit. Med. Assn., 1985. Fellow: Am. Coll. Cardiology, European Soc. Cardiology, Royal Coll. Physicians of Ireland, Soc. of Cardiac Angiography and Intervention; mem.: Am. Coll. Chest Physicians (chmn. Peer Rev. Com.), AMA (chmn. Acute Cardiac Care Com.). Achievements include patents for Methods patent for assessing reperfusion in heart attacks. Office: Duke Univ Med Ctr DUMC 3126 Erwin Rd Durham NC 27710 Office Phone: 919-681-2069. Office Fax: 919-681-0811.

OHN, SUK HOON, medical educator; b. Seoul, Republic of Korea, Apr. 9, 1971; s. Young Kon Ohn and Young Hee Lee; m. Yun Jeong Eom; children: Yoo Na, Joon Sang, Ye Na. MS, Yonsei U., Seoul, 2007. Cert. dr. Korean Med. Assn., 1997. Resident dr. Dept. Phys. Medicine and Rehab., Yonsei U. Severence Hosp., Seoul, 1998—2002, fellow, 2005—06, Dept. Phys. Medicine and Rehab., Samsung Med. Ctr., Seoul, 2006—08; dr. Pub. Health Ctr., Gochang, Iksan, Jeollabuk-do, Republic of Korea, 2002—05; asst. prof. Dept. Phys. Medicine and Rehab., Hallym U. Sacred Heart Hosp., Anyang, Gyeonggi-do, Republic of Korea, 2008—. Contbr. articles to profl. jours. Regular mem. Korean Christian Med. Fellowship, Seoul, 1991—2008. Recipient Excellent Poster award, Korean Acad. PMR, 2006. Home: Dongbucentreville Daechi-dong Gangnam-gu Seoul 135838 Republic of Korea Office: Sacred Heart Hosp Dept Phys Medicine and Rehab Hallym Univ Pyungchon-Dong Dongan-Gu 896 431-796 Anyang Gyeonggi-do Republic of Korea Home Phone: 82-2-562-9346; Office Phone: 82-31-380-6085. Office Fax: 82-31-380-3864. Business E-Mail: myeom@korea.com.

OHNO, KOICHI, pediatric surgeon; b. Osaka, Japan, Nov. 16, 1959; s. Yoshinobu Nishiguchi and Tatsuko Ohno; m. Midori Ohno; children: Ayako, Atsuko, Akiko. MD, Miyazaki Med. Coll., 1985. Cert. surgeon Bd. Japan Surg. Soc., 1989, instr. surgery 2002, surgeon Bd. Japanese Soc. Pediat. Surgeons, 2007, instr. pediat. surgery 2008, pediat. urologist Bd. Japanese Soc. Pediat. Urology, 2008. Resident Dept. Second Surgery, Osaka City U., Sch. Medicine, Osaka, 1985—87, rsch. fellow, 1988—89; surgeon, dept. surgery Haruki Hosp., Kishiwada, Osaka, 1987—88, Osaka City Kitashimin Hosp., 1989—91, Ashihara Hosp., Osaka, 2002—03, Osaka City Sumiyoshi Hosp., 2003—04; pediat. surgeon, dept. surgery Hyogo Children's Hosp., Kobe, Japan, 1991—92, Yodogawa Christian Hosp., Osaka, 1992—97; asst. surgeon Osaka City U., Grad. Sch. Medicine, 1997—2002; asst. chief Dept. Pediat. Surgery, Osaka City Gen. Hosp., 2004—. Contbr. scientific papers. Mem.: Japan Surg. Assn., Pacific Assn. Pediat. Surgeons, Japanese Soc. Pediat. Oncology, Japan Soc. Perinatal and Neonatal Medicine, Japanese Soc. Pediat. Urology, Japanese Soc. Pediat. Surgeons, Japan Surg. Soc. Avocations: travel, movie. Office: Osaka City Gen Hosp 2-13-22 Miyakojima-hondori Miyakojima-ku Osaka 534-0021 Japan Home Phone: 81-6-6794-3457; Office Phone: 81-6-6929-1221. Office Fax: 81-6-6929-1091; Home Fax: 81-6-6794-3457. Business E-Mail: k-ohno@r2.dion.ne.jp, ko8597oh594@yahoo.co.jp.

OHNO, SHINICHI, anatomist, educator; b. Mitaka, Japan, Apr. 9, 1949; s. Minoru and Mayumi (Tanaka) Ohno; m. Sumiko Hayashi, May 3, 1975; 4 children. MD, Shinshu U., 1976, PhD, 1981. From instr. to asst. prof. Shinshu U., Matsumoto, Japan, 1976-81, assoc. prof., 1981-92; fellow NIH, Bethesda, Md., 1981-83; prof. Yamanashi Med. U., Tamaho, Japan, 1992—. Author: Calmodulin and Intracellular Ca-Receptors, 1982, Itnerantl Review of Cytology, 1985, The Thyroid, 1988, Structural Basis for Giomerular Dysfunction, 1991, International Review of Cytology, 1996. Mem.: Microscopy Soc. Am., Japanese Soc. Microscopy, Japan Soc. Histochemistry and Cytochemistry, Japanese Assn. Anatomists. Avocations: skiing, baseball, Karate. Home: 1559-1 Narishima Chuo-City 409-3815 Japan Office: U Yamanashi 1110 Shimokato Chuo-City 409-3898 Japan Home Phone: +81-422-34-0368, 81552740145; Office Phone: +81-55-273-6743. Business E-Mail: sohno@yamanashi.ac.jp.

OHSAKI, KATSUICHIRO, otolaryngologist, researcher, educator; b. Kyoto, Japan, Feb. 13, 1935; s. Kazuo and Tsuya Ohsaki; m. Reiko Miyoshi, Sept. 20, 1964; children: Yohichiro, Mari, Keijiro. MD, Okayama U., Okayama City, Japan, 1959; PhD, Okayama U., 1965; postgrad., NYU, 1962. Intern 6022 USAF Hosp., Japan, 1959-60; resident N.Y. Eye and Ear Infirmary, NYC, 1961-62; otolaryngologist Hiroshima Citizens' Hosp., Japan, 1965-69; from vice chief otolaryngologist to chief otolaryngologist Kobe Nishishimin Hosp., Japan, 1970—75; otolaryngologist-in-chief Okayama Red Cross Gen. Hosp., Japan, 1975-76; prof. otolaryngology sch. medicine U. Tokushima, Japan, 1976—81; prof. divsn. clin. otology Tokushima Univ. Hosp., 1981—2000, prof. emeritus, 2000—. Mem. Sudden Deafness Rsch. Com. Japan organized by Ministry of Health and Welfare of Japanese Govt., 1973-76; hon. chmn. Beijing Internat. Symposium Otolaryngology, 1988; guest prof. Beijing Med. U., 1992—, 4th Mil. Med. U., Xian, China, 1994—; invited lectr. in practical otology U. Toronto, 1999. Author: Sudden Deafness (Japanese edit.), 1985; co-author, co-editor Tinnitus (Chinese edit.), 1994; patentee remedy for sudden deafness and fluctuating sensorineural hearing loss, 1982, test equipment for tinnitus, 1992. Fellow: Am. Acad. Otolaryngology-Head and Neck Surgery (rep. from Japan for Internat. ann. meeting 2003, 2005); mem.: N.Y. Acad. Scis., Otological Soc. Japan (councillor 1991—2000), Japan Soc. Infectious Diseases in Otolaryngology (adminstrn. com. 1991—), European Acad. Otology and Neuro-otology (assoc.), Internat. Soc. of Audiology, Tokushima-ken Med. Soc. (rep. 1994—2000), Oto Rhino Laryngological Soc. Japan (specialist 1994—). Buddhist. Avocations: calligraphy, golf, shogi. Home and Office: 5-25 Nanokaichi-Nishi-Machi Kita Ward Okayama 700 0851 Japan

OHSAWA, MASAKI, internist, cardiologist; s. Kunio and Kimiko Ohsawa. MD, Asahikawa Med. Coll., Japan, 1987; PhD, Iwate Med. U., Morioka City, Japan, 2005. Diplomate Japanese Bd. Internal Medicine. Sr. resident Kumamoto Saiseikai Hosp., Japan, 1994—96, clin. rsch. assoc. Meml. Heart Ctr., Iwate Med. U., Morioka, Japan, 1997—99, rsch. assoc. dept. hygiene and preventive medicine, 2005—; dir. divsn. cardiology Iwate Prefectural Kuji Hosp., Japan, 1999—2001; asst. prof. dept. hygiene and preventive medicine Sch. Medicine, Iwate Med. U., 2006—. Mem.: Japan Epidemiol. Assn. (assoc.), Japanese Soc. Pub. health (assoc.), Japanese Circulation Soc. (assoc.), Japanese Soc. Internal Medicine (assoc.). Office: Iwate Med Univ 19-1 Uchimaru Iwate Prefecture Morioka 020-8505 Japan Office Fax: +81-19-623-8870. Business E-Mail: masakio@iwate-med.ac.jp.

OHSHIGE, KENJI, epidemiologist; b. Kagoshima, Japan, Sept. 4, 1965; s. Tetsuro and Sachiko Ohshige; m. Fumiko Sekiguchi, May 12, 1970; children: Hiyori, Haruto. MB, Saga Med. Sch., 1990; PhD, Yokohama City U., 2000; MSc in Health Econ., U. York, 2001. Lic. Doctor's license Govt. of Japan, 1990. Resident Tokyo Women's Med. Sch. Hosp., 1990—96; lectr. Sch. Medicine, Yokohama City U., Kanagawa, Japan, 2001—06, assoc. prof., 2006—. Contbr. articles to profl. jours. Mem.: Japanese Soc. Pub. Health. Office: Yokohama City Univ Sch Med 3-9 Fukuura Kanazawa-ku Yokohama 236-0004 Japan Office Fax: 81-45-787-2609. Business E-Mail: kenoh@med.yokohama-cu.ac.jp.

OHSHIMA, MITSUHIRO, pharmaceutical & dental educator, researcher; b. Ota-ku, Tokyo, Dec. 21, 1957; s. Ichiji and Sachie Ohshima; m. Kumiko Miyashita; children: Keita, Hiroshi. DDS, Nihon U. Sch. Dentistry, Tokyo, 1982; PhD, Tokyo Med. and Dental U., 1987. Diplomate in dental 1982. Asst. prof. Nihon U. Sch. Dentistry, 1987—; prof. Ohu U. Sch. Pharm. Scis. Vis. rschr. Karolinska Inst. Cancer Ctr., Solna, Stockholm, 2004. Contbr. articles to profl. jours. Grants-in-Aid Sci. Rsch., Japan Soc. Promotion Sci., 2003—05, 2007—. Achievements include patents for test paper strips for screening of periodontal disease. Home: 1-39-12 Kamiikedai Ota-ku Tokyo 145-0064 Japan Office: Ohu University Sch Pharmaceutical Sci Dept Biochemistry Misumido 31-1 Tomitamachi Koriyama Fukushima Koriyama 963-8611 Japan Office Phone: 81-24-932-8611, 81-24-932-9149. Office Fax: 81-24-932-9149. Business E-Mail: m-ohshima@pha.ohu-u.ac.jp.

OHSHIRO, YUZURU, medical researcher, educator; b. Okinawa, Japan, Dec. 4, 1966; s. Kimio and Hiroko Ohshiro; m. Rieko Ohshiro, Oct. 25, 1997; children: Yutaro, Mao. MD, U. Ryukyus, Okinawa, 1994, PhD, 2000. Med. rschr. Joslin Diabetes Ctr., Harvard Med. Sch., Boston, 2003—05; asst. prof. U. Ryukyus, Nishihara, Okinawa, 2001—. Med. instr. Ryukyu U. Hosp., Nishihara, Okinawa, 2001—. Recipient Investigator award, Kanae Med. Found., 2003, Okinawa Med. Sci. Found, 2008. Mem.: Am. Diabetes Assn. (assoc.), Japanese Soc. Internal Medicine (assoc.), Japan Diabetes Soc. (assoc.). Achievements include research in diabetes and obesity. Office: 2d Dept Intern Med U Ryukyus 207 Uehara Nishihara Okinawa 903-0215 Japan Home: Samashita 154-23 Ginowan City Okinawa 901 2216 Japan Office Fax: 81-98-895-1415.

OHTA, HIKOTO, research scientist; b. Yamagata, Japan, 1965; PhD, Tohoku U., 1991. Rsch. scientist, forensic investigation ctr. Nat. Rsch. Inst. Police Sci., Japan, 1996, sr. rsch. scientist, phys. evidence sect., 1997—2001, sr. rsch. scientist, toxicology sect., 2005—06, chief, toxicology sect., 2007—; dir, forensic sci. lab. Aomori Prefectural Police HQ, Japan, 2002—04. Office: 6-3-1 Kashiwa-no-ha Kashiwa City Chiba 277-0882 Japan Business E-Mail: ohta@nrips.go.jp.

OHTA, HIROAKI, retired lab administrator; b. Japan, May 18, 1948; M, Yamaguchi U., DVM, 1971; PhD, Tokyo U., 1986. Dir. CAF Labs. Inc., 1990—2010. Office: 1257-1 Michinoue-Knnnabe Fukuyama Hiroshima 720-214 Japan Office Fax: 81-84-963-4228. Business E-Mail: caf-laboh@pop21.odn.ne.jp.

OHTA, KEN, medical educator; b. Hiroshima, Japan, Oct. 5, 1949; MD, U. Tokyo, 1975, PhD, 1987. Prof., medicine Teikyo U. Sch. Medicine, 1997—. Bd. dirs. Global Initiative Asthma, 2002—11, Japanese Soc. Allergology, 2003—11. Fellow: Japanese Respiratory Soc., Am. Coll. Chest Physician, Japanese Soc. Internal Medicine, Am. Acad. Allergy, Asthma & Immunology; mem.: Am. Thoracic Soc. Avocations: travel, classical music. Office: 2-11-1 Kaga Itabashi-ku Tokyo 173-8605 Japan Office Fax: 81-3-3964-5436. Business E-Mail: kanohta@med.teikyo-u.ac.jp.

OHTA, TOMOHIKO, medical educator; b. Tokyo, Sept. 28, 1960; Japan; MD, St. Marianna U., PhD, 1991. Resident gen. surgery St. Marianna U. Hosp., Kawasaki, Japan, 1985—91; rsch. fellow Roger Williams Med. Ctr. Brown U. Sch. Medicine, Providence, 1991—93; instr. First Dept. Surgery St. Marianna U. Sch. Medicine, 1993—97; rsch. fellow Linberger Cancer Ctr. U. NC Chapel Hill, 1997—99; asst. prof. Divsn. Breast & Endocrine Surgery Dept. Surgery, St. Marianna U. Sch. Medicine, 1999—2004, assoc. prof., 2004—10; prof. dept. translational oncology St. Marianna U. Grad. Sch. Medicine, 2010—. Recipient award, Japanese Breast Cancer Soc., 2000, Tokyo Biochem. Rsch. Found., 2000, Kobayashi Found. Cancer Rsch., 2011. Mem.: Japan Soc. Breast Screening, Japanese Soc. Clin. Surgery, Japanese Surg. Soc., Japan Soc. Cancer Therapy, Japanese Breast Cancer Soc. (councilor), Japanese Cancer Assn. (councilor). Achievements include discovery of RING finger ubiquitin ligase activity; ubiquitin ligase activity of breast cancer susceptibility protein 1. Office: St Marianna University Grad Sch Medicine 2-16-1 Sugao Miyamae-ku Kawasaki Kanagawa 216-8511 Japan Business E-Mail: to@marianna-u.ac.jp.

OHTA, TOMOYUKI, radiologist, department chairman; b. Niigata, Japan, Aug. 21, 1969; MB, Shinshu U. Sch. Medicine, 1997; MD, St. Marianna U. Sch. Medicine, 2008. Chief, dept. radiology Shounandai Hosp., 2010—. Office: Takakura 2345 Fujisawa Kanagawa 252-0802 Japan Business E-Mail: ohta.kent@nifty.com.

OHTA, YOSHIKI, medical technician; b. Nagano City, Japan, Jan. 30, 1959; PhD, Kitasato U., 1983. Cytotechnologist Showa U. Northern Yokohama Hosp., 2000—. Office: Chigasaki-chuo 35-1 Tuzuki-ku Yokohama Kanagawa 224-0032 Japan Business E-Mail: yomareko@cmed.showa-u.ac.jp.

OHTA, YOSHIO, medical educator; b. Okayama, Japan, Jan. 16, 1952; s. Tsuguo and Yukiko Ohta; m. Toko Hamada, Apr. 1, 1984; 1 child, Keisuke. MD, Okayama U., Japan, 1976. Dir. anesthesia rsch. lab. Montefiore Med. Ctr., NYC, 1989—91; assoc. prof. intensive care Okayama U. Hosp., 1996—98, prof. med. informatics, 1998—, chief dept. med. safety, 2001—. Office: Okayama U Hosp 2-5-1 Shikata-cho Okayama 700-8558 Japan Personal E-mail: y.ohta@ieee.org. Business E-Mail: y_ohta@cc.okayama-u.ac.jp.

OHTSU, FUMIKO, pharmacist, educator; b. Kyoto, Mar. 5, 1961; BS, Kobe Pharm. U., 1983; PhD, Meijo U., 2002. Assoc. prof. Meijo U., 2004; chair drug info. com. Japan Pharm. Assn., 2008. Recipient Japan e-Learning prize, Fuji Sankei Bus. Eye. Mem.: Drug Info. Assn. Avocation: travel. Office: Yagotoyama 150 Tempaku-ku Nagoya Aichi 468-8503 Japan Office Fax: 011-81-52-832-8904. Business E-Mail: fohtsu@meijo-u.ac.jp.

OHYAMA, MASAYUKI, pharmacist; b. Osaka, Japan, June 28, 1958; B, Osaka U. Pharm. Scis., 1981. Rschr. Osaka Prefectural Inst. Pub. Health, 1982, sr. rschr., 1995—. Avocation: Go. Office: 1-3-69 Nakamichi Higashinari-ku Osaka 537-0025 Japan Office Fax: 81-6-6972-2393.

OHYAMA, SHIGEKAZU, surgeon, researcher; b. Fukui, Japan, Feb. 21, 1958; MD, Kanazawa U., PhD, 1983. Cancer rschr. Cancer Inst. Hosp., 1994—, dir., dept. GI surgery, 2001. Master: Japan Soc. GI Surgery. Avocation: mountain climbing. Office: 3-10-6 Ariake Koto-ku Tokyo 81 Japan Office Fax: 81-3-3520-0141. Business E-Mail: ohyamas@jfcr.or.jp.

OIKAWA, HIROSHI, parasitologist, researcher; b. Sendai, Miyagi, Japan, June 25, 1932; s. Koushiro and Tomoyo (Isawa) O.; m. Junko Takagi, Mar. 8, 1963; children: Yoko, Wataru. M of Agr., Tohoku U., Sendai, 1958; PhD, Osaka U., Japan, 1975. Rsch. staff Shionogi Pharm. Co. Ltd., Osaka, 1958-70; assoc. dir. Shionogi Aburahi Labs., Shiga, Japan, 1970-92; lectr. Setsunan U. Sch. Pharmacology, Hirakata, Japan, 1985-89; lectr. microbial diseases Osaka U., Suita, 1988-90, lectr. Sch. Medicine, 1993—. Cons. Makki Internat. Acad., Kyoto, Japan, 1994-97. Author: Biology of Dogs, 1969, Parasitology of Dogs and Cats, 1992, Parasitological Situation of Cats and Dogs in Malaysia, 1996; editor: Biological Data Book on Experimental Animals, 1989; patentee in field. Mem. Japanese Soc. Toxicol. Sci. (bd. dirs. 1985—), Japanese Soc. Animal Models for Human Diseases (bd. dirs. 1984—), Kansai Lab. Animal Rsch. Assn. (bd. dirs. 1984—), Japan Malaysia Assn., N.Y. Acad. Scis., Tohoku U. Horseman Club (mgr. West Japan br.). Avocations: flute, sightseeing in malaysia. Home: 1-8-1 Kamigasa 2-chome Shigaken Kusatsu 525-0028 Japan

OISHI, STEPHEN MASATO, physician; b. San Francisco, Mar. 22, 1956; s. Masaichi and Kazumae (Ichiuji) O.; m. Sharon Naomi Oishi. BS in Biology, U. Hawaii, Honolulu, 1978; MS in Physiology, Georgetown U., Washington, 1980, MD, 1984. Diplomate Am. Bd. Internal Medicine. Intern Los Angeles County-U. So. Calif. Med. Ctr., LA, 1984-85; resident LAC-USC Med. Ctr., LA, 1985-87; physician Malad (Idaho) Valley Clinic, 1987-91, Ctrl. Med. Clinic, Honolulu, 1991—; med. dir. CMC Lab., Honolulu, 1996—; asst. clin. prof. medicine John A. Burns Sch. Medicine, U. Hawaii; v.p. MEC Rehab. Hosp. Pacific. Mem. staff Kuakini Med. Ctr., Honolulu, 1995—; advisor Dept. Transp., Honolulu, 1995—; ex officio advisor Hawaii Dept. Transp., v.p. Rehab. Hosp. Pacific. Fellow ACP; mem. Mid Pacific Country Club. Methodist. Avocations: golf, fishing, downhill skiing, bass guitarist-rock. Office: Ctrl Med Clinic 321 N Kuakini St Ste 201 Honolulu HI 96817-2399

OJEDA, JOSEPH A., psychotherapist; b. NYC, Mar. 25, 1950; s. Benigno Ojeda and Maria Luisa Ayala; children: Kenneth, Lorraine. D of Naturopathy, Westbrook U., Weirton, W.Va., 2004; PhD in Hypnotherapy, LaSalle U., Mandeville, La., 2002; DD, U. of Universal Life, Modesto, Calif., 1975; M in Holistic Healing, Westbrook U., 1996. Diplomate Am. Coll. Forensic Examiners, 1997, Am. Psychotherapy Assn., 1998, bd. cert. Am. Acad. of Experts in Traumatic Stress. Psychotherapist/clergy Counseling Ch. of the Universal Living God, Jamaica, NY, 1972—97; psychotherapist Holistic Healing, Hypnotherapy & Psychotherapy Family, Middletown, 1998—. Marriage officiant Counseling Ch. of the Universal Living God, 1976—, counseling, 1976—; free counseling walk-in clinic, Counseling Ch. of the Universal Living God, 1972—97. Author: (book) Re-education & Reprogramming with Hypnotherapy..., 2001, Integration of Behavioral & Relaxation Approaches..., 2002, Application of Self-Hypnosis Reprogramming Procedure..., 2002, Secrets of Clairvoyance, Explanation & Instructions, 2007. Recipient award for poem Mysterious Woman, Nat. Libr. of Poetry, 1997, Medal of Merit for cmty. involvement, Pres. Ronald Reagan, 1986, award letter for emergency control ctr. assistance, Commr. Joseph V. Terrenzio, Dept. of Hosp. Bur., 1970. Fellow: Am. Acad. of Experts in Traumatic Stresss. Home and Office: 27 Sproat Street Middletown NY 10940 Personal E-mail: hypnotex@juno.com.

OJHA, BAL KRISHNA, neurosurgeon; b. Gorakhpur, June 2, 1969; MS in Gen. Surgery, K. G. Med. Coll., Lucknow, Uttar Pradesh, India, 1996; MCh in Neurosurgery, All India Inst. Med. Scis., New Delhi, 2000. Asst. prof. neurosurgery All India Inst. Med. Scis., 2000—03, Chhatrapati Shahuji Maharaj Med. U., Lucknow, 2003—05, assoc. prof. neurosurgery, 2005—09, prof. neurosurgery, 2009, prof., head neurosurgery, 2010—. Mem.: Neurotrauma Soc. India, Delhi Neurol. Assn., Neurol. Soc. India. Home: C-12 Sector-I Aliganj Lucknow Uttar Pradesh 226024 India Personal E-mail: bkojha@rediffmail.com.

OJHA, BUDDHIWARDHAN CHANDRESHWAR, nuclear medicine physician; s. Chandreshwar Indradev Ojha and Pushpakumari Khimji Asher; m. Charu Tripathi, Apr. 5, 1999; children: Sanandan children: Sanak. MBBS, Maharaja Sayajirao U., Baroda, India, 1992; MPH, Tulane U., 1996. Diplomate Am. Bd. Nuc. Medicine, 2000, cert. Am. Soc. Nuc. Cardiology, 2001. Med. officer Primary Health Ctr., Sandhasal and Vadu, Gujarat, India, 1992—94; intern internal medicine Union Meml. Hosp., Balt., 1997—98; resident nuclear medicine U. Ala., Birmingham, 1998—2000, fellow, 2000—01, instr. radiology, 2000—01, asst. prof., 2001—. Dir. clin. PET U. Ala., Birmingham, 2001—. Contbr. articles. Mem.: Am. Coll. Radiology, Soc. Thoracic Radiology, Acad. Molecular Imaging, Soc. Nuc. Medicine (membership com. 2002, grantee 2001—01, 2000—01). Hindu. Achievements include development of a Positron Emission Tomography (P.E.T.) Facility featuring Discovery LS PET-CT system at The Kirklin Clinic, University of Alabama Health System. Avocations: swimming, travel. Home: 330 Crowne Woods Dr Hoover AL 35244 Personal E-mail: bojha@yahoo.com. Business E-Mail: ojha@uab.edu.

OKA, YOSHIHIRO, medical educator; b. Osaka, Japan, Feb. 16, 1955; s. Koichi and Mitsuko Oka; m. Kyoko Imanaga, 1982; children: Mayuko, Natsuko Suenobu, Yoshie. MD, Osaka U., 1980, PhD, 1989. Lic. physician in internal medicine Japan. Resident Osaka U. Hosp., 1980—81, med. staff, 1983—92, Toneyama Hosp., 1981—83; sci. mem. Basel Inst. Immunology, Switzerland, 1992—95; assist. prof. Osaka U., Suita, Japan, 1995—2005, assoc. prof. cancer immunology and cancer immunotherapy and, 2006—. Mem. editl. adv. bd.: Current Medicinal Chemistry. Fellow: Japanese Assn. Cancer Immunology, Japanese Soc. Hematology; mem.: Japanese Soc. Immunology, Japanese Cancer Assn., Japanese Soc. Internal Medicine. Achievements include research with colleagues in the identification of Wilms' tumor, WT1, gene product (WT1 protein) as a novel cancer antigen; research in immune response against cancer antigen; development of cancer vaccine targeting WT1 protein. Avocations: music, baseball, reading. Office: Osaka Univ Grad Sch Medicine Yamada-oka 2-2 Suita Osaka 565-0871 Japan Office Phone: 81 6 6879 3835, 81 6 6879-3676. Office Fax: 81 6 6879 3839. Business E-Mail: yoshi@imed3.med.osaka-u.ac.jp, yoshi@cit.med.osaka-u.ac.jp.

OKA, YOSHINARI, surgeon; b. Okayama, Japan, Apr. 15, 1962; s. Tsuyoshi and Kinko Oka; m. Mayumi Sadamori, June 24, 1990; children: Tomomi, Nanami. Degree, Okayama U., Med. Divsn., 1987, Dr., 1997; MD, 1987. Med. doctor Okayama U. Hosp., 1987, Kagawa Rousai Hosp., Marugame City, Japan, 1987—89, Matsuyama Saiseikai Hosp., Matsuyama City, Japan, 1989—92, Saiwaicho Meml. Hosp., Okayama City Kita-ku, Japan, 1993—. Mem.: Soka Gakkai Internat. Business E-Mail: saiwai@io.ocn.ne.jp.

OKABE, TETSURO, medical educator, researcher; s. Jin-Ichi and Fukiko (Nakazawa) Okabe; m. Miki Sajiki. MD, U. Tokyo, 1973, PhD, 1981. Diplomate Japan Ministry of Welfare and Labor, 1973, Japan Soc. Internal Medicine, 1988, Japanese Respiratory Soc., 1990, Japanese Soc. Oriental Medicine, 2004. Rsch. assoc. 3rd. Dept. Internal Med. U. Tokyo, Bunkyo-ku, 1977—84, asst. prof., 1984—2003; vis. sr. scientist Brown U. Roger Williams Cancer Ctr., Providence, 1987—88; lectr. Chest Disease Rsch. Inst., Kyoto U., Sakyo-ku, Japan, 1989—91; assoc. prof. Dept. Integrated Traditional Med. U. Tokyo, 2003—. Contbr. articles to numerous med. jours. (Incitement award, Japanese Cancer Assn., 1988). Mem.: Japan Soc. Oriental Medicine (standing dir.). Achievements include development of human G-CSF for cancer therapy; monoclonal antibodies for immunodetection and targeting cancer therapy; first to success in non-genetic therapy for genetic, spinocerebellar ataxia; discovery of familial elevation of angiotensin converting enzyme; research in human cell culture in protein-free medium. Office: Univ Tokyo Grad Sch Medicine 7-3-1 Hongo Bunkyo Tokyo 113-8655 Japan Office Phone: 81-3-3400-3288. Business E-Mail: tositm@dentoigaku.org.

OKADA, SHIGERU, medical educator; b. Okayama, Japan, Feb. 15, 1940; s. Keizo and Moyoko (Nishigaki) O.; m. Naoko Kobashi, Nov. 7, 1965; children: Satoru, Rie, Mari. MD, Okayama U., Japan, 1964, PhD, 1969. Chief pathologist Kyoto City Hosp., Japan, 1977-80; lectr. Sch. Medicine Kyoto U., 1980-90; asst. Med. Sch. Okayama U., 1969-71, lectr., 1971-77; prof. Okayama U. Med. Sch., Japan, 1990—2001; dir. Isotope Ctr. Okayama U., Japan, 1995—2001, advisor to the pres., 1999—2001, prof., dean Sch. of Medicine, 2003—05, prof. emeritus, 2005—; prin. Tamano Inst. Health Human Svcs., 2005—. Head radiation protection com. Okayama U., 1991-2001; trustee Kake Ednl. Inst., 2005-; vis. prof. Okayama U., 2005-. Contbr. articles to profl. jours. Mem. Japan Pathol. Soc. Tokyo, Japan Haematological Soc. Kyoto, Internat. Soc. Hematology, Japanese Cancer Assn. Tokyo, NY Acad. Sci. Office: Okayama U Grad Sch Medicine Dentistry and Pharm Scis 2-5-1 Shikata Okayama 700-8558 Japan

OKADA, TAKASHI, neurosurgeon, educator; s. Yosuke and Yoshiko Okada; m. Mayumi Iwata, Mar. 29, 1964. MD, Kanazawa U., Japan, 1991, PhD, 1995. Cert. neurosurgeon Japan Neurosurgical Soc., 1998. Vis. fellow Nat. Human Genome Rsch. Inst. / NIH, Bethesda, Md., 1996—98; postdoctoral fellow Jichi Med. Sch., Minami-kawachi, Japan, 1999—2000, asst. prof., 2000—. Associate board member (reviewer/advisor of the cancer therapy). Grantee, Uehara Meml. Found., 2001, Osaka Cancer Rsch. Found., 2002, The Nakajima Found., 2002; Grants-in-Aid for Sci. Rsch., Ministry of Edn., Culture, Sports, Sci. and Tech. of Japan, 2001-2003. Mem.: The Japan Neurosurgical Soc. (corr.), The Japanese Cancer Assn. (assoc.), Am. Soc. of Gene Therapy (assoc.). Achievements include patents pending for HDAC inhibitor-assisted rAAV-mediated transduction for cancer gene therapy; CAR-SCF fusion protein for rAd-mediated transduction. Avocations: music, driving.

OKADA, TAKASHI, professional athletics coach, physical therapist, educator; MS, Nippon Sport Sci. U. Registered phys. therapist Orgn. Ministry of Health, Labour and Welfare, Japan. Rschr. Nippon Sport Sci. U.; phys. therapist Tokyo-kita Social Ins. Hosp.; asst. prof. Ryotokuji U., Urayashu-shi, Chiba, Japan, 2008—. Contbr. articles to profl. jours. Mem.: Japan Swimming Fedn., All Japan Judo Fedn., Japanese Olympic Com. Achievements include research in associated factors of low back pain in athletes. Office: Ryotokuji Univ 5-8-1 Akemi Urayasu-shi Chiba 279-8567 Japan Home: 1-29-14 Parejute Todaijima Urayasu-shi Chiba 279 0001 Japan Office Phone: 81 47 782 2405. Office Fax: 81-47-382-2017. Personal E-mail: t.okada80@gmail.com. Business E-Mail: t-okada@ryotokuji-u.ac.jp.

OKADA, YOSHITAKA, radiologist; b. Hashima, Japan, Jan. 4, 1959; s. Shoji and Sekiko O.; m. Hitomi, Aug. 16, 1988; children: Naomichi, Eika. MD, U. Tokyo, 1983. Rsch. fellow U. Calif., San Francisco, 1987-88; asst. prof. radiology Kitasato U., Sagamihara, Japan, 1990-92, U. Tokyo, 1996-2000; assoc. prof. radiology Internat. U. Health and Welfare, Otawara, Japan, 2000—03, Dokkyo U. Sch. Medicine, Mibu, 2003—07; prof. radiology Saitama Med. U. Internat. Med. Ctr., 2007—. Mem. Radiol. Soc. N.Am., Japan Radiol. Soc., Am. Roentgen Ray Soc., European Soc. Radiology. Office: Dept Radiology Saitama Med Univ Internat Med Ctr 1397-1 Yamane Hidaka, Saitama 350 1298 Japan Office Phone: 81 42 984 4520. Business E-Mail: okada_y@saitama-med.ac.jp.

OKAFOR, CHIDI, nephrologist; b. Nigeria, June 11, 1976; MD, U. Nigeria, 2001; MPH, U. Tex., 2006. Nephrologist Kidney Specialists Southern Nev., 2011—. Chief fellow U. Va., 2009—11. Named one of America's Top Physicians, Consumers' Rsch. Coun. Am. Mem.: Renal Physicians Assn., Nat. Kidney Found., Am. Soc. Nephrology. Avocation: travel. Office: 500 S Rancho Dr Ste 12 Las Vegas NV 89106 Personal E-mail: crayon487@yahoo.com.

OKAMOTO, HIROSHI, health facility administrator, medical researcher; b. Asahikawa, Hokkaido, Japan, Nov. 3, 1952; s. Ken-ichi and Kimiko Okamoto; m. Rie Haraguchi, Feb. 28, 1956; children: Atsushi, Satoshi, Yui. MD, Asahikawa Med. Coll., 1979; PhD, Hokkaido U., Sapporo, Japan, 1989. Asst. prof. Hokkaido U., 1993—95; dir. in-patient ward Hokkaido U. Hosp., 1995—2001, dir. out-patient ward, 2001—; assoc. prof. Hokkaido U., 2001—. Recipient Hokkaido Heart award, 1994, Japanese Molecular Cadiology award, 96, Kanae Med. award, 1998. Mem.: Japanese Soc. Internal Medicine (bd. dirs. 1993—). Home: Minami-ku Sumikawa 5-jo 12-chome 11-5 Sapporo 005-0005 Japan Office: Hokkaido Med Ctr Kita-ku Kita-15-jo Nishi 4-chome Sapporo 060-8638 Japan Home Phone: +81-11-584-4650; Office Phone: 81116118111. Office Fax: +81-11-6115820; Home Fax: +81-11-584-4650. Business E-Mail: okamotoh@med.hokudai.ac.jp.

OKAMOTO, HIROSHI, physician; b. Japan, May 2, 1962; MD, Juntendo U., 1987, PhD, 1994. Assoc. prof. Tokyo Women's Med. U., 1999—2009; dir. Minami-Otsuka Inst. Tech., Minami-Otsuka Clinic, 2009—. Mem.: Japanese Soc. Allerology, Japan Coll. Rheumatology, Japanese Soc. Internal Medicine. Office: Minami Osaka Clinic 2-41-9 Minami-Otsuka Toshima Tokyo 1700005 Japan

OKAMOTO, MASAHIKO, surgeon; b. Nagoya, Japan, Aug. 11, 1959; MD, Kyoto Prefectural U. Medicine, 1986, PhD, 1996. Assoc. prof. Kyoto Prefectural U. Medicine, 2005—11, vis. lectr., 2011; surgeon Akita Hosp., 2011—. Mem.: Japan Soc. Transplantation, Am. Soc. Transplantation, Transplantation Soc. Avocation: golf. Office: 2-6-12 Takara Chiryu Aichi 472-0056 Japan Business E-Mail: amoto@koto.kpu-m.ac.jp.

OKAMOTO, ROBERTA, medical educator; b. Araçatuba, Brazil, Nov. 24, 1972; d. Tetuo and Júlia Takata Okamoto. MS, Sch. Medicine Ribeirão Preto-USP, 1997, PhD in Scis., 2001. Cert. dentist UNESP, Araçatuba, Brazil, 1994. Rschr. UNESP, 2003—; prof. FUNEC, Santa Fé do Sul, Brazil, 2004—, UNITOLEDO, Araçatuba, 2005—. Contbr. articles to profl. jour. Recipient Honor prize, Ann. Meeting Brazilian Soc. Dentistry Rsch., 2006, 2008. Achievements include research in bone biology.

OKAMOTO, SHIGEKI, ophthalmologist; b. Osaka, Japan, June 12, 1958; MD, Tottori U., 1984; PhD, Osaka U., 1990. Pres. Okamoto Eye Ctr., 2000—. Bd. mem. Japan Cornea Soc., 1998, Japanese Assn. Ocular Infection, 2000, Japanese Soc. Ocular Allergy, 2009; pres. Ehime Eye Bank, 2007. Mem.: Japanese Ophthal. Soc. Avocation: bicycling. Office: 2-7-17 Otemachi Matsuyama Ehime 7900067 Japan Office Fax: 81-89-933-9805. Business E-Mail: okamoto@eyemd.jp.

OKAMOTO, YASUHIRO, physician, consultant; b. Kyoto, Jan. 14, 1960; s. Yasuo and Etsuko Okamoto. MD, Nat. Def. Med. Coll., Tokorozawa Saitama, Japan, 1985. Diplomate Nat. Def. Med. Coll., 1994; cert. occupl. health cons. Flight surgeon and med. adviser JMSDF Air Tng. Regulating Comdr. Hdqs., Kashiwa, Chiba, Japan, 2003—07, JMSDF Fleet Air Force Hdqs., Ayase, Japan, 2007—10;

naval comdr. Japan Maritime Self Def. Force, Ayase, 1985—2010. Contbr. scientific papers. Commodore JMSDF Fleet Air Force, 2006—08, Atsugi Air Base. Fellow: Japanese Soc. Internal Medicine; mem.: Japanese Soc. Circulation. Achievements include research in BMI control in military personnel. Avocation: jogging. Home: Kugenuma Fujigaya Fujisawa Kanagawa 251-0031 Japan Office: JMSDF Fleet Air Foce Atsugi Air Base Ayase Kanagawa 252-1101 Japan Home Fax: 0466-26-0704. Personal E-mail: pgb02665@nifty.com. Business E-Mail: af-n10@inet.msdf.mod.go.jp.

OKAMURA, KAZUHIRO, hospital administrator, pathologist; b. Okayama City, Japan, May 19, 1943; s. Hirota and Ayako Okamura; m. Hisako Noishiki, Apr. 29, 1969; children: Nobuhiro, Tomohisa. MD, Yamaguchi U. Sch. Medicine, Ube City, Japan, 1966; PhD, Yamaguchi U., Ube City, Japan, 1977. Clin. pathologist Tenri Gen. Hosp., Japan, 1969—78; resident pathology Northwestern U. Med. Sch., Chgo., 1972—76; assoc. prof. Kawasaki Med. Sch., Kurashiki City, Japan, 1978—80; chief health exam. dept. Saiseikai Izuo Hosp., Osaka, 1982—88; founder and pres. Okamura Isshindow Hosp., Okayama City, 1988—. Lectr. Tenri Sch. Med. Tech., Japan, 1969—78, Med Tech Sch. VA Lakeside Hosp., Chgo., 1973—76. Recipient First Pl. Hekoen award, Chgo. Pathology Soc., 1975. Office: Okamura Isshindow Hosp 2-1-7 Saidaiji-Minami Okayama 704-8117 Japan Office Fax: +81-86-942-9929.

OKAMURA, NOBUYUKI, internist, researcher; b. Sasayama, Japan, May 9, 1969; s. Hiroyuki and Fujiko Okamura; m. Chikako Nakagawa, Mar. 21, 1999. MD, PhD, Tohoku U., 1998. Cert. Japanese Bd. Internal Medicine, 2001. Intern Nat. Sendai Hosp., Japan, 1994—96; attending staff, dept. geriatric medicine Tohoku U. Sch. Medicine, Sendai, Japan, 1998—2001. Contbr. articles to profl. jours. Grantee, AstraZeneca, 2004. Achievements include patents for amyloid-imaging probe for early diagnosis of Alzheimer's disease. Office: Tohoku University School of Medicine 2-1 Seiryo-machi Aoba-ku Sendai 980-8575 Japan Business E-Mail: oka@mail.tains.tohoku.ac.jp.

OKAN, ABDULLAH, gastroenterologist; b. Istanbul, Turkey, Nov. 27, 1964; Degree, Istanbul U. Cerrahpasa Med. Sch., 1988. Internist, gastroenterologist Dokuz Eylul U., 1989—2001. Mem.: Turkish Gastroenterology Assn. (Izmir). Avocation: painting. Office: 1399 Sok 25 Alsancak Konak Izmir 35220 Turkey Office Fax: 90-232-463-03-71. Personal E-mail: aokan64@hotmail.com.

OKAN, GÖKHAN, dermatologist; b. Istanbul, Bakirköy, Turkey, Mar. 2, 1972; s. Sait Fikret and Inci Okan; m. Funda Oz, 2005. MD, Istanbul U., Turkey, 1995. ECFMG cert. Gen. practitioner Pub. Polyclinics, Corum, Turkey, 1995; resident Istanbul Med. Faculty, Turkey, 1995—98; rsch. fellow Cleve. Clinic Fla., Fort Lauderdale, 1999—2000; dermatologist Acibadem Carousel Hosp., Istanbul, 2000—03, Med. Pk. Bahcellevler Hosp., Istanbul, 2008—. Cons. dermatologist Neomed Co.(MD Formulations), Istanbul, 1996—97; co-investigator Novartis(Sandimmun), Turkey, 1996—98, Dermalabs, Fort Lauderdale, 1999—2000. Contbr. articles to profl. jours. Fellow: Am. Acad. Dermatology; mem.: Internat. Soc. Dermatological Surgery, Turkish Soc. Dermatology, Turkish Med. Assn. Avocations: travel, music. Office: Med Park Bachelievler Hosp Kultur Sokak No 1 Dermatology Dept Istanbul 34160 Turkey Personal E-mail: gokhanokan@hotmail.com.

O'KANE, MARGARET E., non-profit organization executive; children: Katie, Beth. BA in French, Fordham U., 1969; MHS in Health Adminstrn. and Planning, Johns Hopkins U. Sch. Hygiene and Pub. Health. Second grade tchr. St. Ambrose Sch., Bklyn., 1970-72; neurology rsch. asst. Children's Hosp., Boston, 1972-73, respiratory therapist St. Elizabeth's Hosp., Boston, U. Va. Med. Ctr., Charlottesville, Va., Children's Hosp., Washington, DC, 1973-78; program analyst office of planning, evaluation, legislation health svcs. adminstrn. U.S. Dept. Health and Human Svcs., Washington, 1979-81; rsch. assoc. intergovernmental health policy project (IHPP) The George Washington U., Washington, 1981-83; pub. health svc. fellow U.S. Dept. Health and Human Svcs. Nat. Ctr. for Health Svcs. Rsch., Washington, 1983-84, special asst. to dir., 1985-86; dir. med. dirs. divsn. American Assn. Health Plans (formerly Group Health Assn. of America, Inc.), Washington, 1986-89; dir. quality mgmt. Group Health Assn., Inc., Washington, 1989-90; mem. steering com. Nat. Com. Quality Assurance, Washington, pres., 1990—. Elected mem. Inst. of Medicine, 1999; bd. dirs. Nat. Quality Forum, American bd. of Med. Specialties; mem. composite com. US Med. Licensing Examination; co chair Nat. Priorities Partnership; spkr. in field. Featured in Today show, CNN, NBC, ABC, NPR, Wall Street Journal, New York Times and other major daily papers. Bd. dirs. Found. for Informed Med. Decision Making. Named Health Person of Yr. Medicine & Health Journal, 1996; recipient Picker Inst. Individual award for Excellence, 2009, Founder's award American Coll. Med. Quality, 1997, Champion of Prevention award Centers for Disease Control and Prevention; named one of Top 25 Women, 2011, 100 Most Powerful People in Health Care Modern Healthcare. Office: National Committee For Quality Assurance 1100 13th St NW Ste 1000 Washington DC 20005-4056 Office Phone: 202-955-3500. Office Fax: 202-955-3599. *

OKANISHI, TOHRU, neurologist, pediatrician; b. Kanazawa, Ishikawa, Japan, June 8, 1974; s. Yousuke and Junko Okanishi; m. Eri Ishizuka. MD Ministry of Health, Labour and Welfare, Toyama Med. and Pharm. U., Japan, 2001; PhD. Cert. specialist in pediatrics Japan Pediatric Soc., 2007, Japanese Soc. Child Neurology, 2010, Japan Epilepsy Soc., 2010. Attending staff Dept. Pediat., Nagoya City U. Hosp., Aichi prefecture, Japan, 2001; staff Seirei Mikatahara Gen. Hosp., Hamamatsu, Shizuoka prefecture, Japan, 2001—06; attending staff Divsn. Child Neurology, Tottori U. Hosp., Yonago, Tottori prefecture, Japan, 2006—08, Pediats. Divsn. Nagoya City U. Hosp., Nagoya, Aichi prefecture, Japan, 2008—09; staff Seirei Hamamatsu Gen. Hosp., Shizuoka, Japan, 2009—. Liberal. Buddhist. Achievements include research in cerebrovascular malformation, traumatic brain injury; congenital disorder of glycosylation; ACTH therapy in west syndrome, pontocerebellar hypoplasia cortical dysplasia. Avocations: skiing, painting, reading. Office: Seirei Hamamatsu Gen Hosp 2-12-12 Sumiyoshi Hamamatsu Shizuoka 4308558 Japan Home: Nakagama Hosoe Kita-Ku Hamamatsu Shizuoka 4311304 Japan Office Phone: 81-534742222. Personal E-mail: oknsoknsokns@yahoo.co.jp.

OKARMA, THOMAS BERNARD, biotechnology company executive; b. 1946; AB, Dartmouth Coll., 1968; MD, Stanford U., 1972, PhD in Pharmacology, 1974; exec. MBA, Stanford Grad. Sch. Bus., 1997. Asst. prof., dept. medicine Stanford U. Sch. Medicine, 1980—85; scientific founder Applied Immune Sciences, Inc., 1985; v.p. R&D to, chmn., CEO, bd. dir. Applied Immune Sciences, Inc.(acquired by Rhone-Poulene Rorer in 1995); sr. v.p. Rhone-Poulenc Rorer, 1995—96; Joined Geron Corp., Menlo Park, Calif., 1997, v.p., cell therapies, 1997—98, v.p. R&D, 1998—99, pres., CEO, 1999—, pres., oncology drug develop, 2008—. Bd. dirs. Geron Corp., Menlo Park, Calif., 1999—, Geron Bio-Med Ltd., TA Therapeutics, Ltd., BIO (Biotechnology Industry Orgn.); spkr. in field. Contbr. several articles to profl. jours. Chmn., bd. overseers Dartmouth Med. Sch., 2000—07. Achievements include patents in field. Avocations: scuba diving, water and snow skiing, fishing, anything outdoors. Office: Geron Corp 230 Constitution Dr Menlo Park CA 94025 Office Phone: 650-473-7700. Office Fax: 650-473-7750. E-mail: info@geron.com.

OKAWA, AKIHIRO, physician, researcher; b. Yanai, Japan, Sept. 25, 1961; m. Erina Hayashi. MD, Nihon U., Tokyo, PhD, 2003. Asst. prof. Nihon U., 2004—; chief Koishikawa Tokyo Hosp., Tokyo, 2006—08. Office: Koishikawa Toyko Hosp 4-45-16 Otsuka Bunkyo-ku Tokyo 112-0012 Japan Office Phone: 81-3-3946-5151. Business E-Mail: akiokawa@med.nihon-u.ac.jp, akiokawa5@yahoo.co.jp.

OKEANOV, ALEXEY E, oncologist, researcher; b. Vladikavkaz, Russia, June 26, 1949; s. Evgeniy A. Okeanov and Galina F. Okeanova; m. Natalia I. Okeanova, 1972. MD (hon.), North Osetian Med. Inst., 1972; PhD (hon.), Inst. of Oncology and Med. Radiology, 1978, DSc, 1989. Diploma North Osetian Med. Inst./USSA, 1972. Rsch. fellow of epidemiology dept. Inst. of Oncology & Med. Radiology, Minsk, Belarus, 1972—82, head of dept. epidemiolody and cancer svc. mgmt., 1982—92; dir. Ctr. for Med. Tech. and Health Svc., Minsk, Belarus, 1992—97, Rsch. and Clin. Inst. of Radiation Medicine and Endocrinology, Minsk, Belarus, 2001—03; pro-rector on sci. work Internat. Sakharov Environ. U., Minsk, Belarus, 2004—. Pres. Byelorussian Assn. of Oncologists, Minsk, 1990—95; prin. investigator Joint Belarus-USA, 2001—03; expert invited WHO, 1994—98; chmn. Specialized Councile Ecology and Byological Sciences, Minsk, Belarus, 2004—; coord. European Commn., 1991—95; prof. IAEA, Minsk, Belarus. Editor (founder): (journal) Medical and Biologycal Aspects of Chernobyl Accident, Organization and Informatization of Health Care System; contbr. scientific papers. Mem.: Petrov's Acad. of Sci., St. Petersburg (corr.). Avocations: art, literature, travel. Office: Internat Sakharov Environmental Uni Dolgobrodskaya Ulitsa 23 220070 Minsk Minskiy Belarus Office Fax: +375172307332. E-mail: okeanov@nsys.by.

O'KEEFE, SHARON, hospital administrator; b. Chgo., 1952; m. Hal Moore; 1 child, Mackenzie. BA, Northern Ill. U., 1974; MA, Loyola U., Chgo., 1976. Various nursing staff & mgmt. positions Loyola U. Med. Ctr., 1974—79; dir. nursing & surgical services Johns Hopkins Hosp., Balt., 1979—85; assoc. hospital dir. Montefiore Med. Ctr., NYC, 1985—87; sr. mgr. health care Ernst & Whinney, Balt., 1987—89; sr. v.p. ops. U. Md. Med. Sys., Balt., 1989—99; exec. v.p., COO Beth Israel Deaconess Med. Ctr., Boston, 1999—2002; COO Barnes-Jewish Hospital, St. Louis, 2002—09; pres. Loyola U. Med. Ctr., Maywood, Ill., 2009—11, U. Chgo. Med. Ctr., 2011—. Office: University Chicago Medical Center 5841 South Maryland Ave Chicago IL 60637 Office Phone: 773-702-1234. *

ÖKEN, FUAD ÖZDAMAR, physician; b. Ankara, Turkey, Mar. 18, 1968; MD, Ankara U., 1991. Cert. orthop. & traumathology surgeon Ankara Numune Edn. & Rsch. Hosp., 1997. Physician Ankara Numune Edn. & Rsch. Hosp., 1992—. Home: Serdar Sokak 70/3 Yeniçag Mahallesi Yen Ankara 06170 Turkey Personal E-mail: fuadoken@yahoo.com.

OKITA, GEORGE TORAO, retired pharmacologist; b. Seattle, Jan. 18, 1922; s. Kazuo and Fusao (Muguruma) O.; m. Fujiko Shimizu, Nov. 29, 1958; children: Ronald Hajime, Sharon Mariko, Glenn Torao. Student, U. Cin., 1943-44; BA, Ohio State U., 1948; PhD, U. Chgo., 1951. Rsch. asst., rsch. assoc., instr., then asst. prof. U. Chgo., 1949-63; assoc. prof. Northwestern U. Med. Sch., 1963-66, prof. pharmacology, 1966—90, acting chmn. pharmacology, 1968—70, 1976—77; prof. emeritus molecular pharmacology and biol. chemistry, 1990—. Contbr. articles to profl. jours.; Asst. editor: Jour. Pharmacology and Exptl. Therapeutics, 1965-68. Served with AUS, 1944-46. NIH Postdoctoral fellow, 1952 Mem. AAAS, AAUP, Am. Soc. Pharmacology and Exptl. Therapeutics, Internat. Soc. Biochem. Pharmacology, Am. Heart Assn., Cardiac Muscle Soc., Sigma Xi. Achievements include research in med. field. Home: 95-1058 Kihene St Mililani HI 96789 Personal E-mail: gtoki@aol.com.

OKSANEN, TUULA, epidemiologist; b. Helsinki, Finland, June 6, 1963; MD, U. Turku, Finland, 1991, PhD, 2009. Gen. physician City of Turku, 1990—92; occupl. health physician, 1993—2005; occupl. health specialist, rschr. Finnish Inst. Occupl. Health, Turku, 2006—09, team leader,asst. chief med. officer, 2009—; rsch. fellow Harvard Sch. Pub. Health, Boston, 2010—11. Mem., governing bd. Finnish Red Cross, 1988—92, v.p., 1992—97, 1999—2002. Recipient award, Am. Coll. Epidemiology, 2011; Rsch. grant, Finnish Med. Found., Otto A Malm Found., Finnish Work Environment Fund, Local Govts. Pensions Instn. Finland. Mem.: Soc. Epidemiologic Rsch. Avocation: running. Office: Finnish Inst Occupation Health Lemminkahenkatu 14-18 Turku 20520 Finland Business E-Mail: tuula.oksanen@ttl.fi.

OKSHTEYN, MARA, endocrinologist, internist; MD, State U. Medicine and Pharmacy, Moldova, 1980—87. Diplomate Bd. cert. Internal Medicine Am. Bd. Internal Medicine, 1996, Bd. cert. Endocrinology, Diabetes, Metabolism Am. Bd. Internal Medicine, 1998. Internist Polyclinic #12, Kishinev, Moldova, 1988—89, Med. Ctr., 1989—91; endocrinologist Chesapeake and Washington Heart Care, Waldorf, Md., 1998—99, Montgomery Integrative Health and Wellness Ctr., Rockville, 2000—02, Crystal Run Healthcare, Middletown, NY, 2004—. Cons. Heal USA, Rockville, Md., 2001—. Recipient Patient's recognition as Best Physician, Patients. Mem.: AACE, The Endocrine Soc. Office: Crystal Run Healthcare 155 Crystal Run Rd Middletown NY 10941 Home: 1547 W Jonnie DR Willcox AZ 85643-3192

OKTAY, KUTLUK HAN, medical educator, researcher; married. MD, Hacettepe U., Ankara, Turkey, 1986. Diplomate Am. Bd. Ob-Gyn., Am. Bd. Reproductive Endocrinology & Infertility. Assoc. prof. Cornell U. Weill Med. Coll., NYC, 1997—2008; prof. Ny Med. Coll., 2008—. Adv. bd. Fertile Hope, NYC, 2001—; spkr., mem., pres. cancer panel. Exch. scholar, WellBeing Found., 1995—96. Master: Fertility Preservation and Cancer Spl. Interest Group (founder 2002); mem.: Am. Coll. Obstetricians and Gynecologists, Am. Soc. Reproductive Medicine (Rsch. Career Devel. award 1997—2000). Achievements include invention of ovarian tissue transplantation procedure; first in vitro fertilization and embryo development after ovarian transplant; development of IVF for breast cancer patients. Office: New York Medical College Munger Pavillion Rm 617 Valhalla NY 10595 Office Phone: 212-494-4400. Business E-Mail: kokfay@fertilitypreservation.org.

OKUBO, ICHIRO, biology educator, taxonomist; b. Japan, Feb. 26, 1932; Bachelor's degree, Okayama U., 1954; Doctoral degree, Hiroshima U., Japan, 1979. Prof. Shujitsu Jr. Coll., Okayama, Japan, 1975-84, Shujitsu Women's U., Okayama, 1985-96.

OKUBO, KIMIHIRO, otolaryngologist, educator; b. Tokyo, Sept. 8, 1959; 3 children. MD, PhD, Nippon Med. Sch., Tokyo, 1989. Cert. otolaryngologist Tokyo, 2005, allergist 2005. Adj. scientist Niaid, Nih, Rockville Pike, Md., 1989—; assoc. prof., dept. otolaryngology Nippon Med. Sch., Tokyo, 2008—. Chief rschr. Ministry Health, Labour, and Welfare, Tokyo, 2002—08. Recipient Rsch. award, Tokyo Med. Soc., 2000. Mem.: Nippon Med. Sch. Achievements include research in nasal allergy. Office: Dept Otolaryngology Nippon Med Sch Sendagi 1-1-5 Bunkyo-ku Tokyo 113-8603 Japan Office Fax: 81-3-5814-6207. Business E-Mail: ent-kimi@nms.ac.jp.

OKUDA, HARU, hospital administrator; Grad., Brown U.; MD, NY Med. Coll. Assoc. residency dir. Mt. Sinai Sch. Medicine, dir. undergraduate simulation, assoc. prof. Dept. Emergency Medicine; v.p. NY Health and Hosps. Corp., dir. Inst. Med. Simulation and Advanced Learning. Named one of 40 Under 40, Crain's NY Bus., 2010. Office: NYC Health and Hospitals Corporation 125 Worth St, Ste 514 New York NY 10013 Office Phone: 212-788-3321. Office Fax: 212-788-0040. E-mail: haru.okuda@nychhc.org. *

OKUDA, HIROAKI, gastroenterologist; b. Chiba, Japan, Jan. 25, 1950; s. Kunio and Hinae Okuda; m. Kaoru Nakazato, Apr. 19, 1981. MD, Hirosaki U., Japan, 1975; MD (hon.), Tokyo Women's Med. U., 1981. Clin. asst. Inst. Gastroenterology, Tokyo Women's Med. U., 1981—90, asst. prof., 1990—2007, prof., 2007—. Mem.: NY Acad. Scis., Am. Assn. Study Liver Diseases, Internat. Assn. Study Liver. Office: Dept Preventive Medicine Internat U Health and Welfare Mita Hosp 1-4-3 Mita Minato-ku Tokyo 108 8329 Japan Business E-Mail: okuda@iuhw.ac.jp.

OKUDA, KOICHI, research and development company executive; b. Japan, Aug. 5, 1978; MS, Tokyo U. Grad. Sch. Agr. & Tech., 2003; PhD, Kanazawa U. Grad. Sch. Med. Sci., 2011. R & d Toppan Printing Co., Ltd, 2003—06. Mem.: Japanese Soc. Nuc. Cardiology, Japanese Soc. Nuc. Medicine. Office: 13-1 Takara-machi Kanazawa Ishikawa 920-8641 Japan Business E-Mail: okuda@nmd.m.kanazawa-u.ac.jp.

OKUDAIRA, MASAHIKO, pathologist, researcher; b. Hiroshima, Japan, Aug. 28, 1927; s. Minoru and Toshiko (Ohnogi) O.; m. Hiroko Naitou, Apr. 28, 1955; children: Takehito, Tsuneko Okudaira Kumagai. MD, Tokyo U., 1950, PhD, 1958. Rsch. assoc. dept. pathology Tokyo U., 1951-63, lectr. Sch. Medicine, 1963-74; med. examiner Tokyo Met. Govt., 1955-72; rsch. assoc. Jewish Hosp., Cin., 1960-61; prof. pathology Sch. Medicine Kitasato U., Sagamihara, Kanagawa, Japan, 1972-93; dir. hosp. pathology Kitasato U. Hosp., Sagamihara, 1984-93; emeritus prof. Kitasato U., Sagamihara, 1993—; head divsn. pathology Japan Bioassay Rsch. Ctr., Hadano, Kanagawa, 1993-2000. Commr. Ministry of Health, Labor & Welfare, 1996—2009; vis. prof. Sch. Medicine Showa U., Tokyo, 1982-95. Contbr. articles to profl. jours. Mem.: Japan Soc. Portal Hypertension (hon.), Liver Cancer Study Group Japan (hon.; pres. 1989—90), Internat. Soc. Human and Animal Mycology (hon.; v.p. 1991—94), Japanese Med. Soc. Alcohol and Drug Studies (hon.; pres. 1993—94), Japan Soc. Hepatology (hon.; pres. 1984—85, award 1998), Japanese Soc. Med. Mycology (hon.; bd. dir. 1974—94, pres. 1983—84, award 1998), Japanese Path. Soc. (hon.). Home: 3-23-19 Nakano Nakano-ku Tokyo 164-0001 Japan Business E-Mail: md-okudaira@apost.plala.or.jp.

OKUJAVA, VAZHA M., neuroscientist; s. Michael S. Okujava and Nino Modebadze-Okujava; m. Zeinab Antadze, Apr. 18, 1964; children: Natela, Maia, Michael. MD, Tbilisi State Med. U., Georgia, 1956, PhD, 1960; Postgrad., Inst. Physiology, Tbilisi, 1959; DSc, Rsch. Ctr. Exptl. Neurology, Tbilisi, 1966. Cert. in neurology Tbilisi Advanced Tng. Inst. Drs., 1960. Dept. head Rsch. Ctr. Exptl. Neurology, 1961—2000, dir., 2000—05, chmn. sci. coun., 2005—; chief, lab. cellular physiology Inst. Physiology, Georgia, 1978—90; rector I. Javakhishvili Tbilisi State U., 1980—85, head, lab. neurobiology, 1985—, chmn. adv. coun., 2007—. Vis. scientist NINDB, NIH, Bethesda, Md., 1967—68, Max Planck Inst. Brain Rsch., Frankfurt, Germany, 1970; vice-rector Tbilisi Med. U., 1973—75; chmn., divsn. physiology and exptl. medicine Georgian NAS, Tbilisi, 1975—80. Contbr. monographs (Khorezmi Internat. Sci. award, 1999, I. Beritashvili Nat. Sci. award, 1981). Mem.: Internat. League Against Epilepsy, Internat. Bur. Epilepsy, Internat. Brain Rsch. Orgn., Internat. Union Physiol. Scis. Home: Jacob Nikoladze st 6 apt 22 Tbilisi 0179 Georgia Office: Rsch Ctr Exptl Neurology Gudamakari st 2-a Tbilisi 0192 Georgia Business E-Mail: okujava@geo.net.ge.

OKUMURA, MEINOSHIN, surgeon; b. Osaka, Japan, Nov. 22, 1958; s. Meikazu and Kyoko Okumura; m. Sachiko Nishiyama, June 17, 1989; 2 children. MD, Osaka U., 1984, PhD, 1994. Mem. surg. staff Higashi-Osaka Gen. Hosp., 1985—87, Osaka Prefectural Habikino Hosp., 1987—90; clin. rsch. fellow Osaka U. Hosp., 1990—92; asst. prof. Osaka U. Sch. Medicine, 1993; postdoctoral rsch. fellow Howard Hughes Med. Inst., Washington U., St. Louis, 1993—96; asst. prof. Osaka U. Grad. Sch. Medicine, 1996—2002, assoc. prof., 2004—05, prof. dept. surgery, 2007—; mem. surg. staff Nat. Kinki-chuo Hosp. Chest Diseases, 2002—04. Contbr. articles to profl. jours. Recipient Ozawa award, Alumni Assn. Surgery Osaka U., 2000. Avocations: movies, jazz. Office: Osaka University Grad Sch Medicine Dept Gen Thoracic Surgery (L-5) 2-2 Yamada-oka Suita 565-0871 Japan Office Phone: 81-6-6879-3152. Office Fax: 81-6-6879-3164. Business E-Mail: meinosin@thoracic.med.osaka-u.ac.jp.

OKUMURA, YOSHIHIRO, radiologist; b. Japan, Aug. 17, 1961; s. Yoshifumi and Rumi Okumura, Ryouko Okumura (Stepmother); m. Yukiko Watanabe, May 3, 1990. Diploma in medicine, U. Occupl. and Environ. Health, Kitakyushu City, Japan, 1989; MD (hon.), Okayama U., Japan, 2000. Resident, internal med. U. Occupl. Health Japan, Kitakyushu, 1989—90, Toshiba Hosp., Shinagawa-ku, Tokyo, 1990—91; staff physician Clinic Toshiba Himeji Corp., Himeji, Hyogo, 1991—99; rschr. dept. radiology Okayama U. Med. Sch., 1992—99, clin. fellow dept. radiology, 2000—02, asst. dept. radiology, 2003, assos. prof. dept. radiology, 2008—; chmn. PET RI Ctr. Okayama Kyokuto Hosp., 2004—06; dir. radiology Tottori City Hosp., 2007. Contbr. articles to profl. jours. Mem.: Soc. Nuc. Medicine (licentiate), Japan Coll. Radiology (licentiate), Japan Soc. Nuc. Medicine (licentiate), Japan Radiol. Soc. (licentiate). Buddhist. Achievements include research in comparison of diagnostic capabilities of Tl-201 scintigraphy and fine-needle-aspiration of thyroid nodules; usefulness of serum thyroglobulin levels and Tl-201 scintigraphy in diagnosing thyroid follicular lesions; reported the diagnostic capabilities of a quantitative evaluation by Tl-201 scintigraphy in thyroid follicular nodules. Avocations: travel, tennis, reading, spa, singing. Office: Fukuyama City Hospital Department Radiology Zao-cho 5-23-1 Fukuyama 721-8511 Japan Business E-Mail: oku8017@cc.okayama-u.ac.jp.

OKUN, NEIL JEFFREY, vitreoretinal surgeon; b. St. Louis, Nov. 21, 1957; s. Edward and Barbara J. (Braham) O.; m. Joan A. Sosnoff, May 19, 1984; children: David E., Sarah E. AB, Dartmouth Coll., 1980; MD, Washington U., 1984. Diplomate Am. Bd. Ophthalmology. Intern internal medicine Jewish Hosp. at Washington U., St. Louis, 1984-85; resident ophthalmology Washington U. Med. Ctr., St. Louis, 1985-88; fellow vitreoretinal Retina Cons., Ltd., Washington U., St. Louis, 1988-89; vitreoretinal surgeon Fla. Retina Inst., Jacksonville, Fla., 1990-91, Retina Assocs. Ctrl. Fla., Orlando, 1991—2004, Ctrl. Fla. Retina, Orlando, 2004—08, Eye Specialists Mid-Fla., Winter Haven, Fla., 2008—. Instr. dept. ophthalmology Washington U. Sch. Medicine, St. Louis, 1988-89; clin. asst. prof. dept. ophthalmology U. South Fla., Tampa, 1992—; chmn. dept. ophthalmology Fla. Hosp. Orlando, 1996-97 Recipient Upjohn Achievement award for endocrinology and metabolism Washington U. Sch. Medicine, St. Louis, 1984. Fellow ACS, Am. Acad. Ophthalmology; mem. AMA (Physician's Recognition award for continuing med. edn. 1992—), Am. Soc. Retina Specialists, Assn. for Rsch. in Vision and Ophthalmology, Fla. Med. Assn., Fla. Soc. Ophthalmology, Ctrl. Fla. Soc. Ophthalmology, Polk County Med. Soc., Vitreous Soc., Paul Cibis Club. Avocations: music, art. Office: Eye Specialists Mid-Fla 407 Ave K SE Winter Haven FL 33880 Office Phone: 863-294-3504. *

OKUTUCU, SERCAN, cardiologist; b. Diyarbakir, Turkey, Apr. 8, 1983; Degree in Higher Edn., Hacettepe U., 2006. Cardiologist, dept. cardiology Hacettepe U. Faculty Medicine, 2006—. Recipient Ihsan Dogramaci Excellence award, Hacettepe U., 2006; named Seref Zileli, Successful Physician of Yr., 2010. Mem.: European Assn. Cardiovasc. Prevention and Rehab., ESC Working Group Atherosclerosis and Vascular Biology, European Atherosclerosis Soc., Turkish Soc. Cardiology. Avocations: classical music, philosophy. Office: Hacettepe University Faculty Medicine Ankara Altindag 06100 Turkey Personal E-mail: sercanokutucu@yahoo.com.

OKUYAMA, SHIGERU, pharmaceutical executive; b. Nagoya, Japan, Aug. 1, 1953; BE, Meijo U., 1977; PhD, Tohoku U., 1986. Exec. officer Taisho Pharm. Co. Ltd., 2011—. Vis. prof. Yamaguchi U., 1996—2011; councilor Japan Health Scis. Found., 2005. Mem.: Japanese Soc. Neuropsychopharmacology, Japanese Pharmacological Soc. (spl. com. mem. 2008), Soc. Neurosci. Office: 1-403 Yoshino-cho Kita-ku Saitama-shi Saitama 331-9530 Japan Office Fax: 81-48-663-2145.

OLADIPO, ABIODUN, gynecologist, consultant; b. Lagos, Nigeria, Jan. 1, 1957; s. Badmos Oladipo and Ejide Odunbaku; m. Isabel Youdeowei Bekere, Sept. 14, 1991; 1 child, Aramide Anthony. Degree, Fed. Sch. Sci., Lagos, 1976; MBBS, Coll. Medicine, Lagos, 1981. Sr. house officer Royal Gwent Hosp., Newport, England, 1990—92, registrar, 1992—93, Salisbury Hosp., England, 1993—96; registrar to sr. registrar Royal United Hosp., Bath, England, 1996—98; sr. registrar Princess Margaret Hosp., Swindon, England, 1998—99, Southampton U. Hosp., Southampton, England, 1990—2000; cons. gyn. Royal Cornwall Hosp., Truro, England, 2000—, dep. lead oncologist, 2000—; colposcopy Lead, 2000—. Fellow: Royal Coll. Surgeons; mem.: South West Cancer Sci., Royal Coll. Gyn. Avocations: travel, photography, football, cricket, poetry.

OLALLA SAAD, SARA TERESINHA, hematologist, educator; b. São Paulo, June 9, 1956; MD, Faculdade de Medicina de Jundiai, 1979, Faculdade de Ciencias Medicas da UNICAMP, 1989, PhD. Asst. prof. divsn. hematology Hematology & Hemotherapy Ctr., U. Campinas, Hemocentro-Unicamp, 1983—2001, prof. divsn. hematology, 2001—, head divsn. hematology, 2006—. Mem. tchg. distance com. Faculdade de Ciencias Medicas-UNICAMP, 2006; comite de assessoramento de medicina CNPq, 2009—. Recipient Premio De Merito Cientifico, U. Campinas - UNICAMP, 2009—10, Premio de Reconhecimento Acadêmico ZEFERINO VAZ, 2010, Prêmio Análise Medicina, Analise Editl., 2009, Premio Scopus Brasil, Elsevier S&T, 2010. Mem.: Brazilian Acad. Scis., Am. Soc. Hematology. Avocations: movies, travel. Office: Hemocentro-Unicamp R Carlos Chagas 480 Campinas São Paulo 13083-878 Brazil Office Fax: 55 19 3289-1089. Business E-Mail: sara@unicamp.br.

OLATOSI, BANKOLE, healthcare educator; b. Lagos, Nigeria, Oct. 10, 1975; MPH, Twin Cities U. Minn., 2004; PhD, U. SC, 2007. Asst. prof. Mt. Olive Coll., 2008—. Recipient Lucille Packard & Pathfinder Travel award; Grad. Sch. Dera D. Parkinson Trustee fellowship, U. SC. Mem.: APHA, Assn. U. Programs Health Adminstrn., Acad. Health, Am. Coll. Healthcare Execs., Delta Omega. Avocations: reading, soccer. Office: 634 Henderson St Mount Olive NC 28365 Business E-Mail: bolatosi@moc.edu.

O'LAUGHLIN, ELIZABETH M., psychologist, educator; b. Ames, Iowa, Dec. 12, 1964; BA, U. Mo., 1986; PhD, U. Wis., Milw., 1993. Assoc. prof. Ind. State U., 1995—. Lic. psychologist Faculty Practice Plan, 1996—. Recipient Ednl. Excellence award, Ind. State U., Coll. Arts & Scis.; grant, Ind. State U. Ctr. Pub. Engagement and Cmty. Svc., Info. Tech. Innovations grant, Ind. State U. Mem.: APA (mem.

divsn. 53-clin. child psychology). Avocations: bicycling, reading, travel. Office: Ind State University Psychology Dept Terre Haute IN 47809 Office Fax: 812-234-7184. Business E-Mail: lizo@indstate.edu.

OLAUSSON, PER-HÅKAN, surgeon; b. Sweden, Jan. 7, 1973; MD, U. Umeå, Sweden, 2002; MBA, U. Gävle, Sweden, 2008. Dermatologic surgeon SkinDoc, 2011—. Office: Svärdvägen 11 Danderyd Stockholm 18233 Sweden Office Fax: 0855003579. Business E-Mail: ph@skindoc.se.

OLCZAK, PAUL VINCENT, psychologist, educator; b. Buffalo, May 25, 1943; s. Vincent Henry and Helen (Babula) O.; m. Marie Rose Oliveri, Oct. 20, 1973; children: Paul V. II, Patrick J., Drew M. MA, No. Ill. U., 1969, PhD, 1972. Clin. psychologist Family Ct. Psychiat. Clinic, Buffalo, 1975-77, cons. supervisory psychologist, 1977—; supr. psychol. svcs. Hopevale, Inc., Hamburg, NY, 1977-89; clin. psychologist Amherst (N.Y.) Police Dept., 1989—; asst. prof. psychology SUNY, Geneseo, 1977-83, assoc. prof. psychology, 1983-90, prof. psychology, 1990—, chairperson, 1999—, prof. emeritus, 2008; clin. psychologist child and adolescent psychiatry Niagara Falls Meml. Hosp., 1996—, clin. psychologist bariatric medicine program, 2002—; cons. psychologist Batavia (N.Y.) Sch. Dist. Co-editor: Community Mediation, 1991; contbg. author: The POI in Clinical Situations: A Review, 1991, Self-actualization-Polemics Surrounding Its Use, 1991; contbr. articles to profl. jours./publs. Mem. APA, Ea. Psychol. Assn., Midwestern Psychol. Assn., Psychonomic Soc., Soc. Exptl. Social Psychology, Internat. Assn. for Conflict Mgmt., Psi Chi, Sigma Xi. Home: 278 Troy Del Way Buffalo NY 14221-3358 Office: SUNY Dept Psychology Geneseo NY 14454 E-mail: olczak@geneseo.edu.

OLD, LLOYD JOHN, cancer biologist; b. San Francisco, Sept. 23, 1933; s. John H. and Edna A. (Marks) Old. BA, U. Calif., Berkeley, 1955; MD, U. Calif., San Francisco, 1958; MD (hon.), Karolinskia Inst., Stockholm, 1994, U. Lausanne, Switzerland, 1995, Univ. Coll. London, 1997. Rsch. fellow Sloan-Kettering Inst. Cancer Rsch., NYC, 1958—59, rsch. assoc., 1959—60, assoc., 1960—64, assoc. mem., 1964—67, mem., 1967—, acting assoc. dir. research planning, 1972, v.p., assoc. dir., 1973—76, v.p., assoc. dir. sci. devel., 1976—83; rsch. assoc. biology Cornell U. Grad. Sch. Med. Scis., NYC, 1960—62, asst. prof. biology, 1962—66, assoc. prof. biology, 1966—69, prof. biology, 1969—81, prof. immunology, 1981—; assoc. dir. rsch. Meml. Sloan-Kettering Cancer Ctr./Meml. Hosp., NYC, 1973—83, William E. Snee Chair cancer immunology, 1983—. Sci. dir. Ludwig Inst. Cancer Rsch., 1971—86, chmn. sci. com., 1988—2006, bd. dirs., 1989—, dir. NY unit, 1990, CEO, 1995—2004, dir. Cancer Vaccine Collaborative, 2001—, chmn. bd. dirs., 2006—; lectr. Harvey Soc., 1972, G.H.A. Clowes Meml., 1980; assoc. med. dir. NY Cancer Rsch. Inst. Inc., 1970; med. dir. Cancer Rsch. Inst., Inc., 1971—74, dir. sci. adv. coun., 1974—; vis. prof. clin. investigation GM Cancer Rsch. Found., Dana-Farber Cancer Inst.; vis. prof. pathology Harvard U., 1986; fgn. adj. prof. med. faculty Karolinska Inst., 1994—. Adv. editor: Jour. Exptl. Medicine, 1971—76, 1990—95, Progress in Surface and Membrane Sci., 1972—74, assoc. editor: Virology, 1972—74, mem. editl. adv. bd.: Cancer Rsch., 1967—70, Cancer, 1968—71, Recent Results in Cancer Rsch., 1972, mem. editl. bd.: Immunobiology, 1987—. Mem. med. & sci. adv. bd., trustee Leukemia Soc. America Inc., 1970—73; mem. sci. adv. bd. Jane Coffin Childs Meml. Fund Med. Rsch., 1970—75; mem. rsch. coun. Pub. Health Rsch. Inst. NYC, 1977—80, bd. dirs., 1979—89, vice chmn. exec. com., 1984—89; adv. bd. biology divsn. NY Hall of Sci. Recipient Roche award, 1957, Alfred P. Sloan award for cancer rsch., 1962, Lucy Wortham James award, James Ewing Soc., 1970, Louis Gross award, 1972, Founders Tumor Immunology award, Cancer Rsch. Inst., 1975, Rabbi Shai Shacknai Meml. award, 1976, Rsch. Recognition award, Noble Found., 1978, Robert Roesler de Villiers award, 1981, NY Acad. Medicine medal, 1985, Robert Koch prize, 1990, Pres.'s medal, Johns Hopkins U., 2004, Dean's award, Stanford U. Sch. Med., 2004, Charles Rodolphe Brupbacher Cancer Rsch. award, Switzerland, 2007. Mem.: AAAS, NAS, Acad. Cancer Immunology (presdl. mem. 1998—), Inst. Medicine, Am. Assn. Immunologists, Am. Assn. Cancer Rsch. (bd. dirs. 1980—83), Am. Acad. Arts & Scis., NY Acad. Scis., Harvey Soc., Alpha Omega Alpha, Sigma Xi, Phi Beta Kappa. Office: Cancer Rsch Inst Nat Hdqs One Exchange Plaza 55 Broadway Ste 1802 New York NY 10006

OLDEN, KEVIN WILLIAM, medical researcher; b. NYC, Aug. 18, 1948; s. William and Josephine Olden; m. Sylvia Suikam Hom, Apr. 23, 1983; 1 child, Kimberly Jane. AB, NYU, 1971; MD, SUNY Downstate Med. Sch., 1976. Diplomate Am. Bd. of Internal Medicine with subspecialties in gastroenterology and addiction medicine, Am. Bd. of Psychiatry and Neurology. Intern categorical medicine UCLA-San Fernando Valley Med. Program, Sepulveda, Calif., 1976—77, resident internal medicine, 1977—79; resident psychiatry Mass. Gen. Hosp., Boston, 1979—81; postdoctoral fellow substance abuse and gastroenterology DVA Med. Ctr., Palo Alto, Calif., 1981—83; dir. alcohol rehab. unit Calif. Pacific Med. Ctr., San Francisco, 1983—86; asst. prof. medicine and psychiatry U. Calif., Davis, 1986—91, assoc. prof. medicine and psychiatry San Francisco, 1991—98, Mayo Med. Sch., Scottsdale, Ariz., 1998—2005; Levy prof. medicine, chair divsn. gastroenterology U. Ark., Little Rock, 2006—. Cons. Rome Internat. Working Teams on Functional GI Disorders, Rome, 1994—; fellow gastroenterology DVA Med. Ctr., Martinez, Calif., 1988—89; assoc. prof. medicine and psychiatry U. South Ala. Sch. Medicine, Mobile, 2005—06. Editor: (book) Handbook of the Functional Gastrointestinal Disorders, Chronic Abdominal Pain: A Comprehensive Approach; guest editor (med. jour.) Psychiat. Annals, Seminars in Gastroenterology, Jour. Psychosomatic Rsch., editl. bd. Am. Jour. Drug and Alcohol Abuse, Medicine and Psychiatry, Am. Jour. Gastroenterology. Med. advisor Internat. Found. for Functional Gastrointestinal Disorders, Milw., 1997—2003, Cyclic Vomiting Assn., Scottsdale, Ariz., 1998—2003; med. cons. Med. Bd. of Calif., San Francisco, 1986—98; med. advisor Physician Diversion Program State of Calif., 1986—97. Capt. USNR, 1978—2003. Recipient Harvard Macy scholar in Med. Edn., Harvard Med. Sch., 2000, Clin. Scholar award, Am. Coll. of Gastroenterology, 1999, Outstanding Physician Educator (Rsch.), Mayo Clinic Scottsdale, 2000, Outstanding Physician and Educator, St. Mary's Med. Ctr., 1992—93, Clinician Engaged in Edn., Mayo Clinic Scottsdale, 1999—2000. Fellow: Acad. of Psychosomatic Medicine, ACP, Am. Coll. of Gastroenterology, Am. Psychiat. Assn.; mem.: Calif. Soc. Addiction Medicine (pres. 1990—92), Calif.

Med. Assn. (chair chem. dependency 1986—98), Am. Gastroent. Assn. (pres. functional brain-gut rsch. group 2001—03). Avocations: fishing, scuba diving. Office Fax: 501-686-6248. Business E-Mail: kwolden@uams.edu.

OLDER, JAY JUSTIN, ophthalmic plastic surgeon; b. Jersey City, Feb. 7, 1940; m. Lois Rosner; children: Benjamin, Jessica. AB, Rutgers U., 1961; MD, Stanford U., 1966. Diplomate Am. Bd. Ophthalmology. Intern, resident in internal medicine Cornell U./Bellevue Hosp. Ctr., NYC, 1968; resident in ophthalmology Stanford (Calif.) U., 1973; fellow in ophthalmic plastic and reconstructive surgery Stanford U., San Francisco, 1974; pvt. practice Tampa, Fla., 1974—. Clin. prof. ophthalmology U. South Fla. Coll. Medicine, Tampa, 1975—, dir. oculoplastic svc., 1974—99. Author: Eyelid Tumors: Clinical Diagnosis and Surgical Treatment, 1987, 2d edit., 2003. Fellow Am. Acad. Ophthalmology (Sr. Honor award 1995), Am. Soc. Ophthalmic Plastic and Reconstructive Surgery (pres. 1987, sec. 1983-84), ACS; mem. Phi Beta Kappa (v.p. Greater Tampa Bay Assn. 1995-96). Office: Older & Slonim Eyelid Inst 4444 E Fletcher Ave Ste D Tampa FL 33613-4937 Home: 16631 Sedona De Avil Tampa FL 33613

OLDERMAN, GERALD, retired medical device company executive; b. NYC, July 16, 1933; s. Cass and Hilda (Klein) O.; m. Myrna Ruth Schwartz, Aug. 3, 1958; children: Sharon, Neil, Lisa. BS in Chemistry, Rensselaer Poly Inst., Troy, NY, 1958; MS Phys. Chemistry, Seton Hall U., South Orange, NJ, 1971, PhD, 1972. Rsch. chemist Nat. Cash Register, Dayton, Ohio, 1958-61; tech. mgmt. positions Johnson & Johnson, New Brunswick, NJ, 1961-75, dir. R & D, bd. dirs. surg. products hosp. divsn., 1972-75, v.p. R & D, Surgikos divsn., 1975-78; v.p. R & D, bd. dirs. Am. Convertors divsn. Am. Hosp. Supply corp., Evanston, Ill., 1978-85; v.p. internat. R & D Pharmaseal divsn. Baxter Healthcare Corp., Valencia, Calif., 1985-91; v.p. R & D, bd. dirs. cardiopulmonary divsn. C.R. Bard, 1991-96; cons. R.F. Caffrey & Assoc., Inc., Brownsville, Vt., 1996—; exec. v.p. R&D tech. and commercialization, bd. dirs. Quick-Med Techs., Inc., Wilmington, Del., 1998—. With USMC, 1954-56. Recipient Robert Wood Johnson medal, Johnson & Johnson, 1969. Fellow Am. Inst. Chemists; mem. Assn. Advancement Med. Instrumentation, INDA, Assn. Nonwovens Industry (bd. dirs., corp. rep. 1986, 87), Nat. Fire Protection Assn. (industry rep.), Am. Soc. Artificial Internat. Organs. Home: 17 Pickman Dr Bedford MA 01730-1009 Office: RF Caffrey & Assoc Inc PO Box 319 Brownsville VT 05037-0319 also: Quick Med Techs Inc 902 Northwest 4th St Gainesville FL 32601 Office Phone: 781-271-9893, 561-400-6003. Personal E-mail: jolderman@aol.com. Business E-Mail: jolderman@quickmedtech.com.

OLDHAM, JOHN MICHAEL, physician, psychiatrist, educator; b. Muskogee, Okla., Sept. 6, 1940; s. Henry Newland and Alice Gray (Ewton) O.; m. Karen Joan Pacella, Apr. 24, 1971; children: Madeleine Marie, Michael Clark. BS in Engring., Duke U., 1962; MS in Neuroendocrinology, Baylor U., 1966, MD, 1967. Licensed physician NY, NJ, SC, Tex.; diplomate in psychiat. and forensic psychiatry Am. Bd. Psychiatry and Neurology; cert. Am. Psychoanalytic Assn. Intern pediatrics St. Luke's Hosp., NYC, 1967-68; resident psychiat. Columbia U. Dept. Psychiat., N.Y.S. Psychiatric Inst., NYC, 1968-70; chief resident in psychiatry Columbia U., NY State Psychiat. Inst., 1970-71; grad. Columbia Psychoanalytic Ctr., NYC, 1977; dir. psychiatric emergency svcs. Roosevelt Hosp., NYC, 1973-74, dir. residency tng. dept. psychiat., 1974-77; dir. short term diagnostic and treatment unit NY Hosp. Westchester Divsn., White Plains, NY, 1977-80, dir. divsn. acute treatment svcs., 1980-84; deputy dir. NY State Psychiatric Inst., NYC, 1984-89, acting dir., 1989-90, dir., 1990—2002; assoc. chmn. dept. psychiatry Columbia U. Coll. Physicians & Surgeons, NYC, 1986-96, vice chmn., 1996-2000, acting chmn., 2000—02; chief med. officer NY State Office Mental Health, Albany, 1989—2002; prof. psychiatry Med. U. SC, 2002—07, chmn. dept. psychiatry and behavioral sci., 2002—07, exec. dir. Inst. Psychiatry, 2002—07; sr. v.p., chief of staff The Menninger Clinic, 2007—; prof., exec. vice chmn. Menninger dept. psychiatry & behavioral scis. Baylor Coll., 2007. From instr. clin. psychiatry to prof. clin. psychiatry Columbia U. Coll. P&S, 1974-96, 1988-96, Elizabeth K. Dollard profl. clin. psychiatry medicine and law, 1996-2002; asst. prof. psychiatry Cornell U. Med. Coll., NYC, 1977-83, assoc. prof. clin. psychiatry, 1983-84; attending staff dept. psychiatry Roosevelt Hosp., NYC, 1973-77; assoc. attending in psychiatry, NY Hosp., 1977-84, Presbyn Hosp., NYC, 1984-88, attending in psychiatry, 1988-2002; tng. and supervising psychoanalyst Columbia Psychoanalytic Ctr., NYC, 1983-2002; coord. med. student edn., dept. psychiatry Cornell U. Med. Coll., Westchester Divsn., White Plains, NY, 1977-84; coord. clin. clerkships in psychiatry Roosevelt Hosp., Columbia U. Coll. P&S, NYC, 1974-77; spl. adv. bd. Freedom From Fear, Inc.; examiner Am. Bd. Psychiatry and Neurology; chmn. acute divsn. rsch. group, Westchester Divsn., NY Hosp., 1981-84, co-project dir. borderline rsch. group, 1982-84, co-prin. investigator familial transmission DSM III personality disorders, 1982-84; prin. investigator personality disorders in bulimia, NYS. Psychiat. Inst., 1985-90, structured DSM III assessment psychoanalytic patients, Columbia Psychoanalytic Ctr., 1986-91; co-prin. investigator validity DSM III R personality disorders, NY State Psychiat. Inst., 1987-94; co-investigator NIMH, 1996-2002; Hall-Mercer vis. scholar, dept. psychiatry, U. Pa., 2004; Judge Bernard Thompson Meml. Lectr., dept. psychiatry, North Shore U. Hosp., 2004; Albert M. Biele MD vis. prof. in psychiatry, Jefferson Med. Coll., 2005; Wolfe-Adler Lectr., SHeppard Pratt Health Sys., 2006; Ferald R. Klerman MD Meml. Lectr., Payne Whitney Clinic, NYC, 2007. Author: (with L.B. Morris) The Personality Self-Portrait, 1990; editor Jour. Psychia. Practice; editor bd. Jour. Personality Disorders; dep. editor Am. Psychiat. Pub., Inc.; reviewer Arch Gen. Psychiatry, Am. Jour. Psychiatry, Psychiat. Svcs.; contbr. numerous articles to profl. jours.; presentations in field. Major USAF, 1971—73. Recipient John J. Weber prize Excellence in Psychoanalytic Rsch. Columbia Psychoanalytic Ctr., 1990, Dorothea Dix Award Mental Illness Found., 1996, Spl. Comm.'s award NY State Office Mental Health, 1997, Spl. Presdl. commendation Am. Psychiat. Assn., 1999, 2005, Payne Whitney Clin. award for Extraordinary Pub. Svc., 2002; Spl. Citation conferred by Governor George E. Pataki, State of NY, 2002; Paul Hoch award for Disting. Leadership, NY State Office Mental Health, 2002. Fellow Am. Coll. Psychiatrists (pres. 2010-, Bowis award 2007), Am. Psychiat. Assn. (pres. NY County dist. br., 1989-90, com. rsch. psychiat. treatment 1987-93, coun. rsch., steering com. practice guidelines, chmn. sci. program com. 1992-95, chmn. com. quality indicators 1999-2003, chmn. coun. quality care 2003—06, pres. elect 2010-), Am. Psychopath. Assn., NY Acad. Medicine; mem. AMA, Am. Psychoanalytic

Assn. (cert.), Assn. Psychoanalytic Medicine (pres. 1989-91), Internat. Psychoanalytical Assn., NY Acad. Sci., Assn. Rsch. Personality Disorders (bd. dirs.), Internat. Soc. for Study of Personality Disorders (pres. 2000—03), SC Psychiat. Assn. (pres. 2006-07), Houston Psychiatric Soc. Office: Menninger Clinic PO Box 809045 Houston TX 77280-9045 Office Phone: 713-275-5016. Office Fax: 713-275-5117. Business E-Mail: joldham@menninger.edu. *

OLDING, MICHAEL, plastic and reconstructive surgeon; b. Celina, Ohio, July 4, 1950; s. Paul Robert and Virginia Lee (Hierholzer) O. BS, U. Dayton, 1972; MD, U. Ky., 1980. Diplomate Am. Bd. Plastic Surgery. Intern N.Y. Hosp./Cornell Med. Ctr., NYC, 1980-81, resident in surgery, 1981-82, McGill U., Montreal, Canada, 1982-83, fellow, plastic and reconstructive surgery, 1983-85; assoc. prof. surgery divsn. plastic/reconstructive surgery George Washington U., Washington, 1985—; chief divsn. plastic and reconstructive surgery, dir. Cosmetic Surgery & Laser Ctr., George Washington Univ. Med. Faculty Assoc., Washington. Staff privileges George Washington U. Med. Ctr., Sibley Hosp., Children's Hosp., Washington; served on numerous FDA adv. panels; lectr. in field; presenter King Fisal Hosp., Riyadh, Royal Coll. Surgeons Traveling Fellowship and Plastic Surgery Rsch. Coun., London. Author: Clinicians Pocket reference, 1986; contbr. articles to profl. jours. Annals of Plastic Surgery, Plastic Reconstructive Surgery; featured on Discovery Channel, interviewed by CBS, ABC, FOX, WUSA, Washington Post, Washington Times, NY Times Style mag., Boston Globe; quoted in online articles at ABCnews.com, Forbes-.com, CNN.com and participated in an online forum with Washingtonpost.com Bd. dirs. D.C. Ballet Co., 1995—. Named a Top Doc, Washingtonian mag., 1989-, Washington Consumers' Checkbook. Fellow ACS; mem. Northeastern Soc. Plastic Surgery (bd. dirs.), Nat. Capitol Soc. Plastic Surgeons, McGill Plastic Surgery Soc. (bd. dirs.), Am. Soc. Plastic Surgeons, Am. Soc. Aesthetic Plastic Surgeons. Office: George Washington Univ Hosp 2150 Pennsylvania Ave NW Washington DC 20037-3201 Office Phone: 202-741-3241. Office Fax: 202-741-3183.

OLDS, JACQUELINE, psychiatrist, educator; b. Springfield, Mass., Jan. 4, 1947; d. James and Marianne (Ejier) O.; m. Richard Stanton Schwartz, Aug. 26, 1978; children: Nathaniel Leland, Sarah Elizabeth. BA, Radcliffe Coll., 1967; MD, Tufts U., 1971. Diplomate Am. Bd. Psychiatry and Neurology. Resident in adult psychiatry Mass. Mental Health Ctr., Boston, 1974; resident in child psychiatry McLean Hosp., Belmont, Mass., 1976, assoc. attending child psychiatrist, 1979—; psychiatrist-in-charge inpatient unit McLean Hall-Mercer Children's Ctr., Belmont, 1976-79; assoc. child psychiatry Beth Israel Hosp., Boston, 1979—85; cons. in child psychiatry Mass. Gen. Hosp., Boston, 1994—. Instr. psychiatry Harvard U. Med. Sch, Boston, 1976-86; asst. prof. clin. psychiatry, 1986-2000, assoc. clin. prof. psychiatry, 2000—; bd. dirs. Guidance Ctr., Inc. Author: Overcoming Loneliness in Every Day Life, 1996, Marriage in Motion, 2000, The Lonely American: Drifting Apart in the Twenty-first Century, 2009, editor Clin. Challenges column in Harvard Rev. of Psychiatry; contbr. articles to profl. jours.; author (translator into Spanish): Matrimonio in Moviemento. Recipient Mentoring award Mass. Gen. Hosp. Dept. Child Psychiatry, 1998. Disting. fellow Am. Psychiat. Assn.; mem. Mass. Psychiat. Soc. (ethics com. 1988-93, mem. pub. affairs com. 1992—1994), Am. Acad. Child Psychiatry, Am. Psychoanalytic Assn., New England Coun. Child and Adolescent Psychiatry. Democrat. Avocations: piano, writing, cooking, watercolors. Office Phone: 617-547-5920. Business E-Mail: jolds@hms.harvard.edu.

OLEARCHYK, ANDREW, cardiothoracic surgeon, educator; b. Peremyshl, Ukraine, Dec. 3, 1935; s. Symon and Anna (Kravéts) O.; m. Renata M. (Sharan), June 26, 1971; children: Christina N., Roman A., and Adrian S. Grad., Med. Acad., Warsaw, Poland, 1961, U. Pa., Phila., 1970. Diplomate Am. Bd. Surgery, Am. Bd. Thoracic Surgery. Chief divsn. anesthesiology, asst. dept. surgery Provincial Hosp., Kielce, Poland, 1963-66; resident in gen. surgery Geisinger Med. Ctr., Danville, Pa., 1968-73; resident in thoracic, cardiac and vascular surgery Allegheny Gen. Hosp., Pitts., 1980-82; pvt. practice medicine splty. in cardiac, thoracic and vascular surgery Phila. and Camden, NJ, 1982—. Author: A Surgeon's Universe, 2003, 2nd edit., 2006, 3rd edit., 2011; contbr. articles to profl. jours.; author: 3rd edit, 2011. Achievements include description of mimicking of the subclavian steal syndrome (2004); application of the ultrasonic Doppler flow detector to localize an intramyocardial coronary artery to perform coronary artery bypass surgery on a beating heart in the presence of neoplastic pericarditis aiming to preserve cellular immunity (2003); recognition of a triad of the severe atherosclerosis of the aortic valve, a low incidence of coronary artery disease and rheumatic fever in patients with a congenital bicuspid aortic valve (2002); modification of a vertical reduction aortoplasty by a distal external synthetic grafting for surgical treatment of aneurysms of the ascending aorta (2002); treatment of a bullous emphysema of the lung by a conservative resection of bullae and a local application of a biological glue (2001); noted association between congenital diaphramatic defect with peritoneopericardial communication and congenital bicuspid aortic valve (2000); applied a staged treatment of the left subclavian steal syndrome and coronary artery disease by the left carotid-subclavian and coronary artery bypasses (1999); establishing that in patients with coronary artery disease, the causes of congestive heart failure in those with a mild to moderate reduction of the left ventricular ejection fraction were hypertension, myocardial infarction or ischemic insufficiency of the mitral valve, and in those with severe reduction of the left ventricular ejection fraction were left ventricular dysfunction alone, or in combination with ischemic mitral regurgitation (1999); repair of a pseudoaneurysm of the ascending aorta on a beating heart (1997); ligation of bilateral coronary-pulmonary artery fistulas on a beating heart (1996); internal repair of the coronary sinus (Valsalva) aneurysm (1996); grafting of the internal thoracic to coronary arteries without touching the atherosclerotic ascending aorta, on cardiopulmonary bypass with a beating, warm and vented heart and bradycardia induced by beta-blockers (1994); design of Olearchyk R Triple Ringed Cannula Spring Clip to secure vein grafts over blunted cannulas in coronary artery bypass surgery (1989); combined right femoral and iliac retroperitoneal surgical approach to remove retained intraaortic balloon device (1989); technique a side graft during replacement of the ascending aorta in proximal aortic dissection (1989); intro. of endarterectomy and external prosthetic grafting of ascending and transverse aorta under hypothermic circulatory arrest (1987); first to combine insertion of the inferior vena cava filter with a protected iliofemoral venous thrombectomy (Olearchyk's operation, 1986); pioneering promotion of grafting of diffusely diseased coronary arteries with the internal thoracic artery (1980-82) and of the left anterior descending coronary artery sys. during resection of cardiac aneurysms (1979-80); used an inflated Foley balloon catheter to control hemorrhage from cardiac wounds and to infuse fluids through it to replace blood loss before and during suture repair (1978); description of a combined treatment of advanced gastric carcinoma by resection and chemotherapy (1975); recognized that alcoholism and smoking were common habits of patients with stomach cancer (1975); demonstration of safety of simultaneous use of fluothane and curare as gen. anesthesia (1966); description of combined treatment of advanced testicular seminoma with chemotherapy, resection and radiotherapy (1961). Office Phone: 609-519-9316. Personal E-mail: asolearchyk@yahoo.com.

O'LEARY, CLARE, physician, consultant; b. Cork, Ireland, Apr. 10, 1971; d. Kevin O' Leary and Alice O'Leary. BAO, BCH, MB, U. Coll., Cork, Cork, Ireland. Med. cons. South Tipperary Gen. Hosp., Clonmel, Tipperary, Ireland, 2005—; specialist registrar Beaumont Hosp., Dublin, 2003—05. Cons. physician South Tipperary Gen. Hosp., Clonmel, Tipperary, Ireland, 2005—. Achievements include first Irish female to summit Mt Everest, 2004; first Irish female, and fifteenth female in the world, to climb the highest mountain on each of the seven continents, 2005; first Irish female to summit Ama Dablam in the Himalayas, 2006; first Irish female to ski traverse Greenland ice cap, 2007; first Irish female to ski to south pole. Home: Fingerpost Cottage Church Rd Douglas Cork Ireland Office: Cork Univ Hospital Dept Medicine Alimentary Pharmabiotic Ctr Wilton Cork Ireland

O'LEARY, DENNIS SOPHIAN, retired accrediting body executive; b. Kansas City, Mo., Jan. 28, 1938; s. Theodore Morgan and Emily (Sophian) O'L.; m. Margaret Rose Wiedman, Mar. 29, 1980; children: Margaret Rose, Theodore Morgan. BA, Harvard U., 1960; MD, Cornell U., 1964. Diplomate Am. Bd. Internal Medicine, Am. Bd. Hematology. Intern U. Minn. Hosps., Mpls., 1964-65, resident, 1965-66, Strong Meml. Hosp., Rochester, NY, 1966—67, chief resident and hematology fellow, 1967—68; asst. prof. medicine and pathology George Washington U. Med. Ctr., Washington, 1971-73, assoc. prof., 1973-80, prof. medicine, 1980-86, assoc. dean grad. med. edn., 1973-77, dean clin. affairs, 1977-86; pres. Joint Commn., Oakbrook Terrace, Ill., 1986—2007, pres. emeritus, 2008—; chief strategy officer Awarepoint Inc., 2009—. Med. dir. George Washington U. Hosp., 1974-85, v.p. Univ. Health Plan, 1977-85; pres. D.C. Med. Soc., 1983. Chmn. editl. bd. Med. Staff News, 1985-86; contbr. articles to profl. jours. Founding mem. Nat. Capital Area Health Care Coalition, Washington, 1982; trustee James S. Brady Found., Washington, 1982-87; bd. dirs. Nat. Quality Forum, 2001-07, bd. dirs. Nat. Patient Safety Found., 2006-, Nat. Adv. Coun. Agy. for Healthcare Rsch. and Quality, 2002-04., bd. dirs. inst. healthcare Improvement, 2008-, Defense Health Bd., 2008-, Maj. U.S. Army, 1968-71. Recipient Community Service award D.C. Med. Soc., 1981, Key to the City, Mayor of Kansas City, Mo., 1982. Master ACP; fellow Am. Coll. Physician Execs.; mem. AMA (Resolution commendation 1981, Disting. Svc. award 2005), Am. Hosp. Assn. (del. 1984-86, Resolution commendation 1981). Avocation: tennis. Home: 5024 Buena Vista Fairway KS 66205

O'LEARY, JACQUELINE G., medical association administrator; b. Dec. 18, 1973. BS, Stanford U., 1995; MD, Mass. Gen. Hosp., 2006, MPH. Med. dir. inpatient liver & transplant unit Baylor U. Med. Ctr., 2006—. Transplant hepatologist Baylor U. Med. Ctr., 2006. Named Best Doctors, Dallas Mag., 2008—10; fellow fellowship, Am. Assn. Study Liver Disease. Mem.: Am. Gastrointestinal Assn., Am. Assn. Study Liver Disease, Tex. Soc. Gastrointestinal Endoscopy, Internat. Liver Transplant Soc., Am. Soc. Transplantation. Avocations: skiing, travel, scuba diving. Office: 3410 Worth St Ste 860 Dallas TX 75246 Office Fax: 214-820-8168. Business E-Mail: jacquelo@baylorhealth.edu.

O'LEARY, MARY ELIZABETH, retired nursing educator, college dean; b. Holyoke, Mass., Apr. 10, 1932; Diploma, Providence Hosp. Sch. Nursing, 1952; BS in Nursing, Boston Coll., 1954, MS in Nursing, 1958; JD, Western New England Coll., 1966; EdD, U. Mass., 1979. Assoc. degree nursing program, Springfield Tech. CC. Head, practical nursing program Holyoke Pub. Sch. System; dir. edn. Providence Hosp. Sch. Nursing; instr. Boston Coll. Sch. Nursing; clin. instr. med.-surg. nursing Holyoke Hosp. Sch. Nursing; educator Bur. Vocat. Edn., Mass.; staff nurse oper. rm. Mt. Sinai Hosp., NYC, Holyoke (Mass.) Hosp., Providence Hosp., Holyoke; med.-surg. staff nurse St. Elizabeth's Hosp, Brighton, Mass.; med. staff nurse Boston City Hosp.; chairperson Div. Nursing Springfield Tech. CC, Mass., 1969-80, dean Health/Human Svcs. Div., 1980—97, dean emeritus, 1997—; writer, adminstr. practical nursing program City of Holyoke. Rep. Nat. Voc. Edn. Conf., Ohio. 1965, Iowa 1967, Health Issues Adv. Panel Commn. Med. Mal-Practice, 1971; lectr. in field. Author: (with others) Textbook of Practical Nursing, 1974; contbr. articles to profl. jours. Holyoke Health Planning Com., 1960, Holyoke Dept. Health Edn. Com. 1964-68, bd. dirs. Holyoke Mcpl. Home Hosp., 1971-72. Grantee Springfield Tech. C.C. and Coll. Our Lady of Elms, 1989-93, Springfield Tech. C.C.-DNS (LSI)-OTA, 1994-95. Mem. Med. Malpractice Tribunal (sec. 1977), Am. Assn. Law and Medicine, Nat. Assn. Higher Edn. Adminstrs., Sigma Theta Tau. Achievements include research in ultrasound, massage therapy, thirty years successful administration higher education. Home: 159 Homestead Ave Holyoke MA 01040-1033

O'LEARY, PATRICK F., orthopedist, surgeon, educator; MD, U. Coll. Cork, Ireland, 1968. Diplomate Am. Bd. Orthopedic Surgery, lic. NY. Intern Hosp. Univ. of Utah; resident gen. surgery Roosevelt Hosp., 1969—72; resident orthopaedic surgery Hosp. for Spl. Surgery, 1972—75, assoc. attending spine surgeon; fellow spine surgery Toronto East Gen. Orthopedic Hosp., 1975—76; assoc. prof. orthopaedic surgery Weill Cornell Med. Coll. Co-author: (publs.) A Novel Method for the Quantitative Evaluation of Lumbar Spinal Stenosis, 2006, Spontaneous Posterior Iliac Crest Regeneration Enabling Second Bone Graft Harvest: A Case Report, 2009. Named one of Best Doctors, NY Mag., 2009—11, America's Top Doctors, Castle Connolly. Fellow: Am. Coll. of Surgeons, Internat. Coll. of Surgeons, Am. Acad. of Orthopaedic Surgeons; mem.: North Am. Spinal Soc., Cervical Spine Rsch. Soc. Office: Hospital for Special Surgery 1015 Madison Ave New York NY 10021 Office Phone: 212-249-8100. Office Fax: 212-860-8132.

OLENGINSKI, JAN ANTHONY, surgeon; b. West Point, NY, May 29, 1964; s. Jan Anthony and Patricia Ann (Grabowski) O. BS, U. Scranton, 1986; DO, U. Health Scis., 1990. Intern Suburban Gen. Hosp., Norristown, Pa., 1990-91; resident in gen. surgery Phila. Coll. Osteo. Medicine, 1991-95, chief resident, 1994-95, fellow in vascular surgery, 1995-96; attending surgeon gen. and vascular surgery Tenet Hosps., Med. Coll. Pa., Frankford Hosp., Roxborough Hosp., Albert Einstein Med. Ctr., Phila., 1996—; chmn. dept. surgery Parkview Hosp. Chmn. gen. surgery Pa. Osteopathic Med. Assn. (POMA); clin./assoc. prof. gen. and vascular surgery Phila. Coll. of Osteopathic Medicine, active staff Frankford Hosp, Nazareth Hosp. Roxborough Meml. Hosp. Mem. Am. Osteo. Assn., Am. Coll. Osteo. Surgeons, Am. Assn. Osteo. Postgrad. Physicians, Pa. Osteo. Med. Assn. (chmn. subcom. on gen. surgery), Pa. Med. Soc., Phila. County Med. Soc., Phila. County Osteo. Med. Soc. Republican. Roman Catholic. Avocations: golf, sports, running, art. Home: 7 Stevens Ct Lafayette Hill PA 19444 Office: 2701 Holme Ave Ste 100 Philadelphia PA 19152 also: 95021 Roosevelt Blvd Ste 201 Philadelphia PA 19114 Office Phone: 215-533-1200. E-mail: ciraaj@comcast.net.

OLER, ALLISON, internist, educator; BA in Biology, U. Pa., 1990; MD, U. Chgo., 1994. Diplomate Am. Bd. Internal Medicine, 1997, recertification 2007. Intern internal medicine dept. San Francisco Categorical program Univ. of Calif., 1994—95, resident internal medicine dept. San Francisco Categorical program, 1995—97; clin. dir. internal medicine dept. Penn Health for Women Univ. of Pa. Hosp.; assoc. prof. clinical medicine dept. Univ. of Pa. Named one of the Top Doctor, Phila. Mag., 2011. Office: Penn Medicine at Radnor Internal Medicine Department 250 King of Prussia Rd Wayne PA 19087 Office Phone: 610-902-2500. Office Fax: 610-906-2504. E-mail: allison.oler@uphs.upenn.edu.

OLESEN, HANNE VEBERT, pediatrician; b. Naestved, Denmark, Oct. 9, 1965; MD, Aarhus U., 1993, PhD, 2010. Sr. cons. Aarhus U. Hosp., Skejby, 2003—. Co-chmn. steering com. European Cystic Fibrosis Soc. Patient Registry, 2006—10, exec. dir., 2010, mem. organizing com., 2011—. Avocations: reading, gardening. Office: Aarhus University Hosp Skejby Brend Aarhus Region Midtjylland 8200 N Denmark

OLIKER, DAVID WILLIAM, insurance company executive; b. Elkins, W.Va., Mar. 29, 1948; married; 3 children. BA in Sociology and Anthropology, East Carolina U., 1970; MA in Social Anthropology, American U., Washington, DC, 1973, post-master's grad. cert. in health care adminstrn., George Washington U., 1977. Health svcs. specialist United Mine Workers Am. Health and Retirement Funds, 1976-78; health planner Health Sys. Agy. Western Md., Cumberland, 1978-79; ops. mgr. Md.-Individual Practice Assn., Inc., Rockville, 1979-81; project dir. N.Y. Health Maintenance Plan, Inc., NYC, 1981-82, pres., CEO MVP Health Care (merger with Preferred Care), Schenectady, NY, 1982—, Preferred Care (merger with MVP Health Care), Rochester, NY, 2005—. Bd. dirs. America's Health Ins. Plans, mem. policy adv. coun.; bd. dirs. NY State HMO Conf.; former chmn. NY State Health Plans Assn.; mem. bd. MVMA Found., Taconic IPA, MedAllies, Health Advancement Collaborative of Ctrl. NY; chair adv. coun. Grad. Coll. of Union Univ.; adv. bd. mem. Albany Coll. of Pharmacy; president's adv. coun. Exelsior Coll.; chmn. Nat. Managed Care Inc. Bd. dirs. Schenectady 2000, Albany Colonie Regional C. of C., Twin Rivers Boy Scout Coun., Proctor Theatre Bd. Mem.: APHA. Office: MVP Health Care 625 State St PO Box 2207 Schenectady NY 12301-2207 Office Phone: 800-777-4793. *

OLIN, CRAIG H., internist; married; 3 children. Grad. cum laude, Tufts U., 1989; MD, NYU, 1993. Diplomate Am. Bd. Internal Medicine, 1996. Intern and resident internal medicine NY Hosp.-Cornell Med. Ctr., 1993—96; with Internal Medicine Assoc., Prime-Care Med. LLP, Stamford; co-founder Personal Physicians of Conn. Ltd. Liability Co., Stamford, 2007—10; chmn. med. staff Stamford Hosp. Treas. Craig D. Tifford Found.; exec. bd. mem. and bd. dirs. Vis. Nurse and Hospice Care, Southwestern, Conn. Recipient Jack and Bertha Beers award, Stamford Hosp., 1999, Melville G. Magida award, Fairfield County Med. Assn., 2006, Richard and Hinda Rosenthal Found., 2006; named one of Top Doctors in the NY Metro Area, Castle Conolly, 2005—, Top Doctors, Conn. Mag. Mem.: Am. Heart Assn. of Fairfield County (bd. dirs.), Sr. Svcs. of Stamford (bd. dirs.). Office: Stamford Hospital 30 Shelburne Rd Stamford CT 06904 Home: Ste 41043 30 Strawberry HillCourt Stamford CT 06902 Office Phone: 203-276-1000.

OLIN, WILLIAM HAROLD, orthodontist, educator; b. Menominee, Mich., Mar. 7, 1924; s. Harold H. and Lillian (Hallgren) Olin; m. Bertha Spitters, May 6, 1950; children: William Harold, Paul Scott, Jon Edward. DDS, Marquette U., 1947; MS, U. Iowa, 1948. Asst. prof. orthodontics Univ. Hosps., U. Iowa, Iowa City, 1948, assoc. prof., 1963-70, prof., 1970-93, prof. emeritus, 1995—. Chmn. bd. dirs. Hills Bank. Author: (book) Cleft Lip and Palate Rehabilitation, 1960; contbr. articles to profl. jours. Fund raiser, participant Ops. Smile. Served to capt. US Army, 1952—54. Recipient Iowa City Human Rights Comm. award, 2004, Ben Franklyn award, 2007, Disting. Alumni award, Iowa, 2009. Mem.: Am. Cancer Soc. (peer reviwed com. mem. 2004, dist. Iowa alumni 2009), Hope Lodge (adv. bd. mem. 2004, cancer bd. 2009), Boy Scout Coun., Am. Acad. Sports Dentistry (bd. dirs., sec./treas. 1989—95), Am. Cleft Palate Assn. (pres. 1970), Iowa Orthodontic Soc. (pres. 1959), Midwest Orthodontic Soc. (pres. 1968—69), Angle Orthodontic Soc. Midwest (pres. 1982), Univ. Athletic Club (bd. dirs.), Rotary (pres. Iowa City). Republican. Methodist. Avocations: collecting political memorabilia, music box collecting, sports, travel, politics, coin collecting/numismatics. Home: 426 Mahaska Dr Iowa City IA 52246-1610 Personal E-mail: w.olin@mchsi.com.

OLINGER, CARLA D(RAGAN), medical advertising executive; b. Cin., Oct. 8, 1947; d. Carl Edward and Selene Ethel (Neal) Dragan; m. Chauncey Greene Olinger, Jr., May 30, 1981. BA, Douglass Coll., 1975. Mgr. info. retrieval services Frank J. Corbett, Inc., NYC, 1976—77; editor, proofreader, prodn. asst. Rolf W. Rosenthal, Inc., NYC, 1977—78, copywriter, 1978—80, copy supr., 1980—82, v.p. copy dept., 1982—83; v.p., group copy supr., adminstrv. copy supr. Rolf W. Rosenthal, Inc., divsn. Ogilvy & Mather, 1984—89; v.p., assoc. creative dir. RWR Advt., 1989; v.p., copy supr. Barnum & Souza, NYC, 1990—92, Botto, Roessner, Horne & Messinger, Ketchum Comm., NYC, 1992—95, Lyons Lavey Nickel Swift, NYC,

1995—2007, Lyon-Heart, NYC, 2007—. Editor: Antimicrobial Prescribing (Harold Neu), 1979. Mem.: Nat. Inst. Social Scis., St. George's Soc. N.Y., Church Club N.Y. Office: Lyon Heart 220 E 42nd St New York NY 10017-5806

OLIPHANT, CHARLES ROMIG, retired physician; b. Waukegan, Ill., Sept. 10, 1917; s. Charles L. and Mary (Goss) R.; m. Claire E. Canavan, Nov. 7, 1942; children: James R., Cathy Rose, Mary G., William D. Student, St. Louis U., 1936-40, MD, 1943; postgrad., Naval Med. Sch., 1946. Intern Nat. Naval Med. Ctr., Bethesda, Md., 1943; pvt. practice medicine and surgery San Diego, 1947-99; ret., 1999. Bd. dirs. Midway Med. Enterprises; former chief staff Balboa Hosp., Doctors Hosp., Cabrillo Med. Ctr.; chief staff emeritus Sharp Cabrillo Hosp.; mem. staff Mercy Hosp., Children's Hosp., Paradise Valley Hosp., Sharp Meml. Hosp.; sec. Sharp Sr. Health Care, S.D., 1985-98; mem. exec. bd., program chmn. San Diego Power Squadron, 1985-93, 95; charter mem. Am. Bd. Family Practice. Served with M.C., USN, 1943-47. Recipient Golden Staff award Sharp Cabrillo Hosp. Med. Staff, 1990; inducted Wisdom Hall of Fame (Medicine), 2003. Fellow Am. Geriatric Soc. (emeritus), Am. Acad. Family Practice, Am. Assn. Abdominal Surgeons; mem. AMA, Calif. Med. Assn., Am. Acad. Family Physicians (past pres. San Diego chpt., del. Calif. chpt.), San Diego Med. Soc., Pub. Health League, Navy League, San Diego Power Squadron (past comdr.), SAR, San Diego Yacht Club, Douglas County Scottish Soc.

OLIPHANT, URETZ JOHN, physician, surgeon; b. Chgo., May 9, 1953; s. John and Letha (Fryson) O.; m. Mercidita DeJesus, Jan. 11, 1985; children: Michael, Jonathan, Kathryn. AB, Boston U., 1976; MD, U. Minn., 1983. Diplomate Am. Bd. Surgery. Fellow in trauma/critical care Ill. Masonic Hosp./U. Ill., Chgo., 1991-92; attending surgeon Carle Found. Hosp., Urbana, Ill., 1992—, past head divsn. trauma surgery and dept. gen. surgery; clin. prof. dept. surgery U. Ill. Coll. Medicine, Urbana, 1994—, head dept. surgery, 1996—, regional dean, 2011—. Chmn. bd. dirs. Frances Nelson Cmty. Health Ctr., urbana, 1994—; chmn. Region 6 Trauma Com., Urbana, 1995-97. Founding mem. Nat. Safe Kids, Champaign, Ill., 1995—. Recipient Golden Apple Tchg. award U. Ill. Coll. Medicine, 1994, 95, 97, 99, 2006, 07. Fellow ACS, Internat. Coll. Surgeons. Avocations: chess, basketball. Office: University Ill Urbana Champaign Coll Medicine Office of Dean 190 Med Sciences Bldg 506 S Mathews Ave Urbana IL 61801 also: Carle Found Hosp 602 W University Ave Urbana IL 61801-2530 Office Phone: 217-383-3204. Business E-Mail: uretz.oliphant@carle.com. *

OLIVECRONA, GORAN KARL, cardiologist; b. Nykoping, Dec. 28, 1962; MD, Lund U., 1992, PhD, 2007. Resident, cardiology Skane U. Hosp., Lund, 1994—2000, attending physician, 2000—02, cons., 2002—. Fellow: SCAI; mem.: Svenska Lakarforbundet, Swedish Soc. Cardiology (chmn., Working Group PCI 2008), European Assn. Percutaneous Coronary Interventionalists, European Soc. Cardiology. Avocations: snorkeling, golf. Office: Dept Cardiology Skane University Lund Skane 22185 Sweden E-mail: goran.olivecrona@gmail.com.

OLIVEIRA, ANDRÉ LACERDA DE, medical educator, researcher; b. Rio de Janeiro, Nov. 27, 1964; Degree in vet. medicine, U. Fed. Fluminense, 1988; PhD, U. Fed. Rio de Janeiro, 2004. Assoc. prof. U. Estadual Norte Fluminense, 2004—. Pres. Brasilian Coll. Surgery and Anesthesiology Vet., 2008—; rsch. scientist FAPERJ, 2009—. Home: Rua Francisca Carvalho de Azevedo 14/202 Campos dos Goytacazes Rio de Janeiro 28030-355 Brazil Business E-Mail: andrevet@uenf.br.

OLIVEIRA, CARLOS AUGUSTO, physician, otolaryngologist; b. Barras, Piaui, Brazil, Dec. 1, 1942; s. José and Alba Costa Pires Oliveira; m. Videte Pereira, Dec. 4, 1969 (dec. Aug. 1992); children: Marina Pereira Pires Oliveira, Caroline Pereira Pires Oliveira, Maria Helena Pereira Pires Oliveira BSc, Colegio Pedro II, Rio de Janeiro, 1960; MD, Nat. Faculty Medicine, Rio de Janeiro, 1966; PhD Otolaryngology, U. Minn., 1977. Diplomate Am. Bd. Otolaryngology. Resident gen. surgery Brasilia Med. Sch., 1967—68, tchg. asst. gen. surgery, 1969—71; straight surg. intern Washington Hosp. Ctr., 1971—72; resident dept. otolaryngology U. Minn. Med. Sch., Mpls., 1972—77; assoc. prof. dept. otolaryngology Brasilia U. Med. Sch., 1977—96, prof., head dept. otolaryngology, 1997—. Postdoctoral rsch. fellow Mass. Eye and Ear Infirmary/Harvard Med. Sch., Boston, 1989-90; cons. for rsch. in otolaryngology Brazilian Nat. Rsch. Coun., 1990— Contbr. over 80 articles to profl. jours Recipient Physician Recognition award AMA, 1977 Mem. Am. Otological Soc. (assoc.), Otolaryngology Soc. Brasilia (founder, pres. 1987), Internat. Otopathology Soc. (pres.-elect), Prosper Menière Soc., Colegio Brasiliero de Cirurgioes, Neuro-equilibriometric Soc. Roman Catholic. Avocations: jogging, swimming, biking, guitar playing, singing. Office: Centro de Otorrino Brasilia Avda W-3 Sul Quadra 716 Bloco E Sala 202 70390 Brasilia Brazil Office Phone: 55613245183, 551132451837. Business E-Mail: carpoliveira@brturbo.com.br, cobral@brturbo.com.br.

OLIVEIRA, CLARA SLADE, medical researcher; b. Rio de Janeiro, Nov. 27, 1981; DVM, Sao Paulo State U., 2005, M in Vet. Medicine, 2009, PhD student, 2009—. Rsch. fellow U. Cambridge, 2009—. Avocation: dog breeding. Home: Laranjeiras St 525-1401 Laranjeiras Rio de Janeiro 22240002 Brazil Personal E-mail: claraslade@gmail.com.

OLIVEIRA, EVENY CRISTINE LUNA, physician; b. Campo Grande, Aug. 29, 1972; MD, UFMS, 1996, MS, 2009. Physician Núcleo do Hosp. U., 2006—. Mem.: ABHH. Office: R Texaco Campo Grande Mato Grosso do Sul 79080090 Brazil E-mail: evenycristine@yahoo.com.br.

OLIVEIRA, FABRICIO FERREIRA DE, neurologist; b. Campinas, São Paulo, Brazil, Aug. 17, 1976; MD, State U. Rio de Janeiro, 1999; MSc, U. Campinas, 2009. Physician SARAH Network Rehab. Hosp., cons., brain injured patients rehab. program, 2002—03, leader, 2003—04; med. resident, neurology U. Campinas, 2005—07, med. rschr., neurology, 2007—09, Fed. U. São Paulo, 2010—; neurologist Hosp. São Camilo Pompéia, 2007—. Substitute physician Intensive Care Units, Amil Hosp., Rio de Janeiro, 2000—02; med. resident, internal medicine Fed. U. Rio de Janeiro, 2000—02; healthcare cons. Gerson Lehrman Group, 2011. Recipient Internat. Scholarship award, Am. Acad. Neurology, 2009, Prêmio Roberto Melaragno Filho award, Assn. Paulista Medicina, Assn. Paulista Neurologia, 2009; fellowship, World Fedn. Neurology, 2005. Mem.: Assn. Brasileira Medicina Urgência e Emergência, World Stroke Orgn., Acad. Brasileira Neurologia. Avocations: bullfighting, poetry. Home: Rua Leandro Dupret 377/144 Vila Clement São Paulo 04025011 Brazil Personal E-mail: fabricioferreiradeoliveira@hotmail.com.

OLIVEIRA, MARIA DE LOURDES AGUIAR, biologist; b. Rio de Janeiro, Oct. 29, 1964; Degree in Biology, FF Celso Lisboa, 1987; PhD in Cellular and Molecular Biology, Oswaldo Cruz Found., 2008. Technologist Nat. Reference Inst. Quality Control Health, Oswaldo Cruz Found., MoH, 1987—93, head immunodiagnostic svc., 1990—93; technologist pub. health & rsch. Nat. Reference Lab. Viral Hepatitis Oswaldo Cruz Inst., Oswaldo Cruz Found., MoH, 1993—2008, quality mgr. Nat. Reference Lab. Viral Hepatitis, technologist pub. health & rsch., quality mgr. Nat. Reference Lab. Influenza and Measles, 2008—, mem. Com. Reference Lab., 2008. Grant, Ctrs. Diseases Control and Prevention, fellow, Robert Koch Inst., Germany, Deutsche Gesellschaft für Technische Zusammenarbeit, Germany. Mem.: Virored, Programa Iberoamericano de Ciencia y Tecnología para el Desarrollo (Spain) (grant). Avocations: reading, music, movies. Office: Fiocruz HPP SlB105 Ave Brasil 4365 Rio de Janeiro 21040-360 Brazil Business E-Mail: mlaoliveira@fiocruz.br.

OLIVEIRA, MARIA RITA MARQUES, nutritionist, educator; b. Jaú, São Paulo, Brazil, Sept. 20, 1959; Grad. in Nutrition, U. SC, 1983; PhD, USP, 1998. Rsch. prof. U. Estadual Paulista, 2007. Mem.: Inst. Harpia Harpyia. Avocations: reading, travel. Office: University Estadual Paulista Distrito de Ribião Jr Botucatu São Paulo 18 603 560 Brazil Office Fax: 55-14-38116232.

OLIVEIRA, VENEZA BERENICE, medical educator; b. Divinópolis, Minas Gerais, Sept. 14, 1951; Degree, Med. Sch. Fed. U., Minas Gerais, 1976, DPH, 2006. Assoc. prof. Med. Sch. Fed. U., Minas Gerais, 1978—; pub. health rsch. Ctr. Pub. Health Edn. (NESCON), 1984, dir., 2004—05. Mem.: Postgrad. Brasilian Assoc. Pub. Health. Avocations: movies, mountain climbing, travel. Office: Av Alfredo Balena 190 Belo Horizonte Minas Gerais 30.130-100 Brazil Office Fax: 51 31 3409-9675. Business E-Mail: veneza@medicina.ufmg.br.

OLIVER, DAVID JOHN, physician, consultant; b. Oxford, Eng., Feb. 17, 1954; s. Ray and Lucy Leslie (Williams) Oliver; children: Ben, Tom. BSc, U. Coll., London, 1975; MBBS, U. Coll. Hosp., London, 1978. House physician St. Pancras Hosp., London, 1978-79; house surgeon Stoke Mandeville Hosp., Aylesbury, Eng., 1979; gen. practice trainee Swindon, Wiltshire, Eng., 1979-82; registrar St. Christopher's Hospice, London, 1982-83, sr. registrar, 1983-84; cons. physician palliative medicine, med. dir. Wisdom Hospice, Rochester, Kent, Eng., 1984—; med. dir. North Kent Healthcare NHS Trust, 1996-98, Thames Gateway NHS Trust, 1998-99. Adviser palliative care Brit. Nat. Formulary, London, 1984—2006; hon. reader palliative care U. Kent, 1999—; vis. prof. U. Zagreb, Croatia, 2002—. Author: Motor Neurone Disease-A Family Affair, 2011; editor (with G. D. Borasio, D. Walsh): Palliative Care in Amyotrophic Lateral Sclerosis, 2d edit., 2006; author: 3rd edit., 2011. Recipient Thumbs Up award, Motor Neurone Disease Assn. Eng., 1993, Humanitarian award, Internat. Alliance ALS/MND Assns., 2003. Fellow: Royal Coll. Physicians (London), Royal Coll. Gen. Practitioners, Royal Soc. Medicine (London); mem.: Brit. Med. Assn. Avocations: photography, walking. Office: Wisdom Hospice High Bank Rochester ME12NU England Personal E-mail: D.J.Oliver@kent.ac.uk. Business E-Mail: david.oliver1@nhs.net.

OLIVER, GARY J., psychologist, educator; b. Great Falls, Mont., Sept. 20, 1947; m.Linda Ellen Motz, April 3, 2010; children: Nathan, Matthew, Andrew. ThM, Fuller Sem., 1977; MA, U. Nebr., 1980, PhD, 1984. Cert. clin. psychology, Nebr., Colo., Ark. Sr. staff psychologist Lincoln Family Med. Group, Nebr., 1984—86; clin. dir. SW Counseling Assocs., Littleton, Colo., 1986—98; exec. dir., prof. psychology and practical theology The Ctr. for Relationship Enrichment, John Brown U., Siloam Springs, Ark., 1998—. Acad. dir., prof. Denver Sem., 1988—; sr. fellow Coun. Christian Colls. and Univs., 1999-2007 Co-author: (with Carrie Oliver) Raising Sons...And Loving It!, 2000, Mad About Us, 2007, A Woman's Forbidden Emotion, 2005; author: Fears, Doubts, Blues & Pouts, 1999, Real Men Have Feelings Too, 1993; editor Marriage and Family Christian Jour.; contbr. over 250 articles to profl. jours. and popular mags. Mem. APA, ACA, Am. Assn. Christian Counselors (bd. mem.), Am. Assn. for Marriage and Family Therapy, Assn. for Psychol. Type, Nat. Coun. on Family Rels., Christian Assn. for Psychol. Studies, Ctr. Relationship Enrichment. Achievements include Dr. Gary J. Oliver endowed chair for marriage family & relationship studies. Office: Ctr for Relationship Enrichment John Brown Univ 2000 W University St Siloam Springs AR 72761-2112 Office Phone: 479-524-7105. Business E-Mail: cre@jbu.edu.

OLIVER, MICHAEL FRANCIS, physician, consultant cardiologist, educator; b. Wales, July 3, 1925; s. Wilfrid F.L. and Cecilia B. (Daniel) O.; m. Margaret Y. Abbey, Oct. 12, 1948 (div. 1979); children: John (dec.), Sarah, Mark, Paul; m. Helen Louise Daniel, June 28, 1985. MB, U. Edinburgh, Scotland, 1947, MD, 1957; MD (hon.), Karolinska Inst., Stockholm, 1980, Bologna U., Italy, 1986. Personal prof. cardiology U. Edinburgh, 1974-78, Duke of Edinburgh prof. medicine and cardiology, chmn. dept., 1978-89; dir. Wynn Inst. for Metabolic Rsch., London, 1989-93; hon. prof. Nat. Heart and Lung Inst. U. London, 1993-99, emeritus prof., 1999—. Com. mem. Med. Rsch. Coun., London, 1982-86; chmn. panel on cardiac fitness Dept. Transport, 1989-90; cons. Dept. Health, U.K., 1980-99, WHO, Geneva, 1975-2001. Editor 5 books on sci. aspects of heart disease; contbr. over 350 articles on heart disease, biochemistry and epidemiology to med. jours. Decorated comdr. Order Brit. Empire. Fellow Royal Soc. Edinburgh, Royal Coll. Physicians (London), Royal Coll. Physicians (Edinburgh) (pres. 1986-89), Brit. Cardiac Soc. (pres. 1980-84), Athenaeum (London), Garrick (London). Office: Keepier Wharf 12 Narrow St E14 8DH London England E-mail: michaeloliver@mac.com.

OLIVER, STEFAN LYNE, medical researcher; b. Derby, Eng., Jan. 2, 1973; BSc in Immunology, U. East London, 1995; PhD in Vet. Virology, Royal Vet. Coll., Eng., 2003. Rsch. assoc. Stanford U. Sch. Medicine, 2010—. Sci. and Engring. Collaborative grant, Biotech. and Biol. Scis. Rsch. Coun. Mem.: Assn. Vet. Tchrs. and Rsch. Workers, Soc. Gen. Microbiology, Vet. Rsch. Club, Am. Soc. Microbiology, Am. Soc. Virology. Avocation: motorcycling. Office: Stanford University Sch Medicine Stanford CA 94305 Business E-Mail: sloliver@stanford.edu.

OLIVER, STEPHEN PAUL, physiologist, educator; b. Cortland, NY, Oct. 19, 1952; MS, Ohio State U., 1978, PhD, 1980. Asst. prof. U. Mass., 1980—84, U. Tenn., 1984—87, assoc. prof., 1987—92, prof. animal sci., 1992—2010, asst. dean, UT AgResearch, 2010—. Editor-in-chief foodborne pathogens & disease MaryAnn Libert Publs., 2004—11; grant rev. panel USDA, 2005—06; external sci. expert Can. Bovine Mastitis Rsch. Network, 2006—10; bd. dirs. Nat. Mastitis Coun., 2009—10; sci. adv. panel Dairy Mgmt. Inc., 2010—11. Recipient Merck Merial AgVet Dairy Mgmt. Rsch. award, Am. Dairy Sci. Assn., 1998, Land O'Lakes, Inc. award, 2002, Group Recognition award, US FDA, 2003, Chancellor's award, U. Tenn., 2006, Pfizer Animal Health Physiology award, Am. Dairy Sci. Assn., 2006. Fellow: Am. Acad. Microbiology; mem.: Mastitis Rsch. Workers, Nat. Mastitis Coun., Gamma Sigma Delta, Soc. Phi Zeta (Phi chpt.) (hon.). Avocations: boating, fishing, coin collecting/numismatics. Office: 103 Morgan Hall 2621 Morgan Cir Knoxville TN 37996 Office Fax: 865-974-6479. Business E-Mail: soliver@utk.edu.

OLIVER, THORNAL GOODLOE, retired health facility administrator; b. Memphis, Aug. 26, 1934; s. John Robert Oliver and Evelyn Doris Mitchell (Goodloe); m. Pauline Reid Oliver, Oct. 1, 1959. BS, Tenn. State U., Nashville, 1956; MHA, Washington U., St. Louis, 1973. Cert. nursing home adminstr., Mo. Asst. dir. King Meml. Hosp., Kansas City, Mo., 1973—75; evening mgr. Truman Med. Ctr., 1975—77; asst. adminstr. Mid-Am. Radiation Ctr. U. Kans. Coll. Health Sci., Kans., 1977—81; dir. CHS, Inc., Leawood, 1981—82; adminstr. Poplar Bluff Hosp., Mo., 1982—83, Benjamin F. Lee Health Ctr., Wilberforce, Ohio, 1983—86; asst. clin. prof., dept. cmty. medicine Wright State U., Dayton, 1986—89; asst. patent adminstr. Munson Army Hosp., Ft. Leavenworth, Kans., 1987—2004; ret., 2004; cons. Urban Health Assocs., Nashville, 1986—87. Contbr. articles to profl. jours. With US Army, 1957—59, with USAR, 1959—63. Fellow: Am. Coll. Hosp. Adminstrs.; mem.: Mo. League of Nursing Home Adminstrs., Am. Med. Record Assn., Nat. Assn. Health Svcs. Execs., Am. Hosp. Assn. Home: 10641 N Grand Ave Kansas City MO 64155-1655

OLIVERI, EUGENE ALFRED, gastroenterologist; b. NYC, Apr. 30, 1937; children: Gregory, Lisa, Michelle. Student, Bklyn. Coll., 1954-56, 58-60; DO summa cum laude, Kansas City Coll., 1964; LHD, U. Health Scis., 2000; MSc, Trinity So. U., 2003; D of Osteopathic Edn., U. New Eng., Biddeford, Maine, 2007. Diplomate Am. Bd. Internal Medicine, Am. Bd. Gastroenterology. Intern Detroit Osteo. Hosp., 1964-65; resident in internal medicine Botsford/Ziegler Hosps., 1965-67; fellowship in gastroenterology VA Hosp., East Orange, NJ, 1967-68; asst. dean Coll. Osteo. Medicine Mich. State U. Prof. dept. internal medicine sect. of gastroenterology Botsford Gen. Hosp., assoc. program dir. gastroenterology residency emeritus; mem., courtesy staff emeritus dept. of internal medicine Huron Valley Hosp. Trustee Pikeville (Ky.) Coll., 1998—2004, U. New Eng., Biddeford, Maine, 2001—. With US Army, 1956—58. Recipient Highest Acad. Achievement award Mead-Johnson, 1964, Outstanding Alumni Achievement award U. for Health Scis., Coll. Osteo. Medicine, 1991, Dr. J.O. Watson Disting. Lecr. Ohio Osteo. Assn., 1991, Walter Patenge medal for humanitarian svc. MSU, 1999, Galusha Meml. lectr., 1999, FSMB A.T. Still Meml. Lecture award, AOA, 2009, Phillips medal Pub Svc., Ohio U., 2002; named Physician of Yr. Mich. chpt. Ileitis and Colitis Found., 1985, Botsford Profl. Staff, 1994, Riland medal, Pub. Soc. NYIT, 2011. Fellow Am. Coll. Osteo. Internists (pres. 1982-83, Disting. Svc. award 1982, Disting. Lectr. award 1983, Presdl. Leadership award 2010); fellow Am. Coll. Internists (master); mem. Am. Osteo. Assn. (pres. 1999-2000, trustee mem. bd., Disting. Svc. certificat 2005, pioneer medicine 2008), Mich. Assn. Osteo. Physician and Surgeons (pres. 1991-92), Oakland County Osteo. Assn., Am. Coll. Gastroenterology, Am. Soc. Gastrointestinal Endoscopy, Am. Soc. Addiction Medicine, Am. Osteo. Found. (bd. dirs., past pres. bd. dirs., com. on awards), Mich. Osteo. Coll. Found. (chair, trustee, bd. dirs.), Crohn's and Colitis Found. Am. (Physician of Yr. 1991), Psi Sigma Alpha, Sigma Sigma Phi. Avocations: cooking, health policy. Home: 844 Old Milford Farms Milford MI 48381-3363 Personal E-mail: picooliveri@aol.com.

OLKKONEN, SEPPO KULLERVO, physician; b. Perniö, Sami Olkkonen, Finland, Sept. 28, 1947; s. Paavali Olkkonen and Mirjam Sirkiä; m. Eija Raikaslehto, Aug. 7, 1999; children: Elina Vähäkylä, Sami, Mikko Tolvanen. MD, U. Helsinki, Finland, 1978; PhD, U. Kuopio, Eastern Finland, 1993. Pers. med. officer IRCO Contractors Group Finnish Bldg. Firm, Baghdad, Iraq, 1978—80; occupl. health physician Mehiläinen, Helsinki, 1987—88; physician Rehab. Ctr. Korpilampi, Espoo, Finland, 1988—92, chief med. officer, 1992—99, Alfta Rehab Ctr., Hälsingland, Sweden, 1997—98; subs. chief med. officer Imatra Health Ctr., Eastern Finland, 1999—2000; chief med. officer Lappeenrannan työkuntokeskus Oy, Lappeenranta, Finland, 2004—06, Finnish Inst. Occupl. Health, Helsinki, 2000—10; physician Health Ctr. Vantaa, Finland, 1981—84; asst. physician Aurora Hosp., Clinic Surgery, Helsinki, 1984—86; occupl. health physician Mehiläinen, Helsinki, 1987—88. Physician Rd. Accident Investigation Team, Helsinki, 1988—2007; cons. transport and traffic sect Finnish Assn. Indsl. Medicine, Helsinki, 1995—, mem. bd., 2007—. Grants, Swedish Assn. Traffic Medicine, 1994. Mem.: Finnish Assn. Occupl. Physicians (mem. bd. 2007—), Finnish Assn. Traffic Medicine (chmn. 1993—94). Avocations: tennis, golf, photography. Home: Rajasaarentie 7 A 2 Helsinki FI-00250 Finland Office: Finnish Inst Occupl Health Topeliuksenkatu 41 a A Helsinki FI-00250 Finland Office Fax: 358304742008. Personal E-mail: seppo.olkkonen@fimnet.fi. Business E-Mail: seppo.olkkonen@ttl.fi.

OLMEDO, DANIEL GUSTAVO, dentist, researcher; b. Córdoba, Argentina, Feb. 10, 1970; s. Guillermo Olmedo. PhD, Univ. of Cordoba, Argentina, 2001. Tchr. Sch. Dentistry, U. Buenos Aires, 1998; asst. rschr. NRC (CONICET), 2005—. Contbr. scientific papers to profl. jours. Achievements include research in metallic biomaterials - titanium corrosion - macrophages. Home: Fitz Roy 2272 - 1 E Buenos Aires 1425 Argentina Office: Univ Buenos Aires Sch Dentistry Marcelo T de Alvear 2142 - 2 A Buenos Aires 1122 Argentina Business E-Mail: dolmedo@argentina.com.

OLMEZ, NESE, medical educator; b. Milas, Mugla, Feb. 20, 1968; Assoc. prof. Ege U., 1992, Izmir Ataturk Egitim Ve Arastirma Hastanesi, 1993—. Avocations: music, painting, reading. Office: Atatürk Training and Research Hosp Izmir 35360 Turkey E-mail: neseolmez@yahoo.com.

OLNESS, KAREN NORMA, medical educator; b. Rushford, Minn., Aug. 28, 1936; d. Norman Theodore and Karen Agnes (Gunderson) O.; m. Hakon Daniel Torjesen, 1962. BA, U. Minn., 1958, BS, MD, 1961. Diplomate Am. Bd. Pediat., Am. Bd. Med. Hypnosis, Develop. & Behavioral Pediatrics. Intern Harbor Gen. Hosp., Torrance, Calif.; resident Nat. Children's Hosp. Med. Ctr., Washington; asst. prof. George Washington U., Washington, 1970-74; assoc. prof. U. Minn., Mpls., 1974-87; prof. pediat., family medicine and global health Case Western Res. U., Cleve., 1987—. Named Outstanding Woman Physician, Minn. Assn. Women Physicians, 1987; recipient Christopherson award Am. Acad. Pediat., 1998, Aldrich award, Am. Acad. Pediat., 1999, Ann. award Soc. Devel. and Behavioral Pediat., 2003, Outstanding Alumni award U. Minn., 2007, Hon. Doc. award, Khon Kaen U., 2007, Tow Humanism award, 2008, Benjamin Franklin Gold Medal, Inst. Soc. Hypnosis, 2009; named to Cleve. Med. Hall of Fame, 2000. Fellow: Soc. Clin. and Exptl. Hypnosis (pres. 1991—93), Am. Soc. Clin. Hypnosis (pres. 1984—86), Am. Acad. Pediat. (chair internat. health sect. 2001), Am. Acad. Family Physicians; mem.: Internat. Hypnosis Soc. (pres. 2003—06), Northwestern Pediat. Soc. (pres. 1977), Soc. Devel. and Behavioral Pediat. (pres. 1992). Office: Case Western Res U 11100 Euclid Ave Cleveland OH 44106-6038 Office Phone: 216-368-4368.

OLNEY, JOHN WILLIAM, psychiatry professor; b. Marathon, Iowa, Oct. 23, 1931; married, 1957; 3 children. BA, U. Iowa, 1957, MD, 1963. Diplomate Am. Bd. Psychiatry, Am. Bd. Neurology. Intern Kaiser Permanente Found., San Francisco, 1963-64; resident, 1964-68; from instr. to assoc. prof. psychiatry Washington U., St. Louis, 1968-77, prof. psychiatry and neuropathology Sch. Medicine, 1977—. NIMH biol. sci. trainee Washington U., 1966-68; asst. psychiatrist Barnes Hosp., 1968—; cons. psychiatrist Malcolm Bliss Mental Health Ctr., 1968—; elected to Inst. Medicine/NAS, 1996. Recipient Wakeman award Rsch. Neurosci., 1992; co-recipient Charles A. Dana award for Pioneering Achievements in Health, 1994. Mem. APA, Am. Assn Neuropathology, Soc. Neurosci. Assn. Rsch. Nervous & Mental Disorders, Psychiatric Rsch. Soc. Achievements include research in role of excitatory neurotoxins in disorders of the nervous system. Office: Washington U Dept Psychiatry Sch Med Saint Louis MO 63110

OLOFSSON, JAN GUNNAR VILHELM, otolaryngologist, head and neck surgeon, educator, director; b. Malmoe, Sweden, Mar. 28, 1940; s. Gunnar Valdemar and Siri Elisabeth (Persson) Olofsson; m. Margareta Ingegerd Persson, 1973 (div. 1989); children: Charlotta, Matilda, Lovisa, Stefan; life ptnr. Anne Berit Guttormsen, 1990. MD, Lund U., Sweden, 1967; PhD, Linköping U., Sweden, 1973. Specialist in otorhinolaryngology/head and neck surgery. Asst. prof. dept. otolaryngology U. Linköping (Sweden), 1973-75, assoc. prof., 1975-87, head dept. otolaryngology, 1986-87; prof., chmn. dept. otolaryngology/head and neck surgery Univ. Hosp., Bergen, Norway, 1987—, dir. head and neck divsn., 1995-99; dep. CEO Haukeland U. Hosp., Bergen, 2000-2001, med. dir., 2001—02, dir. head and neck divsn., 2003—, chmn. Common Rsch. Ctr., 2001—07; chief med. advisor, dir. Innovest. Mem. editl. bd. Acta Otolaryngologica, 1988-2000, Clin. Otolaryngology, 1980—, Jour. Otolaryngology, 1972-95, Reports of Practical Oncology and Radiotherapy, 2003—, Auris Nasus Larynx, 2005—, Internat. jour. Otolaryngology, 2008-; European Archives Otorhinolaryngology and Head and Neck, 1998-99, mng. editor, 2000—; contbr. over 270 articles to internat. jours., chpts. to textbooks. Mem.: Confederation European ORL HNS (pres. 2009—11), Royal Belg. Soc. ORL (EUFOS pres. 2007—), Internat. Acad. Oral Oncology, European Acad. Otorhinolaryngology Head and Neck Surgery (founding mem.), European Fedn. Otorhinolaryngol. Soc. (pres. 2007—), Internat. Fedn. Otorhinolaryngol. Socs. (chmn. ad hoc. com. laryngology, brnchi, trachea, esophagus), European Head Neck Soc. (founding mem., v.p.), Royal Soc. Medicine Gt. Britain, La Societa de Scienze Mediche di Conegliano Vittorio Veneto, European Laryngological Soc. (past pres., founding mem.), Laryngeal Cancer Assn., Am. Head Neck Soc., European Soc. Surg. Oncology, Soc. Surg. Oncology, Brit. Assn. Head Neck Oncology, Scandinavian Soc. for Head and Neck Oncology (past pres., editor), Can. Soc. Otolaryngology/Head and Neck Surgery, Danish Soc. Head and Neck Oncology, Danish Soc. Otolaryngology/Head and Neck Surgery, Norwegian Med. Soc., Norwegian Otolaryn. Soc. (chmn. spec. com.), Swedish Otolaryn. Soc., Swedish Soc. of Medicine, Swedish Med. Assn., Collegium Oto-Rhino-Laryngologicum Amicitae Sacrum, Royal Belgian Soc. of ORL-HNS (hon.), German Acad. Otorhinolaryngol. Head and Neck Soc. (hon.), German Soc. Otorhinolaryngology Head and Neck Surgery (hon.), Polish Soc. Otorhinolaryngol. Head and Neck Surgery (hon.), Bergenhus Rotary Club (past pres.,). Home Phone: 47 5531 6554; Office Phone: 47-55972669. Office Fax: 47-55974956. Business E-Mail: jan.olofsson@haukeland.no.

OLOMU, ADESUWA B., physician, educator; b. Nigeria, Dec. 8, 1954; MD, U. Benin, Nigeria, 1978; MS, Mich. State U., 2007. Assoc. prof. Mich. State U., 2000—. Attending physician Sparrow Hosp., 2000. Fellow: ACP; mem.: Alpha Omega Alpha Honor Med. Soc. Avocations: travel, reading, music. Office: B329 Clinical Ctr Mich State University East Lansing MI 48824 Business E-Mail: ade.olomu@hc.msu.edu.

OLOPADE, OLUFUNMILAYO FALUSI (FUNMI OLOPADE), geneticist, educator, oncologist, hematologist; b. Nigeria, Apr. 29, 1957; m. Christopher Sola Olopade; 3 children. MD with distinction, U. Ibadan, Nigeria, 1980. Diplomate Am. Bd. Internal Medicine, Am. Bd. Med. Oncology, Am. Bd. Hematology; lic. MD Ill., Ind. Med. officer Nigerian Navy Hosp.; intern in medicine, surgery, pediatrics, ob-gyn. Univ. Coll. Hosp., Ibadan, 1980—81; intern in internal medicine Cook County Hosp., Chgo., 1983—84, resident in internal medicine, 1984—86, chief resident in medicine, 1986; clin. instr. U. Ill. Abraham Lincoln Sch. Medicine, Chgo., 1986—87; postdoctoral fellow jt. sect. hematology/oncology U. Chgo., 1987—91, asst. prof. hematology/oncology, Pritzker Sch. Medicine, 1991—2002, mem. Cancer Rsch. Ctr., 1991—, mem. Cancer Biology com., 1994—, mem. Genetics com., 1996—, assoc. prof. medicine, prof. medicine and human genetics Ill., 2002—, dir. Ctr. for Clinical Cancer Genetics, Cancer Risk Clinic Ill., 1992—, dir. Hematology/Oncology Fellowship Program Ill., 1998—. Attending physician Cook County Hosp., Chgo., 1987; mem. steering com., cooperative family registry for breast cancer studies, Nat. Cancer Inst., also mem. adv. com. Cancer Genetics Network and bd. scientific counselors; mem. adv. bd. Cancerandcareers.org; lectr. in field. Ad hoc reviewer Jour. AMA, Genes, Chromosomes and Cancer, Genomics, Human Molecular Genetics, Cancer Rsch., Blood, Molecular Carcinogenesis, Jour. Clin. Oncology, New Eng. Jour. Medicine; contbr. articles to profl. jours.; contbr. to book chpts. and abstracts on topics including genetics of cancer. Mem. med. adv. bd. Young Survival Coalition. Recipient Sir Samuel Manuwa Gold medal for Excellence in Clin. Sciences, 1980, Scholar award, James S. McDonnell Found., 1992, Doris Duke Disting. Clin. Scientist award, 2000, Phenomenal Women award, 2003, People Are Today's Heroes (PATH), Gov. Rod R. Blagojevich, presented by First Lady Patti Blagojevich, State Ill., 2005, Heroes In Healthcare award, Access Cmty. Network, 2005; named a Top Doctor, Chicago Mag., 1997; named an Outstanding Woman of Achievement, YWCA Metropolitan Chgo., 2008; fellow John D. and Catherine T. MacArthur Found., 2005; Ellen Ruth Lebow Fellowship, Assn. for Brain Tumor Rsch., 1990. Mem. AAAS, Inst. Medicine, Am. Assn. Cancer Rsch. (membership credentialing com. 1994-95, program com. carcinogenesis subcom. 1993; Minorities in Cancer Rsch. Jane Cooke Wright lectureship, 2006), Am. Soc. Clin. Oncology (mem. program com. subcom. tumor biology and genetics 1997, Young Investigator award, 1991), Am. Assn. Preventive Oncology, Women in Cancer Rsch., Am. Soc. Hematology, Am. Coll. Physicians, Am. Soc. Breast Disease, Am. Soc. Hematology, Assn. Am. Professors, Nigerian Med. Assn., Am. Cancer Soc. (adv. com. cancer control investigations, epidemiology, diagnosis, therapy 1994-97). Office: U Chgo Med Ctr 5841 S Maryland Ave # MC2115 Chicago IL 60637-1463 Office Phone: 773-702-1632, 773-702-6149. Office Fax: 773-702-0963. Business E-Mail: folopade@medicine.bsd.uchicago.edu.

O'LOUGHLIN, KATHLEEN T., dental association administrator; BA in Biology, cum laude, Boston U., 1973; DMD summa cum laude, Tufts U. Sch. Dental Medicine, Medford, Mass., 1981; MA in Health Care Mgmt., Harvard Sch. Pub. Health, Boston, 1998. Tchg. cert. Suffolk U., Boston. Pvt. practice gen. dentistry, Medford, 1981—2001; pres., CEO Dental Svcs. Mass. Inc./Delta Dental Mass., 2002—07; chief dental officer, v.p. quality & care mgmt. United Healthcare, Columbia, Md.; exec. dir., COO ADA, 2009—. Asst. clin. prof. Tufts U. Sch. Dental Medicine, 1996—, bd. trustees, 2006—; clin. instr. Boston U. Goldman Sch. Grad. Dentistry; bd. dirs. Children's Dental Health Project, Washington, Oral Health America; past pres. Oral Health Found. Mass. Mem.: ADA, Tufts U. Sch. Dental Medicine Alumni Assn., East Middlesex Dist. Dental Soc., Pierre Fouchard Acad., Mass. Dental Soc., Am. Assn. Women Dentists, Internat. Coll. Dentists, Am. Coll. Dentists, Omicron Kappa Upsilon. Office: ADA 211 E Chgo Ave Chicago IL 60611 Office Phone: 312-440-2500. *

OLSEN, BJORN R., science educator, researcher; MD. PhD, U. Oslo, 1967, PhD (hon.), U. Medicine and Dentistry NJ. Faculty mem. Anatomical Inst., 1967—71; faculty mem., dept. biochemistry to prof. Rutgers Med. Sch. (now U. Medicine and Dentistry NJ-Robert Wood Johnson Med. Sch.), 1971—76; Hersey Prof. Anatomy and Cellular Biology, now changed title to Hersey Prof. Cell Biology Harvard Med. Sch., 1985—; sr. staff mem. Forsyth Inst., 1996—; prof. develop. biology Harvard Sch. Dental Medicine, 1996—, dean rsch., prof. develop. biology, 2005—. Contbr. several articles to profl. jours.; mem. editl. bds. of several profl. jours. Recipient Humboldt Rsch. award, Sr. Rsch. prize, Am. Soc. Matrix Biology. Mem.: Norwegian Acad. Sciences, Internat. Soc. for Matrix Biology (former pres.), ScanBalt Acad. Office: Dept Cell Biology Harvard Medical Sch 240 Longwood Ave Office REB 409 Boston MA 02115 Office Phone: 617-432-1874. Office Fax: 617-432-0638. Business E-Mail: bjorn_olsen@hms.harvard.edu.

OLSEN, CHRISTOPHER MARK, research scientist; b. New Orleans, Aug. 20, 1972; s. David M. and Patricia S. Olsen. BA, Baylor U., Tex., 1994; MS, Tex. Tech U., 1998. Tchg. asst. Tex. Tech U., Lubbock, 1996—97, rsch. asst., 1997—98; grad. rsch. fellow U. of Tex., Austin, 1998—. Sec. Pharmacy Grad. Student Assn. U. of Tex., Austin, Tex., 1999—2000, treas., 2000—01, pres., 2001—02, West Austin I Toastmasters, Austin, 2000—01. Recipient Hon. Mention for Poster, Soc. for Integrative and Comparative Biology, 1996; grantee Grant-in-Aid of Rsch., NAS through Sigma Xi, 1997; fellow Rsch. Fellowship, U. of Tex., 1998—99, Tng. Grant Fellowship, Nat. Inst. on Alcohol Abuse and Alcoholism, 1999—2003. Mem.: Toastmasters Internat., Soc. for Neuroscience, Sigma Xi, N.Y. Acad. of Scis., Phi Kappa Phi. Avocation: mountain biking. Office: U of Tex Bldg ARC 2701 Speedway Austin TX 78712 Personal E-mail: colsen@mail.utexas.edu.

OLSEN, CHRISTOPHER W., molecular virologist; BS, St. Lawrence U., Canton, NY, 1979; DVM, Cornell U., Ithaca, NY, 1982, PhD, 1992. Postdoc. fellowship U. Wis. Sch. Vet. Medicine, Madison, 1992—95, prof. pub. health, 1996—, assoc. dean academic affairs, 2006—. Contbr. articles to profl. jours. Recipient Norden Disting. Tchr. award, U. Wis. Sch. Vet. Medicine, 1996, Walter F. Renk Disting. Prof. award, 2005. Achievements include research in the molecular epidemiology of animal influenza A viruses (especially swine viruses) and studies to determine the genetic factors that control interspecies transmission of influenza A viruses. Office: U Wis Sch Vet Medicine Office 2268 2015 Linden Dr Madison WI 53706 Office Fax: 608-263-2625. E-mail: olsenc@vetmed.wisc.edu, olsenc@svm.vetmed.wisc.edu. *

OLSEN, INGER ANNA, retired psychologist; b. Copper Mountain, BC, Can., Dec. 25, 1926; BS, Wash. State U., 1954, MS, 1956, PhD, 1962. Psychiat. nurse Provincial Mental Health Svcs. B.C., 1947-51, psychologist, 1956-58, Vancouver (B.C.) City Met. Health Svcs., 1958-60; psychologist Student Counseling Ctr., Wash. State U., Pullman, 1960—62; sr. psychologist Met. Health Svcs., Vancouver, 1962-66; instr. psychology Langara Coll., Vancouver, B.C., 1966—87; ret., 1987. Contbr. articles to profl. jours. Docent Vancouver Aquarium Assn.; bd. dirs. Second Mile Soc., 1975—89. Mem. APA, Gerontol. Soc. Am., Can. Assn. Gerontology, Phi Beta Kappa, Sigma Xi, Alpha Kappa Delta. Home: 1255 Bidwell St Apt 1910 Vancouver BC Canada V6G 2K8

OLSEN, LISBETH HØIER, veterinarian, educator; b. Roskilde, Denmark, Mar. 7, 1968; d. Flemming Holger and Inge Høier Jensen; m. Bjarne Ostdal, Sept. 1, 2007; children: Sara Høier, Nina Høier, Aske Høier. DVM, Royal Vet. and Agrl. U., 1996, DSc in Vet. Sci., 2005. Asst. prof. dept. basic animal and vet. scis. Royal Vet. and Agrl. U. (now called U. Copenhagen), 2000—03, assoc. prof., 2003—11, prof. MSO clin. pharmacology & toxicology, 2011—. Lectr. in field; presenter in field. Contbr. articles to profl. jours. Recipient award, Aage and Edith Dyssegaard's Found., 2000, Intervet Scandinavia AS Found., 2000, The Danish Agrl. and Vet. Rsch. Coun., 2000, IAMS, 2001; grantee, various grants, 2000—08, Danish Coun. Independent Rsch., 2006—11. Mem.: European Soc. Vet. Cardiology. Office: University Copenhagen Dept Vet Disease Biology 9 Ridebanevej Frederiksberg 1870 Denmark Office Phone: 45 35332524, 45 35333175. E-mail: liho@life.ku.dk.

OLSEN, MARTIN E., obstetrician, educator, inventor; b. Morgantown, W.Va., 1959; m. Natalie Ann Maschmann, June 25, 1985; 1 child, Karen Rebeca. BS, Muskingum Coll., New Concord, 1981; MD, Med. Coll. Ohio, Toledo, 1981. Diplomate Am. Bd. Ob-Gyn. Resident in family practice Akron (Ohio) Gen. Med. Ctr., 1985-88; resident in ob-gyn. U. Tenn., Chattanooga, 1989-91; mem. faculty E. Tenn. State U., Johnson City, 1992—, chmn. dept. ob-byn., 1999—2009; dir. residency program Johnson City Med. Ctr., 1994—. Contbr. articles to profl. jours. Office: PO Box 70569 Johnson City TN 37614-1707 Office Phone: 423-439-8097. Business E-Mail: olsen@etsu.edu.

OLSEN, ØYSTEIN, physics professor; b. Bodø, Norway, June 3, 1964; PhD, Norwegian U. Sci. and Tech., 2010. Assoc. prof. Sør-Trøndelag U. Coll., 2001—. Mem.: Internat. Soc. Magnetic Resonance in Medicine. Office: Olav Kyrres Gate 9 Trondheim 7000 Norway E-mail: oystein.olsen@hist.no.

OLSEN, RICHARD GALEN, biomedical engineer, consultant; b. Colo. Springs, Colo., Aug. 10, 1945; s. Floyd Edwin and Ruth Elizabeth (Robinson) O.; m. Karen Fidler Brubaker, June 17, 1973 (dec.); children: Kathryn Elizabeth, Nickolas Robert. BSEE, U. Mo., Rolla, 1968; MS, U. Utah, 1970, PhD, 1975. Registered profl. engr., Fla. Engr. Bendix Corp., Kansas City, Mo., 1968-69; elec. engr. Naval Aerospace Med. Rsch. Lab., Pensacola, Fla., 1975-79, chief engring. systems divsn., 1979-82, head bioengring. divsn., 1982-94; head bioengring. dept. Naval Health Rsch. Ctr. Detachment, Brooks AFB, Tex., 1994-2000; cons. in bioelectromagnetics Pensacola, 2001—. Tech. cons. Naval Sea Sys. Command, Arlington, Va., 1989—91, Naval Surface Warfare Ctr., Dahlgren, Va., 1989—95, Armstrong Lab. USAF, 1991—99, Naval Command, Control and Ocean Surveillance Command, San Diego, 1996—97, Selicor, Inc., 2001—04. Contbr. articles to profl. jours. and books. With U.S. Army, 1970-72. Recipient Fred A. Hitchcock award Aerospace Physiologist Aerospace Med. Assn., 1987, Award for Excellence in Tech. Transfer, Fed. Lab. Consortium, 2004; named Engr. of the Yr., N.W. Fla. Engrs. Coun., 1991. Mem. IEEE (life sr., chmn. Pensacola sect. 1982-83, SCC-28 and SCC-34 coms. 1982-2000, cert. of appreciation 1983), Bioelectromagnetics Soc. (charter, editl. bd. 1990-96), Sigma Xi, Eta Kappa Nu, Tau Beta Pi, Phi Kappa Phi. Achievements include conducting the first shipboard measurements of specific absorption rate (SAR) and of electromagnetic pulse (EMP) induced body current; patents in novel garment-mounted diathermy applicator to treat vascular insufficiency, clinically oriented combination system to provided deep muscle stimulation and battery-powered diathermy energy, elastic wire conductor, clinically oriented combination system to provide deep muscle stimulation and battery-powered diathermy energy, RF coil for hypothermia resuscitation, RF dosimetry system, personal microwave and RF detector, and RF warming of submerged extremities. Personal E-mail: olsen116@bellsouth.net.

OLSON, BARBARA FORD, physician; b. Iowa City, June 15, 1935; d. Leonard A. and Anne (Swanson) Ford; m. Robert Eric Olson, 1959 (div. 1973); children: Katherine Gee, Eric Ford, Julie Marie. BA, Gustavus Adolphus Coll., 1956; MD, U. Minn., 1960. Diplomate Am. Bd. Family Medicine, Am. Bd. Geriat. Medicine, added qualification geriat. medicine. Intern St. Paul-Ramsy Med. Ctr., 1960-61; resident in anesthesiology U. Hosp. Cleve., 1961-62, U. Minn. Hosp., Mpls., 1962-63; pvt. practice anesthesiology St. Johns Hosp. and Devine Redeemer Hosp., St. Paul, 1963-67, Mercy Hosp., Coon Rapids, Minn., 1967-74; staff physician Oak Terrace Nursing Home, Minnetonka, Minn., 1974-88; staff physician, med. dir. geriatric evaluation clinic VA Med. Ctr., St. Cloud, Minn., 1988—. Pres. Alpha Epsilon Iota Med. Found., Mpls., 1980—86, bd. dirs., 2003—. Mem. Minn. Med. Assn., Minn. Women Physicians (pres. 1981-82, 2009-, bd. dirs. 81-82, 2004-). Office: VA Med Ctr 4801 8th St N Saint Cloud MN 56303-2015 Home: P O Box 27187 Minneapolis MN 55427 Business E-Mail: Barbara.Olson@va.gov.

OLSON, JACK CONRAD, JR., geriatrician; b. Muskegon, Mich., 1955; BS in Chemistry, Mich. State U., 1977, BA in English, 1977; MD, U. Mich., 1984. Bd. cert. internal medicine, bd. cert. geriatric medicine. Intern U. Wis. Hosps. and Clinics, Madison, 1984—85, resident internal medicine, 1985—87, fellow geriatrics, 1987—89; assoc. med. dir. Mendota Mental Health, U. Wis., 1989—92; dir. Windermere Sr. Health Ctr., U. Chgo., 1992—99; asst. clin. prof., fellowship dir. Rush U. Med. Ctr., Chgo., 1999—. Office: 1725 W Harrison St Ste 955 Chicago IL 60612 Office Phone: 312-942-7030. Business E-Mail: jolson@rush.edu.

OLSON, MAYNARD V., science educator, researcher; Grad., Calif. Inst. Tech.; PhD in Chemistry, Stanford U. Faculty mem. Dartmouth Coll., Washington U., St. Louis; prof. genetics and medicine U. Washington, Seattle, 1992—, adj. prof. computer science and engring. Chmn., Genome Rsch. review com. NIH Genome Rsch. Inst. Recipient Genetics Soc. Am. medal, 1992, Gairdner Found. Internat. award, 2002, Promega Biotech. Rsch. award, American Soc. Microbiology, 2010. Mem.: NAS. Office: U Washington 225 Fluke Hall Genome Ctr Box 352145 Seattle WA 98195 Office Phone: 206-685-7346, 206-685-7336. Office Fax: 206-685-7344. Business E-Mail: mvo@u.washington.edu. *

OLSON, RANDALL J., ophthalmologist, educator; b. Glendale, Calif., Apr. 12, 1947; s. Ferron A. and Donna Lee (Jefferies) Olson; m. Ruth Louise Engstrom, June 10, 1970; children: Jonathan, Patrick, Anthony, Nicole, Monique. BA, U. Utah, 1970, MD, 1973. Diplomate Nat. Bd. Med. Examiners, Am. Bd. Ophthalmology. Intern Bassett Hosp., Cooperstown, NY, 1973—74; resident UCLA, 1974—77; fellow U. Fla., Gainesville, 1977—78; fellow, asst. prof. La State U., New Orleans, 1978—79; assoc. prof. ophthalmology U. Utah, Salt Lake City, 1979—82, prof., chmn. dept. ophthalmology, 1983—; chairperson Sch. Medicine Faculty Practice Orgn., 1996—. Contbr. articles to profl. jours. Bausch & Lomb fellow, 1977, grant, Nat. Eye Inst., 1978, 1981. Fellow: Am. Acad. Ophthalmology; mem.: AMA, Assn. U. Profs. Ophthalmology (sec.-treas. 1982—84), Am. Soc.

Cataract and Refractive Surgery. Republican. Mem. Lds Ch. Office: John A Moran Eye Ctr 65 Mario Capecchi Dr Salt Lake City UT 84132 Business E-Mail: randallj.olson@hsc.utah.edu. *

OLSON, RICHARD DAVID, psychology professor; b. Reading, Pa., Oct. 10, 1944; s. Milton Stuart and Sarah Ellen (Moyer) O.; m. M. Gayle Augustine, Aug. 26, 1967. BA, U. Redlands, 1966; MS, St. Louis U., 1968, PhD, 1970. Lic. psychologist, La. Asst. prof. psychology U. New Orleans, 1970-74, assoc. prof., chmn. dept. psychology, 1974-79, prof., chmn. dept., 1979-81, assoc. dean Grad. Sch., 1981-82, dean, 1982-88, vice chancellor, 1984-88, rsch. prof., 1988—2000, prof. emeritus, 2000—; chmn. dept. psychology, 1995—2000. Cons. psychologist, New Orleans, 1973—2002; pres. Statis. Cons. of New Orleans, 1977-82 Editor: Learning in the Classroom, 1971, The Comma After Love, The Selected Poems of Raeburn Miller, 1994, The Collected Poems of Raeburn Miller, 1997; contbr. articles to profl. jours. Grantee HEW, 1976-81 Fellow APA, Am. Psychol. Soc.; mem. Soc. for Neurosci., Am. Statis. Assn. Home: 40 Infinity Dr Poplarville MS 39470 Office: U New Orleans Dept Psychology Lake Front New Orleans LA 70148 Office Phone: 601-795-4838. Business E-Mail: richardolson@hughes.net.

OLSON, ROBERT EUGENE, physician, biochemist, educator; b. Minn., Jan. 23, 1919; s. Ralph William and Minnie (Holtin) O.; m. Catherine Silvoso, Oct. 21, 1944; children: Barbara Lynn, Robert E., Mark Alan, Mary Ellen, Carol Louise. AB, Gustavus Adolphus Coll., 1938; PhD, St. Louis U., 1944; MD, Harvard, 1951; MD (hon.), Chiang Mai U., Thailand, 1983. Diplomate: Nat. Bd. Med. Examiners, Am. Bd. Nutrition (pres. 1962-63). Postgrad. research asst. biochemistry St. Louis U. Sch. Medicine, 1938-43, asst. biochemistry, 1943-44, Alice A. Doisy prof. biochemistry, chmn. dept. biochemistry, 1965-82, asso. prof. medicine, 1966-72, prof. medicine, 1972-82; vis. prof. (sabbatical) dept. biochemistry U. Freiburg, Breisgau, West Germany, 1970-71; also Hoffman-La Roche Co., Basel, Switzerland, 1970-71; instr. biochemistry and nutrition Harvard Sch. Pub. Health, 1946-47; research fellow Nutrition Found., 1947-49, Am. Heart Assn., 1949-51, established investigator, 1951-52; house officer Peter Bent Brigham Hosp., Boston, 1951-52; prof., head dept. biochemistry and nutrition Grad. Sch. Pub. Health U. Pitts.; lectr. medicine Sch. Medicine, 1952-65; mem. panel malnutrition Japan-U.S. Med. Scis. Program, 1965-69; dir. Nutrition Clinic, Falk Clinic, 1953-65; mem. sr. staff Presbyn. Hosp., dir. metabolic unit, 1960-65; mem. staff St. Louis U. Hosp., 1965-81; prof. biochemistry, prof. medicine, assoc. dean acad. affairs U. Pitts. Sch. Medicine, 1982-84; prof. medicine, prof. pharm. scis. SUNY-Stony Brook, 1984-90, prof. emeritus, 1990—; prof. pediatrics U. South Fla., Tampa, 1994—. Cons. Mercy Hosp., U. Pitts. Med. Center; assoc. in medicine St. Margaret's Meml. Hosp., Pitts., dir. metabolic unit, 1954-60; cons. divsn. rsch. grants USPHS, 1954-69, 72-76; dir. Anemia and Malnutrition Center, Chiang Mai, Thailand, 1967-77; vis. scholar dept. biochemistry Oxford (Eng.) U., 1961-62; vis. prof. dept. biochemistry U. Freiburg, West Germany, 1970-71; food and nutrition bd. NRC, 1977-83; adv. council Nat. Inst. Arthritis, Diabetes, Digestive and Kidney Diseases, 1981-85; William A. Noyes lectr. U. Ill., Urbana, 1980. Author: Perspectives in Biological Chemistry, 1970, Methods in Medical Research, 1970, Protein-Calorie Malnutrition, 1975, Balanced Nutrition, 1989; assoc. editor Nutrition Revs., 1954-56, editor, 1978-88; assoc. editor Am. Jour. Medicine, 1956-65, Circulation Rsch., 1956-76, Am. Heart Jour., 1958-65, Am. Jour. Clin. Nutrition, 1960-66, Methods in Med. Rsch., 1963-70, Biochem. Medicine, 1967-90, Molecular and Cellular Cardiology, 1967-78, Ann. Rev. Nutrition, 1979-84, editor, 1984-94; co-editor: Vitamins and Hormones, 1975-81; author 236 original sci. papers in peer-reviewed jours.; contbr. 114 chpts. in books and major reviews to profl. jours. Bd. dirs. Nat. Nutrition Consortium, 1977-81, Am. Council on Sci. and Health, 1984-91. Lt. (j.g.) USNR, 1944-46. Recipient Fulbright award, 1961-62, Guggenheim Found. award, 1961-62, 70-71, McCollum award, 1965, Joseph Goldberger award, 1974; named Atwater Meml. lectr., 1978; Geiger Meml. lectr., 1979, William A. Noyes lectr. U. Ill., 1980, H. Brooks James lectr. N.C. State U., 1981, Virginia Beal lectr. U. Mass., 1990. Fellow ACP, Internat. Acad. Cardiovasc. Scis., Am. Pub. Health Assn. (chmn. food and nutrition sect. 1960-61), Am. Inst. Nutrition (pres. 1981-82, Conrad Elvehjem award 1998), Assn. Am. Physicians; mem. AAAS (sec. med. scis. N. sect. 1965-67), Am. Assn. Cancer Research, Am. Heart Assn., AMA (mem. council food and nutrition 1959-67, vice chmn. 1962-67), Royal Soc. Health (London), N.Y. Acad. Scis., Am. Fedn. Clin. Research, Am. Soc. Clin. Investigation, Boyleston Med. Soc., Am. Chem. Soc. (pres. biochemistry group Pitts. sect. 1960-61), Am. Soc. Biol. Chemists, Soc. Exptl. Biology and Medicine, Am. Soc. Clin. Nutrition (pres. 1961-62, McCollum award 1965, Herman award 2002), Assn. Med. Sch. Depts. Biochemistry (pres. 1979-80), Pa., St. Louis, Allegheny County med. socs., Am. Soc. Study Liver Diseases, Phi Beta Kappa, Sigma Xi, Phi Lambda Upsilon, Alpha Omega Alpha, Alpha Sigma Nu. Clubs: Cosmos (Washington), Countryside Country Club (Clearwater, Fla.). Office: U South Fla Dept Pediatrics 17 Davis Blvd Ste 200 Tampa FL 33606-3438 Home: 374 Congress St Ste 300 Boston MA 02210-1807 Office Phone: 813-259-8700. Personal E-mail: roberteolsonr@cs.com. Business E-Mail: rolson@hsc.usf.edu.

OLSON, ROBERT WILLIAM, retired counselor, writer; b. Chgo., Feb. 5, 1930; s. Milton Olaf Olson and Leonore Stillman; m. Seiko Itoyama, Jan. 16, 1955. BA, George Williams Coll., 1952; MA, U. Chgo., 1959; 7th yr. cert. counselor-cons., Oreg. State U., 1967. Tchr. 6th grade Matteson Elem. Sch., Ill., 1956—59; cons., sch. counselor elem. schs., jr. and sr. h.s., various cities Ill., Wash., 1959—91; instr. counseling U. Wash., Seattle, 1979—81; family counselor Seattle, 1980—91; ct. apptd. behavariol counselor. Behavioral rschr., U. Wash., 1979-81. Author: Memories with a Christmas Attitude, 1994, Rich Memories with a Christmas Spirit, 2005, Upstaged by Republicans, Uncertain Romantic, Political Potpouri, 2001-2010, Decade to Disaster and Skills Unrealized, 2010, other stories on Amazon Kindle reader; editor FOKUS Newsletter, 1998—; contbr. numerous articles to profl. counseling jours. Vol. Love and Forgiveness Seminar, Monroe Penitentiary, 1996—; pres. King County Guidance Assn., Wash., 1978—79; bd. mem. Children Around the World Resource Ctr. With US Army, 1952—56, Korea and Japan. Mem. NEA (life), Wash. Edn. Assn., Internat. Assn. Near-Death Studies, King County Jail (vol. 1998-), Eastside Writers Assn. (hospitality chmn. 1999—), Northwest Christian Writers Assn. Avocations: ceramics, storytelling, swimming. Home and Office: 252 168th Ave SE Bellevue WA 98008 Office Phone: 425-747-3879. Personal E-mail: membob@comcast.net.

OLSON, STANLEY WILLIAM, physician, educator, dean; b. Chgo., Feb. 10, 1914; s. David William and Agnes (Nelson) O.; m. Lorraine Caroline Lofdahl, June 26, 1936; children: Patricia Ann, Richard David, Robert Dean. BS, Wheaton Coll., 1934, LLD (hon.), 1956; MD, U. Ill., 1938; MS in Medicine (fellow), U. Minn., 1943; ScD, U. Akron, 1979, N.E Ohio U., 1985, Morehouse Sch. Medicine. Diplomate: Am. Bd. Internal Medicine. Intern Cook County Hosp., Chgo., 1938-40; asst. dir. Mayo Found., from 1947; cons. medicine Mayo Clinic, 1947—; instr. medicine grad. sch. U. Minn., 1947-50; dean and prof. coll. medicine, med. dir. Rsch. and Ednl. Hosp. U. Ill., 1950-53; dean and prof. Coll. Medicine Baylor U., Tex. Med. Ctr., Houston, 1953-66; prof. medicine Vanderbilt U.; clin. prof. medicine Meharry Med. Coll., 1966-68; dir. Tenn. Mid-South Regional Med. Program, 1967-68; dir. Div. Regional Med. Programs Svc. USPHS, 1968-70; pres. S.W. Found. for Rsch. and Edn., San Antonio, 1970-73; provost Coll. Medicine N.E. Ohio U., 1973-79, cons. med. edn. Morehouse Coll. Medicine, 1980-81; dean Morehouse Sch. Medicine, Atlanta, 1985-87. Past chmn. med. bd., chief staff Ben Taub Hosp., Jefferson Davis Hosp., Houston; nat. adv. council for health research facilities NIH, 1963-68; rev. panel constrn. med. schs. USPHS, 1964-65; spl. cons. div. Regional Med. Programs NIH, 1966-68; med. cons. bd. trustees. SUNY, 1949; cons. to Hoover Commn., 1954; mem. bd. trustees. Wheaton Coll., Ill., 1953-68. Contbr. articles to profl. jours. Capt., M.C. AUS, 1943-46. Mem. AMA, Houston Philos. Soc. (pres. 1962-63), Tex. Philos. Soc., Assn. Am. Med. Colls., Alumni Assn. Mayo Found., Sigma Xi, Alpha Kappa Kappa, Alpha Omega Alpha. Baptist. Home: 6401 Newburg Rd Apt 128 Rockford IL 61108-4322 *

OLSSON, CARL ALFRED, urologist, department chairman; b. Boston, Nov. 29, 1938; s. Charles Rudolph and Ruth Marion (Bostrom) O.; m. Mary DeVore, Nov. 4, 1962; children: Ingrid, Leif Eric. Grad., Bowdoin Coll., 1959; MD, Boston U., 1963. Diplomate Am. Bd. Urology (trustee 1988-94, pres. 1993-94). Asst. prof. urology Boston U. Sch. Medicine, 1971-72, assoc. prof., 1972-74, prof., chmn. dept., 1974-80; dir. urology dept. Boston City Hosp., 1974-77; chief urology dept. Boston VA Med. Ctr., 1971—75; urologist-in-chief Univ. Hosp., Boston, 1971-80; John K. Lattimer prof., chmn. dept. urology Coll. Phys. and Surgs., Columbia U., NYC, 1980—2005, chmn. emeritus, 2005—. Dir. Squier Urol. Clinic, urology service Presbyn. Hosp., 1980-2005, chief med. officer, 2008-, integrated med. profls, 2008-, NYC; lectr. surgery Tufts U. Sch. Medicine. Boston Interhosp. Organ Bank, 1976-79; mem. working cadre Nat. Prostate Cancer Project, Nat. Cancer Inst., 1979-84; mem. adv. coun. Nat. Inst. Diabetes, Digestive Disease and Kidney; mem. integration panel for prostate cancer rsch. Dept. of Def., 1998-2002, chmn., 2000-01. Editl. bd. Jour. Prostate, World Jour. Urology, Jour. Urodynamics and Neurourology, Jour. Urology; asst. editor Jour. Urology, 1978-2004; contbr. chpts. to books, articles to med. jours. Recipient Disting. Alumnus award Boston U., 1985, Boston U. Alumni award, 2007. Fellow ACS; mem. Am. Urol. Assn. (hon., coord. continuing med. edn. New Eng. sect. 1977-80, del. rsch. com., bd. dirs. 2001-06, exec. com. 2002-06, sec. 2000-06, found. operating bd. 2005-06, Gold Cystoscope award 1979, Grayson-Carroll award 1971, 73, Hugh Hampton Young award 2001), Boston Surg. Soc. (exec. com. 1976-80), Am. Assn. Clin. Urologists, Am. Surg. Assn., Am. Assn. Genitourinary Surgeons (pres. 2007), Clin. Soc. Genitourinary Surgeons (pres. 2009-), Transplantation Soc., Soc. Urologic Oncology (pres. 1993), Soc. Pelvic Surgeons, Soc. Univ. Urologists (pres. 1990), N.Y. Sect. Am. Urol. Assn. (pres. 2002), AMA, Assn. Acad. Surgery, Am. Soc. Artificial Internal Organs, Am. Soc. Transplant Surgeons, Assn. Med. Colls., Can. Urol. Assn., Societe Internationale d'Urologie, Internat. Urodynamics Soc., Mass. Med. Soc., Soc. Govt. Urologists, Australasian Urol. Soc. (hon.), SE. Sect., AUA (hon.), SC. Sect. A (hon.), New Eng. Handicapped Sportsmen's Assn. (exec. com. 1977-81), U.S. Yacht Racing Union, Yacht Racing Union L.I. Sound, N.Y. Yacht Club, Cottage Park Yacht Club, Larchmont Yacht Club, Storm Trysail Club, Alpha Omega Alpha, Am. Found. Urol. Diseases (bd. dirs. 2002-05, exec. coun. 2002-05), NY Acad. Scis. (Valentine award medal 2006). Episcopalian. Office: Columbia-Presbyn Hosp Irving Pavilion 161 Ft Washington Av New York NY 10032-3702 Office Phone: 516-394-9610. Office Fax: 516-869-3015. E-mail: colsson@impplic.com. *

OLSZEWSKI, JUREK, otolaryngologist; b. Kikol, Poland, June 30, 1955; Full prof., Pres. of Republic of Poland, 2001; assoc. prof., Mil. Med. Acad., Lodz, Poland, 1997, asst. prof., 1996, PhD, 1984, MD, 1980. Cons. laryngology Polish Army, Poland, Poland, 1999—2002; carer of students sci. assn. mil. med. acad. Lodz, Poland, 1997—2000; vice-dean faculty medicine physiotherapy Mil. Med. Acad., Lodz, Poland, 2001—02; dean faculty physiotherapy Med. U., Lodz, Poland, 2002—, dir. dept. otolaryngology and phono-audiological rehab., 2003—, dir, chmn. head and neck surgery, 2004—, dir. dept. otolaryngology and laryngol. oncology, 2005—. Rsch. sec. Editl. Com. of Mil. and Med. Survey, Poland, 1998—2002; sub-commander Faculty of Medicine on Didactics, Poland, 2002; mem. med. coun. Mil. Chamber Physicians, Poland, 1997—2001; mem. sen. com. human resources and orgn., student affairs Mil. Med. Acad., 1998—2002; freelance sub-commander of surgery inst., Poland, 1999; polish army laryngology cons., Poland, 1999—2002; freelance sub-commander faculty medicine physiotherapy Mil. Med. Acad., Lodz, Poland, 2001, sec. sci. coun. inst. surgery, 1997—98, sec. coord. cooperation petrochemia plock sa, 1994—99, 2001—02, mem. senate, 1997—2002, Med. U., Lodz, Poland, 2002—. Adviser (19 doctoral dissertations and 17 master's), promoter (25 doctorates, 3 open doctoral dissertat, 55 master's degree), rsch. work (275 publs. and 323 sci. reports). Recipient Rsch. prize, Rsch. Pres. Polish Acad. Scis., 1979, Rector Prize II grade, 1994, Rector Prize III grade, 1996, medal, Commn. on Nat. Edn., 1999, Gold Cross of Merit, 2002, Dr. Henryk Jordan medal, 2003, Individual Prize on Didactics I grade, Rector Med. U. Lodz, 2003, 2004, 2005—07, Distinction of Honor on Health Protection Svcs. II grade, Minister of Health, 1987. Mem.: Polish Rehab. Soc. (mem. bd. Lodz divsn. 2003—), Polish Assn. Otolaryngologists, Head and Neck Surgeons. Achievements include Research Prize on scientific activity by Research president of Polish Academy of Sciences - 1979; research in Rector Prize: II grade - 1994, III grade - 1996; Medal by Commission on National Education - 1999; Gold Cross of Merit - 2002; Doctor Henryk Jordan Medal - 2003; Individual Prize on Didactics I grade by Rector of Medical University in Lodz - 2003; Collective Prize on Didactics I grade by Rector of Medical University in Lodz - 2005; Friend of the Child Medal on community service for children's welfare - 1993; Distinction of Honor on Health Protection Service II grade by Minister of Health - 1987. Avocations: volleyball, ping pong/table tennis. Office: Medical University of Lodz Ul. Stefana Zeromskiego 113 90-549 Lodz Poland Office Phone: 48426393580. Business E-Mail: jolszewski@poczta.onet.pl, jurek.olszewski@umed.lodz.pl.

OLTHOFF, KIM M., surgeon, educator; MD, U. Chgo., Ill. Diplomate Am. Bd. Surgery, cert. Transplantation Surgery. Intern UCLA, resident, fellow; prof. surgery Hosp. of the Univ. Pa. Named one of Top Docs, Phila. Mag., 2006, 2011, Best Doctors in America, 2005—06, 2007—08, 2009—10, America's Top Doctors, 2007—08, 2010. Mem.: Am. Hepato-Pancreato-Biliary Assn., Assn. for the Study of Liver Disease, Am. Soc. Transplant Physicians, Am. Soc. Transplant Surgeons, Soc. Univ. Surgeons, Assn. Acad. Surgeons, Am. Surgical Assn., Am. Coll. Surgeon. Office: Hospital of the University of Pennsylvania Penn Transplant Center 3400 Spruce St Ground Fl Rhoads Pavilion Philadelphia PA 19104 Office Phone: 215-662-6136. Office Fax: 215-662-2244.

OMAE, MASANORI, dentist, educator; b. Japan, Dec. 13, 1975; PhD, Osaka Dental U., 2004. Asst. prof. Okayama U., Japan, 2005—09. Office: Kita Dental Clinic Nakaitashimo 1269-9 Tsuyama Okayama 709-4603 Japan Office Fax: 81-868-57-2025. Business E-Mail: maemae.dds@kpb.biglobe.ne.jp.

O'MALLEY, BERT WILLIAM, cell biologist, educator, physician; b. Pitts., Dec. 19, 1936; s. Bert Alloysius O'M.; m. Sally Ann Johnson; children: Sally Ann, Bert A., Rebecca, Erin K. BS, U. Pitts., 1959, MD summa cum laude, 1963; DSc (hon.), N.Y. Med. Coll., 1979, Nat. U. Ireland, 1985; MD (hon.), Karolinska Inst., Stockholm, 1984. Intern, resident Duke U., Durham, N.C., 1963-65; clin. assoc. Nat. Cancer Inst., NIH, Bethesda, Md., 1965-67, head molecular biology sect., endocrine br., 1967-69; Lucius Birch prof., dir. Reproductive Biology Ctr. Vanderbilt U. Sch. Medicine, Nashville, 1969-73; Tom Thompson prof., chmn. dept. cell biology Baylor Coll. Medicine, Houston, 1973—, Disting. Svc. prof., 1985, dir. Baylor Ctr. for Reproductive Biology, 1973—. Mem. endocrine study sect., NIH, 1970-73, chmn., 1973-74; chmn. CETUS-UCLA Symposium on Gene Expression, 1982; con., mem. coun. rsch. and clin. investigation awards Am. Cancer Soc., 1985-87. Author: (with A.R. Means) Receptors for Reproductive Hormones, 1973, (with L. Birnbaumer) Hormone Action, vols. I and II, 1977, vol. III, 1978, (with A.M. Gotto) The Role of Receptors in Biology and Medicine, 1986; co-author: Methods in Enzymology: Hormone Action: Calmodulin and Calcium-Binding Proteins, 1983, Mechanism of Steriod Hormone Regulation of Gene Transcription, 1994; editor: Gene Regulation: UCLA Symposium on Molecular Cellular Biology, 1982; contbg. author to over 400 publs. Lt. comdr. USPHS, 1965-69. Recipient Ernst Oppenheimer award Am. Endocrine Soc., 1975, Gregory Pincus medal, 1975, Lila Gruber Cancer award, 1977, Disting. Achievement in Modern Medicine award, 1978, Borden award Assn. Am. Med. Colls., 1978, Dickson prize for Basic Med. Rsch., 1979, Philip S. Hench award U. Pitts., 1981, Axel Munthe Reproductive Biology award, Capri, Italy, 1982, Bicentennial Medallion of Distincton U. Pitts., 1987, Carl G.Hartman award, 2007, 2007 Nat. Medal Sci. Mem. AAAS, NAS, Inst. Med. NAS, Am. Soc. Biol. Chemists, Am. Acad. Arts and Scis., Endocrine Soc. (pres. 1985, Fred Conrad Koch medal 1988), Am. Soc. Clin. Investigation, Am. Inst. Chemists, Fedn. Clin. Rsch., Harvey Soc., Alpha Epsilon Delta, Phi Beta Kappa, Alpha Omega Alpha. Democrat. Roman Catholic. Office: Baylor Coll Medicine Interdepartmental Program in Cell & Molecular Biology One Baylor Pla Houston TX 77030 Office Phone: 713-798-6205. Office Fax: 713-798-5599. Business E-Mail: berto@bcm.edu.

O'MALLEY, THOMAS ANTHONY, gastroenterologist, internist; b. St. Helens, Lancashire, Eng., Jan. 21, 1932; s. Michael and Margaret (Melia) O'M.; m. Margaret Mary O'Kane, Apr. 7, 1958 (dec. Apr. 1985); m. Marianne Rapier, Jan. 23, 1988; children: Anne, Patricia, Katherine, Jane, Margaret. MBChB, U. Liverpool, Eng., 1956; Lic. Medicine, U. State N.Y., 1964. Diplomate Am. Bd. Internal Medicine, State Bd. Med. Examiners Fla. House physician Royal Infirmary, Liverpool, 1956-57; house surgeon Royal Liverpool Children's Hosp., 1957; resident in medicine C.S. Wilson Meml. Hosp., Johnson City, NY, 1957-58; fellow internal medicine Lahey Clinic, Boston, 1958-59; USPHS trainee in gastroenterology U. Rochester (N.Y.), Strong Meml. Hosp., 1959-60; chief resident medicine/Segal Watson fellow gastroenterology Genesee Hosp., Rochester, 1960-61; gastroenterologist Cancer Clinic, Regina, Sask., Canada, 1963; asst. dir. med. edn. Genesee Hosp., U. Rochester, 1964—66; pvt. practice Rochester, NY, 1967—72; clin. asst. prof. medicine U. Rochester, 1967—72; clin. assoc. prof. medicine U. South Fla., Tampa, 1972—2008. Chief medicine Sarasota (Fla.) Meml. Hosp., 1973, Doctors Hosp., Sarasota, 1985. With RAF, 1961-62. Recipient Physician of Yr. award Doctors Hosp. Sarasota, 1985; listed among Best Dr.'s of Am., 1998, Lifetime Achievement award, Sarasota Meml. Hosp, Fla., 2008. Fellow: ACP, Am. Coll. Gastroenterology; mem.: Cavalieri del Vini Nobili (amb. 1989—, pres. 1997—, past pres. 2009), Chevalier du Tastevin (comdr. 1985—, officieur comdr. 2001—). Office: O'Malley & Hall MD PA 2650 Bahia Vista St Sarasota FL 34239-2635 Office Phone: 941-366-8960. Personal E-mail: t.omalley10@comcast.net.

OMALU, BENNET IFEAKANDU, pathologist; arrived in US, 1994, permanent resident, 2006; MD, Coll. Medicine, U. Nigeria, Enugu, 1990; MPH in Epidemiology, U. Pitts., 2004; attended, Carnegie Mellon U. Tepper Sch. Bus., Pitts., 2005—08. Diplomate anatomic pathology Am. Bd. Pathology, 2002, clin. pathology Am. Bd. Pathology, 2003, forensic pathology Am. Bd. Pathology, 2004, neuropathology Am. Bd. Pathology, 2005. House physician dept. pediat. Enugu Gen. Hosp., Nigeria, 1990; intern, gen. family practice U. Nigeria Hosp., Enugu, 1991—92; emergency rm. physician Jos U. Hosp., Jos, Nigeria, 1992—94; vis. rsch. scholar dept. epidemiology U. Wash., 1994—95; pathology resident Harlem Hosp. Ctr., NYC, 1995—99; fellowship in forensic pathology Allegheny County Coroner's Office, Pitts., 1999—2000, assoc. forensic pathologist, 2000—02, attending forensic pathologist, 2002—07, attending forensic neuropathologist, 2002—07; fellowship in neuropathology U. Pitts. Med. Ctr., 2000—02; cons. forensic pathologist Cyril H. Wecht and Pathology Assoc. Inc., 2000—05, cons. neuropathologist, 2000—05; clinical assoc. prof. pathology U. Pitts., 2003—07; chief med. examiner San Joaquin County, Calif., 2007—; founding mem., co-dir. W.Va. U. Brain Injury Rsch. Inst., Morgantown. Consulting neuropathologist Conemaugh Meml. Hosp., Johnstown, Pa.; prin. forensic cons. Neo-Forenxis, LLC, Pitts.; prin. health care mgmt. cons. BOGE, LP, Pitts.; adj. asst. prof. epidemiology Grad. Sch. Pub. Health, U. Pitts., Pitts., 2004—07; adj. assoc. prof. pathology U.

Calif., Davis; co-dir., vis. prof. brain injury divsn. W. Va. U. Blanchette Rockefeller Inst. Neuroscience; consulting forensic neuropathologist Commonwealth Va. Office of Chief Med. Examiner, 2007—, Clark County Office of Coroner/Med. Examiner, Las Vegas, 2007—. Contbr. articles to profl. jours. Active St. Benedict the Moor Parish, Pitts., 1999—2006. Fellow: Nigerian Med. Dental Coun., Am. Coll. Epidemiology, Coll. Am. Pathologist, Am. Soc. Clinical Pathologists, Am. Assn. Advancement Sci.; mem.: AMA, Am. Soc. Investigative Pathology, Pa. Assn. Pathologists, Pa. Med. Soc., Alleghany County Pathology Soc., Am. Pub. Health Assn., Am. Assn. Pub. Health Physicians, US and Can. Acad. Pathology, Am. Acad. Forensic Scis., Am. Assn. Med. Examiners, Am. Assn. Neuropathologists, Am. Assn. Physician Execs. Conservative. Roman Catholic. Achievements include copyright ownership forensic case study series. Office: Brain Injury Rsch Inst WVa University Morgantown WV 26506 *

OMAR, SABAH AHMED, biomedical researcher; d. Ahmed Omar Jezan and Zena Said Bakor; m. Feisal Said Feisal, Dec. 19, 1999; 1 child, Khulud Feisal Abeid. MA, U. Nairobi, 1995; PhD (hon.), London Sch. Hygiene and Tropical Medicine, 2002. Rsch. scientist Kenya Med. Rsch. Inst., Nairobi, Kenya, 1995—2002, sr. rsch. scientist, 2002—. Malaria studies Iaea Cons., Khartoum, Sudan, 1998; cons., malaria studies WHO, Kampala, Uganda, 2002. Coun. mem. Moi U., Eldoret, Kenya, 2003—. Fellow, Internat. Atomic Energy, 1995, IAEA, 1995, 2002; scholar, U. Nairobi, 1992—95; Rsch. grant, European Union, 1997—2001. Mem.: Biochem. Soc. Kenya (hon.). Achievements include research in in monitoring antimalarial drug efficacy and molecular mechanisms of resistance.

OMAR, SALEM, physician, gastroenterologist, researcher; b. Kuala Lumpur, Wilayah Persekutuan, Malaysia, Nov. 17, 1968; s. Omar Joni and Salina Abdullah; m. Joanna Abdul Karim, Mar. 22, 1997; 1 child, Edina Salem. MB, BChir with distinction in Pharmacology, U. Malaya, 1993, M in Internal Medicine, 1999. Fellow endoscopic ultrasound Dept. Interdisciplinary Endoscopy U. Hosp. Hamburg-Eppendorf, Germany, 2002—06; lectr. U. Malaya, Kuala Lumpur, 1999—2007, assoc. prof., 2008—. Contbr. articles to profl. jours. Mem.: Parenteral and Enteral Nutrition Soc. Malaysia (asst. sec. 2000—02), Malaysian Soc. Gastroenterology and Hepatology (life). Home: 18 Jalan P8B/2 Presint 8 62250 Putrajaya Malaysia Office Fax: 603-79556936. Personal E-mail: salemomar@yahoo.com.

OMARI, BASSAM O., cardiothoracic surgeon; s. Omar and Munawwar Omari; m. Rana Azhari, Sept. 30, 2004. MD, Am. U. Beirut, 1984. Cert. Am. Bd. Thoracic Surgery, 1996, Am. Bd. Surgery, 1992. Chief divsn. cardiothoracic surgery Harbor-UCLA Med. Ctr., Torrance, Calif., 1994—. Contbr. scientific papers to profl. jours. Fellow: ACS; mem.: Internat. Soc. Minimally Inrasir Cardiothoracic Surgery, Europe Assn. Cardio-Thoraic Surgeons, Western Thoracic Surg. Assn., Soc. Thoracic Surgery. Office: Harbor-UCLA Med Ctr 1000 W Carson St Torrance CA 90509 Office Fax: 310 320 2129. E-mail: bomari@ucla.edu.

OMENN, GILBERT STANLEY, academic administrator, internist, scientist; b. Chester, Pa., Aug. 30, 1941; s. Leonard and Leah (Miller) O.; m. Martha Darling; children: Rachel Andrea, Jason Montgomery, David Matthew. AB, Princeton U., 1961; MD, Harvard U., 1965; PhD in Genetics, U. Wash., 1972. Lic. Mass., Washington, Bd. Internal Medicine Part 1(1970), Part 2, (1972), Specialty Bd. Med. Genetics Clin. Genetics, 1982. Intern Mass. Gen. Hosp., Boston, 1965-66; tchg. fellow in medicine Harvard U., 1966-67; rsch. assoc., Nat. Inst. Arthritis and Metabol Diseases NIH, Bethesda, Md., 1967-69; fellow, divsn. med. genetics U. Wash., 1969-71, asst. prof. medicine Seattle, 1971—74, assoc. prof. medicine, 1974—79, dir., Robert Wood Johnson Clin. Scholars Program, 1975—77, investigator Howard Hughes Med. Inst., 1976-77, prof. medicine, 1979-97, prof. environ. health, 1981—, chmn. dept. environ. health, 1981-83; dean U. Wash. Sch. Pub. Health and Cmty. Medicine, 1982-97, dean emeritus, 1997—; CEO health sys. U. Mich. Health Sys., Ann Arbor, 1997—2002; exec. v.p. med. affairs U. Mich., 1997—2002, prof. internal medicine, human genetics and pub. health, 1997—, dir. ctr. biomedical proteomics, 2002—, dir. ctr. computational medicine and bioinformatics, 2005—. Bd. dirs. Amgen Inc., 1987-, Rohm & Hans Co., 1987-2009, CNA, Armune BioSci., US Civilian Res. & Dev Fedn. Ctr Pub. Integrity, Population Svcs. Internat. Salzburg Global Seminar; sci. adv. bd. 3M, Motorola, Divergence, Compendia Biosci.; attending staff, U. Hosp., Harborview Med. Ctr., VA Hosp. Providence Hosp., cons. staff, Children's Hosp. and Med. Ctr., Seattle, 1971-97, attending staff, U. Mich. Health Sys., 1997-; White House fellow/spl. asst. to chmn. AEC, 1973-74; asst. dir., 1977-78, assoc. dir., for Human Resources and Social and Economic Svcs, Office Sci. and Tech. Policy, The White House, 1977-80; assoc. dir. human resources Office Mgmt. and Budget, 1980-81; vis. sr. fellow Woodrow Wilson Sch. Pub. and Internat. Affairs, Princeton U., 1981; sci. and pub. policy fellow Brookings Instn., Washington, 1981-82; joint mem. Fed Hutchinson Cancer Rsch. Ctr., Seattle, 1983-; cons. govt. agys., Lifetime Cable Network; mem. Nat. Commn. on the Environment, Rene Dubos Ctr. for Human Environments, AFL-CIO Workplace Health Fund., Electric Power Rsch. Inst., Carnegie Commn. Task Force on Sci. and Tech. in Jud. and Regulatory Decision Making, adv. com. to dir., Ctrs. Disease Control, 1992-95, adv. com. Critical Technologies Inst., RAND; mem. Pres. Coun. Nat. Labs., U. Calif., 1992-97; chair, Pres. Congrl. Commn. on Risk Assessment and Risk Mgmt., 1994-97; mem. Nat. Enterprise for the Environment. Coauthor: Clearing the Air, Reforming the Clean Air Act, 1981. Editor: (with others) Genetics, Environment and Behavior: Implications for Educational Policy, 1972; Genetic Control of Environmental Pollutants, 1984; Genetic Variability in Responses to Chemical Exposure, 1984, Environmental Biotechnology: Reducing Risks from Environmental Chemicals through Biotechnology, 1988, Biotechnology in Biodegradation, 1990, Biotechnology and Human Genetic Predisposition to Disease, 1990, Annual Review of Public Health, 1991-97, Clinics in Geriatric Medicine, 1992, Oxford Textbook of Public Health, 1997; editor: Exploring the Human Plasma Proteome, 2006; mem. bd. Jour. Proteome Research, Molecular Cell Proteomics; contbr. articles on cancer prevention including proteomics for cancer biomarkers, human biochem. genetics, prenatal diagnosis of inherited disorders, susceptibility to environ. agts., clin. medicine and health policy to profl. publs. Mem. Pres. Coun. on Spinal Cord Injury; mem. Nat. Cancer Adv. Bd., Nat. Heart, Lung and Blood Adv. Coun., Wash. State Gov.'s Commn. on Social and Health Svcs., Ctr. for Excellence in Govt.; chmn. awards panel Gen. Motors Cancer Rsch. Found., 1985-86; chmn. bd. Environ. Studies and Toxicology, Nat. Rsch. Coun., 1988-91; mem. Bd. Health Promotion and Disease Prevention, Inst. Medicine; mem. adv. com. Woodrow Wilson Sch., Princeton U., 1978-84; mem., Report Review Com., NAS, 2001-10; chair & mem., various com. of Nat. Rsch. Coun. and Inst. Medicine, NAS; trustee Pacific Sci. Ctr., Fred Hutchinson Cancer Rsch. Ctr., Seattle Symphony Orch., Seattle Youth Symphony Orch., Seattle Chamber Music Festival, Santa Fe Chamber Music Festival, Univ. Mus. Soc., Ann Arbor, United Way Washtenaw County, Mich.; chmn. rules com. Dem. Conv., King County, Wash., 1972. Served with USPHS, 1967-69. U.S. Pub. Health Svc. Spl. Fellow, 1969-71, Nat. Genetics Found. Fellow, 1971-72, White House fellow, 1973-74; recipient Research Career Devel. award USPHS, 1972-76. Fellow ACP, AAAS (pres.-elect, pres., chmn. bd. dirs. 2004-07), Hastings Ctr. Inst. Soc., Ethics and Life Sciences, Collegium Ramazzini; mem. Nat. Acad. Social Ins., Western Assn. Physicians, Inst. Medicine of NAS (medal 2008), White House Fellows Assn. (John W. Gardner Legacy of Leadership award 2004), Am. Soc. Human Genetics, Am. Med. Informatics Assn., Assn. Am. Physicians, Am. Acad. Arts and Scis., Am. Assn. for Advancement of Humanities, Am. Occupational Medicine Assn., Phi Beta Kappa, Sigma XiAlpha Omega Alpha. Jewish. Home: 3340 E Dobson Ann Arbor MI 48105-2583 Office: Univ Mich Med Sch 2017 F Palmer Commons 100 Washtenaw Ave Ann Arbor MI 48109-2218 Office Phone: 734-763-7583. Business E-Mail: gomenn@umich.edu.

OMER, ABDELRAHMAN AHMED, colon and rectal surgeon, consultant; s. Ahmed Omer Khalafalla and Firyal Abdelrahman Abdelrahiem Hamid; m. Tayseer Elfaki Mustafa, Jan. 22, 1990; children: Mohammed Abdelrahman Ahmed, Ahmed Abdelrahman Ahmed, Mustafa Abdelrahman Ahmed, Areena Abdelrahman Ahmed. MBBS, Facultu og Medicine Univ. of Khartoum, Khartoum - Sudan, 1982—89; MSc in Surg. Sciences, Univ. London, London, Eng., 1994—96; PhD in health mgmt., Hartford U., U.S.A., 1999—2004. Intercollegiate fellow of the Royal Colleges of Surgery The Royal Colleges Of Surgery U.K. & Ireland, 2004. Rsch. fellow in surgery U. Coll. London, London, 1994—96; gen. & colorectal specialist Oxford and Cambridge Deanery, East Anglia, England, 1996—2004; fellow in colorectal surgery The Cleve. Clinic Found., Fort Lauaderdale, Fla., 2003—04; prof. surgery U. Hartford, 2003—; colorectal specialist and fellow Univ. Cambridge Hosp., Cambridge, England, 2004; cons. colorectal & gen. surgeon The Ipswich Hosp. NHS Trust, Ipswich, England, 2005—. Dir. Golden Dragon Internat. Ltd, Khartoum, Sudan, 1993—; mem. Rotcract, Khartoum, Sudan, 1984—; head of office UDP, London, 1994; advisor Brit. Med. Assn., London, 2004. Contbr. scientific papers. Head of polit. office United Dem. Party, London, United Kingdom, 1994. Fellow: Royal Soc. of Medicine, Internat. Soc. of Univ. Colon & Rectum Surgeon, Internat. Coll. of Surgeon, Royal Coll. of Surgeons of Eng.; mem.: Sudanese Med. assn. (life). Achievements include first to Hunterian Medal; research in peritoneal healing and adhesion histology. Avocations: travel, sports, reading. Office: Ipswich Hosp NHS Trust Heath Rd Suffolk Ipswich IP4 England Personal E-mail: omerab11@aol.com, a.a.omer@gmail.com. E-mail: a.omer@colorectasurgeon.org.uk.

OMER, GEORGE ELBERT, JR., retired orthopaedic surgeon, educator; b. Kansas City, Kans., Dec. 23, 1922; s. George Elbert and Edith May (Hinos) O.; m. Wendie Vilven, Nov. 6, 1949; children: George Eric, Michael Lee. BA, Ft. Hays Kans. State U., 1944; MD, Kans. U., 1950; MSc in Orthopaedic Surgery, Baylor U., Waco, Tex., 1955. Diplomate Am. Bd. Orthopaedic Surgery, 1959, (bd. dirs. 1983-92, pres. 1987-88), re-cert. orthopaedics and hand surgery, 1983, cert. surgery of the hand, 1989. 2nd lt. US Army, 1945, advanced through grades to col., 1967, ret., 1970; rotating intern Bethany Hosp., Kansas City, 1950-51, resident in orthopaedic surgery Brooke Army Hosp., San Antonio, 1952-55, William Beaumont Army Hosp., El Paso, Tex., 1955-56; chief surgery Irwin Army Hosp., Ft. Riley, Kans., 1957-59; cons. in orthopaedic surgery 8th Army, chief orthop. surgery 121st Evacuation Hosp. Republic of Korea, 1959-60; asst. chief orthopaedic surgery, chief hand surgeon Fitzsimons Army Med. Center, Denver, 1960-63; dir. orthopaedic residency tng. Armed Forces Inst. Pathology at Walter Reed Army Med. Ctr., Washington, 1963-65; chief orthopaedic surgery and chief Army Hand Surg. Center, Brooke Army Med. Center, 1965-70; cons. in orthopaedic and hand surgery Surgeon Gen. Army, 1967-70; prof. orthopaedics, surgery, and anatomy, chmn. dept. orthopaedic surgery, chief div. hand surgery U. N.Mex., 1970-90, med. dir. phys. therapy, 1972-90, acting asst. dean grad. edn. Sch. Medicine, 1980-81. Mem. active staff U. N.Mex. Hosp., Albuquerque, 1970—2005, chief of med. staff, 1984-86; cons. staff other Albuquerque hosps.; cons. orthopedic surgery USPHS, 1966-85, US Army, 1970-92, USAF, 1970-78, VA, 1970-2000; cons. Carrie Tingley Hosp. for Crippled Children, 1970-99, interim med. dir., 1970-72, 86-87, mem. bd. advisor 1972-76, chair, 1994-96. Mem. bd. editors Clin. Orthopaedics, 1973-90, Jour. AMA, 1973-74, Jour. Hand Surgery, 1976-81; trustee Jour. Bone and Joint Surgery, 1993-99, sec., 1993-96, chmn., 1997-99; contbr. more than 300 articles to profl. jours., numerous chpts. to books. Decorated Legion of Merit, Army Commendation medal with oak leaf cluster; recipient Alumni Achievement award Ft. Hays State U., 1973, Recognition plaque Am. Soc. Surgery Hand, 1989, Recognition plaque N.Mex. Orthopaedic Assn., 1991, Recognition award for hand surgery Am. Osteo. Acad. Orthopaedics, 1982, Pioneer award Internat. Socs. for Surgery Hand, 1995, Rodey award U. N.Mex. Alumni Assn., 1997, Cornerstone award U. N.Mex. Health Scis. Ctr., 1997; recognized with Endowed Professorship U. N.Mex. Sch. Medicine, 1995; recognized with named Annual Orthop. Seminar and Alumni Day Brooke Army Med. Ctr., 1999. Fellow ACS, Am. Orthopaedic Assn. (pres. 1988-89, exec. dir. 1989-93), Am. Acad. Orthopaedic Surgeons, Assn. Orthopaedic Chmn., N.Mex. Orthopaedic Assn. (pres. 1979-81, 1999-2000), La. Orthopaedic Assn. (hon.), Korean Orthopaedic Assn. (hon.), Peru Orthopaedic Soc. (hon.), Caribbean Hand Soc., Am. Soc. Surgery Hand (pres. 1978-79), Am. Assn. Surgery of Trauma, Assn. Bone and Joint Surgeons, Assn. Mil. Surgeons US, Riordan Hand Soc. (pres. 1967-68), Sunderland Soc. (pres. 1981-83), Soc. Mil. Orthopaedic Surgeons, Brazilian Hand Soc. (hon.), S.Am. Hand Soc. (hon.), Groupe D'Etude de la Main, Brit. Hand Soc. (hon.), Venezuela Hand Soc. (hon.), South African Hand Soc. (hon.), Western Orthopaedic Assn. (pres. 1981-82), AAAS, Russell A. Hibbs Soc. (pres. 1977-78), 38th Parallel Med. Soc. (Korea) (sec. 1959-60); mem. AMA, Phi Kappa Phi, Phi Sigma, Alpha Omega Alpha, Phi Beta Pi. Achievements include pioneer work in hand surgery. Home: 316 Big Horn Ridge Rd NE Sandia Heights Albuquerque NM 87122 Personal E-mail: geoomer@juno.com.

OMI, TOKUYA, dermatologist, allergist, researcher; b. Tokyo, July 9, 1963; m. Asako Omi; 1 child. MD, PhD, Nippon Med. Grad. Sch., Tokyo, 1992. Diplomate Japan Bd. Dermatology, Japan Bd. Allergology. Assoc. lectr. Nippon Med. Sch., 1982—97, lectr. Tokyo, 2000—, prof., 2009—. Mem.: Tokyo Riding Club, Yokohama Country and Athletic Club, Taiheiyo Club, Tokyo Am. Club. Office: Queen's Sq Med Ctr 2-3-5 Minatomirai Yokohama 220-6208 Japan Office Phone: 81-45-682-4112. Office Fax: +81-45-682-4111. E-mail: tomi@olive.ocn.ne.jp.

OMIROS, GEORGE JAMES, medical foundation executive; b. Uniontown, Pa., Oct. 26, 1956; s. Chris George and Alice (Zervoudi) O.; m. Sophia Florent, June 28, 1980; children: Christopher George, Alicia Helene. BS in Politics and Philosophy, U. Pitts., 1978; M, Ctrl. Mich. U., Mount Pleasant, 1982. Campaign coord., program assoc. S.W. Pa. chpt. Am. Heart Assn., Greensburg, 1979, fundraising dir., 1979-80, dir. devel., 1980-84, v.p. devel., ops. We. Pa. chpt. Pitts., 1984-85, dep. exec. v.p., 1985-87, exec. v.p., 1987-88; exec. dir. Leukemia Soc. Am., The Leukemia and Lymphoma Soc., Pitts., 1988—, nat. mktg. rep., 1988—, asst. v.p. nat. office, 1991-93; sr. exec. dir., nat. dir. Don Devel., Pitts., 1993-95, sr. exec. dir., group dir., nat. dir. comm. campaign, 1995—; sr. v.p. Field Devel. Nat. Office, 2008—. Mem. coun., rev. com. Health Sys. Agy. S.W. Pa., Pitts., 1983—87; mem. com. Fayette County Rep. Party; mem. Order St. Andrew-Ecumenical Patriarchate Istanbul, 2001—; cons. devel. Greek Orthodox Archdiocese, Pitts., 1982—, v.p., 1987—, fin. chmn., 1999—; chair Pitts. met. com. Pitts. Metro Com.Internat. Orthodox Christian Charities, Balt., 1993—; mem. parish coun. St. Spyridon Greek Orthodox Ch., Monessen, Pa., 1982—2000; met. chmn. Internat. Orthodox Christian Charities. Decorated Order of St. Andrew, 2001. Mem. AFP Assn. Fundraising Profls. (cert., founder 1980, pres. 1985-87, Outstanding Fundraising Exec. 1990), Oncology Nursing Soc. (chmn. Camp Raising Spirits 1995-2008), Pitts. Planned Giving Coun. (founding com. 1983—), Friends of George C. Marshall (steering com. 1990-92), Uniontown Rotary (local treas. 1985, sec. 1986, v.p. 1987, pres. 1988), Chestnut Ridge Rotary, Pitts. Rotary, Rotary 7330 (dist. gov. Rotary dist. 2003-2004), Masons, Order St. Andrew, Order Jesters, Syria Shrine (pres. Uniontown chpt. 2005). Republican. Greek Orthodox. Avocations: stained glass work, art collections, gardening, antiques. Office: Leukemia and Lymphoma Soc 1311 Mamaroneck Ave White Plains NY 10605

O'MOORE, PAUL V., intervention radiologist; MD, U. Pa., 1983. Diplomate Am. Bd. Radiology-vascular and interventional radiology, Am. Bd. Radiology-radiology, cert. Pa., 1993, NJ, 2003. Resident diagnostic radiology Mass. Gen. Hosp., Boston, 1987, chief resident diagnostic radiology, fellow cardiovasc. radiology; med. staff. Abington Meml. Hosp., 1993—, radiologist dept. of radiology; med. staff. Lansdale Hosp., 2010—, radiologist dept. of radiology. Instl. rev. bd. Abington Meml. Hosp., 1996—, pres. Montgomery County Advanced Med. Imaging, 2008—. Named one of the Top Doctors, Phila. Mag., 2010—11. Office: Abington Memorial Hospital 1200 Old York Rd Abington PA 19001 also: Lansdale Hospital Radiology Department 100 Medical Campus Dr Lansdale PA 19446 Office Phone: 215-481-7305, 215-361-4500. Office Fax: 215-481-2208, 215-361-4872.

O'MORCHOE, CHARLES CHRISTOPHER CREAGH, anatomist, surgeon, educator; b. Quetta, India, May 7, 1931; came to U.S., 1968; s. Nial Francis C. and Jessie Elizabeth (Joly) O'M.; m. Patricia Jean Richardson, Sept. 15, 1955; children: Charles Eric Creagh, David James Creagh. BA, Trinity Coll., Dublin U., Ireland, 1953, MB, BCh, BAO, 1955, MA, 1959, MD, 1961, PhD, 1969, DSc, 1981. Resident Halifax Gen. Hosp., England, 1955-57; lectr. in anatomy Sch. Medicine Trinity Coll., Dublin (Ireland) U., 1957-61, 63-65, lectr. in physiology, 1966-67, assoc. prof. in physiology, 1967-68; instr. in anatomy Harvard Med. Sch., Boston, 1962-63; vis. prof. physiology U. Md. Sch. Medicine, Balt., 1961-62, assoc. prof. anatomy, 1968-71, prof. anatomy, 1971-74; chmn. anatomy bd. State of Md., 1971-73; prof., chmn. dept. anatomy Stritch Sch. Medicine Loyola U., Maywood, Ill., 1974-84; dean Coll. Medicine, U. Ill., Urbana-Champaign, 1984-98, prof. anat. scis. and surgery, 1984-98, emeritus dean and prof., 1998—. WHO cons., vis. prof. physiology Jaipur, India, 1967, S.M.S. Med. Coll., U. Rajasthan, vis. prof. anatomy, 1971; vis. scholar, dept. medicine divsn. oncology U. Wash. Sch. Medicine, 2003-06, affiliate prof., 2007-. Assoc. editor: Anatomical Record, 1978-98, Am. Jour. Anatomy, 1987-91, Lymphology, 2004—; contbr. articles to profl. jours. Elected fellow Trinity Coll., Dublin U., 1966; named faculty mem. of yr. Loyola U., Chgo., 1982. Mem. N.Am. Soc. Lymphology (v.p. 1982-84, pres. 1984-86, sec. 1993-98, Cecil K. Drinker award 1992), Am. Assn. Anatomy Chairmen (emeritus), Am. Assn. Anatomists (dir. placement svc. 1981-91), Internat. Soc. Lymphology (exec. com. 1987-97, pres. 1993-95, Presdl. award 2001), Alpha Omega Alpha. Mem. Church of Ireland. Home: University Wash 5645 NE Lincoln Rd East Poulsbo WA 98370-7756 Office: U Ill Coll Medicine 190 Med Sci Bldg 506 S Mathews Ave Urbana IL 61801-3618 Office Phone: 360-598-2222. Business E-Mail: cccom@uiuc.edu.

OMU, ALEXANDER EMEAKPOR, medical educator; b. Igbide, Delta State, Nigeria, Aug. 8, 1946; s. Larzarus Enyeke and Dorcas Osiunukpere Omu; m. Florence Emadinwe Enenajor; children: Alekuzuazo Ekemona, Tobi Onu, Akomeno Orowo, Efe Azino. MB, U. Ibadan Med. Sch., Nigeria, 1973. Prof. dept. ob-gyn. Kuwait U. Faculty of Medicine, 1992—, departmental chmn.; sr. cons. obstetrician & gynaecologist Maternity Hosp., Ministry Health, Kuwait, 1992—. Dir. Bendel Hosps. Mgmt. Bd., Benin-City, Bendel State, Nigeria, 1988—91; lectr.,sr. lectr., departmental chmn. U. Benin, 1988—90; obstetrician,gynaecologist, U. Benin Tchng. Hosp., 1980—91. Ugbowo lions club chmn. Lions Club Internat., Benin-City, 1986—90. Recipient Best Clin. Poster award, 2008; fellow, Royal Coll. Obstetricians & Gynaecologists, London, 1991. Fellow: West African Coll. Surgeons, Internat. Coll. Surgeons. Achievements include research in antioxidants in male infertility. Avocations: jogging, fishing, gardening. Home: Ghazali Kuwait 13110 Kuwait Office: Dept Ob-Gyn Faculty Medicine KU Jabriya Kuwait 13110 Kuwait Office Fax: 965 5338906. Business E-Mail: omu@hsc.edu.kw.

OMULECKI, WOJCIECH TOMASZ, ophthalmologist, department chairman; b. Wielun, Poland, Mar. 14, 1954; MD, Med. U. Lodz, 1979, PhD, 2008. Head chair dept. ophthalmology Med. U. Lodz, 2000—. Chmn. Polish Soc. Cataract and Refractive Surgeons, 1993—2010, Polish Ophthal. Soc., 2010; mem. Intra-Ocular Implant Club, 2009; co-opted bd. mem. European Soc. Cataract and Refractive Surgeons, 2010. Recipient prize, 11th Ann. Meeting German Ophthalmic Surgeons, 1988. Avocations: tennis, skiing, music, literature, movies. Office: Kopcinskiego 22 Lodz 90153 Poland Office Phone: 48426776800. Office Fax: 48426776801. Business E-Mail: womulecki@poczta.onet.pl.

OMURA, EMILY FOWLER, retired dermatologist; b. Oklahoma City, Okla., Oct. 19, 1938; d. Richard William and Emma (Fraiser) Fowler; m. George A. Omura, Dec. 27, 1962; children: June, Susan, Ann, George F. BA cum laude, Barnard Coll., NYC, 1960; MD, Cornell U. Med. Coll., NYC, 1964. Cert. Am. Bd. Dermatology, Am. Bd. Dermatopathology. Intern mixed-medicine Roosevelt Hosp., NYC, 1965—66; resident dermatology Cornell/N.Y. Hosp., NYC, 1966—69, clin. instr. dermatology, 1969—70; asst. prof. dermatology U. Ala., Birmingham, 1970—75; assoc. prof. U. Ala. Med. Ctr., Birmingham, 1975—83, prof. dermatology, dir. dermatopathology, 1983—99, emeritus prof. dermatology, 1999—; with dermatopathology Skin Path Assocs., Birmingham, 1999—2006, ret., 2006. Dir. dermatopathology fellowship training program U. Ala., Birmingham, 1983-99. Med. Student award for Outstanding Performance in Dermatology established by U. Ala. Birmingham, named for Emily F. Omura, 1999— Fellow Am. Acad. Dermatology, Am. Soc. Dermatopathology (pres. 2000-01). Methodist. Avocations: dance, reading, museum docent.

OMURA, TSUNEO, retired medical educator; b. Shizuoka, Japan, July 29, 1930; s. Bunzo and Yasu Omura; m. Yone Tominaga, Nov. 16, 1957; children: Shigeru, Minoru, Kaoru. BS, U. Tokyo, 1953, DSc, 1962. Instr. Shizuoka U., 1953-60; asst. prof. Osaka U., Japan, 1960-70; prof. Kyushu U., Fukuoka, Japan, 1970-94, prof. emeritus, 1994—. Editor, author: Cytochrome P-450, 1978, 2d edit., 1993. Mem.: Japanese Biochem. Soc., Am. Soc. Biochemistry and Molecular Biology (hon.). Home: 7-17-7 Hinosato Munakata Fukuoka 811-3425 Japan Office: Kyushu U Med Sch Maidashi 3-1-1 Fukuoka 812-8582 Japan

OMURA, YOSHIAKI, medical educator; b. Tomari, Toyama-ken, Japan, Mar. 28, 1934; arrived in U.S., 1959, naturalized, 1979; s. Tsunejiro and Minako (Uozu) Omura; m. Rose Ninon Alexander, Sept. 8, 1962 (separated 1983); children: Alexander Kenji, Vivienne Midori, Richard Itsuma. A degree, Nihon U., 1952—54; BSc in Applied Physics, Waseda U., 1957; MD, Yokohama City U., 1958; postgrad. exptl. physics, Columbia U., 1960—63; ScD (Med.), Coll. Physicians and Surgeons, Columbia U., 1965. Diplomate Internat. Coll. Acupuncture and Electro-Therapeutics, Am. Acad. Pain Mgmt., Am. Bd. Forensic Medicine, Am. Acad. Experts in Traumatic Stress. Rotating intern Tokyo U. Hosp., 1958, Norwalk (Conn.) Hosp., 1959; rsch. fellow cardiovasc. surgery Columbia U., NYC, 1960; resident physician in surgery Francis Delafield Hosp., Cancer Inst., Columbia U., 1961—65; asst. prof. pharmacology and instr. surgery N.Y. Med. Coll., 1966—72; vis. prof. (summers) U. Paris, 1973—77; Maitre de recherche, Disting. Fgn. Scientist program of INSERM Govt. of France, 1977. Rsch. cons. orthop. surgery Columbia U., 1965—66; part-time emergency rm. physician Englewood Hosp., 1965—66; rsch. cons. pharmacology dept. NY Downstate Med. Ctr., SUNY, 1966; co-founder, cons. Lincoln Hosp. Acupuncture Drug Detoxification Program, 1974—75; chmn. Columbia U. Affiliation and Cmty. Medicine com., Cmty. Bd. Francis Delafield Hosp., 1974—75; vis. rsch. prof. dept. elec. engring. Manhattan Coll., 1960—99; chmn. Sci. Divsn. Children's Art & Sci. Workshops, NYC, 1971—92; dir. med. rsch. Heart Disease Rsch. Found., Bklyn., 1972—; adj. prof. dept. pharmacology Chgo. Med. Sch., 1982—93; vis. prof. physiology Sch. Med. Showa U., Tokyo, 1988—96; adj. prof. preventive medicine NY Med. Coll., 1997—; vis. prof. Inst. Anesthesiology and Reanimation U. Padua, Italy, 1999; prof. dept. non-orthodox medicine Ukrainian Nat. Med. U., Kiev, 1993—; attending physician dept. neurosci. LI Coll. Hosp., 1980—88; cons. NY Pain Ctr., 1988—92, NIH Rsch. Grant Evaluation, 1994—96; v.p. Internat. Kirlian Rsch. Assn., 1981—94; mem. NY State Bd. Medicine, 1984—94; mem. alumni coun. Coll. Phys. and Surg. Columbia U., 1986—; vice chair Am. Bd. Forensic Medicine, 2002—07. Author: 7 books; mem. editl. bd. Alternative Medicine, 1985—93, Scandinavian Jour. Acupuncture and Electrotherapy, 1987—, Functional Neurology, 1988—2002; founder, editor-in-chief: Acupuncture & Electro-Therapeutics Rsch. Internat. Jour., 1974—; editl. cons. Jour. Electrocardiology, 1980—86, Am. Jour. Traditional Chinese Medicine, 2006—; contbr. chapters to books, over 220 articles to profl. jours. Recipient Acupuncture Scientist of Yr. award, Internat. Congress of Chinese Medicine, 1989, World 1st Qi Gong Scientist of Yr. award, Internat. Congress of Chinese Medicine & Qi Gong, 1990; grantee, Am. Cancer Soc. Inst., 1961—63, John Polacek Found., 1966—72, NIH, 1967—72, Heart Disease Rsch. Found., 1972—; fellow, Columbia U., 1960. Fellow: Internat. Coll. Angiology, NY Cardiol. Soc., Am. Coll. Angiology, Am. Assn. Integrative Medicine (diplomate) (life; vice chair 2002—07), Am. Coll. Forensic Examiners (life; vice chair sect. forensic medicine 2002—07), Royal Soc. Medicine (life), Internat. Coll. Acupuncture and Electro-Therapeutics (pres. 1980—), Am. Coll. Acupunture (life); mem.: NY Japanese Med. Soc. (pres. 1963—73), Am. Soc. Artificial Internal Organs, Japan Bi-Digital O-Ring Test Med. Soc. (pres. 1990—), Japan Bi-Digital O-Ring Test Assn. (pres. 1986—), NY Acad. Sci., Internat. Assn. for Study of Pain (founding mem. 1975—). Achievements include 7 US and 7 Japanese patents in medical field; originator of Bi-Digital O-Ring test. Home and Office: 800 Riverside Dr Ste 8I New York NY 10032-7400 Office Phone: 212-781-6262. Business E-Mail: icaet@yahoo.com.

OMVIK, PER, medical educator; b. Bergen, Norway, Apr. 11, 1942; MD, U. Bergen, 1966; PhD, U. Oslo, 1976. Fogarty rsch. fellow Cleve. Clinic, 1977—78; cons., dept. cardiac disease Haukeland U. Hosp., 1984; prof. Faculty Medicine and Dentistry, U. Bergen, Norway, 1991—, dean, 2005—10. Chmn. Norwegian Soc. Hypertension, 1999—2002. Mem.: European Soc. Hypertension (Lennart Hansson Meml. Lectr. award 2005). Avocations: hunting, dogs, photography. Office: Haukeland University Hosp Bergen 5021 Norway Office Fax: 4755975836. Business E-Mail: per.omvik@med.uib.no.

ONAL, CEM, medical educator; b. Reyhanli, Turkey, May 4, 1975; MD, Hacettepe U., 1999. Assoc. prof. Baskent U. Faculty Medicine, 2011—. Office: Baskent University Faculty Medicine Adana Yuregir 01120 Turkey Office Fax: 90-322-3444445. Personal E-mail: hcemonal@hotmail.com.

ONAL DARILMAZ, DERYA, research scientist; b. Hannover, Germany, June 16, 1980; PhD, U. Gazi, 2010. Rsch. asst. U. Aksaray, 2008—. Mem. IFT Jour. Food Sci. Office: University Aksaray Faculty Sci Aksaray 68100 Turkey E-mail: derya_onal@yahoo.com.

ONAYA, TOSHIMASA, internal medicine educator; b. Tokyo, May 7, 1935; s. Toshinobu and Kou (Ide) Onaya; m. Michiko Yamamoto, Mar. 7, 1965; children: Jun, Tina. MD, Gunma U., Maebashi, Japan, 1962, PhD, 1971. Intern U.S. Army Hosp. Zama, Sagamihara, Japan, 1962-63; postgrad. Gunma U., 1963-65, 69-71; rsch. fellow U. Calif., Berkeley, 1965-66; rsch. assoc. U. Iowa, Iowa City, 1966-68; postgrad. rsch. endocrinologist UCLA, 1968-69; asst. prof. Shinshu U., Matsumoto, Japan, 1971-73, assoc. prof., 1973-83; prof. medicine U. Yamanashi (Japan) Med. Sch., 1983—2001, prof. emeritus, 2001—. Prof., chmn. Third Dept. Internal Medicine U. Yamanashi Med. Sch., 1983—2001; hon. dir. Enzan Citizens Hosp., Koshu City, Japan, 2001—; hon. pres. Internat. Symposium of Molecular Thyroidology. Contbr. Recipient Daiichi prize, Asia and Oceania Thyroid Assn., 1991. Mem.: Am. Thyroid Assn., Am. Endocrine Soc., Japan Thyroid Assn. (Shichijo prize 1971, Miyake prize 1998), Japan Diabetes Soc., Japan Endocrine Soc., Japanese Soc. Internal Medicine. Home: 12-3 Arigasakidai Matsumoto 390-0867 Japan Business E-Mail: onayatj9@cocoa.plala.or.jp.

ONDERDONK, ANDREW BRUCE, microbiologist; b. Hatford, Conn., July 5, 1947; s. Arthur Bruce and Jacqueline Onderdonk; m. Juliet Ann Wherry, June 2, 1969; children: Mark Andrew, Sara Beghane, Abby Hillman. PhD, U. Mo., 1973; student, Macmurray Coll., 1965—69; BA, Votmo, 1971; MS in Microbiology. Med. dir. clin. microbiology Brigham and Women's Hosp., Boston, 1990; prof. of pathology Harvard Med. Sch., 1990—. Sch. com. Westwood Pub. Schs., Westwood, Mass., 1994—2000; water commr. Dedham Westwood Water, Dedham, Mass., 1989—93; trustee MacMurray Coll., Jacksonville, Ill., 2001. Recipient Alumni of Yr., MacMurray Coll., 2000; Infectious Diseases fellow, USPHS, 1973—75. Office: Brigham and Women's Hosp 75 Francis St Boston MA 02115 Personal E-mail: aonderdonk@partners.org.

ONDRA, STEPHEN LOUIS, neurosurgeon, federal official; b. Belleville, Ill., Mar. 23, 1957; s. Duane Thomas and Shirly Mae (Etling) O.; m. Cynthia Ann Rochon, Sept. 2, 1993; children: Stephanie Lynn, Katherine Maria, Marissa Rose. BA, Ill. Wesleyan U., 1980; MD, Rush Med. Coll., 1984. Diplomate Am. Bd. Neurologic Surgery. Staff surgeon, neurosurgeon William Beaumont Hosp., El Paso, Tex., 1990-91; neurosurgeon, dir. complex spine and skull base surgery Walter Reed Hosp., Washington, 1991-94; asst. prof. neurosurgery Uniformed Services U., Bethesda, 1991—95; clin. prof. neurosurgery U. Mich., Ann Arbor, 1995—96; neurosurgeon Mich. Brain and Spine Inst., Ann Arbor, Mich., 1994—96; prof. neurological surgery Northwestern U., 2006—; mem. Veterans Affairs Group Barack Obama's Presdl. Transition Team, 2008—09; sr. policy adv. for health affairs US Dept. Veterans Affairs, Washington, 2009—. Contbr. chpt. to book and articles to profl. jours. Maj. U.S. Army, 1984-94; served in Operation Desert Shield & Desert Storm, 1990-91 Decorated Bronze star U.S. Army, Saudi Arabia, 1991, US Army Commendation medal Mem. AMA, Am. Assn. Neurol. Surgeons, Congress Neurol. Surgery, Mich. Assn. Neurol. Surgeons, Alpha Omega Alpha. Avocations: horseback riding, skiing, tennis. Office: Northwestern University Feinberg School of Medicine 303 E Chicago Ave Chicago IL 60611 E-mail: sondra@nmff.org. *

ONEGLIA, CARLO, cardiologist; b. Savona, Italy, Mar. 30, 1948; s. Angelo and Marcella (Pasqualini) O.; m. Carla Ricco, May 10, 1980; children: Andrea, Emanuele. MD, U. Padua, Italy, 1973. Intern Padua U., 1973-75; asst. Gen. Hosp., Brescia, Italy, 1977-83; dep. dir. divsn. medicine Iseo (Italy) Hosp., 1983-88; dir. cardiology unit Sant Orsola Hosp., Brescia, 2009—. Contbr. articles to profl. jours. Capt. police Italian mil., 1975-76. Office: S Orsola Hosp Via Vittorio Emanuele II 27 25122 Brescia BS Italy Office Phone: 390302971937. Personal E-mail: carlo.oneglia@teletu.it. Business E-Mail: carlo.oneglia@poliambulanza.it.

O'NEIL, KATHLEEN M., pediatrician, educator; b. Biddeford, Maine, Mar. 9, 1953; BA, Wellesley Coll., 1974; MD, Tufts U. Sch. Medicine, 1978. Asst. prof. pediat. U. Md. Sch. Medicine, 1986—89; assoc. prof. pediat. SUNY at Buffalo Coll. Medicine, 1989—2003; prof. pediat. U. Okla. Health Scis. Ctr., 2003—. Recipient Janet M. Glasgow Achievement award, Am. Med. Women's Assn., Rsch. award, Stetler Found., Johns Hopkins U., Outstanding Tchr. award, Women and Children's Hosp. Buffalo. Fellow: Am. Acad. Pediat., Am. Coll. Rheumatology (Career Re-Entry award); mem.: Childhood Arthritis and Rheumatology Rsch. Alliance, Soc. Pediat. Rsch., Alpha Omega Alpha. Office: 1200 N Phillips Ave Ste 5100 Oklahoma City OK 73104 Office Fax: 405-271-1151. Business E-Mail: kathleen-oneil@ouhsc.edu.

O'NEILL, HELEN CHRISTINE, immunologist, researcher, educator, stem cell biologist; b. Adelaide, South Australia, Australia, Sept. 9, 1951; d. Ewen Keith Lock and Irene Mary Fulton; m. Terence John O'Neill, June 29, 1973; children: Michael Jesse, Connell John. BSc with honors, Adelaide U., 1972; PhD, Australian Nat. U., Canberra, 1980. Rsch. fellow John Curtin Sch. Med. Rsch., Canberra, 1981—89, sr. rsch. fellow, 1990—95; sr. lectr. sch. biochemistry and molecular biology Australian Nat. U., 1996—98, assoc. prof. sch. biochemistry and molecular biology, 1999—2005, prof. immunology sch. biochemistry and molecular biology, 2006—. Contbr. articles to profl. publs. Recipient Vice Chancellor's award, Australian Nat. U., 2004, Citation, Australian Learning and Tchg. Coun., 2009; C. J. Martin fellow, Nat. Health and Med. Rsch. Coun. Australia, 1984—86, Yamagiwa-Yoshida Meml. Internat. Cancer Study fellow, Internat. Union Against Cancer, 1987—88. Office: Australian Nat U Rsch Sch Biology ACT Canberra 0200 Australia Office Phone: 61 2 6125 4720.

O'NEILL, JAMES F., retired health facility administrator; b. Corona, NY, July 3, 1923; s. James Francis O'Neill and Anita Theresa Queroli; m. Wilma Bernice Gallagher, July 17, 1948; children: Sharon, Kevin, Patricia. Med. Technologist, Bethesda Naval Med. Sch., 1943; BSc, L.I. U., 1951, MSc, 1965, postgrad., 1966, Columbia U., 1970. Cert. med. lab. dir. N.Y. State. Owner Shiel Med. Lab., Inc., Queens Village, NY, 1950—56; owner, dir. State of N.Y. Med. Lab., Inc., Queens Village, 1956—89, co-dir. Bklyn., 1990—95; ret., 1998. Cons. in field. With USN, 1942—46. Fellow: Am. Assn Biochemists, Am. Inst. Chemists, Inc. (emeritus 1966); mem.: KC, Rotary. Roman Catholic. Avocations: fishing, gardening, travel, computers. Home Phone: 239-283-1050.

O'NEILL, KATHERINE TEMPLETON, journalist, former nursing educator, museum administrator; b. Moline, Ill., Jan. 13, 1949; d. Morris John and Patricia (Collins) Templeton; 1 child by previous marriage, Carolyn Patricia Coquillette; m. William James O'Neill Jr., July 18, 1987; stepchildren: Alec, Sara, Jessie, Laura. BSN, U. Mich., 1971; postgrad., St. Clare's Hall, Oxford, Eng., 1971-72; MSN, Boston U., 1974. RN Ohio, Mass. Instr. Mass. Gen. Hosp., Boston, 1974-76; assoc. prof. Ursuline Coll., Cleve., 1976-81; dir. devel. and pub. rels. Ohio Coll. Podiatric Medicine, Cleve., 1985-87; dir. Chisholm Halle Costume Wing We. Res. Hist. Soc., Cleve., 1988-90; fashion editor Chagrin Valley Times, 1989-2000, 2009—. Vice-chair bd. dirs., hon. trustee Healthspace Cleve., 1983-2000, Cleve. Music Sch. Settlement, 1983-97. Bd. dirs. Hathaway Brown Sch., 2006—, pres. alumnae bd. dirs., 1984—86; bd. dirs. Cleve. Ballet, 1987—95, Cleve. Inst. Music, 1994—2008, Cleve. Scholarship Programs, 1995—2003, Mus. Arts Assn. The Cleve. Orch., 1995—; mem. adv. bd. Francis Paine Bolton Sch. Nursing and Mandel Sch. Applied Social Scis., Case Western Res. U., Cleve., 1990—2006, GAMUT, Cleve. State U., 1992—93; bd. dirs. Dress for Success, Cleve., 1998—2000, Cleve. Publs. Yearbook, 1993—95, Vis. Nurse Assn.Ohio, 1995—2011, Cleve. Cmty. Bldg. Initiative, 2001—04; founding trustee, vice chair Generation Found., Cleve., 1998—2009; mem. disbursements com. WMJ and Dorothy K. O'Neill Found., 1993—; trustee Cuyanhoga C.C. Found., 2001—; bd. dirs. Cleve. Inst. Art, 2002—08, Gt. Lakes Sci. Ctr., 1999—2009, Ursuline Coll., 1996—, La Confrerie des Chavaliers du Tastevin, 2003, Cleve. State U. Found., 2007—, Commanderie Du Bordeauy, 2010. Recipient Souereign Order St. John Jerusalem Knight award, Malta, 2011. Avocations: singing, gourmet cooking, orchidology. Office: CM Wealth Pepper Pike OH 44124 Office Fax: 440-893-0325.

O'NEILL, WILLIAM WALTER, dean, cardiologist, educator; b. Nov. 24, 1951; BS, U. Mich., 1972; MD, Wayne State U., 1977. Diplomate Am. Bd. Internal Medicine, Am. Bd. Cardiology. Intern internal medicine U. Wis., Madison, 1977—78; resident internal medicine Wayne State U., Detroit, 1978—80; fellow U. Mich., Ann Arbor, 1980-82, instr. internal medicine, 1982-83, asst. prof., 1983-86, assoc. prof., 1986-87; dir. cardiac catheterization lab. U. Mich. Hosp., Ann Arbor, 1984-87; dir. divsn. cardiovascular disease William Beaumont Hosp., Royal Oak, Troy, Mich., 1987—2006, corp. chief cardiology, 2002—06, vice chair Dept. Internal Medicine for Rsch., 2003; co-dir. Beaumont Heart Ctr., 1999—2006; prof. medicine, exec. dean clin. affairs Miller Sch. Medicine, U. Miami, 2006—. Attending cardiologist VA Hosp., Ann Arbor, 1982-90; chmn. govt. rels. subcom. Nat. Cardiovasc. Network; rsch. peer rev. com. Am. Heart Assn. Mich., 1988-89; chmn. publs. com. Mansfield Scientific Balloon Valvuloplasty Registry; bd. govs. William Beaumont Hosp. Rsch. Inst.; presenter in field. Author: Myocardial Revascularization by Coronary Angioplasty or Bypass Surgery During MI in Acute Myocardial Infarction: New Approaches to Evaluation and Therapy, 1986, (chpt.) Acute Coronary Intervention, 1987, Current Perspective in Coronary Care, 1987, Interventional Cardiovascular Medicine, 1994, Acute Coronary Care, 2d edit., 1995; co-author: (chpts.) Cardiovascular Review, 6th edit., 1985, 8th edit., 1987, Tissue Plasminogen Activator in Thrombolytic Therapy, 1987, Techniques and Applications in Interventional Cardiology, 1991, Atherectomy, 1992, Emergency Medicine: A Comprehensive Study Guide, 3d edit., 1992, Adjunctive Therapy for Acute Myocardial Infarction, 1992, Manual of Interventional CArdiology, 1992, Cura Intensiva Cardiologica, Primary Coronary Angioplasty in Acute Myocardial Infarction; author, co-author: (chpt.) Interventional Cardiovascular Medicine, 1994; editl. cons. Jour. Intervention Cardiology; mem. editl. bd. Catheterization Cardiovasc. Diagnosis; contbr. over 400 articles to profl. publs. Grantee Smith/Kline Beecham, 1989-90, 90—, Advanced Cardiovasc. Sys., Inc., 1988-90, 90—, Midwest Heart Rsch. Found., Abbott Labs., 1990—, Duke U., 1990—, William Beaumont Hosp. Rsch. Inst., 1990—. Fellow Am. Coll. Cardiology (chpt. sec.-treas. 1993-94, reimbursement com.), Am. Coll. Chest Physicians, Coun. Clin. Cardiology; mem. AMA, ACP, Internat. Andreas Gruentzig Soc. Office: U Miami / Divsn Cardiology RMSB 1122A 1600 NW 10th Ave Miami FL 33136 Office Phone: 305-243-9483. E-mail: woneill@med.miami.edu.

O'NEIL MUNDINGER, MARY, nursing educator; MA, Columbia U., 1974, DrPH, 1981. Dean Columbia U. Sch. Nursing, 1986—, prof. health policy. Bd. mem. Cell Therapeutics Inc., 1997—, UnitedHealth Group, 1997—, Gentiva, 2002—, Welch Allyn Inc, 2002—. Mem.: NY Acad. of Medicine, Inst. of Medicine, Am. Acad. Nursing. Office: 617 W 168 St Rm 129 New York NY 10032 Office Phone: 212-305-3582. Office Fax: 212-305-1116. E-mail: mm44@columbia.edu.

ONER, AHMET FAIK, pediatrician, educator; b. Bingol, Turkey, Sept. 26, 1959; s. Adil and Hüsna Oner; m. Cigdem Atli; children: Ayse Merve Tat, Mahmut Safa, Hatice Sena, Zeynep Reyyan. Degree in Pediat., Ataturk U. Faculty Medicine, Erzurum, Turkey, 1984. Cert. in pediat. and pediatric hematology Hacettepe U. Ankara, 1997. Prof. pediatric hematology Yuzuncu Yil U. Faculty Medicine, Van, Turkey, 1993—, dir., dept. pediatric hgematology, 1998—; dean Med. Sch.ool, Yuzuncu Yil U., 2009—. Mgr. Management Outbreak Avian Influenza Eastern Turkey, 2006. Recipient Dr. Yr. award, Ministry Health Turkey, 2006. Master: Assn. Voluntary Health (van 2004—08). Moslem. Avocations: swimming, travel. Home: Vali konagi St Van 65100 Turkey Office: Yuzuncu Yil Univ Faculty Medicine Maras Van 65200 Turkey Office Fax: 90 432 2167519. Personal E-mail: afo59@yahoo.com.

ONES, DENIZ S., psychologist, educator; b. Istanbul, Turkey, Aug. 12, 1965; d. Somer and Ulker (Saime) Ones; m. Ates Haner, July 5, 1993; 1 child, Daria M. Haner. BA, Augustana Coll., 1988; PhD, U. Iowa, 1993. Asst. prof. U. Houston, 1993—96; Hellervik Prof. indsl. psychology U. Minn., Mpls., 1996—; founder Thetametrics LLP, Maple Grove, Minn., 2004—. Author: Handbook of Industrial, Work and Organizational Psychology. Recipient Cattell Award for Outstanding Early Career Contbns., Soc. of Multivariate Exptl. Psychology, 2003, Ernest J. McCormick Award for Disting. Early Career Contbns., Soc. for Indsl. and Orgnl. Psychology, 1998; Fellow of Divsn. 14 (Indsl. and Orgnl. Psychology), APA, 1999, Fellow of Divsn. 5 (Measurement, Stats., and Evaluation), 1998. Achievements include research in meta-analyses of integrity tests, managerial selection, police selection, employment testing. Office: Thetametrics LLP 6427 Ranchview Ln N Maple Grove MN 55311 E-mail: ones@thetametrics.com.

ONES, SAIME ULKER, pediatrics educator; b. Ankara, Turkey, Mar. 20, 1939; d. Bahri Vedat and Sukriye (Gurcan) Alpman; m. Somer Ones, Nov. 13, 1964; children: Deniz, Suha Remzi. MD, Med. Faculty Istanbul, Turkey, 1963. Rschr. Inst. Immuno Biology, Paris, 1967—68; asst. prof. Istanbul Sch. Medicine, Turkey, 1968—72, assoc. prof., 1973—79, prof. pediat., 1980, dir. dept. clin. immunology, allergy and infectious diseases, 1980—97, dir. dept. pediatric allergy and chest diseases, 1997—2005, dir. dept. pediat., 2000—. Editor: Jour. Infectious Disease and Clin. Microbiology, Expressions on Allergen Specific Immunotherapy, 1996; contbr. articles to profl. jours. Grantee Inst. Immunobiology Broussais Hosp., Paris. Mem.: European Pediatric Acad. Allergy and Clin. Immunology, European Soc. Immunology, European Acad. Allergy and Clin. Immunology, Am. Acad. Allergy, Asthma and Immunology. Avocations: classical music, archaeology, theater, poetry. Office: Istanbul Med Sch Dept Pediatrics Çapa Istanbul Turkey Home: Tavukcu Fethi Sok No 33-35 Osmanbey 80260 Istanbul Istanbul Turkey Office Phone: 00902122470457.

ONESTI, SILVIO JOSEPH, psychiatrist; b. San Francisco, Jan. 3, 1926; s. Silvio Joseph and Johanna (Kristoffy) Onesti; m. Jean Thomas, May 12, 1956; children: Sally Joanna, Stephen Thomas. BS, Stanford U., 1947; MD, McGill U., 1951. Diplomate Am. Bd. Psychiatry and Neurology. Instr. pediatrics Yale Med. Sch., New Haven, 1956-58; career tchr. psychiatry NIMH, Harvard Med. Sch., Beth Israel Hosp., Boston, 1963-65; head child psychiatry unit Beth Israel Hosp., Boston, 1965-73; dir. child and adolescent psychiatry McLean Hosp., Belmont, Mass., 1973-91, dir. Hall-Mercer Ctr. for children and adolescents, 1973-91; dir. child and adolescent psychiat. tng., 1973-92; dir. clin. svcs. McLean Hosp., Belmont, 1981-83; asst. prof. psychiatry Harvard Med. Sch., Boston, 1969—. Contbr. articles to profl. jours. With USN, 1944—46. Fellow: Am. Coll. Psychiatrists, Am. Acad. Child and Adolescent Psychiatry, Am. Psychiat. Assn.; mem.: Mass. Med. Soc., Boston Psychoanalytic Soc. and Inst. (faculty 1971—81), Group Advancement Psychiatry (bd. dirs. 1987—89, fellow 1959—61), Alpha Omega Alpha. Home: 4 Gray Gdns W Cambridge MA 02138-2312 Office: McLean Hosp 115 Mill St Belmont MA 02478-1048 Home Phone: 617-354-3704; Office Phone: 617-855-2801.

ONG, ALVIN CHUA, orthopaedic surgeon; MD with honors, State U. NY, 1994. Lic. Pa., 1997, diplomate Am. Bd. Orthopaedic Surgery. Intern Univ. Pa., resident orthop. surgery, 1999; fellow orthop. surgery Carolinas Med. Ctr., 2001, Rothman Inst., 2002; hosp. affiliations include Thomas Jefferson Univ. Hosp., AtlantiCare Regional Med. Ctr. Contbr. articles Clinical Orthopaedics and Related Research: Homepage, 2002, Periprosthetic patellar fractures, 2006, A Comparison Between Total Hip Replacement for Osteonecrosis and Degenerative Joint Disease, 2008, Management of Postoperative Hematomas, 2009. Named one of the Top Doctors, Phila. Mag., 2010—11. Mem.: Am. Acad. Orthop. Surgeons, Am. Assn. hip and Knee Surgeons, Pa. Orthop. Soc. Office: AtlantiCare Regional Medical Center Bldg 1300 2500 English Creek Ave Egg Harbor Township NJ 08234 Office Phone: 800-321-9999. Office Fax: 267-479-1321.

ONG, KIM-THANH, physician; b. Vietnam, July 23, 1974; MD, U. Medicine & Pharmacy, Hochiminh, Vietnam, 2002; attending, Paris-Descartes U., France. Tchg. asst., dept. paediatrics U. Medicine & Pharmacy, Hochiminh, 2002—03; resident Assistance Publique - Hôpitaux de Paris, Hôpital Necker, France, 2003—04; physician Assistance Publique - Hôpitaux de Paris, Hôpital Européen Georges Pompidou and Hôpital Louis Mourier; INSERM U970, 2006—. Mem.: European Soc. Hypertension, French Soc. Pharmacology & Therapeutics. Avocations: reading, jogging. Office: 20 Rue Leblanc Paris 75015 France Office Fax: 33 1 56 09 39 92. E-mail: kim-thanh.ong@egp.aphp.fr.

ONG, LAWRENCE, interventional cardiologist, educator; MD, U. Calif., 1976. Diplomate Am. Bd. Internal Medicine, Am. Bd. Internal Medicine-cardiovascular disease, Am. Bd. Internal Medicine-interventional cardiology. Assoc. prof. medicine Sch. of Med. NYU; resident in internal medicine North Shore Univ. Hosp., Manhasset, NY, 1976—79, fellow in cardiovascular disease, 1979—81, cardiologist. Office: North Shore University Hospital 300 Community Drive Manhasset NY 11030 Office Fax: 516-562-4100.

ONG, PECK Y., physician; b. Malaysia, June 26, 1965; MD, Loma Linda U., Calif., 1996. Attending physician Children's Hosp. LA, USC Keck Sch. Medicine, 2004—. Fellow: Am. Acad. Allergy, Asthma & Immunology. Office: 4650 Sunset Blvd MS 75 Los Angeles CA 90027 Office Fax: 323-361-1191. Business E-Mail: pyong@chla.usc.edu.

ONG, WILLIE TAN, cardiologist; b. Manila, Philippines, Oct. 24, 1963; s. Yong and Juanita Tan Ong; m. Anna Liza Ramoso Ong, Oct. 24, 1993; children: Anjelica Co Ramoso, Catherine Co Ramoso. MD, De La Salle Coll. Medicine, Cavite, Philippines, 1992; speciality in internal medicine, Manila Doc. Hosp., Manila, 1994—96; speciality in cardiology, U. Philippines, Manila, 1997—99, MPH (hon.), 2001. Med. dir. Pasay Filipino-Chinese Charity Health Ctr., Inc., Pasay City, Philippines, 1998—. Cardiology cons. Manila Doc. Hosp., 2001—, Makati Med. Ctr., Makati City, Philippines. Author: Medicine Blue Book, Cardiology Blue Book, Ideals and Inspirations for Doctors, Expanded Medicine Blue Book, Philippine College of Physicians Through 50 Years: Fulfilling The Vision; editor; author: Altapresyon at Tamang Pangangalaga sa Inyong Puso; contbr. articles to profl. jours. Founder Movement of Idealistic and Nationalistic Doc., Manila, 2005—05. Fellow: Philippine Coll. Cardiology, Philippine Coll. Physicians (Presdl. award 2003, 2005); mem.: Soc. Philippine Health History, Inc. (chairperson 2003—, founder). Roman Catholic. Achievements include founder of Co Tec Tai Medical Museum. Home: 5320 Amorsolo St Dasmarinas Village Makati City 1222 Philippines Office: Soc Philippine Health History Inc 2652 Taft Ave Pasay City 1300 Philippines Office Fax: 632-831-1866; Home Fax: 632-831-1866. Personal E-mail: willietong@netasia.net. E-mail: willietong@gmail.com.

ONIPCHENKO, VLADIMIR GERTRUDOVICH, biologist, educator; b. Moscow, Sept. 19, 1957; s. Gertrud Fedorovich and Valentina Stepanovna (Tyulpakova) Onipchenko; m. Olga Vital'evna Yurtseva, Jan. 19, 1980 (div. Nov. 2001); 1 child, Elena; m. Assem Aliyakpa-rovna Akhmetzhanova, Nov. 13, 2005; 1 child, Timur. MS, Moscow State U., 1980, PhD, 1984, D in Biol. Sci., 1996. Biologist diplomate. Sci. rschr. Moscow State U., 1984-90, assoc. prof., 1991-96, prof., 1997—. Editor, co-author: Experimental Investigation, 1994, Alpihe Ecosystems, 2004; contbr. articles to profl. jours. Named William Evans vis. fellow, New Zealand, 2002; grantee, Russian Found. Fundamental Rsch., Moscow, 1993—, Sweden Acad. Sci., 1994—96, J. and K. MacArthur Found., Moscow, 1995, Netherlands Orgn. for Sci. Rsch., 1996—2000, 2005—, NATO Sci. Programme, 2000—01. Mem.: Internat. Assn. for Vegetation Sci., Brit. Ecol. Soc., Moscow Soc. Naturalist, Ecol. Soc. Am. Office: Moscow State Univ Dept Geobotany/Biol Fac 119991 Moscow Russia Office Phone: 7 495 9394310. Personal E-mail: vonipchenko@mail.ru.

ONISHI, KATSUYA, cardiologist; b. Tsu, Mie, Japan, Aug. 12, 1965; MD, Mie U. Sch. of Medicine, Tsu, Japan, 1990, PhD, 1996. Resident internal medicine Mie U. Sch. Medicine, Tsu, Japan, 1990—91, resident cardiology, 1992—96; asst. prof. Mie U. Hosp., Tsu, Mie, Japan, 2001—03, Dept. of Lab. Medicine, Mie U. Sch. of Medicine, Tsu, Mie, Japan, 2003—; dir. Heart Filure Clinic, Mie U. Hosp., Tsu, Mie, Japan, 2002—, Echo Lab., Tsu, Mie, Japan, 2003—. Recipient Grant-in-aid for young scienteist, Grant-In-AID for young scientist, 2002—03. Fellow: Am. Coll. Cardiology. Office: Mie U Sch Medicine 2-174 Edobashi Mie Tsu 514-8507 Japan Office Fax: 81-59-231-5250. E-mail: katsu@clin.medic.mie-u.ac.jp.

ONISHI, YASUHIKO, engineering company executive; b. Hagima, Gifu, Japan, Jan. 25, 1945; PhD, Hiroshima U., 1967, DSc, 1979. CEO Ryujyu Sci. Corp., 2006—. Prof. Nippon Bunri U., 2000—02. Mem.: Soc. Polymer Sci. (Japan), Japanese Soc. Gene Design and Delivery. Office: 39-4 Kosora-cho Seto Aichi 4890842 Japan Office Fax: 0561-84-3227. Business E-Mail: vyx00545@nifty.com.

ONITSUKA, HIDEO, radiologist, health facility administrator; b. Fukuoka, Japan, July 7, 1947; s. Toshio and Teru (Hida) O.; m. Kumiko Sato, Sept. 15, 1973; children: June, Ryo, Ken. MD, Kyushu U., Fukuoka, Japan, 1972, D of Med. Sci., 1989. Diplomate Am. Bd. Radiology. Resident U. Mich., Ann Arbor, 1975—79; instr. Kyushu U., 1979—84, lectr., 1984—90, assoc. prof. radiology, 1990—92; dir. dept. radiology Iizuka (Japan) Hosp., 1992—98, v.p., 1997—98, Tanushimaru Ctrl. Hosp., Japan, 1998—2000, pres., 2000—. Cons. Radiation Effects Rsch. Found., Hiroshima, Japan, 1979-89; vis. lectr. Kyushu U., 1992-2003. Mem. Japan Radiol. Soc., Radiol. Soc. N.Am., Am. Coll. Radiology, Am. Roentgen Ray Soc., European Congress Radiology. Avocations: computer, camera, travel. Home: Gojo 2-23-5 Dazaifu 818-0125 Japan Office: Tanushimaru Ctrl Hosp 892 Masuoda Tanushimaru Kurume Fukuoka 839-1213 Japan Office Phone: 81-943-72-2460. E-mail: onitsuka@intermix.ne.jp, hideo1947@seihoukai.or.jp.

ONN, AMIR, medical educator, researcher; b. Rehovot, Israel, Nov. 19, 1959; arrived in U.S., 2000; s. Itzhak and Nitza Onn; m. Elizabeth E. Half, July 18, 1989; children: Lior, Dana, Alon, Yuval. BA, Hebrew U., Jersalem, MD, 1990. Intern Tel-Aviv Med. Ctr., Tel Aviv Sch. Medicine, resident internal medicine, fellow pulmonary medicine; postdoctoral fellow U. Tex. MD Anderson Cancer Ctr., Houston, fellow interventional pulmonary oncology; asst. prof. medicine and cancer biology U. Tex. M.D. Anderson Cancer Ctr., Houston, 2000—. Recipient Physician Scientist award, U. Tex. MD Anderson Cancer Ctr., 2004—. Home: 4926 N Braeswood Blvd Houston TX 77096 2708 Office Fax: 713-794-4922, Home Fax: 713-729-8700. Business E-Mail: amironn@mdanderson.org.

ONO, KEN, radiologist; b. Toyonaka city, Osaka, Japan, Dec. 18, 1969; s. Hiroaki and Yasuko Ono; m. Ikumi Nakatsubo, Apr. 24, 1999; children: Keita, Haruka. M, Kumamoto U., 1994. Cert. physician Japan, 1995. Med. staff radiology Shin-Koga Hosp., Kurume city, 2004—. Contbr. articles to profl. jours. Office: Shin-Koga Hosp 120 Tenjin-cho Kurume City Fukuoka 830-8577 Japan Office Fax: 81-942-38-2248.

ONO, MASAFUMI, medical educator; b. Japan, Apr. 22, 1963; MD, Kochi Med. Sch., 1990, PhD, 1998. Lectr. Kochi Med. Sch., 2007—. Office: Kochi Med Sch Kohasu Oko-cho Nankoku 783-8505 Japan Office Fax: 81-88-880-2338. Business E-Mail: onom@kochi-u.ac.jp.

ONO, TAKAHIRO, dentist, educator; b. Ashiya, Japan, Apr. 3, 1957; DDS, Hiroshima U., 1983; PhD, Osaka U., 1987. Assoc. prof., faculty dentistry Osaka U., 1998—2000, assoc. prof., Grad. Sch. Dentistry, 2000—, assoc. prof., Ctr. Advanced Med. Engrng. and Informatics, 2005, assoc. prof., Ctr. Advanced Sci. and Innovation, 2009—. Guest prof. Hokkaido U. Grad. Sch. Dentistry, 2004; councilor, career specialist, gerodontology U. Uruguay, 2009—10, U. Concepcion, 2009—10. Recipient Yumikura Meml. Academic award, Osaka U., 2008. Fellow: Japanese Assn. Geriatric Dentistry, Japanese Assn. Maxillofacial Prosthetics, Japanese Assn. Prosthetic Dentistry, European Coll. Gerodontology (GABA Rsch. award 2006); mem.: Internat. Assn. Dental Rsch. Avocation: architecture. Office: 1-8 Yamada-oka Suita Osaka 562-0023 Japan Office Fax: 81-6-6879-2957. Business E-Mail: ono@dent.osaka-u.ac.jp.

ONO, YOSHINARI, urologist, educator; b. Nagoya, Japan, Dec. 18, 1948; MD, Sch. Medicine, Nagoya U., 1973; PhD, Postgrad. Sch. Nagoya U., 1983. Chmn. dept. urology Komaki Shimon Hosp., 1985—97; assoc. prof., dept. urology Nagoya U. Hosp., 1997—2007; prof. Sch. Med. Welfare, Aichi Shukutoku U., 2007—. Recipient Heisei 12th Clin. Application of Laparoscopy prize, Japan Med. Assn., 2000. Mem.: Japanese Soc. Endourology, Endourol. Soc. Achievements include developed laparoscopic radical nephrectomy (LRN) and established the usefulness of LRN both in its minimal invasiveness and its compatibility for cancer control in comparison to its open surgical counterpart. Avocation: golf. Home: 4-225 Kamiyashiro Meito-ku Nagoya Aichi 465-0025 Japan Home Fax: 81 527050391. Business E-Mail: onoy@asu.aasa.ac.jp.

ONODERA, HIROKAZU, medical association administrator; b. Japan, Jan. 13, 1965; M, Kanazawa U., 1991; PhD, Nara Inst. Sci. and Tech., 2008. Mgr. Asahikasei Kuraray Med. Co. Ltd. R & D Lab., 1991—2005, Asahi Med. Co. Ltd. Develop and Sci. Affair, 2005—. Home: 14-3 Senjukotobukicyo Adachi-ku Tokyo 120-0033 Japan Business E-Mail: onodera.hc@om.asahi-kasei.co.jp.

ONORATI, FRANCESCO, cardiologist, surgeon, researcher; b. Napoli, Italy, Apr. 22, 1975; s. Pasquale Onorati and Rosaria Ciarfaglia. MD, Second U., Naples, 1999, degree in Cardiac Surgery, 2004. Internship Second U., Pediat. Cardiac Surgery Unit, 1997—99; residency Second U., Cardiac Surgery Unit, 1999—2004; mem. staff cardio-vascular surgery Magna Graecia U., Catanzaro, Italy, 2004—. Mem.: European Assn. Cardiothoracic Surgery. Home: Viale dei pini 28 Naples 80131 Italy Office: Magna Graecia Univ Viele Europe Catanzaro 88100 Italy Business E-Mail: frankono@libero.it.

ONORATO, EUSTAQUIO MARIA, cardiologist, consultant; b. Caracas, Venezuela, Feb. 7, 1952; s. Joseph Onorato and Gerardine Venutolo; m. Barbara Clara Buraggi, Apr. 28, 1990; children: Marta Clara, Cecilia Maria. A Level in Humanistic Studies, Inst. Leone XIII, Milan, 1971; degree with honors, U. Milan, Sch. Medicine, 1977. Bd. cert. in cardiology U. Sch. Caracas, Venezuela, 1984. Co-dir. cardiovasc. catheterization lab. Centro E. Malan, San Donato Hosp., U. Milan, San Donato Milanese, 1989—97; dir. cardiology dept. and catheterization lab. Clinica San Rocco, Brescia, 1997—2002; dir. cardiology dept. Humanitas Gavazzeni Clinic, Bergamo, Italy, 2002—06; dir. cardiology dept. and catheterization lab. S. Orsola Hosp. FBF, Brescia, Italy, 2006—. Sci. cons., adult and pediatric cardiovasc. interventions 13 Interventional Cardiology Units, Italy, 1999—2008; internat. guest faculty Internat. Workshop Catheter Interventions Congenital and Structural Heart Disease, Frankfurt, Germany, 2001—, Pediatric Interventional Cardiac Symposium, Chicago, 2001—, Moscow's Course Endovascular Surgery Congenital and Acquired Heart Diseases, Coronary and Vascular Pathology, Moscow, 2002—, Transcatheter Cardiovasc. Therapeutics, 2003—. Fellow: Associazione Nazionale Medici Cardiologi Ospedalieri, Sci. Coun. Cardio-Thoracic Ctr. Monaco, Soc. Cardiac Angiography and Interventions, Russian Sci. Soc. Interventional Radiology and Endovascular Surgery (Hon. Membership). Office: Cardiology Dept SOrsola Hosp Via Vittorio Emanuele II 27 Brescia 25122 Italy Home Fax: 39-030-2771430. Personal E-mail: eonorato@libero.it.

ONTJES, DAVID AINSWORTH, medicine and pharmacology educator; b. Lyons, Kans., July 19, 1937; s. Max S. and Elizabeth (Ainsworth) O.; m. Joan Troy Ontjes, Aug. 26, 2006; children: Linden F., Sarah E., Ethan A., Jason A. BA, U. Kans., 1959; MA, Oxford U., 1961; MD, Harvard U., 1964. Am. Bd. Internal Medicine, sub-board endocrinology. Intern, resident Boston City Hosp., 1964-66; research assoc. NIH, Besthesda, Md., 1966-69; asst. prof. dept. medicine and pharmacology U. N.C., Chapel Hill, 1969-72, assoc. prof., 1972-76, prof., 1976—, Eunice Bernhardt Disting. prof., 1982—. Contbr. articles in field to profl. jours. Served with USPHS, 1966-69. Rhodes scholar Oxford U., 1959-61; USPHS grantee Nat. Insts. Arthritis and Metabolic Diseases, NIH, 1969-82; recipient Basic Sci. Teaching award U. N.C., 1978. Fellow ACP; mem. Endocrine Soc., Am. Soc. Clin. Investigation, Am. Soc. Pharmacology and Exptl. Therapeutics, Assn. Profs. Medicine Republican. Presbyterian. Office: U NC Sch Medicine Dept Medicine Chapel Hill NC 27599-0001 Office Phone: 919-966-3336. Business E-Mail: david_ontjes@med.unc.edu.

ONUCHIC, LUIZ FERNANDO, medical educator, scientist; b. Sao Paulo, Brazil, Dec. 13, 1960; s. Nelson and Lourdes de la Rosa Onuchic; m. Maria Helena Flesch, June 28, 1986; children: Ana Claudia, Laura, Fernando. MD, U. Sao Paulo, 1984, PhD, 1992. Med. resident Hosp. das Clinicas, U. Sao Paulo Sch. Medicine, 1985—88; asst. prof. medicine dept. medicine divsn. gen. medicine U. Sao Paulo Sch. Medicine, 1988—92, asst. prof. medicine dept. medicine divsn. nephrology, 1999—2003, assoc. prof. medicine dept. medicine divsn. nephrology, 2003—; rsch. assoc. Yale U. Sch. Medicine, New Haven, 1992—93; clin. and sci. fellow in nephrology Johns Hopkins U. Sch. Medicine, Balt., 1994—99. Head med. ICU Hosp. das Clinicas - U. Sao Paulo Sch. Medicine, 1989—92. Contbr. articles to profl. jours. Grantee, Fundação de Amparo a Pesquisa do Estado de Sao Paulo, Brazil, 2000—04, 2004—06. Mem.: Am. Soc. Nephrology (corr.), Brazilian Soc. Biophysics (assoc.), Brazilian Soc. Nephrology (assoc.). Roman Catholic. Achievements include discovery of PKHD1 which is the gene mutated in the autosomal recessive polycystic kidney disease; discovery of a novel cytokine, ML-1, and characterization of its expression in subjects with asthma; discovery of and characterization of PKHD1 (Polycystic Kidney and Hepatic Disease 1), the gene mutated in autosomal recessive polycystic kidney disease; research in elucidation of the molecular basis of focal cyst formation in human autosomal dominant polycystic kidney disease type I; biochemical characterization of the polycystin-1 protein in vitro and in vivo; polyductin, the PKHD1 gene product, comprises isoforms expressed in plasma membrane, primary cilium, and cytoplasm; development of a system that shows that polycystin-1, the gene product of PKD1 that induces resistance to apoptosis and spontaneous tubulogenesis in MDCK cells; identification and characterization of Pkhd1, the mouse orthologue of the human ARPKD gene and construction of an integrated genetic and physical map of the autosomal recessive polycystic kidney disease region; construction of an integrated genetic and physical map of the autosomal recessive polycystic kidney disease region. Home: Rua Francisco Farel 287 05436-070 São Paulo Brazil Office: Faculdade de Medicina da USP Avenida Doutor Arnaldo 455 - Sala 3310 01246-903 São Paulo SP Brazil Office Fax: 55-11-3088-2267. Personal E-mail: lonuchic@usp.br. Business E-Mail: lonuchic@lim12.fm.usp.br.

ONUFREY, VICTOR GEORGE, oncologist; b. NYC, June 16, 1958; s. Serge and Sylvia Onufrey; m. Natalia Fedorova, June 1, 1991; children: Irene Victoria, Paul Michael. BS, Pa. State U., 1979; MD, Jefferson Med. Coll., 1981. Bd. cert. therapeutic radiology Am. Bd. Radiology, 1986. Resident radiation oncology Thomas Jefferson U. Hosp., Phila., 1981—85; staff radiation oncologist David Grant USAF Med. Ctr., Travis AFB, Calif., 1985—87, chief radiation oncology, 1987—90; staff physician dept. radiation oncology Western Pa. Hosp., Pitts., 1990—; state air surgeon, 2004—. Chief brachytherapy svcs. Western Pa. Hosp., Pitts., 2001—. Mem. edit. bd.: Ukrainian Jour. Radiology, 1999—2003; contbr. articles to profl. jours. Treas. St. Peter and Paul Mus., Pitts., 1995—2003. Col. US Air N.G., 2005—, lt. col. U.S. Air Nat. Guard, 1990—. Decorated Meritorious Svc. medal USAF, Air Force Commendation medal; fellow, Am. Cancer Soc., 1980—81. Mem.: Am. Brachytherapy Soc., Am. Soc. Clin. Oncology, Am. Soc. Therapeutic Radiology and Oncology, Am. Coll. Radiology. Eastern Orthodox. Avocations: reading, travel, collecting American Indian art, history. Office: Western Pennsylvania Hospital 4800 Friendship Ave Pittsburgh PA 15224 E-mail: jgonufre@wpahs.org.

ONYA, HANS ELEM, public health service officer, director; b. Afikpo, Nigeria, Dec. 25, 1953; BA, Osmania U., Hydrabad, India, 1985; diploma in Pub. Health Engring., U. Madurai, India; MPH, U. Philippines, 1987. Pub. health supt. Ministry of Health, Owerri, Imo, Nigeria, 1977—82; pub. health edn. specialist UN Devel. Programme, Gaborone, Botswana, 1992—95; dir., head dept. pub. health practice & health promotion U. Limpopo, South Africa, 1995—. Commonwealth scholarship. Mem.: Assn. Child and Adolescent Psychiatry and Mental Health (mem., rsch. sector), South African Nat. AIDS Coun., Internat. Union of Health Promotion and Edn., U. Limpopo Senate. Avocations: travel, photography, reading. Home: Thabo Mbeki 89 Polokwane Limpopo 0699 South Africa Home Fax: 27 15 263 6432. Personal E-mail: ho7@mweb.co.za.

OOI, ENG HOOI, surgeon, otolaryngologist; b. Kuala Lumpur, Malaysia, Dec. 9, 1972; s. Kah Chuan Ooi and Beng Tin Ang; m. Li Lian Cheah, May 2, 1974; children: Sean, Marcus. MBBS, U. Adelaide, Australia, 1997, PhD, 2007; postgrad., Queen Elizabeth Hosp., 2003—. Intern Royal Adelaide Hosp., Australia, 1998; surg. trainee Flinders Med. Ctr., 1999—99, Queen Elizabeth Hosp., 2000—01, registrar otolaryngology surg., 2003—08, Royal Darwin Hosp., 2002—02; surg. trainee Royal Adelaide Hosp., Women's and Children's Hosp., Flinders Med. Ctr. Student mem. bd. conduct U. Adelaide, 1992—93; ENT surgeon and vis. med. specialist Queen Elizabeth Hosp.; vis. med. specialist Flinders Med. Ctr. Contbr. articles to profl. jours. Recipient RP Jepson medal, Royal Australasian Coll. Surgeons, 2005; scholar, Garnett Passe and Rodney Williams Meml. Found., 2003—05, U. Adelaide Faculty Health Scis., 2003; Margorie Hooper and Mark Jolly Travelling scholarship. Fellow: Royal Australasian Coll. Surgeons. Achievements include research in Innate Immune Responses in Chronic Rhinosinusitis patients. Home: PO Box 4071 Tranmere North SA 5073 Australia Office: Flinders Pvt Hosp Ste 200 Bedford Park SA 5042 Australia Office Phone: 61 88 2770288. Personal E-mail: eooi.entsurgery@gmail.com.

OOI, SHIRLEY, emergency physician, consultant; d. Guan Chye Ooi and Keow Kim Ch'ng; m. Keng Yeow Tan, Jan. 1, 1991; children: Samuel Tan, Joshua Tan, Janice Tan. MB, BS, Nat. U. Singapore, 1987. FRCS in Emergency Medicine Edinburgh, 1992, cert. specialist registration in emergency medicine Singapore Med. Coun., specialist accreditation in emergency medicine Singapore Ministry of Health. Intern Ministry of Health, 1987—88; resident Nat. U. Hosp., 1988—93, registrar, 1993—95, sr. registrar, 1996—97, cons., 1998—2003, sr. cons., 2003—, chief dept. emergency medicine, 2006—; fellow in trauma U. Cin., 1996—97. Clin. assoc. prof. Yong Loo Lin Sch. of medicine Nat. U. Singapore, 2004—; adj. prof. dept. emergency medicine U. Kebangsaan, Malaysia, 2007—. Editor: Guide to the Essentials in Emergency Medicine, 2004; co-author (Catherine Tay, Shirley Ooi): (book) Medico-Legal Issues in Emergency Medicine and Family Practice: Case Scenarios, 2007; mem. editl. bd.: Singapore Med. Jour., 2006—. Recipient Young Investigator award, Am. Coll. Emergency Physicians, 1997, Postgrad. Tchg. Excellence award, Nat. U. Hosp., 2002, Recognition award, Singapore Med. Jour., 2005; scholar Govt. Singapore, 1980—81; Merit scholar, Pub. Svc. Commn., Singapore, 1982—87, rsch. grantee, Nat. Med. Rsch. Coun., 1998—2001, 2003—. Fellow: Acad. Medicine Singapore (chair specialist tng. com. in emergency medicine 2008—), Royal Coll. Surgeons in Emergency Medicine (Edinburgh). Avocation: reading. Office: Emergency Medicine Dept Nat U Hosp 5 Lower Kent Ridge Rd Singapore 119074 Singapore Office Fax: 65-67758551. Business E-Mail: shirley_ooi@nuhs.edu.sg.

OOMMAN, ABRAHAM, cardiologist, researcher; b. Kottayam, Kerala, India, Dec. 25, 1966; s. Maliyil Chummar and Annamma Oomman; m. Soosan Jacob, Feb. 1, 1997. MBBS, MD, Med. Coll. Kottayam, India, DM in Cardiology, DNB in Cardiology, Med. Coll. Kottayam, India, MNAMS, 1998. Sr. resident Jawaharlal Inst., Pondicherry, India, 1994—95; trainee Med. Coll. Kottayam, 1996—98; sr. cons. cardiologist Apollo Hospitals, Chennai, Tamil Nadu, India, 1998—, Apollo Hospitals Tondiarpet, Chennai, Tamil Nadu, India, 2000—, Agarwal's Med. Enclave, Chennai, 2003—, Apollo Hosp. Sowcarpet, Chennai, Tamil Nadu, India, 2003—. Founding mem., trustee Medicaid Trust, Chennai, 2001—. Author: Cardiology Update, Medical Update; contbr. articles to profl. jours. Recipient Second Best Paper award, Cardiology Soc. India, 1997; Nat. Talent Search scholar, NTSC, 1982—. Mem.: Nat. Acad. Med. Sci. (life), Indian Acad. Med. Speciality (life), Indian Med. Assn. (life), Chitradarshana Film Soc. Office: Apollo Hosp Greams Rd Tamil Nadu Chennai 600006 India E-mail: dr-oomman@lycos.com.

OOSTHUIZEN, MARIA KATHLEEN, physician; b. South Africa, June 6, 1977; BSc in Zoology, U. Pretoria, 1997, PhD, 2007. Physician U. Pretoria, 2007—. Grant, Mellon Found. Avocation: photography. Office: Dept Zoology & Entomology University Pretoria Gauteng 0002 South Africa Business E-Mail: moosthuizen@zoology.up.ac.za.

OPEL, WILLIAM, medical research administrator; BA, Pepperdine U., Malibu, Calif., 1968; MBA, U. So. Calif., LA, 1993; PhD, Claremont Grad. U., Calif., 1998. Staff Pasadena Found. Med. Rsch., Calif., 1961-63, rsch. assoc., 1964-70, asst. to dir., 1970-72, adminstr., 1972-76, exec. dir., 1976-82; acting exec. dir. Huntington Med. Rsch. Inst., Pasadena, 1978-82, exec. dir./pres., 1982—. Lectr. tech. mgmt. Pepperdine U.; adj. prof. tech. mgmt. Claremont Grad. U.; bd. dirs. Pasadena Biosci. Collaborative. Pres. Pasadena City Coll. Found. Mem.: Phi Kappa Phi, Beta Gamma Sigma. Achievements include launch of one of the country's first clinical magnetic resonance programs, which has won great acclaim in imaging applications development and in clinical spectroscopy, as well as in training of radiologists and other clinicians. Office: Huntington Med Rsch Insts 734 Fairmount Ave Pasadena CA 91105-3104 *

OPHIR, AVINOAM, ophthalmologist; b. Tel-Aviv, Aug. 30, 1945; MD, Hadassah Med. Sch., Jerusalem, 1973. Chmn. divsn. ophthalmology Hillel-Yaffe Med. Ctr., 1993—. Recipient Award of Excellence, Ministry of Health. Office: 84 Sokolov Ramat-Hasharon 47230 Israel Office Fax: 972-35409222. Business E-Mail: ophthalmology@hy.health.gov.il.

OPITZ, JOHN MARIUS, clinical geneticist, pediatrician; b. Hamburg, Germany, Aug. 15, 1935; came to the U.S., 1950, naturalized, 1957; s. Friedrich and Erica Maria (Quadt) O.; m. Susan O. Lewin; children: Lea, Teresa, John, Chrisanthi, Felix(dec.), Emma; Marian C. Ohden. BA, State U. Iowa, 1956, MD, 1959; DSc (hon.), Mont. State U., 1983, Ohio State U., 2007; MD (hon.), U. Kiel, Germany, 1986, U. Bologna, Italy, 1999, U. Copenhagen. Diplomate Am. Bd. Pediat., Am. Bd. Med. Genetics. Intern State U. Iowa Hosp., 1959-60, resident in pediat., 1960-61; resident, chief resident in pediat. U. Wis. Hosp., Madison, 1961-62; fellow in pediat. and med. genetics U. Wis., 1962-64, asst. prof. med. genetics and pediat., 1964-69, assoc. prof., 1969-72, prof., 1972-79; founder dir. Wis. Clin. Genetics Ctr., 1974-79; clin. prof. med. genetics and pediat. U. Wash., Seattle, 1979—; prof. pediat., human genetics, pathology and ob-gyn. U Utah, SLC, 1997—. Adj. prof. medicine, biology, history and philosophy, vet. rsch. and vet. sci. Mont. State U., Bozeman, 1979-94, McKay lectr., 1992, univ. prof. med. humanities, 1994—; adj. prof. pediat., med. genetics U. Wis., Madison, 1979—, Class of 1947 Disting. prof., 1992; coord. Shodair Mont. Regional Genetic Svcs. Program, Helena, 1979-82; chmn. dept. med. genetics Shodair Children's Hosp., Helena, 1983-94; dir. Found. Devel. and Med. Genetics, Toledo, Ohio, 1994-96; pres. Heritage Genetics P.C., Helena, 1996; Farber lectr. Soc. Pediat. Pathology, 1987; Joseph Garfunkel lectr. So. Ill. U., Springfield, 1987, McKay lectr. Mont. State U., 1992; Warren Wheeler vis. prof. Columbus (Ohio) Children's Hosp., 1987, 2001; Bea Fowlow lectr. in med. genetics U. Calgary, 1996; 1st vis. prof. Hanseatic U. Found. of Lübeck, 1996; Lew Barness lectr. U. South Fla., 2001; Enid Gilbert Barness lectr. U. Wis., 2001; vis. prof. U. Cattolica del Sacro Cuore, Rome, 2001-02. Editor, author 14 books; founder, editor in chief Am. Jour. Med. Genetics, 1977-2000, emeritus assoc. editor; mng. editor European Jour. Pediat., 1977-85; contbr. numerous articles on clin. genetics. Chair Mont. Com. for Humanities, 1991. Recipient Pool of Bethesda award for excellence in mental retardation rsch. Bethesda Luth. Home, 1988, Med. Alumni citation U. Wis., 1989, Disting. Alumni award, U. Iowa, 2009 Col. Harlan Sanders Lifetime Achievement award for work in field of genetic scis. March of Dimes, 2010, Purkinje medal Czech Soc. Medicine, Mendel medal Czech Soc. Med. Genetics, 1996, Internat. prize Phoenix-Anni Verdi for Genetic Rsch., 1996. Fellow AAAS, Am. Coll. Med. Genetics (founder); mem. German Acad. Scis. (Leopoldina), Brazilian Acad. Sci., Am. Soc. Human Genetics, Am. Pediat. Soc., Soc. Pediat. Rsch., Am. Bd. Med. Genetics, Am. Inst. Biol. Scis., Am. Soc. Zoologists, Teratology Soc., Genetic Soc. Am., European Soc. Human Genetics, Soc. Study Social Biology, Am. Acad. Pediat., German Soc. Pediat. (hon.), Western Soc. Pediat. Rsch. (emeritus), Italian Soc. Med. Genetics (hon.), Israel Soc. Med. Genetics (hon.), Russian Soc. Med. Genetics (Hon.), So. Africa Soc. Med. Genetics (hon.), Japanese Soc. Human Genetics (hon.), Sigma Xi, German Soc. Human Genetics-(honor medal), Soc. Pediat. Pathol.(hon.) Democrat. Roman Catholic. Achievements include First Evangeline Heaton lectr. in human genetics, U. Colo. Med. Ctr. Home: 2930 E Craig Dr Salt Lake City UT 84109-3636 Office: U Utah Sch Medicine 50 N Mario Capecchi Dr Salt Lake City UT 84132 E-mail: john.opitz@hsc.utah.edu.

OPIYO, WILSON JWE, orthopedist, surgeon; b. Gulu, Uganda, Dec. 12, 1948; s. Modikayo Jwe and Abe Aero; m. Jolly Adereda Alwoch, June 22, 1975; children: Faith Aero, Charles Ochan, Patience Lamunu, Oola Otto. MB, ChB, Makere U., Kampala, Uganda, 1974. Med. officer Friends Hosp. Kaimosi, Tiriki, Kenya, 1977-78; surg. registrar Craigavon, 1979-81; lectr. U. Zambia, Lusaka, 1982-86, sr. lectr., 1986-88; specialist, cons. Govt. of Botswana, Gaborone, 1989-93, specialist Francistown, 1994-97, cons., 1997-98, sr. cons., 1999—2003; mem. staff Gaborone Pvt. Hosp., 2003—. Sec. Zambia Physicians for Prevention of Nuclear War, Lusaka, 1986. Fellow Royal Coll. Surgeons Ireland, Assn. Surgeons East Africa (mem. coun. 1987); mem. Botswana Med. and Dental Assn., Assn. Osteosynthesis, Alumni Assn. Mem. Ch. of Uganda. Avocations: swimming, debating. Office: Gabarone Pvt Hosp Pvt Bag BR 130 Broadhurst Gaborone Botswana Address: PO Box 1342 Francistown Botswana

OPLETALOVA, VERONIKA, pharmaceutical chemistry educator, researcher, consultant; b. Kutna Hora, Czech Republic, Aug. 18, 1955; d. Kvetoslav Slejtr and Veronika Slejtrova; m. Lubomir Opletal, Oct. 4, 1980; children: Kristina, Veronika. RNDr., Charles U., Faculty Pharmacy, Hradec Kralove, 1979. Jr. lectr. Charles U., Faculty Pharmacy, 1979—82, sr. lectr., 1982—2007, assoc. prof., 2008—. Mem.: Czech Christian Acad., Czech Pharm. Soc. Roman Catholic. Avocations: classical music, travel, reading. Office: Charles Univ Faculty Pharmacy Heyrovskeho 1203 500 05 Hradec Králové Czech Republic

OPOCHER, ENRICO, surgeon; b. Treviso, Italy, July 2, 1952; Degree, U. Padova, 1977, degree in Surgery, 1983. Chief, surgery dept. U. Milano San Paolo Hosp., 2007—. Home: via Fontana 17 Milan 20122 Italy Home Fax: 0039 0250323075. Personal E-mail: enrico.opocher@unimi.it.

OPPENHEIM, JEFFREY SABLE, neurosurgeon, educator; b. Queens, NY, Jan. 31, 1962; m. Ann Oppenheim; children: Samuel, Gabrielle, Julius. AB summa cum laude, Princeton U., 1984; MD, Cornell U., 1988. Diplomate Am. Bd. Neurol. Surgery. Resident in neurosurgery Mt. Sinai Hosp., NYC, 1989-93, chief resident in neurosurgery, 1993-94; instr. Coll. Physicians and Surgeons Columbia U., NYC, 1994—; attending physician Nyack (N.Y.) Hosp., 1994—, Good Samaritan Hosp., Suffern, NY, 1994—, Arden Hill Hosp., Goshen, NY, 1996—, Horton Hosp., Middletown, NY, 1997—, Mercy Cmty. Hosp., Port Jervis, NY, 1997—. Bd. trustees Good Samaritan Hosp., Suffern, NY. Active Rockland County Bd. Health, 2001—, pres., 2007—; trustee Village of Montbello, NY, 2003—07, mayor, 2007—. Mem.: Med. Soc. State N.Y. (councillor 1999—), Rockland County Med. Soc. (pres. 1998—99), Am. Jewish Hist. Soc. (trustee 1995—). Office: 222 Route 59 Ste 205 Suffern NY 10901-5206 also: 30 Mathews St Ste 302 Goshen NY 10924-1963 Office Phone: 845-368-0286.

OPPENHEIM, JOOST J., allergist, immunologist, researcher; b. Venlo, The Netherlands, Aug. 11, 1934; MD, Columbia U., 1960. Diplomate Am. Bd. Allergy & Immunology. Intern King County Hosp., Seattle, 1960-61; resident U. Wash. Hosp., Seattle, 1961-62; fellow in immunology U. Birmingham, England, 1965-66; sr. investigator Lab. Biochemistry Nat. Inst. Dental Rsch., NIH, 1966, chief Cellular Immunology Sect., 1970—83; chief Lab. Molecular Immunoregulation Ctr. Cancer Rsch., Nat. Cancer Inst., NIH, Frederick, Md., 1983—, head Cellular Immunology Group, dep. chief Cancer and Inflammation Program. Mem. Am. Acad. Immunology, Assn. Am. Physicians, Am. Soc. Clin. Investigation, Rsch. Soc. Office: Ctr Cancer Rsch Lab Molecular Immunology PO Box B Bldg 560 Rm 21-89A Frederick MD 21702-1201 Office Phone: 301-846-1551. Office Fax: 301-846-7042. E-mail: oppenhei@ncifcrf.gov. *

OPPENHEIM, WILLIAM L., pediatric orthopedist; b. Bangor, Maine, Jan. 4, 1945; BS in Chemistry, U. Md., Coll. Park, 1966; MD magna cum laude, Georgetown U., Washington, DC, 1970. Cert. Am. Bd. Orthop., 1980. Intern in surgery San Francisco Gen. Hosp.; resident in orthop. surgery U. Wash., Seattle; fellow Nuffield Orthop. Ctr., Oxford, England, 1977; fellow in pediatric orthopedics LA Orthop. Hosp., 1979; dir. UCLA/Orthopaedic Hosp. Ctr. Cerebral Palsy; Margaret Jones Kanaar chair, cerebral palsy UCLA Sch. Medicine, prof., chief pediatric orthopedics; cons. LA Shriner's Hosp. Mem. bd. dirs. Temple Beth Shir Shalom, Santa Monica, LA Soc. for Prevention of Cruelty to Animals, 1990—2000. Recipient White Swan award, Abilities First/Jones Kennar Found., 2000; named to America's Best Doctors, 1999, 2004. Fellow: Am. Orthop. Foot and Ankle Soc., Am. Acad. Cerebral Palsy and Devel. Medicine (mem. bd. dirs., sec., webmaster), Am. Acad. Orthop. Surgery, Am. Acad. Pediat. (mem. bd. dirs.), Pediatric Orthop. Soc. North America; mem.: Am. Orthop. Assn., State Orthop. Soc., State Med. Soc., AMA, Western Orthop. Assn. LA Chpt. (pres.). Office: Luskins Children's Clinic La Orthop Hosp 1530 Arizona St Santa Monica CA 90404 Office Phone: 310-206-6345, 310-395-4814. Business E-Mail: woppenhe@ucla.edu.

OPPERMAN, DAVID ANDREW, otolaryngologist; b. Englewood, Colo., Sept. 25, 1973; BS, Tufts U., 1996; MD, Jefferson Med. Coll., 2001. CEO Colo. Voice Clinic, PC, 2007—. Office: 930B W 7th Ave Denver CO 80123 Office Fax: 303-844-3002. Personal E-mail: voicedoc@att.net.

OPREAN, LETITIA G., microbiologist, educator; b. Sibiu, Romania, Jan. 23, 1948; d. Gheorghe and Letitia Rau; m. Constantin Oprean, June 29, 1971; children: Cristina Roxana Tanasescu, Camelia. BA in Biology, Babes-Bolyai U., 1971, PhD in Microbiology, 1998. Tchr. Med. H.S., Sibiu, Romania, 1971—85; insp. H.S. Inspectorate, Sibiu, 1986—92; from lectr. to prof. Lucian Blaga U., Sibiu, Romania, 1992—2002, prof., 2002—. Mem. sci. com. acta univs. cibiniensis jour. Lucian Blaga U., 1998—; expert Nat. Coun. Sci. Rsch., Bucharest, Romania, 2005—; phd advisor in biotechnology Agrl. and Vet. Medicine U., Cluj-Napoca, Romania, 2005—. Author: Parazitology. Practical Papers, 1995, Microbiological Analyses of Environmental Factors, 1995, Microbiology-Parazitology, 1998, General Microbiology, 2000, Food Microbiology, 2000, Microbiology of Milk, 2001, Microbiology of Wine, 2001, Microbiological analyses of food, 2002, Industrial Yeasts, 2002, Microbiology and Control of Aliments' Microbiological Quality, 2003, Microbiological Processes in Beer Industry, 2003, Microbiological Processes in Bakery Industry, 2003. Pres. Red Cross, Sibiu, Romania, 1990—2005. Recipient Gold medal, Internat. Salon Tech. Achievements Inventa '99, Bucharest, Romania, 1999. Master: Nat. Soc. Celular Biology, Sibiu Br., Sci. Rsch. Ctr. Microbiology; mem.: Etnofarmacology Assn. Romania, Assn. Ecosanogenesis Romania (hon.), Sci. Rsch. Ctr. Quality Mgmt., Gen. Assn. Tchrs. Romania. Achievements include patents for product zoovita. Avocations: literature, travel. Office: Luc ian Blaga Univ 10 Bvd Victoriei Sibiu 550024 Romania Home: Strada Florilor 16 550097 Sibiu Romania Personal E-mail: oprean_letitia@yahoo.com.

O'QUINN, JOSIE LU, nursing educator; BSN, Tex. Christian U., 1960; MS in Nursing, U. Tex., 1976, PhD, 1989. Nurse cons. Bd. Nurse Examiners, 1977-87; assoc. prof. Sch. Nursing U. Tex., Arlington, 1988—2004, dir. BSN progrm, 1996—2000, assoc. dean, 2000—04; ret., 2004. Adj. assoc. prof. U. Tex., Arlington, 2004—09; cons., presenter in field. Contbr. articles to profl. jours. Mem. Tarrant County Clin. Coordinator Coun., 1988-2000, chair, 1989-92, 97—2000; Sch. Nursing rep. United Way, 1989; active adminstrv. bd. Trinity United Meth. Ch., Arlington, 1993-95, mem. mental health task force, 1992, 93, greeter/usher, 1992—00, mem. mental health bd., 1994; mem. nursing rsch. com. Parkland Meml. Hosp., 1989-96; bd. dirs. Arlington adv. com. Tarrant County chpt. ARC, 1989-95, mem. health svcs. of Tarrant County chpt., 1988-95, sec., 1992; team capt. heart walk Am. Heart Assn., 1991; elected mem. Leadership Arlington, 1992-93, chair Parks and Recreation com.; pres. Sunday sch. class First United Meth. Ch., 1989-90, greeter, 1988, 89, 90, 91, mem. adult-family coun., 1990, 91, chair parish nurse ministry panel, 1991-92; bd. dirs. ARC, 1989-95, sec., 1992-93, mem. exec. com., 1992-95; bd. dirs. Cancer Survivors Day Am. Cancer Assn., 1994, 95, Arlington Hist. Soc., 1999—. Recipient Svc. award ARC, 1994, Faculty Recognition award, 1993, U. Tex.-Arlington Recognition award, 1994; named one of Great 100 Nurses, 1996, named to Acad. Disting. Tchrs., U. Tex.-Arlington, 2003, named Ft. Worth Bus. Press Health Care Hero, 2004; grantee Jr. League of Arlington, 1991. Mem. ANA, Nat. League Nurses, Tex. Nurses Assn. (mem. govt. affairs com. 1990-91, chair dist. 3 bylaws com. 1991-92, mem. membership com. 1990, elected mem. nominating com. 1992-93, elected del. 1993, 2001, elected chair nominating com. 1993-94), Tex. League Nurses (mem. membership com. 1989-90), So. Nursing Rsch. Soc., Alumni Assn. Sch. of Nursing, Phi Kappa Phi, Sigma Theta Tau (elected mem. nominating com. 1993-94), UTA Retirees Club (treas. Newletters editor, 2008-10, pres. 2010-). Avocations: self-development, aerobics, gardening, bowling, golf. Home: 1003 W Lovers Ln Arlington TX 76013-3945

O'QUINN, MARVIN, insurance company executive; B in Biology, U. Wash., M in Health Adminstrn. Held positions with other hosp. and med. centers in Portland, Fresno and Seattle; exec. positions NY Presbyterian Health Sys., Providence Med. Ctr., Providence Milwaukee Hosp., Portland, Oreg.; exec. v.p., COO Atlantic Health Sys., Florham Park, NJ; pres., CEO Jackson Health System, Miami, Fla., 2003—08; sr. exec. v.p., COO Catholic Healthcare West, 2009—. Office: Catholic Healthcare West 185 Berry St Ste 300 San Francisco CA 94107 *

O'RAHILLY, STEPHEN PATRICK, clinical endocrinologist, researcher, educator; b. Dublin, Apr. 1, 1958; s. Patrick Francis and Teresa Emer (Hyland) O'R.; m. Suzy Oakes, Sept. 9, 1990. MBBCh, BAO, Nat. U. Ireland, Dublin, 1981, MD, 1987; DSc (hon.), U. Coll., Dublin, 2008, U. Warwick, 2009. Fellow Royal Coll. Physicians (U.K.), Royal Coll. Physicians of Ireland. Rsch. fellow in endocrinology Oxford (Eng.) U., 1984-87; clin. registrar John Radcliffe Hosp., Oxford, 1987-88, Radcliffe Infirmary, Oxford, 1988-89; med. rsch. coun. traveling fellow Harvard U. Med. Sch., Cambridge, Mass., 1989-91; Wellcome Trust sr. rsch. fellow in clin. sci. Cambridge

(Eng.) U., 1991-95, prof. metabolic medicine, 1996—2002, prof. clin. biochemistry and medicine, 2002—; dir. Inst. Metabolic Sci. Metabolic Rsch. Labs. Panel mem. Wellcome Trust Clin. Interest Group, London, 1996—2002; lectr. in field; chmn. Med. Rsch. Soc., MRC Translational Rsch. Overview Group; mem. MRC Strategy Bd.; fgn. assoc. Nat. Acad. Scis., 2011. Contbr. over 100 articles to profl. jours. Redcliffe-Maud fellow, Brit. Diabetic Assn., 1986, R.D. Lawrence lectr., 1996, 18th Andrew Marble lectr. Joslin Clinic, Boston, 2001; recipient Medal Soc. for Endocrinology, Graham Bull prize Royal Coll. Physicians Eng., 2000, prize European Jour. Endocrinology, 2001, Novartis award for diabetes rsch., 2001, Heinrich-Wieland prize, 2002, Carl Gottschalk award, 2003, HC Jacobaeus award, 2004, Rolf Luft award, 2005, Feldberg prize, 2007, Solomon Berson award, 2007, Clin. Investigator award, Endocrine Soc., 2007, Sr. Investigation award, Nat. Inst. Health Res., 2008, Dale medal, Soc. Endocrinology, 2010, In Bev Baillet Latour Health prize, 2010. Fellow Acad. of Med. Scis., Royal Soc.; mem. Assn. Am. Physicians (hon.). Office: Inst Metabolic Sci Metabolic Rsch Labs Addenbrookes Hosp Box 289 Keith Day Rd Cambridge CB2 0QQ England Business E-Mail: so104@medschl.cam.ac.uk.

ORAKA, EMEKA, medical researcher; b. Ishpeming, Mich., Nov. 6, 1980; BS, Pa. State U., 2004; MPH, Ga. State U., 2006. Health rsch. analyst 3 Northrop Grumman, 2010—. Home: 315 Old Preston Ct Alpharetta GA 30022 Personal E-mail: eoraka@yahoo.com.

ORATZ, RUTH, physician; d. Murray and Rosalyn Oratz. AB in History and Philosophy of Sci., Harvard U., 1977; MD, Albert Einstein Coll. Medicine, 1982. Diplomate in internal medicine and med. oncology Am. Bd. Internal Medicine. Assoc. prof. clin. medicine NYU Sch. Medicine, NYC, 1997—. Mem. adv. bd. breastcancer.org, cancerandcareers, sharsheret. Named Physician of Yr., Cancer Care, 2005. Fellow: ACP; mem.: Am. Assn. for Cancer Rsch., Am. Soc. Clin. Oncologists. Office: Womens Oncology and Wellness Practice Ste 202 345 E 37th St New York NY 10016 E-mail: contact@thewomenspractice.org.

ORCES, CARLOS H., internist, educator; b. Guayaquil, Ecuador, Oct. 19, 1963; MD, U. Catolica Guayaquil, 1988; MPH, U. Tex., 2005. Physician Laredo Med. Ctr., 2003—. Asst. prof., medicine U. Tex. Health Sci. Ctr. San Antonio, 2000—03. Recipient award, Am. Coll. Rheumatology, 2009. Mem.: ACP. Avocations: reading, cooking. Office: 702 E Calton Laredo TX 78041

ORCHARD, GUY EDWARD, lab administrator; b. London, Eng., Oct. 31, 1964; s. Jack Ernest and Betty Claire Orchard; m. Sarah Anne May, July 21, 1990; 1 child, Ross Robin. MS, U. Surrey, Epsom, 1994. Charterd scientist Fellow Inst. Biomed. Scis., 1990. Lab. mgr. Guy's & St. Thomas' NHS Trust, London, 1999—. Contbr. articles to profl. jours. Rugby coach, referee Beccahamian's Rugby Football Club, West Wickham, London, 2002—08. Fellow: Inst. Biomed. Scis. (sci. adv. panel mem. histopathology 2007—08, R J Lavington prize 1990). Office: Guy's & St Thomas' NHS Trust 2 Lambeth Palace Road SE1 7EP London England Office Fax: 0207 7188 6382. Business E-Mail: guy.orchard@gstt.nhs.uk.

ORCHARD, PAUL JOHN, physician, educator; b. Bismarck, ND, Aug. 8, 1958; MD, Brown U. Program in Medicine, 1984. Assoc. prof. U. Minn., 1990—. Office: 660B Masonic Cancer Research Bldg 4 Minneapolis MN 55455 Office Fax: 612-626-4074. Business E-Mail: orcha001@umn.edu.

ORCI, LELIO, cell biologist; BA, Veroli, Italy; MD, U. Rome; DSc (hon.), McGill U., Montreal, Que., Can., 1999. Chmn. dept. morphology U. Geneva Med. Sch., Switzerland, prof. emeritus. Contbr. articles to profl. jours. Recipient Mack-Foster award, European Soc. Clin. Investigation, David Rumbough award, Am. Juvenile Diabetes Found., Dale medal, Brit. Endocrine Soc., Banting medal, Am. Diabetes Assn. Mem.: Accademia Nazionale dei Lincei, Am. Acad. Arts & Sciences. Office: Univ Geneva/Med Sch Univ Med Ctr/Dept Morphology 1211 Geneva Switzerland Business E-Mail: lelio.orci@medecine.unige.ch.

ORDAN, MARK S., personal care industry executive; s. Harry and Doris Ordan; m. Kathryn Ann Sklar, Nov. 12, 1983. BA, Vassar Coll., 1979; MBA, Harvard Bus. Sch. Equities divsn. Goldman Sachs & Co.; co-founder, pres. then CEO Fresh Fields (sold to Whole Foods Market for $135 million in 1996), Md., 1991—96; co-founder (with Ken Brody) Chartwell Health Mgmt., Bethesda, Md., 1997; chmn. Federal Realty Investment Trust, Arlington, Va., 2003—06; CEO Sutton Place (changed name to Balducci's), Bethesda, Md., 2003—06; COO The Mills Corp., Chevy Chase, Md., 2006, CEO, pres., 2006—08; chief adminstrv., investment officer Sunrise Sr. Living, Inc., McLean, Va., 2008; CEO Sunrise Senior Living, Inc., 2008—. Bd. dirs. Fidelity & Trust Bank, Federal Realty Investment Trust, Sunrise Sr. Living. Exec. com. bd. trustees Vassar Coll.; bd. dirs. Cystic Fibrosis Found. Met., Washington. Mem.: Young President's Assn. Office: Sunrise Sr Living 7900 Westpark Dr Ste T900 Mc Lean VA 22102-4217 Office Phone: 703-273-7500. Office Fax: 703-744-1601. *

ORDOG, TAMAS, research scientist, educator; b. Nagykanizsa, Hungary, Feb. 8, 1964; arrived in US, 1992, permanent resident, 1996; s. Ferenc Ordog and Julianna Domjan; m. Katalin Malek; 1 child, Norbert. MD, U. Pecs, Hungary, 1988. Rsch. fellow neurophysiology rsch. group Hungarian Acad. Scis., Pecs, 1989—92; rsch. fellow U. Tex.-Houston Health Sci. Ctr., 1992—95, sr. rsch. fellow, 1995—97; rsch. asst. prof. U. Nev. Reno Sch. Medicine, 1997—2003, asst. prof., 2003—06; sr. assoc. cons., assoc. prof. Mayo Clinic, Rochester, Minn., 2006—. Contbr. articles to profl. jours. Recipient Young Investigator award, Am. Motility Soc., 2000, 2002, Alvarez award, Internat. Electrogastrography Soc., 2005, Masters award for basic or clin. rsch. digestive scis., 2008, PriCara Eisai; grantee, Am. Motility Soc. and Janssen Pharmaceutica, 2002—03, NIH, 2002—; scholar, Republic of Hungary, 1984—88; Rsch. fellow, Hungarian Acad. Scis., 1989—91. Mem.: AAAS, Soc. for Neuroscience, Internat. Electrogastrography Soc. (treas.), Am. Neurogastroenterology and Motility Soc., Am. Gastroenterol. Assn., The Endocrine Soc. Achievements include research in gastrointestinal cell biology; Diabetic gastroenteropathy; neuroendocrine regulation of reproduction. Office: Mayo Clinic Guggenheim 10 200 1st St SW Rochester MN 55905 Business E-Mail: ordog.tamas@mayo.edu.

ORDON, ANDREW PAUL (DREW ORDON), plastic surgeon; b. Chgo., Dec. 9, 1950; s. V. Anthony and Jay Mary (Lacka) O.; m. Robyn Lee, July 20, 1985; children: Matthew, Shannon. BS with honors in Biol. Scis., U. Calif., Irvine, 1972; MD with honors, U. So. Calif. Medicine, 1979. Diplomate Am. Bd. Plastic Surgery, Am. Bd. Otolaryngology, Head and Neck Surgery, Am. Bd. Cosmetic Surgery, Am. Bd. Med. Examiners. Gen. surgery resident U. So. Calif., LA, 1979-80; otolaryngology, head and neck surgery, facial surgery resident Loma Linda-White Meml., LA, 1980-82, otolaryngology, head and neck surgery, facial surgery chief resident, 1982-83; plastic surgery resident Lenox Hill Hosp., NYC, 1983-84, plastic surgery chief resident, 1984-85; asst. prof. head and neck N.Y. Med. Coll., 1987-90; asst. clin. prof. plastic surgery U. Conn. Sch. Medicine, Farmington, 1990—, UCLA Sch. Medicine, 2004—, Darthmouth Med. Coll., 1999—2004. Fellow aesthetic surgery Beverly Hills Med. Ctr., 1983; chief plastic surgery Med. Arts Ctr. Hosp., N.Y.C., 1985-90; attending surgeon Lenox Hill Hosp., N.Y.C., 1987, N.Y. Eye and Ear Infirmary, N.Y.C., 1987, Beth Israel North Med. Ctr., N.Y.C., 1987. Author: Revealing the New You, A Guide to Plastic Surgery, 1994, Everything You Wanted to Know About Plastic Surgery, 1988, Otoplasty in Facial Aesthetic Plastic Surgery; guest appearances on 20/20, 48 Hours, CNN, Sally Jesse Raphael, Phil Donahue, Leeza, Maury Povitch, Entertainment Tonight, Inside Hollywood, NBC News, ABC News, British Broadcasting Corp., USA Today, Allure, Glamour, Mademoiselle, On-line surgery.com; co-star The Doctors, 2008-. Grantee NSF, 1972. Fellow ACS, Internat. Coll. Surgeons, Am. Acad. Facial Plastic and Reconstructive Surgery, Liposuction Soc. Am., mem. Am. Soc. Plastic/Reconstructive Surgeons, Am. Soc. Plastic Surgeons, Am. Soc. Aesthetic Plastic Surgery, Internat. Soc. Aesthetic Plastic Surgery, Phi Beta Kappa (calif. Chpt.) Republican. Episcopalian. Avocations: tennis, golf, skiing, boating, travel. Office: 465 N Roxbury Dr #1001 Beverly Hills CA 90210 Office Phone: 310-248-6250. Office Fax: 310-248-6258. *

ORDORICA, STEVEN ANTHONY, obstetrician, gynecologist, educator; b. NYC, Jan. 4, 1957; s. Vincent and Rose (Goiricelaya) O. BA magna cum laude, NYU, 1979; MD, Stony Brook U., 1983. Diplomate Am. Coll. Obstetrics and Gynecology, speciality cert. maternal-fetal medicine; lic. Nat. Bd. Med. Examiners. Resident obstetrics and gynecology NYU-Bellevue Hosp. Ctr., 1983-87, fellow maternal-fetal medicine, 1987-89, instr. obstetrics-gynecology, 1989-91; clin. instr. obstetrics-gynecology NYU, 1986-89, asst. prof. ob/gyn., 1989—2001, clin. assoc. prof. ob/gyn., 2001—; dir. perinatal clinics and prenatal diagnostic unit Gouverneur Hosp., NYC, 1989-94. Perinatal cons. Bellevue Hosp. Ctr., N.Y.C., 1989—; faculty mem. perinatal div. NYU Med. Ctr., 1989—; presenter in field. Contbr. articles to Surgery, Am. Jour. Obstetrics and Gynecology, Am. Jour. Perinatal, Surgery, Obstetrics and Gynecology, Jour. Reproductive Medicine, Acta Geneticae Medicae et Gemellologiae, Jour. Rheumatology. Recipient Founder's Day award, NYU, Wash. Sq. Alumni award; named NYU scholar. Mem. Am. Coll. Obstetrics and Gynecology, Soc. Perinatal Obstetricians, N.Y. Acad. Scis., N.Y. State Perinatal Soc., AMA, Phi Beta Kappa, Beta Lambda Sigma. Achievements include research in investigating aspects of maternal-fetal physiology. Office: NYU Med Ctr 530 1st Ave Ste 10Q New York NY 10016 6402

ORDWAY, ELLEN, biologist, educator, entomologist, researcher; b. NYC, Nov. 8, 1927; d. Samuel Hanson and Anna (Wheatland) Ordway. BA, Wheaton Coll., Mass., 1950; MS, Cornell U., 1955; PhD, U. Kans., 1965. Field asst. N.Y. Zool. Soc., NYC, 1950-52; rsch. asst. Am. Mus. Natural History, NYC, 1955-57; tchg. asst. U. Kans., Lawrence, 1957-61, rsch. asst., 1959-65; asst. prof. U. Minn., Morris, 1965-70, assoc. prof. biology, 1970-85, prof., 1986-97, prof. emeritus, 1997—2005, acad. advisor, 1997—2007. Cooperator, cons. USDA Bee Rsch. Lab., Tucson, 1971, Tucson, 1983—. Contbr. articles to profl. jours. Lectr. Morris area svc. clubs, 1972—2004; mgr. preserves Nature Conservancy, Mpls., 1975—2007; bd. dirs. county chpt. ARC, 1998—2003; vol. Stevens County Hist. Mus., 2005—08; bd. dirs. U. Minn. Morris Retirees Assn., 1997—2003, sec., treas., 1998—2003. Mem.: AAAS, Ecol. Soc. Am., Internat. Bee Rsch. Assn., Kans. Entomol. Soc., Sigma Xi. Episcopalian. Avocations: travel, photography.

O'REGAN, RUTH, oncologist, educator; b. Dublin; MD, U. Coll., Dublin. Resident & fellow Mater Hosp., Dublin; fellow Northwestern U.; asst. prof. Northwestern U. Hosp.; assoc. prof. hemtology & oncology Emory U.; dir. translational breast cancer rsch. program Winship Cancer Inst. Recipient Compassionate Care award, Women's Bd. Northwestern Hosp., NSABP Young Clinical Investigator award, 2001. Mem.: Am. Soc. Clinical Oncology (breast cancer scientific com.). Office: 1365 Clifton Rd Bldg C Atlanta GA 30322 also: Emory University School of Medicine Department of Biomedical Engineering 101 Woodruff Cir Ste 2007B Atlanta GA 30322

O'REILLY, BARRY AIDAN, obstetrician, gynecologist, consultant; married. MB, BCh, Royal Coll. Surgeons Ireland, BAO, 1991; MD, Nat. U. Ireland, 2000. Cons. ob-gyn., subspecialist urogynaecology Cork U. Maternity Hosp., Ireland, 2004—. Chmn. Continence Found. Ireland, 2005. Master: Royal Coll. Obstetricians and Gynaecologists; fellow: Royal Australian and New Zealand Coll. Obstetricians and Gynaecologists. Achievements include research in urogynecology and pelvic floor reconstructive surgery. Office: Cork Womens Clinic Cardinals Way Wilton Cork Ireland Office Fax: 353 21 4348949.

O'REILLY, EILEEN MARY, gastrointestinal medical oncologist; MD, Trinity Coll., Ireland, 1990. Diplomate Am. Bd. Internal Medicine, Am. Bd. Internal Medicine-med. oncology, registered NY, 1997. Resident in internal medicine St. Vincent's Hosp., 1994, fellow in hematology, 1995; fellow in med. oncology Meml. Sloan-Kettering Cancer Ctr., NY, 1997, gastrointestinal med. oncologist; hosp. affiliation includes NY Presbyn. Hosp. Author: (articles) Refinement of Adjuvant Therapy for Pancreatic Cancer, 2010, A 67-Year-Old Woman with BRCA 1 Mutation Associated with Pancreatic Adenocarcinoma, 2010, Targeting Mutated K-ras in Pancreatic Adenocarcinoma Using an Adjuvant Vaccine, 2010, Multicenter Phase II Trial of Adjuvant Therapy for Resected Pancreatic Cancer Using Cisplatin, 5-fluorouracil, and interferon-alfa-2b-based chemoradiation: ACOSOG Trial Z05031, 2010, Pain and emotional well-being outcomes in Southwest Oncology Group-directed intergroup trial S0205: a phase III study comparing gemcitabine plus cetuximab versus gemcitabine as first-line therapy in patients with advanced pancreas, 2010. Named one of Best Doctors, NY Mag., 2010. Office: Memorial Sloan-Kettering Cancer Center 1275 York Ave New York NY 10065 Office Phone: 212-639-6672.

O'REILLY, MARY, environmental scientist, educator; b. NYC, Aug. 3, 1948; d. Luke Edward and Regina O'Reilly; m. Jonathan Haney; children: Robert Brophy, Sara Brophy, Lena Reid. Student, Fordham U., 1966—68; BS, U. Mich., 1970, MS, 1972, PhD, 1979. Rsch. asst. prof. Health Sci. Ctr., Syracuse, NY, 1979-84; environ. toxicologist Syracuse Rsch. Corp., 1984-86; pres. ARLS Cons., Inc., Syracuse, 1993—; sr. indsl. hygienist N.Y. State Dept. Labor, Syracuse, 1987—2000; environ. specialist N.Y. State Dept. Transp., Binghamton, 2000—10; indsl. hygieist Cranesville Block Co., 2011—; mem. ZIO Com. Am. Nat. Stads. Inst., 2001—. Adj. asst. prof. SUNY Sch. Pub. Health, Albany, 1990—; dir. Am. Bd. Indsl. Hygiene, Lansing, Mich., 1995—2001; adj. prof. chemistry LeMoyne Coll., 2000; mem. Z10 com. Am. Nat. Stds. Inst., 2001—05; mem. adv. bd. N.Y. State Inst. Health and Environment, 2001—; bd. dirs. Am. Conf. Govt. Indsl. Hygienists, 2006—09; mem. NY State Occupl. Health Clinics Oversight Commn., 2009—; adj. prof. Fundlay U., 2008—. Author: An Ergonomics Guide to VDTs, 1994; author: (with others) Occupational Ergonomics, 1996; co-author: ILO's Encyclopedia of Occupational Health and Safety, 1998, Implications of Hormesis for Industrial Hygienists, 2003, Health Risk Assessment at Brownfield Redevelopment Sites, 2003, Groundwater Effects from Highway Tire Shreds, 2004, An Ergonomics Guide to Computer Workstations, 2007, Canasawacta Creek Watershed Initiative, 2007, Phytoremediation of TCE, 2009, others; contbr. articles to profl. jours.; author: Ergonomics Intervention Follow Up With Symptom Survey, 2010, Human Health Risk Assessment, 2011. Mem. Syracuse Peace Coun. Mem.: ANSI, Human Factors and Ergonomics Soc., Am. Assn. Govtl. Indsl. Hygienists, Am. Indsl. Hygiene Assn. Avocations: Karate, fly fishing, irish harp. Home: 7705 Farley Ln Manlius NY 13104-9571 Office: Cranesville Block Co Inc 434 E Brighton Ave Syracuse NY 13210 Home Phone: 315-682-3064; Office Phone: 607-721-8138, 315-478-4101. Business E-Mail: moreilly@cranesville.com, moreilly@albany.edu.

O'REILLY, RICHARD JOHN, pediatrician; b. Bklyn., Apr. 29, 1943; s. John Russell and Margaret (Cronin) O'R.; m. E. Jean Capitano, Nov. 1984; children from previous marriage: John, Steven. BS, Coll. Holy Cross, 1964; MD, U. Rochester, 1968. Diplomate Am. Bd. Pediat. Intern U. Minn. Hosp., Mpls., 1968-69; resident in pediatrics Children's Hosp. Med. Ctr. and Beth Israel Hosp., Boston, 1971-72; with dept. pediatrics Meml. Sloan Kettering Cancer Ctr., NYC, 1973—; attending pediatrician, chmn. dept. pediatrics Meml. Hosp., NYC, 1986—; mem. dept. immunology Sloan-Kettering Inst. Cancer Research; prof. pediatrics Cornell U. Med. Coll., 1980, Lila Acheson Wallace prof. pediatric research, 1980, Claire L. Tow, chair in pediat. oncology rsch., 2004; chief marrow transplantation svc. Meml. Sloan-Kettering Cancer Ctr., 1981—. Pres. Damon Runyon-Walter Winchell Cancer Fund, 1991-96. Editor-in-chief BBMT, 1995-2001; assoc. editor Cancer Rsch., Clin. Cancer Rsch., 1994-2002. Served with USPHS, 1969-71. Recipient Louise and Allston Boyer-Young Investigator award for clin. rsch., 1980, Boarhaave medal Leiden U., Pediat. Oncology award ASCO, Lifetime Achievement award ASEMT. Mem. AAAS, Am. Pediatric Soc., Am. Assn. Immunologists, Am. Acad. Pediat., Am. Assn. Pathologists, Soc. Pediatric Rsch., NY Transplantation Soc., NY Acad. Scis., Am. Assn. Clin. Radiology, Am. Soc. Hematology, Am. Soc. Blood and Marrow Transplantation (sec. 1993-95, v.p.-elect 1999, pres. 2001). Democrat. Roman Catholic. Achievements include first successful application of marrow transplantation from unrelated donors and from genetically mismatched donors, 1973. Office: Meml Sloan-Kettering Cancer Ctr 1275 York Ave New York NY 10021-6094

OREKONDY, SIDDALINGESWARA, ophthalmologist, consultant; b. Gadag, India, May 1, 1943; arrived in Australia, 1975; s. Shivayogappa and Gowradevi (Kololgi) O.; m. Nalini (Basappa), Sept. 14, 1972; children: Vinita, Kavita, Vinayak. MBBS, Mysore U., India, 1965; DO, U. London, 1972, Dublin U., Ireland, 1971. Clin. asst. Eye Infirmary, Sunderland, Eng., 1974-75; cons. Dryburn Hosp., Durham, Eng., 1974-75; pvt. practice Sydney, Australia, 1975. Dir. Nalini Office Svcs., Sydney, 1980—; coord. Kannada Radio Program S.B.S. Radio Australia, 1984-94; chmn., Asia Pacific Kannada Okkuta, 2007. Contbr. articles to profl. jours. Pres. India League Australia, Sydney, 1992, Kannada Balaga, Sydney, 1994; v.p. Basava Samithi Australasia, 1998, pres., 2000, 2001; v.p. Overseas Med. Graduates Assn., 2003, pres. 2003-05; chmn. United Indian Assn. Australia, v.p. 2003, chmn. 2004-05; coord. Kannada Radio Programming SBS Radio, Australia, 1984-94, with Free Eye Camp Rishikesh India, 2007, Justice of Peace, NSW, Australia, 2008. Fellow Royal Australian Coll. Ophthalmologists (cert.), Internat. Coll. Surgeons; mem. Am. Acad. Ophthalmology, All India Inst. Ophthalmology, Am. Soc. Cataract and Refractive Surgery. Avocation: meditation. Office: Campsie Specialist Ctr 77 Evaline St Campsie 2194 NSW Australia Office Phone: 61-02-9789-4000. Business E-Mail: sorekondy@hotmail.com.

OREL, VALERI EMMANUILOVICH, medical physicist; b. Tehran, Iran, Aug. 11, 1945; s. Emmanuil Michelevich and Polina Grigorievna (Zlotnik) O.; m. Rozalia Konstantinovna Vesnovskay, July 30, 1985; 1 child, Irina Valerievna. B, Tech. Coll. Kiev, 1964; M, Kiev Polytechnick Inst., 1974; PhD, Kiev Inst. Problems Oncology, 1978, Dr. Hab. Biology Sci., 1987. Chief med. physicist, bioengineering dept. Nat. Cancer Inst., Kiev, 1973—. Prof. Internat. U. Solomon, Kiev, Ukraine, 1993—2008, Nat. Tech. U. (Kyiv Poly. Inst.), Kiev, 2004—. Author: Peroxide Oxidation and Radiation, 1991, Chemiluminescence in Oncology, 1984, Chaos and Cancer, 2002, Electromagnetic Field of Radiowaves in Oncology, 2005. Mem. Internat. Orgn. Med. Physicists, Assn. Med. Physicists Ukraine (v.p. 1993-), Literat Club Eng. Achievements include patents in field. Avocation: sports. Office: Nat Cancer Inst 33/43 Lomonosov str 03022 Kiev Ukraine Office Phone: 38044-257-60-68.

ORELLANA RIOS, JORGE ANDRES, ophthalmologist; b. Concepcion, Chile, Sept. 25, 1974; s. Jorge Eduardo Orellana Verdugo and Graciela Del Carmen Rios Ibarra; m. Marcia Andrea Segovia Vera, Jan. 26, 2002. MD, U. Sch. Medicine, Concepcion, 1998. Cert. specialty in ophthalmology 2002. Ophthalmologist Ophthalmology Svc. Antofagasta (Chile) Pub. Hosp., 2002—03. Ophthalmology prof. U. Antofagasta Med. Sch., 2002—03. Mem.: Chilean Soc. Ophthalmology. Office: Hosp Regional de Antofagasta Av Argentina 1962 Antofagasta Chile Home: Manuel Antonio Matta 1839 1271714 Antofagasta Chile

OREM, WILLIAM HENRY, chemist; b. Balt., Apr. 12, 1952; BS, Lehigh U., 1974; PhD, U. NH, 1982. Postdoc. assoc. NRC, 1982—84; chemist US Geol. Survey, 1984—. Adj. faculty U. Md., 1982—89. Recipient Superior Svc. award, US Dept. Interior, Star Awards, US Geol. Survey. Mem.: Am. Chem. Soc., Internat. Med. Geology Assn. Avocations: sailing, running, bicycling. Office: US Geol Survey 12201 Sunrise Va Reston VA 20192 Office Fax: 703-648-6419. Business E-Mail: boem@usgs.gov.

ORENS, JONATHAN B., pulmonologist; MD, U. Md., Balt., 1987. Assoc. dir., divsn. pulmonary and critical care medicine Johns Hopkins U. Sch. Medicine, Balt., 1998—. Office: Johns Hopkins Sch Medicine 1830 E Monument St 5th fl Baltimore MD 21205 Office Fax: 410-955-0036.

ORFIELD, ANTONIA MARIE, optometrist, researcher; d. Alfred Anthony and Eva Swenson Stoll; m. Gary Allan Orfield, May 24, 1963 (div. 2005); children: Amy Elizabeth, Sonia Marie, Rosanna Antonia. BA in History, Smith Coll., 1963; MAT in History/Social Studies, U. Chgo., 1966; BS in Visual Sci., Ill. Coll. Optometry, 1987, OD, 1989. Lic. Mass. Bd. Optometry. Optometrist Michael Reese HMO, Chgo., 1989—91, Eye Exam 2000, Chgo., 1989—91; behavioral optometrist Harvard U. Health, Cambridge, Mass., 1991—. Asst. prof. New Eng. Coll. Optometry, Boston, 1991—2000, dir., chief investigator, clin. preceptor Mather Sch. Vision and Learning Rsch./Svc. Clinic, 1993—99; pvt. practice behavioral optometrist, Cambridge, 1996—; spkr. in field. Author: Eyes for Learning: Preventing and Curing Vision Related Learning Problems, 2007; contbr. articles to profl. jours. Parent rep. Kenwood Acad. Sch. Coun., Chgo., 1989—91. Grantee, State Street Bank, N.E. Congress Optometry, Mass. Soc. Optometrists, Am. Found. Vision Awareness, Friends of the Sensorily Deprived. Fellow: Coll. Optometrists in Vision Devel., Am. Acad. Optometry; mem.: Neurooptometric Rehab. Assn. (charter), Internat. Coll. Applied Kinesiology. Democrat. Achievements include research in children in poverty have a great number of vision problems that interefere with learning; near point glasses can raise test scores; tracking problems are correlated with reading failures; vision therapy is correlated with improvement in grades. Avocations: study of homeopathic medicine, sports vision training, study of educational kinesiology, study of nutrition and vision, swimming. Office: Harvard Univ Health Svc 75 Mt Auburn St Cambridge MA 02138 also: Ste 205 678 Massachussetts Ave Cambridge MA 02139 also: 312 Maryland Ave NE Washington DC 20002-5712 Personal E-mail: antoniaorfield@yahoo.com.

ORFORD, ROBERT RAYMOND, physician, consultant; b. Winnipeg, Manitoba, Can., Apr. 18, 1948; came to U.S., 1988; s. Robert Raymond and Sarah Gloria L. (Gullden) O.; m. Dale Laura Stuart, June 2, 1972; children: Carolyn Tiffany, Andrew Craig, Loren Brent. BS, McGill U., 1969, MD, 1971; MS, U. Minn., 1975; MPH, U. Wash., 1976. Assoc. prof. cmty. medicine U. Alberta, Edmonton, Can., 1978-88; dir. med. svcs. Govt. of Alberta, Edmonton, Can., 1979-81, exec. dir. occupational health svcs., 1981-85, deputy min. cmty. occupational health, 1985-88; med. dir. employee health U. Alberta Hosp., Edmonton, Can., 1988; sr. assoc. cons. Mayo Clinic, Rochester, Minn., 1988-91, cons. preventive medicine, 1991-96, Scottsdale, Ariz., 1996—. Asst. prof. Mayo Med. Sch., Rochester, 1988—; mem. Alberta Energy Resource Conservation Bd., 1988-89; chmn. divsn. preventive and occupl. medicine, dir. exec. health program, Mayo Clinic, Scottsdale, 1999-2007, cons. exec. health program, 2008—. Contbr. articles to profl. jours. Govt. of Can. Nat. Health fellow, 1975-76. Fellow Royal Coll. Physicians and Surgeons Can., Am. Coll. Occupational and Environ. Medicine (pres. 2008-09), Am. Coll. Preventive Medicine, Aerospace Med. Assn., Airlines Med. Dirs. Assn.; mem. Internat. Commn. Occupl. Health Medicine (nat. sec. 2001—), Ariz. Med. Assn. (pres. 2011-). Presbyterian. Avocations: languages, fitness, travel. Home: 15516 E Acacia Way Fountain Hills AZ 85268-3158 Office: Mayo Clinic Scottsdale Divsn Preventive Medicine 13400 E Shea Blvd Scottsdale AZ 85259-5499 Office Phone: 480-301-7379. Office Fax: 480-301-7569. Business E-Mail: rorford@mayo.edu.

ORIANS, GORDON HOWELL, biology professor; b. Eau Claire, Wis., July 10, 1932; s. Howard Lester and Marion Meta (Senty) O.; m. Elizabeth Ann Newton, June 25, 1955; children: Carlyn Elizabeth, Kristin Jean, Colin Mark. BS, U. Wis., 1954; PhD, U. Calif., Berkeley, 1960. Asst. prof. zoology U. Wash., Seattle, 1960-64, assoc. prof., 1964-68, prof., 1968-95, prof. emeritus, 1995—. Active Wash. State Ecol. Commn., Olympia, 1970-75, ecology adv. com. EPA, Washington, 1974-79; assembly life scis. NAS/NRC, Washington, 1977-83, environ. studies and toxicology bd., 1991—2003. Author: Some Adaptations of Marsh Nesting Blackbirds, 1980, Blackbirds of the Americas, 1985, Life: The Science of Biology, 2003; editor: Biodiversity and Ecosystem Processes in Tropical Forests, 1996. 1st lt. U.S. Army, 1955-56. Mem. AAAS, NAS, Am. Inst. Biol. Scis. (Disting. Svc. award 1994), Am. Ornithologists Union (Brewster award 1976), Am. Soc. Naturalists, Animal Behavior Soc., Royal Netherlands Acad. Arts and Scis., Orgn. for Tropical Studies (pres. 1988-94), Ecol. Soc. Am. (v.p. 1975-76, pres. 1995-96, Eminent Ecologist award 1998). Avocations: hiking, opera. Office: U Wash Dept Biology PO Box 351800 Seattle WA 98195-1800 Home Phone: 206-364-5743. E-mail: blackbrd@serv.net.

ORIFICI, CARMELO, dermatologist, consultant; b. Messina, Italy, June 2, 1940; s. Antonino Orifici and Giuseppina Trusso; m. Anna Maria Fasanelli, Aug. 31, 1968; children: Gian-Luca, Marco. Laurea in Medicine, U. Messina, Italy, 1964; specializatto in Dermatology, U. Pisa, Italy, 1967; degree in Occupl. Medicine, U. Genoa, Italy, 1970. Physician Hosp. Roma, Rome, 1956—66; dermatologist Military Hosp., La Spezia, 1967—77; sanitary dir. Nat. Sanitary, La Spezia and Carrara, 1967—80; cons. dermatologist La Spezia, 1967—. Fellow: Am. Acad. Dermatology; mem.: Italian Soc Dermatology. Avocations: reading, gardening. Office: Via Vittorio Veneto 104 19100 La Spezia Italy Home: Localitß Tre Strade 4A 19032 Lerici Italy Office Phone: 39-3470063797. Personal E-mail: Carmelo.Orifici@libero.it, corifici@gmail.com.

ORIGITANO, THOMAS CHARLES, neurological surgeon; BS in Chemistry and Biology, MacMurray Coll., 1976; PhD, Loyola U., Chgo., 1981; MD, Loyola-Stritch U., Maywood, Ill., 1984. Diplomate Am. Bd. Neurol. Surgery, 1995. Intern gen. surgery Loyola U. Med. Ctr., Maywood, 1984—85, resident neurol. surgery, 1985—90, asst. prof., 1990—96, assoc. prof., 1996—98, prof., 1998—, chmn. neurol. surgery med. ctr., 1998—. Home and Office: Loyola Univ Med Ctr 2160 South First Ave Maywood IL 60153

ORLACCHIO, ANTONIO, neurologist; s. Aldo Orlacchio and Rosa Flagiello. MD, U. Perugia Med. Sch., Italy, 1996; PhD, U. Rome "Tor Vergata", 2004. Bd. cert. neurologist Italian Bd. neurologists, 2000. Post-doctoral fellow, ctr. rsch. in neurodegenerative diseases U. Toronto, Ontario, Canada, 1997—2002; head Lab. Neurogenetica, Centro Europeo di Ricerca sul Cervello-Inst. Ricovero e Cura e Carattere Sci. Santa Lucia, Rome, 2002—; attending neurologist, dept. neurosci. U. Rome "Tor Vergata", 2002—, instr. in neurology, 2002—05, asst. prof. neurology, dept. neurosci., 2006—. Recipient Awesome Dude award, Common Cause Found., 1999, Franco Pietrandrea award, Rotary Club, Rome, 2005, award, European Neurol. Soc., 2000, 2003; Rsch. fellow, U. Perugia, 1997, 1999, Italian Nat. Rsch. Coun., 1998—99, 1999, 2000, Various Rsch. grants, Italian Ministry Health, 2002—, Telethon Found., 2003, Sr. Rsch. Fellow, NATO, Italian Nat. Rsch. Coun., 2003, Rsch. fellow, Italian Nat. Rsch. Coun., Can. Inst. Health Rsch., 2004, 2006—07, Rsch. grant, Lundbeck, 2005—, U. Rome "Tor Vergata", 2006—, Telethon Found., 2006—. Mem.: Nat. Ctr. Rare Diseases, Network Excellence on Rare Diseases, Rome Inst. Superiore di Sanità, European Neurol. Soc., Assn. Alzheimer's Disease Scientists", Italian Order Physicians and Surgeons. Achievements include genetic mapping of the SPG29 and SPG38 loci in Hereditary Spastic Paraplegia; discovery of first founder mutation in Hereditary Spastic Paraplegia (SPG4); narrowing the SPG12 locus in Hereditary Spastic Paraplegia. Office: CERC-IRCCS Santa Lucia Neurogenetica Via del Fosso di Fiorano 64 143 Rome RM Italy Office Fax: 39 06 501703312. Business E-Mail: a.orlacchio@hsantalucia.it.

ORLANDO, LORI ANN, medical researcher, educator, physician; d. Geraldine Sainthill and Roy Charles Orlando; m. Bradley F. Mann, May 19, 1995. BS, U. N.C., 1990—2001; MD, Tulane Med. Ctr., 1998; M in health sci., Duke U. Med. Sch., 2004. Diplomate Am. Bd. Internal Medicine. Resident in internal medicine Tulane Med. Ctr., New Orleans, 1998—2001, chief resident in internal medicine, 2001—02; internal medicine fellow Duke U. Med. Ctr., Durham, NC, 2002—04, assoc. in medicine, 2004—06, asst. prof. in medicine, 2006—; rsch. assoc. Durham VA Med. Ctr., NC, 2002—. Contbr. articles to profl. jours. Recipient Rsch. internship, Harvard U., Brigham and Women's Hosp., Dept. of Pathology, 1987, Med. Student Achievement award, Endocrine Soc., 1998, Owl Club award for Outstanding Med. Resident, 2000, 2001, Outstanding Trainee award, so. sect. Am. Fedn. Med. Rsch., 2002, Milton W. Hamolsky award, 2005, Best Sci. Abstract award, 2005. Mem.: Soc. of Gen. Internal Medicine (assoc.; chair planning com.). Achievements include research in describing chronic kidney disease and evaluating interface between generalist and specialist care.

ORLOW, SETH J., dermatologist; b. Bklyn., Dec. 23, 1958; AB magna cum laude, Harvard Coll., 1979; MD, PhD Molecular Pharmacology, Albert Einstein Coll. Medicine, 1986. Diplomate Nat. Bd. Dermatology, Nat. Bd. Med. Examiners. Intern in pediat. Mt. Sinai Med. Ctr., NYC, 1986-87; resident in dermatology Yale-New Haven Hosp., New Haven, 1987-89, fellow in dermatology, 1989-90; asst. prof. dermatology and cell biology NYU Sch. of Medicine, NYC, 1990-94, assoc. prof. dermatology and cell biology, 1994—2000; Weinberg prof. pediat. dermatology, prof. cell biology and pediat. NYU Sch. Medicine, NYC, 2000—, vice chair for rsch. dermatology, 2004—07. Dir. pediat. dermatology, Tisch Hosp., NYC, 1990-2007, chmn. dept. dermatology, 2006—; dir. pediat. dermatology Bellevue Hosp., NYC, 1990—, Lenox Hill Hosp., NYC, 1994—. Editorial bd. Archives of Dermatology, Boston, 1995—05, Pediatric Dermatology, 1999-2006, Pigment Cell Rsch., 1995—05; ad hoc jour. reviewer numerous publs. Rsch. grantee William T. Morris Found., 1990-92, Evans Found., 1991-92, NIH, 1993-; recipient Irma T. Hirschl Career Scientist award, 1995-2000, others. Fellow Am. Acad. Dermatology, Am. Acad. Pediat.; mem. Soc. Investigative Dermatology (bd. dirs. 1988-90), Soc. Pediatric Dermatology, Pan Am. Soc. Pigment Cell Rsch., NY Dermatologie Soc., Dermatol. Soc. Greater NY, others. Office: NYU Med Ctr SKI 7 Ste 7R 530 First Ave New York NY 10016 Office Phone: 212-263-5889.

ORMISSON, ANNE, pediatrician, educator; b. Tartu, Estonia, Nov. 19, 1942; MD, U. Tartu, 1967, PhD, 1975. Postgrad. fellow, dept. pediat. U. Tartu, 1972—75, asst. prof., 1979—84, assoc. prof., 1984—2008; head neonatal unit Children's Clinic, Tartu U. Hosp., 2000—07; assoc. prof. emeritus, dept. pediat. U. Tartu, Children's Clinic, Tartu U. Hosp., 2008—, cons. pediatrician. Head cons. neonatologist Ministry of Health, Estonia, 1982—92; pres. Estonian Pediatric Soc., 1990—94; v.p. Union Nat. European Pediatric Socs. & Assns., 1992—98; pres. Estonian Perinatal Soc., 1995—99; bd. mem. Internat. Children's Ctr., 1999—2003. Recipient Nat. Sci. award, Govt. of Estonia, 1994; Ihsan Dogramaci Family Health Found. fellowship, WHO. Mem.: Estonian Perinatal Soc. (Mem. Honoris Causa 2010), European Pediatric Soc., Estonian Pediatric Soc. (Mem. Honoris Causa 2001). Avocations: gardening, travel. Office: Lunini 6 Tartu 51014 Estonia Office Fax: 372 7319608. E-mail: anne.ormisson@kliinikum.ee.

ORMOND, PAUL A., healthcare company executive; b. Aurora, Ill. B in economics with honors, Stanford U., 1971, MBA, 1973. Mem. corp. staff, positions with glass container divsn. Owens-Ill., Inc., 1973-77, nat. mktg. mgr. soft drinks, glass container divsn., 1977-78; mgr. Atlanta sales dist., glass container divsn. Owens-Ill. Inc., 1978-80, asst. gen. mgr. Gerresheimer Glas (internat. affiliate Owens-Ill. Inc.) Germany, 1980-82, v.p. glass container group, 1982-84, v.p. packaging ops., dir. market strategy and devel., 1984-91, corp. v.p., 1986-91; pres., CEO Health Care and Retirement Corp. (HCR) (subs. Owens-Ill. Inc.), Toledo, 1986-91; chmn., pres., CEO Health Care and Retirement Corp. (HCR) (now ind. co.), Toledo, 1991—98; pres., CEO HCR Manor Care Inc., Toledo, 1998—99, Manor Care, Inc., Toledo, 1999—2001, chmn., pres., CEO, 2001—. Office: Manor Care 333 N Summit St Toledo OH 43604-2617 *

ORNATO, JOSEPH P., emergency physician, educator; MD, Boston U. Cert. Internal Medicine, 1974, Cardiovascular Disease, 1977, Emergency Medicine, 1997. Resident in internal medicine Mt. Sinai Hosp., NYC; fellow in cardiology Cornell U.; prof. and chair emergency medicine Va. Commonwealth U., Richmond; med. dir. Richmond Ambulance Authority. Mem.: Inst. Medicine. Office: Va Commonwealth U Med Ctr Dept Emergency Medicine 1200 Marshall Ave Richmond VA 23223 E-mail: jornato@mcvh-vcu.edu.

ORNE, EMILY CAROTA, psychologist, researcher; b. Boston, Sept. 7, 1938; d. Emil and Ruth (Farrell) Carota; m. Martin T. Orne, Feb. 3, 1962; children: Franklin Theodore, Tracy Meredith. BA, Bennington Coll., 1959. Rsch. assoc. Mass. Mental Health Ctr., Boston, 1963-64; rsch. psychologist Unit for Exptl. Psychiatry, Phila., 1964-79, sr. rsch. psychologist, 1979-83, co-dir., 1982—; rsch. assoc. psychology U. Pa. Sch. Medicine, Phila., 1983—. Trustee Inst. Exptl. Psychiatry Rsch. Found., Mass., 1964—, assoc. co-dir., 1987-97, exec. dir., 1998—; bd. dirs. False Memory Syndrome Found., 1995- Contbr. articles to profl. jours.; assoc. editor Internat. Jour. Clin. and Exptl. Hypnosis, 1977- Recipient Benjamin Franklin Gold medal Internat. Soc. Hypnosis, 1982, Roy M. Dorcus award Soc. Clin. and Exptl. Hypnosis, 1985, Bernard B. Raginsky award, 1993, Morton Prince award Soc. Clin. and Exptl. Hypnosis and APA, 1994 Avocations: fishing, swimming, reading. Office: U Pa Sch Medicine 1013 Blockley Hall 423 Guardian Dr Philadelphia PA 19104-6021

ORNISH, DEAN, medical association administrator and educator; MD, Baylor Coll. Medicine. Resident in internal medicine Mass. Gen. Hosp., Boston, 1981-84; clin. fellow in medicine Harvard Med. Sch., 1981-84; clin. prof. medicine U. Calif., San Francisco, 1984—; founder, pres. Preventive Medicine Rsch. Inst., Sausalito, Calif., 1984—; also bd. dirs. Physician cons. to Pres. Bill Clinton, U.S. Congress, others; U.S. bd. dirs. UN High Commn. on Refugees. Author: 5 books including Dr. Dean Ornish's Program for Reversing Heart Disease, 1990, Eat More, Weigh Less, 1993, Love & Survival: The Scientific Basis for the Healing Power of Intimacy, 1998; contbr. numerous articles to profl. jours. Bd. dirs. Quincy Jones Listen Up Found. Recipient Outstanding Young Alumnus award U. Tex., 1994, U.S. Army Surgeon Gen. medal, Beckmann medal German Soc. Prevention and Rehab. Cardiovascular Diseases, 1996. Mem. Calif. Acad. Medicine. Office: Preventive Med Rsch Inst 900 Bridgeway Sausalito CA 94965-2100 Office Phone: 415-332-2525. Fax: 415-332-5730. Business E-Mail: info@pmri.org.

ORNSTEIN, EWALD ANDERS, hospital administrator, physician; b. Malmioe, Sweden, Apr. 9, 1952; MD, U. Lund, 1980, PhD, 2002. Hosp. mgr., Scania, Ukraine, 1999—. Office: Esplanadgatan 5 Haessleholm Scania 281 25 Sweden Office Fax: 46 451 29 64 15. Business E-Mail: ewald.ornstein@skane.se.

O'ROURKE, DONALD M., neurosurgeon, educator; AB in Biochemistry and Molecular Biology magna cum laude, Harvard U., 1983; MD, U. Pa., 1987, MA, 2002. Diplomate Nat. Bd. Med. Examiners, 1988, Am. Bd. Neurol. Surgery, 1998. Intern in gen. surgery Hosp. Univ. Pa., 1987—88; resident in neurosurgery Univ. Pa., 1988—94, rsch. fellow sch. medicine pathology and lab. medicine, 1994—96; faculty mem. neurosurgery dept. Penn Neurol. Inst. Hosp. Univ. Pa.; faculty mem. neurosurgery dept. Pa. Hosp.; faculty mem. Abramson Family Cancer Ctr. Univ. Pa., founding mem. Ctr. for Cancer Pharmacology, assoc. prof. neurosurgery Abramson Cancer Ctr. Perelman sch. medicine, dir. human brain tissue bank; hosp. affiliations include Pa. Hosp., Hosp. Univ. Pa. Co-author: Role of Monocyte Chemoattractant Protein-1 (MCP-1/CCL2) in Migration of Neural Progenitor Cells Toward Glial Tumors, 2009, Magnetic resonance perfusion-weighted imaging defines angiogenic subtypes of oligodendroglioma according to 1p19q and EGFR status, 2009, The protein tyrosine phosphatase SHP-2 is required for EGFRvIII oncogenic transformation in human glioblastoma cells, 2009, Activated EGFR signaling increases proliferation, survival, and migration and blocks neuronal differentiation in post-natal neural stem cells, 2010, Role of Proton Magnetic Resonance Spectroscopy in Differentiating Oligodendrogliomas from Astrocytomas, 2010, various others. Named one of Best Doctors in America, 2005—08, Top Doctors, Phila. Mag., 2005—11, America's Top Doctors, 2007—08, 2010. Office: Hospital of the University of Pennsylvania 3 Silverstein 3400 Spruce St Philadelphia PA 19104 Office Phone: 215-662-3490. Office Fax: 215-349-5534. Business E-Mail: donald.orourke@uphs.upenn.edu.

O'ROURKE, ROBERT A., cardiologist, educator; b. San Francisco, Calif., June 12, 1936; m. Suzann Reiter, June 8, 1963; children: Michael, Kevin, Sean, Kathleen, Ryan. Student, Santa Clara U., 1954-55; BS, Creighton U., 1957, MD, 1961. Diplomate Am. Bd. Internal Medicine, 1968, Am. Bd. Cardiology, 1969. Straight med. internship Georgetown U. Hosp., Washington, 1961-62, jr. asst. resident internal medicine, 1962-63, sr. asst. resident internal medicine, 1963-64, med. houseofficer internal medicine, 1961-65, fellow cardiology dept., 1964-65; fellow U. Calif Cardiovasc. Rsch. Inst., Washington, 1965-66; staff cardiologist Madagan Army Hosp., Washington, 1966-68; instr. in medicine cardiology Georgetown U. Hosp., Washington, 1968-69; asst. prof. medicine cardiology coll. medicine U. Ariz., Tucson, 1969-70; asst. prof. medicine cardiology, dir. clin. cardiology section, dir. heart station U. Calif., San Diego, 1970-73, assoc. prof. medicine cardiology, dir. clin. cardiology section, dir. coronary care unit, assoc. dir. myocardial infarction rsch. unit, 1973-76; acting chief medicine Audie L. Murphy Vets. Adminstrn. Hosp., 1977-78; Charles Conrad Brown disting. prof. cardiovasc. disease, dir. cardiovasc. divsn. U. Tex. Health Sci. Ctr., San Antonio, 1976—. Cons. in field for various hosps.; vis. professorships to various med. ctrs./univs. Mem. editl. bd.: Jour. Am. Coll. Cardiology, 1983-87, Am. Jour. Cardiology, 1976-81, 83—, Am. Heart Jour., 1980—, Clin. Cardiology, 1985—, Jour. Intensive Care Medicine, 1985—, Internat. Jour. Cardiology, 1981—, Annals of Internal Medicine, 1979-82, Med. Month, 1983—, Weekly Update: Cardiology, 1978-80, Cardiovasc. Medicine, 1976-80, Cardiologic Consultation, 1980—, Cardiovasc. Drugs and Therapy, 1989-90, Coronary Artery Disease, 1990—, Cardiology, 1990—, Jour. Heart Valve Disease, 1992, Current Problems in Cardiology, 1975—, assoc. editor, 1980-83, editor-in-chief, 1984—, Circulation, 1977-80, 81-83, 83-86, 86—, consulting editor, 1993, Yr. Book Cardiology, 1986-92, assoc. editor, 1986-92; assoc. editor: Jour. Applied Cardiology, 1985-90, Am. Jour. Cardiovasc. Pathology, 1985—. Recipient Sinsheimer award for Cardiovasc. Rsch., 1969-70; grantee from various sponsors. Fellow Am. Coll. Physicians, Am. Coll. Cardiology; mem. Am. Soc. Clin. Investigation, Am. Fedn. Clin. Rsch., Am. Heart Assn., Am. Physiological Soc., Assn. Army Cardiologists, Southern Soc. Clin. Rsch., Am. Soc. Echocardiography, Assn. U. Cardiologists, Alpha Omega Alpha, others. Office: The Univ Tex Health Sci Ctr VAH Rm C644 7703 Floyd Curl Drive San Antonio TX 78229-3900 Office Phone: 210-617-5100. Office Fax: 210-567-4687.

OROZCO, JORGE, rehabilitation hospital administrator; Physical therapist Rancho Los Amigos Nat. Rehab. Ctr., Downey, Calif., 1989, chief of rehab. therapy, 2001, COO, 2005, interim CEO, 2007, CEO, 2008—. Adj. instr. Clinical Physical Therapy USC, mem. bd. councilors, divsn. biokinesiology and physical therapy, 2002—. Recipient Diversity award, American Physical Therapy Assn., 2003. Office: Rancho Los Amigos 7601 E Imperial Hwy Downey CA 90242

ORR, EMMA JANE, pharmacist, educator; b. Pennington Gap, Va., Sept. 30, 1956; d. Clyde Wilson and Monnie Lee (Daugherty) O.; m. Allen Emerson Clark, Oct. 24, 1981; 1 child, Katherine Wilson. BS in Pharmacy, Med. Coll. Va., 1979; D of Pharmacy with highest hons., U. Ky., 1981. Registered pharmacist, Va., Ky., Tenn. Asst. dir. pharmacy St. Mary's Hosp., Norton, Va., 1980-84, Norton Community Hosp., 1984-90; clin. coord. Hoston Valley Hosp., Kingsport, Tenn., 1990—; asst. clin. preceptor Sch. Pharmacy, East Tenn. State U., Johnson City; ch. choir dir. 3 bells Units Methodist Ch. Adj. faculty Mountain Empire C.C., Big Stone Gap, Va., 1981—; asst. clin. prof. dept. pharmacy and pharmaceutics Med. Coll. Va., Richmond, 1982—; clin. prof. So. Sch. Pharmacy Mercer U.; mem. pharmacy coll. admission and curriculum coms. East Tenn. State U., 2005—. Tchr., children's spkr. Ch. United Meth. Ch., Duffield, Va., Mountain Empire Older Citizens, Wise, Va., 1983-85; leader Girl Scouts, Duffield, Va. Named Young Career Woman of Yr. Bus. and Profl. Women's Club, 1983. Mem.: Va. Soc. Hosp. Pharmacists, Am. Soc. Hosp. Pharmacists. Methodist. Avocations: reading, needlecrafts, skiing, swimming. Home: 100 Cecil D Quillen Dr Duffield VA 24244 Home Phone: 276-431-4291; Office Phone: 423-224-5601. Business E-Mail: ejane.orr@wellmont.org. E-mail: ejo@adelphia.net.

ORR, KEVIN BRIDSON, retired surgeon, medical educator; b. Balmain, Sydney, Australia, July 17, 1927; s. Clarence Montague and Vera Ruth (Bridson) O.; m. Shirley Hope Frost, Dec. 16, 1950; children: Sandra Carol, Karen Elizabeth, Diane Margaret, Stuart Kelvin Ross, Iain Phillip Angus. MB, BChir, U. Sydney, 1950. Registered med. practitioner, U.K. and NSW. Resident med. officer Grafton Base Hosp., NSW, 1950—51; surg. registrar Red Hill County Hosp., Surrey, England, 1954—56, Essex County Hosp., Colchester, England, 1956—58; sr. lectr. in surgery U. NSW and St. George Hosp., Sydney, 1999—2006, emeritus sr. lectr., 2005—06. Vis. med. officer St. George Hosp., Sydney, 1963, 2006, sec. planning com. med. staff coun., 1965-70, sec. dept. surgery, 1965-75, chmn. med. staff coun., 1983-85, chmn. dept. gastrointestinal surgery, 1992-96. Contbr. articles to profl. jours. Fellow ACS, Royal Coll. Surgeons Eng., Royal Australasian Coll. Surgeons; mem. Australian Med. Assn. Liberal. Presbyterian. Avocations: music, photography, theological science. Home: 42 Castle St Blakehurst NSW 2221 Australia Personal E-mail: kboshorr@eftel.net.au.

ORR, MARCIA, primary school educator, consultant, director; b. Anamosa, Iowa, Mar. 2, 1949; d. Harold Edward Eiben and Clara Elizabeth (Hubbard) E.; m. Robert J. Orr, Sept. 6, 1969; 1 child, Jennifer. Student, U. Iowa, 1977; BS, St. Xavier U., Chgo., 1981; MEd in Early Childhood Leadership, Nat. Louis U., 1996. Bookkeeper Monticello State Bank, 1967-69; exec. sec. Davenport Bank and Trust, 1969-73; asst. educator Elisabeth Ludeman Devel. Ctr., Park Forest, Ill., 1979; tchr. Flossmoor Hills (Ill.) Elem. Sch., 1980-1984; exec. dir. Co-Care, Inc., Park Forest, 1984-89; child devel. rschr., Flossmoor, Ill., 1989—; tchr. Nazarene Nursery Sch. and Kindergarten, Chicago Heights, Ill., 1991; child care ctr. cons. Matteson Sch. Dist. 162, Park Forest, 1991—, adv. mem. project early start, 1991—, home-sch. coord., 1992—; founder, pres., exec. dir. Before and After Sch. Enrichment, Park Forest, 1991—. Grant writer Matteson Sch. Dist. 162 and Before and After Sch. Enrichment, Inc., founder, pres., exec. dir. Child Care Enrichment Ctr. and pre-sch.; officer Boleo Childcare Ctr., Iowa City, 1975-77; mentor to dirs. child care programs early childhood edn. dept. Nat.-Louis U., Ill, 1994—; co-founder Reaching New Horizons, Inc., 1996—; mem. oversight and coord. com. Ill. State Bd. Edn. Early Learning Coun., 2007-, adv. mem. evaluation Com. Early Childhood Programe, State Ill. Contbr. articles pub. to profl. jour. Tchr. religion Infant Jesus of Prague Ch., Flossmoor, Ill., 1982—; mem. Flossmoor PTO, 1987-89; music chmn. Dist. 161 PTO, 1980-90; exec. dir. Before and After Sch. Enrichment, Inc.; parent resource coord. Matteson Sch. Dist. 162. McCormick fellow, 1995—; recipient Golden Achievement award Nat. Sch. Pub. Rels. Assn., 2001; named Best Practices and Rsch. honoree Louis U., Evanston, Ill., 2001. Mem. NAFE, Nat. Assn. for Edn. Young Children (validator), Women Employed Orgn., Internat. Platform Assn., Parent Inst., South Suburban Small Bus. Assn. (charter). Democrat. Roman Catholic. Avocations: piano, classical music, travel. Office: Before and After Sch Enrichment 210 Illinois St Park Forest IL 60466-1100 Home: PO Box 6553 Galena IL 61036-6553 Office Phone: 708-606-5426. Business E-Mail: base@base-inc.net.

ORR, RHONDA, healthcare educator; b. Australia, Aug. 12, 1954; B in Pharmacy, U. Sydney, 1976, PhD, 2008. Sr. lectr. U. Sydney, 1990—, undergrad. course coord., 2000—07, undergrad. course dir., 2009—11. Grant, Australian Govt. Dept. Health and Ageing, 2008, Clive and Vera Ramaciotti Founds., 2008, Nat. Health and Med. Rsch. Com. Equipment, 2011. Mem.: Sports Medicine Australia, Gerontol. Soc. America (Health Scis. Rsch. award 2010). Avocations: kayaking, resistance training, dance. Office: University Sydney 75 East St Lidcombe Sydney NSW 2141 Australia Office Fax: 612 93519204. Business E-Mail: rhonda.orr@sydney.edu.au.

ORR, RICHARD KENNETH, oncologist, director; b. Ft. Wayne, Ind., Aug. 1, 1952; BA, Vanderbilt U., 1974; MD, U. South Fla., 1977; MPH, U. Mass., 1995. Asst. prof., surg. oncology U. Miami, 1984—86; dir., surg. oncology Fallon Clinic, 1986—97, Spartanburg Regional Med. Ctr., 1999—, program dir., surg. residency, 2001—09; surg. oncologist Marshfield Clinic, 1997—99. Assoc. prof., clin. surgery Med. U. SC, 2004—10, prof., clin. surgery, 2010; exec., mgmt. team Gibbs Regional Cancer Ctr., 2006; assoc. prof., surgery Edward Via Coll. Osteo. Medicine, 2009. Recipient Surg. Residency Recognition award, Spartanburg Regional Med. Ctr., 2010; named Rschr. of Yr., Fallon Clinic, Worcester, Mass., 1991, Tchr. of Yr., 1990, U. Mass. Med Ctr. Dept. Surgery, 1997. Fellow: ACS; mem.: Am. Hepatopancreaticobiliary Assn., Spartanburg County Med. Soc., Soc. Surg. Oncology, Am. Assn. Endocrine Surgeons. Avocation: painting. Office: Surgical Oncology Gibbs Cancer Ctr Spartanburg SC 29303 Personal E-mail: rick1841@yahoo.com.

ORR, ROBERT DAVID, clinical ethicist, educator, physician; b. Mooers, NY, Mar. 16, 1941; s. Willard Joseph and Nina Elizabeth (Bell) O.; m. Joyce Lorraine Wirick, June 9, 1962; children: Shirley Ann, Ronald Lee, Robin Lisabeth. BS cum laude, Houghton Coll., 1962; MD, Chirurgee Magistrum, McGill U., Montreal, Que., Can., 1966. Diplomate Am. Bd. Family Practice. Intern U.S. Naval Hosp., Bethesda, Md., 1966-67, resident Jacksonville, Fla., 1967-69, med. officer Roosevelt Roads, P.R., 1969-71; pvt. practice Brattleboro, Vt., 1971-89; fellow clin. ethics U. Chgo., 1989-90; prof. Loma Linda U., Calif., 1990—. Clin. co-dir. Ctr. for Christian Bioethics, Loma Linda, 1991—; chair adv. bd. Ctr. Bioethics and Human Dignity, Bannockburn, Ill., 1994—; prof. U. Vt., 2000-, Grad. Coll., Union U., Schenectady, NY, 2005-. Co-author: Life and Death Decisions, 1990, The Changing Face of Health Care, 1998, Medical Ethics: A Primer for Students, 2001, Aging, Death and the Quest for Immortality, 2004, Basic Questions on Healthcare, 2004; author: Medical Ethics of the Faith Factor, 2009; contbr. numerous articles to profl. jours., chapters to books. Pres. Brattleboro Area Hospice, 1981-84; mem., elder Cmty. Luth. Ch., Burlington, Vt. Lt. comdr. USN, 1966-71. Named Vt. Family Dr. of Yr., Vt. State Med. Soc., 1989. Mem. AMA (Isaac Hayes and John Bell award, 1999), Christian Med. and Dental Soc. (bd. & trustee, mem. ethics commn., chmn. ethics commn. 1991-94, Servant Christ award 2009), Calif. Med. Assn. (mem. com. on bioethics), Soc. for Bioethics Cons. (bd. dirs. 1996—99), Sch. Residence C. S. Lewis Found., Christian Med. Dental Assoc. Avocations: skiing, reading, racquetball. Business E-Mail: rorr@llu.edu.

ORRENIUS, STEN GOSTA, toxicologist, educator; b. Motala, Sweden, Feb. 14, 1937; MB, Karolinska Inst., Stockholm, 1960, PhD, 1965, MD, Lic., 1967; PhD (hon.), U. Stockholm, 1982; MD (hon.), U. Turin, Italy, 1992; PhD (hon.), U. Konstanz, 1997, U. Buenos Aires, 2001; Dr. Honoris Causa (hon.), U. Rene Descartes Paris V, 2000; D (hon.), U. Milan, 2007. Rsch. assoc. Wenner-Gren Inst. for Exptl. Biology, Stockholm, 1965—67; rsch. assoc. dept. biochemistry U. Stockholm, 1967—71; prof., chmn. dept. forensic medicine Karolinska Inst., Stockholm, 1971—84, dean Med. Sch., 1983—90, prof. toxicology, 1984—2003. Sterling Winthrop vis. prof. U. Ky., 1994; Hans Selye vis. prof. U. Calif., Irvine, Calif., 2000. Mem. editl. bd.: European Jour. Biochemistry, 1969—78, Archives of Biochemistry and Biophysics, 1974—2000, Chem. Rsch. in Toxicology, 1988—91, Exptl. Cell Rsch., 1994—2007, Biochem. and Biophys. Rsch. Comms., 1995, Cell Death & Disease, 2009—. Recipient Claude Bernard medal, U. Montreal, 1972, City of Milan medal, 1974, Poulsson medal, Norwegian Soc. Pharmacology and Toxicology, 1984, John Barnes prize, Brit. Toxicology soc., 1991, John A. Muntz Meml. award, Albany Med. Coll., 1995, Merit award, Assn. European Toxicologists and Socs. of Toxicology, 1997, Sci. and Humanity prize, Oxygen Club Calif., 2000, Career award, ECDO, 2003, Dist. Lifetime Toxicology award, Am. Soc. Toxicology, 2005. Mem.: Royal Swedish Acad. Scis., Academia Europaea, Swedish Biochem. Soc., Swedish Med. Assn., Am. Soc. Biochem. & Molecular Biology (hon.), Italian Soc. Toxicology (hon.), Soc. Toxicology USA (hon.), Royal Spanish Acad. Pharmacy (hon.), Am. Soc. for Pharmacology and Exptl. Therapeutics (hon.), Swedish Soc. Toxicology (hon.), NAS, Inst. Medicine (assoc.). Achievements include research in molecular toxicology and cell biology; regulation and mechanisms of cell death, oxidative stress and cellular deference systems and Ca signaling and role in cell toxicity and death. Office: Karolinska Inst Inst Environ Medicine Nobels Vag 13 Box 210 171 77 Stockholm Sweden Office Phone: 46 0 8 335874, 46705933003. E-mail: sten.orrenius@ki.se.

ORRINGER, JEFFREY S., dermatologist, educator; b. Balt., Dec. 7, 1967; s. Mark B. and Susan M. Orringer; m. Kelly A. Orringer, May 1, 1994; children: Matthew J., Kate A. BA with honors, Brown U., 1990; MD, Harvard Med. Sch., 1994. Diplomate Am. Bd. Dermatology. Resident U. Mich., Ann Arbor, 1994—2000, fellowship in Mohs surgery and cosmetic dermatology, 2000—02, assoc. prof. dept. dermatology, 2002—; dir. Cosmetic Dermatology and Laser Ctr., Ann Arbor, 2002—. Contbr. articles to profl. jours. Recipient Cutting Edge Rsch. grant, Am. Soc. Dermatologic Surgery, 2009—; Patient-Directed Investigation grantee, Dermatology Found., 2001—02, Clin. Career Devel. grantee, 2002—05. Fellow: Am. Acad. Dermatology, Am. Soc. Dermatologic Surgery, Am. Coll. Mohs Micrographic Surgery and Cutaneous Oncology, Am. Soc. Laser Medicine and Surgery; mem.: Assn. Acad. Dermatologic Surgeons. Achievements include research in laser therapy and cosmetic dermatology. Office: U Mich Dept Dermatology 1500 E Medical Center Dr Ann Arbor MI 48109 *

ORR-URTREGER, AVI, medical geneticist; b. Israel, Mar. 6, 1952; MD in Health Sci., Ben-Gurion U. Beer-Sheva, Israel, 1981; PhD, Weizmann Inst. Sci., Rehovot, Israel, 1992. Pediat. resident, pediat. specialist Chaim-Sheba Med. Ctr. Tel Hashomer, 1982—87; clin. genetics, postdoc. fellow, dept. molecular and human genetics Baylor Coll. Medicine, Houston, 1992—96; sr. geneticist, acting dir. Genetic Inst., Tel-Aviv Sourasky Med. Ctr., 1997—99, dir., 1999—. Assoc., dept. molecular and human genetics Howard Hughes Med. Inst., Houston, 1982—87; with Nat. Com. Human Med. Rsch., Ministry of Health, Israel, 1998—. Parkinson Disease Genetic Rsch. grant, Michael J. Fox Found., Chief Scientist Dept. Health Israel, Disease Genetic Rsch. grant, ALS Assn., Parkinson Disease Genetic Rsch. grant, Israel Sci. Found. Legacy Heritage Fund, Genetic grant, Kahn Found. Israel. Mem.: Israel Soc. Clin. Genetics, Am. Soc. Human Genetics. Avocations: gardening, travel. Office: Weizmann 6 Tel Aviv 64239 Israel Office Fax: 972-3-6974555. Business E-Mail: aviorr@tasmc.health.gov.il.

ORSHER, STUART, internist; m. Gladys George. MD, Hahnemann Med. Hosp., 1975. Diplomate Am. Bd. Intternal Medicine. Intern Lenox Hill Hosp., NY, resident, internist. Recipient Gay ClarkStoddard Meml. award, Greater NYC, 2006. Mem.: AMA, NYC County Med. Soc., Med. Soc. State of NY. Office: Lenox Hill Hospital 100 E 77th St New York NY 10075 Home: 9 E 79 St New York NY 10075 Office Phone: 212-434-2000. *

ORSI, ANTONIO MARCOS, medical educator, researcher; b. Sales Oliveira, São Paulo, Brazil, July 25, 1947; s. Reynaldo and Amália Bergamo Orsi; m. Maria de Fátima Castilho, Feb. 1, 1975; children: André Castilho, Daniela Castilho, Alessandra Castilho. MS in Morphology and Biomed. Sci., UNESP, Botucatu, São Paulo, PhD in Morphology and Biomed. Sci., 1970. Cert. biomed. scientist CRBM, 1982. Lectr. UNESP, 1971—2003, dean's asst. HR commn., 1983—84, asst. prof., 2009—; assoc. coll. prof. UNIMAR, Marília, São Paulo, Brazil, 2004—09. Rsch. referee FAPESP, CNPQ, São Paulo, 1986—2003; referee, assoc. editor Brazilian Jour. Vet. Rsch. and Animal Sci. Contbr. scientific papers to profl. jours. Sci. Devel. grant, Nat. Coun. Rsch., 2000—04, FAPESP, São Paulo Rsch. Assn., 2003—05. Mem.: Brazilian Soc. Anatomy (mem. 1972—2009, Renato Locchi award 1986, 1999, 2002, named one of Best 5 Anathomists São Paulo State 2008, Renato Locchi award 1994). Office: UNESP Rubião Jr PO Box 510 Botucatu São Paulo 18611-000 Brazil Office Phone: 55-14-3811-6040. Personal E-mail: amorsi47@gmail.com. Business E-Mail: anatomia@ibb.unesp.br.

ORSINI, CAMILLO, surgeon; b. Adria, Rovigo, Italy, Mar. 12, 1959; Degree in Medicine and Surgery, Padua U., 1985, degree in Surgery, 1990. With surgery dept. Camposampiero Hosp., Padua, 2000—. Mem.: AFI, ACOI. Avocations: music, bicycling. Office: via P Cosma 1 Camposampiero Padua 35012 Italy Office Fax: 39 049 9324423. Business E-Mail: camillorsini@libero.it.

ORTALDO, JOHN R., immunologist, researcher; b. West Chester, Pa., Apr. 22, 1945; BS, St. Francis Coll., Loretto, Pa., 1967; MS in microbiology, Villanova U., 1969; PhD in microbiology/immunology, George Washington U., 1979. Mil. svc. in immunohematology Walter Reed Army Inst., 1969—71; microbiologist Dept. Agriculture, Dover, Del.; rsch. biologist Cellular and Tumor Immunology Sect., Lab. Cell Biology Nat. Cancer Inst., NIH, 1971, post-doctoral training Lab. Immunodiagnosis, named sr. investigator Lab Immunodiagnosis, 1980, head Natural Immunity Sect., Biol. Therapeutics Br. Frederick, chief Lab. Exptl. Immunology, 1985, acting head Leukocyte Cell Biology Sect. Mem.: Soc. Natural Immunology, Soc. Biol. Therapy, Reticuloendothelial Soc., Am. Assn. Immunology, Am. Assn. Cancer Rsch. Office: Lab Exptl Immunology Nat Cancer Inst at Frederick PO Box B Bldg 560 Rm 31-93 Frederick MD 21702-1201 Office Phone: 301-846-1323. Office Fax: 301-846-1673. E-mail: ortaldo@ncifcrf.gov.

ORTEGA-CALVO, MANUEL, physician, researcher; b. Sevilla, Spain, July 23, 1956; BS in Medicine, Seville's Medicine Sch., 1979, MD, 1985; postgrad., Nat. Hosp. Neurology and Neurosurgery, London, 1988; postgrad. in Epidemiology, Andalusian Sch. Pub. Health, 2010. Familiy physician trainee Virgen Macarena Tchg. Hosp., 1980—82; adj. prof., medicine dept. Seville's U., 1983—90; familiy physician, rschr. Andalusian Health Svc., 1990—. Vis. prof., neurology dept. Oxford U. John Radcliffe Infirmary, England, 1986; reviewer GUT BMJ Jours., 2009. Mem.: Andalusian Sch. Pub. Health Courses (Granada, Spain), Epidemiology Spanish Soc. Avocations: reading, walking. Home: Avda Cruz del Campo 36 Bl 1 2 A Sevilla Andalucía 41005 Spain Personal E-mail: ortegacalvo@terra.es.

ORTENZIO, ROBERT A., health and medical products executive; V.p. Rehab Hosp. Svcs. Corp.; sr. v.p. Continetal Med. Systems, Inc., Mechanicsburg, Pa., 1986—88, COO, 1988—95, pres., 1995—96; exec. v.p., dir. Horizon/CMS Healthcare Corp.; co-founder, pres., COO Select Medical Holdings Corp., Mechanicsburg, Pa., 1997—2001, pres., 2001—04, CEO, 2001—. Bd. dir. US Oncology, Inc. Office: Select Medical 4716 Old Gettysburg Rd Mechanicsburg PA 17055 Office Phone: 717-972-1100. *

ORTENZIO, ROCCO ANTHONY, health products executive; b. Steelton, Pa., Nov. 28, 1932; s. Rocco and Minnie Ortenzio; m. Nancy Miller, Jan. 29, 1955; children: John, Robert, Martin. BS, West Chester U., 1955; postgrad., U. Pa., 1955—56. Pvt. practice phys. therapy, Harrisburg, Pa., 1957—69, founder, pres., CEO Rehab. Corp., Harrisburg, 1969—77, Pa. Health Corp., Mechanicsburg, Pa., 1977—79, Rehab. Hosp. Svc. Corp., Mechanicsburg, 1979—85; co-founder, chmn, CEO Continental Med. Sys., Inc. (merged with Horizon Healthcare Corp.), Mechanicsburg, 1986—95, Select Medical Holdings Corp., Mechanicsburg, Pa., 1997—2001, exec. chmn., 2001—. Bd. dirs. Continental Med. Sys., Inc., PNC, N.A., AMSCO Internat., Quorum Health Group, Inc. Mem.: World Pres. Orgn. Republican. Roman Catholic. Office: Select Material 4716 Old Gettysburg Rd Mechanicsburg PA 17055 Office Phone: 717-972-1100. *

ORTH, DAVID NELSON, endocrinologist, educator, sculptor, potter; b. East Orange, NJ, Mar. 5, 1933; s. John Joseph and Marjorie Adelaide (Wauters) O.; m. Linda Diana D'Errico, June 9, 1979; children by previous marriage: John Randall (dec.), Jennifer Stewart, Julie Thomas. ScB in Chemistry, Brown U., 1954; MD, Vanderbilt U., 1962. Intern, Osler med. service Johns Hopkins Hosp., Balt., 1962-63, fellow in medicine, 1962-65; asst. resident John Hopkins Hosp., Balt., 1963-65; mem. faculty dept. medicine Vanderbilt U. Sch. Medicine, Nashville, 1965—, prof., 1975-98, prof. emeritus, 1998—, joint dir. endocrinology div. dept. medicine, 1968-81, dir. cancer research and treatment ctr., 1972-77, dir. div. endocrinology, 1984-96; sculptor and potter, 1998—. Scholar-in-residence Rockefeller Found. Bellagio Study and Conf. Ctr., Italy, 1989; vis. scientist Vollum Inst. for Advanced Biomed. Rsch., Oreg. Health Scis. U., Portland, 1993-94. Contbr. numerous articles in field of endocrinology to med. jours. Served with U.S. Navy, 1954-57. John and Mary R. Markle scholar, 1968-73; Howard Hughes Med. Inst. investigator, 1969-75 Mem. AAUP, AAAS, ACP, Assn. Am. Physicians, Am. Soc. Clin. Investigation, Endocrine Soc. (sec.-treas. 1989-94, pres. 1997-98), N.Y. Acad. Scis., Am. Fedn. Clin. Rsch., So. Soc. Clin. Investigation. Personal E-mail: orth@comcast.net. *

ORTIZ, JUAN CAMILO, cardiologist; b. Medellin, Colombia, Aug. 22, 1980; B, San Ignacio De Loyola, 1996. Physician U. Ces, 1997—2002; internal medicine U. Pontificia Bolivariana, Pablo Tobon Uribe Hosp., 2004—07; cardiology U. Pontificia Bolivariana, Cardiovasc. Clin., 2007—09, interventional cardiology, 2009—. Emergency rm. gen. physician Gilberto Mejia Hosp., 2003, Pablo Tobon Uribe Hosp., 2003—04. Recipient award, Santo Domingo Found., Mt. Sinai Hosp., Bbva Hosp. Clin., Barcelona. Fellow: Sociedad Colombiana de Cardiologia Intervencionista (Miguel Nassif award); mem.: Sociedad Colombiana de Medicina Interna, Sociedad Colombiana de Cardiologia. Avocations: sports, travel. Home: Cra 39 13 Sur-80 Medellin Antioquia Colombia Business E-Mail: camiloou@une.net.co.

ORUC, ELIF, biology professor; b. Van, Turkey, Nov. 29, 1969; Degree in Biology, Cukurova U., Adana, Turkey, 1990, degree, 1998. Assoc. prof. Cukurova U., 2005—. Editl. bd. mem. ISRN Toxicology, 2011. Recipient Recognition Cert., Elsevier Pub.; Rsch. grant, Sci. and Tech. Rsch. Coun. Turkey. Fellow: Sci. and Tech. Rsch. Coun. Turkey; mem.: Turkish Soc. Biochemistry, Soc. Toxicology. Avocations: swimming, tennis. Office: Cukurova University Faculty Sci

Dept. Biology Balcali Adana 01330 Turkey Office Fax: 90 322 3386070. Business E-Mail: eozcan@cu.edu.tr.

ÖRVELL, CLAES GUNNAR, virologist, researcher, physician, educator; b. Stockholm, Apr. 22, 1945; s. Gunnar Emanuel and Margit (Borg) Örvell; m. Eva Reimert, May 5, 1987; 3 children. MD, Karolinska Inst., Stockholm, 1973, PhD, 1977. Lic. physician, virologist. Rschr. dept. virology Karolinska Inst., Stockholm, 1978-79; rschr. in virology Nat. Bacteriological Lab., Stockholm, 1980-92; sr. physician Stockholm County Coun., 1992—. Assoc. prof. virology Karolinska Inst., Stockholm, 1988—. Contbr. articles to profl. jours. Recipient Internat. Order of Merit award, 2000, Lifetime Achievement award, 2001, Presdl. Seal of Honor, 2001, Order of Internat. Fellowship, 2001, Outstanding Achievement award, United Cultural Conv., 2001, World Biographee Day, Am. Biog. Inst., 2001, Min. of Culture, Am. Biog. Inst., 2003, Internat. Peace prize, United Cultural Conv., 2004, Order of Distinction, 2004, Order Am. Ambassadors, 2006; named Amb. Grand Eminence, Am. Biog. Inst., 2002, founding mem., Am. Order Excellence, 2002; named to Hall of Fame, Am. Biog. Inst., 2002, Internat. Biog. Ctr., 2006. Avocations: golf, literature. Office: Huddinge Univ Hosp Dept Clin Virology 141 86 Huddinge Sweden Office Phone: 46 8 5858 1307, 4670-0021178. Personal E-mail: claes.orvell@karolinska.se.

ORWA, JENNIFER AKINYI, research scientist, director; d. Wilson Walter and Tabitha Owiti Aluoch; m. Moses Wandaga Orwa, 1980; children: Tabitha Owiti, Marianne Adhiambo, Michael Orwa. BS in Pharmacy, Sch. Pharmacy, U. Nairobi, Kenya, 1979; MSc, U. London, 1984; PhD, Katholieke U. Leuven, Belgium, 2000. Registered pharmacist Pharmacy and Poisons Bd., Nairobi, 1980, tng. participant WHO, Tropical Diseases Rsch. Divsn., 2003, cert. tng. facilitator Internat. Network Rational Drug Use, 2004, seminar participant Kenya Bur. Standards, 2008. Hosp. pharmacist Kenyatta Nat. Hosp., Nairobi, 1980—83, chief pharmacist, 1984—85; rsch. officer Kenya Med. Rsch. Inst., Nairobi, 1985—2000, sr. rsch. officer, 2001—04, prin. rsch. officer, 2004—, acting dir., ctr. traditional medicine and drug rsch., 2008—. Lead cons., report pharm. situation WHO, Nairobi, 2003; cons. trainer drug quantification in Seychelles UN Devel. Program, Nairobi, 2005; cons. drug registration Pharmacy and Poisons Bd., 2005; assoc. lead person, ethnobotany rsch. Lake Victoria Rsch. Initiative, Kampala, Uganda, 2006—. Contbr. articles to profl. jours. and publs. Mem. Nat. Coun., Legal and Ethics Com., Edn. Com., 2004—07. Rsch. Grant, Sida/SAREC, 2006, PhD fellowship, Belgian Govt., 1996—2000. Mem.: Internat. Network Rational Use Drugs (treas. 2004—08), Natural Products Rsch. Network Eastern and Ctrl. Africa, Pharm. Soc. Kenya (nat. coun. mem. 2004—08). Office: Kenya Med Rsch Inst Mbagathi Rd PO Box 54840 Nairobi 00200 Kenya Office Fax: 254(0)202720030. Personal E-mail: jenorwa@yahoo.co.uk. Business E-Mail: jorwa@kemri.org.

ORY, MARCIA GAIL, social science researcher; b. Dallas, Feb. 8, 1950; d. Marvin Gilbert and Esther (Levine) O.; m. Raymond James Carroll, Aug. 13, 1972. BA magna cum laude, U. Tex., 1971; MA, Ind. U., 1972; PhD, Purdue U., 1976; MPH, Johns Hopkins U., 1981. Rsch. asst. prof. U. N.C., Chapel Hill, 1976-77, from adj. asst. prof. to assoc. prof. sch. pub. health, 1978-88; rsch. fellow U. Minn., Mpls., 1977-78; asst. prof. Sch. Pub. Health U. Ala., Birmingham, 1978-80; program dir. biosocial aging and health Nat. Inst. on Aging, Bethesda, Md., 1981-86, chief social sci. rsch. on aging, 1987—2001; prof. Sch. Rural Pub. Health Tex A&M U. Sys., College Station, 2001—, regent prof., 2007—. Dir. RWJF Nat. Program Office on Increasing Phys. Activity in the 50 Plus, 2001—09. Contbr. articles, editor vols. to profl. jours. Mem. several nat. task forces on aging and health issues; leadership coun., Healthy Aging Rsch. Collaborative, Health Found. South Fla.; bd. dirs. Ctr. for Health Improvement. Recipient Dept. HHS award, 1984, 1985, 1988, Dir.'s award, NIH, 1995, Merit award, 1999, 2001, Dir's Lifetime Achievement award, 2000, Polisher award, Gerontol. Soc. Am., 2001, Excellence in Program Innovation award, Archstone Found., 2005, Excellence in Rsch. award, Sch. Rural Pub. Health, 2005—06, Disting. Mentor award, Gerontological Soc. Am., 2007, Betty J. Cleckley Excellence in Minority Health and Ageing Hon. Mention award, 2007, Highest Cited Paper, Excellence in Program award, Erickson Found., 2009; named Disting. Alumna, Purdue U.; named one of 5 Industry Innovators in Active Aging, Internat. Coun. on Active Aging, 2003; named to McKnights Long Term Care News 100, 1997; fellow, Inst. for Advanced Study, LATrobe U.,vMelbourne, Australia, 2004. Fellow: Am. Acad. Health Behavior, Soc. Behavioral Medicine (program chmn. pub. health track 1988—89, program com. 1991—92, program chair lifespan/devel. track 2001—02), Acad. for Behavioral Medicine Rsch., Gerontol. Soc. Am.; mem.: APHA (program chmn. 1986, gov. coun. 1986—88, chmn.-elect 1989—91, chmn. 1992—93, leadership group 1996—, chair, Polisher Award Com. 2009—, chair, Womens Group 2009—, chair older women's interest group 2000—10, chair rural and environ. health group 2010—, Philip G. Weiler Leadership award 2010), Am. Sociol. Assn. (regional reporter 1984—94, program com. 1986, nominations com. 1987, councilor-at-large 1992—93), Delta Omega, Omicron Nu, Phi Kappa Phi. Avocations: walking, birding, travel. Office: Sch Rural Pub Health 1266 TAMU College Station TX 77843-1266 Office Phone: 979-458-1373.

ORY, STEVEN JAY, physician, educator; b. Houston, Aug. 4, 1950; s. Edwin Marvin and Norma Gertrude O.; m. Kathleen Higgins, Jan. 10, 1981; children: Eleanor Claire, Edward Michael. BA, Washington and Lee U., 1972; MD, Baylor Coll., 1976. Diplomate Am. Bd. Obstetrics and Gynecology, subsplty. cert. in Reproductive Endocrinology and Infertility. Asst. prof. Duke U., Durham, NC, 1981-82, Northwestern U., Chgo., 1982-85; assoc. prof., cons. Mayo Clinic, Rochester, Minn., 1985-95, chmn. sect. reproductive endocrinology and infertility, 1985-95; pvt. practice reproductive endocrinology and infertility; mem. ob-gyn. staff Internat. U., Margate, Fla., 1995—; prof. ob-gyn. Fla. Internat. U., Miami, 2008—; vol. assoc. prof. obstets. and gyn. U. Miami, Fla., 1999—. Assoc. dir. Am. Soc. Reproductive Medicine, Birmingham, Ala., 1986-87; bd. trustees Northwest Med. Ctr., Margate, Fla., 2003—09. Asst. editor: Fertility and Sterility, 1988-96, assoc. editor, 2009-11; contbr. articles to profl. jours. Mem.: Ft. Lauderdale Ob-Gyn. Soc. (pres. 1998—2000), Soc. Reproductive Endocrinologists (sec.-treas., pres. 2001—02), Am. Soc. Reproductive Medicine (chmn. practice com. 1998—2000, bd. dirs. 1999—2002, v.p. 2004—05, pres.-elect 2005—06, pres. 2006—07, past pres. 2008—09, bd. dirs. 2010—), Soc. for Humanism in Medicine (bd. dirs. 1999—2002, v.p. 2004—05, pres.-elect 2005—06, pres. 2006—07). Office Phone: 954-247-6200.

ORZALESI, NICOLA, retired physician; b. Florence, Sept. 6, 1938; MD, U. Bari, 1961. Prof. U. Milan, 1984—2011. Mem.: ARVO. Office: Boccaccio 45 Milan 20123 Italy Business E-Mail: nicola.orzalesi@unimi.it.

OSA, TETSUO, retired pharmaceutical science educator; b. Tokyo, Aug. 6, 1932; s. Jiro and Mine (Irie) O.; m. Reiko Uemura, Oct. 26, 1960; children: Minako, Yumiko. B Engring., U. Tokyo, 1955, M Engring., 1957, D Engring., 1964. Sr. researcher Coal Chem. Lab., Hokkaido Colliery and Steamship Co., Toda-shi, Japan, 1957-62; assoc. prof. faculty engring. U. Tokyo, 1962-74; prof. Pharm. Inst. Tohoku U., Sendai, Japan, 1974-96; R&D advisor ctrl. lab. Asahi Glass Co., Yokohama-shi, Japan, 1996—2001. Recipient Purple ribbon Japanese Govt., 1997. Mem. Pharm. Soc. Japan (v.p. 1994), The Japan Petroleum Inst. (bd. dirs. 1989-96, Soc. award 1989), Chem. Soc. Japan (Soc. award 1994), Soc. Cyclodexcrins Japan (pres. 1996-98, society award 1999). Avocation: travel. Home Phone: 81-22-278-4814.

OSAKA, NAOYUKI, psychology professor; b. Kyoto, Dec. 16, 1946; s. Ryoji and Ritsuko Osaka; m. Mariko Yamamoto. BA, Kyoto U. Edn., 1971; MA, Kyoto U., 1973, PhD, 1979. Asst. prof. Otemon-Gakuin U., Osaka, Japan, 1977-81, assoc. prof., 1981-87, adj. prof. to emeritus prof., 2010—; assoc. prof. Kyoto U., 1987-94, prof., 1994—2010, chmn. psychology dept., 1994—, dean, 2008—, prof. emeritus, 2010—; assoc. edit. Japanese Jour. of Psychonomic Soc., Japanese Jour. Cognitive Psychology; pres. Japanese Soc. Working Memory, 2003—, Kansai Psychol. Editor Japanese Psychol. Rev., 1994—. Mem. Japan Color Sci. Assn. (pres. 1998-), Japan Sci. Coun. (dean Grad. Sch. Letters, 2008-), Japanese Psychol. Assn., Psychonomic Soc. U.S., Sci. Coun. Japan., Kansai Psychol. Assn. (pres. 2005—). Avocations: tennis, skiing, travel. Home: 3-28-1 Minegadocho Goryo Nishikyo-ku Kyoto 610-1103 Japan Office: Kyoto U Dept Psychology Grad Sch Letters Kyoto 606-8501 Japan

OSAKI, TOMOHIRO, surgeon, educator; b. Hiroshima, Japan, May 23, 1976; D, Hokkaido U., 2006. Prof. Hokkaido U., Vet. Tchg. Hosp., 2006—10; prof. vet. surgery Tottori U., 2010—. Office: Koyamaminami 4-101 Tottori 680-8553 Japan Business E-Mail: tosaki@muses.tottori-u.ac.jp.

OSAMU, YAMAZAKI, surgeon; b. Osaka, Japan, June 30, 1955; MD, Grad. Sch. Medicine, Osaka City U., PhD, 1986. Staff surgeon, dept. surgery Osaka City Momoyama Hosp., 1986—93; surgeon-in-chief Osaka City Gen. Hosp., Dept. Surgery, 1993—95, co-dir., 1995—2004, dir., 2004—07; exec. v.p. Osaka City Juso Hosp., 2007—. Part-time instr. Osaka City U., Sch. Medicine, 1991. Mem.: Japanese Soc. Gastroenterology, Japan Soc. Hepatology, Japanese Soc. Hepato-Biliary-Pancreatic Surgery, Japanese Soc. Gastroent. Surgery, Japan Surg. Soc. Office: 2-12-27 Nonaka-kita Yodogawa-ku Osaka 532-0034 Japan Office Fax: 81-6-6150-8680. Business E-Mail: o-yamazaki@byouin.city.osaka.lg.jp.

OSBAHR, ALBERT J., hospital administrator; s. Albert J. and Jeanne Osbahr. BA, MD, U. NC; MS in Cmty. Medicine, Marshall U., W.Va. Cert. American Bd. Family Medicine, in occpl. medicine and preventive medicine/pub. health American Bd. Preventive Medicine, American Bd. Ind. Med. Examiners, med. rev. officer American Assn. Med. Rev. Officers. Resident in family medicine Marshall U. Joan C. Edwards Sch. Medicine; resident in occupl./preventive medicine U. Ky.; pvt. practice family health practitioner in preventive medicine; occupl. health dir. Haywood Regional Med. Ctr., Clyde, NC; med. dir. occupl. health services Catawba Valley Med. Ctr., Hickory, NC. Lab dir., med. cons. Haywood County Health Dept.; med. reviewer Carolinas Ctr. Med. Excellence, ExamWorks, Inc., NC Dept. Disability Services. Mem. fed. motor carriers safety adminstrn. med. rev. bd. US Dept. Transp.; mem. rev. panel NC Med. Bd.; mem. NC Gov. Task Force on Pub. Health; bd. dirs. One Health Commn. Mem.: AMA (NC del. 1988—, mem. coun. sci. and health 2004, 2008, chmn. coun. sci. and health 2010—11, bd. trustees 2011—, mem. coun. on med. svc.), NC Med. Soc. (pres. 2008—09, mem. indsl. commn. liaison com., mem. hosp. med. staff com.). Office: Catawba Valley Med Ctr 810 Fairgrove Ch Rd SE Hickory NC 28602 Office Phone: 828-326-3800. *

OSBORN, JUNE ELAINE, pediatrician, microbiologist, educator, foundation administrator; b. Endicott, NY, May 28, 1937; d. Leslie A. and Dora W. (Wright) Osborn; children: Philip I. Levy, Ellen D. Levy, Laura A. Jana. BA, Oberlin Coll., Ohio, 1957; MD, Western Res. U., 1961; DSc (hon.), U. Med. Dental Sch. N.J., 1990, Emory U., 1993, Oberlin Coll., 1993, Rutgers U., 1994, Case Western Res. U., 1997, SUNY, Stony Brook, 1999, U. Wis., 2004; DMS (hon.), Yale U., 1992; LHD (hon.), Med. Coll. Pa., 1994. Intern, resident in pediatrics Harvard U. Hosp., 1961—64; fellow Johns Hopkins, 1964—65, U. Pitts., 1965—66; prof. med. microbiology and pediat. U. Wis. Med. Sch., Madison, Wis., 1966—84, prof. pediat. and microbiology, 1974—84, assoc. dean Grad. Sch., 1975—84; dean Sch. Pub. Health U. Mich. Sch. Pub. Health, 1984—93; prof. epidemiology, pediat. and communicable diseases U. Mich. Sch. Pub. Health and Med. Sch., 1984—96, prof. emeritus, 2008—. Pres. Josiah Macy, Jr. Found., 1997—2007; pres. emeritus, 2008—; mem. rev. panel viral vaccine efficacy FDA, 1973—79, mem. vaccines and related biol. products adv. com., 1981—85; mem. exptl. virology study sect. Divsn. Rsch. Grants, NIH, 1975—79; mem. med. affairs com. Yale U. Coun., 1981—86; mem. life scis. associateships rev. panel NRC, 1981—84; mem. U.S. Army Med. R&D Adv. Com., 1983—85; chmn. working group on AIDS and the Nation's Blood Supply NHLBI, 1984—89; chmn. WHO Planning Group on AIDS and the Internat. Blood Supply, 1985—86. Contbr. articles to profl. jours.; mem. editl. bd.: Jour. AMA, 2002—11. Active task force in AIDS, Inst. of Medicine, 1986; adv. com. Robert Wood Johnson Found. AIDS Health Svcs. Program, 1986—91; nat. adv. com. on health of pub. program Pew and Rockefeller Founds.; active Global Commn. on AIDS, WHO, 1988—92; chmn. Nat. Commn. on AIDS, 1989—93; trustee Kaiser Found., 1990—98, Case Western Reserve U., Cleve., 1993—97; nat. vaccine adv. com. HHS, 1995—98; adv. coun. Nat. Inst. on Drug Abuse, 1995—98; internat adv. bd. Nat. Acads., 2002—05; bd. dirs. Legal Action Ctr., 1994—2001, Ctr. for Health Care Strategies, 1998—2003, The Mind Inst., 2003—05, US Pharmacopeia Bd., 2005—10. Recipient NIH Pub. Svc. award, 2000, Scientific Freedom and Responsibility award, AAAS, 1994, Lifetime Achievement award, Nat. Med. Fellowships, 2008; grantee NIH, 1969, 1972, 1974—75, Nat. Multiple Sclerosis Soc., 1971. Fellow: Infectious Diseases Soc. Am., Am. Acad. Microbiology, Am. Acad. Arts and Scis., Am. Acad. Pediat.; mem.: Inst. Medicine (health promotion and disease prevention bd. 1987—90, coun. mem. 1995—2000), Soc. Pediat. Rsch., Am. Assn. Immunologists. Personal E-mail: jeosborn@aol.com.

OSBORN, LUCY MORIN, pediatrician, educator; b. Kansas City, Mo., 1946; MD, Northwestern U., Evanston, Ill., 1972. Cert. in pediat. Am. Bd. Med. Specialties, in pub. health & gen. preventive medicine Am. Bd. Med. Specialties, 1984. Intern in pediat. U. Wash., Seattle, 1972—73, resident, 1973—74; resident in preventative medicine U. Utah, Salt Lake City, 1974—75, fellow, 1978—80; pediatrician U. Utah Med. Ctr.; prof. pediat. U. Utah Health and Sci. Ctr. Mem.: Am. Acad. Pediat.

OSBORNE, C. KENT, oncologist, educator; AB, U. Mo.; MD, U. Mo. Med. Sch. Cert. Nat. Bds. Parts 1, 2 & 3, diplomate Am. Bd. Internal Medicine, 1975, medical oncology Am. Bd. Internal Medicine, 1977. Intern & resident Johns Hopkins Hosp.; dir. Baylor Coll. Medicine Breast Ctr., Baylor Cancer Ctr.; prof. medicine & cellular & structural biology Baylor Coll. Medicine. Recipient Breull Meml. award, Cleveland Clinic, 1992, Belsky Meml. award, NYU, 1994, Scientific Distinction award, Susan G. Komen Breast Cancer Assn., 1994. Fellow: Nat. Cancer Inst.; mem.: Am. Soc. Clinical Oncology, Am. Assn. Cancer Rsch., Assn. Am. Physicians, Endocrine Soc., Alpha Omega Alpha, Phi Beta Kappa. Office: Lester & Sue Smith Breast Center One Baylor Plaza BCM-600 Houston TX 77030 Office Phone: 713-798-1641. Office Fax: 713-798-1642. E-mail: kosborne@breastcenter.tmc.edu.

OSBORNE, TIMOTHY F., biology professor, researcher; b. Ouray, Colo., Sept. 9, 1955; AB, U. Calif., Santa Barbara, 1978; PhD, U. Calif., LA, 1983. Prof., dept. molecular biology and biochemistry U. Calif., Irvine, 1998—2010, acting chair, dept. molecular biology and biochemistry, 2000, vice chmn., dept. molecular biology and biochemistry, 2001—04, charman, dept. molecular biology and biochemistry, 2004—09; prof., dir. metabolic signaling & disease program Sanford Burnham Med. Rsch. Inst., 2009—. Ad hoc mem. NIH Integrated Nutrition and Metabolic Processes Study Session, 2004; external reviewer Pennington Biomedical Rsch. COBRE Program, 2006; bd. dirs. Deuel Conf. Lipids, 2010; reviewer NIH Coll. Ctr. Sci., 2010; internat. adv. bd. mem. Danish PhD Sch. Molecular Metabolism, 2010. Grant, Nat. Heart Lung and Blood Inst. Mem.: AAAS, ASBMB, AChems. Office: 6400 Sanger Rd Orlando FL 32827 Office Fax: 407-745-2032. Business E-Mail: tosborne@sanfordburnham.org.

OSCHMANN, STEFAN, pharmaceutical executive; b. Würzburg, Germany; married; 2 children. Degree in veterinary medicine, U. Munich, PhD. Academic rschr. Tech. U. Munich; with Internat. Atomic Energy Agency, 1985—89; joined regulatory affairs and sci. policy Merck & Co., Inc., 1989, gen. mgmt. positions Belgium, Netherlands, Austria, v.p. ctrl. and ea. Europe, 1998—99, v.p. Europe, 1999—2005, sr. v.p. worldwide human resources, 2005—06, pres. Europe, Mid. East, Africa and Can., 2006—09, pres. emerging markets, 2009—11; gen. ptnr., mem. exec. bd. Merck KGaA, 2011—; pres. Merck Serono SA, 2011—. Office: Merck Serono SA 9 chemin des Mines Case postale 54 1211 Geneva Switzerland *

OSE, LEIV, physician, researcher; b. Skien, Norway, May 1, 1944; s. Anders and Synnøve Ose; m. Turid Ose. MD, U. Gøttingen, Germany, 1969, PhD, U. Oslo, 1981. Fellow Johns Hopkins U.; rschr. U. Oslo, 1977—80; fellow dept. medicine Coll. Physicians and Surgeons Columbia U., 1981—82; cons. dept. pediat. Rikshospitalg, Oslo, 1987—89, cons. lipidology, med. dir., 1989—, prof. dept. nutrition, 2010; prof. nutrition U. Oslo, 2010. Office: Rikshospitalet Lipid Clinic Forskningsveien 2B Oslo 0027 Norway Home: Ekebergveien 165E 1177 Oslo Norway Office Fax: 47 23075610. Business E-Mail: leiv.ose@rikshospitalet.no.

OSGOOD, NANCY JEAN, medical educator, writer; b. July 6, 1951; d. Jack Kent and Lois Emma (Stober) Luttrell; m. Raymond Clifford Jordan, Jr., Oct. 13, 1984. BA in Sociology and Spanish, Yankton Coll., 1972; MA in Sociology, Drake U., 1974; cert. in gerontology, Syracuse U., 1979; PhD in Sociology, 1979. Rsch. assoc. Syracuse Rsch. Corp., NY, 1975—78; asst. prof. SUNY, Cortland, 1979—80, Med. Coll. Va., Richmond, 1980—92, prof., 1992—. Mem. Nat. Com. on Vital and Health Stats., Washington, 1982—84. Author: Senior Settlers: Social Integration in Retirement Communities, 1982, Suicide in the Elderly: A Practitioner's Guide to Diagnosis and Mental Health Intervention, 1985, Suicide Among the Elderly in Long-Term Care Facilities, 1991; editor: Life after Work: Retirement, Leisure, Recreation and the Elderly, 1982; co-author: Seniors on Stage: The Impact of Applied Theatre on the Elderly, 1985, Suicide and the Elderly: An Annotated Bibliography and Review, 1986; co-editor: Dynamic Leisure Programming with Older Adults, 1987, The Science and Practice of Gerontology: A Multi-disciplinary Guide, 1989, Alcoholism and Aging: An Annotated Bibliography and Review, 1995, Treating Alcohol and Drug Abuse in the Elderly, 2002. Selection com. King William HS, Va., 1985; active Va. State Rehab. Bd., Am. Cancer Soc. Recipient acad. scholarship, Yankton Coll., 1969—72, N.Y. State Dept. Mental Hygiene Rsch. fellowship, 1974—75, Nat. Inst. Edn. award, 1975—78, NIMH award, 1977—79, Presdl. Invitation to White House, 1984, 1991; grantee Va. Commonwealth U., 1981—82. Fellow: Gerontol. Soc. Am.; mem.: Internat. Platform Assn., So. Gerontol. Soc., Am. Sociol. Assn., Am. Assn. Suicidology. Avocations: playing piano and clarinet, gourmet cooking, parrots. Home: PO Box 245 Manquin VA 23106-0245 Personal E-mail: osgoodn@yahoo.com.

OSGOOD, RICHARD MAGEE, JR., electrical engineering professor, researcher; b. Kansas City, Mo., Dec. 28, 1943; s. Richard Magee and Mary Neff (Russell) O.; m. Alice Rose Dyson, June 25, 1966; children: Richard Magee, III, Nathaniel David, Jennifer Anne BS in Engring., U.S. Mil. Acad., 1965; MS in Physics, Ohio State U., 1968; PhD, MIT, 1973. Rsch. assoc. dept. physics MIT, Cambridge, Mass., 1969-72, rsch. staff Lincoln Lab., 1973-80, project leader Lincoln Lab., 1980-81; assoc. prof. applied physics and elec. engring. Columbia U., NYC, 1981-82, prof., 1982-91, Higgins prof., 1989—. Assoc. dir. Brookhaven Nat. Lab., Upton, NY, 2000—03; dir. Microelectronics Sci. Labs., 1984—90; mem. Army Sci. and Tech. Basic Energy Scis. Adv. Com., Def. Scis.-Advanced Rsch. Projects Agy.; cons. Los Alamos Nat. Lab.; mem. ad hoc com. Air Force Sci. Adv. Bd. Editor: Laser Diagnostics and Photochemical Processing of Semiconductor Devices, 1983; contbr. articles to profl. jours.; patentee in field Served to capt. USAF, 1965-69 Recipient Samuel Burka award USAF

Avionics Lab., 1968, Leos Travelling Lectr. award, 1986-87, Disting. Travelling Lectr. APS, R.W. Wood Prize, 1991, Optical Soc. Am.; John Simon Guggenheim fellowship, 1989. Fellow IEEE, Am. Phys. Soc., Optical Soc. Am. (R.W. Wood award, 1991); mem. Am. Chem. Soc., Materials Rsch. Soc. (councillor 1983-86), Optical Device Assn. (Japanese hon. lectr. 1990), Am. Phys. Soc. (travelling lectureship 1992).

OSGUTHORPE, JOHN, medical educator; b. Fairbanks, Alaska, June 15, 1948; MD, U. Utah, 1973. Prof. Med. U. SC, 1979—. Fellow: Am. Rhinologic Soc., Am. Laryngol. Assn., ACS, Am. Acad. Otolaryngic Allergy (Pres.'s award 1999, 2003, 2008, Golden apple award 2006), Am. Acad. Otolaryngology-Head and Neck Surgery (Disting. Svc. award 1994, 2004, Bd. Govs. award 1999, 2001, 2007). Avocations: scuba diving, fishing. Office: 135 Rutledge Ave PO Box 250550 Depa Charleston SC 29425 Office Fax: 843-792-0546. Business E-Mail: osguthjd@musc.edu.

OSGUTHORPE, JOHN DAVID, otolaryngologist, educator; b. Fairbanks, Alaska, 1948; MD, U. Utah, 1973; grad., Med. Ed. in Otolaryngology. Intern UCLA, 1973-74, resident surgery, 1974-75, resident otolaryngology, 1975-78; prof. Med. U. SC, Charleston, SC, 1979—, surg. dir., 2005—10; otolaryngologist Med. U. Hosp., Charleston, SC. Accreditation coun. Skull Base fellowship U. Zurich. Mem.: HNS, AMA (del. 1998—2005), ACGME (residence rev. comm. 1998—2004, chair, residence rev. comm. 2002—04, bd. mem. 2004—06), Sinus Allergy Health Partnership (bd. dir. 1998—, pres. 2004), Am. Rhinologic Soc. (bd. dir. 1998—2001, editor 1998—2001), Am. Laryngological Assn., Am. Acad. Otolaryngologic Allergy (pres. 1995, pres. award 1999, 2003, 2008), Am. Acad. Otolaryngology, Head and Neck Surgery (bd. dirs. 1997—, coord. continuing edn. 2000—08, Disting. Svc. award 1995, 2004, Pres. award 2004). Office: Med Univ SC Dept Otolaryngology 150 Ashley Ave Charleston SC 29401-5803 Office Phone: 843-792-3533. Business E-Mail: osgethjd@mesc.edu. *

O'SHAUGHNESSY, ROSEMARIE ISABELLE RAO, retired clinical nutritionist; b. NYC, Sept. 25, 1940; d. Dr. John O. and Maria Wellmann (Larranaga) Rao; m. John Michael O'Shaughnessy, 1961 (div. 1976); children: Michelle Marie, Chevonne Eileen, Melany Rose; m. Louis L. Feldman, May 3, 1980 (dec. Nov. 17, 2002). BA, St. Mary's Coll., Notre Dame, Ind., 1961; MS, Union U., LA, 1978; PhD, Donsbach U., LA, 1979; postdoctoral, Union for Experimenting Colls. and Univs., Cin., 1987. Cert. clin. nutritionist, 1991. Pvt. practice clin. nutrition, Orlando, Fla., 1979-92, Kissimmee, Fla., 1992—96; ind. dir. Beauticontrol Cosmetics Inc., Orlando, Fla., 1992-94, dir., 1992—2002, RAO Properties, Kissimmee, Fla., 2000—05; pres. Wonderland Inn Inc., 2000—07, Maria W. RAO Bus. Inc., 2000—11. Expert witness for clin. nutritionists and nutritional cons. testimony before state legis. coms. State of Fla., Tallahassee, 1983-88; speaker in field. Interviewee numerous TV and radio programs. Fellow Am. Coun. Applied Clin. Nutrition; mem. Internat. and Am. Assn. Clin. Nutritionists (founder 1987, bd. dirs. 1987-91, co-founder Fla. chpt. 1983, bd. dirs. 1986-91, exec. dir. 1986-90, pres. 1991; founding dir. life), Internat. Acad. Nutrition and Preventive Medicine (bd. dirs. 1987-89), N.Am. Acad. Nutrition and Preventive Medicine. Republican. Roman Catholic. Avocation: public speaking. Home: 8743 The Esplanade Blvd Ste 33 Orlando FL 32836 Personal E-mail: rosemarieo33@yahoo.com.

O'SHEA, MICHAEL, pediatrician, educator; b. Durham, NC, Aug. 4, 1952; BA, U. NC, 1974, MD, MPH, 1980. Asst. prof., pediat. Duke U. Sch. Medicine, 1986—88; prof., pediat. Wake Forest Sch. Medicine, 1990—. Mem.: Am. Acad. Pediat., Soc. Pediatric Rsch., Am. Pediatric Soc. Office: Med Ctr Blvd Winston Salem NC 27157 Business E-Mail: moshea@wakehealth.edu.

OSHIMA, IWAO, dean, educator; b. Bibai, Hokkaido, Japan, May 10, 1955; m. Keiko Oshima. PhD, U. Tokyo. Prof. & chair Dept. Mental Health and Welfare, Kiyose, Tokyo, 2006; dean Grad. Sch. Social Welfare, Japan Coll. Social Work, Kiyose, 2008—. Exec. pres. Cmty. Mental Health & Welfare Bonding Orgn., Ichikawa, Chiba Prefecture, Japan, 2007—. Mem. Japanese Assn. Psychiat. Rehab., Tokyo, 1997, Japan Evaluation Soc., Tokyo, 2006. Home: 3-4-22 Miyakubo Ichikawa Chiba Prefecture 272-0822 Japan Office: Japan Coll Social Work 3-1-30 Takeoka Kiyose Tokyo 204-8555 Japan Personal E-mail: iwao_oshima@yahoo.co.jp.

OSHIMA, MASAYUKI, anesthesiologist, educator; b. Tokyo, Feb. 22, 1962; MD, PhD, Nippon Med. Sch., Tokyo, 1987. Cert. Japanese Soc. Anesthesiologists. Asst. prof. Nippon Med. Sch., 2003—05; assoc. prof. Juntendo U., Tokyo, 2005—.

OSIN, PETER, pathologist, researcher; b. Novosibirsk, Russia, Sept. 15, 1966; s. Galina Osin; life ptnr. Warwick Thompson. MD Cum Laude, Novosibirsk State Med. Inst., Russia, 1983—89; MD, U. London, 1998—2000. Cert. Path. Anatomy Dept. Health USSR, 1990, State Bd. (1) Pathology Supreme Sci. Coun., Israel, 1997, registered Full Specialist Gen. Med. Coun., UK, 2001. Lectr. Inst. Pathology, Hebrew U. Jerusalem, 1992—97; clin. rsch. fellow Inst. Cancer Rsch., London, 1997—2001; sr. lectr. U. Coll. London, 2001—02; cons. breast pathologist/cytopathologist Royal Marsden Hosp., London, 2002—. Ctrl. pathologist Internat. Breast Cancer Study Group, Basel, Switzerland, 1998—2001; mem. cytopathology working group European Soc. Pathology, Paris. Author: (sci. pubs./leading med. jours.) The Lancet, Oncogen, Cancer Rsch., Am. Jour. of Human Genetics, Br. Jour. of Cancer, European Jour. of Cancer, Internat. Jour. of Cancer; author: (with Gusterson BA et al) (textbook) Oxford Textbook of Oncology, The Basic Pathology of Human Breast Cancer (Mammary Gland Biology and Neoplasia). Mem. New London Opera, London, 2003; patron Opera A la Carte, London, 2004; supporter Royal Opera Ho. Covent Garden, London, 2001; patron/supporter Riverside Studio Young Artists, London, 2002. Grantee rsch. grant, Barclay Found., 1999; fellow The Breakthrough Fellowship, The Breakthrough Cancer Rsch., 1999; The Gilbert Fellowship, The Gilbert Family Found., 1997. Mem.: Brit. Soc. Clin. Cytologists, Royal Coll. Pathologists. Achievements include research in pathology and genetics of cancer. Innovative studies of molecular pathology of familial breast cancer, works on molecular genetics of testicular and prostate cancer. Avocations: antiques, art. Office: Royal Marsden Hosp NHS Trust Fulham Rd London SW3 6JJ England Business E-Mail: peter.osin@rmh.nhs.uk.

OSINSKI, MARTIN HENRY, healthcare consultant; s. Stanley and Shirley (Bobick) Osinski; m. Margie Osinski; children: Ashley, Brett, Justin, Kevin. BBA in Acctg., U. Miami, Coral Gables, Fla., 1975, MBA, 1977. Cert. Accredited Valuation Analyst Nat. Assn. Cert. Valuation Analysts. Grad. asst. U. Miami, Fla., 1975-77; staff acct. Ernst & Ernst, CPA, Miami, 1977-78; asst. buyer, dept. mgr. Burdines Dept. Stores, Miami, 1978-80; buyer menswear Jefferson Ward Dept. Stores, Miami, 1980-82, Richway Dept. Stores, Atlanta, 1982-84; pres. Nat. Health Search, Inc., Miami, 1984-95; chief oper. officer MD Resources, Inc., Miami, 1989-95; prin. Am. Med. Consultants, Inc., Miami, 1996—; pres. Nephrology USA, 2002—. Mem. editl. adv. bd. Nephrology News and Issues, 2004—; contbr. articles to profl. pubs. Recipient Disting. Svc. award, 2010. Mem.: Am. Soc. Nephrology, Nat. Assn. Physician Recruiters (bd. dirs. 1989—96, v.p. 1990—91, pres. 1991—92, ethics com. 2001—, bd. dirs. 2004—, v.p. 2006—, pres. 2008—09, Presdl. award 1991, 2006, Disting. Svc. award 2009—10), Iron Arrow Soc. U. Miami, Mens Club (pres. 1992—94). Office: Am Med Consultants Inc 14707 South Dixie Hwy Ste 320 Miami FL 33176 Office Phone: 305-271-9225. Personal E-mail: amcmo@bellsouth.net. Business E-Mail: mo@nephrologyusa.com.

OSIPOW, SAMUEL HERMAN, psychology educator; s. Louis Morris and Tillie Osipow; m. Sondra Beverly Feinstein, Aug. 26, 1956; children: Randall A., Jay I., Reva S., David S. BA, Lafayette Coll., Easton, Pa., 1954; MA, Columbia U., 1955; PhD, Syracuse U., 1959. Lectr. U. Wis., Madison, 1961; psychologist, asst. prof. Pa. State U., 1961-67; mem. faculty Ohio State U., Columbus, 1967-98, prof. psychology, 1969-98, chmn. dept., 1973-86, prof. emeritus, 1998—. Vis. prof. Tel Aviv U., 1972, U. Md., 1980—81; vis. rsch. assoc. Harvard U., 1965; cons. to govt. Author: Strategies in Counseling for Behavior Change, 1970, Theories of Career Development, 1968, 4th edit. 1996, Handbook of Vocational Psychology, 2 vols., 1983, 2d edit. 1995, A Survey of Counseling Methods, 1984; editor: Jour. Vocat. Behavior, 1970-75, Jour. Counseling Psychology, 1975-81, Applied and Preventive Psychology, 1993-99. Served to 1st lt. US Army, 1959—61. Erskine fellow U. Canterbury, New Zealand, 1997, Leona Tyler award Divsn. Counseling Psychology, 1989, Eminent Career award Nat. Career Devel. Assn., 2001. Mem. APA (bd. dirs. 1985-88), Nat. Register Health Svc. Providers in Psychology (bd. dirs. 1982-89, chmn. 1986-89). Achievements include development of instruments to measure occupational stress, career indecision and career self-efficacy. Home: 330 Eastmoor Blvd Columbus OH 43209-2022 Personal E-mail: sosipow@aol.com.

OSMAN, ALI, medical educator, researcher; b. Kluang, Malaysia, Oct. 23, 1955; s. Buntar and Mohd-Amin (Sabidah) O.; m. Abd Manaf Rabitah; children: Marina, Mohd Helmi, Mohd Hamidi, Juliana, Suriana, Mohd Hazimi. MD, Univ. Kebangsaan, Malaysia, 1981; MPH, Tulane Univ., 1984; PhD, Univ. Kebangsaan, 1994. Medical officer Min. of Health, Malaysia, 1981-84; lectr. U. Kebangsaan, Malaysia, 1984-94, assoc. prof., head dept., 1992-94, prof., head dept., 1994—2001; dean Med. Sch. U. Malaysia Sabah, 2003—. Recipient Annual Rsch. award Royal Coll. Physicians, 1994. Fellow Acad. of Medicine; mem. Pub. Health Soc. Malaysia (pres.), Asia Pacific Clin. Nutrition Soc. (treas.). Avocations: writing, reading. Business E-Mail: osmanali@ums.edu.my.

OSMAN, DONMEZ, pediatrician; b. Turkey, July 10, 1965; Lic. 1982. Pediatric nephrologist, rheumatologist Uludag U., 1994—. Office: Uludag University Faculty Medicine Bursa 16059 Turkey Business E-Mail: odonmez@uludag.edu.tr.

OSMAN, ESSAM AHMED, ophthalmologist, educator; b. Jan. 8, 1958; Cons., chief glaucoma unit King Saud U., 1997—, asst. prof., 2006—. Cons., chief glaucoma unit King Saud U., 1997. Named Best Dr., Egypt, 1986—87. Fellow: RCS (Edinburgh); mem.: Saudi Ophthalmology Soc. Avocations: football, swimming, walking. Home: Morabh Riyadh 11411 Saudi Arabia Home Fax: 0096614775724. Personal E-mail: essam.osman065@gmail.com.

OSMERS, RUDIGER GEORG WALTER, obstetrician, gynecologist; b. Bremen, Germany, Oct. 30, 1953; s. Wilhelm H. and Margarete (Kruger) O.; m. Margot S. Voelksen; Oct. 27, 1993; children: Robert, Anthea-Margaux, Alexander, Laura, Maximilian. MD, U. Göttingen, Germany, 1986, PhD, 1991. Resident Cmty. Hosp., Gifhorn, Germany, 1981-84, Univ. Hosp., Göttingen, 1985-87, cons. ob-gyn., 1987, asst. med. dir., 1987-90, asst. prof., 1991-95, assoc. prof., vice dir., 1995-99; head, chair dept. ob-gyn. Acad. Hosp. U. Hannover, 2000—06; internat. health care cons. Hosp. Bethanien Moers, 2007—, head dept. ob-gyn. Treas. ESEGO, London, 1993-98. Author: Ultrasound and the Uterus, 1995; mem. editl. bd. Jour. Ultrasound in Obstetrics and Gynecology, 1991—, ICON, 1990—. Mem. AIUM (sr.), ISUOG, DEGUM, German Soc. Ob-gyn, FMF Germany Avocations: literature, art, music.

OSMOND, DENNIS GORDON, anatomist, researcher, medical educator; b. NYC, Jan. 31, 1930; s. Ernest Gordon and Marjorie Bertha (Milton) O.; m. Anne Welsh, July 30, 1955; children: Roger Gordon, Martin Henry, David Richard. BSc with first class honors, U. Bristol, Eng., 1951, MB, ChB, 1954, DSc, 1975. House surgeon Royal Gwent Hosp., Newport, England, 1954-55; house physician Bristol Royal Infirmary, 1955; demonstrator, lectr. anatomy U. Bristol, 1957-60, 61-64; instr. anatomy U. Wash., Seattle, 1960-61; assoc. prof. anatomy McGill U., Montreal, Que., Canada, 1965-67, prof., 1967-74, Robert Reford prof. anatomy, 1974-00, chmn. dept. anatomy and cell biology, 1985-95, Robert Reford emeritus prof. anatomy, 2000—. Vis. scientist Walter and Eliza Hall Inst. Med. Research, Melbourne, Australia, 1972-73; hon. sr. research fellow U. Birmingham, Eng., 1979; vis. scientist Basel Inst. Immunology, Switzerland, 1980, 96; Gaylord scholar Okla. Med. Rsch. Found., 1995. Contbr. numerous articles to profl. jours. Served with Royal Army Med. Corps, 1955-57. Fellow Royal Soc. Can.; mem. Am. Assn. Anatomists, Can. Assn. Anatomists, Anat. Soc. Gt. Britain and Ireland, Am., Can. assns. for immunology, Am. Assn. Immunology, Internat. Soc. for Exptl. Hematology, Order of Can. Home: 1380 Revell Dr Manotick ON Canada K4M 1K7 Personal E-mail: dennisosmond@rogers.com.

OSO, OLUMUYIWA OLUFEMI, pediatrician; b. Ibadan, Ibarapa, Nigeria, Jan. 10, 1962; s. Afolabi and Phebean Oso; m. Olubunkola Temitayo Abiodun, Nov. 23, 1966; children: Oluwatobi Tolulope, Oluwatosin Olabisi. MBBS, U. Ibadan, Nigeria, 1985. Cert. Diploma in Child Health Royal Coll. Pediat. and Child Health, UK, 1999. Registrar U. Coll. Hosp., Pediat. Dept., Ibadan, Ibarapa, Nigeria, 1992—93, sr. registrar, 1993—95; sr. ho. officer (pediat.) North Kent Hospitals NHS Trust, Dover, Kent, England, 1995—96, Ashford, Kent, England, 1996—96, Kent and Caterbury Hospitals NHS Trust, Canterbury, Kent, England, 1996—97, North Glamorgan Nat. Health Svc. Trust, Merthyr Tydfil, Merthr Tydfil, Wales, 1997—98; staff grade pediatrician Hereford Hospitals Nat. Health Svc. Trust, Hereford, Herefordshire, England, 1998—. Cons. Hereford Hospitals NHS Trust, 1998—. Author: (reviewer) numerous papers for profl. jours.(European Jour. Clin. Nutrition, 2003-04). Grantee Rsch., R & D Consortium, Hereford, 2003. Fellow: Med. Coll. Pediatrics; mem.: Royal Coll. Pediatrics and Child Health, Royal Coll. Physicians U.K., Herefordshire Diabetic Club, Midland Regional Pediat. Soc., Brit. Med. Assn. Office Fax: 01432 364036. E-mail: muyiwaoso@hotmail.com.

OSOLIND, KIRSTEN, marketing executive; BA in Pers. Adminstrn., Mich. State U., 1986—90; MBA in Mktg., Branding, Strategy, Duke U., 1993—95. Mktg. exec. Fortune 500; mktg. columnist Entrepreneur Media, 2006—08; pres. and founder RE:INVENTION Inc., 2002—. Mem.: Am. Mktg. Assn., YWCA San Diego, YWCA Chgo. (jr. bd. dirs. 2007), Nat. Assn. of Women Bus. Owners (NAWBO) Chgo. (bd. dirs. 2006), Internat. Stevie Awards for Women in Bus. (bd. dirs.), Kappa Kappa Gamma Sorority. Avocations: gourmet cooking, art, sailing. Office: RE:INVENTION Incorporated Ste 602 826 Orange Ave San Diego CA 92118 Office Phone: 619-342-4411. E-mail: kirsten@reinventioninc.com.

OSORIO, JOSE HENRY, medical educator; b. Manizales, Colombia, Mar. 21, 1964; DVM, U. Caldas, 1988; PhD, U. Valle, 2006. Prof. U. Caldas, 1993. Office: Calle 65 26-10 Manizales Caldas 2575 Colombia Personal E-mail: josheno@yahoo.com.

OSOWIEC, DARLENE ANN, clinical psychologist, educator, consultant; b. Chgo., Feb. 16, 1951; d. Stephen Raymond and Estelle Marie Osowiec; m. Barry A. Leska. BS, Loyola U., Chgo., 1973; MA with honors, Roosevelt U., 1980; postgrad. in psychology, Saybrook Inst., San Francisco, 1985—88; PhD in Clin. Psychology, Calif. Inst. Integral Studies, 1992. Lic. clin. psychologist, Mo., Ill., Calif. Mental health therapist Ridgeway Hosp., Chgo., 1978; mem. faculty psychology dept. Coll. Lake County, Grayslake, Ill., 1981; counselor, supr. MA-level interns, chmn. pub. rels. com. Integral Counseling Ctr., San Francisco, 1983—84; clin. psychology intern Chgo.-Read Mental Health Ctr. Ill. Dept. Mental Health, 1985—86; mem. faculty dept. psychology Moraine Valley C.C., Palos Hills, Ill., 1988—89; lectr. psychology Daley Coll., Chgo., 1988-90; cons. Gordon & Assocs., Oak Lawn, Ill., 1989; adolescent, child and family therapist Orland Twp. Youth Svcs., Orland Park, Ill., 1993; psychology fellow Sch. Medicine, St. Louis U., 1994-95; pvt. practice Chgo., Geneva, Ill., 1996, San Francisco, 2008—; founder Maximum Potential, Chgo., 1996—. Contbr., author: Transpersonal Hypnosis, 1999. Ill. State scholar, 1969-73; Calif. Inst. Integral Studies scholar, 1983. Mem. APA (chair edn. and tng. com. divsn. 30 1998-2000, chair mem. svcs. 2001-05), Am. Psychol. Soc., Ill. Psychol. Assn., Calif. Psychol. Assn., Mo. Psychol. Assn., Internat. Assn. Cognitive Psychotherapy, Am. Soc. Clin. Hypnosis, Internat. Soc. Hypnosis, Soc. Clin. and Exptl. Hypnosis, NOW (chair legal adv. corps, Chgo. 1974-76), Lincoln Park Bus. Devel. Inst. (chair program com. 2003—). Avocations: playing piano, gardening, reading, backpacking, writing. Address: 1150 Ballena Blvd Ste 202 Alameda CA 94501 Office Phone: 630-845-8740.

OSSER, DAVID NEAL, psychiatrist, educator; b. NYC, Aug. 30, 1946; s. Abe A. and Edna (Meisel) Osser; m. Stephanie D. Fleischer; children: Roselin Emily, Daniel Alexander. BA, Amherst Coll., 1968; MD, SUNY, Syracuse, 1972. Intern in psychiatry U. So. Calif., LA, 1972-73; resident in psychiatry Mass. Mental Health Ctr. Harvard U., Boston, 1973-76; pvt. practice Needham, Mass., 1976—; assoc. prof. psychiatry Harvard U. Med. Sch., Boston, 1999—. Lectr. Tufts U. Med. Sch., 1978—, Taunton State Hosp., 1976—, Faulkner Hosp., 1976—, Brockton VA Med. Ctr., 1995—. Author: internet decision support software for psychopharmacology; contbr. to pharmacol. websites, internat. psychopharmacology algorithm project, articles to profl. jours. Recipient Lundbeck Internat. Neuroscience Found. prize, 2004, Journalism award, Kantar Found., 2001, award of excellence in edn., Internat. Psychopharm. Algorithm Project, 2006. Fellow: Am. Psychiat. Assn. (life; disting. mem.); mem.: Internat. Coll. Neuropsychopharmacologicum, Mass. Psychiat. Soc. (pres. 2001—02), Am. Soc. Clin. Psychopharmacology. Democrat. Jewish. Avocations: classical music, opera, piano, canoeing, hiking. Office: 150 Winding River Rd Needham MA 02492-1025 Office Phone: 781-237-7444.

OSSOFF, ROBERT HENRY, otolaryngologist, surgeon; b. Beverly, Mass., Mar. 25, 1947; s. Michael Max and Eve Joan (Kladky) G.; m. Lynn Spilman, 1984; 2 children: Leslin, Jacob. BA, Bowdoin Coll., Brunswick, Maine, 1969; DMD, Tufts U., Medford, Mass., 1973, MD, 1975; MS in Otolaryngology, Northwestern U., Evanston, Ill., 1981. Diplomate Am. Bd. Otolaryngology. Intern Northwestern Meml. Hosp., Chgo., 1975-76; resident in otolaryngology and maxillofacial surgery Northwestern U. Med. Sch., Chgo., 1976—80, NIH rsch. fellow dept. otolaryngology and maxillofacial surgery, 1977-78, clin. fellow in head and neck surgery, 1980-81; jr. faculty clin. fellow Am. Cancer Soc. Northwestern Med. Sch., Chgo., 1981-84; faculty practice, otolaryngology, head and neck surgery, laryngology and care of profl. voice Northwestern Med. Sch., Chgo., 1981—86, Vanderbilt U. Med. Ctr., Nashville, 1986—, prof., chmn. dept. otolaryngology, 1986—2008, prof., otolaryngology, 2008—; exec. med. dir. Vanderbilt Voice Ctr., 1991—. Attending physician Cook County Hosp., Chgo., 1981—83, cons. physician, 1983—86; attending physician Northwestern Meml. Hosp, Chgo., 1981—86, Children's Meml. Hosp., Chgo., 1981—86; attending physician, chief otolaryngology svc. VA Lakeside Hosp., Chgo., 1982—85; attending physician, head divsn. otolaryngology head and neck surgery Evanston Hosp., 1983—86, chief divsn. otolaryngology, 1983—86; asst. prof. Northwestern U. Dental Sch., Chgo., 1980—86, Northwestern U. Med. Sch., Chgo., 1981—85, assoc. prof., 1985—86; attending surgeon, otolaryngologist-in-chief Vanderbilt U. Hosp., Nashville, 1986—, chief staff, 1995—97; attending surgeon VA Hosp., Nashville, 1986—; Guy M. Maness prof., chmn. dept. otolaryngology Vanderbilt U. Med. Ctr., Nashville, 1986—2008, assoc. vice chancellor health affairs, 1995—2005; assoc. dir. Vanderbilt Free-Electron Laser Ctr. Med. and Materials Rsch., Nashville, 1992—95; dir. Vanderbilt Bill Wilkerson Ctr. Otolaryngology Communication Scis., Nashville, 1997—2008; asst. vice chancellor, compliance and corp. integrity Vanderbilt Med. Ctr., 2008—. Sr. editor Lasers in Surgery and Medicine, 1987—94, editor-in-chief, 1995—2005, laryngology sect. editor Otolaryngology-Head and Neck Surgery, 2005—, mem. editl.

bd. Clin. Laser Monthly, 1984—, Jour. Voice, 1987—, The Laryngoscope, 1988—2003, Jour. of Laser Applications, 1988—2004, Otolaryngology-Head and Neck Surgery, 1988—, mem. editl. adv. bd. Gen. Surgery News, 1990—97, mem. editl. bd. Archives of Otolaryngology, 2006—, assoc. editor Diagnostic and Therapeutic Endoscopy, 1992—2000; co-editor: Complications in Head and Neck Surgery, W.B. Saunders Co., 1993, The Larynx, Lippincott Williams and Wilkins, 2002; contbr. over 160 articles to profl. jours., 60 chpts. in books; editor, co-editor (8 books in field). Bd. dirs. Laser Inst. Am., 1984—90; trustee Midwest Biolaser Inst., Chgo., 1981—86, Leadership Nashville, 1988—89, Nashville Leadership Music, 2008—09; bd. dirs. MDR, Performing Arts Ctr., 2010—, MDR, HCCA, 2011—. Recipient Nat. Rsch. Svc. award, NIH, 1977-78; Francis L. Lederer-Norval H. Pierce award, Chgo. Laryngol. and Otol. Soc., 1978, Hon. mem., 1986; Guest of Honor, First European Carbon Dioxide Laser Surgery Coruse and Workshop in Otolaryngology Head and Neck Surgery, Roskilde, Denmark, 1984; named a Prin. Investigator, NIH, 1977-78; Am. Cancer Soc., Ill. Divsn., 1981-82; VA Merit Rev., 1884-85; Nat. Cancer Inst., 1985-88; Office Naval Rsch., 1987-90, 91-94; A. Ward Ford Found., 1989-90. Fellow: ACS (bd. govs. 1996—2002, adv. coun. Otorhinolarygology 1996—2003), Am. Laryngol. Assn. (chmn. rsch. support task force 1994—96, coun. mem. 1996—2008, sec. 1998—2003, Daniel C. Baker Jr. lectr. 2001, v.p., pres. elect 2003—04, pres. 2004—05, presdl. citation 2008, historian 2010—, coun. mem. 2010—, Guest of Honor 2002, Presdl. citation 2003, DeRoaldes medal 2004, James Newcomb award 2007), The Triological Soc. (nat. nominating com. 1993, coun. mem. 1996—99, thesis adv. com. 1998—99, v.p. so. sect. 2002—03, coun. mem. 2002—03, 2005—, dir., CME 2005—, Presdl. Citation 2008, pres. elect 2010, pres. 2011, Presdl. Citation 2006), Am. Soc. Head and Neck Surgery (coun. mem. 1991—94); mem.: AMA, Soc. Univ. Otolaryngologists Head and Neck Surgeons (coun. mem. 2002—05, pres.-elect 2004—05, pres. 2005—06), Assn. Academic Depts. Otolaryngology Head Neck Surgery (sec.-treas. 1996—98, pres. elect 1998—2000, pres. 2000—02, coun. mem. 2002—04), Am. Laryngol. Voice Rsch. Edn. Found. (bd. dirs. 1996—2007, sec. 1998—2003), Am. Bd. Otolaryngology (task force for new materials mem. 1985—89, assoc. examiner 1994—97, dir. 1995—2007), Cartesian Soc., Am. Broncho-Esophagological Assn. (coun. mem. 1987—90, treas. 1990—94, pres.-elect 1994—95, pres. 1995—96, Chevalier Jackson award 1997, Guest of Honor 2000), Soc. Head and Neck Surgeons, Am. Soc. Laser Medicine and Surgery (bd. dirs. 1985—88, chmn. program com. 1986—87, pres.-elect 1988—89, pres. 1989—90, nominating com. 1990—91, William B. Mark award 1992, Presdl. citation 2003), Am. Acad. Otolaryngology-Head and Neck Surgery (chmn. laser surgery com. 1983—89, chmn. self instl. package com. 1990—96, bd. dirs. 1992—95, coord. for devel. 2001—06, Cert. of Honor 1984, Disting. Svc. award 1995, Presdl. citation 1999, Disting. Svc. award 2004, Presdl. citation 2005), Am. Acad. Oral Pathology, Am. Acad. Oral Medicine, Sigma Xi, Omicron Kappa Upsilon. Achievements include reestablishment of department of otolaryngology at Vanderbilt University Medical Center in 1986; establishment of the Vanderbilt Voice Center in 1991; establishment of an advanced training laryngology fellowship program at Vanderbilt University Medical Center in 1992. Avocations: boating, skiing, fly fishing, golf, photography. Office Phone: 615-343-0429. Business E-Mail: robert.ossoff@vanderbilt.edu.

OST, DAVID EDWARD, medical educator; b. Pa., June 10, 1967; BS, Pa. State U., 1986; MD, Thomas Jefferson U., Phila., 1990; MPH, Harvard Coll., Cambridge, Mass., 2005. Asst. prof., medicine North Shore U. Hosp., 1996—2005, dir., interventional pulmonology, 1997—2005; assoc. prof., medicine, dir., interventional pulmonology NYU Sch. Medicine, 2005—08; assoc. prof., medicine U. Tex. MD Anderson Cancer Ctr., 2009—. Dir., clin. rsch. Pulmonary Dept. MD Anderson Cancer Ctr., 2010. Recipient Pres.'s Freshman award, Pa. State U. Fellow: Am. Coll. Chest Physicians (chmn., quality improvement registry, evaluation, and edn. 2008, Alfred Sofer award, Young Investigators award); mem.: Am. Assn. Bronchology and Interventional Pulmonology (bd. dirs. 2001—09), Am. Thoracic Soc. Avocations: running, snowboarding, hiking. Office: 1515 Holcombe Blvd Dept Pulmonary Houston TX 77030 Business E-Mail: dost@mdanderso.org.

OSTEEN, DEBRA K., healthcare company executive; Various positions Universal Health Svcs. Inc., 1984, v.p., 2000, v.p., Behavioral Health Divsn., 2001—05, sr. v.p., pres., Behavioral Health Care Divsn., 2005—; dir., pres. Psychiatric Solutions Inc., Franklin, Tenn., 2010—. Named one of the Top 25 Women in Healthcare, Modern Healthcare Mag., 2011. Office: Universal Health Services Inc PO Box 61558 367 S Gulph Rd King of Prussia PA 19406 Office Phone: 610-768-3300. Office Fax: 610-768-3336. Business E-Mail: debra.osteen@uhsinc.com. *

O'STEEN, WENDALL KEITH, anatomist, neurologist, educator; b. Meigs, Ga., July 3, 1928; s. Wellna Hubert and Lillian (Powell) O'S.; m. Sandra Lynn Kraeer, July 30, 1983; children: Lisa Diane, Kerry Keith, Buckley Powell. BA, Emory U., 1948, MS, 1950; PhD, Duke U., 1958. Asst. prof. Emory U. Jr. Coll., Valdosta, Ga., 1948-49; instr. Emory U., Atlanta, 1950-51; prof. Emory U. Sch. Medicine, Atlanta, 1968-77; from asst. prof. to prof. med. br. U. Tex., 1958-67; asst. prof. Wofford Coll., Spartanburg, SC, 1951-53; prof., chmn. dept. neurobiology and anatomy, Bowman Gray Sch. Med. Wake Forest U., Winston-Salem, NC, 1977-93, prof. emeritus, 1993—. Mem. anatomy com. Nat. Bd. Med. Examiners, Phila., 1982-87. Contbr. over 150 articles to books, nat. and internat. jours. Lt. col. USAR. Recipient Golden Apple teaching award Med. Br. U. Tex., Galveston, 1967, Outstanding Tchr. award Emory U., 1973, Williams Disting. Teaching award Emory U., 1974, award for teaching excellence Bowman Gray Sch. Medicine, Wake Forest U. Mem. Am. Assn. Anatomists (exec. com. 1980-84, v.p. 1990-92), Assn. Anatomy Chairmen (exec. com. 1982-84, pres. 1990-91), So. Soc. Anatomists (pres. 1975-76), Soc. for Neurosci., N.C. Soc. Neurosci. (pres. 1980-81), Western N.C. Soc. Neurosci. (pres. 1987-88), Assn. Rsch. in Vision and Ophthalmology, Alpha Omega Alpha. Republican. Methodist. Avocations: gardening, music. Office: Wake Forest U Bowman Gray Sch Medicine Dept Neurobiology and Anatomy Winston Salem NC 27157-0001

OSTELL, JAMES M., library and information scientist, biotechnologist; BS in zoology, MS in zoology, U. Mass.; PhD in molecular biology, Harvard U. Founding mem. and chief info. engring. br., Nat. Ctr. Biotechnology Info. NIH Nat. Libr. Medicine, Bethesda, Md., 1988—. Mem.: Inst. Medicine. Office: Nat Ctr Biotechnology Info US Nat Libr Medicine 8600 Rockville Pike Bethesda MD 20894 E-mail: ostell@ncbi.nlm.nih.gov.

OSTERGREN, JAN B., physician, researcher; b. Stockholm, June 7, 1950; s. Bertil and Birgitta (Andersson) O.; m. Elisabeth Svensson, May 9, 1973; children: Fredrik, Henrik, Anna. MD, Karolinska Inst., Stockholm, 1976, PhD, 1984. Cert. specialist in internal medicine and cardiology. Intern, Stockholm, 1976-78; specialist tng., 1978-87; cons., asst. prof. Soderhosp., Stockholm, 1988-93; dir. studies, head cardiovascular medicine Karolinska Hosp., Stockholm, 1994-97, sr. lectr. and cons. dept. medicine, 1997—. Med. editor Lakartidningen, Jour. Swedish Med. Assn., 1997-, First Court Physician, 2005-; contbr. more than 100 sci. articles to profl. jours. Mem. Swedish Soc. Med. Angiology (chmn. 1995-99), Internat. Soc. Hypertension. Office: Karolinska Hosp Dept Medicine 17176 Stockholm Sweden Home: Floragatan 22 Stockholm 11431 Sweden Office Phone: 46851775473. Business E-Mail: jan.ostergren@karolinska.se.

OSTERHOLM, MICHAEL T., epidemiologist, public health service officer; b. 1953; BA in Biology & Polit. Sci., Luther Coll., 1975; MS in Environmental Health, U. Minn., 1976, MPH in Epidemiology, 1978, Ph.D in Environmental Health, 1980. Various positions Minn. Dept. Health, 1975—84, state epidemiologist & chief of acute epidemiology sect., 1984—99; dir. Ctr. Infectious Disease Rsch. & Policy (CIDRAP) U. Minn., Mpls.; prof. U. Minn. Sch. Pub. Health, Mpls. Mem. World Econ. Forum Working Group on Pandemics, 2008—. Author: Living Terrors: What America Needs to Know to Survive the Coming Bioterrorist Catastrophe, 2001; editorial bd. Infection Control & Hosp. Epidemiology, Microbial Drug Resistance; contbr. articles, chapters to books, columns in newspapers, scientific papers. Spl. advisor to sec. US Dept. Health & Human Services, 2001—05, mem. nat. sci. adv. bd. on biosecurity, 2005—; mem. interim mgmt. team Centers for Disease Control (CDC), 2002—03; mem. U. Minn. Acad. Health Center's Acad. of Excellence in Health Rsch., 2008—. Recipient Pump Handle award, Charles C. Shepard Sci. award, Centers for Disease Control (CDC), Harvey W. Wiley medal, FDA, Wade Hampton Frost Leadership award, Am. Pub. Health Assn. (APHA). Fellow: Infectious Diseases Soc. America, Am. Coll. Epidemiology; mem.: Am. Soc. Microbiology (mem. pub. & scientific affairs bd., chmn. pub. health com., mem. task force on biological weapons, mem. task force on antibiotic resistance), Coun. State & Territorial Epidemiologists (past pres.), Inst. Medicine. Office: Ctr Infectious Disease Rsch & Policy MMC 263 Mayo 8263 420 Delaware St SE Minneapolis MN 55455 Office Phone: 612-626-6770, 612-625-3908. Office Fax: 612-626-6783. E-mail: mto@umn.edu.

OSTERKAMP, DALENE MAY, psychology educator, artist; b. Davenport, Iowa, Dec. 1, 1932; d. James Hiram and Bernice Grace Simmons; m. Donald Edwin Osterkamp, Feb. 11, 1951 (dec. Sept. 1951). BA, San Jose State U., 1959, MA, 1962; PhD, Saybrook Inst., 1989. Lectr. San Jose (Calif.) State U., 1960—65, U. Santa Barbara (Calif.) Ext., 1970-76; prof. Bakersfield (Calif.) Coll., 1961-87, prof. emerita, 1987—; adj. faculty, counselor Calif. State U., Bakersfield, 1990—95. Gallery dir. Bakersfield Coll., 1964-72. Juried group shows include Berkeley (Calif.) Art, Ctr., 1975, Libr. of Congress, 1961, Seattle Art Mus., 1962; permanent collections include Archives of Nat. Mus. Women in the Arts. Founder Kern Art Edn. Assn., Bakersfield, 1962, Bakersfield Printmakers, 1976. Staff sgt. USAF, 1952-55. Recipient 1st Ann. Svc. to Women award Am. Assn. Women in C.C., 1989. Mem. APA, Assn. for Women in Psychology, Assn. for Humanistic Psychology, Calif. Soc. Printmakers. Home: PO Box 387 Glennville CA 93226-0387 Office: Calif State Univ Stockdale Ave Bakersfield CA 93309

OSTERMAN, A. LEE, orthopedist, educator; b. Wheeling, W.Va., June 20, 1947; MD, U. Pa., 1973, degree in Orthopedics Surgery, 1979. Assoc. prof. orthopedics U. Pa., 1981—93; pres. Phila. Hand Ctr., King Of Prussia, 1993—. Prof. orthop. & hand surgery Thomas Jefferson U., 1993. Named one of America's Top Drs., Castle Connolly, Top Drs., Phila. Mag. Fellow: Am. Soc. Reconstructive Microsurgery, Arthroscopy Assn. N.Am., Am. Acad. Orthop. Surgery (Outstanding Contbn. award); mem.: Am. Assn. Hand Surgery, Am. Soc. Surgery Hand (Sumner L. Koch Award). Avocations: photography, bicycling, travel. Office: Phila Hand Ctr 700 S King Of Prussia PA 19406 Office Fax: 610-527-0964. Business E-Mail: loster51@bellatlantic.net.

OSTERMANN, MARLIES, medical consultant; MD, Georg-August U., Goettingen, 1990; PhD, Georg-August U. Cert. European Soc. Intensive Care. Cons. critical care and nephrology Guy's & St Thomas' Hosp., London, 2003. Fellow: RCP (UK). Achievements include research in acute kidney injury and critical care nephrology. Office: Guy's & St Thomas' Hosp Westminster Bridge Rd London SE1 7EH England Personal E-mail: marlies@ostermann.freeserve.co.uk. Business E-Mail: marlies.ostermann@gstt.nhs.uk.

OSTLIND, DAN A., retired parasitologist; b. McPherson, Kans., June 19, 1936; s. Harry Dewey and Laura (Bartles) O.; m. Eleanor Ruth Ahlstedt, Oct. 5, 1958; 1 child, Dyanne Dee. MS, Kans. State U., 1962, PhD, 1966. Parasitologist Moorman Mfg. Co., Quincy, Ill., 1966-67; sr. rsch. parasitologist Merck & Co., Rahway, NJ, 1967-69, rsch. fellow, 1969-77, sr. rsch. fellow, 1977-86, sr. investigator, 1986-96. Office Phone: 908-236-9238. Personal E-mail: stanton94@embarqmail.com.

ÖSTMAN, PÄR-OLOV, medical educator; b. Falun, May 4, 1968; DDS, Umeå U., 1992; PhD, Gothenburg U., MD, 2007. CEO Team Holmgatan, 1995—; cons. Biomet 3I, 2005—; asst. prof. Gothenburg Biomaterial group, 2007—. Mem.: AO, EAO. Avocation: golf. Office: Holmgatan 30 Falun 791 71 Sweden Business E-Mail: po@holmgatan.se.

OSTRER, HARRY, clinical geneticist, educator; Attended, Columbia U., 1976. Cert. clin. genetics 1984, clin. cytogenetics 1990, clin. molecular genetics 2006, diplomate Am. Bd. Pediatrics, 1985. Clin. fellowships in molecular genetics Nat. Inst. of Health, 1978—81; internship pediat. Johns Hopkins Hosp., 1976—77, resident pediatrician, 1976—78, residency tng. pediat., 1977—78, clin. fellowships in med. genetics, 1981—83; prof. pediat. dept. NYU, divsn. dir. human genetics. Co-author: (publs.) Increased resolution of Y chromosome haplogroup T defines relationships among populations of the Near East, Europe, and Africa, 2011, The history of african gene flow into southern europeans, levantines, and jews, 2011, Integrative genomics identifies molecular alterations that challenge the linear model of melanoma progression, 2011, Minor Abnormalities of Testis Development in Mice Lacking the Gene Encoding the MAPK Signalling Component, MAP3K1, 2011, and numerous others. Office: Langone Medical Center 550 1st Ave MSB 136 New York NY 10016 Office Phone: 212-263-5746. Office Fax: 212-263-7590.

OSTRIKER, GLENN, ophthalmologist, educator; Attended, NYU Med. Ctr., 1982. Diplomate Am. Bd. of Ophthalmology, 1987. Intern NYU Downtown Hosp., 1982—82; resident NYU, 1983—83, clin. fellow, 1983—83; resident NYU Med. Ctr., 1983—86; clin. assoc. prof. dept. of ophthalmology NYU Langone Med. Ctr. Contbr. (publs.) Tensor network theroy applied to the oculomotor system, Generation and modification of neuronal networks acting as metric tensors: a computer demonstration of the process of organizing, Tensorial computer model of gaze--I. Oculomotor activity is expressed in non-orthogonal natural coordinates, Epibulbar conjunctival fibroma, Tensorial Computer Movie Display of the Metaorganization of Oculomotor Metric Network. Office: NYU Langone Medical Center and School of Medicine 550 1st Ave New York NY 10016 Office Phone: 212-263-7300.

OSTROV, BARBARA E., physician; b. Bklyn., Aug. 6, 1978; SB, MIT, Cambridge, Mass., 1979, SM; MD, SUNY Buffalo Sch. of Medicine, 1983. Cert. in Rheumatology Am. Bd. of Internal Medicine, 1990, in pediat. rheumatology Am. Bd. Pediat., 1994. Clin. asst. prof. Children's Hosp. Phila., 1989—91; asst. prof. to prof., pediat. and medicine Pa. State Hershey Med. Ctr., 1991—, dir., 1994—2004, vice chair, 2006—. Bd. mem. Am. Juvenile Arthritis Orgn., Atlanta, 2001—05; mem., pediatric rheumatology sub bd. Am. Bd. Pediat., Chapel Hill, NC, 2007—, sub bd. mem.; mem., local bd. Ctrl. Pa. Arthritis Found., Harrisburg, 1991. Recipient Distinguished Educator award, Woman of Excellence award, YWCA. Mem.: Am. Acad. Pediat., Am. Coll. Rheumatology. Office: Penn State Hershey Children's Hosp 500 University Dr Hershey PA 17033 Office Fax: 717-531-0135. Business E-Mail: bostrov@psu.edu. *

OSTROV, GERALD MARTIN, pharmaceutical executive; b. Bklyn., Oct. 29, 1949; s. Joshua and Harriet (Theaman) O.; m. Aimee Ostrov; children: Betsy, David. BS in Indsl. Engring. and Ops. Rsch., Cornell U., 1971; MBA, Harvard U., 1973. Product mgr. Proctor & Gamble, Cin., 1973-76; pres. CIBA Consumer Pharm., Ciba-Geigy AG, Edison, NJ, 1985—91; pres. personal products Johnson & Johnson, 1991, group chmn. N.Am. comsumer and personal care, group chmn. worldwide vision care, 1998—2006; chmn., CEO Bausch & Lomb, Inc., 2008—. Bd. dirs. NuLens Ltd. Mem. Proprietary Assn. (bd. dirs. 1987—). Jewish. Avocation: marathon running. Office: Bausch & Lomb Inc One Bausch & Lomb Pl Rochester NY 14604-7201 Office Phone: 585-338-6000. Office Fax: 585-338-6007.

OSTROVSKII, VICTOR EPHIM, chemical engineer; b. Moscow, Feb. 25, 1935; s. Ephim (Ephroim) Ostrovskii and Anna-Emilia Shaphir-Ostrovskaia; m. Elena Abel Kadyshevich, Aug. 13, 1993; children: Ephim Victor, Evgeny Victor. Engineer-Researcher, Lomonosov U. of Thin Chem. Tech., Moscow, 1952—57; Dr, Karpov Inst. of Phys. Chemistry, Moscow, 1957—64. Dr. in the field of Physical Chemistry, Karpov Inst. of Phys. Chemistry, 1964. Jr. sci. worker, sci. worker, and sr. sci. worker of the lab. of chem. kinetics. Karpov Inst. of Phys. Chemistry, Moscow, 1957—81, chief of sector of calorimetry in adsorption and catalysis, 1981—. Lectr. of the univ. of profes. refreshing of engineers and invited lectr. in universities, supr. of grad. and post-graduate students Univs. Moscow, Alma-Ata, and Tomsk (former Soviet Union), Russia, 1970—90. Principal creator of sci instruments (design and production) Original Microcalorimeters (Medal of the Nat. Exhbn. (NE) of the former USSR., 1989). Scientist and organizer of sci. confs., Moscow, Novosibirsk, Alma-Ata., Former Soviet Union, 1980—91. Recipient Christensen award, Cal Con, NIST, 2005; grantee Soros Found. (Travel), CRDF (US), DFG (Germany) 3 times, Nagase&Co., RFBR (Russia) 18 times, and others, $250,000, 1991—. Achievements include invention of sensor for hermeticity of chambers, medal of NE and honore title, 1987; expert in the field of the theoretical grounds, calorimetry, kinetics, mechanisms of heterogeneous catalytic and absorption processes, and life origination; author hypothesis of life origination. Avocations: books, art museums, travel. Office: Karpov Institute of Physical Chemistry ul Vorontsovo Polye 10 105064 Moscow Russia Office Fax: 007 (095) 975-2450. Business E-Mail: vostrov@cc.nifhi.ac.ru. E-mail: victor@ostrovskiy.net.

OSTROW, JAY DONALD, gastroenterology educator, researcher; b. NYC, Jan. 1, 1930; s. Herman and Anne Sylvia (Epstein) O.; m. Judith Fargo, Sept. 9, 1956; children: George Herman, Bruce Donald, Margaret Anne. BS in Chemistry, Yale U., 1950; MD, Harvard U., 1954; M.Sc. in Biochemistry, Univ. Coll., London, 1970. Diplomate Am. Bd. Internal Medicine, Am. Bd. Gastroenterology. Intern Johns Hopkins Hosp., Balt., 1954—55; resident Peter Bent Brigham Hosp., Boston, 1957—58; NIH trainee in gastroenterology, 1958—59; NIH trainee in liver disease Thorndike Meml. Lab. Boston City Hosp., 1959—62; instr. in medicine Harvard U., Boston, 1959—62; asst. prof. medicine Case-Western Res. U., Cleve., 1962—70; assoc. prof. U. Pa., Phila., 1970—76, prof., 1977—78; Sprague prof. medicine Northwestern U., Chgo., 1978—89, prof. medicine, 1989—95, prof. emeritus, 1995—, chief gastroenterology sect., 1978—87; vis. prof. gastroenterology and hepatology dept. Acad. Med. Ctr., U. Amsterdam, Netherlands, 1995—98; affiliated prof. medicine GI/Hepatology divsn. U. Wash., Seattle, 1999—. Med. investigator VA Hosp., Phila., 1973-78, VA Med. Ctr. Lakeside, Chgo., 1990-95. Editor, contbg. author: Bile Pigments and Jaundice, 1986. Asst. scoutmaster Valley Forge coun. Boy Scouts Am., Merion, Pa., 1972-78, asst. scoutmaster N.E. Ill. coun., 1978-81; vestryman St. Matthew's Episcopal Ch., Evanston, Ill., 1979-82, Christ Episcopal Ch., Seattle, 2004-07; treas. Classical Children's Chorale, Evanston, 1982; mem. Sacred Music Chorale, Seattle, 1999-, bd. dirs., sec. and editor, 2002-05, mng. dir., 2005—08, vice chair bd., 2008- Advanced from lt. j.g. to lt. comdr. med. corps. USN, 1955—57, with USNR, 1957—63. Recipient Gastroenterology Rsch. award Beaumont Soc., El Paso, 1979, Sr. Disting. Scientist award Alexander von Humboldt Found., Germany, 1989-90; NIH fellow, 1958-62, grantee, 1962-92; VA grantee, 1970-95. Mem. Am. Assn. Study Liver Diseases (councillor 1983-85, v.p. 1985-86, pres. 1987), Am. Gastroent. Assn. (chmn. exhibit com. 1969-72, mem. undergrad. tchg. project 1972-88), Am. Soc. Clin. Investigation, Am. Physiol. Soc. (asst. editor 1979-84), Internat. Assn. Study Liver, Seattle Audubon Soc. (co-chair membership com.

1999-2004). Avocations: birdwatching, singing. Office: GI/Hepatology Divsn HSB AA 103-F Box 356424 Univ Wash Sch Medicine 1959 NE Pacific St Seattle WA 98195-6424 Office Phone: 206-221-6147. Business E-Mail: jdostrow@medicine.washington.edu.

OSTROWSKI, MARY LEE, physician, consultant, pathologist, cytologist, researcher; b. Providence, June 8, 1953; d. Ralph Ernest Haggstorm and Mary Lorraine MacIntyre; m. Zbigniew Marcus Ostrowski, Apr. 25, 1981; children: Andrew Marcus, Bethany Grace. BA, Univ. R.I., Kingston, RI, 1975; MD, Tufts Univ. Sch. of Medicine, Boston, 1980. Cert. anatomic & clin. pathology 1986, cytopathology 1991. Intern Univ. Fla., Gainesville, 1980—81, resident, 1981—84; fellow surg. Mayo Clin., Rochester, Minn., 1984—85; asst. prof. Univ. Fla., Jackonville, 1985—91, Baylor Coll. of Medicine, Houston, 1992—2001, assoc. prof., 2001—. Contbr. articles to profl. jour.; editor: (jour.) Atlas/Pulmonary Pathology. Mem.: Am. Soc. Cytopathologists, U.S. & Can. Acad. Pathologists, Coll. Am. Pathologists. Avocations: reading, skiing, walking. Business E-Mail: mostrowski@brownpathology.com.

OSTROWSKI-MEISSNER, HENRY, nutritional biochemist, educator, research and development company executive; b. Grochowce, Poland, Apr. 18, 1940; arrived in Australia, 1977; s. Tadeusz-Alfred and Janina (Sliwiak) O.; m. Teresa Krystman, Aug. 15, 1973; children: Misia, Henia, Rysia, Witold; m. Dorota Renata Szyszka, June 21, 2000. BS, Agrl. Coll. Cracow U., 1961, MS in Environ. Physiology, 1963, PhD in Nutritional Biochemistry, 1968. Rsch. asst. Nat. Inst. Animal Production, Cracow, Poland, 1963-70; head feed divsn. Nutritional Biochemistry Lab., Balice-Cracow, Poland, 1966-70; dept. head Quality Ctrl. Lab. Feed Industry, Lublin, Poland, 1970-72, 76; project leader protein extraction and herbal biomass fractionation Ruakura Rsch. Ctr., Hamilton, New Zealand, 1973-76; sr. lectr. dept. biochemistry Bendigo (Australia) Coll. Advanced Edn. (now LaTrobe U.), 1977-78; lectr. U. Sydney (Australia), 1978-79; program leader Ctr. Animal Rsch. and Devel., Bogor, Indonesia, 1979-82; sr. rsch. scientist CSIRO, Blacktown-Sydney, Australia, 1979-92; dir. AFIC Nat. Facilities, Sydney, 1984—; exec. dir. rsch. & devel. TTD Internat., Sydney, 1986—; sr. tech. advisor China Internat. Ctr. for Econ. Tech Exch., UN Devel. Program, Beijing, China, 1995-99. Vis. prof. U. Nagoya (Japan), 1992-96; guest prof. Hubei Agrl. Coll., China, 1993-98; chief rsch. scientist joint rsch. project Chinese Acad. Scis., Beijing, 1995-2000; exec. dir. R&D Ecotech Labs., Melbourne, Australia, 1995-96; dir. R&D Nutriceutical Devel., Melbourne, 1997-98, Wild Herbs Australia Pty. Ltd., Sydney, 1998-2000; mem. exec. com., regional coord. Asia-Pacific INFIC, Sydney, 1984—; sr. internat. cons. UN Indsl. Devel. Orgn. Investment Promotion Svc., Beijing, 1996-98; rsch. coord. joint aquaculture project Oceanic Inst., Hawaii, 1992-96; project coord. Joint Australian-Polish rehab. and recreation project Copper Mining Region, Legnica, Poland, 1995-98; sr. R&D cons. in functional foods Freedom Foods, Melbourne, 1995—; cons. herbal therapeutics Regional Pharms., Sydney, 1995-99; internat. exec. project coord. Joint China-Australian Environ. Project on Ecol. Rehab. and Regeneration, Beijing, 1996-99; prof., hon. rsch. Inst. Animal Sci., Chinese Acad. Agrl. Sci., Beijing, 1996-99; dir. rsch. and devel. Wild Herbs Australia Pty. Ltd., Sydney, 1998-2000; chmn. Therapeutics Rsch., Charles Sturt U. Found., Bathurst, Australia, 1999-2001; assoc. prof. therapeutic rsch. Charles Sturt U., Bathurst, 1999-2001; internat. project coord. Camptotheca acuminata-Xi-Shu for cancer cure and prevention Open Rsch. Lab. N.E. U., Harbin, China, 1999—; internat. coord. distant edn. program, govt. accredited courses in marketing herbal therapeutics and herbal-based medications Rsch. Inst. for Medicinal Plants, Poznan, Poland, 2001-03; dir. R&D Nature Corp., Sydney, 2001-04, Natural Health Internat. San Francisco, 2006-; chmn. Therapeutic Rsch. Oceania, Sydney, 2001-05; internat. coord. advanced diploma in clin. and applied phytotherapies, integrated medicine program, Pomeramian Acad. of Medicine, Szczecin, Poland, 2001-03; internat. cons. MDD Food Specialties, Kuala Lumpur, Malaysia, 2003-04; mem. expert panel Freedom Foods Co., 2003-05; internat. coord. for clin. study on use of phytopharmaceuticals as an alternative to Hormone Replacement Therapy in early premenopausal and postmenopausal women; cons. Goody Environ. Pty., Ltd., Adelaide, Australia, 2005—. Author: 18 books; contbr. over 300 articles to profl. jours. Pres. Soc. for Green Vegetation Rsch., Calcutta, India, 1991-96; hon. mem. Internat. Editl. bd. Acta Poloniae Pharmaceutica, Warsaw, Poland, 2002—; exec. editor Internat. Jour. Biomed. Sci., Calif. Rsch. fellow Rowett Rsch. Inst., Bucksburn, Aberdeen, 1968, Rsch. Adv. Coun. fellow Ruakura Rsch. Inst., Hamilton, New Zealand, 1972-76. Roman Catholic. Achievements include design of functional dietary preparations, health and herbal therapeutic products and establishment of commercial-scale extraction and fractionation technologies; establishment of installations to recover functional dietary supplements and refined biologically-active pharmaceutical compounds for dietary, therapeutic, and medicinal use; design, establishment and coordination of multi-disciplinary international environmental projects for ecological rehabilitation and sustainable agro-industrial development; design and implementation of computerized system for quality control and standardisation of traded agri-commodities; establishment of commercial-scale production of preventive therapeutics, functional foods and refined pharmaceuticals to deal with such disorders as insulin non-dependent diabetes, obesity, hyper-cholesterolemia, vitamin A deficiency, osteoarthritis, various dermatological conditions, coeliac disease and others; design lines of functional food products for prevention and health products; design and coordination of distant education courses in herbal therapeutics and complementary medicine; established Therapeutic Research Oceania, a not-for-profit organization dealing with phytotherapies derived from medicinal plants; research on Andean and Amazonian herbs and medicinal plant and lepidium perurianum in particular Maca for medicinal and therapeutic purposes; designed, conducted and coordinated a series of clinical studies on Maca in peri- and early post-menopausal women as a potential substitute for hormone replacement therapy; coordination of Maca project and its practical applications as dietary supplement, functional food and therapeutic for prevention and alleviation of symptoms associated with "menopausal discomfort;" design of advanced systems for bio-remediation and environmental photo-oxidative and biological degradation of thermoplastic polymers for commercial applications, implementing procedures for adoption of biodegrading plastic additives by industry and commercial application of production technologies based on reduced plastic components and plasticized starch, as a direction to be promoted for the future of plastic industry. Office: TTD Internat GPO Box 4792 Sydney 2001 Australia Home: 26 3 15 Christie St 2065 Sydney Australia E-mail: hmeissner@ttdintnl.com.au.

OSTRUM, ROBERT F., orthopaedic surgeon; b. Phila., Pa., 1955; MD, Temple U., 1980. Cert. Orthopaedic Surgery. Resident, gen. surgery Albert Einstein Med. Ctr., Phila., 1980—81, resident, orthop., 1981—85; fellow, trauma AONA/ Assn. for the Study of Internal Fixation, 1985; assoc. dir. orthop. trauma, dir. trauma rsch. Ohio State Univ., Columbus, asst. prof. orthop. surgery; med. staff Grant Med. Ctr., Columbus, Ohio; dir., orthop. trauma surgery Cooper Bone & Joint Inst., Camden; assoc. prof. Cooper Univ. Hosp., Camden, NJ. Lectr. in field. Contbr. articles to profl. jours. Named Top Doctor, Columbus Mag. Mem.: Orthop. Trauma Assn., Am. Acad. Orthop. Surgery, Am. Bd. Orthop. Surgery. Office: Three Cooper Plz Ste 403 Sells AZ 85634 Address: 401 S Kings Hwy Ste 3A Cherry Hill NJ 08034 Office Phone: 856-342-3159.

OSUGA, TOSHIAKI, research scientist; b. Okayama, Sept. 10, 1958; BD, Nagoya U., 1981; PhD, Osaka U., 1986. With rsch. ctr. frontier med. engring. Chiba U., 1990—. Mem.: Japanese Soc. Artificial Organs (Rsch. grant 2006). Office: 1-33 Yayoi Inage Chiba 263-8522 Japan Office Fax: 043-290-3123. Personal E-mail: artisankoshik@yahoo.co.jp.

O'SULLIVAN, DUDLEY JOSEPH, neurologist, consultant; b. Sydney, Jan. 12, 1935; MBBCh, U. Sydney, 1960. Post grad. fellow, academic registrar, sr. house physician, sr. registrar Nat. Hosp. Nervous Diseases, Queen Sq., London, 1965—68; jr. & sr. med. officer, med. & neurology registrar St. Vincent's Hosp., Sydney, 1960—65, neurologist, staff specialist neurologist, 1969—78, vis. med. officer neurology, 1978—2002, chmn. dept. neurology, 1983—88, chmn. divsn. medicine, 1988—89, chmn. med. bd., mem. bd. dirs., 1989—91, cons. neurologist, 1978—, Sacred Heart Hosp., Sydney, 1978—. Mem. med. credentials and appointment com. St. Vincent's Pvt. Hosp., Sydney, 1995—98; mem. sci. com. St. Vincent's Clinic, Sydney, 2000—11. Fellow: Royal Australasian Coll. Physicians; mem.: Movement Disorder Soc. Australia, Movement Disorder Soc. Internat., Australian Med. Assn., Australian and New Zealand Assn. Neurologists. Avocations: golf, swimming, travel. Home: 36 Glen Ave Randwick NSW 2031 Australia Personal E-mail: dudleyo@bigpond.com.

O'SULLIVAN, RENEE BENNETT, plastic surgeon; b. Boston, July 13, 1929; d. Paul Lloyd and Jessie Bennett O'Sullivan; children: Rebecca Bennett Hunnewell, Jennifer Letitia Pogue, Kimberley Lloyd. BA, Bennington Coll., Vt., 1951; MD, Drexel U. Coll. Medicine, 1955. Diplomate Am. Bd. Plastic Surgery, lic. Calif., 1965, Mass., 1965. Pathology intern. Children's Hosp. Med. Ctr., Boston, 1955—56, asst. resident surgeon, 1957—58; asst. resident pediat. Mass. Gen. Hosp., Boston, 1956—57; tchg. fellow Harvard Med. Sch., Boston, 1957—58, asst. surg., 1971—72, clin. instr. surg., 1972—2011; asst. resident surg. Boston VA Hosp., 1958—60; sr. resident plastic surg. NY Hosp-Cornell Med. Ctr., NYC, 1960—62, cons. plastic surg. U. Indonesia Sch. Med., Djakarta, Indonesia, 1962—64, Am. Embassy Med. Dept., Djakarta, Indonesia, 1962—64; surg. svc. Boston City Hosp., 1965—81; staff Newton-Wellesley Hosp., Mass., 1965—2011, Faulkner Hosp., 1965—2011, Beth Isreal Deaconess Hosp., Needham, Mass., 1965—2011, Metro W. Med. Ctr., Natick, Mass., 1965—2007, Cambridge City Hosp., Boston, 1966—77, MIT, Cambridge, Mass., 1966—80, New Eng. Med. Ctr. Hosp., Boston, 1968—76, St. Elizabeth's Hosp., Brighton, Mass., 1968—2004, Emerson Hosp., Concord, Mass., 1971—83; cons. plastic surg. Mt. Auburn Hosp., Cambridge, Mass., 1972—99. Trustee Ada Draper Trust, 1998—2011. Fellow: ACS, Boston Med. Libr. (trustee 1992—97, 2006—10); mem.: Wellesles Town Meetings, Royal Soc. Medicine, Northeastern Soc. Plastic Surgeons (charter mem. 1983), New Eng. Soc. Plastic and Reconstructive Surgery, Mass. Soc. Plastic Surgery, Charles River Dist. Med. Soc., Mass. Med. Soc., Found. Am. Soc. Plastic and Reconstructive Surgery, Am. Embassy Med. Dept. Djakarta, Indonesia, Conway Soc., Charles River Dist. Med. Soc., Boston Surg. Soc., Assn. Women Surgeons, Am. Trauma Soc. (founding mem., v.p. Mass. chpt. 1974—75), Am. Soc. Plastic and Reconstructive Surgeons, Am. Soc. Aesthetic Plastic Surgery, Am. Med. Women's Assn. (v.p. New Eng. br. 1969—70, pres. New Eng. br. 1970—71), Am. Med. Assn., Am. Assn. Hand Surgery, White Mountain Ski Runners, Wellesley Coll. Club, Woods Hole Golf Club, Harvard Club (Boston), Quissett Yacht Club (Wellesley, Mass.) (historian, town meeting mem.), Woods Hole Yacht Club. Republican. Episcopalian.

OTHERSEN, HENRY BIEMANN, JR., surgeon, physician, educator; b. Charleston, SC, Aug. 26, 1930; s. Henry and Lydia Albertine (Smith) Othersen; m. Janelle Lester, Apr. 4, 1959; children: Megan, Mandy, Margaret, Henry Biemann III. BS, Coll. Charleston, 1950; MD, Med. Coll. S.C., 1953. Diplomate Am. Bd. Surgery, Am. Bd. Thoracic Surgery, Am. Bd. Pediatric Surgery. Intern Phila. Gen. Hosp., 1953-54; postgrad. U. Pa., 1956-57; resident in gen. surgery Med. Coll. S.C., Charleston, 1957-62; resident in pediatric surgery Ohio State U. and Columbus Children's Hosp., 1962-64; research fellow Harvard U., Mass. Gen. Hosp., Boston, 1964-65; from asst. prof. to assoc. prof. pediat. surgery Med. U. SC, Charleston, 1965—72, prof., 1972—, chief pediat. surgery, 1972-98; med. dir. Med. U. S.C. Hosp., 1981-85, Children's Hosp., 1985—2001, med. dir. profl. staff, 1996—2001, physician liaison documentation, 2002—03; acting chief surgery VA Hosp., 2002—04. Editor: The Pediatric Airway; mem. editl. bd. Jour. Pediatric Surgery, Jour. Parenteral and Enteral Nutrition; contbr. articles to profl. jours. Bd. Children's Hosp. Fund; bd. dirs., pres. S.C. divsn. Am. Cancer Soc., 1977—79; bd. dir. SC Safe Kids. With USN, 1954—56, Korea. Fellow: ACS, Am. Acad. Pediat.; mem.: Charleston County Med. Soc. (pres. 1981—83), Am. Trauma Soc., SC Surg. Assn. (pres. 1991—92), Am. Surg. Assn., Brit. Assn. Pediatric Surgeons (overseas coun. 1995—99), Am. Pediatric Surg. Assn. (pres. 1998—99), Alpha Omega Alpha (councilor 1978—93). Republican. Lutheran. Achievements include first academic pediat. surgeon in SC; first to establish divsn. pediat. surgery and children's hosp. Med. U. SC. Avocation: water sports. Home: 3 West St Charleston SC 29401-1929 Home Phone: 843-722-5939. Personal E-mail: jnbothersen@bellsouth.net.

OTHMAN, IBRAHIM, surgeon, educator; b. Egypt, Oct. 23, 1965; MBChB, Tanta U., 1989, MD in Surgery, 2001. Resident dept. surgery Tanta U. Hops., 1990—94; asst. lectr. Dept. Sugery, Tanta U., 1994—2002, lectr., 2002—07, assoc. prof., 2007—; cons. surgery, med. dir. Ghodran Hosp., Saudi Arabia, 2003—. Contbr. scientific papers to profl. jours. Master: European Inst. Tele-Surgery (Strasbourg, France). Avocations: reading, research, reading. Office: P O Box 14 Baljurashi Baha 22888 Saudi Arabia Office Fax: 0096677224470. Personal E-mail: ibrahimothman000@yahoo.com.

O'TOOLE, TARA JEANNE, federal agency administrator, medical educator; b. Newton, Mass., May 3, 1951; d. Harold J. and Jeanne (Whalen) O'T. BA, Vassar Coll., 1974; MD, George Washington U., 1981; MPH, Johns Hopkins U., 1988. Diplomate Am. Bd. Internal Medicine, Am. Bd. Preventive/Occupational Medicine. Rsch. asst. Sloan-Kettering Cancer Inst., NYC, 1974-77; resident in internal medicine Yale New Haven (Conn.) Hosp., 1981-84; physician Balt. Cmty. Health Ctrs., 1984-87; fellow in occupational medicine Johns Hopkins U., Balt., 1987-89; sr. analyst Office Tech. Assessment, Washington, 1989-93; asst. sec. energy for environ., safety and health US Dept. Energy, Washington, 1993-97; dep. dir. Johns Hopkins U. Ctr. Civilian Biodefense Studies, 1998—2001, dir., 2001—03; prof. medicine U. Pitts., 2003—09; CEO Ctr. for Bio Security, U. Pitts. Medical Ctr., 2003—09; under sec. for sci. & tech. US Dept. Homeland Security, Washington, 2009—. Chmn. Bd. Fedn. Am. Scientists, 2004—. Democrat. Office: US Dept Homeland Security 3801 Nebraska Ave NW Washington DC 20393

OTS ROSENBERG, MAI, nephrologist, educator; b. Tartu, Estonia, Sept. 28, 1958; MD, U. Tartu, Estonia, 1984, DMS, 1998. Assoc. prof. dept internal medicine U. of Tartu, 1999—. Recipient Internat. Soc. of Nephrology Fellowship award, Harvard Med. Sch.; fellowship, Internat. Soc. Nephrology, 1995—97. Master: Estonian Soc. Nephrology (assoc.; pres.); mem.: European Renal Assn. (corr.), Am. Soc. Nephrology (corr.), Internat. Soc. Nephrology (corr.). Business E-Mail: mai.ots@kliinikum.ee.

OTSUKA, KOTARO, psychiatry lecturer; MD, Iwate Med. U. Sch. Medicine, Morioka, Japan, 1997, PhD, 2001. Instr. Iwate Med. U. Sch. Medicine, 2001—05, lectr., 2005—. Co-author: (book) Haizmann's Madness: The Concept of Bizzareness and the Diagnosis of Schizophrenia. Recipient Excellent Study award, Japanese Soc. Social Psychiatry, 2006, Cert. of Merit, RSNA, 2006; grantee, Ministry of Edn., Culture, Sports, Sci. and Tech., 2007—10. Office: Iwate Med Univ 19-1 Uchimaru Morioka Iwate 0208505 Japan

OTT, HELMUT WERNER, psychologist, physician; b. Bad Wimpfen, Germany, Apr. 18, 1965; s. Werner and Gertrud Ott; life ptnr. Brigitte Rohregger. MD, U. Innsbruck, 2001; degree, U. Graz, Austria, 2004; MS in Clin. Rsch., U. Graz, 2003; MS in Psychology, Sexualmedicine and Sexualtherapy, U. Innsbruck, 2004. Rsch. asst. Univ. Hosp. of Gynecology and Obstetrics, Innsbruck, Austria, 1998—2001; physician Univ. Hosp. Innsbruck, 2001—04; psychologist Med. U. Innsbruck, 2005—, clin. rsch. physician. Leader rsch. lab. Clin. Divsn. of Gynecol. Endocrinology and Reproductive Medicine, Innsbruck, 2004—. Recipient rsch. prize, Austrian Cancer Rsch. Soc., 2003. Master: Austrian Soc. Sexual Medicine and Sexual Therapy, mem.: Austrian Soc. Behavior Therapy, Austrian Soc. Endocrinology and Reproductive Medicine, Ethics in Medicine. Achievements include pioneering work in ciliary tubal transport. Home: Salurnerstrasse 14/Top 15 A-6020 Innsbruck Austria Office: Med U of Innsbruck Anichstrasse 35 A-6020 Innsbruck Austria Office Fax: 0043 512 23277; Home Fax: 0043 512 238197. Personal E-mail: helmuto@hotmail.com. E-mail: helmut.ott@uibk.ac.at.

OTT, PETER, physician; b. Kolding, Denmark, Feb. 2, 1952; MD, Copenhagen, 1979, DSc, 1991. Cert. specialist in hepatology and internal medicine. Head dept. Aarhus U. Hosp., 2004—. Asst. prof. Aahus U., 2004. Contbr. to profl. publs. Mem.: European Assn. Study Liver, Am. Assn. Study Liver. Avocation: fishing. Office: Aarhus University Hosp Norrebrogade Aarhus 8000 Denmark Business E-Mail: peterott@rm.dk.

OTTENSMEYER, DAVID JOSEPH, neurosurgeon, retired health facility administrator; b. Nashville, Jan. 29, 1930; s. Raymond Stanley and Glenda Jessie Ottensmeyer; m. Mary Jean Langley, June 30, 1954; children: Kathryn Joan, Martha Langley BA, Wis. State U., Superior, 1951; MD, U. Wis., Madison, 1959; MS in Health Svcs. Adminstrn., Coll. St. Francis, 1985. Diplomate Am. Bd. Neurological Surgery. Intern then resident in gen. surgery Univ. Hosps., Madison, Wis., 1959-61, resident in neurol. surgery, 1962—65; staff neurosurgeon Marshfield Clinic, Wis., 1965-76; from instr. of neurol. surgery to clin. asst. prof. U. Wis. Med. Sch., Madison, 1964-77; CEO Lovelace Med. Ctr., Albuquerque, 1976-86, chmn., 1986-91; clin. prof. community medicine U. N.Mex., Albuquerque, 1977-79, clin. prof. neurol. surgery, 1979-92; exec. v.p., chief med. officer Equicor, 1986-90; pres., CEO The Lovelace Inst., Biodmedical Rsch., Albuquerque, 1991—95. Bd. dirs. AABC; v.p. Marshfield Clinic, 1970-71, pres., CEO, 1972-75; pres., CEO The Lovelace Insts., 1991-96; sr. v.p., chief med. officer Travelers Ins. Co., 1990-91. Contbr. articles to profl. jours. Col. USAR, 1960-90. Fellow ACS, Am. Coll. Physician Execs. (pres. 1985-86); mem. Am. Group Practice Assn. (pres. 1983-84), Am. Bd. Med. Mgmt. (bd. dirs. 1989-95, chmn. 1995). Republican. Episcopalian. Avocations: flying, golf, travel. Home: 20 Bradbury Pl Huntsville AL 35801-2863 Home Phone: 251-990-4505. Personal E-mail: ottensmeyer@msn.com.

OTTESEN, BENT SMEDEGAARD, obstetrician and gynecologist, educator; b. Frederiksberg, Denmark, Nov. 10, 1949; s. Frede Smedegaard and Gerda Edith (Hansen) O.; m. Anne Marie Jacobsen, Dec. 15, 1979; children: Casper, Anna, Marie. MD, Copenhagen U., 1976, DSc, 1984, Specialist in Ob-Gyn., 1988. Physician Copenhagen Hosps. and Copenhagen Count Hosps., 1976-90; head dept. ob-gyn. Copenhagen Count Hosp. Glostrup, U. Copenhagen, 1990-91; prof., head dept. ob-gyn. Hvidovre Hosp., U. Copenhagen, 1991—; dir., prof. Juliane Marie Ctr. Rigshospitalet. Mem. med. faculty coun. U. copenhagen, 1992—; mem. Rsch. Coun. Copenhagen, 1992—; pres. Danish Medico-Legal Coun; mem. bd. King Christian Xth's Found., Cart Petersens Found., Nat. Coun. Drs. Edn. Med. Specialidies; chmn. Danish Keysterechomy Database. Author: Operative Gynaecology, 1989, Obstetrics, 1993; editor: Practical Operative Gynecology, 1992; contbr. over 200 articles to profl. jours. Recipient Martha Margrethe and Christian Hermansens award, 1986, Generalkonsul Valdemar Joseph Glückstadts award, 1988, Medal of Honor Her Majesty The Queen, Knight Order, 2004, Coaain prize, 1996, August Krogh award, 2009. Mem. Danish Med. Assn., Danish Soc. for Ob-Gyn., Danish Soc. for Endocrinology (bd. dirs. 1987-91), Copenhagen Med. Soc.,

Nordic Soc. for Ob-Gyn. (bd. dirs. 1990-91, mem. rsch. com. 1991—), Soc. for Study of Fertility, Soc. Biology, Soc. for Theoretical and Applied Therapy. Office Phone: 0(045)35454769. Business E-Mail: bent.ottesen@rh.region.dk.

OTTINGER, MARY LOUISE, podiatrist; b. Valley City, ND, July 8, 1956; d. Roy A. and Harriet A. Ottinger. BS, N.D. State U., 1978; D of Podiatric Medicine, Scholl Coll. Podiatric Med., 1983. Diplomate Am. Bd. Podiatric Surgery. Resident in podiatric medicine J.A. Haley VA Hosp., Tampa, Fla., 1983—84; podiatrist Med. Ctr. Podiatry Group, Augusta, Ga., 1984—. Author: (with others) Podiatric Dermatology, 1986. Fellow Am. Coll. Foot Surgeons; mem. Am. Podiatric Med. Assn., Ga. Podiatric Med. Assn., Am. Diabetes Assn. Methodist. Avocation: photography. Office: Foot and Ankle Group PC 1519 Laney Walker Blvd Augusta GA 30904

OTTO, CATHERINE MARY, cardiologist, educator; BA, Reed Coll., Portland, Oreg., 1975; MD, U. Wash. Sch. Medicine, Seattle, 1979. Lic. physician Wash., 1982, cert. Am. Bd. Internal Med., 1982, Am. Bd. Internal Med., Cardiovascular Diseases, 1985. Intern The NY Hosp. Cornell Med. Ctr., NYC, 1979—80, resident, internal medicine, 1980—82; cardiology fellow U. Wash. Sch. Medicine, 1982—85, prof. medicine, 1999—, J. Ward Kennedy-Hamilton endowed prof. cardiology, 2005—; assoc. dir. echocardiography U. Wash. Med. Ctr., 1987, co-dir. adult congenital heart disease clinic, 1992, dir. tng. programs in cardiovasc. disease, 1993—. Editor-in-chief, cardiology sect. Up To Date, Waltham, Mass., 2006—. Author: The Textbook of Clinical Echocardiography, 2004, Valvular Heart Disease, 2004; co-author (with Becky Schwaegler): Echo Review Guide, 2007; co-author: (with Don Oxorn) Atlas of Intraoperative Echocardiography, 2007; editor: The Practice of Clinical Echocardiography, 2007. Mem.: Alpha Omega Alpha. Office: Univ Wash Med Ctr 1959 NE Pacific St Box 356422 Seattle WA 98195-6422 Office Fax: 206-616-4847. Business E-Mail: cmotto@u.washington.edu.

OTTO, HANS F., physician; b. Ohio, Jan. 30, 1974; BS in Biology with honors, Wright State U., 1997; MD, Ohio State U., 2001. Chief, internal medicine Osan AB Med. Ctr. USAF, Republic of Korea, 2004—05, chief, internal medicine Spangdahlem AB Med. Ctr. Germany, 2005—07, chief, allergy, immunology, 2009—. Asst. prof., dept. internal medicine Wright State U. Boonshoft Sch. Medicine, 2009—, Uniformed Svcs. U. Health Scis., Sch. Medicine, 2009—. Recipient PACAF's Best Splty. Clinic of Yr. award, USAF, 2005, Med. Svc. Primary Care Clinic of Yr. award, 2007. Fellow: ACP, Am. Coll. Allergy, Asthma & Immunology; mem.: Joint Counsel Allergy, Asthma & Immunology, Am. Acad. Allergy, Asthma & Immunology. Office: 88 MDOS/SGOMA 4881 Sugar Maple Dr Wright Patterson AFB OH 45433 Business E-Mail: hans.otto@wpafb.af.mil.

OTTO, RANDAL ALLEN, otolaryngologist, educator; b. Sheboygan, Wis., June 17, 1954; MD, U. Mo., 1981. Diplomate Am. Bd. Otolaryngology. Resident in pathology Queens Med. Ctr., Honolulu, 1981-82; resident in otolaryngology U. Mo., Columbia, 1982-87; asst. prof. dept. otolaryngology U. Tex. Health Sci. Ctr., San Antonio, 1989—90, acting chmn. dept. otolaryngology, 1989—90, assoc. prof. with tenure, 1992—97, prof., 1997—, interim chmn., 1999-2001, prof., chmn., 2001—; asst. prof. dept. otolaryngology U. Fla., Gainesville, 1987—89; physician U. Tex. Cancer Therapy & Rsch. Ctr., chief physician, 2008—. Fellow ACS, Am. Acad. Otolaryngology-Head and Neck Surgery, Triologic Soc.; mem. AMA, Am. Soc. for Head and Neck Surgeons, Tex. Med. Assn. Office Phone: 210-567-5662. E-mail: otto@uthscsa.edu.

OTTO, WILLEM STEPHANUS, internist, consultant; b. Boshoff, South Africa, Oct. 29, 1953; MBChB, U. Free State, 1979, MS in Internal Medicine, 1993. Cons., head clin. unit Free State Provincial Govt., U. Free State, 1994—2011, prin. specialist, 2000—. Avocations: running, travel, reading. Home: 71 Lucas Steyn St Heuwelsig Bloemfontein Free State 9301 South Africa Home Fax: 27514443138. Personal E-mail: ottowsj@ufs.ac.za.

OTTO, WŁODZIMIERZ JOZEF, surgeon, educator; b. Warsaw, July 10, 1949; s. Włodzimierz Franciszek and Halina (Łukaszewska) O.; m. Małgorzata Halina Szelagowska, Aug. 29, 1970 (div. Mar. 1994); children: Patrycia, Dagmara; m. Janina Kazimiera Berson, Dec. 10, 1994. Physician diploma, Med. U. Warsaw, 1973, MD, 1980, Habilitation in Med. Sci., 1996. Cert. specialist in surgery. Asst. dept. surgery Ctrl. Rlwy. Hosp., Warsaw, 1974-77; rsch. fellow Surg. Med. Rsch. Inst., U. Alta., Edmonton, Can., 1977-78; sr. asst. dept. gen. and plastic surgery Med. U. Warsaw, 1979-81, adj. dept. gen. and liver surgery, 1982-96, lectr., 1996—, prof. surgery, 2009. Hon. res. dept. surgery U. Alta. Hosp., 1977-78; vis. physician dept. surgery Cath. U. Louvain, Belgium, 1989, Queen Mary Hosp., U. Hong Kong, 1990; chmn. med. judicature Nat. Ins. Co., Warsaw, 1981-97, expert in med. judicature, 1997—; vice-dean faculty postgrad. med. edn. Med. U. Warsaw, 2005, 09-. Editor, author: Outline of Clinical Application of Lasers, 1995; contbr. articles to profl. jours. Active Dist. Med. Coun., Warsaw, 1997—, chmn. bd. edn., 1998—; bd. bioethics Supreme Med. Coun., Warsaw, 1998—; chmn. sci. bd. Ctrl. Med. Libr., Warsaw, 2003 Mem. Polish Surgeons Soc., Internat. Hepato-Pancreato-Biliary Assn., Internat. Gastro-Surg. Club, European Assn. Endoscopic Surgeons. Roman Catholic. Avocations: skiing, windsurfing, optoelectronics, organization of health care, fishing. Office: Med Univ Warsaw Dept Gen Transpl and Liver Surgery Banacha 1A 02-097 Warsaw Poland Office Phone: 48-22-599-2542, 4822 599 2546. Personal E-mail: wotto@gsystem.pl.

OU, CHE-WEI RYAN, gynecologist; b. Taiwan, Jan. 24, 1965; MB, Nat. Taiwan U., 1989; PhD, U. Toronto, 1998. Staff York Ctrl. Hosp., 2006—. Fellow: Royal Coll. Physicians & Surgeons Can. Avocation: golf. Office: 9651 Yonge St Richmond Hill Ont Canada L4C 1V7 Office Fax: 905-918-0524. E-mail: cheweiou@rogers.com.

OU, CHUNG-MING, engineering educator; b. Taichung, Taiwan, July 7, 1965; PhD, Iowa State U., 1996. Assoc. prof. Kainan U., 2008—. Mem.: IEEE. Office: 1 Kainan Rd Dept Info Mgmt Luchu Taoyuan 33857 Taiwan Business E-Mail: cou077@mail.knu.edu.tw.

OU, LO-CHANG, physiology educator; b. Shanghai, Oct. 16, 1930; came to U.S., 1964; m. Cynthia Chin Ou, June 10, 1960; children; Winnie, Edward, Emily, Joseph. BS, Peking U., Beijing, 1954; PhD, Dartmouth Coll., 1971. Tchg. asst., dept. biochemistry Peking U., Beijing, 1954-60, lectr., dept. biochemistry, 1960-62; demonstrator, dept. physiology Hong Kong U., 1962-64; asst. prof. dept. physiology Dartmouth Med. Sch., Hanover, N.H., 1977-80, assoc. prof., 1980-85, rsch. prof., 1985—, prof. emeritus (active), 1998—. NIH rsch. grantee, 1977-94. Mem. Am. Physiol. Soc. Achievements include research on pathophysiology of high altitude. Office: Dartmouth Med Sch Dept Physiology Lebanon NH 03756 Office Phone: 603-650-7729. Business E-Mail: Lo.Chang.Ou@Dartmouth.edu.

OUDIZ, RONALD, cardiologist; BA, U. Calif., San Diego, 1985; MD, U. So.Calif., LA, 1987—89. Diplomate Calif., 1989. Academic physician dept. med. edn. St. Mary Med. Ctr., Long Beach, Calif., 1996—2002; clin. instr. UCLA Sch. Medicine, 1995—96, asst. prof., 1996—2002; co-dir. Liu Ctr. for Pulmonary Hypertension Harbor-UCLA Med. Ctr., Torrance, 1998—99, dir. Liu Ctr. for Pulmonary Hypertension, 1999—; prof. divsn. cardiology David Geffen Sch. Medicine, UCLA, 2003—. Office: LA Biomed Rsch Inst UCLA Med Ctr 1124 W Carson St Torrance CA 90502 Office Fax: 310-787-0448. Business E-Mail: roudiz@labiomed.org. *

OUELLET, ROBERT, radiologist; b. Longueuil, Quebec, Can. MD, U. Montreal Faculty Medicine, 1970. Cert. in diagnostic radiology U. Montreal, 1975. Staff dept. radiology Trois-Rivieres Regional Med. Hosp., St.-Marie Pavilion, Quebec, 1975, St.-Joseph Hosp., La Tuque, Quebec, 1975; founder, dir. Clinique de radiologie des Recollets, Trois-Rivieres, 1978—84; staff. dept. radiology City de la Sante de Laval/L.H.-Lafontaine Hosp., Montreal, 1984, head dept. radiology, 1985; co-founder, dir. Tomo Concorde Inc., Laval, 1987—, Reso-Concorde, Laval, 1997—, Reso-Carrefour, Laval, 2000—; dir. Radiologie Concorde, Laval, 2004—, Imagerie Terrebonne, 2004—. Mem.: Can. Med. Assn. (pres. 2008—09). Office: Reso Concorde 300 boul de la Concorde Est Laval PQ Canada H7G 2E6 *

OUELLETTE, EILEEN MARIE, retired pediatric neurologist; b. Cambridge, Mass., Aug. 10, 1936; d. Leo A. and Audna M. (La Fortune) Ouellette. AB cum laude, Smith Coll., Northampton, Mass., 1958; MD, Harvard U., 1962; JD, Suffolk U., Boston. Diplomate Am. Bd. Pediat., Am. Bd. Psychiatry & Neurology. Intern pediat. Mass. Gen. Hosp./Harvard U. Med. Sch., Boston, 1962-63, asst. resident pediat., tchg. fellow pediat., 1963-64, clin. fellow pediat., 1964-66, rsch. fellow, asst. resident neurology, 1968, clin. rsch. fellow, acting asst. resident neuropathology, 1968-69, clin. rsch. fellow, acting asst. resident neurology, 1968-70, clin. fellow in neurology, 1969-70; asst. pediat. Harvard U. Med. Sch., 1965-70, instr. pediat., 1967-68, instr. neurology, 1971-76, asst. prof., 1976; asst. neurologist Mass. Gen. Hosp., 1976, asst. pediatrician, 1978; spl. fellow neurology Nat. Insts. Neurol. Diseases & Stroke, NIH, Washington, 1968-70; asst. prof. pediat. Boston U. Sch. Medicine, 1971-75, asst. prof. neurology, 1971-76, assoc. prof. pediat., 1975-76, assoc. prof. neurology, 1975-76; pediatric neurologist & encephalographer Emerson Hosp., Concord, Mass., 1975; dir. pediat. Eunice Kennedy Shriver Ctr. Hosp., Waltham, Mass., 1976-79; assoc. attending pediatric neurologist McLean Hosp., Belmont, Mass., 1981; ret. North Shore Children's Hosp., Salem, Mass. Vis. prof. child neurology Children's Hosp. DC/George Washington U. Med. Sch., 1975—76, La. State U., 1983; mem. exec. com. Mass. Devel. Disabilities Coun. Mem. editl. bd. Jour. Am. Assn. Mental Deficiency, 1977—80; contbr. articles to profl. jours., chapters to books. Bd. dirs. Newton Hist. Soc., Mass., Greater Waltham Assn. Retarded Citizens, Project Pact Prog. for Alcoholic Women. Fellow: Am. Acad. Pediat. (nat. pres. 2005—07, mem. exec. com. New Eng. chpt.); mem.: ABA, Am. Epilepsy Soc., Am. Acad. Neurology, Internat. Child Neurology Assn., Child Neurology Soc., Am. Soc. Human Genetics, New Eng. Pediatric Soc., Mass. Med. Soc.

OUYANG, QIN, medical association administrator; b. Chongqing, China, Dec. 22, 1940; Degree, Sichuan Med. Coll., 1963. Hon. moderator Chinese Orgn. Inflammatory Bowel Disease, 2010. Cons. Chinese Diagnostic Tchg. Cons. Soc., 1993—. Recipient Nat. Hon. Tchr. award, Ministry of State Edn. Mem.: Chinese Med. Assn. Avocation: swimming. Office: Guoxue St 37 W China Hosp Chengdu Sichuan 610041 China Office Fax: 862885423389. Business E-Mail: qin.ouyang@163.com.

OUZTS, EUGENE THOMAS, minister, secondary education educator; b. Thomasville, Ga., June 7, 1930; s. John Travis and Livie Mae (Strickland) O.; m. Mary Olive Vineyard, May 31, 1956. BA, Harding U., Searcy, AR, 1956, MA, 1957; postgrad., Murray State U., KY, U. Ark., U. Ariz., Ariz. State U., No. Ariz. U. Cert. secondary tchr., Ark., Mo., Ariz.; cert. c.c. tchr., Ariz.; ordained minister Church of Christ, 1956. Min. various chs., Ark., Tex., Mo., 1957—65; tchr. various pub. schs., 1959—92; min. Ch. of Christ, Ariz., 1965—; 1st lt. CAP USAF, 1980, advanced through grades to lt. col., 1989, chaplain Ariz., 1982—2008, asst. wing chaplain, 1985—2008. Adviser student activities Clifton (Ariz.) Pub. Schs., 1965-92; bd. dirs. Ariz. Ch. of Christ Bible Camp, Tucson, 1966-2005. Mem. airport adv. bd. Greenlee County, Clifton, Ariz., 1992—. Recipient Meritorious Svc. award, 1994, Exceptional Svc. award, 1997, Civil Air Patrol; named Ariz. Wing Chaplain of Yr, 1984, Thomas C. Casaday Unit Chaplain of Yr., 1985, Ariz. Wing Safety Officer of Yr., 1989, Ariz. Wing Sr. Mem. of Yr., 1994, Southwest Region Sr. Mem. of Yr., 1995, Civil Air Patrol. Mem. Mil. Chaplains Assn., Air Force Assn., Disabled Am. Vets., Am. Legion, Elks. Democrat. Avocations: flying, building and flying model aircraft, reading. Home and Office: 739 E Cottonwood Rd Duncan AZ 85534-8108

OVALI, FAHRI, pediatrician; b. Istanbul, June 6, 1960; MD, Istanbul Sch. Medicine, 1985. Prof. pediat., 2003; chief Zeynep Kamil Maternity & Childrens Tng. & Rsch. Hosp., Neonatal ICU, 2005—; mem. Neonatal Care Turkey. Pres. Dept. Pediat., Afyon Kocatepe U. Med. Sch., 2003—05. Mem.: NY Acad. Scis., Neonatal Orgn. Com. Ministry of Health, Turkey, Mother & Child Care Found. Avocations: history, philosophy. Home: Balkan Cad No 55 Yesilvadi Konakl Istanbul 34664 Turkey Personal E-mail: fovali@yahoo.com.

OVERGAARD, DORTHE, nurse, researcher; b. Korsoer, Zealand, Denmark, Jan. 12, 1953; d. Axel and Edith Jensen; m. Hans Boje Nielsen, Jan. 12, 2008; children: Anne, Karen, Morten, Jakob. MSc in Nursing Sci., Aarhus U., 1998; PhD, Copenhagen U., 2005. RN DNO, 1974. Lectr. U. Coll., Herlev, Denmark, 1990—2007; rsch. leader U. Hosp. North, Roskilde, Zealand, Denmark, 2007—. Author: (non fiction book) Clinical Research, Health Care. Mem.: Zonta- Internat. Office: Hosp North Munkesoevej 18 Roskilde Zealand 4000 Denmark Home: Hoejskolevej 8 Vedskoelle 4600 Koege Denmark Personal E-mail: dorthe@overgaard.mail.dk.

OVERHAGE, J. MARC, medical educator, research scientist; BA in Physics, Wabash Coll., Crawfordsville, Ind.; MD, Ind. U. Sch. Medicine, PhD in Biophysics. Asst. dept. physics Wabash Coll., 1978; rsch. assoc. divsn. chemistry Argonne Nat. Lab., Ill., 1978—79; grad. asst. dept. pharmacology Ind. U. Sch. Medicine, 1980—81, intern dept. internal medicine, 1988—89, resident dept. internal medicine, 1989—90, rsch. fellow clin. pharmacology, 1990—92, prof. medicine, 1994—, Regenstrief prof. med. informatics, 2006—. Clin. fellow med. informatics, divsn. gen. internal medicine Regenstrief Inst., Indpls., 1990—92, rsch. scientist, 1994—, dir. med. informatics, 2006—; chief med. resident Wishard Meml. Hosp., Indpls., 1992—93, med. staff, 1992—; pres., CEO Ind. Health Info. Exch., 2004—. Contbr. articles to profl. jours. Recipient Davies Recognition award for excellence in computer-based patient recognition, Healthcare Info. & Mgmt. Systems Soc., 1997. Fellow: ACP, American Coll. Med. Informatics; mem.: Inst. Medicine. Achievements include recognition as a pioneer of medical informatics; development of the Indiana Network for Patient Care, an electronic patient record system containing data from laboratories, pharmacies, hospitals and long term care facilities throughout Indiana, now the highest volume health information exchange in the nation. Office: Ind Univ Sch Medicine 1050 Wishard Blvd RG 5th Fl Indianapolis IN 46202 also: Regenstrief Inst Inc 410 W 10th St Ste 2000 Indianapolis IN 46202 *

OVERLAND, KEITH S., chiropractor; Cert. chiropractic sports physician, sports medicine trainer. Pvt. practice chiropractic physician, 1981—; mng. mem. Allcare Ctr. Integrative Health Care, 1981—2004. Chiropractic cons. NY Mets, 1995—99, US Olympic Speedskating Team, US Olympic Tng. Ctr.; adj. prof. NY Chiropractic Coll., 1988—94; post grad. faculty, adj. prof. U. Bridgeport Coll. Chiropractic, 1995—; post grad. faculty Cleve. Coll. Chiropractic, 2002—. Editor: New Eng. Tennis Mag., 2003—; contbr. articles to profl. jours. Fellow: Internat. Coll. Chiropractors; mem.: American Chiropractic Assn. (chmn. pub. rels. com. 2003—07, chmn. polit. action com. 2003—, v.p. coun. dels. 2005—07, pres. coun. dels. 2007—, chmn. membership 2007—, v.p. 2009—11, pres. 2011—, Conn. del. 1997—), New Eng. Chiropractic Coun. (pres. 1991—94), Conn. Chiropractic Assn. (bd. dirs. 1985—91, pres. 1989—91). Office: 83 East Ave Ste 313 Norwalk CT 06851-4902 Office Phone: 203-838-9795. Office Fax: 203-853-2078. Business E-Mail: doco57@aol.com. *

OVERTON, EDWIN DEAN, retired campus minister, educator; b. Dec. 2, 1939; s. William Edward and Georgia Beryl (Fronk) O. BTh, Midwest Christian Coll., 1963; MA in Religion, Ea. N.Mex. U., 1969, EdS, 1978; postgrad., Fuller Theol. Sem., 1980. Ordained to ministry Christian Ch., 1978. Min. Christian Ch., Englewood, Kans., 1962-63; youth min. 1st Christian Ch., Beaver, Okla., 1963-67; campus min. Cen. Christian Ch., Portales, N.Mex., 1967-68, Christian Campus House, Portales, 1968—2005; acting chmn. religion dept. Ea. N.Mex. U., Portales, 2000, tchr. religion, philosophy, counseling, 1970—2005; ret. Dir. Christian Campus House, 1980-2005; farm and ranch partner, Beaver, Okla., 1963—; guide Beaver HS Cl. 57 Bus Tour, 2008; power-of-atty. Older Sister, 2009-. Editor: (book) The Christian Campus House at Eastern New Mexico University (1968-2005), 2008. State dir. Beaver Jr. C. of C., 1964-65; pres. Beaver H.S. Alumni Assn., 1964-65; elder Cen. Christian Ch., Portales, 1985-88, 90-93; chmn. Beaver County March of Dimes, 1966; neighborhood chmn. Portales March of Dimes, 1997; pres. Portales Tennis Assn., 1977-78. Mem. U.S. Tennis Assn., Am. Assn. Christian Counselors, Ea. N.Mex. U. Faith in Life Com., Lions Club. Republican. Home: 1129 Libra Dr Portales NM 88130-6123 Home Phone: 575-359-0608. E-mail: campusmin@juno.com.

OVERTON, PAUL GEOFFREY, science educator; b. Leicester, Eng. s. Geoffrey Raymond and Dorothy Overton. PhD, U. Sheffield, 1986. Lectr. U. Sheffield, 2001—. Mem.: Brit. Neuroscience Assn. (life). Office: Univ Sheffield Western Bank Sheffield S10 2TP England Business E-Mail: p.g.overton@sheffeild.ac.uk.

OVERWEG, NORBERT IDO ALBERT, physician; b. Enschede, Netherlands; arrived in USA, 1961, naturalized, 1988; s. Ido and Bella Theresa (Lievenboom) Overweg; m. Angelique de Gorter; children: Eleanore, Elizabeth, Harold. MD, U. Amsterdam, 1957. Specialist in clin. hypertension ASH Specialists Program Inc. in affiliation with Am. Soc. Hypertension (ASH), 2003. Intern U. Amsterdam Hosp., 1958-60; resident Rochester Gen. Hosp., NY, 1961-62; postdoctoral fellow dept. pharmacology Coll. Physicians and Surgeons Columbia U., 1962-65, instr. dept. public health, 1965-66, rsch. assoc. dept. surgery Coll. Physicians and Surgeons, 1967-71; rsch. collaborator, asst. attending physician Brookhaven Nat. Lab., 1966-67; asst. prof. dept. physiology and pharmacology NYU, 1971-78; cons. Lung Rsch. Ctr. Yale U. Sch. Medicine, New Haven, 1972-73; pvt. practice medicine specializing in internal medicine NYC, 1967—2008; Internist NY Hotel Trades Coun. Health Ctr., 1993—. Past attending staff St. Vincent's Midtown Hosp., Cabrini Med. Ctr.; clin. investigator antihypertension, anti-depressant, anti-anxiety, Alzheimer's Disease, migraine headache, panick attack, and gastro-intestinal drugs. Contbr. articles to profl. jours. NIH fellow, 1964—65. Mem. AAAS, AAUP,Am. Soc. Pharmacology and Exptl. Therapeutics, Am. Physiol. Soc., Am. Soc. Hypertension (cert. specialist in clin. hypertension), Am. Coll. Clin. Pharmacology, Am. Soc. Hypertension, N.Y. Acad. Scis., Royal Dutch Soc. Advancement of Medicine, Harvey Soc., N.Y. County Med. Soc., N.Y. State Med. Soc., Netherlands Club of N.Y., Sigma Xi. Avocations: classical music, opera, painting, travel. Personal E-mail: norbertoverweg@msn.com.

OVESEN, THERESE, otolaryngologist; b. Esbjerg, Jutland, Denmark, Oct. 28, 1959; d. Helge Markus and Edith Kirstine Ovesen. MD, Aarhus U., Denmark, 1986, MDSci, 1996, prof., 2002. Resident dept. ear, nose, and throat Aarhus Univ. Hosp., 1986—88, resident dept. neurosurgery, 1986—88, rschr. dept. ear, nose, and throat, 1988—92, resident dept. ear, nose, and throat Aarhus-Aalborg, 1992—96, ear, nose, and throat specialist dept. ear, nose, and throat, 1997—2001, ear, nose, and throat cons. dept. ear, nose, and throat, 2001—, prof. dept. ear, nose, and throat, 2002—. Office: Ear Nose and Throat Dept Nörrebrogade 44 8000 Aarhus Denmark Office Phone: 45 89 49 31 75.

OVIDIO, BERMUDEZ B., pediatrician, educator; Grad., Dominican Republic, 1985. Diplomate Am. Bd. Pediatrics, 2005, Am. Bd. Pediatrics-adolescent medicine, 2009. Resident pediat. Med. Coll. Penn Hosp., Phila., 1986—88; fellow adolescent medicine Univ. Ala., Birmingham, 1988—90; clin. prof. pediat. Univ. Okla. Coll. Med.; with Eating Recovery Ctr. Office: Eating Recovery Center 8140 E Fifth Ave Denver CO 80230 Office Phone: 918-491-3702.

OVITT, KIMBERLY, medical researcher; AA in Communication, Ctrl. Ariz. Coll.; BA in Communicatio, Ariz. State U. Accredited in Pub. Rels. (APR) Pub. Rels. Soc.of Am. (PRSA). Mktg./pub. rels. mgr. Baptist Hosps. and Health Sys., 1983—86; mktg./pub. rels. coord. City of Mesa, Ariz., 1986—95; communication dir. Phoenix Children's Hosp., 1995—2004; communication dir., the Biodesign inst. Ariz. State Univ., 2004—10, dir. strategic affairs, the Biodesign inst., 2004—10, communication dir., complex adaptive sys. initiative, 2010—11; sr. v.p. pub. rels. St. Jude Children's Rsch. Hosp., 2011—. Mem. Green Collar Ariz. Recipient four nat. collegiate speaking awards, 1978—79. Mem.: Ariz. Tech. Coun., Ariz. BioIndustry Assn. (AZBio), Publ. Rels. Soc. of Am. (PRSA Nat.) (PERCY award 1993), Econ. Club of Phoenix. Office: St. Jude Children's Research Hospital 262 Danny Thomas Pl Memphis TN 38105 Office Phone: 901-595-3300.

OVIZE, MICHEL OVIZE, cardiologist, educator; b. La Mulatière, France, Sept. 7, 1958; MD, Lyon Sch. Medicine, 1990; PhD, Lyon U., 1993. Prof., chief non invasive stress testing dept. Lyon Hospices Civils Cardiology Hosp., 1998—. Dir. unit cardioprotection Inserm, 2002—11. Mem.: European Soc. Cardiology. Avocations: sports, reading. Office: 59 Bd Pinel Lyon Rhone Alpes 69394 France Business E-Mail: michel.ovize@chu-lyon.fr.

OVSYSHCHER, I. ELI, cardiologist; b. Gomel, USSR, May 30, 1936; s. Aaron S. and Helen J. (Doith) O.; m. Lili Markow, May 13, 1964; children: Masha, Raya. MD, 2d Med. Inst. Leningrad, 1960; PhD, Med. Sch. Leningrad, 1971. Cert. in cardiology. Intern, resident in cardiology Hosp. Kostroma, Pskov, Leningrad, 1969—70; head cardiac unit Sestroretsk Hosp., Leningrad, 1969—72; sr. cardiologist Soroka Med. Ctr., Beer-Sheva, Israel, 1973—81, dir. EP and Pacemaker Labs., 1981—; prof. Ben Gurion U., Beer-Sheva, 1993—. Dir. Arrhythmia Svc., 1996. Contbr. articles to profl. jours. Mem. Heart Rate Soc., Am. Coll. Cardiology, Am. Heart Assn., Israel Heart Soc., N.Y. Acad. Scis., Fellow European Soc. Cardiology Office: Soroka Med Ctr Cardiology 84100 Be'er Sheva Israel Business E-Mail: eliovsy@bgu.ac.il.

OWEN, DUNCAN SHAW, JR., internist, retired educator; b. Fayetteville, NC, Oct. 24, 1935; s. Duncan S. and Mary Gwyn (Hickerson) O.; m. Irene Lacy Rose, Oct. 22, 1966; children: Duncan Shaw III, Robert Burwell, Frances Gwyn. BS in Medicine, U. N.C., 1957, MD, 1960. Diplomate Am. Bd. Internal Medicine (proctor 1977-97). Intern Med. Coll. Va., Richmond, 1960-61, jr. asst. resident in medicine N.C. Meml. Hosp., Chapel Hill, 1961-62; asst. resident in medicine Med. Coll. Va., Richmond, 1964-65, fellow in rheumatic diseases, 1965-66; internal medicine and rheumatology physician Richmond, Va., 1966—; from instr. in medicine to assoc. prof. Med. Coll. Va., Richmond, 1966-78, prof. dept. internal medicine, 1978—; Tallaferro/Scott Disting. prof. internal medicine Med. Coll. Va., Va. Commonwealth U., 1989-2000, emeritus prof., 2000—; dir. residency tng. Med. Coll. Va. Hosp.; dir. rheumatology clinics. Dir. clin. tng. divsn. rheumatology, allergy, immunology, 1975-98, chmn. clin. activities comm., dept. internal medicine, 1970-90; chmn. med. adv. com. Richmond br. Arthritis Found., 1966-75, nat. patient edn. com., 1979-80; med. advisor Social Security Adminstrn., HHS, 1967-2004; co-chmn. arthritis project Va. Regional Med. Program, 1975-76; prodr. Your Health TV series Va. Ednl. TV, 1978-79; prodr. Update in Medicine, Good Morning Virginia TV show, 1980; cons. McGuire VA. Contbr. articles to profl. jours.; assoc. editor: Va. Med., 1978-98; editl. reviewer Jour. AMA, 1979—, Arthritis Rheumatism, 1981-2004, Jour. Rheumatology, 1984—. Mem. usher's guild First Presbyn. Ch., Richmond, Va., 1966-70, deacon, 1974-77, chmn. of diaconate, 1976-77, elder, 1978—, chmn. witness com., 1978-80; co-chmn. physicians statewide capital funds campaign Va. Commn. U., 1986-87; bd. dirs. Mooreland Farms Assn., 1971-73, 77-81, Va. chpt. Arthitis Found., 1970-85; mem. Va. Mus., Richmond Symphony; bd. dirs. Richmond Area Health Care Coalition, 1980-84. Med. officer US Army, 1962—63, Womack Army Hosp., Fort Bragg, NC, post surgeon, asst. divsn. surgeon US Army, 1963—64, Camp Kaiser, Korea. Decorated Army Commendation medal; recipient Gerard B. Lambert award, 1974-75, Disting. Svc. award Arthritis Found., 1971, U. N.C., Chapel Hill, 1999; Nat. Inst. Arthritis and Metabolic Diseases fellow, 1965-66 Fellow ACP (Laureate award 1997), Am. Coll. Rheumatology; mem. AMA (expert on diagnostic and therapeutic tech. assessment program 1990-99), Am. Rheumatism Assn. (exec. com. 1979-80), Richmond Acad. Medicine (pres. 1982, chmn. bd. 1983, parliamentarian 1988-99), Med. Soc. Va. (com. on aging 1980-89, v.p. 1973, 75, del. 1972-99, scholarship com. 1980-89), Richmond Soc. Internal Medicine (bd. dirs. 1971-73), Met. Richmond C. of C. (bd. dirs. 1981-84), Jr. Clin. Club (emeritus), Custis Hunting and Fishing Club, Alpha Omega Alpha Honor Med. Soc. Presbyn. Achievements include development of techniques for arthrocenteses; cellophane tape polarizing microscopic compensator for identifying crystals in joint fluid. Avocations: hunting, fishing, photography, amateur radio. Home: 8910 Brieryle Rd Richmond VA 23229-7704 Personal E-mail: dowen75089@aol.com.

OWEN, EOGHAN RONAN THOMAS C., surgeon, consultant; b. Dublin, Jan. 21, 1955; s. William Mervyn and Anne (Daly) O. MB, ChB, Liverpool U., 1978; F.R.C.S., Royal Coll. Surgeons, Edinburgh, 1984; FRCSI, Royal Coll. Surgeons, Ireland, 1984, FRCS Gen., 1991. House officer Broadgreen Teaching Hosp., Liverpool, 1978-79, sr. house officer in gen. surgery, 1979-80; sr. house officer in orthopedics Royal Liverpool Hosp., 1980-81; sr. house officer in gen. surgery Chester Royal Infirmary, 1981-82; registrar in surgery Liverpool Rotation, 1982-84; registrar and rsch. fellow in gen. surgery Northwick Park Hosp., London, 1985-88; sr. registrar in surgery St. Mary's Hosp., London, 1988-89, West Middlesex U. Hosp., London, 1989-90; ret., 2011. Sr. registrar in surgery Hammersmith Hosp., London, 1990-91, Ctr. Middlesex Hosp., London, 1991-92; cons. surgeon, Queen Victoria Hosp. 1992-95, Survey and Sussex NHS Trust Crawley Horsham and east Surgey Hosp., 1992-2011, Queen Victoria Hosp.; sr. registrar, resident surg. officer St. Mark's Hosp., 1992. Assoc. editor: Obesity Surgery, 1991. Fellow Royal Coll. Surgeons; mem. Am. Soc. Bariatric Surgery (hon.), Brit. Med. Assn., Brit. Soc. Gastroenterology, Surg. Rsch. Soc., Royal Soc. Medicine, Assn. Surgeons Gt. Britain and Ireland, Royal Soc. Health, Assn. Coloproctology Gt. Britain and Ireland. Roman Catholic. Avocations: music, reading, sport, gardening, photography. Office: Surrey and Sussex NHS Trust West Green Dr Crawley RH11 7DH England Office Phone: 01403 242904. Business E-Mail: eoghan.own@pipersholbe.plus.com. E-mail: e.owen@onetel.net.

OWEN, JOHN, gynecologist, educator; b. Miami, Fla., Jan. 20, 1953; BEE, Ga. Tech, 1975; MD, Southwestern Med. Sch., 1982. Instr., fellow, maternal-fetal medicine U. Ala., Birmingham, 1986—88, asst. prof., ob-gyn., maternal-fetal medicine, 1988—93, assoc. prof., 1993—2001, prof., 2001—, program dir., maternal-fetal medicine fellowship, 1995—, Bruce A. Harris, Jr. endowed prof., dept. ob-gyn., 2009—. Mem.: Charles E. Flowers Jr. Soc., Greater Birmingham Ob-Gyn Soc., Jefferson County Med. Soc., Soc. Maternal-Fetal Medicine, Am. Coll. Obstetricians & Gynecologists, Phi Kappa Phi Honor Soc., Alpha Omega Alpha. Avocation: backpacking. Office: 619 19th St S 176F 10270 Birmingham AL 35249 Office Fax: 205-975-9858. Business E-Mail: johnowen@uab.edu.

OWEN, JOHN ATKINSON, JR., internist, educator; b. South Boston, Va., Sept. 24, 1924; s. John Atkinson and Mary Helen (Carrington) O.; m. Wanda Earle Reamy, Nov. 29, 1952; children—John Atkinson III, Ryland R. BS, Hampden-Sydney Coll., 1944; MD, U. Va., 1948. Intern Cin. Gen. Hosp., 1948-49; resident, fellow U. Va. Hosp., 1950-52; rsch. fellow Duke Med. Center, 1954-56; asst. prof. medicine Med. Coll. Ga., 1956-58, George Washington U. Med. Sch., 1958-60; mem. faculty U. Va. Sch. Medicine, 1960-96, prof., 1970-96, vice chmn. dept. internal medicine, 1972-74, James M. Moss prof. diabetes, sr. assoc. dean, 1995-96, prof. emeritus, 1997—. Mem. Va. Vol. Formulary Bd.; mem. exec. com. U.S. Pharmacopeia, 1970-75, pres., 1975-80, trustee, 1975-85. Mem. editorial bd.: Jour. Clin. Pharmacology, 1971-84; editor-in-chief: Hosp. Formulary, 1974-83. Capt. MC, USNR, 1942-45, 48-50, 52-53, ret. Recipient Raven award U. Va., 1948; co-recipient Horsley Research prize, 1962, Walter Reed Disting. Achievement award, 1998; laureate ACP, 1998. Mem. AMA, ACP, Am. Fedn. Clin. Rsch., So. Soc. Clin. Investigation, Med. Soc. Va. (pres. 1990-91), Am. Diabetes Assn., Endocrine Soc. Presbyterian. (elder 1965—). Home: 106 Tally Ho Dr Charlottesville VA 22901-2034

OWEN, RANDALL P., surgeon, researcher; b. LA, Jan. 16, 1968; s. Timothy and Edie Owen; m. Jane Weber, Aug. 20, 1994; 1 child, Timothy. MD, Columbia U. Coll. Physicians & Surgeons, NYC, 1994. Intern/resident in gen. surgery Albert Einstein Coll. Medicine, Yeshiva U., NYC; surgeon Montefiore Med. Ctr., Bronx, NY, 1999—. Asst. prof. dept. otolaryngology-head and neck surgery Albert Einstein Coll. Medicine. Contbr. articles to profl jours. Grantee MAP Internat. Fellowship, 1994. Achievements include invention of radiofrequency ablation of head and neck tumors. Office: Montefiore Med Ctr 3400 Bainbridge Ave 4th floor Bronx NY 10467 Office Fax: 718-655-5047. E-mail: rowen@montefiore.org.

OWEN, RAY DAVID, biology professor; b. Genesee, Wis., Oct. 30, 1915; s. Dave and Ida (Hoeft) O.; m. June J. Weissenberg, June 24, 1939; 1 son, David G. BS, Carroll Coll., Wis., 1937, ScD, 1962; PhD, U. Wis., 1941, ScD, 1979, U. of Pacific, 1965, Ohio State U., 2002. Asst. prof. genetics, zoology U. Wis., 1944-47; Gosney fellow Calif. Inst. Tech., Pasadena, 1946-47, assoc. prof. div. biology, 1947-53, prof. biology, 1953-83, also chmn., v.p. for student affairs, dean of students, prof. emeritus, 1983—. Research participant Oak Ridge Nat. Lab., 1957-58; Cons. Oak Ridge Inst. Nuclear Studies; mem. Pres.'s Cancer Panel. Author: (with A.M. Srb) General Genetics, 1952, 2d edit. (with A.M. Srb, R. Edgar), 1965; Contbr. articles to sci. jours. Recipient Gregor Mendel medal Czech Acad. Scis., 1965, Medawar prize The Transplantation Soc., 2000, President's Disting. Achievement award, Am. Soc. Transplantation, 2005. Fellow AAAS; mem. Genetics Soc. Am. (pres., Thomas Hunt Morgan medal 1993), Am. Assn. Immunologists (Excellence in Mentoring award 1999), Am. Soc. Human Genetics, Western Soc. Naturalists, Am. Soc. Zoologists, Am. Genetics Assn., Nat. Acad. Scis., Am. Acad. Arts and Scis., Am. Philos. Soc., Am. Acad. Allergy and Immunology (hon.), Internat. Soc. Animal Genetics (hon.), Sigma Xi. Home: 1583 Rose Villa St Pasadena CA 91106-3524 Office: Calif Inst Tech # 156-29 Pasadena CA 91125-0001 Office Phone: 626-395-4960.

OWEN, WILLIAM FRANKLIN, JR., academic administrator, former research and development company executive; b. Memphis, Nov. 11, 1955; m. Alice Crosby Owen; children: Lauren Leslie, William Franklin III. MD, Tufts U., 1980. Cert. nephrology Am. Bd. Internal Medicine, 1985, internal medicine Am. Bd. Internal Medicine, 1984. Dir. dialysis svcs. Brigham and Women's Hosp., Boston, 1996—99; dir. Duke Inst. Renal Outcomes Rsch. Duke U. Med. Ctr., Durham, NC, 1999—2001; tenured prof. medicine Duke U. Sch. Medicine, Durham, 2001—01, adj. prof. medicine, 2002—; chief scientist Baxter Healthcare Corp., Renal, Deerfield, Ill., 2002—05; chancellor, v.p, health affairs U. Tenn. Health Sci. Ctr., Memphis, 2005—07; pres. U. Medicine and Dentistry NJ, Newark, 2007—. Chmn. internat. med. adv. bd. Nat. Kidney Found. Singapore, 1998; bd. sci. counsilors NIH, Bethesda, Md., 1998—2001; sci. adv. bd. U.S. Renal Data Sys., Bethesda, 2000—01; pres. Renal Physicians Assn., Bethesda, 2001—03; mem. medicare coverage adv. com. Ctrs. for Medicare and Medicaid Svcs., Balt., 2003—. Contbr. articles to profl. jours. Mem. site based com. Hillandale Elem. Sch., Durham, 1999—2000. Grantee, NIH, 1984—; fellow, Robert Wood Johnson Found., 1985—89. Avocation: astronomy. Office: U Medicine and Dentistry NJ Office of Pres 65 Bergen St Newark NJ 07103 *

OWENS, DOUGLAS K., physician, researcher; s. Richard C. and Dorothy D. Owens; m. Sara H. Cody. BS, Stanford U., Stanford, California, 1978; MS, Stanford U., Stanford, Calif., 1991; MD, U. Calif., San Francisco, 1982. Diplomate Am. Bd. of Internal Medicine, 1985. Prof. medicine Stanford U., 2006—, assoc. prof. medicine, 1997—2006, asst. prof. medicine, 1991—97. Trustee Soc. for Med. Decision Making, Phila., 1995—97, pres., 1998—99; chair, clin. efficacy assessment com. ACP, Phila., 2005—. Recipient Rsch. Assoc. Career Devel. Award, Dept. Vet. Affairs, 1992-1995, Sr. Rsch. Assoc. Career Devel. Award, 1995 to 1999, Under Secs. award for outstanding achievement in health svcs. rsch., Dept. Vet. Affairs, 2007; Fellowship Health Care Rsch. and Health Policy, Stanford U., 1998-1991. Mem.: Soc. for Med. Decision Making (pres. 1998—99, Lee Lusted Prize 1991), ACP (chair, clin. efficacy assessment com. 2005), Phi Beta Kappa. Office: Stanford U 117 Encina Commons Stanford CA 94305-6019 *

OWENS, FREDRIC NEWELL, animal nutritionist, educator; b. Hammond, Wis., Sept. 1, 1941; s. Fred Newell and Stella Elvera Owens; m. Christa F. Hanson, Dec. 1983; children: Gwen, Eric, Crystal. Student, Wis. State U., River Falls, 1959-61; BS, U. Minn., 1964, PhD, 1968. Asst. prof. animal sci. U. Ill., Urbana, 1968-74; prof. animal sci. Okla. State U., Stillwater, 1974-86, Regents prof., 1986-90, Regents prof., Sarkeys Disting. prof., 1990—; sr. rschr. Pioneer Hi-Bred Internat., Johnston, Iowa, 1998—. Lectr. Sigma Xi, 1990, numerous other invted lectures; mem. com. on animal nutrition NRC, 1985-88. Contbr. chpts. to 13 books, more than 180 articles to profl. jours.; sect. editor Jour. Animal Sci., 1975-78, editor-in-chief, 1987-90. Recipient Tyler award Okla. State U., 1980, Am. Feed Industry Nutrition Rsch. award, 1986, Elmo Baumann Prof. award Okla. State U., 1990; NSF fellow, 1966-68. Mem. Am. Soc. Animal Soc. (pres. 1992, Morrison award 1996), Am. Inst. Nutrition, Am. Dairy Sci. Asns., Nutrition Soc. Lutheran. Home: 5004 Brookview Dr West Des Moines IA 50265-2733 Office Phone: 515-334-6416. Business E-Mail: fred.owens@pioneer.com.

OWENS, MICHAEL HOWARD, otolaryngologist; b. Evanston, Ill., Jan. 15, 1958; MD, U. South Fla., Tampa, 1984. Diplomate Am. Bd. Otolaryngology, 1990. Intern in otolaryngology U. South Fla., 1984—86, resident in gen. surgery and otolaryngology, 1986—90; otolaryngologist Miami Children's Hosp., Bapt. Health South Fla.; clinical asst. prof. U. Miami. Office: Miami Childrens Hosp #204 4675 Ponce De Leon Blvd Coral Gables FL 33146 Office Phone: 305-666-0203. Office Fax: 305-666-0535.

OWENS, WILLIAM DON, anesthesiology educator; b. St. Louis, Dec. 12, 1939; s. Don and Caroline Wilhemena (Raaf) Owens; m. Patricia Gail Brown, Dec. 12, 1964; children: Pamela, David, Susan. AB, Westminster Coll., 1961; MD, U. Mich., 1965. Diplomate Am. Bd. Anesthesiology. Resident and fellow Mass. Gen. Hosp. and Harvard Med. Sch., Boston, 1969—72; instr. Harvard Med. Sch., Boston, 1972—73; asst. prof. anesthesiology Washington U. Sch. Medicine, St. Louis, 1973—76, assoc. prof., 1976—82, prof., 1982—2004, prof. emeritus, 2004—, chmn. dept., 1982—92. Trustee Barnes Hosp., St. Louis, 1987—89; bd. dirs. Anesthesia Found., 1994—, pres., 1999—; sec.-treas. Am. Bd. Anesthesiology, 1991—94, pres., 1995—96, bd. dirs., 1984—96, Found. Anesthesia Edn. and Rsch., 1990—95, pres., 1994—95; mem. Mo. State Bd. Healing Arts, 2003—04. Assoc. editor Survey of Anesthesiology, 1977—92; contbr. numerous articles to profl. jours. and chpts. to books. Served to lt. comdr. USN, 1966—69. Fellow: Am. Coll. Anesthesiology; mem.: Assn. Univ. Anesthesiologists, Acad. Anesthesiology, Internat. Anesthesia Rsch. Soc., Am. Soc. Anesthesiologists (bd. dirs. 1989—99, 1st v.p. 1995—96, pres. 1997—98, assoc. mem.). Office: Washington U Sch Med Dept Anesthesiology 660 S Euclid Ave Saint Louis MO 63110-1010

OWNBY, DENNIS RANDALL, pediatrician, allergist, educator, researcher; b. Athens, Ohio, July 14, 1948; s. Dillard Ralph and Miriam (Lee) Ownby; m. Helen Louise Engelbrecht, May 24, 1970; children: David Randall, Kathryn Louise. BS, Ohio U., 1969; MD, Med. Coll. Ohio, 1972. Diplomate Am. Bd. Allergy and Immunology (bd. dirs. 1993-98, chair 1998, residency rev. com. 1995-2000), Am. Bd. Pediat., Nat. Bd. Med. Examiners. Intern and resident Duke U. Sch. Medicine, Durham, NC, 1972—74, asst. prof., 1977—80; staff physician Henry Ford Hosp., Detroit, 1980—97, dir. Allergy Rsch. Lab., 1986—97; prof. pediat. Case Western Res. U., Cleve., 1997; prof. pediat. and medicine Med. Coll. Ga., Augusta, 1998—. Clin. asst. prof. pediat. U. Mich., Ann Arbor, 1980—86, clin. assoc. prof. pediat., 1986—95. Contbr. articles to med. jours., chpts. to books. Fellow: Am. Acad. Allergy, Am. Acad. Pediat. Office: Med Coll of Georgia Sect Allergy & Immunology BG-1019 Augusta GA 30912-3790 Home Phone: 706-651-9229; Office Phone: 706-721-3531. Business E-Mail: downby@mcg.edu.

OWSLEY, FREDERICK MARK, plastic surgeon; b. July 29, 1959; BA in Sci., Carroll Coll., Helena, Mont., 1981; MD, St. Louis U. Med. Sch., 1986. Cert. Am. Bd. Plastic Surgery, lic. Idaho. Resident, gen. surgery U. Tex., 1986—92, resident, plastic surgery, 1992—95, private practice Idaho, 1995—; staff mem., med. dir. Northwest Specialty Hosp., Idaho; staff mem. Bonner Gen. Hosp., Kootenai Med. Ctr. Mem.: Soc. Plastic Surgery. Achievements include being the first surgeon to bring free flap reconstruction & tram flap reconstruction of the breast, and endoscopic breast augmentation to Kootenai County. Avocations: camping, fishing, hiking, rides mules. Office: North Idaho Plastic and Reconstructive Surgery 750 N Syringa St Ste 204 Post Falls ID 83854 Office Phone: 208-777-7830, 800-873-3823. Office Fax: 208-777-7850.

OWSLEY, JOHN QUINCY, IV, plastic surgeon, educator; b. Manila, Luzon, Philipines, Oct. 2, 1928; came to US, 1930; s. John Quincy Owsley III and Sara Christine Maxwell; m. Mary Leslie Marriott, Apr. 27, 1957 (div. 1969); children: John Quincy V, Sara Elizabeth; m. Sharon Theresa Anton, Jan. 2, 1971. BA, Vanderbilt U., 1950; MD, Vanderbilt U. Sch. Medicine, 1953. Intern, surgery U. Calif. Med. Ctr., San Francisco, 1953—54, asst. resident in surgery, 1956—58, asst. resident, chief resident plastic surgery, 1959—60, clin. instr. to asst. prof. to assoc. prof., clin. prof. surgery, 1960—80, disting. prof. surgery, 2009—; resident Franklin Hosp., 1958—59; pvt. practice San Francisco, 1960—. Dir. Esthetic Surgery Inst. San Francisco Fellowship, 1989—; vis. prof. Columbia U. Coll. of Physicians and Surgeons, 1989, Divsn. of Plastic Surgery U. Pa., 1993; Donald P. Hause Meml. lectr. U. Calif., Davis Med. Ctr., 1993; guest reviewer Jour. of Plastic and Reconstructive Surgery; founder, dir. ann. aesthetic surgery symposium U. Calif., San Francisco, 1989-2002; past chmn., dept. plastic surgery, Davies Med. Ctr., San Francisco, Calif. Author: Aesthetic Facial Surgery, 1994; contbr. chpts. to books and articles to profl. publs. Fellow ACS; mem. Am. Soc. of Plastic Surgeons (chmn. ethics com. 1973-76, Plastic Surgery Ednl. Found. award for spl. recognition for innovation and excellence in edn., 2003), Am. Soc. for Aesthetic Plastic Surgery (gen. sec. 1975-77), Am. Assn. of Plastic Surgeons, Am. Soc. Plastic and Reconstructive Surgeons (past chmn. ethics com.), Am. Cleft Palate Assn. (pres. 1977-78), Internat. Soc. for Aesthetic Plastic Surgery, Bohemian Club, Pacific Union Club Avocations: sailing, bird hunting, travel. Office: 45 Castro St Ste 111 San Francisco CA 94114 Office Phone: 415-861-8040. Office Fax: 415-861-0626. Business E-Mail: owsley@drjohnowsley.com.

OXENDALE, ROGER A., hospital administrator; m. Diane Oxendale; 3 children. BA, Clarion U., MA in Bus. Adminstrn. Sr. audit mgr. with PricewaterhouseCoopers, Pitts.; sr. fin. exec. Allegheny Health, Edn. and Rsch. Found.; CFO Children's Hosp. Pitts., 1995—2000, exec. v.p., COO, 2000—05, pres., CEO, 2005—. Bd. mem. Pittsburgh

Project, Mission Meadows, Coalition for Christian Outreach, Covenant Bible College Found., Lawrenceville Devel. Corp. Office: Children's Hosp of Pitts 3705 Fifth Ave Pittsburgh PA 15213 Office Phone: 412-692-5325.

OXMAN, THOMAS ELLIOT, psychiatrist; b. Denver, May 15, 1949; s. Albert Charles and Leah (Hurwitz) O.; m. Judy Ann Heldman, May 27, 1971; children: Elliot Warren, Robert Charles, Annaleah H. AB in Philosophy, Dartmouth Coll., 1971; MD, U. Colo., 1975. Diplomate in psychiatry and geriatric psychiatry Am. Bd. Psychiatry and Neurology (mem. test com. 1987-95). Intern Mt. Zion Med. Ctr., San Francisco, 1976; resident in psychiatry Dartmouth Med. Sch., Hanover, N.H., 1979, fellow in consultation/liaison and cancer psychiatry, 1979-80; asst. prof. psychiatry and family medicine U. Cin. Med. Ctr., 1980-83; asst. prof. Dartmouth Med. Sch., Hanover, 1983-87, assoc. prof. psychiatry and family and cmty. medicine, attending, 1987-95, prof., 1995—2007, prof. emeritus, 2007—. Assoc. dir. consultation liaison psychiatry svc. Dartmouth Hitchcock Med. Ctr., Hanover, 1983-90, dir. geriatric psychiatry, 1988-2008, mem. sci. rev. com. Hitchcock Found., 1988-95; mem. Mental Disorders of Aging rev. group NIMH, 1995-99; med. dir. glencliff Home for the Elderly, NH, 1996-; assoc. chair MacArthur Found. Initiative on Depression in Primary Care, 2000-2007; ptnr. 3CM, LLC, 2006—. Editor Internat. Jour. Psychiatry in Medicine, 1996-2000, Online Abstract Svc. Am. Assoc. Geriatric Psychiatry, 2005-07; contbr. articles to profl. jours Recipient Merrell Resident Rsch. award Dartmouth Med. Sch., 1978; Rufus Choate scholar Dartmouth Coll., 1971; Mental Health Acad. awardee NIMH, 1987-90, Aging, Social Support and Phys. and Emotional Disability grantee, 1990-95; MacArthur Found. and Hartford Found. Depression in Primary Care grantee, 1995—2005. Dist. fellow Am. Psychiat. Assn. (liaison com. on consultation/liaison psyhciatry 1982-88,)bd. dirs. Am. Assn. Geriatric Psychiatry, 2002-2006 (sec.-treas. 2007-09); mem. Phi Beta Kappa. Avocation: running. Office: Dartmouth Med Sch Dept Psychiatry Lebanon NH 03756

OXNARD, CHARLES ERNEST, anatomist, anthropologist, biologist, educator; b. Durham, Eng., Sept. 9, 1933; arrived in Australia, 1987; s. Charles and Frances Ann (Golightly) O.; m. Eleanor Mary Arthur, Feb. 2, 1959; children: Hugh, David. BSc with 1st class honors, U. Birmingham, Eng., 1955, MB, BChir in Medicine, 1958, PhD, 1962, DSc, 1975. Med. intern Queen Elizabeth Hosp., Birmingham, 1958-59; rsch. fellow U. Birmingham, 1959-62, lectr., 1962-65, sr. lectr., 1965-66, court govs., 1958-66; assoc. prof. anatomy, anthropology and evolutionary biology U. Chgo., 1966—78, prof., 1970-78, gov. biology collegiate div., 1970-78, dean coll., 1973-77; dean grad. sch. U. So. Calif., Los Angeles, 1978-83, univ. rsch. prof. biology and anatomy, 1978-83, univ. prof., prof. anatomy and cell biology, prof. biol. scis., 1983-87; prof. anatomy and human biology U. We. Australia, 1987-98, dir. ctr. for human biology, 1989-99, head div. agr. and sci., 1990-92, prof. emeritus, 1998—, sr. rsch. fellow, 1998—, adj. prof. forensic sci., 2007—; Leverhulme prof. U. Liverpool (U.K.), Univ. Coll., London, 2000—03; hon. prof. U. Hull, England, 2004—, Hull York Med. Sch., 2004—. Rsch. assoc. Field Mus. Natural History, Chgo., 1967; overseas assoc. U. Birmingham, 1968—; Lo Yuk Tong lectr. U. Hong Kong, 1973, 94, 97, 2003, hon. prof., 1978, Chan Shu Tzu lectr., 80, vis. scholar, 95, 96; Octagon lectr. U. Western Australia, 1987; Latta lectr. U. Nebr., Omaha, 1987; Stanley Wilkinson orator, 91; rsch. assoc. L.A. County Natural History Mus., 1984—, George C. Page Mus., LA, 1986; vis. scholar Shaw Coll. Chinese U. of Hong Kong, 1995; bd. dirs. U. Western Australia Press, 1993—95; advisor on human biology World Sci. Pub. Co., 1993—; vis. prof. Northwestern U., Xian, China, 1999, U. York, England, 2003, hon. prof., 2004—, Hull York Med. Sch., 2004—; hon. prof. bioengring. U. Hull, 2004—. Author: Form and Pattern in Human Evolution, 1973, Uniqueness and Diversity in Human Evolution, 1973, Human Fossils: The New Revolution, 1977, The Order of Man, 1983, Humans, Apes, and Chinese Fossils, 1985, Fossils, Teeth and Sex, 1987, Anatomies and Lifestyles, 1990; series editor Recent Advances in Human Biology Series World Sci. Pub., Vol. I, The Origin and Past of Modern Humans, 1995, Vol. 2, Bone Structure and Remodeling, 1995, Vol. 3 The Origins and Past of Modern Humans: Towards Reconciliation, 1998, Vol. 4 The Natural History of the Doucs and Snub-nosed Langurs, 1998, Vol. 7 Morphometrics for the Life Sciences, 2000, Perspectives in Human Biology, Vol. 1 Genes, Ethnicity and Aging, 1995, Vol. 2 Humans in the Australasian Region, 1996, Vol. 3 Human Adaptability: Future Trends and Lessons from Past, 1998, Vol. 4, Is Human Evolution a Closed Chaptr, 1999, Vol. 4, Child Growth, Secular Trends and Continuing Human Evolution, Vol. 4, Dento-Facial Variation in Perspective, 1999, Vol. 5 Towards Consilience, 2000, Dedicatee, Shaping Primate Evolution, 2004, Anatomical Terms and their Derivation, World Sci., 2007, Ghostly Muscles, Wrinkled Brains, Heresies and Holbits, World Sci., 2008; mem. editl. bd. Annals of Human Biology; cons. editor: Am. Jour. Primatology, Jour. Human Biology, Jour. Human Evolution: Australia com. mem. Ency. Britannica, 1991-99; bibliographic referee Britannica On-Line, 1994-99; contbr articles to anat. and anthrop. jours. Mem. Pasteur Found., 1988; bd. dirs. West Australian Inst. for Child Health, 1991-98; mem. electoral bd. Freemantle Hosp., 1991-94. Recipient Book award, Hong Kong Coun., 1984, S.T. Chan Silver medal, U. Hong Kong, 1980, Charles Darwin Lifetime Achievement award, Am. Assn. Phys. Anthropology, 2001, Chancellor's medal, U. Western Australia, 2008; grantee, USPHS, 1960—71, NIH, 1974—87, NSF, 1971—87, Raine Found., 1988—91, Viertel Found., 1993—94, Australian Acad. Sci., 1995, Leverhulme Trust, Eng., 2003—06; Marie Curie Evan Rsch. Tng. grantee, 2005—, Marie Curie Palaeo Rsch. Tng. grantee, 2005—. Fellow N.Y. Acad. Sci., AAAS, So. Calif. Acad. Sci. (bd. dirs. 1985); mem. Chgo. Acad. Soc. (hon. life), Australasian Soc. for Human Biology (pres. 1987-90), Australian and New Zealand Anat. Soc. (pres. 1989-90), Anat. Soc. Gt. Britain and Ireland (councillor 1992-94), Nat. Health and Med. Rsch. Coun. (grantee 1994-97), Australian Rsch. Coun. (grantee 1988—), Med. and Health Infrastructure Fund, Western Australia (grantee 2001-03, Leverhulme Trust Rsch. grant, 2003-06, Marie Curie awards 2005-, BBSRC Rsch. grant, 2007—), Soc. Study Human Biology (treas. 1962-66), Sigma Xi (pres., nat. lectr. 1990), Phi Beta Kappa (pres. chpt.), Phi Kappa Phi (pres., Book award 1984). Office: U Western Australia Nedlands WA 6009 Australia Business E-Mail: coxnard@cyllene.uwa.edu.au.

OYAMA, LESLIE, medical educator; b. Hawaii, July 14, 1968; BA, USC, 1991; MD, Boston U., 2002. Asst. clin. prof. UCSD, 2006—. Office: 200 West Arbor Dr MC8676 San Diego CA 92103 Office Phone: 619-543-6463. Business E-Mail: leslie.oyama@gmail.com.

ØYEN, JANNIKE, medical researcher; b. Molde, Norway, Apr. 24, 1971; MSc, Norwegian U. Sci. & Tech., 2005; PhD, U. Bergen, Norway, 2007—. Postdoc. fellow, dept. pub. health & primary health Care U. Bergen, 2011; postdoc. fellow, dept. rheumatology Haukeland U. Hosp., 2011—. Rsch. worker Bergen Surg. Hosp., 2005—. Avocations: skiing, running. Office: Kalfarveien 31 Bergen 5018 Norway Home Phone: (47)95773490; Office Phone: (47)55588523. Business E-Mail: jannike.oyen@isf.uib.no.

OYEYEMI, ADETOYEJE YOONUS, physical therapist, educator; b. Offa, Nigeria, Dec. 14, 1959; BS in Physiotherapy, Obafemi Awolowo U., Ile-Ife. Nigeria, 1982; D in Health Sci., U. St. Augustine, Fla., 1996. Assoc. prof. Dominican Coll. Blauvelt, 2000—. Dir. rehab. svcs. Susan Smith McKinney Nursing and Rehab. Ctr., 2004—. Contbr. articles to profl. jours. & publs. Recipient Disting. Author award, Assn. Schs. Allied Health Professions; named one of Phys. Therapist Practitioner of Yr., Meridian Publ., 2008. Fellow: Nigeria Soc. Physiotherapy; mem.: NY Acad. Scis., Am. Phys. Therapy Assn. (Geriat. Sect. Clin. Educator award). Avocations: reading, exercise. Office: 594 Albany Ave Brooklyn NY 11203 Business E-Mail: adetoyeje.oyeyemi@nychhc.org.

OYLER, ANNE, audiologist; Assoc. dir. audiology profl. practices Am. Speech-Language Hearing Assn. Office: 2200 Research Blvd #305 Rockville MD 20850-3289 Office Phone: 301-296-5700. E-mail: aoyler@asha.org.

OZ, MEHMET CENGIZ, cardiac surgeon; b. Cleve., June 11, 1960; s. Mustafa and Suna (Atabay) Oz; m. Lisa Oz; children: Daphne, Arabella, Zoe, Oliver. BA magna cum laude, Harvard U., 1982; MD, U. Pa. Sch. Medicine, 1986; MBA, U. Pa. Wharton Bus. Sch., Phila., 1986; doctorate (hon.), Istanbul U. Diplomate Am. Bd. Surgery, Am. Bd. Thoracic Surgery. Intern/resident gen. surgery Columbia-Presbyn. Med. Ctr., NYC, 1986—90, chief resident gen. surgery, 1990—91, resident cardiothoracic surgery, 1991—93; attending surgeon NY Presbyn. Hosp./Columbia U. Med. Ctr., 1993—; Irving asst. prof. surgery Columbia U. Coll. Physicians & Surgeons, NYC, 1994—2000, assoc. prof. surgery, 2000—01, prof. surgery, 2001—; vice-chmn. cardiovasc. svcs., dir. Cardiovasc. Inst, dept. surgery Columbia U. Med. Ctr., 2001—. Bd. dirs. Siga Corp.; med. class chmn. U. Pa. Sch. Medicine, 1982—83, med. sch. pres., 1984—85; dir., Cardiac Assist Device Program Columbia-Presbyn. Med. Ctr., 1994—2001, founder, Complementary Medicine Program; mem. Thoracic Surgical Workforce Com., 1998. Author: Healing from the Heart: A Leading Surgeon Combines Eastern and Western Traditions to Create the Medicine of the Future, 1998 (Books for a Better Am. award, 1999), YOU: The Owner's Manual Diet, 2009; co-editor (with Daniel J. Goldstein): Minimally Invasive Cardiac Surgery, 1998 (Voted the best health sci. book, Doody, 2000), Minimally Invasive Cardiac Surgery, 2nd edit., 2004, Cardiac Assist Devices, 2000; co-author (with Michael F. Roizen): YOU: The Owner's Manual: An Insider's Guide to the Body That Will Make You Healthier and Younger, 2005, YOU: The Smart Patient: An Insider's Handbook for Getting the Best Treatment, 2006, YOU: On a Diet- The Owner's Manual for Waist Management, 2006, YOU: Staying Young: The Owner's Manual for Extending Your Warranty, 2007, YOU: Being Beautiful: The Owner's Manual to Inner and Outer Beauty, 2008, YOU: The Owner's Manual: An Insider's Guide to the Body That Will Make You Healthier and Younger (revised and expanded edition), 2008, YOU: Having a Baby: The Owner's Manual to a Happy and Healthy Pregnancy, 2009, YOU: On a Diet: YOU: On a Diet- The Owner's Manual for Waist Management (revised), 2009, (compact disc) YOU: on a Walk, 2007, YOU: Breathing Easy: Meditation and Breathing Techniques to Help You Relax, Refresh and Revitalize, 2008, YOU: The Owner's Manual for Teens-A Guide to a Healthy Body and Happy Life, 2011; host (TV series) Second Opinion with Dr. Oz, Discovery Health Channel, 2003—04, Ask Dr. Oz on The Oprah Winfrey Show, 2004—09, (syndicated TV series) The Dr. Oz Show, 2009— (Daytime Entertainment Emmy award for Outstanding Talk Show Host, Nat. Acad. of Television Arts & Sciences, 2011), numerous programs for Discovery Health Channel, regular contbr. Oprah & Friends, XM Satellite Radio, 2006—, numerous network news appearances. Recipient Blakemore Rsch. prize, Columbia U. Coll. Physicians & Surgeons, 1988—91, P & S Club Outstanding House Officer award, 1991, 25th Anniversary Silver award, Bastyr U., 2004; named Turkish-Am. of Yr., Assembly Turkish-Am. Assns., 1996; named a Doctor of Yr., Hippocrates mag.; named one of The Best and Brightest, Esquire mag., Healers of the Millenium, Healthy Living mag., Best Doctors of Yr., NY Mag., Global Leaders of Tomorrow, World Econ. Forum, 1999, the 100 Most Influential People in the World, TIME mag., 2008; named to Castle Connolly Guide America's Top Doctors. Fellow: ACS, Am. Coll. Cardiology; mem.: Am. Coll. Angiology (mem. scientific coun.), Am. Soc. Laser Medicine & Surgery (Rsch. award 1991), Internat. Soc. Optical Engring., Assn. Turkish-Am. Scientists, NY Soc. Thoracic Surgery, NY State Soc. Surgeons, 21st Century Cardiac Surg. Soc., Found. Advancement of Cardiac Therapies (bd. dirs.), Am. Turkish Soc. (bd. dirs.), Am. Soc. Artificial Internal Organs, Am. Heart Assn. (mem. scientific coun.), Turkish-Am. Physicians Assn., Assn. Acad. Surgery, Internat. Soc. Heart & Lung Transplantation, Am. Bd. Surgery, Am. Bd. Thoracic Surgery, Am. Assn. Thoracic Surgery (Robert E. Gross Rsch. scholarship 1994—96). Achievements include patents in field. Office: NY Presbyn Hosp Columbia Med Ctr 177 Fort Washington Ave MHB 7 435 New York NY 10032 Office Phone: 212-342-3520. Office Fax: 212-305-4434. E-mail: mco2@columbia.edu. *

OZAKI, KATSUTOSHI, hematologist, educator; b. Osaka, Japan, May 6, 1967; MD, Keio U. Sch. Medicine, 1992, PhD, 1996. Asst. prof. Jichi Med. U., 2002—. Mem.: Japan Soc. Hematology, Am. Soc. Hematology. Office: 3311-1 Yakushiji Shimotsuke Tochigi 329-0498 Japan Office Fax: 81-285-44-5258. Business E-Mail: ozakikat@jichi.ac.jp.

OZAKI, MASAYUKI, physician, anesthesiologist; MD, U. Occupl. and Environ. Health, Kitakyushu-shi, Japan, 1998; diploma in occupl. health, U. Occupl. and Environ. Health, 1998; PhD, U. Occpl. & Environ. Health, 2010. Resident U. Occupl. and Environ. Health, Kitakyushu-shi, 1998—99, instr., 2004—04; resident Nippon Steel Hirohata Hosp., Himeji-shi, Hyogo-ken, Japan, 1999—2001, Kyushu-koseinenkin Hosp., Kitakyushu-shi, 2002—03; occupl. physician Toray Industries, Inc, Otsu-shi, Shiga-ken, Japan, 2005—09. Anesthesiologist Shiga U. Med. Sci., Otsu-shi, Japan, 2006—10; physicain Dept Emergency & Critical Care Med. St. Marianna U. Sch. Medicine Hosp., Kawasaki, Japan, 2010—. Mem.: Japan Med. Assn., Japanese Soc. Anesthesiologists (bd. cert. anesthesiologist). Achievements include first to use of the Laryngeal Mask Airway in one-lung ventilation; research in role of nitric oxide in the hypothalamic neurons; effects of ethanol on host defence; prevention of thrombosis with prostaglandin E1 in a patient with catastrophic antiphospholipid syndrome. Home: 428-1-B102 Suenaga Takatsu-ku Kawasaki Kanagawa 2130013 Japan Office: St Marianna University Sch Medicine Hosp Dept Emergency Critical Care Medicine Sugao Kawasaki Kanagawa 216-8511 Japan Office Phone: 81 44 977 8111. Personal E-mail: ozaki.masayuki@nifty.com.

OZAKI, MICHAEL FRED, pediatrician; b. San Francisco, June 13, 1950; s. Toshiye and Nobuo Ozaki; m. Darcy Mulville, Sept. 7, 1990. BA, U. Calif., Berkeley, 1974; MD, U. Calif., Irvine, 1983. Diplomate Am. Bd. Pediat., 1993. Staff pediatrician Columbia Pediat., Long Beach, Calif., 1986—92, Meml. Pediat., Westminster, Calif., 1992—94; instr. pediat. Riverside Regional Med. Ctr., Newport News, Va., 1994—95; sr. pediatrician Bristol Pk. Med. Group, Fountain Valley, Calif., 1995—, also bd. dirs., 2005—, treas., 2007—, v.p., 2009—. Chmn. pediatics Long Beach Meml. Hosp., 1992—93; exec. com. Miller Children's Hosp. Long Beach Meml., 1992—93. Recipient Outtanding Svc. award, U. Calif. Sch. Medicine, Irvine, 1978, Mereck award, 1982—83, Outstanding Svc. award, Long Beach Meml. Hosp., 1992—93, Outstanding Faculty award, Long Beach Meml. Family Practice Residency Program, 1994, 2003, Riverside Regional Med. Ctr., 1994, Excellence in Tchg. award, U. Calif., Irvine, 2005, Physician of Excellence award, Orange Coast Mag. and Orange County Med. Assn., 2005—07, Barton award, Bristol Pk. Med. Group, 1995, 2002—03, Hagadorn award, 1996—97, 1999—2000; named Most Outstanding Student in Pediat., U. Calif. Sch. Medicine and Orange County Med. Soc., 1983, Outstanding Tchr., U. Calif. Irvine Sch. Medicine, 1987, 1990, Physician of Yr., Nursing Staff Long Beach Meml. Hosp., 1989, 1993, Super Doc, LA Mag., 2010; named one of America's Top Pediatricians, Coun. on Consumer Rsch., 2007; nominee Pediat. Hero award, Am. Acad. Pediat., 2009; grantee, Healthnet, 2004; McKenzie scholar, U. Calif. Sch. Medicine, Irvine, 1982—83. Fellow: Am. Acad. Pediat.; mem.: Orange County Med. Assn. Achievements include research in radionucleotide excretion in breast milk; effect of vitamin C on prevention of dilantin induced gingival hyperplasia. Office: Bristol Park Med Group 11420 Warner Ste B Fountain Valley CA 92708 Office Phone: 714-549-1300. Business E-Mail: mozaki@bristolparkmed.com.

OZAKI, YUKIO, cardiologist, medical educator; s. Teruzo and Kazuko Ozaki; m. Atsuko Watanabe, June 1, 1986; children: Reina, Yuri. MD, Nagoya U., 1981. Lic. physician Ministry of Health and Welfare, Tokyo, Japan, 1981. Internal medicine resident Anjo Kosei Hosp., Japan, 1981—83, cardiology resident, 1983—85, staff cardiologist, 1985—92; clin. rsch. fellow Thoraxcenter Med. Ctr., Erasmus U., Rotterdam, Netherlands, 1993—95, assoc. dir. of angiographic rsch. lab., 1995—96; asst. prof., chief of cath. lab. dept. cardiology Aichi Med. U. Hosp., Nagakute, Japan, 1997—. Dir. Aichi Med. U. Coronary Imagning Analysis Ctr. (AMAC), Nagakute, Japan, 1997—. Author: (book chpt.) Vascular Remodeling and Restenosis, 1997; mem. editl. bd.: Japanese Jour. of Interventinal Cardiology. Assoc. pres. PTA of Meiwa H.S., Nagoya, Japan, 2003—. Rsch. grant, Aichi Med. U., 1998, Suzuken Meml. Found., 2000, Grant-In-Aid for Sci. Rsch., Japanese Govt., 2001-1003. Fellow: Japanese Coll. Cardiology, Japanese Soc. Interventional Cardiology, Am. Coll. Cardiology, European Soc. Cardiology; mem.: Am. Heart Assn. Avocations: tennis, golf, swimming, travel. Office: Aichi Med Univ Hosp Nagakute Aichi Nagakute 480-1195 Japan Office Fax: 81-56-163-1183; Home Fax: 81-52-917-3169. E-mail: ozakiyuk@aichi-med-u.ac.jp.

OZASA, HIROSHI, gynecologist, educator, obstetrician; b. Moriguchi, Osaka, Japan, Dec. 21, 1947; s. Seiji and Shigeko Ozasa; m. Tomiko Ono, Feb. 16, 1969; children: Ami, Neiko. MD, Kyoto U., Japan, 1972, PhD, 1980. Resident Kyoto U., 1972—74, asst. prof., 1984—89; vis. asst. prof. Emory U., Atlanta, 1980—82; dept. head Otsu Red Cross Hosp., Otsu, Japan, 1990—. Lectr. Kyoto U., 1995—, clin. prof., 2003—, Shiga U. Med. Scis., Japan, 2002—. Fellow: Japanese Endocrine Soc.; mem.: Japanese Soc. Ob-Gyn. (councilor 2003—), Endocrine Soc. Office: Otsu Red Cross Hosp 1-1-35 Nagara Otsu 520 8511 Japan

OZAWA, MARTHA NAOKO, social work educator; b. Ashikaga, Tochigi, Japan, Sept. 30, 1933; arrived in US, 1963; d. Tokuichi and Fumi (Kawashima) O.; m. May 1959 (div. May 1966). BA in Econs., Aoyama Gakuin U., 1956; MS in Social Work, U. Wis., 1966, PhD in Social Welfare, 1969. Asst. prof. social work Portland State U., Oreg., 1969-70, assoc. prof. social work, 1970-72, 1975-76; assoc. rsch. prof. social work NYU, 1972-75; prof. social work Washington U., St. Louis, 1976-85, Bettie Bofinger Brown prof. social policy, 1985—2003, Bettie Bofinger Brown Disting. prof. social policy, 2003—; dir. Martha N. Ozawa Ctr. Social Policy Studies, 2005—. Vis. fellow social devel. Adelphi U. Sch. Social Work, 1982; Ellen Winston lectr. NC State U., 1984; Seabury lectr. Sch. Social Welfare, U. Calif., Berkeley, 1985; endowed chair Bettie Bofinger Brown Wash. U., St. Louis, 1985; Leon and Josephine Winkelman meml. lectr. U. Mich., 1996; Carl A. Scott Memorial Fund lectr. Coun. Social Work Edn., Kans. City, Mo., 1992; keynote spkr. U. Wis. Sch. Social Work, 1997; mem. bd. advisors Tokyo U. Socail Welfare, Japan, 1998—; guest prof. Japan Coll. Social Work, 1998—; hon. advisor Pavazzin Ctr. Social Work Rsch. Aging, Fordham U., NYC, 1999—; lectr. U. Ala. Sch. Social Work Colloquium Series, 2002—03; mem. Jour. Population Ageing, 2011—; co-editor-in chief Asian Social Work & Policy Review, 2005—; mem. editl. bd. Jour. Social Work Edn., 2006—, Special Issue Challenges Aging US, 2005, Jour. Poverty Innovations Social, Political & Economic Inequalities, 1995—2004, Social Work Rsch., 1994—97, Children & Youth Svcs. Review, 1991—; prin. investigator Ministry Health & Welfare Japan, 1996—97; co-investigator Gateways & Pathways Project, 1997—99; co-prin. investigator TRANS ADAMHA HHS, 1989—92; prin. investigator Rsch. Fund Wash. U., 1977—78, St. Louis, 1980—81. Author: Income Maintenance and Work Incentives, 1982; editor: Women's Life Cycle: Japan-U.S. Comparison in Income Maintenance, 1989, Women's Life Cycle and Economic Insecurity: Problems and Proposals, 1989, Women's Life Cycle: Shotoku Hoshou no Nichibei Hikaku, 1992; editl. bd. Social Work, Silver Spring, Md., 1972-75, 85-88, New Eng. Jour. Human Svcs., Boston, 1987-95, Ency. of Social Work, Silver Spring, 1974-77, 91-95, 99-2003, Jour. Social Svc. Rsch., 1977-97, Children and Youth Svcs. Rev., 1991—, Social Work Rsch., 1994-97, Jour. Poverty, 1997-2004; co-editor-in-chief Asian Social Work and Policy Rev., 2005—; contbr. chapter to books, articles to profl. jours. Grantee Adminstrn. on Aging, Washington, 1979, 84, NIMH, 1990-93, grant, Coun. Gerontol. Soc. America, 1992, Disting. Achievement award, 2007, Bettie Bofinger Brown Disting. Prof. award, Annual Outstanding Faculty Mentor award, Wash. U. St. Louis, 2002, Disting. Faculty award, George Warren Brown Sch. Social Work Alumni Assn., 2000, Excellence award, Nat. Assn. Social Worker, 1995, Appreciation Cert. award, Nat. Assn. Social Workers, 1985-88, Disting. Faculty award, Bd. Govs., Wash. U. Alumni Assn., wash. U. Founders Day, 1988. Mem. Nat. Assn. Social Workers (presdl. award 1999), Nat. Acad. Social Ins., Nat. Conf. on Social Welfare (bd. dirs. 1981-87), The Gerontol. Soc. Am., Soc. for Social Work and Rsch., Washington U. Faculty Club (bd. dirs. 1986-91). Avocations: photography, tennis, swimming, gardening. Home: 13018 Tiger Lily Ct Saint Louis MO 63146-4339 Office: PO Box 1196 Saint Louis MO 63130-4899 Office Phone: 314-935-6615. Business E-Mail: ozawa@wustl.edu.

OZAWA, SHUTARO, surgeon; b. Tokyo, Dec. 13, 1965; PhD, Saitama Med. U., 1990. Assoc. prof. Saitama Med. U. Internat. Med. Ctr., 2010; surgeon Chichibu Hosp., 2010—. Recipient Ochiai Meml. award, Saitama Med. U.; Young Scientists grant, Ministry of Edn., Culture, Sports, Sci. and Tech. Mem.: Japanese Soc. Gastroent. Surgery, Japan Surg. Soc. Office: 20 Izumicho Chichibu-shi Saitama 369-1874 Japan Business E-Mail: shutaro@saitama-med.ac.jp.

OZAWA, TOSHIO, geriatrician; b. Tokyo, Mar. 13, 1929; s. Mamoru and Chiyo Ozawa; m. Kuniko Iwasa, Oct. 9, 1960; children: Takeyuki, Akihiro. MD, U. Tokyo, 1953, D of Med. Scis., 1960. Med. diplomate. From asst. prof. to assoc. prof. U. Tokyo, 1968-81; prof. Kochi (Japan) Med. Sch., 1981-93, prof. emeritus, 1993—; dir. Tokyo Met. Geriatric Hosp., 1993-97; dir. emeritus, 1999—; cons. Tokyo Met. Geriatric Hosp., 1997-99; dir. emeritus, 1999—. Pres. Japan Gerontol. Soc., 2008—09. Editor Japan Jour. Geriatrics, 1982-93, Japanese Circulation Jour., 1991-94. Recipient Erwin Von Baelz prize C.H. Boehringer Sohn Ingelheim Am Rhein, 1964. Mem. Japan Geriatric Soc. (bd. dirs. 1982—), Japanese Circulation Soc. (bd. dirs. 1991-94). Office Phone: 03 3964 1141. Business E-Mail: ozwt@js9.so_net.ne.jp.

OZAWA, TSUKASA, surgeon, educator; b. Tokyo, Sept. 7, 1965; MD, Toho U., 1990, PhD, 2000. Rsch. fellow Divsn. Cardiac Surgery, Toronto Gen. Hosp., U. Toronto, 2000—02; clin. observer, dept. cardiovasc. surgery Hosp. Sick Children, Toronto, 2002; surgeon Sakakibara Heart Inst., 2003; pediat. cardiac surgeon chief, asst. prof. Dept. Cardiovasc. Surgery, Toho U. Omori Med. Ctr., 2004—11, assoc. prof., pediat. cardiac surgeon chief, 2011—. Councilor Japanese Soc. Pediatric Cardiology and Cardiac Surgery, 2005; infection control dr. Japan Soc. Surg. Infection, 2010; rschr. Regenerative Medicine Cardiovasc. Surgery Toho U., 2002. Recipient Toho U. Med. award. Mem.: Japan Surg. Soc., Japanese Soc. Cardiovasc. Surgery, Japanese Assn. Thoracic Surgery, Cardiothoracic Surgery Network, Asian Soc. Cardiovasc. and Thoracic Surgery. Avocations: history, basketball, surfing. Office: Omorinishi 6-11-1 Ota-ku Tokyo 143-8541 Japan Office Fax: 81-3-3766-7810. Business E-Mail: cbc02537@nifty.com.

OZAWA, YASUNORI, endocrinologist, researcher; b. Toyama, Japan, Mar. 11, 1944; m. Midori Ohuchi, June 1976; children: Noriko, Satoko, Naoko. MD, Gunma U., 1969; PhD, Tokyo U., 1980. Rschr. Okinaka Meml. Inst. for Med. Rsch., Tokyo, 1990—, chmn. dept. endocrinology and metabolism Toranomon Hosp., Tokyo, 1993—2004, exec. rep. clin. medicine divsn.; dir. gen. clinic Ministry Economy, Trade and Industry Japan, Chiyodaku, 2004—. Clin. fellow UCLA, 1976—78; vis. rschr. U. Minn., 1986—87; vis. lectr. Iwate Med. Sch., Tokyo, 1990—; vis. prof. Tokyo U., 2001—. Author: Therapy of Endocrine Diseases, 1999, Thyroid Desease, 2002; contbr. articles to profl. jours. Office: Toranomon Ozawa Clinic Toranomon Hoso Bldg 1 F 1-20-3 Nishishinbashi Minatoku Tokyo 105-0003 Japan Office Phone: 3-3507-1101. Office Fax: 3-3507-1102.

OZBEK, BERNA, biology professor; b. Istanbul, Sept. 25; MSc, Istanbul U., 1999, PhD, 2005. Asst. prof. Istanbul U., 2007—. Grant, 2007. Mem.: FEMS. Office: Istanbul University Faculty Pharmacy Istanbul Fatih-Beyazit 34160 Turkey Office Fax: 00212 4400257. Personal E-mail: bernaozbek@hotmail.com.

OZCAN, IPEK, pharmacist; b. Denizli, Apr. 20, 1979; PhD in Pharm. Tech., Ege U., 2008. Rsch. scientist, dept. pharm. tech. Ege U., Faculty Pharmacy, 2000—. Mem.: Controlled Release Soc. Office: Ege University Faculty Pharmacy Izmir Bornova 35040 Turkey Office Fax: 00902323885258.

OZCAN EDEER, AYSE, physical therapist; b. Turkey, Aug. 1, 1970; B, Hacettepe U. Sch. Phys. Therapy, 1992; PhD, Dokuz Eylul U., 2000. Assoc. prof. Dokuz Eylul U. Sch. Phys. Therapy, 2006—09; therapist Access Phys. Therapy, 2011—. Rater MORE, 2009—11. Geriatric Rehab. Project grant, Tubitak. Mem.: Turkish Phys. Therapy Assn. Home: 5 Hamburg Tpke Butler NJ 07405 Personal E-mail: ayseozcan1@gmail.com.

ÖZDEMIR, BINNAZ HANDAN, pathologist, educator; b. Buffalo, Feb. 27, 1968; d. Abdullah Ilhan and Güray Özdemir. Associate Prof., Baskent U., Med. Sch., Ankara, Turkey, 2002—03. Specialist cert. Ministery of Health, 1996, assoc. prof. cert. Com. of Univ., 2002. With Hacettepe U. Faculty Medicine, Ankara, Turkey, 1985—91; pathologist Ankara U. Med. Sch., Turkey, 1992—99, Zekai Tahir Women Hosp., Ankara, 1997—98; asst. prof. Baskent U. Med. Sch., Ankara, 2000—02, assoc. prof., 2002—. Fellow nephropathology tng. Cleve. Clininc Found. Hosp., 1998—99. Contbr. articles to profl. jours. Sec. Hypertansion and Kidney Found., Ankara, 1992—2003. Recipient First award in painting, 1972, 1984, First award in poem, 1981. Mem.: European Soc. Pathology (corr.). Office: Baskent Univ Faculty Medicine 12 Sokak 7/4 Bahcelievler Ankara 06490 Turkey Office Fax: +90-312-212 75 72; Home Fax: +90-312-212 75 72. E-mail: handan27@hotmail.com.

ÖZDEMIR, ÖNER, pediatrician; b. Kdz Eregli, Zonguldak, Turkey, Sept. 18, 1965; MD, Istanbul U., 1989. Chief pediat. Göztepe Rsch. and Tng. Hosp., 2010—. Home: Orhantepe mah Defne sok Özer Apt 86 Dragos Kartal Istanbul 89530 Turkey Personal E-mail: oner.ozdemir.md@gmail.com.

ÖZEL, HALIL ERDEM, otolaryngologist; b. Turkey, Aug. 3, 1977; MD, Gazi U., 2001. ENT specialist 2007. Physician, ENT dept. Iskenderun Devlet Hastanesi, 2009—. Office: Dumlupinar mah Iskenderun De Hatay Iskenderun 31200 Turkey E-mail: heozel@yahoo.com.

ÖZENOGLU, ALIYE, nutritionist, educator; b. Konya, Turkey, Sept. 12, 1963; PhD, Istanbul U., 1999. Cerrahpasa med. faculty Istanbul U., 1997—2008, Ondokuz Mayis U., 2008—, head dietetics dept., 2009. Mem.: Tukish Dietetics Assn. Office: Ilkadim Lise caddesi Samsun Blacsea 55070 Turkey

ÖZGER, NAIL HARZEM, medical educator; b. Trabzon, Jan. 7, 1955; Degree, 1st U. Faculty Medicine Orthop. Clinics, 1973. Prof. med. 1st Clinic Orthop., 1979—. Mem.: TMSTS, APMSTS, EMSOS, ISOLS. Avocation: travel. Home: Konak mah 1cad 122 Zekeriyakoy Sariyer Istanbul 33450 Turkey Home Fax: 00902122910488. Personal E-mail: harzemo@yahoo.com.

ÖZKALE, M. REVAN, science educator; b. Kadirli, Sept. 24, 1979; PhD, Cukurova U., 2007. Rsch. asst. Cukurova U., 2002—07, asst. prof., 2007—10, assoc. prof., 2010. Office: Cukurova University Faculty Sci & Letters Adana 01330 Turkey Business E-Mail: mrevan@cu.edu.tr.

OZKAYA, SEVKET, medical educator; b. Samsun, Turkey, Feb. 27, 1976; Degree, Samsun Ondokuzmayis U., 1999; MD in Pulmonary Medicine, 2005. Cert. pulmonologist. Asst. prof. Rize U. Faculty Medicine, 2009—10, Dr. Suat Seren Edn. and Rsch. Hosp., 2010—. Office: Doctor Suat Seren Gögüs Hast EAH Izmir 35100 Turkey Personal E-mail: ozkayasevket@yahoo.com.

ÖZTÜRKMEN, YUSUF, surgeon, educator; b. Istanbul, Turkey, Oct. 13, 1964; Assoc. prof. Istanbul Med. U., 1989; orthop. surgeon Health Ministry, 1997. Home: Ataköy 7-8-9-10 Mahalle Palmiye Sk Istanbul 34158 Turkey Personal E-mail: yozturkmen@gmail.com.

OZUMBA, BENJAMIN CHUKWUMA, obstetrician, gynecologist, educator; b. Onitsha, Anambra, Nigeria, Mar. 21, 1954; s. Arthur Nwabunwanne and Alice chiebonam (Igebuike) O.; m. Chinelo Obianuju Udokwu, Jan. 29, 1994; children: Benjamin Chukwumdindu, Sarah Onyinyechukwu, Elizabeth Chimfumnanya, Rachel Chidinma. MB, BChir, U. Lagos, Nigeria, 1979; FMCOG, Post Grad. Med. Coll., Nigeria, 1987; MRCOG, Royal Coll. Ob.-Gyn., London, 1993; FICS, Internat. Coll. Surgeons, U.S., 1991; FWACS, W. African Coll. Surgeons, Lagos, Nigeria, 1993. Intern Lagos U. Tchg. Hosp., 1979—80; med. officer Coll. of Edn., Minna, Nigeria, 1980—81; sr. house officer Univ. Nigeria Tchg. Hosp., Enusu, 1981—82, registrar, 1982—83, sr. registrar, 1983—88, sr. lectr./ cons., 1988—93; prof. ob./gyn. U. Nigeria, Nsukka, 1993—, dean faculty med. scis. and dentistry, 2002—04, provost Coll. Medicine, 2004. Chmn. Enugu Med. Soc., 1993-95; coord. Tutorial System Internat., Nigeria, 1993-95; dean medicine U. Nigeria. Editor: Tropical Pediatrics and Child Health, 1999; assoc. editor Orient Jour. Medicine, 1988—, Nigerian Jour. Surgical Scis., 1991—, contbr. articles to profl. jours. V.p. Enugu chpt. Full Gospel Businessmen's Fellowship Internat., 1994-95, chpt. pres., 1997—; chmn. Harvest and Love Feast Com., Chapel of Redemption, Enugu, Nigeria, 1994-95. Takemi fellow Internat. Health Harvard U., 1995-96. Fellow Internat. Coll. Surgeons, W. African Coll. of Surgeons, Nigerian Postgrad. Med. Coll.; mem. AAAS (internat. mem.), Royal Coll. Obstetricians and Gynecologists. Born Again Christian. Achievements include measuring: serum concentrations of alphafetoprotein in mormal pregnancy and in pregnancy induced hypertensions; ivermectin levels in human breast milk. Office: Univ Nigeria Teaching Hosp Dept Ob-gyn Enugu Anambra Nigeria Mailing: 45 Duffield Dr South Orange NJ 07079 Home Phone: 236 42 253496. Personal E-mail: BenOzumba@hotmail.com.

PÄÄBO, SVANTE, molecular biologist, biochemist; b. Stockholm, 1955; PhD in Molecular Immunology, Uppsala U., 1986; PhD (hon.), U. Zurich, 1994, U. Helsinki, 2000. Postdoctoral rsch. Inst. Molecular Biology, U. Zurich., 1986—87, U. Calif., Berkeley, 1987—90; rsch. scientist U. California; prof. biology U. Munich, 1990—98; dir. Max Planck Inst. for Evolutionary Anthropology, Leipzig, Germany, 1997—; hon. prof. genetics and evolutionary biology U. Leipzig, 1999—. Guest prof. comparative genomics Uppsala U., Sweden, 2003. Recipient Leibniz prize, Deutsche Forschungsgemeinschaft, 1992, Max Delbruck medal, 1998, Carus medal, 1999, Rudbeck prize, Uppsala, 2000, Leipzig Sci. prize, 2003, Ernst Schering prize, 2003, Louis Jeantet prize for medicine, 2005, Virchow medal, U. Würzburg, Germany, 2005; named an The World's Most Influential People, TIME mag., 2007. Mem.: NAS (fgn. assoc.), Finnish Soc. Arts & Letters, Saxonian Acad. Scis., Deutsche Akademie der Naturforscher Leopoldina, Berlin-Brandenburg Acad. Scis., Royal Swedish Acad. Scis., Academia Europaea. Achievements include pioneering ancient DNA extraction studies. Office: Max Planck Inst Evolutionary Anthropology Deutscher Platz 6 04103 Leipzig Germany

PAASKE, WILLIAM PETERSEN, vascular surgeon; b. Nykøbing Falster, Denmark, June 12, 1948; s. Frank and Jonna Lüthans (Simonsen) P.; m. Vibeke Castenschiold, Apr. 2, 1981 (div. 2003); children: Alexandra Elizabeth, Ulrich William Holten. MD, U. Copenhagen, 1974, D of Med. Sci., 1979. Cert. specialist in vascular surgery, specialist in gen. surgery, Denmark. Rsch. fellow U. Copenhagen, 1974-77; resident Copenhagen Hosps., 1977-81; surgeon-in-tng. Rigshospitalet, Copenhagen, 1981-83, sr. resident Copenhagen, Hoersholm and Odense, Denmark, 1983-90; chief vascular surgeon Skejby Hosp., U. Aarhus, Denmark, 1990—; assoc. prof. surgery U. Aarhus, 1992-95, prof. vascular surgery, 1996—. Instr. physiology U. Copenhagen, 1971-85. Editor: (supplement) Acta Physiologica Scandinavica, other books; mem. editl. bds.; contbr. sci. papers to sci. and profl. jours. Chmn. Danish Med. Students Union, Copenhagen, 1968; vice-chmn. Students Coun., Univ. Copenhagen, 1968. Named Knight Order of Dannebrog, 2007; rsch. grantee, 1971—. Fellow Royal Soc. Medicine (Eng.), Royal Coll. Surgeons (Eng.), Royal Coll. Surgeons (Edinburgh), Am. Coll. Surgeons; mem. European Soc. Vascular Surgery (councillor, treas. 1992-97, trustee 1996-99, treas. endorsement and cert. com. 1996-99, pres.-elect 1999, pres. 2000), European Union Med. Specialists (divsn. vascular surgery 1992-97), European Bd. Vascular Surgery (pres. divsn. vascular surgery 1997-99), Coun. Vascular Surgeons in European Union (councillor, vice-chmn. 1993—), Hellenic Angiology Soc. (hon.), Soc. Clin. Vascular Surgery US (hon.), Vascular Surg. Soc. Gt. Britain and Ireland (hon.), Soc. Vascular Surgery, Athenaeum, London, Internat. Soc. Vascular Surgeons (mem. coun.). Achievements include research in circulation physiology including microcirculation; clinical vascular surgery. Avocations: literature, music, art. Office: Dept Cardio & Vasc Surgery Aarhus U Hos Skejby Sygehus DK-8200 Aarhus Denmark

PAAVOLA, FRED G., pharmacist; s. George W. and Eleanor M. Paavola; m. Linda M. Kane, June 25, 1977; children: Nicholas, Chad, Heather. BS, Mont. State U., Bozeman, 1967, ND State U., Fargo, 1970, DSc, 2002. Chief pharmacy officer Indian Health Svc., Eagle Butte, SD, 1981—88, area pharmacy officer, 1987—88; pharmacy manpower analyst Bur. Health Professions, Rockville, Md., 1988—90, chief allied and assn. health professions, 1990—95, chief peer rev., 1995—2000; chief pharmacist officer USPHS, Rockville, Md., 1996—2000; team comdr. Ariz. One Disaster Med. Assistance Team, Tucson, 2003—11. Asst. chief Ft. Benning, Ga., 1972—73; chair pharmacist Ft. Wainwright, Ark., 1973—76, Ft. Sill, Okla., 1977—79; chair pharmacy nat. adv. bd. ND State U. Coll. Pharmacy, Fargo, 2005—10. Author: Remington, 2000; contbr. articles to profl. jours. Nat. cert. swim ofcl. Ariz. Swimming, Tucson, 2000—10; v.p. Monument Vista Homeowners Assn., Tucson, 2001—04; dir. emergency svcs. El Tour de Tucson, 2003. With US Army, 1970—80, with USPHS, 1980—2000. Recipient Exemplary Svc. award, Surgeon Gen., 1993, 1997, 2000; named Pharmacist of Yr., Drug Topics, 2000; named to Wall of Fame, ROTC ND State U., 2003. Fellow: Am. Pharmacists Assn.; mem.: ASHP (exec. v.p., Courageous Svc. award 2006), Assn. Mil. Surgeons US (life), NDMS (mem. sr. med. workgroup 2008, chair human capital working group 2009—11), ND State U. Alumni Assn., George F. Archambault Found., Commd. Officers Assn. (life).

PABLOS-MÉNDEZ, ARIEL, federal agency administrator, epidemiologist, educator; b. 1961; MD, U. Guadalajara; MPH, Columbia U. With Rockefeller Found., NYC, 1998—2004, mgr. Joint Learning Initiative on Human Resources for Health, dep. and interim dir. health equality; assoc. attending physician medicine NY-Presbyn. Hosp., NYC; dir. knowledge mgmt. and sharing WHO, Geneva, 2004—07; prof. clin. epidemiology Mailman Sch. Pub. Health Columbia U., NYC, prof. clin. medicine Coll. of Physicians; mng. dir. Rockefeller Found., 2007—11; asst. adminstr. global health bur. US Agy. for Internat. Development (USAID), Washington, 2011—. Founding bd. mem. Global Alliance for Tuberculosis Drug Devel., 2000—06; adv. bd. mem. Fogarty Internat. Ctr. NIH, 2008—. Editl. reviewer Internat. Jour. of Tuberculosis and Lung Disease, Jour. of AMA; contbr. articles to med. journals. Founding com. mem. Noguchi Africa Prize, 2007—08. Recipient Jalisco Award in Health Sciences, U. Guadalajara, 2004. Mem.: American Soc. Clin. Investigation. Office: US Agency for International Development 1300 Pennsylvania Ave, NW Washington DC 20523 *

PAC, MALGORZATA MARIA, medical educator; b. Drawsko Pomorskie, Jan. 5, 1960; MD, Med. U., 1984; PhD, Children's Meml. Health Inst., 1991. Asst. prof. CMHI, 1998—. Cons. LUXMED, 2001. Recipient Excellent worker, Ministry of Health. Mem.: PTIDIK, PTP. Avocations: skiing, bicycling. Office: Av Dzieci Polskich 20 Warsaw Mazovia 04 730 Poland Office Fax: 48 815 73 82. E-mail: malgorzata.pac@wp.pl.

PACAUSKIENE, INGRIDA MARIJA, periodontist, educator; b. Lithuania, Sept. 8, 1968; MD, PhD, Kaunas U. Medicine, 1992. Asst. prof. Kaunas U. Medicine, 1993—2002, lector, 2002—05; assoc. prof. Kaunas Acad. Medicine, 2005—. Mem.: Assn. Periodontists Lithuania. Avocations: travel, music, gardening, cooking. Home: Visinskio 16-2 Kaunas LT 44173 Lithuania Personal E-mail: ingridapacauskiene@takas.lt

PACE, CHARLES ROBERT, psychologist, educator; b. St. Paul, Sept. 7, 1912; s. Charles N. and Lenore (Lee) P.; m. Rosella Gaarder, Dec. 18, 1937; children: Rosalind, Jenifer. BA, De Pauw U., 1933; MA, U. Minn., 1935, PhD, 1937. Instr. in gen. coll. U. Minn., 1937-40; research asso. Am. Council Edn., 1941-42; research psychologist Bur. Naval Personnel, Navy Dept., 1943-47; mem. faculty Syracuse U., 1947-61, asso. dir., then dir. evaluation service center, 1947-52, asst. to chancellor, 1948-52, prof. psychology, chmn. dept., dir. psychol. research center, 1952-61; prof. higher edn. UCLA, 1961-82, prof. emeritus, 1982—. Mem. adv. coms. Am. Council Edn., Coll. Entrance Exam. Bd., Social Sci. Research Council. Author: They Went to College, 1941, (with M. E. Troyer) Evaluation in Teacher Education, 1944, The Junior Year in France, 1959, (with F.H. Bowles and J.C. Stone) How to Get Into College, 1968, College and University Environment Scales, 2d edit, 1969, Education and Evangelism, 1972, The Demise of Diversity?, 1974, Measuring Outcomes of College, 1979, Measuring the Quality of College Student Experiences, 1984, CSEQ: Test Manual and Norms, 1987, The Undergraduates, 1990. Post-doctoral fellow Rockefeller Found., 1940-41; fellow Center Advanced Study Behavioral Scis., 1959-60; recipient citation for meritorious civilian service Navy Dept., 1946, E.F. Lindquist award Am. Ednl. Research Assn. and Am. Coll. Testing Program, 1984, Suslow award for outstanding svc. Assn. for Instl. Rsch., 1989. Mem. APA, Am. Ednl. Rsch. Assn. (Disting. Rsch. award divsn. postsecondary edn. 1992), Assn. for Study Higher Edn. (Disting. Career award 1989), Am. Assn. Pub. Opinion Rsch. Office Phone: 707-822-1204. Business E-Mail: crp7001@axe.humboldt.edu. *

PACHINGER, OTMAR M., cardiologist, educator; b. Wels, Austria, Mar. 29, 1944; MD, Med. U. Vienna, 1968. Prof. Med. U. Innsbruck, 1997—. Chief, cardiology, chmn., dept. internal medicine U. Innsbruck, 1997. Fellow: Internat. Coll. Angiology, Am. Heart Assn., European Soc. Cardiology, Austrian Soc. Cardiology. Avocations: travel, skiing, languages. Office: Anichstrasse 35 Innsbruck A-6020 Austria Office Fax: 0043-512-504-25622. Business E-Mail: otmar.pachinger@uki.at.

PACHMAN, LAUREN M(ERLE), physician, pediatrician; b. Durham, NC, Mar. 16, 1937; d. Daniel James and Vivian Allison P.; m. Mark A. Satterthwaite; children: Emily Ann, Theodore Daniel. BA, Wellesley Coll., 1957; MD, U. Chgo., 1961. Diplomate: Am. Bd. Pediatrics, Am. Bd. Allergy and Clin. Immunology. Intern Phila. Gen. Hosp., 1961-62; resident Babies Hosp., NYC, 1962-64; asst. prof. Hosp. of Rockefeller U., 1964-66; asst. dept. pediatrics Columbia U., 1964-66; instr. dept. pediatrics LaRabida-U. Chgo., 1966-69, asst. prof., 1969-71; assoc. prof. pediatrics Northwestern U., 1971-78, prof., 1978—. Head div. immunology and rheumatology Children's Meml. Hosp., 1971—2002; mem. study group A Nat. Inst. Arthritis, Diabetes and Digestive Diseases, 1980-84; mem. subcom. A Nat. Inst. Arthritis and MS, 1985-89; mem. arthritis adv. com. FDA, 1986-90;

mem. rsch. com. Arthritis Found., 1986-88; vis. prof.; dir. Curesm Program Excellence Myositis Rsch., 2007-, Focis Ctr. Excellence Clin. Immunology, 2008-. Contbr. articles to profl. jours. Mem. Arthritis Found. (profl. edn. com. 1994-96, blue ribbon rsch. com. 1996) Nat. Found. fellow, 1958; NIH fellow, 1964-66. Fellow Am. Acad. Pediatrics; mem. AAAS, Soc. Pediatric Research, Am. Assn. Immunologists, Am. Rheumatism Assn. (pres. pediat. rheumatism coun. 1983-84), Midwest Soc. Pediatric Rsch. (pres. 1980-81), Am. Coll. Rheumatology (edn. com. 1994-97), Am. Bd. Pediat. (rheumatology subspecialty bd. 1990-94). Office: Childrens Memorial Hops Box 212 2300 N Childrens Plz Chicago IL 60614-3363 *

PACHOLCZYK, MAREK JERZY, surgeon; b. Warsaw, June 23, 1962; MD, Warsaw Med. U., 1986, PhD, 1993. Sr. lectr. Warsaw Med. U., 2000—. Cons. Liver Transplant Program Ctr., 2000—11. Home: Krzywa 10a Lomianki Mazowieckie 05-092 Poland Home Fax: 225022155. Personal E-mail: pacholczykm@interia.pl.

PACHT, ERIC REED, pulmonary and critical care physician; b. Madison, Wis., Mar. 24, 1954; s. Asher Roger and Perle (Landau) P.; m. Karen Sue Dalpiaz, Aug. 7, 1982; children: Ben, Lora. BA summa cum laude, Lawrence U., 1976; MD cum laude, U. Wis., Madison, 1980. Diplomate Nat. Bd. Med. Examiners, Am. Bd. Internal Medicine. Intern, resident Ohio State U. Hosps., 1980-83, fellow in pulmonary and critical care medicine, 1983-86; asst. prof. Ohio State U., 1986-91, assoc. prof., 1991-99; staff phys. Mt. Carmel Med. Ctr. and St. Ann's Hosp., Columbus, Ohio, 1999-01, Licking Meml. Heatlh Profls., Columbus, Ohio, 2001—. Asst. dir. pulmonary and critical care Ohio State U., 1988-96, dir. pulmonary and critical care fellowship tng. program, 1988-99, med. sch. rep. to Am. Fedn. for Clin. Rsch., 1990-94, med. dir. lung transplantation program, 1992-95, dir. clin. rsch., 1993-99. Contbr. articles to profl. jours. Vol. Am. Lung Assn., Columbus, Ohio, Columbus Cancer Clinic. Recipient numerous rsch. awards. Fellow Am. Coll. Chest Physicians; mem. Am. Thoracic Soc., Ohio Thoracic Soc., Am. Fedn. Clin. Rsch., Phi Beta Kappa. Achievements include description of new form of respiratory failure and emphysema in patients with HIV. Home: 1224 Leicester Pl Columbus OH 43235-2181 Office Phone: 740-348-1805. Personal E-mail: EPacht@aol.com.

PACHTER, HERSCH LEON, surgeon, educator; MD, NYU, 1971. Diplomate Am. Bd. Surgery, 1999. Intern NYU Med. Ctr., 1971—72, resident in surgery, 1972—76; George David Stewart prof. of surgery NYU; chair NYU Langone Med. Ctr. Author: Low dose heparin: bleeding and wound complications in the surgical patient. A prospective randomized study, 1977, Heparin, 1977, Experience with routine open abdominal paracentesis, 1978, Traumatic injuries of the portal vein. The role of acute ligation, 1979, Simplified distal pancreatectomy with the Auto Suture stapler: preliminary clinical observations, 1979, Recent concepts in the treatment of hepatic trauma: facts and fallacies, 1979, The radiation-injured bowel, 1979, Open and percutaneous paracentesis and lavage for abdominal trauma: a randomized prospective study, 1981, Evolving concepts in splenic surgery: splenorrhaphy versus splenectomy and postsplenectomy drainage: experience in 105 patients, 1981, Iatrogenic intussusception: a complication of long intestinal tubes, 1982, various publs. Office: New York University Langone Medical Center 530 1st Ave Ste 6C New York NY 10016 Office Phone: 212-263-7302. Office Fax: 212-263-7511.

PACIA, STEVEN V., neurologist, educator; MD, Yale U., 1989. Diplomate Am. Bd. Neurology, 1992, Am. Bd. Psychiatry and Neurology-clin. neurophysiology, 2007. Intern St. Vincent's Med. Ctr., 1988—91; resident Yale- New Haven Hosp., Conn., 1988—91, clin. fellow, 1991—92, fellow in epilepology, 1991—93; dir. neurology Lenox Hill Hosp.; assoc. prof. neurology NYU, asst. prof. neurophysiology; dir. neurophysiology NYU Langone Med. Ctr., prin. investigator. Author: The timing of post-surgical seizures after epilepsy surgery predicts subsequent seizure recurrence and long-term outcome, 2005, Predicting long-term seizure outcome after resective epilepsy surgery: the multicenter study, 2005, Changes in depression and anxiety after resective surgery for epilepsy, 2005, Time-frequency analysis as an adjunct to intracranial EEG interpretation, 2005, Magnetic source imaging for pre-surgical lateralization of refractory epilepsy, 2006, Patient-perceived impact of resective epilepsy surgery, 2006, Inter- and intra-modality reliability of magnetoencephalographic somatosensory localization utilizing pneumatic digit and median nerve stimulation, 2006, Race/ethnicity, sex, and socioeconomic status as predictors of outcome after surgery for temporal lobe epilepsy, 2006, Employment outcomes following resective epilepsy surgery, 2007, A subcortical network of dysfunction in TLE measured by magnetic resonance spectroscopy, 2007, Epilepsy in Treated Brain Tumor Patients, 2009, numerous publs. Office: New York University Langone Medical Center 223 E 34th St New York NY 10016 Office Phone: 646-558-0867. Office Fax: 646-385-7164.

PACIFICO, ALBERT DOMINICK, cardiovascular surgeon; b. Bklyn., Sept. 24, 1940; s. Dominick Vincent and Amelia Catherine (Jannelli) P.; m. Vicki Lynne Overton, May 16, 1980; children: Albert D., Nicole M., Paul V. BS, St. Johns U., 1960; MD, N.J. Coll. Medicine, 1964. Diplomate Am. Bd. Surgery, Am. Bd. Thoracic Surgery. Med. intern Jersey City Med. Ctr., Seton Gall Coll. Medicine, 1964-65; asst. resident in surgery Mayo Clinic, Rochester, Minn., 1965-67; research fellow in surgery U. Ala., Birmingham, 1967-69, sr. resident, then chief resident surgery, resident in thoracic and cardiovascular surgery, 1968-72, mem. faculty dept. surgery, 1970—2006, prof. surgery, 1978-83, John W. Kirklin prof. cardiovascular surgery, 1983—2006, vice chmn. dept. surgery, 1990, dir. divsn. cardiothoracic surgery, 1984—2006, dir. Congenital Heart Disease Diagnosis and Treatment Ctr., 1985—2006; ret., 2006. Mem. staff gen., thoracic and cardiovascular surgery Univ. Hosp., Birmingham, 1972-2006, VA Hosp., Birmingham, 1972-2006; mem. staff Children's Hosp., Birmingham, 1971-2006, chief gen., thoracic and cardiovascular surgery, 1984-2006. Author: (with others) Pediatric Cardiac Surgery, 1985, Cardiology, 1985, Textbook of Surgery, 13th edit., 1986, The Treatment of Congenital Cardiac Anomalies, 1986, Perspectives in Pediatric Cardiology, 1988, Current Therapy in Cardiothoracic Surgery, 1989, Decision Making in Surgery of the Chest, 1989, Cardiac Surgery: Cyanotic Congential Heart Disease, 1989, Reoperation in Cardiac Surgery, 1989, others; mem. editorial bd. Am. Jour. Cardiology, 1983-2006, Heart and Vessel, 1985-2006, Jour. Cardiac Surgery, 1985-2006; cons. editorial referee Ala. Jour. Med. Scis., 1974-75; contbr. articles to med. jours. Fellow ACS, Am. Coll. Cardiology, Am. Surg. Assn.; mem. AMA, Ala. State Med. Soc., Jefferson County Med. Soc., Am. Heart Assn. (Paul Dudley White Internat. Svc. Citation 1977), Am. Assn. Thoracic Surgery, Soc. Thoracic Surgeons, Am. Surg. Soc., Internat. Coll. Pediatrics, John Kirklin Soc., Congentital Heart Surgeons Soc., Assn. Acad. Surgery, Ala. chpt. Mayo Clinic Alumni Assn., Panamanian Soc. Cardiology (hon.), Peruvian Soc. Thoracic and Cardiovascular Surgery (hon.), Soc. Nat. Inst. Cardiology Mex. (hon.), Cardiac Soc. Australia and New Zealand (corr.), Peruvian Soc. Cardiology (corr.), Alpha Omega Alpha. Republican. Roman Catholic.

PACKARD, JOHN MALLORY, physician, researcher; b. Saranac Lake, NY, Sept. 25, 1920; s. Edward Newman and Mary Bissell (Betts) P.; m. Ann Maurine Schoonover, June 15, 1944; children: Michael David, John Mallory, Ann Maurine, Mary Betts, Charles Edward, Kris Asvananda, Frank Schoonover, Charlotte Mellen. BA, Yale U., 1942; MD, Harvard U., 1945. Diplomate Am. Bd. Internal Medicine. Intern Presbyn. Hosp., NYC, 1945-46; resident in internal medicine Peter Bent Brigham Hosp., Boston, 1948-49; practice medicine specializing in internal medicine and cardiology Pensacola, Fla., 1954-68; prof. medicine, assoc. dean Med. Sch. U. Ala., Birmingham, 1968-76; exec. dir. Ala. Regional Med. Program, Birmingham, 1968-73; corp. v.p. med. edn. Bapt. Med. Centers, Birmingham, 1976-92; ret., 1992. Contbr. articles to med. jours. Served with USN, 1946-54. Fellow ACP, Am. Coll. Cardiology, AHA; mem. Jefferson County Med. Soc., Med. Assn. Ala., AMA, Am. Soc. Internal Medicine, Ala. Soc. Internal Medicine (pres. 1981-82), Alpha Omega Alpha. Republican. Episcopalian. Personal E-mail: jmpackard@juno.com.

PACLT, IVO, psychiatrist, educator; b. Prague, Czech Republic, Feb. 1, 1949; MD, Charles U. Prague, 1973. Assoc. prof., psychiat. dept., 1st med. faculty Charles U., 1992—2011. Office: Ke Karlovu 11 Prague 128 00 Czech Republic Business E-Mail: ivopaclt@seznam.cz.

PACLT, JURAJ, research scientist; b. Prague, Czechoslovakia, Jan. 15, 1925; s. Emil and Marie (Srámková) P.; m. Viera Vanecková, June 8, 1949; children: Helena, Roman, Eva. D Natural Scis., Charles U., Prague, 1949; PhD, Slovak Acad. Scis., Bratislava, 1972. Researcher Forest Products Rsch. Inst., Bratislava, Slovakia, 1949-54; jr. rsch. scientist Slovak Acad. Scis., Biol. Inst., Bratislava, 1954-62; sr. rsch. scientist Slovak Acad. Scis., Inst. Exptl. Phytopathol. and Entomol., Ivanka pri Dunaji, 1962-89. Author: Technique of Biological Wood Exploring, 1953, Wood Defects, 1954, Biologie der primär flügellosen Insekten, 1956, Farbenbestimmung in der Biologie, 1958; contbr. over 300 articles to profl. jours.

PADBERG, FRANK T., JR., surgeon, educator; b. Chgo., Aug. 30, 1947; BA, Vanderbilt U., 1969; MD, U. Ark., 1973. Prof. surgery UMDNJ-NJ Med. Sch. Surgery, 1981—. Chief, sect. vascular surgery VA-NJ Healthcare Sys., 1981. Named one of Best Doctor's, Castle Connolly. Fellow: ACS, Soc. Vascular Surgery; mem.: Am. Assn. Surgery Trauma, Peripheral Vascular Surgery Soc., Am. Venous Forum. Avocations: cartography, photography. Office: UMDNJ-NJ Med Sch Ste 740 Newark NJ 07103-2499 Office Fax: 973-972-9375. E-mail: padbergjr@aol.com.

PADILLA, MEDINA JOSE ALFREDO, electrical engineer, researcher; b. Iguala, Guerrero, Mexico, Apr. 21, 1969; s. Barrera Jose Padilla and Honorato Esther Medina; m. Rodriguez S. Araceli Montoya, Dec. 21, 1997; 1 child, Montoya Itzeen Araceli. Degree in elec. engring., Technol. Inst. Celaya, 1991; MS, Guanajuato U., 1995; D, Rsch. Ctr. In Optics, 2002. Tech. supr. Grupo Gamesa, Celaya, Guanajuato, Mexico, 1994—95; prof. Benavente U., Leon, 1999—2001; assoc. rschr. Rsch. Ctr. In Optics, 1997—2002; chief of electronic lab. Technol. Inst. Celaya, 1995—96, postgrad. coord., 2003—; tech. chair Internat. Power Electronics Congress, 2002—. Co-author: (chapter of book) Intelligent Sensory Evaluation; contbr. articles to profl. jours. Achievements include research in Design Of Software To The Evaluation Of Visual Capabilities Of Human Observers Using Roc (Receiver Operating Characteristic) Theory And Fuzzy Logic; Software To Detect Psychomotricity Visual Problems In Children; Software To Detect Visual Capabilities Of Human Observers In A Task Of Quality Control; An Analisys Of The Roc Theory Under The Assumptions Gaussian And Exponential; An Analisys Of The Detectability Index Under The Roc (Receiver Operating Characteristic) Theory Using Fuzzy Logic. Avocations: soccer, chess, camping. Home: Matamoros Prolongation # 203 Guanajuato Juventino Rosas 38000 Mexico Office: Technological Institute Of Celaya Avenida Tecnologico Y Cubas S/N Guanajuato Celaya 38010 Mexico Office Fax: 461 611 79 79. Business E-Mail: apadilla@itc.mx.

PADLAN, EDUARDO AGUSTIN, retired immunologist; b. Manila, Philippines, Aug. 31, 1940; s. Feliciano Macaraeg Padlan and Aida Almeda Agustin; m. Rosemarie Dino, Dec. 10, 1960; children: Josefina Padlan Simpson, Ramon Eduardo, Cristina Padlan Packard, Anna Maria, Cecilia Padlan Mikita. BS, U. of the Philippines, Diliman, Quezon City, 1960; PhD, Johns Hopkins U., Balt., 1968. Asst. prof. U. The Philippines, Quezon City, Philippines, 1968—69, adj. prof., 2002—; rsch. scientist Johns Hopkins U., Balt., 1978—83, rsch. assoc., 1969—71; vis. scientist NIH, Bethesda, Md., 1971—78, rsch. physicist, 1983—2000. Editor: ImmunoMethods vol. 1 no. 2, 1992; co-editor: Current Opinion in Biotechnology vol. 8, 1997; mem. editl. bd.: Molecular Immunology, 1980—99, Receptor, 1990—96, Macromolecular Structures, 1993—97; author: (book) Antibody-Antigen Complexes, 1994; contbr. articles to more than 140 sci. publs. Mem.: Am. Soc. for Biochemistry and Molecular Biology, Am. Assn. Immunologists, Philippine Am. Acad. Sci. and Engring., Nat. Acad. Sci. and Tech. Philippines (corr.). Achievements include patents in field; patents pending in field. Home: 4006 Simms Dr Kensington MD 20895 Office: Univ of the Philippines Velasquez St Diliman Quezon City 1101 Philippines Personal E-mail: edpadlan@aol.com. Business E-Mail: epadlan@upmsi.ph.

PADMAN, REMA, engineering educator, researcher; b. Doha, Qatar, June 1, 1958; PhD, U. Tex., Austin, 1986. Prof., mgmt. sci. & healthcare informatics Carnegie Mellon U., 1989—. Mem.: Assn. Computing Machinery, Inst. Ops. Rsch. and Mgmt. Sci., Am. Med. Informatics Assn. Office: Carnegie Mellon University H John Heinz III Sch Pub Policy & Mgmt 5000 Forbes Ave Pittsburgh PA 15213 Business E-Mail: rpadman@cmu.edu.

PADMANABHAN, VIVEK, dentist, educator; b. Bangalore, Karnataka, India, Dec. 11, 1978; BDS, Govt. Dental Coll. and Hosp., 2002; MDS, A.B.Shetty Inst. Dental Scis. and Hosp., 2008. Asst. prof. Vyas Dental Coll. and Hosp., 2008—11, Triveni Dental Coll. and Hosp., 2011—, adj. prof., 2011. Recipient Best Poster award, Indian Soc. Pedodontics and Preventive Children Dentistry. Avocations: music, photography. Office: Triveni Dental Coll and Hosp Bilaspur Chattisgarh 495001 India E-mail: vivek_pdr@rediffmail.com.

PAE, CHI-UN, psychiatrist, researcher; b. Pusan, Republic of Korea, May 1, 1967; s. Seok-Hyun Pae and Soon-Ahk Jang; m. You-Jeong Lee; 1 child, Ga-Young. MD, MS, Cath. U. Korea, 1992. Lic. physician The Korean Bd. Medicine Korean Med. Assn., 1992. Asst. prof. The Cath. U. Korea, Seoul, 2000—. Dir. Lab. Psychiatry Catholic U. Med. Coll., Seoul, Republic of Korea, 2002—. Contbr. articles to profl. jours. Grantee, Korea Inst. of S & T Evaluation and Planning, 2002, GlaksoSmithKline, 2003, Ministry Pub. Health and Welfare, 2003, AstraZeneca Internat., 2004, Eli Lilly, 2004. Mem.: Korean Neuropsychiatric Assn. (sec. acad. divsn. 2002—, Young Investigator award 2002), Korean Coll. Neuropsychopharmacology (sec. 2003—, Young Investigator award 2003), Korean Soc. Biol. Psychiatry (sec. academic divsn. 2003—), Korean Soc. Depressive and Bipolar Disorders (sec. 2003—). Achievements include research in psychiatric genetics and clinical trials of psychopharmacology. Office: Kangnam St Mary's Hospital (Psychiatry) 505 Banpo Dong Seocho Gu Seoul 137 701 Republic of Korea Office Fax: 82-2-536-8744. Business E-Mail: pae@catholic.ac.kr.

PAES, FABIO M., radiologist; b. Brazil, Oct. 30, 1980; MD, U. Fed. da Bahia, 2005. Physician U. Miami, Jackson Meml. Hosp., 2006—. Mem.: Am. Bd. Radiology, SNM, Radiol. Soc. N.Am. Office: 1611 NW 12th Ave WW-279 Miami FL 33131 Office Fax: 305-585-5743. Personal E-mail: fabiompaes@yahoo.com.

PAEZ, DAVID, oncologist; b. Madrid, Nov. 29, 1979; MD, U. Autonoma Barcelona, 2003. Med. oncologist Hosp. de la Santa Creu i Sant Pau, 2004—. Rio Hortega fellow. Mem.: SEOM. Home: C/ Valencia 329 4 2a Barcelona 08009 Spain Business E-Mail: dpaez@santpau.cat.

PAFROELICHER, VIC, medical educator; b. Pa., Nov. 3, 1941; MD, PITT, 1967. Prof. Stanford U., 1992—. Fellow: ACC. Home: 1028 Ringwood Ave Menlo Park CA 94025 Personal E-mail: vicmdatg@gmail.com.

PAGÁN, GILBERTO, JR., psychologist; b. San Juan, Dec. 30, 1950; Exch. student, SUNY, Albany, 1969-70; BA in Psychology magna cum laude, U. P.R., 1972; MS in Devel. Psychology, Rutgers U., 1974, PhD in Clin. Psychology, 1984. Lic. psychologist, N.J.; cert. sch. psychology. Psychometrician Well Baby Clinic of New Brunswick, N.J., 1972-73; staff psychologist Community Orgn. for Mental Health and Retardation, Inc., Phila., 1976-77; intern in clin. psychology Multimodal Therapy Inst., Kingston, NJ, 1979-80; sch. psychologist New Brunswick Pub. Sch. System, 1980-83; mental health clinician Community Mental Health Ctr. U. Medicine and Dentistry N.J., Piscataway, 1983-93; sch. psychologist Perth Amboy Pub. Sch. Sys., 1993-95; pvt. practice clin. psychology Newark, 1988—2011; sch. psychologist Jersey City Pub. Sch. Sys., 1995-98, Elizabeth (N.J.) Pub. Sch. Sys., 1998—2009. Assoc. in psychiatry Univ. of Medicine and Dentistry of N.J., Piscataway, 1988-98; field supr. Rutgers U., New Brunswick, N.J., 1988—; cons. in field to clients including Bloomfield Pub. Sch. System, Div. of Youth and Family Svcs. of State of N.J., Project Head Start, Plainfield, N.J. Columnist San Juan Star, 1990-93, 97-98, El Hispano, Phila., 1977-78; contbr. profl. publs.; presenter in field. Pres. N.J. chpt. Nat. Com. for Puerto Rican Statehood, 1990-95; mem. U.S. Coun. for Puerto Rico Statehood, 2004-. NIMH fellow, 1978-79; predoctoral rsch. fellow Inst. for Rsch. in Human Devel., Divsn. Psychol. Studies of Ednl. Testing Svc., Princeton, N.J., 1974-75; recipient P.R. Psychol. Assn. award, 1972, Puerto Rican Action Bds. Parents Assn. award 1985; inducted into Nat. Honor Soc. in Psychology, 1973. Mem. APA, NEA, N.J. Edn. Assn. Democrat. Roman Catholic. Avocation: swimming. Office: 467 Mount Prospect Ave Newark NJ 07104-2907 Home Phone: 732-324-2322; Office Phone: 973-483-0448.

PAGANELLI, CHARLES VICTOR, physiologist, educator; b. NYC, Feb. 13, 1929; s. Charles Victor and Mary Paganelli; m. Barbara Harriet Slauson, Sept. 18, 1954; children: William, Kathryn, Peter, Robert, John. AB, Hamilton Coll., Clinton, NY, 1950; MA, Harvard U., Cambridge, Mass., 1952, PhD, 1957. Instr. physiology U. Buffalo, 1958-60, asst. prof., 1960-63; assoc. prof. SUNY, Buffalo, 1963-71, prof. physiology, 1971-97, disting. svc. prof., 1997—. Interim chair SUNY, Buffalo, 1991-98, emeritus, 1998. Editor: Physiological Function in Special Environments, 1990; contbr. articles to profl. jours. Recipient Elliott Coues award Am. Ornithologists Union, 1981, Newman award 1998. Mem.: Am. Physiol. Soc., Gold Humanism Honor Soc., Phi Beta Kappa, Sigma Xi, Alpha Omega Alpha. Office Phone: 716-829-2738. Business E-Mail: cvp@buffalo.edu.

PAGE, DAVID C., biologist, educator; MD magna cum laude, Harvard Med. Sch. Mem. Whitehead Inst. for Biomedical Rsch., 1986—, interim dir., 2004—05, dir., 2005—; prof. biology MIT; investigator Howard Hughes Med. Inst. Editor Current Opinion in Genetics and Develop.; assoc. editor Ann. Rev. Human Genetics and Genomics. Recipient Searle Scholar's award, 1989, Amory prize, Am. Acad. Arts and Sciences, 1997, Curt Stern award, Am. Soc. Human Genetics, 2003; MacArthur Found. prize fellowship, 1986. Mem.: NAS, Inst. Medicine. Achievements include mapping and cloning the Y chromosome; publishing the complete sequence of Y chromosome. Office: Whitehead Institute Nine Cambridge Ctr Cambridge MA 02142-1479 Office Phone: 617-258-5203. E-mail: page_admin@wi.mit.edu. *

PAGE, ERNEST, retired medical educator; b. Cologne, Germany, May 30, 1927; came to US, 1936, naturalized, 1942. s. Max Ernest and Eleanor (Kohn) P.; m. Eva Veronica Gross, June 5, 1967; 1 son, Thomas J. AB, U. Calif., Berkeley, 1949; MD, U. Calif., San Francisco, 1952. Intern Peter Bent Brigham Hosp., Boston, 1952-53, resident, 1953-54, 57-58; rsch. assoc. Harvard Med. Sch., 1957-65; assoc. prof. medicine and physiology U. Chgo. Med. Sch., 1965-69, prof. physiology & cardiology, 1968—98, prof. emeritus, 1998—. Editor: (jour.) Am, Jour. Physiology: Heart and Circulatory Physiology, 1981—86; editor: (sects.) Handbook of Physiology Vol. I The Heart, 2002. Served with AUS, 1945-46. Established investigator Am. Heart Assn., 1959-65. Mem. Am. Physiol. Soc., Biophys. Soc., Am. Soc. Cell Biology, Soc. Gen. Physiologists, Assn. Am. Physicians. Home: ALFASI 33 APT 7 Jerusalem 92302 Israel Personal E-mail: pageeva@yahoo.com.

PAGE, JOHN GARDNER, toxicologist, consultant; b. Milw., Wis., Sept. 14, 1940; s. Raymond G. and Leone B. (Churchill) P.; m. Joyce Ann Krueger, July 7, 1962; children: Teresa Ann, Kimberly Christine. BS, U. Wis.-Madison, 1963, MS, 1966, PhD, 1967. Diplomate Am. Bd. Toxicology. Sr. scientist NIH, Bethesda, Md., 1967-69, Eli Lilly Co., Indpls., 1969-77; dir. toxicology and pathology Rhone Poulenc, Inc., Ashland, Ohio, 1977-79; dir. toxicology Toxigenics, Inc., Decatur, Ill., 1979-83; sr. rsch. advisor Battelle Meml. Inst., Columbus, Ohio, 1983-87; dir. preclin. toxicology So. Rsch. Inst., Birmingham, Ala., 1987—2004; dir. NGVL-Nat. Toxicology Ctr., 2001—06; disting. scientist So. Rsch. Inst., Birmingham, Ala., 2004—06; CEO, chief scientist Rockhill Toxicology Cons. LLC, 2006—. Adj. prof. U. Ill., 1981-83, ctr. for AIDS rsch., U. Ala., Birmingham, 1987—, sch. pub. health, 1988—, sch. medicine, 1997—. Contbr. articles to profl. jours. Bd. dirs. Am. Cancer Soc., Greenfield, Ind., 1973-77. Recipient Rennebohm Outstanding Tchr.'s award U. Wis., 1964. Mem. AAAS, Fedn. Am. Socs. Exptl. Biology, Am. Soc. Pharm. Exptl. Therapeutics, Soc. Toxicology, Am. Coll. Toxicology, Internat. Soc. for Study Xenobiotics, Sigma Xi, Rho Chi. Avocations: photography, hiking, fishing. Home and Office: 3700 Rockhill Rd Birmingham AL 35223-1562 Office Phone: 205-967-2776. Personal E-mail: toxman1@bellsouth.net.

PAGE, LARRY KEITH, neurosurgeon, educator; b. Rayville, La., July 7, 1933; s. Ardie Lee and Edris Estelle (Chaney) P.; m. Joan Marie Doherty, Aug. 27, 1960; children: Matthew, Elizabeth, Jennifer. BS, La. State U., 1955, MD, 1958. Diplomate: Am. Bd. Neurol. Surgery. Intern Grad. Hosp., U. Pa., Phila., 1958-59; resident Children's Hosp. and Peter Bent Brigham Hosp., Boston, 1962-66; assoc. neurosurgeon Children's Hosp., assoc. surgeon Peter Bent Brigham Hosp., 1966-71; cons. Beverly Hosp., Mass., Robert Breck Brigham Hosp., Boston, Pondville Hosp., Boston, West Roxbury VA Hosp., Boston VA Hosp.; clin. instr. neurosurgery Harvard U., Boston, 1966-71; prof., vice chmn. dept. neurosurgery U. Miami, Fla., 1971-95, prof. emeritus Fla., 1995—, chief div. pediatric neurosurgery Fla., 1971-95; neurosurgeon VA Hosp., Miami, 1971-88, Jackson Meml. Hosp., Miami, 1971-95, dir. neurosurgery, 1994-95; chief neurosurgery Mt. Sinai Hosp., Miami, 1990-94. Chmn. CSF Shunt Standard Com. for ASTM, ISO, AANS & CNS, 1974-86, cons. neurosurg. FDA, 1976-79, NASA, 1979-80 Mem. editorial bds., contbr. articles to profl. jours. Served to lt. USN, 1959-62. Mem. ACS, Am. Acad. Pediatrics, Am. Assn. Neurol. Surgeons, Internat. Soc. Pediatric Neurosurgery, Am. Soc. Pediatric Neurosurgery, Congress Neurol. Surgeons, Fellowship of Acad. Neurosurgeons, Internat. Neurosurg. Forum, Royal Soc. Medicine, Soc. for Rsch. in Hydrocephalus and Spina Bifida, New Eng. Neurosurg. Soc., Fla. Neurosurg. Soc. (pres. 1989-90), Mass. Med. Soc., Dade County Med. Assn., Internat. Palm Soc., Alpha Omega Alpha. Roman Catholic. Home and Office: 13845 SW 73rd Ct Miami FL 33158-1213

PAGE, LESLEY ANN, nurse midwife, educator; d. Leslie Edwin and Ivy Page; m. Mark David Starr, Aug. 23, 1986; 1 child, David Edwin Page-Starr; m. Philip McDonald Weatherston, Mar. 28, 1968 (div. Mar. 1, 1985); children: Leslie Iain Page Weatherston, Anna Isobel Weatherston. BA, Open U., Eng., 1977; MS, U. Edinburgh, 1978; PhD, U. Tech. Sydney, 2005. Cert.: Cardiff Law Sch. U. Cardiff (expert witness) 2008; RN Nursing and Midwifery Coun., 1965, registered midwife, 1966, RN tchr., 1978, registered midwife tchr., 1994. Staff nurse St. Bartholomews Hosp., London, 1966—67; night sister Royal Infirmary, Edinburgh, 1967—68; ward sister Western Gen. Hosp., Edinburgh, 1968—72; coord. continuing edn. Grace Hosp., Vancouver, BC, Canada, 1980—86; dir. midwifery John Radcliffe Maternity Svc., Oxford, England, 1986—92, prof. midwifery practice Thames Valley U. and Queen Charlotte's Hosp., 1992—2000; head dept. midwifery Children's and Women's Health Ctr. and Midwifery Dept. Providence Health Care, Vancouver, 2000—01; head midwifery Royal Free NHS Trust, London, 2002—03, Guy's and St. Thomas' NHS Trust, 2003—06; vis. prof. midwifery King's Coll., London, 2004—; midwife Oxford Radcliffe Hosps. Trust, England, 2006; adj. prof. U. Tech. Sydney, 2006—. Expert maternity group Dept. Health, London, 1992—93; dep. chmn. English Nat. Bd. Nursing Midwifery and Health Vis., London, 1993—99; adviser House Commons Health Select Com., London, 2002—03, King's Fund, London, 2006—08. Editor: (book) The New Midwifery: Science and Sensitivity in Practice, The New Midwifery: Science and Sensitivity in Practice 2nd edition, Effective Group Practice In Midwifery:Working with Women in Childbirth. Adviser Cross Rds. Women's Ctr., London, 2002; patron Douglas Homerton Prison, London, 2002. Recipient Jubilee award for Nursing, Hammersmith Hosp. Sch. Nursing. Fellow: Royal Coll. Midwives, Royal Soc.Medicine (coun. mem. newborn and maternity forum 2002, pres. elect maternity and newborn forum 2009); mem.: Med. Justice. Labor. Mem. Ch. Eng. Achievements include research in evaluation of one-to-one midwifery. Avocations: reading, walking, swimming, skiing, travel.

PAGE, RICHARD LEIGHTON, cardiologist, medical educator, researcher; b. San Diego, Mar. 8, 1958; s. Ellis Batten and Elizabeth Latimer (Thaxton) P.; m. Jean Reynolds, Oct. 12, 1985; children: Franklin Reynolds, Gillian Grace, Edward Batten. BS in Zoology magna cum laude, Duke U., 1980, MD, 1984; degree in Med. Mgmt., U. Wash. Ext., Seattle, 2007. Diplomate Nat. Bd. Med. Examiners, Am. Bd. Internal Medicine, subspecialties cardiovascular disease and clin. cardiac electrophysiology; lic. physician, Wis. Rsch. fellow in pharmacology Columbia Presbyn. Med. Ctr., 1982-83; intern dept. medicine Mass. Gen. Hosp., Boston, 1984-85, resident dept. medicine, 1985-87; cardiology fellow clin. electrophysiology Duke U. Med. Ctr., Durham, N.C., 1987-89, clin. cardiology fellow, 1989, lectr. medicine divsn. cardiology, 1989-90, assoc. in medicine, 1990, asst. prof., dir. clin. electrophysiology lab., 1990-92; asst. prof. medicine U. Tex. Southwestern Med. Ctr., Dallas, 1992-95, assoc. prof., 1995-2001, tenured prof., 2001—02; tenured prof. and head cardiology U. Wash. Sch. Medicine, Seattle, 2002—09, Robert A. Bruce endowed chair in cardiovascular rsch., 2002—09; chmn. dept. medicine U. Wis. Sch. Medicine and Pub. Health, 2009—; George R. and Elain Love tenured prof. medicine, 2009—. Dir. sect. clin. electrophysiology U. Tex. Southwestern Med. Ctr., Dallas, 1992; dir. clin. electrophysiology lab., arrhythmia and pacemaker svc., Parkland Meml. Hosp., Dallas, 1992; holder Dallas Heart Ball Chair in Cardiac Arrhythmia Rsch., 1997; dir. Stanley J. Sarnoff Endowment for Rsch. in Cardiovasc. Sci., Inc., Bethesda, Md., 1990, co-chmn., 1992; Dallas Heart Ball chair in Cardiac Arrhythmia Rsch., 1997. Mem. editl. bd. Cardiac Chronicle, 1993, Am. Heart Jour., 1998—, Am. Jour. Cardiology, 1999—, Circulation 2001-, Pacing and Clinical Electrophysiology, 2004-, Journal Cardiovascular Electrophysiology, 2004-, Heart Rhythm Journal, 2007-; author: (with others) Manual of Clinical Problems in Cardiology, 5th edit., 1995; contbr. articles to profl. jours., chpt. to book. Alpha Omega Alpha, 1984; Sarnoff Endowment fellow, 1982, Sarnoff scholar, 1987. Fellow Stanley J. Sarnoff Soc., Am. Heart Assn., Am. Coll. Cardiology, Heart Rhythm Soc. (pres., 2009-2010), ACP, Alpha Omega Alpha; mem. Assn. U. Cardiologists, Am. Clin. and Climatol. Assn., Assn. Profs. Medicine. Episcopalian. Avocations: tennis, sailing. Office: University Wisconsin Sch Medicine & Public Health 1685 Highland Ave Suite 5000 Madison WI 53705-2281

PAGE, ROY CHRISTOPHER, periodontist, scientist, educator; b. Campobello, SC, Feb. 7, 1932; s. Milton and Anny Mae (Eubanks) P. BA, Berea Coll., 1953; DDS, U. Md., 1957; PhD, U. Wash., 1967; ScD (hon.), Loyola U., Chgo., 1983. Cert. in periodontics. Pvt. practice periodontics, Seattle, 1963-98; asst. prof. U. Wash. Schs. Medicine and Dentistry, Seattle, 1967-70, prof., 1974—2002, Disting. prof. dentistry, 1996-98, dir. Ctr. Research in Oral Biology, 1976-96; dir. grad. edn. U. Wash. Sch. Dentistry, 1976-80, dir. rsch. Seattle, 1976-94, dir. Regional Clin. Dental Rsch. Ctr., 1990—2008, assoc. dean rsch., 1994-2000, prof. emeritus, 2003—. Vis. scientist MRC Labs., London, 1971-72; cons., lectr. in field; fellow Pierre Fauchard Acad. Author: Periodontal Disease, 1977, 2d edit., 1990, Periodontitis in Man and Other Animals, 1982. Recipient Gold Medal award U. Md., 1957; recipient Career Devel. award NIH, 1967-72, Disting. Alumnus award U. Wash. Sch. Dentistry, 2000. Fellow Internat. Coll. Dentists, Am. Coll. Dentists, Am. Acad. Periodontology (Gies award 1982, fellowship award 1989, spl. citation 1998); mem. ADA (Norton Rose award for clin. rsch. 1998), Am. Assn. Dental Rsch. (pres. 1982-83, disting. scientist award 2001), Am. Soc. Exptl. Pathology, Internat. Assn. Dental Rsch. (pres. 1987, basic periodontal rsch. award 1977). Home: 5583 171st Ave SE Bellevue WA 98006-5503 Office Phone: 206-543-5599. E-mail: roypage@u.washington.edu.

PAGEL, PAUL STANLEY, cardiac anesthesiologist; b. Madison, Wis., Dec. 6, 1957; s. Gerald Gordon and Mary Ellen (Young) P.; m. Judith A. May, Sept. 13, 1996. BS, Carroll Coll., 1979; MD, Med. Coll. Wis., 1986, MS, 1991, PhD, 1994. Cert. Am. Bd. Anesthesiology, 1991, Nat. Bd. Echocardiography, 1998. Intern in medicine St. Josephs Hosp., Milw., 1986-87; anesthesiology resident Med. Coll. Wis., Milw., 1987-90, fellow in anesthesiology rsch., 1990—93, instr. cardiac anesthesiology, 1990—93, asst. prof., 1994—96, assoc. prof., 1996—99, prof. and dir. cardiac anesthesia, 1999—. Assoc. examiner Am. Bd. Anesthesiology, 2000—; sr. editor ABA/ASA Written Exam., 2005—. Contbr. articles to profl. jours.; editl. bd. Anesthesiology, Jour. of Cardiothoracic and Vascular Anesthesia, Anesth Analg Faculty 1000 Medicine. Disting. Alumnus award, Carroll Coll., 2004; named one of Best Drs. in America, 2009. Fellow: European Soc. Cardiology, Am. Soc. Echocardiography, Am. Heart Assn., Am. Coll. Chest Physicians, Am. Coll. Cardiology. Office: Zablocki VA Med Ctr 5000 W National Ave Milwaukee WI 53295 Office Phone: 414-384-2000 Ext. 42417. Office Fax: 414-384-2939. Business E-Mail: pspagel@mcw.edu.

PAGÈS, JEAN-MARIE, microbiologist, director; b. Marseille, France, Nov. 15, 1951; MD, PhD, U. Aix Marseille II, 1975, degree, 1983. Dir. U. Rsch. Team, 2002—08, UMR-MD1, Membrane Transporters, Chemoresistance and Drug-Design, 2008—. Dir. rsch. INSERM-Nat. Inst. Health, France, 2006. Decorated Honour medal Ministére de Défense; recipient Eloi Collery prix, Acad. Nat. Médecine; grant, Astra/Zeneca/ESMID. Mem.: Soc. Française Microbiology, Am. Soc. Microbiology. Avocations: history, reading, mountain climbing. Office: Faculté Médecine 27 Bd Jean Moulin Marseille 13385 France Business E-Mail: jean-marie.pages@univmed.fr.

PAGNANI, MICHAEL JOSEPH, orthopaedic surgeon; b. Endicott, NY, Apr. 23, 1961; s. Bruno and Patricia Ann Connors P.; m. Kelly Jackson, May 14, 1988; children: Sarah, Connor. MD, Vanderbilt U., 1987. Diplomate Am. Bd. Orthopaedic Surgery. Intern Baylor U., Dallas, 1987-88; resident in orthop. surgery The Hosp. for Spl. Surgery-Cornell U., NYC, 1988-92, fellow in sports medicine, 1992-93; pvt. practice The Lipscomb Clinic, Nashville, 1993, Nashville Knee & Shoulder, Nashville; attending orthop. surgeon Centennial Med. Ctr., Nashville, 1993—, St. Thomas Hosp., Nashville, 1993—; clin. asst. prof., orthop., rehabilitation Vanderbilt U., Nashville, 1993—2002. Bd. dir. Nashville Sports Coun., 1997-2002; asst. orthop. cons. St. John's U., 1992-93; orthop. cons. Tenn. Technological U., 1993-94, Nashville Xpress Baseball Team, 1994, Chgo. White Sox Baseball Orgn., 1995-97, Pitts. Pirates Baseball Orgn., 1998-2003, Miami Dolphins, 2001-; team physician NY Pub. Sch. Athletic League, 1988-92, numerous Nashville area high schools, 1993-, Elite Runners, Country Music Marathon, 2000-2003; orthop. team physician, Nashville Sounds Baseball team, 1994-2003; asst. team physician, NY Giants Football team, 1992-93, NY Mets, 1992-93; med. cons. Ohio Valley Conf. Basketball Tournament, 1994-2000, NCAA Sectional Basketball Tournament, 2000; med. staff mem. US Open Tennis Championships, 1989-92; US Figure Skating Championships, 1997; head team physician, Nashville Kats arena football team, 1997-2002, Tenn. State Univ., 1993-, Nashville Predators Hockey team, 1997-2007. Cons. Am. Journal of Sports Medicine, Journal of Bone and Joint Surgery. Named Tenn. Sports Medicine Person of Yr., Tenn. Athletic Trainers' Soc., 2004. Fellow, Am. Acad. Orthop. Surgeons (mem. program com.), mem. Am. Orthop. Soc. Sports Medicine (rsch. com., 1997-), Nat. Hockey League Team Physicians' Soc., Arthroscopy Assn. N. Am., Nashville Acad. Medicine, Tenn. Med. Assn., Am. Shoulder and Elbow Surgeons (mem. program com.). Office: Nashville Knee And Shoulder Center Pllc 345 23rd Ave N Ste 301 Nashville TN 37203-1513 Office Fax: 615-329-3530.

PAGON, ROBERTA ANDERSON, pediatrician, educator; b. Boston, Oct. 4, 1945; d. Donald Grigg and Erna Louise (Goettsch) Anderson; m. Garrett Dunn Pagon Jr., July 1, 1967; children: Katharine Blye, Garrett Dunn III, Alyssa Grigg, Alexander Goettsch. BA, Stanford U., 1967; MD, Harvard U., 1972. Diplomate Am. Bd. Pediat., Am. Bd. Med. Genetics. Pediatric intern U. Wash. Affiliated Hosp., Seattle, 1972-73, resident in pediat., 1973-75; fellow in med. genetics U. Wash. Sch. Medicine, Seattle, 1976-79, asst. prof. pediat., 1979-84, assoc. prof., 1984-92, prof., 1992—. Prin. investigator, editor in chief GeneTests (www.genetests.org), Seattle, 1992—; pres. Am. Bd. Med. Genetics, 2002, 03; bd. sci. counselors Nat. Human Genome Rsch. Inst., NIH, 2000—04. Sponsor N.W. region U.S. Pony Club, 1985-94. Mem. Am. Soc. Human Genetics (bd. dirs. 2005-2007, Excellence award in Edn. 2006), March of Dimes (Col. Harland Sanders Lifetime Achievement award 2009), Am. Coll. Med. Genetics, Western Soc. Pediat. Rsch., Phi Beta Kappa. Avocations: hiking, backpacking, horseback riding. Office: Gene Tests 9725 Third Ave NE Ste 602 Seattle WA 98115 Office Phone: 206-221-4674. Business E-Mail: bpagon@u.washington.edu.

PAHISA, JAUME, oncologist; b. Sant Cugat del Valles, Barcelona, Spain, May 30, 1951; MD, U. Barcelona, 1976, PhD, 1987. Med. asst. Hosp. del Mar, Barcelona, 1986—89, Hosp. Clinic, Barcelona, 1989—97, med. cons., 1998—2002, head, sect. gynecologic oncology, 2003—10, sr. cons., 2003—, head, unit gynecologic oncology, 2010—. Assoc. med. prof. Sch. Medicine, U. Autonoma Barcelona, 1986—; assoc. editor Jour. Progresos en Obstetricia y Ginecologia, 2007—; assessor Nat. Evaluation and Foresight ANEP, Spain, 2009—. Recipient First prize, Catalan-Balear Soc. Oncology. Acad. Med. Scis. Catalonia and Balearics; grant, Ministry of Health, Health Rsch. Fund FIS PI, 2006—. Mem.: European Soc. Gynecol. Oncology, Soc. Española Cirugía Oncológica, Internat. Soc. Senology, Internat. Fedn. Ob-Gyn., Soc. Española Obstertricia y Ginecologia. Office: Villarroel 170 Barcelona 08036 Spain Office Phone: 0034932275436. Office Fax: 0034932279325. Business E-Mail: jpahisaf@ub.edu, jpahisa@clinic.ub.es.

PAHL SCHUETTE, ELFRIEDE, pediatric transplant cardiologist; d. Adam and Rosalia Pahl; m. Michael Allen Schuette, Sept. 9, 1989. MD, Northwestern U. Med. Sch., Chgo., 1983. Diplomate in pediat. cardiology Am. Bd. Pediat., 1988. Med. dir., heart transplantation Children's Meml. Hosp., Chgo., 1994—; prof. pediat. Feinberg Northwestern Sch. Medicine, Chgo., 2001—. Contbr. articles to med. jours. Fellow: Am. Acad. Pediat., Am. Coll. Cardiology; mem.: Pediat. Coun. (pres. 2010—), Internat. Soc. Heart and Lung Transplantation, Am. Transplant Soc., Am. Heart Assn., Pediatric Heart Transplant Study (sec. 2008—, treas. 2008—). Avocations: piano, travel, bicycling. Office: Children's Memorial Hosp 2300 Children's Pl Chicago IL 60614 *

PAHOR, DUSICA, ophthalmologist, consultant; b. Murska Sobota, Slovenia, Oct. 29, 1957; d. Venčeslav and Irena (Rogl) Svatina; m. Artur Pahor, Dec. 19, 1981; 1 child, Jan. MD, Med. Faculty Ljubljana, Slovenija, 1981; MS, Med. Faculty Zagreb, Croatia, 1994, PhD in Medicine, 1997. Gen. practitioner Health Inst., Maribor, Slovenia, 1981-85, pediatric ophthalmologist, 1990-92; specialist in ophthalmology Eye Clinic, Ljubljana, 1986-90; cons. in ophthalmology Teaching Hosp. Maribor, 1992—. Lectr. High Med. Sch., Maribor, 1995—; assoc. prof. med. faculty U. Ljubljana, 2001—, U. Maribor, 2004—06, prof., 2006—; vice-dean Faculty Medicine, U. Maribor, 2004—; editor-in-chief Acta Medico-Biotech., 2008—. Contbr. articles to profl. jours. Grantee European Soc. Ophthalmology, Milan, Italy, 1995. Mem. Austrian Ophthalmol. Assn., N.Y. Acad. Scis., European Soc. Cataract and Refractive Surgeons (award 1996), German Ophthalmol. Assn. Avocation: classic guitar. Home: Presernova 11 2000 Maribor Slovenia Office: Teaching Hosp Opthalmol Dpt Ljubljanska 5 2000 Maribor Slovenia Office Phone: 00386-2-321-1630. Personal E-mail: d.pahor@sb-mb.si. Business E-Mail: d.pahor@ukc-mb.si.

PAIK, CHANG NYOL, medical educator; b. Seoul, Republic Of Korea; Lic. in medicine Ministry Health, Welfare & Family Affairs, Korea, 1997, cert. in internal medicine Ministry Health, Welfare & Family Affairs, Korea, 2002, Korean Assn. Internal Medicine, 2007, cert. in gastrointestinal endoscopy Korean Soc. Gastrointestinal Endoscopy, 2006. Intern St. Mary's Hosp., Seoul, 1997—98; resident Kangnam St. Mary's Hosp., 1998—2002, clin. & rsch. fellow, 2005—07; clin. asst. prof. St. Vincent's Hosp., Suwon-si, Kyunggido, Republic of Korea, 2007—09, asst. prof., 2010—, St. Vincents Hosp. Swoon-Si Kyunggido, Republic of Korea. Office: St Vincent's Hosp Ji dong Paldalgu Suwon Kyunggido 442-723 Republic of Korea Office Fax: +82-31-253-8898. Business E-Mail: cmcu@catholic.ac.kr.

PAIK, HAE-JUNG, physician, educator; b. Seoul, Republic of Korea, Oct. 8, 1962; MD, Korea U. Med. Coll., PhD, 1987. Chmn. & prof. Gachon U. Gil Hosp. Dept. Ophthalmology, 1984—. Mem.: Korean Pediat. Ophthalmology and Strabismus Assn., Korean Ophthalmology Soc. Avocation: swimming. Office: Guwoul-dong 1198 Namdong-gu Incheon 405-760 Republic of Korea Office Fax: 82-32-460-3358.

PAIK, NAM-JONG, physiatrist, medical educator; b. Seoul, Republic of Korea, Jan. 9, 1966; MD, Seoul Nat. U., 1990, MS, 1995, PhD, 2000. Lic. Korean Bd. Rehab. Medicine, 1995, Korean Bd. Geriatric Medicine, 2001, cert. Am. Bd. Electrodiagnostic Medicine, 1998. Intern Seoul Nat. U. Hosp., 1990—91, resident, 1991—95, clin. fellow, 1998—2000; asst. prof. Seoul Nat. U., 2001; med. dir. Ctrl. Hosp. Workers Accident Med. Corp., Inchon, Republic of Korea, 1999—2001; chief dept. rehab. medicine Seoul Nat. U. Bundang Hosp., Seongnam, Republic of Korea, 2003—, coord. edn., 2003—10, dir. med. info. and media ctr., 2004—10, chief, dept. clin. support and referral ctr., 2011—; asst. dean acad. affairs Seoul Nat. U. Coll. Medicine, 2004—10, assoc. prof., 2005—, tenured prof., 2011—. Adj. instr. Seoul Nat. U. Coll. Medicine, 2000—01; postdoctoral rsch. fellow NIH, Bethesda, Md., 2005—06. Author: (online book) Dysphagia, 2006.

PAIK, SOON-YOUNG, microbiologist, educator, virologist; b. Seoul, Republic of Korea, Aug. 5, 1955; s. Sung-Yong Paik and Han-Hee Yang; m. Jae-Shin Lee, May 1, 1982; children: Bomina, Namina. BS, Korea U., 1979, MS, 1981; PhD, Hiroshima U., 1990, Korea U., 1992. Asst. prof. Hiroshima U., Japan, 1990—91; postdocdral fellow NIH, Bethesda, Md., 1991—96; asst. prof. Cath. U. Korea, 1996—2000, assoc. prof., 2000—06, prof., 2006—. Cons. FDA, Seoul, Republic of Korea, 2002—04, Nat. Inst. of Environ., Seoul, 2002—, KHIDI, Seoul, Republic of Korea, 2005—07, KCDC, Seoul, Republic of Korea, 2007—08. Editor: (book) Medical Microbiology; author: Technical Advances in AIDS Research in Human Nervous System. Exec. sec. Korean Soc. of Wash. DC and Met. Area, Md., 1995—96. Recipient Fgn. Student award, Ministry of Edn., 1986—90. Mem.: Microbiological Soc. of Korea, Korean Soc. of Microbiology, Korea Soc. of Virology (pres. 2011). Achievements include patents in field. Avocation: tennis. Office: Catholic Univ of Korea 505 Banpodong Seoul 137-701 Republic of Korea Home: 790 Yongdu-dong Dongdaemun-gu Seoul Republic of Korea Home Phone: 82-2-963-6473; Office Phone: 82-2-2258-7342. Office Fax: 82-2-535-6473. Business E-Mail: paik@catholic.ac.kr.

PAINELLI, VITOR DE SALLES, physical education educator, researcher; b. Sao Paulo, Dec. 12, 1988; Degree in Phys. Edn., U. Sao Paulo, 2010. Sci. & phys. tng. coord. Rheumatology Assessment and Conditioning Lab., 2008—10. Avocation: exercise. Office: 65 Prof Melo de Morais Ave Sao Paulo 5508-030 Brazil Business E-Mail: vitor.painelli@usp.br.

PAINTER, ROBERT LOWELL, surgeon, educator; b. Winchester, Ind., Jan. 13, 1934; s. Lowell Walter and Lillian Genevieve (Pierson) P.; m. Esther Lillian Reece, Sept. 21, 1957 (div. Sept. 1977); children: Elizabeth Haines, Bradley, Robert R., Andrew, Jane Macy-Painter; m. Nancy Sue Macy, Feb. 10, 1980. BA, Earham Coll., Richmond, Ind., 1955; MD, Ind. U., 1959. Intern and resident Hartford (Conn.) Hosp., 1959-65; resident Baylor U. Sch. Medicine, Houston, 1967-68; attending surgeon Day Kimball Hosp., Putnam, Conn., 1962-91; chmn., dir. surgery St. Francis Hosp., Hartford, 1991-98; med. practice, cons., 1999—2001. Cons. Hartford Hosp., 1969-99; assoc. prof. surgery U. Conn., 1991-99, anatomy instr., 2000—. Councilman Ct. Common Coun., Hartford, Conn., 2001—. Capt. USAF, 1965—67. Fellow ACS, Am. Coll. Physician Execs.; mem. New Eng. Surg. Soc., New Eng. Vasc. Soc., Soc. Thoracic Surgery. Republican. Avocations: hiking, gardening, bicycling, birdwatching. Home: 12 Babcock St Hartford CT 06106-1301 *

PAINTER, THEOPHILUS SHICKEL, JR., internist, allergist; b. Austin, Tex., Apr. 29, 1924; s. Theophilus Shickel and Anna Mary (Thomas) P.; m. Dorothy Bulkley, July 11, 1957; children: Dana Parkey, Amy Hur, Theophilus III. BA, U. Tex., 1944, MD, 1947. Diplomate Am. Bd. Internal Medicine, Am. Bd. Allergy and Immunology. Rotating intern Univ. Hosp., U. Mich., Ann Arbor, 1947-48, resident in internal medicine, 1948-51, fellow, jr. clin. instr., 1956-58; pvt. practice, Austin, Tex., 1958—. Capt. USAF, 1951-53. Fellow ACP, Am. Coll. Allergy and Immunology, Am. Acad. Allergy and Immunology. Avocations: fishing, carving, hunting, painting. Home: 3222 Tarryhollow Dr Austin TX 78703-1639 Office: 800 W 34th St Ste 201 Austin TX 78705-1146 Office Phone: 512-454-5821. Personal E-mail: tspainterjr@gmail.com.

PAIROJKUL, SRIVIENG, pediatrician, educator; b. Bangkok, Feb. 1, 1952; MD, Mahidol U., 1976. Cert. in pediat. pulmonolgy Royal Hosp. Sick Children, Edinburgh, 1987. Assoc. prof. Khon Kaen U., Faculty Medicine, 1981—, dir., Srinagarind Pallaitive Care Unit, 2010—. Adj. prof. Case Western Res. U., 2000—; co-chair tech. adv. com. on children in humanitarian emergencies Internat. Pediat. Assn., 2007—. Mem.: Asia Pacific Hospice Palliative Care Network, Internat. Assn. Hospice and Palliative Care. Office: Khon Kaen University Dept Pediatrics Faculty Medicine Muang Khon Kaen 40002 Thailand Office Phone: 66-81-7087909. Office Fax: 66 43 348382. Business E-Mail: srivieng@kku.ac.th.

PAJNO, GIOVANNI BATTISTA, allergist, pediatrician; b. Valdina, Italy, July 5, 1955; s. Felice Pajno and Maria Viglianti; m. Graziella Antonina Cucinotta, Dec. 17, 1963; children: Valentina, Cristina. MD, U. Messina, Italy, 1982. Resident in pediats. U. Messina, 1986, resident in respiratory medicine, 1990, asst. pediatrician, 1989-96, reader in pediats., 1992-99; cons. pediatrician Messina, 1996—. Hon. cons. physician Royal Brampton Hosp., London, 1996-97; hon. rsch. fellow dept. allergy and respiratory medicine Guy's Hosp., London, 1997. Mem. Italian Soc. Pediats. (exec. com. respiratory diseases 1999), European Acad. Allergy and Clin. Immunology. Roman Catholic. Home: Via Marche 12/7 98124 Messina Italy Office: Messina U Inst Pediats Via Consolare Valeria 98124 Messina Italy

PAK, JAYOUNG, neurologist, pediatrician, educator; MD, Ewha Womans U. Med. Sch., Seoul, Korea, 1978. Diplomate Am. Bd. of Psychiatry & Neurology, 1993, Am. Bd. of Pediatrics. Internship Ewha Women's Univ. Hosp., Republic of Korea, 1978—79, resident, 1979—83; asst. prof. neurosciences & pediat. NJ Med. Sch.; with UMDNJ - Univ. Hosp. Office: The University Hospital 150 Bergen St C 431 Newark NJ 07103 Office Phone: 973-972-4300.

PAKOS, EMILIOS E., orthopedist; b. Ioannina, Greece, May 20, 1974; s. Eleftherios Pakos and Vasiliki Karra; m. Efstathia Kalogirou, May 19, 2007. MD, U. Ioannina, 1999, PhD, 2006. Physician Health Sta. Village Manteio, Ioannina, 2000—01, Ctr. Open Protection of Elderly People, Ioannina, 2000—01; resident, gen. surgery U. Hosp. Ioannina, 2001—02, resident, radiation oncology, 2002—03, resident, orthop., 2004—09; clin. fellow orthop. oncology Royal Orthop. Hosp., Birmingham, 2008, 2010. Sci. co-operator, dept. hygeine, epidemiology U. Hosp. Ioannina, 2001—, sci. co-operator, dept. radiation oncology, 2004—. Author sci. rsch. papers. Achievements include research in combined radiotherapy and indomethacin as effective in the prevention of heterotopic ossification after THA; p-glycoprotein positivity increaed the risk of disease progression in patients with osteosarcoma; patellar resurfacing reduces the risk of re-operation and anterior knee pain after total knee arthroplasty; effectiveness of wrist arthrodesis for brachial plexus palsy using an external fixator and a cannulated screw; effect of interlaminar epidural steroid injection in acute and subacute pain due to lumbar disk herniation; prognostic factors and outcomes for osteosarcoma; absence of correlation of clinical infection with intra-operative hamstring tendon graft contamination in ACL reconstruction; AGS with monoclonal antibodies had high discriminating ability to identify prosthesis infection in patients who underwent total joint arthroplasty. Personal E-mail: epakos@yahoo.gr.

PAKTER, JEAN, maternal and child health consultant; b. NYC, Jan. 1, 1911; d. David and Lillian (Kunitz) P.; m. Arnold L. Bachman, Sept. 17, 1939 (dec. Dec. 1992); children: Ellen Bachman Mendelson, Donald M. Bachman. BS, NYU, 1931, MD, 1934; MPH, Columbia U., 1955. Diplomate Am. Bd. Pediat. Intern Mt. Sinai Hosp., NYC, 1934-36, resident in pediat., 1937-39; pvt. practice, NYC, 1939-43; dir. Bur. Dept. Health, Maternity, Newborn and Family Planning, NYC, 1950-82; cons., lectr. maternity, child health Columbia U. Sch. Pub. Health, NYC, 1984—, dep. dir. maternal and child health program, 1984-94, lectr. maternity, child health, 1970—. Contbr. numerous articles to profl. med. jours. Advisor March of Dimes, N.Y.C., 1975—. Recipient Fund for City of N.Y. Pub. Svc. award, 1974, Jacobi medal Mt. Sinai Hosp., 1975, N.Y. State Med. Soc. award, 2006. Fellow APHA (Martha May Eliot award 1990), Am. Acad. Pediatrics, N.Y. Acad. Medicine (trustee 1979-83), N.Y. Obstet. Soc. (assoc.); mem. Pub. Health Assn. N.Y.C. (bd. dirs. 1992-96, The Haven Emerson award 2006), Women's City Club, Alpha Omega Alpha. Avocations: concerts, opera, theater, reading. Home: 1175 Park Ave New York NY 10128-1211

PAL, KUNAL, engineering educator; b. Kolkata, Oct. 15, 1980; BS in Pharmacy, Delhi U., 2002; ME in Biomed., Jadavpur U., 2004. Rsch. assoc. Indian Inst. Tech. Delhi, 2006—07; postdoc. fellow Ryerson U., 2007—09; asst. warden, MSS Hall Residence Nat. Inst. Tech. Rourkela, 2009, asst. prof., 2009—. Vice chair AFMNet Ctr. Excellence, 2008—09. GATE fellowship, UGC, India, Fgn. Travel grant, AICTE, India, DST, India, fellowship, Indian Inst. Tech., Kharagpur, AFMNet Ctr. Excellence. Mem.: Soc. Biomed. Engrs. (India), Indian Pharm. Assn., Soc. Biomaterials & Artificial Organs (India), Indian Pharmacy Grads. Assn. Avocation: music. Office: Dept Biotech and Med Engineering Rourkela Orissa 769008 India Office Phone: 661-246-2280. E-mail: pal.kunal@yahoo.com.

PAL, MANIDIP, gynecologist, educator; b. Dharmanagar, Tripura, India, Jan. 26, 1972; MBBS, RIMS, Imphal, Manipur, India, 1995, MD in Ob-Gyn., 2000. Registrar, obgyn Ramakrishna Mission Seva Pratishthan, Kolkata, West Bengal, India, 2001—04; asst. prof., obgyn G.S.L. Med. Coll. & Gen. Hoapital, Rajahmundry, Andhrapradesh, India, 2004—10; assoc. prof., obgyn Coll. of Medicine & J.N.M. Hosp., Kalyani, Nadia, West Bengal, India, 2010—. Mem.: Fedn. Obstetrics & Gynecol. Socs. India, Urogynecology & Reconstructive Pelvic Surgery Soc. India, Internat. Urogynecol. Assn. Avocation: singing. Home: Block C 2nd Fl B/1 Tolly twin Kolkata West Bengal 700104 India Personal E-mail: manideep2b@yahoo.com.

PAL, MANOJIT, medical researcher; s. Chitta Ranjan and Hasi Pal; m. Sarbani Das, May 18, 1994; 1 child, Parthajit. PhD, Indian Assn. for Cultivation Sci., Calcutta, 1994. Jr. rsch. fellow Indian Assn. for Cultivation Sci., Calcutta, 1989—91, sr. rsch. fellow, 1991—94, rsch. assoc., 1994—95; rsch. officer microbial and develop. Alembic Chem. Works Co. Ltd., Vadodara, Gajarat, India, 1995—97; exec. organic synthesis Sun Pharma Advanced Rsch. Ctr., Vadodara, 1997—98; sr. scientist Dr. Reddys Lab. Ltd., Hyderabad, Andhra Pradesh, India, 1998—2001, prin. scientist, 2001—03, assoc. rsch. dir., 2003—05, rsch. dir., 2005—. Contbr. articles to profl. jours. Recipient Merit cert.; fellow, Coun. Sci. and Indsl. Rsch., New Delhi, 1989, Sr. Rsch. Fellowship, 1991. Achievements include identification of Cyclooxygenase-2 inhibitors for oral and injectable formulation; development of process for clarithromycin a semisynthetic erythrromycin, a derivative of macrolide antibiotic; impurity profile for marcolide antibiotic like roxithromycin and azithromycin; discovery of new molecules having anti-inflammatory activites for the treatment of atherosclerosis and arthritis; development of palladium catalyzed reactions in organic synthesis. Home: Bollaram Rd Miyapur Andhra Pradesh Hyderabad 5000 49 India Office: Dr Reddys Lab Ltd Bollaram Rd 500 049 Hyderabad 5000 49 India Office Fax: 91 40 2304 5438. E-mail: manojitpal@rediffmail.com.

PALACIOS, RONALD, immunologist; b. Camiri, Bolivia, Jan. 11, 1953; came to U.S., 1992; s. Enrique and Leddy (Castrillo) P.; m. Patricia Ibarra, June 4, 1977; children: Catherine, Patricia. B Humanities, Colegio Sagrado Corazon, Sucre, 1970; MD with distinction, U. Nat. Autonoma de Mex., Mexico City, 1976, degree in internal medicine splty., 1979; PhD, Karolinska Inst., Stockholm, 1982. Cert. Mexican Bd. Internal Medicine. Instr. histology U. Nat. Mexico, Mexico City, 1973, asst. prof. introduction to medicine; fellow immunology Inst. Nat. Nutrition, Mexico City, 1979-80; mem. Basel (Switzerland) Inst. Immunology, 1982-92; prof., dep. chmn. dept. immunology U. Tex. M.D. Anderson Cancer Ctr., Houston, 1992—. Contbr. articles to profl. jours., chpts. to books. Fellow Swedish Inst., Stockholm, 1980-82, WHO, 1980-81. Fellow Mexican Bd. Internal Medicine; mem. AAAS, Am. Assn. Hematology, Assn. Medicos Internistas Mexico, Assn. Medicos Instituto Nat. Nutrition, Am. Assn. Immunology, Am. Assn. Microbiology, Scandinavian Soc. Immunology, U. Tex. M.D. Anderson Assocs., N.Y. Acad. Scis. Home: PO Box 2795 Santa Cruz Bolivia

PALAMARA, SHERRY A., psychologist; b. Detroit, Sept. 21, 1962; d. Ronald Dominic and Margot Cathrine Palamara. BA in Psychology cum laude, St. Leo Coll., Fla., 1984; MS, Butler U., 1987, Carlos Albizu U., 2000, D in Psychology, 2000. Lic. massage therapist 1991. Behavior specialist Behavior Therapy and Learning Ctr., Long Beach, Calif., 1988—89; program coord. Geriatric Residentail Treatment Sys., Miami, Fla., 1989—95; addictions therapist Families in Transition, Miami, 2002—03, child devel. specialist, 2003—06; pvt. practice clin. and neuro psychology Miami Beach, Fla., 2005—. Counselor Exceptional Children's Found., LA, 1988—89; adj. faculty Miami-Dade Coll., 1999—, Fla. Internat. U., Miami, 2001—; clin. and neuropsychologist Dr.'s and Assocs., Doral, Fla., 2006—. Contbr. articles to profl. jours. Counselor Exceptional Childrens Found., LA, 1988—89. Mem.: APA. Achievements include research in infant massage, trauma, addictions, motivation, employee relations. Avocations: meditation, running, swimming, writing. Office: 407 Lincoln Rd Ste 6L Miami Beach FL 33139 Office Phone: 305-450-1470. Office Fax: 305-271-1633. Personal E-mail: shpalamara@aol.com.

PALANIVELU, SHANTHI, medical educator; d. Palanivelu Kuppanna and Sarojini Palanivelu; m. Chandrasekaran Kolandaisamy; 1 child, Gayathrisai Chandrasekaran. MBBS, U. Madras, Vellore, 1978, MD in Pathology, 1983, PhD, 2008. Lectr. Dr. AL Mudaliar PG Inst Basic Med. Scis., U. Madras, 1984—92, reader, 1992—98, prof., 1998—. Contbr. articles to numerous profl. jours. ICRETT fellowships, Union Internat. Ctr. Cancer, Geneva, 1989, Academic Exch. fellowship, Assn. Commonwealth Univs. London., 1993, fellowship, Indian Assn. Biomed. Scientists, 2004. Fellow: Indian Assn. Biomed. Scientists (treas. 2004); mem.: Internat. Acad. Pathology (Indian Divsn.), Indian Assn. Hematology and Blood Transfusion, Indian Assn. Pathologists and Microbiologists. Achievements include research in the fields of human hematology and phytotherapy in experimental malignant tumors. Office: DRALMPGIBMS Univ Madras Taramani Chennai Tamilnadu 600113 India Office Phone: 91-044-24547121. Personal E-mail: shanthipalanivelu@gmail.com.

PALEOLOGOS, NINA A., physician; b. Mar. 25, 1958; BS in Biology, Northeastern Ill. U., 1980; MD, Rush U. Med. Sch., 1985. Physician North Shore U. Health Sys., 1992—. Office: 2650 Ridge Ave Evanston IL 60201 Office Fax: 847-570-2073. Business E-Mail: npaleologos@northshore.org.

PALEP, JAYDEEP H., gastrointestinal laparoscopic & robotic surgeon; b. Mumbai, Nov. 30, 1973; MS in Surgery, B.Y.L.Nair Charitable Hosp. and T. N. Med. Coll., 2001. Assoc. prof. Grant Med. Coll. & Sir. J. J. Group Hosp., 2007—. Mem.: CRSA. Achievements include first to robotic gastrointestinal surgery in India in 2009. Office: Dr Palep's Nursing Home Manoj CHS S Mumbai Maharashtra 400025 India Personal E-mail: surgeonjay@gmail.com.

PALESE, MICHAEL A., urologist, educator; MD, Mt. Sinai Sch. of Medicine, 1997. Diplomate Am. Bd. of Urology. Resident surgery Univ. of Md. Med. Ctr., Balt., 1998—99, resident urology, 2000—03; fellow urologic oncology NY Presby-Cornell Med. Ctr., 2003—04, fellow robotic surgery, 2003—04; fellow Weill Med. Coll. Cornell Univ.; dir. dept. of urology Mt. Sinai Hosp., course dir.; instr. basic laproscopy course The Am. Urol. Assn., Houston, co-dir., 2007. Assoc. prof. urology Mt. Sinai Sch. of Medicine. Author: (books) several book chpts., (publs.) several publs. Recipient Outstanding Achievement award, Soc. of Laparoendoscopic Surgeons, Pfizer Scholar award, Gerald P. Murphy Scholar award. Office: 5 East 98th St 6th Fl New York NY 10029 Office Phone: 212-241-4812. Office Fax: 212-987-4675. E-mail: michael.palese@mountsinai.org.

PALESTRO, CHRISTOPHER J., physician; m. Lynnette V. Stevens, May 24, 1985; children: Christopher J., Sarah Alice, Alexander Steven, Lissette Halle, Vincent Giancarlo. MD, Universidad Autonoma de Guadalajara, Mex., 1975. Diplomate Am. Bd. Nuc. Medicine, 1982. Chief nuc. medicine Norwalk Hosp., Conn., 1982—85; nuc. medicine physician Mt. Sinai Med. Ctr., NYC, 1985—92; chief nuc. medicine LI Jewish Med. Ctr., New Hyde Park, 1992—2007, North Shore U. Hosp., Manhassett, NY, 2006—07; chief nuc. medicine and molecular imaging North Shore LI Jewish Health Sys., 2007—. Prof. nuc. medicine and radiology Albert Einstein Coll. Medicine, Bronx, NY, 1996—; chmn. Am. Bd. Nuc. Medicine, 2006; mem. residency rev. com. for nuc. medicine Accreditation Coun. Grad. Med. Edn., 2007—; mem. editl. bd. Quar. Jour. Nuc. Medicine and Molecular Imaging. Assoc. editor: Radiology; contbr. articles to profl. jours. including Jour. Nuc. Medicine, Radiology, RadioGraphics. Fellow: Am. Coll. Nuc. Physicians; mem.: NY Acad. Medicine, Internat. Skeletal Soc., Radiol. Soc. N.Am., Soc. Nuc. Medicine. Office: Long Island Jewish Med Ctr 270-05 76th Ave New Hyde Park NY 11040 Business E-Mail: palestro@lij.edu.

PALFREY, JUDITH S., pediatrician; b. El Paso, Tex., Nov. 5, 1945; d. Maurice and Beatrice Adams Sullivan; m. John G. Palfrey, Sept. 9, 1967; children: John G. Palfrey Jr., Quentin A., Katharine E. AB, Harvard U., 1967; MD, Columbia U., 1971. Intern, resident Albert Einstein, Bronx, 1971—74; dir. cmty. svcs. program Children's Hosp., Boston, 1976—86, chief divsn. gen. pediatrics, 1986—2007, dir. global health Dept. Medicine; T. Barry Brazelton prof. pediatrics Harvard Medical Sch., 1996—; exec. dir. Let's Move!, 2011—. Master Adams House Harvard Coll., 2000—. Author: Community Child Health, 1994; co-author: Disney Ency. Pedia of Child Health, 1994, Guidlines for Care for Children Assisted by Medical Technology. Recipient Milton J.E. Senn award, American Acad. Pediatrics, Bright Future award, Nat. Ctr. Edn. Health, Arlington, Va., 2000, Millie & Richard Brock award, NY Acad. Medicine, Marie Felton award, Boston Ctr. for Ind. Living; Cmty. Child Health fellow, Children's Hosp., Boston, 1974—75. Mem.: American Pediatric Soc., Ambulatory Pediatric Assn. (pres. 1995), American Acad. Pediatrics (pres. 2010—11). Democrat. Episcopalian. Avocation: clam digging. Office: Harvard School Public Health 677 Huntington Ave Kresge Bldg 6th Fl Boston MA 02115 Office Phone: 617-432-6714. E-mail: palfrey@fas.harvard.edu. *

PALISI, ANTHONY THOMAS, psychologist, educator; b. Rahway, NJ, Mar. 8, 1930; s. Anthony Francis and Marianne Catherine (Picone) P.; m. Dyane Cassidy, Apr. 19, 1954; children: Jane, Anthony Francis II, Phyllis, Damian-Marie. BS, Seton Hall U., 1951, MA, 1958; EdD, Temple U., 1973. Cert. secondary tchr., elem. prin., psychologist, rehab. counselor, N.J.; mem. Nat. Register Health Care Profls. in Psychology. Tchr., coach pub. schs., Rahway, 1953-60; sports editor Rahway News-Record, 1950-60; prin. elem. pub. sch. Franklin Twp., NJ, 1960-65; asst. prof. edn. Seton Hall U., 1965-73, assoc. prof., 1974-77, prof., 1977-82, acting grad. dean, 1976-77, dir., 1969-80, indsl. cons. group dynamics, 1967-97; pvt. practice psychology, 1977; dir. cons. divsn. FormTech Graphics, Inc., 1997—. Adj. faculty Brookdale C.C., 2005—, Prevention, Inc. Co-author and co-prodr.: (documentary film) Madison School, The Early Years, 2008; contbr. articles and short stories to profl. jours. and popular periodicals. Mem. Rahway Bd. Edn. 1961-62; trustee Rahway Libr., 1961-68, pres. 1967-68. Recipient award N.J. Sportswriters' Assn., 1953. Mem. APA, ACA, Am. Mgmt. Assn. (co-author video tng. program), N.J. Psychol. Assn., Assn. for Specialists in Group Work (mem. rsch. com. 1980-82), N.Y. Acad. Scis., Nat. Acad. Counselors and Family Therapists (chmn., exec. dir. 1988-93, co-editor Family Letter 1985-93), Nat. Register of Health Svc. Providers in Psychology, Am. Coll. Counselors., Clin. Hypnosis Soc. NJ. Roman Catholic. Business E-Mail: atpalisi@optonline.net.

PALL, MARTIN LAWRENCE, science educator, researcher; b. Montreal, Que., Can., Jan. 20, 1942; arrived in US, 1947; s. Gordon and Eleanor (Dresdner) Pall; m. Linda Blackwelder Pall, May 30, 1970 (div. 1983); 1 child, Zachary Aaron. BA in Physics, Johns Hopkins U., 1962; PhD in Biochemistry & Genetics, Calif. Inst. Tech., 1967. Asst. prof. Reed Coll., Portland, Oreg., 1967—72, Wash. State U., Pullman, 1972—75, coord. scis. Vancouver; assoc. prof., 1975—83; prof. genetics, cell biology, biochemistry, 1983—; adj. prof. U. Calif., San Francisco, 1985. Vis. assoc. prof. Yale U., New Haven, 1979—80. Contbr. articles to numerous profl. jours. Rsch. com. Am. Heart Assn. Wash., Seattle, 1979—84. Fellowship, Arthur McCallum, 1962—64, Nutrition Found., 1964—67. Mem.: Genetics Soc. Am., Am. Soc. Biol. Chemistry, Phi Beta Kappa, Sigma Xi. Office: Wash State U Dept Genetics Cell Bio Pullman WA 99164-0001

PALLA, PIERO, medical association administrator; b. Pisa, Italy, Mar. 18, 1954; Scuola Superiore, Liceo Classico, 1973; degree, U. Medicina e Chirurgia, 1979. Dir. Blood Bank, 2009—. Avocation: motorcycling. Home: c/o Ospedale di Livorno VAlfieri n36 Livorno 57100 Italy Home Fax: 00390586223451. Personal E-mail: p.palla@usl6.toscana.it.

PALLAGHY, CHARLES KALMAN, retired biologist, chief research scientist agricultural and industrial effluents; b. Kecskemet, Hungary, Nov. 5, 1939; s. Kalman and Elizabeth Pallaghy; m. Milena

Bozena Kouril, Mar. 2, 1963; children: Paul, Jenny. BSc with honors, U. Melbourne, Australia, 1962; PhD, U. Tasmania, Australia, 1967. Rsch. scientist divsn. land rsch. Commonwealth Sci. and Indsl. Rsch. Orgn., Canberra, Act, Australia, 1967—70; post doctoral rsch. fellow Mich. State U., East Lansing, 1970—71; sr. lectr. La Trobe U., Melbourne, 1971—2004; ret., 2004. Author six ch. backed publs. on sci. matters Melbourne Christian Fellowship, 1984—. Contbr. articles to profl. jours., chapters to books. Mem.: Australian Soc. Plant Scientists (assoc.). Achievements include research in plant physiology, virology and molecular biology; patent on manipulation of leaf senescence. Home: 83/120 Clegg Rd Mount Evelyn VIC 3746 Australia Personal E-mail: c.pallaghy01@optusnet.com.au, charles.pallaghy@bigpond.com.

PALLOTTA, JOHANNA ANTONIA (JOHANNA STEPHEN), endocrinologist, educator; b. Boston, May 7, 1937; d. John and Antonia (Lanni) P.; m. Michael John Stephen, Aug. 13, 1966; children: Jacqueline, Antonia, Michael, Andrew. BS in Chemistry magna cum laude, Boston Coll., 1958; MD, N.Y. Med. Coll., 1962. Diplomate Am. Bds. Internal Medicine, Endocrinology and Metabolism; lic., Mass., Calif. Intern St. Elizabeth's Hosp., Boston, 1962-63; resident in medicine N.Y. Med. Coll. Metro. Hosp., NYC, 1963-64; resident in medicine, fellow radioisotope svc. VA Hosp., Bronx, 1964—66; fellow metabolism and endocrinology Yale U. Sch. Medicine, New Haven, 1966-67; instr. medicine Harvard Med. Sch., Boston, 1967-69, Beth Israel Deaconess Hosp. Harvard Med. Sch., 1969-70; asst. prof. medicine Harvard Med. Sch., 1970—2003, assoc. prof. medicine, 2004—. Tutor med. scis. Harvard Med. Sch., 1972-73; dir. endocrinology clinic Beth Israel Deaconess Hosp., Boston, 1967—, dir. radioimmunoassay lab., 1972-83, clin. cons., 1984—, asst. in medicine, 1967-69, assoc. in medicine, 1969-70, asst. physician, 1970-79, assoc. physician, 1979-87, sr. physician, 1987—, dir. clin. rsch. ctr. core radioimmunoassay lab., 1984-93; cons. staff Mount Auburn Hosp., Cambridge, 1974-90; mem. numerous other coms., 1969—. Rschr. in field; contbr. articles to profl. jours. Recipient S. Robert Stone Harvard Med. Sch.-BIDMC tchg. award, 1998; named Carl Shapiro scholar, BIDMC-Harvard Med. Sch., 2000—. Fellow: ACP, Am. Assn. Clin. Endocrinologists (Outstanding Clin. Endocrinologist award 2010), mem.: Am. Fedn. Clin. Rsch., Am. Thyroid Assn., Endocrine Soc., Harvard Aesculapian Club, Alpha Omega Alpha. Roman Catholic. Home: 16 Fresh Pond Ln Cambridge MA 02138-4616 Office: Beth Israel Hosp Harvard Med Sch 330 Brookline Ave Boston MA 02215-5491 Home Phone: 617-868-1494; Office Phone: 617-667-4016. Business E-Mail: jpallott@bidmc.harvard.edu.

PALMAZ, JULIO C., cardiologist, radiologist, educator; b. Buenos Aires, Dec. 13, 1945; m. Amalia Palmaz; children: Florencia, Christian. MD, Nat. Univ. La Plata, Argentina, 1971. Vascular radiologist, chief of angiography San Martin Univ. Hosp., La Plata, Argentina, 1974—77; radiology tng. Martinez VA Med. Ctr., U. Calif., Davis, 1977—80, chief spl. procedures, 1981; chief of angiography & spl. procedures U. Tex. Health Sci. Ctr., San Antonio, 1983—99, Stewart R. Reuter disting. prof., chief cardiovasc. & interventional radiology rsch., 1999—2005, Ashbel Smith prof., 2006—. Co-owner Palmaz Vineyards, Napa, Calif., 1997—; co-founder Advanced Bio Prosthetic Surfaces Ltd, San Antonio, 1999; co-founder, chief scientist, chmn. bd. dirs. Palmaz Scientific Inc., Dallas, 2008—. Mem. editl. bd. Circulation; contbr. articles to profl. jours., chapters to books. Recipient Presdl. Disting. Scholar award, U. Tex. San Antonio, 2003; named a Disting. Scientist, Am. Heart Assn., 2005; named to Nat. Inventors Hall of Fame, 2006. Fellow: Am. Inst. Med. & Biol. Engring.; mem.: Internat. Soc. Endovascular Surgery, Soc. Interventional Radiology. Achievements include invention of a balloon-expandable stent (the Palmaz-Schatz stent), a tiny, expandable stainless steel tube which holds heart arteries open following angioplasty; patents in field. Office: U Tex Health Sci Ctr Dept Radiology 7703 Floyd Curl Dr MS 7800 San Antonio TX 78229 also: Palmaz Vineyard 4029 Hagen Rd Moraga CA 94556 Office Phone: 210-567-5544. Office Fax: 210-567-5541. E-mail: palmaz@uthscsa.edu.

PALMER, BEVERLY BLAZEY, psychologist, educator; b. Cleve., Nov. 22, 1945; d. Lawrence E. and Mildred M. Blazey; m. Richard C. Palmer, June 24, 1967; 1 child, Ryan Richard. PhD in Counseling Psychology, Ohio State U., 1972. Lic. clin. psychologist, Calif. Adminstrv. assoc. Ohio State U., Columbus, 1969—70; rsch. psychologist Health Svcs. Rsch. Ctr. UCLA, 1971—77; commr. pub. health L.A. County, 1978—81; pvt. practice Torrance, Calif., 1985—; prof. psychology Calif. State U., Dominguez Hills, 1973—2006; faculty Saybrook U., 2005—. Author: Interpersonal Skills for Helping Professionals Online Course, 2001, 04, reviewer manuscripts for numerous textbook pubs; contbr. articles to profl. jours. Recipient Proclamation, County of L.A., 1972, 1981, Outstanding Prof. award, Calif. State U., 1995; Fulbright scholar, Borneo, 2001, Fulbright Sr. scholar, Malaysia, 2004—05, Fulbright scholar, Barbados, 2005. Mem. APA. Office: Calif State U Dominguez Hills Dept Psychology Carson CA 90747-0001 Office Phone: 310-373-6691 ext. 2.

PALMER, CAMERON SCOTT, hospital administrator; b. Melbourne, Apr. 28, 1975; B in Orthoptic with hons., LaTrobe U., 1996; Grad Dip in Clin. Epidemiology, Monash U., 2005. Orthoptist South Ea. Eye Surgery, 1997—2000, Blackburn South Eye Clinic, 2001; trauma data mgr. Royal Children's Hosp. Melbourne, 2002—. Chair Nat. Trauma Registry Consortium Nat. Minimum Dataset Working Party, 2005; mem. Victorian State Trauma Com. Quality Subcommittee, 2008, RACS Trauma Com. Quality Improvement Subcommittee, 2009. Office: Royal Children's Hosp Melbourne 50 Parkville Victoria 3052 Australia Office Fax: 61 3 9345 6668. Business E-Mail: cameron.palmer@rch.org.au.

PALMER, CHRISTOPHER RALPH, medical statistician; b. Maidstone, Kent, Eng., Aug. 11, 1961; s. Ralph George and Joyce (Herd) P.; m. Cathy-Joan MacDonald, Dec. 30, 1989; children: Laura, Carolyn, David. BA, U. Oxford, Eng., 1982, MA (hon.), 1987; MS, U. N.C., Chapel Hill, 1986, PhD, 1988; MA (hon.), U. Cambridge, Eng., 2001. Lectr. applied statistics U. Reading, Eng., 1989-91; sr. rsch. asst. U. Cambridge, Eng., 1991-97, dir. ctr. applied med. statistics, 1996—, asst. dir. rsch., 1997—. Dep. editor Stats. Medicine, 1996-2001; European office acting editor Stats. Medicine, 1999-2000; statis. referee The Lancet, 1992—; contbr. articles to profl. jours. Harvard U. fellow, 1988-89, Hughes Hall fellow U. Cambridge, 1993—. Fellow Royal Statis. Higher End. Acad.; mem. Soc. Clin. Trials, Internat. Soc. Clin. Biostats., World Assn. Med. Editors. Office: U Cambridge Inst Pub Health University Forvie Site Robinson Way CB2 0SR Cambridge England Business E-Mail: chris.palmer@medschl.cam.ac.uk.

PALMER, EARL A., ophthalmologist, educator; m. Carolyn Mary Clark. BA, Ohio State U., 1962; MD, Duke U., 1966. Diplomate Am. Bd. Pediat., Am. Bd. Ophthalmology. Resident in pediat. U. Colo. Med. Ctr., Denver, 1966-68; resident in ophthalmology Oreg. Health & Scis. U., Portland, 1971—74, prof., 1979—; fellow Baylor Coll. Medicine, Houston, 1974-75; asst. prof. Pa. State U., Hershey, 1975-79. Eye alignment specialist; expert in retinopathy of prematurity; chnm., prin investigator, ROP, 1985-2002, exec. com. mem Early Treatment, 2001-2010. Contbr. articles to profl. jours. Fellow: Am. Acad. Ophthalmology (Honor award); mem.: Am. Assn. Pediatric Ophthalmology and Strabismus (pres. 1996—97, Honor award). Avocation: golf. Office: Casey Eye Inst 3375 SW Terwilliger Blvd Portland OR 97239-4197 Home Phone: 503-635-4004; Office Phone: 503-494-7675. Business E-Mail: palmere@ohsu.edu. *

PALMER, EDWARD L., psychologist, educator, writer; b. Hagerstown, Md., Aug. 11, 1938; s. Ralph Leon and Eva Irene (Brandenburg) P.; children: Edward Lee, Jennifer Lynn. BA, Gettysburg Coll., 1960; BD, Luth. Theol. Sem., Gettysburg, 1964; MS, Ohio U., 1967, PhD, 1970. Asst. prof. Western Md. Coll., Westminster, 1968-70, Davidson Coll., NC, 1970-77, assoc. prof. NC, 1977-86, chair, 1985—99, prof. NC, 1986—, Watson prof. NC, 1991—, Watson prof. chair, 2009—. Guest rschr. Harvard U., Cambridge, Mass., 1977; vis. scholar UCLA, 1984, UNC Chapel Hill, 1991, U. Exeter, 2000, U. Ala., 2005; cons. Council on Children, Media, Merchandising, 1978-79, 1st Union Bank Corp., Charlotte, N.C., 1975-79; NSF proposal reviewer, 1978—. Editl. reviewer Jour. Broadcasting and Electronic Media, 1978—, editl. bd. Media Psychology; editor: Children and the Faces of TV, 1980, Faces of Televisual Media, 2003; author: Children in the Cradle of TV, 1987; contbr. to Wiley Ency. of Psychology, 1984, 2002, Lawrence Erlbaum Assocs., 1991, Sage Pub., 1993-96; author jour. articles and book chpts. Sec. Mecklenburg Child Devel. Assn., Davidson and Cornelius, N.C., 1974-78; bd. mem. pub. radio Sta. WDAV, 1970-90, Telecomms. task force Rutgers U., 1981. Recipient Thomas Jefferson Tchg. award Robert Earl McConnell Found., 1993, Deptl. Psychology in Svc. award, 2007. Mem. APA, Am. Psychol. Soc., Assn. Heads Depts. Psychology (chair 1994-96), Am. Psychol. Assn. (task force on advt. and children 2001-03), Southeastern Psychol. Assn., Southeastern Soc. Social Psychologists, Phi Beta Kappa (pres. Davidson chpt. 1985-86). Avocations: sunrise and sunset walks, poetry, hiking, birdwatching, music. Office: Davidson Coll PO Box 7007 Davidson NC 28035-7007 Office Phone: 704-894-2882. E-mail: edpalmer@davidson.edu.

PALMER, HAZEL D., medical association administrator, writer; b. Ely, Cambridgeshire, Eng., Dec. 1, 1968; BSc in Applied Biology with honors, Sunderland U., 1991; MSc in Nutritional Biochemistry, Nottingham U., 1992. Dir. Scius Solutions Pty Ltd., 2004—. Accredited med. edn. provider Royal Australian Coll. Gen. Practitioners, 2004. Recipient Pyramid award, GlaxoSmithKline Consumer Healthcare, 2002, 2004—05, Best Promotion award, Australian Self Medicine Industry, 2006, Best Campaign award, 2007, Best Self-Care Programme award, 2009, Best Pharmacist award, Australian Jour. Pharmacy, 2009. Mem.: Internat. Soc. Med. Publ. Profls., ARCS Australia. Avocations: yoga, painting, writing. Office: Scius Solutions Pty Ltd Level 1 357 Military Rd Mosman NSW 2088 Australia Office Fax: 61 2 9904 1322. Business E-Mail: hazel@scius.com.au.

PALMER, JEFFREY BRUCE, physiatrist, researcher; b. NYC; s. Walter and Barbara Horna (Doctor) P.; m. Sara Sarnoff, July 5, 1975; children: Joshua Henry, Noah Gabriel. BA, NYU, 1976, MD, 1980; M in Rehab. Medicine, U. Wash., 1983. Diplomate Am. Bd. Phys. Medicine & Rehab., Am. Bd. Electrodiagnostic Medicine. Resident U. Wash., Seattle, 1980-83; asst. prof. Johns Hopkins U., Balt., 1983-92, assoc. prof., 1992—; assoc. Harvard U., Cambridge, Mass., 1990—94. Mem. editorial bd. Arch. Phys. Medicine Rehab., 1994 95, 2001-; guest editor Physical Medicine and Rehabilitation Clinics of America, 2008; editorial adv. bd. Dysphagia, 1986—; mem. editorial bd. Jour. Thermology, 1989—; contbr. (co-author) Spinal Cord Injury: A Guide for Living, Eds. 1 and 2; contbr. (chpt.) Normal and Abnormal Swallowing, 1991, 2003; Rehabilitation Medicine: Principles and Practice (Ed. 3 and 4), 1998 and 2005; Encyclopedia of Disability, 2005; Essentials of Physical Medicine and Rehabilitation (Eds. 1 and 2), 2002 and 2008; Physical Medicine and Rehabilitation, 2007; Physical Medicine and Rehabilitation Secrets (Ed. 3), 2008; Stroke Recovery and Rehabilitation, 2009. NIH grantee, 1987-2008. Fellow Am. Acda. Phys. Medicine and Rehab., Am. Assn. Electrodiagnostic Medicine; mem. Assn. Acad. Psychiatrists, Phi Beta Kappa. Office: Johns Hopkins U 600 N Wolfe St Phipps 160 Baltimore MD 21239 Office Phone: 410-502-2446. Office Fax: 410-502-2420. Business E-Mail: jpalmer@jhmi.edu.

PALMER, JOHN DERRY, physiology educator; b. Chgo., May 26, 1932; s. John and Florence (Eley) P.; m. Carla Bianchi, Sept. 15, 1960; 1 child, John Charles. BA, Lake Forest Coll., 1957; MS, Northwestern U., 1959, PhD, 1962. Asst. prof. U. Ill., Chgo., 1961-63; fellow NSF, U. Bristol, Eng., 1963-64; prof., dept. chmn. NYU, 1964-74; prof. U. Mass., Amherst, 1974—, dept. chmn., 1974-80. Edit. bd. Marine Behavior and Physiology, 1988—, Chronobiology Internat., 1986—; author: Textbook of Modern Biology, 1968, The Biological Clock: Two Views, 1970, Biological Clocks in Marine Organisms: The Control of Physiological and Behavioral Tidal Rhythms, 1974, An Introduction to Biological Rhythms, 1976, (with others) Biological Rhythms and Living Clocks, 1977, Human Biological Rhythms, 1983, The Biological Rhythms and Clocks of Intertidal Animals, 1995, The Living Clock, 2000, The Biological Clock, 2003; contbr. articles to profl. jours. With U.S. Army, 1953-55. Fellow AAAS, Explorers Club; mem. Internat. Soc. of Chronobiology, Nat. Assn. of Scholars, Marine Biol. Lab., Phi Beta Kappa, Sigma Xi (pres., v.p., treas. N.Y. chpt., Disting. Rschr. award 1968). Avocation: trout and saltwater fishing. Office: U Mass Dept Biology 611 North Pleasant St Amherst MA 01003 Home: 98 January Hill Rd Amherst MA 01002 Office Phone: 413-545-4400. Business E-Mail: ftodd@bio.umass.edu.

PALMER, PHILIP EDWARD STEPHEN, radiologist; b. London, Apr. 26, 1921; MBBS, U. London, 1944, DMR, 1946, DMRT, 1947; MD (hon.), U. Tirgu Mures, Romania, 2004. Intern, then resident Westminster Hosp.; cons. radiologist West Cornwall (Eng.) Hosp. Group, 1947-54; sr. govt. radiologist Matabeleland, Rhodesia-Zimbabwe, 1954-64; prof. radiology U. Cape Town, South Africa, 1964-68; prof. U. Pa., 1968-70; prof. diagnostic radiology and vet. radiology U. Calif., Davis, 1970—. Dir. Bd. World Health Imaging; WHO cons. in field. Author: The Imaging of Tropical Diseases, 1980 and 2nd edit.: 2000, Diagnostic Imaging in the Community, 2011; contbr. 200plus articles to profl. publs. Recipient German Röentgen award, 1993, 1st Béclère medal Internat. Soc. Radiology, 1996, 1st Antoine Béclère lectr. Internat. Soc. Radiology, 1996, Presdl. award Radiol. Soc. N.Am., 2000. Fellow Calif. Radiol. Assn., Royal Coll. Physicians (Edinburgh), Royal Coll. Radiologists (Eng.), Romanian Soc. Radiol. and Nuclear Med.; mem. Brit. Inst. Radiology, Brit. Med. Assn., Calif. Med. Assn., Internat. Skeletal Soc., Assn. Univ. Radiologists, Radiol. Soc. N.Am. (Spl. Pres.'s award 2000), Kenya Radiol. Soc., South African Coll. Medicine, Egyptian Soc. Radiology and Nuclear Medicine, Yugoslav Assn. for Ultrasound, West African Assn. Radiologists. Address: 821 Miller Dr Davis CA 95616-3622

PALMER, ROGER D., pediatrician, researcher; b. Durham, Eng. s. Clive Alistair and Rosemary Palmer; m. Eira Siobhan Palmer, Nov. 18, 2000; children: Sarah Jane, Thomas James, Laurence Anthony. BSc, U. St. Andrews, 1991; MBBChir, U. Cambridge, 1993. Ho. surgeon West Suffolk Hosp., Bury St. Edmonds, England, 1994; ho. physician Addenbrooke's Hosp., Cambridge, 1994—95; with Newcastle Upon Tyne Hosps., 1995—99; specialist registrar pediat. East Anglia Deanery, Cambridge, 1997—2004; specialist registrar pediat. oncology Great Ormond St. Hosp., London, 2004—05; clin. rsch. tng. fellow Med. Rsch. Coun., Cambridge, 2005—. Mem.: Royal Coll. Pediatrics and Child Health, Royal Coll. Physicians Edinburgh.

PALMER, WALTER J., cosmetic dentist; married; 2 children. BS in Human Physiology with honors, U. Minn., 1982. Postgrad. tng. Las Vegas Inst.; clin. staff River Bluff Dental, Minn., co-owner, 1997. Regular guest (lifestyle show) Showcase Minn. Named Top Dentist, Mpls. St.Paul Mag. Mem.: Minn. Detal Assn., Mpls. Dist. Dental Soc., Am. Acad. of Cosmetic Dentistry, ADA. Avocations: drawing, painting. Office: River Bluff Dental 10851 RI Ave S Bloomington Minneapolis MN 55438 Office Phone: 952-884-5361.

PALMISANO, DONALD J., general and vascular surgeon, medical educator; b. New Orleans, 1939; m. Robin Palmisano; 3 children. MD, Tulane U., 1963; JD, Loyola U., 1982. Diplomate Am. Bd. Surgery; bar: La. Intern Charity Hosp., New Orleans, 1963-64, resident in surgery, 1964-68, Lallie Kemp Charity Hosp., Independence, 1967-68; pvt. practice; clin. prof. surgery, clin. prof. med. jurisprudence Tulane U. Sch. Medicine; founder, pres. Intrepid Resources. Mem. Gov.'s Commn. on organ donations; chair La. Med. Disclosure Panel; founding mem. La. Med. Mutual Ins. Co., bd. dirs. 1982-89; commr. on the bd. Joint Com. on Accreditation of Healthcare Organizations, 1999-2003; selected as one of 60 Americans "opinion-leaders" chosen by Dept. Def. to participate in the Joint Civilian Orientation Conf. (JCOC 63), 2000; bd. dirs. Nat. Patient Safety Found., chair develop. com. responsible for fund raising; bd. govs. Tulane U. Health Svcs. Ctr., 2005-, The Doctors Company, 2004-; mem. Nat. Advisory Council, Annenberg Ctr. Health Sci.; adj. prof., dept. health sys. mgmt., Tulane Sch. Pub. Health and Tropical Medicine, 2005; lectr. in field; keynote spkr. on leadership. Author On Leadership: Essential Principals for Success, 2008; chair comm. prog., 2000; editl. bd. Journal of Patient Safety; guest appearances on Good Morning America, Today Show, debate on Nightline. World News Tonight, CNN Talk Back Live, Hardball with Chris Matthews, CNN Crossfire, John McLaughlin One on One, Fox News with Tony Snow, Aaron Brown's NewsNight; featured on CNN The Capital Gang; contbr. articles to profl. publs. With USAF. Recipient Air Force Commendation medal, award for the Advancement of Patient Safety, The Doctors Co., 2005, Dr. Edward Annis Med. Leadership award, Honolulu, 2007; named one of top doctors in New Orleans, 2001. Fellow ACS, AMSUS, SAFCS; mem. AMA (bd. trustees 1996-2005, chair devel. com., Physician Outreach awards, exec com. mem. 1999, sec-treas 2001, pres-elect 2002, pres. 2003-04, chair La. delegation), La. State Med. Soc. (pres. 1984-85, elected to Hall of Fame 2000), Tulane Sugical Soc. (pres. 2000). Republican. Achievements include playing a key role in the passage of the landmark Louisiana Medical Malpractice Act of 1975. Avocation: photography. Office: Intrepid Resources 5000 W Esplanade Ave #432 Metairie LA 70006 Office Phone: 504-455-5895. Office Fax: 504-455-9392. Business E-Mail: djp@intrepidresources.com. *

PALOMO, JUAN MARTIN, dental educator, director, orthodontist; arrived in US, 1995, permanent resident, 2003; s. Jorge Alberto and Maria Cristina Sere de Palomo; m. Leena Bahl, Oct. 8; 1 child, Veda Caroline. MS, Case Western Res. U., Cleve., 1997. Cert. orthodontics Case Western Res. U., 1997, diplomate Am. Bd. Orthodontics, 2008, cert. Oral & Maxillofacial Radiology Assns. Clinic dir. Case Western Res. U., 1998—2003, tenured assoc. prof., 2007—, program dir., orthodontics, 2008; dir. Craniofacial Imaging Ctr., Cleve., 2005—. Dir. orthodintics Craniofacial Imaging Ctr., Case Western Res. U. Cleve. Contbr. numerous sci. articles & chpts. Recipient Rsch. award, Am. Assn. Orthodontists Found., 1999, 2001, 2006, Am. Soc. Anesthesiologists, 2006—07. Mem.: Computer Assisted Radiology & Surgery, Computed Maxillofacial Imaging, Internat. Assn. Dental Rsch., Conselho Regional de Odontologia Brazil, Coll. Diplomates Am. Bd. Orthodontics, Charles H. Tweed Internat. Found., Bolton-Brush Study Growth Ctr., Am. Dental Edn. Assn., Am. Acad. Oral & Maxillofacial Radiology, Am. Bd. Orthodontics, Am. Assn. Orthodontists, Omnicron Kappa Upsilon National Honor Dental Soc. Office: Case Western Res Univ 10900 Euclid Ave Cleveland OH 44106 Office Fax: 216-368-3204. Business E-Mail: palomo@case.edu.

PAMPADYKANDATHIL, LIZYMOL PHILIPOSE, research scientist; b. Kottayam, India, May 28, 1967; MSc, Mahatma Gandhi U., 1989, PhD, 1998. INSA vis. fellow Mahatma Gandhi U., 1998; prin. investigator SCTIMST, 2001—04, tchg. fellow, 2009—; scientist Sree Chitra Tirunal Inst. Med. Scis. and Tech., 2007—. Recipient Young Scientist award, Govt. of Kerala; Rsch. grant, Govt. of India, CSIR JRF, fellow, Ministry of HRD, India. Avocations: painting, sewing, reading. Office: Poojappura Thiruvanathapuram Kerala 695012 India Office Fax: 91-471-2341814.

PAN, JAMES CHUAN-HSIN, ophthalmologist; b. Singapore, Nov. 24, 1971; s. Yu-Chang Pan and Kim Seng Wong; m. Anne Regina Chu Hui Tan, Mar. 1, 1997; children: Joshua Ethan, Jason Timothy, Allyson Joy. MBBS, Nat. U. Singapore, 1995, MMed in Ophthalmology, 2001. Specialist accreditation in Ophthalmology Ministry Health, Singapore, 2004. Med. officer Ministry Health, Singapore, 1995—97, Nat. Healthcare Group, Singapore, 1999—2001, registrar, 2001—04; assoc. cons. The Eye Inst., NHG, Singapore, 2004—06; cons. eye surgeon Nat. Healthcare Group Eye Inst., Singapore, 2006—. Chmn., SAF med. bd. Singapore Armed Forces, 1998—. Contbr. articles to profl. jours. Councillor Ctrl. Singapore Cmty. Devel. Coun., 2005—;

mem. Citizen Consultative Com., Sengkang West, Singapore, 2005—. Med. officer, capt. Singapore Armed Forces, 1997—99, with Med. Classification Ctr. Singapore Armed Forces, 1998—99. Decorated Defence Adminstrn. Group Excellence award Ministry Defence; recipient Book prize, Ob-Gyn. Soc., Singapore, 1994, Dean's List award, Nat. U. Singapore, 1995, Courage Star award, Singapore Govt., 2003, Best Rsch. Paper award, Soc. Emergency Medicine, Singapore, 2004, Best Poster award, Nat. Healthcare Group, 2005; grantee Rsch. grant, Tan Tock Seng Hosp., 2002. Fellow: Lions Eye Inst., Perth, Australia, Royal Coll. Surgeons Edinburgh (Travel Grant award 2005), Acad. Medicine Singapore; mem.: European Soc. Cataract & Refractive Surgeons, Am. Soc. Cataract & Refractive Surgery, Singapore Soc. Ophthalmology, Singapore Med. Assn., Asia Cornea Soc.

PAN, JING, medical educator; b. China, June 30, 1965; MD, Shangxi Med. Sch., 1987; PhD, Health Sci. Ctr., Beijing U., 1994. Assoc. prof. Tex. A&M U. Health Sci. Ctr., Coll. Medicine, 2003—. Fellowship, Japan Sci. & Tech. Promoting Assn., BGIA grant, Am. Heart Assn., Rsch. grant, Scott & White Hosp. Rsch. Found. Mem.: AHA. Avocations: painting, reading. Office: 1901 S 1st St Bldg 205 Temple TX 76504 Business E-Mail: jpan@medicine.tamhsc.edu.

PAN, MIN HSIUNG, nutritionist, researcher; b. Ping-Tung, Taiwan, Apr. 15, 1968; s. Fon Ton Pan; m. Shu Ping Pan-Chen, June 10, 1971; 1 child, Chi Yo. PhD, Nat. Taiwan U., Taipei, 2000. With Kaohsiung Marine U., Kaoshiung, Taiwan, 2001—. Achievements include research in induction of apoptosis by hydroxydibenzolymethane through coordinative modulation co cyclin D3, Bcl-Xl, and Bax, release of cytochrome c, and sequential activtion of caspases in human cancer cells. Home: Tsoying Kaoshiung 830 Taiwan Office: Nat Kaohsiung Marine U 142 Hai-Chuan Rd Nan-Tzu Kaohsiung Kaohsiung 142 Taiwan Office Fax: 886-7-3611261; Home Fax: 886-7-3611261. Business E-Mail: mhpan@mail.nkmu.edu.tw.

PAN, YA-HUI LAURIE, toxicologist, director; m. Larry Swales. BS in Biology & Chemistry, Bethel Coll., N.Newton, Kans., 1983—87; PhD in Toxicology, U. Kans. Med. Ctr., Kans. City, 1987—92. Diplomate of American Board of Toxicology Am. Bd. of Toxicology/North Carolina, 1996. Human safety toxicologist Proctor & Gamble, Co., Hunt Valley, Md., 1992—94; sr. scientist product safety Mary Kay, Inc., Dallas, 1994—95, group leader product safety, 1995—2000, mgr. product safety, 2000—05; dir. regulatory affairs Sally Beauty Supply LLC, Denton, Tex., 2006—. Chmn. safety & regulatory toxicology com. Cosmetic, Toiletry & Fragrance Assn., DC, 2002—04. Mem.: Am. Contact Dermatitis Soc. (assoc.), Am. Acad. Dermatology (assoc.), Soc. Toxicology (assoc.).

PANAGIA, CARLO, anesthesiologist; b. Rome, Mar. 30, 1945; s. Antonino Panagia and Angela Carmela Capua; m. Nadia Fenici, July 29, 1971; children: Patrik, Paola. Degree in Medicine and Surgery, U. Cattolica del S. Cuore, Rome, 1970. Asst. Pneumologia Osp S. Filippo, Rome, 1970—71, Pronto Soccorso Osp Lecco, Italy, 1972—74, Anestesia-Rianimaz Osp Magg, Bergamo, Italy, 1975—77, anesthesiologist, 1977—93; med. dir. Osservaz Rianim, Pronto Soccorso Osp Riun Bg, Bergamo, Italy, 1993—. Avocations: hockey, classical music. Home: Via Guglielmo Mattioli 16/E 24129 Bergamo BG Italy Home Phone: 3935 258118; Office Phone: 3935 269817. Fax: 035-266672. Business E-Mail: cpanagia@ospedaliriuniti.bergamo.it.

PANAGOULIAS, GEORGE SPIRIDON, physician; b. Athens, Greece, Aug. 28, 1975; Degree in Medicine, Aristotle U. Thessaloniki Corps Officers Mil. Acad., 2000. Cert. specialist in internal medicine Nat. and Kapodistrian U. Athens, 2009. Head med. officer 21 Tank Brigade Gen. Armed Forces, 2001—03; resident 401 Gen. Mil. Hosp. Athens, 2003—05, Nat. and Kapodistrian U. Athens Laiko Gen. Hosp., 2005—09; head, med. sect. Signals Officers Sch., 2009—10; head, med. office greek army staff Gen. Army Staff 417 Vets. Adminstrn. Hosp., cons., 2nd clinic internal medicine; pvt. practice, 2010—. Decorated Gold Cross of Phoenix Gen. Army Staff, Mil. Value 3rd Class medal. Mem.: Hellenic Med. Assn. Obesity EIEP, Hellenic Diabetes Assn. EDE, Hellenic Soc. Infectious Diseases, Med. Assn. Athens. Avocations: literature, bicycling. Office: Chrisostomou Smirnis Ave 4 Athens Attica GR-16232 Greece Office Fax: 30-210-760-8539. Business E-Mail: gpanago@med.uoa.gr.

PANCHANADHAM, SACHDANANDAM, biochemist, educator; b. Thanjur, India, Feb. 23, 1952; s. Panchanadham and Madhikkadhammal; m. Vijayamala Panchanadham, July 9, 1989; 1 child, Brindha. BSc in Chemistry, U. Madras, 1972, MSc in Biochemistry, 1975, MPhil in Biochemistry, 1977, PhD in Biochemistry, 1980. From lectr. to prof. U. Madras, India, 1982—96, prof., 1996—. Lectr. in field. Mem. editl. bd.: Indian Jour. Human Scis.; contbr. articles to profl. jours. Recipient Rashtriya Govruav award, India Internat. Friendship Soc., Best Paper award, Ayurveda 2000, Internat. Symposium, Udaipur, India, 1997. Fellow: Tamil Nadu (India) Acad. Scis., Indian Assn. Biomed. Scientists, Indian Chem. Soc.; mem.: Internat. Coenzyme Q10 Soc., Soc. Biol. Chemists, N.Y. Acad. Scis. (assoc.), Soc. Reproductive Biology and Comparative Endocrinology (life). Office: Dept Med Biochem DR ALM P-G IBMS Univ Madras Taramani Campus Chennai 600113 India Home: 19-2A Thirumurugan Street 600 090 Chennai India

PANCHOVSKA, MARIA STOJANOVA, rheumatologist, physician; b. Panagurischte, Bulgaria, Apr. 17, 1962; married; 1 child, Georgi Martinov Mochew. Degree, Med. U., Plovdiv, Bu;garia, 1986, MD, attending, 1988—; degree in Internal Disease, Med. U., Sofia, 1991, degree in Rheumatology, 1994. Diplomate Med. U., Plovdiv, 1986. Asst. prof. Med. U., Plovdiv, 1988—2004, cons., rheumatologist, dept. internal diseases, 1996—, assoc. prof., 2004—, cons., rheumatologyst, dept. gen. practitioners, 2006—. Contbr. articles to profl. jours. Mem. Poem, Plovdiv, 1988. Achievements include research in Rheumatology And Internal Diseae. Home: 10 Alen mak Plovdiv 4003 Bulgaria Office: Med University 15 A Vasil Aprilov Plovdiv 4000 Bulgaria Office Phone: 35932602395. Business E-Mail: panchovska@abv.bg.

PANDA, SUNAKAR, chemistry professor; b. May 25, 1960; MSc, Sambalpur U., 1983, PhD, 1989. Prof., P.G. dept. chemistry Berhampur U., 2006—, head dept., 2009. Fellowship, CSIR, India. Fellow: Internat. Congress Chemistry & Environment; mem.: Odisha Chem. Soc. Avocations: reading, sightseeing. Office: Berhampur University PG Dept Chemistry Bhanjabihar Odisha 760007 India Personal E-mail: sunakar_bu@yahoo.co.in.

PANDE, PRAKASH NARAIN, cardiologist, educator, consultant; b. Basti, UP, India, Jan. 1, 1942; came to U.S., 1971; s. Bhawnath and Chandra (Misra) P.; m. Lora Joann Kargina, June 19, 1974; children: Jennifer, Robby. BSc, Lucknow U., India, 1958, MBBS, 1964, MD in Internal Medicine, 1968. Diplomate Am. Bd. Internal Medicine, Am. Bd. Cardiovascular Diseases. Rotating house officer Associated Hosps. Med. Coll. (India) Kanpur, 1964-66, resident med. officer, 1966-67; sr. house officer Bury and Rosendale Hosp., Eng., 1969-71; resident in medicine Rochester (N.Y.) Gen. Hosp., 1971-73; trainee in cardiology U. Rochester, 1973-75; cons. cardiology, attending physician Rochester (N.Y.) Gen. Hosp., 1975-98, dir. cardiac catheterization labs., 1982-90, head cardiology unit, 1990-97; from clin. asst. prof. medicine to clin. prof. U. Rochester, 1980-97, adj. prof., 1998—99; prof. clin. medicine, cardiology Ind. U. Sch. Medicine, Indpls., 1998—2010, prof. emeritus clin. medicine, 2011—. Cardiologist Krannert Inst. Cardiology, Indpls., 1998-2010; hon. chmn. Physicians' Adv. Bd. Nat. Rep. Congl. com., 2003-04; dir. Johnson Meml. Homecare, 1998-2003, chair credentials com., 2001-2004; dir., continuing med. edn. for physicians, Johnson Meml. Hosp., 1999-2004; chmn. dept. medicine, 2003-2004, dir. cardiology and cardiac rehab., 2003-06. Editor Clarian Cardiology newsletter, 1998-2003. Fellow Sr. rsch. fellow, Coun. Scientific and Indsl. Rsch., 1968. Fellow ACP, Am. Heart Assn. (coun. clin. cardiology 1990), Am. Coll. Cardiology (Ind. councilor 1994, 1996), Soc. Cardiac Angiography and Interventions (sr.), Coun. Geriatric Cardiology.

PANDEY, GIRDHAR KUMAR, molecular biologist; b. Almora, Utter Paradesh, India, Feb. 15, 1972; arrived in US, 2000; s. Kishan Chand and Kamala Devi Pandey; m. Amita Tyagi, Dec. 3, 1997; children: Daksh, Aryan. BSc in Biochemistry, Jawaharlal Nehru U., New Delhi, 1992; MSc in Biotech., U. Delhi South Campus, 1994; PhD in Life Scis., Plant Molecular Biology and Biotech., Jawaharlal Nehru U., 1999. Postdoctoral fellow U. Calif., Berkeley, 2000—06; lead scientist Delmonte Fresh Produce Co., Richmond, Calif., 2006—08; assoc. prof. plant molecular biology and genetic engring. dept. U. Delhi, New Delhi, 2008—. Assoc. editor, editl. bd. mem. e-Jour. Biol. Scis., Plant Signaling and Behaviour, Jour. Biomed. Sci. and Engring. Contbr. articles to profl. jours. Moderator, vol. Sch. and Edn. Bd., El Cerrito, Calif., 2004—06. Grantee, NSF, 2003; fellow, Dept. Bio-Tech., India, 1992, Coun. Sci. and Indsl. Rsch., India, 1994, USDA, 1998, Indo-Srilankan Rsch. Com., 1999; Rsch. Project grant, DBT, DST, CSIR, UGC, DU-PURSE. Mem.: NY Acad. Sci., Calif. Acad. Sci., Am. Soc. Plant Biologist. Independent. Hindu. Achievements include two patents for developing strees tolerant plants. Avocations: reading, writing, gardening, cricket, golf. Office: Univ Delhi Dept Plant Molecular Biology South Campus 110 021 New Delhi India Office Phone: 91-9718318329. Personal E-mail: giridhar98@gmail.com. Business E-Mail: gkpandey@south.du.ac.in.

PANDEY, KISHOR, research scientist; b. Parbat, Nepal, July 24, 1975; PhD, Nagasaki U., 2008. Project rsch. U. Tokyo, 2008—10; rschr. Nepal Devel. Rsch. Inst., 2011—. Recipient Vidhya Bhusan award, Nepal Govt.; scholarship, Japanese Govt. Avocations: writing, music, reading. Office: Everest Internat Clinic and Research Ctr Kathmandu 9045 Nepal Personal E-mail: pandey_kishor@hotmail.com.

PANDEY, RABINDRA, cardiologist; b. Rupendehi, Nepal, June 23, 1977; MD in Cardiology, Tongji U., Shanghai, 2009. Registrar cardiologist Sahid Gangalal Nat. Heart Ctr., 2009—. Mem.: Cardiac Soc. Nepal. Office: Bansbari Kathmandu 11360 Nepal E-mail: rabinxmu@yahoo.com.

PANDEY, SIDDHARTH, chemistry professor; b. Allahabad, India, Oct. 6, 1970; PhD, U. North Tex., 1998. Prof. Indian Inst. Tech., 2004—. Recipient NASI SCOPUS award, Elsevier. Mem.: ACS. Office: Indian Inst Tech Dept Chemistry New Delhi Delhi 110016 India Business E-Mail: sipandey@chemistry.iitd.ac.in.

PANDHI, DEEPIKA, medical educator; b. India, Nov. 15, 1972; MBBS, Lady Hardinge Med. Coll. Delhi, 1994; MD in Dermatology, Maulana Azad Med. Coll., Delhi, 1999. Lectr. Dept. Dermatology & STD U. Coll. Med. Scis. U. Delhi, 2002—03, sr. lectr., 2003—07, reader, 2007—. Cons. Nat. Bd. Exams., 2004—06; editl. bd. mem. Indian Jour. Sexually Transmitted Diseases, 2006—11. Contbr. numerous articles to profl. jours. Recipient Gold medal, U. Delhi; Attending Conf. fellow, European Assn. Dermatology and Venereology. Mem.: Soc. Pediatric Dermatology, Indian Assn. Leprosy, Indian Assn. Study Sexually Transmitted Diseases and AIDS, Indian Assn. Dermatology, Venereology and Leprosy. Avocations: reading, travel, music. Home: B-1 1101 Vasant Kunj New Delhi 110070 India Office Phone: 22586262 2594. Office Fax: 911122590495. Personal E-mail: deepikapandhi@rediffmail.com.

PANDIT, HEMANT, orthopedist, surgeon, research scientist; b. Bombay, Sept. 3, 1964; s. Govind and Pushpa Pandit; m. Medha Vanarase; 1 child, Gargi. MBBS, Seth GS Med. Coll., 1988; MS, U. Bombay, 1990. Diplomate Nat. Bd., New Delhi, 1991. Intern KEM Hosp., Bombay, 1987, resident, 1988—90; specialist registrar in trauma orthops. Wessex Region, Hampshire, England, 1996—2001; clin. and rsch. fellow Nuffield Orthop. Ctr., Oxford, England, 2001—. Contbr. articles to profl. jours. Recipient Best Registrar award, KEM Hosp. U. of Bomaby, 1989; scholar, Govt. India, 1980. Fellow: Royal Coll. Surgeons; mem.: Brit. Assn. Surgery of Knee, Brit. Orthop. Rsch. Soc. Home: 2 Powell Close Forest Hill Oxford OX33 1EN England Office: Nuffield Orthopaedic Centre Windmill Rd Headington Oxford OX3 7LD England Office Fax: 0044-1865-227671. Personal E-mail: hgargi@aol.com. Business E-Mail: hemantpandit@hotmail.com.

PANDIT, NYMPHEA, dental educator; b. Jammu & Kashmir, India, Apr. 10, 1968; BDS, S.C.B Med. Coll. Cuttack, Orissa, 1993; MDS, Govt. Dental Coll., Ahmedabad, Gujrat, 1999. Postgrad. thesis guide D.A.V Dental Coll., Yamuna-Nagar, Haryana, 2002, prof., head, 2009—. Contbr. articles to profl. jours. Mem.: Indian Dental Assn., Indian Soc. Periodontology. Avocations: badminton, music. Home: #9 Professor Colony Behind Telephone Exchange Yamuna-Nagar Haryana 135001 India Home Fax: 91-1732-227155. Personal E-mail: drpanditynr@rediffmail.com, drnymphea@yahoo.com.

PANDOLFI, FRANCES, health facility administrator; b. NYC, Sept. 7, 1944; d. Frank Pandolfi and Rose McGinn; m. Edmund Lewiska Menelik Bobbitt, May 19, 1973. BA, Vassar Coll., 1965; MPA, NYU, 1990. Health planner N.Y.C. Dept. City Planning, 1965-74; planner West Midlands County Coun., Birmingham, Eng., 1974-81, dir. recreation and tourism planning, 1981-85, dir. strategic planning, 1985-86; dep. dir. housing coord. N.Y.C. Mayor's Office, 1987-89; dir. nurses housing N.Y.C. Health & Hosps. Corp., 1989-92, exec. asst. to v.p., 1992-94, asst. v.p., 1994-97; chief of staff N.Y.C. Health and Hosps. Corp., 1998-2001, chief info. officer, 2001—09, restructuring project dir., 2009—11. Dir. Women in Housing and Fin., N.Y.C., 1990-96. Mem.: Am. Soc. Pub. Adminstrn.

PANESAR, KANWAR JIT SINGH, surgeon, consultant; b. Dosanju Kalan, Jallandhar, India, Apr. 22, 1941; arrived in Northern Ireland, 1975; s. Bhagat Singh Panesar and Sukhjit Kaur Lehall; m. Iqbal Kaur; children: Deshpal Singh, Tej Paul Singh. MBBS, Amritsar Punjab U., India, 1965. Trained lead assessor profl. performance procedures Gen. Med. Coun. Cons. surgeon Altnagelvin Area Hosps., London, 1977—. Examiner surgery Queens' U., Belfast, Northern Ireland, 1991—. Specialist advisor surgery to assessment referral com. Gen. Med. Coun., 2002—; founder, pres. No. Ireland Sikh Assn. Named Officer of the Most Excellent, Order of the British Empire, 2004. Fellow: Assn. Surgeons Gt. Britian and Ireland, Royal Coll. Surgeons Edinburgh (examiner 1999—), Royal Coll. Surgeons; mem.: Brit. Med. Assn. (mem. ctrl. cons. and specialists com. 1993—, chmn. No. Ireland cons. com. 2001—05), Royal Coll. Surgeons Ireland (examiner anatomy 1989—), Royal Coll. Physicians. Avocation: golf. Home: Hinton House 1 Clooney Park W Londonderry BT47 6LA Northern Ireland Office: Altnagelvin Area Hosps Glenshane Rd Londonderry BT47 68B Northern Ireland Office Phone: 07803-201-777. Personal E-mail: panesarfrcs@gmail.com.

PANETTA, JILL, foundation administrator; PhD in Organic Chemistry, Dartmouth Coll., Hanover, NH. Postdoctoral fellowship U. Calif., Berkeley; sr. rsch. scientist, group leader in drug discovery Eli Lilly and Co., dir. Lilly Ctr. Women's Heath; co-founder, chief sci. officer InnoCentive, Inc.; chief sci. officer Polycystic Kidney Disease Found., Kansas City, Mo., 2010—, interim CEO, 2011—. Co-editor: Psychiatric Illness in Women; contbr. articles to profl. jours. Mem. com. on understanding the biology of sex and gender differences Inst. Medicine; bd. dirs. Soc. Women's Health Rsch. Achievements include patents in field. Office: PKD Found 8330 Ward Pky Ste 510 Kansas City MO 64114-2000 Office Phone: 816-931-2600. Office Fax: 816-931-8655. *

PANETTA, JOSEPH DANIEL, biotechnologist, director; b. Syracuse, NY, Mar. 1, 1954; s. Salvatore and Josephine Mary (Sbardella) P.; m. Karin Ann Hoffman, Oct. 21, 1978; children: Lauren Marie, Christopher Daniel. BS, LeMoyne Coll., 1976; MPH, U. Pitts., 1979. Environ. protection specialist EPA, Washington, 1979-82, sr. policy analyst, 1982-84; project leader Schering Corp./NorAm Chem Co., Wilmington, Del., 1984-85; mgr. regulatory affairs agrchems. divsn. Pennwalt Corp., Phila., 1985-88; mgr. corp. regulatory affairs Mycogen Corp., San Diego, 1988-90, dir. corp. regulatory affairs and quality assurance, 1990-92, dir. corp. regulatory, environ. affairs San Diego, 1992-97, v.p. govt. and pub. affair, 1998-99; pres., CEO BIOCOM, San Diego, 1999—. Bd. dirs. Gene Therapy Sys., San Diego (Calif.) Econ. Devel. Corp., eStudy Site; chmn. agr. and environment subcom. Internat. Bioindustry Forum; guest lectr. biotech. U. Calif., San Diego, and Calif. Western Law Sch.; advisor bd. on agr. NAS; mem. San Diego Pub. Utilities Adv. Commn., 2002—06; adv. Com. Calif. Food Biotech., 2002-2004, U. Calif. Sch. Pharm. Sci., San Diego, Calif., 2003—; mem. adv. coun. Keck Grad. Inst., 2003—07; vice chmn. Coun. State Biotech Assocs., 2002—04, chmn. Coun. State Biotechnology Assn., 2004-06, Calif. Biotechnology Found., 2006-. Columnist San Diego Daily Transcript, 1999—2003; contbr. articles to profl. jours. Mem. Rep. State Com. Del., 1987; bd. dirs., chmn San Diego Work Force Partnership, 2008; mem. exec. com. Calif. Cmty. Colls. Econ. Devel. Network; mem. adv. bd. UCSD-Connect; bd. dirs. San Diego C. of C.; commissioner San Diego City Pub. Utilities commn., 2002—06. Mem. Am. Crop Protection Assn. (chmn. com. biotech.), Nat. Agrl. Chems. Assn. (mem. registrations com. 1986-89), Biotech. Industy Orgn. (mem. food and agr. steering com., chmn. bipesticides com., internat. affairs com.), Calif. Indsl. Biotech. Assn. (mem. agrl. affairs com.), Am. Chem. Soc. (mem. agrl. div.), Am. Seed Trade Assn. (chmn. steering com. biotech.), Gov.'s Biotech. Coun. (Calif.), San Diego C. of C. (mem. pub. policy com.), San Diego Workforce Partnership (mem. youth coun.), CA Comn. Econ. Devl.(biotech. adv. com, 2008-) Roman Catholic. Avocations: yachting, skiing, classical piano. Home: 5459 Shannon Ridge Ln San Diego CA 92130-4808 Office: BIOCOM San Diego 4510 Executive Dr San Diego CA 92121-3025 Home Phone: 858-481-5336. E-mail: jpanetta@biocom.org.

PANG, JIE, food scientist, educator; b. Yibin, Sichuan, China, Nov. 9, 1965; PhD, Xinan U., 1999. Asst. to pres. Fujian Agr. & Forestry U., 2001—. Recipient award, Fujian Agr. & Forestry U., Innovation Gardener award. Mem.: China Konjac Assn., China Beverage Industry Assn. Office: Fujian Agriculture & Forestry University Fuzhou Fujian 350002 China Office Fax: 86 591 837 05076. Business E-Mail: pang3721941@163.com.

PANG, JIJIE, medical educator; MD, Xi'an JiaoTong U., 1986, PhD, 1995. Asst. prof. Baylor Coll. Medicine, 2009—. Mem.: Soc. Neurosci. (Washington), Assn. Rsch. Vision and Ophthalmology (Md.), Royal Soc. Medicine (London). Avocations: photography, music, gardening. Office: One Baylor Plz NC205 Houston TX 77030 Personal E-mail: pangjijie@yahoo.com.

PANG, MYUNG-GEOL, reproductive physiologist, educator; b. Seoul, Republic of Korea, Aug. 25, 1961; s. Dong-Soon Shin; m. Young-Ju Kim; children: Won-Kee, Jun-Kee. BS in Animal Scis., Chung-Ang U., Seoul, 1985, MS in Animal Scis., 1987; PhD in Endocrinology and Reproductive Biology, Ea. Va. Med. Sch., Norfolk, Va., 1996. Sr. rschr. Med. Rsch. Ctr., Seoul Nat. U., 1997—98, Biomedical Rsch. Ctr., Korea Advanced Inst. Sci., Taejeon, 1998—2000; rsch. assoc. IRMP, Seoul Nat. U., 1998—2003; CEO GenDix, Inc., Seoul, Republic of Korea, 2000—03; prof., dept. animal sci. & tech. Chung-Ang U., Ansung, Republic of Korea, 2003—. Co-host World Forum Fedn., 2009. Recipient Outstanding Performance Project award, Korean Ministry Health & Welfare, 1998, Human Right award, Nat. Orgn. Circumcision Info. Resource Ctrs., 2000, Excellent Presentation award, Third Internat. Symposium Devel. Biotech., 2003, 12th AAAP Animal Sci. Congress, 2006, 9th Internat. Symposium Devel. Biotech., 2009, Amb. of Korea, World Forum, 2009, Internat. Einstein award, Internat. Bibliog. Ctr., 2009, Hon. award, Am. Soc. Reproductive Medicine, 2010; named Foremost Scientist of World, Internat. Bibliog. Ctr. Eng., 2008; named one of

Top 100 Scientist of World, 2008. Independent Thinkers. Achievements include development of IVF-ET in rabbit; transgenic goat secreting human granulocyte colony stimulating factor. Home: 120-902 Mokdong 1 Danji Apt Seoul 158-751 Republic of Korea Office: Chung-Ang U Dept Animal Sci & Tech 1 Nae-Ri Daeduk-Myun Gyeonggi-do 72 456-756 Anseong Gyeonggi-do Republic of Korea Office Phone: 82 31 670 4841. Office Fax: 82 31 675 9001. Personal E-mail: mgpang@hotmail.com.

PANI, ALESSANDRA, virologist, educator; b. Rome, July 14, 1953; d. Salvatore Pani and Giovanna Mangiarotti; m. Giancarlo Zanoli, Mar. 6, 1954; 1 child, Giovanni Zanoli. PhD in Biology, U. Cagliari, Italy, 1977. Rschr. U. Cagliari, 1990—2003, assoc. prof. Monserrato - Cagliari, Italy, 2003—. Editor: Cell Growth and Cholesterol Esters. Post-doctoral fellow, CNR, Italy, 1978—80, U. London, 1980—81, U. Conn., 1984—86. Achievements include patents for antiviral/antiproliferative agents. Office: Univ Cagliari Cittadella Universitaria 09042 Monserrato Italy Office Fax: 00 39 070 675 4210. Business E-Mail: pania@unica.it.

PANICEK, DAVID, radiologist; b. Johnson City, NY, Oct. 7, 1954; MD, Cornell U., 1980. Cert. diagnostic radiology 1984. Intern Lenox Hill Hosp., NYC, 1980—81; resident NY Hosp. Cornell Med. Ctr., NYC, 1981—84; radiologist U. Hosp., Syracuse, NY, 1984—88; asst. prof. radiology SUNY Health Sci. Ctr., Syracuse, 1984—88, Cornell U. Med. Coll., 1988—93; radiologist Meml. Sloan-Kettering, NYC, 1988—; assoc. prof. radiology Cornell U. Med. Coll., 1993—98, prof. radiology, 1999—; vice chair, Clin. Affairs, Radiology Meml. Sloan-Kettering, NYC. Fellow: Am. Coll. Radiology; mem.: Am. Roentgen Ray Soc., Radiological Soc. N.Am., Internat. Skeletal Soc. Office: Meml Sloan-Kettering Cancer Ctr 1275 York Ave New York NY 10021-6007

PANITZ, LAWRENCE, physician; b. Apr. 30, 1928; s. Max and Gussie (Gorenstein) Panitz; m. Adrienne Ruth Luke, June 20, 1965; children: Jennifer, Michael. BA, NYU, 1962; MD, Upstate Med. U., Syracuse, 1966. Diplomate Am. Bd. Family Practice. Intern St. Joseph's Hosp., Syracuse, NY, 1966—67; pvt. practice gen. medicine Elmsford, NY, 1967—90, Hawthorne, NY, 1968—. Affiliated with Docs Physicians Beth Israel Med. Ctr., NYC, Shrub Oak, NY, Hartsdale, NY, Larchmont, NY, Yonkers, NY, Thornwood, NY, Crestwood, NY, New City, West Haverstraw, NY; mem. staff New Rochelle Hosp., NY, St. Agnes Hosp., White Plains, NY, Westchester County Med. Ctr., Valhalla, NY, N.Y. Dobbs Ferry Hosp., Beth Israel Hosp. Med. Ctr., NYC, Sound Shore Med. Ctr., Phelps Meml. Hosp., Sleepy Hollow, NY, dep. dir. dept. family practice, North Tarrytown, NY; dir. Elmsford Med. Ctr.; police surgeon, Tarrytown, North Tarrytown, Sleepy Hollow, Elmsford, Town of Greenburgh; med. dir. Margaret Chapman Sch. Exceptional Child, Hawthorne; med. dir., prin. rschr. Clin. Tech. Assoc., Elmsford, CNS Bioservices, Pleasantville, NY; physician Westchester County Correctional Health Dept., Valhalla; sch. physician, Elmsford; cons., expert witness Vogel & Rosenberg, NYC, Britcher, Leone & Roth, LLC, Glen Rock, NJ; cons. on malpractice litig. for law firms. With US Army, 1946—48, with US Army, 1982—88, lt. col. Med. Corps USAR. Fellow: AMA, Am. Acad. Family Physicians; mem.: Westchester Acad. Medicine, Westchester County Med. Soc., Med. Soc. State NY, Jewish War Vets., Masons, Shriners. Jewish. Home and Office: Riveredge 3 David Ln Ste 2P Yonkers NY 10701-1122 Office: 132 S Central Ave Elmsford NY 10523 Home Phone: 914 968 6033; Office Phone: 914 968 6135. E-mail: lp711md@aol.com.

PANIZZON, RENATO G., physician, researcher; b. Basel, Switzerland, Dec. 12, 1944; s. Leandro R. Panizzon and Marguerite E. Schweizer; m. Nicole M. Guisan, Sept. 30, 1972; children: Marion, Francoise, Philippe. MD, U. Basel, Switzerland, 1971. Bd. cert. in dermatology and dermatopathology, bd. cert. in angiology. Asst. prof., Zurich, Switzerland, 1986-92; assoc. prof., 1992-96; prof./chmn. Lausanne, Switzerland, 1996—. Author: Radiation Therapy and Radiation Reactions in Dermatology, 2004. Col. Sanitary Troops. Recipient Poster award, 1982. Mem.: German Soc. Dermatology, Internat. Dermatol. Radiotherapy Soc. (past. pres.), French Soc. Dermatology, Swiss Soc. Dermatology and Venerology (past pres.), Swiss Med. Assn., Internat. Soc. Dermatopathology, Am. Soc. Dermatopathology, Am. Acad. Dermatology, Swiss Group for Cancer Rsch. (past pres.). Office: CHUV Dept Dermatology & Venerology Ch 1011 1015 Lausanne Switzerland Office Phone: 41213143262. Business E-Mail: renato.panizzon@chuv.ch.

PANKEY, GEORGE ATKINSON, internist, educator, researcher; b. Shreveport, La., Aug. 11, 1933; s. George Edward and Annabel (Atkinson) P.; m. Patricia Ann Carreras, Sept. 22, 1972; children: Susan Margaret, Stephen Charles, Laura Atkinson, Edward Atkinson. Student, La. Poly. Inst., 1950-51; BS, Tulane U., 1954, MD, 1957; MS, U. Minn., 1961. Diplomate Am. Bd. Internal Medicine, Am. Bd. Infectious Disease. Intern U. Minn. Hosps., 1957-58, resident in internal medicine, 1958-60, Mpls. VA Hosp., Mpls. Gen. Hosp., 1960-61; asst. vis. physician Charity Hosp. La., New Orleans, 1961-62, vis. physician, 1962-75, sr. vis. physician, 1975-95; ptnr. Ochsner Clinic, New Orleans, 1968—99; head sect. infectious diseases Ochsner Clinic Found., 1972—94, dir. infectious disease training program, 1972—94, dir. infectious disease rsch., 1999—; instr. dept. medicine, div. infectious diseases Tulane U. Sch. Medicine, New Orleans, 1961-63, clin. instr., 1963-65, clin. asst. prof. medicine, 1965-68, clin. assoc. prof., 1968-73, clin. prof., 1973—. Dir., founder Century Nat. Bank, New Orleans; medicine test com. Nat. Bd. Med. Examiners, 1979-83; infectious diseases adv. bd. Hoffman-LaRoche, 1982-92; dir. Nat. Found. Infectious Diseases, 2004—10, trustee, 2010-. Author: A Manual of Antimicrobial Therapy, 1969; co-author: (with Charles W. Gross and Michael G. Mendelsohn) Contemporary Diagnosis and Management of Sinusitis, 1997, 4th edit., 2004; (with Julia Garcia-Diaz and Layne O. Gentry) Contemporary Diagnosis and Management of Diabetic Foot Infections, 2006; editor: Infectious Diseases Digest, 1983-95, So. Med. Assn. Program for Infectious Diseases Dial-Access, 1983-92, Ochsner Clinic Reports on Serious Hosp. Infections, 1985-2005, Ochsner Clinic Reports on Geriatric Infectious Diseases, 1990-93, Ochsner Clinic Reports on the Mgmt. of Sepsis, 1991-93, Infectious Disease Clinics of N.Am., 1994; co-editor: (with Geoffrey A. Kalish) Outpatient Antimicrobial Therapy - Recent Advances, 1989; contbg. editor: Antimicrobial Therapy Guide, 18th edit., 2006; mem. editl. bd. Patient Care, 1969-75, Today in Medicine, 1990, Nat. Infectious Disease Info. Network, 1983, Compendium Continuing Edn. in Dentistry, 1984-2004, Quinolones Bull., 1985-93, Ochsner Jour., 1999-2003, Infectious Disease News, 2001—; contbr. articles to profl. jours. Dir. Camp Fire Inc.; Pres. New Orleans Young Republican Club, 1969-71; adv. bd. Angie Nall Sch. Hosp., Beaumont, Tex.; trustee Nall Found. for Children, Beaumont. Recipient cert. merit Am. Acad. Gen. Practice, 1969, 70, 2002. Master ACP-ASIM (laureate award La. chpt. 1997); fellow Am. Coll. Preventive Medicine, Infectious Disease Soc. Am. (Clinician award 1996), Am. Coll. Chest Physicians, Royal Soc. Medicine; mem. Am. Soc. of Transplantation, Assn. Contamination Control (chpt. pres. 1968-70), Am. Fedn. Med. Rsch., So. Med. Assn. (certificate of award 1970), Am. Soc. Internal Medicine (del. ann. meeting 1971-72), Am. Soc. Microbiology, Am. Thoracic Soc., New Orleans Acad. Internal Medicine (pres. 1977-78, 96-97), AMA, Aerospace Med. Assn., Am. Soc. Tropical Medicine and Hygiene, Am. Venereal Disease Assn., Am. Soc. Parasitologists, Internat. Travel Medicine Soc., La. Soc. Internal Medicine (pres. 1972-73), La. Med. Soc., La. Thoracic Soc. (chmn. program com. 1968, governing council 1976-80), Surg. Infection Soc., Immunocompromised Host Soc., Musser Burch Soc., Orleans Parish Med. Soc., N.Y. Acad. Scis., Pan Am. Med. Assn. (diplomate mem. sect. internal medicine 1971, sect. pres. infectious diseases and virology 1978-85), SAR, Huguenot Soc. Founders Manakin in Colony of Va., Aviation Med. Examiner, Federal Air Surgeon(inf. dis cons.), Masons (32 deg), Shriners. Home: 5910 Prytania St New Orleans LA 70115-4348 Office: Ochsner Clinic Found 1514 Jefferson Hwy New Orleans LA 70121-2483 Office Phone: 504-842-4006. Personal E-mail: gpankey@ochsner.org.

PANKOV, YURI A., molecular biologist, biochemist; b. Leningrad, Russia, Feb. 10, 1930; s. Alexandr Alexeevich and Anna Kusminichna (Ershova) Pankov; m. Svetlana Sergeevna Chumachenko, Oct. 6, 1964; children: Denis, Darya. Diploma in Biochemistry, State U., Leningrad, 1953; PhD, Sci. Coun. Acad. Med. Scis., Moscow, 1963, D in Biol. Scis., 1968. Jr. scientist Inst. Biol. and Med. Chemistry, Moscow, 1953-65; sr. scientist Inst. Exptl. Endocrinology and Hormone Chemistry, Moscow, 1965-70, deputy dir., 1970-83, dir., 1983-90; head of lab. Endocrine Rsch. Ctr., Moscow, 1990—. Dir. Collaborating Ctr. Spl. Program Rsch. Devel. and Rsch. Tng. Human Reproduction WHO, Moscow, 1984—97, dir. Collaborating Ctr. Epidemiology Care and Prevention Diabetes, 1984—90; mem. Sci. and Tech. Adv. Group Spl. Program Rsch. Devel., and Rsch. Tng. Human Reproduction, Geneva, 1985—90; adj. prof. spl. ednl. program biochemistry, immunology, molecular and cellular biology A. N. Belozersky Inst., Moscow State U., 1999; mem., rep. of Russia Order Internat. Fellowship, 2000. Author: (book) Biochemistry of Hormone and Hormonal Regulation, 1976; contbr. scientific papers in field, articles to profl. jours. Named Hon. Citizen, Lexington Urban Govt., 1987, grantee, Internat. Sci. Found., 1994. Mem.: Russian Acad. Med. Scis., Planetary Soc., Endocrine Soc., Cuba Endicronology Soc. (hon.). Avocations: boating, fishing, skiing, vegetable growing. Office: Endocrine Rsch Ctr Moscvorechye St 1 115478 Moscow Russia Office Phone: (78495) 324-9315. Personal E-mail: ercentre@yahoo.com.

PANKOVA, NATALIYA BORISOVNA, physiologist, researcher; b. Golygino of Serpukhov distr., Moscow region, Russia, Sept. 1, 1962; d. Boris Sergeevich Oknin and Rimma Mikhaylovna Oknina; m. Oleg Yurievich Pankov; children: Vyacheslav Olegovich Pankov, Ekaterina Olegovna. Magister, Lomonosov State U., Moscow, 1984, PhD, 1988. Rschr. Inst. Gen. Pathology and Pathophysiology, Moscow, 1988—, prof., 2009—. Tchg. Moscow Inst. Open Edn., Russia, 1999—. Contbr. scientific papers. Office: Inst Gen Pathol and Pathophysiol Baltiyskaya 8 Moscow 125315 Russia Office Fax: (495) 601 21 83; Home Fax: (495) 601-21-83. Personal E-mail: nbpankova@gmail.com.

PANNEERCHELVAM, SUNDARARAJULU, health facility administrator; b. Villupuram, Tamilnadu, India, June 28, 1951; s. Sundararajulu Muthu and Mangalakshimi Sundararajulu; m. Banumathi Panneerchelvam, Mar. 15, 1953; children: Sairaj, Kishorekumar, S.P. Preethy. MSc in Zoology, Annamalai U., Tamilnadu, 1974; LLB, Madras U., Tamilnadu, 1993. Sci. asst. grade 1 Tamilnadu Forensic Sci. Lab., 1974—87; sci. officer Forensic Scis. Dept., Tamilnadu, 1987—98, asst. dir., 1998—2001; lectr. U. Sains Malaysia, 2001—. Contbr. articles to profl. jours. Gen. sec. Tamilnadu Forensic Sci. Staff Welfare Assn., Chennai, India, 1996—99. Mem.: Assn. for the Promotion of DNA Fingerprinting and Other DNA Techs. (life). Hindu. Avocations: badminton, movies, reading, travel. Office: USM Sch Health Scis Jalan Hosp Kuban G Iserian 16150 Malaysia Home: 10 Kamaraj Street 600 078 Chennai India Office Phone: 0609 7663921.

PANNILL, MALCOLM HART, physician assistant, organist, consultant; s. Harry Lee and Louise Lyon Pannill; m. Linda Jane Pannill, May 11, 1985; children: Catherine Elizabeth, Sarah Louise. BS, Guilford Coll., Greensboro, NC, 1986; Ms of Physician Asst. Studies (MPAS), U. Nebr. Coll. Medicine, Omaha, 1998. Cert. Physician Asst. Wake Forest U. Sch. Medicine Physician Asst. Program, 1988, Physician Assistant Nat. Commn. Certification of Physician Assistants (NCCP), 1999; Service Playing Exam Am. Guild Organists, 1992, cert. Certificado Merito Healthcare Spanish Esperanza Ednl. Services, 1997. Physician asst. WakeMed Faculty Physicians Ob/Gyn, Raleigh, NC, 1988—; cons. assoc. dept. cmty. family medicine Duke U. Med. Ctr., Durham, 1989—; ch. organist White Plains United Meth. Ch., Cary, 1990—; physician extender So. Regional Ctr. Wake County Human Services, Raleigh, 1998—. Author: (journal article) Surgical Physician Assistant, Medscape. Sub-dean Ctrl. NC Chpt. Am. Guild Organists, Raleigh, 1991—92. Recipient Circle Quality Svc., WakeMed, 1998. Fellow: NC Acad. Physician Assistants, Am. Acad. Physician Assistants; mem.: Am. Guild Organists (Colleague (CAGO) 1998). Achievements include Bilingual Provider. Avocations: tennis, reading, music. Office: WakeMed Faculty Physicians Ob/Gyn 3024 New Bern Ave Suite 306 Raleigh NC 27610 E-mail: mhp@med.unc.edu.

PANOSIAN, CLAIRE B. (CLAIRE PANOSIAN DUNAVAN), internist, epidemiologist; m. Patrick Dunavan. MD, Northwestern U. Med. Sch., 1976. Cert. Am. Bd. Internal Medicine, Am. Bd. Internal Medicine, Infectious Disease. Intern, internal medicine Northwestern U. Med. Sch., 1976—77, resident, internal medicine, 1977—80; fellow, tropical medicine London Sch. Hygiene & Tropical Medicine, 1979; fellow, infectious disease Tufts-New England Med. Ctr., 1980—83; chief, infectious diseases LA County-Olive View Med. Ctr., 1984—86; founder, dir., Travel and Tropical Medicine Program UCLA Med. Ctr.; with UCLA, 1984—, prof. medicine and infectious diseases, co-founder, co-dir. program for pub. health. Taught courses on tropical medicine, internat. health, and health and human rights David Geffen Sch. Medicine, UCLA, UCLA Coll. of Letters and Sci. & UCLA Grad. Sch. Edn., 1987—; vis. prof., health cons. in Albania, Armenia, Indonesia, Pakistan, Philippines, Taiwan, Tanzania, and Vietnam; sr. cons.-writer Bd. on Global Health, Inst. Medicine. Med. editor, reporter Lifetime TV, created & launched a med. column, The Doctor Files, LA Times, 1989;, prodr. (with husband TV program on hepatitis B); frequent contbr. to LA Times, Scientific American, and Discover Mag., 1987—, columns and articles have appeared in the NY Times, Washington Post, International Herald Tribune, Baltimore Sun, and Chicago Tribune, profl. articles have appeared in Nature, New England Journal of Medicine, Journal of the American Medical Association, and Health Affairs. Mem.: Am. Soc. Tropical Medicine and Hygiene (past pres. 2008, councilor). Office: David Geffen Sch Medicine at UCLA UCLA Program in Global Health 10940 Wilshire Blvd Ste 1220 Los Angeles CA 90024-7230 Office Phone: 310-794-6053. Office Fax: 310-794-2795. Business E-Mail: cpanosian@mednet.ucla.edu.

PANOSSIAN, ANDRE, plastic surgeon, educator; b. Tehran, Iran, June 5, 1971; MD, Tufts U. Sch. Medicine, 2000. Pvt. practice, 2007—; asst. prof. surgery Keck Sch. Medicine, U. SC, 2007—11. Fellow: ACS, Am. Acad. Pediat.; mem.: Am. Cleft Palate-Craniofacial Assn., Am. Soc. Reconstructive Transplantation, Am. Soc. Reconstructive Microsurgery, Alpha Omega Alpha Honor Soc. Avocations: travel, guitar. Office: 800 S Fairmount Ave Ste 207 Pasadena CA 91105 Office Fax: 626-564-0009. Personal E-mail: drpanossian@gmail.com.

PANSINI, JILL ANNE, medical/surgical nurse, consultant; b. Pompton Plains, NJ, June 14, 1965; d. Charles Carmen and Joyce Martha (Hagen) Cullari; m. David Anthony Pansini, May 5, 1991; children: Stephanie Rianne, Sloane Marie, Madison Taylor. AAS, Bergen C.C., 1986; BSN (hon.), Pace U., 1989; cert. in Legal Nurse Consulting (hon.), Fairleigh Dickenson U., 1998. Lic. practical nurse, N.J., 1987, RN N.J., 1988. Staff nurse The Valley Hosp., Ridgewood, NJ, 1986—91; nurse mgr. surg. ICU Clara Maass Med. Ctr., Belleville, NJ, 1991—94; nurse mgr. Post Anesthesia Care Unit St. Barnabas Med. Ctr., Livingston, NJ, 1994—97, perioperative clin. coord., 1997—99; pre-operative staff and charge nurse St. Barnabas Ambulatory Care Ctr., Livingston, 1999—. Tchr. religious edn. St. William the Abbot, Howell, NJ, 2004. Mem.: Am. Assn. Legal Nurse Cons. (assoc.), Sigma Theta Tau (assoc.). Office: 200 S Orange Ave Livingston NJ 07039 Personal E-mail: jillpansini@optonline.net.

PANT, KAMLESH KUMAR, pharmacologist, educator; b. Almora, Oct. 14, 1953; MBBS, King George's Med. Coll., 1975, MD in Pharmacology, 1978; MS, Nat. Acad. Med. Scis., 2010. Tchr. rsch. adminstrn. C.S.M. Med. U., 1978—, prof., head, 2006—. Guest referee Brain Rsch. Jour.; mem. new drug adv. com. Ministry of Health & Family Welfare, New Delhi. Recipient Shakuntala Amir Chand award, Indian Coun. Med. Rsch., 1986; Alta. Heritage fellowship, U. Alta., Edmonton, Can. Mem.: IUPHAR, Indian Pharmacol. Soc., Nat. Acad. Med. Scis. (India). Avocations: computers, reading. Office: Dept Pharmacology & Therapeutic Lucknow Uttar Pradesh 226003 India Home Phone: 0522-4021208. Office Fax: 2257448. E-mail: pant.kamlesh@gmail.com.

PANTEL, JACQUES J., medical educator; b. Cognac, Jan. 17, 1968; PharmD, Paris-Descartes U., 1995, PhD, 1997. Resident Assistance Publique des Hopitaux de Paris, France, 1991—97; postdoc. rschr. INSERM, 1998—2000, assoc. prof., 2001—, adj. assoc. prof. Vanderbilt Med. Ctr., 2008. Rsch. grant, NIH Dk R01, 2010—. Mem.: European Soc. Paediatric Endocrinology. Office: 2ter Rue d Alesia Paris 75014 France Business E-Mail: jacques.pantel@vanderbilt.edu.

PANTELL, ROBERT HOWARD, pediatrician, educator; b. NYC, Oct. 6, 1945; s. Milton and Rose (Rappaport) P.; m. Marcia Ruth Snell, Oct. 30, 1971 (div. 1980); m. Maureen Theresa Shannon, Aug. 29, 1982; children: Matthew Shannon, Gregory Michael, Megan Elizabeth. BA, Columbia U., 1965; MD, Boston U., 1969. Cert. in pediat. Am. Bd. Med. Specialties, 1974. Intern in pediat. NC Meml. Hosp., Chapel Hill, resident in pediat., 1969-72; fellow in health svcs. rsch., behavioral pediat. Stanford U.; pediatrician, med. dir. Cmty. Health Clinics, Nampa, Idaho, 1972-74; Robert Wood Johnson Found. clin. scholar Stanford (Calif.) U., 1974-77; asst. prof. med. U. SC, Charleston, 1977-80; prof., dir. divsn. gen. pediat. U. Calif.-San Francisco, 1980—. Cons. for fed. and pvt. founds. Author: Taking Care of Your Child, 1977, 8th edit., trans. to Japanese, 1982, Spanish, 1983, Italian, 1990, Chinese, 2007, (Book of Yr. award Am. Med. Writers Assn. 1978); author, editor: Parents' Pharmacy, 1982, Pediatrics: A Study Guide, 1987, The Common Sympton Guide, 1977, 7th edit., 2009; contbr. articles to profl. publs. Grantee HHS, David and Lucile Packard Found., Nat. Ctr. Health Svcs. Rsch., Investigator award Am. Assn. Med. Colleges, 1986. Fellow Am. Acad. Pediat.; mem. Ambulatory Pediatric Assn. (bd. dirs. 1988, Tchg. award Cmty. Program, 1998), Am. Pediat. Soc. Office: Divsn Gen Pediat U Calif Box 0503 3333 California St Ste 245 San Francisco CA 94118 Home: 11 Piedmont St San Francisco CA 94117 Office Phone: 415-476-4349. Office Fax: 415-476-6106. Business E-Mail: pantellr@peds.ucsf.edu.

PANTHAKI, ZUBIN JAL, medical educator, plastic surgeon; b. Bombay, Feb. 26, 1968; arrived in U.S., 2000; s. Jal Minocher Panthaki and Nergish Nanabhoy Sethna; m. Dimple Panthaki; children: Karl, Kayaan. B in Engring., McGill U., Montreal, Quebec, 1991, MD, 1995. Diplomate Am. Bd. Plastic Surgeons, cert. for hand surgery Am. Bd. Plastic Surgeons, lic. N.H., Fla. Resident in surgery McGill U., Montreal, 1995—2000; microsurgery and hand surgery fellow Buncke Clinic, San Francisco, 2000—01; assoc. prof. plastic surgery U. Miami, Fla., 2001—, program dir. plastic surgery, 2005—. Cons. Miami Children's Hosp., Jackson Meml. Hosp., 2001—, Miami Vets. Hosp., West Palm Beach Vets. Hosp., U. Miami Hosps., chief hand surgery, plastic surgery; editor Plastic Surgery Hyperguide, 2009—. Editor: Jour. Craniofacial Surgery, 2004—. Vol. Interplast, 2003—; trustee Stanstead Coll., 2007—. Capt. mil. engrs., 1987—2000, Can. Fellow: Royal Coll. Surgeons; mem.: Am. Soc. Surgery Hand, Am. Soc., Miami Soc. Plastic Surgeons (pres. 2007—), Fellow Am. Coll. Surgeons, Fla. Soc. Plastic Surgeons, Nat. Bd. Med. Examiners, Am. Soc. Plastic Surgeons. Avocation: computers. Home: 6002 SW 58th St South Miami FL 33143 Office: University Miami Clin Research Bldg 1120 NW 14th St 4th Fl Miami FL 33136 Home Phone: 305-531-0601; Office Phone: 305-243-4500. Office Fax: 305-243-4535. Business E-Mail: zpanthaki@med.miami.edu.

PANULA, PERTTI AARRE JUHANI, anatomy and cell biology educator, scientist; b. Helsinki, Finland, Mar. 1, 1952; s. Aarre Erkki and Eine Irene (Hongisto) P.; m. Ann-Charlotte Lassenius, May 25, 1962; children: Jonatan Mikael, Hanna Miranda, Julian Sebastian, Ellen Matilda. MD, U. Helsinki, 1977, PhD, 1980. Instr. U. Helsinki, 1977-81; vis. fellow NIH, Washington, 1981-83; sr. lectr. U. Helsinki, 1983-85, assoc. prof., 1986-87; sr. scientist Acad. Finland, 1986-92; prof. cell biology Åbo Akademi U., Turku, Finland, 1992—; prof. biomedicine U. Helsinki, 2000—. Sec. gen. VII Internat. Congress Histochemistry and Cytochemistry, Helsinki, 1984; sec. Soc. for Histochemistry and Cytochemistry, Finland, 1978-79. Author: Protection of Birds, 1970; editor: Neurohistochemistry, 1986; contbr. articles on neurobiology to profl. jours. Lt. Finnish Navy, 1980-81. Lutheran. Research interests include biology of neuropeptides and histamine, development and function of neurotransmission. Home: Finntraskinsalmi 31 Jorvas 02420 Finland Office: Inst of Biomedicine Haartmaninkatru 8 00270 Helsinki Finland Office Phone: 358919125263.

PAO, LINCOLN K., oncologist, educator; s. James and Sandra Pao; 1 child, Sophia. MD, Johns Hopkins, Baltimore. Diplomate Am. Bd. Radiology, 1995. Asst. prof. Cornell U., NYC, 2004—, Columbia U., NYC, 2004—; with Johns Hopkins Alumni Exe. Com., NY Chpt., 2008—; admission interviewer U. Pa., 2009—, Nat. Arts Club, 2010—. Chmn., radiation oncology NY Roentgen Soc., NYC, 2005—06; bd. advisors Am. Cancer Soc., NYC, 2004—; councilor Am. Coll. Radiology, NYC, 2007—; chmn. radiation oncology NY State Radiol. Soc., NYC, 2008—. Bd. mem., arts com. Redeemer Presbyn., NYC, 2006. Named Top Dr. in US, CRC, 2005—. Mem.: Am. Soc. Therapeutic Radiology & Oncology, Nat. Arts Club. Personal E-mail: radcare@yahoo.com. Business E-Mail: pao@jhu.edu.

PAOLAGGI, JOSEPH ANTOINE, internist, medical educator; b. Santa Maria Sicche, Corse, France, Oct. 11, 1925; s. Dominique and Jeanne (Massimi) P. MD, Faculty of Medicine, Paris, 1955, Prof Agrege, 1966. Diplomate in medicine. Chief of clinic Faculty of Medicine, Paris, 1956-58; med. asst. Hosps. of Paris, 1961-66, physician, 1966-94; chief of svc. Hosp. Beaujon, Paris, 1975-91; med. cons. Hosp. Bichat, Paris, 1991-94, med. conciliator, 1995-97. Contbr. more than 400 articles to profl. jours. Decorated officer Nat. Order Legion of Honor (France). Mem. Assn. Charles Debray (pres. 1990—), Club Francais d'Echoendoscopie (pres. 1988-95). Roman Catholic.

PAOLICCHI, JULIANN MARIE, neurologist, educator; b. Chgo., May 22, 1959; MA, MD, Johns Hopkins U., 1988. With Nationwide Children's Hosp., Columbus, 1997—2007; assoc. prof. Monroe Carell Jr. Children's Hosp., Vanderbilt, 2008—. Vol. dept. drama & music Brentwood HS, Tenn. Grant, NINDS, Katherine Dodd Tchg. Soc., Dept. Pediat., Monroe Carell Jr. Children's Hosp. Mem.: Am. Neurol. Assn., John Hopkins Med. and Surg. Assn., Am. Acad. Neurology, Am. Epilepsy Soc. (Pediatric content adv. com. mem. 2010—), Child Neurology Soc. (long-term planning com. mem. 2010—, prof.). Office: 2200 Children's Way DOT 11212 Nashville TN 37232 Office Fax: 615-343-8407. Business E-Mail: juliann.paolicchi@vanderbilt.edu.

PAOLINO, RONALD MARIO, clinical psychologist, consultant, psychopharmacologist, pharmacist; b. Providence, Mar. 15, 1938; s. Lawrence and Mary Corinne (Guglielmi) P.; m. Eileen Frances Quimby, June 18, 1960; children: Lisa Katherine, David Lawrence. Student, Providence Coll., 1955—56; BS in Pharmacy, U. R.I., 1959, MS, 1961; PhD in Pharmacology/Toxicology, Purdue U., 1963; postdoctoral studies Exptl. Psychology, Yale U., 1963—65; doctoral studies in clin. psychology, Purdue U., 1972—74; postdoctoral studies in existential analytic psychotherapy, Okla. Inst. Existential Analysis and Psychotherapy, 1974—75; Hostage Negotiation, FBI, 1991, Advanced Hostage Negotiation, 1995; Crisis Negotaition, FBI Acad., 1994; MA (hon.), Brown U., 1977. Lic. psychologist, R.I., pharmacist R.I.; nat. registered health svc. provider in psychology; cert. arbitrator; cert. nat. registered group psycho-therapists; cert. edn. provider N.Y.; diplomate Am. Bd. Forensic Examiners, Am. Bd. Forensic Medicine; nat. cert. mediator Dept. Vet. Affairs, 2007. Intern dept. psychiatry and behavioral scis. U. Okla. Health Scis. Ctr., 1974—75, NIMH fellow in clin. psychology, 1974-75; David Ross predoctoral fellow dept. pharmacology/toxicology Purdue U., West Lafayette, Ind., 1961—63, assoc. prof. psychopharmacology, 1967—74; NIMH postdoctoral fellow in psychology dept. psychology Yale U., 1963—65; asst. prof. pharmacology U. Conn. Sch. Pharmacy, 1965—67; coord. group psychotherapy tng. program Brown U. Program in Medicine, 1983—85, assoc. prof. psychiatry and human behavior, 1976—90; pvt. practice; chief drug dependency treatment program VA Med. Ctr., Providence, 1975—87, dir. biofeedback clinic, 1977—87, primary hostage negotiator, 1991—. Psychiatric cons. VA Police, alternative Dispute Resolution Mediator, New Eng. Veterans Integrated Svc. Network, 1996—, pain mgmt. bd., 1999—; mem. Pharmacology and Therapeutic Agts. Com., 1979-87, VA Med. Ctr., coord. VA Contracted Half-Way Project for Substance Dependent Vets., 1981-85, chmn. Pain Mgmt. Task Force, 1984-85, mem. Supervisory Level Pharmacy Profl. Standards Bd., 1990—, mem. Mgmt. Suicidal and Violent Patient Task Force, 1990-91, chmn. Com. Prevention & Mgmt. of Disturbed Behaviors, 1991—, chief crisis mgmt. program, 1993-96, advisor FBI Hostage Negotiations, 1991—, Instr. R.I. State Police Acad., 1994, Instr., Drug Recognition Experts Recert PRGM, R.I. Dept Health, 1995, Faculty, Law Enforcement Mgmt. Command Sch. U.R.I., 1991—, Va. Nat. Law Enforcement Tng. Ctr., 1997; chmn. Outpatient Psychiatry Svcs. Reorganization Task Force, 1991, mem. VA DOD Desert Storm Emergency Plan Com., 1991; advisor OSHA Dept. Labor for Violence in the Work Place, 1994-95; mem. E. Prov. Clergy & Mental Health Providers Alliance, 1995—; mem. substance abuse and prevention grant application rev. com. R.I. Adv. Coun. on Substance Abuse, 1982-92, prevention, edn. and tng. com. on substance abuse, 1981—, chmn. 1981-82; adj. assoc. prof. psychology, U. R.I., 1982—, clin. prof. pharmacy U. R.I., 1998—; mem. planning com. State Conf. on Substance Abuse in the Hispanic Community, 1986; mem. alcohol awareness commn. Episc. Diocese of R.I., 1983-85; gubernatorial appointee Gov.'s Permanent Coun. on Drug Abuse Control, 1978-82; mem. rev. com. for funding of state drug abuse programs R.I. Single State Agy. on Drug Abuse, R.I. Dept. Mental Health Retardation and Hosps., 1978-82; cons. Nurses Renewal Com., 1980-81, substance abuse prevention edn. for elem. sch. children R.I. chpt. ARC, 1977, mem. suicide prevention steering com., 1977; mem.Interagy. Drug Abuse Steering Com., Lafayette, Ind. 1969-72; bd. dirs. Providence VA Med. Ctr. Credit Union; mem. bd. cert. for alcoholism counselors R.I. Assn. Alcohol Counselors, 1979-81; mem. Gov.'s Task Force on Substance Abuse at Adult Correctional Instn., 1977-78, Gov.'s Task Force on Mental Health Svcs. at Adult Correctional Instn., 1977-78, chmn. reclassification of inmates com., 1977-78; chmn. com. on edn. and cert. biofeedback practioners Conn. Biofeedback Soc., 1977-78; summer faculty fellow U. Conn., 1967; vis. scientist lectr. Assn. Am. Colls. Pharmacy, 1972-73; cons. to bus., unions, law enforcement. Author: (2 chpts.) Drug Testing: Issues and Options, 1991; contbr. 37 articles to profl. jours. Bd. dirs. R.I. chpt. Samaritans Internat. Suicide Prevention Orgn., 1978-84; v.p. Experience Jesus Inc.; mem. com. adv. bd. Cpina Bifida Assn. R.I., 1980-83; mem. R.I. East Bay Interfaith Mental Health Alliance; congressman appointee (Patrick J. Kennedy); mem. veterans adv. commn., 1995—. Recipient Citation award for svc. and contbns. to formulation of state policy for treatment and prevention of drug abuse Gov. R.I., 1983, Letter of Commendation, Gov.'s R.I. Adv. Coun. on Substance Abuse, 1986, vc. Recognition award DAV, 1990, Spl. Contbn. award Providence VA Med Ctr., 1990, 98, 99, 2000, 05, 10, Outstanding Performance award, 1991, 92, 93, 94, 97, 11, cert. appreciation for continued excellence in patient care, 1999; named to Cranston Hall of Fame, 2001. Fellow Am. Coll. Forensic Examiners; mem. AMA, Am. Psychotherapy Assn., Am. Soc. Pharmacology Exptl. Therapeutics, Internat. Brain Rsch. Orgn., Internat. Narcotic Enforcement Officers Assn., R.I. Group Psychotherapy Soc. (pres. 1991-93, continuing edn. dir. psychologists 1990-95, exec. bd. 1986—, tng. faculty 1985—, co-dir. tng. 1986-87, tng. adv. bd. 1985-86), R.I. Psychol. Assn. (chmn. substance abuse ins. subcom. 1986-87, rep. Gov.'s Coun. on Mental Health State Plan Com. 1982-84), Hostage Negotiators Am. Office: Mental Health and Behavioral Scis Svc VA Med Ctr Providence RI Office Phone: 401-457-3083. E-mail: ronald.paolinophd@med.va.gov.

PAOLO, BECK-PECCOZ, endocrinologist, educator; b. Gressoney Saint Jean, Aosta, Sept. 5, 1943; MD, U. Turin, 1969. Prof. endocrinology U. Milan, 1990. Recipient ETA Merck prize, European Thyroid Assn. Avocations: skiing, birdwatching. Office: Via F sforza 35 Milan Lombardy 20122 Italy Business E-Mail: paolo.beckpeccoz@unimi.it.

PAOLUCCI, GABRIELLA, cosmetic dentist; Grad., Loyola U., Chgo., 1988. Featured in Chgo. Mag., New Beauty Mag. Mailing: 1960 Essington Rd Joliet IL 60435 Office Phone: 815-436-8660. Office Fax: 815-577-0189.

PAPACONSTANTINOU, ANTHONY, pulmonologist; b. Athens, Greece, May 7, 1949; s. Periklis and Niki Papaconstantinou; m. Urania Spyrakou, Oct. 10, 1976; children: Periklis, Danai. MD, Med. Sch. Athens, 1973; tng. in allergy-immunology, Sotiria Hosp. Chest Diseases, Athens, 1983—85. Cert. pneumology specialist Greek Ministry Health. Intern 401 Gen. Army Hosp., Athens, 1975—76; resident Syros Gen. Hosp., Greece, 1976—78; fellow Sotiria Hosp. Chest Diseases, Athens, 1979—81, registrar, 1981—85; assoc. prof. Athens Technol. Inst., 1985—97; dir. IDEA Med. Diagnostic Labs., Athens, 1987—. Author: Physiology, 1977, Tuberculosis, 1986; contbr. articles to profl. jours. Mem.: Interasma, Am. Thoracic Soc., Panhellenic Assn. Health Scientists (pres. 1995—). Achievements include patent for IAST (Inhalation Allergy Screen Test) method of in vitro diagnosis of respiratory allergy. Office: IDEA Med Diagnostic Labs Skufa 27 106 73 Athens Greece Office Phone: 30210-3609363. Fax: 302103601762. E-mail: idea@hol.gr.

PAPADAKIS, EMMANOUEL GEORGE, surgeon; b. Ierapetra, Greece, June 7, 1953; s. George Emmanouel Papadakis and Maria Emmanouel Lambrakis. DDS, U. Athens, 1978; MD, U. Thessaloniki, 1984; PhD, U. Athens, 1992. Diplomate European Bd. Thoracic and Cardiovasc. Surgeons, 2002, cert. in thoracic and cardiovascular surgery Hellenic Ministry Health, 1992. Gen. surgery program A. Fleming State Gen. Hosp., Athens, 1984—87; thoracic surgeon Metaxa Anticancer Hosp., Athens, 1987—89; cardiac surgeon Evagelismos Gen. Hosp., Athens, 1989—93, Onasis Cardiac Surgery Ctr., Athens, 1993—. Cons. Hellenic Surg. Soc., Athens, 1999—. Contbr. articles to profl. jours. Recipient Surg. Skill award, Hellenic Surg. Soc., 2003; grantee, Hellenic Ministry Health, 1992. Fellow: ACS; mem.: Brit. Gen. Med. Coun. (mem. gen. med. coun. 1987—2005), Athens Med. Assn., European Soc. Cardiovasc. Surgery. Avocations: music, gymnastics, sailing, nature and environment, philosophy. Home: Korai 43 N Smirni Athens 171 22 Greece Office: Onasis Cardiac Surgery Centre Sygrou Ave 356 Kallithea Athens 176 74 Greece Address: Nikomidias 40 N Smirni 171 24 Athens Greece Office Fax: 210 9493331; Home Fax: 210 9493331.

PAPADAKIS, STAMATIOS A., orthopedist, surgeon, consultant; s. Alexandros Napoleon and Lemonia Paraskevi Papadakis. BS in Medicine and Surgery, Nat. and Kapodestrian U. Athens, 1990; DSc, Med. Sch. Athens U., Greece, 2003. Cert. full registration Athens Med. Assn., 1991, Orthop. Surgery Bd., 1998. Lt. physician civil res. Greek Army M.C., Corfu, Greece, 1991—92, gen. practitioner ministry health, 1991—92; resident gen. surgery Patission Gen. Hosp., Athens, 1993—94; resident dept. orthops. Athens U., 1994—98, fellow spinal surgery dept. orthops. spinal unit, 1998—2000; fellow osteoporosis Nat. Ctr. Metabolic Diseases, Athens, 1996; fellow dept. microsurgery G.H.A. KAT, Athens, 1997; fellow endoscopic spinal surgery Orthop. Clinic Kassel, Germany, 1998; cons. orthopaedics Didimoticho Gen. Hosp. Nat. Health Sys., Greece, 2000—03, cons. orthops. health ctr. Myconos Greece, 2003—04, cons. orthops. Gen. Hosp. Atika Athens, 2007—; cons. orthops. Thriasio Gen. Hosp., Elefsina, Greece, 2004—06. Coord. Ministry Health, Athens, 2004—; treas. Sector Spinal Diseases, Athens, 2007—; sec. sci. com. Gen. Hosp. Didimoticho, 2000—01; mem. Health Adv. Bd., Didimoticho, 2003—03; clin. rsch. fellow trauma svc. dept. orthop. surgery Keck sch. medicine U. So. Calif., LA, 2001—02; reviewer profl. jours. Contbr. chapters to books, articles to profl. jours. Recipient Remarkable Social Offer and Activity cert., Pres. Corfu G. P. Hosp., 1992, Social Offer Onorary medal, Mayor Poros, 1999, Remarkable Offer Onorary medal, V.P. Spl. Olympics, 1999. Fellow: Hellenic Med. Acupuncture Soc. (licentiate), Hellenic Found. Osteoporosis (hon.); mem.: Hellenic Soc. Crisis and Disaster Medicine (pres. 2005—), Hellenic Soc.Study Bone Metabolism (assoc.), Hellenic Spine Soc. (life), Greek Friends Meth. Hosp. (assoc.), Hellenic Assn. Orthop. Surgery and Traumatology (assoc.; dep. sec. 2006—07, Acad. award 2002), Hellenic Med. Assn. Arts and Dance (corr.), Rotary (pres. Pendeli chpt. 1998—99, 2003—04), Hellenic Assn. Rd. Traffic Victim Support (life). Avocations: guitar, chess, swimming, modelism, scuba diving. Home: 28th Octovriou Street 54 Attika Nea Penteli 152 36 Greece Office: General Hosp Attika KAT 2 Nikis Street Attika Kifissia 145 61 Greece Personal E-mail: snapmd@gmail.com.

PAPADAKOS, PETER JOHN, critical care physician, educator; b. Bklyn., Feb. 4, 1957; s. John and Irene (Vahaviolos) P.; m. Susan E. Dantoni; children: Yanni, Ava René BA, NYU, 1979; MD, Mt. Sinai Sch. Med, CUNY, 1983. Intern, then resident in surgery Roosevelt Hosp., NYC, 1983-85; resident in anesthesiology Mt. Sinai Hosp., NYC, 1985-87, fellow in critical care medicine, 1987-88; from asst. prof. to prof. anesthesiology and surgery U. Rochester (N.Y.) Sch. Medicine, 1988—2003, prof. anesthesiology, surgery, and neurosurgery, 2003—, dir. divsn. critical care medicine, 2000—. Prof. respiratory care SUNY, 1996—. Editor: (textbooks) The Intensive Care Manual, 2001, Requisites in Anesthesiology Critical Care Medicine, 2005, Mechanical Ventilation Principals and Pathophysiology, 2007, Mechanical Ventilation Critical Care Clinics, 2007; editor-in-chief Controversies in Critical Care; sect. editor Intensive Care Medicine Jour. Applied Cardiopulmonary Pathophysiology, Internet Jour. Emergency and Intensive Care Medicine, Intensive Care & Shock, Jour. Neurocritical Care; mem. adv. bd. Anesthesiology News; contbr. articles to profl. jours., numerous chpts. to books. Trustee Incurable Illness Found., N.Y.C., 1986-88. Recipient rsch. award USN, 1975, Pres.'s citation Soc. Critical Care Medicine, 1996. Fellow Coll. Critical Care Medicine, Am. Coll. Chest Physicians; mem. Shock Soc., Soc. Critical Care, Thoracic Soc. Achievements include research on effect of inverse ratio ventilation and pressure regulated volume control on acute respiratory distress syndrome, research on septic shock and oxygen delivery, basic science work on pulmonary pathophysiology of acute lung failure; research on nitric oxide in treatment of lung failure and acute respiratory distress syndrome; research on open lung concept. Office: U Rochester 601 Elmwood Ave Rochester NY 14642-0001 Office Phone: 585-273-4750. Business E-Mail: peter_papadakos@urmc.rochester.edu.

PAPADATOU PASTOU, MARIETTA, psychologist, researcher, educator; b. Athens, Attiki, Greece, Oct. 7, 1980; d. Maria Papadatou-Pastou and Ioannis Papadatos. BSc in Psychology, Panteion U., Athens, 2003; MSc in Psychology, U. Oxford, Eng., 2004, DPhil in Neuropsychology, 2008. Cert. psychologist Greece, 2003. Rsch. assoc., Ctr. Study Psychophysiology and Edn. U. Athens, Athens, 2003—09, lectr. in neuropsychology-lang. functions, 2009—. Contbr. scientific papers. Scholarship, Greek State Scholarship Found., 2003—08, grant, A.G. Leventis Found., 2006. Mem.: Hellenic Soc. Neurosciences, Hellenic Psychol. Soc., Internat. Brain Rsch. Orgn., Fedration European Neuroscience Socs., Brit. Neuroscience Assn., Brit. Psychol. Soc. Personal E-mail: marietta.papadatou@gmail.com.

PAPADIA, FRANCESCO SAVERIO, medical educator; b. Genoa, Italy, Mar. 25, 1973; s. Salvatore Papadia and Mariangela Marcenaro. MD, U. Genoa, 1998. Affiliate Surgeon Am. Soc. Bariatric Surgery, 2003. Resident surgeon U. Genoa Med. Sch., Genoa, Italy, 1998—2003, asst. prof. surgery, 2003—. Mem. Rotaract Internat., Genoa, 1992—94. Scholar, Deutsches Akademisches Austauschdienst, 1992, Uehara Meml. Found., 2002. Mem.: Internat. Hepato-Pancreato Billary Assn., Soc. Polispecialistica Italiana Giovani Chirurghi, Soc. Italiana Chirurghi Univ., Am. Soc. Bariatric Surgery, Yacht Club Italiano. Roman Catholic. Achievements include research in hepato-pancreato-biliary surgery and obesity surgery, published in internationl medical journals. Avocations: sailing, skiing, travel. Office: Clinica Chirurgica Univ Genoa Lgo Rosanna Benzi 8 Genoa 16100 Italy Home: 3 Piazza Raffaele Rossetti 5 16129 Genoa GE Italy Home Fax: +39-010-502754. Personal E-mail: francesco.papadia@unige.it.

PAPADIMITRIOU, GEORGE MARIOS, rheumatologist, educator; b. Thessaloniki, Makedonia, Greece, Dec. 1, 1940; s. Marios Ioannis Papadimitriou and Niki Georgios Mantalla; m. Evangelina Christos Zachariadou, Apr. 30, 1976; children: Marios, Christos. MD, U. Thessaloniki, 1965; diploma in Internal Medicine, Hippocration Hosp., Athens, Greece, 1973; diploma in Rheumatology, Royal Nat. Hosp. Rheumatic Diseases, Bath, Eng. and Athens, 1980; diploma in Aerospace Medicine, Sch. Aerospace Medicine, San Antonio, 1970. Mil. physician Greek Air Force, Greece, 1965—78; registrar in rheumatology Royal Nat. Hosp. Rheumatic Diseases, Bath, 1978—79, 251 Gen. Air Force Hosp., Athens, 1980—83, dir. dept. rheumatology, 1984—92; prof. Athens U., 1989—. Cons. Hygeia Hosp., Athens, 2003—. Contbr. chapters to books, articles to profl. jours. Recipient award, Athens Acad. Fellow: Royal Coll. Physicians; mem.: Brit. Soc. Rheumatology, Hellenic Soc. Rheumatology (v.p. 1997—98, pres. 1999—2000). Avocation: classical music. Office: 28th Oktovriou 8 St Agia Paraskevi 15341 Athens Greece Office Phone: 30 210-6560255. Business E-Mail: gmpap@otenet.gr.

PAPADOPOULOS, CONSTANTINE L., cardiology educator; b. Pyrgos, Greece, Feb. 6, 1939; s. Leonidas and Anna (Diamantopoulou) Papadopoulos; m. Malamati Lioliopoulou (div. 1985); children: Leonidas, Paul. MD, PhD, Aristotle U., Thessaloniki, Greece, 1963. Asst. resident, sr. resident 2nd dept. internal medicine Aristotle U., Thessaloniki, 1963-69, lectr. 2nd dept. internal medicine, 1970-75, sr. lectr., 1975-78, asst. prof., 1978-85, commd. spl. scientist, 1980—85, assoc. prof. of cardiology, 1985-2000, prof. cardiology, 2000—06, prof. emeritus, 2006—. Head sect. cardiology 2d univ. dept. internal medicine Hippokration Gen. Hosp., Thessaloniki, 1969—80, dir. 2d univ. dept. cardiology, 1985—2006, vice chmn. divsn. internal medicine, 1999—2006; dir. dept. cardiology Gen. Pref. Hosp., Larissa, Greece, 1973—74; head sect. cardiology 1st univ. dept. cardiology Ahepa Gen. Hosp., Thessaloniki, 1980—85. Co-editor and author: (V. Kokkas, C. Papadopoules) Issues of molecular Pharmacology of the Cardiovascular System, 2011, Molecular Pharmacolgy of Inflammation in Relation to the Cardiovascular System, 2006, Molecular Pharmacology of the Vascular Tone, 2008, contbr. chapter to books, numerous articles to profl. jours. Fellow Internat. Coll. Angiology, Internat. Coll. Chest Physicians and Surgeons, European Hypertension Soc., European Soc. Cardiology (working group on nuc. cardiology and magnetic resonance imaging), Am. Coll. Angiology, Am. Coll. Chest Physicians, Am. Coll. Cardiology; mem. Internat. Soc. on Thrombosis and Haemostasis, Internat. Soc. on Mechanocardiology, European Soc. on Mechanocardiology, N.Am. Soc. Pacing and Electrophysiology, Am. Soc. Nuc. Cardiology, Mediterranean League on Thrombosis and Haemostasis, Union Med. Balcanique, Am. Heart Assn. (clin. cardiology coun.), Hellenic Soc. Cardiology (former v.p.), Hellenic Soc. Hypertension (former pres.), Cardiol. Soc. No. Greece (former pres.), Hellenic Soc. Pediat. Cardiology, Hellenic Soc. Nephrology, Hellenic League Thrombosis Hemost, Hellenic Soc. Respiration Physiopathology, Hellenic Soc. Biochemistry, Hellenic Soc. Study and Application Ultra-sounds in Medicine and Biology, Hellenic Soc. Pharmacology, Hellenic Soc. Atherosclerosis, Med. Soc. Thessaloniki (past gen. sec.), N.Y. Acad. Scis. Greek Orthodox. Avocations: astronomy, palaeontology, philosophy, painting. Office: Hippokration Gen Hosp Constantinoupoleos 49 54642 Thessaloniki Greece Home: Vasilissis Olgas 83 546 42 Thessaloniki Greece Office Phone: 0030.2310.81710.

PAPADOPOULOS, EMMANUEL STAVROS, physical therapist; b. Athens, Attika, Greece, July 20, 1967; s. Stavros Emmanuel Papadopoulos and Despina Anastasios Papadopoulou; m. Maria Dimitrios Cherouvim, June 19, 1999; 1 child, Marina Emmanual Papadopoulou; children: Polixeni Emmanuel Papadopoulou, Despina Emmanuel Papadopoulou. Diploma in Phys. Therapy, Technol. Ednl. Inst. Athens, 1989; diploma in Physiotherapy for Sports, U. London, 1992; MS in Rehab. Studies, U. Southampton, UK, 1993; PhD, U. Athens, 2006. Registered physiotherapist Health Professions Coun., 1995. Physiotherpist Ealing Hosp. NHS Trust, London, 1990—91; sr. physiotherapist Ctrl. Middlesex Hosp., London, 1992, Southampton Gen. Hosp., Hampshire, 1992—93; head physiotherapist Anaplasis Rehab. Ctr., Athens, 1996—97; sr. physiotherapist Evangelismos Gen. Hosp., Athens, 1999—. Physiotherapy lectr. Technol. Ednl. Inst. Of Lamia, Lamia, Fthiotida, Greece, 1995—96, Technol. Ednl. Inst. Athens, 1997—. Editor (reviewer): Physical Therapy Themes (Contbn. Award in the 'Phys. Therapy Thenes' Jour., 2001, 2008); contbr. articles to med. sci. jours. With marine svc. Greece Army, 1994—95. Named one of Top 100 Health Profls., 2007. Mem.: European Tissue Repair Soc., Greek Physiotherapy Soc., Soc. Orthopaedic Medicine. Greek Orthodox. Avocations: sports, singing, music. Office: Evangelismos Gen Hospl 42-44 Ipsilantou St Attika Athens 10675 Greenland Home: Irinis Leof. 37 185 47 Piraeus 18547 Greece Office Fax: 0103210 7244941. Personal E-mail: epapas@in.gr. Business E-Mail: epapadop@phed.uoa.gr.

PAPADOPOULOS, NIKOLAOS M., internist; b. Athens, Attiki, Greece, Dec. 13, 1971; D, Aristotelion U. Thessaloniki, 1996. Internist, hepatic disorders specialist 401 Gen. Army Hosp. Athens, 2005—. Mem.: EASL. Office: Ravine 14-16 Athens Attiki 11521 Greece Personal E-mail: npnck7@yahoo.com.

PAPADOPOULOS, NIKOLAOS THEOLOGOS, medical educator; b. Drama, Macedonia, Greece, Oct. 15, 1945; Degree in Medicine, 1970. Prof. Aristotle U. Thessaloniki, 1978—. Mem. bd. dirs. Ophthal. Clinic AHEPA Hosp., 2000—. Master. Ophthal. Clinic, fellow. European Bd. Ophthalmology. Avocations: painting, music, fishing, gardening. Home: 3 Nestoros Typa Thessaloniki Macedonia 546 46 Greece Home Fax: 00302310242542.

PAPADOPOULOS, STEPHEN M., neurosurgeon; m. Penelope Papadopoulos; children: Michael, Mathew, Marcus. BS, U. Calif., San Diego, 1978, MS, U. Tex., Houston, 1982. Cert. MD Tex., 83, bd. cert. 91. Intern U. Mich., Ann Arbor, 1982—83, resident, 1983—88, neurosurgeon, 1989—2000, program dir. image guided surgery, 2000—01, Barrow Neurosurg. Assoc., 2001—, neurosurgeon, 2001—. Bd. mem. St. Joseph's Hosp. and Med. Ctr., Phoenix, 2004—. Editor: Spinal Arthroplasty - The Preservation of Motion, 2007. Recipient Young Investigator award in Stroke, Am. Heart Assn., 1989, Resident Rsch. award, Joint Cerebrovascular Sect., 1987, Rehab. Act Title II, US Dept. Edn., 1991—2001. Mem.: Congress Neurol. Surgeons, Am. Assn. Neurol. Surgeons/Congress Neurol. Surgeons Joint Sect. Disorders Spine and Peripheral Nerves, Am. Assn. Neurol. Surgeons. Achievements include patents for an anterior cervical plating system, an adjustable surgical guide and method of treating vertebral members. Office: Barrow Neurosurg Assn 2910 N 3rd Ave Phoenix AZ 85013 Office Phone: 602-406-3159. Office Fax: 602-406-3167.

PAPADOPULOS, NIKOLAOS A., assistant medical director, researcher, physician; b. Zevgolatio, Serres, Greece, Mar. 10, 1966; s. Apostolos M. Papadopoulos and Maria N. Papadopoulou. MD, U. Naples and Perugia, Italy, 1991; Dr Med., Tech. U. Munich, Germany, 1999, PhD, 2003. Cert. specialist in plastic surgery Tech. U., Munich, 2001. Resident physician dept. traumatology Clinic Neuss, Germany, 1993—94; asst. prof. dept. plastic surgery, resident MD dept. plastic surgery Tech. U. Munich, 1994—96, asst. prof. dept. plastic surgery, resident physician, 1997—2000, prof. plastic surgery, 2009, sci. collaborator dept. plastic surgery, 2000—02, physician dept. plastic surgery, asst. med. dir. dept. plastic surgery, 2002—, prof. plastic surgery, 2009; rsch. fellow Ctr. Surg. Techs. Cath. U. Leuven, Belgium, 1996—97; physician dept. plastic surgery, asst. med. dir. dept. plastic surgery Klinikum Dachau, Bavaria, Germany, 2001—02; prof. plastic surgery, 2009. Guest med. physician dept. surgery State Clinics Neuss, 1992—93. Contbr. articles, letters, and abstracts to profl. jours. Student grantee, ERSU Perugia Italy, 1986—91, Residency grantee, Ctrl. European Divsn. Hellenic Orthodox Ch., 1994—96, 1997—98, Rsch. grantee, Rsch. Coun. Tech. U. Munich, 1998—2001, 2001—, 2003—, Karl Storz Endoskope, Tuttlingen, Germany, 2002—, Rsch. fellow, Med. Faculty Cath. U. Leuven, 1996—97, others. Mem.: European Assn. Plastic Surgeons, Assn. Bavarian Surgeons, Hellenic Acad. Munich Germany, German Soc. Plastic and Reconstructive Surgery, World Soc. Reconstructive Microsurgery, Hellenic Soc. Hand Surgery, Hellenic Med. Assn., German Med. Assn., Greek Maternalfetal Med. Soc., Balcan Assn. Plastic, Reconstructive and Aesthetic Surgery, German Soc. Senology, Hellenic Soc. Reconstructive Microsurgery, Internat. Fetal Medicine and Surgery Soc., Hellenic Soc. Plastic, Reconstructive and Aesthetic Surgery, German Soc. Surgery, Assn. German Plastic Surgeons. Office: Tech U Munich Dept Plastic Surgery Ismaningerstr 22 Bavaria Munich D-81675 Germany Office Phone: +49 89 4140 2171. Office Fax: +49 89 4140 4869. Business E-Mail: n.papadopulos@lrz.tum.de.

PAPAIOANNOU, SPYROS, gynecologist, researcher; b. Thessaloniki, Thessaloniki, Greece, Mar. 5, 1967; s. Nicholas and Kathryn Papaioannou; m. Vicky Matiopoulou, May 29, 1997; 1 child, Nicholas. Ptychion Iatrikes, U. Thrace, 1990. Clin. rsch. fellow Birmingham Women's Hosp., West Midlands, England, 2000—02, cons. ob-gyn. West Midlands, England. Presenter to med. and sci. group meetings both nat. and internat. Contbr. articles to profl. jours. Master: Royal Coll. Ob-Gyn.; mem.: European Soc. Human Reprodn. and Embryology. Home: 142 Harborne Park Rd West Midlands Birminhgam B17 0BS England Office: Heartlands and Solihull Hosp Bordesly Green E West Midlands Birmingham B9 5SS England Personal E-mail: spyrospap@talk21.com.

PAPAIOANNOU, VASILIOS EFTHYMIOS, preventive medicine physician; b. Thessaloniki, Greece, Mar. 10, 1969; s. Efthimios and Liza Tsipa Papaioannou; m. Efimia Petkou, Sept. 20, 2000; children: Efthimios, Mariliza. MD, Aristotle U. Thessaloniki, Greece, 1993, MSc, 2001, PhD, 2004. Residency in anesthesiology G. Gennimatas Hosp., Thessaloniki, 1998—2003; fellowship in critical care medicine AHEPA U. Hosp., Thessaloniki, 2003—05; lectr. critical care medicine Democritus U. Thrace, Med. Sch., Alexandroupolis, Greece, 2006—. Translator: (research project) Using heart rate variability and its relation with Th1/Th2 balance as early indicators of severe sepsis and septic shock; contbr. articles to numerous sci. jours. Mem.: NY Acad. Sci., Am. Chem. Soc., Soc. Complexity Acute Illness, European Soc. Intensive Care Medicine (Minimally Invasive Heamodynamics award 2007). Progressive. Orthodox. Achievements include design of relation between autonomic nervous system and cytokine kinetics in critical illness. Avocation: travel. Office: Alexandroupolis Univ Hosp Dragana Alexandroupolis 68100 Greece Home: Poliviu 6-8 543 51 Thessaloniki Greece Business E-Mail: papabil69@vodafone.net.gr.

PAPAKOCA, KIRO, dental educator; b. Krushevo, Macedonia, Apr. 28, 1978; Degree in Dentistry, UMF Carol Davila, Bucharest, 2003, degree in Oral Surgery, 2006. Asst. prof., faculty med. scis. U. Goce Delcev Shtip, 2008—. Home: Str Dzemal Bijedik 50/11 Shtip Macedonia 002 Macedonia Personal E-mail: drpapakoce@yahoo.com.

PAPANICOLAOU, ANDREW C., neuroscientist, educator; b. Sikyon, Greece, July 8, 1950; U.S. s. Constantinos A. and Photeini C. Papanicolaou; m. Nora Kapouralis, Nov. 21, 1950; children: Constantinos, Anastasia. Student, U. Athens, 1968—70; BS, Xavier U., 1972, MA, 1974; PhD, So. Ill. U., 1978. Asst. prof. U. Tex., Galveston, 1980—86, assoc. prof., 1986—90, prof. neurosurgery, 1990—93; prof., dir. divsn. clin. neurosci. U. Tex., Houston Med. Sch., 1993—. Dir. Vivian L. Smith advanced studies Inst. Internat. Neuropsychol. Soc., Houston, Xylocastro, Greece. Author: Emotion: A Reconsideration of the Somatic Theory, 1989; editor: Bergson and Modern Thought: Towards A Unified Science, 1987; author: Fundamentals of Functional Brain Imaging, 1998, Plato: 4 Critique of Pragmatism (in Greek), 2002; co-author: The Amnesias: A Clinical Textbook of Memory Disorders, 2006. Grantee, NIH, 1999—, 2000—, NSF, 2001—. Mem.: APA, AAAS, Soc. Psychophysiological Rsch., NY Acad. Sciences, Internat. Neuropsychological Soc., Hellenic Psychological Assn., Am. Soc. Neurophysiological Monitoring. Office: Univ Tex Houston Med Sch 1333 Moursund Ste H114 Houston TX 77030

PAPANTONIOU, VASSILIOS I., nuclear medicine physician; b. Athens, Apr. 8, 1954; MD in Gen. Medicine, U. Athens, Greece, 1979, PhD, 1993. Nuc. medicine trainee Alexandra U. Hosp., 1981—85; sr. registrar B Dept. Nuc. Medicine, Alexandra U. Gen. Hosp., 1988—93, sr. registrar A, 1993—2005, assoc. head, 2005—08, head, 2008—. Chief investigator Internat. Atomic Energy Assn., Vienna, 1997—2000. Recipient award, European Jour. Nuc. Medicine and Molecular Imaging. Mem.: Greek Soc. Nuc. Medicine and Biology, Greek Soc. Nuc. Medicine, European Assn. Nuc. Medicine, Am. Soc. Nuc. Medicine. Achievements include research in imaging and therapeutic applications with radiolabelled substances; in vivo imaging of the underlying mechanism INV. Avocations: motorcycling, music, swimming. Office: 80 Vas Sofias Ave Athens 11528 Greece Office Fax: 00302103381785. Personal E-mail: vpapantoniou@gmail.com.

PAPAS, ATHENA S., dental educator; b. Athens, Greece, Oct. 13, 1945; PhD, MIT, 1971; DMD, Harvard U., 1974. Johansen prof. dental rsch. Tufts U., 1974—, head divsn. pub. health rsch. & oral medicine. Past pres. Hellenic Women's Club. Recipient Disting. Scientist award, Internat. Assn. Dental Rsch., award, Pierre Fouchard Acad. Avocation: gardening. Office: Tufts Sch Dental Medicine 1 Knee Boston MA 02111 Office Fax: 617-636-4083. Business E-Mail: athena.papas@tufts.edu.

PAPATHEODORIDIS, GEORGE V., medical educator; b. Kalamata, Greece, Feb. 6, 1963; s. Vassilios G. Papatheodoridis and Margarita Papatheodoridi; m. Spybidoula S. Dimadi, Feb. 3, 1990; children: Margarita, Maria-Alkistis. MD, Athens U., 1986, MD, 1996. Specialist gastroenterology, Athens, Greece, 1991—97; clin. rschr. hepatology Royal Free Hosp., London, 1997—99; assoc. prof. medicine and gastroenterolgoy Med. Sch. Athens U., Hippokration Hosp., 2000—. Mem. ethics sci. com. Tzaneion Hosp., Piraeus, Greece, 1985—87; mem. sci. com. for viral hepatitis Greek Ctr. for Control of Specific Infections, Athens, 2002; sec., mem. organizing coms. several med. meetings. Reviewer: various Greek and internat. jours., 1993—, asst. editor: Annals of Gastroenterology, 1999—; contbr. chapters to books, articles to profl. jours. Recipient various awards for best presentation, Liver and Gastroenterology Meetings, 1994—2007; scholar, Greek Govt., 1981—86, Hellenic Liver, Gastroenterology Assn., 1997—98. Mem.: European Assn. Study of the Liver (gov. bd. mem.), Am. Gastroenterol. Assn., Am. Assn. for the Study Liver Disease. Avocations: tennis, ping pong, basketball. Home: 1 Ath Diakou St 15235 Vrilissia Athens Greece Office: Hippokration Hosp Acad Dept 114 Vas Sofias Ave 11527 Athens Greece Office Phone: 30 6946 330639. Business E-Mail: gepapath@med.uoa.gr.

PAPAZAHARIADOU, MARGARITA, parasitologist, educator; b. Florina, Greece, Dec. 17, 1952; d. George and Maria Papazahariadou. DVM, Aristotle U., Thessaloniki, Greece, 1977, PhD, 1988. Rsch. asst. Parasitology Lab. Faculty of Vet. Medicine Aristotle U., Thessaloniki, Greece, 1980—88, lectr., 1989—99, asst. prof., 1999—2004, assoc. prof., 2004—07. Post doc. rschr. Liverpool Sch. Tropical Medicine, England, 1991—92; sec. Assn. Scientist Women of Thessaloniki, 1990—2000. Author: Parasites and Parasitic Diseases of Ostrich, 2002; co-author: Parasitic Diseases of Domesticated Animals, 2001; contbr. scientific papers, articles to profl. jours. Mem.: Greek Soc. Parasitology, Greek Soc. Hydatidosis and Echinococcosis, Greek Vet. Med. Assn., Brit. Soc. Parasitology, European Veterinary Parasitology Coll., World Assn. Advancement of Veterinary Parasitology. Office: Lab Parasitology and Parasitic Disease Aristotle U Thessaloniki 54124 Thessaloniki Greece Home: Brecht 3 Polihni 565 32 Thessaloniki Greece Office Phone: +30-2310-999917. Business E-Mail: ritap@vet.auth.gr.

PAPENDIECK, CRISTOBAL MIGUEL, pediatrician, pediatric surgeon, pediatric phlebolymphologist, educator; b. Glücksburg, Germany, May 5, 1942; arrived in Argentina, 1949; s. Joachim Christoph and Inés (von Koschitzky) P.; m. Laura Gruñeiro, Oct. 16, 1968; children: Andrea Inés, Patricia, Marina, Laura, Sabina, Cristobal Sebastian. MD, U. Del Salvador, Buenos Aires, 1967, PhD, 1987. Cert. pediatricsurgeon Pediat. Surgeon Otamendi-Miroli Clinic, Sanat. Anchorena, 2003. Resident pediat. surgery Childrens Hosp., Buenos Aires, 1968-74, head instr. pediat. surgery, 1974—78; pediat. surgeon Otamendi-Miroli Clinic, Buenos Aires, 1977—2003; cons. pediat. surgeon German Hosp., Buenos Aires, 1980—99; prof. pediat. phlebolymphology Cath. U., Buenos Aires, 1980—2002, dir. doctorates, 1999—2002; prof. pediat. surgery U. Del Salvador, 1995—, assoc. prof. phlebolymphology, angiodysplasias, pediat. post grade career, 2000—; pediat. surgeon, head dept. pediat. surgery German Hosp., Buenos Aires, 1996-2000; prof. phlebolymphology U. Córdoba, Mendoza, Argentina. Head pediat. surgery French Hosp., Buenos Aires, 1977—79, Pediat. Found. CENI, Buenos Aires, 1984—86, German Hosp., Buenos Aires, 1996—2000; prof. pediat. surgery U. Del Salvador, Buenos Aires, 1988, Buenos Aires, 1995—, dean Sch. Medicine, 1974—76, Buenos Aires, 1988—94, rector, 1975; prof. pediat. phlebolylmphology Cath. U., Argentina, 1992—2002, prof. phlebolylmphology and anglodysplasias in pediat. postgrad. career phlebolylymphology, 1995—2002; cons. German Hosp., Buenos Aires, 1989—95, Ctrl. Mil. Hosp., Buenos Aires, 1989—95; dir. Centro Buenos Aires Angiodisplasias en Pediatria. Author: Angiodysplasias in Pediatrics, 1988 (E. Stahlschmidt award 1988), Pediatric Angiology Subjects, 1992 (A.L. Stein award 1992); contbr. chpt. to books. Mem. Lymphatic Rsch. Found. NIH, Washington; mem. coun. Liga Argentina de Lucha contra el Cancer. Grantee Rsch. in Transnodal Lymphography in Pediat., Buenos Aires, 1973-74, Rsch. in Oncology in Pediat., Buenos Aires, 1975-76. Fellow ACS; mem. AMA (hon.), Am. Venous Forum, Groupement Européen de Lymphologie, Argentine Soc. Pediat., Curatorium Angiologicae Internat. (pres. 1999-2001), Internat. Soc. Lymphology (pres. 1999-2001, exec. com.), Argentine Acad. Surgery (titular mem.), Argentine Soc. Pediat. Surgery, Argentine Coll. Phlebo and Lymph Surgery (pres. 2002-04), Congreso Internat. de Flebologia y Linfologia, Buenos Aires (pres.), Acad. Medicine Brazil, Assn. Argentine Surgery, Argentine Soc. Phlebolymphology, Club Español Linfologia, Capitulo Latinomediterráneo de Linfologia de la ISL (v.p. 2003-, co-fund fronteres de lalinfologia, dir. Angio Pediat. Buenos Aires). Avocations: painting, photography. Office: Arenales 3605 Pb 1 1425 Buenos Aires Argentina Office Phone: 00541147990740. Office Fax: 00541147990740. Business E-Mail: cpapen@intramed.net.ar, cmpapendieck@angiopediatria.com.ar.

PAPP, JULIUS GYULA, pharmacologist, researcher; b. Szigetvár, Baranya, Hungary, Aug. 29, 1937; s. Gyula Papp and Magdolna Eberhardt; m. Ilona Mária Németh, Dec. 13, 1943; children: Andrea, Eszter. BSc, Oxford U., Eng., 1969; MD, Pécs U., Hungary, 1961; PhD, Hungarian Acad. Scis., Budapest, Hungary, 1968, DSc, 1984. Diplomate Med. Chamber, Hungary. Asst. prof. Med. Sch. U. Pécs, Pécs; rsch. fellow U. Oxford, England, 1968—70; assoc. prof. Med. U., Szeged, Hungary, 1970—79; prof. and chmn. dept. pharmacology Albert Szent-Györgyi Med. U., Szeged, 1991—2001; rsch. prof. div. cardiovasc. pharmacology Hungarian Acad. Scis., Budapest-Szeged, Hungary, 2001—. Sci. advisor Internat. Inst. Therapeutic Rsch., Oslo, 1986—96; chmn. com. clin. pharmacology and drug trials Min. Health, Budapest, 1992—2006; adviser, mem. Med. Rsch. Coun., Budapest, 1997—2006; gen. sec. World Heart Fedn., Geneva, 1999—; vis. prof. U. Paris, 1990. Author: Experimental Cardiac Arrhythmias and Antiarrhythmic Drugs, 1971; editor: Clinical Cardiac Electrophysiology and Arrhythmology, 1999 (Academic Niveau prize, 2000); contbr. articles to profl. jours.; mem.: numerous editl. bds.; contbr. chapters to books. Recipient Order of Merit, Pres. Hungary, 1996, Széchenyi prize, 1999, Issekutz prize, Hungarian Soc. Exptl. and Clin. Pharmacology, 1996, Batthyany-Strattmann prize, Hungarian Min. Health, 2003, Hippocrates award, 2009; named to White Rose Order, Pres. Finland, 1995. Fellow: Royal Soc. Medicine (fellow), European Soc. Cardiology (councillor 1984—88, bd. dirs. 1984—94, mem. sci. com. 1984—96, treas. 1988—92, v.p. 1992—94, chmn. working group on drug therapy in cardiology 1992—94, mem. rsch. and tng. fellowship com. 1992—94, mem. nominating com. 1996—98, mem. sci. com. 1999—, Medal for Soc. 1988, Medal for Svc. 1994); mem.: Internat. Soc. Heart Rsch., Hungarian Physiol. Soc., Brit. Pharmacol. Soc., Deutsche Gesellschaft Pharmakologie, N.Y. Acad. Scis., Hungarian Profl. Coun. Cardiology, Hungarian Soc. Exptl. and Clin. Pharmacology (pres. 1999—2001, hon. life pres. 2006—), Hungarian Nat. Heart Found. (bd. dirs. 1993—98), Czech Soc. Cardiology (hon. Diploma of Merit 1995), Croatian Soc. Cardiology (hon. Diploma of Merit 1995), Hellenic Soc. Cardiology (hon. Diploma of Merit 1993), Italian Soc. Cardiology (hon. Diploma of Merit 1996), Romanian Soc. Cardiology (hon. Diploma of Merit 1994), Slovak Soc. Cardiology (hon. Diploma of Merit 1994), Slovenian Soc. Cardiology (hon. Diploma of Merit 1996), Portuguese Soc. Cardiology (corr.), Spanish Soc. Cardiology (corr.), Hungarian Soc. Cardiology (bd. dirs. 1976—, pres.-elect 1990—92, pres. 1992—95, past pres. 1992—95, chmn. sci. com. 1998—2005, hon. life-pres. 1998—, Pro Societate medal 1995, Einthoven prize 2007, Hippocrates award 2009), Alpe Adria Assn. Cardiology (mem. exec. bd. 1992—98, pres. 1994—95), Internat. Cardiol. Inst. Therapeutic Rsch. (bd. dirs. and sci. adviser 1986—96), Internat. Soc. and Fedn. Cardiology (mem. drug com. 1990—93), Internat. Soc. Cardiovasc. Pharmacotherapy (mem. exec. bd. 1997—, first v.p. 1999—2001), Am. Heart Assn. (internat. fellow), Hungarian Acad. Scis. (mem. drug com. 1974—2005, corr. mem. 1993—98, full mem. 1998—), Histamine Club. Achievements include patents in field. Avocations: classic music, tourism. Home: Nemestakács 10 H-6722 Szeged Hungary Office: Hungarian Acad Scis and U Szeged Dóm tér 12 PO Box 427 H-6701 Szeged Hungary Office Phone: 36-62-545681. Office Fax: 36-62-544565. Business E-Mail: papp.gyula@med.u_szeged.hu.

PAPPA, HELEN, physician; b. Athens, Greece, Oct. 23, 1963; MD, U. Athens, 1988; MPH, Harvard Sch. Pub. Health, 2004. Physician Children's Hosp., Boston, 2000—. Rschr. IBD Ctr., 2004—11. Grant, NIH. Mem.: NASPGHAN. Avocation: piano. Office: 300 Longwood Ave Boston MA 02115 Business E-Mail: helen.pappa@childrens.harvard.edu.

PAPPAS, CHARLES ENGELOS, plastic surgeon; b. Phila., May 20, 1946; s. Engelos George and Angelina (Biniaris) Pappas; m. Aprille Pappas; children: Evan, Angela, Chrysten. BA, BS, U. Pa., 1968; MD, Temple U., 1972. Intern, then resident in gen. surgery

Johns Hopkins Hosp., Balt., 1972-75; resident in gen. surgery Temple U. Hosp., Phila., 1975-76, resident in plastic surgery, 1976-78, clinical fellow cardiac sugery, 1972-73; clinical fellow transplant Harvard Med. Sch., 1973; chmn. dept. plastic surgery Temple U. Hosp., Phila., 1978-81, clin. assoc. prof. surgery, 1981—; chief dept. plastic surgery Meml. Hosp., Phila., 1986—; clin. assoc. plastic surgery Chestnut Hill Hosp., Phila., 1979—, chief/dir. dept. plastic surgery, 1994—; med. dir. Ft. Washington Surgery Ctr., 1994—. Dir. Inst. for Aesthetic Plastic Surgery, Ft. Washington, Pa., 1985—; chmn. bd. Am. Gaming Industries, 1984—; dir., ptnr. Tristate Quicklube Co., 1982-91, Medars; pres., dir. two carwash cos., Phila., 1989—; med. dir. Fort Washington Surgery Ctr., 1995—, dir., trustee, 1996—; med. dir. Aesthetica, Inc., 1996—; nat. med. dir. Aesthetics Med. Mgmt., Inc., 1996—, med. advisor, 1997—; dir., CEO Spa Aesthetika, 1998—; CEO, dir. Aesthetic Health Care Ctrs., 1999—, SPA Aesthetika, 1999—; founder, CEO Papco Ventures, Inc., 2000-; med. dir. Joseph Anthony Med. Day SPA, 2008. Contbr. articles to profl. jours. Trustee Germantown Acad., Ft. Washington, 1986—, Commonwealth Nat. Country Club, Horsham, 1988—, Patrons' Charity Found. Fellow ACS, Royal Coll. Surgeons; mem. Am. Soc. Plastic Reconstructive Surgeons (diplomate), Am. Soc. Aesthetic Plastic Surgeons (diplomate), Phila. Soc. Plastic Surgeons (pres. 1990-92). Greek Orthodox. Avocations: golf, tennis, development and investing, skiing. Office: The Aesthetic Health Care Ctr 467 Pennsylvania Ave Ste 202 Fort Washington PA 19034-3420 Personal E-mail: cepmd@att.net.

PAPPAS, THOMAS, cardiologist; Attended, Cornell U.-Weill Med. Coll., 1983. Diplomate Am. Bd. Cardiology-cardiovascular disease, Am. Bd. Cardiology-interventional cardiology, Am. Bd. Internal Medicine. Intern Cornell Med. Ctr., resident, fellow; resident in internal medicine NY Hosp., 1984—86; fellow in cardiovascular disease NY Hosp. - Cornell, 1986—88; fellow in interventional cardiology NYU Med. Ctr., 1989—90; cardiologist heart ctr. St. Francis Hosp. Office: Saint Francis Hospital Heart Center 100 Port WA Blvd Roslyn NY 11576 Office Phone: 516-390-9640. Office Fax: 516-390-9650.

PAPPAS, VIRGINIA M., medical association administrator; m. Bill Pappas; 1 child. BA in Mgmt., George Mason Univ. Various leadership positions to dep. exec. dir. Soc. Nuclear Medicine, Reston, Va., 1978—2002, exec. dir., 2002—. Office: Soc Nuclear Medicine 1850 Samuel Morse Dr Reston VA 20190-5316 Office Phone: 703-708-9000. *

PAPROSKY, WAYNE G., orthopedist; BA in Physiology, Univ. Western Canada, London, On., 1972; MD, McMaster Univ. Sch. Med., Hamilton, On., 1975. Cert. Am. Bd. Orthopaedic Surgeons, 1982, Am. Acad. Orthopaedic Surgeons, 1985, Am. Coll. Surgeons, 1986. Staff Edwards Hosp., Naperville, Ill., Ctrl. Dupage Hosp., Winfield, Ill., Rush Presbyterian-St. Luke's Med. Ctr., Chgo. Assoc. prof., adult joint reconstruction Rush Presbyn.-St. Luke's Med. Ctr., Chgo. Mem.: The Hip Soc., Ontario Med. Assn., Mid-America Orthopaedic Assn., Ill. State Med. Soc., Ill. Orthopaedic Soc., Dupage Co. Med. Soc., Can. Orthopaedic Soc., Can. Med. Soc., Assn. Arthritic Hip and Knee Surgery, Am. Med. Soc., Am. Acad. Orthopaedic Surgeons. Office: Rush Presbyn St Lukes 1653 W Congress Pkwy Chicago IL 60612 Office Phone: 630-339-2227.

PAPS, BETTY LOU, nursing educator; b. Chrisman, Ill., Nov. 17, 1937; d. Robert Bertram Bonwell and Katherine Carol (Hess) Buchanan; m. Peter George Paps, Apr. 22, 1989 (dec.); children: Jill Stuebe Thompson, Nena Carol Mihailovic. RN, Lakeview Hosp. Sch. Nursing, 1958; BSN, U. Ill., Chgo., 1965; MSN, DePaul U., 1970; PhD, LaSalle U., 1998. Nurse educator Danville Jr. Coll., Ill., 1963-65, Chgo. Pub. Schs., 1966-68, Mt. Sinai Hosp. Sch. Nursing, Chgo., 1970; prof. nursing Kennedy King Coll., Chgo., 1970—96; chief nurse 63d Aeromedical Evacuation Squadron, 1980—92, troop comdr. Persian Gulf War, 1991; evaluator Nat. League Nursing, 1994—98. Col. USAFR, 1974—94. Decorated Commendation award, Air medal, Meritorious Svc. award, Southeast Asia award, Kuwait Liberation medal, Chief Nurse's badge, Chief Flight Nurse award, Nat. Def. medal. Mem.: VFW, Air Force Assn., Res. Officers Assn., Aerospace Med. Assn., Mil. and Hospitallar Order of St. Lazarus of Jerusalem (Dame, Silver medal), Am. Legion, Order of The Eastern Star. Personal E-mail: bpaps@aol.com.

PÃQUIN, TRUDY, gerontological nurse; b. Wantagh, NY, May 23, 1954; d. William Carl and Gertrude Mary (Kryl) Bauer; m. Alfred Joseph Pãquin III, July 30, 1977. AAS, John Tyler C.C., Chester, Va., 1982; BA magna cum laude, So. Conn. State U., New Haven, 1993, MS in Sociology, 2003; gerontol. nurse cert., U. Conn., Storrs, 1994, nurse mgmt. cert., 1995. cert. psychiat. and mental health nurse, cert. rehab. nurse, 2010. Animal trainer, 1972—; pet therapist, 1974—; rschr. Alzheimer's, 1995; therapy dog tng., educator, 1983—; adj. faculty dept. sociology So. Conn. State U., 2001—10. Mem. Antarctic Expdn., 1996; qualitative rsch. on psychiat. patient interaction, 2002. Author: Pet Therapy Handbook, 1998, One Man's Journey to America, 1996; composer numerous musical works. Avocations: swimming, running, hiking. Office: Apple Rehab Guilford 10 Boston Post Rd Guilford CT 06437 Office Phone: 203-453-3725. Personal E-mail: trudy@prodigy.net.

PARADA, LUIS FERNANDO, science educator; b. Santa Fe de Bogota, Colombia, July 18, 1954; s. Alfonso and Clara Parada. BS in Molecular Biology, U. Wis., Madison, 1979; PhD in Biology, MIT, 1985. Damon Runyon postdoc. fellow Pasteur Inst., Paris, 1985—86, Helen Hay Whitney postdoc. fellow, 1986—87; head molecular embryology group Mammalian Genetics Lab., Nat. Cancer Inst., Frederick, Md., 1987—94; prof., dir. Ctr. Devel. Biology, U. Tex. Southwestern Med. Ctr., Dallas, 1994—2006, dir. Kent Waldrep Ctr. Nerve Regeneration, 1995—, Southwestern Bell disting. chair basic neurosci. rsch., 1998—, Amer. Cancer Soc. rsch. prof., 2003, Dana & Richard C. Strauss disting. chmn. devel. biology, 2006—. Mem. nat. adv. coun. Nat. Inst. Neurol. Disorders & Strokes; mem. sci. adv. bd. Rett Syndrome Rsch. Trust; sci. rev. bd. Howard Hughes Med. Inst.; adv. bd. Pews Scholars Found. Recipient Peter A. Steck Memorial ward, Soc. Neuro-Oncology, 2000, Friedrich von Recklinghausen award, Children's Tumor Found., 2009, Javits Neuroscience Investigator award, NIH. Fellow: AAAS; mem.: NAS, American Assn. Cancer Rsch., Soc. Devel. Biology, Soc. Neuroscience, Inst. Medicine, American Acad. Arts & Scis. Achievements include research in the elucidation of regulatory pathways that control the complex process of nervous system development and the consequences of inappropriate development which can include behavioral and mood disorders as well as cancer. Office: U Tex Southwestern Med Ctr 5323 Harry Hines Blvd Dallas TX 75390-9133 Office Phone: 214-648-1822. E-mail: luis.parada@utsouthwestern.edu. *

PARADISE, LOUIS VINCENT, education educator, dean; b. Scranton, Pa., Apr. 19, 1946; s. Louis Benjamin and Lucille P.; children: Christopher, Gabrielle,Victoria. BS, Pa. State U., 1968; MS, Bucknell U., 1974; PhD, U. Va., 1976. Lic. psychologist, profl. counselor; cert. sch. psychologist. Assoc. prof. Cath. U. Am., Washington, 1976-83; prof. edn., chmn. edn. leadership U. New Orleans, 1983-90, dean Coll. Edn., 1990-92, univ. vice chancellor, provost, 1992-94, exec. vice chancellor, provost, 1994—2003, prof. Dept. Ednl. Leadership, Counseling, and Found., 2003—. Author: Ethics in Counseling and Psychotherapy, 1979, Questioning: Skills for the Helping Process, 1979, Counseling in Community College, 1982. 1st lt. U.S. Army, 1968-72. DuPont scholar U. Va., 1974. Mem. APA, ACA (ethics com. 1986-89), Am. Edn. Rsch. Assn., So. Assn. Counselor Edn. (chmn. ethics com. 1988-89), Acad. Counseling Psychology, Chi Sigma Iota (founding chpt. pres. 1985-87). Roman Catholic. Avocations: running, bicycling, music. Office: U New Orleans Dept Ednl Leadership Counseling & Found New Orleans LA 70148-0001 Office Phone: 504-280-6026. Business E-Mail: louis.paradise@uno.edu.

PARAF, FRANCOIS, pathologist, educator; b. Boulogne-Billancourt, France, Feb. 13, 1961; s. André Paraf and Marie-Jeanne Couroucé; m. Agnes Peyclit, May 11, 2002; children: Caroline, Eugénie, Joséphine. MD, degree, U. Paris, 1990; PhD in Biology, U. Limoges, France, 2001, Habilitation, 2000. Diplomate pathology U. Paris 7, 1990, cert. in capacité pratiques médico-judiciaires U. Limoges, 2006. Rsch. assoc., dept pathology McGill U., Montreal, Canada, 1990—91, vis. asst. prof., dept pathology, 1991; asst. hospitalier U. Paris, 1991—94, asst. hospitalier, faculté médecine, 1994—96; praticien hospitalier U. Limoges, 1996—2001, prof. pathology, forensic medicine, 2001—; head dept forensic medicine Ctr. Hosp. U. Dupuytren, 2010—. Expert près la Cour d'appel, Limoges, 2002—; editl. bd. mem. Annales Pathologie, Paris, 2001—, Gastroenterologie Clin. Biologique, Paris, 1988—2009. Contbr. scientific papers. With Svc. Santé Des Armées, 1988—89, Paris. Mem.: European Assn. Cadiovasc. Pathology, Soc. Française Médecine Légale, Soc. Nat. Française Gastroentérologie, Club d'Histopathologie Digestive Hépatique (pres. 2002—), Soc. Française Pathologie. Avocations: history, genealogy. Office: Ctr Hosp Univ Dupuytren 2 Ave Martin Luther King Limoges 87042 France Office Phone: 0555056168. Office Fax: 0555056699. Personal E-mail: francois.paraf@chu-limoges.fr.

PARAMOTHAYAN, NIRANJALA SHANTHIMANOHARIE, medical researcher, consultant; arrived in Eng., 1974; s. Kanthappoo Paramothayan and Ivy Kamala Padmasundary Navaratnasingam; m. Rajapillai Velupillai Ahilan, Aug. 25, 1988; children: Arjunan, Sanjeevan. BSc in Med. Biochemistry with honors, U. Birmingham, Eng., 1984; PhD, U. Cambridge, Eng., 1988; MBBS in Medicine with honors, U. London, 1993. Tng. St. Bartholomew's Hosp. Med. Sch., 1988—93; reviewer Cochrane Airways Group, London, 1997—2003; cons. respiratory physician Kingston (Eng.) Hosp., 2003, Epsom & St. Helier NHS Trust, England, 2003—; hon. sr. lectr. St. Helier U. Hosp., Carshalton, England, 2003—. Assoc. tutor St. Helier Hosp., Carshalton, 2000—01. Contbr. articles to profl. jours. Recipient George Burrows prize in pathology, 1992, Walsham prize in surg. pathology, 1992, prize in rheumatology, Arthritis and Rheumatism Coun., 1993; scholar, Sci. and Engring. Rsch. Coun., 1984—87. Mem.: Brit. Med. Assn., Brit. Thoracic Soc., Royal Coll. Physicians (Eng.). Avocations: piano, acting, creative writing. Business E-Mail: NSParam@thelighthouse.freeserve.co.uk.

PARASHER, GULSHAN, medical educator; b. New Delhi, Dec. 23, 1968; MBBS, U. Delhi, 1993. Resident physician internal medicine Maimonides Med. Ctr. Bklyn., 1995—98; gastroenterology & hepatology fellow State U. NY Health Scis. Ctr., 1998—2001; clin. instr., advanced endoscopy fellow U. Calif. Med. Ctr., Irvine, 2001—02; asst. prof. medicine, dir. endoscopic ultrasound & therapeutic endoscopy U. N.Mex. Sch. Medicine, 2002—09, med. dir., assoc. prof. medicine gastroenterology, 2002—, assoc. prof. medicine, dir. endoscopic & clin. ops., 2009—. Recipient Outstanding Physician House Staff award, Maimonides Med. Ctr., Excellence award, Indian Acad. Pediat., Outstanding Faculty award, Dept. Internal Medicine U. N.Mex. Fellow: ACP, Am. Coll. Gastroenterology (gov. N.Mex. chpt. 2006—); mem.: Am. Gastroenterology Assn., Am. Soc. Gastrointestinal Endoscopy. Avocations: golf, reading, antiques. Home: 9005 Walter Bambrook PL NE Albuquerque NM 87122 Home Fax: 505-925-6160. Business E-Mail: gparasher@salud.unm.edu.

PARASTA, AMIR-MOBAREZ, ophthalmologist, consultant; MD, PhD, U. Munich. Diplomate German Bd. Ophthalmology. Attending physician U. Eye Clinic, Munich, 2000—05. Cons. Rosenheim Eye Ctr., Rosenheim, Germany; cons. telemed. applications Epitop Med. Ltd., Munich, med. dir. Mem.: European Assn. Vision and Eye Rsch. (corr.), Am. Assn. Rsch. Vision and Ophthalmology (corr.), German Ophthalmology Soc. (corr.), Iranian Soc. Ophthalmology (assoc.). Achievements include first to telemedical networks and applications in Germany. Home: Spilhofstr 49 Munich D-81927 Germany Office: Munich Retina Inst Einsteinstr 1 81675 Munich Germany Personal E-mail: a.parasta@gmx.de.

PARASURAMAN, RAVI KUMAR, nephrologist; b. Karnataka, India, Dec. 10, 1958; s. Parasuraman and Pattammal; m. Sathya Ramanujam, Feb. 4, 1987; 1 child, Emmanuel Kumar. MD, U. Bangalore, India, 1982. Lic. Am. Bd. Internal Medicine, 1996. Sr. staff, transplant nephrologist Henry Ford Hosp., Detroit, 1998—, med. dir. kidney and pancreas transplant program, 2002—; assoc. prof. medicine Wayne State U., Detroit, 2006—; with Beaumont Hosp. Royal Oak, Mich. Contbr. articles to profl. jours. Mem.: Royal Coll. Physicians. Office Fax: 313-916-2554. Business E-Mail: rparasu1@hfhs.org.

PARDA, DAVID S., radiation oncologist, educator; MD, U. South Fla. Diplomate Am. Bd. Internal Medicine, Am. Bd. Radiology-radiation oncology. Practice West Pa. Allegheny Health System Radiation Oncology Network; intern Cleveland Clin. Found., resident; assoc. prof. radiation oncology Drexel Univ.; chmn. Allegheny Gen. Hosp., residency dir. dept. radiation oncology. Named one of Top Doctors, Pitts. mag., 2011. Office: Allegheny General Hospital 320 E N Ave Pittsburgh PA 15212 Office Phone: 412-359-3131. Office Fax: 412-359-4108.

PARDEE, ARTHUR BECK, biochemist, educator; b. Chgo., July 13, 1921; s. Charles A. and Elizabeth B. (Beck) Pardee; m. Ruth Sager (dec.); m. Ann Goodman; children: Michael, Richard, Thomas. BS, U. Calif., Berkeley, 1942; MS, Calif. Inst. Tech., 1943, PhD, 1947; D (hon.), U. Paris, 1993. Merck postdoctoral fellow U. Wis., 1947—49; mem. faculty U. Calif., Berkeley, 1949—61, assoc. prof., 1957—61; NSF fellow Pasteur Inst., 1957—58; prof. biology, chmn. dept. biochem. scis. Princeton (NJ) U., 1961—67, prof. biochemistry, 1961—75, Donner prof. sci., 1966; prof. Dana Farber Cancer Inst. and biochem. pharmacology dept. Harvard Med. Sch., Boston, 1975—. Co-author: Experiments in Biochemical Research Techniques, 1957; editor: Biochemica et Biophysica Acta, 1962—68; contbr. over 500 articles to publs. Mem. rsch. adv. coun. Am. Cancer Soc., 1967—71; trustee Cold Spring Harbor Lab. Quantitative Biology, 1963—69. Recipient Young Biochemists travel award, NSF, 1952, Krebs medal, Fedn. European Biochem. Socs., 1973, Rosenstiel award, Brandeis U., 1975, 3M award, Fedn. Am. Socs., Exptl. Biology, 1980, CIIT prize, 1993, Disting. Alumnus award, Calif. Inst. Tech., 1999; named Princess Takamatu lectr., 1990, hon. faculty mem., Nanjing U., 1999; fellow, Internat. Inst. for Advanced Studies, 1999. Fellow: AAAS; mem.: NAS (editl. bd. proc. 1971—73, com. on scis. and pub. policy 1973—76), Chem. Industry Inst. Toxicology (Founders award, Boehringer-Mannheim award 1998), Ludwig Inst. Cancer Rsch. (sci. com. 1988—), Japanese Biochem. Soc., Am. Philos. Soc., Am. Soc. Microbiologists, Am. Assn. Cancer Rsch. (pres. 1985—86), Am. Soc. Biol. Chemists (treas. 1964—70, pres. 1980—81), Am. Chem. Soc. (Paul Lewis award 1960). Office Phone: 617-632-3372. Business E-Mail: arthur_pardee@dfci.harvard.edu.

PARDES, HERBERT, psychiatrist, educator, former hospital administrator; b. Bronx, NY, July 7, 1934; s. Louis and Frances (Bergman) P.; m. Juidith Ellen Silber, June 9, 1957; children: Stephen, Lawrence, James. BS, Rutgers U., 1956; MD, SUNY-Downstate Med. Center, Bklyn., 1960; DSc (hon.), SUNY, 1990. Straight med. intern Kings County Hosp., 1960-61, intern & resident in psychiatry Bklyn., 1961-62, 64-66; asst. prof. psychiatry Downstate Med. Ctr., Bklyn., 1968-72, prof., chmn. dept., 1972-75; dir. psychiat. svcs. Kings County Hosp., Bklyn., 1972-75; prof., chmn. dept. psychiatry U. Colo. Med. Sch., 1975-78; dir. psychiat. svcs. Colo. Psychiat. Hosp., Denver, 1975-78; dir. NIMH, Rockville, Md., 1978-84; asst. surgeon gen. USPHS, 1978-84; prof. psychiatry Columbia University, NYC, 1984—, chmn. dept., 1984; dir. Psychiat. Svc. Presbyn. Hosp. (now Columbia Presbyn. Center of NY Presbyn. Hosp.), NYC, 1984-89; dir. NY State Psychiatric Inst., 1984—89; v.p. for health scis., dean faculty medicine Columbia University, NYC, 1989—99; pres., CEO New York-Presbyterian Hospital & Healthcare Systems, NYC, 2000—11. Bd. trustees Healthcare Leadership Coun.; bd. dirs. Value Line, Inc., 2000—. Contbr. articles to med. jours. Pres. sci. bd. Alliance for Rsch. on Schizophrenia and Depression. Capt. M.C., AUS, 1972-74. Named Ann. Hon. Lectr. Downstate Med. Ctr. Alumni Assn., 1972; recipient Alumni Achievement medal, 1980, William Menninger award ACP, 1992, Dorothy Dix award Mental Illness Fedn., 1992, Vester Mark award, 1994, Salmon award, 1996. Mem. Assn. American Med. Colls. (chair 1995-96), American Psychiat. Assn. (v.p. 1986-88, pres. 1989-90, Disting. Svc. award 1993), Inst. Medicine, American Psychoanalytic Assn., Coun. of Deans (adminstrv. bd., chair-elect 1993-94, chair 1994-95), Assoc. Med. Schools NY (pres. 1995-2000), Phi Beta Kappa, Alpha Omega Alpha. Office Phone: 212-305-8000. Business E-Mail: pardesh@nyp.org. *

PARDUE, A. MICHAEL, retired plastic and reconstructive surgeon; b. Nashville, June 23, 1931; s. Andrew Peyton and Ruby (Fly) P. BS, Sewanee U. of the South, 1953; MD, U. Tenn., 1957. Resident in gen. surgery Pittsfield (Mass.) Affiliated Hosps., 1966; resident in plastic surgery N.Y. Hosp./Cornell Med. Ctr., 1968; plastic surgeon A. Michael Pardue, M.D., Thousand Oaks, Calif., 1968-98; ret., 1995. Lt. comdr. USN, 1956-62. Fellow ACS; mem. Am. Soc. Plastic Surgeons, Am. Soc. Aesthetic Plastic Surgery, Calif. Soc. Plastic Surgeons. Episcopalian. Avocations: fly fishing, skiing, golf. Home (Summer): 3217 Augusta Dr Bozeman MT 59715-8792 Personal E-mail: amikepardue@gmail.com.

PARES, ALBERT, physician, educator; b. Calonge, Dec. 17, 1950; MD, PhD, U. Barcelona, 1974. Prof. medicine, sr. cons. hepatology Hosp. Clínic, U. Barcelona, 2002—. Mem.: EASL, AASLD. Office: Villarroel 170 Barcelona 08017 Spain Business E-Mail: pares@ub.edu.

PARFITT, RICHARD C., facial plastic surgeon, educator; MD, U. Wis. Diplomate Am. Bd. Facial Plastic Surgery, Am. Bd. Otolaryngology. Fellow in facial plastic surgery, Beverly Hills; resident Naval Hosp., San Diego, 1993; surgical instr. in cosmetic facial plastic surgery UCLA, 1995—96; founder Parfitt Facial Cosmetic Surgery Ctr., Wis., 1996, plastic surgeon; founder AestheticA Skin Health Ctr., 2001, plastic surgeon. Fellow: Am. Acad. Cosmetic Surgeons; mem.: Wis. Better Bus. Bur., Botox Cosmetic. Office: Parfitt Facial Cosmetic Surgery Center 2261 Deming Way Middleton WI 53562 Office Phone: 608-831-3991. Office Fax: 608-831-4021.

PARHAM HOPSON, DEBORAH, federal agency administrator; b. Glouster, Ohio, Apr. 20, 1955; m. Kevin M. Hopson; 1 child, William M. Hopson. BSN, U. Cin., 1977; MS in Pub. Health, U. NC, Chapel Hill, 1979, PhD in Pub. Health, 1990. Former White House intern & Presdl. mgmt. intern; rsch. assoc. Inst. Medicine, NAS; officer Commd. Corps., USPHS, 1984—, asst. surgeon gen., rear adm.; dep. assoc. adminstr. HIV/AIDS Bur. Health Resources & Services Adminstrn., US Dept. Health & Human Services, 2000—02, assoc. adminstr. HIV/AIDS Bur., 2002—. Bd. dirs. Patient Adv. Found., Hampton, Va. Recipient Chief Nurse Officer award, USPHS, Meritorious Svc. Medal, Hildrus A. Poindexter award, Black Commd. Officers' Adv. Group, Exceptional Svc. Medal, Uniformed Services Univ. Health Scis. Fellow: Nat. Academies. Practice, American Acad. Nursing; mem.: APHA, ANA, Assn. Mil. Surgeons US, Commd. Officers Assn., Assn. Nurses in AIDS Care, Md. Nurses Assn. Baptist. Office: US Dept Health and Human Svcs Health Resources Svcs Adminstrn 5600 Fishers Ln LKLN 7 05 Rockville MD 20857 Office Phone: 301-443-1993. Business E-Mail: dparham@hrsa.gov. *

PARIENTE, RENÉ GUILLAUME, physician, educator; b. Sept. 1, 1929; s. Jules and Vera (Guttieres) P.; m. Dominique Savary, Dec. 26, 1971; children: Pierre, David, Benjamin. MD, U. Paris, 1962. Prof. medicine U. Paris, 1966—, head dept. intensive care and chest disease. Dir. Inst. Nat. du Recherche Med., emeritus. Mem.: Am. Thoracic Soc., NY Acad. Scis., Am. Soc. Chest Physician, Soc.

Française de Microscopie Electronique, Soc. de la Tuberculose, Soc. de Pathologie Respiratoire, Soc. Française de Cardiologie. Home: 12 rue de la Neva 75008 Paris France Office: Bichat Hosp 16 Rue H Huchard 75018 Paris France Personal E-mail: renepariente@yahoo.fr, parienterene@gmail.com.

PARIETTI-WINKLER, CÉCILE, medical educator; b. Jan. 9, 1971; MD, U. Nancy, PhD, 2006. Prof., ENT dept. U. Hosp. Nancy, 2010—. Office: Service ORL CHU-Hopital Ctrl Nancy 54035 France Business E-Mail: c.parietti@chu-nancy.fr.

PARIKH, JAY R., radiologist; s. Rajendra Somalal and Minaxi Rajendra Parikh; m. Niyati Parikh, July 5, 1992; children: Miti children: Viraj, Rajan. MD, U. Ottawa, Ontario, Can., 1990. Cert. physician exec. Am. Coll. of Physician Execs., 2005. Med. dir. Women's Diagnostic Imaging Ctr., Seattle, 2003—. Pres. Nat. Consortium of Breast Ctrs., Warsaw, 2005—07; cons., sci. adv. panel Hologic, Bedford, Mass. Contbr. articles to profl. jours. Asst. scoutmaster, Pack 624 Boy Scouts Am., Seattle, 2009—. Named Honorary Texan, Gov. Tex., 2006, Seattle Top Doctors, Seattle Mag., 2011; Leadership Conf. scholar, WSMA, 2004. Fellow: Am. Coll. Physician Execs., Soc. Breast Imaging, Am. Coll. Radiology (clin. image rev., nat. mammography accreditation program 2005—, clin. image rev. nat. breast ultrasound accreditation program 2006—), Royal Coll. Physicians and Surgeons Can. (licentiate); mem.: Wash. State Med. Assn. (trustee 2004—), Pacific NW Radiol. Soc. (pres. 2007—08), Hawaii Breast Soc. (hon.; life), Alaska State Soc. Radiol. Technologists (hon.), Ariz. State Soc. Radiol. Technologists (life), Am. Assn. Radiologists of Indian Origin (life), Hawaii Radiol. Soc. (hon.), Western Wash. Mammography Soc. (hon.), Wash. State Radiol. Soc. (pres. 2004—06), Radiol. Soc. N.Am., Am. Roentgen Ray Soc., King County Med. Soc., Am. Coll. Physician Execs. Office: Women's Diagnostic Imaging Center 1221 Madison St Seattle WA 98104 Home: 2259 66th Ave SE Mercer Island WA 98040 Office Fax: 206-215-3909.

PARIKH, KEYUR HARSHADRAY, cardiologist, researcher; b. Daresalaam, Tanzania, June 18, 1958; s. Harshadray and Surabala Parikh; m. Reeta K. Shah, Sept. 6, 1981; children: Shivam Keyur, Roosha Keyur, Parth Keyur. MD, U. So. Calif., 1985. Diplomate Am. Bd. Internal Medicine, Am. Bd. Cardiology, Am. Bd. Interventional Cardiology. Chief of cardiology, cardiac cath lab. St. Rose Hosp., San Francisco, 1990—91, chief of medicine, 1992—93; chmn. Care Cardiology Cons., Ahmedabad, Gujarat, India, 2001—. Contbr. articles to profl. jours. Fellow: Cardiol. Soc. India (life), Soc. for Cardiac Angiography and Interventions (life), Am. Coll. Cardiology (life Internat. Svc. award 2004); mem.: Indian Med. Assn. (life), Order of William Harvey. Hindu. Office: Heart Care Clinic 201 Balleshwar Ave Bodakdev Ahmedabad 380054 India Home: Satyagrah Chhavani 380 015 Ahmedabad 380015 India Office Phone: 919825066664. Office Fax: 0091-76-26872620 Personal E-mail: keyurparikh@gmail.com.

PARIKH, MANISH A., interventional cardiologist, educator; MD, U. Medicine and Dentistry of NJ-Sch. Health Related Prof, 1990. Diplomate Am. Bd. Internal Medicine cardiovascular disease, Am. Bd. Internal Medicine-interventional cardiology, lic. NY. Asst. prof. medicine Cornell Univ.- Weill Med. Coll.; interventional cardiologist Lenox Hill Hosp.; resident in internal medicine NY Hosp., 1991—93, fellow in cardiovascular disease, 1993—97, interventional cardiologist. Office: New York Hospital 16 E 60th St Ste 322 New York NY 10022 Office Phone: 212-326-8532.

PARINI, PAOLO, medical researcher; b. Rimini, Italy, July 20, 1964; MD, U. Bologna, Italy, 1990; PhD, Karolinska Inst., 1999. Head divsn. Karolinska Inst., 2010—. Chmn. Scandinavia Soc. Atherosclerosis Rsch., 2011. Recipient Alvarenga's prize, Swedish Med. Soc. Avocation: sailing. Office: Karolinska University Hosp Huddinge Stockholm 141 86 Sweden Office Fax: 46 8 58581260. Business E-Mail: paolo.parini@karolinska.se.

PARIS, MARGARITIS, medical researcher, educator; b. Thessaloniki, Greece, July 12, 1973; BSc, U. Newcastle-upon-Tyne, Eng., 1995; PhD, U. Oxford, Eng., 2000. Postdoc. fellow Children's Hosp. Phila., 2000—05, rsch. assoc., 2005—08, sr. rsch. assoc., 2008—09; rsch. asst. prof. pediat. U. Pa., 2010—. Recipient Early Career Investigator award, Bayer Pharms., John Corran Book prize, U. Newcastle-upon-Tyne. Mem.: Faculty 1000 Medicine, Internat. Soc. Thrombosis and Hemostasis, Am. Soc. Gene and Cell therapy, Am. Soc. Hematology. Business E-Mail: margaritis@email.chop.edu.

PARISER, DAVID MICHAEL, dermatologist, educator; b. Norfolk, Va., Sept. 8, 1946; s. Harry and Alice Pariser; m. Carol Odessky, Mar. 25, 1975; children: Michael Steven, Jana Robin. MD, Med. Coll. Va., Richmond, 1972. Cert. Am. Bd. Dermatology, 1977, Va. State Bd. Med. Examiners, Nat. Bd. Med. Examiners, Am. Bd. Pathology, spl. competence in dermatopathology. Intern Med. Coll. Va., Richmond; resident Univ. Miami Sch. Medicine/Jackson Meml. Med. Ctr., 1973—76; prof., dept. dermatology Ea. Va. Med. Sch., Norfolk, 1995—; sr. physician Pariser Dermatology Specialists, Ltd., Norfolk, Va. Spkr. in field. Contbr. articles to profl. jours.; review coms. of several peer-reviewed jours., mem. editl. bds. of several peer-reviewed jours. Pres. Ea. Va. Dermatology Found., Norfolk, 2001—07, bd. dirs., Sentara Health Mgmt., Dermatology Services, Inc., Nat. Psoriasis Found. Recipient Gold Triangle award, Am. Acad. Dermatology, 2007. Fellow: Am. Soc. for Laser Medicine and Surgery, Am. Soc. for Dermatologic Surgery, Am. Acad. Dermatology (secretary-treasurer 2003—06, pres. elect 2008—, bd. dirs., Gold Triangle award for outstanding dedication to isotretinoin awareness initiatives 2002, (9) Continuing Med. Edn. award, (4) Presdl. Citations); mem.: Med. Soc. Va., Am. Soc. for Dermatologic Surgery, AMA (Physician's Recognition award 2004), Internat. Hyperhidrosis Soc. (pres., founding mem., bd. dirs. 2003—). Office: Ea Va Med Sch Pariser Dermatology SpecialistsLtd 601 Medical Tower Norfolk VA 23507 Office Fax: 757-625-6940.

PARISH, JAMES MICHAEL, medical educator; BS in Biology with honors, U. Ill., 1974; MD, U. Ill., Chgo., 1978. Diplomate Am. Bd. Internal Medicine, Am. Bd. Pulmonary Medicine. Resident internal medicine Mayo Clinic, 1978—81, fellow pulmonary medicine, 1981—84; pulmonary and critical care specialist Sharp Meml. Hosp., San Diego, 1984—87; cons., Assoc. Prof. Mayo Clinic Coll. Medicine, Scottsdale, Ariz., 1987—; chair Divsn. Pulmonary Medicine, Mayo Clinic, Ariz.; bd. dir. Nat. Assn. Med. Direction Respiratory Care. Fellow: ACP, Am. Acad. Sleep Medicine, Am. Coll. Chest Physicians; mem.: AMA, Am. Thoracic Soc. Achievements include research in sleep disorders. Office: Mayo Clinic 13400 Shea Blvd Scottsdale AZ 85259

PARISI, VALERIE MARIE, dean, medical educator; b. Bklyn., 1952; m. Gary Strong. BS in Biology, Brown U., 1972, MD, 1975; MPH, U. Calif. Sch. Pub. Health, 1980; MBA, U. NC, 2004. Lic. Calif., 1979, Tex., 1984, NY, 1994, NC, 1998, diplomate Nat. Bd. Med. Examiners, 1976, Am. Bd. Ob-gyn., 1981, Am. Bd. Ob-gyn. Divsn. Maternal-Fetal Medicine, 1987. NIH rsch. fellow, Dept. Chemistry and Physics Brown U., Providence, 1970, Noyes Found. rsch. fellow, Dept. Sociology & Divsn. Reproductive Biology and Medicine, 1971; Noyes Found. rsch. fellow, Dept. Ob-gyn. Women and Infants Hosp. RI, Providence, 1972; intern in categorical gen. surgery Brown U. Affiliated Hospitals, RI Hosp., Providence, 1975—76; resident in ob-gyn. Women and Infants Hosp. of RI, Providence, 1976—79; fellow divsn. maternal-fetal medicine, Dept. Ob-gyn. U. Colo. Health Sci. Ctr., Denver, 1982—83, U. Wis. Ctr. for Health Sciences, Madison, 1983—84; instr. Dept. Human Growth and Reproduction Brown U., 1976—79; lectr., divsn. maternal child health U. Calif. Sch. Pub. Health, Berkeley, 1980—81; clin. instr. Dept. Ob-gyn. and Reproductive Sciences, U. Calif., San Francisco, 1980—81, clin. asst. prof., 1981—82; asst. prof. Dept. Ob-gyn. U. Colo. Health Sci. Ctr., Denver, 1982—83, U. Wis. Health Sci. Ctr., Madison, 1983—84; asst. prof. Dept. Ob-gyn. and Reproductive Sciences U. Texas Med. Sch., Houston, 1984—89, assoc. prof. Dept. Ob-gyn. and Reproductive Sciences, 1989—94, dir. divsn. maternal-fetal medicine, 1984—94, asst. prof. Dept. Pediatrics, 1987—89, assoc. prof. Dept. Pediatrics, 1989—94, co-dir. maternal-fetal medicine fellowship program, 1987—94; vis. prof. divsn. neonatology Dept. Pediatrics U. Cin. Med. Ctr., 1991—92; prof. & chair Dept. Ob-gyn. and Reproductive Medicine U. Med. Ctr. at Stony Brook, NY, 1994—97; Robert A. Ross prof. & chair Dept Ob-gyn. U. NC, Chapel Hill, 1997—2004, residency program dir. Dept. Ob-gyn., 1999—2004, rsch. fellow Cecil G. Sheps Ctr. for Health Sciences Rsch., 2003—; dean medicine U. Tex. Med. Branch, Galveston, 2004—06, chief acad. officer, v.p. acad. program adminstrn. and services, 2004—06, adv., 2006; vice dean hosp. relations and clinical affairs, sr. advisor to chmn. CEO, U. Physician Group Wayne State U. Sch. Medicine, Detroit, 2007—10, prof. dept. obstetrics and gynecology, 2007—, dean, 2010—. Attending staff Providence Neighborhood Health Centers, RI, 1977—79; dir. Ob-gyn. Services Bristol County Cmty. Med. Ctr., RI, 1977—79; dir. gynecological services Brown U. Student Health Services, 1978—79; consulting staff Letterman Army Med. Ctr., Presidio of San Francisco, 1979—82; attending staff Kaiser Found. Hosp., Oakland, Calif., 1980, San Francisco, 1980—82; clin. staff Moffitt Hosp. U. Calif. San Francisco Med. Ctr., 1980—82; med. dir. Ambulatory Care Ctr. Dept. Ob-gyn. U. Colo. Health Sci. Ctr., Denver, 1982—83; attending staff Madison Gen. Hosp., Wis., 1983—84, U. Wis. Clin. Sciences Ctr., Madison, 1983—84; consulting staff St. Mary's Med. Ctr., Madison, Wis., 1983—84; attending staff Hermann Hosp., Houston, 1984—94, dir. Maternal-Fetal Spl. Care Unit, 1985—92, obstetrical dir. labor and delivery, 1987—88, Houston, 1992—94, med. dir. Family Ctr., 1992—94; consulting staff St. Joseph's Hosp., Houston, 1987—94, Meml. Southwest Hosp., Houston, 1990—94; active staff Lyndon Baines Johnson Hosp., Houston, 1990—94; ob-gyn. chief U. Hosp., Stony Brook, NY, 1994—97; consulting staff Southampton Hosp., NY, 1995—97, St. Charles Hosp., Port Jefferson, NY, 1996—97, obstetrician-gynecologist-in-chief NC Women's Hosp., Chapel Hill, 1997—2004; attending staff Dept. Ob-gyn REX Hosp., 2002—04. Bd. dirs. Am. Bd. Family Practice, 1999—2004; fin. and investment com., nominating com. Am. Bd. Med. Specialties, 2004; basic examiner Am. Bd. Obstetrics and Gynecology, 1990—, maternal and fetal medicine examiner, 1992—, divsn. maternal and fetal medicine, 1996—2002, bd. dirs. and divsn. chief maternal and fetal medicine, 1998—2002, exec. com., 1999—2002, fin. com., 2004—09, sec., treas., 2009—; mem. Coun. on Residency Edn. in Ob-gyn., 1995—2000; bd. dirs. Planned Parenthood of Suffolk County, 1994—97; exec. bd. Western Perinatal Collaborative Group, 1986—92, chair membership com., 1986—88, vice pres. & pres.-elect, 1988—90, pres., 1990—92. Fellow: Am. Gynecologic and Obstetrical Soc. (nominating com. 1992, fellowship com. 1992—95), Am. Assn. Advancement Sci.; mem.: Tex. Perinatal Assn., Tex. Med. Found., Tex. Med. Assn., Tex. Assn. Obstetricians and Gynecologists, Soc. for Study of Reproduction, Soc. Obstetric Anesthesia and Perinatology (bd. dirs. 1995—99), Soc. for Maternal Fetal Medicine (bd. dirs. 1989—92, scientific program chair 1993, pres.-elect 1993—94, pres. 1994—95), Soc. Gynecological Investigation, Perinatal Rsch. Soc. (exec. coun. 1993—95), NY Obstetrical Soc., Internat. Soc. for Study of Hypertension in Pregnancy, Houston Gynecological and Obstetrical Soc., Harris County Med. Soc., Assn. Reproductive Health Professionals, Assn. Professors of Gynecology and Obstetrics, Am. Med. Women's Assn., AMA, Am. Coll. Obstetricians and Gynecologists (patient edn. com. 1989—91, scientific program com. 1993, edn. commn. 1995—97), Sigma Xi. Office: Wayne State University Sch Medicine Office of Dean 1241 Scott Hall 540 E Canfield Ave Detroit MI 48201 Office Phone: 313-577-7742. Office Fax: 313-577-8777. Business E-Mail: vparisi@med.wayne.edu. *

PARK, CHAN BEOM, surgeon; b. WonJu, Kangwondo, Republic Of Korea, Dec. 25, 1970; s. Hee Seo Park and Sook Ja Lee; m. Il Jim Cho; 1 child, Si Woo. PhD, Cath. U. Korea, Seoul, 2007. Cert. physician Min. Health & Welfare, 1996. Asst. prof. Cath. U. Korea, 2007—08; staff cardiothoracic surgeon St. Paul's Hosp., Seoul, 2003—. Mem.: Korean Soc. Thoracic & Cardiovasc. Surgery. Business E-Mail: drcs5223@daum.net.

PARK, CHAN HONG, physician; b. Daegu, Republic of Korea, Nov. 5, 1965; MD, Keimyung U., 1990; PhD, Kyungngpook U., 2003. Assoc. prof. Daegu Cath. U. Med. Ctr., 2000—08, bd. dir., 2005—06; vis. scholar Duke U. Med. Ctr., 2007—08; physician Daegu Wooridul Spine Hosp., 2008—, bd. dir., 2008—. Reviewer Korean Pain Soc., 2004—, Korean Soc. Anesthesiologist, 2005—08. Avocation: tennis. Office: 50-3 Dongin Jung-gu Daegu 700732 Republic of Korea

PARK, CHAN HYUNG, cell biologist, physician; b. Seoul, Korea, Aug. 16, 1936; s. Chung Suh and Yoon Sook Yuh; m. Mary Hyungrok Kim, Apr. 16, 1966; 1 child, Christopher Myungwoo. MD, Seoul Nat. U., 1962, MS, 1964; PhD, U. Toronto, 1972. Diplomate in internal medicine and med. oncology Am. Bd. Internal Medicine. Asst. prof. U. Kans. Med. Ctr., 1974—80, assoc. prof., 1980—86, prof., 1986—89; prof., chief divsn. oncology/hematology, dept. internal med. Tex. Tech U. Health Scis. Ctr., 1989—94; dir. Cancer Ctr. Samsung Med. Ctr., Seoul, 1994—2001, head divsn. hematology/oncology dept. medicine, 1994—99; sr. rsch. scientist Ctr. for Improvement of Human Functioning Internat., Inc., Wichita, Kans., 2001—; prof. medicine Sungkyn-Kwan U. Med. Sch., 1997—2001, prof. emeritis, 2007—. Cancer ctr. cons. 2001; adv. com. Samsung Cancer Ctr., 2006—. Transl. novel from German to Korean; mem. editl. bd. Jour. Nutrition, Growth and Cancer, 1986-87; mem. editl. bd. Internat. Jour. Hematology, 1999—; contbr. articles to biomed and sci. jours. Recipient Rsch. Career Devel. award USPHS, NIH, 1979-84. Fellow: ACP; mem.: Am. Soc. Hematology, Internat. Soc. Exptl. Hematology, Am. Soc. Clin. Oncology, Am. Assn. Cancer Rsch. Office: The Ctr for the Improvement Human Functioning Internat Inc 3100 N Hillside Wichita KS 67219 Home: 22226 Cliff Ave S 304 Des Moines WA 98198 Personal E-mail: park.chanh@gmail.com.

PARK, CHANG SUK, medical educator; b. Busan, Republic of Korea, July 15, 1972; d. Jong-Min Park and Jung-Lye Kim; m. Il-Kyu Kim; children: Yeon-Soo Kim, Min-Sung Kim. MD, Busan Nat. U., 1997; MS, Dong-A U. Korea, 2002; D, Cath. U. Korea, 2010. Cert. specialist in radiology Korean Bd. Radiology, 1995, lic. Nat. Med. Bd. Korea, 1997. Intern Dong-A U. Hosp. Coll. Medicine, 1997—98, resident, 1998—2002; fellow dept. radiology Bucheon St. Mary Hosp. Coll. Medicine, Cath. U. Korea, Seoul, 2002, 2003—04; instr. dept. radiology Incheon St. Mary Hosp. Coll. Medicine, Cath. U. Korea, 2005—08, asst. prof. dept. radiology, 2008—. Mem.: Korean Soc. Breast Radiology, Korean Radiol. Soc., Korean Med. Assn. Office: Incheon Saint Mary Hosp Coll Medicine Cath University Korea 665-8 Bupyeong 6-dong Bupyeong Incheon 403-720 Republic of Korea Office Phone: 82-32-280-5183. Office Fax: 82-32-529-0964, 82-280-5192. E-mail: blounse@catholic.ac.kr.

PARK, CHANG-SOO, pathologist, educator; b. Chonnam, Republic of Korea, July 10, 1953; m. Jung-Ok Kwon, May 5, 1953; children: So-Yeon, Yong-Jin. MB, Chonnam Nat. U. Med. Sch., Kwangju, Korea, 1978, M in Medicine, 1981, MD, 1987. Lic. MD Korea, 1978, bd. cert. clin. pathology, 1983, anat. pathology, 1988. Prof. pathology Chonnam Nat. U. Med. Sch., Kwangju, Republic of Korea, 1997—. Mem.: Korean Soc. Pathologists (licentiate). Office: Chonnam Nat U Med Sch Hakdong Dongku # 5 501-746 Gwangju Republic of Korea Office Fax: 062-225-0480.

PARK, CHUNG-GYU, medical educator; b. Daegu, Republic of Korea, July 1, 1962, MD, Seoul Nat. U., 1987, PhD, 1993. Rsch. fellow Harbor UCLA Rsch. and Edn. Inst. Gen. Clin. Rsch. Ctr., Calif., 1997; rsch. assoc. Chgo. U. Ben May Inst., Ill., 1998—2000; asst. prof. Seoul Nat. U. Coll. Medicine, 1998—2004, assoc. prof., 2004—09, prof., 2009—, assoc. dean, rsch. affairs, 2010. Mem.: Korean Soc. Transplantation, Am. Soc. Transplantation, Transplantation Soc., Internat. Xenotransplantation Assn., Am. Assn. Immunologists. Office: 103 Daehak-ro Jongno-gu Seoul 110-799 Republic of Korea Office Fax: 82-2-743-0881. Business E-Mail: chgpark@snu.ac.kr.

PARK, DAEHWAN, plastic surgeon; b. Daegu, Republic of Korea, Sept. 1, 1954; s. Gudong Park and Jinchan Lee; m. Heesuk Bae, July 14, 1939; children: Soyoung, Kisoo. MD, Kyungpook Nat. U., Republic of Korea, 1980, PhD, 1989. Bd. Cert. Plastic Surgeon Health Adminstrn., Republic of Korea, 1985. Prof. Daegu (Republic of Korea) Cath. U., Republic of Korea, 1991—, chmn. plastic surgery Daegu (Republic of Korea) Cath. U. Med. Ctr., 1988—; dir. tissue engrng. ctr. MSCUD, Daegu, 2001—; dir. osmidrosis ctr. DCUMC, Daegu, Republic of Korea, 2002—, dir. cosmetic surgery ctr., 2002—, dir. oculoplastic surgery ctr., 2002—. Editor: Textbook of Ophthalmic Plastic Surgery (Academic prize of Daegu Med. Assn., 2001); author: (book) Treatment of Osmidrosis and Hyperhidrosis, (presentation) No-reflow Phenomenon in Rabbit (Best Scientic Paper, 1994); contbr. Mem. Daegu Cath. Doctor's Assn., 2001—03; dir. Goechon Scholarship Found., Ulsan, 1997—2003. Capt. Army Physician, 1985—88, Korea. Recipient Sci. Achievements, Korea Soc. of Microsurgery, 1994; grantee Rsch. Fund for Tissue Engring., Korea Sci. Found., 2001, Rsch. Fund, Korean Scholar Promoting Found., 2001; fellow, ACS, 1996; Scholarship, Jungsoo Scholarship Found., 1976. Mem.: Korean Soc. Plastic Surgery (dir. 1996—), Total Cosmetic Acad. (pres. 2003—), Korean Soc. of CPCA (dir. 1999—), Korean Soc. Aesthetic Plastic Surgery (dir. 1999—), Internat. Soc. Aesthetic Plastic Surgery, Am. Soc. of Plastic Surgery (corr.), Am. Soc. Aesthetic Plastic Surgery (corr.), Dalseo Lions Club (life). Roman Catholic. Achievements include first to Alginate engrng. by Korean seaweed. Avocations: golf, tennis, travel. Office: Daegu Cath Univ Med Ctr Plastic Surgery 3056-6 Daemyung 4-Dong 705-718 Daegu Daegu Republic of Korea Office Fax: 82-53-650-4584. E-mail: dhpark@cu.ac.kr.

PARK, DEOKHOON, medical products executive, biologist; b. Jeju, Republic of Korea, Feb. 20, 1965; s. Suseun Park and Sukja Hong; m. Myeongok Kim, May 5, 1994; children: Jiseob, Hyunjeong. BS, Kyungbuk Nat. U., Taegu City, Republic of Korea, 1987; MS, Kyungbuk U., Taegu City, Republic of Korea, 1989; PhD, Kyungbuk Nat. U., Taegu City, Republic of Korea, 1992. Sr. scientist Pacific Rsch. and Devel. Ctr, Yongin, Kyunggi-Do, Republic of Korea, 1992—97; prin. scientist Postech, Pohang, Kyungbuk, 1997—99; dir. Genomine, Inc., Pohang, 1999—2000; CEO BioSpectrum, Inc., Gunpo, Kyunggi-Do, 2000—. Mem. adv. bd. BK21 Bus. Team, Jeju, Jeju-Do, 2004—, Youngnam Agr. Rsch. and Devel. Ctr., Mulyang, Jyungbuk, 2005—. Contbr. articles to profl. jours. Grantee, Ministry of Agr. and Forestry, Seoul, 2003, Ministry of Commerce, Industry and Energy, Seoul, 2004. Avocations: golf, inline skating, tracking. Office: BioSpectrum Inc 101-701 Sk Ventium Dangjung-Dong 435-776 Gunpo Gyeonggi-do Republic of Korea Office Phone: +82 31 436 2090.

PARK, DONG IL, gastroenterologist, researcher; b. Seoul, Republic of Korea, Feb. 5, 1967; s. Jae Sik Park and Eun Young Joh; m. Se Eun Kim, Nov. 20, 1994; children: Ji Ho, Jae Yeon. MD, Hanyang U., Seoul, PhD, 2001. Asst. prof. Kanbuk Samsung Hosp., Sungkyunkwan U., Seoul, 2003—. Assoc. editor: Korean Jour. Gastroent. (ACS fellowship for Beginning Investigator, 2001). Fellow, Samsung Med. Ctr., Seoul, 1999—2001, U. Pitts. Med. Ctr., 2001—03, Union Internat. Cancer Ctr., Geneva, 2001—02. Mem.: Korean Soc. Gastrointestinal Endoscopy (life), Korean Soc. Gastroent. (life). Achievements include research in HER-2/neu overexpression is an independent prognostic factor in colorectal cancer. Office: Kangbuk Samsung

Hospital 108 Pyung-dong Jongro-gu Seoul 110-746 Republic of Korea Office Phone: 82-2-2001-2059. Office Fax: 82-2-2001-2610. Business E-Mail: diksmc.park@samsung.com.

PARK, DONG-SUK, medical educator; b. Busan, Republic of Korea, Aug. 24, 1949; s. Park Kee-Taek and Cho Tae-Sook; m. Eun-Ok Lee; children: Hye-Jean, Tae-Hee, Young-Wook. B, KyungHee U., Seoul, Republic of Korea, 1974, M, 1976, MD, 1983. Cert. Oriental med. Dr. Min. Health and Welfare, 1974. Prof. KyungHee U., Seoul, Republic of Korea, 1979—, pres. East-West Med. grad. sch., 2005—06, dir. Oriental Med. Hosp., East-West Neo Med. Ctr., 2006—08; chmn. Korean Acupuncture & Moxibustion Soc., Seoul, Republic of Korea, 1997—99, Korean Oriental Med. Soc., Seoul, 2003—06; dir. Oriental Med. Hosp. Kyung Hee U. Hosp., Gangdong, 2011—; chmn. Korean Oriental Medicine Edn. and Evaluation Inst., 2011—. Med. adv. com. Ministry Nat. Def., Seoul, 2002—07; pvt. sector commr. Presdl. com. Healthcare Industry Innovation, 2006—07. Contbr. scientific papers to profl. jours. Med. adv. com. Min. Nat. Def., Seoul, Republic of Korea, 2002—07; pvt. sector commr. Presdl. Com. on Healthcare Industry Innovation, 2006—07. Co. grade civil defense, 1977—99, Seoul. Recipient Med. award, KyungHee U., 2006, award, Min. Health and Welfare, 2006, 2011. Master: Korean Oriental Med. Soc. (hon.). Presbyterian. Achievements include patents for development of aroma acupuncture; patents pending for herbal medicine in arthritis; herbal medicine in fracture healing; herbal medicine in angiogenesis; herbal medicine in arthritis prevention; research in treatment of incurable diseases; acupunctural mechanism in chronic pain; development of herbal medicine in bone and joint disease. Avocations: golf, tennis, billiards, travel. Office Fax: 82-2-440-7705. Personal E-mail: dspark49@yahoo.co.kr.

PARK, EUI-SOO, dermatologist, consultant; b. Daegu, Republic of Korea, Feb. 16, 1953; s. Nam-Ho Park and Sung-Hyea Kim; m. Hyea-Myung Cho, Jan. 18, 1977; children: Sung-Eun, So-Eun, Sung-Min. MD, Kyungpook Nat. U., Daegu, Korea, 1978, MA, 1982, PhD, 1985. Lic. Korean Med. Bd. Medicine, 1978, Korean Bd. Dermatology, 1983. Instr. sch. medicine Keimyung U., Daegu, 1983—87, asst. prof. sch. medicine, 1988—91, assoc. prof. sch. medicine, 1992—94; fellow dermatology U. Toronto, 1992; dir. Bosung Skin & Laser Clinic, Daegu, 1995—96, Dr. Park's Skin & Laser Clinic, Daegu, 1997—. Med. cons. sch. medicine Keimyung U., 2000—04. Contbr. articles to profl. jours. Elder The Presbyn. Ch., Daegu, 2002—07. Maj. Korean Army, 1986—88. Fellow: Am. Acad. Dermatology; mem.: Korean Assn. Practitioners Dermatology (chmn. 2001—02, mem. com. 2005—), Soc. Investigative Dermatology. Achievements include research in effects of UVB-inducible cytokines on melanoma growth; serum testosterone levels on leprosy patients; serum angiotensin converting enzyme levels on leprosy; expression of epidermal growth factor receptor in malignant epidermal tumors; mutant p53 protein expression squamous cell carcinoma. Avocations: travel, tennis, mountain climbing. Home: 101-402 Dalim E Pyunhan Sesang Apt Suseong-dong 4-ga Suseong-gu Daegu 706926 Republic of Korea Office: Skin & Laser Clinic Ste 402 1431-4 Dowon-Dong Dalseo-gu Daegu 704380 Republic of Korea Office Phone: 82-53-637-7477. Office Fax: 82-53-636-2123. Personal E-mail: parkpes7977@hanmail.net.

PARK, EUN-KEE, government agency administrator, researcher, environmental scientist, educator; b. Seoul, Republic of Korea, Oct. 21, 1966; arrived in Australia, 1994, permanent resident; s. Jang-Won Park and Ul-Sup Kim; m. Sylvia Kim, Nov. 3, 1994; children: Justin Jong-Min, Joshua Jong-Wu. BAS, Korea U., Seoul, 1989; M Applied Sci., U. NSW, Sydney, 1993; PhD in Environ. Sci. and Toxicology, U. Sydney, 2000. Rsch. fellow Waters Co. Ltd., Seoul, 1993—94; tech. officer U. Sydney, 1996—99, rsch. asst., 1997—99, postdoc. fellow, 1999—2000; rsch. assoc. U. Calif., 2001—02, rschr., 2003—05; vis. rsch. fellow U. NSW, 2005—; sr. project mgr. Workers' Compensation Dust Diseases Bd., Sydney, 2005—09; prof. Dept. Environ. Epidemiolgy Inst. Indsl. Ecol. Sci. U., 2009—11; prof. dept. humanities and social medicine Kosin U. Coll. Medicine, Busan, Republic of Korea, 2011—. Contbr. scientific papers to profl. jours. Ch. Sunday sch. coord., 2008. Recipient Internat. Health award; Norman Scott Noble scholarship, U. Sydney, 1996. Conservative. Achievements include screening of clinical biomarkers to identify mesothelioma and lung cancer in a population exposed to asbestos; monitoring of endocrine-disrupting compounds in biological and environmental samples; evaluation of in cell model; human pesticide exposure assessment in farm workers; monitoring and removal of heavy metals from aqueous solutions; bioremediation of heavy metals and pesticides; estimation of asbestos exposure in non-occupational setting; indoor air quality monitoring; evaluation of natural products. Avocations: tennis, baseball, travel. Office: Kosin University Coll Medicine Dept Humanities and Social Medicine 34 Anandong Seoga Busan 602-102 Republic of Korea Personal E-mail: bioremediation@hotmail.com.

PARK, EUN-MI, neurologist, researcher, medical educator; d. Jong-Tae Park and Soon-Yei Kim. MD, Ewha Womans U., Seoul, 1993, PhD, 1999. Cert. neurologist Ministry Health and Welfare, 1998. Intern Ewha Womans U. Hosp., Republic of Korea, 1993—94, neurology resident, 1994—98, clin. fellow in neurology, 1999—2000, asst. prof. dept. pharmacology Sch. Medicine, 2004—08; clin. fellow in neurology Seoul Nat. U. Hosp., 1998—99; rsch. scholar Burke Med. Rsch. Inst., White Plains, NY, 2000—02; postdoctoral assoc. Weil Med. Coll., Cornell U., NYC, 2002—04; assoc. prof. Dept. Pharmacology Sch. Medicine, 2008—. Contbr. articles to profl. jours. Scholar, Keystone Symposia, 2002. Mem.: Korean Med. Assn., Korean Neurol. Assn., Soc. Neuroscience. Office: Sch Medicine Ewha Womans Univ Bldg A 306 Dept Pharm 911-1 Mok6dong Yangcheongu Seoul 158-710 Republic of Korea Business E-Mail: empark@ewha.ac.kr.

PARK, EUNOK, healthcare educator; d. Heechul Park and Yoongyu Song; m. Byung-Wang Jun; children: Minhyung Jun, Minjae Jun. BSN, Seoul Nat. U., Korea, 1991; MPH, Seoul Nat. U., 1994, PhD in Pub. Health, 1999. Cert. health tchr. Ministry, Edn. and Human Resources, 1991; R.N., Ministry, Health and Welfare, South Korea, 1991. Nurse Seoul Nat. U. Hosp., 1991—92; tchr. asst. Red Cross Coll. Nursing, Seoul, 1994—96; parttime instr. Suwon Women's Coll., Suwon, Gyeonggido, Republic of Korea, 1996—96, Gyungin Women's Coll., Suwon, 1997—98, Dongnam Health Coll., Suwon, 1998, Gyonggi U., Suwon, 1999—2000; spl. rschr. Seoul Nat. U. Inst. Health and Environ. Sci., Seoul, 1998—2000; instr. Jeju Nat. U., Jejudo, Republic of Korea, 2000—02; asst. prof. Cheju Nat. U., Jejudo, Republic of Korea, 2002—06, assoc. prof., 2006—11; postdoc. fellow U. Colo. Health Scis. Ctr., Denver, 2002—03; adv. com. mem. Case Mgmt. Med. Aid Beneficiary, Jeiudo, 2010; mem. Civil Affairs & Sys. Renovation Com., Ministry of Health & Welfare, 2010—, Social Interchange Seoul Internat. Conferences Cmty. Health Nursing Rsch., 2010—, Bd. Sch. Health, Jeiudo, 2008—, Ministry of Edn., Sci. & Tech., 2008—; prin. investigator Devel. & Evaluation Depression Mgmt. Program Vulnerable Elderly, 2010, Planning Local Pub. Health Care Jeju Spl. Gov. Province, 2010—11, assoc. prof., 2006—11; prof. Coll. Nursing Jeju Nat. U., 2011—. Exec. mem. Korean Acad. Soc. Occupl. Nursing, Seoul, 2001—04; chief editor Jour. Korean Soc. Sch. Health, Seoul, 2004—05, editor, 2006—07; exec. mem. Korean Acad. Soc. Sch. Health, Seoul, 2004—05; bd. mem. Bukjeju County Bd. Assn. Health Promotion, Jejudo, 2004—06, Water Evaluation Com. Jejudo, 2006—; pres. Jeju Pub. Health Nurses Assn., Jeju, Jejudo, 2006—07; vice dir. Bd. Sch. Health, Jejudo, 2006—; exec. mem. Korean Academic Soc. Rural Health Nursing, Seoul, 2006—; dir. Jeju Mgmt. Ctr. Health Promotion, Jejudo, 2007—; prin. Jeju Ctr. Health Promotion Field Mgmt. Tng. Program, Jejudo, 2007—09; prin. investigator Jeju Ctr. Customer Centered Home Vis. Health Care Field Mgmt. Tng. Program, Jejudo, 2008—09; reviewer Jour. Korean Acad. Cmty. Health Nursing, Seoul, 2008—, Jour. Korean Acad. Nursing, 2009—, Korean Academic Soc. Sch. Health, 2010—; exec. mem. Korean Soc. Customized Vis. Healthcare, 2009—. Contbr. articles to profl. jours. Supporter Jeju Yeominhoi, Jejudo, 2001—02; mem. Soc. Christian Young Adults Health Profls., Seoul, 2001—09; supporter Plan Korea, Seoul, 2006—09, YMCA, Jeju, Jejudo, 2007—09. Grantee Disease prevalence and health promotion strategy for rural women elderly, Korea Inst. for Health and Social Affairs, 2007, Devel. of servces delivery model for the elderly in the cmty., Ministry of Health and Welfare, 1999—2000, Policy devel. for preventive health care in Gyeonggido, Gyeonggi Province, 1999, Task analysis and workload estimation of pers. in urban pub. health ctr. br. in South Korea, Ministry of Health and Welfare, 2007, A survey on depression prevalence in Jeju, Jejudo, 2007, The risk factors of suicidal attempt in youth, Cheju Nat. U., 2007—08, A need assessment of health and welfare among the disabled for cmty. based rehab. in Jeju, South Korea, Korea Assn. of Health Promotion Jeju Br., 2006, A Jeju health survey 2005, Jejudo, 2005, Strengthening strategies of sch. health in Korea, Ministry of Health and Welfare, 2004—05, A study on a pub. health workforce tng. scheme for developing health promotion policy for the future, Ministry of Health and welfare, 2004, A meta-analysis of the effects of smoking prevention programs in Korea, Korea Rsch. Found., 2002—03, Devel. Health City Indicator & City Project, Jejudo, 2008, Devel. Case Mgmt. Program, 2008, Program Devel. Frail Elderly, 2008, Devel. and Evaluation of Depression and Mgmt. Program for the Vulnerable Elderly, Jeju Province, 2010, Planning of Local Public Health Care in Jeju Spl.-Governing Province, 2010—11. Mem.: Jeju Women Spl. Bd. (Jejudo) (mem. bd. 2008—), Korean Assn. Agrl. Medicine & Cmty. Health (exec. mem. 2007—), Jeju Pub. Health Nurses Assn., Korean Nurses Assn., Korean Academic Soc. Cmty. Health nursing, Korean Academic Soc. Nursing, Korean Academic Soc. Occupl. Nursing, Korean Academic Soc. Sch. Health, Korean Academic Soc. Rural Health Nursing. Achievements include devel. education promams for visiting health nurses; Development Depression Management Promam for the Vulnerable Population. Office: Jeju National University Jejudaehakro 66 Ara1dong 690-756 Jeju Jeju-do Republic of Korea Office Fax: +82-64-702-2686. Business E-Mail: eopark@jejunu.ac.kr.

PARK, EUN-YOUNG, medical educator; b. Daegu, Gyeongsangbuk-do, Republic of Korea, Dec. 19, 1968; d. Su-Kyu Park and Ki-Yeon Nam. MD, Hanyang U., Seoul, 1993, PhD, 2000. Instr. Hallym U. Coll. Medicine, Chuncheon, Gangwon-do, Republic of Korea, 2002—04, asst. prof., 2004—05; pediatrician Mizmedi Hosp., Seoul, 2006—08, Seoul Red Cross Hosp., 2008—. Contbr. articles to profl. jours. Mem.: Korean Pediat. Assn. Personal E-mail: neonatol@hanmail.net.

PARK, GAB MAN, parasitologist, educator; s. Park Su Cheun and Yoon Oak Soon; m. Park Gab Man, Apr. 21, 1985; 1 child, Park Jae Ho. BSc in Biology, Kangweon Nat. U., Chuncheon, Republic of Korea, 1983, MSc in Biology, 1985, PhD, 1991. With U. Mich., Ann Arbor, 1993—95, Gangweon Nat. U., Chuncheon, 1996—97, Yonsei U., Seoul, Republic of Korea, 1999—2001; prof. Kwandong U. Coll. Medicine, Gangneung, 2002—. Editor-in-chief Korean Jour. Malacology, 2008. Dir. Found. Simwon HakSul Jaedan, Gangneung, 2003—07. With Korean Army, 1979—81. Grantee, Ministry Commerce, Industry and Energy, 2004—06. Master: Marine Med. Resources Rsch. Ctr. Achievements include patents for a composition containing Ecklonia stolonifera extract for skin external application. Office: Kwandong Univ Coll Med/Dept Parasitology Naegok-Dong 522 210-701 Gangneung Gangwon-do Republic of Korea Office Phone: 82-33-649-7485. Office Fax: 82-33-641-1074. Business E-Mail: gmpark@kd.ac.kr.

PARK, GUN, dermatologist, hair transplantation surgeon; b. Daegu, Korea, Oct. 27, 1973; MS, Cath. U. Daegu Hyusung, 2000. Chief physician 2080 Dermatologic Clinic, 2008—11. Recipient Exemplary award, Daegu Metropolit. Office Edn. Mem.: Korean Dermatol. Assn., Assn. Korean Dermatologist. Avocations: reading, scuba diving. Office: Buk-gu Chimsan-dong 285-5 Myungsung Daegu 702-502 Republic of Korea Business E-Mail: 2080skin@naver.com.

PARK, HEE-JUHN, pharmacist, researcher; b. Changwon, Gangwon-do, Republic Of Korea, July 2, 1960; s. Hong-Sik Park and Wi-Jo Kim; m. Hearan Sean, Apr. 9, 1989; children: Kyung-Jin, Myung-Gon. PhD, Pusan Nat. U., 1991. Lic. pharmacist Korea, 1983. Prof. Sangji U., Wonju, Republic of Korea, 1991—2008. Editor-in-chief: Korean Soc. of Pharmacognosy. 2d lt. Land Forces, 1985—86, Youngcheon. Recipient Best Paper award, Korean Soc. Pharmacognosy, 1985. Liberal. Achievements include patents for bioactive compounds isolated from medicinal herbs. Avocations: tennis, golf. Home: Dangye-dong Gangwon-do Wonju 220-100 Republic of Korea Office: Sangji U Woosan-Dong 220-702 Wonju Gangwon-do Republic of Korea Office Fax: 82 33 730 0564.

PARK, HEUNG JAE, urologist, medical researcher; b. Seoul, Dec. 17, 1962; s. Chang Gun Park and Yeon Ok Han; m. Mi Young Song, Feb. 2, 1989; children: Jung We, Jeoung Won. Bachelor, Korea U., Seoul, 1987, Master, 1992, PhD, 1994. Cert. physician Korea, Korean Bd. Urology. Assoc. prof Sungkyunkwan U. Sch. Medicine, Seoul, 2001—, asst. prof., 1997—2000; rsch. fellow dept. urology Harvard U. Children's Hosp., Boston, 1997—98; staff urologist Koryo Gen. Hosp., Seoul, 1993—97; resident in urology Korea U. Med. Ctr., Seoul, 1989—93; intern Seoul Adventist Hosp., 1988—89. Dir. various rsch. projects. Contbg. author: several textbooks; contbr. articles to profl. jours. Soldier land forces, 1987—87, Anyang, Kyungki-Do, Korea. Grantee, Korea Sci. and Engring. Found., 2001—, Samsung Biomed. Rsch. Inst., 2000—02. Mem.: Korean Endourol. Assn. (licentiate), Korean Continence Soc. (licentiate), Korean Andrological Soc. (licentiate), The Korean Urol. Assn. (licentiate), The Korean Med. Assn. (licentiate), Korea Tissue Engring. Soc. (assoc.), Internat. Tissue Engring. Soc. (assoc.), Korean Female Sexual Dysfunction Soc. (assoc.). Office: Kangbuk Samsung Hosp 108 Pyung-Dong Jongro-Gu Seoul 110-102 Republic of Korea Office Fax: 82-2-2001-2247. Personal E-mail: tigerhj@dreamwiz.com.

PARK, HONG SEOK, urologist, educator; b. Pusan, Republic of Korea, May 1, 1967; s. Hyun Chul Park and Kyung Ja Kim; m. Hyun Yee Cho; 1 child, Tae Young. PhD, Korea U. Med. Coll., Seoul, Republic of Korea, 1999. Cert. physician Urology Bd., Republic of Korea, 1996. Dir., dept. urology Korea U. Ansan Hosp., Kyungki-do, 2003—; assoc. prof. Korea U. Med. Coll., Seoul, 2003—. Contbr. articles to med. jours. Capt., flight surgeon 5th Airbase Hosp. Republic of Korea Air Force, 1996—99, Pusan. Office: Urology Korea Univ Ansan Hosp Kojan-Dong Danwon-Ku 425-707 Ansan Kyungki do Republic of Korea Office Fax: 82-31-412-5194. Business E-Mail: dr4you@korea.ac.kr.

PARK, HWA JIN, biomedical engineer, researcher, educator; b. Sam-Ga-Myoun, Republic of Korea, Jan. 29, 1952; s. Hee Cheol Park and Sam Soon-Yi Kim; m. Young Jin Cho, Jan. 3, 1984; children: Min Wook, Min Gyu. BS, Kon-Kuk U., Seoul, Korea, 1979; MS with honors, Obihiro U. Agr. and Vet. Medicine, Obihiro, Japan, 1983; PhD with honors, Kyoto U., Japan, 1986. Postdoctoral fellow dept biochemistry Chung-Buk Nat. U., Cheong-Ju, Republic of Korea, 1987—88; asst. prof. dept. food nutrition Coll. Chung-Cheung, Cheong-Ju, 1988—89; postdoctoral fellow dept. chemistry U. Nebr., Lincoln, 1989—90; head dept. biomedical pharmacology Korea Ginseng and Tobacco Rsch. Inst., Taejon, Republic of Korea, 1990—96; concurrent prof. Chung Nam U., Taejon, Republic of Korea, 1992—96; prof. coll. biomedical sci. and engring. Inje U., Gimhae, Republic of Korea, 1996—, vice dean coll. biomedical sci. and engring., 2001—03. Mem. evaluation com. sci. and tech. Ministry Sci. and Tech., Seoul, 2006—; vis. prof. Kyoto U., 2000—01. Contbr. articles to profl. jours. Recipient The Excellent Treatise Sci. Tech. prize, All the Union Pres. Assn., Korean Sci. Tech., 1991, Pres. Korean Soc. Ginseng, 1993; scholar, Ministry Edn., Japan, 1980—86. Mem.: Korean Soc. Biomedical Lab. Sci. (vice chmn. 2006—). Achievements include patents for novel substances PF-01, PF-02, OF-03; antithrombotic cordycepin from cordyceps; antihyperlipidemic substance from chlorella; Antihepatotoxicitic sbustance from chlorella; development of antithrombotic and antihyperlipidemic substances from ginseng. Avocations: reading, music. Business E-Mail: mlsjpark@inje.ac.kr.

PARK, HYE SOON, physician, educator; d. Chun Bong Park and Eui Bum Lee; m. Jung Yul Park, Oct. 11, 1985; children: Min Young, Sung Joon. MD in Medicine, Korea U., Seoul, 1985, PhD, 1992; MPH, Grad. Sch. Pub. Health Seoul Nat. U., 2004. Lic. Korean Med. Assn., 1985, diplomate Korean Bd. Family Medicine, 1988. Asst. prof., dept. family medicine U. Ulsan Coll. Medicine, Seoul, 1994—99, assoc. prof., dept. family medicine, 1999—2004, prof., dept. family medicine, 2004—, chair family medicine, 2006—; vis. prof., dept. medicine Cardiovascular Risk Factor Modification Ctr., Toronto U. Sch. Medicine, 1999—2000; vice chair family medicine Asan Med. Ctr., Seoul, 2000—06, chair family medicine, 2006—. Exec. sec. com. Korean Soc. Cmty. Nutrition, 1997—2001; chair Soc. Rsch. Obesity, 1997—2001; nutrition com. Asan Med. Ctr., 2001—, mem. Instl. Rev. Bd., 2003—06; spl. advisor evaluation rev. bd. academic rsch. Korea Rsch. Found., 2003—06; mem. edn. com. U. Ulsan Coll. Med., 2006—, 2006—; chair Soc. Rsch. Metabolic Syndrome, 2006—; spl. advisor, project health promotion disease prevention Seoul Met. City, 2006—07; spl. advisor, project mgmt. metabolic syndrome Korean Med. Assn., 2006—07; cons. in field. Contbr. scientific papers; author: Family Medicine Principal, 2003, Diagnosis and Treatment Obesity, 2003, Guideline of Treatment Obesity, 2003, Dyslipidemia and Atherosclerosis, 2003, Guideline of Treatment Dyslipidemia, 2003, Health Promotion among Koreans, 2004, Metabolic Syndrome, 2005, 2007, Metabolic Syndrome Practical Guide, 2005, Pathophysiological Molecular Biology of Metabolic Syndrome, 2005, Clinical Obesity, 2008. Recipient Korean Med. Women's Assn. award, 2005. Mem.: Korean Soc. Lipidology Atherosclerosis (vice-chair info. com. 1998—2005), Internat. Soc. Study Obesity (assoc.), Korean Soc. Food Sci. Nutrition (assoc.), Korean Soc. Study Obesity (life; vice-sec. 2000—02, vice-chair, tng. com. 2000—02, vice-chair 2002—04, chair metabolic syndrome task force 2004—06, vice-chair 2006—, chairperson 2008—, award 2003, 2008), Korean Acad. Family Medicine (life; mem. sci. com. 1992—94, mem. exam. com. 1994—96, mem. sci. com. 1996—98, chair 1997—2001, pub. com. 2000—01, bd. mem. 2006—, chair 2006—, exec. bd. mem. 2006—, award 1992, 1993, 1995, 2006), Korean Med. Assn. (life). Achievements include research in the fields of obesity, metabolic syndrome, health promotion, and epidemiology. Office: Asan Med Ctr Dept Family Medicine 388-1 Pungnap-2dong Songpa-gu Seoul 138-736 Republic of Korea Office Fax: 82-2-3010-3815. Business E-Mail: hyesoon@amc.seoul.kr.

PARK, HYE-KYUNG, health facility administrator; b. Seoul, Republic Of Korea, Feb. 17, 1960; d. Jee-Young Park and Ok-Jung Oh; m. Young-Kook Ham, Oct. 26, 1991; children: Hyun-Joo Ham, Soo-Yon Ham. BA, Sook Myung Womans U., Seoul, 1982; MA, Korea U., Seoul, 1985, PhD in Food Chemistry and Applied Nutrition, 1991. Cert. dietitian Ministry Health Soc., 1982, mid. & HS tchr. Ministry Edn., 1982. Rschr. Nutrition Rsch. Inst. Hallym U., Chunchon, Republic of Korea, 1988—91; rsch. officer Korea Nat. Inst. Health, Seoul, 1991—96; dep. dir. Korea Food & Drug Adminstrn., Seoul, 1996—2003, dir., 2003—. Cyber lectr. Sookmyung Womens U., 2000—01; lectr. Dankook U., Seoul, 2002—03; concurrent prof. Yonsei U., Seoul, 2004—05. Contbr. articles to jours. Korean del. CODEX, Republic of Korea, 2001—05. Named Saettugi, Joonang Daily Korea, 2007; named to Presdl. Citation, Ministry Pub. Adminstrn. and Security, 2007; Internat. Visitor grant, Dept. 2State USA, 2002. Mem.: Korean Nutrition Soc., Korean Soc. Lipidology and Atherosclerosis, Korean Soc. Food Hygiene and Safety. Consumer. Achievements include policy for reducing trans fat contents, safe foods and better nutrition; patents for low temperature interesterification. Office: Korea Food & Drug Adminstrn 194 Tongil-ror Seoul 122-704 Republic of Korea Office Phone: 82-2-380-1677. Office Fax: 82-2-354-1399. Personal E-mail: aqua60@paran.com. Business E-Mail: phkfda@kfda.go.kr.

PARK, HYUN CHUL, biotechnologist; b. Suseong-gu, Daegu, Republic of Korea, Jan. 23, 1970; s. Mu Ung Park and Duck Soon Kim. B, Yeungnam U., Gyeongsan-si, 1998, M, 2001. Rschr. Nat. Inst. Toxicological Rsch., Eunpyeong, Seoul, Republic of Korea, 2001—04; mgr. CSM, Buck Gu, Daegu, Republic of Korea, 2006—06; rschr. Jung San Biotech., Asan, 2006—. Contbr. articles to profl. jours. Staff sgt. US Army, 1992—94. Recipient Encouragement prize, Daegu Technopark, Daegu City Hall, 2009. Mem.: Pharm. Soc. Korea. Achievements include patents pending in field. Office: R & D Ctr Jung San Biotech Sinin-Dong 336-140 Asan Si Chungcheongnam-do Republic of Korea

PARK, HYUN JEONG, dermatologist, educator; b. Seoul, Republic Of Korea, Nov. 4, 1969; d. Il Nam Park and Young Nam Bae; m. Dae Ho Cho, Nov. 9, 1997; 1 child, Won Chang Cho. MD, Cath. U. Korea, 1994, MSc, 1997; PhD, Cath. U. Korea, Seoul, 2000. Cert. Korean Bd. Dermatology, 1999. Internship Cath. U., St. Mary's Hosp., 1994—95; residency dept. dermatology, St. Mary's Hosp., 1995—99; fellow, dept. dermatology Kangnam St. Mary's Hosp., 1999—2001; instr. dept. dermatology, St. Mary's Hosp., Seoul, 2001—04, asst. prof., 2004—07, assoc. prof., 2008—, chief, 2009—. Contbr. articles to profl. jours. Recipient Internat. Young Dermatologist Achievement award, 2007. Mem.: Am. Acad. Dermatology (assoc.). Achievements include research in stress dermatology. Home: 211-110 Hyun Dai Apt Apkujungdong Seoul 135-789 Republic of Korea Office: St Marys Hosp Dept Dermatology 62 Youidodong Youngdeunpogu Seoul 150-713 Republic of Korea Office Phone: 82 23779 1230. Business E-Mail: hjpark@catholic.ac.kr.

PARK, HYUN SU, dermatologist, laser therapist, educator; s. Jeong Do Park and Bok Im Kim; m. Su Jin Gu, Sept. 23, 2000; children: Jisung, Jina, Jiye. MS, Grad. Sch. Inje U., Seoul; MD, Inje U. Coll. Medicine, Seoul. Lic. MD Ministry Health and Welfare, 2000, bd. dermatology Ministry Health and Welfare, 2005. Intern Inje U. Sanggye Paik Hosp., 2000—01, resident, dept. dermatology, 2001—05, fellow, dept. dermatology, 2005—06, instr., dept. dermatology, 2006—08, asst. prof., dept. dermatology, asthma & allergy ctr., 2008—, chief dept. dermatology, 2011—. Reviewer European Jour. .Dermatology, 2008, Pediat., 2008, Annals Dermatology, 2009—, Korean Jour.Dermatology, 2009—; editl. staff Korean Soc. Aesthetic & Dermatologic Surgery, 2009—; examiner Korean Bd. Dermatology Certifying Exam., 2008—10. Contbr. to numerous rsch. papers, articles to profl. jours. Mem. Internat. Christian Med. and Dental Assn., KwaZulu-Natal, South Africa, 2004. Korean Christian Med. fellowship, Seoul, 2000. Mem.: Korean Photomedicine Rsch. Group Assn. Korean Dermatologists, Korean Soc. Psoriasis, Korean Soc. Acne Rsch., Korean Atopic Dermatitis Assn., Am. Acad. Dermatology, Korean Dermatol. Assn., Korean Med. Assn, Mem. Christian Ch. Avocation: travel. Office: Dept Dermatology Sanggye Paik Hosp 761-1 Sanggye-7-Dong Nowon-Gu Seoul 139-707 Republic of Korea Office Fax: 82-2-931-8720. Business E-Mail: gajfirst@empal.com.

PARK, HYUNG BIN, medical educator, consultant; b. Jinhae, Kyung Nam, Republic of Korea, Aug. 14, 1963; s. Duk Choo Park and Young Ja Cho; m. Pil Yeob Choi, Dec. 26, 1965; children: Eun Sang, Se Hyuk. MD, Gyeong Sang Nat. U., 1989. Assoc. prof. Gyeong Sang Nat. U., Jinju, Kyung Nam, Republic of Korea, 1999 . Lt. comdr. Korean Navy, 1994—97. Mem.: Korean Shoulder and Elbow Assn. (assoc.). Avocation: travel. Office: Gyeong Sang Nat U Hosp Chilam-dong 90 660-702 Jinju Gyeongsangnam-do Republic of Korea Office Fax: 82-55-7624640. Personal E-mail: hbinpark@gnu.ac.kr.

PARK, IL-JUNG, medical educator; b. Seoul, Republic of Korea, May 26, 1974; MD, Cath. U. Korea, 1999, M in Med. Sci., 2004. Instr., dept. orthopaedic surgery Cath. U. Korea, Bucheon St. Mary's Hosp., 2007—08, asst. prof., 2009—. Recipient highest award, Korean Fracture Soc., 2007, Korean Soc. Surgery Hand, 2008, Korean Soc. Microsurgery, 2010; named Invited lectr., 7th Congress Asian Pacific Fedn. Societies Surgery Hand; Spl. grant, Korean Soc. Surgery Hand. Master: Cath. U. Korea. Avocations: soccer, piano. Office: 2 Sosa-dong Wonmi-gu Bucheon City Kyounggi-Do 420-717 Republic of Korea Office Fax: 82-32-340-2671. Business E-Mail: jikocmc@naver.com.

PARK, IN SUH, internist, educator; b. Seoul, South Korea, May 27, 1937; s. Jun Keun Park and Jung Won Kim; m. Soon Doe Park, Mar. 27, 1967. MD, Yonsei U., Seoul, 1962, M in Med. Sci., 1967; PhD, Yonsei U. Coll. of Medicine, Seoul, 1978. Intern, resident Severance Hosp., Seoul, 1962—66; prof. Yonsei U. Coll. Medicine, 1970—, prof. emeritus, 2002—; prof. medicine, dir. digestive disease ctr. Myungi Hosp. Kwandong U., Republic of Korea. Fellow Med. Cancer Inst. Hosp., Tokyo, 1972; vis. prof. Tech. U. Munchen, Germany, 1991; chief gastroenterology Yonsei U. Med. Ctr., Seoul, 1991—97; dir. Inst. Gastroent. Yonsei U., Seoul, 1992—97. Author: (book) Gastritis, 1998; contbr. articles to profl. jours. Maj. Korean Air Force, 1967—69. Recipient Acad. award, Korean Soc. Internal Medicine, 1977, 1989. Fellow: Am. Gastroenterological Assn.; mem.: Korean Assn. Internal Medicine (v.p. 1999—2000), Nat. Acad. Medicine Korea, Korean Coll. H.pylori Rsch. (pres. 1999), Korean Soc. Gastrointestinal Motility (pres. 1997—99), Korean Soc. Gastroenterology (pres. 1998—99, Acad. award 2000), Korean Soc. Gastrointestinal Endoscopy (pres. 1993—94), Am. Gastroenterology Assn.

PARK, INHO, physician; b. Gyeonggi, Republic of Korea, Dec. 5, 1968; MS, Grad. Sch. Pub. Health, Yonsei U., 2001. Chief profl. svc. Armed Forces Seoul Hosp., 2007—10. Home: Gangnam-gu Daechi-dong 901-51 Seoul 135-280 Republic of Korea Personal E-mail: park.afmc@gmail.com.

PARK, IN-SEOP, orthopedist, researcher; b. Seoul, Republic Of Korea, Mar. 24, 1964; s. Sang-Soon Park and Ok-Lim Yoon; m. Gi-Un Kim, Apr. 26, 1992; children: U-Jin, U-mi. Attended, Seoul Nat. U., 1984—90; M in Medicine, Gangwon Nat. U., 2006. Diplomate Seoul Nat. Med. U., 1990. Internship Nat. Med. Ctr., Seoul, 1991, resident, 1992—95; gen. orthopaedic dr. Yong-Dong Hosp., Jeonbuk, Republic of Korea, 1995—2002; arthroscopist, orthopaedic dept. Gangnam Hosp., Yongin-si, Gyeonggi-do, Republic of Korea, 2002—. Rschr. Severance Joint & Arthroscopy Rsch. Inst., Seoul, 2001—. Contbr. articles to profl. jours. Recipient Douglas W. Jackson award, Severance Joint & Arthroscopy Rsch. Inst., 2004. Office Phone: 82 31 300 0110, 82 31 300 0106. Business E-Mail: kju0115@naver.com.

PARK, JAE HYUN, orthodontist, educator; b. Seoul, Republic Of Korea, Nov. 30, 1963; s. Tae Sup Park and Young Whan Kho; m. Eun Mi Jung, Dec. 29, 1993; 1 child, Sung Ho. MS, MSD, DMD, NY U., NYC, PhD in Orthodontics, 2006. Pres. Ariz. Orthodontic Ctrs., Avondale; assoc. prof. & chair Ariz. Sch. Dentistry & Oral Health, Mesa, 2008—. Mng. orthodontist Western Dental Svcs., Inc., Phoenix, 2006—09. With Sungnam Dental Assn., Sungnam, 2000—02. Recipient Award, Pres. of KyungHee U., 1995, Gov. of Kyoungi Province, 1999, Pres. Korean Acad. Oral Anatomy, 1999. Mem.: Korean Dental Assn., World Fedn. Orthodontists, Am. Bd. Orthodontics, Minn. Dental Assn., Ariz. Dental Assn. Avocations: swimming, travel, hiking, golf, movies. Home: 5519 E Beryl Ave Paradise Valley AZ 85253 Office: Arizona Sch Dentistry & Oral Healt 5855 E Still Cir Mesa AZ 85206 Office Phone: 480-248-8165. Office Fax: 480-248-8117; Home Fax: 480-668-3081. E-mail: jpark@atsu.edu.

PARK, JAI SOUNG, radiologist, educator; b. Daejeon, Chungcheongnam-do, Republic Of Korea, Mar. 16, 1959; s. Kyung Won Park and Jeong Hee Kim; m. Sin Won Park; children: Jong Beom, Jong Yoon. MD, Soonchunhyang U., Asan, Chungcheongnam-do, 1983, MS, 1986, PhD, 1995; MD, Ministry Health and Welfare, Republic Of Korea, 1984. Cert. radiologist Ministry Health and Welfare, 1989. Prof. Dept. Radiology, Soonchunhyang U. Sch. Medicine, 1991—; radiologist Dept. Radiology, Soonchunhyang U. Hosp., Seoul, Republic of Korea, 1991—2000, Bucheon, Gyeonggi-do, Republic of Korea, 2001—; fellowship Dept. Radiology, U. Colo. Health Scis. Ctr., Denver, 1997—98; vis. prof. Dept. Radiology, Nat. Jewish Med. and Rsch. Hosp., Denver, 1997—98. Reviewer jour. Am. Coll. Chest Physicians, Northbrook, Ill., 2006—; expert advisor Nat. Evidence Based Healthcare Collaborating Agy., 2009. Expert adviser Judging Com. Epidemiologic Evaluation; mem. practical affairs Quality Mgmt. Com. Health Care Pneumoconiosis, Seoul, 2004, Quality Mgmt. Com. Spl. Health Care, Seoul, 2004; publ. Korean Fedn. Med. Imaging, Seoul, 2006; judge Judging Com. Compensation Pneumoconiosis, Seoul, 2005; expert adviser Com. Health Tech. Assessment, Seoul, 2009, Nat. Evidence Based Healthcare Collaborating Agy. Capt. Army. Mil., 1989—91, Korea. Recipient Cert. Merit, Radiologic Soc. N.Am., 2005, Bronze medal, Korean Soc. Ultrasound Medicine, 2004; grantee, Korea Sci. and Engring. Found., 1999, Korean Occupl. Safety and Health Agy., 2007. Mem.: Korean Soc. Magnetic Resonance in Medicine, Korean Soc. Ultrasound in Medicine, Korean Soc. Radiology (reviewer jour. 2002—), European Radiologic Soc., Radiologic Soc. N.Am., Korean Soc. Lung Cancer, European Soc. Thoracic Radiology, Asian Soc. Thoracic Radiology (sec. gen. 2005—07), Korean Soc. Thoracic Radiology (sec. gen. 2005—06), Korean Soc. PACS. Achievements include experimental study of renal artery stenosis in rabbits using doppler ultrasonography; experimental study and clinical value of single photon emission computed tomography; research in study of in-stent stenosis. Avocations: travel, sports, movies. Home: 338-807 Hanshin Apt Jamwon-dong Seocho-gu Seoul 137-951 Republic of Korea Office: Soonchunhyang Univ Hosp 1174 Jung dong Wonmi-gu Bucheon Gyeonggi-do 420-767 Republic of Korea Home Phone: 82-2-591-8118; Office Phone: 82-32-621-5851. Office Fax: 82-32-621-5874. Business E-Mail: jspark@schbc.ac.kr.

PARK, JE HOON, surgeon; b. Seoul, Republic of Korea, Oct. 29, 1966; MD, Yonsei U., 1995; PhD, Kyunghee U., 2009. Residentship Dept. Surgery, Samsung Med. Ctr., 1997—2001, fellowship, 2001—03, instr. Dept. Surgery, Inje U. Ilsan Paik Hosp., 2003—06, asst. prof., 2006—, chief organ transplant ctr., 2007—. Mem.: Korean Soc. Critical Care Medicine, Korean Soc. Traumatology, Korean Surg. Soc., Korean Soc. Vascular Surgery, Korean Soc. Transplantation. Avocations: skateboarding, bicycling. Office: Inje University 2240 Daehwa-dong Ilsanseo-gu Goyang Gyonggi-do 411-706 Republic of Korea Business E-Mail: ceccil@paik.ac.kr.

PARK, JEONG BAE, medical educator, researcher; b. Daegu, Kyungsangbukdo, Republic Of Korea, Oct. 23, 1961; s. Hee Tae Park and Young Soon Lee; m. So Yeun Kim, Mar. 22, 1963; children: Yeun Joo, Ji Eun. MD, Kyungbuk Nat. U., Daegu, Republic of Korea, 1986, PhD, 2003. Prof. medicine Kwandong U., Coll. Medicine, 2007—, Cheil Gen. Hosp., Kwang-dong U.; forum officer, co-chair Internat. Soc. Hypertension, Internat. Forum. Vis. prof. Montreal U., Que., 1998—2000; vis. scientist IRCM, Montreal, 1998—2000. Capt. Korean Mil., 1990—93. Fellow, Am. Heart Assn., 2003. Fellow: European Soc. Cardiology, Korean Soc. Cardiology (assoc.); mem.: ISH Internat. Forum (officer 2011—). Home: 225 Bangyi-1dong Songpa-gu Seoul 138-836 Republic of Korea Office: Cheil Gen Hosp Kwandong Univ 1-19 Mukjung-dong Jung-ku Seoul 100-380 Republic of Korea Office Fax: 822-2000-7152.

PARK, JEONG MEE, research scientist; b. Republic of Korea, Dec. 30, 1969; PhD, Korea U., 2000. Prin. rschr. Korea Rsch. Inst. Biosci. and Biotech., 2002—. Office: 111 Gwahangno Yusong-gu Daejeon 305-806 Republic of Korea Office Fax: 82-42-860-4468. Business E-Mail: jmpark@kribb.re.kr.

PARK, JI KANG, radiologist, educator; b. Pusan, Mar. 9, 1971; MD, Yonsei U., 1996. Assoc. prof. Jeju Nat. U. Sch. Medicine, 2005—. Office: 1753-3 Ara-1-dong Jeju 690-716 Republic of Korea Business E-Mail: jkcontrast@naver.com.

PARK, JI WON, physician; b. Busan, Republic of Korea, Nov. 18, 1976; M, Chungbuk Nat. U., 2008. Physician Nat. Cancer Ctr., 2008—. Office: 323 Ilsan-ro Ilsandong-gu Goyang-si Gyeonggi-do 410-769 Republic of Korea Business E-Mail: sowisdom@ncc.re.kr.

PARK, JIN BONG, medical educator; b. Choongju, Republic of Korea, July 28, 1967; s. Yoon Dal Park and Jeong Soon Shin; m. Yoon Jeong Kim; children: Han Ung, Han Ah. MS, Seoul Nat. U., 1991, PhD, 1996. Cert. DVM Ministry Food, Agr., Forestry and Fisheries, 1989. Rinstr. Dept. Physiology, Coll. Medicine, Chungnam Nat. U., Daejeon, 1999—2001, asst. prof., 2001—05, assoc. prof., 2005—, dept. chmn., 2008—. Contbr. scientific papers. Mem. evaluation com. Korea Occupl. Safety & Health Agy., Daejeon, 2008. Recipient NCAR Rsch. Recognition Awards, 2005; grantee, KOSEF, 2008, KRF, 2008. Mem.: SFN. Home: Burdnae Apt 207-1503 Taepyoung-dong Daejeon 301-780 Republic of Korea Office: Coll Medicine Chungnam Nat Univ Munhwa-Dong Joong-Gu 6 301-747 Daejeon Daejeon Republic of Korea Office Fax: 82-42-585-8440.

PARK, JIN-WOO, dentist, educator; b. Daegu, Republic of Korea, July 25, 1966; s. Jae-Hoon Park and Young-Ok Kwon; m. Shin-Jung Oh; children: Ji-Won, Ji-Hyun. BS in Dentistry, Kyungpook Nat. U., Republic of Korea, 1994, MSD, 1997; PhD, Chonnam Nat. U., Republic of Korea, 2005; PhD in Biomaterials, Tokyo Medical Dental U., 2010. DDS Ministry Health, Welfare, Republic of Korea, 1994. Resident dentist Kyungpook Nat. U. Hosp., Daegu, 1994—97, clin. prof., 2002—03, prof, Sch. Dentistry, 2003—; dir. Pvt. Dental Clinic, Daegu, 1997—2002; invited prof. Tokyo Med. & Dental U., 2010—11. Vis. rsch. prof. Materials Sci. Engring., Pohang Univ. Sci. & Tech., 2006—07. Contbr. articles to numerous sci. jours. Pres. Osteophil Co. Ltd., Daegu, 2007—08. Recipient Academic award New Figure, Korean Acad. Periodontology, 2007. Mem.: Korean Acad. Periodontology, European Assn. Osseointegration, Soc. Biomaterials. Office: Dental Sch Kyungpook Nat Univ 188-1 Samduk-2ga Jung-Gu 700-412 Daegu Daegu Republic of Korea Office Phone: 82-53-600-7523. Office Fax: 82-53-257-6883. Business E-Mail: jinwoo@mail.knu.ac.kr, jinwoo@knu.ac.kr.

PARK, JIN-WOO, physiatrist, educator; b. Seoul, Republic of Korea, July 17, 1972; m. Bo-Sun Jung. MD, Seoul Nat. U., 1997, MS, 2002. Resident, dept. rehab. medicine Seoul Nat. U. Hosp., 1998—2002; specialist stroke rehab. Nat. Rehab. Ctr., 2002—05; asst. prof., dept. physical medicine and rehab. Dongguk U. Ilsan Hosp., Goyang-si, Gyeonggi-do, Republic of Korea, 2005—. Contbr. articles to profl. med. jours. Mem.: Dysphagia Rsch. Soc. Office: Dongguk Univ Ilsan Hosp Siksa-Dong Ilsandong-Gu 814 411-773 Goyang-si Gyeonggi-do Republic of Korea Office Fax: 82-31-961-7488. Business E-Mail: jinwoo.park.md@gmail.com.

PARK, JI-YOUNG, pharmacologist, educator; b. Soonchun, Republic of Korea, Oct. 11, 1968; B of Med. Sci., Pusan Nat. U., 1994, MS, 1997; PhD, Inje U., 2002. Lic. physician Korea, 1994. Intern Pusan Nat. U. Hosp., Busan, Republic of Korea, 1994—95; asst. dept. pharm. Pusan Nat. U., Coll. Medicine, 1995—97; physician Korean Army Med. Sch., Daejeon, 1997—2000. Rsch. instr. dept. pharm. Gachon Med. Sch., Incheon, Republic of Korea, 2000—01, asst. prof. dept. pharm., 2001—06, Korea U. Coll. Medicine, Seoul, 2006—06, Seoul, 2006—. Mem.: Am. Soc. Clin. Pharm. and Therapeutics. Office: Korea Univ Dept Pharm 126-1 Anam-Dong 5-Ga 136-701 Seongbuk-gu Seoul Seoul Republic of Korea Office Fax: +82 2 972 0824. Personal E-mail: seripham@hitel.net. Business E-Mail: jypark21@korea.ac.kr.

PARK, JONG HO, thoracic surgeon, department chairman; b. Seoul, Republic of Korea, Aug. 15, 1961; MD, Seoul Nat. U., 1986, PhD, 1998. Chair Lung Cancer Ctr. Korea Cancer Ctr. Hosp., 2000—, chair dept. thoracic surgery, 2008. Mem. bd. dir. Korean Assn. Study Lung Cancer, 2005, Korean Assn. Thoracic Surg. Oncology, 2009. Recipient Dr. C. Walton Lillehei Merit award, Korean Thoracic and Cardiovasc. Soc.; named Internat. Health Profl. of the Yr., Internat. Biog. Ctr., 2006. Mem.: ASCO, European Soc. Thoracic Surgeon, Internat. Soc. Disease Esophagus, Soc. Thoracic Surgeon, Internat. Assn. Study Lung Cancer. Achievements include research in diagnostic & therapeutic methods. Avocations: golf, mountain climbing. Office: 215-4 Nowon-Ku Gongneung-Dong Seoul 139-706 Republic of Korea Business E-Mail: jhpark@kcch.re.kr.

PARK, JONG JU, plastic surgeon; Grad., Seoul Nat. U. Med. Coll.; PhD, Seoul Nat. U. Bd. cert. tng. plastic surgery dept. Seoul Nat. Univ. Hosp., fellowship plastic surgery dept., Seoul Nat. Univ. Bundang Hosp.; rsch. mem. plastic surgery dept. stencell lab. Seoul Nat. Univ. Hosp.; dir. Dream Plastic Surgery Clinic. Mem.: Internat. Craniofacial Assn., Korean-Japan Assn., Internat. Confederation Plastic reconstructive and Aesthetic Surgery, Korean Cleft-Palate-Craniofacial Assn., Korean Microsurgical Soc., Korean Soc. Reconstructive Hand Surgery, Korean Med. Assn., Korean Soc. Aesthetic Plastic Surgery, Korean Soc. Plastic and Reconstructive Surgeons. Office: Dream Plastic Surgery Clinic Apkujung Subway Sta Seoul Republic of Korea Office Phone: 8225461616. Office Fax: 8225461614. *

PARK, JONG YEON, anesthesiologist, educator; s. Chang Jin Park and Seung Gyun Lee; m. Hyun Ah Yim; children: Se Il, Se Yoon. PhD, U. Ulsan, Coll. Medicine, Seoul, Republic of Korea, 2002. Lic. in practice medicine & surgery Korean Med. Assn., 1992, cert. Korean Soc. Anesthesiologists, 2001. Assoc. prof. ASAN Med. Ctr., Seoul, Republic of Korea, 2008—, U. Ulsan, Republic of Korea, 2008—. Capt. Korean Army, 1994—97. Mem.: Korean Soc. Anesthesiologists. Office: ASAN Med Ctr 388-1 Pungnap-2dong Songpa-gu Seoul 138-736 Republic of Korea Office Phone: 82-10-6824-3867. Office Fax: 82-2-470-1363. Business E-Mail: jongyeon_park@amc.seoul.kr.

PARK, JONG-HO, neurologist; b. Seoul, Republic of Korea, Oct. 10, 1968; s. Park In-Soo and Moon Myung-Sook; m. Choe Soo-Im, Apr. 11, 1999; children: Park Seung-Jun, Park Chae-Bin. MD, Hallym U. Coll. Medicine, Seoul, 1995; PhD, Hallym Med. Grad. Sch., Kangwon, Republic of Korea, 2010. Cert. MD Korean Med. Assn., 1995, in neurology Korean Neurol. Assn., Seoul, 2000, in critical care medicine Korean Soc. Critical Care Medicine, Seoul, 2009. Intern. Hallym U. Kangdong Sacred Heart Hosp., Seoul, 1995—96; resident. dept. neurology Hallym U. Med. Ctr., Seoul, 1996—2000; pub. health dr. Dept. Neurology, Kangwha Cmty. Hosp., Incheon, Republic of Korea, 2000—03; clin. instr. Dept. Neurology, Gil Med. Ctr., Gachon Med. Sch., Incheon, 2003—05; fellowship stroke Dept. Neurology, Seoul Nat. U. Hosp., 2005—06, asst. prof., 2006—08; assoc. prof. Neurology, Myongji Hosp., Kwandong U. Coll. Medicine, 2009—; dir. Stroke Ctr., Myongji Hosp., 2009—. Editl. bd. mem. ISRN Nuerology, Case Reports Neurol. Medicine, Neurology Internat. Contbr. articles to profl. jours. Capt. Pub. Health Korean Army, 2000—03, Incheon. Mem.: Am. Stroke Assn., Korean Stroke Soc., The Korean Neurol. Assn., Korean Med. Assn., Korean Headache Soc. Avocation: travel. Home: RICENZ Apt 211-1501 Jamsil 2-Dong Seoul Republic of Korea Office: Kwandong Univ Myongji Hosp 697-24 Hwajeong-Dong Deokyang-Gu 412-270 Goyang Gyeonggi-do Republic of Korea Office Phone: 82-31-810-5417. Personal E-mail: neurocraft.jhp@gmail.com. Business E-Mail: neurocraft@kd.ac.kr.

PARK, JOON BU, biomedical engineer, researcher, educator; b. Pusan, Republic of Korea, June 20, 1944; arrived in U.S., 1964; s. Sung Sub and Jung Ju (Kim) P.; m. Hyonsook Yoo, Apr. 15, 2000; children: Misun, Yoon Ho, Yoon Il, Lajong. Student, Seoul Nat. U., 1962—64; BS, Boston U., 1967; MS, MIT, 1969; PhD, U. Utah, 1972.

NIH postdoctoral fellow U. Wash., Seattle, 1972—73; vis. asst. prof. U. Ill., Urbana, 1973—76; asst. prof., assoc. prof. Clemson U., SC, 1976—81; prof. Tulane U., New Orleans, 1981—83; prof. biomed. engring. U. Iowa, Iowa City, 1983—. Advisor, cons. FDA, Rockville, Md., 1980—. Author: Biomaterials: An Introduction, 1979, 3rd edit., 2007, Biomaterials Science and Engineering, 1984, Biomaterials: Principles and Applications, 2002, Bioceramics: Properties, Characterizations and Applications, Springer, NY, 2008; contbr. articles to profl. jours. Fellow Am. Inst. Med. and Biol. Engring.; mem. Soc. for Biomaterials (founding mem.), Biomed. Engring. Soc., Orthop. Rsch. Soc., NY Acad. Scis. Achievements include patents in field. Home: 1810 Country Club Dr Coralville IA 52241-1183 Office: Univ Iowa Dept Biomed Engring Iowa City IA 52242 Office Phone: 319-335-5636. Business E-Mail: joon-park@uiowa.edu.

PARK, JUNG YUL, neurosurgeon, educator; b. Seoul, Republic of Korea, Dec. 27, 1958; s. Sa Pil Park and Sun Myung Kang; m. Hye Soon Park, Oct. 11, 1985; children: Min Young, Sung Joon. MD, Korea U., Seoul, 1985; PhD, Korea U., 1995. Diplomate Korean Bd. Neurosurgery Korean Neurosurgery Soc., 1990, med. practice cert. Ont. Med. Assn., Can., 1998. Rsch. and clin. fellow Med. Sch. Toronto U., Ont., Canada, 1998—2000; dir. and chmn. dept. neurosurgery Ansan Hosp. Korea U. Med. Ctr., Ansansi, Kyungki-Do, Republic of Korea, 2002—, dir. tng. and edn. Ansan Hosp., 2005—, dir. minimal invasive surgery ctr. Seoul, 2005—, dir. ICU Ansan Hosp. Ansansi, 2005—; dir. med. informatics Korea U. Med. Coll., Seoul, 2000—. Spkr. in field; pres. Ctr. Minimal Invasive Surgery, 2005—; v.p. Korea U. Med. Ctr. Ansan Hosp., 2008—; editor-in-chief Jour. Neurosurg. Soc.; chmn. dept. med. edn.; gen. sec. AMEWPE; pres. KAME, Korean Assn. Thermology. Author: (books) Infrared Secrets, Interventional and Surgical Management of Pain, Management of Spinal Pain, Diagnosis & Treatment of Spinal Stenosis, Clinical Application of Infrared Thermogrpahy, Differential Diagnosis of Movement Disorder, numerous others; contbr. articles to profl. jours.; mem. editl. bd.: World Fedn. Neurosurgical Soc., 2004—. Del. World Fedn. Neurosurgery & Asta-Austr. Soc. Neurosurgery; pres. Korea Assn. Thermology. Capt. Korean Army, 1990—93. Mem.: Korean Soc. Study of Spinal Pain (sci. chmn. 2004—), Internat. Assn. Study of Pain (sci. chmn. Korean chpt. 2005—), Korean Soc. Functional and Stereotactic Neurosurgery (mem. exec. com. 1998—, pres.), Korean Neurosurgical Soc. (del. 2000—), Korean Soc. Geriatric Neurosurgery (editor-in-chief 2005—), Korean Soc. Pediat. Neurosurgery (editor-in-chief 2006—), Korean Soc. Spinal Neurosurgery (mem. exec. com. 2002—). Home: # 215-101 Family Apt Moonjung-Dong Seoul 138-200 Republic of Korea Office: Korea Univ Medical Center Ansan Hospita Gojan-Dong Danwon-Ku # 516 425-700 Ansan Kyungki-do Republic of Korea Home Phone: 82-2-403-9912; Office Phone: 82-31-412-5002, 82-10-8921-9912, 82314124890. Office Fax: 82-412-5054; Home Fax: 82-31-412-5054. Business E-Mail: jypark@kumc.or.kr.

PARK, JUNG-HAN, medical educator; b. Kyungpook, Republic of Korea, Aug. 8, 1945; s. Joo-Whan Park and Sung-Eu Bae; m. Jeong-Ok Hah, Nov. 18, 1972; children: Eun-Young, Eun-Jin, Sun-Joo. MD, Kyungpook Nat. U., Daegu, Korea, 1970, MS, 1973; MPH, Johns Hopkins U., 1975, DrPH, 1979. Diplomate Am. Bd. Preventive Medicine, Korean Bd. Preventive Medicine. Chief dept. advanced preventive medicine studies Walter Reed Army Inst. Rsch., Washington, 1979-81; asst. prof. Sch. Medicine Uniformed Svcs. U. Health Scis., Bethesda, Md., 1979-81; prof. Sch. Medicine Kyungpook Nat. U., 1981-92, assoc. dean Sch. Pub. Health, 1984-88; prof. Cath. U. Daegu Sch. Medicine, Daegu, 1992—2010, dean, 1992—97, 2001—07; v.p. Cath. U. Daegu, 2010—11, disting. prof., 2010—. Temp. adv. WHO Western Pacific Regional Office, Manila, 1983, 1985—86, 1989; cons., 88; vis. prof. Johns Hopkins Sch. Pub. Health, 1990—91; rep. to policy and coordination com. for reproductive health Govt. of Republic of Korea for WHO, 1998—2000; chmn. subcom. environment and welfare Com. for 21st Century, Daegu, Republic of Korea, 1995—97; health reform com. Prime Min., Seoul, Republic of Korea, 1996—97; policy advisor for min. of health and welfare Republic of Korea, 1998—99; ombudsman Ministry Health and Welfare, 1999—2001; mem. presdl. com. aging Soc. Population Policy, Republic of Korea, 2005—07; sci. tech. adv. group for reproductive health and rsch. WHO, 2004—10; v.p. biomed. scis. Cath. U., 2010; disting. prof. preventive medicine Cath. U. Daegu, 2011—. Co-author: Preventive Medicine and Public Health, 1995, National Health Promotion Targets and Strategies, 1995, Health Promotion of Women and Children-A Guideline for Field Workers, 2002, Preventive medicine and Public Health, 2010; contbr. over 140 articles to profl. jours. Maj. Walter Reed Army Inst. Rsch., 1979-81. Recipient Meritorious Svc. medal Dept. Army Dept. of Def., 1982, Outstanding Internat. Alumnus award pub. health pratice Soc. Alumni Johns Hopkins Sch. Hygiene and Pub. Health, 1997, Nat. Decoration Camellia medal Korean Govt., 1998, Indang Grand prize, Korean Soc. Med. Edn., 2009; tng. grantee USPHS, 1974-79; Fulbright sr. rsch. grantee Korea-Am. Edn. Coun., 1990. Fellow Am. Coll. Preventive Medicine; mem. Korean Soc. for Preventive Medicine ((trustee 1989—, sec. gen. 1987-89, chief editor 1994-96, chmn. bd. examiners 1997-2000, exec. dir., chmn. bd. dirs. 2004—2006), Korean Soc. Maternal and Child Health (trustee, pres. 1996-2000, chmn., 2001-2004), Nat. Acad. Medicine of Korea (charter mem. 2004—), Daegu Health and Welfare Forum(pres., 2006-), Inst. Future Daegu Gyeongbuk (pres. 2011-). Roman Catholic. Avocation: mountain climbing. Home: 100 Whang Gum Dong Garden Heights Apt 202-102 706-794 Daegu Republic of Korea Office: Cath U Daegu Sch Medicine 3056-6 Daemyung 4 Dong 705-718 Daegu Republic of Korea Office Phone: 82-53-650-4474. Business E-Mail: jhpark@cu.ac.kr.

PARK, JUNG-MI, medical educator; b. Seoul, Republic of Korea, June 20, 1965; OMD, Kyung Hee U., 1990, PhD, 1997. Assoc. prof. CHA U., Coll. Medicine, 1998—2006; prof. Kyung Hee U., 2006—. Recipient awards, Acupuncture & Merdian Studies. Office: KyungHee University Hosp Gangdong Seoul 134-727 Republic of Korea Business E-Mail: pajama@khu.ac.kr.

PARK, KAP JOO, biologist, researcher; b. Seoul, Republic of Korea, Nov. 19, 1956; s. Young Hwan Park and Ki Cho Lee; m. Myung Soon Lee, May 11, 1991; children: Seo Wan, Seo Young. BS, Konkuk U., Republic of Korea, 1986; MS, Konkuk U., 1988; PhD, Konkuk U., Republic of Korea, 1994. Sr. rschr. Korea Inst. Oriental Med., Seoul, Republic of Korea, 1995—99; chief rschr. Konkuk U., Seoul, Republic of Korea, 1999—2001, rsch. prof., 2001—. Bd. mem. Korea Soc. of Virology, Seoul, 1996—, bd mem., 1996—; editor Korea Soc. of Environ. Biol., Seoul, Korea (South), 2002—; bd. mem. Korea Assn. for Creation Rsch., Seoul, 2002—. Contbr. articles various profl.jours. Deacon Somang Presbyn. Ch., Seoul, 2000—05. Cpl., 1978—81, Seoul. Grantee, Korea Ministry of Health and Welfare, 1995-1998, 1996—98, 1997, Korea Ministry of Agr. and Forestry, 2000-2002, 2001-1004, 2002-2004, Korea Rsch. Found., 2002-2005. Achievements include patents for anti-viral drug for Influenza; anti-viral functional food for influenza; new Tofu congelator using Korean medicinal herbs; patents pending for drug for hematopoiesis using Korean medicinal herbs; functional cosmetics using Korean medicinal herbs; drug for Anti-Hyperlipidemia and Liver cell protection; soyembrio tofu and 11s protein tofu for Anti-Hyperlipidemia and Liver cell protection; soymilk and 11s protein milk for Anti-Hyperlipidemia and Liver cell protection; patents for functional tofu using new tofu congelator. Avocations: golf, travel, piano. Home: Kangnam-gu Chungdam-dong 19-36 Seoul 135-949 Republic of Korea Office: Dept Biological Scis Konkuk U Kwangjin-gu Hwayang-dong 1 Seoul 143-701 Republic of Korea Office Fax: 82-2-3436-5432. Personal E-mail: kkupkj@chol.com. Business E-Mail: kkupkj@konkuk.ac.kr.

PARK, KEEHYUN, otolaryngologist, director; b. Daegu, Republic of Korea, Dec. 25, 1951; s. Chanseng Park and Shinja (Park) Hur; m. Yoonhee Park, Oct. 14, 1979; children: Kate, Sally. MD, Yonsei U., 1976, PhD, 1982. Lic. physician Korea, otolaryngological specialist Korea. Resident dept. ENT Severance Hosp., Seoul, Republic of Korea, 1976—81; with Gen. Hosp. Capital Armed Forces, Seoul, 1982—85; instr. asst. Med. Ctr. Dept. ENT Yonsei U., Seoul, 1985—94; rsch. fellow Otol. Rsch. Lab. Ohio State U., Columbus, Ohio, 1989—91; prof., chmn. Med. Ctr. Dept. ENT Ajou U., Suwon, Republic of Korea, 1994—2005, dean Sch. Medicine, 1999—2001, pres. Sch. Medicine, 2005—. Author: Middle Ear Disease, 2002; contbr. over 200 articles to profl. jours. Maj. US Army, 1982—85, Korea. Mem.: Korean Audiological Soc. (pres. 2005—), Korean Otol. Soc. (auditor 2004—), Korean Soc. Otolaryngology (trustee 1991—, Gold medal 2004), Am. Acad. Otolaryngology-Head and Neck Surgery, Am. Assn. Rsch. in Otolaryngology, Collegium Oto-Rhino-laryngologicum Amicitiae Sacrum (assoc.). Home: 102-1402 LG Village 155 Sungbock-Dong Yong-In Gyeonggi 449-980 Republic of Korea Office: Ajou University Medical Center 5 Woncheon-Dong Yeongtong-Gu Suwon Gyeonggi 443-721 Republic of Korea Office Fax: 82-31-216-6380. Business E-Mail: parkkh@ajou.ac.kr.

PARK, KOOK IN, physician, researcher; b. Pusan, Republic of Korea, July 27, 1956; m. Seung Hee Yoo, Nov. 19, 1983; children: Yoo Kyung, Jae Hyung. MD, Yonsei U., Republic of Korea, 1982; Masters, Yonsei U. Coll. of Medicine, Republic of Korea, 1986; PhD, Yonsei U., Republic of Korea, 1992. Diplomate Korean Med. Assn., 1982, Bd. of Pediats. Korean Acad. of Pediat., 1986. Asst. prof. Yonsei U. Coll. of Medicine, Seoul, Republic of Korea, 1993—98, assoc. prof., 1998—2002, prof., 2003—. Recipient Jin Am Maeil Academic award, Korean Acad. of Neonatology, 2002, Pfizer Rsch. award, Med. Newspaper Office, 2003; grantee Stem Cell Rsch. Program, Korean Ministry of Sci. and Tech., 2008. Mem.: Soc. for Neuroscience (life). Office: Severance Hosp Seodaemoon-Ku Shinchon-Dong 134 Seoul 120-752 Republic of Korea Office Fax: 822-393-9118. Business E-Mail: kipark@yuhs.ac.

PARK, KWANG JOO, medical educator; b. Masan, Republic of Korea, Nov. 15, 1963; s. Park and Choi; m. Ji Hyun Kim, Nov. 11, 1990; children: Hyun Min, Seung Min. PhD, Yonsei U., Seoul, Korea, 2000. Diplomate med. Korean Med. Assn. Prof., chmn. Ajou U. Sch. Medicine, Suwon, Republic of Korea, 2005—, chmn. dept. pulmonary & critical care medicine. Com. mem. Med. acad, 2008—. Officer med. Army. Recipient award, Ajou U. Sch. Medicine. Achievements include research in med. field. Home: Hyundai Apt 77-1404 Abgujeong-dong Seoul 135-788 Republic of Korea Office: Ajou Univ Sch Medicine Wonchon-dong Youngtong-gu Suwon 443-721 Republic of Korea Office Phone: 82-31-219-5121. Office Fax: 82-31-219-5124. Personal E-mail: parkkjmd@hanmail.net. Business E-Mail: parkkj@ajou.ac.kr.

PARK, KWANG MIN, surgeon, educator; b. Busan, Sept. 9, 1959; MD, Hanyang U., 1984; PhD, Yonsei U., 1992. Prof. divsn. hepatobiliary and pancreatic surgery, dept. surgery Asan Med. Ctr., 1995—. Mem. bd. com. Korean Assn. Hepatobiliary and Pancreatic Surgery, Korean Soc. Transplantation, 2007—11. Recipient Presentation award, Korean Hepatobiliary and Pancreas Surgery Congress. Avocation: golf. Office: Asan Med Ctr Poong-nap dong Seoul 138-736 Republic of Korea Office Phone: 82-2-3010-3493. Office Fax: 82-2-3010-6701. Business E-Mail: kmpark@amc.seoul.kr.

PARK, KWIDEOK, biomedical engineer, researcher; b. Ulsan, Korea, Dec. 20, 1967; s. Wonho Park and Ockjo Kim; m. Hwasoon Kim, May 5, 1996; children: Erin, Brian. BS, Hanyang U., Seoul, Korea, 1993; MS, Hanyang U., Ansan, Korea, 1996; PhD, U. Iowa, 2001. Rsch. asst. U. Iowa, 1997—2001; postdoctoral fellow U. Memphis, 2001—. Reviewer Jour. Biomed. Mat. Res. (Part B), Springfield, NJ, 2002—, Jour. Applied Polymer Sci., Cleve., 2003—. Contbr. articles to profl. jours. Recipient Student Travel and Profl. Devel. award, Soc. for Biomaterials, 2001. Mem.: Orthop. Rsch. Soc. Achievements include development of PMMA pre-coated UHMWPE acetabular component in total hip arthroplasty (THA); scaffold-free chondrocytes/ECM neocartilage construct for cartilage injury repair; PLGA-based composite scaffold with biomimetic ECM substrate for bone tissue engineering; temporal control dexamethasone for chondrogenesis of MSCs. Home: 303-1201 Hyosung Fountain Ville Nowon Seoul 139-853 Republic of Korea Office: Korean Inst Sci and Tech Biomat Rsch Ctr Seoul Cheongnyang PO Box 131 130-650 Seoul Republic of Korea E-mail: kpark@kist.re.kr.

PARK, KYONG SOO, medical educator; married. MD, Seoul Nat. U. Coll. Medicine, 1984; PhD, Seoul Nat. U., 1993. Diplomate Ministry health and welfare, Republic of Korea, 1984, cert. in internal medicine Korean Med. Assn., 1988. Postdoc. fellow U. Calif. San Diego, 1995—97; asst. prof. Dept. Internal Medicine, Seoul Nat. U. Coll. Medicine, 1995—99, assoc. prof., 1999—2003, prof., 2003—. Sec. gen. Korean Soc. Endocrinology, Seoul, 2001—02; dir. Genome Rsch. Ctr. Diabetes and Endocrine Disease, Seoul, 2000—11; chair Divsn. Endocrinology and Metabolism, Seoul Nat. U. Hosp., 2006—. Contbr. articles to profl. jours. Capt. Korean army, 1988—91. Recipient award, Seoul Nat. U. Coll. Medicine, 1984, Namkok Sci. Achievement award, Korean Soc. Endocrinology, 2007; Genome Rsch. Ctr. Diabetes and Endocrine Disease grant, Ministry Health and Welfare, Republic of Korea, 2000—11. Mem.: Endocrine Soc., Korean Diabetes Assn., Am. Diabetes Assn. Office: Seoul Nat Univ Hosp 28 Yongon-Dong Chongno-Gu Seoul 110-744 Republic of Korea Business E-Mail: kspark@snu.ac.kr.

PARK, KYUNG SOOK, cognitive scientist, computer science professor, researcher; b. Masan, Republic of Korea, June 26, 1964; d. Sung-Jae Park and Young-Nam Kwon; m. Jae-Hong Lim, Mar. 25, 2000; 1 child, Se-Vin Lim. PhD, Yonsei U., Korea, 2000. Lectr. Kyung-Nam U., Masan, 1988—95; prof. Hyejeon coll., HongSung, 1995—2005; vis. prof. KAIST, Daejeon, Republic of Korea, 2005—07; rsch. prof. Yonsei U., Seoul, Republic of Korea, 2007—09, SungKyunKwan U., Republic of Korea, 2009—; rschr. Bhgoo Transformation Inst., 2010—. Sec. IEEE Ro-Man, Jeju, 2005—07. Author: (book) Computational Mathematics, 2011; contbr. scientific papers. Vol. Voluntary Ctr., Koyang, 2003—05. Mem.: IEEE, SMC. Office: SungKyunKwan Univ 300 Chunchun-dong, Jangan-gu, Suwon 440-746 Gyeonggi Republic of Korea Business E-Mail: sevinmo@hanmail.net.

PARK, KYUNG WON, neurologist; b. Busan, Republic of Korea, Mar. 14, 1968; s. Sang Geun Park and Jung Soon Kim; m. Hye Jin Son, July 17, 1993; children: Ye-Eun, Min-Kyu. MD, Dong-A Coll. Medicine, Busan, South Korea, 1993; PhD, Inje U. Coll. Medicine, Busan, 2004. Diplomate in med. Ministry Health & Welfare, 1993, med. specialist neurology Ministry Health & Welfare, 1997. Assoc. prof. Dong-A U. Coll. Medicine, 2001—; med. specialist dept. neurology Dong-A Med. Ctr., 2001—; asst. prof. Dept. Neurology, Coll. Medicine, Dong-A U., 2003—07; postdoc. rsch. fellow Alzheimer's Disease & Memory Disorder Ctr., Dept. Neurology, Baylor Coll. Medicine, Houston, 2005—07. Contbr. articles to profl. sci. jours. Recipient Korean Dementia Assn. award for Sci. Rsch., 2004, Korean Dementia Assn. award for Execellent Publ. Article, 2007; grant, Korean Gereiatic Soc. Rsch. Fund, 2005, Dong-A U. Rsch. Program Fund, 2007, Alzheimer's Assn. award for Trevel fellowship, 2006. Mem.: Korean Geriat. Soc., Korean Stroke Soc., Korean Dementia Assn., Korean Neurol. Assn. Achievements include research in neuropsychological assessment and treatment of Alzheimer's disease, vascular dementia, frontotemporal dememtia and dementia with lewy bodies, functional neuroimaging in dementia patients. Office: Dong-A Univ Coll Medicine 1-3 Ga Dongdaesin-Dong 602-715 Busan Seo-Gu Republic of Korea Office Fax: 82512448338. Business E-Mail: neuropark@dau.ac.kr.

PARK, KYUNG-YEON, nursing educator; b. Busan, Republic of Korea, Nov. 15, 1965; PhD, Busan Nat. U., 2006. Asst. prof. Silla U., 2007—. Office: Silla University San 1-1 Gwaebeop-dong Busan Sasang 617-736 Republic of Korea Business E-Mail: kypark@silla.ac.kr.

PARK, LEE CRANDALL, psychiatrist, physician; b. Washington, July 15, 1926; s. Lee I. and Alice (Crandall) P.; m. Barbara Ann Merrick, July 1, 1953; children: Thomas Joseph, Jeffrey Rawson; m. Mary Woodfill Banerjee, Apr. 27, 1985; stepchildren: Stephen K., Scott K. Grad., Putney Prep. Sch., Vt.; BS in Zoology, Yale U., 1948; MD, Johns Hopkins U., 1952. Diplomate Nat. Bd. Med. Examiners, Am. Bd. Psychiatry and Neurology. Intern medicine Johns Hopkins Hosp., Osler Svc., Balt., 1952—53; resident psychiatry USN Hosp., Oakland, Calif., 1953—54, Henry Phipps Psychiat. Clinic, Johns Hopkins Hosp., Balt., 1955—59, asst. psychiatrist, 1955—59, staff dept. medicine, 1970—91, hon. staff dept. medicine, 1991—, dir. psychiat. outpatient svcs. and cmty. psychiatry program, 1972—74, asst. dir. clin. svcs. dept. psychiatry, 1973—74, mem. departmental coun., 1972—75, staff psychritrist, 1959—2008. Rsch. fellow psychiatry Johns Hopkins U., 1955-59, faculty in psychiatry, 1959—,physician charge psychiat. svcs. student health svc., 1961-73, assoc. prof., 1971—2008, emeritus assoc. prof., 2008-; vis. psychiatrist Balt. City Hosp., 1960-61; co-prin., prin. investigator NIMH Psychopharmacology Rsch. Br. Outpatient Study of Drug-Set Interaction, 1960-68, co-dir. (with Eugene Meyer) Time-Limited Psychotherapy Rsch. Grant, 1969-73; pvt. practice psychiatry, 1964—; cons. Met. Balt. Assn. Mental Health, 1961-63, Bur. Disability Ins., Social Security Adminstrn., 1964-81; attending staff Seton Psychiat. Inst., 1966-73, exec. bd., 1970-73; staff Sheppard and Enoch Pratt Hosp., 1974—2000. Co-author: A Primer on Mental Disorders: A Guide for Educators, Families and Students, 2001; contbr. articles to profl. jours.; contbr. chpts. to books. Served to lt. M.C., USNR, 1953-55, div. psychiatrist 1st Marine Div., Korea with Letter of Appreciation from Commanding Officer "Outstanding Performance of Duty", staff psychiatrist USN Hosp., Camp Pendelton, Calif., 1954-55; mem. Md. Interdisciplinary Coun. for Children and Adolescents, 1978-98, treas., 1980-87. Fellow: AAAS, Am. Psychiat. Assn. (mem. assembly 1983—93, Psychiat. Rsch. Network 1994—2002, Disting. life fellow); mem.: AAUP, AMA, Ancient & Hon. Mech. Co. Balt., Johns Hopkins Med. and Surg. Assn., Balt. County Med. Assn., Balt. City Med. Soc., Med. and Chirurg. Faculty Md., Group Therapy Network, N.Y. Acad. Scis., Soc. Psychotherapy Rsch., Md. Psychiat. Soc. (pres. 1978—79), Md. Assn. Pvt. Practicing Psychiatrists, Am. Assn. Pvt. Practicing Psychiatrists, Am. Coll. Neuropsychopharmacology, Am. Soc. Adolescent Psychiatry, Internat. Soc. Study Personality Disorders, Am. Psychosomatic Soc., Md. Found. Psychiatry (bd. dirs. 1995—2003, pres. 2000—03), St. George's Soc., Avery Assn., Denison Soc., Crandall Assn., Van Kouwenhoven-Conover Assn., Van Voorhees Assn., Parke Soc., Nat. Soc. Sons and Daus. of Pilgrims (gov. State of Md. 2006—08), Gen. Soc. War 1812 (pres. State Md. 2004—06, v.p. gen. 2006—08, asst. surgeon gen. 2008—11, surgeon gen. 2011—), Nat. Huguenot Soc. (surgeon gen. 2005—08), Descendants Mexican War Vets, Sons Union Vets. Civil War, SAR (surgeon State of Md. 2006—, surgeon gen. 2009—11), Gen. Soc. Colonial Wars, S.R. (bd. mgrs. State of Md. 2006—08), Yale Club NYC, Farmington Country Club (Va.), Met. Club (Washington), Johns Hopkins Club (Md.), Chevy Chase Country Club (Md.), Phi Beta Pi. Episcopalian. Achievements include research in borderline and narcissistic conditions; long-term effects of childhood emotional abuse and neglect; psychotherapy; interrelationships of psychotherapy and pharmacotherapy; genesis and nature of social, personal and emotional intelligence. Home: 308 Tunbridge Rd Baltimore MD 21212-3803 Office: 1205 York Rd Ste 35 Lutherville Timonium MD 21093-6268 Office Phone: 410-321-1276. E-mail: lpark3@jhmi.edu.

PARK, MELBURN, medical educator; b. Santa Ana, Calif., Oct. 8, 1944; m. Elizabeth Haskell, June 11, 1966; children: Geoffrey Haskell, Carolyne Elizabeth Krupa. AB in Biology, Stanford U., Palo Alto, 1966; PhD in Physiology, SUNY Buffalo, 1973. Asst. prof. Mich. State U., Dept. Anatomy & Neurobiology, East Lansing,

1978—83; assoc. prof. U. Tenn. Ctr. Health Scis., Dept. Anatomy & Neurobiology, Memphis, 1983—. Dir. Cave Rsch. Found., 1988—94, pres., 1992—94; dir., med. gross anatomy U. Tenn. Ctr. Health Scis., Memphis, 2004—, vice chair med. admissions, 2007—. Contbr. articles to profl. jours. Office: University Tenn Health Scis Ctr 855 Monroe Ave Memphis TN 38163 Business E-Mail: mpark@uthsc.edu.

PARK, MI-HYUN, engineering educator; b. Seoul, Republic of Korea, Apr. 18, 1973; PhD, UCLA, 2004. Asst. prof. U. Mass., 2008. Office: Civil & Environ Engineering Dept Amherst MA 01003 Business E-Mail: mpark@ecs.umass.edu.

PARK, MOON HO, medical educator; b. Uiwang, Gyeonggi-do, Republic Of Korea, July 27, 1972; s. Yong-Il Park and Yun-Ja Kim; m. Joo Young Min, Nov. 30, 2002; children: Ye-Chan, Ye-Gang. PhD, Korea U., Seoul, 2006. Registered in medicine Ministry for Health, Welfare, Family Affairs, Republic of Korea, 1997. Asst. chief Geriatric Health Clinic Rsch. Inst., Ansan, Gyeonggi-do, 2005—; asst. prof. Korea U. Coll. Medicine, Seoul, 2006—. Rsch. dir. Geriatric Health Clin. and Rsch. Inst., Ansan city, Gyeonggi-do, 2005—. Contbr. scientific papers to profl. jours. (Academic prize, Korea U. Coll. Medicine Alumni, 2005, Young Investigator award, 2006). Mem.: Korean Med. Assn. Office: Korea Univ Coll Medicine Neurology Korea Univ Ansan Hosp Ansan Gyeonggi-do 425-707 Republic of Korea

PARK, MOON SOO, orthopedist; MB, Yonsei U. Coll. Medicine, Seoul, South Korea, 1995; MSc in Med. Sci., Postgrad. Sch. Yonsei U., Seoul, 2002, DMS, 2006. Diplomate South Korea, 1995, cert. orthop. surgery 2000. Rotating internship Severance Hosp., Yonsei U. Coll. Medicine, Seoul, 1995—96, residency, orthop. surgery, 1996—2000, clin. fellowship, spine sect. orthop. surgery, 2000—02; rsch. fellowship, spine sect. orthop. Emory U. Sch. Medicine, Atlanta, 2002—03; clin. asst. prof., spine divsn. orthop. surgery Ulsan U. Hosp., Republic of Korea, 2003—05; asst. prof., spine divsn. orthop. surgery Ulsan U. Coll. Medicine, 2005—07, Hallym U. Coll. Medicine, Seoul, 2007—. Contbr. scientific papers to profl. jours. Recipient Hibbs award, Scoliosis Rsch. Soc., 2004. Mem.: Korean Soc. Spine Surgery, Soc. Internat. Chirurgie Orthop. Traumatologie, North Am. Spine Soc. Office: Med Coll Hallym Univ 94-200 Yeongdeungpodong Seoul 150-719 Republic of Korea

PARK, MOON SUH, otolaryngologist; b. Seoul, Republic of Korea, Feb. 25, 1954; s. Geun Ju Park and So Yon Eum, m. Hye Ki Han, Dec. 17, 1979; children: Eun Jung, Jun Woo. BS, Kyung Hee U., 1978, MS, 1982, DSc, 1989. Cert. Korean Bd. Otolaryngology, 1983. Resident Kyung Hee Univ. Hosp., Seoul, 1979-82; instr. Hallym U., Seoul, 1983-86, asst. prof., 1986-91; vis. prof. Bonn U., Germany, 1986-87; from assoc. prof. to prof. Hallym U., 1987—2002; dir. Dain ENT Clinic, Republic of Korea, 2002—04, Park's ENT Clinic, 2005—06; prof. Kyung Hee U., Republic of Korea, 2006—; dir. Kyung Hee U. Hosp. Gang Dong, Seoul, 2011—. Chmn. dept Ear Nose and Throat Choonchun Sacred Heart Hosp., Hallym U., Republic of Korea, 1987—88, Hangang Sacred Heart Hosp., Hallym U., Seoul, 1989—2001; chmn. resident training com. Hallym Med. Ctr., Seoul, 1999—2001; chmn. Ear Nose and Throat Ctr. East West Neo Med. Ctr., Kyung Hee U., Seoul, 2006—; dir. Kyung Hee U. Hosp., Gang-dong. Author: Otorhinolaryngology- Head & Neck Surgery, 1995, Principles and Practices of Hearing Aids, 1998, Otorhinolaryngology - Head & Neck Surgery, 2002. Scholar Alexander von Humboldt Found., Bonn, Germany, 1986. Mem. Internat. Soc. Audiology, NY Acad. Scis., Am. Otolaryngol Soc., Politzer Soc. (Active Fellow), Korean Audiol. Soc. (councilor 1996-2001), Korean Otol. Soc. (councilor 1997-2001, dir. 2007—). Avocations: travel, swimming. Home: Dept Ent 149 Sangil-Dong Seoul Gangdong-ku 134-727 Republic of Korea Personal E-mail: pmsuh@yahoo.co.kr.

PARK, MYUNG KUN, medical educator; b. Suhung, Hwanghae, Republic of Korea, Sept. 30, 1934; arrived in U.S., 1962; s. Jung-Jin and Sonnyu (Lee) Park; m. Issun Kim, Jan. 21, 1967; children: Douglas Yongwoon, Christopher Yongchul, Warren Yongsun. Diploma, Seoul Nat. U., Republic of Korea, 1956, MD, 1960. Intern Vassar Brothers Hosp., Poughkeepsie, NY, 1962—63; pediat. resident Georgetown U., Washington, 1963—64; chief resident Univ. Hosp., Morgantown, W.Va., 1964—65; pediat. cardiology fellow U. Washington, Seattle, 1965—68; asst. prof. U. Kans. Coll. Medicine, Kansas City, 1973-76; assoc. prof. U. Tex. Med. Sch., San Antonio, 1976-83, prof., 1983—2003, prof. emeritus, 2003—; prof., chmn. pediat. Arabian Gulf U. Med. Coll., Bahrain, 1995-98. Author: (book) How to Read Pediatric ECG, 1982, 4th rev. edit., 2006, Pediatric Cardiology for Practitioners, 1984, 5th rev. edit., 2008, The Pediatric Cardiology Handbook, 1991, 4th rev. edit., 2010; contbr. articles to profl. jours. Postdoctoral fellow, NIH, 1965—68, Rsch. fellow, 1971—73, Rsch. grantee, Maternal and Child Health Bur., 1991—95. Fellow: Am. Acad. Pediat., Am. Coll. Cardiology; mem.: Am. Assn. Pharmacology Therapy, Soc. Pediatric Rsch. Personal E-mail: drmpark@satx.rr.com.

PARK, NOH HYUCK, medical educator; b. Chungdo, Kyungpook, Sept. 4, 1969; s. Seung Sik Park and Jae Hwa Song; m. Rho Tae Yeon, Dec. 26, 1994; children: So Hyun, Joon Woo. BS in Med., Med. Coll. Kyungpook Nat. U., Daegu, 1993, MS in Radiology, 1996. Lic. MD Republic of Korea, 1993, in radiology Republic of Korea, 1998. Intern Kyungpook Nat. U. Hosp., Daegu, Republic of Korea, 1993—94, residency radiology, 1994—98, clin. prof., dept. radiology, 2002—03; dr. Woolin and Seongju Pub. Health Ctr., Republic of Korea, 1998—2001; assoc. prof. Myongji Hosp, Kwandong U. Coll. Medicine, Koyang, Kyunggi, Republic of Korea, 2003—. Capt. Korean AF, 1998—2001. Achievements include research in pediatric, cardiac imaging. Office: Myongji Hosp Kwandong Univ 697-24 Hwajungdong Dukyang-ku Kyunggi 412-270 Republic of Korea Business E-Mail: nhpark904@kd.ac.kr.

PARK, RAE WOONG, medical educator; b. Kwangju, Republic of Korea, Feb. 4, 1969; s. Bong Gu Park and Byum Geum Kim; m. Sung Ae Hwang; children: Ye Jin, Dong Hyun. MD, Ajou U., Suwon city, Kyunggi-do, Republic Of Korea, 1995, MS, 1999; PhD, Chungbuk Nat. U., 2006. Cert. med. dr. Ministry Health and Welfare, 1995, pathologist 2000. Internship Ajou U. Hosp., 1995—96, resident, Pathology, 1996—2000; rsch. fellow Dept. Med. Informatics, Ajou U., 2004—05, asst. prof., 2005—; dir. Inst. U. Health Info. Rsch., Ajou U. Med. Ctr., 2007—. Sec. publ. Korean Soc. Med. Informatics, 2006—08, sec. pub. rels., Republic of Korea, 2008—. Contbr. chapters to books, articles to profl. jours.; co-author (with SP Chen and CK Park): (book) U-Health: Issues on the Health and Medical Service Providers in the U-Health Environments. Capt. US Army, physician Human Remains Exhumation Team Army Hdqs., 2000—01, physician Spl. Investigation Team Mil. Death Cases MND, 2001, Republic Of Korea, physician, pathology Armed Forces Capital Hosp., 2001—03. Recipient Alumni Assn. award, Ajou U., 1995, Outstanding Brief Report, APIII, 2002, Korean Fedn. Sci. and Tech., 2006. Mem.: Korean Med. Assn., Korean Soc. Pathologists, Am. Med. Informatics Assn., Korean Soc. Med. Informatics. Office: Ajou Univ Dept Med Informatics Woncheon-dong Yeoungtong-gu Suwon Kyounggi-do 443-721 Republic of Korea Office Fax: 82-31-219-4472. Business E-Mail: veritas@ajou.ac.kr.

PARK, SANG ICK, biomedical researcher, director; b. Inje-Gun, Kangwon-Do, Republic of Korea, July 10, 1961; m. Hyung Ok Sohn, Nov. 23, 1990; 1 child, Sooin. PhD in Biochemistry, Seoul Nat. U., 1994. Dep. dir. Ctr. Biomed. Sci., Korean Nat. Inst. Health, Seoul, 2007—08, dir. divsn. intractable disease, 2004—. Vis. prof. Sch. Life Sci. and Biotechnology, Korea U., Seoul, 2001—; adj. prof. Coll. Med. Sch., Korea U., Seoul, 2002—. Contbr. articles to profl. jours. Coord. Nat. Inst. Health in Korea, 2007—07, rep., 2007—07; rsch. presentator Rsch. Soc. Alcoholism, Chicago, 2007—07. Recipient Excellent project award, Nat. Inst. Health in Korea, 2001, Bum-Suk Academic Grand award, 2002; scholar Excellent student, TongCheun Scholarship Found., 1983—84. Mem.: Korean Soc. Molecular and Cellular Biology (mem. rsch. ethical com.), Korean Soc. Applied Biol. Chemistry (exec. sec.). Roman Catholic. Avocations: tennis, travel. Office: Korean Nat Inst Health Ctr Biomed Sci 194 Tongil-Lo 122-701 Seoul Eunpyung gu Republic of Korea Office Phone: 82-2-380-1528. Office Fax: 82-2-388-0924. Business E-Mail: parksi@nih.go.kr.

PARK, SANG-YOUEL, science educator; b. Jeonju, Jeonbuk, Republic of Korea, Mar. 1, 1970; s. Ik-Soo Park and Bo-Soon Lee; m. You-Jin Lee, Nov. 3, 1996; children: E-Whan, Ki-Whan. PhD, Chonbuk Nat. U., Republic of Korea, 2000. Tchg. asst. Chonbuk Nat. U., Jeonju, Jeonbuk, Republic of Korea, 1998—2000, instr., 2002—04, asst. prof., 2004—. Vis. prof. U. Sydney, 2006—. Contbr. articles to profl. jours. Sgt. Korean Army, 1991—93. Grantee, Ministry Agr. and Forestry, 2003—05, Ministry Edn., 2003—06, Ministry Sci. and Tech., 2005—07; fellow, U. Pitts., 2000—02. Mem.: Korean Vet. Assn., AACR. Avocations: travel, tennis. Home: Kyodong 80-13 Jeonju 560-070 Republic of Korea Office: Chonbuk National University Duk-jin dong 664-14 Jeonju 561-756 Republic of Korea Business E-Mail: sypark@chonbuk.ac.kr.

PARK, SE HOON, oncologist, educator; b. Seoul, Republic of Korea, Feb. 7, 1969; m. Chun Kyung Yoo, Nov. 29, 1994; children: He Won, Je In. MD, Sungkyunkwan U., 2003. Cert. in medicine Korea Med. Assn., Seoul, 1994. Clin. fellowship oncology Samsung Med. Ctr., Seoul, Republic of Korea, 2002—03; assoc. prof. Gil Med Ctr. Gachon Med Sch., Incheon, Republic of Korea, 2003—. Contbr. articles to profl. jours. Lt. med. corps. Korean Army, 1994—97. Mem.: Am. Soc. Clin. Oncology (assoc.). Home: 1714-102 Keonyoung Apt Kyunggi Bucheon 420 020 Republic of Korea Office: Gachon Med School Gil Med Center Kuwol-Dong 405-760 Incheon Incheon Republic of Korea Office Fax: 82 32 460 3233. Personal E-mail: hematoma@gmail.com.

PARK, SEONG-WOOK, hospital administrator; MD, Seoul Nat. U., Korea. Intern Seoul Nat. Univ. Hosp., Seoul, resident, vis. prof. Wash. Hosp. Ctr., Wash.; prof. Univ. of Ulsan Coll. of Medicine / Asan Med. Ctr., ctr. for angina pectoris and myocardial infarctio dir.; pres. Asan Med. Ctr., Seoul, Republic of Korea. Fellow in Dept. of Cardiology, Baylor Coll. of Medicine. Mem.: Korean Soc. Interventional Cardiology, Korean Soc. Cardiology, Fellow of Am. Coll. Cardiology. Office: Asan Medical Center 388-1 Pungnap-2 Dong Songpa-Gu Seoul Republic of Korea Office Phone: 82230107941. *

PARK, SEUNG HA, medical educator; b. Seoul, Republic Of Korea, May 28, 1957; s. Eun-ook Park; m. Jin-sam Lee Park; children: Ji-hyun, Sang-eun. MD, Seoul, 1982; PhD, Korea U., Seoul, 1991. Prof. Korea U., 1991—. Dir. head, dept. plastic surgery Korea U. Med. Ctr., 1998—2005, v.p., 2003—07; vice dean Korea U. Med. Coll., 2000—02. Contbr. articles (Hon. Pres. award, 2008). Capt., med. officer Korea Army, 1987—90, South Korea. Mem.: Inernat. Soc. Plastic and Reconstructive Surgeon, Korean Soc. Laser Medicine (editor in cheif, award 2008), Korean Soc. Plastic and Reconstructive Surgery (chmn. internal affairs 2008). Roman Catholic. Office: Korea Univ Med Ctr 126 Anam-dong Sungbuk-ku Seoul 136-705 Republic of Korea Office Phone: 82-2-920-5440. Office Fax: 2-921-4291; Home Fax: 2-3461-5803. Personal E-mail: parksha@unitel.co.kr. Business E-Mail: shp98@korea.ac.kr.

PARK, SOONG-KOOK, internist, researcher; b. Pyung-Yang, Korea, Aug. 9, 1938; s. Tae-Soo and Wha-Sil (Lee) P.; m. Sine-Ja, Oct. 9, 1965; children: Han-Kil, See-Nae, Han-Sol. BA, MD, Kyung-Pook Nat. U., Daegu, Korea, 1963. Med. diplomate. Surgeon gen. Republic of Korea, 1963-67; hosp. intern Bklyn. Jewish Hosp., 1968-69; resident in internal medicine Grassland Hosp., Valhalla, NY, 1969-72; fellow in gastroenterology Lahey Clinic, Boston, 1972-74; chief internal medicine Dongsan Presbyn. Hosp., Daegu, 1974-76; cons. in internal medicine, chief staff Mariana Med. Ctr., Guam, 1977-78; chief internal medicine Bak Hosp., Seoul, Korea, 1978, Dongsan Presbyn. Hosp., Daegu, 1978-90; prof. Keimyung U. Med. Sch., Daegu, 1980—2003, prof. emeritus, 2003—; pres. Andong Sungso Presbyn. Hosp., 2011—. Supt. Dongsan Med. Ctr., Daegu, 1990—94, Kyungju Dongsan Hosp., Kyungju, Republic of Korea, 1994—96; v.p. for med. affairs Keimyung U., 1996—98; dir. Dongsan Med. Ctr., 1996—98; supt. Andong (Korea) Presbyn. Hosp., 2003—; pres. Korea Oversea Med. Missionary Soc., 2010—. Elder Sungji Presbyn. Ch., Daegu, 1976—; bd. dirs. YMCA, Daegu, 1980—, chmn., 1999-2001; dist. gov. Y's Men's Internat., Daegu, 1987-88; regional dir. Korea East region Y's Men's Internat., 2001-2002; internat. svc. dir. Internat. Bro. Club, Y's Men's Internat., 2002-2003; comdt. Med. Drs. Soccer Team, Daegu, 1990-94, 96-2003; pres. Korea Christian Hosp. Assn., 1997-98. Mem. Korean Assn. Internal Medicine (councilor 1980—, v.p. 1999), Korean Assn. Gastroenterology (councilor 1980—), Korean Soc. Gastrointestinal Endoscopy (coun. 1988—, pres. 1996), Korean Soc. Gastrointestinal Motility Study (pres. 1993), Am. Coll. Gastroenterology (internat.) N.Y. Acad. Scis. Presbyterian. Avocations: tennis, soccer, choir. Home: Eunhatown 101-1708 Sangin-Dong 42 Dalseo-Ku Daegu 704-370 Republic of Korea Home Phone: 82-53-632-3751; Office Phone: 82-54-850-8200. E-mail: skpark@dsmc.or.kr. *

PARK, SOO-SUNG, orthopaedic surgeon, educator; b. Busan, Republic of Korea, Sept. 26, 1963; MD, Seoul Nat. U., 1988; PhD, Chungbuk Nat. U., 2005. Prof., dept. orthop. surgery Asan Med. Ctr., Coll. Medicine Ulsan U., 1999—, dir., 2011. Mem.: Korean Orthop. Assn., Korean Pediatric Orthop. Soc. Office: 88 Olympic-ro 43-gil Songpa-gu Seoul 138-736 Republic of Korea Office Phone: 82 2 3010 3530. Office Fax: 82-2-488-7877. Personal E-mail: hibone1@gmail.com. Business E-Mail: sspark@amc.seoul.kr.

PARK, SUENIE, government agency administrator, researcher; b. Republic of Korea, July 4, 1954; BS, Wash. State U., 1975; MS, Seoul Nat. U., 1979; PhD, Wash. State U., 1987. Lab chief, virus and oncology team Korea Rsch. Instn. Biosci. & Bioengring., 1987—99; dir., hazardous substances analysis divsn. Korera Food & Drug Adminstrn., 1999—. Profl. advisor WHO, 2000—05, expert panel mem., biols. standardization, 2005—10; adv. group mem., toxicogenomics program OECD, 2006—, subgroup leader, cancer epigenetic subgroup, 2009—; adj. prof. Korea U.; liason USTDA NCTR KEDA NTTR, 2008—. Contbr. chapters to books, articles to numerous sci. profl. publs. Recipient Nat. Laureate award, Korea Govt., Pres. Korea, Best Mentor award, Womens Sci. & Engring., Supporting Instn., 2006; grant, Govt. Fellow: Korea Soc. Microbiology, Korea Soc. Biomolecular and Biochemistry, Korea Soc. Virology; mem.: Internat. Papillomavirus Soc. (bd. mem. 2004—). Avocations: singing, mountain climbing. Office: 900-12 Mok-Dong Yangcheon-Gu Seoul 158-050 Republic of Korea Office Fax: 82-02-2640-1364.

PARK, SUNG-PA, neurologist, educator; b. Daegu, Republic of Korea, May 9, 1959; s. Cheol-Bong Park and Young-Ja Kim; m. Gook-Sun Hwang, Sept. 29, 1984; children: So-Yoon, Jung-Yoon. BS, Kyungpook Nat. U., Daegu, 1984; MS, Keimyung U. Sch. Medicine, Daegu, 1990, D, 1994. Diplomate Korean Med. Assn., 1984. Internship Keimyung U. Dongsan Hosp., Daegu, 1984—85, residency, 1989—92; physician Kaya Hosp., Daegu, 1993—94; instr. Dept. Neurology, Sch. Medicine, Kyungpook Nat. U., 1994—96, asst. prof., 1996—2000, assoc. prof., 2000—05, chmn., 2003, head prof., 2003, prof., 2005—. Dir. Epilepsy and Headache Clinic, Kyungpook Nat. U. Hosp., 1998. Exhibitions include Long-term cognitive effects of topiramate monotherapy in epilepsy. Mem.: Korean Neurol. Assn., Korean Epilepsy Soc. Achievements include research in cognitive and psychiatric comorbidities in epilepsy and problems in migraine. Office: Kyungpook Nat University Hosp Samdeok-Dong 2-Ga Jung-Gu 50 700-721 Daegu Daegu Republic of Korea Office Fax: 82-53-422-4265. Business E-Mail: sppark@mail.knu.ac.kr.

PARK, TAE-SOO, medical educator; b. Busan, Republic of Korea, Dec. 4, 1956; s. Joo-Ho Park and Jong-Suck Lee; m. Young-Mi Wang, Nov. 30, 1985; 1 child, Ja-Eun. MD, Hanyang U. Coll. Medicine, Seoul, Republic of Korea, 1981, MS, 1989, PhD, 1994. Cert. in med. course Hanyang U. Coll. Medicine, 1977, in premed. course Hanyang U. Coll. Medicine, 1981. Intern Hanyung U. Coll. Medicine, 1984—85, orthop. surgery resident, 1985—89; staff, dept. orthop. surgery Hanil Gen. Hosp., Seoul, 1993—94; instr. Seoul Hosp. Hanyang U. Coll. Medicine, Dept. Orthop. Surgery, 1994—96, Guri Hosp. Hanyang U. Coll. Medicine, Dept. Orthop. Surgery, 1994—96, asst. prof., 1996—2000, assoc. prof., 2000—05, chmn., 2003—07, prof., 2005—. Bd. editor Jour. Korean Orthop. Assn., Seoul, 2000—03; bd. editor-in-chief Jour. Korean Orthop. Soc. Sports Medicine, Seoul, 2005—08; rsch. bd. advisors Am. Biog. Inst., Seoul, 2007—. Contbr. articles to profl. jours., numerous presentations. Bd. trustee Korean Shoulder and Elbow Soc., Seoul, 2000—, Korean Orthop. Ultrasound Soc., Seoul, 2006—; pres. Korean Shoulder and Elbow Soc., 2007—08; trustee Hanyang U. Alumni Assn., Seoul, 2006—; auditor Gyunggi Br. Korean Orthop. Assn., Republic of Korea, 2004—; specialist Auto Ins. Med. Fee Review Coun., Seoul, 2008—, Ctrl. Pharm. Affairs Coun., Seoul, 2008—; med. advisor Uijeongbu Dist. Ct., Republic of Korea, 2005—; med. counsellor Uijeongbu Dist. Prosecutors' Office, 2005—. 1st lt. Med. Officer Korean Army, 1981—84. Mem.: Am. Shoulder & Elbow Surgeons, Korean Arthroscopy Assn. (bd. editor 1999—2009, auditor 2009—), Korean Shoulder Elbow Soc., Korean Orthop. Assn. (bd. trustees 2010—), Korean Soc. Sports Medicine, Asia Pacific Orthop. Assn., Internat. Soc. Arthroscopy, Knee Surgery & Orthop. Sports Medicine (arthroscopy com.), Soc. Internat. Chirurgie Orthop. et de Traumatologie, Asian Shoulder Assn., Am. Acad. Orthop. Surgeons, Korean Soc. Fractures, Korean Orthop. Soc. Sports Medicine (auditor 2008), Korean Knee Soc., Korean Med. Assn. Avocations: golf, travel. Office: Hanyang Univ Guri Hosp Dept Orthop 249-1 Gyomoon-dong Guri-city Gyunggi-do 471-701 Republic of Korea Office Fax: 82 31 557 8781. Business E-Mail: parkts@hanyang.ac.kr.

PARK, THOMAS JOSEPH, biology researcher, educator; b. Balt., June 8, 1958; s. Lee Crandall and Barbara Ann (Merrick) P.; m. Stephanie Suzanne Reynolds, June 22, 1985; 1 child, Nicholas Timothy. BA in Psychology, Johns Hopkins U., 1982; MSc in Exptl. Psychology, U. Md., 1984, PhD in Exptl. Psychology, 1988. Postdoctoral fellow Inst. Cellular and Molecular Embryology, Paris, 1989; postdoctoral rsch. assoc. dept. zoology U. Tex., 1989—94; faculty dept. biol. scis. U. Ill., Chgo., 1994—, prof. dept. biol. scis., 2009—. Contbr. articles and chpts. to profl. jours. and books. Grantee NIMH, 1986-88, Nat. Ctr. Sci. Rsch., Paris, 1989, NIH, 1989-90, 1997-2003, Nat. Orgn. Hearing Rsch., 1996-97, NSF, 2009-; Alexander von Humboldt Rsch. fellowship, Zool. Inst., U. Munich, 1993-94, Max Planck Inst. Neurobiology, Munich, 2001-02. Mem. AAAS, Soc. Neurosci., Assn. Rsch. in Otolaryngology. Achievements include research in neurobiology of sensory information processing and sensorimotor integration. Office: Univ Ill Chgo Dept Biol Sci Neurobiology Group 840 W Taylor St Chicago IL 60607 Business E-Mail: tpark@uic.edu.

PARK, WANSU, medical educator, dean; b. Seoul, Republic of Korea, Jan. 12, 1969; MD in Oriental Medicine, Kyung-Hee U., 1994, PhD in Oriental Medicine, 2002. Dean Coll. Oriental Medicine, Kyungwon U., Republic of Korea, 2008—. Contbr. scientific papers to profl. jours. Maj. Republic of Korea Army, 2007. Recipient Prime Min. award, South Korean Govt. Methodist. Office: Coll Oriental Medicine Kyungwon University Seongnam Kyung-gi 461-701 Republic of Korea Office Phone: 82-31-750-8821. Business E-Mail: hangl98@naver.com.

PARK, WON-HEE, urologist, educator; b. Seoul, Republic Of Korea, Aug. 25, 1954; s. Jung-Ja Oh; m. Jung-Joo Doh; children: Jung-Hong, So-Young. BA, Seoul Nat. U., 1979, MA, 1982, PhD, 1989. Intern and resident Seoul Nat. U. Hosp., 1979—82; med. staff dept. urology Korea Vets. Hosp., 1986—95; head dept. urology Sungnam Inha Gen. Hosp., Inha U., Incheon, Republic of Korea, 1995—2003; assoc. prof. Coll. Medicine, Inha U., Incheon, Republic of Korea, 1995—2000, prof., 2000—, prof.-in-charge dept. urology, 2002—08; prof. dept. urology Inha U. Hosp., Incheon, Republic of Korea, 2003—, head dept. urology, 2004—08. Cons. prof. Samsung Ins. Co., Seoul, 2001—04. Capt. Republic of Korea Army, 1983—86. Mem.: Korean Assn. Spinal Cord Injury (dir.), Internat. Soc. Urology, Internat. Continence Soc., Korea Urol. Assn. (bd. dirs. 2005—, dir., Best Sci. Paper award 2006), Korea Continence Soc. (dir., pres. 2000—03, Best Sci. Paper award 2004, 2006), Am. Urol. Assn. (corr.). Home: 102-1402 Sangnokmauel Jeongja-Dong Kyunggi-Do Bundang-Ku, Songnam-Si Republic of Korea Office: Inha U Hosp Dept Urology 7-206 3-Ga Sinheung-Dong Jung-Ku 400-711 Incheon Incheon Republic of Korea Office Fax: +82328903560; Home Fax: 82317154315. Business E-Mail: drwonhee@inha.ac.kr.

PARK, WOO-HYUN, medical researcher, educator; b. Jeonju, Jeonbuk, Republic Of Korea, June 4, 1971; s. Park and Kim; m. Eun-Young Jeon, Dec. 2, 2000; children: Kwan Jun, Eunice Kwan Chae. PhD, Seoul Nat. U., Republic Of Korea, 2000. Cert. scientist Chonbuk. Postdoc. rsch. Havard Med. Sch., Boston, 2003—05; asst. prof. Chonbuk Nat. U., Jeonju, Republic of Korea, 2005—. Decorated Postdoc. award US Army. Office: Chonbuk Nat Univ san 2-20 Geumam-dong Jeonju Jeonbuk 561-180 Republic of Korea Office Fax: 820632749892. Business E-Mail: parkwh71@chonbuk.ac.kr.

PARK, YANG SOO, plastic surgeon; Grad., Seoul Nat. U. Med. Coll.; postgrad., Seoul Nat. U. Bd. cert. tng. plastic surgery dept. Seoul Nat. Univ. Hosp.; fellowship plastic surgery dept. samsung med. ctr. Samsung Seoul Hosp.; dir. plastic surgery dept. Kim Soo Shin Aesthetic Clinic; chmn. plastic surgery dept. Seoul Hosp.; surgeon Dream Plastic Surgery Clinic. Clin. prof. samsung med. ctr. Sungkyunkwan Univ. Med. Coll.; clin. prof. Seoul Nat. Univ. Hosp.; chief prof. plastic surgery dept. Chungbook Univ. Med. Coll. Fellow: Am. Soc. Laser Medicine and Surgery; mem.: European Acad. Cosmetic Surgery, Japan Soc. Aesthetic Surgery, Internat. Confederation Plastic Reconstructive and Aesthetic Surgery, Korean Cleft Palate-Craniofacial Assn., Korean Microsurgical Soc., Korean Soc. Reconstructive Hand Surgery, Korean Med. Assn., Korean Soc. Aesthetic Plastic Surgery, Korean Soc. Plastic and Reconstructive Surgeons. Office: Dream Plastic Surgery Clinic Apkujung Subway Sta Seoul Republic of Korea Office Phone: 8225461616. Office Fax: 8225461614. *

PARK, YIKYUNG, epidemiologist, oncologist; Staff scientist Nat. Cancer Inst. Office: NCI Public Inquiries Office 6116 Executive Blvd Room 3036A Bethesda MD 20892-8322 E-mail: parkyik@mail.nih.gov.

PARK, YONG WON, pediatrician, educator; b. Seoul, Republic of Korea, July 6, 1958; s. Eui Byung Park and Sang Jip Choi; m. Sun Joo Lee, Oct. 21, 1983; children: Soon Won, Yoon Kyung. MD, Seoul Nat. U., 1987, PhD, 1995. Lic. med. doctor Republic of Korea, 1983. Intern Seoul Paik Hosp., 1983, pediatric resident, 1984—86; fellow in pediatric neonatology Seoul Nat. U. Children's Hosp., 1990, fellow in pediatric cardiology, 1991; prof. Seoul Paik Hosp. Inje U., Republic of Korea, 1994—2006. Contbr. articles to profl. jours. Capt. MC Korean Army, 1987—89. Achievements include epidemiologic survey of Kawasaki disease in Korea. Office: Inje Univ Seoul Paik Hosp 85 2-ga Jeo-dong Jung-gu Seoul 100-032 Republic of Korea Office Fax: 82-2-2270-0264. Personal E-mail: yongpw@hanmail.net.

PARK, YONG-MOON, preventive medicine physician, educator; b. Seoul, Republic of Korea, Mar. 1, 1969; s. Kyun-Hee Park and Young-Sun Lee; m. Janette Heejin, July 5, 2003; children: Edward Jiho, Clara Jimin, Olivia Seyoung. MD in Medicine, Cath. U. Korea, 1996, MMSc in Preventive Medicine, 1999, PhD, 2005; MS in Genetic Epidemiology, Washington U., St. Louis, 2008. Diplomate Korean Bd. Preventive Medicine. Instr. dept. preventive medicine Cath. U. Korea, 2003—05, asst. prof. dept. preventive medicine, 2005—10, assoc. prof. dept. preventive medicine, 2011—. Mem. com. on diabetes treatment Korean Diabetes Assn., 2005—07; mem. institutional review bd. Catholic Med. Ctr., 2009—; bd. dirs. Korean Soc. Epidemiology, 2009—, Korean Soc. Preventive Medicine, Korean Diabetes Assn., Korea Soc. Genomic Epidemiology, Korea Genome Orgn., Internat. Genetic Epidemiology Soc.; bd. mem. Sanoti Aventis Korea, Korean Soc. Hypertension, Korean Soc. Cardiovascular Disease Prevention; ad-hoc reviewer Korean Jour. Occupl. Health, 2005—07, Korean Jour. Epidemiology, 2006, Tohoku Jour. Exptl. Medicine, 2010, Jour. Preventive Medicine and Pub. Health, 2010, Blood Pressure, 2010, Experimental and Molecular Medicine, 2010, Epidemiology & Health, 2010; statis. advisor Jour. Korean Soc. Endocrinology, 2005—07, Korea Ctr. Disease Control and Prevention, 2010—, Korean Diabetes Jour., 2010—; ad-hoc reviewer African J. Biotechnology, 2011. Pub. health doctor Ministry of Health and Welfare, 2000—03, Republic of Korea. Recipient award, Washington U., 2008; Alumni grant, Cath. U. Korea, 2005, grant, Korean Med. Assn., 1998, Korea Inst. Health and Social Affairs, 2005, Korea Rsch. Found., 2005. Mem.: Sanofi-aventis Korea, Cath. Med. Ctr. Rsch. Found. Achievements include research in epidemiologic characteristics of hypertension, metabolic syndrome, and diabetes mellitus in Korean population; the identification of genetic epidemiologic characteristics of metabolic syndrome. Avocations: travel, golf, Go, classical music, photography. Office: Dept Preventive Medicine Coll Medicine Cath University Korea 505 Banpo-Dong Seocho-Gu Seoul 137-701 Republic of Korea Office Phone: 82-2-2258-7369. Office Fax: 82-2-532-3820. Personal E-mail: markympark@gmail.com. Business E-Mail: mark@catholic.ac.kr.

PARK, YOUNG HA, nuclear medicine physician, radiologist; s. Kyu Hyun Park and Soo Bok Park (Kim); m. Sang Youl Hann, Jan. 13, 1956; children: Eun Hyoung, Eun Jin. MD, Cath. U. Korea, 1978, M in Med. Sci., 1990, PhD in Med. Sci., 1995. Physician Min. of Health & Social Affairs/Republic of Korea, 1978, Diagnostic Radiology Min. of Health & Social affairs, Republic of Korea, 1989, Nuclear Medicine Min. of Health & Social Affairs, Republic of Korea, 1997. Intern Yongdong Severance Hosp., Yonsei Univer., Seoul, 1985—86; resident diagnostic radiology Kangnam St. Mary's Hosp., Cath. U. Korea, 1986—89, fellow, 1989—90; instr. radiology Cath. U. Korea, 1990—95, asst. prof. radiology, 1995—99, assoc. prof. radiology, 1999—2004, prof. radiology, 2004—; fellow nuc. medicine Ind. U. Hosp., 1995—96. Chief dept. radiology and nuc. medicine St. Vincent's Hosp., Cath. U. Korea, 1991—2004. First lt. Republic of Korea Army, 1978—81. Mem.: EANM, ECR, Soc. Nuc. Medicine, Radiol. Soc. N.Am. Office Fax: 82-31-247-5713. Business E-Mail: yhpark@catholic.ac.kr. E-mail: yparkh@catholic.ac.kr.

PARKE, DAVID WILKIN, II, ophthalmologist, educator, health facility administrator; b. Columbus, Ohio, May 19, 1951; s. David William Parke and Eunice Joyce Erikson; m. Julie Diane Thorne, Sept. 15, 1975; children: David W. III, Laura Thorne, Lindsey Diane. AB, Stanford U., 1973; MD, Baylor Coll. Medicine, 1977. Diplomate Am. Bd. Ophthalmology. Resident in internal medicine Baylor Coll. Medicine, Houston, 1977-78, resident in ophthalmology, 1978-81, fellow in med. retina, 1981-82, asst. prof., 1983-90, assoc. prof., 1990-92; fellow diseases and surgery of the retina and vitreous Med. Coll. of Wis., 1982-83; prof., chair dept. ophthalmology U. Okla., Oklahoma City, 1992—; pres., CEO McGee Eye Inst., Oklahoma City, 1992—. Chmn., bd. dirs. Medem, Inc., 2004—; vice chair Ophthalmic Mut. Ins. Co., 2005—. Active Okla. Econ. Devel. Found., 1992, Okla. Health Ctr. Found., 1992—; trustee Presbyn. Health Found., 1995-2006, Casady Sch., 1997-2004, vice chair, 1999-2004; mng. dir. Stephenson Laser Ctr., 1996—; bd. mgrs. Okla. Health Alliance, 1995-97; dir. Oklahoma City C. of C. Fellow: Am. Acad. Ophthalmology (assoc. sec. 1983—92, trustee 2000—, sr. sec. for ophthalmic practice 2002—, pres. 2007—08, Honor award 1980, Sr. Honor award 1998); mem.: Am. Soc. Ret. Specialists, Retina Soc., Assn. Univ. Profs. Ophthalmology (trustee 1997—2003, pres. 2001—02), Greater Oklahoma City C. of C. (bd. dirs. 1998—99, 2004—), Alpha Omega Alpha. Office: Dean A McGee Eye Institute 608 Stanton L Young Blvd Oklahoma City OK 73104-5065 E-mail: david-parke@ouhsc.edu.

PARKER, BRENT MERSHON, retired medical educator, internist, cardiologist; b. St. Louis, July 3, 1927; s. William Bahlmann and Florence (Mershon) P.; m. Martha Shelton, Aug. 1, 1953; children: Martha Parker Burgess, Elizabeth, Margaret. MD cum laude, Wash. U., St. Louis, 1952. Diplomate Am. Bd. Internal Medicine. Intern and asst. resident N.Y. Hosp.-Cornell, NYC, 1952-54; asst. resident, fellow Barnes Hosp., Wash. U., St. Louis, 1954-57; cardiology sect. chief VA Hosp., U. Oreg., Portland, 1957-59; asst. prof. to assoc. prof., co-dir. cardiovascular div., chief adult cardiac catherization Wash. U. Sch. Medicine, St. Louis, 1959-73; prof. medicine U. Mo., Columbia, 1973-89, prof. emeritus, 1989-94, chief of staff, assoc. dean, 1976-82, chief of cardiology, 1983-89. Mem. colloquium faculty Merck, Sharp and Dohme, West Point, Pa., 1980-86. Author or co-author 58 papers in referred jours., 6 book chpts., teaching papers, others. Bd. dirs. St. Louis Heart Assn., 1962-73, v.p. 1972-73; bd. dirs. Mo. Heart Assn., 1965-75, pres. 1970-71. Served with USN, 1945-46. Recipient Arthur Strauss award St. Louis Heart Assn., 1973, 3 teaching awards U. Mo. Sch. Medicine, 1974, 75, 86, Preventive Cardiology Acad. award, Nat. Heart Lung and Blood Inst., 1982-87, Alumni Achievement award Washington Univ. Sch. Medicine, 1992; Brent Mershon Parker professorship estab. in honor U. Mo., 1989. Fellow ACP, Am. Coll. Cardiology (Mo., Kans. council rep. 1973-77), Clin. Cardiology Soc. Am. Heart Assn.; mem. Am. Fedn. Clin. Research, Cen. Soc. for Clin. Research, Alpha Omega Alpha, Sigma Xi. Episcopalian. Avocations: choral singing, jogging, camping, back packing.

PARKER, GERALD M., osteopath, researcher; b. Olean, NY, Nov. 20, 1943; s. Richard and Kathleen (Manwaring) P.; m. Linda Kay Stuart, Dec. 28, 1968; children: Kimberly, Gerald, Cassandra, Kevin. BA, Western Wash. U., 1965; DO, Kirksville Coll. Osteopathy & Surgery, 1969. Intern Art Centre Hosp., Detroit, 1969-70; ptnr. Doctor's Clinic, Amarillo, Tex., 1970. Dir. S.W. Inst. Preventive Medicine, Amarillo, 1978—, Hyperbaric Oxygen Ctr., Amarillo, 1979—; appeared on That's Incredible TV show, 1982. Contbr. articles to profl. jours. Pres. S.W. Amarillo Little Dribblers Assn., 1979—; coach Girls Nat. Champion Basketball Teams, 1981, 83-87, 89. Named Physician of Yr., Nat. Rep. Com. Physician Adv. Bd., 2003. Fellow Am. Acad. Med. Preventics; mem. S.W. Acad. Preventive Medicine (pres. 1980—), Am. Osteo. Assn. Methodist. Avocation: athletics. Office: Doctors Clinic 4714 S Western St Amarillo TX 79109-5950 Office Phone: 806-355-8263.

PARKER, KATHY P., dean, nursing educator; ADN, We. Ky. U., Bowling Green, 1970; BSN, Columbia U., NYC, 1973; MN, Emory U., Atlanta, 1977; PhD in Family and Cmty. Nursing, Ga. State U., Atlanta, 1990. Diplomate Am. Bd. Sleep Medicine, 2001; RN Ga., 1974, cert. adult nurse practitioner, Am. Nurses Credentialing Ctr., 1981, clin. nurse specialist, Am. Nurses Credentialing Ctr., 1982, in med./surg. nursing, Am. Nurses Credentialing Ctr., 1982; in French U. Paris Coll. Sorbonne, 1974. Staff nurse, charge nurse Columbia Presbyn. Med. Ctr., NYC, 1970—73; staff nurse Ga. Meml. Hosp., Atlanta, 1973—74; instr., advanced med./surg. nursing Ga. Bapt. Hosp. Sch. Nursing, Atlanta, 1974—76; head nurse, dialysis unit VA Med. Ctr., Atlanta, 1977—79; ops. officer, nurse practitioner nephrology Veterans Affairs Med. Ctr., Atlanta, 1979—87, clin. nurse specialist, nurse practitioner nephrology, 1989—93; rsch. asst. Ga. State U. Sch. Nursing, Atlanta, 1987—89; rsch. assoc. Emory U. Nell Woodruff Sch. Nursing, Atlanta, 1987—88, clin. track assoc. prof., 1989—93, assoc. prof., 1993—2003, tenured, 1998, prof., 2000—08, Edith F. Honeycutt endowed chair, 2003—08; nurse practitioner, Sleep Disorders Ctr. Emory U., Atlanta, 1993—2008, co-dir. Emory sleep program, dept. neurology, 2006—08; prof., dean U. Rochester Sch. Nursing, NY, 2008—. Cons. in field; vis. prof. U. Pitts. Renal Divsn. Contbr. articles to profl. jours. Recipient Disting. Alumni in Nursing award, Emory U., 2000; named Grad. Clin. Preceptor of Yr., Ga. State U., 1982; fellow, Woodruff Leadership Acad., 2003. Fellow: Am. Acad. Nursing, Am. Acad. Sleep Medicine; mem.: ANA, Am. Acad. Nurse Practitioners, Sleep Rsch. Soc., Am. Nephrology Nurses Assn. (Nephrology Nurse Rschr. award 2000), Ga. Nurses Assn., Sigma Theta Tau. Office: Univ Rochester Med Ctr Sch Nursing 601 Elmwood Ave Rochester NY 14627 Office Phone: 585-275-8902. Business E-Mail: kathy_parker@urmc.rochester.edu.

PARKER, LEE BRYAN, retired physician; b. Dermott, Ark., May 10, 1929; s. Lee Bryan and Viola Lee Parker; m. Beverly Edith Brosell, Dec. 23, 1951; children: Susan Leigh Brewer, Elizabeth Ann Beecher, Steven Lee, Edith Lynn Hegwood. BS, U. Ark., Fayetteville, 1950; MD, U. Ark., Little Rock, 1954. Lic. physician Ark., 1954. Intern Crawford Long Hosp., Atlanta, 1954—55; pvt. practice Dermott, 1957—59, McGehee, Ark., 1959—67; gen. practice Doctor's Bldg., Fayetteville, Ark., 1967—74; dir. U. Ark. Med. Scis., Area Health Edn. Ctr. NW, Fayetteville, 1974—96; ret., 1996. Chief med. staff S.t Mary's Hosp., Dermott, 1964—65, McGehee Desha Hosp., Ark., 1965—67, Fayetteville City Hosp., 1975—76, Wash. Regional Med. Ctr., Fayetteville, 1980—81; vis. prof. Kaohsiung Med. U., Taiwan, 1986; bd. dirs. Ark. Regional Med. Program, Little Rock, 1967—70, Butterfield Trail Village, Fayetteville, 2001—06; dir. continuing med. edn. U. Ark. Sch. Medicine, Little Rock, 1970—74, adj. prof., 1996—; adv. bd. U. Ark. Sch. Medicine, Area Health Edn. Ctr. NW, Fayetteville, 2004—. Sec. Wash. County Med. Soc., Fayetteville, 1973—74. Capt. USAF, 1955—57. Recipient Disting. Svc. award, McGehee Jaycees, 1963, Distinguised Svc. award, U. Ark. for Med. Scis. Coll. Medicine, 1992, Founders Soc. award, U. Ark. for Med. Scis., 1996, Eagle award, Wash. Regional Med. Found., 1999, Diamond Soc. award, Ark. Cmty. Found., 2004, Doyne Soc. award, U. Ctrl. Ark., 2004, Legacy Soc. award, U. Ark. for Med. Scis., 2005. Mem.: Ark. Acad. Family Physicians (life; bd. dirs. 1962—67, chmn. continuing edn. com. 1971—89, pres. 1982—83, alt. del. 1984—89, Family Dr. of Yr. 1993), Ark. Med. Soc. (life; councilor 4th dist. 1965—67, jour. editor 1993). Independent. Methodist. Avocations: hunting, fishing, golf, gardening. Office: University Ark Med Sci 1125 N Coll Fayetteville AR 72701

PARKER, SUSAN BROOKS, government agency administrator; b. Newport, NH, Nov. 7, 1945; d. Ronald Elliott and Elizabeth Louise (Wiggins) P.; m. Allen D. Avery, 1967 (div. 1978); children: Jeffrey Roberts Avery, Mark Brooks Avery. BS in English and French, U. Vt., 1968; MSW/MSP, Boston Coll., 1978. EMT Vt., 1973-76. Resort hotel mgr., retail buyer Avery Vt. Inns, 1967-75; psychiat. social worker Orange County Mental Health, Bradford, Vt., 1974-76; exec. dir. Grafton County Planning Coun., Lebanon, NH, 1978-80, NH Developmental Disabilities Planning Coun., Concord, NH, 1980-87; commr. Dept. of Mental Health, Augusta, Maine, 1987-89; disability commr. US Social Security Adminstrn., Balt., 1989-93; sec. gen. Rehab. Internat., NYC, 1993—98; sr. adv., interim dir. disability program Internat. Labor Office, Geneva, 1998—2002; dir. policy and devel. Office Disability Employment Policy US Dept. Labor, Washington, 2002—11. Cons. Nat. Gov.'s Assn., Washington, 1985-86, Office of Health and Devel. Svcs., Washington, 1987; bd. dirs. Nat. Assn. Devel. Disabilities, Washington, 1983-87, Ctrl. NH Mental Health Ctr., Concord, 1985-87, World Com. Disability, Washington, 1997-2007, Roeher Inst., Toronto, 1997-2000, Orah.com, Geneva, 2002-08, NH Devel. Disabilities Coun., 2002—05; hon. coun. Rehab. Internat., mem. World Assembly, NYC, 1998-, elected vice chmn. Policy & Svcs. Commn., 2008-, consuler mem., Am. Occpl. Therapy Assoc., 2010; chairperson Knapp Scholarship Fund, So. NH U., 2007-. Author: poetry; contbr. articles to newspapers and profl. jours. Pres. Parent Tchr. Orgn., Fairlee, Vt., 1972-73; founder and dir. Fairlee Ford Sayre Ski Program, Dartmouth Coll. Skiway, Fairlee, 1972-76, United Way, Concord, 1983-86; bd. dirs. PTO Rundlett Jr. HS, Concord, 1982-85; pres. US Coun. for Internat. Rehab., Washington, 1993. Recipient Children's Disability Pub. Policy award, Assn. Retarded Citizens, 1992, Kathryn C. Arneson award, People to People, 1992, Commr.'s citation, US Social Security Adminstrn., 1992, Commn.'s citation, 1993, Secretary's Exemplary Achievement awards, US Dept. Labor, 2003—10, Appreciation award Dept. State, CFC, 2007, award, Steering Com. Roosevelt Internat. Disability Rights., 2011—; named Outstanding Alumnae, Boston Coll., 1991. Avocations: skiing, gardening, boating, reading, film and performing arts.

PARKER, WILLIAM HOWARD, obstetrician-gynecologist; b. NYC, 1948; BA, Rutgers U., 1970; MD, SUNY Downstate Med. Sch., 1974. Diplomate Am. Bd. Ob-Gyn; cert. Accreditation Coun. Gynecologic Endoscopy. Intern U. Calif.-San Diego Med. Ctr., 1974-75, resident in ob-gyn., 1975-78; tchg. faculty Houston Laser Inst., Tex., 1988—93; asst. clin. prof. UCLA Sch. Medicine, Calif., 1979—91, assoc. clin. prof. Calif., 1992—95, clin. prof. Calif., 1995—; vice-chmn., obstetrics and gynecology Santa Monica-UCLA Med. Ctr., Calif., 1985—91, chmn., gynecologic laser/pelviscopy subcommittee Calif., 1988—96, chmn., interdisciplinary advanced tech. com. Calif., 1990—96, chmn. dept. obstetrics and gynecology Calif., 1992—99, mem. exec. med. bd. Calif., 1992—99; vice-chmn., obstetrics and gynecology St. John's Hosp. and Health Ctr., Santa Monica, Calif., 2003—04, chmn., dept. obstetrics and gynecology, 2004—09, mem. med. exec. com., 2004—05; pvt. practice ob-gyn. Santa Monica, Calif., 1978—. Supervisong attending physician, Santa Monica Rape Treatment Ctr., 1990-2007; scientific program chmn., Global Congress of Gynecologic Endoscopy, 1999; med. cons. OBGYN.net; cons. Nat. Women's Health Resource Ctr., Women's Health Adv. Coun., Found. for Informed Med. Decision Making -Fibroids, Abdominal Bleeding-Benign Uterine Conditions, Women's Health and Hysterectomy Project, The Rand Corp., 1997; lectr. in field. Ad hoc reviewer Jour. Am. Assn. Gynecologic Laparoscopists, 1993—95, mem. editl. bd., 1995—96; editor: Jour. Am. Assn. Gynecologic Laparoscopists, 1997—2003; mem. editl. adv. bd. OB/GYN and Endoscopy News, 1995—96, ad hoc reviewer Obstetrics and Gynecology, 1992—, Jour. Gynecologic Techniques, 1994—, New England Jour. Medicine, 1996—, Fertility and Sterility, 1997—, reviewer Jour. Gynecologic Techniques & Am. Jour. Obstetrics and Gynecology, mem. editl. bd. Jour. Minimally Invasive Gynecology, 2003—05; editor: Jour. Minimally Invasive Gynecology, 2006—; author: A Gynecologist's Second Opinion: The Questions and Answers You Need to Take Charge of Your Health, 1996, A Gynecologist's Second Opinion: The Questions and Answers You Need to Take Charge of Your Health, 2nd edit., 2003; co-author (with Amy Rosenman): The Incontinence Solution: Answers for Women of All Ages, 2002; featured guest spkr. Lifetime Med. Network, Laparoscopic Ovarian Surgery, 1991, med. editor Lifetime Med. Network, Gynecologic Surgical Procedures, 1993. Named one of Best Doctors in Am.; named to Top Doctor's Book. Fellow ACOG; mem. AMA, Calif. Med. Assn., L.A. County Med. Assn., Am. Assn. Gynecological Laparoscopists (adv. bd. mem. 1994-95, bd. trustee, 1995-96, sec.-treas., 1998, v.p., 1999, pres. 2000), LOS Angles Ob-Gyn Soc. (pres. 2009). Address: 1450 10th St Ste 404 Santa Monica CA 90401 Office Phone: 310-451-8144.

PARKERSON, GEORGE ROBERT, JR., medical educator; s. George Robert and Nettie Sue Parkerson; m. Mary McCowen, June 4, 1949 (dec. 2006); children: Sue, George Robert III, Ann Jones, Lyn Carpenter. MD, Duke U. Sch. Medicine, Durham, NC, 1953; MPH in Epidemiology, U. NC Sch. Pub. Health, Chapel Hill, 1977. Diplomate Am. Bd. Family Practice, 1984. Pvt. practice, Winder, Ga., 1955—73;

dir. family practice residency program Med. Ctr. Ctrl. Ga., Macon, 1973—74. Asst. prof. family practice Med. Coll. Ga., Augusta, 1973—74; asst. prof. cmty. family medicine Duke U. Sch. Medicine, Durham, NC, 1974—80, assoc. prof. cmty. family medicine, 1980—88, chmn., 1985—94, prof., 1988—; adj. asst. prof. U. NC Sch. Pub. Health, 1978—83, adj. assoc. prof., 1983—89, adj. prof., 1989—; chmn. Instl. Rev. Bd. Clin. Investigations, Duke U. Health Sys., Durham, NC, 2000—. Contbr. scientific papers. Seaman first class USN, 1945—46, Bainbridge, Newport, Boston, destroyer duty on USS Robert L. Wilson. Mem.: North Am. Primary Care Rsch. Group, NC Acad. Family Physicians, Soc. Teachers Family Medicine, Am. Acad. Family Physicians (life). Office: Duke Univ Med Ctr Durham NC 27710

PARKEY, ROBERT WAYNE, radiology and nuclear medicine educator, research radiologist; b. Dallas, July 17, 1938; s. Jack and Gloria Alfreda (Perry) P.; m. Nancy June Knox, Aug. 9, 1958; children: Wendell Wade, Robert Todd, Amy Elizabeth. BS in Physics, U. Tex., 1960; MD, S.W. Med. Sch., U. Tex., Dallas, 1965. Diplomate Am. Bd. Radiology, Am. Bd. Nuclear Medicine. Intern St. Paul Hosp., Dallas, 1965-66; resident in radiology U. Tex. Health Sci. Ctr., Dallas, 1966-69, asst. prof. radiology, 1970-74, assoc. prof., 1974-77, prof., chmn. dept. radiology, 1977—, Effie and Wofford Cain Disting. chair in diagnostic imaging, 1994—. Chief nuc. medicine Parkland Meml. Hosp., Dallas, 1974-79, chief dept. radiology, 1977—. Contbr. numerous chpts., articles and abstracts to profl. publs. Served as catp. M.C., Army N.G., 1965-72. NIH fellow Nat. Inst. Gen. Med. Sci., U. Mo., Columbia, 1969-70; Nat. Acad. Scis.-NRC scholar in radiol. rsch. James Picker Found., 1971-74. Fellow Am. Coll. Cardiology, Am. Coll. Radiology; mem. Am. Coll. Nuclear Physicians (charter, ho. of dels. 1974—), Coun. on Cardiovascular Radiology of Am. Heart Assn., AMA, Assn. Univ. Radiologists, Dallas County Med. Assn., Dallas Ft. Worth Radiol. Soc., Radiol. Soc. N.Am., Soc. Chmn. of Acad. Radiology Depts., Soc. Nuclear Medicine (acad. coun.), Tex. Med. Assn., Tex. Radiol. Soc., Sigma Xi, Alpha Omega Alpha. Achievements include Achievements include academic research on nuclear cardiology, development of new imaging technologies, medical education. Avocations: gardening, golf, tennis. Office: U Tex Southwestern Med Ctr Dept Radiology 5323 Harry Hines Blvd Dallas TX 75390-8896

PARKINS, FREDERICK MILTON, dental educator, dean; b. Princeton, NJ, Sept. 8, 1935; s. William Milton and Phyllis Virginia (Plyler) P.; m. Carolyn V. Rude; children: Bradford, Christopher, Eric. Student, Carleton Coll., 1953-56; D.D.S., U. Pa., 1960; MSD in Pedodontics, U. N.C., Chapel Hill, 1965; PhD in Physiology, 1969. Instr. pedodontics U. N.C., 1965-67; asst. prof. pedodontics U. Pa., 1967-68, dir. Dental Aux. Utilization program, chmn. pedodontics, 1968-69; assoc. prof., head pedodontics U. Iowa, Iowa City, 1969-72, prof., head pedodontics, 1972-75; asst. dean acad. affairs U. Iowa (Coll. Dentistry), 1974-75, asso. dean acad. affairs, 1975-79, dir. continuing edn., 1975-77; prof. pedodontics, dean Sch. Dentistry, U. Louisville, 1979-85, prof. pediatric dentistry, 1985—2003, prof. pediatric dentistry emeritus, 2003—. Mem. Hillenbrand Fellowship adv. com. Am. Fund Dental Health, 1980-85; cons. Div. Dental Health USPHS, 1969-72; dental cons., med. staff Children's Hosp. Phila., 1968-71, med. staff Kosair Children's Hosp. Louisville, 1980—, cons., mem. pedodontic adv. com. Council Dental Edn., 1974-80, chmn. pedodontic adv. com., 1978-80, cons. council on legislation, 1978-79; dental cons. Aux. Utilization VA, 1968-69; cons. Bur. Health Resources Devel., 1974-76, Dept. Army, 1980-, numerous others Assoc. editor Jour. Preventive Dentistry, 1973-79, mem. editl. bd., 1980-83; editl. reviewer Jour. Pediatrics, 1969-, Jour. Dental Edn, 1978-, Jour. AMA, 1979-; assoc. editor Jour. Clin. Preventive Dentistry, 1979-84; mem. editl. bd. Jour. Clin. Laser Medicine and Surgery, 1999-; contbr. chpts. to textbooks, articles to profl. publs. Bd. govs. Youth Performing Arts Coun., Louisville-Jefferson County Sch. Dist., 1980-89, pres., 1986-88; bd. govs. Regional Cancer Ctr., U. Louisville, 1979-84, Univ. Hosp., 1979-84, mem. human studies com. U. Louisville, 1988-90. Robert Wood Johnson Congl. fellow Inst. of Medicine, 1977-78; USPHS postdoctoral fellow, 1963-67; NIH grantee, 1971-75; Recipient Earle Banks Hoyt Teaching award, 1969 Fellow AAAS, Am. Acad. Pediat. Dentistry (chmn. rsch. com. 1972-73, Ann. Rsch. award 1968, chmn. advanced edn. com. 1974-75, chmn. dental care programs com. 1978-80); mem. ADA, Am. Coll. Dentistry, Am. Soc. Dentistry for Children (exec. bd. Iowa unit 1969-75, award com. 1973-76, edn. com. 1974-77, chmn. rsch. adv. com. 1973-76), Biophys. Soc., Internat. Assn. Dental Rsch., N.Y. Acad. Dentistry, Ky. Dental Assn. (exec. bd. 1979-84), Am. Assn. Dental Schs. (coun. deans 1979-85, chmn. pedodontics sect. 1976, chmn. continuing edn. sect. 1979, legis. com. 1978-83), Louisville Dental Alumni Assn. (bd. govs. 1979-84), Am. Assn. Dental Rsch. (nat. affairs com. 1978-85), Acad. Laser Dentistry (co-chmn. rsch. and edn. 1997, chair 1998-2003, bd. dirs. 1997-2003, cert. com., T.H. Maiman award for excellence in dental laser rsch.), U.S. Power Squadron (bd. govs. 1987-93, sec. 1989, adminstrv. officer 1990, exec. officer 1991, comdr. 1992), Aircraft Owners and Pilots Assn., Omicron Kappa Upsilon (pres. Wa. chpt. 1991-92), Rotary. Unitarian Universalist. Home: 6424 Marina Dr Prospect KY 40059-8846 Office: U Louisville Sch Dentistry Dept Orth and Pediatric Dentistry Rm 240N Louisville KY 40292 Office Phone: 502-228-3389. Business E-Mail: fmpark01@louisville.edu.

PARKINSON, MARK VINCENT, former Governor of Kansas, health science association administrator; b. Wichita, Kans., June 24, 1957; s. Henry Filson and Barbara Ann (Gilbert) Horton; m. Stacy Abbott Parkinson, Mar. 7, 1983; children: Alex Atticus, Sam Filson, Kit Harlan. BA in Edn., summa cum laude, Wichita State U., 1980; JD, Kans. U., 1984. Assoc. Payne & Jones Law Firm, Olathe, Kans., 1984-86; ptnr. Parkinson, Foth & Reynolds, Lenexa, Kans., 1986—96; mem. Kans. House of Reps., 1990-92, Kans. State Senate, 1993-97; chmn. Kans. Republican Party, 1999—2003; lt. gov. State of Kans., Topeka, 2007—09, gov., 2009—11; CEO American Health Care Assn., 2011—. Chmn. Shawnee Area C. of C., 2004—05. Mem.: ABA, Johnson County Bar Found. (past pres.), Kans. Bar Assn. Democrat. Avocations: travel, running, movies. Office: American Health Care Association 1201 L St NW Washington DC 20005 Office Phone: 202-842-4444. Office Fax: 202-842-3860. *

PARKINSON, ROBERT L., JR., medical products executive, health facility administrator; BBA, MBA, Loyola U., Chgo. With Abbott Laboratory, Inc., Abbott Park, Ill., 1976, v.p. European ops., 1990-93, sr. v.p. chem. and agrl. products, 1993-95, pres. internat. divsn., 1995-98, bd. dirs., 1998, pres., COO, 1999-2001; dean Loyola U. Chgo.'s Sch. of Bus. Adminstrn. and Grad. Sch. of Bus., 2002—04; chmn., CEO Baxter International, Inc., 2004—. Chmn. Geneva (Switzerland) Proteomics, 2001; bd. trustees Healthcare Leadership Coun. Bd. dirs. Northwestern Mem. Hosp., Northwestern Mem. Found. Office: Baxter Internat Inc One Baxter Pkwy Deerfield IL 60015 Office Phone: 847-948-2000. *

PARKS, JOHN SCOTT, pediatric endocrinologist; b. Washington, Oct. 14, 1939; s. John Louis and Mary Dean (Scott) P.; m. Georgia Bigley, May 7, 1959, (dec.) Sept 25, 2008; children: Stephanie Dean, Paige Wallace Parks Adams, John Thurston. AB in Am. Studies magna cum laude, Amherst Coll., 1961; MD, U. Pa., 1966, PhD in Biochemistry, 1971. Diplomate Nat. Bd. Med. Examiners, Am. Bd. Pediat. Intern in pediat. Children's Hosp. Phila., 1967-68, resident in pediat., 1968-69; clin. assoc. endocrinology br. Nat. Cancer Inst. NIH, Bethesda, Md., 1969-71; endocrinology fellow Children's Hosp. Phila., 1971-73; from instr. pediat. to assoc. prof. pediat. U. Pa., 1971-83; asst. physician, asst. endocrinologist Children's Hosp. Phila., 1972-74, assoc. physician, assoc. dir. endocrinology, 1974-80, assoc. endocrinologist, 1974-82, dir. hypothyroidism program, 1978-81, sr. physician, dir. adolescent medicine, 1980-82; prof. pediat. Emory U., Atlanta, 1982—, assoc. prof. biochemistry, 1983—, dir. divsn. pediat. endocrinology and diabetes, 1982—; pediat. endocrinologist Henrietta Egleston Hosp., 1982—, Grady Meml. Hosp., 1982—. Lectr. in field. Author books; contbg. author over 50 book chpts.; contbr. over 65 articles to profl. jours. Bd. dirs. Spruce Hill Cmty. Assn., 1967-69, Hill Top Prep. Sch., 1977-81. Recipient fellowship NIH, 1963-64, 66-67, 75-80, GM Nat. scholarship, 1957-61, Ford Found. fellowship, 1960-61, Am. Cancer Soc. fellow, 1962-63, Morton McCutcheon award, 1963, Merck award, 1966, numerous rsch. awards, 1964—. Mem. Am. Pediat. Soc., Endocrine Soc. (organizing com. 1990), Soc. for Pediat. Rsch., Coll. Physicians and Surgeons of Phila., Lawson Wilkins Pediat. Endocrine Soc. (program com. chair 1983-87, bd. dirs. 1990-93, pres. 1996-97), Spinx Soc., Scarab Soc., Phi Beta Kappa, Psi Upsilon. Office: Emory U Sch Medicine Dept Pediat 2015 Uppergate Dr NE Atlanta GA 30322 Office Phone: 404-778-2400. Office Fax: 404-727-9834. Business E-Mail: jparks@emory.edu.

PARLE, MILIND, pharmacologist, educator; b. Karad, Maharashtra, Jan. 9, 1958; B in Pharmacy, Govt. Coll. Pharmacy, Karad, PharmM; PhD, Govt. Coll. Pharmacy, 1980; degree, Panjab U., Chandigarh, 1986. Prof. pharmacology Guru Jambheshwar U. Sci. and Tech., Hisar, Haryana, India, 1997—, chmn. dept. pharm. scis., 2008—11. Prin. SCS Coll. Pharmacy, Karnataka, 1987—91; dep. dir. AICTE, New Delhi, 1994—97. Recipient Best Rsch. Paper award, UGC, ICMR, New Delhi. Mem.: IPS, IPGA, APTI, IPA. Avocation: chess. Home: Guru Jambheshwar University Sci and Technology F-8 Guru Jambheshwar University Campus Hisar Haryana 125001 India Personal E-mail: mparle@rediffmail.com.

PARMELEE, ARTHUR HAWLEY, JR., pediatric medical educator; b. Chgo., Oct. 29, 1917; s. Arthur Hawley and Ruth Frances (Brown) P.; m. Jean Kern Rheinfrank, Nov. 11, 1939; children: Arthur Hawley III, Ann (Mrs. John C. Minahan Jr.), Timothy, Ruth Ellen. BS, U. Chgo., 1940, MD, 1943. Diplomate Am. Bd. Pediatrics (examiner 1966—). Intern U.S. Naval Hosp., Bethesda, Md., 1943-44; extern Yale Inst. Child Devel., 1947, New Haven Hosp., 1947-48, L.A. Children's Hosp., 1948-49, mem. faculty UCLA Med. Sch., 1951—, prof. pediat., 1967-88, prof. emeritus, 1988, dir. divsn. child devel., 1964-88; mem. Brain Rsch. Inst., 1966-88, Mental Retardation Rsch. Ctr., 1970-88. Rsch. prof. pediat. U. Göttingen, Germany, 1967-68; mem. com. child devel. rsch. and pub. policy NRC, 1977-81; cons. Nat. Inst. Child Health and Human Devel., 1963-70, Holy Family Adoption Svc., 1949-80. Author articles, chpts. in books. Trustee Los Angeles Children's Mus., 1979. Served with USN, 1943-47. Recipient C. Anderson Aldrich award in child devel., 1975; Commonwealth fellow Centre de Recherches Biologiques Neonatales, Clinique Obstetricale Baudelocque, Paris, 1959-60; fellow Ctr. Advanced Study in Behavioral Scis., Stanford U., 1984-85; hon. lectr. Soc. for Developmental and Behavioral Pediat., 1996. Mem. AMA, Am. Pediat. Soc., Soc. Pediat. Rsch., Western Soc. Pediat. Rsch., Am. Acad. Pediat. (chmn. com. sect. child devel. 1966), Assn. Ambulatory Pediat. (mem. coun. 1966-69), Soc. Rsch. in Child Devel. (pres. 1983-85, Disting. Sci. Contbns. to Child Devel. award 1993), Assn. Psychophysiol. Study of Sleep, Los Angeles County Med. Soc., Phi Beta Kappa. Home: 764 Iliff St Pacific Palisades CA 90272-3927 Office: Univ Calif Dept Pediatrics Los Angeles CA 90024

PARMELEE, WALKER MICHAEL, psychologist; b. Grand Haven, Mich., Apr. 26, 1952; s. Walker Michael and Evelyn Mae (Essenberg) P.; m. Gayle Ann Klempel, Jan. 11, 1975; children: Morgan Christine, Kathryn Ann, Elizabeth Mae. BS, Ctrl. Mich. U., 1974, MA, cert. specialist in psychology, 1977; D in Counseling Psychology, Western Mich. U., 1986. Lic. psychologist, Mich. Sch. psychologist Oakridge Pub. Schs., Muskegon, Mich., 1977—82, Ravenna (Mich.) Schs., Muskegon Heights (Mich.) Schs., 1982—84; sr. staff therapist Steelcase Counseling Svcs., Grand Rapids, Mich., 1984—90; prin., psychologist Parmelee and Assocs. Psychol. Cons., Grand Haven, 1989—. Consulting psychologist Cross Rds. Family Ctr., Grand Haven, 1989—2000. Contbr. articles to profl. jours. Bd. dirs. Planned Parenthood, Muskegon, 1979-82, Harbinger Inc., Grand Rapids, 1986-90, Tri Cities Ministries Counseling, 2003-07; elder 2d Ref. Ch., Grand Haven, 1989-92, 2006-10; mem. women and families adv. group Allegan, Muskegon, Ottawa Substance Abuse Agy., 1992-95; mem. support team ARC, 2005-07. Mem. Nat. Assn. Child Alcoholics, Mich. Psychol. Assn., Mich. Sch. Psychologists. Avocations: woodworking, skiing, running, tennis, camping. Home: 215 Howard St Grand Haven MI 49417-1806 Office: Parmelee and Assocs Psychol Cons 321 Fulton Ave Grand Haven MI 49417-1231 Office Phone: 616-842-4772. Personal E-mail: parmeleenet@aim.com.

PARMLEY, RICHARD TURNER, pediatric hematologist, oncologist; b. Madison, Wis., Sept. 10, 1949; BA, U. Va., 1970; MD, Med. U. S.C., 1973. Diplomate in pediatrics and in pediatric hematology/oncology Am. Bd. Pediatrics; diplomate in hematopathology Am. Bd. Pathology. Intern Med. U. S.C., Charleston, S.C., 1973, resident in pediats., 1974-75; fellow in pediat. hematology-oncology St. Jude Children's Rsch. Hosp., Memphis, 1976-77, U. Ala., Birmingham, 1977; clin. fellow in med. oncology bone marrow transplant svc. Fred Hutchinson Cancer Rsch. Ctr., Seattle, 1986; dir. electron microscopy and histology unit inst. dental rsch. U. Ala., Birmingham, 1978-83, assoc. scientist Comprehensive Cancer Cancert Ctr., 1978-83, asst. prof. pediats. and pathology, 1978-82, assoc. prof. pediats., 1982-83; assoc. prof. pediats. and pathology U. Tex. Health Sci. Ctr., 1983-88, prof. pediats., 1988-94; dir. divsn. pediat. hematology/oncology Carolinas Med. Ctr., Charlotte, NC, 1994—2000; clin. prof. pediat. U. NC, Chapel Hill, 1994—2000; mem. med. staff Spartanburg Reg. Med. Ctr., SC, 2000—07; clin. prof. pediat. Med. Univ. SC, Charleston, 2000—07; pediat. hematologist-oncologist Nemours Children's Clinic, Pensacola, Fla., 2007—; clin. prof. Fla. State U., 2007—. Mem. Am. Soc. Pediatric Hematology/Oncology, Am. Acad. Pediat., Am. Pediatric Soc., Soc. Pediatric Rsch., Alpha Omega Alpha. Office Phone: 850-505-4790. Personal E-mail: rparmley@nemours.org.

PARNELL, FRANCIS WILLIAM, JR., otolaryngologist; b. Woonsocket, RI, May 22, 1940; s. Francis W. and Dorothy V. (Lalor) P.; m. Diana DeAngelis, Feb. 27, 1965; children: Cheryl Lynn, John Francis, Kathleen Diana, Alison Anne, Thomas William. Student, Coll. Holy Cross, 1957-58; AB, Clark U., 1961; MD, Georgetown U., 1965. Diplomate: Nat. Bd. Med. Examiners, Am. Bd. Otolaryngology. Intern Univ. Hosps., Madison, Wis., 1965-66, resident in gen. surgery, 1966-67, otolaryngology, 1967-70; pvt. practice medicine specializing in otolaryngology San Rafael, Calif., 1972-75, Greenbrae, Calif., 1978—2000; chmn., pres., CEO Parnell Pharms., San Rafael, Calif., 1982—. Cons. corp. med. affairs, 1978-82; corp. med. dir. Becton, Dickinson & Co., Rutherford, N.J., 1976-78; clin. instr. U. Calif. at San Francisco, 1972-75, asst. clin. prof., 1975-76; Alt. del., U.S. Del. 27th World Health Assembly WHO, Geneva, 1974. Contbr. articles to profl. jours. Candidate Calif. State Assembly, 1988; bd. dirs. Marin Coalition, 1980-96, 97-01, chmn., 1986-87; trustee Ross (Calif.) Sch. Dist., 1981-89; mem. governing bd. Marin Cmty. Coll. Dist., 1995-03, pres., 1999-00, 02-03; dir. Coll. Marin Found., 2004-10, pres., 2006-10. Maj. M.C. AUS, 1970-72, lt. col. M.C., USAR, 1985-93. Fellow ACS (gov. 1988-94), Am. Acad. Otolaryngology. Home: PO Box 998 Ross CA 94957-0998 Office: 1100 S Eliseo Dr Greenbrae CA 94904-2017 Office Phone: 415-256-1800.

PARNEY, IAN, neurosurgeon, educator; b. Calgary, Alta., Can., May 13, 1969; MD, U. Alta., 1993, PhD, 1999. Assoc. prof. neurologic surgery Mayo Clinic, 2008. Office: 200 First St Rochester MN 55905 Business E-Mail: parney.ian@mayo.edu.

PARNHAM, MICHAEL JOHN, pharmacologist, researcher; b. London, Mar. 13, 1951; arrived in Croatia, 1998; s. Walter and Sheila Jean (Horsman) Parnham; m. Elaine Cordelia Whitehead, Aug. 9, 1975; children: Philip, Joanna, Ian, Simon. BSc, London U., 1973; PhD, Bristol U., Eng., 1976; Habil. Pharmacology and Toxicology, Frankfurt U., Germany, 1990. Rsch. fellow Erasmus U., Rotterdam, Netherlands, 1976—80; rsch. scientist A. Nattermann & Cie. GmbH, Cologne, Germany, 1980—82, head immunopharmacology, 1982—85; dir. gen. biology Rhône-Poulenc, Cologne, 1985—90, mgr. internat. project, 1985—90; founding pres. Parnham Adv. Svcs., Bonn, Germany, 1990—98, FIRE GmbH, Bonn, 1992—97; dir. pharmacology and toxicology PLIVA, Zagreb, Croatia, 1998—2002, sr. sci. advisor, 2002—06; dir. preclinical discovery GlaxoSmithKline Rsch. Ctr., Zagreb, 2007—08. Adj. prof. Goethe U., Frankfurt/Main, Germany, 1990—. Editor: Discoveries in Pharmacology, 1983—86, Progress in Inflammation Rsch., 1996—, Milestones in Drug Therapy, 1997—; mng. editor: Inflammation Rsch., 1991—, news editor: Experientia, 1992—95, editor-in-chief: Encyclopedia of Inflammatory Diseases, 2007—. Elder, Bible sch. tchr. Christliche Gemeinde Köln, Cologne, 1986—97; deacon Zagreb Bapt. Ch., 1999—2001. Recipient Gosling prize, Dutch Rheumatology Assn., 1980, Galenus prize, German Med. Assn., 1990, PLIVA award, 2002, 2004. Mem.: European Assn. Sci. Editors, Internat. Assn. Inflammation Socs. (com. 1992—), European Inflammation Soc. (sec. 1980—88, 1995—99), German Soc. Pharmacology and Toxicology, Inst. Biology (U.K.), Brit. Pharmacol. Soc. Achievements include co-invention of EBSELEN; contribution to first biogeneric drug in Europe. Avocations: church activities, movies, walking, photography. Home and Office: Pozarinje 7 10-000 Zagreb Croatia Personal E-mail: mjparnham@yahoo.co.uk.

PARODI, ANDRÉ LAURENT MARIE, veterinary medicine educator; b. Sidi-Bel-Abbès, Algeria, Aug. 6, 1933; m. Monique Blanchard-Gaillard; 2 children. DVM, Pasteur Inst.; D honoris causa, U. Cordoba, U. Bucharest. Diplomate veterinary medicine. Prof. vet. pathology Ecole Nationale Vètèrinaire, Alfort, France, 1977—2001, dean, 1992—98; mem. sci. com. on animal health European Union, 1997—2003. Mem. WHO Expert Group Animal Tumors Classification, 1974—75, European Cmty. Expert Group Enzootic Bovine Leukosis, 1974—82; hon. dir. Ecole Nationale Vètèrinaire dAlfort, 1998—, prof. emeritus, 2001—, internat. affairs dep., 2004—08; pres. Nat. Com. for Ethics in Animal Experimentation, 2006—10. Contbr. over 150 articles to profl. jours. Decorated chevalier Ordre Nat. Merite, comdr. Ordre Palmes Academiques, officer Ordre Merite Agr., Ordre Legion d'honneur. Mem. World Assn. Vet. Pathologists (pres. 1986-98), Internat. Assn. for Comparative Rsch. on Leukemia and Related Diseases, European Coll. Vet. Pathologists (pres. 1999-2000) Am. Coll. Vet. Pathologists, Vet. Acad. France (pres. 2000), Nat. Acad. Medicine, Am. Soc. Toxicol. Pathology. Achievements include research in animal and comparative oncology. Office: Ecole Nat Vet Dept Anat-Path 94704 Maisons-Alfort France Office Phone: 33 1 43967260. E-mail: alparodi@vet-alfort.fr.

PARR, GRANT VAN SICLEN, surgeon; b. NYC, Dec. 30, 1942; s. Ferdinand Van Siclen and Helene H. P.; m. Helen Mushat Frye, July 1, 1967; children: Kathleen Gage, Helen Johnston. AB with honors, Wesleyan U., 1965; MD, Cornell U., 1969. Diplomate Am. Bd. Thoracic Surgery, Am. Bd. Surgery. Intern, resident U. Hosps. of Cleve., 1969-71; resident in surgery U. Ala. Hosps., Birmingham, 1971-74, chief resident in surgery, 1974-75, resident in cardiovascular and thoracic surgery, 1975-77; practice medicine specializing in thoracic surgery Hershey, Pa., 1978-82; mem. staff Presbyn.-U. Pa. Med. Ctr., Phila., 1982-88, chief div. Thoracic surgery, 1984-88, acting chmn. Dept. Surgery, 1988, chief cardiovascular surgery, 1984-88; asst. prof. cardiothoracic surgery M.S. Hershey Med. Center, Hershey, Pa., 1987-88; chief cardiovascular surgery Morristown (N.J.) Meml. Hosp., 1988-97, co-chmn. dept. cardiovasc. scis., 1997—2004, chmn. dept. cardiovasc. medicine, 2004—06, med. dir. Cardiac Svc. Line, 2004—; asst. prof. Pa. State U., 1978-82; clin. assoc. prof. surgery U. Pa., 1982-89; assoc. prof. clin. surgery Columbia U., 1992—2010; physician in chief Gagnon Cardiovascular Inst., 2007—. Chief cardiovasc. surgery Overlook Hosp., 1988—, Morristown Meml. Hosp., 1988—98; chmn. cardiovasc. surgery Atlantic Health Sys., 1998—, trustee, 1998—2011, med. dir. cardiac svcs., 2004—;

vice chair Morris Township Parks and Recreation Found., 2005—; bd. mem. Homeless Solutions Inc., 2007—, Morristown Meml. Health Found., 2008—. Contbr. articles to profl. jours. Fellow Am. Coll. Cardiology, ACS, Am. Coll. Chest Physicians, Phila. Coll. Physicians, Royal Soc. Medicine; mem. AMA, Internat. Cardiovascular Soc., Assn. of Acad. Surgeons, Am. Assn. Thoracic Surgery, County Med. Soc., Soc. Thoracic Surgeons, Soc. Critical Care Medicine Pa., Thoracic Surg. Soc., John W. Kirklin Soc., Morris County Med. Sch., NJ Soc. Thoracic Surgery, N.Y. Soc. Thoracic Surgery, Morris County Golf Club, NYU Club, Beaverkill Trout Club (pres., 2005-11). Office: 100 Madison Ave Morristown NJ 07960-1956 Office Phone: 973-971-5597.

PARRILLO, JOSEPH EDISON, JR., cardiologist, allergist, immunologist; b. Paterson, NJ, Jan. 5, 1947; MD, Cornell U., 1972. Diplomate Am. Bd. Allergy and Immunology, Am. Bd. Internal Medicine, Am. Bd. Cardiology. From intern to resident in medicine Mass. Gen. Hosp., Boston, 1972-74, fellow in cardiology, 1978-80; resident in medicine N.Y. Hosp.-Cornell Med. Ctr., NYC, 1977-78; resident in allergy & immunology and infectious disease Clin. Ctr. Nat. Inst. Allergy and Immunology Disease, Bethesda, Md., 1974-77; med. staff Rush-Presbyn.-St. Lukes Med. Ctr., Chgo.; chief divsn. cardiology and critical care medicine Rush Heart Inst.; dir., chief medicine Cooper Heart Inst.; Edward Viner chmn. Dept. Med. Cooper U. Hosp.; and prof. medicine UMDNJ-RWJMS at Camden. Mem. Am. Coll. Cardiology, Am. Fedn. Clin. Rsch., Am. Heart Assn., Am. Soc. Clin. Investigation, Assoc. Am. Phys., Am. Coll. Critical Care Medicine, Am. Coll. Chest Physicians, Soc. Critical Care Medicine, Alpha Omega Alpha. Office: Cooper Univ Hosp Dorrance Bldg 3d Fl One Cooper Plaza Camden NJ 08103 Office Phone: 856-968-8349. Business E-Mail: Parrillo-Joseph@cooperhealth.edu.

PARRISH, EARL H., plastic surgeon, educator; Attended, U. Ill.; MD, Wash. U., St. Louis. Diplomate Am. Bd. Plastic Surgery, Am. Bd. Surgery. Intern surgery Ind. Univ. Med. Ctr.; resident gen. surgery Strong Meml. Hosp.; resident plastic surgery Univ. Rochester, NY; clin. assoc. prof. surgery Oreg. Health Sciences Univ.; cons. Child Devel. and Rehab. Ctr., Oreg.; staff mem. Rogue Valley Med. Ctr., Ashland Cmty. Hosp.; Emeritus staff Providence Medford Med. Ctr. Mem.: Oreg. Med. Soc., Am. Med. Soc., Lipoplasty Soc., Am. Soc. of Plastic Surgeon, Am. Soc. for Aesthetic Plastic Surgery. Office: Parrish Cosmetic & Plastic Surgery Center 701 Golf View Dr Medford OR 97504 Office Phone: 800-458-0684.

PARRISH, MATTHEW DENWOOD, psychiatrist; b. Washington, Apr. 1, 1918; s. Forrest Denwood and Alice Lorena (Flynn) P.; m. Virginia John Bennet, Sept. 24, 1944 (div.); children: Denwood, John, Stephen; m. Marilyn Kay Arney, May 29, 1978; children: Megan, Maxwell. BA, U. Va., 1939; MD, George Washington U., 1950. Diplomate Am. Bd. Psychiatry. Intern Letterman Hosp., San Francisco, 1950-51; resident in psychiatry Walter Reed Hosp., Washington, 1951-54; commd. 2d lt. U.S. Army, 1941, advanced through grades to col., 1967, ret., 1971; chief tng. Ill. Dept. Mental Health, Chgo., 1972-74; supt. Singer Mental Health Ctr., Rockford, Ill., 1974-85, med. dir., 1985-93; child and adolescent psychiatrist, 1986-95; ret., 1996. Clin. prof. psychiatry U. Ill., Chgo., 1972-76; clin. asst. prof. psychiatry Coll. Med., Rockford, 1976—. Editor in chief: U.S. Army Vietnam Medical Journal, 1967-68. Decorated Legion of Merit (2). Fellow Am. Psychiat. Assn. (life); mem. Soc. Med. Cons. in Armed Forces, Assn. Mil. Surgeons U.S. Avocations: writing, photography, painting, linguistics, electronics. Office Phone: 815-399-4504.

PARRISH, OVERTON BURGIN, JR., pharmaceutical corporation executive; b. Cin., May 26, 1933; s. Overton Burgin and Geneva Opal (Shinn) P. BS, Lawrence U., 1955; MBA, U. Chgo., 1959. With Pfizer, Inc., 1959-74; salesman Pfizer Labs., Chgo., 1959-62, asst. mktg. product mgr. NYC, 1962-63, product mgr., 1964-66, group product mgr., 1966-67, mktg. mgr., 1967-68, v.p. mktg., 1969-70, v.p., dir. ops., 1970-71; exec. v.p. domestic pharm. div. Pfizer Pharms., 1971-72; exec. v.p., dir. Pfizer Internat. Divsn., 1972-74; pres., chief operating officer G.D. Searle Internat., Skokie, Ill., 1974-75, pres., chief exec. officer, 1975-77; pres. Worldwide Pharm./Consumer Products Group, 1977-86; pres., chief exec. officer Phoenix Health Care, Chgo., 1987—; chmn., CEO, bd. dirs. Wis. Pharmiacal Co., Inc., 1990-96; co-chmn. Inhalon Pharms., 1991-95, also bd. dirs.; chmn. ViatiCare Financial Services, LLC, 1993—, also bd. dirs.; chmn., CEO, bd. dirs. Female Health Co., 1996—. Bd. dirs., chair Abiant Inc.; dir. Pharms. Inc., 2007—. Author: The Future Pharmaceutical Marketing; International Drug Pricing, 1971. Trustee Mktg. Sci. Inst.; trustee Food and Drug Law Inst., 1979-86, Lawrence U., 1983-87, 98—. Served to 1st lt. USAF, 1955-57. Mem. Beta Gamma Sigma, Phi Kappa Tau.

PARROTT, SHARON, federal agency administrator; BA in Economics, U. Mich., Ann Arbor, MA in Social Work. Positions to dir. welfare reform and income support policy Ctr. Budget & Policy Priorities, 1993—99, 2001—09; sr. policy advisor DC Dept. Human Svcs., 1999—2000; counselor to sec. for human svcs. policy US Dept. Health & Human Services, Washington, 2009—. Office: HHS 200 Independence Ave SW Rm 600E1 Washington DC 20201 Office Phone: 202-690-5400. E-mail: sharon.parrott@hhs.gov. *

PARRY, TREVOR STEWART, pediatrician; b. Perth, Australia, July 1, 1939; s. Clifford Foster and Margaret Bold Parry; m. Elizabeth Jean Rippingale, Dec. 19, 1965; children: Bronwyn Margaret, David Stewart. MBBS, U. We. Australia, 1962; DPH, U. Bristol, 1970; DS in Cmty. Health, U. London, 1970; postgrad, Eng., 1973. Registered physician Royal Australian Coll. Med. Administrs., 1976; Med. Bd. Western Australia, 1963. Resident Royal Perth Hosp., Perth, Australia, 1964, Princess Margaret Hosp. Children, 1965; med. officer Ba (Fiji) Meth. Hosp., 1966; divisional med. officer Govt. Sarawak, Limbang, Malaysia, 1967—69; sr. med. officer Health Dept. We. Australia, Perth, Australia, 1973—76, sr. devel. paediatrician, dir. State Child Devel. Ctr. Women's and Children's Health Svc., 1976—2004, head Dept. Cmty. and Developmental Pediats. Women'sand Children's Health Svc., 1999—2004, emeritus cons. Women's and Children's Health Svc., 2004—. Pediatrician Ngala-a Mothercraft Home and Tng. Ctr., 1972—81; pediatrician Assessment Clinic Princess Margaret Hosp., 1973—2000, physician Neurology Clinic, 1975—95; physician Developmental Pediat. Clinic King Edward Meml. Hosp. Women, Australia, 1977—90; from adj. sr. lectr. to clin. assoc. prof. Sch. Paediatrics and Child Health U. We. Australia, 1992—2000, clin. assoc. prof. Sch. Paediatrics and Child Health, 2000—; cons. in field. Lay preacher Uniting and Anglican Chs., Perth, 1959; youth work and spkr. Scripture Union Meth Uniting Ch., Perth, 1957—2000; pastoral asst. Anglican Ch. Diocese Perth, Perth; chmn. Family Partnership Tng. Australia, Perth, 2003. Recipient Children and Young People's Lifetime Achievement award, 2010; named West Australian Litig. of Yr., 2010; fellow, Nestles Corp., 1971, WHO, 1976. Fellow: Royal Australian Coll. Physicians (John Sands medal 2006); mem.: Autism Assn. We. Australia (bd. dirs. 2004, dep. chair 2008), National Investment for the Early Years Australia (chmn. West Australia chpt. 2002). Achievements include development of one of the first (if not the first) community based and hospital linked multdisciplinary Child Development Centres in Australia with postgraduate training; postgraduate curriculum development in community paediatrics for College; first to introduction in Australia of family partnership training; introduction in Australia of the emotional literacy program, roots of empathy; establishment of other child development centres in Western Australia; development of follow-up of low birth weight infants in Western Australia; training in the Griffiths developmental scales for children into Western Australia; Stycar Screening/Developmental screening for commuity nursing in Western Australia. Avocations: singing, music, theater, reading, walking. Office: 64 Churchill Avenue Subiaco Western Australia Perth 6019 Australia Office Fax: 61.08.93814522. Business E-Mail: trevor@cyllene.uwa.edu.au.

PARSA, FEREYDOUN DON, plastic surgeon; b. Tehran, Iran, May 20, 1942; came to U.S., 1970; s. Issa and Zahra (Bismark) P.; m. Touri Akhlaghi, June 17, 1972; children: Natalie, Alan, Sean. MD, Lausanne U., Switzerland, 1969. Diplomate Am. Bd. Plastic Surgery. Chief of plastic surgery, prof. surgery U. Hawaii, Honolulu, 1981—. Contbr. articles to profl. jours. Mem. AMA, Am. Soc. Plastic Surgeons, Hawaii Med. Assn. Avocation: painting. Office: U Hawaii Sch Med Surgery 1329 Lusitana St 807 Honolulu HI 96813-2421 Office Phone: 808-526-0303. Personal E-mail: hawaiiplasticsurgery@yahoo.com.

PARSONS, CHRIS HAMILTON, medical educator; b. Columbus, Ohio, Dec. 14, 1970; MD, Case Western Res. U. Sch. Medicine, 1998; degree in Internal Medicine, Johns Hopkins Sch. Medicine, 2001. Asst. prof. medicine and craniofacial biology Med. U. SC, 2006—. Recipient award, Infectious Diseases Soc. Am.; Investigator-Initiated Rsch. Project grant, Nat. Cancer Inst., grant, Nat. Inst. Allergy and Infectious Diseases. Mem.: Am. Soc. Microbiology, Am. Assn. Cancer Rsch., Infectious Diseases Soc. Am. Home: 1394 Crystal Shore Ct Charleston SC 29412 Business E-Mail: parsonch@musc.edu.

PARSONS, ROSALEEN BRIDGETTE, diagnostic radiologist; MD, Med. Coll. of Phila., 1986. Diplomate Am. Bd. of Radiology-diagnostic radiology. Intern internal medicine Albert Einstein Med. Ctr., 1987; resident diagnostic radiology Hosp. of the Univ. of Pa., 1991; chair dept. of diagnostic imaging Fox Chase Cancer Ctr. Mem. edtl. bd. Journal of Women's Imaging; manuscript reviewer Radiology, Radiographics, Am. Journal of Radiology, Acta Radiology; counselor Am. Coll. of Radiology; assoc. prof. radiology Mt. Sinai Med. Ctr. Fellow: Am. Coll. of Radiology (bd. examiner 1997—); mem.: Internat. Soc. of Oncologic Imaging, Soc. of Uroradiology, Radiol. Soc. of N. Am., Am. Roentgen Ray Soc. Office: Fox Chase Cancer Center 7701 Burholme Ave Philadelphia PA 19111

PARSONS, WILLIAM JONATHAN, cardiologist; b. Apr. 3, 1955; married; 3 children. BA, Dartmouth Coll., 1977, MD, 1980. Diplomate Am. Bd. Internal Medicine, Am. Bd. Cardiovascular Diseases, Am. Bd. Nuclear Cardiology, Nat. Bd. Echocardiography. Resident in internal medicine Strong Meml. Hosp. U. Rochester (N.Y.), 1983-85; cardiology fellow Duke U. Med. Ctr., Durham, 1985-88, asst. prof., 1988-91; asst. prof. medicine Southwestern Med. Ctr. U. Tex., Dallas, 1991-93; attending cardiologist Baylor U. Med. Ctr., Dallas, 1993—2001, WakeMed Health & Hosps., Raleigh, NC, 2001—. Contbr. articles to profl. jours. Gen. med. officer USPHS-IHS, 1981-83. Fellow Am. Coll. Physicians, Am. Coll. Cardiology, Am. Soc. Echocardiography, Am. Soc. Nuc. Cardiology. Office: Carolina Cardiology WakeMed 3324 Six Forks Rd Raleigh NC 27609 Home Phone: 919-845-6743; Office Phone: 919-781-7772. Personal E-mail: sereneparsons@aol.com. *

PART, HOWARD MITCHELL, dean; b. NYC, Apr. 26, 1949; m. Kristine Kunesh-Part. BS, Ohio U.; MD, Ohio State U., 1982. Cert. Am. Bd. Internal Medicine. Intern Ohio State U. Hospitals, Columbus, 1982—83, resident in internal medicine, 1983—85; voluntary faculty mem. Wright State U. Sch. Medicine, Dayton, Ohio, 1986—88, mem. faculty, 1988—, chief of gen. medicine consult svc., dir. internal medicine residency program Dayton VA Med. Ctr., assoc. dean faculty and clin. affairs, 1995—98, acting dean, 1998—99, dean, 1999—. Recipient Dean's Award for Excellence in Med. Edn., Wright State U. Sch. Medicine, 1992, Disting. Teaching award, 1996, Master Teacher of Medicine award, Am. Coll. of Physicians, 2000. Fellow: Am. Coll. Physicians (Gov.'s Award - Ohio Chpt.); mem.: Am. Bd. of Internal Medicine. Office: Wright State University Boonshoft Sch Medicine Office of Dean Univ Park 3817 Colonel Glenn Hwy Dayton OH 45435 Office Phone: 937-775-2933. Office Fax: 937-775-2211. *

PARTAIN, CLARENCE LEON, radiologist, nuclear medicine physician, educator, health facility administrator; b. Memphis, July 12, 1940; s. Archie Leon and Vergie (Young) P.; m. Judith Stafford, Jan., 1964; children: David Blane, Teri Ellyn, Amy Leigh. BSNE, U. Tenn., 1963; MSNE, Purdue U., 1965, PhD in Nuc. Engring., 1967; MD, Washington U., St. Louis, 1975. Diplomate Am. Bd. Nuc. Medicine, Am. Bd. Radiology; registered profl. engr., Mo. Asst. prof. nuc. engring. U. Mo.-Columbia, 1968-71, assoc. prof., 1971-75; resident NC Meml. Hosp., Chapel Hill, 1975-79; assoc. prof. radiology U. NC-Chapel Hill, 1978-79; assoc. prof. Vanderbilt U., Nashville, 1980-85, prof. radiology and biomed. engring., 1985—, vice chmn. radiology, 1989-92, dir. nuc. medicine, 1981-85, dir. magnetic resonance imaging, 1983-92, chmn. radiology, radiologist in chief, 1992-2000, dir. Ctr. for Imaging Rsch., 2000—; cons. NIH, Bethesda, Md., 1980—; Carol D. and Henry P. Pendegrass prof. radiology and radiol. scis. Vanderbilt U., 1997—. Pres. SE chpt., Soc. Nuc. Medicine, 1984—85; editor, jour. MRI Internat. Soc. Magnetic Resonance Imaging, 2000—; bd. dirs. Internat. Soc. MRI, 2000—, Rad Soc. N.Am., Rsch. and Edn. Found., 2003—09; pres. Radiology Rsch. Alliance, Assoc. U. Radiologists, 2004—05; Paul Ross lectr. U. Mich. Author: Nuclear Magnetic Resonance (NMR) Imaging, 1983, NMR Imaging: Clinical Utility and Correlation, 1984, Thyroid and Parathyroid Imaging, 1986, Magnetic Resonance Imaging, 2d edit., 1988, Correlative Image: Nuclear Medicine, Magnetic Resonance, Computer Tomography, Ultrasound, 1988; editl. bd. Acad. Radiology, Magnetic Resonance Imaging, Jour. Magnetic Resonance Imaging, Jour. Nuclear Medicine; editor-in-chief Jour. of Magnetic Resonance Imaging. Scientific adv. coun. Whitaker Found. AEC Spl. fellow, 1964-66; grantee Nat. Inst. Neurosci., Communicative Diseases and Stroke, 1977-78 Fellow Am. Coll. Nuc. Physicians, Am. Coll. Radiology, Soc. Magnetic Resonance Imaging (bd. dirs.), Internat. Soc. of Magnetic Resonance in Medicine, Accreditation Coun. for Grad. Med. Edn., Residency Rev. Com. Nuc. Medicine; mem. AMA, IEEE, Radiol. Soc. N.Am. (chair rsch. devel. com., trustees, R&E Found.), Assn. Univ. Radiologists (exec. com.), Radiology Rsch. Alliance (pres.), Soc. Nuc. Medicine (trustee, Benedict Casson lectr. 1981), Am. Roentgen Ray Soc. (exec. coun.), Soc. Magnetic Resonance in Medicine (trustee), Internat. Soc. Magnetic Resonance in Medicine (governance coun., bd. dirs.), Soc. Chmn. Acad. Radiology Depts. (bd. dirs.), Am. Bd. Radiology (examiner in nuc. medicine, Disting. Svc. award), Sigma Phi Epsilon. Baptist. Avocation: travel. Office: Vanderbilt U Med Ctr Dept Radiology RM RR-1223 MCN Nashville TN 37232-0001 Home: 6224 Belle Rive Dr Brentwood TN 37027

PARTHEMORE, JACQUELINE GAIL, internist, educator, hospital administrator; b. Harrisburg, Pa., Dec. 21, 1940; d. Philip Mark and Emily (Buvit) Parthemore; m. Alan Morton Blank, Jan. 7, 1967; children: Stephen Eliot, Laura Elise. BA, Wellesley Coll., 1962; MD, Cornell U., 1966. Diplomate Am. Bd. Internal Medicine. Resident in internal medicine N.Y. Hosp./Cornell U., 1966-69; fellow in endocrinology Scripps Clinic and Rsch. Found., La Jolla, Calif., 1969-72; rsch. ednl. assoc. VA Hosp., San Diego, 1974-78; staff physician VA San Diego Health Care Sys., 1978-79, asst. chief, med. svc., 1979-83, acting chief, med. svc., 1980-81, chief of staff, 1984—2009, vol. staff physician, 2009—; asst. prof. medicine U. Calif. Sch. Medicine, San Diego, 1974-80, assoc. prof. medicine, 1980—85, prof. medicine, assoc. dean, 1985—2009, clin. prof. medicine, 2009—. Mem. nat. rsch. resources coun. NIH, Bethesda, Md., 1990—94; mem. Blue Ribbon Panel Acad. Affiliations, 2007—09. Contbr. chapters to books, articles to profl. jours. Mem. adv. bd. San Diego Opera, 1993—2009; mem. Roundtable and Channel 10 Focus Group, San Diego Millennium Project, 1999; v.p. bd. dirs. San Diego Vets. Med. Rsch. Found., 1989—2009; mem. Vet. Rsch. Coun., 2009—. Recipient Bullock's 1st Annual Portfolio award, 1985, San Diego Pres.'s Coun. Woman of Yr. award, 1985, YWCA Tribute to Women in Industry award, 1987, San Diego Women Who Mean Bus. award, 1999, Excellence in Leadership award Am. Hosp. Assn., 2002, Local Legend award AMWA/Nat. Libr. Medicine, 2005. Fellow ACP (gov. 2005-09, mem. edn. com. 2006-09, vice-chair edn. com. 2008-09), Am. Assn. Clin. Endocrinologists; mem. Endocrine Soc., Nat. Assn. VA Chiefs Staff/Physician Execs. (pres. 1989-91), Assn. Am. Med. Colls. (mem. steering group chief med. officers, 2005—09), Wellesley Coll. Alumnae Assn. (1st v.p. 1992-95), San Diego Wellesley Club (pres. 1997-99), San Diego Herb Soc. (co-pres. 2003-04), Nat. Assn. VA Rsch. and Ednl. Fedn. (bd. mem., 2003—09), Nat. Ctr. Leadership in Academic Medicine (mem. bd. UCSD 1998-). Avocations: gardening, reading, sailing, cooking, travel. Office: VA San Diego Healthcare Sys 3350 La Jolla Village Dr San Diego CA 92161-0002 Home Phone: 858-756-2917; Office Phone: 858-552-7419. Business E-Mail: jparthemore@ucsd.edu.

PARTHIER, BENNO, biologist; b. Holleben, Germany, Aug. 21, 1932; s. Hermann and Helene (Bielig) P.; m. Christiane Luecke, Aug. 19, 1968; children: Juliane, Christoph, Dorothea. Diploma in Biology, U. Halle, Germany, 1958, D of Natural Scis., 1961, D of Habilitation, 1967. Rsch. asst. U. Halle, 1958-61, docent, 1962-66; dept. head Acad. Scis. German Dem. Rep., Halle, 1967-90, prof. biology, 1975; dir. Fed. State Inst. Plant Biochemistry, Halle, 1990-97; prof. U. Halle, 1993. V.p. Deutsche Akademie Naturforsch Leopoldina, Halle, 1987-90, pres., 1990-2003; chmn. sci. commn. Sci. Coun., Koeln, Germany, 1991-97. Author: Die Leopoldina, 1994; editor (encyclopedia) Plant Physiology, 1982; editor Biochemie Physiol. Pflanzen jour., 1971. Mem. Saechsische Akad. Wissensch., Bayerische Akad. Wissensch., Academia Europaea, Berlin Akad. Wissenschaft. Avocation: gardening. Home: Am Birkenwaeldchen 12 D-06120 Halle Germany Office: Deutsche Akad der Naturforsch Leopoldina Emil Abderhalden Str 37 D-06108 Halle Germany Office Phone: 0049-345-4723915. Business E-Mail: parthier@leopoldina-halle.de.

PARULKAR, GURUKUMAR BHALCHANDRA, surgeon, consultant, medical educator; b. Bombay, Dec. 1, 1931; s. Bhalchandra Jivaji and Shantabai Bhalchandra (Bhandarkar) Parulkar; m. Vidya Dattatraya Telang, May 17, 1957; 2 children. MB BS, G.S. Med. Coll., Bombay, 1955, MS, 1958. Diplomate Med. Coun. India. Resident in surgery and cardiovasc. surgery G.S. Med. Coll./KEM Hosp., Bombay, 1955—58; lectr. in surgery G.S. Med. Coll., 1959—62; asst. prof. surgery G.S. Med. Coll./KEM Hosp., 1962-64, prof. surgery, 1964-74, dir. surgery, 1974-84, dean, dir., 1984-89; chmn. rsch. coun. Heart Inst., Bombay, 1990—. Cons. WHO, Geneva, 1975—95; bd. dirs. KEM Hosp., 1974—89, Heart Inst., 1990—, Khorakiwala Found., Bombay, 1992—. Contbr. articles to profl. jours. Mem. faculty Mcpl. Corp., Bombay, 1959—89; advisor Union Pub. Svc. Commn., New Delhi, 1975—89; mng. trustee G. M. Charitable Mission, Bombay, 1995—. Recipient US Pub. Health award, NIH, 1966, Dr. Evarts A. Graham award, Am. Assn. Thoracic Surgery, 1967, Dr. B. C. Roy Nat. award, Med. Coun., India, 1983, Eminent Med. Man. of Yr. award, Med. Coun. India, 1997, Sr. Brit. Commonwealth award, Brit. Coun., 1987, Padmabhushan award, Pres. of India, 1998. Mem.: Assn. Cardiovasc. Surgeons India, Assn. Cardiovasc. Surgeons Asia (pres. 1982—83, 1980—81, Presdl. medal of Lifetime Achievement 1982), Indian Assn. Surgeons, Indian Edn. Soc. (pres. 1983—84). Achievements include research in open heart surgery; heart transplantation; nonspecific aortoarteritis; discovery of online electrical impedence plethysmography. Home: KK Marg 4-31 Haji Ali Officers Qtrs 400034 Bombay India Office: Heart Inst 95 August Krant Marg 400 036 Bombay India Office Phone: 91-9820289391. Personal E-mail: gurukumar@gmail.com.

PARUNGAO, ALLAN J., plastic surgeon; BA, Wash. U., St. Louis; MA in Physiology, Chgo. Med. Sch.; MD, So. Ill. U. Diplomate Am. Bd. Plastic Surgery. Chief resident plastic surgery Southern Ill. Univ. Sch. Medicine. Author: A Woman's Guide to Cosmetic Breast Surgery and Body Contouring; contbr. chapters to books Bds. Rev. Series: Surgery. Plastic surgeon med. mission, Dumaguete, Philippines, 2001. Fellow: Am. Acad. Cosmetic Surgery, Am. Coll. Surgeons; mem.: Chgo. Soc. Plastic Surgeons, Am. Acad. Facial, Plastic and Reconstructive Surgery, Am. Soc. Plastic Surgeons. Avocations: running, triathlete. Office: Parungao Plastic Surgery 2425 W 22nd St Ste 213 Oak Brook IL 60523 Office Phone: 630-794-0700.

PARVATANENI, RADHIKA, medicinal chemist, researcher; d. Srinivasa Rao and Syamala Devi Parvataneni; m. Naga Prasad Tummala, May 5, 1993; children: Vishal Tummala, Vindhya Tummala. PhD, Andhra U., Visakhapatnam, India, 1997. From jr. rsch. fellow to rsch. assoc. Andhra U., 1993—2003, sr. rsch. assoc., 2003—06, asst. prof. dept. biochemistry, 2006—. Instr. Andhra U., 1993—. Contbr. articles to profl. jours. Bd. dirs. Vikas Ednl. Institutions Ltd., Visakhapatnam, 1998—2005. Scholar Telugu Vignana Parithoshikam, Govt. of Andhra Pradesh, 1986—89; Nat. Merit scholar, Ministry of Edn. and Culture, Govt. of India, 1984—92. Achievements include discovery of new and novel bio-active molecules. Home: 10-1-28 Asilmetta Andhra Pradesh Visakhapatnam 530003 India Office: Andhra Univ Andhra Pradesh Visakhapatnam 530003 India Home Fax: 8912755580. Personal E-mail: radhika_parvataneni_in@yahoo.com.

PARVATHI, AMMINI, oceanographer; b. Alappuzha, Kerala, India, Apr. 28, 1977; MSc, U. Agrl. Scis., 2002; PhD, Mangalore U., 2006. Scientist Nat. Inst. Oceanography, Regional Ctr., Kochi, India, 2007—. Recipient Young Scientist award, Assn. Microbiologists India, Fast Track Young Scientist award, Dept. Sci. and Tech., India. Mem.: Profl. Fisheries Graduates Forum (Mumbai), Assn. Microbiologists India. Home: Nat Inst Oceanography Kochi Kerala 682018 India Home Fax: 04842390614. Personal E-mail: parubfsc@yahoo.co.in.

PARVEZ, TARIQ, oncologist, consultant, department chairman; b. Multan, Pakistan, Apr. 5, 1952; s. Sheikh Muhammad Shafi and Sardar Begum; m. Kaniz Akhter, Nov. 14, 1976; children: Khurram, Babar, Amina. BSc in English Lit., Pakistan, 1975; MBBS, Nishtar Med. Coll., Pakistan, 1976; diploma in DMRT, Punjab U., 1988; MCPS in Radiation Oncology, Coll. Physician and Surgeon, Pakistan; MD USMLE Qualified, US, 1994. Cert. radiation oncologist. Demonstrator Allama Igbal Med. Coll., Lahore, Pakistan, 1979—85, asst. prof. radiation oncology, 1988—90; radiation oncologist Sir Ganga Ram Hosp., Lahore, 1990—97, Svcs. Hosp., Lahore, 1997—2001; cons. oncologist King Fahad Hosp., Madina Munawra, Saudi Arabia, 2001—06; med. dir. oncology PRA Internat., Charlottesville, Va., 2006—. Chmn. Pakistan Soc. Cancer Prevention, Lahore, 1993—. Author: Cancer No More A Threat, 1989, Cancer is Treatable, 1990, Cancer Treatments, Side Effects and Their Remedies, 1992, Diet and Cancer, 1993, Prevention of Cancer, 1994, Psychosocial Issues of Cancer Patients Family, 1995, Chemical Occupation and Cancer, 1997, Certain Facts About Breast Cancer, 2001; contbr. articles to rsch. publs. on cancer. Capt. Army M.C., 1976—79, Thal and Jhelum. Decorated Quaid-e-azam medal Pakistan Army; recipient Pres. Pakistan Gold medal, 1997, Disting. Leadership award, ABA, 1999, Hall of Fame award, 2000, Yr. 2000 Millennium medal of honor, 2000; fellow, Union Internat. Cancer Care, 1999. Mem.: Am Soc Clin Oncology, Radiol. Soc. Pakistan (life), Clin. Oncology Soc. (life). Avocations: movies, gardening. Home: 4617 Jalbert Dr Glen Allen VA 23060 Office: 4105 Lewis and Clark Dr Charlottesville VA 22911 Office Phone: 804-332-6465. Office Fax: 804-332-5577. Personal E-mail: tariq_parvez52@hotmail.com.

PASCERI, VINCENZO, cardiologist, researcher; b. San Nicola da Crissa, Italy, July 14, 1968; s. Rocco Pasceri and Giovanna Renda. MD, Cath. U. Sacred Heart, 1992, PhD, 2000. Lic. physician Italian Bd. Medicine, 1992, cert. in cardiology Italian Bd. Medicine, 1996. Resident cardiology Cath. U. Sacred Heart, Rome, 1992—96; rsch. fellow Tex. Heart Inst., Houston, 1998—2000, fellow interventional cardiology, 2000—01; attending cardiologist San Filippo Neri Hosp., Rome, 2002—. Chmn. study group Atorvastatin for Reduction of Myocardial Damage During Angioplasty, Rome, 2003—; cons. San Cosma Med. Assn., Rome, 2002—. Recipient Agostino Gemelli Grad. of Yr. award, Cath. U. Sacred Heart, 1992, Samuel A. Levine Young Clin. Investigator award, Am. Heart Assn., 1997. Fellow: Tex. Heart Inst. Cardiac Soc., Italian Soc. Interventional Cardiology, Am. Coll. Cardiology; mem.: Soc. for Cardiac Angiography Interventions. Roman Catholic. Achievements include research in role of C-reactive protein in atherosclerosis and coronary disease. Avocations: skiing, travel, history, archaeology. Office: San Filippo Neri Hospital Via G Martinotti 20 Rome 00135 Italy Home: Via Bartolomeo Avanzini 12 163 Rome RM Italy Office Fax: +390633062516. Personal E-mail: vpasceri@hotmail.com.

PASCHE, BORIS CLAUDE ROGER, hematologist, oncologist, educator; b. Lausanne, Vaud, Switzerland, Aug. 5, 1961; arrived in US, 1989; s. Rene Charles Edouard and Marina (Guidetti) Pasche. MD, Karolinska Inst., Stockholm, 1986, PhD, 1989; MD, U. Lausanne, Switzerland, 1987. Diplomate Am. Bd. Internal Med., Am. Bd. Med. Oncology, Am. Bd. Hematology, lic. NY, Ill., Ala. Rsch. fellow cardiovasc. medicine Brigham & Women's Hosp./Harvard Med. Sch., Boston, 1989-92; intern medicine NY Hosp./Cornell Med. Ctr., NYC, 1992-93, resident medicine, 1993-94; fellow hematology/oncology Meml. Sloan-Kettering Cancer Ctr., NYC, 1994—97; rsch. fellow cell biology Howard Hughes Med. Inst., Chevy Chase, 1996—2000; asst. prof. medicine Northwestern U. Feinberg Sch. Medicine, Chgo., 2001—05, assoc. prof. medicine, 2006—08; prof. medicine, dir. divsn. hematology/oncology U. Ala., Birmington, 2008—, Martha Ann & David L. May endowed chair cancer rsch., 2008—; assoc. dir. transnational rsch. U. Ala. Comprehensive Cancer Ctr., 2008—09, dep. dir., 2009—. Asst. physician NY Hosp./Meml. Sloan-Kettering Cancer Ctr., 1993—2000; attending physician Northwestern Meml. Hosp., 2001—08; co-leader cancer genes & molecular targeting program Robert H. Lurie Comprehensive Cancer Ctr., Chgo., 2006—07. Editor: Oncology, Genetics & Molecular Medicine, 2003—, Jour. Exptl. & Clin. Cancer Rsch., 2004—; contbr. articles to profl. jours. Recipient K12 Physician Scientist award, Nat. Cancer Inst., 1995—98, Human Cancer Genetics Program Commemorative Medal, Ohio State U., 2005; grantee Swiss Academic Soc. fellowship, 1983, Rsch. fellowship, Lausanne Academic Soc., 1984—86, Clin. Oncology fellowship, Am. Cancer Soc., 1994. Fellow: ACP; mem.: AMA, AAAS, Am. Soc. Clin. Investigation, Am. Fedn. Clin. Rsch., Am. Soc. Human Genetics, Am. Assn. Cancer Rsch., Am. Soc. Clin. Oncology, Am. Soc. Hematology, Internat. Soc. Thrombosis & Haemostasis (Young Scientist Merit award 1989, Young Investigator Merit award 1991), Bioelectromagenetics Soc., Nat. Inst. Electromed. Info., European Bioelectromagnetics Soc. Achievements include invention of electronic system for influencing cellular functions. Avocations: skiing, windsurfing, classical music, fine arts. Office: U Ala Divsn Hematology Oncology 1802 6th Ave S NP 2566 Birmingham AL 35294 Office Phone: 205-934-9591. Business E-Mail: uifcftu@uab.edu.

PASCHER, ANDREAS, medical educator, consulting surgeon, researcher; MD, Ludwig Maximilians U. Munich, 1991—97, PhD. Resident Dept. Abdominal and Transplant Surgery Med. Sch. Hannover, Germany, 1997—98; prof. dept. visceral and transplant surgery Charité U., Berlin, 1998—2004, sr. surgeon dept. visceral and transplant surgery Virchow, 2005—, dir. intestinal and multivisceral transplant program, 2005—, co-dir. kidney and pancreas transplantation, 2007—. Recipient Rsch. award, U. Munich, 1995, Excellence award, Cong. Immunosuppression, 2004; grantee David Geffen Sch. Med. UCLA, 4th Internat. Congress, 1997; fellow, Deutsche Forschungsgemeinschaft, 2004—. Fellow: German Coll. Surgeons. Office: Dept Surgery Charité Campus Virchow Augustenburgerplatz 1 Berlin 13353 Germany Office Fax: 004930450552900. Business E-Mail: andreas.pascher@charite.de.

PASCOTTO, RENATA CORRÊA, medical educator; b. Jaú, São Paulo, Brazil, Sept. 12, 1966; Degree in Odontology, U. São Paulo, 1987, PhD, 1995. Prof. State U. Maringá, 1991, assoc. prof., 2006. Mem.: Brazilian Soc. Aesthetic Dentistry, Internat. Assn. Dental Rsch. Avocation: reading. Home: 226 Saint Hilaire St Maringá Paraná 87015-160 Brazil Home Fax: 55 44 32623499. Personal E-mail: rpascotto@uol.com.br.

PASCUAL, RODOLFO M., pulmonologist, educator; b. Mar. 15, 1968; MD, Jefferson Med. Coll., 1994. Asst. prof. Wake Forest Bapt. Health, 2003—. Fellow: Am. Coll. Chest Physicians. Office: Nutrition Rsch Bldg Medical Center Blvd Winston Salem NC 27157 Business E-Mail: rpascual@wakehealth.edu.

PASCUZZI, ROBERT MARK, neurologist; b. Council Bluffs, Iowa, Oct. 1, 1953; s. Chris A. and Janice (Mayne) P.; m. Karen L. Roos; children: Anna, Janice. AB, Ind. U., Bloomington, 1976; MD, Ind. U., Indpls., 1979. Diplomate Am. Bd. Psychiatry and Neurology, Am. Bd. Electrodiagnostic Medicine. Intern Ind. U. Med. Ctr., Indpls., 1979-80; resident in neurology U. Va. Med. Ctr., Charlottesville, 1980-83, fellow in neuromuscular disease, 1983-85; prof. in neurology Ind. U. Sch. Medicine, Indpls., 1995—, vice chmn. edn., 1995, vice chmn. neurology, 1996—. Mem. med. staff Ind. U. Hosps., 1985—; chief neurol. svc. Wishard Meml. Hosp.; mem. med. adv. bd. Nat. Myasthenia Gravis Found., 1988—; lectr. in field; presenter at profl. confs. Editor-in-chief Seminars in Neurology, 1998; contbr. papers to profl. publs. Mem. Am. Acad. Neurology, Am. Assn. Electrodiagnostic Medicine, Ind. Neurol. Soc., Ctrl. Soc. Neurol. Rsch. Office: Ind Univ Sch Medicine Regenstrief Health Ctr 1050 W Walnut St Indianapolis IN 46202-5254

PASETTI, LOUIS OSCAR, retired dentist; b. Tampa, Fla., Dec. 27, 1916; s. Joseph G. and Carmen (Gonzalez) P.; m. Mary Mendez, Jan. 11, 1942; children: Louis M., Arleen Pasetti Mariotti. BS, U. Fla., 1937; DDS, Emory U., 1941; postgrad., U. Pa., 1978. Capt. U.S. Army, 1942—46; pvt. practice Tampa, Fla., 1947—2002; ret., 2002. Contbr. articles on Differential Diagnosis of Dental Pain. Past. pres. Tampa Civitan Club, 1953; past lt. gov. Civitan Clubs of Tampa, 1962; past dep. gov. Civitan Internat., Fla., 1964; fin. officer Am. Legion Post 248. Named Fla. Dentist of the Yr., Fla. Acad. Gen. Dentistry, 1983; recipient meritorious Svc. award Fla. Acad. Gen. Dentistry, 1989, Disting. Svc. award, 1985, finalist Nat. Competetion Humanterian award. Fellow Acad. Gen. Dentistry (Lifetime Achievement award 2004), Am. Coll. Dentists, Internat. Coll. Dentists, Acad. Dentistry Internat.; mem. ADA, Fla. Dental Assn., Fla. Acad. Gen. Dentistry (pres. 1981, Lifetime Achievement award 1996, mem. emeritus 2002), Tampa Bay Acad. Gen. Dentistry (pres. 1977-78), Elks, Round Table of Civic Clubs of Tampa (sec. 1953), Palma Ceia Golf and Country Club. Democrat. Roman Catholic. Avocations: photography, orchid culture. Home: 10023 Hampton Pl Tampa FL 33618-4227

PASHANKAR, FARZANA, hematologist, oncologist; b. Pune, India, Aug. 23, 1965; MBBS, Byramjee Jeejeebhoy Med. Coll., MD, 1988. Asst. prof. Yale U. Sch. Medicine, 2005—. Mem.: RCP (Eng.), Children's Oncology Group. Office: 333 Cedar St New Haven CT 06520 Business E-Mail: farzana.pashankar@yale.edu.

PASKAWICZ, JEANNE FRANCES, pain specialist; b. Phila., Mar. 3, 1954; d. Alex and Lillian (Pyluck) P. BSc, Phila. Coll. Pharmacy; MA, Villanova U., 1973; postgrad., St. Joseph U., 1979; PhD, Kensington U., 1984. Mem. anesthesiology staff Einstein Med. Ctr., Phila., 1990-94, Temple U. Hosp., 1994—; mem. detox./rehab. staff Presbyn. Med. Ctr., Phila., 1984—; house officer Tenet Hosps., Elkins Park, Pa., 1990—; mem. psychiatry staff Hahnemann U. Hosp., Phila., 1984-90; hostage negotiator Office of Mental Health, Phila., 1984-90; mem. surgery/anesthesiology staff Mt. Sinai Hosp., Phila., 1989-91; lectr. Drexel U., 2009—. Contbr. articles to profl. jours. Bd. dirs. Phila. Coll. Pharmacy, St. Joseph U. Mem. NAFE, Am. Pain Soc., Lambda Kappa Sigma.

PASKETT, ELECTRA, epidemiologist, oncologist, educator; PhD in Epidemiology, U. Wash. Prof. cancer rsch. divsn. epidemiology Ohio U. Sch. Pub. Health, assoc. dir. population sciences; co-program leader cancer control program Ohio U. Comprehensive Cancer Ctr.; dir. diversity enhancement program James Cancer Hosp.; chmn. cancer ctrl. & health outcomes com. Cancer & Leukemia Group B. Fellow: Am. Assn. Advancement Sci.; mem.: Am. Soc. Preventive Oncology (pres. elect). Office: Ohio State University Comprehensive Cancer Center 320 W 10th Ave Columbus OH 43210 Office Phone: 614-293-3917. Office Fax: 614-293-5611. E-mail: cansrp@gwumc.edu.

PASNOOR, MAMATHA, physician; b. India, Dec. 30, 1971; MD, Osmania Med. Coll., 1996. Physician U. Kans. Med. Ctr., 2002—, asst. prof. Mem.: Muscle Study Group, Neuropathy Assn., Myasthenia Gravis Found. Assn. Kans. City, Peripheral Nerve Soc., Am. Acad. Neurology. Avocation: travel. Office: 3599 Rainbow Blvd Kansas City KS 66160 Personal E-mail: mamathapasnoor@hotmail.com.

PASQUALOTTO, FABIO FIRMBACH, urologist, educator; b. Caxias do Sul, Rio Grande do Sul, Brazil, May 21, 1971; s. Arno Luiz and Marilena Firmbach Pasqualotto; m. Eleonora Bedin, Apr. 5, 1997; 1 child, Lucas Bedin. MD, U. Caxias do Sul, Brazil, 1993; MsC, U. São Paulo, Brazil, 2001, PhD, 2002. Prof. urology U. Caxias do Sul, 2003—; prof. clin. andrology Sapientae Inst., São Paulo, 2003—. Bd. dirs. Conception-Ctr. for Reproduction, Caxias do Sul; assoc. rschr. Ctr. for Advanced Rsch. in Human Reproduction, Fertility & Sexual Function, Cleve. Clinic Found., Cleve., 2003—; pres. andrology commn. Brazilian Soc. for Human Reproduction, São Paulo, Brazil, 2000—. Recipient Am. Soc. for Reproductive Medicine award, 1999, Internat. Soc. Andrology award, 2001. Avocation: travel. Office: Conception-Ctr for Reproduction Rua Pinheiro Machado 2569 Sl 23/24 95020-172 Caxias do Sul Rio Grande do sul Brazil Office Fax: 55 54 3215 1695. Business E-Mail: fabio@conception-rs.com.br.

PASQUARIELLO, JULIUS ANTHONY, pharmacist; b. Schenectady, NY, Aug. 3, 1960; s. Julius and Maria (Cervera) P. BS in Pharmacy, Albany Coll. Pharmacy, 1983. Cert. in geriatric pharmacy 2001, mem. 2010. Supervising pharmacist Brooks Pharmacy # 727, Schenectady, 1983-88, NRX Svcs. Inc., Guilderland, N.Y., 1988-90, Cmty. Health Plan, Delmar, N.Y., 1990-93; staff pharmacist, oncology pharmacist Kaiser Permanent, Latham, N.Y., 1993-99, Family Meds. Pharmacy, 1999-2000, Albany (N.Y.) Med. Ctr. Hosp. Pharmacy, 2000—04; staff pharmacist N.Y. State Dept. Health/Office Health Insurance Program, Albany, 2004—; pharmacist St. Peter's Hosp. Pharmacy, Albany, 2005—. Cons. pharmacy edn. com. Am. Cancer Soc., Albany, 1993—, N.Y. State Dept. Health, Medicaid Mgmt. Bur., Albany, N.Y. Avocations: golf, weightlifting, saxophone, running. Home: 345 Dolan Dr Schenectady NY 12306-1012 Office: 1 Commerce Plz Albany NY 12210

PASQUARIELLO, PATRICK S., JR., pediatrician; b. Phila., Mar. 29, 1930; MD, Jefferson Med. Coll., 1956. Cert. in pediat. Am. Bd. Pediat., 1963. Intern St. Joseph's Hosp., Phila., 1956—57; resident in pediat. Children's Hosp. of Phila., 1961—63, acting chief divsn., 1997—2000, dir. diagnostic ctr., dir. spina bifida program; prof. U. Pa. Sch. Medicine. Co-investigator Spina Bifida Rsch. Resource. Office: Childrens Hosp Phila Diagnostic Ctr 34th St and Civic Ctr Blvd Philadelphia PA 19104 also: Joseph Stokes Jr Rsch Inst Childrens Hosp Phila 1120 Wood Bldg Philadelphia PA 19104 Office Phone: 215-590-4020, 215-590-1760.

PASQUINI, MASSIMO, psychiatrist, researcher; b. Rome, July 20, 1973; MD, U. La Sapienza of Rome, 1998. Resident in psychiatry U. La Sapienza, Rome, 2002; cons. U. La Sapienza of Rome, 2002—05, San Camillo- Forlanini Hosp., Rome, 2003—05; psychiatrist Psychiatric Emergency Svcs., Policlinco Umberto I, Rome, 2006—; dir. Psychiatric Consultation and Liason Svcs., 2007—. Cons. S'Alessandro Clinic, Rome, 2002—06, 2006—. Recipient Pacini Sopsi award, 2004. Fellow: Am. Italian Cancer Found.; mem.: Assn. European Psychiatrists, Italian Soc. Psico-oncologia, Italian Soc. Psicopatologia. Office: University La Sapienza of Rome viale dell'Università 30 Rome Italy Office Fax: 0649914591. Personal E-mail: maxpasquini@tiscalinet.it. Business E-Mail: massimo.pasquini@uniromo1.it.

PASS, CAROLYN JOAN, dermatologist; b. Balt., May 14, 1941; d. Isidore Earl and Rhea (Koplowitz) P.; m. Richard Malcolm Susel, June 23, 1963; children: Steven, Gary. BS, U. Md., 1962, MD, 1966. Diplomate Am. Bd. Dermatology. Rotating intern USPHS Hosp., Balt., 1966-67; med. resident St. Agnes Hosp., Balt., 1967-68; dermatology resident and fellow U. Md. Sch. Medicine Hosps., 1968-71; pvt. practice specializing in dermatology Balt. and Ellicott City, Md., 1971—. Mem. staff St. Agnes Hosp.; vol. dermatology clinics U. Md., St. Agnes hosps.; asst. clin. prof. dermatology U. Md. Sch. Medicine, 1978—; mem. exec. com. adv. bd. Nat. Program in Dermatology, 1975. Mem. AMA, Med. and Chirurgical Soc. State Md. (del.), Balt. City Med. Soc. (del 1974, pub. rels. com., 1992-94, alternate del. 1994—), Am. Women's Med. Assn., Am. Acad. Dermatology (award exhibit 1970), Soc. Investigative Dermatology, Md. Dermatology Soc. (sec.-treas. 1974-76, pres. 1976-77), U. Md. Sch. Medicine Alumnae Assn. (bd. dirs. 1987—), Woodholme Country Club, Country Garden Club. Jewish. Avocations: gourmet cooking, gardening, art, golf. Office: Pine Heights Med Ctr 1001 Pine Heights Ave Ste 301 Baltimore MD 21229-5285 *

PASS, ROBERT, pediatrician; BS in chemistry, U. Ala., 1969, MD, 1973. Intern and resident in pediat. Stanford U. Med. Ctr., 1973—76; fellow in pediatric infectious diseases U. Ala., Birmingham, 1976—79, faculty in pediat., 1979—, prof. pediat. and microbiology. Fellow: Infectious Diseases Soc. America; mem.: Am. Soc. Virology, Am. Soc. Microbiology, Am. Pediatric Soc., Soc. Pediatric Rsch., Alpha Omega Alpha, Phi Beta Kappa. Office: Childrens Harbor Bldg 309 1530 3rd Ave S Birmingham AL 35294-0011 Office Phone: 205-934-2441, 205-996-4104. Office Fax: 205-934-2370. E-mail: rpass@peds.uab.edu.

PASSANTINO, ANNAMARIA, veterinarian, educator; b. Messina, Italy, Dec. 4, 1969; d. Michele Passantino and Felice Maria Rosa Montaperto; m. Carmelo Neal Giuseppe Russo, July 19, 2001. DVM with honors, U. Messina, 1993; PhD in Vet. Medicine, Dept. Vet. Medicine and Pharmacology, 1995. Rschr. Faculty Vet. Medicine, Messina, 1996—2001, prof., 2001—. Lectr. in field. Contbr. over 50 articles to profl. jours. Mem.: Leo Club (pres. Messina Iona chpt. 1996—97), Lions Club (pres. 1998—2000, dist. vice tail twister 2000—01, pres. com. dist. organ and bone marrow donation 2002—03, chmn. zone 2003—04, sec. Spadafora Tyrrhenum dist. 2004—05, region sec. 2005—06). Roman Catholic. Avocations: stamp collecting/philately, travel. Office: Faculty Vet Medicine Polo Universitario Annunziata 98168 Messina Italy Home: Salita Fosse 98168 Messina ME Italy Office Phone: 0039 090-3503742.

PASSEY, GEORGE EDWARD, psychologist, educator; b. Stratford, Conn., Sept. 28, 1920; s. Henry Richard and Elizabeth (Angus) P.; m. Algie Aldridge Ashe, Nov. 18, 1950; children— Richard Ashe, Elizabeth Aldridge, Mary Louise. BS, Springfield Coll., 1942; MA, Clark U., 1947; PhD, Tulane U., 1950. Asst. prof. U. Ala., Tuscaloosa, 1952-55, assoc. prof., 1955-56, 57-59, prof., 1959-63, prof. psychology, chmn. div. social and behavioral scis. Birmingham, 1967-73, prof. engring., 1969-84, Disting. Service prof. psychology, 1984-85, Disting Service prof. emeritus, 1985—; dean U. Ala. (Sch. Social and Behavioral Scis.), Birmingham, 1973—84. Research scientist Lockheed Ga. Co., Marietta, Ga., 1956-57, 63-65, cons., 1965-67; prof. Ga. Inst. Tech., 1965-67 Served with USNR, 1942-46, PTO; with USAF, 1951-52, lt. col. USAF, 1980 Fellow Am. Psychol. Assn.; mem. So.

Soc. for Philosophy and Psychology, Southeastern Psychol. Assn., Ala. Psychol. Assn., Sigma Xi. Home: 400 University Pk Dr Apt G15 Birmingham AL 35209-6787 E-mail: gpassey3299@charter.net, gpassey@connectedliving.com.

PASSLEY, JOSEF ANTONIO, psychologist, educator, writer; b. Kingston, Jamaica, Oct. 22, 1974; s. Harold Arnold and Yvonne Claire Passley; m. Staci Latreese Manago, July 29, 2005. AS, Lancaster Bible Coll., 1995, BS, 1996; MA, Towson U., Md., 1999; PhD, Walden U., 2004. Licensed Clinical Professional Counselor Md., 2004. Mental health worker Sheppard and Enoch Pratt Hosp., Towson, 1996—99, spl. edn. tchr., 1999—2000; child adolescent therapist Johns Hopkins Bayview Med. Ctr., Balt., 2000—05, sr. child, adolescent therapist Baltimore, Md., 2005—09; psychotherapist Cedar Ridge Counseling Ctr., Eldersburg, Md., 2005—08; owner, psychotherapist, cons. Passley Consulting & Psychol. Svcs., 2008—. Radio guest WOLB Radio, Lanham, Md., 2004—08; cons. Johns Hopkins Hosp., Balt., 2005—08; adj. prof. Lancaster Bible Coll., Pa., 2004—, U. Balt., 2005—; assoc. prof. Ctrl. Mich. U., 2006—; faculty assoc. Johns Hopkins U., 2006—, 2006—. Co-author: (tng. manual) Keeping Families Strong: A Clinic Based Intervention, Single Parenting in the 21st Century and Beyond; author (books), 2006, From Depression to Aggression: Understanding the Violent World of Urban Males, 2008. Recipient Psi Chi Nat. Honor Soc., Walden U., 2000, Outstanding Clinician award, Johns Hopkins Bayview Med. Ctr., 2003, Employee Excellence award, 2003. Mem.: Media Psychology (assoc.), Soc. Child and Adolescent Psychology (assoc.), Am. Assn. Christian Counselors (assoc.), APA (assoc.). Avocations: reading, travel. Office: Johns Hopkins Bayview Med Ctr 4940 Eastern Ave Baltimore MD 21224 Business E-Mail: jasphd1@yahoo.com.

PASTA, JIRI, physician, ophthalmologist, researcher; b. Turnov, Czech Republic, Dec. 1, 1952; s. Frantisek Pasta and Jitka Pastova; m. Miluse Jedlickova, Sept. 18, 1976 (div. Feb. 7, 1984); 1 child, Lenka Paikertova; m. Yveta Chvojkova, July 6, 1985; children: Eva Pastova, Barbora Pastova, Zuzana Pastova. MD, Charles U., Hradec Kralove, Czech Republic, 1978; PhD, Charles U., Prague, Czech Republic, 1992. Cert. first attestation ophthalmology-gen. ophthalmology, second attestation ophthalmology-ophthalmic surgery and leadership. Ophthalmologist dept. opthalmology Ctrl. Mil. Hosp., Prague, 1980—83, dep. head dept. ophthalmology, 1983—93, head dept. ophthalmology, 1993, head eye clinic, 2004. Asst. prof. first med. faculty Charles U., Prague, 1999—. Co-author: Head Imaging, 2000 (Hlavka prize, 2001). Col. Czech Army. Mem.: World Cataract Surgeons Soc., Czech Ophthalmic Soc., Can. Implant and Refractive Keratoplasty Assn., Am. Soc. Cataract and Refractive Surgery, Am. Acad. Ophthalmology. Avocations: chess, literature, computer games. Office: Ctrl Mil Hosp Eye Clinic U vojenske nemocnice 1200 Prague 169 02 Czech Republic Home: Vondrousova 1157/7 Prague 163 00 Czech Republic Office Fax: +420 224 314 098. E-mail: Jiri.Pasta@uvn.cz.

PASTAN, IRA HARRY, medical researcher; b. Winthrop, Mass., June 1, 1931; s. Jacob and Miriam (Ceder) Pastan; m. Linda Olenik, June 14, 1953; children: Stephen, Peter, Rachel. BS magna cum laude, Tufts U., Medford, Mass., 1953; MD magna cum laude, Tufts U. Sch. Medicine, 1957. Intern, asst. rschr. medicine Grace-New Haven Hosp., Yale U. Sch. Medicine, 1957-59; clin. assoc. Nat. Inst. Arthritis & Metabolic Disease (NIAMD), NIH, Bethesda, Md., 1959-61, postdoc. fellow lab. cellular physiology, Nat Heart & Lung Inst., 1961-62, sr. investigator sect. endocrine biochemistry, clin. endocrinology br. NIAMD, 1963-69; chief Lab. Molecular Biology, head molecular biology sect. Nat. Cancer Inst., NIH, Bethesda, Md., 1970—. Mem. sci. coun. Internat. Inst. Cellular & Molecular Pathology, Brussels, 1979—. Author, editor An Atlas of Immunofluorescence, 1985, Endocytosis, 1985; contbr. articles to profl. jours. Recipient Van Meter prize, Am. Thyroid Assn., 1971, Superior Svc. award, HHS, 1973, Meritorious Svc. medal, USPHS, 1983, Pierce Immunotoxin award, 1988, Internat. Antonio Feltrinelli prize for medicine, Accademia dei Lincei, Italy, 2009. Fellow: AAAS, Am. Soc. Microbiology; mem.: NAS, Inst. Medicine, Molecular Medicine Soc., Am. Acad. Arts & Scis., Am. Assn. Physicians, Am. Soc. Cell Biology, Am. Soc. Biol. Chemists, Am. Soc. Clin. Investigation, Peripatetic Club, Alpha Omega Alpha. Office: NCI Lab Molecular Biology Bldg 37 Rm 4E16 37 Convent Dr MSC 4255 Bethesda MD 20892 Office Phone: 301-496-4797. Office Fax: 301-402-1344. E-mail: pastani@mail.nih.gov, pasta@helix.nih.gov. *

PASTERNAC, ANDRÉ, cardiologist, educator; b. Toulouse, France, July 22, 1937; came to Can., 1971, naturalized, 1978. s. Jacques and Régine P. Adv. math., Lycée Henri IV, Paris, 1956; BA in Polit. Sci., Toulouse U., 1963, MD Med. Sch., 1968; grad. in Mgmt. Program, Columbia U., 2000. Cert. Ins. and Disability Assessment U. Montreal, 2002. Intern Toulouse Univ. Hosp., 1962-63, resident, 1963-64, Edouard-Herriot Hosp., Lyon, France, 1965-66; Fulbright scholar in cardiology Harvard U., 1968-71; research fellow Peter Bent Brigham Hosp., Boston, 1968-69; Milton fellow Children's Hosp., Boston, 1969-71; fellow in cardiology Toronto (Ont., Can.) U., 1971-72; staff cardiologist Montreal (Que., Can.) Heart Inst., 1972—; asst. prof. medicine U. Montreal, 1972-78, clin. assoc. prof., 1978—, clin. prof. medicine, 1994—. Vis. lectr. U. Liège (Belgium), 1977, U. Madrid, 1977, U. Warsaw, 1979, 83; cons. Harley St. Clinic, Cromwell Hosp., Wellington Hosp., London; vis. assoc. prof. McGill U., Montreal, 1975-76; medico-legal and ins. expert U. Montreal, 2002. Contbr. articles to profl. jours. Bd. dirs. Heart-Brain Rsch. Found. Inc., NYC, Cardiostat Canada Inc., Montreal, Cardiostat USA Inc., West Palm Beach, Fla. Am. Field Svc. grantee, Oreg., 1954-55. Mem. French Cardiac Soc., European Soc. Cardiology, Canadian Cardiovasc. Soc., Am. Coll. Cardiology, Am. Heart Assn., Internat. Soc. Heart Rsch., Am. Fedn. Clin. Rsch., NY Acad. Scis. Research in stress-related myocardial ischemia and dysfunction, mitral valve prolapse, cardiovascular drugs, cardiomyopathies, catecholamines, neuroendocrine control of the heart, stress and the heart, prevention of cardiovascular disease. Office: Westmount Square Health Group 1 Westmount Square Suite 550 Westmount PQ H3Z2PG Canada also: Ctr for Cardiovascular Disease Prevention 200 Butler St Ste 61 West Palm Beach FL 33407 also: Cardiovascular Disease Prevention Ctr 1045 95th St Ste 10 Bay Harbor Islands FL 33154 also: Balmoral Ste 7G 9801 Collins Ave Bal Harbour FL 33154 Office Phone: 561-659-6756. Personal E-mail: aparternac@gmail.com. E-mail: apasternac@aol.com.

PASTERNACK, STEFAN ALAN, psychiatrist, psychoanalyst; b. Jersey City, Nov. 5, 1939; BA, Cornell U., 1961; MD, Georgetown U., 1965. Diplomate in psychiatry Am. Bd. Neurology and Psychiatry; lic. physician, D.C., Md. Resident in psychiatry U. Cin. Gen. Hosp., 1966-69; psychiat. cons. North Cmty. Mental Health Ctr., Washington, 1971-97; asst. prof. psychiatry Georgetown U. Sch. Medicine, Washington, 1971-79, assoc. clin. prof. psychiatry, 1979-86, clin. prof. psychiatry, 1986—, co-dir. advanced studies prog. in psychiatry/psychoanalysis, 1995—; clin. prof. biomed. sci. Fla. Atlantic U., 2007—; tchg. analyst Fla. Psychoanalytic Inst., 2008—. Pvt. practice psychiatry and psychoanalysis, Washington, 1978-2005; Fla., 2005; faculty, Fla. Psychoanalytic Inst., 2006; clin. prof. psychiatry, Fla. Atlantic U., 2007. Editor: Violence and Victims, 1975; contbr. articles to profl. jours. Bd. dirs. Nat. Capital Med. Found., Washington, 1973-76, Forum for Psychoanalytic Study of Film, Washington, 1989—, vol. clin. prof. psychiatry U. Miami Miller Sch. Medicine, 2007-. Lt. comdr. USN, 1969-71. Mem.: Fla. Psychiat. Soc., Washington Psychiat. Soc. (mem. coun. 1987—99), Am. Psychoanalytic Assn., Am. Psychiat. Assn. (disting. life fellow), Cosmos Club. Avocations: motorboating and yachting, piano, writing. Home: 6924 Balboa Island Ct Delray Beach FL 33446-5641 Office: Ste 2004 950 Pa Corp Cir Boca Raton FL 33487 Office Phone: 561-706-9584. Personal E-mail: sp39@aol.com.

PASTERNACKI, LINDA LEA, critical care nurse; b. Green Bay, Wis., May 26, 1947; d. Paul John and Marion M. (Zagzebski) P.; (div.); children: Sam, Dan, Rachel Marie. Nursing diploma, St. Francis Sch. Nursing, Wichita, Kans., 1968; BS, Coll. St. Francis, Joliet, Ill., 1981, MS in Health Adminstrn., 1986. Cert. ACLS, PALS. Med.-surg. nurse geriatrics, psychiatry St. Francis Hosp., Wichita, 1968-70; nurse Critical Care Unit Sunrise Hosp., Las Vegas, Nev., 1970-72; nurse orthopedics Coronary Care Unit Presbyn. Hosp., Albuquerque, 1972-75, nurse cardiac and intensive care, 1986—94; nurse intensive care and coronary care VA Hosp., Albuquerque, 1976-81; nurse emergency rm. Univ. Heights Hosp., Albuquerque, 1981-82; nurse Critical Care Unit Lovelace Med. Ctr., Albuquerque, 1982-86; nurse emergency rm., Critical Care Unit St. Joseph Med. Ctr., Albuquerque, 1990—94; nurse, PRN staffing James Healthcare Staffing Agy., 1990—2000; nurse intensive care Transitional Hosp. Corp., Albuquerque, 1994-97, admissions coord., 1995; nurse Health-South, Albuquerque, 1997-98, Bernalillo County Juvenile Detention Ctr., 1997—99, Bernalillo County Detention Ctr., 1999—2000; nurse for Dr. R. Schwend, Chief of Pediatric Orthopedics Carrie Tingley Children's Hosp., U. N.Mex. Hosp., 2000—02; nurse cardiac care Heart Hosp. of N.Mex., 2002—04; dialysis nurse Fresenius Med. Care, Albuquerque, 2004—05; nurse PRN staffing Maxim Healthcare Staffing Agy., Albuquerque, 2005; clin. nurse cons. LifeMasters Supported Self-Care, Inc., 2005—09; quality mgr. Vista Care Hospice, 2009; case mgr., clin. supr. Maxim Healthcare Staffing Agy., 2011—; pvt. practice nursing Cowen Home Care, 2011—. Hyperbaric therapy instr. Presbyn. Hosp., Albuquerque, 1975; clin. instr. U. N.Mex. EMT Sch., Albuquerque, 1980. Camp nurse Easter Seals Camps in Calif. and Wash., 2005. Mem. AACN, N.Mex. Nurses Assn. Home: 10605 Central Park Dr NE Albuquerque NM 87123-4844

PASTERNAK, JEFFREY JOHN, anesthesiologist, educator; b. Elizabeth, NJ, Nov. 9, 1968; MS, U. Mich., 1992; MD, U. Medicine and Dentistry NJ, 1998. Asst. prof. anesthesiology Mayo Clinic, 2002—. Office: Mayo Clinic Dept Anesthesiology 200 First St SW Rochester MN 55905 Business E-Mail: pasternak.jeffrey@mayo.edu.

PASTERNAK, TATIANA, biology professor; b. Riga, Latvia, June 01; PhD, U. Copenhagen, 1977. Prof. U. Rochester, 1996—. Mem.: Vision Scis. Soc., Soc. Neuroscis. Office: Dept Neurobiology & Anatomy Box 603 Rochester NY 14642 Business E-Mail: tania@cvs.rochester.edu.

PASTEUR, GEORGES AUGUSTE, biologist, educator; b. Paris, Feb. 26, 1930; s. Louis Leon and Simone Andree (Jamet) Pasteur; m. Nicole Mercier, Aug. 25, 1965; 1 child, Aude; children: Jean Louis, Isabelle, Bertrand. Lic. scis., Sorbonne U., 1953, D of Scis., 1964. From asst. zoologist to assoc. prof. Morocco Sci. Inst., Rabat, 1953-67; rsch. assoc. Rockefeller U., NYC, 1967-69; assoc. prof. Ecole Pratique des Hautes Etudes, Montpellier, France, 1973-78, prof. Montpellier and Paris, 1978-93; freelance sci. writer, 1993—. Vis. prof. Southwestern Med. Sch., Dallas, 1969—72; cons. Japan Soc. for Promotion of Sci., Tokyo, 1985—, Commn. of European Communities, Brussels, 1987—, Inamori Found., Kyoto, 1992—, Found. for Rsch. Devel., Pretoria, South Africa, 1996—; hon. guest 1st congress Mediterranean Herpetology, Marrakesh, 2007. Author: Les Batraciens du Maroc, 1959, Le Mimetisme, 1972, Practical Isozyme Genetics, 1988; editor: Systematique et Societe, 1993, Biologie et Mimétismes, 1995, Laureate Academie Francaise, 1996. Rsch. scholar, U. Calif., Irvine, 1998—99. Fellow: French Zool. Soc. (editl. bd. mem. 1970—80, Charles Bocquet prize 1992), French Soc. Systematics (v.p. 1990—93), Internat. Soc. for Philosophy of Biology (editl. bd. mem. 1986—95), Soc. for Study of Amphibians and Reptiles (editl. bd. mem. 1980—95); mem.: Soc. Oceanistes, Species Survival Commn. Internat. Union for Conservation of Nature, Genetica The Netherlands (editl. bd. mem. 1983—89). Home: 15 Rue Buffon 75005 Paris France Office: Inst des Scis de l'Evolution Université Montpellier 2 34095 Montpellier France Office Phone: 33-0145351801. Business E-Mail: gpast@mnhn.fr.

PASTIN, MARK JOSEPH, health science association administrator, educator; b. Ellwood City, Pa., July 6, 1949; s. Joseph and Patricia Jean (Camenite) Pastin; m. Joanne Marie Reagle, May 30, 1970 (div. Mar. 1982); m. Carrie Patricia Class, Dec. 22, 1984 (div. June 1990); m. Christina M. Brecto, June 15, 1991. BA summa cum laude, U. Pitts., 1970; MA, Harvard U., 1972, PhD, 1973. Asst. prof. Ind. U., Bloomington, 1973-78, assoc. prof., 1978-80; founder, bd. Compliance Resource Group, Inc., 1983—; chmn., CEO, pres. Coun. Ethical Orgns., Alexandria, Va., 1986—; prof. mgmt., dir. Ariz. State U., Tempe, 1988-92, prof. emeritus, 1996—; chair Health Ethics Trust, 1995—. Dir. Learned Nicholson, Ltd., 1990-91; bd. Japan Am. Soc. Phoenix, Found. for Ethical Orgns.; cons. GTE, Interim Healthcare, 1997-2000, U.S. Dept. Edn., 2002, Tex. Instruments, MicroAge Computers, Med-Tronic, Blood Sys., Inc., Opus Corp., GTE, NyNex, Am. Express Bank, Kaiko Bussan Co., Japan, Arex Co., Japan, Century Audit Co., U.S. Dept. Edn., Japan, Scottsdale Meml. Hosp., Cosanti Found., Lincoln Electric Co., Tenet Healthcare, The Williams Co.; vis. faculty Harvard U., 1980; presenter Australian Inst. Mgmt., Nippon Tel. & Tel., Hong Kong Commn. Against Corruption, 1984, Young Pres.'s Orgn. Internat. U., 1990, Nat. Assn. Indsl. & Office Parks, 1990, ABA, 1991, Govt. of Brazil, 1991; columnist Jour. Clin. Medicine. Author: Hard Problems of Management, 1986 (Book of Yr. Armed Forces Mil. Comtrs. 1986, Japanese edit. 1994), The Hotline Handbook, 1996, Planning Forum, 1992; editor: Public-Private Sector Ethics, 1979; mem. editl. bd. Report on Medicare Compliance; pub. Pastin Report on Best Compliance Practices, 1998—, Columnist jours. clin. medicine; Guerin Lect. on Philanthropy, 1996. Founding bd. mem. Tempe Leadership, 1985-89; bd. mem. Ctr. for Behavioral Health, Phoenix, 1986-89, Tempe YMCA, 1986—, Valley Leadership Alumni Assn., 1989-92; mem. Clean Air Com., Phoenix, 1987-90. Nat. Sci. Found. fellow, Cambridge, Mass., 1971-73; Nat. Endowment for the Humanities fellow, 1975; Exxon Edn. Found. grant, 1982-83. Mem.: Am. Assn. Physician Specialists (exec. com.), Found. Ethical Orgns. (chmn. 1988, pres.), Am. Soc. Assn. Execs. (presenter 1987—97), Harvard Club D.C., Phi Beta Kappa, Golden Key. Avocations: golf, running. Office: 214 S Payne St Alexandria VA 22314-3530 Home: 7205 Regent Dr Alexandria VA 22307-2044 Office Phone: 703-683-7916. Personal E-mail: councile@aol.com, markpastin@gmail.com.

PASTOR, JESÚS EDUARDO, clinical neurophysiologist, researcher; b. San Bartolomé de Pinares, Ávila, Spain, Oct. 11, 1966; s. Jesús Pastor and Josefa Gómez; m. Mónica Domínguez, May 16, 1997; children: Eugenia, Gonzalo. MD, U. Salamanca, Spain, 1990; PhD cum laude, U. Alicante, Spain, 1995. Cert. in clin. neurophysiology Ministry Health, Spain, 2000. Med. staff Clin. Neurophysiology, Hosp. La Princesa, Madrid, 2001—, Clin. Neurophysiology, Hosp. Monteprincipe, Boadilla del Monte, Madrid, 2001—, Clin. Neurophysiology, Hosp. Madrid-Norte, Sanchimarro, 2008; invited expert Soc. Iberoamericana Info. Científica, Buenos Aires, 2003—; rschr. Found. Biomed. Rsch. Hosp. U. La Princesa, 2004—, tutor med. residents, 2005—. Peer reviewer Revista de Neurología, Barcelona, 2002—10, Brain Rsch. Bulletin, Cardiff, 2002—09, Epilepsia, 2010; clin. neurophysiology cons. Medtronic, Madrid, 2003; lectr. medicine San Pablo Ceu U., Madrid; founder Neuromonitorizacion S.L., 2008. Recipient award, U. Alicante, 1997, Sci. Rsch. award, Neurosci. Inst. F. Oloriz, Granada, Spain, 1997, Pedro Mata award, Coll. Neurosurgeons, Madrid, 2008, 2009. Mem.: Spanish Soc. Neurosci., Acad. Medicine Andalucía Oriental, Clin. Neurophysiology Spanish Soc., Spanish League Against Epilepsy. Home: Maudes 36 4D Madrid 28003 Spain Office: Hosp Univ La Princesa Calle Diego de Leon 62 28006 Madrid Spain Office Phone: 34-91-5202213. Office Fax: 34-91-4013582.

PASTOR COLON, CARMEN NINA, medical educator, researcher; b. Mexico City, Apr. 1, 1967; PhD, Mt. Sinai Sch. Medicine, 1997. Prof., investigador, tiempo completo U. Autónoma del Estado de Morelos, 1997—. Fulbright scholarship, ONACyT. Mem.: Am. Chem. Soc., Biophysical Soc. Avocations: swimming, reading. Office: Av Universidad 1001 Col Chamilpa Cuernavaca Morelos 62209 Mexico Office Fax: 52 777 3297040. Business E-Mail: nina@uaem.mx.

PASTORE, DANIEL, radiologist; b. São Paulo, Brazil, Sept. 4, 1976; s. Ayrton Roberto and Luci Beatriz Malagoni Pastore; m. Paula Christina Falcão Pastore, May 22, 2004. MD, FAMERP, São José do Rio Preto, Sao Paulo, 2000; PhD, Med. Coll. U. São Paulo, FMUSP, São Paulo, 2009. Cert. radiologist Brazilian Coll. Medicine, São Paulo, 2004. Radiologist CTC- Gênese, São Paulo, 2005—, Fleury Medicina e Saúde, São Paulo, 2008—. Mem.: Brazilian Coll. Medicine (assoc.), RSNA (assoc.). Achievements include research in tibialis posterior tendon, triceps brachii tendon; configuration and extension of normal fluid collections within Kager's fat; ligaments of the posterior and lateral talar processes. Office: Fleury Medicina e Saúde Rua Cincinato Braga 282 São Paulo 01333-910 Brazil Office Phone: 55 11 50146813. Office Fax: 55 11 50146813. Personal E-mail: dampastore@hotmail.com. Business E-Mail: daniel.pastore@fleury.com.br.

PASTORE, FRANCESCO SAVERIO, neurosurgeon, educator; b. Rome, Feb. 29, 1956; Laurea in Medicine & Surgery, U. La Sapienza, Rome, 1980, cert in Neurosurgery, 1987. Asst. prof. neurosurgery U. Rome Tor Vergata, 2001—. Avocations: skiing, music. Office: viale Montpellier 1 Rome Latium 00133 Italy Office Fax: 06 20903056. E-mail: pastore@uniroma2.it.

PASTOREK, NICHOLAS JOSEPH, psychologist; b. Ill., Dec. 3, 1976; PhD, U. Houston, 2004. Clin. neuropsychologist Michael E. DeBakey VA Med. Ctr., 2006—. Asst. prof. dept. phys. medicine and rehab. Baylor Coll. Medicine, 2008. Mem.: Houston Neuropsychol. Soc., Internat. Neuropsychol. Soc., Am. Bd. Profl. Psychology. Office: 2002 Holcombe Blvd RCL 117 Houston TX 77030 Business E-Mail: nicholas.pastorek@va.gov.

PASTOREK, NORMAN JOSEPH, facial plastic surgeon; b. Moline, Ill., Feb. 8, 1939; s. Joseph Andrew and Rose (Faurone) P.; m. Janice Marie Gloss, Apr. 27, 1986; children: Kate Haviland, Kelly Taylor. AB, Augustana Coll., 1960; MD, U. Ill., Chgo., 1964. Diplomate Am. Bd. Otolaryngology, Am. Bd. Facial Plastic and Reconstructive Surgery. Intern San Francisco Gen. Hosp., 1964-65; resident U. Ill. Hosps., Chgo., 1965-69; pvt. practice medicine specializing in facial plastic surgery NYC; clin. asst. prof. N.Y. Hosp. Cornell Med. Coll., 1971-83, dir. div. facial plastic surgery dept. otolaryngology, 1977—2008, clin. assoc. prof., 1983-91, clin. prof., 1991—; clin. prof. dept. otolaryngology NYU Sch. Medicine, 2003—, dir., facial plastic surgery fellowship, 2003—. Examiner Am. Bd. Otolaryngology, 1971, 91-93; mem. bd. surgeon dirs. Manhattan Eye, Ear and Throat Hosp., N.Y.C., 2005. Author: Blepharoplasty, 1983, 3d edit., 1994; editor: Aesthetic Facial Surgery, 1990; editor for beauty: Archives of Facial Plastic Surgery, 1999. Lt. comdr. USN, 1969—71. Named Best Drs. America; named one of Top Doctors in America, 1997—2010. Fellow Am. Acad. Otolaryngology, Am. Bd. Otolaryngology (examiner 1991—), Am. Acad. Facial Plastic and Reconstructive Surgery (v.p. eastern region 1982-86, pres.-elect 1989-90, pres. 1990-91, pres. founders club 1996—), ACS; mem. Alpha Omega Alpha, European Soc. Facial Plastic Surgery, Canadian Acad. Facial Plastic Surgery, NY Acad. Medicine Republican. Episcopalian. Office Phone: 212-987-4700. Personal E-mail: drnormanpastorek@nyc.rr.com, pastorekmd@gmail.com.

PASTORES, STEPHEN M., internist; b. NYC, Sept. 5, 1958; s. Jovito Camara and Annie McCarthy Pastores; m. Maria Teresa Desancho; children: Steven Michael, Monica Cristina. MD, Lyceum Northwestern Coll. Medicine, Philippines, 1982. Diplomate Am. Bd. Internal Medicine, Am. Bd. Pulmonary Disease, Am. Bd. Critical Care Medicine. Resident Met. Hosp. Ctr., 1989; attending critical care physician Montefiore Med. Ctr., Bronx, NY, 1993—96; dir. emergency svcs. Dept. VA Med. Ctr., Bronx, 1996—99, asst. dir. surg. ICU,

1996—99; attending critical care physician Meml. Sloan-Kettering Cancer Ctr., NYC, 1999—, dir. critical care rsch. and critical care fellowship program; prof. medicine and anesthesiology Weill Med. Coll. Cornell U., NYC, 2001—. Editor: (book) Intensive Care of the Cancer Patient, 2010; contbr. articles to profl. jours. Fellow: ACP (2000-Present), Am. Coll. of Critical Care Medicine, Am. Coll. Chest Physicians (1997-Present). Office: Meml Sloan-Kettering Cancer Ctr 1275 York Ave C-1179 New York NY 10065 Business E-Mail: pastores@mskcc.org.

PASTORINO, FABIO, research scientist; b. Genoa, Aug. 2, 1973; Degree in Biol. Scis., 1998, PhD in Clinical Pathology, 2005. Sr. scientist G. Gaslini Children's Hosp., 2006—. Office: Largo G Gaslini 5 Genoa 16148 Italy E-mail: fabiopastorino@ospedale-gaslini.ge.it.

PATAKY, ZOLTAN, internal medicine physician; b. Kralovsky Chlmec, Slovak Republic, Aug. 29, 1971; s. Zoltan and Susan Pataky; children: Patrick, Robert. Degree in Medicine, 1995; MD, postgrad., U. Geneva, 1999—. Cert. in internal medicine Acad. Medicine, Slovakia, 2002. Resident U. Hosps. Geneva, 1995—99, Regional Hosp., Chateau-d'Oeux, Switzerland, 1999—2000, Riaz, Switzerland, 2000—01, U. Hosp., Bratislava, Slovakia, 2001—02, chief physician Geneva, 2002—. Cons. in field. Rewiever Diabetes Care, Brit. Med. Jour., Jour. Dermatol. Sci., Journ. Lower Extremity Wounds; contbr. articles to profl. jours. Recipient Denber-Pinard award, 2000. Mem.: Assn. Langue Française L'étude Diabète et Maladies Métaboliques, Am. Diabetes Assn. Achievements include research in diabetes and diabetic foot. Office: Univ Hosps Geneva Micheli-du-crest 24 CH-1211 Geneva Switzerland Office Fax: 41223729715. Business E-Mail: zoltan.pataky@hcuge.ch.

PATANAPORN, VIRUSH, dental educator; b. Pichit, Thailand, June 24, 1955; s. Pipop and Pilaiwan Patanaporn; m. Kobkul Patanaporn, Nov. 17, 1980; children: Rushkul, Parin. DDS, Chiang Mai U., Thailand, 1979; MS in Orthodontics, Chulalongkorn U., Thailand, 1983. Cert. Thai Bd. Orthodontics, Dental Coun., 1998, Loma Linda U., 1987. Assoc. prof. orthodontics, faculty dentistry Chiang Mai U., 1996—, dean, faculty dentistry, 1998—2006. Pres. Lanna Thai Pub. Speaking Club, Chiang Mai, 1999—2000; mem. dental profession Parliament of Senate, Bangkok, 2008. Named one of Best Alumni, Faculty Dentistry, Chiang Mai U., 2006; grantee, King's Sister Fund, 2000. Mem.: Dental Faculty Consortium Thailand (Chiang Mai) (gen. sec., faculty dentistry 2006—), Rotary Club (Chiang Mai). Buddhist. Achievements include development of Dental Science Museum in facalty of dentistry, Chiang Mai University; organizing dental mobile team to take care and do the dental service for the people in the rural area and on the mountain. Avocations: ping pong/table tennis, reading, walking, travel, exercise. Office: Faculty Dentistry Suthep Rd 50200 Chiang Mai Thailand Home Phone: 6681-6715125; Office Phone: 6653 282592. Office Fax: 6653 222844; Home Fax: 6653-276170. Business E-Mail: dnoti003@chiangmai.ac.th.

PATCHEFSKY, ARTHUR S., pathologist; MD, Hahnemann Med. Coll., 1963. Diplomate Am. Bd. Pathology, Am. Bd. Pathology-anatomic pathology. Resident pathology Johns Hopkins Hosp., Hosp. of the Univ. of Pa.; fellow Meml. Sloan-Kettering Hosp.; joined Fox Chase Cancer Ctr., 1994, chmn. pathology dept. Co-author: (publs.) Pleiotrophin expression correlates with melanocytic tumor progression and metastatic potential, 2005, Fiberoptic ductoscopy findings in women with and without spontaneous nipple discharge, 2005, Localized diseases of the bronchi and lung. In Principles and Practice of Surgical Pathology and Cytopathology, 2009, Sentinel lymph node metastasis in breast cancer. Is completion axillary dissection mandated in all patients breast, and other numerous publications. Named one of Top Doctors, Phila. Mag., 2011. Mem.: Am. Soc. for Clin. Pathology, Am. Assn. for Cancer Rsch. Office: Fox Chase Cancer Center 333 Cottman Ave Philadelphia PA 19111-2497 Office Phone: 215 728 3675.

PATCHETT, ARTHUR ALLAN, retired pharmaceutical executive, medicinal chemist; b. Middletown, NY, May 28, 1929; s. Arthur Allan and Anna Gertrude (Vossler) P.; m. Lois Rhoda Mc Neil, Aug. 18, 1962; Thomas John, Steven Edward. BA, Princeton U., 1951; PhD, Harvard U., 1955; DSc (hon.), Bloomfield Coll., 2001. Rsch. assoc. NIH, Bethesda, Md., 1955-57; rsch. chemist Merck Rsch. Labs., Rahway, NJ, 1957-62, dir. synthetic chem. rsch., 1962-69, sr. dir. synthetic chem. rsch., 1969-71, sr. dir. new lead discovery, 1971-76, exec. dir. new lead discovery, 1976-88, v.p. exploratory chemistry, 1988-95, v.p. medicinal chemistry, 1995-2000, cons., 2000—. Contbr. over 180 papers to profl. jours., sci. confs. Recipient Discoverers award, Pharm. Mfrs. Assn., 1992, Smissman Bristol-Myers Squibb award, 2001, NAS award for Chemistry in Svc. to Soc., 2007; named to, N.J. Inventors Hall of Fame, N.J. Inst. Tech., 1990. Fellow AAAS; mem. Am. Chem. Soc. (chmn. div. medicinal chemistry 1971, E.B. Hershberg Important Discoveries in Medicinally Active Substances award 1993, Alfred Burger award in medicinal chemistry 2002, Nat. Acad. Sci. award for chemistry in svc. to soc. 2007). Achievements include 180 U.S. patents (co-holder); co-inventor antihypertensive drug Vasotec; key contbr. to discovery of cholesterol lowering drug Mevacor.

PATCHIN, REBECCA J., anesthesiologist, educator, administrator; b. Detroit, Dec. 8, 1949; d. Robert Ira and Doris J. (Hubert) P.; m. Carl W. Anderson, 1988 (dec.) ASN, Pacific Union Coll., 1969; BSN, Walla Walla Coll., 1971; MD, Loma Linda U., 1989. Diplomate in anesthesiology and pain mgmt. Am. Bd. Anesthesiology. Resident internal medicine Loma Linda U. Med. Ctr., Calif., 1989-90, resident anesthesiology Calif., 1990-93, fellow pain mgmt. Dept. Anesthesiology Calif., 1993-94, asst. prof. anesthesiology, 1994—; assoc. med. dir. Ctr. for Pain Mgmt., Loma Linda, 1995—; pvt. practice Riverside, Calif. Appointed to Joint Commn. on Accreditation od Healthcare Organizations' Standards and Surveys Coms., 2006; mem. Accreditation Coun. Grad. Med. Edn. (mem. liaison com. med. edn., co-chair 2001-2002); presenter in field. Contbr. abstracts to profl. jours. Mem. AMA (mem. credentials com. 1986-, mem. bd. nominations and awards com. 1988-89, chair, Med. Liability Task Force, del. ho. of dels. 1990-99, mem. reference com. 1994-, mem. coun. on med. edn. 1996-2003, chair, 2002-03, mem. bd. trustee 2003-11, sec. 2006-07, liasion polit. action com., mem. young physician sect., chair, membership com., bd. audit, mem. orgn. and ops. com., chair-elect 2008-09, chair 2009-10, immediate past chair, 2010-11), Internat. Anesthesiology Rsch. Soc., Internat. Assn. for Study of Pain, Am. Soc. Anesthesiology, Am. Pain Soc., Am. Soc. Regional Anesthesia, Am. Acad. Pain Medicine, Calif. Soc. Anesthesiology (del. resident component 1991-93, mem. com. on young physicians 1994—96, chair com. on young physicians 1996—), Calif. Med. Assn. (mem. reference com. 1988, trustee 1991-93, mem. com. on health professions and licensure 1992-, chair com. on health professions and licensure 1993-96, mem. coun. on legislation 1995-96, chair coun. on legislation, liaison com. on specialty bds., bd. dir.), So. Calif. Cancer Pain Initiative, Riverside County Med. Assn. (sec.-treas 2002, pres. 2004), San Bernardino County Med. Soc. Avocation: sailing. Office Phone: 951-413-0200. *

PATE, GORDON ERIC, cardiologist, consultant; b. Dun Laoghaire, County Dublin, Ireland, July 5, 1966; s. Alexander Roberts and Eleanor Marion Pate; m. Ebba Kinberg, Feb. 23, 2002; children: Alexandra Ingrid, Eric George William, Robert Bjom. MB, BCh, Trinity Coll., Dublin, 1990, MSc, 2000. Cert. European Soc. Cardiology, 2004. Cons. cardiologist Galway Clinic, Doughiska, Ireland, 2005—. Contbr. articles to profl. jours. IMPACT fellow, Can. Insts. Health Rsch., 2004—05, Heart and Stroke Found. Can., 2004—05. Mem.: Royal Coll. Physicians Ireland. Office: Ste 28 Galway Clinic Doughiska Galway Galway Ireland Office Fax: 0035391720141. Business E-Mail: cardiology@galwayclinic.com.

PATE, ROBERT HEWITT, JR., retired counselor educator; b. Abingdon, Va., Apr. 5, 1938; s. Robert Hewitt and Esther Frances (Kirk) P.; m. Ellen O'Neal Pope, Dec. 11, 1960; children: Robert Hewitt III, Mary Ellen Pate Barton. AB, Davidson Coll., 1960; MEd, U. Va., 1965; PhD, U. N.C., 1968. Lic. prof. counselor, Va. Marketer Sinclair Refining Co., Abingdon, Va., 1960-61, 63-64; counselor St. Andrews Presbyn. Coll., Laurinburg, NC, 1965-66; counselor educator U. Va., 1968—2008, interim dean, 1994-95, assoc. dean, 1995—2007, prof. edn., emeritus, William Clay Parrish Jr. prof. edn., 2003—08. Author: Being A Counselor, 1983. Sr. warden, St. Paul's Ivy, Va., 2010. 1st lt. U.S. Army 1961-63. Mem. ACA, Va. Counselors Assn. (pres. 1983-84), Ctr. Credentialing and Edn.(dir., sec.), Nat. Bd. Cert. Counselors (chair 1996-97). Avocation: reading. Home: 552 Dryden Pl Charlottesville VA 22903-4666

PATE, RUSSELL R., exercise physiologist; b. NY; BS in Physical Edn., Springfield Coll., 1968; MS, U. Oreg., 1973, PhD in Exercise Physiology, 1974. Faculty Arnold Sch. Pub. Health, U. SC, Columbia, 1974—, prof. dept. exercise sci., assoc. v.p. health scis., dir. Children's Phys. Activity Rsch. Group. Apptd. mem. SC Gov.'s Coun. Phys. Fitness, 1988—; panel mem. US Dietary Guidelines Adv. Com., NAS Inst. Medicine, 2003—04; past pres. Nat. Coalition Promoting Phys. Activity; past faculty mem. U. Va., Med. Coll. Ga. Author: Scientific Foundations of Coaching, 1984, Training for Young Distance Runners, 1996; editor: Health & Fitness through Physical Education, 1994; contbr. articles to profl. jours. Recipient Alliance Scholar award, Am. Alliance Health, Phys. Edn., Recreation & Dance, 1999, Sci. Honor award, Pres.'s Coun. Phys. Fitness & Sports, 2008. Fellow: Am. Acad. Kinesiology & Phys. Edn.; mem.: Am. Coll. Sports Medicine (pres. 1993—94, Citation award 1996), Am. Dietetic Assn. (hon.), Carolina Marathon Assn. (bd. dirs., past. pres.). Achievements include coordinating the effort leading to the development of the recommendation on physical activity and public health of the US Centers for Disease Control and Prevention and the American College of Sports Medicine; competing in three US Olympic Trials marathons and placing twice among the top ten finishers in the Boston Marathon. Office: Arnold Sch Pub Health U SC 800 Sumter St Columbia SC 29208 Office Phone: 803-777-5032. Office Fax: 803 777 4783. Business E-Mail: rpate@mailbox.sc.edu. *

PATEL, AMIT N., surgeon, researcher; b. Dallas, Dec. 8, 1972; s. Nilkanth and Manjula Patel. BS, Youngstown State U., 1993, MS in Immunology, 1994; MD, Case Western Res. U., 1998. Surgery resident Baylor U. Med. Ctr., Dallas, thoracic and cardiovasc. surgery rsch. fellow, dir. cardiac surgery rsch., 2002—03; cardiothoracic surgery fellow U. Pitts. Med. Ctr.; clin. rsch. fellow dept. thoracic and cardiovasc. surgery Cleve. Clinic Found.; dir. cardiac cell therapy U. Pitts. Med. Ctr., McGowan Inst. of Regenerative Medicien; assoc. prof. surgery U. Utah Sch. Medicine, 2008—. National principal investigator Phase II Impact-DCM clinical trial Aastrom Biosciences Inc. Author (with Dr. Urschel Jr.): Atlas of Thoracic Surgery 2nd ed.; author: (with Dr. F. Benetti) Atlas of Off Pump Cardiac Surgery; contbr. articles to profl. jours. Recipient First Pl. - Paravertebral Blocks in Thoracic Surgery, Inst. Surg. Pain Mgmt.; named Best Resident in Am., Am. Assn. Physicians Indian Origin. Mem.: ACS (Best Overall Presentation award 2001, 2002, 2003, 2005), Soc. Thoracic Surgeons, Internat. Soc. Minimally Invasive Cardiac Surgery. Achievements include patents for Patel Minimally Invasive Cardiac Retractor; first to first surgeon to perform epicardial defibrillation for postoperative atrial fibrillation in America; first Surgeon to implant human stem cells in the heart in America. Office: U Utah Cardiovascular Ctr 50 N Medical Dr Salt Lake City UT 84132 Personal E-mail: anpatel72@hotmail.com.

PATEL, ANAND CHAMPAK, medical educator; b. Hackensack, NJ, Aug. 3, 1973; MD, Rush Med. Coll., 1999; MS in Bioinformatics, Johns Hopkins U., 2010. Instr., pediat. Wash. U. Sch. Medicine, 2005—08, asst. prof., pediat., 2008—10, asst. prof., pediat. and medicine, 2010—. Editl. bd. mem. Am. Jour. Respiratory Cell and Molecular Biology, 2010. Recipient Mentored Clin. Scientist Devel. award, NIH & NHLBI. Mem.: Am. Thoracic Soc. Office: 660 S Euclid Ave Campus Box 8052 Saint Louis MO 63110 Office Fax: 314-454-2515. Business E-Mail: patel_an@kids.wustl.edu.

PATEL, ANIL S., biomedical engineer, researcher, medical products executive; b. Baroda, India, June 28, 1939; came to US, 1961, naturalized. s. Shankerbhai S. and Gangaben T. Patel; children: Ravi, Sunil; m. Asha Rairkar, Aug. 22, 1992. BS, U. Baroda, 1960; MS, Purdue U., 1963; PhD, Northwestern U., 1966; postgrad., Stanford U., 1993. Sr. rsch. scientist Baxter Travenol Labs. Inc., Morton Grove, Ill., 1968-74; chief scientist Cavitron Corp., NYC, 1974-79; chief scientist, mgr. advanced prodcts rsch. Cooper Vision Sys. divsn. Cooper Vision Inc. (formerly Cavitron Corp.), Irvine, Calif., 1979-83, Bellevue, Wash., 1983-86; dir. advanced product rsch., chief scientist Cooper Vision CILCO divsn. Cooper Cos., Inc., Bellevue, 1986-89; dir. rsch. intraocular lens Alcon Labs., Inc., Ft. Worth, 1989-92, sr. dir. rsch. surg. products, 1993-2000, v.p. rsch. surg. products, 2001—02; cons. Global Healthcare, Seattle, 2003—. Contbr. articles to profl. jours.; patentee in field. Organizer Highland Park (Ill.) Chess Club, 1970-74, White Plains (N.Y.) Chess Club, 1974-77. Recipient free passage from India to U.S., Indian Ministry Sci. and Cultural Affairs, 1961; NIH postdoctoral fellow Northwestern U., 1966-67, named to Alcon Hall of Fame, 2009. Fellow Am. Soc. Laser Medicine and Surgery (founder); mem. AAAS, IEEE, Assn. for Advancement Med. Instrumentation (chmn. infrared warmers and incubators stds. com. 1978-80, pulmonary function devices-spirometer stds. subcom. 1978-80), Am. Nat. Stds. Inst. (com. intraocular lenses std. 1988-94, viscoelastic ophthalmic devices 1992—2002, apptd. tech. expert del. U.S.A. tech. adv. group Internat. Stds. Orgn. tech. com. 1992—, vice elastic ophthalmic devices 1992-2002), Am. Soc. Cataract and Refractive Surgery, Assn. Rsch. in Vision and Ophthalmology, Internat. Soc. Refractive Keratoplasty, Soc. Biomaterials, Sigma Xi. Avocations: travel, chess, literature. Home Phone: 206-525-9765; Office Phone: 206-525-9765. Personal E-mail: anilasha@aol.com.

PATEL, ANUPA, endocrinologist; b. NJ, Mar. 27, 1978; MD, Med. U. Silesia, 2004. Endocrinology staff Scott & White Meml. Hosp., 2011—. Asst. prof. Tex. A&M U. Health Scis. Ctr., 2011. Mem.: AMA, Am. Assn. Clin. Endocrinologists, Endocrine Soc. Home: 3009 Ira Young Dr Apt 408 Temple TX 76504 Personal E-mail: dr_anupa@yahoo.com.

PATEL, DASHARATH M., pharmacist, educator; b. Manekpur, June 1, 1971; BPharm, L. M. Coll. Pharmacy, Ahmedabad, 1997; PhD, North Gujarat U., Patan, 2005. Lectr. to asst prof. Shri B. M. Shah Coll. Pharm. Edn. & Rsch., Modasa, 2002—06; asst. prof. to prof. Shri Sarvajanik Pharmacy Coll., Mehsana, 2007—. Formulation devel. officer Claris Life Scis. Ltd., Ahmedabad, 1999—99; tchr. Rofel Coll. Pharmacy, Vapi, 2000—01. Avocations: music, cricket, reading. Office: Shri Sarvajanik Pharmacy Coll Near Arvind Baug B/H Bus Stand Mehsana Gujrat 384 001 India Office Fax: 91-2762-247712. E-mail: justdmpatel@rediffmail.com.

PATEL, MAMTA, lab administrator; b. India, May 14, 1970; BSc, S.P. U., India, MT, 1990, M in Microbiology, 1992. Adminstrv. lab. dir. Rockford Health System, 2008—. Office: 2400 N Rocton Ave Rockford IL 61103 Business E-Mail: mpatel@rhsnet.org.

PATEL, MANISHKUMAR BHIKHALAL, pharmacologist, educator; b. India, Feb. 19, 1982; PharmM, KB Inst. Pharm. Edn. and Rsch., 2005. Asst. prof., career counselor Shri Sarvajanik Pharmacy Coll., 2006—11. Mem.: Assn. Pharmacy Tchrs. India, Indian Pharmacological Soc. Avocations: surfing, reading. Home: Apt #806 20-Tuxedo CRT Scarborough Toronto ON M1G3S5 Canada Personal E-mail: manish_pharma2005@yahoo.com.

PATEL, MITUL SURESH, surgeon; b. LA, Nov. 26, 1979; MD, NY Med. Coll., 2005. Gen. surgery resident Cooper U. Hosp., 2005—. Home: 1509 Lakeside Dr Palmyra NJ 08065 Business E-Mail: patel-mitul@cooperhealth.edu.

PATEL, MULCHAND SHAMBHUBHAI, biochemist, researcher; b. Sipor, India, Sept. 9, 1939; came to U.S., 1965; s. Shambhubhai J. and Puriben (Patel) P.; m. Kankuben M. Patel; children: Sumitra, Yashomati, Mayank. BS, Gujarat U., 1961; MS, U. Baroda, 1964; PhD, U. Ill., 1968. Asst. prof. pediat. rsch. Sch. Medicine Temple U., Phila., 1970-72, rsch. asst. prof. medicine, 1972-75, rsch. asst. prof. biochemistry, 1970-75, rsch. assoc. prof. biochem. medicine, 1975-78; assoc. prof. biochemistry Sch. Medicine Case Western Res. U., Cleve., 1978-86, prof., 1986-93; prof., chmn. biochemistry SUNY, Buffalo, 1993-98, assoc. dean biomed. rsch. edn., 1999—, prof., 1999, UB disting. prof., 2004—, disting. prof., 2008—. Mem. NIH biochem. study sect. 2, 1984 88; mem. editl. bd. Jour. Biol. Chem., 1991 97, 99-2004, 06-11. Contbr. articles to profl. jours. Recipient gold medal in biochemistry U. Baroda, 1973, Fulbright Rsch. Scholar award to India, 1987; prin. investigator, rsch. grantee NIH. Mem. Am. Soc. for Biochemistry and Molecular Biology, Am. Soc. Nutritional Scis. Office: SUNY-Dept Biochemistry Sch Medicine 140 Farber Hall 3435 Main St Buffalo NY 14214-3001 Office Phone: 716-829-3074. Business E-Mail: mspatel@buffalo.edu.

PATEL, RAJESH MANILAL, pharmacist, educator; b. Jasalpur, Sept. 17, 1978; PharmM, J.S.S. Coll. Pharmacy, 2004. Lectr. S.K. Patel Coll. Pharm. Edn. & Rsch., 2004—05, tchr., guide rsch. students, 2005—. Recipient award, B.V. Patel PERD Ctr., Ahmedabad. Mem.: Indian Pharm. Assn., Assn. Pharm. Tchr.'s. India. Avocations: cricket, literature. Home: B-13 Karnavati Soc K K Nagar Ahmedabad Gujarat 380061 India Home Phone: 91-9427375242. Personal E-mail: rajmit_120@rediffmail.com.

PATEL, RAJUL, pharmacist, educator; b. Panorama City, Calif., Mar. 2, 1972; BA BS, Johns Hopkins U., 1993; PharmD, U. Pacific, 2003. Assoc. prof. U. Pacific Sch. Pharmacy & Health Scis., 2005—. Named Pharmacy Tchr. of Yr., U. Pacific Sch. Pharmacy and Health Scis.; grant, U. Pacific. Mem.: APHA, Am. Assn. Colls. Pharmacy, ISPOR. Avocations: basketball, golf. Office: 751 Brookside Rd Stockton CA 95211 Business E-Mail: rpatel@pacific.edu.

PATEL, SAMEER ANILKUMAR, plastic surgeon; b. Nov. 19, 1973; BS in Chem. Biology, Stevens Inst. Tech.; MD, NJ Med. Sch. Univ. Medicine and Dentistry, Newark, NJ, 1998. Cert. Am. Bd. Surgery, 2005. Resident, gen. surgery and plastic and reconstructive surgery Montefiore Med. Ctr./Albert Einstein Coll. Medicine, Bronx, NY; fellowship, microsurgical reconstruction U. tex. MD Anderson Cancer Ctr., Houston; attending plastic and reconstructive surgeon, dept. surgical oncology Fox Chase Cancer Ctr., Phila., 2007—. Office: Fox Chase Cancer Ctr 333 Cottman Ave Philadelphia PA 19111-2497

PATEL, SANJAY, pulmonologist, educator; AB in Mathematics, Princeton U.; MD, Harvard Med. Sch. Resident U. Pa. Hosp; fellow in pulmonary & critical care Harvard U.; former instr. Harvard Med. Sch.; clinical staff divsn. sleep Brigham & Women's Hosp.; staff divsn pulmonary, critical are & sleep medicine Beth Israel Deaconess Med. Ctr.; prof. divsn. clinical epidemiology Case Western Reserve U., asst. prof. divsn. pulmonary, critical care & sleep medicine, 2005—. Mem.: Am. Acad. Sleep Medicine, Am. Thoracic Soc., Am. Coll. Chest Physicians, Mass. Med. Soc. Office: 11100 Euclid Ave Ste WRM5067 Cleveland OH 44106

PATEL, SUNITA K., researcher; b. Kenya, Oct. 17, 1964; PhD, CSPP, LA, 1996. Asst. prof. City Hope Med. Ctr. and Beckman Rsch. Inst., 2006—. Grant, NCI. Mem.: Childrens Oncology Group Behavioral Sci. Steering Com. Avocation: hiking. Office: #173 1500 E Duarte Rd Duarte CA 91011 Business E-Mail: spatel@coh.org.

PATEL, VAIBHAV B., medical researcher; b. India, Dec. 19, 1983; PharmD, Maharaja Sayajirao U. Baroda, 2011. Postdoc. fellow, dept. medicine U. Alta., 2011—. Recipient Prof. Saroj Sharma prize, Indian Pharmacological Soc., 2nd prize, GUJCOST, India. Avocations: sports, dance. Home: 11009- 81 Ave Edmonton Alberta T6G0S3 Canada Personal E-mail: vab.patel@gmail.com.

PATEL, VIKRAM B., medical association administrator; b. India, Oct. 20, 1959; MD, B. J. Med. Coll., Ahmedabad, India, 1984. Med. dir. Ctrl. Ill. Pain Ctr., St Mary's Hosp., Decatur, Ill., 1998—2000; asst. & assoc. prof. Loyola U. Med. Ctr., 2000—07, program dir., pain fellowship program Chgo., 2000—07; pres. & med. dir. ACMI Pain Care, LLC, 2007—. Bd. dirs. Midwest Pain Soc., 2007—10; bd. dirs., sec. & treas. McHenry County Med. Soc., 2008; bd. examiners World Inst. Pain, FIPP Exam., 2008. Mem.: McHenry County Med. Soc., World Inst. Pain, Ill. Soc. Anesthesiologists, Am. Soc. Interventional Pain Physicians, Am. Soc. Anesthesiologists. Avocation: hobbies: computer graphics, sports, kung-fu. Office: 1479 Commerce Dr Algonquin IL 60102 Personal E-mail: vikpatel1@yahoo.com.

PATERSON, DENNIS CRAIG, retired orthopedist, educator; b. Adelaide, Australia, Oct. 14, 1930; MBBS, U. Adelaide, 1953; MD, 1958. Prof., dir., chief orthopedic surgeon Adelaide Childrens, Royal Adelaide, Modbury Hosps., 1966—97. Pres. Crippled Childrens Assn. South Australia, 1968—84; bd. dirs. Australian Orthopaedic Assn., 1972—84; mem. bd. dirs. Adelaide Childrens Hosp., 1976—86; pres. Internat. Soc. Orthopaedic Surgery & Traumatology, 1987—90. Recipient Queen's Jubilee Medal, Australian Govt., 1977, L O Betts Medal, Australian Orthopaedic Assn., 1980; named Knight Bachelor, Her Majesty, Queen Elizabeth 11, 1976; named to Order of the Yugoslav Flag with Golden Wreath, Govt. of Yugoslavia. Fellow: Royal Australasian Coll. Surgeons, Royal Coll. Surgeons. Avocations: golf, gardening, reading, winemaking. Home: 26 Queen St Glenunga South Australia 5064 Australia Business E-Mail: paterson@awam.com.au.

PATHAK, ATUL, cardiologist, pharmacologist; b. Bremen, Germany, Feb. 19, 1972; s. Bal Krishna Pathak and Manju Sharma; m. Santoshi Dubey, Mar. 13, 1999; children: Mayanka, Ved. MSc in Pharmacology, U. Paris Sud XI, 1999; MD magna cum laude, U. Paul Sabatier, 2001, PhD. Rsch. fellow Cleve. Clinic (Ohio), 1998; fellow cardiology Rangueil U. Hosp., Toulouse, France, 1996—2001; rsch. fellow French Inst. Health, Toulouse, 2001—02; asst. prof. clin. pharmacology Toulouse (France) U. Hosp., 2002—. Cons. Bristol Myer Squib, Paris, 2001—, Astra-Zeneca Pharms., Paris, 2002—, Pfizer, Paris, 2002—. Co-author: Textbook of Cardiology, 1999, QT Dispersion, 1999; assoc. editor: Panorama du Medecin, 2002. Mem.: Soc. Cardiology, European Fedn. Autonomic Sys., Am. Soc. Heart Failure, French Soc. Hypertension, French Soc. Cardiology (Thesis prize 2003), French Soc. Pharmacology (Travel prize 1999, 2003). Office: Faculté Medecine Lab Pharmacology 37 Allées Jules Guesde 31000 Toulouse France

PATIL, NAISHADH PRABHAKAR, otolaryngologist; b. Bombay, Sept. 8, 1960; s. Prabhakar Babaji and Vimla (Gersoppa) P.; m. Anita Vishwas Barde, Dec. 25, 1991; children: Anish, Aishan. CM, G.S. Med. Coll., Bombay, India, 1986; MD, U. Wurzburg, Germany, 1988. Approved Alien Extraordinary Ability, US Immigration and Naturalization Svc. Clin. fellow U. Tubingen, Germany, 1987, U. Wurzburg, Germany, 1987-88; clin. tutor otolaryngology U. Galway, Ireland, 1993-99; lectr. otolaryngology Royal Coll. Surgeons, Dublin, Ireland, 1999—. Pres. Club Mac, Bombay, 1989, No. Ireland Mac User Group, Belfast, 1991; internet rev. CME-H/N Bull., Eng., 1997—; internat. rev. ENT News, 1995—. Co-author: (textbook) Clinical Atlas of ENT, 1992; asst. editor: Proceedings XI and XII/XIII Internat. Congresses of the NES, 1988; mem. editl. bd. Indian Jour. Otolaryngology, 1989-90 Intercollegiate fellow Otorhinolaryngology-Head & Neck Surgery, 1998. Fellow Royal Coll. Surgeons (Edinburgh); mem. Neurotological & Equilibriometric Soc., Politzer Soc. Hindu. Avocations: medical informatics, languages, health and nutrition, writing.

PATIL, NITIN T., chemist; b. Jalgaon, Maharashtra, May 22, 1975; MSc, North Maharastra U., India, 1997; PhD, U. Pune, India, 2002. Postdoc. fellow U. Göttingen, Germany, 2002; JSPS fellow to asst. prof. Tohoku U., Japan, 2002—06; rsch. fellow Inst. Chem. and Engring. Sci., Singapore, 2006—07, Scripps Rsch. Inst., 2007—08; rschr., group leader Indian Inst. Chem. Tech., 2008—. Recipient INSA Young Scientist medal, Indian Nat. Sci. Acad., India, 2010, Found. Day Young Scientist award, Alkyl Amine - ICT, 2010. Mem.: Indian Acad. Sci. (Bangalore). Office: IICT Habsiguda Tarnaka Hyderabad Andhra Pradesh 500607 India Personal E-mail: patilnitint@yahoo.com.

PATIL, SHARAN SHIVRAJ, orthopedic surgeon; b. Karnataka, India, Apr. 13, 1965; m. Meena Patil; 2 children. Completed med. sch. with academic distinction, M.R. Med. Coll., Gulbarga; grad., Kasturba Med. Coll., Manipal, 1990; MS in Orthop., 1991; Mch in Orthop., Liverpool U., 1995. Attended premedical sch. tng. MES Coll., Bangalore; with St. Martha's Hosp., Gulbarga; tng. Alder Hey Children's Hosp., Royal Liverpool Univ. Hosp. Hope Hosp., Manchester, Warrington District Gen. Hosp.; joined Manipal Hosp., Bangalore, 1996; chmn. Sparsh Hosp., chief orthop. surgeon, cons. Invited presenter in field. Pro bono work conducting free arthritis camps and camps for disabled children. Recipient Rajyotsava award, State of Karnataka, 2007, Suvarna Kannada Rajyotsava Prashasthi, Karnataka Cultural Acad., Bangalore, 2007, Belli Chukki, Karnatake Prathibhavardhaka Acad., Bangalore, 2007, Sadhana Rathna award, Sri Guru Cultural Acad., Bangalore, Vishwa Manya Kannadiga award, Vachana Sahithya Parishath, Dr. P.S. Shankar Vaidyashree award, Dr. P.S. Shankara Prathishtana, Gulbarga, Winnova Vaidyashree award, Winnova World, Bangalore. Mem.: Karnataka Orthop. Soc., Indian Orthop. Soc., Assn. Trauma Care of India. Achievements include being the lead surgeon of a team of doctors who performed the successful separation of the parasitic twin (8 limbs) from the body of Lakshmi Tatma in 2007; has performed several thousand major surgeries which include complex pediatric orthopedics surgeries, accidents/poly trama, total joint replacement of hip, knees and shoulder; one of the pioneers in establishing basic ground rules for safe trauma care in India; contributed to the development of the Sparsh Foundation. Avocation: sportsman. Office: Sparsh Hospital Unit of Shiva & Shiva Orthopedic Hospital Health City Industrial Lane 560 079 Bangalore India

PATINKIN, TERRY ALLAN, physician; b. Oak Park, Ill., Feb. 1, 1950; s. Lester D. and Marcella Jaqueline (Steynburg) P.; m. Sandra Lee Friedman, Apr. 21, 1985; children: Jonathan, Zachary. BS, U. Ill., 1971; MD, U. Calif., San Francisco, 1975; MPH in Health Care Mgmt., Harvard U., 1996. Diplomate Am. Bd. Emergency Medicine, Am. Bd. Family Medicine; cert. physician exec. Intern, resident in family practice U. Calif. San Francisco/Natividad Med. Ctr., Salinas, Calif., 1975-78, assoc. dir. family medicine residency program, 1978-90; dir. emergency dept. Natividad Med. Ctr., Salinas, 1985-91, dir. continuing med. edn., 1978-91, dir. undergrad. edn., 1978-90, emergency physician, 1979-91, Sturdy Meml. Hosp., Attleboro, Mass., 1991-94; dir., chmn. emergency dept. Roger Williams Hosp., Providence, 1994-99, Landmark Med. Ctr., Woonsocket, RI, 2000—02; med. dir. urgent care East Boston Neighborhood Health Ctr., 2002—. Asst. clin. prof. U. Calif., San Francisco, 1981-88, assoc. clin. prof., 1988-91; clin. asst. prof. Stanford U., 1990-93; asst. clin. prof. Brown U., Providence, 1995—, Boston U., 1999—. Fellow Am. Coll. Emergency Physicians; mem. Am. Coll. Physician Execs., Mass. Coll. Emergency Physicians, Mass. Med. Soc., U. Ill. Alumni Assn. (life), U. Calif. San Francisco Alumni Faculty Assn. Home Phone: 617-332-3752; Office Phone: 617-568-4639. Business E-Mail: patinkit@ebnhc.org.

PATINO-BRANDFON, SYLVIA, retired psychologist; d. Alfonso and Zenobia Moeller Patino; children: Andrea, Thea. AB in English, U. N.Mex., 1956; MS in English, Wis. U., 1958; student, Tavistock Inst., London, 1970—71; MA in Child Study, Tufts U., 1975; PhD in Psychology, Boston Coll., 1980; student in Psychopharmacology, Internat. Coll. Prescribing Psychologists, 1995—97. Lic. psychologist Mass., 1981. Intern psychotherapy Judge Baker Guidance Ctr., Boston, 1972—74; intern McLean Hosp., Belmont, Mass., 1979—80, post doctoral fellow, 1980—81; pvt. practice Quincy and Taunton, Mass., 1982—99; ret., 1999. Spkr. in field. Author: (newsletter) ADHD and Other Behavior Problems, 1994—98. Mem. com. superior cts. Ariz. Supreme Ct., 2004—, mem. jud. performance rev. commn., 2004—, bd. overseeing reporters, 2004; mem. Ariz. Commn. Jud. Conduct, 2007—. Fellow: APA (life).

PATLAS, MICHAEL NATHAN, radiologist, researcher; b. Leningrad, Russia, Mar. 24, 1969; s. Nathan and Ludmila Patlas; 1 child, Michal. MD, Hebrew U., 1993. Lic. physician Israeli Med. Assn., 2000. Intern Hadassah U. Hosp., 1994; resident ob-gyn. Shaare Zedek Med. Ctr., Jerusalem, 1995—96, resident radiology, 1996—2000, staff radiologist, 2000—01; fellow radiology Montefiore Hosp., NYC, 2001; fellow U. Toronto, Canada, 2002—04, McMaster U., Hamilton, Canada, 2004—04; staff radiologist Hamilton Gen. Hosp., 2004—. Ptnr. Barton Radiologists, Hamilton, 2005—; asst. prof. McMaster U., 2004—08, assoc. prof., 2008—. Recipient Hon. Mention award, AIUM, 2004, Pres. award, Hamilton Health Scis. Med. Staff Assn., 2011; Program Dir. Radiology fellowship, 2008—. Mem.: Can. Assn. Radiologists (Investigator award 2009), Ont. Coll. Physicians, Am. Roentgen Ray Soc., Radiologic Soc. N.Am. (ednl. exhibits com. mem.). Office: Hamilton General Hos Dept of Radiology 237 Barton St E Hamilton ON Canada L8L 2X2

PATNI, PALLAV MAHESH, endodontist; b. Indore, India, June 15, 1977; MDS, St.Pauls U., Indore, 2001, S.P.D.C. Wardha Nagpur U., 2006. Physician SAIMS, 2001—. Contbr. articles to profl. jours. Office: 27/2 Manoramaganj Indore Madhya Pradesh 452001 India Personal E-mail: pallavpatni@yahoo.com.

PATRADUL, ADISORN, dean, hospital administrator; b. Mar. 17, 1951; MD, Chulalongkorn U., Bangkok, 1975; diploma in Orthopaedic Surgery, Med. Coun. Thailand, 1980. Resident King Chulalongkorn Meml. Hosp.; hand & microsurgery fellowship U. Singapore; asst. prof. orthopedics dept. Faculty Medicine, Chulalongkorn U., 1990—93, assoc. prof., 1993—2009, asst. dean planning & devel., 1999—2007, dean Faculty Medicine, 2007—, prof., 2009—; dir. King Chulalongkorn Meml. Hosp., 2008—. Asst. sec. gen. in medicine Thai Red Cross Soc. Mem.: Royal Coll. Orthop. Surgeon Thailand (pres. 2010—). Achievements include recognition as the first doctor in Thailand to perform microsurgical toe to thumb transplantation for traumatic thumb loss. Office: Chulalongkorn Univ Faculty of Medicine 1873 Rama 4 Rd Pathumwan Bangkok 10330 Thailand Office Phone: 6622564244. Business E-Mail: adisorn.p@chula.ac.th.

PATRAS, JAMES, psychiatrist; b. Chgo., Feb. 14, 1951; m. Angie Z. Zaharopoulos, Sept. 16, 1979; 1 child, Simone. BA in Psychology, U. Ill., Chgo., 1973, BS in Biol. Scis., 1973; MD, U. Athens Sch. Medicine, 1981. Diplomate Am. Bd. Psychiatry and Neurology, 1986. Intern Mt. Sinai Med. Ctr., Chgo., 1981—82; resident Ill. State Psychiat. Inst., Chgo., 1982—85; v.p. med. svcs. Resurrection Behavioral Health, Chgo., 1997—2001, dir. med. svcs., 2001—; med. dir. dept. psychiatry Westlake Hosp., Melrose Park, Ill., 2002—. Asst. prof. clin. psychiatry U. Ill. Sch. of Medicine, Chgo., 1992—. Mem.: Hellenic Med. Soc. Chgo., Ill. Psychiat. Soc., Am. Psychiat. Assn. Office: 7627 W Lake St River Forest IL 60305-1878

PATRICK, CHRISTOPHER JOHN, psychology educator; b. Regina, Sask., Can., July 16, 1958; s. Donald Arthur and Susan Elsie (Sorokowsky) P.; m. Deborah Lynn Dixson, Apr. 18, 1981. BSc in Psychology with honors, Calgary U., Can.; PhD in Psychology, U. B.C., 1987. Psychology resident Alberta Hosp. Edmonton, Can., 1986-87; postdoctoral fellow U. Fla., Gainesville, 1987-90; asst. prof. Fla. State U., Tallahassee, 1990-95, assoc. prof., 1995—. Mem. editorial bd. Jour. Abnormal Psychology, 1994—, Jour. Applied Psychology, 1994—; contbr. chpt. to book, articles to profl. jorus. Social Scis. and Humanities Rsch. Coun. Can. scholar U. B.C., 1980-81, Univ. Grad fellow U. B.C., 1981-83, J.W. Killam fellow U.B.C., 1983-85, Social Scis. and Rsch. Coun. Can. doctoral fellow, 1983-87; NIMH 1st awardee Fla. State U., 1992-96. Fellow AAAS, APA, Soc. Psychophysiol. Rsch. (program com. 1989, pres.-elect, 2010-11, pres. 2011-, Disting. Sci. award 1993), Soc. Rsch. in Psychopathology. Achievements include identification of facial movements associated with pain; discovery of high error rate of lie detection with innocent suspects in real life criminal cases; research on accuracy of polygraph tests with criminal psychopaths; evidence for emotional abnormalities in criminal psychopaths. Office: Fla State U Dept Psychology 1107 W Call St Tallahassee FL 32306 Office Phone: 850-645-9315. Business E-Mail: cpatrick@psy.fsu.edu. *

PATRICK, SHARON, obstetrician-gynecologist, educator; BA, Coll. of Wooster, Ohio, 1982; MD, Case Western Reserve U., Cleve., Ohio, 1986. Diplomate Am. Bd. Ob-Gyn, cert. maternal and fetal medicine. Resident obstetrics and gynecology Columbia Presbyn. Hosp., NY, 1987—90, fellow maternal and fetal medicine, 1990—92; faculty attending physician roosevelt divsn. St. Luke's - Roosevelt Hosp. Ctr. Asst. clin. prof. obstetrics and gynecology Columbia Univ. Coll. of Physicians and Surgeons. Office: St. Luke's Roosevelt 800 A Fifth Ave 61st St Ste 503 New York NY 10021 Office Phone: 212-230-1785.

PATRIZI, ANNALISA, dermatologist; b. Bologna, Oct. 16, 1952; Degree in Medicine and Surgery, U. Bologna, 1977, degree in Dermatology and Venereology, 1981. Prof., dir. dermatology U. Bologna-Ospedale S.Orsola Malpighi, 2008—. Office: via Massarenti 1 Bologna Emilia-Romagna 40138 Italy Business E-Mail: annalisa.patrizi@unibo.it.

PATTANAGUL, PATCHAREE, medical researcher; b. Thailand, Jan. 1, 1978; D, Chiang Mai, 2005. Rschr. Elsie Inglis, 2009—. Home: 24 Gilmore Pl Edinburgh EH3 9NQ Scotland Personal E-mail: mrsupavej@hotmail.com.

PATTEN, BERNARD MICHAEL, neurologist, writer, educator; b. NYC, Mar. 23, 1941; s. Bernard M. and Olga (Vaccaro) P.; m. Ethel Doudine, June 18, 1964; children: Allegra, Craig. AB summa cum laude, Columbia Coll., 1962; MD, Columbia U., 1966. Med. intern N.Y. Hosp. Cornell Med. Ctr., NYC, 1966-67; resident neurologist Columbia Presbyn. Med. Ctr., NYC, 1967-69, chief resident neurologist, 1969-70; assoc. prof. neurology Baylor Coll. Medicine, Houston, 1973-95; ret., 1995. Asst. chief med. neurology NIH, Bethesda, Md., 1970-73; mem. med. bd. Nat. Myasthenia Gravis Found., 1973—, Nat. AmyoTrophic Lateral Sclerosis Found., 1982—, Nat. Myositis Assn., 1995—; invited faculty Rice U., 1999—; faculty Women's INst. Houston. Author: One or Two Things I Remember About Her, 1999, Tristan and Iseult: Modern Version, 2000, Investment Pearls for Modern Times Expressed in Meter and in Rhymes, 2000, The Great Cotzias, 2001, Ascent to Heaven, 2001, Quia Imperfectum, 2001, Truth, Knowledge or Bull: How to Tell the Difference, 2004, The Blood of a Million Christs, 2004, Cruising Around the World on the Queen Elizabeth 2, 2006, The Logic of Alice: Clear Thinking in Wonderland, 2009, Colossal Workers, 2011; contbr. articles to profl. jours. With USPHS, 1970-73. Rsch. grantee NIH, pvt. founds., nat. health orgns. Fellow ACP, Royal Coll. Physicians, Tex. Neurol. Soc. Achievements include discovery (with others)of L-Dopa for Parkinson's disease; pioneered use of immune suppression for myasthenia gravis, diagnosis and treatment of medical and neurologcal complications of breast implants. Home: 1019 Baronridge Dr Seabrook TX 77586-4001 Office Phone: 713-252-1306. Personal E-mail: dadpatten@aol.com.

PATTERSON, HEIDE CHRISTINE, medical researcher; b. Dinslaken, Germany, Apr. 7, 1973; MD, Ludwig Maximilians U., Germany, 1999, Johannes Gutenberg U., 1999. Resident, medicine Ludwig Maximilians U. Hosp., Germany, 1999—2000, Freiburg U. Med. Ctr., Germany, 2000—01; rsch. fellow Immune Disease Inst. Harvard Med. Sch., 2001—08; resident, clin. pathology Brigham and Women's Hosp. Harvard Med. Sch., 2008—11; vis. scientist Whitehead Inst. Biomed. Rsch. MIT, 2010—. NRSA fellowship, Joint Program Hematology and Transfusion Medicine. Mem.: AAAS, Soc. Clin. and Translational Sci., Mass. Med. Soc., Acad. Clin. Lab. Physicians and Scientists (Paul E. Strandjord Young Investigator award). Home: 162 Dedham St Newton MA 02461 Personal E-mail: kiki.kunst@gmail.com.

PATTERSON, JAMES RANDOLPH, physician; b. Lancaster, Pa., Jan. 30, 1942; m. Linda Lewis Patterson, Nov. 22, 1969. AB, U. Pa., 1964; MD, Columbia U., 1968. Diplomate Nat. Bd. Med. Examiners, Am. Bd. Internal Medicine, Subsplty. of Pulmonary Disease. Pulmonary and critical care specialist The Oreg. Clinic, Portland, 1975—; clin. prof. medicine Oreg. Health Scis. U., Portland, 1978—. Mem. Am. Bd. Internal Medicine, Phila., 1995—, sec.-treas., 2002--; trustee Collins Med. Trust, Portland, Oreg., 1992—, chair subsplty. bd. pulmonary disease, 1998-2002. Contbr. numerous articles to profl. jours. Recipient Class of 1964 award U. Pa., Van Loan award Am. Lung Assn. Oreg., 1990, Meritorious Achievement award Oreg. Health Scis. U., 1991; named Class Pres. Coll. Physicians and Surgeons of Columbia U., 1968, Tchr. of Yr. Providence Med. Ctr., Portland, Oreg., 1976, Internist of Yr., 1983, Best Doctors in Am., 1992—, Consumers Guide to Top Doctors, 2002-. Mem. AMA, Am. Thoracic Soc. (Clinician Tchr. of Yr. 2009), Am. Coll. Chest Physicians, Oreg. Lung Assn., North Pacific Soc. of Internal Medicine, Pacific Interurban Clin. Club, Multnomah County Med. Soc., Oreg. Med. Assn., Oreg. Soc. Critical Care Medicine. Office: The Oregon Clinic 1111 NE 99th St Ste 200N Portland OR 97220 Office Phone: 503-963-3030. Business E-Mail: jpatterson@orclinic.com.

PATTERSON, JAMES WILLIS, medical educator; b. Takoma Park, Md., Dec. 29, 1946; s. James Clark and Helen (Hendricks) Patterson; m. Julie Wyatt, Dec. 30, 1989; 1 child, James Wyatt. BA, Johns Hopkins U., 1968; MD, Med. Coll. Va., 1972. Diplomate Am. Bd. Dermatology, Am. Bd. Dermatopathology, Nat. Bd. Med. Examiners. Rotating intern in medicine Med. Coll. Va., Richmond, 1972-73, resident in dermatology, 1973-76, assoc. prof. pathology and dermatology, 1982-89, dir. dermatopathology, 1982-92, prof., 1989-92, clin. prof. pathology, 1992—; fellow dermatopathology Armed Forces Inst. Pathology, Washington, 1979—80; clin. instr. dermatology U. Colo. Med. Ctr., Denver, 1980—82; with Dermatology Assocs. Va., 1992-96, Va. Dermatopathology Svcs., Richmond, 1992-96; prof. pathology and dermatology U. Va., 1996—. Cons. in pathology McGuire VA Hosp., Richmond, 1982—92; cons. in pathology and dermatology Kenner Army Hosp., Ft. Lee, Va., 1982—95. Co-author: Dermatology: A Consise Textbook, 1987, Non-Melanocytic Tumors of the Skin, 2006; asst. editor: Jour. Cutaneous Pathology, 1989—94, editor-in-chief:, 2005—; contbr. articles to profl. jours. Mem. nat. alumni schs. com. Johns Hopkins U., 1986—. With MC US Army, 1976—82, col. USAR. Recipient Recipient Stuart McEwen award, Assn. Mil. Dermatologists, 1980, 1982; named to Best Doctors in Am., 2005—. Fellow: ACP, Am. Soc. Dermatopathology (sec.-treas. 2001—05, pres.-elect 2005—06, pres. 2006—), Am. Acad. Dermatology; mem.: Am. Bd. Dermatology, Am. Dermatol. Assn., Va. Dermatol. Soc. (sec.-treas. 1984—88, v.p. 1988—89, pres. 1989—90), Johns Hopkins U. Alumni Assn. (pres. ctrl. Va. chpt. 1989), Res. Officers' Assn. (life), Colonnade Club (bd. govs. 2004—08), Tau Epsilon Phi (life). Republican. Presbyterian. Avocations: history, baseball, golf. Business E-Mail: jwp9e@virginia.edu.

PATTERSON, NEAL L., information technology executive; BS in Fin., Okla. State U., MBA. Info. sys. cons., mgr. Arthur Andersen & Co., Kansas City, Mo.; co-founder, exec. dir. First Hand Found.; co-owner, Maj. League Soccer franchise Sporting KC, Kansas City; co-founder, CEO, chmn. Cerner Corp., 1979—, pres., 1999, 2010—. Lifetime dir., horse show and rodeo Am. Royal livestock. Trustee Midwest Rsch. Inst.; mem. steering com. Coun. Growing Cos. Named Entrepreneur of Yr., Ernst & Young, 1991; named one of 100 Most Powerful People in Healthcare award, Modern Healthcare, 4th America's Best-Performing Bosses, Forbes, 2010. Mem. Health Execs. Network. Office: Cerner Corp 2800 Rockcreek Pky Ste 601 Kansas City MO 64117 Office Phone: 816-201-1024. Office Fax: 816-474-1742. Business E-Mail: neal.patterson@cerner.com. *

PATTI, GIUSEPPE, cardiologist; b. Reggio Calabria, Italy, Oct. 31, 1967; MD, Cath. U. Rome, 1992. Cert. cardiologist Cath. U. Rome, 1997. Asst. prof. cardiology Campus Bio-Medico U. Rome, 2001—, prof. Sch. in Endocrinology & Cardiology, 2004—, chief instrumental cardiological svc. divsn., 2011—. Recipient Ippocrate Nat. award, 2007, Bronzi di Riace, 2009, Melvin Jones award, Lions Club Found., Chgo., 2010. Fellow: Italian Soc. Interventional Cardiology (Ann. award 2000), Am. Coll. Cardiology; mem.: Nat. Coun. Italian Soc. Cardiovasc. Rschs., Working Group on Atherosclerosis, Thrombosis and Vascular Biology Italian Fedn. Cardiology, European Soc. Cardiology. Avocations: music, tennis, volleyball. Office: Via Alvaro del Portillo 200 Rome 00128 Italy Office Fax: 39-06-225411638. Business E-Mail: g.patti@unicampus.it.

PATTI, MITCHELL J., internist; MD, SUNY, Brooklyn, 1986. Diplomate Am. Bd. Internal Medicine, Am. Bd. Internal Medicine-critical care medicine, Am. Bd. Internal Medicine-pulmonary disease. Resident Univ. Pitts. Med. Sch., fellow; hospital affiliation Univ. Pitts. Med. Ctr. St. Margaret. Office: University of Pittsburg Medical Center St Margaret Medical Arts Bldg 200 Delafield Rd Ste 2040 Pittsburgh PA 15215 Office Phone: 412-784-5888.

PATTISON, CHARLES WILLIAM, cardiac surgeon; b. Bedford, Eng., Nov. 3, 1956; MB ChB, U. Birmingham, 1980. Pvt. practice cardiac surgery, London, 1990—; dir. Wimpole St. Cardiac Practice, London. Chmn. cardiac com. Harley St. Clnic; mem. coun. Ind. Drs. Forum. Fellow: Soc. Cardiothoracic Surgeons, Royal Coll. Surgeons (Edinburgh), Royal Coll. Surgeons (Eng.); mem.: Soc. Cardiothoracic Surgeons of Gt. Britain. Avocations: sailing, skiing. Home: 42 Wimpole St London W1G 8YF England Home Phone: 00-44-207-486-7416; Office Phone: 00-44-207-486-7416. Fax: 00-44-207-487-2569.

PATTISON, JOHN EDWARD, medical and health physicist, researcher; b. Melbourne, Australia, Aug. 14, 1943; s. Robert McCorrie Pattison and Elsie May King; m. Annette Leone Morrison, July 11, 1969 (div.); children: Rebecca Ursula, Veronica Natasha, Benjamin John, Amanda Jayne. BSc, Australian Nat. U., 1966; MSc, U. Adelaide, 1971; MA, U. London, 1974, grad. in Edn., 1991. Cert. in archaol. Flinders U., 2010. Exptl. officer Defence Stds. Labs., Melbourne, Victoria, Australia, 1964—66; sr. tutor, lectr. South Australian Inst. of Tech., Adelaide, Australia, 1967—97; sr. lectr. U. of South Australia, Adelaide, Australia, 1997—2009. Sr. rsch. scientist Royal Adelaide Hosp., Australia, 1995; radiation safety officer U. South Australia, Adelaide, 1997—2009; vis. prin. scientist Queen Elizabeth Hosp., Birmingham, England, 1999—2000, 2006; adj. sr. rsch. fellow U. South Australia, Adelaide, Australia, 2009—. Editor: Australasian Phys. and Engr. Sci. in Medicine, 2002—05; guest assoc. editor: Med. Physics, 1998—99; assoc. editor Australasian Phys. and Engr. Sci. in Medicine, 2006—; contbr. articles to profl. jours. Justice of the peace, Australia, 1975—. Fellow, Royal Melbourne Inst. Tech., 1965. Fellow Coll. Biomedical Engring Engrs., Australia, Royal Soc. South Australia (councillor, comm. officer, webpage editor 1998—2005), Australian Inst. Physics (br. com. mem. 1990, 2000); mem.: Australasian Radiation Protection Soc. (mem. accrediation bd. 2011—), Australasian Coll. Phys. Scientists and Engrs. in Medicine (br. chmn., nat. registrar.continuing professional devel. 1997—2002), Skeptics Soc. South Australia (coord. $100,000 challenge 1996—2005). Achievements include development of method to estimate levels of inbreeding in large human populations over historic times. Avocations: ballroom dancing (medalist), astronomy, genealogy, heraldry, skeptic. Office: Univ South Australia EIE Applied Physics Mawson Lakes SA 5095 Australia Office Fax: 61-8-8302-3389. E-mail: john.pattison@unisa.edu.au.

PATTISON, TEALA ANN, nurse; b. Marion, Ind., Dec. 21, 1972; LPN, Marion Cmty. Sch. Practical Nursing, 2004. Pediat. office nurse Ea. Shore Children's Clinic, 2005—06, Pediat. by the Bay, 2006—09, Vols. America, 2009; nurse Infirmary West, 2009; office mgr. Ea. Shore Gastroenterology, 2009—. Grant, Marion Cmty. Sch. Practical Nursing. Mem.: Destiny Ch. Internat. Home: 599 Ridgewood Dr Daphne AL 36526 Office Phone: 251-279-4600. Personal E-mail: sweetnurse1972@yahoo.com. Business E-Mail: tpattiscan@imdsinc.com.

PATTON, GERALD M., vascular surgeon; MD, U. Miami. Diplomate Am. Bd. Surgery-vascular surgery, 1994, Am. Bd. Surgery-gen. surgery, 1993. Intern Thomas Jefferson Univ. Hosp., resident; fellow Univ. of Kansas Med. Ctr.; staff Bryn Mawr Hosp., 1995, Paoli Hosp., 1996; attending physician. Named one of the Top Doctor, Phila. Mag., 2011. Mem.: ACS, AMA, Internat. Soc.of Endovascular Specialists, Del. Valley Vascular Soc., Montgomery County Med. Soc., Pa. Med. Soc. Office: Bryn Mawr Hospital MOB N Ste 300 830 Old Lancaster Rd Bryn Mawr PA 19010 Office Phone: 610-527-1185. Office Fax: 610-527-1940.

PATTON, JACK THOMAS, physician; b. Rogers, Ark., Feb. 18, 1941; s. Jack Marcus and Jewell Selah (Pense) P.; m. Lynette Anne Carr, Sept. 2, 1960; children: Robert, John, Mark, Christopher. BA in History, Calif. State U., Long Beach, 1963; MA in History, Calif. State U., Fresno, 1993; MD in Medicine, U. Southern Calif., 1967; MA in Bibl. Studies, Mennonite Brethren Bib. Sem., Fresno, Calif., 1980. Cert. Bd. Med. Examiners, Calif., Hawaii., diplomate Am. Bd. Family Medicine. Intern Tripler Army Med. Ctr., Honolulu, 1967—68; resident in gen. practice Walson Army Hosp., Ft. Dix, NJ, 1968—70; med. supt. Nazarene Hosp., Papua New Guinea, 1973—80; chmn. family practice dept. Sharp Rees-Stealy, San Diego, 1981—86; chmn. occupl. medicine Kaiser Permanent, Fresno, 1986—87; assoc. med. dir. Sharp Rees-Stealy, San Diego, 1987-92; med. dir. Summer Inst. Linguistics, Papua New Guinea, 1993—94; with family practice dept. Sharp Rees-Stealy Med. Group, San Diego, 1994—97, Northwest Med. Group, Fresno, Calif., 1997—2007; chmn. dept. family practice St. Agnes Med. Ctr., 2002—05, family medicine cons. Sanger, Calif., 2007—. Family practice residency liaison Tripler Army Med. Ctr., Honolulu, 1972-73; chief medicine, dep. commr. Schofield Army Med. Clinics, Wahiawa, Hawaii, 1970-72; lectr. Calif. State U., Fresno, 1978-79, Pt. Loma Nazarene Coll., 1982-85, San Jose Christian Coll., 1997-2003; v.p. Patton Industries, Inc., 2005—. Mem. med. sch. support Salerni Collegium, U. Southern Calif. Sch. Medicine, 1967-85; lectr. Ch.-Mission Inst., Mennonite Brethren Bib. Sem., 1984-92; sec. S.E. Asian Task Force Mennonite Brethren Ch. Fresno, 1990-93. Maj. US Army, 1966-73. Mackenzie scholar U. Southern. Calif. Sch. Medicine, 1966-67; decorated Meritorious Svc. medal. Fellow Am. Acad. Family Physicians(life); Calif. Acad. Family Physicians, Royal Soc. Medicine (assoc., London). Republican. Baptist. Avocations: history, travel, hiking. Home: 847 Rosewood Ave Sanger CA 93657-5400 Office: 831 Rosewood Ave Sanger CA 93657-5400 Office Phone: 559-875-9791. Personal E-mail: dr_jack@verizon.net.

PATTON, REBECCA M., nursing administrator; BSN, Kent State U.; MSN, Case Western Res. U. RN, CNOR. Clin. instr. Frances Payne Bolton Sch. Nursing, Case Western Res. U.; dir. nursing, dir. surgical services, dir. ambulatory ops. U. Hospitals Health System; dir. perioperative services EMH Regional Healthcare System, Elyria, Ohio; Atkinson vis. instr. in perioperative nursing Case We. Res. U. Frances Payne Bolt Sch. Nursing, Cleve., 2011—. Recipient Cmty. Involved Polit. Action award, Sigma Theta Tau, Delta Xi chapt., Kent State U., 2000. Mem.: ANA (bd. dirs. 1994—98, treas. 1998—2002, del. 2003—05, pres. 2006—10), Ohio Nurses Assn. (first v.p. 1990—92, fin. com. 2003—05, del. 2005—06, Dorothy E. Cornelius Leadership Congress award 1999). Office: Frances Payne Bolton Sch Nursing Case We Res Universtiy 10900 Euclid Ave Cleveland OH 44106-4904 Office Phone: 216-368-3125. Business E-Mail: rmp9@case.edu. *

PATTON, THOMAS JAMES, marketing and sales executive; b. Cleve., Nov. 2, 1948; s. Michael Anthony and Delores (Bammerlin) Patton; m. Thomasina Bernadette Cavallaro, Aug. 9, 1969; children: Thomasina, Thera V. A in Transp., Cleve. State U., 1971, BA in Mktg., 1973; BA, SUNY, Empire State, 1994. CLU; ChFC; registered health underwriter; registered employee benefit cons. Ins. salesman Manulife, Cleve., 1972-75, Mass. Mut., Cleve., 1976-80, Patton Ins. Assn., Inc., Avon Lake, Ohio, 1976—; ins. cons. Diversified Benefit Plans, Inc., Avon Lake, 1978-93, dir. sales and mktg., 1993—; pres. commerce Benefits Group, Inc. and Ins. Mktg. Group, Inc., 1995; prin. Cmty. Health Ptnrs., Ltd., Ill., 1994. Pres. Commerce Benefits Group, Inc.; cons. Regional Sch. Consortium, Lorain County, Ohio, 1986—, County of Lorain, 1984—, City of Lorain, 1986—, County of Lorain, 1984—, City of Lorain, 1984—; prin. Comty. Health Ptnrs. Ltd.; bd. Italian Cultural Found.; founder 1-888 Ohiocomp w/c MCO-Ohio, 1997; co-founder VocRehabOne, Ltd., w/c Vocat. Rehab. Co.; founder MedAudits Inc., Cardinal Utilization Mgmt., Cardinal Preferred Care, Imaging Workflows Sys. Pres. Lake Erie Rate Coun., Cleve., 1970-71; mem. Lorain County Dem. Ctrl. Com., Avon Lake, Ohio, 1986 ; mem. com. Cleve. Leukemia Soc., 1985; bd. dirs. Villa Serena Sr. Housing, St. Francis Soc., Italian Cultural Found.; bd. trustees Found. Am. Coll., Bryn Mawr, Pa., 2002—. Mem. Nat. Assn. Life Underwriters, Profl. Ins. Agts. Assn., Cert. Profl. Ins. Agts. Soc., Soc. Benefit Plan Adminstrn., Lorain County Life Underwriters, Irish Heritage, Order Italian Sons and Daus., Profl. Assn. Dive Instrs./Nat. Assn. Underwater Instrs. (SCUBA diving instr.). Roman Catholic. Avocations: fishing, skin and scuba diving, photography. Office: Commerce Group PO Box 900 Elyria OH 44036-0900 Office Phone: 440-930-7500 ext. 203. Business E-Mail: tompatton@thecommercegroup.com.

PATTON, W. DAVID, public health service officer, state official; BS in Economics & Polit. Sci., Brigham Young U., MPA; PhD, U. Utah. Dir. ctr. for pub. policy and adminstrn. Univ. Utah, tchr., Boise State Univ.; exec. dir. Utah Policy Partnership; spl. adviser to Gov-elect Jon Huntsman Jr. Govt. of Utah; COO Utah Dept. Health, 2009, interim exec. dir., exec. dir., 2011—. Office: Utah Department of Health Cannon Health Bldg 288 North 1460 West Salt Lake City UT 84114 also: PO Box 141000 Salt Lake City UT 84114 Office Phone: 801-538-6111. *

PAU, HENRY POON HANG, otolaryngologist, researcher, professor; b. Hong Kong, Aug. 31, 1970; s. Chi Keung Pau and Vera Lai Ying Pau Wong; m. Hannah King, Sept. 6, 1997; children: Olivia Wymay children: Joshua Wyjing. MBChB, Leicester U., Eng., 1994; MD, U. Liverpool, 2004. Sr. ho. officer surgery and otorhinolaryngology, Leicester, England, 1994—99; specialist registrar otorhinolaryngology Liverpool, England, 1999—2001, 2003—05; fellow Med. Rsch. Coun. Inst. Hearing Rsch., Nottingham, England, 2001—03; fellow otology Sydney (Australia) Cochlear Implant Centre, 2005—06; cons. otorhinolaryngologist Alder Hey Children's Hosp., Liverpool, 2006. Cons. otorhinolaryngologist U. Hosp. Leicester, 2006—; hon. sr. lectr. Leicester U. Med. Sch., 2006—; vis. prof. Loughborough U., England, 2009—. Recipient award, Leicester U. Med. Sch., 1991, The Philip Stell prize, Otorhinolaryngology Rsch. Soc., 2002; fellow, Ctr. Rsch. and Studies Amplifon, Milan, Italy, 2000, St Vincent Hosp., Sydney, 2005; Graham Fraser Meml. fellow, 2005, European Soc. Paediatric Otorhinolaryngology scholar, 2002, TWJ Found. grantee, 2003. Fellow: Royal Coll. Surgeons (Eng.), Royal Coll. Surgeons (Edinburgh) (Ethicon Travel grantee 2005); mem.: British Soc. Audiology (mem. coun. 2008—), Royal Soc. Medicine (mem. coun. otology sect. 2004—, Rhinology Rsch. prize 2001, Ellison Cliffe Travelling fellow 2005, scholar 2002), Otorhinolaryngological Rsch. Soc. (mem. coun. 2003—). Personal E-mail: henry.pau@clara.co.uk.

PAUL, ABRAHAM DILIP, pharmacologist, researcher; s. Abraham and Rosie Paul; m. Lilly Mathew, Apr. 25, 1977; children: Teena, Neeta. MSc in Medicine, Christian Med. Coll., 1970; PhD in Medicine, Lokmanya Tilak Mcpl. Med. Coll., Mumbai, 1998. Lectr. pharmacology Christian Med. Coll., Vellore, India, 1970—71; gen. mgr. Boots Pharma and Knoll Pharma and Abbott India Ltd., Mumbai, India, 1972—2002; sr. dir. Dr. Reddy's Labs. Ltd., Hyderabad, India, 2002—. Dir., chmn. YMCA, Mumbai, 1980—2001. Fellow: Royal Soc. Health; mem.: Indian Pharmacological Soc. (life). Avocations: stamp collecting/philately, writing. Office: Dr Reddy's Labs Ltd CMS Srinivasa Complex Ameerpet Hyderabad 500016 India Home: 69 501 Krishna Kasturi 500 016 Hyderabad India Office Fax: 91-40-55511536. Personal E-mail: dradpaul@gmail.com.

PAUL, CHARLOTTE PATRICIA PEGGRAM, nursing educator; b. Clarendon, Texas, Jan. 13, 1941; d. William Clyde Peggram and Sibyl (Rattan) Jones; m. Robert M. Paul, Apr. 4, 1964; children: Peter, Lauraine. Attended, Amarillo Coll., Tex., 1958-65; diploma, St. Anthony's Hosp. Sch. Nursing, Amarillo, Tex., 1961; BS, Syracuse U., NY, 1972, MS, 1973, PhD in Edn. adminstrn., 1979; post grad., Wright State U., 1977-79, U. Tex., El Paso, 1983-86. Nurse St. Anthony's Hosp., Amarillo, Tex., 1961-65; evening charge nurse VA Hosp. Gen. Hosp., Syracuse, NY, 1965-66, Upstate Med. Ctr. State Univ. N.Y., Syracuse, NY, 1966-68; asst. to head nurse Meml. Hosp., Syracuse, NY, 1966-68; nurse IV therapy Cmty. Gen. Hosp., Syracuse, NY, 1968-72; instr. Syracuse Ctr. Sch. Sys., NY, 1972; instr. in svc. edn. House of Good Samaritan Hosp., Watertown, NY, 1973-74; instr. State Univ. N.Y. Sch. Nursing, Syracuse, NY, 1974-75, Syracuse U. Sch. Nursing, NY, 1975-76; asst. dean Wright State Univ., Dayton, Ohio, 1977-79; assoc. prof. Edinboro Univ., Pa., 1979-86, prof. Pa., 1986—2001, chairperson, dept. grad. studies Pa., 1980-82, chairperson dept. nursing Pa., 1987-89. Spl. project officer William Beaumont Army Med. Ctr., Ft. Bliss, Tex., 1982—85; adj. assoc. prof. U. Tex., El Paso, 1982—85; cons. in field. Contbr. articles and papers to profl. jour. Bd. dir. ARC, Syracuse, NY, 1970—77; cons. Erie County Emergency Mgmt. Agy., 1987—89; mem. Coun. on Aging Com. on Long Term Care, Dayton, Ohio, 1977—78; instr. U. Pheonix, Ariz., 2008—. Lt. col., ret. USAR, 1977—2001. Recipient Unit Citation Award, CAP, 1968, Excellence in Nursing Edn. Award, 1992, Leadership and Svc. Award, Lake Area Health Edn. Ctr., 1994, Comdr. Commendation Award, 1995; named to Hall of Fame, Internat. Bus. and Profl. Women, 1994; grantee Gladys Post scholar, 1958—61, Nellie Hurly scholar, 1971—72, Rodney Horle scholar, 1971—72, HEW, 1977, Wright State Univ., 1977—78, Edinboro Univ., 1979—80, William Beaumont Army Med. Ctr., 1986; fellow Nightingale Soc. fellow, 1988. Mem.: U.S. Nightingale Soc., Syracuse Univ. Alumni Assn., St. Anthony's Hosp. Sch. Nursing Alumni Assn., Res. Officers Assn. (life), Assn. Mil. Surgeons (life), Nat. Ski Patrol (life), Kiwanis (v.p. 1987—88, bd. dirs. Edinboro chpt. 1987—89, pres. 1988—89), Sigma Theta Tau (advisor 1987—94), Pi Lambda Theta (life; pres. local chpt. 1973—75). Republican. Office: Edinboro Univ Pa 139 Centennial Hall Edinboro PA 16412 E-mail: peggram_01@yahoo.com.

PAUL, DAVID ANDREW, medical association administrator; b. Pitts., June 28, 1962; MD, Hahnemann U., 1988. Assoc. dir. Christiana Neonatology Assoc., 2010—. Chair Del. Healthy Mother Infant Consortium, 2005; prof. pediat. Thomas Jefferson U. Med. Coll., 2010. Recipient Katherine Esterly Health Care award, Mar. of Dimes. Office: 4745 Ogletown Stanton Rd Newark DE 19713 Office Fax: 302-733-2602. Business E-Mail: dpaul@christianacare.org.

PAUL, FLORIN, surgeon; b. Simeria, Hunedoara, Romania, Dec. 16, 1953; s. Nicolae and Ileana Paul; m. Liliana Hodojeu, July 26, 1980; children: Emilian Simion, Oana Maria. PhD (hon.), U. of Medicine, Bucharest, Romania, 2000; MPH (hon.), U. of Medicine Carol Davilla, Bucharest, 2004. Lic. MD Ministry of Edn., Romania, sr. epidemiologist U. of Medicine, Bucharest, infectious diseases specialist U. of Medicine, Bucharest, mgmt. of med. svcs. U. of Medicine, Bucharest. Med. officer Air Force unit Ministry of Nat. Def., Bucharest, 1984—85; med. officer occupl. and environ. dept. Ctr. of Preventive Medicine, MOD, Romania, 1985—94; dep. dir., sr. rschr. Army Ctr. for Med. Rsch., Bucharest, 1995—2001; dep. comdr. officer Ctr. for Med. Rsch., MOD, Romania, 1995—2001; dep. surgeon gen. Med. Directorate, MOD, Bucharest, 2001—. Force med. officer UN Mission in Angola - UNAVEM, Luanda, Angola, 1995—96; sr. epidemiologist Med. Rsch. Ctr., MOD, Bucharest, Romania, Romania, 1995—. Contbr., dir., transl.: R&D Medical Protection in Biological Crisis. Col. Med. Directorate, 1974—2004, Romania. Decorated Mil. Virtue, Knight Pres. of Romania. Master: Romanian Assn. for Antimicrobials (mem. of bd. 1998—2004); mem.: Romanian Mil. Med. Assn., Romanian Soc. of Epidemiology and Infection Control. Home: 7 Burdujeni bloc B2 scA apt35 Bucharest 7000 Romania Office: Med Directorate MOD 3-5 Institutul Medico-Militar Bucharest 7000 Romania Office Fax: 00 40 21 2205453. Personal E-mail: paulf@pcnet.ro.

PAUL, IAN M., pediatrician, educator; BA in Chemistry with honors, Franklin and Marshall Coll.; MSc in Medicine and Health Evaluation Scis., Pa. State Univ.; MD, Pa. State U. Coll. Medicine. Intern Duke Univ. Med. Ctr. and Children's Hosp.; asst. prof. pediatrics and pub. health scis. Pa. State Univ. Coll. Medicine, pediatrician, health svcs. rschr., dir., pediatric clin. rsch. Co-investigator Nat. Heart, Lung and Blood Inst., Childhood Asthma Rsch. and Edn. (CARE) Network; mem. exec. com. Am. Acad. Pediatrics' Sect. Clin. Pharmacology and Therapeutics. Office: Univ Physicians Group Cherry Drive (Peds) UPG-Cherry Drive HS05 670 Cherry Dr Ste 102 Hershey PA 17033 Fax: 717-531-3527.

PAUL, LEENDERT CORNELIS, medical educator; b. Zevenhuizen, The Netherlands, Jan. 31, 1946; married; 2 children. Student, Leiden State U. Med. Sch., The Netherlands, 1964-69; MD cum laude, State U. of Leiden, The Netherlands, 1969, PhD cum laude, 1979. Cert. gen. med. lic., The Netherlands; Ednl. Coun. Fgn. Med. Grads.; cert. specialist in internal medicine, The Netherlands, cert. specialist in internal medicine. Rotating intern U. Hosp. Leiden, 1969-72, resident in internal medicine, 1972-77, clin. fellow in nephrology, 1977-79, rsch. fellow in transplantation immunology, 1977-79, staff nephrologist, 1979-87, chef de policlinique Renal divsn., 1979, chef de clinique Renal Transplant unit, 1981-87; rsch. fellow in transplantation immunology & immunogenetics Renal divsn. Brigham and Women's Hosp./Harvard Med. Sch., Boston, 1979-81; from asst. prof. to assoc. prof. medicine Leiden U., 1979-87; prof. medicine U. Calgary, Can., 1987-93, head divsn. nephrology, 1989-93; staff nephrologist Foothills Hosp., Calgary, Can., 1987-93, dir. Clinic for Organ Transplantation, 1987-93, chief renal divsn., 1989-93; prof. medicine U. Toronto, Can., 1993—; chief nephrology St. Michael's Hosp., Toronto, 1993—1998. Guest prof. Free U., Brussels, 1987-90, 96—; med. dir. Human Orgn. Procurement and Exch. Program, South Alberta, 1991-92, chmn. immunol. scis. rsch. group, 1991-92; adv. bd. Eurotransplant, 1984-87; sci. coun. Dutch Kidney Found., 1984-87; adv. bd. Dutch Soc. Cardiac Transplant Recipients, 1984-87; mem. panels Dutch Orgn. for Fundamental Med. Rsch., 1985, 86-87; sec. Bd. Dutch Renal Failure Register, 1986-87; mem. adv. bd., fellowship com. Kidney Found. Can., 1989—, sci. coun., 1990—, scholarship and fellowship com., 1993-96; chmn. Provincial Renal Programs Adv. Com., Alta., Can., 1990-93; mem. com. on immunology and transplantation Med. Rsch. Coun., 1991-94; Keenan chair medicine U. Toronto, 1993—; lectr. at internat. meetings and symposia. Editor several books in field; editor-at-large Marcel Dekker, Inc., 1992—; mem. editl. bd. Transplantation, 1986—, Transplant Revs.; mem. internat. bd. Transplant Internat.; contbr. numerous chpts. to books, also articles and abstracts to profl. jours. Recipient Anna Overwater award for sci. contbns. in immunology of human kidney transplantation, 1983, Alta. Heritage Found. for Med. Rsch. Scientist award, 1988—. Achievements include research in organ transplantation and mechanisms of rejection, histocompatibility antigens, immunosuppressive drugs, mechanism of actions, side effects; mechanisms of progressive loss of renal function. *

PAUL, MALCOLM DAVID, plastic and reconstructive surgeon; b. Balt., Nov. 8, 1943; s. William and Rose (Friedman) P.; m. Pamela Sisk Paul, May 15, 1981; children: Stephen, Scott, Jacquie, Matthew. BS, U. Md., 1965; MD, U. Md., Balt., 1969. Cert. Am. Bd. Platic Surgery, 1976. Intern Mt. Sinai Hosp., NYC, 1969-70, resident, 1970-71, George Washington U., Washington, 1971-75; practice medicine specializing in plastic surgery Fountain Valley, Calif., 1975—. Asst. clin. prof. to assoc. prof. clin. surgery, divsn. plastic surgery U. Calif., Irvine, 1976-; bd. dirs. CAP-MPT; adv. bd. mem., med. spa advisor Cosmetic Surgery Exposition Group; mem. adv. bd. Cosmetic Enhancement Expo. Named to Best Doctors in America, Orange County Top Doctors, Guide to Top Doctors. Mem. Am. Soc. Plastic and Reconstructive Surgery, Am. Soc. Aesthetic Plastic Surgery, Inc. (past pres., chmn. bd. trustees), Am. Bd. Plastic Surgery (past dir.), Orange County Soc. Plastic Surgeons, Inc. (past pres.), Am. Assn. Plastic Surgeons, Am. Soc. Plastic Surgery, Inc.(bd. trustee, 2009), Aesthetic Surgery Edn. and Rsch. Found., Internat. Soc. Aesthetic Plastic Surgery (past US Nat. sec.), Calif. Soc. Plastic Surgeons Republican. Jewish. Office: 1401 Avocado Ave Ste 810 Newport Beach CA 92660-8708 Office Phone: 949-760-5047.

PAUL, MITRUT, gastroenterologist; b. Romania, Feb. 2, 1959; D, U. Medicine And Pharmacy Craiova, Dolj, Romania, 1985; M in Health Mgmt., U. Bucharest, 2009. Master conf. dept. internal medicine U. Medicine And Pharmacy Craiova, 1990—. Mgr. Med. Ctr. Renasterea Srl, 2007; founder Med. Rsch. Ctr.-Renasterea. Mem.: Romanian Soc. Phlebology, Romanian Soc. Gastroenterology And Hepatology, European Soc. Gastrointestinal Endoscopy. Avocations: travel, sports, music. Home: Aries St 36 Craiova Dolj 200384 Romania Home Fax: 251533020. Business E-Mail: centrul_renasterea@rdscv.ro.

PAUL, NORMAN LEO, psychiatrist, educator; b. Buffalo, July 5, 1926; s. Samuel Joseph and Tannie (Goncharsky) P.; m. Betty Ann Byfield, June 6, 1951 (dec. May 1994); children: Marilyn, David Alexander; m. Janet Athos, Aug. 16, 2002. MD, U. Buffalo, 1948. Fellow pharmacology U. Cin. Coll. Medicine, Ohio, 1949-50; resident psychiatry Mass. Mental Health Ctr., Boston, 1952-55; fellow child psychiatry James Jackson Putnam Children's Ctr., Boston, 1957-59, Mass. Gen. Hosp., Boston, 1958-59; chief psychiatrist Day Hosp. Mass. Mental Health Ctr., Boston, 1960-64; dir. conjoint family therapy Boston State Hosp., 1964-65, cons. in family psychiatry, 1965-70; assoc. clin. prof. dept. neurology Boston U. Sch. Medicine, 1977—. Cons. Mental Health Ctr., Alaska Native Hosp., Anchorage, 1967-68; cons. family psychiatry Boston VA Hosp., 1967-71, Mass. Soc. for the Prevention of Cruelty to Children, Boston, 1993—; vis. family therapist St. George's Med. Sch., London, 1996-97; lectr. in psychiatry Harvard Med. Sch., Boston, 1976-2003; faculty assoc. Mgmt. Analysis Corp., Cambridge, Mass., 1979-82; presenter Internat. Conf. on Telemedicine and Telecare, London, 1996 Family therapist: (tv documentary) PBS-Trouble in the Family, 1965 (George Foster Peabody award 1965); co-author A Marital Puzzle, 1977, 86, German edit., 1987, French edit., 1995, Chinese edit., 1997, contbr. articles to profl. jours. Sponsor Mass. Orgn. to Repeal Abortion Laws, Boston, 1965-70; chair Audio Unit of Child Devel. and Mass Media, White House Conf. on Children and Youth, Washington, 1970; bd. trustees Cambridge (Mass.) Coll., 1977-89; bd. dirs. Let's Face It, 1990—, Ctr. for Family Connections, 1998—2002. Capt. USAF, 1950-52. Recipient Edward A. Strecker, M.D. award for young psychiatrist of yr., 1966, Cert. of Merit, Mass. Coun. on Family Life, Boston, 1967, Cert. of Commendation, Mass. Assn. for Mental Health, Boston, 1967, Disting. Achievement award Soc. for Family Therapy and Rsch., Boston, 1973, Lifetime Achievement award Mass. Assn. for Marriage and Family Therapy, 1998, Disting. Svc. award Physician Health Svcs., 1998. Fellow Royal Soc. Medicine, Am. Psychiat. Assn. (life); mem. Am. Assn. Marriage and Family Therapy (bd. dirs. 1983-86), Am. Family Therapy Assn. (v.p. 1982-83, Disting. Contbn. award 1984), Assn. for Rsch. in Nervous and Mental Disorders, Group for the Advancement Psychiatry (chair com. on the family 1982-84). Avocations: study of codes, travel. Home and Office: 17 Highwood Ln Ipswich MA 01938-3024 Office Phone: 978-369-3754. Personal E-mail: nlpaul@aol.com.

PAUL, STEVEN M., retired pharmaceutical executive; BA magna cum laude in Biology and Psychology, Tulane U., New Orleans, 1972, MS in Anatomy and Neuroanatomy, 1975, MD, 1975. Intern neurology Charity Hosp., New Orleans; resident psychiatry, instr. dept. psychiatry U. Chgo. Pritzker Sch. Medicine; prof. psychiatry Tulane U. Sch. Medicine; chief clin. neuroscience br., chief preclinical studies sect. NIH NIMH, Bethesda, sci. dir. intramural rsch. program; v.p. ctrl. nervous sys. discovery and decision phase med. rsch. Lilly Rsch. Labs. Eli Lilly & Co., Indpls., 1993—96, v.p. therapeutic area discovery rsch. and clin. investigation Lilly Rsch. Labs., 1996—98, group v.p. therapeutic area discovery rsch. and clin. investigation Lilly Rsch. Labs., 1998, exec. v.p. sci. and tech., pres. Lilly Rsch. Labs., 2003—10, mem. corp. policy and strategy, ops. coms., mem. sr. mgmt. coun. Chmn. exec. bd. Pharm. Rsch. and Mfrs. Am. Sci. and Regulatory Com.; bd. mem. Biotechnology Industry Orgn. Contbr. articles to profl. jours., chapters to books. Bd. dirs. Lilly Found., Found. of NIH, Butler U., Indpls., Indpls. Zoological Soc. Recipient A.E. Bennett award, Soc. Biol. Psychiatry, Foundations' Fund prize for Rsch., Am. Psychiat. Assn., Disting. Svc. medal, US; named Chief Sci. Officer of Yr., 2005. Mem.: NAS Inst. Medicine, Tulane Scholars and Fellows, Alpha Omega Alpha Med. Soc., Phi Beta Kappa, Sigma Xi, Alpha Epsilon Delta, Phi Eta Sigma.

PAUL, WILLIAM ERWIN, immunologist; b. Bklyn., June 12, 1936; s. Jack and Sylvia (Gleicher) Paul; m. Marilyn Heller, Dec. 25, 1958; children: Jonathan M. Carmel, Matthew E. BA summa cum laude, Bklyn. Coll., 1956; MD cum laude, SUNY, Bklyn., 1960, DSc (hon.), 1991; PhD (hon.), Hebrew U., Jerusalem, 2003, Med. U. Cluj-Napoca, Romania, 2003, Nat. U. Athens, Greece, 2007; Laurea hon. causa, U. Rome, 2005. Intern, asst. resident Mass. Meml. Hosp., Boston Med. Ctr., 1960—62; clin. assoc. Nat. Cancer Inst., NIH, Bethesda, Md., 1962—64; post doctoral fellow, instr. NYU Sch. Medicine, NYC, 1964—68; prin. investigator lab. immunology Nat. Inst. Allergy and Infectious Diseases, NIH, Bethesda, Md., 1968—70, chief lab. immunology, 1970—; dir. office of AIDS rsch. NIH, Bethesda, Md., assoc. dir. AIDS rsch., 1994—97, disting. investigator, 2007—. Awards jury mem. Albert Lasker Med. Rsch. Awards Program, 1993—; chmn. selection com. Irene Diamond Fund Professorship in Immunology, 1997—2005; Sackler sr. prof. Tel Aviv U., Israel; chair sci. adv. bd. Lupus Rsch. Inst.; mem. Novartis Sci. Bd., 2001—05; adj. prof. U. Pa., 2002—; governing dir. Am. Found. for AIDS Rsch., 2002—05, mem. program adv. bd., 2006—; chair visiting com. assessment of basic biomed. rsch. Israel Acad. Sci. and Humanities, 2007; mem. sci. adv. bd. Trudeau Inst. Adv. editor Jour. Exptl. Medicine, 1974—2006; editor: Ann. Rev. Immunology, Volumes 1-28, 1983—, Fundamental Immunology, 1st - 6th edits., 1984—, Immunity, 2003—06; assoc. editor Cell, 1985—96, transmitting editor Internat. Immunology, 1989—96, corr. editor Procs. Royal Soc. Series B, 1989—93, mem. editl. bd. Molecular Biology of Cell, 1990—93; contbg. editor: Procs. NAS U.S.A., 1992—94; mem. editl. bd. Procs. NAS U.S.A., 2004—; contbr. numerous articles to sci. journals. With USPHS, 1962—64, with USPHS, 1975—96. Recipient Founders' prize, Tex. Instruments Found., 1979, Alumni medal, SUNY Downstate Med. Ctr., 1981, DSM, USPHS, 1985, Life Sci. Award, 3M, 1988, Tovi Comet - Wallerstein prize, CAIR Inst., Bar Ilan U., 1992, 6th ann. Excellence Award in Immunologic Rsch., Duke U., 1993, Alumni Honors, Bklyn. Coll., 1994, Abbott Labs. Award in Clin. and Diagnostic Immunology, Am. Acad. Microbiology, 1998, Lifetime Achievement award, Am. Assn. Immunologists, 2002, Sci. Achievement in award, The Irvington Inst., 2002, Rsch. in Action award, Treatment Action Group, 2003, Scientific Leadership award, Lupus Found., 2005, Hon. Lifetime Achievement award, Internat. Cytokine Soc., 2007. Fellow: Am. Acad. Arts and Sci.; mem.: NAS, Am Assn. Immunologists (pres. 1986—87, Lifetime Achievement award 2002, Mex Delebruck medal 2008), Assn. Am. Physicians, Scandinavian Soc. Immunology (hon.), Am. Soc. Clin. Investigation (pres. 1980—81), Inst. Medicine NAS. Achievements include discovery of interleukin-4 and demonstration of its central role in allergic inflammatory responses; determination of mechanisms of Th2 differentiation. Office: NIH Bldg 10 Rm 11n311 Bethesda MD 20892-1982 Office Phone: 301-496-5046. Business E-Mail: wpaul@niaid.nih.gov.

PAUL, WILLIAM S., city health department administrator; b. Chgo. m. Tonya Paul; 3 children. BS, Stanford Univ.; MD, MPH, Univ. Ill. Cert. internal med. & infectious diseases. Positions through dep. commr. & chief med. officer Chgo. Dept. Pub. Health, 1992—2007; dir. health Metro. Bd. Health Nashville/Davidson County, 2007—. Office: Metro Bd Health 311 23d Ave Nashville TN 37203 Office Phone: 615-340-5622. Office Fax: 615-340-2131.

PAULINO, LEONARDO VERRI, ophthalmologist, educator; b. São Paulo, Brazil, Nov. 15, 1973; B, Faculdade de Medicina do ABC, 1998; M, Escola Paulista de Medicina, 2000. Prof. Faculdade de Medicina do ABC, 2003—. Cataract and refractive surgeon Inst. Olhos Dr. Eduardo Paulino, 2005—11; psychotherapist Citara Saúde, 2008—11. Recipient 2nd prize, V Brazilian Cataract and Refractive Congress SBCR e SBCII Photography Contest, 2009, 1st prize, VII ABC Winter Video Festival Ophthalmology, 2010. Mem.: Brazilian Coun. Ophthalmology, Brazilian Soc. Refractive Surgery, Brazilian Soc. Cataract and Ocular Implants. Avocation: music. Office: Av Washington Luiz 451 Santos São Paulo 11055-001 Brazil Personal E-mail: leonardovpaulino@hotmail.com.

PAULISSEN, JAMES PETER, retired pediatrician, county official; b. Chgo., Aug. 14, 1928; s. Joseph Edward and Louise Catherine (Muno) P.; m. Lorraine Antoinette Polly, Sept. 11, 1954; children: Linda, Steven, Mark, Daniel. Student, Loyola U., 1946-49, MD cum laude, 1953; MPH, Johns Hopkins U., 1966. Diplomate Am. Bd. Pediat. Intern Milw. County Hosp., 1953-54; resident Milw. Children's Hosp., 1957-58; practice medicine specializing in pediats. Wauwatosa Children's Clinic, Wis., 1959-65; pediat. fellow Johns Hopkins U., 1965—66; chief Bur. Maternal and Child Health Ill. Dept. Pub. Health, Springfield, 1966-70, chief Divsn. Family Health, 1970-76; exec. dir. DuPage County Health Dept., Wheaton, Ill., 1976-93. Bd. dirs., mem. exec. com. Suburban Cook-DuPage Health Sys. Agy., Oak Park, Ill., 1976-82; bd. dirs., past pres. Comprehensive Health Coun. Met. Chgo., 1977-87; dir. Sr. Home Sharing, Inc., Wheaton, 1981-83; mem. Ill. Commn. on Children, 1971-85, vice chmn., 1983-85; chmn. Ill. Perinatal Adv. Com., 1981-84, mem., 1981-92; mem. Ill. Sch. Health Adv. Com., 1982-93, Gov.'s Adv. Coun. on Devel. Disabilities, 1973-76, Ill. Med. Determinations Bd., 1985-93; vice chmn. Ill. Pub. Health Advisors, 1988-91; mem. adv. bd. divsn. Svcs. Crippled Children U. Ill., 1986-94; trustee DuPage County Med. Found., 1976-82, 86-92, 1999-2006, treas. 2002-06; bd. dirs. DuPage Cmty. Clinic, 1993-2008, Cmty. Nursing Svc. of DuPage, 1993-99, vice chair, 1997-99; mem. cmty. health com. Ctrl. DuPage Health Sys., 1993-98; del. White House Conf. for Children, 1970. Capt. USAF, 1954-56. Recipient Dir.'s award for Sustained Excellence Ill. Dept. Pub. Health, 1988, Ill. Pediatrician of Yr. award, 1992, Humanitarian award DuPage County Health Planning Coun., 1994. Fellow Am. Acad. Pediats. (exec. com. Ill. chpt. 1978-81, sec. 1988-92), APHA, Am. Coll. Preventive Medicine; mem. Ill. Pub. Health Assn. (pres. 1977-78, Disting. Svc. award 1983), Ill. Assn. Maternal and Child Health (pres. 1975-76). Avocation: model building. Home: 28w660 Hawthorne Ln West Chicago IL 60185-2472

PAULSON, GWEN O., career and leadership coach, government relations consultant; b. Detroit, Mar. 16, 1945; d. Maurice V. and Lilyan Victor; div.; children: Jill Susan, Mindy Beth; m. Jerome A. Paulson, July 2, 1989. BA, Mich. State U., 1966; MA, Wayne State U., 1974; postgrad., U. Mich., 1981; cert. in Leadership Coaching, Georgetown U., 2005. Profl. cert. coach. Lectr. Oakland U., Mich., 1979—80, U. Mich., Ann Arbor, 1981; legis. asst. U.S. Rep. Pete Stark, Washington, 1982—85; mem. profl. staff, ways and means health subcom. U.S. Ho. of Reps., Washington, 1985—89; v.p. for health Capitol Assocs., Washington, 1989—90; pres. Congl. Cons., Washington, 1990—2005, Coaching and Cons. LLC, 2005—. Author: Women and the Structure of Society, 1984. Edward S. Beck fellow U. Mich., Ann Arbor, 1978-79; Rackham Dissertation grant U. Mich., Ann Arbor, 1980. Mem. Partnership Pub. Svc., Soc. Industry Leaders, Internat. Coach Fedn., The Mind Tools Career Excellence Club (assoc. coacher), Phi Alpha Theta, Tau Sigma. Avocations: collecting contemporary glass, travel, history, politics, reading. Office: Coaching and Consulting LLC 1113 N Howard St Alexandria VA 22304-1627 Office Phone: 703-461-7683. Personal E-mail: gwencc@comcast.net.

PAULSON, HENRY L., medical educator; b. Raleigh, NC, July 6, 1959; MS, Yale U., 1981, MD, PhD, 1990. Neurology prof. U. Mich., 2007—. Head neuroedegenerative disease programs, Mich., 2007. Mem.: ANA, AAN. Office: University Mich 109 Zina Pitcher Pl Ann Arbor MI 48109 Business E-Mail: henryp@umich.edu.

PAULSON, JEROME AVROM, pediatrician; b. Balt., July 31, 1949; s. Robert R. and Edna (Brenner) P.; m. Susan Miller, 1973 (div. 1986); m. Gwen Victor Gampel, July 2, 1989. BS in Biochemistry, U. Md., 1971; MD, Duke U., 1974. Diplomate Am. Bd. Pediatrics, Nat. Bd. Med. Examiners. Resident in pediatrics Johns Hopkins Hosp., Balt., 1974-76, Sinai Hosp., Balt., 1976-77, fellow in ambulatory pediatrics, 1977-78; asst. prof. pediatrics Case Western Res. U., Cleve., 1978-86; dir. sci. rsch. and pub. policy devel. Joseph P. Kennedy Jr. Found., Washington, 1986-87; dir. pediatrics Regional Inst. for Children and Adolescents, Rockville, Md., 1987-89; clin. assoc. prof. pediatrics Georgetown U., Washington, 1987—; exec. dir. Research!America, Alexandria, Va., 1989-90; assoc. prof. medicine (formerly healthcare scis.) George Washington U., Washington, 1990—2002, assoc. prof. pediats., 1991—, fellow Ctr. Health Policy Rsch., 1991—98, assoc. prof. prevention and cmty. health, 1997—, assoc. rsch. prof. environ. health sci. & policy, 2003—; dir. Mid-Atlantic Ctr. for Children's Health and the Environment Children's Nat. Med. Ctr., 2000—; med. dir. Nat. Global Affairs, Children's Health Adv. Inst., 2008—. Mem. conf. on methodology and std. definitions for childhood injury rsch. Nat. Inst. Children & Human Devel., 1989; health adv. com. Congressman James Moran, 8th Congl. Dist., Va., 1992—94; mem. benefits working group Nat. Drinking Water Adv. Coun. EPA, 1989—99; adv. Health Pages, 1994—97; spl. asst. to dir. Nat. Ctr. for Environ. Health, Ctrs. for Disease Control, Washington, 1999—2001; Soros advocacy fellow Children's Environ. Health Network, 2000—02; bd. dirs. Crative Glass Ctr. Am. Author: Pediatrics: Review for New National Boards, 2000; editor Pediat. Clinics N.Am., 2001, 07; contbr. articles to profl. jours., chpts. to books. Profl. adv. bd. Nat. Safety Town Ctr., Cleve., 1981-85; bd. dirs., pres. James Renwick Alliance, Washington, 1986-93, 95-98; bd. dirs. Jewish Social Svcs. Agy Greater Washington, 2002—08, chmn. No. Va. com., 2002—08, adv. com. mem. Child Health Protect, USEPA, 2007-. Recipient Cert. for Ednl. and Pub. Policy Activity, Ohio State Senate/Ho. of Reps., 1985; Robert Wood Johnson Health Policy fellow, 1985-86, Soros Advocacy fellowship 2000-02. Fellow Am. Acad. Pediat. (chair exec. com., coun. on environ. health 2011-); mem. Acad. Pediatric Assn. Jewish. Office: Children's Health Adv Inst 2233 WI Ave NW Washington DC 20007 Home Phone: 703-461-7683; Office Phone: 202-471-4891. Business E-Mail: jpaulson@cnmc.org.

PAULSON, PAMELA E., psychology professor, researcher; b. Osage, Iowa, Aug. 7, 1954; Degree in Biopsychology, U. Wis., LaCrosse, 1987, U. Mich., 1995. Rschr., asst. prof. U. Mich., Ann Arbor, 1995—. Mem.: Am. Psychol. Soc., Am. Pain Soc., Internat. Assn. Study Pain, Soc. Neurosci. Avocations: motorcycling, reading, gardening. Home: 613 Palm Blvd Laguna Vista TX 78578 Business E-Mail: plein@umich.edu.

PAULSON, RICHARD JOHN, obstetrician, gynecologist, educator; b. Prague, Czech Republic, Feb. 2, 1955; came to U.S., 1966, naturalized citizen, 1972. m. Lorraine M. Cummings, Oct. 11, 1987; children: Jessica, Jennifer, Philip, Erika, Josef. BS in Physics magna cum laude, UCLA, 1976, MD, 1980; MS, U. So. Calif., 1998. Diplomate Am. Bd. Ob-Gyn., Reproductive Endocrinology and Infertility. Rotating intern Harbor-UCLA Med. Ctr., Torrance, 1980-81, resident in ob-gyn., 1981-84; clin. rsch. fellow dept. ob-gyn. Los Angeles County/U. So. Calif. Med. Ctr., LA, 1984-86, mem. staff, 1984—; clin. instr. ob-gyn. Sch. Medicine U. So. Calif., LA, 1984-86, asst. prof., 1986-91, assoc. prof., 1991-96, prof. clin. ob-gyn., 1996—; affiliate staff mem. Calif. Med. Ctr., LA, 1986—; staff mem. L.A. Clin. & U. So. Calif. Med. Ctr., 1986—, dir. clin. infertility program, 1986—; chief divsn. reproductive endocrinology and infertility Keck Sch. Medicine U. So. Calif., LA, 1996—; med. dir. U. So. Calif. Fertility. Vis. prof. in vitro fertilization lecture series Clinica Kennedy, Guayaquil, Ecuador, 1980; presenter at numerous profl. confs., symposia and grand rounds. Co-editor Infertility, Contraception and Reproductive Endocrinology, 4th edit., 1996; contbr. chpt. to Management of Common Problems in Obstetrics and Gynecology, 2nd. edit., 1988, 3rd edit., 1994, Infertility, Contraception and Reproductive Endocrinology, 1991; co-author several book chpts.; co-author (lay book) Rewinding Your Biological Clock: Motherhood Late in Life, 1998; technical reviewer for Infertility for Dummies, 2007; contbr. or co-contbr. several articles to sci. jours.; mem. editl. bd. Jour. of Assisted Reprodn. and Genetics, Jour. Soc. for Gynecologic Investigation; mem. ad hoc editl. bd. Fertility and Sterility, Am. Jour. Ob-Gyn., Jour. of AMA, Contraception, Am. Jour Reproductive Immunology, others. Co-recipient Wyeth award 1985, recipient, 1989; co-recipient Serono award, 1991, 92, 93, Poster award 1994, Excellence in Tchg. award-Keck Sch. Medicine U. So. Calif., Assn. Professors of Gynecology and Obstetrics, 2004; rsch. grantee Ortho Pharm. Corp., 1986-87, Tap Pharmas., 1989-91, Irvine Sci., 1990-91, Syntex, 1990-92, Serono, 1992-93; named one of Best Doctors in America, 1994-, America's Top Doctors, 2002-; named Best Doctors for Women, 1997. Fellow ACOG (mem. PROLOG task force for reproductive endocrinology 1993), L.A. Obstetrical and Gynecologic Soc.(bd. dirs.); mem. Pacific Coast Fertility Soc. (bd. dirs. 1992, past pres.), Am. Fertility Soc., Am. Fertility Assn. (bd. mem., Howard and Georgeanna Jones Lifetime Achievement award, 2005), Soc. Reproductive Surgeons, Soc. for Assisted Reproductive Tech., Soc. Reproductive Endocrinologists, Soc. for Reproductive Endocrinology and Infertility (past pres.), Am. Soc. Reproductive Medicine (past bd. mem.), Soc. for Gynecologic Investigation, Endocrine Soc. Office: USC Fertility 1127 Wilshire Blvd Ste 1400 & 1410 Los Angeles CA 90017

PAULY, JOHN EDWARD, retired anatomist; b. Elgin, Ill., Sept. 17, 1927; s. Edward John and Gladys (Myhre) P.; m. Margaret Mary Oberle(dec.), Sept. 3, 1949; children: Stephen John (dec.), Susan Elizabeth, Kathleen Anne, Mark Edward; m. Dola S. Thompson, Jan. 7, 2006. BS, Northwestern U., 1950; MS, Loyola U., Chgo., 1952, PhD, 1955. Grad. asst. gross anatomy Stritch Sch. Medicine, Loyola

U., 1953-54; rsch. asst. anatomy Chgo. Med. Sch., 1952-54, rsch. instr., 1954-55, instr. in gross anatomy, 1955-57, assoc. in gross anatomy, 1957-59, asst. prof. anatomy, 1959-63, asst. to pres., 1960-62; assoc. prof. anatomy Tulane U. Sch. Medicine, 1963-67; prof., head dept. anatomy U. Ark. for Med. Scis., Little Rock, 1967-83, prof., head dept. physiology and biophysics, 1978-80, vice chancellor for acad. affairs and sponsored rsch., 1983-92, assoc. dean Grad. Sch., 1983-92, prof. anatomy, 1967—95, prof. emeritus, 1995—. Flight instr. Ctrl. Flying Svc., Little Rock, 1997—2002; tech. adviser Ency. Brit. Films, 1956; mem. safety and occupl. health study sect. Nat. Inst. Occupl. Safety and Health, Ctr. for Disease Control, 1975—79; vis. prof. faculty medicine Kuwait U., 1993, 94; vis. prof. anatomy U. Nev., 1996; chief of staff Ark. wing Civil Air Patrol, 2002—05. Author: (with Hans Elias) Human Microanatomy, 1960, 3d edit. 1966, (with Elias and E. Robert Burns) Histology and Human Microanatomy, 1978; editor: (with Lawrence E. Scheving and Franz Halberg) Chronobiology, 1974, (with Heinz von Mayersbach and Lawrence E. Scheving) Biological Rhythms in Structure and Function, 1981, The American Association of Anatomists, 1888-1987. Essays on the History of Anatomy in America and a Report on the Membership-Past and Present, 1987, (with Lawrence E. Scheving) Advances in Chronobiology, 1987, (with Dora K. Hayes and Russel J. Reiter) Chronobiology: Its Role in Clinical Medicine, General Biology and Agriculture, 1990; editor Am. Jour. Anatomy, 1980-92; co-mng. editor Advances in Anatomy, Embryology and Cell Biology, 1980-95; mem. adv. editl. bd. Internat. Jour. Chronobiology, 1973-83; contbr. articles to profl. jours. Chief of staff, mission pilot, instr. pilot and check pilot Ark. Wing Civil Air Patrol, 2002—05. With USNR, 1945—47. Recipient merit certificates AMA, 1953, 59; Bronze award Ill. Med. Soc., 1959; Lederle Med. Faculty award, 1966, Coll Medicine Hall of Fame, U. Ark. medical Sci., 2007. Fellow AAAS, Am. Assn. Anatomists (sec.-treas. 1972-80, pres. 1982-83, Centennial award 1987, Henry Gray award 1995); mem. So. Soc. Anatomists (pres. 1971-72), Assn. Anatomy Chmn. (sec.-treas. 1969-71), Am. Physiol. Soc., Internat. Soc. Chronobiology, Pan-Am. Assn. Anatomy, Internat. Soc. Electrophysiol. Kinesiology, Internat. Soc. Steriology, Consejo Nacional de Profesores de Ciencias Morfologicas (hon.), Quiet Birdmen, Sigma Xi, Sigma Alpha Epsilon. Roman Catholic. Personal E-mail: flydoc1@comcast.net.

PAVAN, FERNANDO ROGÉRIO, medical researcher; b. Bauru, Brazil, Nov. 17, 1981; Degree in Biomedicine, CUBM, 2004. Rsch. fellow UNESP, 2009—. Office: Rd Araraquara-Jaú Km 01 Araraquara Sao Paulo 14-800-902 Brazil

PAVELY, STUART JOHN, physical therapist; b. Pershore, Eng., Mar. 26, 1970; BA with honors, U. Manchester, BSc with honors, 1995; PhD student in Physiotherapy, U. Sydney. Head physiotherapist Sheffield Utd FC, 1997—99, Sydney U. Football Club, 2001—05; rehab. and head physiotherapist NSW Waratahs, 2003—08; prin. physiotherapist Sports Clinic, U. Sydney, 2011—. Mem.: Australian Physiotherapy Assn. Avocation: running. Office: University Sydney Sports Clinic Western Ave Sydney NSW 2006 Australia Office Fax: 02-93510123. Personal E-mail: stupavely@gmail.com. Business E-Mail: stuartpavely@thesportsclinic.com.au.

PAVLICK, ANNA CATHERINE, oncologist, hematologist; b. Passaic, NJ, July 25, 1962; d. Donald Stephen and Patricia Ann Pavlick. BS, Fairfield U., 1984; MS, Fairleigh Dickinson U., 1990; DO, UMDNJ, 1990. Resident UMDNJ/Hackensack Med. Ctr., 1990-93; hematology/oncology fellow Meml. Sloan-Kettering Cancer Ctr., NYC, 1993—96; asst. prof. medicine, dir. clin. oncology UMDNJ, Newark, 1996—99; asst. prof. medicine NYU Kaplan Comprehensive Cancer Ctr. (now Langone Med. Ctr.), NYC, 1999—. Mem. NYU Med. Oncology Associates. Office: Clin Cancer Ctr 9 0936 160 E 34th St New York NY 10016 Office Phone: 212-731-5431.

PAVLIDIS, ANTONIOS N., cardiologist; b. Montgomery, Aug. 9, 1979; MD, Athens Med. Sch., Greece, 2004, PhD, 2011. Mem.: European Soc. Cardiology. Home: P Tsaldari 10A1 Kifissia Athens Attiki 14561 Greece Home Fax: 302106205330. Personal E-mail: antonispav@yahoo.com.

PAVLOU, SPYROS N., endocrinologist, researcher; b. Athens, Greece, Apr. 26, 1951; s. Nikolaos Pavlou and Xeni Christodoulou; m. Vanessa Graham, Oct. 21, 1981 (div. Mar. 3, 2003); children: Nicholas, Alexander, Lysander, Stephan. MD, U. Athens, 1976; diploma in bioChemistry and physiopathology, U. René Descartes, Paris, 1979. Lic. physician Tenn., Mass. Resident in internal medicine Hosp. Cochin U. René Descartes, Paris, 1976—79, rschr. Coll. de France, 1977—79; fellow in residence The Population Coun., Rockefeller U., NYC, 1981—84; clin. fellow in endocrinology dept. medicine Vanderbilt U. Sch. Medicine, Nashville, 1984—86, 1984—86, clin. assoc. physician gen. clin. rsch. ctr., asst. prof. medicine, 1986—90, assoc. dir. The Vanderbilt Nutrition and Metabolic Ctr., 1986—90; assoc. prof. medicine and ob-gyn. Harvard Med. Sch., Mass. Gen. Hosp. and Beth Israel Hosp., Boston, 1990—97; assoc. in medicine, dir. RIA Hormone Core Facility of the Beth Israel Clin. RSch. Ctr. Beth Israel Hosp., 1990—97; dir. endocrinology, Boston IVF, staff endocrinologist reproductive unit Harvard Med. Sch., 1990—97; assoc. dir. Nat. Ctr. Infertility Rsch. Mass. Gen. Hosp., 1990—97; dir. reproductive endocrinology, infertility and IVF unit Mitera Maternity and Surg. Hosp., Maroussi, Greece, 1997—98; dir. endocrinology and metabolism Athens Med. Ctr., 1997—, Apollonio Hosp., Athens, 1999—; dir. Endocrine Clinics, Athens, 2000—. Vis. prof. medicine U. Pierre et Marie Curie, Paris, 1991—; mem. rev. com., specialized population site visitor, mem. spl. rev. com. on contraceptive ctrs., spl. rev. com. on infertility ctrs. NICHD; advisor steering com. of task force on methods for regulation of male fertility, del. to China WHO; symposium organizer IXth INternat. Congress Endocrinology, Paris, 1992; lectr., presenter in field. Contbr. articles to profl. jours., chapters to books; assoc. clin. editor Jour. Andrology, 1987—89, mem. editl. bd. Endocrinology, 1992—96, Références en Gynécologie Obstétrique, 1993—, Endocrine Jour., 1993—96. Recipient Horemion prize, Greek Soc. Pediat., 1976; fellow, French Govt., 1977—79. Mem.: Med. Soc. Athens, European Soc. Human Reprodn. and Embryology (organizer reproductive endocrinology course 2001), European Soc. Gynecology, The Endocrine Soc., Am. Fertility Soc., Am. Soc. Andrology, Am. Fedn. Clin. Rsch. Achievements include development of first effective male contraceptive; first GnRH antagonist for use in ovulation induction and IVF. Office: Endocrine Clinics Vasilissis Sofias 98 115 28 Athens Greece Office Fax: (+30 210) 77 09 567. E-mail: pavlou@attglobal.net.

PAVLOVA, SVETLANA, cytologist; b. Pavlovo, Russia, Jan. 14, 1981; PhD, Ipee Ras, 2007. A.n. severtsov inst. ecology and evolution Russian Acad. Scis., 2007—11. Disting. Young Scientists grant, Russian Govt. Office: 33 Leninskij pr Moscow 119071 Russia Office Fax: 7 4959523584. Business E-Mail: swpavlova@mail.ru.

PAVLOVSKY, ALEXANDER VASILIEVICH, surgeon; b. Kalingrad, Russia; s. Vasily Vasilievich Pavlovsky and Nina Ivanovna Pavlovskaya; m. Irina Eugenievna Zazerskaya, Apr. 23, 1983; children: Eugenia, Vasily. Grad., Pavlov Med. Inst., Leningrad, Russia, 1983. Resident Pavlov Med. Inst., Leningrad, Russia, 1983—85, lectr., 1985—91, asst. prof. St. Petersburg, 1991—99, assoc. prof., 1999—; cons. Ctrl. Rsch.Inst., St. Petersburg, 1999—. Contbr. articles to profl. jours. Achievements include patents for for pancreas cancer treatment. Office: Ctrl Rsch Inst Leningradskey 20 197758 Pesochni, St. Peters Russia Home: Flat 15 ul. Millionnaya 15 191186 St Petersburg Sankt-Pyetyerburg Russia Home Phone: 8 812 594 95 37; Office Phone: 8 812 596 85 96. Personal E-mail: avpavlovsky@yahoo.com.

PAVLOVYCH, SVITLANA IVANIVNA, medical researcher; b. Ternopil, Ukraine, Oct. 16, 1947; Diploma, Med. Scientifical Soc. Microbilogists; PhD, Nat. U. Taras Shevchenko, Kiev, 1970. Rschr. Inst. Infectious Diseases, 1970—81; sr. rschr. Inst. Pediatry, Obs. and Gyneacology Health, 1981—83; sr. rsch. fellow A.A. Bogomoletz Inst. Phisiology NASU, 1991—. Dir., immunology dept. Scientifical Acad. Young Rschrs., 1986—95. Recipient Hon. award, NASU, 2004. Fellow: Pathophisiology Soc. Avocations: travel, sports, gardening. Office: Bogomoltsa Str 4 311 Kiev 01024 Ukraine Office Fax: 380442562000. Business E-Mail: spavl@biph.kiev.ua.

PAVLU, JIRI, hematologist; b. Liberec, Bohemia, Czech Republic, Aug. 28, 1973; s. Jiri and Jitka Pavlu. MD, First Med. Faculty, Charles U., Czech Republic, 1998. Med. resident Inst. of Hematology, U. Gen. Hosp., Prague, Bohemia, Czech Republic, 1998—2000; sr. ho. officer in hematology Lothian U. Hosp., Edinburgh, Scotland, England, 2000—01; sr. ho. officer, internal medicine Birmingham U. Hosp., Birmingham, England, England, 2001—02; specialist registrar, hematology North Thames Tng. Program, Hammersmith and Royal Free Hosp. Rotation, London, England, 2002—07; locum cons. Imperial Coll. Healthcare, London, 2008—. Contbr. articles various profl. jours. Recipient award, Rector of the Charles U., Prague, 1998, Min. of Edn. prize, Ministry of Edn., Czech Republic, 1998, Josef Hlavka prize, Hlavka Found., Prague, 1997. Mem.: Royal Coll. Pathologists, Royal Coll. of Physicians of London. Office: Hammersmith Hosp Du Cane Rd England London W12 0HS England E-mail: pavluj@yahoo.com.

PAVONE, MARY ELLEN, physician; b. Albany, NY, May 11, 1977; BA, Boston U., 1999, MD, 2003. Asst. prof. Northwestern U., 2010—. Scholar WHRH. Mem.: ACOG, SGI, ASRM (Career Devel. award). Avocations: ballet, running. Office: 303 E Superior St Lurie 4-200 Chicago IL 60611 Office Fax: 312-503-0095. Personal E-mail: mepavone@yahoo.com.

PAVORD, IAN DOUGLAS, physician, consultant; b. Abergavenny, Wales, July 3, 1961; s. Anthony Dwelly and Janet Rosslyn Pavord; m. Susannah Ruth Harris, June 24, 1989; children: Matthew John Christopher, Molly Rose, Iwan Anthony. MBBS, London U., 1984; MD, U. Nottingham, 1992. Cons. physician, prof. medicine U. Hosps. Leicester, England, 1995—. Joint editor Thorax; chief med. advisor Asthma, UK. Recipient Cournand Lectr. award, European Respiatory Soc., 2004; named NIHS Sr. Investigator, 2011. Master: RCP (UK); fellow: RCP (London). Achievements include research in clinical aspects of airway diseases. Avocation: golf. Office: Glenfield Hospital Groby Road LE3 9QP Leicester England Home: House Hill Nanhill Dr Woodhouse Eaves Loughborough LE12 8TC England Office Fax: 0044 116 2367768; Home Fax: 0044 116 2367768. Business E-Mail: ian.pavord@uhl-tr.nhs.uk.

PAWINSKA, ALICJA DANUTA, microbiologist, epidemiologist; b. Korsze, Poland, Apr. 19, 1960; d. Jan Danielewicz and Janina Mozejko; m. Adam Pawinski, Apr. 12, 1982; children: Oleg, Ewa. Master analyst, Med. Acad., Poland, 1983; PhD, Nat. Inst. Hygiene, Warsaw, 1998. Asst. Inst. Pediatry MA, Biatystok, Poland, 1984—88, Grochowski Hosp., Warsaw, 1988—93, The Children's Meml. Health Inst., Warsaw, 1993—, head infection control team, 2000—. Author: (book chpt.) Hospital Infections, 1999, Prevention of Central-Venous Catheter-Related Infection, 2004; co-author: (book chpt.) Intensive Care, 2002, Infectious and Parasitic Diseases, 2003. Achievements include research in hosp. infections related to catheters and other biomaterials. Office: The Children's Meml Health Inst Al Dzieci Polskich 20 04-730 Warsaw Poland Home: Ul. Listonoszy 6 04-431 Warsaw Poland Home Phone: 48 22 812 9635; Office Phone: 48 22 8157174. Fax: 48 22 8157275. E-mail: pawinska@poczta.onet.pl.

PAWLIK, KURT F., psychologist, science educator; b. Vienna, Mar. 16, 1934; PhD in Psychology magna cum laude, U. Vienna, 1959. Sci. asst. U. Vienna, 1956—60, 1962—65; rsch. assoc. U. Ill., Urbana, 1960-62; acting prof. psychology U. Graz, Austria, 1965-66; prof. psychology U. Hamburg, Germany, 1966—. Pres. Criminology Sci. Coun., Coun. Europe, France, 1978-92, Internat. Social Sci. Coun., Paris, 1998—; sec. gen., pres. Internat. Union Psychol. Sci., Montreal, Man., Can., 1992-96. Contbr. over 180 articles to profl. jours. and 17 books. Recipient Austrian Cross of Honors 1st Class. Mem. German Soc. Psychology (hon. mem.), Austrian Psychologial Assn., Am. Psychol. Assn., Chinese Psychol. Soc. (fellow); mem. J. Jungius Soc. Sci. (pres. 2000—2007), Acad. Europaea, European Acad. Sci. & Arts, Am. Psychol. Assn., Psychometric Soc., Soc. Neurosci., Am. Assn. Advancement Sci., Internat. Assn. Applied Psychology, Assn. Psychol. Sci. (fellow), Acad. Sci. Hamburg (hon. mem.). Achievements include psychological research in individual differences, learning and memory processes, experimental and clinical neuropsychology, psychometrics; psychological assessment, environmental psychology, international psychology, history of psycholog. Avocations: music, art, skiing, travel. Office: University Hamburg Von-Melle-Park 11 20146 Hamburg Germany Office Phone: 001-4940-42838-4722. Business E-Mail: pawlik@uni-hamburg.de.

PAWLIKOWSKA-HADDAL, ANNA, medical educator; b. Lodz, Poland, Nov. 11, 1958; MD, Med. Sch., Lodz, 1983; PhD, Inst. Endocrinology, Med. Sch., Lodz, 1989. Assoc. prof. Mattel Children's Hosp., UCLA, 2003—, clin. dir. divsn. pediat. endocrinology, 2006. Recipient Found. award, Endocrine Soc., award, Human Growth Soc., Tng. award, Elli Lilly & Co., Ann. Rsch. award, U. W.Va., Charleston Divsn., Calif. State Newborn Screening Program Ann. award. Mem.: Pediat. Endocrine Soc. Avocations: art, history, running. Home: 359 Beloit Ave Los Angeles CA 90049 Office Phone: 310-825-6244. Home Fax: 310-206-5843. Business E-Mail: ahaddal@mednet.ucla.edu.

PAWLOWICZ, ANNA, physician, consultant; d. Ireneusz Kazimierz Pawlowicz and Janina Maria Bogusz. MD, Acad. Medicine, Warsaw, 1978, PhD, 1985. Specialization in internal medicine Ministry Health and Social Security, 1982. Clin. asst. internal medicine and pneumonology Acad. Medicine, Warsaw, 1978—85, lectr., 1986—87; clin. rsch. fellow in respiratory medicine Llandough Hosp., Cardiff, Wales, 1987—88, specialist registrar internal and respiratory medicine, 1989—95; locum cons. respiratory medicine Addenbrooke's Hosp., Cambridge, England, 1996—97; cons. internal and respiratory medicine Queen Elizabeth Hosp., King's Lynn, Norfolk, England, 1997—. Sec. Polish Allergology Soc., Warsaw, 1985—87; tchg. physician U. Cambridge/Med. Sch.; chief physician for lung cancer at Queen Elizabeth Hosp. Cambridgeshire Lung Cancer Network, Cambridge, 1997—; lead clinician for clin. governance in respiratory medicine Queen Elizabeth Hosp., England, 1999—; rschr. internat. multi-ctr. clin. trials, respiratory medicine Cambridge Clin. Rsch., 2000—05; editor/clin. abstracts European Respiratory Symposium, Stockholm, 2002, Vienna, 03; prin. investigator Queen Elizabeth Hosp. for matrex study U. East Anglia, Norwich, 2005—. Co-author: Medical Masterclass/Respiratory Medicine, 2nd Edit., 2008; author: Progress in Pneumonology/Mucolytic Drugs, Progress in Pneumonology/Adult Respiratory Distress Syndrome; contbr. articles to profl. jours. Recipient Best Article Pub. by Jr. Rschr. in Jour. Pulmonologia Polska award, Polish Acad. Sci., 1986; named COPD Mgmt. Team of the Yr., Hosp. Dr. Award (UK), 2005, Best PhD Thesis of the Yr., Dean Acad. Medicine, 1985; fellow, Wellcome Trust, 1987. Fellow: Royal Coll. Physicians London (hon.); mem.: European Respiratory Soc. (corr.), Brit. Med. Assn. (corr.), Ea. Region Thoracic Soc. (corr.), Ea. Anglian Asthma Mortality and Severe Morbidity Group (hon.), Cambridge Clin. Rsch. (hon.). Achievements include research in asprin induced asthma. Avocations: classical music, skiing, travel. Office: The Queen Elizabeth Hospital Gayton Road PE30 4ET Kings Lynn England Office Fax: 44 1553 613984. Business E Mail: Anna.Pawlowicz@qehkl.nhs.uk.

PAWSON, ANTHONY J., molecular biologist; b. Maidstone, Eng., Oct. 18, 1952; BA in Biochemistry, Cambridge U., 1973; PhD in Molecular Biology, London U., 1976. Postdoc. rsch. fellow U. Calif., Berkeley, 1976—80; asst. prof. dept. microbiology U. Brit. Columbia, Vancouver, Canada, 1981—85; sr. scientist Nat. Cancer Inst. Can., 1985—88, Terry Fox cancer rsch. scientist, 1988—99; assoc. prof. dept. med. genetics U. Toronto, Canada, 1985—88, prof. dept. med. genetics & microbiology, 1989—, sr. fellow Massey Coll., 2003—; sr. investigator Samuel Lunenefeld Rsch. Inst., Mount Sinai Hosp., Toronto, 1985—, Apotex chair molecular oncology, 1991, head rsch. molecular biology & cancer, 1994—, dir. rsch., 2002—06. Mem. sci. adv. bd. Inst. Molecular & Cell Biology, Singapore, 1998—2004, Jane Coffin Childs Meml. Fund Med. Rsch., 1997—2004, MGH Cancer Ctr., 1999—, Argonex Discovery Inc., 1999—; mem. sci. planning com. Nat. Human Genome Rsch. Inst., 1997—98; mem. sci. review bd. Howard Hughes Med. Inst., 1997—2000; mem. med. adv. bd. Gairdner Found., 1998—; mem. adv. bd. Ariad Pharm. Inc., 1992—97. Mem. editl. bd.: Trends in Genetics, Oncogene, Molecular & Cellular Biology, Cell Growth & Differentiation, Chemistry & Biology, Current Opinion in Cell Biology, Developmental Cell, Molecular Biology of the Cell, European Jour. Biochemistry; editor: Jour. Cellular Physiology, Progress in Biophysics & Molecular Biology. Decorated Officer Order of Can.; recipient Gairdner Found. Internat. award, 1994, Robert L. Noble prize, Nat. Cancer. Inst. Can., 1995, George Drummond Meml. award, U. Alberta, 1995, John Colter award, U. Calgary, 1996, Boehringer Mannheim prize, Can. Soc. Biochemistry & Molecular & Cellular Biology, 1997, Disting. Sci. award, Med. Rsch. Coun., 1998, Dr. H.P. Heineken prize for biochemistry/biophysics, Royal Netherlands Acad. Arts & Scis., 1998, Henry Friesen award, Can. Soc. Clin. Investigation, 1998, Pezcoller Internat. award for cancer rsch., Am. Assn. Cancer Rsch./Pezcoller Found., 1998, J. Allyn Taylor Internat. prize in medicine, U. Western Ont., 2000, Killam prize for health scis., 2000, Michael Smith prize in health rsch., 2002, Prix Galien, Can., 2002, Ernst W. Bertner Meml. award, MD Anderson Cancer Ctr., 2004, Louisa Gross Horwitz prize, 2004, Disting. Investigator award, Can. Inst. Health Rsch., 2004, Poulsson medal, Norwegian Soc. Pharmacology & Toxicology, 2004, Louisa Gross Horwitz prize, Columbia U., 2004, Wolf prize in medicine, Jerusalem, 2005, Daniel Nathans Meml. award, Van Andel Rsch. Inst., 2005, Wolf Found. prize in medicine, Israel, 2005, Howard Taylor Ricketts award, U. Chgo., 2007, Kyoto prize for lifetime achievement in basic scis., Inamori Found., 2008; internat. rsch. scholar, Howard Hughes Med. Inst., 1991—2001. Fellow: Am. Acad. Microbiology, Royal Soc. Can. (Flavelle medal 1998), Royal Soc. London (Royal medal 2005); mem.: NAS (assoc.), EMBO (assoc.; mem. editl. bd.), Japanese Biochem. Soc. (hon.), Am. Acad. Arts & Scis. (hon.; fgn.). Office: Mt Sinai Hosp 600 University Ave Rm 1084 Toronto ON Canada M5G 1X5 Mailing: Samuel Lunenfeld Rsch Inst Mt Sinai Hosp 600 Univ Ave Rm 1084 Toronto ON M5G 1X5 Canada Office Phone: 416-586-4800 ext. 8262. Office Fax: 416-586-8869. E-mail: pawson@lunenfeld.ca.

PAXTON, RAHEEM, medical researcher, educator; b. Savannah, Ga., June 25, 1978; PhD, U. SC, 2005. Rsch. asst. prof. U. Houston, 2011—. Office: 1155 Herman P Pressler Unit 1365 Houston TX 77030 Business E-Mail: rjpaxton@mdanderson.org.

PAYNE, ANITA HART, reproductive endocrinologist, researcher; b. Karlsruhe, Baden, Germany, Nov. 24, 1926; came to U.S., 1938; d. Frederick Michael and Erna Rose (Hirsch) Hart; widowed; children: Gregory Steven, Teresa Payne-Lyons. BA, U. Calif., Berkeley, 1949, PhD, 1952. From rsch. assoc. to prof. U. Mich., Ann Arbor, 1961-96, prof. emeritus, 1996—; assoc. dir. U. Mich. Ctr. for Study Reproduction, Ann Arbor, 1989-94; sr. rsch. scientist Stanford U. Med. Ctr., Calif., 1995—2007. Vis. scholar Stanford U., 1987-88; mem. reproductive biology study sect. NIH, Bethesda, Md., 1978-79, biochem. endocrinology study sect., 1979-83, population rsch. com. Nat. Inst. Child Health and Human Devel., 1989-93. Assoc. editor Steroids, 1987-93; contbr. book chpts., articles to profl. jours. Recipient award for cancer rsch., Calif. Inst. for Cancer Rsch., 1953, Acad. Women's Caucus award, U. Mich., 1986, Mentor award, Women in Endocrinology, 1999. Mem. Endocrine Soc. (chmn. awards com. 1983-84, mem. nominating com. 1985-87, coun. 1988-91), Am. Soc. Andrology (exec. coun. 1980-83), Soc. for Study of Reproduction (bd. dirs. 1982-85, sec. 1986-89, pres. 1990-91, Carl G. Hartman award 1998, Disting. Svc. award 2004).

PAYNE, ANN MARTINA, psychiatrist, consultant; MA in Behavioural & Cognitive Psychotherapy, U. Coll. Cork, Ireland, 2005, MB, BCh, U. Coll. Cork, Ireland, 1987. Registrar, anaesthesia Cork U. Hosp., 1987—91, registrar, emergency medicine, 1997—2001; cons. psychiatrist St. Mary's Orthop. Hosp., Cork, 2006—, Kerry Gen. Hosp., Ireland, 2009—. Contbr. articles to profl. jours. Master: RCP. Office: Kerry Gen Hosp Tralee Kerry Ireland Business E-Mail: ann.payne@hse.ie.

PAYNE, CHRISTOPHER JESS, medical educator; b. Mpls., May 29, 1972; BS, U. Wash., 1994; PhD, Oreg. Health & Sci. U., 2003. Asst. prof. Northwestern U. Children's Meml. Rsch. Ctr., 2009—. Recipient Disting. Svc. award, FIR Bd. Dirs. and Burroughs Wellcome Fund, Pathway to Independence award, NIH. Mem.: Am. Soc. Andrology, Soc. for Study of Reproduction, Internat. Soc. Stem Cell Rsch. Office: 2300 Children's Plz Box 211 Chicago IL 60614 Office Fax: 773-755-6593. Business E-Mail: c-payne@northwestern.edu.

PAYNE, CHRISTOPHER KENNERLY, urologist, educator; b. Kinston, NC, Nov. 8, 1959; BA, U. Va., 1981; MD, Vanderbilt U., 1986. Prof. urology Stanford U. Med. Sch., 1993—, dir. female urology & neurourology, 1993. Office: Stanford University Med Sch 300 Pasteur Dr A260 Stanford CA 94305 Office Fax: 650-724-9608. Business E-Mail: cpayne@stanford.edu.

PAYSON, NORMAN C., healthcare services company executive; Grad., MIT, 1970; MD, Dartmouth U., 1973. Physician; founder, pres., CEO Healthsource, Inc., 1985—97; CEO Oxford Health Plans, Inc., Norwalk, Conn., 1998—2002, chmn., 1999—2002; exec. chmn., CEO Apria Healthcare, 2008—. Mem. bd. dirs. American Assoc. of Health Plans, Washington; mem. faculty Dartmouth Med. Sch., Columbia U. Mailman Sch. Pub. Health, U. Chgo. Booth Sch. Bus. Bd. dirs. City of Hope, Medicine in Need; bd. overseers Dartmouth Med. Sch. Office: Apria Healthcare 26220 Enterprise Ct Lake Forest CA 92630 *

PAYTON, FAY COBB, engineering educator; BS in Indsl. & Sys. Engring., Ga. Inst. Tech.; PhD in Info. & Decision Sys., Case Western Res. U. Assoc. prof., info. sys., tech. NC State U., Raleigh, 1998—. Recipient award, Am. Coun. Edn. Avocation: exercise. Office: NC State University Coll Mgmt Campus Box 7229 Raleigh NC 27695 Business E-Mail: fay_payton@ncsu.edu.

PAZ, GEORGE, health products executive; b. St. Louis, Aug. 27, 1955; s. Geronimo and Collen May (Hart) P.; m. Georgene Marie Wade, July 27, 1974; children: Stacy, Kelly, Rebecca. BSBA, U. Mo., St. Louis, 1982. CPA, Mo. Jr. acct. Gen. Am., St. Louis, 1980-82, sr. acct., 1982-83, acctg. adminstr., 1983-85, tax planning analyst, 1985-87, dir. tax planning, 1987; ptnr. Coopers & Lybrand, 1988—93, 1996—98; exec. v.p., CFO Life Ptnrs. Group, 1993—95; sr. v.p., CFO Express Scripts, Inc., St. Louis, 1998—2003, pres., 2003—, bd. dirs., 2004—, CEO, 2005—, chmn., 2006—. Bd. dirs. Gen. Am. Employees Fed. Credit Union, 1985. Fellow Life Office Mgmt. Assn.; mem. AICPA, Mo. Soc. CPA, Pharm. Care Mgmt. Assn. Lutheran. Avocations: golf, running, softball. Office: Express Scripts Inc 14000 Riverport Dr Maryland Heights MO 63043-4805 Office Phone: 314-770-1666. Office Fax: 314-702-7037. *

PAZ, HAROLD LOUIS, hospital administrator, dean, internist; b. NYC, Jan. 3, 1955; BA in Biology and Psychology, U. Rochester, 1977, MD, 1982; MS in Life Sci. Engring., Tufts U., 1979. Diplomate subspecialty in pulmonary medicine Am. Bd. Internal Medicine. Intern in internal medicine Northwestern U. Med. Ctr., Chgo., 1982—83, resident in internal medicine, 1983—85, chief med. resident, 1985—86; instr. clin. medicine Northwestern U., Chgo., 1985—86; fellow in pulmonary and critical care Johns Hopkins U., Balt., 1986—88, fellow in environ. health scis., 1986—88; asst. prof. medicine Hahnemann U., Phila., 1988—92, asst. prof. anesthesia, 1989—92, assoc. dean grad. med. edn., 1992—94, assoc. prof. medicine, 1992—94, dir. med. ICU, 1988—94, assoc. hosp. med. dir., 1992—94, dir. Ctr. for Clin. Outcomes, 1992—94; med. dir., assoc. dean for clin. affairs U. Medicine and Dentistry NJ Robert Wood Johnson Med. Sch., New Brunswick, 1994—95, assoc. prof. medicine, 1994—2003, dean, 1995—2006, CEO, 1995—2006, prof. medicine, 2003—06; CEO Penn State Milton S. Hershey Med. Ctr., 2006—; dean Penn State Coll. of Medicine, 2006—; sr. V.P. Health Affairs Pa. State Coll. of Medicine, 2006—. Editor: Jour. Undergrad. Rsch., 1976, Med. Staff News newsletter, 1992—94; cons.: Annals Internal Medicine, Clin. Immunology and Immunopathology, Chest, Intensive Care Medicine, Physician Execs., NY State Med. Jour., mem. editl. bd.: Jour. Disease Mgmt. and Clin. Outcomes, 1996—, Chest, 1998—2003. Recipient Disting. Svc. award, Motolinsky Rsch. Found., 1998, Cmty. Leaders of Distinction award, County C. of C., 1999, Sir William Oster Humanitarian award, 2005, Hon. Alumni award, UMDNJ-Robert Wood Johnson Med. Sch. Alumni Assn., 2005, Alumni Merit award, Northwestern U. Alumni Assn., 2007; named to Gold Humanism Honor Soc., 2005; Eudowood fellow, Johns Hopkins U., 1987—88, U. Rochester scholar, 1979. Fellow: ACP, Am. Coll. Chest Physicians; mem.: AMA, Laennec Soc. (pres. 1994—95), Philip Drinker Soc. for Critical Care (pres. 1992—94), Am. Thoracic Soc. Office: Penn State Hershey Med Ctr 500 University Dr Mail Code H162 Hershey PA 17033 Office Phone: 717-531-8323. *

PEABODY, LAURA S., lawyer, insurance company executive; b. 1958; m. Robert Peabody, 1986. BA, SUNY, Binghamton; JD, Boston U. V.p., dep. gen. counsel Blue Cross and Blue Shield, Mass.; atty. health care group Choate Hall and Stewart, 1988—; sr. v.p., gen. counsel, chief legal officer Harvard Pilgrim Health Care, Wellesley, Mass., chair Harvard Pilgrim Health Care Found. Mem., trustee New Eng. Chpt. Bd. US Found. for UNICEF, 2005—; trustee Eliot Sch. of Fine and Applied Arts, Jamaica Plain. Mem.: Bars of the Commonwealth of NY, Bars of the Commonwealth of Mass., Mass. Women's Bar Found. (bd. dirs. 2005—08). Office: Harvard Pilgrim Health Care 93 Worcester St Wellesley Hills MA 02481 Office Phone: 617-509-1000. Office Fax: 617-730-4765. E-mail: laura_peabody@hphc.org. *

PEABODY EHLERS, ARLENE L. HOWLAND BAYAR, retired enterostomal therapy nurse; b. Deposit, NY, June 26, 1931; d. Burt and Olive (Oralls) Howland; m. Atilla C. Bayar, Dec. 8, 1956 (div.); m. Norman R. Peabody, Feb. 1, 1975 (dec.); children: Tildy Anne Bayar Sparrow, Carol A. Digilio; m. Robert A. Ehlers, Feb. 15, 2003. Diploma, Ridley's Sec. Sch., Binghamton, NY, 1949, Binghamton Sch. Practical Nursing, 1970, Harrisburg Hosp. Sch. Enterostomal Therapy, Pa., 1971; AAS, Empire State Coll., Saratoga Springs, NY, 1985; BS in Edn., SUNY, Oneonta, 1990. RN, N.Y.; cert. therapeutic touch practitioner, natural force healing practitioner, enterostomal nurse. Sec. pres.'s office Cornell U., Ithaca, NY, 1949—55; exec. sec. Rudolph Lang, Office Execs. Assn. N.Y. and Prestige Expositions Inc., NYC, 1955—69; enterostomal therapy nurse M.I. Bassett Hosp., Cooperstown, NY, 1972—89; pvt. practice enterostomal therapy nurse Oneonta, NY, 1989—2002. Spkr. in field. Vol. Am. Cancer Soc., 1972-2002, Catskill Area Hospice, 1990-02, Glimmerglass Opera, 1975-2002; bd. dirs. Del. Heritage Inc., 1996-2002; trustee Unitarian Universalist Soc.; active Storytelling Ctr. of Oneonta, Oneonta Concert Assn., Oneonta Contradance. Mem. AARP (bd. dirs. 1986-2002), N.Y. State Hist. Assn., Delaware County Hist. Soc., Wound Ostomy and Continence Nurses Soc., United Ostomy Assn. (N.Y. state field svcs. rep.), Order Ea. Star. Avocations: dance, quilting, music. Home: 13511 Pebblebrook Dr Houston TX 77079-6023 Home Phone: 713-467-7191.

PEACHEY, LEE DEBORDE, biology professor; b. Rochester, NY, Apr. 14, 1932; s. Clarence Henry and Eunice (DeBorde) P.; m. Helen Pauline Fuchs, June 7, 1958; children: Michael Stephen, Sarah Elizabeth Keating, Anne Palmer Lorenz. BS, Lehigh U., 1953; postgrad., U. Rochester, 1953-56; PhD (Leitz fellow), Rockefeller U., 1959; MA (hon.), U. Pa., 1971. Research asso. Rockefeller U., 1959-60; asst. prof. zoology Columbia U., 1960-63, asso. prof., 1963-65; asso. prof. biochemistry and biophysics U. Pa., Phila., 1965-70, prof. biology, 1970-2000, prof. emeritus, 2000—; adj. prof. molecular, cellular and developmental biology U. Colo., 1969-84; mem. molecular biology study sect. NIH, 1969-73. Internat. vis. prof. Ministry Edn., Sci. and Culture Gunma (Japan) U. Med. Sch., Maebashi, 1992-95; biomed. rsch. tech. rev. com. NIH, 1994-2000; mem. Mayor's Sci. and Tech. Adv. Coun., Phila., 1972-80; chmn. Gordon Rsch. Conf. on Muscle, 1983; ext. evaluation com. Nat. Inst. Physiol. Sci., Okazaki, Japan, 1997; cons. Leica Microsys., 2002—09. Editor: Third and Fourth Conferences on Cellular Dynamics, N.Y. Acad. Scis., 1967, First and Second Confs. on Cellular Dynamics, 1968, Am. Physiol. Soc. Handbook on Skeletal Muscle, 1983; mem. editl. bd. Tissue and Cell, 1969—, Jour. Cell Biology, 1970-73, Pitman Series in Cellular and Development Biology, 1977-2000, Microscopy Rsch. and Technique, 1982-93, Advances in Optical and Electron Microscopy, 1983—, Neuroimage, 1991—95, Jour. Microscopy, 1992-96, Bioimages, 1993—; contbr. articles to profl. jours. Trustee Keith R. Porter Endowment for Cell Biology, Merion Station, Pa., 1981—2004 Guggenheim and Fulbright-Hays fellow, 1967-68, Overseas fellow Churchill Coll., Cambridge, Eng., 1967-68, Fogarty Sr. Internat. fellow, 1979-80, hon. rsch. fellow U. Coll., London, 1979-80; Royal Soc. (London) guest rsch. fellow, Cambridge, 1986; grantee NSF, 1960-72, NIH, 1973-2002, Muscular Dystrophy Assn. Am., Inc. 1973-91. Fellow AAAS, Electron Microscopy Soc. Am. (council 1975-78, pres. 1982), Am. Soc. Cell Biology (program chmn. 1965, coun. 1966-69), Biophys. Soc. (program chmn. 1976, coun. 1976-80, exec. com. 1976-82, pres. 1981-82), Internat. Union Pure and Applied Biophysics (coun. 1978-84, v.p. 1984-87, pres. 1987-90, chmn. commn. on cell and membrane biophysics 1981-84, hon. v.p. 1990-93), Physiol. Soc. (Eng.).; mem. Internat. Soc. Stereology (internat. stereology software com. 1982-94), Soc. Gen. Physiologists. Achievements include research in mechanisms of muscle cell contraction; development of methods in light and electron microscopy; development of computer graphic methods for three-dimensional image analysis and reconstruction. Home: 524 Revere Rd Merion Station PA 19066-1033 Office: U Pa Dept Biology Philadelphia PA 19104-6018 Home Phone: 610-664-0478; Office Phone: 215-898-5788. Business E-Mail: lpeachey@sas.upenn.edu.

PEACOCK, ERLE EWART, JR., surgeon, lawyer, educator; b. Durham, NC, Sept. 10, 1926; s. Erle Ewart and Vera Louise (Ward) P.; m. Mary Louise Lowrey, Apr. 17, 1954; children: James Lowrey, Susan Louise, Virginia Gayle. Cert. in Medicine, U. N.C., 1947, BS, 1990, JD, 1999; MD, Harvard U., 1949. Bar: N.C. 1993. Intern, asst. resident surgery Roosevelt Hosp., NYC, 1949-51; from asst. resident gen. surgery U. N.C. Hosps., Chapel Hill, 1953-54, chief resident gen. surgery, 1954-55; resident in plastic surgery Barnes Hosp., St. Louis, 1955-56; mem. faculty dept. surgery U. N.C., Chapel Hill, 1956-69, prof. surgery, head divsn. plastic surgery, 1965-69; prof., chmn. dept. surgery U. Ariz., Tucson, 1969-77; prof. surgery Tulane U., New Orleans, 1977-82; pvt. practice surgery Chapel Hill, 1982-93; vis. prof. surgery U. Va., Charlottesville, 1988-97; clin. prof. surgery U. N.C., Chapel Hill, 1996—. Chief hand surgery Valley Forge Army Hosp., Phoenixville, Pa., 1951-53. Author: Wound Repair, 1977, 3d edit., 1982; assoc. editor: Am. Jour. Surgery, 1967—, Surgery Yearbook, 1970-89, Plastic and Reconstructive Surgery, 1972-78; asst. editor: Jour. Surg. Rsch., 1970-76. Served with U.S. Navy, 1945-46; served to capt. M.C. U.S. Army, 1951-53. Recipient Yandell medal Louisville Surg. Soc., 1972, McGraw medal Detroit Surg. Soc., 1973, Disting. Svc. award U. N.C., 1979, Jacob Markowitz award Acad. Surg. Rsch., 1993, Lifetime Achievement award Wound Healing Soc., 2004. Mem. AAAS, ACS, ABA, Womack Sur. Soc. (pres. 1979-80), Soc. U. Surgeons (treas. 1965-68), Plastic Surgery Rsch. Coun. (pres. 1966), Am. Surg. Assn., Am. Bd. Plastic Surgery (pres. 1976), Am. Bd. Gen. Surgery, Am. Assn. Plastic Surgeons (Clinician of Yr. 1985), Am. Soc. Surgery Hand, Internat. Soc. Surgeons, So. Surg. Assn., Am. Coll. Legal Medicine, Rotary, Alpha Omega Alpha. Republican. Methodist. Mailing: 425 Cedar Club Cir Chapel Hill NC 27517 Home Phone: 919-967-0347. E-mail: eepeacockmd@aol.com. *

PEACOCK, MUNRO, medical researcher, educator; b. Darvel, Scotland, Apr. 9, 1936; MBChB, Glasgow U., 1960, DSc, 2007, Purdue U. Clin. scientist Med. Rsch. Coun., 1965—; prof. medicine Ind. U., 1985, physician Health Physicians, 2011. Fellow: RCP (London); mem.: Internat. Bone and Mineral Soc., Am. Soc. Nephrology, Endocrine Soc., Am. Soc. Bone and Mineral Rsch. Avocations: music, art. Office: CL 368 541 Clinical Dr Indianapolis IN 46202 Business E-Mail: mpeacock@iupui.edu.

PEAKE, JAMES BENJAMIN, information technology executive, former United States Secretary of Veterans Affairs; b. St. Louis, June 18, 1944; m. Janice M. Peake; children: Kimberly, Thomas. BS, U.S. Mil. Acad., 1966; MD, Cornell U., 1972; grad., U.S. Army War Coll., 1988. Commd. 2nd lt. inf. US Army, 1972, advanced through grades to lt. gen., 1995, ret., 2004; gen. surgery resident Brooke Army Med. Ctr., Ft. Sam Houston, asst. chief cardiothoracic surgery; staff gen. surgeon, chief gen. surgery clinic DeWitt Army Hosp., Ft. Belvoir, Va.; dep. comdr. for clin. svcs. Tripler Army Med. Ctr., Honolulu; comdr. 18th Med. Command and 121st Evacuation Hosp. US Army, Seoul, Republic of Korea, dep. dir., profl. svcs. chief, cons. Office Surgeon Gen., commdg. gen. 44th Med. Brigade/Corps Surgeon XVIII Airborne Ft. Bragg, NC; commdg. gen. Madigan Army Med. Ctr./N.W. Health Svc. Support Activity, Tacoma; dep. comdr. US Army Med. Command, 1996-97; installation comdr. US Army, Ft. Sam Houston, 1996; comdr. US Army Med. Dept. Ctr. & Sch., 1996-2000, US Army Med. Command, Ft. Sam Houston, Tex., 2000—04; surgeon gen. US Army, 2000—04; exec. v.p., COO Project HOPE, 2004—06; chief med. officer, COO QTC Mgmt. Inc., 2006—07; sec. US Dept. Veterans Affairs, Washington, 2007—09; sr. v.p. for health industry CGI Group, Inc., Fairfax, Va., 2009—. Chmn. Med. Advisory Bd. The BrainScope Co., Inc., 2009—. Contbr. articles to profl. jours. Decorated Order of Mil. Med. Merit, Silver Star, Def. Superior Svc. medal, Legion of Merit with three oak leaf clusters, Bronze Star with V device and oak leaf cluster, Purple Heart with oak leaf cluster, Meritorious Svc. medal with two oak leaf clusters, Air medal, Joint Svc. Commendation medal, Army Commendation medal with V device and oak leaf cluster, Humanitarian Svc. medal, Armed Forces Expeditionary medal, Joint Meritorious Unit award with oak leaf cluster. Fellow ACS, Soc. Thoracic Surgeons, Am. Coll. Cardiology; mem. Korean Med. Assn. (hon.), Assn. Mil. Surgeons U.S., Soc. Med. Cons. of the Armed Forces. Republican. Office: CGI Group Inc 12601 Fair Lakes Cir Fairfax VA 22033

PEARCE, ELIZABETH NIEWOEHNER, endocrinologist, researcher; arrived in U.S., 1968; d. Dennis Erwin and Catherine Beattie Niewoehner; m. Richard A. Pearce, May 24, 1997; children: Alexander, Ian. BA, Harvard U., Cambridge, Mass., 1990; student, Bryn Mawr Coll., 1991—92; MD, Harvard U., 1997; MSc in Epidemiology, Boston U., Mass., 2004. Diplomate internal medicine, endocrinology, diabetes and metabolism. Intern internal medicine Beth Israel Deaconess Med. Ctr., Boston, 1997—98, resident internal medicine, 1998—2000; from fellow in endocrinology to asst. prof. medicine Med. Ctr. Boston (Mass.) U., 2000—04, assoc. prof. medicine Med. Ctr., 2009—. Mem. editl. bd. Thyroid, Endocrine Practice, & Jour. Clin. Endocrinology & Metabolism. Contbr. chapters to books, articles to profl. jours. Recipient K-23 Mentored Career award, NIH, 2003, Von Meyer award, Am. Thyroid Assn., 2011; grantee Pfizer Scholars in Endocrine, 2002. Mem.: Internat. Coun. Control Iodine Deficiency Disorders (bd. dirs. 2009—), Mass. Med. Soc., Am. Thyroid Assn. (chair pub. health com. 2008—09, bd. dirs. 2009—), Endocrine Soc. Avocation: singing. Office: Boston Med Ctr Evans 201 88 E Newton St Boston MA 02118 Business E-Mail: elizabeth.pearce@bmc.org.

PEARL, HARVEY, rehabilitation psychologist; b. NYC, July 11, 1930; s. Louis and Blanche (Birnbaum) P.; m. Dorothy Morrison, June 20, 1953; children: Stuart Ray, Lesley, Andrea. BS, NYU, 1953, MA, 1957; PhD, Syracuse U., 1970. Cert. rehab. counselor. Tchr. indsl. arts Pub. Schs. Elizabeth (N.J.), 1955-56; workshop supr. United Cerebral Palsy Assn., Roosevelt, N.Y., 1956-58; workshop dir. Jewish Vocat. Service, Cin., 1958-61; dir. work tng. center Assn. Retarded Children, Rochester, N.Y., 1961-63; asst. exec. dir. Consol. Industries Greater Syracuse (N.Y.), 1965-96, rehab. cons., 1996—. Instr. Cornell U., Ithaca, NY, 1970—; cons. Social Security Adminstrn., 1962—2000. Author: (with A. Speiser, A. Staniec) Bibliography of Work Evaluation in Vocational Rehabilitation, 1966; Comparison of Personal Values and Worker Assessments of Work Evaluators in Rehabilitation and Industrial Settings, 1970. Pres. Jewish Family Service Bur., 1974-82; adv. council Cazenovia Coll., 1977—, Occupational Edn., Syracuse City Sch. Dist., 1971—2002, Onondaga-Madison County Bd. Cooperative Ednl. Svcs., 1971—, Onondaga Citizens League., 1985-, Syracuse Thursday Morning Roundtable, 1990-; chair, Allen Speiser Meml. Fund Cmty. Found., 2005-. Served with US Army, 1953—55, European Tour of Duty. Recipient citation of merit Syracuse U. Sch. Social Work, 1972; cert. rehab. counselor. Mem. Nat. Rehab. Assn., Am. Counseling Assn., Am. Rehab. Counseling Assn., Nat. Career Devel. Assn., Am. Psychol. Assn., Am. Wine Soc. Home and Office: 227 Wellington Rd De Witt NY 13214-2225 Personal E-mail: hpearl@twcny.rr.com.

PEARL, ROBERT M., plastic surgeon; MD, Yale U. Cert. plastic and reconstructive surgery. Exec. dir., CEO, Med. Group, Mid Atlantic States, Northern Calif. Kaiser Permanente, 1998—. Currently serving as clin. prof., plastic surgery Stanford U.; currently serving as faculty Stanford Grad. Sch. Bus. Former vis. prof. Duke U. Sch. Medicine, Haas Sch. Bus., Harvard Sch. Pub. Health. Named one of Most Powerful Physician Leaders in the Nation, Modern Healthcare. Avocation: writing. Office: Kaiser Permanente Fl 18 1950 Franklin St Oakland CA 94612 Office Phone: 510-987-3118. Personal E-mail: Robert.Pearl@KP.org. *

PEARSE, WARREN HARLAND, obstetrician, gynecologist, medical association administrator; b. Detroit, Sept. 28, 1927; s. Harry Albridge and Frances (Wressell) P.; m. Jacqueline Anne Langan, June 15, 1950; children: Kathryn, Susan, Laurie, Martha. BS, Mich. State U., 1948; M.B., MD, Northwestern U., 1950. Intern. Univ. Hosp., Ann Arbor, Mich., 1950-51; resident obstetrics and gynecology, 1951-53, 55-56; practice medicine specializing obstetrics and gynecology Detroit, 1956-58; mem. faculty U. Nebr. Med. Ctr., Omaha, 1959-71, Found. prof., chmn. dept. obstetrics and gynecology, 1962-71, asst. dean, 1963-71, mem. residency rev. com. obstetrics and gynecology, 1968-93; dean Med. Coll. Va., Richmond, Va., 1971-75; exec. dir. Am. Coll. Obstetrics and Gynecology, 1975-93; cons., 1993—; editor Women's Health Issues, Washington, 1993—. Author: (with V.L. Seltzer) Primary Health Care for Women, 1999; contbr. chpts., articles tech. lit. Served from 1st lt. to capt. AUS, 1953-55. Mem. Am. Coll. Obstetrics and Gynecology (dist. sec., treas. 1964-68, vice chmn. 1968-71), Am. Gynecology Soc., Soc. Gynecology Investigation, Assn. Profs. Gynecology and Obstetrics (sec., treas. 1969—), Alpha Omega Alpha. Home: #5005 10450 Lottsford Rd Bowie MD 20721-3301

PEARSON, JOHN WILLIAM, cardiologist; b. Apr. 25, 1950; MD, Univ. Missouri Columbia Sch. Med., 1976. Cert. Am. Bd. Internal Med., 1979, Am. Bd. Internal Med., Cardiovascular Disease, 1981. Intern Univ. Iowa Hosp. & Clinics, 1976—77, resident in cardiology, 1977—79; fellow in cardiology Med. Coll. Va., Richmond, 1976—81; attending physician Ctrl. Suffolk Hosp., Riverhead, NY; cardiologist

East End Cardiology PC, Riverhead, NY, 1994—. Office: East End Cardiology PC 1279 E Main St Riverhead NY 11901 Office Phone: 631-727-2100. Office Fax: 631-727-2646.

PEARSON, LUWEI, public health professional; b. Beijing, July 23, 1959; MSc, LSHTM, 2003, China Academi Sci., 1987. Health programme officer UNICEF Paksitan, 1992—96; rsch. asst. CIET Internat., Nepal, 1996—2002; mnh advisor, Unicef Esaro, 2003—07; chief health UNICEF, 2007—. Mem.: Am. Pediatric Soc. Office: UNICEF Ethiopia PO Box 1169 Addis Ababa 1169 Ethiopia Business E-Mail: lpearson@unicef.org.

PEARSON, STEPHEN JOHN, physiologist, educator; s. John and Rita Pearson; m. Gladys Onambele, Dec. 6, 2003; 1 child, William Blake. BSc with honors, U. Sunderland, Eng., 1996; PhD, U. Coll. London, 2002. Lectr. U. Salford, Manchester, England, 2002—. Contbr. articles to profl. jours. Mem.: Physiol. Soc. Mem. Labor Party. Achievements include research in human aging and the changes in skeletal muscle characteristics. Office: U Salford Allerton Building Frederick Road M6 6PU Manchester England Business E-Mail: s.pearson@salford.ac.uk.

PEARSON, THOMAS ARTHUR, epidemiologist, educator; b. Berlin, Wis., Oct. 21, 1950; married; 2 children. BA, Johns Hopkins U., 1973, MD, MPH, Johns Hopkins U., 1976, PhD in Epidemiology, 1983; MA (hon.), U. Umeå, 2002. Fellow in cardiology Johns Hopkins Sch. Medicine, Balt., 1981-83, from asst. prof. to assoc. prof. medicine, epidemiology, 1983-88; prof. epidemiology Columbia U., 1988-97, prof. medicine, 1995-97, prof. medicine, Jane Forbes Clark chair in health rsch. NYC, 1995-97; dir. Mary Imogene Bassett Rsch. Inst., 1988-97; Kaiser prof. epidemiology, cmty. and preventive medicine U. Rochester, NY, 1997—, sr. assoc. dean for clin. rsch., 2002—. Mem. clin. applications and prevention commn. NIH, 1987—91, chmn., 1990; dir. Rochester Prevention Rsch. Ctr., 2004—; bd. dirs. World Heart Fedn. Co-editor: Scandinavian Jour. Pub. Health, 2000—. Mem. ACP, Am. Heart Assn. (nat. rsch. com. 1987-92, coun. epidemiology 1987—, vice chmn. 1994-95, chmn. 1996-98), Am. Fedn. Clin. Rsch., Am. Coll. Epidemiology, Am. Coll. Preventive Medicine, Am. Coll. Cardiology (prevention com.), Soc. Epidemiol. Rsch. (rsch. prize 1978). Achievements include research in the etiology and pathogenesis of atherosclerosis. Office: U Rochester Sch Medicine Dept Cmty Preventive Med 601 Elmwood Ave Box 644 Rochester NY 14642-0001 Office Phone: 585-275-2191.

PEASE, WILLIAM STOESS, physiatrist, educator; b. Cin., Jan. 7, 1955, s. Burton Reiman and Elizabeth Stoess Pease; m. Margaret E. Ginn, Dec. 29, 1979; children: James Burton, Katherine Elizabeth. MD, U. Cin., 1977—81. Lic. dr. Am. Bd. Phys. Medicine & Rehab., 1985, Am. Bd. Electrodiagnostic Medicine, 1989. Resident phys. medicine and rehab. Ohio State U. Med. Ctr., 1981—84; faculty Ohio State U. Coll. Medicine, Columbus, 1984—94, prof., dept. chair, 1991—2009. Bd. dir. Am. Bd. Electrodiagnostic Medicine, Rochester, Minn., 2003—. Editor: (medical textbook) Johnson's Practical Electromyography, 2006, Am. Jour. Phys. Medicine & Rehab., 2005—; contbr. chapters to books. Bd. mem. St. Joseph Montessori Sch., Columbus, 1999—2001. Recipient Faculty Tchg. award, Ohio State U. Coll. Medicine, 2005, Disting. Clinician award, Am. Acad. Phys. Medicine & Rehab., 2006. Fellow: Am. Assn. Neuromuscular & Electrodiagnostic Medicine, Assn. Academic Physiatrists, Am. Acad. Phys. Medicine & Rehab.; mem.: AMA (alt. del., ho. delegates 2004—), Tau Beta Pi (life), Beta Theta Pi (pres. 1976—76). Meth. Office: Ohio State Univ Med Ctr 480 Medical Center Dr Columbus OH 43210

PECHET, TAINE T.V., thoracic surgeon, educator; MD, Harvard Coll., Cambridge, Mass., 1992. Diplomate Am. Bd. Surgery, Am. Bd. Thoracic Surgery, 2002, lic. Mass., 1993, NJ, 2001, Pa., 2001. Intern Brigham & Women's Hosp., resident; fellow Barnes Jewish Hosp., 2001; asst. prof. surgery; vice chief surgery Pa. Hosp. Named one of Top Doctors, Phila. Mag., 2011. Fellow: ACS; mem.: Pa. Med. Soc., Phila. County Med. Soc., Internat. Soc. of Heart and Lung Transplantation, Am. Coll. of Chest Physicians, Mass. Med. Soc., Am. Assn. for Thoracic Surgery, Soc. of Thoracic Surgeons, Soc. of Am. Gastrointestinal and Endoscopic Surgeons, Gen. Thoracic Surg. Club, Gen. Thoracic Biology Club. Office: Pennsylvania Hospital Garfield Duncan Bldg Ste 305 700 Spruce St Philadelphia PA 19106 Office Phone: 800-789-7366.

PECK, GARNET EDWARD, pharmacist, educator; b. Windsor, Ont., Can., Feb. 4, 1930; s. William Crozier and Dorothy (Marentette) P.; m. Mary Ellen Hoffman, Aug. 24, 1957; children: Monique Elizabeth, Denise Anne, Philip Warren, John Edward. BS in Pharmacy with Distinction, Ohio No. U., 1957; MS in Indsl. Pharmacy, Purdue U., 1959, PhD, 1962. Sr. scientist Mead Johnson Research Center, 1962-65, group leader, 1965-67; assoc. prof. indsl. and phys. pharmacy Purdue U., West Lafayette, 1967—73, prof., 1973—2003, dir. indsl. pharmacy lab., 1975—, assoc. dept. head, 1989-96, prof. emeritus, 2003—. Cons. in field. Contbr. articles to profl. jours. Mem. West Lafayette Mayor's Advisory Com. on Community Devel., 1973-; mem. West Lafayette Citizen's Safety Com., 1974-81; mem. West Lafayette Park Bd., 1981-2010, pres., 1983-96. Served with U.S. Army, 1951-53. Recipient Lederle Faculty award Purdue U., 1976 Fellow APHA, AAAS, Am. Inst. Chem., Am. Assn. Pharm. Scientists; mem. Am. Chem. Soc., Acad. Rsch. and Sci. (Sidney Riegelman award 1994), Am. Assn. Colls. Pharmacy, Cath. Acad. Sci. (founding mem.), KC, Knight of Holy Sepulchre, Sigma Xi, Rho Chi, Phi Lambda Upsilon, Phi Kappa Phi, Phi Sigma Lambda, Phi Lambda Sigma. Roman Catholic. Office: Purdue University Coll Pharmacy Dept Industrial & Phys Pharm West Lafayette IN 47907 Office Phone: 765-494-1400. Business E-Mail: gepeck@pharmacy.purdue.edu.

PECK, KYUNG K., medical researcher; b. Seoul, Republic of Korea, June 30, 1966; MSc, U. Birmingham, Eng., 1996; PhD, U. Nottingham, Eng., 2001. Asst. attending Meml. Sloan-Kettering Cancer Ctr., 2003—. Mem.: Internat. Soc. Magnetic Resonance in Medicine. Avocations: reading, ping pong/table tennis, soccer. Office: BOX 84 1275 York Ave New York NY 10065 Business E-Mail: peckk@mskcc.org.

PECK, SHELDON, orthodontist, educator, dental anthropologist, art collector; b. NYC, Sept. 12, 1941; s. Max A. and Sylvia Peck; m. Leena Kataja, Apr. 20, 1986; children: Mark Alvar, Anya Elizabeth. BS, U. NC, Chapel Hill, 1963, DDS, 1966; MSc in Dentistry, Boston U., 1968. Pvt. practice orthodontics Doctors Peck, Peck and Savusalo, Boston, Newton, 1968—; asst. prof. Boston U., 1971—75, adj. prof., 1976—80; asst. prof. Harvard U., Boston, 1992—99, assoc. prof., 1999—2006, clin. prof. devel. biology, 2007—. Exec. sec. The Angle Soc., 1995—2009. Author: Rembrandt Drawings: Twenty-Five Years in the Peck Collection, 2003; co-author: Fresh Woods and Pastures New: Seventeenth-Century Dutch Landscape Drawings from the Peck Collection, 1999; editor: The World of Edward Hartley Angle, MD, DDS, His Letters, Accounts and Patents, 2007; assoc. editor: The Angle Orthodontist, 1997—. Adv. bd. mem. Met. Mus. Art, NYC, Mus. Fine Arts, Boston, Ackland Art Mus., Chapel Hill, NC, Harvard U. Art Museums, Cambridge, Mass. Mem.: St. Botolph Club (gov. 2005), Omicron Kappa Upsilon, Phi Beta Kappa, Alpha Chi Sigma, Phi Eta Sigma. Achievements include discovery of genetic linkage in dental anomaly patterns; research in radiographic and graphic-stroke analysis of old artworks; orofacial morphogenetic fields; dental anthropology. Office: 1400 Centre St Newton Center MA 02459 *

PECK, WILLIAM ARNO, internist, educator, dean, academic administrator; b. New Britain, Conn., Sept. 28, 1933; m. Patricia Hearn, July 10, 1982; children by previous marriage: Catherine, Edward Pershall, David Nathaniel; stepchildren: Andrea, Elizabeth, Katherine. AB, Harvard U., 1955; MD, U. Rochester, NYC, 1960; DSc (hon.), U. Rochester, 2000. Intern, then resident in internal medicine Barnes Hosp., St. Louis, 1960-62; fellow in metabolism Washington U. Sch. Medicine, St. Louis, 1963; mem. faculty U. Rochester Med. Sch., 1965-76, prof. medicine and biochemistry, 1973-76, head divsn. endocrinology and metabolism, 1969-76; John E. and Adaline Simon prof. medicine, co-chmn. dept. medicine Washington U. Sch. Medicine, St. Louis, 1976-89; physician in chief Jewish Hosp., St. Louis, 1976-89; prof. medicine and exec. vice chancellor med. affairs, dean sch. medicine, pres. univ. med. ctr. Washington U., St. Louis, 1989—2003, Wolff disting. prof., dean emeritus and dir. ctr. for health policy, 2003—. Chmn. endocrinology and metabolism adv. com. FDA, 1976-78; chmn. gen. medicine study sect. NIH, 1979-81; chmn. Gordon Conf. Chemistry, Physiology and Structure of Bones and Teeth, 1977, Consensus Devel. Conf. on Osteoporosis, NIH, 1984; co-chmn. Workshop on Future Directions in Osteoporosis, 1987; chmn. Spl. Topic Conf. on Osteoporosis, U.S. FDA, 1987; bd. dirs. Allied Healthcare Products, St. Louis Regional Chamber and Growth Assn., TIAA-CREF Trust Co., Centene Health Policy Adv. Coun. Editor Bone and Mineral Rsch. Anns., 1982-88. Pres. Nat. Osteoporosis Found., 1985-90. Served as med. officer USPHS, 1963-65. Paul Harris fellow Rotary Found., 2001; recipient Lederle Med. Faculty award, 1967, Career Program award NIH, 1970-75, Commr.'s Spl. citation FDA, 1988, Humanitarian award Arthritis Found. Ea. Mo., 1995, Crohn's and Colitis Fedn. Am., 1999, Founders award Nat. Osteoporosis Found., 1996, Huntington Disease Soc. Am. award, 2002, Juvenile Diabetes Rsch. Found. Lifetime Achievement award, 2003, Internat. Brotherhood award Bikur Cholim Hosp., Jerusalem, 2003, Nat. Children's Cancer Soc. Legacy award, Disting. Svc. award Washington U. Sch. Medicine, Lifetime Achievement award health care. Fellow AAAS, ACP; mem. Internat. Bone & Mineral Soc., Royal Soc. Medicine, Am. Assn. Clin. Endocrinologists, Am. Geriatrics Soc., Am. Soc. Biochemistry & Molecular Biophysics, Am. Soc. Bone and Mineral Rsch. (councllor 1978-81, pres.-elect 1982-83, pres. 1983-84), Am. Soc. Clin. Investigation, Am. Soc. Internal Medicine, Assn. Am. Med. Colls. (coun. deans adminstrv. bd. 1992—, chmn. 1996-97, chair elect 1997-98, chair 1998—, immediate past chair 1999), Assn. Am. Physicians, Endocrine Soc., Orthopaedic Rsch. Soc., Soc. Med. Adminstrs., St. Louis Metro. Med. Soc., St. Louis Soc. Internal Medicine (pres. 1986), Inst. Medicine Nat. Acad. Sci., Washington U. Health Adminstrn. Program Alumni Assn. (hon.), Research! Am. (vice chair 1999—), Pi Theta Epsilon (hon.), Sigma Xi, Alpha Omega Alpha (bd. dirs 1992-95). Home: 32 Huntleigh Downs Saint Louis MO 63131 Office: Washington U Sch Medicine #1 Brookings Dr Box 1133 Saint Louis MO 63130

PECORA, ANDREW LOUIS, hematologist, oncologist; b. Newark, 1957; B magna cum laude, Seton Hall U.; MD, U. Medicine and Dentistry NJ, 1983. Diplomate Am. Bd. Internal Medicine, Am. Bd. Hematology, Am. Bd. Med. Oncology. Intern NY Hosp.-Cornell Med. Ctr., NYC, 1983—84, resident in internal medicine, 1984—86; fellow in hematology and oncology Meml. Sloan Kettering Cancer Ctr., NYC; asst. dir. adult stem cell/bone marrow transplantation program Hackensack U. Med. Ctr., NJ, 1990—93, chief, program dir., 1993—, dir. stem cell collection and storage svc., 1993—, chmn., 1999—, chmn., dir. Cancer Ctr., 2001—. Prof. medicine U. Medicine and Dentistry NJ Med. Sch.; chmn. & CEO Progenitor Cell Therapy; chmn. techs. Amocyte; chmn., exec. adminstrn. devel. John Theurer Cancer Ctr. Named one of Top Drs. in America, 2005—, NY Met. Area, NJ, 2003—10. Home: 92 2nd St Hackensack NJ 07601-2105

PECORA, DAVID VICTOR, retired surgeon; b. Yonkers, NY, Oct. 2, 1916; s. Cavaliere Michael and Tulia (Muzi) Pecora; m. Dorothy Edith Beavers, July 22, 1944; children: Ann Charlene Diamond, Michele. BA, Columbia U., 1937; MD, Yale U., 1941. Diplomate Am. Bd. Gen. Surgery, Am. Bd. Thoracic Surgery. Intern Lakeside Hosp., Western Res. U., Cleve., 1941-42; grad. fellow in surgery NY Med. Coll., NYC, 1946-47; asst. resident in surgery Sch. Medicine, Yale U., New Haven, 1947-49, resident surgeon in thoracic surgery Uncas-on-Thames, Conn., 1949-51; chief thoracic surgery, sect. chief second surg. svc. VA Hosp., Providence, 1951-54, McGuire VA Hosp., Richmond, Va., 1967-72; prin. thoracic surgeon Ray Brook State Tb Hosp., NY, 1954-65; chief surgery Sunmount VA Hosp., Tupper Lake, NY, 1964-65, VA Hosp., Altoona, Pa., 1965—67; chief surg. svc. VA Ctr., Wilmington, Del., 1972-82; pvt. practice in thoracic, vascular and gen. surgery Newark, Del.; mem. staff Med. Ctr., Wilmington, Del., Cmty. Hosp., Chester, Pa., Crozer-Chester Hosp., Pa., Union Hosp., Elkton, Md., Riverside Hosp., Wilmington; ret., 1995. Instr. in surgery Boston U., 1953-54; clin. assoc. prof. in surgery SUNY, Syracuse, NY, 1961-70; asst. prof. surgery Med. Coll. Va., Richmond, 1967-70, assoc. prof. surgery, 1970-72; prof. surgery Thomas Jefferson U., Phila., 1972—; adj. prof. surgery Hahnemann U., Phila., 1988—; supv. tng. surg. residents numerous hosps. Mem. editl. bd. Del. Med. Jour.; author: Memoir: Between the Raindrops, 1998; contbr. over 130 articles to sci. jours. Capt. med. corps U.S. Army, 1942-46. Fellow ACS (instr. advanved trauma life support); mem. AMA, IEEE, Am. Assn. for Thoracic Surgery, Am. Coll. Chest Physicians, Am. Thoracic Soc., Am. Soc. Microbiology, Am. Med. Writers Assn., Am. Lung Assn. (eastern sect.), Royal Soc. Medicine, Pa. Assn. Thoracic Surgery, Del. Valley Vascular Soc., Md. State Med. Assn., Del. State Med. Assn., Del. Acad. Medicine, Va. Thoracic Soc., New Castle County Med. Assn., Phila. Acad. Surgery, Phila. Coll. Physicians, So. Thoracic Surg. Assn., Soc. Thoracic Surgeons (founder), Soc. Laparoendoscopic Surgeons, Soc. Neurovascular Surgery, Upstate NY Soc. Thoracic Surgery (past pres.), Saranac Lake Med. Soc. (past pres.).

PECORINO, LAUREN TERESA, biologist; b. Bronx, June 17, 1962; d. Joseph Salvatore and Raffaela (Rapillo) P. BS in Biology, SUNY, Stony Brook, 1984, PhD, 1990. Postdoctoral fellow Ludwig Inst. for Cancer Rsch., London, 1991-96; prin. lectr., biosci. program leader U. Greenwich, England, 1996—, dir. quality and learning, 2002—03. Cons. for cogent neurosci., 2001. Author: Molecular Biology of Cancer: Mechanisms, Targets and Therapeutics, 2005, 2nd edit., 2008, Why Millions Survive Cancer: The Success of Science, 2011; contbr. articles to profl. jours. Postdoctoral fellow European Molecular Biology Orgn., 1991-93, NATO, 1993-95. Fellow: Royal Soc. Medicine; mem.: AAAS, Soc. Biology, Am. Assn. Cancer Rsch., Biochem. Soc., NY Acad. Scis., Sigma Xi. Avocations: swimming, travel. Home: 1422 San Mateo Ave Lady Lake FL 32159-8661 Office: U Greenwich Medway Campus Chatham Kent ME4 4TB England Office Phone: 011 44 208 331-8210. Personal E-mail: lpecorino@aol.com. Business E-Mail: l.pecorino@gre.ac.uk.

PEDERSEN, BENTE KLARLUND, physician, educator, medical association administrator; b. Copenhagen, F, Denmark, Nov. 8, 1956; d. Knud and Inger Elise Pedersen; m. Kim Klarlund, Apr. 3, 1982; children: Dean Tuladhar, Diana Bonnen, Dorte Tuladhar, Andreas Klarlund. MD, U. Copenhagen, 1983. Sr. physician Rigshospitalet U. Copenhagen, 1996—, prof., 2001—. Dir. Nat. Coun. Pub. Health Ministry Health, Copenhagen, 2004—, Ctr. Inflammation and Metabolism U. Copenhagen, 2005—. Recipient Hagedorn award, 2004, Odd Fellow award, 2005, Frimurerlogens award, 2003, Tagea Brandt award, 2005. Home: Gråbrødre Torv 11 K Copenhagen 1054 Denmark Office: Univ Copenhagen Rigshospitalet Blegdamsvej 9 2100 Copenhagen 2100 Denmark Business E-Mail: bkp@rh.dk.

PEDERSEN, METTE, otolaryngologist, consultant; d. Katharina Wagner and Johannes Magelund; children: Christian, Michala. MD, U. Conpenhagen, Denmark, 1965; DMS, Oulu U., Finland, 1997; MD (hon.), U. Fienze, Italy, 2006. Con. ENT Surgeon Danish Med. Orgn., 1974. Ear nose throat specialist edn. Sundby Hosp., Copenhagen, 1973—75, Gentofte U. Hosp., 1975—76; ent specialist Strandgade 21, 1977—83; ear- nose- throat specialist edn. Bispebjerg Hosp., Bispebjerg, Denmark, 1966—68, Madison Vet. Hosp., Wis., 1968—69, rsch. fellow Wis., 1969—69; radiologist Finsens Inst., Copenhagen, 1969—70; lung surgeon Bispebjerg Hosp., 1970—71; plastic surgeon Diakonissestiftelsen, 1971; ear nose throat specialist edn. Glostrup Hosp., Glostrup, Copenhagen, Denmark, 1971—72; ent specialist Med. Ctr., 1983—; cons. phoniatrician Allergy Clinic, The Pvt. Hosp., 1998—2007; extern lectr. U. Copenhagen, 2009—. Enxaminer, censor U. of Copenhagen, 1974—83; cons. phoniatrician Copenhagen Sch. of Music, 1974—85; adv. physician to singers in the devel. of their voices Med. Ctr., 1983—; chair pub. rels. European Union Advanced Voice Assessment, 2006; spkr. in field; lectr. U. Copenhagen; bd. mem. Bioengring. Application in Performing Arts, Calif., Phonoscop e Jour. Prodr.(prodr., developer): (1st computerized phonetography) (Funded by Shering Plough); contbr. articles to profl. jours. Voluntary support to victims After the Chernobyl disaster, Russia, 1991; chmn. Christian Med. Student Soc., Copenhagen; mem. Sooptimists, 1980—88; elected Danish rep. European Union, 2005. Fellow: Royal Coll. Medicine; mem.: Danish Phoniatric Soc. (founder), European Union Advanced Assessment, Danish ENT Soc. (assoc.), Danish Sci. and Mgmt. Cmty., European Union Phoniatricians (bd. mem. 1976—, chmn. group 5 pub. rels. 2006—09, mem. European union advanced voice acoustical assessment). Achievements include invention of building the first diagnostic laboratory for voice disorders in Denmark; research in introducing evidence based medicine into voice medicine; relating developement of voice to biological developement; invention of synchronising stroboscopy with other measures. Home: Falkoner Allé 20 Copenhagen 1100 Denmark Office: The Med Ctr Voice Unit Østergade 18 Copenhagen 3 DK 1100 Denmark Office Fax: 45 33 13 77 05. Personal E-mail: m.f.pedersen@dadlnet.dk.

PEDERSEN, OLE LEDERBALLE, cardiologist; s. Peder Christian Lederballe and Margrethe Kirstine Pedersen; m. Else-Marie Kofod, Oct. 29, 1998; children: Thomas Lederballe, Lotte Sophie Lederballe, Rasmus Lederballe. MD, U. Aarhus, Denmark, 1971, DMSci, 1981. Cons. Regionshospitalet Viborg, Denmark, 1988—. Contbr. articles to profl. sci. jours. Recipient Astra-Zeneca award, Danish Soc. Cardiology, 2002, Danish Hypertension Soc., 2003. Achievements include research in hypertension and clinical pharmacology. Office: Regionshospitalet Viborg Heibergs Allé Viborg DK-8800 Denmark Business E-Mail: ole.lederballe@viborg.rm.dk.

PEDERSEN, SUSAN HELENE, physician; b. Copenhagen, June 26, 1973; MD, U. Copenhagen, 2001; PhD, Rigshospitalet, Copenhagen U. Hosp., 2005. Physician Glostrup U. Hosp., Copenhagen U., 2008—. Contbr. articles to sci. publs. Home: Fredensvej 27A Charlottenlund 2920 Denmark Personal E-mail: susanpedersen@dadlnet.dk.

PEDERSEN, WESLEY NIELS M., public relations and public affairs counselor; b. South Sioux City, Nebr., July 10, 1922; s. Peder Westergaard and Marie Gertrude (Sorensen) P.; m. Angeline Kathryn Vavra, Oct. 17, 1948; 1 son, Eric Wesley. Student, Tri-State Coll., Sioux City, Iowa, 1940-41; BA summa cum laude, Upper Iowa U., Fayette; postgrad. in Russian, George Washington U., 1958—59. Editor, writer Sioux City Jour., 1941-50; corr. N.Y. Times, Life, Time, Fortune, 1948-50; editor Dept. State, 1950—52, fgn. svc. officer Hong Kong, 1960-63; fgn. affairs columnist, roving corr., counselor summit meetings and fgn. ministers confs. USIA, 1952—60, chief, worldwide spl. publs. and graphics programs, 1963-69; chief Office Spl. Projects, Washington, 1969-78, Office Spl. Projects, Internat. Comm. Agy., 1978-79; v.p. Fraser Assocs., pub. rels., Washington, 1979-80; dir. comm. and pub. rels. Pub. Affairs Coun., Washington, 1980—2006; prin. Wes Pedersen Comms., 2006—. Lectr. creative comm. Upper Iowa U., 1975; chmn., Europe, Ambassadorial Internat. Affairs Seminar, Fgn. Svc. Inst., 1975; lectr. internat. pub. rels. Pub. Rels. Inst., Am. U., 1976; lectr. bus. and mgmt. divsn. NYU, 1976-78; cons. pub. rels., editl. and design; del. founding sessions 1st Amendment Congress, Phila. and Williamsburg, Va., 1980, exec. com., 1980; columnist O'Dwyer Pub. Relations Newsletter, 2008-, O'Dwyer's Magazine, 2008-. Columnist: (as Paul L. Ford) The World Today, 1952-60; (as Benjamin E. West) Behind the Curtain, 1952-60; White

House Report, 1966-69 (as Wesley Pedersen), Washington Report-Pub. Rels. Jour., 1980-85; author: Mr. President: Lyndon B. Johnson, 1964, Legacy of a President: The Memorable Words of John F. Kennedy, 1964, Journey to the Pacific, 1965, decision '68', How Am. Elect Their Pres., Mr. President: Richard M. Nixon, 1969, Pres. Nixon in Europe, 1969, American Heroes of Asian Wars, 1969; co-author: Effective Government Public Affairs, 1981; editor: The Imam's Story, 1961, Escape at Midnight and Other Stories (Pearl S. Buck), 1962, Exodus From China (Harry Redl), 1962, Macao, 1962, The Dividing Line (Arturo Gonzalez), 1962, China's Men of Letters (K.E. Priestley), 1963, Children of China (Pearl S. Buck and Margaret Wylie), 1963, Destination the Moon (William Howard), 1964, Man on the Moon, 1964, Nine From Little Rock, 1964, We Shall Overcome, 1964, To the Moon and Beyond, 1965, Bounty From the Land, 1965, Workers Paradise Lost (Eugene Lyons), 1967, The Americans and the Arts (Howard Taubman), 1969, The Dance in America (Agnes de Mille), 1969, Getting the Most From Grassroots Public Affairs Programs, 1980, Computer Applications in Public Affairs, 1984, Cost-Effective Management for Today's Public Affairs, 1984, Making Community Relations Pay Off: Tools and Strategies, 1988, Winning at the Grassroots: How to Succeed in the Legislative Arena by Mobilizing Employees and Other Allies, 1989, Leveraging State Government Relations, 1990, Managing the Business-Employee PAC, 1992, Adding Value to the Public Affairs Function, 1994, Winning at the Grassroots (with Tony Kramer), 2000, Managing the Corporate Political Action Committee, 2001; Pub. Affairs Rev. Mag., 1980-86, 2000-05, Impact newsletter Columnist O'Dwyer Pub. Rels. Newsletter, 2008-; on nat. and internat. pub. affairs, 1980-2006; contbr. to The Commissar, 1972, Informing the People: A Public Affairs Handbook, 1981, The Practice of Public Relations, 1984, 2d edit., 2003, Legislative Careers: Why and How We Should Study Them, 1999, Encyclopedia of Public Relations, 2004, Corporate Public Affairs: Interacting with Interest Groups, Media, and Government, 2006, Implausible Deniabilities, 2007; mem. editl. bd. Pub. Rels. Quar., 1975—, Washington editor, Pub. Rels. Quar., 1998—, Fgn. Svc. Jour., 1975-81; mem. editl. adv. bd. Pub. Rels. News, 1991-98, contbg. editor Pub. Affairs News Mag., London, 2004—; author scripts Uncle Walter's Doghouse radio show, 1938; contbr. articles to profl. jours. Founding chmn. bd. dirs. Nat. Inst. for Govt. Pub. Info. Rsch., Am. U., 1977-80. Served with Air Corps, US Army, 1943-46. Recipient 3 awards A.P. Mng. Editors Assn., Iowa, 1948-49, Meritorious Svc. award USIA, 1963, Superior Svc. award USIA, 1964, Presdl. commendation, 1964, 70, 1st prize Fed. Editors Assn., 1970, 74-75, Agy. Dir.'s citation USIA, 1965, 74, 78, Soc. Tech. Comm., 1974-76, Gold award Internat. Newsletter Conf., 1982, Silver award, 1985, Eddi award for design excellence Editor's Workshop, 1983, Gold Circle award Am. Soc. Assn. Execs., 1983-89, 97-2000, Ten Cool award Am. Soc. Assn. Execs., 2001, Editors' Forum award, 1988-90, 94-96, Assn. Trends award, 1989-2005, Lifetime Great Assn. Communicator award, Assn. Trends, 1999, Best of Century Comm. award, Assn. Trends, 2001, spl. citation Assn. Trends, 2001, 07, PR Week 2008, Silver award 2004, 05, Gold award, 2004, Excellence award, 2006, Grand prize Internat. Ann. Report Conf., 1989, Gold award 1997, Comm. Concepts awards, 1989-2006, Grand Comm. Concepts awards, 1992, 95, 2000, 02, 04-06, MerComm awards, 1990-2000, Nat. Media Conf. award, 1989-90, Internat. Acad. Comm. Arts and Scis. award, 1994-98, 2000, Grand prize, 1995, awards Printing and Graphic Assn., 1987, 91, 96-97, 2000, Excell award Soc. of Nat. Assn. Publishers, 2000, Judges' award 2000; named Most Outstanding Info. Officer in Exec. Br. Govt. Info. Orgn., 1975, Ky. Col. and Adm. Nebr. Navy, 1984. Mem. DAV, Am. Fgn. Svc. Assn., Am. Legion, Internat. Assn. Bus. Communicators (Communicator of Yr. Washington chpt. 1978, various awards 1973, 76-78, 84, 90, 94-2004, Winners' Circle awards dist. III 1996-2003), Nat. Assn. Govt. Communicators (pres. 1978-79, Communicator of Yr. 1977, Disting. Svc. award 1978), Pub. Rels. Soc. Am. (mem. Counselor's Acad. 1980—, chmn. 1st Amendment task force 1980-81, hall of fame steering com. mem., 2008-2009, co-recipient Thoth award 1980-81, 94, twin Thoth awards 1995-97, 2003, Thoth awards 1998-2003, Bronze Anvil award 2000, named to Hall of Fame 2005), Am. Soc. Profl. Communicators (Colonial award 2002, Masters award 2004), World Affairs Coun., Soc. Profl. Journalists, The Acad. Polit. Sci. Episcopalian. Office: Wes Pedersen Comms and Pub Rels 4701 Willard Ave Ste 1007 Chevy Chase MD 20815-4622 Office Phone: 301-718-9191. Personal E-mail: wesped@comcast.net, editorwes@hotmail.com. *

PEDERSON, WILLIAM CHRISTOPHER, plastic surgeon; b. Texas City, Tex., July 15, 1952; s. Alton Curtis and Lucy Vernor (Windham) P.; m. Cynthia Lea Anderson, June 17, 1978; children: Liv, Anton, Candice. BA, U. Tex., 1974, MD, 1978. Hand fellow U. Louisville, 1984; rsch. fellow Duke U. Med. Ctr., Durham, N.C., 1985; microsurgery rsch. fellow St. Vincent's Hosp., Melbourne, 1986; asst. prof. plastic surgery Duke U. Med. Ctr., Durham, 1087-89; chief of plastic surgery U. Tex. Health Sci. Ctr., San Antonio, 1989—; intern, resident surgery U. Tex., San Antonio, 1978—83, resident plastic surgery, 1983—85; pres. Am. Soc. Reconstructive Microsurgery, 2005—06. Contbr. articles to profl. jours. Fellow ACS (assoc.); mem. Am. Soc. Plastic and Reconstructive Surgery, Am. Assn. Hand Surgery, Am. Soc. Reconstructive Microsurgery.

PEDINI, EGLE DAMIJONAITIS, radiologist; b. Kaunas, Lithuania, July 22, 1943; d. Vytautas and Elena Damijonaitis; m. Kenneth Pedini, June 4, 1966; children: David Durand, Julian Adam. BA cum laude, Boston U., 1967, MD, 1967. Diplomate Am. Bd. Radiology. Intern St. Elizabeth's Hosp., Brighton, Mass., 1967—68; resident in radiology Boston City Hosp., 1968—71; radiologist St. John's Hosp., Lowell, Mass., 1972, Chelmsford X-Ray, Mass., 1979—80, Amesbury Hosp./Amesbury Health Ctr., Mass., 1973—98, New Eng. Meml. Hosp./Boston Regional Med. Ctr., Stoneham, Mass., 1973—98, Anna Jacques Hosp., Newburyport, Mass., 1973—98. Ptnr. NE Radiology Assocs., Brockton, Mass., 1980-98; chief radiology Anna Jacques Hosp., Newburyport, Mass., 1984, Amesbury Hosp., 1988-90. Founder, bd. dirs. Andover Sch. Montessori, Mass., 1974-79; parent ann. fundraising com. Phillips Exeter (N.H.), 1985, 86, 87. Mem. Am. Coll. Radiology, Mass. Radiol. Soc., New Eng. Roentgen Ray Soc., Pelican bay Womens League(Naples, Fla.), Greater Naples Leadership, Eastward Ho Country Club, Naples Garden Club, Allen Harbor Yacht Club.

PEDINI, KENNETH, radiologist; b. Hartford, Conn., Mar. 19, 1940; s. Daniel Victor and Elizabeth Catherine Pedini; m. Egle Damijonaitis; children: David D., Julian A. AB in Philosophy, Trinity Coll., 1962; MD, Boston U., 1966. Diplomate Nat. Bd. Med. Examiners, Am. Bd. Radiology. Resident in radiology Boston City Hosp., 1967—70, chief resident in radiology, 1969—70, jr. staff radiologist, 1970—71, U. Hosp., Boston, 1970—71; ptnr. Shawsheen Radiology, Andover, Mass., 1971—98; sr. radiologist Lawrence Gen. Hosp., Mass., 1971—, dir. radiology, 1976—87; sr. radiologist Melrose-Wakefield Hosp., Mass., 1971—99, chief radiologist, 1993—97, emeritus staff, 1999; pres. L & M Radiology Inc, Andover, Mass., 1994—98. Bd. trustees Lawrence Gen. Hosp., 1984-89, fin. com., 1986-03. Mem. Townwide Water Quality Mgmt. Task Force, 2001—04; mem., bd. dirs. Italian Cultural Soc. Naples, Fla. Incv., 2009—; mem. Class XI, Greater Naples Leadership, Inc., 2006; trustee Lawrence Gen. Hosp. Health Enterprises, Inc., 1990—93; mem. fin. com. Lawrence Gen. Regional Health Sys., 1996—2003; mem. alumni adv. com. Trinity Coll., 1995; co-founder Andover Sch. Montessori, 1975—; bd. dirs. The Bach Ensenble Naples, Fla., 2011—. Fellow Am. Coll. Radiology (councilor 1979-81); mem. New Eng. Roentgen Ray Soc., Mass. Radiol. Soc. (pres. 1985-86, pres.-elect 1984-85, v.p. 1983-84, exec. com. 1977-87), Mass. Med. Soc., Algonquin Club, Allen Harbor Yacht Club, Eastward Ho! Country Club.

PEDLEY, TIMOTHY ASBURY, IV, neurologist, educator, researcher; b. Phoenix, Aug. 31, 1943; s. Timothy Asbury Pedley III and Mary Adele (Newcomer) Melis; m. Barbara S. Koppel, Mar. 17, 1984. BA, Pomona Coll., 1965; MD, Yale U., 1969. Cert. neurology, electroencephalography, clin. neurophysiology; diplomate Am. Bd. Psychiatry and Neurology. Intern Stanford U. Hosp., 1969-70, resident in neurology, 1970—73, postdoctoral fellow, 1973-75; asst. prof. neurology Stanford U., 1975-79; from assoc. prof. neurology to prof., vice chmn. Columbia U., 1979-98, Henry and Lucy Moses prof., chmn. neurology, 1998—; neurologist-in-chief Columbia U. Med. Ctr., NYC, 1998—. Dir. comprehensive epilepsy ctr. Columbia U. Med. Ctr., 1983-97. profl. adv. bd. Epilepsy Found Am., 1984-98, chmn. profl. adv. bd., 1985-87, pres. bd. dirs., 1991-93, chmn. 1993-95, mem. rev. com. NIH Nat. Inst. Neurol. and Chronic Diseases and Strokes, 1985-89, chmn., 1988-89, mem. Nat. Advisory Neurological Disorders & Stroke Coun. (NINDS/NIH), 2007-; various adv. coms. NIH/NINDS, 1990-98; vis. fellow in exptl. neurology Inst. Psychiatry, London, 1978-79; mem. merit rev. bd. neurobiology rsch., VA, 1992-96, chmn., 1995-96; vis. prof. various univs., U.S. and abroad. Editor-in-chief: Epilepsia, 1993—2001; contbr. articles to profl. jours. Fellow AAAS, 2000, N.Y. Acad. Medicine; Recipient various honors and awards. Fellow Am. Acad. Neurology (bd. trustees 2001—, sec., 2003-07), Am. Electroencephalographic Soc. (pres. 1989-90, bd. dirs. 1981-85), Royal Soc. Medicine; mem. Am. Neurol. Assn. (coun. 1992-94, treas. 1995-98, 1st v.p. 2003-04, pres. 2007-09), Am. Epilepsy Soc. (treas. 1980-83, pres. 1991-92), Soc. Neurosci., Internat. League Against Epilepsy (exec. com. 1994-02), Inst. Med. Nat. Acad. Sci., Vidonian Club, Yale Club, N.Y. Med. Surg. Soc., Shenorock Shore Club, Alpha Omega Alpha. Office: The Neurological Inst 710 W 168th St New York NY 10032-2603 Office Phone: 212-305-6489. Office Fax: 212-305-6978. Business E-Mail: tap2@columbia.edu.

PEDOWITZ, ROBERT ALAN, orthopaedic surgeon, researcher; b. NYC, Aug. 1, 1959; s. Irving and Beverly Pedowitz; m. Loraine Pedowitz, Sept. 28, 1986; children: Rachel, Jason. BS in Psychobiology, UCLA, 1981; MD, U. Calif., San Diego, 1985; PhD, U. Gothenburg, Sweden, 1991. Diplomate Am. Bd. Orthop. Surgery. Resident, orthop. surgery U. Calif., San Diego, 1985—92; fellow, sports medicine Duke U., Durham, NC; faculty, dept. orthopaedics U. Calif., San Diego, 1992—, chief sports medicine, 1998—2006, residency dir., dept. orthop., 2001; co-dir. San Diego Arthroscopy and Sports Medicine Fellowship, San Diego, 2001—06; chmn., dept. orthop. surgery Univ. S. Fla. Coll. Medicine, Tampa, 2007—. Cons. Orthop. Mfg. Cos., 1995—2003; internat. adv. bd. Doha Orthop. and Sports Medicine Hosp., Qatar. Author; contbr. articles to profl. jours. Named a San Diego Top Doctor, 2005—06. Fellow: Am. Acad. Orthop. Surgeons; mem.: Orthop. Rsch. Soc., Arthroscopy Assn. N.Am., Am. Orthop. Soc. Sports Medicine, Am. Orthop. Assn. Avocations: golf, travel, skiing.

PEDRO, AMARILES, pharmacist; b. Medellin, Sept. 20, 1967; PhD, U. Granada, 2008, PharmaD. Cert. pharmacist U. Antioquia, 1994. Pharmacist Hosp. la Meced, 1994—95; clin. pharmacy & pharmacology prof. U. Antioquia, 1995—, bd. dirs., 2001—03, dean, 2010—. Mem.: Rsch. Group Pharm. Care, OFIL. Office: Aa 1226 Medellin Antioquia 1226 Colombia Business E-Mail: pamaris@farmacia.udea.edu.co.

PEEL, DEBORAH C., medical privacy organization executive; Practicing physician; nat. expert on med. privacy; founder, chairwomen Patient Privacy Rights Found., Tex., 2004—. Formed Coalition for Patient Privacy, 2006. Mem.: American Psychoanalytic Assn. (co-chair com. on govt. relations). Office: Patient Privacy Rights Foundation PO Box 248 Austin TX 78767

PEEL, MARGARET MARY, microbiologist, public health service officer; b. Kingaroy, Queensland, Australia; d. Percy Desmond and Ann Margaret (Moriarty) Peel. BSc, U. Queensland, 1966; diploma in bacteriology, U. London, 1972, PhD, 1975; DSc, U. Queensland, 2009. Lectr. Queensland U. Tech., Brisbane, 1966—71; rsch. tng. fellow Wellcome Pty. Ltd./London U., 1973—75; prin. microbiologist Microbiol. Diagnostic Unit U. Melbourne, Australia, 1976—2000; ret., 2000. Hon. lectr. microbiology U. Melbourne, 1985—95, acad. assoc. microbiology, 1986—2000; lectr. epidemiology Swinburne U. Tech., Melbourne, 1977—96; invited spkr. confs. microbiology and infection control; cons. infection and contamination control and biosafety. Author (with J. F. Gardneau): Sterilization, Disinfection and Infection Control, 1986, 3d edit., 1998; contbr. over 70 articles to profl. jours. Rep. polio survivors, Queensland. Jubilee fellow, Queensland Assn. Univ. Women, 1972—73, Travel grantee, Australia-China Soc., 1985. Fellow: Australian Soc. Microbioloby; mem.: ASM (mem. standing com. biosafety 1989—99), Grad. Women Queensland (nat. sec. 1979—80, convener for health 2006, minutes sec. 2008), Sterilizing Rsch. Adv. Coun. Australia (hon.). Roman Catholic. Avocations: amateur astronomy, singing, sugar craft, cake decorating. Home: 27A Levant St Albany Creek Queensland 4035 Australia

PEERAPITTAYAMONGKOL, CHAYANON, physician, educator; b. Bangkok, Jan. 21, 1971; PhD, Mahidol U., Bangkok, MD, 1999. Lectr., faculty medicine Siriraj Hosp., Mahidol U., 1999—; postdoc. rschr. Inst. Pasteur, Paris, 2003. Scholar Monbusho, Japanese Govt.; Postdoc. fellowship, INSERM, France. Avocation: movies. Office: Mahidol University Siriraj Hosp 2 Prannok Rd Bangkoknoi Dist Bangkok 10700 Thailand Business E-Mail: sicpr@mahidol.ac.th.

PEIHUA, LU, surgeon; b. Jiangsu, China, Aug. 21, 1980; MD, Nanjing Med. U., 2007. With gen. surgery Wuxi People's Hosp., 2007—. Home: Wuxi Qingyang Rd Wuxi Jiangsu Province 214023 China Personal E-mail: lphty1_1@yahoo.com.cn.

PEIKIN, STEVEN R., gastroenterologist, educator; Grad. in Math., Temple U.; MD magna cum laude, Thomas Jefferson U., 1974. Diplomate Am. Bd. Internal Medicine, Am. Bd. Internal Medicine-gastroenterology. Prof. Medicine Univ. Medicine and dentistry of NJ, head gastroenterology and liver diseases divsns.; intern internal medicine Univ. Calif., San Francisco, resident internal medicine; fellow gastroenterology NIH, Mass. Gen. Hosp., Harvard Univ.; Asst. prof. Medicine Thomas Jefferson Univ., assoc. prof. Medicine, acting dir. gastroenterology and hepatology divsns., 1985—86; prof. Medicine Cooper Univ. Hosp., head gastroenterology and liver diseases divsns., physician. Author: Gastrointestinal Health (best selling book); co-author: numerous papers. Recipient Golden Apple Tchg. award, 1997—2001, Alumni award, surgery and medicine prizes; named Top Dr., Phila. Mag., NJ Mag. Mem.: Alpha Omega Alpha (pres.). Office: Cooper University Hospital Ste101 501 Fellowship Rd Mount Laurel NJ 08054 Office Phone: 856-642-2133. Office Fax: 856-642-2134.

PEIXOTO NETO, JOSE ULYSSES, internist, researcher; b. Crato, Ceará, Brazil, Aug. 29, 1930; s. Adérito de Aquino Silva and Adelite Alencar Peixoto; m. Maria Isolda Teles Cartaxo, May 23, 1958; children: Jose Ulysses Peixoto Filho, Eunice Ulysséia Peixoto Maia, Jorge André Cartaxo Peixoto. 1st degree, State Coll. Goias, Brazil, 1942, postgrad., 1942-49; 2d degree, St. John Coll., Fortaleza, Brazil, 1949; postgrad., Fed. U., Recife, Brazil, 1955; Laurel, Cearense Med. Ctr., 1994. Med. resident St. Michael Hosp., Rio de Janeiro, 1956; intern St. Anthony Hosp., Iguatú, Ceará, 1957; founder Social Providence, Crato, Ceará, 1958-64; attendent St. Frances Hosp., Crato, 1958-69; founder St. Michael Hosp., Crato, 1967-93, pres., dir., 1983-93, internist, researcher, 1993—; founder Faculty of Law, Crato, 1977-78. Lectr. faculty of medicine The Fed. U. of Ceará, 1976—. Recipient Good Svc. award Lyons Club, 1992, Laurel Cearense Med. Ctr., 1994, Cert. Merit Health Care Profls. Juazeiro North Profl. Health Assn., 1998, Gold Medal of Profl. Merit, Ceara Estate Regional Coun. Medicine, 1999, Plaque of profl. merit Cariri sect. Coun. of Ceara, 2002, Diploma of Ethical Profl. Merit Fed. Medicine Coun., 2006, Jubilee of Gold, Diploma of Fifty Yrs. as Med. Doctor, Medice Meml. Pernam Buco, 2006. Fellow Brazilian Med. Assn. (specialist); mem. AAAS, ACP, Brazilian Soc. Clin. Medicine (specialist), NY Acad. Sci. Roman Catholic. Avocations: reading, walking, movies, farming.

PELARGONIO, SALVATORE, physician; b. Taranto, Italy, Dec. 5, 1927; s. Gaetano Pelargonio and Irene Campisi; m. Eleonora Cassinari, Dec. 28, 1966; 3 children. MD, Rome U., 1952, Bd. Med. Examiners, Md., 1962; Cardiologist, U. Turin, Italy, 1969. Diplomate Specialist in cardiology and paediatric cardiology. Intern U. Rome, 1952—53; rotating intern Newton Wellesley Hosp., Boston, 1953—54; resident in pediat. Children's Hosp. - Wayne U., Detroit, 1954—56, Boston City Hosp., 1956—57; resident in pediatric cardiology and cardiorheumatology Harvard Med. Sch., Boston, 1957—58; tchg. fellow in pediatric cardiology Johns Hopkin Hosp. Med. Sch., Balt., 1958—59; tchg. fellow in med. rsch. Harvard Med. Sch./Children's Hosp., Boston, 1959—63; asst. in pediat. and pediatric cardiology U. Rome, 1960—72, prof. pediat. and pediatric cardiology, 1971—72; prof. pediatric cardiology Cath. U., Rome, 1972—95, dir. autonomous sect. pediat. cardiology, assoc. prof., 1981—95. Mem. coun. U. Assn. for Internat. Cooperation, Rome, pres., 1982—2005. Fellow: Am. Coll. Cardiology (emeritus); mem.: Umanitary Assn. Dr. against Torture, Italian Soc. Migration Medicine, N.Y. Acad. Scis., Italian Soc. Sport Cardiology, Italian Soc. Pediat. Cardiology (founding and hon. mem.), Italian Soc. Cardiology, Assn. European Pediat. Cardiology (founding mem.), Assn. for Internat. Cooperation Study and Work (pres. 1987—). Office: ACISEL Via Amantea 89 00178 Rome Italy Personal E-mail: salvatorepelargonio@yahoo.it.

PELECHANO, VICENTE, psychologist, educator; b. Algemesi, Spain, June 18, 1943; s. Vicente and Consuelo (Barbera) P. Psychologist, Sch. Psychology Madrid, 1968; behavior therapist, Max Planck Inst. Psychiatry, 1971; PhD of Philosophy, Faculty of Philosophy Madrid, 1972. Lectr. psychology U. Complutense, Madrid, 1968-69, 71-74; prof. psychology U. La Laguna, Spain, 1974-77, Tenerife, Canary Islands, Spain, 1983—, U. Valencia, Spain, 1977-83, U. La Laguna, Tenerife, Canary Islands, Spain, 1983—; state clin. psychologist Spanish Health Ministry, 2006. Pres. Acreditation Commn. for Social and Juridical Sci., Valencia, Spain. Patentee in field; editor, contbr. Analysis and Behavior Modification Jour., 1975-; editor Psychologemas Jour., 1987—2005; contbr. chpts. in books and articles to profl. jours. Mem. APA, Spanish Soc. Psychology (exec. com. 1972-75, Jose Germain award 1968, Luis Simarro award 1970, Pilar Sangro award, 1972), Internat. Soc. for Personality and Individual Differences, Valencian Soc. Behavior Analysis (pres. 1980-82, editl bd.), Spanish Soc. of Psychopathology and Clin. Psychology (hon.), Spanish Soc. of Individual Differences (hon.), Spanish Soc. Rsch. Individual Differences (hon. pres.), European Congress Behavioral and Cognitive Therapies (hon. pres.), European Soc. for Personality. Office: U La Laguna Psychol Dept Campus de Guajara Tenerife Spain Business E-Mail: vpelecha@ull.es.

PELHAM, JUDITH, health system administrator; b. Bristol, Conn., July 23, 1945; d. Marvin Curtis and Muriel (Chodos) Pelham; m. Jon N. Coffee, Dec. 30, 1992; children: Rachel Welch, Molly, Edward. BA, Smith Coll., 1967; MPA, Harvard U., 1975. Various govt. postions, 1968-72; prin. analyst Urban Systems, Cambridge, Mass., 1972-73; dir. devel. & planning Roxbury Dental & Med. Group, Boston, 1975-76; asst. to dir. for gen. medicine and ambulatory care Peter B. Brigham Hosp., Boston, 1976-77, asst. dir. ambulatory care, 1977-79; asst. v.p. Brigham & Women's Hosp., Boston, 1980-81; dir. planning and mktg. Seton Med. Ctr., Austin, Tex., 1980-82, pres., 1982-92, CEO, 1987-92; pres., CEO Daughters of Charity Health Svcs., Austin, 1987-92, Mercy Health Svcs., Farmington Hills, Mich., 1993—2000, Trinity Health (merger of Mercy Health Svcs. and Holy Cross Health Sys.), Novi, Mich., 2000—04, pres. emeritus, 2005—. Bd. dirs. Amgen, 1995—, Cath. CEO Healthcare Connection, 1998—2004, Eclipsys Corp., 2009—; cons. Robert W. Johnson Found., 1979—80; mem. mgmt. bd. Inst. for Diversity in Health Mgmt., 1994—97; chair Coalition for Non-Profit Healthcare, 1997—2000, exec. com., 1997—2002; mem. Healthcare Rsch. and Devel. Inst., 1998—2005, bd., 2003—05; mem. adv. com. RAND

Health Compare Strategic Policy, 2005—; mem. strategic adv. bd. Shattuck Hammond, 2005—; mem. strategic adv. com. for comprehensive assessment of reform efforts RAND Corp., 2006—. Contbr. articles to profl. jours. Trustee A. Shivers Radiation Therapy Ctr., Austin, 1982—92, Marywood Maternity and Adoption Agy., 1982—86; bd. dirs. Quality of Life Found., Austin, 1985, Austin Rape Crisis Ctr., adv. bd. mem., 1986—88; bd. dirs., trustee League House, 1992—93, Seton Fund, 1982—93, Greater Detroit Area Health Coun.; mem. Gov.'s Job Tng. Coordinating Coun., 1983—85; mem. adv. coun. U. Tex. Social Work Found., 1983—85; charter mem. Leadership Tex., Austin, 1983—93; trustee Smith Coll. Recipient Leadership award, YWCA Austin, 1986, CEO IT Achievement award, Modern Healthcare, Healthcare Info. Mgmt. Sys. Soc., 2004; named one of Detroit's 100 Most Influential Women, Crain's Detroit Bus., 1997, 2002. Fellow: Am. Hosp. Assn., Am. Coll. Healthcare Execs. (bd. dirs. 1987—95); mem.: Cath. Health Assn. (sec., treas. 1982—95, com. on govt. rels. 1984—91, chair fin. com. 1992—95, bd. dirs. 1987—95), Tex. Conf. Health Facilities (bd. dirs. 1985—89, pres. 1988), Austin Area Rsch. Orgn., Tex. Hosp. Assn. (various couns. 1982—87).

PELISSIER, EDOUARD-PIERRE, retired surgeon; b. Bastia, Corse, France, Sept. 1, 1937; s. Jean-Baptiste and Francoise (Geronimi) P.; m. Sylvie Geoffroy-Emmanuelli, Feb. 9, 1967 (div.); m. Penelope Willard July 25, 2009; children: Emmanuelle, Pierre, Francois, Anne-Catherine. MD, U. Paris, 1968. Ancien interne Hopitaux de Paris, 1963-67; attache cons. Centre Hospitalier Universitaire de Besancon, France, 1975; surgeon Clinique St. Vincents, Besancon, 1968—2011. Sec. conseil de l'Ordre des Medecins, Doubs., France, 1980-83. Contbr. articles to med. revs. With French Marine Corps., 1961-63. Fellow ACS; mem. Academie Nat. de Chirurgie, Collegium Internationale Chirurgiae Digestivae, Société Nationale Francaise de Gastro-Enterologie, Assn. Française de Chirurgie, Internat. Soc. Surgery, N.Y. Acad. Scis. Home: 10 Rue de Poulampont Conde-sur-Vesgre 78113 France Personal E-mail: pelissier.edouard@wanadoo.fr.

PELKOVA, JANA, hematologist, educator; b. Zlin, Czech Republic, Jan. 13, 1968; 2 children. D, Masaryk U. Brno, 1992. Lectr. Tomas Bata U. Zlin, 2008; specialist haematology and transfusion medicine Bata Region Hosp. Zlin, 1994—. Mem.: Czech Med. Soc. Avocations: music, sports. Home: Ceska 4755 Zlin 76005 Czech Republic Home Fax: 420577552327. Business E-Mail: pelkova@bnzlin.cz.

PELL, SIDNEY, epidemiologist; b. NYC, Dec. 13, 1922; m. Lola May, July 2, 1950. MBA, CCNY, 1952; PhD, U. Pitts., 1956. Biostatistician E.I. Du Pont de Nemours and Co., Wilmington, Del., 1955-76, mgr. epidemiology sect., 1976-82, sr. cons., 1982-85; epidemiology cons. Wilmington, 1985—. Epidemiology cons. Del. Divsn. Pub. Health, Dover, 1986-95. Contbr. articles to New Eng. Jour. Medicine, Jour. Occupational Medicine, Jour. AMA. With U.S. Army, 1943-45, ETO. Recipient Merit in Authorship Hon. Mention, Inds. Med. Assn., 1959. Fellow Am. Coll. Epidemiology, Am. Heart Assn., Am. Pub. Health Assn., Delta Omega. Home: 1416 Emory Rd Wilmington DE 19803-5120 E-mail: pell104@aol.com.

PELLEGRINO, EDMUND DANIEL, internist, educator, retired academic administrator; b. Newark, June 22, 1920; s. Michael J. and Marie (Catone) Pellegrino; m. Clementine Coakley, Nov. 17, 1944; children: Thomas, Virginia, Michael, Andrea, Alice, Leah. BS, St. John's U., 1941, DSc (hon.), 1971; MD, NYU, 1944; 39 hon. degrees. Diplomate Am. Bd. Internal Medicine. Intern Bellevue Hosp., NYC, 1944—45, asst. resident medicine, 1948—49; resident medicine Goldwater Meml. Hosp., NYC, 1945—46; fellow medicine NYU, 1949—50; supervising Tb physician Homer Folks Hosp., Oneonta, NY, 1950—53; dir. internal medicine Hunterdon Med. Center, Flemington, NJ, 1953—59, med. dir., 1955—59; prof., chmn. dept. medicine U. Ky. Med. Center, 1959—66; prof. medicine SUNY, Stony Brook, 1966—72, v.p. for health scis., dir. Health Scis. Center, 1968—73, dean Sch. Medicine, 1968—72; v.p. health affairs U. Tenn. System; chancellor U. Tenn. Med. Units, Memphis, 1973—75; prof. med. Yale U., New Haven, 1975—78; pres. Yale-New Haven Med. Center, 1975—78, Cath. U. Am., Washington, 1978—82, prof. philosophy and biology, 1978—82; John Carroll prof. medicine and med. ethics Georgetown U., Washington, 1982—; dir. Kennedy Inst. Ethics, Washington, 1983—88; dir. Ctr. for Advanced Study Ethics Georgetown U., Washington, 1988—94, dir. Ctr. for Clin. Bioethics, 1991—, acting chief Divsn. Gen. Internal Medicine, 1993—94, chief Gen. Internal Medicine, 1995. Founding editor: Jour. Medicine and Philosophy, 1983—. Chmn. Pres.'s Coun. on Bioethics, Washington, 2005—. With USAF, 1946—48. Master: ACP; fellow: N.Y. Acad. Medicine; mem.: Inst. Medicine NAS, AMA, Am. Clin. and Climatol. Assn., Assn. Am. Physicians (chmn. pres. coun. 2005—). Office: Georgetown U Ctr for Clin Bioethics Washington DC 20007

PELLEGRINO, PETER, retired surgeon; b. Camden, NJ, July 7, 1934; s. Peter and Alice (Alchin) Pellegrino; m. Barbara Ann Holden, June 18, 1960; children: Peter Scott, Kathleen Ann, Lisa Marie. AB in Psychology, Franklin & Marshall Coll., Lancaster, Pa., 1960; MD, Hahnemann Med. Coll., Phila., 1960. Diplomate Am. Bd. Surgery. Intern Hahnemann Hosp., Phila., 1960—61, surg. resident, 1961—62, 1965—67, 1968, attending surgeon, 1969—2006; chief dept. surgery Kessler Hosp., Hammonton, NJ, 1969—2006. Assoc. prof. surgery Hahnemann Hosp., Phila., 2003—06. Capt. US Army, 1962—65. Fellow: ACS; mem.: N.J. Med. Soc., Hahnemann Alumni Assn. (1st v.p. 1984). Republican. Office Phone: 856-767-8980.

PELLETIER, GLENN JEFFREY, cardiologist, educator; b. Webster, Mass., Mar. 17, 1965; BA, Coll. Holy Cross, 1987; MD, Dartmouth Med. Sch., 1991. Cardiac surgeon Nemours Cardiac Ctr., Alfred I. duPont Hosp. Children, 2010—. Asst. prof. cardiothoracic surgery Drexel Coll. Medicine, 2004—. Mem.: Soc. Thoracic Surgeons. Avocation: painting. Office: 1600 Rockland Rd Wilmington DE 19803 Business E-Mail: gpelleti@drexelmed.edu.

PELLICCI, PAUL M., orthopedist, surgeon, educator; MD, Weill Cornell Med. Coll., 1975. Cert. orthopaedic surgery, lic. NY. Resident surgery NY Hosp., 1976—77; resident orthopaedic surgery Hosp. for Spl. Surgery, 1977—80, attending orthopedic surgeon; fellow adult reconstructive surgery Brigham & Women's Hosp., 1980—81; prof. clin. orthopaedic surgery Weill Cornell Med. Coll. Author: (publs.) Arthritis of the Hip - Overview, 2002, HSS Manual Ch. 28 - Bursitis and Tendinitis, 2006; co-author: Varus Rotational Osteotomies for Adults with Hip Dysplasia, 2007, Randomized Trials to Modify Patients' Preoperative Expectations of Hip and Knee Arthroplasties, 2008, and other numerous publications. Recipient Lewis Clark Wagner award, Hosp. for Spl. Surgery, 1980, Teaching award, 1996, 2005, Otto AuFranc award, Hip Soc., 1991, Patients Choice Physician award, 2010, and other numerous award.; named one of Best Doctors, NY Mag., 2002—11. Office: Hospital for Special Surgery 3rd Fl 535 E 70th St New York NY 10021 Office Phone: 212-606-1010. Office Fax: 212-744-9145.

PELLICER, ANTONIO, gynecologist; b. Gandia, Valencia, Spain, Apr. 10, 1955; MD, Faculty Medicine & Odontology, 1980. Pres., dir. Inst. Valenciano De Infertilidad I.u., 1990; pres. Ivi Found., 1998; disting. prof. Faculty Medicine, Area Ob-Gyn., Valencia, 1999, assoc. prof., 1986—99; dean Faculty Medicine & Odontology, U. Valencia, 2006—; chmn. dept. ob-gyn. Hosp. U. La Fe, Valencia, 2009. Dir. Reproducción Humana, IVI Valencia, Biotech. de la Reproducción Humana Asistida, IVI Valencia; co-editor Jour. Fertil & Sterility. Recipient King James award, 2004, award, Found. Lilly Investigation Biomed. Clinic, 2008, Gold medal, Valencia, 2006, Royal Coll. Physicians, 2006, Llama Rotaria, 2007, Rotary Club Valencia, 2007. Avocations: bicycling, swimming, classical music. Office: Plz De La Policia Local N°3 Bajo Valencia 46015 Spain Office Fax: 34 963050998. Business E-Mail: apellicer@ivi.es.

PELSER, DEBORAH, science administrator; b. South Africa, Apr. 7, 1961; BSc, UCT, 1983; MBBCh, 1995. Mgr. sci. affairs Lundbeck, 2000. Office: Ground Fl 1 Innovation Rd North Ryde NSW 2113 Australia Business E-Mail: depe@lundbeck.com.

PELTOLA, JAAKKO SAKARI, retired oral radiology professor; b. Oulu, Finland, Sept. 9, 1944; s. Lauri Jalmari and Raakel Peltola; m. Tuija Marjatta Susiaho, June 3, 1968; children: Timo Jaakko, Sanna Marjukka. DDS, PhD, U. of Helsinki, Finland, 1996, degree in Oral Radiology, 2006. Dentist Communal Health Ctr., Jurva, Jurva, Finland, 1971—76; pvt. practice in dentistry Helsinki, 1976—91; asst. Inst. Dentistry, Helsinki, 1982—95, assoc. prof., 1995—2001, prof., 2009—, head dept. oral radiology Helsinki, 2001—, prof. oral radiology, 2009; ret. Contbr. articles to sci. publs. Recipient tchg. award, Med. Faculty, U. of Helsinki, 1994. Mem.: Finnish Dental Soc. (licentiate; mem. edn. com. 2002—05, pres. radiologic sect. 1992—94). Avocations: travel, reading, skiing. Office Fax: 358 9 19127230. Personal E-mail: jaakko.peltola@saunalahti.fi.

PENA, RENE PROSIA, surgeon, radiologist; b. Cebu, The Philippines, 1942; s. Jesus and Casilda (Prosia) P.; m. Lydia Tanero, Apr. 14, 1968; children: Roehl, Ananette, Brian. MD, Coll. Medicine Cebu Inst., 1965. Diplomate Am. Bd. Surgeons, Am. Bd. Radiology. Intern Overlook Hosp., Summit, N.J., 1969; resident in surgery Lutheran Med. Ctr., Bklyn., 1970-74; surgeon Lake Mead (Nev.) Hosp., 1974—, Valley Hosp., 1974—, Sun Rise Hosp., 1974—, Sunrise Mountain View Hosp., Las Vegas, 1974—. Fellow Am. Coll. Surgeons; mem. Nev. State Med. Assn., Soc. Philosophy South Am. Office: 2031 Mcdaniel St Ste 230 North Las Vegas NV 89030-6309 *

PEÑALVER, FRANCISCO-JAVIER, hematologist; b. Madrid, May 18, 1962; MD, U. Autónoma Madrid, 1990. Cert. hematologist 1996. Head hematology unit Hosp. Inversitario Fundación Alcorcon, 2010—. Mem.: Assn. Española Hematologia Y Hemoterapia. Avocations: sports, football, writing, horseback riding. Office: Budapest 1 Alcorcón Madrid 28922 Spain Office Fax: 34916219896. Business E-Mail: fjpenalver@fhalcorcon.es.

PEÑA QUINTANA, LUIS, pediatrician, educator; b. Teror, Las Palmas, Spain, June 19, 1956; MD, U. La Laguna, 1979, degree in Pediat., 1983, U. Barcelona, 1983. Head unit pediat. gastroenterology, hepatology and nutrition Hosp. U. Materno Infantil Las Palmas, Spain, 1984—; prof. pediat. U. Las Palmas De Gran Canaria, Spain, 1991, head svc. clinic sci. dept., 2009. Pres. Spanish Soc. Pediat. Gastroenterology, Hepatology And Nutrition; sec. Spanish Academic Nutrition, v.p. Mem.: Non Govtl. Orgn. Nutrición sin fronteras (Barcelona), European Working Group Cystic Fibrosis, L.Am. Soc. Pediat. Gastroenterology, Hepatology and Nutrition, Spanish Assn. Pediat., European Soc. Pediat. Gastroenterology, Hepatology And Nutrition. Office: C/ Cebrián 74 Bajo Las Palmas De Gran Canaria Las Palmas 35003 Spain Business E-Mail: lpena@dcc.ulpgc.es.

PENCE, LORENZO L., dean, osteopath, educator; BS, Bluefield State Coll., W.Va.; MD, W.Va. Sch. Osteo. Medicine, Lewisburg, 1985. Resident in family medicine Parkview Hosp., Toledo; dir. med. edn. The Toledo Hosp., St. Vincent Mercy Med. Ctr., Toledo, Greenbrier Valley Med. Ctr., Ronceverte, W.Va.; prof. family medicine W.Va. Sch. Osteo. Medicine, assoc. dean grad. med. edn., 2003—, v.p. academic affairs, dean, 2011—, chief academic officer Mountain State Osteo. Postdoctoral Tng. Institutes; chmn. bd. dirs. Southeastern Area Health Edn. Ctr. Office: WVa Sch Osteo Medicine C203 C Bldg 400 N Lee St Lewisburg WV 24901 Office Phone: 304-647-6237. Office Fax: 304-793-6810. Business E-Mail: lpence@osteo.wvsom.edu. *

PENCO, SILVIA, medical educator; b. Italy, Oct. 5, 1975; Degree in Medicine and Surgery, U. Milan, 2000. Asst. prof. European Inst. Oncology, 2000—. Mem.: SIRM. Avocation: travel. Office: Via Ripamonti 435 Milano 20100 Italy Business E-Mail: silvia.penco@ieo.it.

PENDERS, JOHANNES MATHYS A., pharmaceutical physician; b. Bandoeng, The Netherlands, July 10, 1942; s. J.M.A. and M.A. (Bleys) P.; m. Anneke H. Nomden, Dec. 5, 1973; children: Frank, Thys. MD, U. Leiden, 1970; Diploma in Pharm. Medicine, Royal Coll. Physicians Glasgow, UK, 1980. Head med. dept. Sterling Winthrop, Haarlem, The Netherlands, 1973-74; clin. rsch. asst. Hoffmann-La Roche, Mydrecht, The Netherlands, 1974-76; coord. reuma rsch. Coun. Health Rsch., The Hague, The Netherlands, 1976-78; head rsch. dept. Hoffmann-La Roche, Mydrecht, The Netherlands, 1978-81; med. dir. Pfizer, Rotterdam, Netherlands, 1981—98; med. consl., 1998—. Editor Jour. Drug Rsch., 1988. 1st lt. Air Force, 1971-72, The Netherlands. Fellow Faculty Pharm. Medicine, U.K., 1998. Mem. NVFG, Faculty Pharm. Medicine London, Royal Dutch Soc. Physicians, Vereniging Nederland China (bd. mem.). Liberal. Avocations: golf, tennis. Home: Heemsteedse Dreef 173 2101 KD Heemstede Netherlands Office Phone: 31235476664. Fax: 023-5478627. E-mail: th.penders@planet.nl.

PENDLETON, ROBERT GRUBB, pharmacologist; b. Kans. City, Mo., Apr. 24, 1939; AA, Kansas City Jr. Coll., 1959; AB in Chemistry, U. Mo., 1961; PhD in Pharmacology, U. Kans. Med. Ctr., 1966. Sr. scientist SmithKline and French, Phila., 1966-67, assoc. sr. investigator, 1967-69, sr. investigator, 1969-74, asst. dir., 1974-79, assoc. dir., 1977-80, dir. pharmacology, 1980-81; dir. gastroenterology Merck, West Point, 1981-86; dir. pharmacology Rorer Ctrl. Rsch., King of Prussia, 1986-90, Sepracor, Marlborough, Mass., 1991—96; assoc. prof. Temple U., Phila., 1993—; lectr. Thomas Jefferson U., 1997—2006, CCP, 1991—2009. Lab. sci. cons. Office Surgeon Gen., U.S. Army, Washington, 1989—96, Ft. Detrick, Md., 1996—99. Col. US Army. Decorated Legion of Merit. Mem.: Soc. Armed Forces Med. Lab. Scientist, Am. Chem. Soc., Am. Soc. Pharmacology and Exptl. Therapeutics, Sigma Xi, Phi Beta Kappa. Achievements include discovery of new drugs to activate dopamine receptors in CNS and kidney; PNMT inhibitors, new drugs to inhibit epinephrine biosynthesis in adrenal gland and CNS; new drugs to block histamine receptors insurmountably including Pepcid; tricyclic antidepressant DMI acts in CNS to decrease gastric acid secretion; roles of CCK in gut; a potential use for allosteric GABA-B receptor agonists in the treatment of PD; research in pharmacology of chiral molecules including Xopenex and in transgenic Drosophila models of Parkinson's disease(PD) and neurodevelopment. Avocation: ballroom dancing. Home and Office: 1312 Sumneytown Pike Lower Gwynedd PA 19002-1303 Office Phone: 215-654-5022. Personal E-mail: robertpendleton@comcast.net.

PENDRED, PIERS, health science association administrator; Grad., Cambridge U. Positions of increasing responsibility including dir. of pub., dir. pub. rels., asst. dir. gen., dir. of edn. Brit. Coun., 1976—2000; dir. gen. Internat. Psychoanalytic Assn., London, 2000—07, interim dir. gen., 2010—. Office: Internat Psychoanalytic Assn Broomhills Woodside Lane London N12 8UD England Office Phone: 44 0 20 8446 8324. Business E-Mail: piers@iap.org.uk. *

PENDYALA, RAMARAO, chemist, educator; b. Guntur, Andhra Pradesh, India, Aug. 1, 1964; s. Hanumaiah and Ramulamma Pendyala; m. Sri Latha Devi Miriampalli; children: Chandra Jvss, Sindhura Rupa. BS, Andhra U., Waltair, India, 1984, M of Pharmacy, 1991; B of Pharmacy, Gulbarga U., India, 1988; PhD, Osmania U., Hyderabad, India, 1998. Registered pharmacist. Exec. R&D NATCO Pharma Ltd., Hyderabad, 1998—99, scientist R&D, 1999—2001, dep. mgr. R&D, 2001—02, mgr. R&D, 2002—03; scientist UPM Pharms., Balt., 2004—08. Rsch. guide for PhD Jawaharlal Nehru Tech. U., Hyderabad, 1999—; dissertation guide for MPharm Annamalai U., India, 2000—03; examiner Gulbarga U., India, 1991—96; lectr. in pharmacy Vutkoor Laxmaiah, India, 1991—94. Contbr. articles to profl. jours., 20 rsch. papers in various internat. and nat. jours. Ency. Pharm. Tech. Social worker Nat. Cadet Course, Guntur, 1982—84. Sr. rsch. fellow, Coun. Sci. and Indsl. Rsch., 1994. Fellow: Instn. Chemists; mem.: Indian Pharm. Assn. (life; mem. sci. com. 2000). Achievements include 12 patents, India and abroad. Avocations: chess, reading, music. Personal E-mail: Pendyala_ramarao@hotmail.com.

PENG, ROGER D., biostatistics professor; BS in Applied Math., Yale U., 1999; MS in Stats., UCLA, 2001, PhD in Stats., 2003. Software engr. Kencast Inc., 1997, 1999; software engr., UnderSea Warfare Systems and Cartography Logicon INRI/Northrop Grumman, 1998; grad. student rschr. stats. dept. UCLA, 2000—03, tchg. asst., 1999—2001, tchg. asst. coordinator, 2000—01; dir. biostatistics core Johns Hopkins Ctr. for Urban Environ. Health, 2009—; dir. data mgmt. core Johns Hopkins Particulate Matter Rsch. Ctr., 2010—; co-dir. data mgmt. and stats. core Johns Hopkins Children's Ctr. for Asthma in the Urban Environment, 2010—, stats. dept. rep. Johns Hopkins Bloomberg Sch. Pub. Health, com. mem. Biostatistics Info. Tech., co-instr. biostatistics dept., primary instr. biostatistics dept.; postdoc. fellow biostatistics dept. Johns Hopkins Bloomberg Sch. of Pub. Health, 2003—05; asst. prof. biostatistics dept. Johns Hopkins Bloomberg Sch. Pub. Health, 2005—10, co-dir. Tng. Program in Environ. Biostatistics, 2010—, assoc. prof. biostatistics dept., 2010—. Co-author: Model choice in time series studies of air pollution and mortality, 2005—08 (no.1 most cited paper, 2006), Particulate air pollution and mortality in the United States: Did the risks change from 1987 to 2000?, 2007 (Nat. Inst. of Environ. Health Sciences Extramural Paper of the Month, 2007), Coarse particulate matter air pollution and hospital admissions for cardiovascular and respiratory diseases among Medicare patients, 2008 (Nat. Inst. of Environ. Health Sciences Extramural Paper of the Month, 2008), Emergency admissions for cardiovascular disease and ambient levels of carbon monoxide: Results for 126 U.S. urban counties., 2009; author: Discussion of Keiding, 2010; various positions numerous publs., regular contbr.to the R-help and R-devel. mailing lists, assoc. editor Jour. of Statis. Software, 2004—06, Reproducible Research, Biostatistics, 2006—, Jour. of Agrl., Biol. and Environ. Stats., 2010—, BMC Public Health, 2010—, reviewer for several publs. Mem. Free Software Found., Electronic Frontier Found., R Found. for Statis. Computing. Recipient Dissertation of the Yr. Fellowship, UCLA, 2002, Charles E. and Sue K. Young Grad. Student award, 2003, Faculty Innovation Fund award, Johns Hopkins Bloomberg Sch. of Pub. Health, 2006; named Tchg. Asst. of the Yr., UCLA Stats. Dept., 2000, winner, Am. Statis. Assn. Student paper Competition in Statis. Computing and Graphics, 2002. Mem.: Internat. Biometric Soc., Am. Statis. Assn., Environ. Biostatistics and Epidemiology Group. Avocation: violin. Office: Johns Hopkins Bloomberg School of Public Health Office E3535 615 N Wolfe St Baltimore MD 21205 Office Phone: 410-955-2468. Office Fax: 410-955-0958. Business E-Mail: rpeng@jhsph.edu.

PENG, XIONGQI, engineering educator; b. China, May 2, 1970; BS, Northwestern Poly. U., China, 1992; PhD, Northwestern U., 2003. Prof. Northwestern Poly. U., 2006—10, Shanghai Jiao Tong U., 2010—. Fellow: Chinese Soc. Composite Materials; mem.: Am. Soc. Composites. Office: 1945 Huashan Rd Shanghai 200030 China Personal E-mail: xqpeng70@gmail.com.

PENG, ZHANG, medical researcher, educator; b. Tai'an City, Shandong Province, Feb. 10, 1980; PhD, Shang Hai Jiao Tong U., 2008. Postdoc. fellow Zhe Jiang U., 2008—09; rsch. asst. Chinese U. Hong Kong, 2009—10; asst. rsch. prof. Shen Zhen Insts. Advanced Tech., Chinese Acad. Scis., 2010—, MA student adviser, 2011—. Contbr. chapters to books, articles to sci. profl. jours. Recipient Second prize, Com. 5th Internat. Summit; grant, Com. Nat. Natural Sci. Found. China. Mem.: Internat. Chinese Hard Tissue Soc. Avocations: football, singing, reading. Office: 1068 Xueyuan Ave Shen Zhen Guang Dong 518055 China Office Phone: 86-0755-86392258. Business E-Mail: peng.zhang@siat.ac.cn.

PENGO, VITTORIO, medical educator; b. Lendinara, Rovigo, Italy, Nov. 30, 1948; MD, U. Padova, 1974, specialist, 1985. Assoc. prof. cardiology U. Padova, 1988—. Office: via Giustiniani 2 Padua 35128 Italy Business E-Mail: vittorio.pengo@unipd.it.

PENHOET, EDWARD E., retired foundation administrator, former biochemicals company executive, former dean; b. Oakland, Calif., Dec. 11, 1940; AB in Biology, Stanford U., 1963; PhD in Biochem., U. Wash., 1968. Prof. biochem. U. Calif., Berkeley, 1971—81; co-founder, CEO Chiron Corp., 1981—98; dean Sch. Pub. Health U. Calif., Berkeley, 1998—2002, dean emeritus, 2002—; sr. dir., Sci. & Higher Education Gordon and Betty Moore Found., 2002—04, pres., 2004—08, bd. trustees. Bd. dirs., sr. adv. to CEO Chiron Corp. Recipient Outstanding Philanthropist award, Assn. of Fundraising Professionals, No. Calif. Entrepreneur of the Yr. award, Ernst & Young and Inc. Mag. Mem.: Am. Soc. of Biological Chemists, Nat. Acad. of Sci., Inst. Medicine. Office: Chiron Corp 4560 Horton St Emeryville CA 94608-2900 also: Gordon and Betty Moore Found Presidio of San Francisco 1661 Page Mill Rd Palo Alto CA 94304-1209

PENHOLLOW, TINA MARIE, health science researcher, educator; b. Dunkirk, NY, Sept. 24, 1980; d. Duane Wesley and Christine Ann Penhollow. BS, SUNY Coll. Fredonia, 2001; MS, U. West Fla., Pensacola, 2003; PhD, U. Ark., Fayetteville, 2006. Cert. health edn. specialist Nat. Commn Health Education Credentialing Inc., 2011, master cert. health edn. specialist. Grad. tchg. and rsch. asst. U. West Fla., 2001—03; health educator women infants and children program Escambia County Health Dept., 2002—03; doctoral acad. fellow and sr. grad. asst. U. Ark., Fayetteville, 2003—06; asst. prof. health promotion Fla. Atlantic U., Boca Raton, 2006—. Presenter in field. Author: (book) Aging and Sexuality: A Study of Active Older Adults, 2007—; contbr. scientific papers, articles to nat. and internat. periodicals, in profl. jours.; author: (book) Sexuality, Longevity & Quality of Life: A Study of America's Largest Active Retirement Community, 2010. Recipient Outstanding Doctoral Student in Health Sci. award, U. Ark., 2005; scholar, Western Divsn. Credit Union NY, 1997—98; Pace Grad. scholar, U. West Fla., 2001—03. Mem.: AAHPERD, Soc. Sci. Study of Sexuality, Am. Assn. Health Edn. (Horizon Award 2007). Achievements include youngest PhD graduate from the University of Arkansas's program in Health Science. Office: Florida Atlantic Univ Dept Exercise Sci & Health Promotion 777 Glades Rd FH 11-25B Boca Raton FL 33431 Office Phone: 561-297-2643. Business E-Mail: tpenholl@fau.edu.

PENICK, ELIZABETH C., psychologist; b. New Orleans, July 17, 1934; d. Rawley M. Penick and Marie G. Sells. BA, Newcomb Coll., 1957; MS, Tulane U., 1960; PhD, Washington U., St. Louis, 1975. Diplomate clin. psychology Am. Bd. Profl. Psychology. Prof. dept. psychiatry Kans. U. Med. Ctr., Kansas City, 1980—, dir. divsn. psychology. Rsch. grantee Nat. Assn. Alcohol Abuse and Alcoholism, Washington, 1980-97. Mem. APA, Kans. Psychol. Assn. (dir.). Home: 12231 Charlotte Kansas City MO 64146 Office: Kans U Med Ctr Dept Psychiatry 3901 Rainbow Blvd Kansas City KS 66160 Office Phone: 913-588-6463. E-mail: epenick@kumc.edu.

PENKERT, GOETZ RUDOLF WILHELM, neurosurgeon; b. Remscheid-Lennep, Germany, Mar. 17, 1949; s. Waldemar and Helga (Wilms) P.; m. Ortrud Elisabeth Seuthe, Nov. 3, 1976; children: Daniel, Judith. MD, U. Frankfurt, 1973; PhD, U. Hannover Med. Sch., 1989. Guest physician plastic surgery dept. U. Hosp. Vienna, Austria, 1977-78; neurosurgeon Altona Hosp., Hamburg, Germany, 1978-81, Nordstadt Hosp., Hannover, 1981-87, asst. prof., vice chmn., 1987-98; chmn. neurosurg. dept. Friederiken Hosp., Hannover, 1999—. Author: Peripheral Nerve Lesions, 2004. Mem. Am. Soc. Peripheral Nerve. Home: Kneippweg 1 D-30459 Hannover Germany Office Phone: +49-511-14142. E-mail: goetz.penkert@gmx.net.

PENKOWA, MILENA, professor; b. Odense, Fyn, Denmark, Apr. 15, 1973; d. Niels Kr. Egholm Pedersen and Pirinka Ignatova Penkowa. MD, PhD, DMSc, U. Copenhagen. Cert. med. sci. U. Copenhagen. Prof., head sect. neuroprotection U. Copenhagen, 1992—. Inventor, Copenhagen. Bd. mem. Neuro Cluster, U. Copenhagen. Recipient Award, Marie Curie - Cosmopolitan, 2008, Internat. Soc. Neurochemistry, 2005, NAGE, 2007, Videnskabsministeriet & Det Frie Forskningsråd, 2009, EliteForsk rsch. awards, Ministry of Tech., Sci. & Innovation, 2009, Talentpris award, Lundbeckfonden, 2002; named Outstanding Young Person, Jr. Chamber Internat., 2007. Mem.: Soc. Neurosci.

PENLEY, JULIE ANNE, psychologist, educator; d. John and Marcheta Isabelle Dietzen; m. Howard Lawson Penley. PhD, U. Tex., 2001. Tchg. asst. U. Tex., El Paso, 1995—96, rsch. asst., 1996—2001; instr. Dona Ana CC, Sunland Park, N.Mex., 1999; part-time instr. El Paso CC, 2000—02, asst. prof., 2002—07, assoc. prof., 2007—; evaluation coord. U. Tex., El Paso, 2001—02. Mem.: APA, STP, Psychology Tchrs. at CCs., PTCC, Assn. Women in CC. Lutheran. Office: El Paso Community Coll PO Box 20500 El Paso TX 79998-0500 Office Phone: 915-831-3210. Business E-Mail: jpenley@epcc.edu.

PENLEY, VIRGINIA LONG, social worker; b. Statesville, NC, July 3, 1955; d. Robert Long and Mary Joyce Broussard; m. Jeffrey Michael Penley. AA, Mitchell C.C., 1975; BA in Social Work, Greensboro Coll., 1977. LCSW; cert. Dir. Vol. Svcs. Social worker Moses H. Cone Hosp., Greensboro, 1987—94; dir. vol. svcs. and patient rels. Women's Hosp. Greensboro, NC, 1994—. Mem.: NASW (Piedmont rep. 1991—92), N.C. Soc. Dirs. Vol. Svcs. (chair publicity 2000—, corr. sec., edn. co-chair 1997—99), N.C. Zoologica. Presbyterian. Avocations: travel, antiques, reading. Office: Women's Hosp Greensboro 801 Green Valley Rd Greensboro NC 27408 Home Phone: 336-855-0353; Office Phone: 336-832-6586. Business E-Mail: ginger.penley@mosescone.com.

PENN, AUDREY S., federal agency administrator; BA, Swarthmore Coll., Pa., 1956; MD, Columbia U., NYC, 1960. Intern, asst. resident Bronx Mcpl. Hosp. Ctr., Albert Einstein Coll. Medicine, 1960—62; asst. resident in neurology, Neurol. Inst. Columbia Presbyn. Med. Ctr., NYC, 1962—64, neurologist; asst. and instr. in neurology Coll. Physicians and Surgeons, Columbia U., NYC, 1964—67, assoc. prof. neurology, 1973—82, assoc. prof. to prof. neurology, 1973—95; dep. dir. Nat. Inst. Neurol. Disorders and Stroke, NIH, 1995—, acting dir., 1998, 2001—03. Bd. dirs. Am. Bd. Psychiatry and Neurology, 1975—82, exec. com, 1981—82; mem. immunological soc. study sect. NIH, 1982—86; mem. rev. panel for rsch. tng. fellowships Howard Hughes Med. Inst., 1989—91, chair rev. panel, 1992—94; mem. nat. adv. neurol. disorders and stroke coun. NIH, 1992—95. Mem.: AAAS, Assn. Rsch. in Nervous and Mental Disease, Harvey Soc., Am. Acad. Neurology, Am. Neurol. Assn. (pres. 1994). Office: Nat Inst Neurol Disorders & Stroke Bldg 31 8A52 31 Center Dr Bethesda MD 20892-2540 Office Phone: 301-496-3167.

PENNEBAKER, JAMES WHITING, psychologist, researcher; b. Midland, Tex., Mar. 2, 1950; s. William Fendall and Elizabeth (Whiting) P.; m. Ruth Burney, Dec. 30, 1972; children: Catherine Teal, Nicholas Clift. BA, Eckerd Coll., 1972; PhD, U. Tex., Austin, 1977; DCS (hon.), Catholic U., Louvain-La-Neuve, Belgium, 1993. Asst. prof. U. Va., Charlottesville, 1977-83; assoc. prof. So. Meth. U., Dallas, 1983-87, prof. dept. psychology, 1987-97, U. Tex., Austin, 1997—, assoc. chmn. dept. psychology, 2004—05, chmn. dept. psychology, 2005—; internat. prof. psychology U. Ctrl. Lancashire, England, 2005—. Chmn. dept. psychology So. Meth. U., 1995-97; cons. Dallas Hist. Assn., 1988—; Hilgard vis. prof. Stanford U., Palo Alto, Calif., 1989. Author: Psychology of Physical Symptoms, 1982, Opening Up, 1990; editor: Collective Memory of Political Events, 1997; cons. editor various psychol. jours. Grantee NIH, 1984-86, 96—, NSF, 1987-97; recipient Pavlovian Soc. award, 1995. Achievements include development of theories that writing or talking about traumas improves physical health, that coping with earthquake, Persian Gulf War or other traumas follows a predictable 3-phase path, that men and women rely on different cues in defining emotion. Office: Dept Psychology Univ Texas at Austin 1 University Station A8000 Austin TX 78712 Office Phone: 512-232-2781. E-mail: pennebaker@mail.utexas.edu.

PENNELL, DANNY JOE, social worker; b. Aug. 31, 1945; s. Donald Louis and Lela Geneva (Murray) P.; m. Janis Evelyn Reynolds, Dec. 26, 1984; children: Joel, Jason, Jaime, Chad, Colter. BA, U. Ill., 1970, MSW, 1972. Social worker Dept. Child and Family Svcs., Danville, Ill., 1971-72, social worker supr. Rockford, Ill., 1972-74; instr. Rockford Coll., 1977-78; pres., CEO Goldie B. Floberg Ctr., Rockton, Ill., 1974—. Exec. dir. Found. Ft. Lewis Coll., Durango, Colo., 1986-87; bd. dirs. Winnebago County Child Protection Assn., Rockford, 1974-76; bd. dirs., mem. legis. affairs com., chmn. mental health devel. disabilities com., spl. edn. com. Child Care Assn. Ill., Springfield, Ill., 1980—; mem. child welfare adv. com. Ill. Dept. Children and Family Services; mem. devel. disabilities adv. com. Dept. Mental Health, mem. children's svcs. subcom.; cons. in field. Bd. dirs., v.p. H.O.P.E. Found., 2001—. Grantee Ill. Dept. Children and Family Svcs., 1970-72. Mem. Nat. Soc. Fund Raising Execs. (bd. dirs., sec. 1984-85, v.p. 1986-87), Nat. Soc. Fund Raising Dirs. (pres. bd. dirs. 1988, v.p. 1987, v.p. 1986, bd. mem. various coms. 1984, 85), Am. Assn. Mental Deficiency, Nat. Assn. Retarded Citizens, Coordinating Council for Handicapped Children, Nat. Assn. Devel. Disabilities Mgrs., Roscoe C. of C. (bd. dirs. 2000—). Home: 12080 N Ledges Dr Roscoe IL 61073-9600 Office: Goldie B Floberg Ctr PO Box 346 Rockton IL 61072-0346 Personal E-mail: dpenn58@aol.com.

PENNEY, J. NICHOLAS, medical researcher; b. Manchester, Eng., Apr. 3, 1957; BSc with honors, Brit. Coll. Osteo. Medicine, 2001; PhD, U. Queensland Sch. Medicine, 2009. Rsch. assoc. Spinal Rsch. Unit, 2001—. Expert panel mem. low back pain Nat. Health and Med. Rsch. Coun., 2001—10; multidisiplinary rev. com. Australian and New Zealand Coll. Anaesthetists and Faculty Pain Medicine, 2004—10. Mem.: Australian Osteo. Assn., Australian Pain Soc., Assn. Contextual Behavioral Sci., Internat. Assn. Study Pain. Avocations: meditation, golf, running. Office: 30 Queen St Huddersfiled West Yorkshire HD1 2 SP England Business E-Mail: nickpenney@theosteopath.net.au.

PENNINGTON, DAVID GEORGE, plastic surgeon; b. Sydney, Aug. 26, 1947; s. Victor Warren and Dorothy Isobel Pennington; m. Delma Alice Standish, July 12, 1972; children: Andrew Victor, Thomas Edward. MBBS, Sydney U., 1970. Lic. NSW Med. Bd., 1971. Surg. registrar Sydney Hosp., 1974—76, hand surgery registrar, 1976; sr. house officer in plastic surgery South Wales Plastic Surgery Unit, Chepstow, 1976—77; plastic surgery registrar Southeast Scottish Plastic Surgery Unit, Bangour, 1977—79; microsurgery registrar Prince of Wales Hosp., Sydney, 1979—80; vis. med. officer Royal Prince Alfred Hosp., Sydney, 1980—, head dept. plastic surgery, 1987—2007. Capt. Royal Australian Army MC, 1972—72, Ingleburn. Recipient Australian Centenary medal, Commonwealth Govt. Australia, 2004. Fellow: Royal Coll. Surgeons (Edinburgh), Royal Australasian Coll. Surgeons (Edin.). Achievements include first person in world to replant severed ear by microsurgery. Office: DG Pennington Pty Ltd 1204/135 Macquarie St 2000 Sydney NSW Australia Office Phone: 0292471066.

PENNISI, LIZ, women's health nurse; b. Bklyn., Nov. 20, 1953; d. Alexander and Marjorie (Soviero) Perillo; children: Stephen, Scott, Greg. Diploma, Beth Israel Sch. Nursing, NYC, 1974. RN, N.Y.; cert. ambulatory women's health nurse. Staff nurse Montefiore Hosp., Bronx, NY, 1974-75; mem. staff Beth Israel Med. Ctr., NYC, 1975-77; office nurse Martin Kurman, M.D., NYC, 1977-80, Adam Romoff, M.D. and Suzanne Yale, M.D., P.C, 1984—. Mem. AWHONN. Avocations: horseback riding, reading. Office: Drs Romoff and Yale 16 E 82 St New York NY 10028 Personal E-mail: lizpennisi@hotmail.com.

PENSHORN, JOHN S., insurance company executive; Stock analyst Piper Jaffray; dir. Capital Markets Comm. and Strategy UnitedHealth Group, Inc., Minnetonka, Minn., 1998—, sr. v.p. Office: UnitedHealth Grp 9900 Bren Rd E Minnetonka MN 55343

PENSLER, JAY MICHAEL, plastic surgeon, educator; b. Detroit, Apr. 29, 1954; BS Microbiology, U. Mich., 1976; MD, U. Chgo., 1980. Diplomate Am. Bd. Plastic Surgeons, Nat. Bd. Med. Examiners; lic. N.Y., Calif., Mass., Ill. Resident gen. surgery NYU Med. Ctr., 1980-83; resident plastic surgery U. Tex. Med. Br., Galveston, 1983-86; fellow craniofacial surgery Harvard U., Boston, 1986-87; plastic surgeon Northwestern Meml. Hosp., Chgo., 1987—; and assoc. prof. clin. plastic surgery Northwestern Univ. Med. Sch., Chgo. Assoc. prof. surgery Northwestern U., Chgo., 1987-93; plastic surgeon Children's Meml. Hosp., Chgo., 1987—; surf. staff Columbus-Cabrini Med. Ctr., Chgo., 1990—, Evanston (Ill.)-Glenbrook Hosps., 1992—. Featured on NBC, CBS, ABC, Fox-TV; contbr. more than 100 articles to profl. jours. Named one of Chgo.'s Top Doctors, Chgo. mag., 2003. Fellow Am. Coll. Surgeons (Met. Chgo. chpt.), Internat. Coll. Surgeons (Plastic Surgery); mem. AMA, Am. Acad. Pediatrics, Am. Assn. Pediatric Plastic Surgeons, Am. Burn Assn., Am. Cleft Palate-Craniofacial Assn., Am. Fedn. Clin. Rsch., Am. Soc. Bone and Mineral Rsch., Am. Soc. Maxillofacial Surgeons, Am. Soc. Plastic and Reconstructive Surgeons, Bioelec. Repair and Growth Soc., Blocker-Lewis Plastic Surgery Soc., Midwestern Assn. Plastic Surgeons, Chgo. Med. Soc., Chgo. Soc. Plastic Surgery. Office: 680 N Lake Shore Dr Ste 1125 Chicago IL 60611-8701

PENTELÉNYI, THOMAS JOHN, neurosurgeon; b. Budapest, Hungary, Feb. 25, 1939; s. László and Anna Maria (Bohuniczky) P.; m. Mary P. Pálfalvy, Dec. 19, 1947; children: Marianne, Kinga. MD, Semmelweiss Medical Sch., Budapest, 1963, specialist of surgery, 1967; specialist of neurosurgery, Haynal Imre Univ., Budapest, 1974; PhD, Hungarian Acad. of Scis., 1978. Resident of surgery Szovetség Hosp., Budapest, 1964-66, Bajcsy Hosp., Budapest, 1966-68; resident of neurosurgery Nat. Inst. of Traumatology, Budapest, 1968-73, scientific co-worker, 1974-86, head of neurosurgery, 1986—2005; prof., chmn. of neurosurgery Nat. Inst. of Traumatology, Haynal Imre Univ., Budapest, 1987—2005; head, chmn. dept. neurosurgery Nat. Inst. of Traumatology, Budapest, 1986—; prof. of neurotraumatology Semmelweis U., Budapest, 1986—. Pres. Internat. Conf. on Lumbar Fusion and Stabilization/ICLFS Movement, Budapest, 1995—; internat. adv. bd. Paraplegia and Spinal Cord, 1992—, editl. bd. Clinical Neuroscience, 1992—; vis. prof. U. Chgo. Med. Sch., 1990, U. Tenn., 1989, Temple U., Phila., 1990, Thomas Jefferson U., Phila., 1990, U. Calif., Davis, 1990, U. Calif., Sacramento, 1990, U. Xaveriana, Bogota, Columbia, 1990; coord. Ctrl.-European Internat. Brain Injury Data-Base, 1997—; sr. cons. bd. Memphis Neuroscis. Ctr., 1989-96; head Hungarian-Japanese Intergovtl. Neurotrauma Sci. Rsch. Project. Hungarian coord. Ctrl. European Internat. Brain Injury Data Base. Recipient Highest Medical Profl. award Min. of Health, 1987, Budapest, Felicitation Medalist of Indian Neurology Soc., 1994. Mem. WHO (steering com.), World Fedn. Neurosurg. Socs. (neurotraumatology com., chmn. subcom. edn.), Internat. Med. Soc. of Paraplegia, Scientific Program Com. (coun. mem.), European Fedn. Neurol. Soc. (scientist panel 1994—), Euroacad. Multidisciplinary Neurotramatology (exec. com.), Hungarian Spine Soc. (pres. 1993-95), U. Padova (hon.), Purkinje Med. U. (hon.), N.Y. Acad. Scis. (diploma), Indian Neurology Soc. (hon.), Internat. Biographical Ctr., Cambridge Eng. (diploma achievement medicine and healthcare, 2005, dep. dir. gen., 2006), Am. Biographical Inst., NC Avocations: music, philosophy, art. Office: Nat Inst of Traumatology Dept Neurosurgery VIII Fiumei ut 17 1081 Budapest Hungary

PEPE, FRANK A., cell and developmental biology educator; b. Schenectady, May 22, 1931; s. Rocco and Margherita (Ruggiero) P. BS, Union Coll., 1953; PhD, Yale U., 1957. Instr. anatomy U. Pa., Phila., 1957-60, assoc. in anatomy, 1960-63, asst. prof., 1963-65, assoc. prof., 1965-70, prof., 1970-92, chmn. dept. anatomy, 1977-90, prof. cell. and devel. biology, 1992-96, emeritus prof., 1996—. Editor: Motility in Cell Function, 1979. Recipient Rsch. Career Devel. award USPHS, 1968-73, Raymond C. Truex Disting. Lecture award Hahneman U., 1988. Fellow AAAS; mem. Am. Assn. Anatomists, Am. Chem. Soc., Biophys. Soc., Microscopy Soc. Am., Sigma Xi. Mailing: University Pa Sch Medicine 4614 Pine St Philadelphia PA 19143-1808 E-mail: fpepe@mail.med.upenn.edu.

PEPE, GERALD J., dean, physiologist; b. RI; m. Catherine Pepe; 2 children. BA, Providence Coll., 1965; MS, Northeastern U., 1967; PhD, U. Kans., 1970. Sr. staff fellow Divsn. Child Health NIH, Bethesda, Md., 1972—78; assoc. prof. physiology Eastern Va. Med. Sch., Norfolk, Va., 1978—84, interim chmn. dept. physiology, 1982—84, prof. and chmn. dept. physiology, 1985—2004, assoc. dean rsch., 1995—97, prof., chmn. physiol. sciences, 1997—, interim dean and provost, 2004—05, dean and provost, 2005—. Office: Office of Dean and Provost East Virginia Med Sch Lewis Hall 2021A PO Box 1980 Norfolk VA 23501 Office Phone: 757-446-5616. E-mail: pepegj@evms.edu. *

PEPINE, CARL JOHN, physician, educator; b. Pitts., June 8, 1941; s. Charles John and Elizabeth (Hovan) P.; m. Lynn Dives, Aug. 3, 1963; children: Mary Lynn, Anne, Elizabeth. BS, U. Pitts., 1962; MD, N.J. Coll. Medicine (UMDNJ), 1966. Cert. Am. Bd. Internal Med., 1971, Am. Bd. Internal Med., Cardiovascular Disease, 1973. Intern Allegheny Gen. Hosp., U. Pitts., 1966-67; resident in internal medicine Jefferson Med. Coll. Hosp., Phila., 1967-68, naval med. ctr., 1968-69, fellow in physiology and cardiovasc. disease, 1969-71; asst. prof. medicine Jefferson Med. Coll., Phila., 1972-74, U. Fla., Gainesville, 1974-75, assoc. prof., 1975-79, prof., 1979—, co-dir. divsn. cardiovasc. medicine, 1982-88; chief cardiology VA Regional Med. Ctr., Gainesville, 1979-94, chief divsn. cardiovasc. medicine, 1998—2008. Dir. cardiology catheterization lab. Shands Hosp., U. Fla., Gainesvile, 1974-86. Mem. editl. bds. Am. Heart Jour., 1997—, Am. Jour. Cardiology, 1981-94, 97—, Am. Jour. Geriat. Cardiology, 1992—96, Clin. Cardiology, 1995—, Circulation, 1980-83, 93—, Cardiac Chronicle, 1986—90, Heart Disease: A Jour. of Cardiovasc. Medicine, 1999—2003, Hypertension, 1999—2001, Jour. Am. Coll. Cardiology, 1981-85, 91-95, 98—2004, Jour. Preventive Cardiovasc. Medicine, 1997, Preventive Cardiology, 1998-2000; chief med. editor Cardiology Today, 1997—; contbr. articles to profl. jours.; developer catheters to measure blood flow and heart circulation. Comdr. USN, 1968-74. Recipient 7th Ann. Funk award for contrbn. to cardiovascular rsch., Soc. Federated Med. Agencies, 1974, clin. faculty Rsch. prize, U. Fla., 1989-90, Profl. Excellence Program (PEP) award, 1996-97, Disting. Internat. Educator, 2005, Pioneer Investigator award Internat. Soc. for Holter Monitoring, 1990, Rsch. Achievement awards U. Fla., 1990-93, Rsch. Found. Professorship award, 1999-2001, Paul Dudley White award Assn. Mil. Surgeons US, 1991, grantee Dept. of Def., 1971-74, VA, 1975-90, NHLBI, 1985-; named to America's Top Doctors, The Best Doctors in Am. and Am. Men and Women of Sci. Fellow Am. Coll. Cardiology (master, 1999, trustee 1986-88, 90-95, 2001—, v.p. 2001—, chmn. cardiac catheterization com. 1990-96, chmn. Fla. chpt. found. 1992—, chmn. bd. govs. 1986-87, chmn. ann. sci. sessions 1990, pres. 2003-04, Gifted Tchr. award (Fla. Chpt.), 2001), Am. Heart Assn. (coun. on clin. cardiology and on circulation, (Fla. affiliate bronze award for svc. recognition, 1983, Suncoast Chpt. for cardiovascular rsch. named Eminent Scholar of an endowed chair, 2001), Am. Fedn. Clin. Rsch., Soc. Cardiac Angiography, Am. Soc. Clin. Investigation; mem. Assn. Univ. Cardiologists, Am. Clin. and Climatol. Assn. (Theodore E. Woodward award 1998), Assn. of Profs. of Cardiology, European Soc. Cardiology, Pi Kappa Alpha, Alpha Omega Alpha. Office: U Fla 1600 SW Archer Rd PO Box 100277 Gainesville FL 32610-0277 Office Phone: 352-846-3292. Office Fax: 352-371-0370. Business E-Mail: pepincj@medicine.ufl.edu.

PEPKE-ZABA, JOANNA, chest physician, consultant; d. Wiktor and Halina Pepke; m. Jerzy Marcin Zaba, May 11, 1980; 1 child, Marcin Jerzy Zaba. MD, Med. Acad., Warsaw, 1977; PhD, Inst. TB and Lung Diseases, Warsaw, 1995. 1st degree specialization in internal medicine Ministry Health and Social Security, Poland, cert. specialist in internal medicine Ministry Health and Social Security, Poland, specialist in gen. medicine and respiratory medicine Gen. Med. Coun., London. Asst. in gen. medicine Inst. of Tb, Warsaw, 1977—84, sr. asst. specialist in internal medicine, 1984—87; rsch. fellow, hon. registrar Papworth Hosp. & Addenbrookes Hosp., Cambridge, England, 1988—92, sr. rsch. fellow, hon. registrar, 1992—94; staff physician Papworth Hosp., Cambridge, 1994—98, assoc. specialist in respiratory medicine, 1998—2003, cons. physician in respiratory medicine, 2003—. Dir. pulmonary vascular diseases unit Papworth Hosp., 2003—; sci. organizer 1st Internat. Meeting on Pulmonary Hypertension, Cambridge, 2003; chmn. Assn. Pulmonary Hypertension Ctrs. UK, 2007. Chmn. physician com. Nat. Pulmonary Hypertension Ctr., UK, Ireland. Mem.: European Respiratory Soc. (corr.), Brit. Thoracic Soc. (corr.). Roman Catholic. Avocations: travel, music. Office: Papworth Hosp Found Trust Papworth Everard CB23 3RG Cambridge England E-mail: joanna.pepkezaba@papworth.nhs.uk.

PEPPAS, NICHOLAS ATHANASSIOU, chemical and biomedical engineering educator, consultant; b. Athens, Greece, Aug. 25, 1948; s. Athanassios Nikolaou Peppas and Alice Petrou Rousopoulou; m. Lisa Brannon, Aug. 10, 1988; children: Katherine, Alexander. Diploma in Engring., Nat. Tech. U., Athens, 1971; ScD, MIT, 1973; D honoris causa, U. Parma, Italy, 1999, U. Ghent, Belgium, 1999, U. Athens, 2000. Asst. prof. chem. engring. Purdue U., West Lafayette, Ind., 1976-78, assoc. prof., 1978-81, prof., 1981—2002, Showalter Disting. prof. of chem. and biomed. engring., 1993—2002; prof. chem. engring. U. Tex., Austin, 2003—, prof. biomed. engring., 2003, prof. pharmaceutics, 2003—, Fletcher S. Pratt disting. prof., 2003—, chair biomed. engring., 2009—. Vis. prof. U. Geneva, 1982-83, Calif. Inst. Tech., Pasadena, 1983, U. Paris, 1986, Hoshi U., Japan, 1994, Hebrew U., Jerusalem, 1994, U. Naples, 1995, Free U. Berlin, 2001, Complutense U. Madrid, 2001, Nanyang U., Singapore, 2007; adj. prof. U. Parma, Italy, 1987; cons. in field; mem. adv. bd. several cos. Author: Biomaterials, 1982, Hydrogels in Medicine and Pharmacy, 1987, One Hundred Years of Chemical Engineering, 1989, Pulsatile Drug Delivery, 1993, Biopolymers, 1993, Superabsorbent Polymers, 1994, Biomaterials for Drug and Cell Delivery, 1994, Polymer/Inorganic Interfaces, 1995, Physicochemical and Cellular Foundations of Biomaterials, 2004, Nanotechnology in Therapeutics, 2007; contbr. over 1100 articles and over 450 abstracts to jours.; editor: Biomaterials, 1982-2002; assoc. editor: AIChE Jour., 2008-, Biomedical Microdevices, 2007-, Pharmaceutical research, 2004-. Active Austin Symphony Orch., Transfiguration Orthodox Ch. Austin. Recipient APV medal, Herbert McCoy award Purdue U., 2000, Hamilton Book award, 2004; Career Rsch. Excellence award U. Tex., 2007 Fellow: AIChE (chmn. materials divsn. 1988—90, dir. bioengring. divsn. 1994—97, bd. dirs. 1999—2002, Inst. lectr. 2007, elected engr. modern era 2008, Materials Engring. Sci. award 1984, Bioengring. award 1994, Best Paper award 1994, William Walker award 2006, Jay Bailey award 2006, Founders award 2008, Top 100 Engrs. Modern Era 2008, Founders award 2008), Biomed. Engring. Soc. (Best Rsch. award 2002, Disting. Rsch. award 2010), Am. Soc. Engring. Edn. (AT&T award 1982, Curtis McGraw award 1988, G. Westinghouse award 1992, GE Sr. Rsch. award 2002, Dow Chem. Engring. award 2006), Am. Phys. Soc., Controlled Release Soc. (pres. 1987—88, Founders award 1991, Eurand award 2002), Soc. Biomaterials (pres. 2002—03, 2003—04, Clemson award 1992, Founders award 2005, W. Hall award 2010), Am. Inst. Med. Biol. Engrs. (Pierre Galletti award 2008), Am. Assn. Pharm. Scientists (Rsch. Achievements Pharm. Tech. award 1999, Dale Wurster award 2002), Am. Phys. Soc., Italian Soc. Medicine and Scis.; mem.: Acad. Biometerial (Gold medal 2010), Nat. Acad. Engring., Inst. Medicine, Inst. Medicine Nat. Acads., Tex. Acad. Scis., French Acad. Pharmacy, Polymer Pioneer, Soc. Biomaterials, Am. Chem. Soc. (Newsmaker of Yr. award 2002), Sigma Xi (South U. Rsch. award 2010, Maurice Janot award 2010). Avocations: linguistics, opera, rare maps, classical record collecting. Office: U Tex Dept Chem Engring Austin TX 78712 Office Phone: 512-471-6644. Business E-Mail: peppas@che.utexas.edu.

PERACCHIA, CAMILLO, retired physiologist, biophysicist, researcher, medical educator; b. Milan, Mar. 31, 1938; s. Luigi Peracchia and Ida Magnocavallo; m. Lillian Mae Leverone; children: Luigi Francesco, Carla Maria, Tanya Elena. MD summa cum laude, U. Milan, 1962. Cert. dr. in medicine and surgery 1962, Ednl. Coun. Fgn. Med. Grad. 1967. Asst. prof. physiology U. Rochester, Med. Ctr., NY, 1970—75, assoc. prof. physiology, 1975—79, tenured assoc. prof. physiology, 1979—83, prof. physiology, 1983—96, acting chair dept. physiology, 1995, prof. pharmacology and physiology, 1996—2007, prof. emeritus pharmacology and physiology. Vis. assoc. prof. anatomy Harvard U., Med. Ctr., Boston, 1978; mem. cell biology and physiology study sect. NIH, Bethesda, Md., 1991—94, nat. reviewers res., 1994—. Editor: Biophysics of Gap Junction Channels, Handbook of Membrane Channels - Molecular and Cellular Physiology, Gap Junctions - Molecular Basis of Cell Communication in Health and Disease. Recipient Tchg. Commendation award, U. Rochester Med. Ctr., 1995, 1996, 1999, 2002, 2005, Adolph medal, 2004, Goldman award, 1998; grantee Rsch. grant, NIH, Inst. Gen. Med. Sci., 1974—2007, Rochester Eye and Human Parts, Inc., 1986—89; Travel grant, Italian Nat. Coun. Rsch., CNR, 1993—94. Mem.: Biophysical Soc., Am. Soc. Cell Biology. Roman Catholic. Avocations: skiing, windsurfing, travel. Office: Univ Rochester Med Ctr 601 Elmwood Ave Rochester NY 14642-8711 Office Fax: 585-273-2652. Business E-Mail: camillo_peracchia@urmc.rochester.edu.

PERALTA, PERRY ISHMAEL GARCIA, emergency physician; b. Madison, Wis., Apr. 24, 1960; s. Francisco Mateo Peralta and Yolanda Crisostomo Garcia; m. Diana Concepcion Hernandez, Dec. 14, 1988; children: Justine Franco H., Perry Danico H., Ashley Brianna H. BS in Gen. Sci., accelerated, U. Santo Tomas, Manila, 1979, MD, 1983. Registered physician Profl. Regulation Commn., Philippines, diplomate Philippine Bd. Emergency Medicine. Co. physician Hotel Intercontinental, Manila, 1989—92, Pilipinas Shell, Manila, 1989—92; asst. emergency dept. officer Makati Med. Ctr., Manila, 1989—92, program dir. emergency medicine residency tng. program, 1989—92; clinic physician Ayala Alabang Village Assn. Clinic, Manila, 1990; med. dir. Makati Specialists and Svcs. Group, Inc., Manila, 1991—95, SecurAir Svcs., Manila, 1993—2002; emergency medicine cons. Vets. Meml. Med. Ctr., Manila, 1994—2002; program dir. emergency medicine residency tng. program Ospital Ng Makati, Manila, 1994—2004, emergency med. svcs. fellowship dir., 1999—, chair dept. emergency medicine, 2003—, adminstr. Acute Care Ctr., 2004—; clin. dir. Makati Emergency Med. Svcs. Sys., Manila, 1995—; asst. v.p., med. dir. Health + Plus, Inc., Manila, 1996—97; chair dept. emergency medicine San Juan Med. Ctr., Manila, 1996—2003; first v.p., med. dir. Insular Life Health Care, Inc., Manila, 1997—2006; adminstr. P & D Peralta Med. Clinic, Manila, 2000—; med. dir. Asia Pacific Med. Diagnostics, Inc., Manila, 2001—; hosp. dir. Hosp. NG Nakati, 2008—. Tng. cons. Philippine Nat. Red Cross, Manila, 1988, Bur. Fire Protection, Dept. Interior and Local Govt., Manila, 1993—96; cons. Exxon, Manila, 1990—92, Com. on Health and Demography, Senate of the Philippines, Manila, 1996—98, Philippine Health Ins. Corp., Manila, 1999; chair Philippine Bd. Emergency Medicine, Manila, 1994—96; chair disaster preparedness com. San Juan Med. Ctr., Manila, 1999—2003; sr. med. advisor Ibero Assistencia, Manila, 1999—; med. program evaluator Philippine Ctr. for Advanced Maritime Simulation and Tng. Inc., Manila, 2000—02; sr. med. advisor MediPhone, Manila, 2003—; mem. organizing com. Makati Command and Control Ctr., Emergency Alert and Response Sys., Manila, 2005—. Contbr. articles to profl. jours. Coord. Mass Casualty Task Force, World Youth Day, Manila, 1995; mass casualty task force coord. World Culture and Sports Festival, Manila, 1995; regular co-host Radyo Klinica Program Sta. DWIZ, Manila, 1995—97; emergency med. svcs. coord. Internat. Prayer Rally for World Peace, Manila, 1996, Espinosa-Sotto Boxing Bout, Manila, 1996; coun. mem. cardiopulmonary resuscitation coun. Philippine Heart Assn., Manila, 1996—2002; bd. mem. San Juan Med. Ctr. Med. Staff Assn., Manila, 1997—2003; regional liaison for the Philippines, Emergency Internat., Balt., 1997—; internat. Philippine del. Global Med-Net, Inc., Naperville, Ill., 1998—; bd. dirs. Asian Mobile Med. Svc. Mission, Inc., Manila, 2001—. Recipient Svc. award, Cath. Bishops Conf. Philippines, 1995, Asian Devel. Bank, 1995, Radyo Klinica, DWIZ, 1995. Fellow: Philippine Soc. Critical Care Medicine (Svc. award 1996), Philippine Coll. Emergency Medicine and Acute Care (regent 1988—96, charter mem., past pres., Svc. award 1991, Pres. award 2000); mem.: Philippine Soc. Emergency Med. Technicians (nat. exec. coun. mem. 1999—), Makati Med. Soc. (councilor 1994—97, chmn. disaster com. 1994—97, vice chair com. on calamities and disasters 1997—98, Svc. award 1996, 1998), Asian Hosp. and Med. Ctr. Med. Staff Assn., Ospital Ng Makati Med. Staff Assn., Philippine Med. Assn. (life; gen. coord. emergency and disaster com. 1992—93, co-chmn. com. on emergency, disaster and nat. goals 1993—94, Svc. award 1993, Presdl. award 1994), Rizal Med. Soc. (life), Am. Coll. Emergency Physicians, Makati Med. Ctr. Med. Staff Assn., Makati Med. Ctr. Alumni Assn., U. Santo Tomas Med. Alumni Assn. Roman Catholic. Avocations: reading, movies, computers, painting. Home: Ayala Hillside Estates Capitol Hills Dr 47 Watson St Old Balara Guezon City Philippines Office: P&D Peralta Med Clinic 14/F Jaka 6780 Ayala Ave 1200 Makati National Capital Region Philippines Office Phone: 632 810 0820. Personal E-mail: pgperaltamdatwork@yahoo.com.

PERANTONI, ALAN O., medical researcher; PhD in Cell Biology, Catholic U., 1983. Asst. prof. Pathology Dept. U. Colo. Med. Sch.; joined Ctr. Cancer Rsch., Nat. Cancer Inst., NIH, Frederick, Md., 1992, chief Cancer and Devel. Biology Lab., head differentiation and neoplasia sect. Spkr. in field. Office: Nat Cancer Inst at Frederick Bldg 538, Rm 224 PO Box B Frederick MD 21702-1201 Office Phone: 301-846-6529, 301-846-5946. E-mail: peranton@ncifcrf.gov. *

PERCY, HELEN SYLVIA, physician; b. Atlanta, May 7, 1923; d. George L. and Sophia (Toulchin) P.; 1 child, Valentina Stewart-Watson. BS, U. San Francisco, 1951; MD, Med. Coll. Pa., 1958. Intern Harbor Gen. Hosp., Torrance, Calif., 1958-59, resident, 1959; physician Maui Med. Group, Lahaina, Hawaii, 1968—; asst. prof. medicine U. Hawaii, Honolulu, 1978—2000. Adv. bd. Maui Community Health Ctr., 1986-89; v.p. Maui AIDS Found., 1986-89. Mem. AMA, Maui County Med. Soc. (pres. 1988-1989), Hawaii Med. Assn. (Maui councilor). Democrat. Buddhist. Avocation: dance. Office: Maui Med Group 130 Prison St Lahaina HI 96761-1247 Office Phone: 808-661-0051.

PERDETZOGLOU, DIMITRIOS, pharmacist, researcher, pharmacy director; b. Serres, Greece, July 16, 1961; s. Kyriakos and Fani Perdetzoglou; m. Evangelia Moraitaki, July 3, 1994; 2 children. Degree in Pharmacy, U. Athens, 1986; PhD in Pharm., Sch. Pharmacy, Athens, 1994; degree in Tech. Pedagogics, Pedagogical Sch., Athens, 1999. Asst. rsch. prof. Inst. Biology, Bot. Lab., Copenhagen, 1994—95; prof. pharmacology, interpersonal relationships, etc. Sch. Paramedical Studies, Athens, Greece, 1991—94, 1996—97; prof. pharmacology Nursing Sch. Athens, 1998—98; prin. pharmacist Apothecary, 1999—99; spl. scientist U. Athens, Sch. Pharmacy, 1998—99, rschr., 1994—; hosp. pharmacist dir. Maternity Hosp., 1999—2010, Gen. Hosp. Gennimatas, 2010—. Contbr. articles to profl. jours. With Greek Army, 1990—91. Grantee, European Cmty., 1994—95; fellow, U. Athens, Sch. Pharmacy, 1988—94. Mem.: Hellenic Pharm. Soc. (life), Panhellenic Pharm. Soc. (life). Avocations: photography, computers, Greek & ancient philosophy, history, astronomy. Home: Synesiou Kyrinis 3-7 114 71 Athens Greece Personal E-mail: dpathens@yahoo.gr.

PERDUE, BEVERLY EAVES, Governor of North Carolina; b. Grundy, Va., Jan. 14, 1948; d. Alfred P. and Irene E. (Morefield) Moore; m. Gary Perdue, 1970 (div. 1974); children: Garrett, Emmett; m. Robert W. Eaves, Jr., 1997. BA, U. Ky., 1969; MEd, U. Fla., 1974, PhD, 1976. Pvt. lectr., writer, cons., 1980-86; pres. The Perdue Co., New Bern, NC; mem. from Dist. 3 NC House of Reps., Raleigh, 1987—91, NC State Senate, 1991—2001; lt. gov. State of NC, Raleigh, 2001—09, gov., 2009—. Toll fellow Nat. Conf. State Legislators, Lexington, Ky., 1992; bd. dirs. Nations Bank, New Bern. Exec. mem. NC Democratic Party; mem. NC travel bd. Nat. Conf. State Legislators; bd. dirs. NC United Way, Greensboro, 1990—92. Named Outstanding Legislator, NC Aging Network, 1989, 1992. Mem.: Bus. & Profl. Women, Rotary. Democrat. Episcopalian. Office: Office of Governor 20301 Mail Service Ctr Raleigh NC 27699 Office Phone: 919-733-4240. Office Fax: 919-733-2120. E-mail: bperdue@ncmail.net.

PEREDO, MARINA I., dermatologist; MD, Mt. Sinai Sch. of Medicine. Diplomate Am. Bd. Dermatology. Internal medicine internship Columbia-Presbyterian Med. Ctr.; dermatology residency NY Hospt.-Cornell Med. Ctr.; assoc. clin. prof. dermatology Mt. Sinai Hosp., NY. Mem. The Skin Cancer Found. Fellow: The Am. Acad. of Dermatology; mem.: Am. Soc. for Dermatologic Surgery, Nat. Physician Trainer for Medicis Aesthetics, Suffolk County Dermatologic Soc. Office: Marina I Peredo Ste 208 260 Middle Country Rd Smithtown NY 11787 Mailing: Spatique Ste 112 260 Middle Country Road Smithtown NY 11787 Office Phone: 631-863-3223, 631-724-7720.

PEREGO, KENNETH LEE, II, urologist; b. Vinton, La., June 30, 1969; BS, La. Coll., 1991; MD, La. State U. Med. Ctr., 1995; Gen. Surgery, Tex. A & M, 1997. Cert. Urology Scott & White Meml. Hosp., 2001, Diplomate Am. Bd. Urology 2003. Resident gen. surgery Tex. A&M, Temple, 1995—97; resident adult & pediatric urology Scott & White, Temple, 1997—2001; pediatric urology tng. Children's Hosp., Dallas, 2000; urologist The Urology Clin., Alexandria, La., 2001—. CEO Innovative Med. Therapies, Baton Rogue, 2002—; cons. laparoscopic urology. Recipient Pfizer Scholars in Urology award, 2001. Mem.: Endocrological Soc., Am. Assn. Clin. Urologist, Am. Urologic Assn.

PEREIRA, FRANCISCO J., dentist; b. Rio de Janeiro, Nov. 29, 1966; DDS, Fed. U. Rio de Janeiro, 1989; PhD, Lund U., 1995. Chmn., dept. tmd and orofacial pain UNESA, 1996—2006; dir., master program UNIGRANRIO, 2002—05, chmn., dept. occlusion and tmd, 1998—2008. Mem.: Internat. Assn. Study Pain. Avocations: swimming, travel, winemaking. Office: Rua Visconde de Piraja 595/702 Ipane Rio de Janeiro 22410-003 Brazil Office Fax: 55 21 2511-1513. Business E-Mail: francisco@oclusaoedtm.com.br.

PEREIRA, GERSON ALVES, JR., surgeon, educator; b. São José do Rio Preto, Brazil, Jan. 20, 1968; s. Aparecida Rincon Alves and Gerson Alves Pereira; life ptnr. Rejane Maira Góes; 1 child, João Pedro Góes Alves. Physician, São Paulo U., 1991. Gen. Surgery Specialist Brazillian Coll. of Surgeons, 1996, Trauma Surgery Specialist Brazillian Coll. of Surgeons, 1999, Digestive Surgery Specialist Brazillian Coll. of Digestive Surgery, 1996, Intensive Care Specialist Brazilian Intensive Care Assn., 1997. Med supr. ICU Emergency Unit, Hosp. das Clínicas, Ribeirão Preto, Brazil, 1998—2003; med. coord. ICU Santa Casa de Sertãozinho, Sertãozinho, Brazil, 2002; med. supr. habilities lab. Ribeirão Preto U. (UNAERP), Ribeirão Preto, Brazil, 2002, med. coord. emergency medicine, trauma and intensive care league, 2002. Prof. emergency and intensive care medicine Ribeirão Preto, Ribeirão Preto, São Paulo, 2000; trauma surgeon São Paulo U., São Paulo, 1997. Physician Brazilian Air Force, Santos, Brazil, 1992—93. Lt. Brazilian Air Force, 1992—93, Santos. Recipient Good Services, Ribeirão Preto's City, 2002. Mem.: Brazilian Coll. of Surgeons (cert. Gen. Surgery Specialist 1996, cert. Trauma Surgery Specialist 1999), Brazillian Coll. of Digestive Surgery (cert. Digestive Surgery Specialist 1996), Brazilian Intensive Care Assn. (cert. Intensive Care Specialist 1997). Achievements include research in renal trauma; trauma scores; emergency and intensive care medicine. Home: Rua Iguape 747 apto 31-M Ribeirão Preto São Paulo 14090-090 Brazil Office: Ribeirão Preto Univ Av Costabile Romano 2201 Ribeirão Preto São Paulo 14096-380 Brazil Office Fax: (16) 3603 - 6794; Home Fax: (16)- 3610 - 2229. Personal E-mail: gersonapj@netsite.com.br.

PEREIRA, LEILA MM BELTRÃO, gastroenterologist, educator; b. Brazil, Oct. 10, 1959; MD, U. Fed. Pernambuco, 1983; PhD, U. London, 1994. Prof. gastroenterology U. Pernambuco, 2000—. Head hepatology unit U. Hosp., 1994. Mem.: AASLD. Avocations: music, tennis. Office: Rua Arnóbio Marques 282 Recife Pernambuco 50100-130 Brazil Office Fax: 558130352073. Business E-Mail: leilapereira@pq.cnpq.br.

PEREIRA, MARCELO PINTO, physical therapist, educator; b. Piracicaba, Jan. 29, 1982; Degree, UNIMEP, 2003; M, São Paulo State U., 2008, attending, 2010—. Prof. Rio Claro Anhanguera Coll., 2008—10. Mem.: Brazilian Biomechanics Soc. Home: Rua Napoleão Laureano 72 Piracicaba São Paulo 131418-160 Brazil Personal E-mail: mppereir@yahoo.com.br.

PEREIRA, ROSANGELA ALVES, nutritionist, educator; b. Rio de Janeiro, May 3, 1955; Degree in Nutrition, U. Fed. Fluminense, 1977; DSc, Nat. Sch. Pub. Health, 2000. Nutritionist Ministry Health, Mozambique, 1979—80; asst. prof. Fed. U. Mato Grosso, Brazil, 1981—93, Fed. U. Rio de Janeiro, 1993—, coord. nutrition grad. program, 2009—. Rsch. fellowship, Nat. Coun. Sci. and Technol. Devel.-CNPq. Fellow: Brazilian Soc. Food and Nutrition. Office: Ave Carlos Chagas Filho 373 Bloco J 2 Rio de Janeiro 21941-902 Brazil Office Fax: 55 21 2280-8343. E-mail: roapereira@gmail.com.

PEREIRA, SÉRGIO LUÍS DA SILVA, dental educator; b. Itapetininga, São Paulo, Brazil, Mar. 17, 1971; Degree in Dentistry, FOA Unesp Araçatuba, São Paulo, 1993; postgrad., FOP Unicamp, 1999. Prof. U. Fortaleza, 1998—. Pvt. practice, 1998; editl. bd. Perio Jour., 2007, Revista Periodontia Jour., 2005, Brazilian Health Promotion Jour., 2005. Mem.: Periodontology Brazilian Soc. Avocations: movies, football, travel. Home: Ave Engo Leal Lima Verde 2086 Fortaleza Ceará 60830-055 Brazil Home Fax: 85 34773055.

PEREIRA, SIMONE PINHEIRO, chemistry professor; b. Belém, Pará, Brazil, Apr. 17, 1957; Degree in Chem. Engring., Pará Fed. U., 1982; PhD in Analytical & Environ. Chemistry, Bahia Fed. U., 1997. Assoc. prof. Pará Fed. U., 1985—. Cons. Amapá Health Dept. (SESA-AP), 2000—03, Amapá Environment Dept. (SEMA-AP), 2000—03, Environment Nat. Coun. (CONAMA), 2004—04, Pará Health Dept., Pará State Health. Secretariat, 2007—09, Pará Environment Dept., Secretaria de Estado do Meio Ambiente, 2007—09. Master: Police Sta. Environment; mem.: Internat. Coun. Engring. and Tech. Edn., Environment Nucleus Pará Fed. U. Avocations: movies, surfing. Home: Alferes Costa 800 Bairro Pedreira Belém Pará 66083040 Brazil Home Fax: 559132444337. Business E-Mail: simonefp@ufpa.br.

PEREIRA, TELMO, medical educator; b. Coimbra, Portugal, June 23, 1976; MSc, U. Coimbra, 2006, PhD, 2011. Prof. Superior Coll. Health Techs., 2005—. Cons. Cardiovasc. Rsch. Inst., 2000—; cons. rschr. Psychology Faculty, U. Coimbra, 2006—. Recipient Teixeira Lopes award, Rotary Club Coimbra, Best Sci. Communication award, Sci. Com. Portuguese Congress Hypertension, 2010—, Sci. Com.

Cardiorhythm Meeting Hong-Kong, 2011. Fellow: Cardiopneumologist Assn.; mem.: Portuguese Soc. Hypertension, Portuguese Soc. Cardiology. Avocations: guitar, sports, reading, films. Home: Rua Gen Humberto Delgado 102 Lousã Coimbra 3200-107 Portugal Personal E-mail: telmo@estescoimbra.pt.

PEREIRA NUNES, TERESA LÚCIA SILVA, pharmacologist; b. Funchal, Portugal, Sept. 7, 1977; m. Nino Sancho Sampaio Martins Pereira, Oct. 5, 2002. MD, U. Coimbra, Portugal, 2001. Gen. intern Hosp. Senhora da Oliveira, Guimarães, Portugal, 2002—03; med. advisor, clin. trials monitor Bial - Portela e Companhia SA, S. Mamede do Coronado, Portugal, 2003—04, project mgr. Phase II trials, 2004—05, study ops. coord. human pharmacology unit, 2004—, med. monitor Phase I, II, III clin. trials, 2005—. Mem. adminstrn. bd. Ho. of Madeira in Coimbra, 1996—97. Mem.: Ordem dos Médicos (assoc.). Avocation: travel. Home: R Pedro Alvares Cabral n°99 3°dto 4835 Guimarães Portugal Office: Bial- Portela e Companhia SA Ave da Siderurgia Nacional Apt 19 4745-457 South Mamede do Coronado Portugal E-mail: teresa.nunes@bial.com.

PEREL, JAMES MAURICE, pharmacology and healthcare educator, researcher; b. Buenos Aires, Mar. 30, 1933; came to U.S., 1947, naturalized, 1954; s. Aria and Bella (Silverberg) P.; m. July 18, 1959 (div. 1971); 1 child, Allan B.; m. Audrey Feldman, Apr. 9, 1972; children: Alissa A., Stephen M. BS, CUNY, 1956; MS, NYU, 1961, PhD, 1964. Nuclear chemist NY Naval Shipyard Lab., Bklyn., 1956—58; assoc. rsch. scientist Goldwater Meml. Hosp. NYU, 1964—67; asst. prof. medicine and chemistry Emory U., Atlanta, 1967-70; asst. prof. psychiatry, pharmacology Columbia U. Coll. Physicians and Surgeons, NYC, 1970-76; assoc. rsch. scientist NY State Psychiat. Inst., NYC, 1970—76, assoc. prof. clin. pharmacology, chief psychiat. rsch., 1976-80; chief clin. pharmacology VA Med. Ctr. Highland Drive, Pitts., 1979-83; prof. psychiatry U. Pitts. Sch. Medicine, 1980—2001, acting chmn. dept. pharmacology, 1985-88, prof. pharmacology, 1980—2008, prof. pharmacology and chem. biology, 2008—, prof. emeritus psychiatry, 2001—; dir. clin. pharmacology Western Psychiat. Inst. & Clinic, Pitts., 1980—; prof. grad. neurosci., 1988—; postdoctoral fellow in clin. pharmacology NIH, 1964-67, NYU. Adj. faculty in chemistry CUNY, 1963-67; cons., mem. grant-awarding study sects. NIH, NIMH. Mem. editorial bd. Psychopharmacology, Neuropsychobiology, Therapeutic Drug Monitoring, Focus on Schizophrenia and Bipolar Disorders, Applied PHarmacokinetics and Pharmacodynamics, 4th edit.; contbr. over 450 peer-reviewed articles to sci. jours., chpts. to books. Recipient Founders Day award, NYU, 1974, Julius Koch Meml. award, Rho Chi, 1983; named Psychopharmacologist of Yr., U. Toronto, 1993; named to Honor Roll, Century of Therapeutics and Sci. 1900-2000, Am. Soc. Clin. Pharmacology and Therapeutics; predoctoral fellow, NSF, 1958—60, numerous rsch. grants, including NIH, NIMH, Founds. Fund for Rsch. in Psychiatry, pharm. cos., pvt. founds. Fellow: Am. Inst. Chemists; mem. Am. Chem. Soc., World Fed. Neurology (co-founder, mem. neurotoxicology group), Internat. Assn. Therapeutic Drug Monitoring and Clin. Toxicology (com. chair), Am. Soc. Pharmacology and Exptl. Therapeutics, Am. Soc. Clin. Pharmacology and Therapeutics (sect. chair), Sigma Xi Jewish. Achievements include discovery of several widely-used pharmacotherapeutic agents. Office: U Pitts Sch Medicine 3811 Ohara St Pittsburgh PA 15213-2593 Office Phone: 412-246-6600. Business E-Mail: pereljm@upmc.edu, pereljm@pitt.edu.

PERELSTEIN, EDUARDO M., pediatric nephrologist; b. Buenos Aires, Dec. 11, 1951; BA; U. Buenos Aires, 1968, MD, 1974. Cert. Am. Bd. Pediat., 1996, Am. Bd. Pediatric Nephrology, 1997. Resident in pediat. Children's Hosp., Buenos Aires, 1975—84; fellow in pediatric nephrology Saint Christopher's Hosp. for Children, Phila., 1984—87; assoc. attending pediatrician Weill Cornell Med. Coll., NYC, 1998—, assoc. prof. clinical pediat., 1998—. Recipient Chief Resident's award, NY Hosp. Pediatric Housestaff, 1995—96, Faculty award for Excellence in Tchg., NY Presbyn. Hosp.-Weill Cornell Med. Coll. Cornell U. Pediatric Housestaff, 2000, Excellence in Tchg. award, Joan and Sanford I. Weill Med. Coll. Cornell U., 2001—02, Outstanding Tchg. award, Weill Med. Coll. Pediatric Housestaff, 2002—03; named Tchr. of Yr., NY Hosp. Pediatric Housestaff, 1992—93, Physician of Yr., Wetll Cornoil, Divsn. Nursing, 2005, Top Drs., NY, 2008; named to Best Doctors in America, 2007—08. Office: Dept Pediat Weill Cornell Med Coll 525 E 68th St New York NY 10065 Office Phone: 212-746-3260. Office Fax: 212-746-8861. Business E-Mail: emperels@med.cornell.edu.

PERERA, DAYASHAN SHEVANTHA, colon and rectal surgeon; b. Sri Lanka, Apr. 9, 1968; MBBCh, Auckland Med. Sch., 1991. Cons. surgeon Sydney Colorectal Assoc., 2002—. Fellow: Colorectal Surg. Soc. Australia, Royal Australasian Coll. Surgeons. Avocations: skiing, music. Office: 37 Gloucester Rd Hurstville NSW 2220 Australia Office Fax: 61295538456. Business E-Mail: shevyperera@sydneycolorectal.com.au.

PERES, FLÁVIO GODOY, dentist, educator; b. Rio de Janeiro, Jan. 8, 1967; DDS, São Paulo U., 1992; PhD, São Paulo Fed. U., 2006. Dentist Prefeitura Mcpl. São Sebastião, 1996—. Prof. Inst. Praxis, 2008—11. Avocation: gymnastics. Home: Rua Padre Anchieta 350 Pindamonhangaba São Paulo 12420510 Brazil Personal E-mail: professor.peres@gmail.com.

PERES, LUIS ALBERTO BATISTA, nephrologist, educator; b. Sao Paulo, Brazil, Jan. 10, 1961; Degree in Medicine, FAMEMA, 1985; MD, UEL, 2007. Prof. UNIOESTE, 1999—. Adj. prof. State U. West Paraná, 2007. Home: São Paulo 769 Cascavel Paraná 85801020 Brazil Home Fax: 55 45 3327 2295. Personal E-mail: peres@certto.com.br.

PERESUNKO, ALEXANDR PETROVICH, medical researcher, physician, gynecologist, oncologist; b. Chernovtsy, Ukraine, Dec. 29, 1963; s. Petr Nazarovich and Tamara Panteleyevna P.; m. Olga Nikolayevna Sakhnenko, Mar. 7, 1987; 1 child, Katerina. Student, Chernovtsy Med., 1987; clin. degree, Inst. Dept. Ob-Gyn., Chernovtsy, 1989; Candidate of Med. Sci., Petrov Sci.-Rsch. Inst. Oncology, St. Petersburg, 1993; MD, Odessa Med. U., Ukraine, 2001. Clin. ordinator Chernovtsy Med. Inst., 1987-89, asst., 1989-2000; assoc. prof. dept. oncology Bukovinian Med. Acad., Chernovtsy, 2000—. Head sci. lab. Bukovinian Med. Acad., Chernovtsy, 1996—. Cons. editor The Contemporary Who's Who Am. Biog. Inst., 2003; contbr. articles to profl. jours Recipient prize for Best Sci. Work, Acad. Med. Sci. of Ukraine, Kiev, 2000. Mem. Students' Sci.-Rsch. Club on Ob-Gyn. (head 1993—). Achievements include research in genetic approaches to early diagnostics, screening, prevention of cancer of female reproductive sphere (problems of clinical and population oncogenetics); new technical methods of early diagnostics of cancer. Home: 1 Pivdenno-Kiltseva St Apt 16 58013 Chernivtsi Ukraine Office: Bukovinian State Med Univ 2 Teatralna Sq 58000 Chernivtsi Ukraine Home Phone: 8 (0372) 514469.

PERET, KAREN KRZYMINSKI, health facility administrator; b. Springfield, Mass., Mar. 8, 1950; d. Edward S. and Doris L. (Beaudry) Krzyminski; m. Robert J. Peret, June 19, 1971 (div. Sept. 2003); children: Heather, James, Kaitlin, Matthew. BSN, St. Anselm's, 1972; MS in Nursing Adminstrn., Boston U., 1980; EdD in Orgnl. Devel., U. Mass., 1993. RN, Mass. Staff nurse Boston VA's Hosp., 1972—73; staff nurse pediat. Harrington Meml. Hosp., Southbridge, Mass., 1973—74, instr. edn., 1974—75, relief day asst. dir. nursing, 1975; coord. continuing edn. Ctrl. Maine Med. Ctr., Lewiston, 1975—76; asst. dir. nursing Monson Devel. Ctr., Palmer, Mass., 1977—83, DON, 1983—94; exec. nursing cons. Liberty Healthcare, Waltham, Mass., 1994—98, v.p. ops. Phila., 1998—; ind. mgmt. cons., 1993—. Instr. Quinsigamond Cmty. Coll., Worcester, Mass., 1972-73. Contbr. articles to profl. jours. Mem. ANA, Mass. Nurses' Assn., Am. Assn. on Mental Retardation, Sigma Theta Tau. Home: 79 Sturbridge Rd Holland MA 01521-3123 Office: 401 E City Ave Ste 820 Bala Cynwyd PA 19004-1130 Home Phone: 413-245-9452; Office Phone: 800-331-7122. Personal E-mail: karenperet@aol.com.

PEREZ, JOSEPHINE, psychiatrist, educator; b. Tijuana, Mex., Feb. 10, 1941; came to the U.S., 1960, U.S. citizenship, 1968. BS in Biology, U. Santiago de Compostela, Spain, 1971, MD, 1975. Nuc. medicine technician, EEG technician, supr. Electrographic Labs., Encino, Calif., 1963—69; clerkships in internal medicine, gen. surgery, otorhinolaryngology, dermatology and venereology Gen. Hosp. of Galicia, Spain, 1972-75; resident in gen. psychiatry U. Miami, Jackson Meml. Hosp. and VA Hosp., Miami, Fla., 1976-78; practice medicine specializing in psychiatry, marital and family therapy, individual psychotherapy Miami, 1979—. Emergency room physician Miami Dade Hosp., 1975; attending psychiatrist Jackson Meml. Hosp., 1979—, asst. dir. adolescent psychiat. unit, 1979-83; mem. clin. faculty U. Miami Sch. Medicine, 1979—, clin. instr. psychiatry, 1979—. Mem. AMA (Physicians' Recognition award 1980, 83, 86, 89, 98, 2000, 01, 05), Am. Assn. for Marital and Family Therapy (cert. clin. mem., treas. 1982-84, pres.-elect 1985-87, pres. 1987-89), Am. Psychiat. Assn., Am. Med. Women's Assn., Assn. Women Psychiatrists, Fla. Psychiat. Soc., South Dade Women Physicians Assn. Office: 420 S Dixie Hwy Ste 4A Coral Gables FL 33146-2228 Office Phone: 305-666-7766, 305-857-9250.

PEREZ, LOUIS ANTHONY, radiologist; b. NYC, June 11, 1939; s. Salvatore Lawrence and Valvadina Rose (Ruscillo) P.; divorced, 1988; children: Lisa, Gregg, Nicole; m. Patricia Ann McVey, May 19, 1990; 1 child, Kelsey. BEE, Manhattan Coll., 1962; MD, SUNY, Bklyn., 1966. Diplomate Am. Bd. Radiology (oral examiner), Am. Bd. Nuclear Medicine. Chief nuc. medicine Misericordia Hosp., Bronx, 1973-75, Norwalk Hosp., Conn., 1975-82; cons. Manhattan Coll., Radiology Inst., Riverdale, N.Y., 1974-81; dir. radiology Lawrence Hosp., Bronxville, NY, 1982—2004; asst. clin. prof. radiology Columbia U. Coll. Physicians and Surgeons, NYC, 1995—2006; with NE Radiology, Brewster, 2006—. Contbr. articles to profl. jours., chpts. to books. Lt. comdr. USN, 1963-77. Grantee, Am. Cancer Soc., 1968-70, USPHS, 1974-75. Fellow Am. Coll. Radiology; mem. Soc. Nuc. Medicine (trustee 1985-89, 92—, chmn. sci. subcom. 1988—, chpt. pres. 1982), NY State Med. Soc. Independent. Roman Catholic. Office: 6 Dover Cir Newtown CT 06470

PEREZ, VICTOR MANUEL, physician, plastic surgeon; b. Cosamaloapan, Veracruz, Mex., Aug. 18, 1967; s. Tomas and Manuela Perez; m. Diana Marie Bobovnyik, July 14, 2000; children: Victor Manuel Jr., Ava Elizabeth. BS, U. Autonomous Nuevo Leon, Guadalupe, N.L. Mex., 1990. Cert. Am. Bd. Plastic Surgery, 2003. Gen. practitioner Ministry of Health, Benito Juarez, Nuevo Leon, Mexico, 1990—91, Mexican Inst. Social Security, Pal, Coahuila, 1991—92; resident Cook County Hosp., Chgo., 1994—95; resident in gen. surgery Western Res. Care Sys., Youngstown, Ohio, 1995—98; burn surgery fellow Shriners Burn Hosp., Galveston, Tex., 1998—99; resident in plastic surgery Loma Linda U. Med. Ctr., Calif., 1999—2002; chief, plastic surgery sect. VA Hosp., Kansas City, Mo., 2002—; asst. prof. plastic surgery U. Kans. Med. Ctr., Kansas City, 2002—. Presenter in field. Contbr. articles to profl jours. and book chpts. in field. Grant, Plastic Surgery Ednl. Found., 2001. Fellow: ACS; mem.: Kans. City Plastic Surgery Soc., Am. Burn Assn., Am. Soc. Plastic Surgeons. Roman Catholic. Achievements include invention of new techniques in abdominoplasty-umbilical inset. Avocation: dog shows. Office: Univ Kansas Medical Ctr 3901 Rainbow Blvd Kansas City KS 66160 Office Fax: 913-588-2061. Business E-Mail: vperez@kumc.edu.

PEREZ-BARCENA, JON, emergency physician; b. Bilbao, Spain, Apr. 22, 1971; MD, U. de Navarra, 1995; PhD, U. Autónoma de Barcelona, 2009. Intensive care physician Intensive Care Dept. Son Espases U. Hosp., 2001—. Asst. clinic cons. U. Autonoma de Madrid, 2010. Office: Carretera de Valdemossa 79 Palma Mallorca Islas Baleares 07010 Spain Office Fax: 34-871909970. Business E-Mail: juan.perez@ssib.es.

PEREZ-CRUET, JORGE, geriatric psychiatrist, researcher; b. Santurce, PR, Oct. 15, 1931; s. Jose Maria Perez-Vicente and Emilia Cruet-Burgos; m. Anyes Heimendinger, Oct. 4, 1958; children: Antonio, Mick, Graciela, Isabelle. BS magna cum laude, U. PR, 1953, MD, 1957; diploma in psychiatry, McGill U., Montreal, Que., Can., 1976. Diplomate Am. Bd. Geriat. Psychiatry, Am. Bd. Psychiatry and Neurology, Nat. Bd. Med. Examiners, lic. Can. Coun. Med. Examiners, Med. Coun. Can., cert. in quality assurance, profl. in healthcare quality Health Quality Cert. Bd., eligible Am. Bd. Psychiatry and Neurology, psychiatrist Am. Bd. Psychiatry and Neurology, 1980, in Geriatric Psychiatry Am. Bd. Psychiatry and Neurology, 1991, re-cert. Am. Bd. Psychiatry and Neurology, 2001, in Addiction Psychiatry Am. Bd. Psychiatry and Neurology, 2006. Rotating intern Michael Reese Hosp., Chgo., 1957-58; fellow in psychiatry Johns Hopkins U. Med. Sch., 1958-60, instr., then asst. prof. psychiatry, 1962-73; psychiatrist neurophysiology and psychosomatic lab. Walter Reed Army Inst. Rsch., Washington, 1960—62, cons., 1963-65; rsch. assoc. lab. chem. pharmacology Nat. Heart Inst., NIH, Bethesda, Md., 1969-71; med. dir. USPHS adult psychiatry sect. lab. clin. sci. NIMH, Bethesda, 1971-73; psychiatry resident diploma course in psychiatry McGill U. Sch. Medicine, Montreal Gen. Hosp., 1973-76, Montreal Children's Hosp., 1975; prof. psychiatry, chief psychopharmacology lab. U. Mo.-Mo. Inst. Psychiatry, St. Louis, 1976—78; chief psychiatry svc. San Juan VA Hosp., PR, 1978—92, pharmacy and therapeutic com., 1978—2004; prof. psychiatry U. PR Med. Sch., 1978-92, U. Okla. Health Sci. Ctr., 1992—2004, Okla. City VA Med. Ctr., 1992—2004; pvt. practice. Spl. cons. NASA, Moffettfield, Calif., 1965-69; cons. divsn. narcotic addition and drug abuse NIDA, 1972-73; drug adv. com. FDA/NIDA, 1976-80, pharmacy and therapeutic com., 1992—; local organizer Internat. Coll. Neuropsychiatry, San Juan, PR, 1986, CINP, 1986; spl. advisor mental health PR Senate, PR sec. health, 1989; prin. investigator NASA biosatellite project JH Sch. Med., 1963-65.; staff sr. psychiatrist and supt. psychiatry ward, VA Med. Ctr., Oklahoma City, 1992-1995, sr. staff psychiatrist and physician substance abuse clinic, 1995-2004, med. dir. Opioid Treatment Ctr., 1995-2004. Editor: Catholic Physicians Guild Archiocese of Okla., 1997-98. Mem. Rep. Nat. Com., 1995; mem. Eisenhower Commn., 2001. Capt. M.C. USAR, 1960-62; sr. surgeon USPHS, 1969-71, med. dir., 1971-73. Recipient Coronas award, 1957, Ruiz-Arnau award, 1957, Diaz-Garcia award 1957, Geigy award, 1975, 76, AMA Recognition award 1971, 76, 81, Horner's award 1975, 76, Pavlovian award, 1978, Recognition cert. VA Svc. awards and commendations, 1980-98, Senate of PR, 1986, Cert. of Merit Gov. of PR, 1986, Cert. Recognition, Sec. Health, San Juan, Puerto Rico, Appreciation plaque Fifth World Congress of IRMA, Manila, Philippines, Eisenhower Commn., 1995; nominee Eisenhower Commn. award, 1995, 2001. Fellow Interam. Coll. Physicians and Surgeons, Royal Coll. Physicians and Surgeons Can. (sr., cert.), Am. Psychiat Assn. (Disting., life, 2001); mem. AAAS, Am. Coll. Med. Quality (bd. dirs. 2004), Am. Physiol. Soc., Am. Coll. Psychiatrists, Pavlovian Soc., Am. Fedn. Clin. Rsch., Am. Fedn. Med. Rsch., Am. Assn. Geriat. Psychiatry, Am. Geriat. Soc., Am. Coll. Preventive Medicine, Am. Soc. Clin. Pharmacology and Therapeutics, Am. Soc. Pharmacology and Exptl. Therapeutics, Am. Soc. Addiction Medicine (cert.), Am. Acad. Addiction Psychiatry (dir. Area VIII, 2002-), Soc. Neurosci., Nat. Assn. Healthcare Quality (mem. editl. bd. Jour. Health Quality, 2005), Internat. Soc. Rsch. Aggression, Okla. Psychiat. Assn., Am. Soc. Clin. Psychopharmacology, Menninger Found., Charles F. Menninger Soc., Okla. Assn. Health Care Quality, Alumni, UPR Sch. Med., Johns Hopkins Med. Surg. Inst., NY Acad. Scis., NIH Alumni (life), McGill, Okla. Hist. Soc.(life). Republican. Roman Catholic. Avocations: painting, writing. Home: 307 Tano Rd # 8 Santa Fe NM 87506-8823 Personal E-mail: jperezcrue@aol.com.

PEREZ-CRUET, MICK JORGE (MIGUELANGELO JORGE PEREZ-CRUET), neurosurgeon, educator; b. Washington, May 3, 1961; s. Jorge Fortunato and Anyes Lilly Perez-Cruet; m. Donna Jeanne Roggenbuck, July 9, 1994; children: Kristin Magdalene, Joshua Michael, Rachel Elizabeth, David Gabriel. BA, Grinell Coll., 1983; MSc in Chemistry, U. South Fla., 1986; MD, Tufts U., 1991. Commd. 2d lt. USAF, 1987, advanced through grades to maj., 1997, ret., 2001; intern surg. svc. Baylor Coll. Medicine, Houston, 1991-92, resident in neurosurgery, 1992-97; attending neurosurgery, v. chmn. Wilford Hall Med. Ctr., San Antonio, 1997—2001; spinal fellow Rush U./CINN, Chgo., 2001—02; asst. prof., dir. minimally invasive spine surgery Rush U., Chgo., 2002—03; assoc. dir. Inst. Spine Care/CINN; dir., spinal surgery Mich. Head and Spine Inst., 2003—; prof. Oakland U. William Beaumont Med. Sch.; dir. minimally invasive spine surgery, Providence Med. Ctr. William Beaumont Hosp., 2003—, vice chair dept. neurosurgery, dir. spine fellowship program, Providence Med. Ctr., 2004—10; pres., CEO, MI4Spine, LLC; founder, pres. Minimally Invasive Neurosurg. Soc., 2009—; chief med. officer Thompson Mis. Prin. investigator clin. trials; presenter in field; appointee Coun. State Neurosurg. Socs., 1997, chmn. young physicians com., chmn. workforce com., corr. sec., publs. com.; mem. sci. adv. bd. Neospine; founding surgeon US Spine CNS Publs. Com., 2002—; dir. socioecon. peer rev. articles AANS Bull.; med. dir. Thompson MIS. Editor: (textbooks) Outpatient Spinal Surgery, An Anatomical Approach to Minimally Invasive Spine Surgery, (DVD) AANS Minimally Invasive Spine Techniques, Minimally Invasive Spine Fusion: Techniques and Operative Nuances; asst. editor: AANS Bull. Com.; contbr. chapters to books, articles to profl. jours. Chmn. class reunion Tufts Sch. Medicine, 1995-96; dir. class fund Grinnell Coll., 1999—. Air Force Health Professions scholar, 1987—91, Translational Rsch. grant, NASS, 2010. Mem. AMA, ACS, AAAS, AANS (fel), Congress Neurol. Surgeons, Am. Assn. Neurol. Surgeons (dir. spine courses, editor-in-chief AANS Bull. Socioecon. Jour. 2005—), Mich. Med. Soc., Mich. Assn. Neurol. Surgeons (treas., pres. 2006-08), Sigma Xi (grantee 1985). Achievements include invention of spine instrumentation; patents in field. Avocations: hunting, fishing, scuba diving, archery, poetry. Office: Mich Head and Spine Inst 3577 W 13 Mile Rd Ste 206 Royal Oak MI 48073 Personal E-mail: perezcruet@yahoo.com.

PEREZ-JARA, JAVIER, physician, consultant; b. Madrid, Dec. 6, 1965; Diploma in medicine, U. Complutense, Madrid, 1989. Specialization in geriatrics Hosp. Clinico San Carlos, Madrid, 1994. Cons. geriat. Hosp. Del Bierzo, Ponferrada, Spain, 1995—. Dir., mem. Assn. Alzheimer Bierzo, Ponferrada, Spain, 1997—2003. Recipient First prize, Soc. Espanola Geriatria Barcelona, 2000, 2003. Office: Geriatria Hosp Del Bierzo c/Médicos sin Fronteras s/n 24411 Ponferrada Spain Office Phone: 987 455200. Fax: 987 455300. Personal E-mail: jperezjarac@gmail.com. E-mail: jperezjara@wanadoo.es.

PERGOLIZZI, JOSEPH VINCENT, anesthesiologist; b. Bklyn., Mar. 23, 1967; MD, Ross U. Sch. Medicine, 1996. Dir. bus. devel., clin. trials unit Johns Hopkins U. Sch. Medicine, 1997—2000, adj. asst. prof., dept. medicine, 2000; COO NEMA Rsch. Inc., 1997—2011; anesthesiology resident Georgetown U. Sch. Medicine, 2000, adj. faculty, dept. anesthesiology and pain medicine, 1999—2011; CEO CreoMed Inc., 2004—11; mng. dir. RTU Pharmaceuticals, 2010—11; chief med. officer Tigris Pharmaceuticals, 2011—. Faculty, steering com. Pan European Initiative, 2008—11; bd. dirs., chmn. Assn. Chronic Pain Patients, Tex., 2010—11; safe use initiative, steering com. FDA, 2010—11. Recipient Charles Fazio award, Georgetown U., Physicians Recognition award, AMA. Master: Nat. Inst. Pain, Georgetown U. Alumni Assn., Johns Hopkins Alumni Assn.; fellow: Internat. Pain Rsch. and Treatment Found.; mem.: Am. Chem. Soc. Avocations: skiing, travel, target shooting. Office: 840 111th Ave North Ste 7 Naples FL 34108 Office Fax: 239-597-7566.

PERHACH, JAMES LAWRENCE, pharmaceutical executive; s. James Lawrence and Elizabeth Louise (Hoffman) P.; m. Judith Irene Selter, Apr. 15, 1967; children: Laura Anne, Amy Elizabeth. BS, U.

Dayton, 1966; MS, U. Pitts., 1969, PhD, 1971. Sr. scientist dept. pharmacology Mead Johnson Rsch. Ctr., divsn. Bristol Myers, 1971—74, sr. investigator dept. biol. rsch., 1974—76, sr. rsch. assoc. dept. biol. rsch., 1976—77, sr. rsch. assoc. dept. pathology and toxicology, 1977—78, prin. rsch. assoc. dept. pathology and toxicology, 1978—80; from dir. pharmacology to dir. biol. rsch. to dir. clin. investigation Wallace Labs. Divsn. Carter-Wallace, Inc., Cranbury, NJ, 1980—87, v.p. clin. pharmacology and pharmacokinetics, 1987—2001; sr. dir. clin. pharmacology Purdue Pharma, L.P., 2001—04; sr. dir. CNS Therapeutic Area Forest Rsch. Inst, 2004—05, exec. dir. clin. devel., 2005—. Adj. asst. prof. dept. pharmacy practice and adminstrn. Ernest Mario Coll. Pharmacy Rutgers U., 1993—; adv. bd. clin. rsch. ctr. U. Medicine and Dentistry NJ Robert Wood Johnson Med. Sch., 1995-2003; drug utilization rev. coun. State of NJ, 1983-2003, med. pharmacologist, 1983, sec., 1984, chmn., 1985-87. Fellow: Am. Coll. Clin. Pharmacology; mem.: Am. Soc. Pharmacology and Exptl. Therapeutics, Am. Soc. Clin. Pharmacology and Therapeutics. Achievements include research in drug discovery, elucidation of mechanism of action and safety evaluation of new therapeutic agents. Office: Forest Rsch Inst Harbor Side Fin Ctr Plaza V Jersey City NJ 07311 Home Phone: 609-716-9228; Office Phone: 201-427-8465. Business E-Mail: james.perhach@frx.com.

PERINPANAYAGAM, NOEL I., hospital administrator; MD, U. Colombo, Sri Lanka. Diplomate Am. Bd. Neurol. Surgery. Intern gen. surgery, emergency medicine St. Helier's Hosp., England; gen. surgery orthopedics Chelmsford, Essex and Broomfield Hosps., England; senior house officer neurosurgery The Middlesex Hosp., London, fellow/ registrar neurosurgery; resident neurosurgery NYU Med. Ctr., neuro and ortho fellow spinal surgery; fellow Complex Cervical Spine Surgery, Osnerbruk, Germany; asst. prof. dept neurosurgery Univ. Cin.; dir. neuro-trauma and spine Mayfield Neurol. Inst.; assoc. prof. dept. neurosurgery Mt. Sinai Sch. Med., Manhattan, NY; dir. spinal neurosurgery Elmhurst Hosp., Queens, NY, St. Joseph's Hosp., Patterson, NJ; dir. ctr. for spine and minimally invasive surgery St. Luke's-Roosevelt Hosp. Ctr., dir. dept. neurosurgery; physician The Ctr. For Cranial Base Surgery. Author: (publs.) The effect of isovolaemic hemodilution and intra-venous glycerol on the sequele of middle cerebral artery occlusion in the rat, 1986; co-author: Quantitative three-dimensional anatomy of the subaxial cervical spine: Implication for anterior spinal surgery, 1996, Vertical fractures of the odontoid process, 1996, Paraspinal calcinosis associated with progressive systemic sclerosis, 1997, Arthritic and bone softening diseases of the craniocervical junction, 1998, Somatosensory evoked potential monitoring in Anterior Thoracic Vertebrectomy, 2000, varies others. Mem.: Royal Coll. of Surgeons, ACS, Am. Bd. Neurological Surgeons. Office: St Lukes Roosevelt Hospital Center 1000 Tenth Ave New York NY 10019 Office Phone: 212-523-4000.

PERIS-BONET, RAFAEL, medical educator, researcher; b. Valencia, Spain, Nov. 18, 1946; m. Neus Campillo-Iborra, Aug. 10, 1970; 1 child, Paula Peris-Campillo. PhD, U. Valencia, Spain, 1974. Registered dr. U. Valencia, 1969. Med. staff Hosp. Info. Sys. Unit, U. Hosp., Valencia, Spain, 1972—75; asst. prof. Faculty Medicine, U. Valencia, 1971—83; dir., hosp. info. sys. unit U. Hosp., Valencia, 1998—; lectr. Faculty Medicine, U. Valencia, Valencia, Spain, 1983—2001, prof., 2001—; dir. Nat. Childhood Cancer Registry Spain, Valencia, 1980—. Sci. dir. Childhood Tumours Registry, Valencia, Spain, 1986—96. Author: (book) El cáncer infantil de sistema nervioso central en España; contbr. articles to numerous sci. jours. Mem.: Spanish Soc. Epidemiology, Spanish Soc. Hematology and Oncology. Office: Faculty Medicine Univ Valencia Avda Blasco Ibañez 15 Valencia 46010 Spain Office Phone: 34963864951, 34963864161. Business E-Mail: rafael.peris@uv.es.

PERKIN, RONALD MURRAY, pediatrician, educator; b. Denver, July 31, 1948; s. Robert Murray and Marion Kathryn (Thompson) P.; m. Susan Renee Sheer; children: Matthew Murray, Jeffrey Jay, Nickolas James, Thomas Mitchell, Benjamin Sheer, Savannah Paige. BS in Engring., U. Colo., 1970; postgrad., Johns Hopkins U., 1970-71; MD, U. South Fla., 1976; MA, Loma Linda Univ., 1997. Diplomate Am. Bd. Pediatrics. Resident in pediatrics Children's Med. Ctr., Dallas, 1976-79, fellow in pediatric intensive care, 1979-81, asst. dir. pediatric intensive care, 1981; clins. asst. prof. pediatrics U. Tex. Health Sci. Ctr. Southwestern Med. Sch., Dallas, 1981; asst. adj. prof. pediatrics U. Calif. Sch. Medicine, San Diego, 1982-84, co-dir. pediatric intensive care, 1982-84; dir. pediatric ICU attending physician Childrens Hosp. Orange (Calif.) County Hosp., 1984-88; attending physician newborn ICU St. Joseph's Hosp., Orange, 1984-88; assoc. prof. pediatrics Loma Linda Univ., 1988-90, prof. pediatrics, 1990-2000; prof., chmn. dept. pediats. Brody Sch. Medicine, East Carolina U., Greenville, NC, 2000—. Cons. Naval Hosp., San Diego, 1983-84; asst. adj. prof. pediatrics U. Calif., Irvine, 1984-88; dir. pediat. intensive care fellowship program U. Calif. Irvine and Children's Hosp. Orange County, 1984-88; critical care adv. com., critical care coun., Extra Corporeal Membrane Oxygenation found. So. Calif., emergency dept. com., ethics com., ethics cons. svc. critical care com., resident evaluation sub-com., respiratory care com.; dir. pediat. critical care Loma Linda U. Children's Hosp., 1988-2000, assoc. chair pediat. Sch. Medicine, 1993-2000; lectr. in field. Editor: (with others) Brain Insults in Infants and Children: Pathophysiology and Management; Emergency Management of the Critically Ill Child; Pediatric Hosp. Medicine: A Textbook of Inpatient Care, 2003, 2d edit., 2008, Primer on Pediatric Palliative Care, 2005, Pediatric Emergency Medicine Manual, 2007, The PICU Book, 2011; reviewer Capistrano Press, Ltd., 1982-84, Jour. Pediatrics, 1982—; contbr. articles to profl. jours. With USN, 1971—73. Recipient student awards U. South Fla. Coll. Medicine, faculty awards U. Calif., Irvine, Lange Ann. award Lange Book Co., 1974; Mosby scholar Mosby Book Co., 1975-76. Fellow Am. Acad. Pediatrics, Am. Coll. Critical Care Medicine, Am. Acad. Sleep Medicine; mem. Soc. Critical Care Medicine, Calif. Children Svcs. (adv. com. rev. pediatric ICU's 1986-2000). Office: 3E-142 Brody Med Scis Bldg Greenville NC 27858-4354 Office Phone: 252-744-2540. Office Fax: 252-744-1376. Business E-Mail: perkinr@ecu.edu.

PERKINS, BOB S., cosmetic dentist; Grad., Las Vegas Inst. Dentist Malibu Dental Group. Office: Malibu Dental Group 29350 Pacific Coast Hwy Ste 3 Malibu CA 90265 Office Phone: 310-419-6900.

PERKINS, HERBERT ASA, hematologist, educator; b. Boston, Oct. 5, 1918; s. Louis and Anna (Robinson) P.; m. Frances Snyder, Sept. 2, 1942; children: Susan, Deborah, Dale, Karen, Ronnie. AB cum laude, Harvard U., 1940; MD summa cum laude, Tufts U., 1943. Intern Boston City Hosp., 1944, resident, 1947-48; practice medicine specializing in transfusion medicine; clin. instr. Stanford Med. Sch., 1953-57, asst. clin. prof., 1957-58; hematologist Open Heart Surgery Team, Stanford Hosp., San Francisco, 1955-58, Jewish Hosp., St. Louis, 1958-59; dir. rsch. Irwin Meml. Blood Ctrs. (now Blood Ctrs. of the Pacific), San Francisco, 1959-78, med. and sci. dir., 1978-90, exec. dir., 1987-91, pres., 1991-93, sr. med. scientist, 1993—. Asst. prof. medicine Washington U., St. Louis, 1958-59, U. Calif., San Francisco, 1959-66, assoc. prof., 1966-71, clin. prof., 1971—. Coeditor: Hepatitis and Blood Transfusion, 1972. Maj. M.C., U.S. Army, 1944-47. Mem. AAAS, Am. Assn. Blood Banks (chmn. sci. adv. com. 1972-73, chmn. stds. com. 1968-71, chmn. com. on organ transplantation and tissue typing 1970-80, bd. dirs. 1982-86), Am. Soc. Hematology, Internat. Transfusion Soc., Am. Soc. Histocompatibility and Immunogenetics (pres. 1985-86), Nat. Marrow Donor Program (chair bd. dirs. 1995-96, chmn. com. on stds. 1987-94, chmn. fin. com. 1987-94). Office: Blood Ctrs of the Pacific 270 Masonic Ave San Francisco CA 94118-4417 Home: 10 Wolfback Ridge Rd Sausalito CA 94965-2052 E-mail: hperkins@bloodcenters.org. *

PERKINS-BANAS, MELISSA VERONICA, neuropsychologist; d. Roy Dennis and Marian Dana Perkins; m. Joseph Paul Banas, July 3, 1999. BA, U. RI, 1992; MA, U. Hartford, 1995, MS, 1996; PsyD, Yeshiva U., 2004. Cert. Psychologist 1999. Sch. psychologist Norwich Pub. Schools, Norwich, Conn., 1999—2003; neuropsychologist Wheeler Clinic, Conn., 2003—. Post- doctoral neuropsychology fellowship Fielding Inst., NYC, 2004—. Sponsored athlete Adidas Woodbridge Racing Team, Woodbridge, Conn., 2000—02. Recipient Conn. Distance Runner of the Yr., Hi Tek Racing Team, 2001; Cecilia Rothenberg scholarship, Yeshiva U., 2002—03. Mem.: Assn. Advancement of Applied Sport Psychology, Conn. Assn. Sch. Psychologists, NASP, Am. Psychology Assn. (Divsn. 60, clin. neuropsychology), Psi Chi Nat. Honor Soc. Psychology. Roman Catholic. Office: Wheeler Clinic 91 Northwest Dr Plainville CT 06062 Home: 1 Upper Downs Dr Danielson CT 06239-3220

PERKINSON, ROBERT RONALD, psychologist, consultant; b. Richmond, Va., Aug. 8, 1945; s. Gordon Archibald and Sarah (Haskins) P.; m. Elizabeth Godfrey Fly, July 27, 1968 (div. 1984); children: Robert Reps, Nyshie Page, Shane William; m. Angela Kaufman, Sept. 20, 1991. BS, Colo. State U., 1968; MS, Ea. Wash. State U., 1970; PhD, Utah State U., 1974. Lic. psychologist, S.D.; cert. chem. dependency counselor level III, S.D.; nat. cert. gambling counselor; nat. cert. alcohol and drug counselor; lic. marriage and family counselor, S.D. Juvenile ct. psychologist, Cedar City, Utah, 1971-72; psychologist in pvt. practice Jackson, Wyo., 1974-83; dir. psychol. svcs. Western Wyo. Mental Health Assn., Jackson, 1977-78, psychologist, 1983—; psychologist, clin. dir. Keystone Treatment Ctr., 1988—. Cons. in field; chief psychologist Grand Teton Nat. Pk., Teton County Sheriff's Office and Police Dept. Copyrights: The Yellowstone Park Game, The Good Health Game, The Grizzly Control Team, Communication from God, Chemical Dependency Counseling, The Mystics, God Talks CD, Peace Will Come CD, The Treatment of Pathological Gambling: A Step By Step Approach. Author: Chemical Dependency Counseling: A Practical Guide, 1997, 2nd edit., 2002, 3rd edit, 2008, The Chemical Dependency Treatment Planner, 1998, God Talks to You, 2000, The Addiction Treatment Planner, 2001, 3rd edit., 2006, 4th edit., 2009, The Alcoholism and Drug Abuse Patient Workbook, 2003, The Gambling Addiction Patient Workbook, 2003, Treating Alcoholism: Helping Your Clients Find the Road to Recovery, 2004; contbr. articles to profl. jours. Mem. APA, S.D. Psychol. Assn., S.D. Chem. Dependency Assn., Biofeedback Soc. Am. (bd. dirs. Wyo. br.), Wyo. Bd. Psychologist Examiners (pres. 1997, bd. dirs. S.D. coun. problem gambling), Nat. Registere of Health Svc. Providers in Psychology. Address: PO Box 159 Canton SD 57013-0159 Personal E-mail: perk@iw.net.

PERKONIGG, AXEL, psychologist, researcher; b. Vaihingen, Enz, Germany, Nov. 11, 1959; s. Rudolf Perkonigg and Annerose Irmgard Perkonigg, geb. Siegert. MS, PhD, Paris Lodron U. Salzburg, Austria, 1991. Cert. clin. psychologist U. Salzburg, 1991. Rsch. asst. Max Planck Inst. Psychiatry, Munich, 1992—97, vis. scientist, 2002—07; sci. asst. U. Regensburg, Dept. Psychiatry, Germany, 1997—2000; sr. scientist Tech. U. Dresden, Germany, 2001—09, Protest U., Ludwigsburg, Germany, 2009—. Achievements include research in first European epidemiological, general population study on traumatic events and posttraumatic stress disorder as well as knowledge transfer and consulting of substance abuse services. Office: Protest University Ludwigsburg Paulusweg 6 Ludwigsburg 71638 Germany Office Phone: 004971419745241. E-mail: axelp11@gmx.net.

PERL, DANIEL PETER, neuroscientist, medical educator; b. NYC, June 9, 1942; s. Alan and Florence Perl; m. Eleanor Perl; children: Erica, Alexander. BA, Columbia U., 1963; MD, SUNY Downstate Med. Ctr., 1967. Diplomate Nat. Bd. Med. Examiners, Am. Bd. Pathology, cert. in neuropathology and anatomic pathology. Intern pathology Yale-New Haven Hosp., 1967—68, resident pathology, 1968—69; tchg. assoc. Yale U. Sch. Medicine, 1968-70, postdoc. fellow neuropathology, 1969—70; clin. instr. dept. pathology & lab. medicine Emory U. Sch. Medicine, Atlanta, 1970-72; asst. prof. Brown U., Providence, 1972-76; assoc. prof. pathology U. Vt. Coll. Medicine, Burlington, 1976-83, prof. pathology, 1983-86; prof. pathology, psychiatry & neuroscs. Mt. Sinai Sch. Medicine, NYC, 1986—; dir. neuropathology Mt. Sinai Med. Ctr., NYC, 1986—. Rsch. pathologist Centers Disease Control, Atlanta, 1970—72; attending pathologist Miriam Hosp., Providence, 1972—76; cons. neuropathologist Office Med. Examiner, State of RI, 1972—76, State of Vt., 1976—86; cons. neuropathologist Eastern Maine Med. Ctr., Bangor, 1976—86, Dartmouth-Hitchcock Med. Ctr., Hanover, NH, 1981—86, Pilgrim Psychiat. Ctr., Brentwood, NY, 1994—; attending pathologist Mt. Sinai Hosp., 1986—. Contbr. articles to profl. jours. Surgeon, lt. comdr. USPHS, 1970—72. Mem.: Movement Disorder Soc., Soc. Neuroscis., Am. Acad. Neurology, Am. Neurol. Assn., Am. Assn. Investigative Pathologists, Internat. Soc. Neuropathologists, Am. Assn. Neuropathologists, Alpha Omega Alpha. Office: Mt Sinai Med Ctr Annenberg Bldg Fl 15 Rm 76A 1468 Madison Ave New York NY 10029-6500 E-mail: daniel.perl@mssm.edu. *

PERLER, BRUCE ALAN, vascular surgeon; b. New Bedford, Mass., Mar. 12, 1950; s. J. Leonard and Muriel Marcia (Katzman) P.; children: Mason, Rachel. AB in Zoology summa cum laude, Duke U., Durham, NC, 1972, MD, 1976; MBA, Johns Hopkins U., Balt., 2004. Diplomate Am. Bd. Gen. Surgery, cert. spl. qualificatons in gen. vascular surgery; lic. physician, Mass., Md. Surg. intern Mass. Gen. Hosp., Boston, 1976-77, surg. resident, 1977-81, clin. and rsch. fellow in vascular surgery, 1981-82; clin. fellow surgery Harvard Med. Sch., 1977-82; asst. prof. surgery Johns Hopkins U. Sch. Medicine, Balt., 1982-88, assoc. prof., 1988—97, prof., 1997—; asst. surgery Mass. Gen. Hosp., Boston, 1981-82; dir. noninvasive lab., mem. med. bd., vice-chmn. med. staff com. Johns Hopkins Hosp., Balt., 1982—, chief divsn. vascular surgery, 2002—, attending vascular surgeon, 1982—, med. dir. intermediate care unit, 1989-91, mem. med. bd., 1995—99; Julius H. Jacobson II prof. Johns Hopkins U. Sch. Medicine, Balt., 2002—. Cons. vascular surgery Johns Hopkins Bayview Med. Ctr., Balt., 1982—, circulatory system devices panel Ctr. Devices and Radiologic Health, FDA, Washington, 1989—, Rsch. Adv. Group, VA, Washington, 1993—; mem. diagnostic and therapeutic tech. assessment panel AMA, 1991; lectr. throughout U.S. and Can. Mem. editl. bd. Jour. Vascular Surgery, asst. editor, assoc. editor, 2006—, editor, 2009-; editl. bd. Jour. Vascular Endovascular Surgery, Annals of Vascular Surgery; contbr. articles to profl. jours., chpts. to books. Rsch. grantee NIH, 1986-87, 92-94. Mem. ACS, Am. Surg. Assn., Soc. Vascular Surgery (bd. dirs.), So. Assn. Vascular Surgery (program com. 1992-95, exec. coun. 2004—, pres 2009-), Ea. Vascular Soc. (membership com. 1991-94, sec. 2001-, pres. 2004-05), Soc. Univ. Surgeons, Assn. Acad. Surgery, Chesapeake Vascular Soc. (pres. 1992-93), Balt. Acad. Surgery, Duke Med. Alumni Assn., Phi Beta Kappa. Office: Johns Hopkins Hosp - Harvey 611 Dept Surgery 600 N Wolfe St Dept Surgery Baltimore MD 21287-8611 Office Phone: 410-955-2618.

PERLIN, JONATHAN BRIAN, hospital administrator; b. 1961; s. Seymour Perlin; m. Donna Perlin; 2 children. MS in Health Adminstrn., Va. Commonwealth U., Ph.D in Pharmacology & Toxicology, MD. Med. dir., quality improvement, Med. Coll. Va. Hosps. Va. Commonwealth U., assoc. dir., internal medicine residency tng. prog., adj. prof., health adminstrn.; CEO Veterans Health Adminstrn. (VHA); chief quality officer & chief performance officer US Dept. Veterans Affairs, Washington, 1999—2002, dep. under sec. health, 2002—04, acting chief rsch. officer & chief devel. officer, 2003—04, acting under sec. for health, Veterans Health Adminstrn., 2004—05, under sec., health, 2005—06; sr. v.p. quality HCA Inc., 2006, pres., clin. svcs., chief med. officer, 2006—. Adj. prof., medicine & biomedical informatics Vanderbilt U. Contbr. articles to profl. jours. Bd. dirs. Nat. Quality Forum, Joint Commn., Meharry Med. Coll., Am. Health Info. Cmty.; fellow Am. Coll. of Physicians, Am. Coll. of Med. Informatics. Recipient Disting. Alumnus, Founders Medal, Assn. of Mil. Surgeons of the US; named one of 15 Most Influential Physician Execs. in US, Modern Healthcare, nine hon. mems., Spl. Forces Assn. & Green Berets. Fellow: ACP. Office: HCA Inc One Park Plz Nashville TN 37203 Office Phone: 615-344-9551. Business E-Mail: jonathan.perlin@hcahealthcare.com. *

PERLIN, SEYMOUR, psychiatrist, educator; b. Passaic, NJ, Sept. 27, 1925; s. Samuel and Fanny (Horowitz) P.; m. Ruth Joan Rudolph, Aug. 21, 1958; children: Jonathan Brian, Steven Michael, Jeremy Francis. Student, Johns Hopkins U., 1943-44; BA summa cum laude, Princeton U., 1946; MD, Columbia U., 1950; grad., Washington Psychoanalytic Inst. Diplomate Am. Bd. Psychiatry and Neurology. Intern Univ. Hosp., Ann Arbor, Mich., 1951-52; resident N.Y. State Psychiat. Inst., 1950-51, 53-54, Manhattan State Hosp., 1952; practice medicine specializing in psychiatry and psychoanalysis Bethesda, Md., 1954-59, Stanford, Calif., 1959-60, NYC, 1960-63, Balt., 1964-72, Bethesda, 1974—; chief div. psychiatry Montefiore Hosp., 1960-63; dir. clin. care and tng. Henry Phipps Psychiat. Clinic, Johns Hopkins Hosp., 1964-72; sr. research scholar Ctr. for Bioethics, Kennedy Inst., Georgetown U., Washington, 1974-78; clin. prof. psychiatry UCLA Sch. Medicine, 1973-74, George Washington U. Sch. Medicine, 1974-76, prof. to prof. emeritus, 1977-97, 97—, also dir. residency tng., 1977-93; lectr. psychiatry Columbia U., 1963-64; assoc. prof. psychiatry Johns Hopkins Sch. Medicine, 1964-65, prof., 1966-72, dep. chmn. dept. psychiatry and behavioral scis., 1969-72; program dir. Fellowship Program in Suicidology, 1967-72; adv. council Univ. health services Princeton, 1970-82. Vis. fellow Princeton U., 1973, Oxford U., 1974; Joseph P. Kennedy fellow medicine, law and ethics, 1974-75; chief sect. psychiatry Lab. Clin. Sci., NIMH, 1955-59, mem. clin. program-project com., 1967-70; fellow Ctr. Advanced Study in Behavioral Scis., 1959-60; chmn. mental health study sect. B, div. research grants NIH, 1964-66; cons. Community Mental Health Services, Md. Dept. Mental Hygiene, 1964-72; chmn. bd. dirs. Youth Suicide Nat. Ctr., 1985-87. Cons. editor: Jour. Suicide and Life Threatening Behavior, 1970-89; editorial bd.: Johns Hopkins Med. Jour, 1970-72; editor: Handbook for the Study of Suicide; co-editor: Ethical Issues in Death and Dying; contbr. numerous articles to med. jours. Served with USNR, 1944-46, with USPHS, 1954-58. Recipient Meirhoff award in pathology, 1950, Bicentennial Silver medal for achievement in psychiatry, 1967, both Coll. Phys. and Surg. Columbia. Fellow Am. Psychiat. Assn. (named Disting. Life fellow 2003); mem. Am. Coll. Psychiatry, Washington Psychoanalytic Soc., Med. Soc. D.C., Washington Psychiat. Soc., Am. Assn. Suicidology (pres. 1969-70, Dublin award 1978, ann. lectr. in suicidology in his name George Washington U. 1995), Phi Beta Kappa. Home and Office: 5125 Westbard Ave Bethesda MD 20816-1413 Office Phone: 301-229-5330.

PERLITZ, YURI, gynecologist; b. Romania, May 19, 1960; MD, Technion, Israeli Inst. Tech., Haifa, 1989. Dept. ob-gyn. dir. maternal fetal medicine unit Baruch Padeh Med. Ctr., Poria, 2010—. Clin. lectr. Technion, Israel Inst. Tech., 2005. Named Outstanding Physician, Baruch Padeh Med. Ctr., Outstanding Lectr., Technion, Israel Inst. Tech. Mem.: Israeli Maternal Fetal Medicine Orgn. (bd. dirs. 2007—). Avocations: skiing, gardening, hiking. Office: MPO Galil Hatachton Tiberias 15208 Israel Office Fax: 972-4-6652487. Business E-Mail: yperlitz@poria.health.gov.il.

PERLMAN, JOEL A., hospital administrator; CPA. Various positions Ernst & Young LLP; CFO St. Francis Med. Ctr., NJ; sr. v.p. finance dept. Montefiore Med. Ctr., exec. v.p. finance dept., CFO. Office: Montefiore Medical Center 111 E 210th St Bronx NY 10467 Office Phone: 718-920-4964. Office Fax: 718-515-5315.

PERLMUTTER, DAVID H., physician, educator; b. Bklyn., May 11, 1952; s. Herman Arthur and Ruth (Jacobs) P.; m. Barbara Ann Cohlan, Feb. 7, 1981; children: Andrew, Lisa. BA, U. Rochester, 1974; MD, St. Louis U., 1978. Cert. Pediatrics, 1983, Pediatric Gastroenterology and Nutrition, 1990. Intern then resident in pediatrics U. Pa. Sch. Medicine, Phila., 1978-81; fellow in pediatric gastroenterology Harvard U. Sch. Medicine, Boston, 1981-84, instr.

pediatrics, 1983-85, asst. prof. pediatrics, 1985-86; Donald Strominger prof. of pediatrics Washington U. Sch. Medicine, St. Louis, 1986-89, prof. cell biology, physiology, 1989—2001; dir. gastroenterology and nutrition divsn. St. Louis Children's Hosp., 1992—2001; Vira I. Heinz prof. and chair pediatrics U. Pitts. Sch. Medicine, 2001—, prof. cell biology and physiology, 2001—; physician in chief, sci. dir. Children's Hosp. Pitts., 2001—. Editl. bd.: Hepatology, Am. Jour. Physiology; cons. editor: Pediatric Rsch.; contbr. articles to profl. jours. Recipient Established Investigator award Am. Heart Assn., 1987, Rsch. Scholar award Am. Gastroent. Assn., 1985, RJR Nabisco Co., 1986, E. Mead Johnson award for Rsch. in Pediatrics, 1994. Mem. Inst. Medicine, Am. Pediatric Soc., Assn. Am. Physicians, Am. Assn. for the Study of Liver Disease, Soc. Pediatric Rsch. (coun. rep. 1990—, former pres.), Am. Soc. Cell Biology, Am. Soc. Clin. Investigation. Office: Dept Pediatrics Ste 3300 3705 5th Ave DeSoto Wing Pittsburgh PA 15213 Office Phone: 412-692-8071. E-mail: david.perlmutter@chp.edu.

PERLMUTTER, SAUL, astrophysicist, educator; AB in Physics (magna cum laude), Harvard U., 1981; PhD in Physics, U. Calif. Berkeley, 1986. Postdoctoral rschr. Space Sci. Lab., Lawrence Berkeley Nat. Lab., 1987—88; sr. staff scientist, astrophysicist Lawrence Berkeley Nat. Lab.; prof., physics dept. U. Calif. Berkeley, 2004—. Leader Internat. Supernova Cosmology Project, 1998—. Contbr. articles to profl. jours., to Sky and Telescope mag.; guest appearances Pub. Broadcasting Sys., BBC documentaries on astronomy and cosmology. Recipient Henri Chretien award, Am. Astronomical Soc., 1996, Breakthrough of Yr. award, Science Mag., 1998, E.O. Lawrence award in Physics, Dept. Energy, 2002, John Scott award, 2005, Padua prize, 2005, Feltrinelli Internat. prize, Phys. and Math. Scis., Lincei Acad., Rome, 2006; co-recipient Shaw prize in Astronomy, Shaw Found., Hong Kong, 2006, Gruber Cosmology prize, 2007; named Scientist of Yr., Calif., 2003. Fellow: Am. Acad. Arts & Scis. Achievements include discovery of the universe's accelerating expansion using supernovae as "standard candles" to measure the cosmic expansion rate. Office: Lawrence Berkeley Lab 50-232 Univ Calif 392 LeConte Berkeley CA 94720 Office Phone: 510-486-5203, 510-642-3596. Office Fax: 510-486-5401. Business E-Mail: saul@lbl.gov.

PERLOFF, JOSEPH KAYLE, cardiologist, educator; b. New Orleans, Dec. 21, 1924; s. Richard and Rose (Cohen) P.; m. Marjorie G. Mintz; children: Nancy L., Carey E. BA, Tulane U., 1945; postgrad., U. Chgo., 1946-47; MD, La. State U., New Orleans, 1951; MA (hon.), U. Pa., 1973. Diplomate Am. Bd. Internal Medicine, Am. Bd. Cardiovascular Disease. Intern Mt. Sinai Hosp., NYC, 1951-52, resident in pathology, 1952-53, resident in medicine, 1953-54; Fulbright fellow Inst. Cardiology, London, 1954-55; resident in medicine Georgetown U. Hosp., Washington, 1955-56, fellow in cardiology, 1956-57; from clin. instr. to prof. Georgetown U. Sch. Medicine, Washington, 1957-72, dir. cardiac diagnostic lab., 1959-68, asst. dir. divsn. cardiology, 1968-72; prof. medicine and pediat. U. Pa. Sch. Medicine, Phila., 1972-77, chief cardiovascular sect., 1972-77; prof. medicine and pediatrics UCLA Sch. Medicine, 1977—, Streisand/AHA chair in cardiology, 1983. Cons. Nat. Heart, Blood and Lung Inst.; dir. UCLA Adult Congenital Heart Disease Ctr. Author: The Cardiomyopathies, 1988, Physical Exam Heart and Circulation, 1990, 4th edit., 2009, Clinical Recognition of Congenital Heart Disease, 5th edit., 2003, 6th edit., 2011, Congenital Heart Disease in Adults, 3rd edit., 2009. Ensign USN, 1943—46, PTO. Recipient The Best of UCLA award Chancellor's Selection, 1987; Residency Career Devel. award NIH, 1959-69, Sherman M. Mellinkoff award UCLA Med. Sch., 2000, Extraordinay Merit award, 2004, Fellow ACP, Am. Coll. Cardiology(Lifetime Achievement award 2008); mem. Am. Fedn. Clin. Rsch., Assn. Univ. Cardiologists, Alpha Omega Alpha. Office: UCLA Sch Medicine Cardiology 47 123 Chs Los Angeles CA 90024 Office Phone: 310-825-2019. Personal E-mail: josephperloff@earthlink.net.

PERLOFF, ROBERT, psychologist, educator; b. Phila., Feb. 3, 1921; s. Myer and Elizabeth (Sherman) P.; m. Evelyn Potechin, Sept. 22, 1946; children: Richard Mark, Linda Sue, Judith Kay. AB, Temple U., 1949; MA, Ohio State U., 1949, PhD, 1951; DSc (hon.), Oreg. Grad. Sch. Profl. Psychology, 1984; DLitt (hon.), Calif. Sch. Profl. Psychology, 1985. Diplomate Am. Bd. Profl. Psychology. Instr. edn. Antioch Coll., 1950—51; with pers. rsch. br. Dept. Army, 1951—55, chief statis. rsch. and cons. unit., 1953—55; dir. R & D Sci. Rsch. Assocs., Inc., Chgo., 1955—59; vis. lectr. Chgo. Tchrs. Coll., 1955—56; mem. faculty Purdue U., 1958—59, prof. psychology, 1964—69; 1961field assessment officer univ. Peace Corps Chile III project, 1962; Disting. Svc. prof. bus. adminstrn. and psychology U. Pitts. Joseph M. Katz Grad. Sch. Bus., 1969—90, Disting. Svc. prof. emeritus, 1991—; dir. rsch. programs U. Pitts. Grad. Sch. Bus., 1969—77; dir. Consumer Panel, 1980—83. Bd. dirs. Book Ctr.; adv. com. assessment exptl. manpower R & D labs. NAS, 1972-74; mem. rsch. rev. com. NIMH, 1976-80, Stress and Families rsch. project, 1976-79; cons. in field. Contbr. articles to profl. jours.; editor Indsl. Psychologist, 1963-65, Evaluator Intervention: Pros and Cons; book rev. editor Personnel Psychology, 1952-55; co-editor: Values, Ethics and Standards Sourcebook, 1979, Improving Evaluations; bd. consulting editors Jour. Applied Psychology; bd. advs. Archives History Am. Psychology, Psychol. Svc. Pitts., Recorded Psychol. Jours.; guest editor Am. Psychologist, 1972, Edn. and Urban Soc., 1977, Profl. Psychology, 1977; adv. editor Contemporary Psychology, 1994—. Bd. dirs., v.p. Sr. Citizens Svc. Corp., Calif. Sch. Profl. Psychology; bd. dirs. Greater Pitts. chpt. ACLU, sec., 1997-98; chmn. nat. adv. com. Inst. Govt. and Pub. Affairs, U. Ill., 1986-89, sec. nat. adv. com., 1997—; mem. adv. com. Cornell Inst. for Rsch. on Children, 2002—. Decorated Bronze Star; recipient Legacy award, Greater Pitts. Psychol. Assn., 2001, Hist. Preservation award, City of Pitts., 2002; named in his honor, Robert Perloff Grad. Rsch. Assistantship in Inst. Govt. and Pub. Affairs, U. Ill., 1990, in his honor, Robert Perloff Career Achievement award, Knowledge Utilization Soc., 1991. Fellow: APA (mem.-at-large exec. com. divsn. consumer psychology 1964—67, coun. reps. 1965—68, pres. divsn. 1967—68, chmn. sci. affairs com., divsn. consumer psychology 1968—69, edn. and tng. bd. 1969—72, mem.-at-large exec. com. divsn. consumer psychology 1970—71, coun. reps. 1972—74, dir. 1974—82, chmn. fin. com., treas. 1975—84, chmn. investment com. 1977—82, pres. 1985, adv. bd., bd. sci. affairs 1994—96, task force intelligence and Intelligence Tests, author column Std. Deviations in jour., pres. address selected as one of 50 over 50 yrs.), AAAS, Ea. Psychol. Assn. (dir. 1977—80, pres. 1980—81); mem.: Coun. of Sci. Soc. (found. alumnus, pres. 1998—), Knowledge Utilization Soc. (pres. 1993—95), Soc. Psychologists in Mgmt. (pres. 1993—94, Disting. Contbn. to Psychology Mgmt. award 1989), Am. Evaluation Assn. (pres. 1977—78), Am. Psychol. Found. (v.p. 1988—89, pres. 1990—92, trustee 1995—98, Lifetime Achievement in Psychology Gold Medal award 2000), Assn. for Consumer Rsch. (chmn. 1970—71), Pa. Psychol. Assn. (Disting. Svc. award 1985), Internat. Assn. Applied Psychology, Am. Psychol. Soc., Phi Beta Kappa, Psi Chi, Beta Gamma Sigma, Sigma Xi (pres. U. Pitts. chpt. 1989—91). Home: 815 Saint James St Pittsburgh PA 15232-2112 Office Phone: 412-648-1554. Business E-Mail: rperloff@katz.pitt.edu.

PERLSTADT, HARRY, medical sociology educator; b. Chgo., Aug. 23, 1942; s. Sidney M. and Mildred (Penn) Perlstadt; m. Tari Chrystal Taylor, Aug. 4, 1968; children: Emily, Roger. BA, U. Mich., 1963; MA, U. Chgo., 1966, PhD, 1973; MPH, U. Mich., 1979. Prof. med. sociology Mich. State U., East Lansing, 1968—, dir. program in bioethics, humanities and society, 2003—07; fulbright lectr. Semmelweis U., Budapest, Hungary, 2010. Evaluation cons. Kellogg Found., 1986-97, Mich. Dept. Pub. Health and Mich. State U., 1987-91, COSMOS Corp. and NIMH, Washington, 1988-90, Mott Children's Health Ctr., 1991-95, WHO, 2002-03, Mich. Dept. Cmty. Health and Health Resources and Svcs. Adminstrn., U.S. Dept HHS, 1999-2000. Chair Mich. Coalition Smoking or Health, Lansing, 1984-92; mem. Mich. Tobacco Reduction Task Force, Lansing, 1989, Tobacco Free Mich. Action Coalition, Lansing, 1990-94; chair Commn. on Applied and Clin. Sociology, 1995-2004; rsch. agenda com. Ctrs. for Disease Control, 2005-06. NIMH postdoctoral fellow, U. Mich., 1977-78; recipient Pub. Svc. Achievement award Am. Lung Assn. Mich., 1985. Mem. APHA (governing coun. 1990-95, 2004-06, exec. bd. 2002-04, sci. bd. 2000-08), Am. Sociol. Assn. (chair sociol. practice sect. 1998-99, Soc. Applied Sociology (editor The Useful Sociologist 1987-89), Mich. Pub. Health Assn. (pres. 1988-89), Am. Lung Assn. (nat. coun. 1999-2009, sci. adv. com. 2003-09), Am. Lung Assn. Midland States (chair, 2010-). Avocations: dance, reading, history. Office: Mich State U Sociology/Berkey Hall East Lansing East Lansing MI 48824-1111 Business E-Mail: perlstad@msu.edu.

PERMUT, STEPHEN ROBERT, physician, educator; b. Olympia, Wash., Sept. 24, 1945; s. Max L. and Ruth E. (Epstein) Permut; m. Marylene Quiambao, Apr. 20, 1974; children: Laura, Irene. AB, U. Pa., 1967; MD, Temple U. Sch. Medicine, Phila., 1972; JD, Widener U. Sch. Law, Chester, Pa., 1985. Bar: Pa. 1985; diplomate Am. Bd. Internal Medicine, Am. Bd. Family Medicine. Intern internal medicine Ind. U. Med. Ctr., Indpls., 1972—73, resident, 1973—75; program dir. St. Francis Hosp., Wilmington, Del., 1976-85, v.p. med. affairs, 1993-96; med. dir. Blue Cross Blue Shield Del., Wilmington, 1985-90; spl. counsel Saul, Ewing, Remick & Saul, Phila., 1990-93; prof., chmn. dept. family & cmty. medicine Temple U. Sch. Medicine, Phila., 1994—, asst. dean academic affiliations, 1999—. Contbr. articles to profl. jours. Pres. Children's Bur. Del., Wilmington, 1986—89. Fellow: ACP, Coll. Physicians Phila., American Coll. Legal Medicine, American Acad. Family Physicians; mem.: AMA (mem. coun. legislation 1999—2007, bd. trustees 2010—, bd. dirs. 2010—), ABA, Med. Soc. Del. (bd. trustees 1979—, v.p. 1990—91, pres.-elect 1991—92, pres. 1992—93, Disting. Svc. award1987, Pres.'s award 1989), New Castle County Med. Soc., Pa. Bar Assn. Office: Temple U Sch Medicine 3500 N Broad St Philadelphia PA 19140-5104 Office Phone: 215-707-4610. Business E-Mail: spermut@temple.edu.

PERNA, GIAMPAOLO ROBERT, psychiatrist, researcher; b. Hartford, Conn., Nov. 16, 1964; s. Enrico Roberto Perna and Teiko Ikeda; 1 child, Alessandro John. MD, State U. Milan, 1990, PhD in Psychiatry and Behavioral Scis., 1994. Vice chief Anxiety Clin. and Rsch. Unit San Raffaele Hosp., Milan, 2009; chief, dept. clin. neurosci. San Benedetto Hosp. Hermanas Hospitalarias, 2009—. Asst. prof., psychiatry Faculty Medicine and Surgery Vita-Salute U., Milan, 2000—03; assoc. dir., master, affective neurosci. U. Maastricht, U. Florence, 2004—; vis. prof. Faculty Life Scis., Health and Medicine Maastricht U., 2008—. Contbr. scientific papers to publs. ECNP fellowship, 2007. Mem.: Italian Soc. Psychopathology, Italian Soc. Psychiatry, NY Acad. Scis. Avocations: tennis, computers. Office: San Benedetto Hosp Dept Clin Neuroscis Via Roma 16 Albese con Cassano Como 22032 Italy Office Phone: 0039-0314291539. Personal E-mail: pernagp@tin.it.

PERNAZZA, GRAZIANO, surgeon; b. Rome, Apr. 17, 1974; Degree in Medicine and Surgery, Sapienza U. Rome, 1999; degree in Gen. Surgery, Tor Vergata U. Rome, 2005. Attending surgeon Misericordia Hosp., 2005—08, Az Osp San Giovanni-Addolorata, 2008—. Cons. robotic surgery Az Osp San Camillo-Forlanini, 2007—08; nat. vice-sec. Assn. Chirurghi Ospedalieri Italiani, 2008—11; founding mem. Clin. Robotic Surgery Assn., 2009—11. Mem.: Clin. Robotic Surgery Assn., Soc. Italiana Chirurgia, Assn. Chirurghi Ospedalieri Italiani. Office: Amba Aradam St 9 Rome 00100 Italy Office Phone: +390677055376. Office Fax: +3906770579131. E-mail: gpernazza@gmail.com.

PERNICIARO, CHARLES VINCENT, dermatologist, dermatopathologist, educator, entrepreneur; b. New Orleans, June 15, 1957; s. Ernest Gabriel and Phereby Sheppard Perniciaro; children: Jamie Lynn, Kelly Gabrielle. BS, U. La., Lafayette, 1979; MD, La. State U., New Orleans, 1983. Diplomate Am. Bd. Dermatology, Am. Bd. Dermatology and Pathology. Staff physician Ochsner Clin. of Baton Rouge, La., 1987-90; sr. assoc. cons. and staff dermatologist Mayo Clinic, Jacksonville, Fla., 1990-93, cons., staff dermatologist and dermatopathologist, 1993-99; pvt. practice dermatology Brunswick, Ga., 1999—2008, Neptune Beach, Fla., 1999—2006, Ponte Vedra Beach, Fla., 2006—; dir. dermatopathology Bernhardt Labs. Aurora Diagnostics, Jacksonville, Fla., 2001—. Pres., CEO Holiday Lighting Concepts, Inc., 1996-2000; lectr., presenter in field; adj. clin. assoc. prof. pathology U. Fla. Shands Jacksonville Med. Ctr., 1999-2001. Contbr. articles to profl. jours. Founder, bd. dirs. S.W. La. Skin Cancer Found., 1987. Recipient Outstanding Paper award Noah Worcester Dermatol. Soc., 1993, First Place Poster award 17th Internat. Colloquium Dermatopathology, 1996; named one of Best Doctors, 2000-, How to Find the Best Fla. Doctors, 2000, Am. Top Physicians, 2003-05. Fellow: Am. Soc. Dermatopathology (chmn. membership com., bd. dirs. 2000—01), Am. Acad. Dermatology (com. on preventive dermatology 1988—90, task force on dermatologic oncology 1990—93, environ. coun. 1994—96, adv. coun. 1995—2001, adv. bd. 2006—07); mem.: Noah Worcester Derm Soc. (bd. dirs. 2011—), So. Med. Assn. (vice chair sect. dermatology 1995—96, chair-elect 2001—06, chair 2006—07, Resident-in-Tng. award 1994), Fla. Soc. Dermatology (bd. dirs. 1998—2006, chmn. membership com. 1999—2002, v.p. 2002—03, pres. 2003—04, Practitioner of Yr. 2009), Jacksonville Dermatology Soc. (sec.-treas. 1995, pres. 1996, webmaster 2003—04), Lions (charter, bd. dirs. Ponte Vedra Beach 1997—98). Avocations: tennis, computers. Home: 1750 Beach Ave Atlantic Beach FL 32233 Office: 183 Landrum Lane Ste 201 Ponte Vedra Beach FL 32082 also: 5008 Mustang Rd Jacksonville FL 32216

PERO, ALICE NEUMAN, community health and rehabilitation nurse; b. Phila., May 31, 1941; d. Andrew and Dorothy (Vucetich) Neuman; m. Kenneth E. Pero, Aug. 26, 1961; children: Kristine, Kenneth, Jeffrey. Diploma in nursing, Abington Meml. Hosp., Pa., 1962. RN, Pa. Staff nurse Community Nursing Svc., Phila., 1962-64, 76-89; community health nurse Vis. Nurse Assn. Ea. Montgomery County, Abington, 1989-91; discharge planning nurse Abington Meml. Hosp., 1991-95, case mgr., 1995—2005, case mgmt., 2007—10. Participant pub. health tour, USSR, 1982. Recipient Outstanding Nurse award Vis. Nurse Assn., 1983, Legion of Honor for Community Svc., City of Phila., 1980. Mem. Abington Meml. Hosp. Sch. Nursing Alumni Assn. (pres., co-pres.) Home: 12 Preswyck Ln Seaville NJ 08230

PEROS-GOLUBICIC, TATJANA, pulmonologist; b. V.Greda, Croatia, July 20, 1949; d. Vjekoslav and Milena Peros; m. Zdravko Golubicic; 1 child, Masha Golubicic. MD, Med. Sch. Zagreb, 1974, PhD, 1982. Pulmonary specialist U. Hosp. Lung Disease, Zagreb, Croatia, 1974—88, dept. head, 1998—. Prof. internal medicine U. Zagreb, Med. Sch., Croatia, 1998—. Author: (book) Sarcoidosi Interstitial Lung Disease. Mem.: World Assn. Sarcoidosis and Other Granulomatous Disease, WASOG-World Assn., ERS-European Respiratory Soc. Office: Univ Hosp Lung Disease Jordanovac 104 Zagreb 10000 Croatia Home: Kamaufova Ulica 3 10-000 Zagreb Croatia Office Phone: 38512385141. Office Fax: 38512348345. Personal E-mail: tperos-golubicic@net.hr.

PERPATI, GEORGIA, physician; b. Athens, Greece, Nov. 1, 1970; MD, Plovdiv Med. Sch., 1996; PhD, U. Athens, 2011. Ambulance physician Emergency Med. Transp., Athens, 2004—06; resident, fellow, rsch. assoc. Adult Cystic Fibrosis Unit, 1998—2009, responsible CF physician, 2009—. Med. mgr. Oncology-Lung Cancer-Roche SA, 2006—09; med. affairs physician clin. R & D dept. Wyeth Pharms., 2009. Mem.: ERS, ECFS. Home: Thrasyvoulou 7 Athens Attiki 153 43 Greece Personal E-mail: georgiaperpati@yahoo.com.

PERREAULT, PAUL R., biotechnology company executive; B in Psychology, U. Ctrl. Fla., Orlando; completed advanced bus. mgmt. tng., Kellogg Sch. Bus., Wharton Sch. Bus.; completed, CSL Exec. Leadership Program. Various positions including area bus. dir., mgr. mktg. program and dist. sales mgr. Wyeth-Ayerst Laboratories; v.p., gen. mgr. N.Am. and PR bus. units Aventis Behring Hosp. Products; mgr. environ. and safety health team and corp. mktg. dept. Aventis Bio-Services, v.p., gen. mgr. plasma ops.; v.p., gen. mgr. US comml. ops. CSL Behring, exec. v.p. worldwide comml. ops., pres. Bd. dirs. Plasma Protein Therapeutics Assn. Office: CSL Behring 1020 First Ave PO Box 61501 King Of Prussia PA 19406-0901 Office Phone: 610-878-4000. Office Fax: 610-878-4009.

PERRET, GERARD ANTHONY, JR., orthodontist; b. New Orleans, Feb. 13, 1959; s. Gerard A. and Marie M. (Gamino) P.; m. Catherine J. McMahon, 1996; 1 child, Caroline Marie. BS in Chemistry, U. N.C., 1981; DDS, La. State U., 1986, cert. orthodontics, 1989. Diplomate Am. Bd. Orthodontists. Clin. asst. prof. La. State U. Sch. Dentistry, New Orleans, 1986-87; pvt. practice dentistry Lakeside Dental Group, Metairie, La., 1986-87; pvt. practice orthodontics Jacksonville, Fla., 1989-91, Tampa, Fla., 1991—; founder, pres. Orthogap, Inc., Tampa, 1993—, Rodent Realty, Inc., 2001—. Patentee in field. Active mem. New Tampa C. of C.; chmn. New Tampa Rotary Found., Inc., 2003—11. Mem. Am. Assn. Orthodontists, Fla. Assn. Orthodontists, Hillsborough County Dental Soc., Hillsborough County Dental Rsch. Clinic, So. Assn. Orthodontists, Rotary (pres. New Tampa chpt. 1997-98), Omicron Kappa Upsilon. Avocations: sailing, fishing, music, golf. Home: 16014 Penwood Dr Tampa FL 33647-1137 Office: 15283 Amberly Dr Tampa FL 33647 Home Phone: 813-972-7483; Office Phone: 813-977-2828.

PERRIMON, NORBERT JEAN PAUL, medical geneticist, educator; b. Bosguerard, France, Oct. 24, 1958; naturalized, US, 2005; s. Marcel Perrimon and Francine Ferret; m. Lizabeth A. Perkins; children: Pamela, Sarah. PhD, U. Paris VI, 1983; MS (hon.), Harvard U., 1996. Postdoctoral fellow Case Western Res. U., Cleve., 1983-86; asst. prof. genetics Harvard Med. Sch., Boston, 1986-93, assoc. prof. genetics, 1993-96, prof. genetics, 1996—; asst. investigator Howard Hughes Med. Inst., 1986—93, assoc. investigator, 1993—97, investigator, 1997—; assoc. mem. Broad Inst., Cambridge, Mass., 2006—. Mem. editl. bd. Mechanisms of Devel., 1999-, BioMed Ctrl. Devel. Biology, 2000-, Molecular and Cellular Biology, 2000-, Internat. Jour. Devel. Biology, 2002-, BioMed Ctrl. Genomics, 2005-, Genome Biology, 2008-, Sci. Signaling, 2008-; assoc. editor PLoS Genetics, 2008-. Recipient Chaire d'Etat, College de France, Paris, 2003, George W. Beadle medal, Genetics Soc. America, 2004; Lucille Markey scholar, 1985-86. Fellow: Am. Acad. Arts and Sciences. Office: Howard Hughes Med Inst Dept Genetics Harvard Med Sch 77 Ave Louis Pasteur Boston MA 02115 Office Phone: 617-432-7672. Office Fax: 617-432-7688. E-mail: perrimon@receptor.med.harvard.edu.

PERRIN, EDWARD BURTON, biomedical researcher, public health educator; b. Greensboro, Vt., Sept. 19, 1931; s. J. Newton and Dorothy E. (Willey) P.; m. Carol Anne Hendricks, Aug. 18, 1956; children: Jenifer, Scott. BA, Middlebury Coll., 1953; student in Stats., Edinburgh U., Scotland, 1953—54; MA in Math. Stats., Columbia U., 1956; PhD, Stanford U., 1961. Asst. prof. dept. biostats. U. Pitts., 1959-62; asst. prof. dept. preventive medicine U. Wash., Seattle, 1962-65, assoc. prof., 1965-69, prof., 1969-70, prof., chmn. dept. biostats., 1970-72, prof. dept. health svcs., adj. prof. dept. biostats., 1975-98, chmn. dept., 1983-94, prof. emeritus, 1999—; hon. prof. West China U. of Med. Scis., Szechwan, China, 1988-98; overseas fellow Churchill Coll., Cambridge U., 1991-92; sr. scientist Seattle Vets. Affairs Med. Ctr., 1994—2001. Biometrician VA Co-op Study on Treatment of Esophageal Varices, 1961—73; sr. cons. biostatistics Wash., Alaska regional med. programs, 1967—72; mem. epidemiology & disease control study sect. NIH, 1969—73; clin. prof. dept. cmty. medicine and internat. health Sch. Medicine, Georgetown U., Washington, 1972—75; dep. dir. Nat. Ctr. Health Stats. HEW, 1972—73, dir., 1973—75; rsch. scientist Health Care Study Ctr.

Battelle Human Affairs Rsch. Ctr., Seattle, 1975—76, dir., 1976—78, Health & Population Study Ctr. Battelle Human Affairs Rsch. Ctr., 1978—83; chmn. health svcs. rsch. study sect. HEW, 1976—79; chmn. health svcs. R & D field program rev. panel VA, 1988—91; chmn. health svcs. info steering com. State of Wash., 1993—94; mem. nat. adv. coun. Agy. for Health Care Policy & Rsch. Dept. HHS U.S. Govt., 1994—97; mem. com. on nat. stats. NRC, NAS, 1994—2000; chmn. sci. adv. com. Med. Outcomes Trust, 1994—99; mem. report rev. com. NAS, 2005—. Contbr. articles on biostats., health svcs. and population studies to profl. publs.; mem. editl. bd.: Jour. Family Practice, 1978-90, Pub. Health Nursing, 1992-98. Mem. tech. bd. Milbank Meml. Fund, 1974-76, Health Svcs. and Outcomes Rsch. Methodology, 1999-04. Recipient Outstanding Svc. citation HEW, 1975; Fulbright scholar 1953-54. Fellow AAAS, APHA (Spiegelman Health Stats. award 1970, program devel. bd. 1971, chmn. stats. sect. 1978-80, governing coun. 1983-85, stats. sect. recognition award 1989), Am. Statis. Assn. (mem. adv. com. to divsn. statis. policy 1975-77); mem. Assn. Health Svcs. Rsch. (pres. 1994-95, bd. dirs. 1991-2000), Inst. Medicine of NAS (chmn. membership com. 1984-86, mem. bd. on health care svcs. 1987-96, forum health stats. 1994-95, chmn. com. on clin. evaluation 1990-93), Biometrics Soc. (pres. Western N.Am. Region 1971), Wash. State Acad. Scis. (bd. dirs. 2007-09), U. Wash. Retirement Assn. (bd. dirs. 2006—, v.p. 2009-10, pres. 2011-), Sigma Xi, Phi Beta Kappa. Home: 116 Fairview Ave N Unit 728 Seattle WA 98109-5374

PERRIN, JAMES MARC, pediatrician, researcher; b. Pitts., Oct. 28, 1942; s. Samuel R Perrin, Ethel K Perrin; m. Ellen C Coser; children: Andrew, Benjamin. AB, Harvard Coll., 1964; MD, Case Western Res. U. Sch. Medicine, Cleve., 1968. Diplomate Am. Bd. Pediat. Intern pediat. Strong Meml. Hosp., Rochester, NY, 1968—69, resident, 1971—73, fellow, 1973—74; asst. prof. pediat. Vanderbilt U. Med. Sch., Nashville, 1977—86; dir. divsn. gen. pediat. Mass. Gen. Hosp. for Children, Boston, 1986—, dir. Ctr. Child & Adolescent Health Policy, 1998—; prof. pediat. Harvard Med. Sch., 2001—. Mem. Nat. Commn. Childhood Disability, Washington, 1995, Nat. Adv. Coun. Health Care Quality, Washington, 1998—2002. Author: Home and Community Care for Chronically Ill Children, 1993; founding editor-in-chief: Ambulatory Pediatrics, 1998—; contbr. articles to profl. jours. Recipient Investigator award in health policy rsch., Robert Wood Johnson Found., 1998—2001. Mem.: Am. Acad. Pediat. (chair nat. com. children with disabilities 1992—96, Rsch. award 0208), Ambulatory Pediatric Assn. (pres. 1997—98, Pub. Policy award 2001, George Armstrong award 2004). Office: Mass Gen Hosp Children Child & Adolescent Health Ste 901 50 Staniford St Boston MA 02114 Office Phone: 617-726-8716. Office Fax: 617-726-1886. Business E-Mail: jperrin@partners.org. *

PERRONNET, CAROLINE, research scientist; b. Longjumeau, France, Oct. 24, 1982; PhD, U. Paris-Sud, 2011. Postdoc. rschr. dept. cellular and physiol. scis. U. BC, 2011—. Home: 45 Chemin des Mules S Nazaire 44600 France Personal E-mail: caroline.perronnet@ubc.ca.

PERROS, MANOS, medical researcher; PhD, Inst. Pasteur. Sr. dir., interim head obesity biology Pfizer, Sandwich, England, sr. dir. urology, gynecology and pain biology, v.p., head antiviral rsch., 2007—09; dir. Novartis Inst. Tropical Diseases (NITD), Singapore, 2009—. Avocations: skiing, scuba diving, piano. Office: Novartis Institute for Tropical Deseases 10 Biopolis Rd Chromos # 05-01 Singapore 138 670 Singapore *

PERRY, GEORGE, dean, neuroscientist, educator; s. George Richard and Mary Arlene (George) P.; m. Paloma Aguilar, May 21, 1983; children: Anne, Elizabeth. AA in Liberal Arts, Allan Hancock Coll., Santa Maria, Calif., 1973; BA in Zoology with high honors, U. Calif., Santa Barbara, 1974; PhD in Marine Biology, U. Calif., San Diego, 1979; PhD (hon.), Arturo Prat, Iquique, Chile, 2007. Postdoctoral fellow Baylor Coll. Medicine, Houston, 1979-82; from asst. prof. to prof. pathology Case Western Res. U., Cleve., 1982-94, prof., 1994—2005, interim chair dept., 2001—05; affiliated prof. chemistry and biochemistry U. Alaska, Fairbanks, 2001—; dean Coll. of Sciences U. Tex., San Antonio, 2006—. Tchg. asst. U. Calif., San Diego, 1977, Stanford U., 1978—79; memory task force on Alzheimer's disease Ohio Gov., 1987, 90; mem. sci. adv. bd. Familial Alzheimer's Disease Rsch. Found., 1988—; mem., chair neurology scis. study sect. NIH, Bethesda, Md., 1989—95; cons. Nymox, Inc., Panacea Pharms., Inc., Prion Devel. Labs., Voyager, Takada Pharms., Neurotez Labs., Alzheimer Rsch. Disease and Regeneration Forum, Alzheimer Found. America; mem. Faculty of 1000 Biology, Neurobiology Sect., 2004—; spkr. in field; mem. numerous rev. bds. nationally/internationally. Author: The Neuronal Cytoskeleton, 1992, numerous publs. in field; co-author: Frontiers in Biosciences, 2002, Neurosignals, 2002, Brain Pathology, 2004, Microscopy Rsch. and Technique, 2005, Internat. Jour. Exptl. Pathology, 2005; assoc. editor: Am. Jour. Pathology, 1994-2000, Jour. Biomedicine and Biotechnology, 2004—; sr. assoc. editor: Microscopy Rsch. and Technique, 2002—; mem. editl. bd. Am. Jour. Pathology, 1992—, Alzheimer Disease and Associated Disorders, 1994—, Alzheimer's Disease Rev., 1995-98, Jour. Alzheimer's Disease, 1997—, Jour. Exptl. Neurol., 1997-99, Molecular Chem. Neuropathology, 1997-99, Jour. Neural Transmission, 1998-2003, Investigational Drugs Jour., 1998—, Brain Pathology, 1999—, Jour. Molecular Neurosci., 1999-2001, Antioxidant and Redox Signaling, 2000—, Research Signpost, 2000, Lab. Investigation, 2000—06, Brain Rsch., 2002—, Current Medicinal Chemistry, 2002—, Neurobiology of Lipids, 2003—, Jour. Biomed. Biotech., 2002—, Pathology, 2003—, Pharm. Devel. Regime, 2003—, Med. Chemistry Rev. Online, 2003 05, Current Alzheimer Rsch., 2003—, NeuroSignals, 2003—, Disease Markers, 2003—, Neurobiology Disease, 2004—, Lett Drug Design Discovery, 2004—; reviewer: Expert Review of Neurotherapeutics, 2004—, Mini-Reviews in Medicinal Chemistry, 2005—, Future Neurology, 2005—, Jour. Biological Chemistry, 2006—, Developmental Microbiology and Molecular Biology, 2006—, CNS Agents in Medicinal Chemistry, 2006—, Jour. Clin. Pathology, 2007—, Molecular Neurodegeneration, 2007—, Open Medicinal Chemistry Jour., 2007—, Acta Neuropathol., Alan Liss Publ. Co., Am. Jour. Pathol., Ann Neurol, others; contbr. articles to Exptl. Cell Rsch., Jour Cell Biology, Devel. Biology, Brain Rsch., Am. Jour. Pathology, Jour. Neurosci., European Jour. Cell Biology, Nature, Annals Neurology, Lancet, Acta Neuropathology, Jour. Neurochemistry, Neurosci. Letters, Neuroreport, Med. Hypotheses, Nature Medicine, Neurodegeneration, Sci., others. Pres. Serra Club, 1995-97. Tng. corps. USAR, 1972—74, U. Calif. Santa Barbara. Recipient Bausch and Lomb medal, 1971, Rsch. Career Devel. award, NIH, 1988—93, Temple award, Alzheimer's Assn., 1999, Disting. Am. Portuguese Ancestry award, Portuguese-Am. Hist. Found., Inc., 2001, Mensch award, Alzheimer Rsch. Forum, 2003, Cmty. Svc. award, Cleve. Area Chpt. Alzheimer's Assn., 2004, Zenith award, Alzheimer Assn., 2007, Nat. Honor Plaque Panama, 2011; grantee, NIH, 1985—, Am. Health Assistance Found., 1988—90, 1997—99, Alzheimer's Assn., 1989—90, 1998—2002, 2004—09, United Mitochondrial Disease Fund, 2000—02; fellow, Kennecott Copper, 1974—75, Muscular Dystrophy Assn., 1980—82, Philip Morris, USA, 2003—06. Fellow AAAS,Microscopy Soc. America, Royal Soc. Chemists, Linnean Soc., Royal Soc. Medicine, Biology Soc., Iberoam. Molecular Biology Orgn. ISI Highly Cited Com. Neurosci.; mem. AAUP (case chapter exec. com. 1996—2006, membership chair 1996-98, v.p. 1998-99, pres. 1999—2006), Am. Soc. Cell Biology, Royal Acad. Spain (fgn. corr. mem. 2009), Electron Microscopy Soc. N.E. Ohio (treas. 1986-88, trustee 1988-90, pres. 1990-91), Soc. Neurosci., Am. Assn. Neuropathologists (awards com. 1992-93, 95-2002, chmn. 2001-02, internat. congress neuropathology concilator 1995-2000, sec.-treas. 2003-08, pres. elect. 2007-08, pres. 2008-, past pres. 2009-10, mem. non com. 2010-, chair 2010), Am. Soc. Investigative Pathology (program com. 1998-2001), Am. Soc. Neurochemistry, U.S. and Can. Acad. of Pathology, Hispanic Med. Assn. (com. on status of Portuguese in medicine and sci.), Soc. for Neurosci., Sigma Xi (pres. chpt. 2004-06), Iberoamerican Molecular Biology Orgn., Am. Aging Assn.(Harman Research award, 2008), Soc. Advancements Chicanos and Native Ams. in Scis. (Disting. Profl. Mentor award 2010, Alzheimer award 2010), Dana Alliance Brain Initiatives., Mex. Acad. Scis.(Corr.) Democrat. Roman Catholic. Avocation: genealogy. Office: U Tex San Antonio Coll Scis One UTSA Circle San Antonio TX 78249-0661 Office Phone: 210-458-4450. Business E-Mail: george.perry@utsa.edu.

PERRY, HAROLD OTTO, dermatologist; b. Rochester, Minn., Nov. 18, 1921; s. Oliver and Hedwig Clara (Tornow) P.; m. Loraine Thelma Moehnke, Aug. 27, 1944; children— Preston, Oliver, Ann, John. AA, Rochester Jr. Coll., 1942; BS, U. Minn., 1944, MB, 1946, MD, 1947; MS, Mayo Grad. Sch. Medicine, 1953. Diplomate Am. Bd. Dermatology with spl. competence in dermatopathology. Intern Naval Hosp., Oakland, Calif., 1946-47; resident in dermatology Mayo Grad. Sch. Medicine, 1949-52; practice medicine specializing in dermatology Rochester, 1953-86; mem. staff Mayo Clinic, 1953-86, mem. emeritus staff, 1987—; instr., asst. prof., assoc. prof. Mayo Med. Sch., 1953-86, prof., 1978-83, Robert H. Kieckhefer prof. dermatology, 1978-83, head dept. dermatology, 1975-83, emeritus prof. dermatology, 1987—. Civilian cons. dermatology to surgeon gen. USAF, 1973-. Contbr. articles to med. jours. and, chpts. to books. With USNR, 1943-45, 46-49. Inducted into Rochester (Minn.) C.C. Alumni Hall of Fame, 1993; recipient Disting. Alumnus award Mayo Found., 1995. Mem. AMA, Am. Acad. Dermatology (pres. 1981, Sulzberger internat. lectr. 1986, Gold Medal for visionary leadership 1998), Am. Dermatol. Assn. (bd. dirs. 1985-89, pres. 1989-90), Am. Bd. Dermatology (bd. dirs. 1979-90, v.p. 1989, pres. 1990), Noah Worcester Dermatol. Soc. (pres. 1969), Minn. Dermatol. Soc. (pres. 1967), Chgo. Dermatol. Soc., Internat. Soc. Tropical Dermatology, Minn. Med. Assn., hon. mem. French Dermatol. Soc., Spanish Acad. Dermatology, Brazilian Dermatol. Soc., Ga. Dermatol. Soc., Iowa Dermatol. Soc., Korean Dermatol. Soc., Bolivar Soc. Dermatology, Jacksonville Dermatol. Soc., N.Am. Clin. Dermatol. Soc., Pacific Dermatol. Assn. *

PERRY, HELEN, medical/surgical nurse, secondary school educator; b. Birmingham, Ala., Mar. 4, 1927; d. Van Mary Ellenol (Thornton) Curry, m. Charlie Pitts, May 1960 (div.); 1 child, Charlonia Pitts; m. George Perry (dec. 1989); children: Hattie Mae(dec.), George Jr., Bishop, Jose Sr. Student, LaSalle Extension U., Chgo., 1968; MA in Nat. Security Criminal Justice, Georgetown U., 1979; Doctorate/Mayanuis Mosaic Soc., Duke Univ., San Antonio, 1979; student in Nursing, Syracuse U., 1983; BS in Nursing, Suracuse U., 1989. Cert. paramedic, of completion Ptnrs. in Health Sheperd Ctr. Am. South Side, 2006; LPN, lic. practical nurse, paramedic, Fla. Profl. Acad. Nurse U. Ala., 1955; tchr. Wenona HS City Bd. Edn., Birmingham, 1977—2005, supply tchr., 2005—; founding mem. Internat. Women's Review Bd., 2008; mem. Nation Assn. Profl. Women, 2011—; sr. mem. Jefferson County, 2011. Notary pub., Ala., 1975—; home health nurse U. Ala. Birmingham Hosp., 1988—; math. and reading tutor Princeton Elem. Sch., 2004; founding mem. Review Bd., 2009. Composer: (songs) Twas the Hour of Midnight, 1950. Trustee Nat. Crime Watch, 1989; mem. adv. bd. Am. Security Coun., Va., Washington, 1969—91; mem. Coalition for Desert Storm; others; vol. ARC, Birmingham, 1970—; mem. crime watch Am. Police, Washington, 1989; mem. Hall of Fame Pres. Task Force, Washington, 1983—91, Image Devel. Adv. Bd.; nominee Nat. Rep. Com., Washington, 1991, 1992; selected VIP guest del. Rep. Nat. Conv., Houston, 1992; life mem. Rep. Presdl. Task Force, Washington, 1992; mem. Jefferson Com., 2001; mem. adv. bd. Nat. Congl. Com., Washington; mem. fin. com. fundraiser Middleton for Congress Campaign, 1994, Dist. # 59 Bd. Reps.; mem. exec. com. Jefferson County Rep., chairperson legis. dist. 52; chair Harriet Tubman Rep. Com.; del. Commonwealth of Ky. So. Rep. Leadership Conf., 2000; min. Greater Emmanuel Temple Holiness Ch., Birmingham, 1957—, ordained elder, vice champion mother bd.; apptd. hon. mem. Internat. Women's Review Bd.; apptd. Profl. Women's Adv. Bd.; mem. Nat. Law Enforcement Officer's Assn., 1989. Recipient award, Ala. Sheriff Assn., 1989, Navy League, 1989—91, cert. of appreciation, Pres. Congl. Task Force, 1990, Rep. Nat. Com., 1994, Diamond award, U.S.A. Serve Am., 1992, Rep. Presdl. award, Legion of Merit, 1994, Royal Proclamation, Royal Highness Kevin, Prince Regent of Hutt River Province, 1994, Royal Ceremonial jewel, Svc. award, Ala. Bd. Nursing, Outstanding Sr. Citizen's cert. of recognition, Lifetime Achievement award, Fran Nicholas Law, World Congress Arts Ctr., Ret. Nurse Demonstator Leadership award, UAB Hosp., Svc. award, Ala. Bd. Nursing., Pres. of Ala.; named Good Samaritan, Law Envforcement Officers, Amb., Am. Biog. Inst., Woman of Yr., Cambridge Blue Book; named to Police Hall of Fame, Nat. Crime Watch Pub. Svc.; nominee Presdl. Election Registry, Rep. Presdl. Task Force, 1992. Mem.: Nat. Rep. Com., ICC (clergyman), Am. Assn. Advancement Sci., Pres.'s Task Force, Hon. Sheriff's Assn., Am. Security Coun. (nat. adv. bd.), Nat. Fedn. Rep. Women (trustee bd.), Ala. Nurses Assn., Nat. Assn. Unknown Players, LaSalle Ext. U. Alumni (life), Nat. Rep. Women Assn., Notary Pub. and Notary Soc. Achievements include first ambassador of the US in November 2007. Avocations: singing, writing, reading, gardening. Home: 2321 7th Ave N Apt 321 Pk Pl Birmingham AL 35203-2410 Home Phone: 205-488-9896.

PERRY, JACQUELIN, orthopedist, surgeon; b. Denver, May 31, 1918; d. John F. and Tirzah (Kuruptkat) P. BE, U. Calif., LA, 1940; MD, U. Calif., San Francisco, 1950; DSc (hon.), U. So. Calif., 1996. Intern Children's Hosp., San Francisco, 1950-51; resident in orthop. surgery U. Calif., San Francisco, 1951-55; orthop. surgeon Rancho Los Amigos Hosp., Downey, Calif., 1955—, chief stroke svc., 1972-75; chief pathokinesiology Rancho Los Amigos Med. Ctr., 1961—; mem. faculty U. Calif. Med. Sch., San Francisco, 1966—, clin. prof., 1973—; mem. faculty U. So. Calif. Med. Sch., 1969—, prof. orthop. surgery, 1972—, dir. polio and gait clinic, 1972—. Disting. lectr. for hosp. for spl. surgery and Cornell U. Med. Coll., NYC, 1977-78; Packard Meml. lectr. U. Colo. Med. Sch., 1970; Osgood lectr. Harvard Med. Sch., 1978; Summer lectr., Portland, 1977; Shands lectr.; cons. USAF; guest spkr. symposia; cons. Biomechanics Lab. Centinela Hosp., 1979—. Served as phys. therapist U.S. Army, 1941-46. Recipient Disting. Svc. award Assn. Rehab. Facilities, 1981, Pres.'s award, 1984, Isabelle and Lenard Goldensen award for tech. United Cerebral Palsy Assn., 1981, Jow Dowling award, 1985, Profl. Achievement award UCLA, 1988, Milton Cohen award Nat. Assn. Rehab., 1993, Tribute Pres. award Ruth Jackson Orthop. Soc., 2004; named Woman of Yr. for Medicine in So. Calif. LA Times, 1959, Alumnus of Yr. U. Calif. Med. Sch., 1980, Physician of Yr. Calif. Employment Devel. Dept., 1994; Jacquelin Perry Neuro Trauma Inst. Rancho Clin. Bldg. named in her honor, 1996. Mem. AMA, Am. Acad. Orthop. Surgeons (Kappa Delta award for rsch. 1977, orthop. rsch. svc., 1976), Am. Orthop. Assn. (Shands lectr. 1988), Western Orthop. Assn., Calif. Med. Soc., LA County Med. Soc., Am. Phys. Therapy Assn. (hon. Golden Pen award 1965), Am. Acad. Orthotists and Prosthetists (hon.), Scoliosis Rsch. Soc. (Lifetime Achievement award 2009), LeRoy Abbott Soc., Am. Acad. Cerebral Palsy, Gait & Clin. Movement Analysis Soc. (mem. emeritus, Lifetime Achievement award 2000), Orthop. Rsch. Soc. (Shands award 1998, 99). Home: 12319 Brock Ave Downey CA 90242-3503 Office: Rancho Los Amigos Med Ctr 7601 Imperial Hwy Downey CA 90242-3456 Office Phone: 562-401-7177. E-mail: pklab@larei.org.

PERRY, MALCOLM BLYTHE, biologist, researcher; b. Birkenhead, Cheshire, Eng., Apr. 26, 1930; s. Cyril A. and Hilda P. (Blythe) Perry; m. Eileen M. Perry, Aug. 10, 1956 (dec. Nov. 1981); children: Sara Jane, Judith Anne; m. Philomena C. Kingsley, July 25, 2001. B.Sc., U. Bristol, Eng., 1953; PhD, U. Bristol, 1956, D.Sc., 1969. Banting rsch. fellow Queen's U., Kingston, Ont., Canada, 1955, asst. prof., 1956-60, R.S. McLaughlin research prof., 1960-62; sr. resch. officer Nat. Rsch. Coun., Ottawa, 1962—81, prin. rsch. officer, 1981—2011, MRC rschr. emeritus, 2011. Scientist U. Cambridge, Eng., 1969, U. Paris, 1979; prof. U. Ottawa, 1982 Contbr. articles to profl. jours. Fellow Royal Soc. Can., Royal Inst. Chemistry; mem. Can. Soc. Microbiology (award 1991), Am. Soc. Microbiology, Internat. Endotoxin Soc. (award 2002). Office: NRC 100 Sussex Dr Ottawa ON Canada K1A 0R6 Home: 769 Hemlock Rd Ottawa ON Canada K1K 0K6 Office Phone: 613-990-0837. Business E-Mail: malcolm.perry@nrc.ca.

PERRY, MICHAEL CLINTON, internist, academic administrator, educator; b. Wyandotte, Mich., Jan. 27, 1945; s. Clarence Clinton and Hilda Grace (Wigginton) P.; m. Nancy Ann Kaluzny, June 22, 1968; children: Rebecca Carolyn, Katherine Grace. BA, Wayne State U., 1966, MD, 1970; MS in Medicine, U. Minn., 1975. Diplomate Am. Bd. Internal Medicine, Am. Bd. Hematology, Am. Bd. Oncology. Intern in internal medicine Mayo Grad. Sch. Medicine, Rochester, Minn., 1970-71, resident, 1971-72, fellow, 1972-73, instr. Mayo Med. Sch., Rochester, 1974-75; asst. prof. U. Mo., Columbia, 1975-80, assoc. prof., 1980-85, prof., 1985—, chmn. dept. medicine, 1983-91, sr. assoc. dean, 1991-94, Nellie A Smith chair oncology, dir. div. hematology/oncology, 1994—2008. Prin. investigator Cancer and Leukemia Group B, Nat. Cancer Inst., Chgo., 1982—, exec. com., 1982-84, 1987-90. Author, co author 40 book chpts., editor: Toxicity of Chemotherapy, 1984, The Chemotherapy Source Book, 1992, 96, 2001, 04, Comprehensive Textbook of Thoracic Oncology, 1996; contbr. articles to profl. jours. Recipient Faculty Alumni award U. Mo., Columbia, 1985, Disting. Alumnus award Wayne State U., 1995, Disting. Oncologist of Yr. award So. Assn. Oncology, 2000. Master ACP (profl. oncologist 2010); mem. Am. Soc. Hematology, Am. Soc. Clin. Oncology, Cen. Soc. Clin. Research, Am. Soc. Internal Medicine (Young Internist of Yr. 1981), Sigma Xi, Alpha Omega Alpha. Office: U Mo-Columbia 516 Ellis Fischel Cancer Ctr 115 Business Loop 70 W Columbia MO 65203-3244 Home: 3111 S Bobcat CT Columbia MO 65201-3141 E-mail: perrym@health.missouri.edu. *

PERRY, ROBIN L., physician, obstetrician, gynecologist; MD, U. Medicine and Dentistry of NJ. Diplomate Am. Bd. Ob-Gyn, cert. maternal and Fetal medicine. Fellow Pa. Hosp.; intern Cooper Univ Hosp., resident, med. group physician, assoc. prof. of ob-gyn., chief dept. of ob-gyn. Office: Cooper University Hospital 1230 White Horse-Mercerville Rd Trenton NJ 08619 Office Phone: 609-581-5681. Office Fax: 609-581-5685.

PERSELLIN, ROBERT HAROLD, physician; b. Fargo, ND, July 3, 1930; s. James Harry and Bessie (Hoffman) P.; m. Bonnie Feibleman, June 27, 1957 (dec. 1983); children: Kathleen, Jamie; m. Diane Cummings, June 14, 1986 BS, Northwestern U., 1952, MD, 1956, MS, 1959. Diplomate: Am. Bd. Internal Medicine, Am. Bd. Rheumatology. Intern Charity Hosp., New Orleans, 1956-57; resident in internal medicine Northwestern U. Med. Center, 1957-60; fellow in rheumatology Southwestern Med. Sch., 1962-64; asst. prof. medicine U. Oreg. Med. Sch., 1964-68; prof. medicine, head div. rheumatology U. Tex. Health Sci. Ctr., San Antonio, 1968—81, prof. family practice, 1993—2003. Cons. rheumatology VA Hosps., U.S. Army, Internat. Med. Corps, Kosovo and Republic of Moldova; vis. prof. rheumatology Kingstown Med. Coll.; vis. scholar Corpus Christi Coll., Cambridge U., 1979-80; vis. scientist Strangeways Rsch. Lab., Cambridge. Contbr chpts. to books, articles to profl. jours. Bd. dirs. San Antonio Chamber Music Soc., 1970-75, 80-96, pres., 1983-85; bd. dirs. Friends of Strings, 1972-75, San Antonio Bot. Soc., 1985-87; Dem. precinct committeeman Washington County, Oreg., 1966-68. Served to capt. M.C. U.S. Army, 1960-62. Fellow ACP, Am. Coll. Rheumatology (exec. com. mem.); mem. Arthritis Found. (chmn. med. and sci. com. South Ctrl. Tex. chpt.), Heberden Soc., Am. Fedn. Clin. Rsch., So. Soc. Clin. Investigation, Tex. Rheumatism Assn. (pres.), Nat. Soc. Clin. Rheumatology, Mex. Rheumatology Soc. (hon.). Office: 635 E Olmos Dr San Antonio TX 78212-2504 *

PERSHAD, ASHISH, cardiologist; b. Hyderabad, India, Jan. 7, 1971; s. Kailash and Sheela Pershad; m. Nisha Waghray, Oct. 11, 1970; 1 child, Yash. MD, U. Bombay, 1994. Interventional cardiologist Heart and Vascular Ctr. Ariz., Phoenix, 2001—. Cons. WL Gore Inc, Flagstaff, Ariz., 2002—05, Care Hospitals, Hyderabad, Ap, India, 2003—. Med. adv. bd. Boston Sci. Inc, Natick, Mass., 2003—05. McLennon Acad. scholar, U. Bombay, 1994—95. Mem.: Soc. Coronary Angiography and Interventions, Am. Coll. Physicians, Am. Coll. Cardiology, Maricopa Med. Soc. (licentiate), Ariz. Med. Assn. (licentiate). Office: Heart and Vascular Ctr Ariz 1331 N7th St Ste #375 Phoenix AZ 85006 Office Fax: 602-307-0080. Business E-Mail: apershad1@cox.net.

PERSICHETTI, PAOLO, plastic surgeon, educator; b. Orvieto, Italy, Aug. 5, 1957; s. Ferruccio Persichetti and Arnalda Cerquetelli; m. Maria Gabriella Carrozza, Sept. 5, 1984; children: Giovanni T.M., Maria Flaminia. MD, U. Rome, 1982, PhD, 1998. Diplomate European Bd. Plastic Reconstructive and Aesthetic Surgery. Cons. plastic surgeon Campus Biomedico U. Rome, 1995—97, chief of plastic surgery dept., 1997—, prof. plastic surgery, 2006—. Mem. Interplast Humanitary Missions; assoc. prof. U. Rome. Recipient Publication of Yr. award Book of Plastic Surgery, Hartcourt Health Scis., 2002. Mem.: EURAPS, Italian Soc. Plastic and Reconstructive Surgery, Associação dos Ex-alunos do Prof. Ivo Pitanguy (Rua Dona Mariana 65 - Rio de Janeiro 1985—2002), Rotary Internat. Avocations: collecting greyhound figurines, marionettes. Office: Plastic Surg Hand Surg Micro Surg Via Antonio Bertoloni 19 197 Rome RM Italy Home Phone: +39 068086426; Office Phone: 39 06225411220. Office Fax: 390680662294. Business E-Mail: p.persichetti@unicampus.it.

PERSING, JOHN ARTHUR, surgeon; b. Burlington, Vt., Apr. 16, 1948; s. Raymond Maurice and Natalie (Vespucci) P.; m. Susan Powers Light, June 22, 1971; children: Sarah Merriman, John Scott. BA cum laude, U. Vt., 1970, MD, 1974; MA (hon.), Yale U., 1992. Diplomate Am. Bd. Plastic and Reconstructive Surgery, Am. Bd. Neurol. Surgeons. Resident gen. surgery Hosp. of U. Ariz., Tuscon, 1974-76; resident neurol. surgery Hosp. of U. Va., Charlottesville, 1976-82, resident plastic surgery, 1982-84, dir. cranial base surgery, 1988-92, vice chmn. dept. of plastic surgery, 1988-92, chief divsn. of craniofacial surgery, 1988-92; asst. prof. plastic and neurosurgery U. Va., Charlottesville, 1984-87, assoc. prof. of plastic and neurosurgery, 1987-89, prof. plastic and neurosurgery, 1989-92; prof. plastic surgery and neurosurgery Yale U. Sch. of Medicine, New Haven, Conn., 1992—, chief sect. of plastic surgery, 1992—; fellow Trumbull Coll. Yale U., New Haven, 1994—. Editor: Clinics in Plastic Surgery, July, 1995; co-editor Jour. of Craniofacial Surgery, 1992—, Scientific Foundations and Surgical Treatment for Craniosynostosis, 1989, Neurosurgery Clinics of North America, July, 1991; assoc. editor Plastic and Reconstructive Surgery, 1997-2005. Recipient Donald D. Matson award Am. Assn. of Neurol. Surgeons, 1981. Mem. Am. Assn. Pediatric Plastic Surgeons (pres. 1995-97), Am. Assn. Plastic Surgeons (membership com. 1994-95), Am. Soc. Plastic and Reconstructive Surgeons (trustee 2007-), Am. Cleft Palate-Craniofacial Assn. (coms.), Am. Soc. Maxillofacial Surgeons (coms., v.p. 2000-01,pres. 2002-03, Bernd Speissl award 1991, Maxillofacial Surgeons Found. Rsch. award 1992), Plastic Surgery Edn. Found. (sec. 2005-07, pres. elect 2009), Assn. Acad. Chmn. of Plastic Surgery (plastic surgery residency tng. evaluation com. 1993, chair issues com. 1994, v.p. 2002-03, pres. 2004-05), Northeastern Soc. Plastic Surgeons (program com. 1995), Plastic Surgery Rsch. Coun. (program com. 1991-94), Am. Bd. Plastic Surgery (chmn. 2005). Office: Yale Plastic Surgery 330 Cedar St # 2 New Haven CT 06510-8041 Office Phone: 203-785-2570. Business E-Mail: john.persing@yale.edu.

PERSINGER, DEL LOUIS, pharmaceutical association executive; b. Whiting, Iowa, Aug. 2, 1949; s. Ardell L. and Doris L. Persinger; m. Mary L. Tabor, Sept. 16, 1984; children: Christopher, Benjamin Hammerschlag, Sarah Hammerschlag. BSChemE with distinction, Iowa State U., 1971, MS in Journalism and Mass. Comm., 1975; MBA in Fin., Am. U., 1990. Refinery process engr. Exxon Co., Baton Rouge, 1971-73; environtl. and pub. affairs mgr. Am. Petroleum Inst., Washington, 1975-89, sr. assoc. refining, 1989-92, dep. dir. mfg., distbn. and mktg., 1992-94, dir. mgmt. and budget, 1994-96; v.p. fin. ops. Pharm. Rsch. and Mfrs. of Am. (PhRMA), Washington, 1996—2006, sr. v.p., CFO, 2006—. Pres., CEO PhRMA Found., 1999—. Trustee, past pres. Bethesda Jewish Congregation, 1992—2000. Mem. Fin. Execs. Inst., Am. Soc. of Assn. Execs., Am. Found. for Pharm. Edn. (bd. dirs. 1999—), Phi Kappa Phi, Tau Beta Pi, Omega Chi Epsilon. Office: Pharm Rsch and Mfrs of Am Ste 300 950 F St NW Washington DC 20004 *

PERSOFF, MYRON MAYER, plastic surgeon; b. West Palm Beach, Fla., Apr. 26, 1941; BS, U. Fla., Gainesville, 1963; MD, U. Miami, Fla., 1967. Cert. Am. Bd. Plastic Surgery, 1977. Rotating-2 intern Phila. Naval Hosp., 1967—68; resident gen. surgery U. South Fla. Sch. Medicine, Tampa, 1971—73, St. Joseph Hosp., Houston, 1973—74, resident plastic surgery, 1974—76; fellow Cronin-Brauer Clin. Assn., Houston, 1974—76; staff mem. North Broward Hosp., 1976—90, West Boca Med. Ctr., 1985—94, Northridge Med. Ctr., Ft. Lauderdale, Fla., 1993—95, Mercy Hosp., Coconut Grove, Fla., 1994—, Coral Gables Hosp., Fla., 1998—2001; active staff mem. Boca Raton Cmty. Hosp., Fla., 1976—93; clin. asst. U. Miami Sch. Medicine, 1977—2001. Contbr. articles to med. jours.; featured: magazines Plastic Surgery Products. Orthopedic surgeon USN, 1968—69, Navy Hosp., Pensacola, Fla., sea duty USN, 1968, USS Speigel Grove, attended Flight Surgeons Sch. USN, 1969, Pensacola, Fla., served in USN, 1969—71, US Naval Air Sta., Cubi Point, Philippines. Fellow: Am. Coll. Surgeons; mem.: AMA, Broward County Soc. Plastic Surgeons, Lipolysis Soc. N.Am., Miami Soc. Plastic Surgeons, Dade County Med. Assn., Palm Beach County Med. Soc., Fla. Med. Assn., Palm Beach County Soc. Plastic and Reconstructive Surgeons, Fla. Soc. Plastic and Reconstructive Surgeons, Southeastern Soc. Plastic and Reconstructive Surgeons, Am. Soc. Plastic and Reconstructive Surgeons, Am. Soc. Aesthetic Plastic Surgery. Office: Coconut Grove Plastic Surgery Mercy Output Ctr 4011 Hardie Ave Miami FL 33133-6344 Office Phone: 305-858-5255. Office Fax: 305-858-5235. Business E-Mail: info@drpersoff.com.

PERSSON, EVA, healthcare educator; b. Sweden, Mar. 12, 1953; PhD in Surgery, U. Gothenburg, 2004. RN Sch. Nursing, Gothenburg, 1980. Stoma care nurse colorectal unit Sahlgrenska U. Hosp., Östra, 1990—2007; sr. lectr. Sch. Health Scis., U. Borås, 2007—. Mem.: Nordic Coll. Caring Sci. Avocations: exercise, reading. Home: Kornettgatan 10 Råå Skåne 252 71 Sweden Home Phone: 46 705 691071. Business E-Mail: eva.persson@hb.se, eva.persson@secl.lu.se.

PERSSON, ROLAND S., psychologist, educator; b. Vastra Frolunda, Gothenburg, Sweden, Oct. 7, 1958; s. Sven O. F. and Karin G. (Backlund) P. MFA, Ingesund Coll. Music, Sweden, 1982; PhD in Psychology, U. Huddersfield, UK, 1993. Lic. Personal trainer (IFBB) 1987. Head tchr. Uddevalla Pre-Conservatoire, Sweden, 1986-90; rschr., lectr. U. Huddersfield, 1990-93; assoc. prof. Jonkoping (Sweden) U., 1994-2001, 02—; dir. psychol. test and devel. Psykologiforlaget AB, Stockholm, 2001—02; prof. ednl. psychology, 2008—. Bd. regents Ingesund Coll. Music, 1994-98; nat. rep. European Coun. for High Ability, 1994—, World Coun. for Gifted and Talented Children, 1998; bd. dirs. Ctr. for Psychology, Jonkoping, cons. The Found. Applied Psychology (STP), 2002. Author: Formal Writing and Personal Style, 1996, Psyche, Stress and Artistic Freedom, 1996, In a Different Land: The Psychology of High Ability, 1997, Handbook of Supervising Research, 1999, Differences or Deficits!, 2000, Hungry to Win, Losing Your Mind!, 2004, Big, Bad, Stupid or Big Good and Smart?, 2004; editor-in-chief High Ability Studies, 1998-2002; mem. editl. bd. Edn. Today, London, 2001—, Gifted & Talented Internat., 2010-. Mem. APA, BPS, ECHA. Avocations: civil aviation, philosophy, bodybuilding. Office: Sch Edn & Comm/Jönköping U PO Box 1026 SE-55111 Jönköping Sweden Office Phone: 46 (0)36-101360. Business E-Mail: pero@hlk.hj.se.

PERUMAL SAMY, RAMAR, research scientist; s. Sanku and Valliyammal Ramar; m. Kanakarajan Porselvi, June 7, 2006; 1 child, Swati. PhD, U. Madras, Tamil Nadu, 2000. Diploma in computer application Loyola Bio-informatic Ctr., 1998. Jr. and sr. rsch. fellow Loyola Coll. Autonomus, Chennai, Tamil Nadu, 1995—, rsch. assoc., 1995—, lectr., 1995—; rsch. fellow, grade a Nat. U. Singapore, Singapore, 2003—08; rsch. scientist SERI, 2010—. Contbr. articles to profl. jours. Social activities West Coast Recreation Ctr., Singapore. Sr. Rsch. fellowship, Coun. Sci. Indsl. Rsch., Govt. India, New Delhi, 1997, Rsch. Assoc. fellowship, 2000. Mem.: Internat. Soc. Infectious Diseases. Achievements include patents for development of new antibiotic peptides against human pathogens; anti-flammatory polypeptides. Office: SOW SERI 9 Hospital Drive School of Nursing 169612 Singapore Singapore Office Phone: 6322 4500. Office Fax: 6323 1903. Personal E-mail: rperumalsamy@yahoo.co.uk. Business E-Mail: phyrps@nus.edu.sg.

PEŠÁK, JOSEF, biophysics educator; b. Olomouc, Czech Republic, May 21, 1942; m. Eva Utěšená, Nov. 13, 1965; children: Daniel, Dagmar Flynt, Dita, Perrier. Msc, Palacky U., 1966, Doctorate, 1968; PhD, Tech. U., Brno, Czech Republic, 1985. Researcher Meopta/Tesla, Přerov and Litovel, Czech Republic, 1966-67, 67-74; sr. lectr. NS UP Olomouc, 1974-88, scientist neurol. clin. med. faculty, 1988-92, asst. prof. dept. biophysics med. faculty, 1992—; prof. dept. med. biophysics, faculty medicine Palacký U., Olomouc. Contbr. articles to profl. jours. Mem. Union of Czech Mathematicians and Physicists, Czech Med. Soc., N.Y. Acad. Scis., Czech Acoustical Soc. Achievements include reduction of stuttering through bronchodilatation with B2 sympathomimetic drug tormotetol. Avocation: folklore activities. Office: UP Olomouc Med Fac Dept Biophysics 3 Hnevotínská St Olomouc 775 15 Czech Republic E-mail: pesak@tunw.upol.cz.

PESAVENTO, GARY D., psychologist; b. Pitts., Apr. 15, 1946; s. Edward J. and Johanna M. Pesavento; m. Kaye Kos Pesavento, Aug. 14, 1971; children: Joshua D., Zachary J. BA, Duquesne U., Pitts., 1968; MS in Edn., Ft. Hays Kans. State U., 1969; PhD, US Internat. U., San Diego, 1982. Clin. psychologist pvt. practice, Bonita, Calif., 1983—, Calif. State Dept. Corrections, San Diego, 1992—. Program coord. Positive Parenting Program, YMCA, San Diego, 1980—81; program dir. Juvenile Firesetting Program, San Diego, 1982; vice-chmn. San Diego County Regional Mental Healh Adv. Bd., 1983—85; bd. mem., sec., treas. San Diego County Mental Health Assn., 1983—85; instr. Rise Program, San Diego, 1989—92; mem. adv. group Magellan Health Svcs. Provider, San Diego, 2004—. Bd. mem., sec. Nat. City Cmty. Action, National City, Calif., 1985—87; mem. PTA, Chula Vista, Calif., 1996—2008; mem. patron Tariq Khamisa Found., San Diego, 1996—2009; bd. mem., treas., pres. Interactions for Peace-Peace Patrol, San Diego, 2001—; trustee, union steward AFSCME Local 2620 Bargaining Unit, San Diego, 2004—06. With USAF, 1969—73. Mem.: APA, Calif. Marriage and Family Therapists Assn., Am. Assn. Retired Persons. Avocations: reading, travel, photography. Office: Ste 109 180 Otay Lakes Rd Bonita CA 91902-2439 Office Phone: 619-227-5079. Business E-Mail: gpesavento@cox.net.

PESCHEL, RICHARD, radiation oncologist, educator; MD, Yale U., 1977. Prof. sch. of medicine Yale Univ.; resident in radiation oncology Yale New Haven Hosp., New Haven, 1978—81; radiation oncologist Yale-New Haven Hosp.; therapeutic radiologist Yale Med. Group. Author: A Theoretical Evaluation Of Plastic Dosimetry Phantoms, 1975, A Review Of Time-dose Effects In Radiation Therapy, 1981, "But What If She Should Die?"-- case Histories, Literary Histories: A Discussion Of Maternal Death In Childbirth, 1981, Testicular Tumors in 2 Families, 1981, Optimization Of The Time-dose Relationship, 1981, The Treatment Of Massive Hepatomegaly In Atage IV-S Neuroblastoma, 1981, Long Term Survivors With Small Cell Carcinoma Of The Lung, 1982, Multiple Daily Fractionation Schedules, 1983, Ependymomas Of The Spinal Cord, 1983, Ritual And The Death Certificate: Case Histories, Literary Histories, 1983, The Face Of Death: Case HIstory, Literary Histories, 1983, "Am I In Heaven Now?": Case History, Literary Histories, 1984, Tumor Cure Studies On The Rat Sarcoma BA1112 Using Continuous Low-dose-rate Radiation, 1984, various articles in publs. Recipient Castle Connolly America's Top Doctors for Cancer, 2009—10, Castle Connolly Amreica's Top Doctors for Cancer, 2005—07, Castle Connolly Top Doctors: NY Metro Area, 2006—10. Mem.: Am. Soc. for Therapeutic Radiology and Oncology. Office: Yale-New Haven Hospital 20 York St New Haven CT 06510 Office Phone: 203-688-6937. Office Fax: 203-688-6937.

PESCOVITZ, ORA HIRSCH, health facility administrator, medical educator; b. Carmel, Ind., Sept. 23, 1956; m. Mark David Pescovitz; children: Aliza Beth, Ari Samuel, Naomi Rachel. MS in Med. Edn., Northwestern U., Ill., 1978; MD, Northwestern U. Med. Sch., Ill., 1979. Cert. diplomate Am. Bd. Pediatrics, 1985, Am. Bd. Pediat. Endocrinology and Metabolism, 1986. Med. ward officer Children's Hosp. Nat. Med. Ctr., Washington, 1983—84, instr. pediat. endocrinology/metabolism, 1985—86; asst. prof. pediat. endocrinology, metabolism Dept. Pediat. U. Minn., 1986—97; assoc. prof. pediat., physiology and biophysics Ind. U. Sch. Medicine, 1988—92, prof. pediat., physiology and biophysics, 1992—2009, full mem. grad. sch. faculty, 1993, dir. sect. pediat. endocrinology, diabetology dept., 1990, Edwin Letzter prof. prof. pediat., 1998—2009, exec. assoc. dean rsch. affairs; pres., CEO Riley Hosp. for Children, 2004—09; exec. v.p. med. affairs U. Mich., 2009—; CEO U. Mich. Health Sys., 2009—. Editor (editl. bd.): Jour. Clin. Endocrinology and Metabolism, 1989—93, (jour.) Endocrine Reviews, 1995—98, Hormone Rsch., 1996—, Endocrine, 1997—, Pediat. Endocrinology: The Endocrinologist, 1998—; contbr. to devel. of movie on precocious puberty;, author 150 sci. publs., 101 abstracts. Mem. numerous nat. coms., 1987—; mem. Internat. Consensus Group on Growth Hormone Therapy: Workshop on Current Trends of Growth Related Rsch., 1989, Internat. Growth Forum II Organizing Com., 1996, 1997, Advances in Pediats. Course Planning Com., Mpls., 1985—88, Accident Prevention Com., AAP; mem. com. to draft a mission statement U. Minn., 1986—88, mem. residency selection com. dept. pediat., 1986—88, mem. gen. clin. rsch. ctr. sci. rev. com., 1986—88, mem. pediat. specialists bd. nominating com., 1986—88; mem. numerous coms. Ind. U., 1989—. Recipient Rsch. Career Devel. award, NIH, 1991—96, Forty Under 40, Indpls. Bus. Jour., 1993, Disting. Lectr., Mary E. Culbertson Symposium, Ind. U. Sch. Nursing, 2002; named one of Best Drs. in Am., Woodward and White, 1995, 1996, 1998, Am. Health, 1997, Indpls. Best Drs., 1995, The Influential Women in Indpls., Indpls. Bus. Jour. and Ind. Lawyer, 1999; nominee Women in the Lead, Indpls. Bus. Jour., 2002. Mem.: Women in Endocrinology, Soc. Pediat. Rsch., Midwest Soc. Pediat. Rsch., Lawson Wilkins Pediat. Endocrine Soc., Endocrine Soc., Am. Acad. Pediat. Achievements include patents for Use of GHRH-RP to stimulate stem cell factor production. Office: U Mich M7324 Med Scis Bldg Box 5626 1500 E Medical Center Dr Ann Arbor MI 48109 Office Phone: 734-647-9351. Business E-Mail: opescovi@umich.edu. *

PESEK, KSENIJA, cardiologist, department chairman; b. Krapina, Croatia, May 18, 1955; d. Stjepan and Nevenka Vidovic; m. Tomislav Pesek, Nov. 28, 1981; children: Mirna Pešek, Borna Pešek. MD, Med. U., Zagreb, Croatia, 1980—80. Cert. ESC, France, 2003, CCS, 1994, HLZ, 1981, CSH, 1998, CSI, Croatia, 2000. Chief dept. cardiology Gen. Hosp. Zabok, 1996—2008, chief dept. internal medicine, 2006—08. Contbr. scientific papers to profl. jours. Mem.: European Cardiac Soc. Roman Cath. Avocations: travel, skiing, sailing. Home: Ljubljanska 5 Zabok 49210 Croatia Office: Gen Hosp Zabok Bracak 8 Zabok 49210 Croatia Home Phone: 0038549223784; Office Phone: 0038549204401. Personal E-mail: ksenija.pesek@kr.t-com.hr. Business E-Mail: medicina@bolnica-zabok.hr.

PESKA, DON N., dean, surgeon, educator; b. NY; m. Judith Peska; 3 children. BS in Biology, Bklyn. Coll.; DO, Des Moines Osteo. Coll. Rotating internship and gen. residency Oakland Gen. Hosp; residency in cardiovascular and thoracic surgery Detroit Osteo. and Bi-County Hospitals; clin. practice in thoracic and vascular surgery Ft. Worth, 1982—; assoc. prof. surgery U. North Tex. Health Sci. Ctr. Tex. Coll. Osteo. Medicine, Ft. Worth, 1995—2008, asst. dean clin. edn., 2003, assoc. dean academic affairs, 2003—04, assoc. dean ednl. programs, 2004—, prof. surgery, 2008—, dean, 2009—; dir. osteo. med. edn. John Peter Smith Hosp.; adminstrv. dir. med. edn. Plz. Med. Ctr. Contbr. articles to profl. jours. Mem.: American Coll. Osteo. Surgeons (President's Svc. award 2003, Disting. Osteo. Surgeon award 2007), American Osteo. Assn., Tex. Osteo. Med. Assn., Tarrant County Med. Soc., Tex. Med. Assn., Tex. Med. Found. Studio: University North Tex Health Sci Ctr Tex Coll Osteo Medicine Med Edn Tng Bldg 3500 Camp Bowie Blvd PCC4 Fort Worth TX 76107 Office Phone: 817-735-2244. Office Fax: 817-735-0623. Business E-Mail: don.peska@unthsc.edu. *

PESOLA, GENE RAYMOND, physician; b. Hancock, Mich., Oct. 21, 1952; s. Raymond Lloyd and Helen Eleanor Pesola; m. Helen Rostata, Jan. 5, 1991; children: Gene Richard, Glen Raymond, Gary Roger. BS in Biology magna cum laude, Mich. Technol. U., Houghton, 1974; MD, Wayne State U., 1979; MPH in Biostats. magna cum laude, Columbia U., 1998, MPhil in Epidemiology, 2006. Diplomate Am. Bd. Internal Medicine, also sub-bds. pulmonary medicine and critical care medicine; cert. in pub. health, 2008, BCLS, ACLS, ATLS, PALS. Intern Harlem Hosp., NYC, 1979-80; resident U. Tenn. Affiliated Hosps., Memphis, 1980-82; fellow in pulmonary medicine Mt. Sinai Hosp. and Affiliates, NYC, 1982-84; fellow in critical care medicine Meml. Sloan-Kettering Cancer Ctr., NYC, 1984-85, rsch. fellow, 1985-87; asst. prof. medicine and anesthesia Albert Einstein U., Bronx, NY, 1988-89; attending physician Mt. Vernon Emergency Room, NY, 1989-90; rschr. cell/molecular pharmacology and exptl. therapeutics Med. U. SC, Charleston, 1991-94; attending physician critical care and emergency medicine N.Y. Cmty. Hosp., Bklyn., 1989—; attending physician dept. emergency medicine St. Vincent's Hosp., NYC, 1994—2000; asst. prof. emergency medicine NY Med. Coll., 1995-2000, assoc. prof. emergency medicine, 2000; assoc. attending physician Divsn. Pulmonary and Critical Care Medicine, Harlem Hosp./Columbia U., NYC, 2001—; assoc. clin. prof. medicine Columbia U., NYC, 2001—; co-prin. investigator ACRN, NYC, 2001—04. Mem. editl. bd. Academic Emergency Medicine, 2002—09, assoc. editor, 2006—09, Internet Jour. Asthma, Allergy and Immunology, 2002—; contbr. chapters to books, articles to profl. jours.; reviewer numerous jours. including CHEST, Catheterization and Cardiovasc. Interventions, Annals of Emergency Medicine, The Lancet, Academic Emergency Medicine. Grantee Am. Fedn. Clin. Rsch., 1992; Pharm. Mfr. Found. fellow, 1992-94; named one of Am.'s Top Physicians Consumer's Rsch. Coun., 2004,06; named Tchr. of Yr. Dept. Medicine Harlem Hosp., 2006.

PESSIS, DENNIS AARON, urologist, educator; s. Benjamin Hyman Pessis and Esther Wolinsky; m. Amy Leslie Diamond, Feb. 6, 1971; children: Stefanie, Gwen, David, Jill. BS, U. Ill., Champaign, 1969; MD, U. Health Sci., North Chicago, Ill., 1973. Intern Rush Presbyn. St. Luke's Med. Ctr., Chgo., 1973—74, resident in urology, 1974—78; physician Affiliated Urologists, Chgo., 1980—; assoc. chmn. dept. urology Rush Presbyn. St. Luke's Med. Ctr., Chgo., 1992—, prof. urology, 2002. Merck cons. and lectr., NJ, 1997—; Praecis Corp. cons. for LHRH Antagonist, Boston, 1999—2003; cons. Olympus Corp., LI, NY, 1999—; vis. prof. Northeastern Ohio U., Toledo, 1999, Ann. Oncology Symposium, Youngstown, Ohio, 2000. Mayoral election com., Highland Park, Ill., 2003; senate election com., Sen. Bill Frist Chgo., 1997; Ill. Ho. of Reps. election com. Highland Park, 2002. Recipient Pfizer vis. professorship grant, Chgo.,

2003. Mem.: ACS (pres. Chgo. chpt. 1997—99), Am. Urol. Assn. (treas. North Ctrl. sect. 1999—), Ill. Urol. Soc. (pres. 1994—95), Chgo. Urol. Soc. (pres. 1994—95). Jewish. Avocations: golf, geology, French horn, politics, history. Office: Affiliated Urologists 1725 W Harrison Ste 762 Chicago IL 60612 Home Phone: 847-433-7032; Office Phone: 312-563-3447.

PESTANA, CARLOS, surgeon, retired dean, educator; b. Tacoronte, Tenerife, Canary Islands, Spain, June 10, 1936; came to U.S., 1968, naturalized, 1973; s. Francisco and and Blanca (Suarez) P.; m. Myrna Lorena Serrato, Aug. 25, 1966; children— Becky Elizabeth, George Byron. BS, Nat. U. Mex., 1952, MD, 1959; PhD in Surgery, U. Minn., 1965. Intern St. Mary of Nazareth Hosp., Chgo., 1959-60; resident Mayo Clinic, Rochester, Minn., 1961-65; surgeon Hosp. 20 de Noviembre Mexico City; asst. prof. surgery Nat. U. Mex., 1966-67, U. Tex. Med. Sch. at San Antonio, 1968-70, asso. prof., 1970-74, prof., 1974—, asso. dean for acad. devel., 1971-73, asso. dean for student affairs, 1973-86, assoc. dean acad. affairs, 1986-97, clin. prof. surgery, 1998-2000, prof. emeritus, 2000—. Recipient Edward John Noble Found. award, 1965, Piper Prof. award Minnie Stevens Piper Founds., 1972, Nat. Golden Apple award Am. Med. Student Assn., 1999. Mem. Alpha Omega Alpha (Robert J. Glaser Disting. Tchr. award 1997). Home: 10123 N Manton Ln San Antonio TX 78213-1932 Office: 7703 Floyd Curl Dr San Antonio TX 78284-6200 Office Phone: 210-567-5700.

PESTEL, GUNTHER JÜRGEN, anesthesiologist, researcher; b. Werneck, Germany, Oct. 27, 1963; s. Jürgen Erl Pestel and Margit Dorothea Wittmann; m. Kerstin Westphal, May 5, 2000; children: Dora Henriette Therese Westphal, Mathis Albert Martin Westphal. MD, Friedrich-Alexander U., Erlangen, Germany, 1991; PhD, Johannes Gutenberg U., Mainz, Germany, 2009. Lic. anesthesiologist Bavarian Physicians' Chamber, 1998, intensivist 2002. Assoc. prof. Johannes Gutenberg U., 2007—. Vis. prof. Wash. U. Sch. of Medicine, St. Louis, 2003—04, U. Louisville, 2007. Contbr. articles to profl. jours. Founder Kulturpackt, Schweinfurt, Germany, 1993. Mem.: Am. Soc. Anesthesiologists, Internat. Liver Transplant Soc., Soc. Critical Care Medicine, Internat. Anesthesia Res. Soc., German Soc. Anesthesiology and Critical Care Medicine. Avocations: soccer, travel, history. Office: Dept Anesthesiology Johannes Gutenberg Univ Mainz 55131 Germany Personal E-mail: gunther.pestel@gmx.net.

PETAK, STEVEN M., endocrinologist; m. Karen Petak; children: Kate, Alex. MD, Univ. Ill., 1979; JD magna cum laude, Univ. Houston, 1996. Bar: Tex. Asst. prof. medicine, pharmacology Univ. Tex. Med. Sch., Houston, clin. faculty; assoc. Tex. Inst. Reproductive Medicine and Endocrinology, 1989—, dir. Bone Densitometry Unit and Osteoporosis Ctr. Endocrine cons. NASA, Johnson Space Ctr.; chmn., osteoporosis adv. com. Tex. Dept. Health, 1996—2000. Mem.: Am. Coll. Endocrinology (pres. 2009—), AMA, Am. Assn. Clin. Endocrinologists (pres.-elect 2005—06, pres. 2007—08), Internat. Soc. Clin. Densitometry (pres. 2006—07). Office: Ste 850 7400 Fannin St Houston TX 77054 Office Phone: 713-791-1874.

PETANOVIC, MIRNA, microbiologist; b. Slavonski Brod, Croatia, Jan. 29, 1951; d. Viktor and Katica Cer; m. Zvonko Petanovic, Nov. 18, 1972; children: Berislav, Tomislav. MD, Zagreb Sch. Medicine, Croatia, 1974, MSc, 1983, PhD, 1998. Head serological divsn. microbiology svc. Med. Ctr., Slavonski Brod, Croatia, 1979—90, head dept. microbiology, 1990—94; rsch. asst. Zagreb Sch. Medicine, Slavonski Brod, 1988—; head dept. microbiology Pub. Health Instn. Brod-Posavina County, Slavonski Brod, 1994—. Mem. working group Com. for Nat. Resistance Surveillance, Zagreb, 1996. Contbr. articles to profl. jours. Mem.: Croatian Microbiology Soc. (mem. presidency 1975), Croatian Med. Assn. (HLZ diploma 1992, 1999), Assn. Croatian Univ. Women (mem. presidency). Avocation: exercise. Office: Pub Health Inst Brod-Posavina County V Nazora BB Slavonski Brod 35000 Croatia Home: Andrija Hebrang Biv/7 35-000 Slavonski Brod Croatia Office Phone: +385/35 447228. Office Fax: +385/35 440244. Personal E-mail: zzjzsb@sb.hinet.hr.

PETELENZ, TADEUSZ KAROL, cardiologist; b. Cracow, Poland, Apr. 15, 1925; s. Ignacy and Zofja P.; m. Teresa Wanda Slominska, Aug. 25, 1951; children: Thomas, Michael. Physician, U. Jagiellonica Med. Sch., Poland, 1952; MD, Silesian Med. Sch., Poland, 1961, PhD, 1966. Chmn. dept. internal medicine 1st City Hosp., Zabrze, Poland, 1969—75; chmn. cardiol. dept. specialistic Hosp. No 2, Katowice, Poland, 1975—78; prof., chmn. III Cardiology Clinic Silesian Med. Sch., Ochojec, Poland, 1978—95; chmn. Silesian Cardiol. Ctr. Found., Katowice-Ochojec, Poland, 1995—. Adj. in Clinic of Internal Diseases, Silesian Med. Sch., Zabrze, Poland, 1958-68; chmn. outpatients multispecialists dept. for Dist. Katowice, 1962-75; cons. prof. for cardiology Dist. Czestochowa, Poland, 1977-82, Dist. Katowice, Poland, 1983-91; chmn. 3d Clinic of Cardiology Silesian Cardiol. Ctr in Katowice, 1978-95, pres. Cardiol. Found., 1995—. Contbr. 420 articles to profl. jours. Physician Med. Corps Polish Armed Forces, 1952—57. Recipient prize of 4 World Congress of Cardiology in Mexico City, 1962, Sci. award Polish Cardiol. Soc., 1994, Pres. of Silesian Med. Sch., 1993-94, award for Didactics, 1994, 95. Fellow European Soc. Cardiology; mem. Polish Med. Soc., Cardiol. Soc. Dist. Katowice (pres. bd. dir. 1996—), IEEE. Roman Catholic. Avocations: tennis, sailoring, skiing, swimming, tourism. Office: Silesian Cardiol Ctr 46 Ziolowa Str 40635 Katowice Poland Office Phone: 48-32-2523601. Personal E-mail: slopet@wp.pl. Business E-Mail: fundkard@sum.edu.pl.

PETER, BACH, epidemiologist, pulmonologist; MA in Pub. Policy, U. Chgo.; MD, U. Minn. Med. Sch. Cert. internal med., pulmonary med., critical care med. Resident Johns Hopkins Hosp.; former sr. adv. to adminstr. Centers for Medicare and Medicaid Svcs.; assoc. attending physician Meml. Sloan-Kettering Cancer Ctr.; mem. Health Outcomes Rsch. Group Meml. Sloan-Ketterin Cancer Ctr. Dept. Epidemiology & Biostatistics. Mem. Inst. Medicine's Nat. Cancer Policy Forum, Com. Performance Measurement of the Nat. Com. on Quality Assurance; camp physician Rwandan Civil War Refugee Camp, Goma, Democratic Republic of Congo. Author: (op-ed pieces) Wall St. Jour.; contbr. articles various medical publs. Office: 1275 York Ave New York NY 10065 Office Phone: 646-735-8137. Office Fax: 646-735-0011. E-mail: bachp@mskcc.org.

PETERS, ALAN, anatomy educator; b. Nottingham, Eng., Dec. 6, 1929; came to U.S., 1966; s. Robert and Mabel (Woplington) P.; m. Verona Muriel Shipman, Sept. 30, 1955; children: Ann Verona, Sally Elizabeth, Susan Clare. BSc, Bristol U., Eng., 1951, PhD, 1954; DSc (hon.), U. Edinburgh, 2011. Lectr. anatomy Edinburgh (Scotland) U., 1958-66; vis. lectr. Harvard, 1963-64; prof., chmn. dept. anatomy and neurobiology Boston U., 1966-98, Waterhouse prof., 1998—. Anatomy com. Nat. Bd. Med. Examiners, 1971-75; mem. neurology B Study sect. NIH, 1975-79, chmn., 1978-79; affiliate scientist Yerkes Regional Primate Rsch. Ctr., 1984—. Author (with S.L. Palay and H. deF Webster): The Fine Structure of the Nervous System, 1970, The Fine Structure of the Nervous System, 3rd edit., 1991; author: Myelination, 1970; mem. editl. bd.: Anat. Record, 1972—81, Jour. Comparative Neurology, 1981—97, Neurocytology, 1972—89, 1993—2006, Cerebral Cortex, 1990—2005, Studies of Brain Function, Anat. and Embryology, 1989—92; editor (with E.G. Jones): (book series) Cerebral Cortex, 1984—2000; exec. prodr.(with B. Payne): Cat Visual Cortex, 2001; contbr. articles to profl. jours. Served to 2d lt. Royal Army Med. Corps, 1955-57. Recipient Henry Gray award, 1998, Sanford L. Palay award Jour. Comparative Neurology, 2004; grantee NIH, 1986. Mem. Anat. Soc. Gt. Britain and Ireland (Symington prize anatomy 1962, overseas mem. coun. 1969), Assn. Anatomy Chmn. (pres. 1976-77), Am. Anat. Assn. (exec. com. 1986-90, pres. 1992-93, Henry Gray award 1998), Am. Soc. Cell Biology, Soc. Neurosci., Internat. Primatological Soc., Cajal Club (Harman lectr. 1990, Cortical Discoverer award 1991). Home: 1010 Waltham St # 589 Lexington MA 02421 Office: Boston U Sch Medicine Dept Anatomy and Neurobiology 80 E Concord St Roxbury MA 02118-2307 Home Phone: 781-862-1492; Office Phone: 617-638-4235. Business E-Mail: valan@bu.edu.

PETERS, CALVIN RONALD, plastic and reconstructive surgeon; b. New Orleans, Jan. 27, 1940; s. Arthur Henry and Christine Cecile (Moldaner) P.; m. Pamela Alice Orth, Sept. 4, 1965; children: Brandon Scott, Kendall Kyle. BS, La. State U., 1961, MD, 1964. Diplomate Am. Bd. Surgery, Am. Bd. Plastic Surgery. Intern USN Hosp., Portsmouth, Va., 1964-65; gen. surg. resident Ochsner Clinic, 1968-72; plastic surgery resident Duke U. Med. Ctr., Durham, 1972-75, asst. prof. plastic surgery, 1975-78; program dir., plastic surgery Cleve. Clinic, 1978-79; pres., founder Ctr. for Plastic and Reconstructive Surgery, Orlando, Fla., 1979—. Chmn. dept. plastic surgery, Orlando Regional Med. Ctr., Orlando, 1981-86, Fla. Hosp. Med. Ctr., Orlando, 1981-86. Contbr. numerous articles, chpts. to profl. jours. and textbooks. With USN, 1965-68. Recipient Sr. Resident award Plastic Surgery Ednl. Found., Chgo., 1975. Fellow Am. Coll. Surgeons (bd. govs. 1980-86); mem. Am. Soc. Plastic and Reconstructive Surgeons, Am. Assn. Plastic Surgeons, Am. Soc. Maxillofacial Surgeons, Am. Soc. Aesthetic Plastic Surgeons, Orange County Med. Soc. (pres. 1989—), Fla. Soc. Plastic and Reconstructive Surgeons (pres. 1989—), Fla. Cleft Palate Soc. (pres. 1987-88), Interlachen Country Club, Winter Park Racquet Club. Republican. Episcopalian. Avocations: running, skiing, swimming, boating, golf. Home: 467 Lakewood Dr Winter Park FL 32789-3939 Office: Ctr Plastic/Recon Surgery 2501 N Orange Ave Ste 442 Orlando FL 32804-4642

PETERS, DOUGLAS ALAN, appeals nurse manager; b. Portsmouth, Va., Oct. 4, 1968; s. Terrance Gene and Pamela P. BA in Philosophy, Va. Poly. Inst. and State U., 1992, BSN summa cum laude, James Madison U., 1995; JD, U. Md., Balt., 2003. RN Tenn.; cert. case mgr., legal nurse cons. Photojournalist CVNI/The Greene County Record, Stanardsville, Va., 1992; nursing asst. Rockingham Meml. Hosp., Harrisonburg, Va., 1993-95; clin. nurse Bapt. Hosp., Pensacola, Fla., 1995-96; nurse mgr. quality assurance Escambia County Jail Infirmary, Pensacola, 1996-97; case mgr./U.R. Total Health Care, Balt., 1997-98; case mgr. Blue Cross/Blue Shield of Md., Balt., 1998-2000, appeals analyst, 2000—01, sr. appeals analyst, 2001—04; jud. law clk. 23d Jud. Cir., W.Va., 2004—05; legal cons. CareFirst Blue Cross Blue Shield, 2005; nurse, case mgr. George Washington U. Hosp., 2006—07, Medicare Part D Appeals Grievances Healthspring Inc., Nashville, 2007—09, appeals nurse supervisor, 2009—10, appeals nurse manager, 2011—. Mem.: Greater Nashville Darts Assn., Am. Assn. Legal Nurse Cons., Phi Alpha Delta, Sigma Theta Tau, Alpha Chi Sigma. Avocation: darts. Personal E-mail: dapeters2006@yahoo.com.

PETERS, ELIZABETH ANN HAMPTON, retired nursing educator; b. Detroit, Sept. 27, 1934; d. Grinsfield Taylor Hampton and Ida Victoria (Jones) Hampton; m. James Marvin Peters, Dec. 1, 1956; children: Douglas Taylor, Sara Elizabeth. Diploma, Berea Coll. Hosp. Sch. Nursing, Berea, Ky., 1956; BSN, Wright State U., Dayton, Ohio, 1975; MSN, Ohio State U., Columbus, 1978. Therapist, nurse Eastway, Inc., Dayton, Ohio, 1979-81; therapist, family counseling svc. Good Samaritan-Cmty. Mental Health Ctr., Dayton, Ohio, 1981-83; instr. Wright State U. Sch. Nursing, Dayton, 1983-84; clin. nurse specialist, pain mgmt. program UPSA, Inc., Dayton, 1983-86; staff nurse Hospice of Dayton, Inc., 1985-86, dir. vol. svcs., 1986-89, dir. bereavement svcs., 1986-87; asst. prof. Cmty. Hosp. Sch. Nursing, Springfield, Ohio, 1990-93, prof., 1993—97; ret., 1997; parish nurse Honey Creek Presbyn. Ch., 1998—2003. Co-author (with others): Oncologic Pain, 1987. Mem. Clark County Mental Health Bd., Springfield, 1986-95; mem. New Carlisle (Ohio) Bd. Health, 1990-2003. Mem.: Sigma Theta Tau. Home: 402 Flora Ave New Carlisle OH 45344-1329

PETERS, KENNETH MICHAEL, urologist, researcher; b. Detroit, Apr. 1, 1964; s. William Thomas and Janet Ann Peters; m. Diane Lynn Hogeboom, July 15, 1988; children: Anna Rose, Amanda Leigh. MD, Case Western Res. U. Sch. Medicine, Cleve., 1991. Diplomate Am. Bd. Urology. Resident gen. surgery William Beaumont Hosp., Royal Oak, Mich., 1991—93, resident urology, 1993—97, fellow urology, 1997—98, dir. clin. rsch., dept. urology, 1999—2007, chmn. dept. urology, 2007—; pvt. practice clin. urologist Birmingham Urology Assoc., Mich., 1998—. Contbr. articles to profl. jours., chapters to books. Grantee NIH. Mem.: Internat. Soc. Pelvic Neuromodulation, Internat. Continence Soc., Soc. Urodynamics & Female Urology (Clin. Rsch. award), Mich. Urological Soc., Am. Urological Assn. (mem. rsch. coun.). Achievements include research in nerve rerouting surgery, interstitial cystitis and neuromodulation; the use of neuromodulation for the treatment of interstitial cystitis; pioneering the use of BCG for interstitial cystitis. Office: Comprehensive Urology 31157 Woodward Ave Royal Oak MI 48073-0926 Office Phone: 248-336-0123. Business E-Mail: kmpeters@beaumont.edu.

PETERS, KURT JAMES, retired obstetrician, gynecologist; b. NYC, Jan. 10, 1947; s. John Henry and Gertrude Anna (Lang) Peters; m. Mahafarin Partovi, Nov. 24, 1974; children: Katherine Amy, Suzanne Elizabeth. AB, U. Pa., 1969; MD, Pahlavi Med. Sch., Shiraz, Iran, 1975; diploma, marine radio operator's permit, Chapman Sch. Seamanship, Stuart, Fla., 1997. Intern Boston City Hosp., 1975-76, resident in ob-gyn., 1976-79; clin. instr. ob-gyn. Boston U. Sch. Medicine, 1979-81; pvt. practice Sparta, NJ, 1981-89, Newton, NJ, 1989-97; obstetrician, gynecologist Women's Health Care Assocs., Newton, 2001—11. Mem. attending staff Newton Meml. Hosp., 1981—97, treas. med. staff, 1983—85. Capt. USCG Aux. Mem.: Sussex County Med. Soc., Med. Soc. N.J., Alpha Beta Kappa, Alpha Chi Sigma. Republican. Lutheran. Avocations: boating, scuba diving. Personal E-mail: kurt.peters5@gmail.com.

PETERS, MERCEDES, psychotherapist; b. NYC; BS, L.I. U.; MS, U. Conn.; degree, Am. Inst. Psychotherapy; PhD in Psychoanalysis, Union Inst., 1989. Cert. in psychoanalysis Postgrad. Ctr. Mental Health. Psychotherapist Cmty. Guidance Svc. Postgrad. Ctr. Mental Health; staff affiliate Postgrad. Ctr. for Mental Health, 1974-76; pvt. practice psychoanalysis and psychotherapy, Bklyn.; tchr., supr. psychoanalytic psychotherapy at various psychotherapeutic tng. ctrs., 1975—; cons. to advanced tng. program Jewish Bd. Family and Children's Svcs., 2000—06; mem. Guidance Svc. Tng. Am. Inst. Psychology. Contbr. articles to profl. jours. Past bd. dirs. Brookwood Child Care Assn. Recipient Order in Waith award. Fellow: Am. Orthopsychiat. Assn.; mem.: NASW, LWV, NAACP, Assn. Psychoanalytic Self Psychology, Assn. Psychoanalytic, Nat. Assn. Advancement Psychoanalysis (past bd. dirs., chair UN com.), Wednesday Club. Office: 142 Joralemon St Brooklyn NY 11201-4709 Office Phone: 718-875-9874.

PETERS, THEODORE, JR., emeritus research scientist, consultant; b. Chambersburg, Pa., May 12, 1922; s. Theodore and Miriam (Lenhardt) P.; m. Margaret Campbell, June 9, 1945; children: Theodore D., James C., Melissa Peters Barry, William L. BS in Chem. Engrng. summa cum laude, Lehigh U., 1943; PhD in Biol. Chemistry, Harvard U., 1950. Diplomate Am. Bd. Clin. Chemistry. Grad. asst. MIT, Cambridge, 1943-44; rsch. fellow Harvard Med. Sch., Boston, 1948-50; instr. U. Pa. Sch. Medicine, Phila., 1950-51; biochemist U.S. VA Hosp., Boston, 1953-55; rsch. biochemist Mary Imogene Bassett Hosp., Cooperstown, N.Y., 1955-88, rsch. scientist emeritus, 1988—; vis. scientist Carlsberg Laboratorium, Copenhagen, 1958-59; guest worker NIH, Bethesda, Md., 1971-72; vis. rsch. prof. U. Western Australia, Perth, 1982. Chmn. classification panel FDA, Washington, 1976-79; bd. dirs. Nat. Com. for Clin. Lab. Standards, Villanova, Pa., 1986-87. Author: All About Albumin, Biochemistry, Genetics, and Medical Applications, 1996; chmn. bd. editors Clin. Chemistry, 1979-84; contbr. articles to profl. jours. Mem. Sewer Bd., Cooperstown, 1973—, chmn., 1975-; mem. Water Bd., Cooperstown, 1973—, chmn., 2004-05, mem., Watershed Supervisory Com., Cooperstown, 1999-; chmn. lake com. Otsego County Conservation Assn., Cooperstown, 1972-78. Comdr. USNR, submarine comm. & electronics, 1944-47, 51-53. Recipient Gold medal Biol. div. Electron Microscope Soc. Am., 1966, Conservationalist of Yr. award, Otsego County Conservation Assn., 2006, Outstanding Achievement award, NY Rural Water Assn., 2008. Fellow Am. Assn. Clin. Chemistry (pres. 1988, awards 1976, 77, 91); mem. Am. Chem. Soc., Am. Soc. Biol. Chem. Molecular Biology (emeritus), Am. Soc. for Cell Biology (emeritus), Protein Soc. (emeritus), Nat. Acad. for Clin. Biochemistry (diplomate), Acad. Clin. Lab. Physicians and Scientists, Phi Beta Kappa. Avocations: tennis, hiking, music. Home: 85 Lake St Cooperstown NY 13326-1038 Personal E-mail: tedp@stny.rr.com.

PETERSEN, ANNE C. (CHERYL PETERSEN), foundation administrator, educator; b. Little Falls, Minn., Sept. 11, 1944; d. Franklin Hanks and Rhoda Pauline (Sandwick) Studley; m. Douglas Lee Petersen, Dec. 27, 1967; children: Christine Anne, Benjamin Bradfield. BA, U. Chgo., 1966, MS, 1972, PhD, 1973. Asst. prof., rsch. assoc. Dept. Psychiatry U. Chgo., 1972-80, assoc. prof., rsch. assoc., 1980-82; prof. human devel., head Dept. Individual and Family Studies Pa. State U., University Park, 1982-87, dean Coll. Health and Human Devel., 1987-92, prof. health and human devel., 1987-92; dean grad. sch., v.p. for rsch. throughout state U. Minn., Mpls., 1992-94, prof. adolescent devel. and pediatrics, 1992-96; dep. dir., COO NSF, Arlington, Va., 1994-96; sr. v.p. programs W.K. Kellogg Found., 1996—2005; dep. dir. Ctr. Advanced Study Behavioral Scis. Stanford U., 2006—, prof. Dept. Psychology, 2006—. Vis. prof., fellow Coll. Edn., R&D Psychology, Roosevelt U., Chgo., 1973-74; cons. Ctr. for Health Adminstrn. Studies U. Chgo., 1976-78, Ctr. for New Schs., Chgo., 1974-78, Robert Wood Johnson Found. Mathtech, Inc., 1987-89; coord. clin. rsch. tng. program Michael Reese Hosp. and Med. Ctr., Chgo., 1976-80, dir. Lab. for Study of Adolescence, 1975-82; faculty Ill. Sch. for Profl. Psychology, 1978-79; statis. cons. Coll. Nursing U. Ill. Med. Ctr., 1975-83; assoc. dir. health program MacArthur Found., 1980-82, also cons. health program, 1982-88; chair sr. adv. bd. NIMH, 1987-88; nat. adv. mental health coun. NIH, 1997-2003; trustee Nat. Inst. Statis. Scis., 1998-2004. Author: Sex Related Differences in Cognition Functioning: Developmental Issues, 1979, Promoting Adolescent Health: A Diolog on Research and Practice, 1982, Firls at Puberty: Biological and psychosocial Perspectives, 1983, Brain Maturation and Cognitive Development: Comparative and Cross Cultural Perspectives, 1991, Narrowing the Margins: Adolescent Unemployment and the lack of a social role, 1991, Grofit: A Fortran Program for the Estimation of Parameters of a Human Growth Curve, 1972, Girls at Puberty: Biological and Psychosocial Perspectives, 1983, Adolescence and Youth: Psychological Development in a Changing World, 1984, Youth Unemployment and Society, 1994, Transitions Through Adolescence: Interpersonal Domains and Context, 1996; reviewer Jour. Youth and Adolescence, 1975-80, Devel. Psychology, 1979—, Sci., 1979—, Jour. Edn. Psychology, 1979—, Child Devel., 1980—, Jour. Edn. Measurement, 1980, Ednl. Rschr., 1980, Am. Ednl. Rsch. Jour., 1981—, Jour. Mental Imagery, 1982-92, Sex Roles, 1984—; cons. editor Psychology of Women Quar., 1978-82, assoc. editor, 1983-86; adv. editor Contemporary Psychology, 1985-86; mem. editl. bd. various profl. jours.; contbr. chpts. to books and articles to profl. jours. Bd. overseers Lewis Coll., Ill. Inst. Tech., 1980-82; mem. adv. bd. longitudinal data archive project Murray Ctr., Radcliffe Coll., 1985-91, mem. sci. adv. bd., 1983-91 Fellow: APA (chmn. task force on reproductive freedom 1979—81, program chmn. 1981—82, chmn. task force on long range planning 1986—89, pres. divsn. 7 1992—93), AAAS; mem.: NAS (nat. forum on future children and their families 1987—91, chmn. panel on child abuse and neglect 1991—93, mem. forum on adolescence Inst. of Medicine 1997—2000, chair bd. on behavioral, cognitive and sensory scis. 1997—, mem. nat. academics com. sci., engring., and policy 2003—), Global Phys. Therapy Alliance (pres. 2005—), Soc. for Rsch. on Adolescence (pres. 1990—92, past pres. 1992—94, chmn. nominations com. 1992—94, mem. fin. com.

2004—), Acad. Europaea, Psychometric Soc., Behavior Genetics Assn., Assn. Women in Sci. (bd. dirs. 1996—2000), Am. Ednl. Rsch. Assn. (various offices), Internat. Soc. for the Study of Behavioral Devel. (coun. mem. 1995—, pres.-elect 2002—06, pres. 2006—), Inst. for Medicine. Home: 3715 Blackberry Ln Kalamazoo MI 49008-3333 Office Phone: 650-321-2052. E-mail: globalphilliance@yahoo.com.

PETERSEN, CAROLYN ASHCRAFT, retired psychologist; b. Waxhaw, NC; d. J. Carl and Carolyn (Ray) Wolfe; m. Thomas L. Ashcraft (div. 1973); children: Anne C., Thomas Wolfe; m. Marvin E. Petersen, Nov. 14, 1982. BS, U. N.C.; MA, Vanderbilt U., PhD, 1963. Lic. psychologist, Pa., Fla. Psychologist Peabody Child Study Ctr., Nashville, 1963-64; rschr. U.S. Dept. Edn.-Peabody, Nashville, 1964-65; assoc. prof. Tenn. State U., Nashville, 1965-66; asst. prof. U. Tenn., Nashville, 1966-69, LaSalle Coll., Phila., 1970-72; adj. instr. U. Pa., Phila., 1970-73; clin. psychologist Overbrook Sch. for Blind, Phila., 1974-76, Fla. Sch. for Deaf and Blind, St. Augustine, 1976-78; asst. prof. psychology U. Tampa, Fla., 1979-82; assoc., adj. prof. S.D. State U., Brookings, 1983-89; ret., 1995. Cons. Tenn. Dept. Edn., Cookeville, 1966-69, Charter Hosp., Tampa, 1979-82; organizer symposia for profl. meetings. Contbr. to profl. publs. Bd. dirs. Brookings Hosp. Aux., 1985-88; v.p. S.D. Art Mus. Guild, 1988-89. Fellow Am. Psychol. Soc., Pa. Psychol. Assn.; mem. APA, Southeastern Psychol. Assn., Nat. Register Psychologists. Republican. Avocations: bridge, travel, art. Home: Apt 102 809 Freedom Plaza Cir Sun City Center FL 33573-5289 Personal E-mail: drcarolynpetersen@yahoo.com.

PETERSEN, MAUREEN JEANETTE MILLER, management information technology director, retired nurse; b. Evanston, Ill., Sept. 4, 1956; d. Maurice James and M. Joyce (Mielke) Miller; m. Gregory Eugene Petersen, July 7, 1984; children: Trevor James, Tatyana Brianne. BS in Nursing cum laude, Vanderbilt U., 1978; MS in Biometry and Health Info. Systems, U. Minn., 1984. Nurse U. Iowa Hosps. and Clinics, Iowa City, 1978—82; research asst. Sch. Nursing, U. Minn., Mpls., 1982—83; mgr. Accenture, Mpls., 1984—2001; dir. health info. tech. Park Nicollet, Eden Prairie, Minn., 2003—09, Fair View Health Svcs., 2009—. Mem.: Project Mgmt. Inst. (proj. mgmt. profl.), Mensa. Methodist. Avocation: travel. Home: 494 N Hillscourte Ave Roseville MN 55113-1945 Office: 323 N Stinson Minneapolis MN 55413 Personal E-mail: peters1050@aol.com. Business E-Mail: mpeter49@fairview.org.

PETERSEN, POUL ERIK, dental educator, director; b. Copenhagen, Dec. 9, 1951; m. Vibeke Juul Poulsen; children: Jeppe Juul Petersen, Lotte Juul Petersen. BA, U. Copenhagen, MSc in Sociology, PhD, DDS, 1988. Prof. U. Copenhagen, 1989—; head, global oral health programme WHO, Geneva, 2002—. Achievements include research in epidemiology, sociology, public health and international health. Home: Blvd Epinettes 268 Divona Parc Divonne-les-Bains F01220 France Office: World Health Organization ave Appia 20 1211 Geneva Switzerland Office Fax: 41 22 791 4866; Home Fax: 45 35326780. Personal E-mail: pep@odont.ku.dk. Business E-Mail: petersenpe@who.int.

PETERSEN, ROBERT ALLEN, pediatric ophthalmologist; b. NYC, Dec. 30, 1933; s. Harold Marinus and Elinor Louise (Buckley) P.; m. Veronica Margiana Stinnes, Dec. 22, 1956; children: Anne, Catherine, John. BS, Queens Coll., CUNY, 1955; MD, Columbia U., 1959, DrMedSc, 1964. Diplomate Am. Bd. Ophthalmology. Med. resident Presbyn. Hosp., NYC, 1959-61; USPHS postdoctoral fellow Columbia U. Coll. Physicians and Surgeons, NYC, 1961-62; USPHS preclin. trainee Howe Lab. of Ophthalmology, MEEI, Boston, 1962-63; resident in ophthalmology Mass. Eye and Ear Infirmary, Boston, 1963-66; instr. in ophthalmology to assoc. prof. Harvard Med. Sch., Boston, 1970—; assoc. in Ophthalmology to sr. assoc. Children's Hosp., Boston, 1966—. Contbr. articles to profl. jours. Cons., vision task force Mass. Dept. Pub. Health, 1981-85. Major U.S. Army, 1967-69, South Vietnam. Various rsch. grants NIH, 1961-63, 94—. Fellow Am. Acd. Ophthalmology, Am. Acad. Pediatrics; mem. Am. Assn. for Pediatric Ophthalmology and Strabismus (bd. dirs. 1974-76, edn. com. 1987-93, Costenbader Lectureship com. 1993-96, 97-2000, chair 1995-96, 99-2000, chair site selection com. 1995-97), New Eng. Ophthal. Soc. Mem. Soc. Of Friends. Achievements include rsch. on the genetics of reinoblastoma; first to describe optic nerve hypoplasia in the children of diabetic mothers, to describe eye findings in a variety of systemic anomalies. Office: Children's Hosp 300 Longwood Ave Boston MA 02115-5737 Home Phone: 617-492-0454. E-mail: robert.petersen@childrens.harvard.edu.

PETERSEN, RONALD C., neurologist, educator; BA, Hamline U., St. Paul; PhD, U. Minn.; MD, Mayo Clinic, Rochester, Minn. Cert. Am. Bd. Psychiatry and Neurology. Internship in internal medicine Stanford U. Med. Ctr., Palo Alto, Calif.; residency in neurology, Mayo Grad. Sch. Medicine Mayo Clinic, Rochester, Minn., prof. neurology, dir., Mayo Alzheimer's Disease Rsch. Ctr.; fellowship in behavioral neurology Harvard U. Med Sch./Beth Israel Hosp., Boston. Editor: Memory Disorders, Mayo Clinic on Alzheimer's Disease, Mild Cognitive Impairment: Aging to Alzheimer's Disease, Mayo Clinic Guide to Alzheimer's Disease; contbr. articles to profl. jours. Recipient MetLife award for med. rsch. in Alzheimer's disease, 2004, Potamkin prize, Am. Acad. Neurology, 2005, Leon Thal prize for excellence in dementia rsch., Lou Ruvo Brain Inst., 2007. Mem.: Nat. Alzheimer's Assn. (vice chmn., med. and sci. adv. com. 2005—08), Alzheimer's Assn. (chair, med. & sci. adv. com. 2008, Ronald and Nancy Reagan Rsch. Inst. award 2004). Office: Mayo Clinic 200 First St SW Rochester MN 55905 Office Phone: 507-284-2511, 507-538-0487. Office Fax: 507-284-0161, 507-538-6012.

PETERSON, ALFRED EDWARD, retired family physician; b. Bridgeport, Conn., Mar. 23, 1922; s. Carl Emil Rudolf and Elin Maria (Lindholm) P.; m. June Meadows, May 27, 1944 (dec. Apr. 22, 2007); children: Christina, Elin (dec.), Martha, Amy. BA, Dartmouth Coll., 1946; MD, U. Vt., 1950. Diplomate Nat. Bd. Med. Examiners. Intern Binghamton City Hosp., NY, 1950-51; pvt. practice Binghamton, 1952—2005; ret., 2005. Sch. physician Chenango Forks (N.Y.) Ctrl. Schs., 1953-94; founding mem. Chenango Bridge Med. Group. Bd. dirs. Chenango Emergency Squad, Binghamton, 1980-85, Robert W. Smith Found., Rotary Club, 1980-2003; bd. dirs. med. records Broome CC, Binghamton, 1988-94. Capt. USAAF, 1943-45. Fellow Am. Acad. Family Physicians; mem. AMA, N.Y. State Med. Soc., Broome County Med. Soc., N.Y. State Acad. Family Physicians. Democrat. Avocations: travel, history.

PETERSON, ANN SULLIVAN, physician, consultant; b. Rhinebeck, NY, Oct. 11, 1928; AB, Cornell U., 1950, MD, 1954; MS, MIT, 1980. Diplomate Am. Bd. Internal Medicine. Intern Cornell Med. Divsn.-Bellevue Hosp., NYC, 1954—55, resident, 1955—57; fellow in medicine and physiology Meml.-Sloan Kettering Cancer Ctr., Cornell Med. Coll., NYC, 1957—60; instr. medicine Georgetown U. Sch. Medicine, Washington, 1962—65, asst. prof., 1965—69, asst. dir. clin. rsch. unit, 1962—69; assoc. prof. medicine U. Ill., Chgo., 1969—72, asst. dean, 1969—71, assoc. dean, 1971—72; assoc. prof. medicine, assoc. dean Coll. Physicians and Surgeons, Columbia U., NYC, 1972—80, Cornell U. Med. Coll., NYC, 1980—83; assoc. dir. divsn. med. edn. AMA, Chgo., 1983—86, dir. div. grad. med. edn., 1986—89, v.p. mgmt. cons. corp., 1989—93; ind. cons. Chgo., 1993—2005. Contbr. articles to med. jours. Mem. bd. regents Uniformed Svcs. U. of Health Scis., 1984—90. John and Mary R. Markle scholar, 1965—70, Alfred P. Sloan fellow, MIT, 1979—80. Fellow: ACP; mem.: Mortar Bd., Alpha Omega Alpha, Alpha Epsilon Delta.

PETERSON, BART R. (BARTON R. PETERSON), pharmaceutical company executive, former mayor; b. Indpls., June 15, 1958; m. Amy Minick Peterson; 1 child, Meg. Grad., Purdue U., 1980; JD, U. Mich., 1983. Atty. Ice Miller Donadio & Ryan, Indpls.; exec. asst. environ. affairs to chief staff to gov. Evan Bayh Indpls., 1989—95; pres. Precedent Co., 1995; mayor Indpls., 2000—08; sr. v.p. corp. affairs & comm. Eli Lilly & Co., Indpls., 2009—. Fellow politics John F. Kennedy Sch. Govt., Harvard U., 2008; disting. vis. prof. pub. policy Ball State U., 2008—. Bd. mem. Ind. Nature Conservancy, Regenstrief Found. Democrat. Office: Eli Lilly & Co Lilly Corp Center 893 S Delaware Indianapolis IN 46285 also: Ball State U 2000 W University Ave Muncie IN 47306 Office Phone: 617-495-1360. Office Fax: 617-496-4344. E-mail: bart_peterson@ksg.harvard.edu.

PETERSON, DONNA RAE, health facility administrator, gerontologist, director; b. Wichita, Kans., Aug. 29, 1948; d. Raymond Houston and Edna Brooks (Waddell) Hobbs; m. William E. Peterson, Nov. 7, 1993; 1 child, Shauna Layne Heath. Student, Wichita State U., 1968—70; BS in Mgmt., N.W. Christian Coll., 1996, MA in Interdisciplinary Studies Gerontology, 2000. Adminstrv. asst. postgrad. edn. Med. Sch. U. Kans., Wichita, 1974—80; activity coord. continuing med. edn. Wesley Med. Ctr., Wichita, 1980—84; mgr. support svcs. 9th dist. Farm Credit Svcs., Wichita, 1984—88; mgr. sales and mktg. Amb. Travel, Eugene, Oreg., 1988—93; dir. mktg. Peterson Design Devel., Eugene, 1993—95; pres. Davinci Designs, Eugene, 1996—2000; owner 2d Half Dynamics, 2000—; dir. Alzheimer's program Sunwest Mgmt., Inc., 2002—04; adult/elder specialist, life coach United Behavioral Health, 2004—06; adminstr. Bayberry Commons Assisted Living and Memory Care, Springfield, Oreg., 2006—08; caregiver rels. dir. Home Instead Sr. Care, 2008—10; gerontology Instr. Lane CC, Eugene, Oreg., 2010—; cmty. rels. coord. New Horizons In Home Care, 2011—. Cons. Jr. League Wichita, 1983, Plancon, Inc., Martinsville, NJ, 1987-88, Changing Creatively, 1997; continuing edn. instr. Lane C.C., 2000—; mem. adv. bd. Lane C.C. Ctr. for Leisure and Learning, 2000—. Mem. Wichita Conv. and Visitors Bur., 1987; mem. events com. Wichita Festivals, Inc., 1987; mem. Eugene Conv. and Visitors Bur., 1988—; mem. Eugene Airport Commn., 1991—, chmn., 1992-93; bd. dirs. Campus Life, chmn., 1993-94; mem. steering com. Eugene Celebration, 1991-94, Oreg. Women Bus. Owners Conf., 1997; bd. pres. Of Coun. for Bus. Edn., 1999-2000. Mem. AAUW, Am. Mktg. Assn. (pres. S.W. chpt. 1991—, pres. 1992-94, bd. dirs.), Soc. Travel Agt. in Govt., Adminstrv. Mgmt. Soc., Forum for Exec. Bus. Women, Gt. Plains Bus. Adminstrn. Group, Assn. Travel Exec., Eugene C. of C. (bus. devel. com. 1990-91), The Gerontol. Soc. Am. (student campus rep. 1999, sr. disabled svcs. adv. coun., 2007-), Alzheimers Assn. (Oreg. chpt., edn. com., 2002-, leadership coun., 2008-, LCC adv. coun., 2008-), Eugene High Ground Assn. (chmn.), Delta Gamma Alumni Assn, SW Willimalte Valley Coun. (bd. chmn., 2008-). Republican. Avocations: decorating, writing, skiing, water-skiing, camping. Home: 1460 Olive St Apt 32 Eugene OR 97401-3991 Office Phone: 541-485-2273. Personal E-mail: gerovision@comcast.net, donna@bayberrycommons.com, gerovision@comcast.net.

PETERSON, HERBERT BRYSON, obstetrician, gynecologist, educator; b. Maryville, Tenn., Sept. 24, 1951; BA in biology, Wittenberg U., 1973; MD, U. Pitts., 1977. Cert. Ob-Gyn., 1986, Pub. Health and Gen. Preventative Medicine, 1989. Intern U. NC, Chapel Hill, 1977—79, resident, 1979—81; chief, Epidemiologic Studies br. CDC, chief, Women's Health and Fertility br.; with Dept. Reproductive Health and Rsch. WHO; clin. prof. Emory U., Atlanta, 1994—2002; joint prof. U. NC Sch. Medicine, Chapel Hill, 1994—2004, prof. obstetrics and gynecology, 2004—; prof. and chair maternal and child health U. NC Gillings Sch. Global Pub. Health, Chapel Hill, 2004—, Kenan disting. prof., 2009—; fellow U. NC Cecil B. Sheps Ctr. Health Services Rsch., Chapel Hill. Recipient Disting. Svc. medal, USPHS, 1999. Fellow: Am. Coll. Epidemiology, Am. Coll. Preventive Medicine, Am. Coll. Obstetricians and Gynecologists; mem.: Inst. Medicine, Soc. Gynecol. Investigation, Am. Gynecol. and Obstet. Soc. Office: 430A Rosenau Hall Campus Box 7445 135 Dauer Dr Chapel Hill NC 27599 Office Phone: 919-966-5981. Office Fax: 919-966-0458. E-mail: herbert_peterson@unc.edu.

PETERSON, JAMES ROBERT, engineering psychologist; b. St. Paul, Apr. 16, 1932; s. Palmer Elliot and Helen Evelyn (Carlson) P.; m. Marianna J. Stockvig, June 26, 1954; 1 child, Anne Christine. BA in Psychology cum laude, U. Minn., 1954, MA in Exptl. Psychology, 1958; PhD in Engring. Psychology, U. Mich., 1965. Devel. engr. Honeywell Inc., 1961-65, sr. devel. engr., 1965-67, staff engr., 1967-90, sr. project staff engr., 1990-93, retired, 1993. Honeywell sponsor rep. Shuttle Student Involvement Program, 1982, 84; emeritus Human Factors and Ergonomics Soc. Contbr. articles to profl. jours. With USMC, 1954-57, USMCR, 1957-62. Mem. Air and Space Mus. (charter), Smithsonian Inst., Masons, Am. Legion, Delta Upsilon (life). Achievements include invention of Apollo translation hand controller; participation in development work in all U.S. Manned Space Programs (Mercury, Gemini, Apollo, Lunar Excursion Module, Manned Orbiting Laboratory, Space Shuttle and Space Sta.) as member/manager of associated human factors groups. Home: 3303 San Gabriel St Clearwater FL 33759-3341 Personal E-mail: bpeteputt@aol.com.

PETERSON, JEANNINE DORSEY, healthcare consultant; b. Pitts., July 25, 1951; d. Cornelius H. and Clara M. (Walker) Dorsey; m. William F. Peterson, Nov. 6, 1976; 1 child, Kendra Rose. BA, Mich. State U., 1973; MPA, Pa. State U., 1978. Case worker St. Francis Hosp., Pitts., 1973-74; program analyst Gov. Coun. on Drug and Alcohol Abuse, Harrisburg, Pa., 1974-78, dir. divsn. planning, 1978-80; dir. divsn. intervention Office Drug and Alcohol Programs Dept. Health, Harrisburg, 1980-82, dir. Bur. Program Svcs., 1982-87, dep. sec., 1987-93, dep. sec. Office Health Promotion, Disease and Substance Abuse, 1993-95; prin. Johnson Bassing & Shaw Inc., 1995—. Adj. prof. Lincoln (Pa.) U., 1983-84; med./legal adv. com. Pa. Atty. Gen., 1991-94; cons. CSAP, Washington, 1992, NYU, P.R., 1992, U.S. V.I., 1992, Hawaii, 1993, Birch and Davis, New Orleans, 1994, George Washington U., Tampa, Fla., 1994; active Nat. Adv. Coun. Health Human Svcs. CSAT, 1993—. Active Jack & Jill in Am., 1993—. Mem. Nat. Assn. State Alcohol and Drug Abuse Dirs. (bd. dirs. 1993-95), Alpha Kappa Alpha. Avocations: swimming, reading. Home: 1815 Signal Hill Dr Mechanicsburg PA 17050-1648 *

PETERSON, LANCE ROBERT, physician; b. Mpls., Sept. 2, 1947; s. Alvin Robert and Norma Lorraine (Soderlin) P.; m. LoAnn Charlotte Liukonen, Aug. 24, 1968; children: Anja Kristine, Kari Elizabeth. BS, U. Minn., 1970, MD, 1972. Diplomate Am. Bd. Internal Medicine, Am. Bd. Infectious Diseases, Am. Bd. Med. Microbiology. Intern U. Minn., 1972—73, resident, 1973—75; med. dir. home care VA Med. Ctr., Mpls., 1975—77, staff infectious diseases, 1977—92; dir. clin. microbiology Northwestern Meml. Hosp., Chgo., 1992—2002; dir. microbiology and infectious diseases rsch. NorthShore U., Evanston, 2002—, health care epidemiologist, 2005—. Prof. medicine U. Minn., Mpls., 1990—92, prof. lab. medicine, 1990—92; prof. pathology and medicine Northwestern U., Chgo., 1992—2009; chief microbiology VA Med. Ctr., Mpls., 1979—92, assoc. chief molecular biology, 1987—89; staff infectious diseases Northwestern Meml. Hosp., Chgo., 1992—2002, dir. prevention epicenter, 1999—2002; clin. prof. U. Chgo., 2009—. Co-editor: Diagnostic Microbiology, 9th edit.; editor: The Biologic and Clinical Basis of Infectious Diseases, 5th edit.; contbr. chpts. to books and articles to profl. jours. Pres. Greater Mpls. Day Care Assn., 1985-86; bd. dir. Cmty. Child Care Ctr., Mpls., 1986-89, VA Employees Child Care Ctr., Mpls., 1987-92, chair fundraising com., 1987-92. Grantee, VA Dept., 1978—88, Bayer, Inc., 1985—2006, R.W. Johnson Rsch. Instn., 1990—2004, Ctrs. Disease Control, 1999—2004, Wyeth, Inc., 2003—, Wash. Sq. Health Found., 2003—04, 2006—08, Gene Ohm Scis., 2006—, Cepheid, Inc., 2006—, Nanosphere, Inc., 2006—09, NIH, 2009—, AHRQ, 2010—, others. Fellow: Ctrl. Soc. Clin. Rsch. (chair. infectious diseases sect. 1995—97), Am. Soc. Clin. Pathologists, Infectious Diseases Soc. Am. (regional bd. 1991—92, sec.-treas. Chgo. area 2003—), Am. Acad. Microbiology; mem.: Assn. Molecular Pathology (chair elect., infectious diseases subdivsn. 2010), Am. Soc. Microbiology (BD Rsch. Clin. Microbiology award 2005, NQF Eisenberg award 2007, chair conf. com. 2010—). Avocations: travel, jogging, gardening. Office: NorthShore Univ 2650 Ridge Ave Evanston IL 60201 Home Phone: 847-835-2971. Personal E-mail: lance1@uchicago.edu. Business E-Mail: lpeterson@northshore.org.

PETERSON, LARS GUSTAF, orthopedist; b. Jarna, Sweden; MD, Gothenburg U., 1966, PhD, 1974; PhD (hon.), Helsinki U., Finland, 2010, U. Catolica San Antonio, Spain, 2011. Prof. orthop. Sahlgrenska Acad. Gothenburg U., 2000—07, asst. prof., 1973—83; vis. prof. Hosp. Joint Diseases Orthop. Inst. NYU, 1982—83; head dept. Orthop. Sahlgrenska U. East Hosp., 1983—88; clin. dir. Gothenburg Med. Ctr. Sports Medicine Clinic, 1988—2007. Bd. mem. Swedish Sports Med. Rsch. Coun., 1975—82; pres. Swedish Soc. Sports Medicine, 1985—87; pres. founding mem. Internat. Cartilage Repair Soc., 2001—02; mem. FIFA Med. Com. Fed. Internat. De Football Assn., 1979, FIFA Med. Assessment & Rsch. Ctr. Fedn. Internat. Football Assn., 1994. Recipient award, Harvard Med. Sch. Boston, 1995, Jubilee prize, Silver medal, Swedish Soc. Medicine, Cartilage Repair Lifetime award, Intenat. Cartilage Repair Soc., 2004, Duke Edinburg prize, Inst. Sport Medicine, London, 2010; named Top Ten Med. Advances, 1994, Hall of Fame, Am. Orthop. Soc. Sports Medicine, 2007. Mem.: Internat. Soc. Arthroscopy, Knee Surgery & Orthop Sport Medicine, Am. Acad. Orthop. Surgeons. Avocations: sports, history. Home: Billdals Hagen Vag 41 Billdal Vastra Gotaland 427 37 Sweden Home Fax: 46 31 914161. Personal E-mail: peterson.lars@telia.com.

PETERSON, RALPH E., endocrinologist, researcher; b. Paola, Kans., Aug. 21, 1918; s. William Oscar and Alice Danial Peterson; children: Susan, Merrill, Larry, Patricia, Dean, Sandi. BS, Kans. State U., 1940, MS, 1941; postgrad., Brown U., 1941—42; MD, Columbia U., 1946. Resident U. Minn. Hosp., Mpls., 1946—48; asst. chief dept. chemistry Walter Reed Med. Ctr., Washington, 1950—52; sr. clin. investigator NIH, Bethesda, 1953—58; dir. divsn. endocrinology Cornell U. Med., NYC, 1958—83; prof. med. NY Hosp. Cornell U., NYC, 1958—83; dir. med. rsch. svc. VA, Washington, 1983—90; ret., 1990. Contbr. articles to profl. jours. Recipient Rsch. Career award, NIH, 1962—83, Foster Fuqua award, Am. Acad. Pediat., 1977, Nicholas Pichardo award, Santo Domingo, Dominican Rep., 1980; fellow Fulbright, How Florey Inst., 1964—65. Mem.: AAAS, Endocrine Soc., Am. Assn. Physician, Am. Soc. Clin. Investigation, Am. Fed. Clin. Res., Am. Chem. Soc. Avocation: scultpure. Home: PO Box 10545 El Paso TX 79995-0545

PETERSON, RONALD R., hospital administrator; b. New Brunswick, NJ, 1948; m. Elizabeth Rooney; children: Joey, Susie. MA in Hosp. Adminstrn., Johns Hopkins U., Balt., 1970. Adminstrv. resident Johns Hopkins U., Balt., 1973, adminstr. Henry Phipps Psychiatric Clinic, 1974, adminstr. cost improvement program, 1975, adminstr. Children's Ctr., 1978, adminstr. Balt. City Hosps., 1982, pres. Johns Hopkins Bayview Med. Ctr., 1984—99, exec. v.p., COO Johns Hopkins Health Sys., 1995—97, acting pres. Johns Hopkins Hosp., 1996, acting pres. Johns Hopkins Health Sys., 1996—97, pres., John Hopkins Hosp., 1996—, pres., John Hopkins Health Sys., 1997—. Mem. bus. adv. coun., Balt.; vol. ARC, United Way, Am. Heart Assn. Mem. Md. Hosp. Assn. (mem. exec. com.), Md. C. of C. Office: Johns Hopkins Hosp 600 N Wolfe St Baltimore MD 21287-0005 also: Johns Hopkins U 720 Rutland Ave Baltimore MD 21205-2109 Office Phone: 410-955-5000. *

PETERSON, STEFAN SWARTLING, healthcare educator; b. Sweden, Apr. 16, 1962; MD, Uppsala U., 1990; MPH, Harvard U.; PhD, Uppsala U., 2000. Prof., Global Health Karolinska Inst., 2009—. Office: Global Health IHCAR Nobels Väg 9 Stockholm 17177 Sweden Office Fax: 46 8 311590. Business E-Mail: stefan.peterson@ki.se.

PETERSON, STEPHEN JOSEPH, internist; b. Bellerose, NY, Mar. 17, 1953; s. Robert Francis and Veronica Mae (Burns) P. BS in Biology, Fairfield U., Conn., 1975; MD, Cebu Drs. Coll. Medicine, Cebu City, The Philippines, 1982. Diplomate Am. Bd. Internal Medicine, 1985. Intern internal medicine Met. Hosp. Ctr. N.Y. Med. Coll., 1982—83, resident to chief resident internal medicine Valhalla, NY, 1983—86, dir. medicine clerkship, 1994—2003; assoc. program dir. Met. Hosp. Ctr., NYC, 1986—88; dep. dir. dept. medicine Lincoln Med. & Mental Health Ctr., Bronx, 1988—93; attending physician Westchester Sq. Hosp Med. Ctr., Bronx, 1993—94; dir. internal medicine residency tng. program Westchester Med. Ctr., Valhalla, 1994—2007, chief gen. internal medicine, 1994—. Bd. dirs. St. Agnes Hosp., White Plains, NY, 1995—2003; asst. prof. medicine NY Med. Coll., 1986—96, assoc. prof. clin. medicine, 1996—99, adj. prof. pharmacology, 2001—06; mem. med. edn. coms. N.Y. Med. Coll., Westchester Med. Ctr.; prof. clin. medicine NY Med. Coll., 1999—2006, vice chmn. dept. medicine, 2002—06, exec. vice chair, 2006—, prof. medicine and pharmacology, 2006—, prof. clin. public health, 2006—. Contbr. articles to profl. jours. Recipient Advisor award Med. Explorers Boy Scouts Am., 1986, 88. Master ACP (gov. Hudson Valley region 2004-08); mem. AMA, Clerkship Dirs. Internal Medicine, Assn. Program Dirs. Internal Medicine, Assoc. Chiefs Gen. Internal Medicine, Soc. Gen. Internal Medicine, Assn. Profs. Medicine. Rep. Roman Cath. Avocations: singing, exercise. Office: NY Med Coll Munger Pavillion # 256 Valhalla NY 10595 Home Phone: 914-455-2214; Office Phone: 914-493-8370. Business E-Mail: stephen_peterson@nymc.edu.

PETERSON, STEVEN W., clinical documentation improvement specialist; m. Melissa J. Peterson. AS, Allen County CC, Iola, Kans., 1996; BSN, Baker U., Baldwin City, Kans., 2002; MSN student. RN Kans., cert. legal nurse cons., Kans., critical care RN, neonatal, AACN. Med. advisor Am. Legion Boys State Kans., Topeka, 1994—. Mem.: ANA, AACN, Kans. State Nurses Assn., Assn. Clin. Documentation Improvement Specialist, Am. Assn. Legal Nurse Cons., Kans. Bar Assn., Acad. Neonatal Nursing, Sigma Theta Tau Internat. Home: 2418 SW Pepperwood Cir Topeka KS 66614 Personal E-mail: stevep_rn@yahoo.com.

PETERSON, W(ALTER) SCOTT, ophthalmic surgeon; b. Newton, Kans., Sept. 5, 1944; s. Walter F. and Elizabeth (Wiebe) P.; m. Jean Louise Murray, Dec. 16, 1967; children: James Scott, Hilary Jean. BA summa cum laude, Yale U., 1966, MD, 1971. Diplomate Am. Bd. Ophthalmology. Ophthalmic surgeon OptiCare Eye Health Ctr., 1974—. Mem. tchg. faculty Yale U. Med. Sch., New Haven, 1975—. Author: An Approach to Paterson, 1967. Bd. dirs. Waterbury Found., 1985-2000, pres., 1997-2000; trustee Dickinson Coll., 1993-2000, Internat. Eye Found., 2005—. Recipient Med. Sci. award Am. Diabetes Assn., 1980, Promotion Peace Vision award Internat. Eye Found., 2009. Fellow ACS, Am. Acad. Ophthalmology; mem. MLA, New England Ophthal. Soc., William Carlos Williams Soc., Phi Beta Kappa Assocs. Office: OptiCare Eye Health Ctr 87 Grandview Ave Waterbury CT 06708-2563 Office Phone: 203-574-2020. Business E-Mail: wsp@opticare.pc.net.

PETERSSON, PIA, nurse; b. Svedala, Sweden, Apr. 11, 1961; PhD, Örebro U., 2009. Head primary health care ctr. Primary Care Blekinge, 1996—2010; head nursing program Kristianstad U., 2010—. Office: Kristianstad University Kristianstad 29188 Sweden Business E-Mail: pia.petersson@hkr.se.

PETIET, CAROLE ANNE, psychologist; b. Newport News, Va., Mar. 1, 1952; d. Gaston Kaleski and Ann (Snyder) Pettit Johnson; m. Lawrence Phillip Bischoff III, Dec. 29, 1973 (div. 1979); m. Robert Jomax Brooks, May 4, 1984 (div. 1989); 1 child, Nicole; stepchildren: Gregory, Randall. BS in Nursing, Baylor U., 1975; MA, Calif. Sch. Profl. Psychology, Berkeley, 1980, PhD, 1982. RN Calif.; lic. psychologist Calif., Colo. Charge nurse Elizabeth Knutsson Hosp., Estes Park, Colo., 1975-76; nurse coordinator, staff nurse Alta Bates Hosp., Berkeley, Calif., 1976-83; pvt. practice psychotherapy, cons., sports psychology Berkeley, Calif., 1982—; tng./clin. cons., rsch. cons. Phoenix Recovery Ctrs., Alameda, Calif., 1980-88; staff psychologist Kaiser Permanente Med. Ctr., Vallejo, Calif., 1982-84. Sports psychology cons. Women's Ski Programs, Aspen, Colo., and B.C., Can., 1986-93; co-coord. women's studies splty., mem. faculty Rosebridge Grad. Sch., Walnut Creek, Calif., 1986-94; supr., mem. adj. faculty CSPP, Berkeley/Alameda, 1986-89; intern Eden Youth and Family Svcs., Hayward, Calif., 1978-79, No. Calif. State Correctional Med. Facility, Vacaville, 1979-80, Kaiser Vallejo, 1980-81, Kaiser San Francisco, 1981-82; rschr. in field. Contbr. articles, presentations to profl. publs. Scholar Baylor Hosp. Women's Aux., 1974, Soroptimists, 1981; recipient Am. Coll. Scholarship, 1979. Mem. APA, Assn. Women in Psychology, World Fedn. Mental Health, NOW, Amnesty Internat. Democrat. Achievements include research on neuropsychological effects of altitude on women climbers; participant in the 1986 American Women's Expedition to Mount Kongur, China. Office: 2340 Ward St Ste 105 Berkeley CA 94705-1146 Office Phone: 510-843-6760.

PETILLO, JOHN J., academic administrator; b. Montclair, NJ, Mar. 19, 1947; s. Gennaro and Geraldine (Illaria) Petillo; m. Sabina M. Porcaro; 1 child. Earned undergraduate degree, Seton Hall U., 1969, MA in Counseling, 1971; profl. diploma in counselor edn., Fordham U., 1973, PhD in Counseling and Personnel Services, 1976; M.Div. in Pastoral Theology, Darlington Sch. Theology, 1975; M.P.A., Rutgers U., 1977. Ordained priest Roman Cath. Ch., 1973; left priesthood, 1990; asst. dir. Office Rsch. and Planning Archdiocese Newark, NJ, 1975—77, chancellor for adminstrn. NJ, 1978—83; dep. dir. Cath. Cmty. Services, NJ, 1976—78; asst. to pres. Seton Hall U., South Orange, NJ, 1978, chancellor, CEO, 1983—90, mem. bd. trustees and bd. regents, 1983—; chancellor, CEO Immaculate Conception Sem., 1983; pres., CEO Newark Alliance, 2001—04; chmn. bd. trustee U. Medicine and Dentistry NJ, 2003—, interim pres., 2004, pres., 2004—06; dean. John F. Welch Coll. Bus. Sacred Heart U., Fairfield, Conn., 2009—11, interim pres., 2010—11, pres., 2011—. Mem. Archdiocesan Bd. Adminstrn. Mem. long range-strategic planning com. United Way Am.; bd. dirs. Blue Cross NJ, Nat. Soc. Prevention Blindness, Nat. Commn. on Coop. Edn., Found. Ednl. Alternatives, Ind. Coll. Fund NJ, NJ State Police Meml. Library and Mus. Assn., labor-higher edn. council Am. Council on Edn. and AFL-CIO, Commn. for Pub. Responsibility for Ednl. Success, Washington Ctr. NJ Scholarship Program, Statue of Liberty Centennial Commn. State NJ, NJ Performing Arts Ctr., St. Joseph's Health System, Wachovia Regional Found., Lincoln Educational Svcs.; chmn. bd. Essex County Coll. Found. Mem. Assn. Ind. Colls. and Univs. NJ (bd. dirs.) Office: Sacred Heart University Office of President 5151 Park Ave Fairfield CT 06825-1000 Office Phone: 203-371-7999. *

PETIT, JEAN-YVES, pharmacologist, educator; b. France, Jan. 19, 1945; PhD in Pharmacology, Faculty Pharmacy, Nantes, France, 1975. Prof. U. Nantes, 1972—2009. Pharmacologist referee doping drugs CNOSF, Paris. Contbr. chapters to books. Marine officer. Rsch. grant, Ministry of Health, France. Mem.: French Soc. Pharmacology & Physiology. Achievements include research in mechanisms of action of new anti-inflammatory and immunosuppressive drugs. Home: 34 Rue Felibien 44000 Nantes France Home Phone: 33 2 40 89 76 90. Personal E-mail: jeanpeti@numericable.fr. Business E-Mail: jean-yves.petit@univ-nantes.fr.

PETIT, PARKER HOLMES, investment company executive; b. Decatur, Ga., Aug. 4, 1939; s. James Percival and Ethel (Holmes) P.; m. Janet Lewis; children: William Wright, Patricia Monique, Meredith Katherine. BS in Mech. Engring., Ga. Inst. Tech., 1962, MS in Engring. Mechanics, 1964; MBA, Ga. State U., 1973. Engr. Gen. Dynamics Corp., Fort Worth, Tex., 1966-67; engring. project mgr. Lockheed-Ga. Co., Marietta, 1967-71; pres., founder, CEO Healthdyne, Inc., Marietta, 1971—2008; founder, pres. The Petit Group, Roswell, Ga., 2008—. Bd. dirs. Atlantic S.E. Airlines, Atlanta, Healthdyne Technologies, Inc., Atlanta, Healthdyne Info. Enterprises, Inc., Marietta, Ga., Matria Healthcare, Inc., Marietta, Logility Corp., Atlanta, Intelligent Sys., Norcross, Ga. Author: Primer on Composite Materials, 1968; patentee in field Chmn. bd. dirs. Sudden Infant Death Syndrome Alliance, Washington, 1986; active nat. adv. coun. Emory U. Med. Sch., Coun. fellows for the Emory, Ga. Tech. Biomed. Tech. Rsch. Ctr.; bd. dirs. Ga. Rsch. Alliance, 1995. 1st lt. U.S. Army, 1964-67. Recipient Humanitarian award La Societe Francaise de Bienfaisance, 1981; named Ga. Tech. Acad. Disting. Alumni, 1994; named to Tech. Hall of Fame Ga., 1994, Ga. State Bus. Sch. Hall of Fame, 2007; Internat. Bus. fellow, 1986. Mem. NAE, Health Industry Mfrs. Assn., Cobb County C. of C. (bd. dirs. 1980-82), Atlanta C. of C. (bd. dirs. 1997—), Pi Kappa Phi. Republican. Methodist. Avocations: flying, painting, golf, tennis. Office: The Petit Group 300 Colonial Ctr Pky Ste 130 Roswell GA 30076 Office Phone: 770-650-7570. Office Fax: 770-650-7569. Business E-Mail: pete.petit@thepetitgroup.com. *

PETOIN, DOMINIQUE SYLVAIN, plastic surgeon; b. Apr. 23, 1954; MD, Paris, 1982, degree in surgery, 1984, degree in plastic reconstrn. and aesthetic surgery, 1984; degree in cancerology, 1993. Intern Hopitaux de Paris, 1977, chief clinic Assistant de la Faculte, 1984; specialist Centre Lutte Contre le Cancer, St. Cloud, France, 1987. Contbr. articles to profl. jours. Mem.: Soc. Francaise Senologe, Soc. Francaise Plastique Reconstructive et Esthetique. Address: Chirurgien Plasticien 6 Ave Mac Mahan Paris 75017 France

PETR, NOVAK, microbiologist; b. Ostrava, Czech Republic, May 8, 1974; PhD, Charles U., 2002. With Sandia Nat. Labs., 2002—04; sr. rsch. scientist Inst. Microbiology, 2004—. Mem.: Czech Soc. Mass Spectrometry, Am. Soc. Mass Spectrometry. Avocations: motorcycling, skiing, jogging. Office: Videnska 1083 Prague 14220 Czech Republic Business E-Mail: pnovak@biomed.cas.cz.

PETRAGLIA, ANTHONY LIBERATO, neurosurgeon; BA, U. Chgo., 2002; MD, Sch. Medicine & Dentistry, U. Rochester, 2007. Neurosurgeon, dept. neurosurgery U. Rochester Med. Ctr., 2007—. Rsch. grant, Richter Fund, U. Chgo., NIH, Rsch. fellowship, Howard Hughes Med. Inst. Mem.: Am. Assn. Neurol. Surgeons, Congress Neurol. Surgeons, Sigma Xi, Alpha Omega Alpha. Avocations: golf, bowling, cooking, football. Office: 601 Elmwood Ave Box 670 Rochester NY 14586

PETRAGLIA, FELICE, medical educator; s. Giuseppe Petraglia and Maria Grazia Macellaro; m. Silvia Sardelli, Sept. 3, 1983; children: Maria Grazia, Enrica. MD, U. Siena, Italy, 1980. Lic. U. Siena, 1980. Prof. and chair obstetrics and gynecology U. Siena, 2000—, chair dept. pediat., obstetrics and reproductive medicine, 2002—08, chair residency and PhD program, 2000—; adj. prof. obstetrics and gynecology U. Toronto, 2005—. Grant com. mem. Med. Rsch. Coun. Can., Royal Coll. Obstetrics and Gynecology, Rsch. Grant Coun. Hong Kong, Wellcome Trust; com. med. edn. mem. Ministry Health, Italy; editor in chief Jour. Endometriosis. Contbr. scientific papers to med. jours. Recipient San Marino prize on Reproductive Medicine, Republic of San Marino, 1988, Internat. award Arnaldo Bruno, Accademia Nazionale Lincei, 2001; grantee Mechanisms of Onset of Labor, Italian NRC, 1993—98;, 2006—10. Mem.: European Assn. Gynecologists and Obstetricians (sci. com. mem. 1996—99), European Soc. Human Reproduction and Embriology, Endocrine Soc., European Bd. and Coll. Obstetrics and Gynecology (coun mem. 2006—10), Internat. Soc. Gynacological Endocrinology (exec. com. mem. 1990—2008), Soc. for Gynecologic Investigation (pres. 2008—). Roman Catholic. Achievements include discovery of inhibin and activin in human placenta; follistatin and urocortin in endometriosis; patents for in fields; first to identify neuroendocrine mechanisms regulating placenta and endometrial function; development of non invasive diagnosis for endometriosis. Office: Univ Siena-Sch Medicine Viale Mario Bracci 16 53100 Siena SI Italy Office Fax: 39 0577 233454. Business E-Mail: petraglia@unisi.it.

PETRAKIS, NICHOLAS LOUIS, epidemiologist, medical researcher, educator; b. San Francisco, Feb. 6, 1922; s. Louis Nicholas and Stamatina (Boosalis) P.; m. Patricia Elizabeth Kelly, June 24, 1947; children: Steven John, Susan Lynn, Sandra Kay. BA, Augustana Coll., 1943; BS in Medicine, U. S.D., 1944; MD, Washington U., St. Louis, 1946. Intern Mpls. Gen. Hosp., 1946-47; physician, researcher U.S. Naval Radiol. Def. Lab., San Francisco, 1947-49; resident physician Mpls. Gen. Hosp., 1949-50; sr. asst. surgeon Nat. Cancer Inst., USPHS, San Francisco, 1950-54; asst. research physician Cancer Research Inst., U. Calif., San Francisco, 1954-56; asst. prof. preventive medicine U. Calif. Sch. Medicine, San Francisco, 1956-60, assoc. prof., 1960-66, prof., 1966-91, chmn. dept. epidemiology and internat. health, 1978-88, prof. emeritus, 1991—; prof. epidemiology U. Calif. Sch. Pub. Health, Berkeley, 1981-91. Assoc. dir. G.W. Hooper Edn., U. Calif., San Francisco, 1970-74, acting dir., 1974-77, chmn. dept. epidemiology and internat. health, 1979-89; co-dir. Breast Screening Ctr. of No. Calif., Oakland, 1976-81; cons. Breast Cancer Task Force, Nat. Cancer Inst., Bethesda, Md., 1972-76; chmn. Biometry & Epidemiology Contract Rev. Com., Bethesda, 1977-81; bd. sci. counselors, divsn. cancer etiology Nat. Cancer Inst., Bethesda, 1982-86; scientific adv. com. Calif. State Tobacco-Related Disease Rsch. Program, 1991-93; cons. U. Crete Sch. Medicine, Heraklion, Greece, 1984. Contbr. articles to profl. jours. Eleanor Roosevelt Internat. Cancer fellow Am. Cancer Soc., Comitato Reserche Nucleari, Cassacia, Italy, 1962; U.S. Pub. Health Service Spl. fellow Galton Lab., U. London, 1969-70; recipient Alumni Achievement award Augustana Coll., Sioux Falls, S.D., 1979, Axion award Hellenic-Am. Profl. Soc. of Calif., San Francisco, 1984, Lewis C. Robbins award Soc. for Prospective Medicine, Indpls., 1985, Otto W. Sartorius, MD, award from Susan Love MD Breast Cancer Found., 2001. Mem. Am. Soc. Preventive Oncology (founding, pres. 1984-85, Disting. Achievement award 1992), Soc. for Prospective Medicine (founding), Am. Assn. Cancer Rsch., Am. Epidemiol. Soc., Am. Soc. Clin. Investigation, Am. Bd. Preventive Medicine (cert.). Achievements include research in breast cancer, med. oncology and hematology. Office: U Calif Sch Medicine Dept Epidemiology & Biostats Box 0560 MU420W San Francisco CA 94143-0001 Home: 1450 Post St Apt 415 San Francisco CA 94109

PETRAKOPOULOU, PARASKEVI A., cardiologist; b. Komotini, Greece, Sept. 2, 1977; MD, Ludwig-Maximilians-U., Munich, 2003. Cardiology resident U. Hosp. Grosshadern, Munich, 2003—05, cardiac surgery- heart transplantation resident, 2007—08; cardiology resident Papageorgiou Hosp., Thessaloniki, Greece, 2008—. Achievements include research in cardiac allograft vasculopathy. Home: Vryoulon Str 20 Kalamaria Thessaloniki 55132 Greece Office: Papageorgiou Hosp Ring Rd Thessaloniki 56429 Greece Personal E-mail: ppetrakopoulou@yahoo.gr.

PETRALI, JOHN PATRICK, anatomist, researcher, pathologist; b. Fairview, NJ, July 30, 1933; s. John and Yolanda (Stigliano) P.; m. Sadie Belle Hose, Dec. 7, 1963 (div. 1990). Student, Boston U., 1956-58; BS cum laude, Davis and Elkins, 1955; PhD, U. Md., Balt., 1969. Cert. electron microscopy technologist, Md. Rsch. anatomist, team leader U.S. Army Med. Rsch. Inst., Aberdeen Proving Ground, 1962—. Asst. prof. dept. anatomy U. Md., 1969-72, assoc. prof., 1975-80, adj. assoc. prof., 1990—; advisor/ cons. Md. Optical Assn., Balt., 1985. Editl. bd. Jour. Ophthamology, 1987; contbr. chpt. to book and articles to profl. jours. Bd. dirs. Forward Step, Edgewood, Md., 1978-81; treas., pres., coun. mem. coun. Civic Improvement Assn., Edgewood, 1970-75; treas., mem. coun. Civic Assn., Priestford Hills, Md., 1988-90. With U.S. Army, 1958-60. Recipient Achievement awards U.S. Med. Rsch. Labs., 1990-95, Comdr.'s medal, 1992, Exhibit awards Microscopy Soc. Am., 1994-95. Mem. Chesapeake Soc. Microscopy (pres., v.p., coun.). Avocations: jogging, horseback riding. Home: 204 Goucher Way Churchville MD 21028-1220 Office: US Army Med Rsch Inst Ricketts Point Rd Aberdeen Proving Ground MD 21010-5425 *

PETRELLI, MASSIMILIANO DONATO, endocrinologist; b. Matera, Italy, Feb. 17, 1967; s. Pier Giorgio Petrelli and Angela Rosa Sicolo; m. Gabriella Giuseppina Maria Garrapa, Sept. 13, 1997. MD, U. Ancona, 1992. Postgrad. fellow Dept. Endocrinology, Ancona, Italy, 1992—98; sr. registrar Dept. Dietetic and Clin. Nutrition, Ancona, Italy, 1999—. Catechist Parrish S. Pio X, Fano, Pesaro, Italy, 1980—86. Lt. Italian Air Army, 1995—95. Rsch. fellow, Dept. Medicine, 1996, Rsch. grantee, Italian Soc. Hypertension, 1998. Roman Catholic. Avocations: computer, travel, movie making, reading, drawing. Home: Piave 55 Ancona 60124 Italy Office: Umberto I Hosp Via Conca 1 60126 Ancona AN Italy Office Fax: *39 071 5963586.

PETRIASHVILI, MARINA, physician; arrived in US, 1997; d. Linette Tsertsvadze. MD, Tbilisi State Med. U., Georgia, 1983—89; student, NYU Sch. Medicine. Diplomate Tbilisi State Med. U., 1989, Ednl. Commn. for Foreign Med. Graduates Ednl. Commn. For Fgn. Med. Graduates, 1998, cert. Anesthesiology Residency NY U. Sch. of Medicine/NY, 2004, Fellowship in Cardiac Anesthesiology NY U. Sch. of Medicine, 2005, Am. Bd. of Anesthesiology Written Test Am. Bd. of Anesthesiology, 2004. Attending physician Rehab. Ctr. Kartli, Tbilisi, Georgia, 1990—93, Dimitrov Hosp. and Clinics Found., Tbilisi, Georgia, 1994—97; residency in surgery Albert Einstein Coll. of Medicine, Bronx, 2000—01; residency in anesthesiology NY U. Med. Ctr., NY, 2001—04; fellowship in cardiac anesthesiology NY U. Sch. of Medicine, NY, 2004—05; with Woodhull Med. and Mental Health Ctr., Bklyn. Active mem. Am. Soc. of Anesthesiologists, 2001; mem. Soc. of Cardiovasc. Anesthesiologists, 2004, Am. Soc. of Echocardiography, NY State Soc. of Anesthesiologists, NY, 2001. Recipient Honors Diploma, Tbilisi State Med. U. Mem.: AMA (corr.). Personal E-mail: petrim02@hotmail.com.

PETRICA, LIGIA, nephrologist, educator; b. Zalau, Salaj, Romania, Mar. 20, 1958; d. Augustin and Lucia Popa; m. Maxim Petrica, Aug. 12, 1989; children: Flaviu, Lamia. MD in Medicine, U. Medicine and Pharmacy, Timisoara, Romania, 1983, PhD in Nephrology, 1998. Cert. in abdominal ultrasound U. Medicine and Pharmacy, 1999, nephrologist cons. U. Medicine and Pharmacy, 2000. Asst. prof. nephrology U. Medicine and Pharmacy, 1991—2004, lectr. nephrology, 2004—08, assoc. prof. nephrology, 2008—. Sect. editor nephrology Ctrl. European Jour. Medicine. Author: Cerebrovascular Disease Within the Frames of Chronic Kidney Disease, 2007, Update in Nephrology, 2009; contbr. articles to ISI-quoted med. jours.; reviewer in field:; contbr. chapters to books. Scholar, Medicines sans Frontiers, 1994. Mem.: World Fedn. Socs. Ultrasound Med. Biology, European Fedn. Socs. Ultrasound in Medicine and Biology, European Renal Assn. European Dialysis and Transplant Assn., Internat. Soc. Nephrology. Avocations: literature, classical music, travel. Office: County Emergency Hosp Nephrology 10 I Bulbuca Str Timisoara Timis 380557 Romania Home: Strada Telegrafului C11 Apt 7 Timisoara 300125 Romania Personal E-mail: ligia_petrica@yahoo.co.uk. Business E-Mail: ligiapetrica@rdslink.ro.

PETRIE, WILLIAM MARSHALL, psychiatrist; b. Louisville, Oct. 19, 1946; s. Garner McReynolds and Claire (Samuels) P.; children: Christopher W., Ellen M., Shelley M.; m. Lori L. Molchin, Oct. 1, 1994; 1 child, Halle C. BA, Vanderbilt U., 1968, MD, 1972. Research psychiatrist NIMH, Rockville, Md., 1975-77; asst. prof. dept. psychiatry Vanderbilt Med. Ctr., Nashville, 1977-81, assoc. prof., 1981-82, assoc. clin. prof., 1982-87, clin. prof., 1992—, prof. clin. psychiatry, dir. geriat. psychiatry, 2011; pvt. practice psychiatry Psychiat. Cons., P.C., Nashville, 1982—, pres., 1996—; med. dir. Pavtham Pavilian, 2007—08, Rolling Hills Hosp., 2009—11; prof. clin. psychiatry Vanderbilt Med. Ctr., 2011—. Bd. dirs Psychiat. Solutions, Inc.; clin. instr. Georgetown U. Med. Ctr., 1975—77; cons. psychopharmacology rsch. br. NIMH, 1977—80; rschr. in geriatric psychopharmacology; med. dir. memory Study Ctr., 1987—; chmn. of psychiatry Parthenon Pavilion, 1994—96; bd. trustees Centennial Mutual Ctr., 1994—2000, vice-chmn. bd. trustees, 1998—2000; pres. Columbia Psychiat. Care Network, 1997—98, Psychiat. Cons., PC, 1999—2005; med. dir. Parthenon Pavilion, 2007—, Rolling Hills Hosp., 2009—. Mem. editl. bd. Gen. Hosp. Psychiatry, 1995—, Audio Digest Psychiatry, 1996-99; contbr. articles to profl. jours.; chpts. to books. Fellow Am. Psychiat. Assn. (disting. fellow, pres. mid. Tenn. dist. br. 1986-87); mem. AMA, Tenn. Med. Assn., Am. Assn. Geriatric Psychiatrists, Am. Coll. Psychiatrists, Tenn. Psychiat. Assn. (pres. 1999-2000). Democrat. Methodist. Office: Vanderbilt Med Ctr 1500 21st Ave N Ste 1100 Nashville TN 37212 Home Phone: 615-373-5033; Office Phone: 615-936-3555. Business E-Mail: william.petrie@vanderbitt.edu.

PETRINOVICH, LEWIS FRANKLIN, psychologist, educator; b. Wallace, Idaho, June 12, 1930; s. John F. and Ollie (Steward) Petrinovich. BS, U. Idaho, 1952; PhD, U. Calif., Berkeley, 1962. Asst. prof. San Francisco State Coll., 1957—63; from assoc. to prof. SUNY, Stony Brook, 1963-68; prof. U. Calif., Riverside, 1968-91, chmn. psychology, 1968-71, 86-89, prof. emeritus, 1991—. Bd. dirs. Eastman Med. Products, Cymed Corp., 1997—2008. Author: Understanding Research in Social Sciences, 1975, Introduction to Statistics, 1976, Human Evolution, Reproduction and Morality, 1995, Living and Dying Well, 1996, Darwinian Dominion: Animal Welfare and Human Interests, 1999, The Cannibal Within, 2000; editor: Behavioral Development, 1981, Habituation, Sensitization and Behavior, 1984; cons. editor Behavioral and Neural Biology, 1972-90, Jour. Physiol. and Comparative Psychology, 1980-82, Jour. Comparative Psychology, 1983-90. Bd. dirs. Friends of Big Band Jazz, 2001—07. Fellow APA, Am. Psychol. Soc., Calif. Acad. Scis., Human Behavior and Evolution Soc., Western Psychol. Assn.; mem. Am. Ornithol. Union, Animal Behavior Soc., Sigma Xi Home: 415 Boynton Ave Berkeley CA 94707-1701 Office: U Calif Riverside Psychology Dept Riverside CA 92521-0001 Personal E-mail: lpetrin@aol.com.

PETROIANU, ANDY, surgeon, educator; b. Brăila, Romania, Sept. 2, 1952; arrived in Brazil, 1962; s. Jac and Sonia (Laurian) P.; 1 child, Larissa P.G. Petroianu Student philosophy, Fed. U. Minas Gerais, Belo Horizonte, Brazil, 1972—75; MD, Fed. U. Minas Gerais, Belo Horizonte, 1976, MS Surgery, 1981, MS Physiology, 1983, PhD, 1985, PhD, 1997. Specialist in surgery, docent in surgery. Intern emergency svc. João XXIII Hosp., Belo Horizonte, 1973—76; intern cardiovasc. surgery svc. Felicio Rocho Hosp., Belo Horizonte, 1974—76; resident surgery Fed. U. Minas Gerais, Belo Horizonte, 1979, clin. instr. surgery, 1978—81, asst. prof., 1981—85, assoc. prof., 1985—94, prof., 1994—, chief rsch. group medicine, 1987—, dir. internship surgery, 1995—; free docent surgery Fed. U. São Paulo, Brazil, 1990, U. São Paulo, Ribeirão Preto, Brazil, 1992. Rschr. Nat. Coun. Rsch., 1983—; rsch. fellow, clin. instr. Health Scis. Ctr., Bklyn., 1986-87; dir. surg. group Hosp. of Clinics, 1984—; dir. assessory in medicine Nat. Coun. Rsch. Brasilia, 1996-2000; presenter in field Editor: Clinical and Technics, 1984, Geriatric Surgery, 1997, Clinical and Surgical Geriatry, Surgical Anatomy, Surgical Decision Making, Surgical Deontology, 1998-99, Ethics in Medicine, Tubes and Drains, Endocrinology and Surgical Endocrinology, 2000, Surgical Therapeutics, Surgical Clinics, Clinical and Surgical Emergency, 2001, The Spleen, 2002, Routines in Gastroenterology, 1993, Surgical Lectures, 1997, Topics in Gastroenterology, 1997, Black Book in Surgery, 2008, Surgical Clinics, 2010, Kidney Transplantation, 2010, The Spleen, 2011; contbr. over 480 articles to profl. jours Mem. Brazilian Assn. Medicine (sec. 1979-85), Brazilian Assn. U. Profs., Brazilian Coll. Surgeons (v.p., Best Rschr. in Surgery 1987), Brazilian Assn. Organ Transplants, Acad. Medicine Minas Gerais Avocations: literature, swimming, tourism, writing. Office: Fed U Minas Gerais Medical Sch Avenida Alfredo Balena 190 30130100 Belo Horizonte Brazil Home: Avenida Afonso Pena 1626 - Apt 1901 30130-005 Belo Horizonte MG Brazil Home Phone: 55-31-8884-9192; Office Phone: 55-31-3274-7744. Personal E-mail: petroian@gmail.com. Business E-Mail: petroian@medicina.ufmg.br.

PETRONE, WILLIAM FRANCIS, pediatrician, microbiologist, corporate executive; b. Bklyn., Sept. 12, 1949; s. Arthur Carmen and Helen (Kenny) P.; m. Kathleen Anne Baron, Aug. 25, 1979; children: William Gaetano, Katherine Bridget, Jason Daniel. BA, U. Conn., 1972; MS, U. Mass., 1974; PhD, U. R.I., 1978; MD, U. South Ala., 1984. Diplomate Am. Bd. Pediatrics, Pediatric Emergency Medicine, Gen. Pediatrics. Rsch. assoc. Coll. Medicine U. South Ala., Mobile, 1978-80; resident in pediat. Orlando Regional Med. Ctr., Fla., 1984—85, W.Va. Univ. Med. Ctr., 1985—87; emergency rm. physician, pediat. emergency svcs. Mercy Hosp., Springfield, Mass., 1987—2006, Harrington Meml. Hosp., Southbridge, Mass., 2006—; founder & CEO MediED LCC, 2010—. Med. Simulation Software, Cmty. Pediat. Assoc. Contbr. articles on inflamation and white blood cell function to sci. jours. Fellow Am. Acad. Pediat., Am. Coll. Emergency Physicians; mem. AAAS, AMA, N.Y. Acad. Scis., Sigma Xi. Roman Catholic. Office: Mercy Hosp Emergency Unit PO Box 9012 Springfield MA 01102-9012

PETROSSIAN, GEORGE ARMEN, interventional cardiologist, educator; MD, NYU, 1983. Diplomate Am. Bd. Internal Medicine-cardiovascular disease, Am. Bd. Internal Medicine-interventional cardiovascular. Resident in internal medicine Columbia-Presbyn. Med. Ctr., NYC, 1984—87, fellow in cardiovascular disease, 1987—89; fellow in interventional cardiology Mass. Gen. Hosp., Boston, 1989—90; interventional cardiologist South Nassau Cmtys. Hosp., St. Francis Hosp. Office: St. Francis Hospital 100 Port Washington Blvd Roslyn NY 11576 Office Phone: 516-562-6000. Office Fax: 516-705-6661.

PETROVSKY, NIKOLAI, endocrinologist, researcher; b. Launceston, Tasmania, Australia, May 26, 1959; s. Constantin Petrovsky and Kathleen Maxwell; m. Sharon Pringle; children: Willem, Andrei, Isobella. B of Med. Sci., U. Tasmania, 1979, MBBS, 1982; PhD, U. Melbourne, Victoria, 1998. Dir. Nat. Health Sci. Ctr., Canberra, ACT, Australia, 2000—04; prof. U. Canberra, 2001—; assoc. prof. Australian Nat. U., 2004; dir. endocrinology dept. Flinders Med. Ctr., 2004—; prof. medicine Flinders U., 2004—; chmn. Vaxine Pty. Ltd., 2003—. Fellow: Royal Australasian Coll. Physicians; mem.: Internat. Immunomics Soc. (sec. gen.), Immunology of Diabetes Soc., Australian Diabetes Soc., Australasian Soc. Immunology. Home: 11 Walkley Ave Warradale 5046 Australia Business E-Mail: nikolai.petrovsky@flinders.edu.au.

PETROZZA, PATRICIA H., anesthesiologist; b. Phila., Jan. 5, 1953; d. Thomas B. and Frances (McCarron) Harper; m. Joseph A. Petrozza, Sept. 23, 1978 (div. Oct. 1997); 1 child, Anthony. BS, Chestnut Hill Coll., 1974; MD, Jefferson Med. Coll., 1978. Diplomate Am. Bd. Anesthesiology. Intern Washington Hosp. Ctr., 1978-79; resident in anesthesia U. Md., Balt., 1981-84, fellow in neurol. anesthesia, 1983-84; mem. staff N.C. Bapt. Hosp., Winston-Salem, 1984—, head neurol. anesthesiology, 1993—; prof. anesthesiology Wake Forest U. Sch. Medicine, Winston-Salem, 2000—, assoc. dean for grad. med. edn., 2001—. Mem. AMA, Am. Soc. Anesthesiologists (editor-in-chief 1993-97, self edn. program), So. Med. Assn., Internat. Anesthesia Rsch. Soc., Soc. Neurol. Anesthesia and Critical Care (pres. 1998). Office: Wake Forest U Med Ctr Dept Anes Wake Forest U Sch Medicine Medical Center Blvd Winston Salem NC 27157-0009 Office Phone: 336-716-2965.

PETTERSEN, EIRIK, cardiologist; b. Fredrikstad, Norway, July 7, 1975; MD, U. Oslo, 2001, PhD, 2010. Rsch. fellow Oslo U. Hosp., 2003—07; resident Akershus U. Hosp., 2008—. Mem.: European Soc. Cardiology (Young Investigators' award). Office: Akershus Universitetssykehus Lørenskog Akershus 1478 Norway Business E-Mail: eirik@pettersen-jung.com.

PETTERSON, GOSTA, surgeon; b. Sweden; MD, Gothenburg U., Sweden, 1971, PhD. Bd. cert. in gen. and thoracic surgery Sweden, Denmark, Norway and England, cert. European Bd. Thoracic and Cardiovascular Surgery. Residency in gen. surgery Sahlgrenska U. Hosp., Gothenburg, 1971—76, residency in cardiothoracic surgery, 1977—81, staff cardiothoracic surgeon, 1981—90; clin., rsch. fellowship, dept. surgery U. Ill. Coll. Medicine, Chgo., 1979—80; prof. cardiothoracic surgery U. Copenhagen, 1990; chief surgeon, dept. cardiothoracic surgery State U. Hosp. Rigshospitalet, Copenhagen; chief cardiothoracic surgery Hamlet Pvt. Hosp., 1998—99; staff cardiothoracic surgeon Cleve. Clinic Found., 1999—, vice chmn. dept. thoracic & cardiovascular surgery, surg. dir. lung transplantation. Chmn. endocarditis working group Internat. Soc. Chemotherapy; mem. OPTN/UNOS Thoracic Organ Transplantation Com., Region 10; expert on cardiothoracic surgery Sweden, Denmark; guest prof. China, Romania, US. Author: My Heart Needs Repair, You Have Touched My Heart; contbr. articles to profl. jours. Mem.: Soc. Thoracic Surgeons, Am. Assn. Thoracic Surgery, Internat. Soc. Heart and Lung Transplantation, European Assn. Cardiothoracic Surgery, Finnish Surg. Soc. (hon.), Lithuanian Soc. Cardiothoracic Surgery (hon.), Romanian Acad. Sci. (hon.), Romanian Acad. Med. Sciences (hon.), European Congenital Heart Surgeons Club (hon.). Avocations: running, skiing, horseback riding, hunting. Office: Cleveland Clinic Found 9500 Euclid Ave # F25 Cleveland OH 44195-0002 Office Phone: 216-444-2035. Office Fax: 216-445-3294.

PETTERSSON, GÖRAN, medical researcher; b. Nyköping, Sweden, Sept. 5, 1952; PhD, Linköping U., Sweden, 1985. Rsch. scientist Pharmacia, 1985—93, GE Healthcare, 1993—2006; med. writer Ferring Pharms., 2007—. Avocations: sailing, motorcycling. Office: Kay Fiskers Plads 11 Copenhagen DK-2300 Denmark Business E-Mail: gop@ferring.com.

PETTIGREW, RODERIC I., federal agency administrator, radiologist, researcher; BS in Physics, cum laude, Morehouse Coll., Atlanta, 1972; MS in Nuc. Medicine and Engring., Rensselaer Poly. Inst., Troy, NY, 1973; PhD in Applied Radiation Physics, MIT, 1977; MD, U. Miami, 1979. Intern/resident internal medicine Emory U., Atlanta; resident nuc. medicine U. Calif., San Diego; clin. rsch. scientist Picker Internat.; Robert Wood Johnson Found. fellow Emory U., 1985; prof. radiology, medicine (cardiology) & bioengring. Emory U. Sch. Medicine, dir. Ctr. Magnetic Resonance Rsch.; dir. Nat. Inst. Biomed. Imaging & Bioengring. NIH, Bethesda, Md., 2002—. Contbr. articles to profl. jours. Recipient Benjamin E. Mays award, 1989; named a Most Disting. Alumnus, U. Miami, 1990. Fellow: Am. Inst. Med. & Biomed. Engring., Internat. Soc. Magnetic Resonance in Medicine, Am. Coll. Cardiology, Am. Heart Assn.; mem.: Nat. Acad. Engring., Inst. Medicine, Phi Beta Kappa. Achievements include research in dynamic three-dimensional imaging of the heart using magnetic resonance; development of first computer software package specifically designed for cardiac imaging using MRI. Office: NINIB 6707 Democracy Blvd Bethesda MD 20892 Office Phone: 301-496-8859. Office Fax: 301-480-0679. E-mail: roderic.pettigrew@nih.gov. *

PETTIGREW, THOMAS FRASER, social psychologist, educator; b. Richmond, Va., Mar. 14, 1931; s. Joseph Crane and Janet (Gibb) Pettigrew; m. Ann Hallman, Feb. 25, 1956; 1 child, Mark Fraser. AB in Psychology, U. Va., 1952; MA in Social Psychology, Harvard U., 1955, PhD, 1956; DHL (hon.), Governor's State U., 1979; DSN (hon.), Philipps U., Germany, 2008. Rsch. assoc. Inst. Social Rsch., U. Natal, Republic South Africa, 1956; asst. prof. psychology U. N.C., 1956-57; asst. prof. social psychology Harvard U., Cambridge, Mass., 1957-62, lectr., 1962-64, assoc. prof., 1964-68, prof., 1968-74, prof. social psychology and sociology, 1974-80; prof. social psychology U. Calif., Santa Cruz, 1980-94, rsch. prof. social psychology, 1994—; prof. social psychology U. Amsterdam, 1986-91. Adj. fellow Joint Ctr. Polit. and Econ. Studies, Washington, 1982—; adv. bd. women's studies program Princeton (N.J.) U., 1985-2001; vis. prof. Westfaelishe Wilhelms-U., Germany, 1993, Philipps U., Germany, 2000, 01, 04, 06, Schiller U., Germany, 2002; Glynn Resident scholar, Washington & Lee U., 2008; disting. vis. prof. Flinders U., Australia, 1997; sr. fellow Rsch. Inst. for the Comparative Study of Race and Ethnicity, Stanford U., 2001-02, mem. German govt. adv. com. Intercultural Conflicts and Social Integration, 2003-2006 Author: (with E.Q. Campbell) Christians in Racial Crisis: A Study of the Little Rock Ministry, 1959, A Profile of the Negro American, 1964, Racially Separate or Together?, 1971; (with Frederickson, Knobol, Glazer and Veda) Prejudice, 1982; (with Alston) Tom Bradley's Campaigns for Governor: The Dilemma of Race and Political Strategies, 1988, How to Think Like a Social Scientist, 1996, (with L.R. Troop) When Groups Meet: The Dynamics of Intergroup Contact, 2011; editor: Racial Discrimination in the United States, 1975, The Sociology of Race Relations: Reflection and Reform, 1980; (with C. Stephan & W. Stephan) The Future of Social Psychology: Defining the Relationship Between Sociology and Psychology, 1991; mem. editorial bd. Jour. Social Issues, 1959-64, Social Psychology Quarterly, 1977-80; assoc. editor Am. Sociol. Rev, 1963-65; adv. bd. Integrated Edn, 1963-84, Phylon, 1965-93, Edn. and Urban Society, 1968-90, Race, 1972-74, Ethnic and Racial Studies, 1978-95, Rev. of Personality and Social Psychology, 1980-85, Cmty. and Applied Social Psychology, 1989-2004, Individual and Politics, 1989-93, Jour. Ethnic and Migration Studies, 1994—, 21st Century Afro Rev., 1994—; contbr. articles to profl. jours. Chmn. Episcopal presiding Bishop's Adv. Com. on Race Relations, 1961-63; v.p. Episcopal Soc. Cultural and Racial Unity, 1962-63; mem. Mass. Gov.'s Adv. Com. on Civil Rights, 1962-64; social sci. cons. U.S. Commn. Civil Rights, 1966-71; mem. White House Task Force on Edn., 1967; mem. nat. task force on desegregation policies Edn. Commn. of States, 1977-79; trustee Ella Lyman Cabot Trust, Boston, 1977-79; Emerson Book Award com. United Chpts. Phi Beta Kappa, 1971-73; com. status black Ams. NRC, 1985-88. Guggenheim fellow, 1967-68, Sr. Scientist fellow NATO, 1974, Ctr. Advanced Study in Behavioral Scis. fellow, 1975-76, Sydney Spivack fellow Am. Sociol. Assn., 1978, Netherlands Inst. Advanced Study fellow, 1984-85, Bellagio (Italy) Study Ctr. resident fellow, Rockefeller Found., 1991; Fulbright New Century scholar, 2003-04; recipient Kurt Lewin Meml. award Soc. for Psychol. Study Social Issues, 1987, (with Martin) Gordon Allport Intergroup Rels. Rsch. prize, 1988, Faculty Rsch. award U. Calif., Santa Cruz, 1988, (with Tropp) Gordon Allport Intergroup Rels. Rsch. prize, 2003, Disting. Social Scis. Emeriri Faculty award, U. Calif., Santa Cruz, 2008. Fellow APA (Weiss meml. lectr., 2003), Am. Sociol. Assn. (coun. 1979-82, mem. sociol. practices and pub. sociology sect., William Foot White Distinct Career award, 2011), Internat. Acad. Intercultural Rsch. (Lifetime Achievement award, 2008, U. Calif. Panunzio Disting. award, 2009), Soc. Psychol. Study Social Issues (coun. 1962-66, pres. 1967-68, Disting. Svc. award 1998); mem: Soc. Exptl. Social Psychology (Disting. Scientist award 2002), Soc. Psychol. Study of Pease Conflict & Violence (Ralph White Lifetime Achievement award, 2010), European Assn. Social Psychology, Internat. Soc. Polit. Psychology (Harold Lasswell Lifetime Achievement award 2010). Home: 524 Van Ness Ave Santa Cruz CA 95060-3556 Business E-Mail: pettigr@ucsc.edu.

PETTIT, GEORGE ROBERT, chemist, educator, cancer researcher; b. Long Branch, NJ, June 8, 1929; s. George Robert and Florence Elizabeth (Seymour) P.; m. Margaret Jean Benger, June 20, 1953; children: William Edward, Margaret Sharon, Robin Kathleen, Lynn Benger, George Robert III. BS, Wash. State U., 1952; MS, Wayne State U., 1954, PhD, 1956. Tchg. asst. Wash. State U., 1950-52, lecture demonstrator, 1952; rsch. chemist E.I. duPont de Nemours and Co., 1953; grad. tchg. asst. Wayne State U., 1952-53, rsch. fellow, 1954-56; sr. rsch. chemist Norwich Eaton Pharms., Inc., 1956-57; asst. prof. chemistry U. Maine, 1957-61, assoc. prof. chemistry, 1961-65, prof. chemistry, 1965; vis. prof. chemistry Stanford U., 1965; prof. chemistry Ariz. State U., 1965—, chmn. organic chemistry divsn., 1966-68, disting. rsch. prof., 1978-79, Dalton prof. medicinal chemistry and rsch., 1986—2005, Regent's prof. chemistry, 1990—. Vis. prof. So. African, Univs., 1978; dir. Cancer Rsch. Lab., 1974-75, 2005, Cancer Rsch. Inst., 1975-2005; co-dir. Ariz. Prostate Cancer Task Force, 2000-05; lectr. various colls. and univs.; cons. in field. Contbr. articles to profl. jours. Mem. adv. bd. Wash. State U. Found., 1981—85. With Res. USAF, 1949—53. Recipient Alumni Achievement award, Wash. State U., 1984; named to Academic Hall of Fame, Pub. Schs., City of Long Br., NJ, 2009. Fellow: Am. Inst. Chemists (Guenther award in chemistry of natural products 1998, Pioneer award 1989, Ariz. Gov.'s Excellence award 1993); mem.: Am. Soc. Oncology, Am. Assn. Cancer Rsch., Am. Soc. Pharmacognosy (Rsch. Achievement award 1995), Chem. Soc. London, Am. Chem. Soc. (mem. awards com. 1968—71), Phi Lambda Upsilon, Sigma Xi. Office: Ariz State U Dept Chemistry and Biochemistry Tempe AZ 85287-2404

PETTIT, JOHN W., health facility administrator; b. Detroit, Mar. 6, 1942; s. John W. and Clara (Schartz) P.; m. Kathleen Endres, Aug. 8, 1970; children: Julie, Andrew, Michael. BBA, U. Notre Dame, 1964; MBA, Mich. State U., 1974. CPA, Mich.; CFP, 2001. Acct. Ernst & Ernst, Detroit, 1964-67; chief acct. Detroit Inst. Tech., Detroit, 1967-69; controller, dir. adminstrn. & fin. Mich. Cancer Found., Detroit, 1969-80; chief adminstrv. officer Dana-Farber Cancer Inst., Boston, 1980-94; exec. v.p., chief oper. officer John Wayne Cancer Inst., Santa Monica, Calif., 1995-97; fin. cons. LA, 1998—. Grant reviewer Nat. Cancer Inst., Bethesda, Md., 1979-94. Pres. advanced mgmt. program Mich. State U., 1978-79; mem. adv. bd. Arthritis Found. So. Calif. chpt., 1999—2004; mem. Town Meeting, Wellesley, Mass., 1991-94. Avocations: sailing, woodworking, photography, music. Home and Office: 4518 Winnetka Ave Woodland Hills CA 91364 Office Phone: 818-226-3832. E-mail: john@jwpfinancial.com.

PETZ, THOMAS JOSEPH, internist; b. Detroit, Feb. 10, 1930; s. Arthur J. and Marie (McCarthy) P.; m. Catherine Crowe, June 13, 1959; children: Thomas Jr., William, David, John, Catherine. BS, U. Detroit, 1951; MD, Wayne State U., Detroit, 1955. Diplomate Am. Bd. Internal Medicine and Pulmonary Disease. Intern Harper Hosp., Detroit, 1955-56, resident, 1958-59, 60-62, U. Calif., San Francisco, 1959-60; clin. instr. Wayne State U., Detroit, 1962-72, assoc. prof., 1972-76, clin. assoc. prof., 1976-95, clin. prof., 1996-97, prof. emeritus, 1997—; pvt. practice pulmonary disease and internal medicine Detroit, 1962-72, St. Clair Shores, Mich., 1977-96; med.-legal cons. Northville, Mich., 1996—. Chief pulmonary Wayne State U., Detroit, 1974-76, Harper Hosp., Detroit, 1972-79; dir. med. intensive care unit Harper Hosp., Detroit, 1977-83; chmn. dept. medicine Bon Secours Hosp., Grosse Pointe, Mich., 1984-86; chmn. Gen. Motors human rsch. com., 1995-2010. Bd. govs. Wayne State Sch. of Medicine Alumni Assn., Detroit, 1981-85. Recipient Tchr. of Yr., Harper Hosp. Dept. of Medicine, 1972—73. Fellow Detroit Acad. Medicine (pres. 1982-83), Am. Coll. Chest Physicians, Detroit Med. Acad.; mem. Am. Coll. Physicians, Respiratory Found. SE Mich.(pres.2006-), Detroit Med. Club. Republican. Roman Catholic. Avocation: golf.

PETZEL, ROBERT ANDREW, federal agency administrator; b. Berwyn, Ill., 1943; married; 3 children. Grad., St. Olaf Coll., 1965; MD, Northwestern U., 1969. Cert. Internal Medicine. Chief of staff Minn. VA Med. Ctr., Mpls., 1980—95; network dir. Upper Midwest Health Care Network (VISN 13) US Dept. Veterans Affairs, Mpls., 1995—2002, network dir. Midwest Health Care Network (VISN 23), 2002—09, co-chair Nat. Strategic Planning Coun. and Sys. Redesign Steering Com., acting prin. dep. under sec. for health Veterans Heath Adminstrn., 2009—10, under sec. for heath, 2010—. Faculty mem. U. Minn. Med. Sch. Office: US Dept Veterans Affairs Veterans Health Adminstrn 810 Vermont Ave, NW Washington DC 20420 *

PEWEN, WILLIAM F., legislative staff member; b. Pasadena, Calif. BS in Health Edn., Southern Oreg. State U.; MPH in Epidemiology, U. Pitts., 2001, PhD in Infectious Diseases and Microbiology, 2003.

Sr. health policy advisor, Senator Olympia Snowe US Senate, Washington, 2004—. Congl. fellow, Am. Soc. Microbiology, 2003—04. Republican. Office: 154 Rayburn Senate Office Bldg Washington DC 20515 Office Phone: 202-224-5344. Office Fax: 202-224-1946.

PEZZONE, MICHAEL A., physician, internist, educator; BA in Chemistry and Biochemistr, Cornell U., Ithaca, 1983—87; MD in Neuroimmunology and Stress, U. Pitts., PhD in Neuroimmunology and Stress, 1987—94. Diplomate Am. Bd. Internal Medicine-gastroenterology, Am. Bd. Internal Medicine, cert. Pa., 1996. Intern internal medicine Univ. of Pitts. Med. Ctr. (UPMC), 1994—95; resident internal medicine Univ. Pitts. Med. Ctr., 1995—97, fellow internal medicine; hosp. affiliations include UPMC Mercy South Side Surgery Ctr., UPMC Presbyn. South Surgery Ctr., UPMC Mercy, UPMC Passavant, UPMC Presbyn., UPMC Shadyside, Magee-Womens Hosp. of UPMC; instr. of medicince, pharmacology and chem. biology Univ. of Pitts., 1999—2001, asst. prof. medicine, pharmacology and chem. biology, 2001—08, assoc. prof. medicine, pharmacology and chem. biology, 2008—09, adj. prof. medicine, pharmacology and chem. biology, 2009—. Med. group mem. Pezzone Gastroenterology Assocs. Co-author: (med. rsch.) A model of neural cross-talk and irritation in the pelvis: implications for the overlap of chronic pelvic pain disorders, 2005, Convergence of bladder and colon sensory innervation occurs at the primary afferent level, 2006, Sensitization of pelvic nerve afferents and mast cell infiltration in the urinary bladder following chronic colonic irritation is mediated by neuropeptides, 2007, Management of persistent gastric bleeding in a patient with Glanzmann's thrombasthenia, 2008, Cross-talk and sensitization of bladder afferent nerves, 2010, various med. rsch. includes Mechanisms of polymicrobial sepsis-induced ileus, Colonic postoperative inflammatory ileus in the rat and Functional bowel disorders in inflammatory bowel disease. Named one of the Top Doctors, Castle Connolly, 2008—11, the Top Doctors in Gastroent., Pitts. Mag., 2008—11. Fellow: The Am. Gastroent. Assn. Office: University of Pittsburg Medical Center Presbyterian Manifold Professional Bldg 3 Washington PA 15301 Office Phone: 724-503-4637.

PEZZUTO, JOHN MICHAEL, dean, pharmacology educator; b. Hammonton, NJ, Aug. 29, 1950; s. Michael L. and Elizabeth (Brown) Pezzuto; m. Mimi Rotstein, Aug. 29, 1986; children: John-Henry Albert, Elisabeth Lee, Michael Joseph Ivan; 1 child from previous marriage, Jennifer Anne. AB, Rutgers U., NJ, 1973; PhD, U. Medicine & Dentistry NJ, 1977. Postdoc. assoc. MIT, Cambridge, 1977-79; instr. chemistry U. Va., Charlottesville, 1979-80; asst. prof. U. Ill., Chgo., 1980-84, assoc. prof., 1984-91, prof., Coll. Pharmacy, 1991—2002, prof., Coll. Medicine, 1994—2002, Disting. Univ. prof., 2002; prof. medicinal chemistry/molecular pharmacology Purdue U. Coll. Pharmacy, Nursing & Health Scis., West Lafayette, Ind., 2002—06, dean, 2002—06; founding dean, prof. chemistry U. Hawaii Coll. Pharmacy, Hilo, 2006—. Assoc. dir. U. Ill. Cancer Ctr., 1991—95, dep. dir., 2000—02; head dept. med. chemistry/pharmacognosy U. Ill. Coll. Pharmacy, 1992—95, interim head, 2000—01, dir. prog. collaborative rsch. in pharm. scis., 1995—98, assoc. dean rsch. & grad. edn., 1998—2002; pres., co-founder Internat. Therapeutics Inc., River Forest, Ill. Editor-in-chief Jour. Pharmacognosy, 1991—95, Combinatory Chemistry and High Throughput Screening, 1996—97, Pharmaceutical Biology, 1997—; contbr. articles to profl. jours. Recipient Career Devel. award, NIH, 1984—89; grantee Nat. Inst. Dental Rsch., 1984—85; fellow NIH, 1977—80, Alexander von Humboldt Found., 1990—91. Mem.: AAAS, Am. Soc. Biol. Chemists, NY Acad. Scis., Am. Assn. Cancer Rsch., Am. Soc. Pharmacognosy, Am. Chem. Soc. Office: U Hawaii Coll Pharmacy 34 Rainbow Dr Hilo HI 96720-4091 Office Phone: 808-933-2909. Business E-Mail: pezzuto@hawaii.edu.

PFAFF, WILLIAM WALLACE, medical educator; b. Rochester, NY, Aug. 14, 1930; s. Norman Joseph and Eleanor Blakesley (Wells) P.; m. Patricia Ann Clark; children: Nancy, Karen, Margaret, Mary Catherine. AB, Harvard U., 1952; MD, SUNY, 1956. Intern U. Chgo., 1956-58; sr. asst. surgeon NIH, Bethesda, Md., 1958-60; resident Stanford U. Med. Ctr., Palo Alto, Calif., 1960-65; asst. prof. U. Fla., Gainesville, 1965-68, assoc. prof., 1968-71, prof. surgery, 1971-95, prof. emeritus, adj. prof., 1995—, dir. organ transplant programs, 1971-95. Bd. dirs. United Network for Organ Sharing, Richmond, Va., pres. elect, 1997-98, pres., 1998-99; pres., com. chmn. Southeastern Organ Procurement Found., Richmond, 1973-95. Fellow Am. Coll. Surgeons; mem. Am. Surg. Assn., Am. Soc. Transplant Surgeons, So. Surg. Assn., Transplantation Soc., Alachua County Med. Soc. (pres. 1977-78). Home: 2445 NW 15th Pl Gainesville FL 32605-5148 Office: U Fla Dept Surgery PO Box 100286 Gainesville FL 32610-0286 Personal E-mail: puffer12@aol.com. Business E-Mail: pfaff@surgery.ufl.edu.

PFAFFLIN, SHEILA MURPHY, psychologist; b. Pasadena, Calif., July 31, 1934; d. Leonard Anthony and Honora (Shields) Murphy; m. James Reid Pfafflin, Sept. 7, 1957. BA, Pomona Coll., 1956; MA, Johns Hopkins U., 1958, PhD, 1959. Mem. tech. staff AT&T Bell Labs., Murray Hill, N.J., 1959-75; dist. mgr. AT&T, Morristown, N.J., 1975-98. Chair subcom. on womem Com. on Equal Opportunities in Sci. and Tech., NSF, Washington, 1981-85; mem. adv. coun. Math/Sci. Tchr. Supply and Demand, N.J. Dept. Higher Edn., 1982-83; mem. adv. bd. for Maths., Sci. and Computer Sci. Teaching Improvement Grants, N.J. Dept. Higher Edn., 1984-89. Co-editor: Expanding the Role of Women in the Sciences, 1978, Scientific-Technological Change & the Role of Women in Development, 1981, Psychology & Educational Policy, 1987; contbr. articles to profl. jours. Trustee Ramapo Coll. of N.J., Mahwah, N.J., 1984-96; adv. bd. Project "SMART", Girls Clubs of Am., N.Y.C., 1984-94, Consortium for Ednl. Equity, Rutgers U., New Brunswick, N.Y., 1983-90; pres. Assn. for Women in Sci. Ednl. Found., Washington, 1982-98. Fellow: APA, AAAS, N.Y. Acad. Scis., Assn. for Women in Sci. (pres. 1980—81, Women Scientist award, Met. chpt. 1987); mem.: Phi Beta Kappa, Sigma Xi. Avocation: sailing. Home: 173 Gates Ave Gillette NJ 07933-1719 Office Phone: 908-647-2390. Personal E-mail: sheilpnj@lycos.com, spfafflin@gmail.com.

PFANNSCHMIDT, JOACHIM, surgeon; b. Bremen, Germany, Dec. 13, 1960; s. Walter and Barbara Pfannschmidt; m. Christine Boss, Dec. 12, 1997; children: Tristan-James, Luisa-Marie. MD, U. Munster, Germany, 1988; PhD, U. Heidelberg, Germany, 2006. Fellow in cardiac surgery U. Cologne, Germany, 1989—92; attending surgeon Zentralkrankenhaus Reinkenheide, Bremerhaven, Germany, 1992—99; attending thoracic surgeon Thoraxklinik am Universitätsklinikum, Heidelberg, Germany, 1999—. Avocations: travel, swimming. Office: Thoraxklinik am Universitätsklinikum Amalienstr 5 69126 Heidelberg Germany Office Fax: 49-6221 396 1002. Business E-Mail: joachim.pfannschmidt@thoraxklinik-heidelberg.de.

PFAU, PATRICK, gastroenterologist; b. Milw., Wis., Dec. 28, 1966; MD, Northwestern U., 1994. Chief clin. gastroenterology U. Wis., 2001. Office: 660 Highland Ave Madison WI 53711 Business E-Mail: prp2@medicine.wisc.edu.

PFEFFER, CYNTHIA ROBERTA, psychiatrist, educator; b. Newark, May 22, 1943; d. Edward I. and Ann Pfeffer. BA, Douglas Coll., 1964; MD, NYU, 1968. Assoc. dir. child pyschiatry inpatient unit Albert Einstein Coll. Medicine, Bronx, NY, 1973-79; chief child psychiatry inpatient unit N.Y. Hosp. Cornell Med. Ctr., White Plains, NY, 1979-95; assoc. prof. clin. psychiatry Weill Med. Coll. Cornell U., NYC, 1984—. Prof. psychiatry Cornell U. Med. Coll., 1989—; pres. N.Y. Coun. on Child and Adolescent Psychiatry, N.Y.C., 1989—; dir. childhood bereavement program Weill Med. Coll. Cornell U., 1999—. Author: The Suicidal Child, 1986, Difficult Moments in Child Psychotherapy, 1988; editor: Youth Suicide: Perspectives on Risk and Prevention, 1989, Intense Stress and Mental Disturbance in Children, 1996; co-editor: Child and Adolescent Neurology for Psychiatrist, 1992, 2008, Neurologic Disorders: Developmental and Behavioral Sequelae for Child and Adolescent Psychiatric Clinics of North America, 1999. Recipient Erwin Stengel award Internat. Assn. Suicide Prevention, 1987, Wilford Hulse award N.Y. Coun. on Child & Adolescent Psychiatry, 1989, Sigmund Freud award Am. Soc. Psychoanalytic Physicians, 1994., William Shonfeld award Am. Soc. Adolescent Psychology, 2009 Fellow Am. Psychiat. Assn., Am. Acad. Child and Adolescent Psychiatry (councillor-at-large 1989—, Norbert Rieger award 1988), Am. Psychopathological Assn.; mem. Am. Assn. Suicidology (pres. 1987, Young Contbrs. award 1981, 82). Office: NY Hosp Westchester Div 21 Bloomingdale Rd White Plains NY 10605-1504 also: 1100 Park Ave Ste 1B New York NY 10128-0327 Business E-Mail: cpfeffer@med.cornell.edu.

PFEFFER, LAWRENCE MARC, cell biologist; b. NYC, Nov. 28, 1951; s. Paul and Bess (Wilkins) P.; m. Susan Ritterstein, Sept. 19, 1976; children: Jessica Rachel, Elyssa Danielle. BS (magna cum laude), SUNY, Albany, 1972; PhD, Cornell U., 1977. Undergrad. fellow SUNY, Albany, 1971-72; grad. fellow Cornell U. Grad. Sch. Med. Sci., NYC, 1972-77; postdoctoral fellow Rockefeller U., NYC, 1977-80, rsch. assoc., 1980—81, asst. prof., 1981-87, assoc. prof., 1987-91; assoc. prof. dept. pathology U. Tenn. Coll. Medicine, Memphis, 1991-92, prof., 1992—, Muirhead prof., 2002—; dir. Ctr. Cancer Rsch., 2007—. Ad hoc reviewer for Sci. Procs. NAS, Cancer Rsch., Interferon Rsch., Jour. Immunology, Molecular Cellular Biology. Editor: Mechanisms of Interferon Actions, 1989; mem. editl. bd. Jour. Interferon Cytokine Rsch., 1992—, Jour. Biol. Chemistry, 2002-08, 2010-. Recipient Jr. Faculty Rsch. award Am. Cancer Soc., 1982-85, Leukemia Scholar award Leukemia Soc. Am., 1986-91. Mem. Harvey Soc., Interferon Soc., Sigma Xi, Am. Soc. for Microbiology. Democrat. Jewish. Achievements include research on signal transduction of cytokines, cytokine receptors, mechanism of interferon action, and regulation of gene expression by interferon. Office: Univ Tenn Dept Pathology Coll Medicine 19 South Manassas Ave Rm 154 Memphis TN 38103-3400 Home Phone: 901-758-0624; Office Phone: 901-448-7855.

PFEFFERBAUM, BETTY JANE, psychiatrist, educator; b. Seattle, Sept. 7, 1946; d. Lois (Yager) P.; m. Richard L. Van Horn, May 29, 1988. BA, Pomona Coll., 1968, MD, U. Calif., San Francisco, 1972; JD, U. Okla., Norman, 1993. Bar: Okla. 1993; diplomate Am. Bd. Psychiatry and Neurology with subspecialty in child psychiatry. Intern pediatrics Martin Luther King Jr. Gen. Hosp., Compton, Calif., 1972-73; resident in psychiatry Neuro Psychiat. Inst., UCLA, 1973-76, fellow in child psychiatry, 1975-77; pvt. practice psychiatry, LA, 1977-78; prof. U. Tex. Med. Sch., Houston, 1978-89; v.p. for edn. U. Tex. Health Sci. Ctr., Houston, 1987-89; prof., chief child sect. dept. psychiatry U. Okla. Health Scis. Ctr., Oklahoma City, 1989-96, chair dept. psychiatry, 1996—; adj. prof. Oklahoma City U. Sch. Law, 1994-95. Mem. Okla. Indigent Def. Sys. Bd., 1992-93, Okla. Bd. Mental Health and Substance Abuse Svcs., 1993-99. Contbr. articles to profl. jours. Grad. Leadership Tex., 1988, Leadership Okla., 1995. Fellow Am. Psychiat. Assn., Am. Acad. Child and Adolescent Psychiatry, Group for Advancement Psychiatry; mem. ABA, Order of Coif, Phi Beta Kappa, Pi Mu Epsilon. Jewish. Office: U Okla Health Scis Ctr William Pavilion Rm 3470 920 S L Young Blvd PO Box 26901 Oklahoma City OK 73104-5020 Home: 2517 Stratton Dr Edmond OK 73013 Office Phone: 405-271-5121. Business E-Mail: betty-pfefferbaum@ouhsc.edu.

PFEIFER, MICHAEL, physician, researcher, consultant, director; b. Kehl, Baden, Germany, May 16, 1963; MD, Heidelberg U. Med. Sch., Germany, 1991. Head clin. rsch. Inst. Clin. Osteology Gustav Pommer, Bad Pyrmont, Lower Saxony, Germany, 2000. Cons. various pharm. cos., Germany, 2000, United States, 00. Author: med. text books on osteoporosis, German transl., 1996, Italian transl., 1998, Spanish transl., 2003. Mem.: German Bone and Joint Soc., Internat. Bone and Mineral Soc., Am. Soc. Bone and Mineral Rsch. Avocations: German literature of the 20th Century, travel. Office: Inst Clin Osteology Gustav Pommer Am Hylligen Born 7 Bad Pyrmont 31812 Germany Office Phone: +49 5281-151414. Office Fax: +49 5281-151100. Business E-Mail: iko_pyrmont@t-online.de.

PFEIFER, ROMAN, orthopedist; b. Frunse, May 18, 1980; MD, Hannover Med. Sch., 2009. With dept. orthop. trauma surgery Rheinisch-Westfälische Technische Hochschule Aachen U., U. Aachen Med. Ctr., 2010—. Mem.: Marburger Bund, German Soc. Orthopaedics and Trauma (mem. Sect. Fundamental Rsch.). Avocation: travel. Office: Pauwelsstrasse 30 Aachen Nordrhein-Westfalen 52074 Germany Business E-Mail: romanpfeifer@aol.com.

PFEIFFER, ALBRECHT, gastroenterologist; b. Trostberg, Germany, Feb. 8, 1957; s. Alfred and Helene Pfeiffer; m. Juliane Pfeiffer, May 11, 1958; children: Johannes, Julia, Christian. MD, Ludwig-Maximilians U., Munich, Germany, 1982. Mil. physician Deutsche Bundeswehr, Mittenwald, Germany, 1983; intern Hosp. Saint-Lazare, Paris, 1984—85; resident Hosp. Bogenhausen, Munich, 1985—91, sr. registrar, 1991—97; chief dept. Klinikum Memmingen, Memmingen, 1997—; asst. prof. Ludwig-Maximilians U., Munich, 1997—2001, prof. medicine, 2002—. Contbr. articles to profl. jours. Mem.: European Soc. Neurogastroenterology & Motility, German Soc. Gastroenterology, French Soc. Gastroenterology. Roman Catholic. Office: Klinikum Memmingen Bismarck Str 23 D 87700 Memmingen Germany Office Phone: 08331 70-2367. Personal E-mail: albrecht-pfeiffer@gmx.de.

PFEIFFER, ERIC ARMIN, psychiatrist, gerentologist, author; b. Rauental, Germany, Sept. 15, 1935; came to U.S., 1952; naturalized, 1957; s. Fritz and Emma (Saborowski) P.; m. Natasha Maria Emerson, Mar. 21, 1964; children: Eric Alexander, Michael David, Mark Armin. AB, Washington U., 1956, MD, 1960. Intern Albert Einstein Coll. Medicine, Bronx, NY, 1960-61; resident in psychiatry U. Rochester, NY, 1961-64; practice medicine specializing in psychiatry Durham, NC, 1966-76, Denver, 1976-78; asst. prof. Duke U., Durham, 1966-69, assoc. prof., 1969-72, prof., 1973-76, project dir., 1971-76, assoc. dir., 1974-76; dir. Davis Inst. Care and Study Aging, Denver, 1976-77; prof. psychiatry U. Colo., Denver, 1976-78; prof. psychiatry, chief div. geriatric psychiatry U. South Fla. Coll. Medicine, Tampa, 1978—2008, dir. Suncoast Gerontology Ctr., 1980—2008. Chief psychiatry svc. Tampa VA Med. Ctr., 1979-80; cons. in field; chmn. bd. Social Systems, Inc., 1975-76; chmn. com. on mental health and mental illness of elderly HEW, 1976-77. Author: Disordered Behavior, 1968, (with E.W. Busse) Behavior and Adaptation in Late Life, 1970, 3d edit., 1977, Successful Aging, 1974, Multidimensional Functional Assessment, 1977, Alzheimer's Disease, 1989, 14 Winning Strategies for Successful Aging, 2010, Under One Roof Poems, 2010, The Art of Caregiving in Alzheimer Disease, 2011. With USPHS, 1964-66. Markle Found. scholar acad. medicine, 1968-73; Eric Pfeiffer Chair in Alzheimer's Disease Rsch. named in his honor, U. S. Fla., 1985. Fellow Gerontol. Soc. (chmn. clin. medicine sect. 1975-76), Am. Psychiat. Assn.; mem. Am. Geriatrics Soc. (Allen Gold medal 1977), So. Psychiat. Soc., Phi Beta Kappa. Office Phone: 813-839-5769. Business E-Mail: epfeiffe@health.usf.edu.

PFEIFFER, RONALD FREDERICK, neurologist, researcher; b. Racine, Wis., Aug. 11, 1947; s. Benjamin and Irene Pfeiffer; m. Brenda Elaine Pfeiffer; children: Aaron, Gretchen. BS, U. Nebr., Lincoln, 1969; MD, U. Nebr. Med. Ctr., Omaha, 1973; LLD (hon.), Concordia U., Seward, Nebr. Bd. cert. Am. Bd. Psychiatry and Neurology, 1980. Intern Walter Reed Army Med. Ctr., Washington, 1973—74, resident neurology, 1974—77; neurologist U.S. Army Hosp., Nuremberg, Germany, 1977—79, Landstuhl, 1979—80; asst. prof. neurology and pharmacology U. Nebr. Med. Ctr., Omaha, 1980—85, assoc. prof. neurology and pharmacology, 1985—93, chief neurology sect., 1986—93, prof. neurology and pharmacology, 1993—94; dir. divsn. neurodegenerative diseases U. Tenn., 1994—, prof. dept. neurology, 1994—, vice chair dept. neurology, 1996—. Mem. bd. dirs. Wheat Ridge Ministries, Itasca, Ill., 1999—2006; bd. regents Concordia U., Seward, Nebr., 2001—10. Maj. US Army, 1973—80. Mem.: Parkinson Study Group, Movement Disorders Soc., Am. Acad. Neurology, Am. Neurol. Assn., Phi Beta Kappa. Office: Dept Neurology U Tenn HSC 855 Monroe Ave Memphis TN 38163 Office Phone: 901-448-5209.

PFISTER, ALFRED KARL, internist, educator; b. Wheeling, W.Va. s. Alfred and Anna Seeger Pfister; m. Nancy Ann Taylor, June 24, 1989; children: Alfred, Constance, Philip. BA, Washington & Jefferson U., Pa., 1958; MD, George Washington U., Wash., 1962. Diplomate Am. Bd. Internal Medicine. With Charleston Med. Group, W.Va., 1969—96, Integrated Healthcare, 1997—2002; prof. Sch. Medicine W.Va. U., 2003—. Contbr. articles to profl. jours. Lt. comdr. USPHS, 1966—68. Recipient Laureate award, W.Va. ACP, 1992. Republican. Unitarian. Avocations: running, plant biology. Home: 1 Beta Lane Charleston WV 25304 Office: University Health Assocs 4522 MacCorkle Ave SE Charleston WV 25304 Business E-Mail: apfister@hsc.wvu.edu.

PFISTER, DAVID GERARD, medical oncologist; MD, U. Pa., 1982. Diplomate Am. Bd. Internal Medicine, Am. Bd. Internal Medicine-med. oncology, registered NY, 1987. Intern Pa. Hosp., 1983, resident in internal medicine, 1985; fellow Yale New Haven Hosp., 1987; fellow in hematology Meml. Sloan-Kettering Cancer Ctr., NY, 1989, hosp. affiliation includes. Author: (articles) Concurrent Cisplatin and Radiation Versus Cetuximab and Radiation for Locally Advanced Head-and-Neck Cancer, 2010, Hypofractionated Dose-Painting Intensity Modulated Radiation Therapy with Chemotherapy for Nasopharyngeal Carcinoma: A Prospective Trial, 2010, A phase 2 study of pemetrexed plus gemcitabine every 2 weeks for patients with recurrent or metastatic head and neck squamous cell cancer, 2010, Optimizing treatment of advanced testicular germ cell tumors, 2010, American Society of Clinical Oncology Clinical Practice Guideline update on chemotherapy for stage IV non-small-cell lung cancer, 2010. Named one of Best Doctors, NY Mag., 2010. Office: Memorial Sloan-Kettering Cancer Center 1275 York Ave New York NY 10065 Office Phone: 212-639-8235.

PFLUM, BARBARA ANN, retired allergist; b. Cin., Jan. 10, 1943; d. James Frederick and Betty Mae (Doherty) P.; m. Makram I. Gobrail, Oct. 20, 1973 (dec.); children: Christina (dec.), James. BS, Coll. Mt. St. Vincent, 1967; MD, Georgetown U., 1971; MS, Coll. Mt. St. Joseph, 1993. Cons. Children's Med. Ctr., Dayton, Ohio, 1975—2006, dir. allergy clinic, 1983-89; dir. allergy divsn. Hopeland Splty. Clinic, Dayton, 1998-2000; ret., 2006. Fellow Am. Acad. Pediatrics, Am. Acad. Allergy and Immunology, Am. Coll. Allergy and Immunology; mem. Ohio Soc. Allergy and Immunology, Western Ohio Pediatric Soc. (pres. 1985-86) Roman Catholic. Home Phone: 937-293-2079. Personal E-mail: bapflum@hotmail.com.

PFLUM, WILLIAM JOHN, retired physician; b. NYC, July 30, 1924; s. Peter Arthur and Caroline (Schmidt) P.; m. Roseann Sarah Stubing, Oct. 13, 1956; children: Carol Jean, Jeanine, Suzanne, Denise, Peter. BS, Georgetown U., 1947; MD, Loyola U., Chgo., 1951. Diplomate Am. Bd. Allergy & Immunology. Intern St. Vincent's Hosp, NYC, 1951-52; resident in internal medicine NYU div. Goldwater Meml. Hosp., NYC, 1952-53; resident in allergy Inst. Allergy Roosevelt Hosp., NYC, 1956; attending internist allergy & immunology Overlook Hosp., Summit, NJ, 1958—. Assoc. attending Inst. Allergy, Immunology and Infectious Diseases, Roosevelt Hosp., N.Y.C., 1957-92; pvt. practice medicine, specializing in allergy and immunology, Summit, 1957-92; ret.; cons. in field. With USAAF, 1943—45, ETO. Decorated Purple Heart, air medal with two clusters, POW medal. Fellow Am. Acad. Allergy, Am. Coll. Allergists, Am. Assn. Clin. Immunology and Allergy; mem. Summit Med. Soc., Am. Assn. Clin. Immunology and Allergy (pres. Mid-Atlantic region 1975-76), Disabled Am. Vets., Mil. Order Purple Heart, Am. Ex-

Prisoners of War, 8th Air Force Hist. Soc., World Marathon Runners Assn., Robert A. Cooke Allergy Alumni Assn. Achievements include completion of 26 consecutive Boston Marathons, 1971-1996 with Am. Med. Athletic Assn. Home: 1104 Presa Pl Lady Lake FL 32159 Home Phone: 352-205-8186.

PHALEN, ROBERT NORMAN, industrial hygienist, educator; b. Rochester, NY, Aug. 2, 1969; BA in Biology, Calif. State U., Fullerton, 1995; PhD in Environ. Health Sci., UCLA, 2006. Indsl. hygienist, mgr., loss prevention and control Stockman Group, 1997—2001; environ. health and safety specialist UCLA, 2001—06; asst. prof. Calif. State U., San Bernardino, 2006—. Indsl. Hygiene fellowship, Nat. Inst. Occupl. Safety and Health, Southern Calif. Edn. and Rsch. Ctr. Mem.: Air and Waste Mgmt. Assn., Am. Indsl. Hygiene Assn., Delta Omega Soc. (Iota chpt., elected mem.). Office: 5500 University Pky San Bernardino CA 92407 Business E-Mail: phalen@csusb.edu.

PHAM, SI MAI, cardiothoracic surgeon; b. Ninh Hoa, Khanh Hoa, Vietnam, Oct. 6, 1955; arrived in US, 1975; s. Tro Pham and Nhung Thi Mai; m. Marie Christine Pham, Sept. 9, 1987; children: Benjamin Bartley, Anthony Ninh, Vivienne Elisabeth, Victoria B.H. Student, U. Saigon Sch. Pharmacy, Vietnam, 1973-75; BS in Chem. magna cum laude, Lebanon Valley Coll., Annville, Pa., 1979; MD, U. Pitts., 1983; D (hon.), U. Morón, 2002. Diplomate, surg. critical care Am. Bd. Surgery, Am. Bd. Thoracic Surgery. Intern, resident gen. surgery U. Pitts., 1983-86, rsch. fellow, cardiothoracic surgery, 1986-87, sr. and chief resident gen. surgery, 1987-89, resident cardiothoracic surgery, 1989-92, asst. prof. surgery, Sch. Medicine, 1992—98, dir. adult cardiac transplant program, Sch. Medicine, 1993-97, assoc. dir. heart transplant and artificial heart program, 1997-98, dir. cardiothoracic transplant rsch., 1997-98; dir. extracorporeal membrane oxygenation svc. Presbyn. U. Hosp., Pitts., 1993-98; dir. cardiopulmonary transplantation and artifical heart program, divsn. cardiothoracic surgery U. Miami Sch. Medicine, 1998—; assoc. prof. surgery U. Miami Sch. Medicine, 1998—2002, prof. surgery, 2002, prof. surgery & biomed. engring., 2010. Reviewer various med. jours. Contbr. articles to profl. jours., chapters to books, scientific papers. Recipient Am. Chem. award, 1979, Radiology award U. Pitts., 1983, Dalsemer rsch. scholar award Am. Lung Assn., 1997-99; ACS Faculty fellowship award, 1994-96, Health Care Heroes award Greater Miami C. of C., 2007; grantee Children's Hosp. Pitts., 1987, Am. Heart Assn., 1987-89, 94-96, 96-99, Thoracic Surgery Found., 1996-97, 97-98, Am. Lung Assn., 1997—, Presbyn. U. Hosp., 1987-89, NIH, 1999—, Vietnamese Am. Med. Rsch. Found. sci. award, 2005. Fellow Am. Coll. Surgeons, Am. Heart Assoc. (cmty. bd. mem.); mem. Am. Soc. Artificial Internal Organs, Internat. Soc. Heart and Lung Transplantation, Soc. Critical Care Medicine, Am. Assn. Advancement of Sci., Am. Soc. Transplant Surgeons, Soc. Thoracic Surgeons, Am. Assn. Thoracic Surgery, Extracorporeal Life Support Organization, Assn. for Acad. Surgery, Phi Alpha Epsilon, Transplant Found. South Fla. (adv. bd. mem.). Avocations: reading, gardening. Office: U Miami Sch Medicine Highland Profl Bldg 1801 NW 9th Ave Ste 5th Fl Miami FL 33136 Office Phone: 305-355-5070. Business E-Mail: spham@med.miami.edu.

PHAM DANG, CHARLES, anesthesiologist; b. Hanoi, North Viet-Nam, July 27, 1951; s. Duong Van Pham and Nam Thi Dang; m. Isabelle Gavard; children: Benoît, Anne, Olivier. MD, Faculty Medicine, Montpellier, France, 1981. Cert. anesthesiology and resuscitation Faculty Medicine, 1984. Resident anesthesiology and resuscitation Faculty Medicine, 1980—; state practitioner anesthesiology and resuscitation U. Hosp., Nantes, Loire-Atlantique, France, 1986—. Staff Francovietnamese Hosp., Ho Chi Minh, South Vietnam, 2003—. Mem.: SFAR, ASRA. Catholic. Achievements include development of stimulating catheter to verify the correct positioning of the perineural catheter to improve continuous regional analgesia; design of side handle for holding the needle during ultrasound guided block. Avocations: hiking, skiing, travel. Home: 10 rue de la Carrière Orvault Loire-Atlantique 44700 France Office: Univ Hosp Pl Alexis Ricordeau Nantes Loire-Atlantique 44093 France Office Fax: 33 2 40 08 44 59. Personal E-mail: cphamdang@aol.com. Business E-Mail: charles.phamdang@chu-nantes.fr.

PHAN, HAI VU THANH, physician; b. Vietnam, Dec. 21, 1979; D, Hue Med. Coll., 2003; MPhil, U. Queensland, 2009. Physician Da Nang Hosp., 2003—. Home: K402/1 Trung Nu Vuong Da Nang Hai Chau 84 Vietnam Personal E-mail: drthanhhaient@yahoo.com.

PHARAON, HASAN MUSA, pediatrician, consultant; b. Jaffa, Palestine, May 1, 1920; arrived in Jordan, 1957; s. Musa Ra'fat Abdel Majid and Badrieh Kheir P; m. Hildur Bech Jensen, Oct. 29, 1935; children: Ali, Omar, Tareq. MD, Am. U., Beirut, Lebanon, 1943; diploma in child health, Fuad U., Cairo, Egypt, 1947; degree in pediat., Paris U., 1957. Clin. asst. Govt. Hosp., Jaffa, Palestine, 1943-45; resident doctor Children's Hosp., Cairo, Egypt, 1945-47, Hadassah Hosp., Tel Aviv, Israel, 1953-55, Hosp. Enfants Malades, Paris, 1955-57; sr. pediatrician Children's Hosp., Amman, Jordan, 1958-72; gen. dir. Univ. Hosp., Amman, Jordan, 1972-73. Dir. study on nutritional status of infants and preschool children in Jordan, 1963-64, study/nutrition survey of Palestinian refugees in Jordan after 1967 war, 1968-69, study on vitamin A in infants in Jordan, in assn. with WHO, 1965-66; establisher First Pediat. Hosp., Ministry of Health, Jordan, 1958; cons. child health World Health Orgn., 1979. Editor Jordan Med. Jour., 1965-75, booklets in pediat. pub. health; contbr. articles to med. jours. Liaison officer Internat. Red Cross Orgn., Jaffa, 1948-53; mem., pres. Save the Children Fund, Jordan, 1960-75. Mem. Jaffa Med. Soc. (sec. gen. 1947-48), Jordan Med. Assn. (asst. gen. sec., v.p. 1957-75), Jordan Pediat. Soc. (establisher 1962), Union of M-E and Med. Pediat. Soc. (asst. gen. sec., treas. 1966-96), Internat. Pediat. Assn. (mem. standing com. 1977-87), Am. U. Beirut Alumni Assn. Muslim. Avocation: archaeology. Home: Shmeisani Area PO Box 9215 Amman 11191 Jordan Office: Pvt Clinic PO Box 9215 Amman 11191 Jordan Office Phone: 962-6-5665588. Personal E-mail: hildurph@gmail.com.

PHELAN, MICHAEL WILLIAM, medical educator; b. Quincy, Mass., Apr. 29, 1966; MS, Boston U., 1996. Asst. prof. U. Md. Sch. Medicine, 2003—, faculty senate, 2009—. Mem. Cancer Com. Veterans Adminstrn., Balt., 2005—11. Mem.: Mid-Atlantic Section Am. Urologic Assn., Am. Urologic Assn., Am. Bd. Urology. Avocations: hockey, skiing, running. Office: 29 South Greene St 5th Fl Baltimore MD 21201 Business E-Mail: mphelan@smail.umaryland.edu.

PHELPS, CHARLES ELLIOTT, economics professor, director; b. NYC, Apr. 20, 1943; s. McKinnie L. and Carolyn (McCleery) P.; m. Dale L. King, Sept. 2, 1967; children: Darin H., Teresa A. BA in Math., Pomona Coll., 1965; MBA in Hosp. Adminstrn., U. Chgo., 1968, PhD in Bus Economics, 1973. Rsch assoc., Ctr. for Health Adminstrn. Studies U. Chgo., 1969—71; rsch. economist, economics dept. RAND Corp., Santa Monica, Calif., 1971—79, dir., regulatory policies and institutions program, sr. staff economist, faculty mem., RAND Grad. Inst., 1979—84; prof. polit. sci. & econs. U. Rochester, NY, 1984—, dir., pub. policy analysis program NY, 1984—89, faculty mem., Rochester Ctr. for Economics Rsch. NY, 1984—, prof., cmty. and preventative medicine, Sch. Medicine and Dentistry NY, 1989—, chair, cmty. and preventative medicine, Sch. Medicine and Dentistry NY, 1989—94, provost NY, 1994—. Cons. JUREcon, Inc., LA, 1977-86; pvt. cons., Rochester, NY, 1986-; dir., pub. policy analysis program, U. Rochester, 1984-89, chair, health and soc. com., 1984-94, mem. academic computing exec. com., 1988-94, mem. exec. com. and informal exec. com., Sch. Medicine and Dentistry, 1989-94, chair, dept. cmty. and preventive medicine, 1989-94, chair, faculty adv. com. for presdl. search, 1993; mem. Nat. Adv. bd. Leonard Davis Inst. Health Economics, U. Pa., 1988-93; commr. Rochester Health Commn., 1995-2000; bd. trustee, Ctr. for Governmental Rsch., 1998-99; mem. Nat. Adv. Commn. for Digital Strategies, Libr. Congress, 2001-02; mem. report review com., NRC, 2002-. Co-editor Transforming Ideas: Selected Profiles in University of Rochester Research and Scholarship, 2000; Author Health Economics, 1st edit 1992, 2nd edit. 1997, 3rd edit., 2002; mem. editl. bd. Journal Health Economics, Journal Risk and Uncertainty, 1990-2000; founding assoc. editor, Economic Bulletin, 2000; contbr. articles to profl. jours. Mem. Greater Rochester Fights Back Against Drugs, 1990—91. Assoc. Nat. Bur. for Econ. Rsch.; mem. Inst. Medicine(mem. com. on med. technologies, 1985-86, com. for priority setting in med. tech., 1989-90, com. on Gulf War illnesses, 1999-2000), Am. Econ. Assn., Nat. Acad. Social Ins., Soc. for Med. Decision Making (trustee 1990-92), Assn. for Pub. Policy Analysis and Mgmt.(sec. 1980-91), Agy. for Health Care Policy and Rsch. (health care tech. study sect 1990-94). Avocations: photography, archery, astronomy, canoeing, woodworking. Home Phone: 585-381-2429; Office Phone: 585-275-5931. Office Fax: 585-461-1046. Business E-Mail: charles.phelps@rochester.edu.

PHELPS, JUDSON HEWETT, retired health facility administrator, marketing professional; b. Evanston, Ill., Oct. 18, 1942; s. Sidney Norman and Mary Schuyler (Coons) Phelps; m. Barbara Ann Ray, Dec. 21, 1963; children: Wyeth Hewett, Christopher Ashley, Whitney Magee. BA, Williams Coll., 1964; MS, Springfield Coll., 1993. Lic. alchohol, drug counselor. Asst. brand mgr. Procter & Gamble Co., Cin., 1968—70; brand mgr. Memorex, Santa Clara, Calif., 1970—72; product mgr. Chesebrough Ponds Inc., Greenwich, Conn., 1972—76; v.p. mktg. L'Oreal subs. Cosmair Inc., NYC, 1976—77; v.p. sales Bio Products, Inc., Norwalk, Conn., 1978, exec. v.p., 1979, pres., 1980—86; corp. v.p. Ketchum & Co. parent co. Bio Products, Norwalk, 1982—86; mng. dir. Dameon Ptnrs. Inc., Wilton, Conn., 1987—88; pres. Theracom Corp., Rye, NY, 1988—89; v.p. Promotion Info. Bur., Norwalk, 1990; prin. Daniel Adams Co., Danbury, Conn., 1991—92; clin. coord., addictions therapist, counselor Ctr., Bridgeport, Conn., 1993—97; program dir. Gosnold-Thorne Counseling, Hyannis, 1997—2008; dir. ops. L.I.F.E., Inc., Hyannis, 2009—10. Adj. faculty Housatonic Cmty. Tech. Coll., Bridgeport, 1995—97. Family counselor Caregivers, Assn. Religious Communities, Danbury, Conn., 1975—79; leader, treas. Ridgefield Emmaus Teenage Christian Retreats, Conn., 1983—92; vestry St. Mary's Ch., Barnstable, Mass., 2007—10; pres. Camp Dudley (YMCA) Alumni Assn., Westport, NY, 1974—79; chmn. Ridgefield Alcohol and Drug Use Commn., 1992—97. Lt. USNR, 1964—68. Home: 53 Gingerbread Ln Yarmouth Port MA 02675-1110

PHIBBS, CLIFFORD MATTHEW, surgeon, educator; b. Bemidji, Minn., Feb. 20, 1930; s. Clifford Matthew and Dorothy Jean (Wright) P.; m. Patricia Jean Palmer, June 27, 1953; children— Wayne Robert, Marc Stuart, Nancy Louise BS, Wash. State U., Pullman, 1952; MD, U. Wash., Seattle, 1955; MS, U. Minn., 1960. Diplomate Am. Bd. Surgery. Intern Ancker Hosp., St. Paul, 1955—56; resident in surgery U. Minn. Hosps., 1956—60; practice medicine specializing in surgery Oxboro Clinic, Mpls., 1962—, pres., 1985—; cons. to health risk mgmt. corps., 1994—. Mem. Children's Hosp. Ctr., Northwestern-Abbott Hosp., Fairview-Southdale Hosp., Fairview Ridges Hosp.; clin. asst. prof. U. Minn., Mpls., 1975-78, clin. assoc. prof. surgery, 1978—; med. dir. Minn. Protective Life Ins. Co. Contbr. articles to med. jours. Bd. dirs. Bloomington Bd. Edn., Minn., 1974—, treas., 1976, sec., 1977-78, chmn., 1981-83; mem. adv. com. jr. coll. study City of Bloomington, 1964-66, mem. cmty. facilities com., 1966-67, advisor youth study commn., 1966-68; vice chmn. bd. Hillcrest Meth. Ch., 1970-71; mem. Bloomington Adv. and Rsch. Coun., 1969-71; bd. dirs. Bloomington Symphony Orch., 1976—, Wash. State U. Found., trustee, 1990—; dir. bd. mgmt. Minnesota Valley YMCA, 1970-75; bd. govs. Mpls. Met. YMCA, 1970—; bd. dirs. Bloomington Heart-Health Found., 1989—, Martin Luther Manor, 1989; pres. Oxboro Clinics, 1985—; bd. dirs. Bloomington History Clock Tower Assn., 1990—; bd. dirs. Fairview Hosp. Clinic, 1994—, Bloomington Sister city Orgn., 1999-, Bloomington Cmty. Found., 1997-, v.p., Bloomington Health Adv. Bd., 2000-, MMA Minority and Cross-Cult. Affairs Com., 2000-, Com. on Cult. Competence Minnesota Med. Assn., 1986. Capt. MC, US Army, 1960-62; mem. Minn. Med. Assn. Minority and Cultural Affairs Com., 2007. Recipient Minority Affairs Meritorious Svc. award, Minn. Med. Assn., 2007, Bloomington Health Promotional award, Bloomington Adv. Bd. Health, 2011. Mem. ACS, AMA (Physician Recognition awards 1969, 73, 76, 79, 82, 85, 88, 91, 94), Assn. Surg. Edn., Royal Soc. Medicine, Am. Coll. Sports Medicine, Minn. Med. Assn. (del. 1991-94, Minority Affairs Meritorius Svc. award, 2007), Minn. Surg. Soc., Mpls. Surg. Soc., Hennepin County Med. Soc., Pan-Pacific Surg. Assn., Jaycees, Bloomington C. of C. (chmn. bd. 1984, chmn. 1985-86), Bloomington Adv. Bd. health, Bloomington Sister City Bd., Bloomington Cmty. Found. (bd. dirs. 1996-). Achievements include development of program for Bloomington Public Schools to encourage minority students interest in careers in healthcare fields. Home: 9613 Upton Rd Minneapolis MN 55431-2454 Office: 600 W 98th St Minneapolis MN 55420-4773 Office Phone: 651-259-7828. Personal E-mail: kphiibs@aol.com.

PHILIP, IVAN, anesthesiologist; b. Paris, Apr. 12, 1959; Degree in Medicine, 1982. Anesthesiologist Inst. Mutualiste Montsouris, 2009. Avocations: music, sports. Home: Rue De La Cerisaie Charenton 94220 France Personal E-mail: ivan.philip@imm.fr.

PHILIPP, CLAIRE S., hematologist, educator, oncologist, internist; MD, Brown U., Providence, 1978. Diplomate Am. Bd. Internal Medicine, 1981, Am. Bd. Internal Medicine-hematology, 1984, Am. Bd. Internal Medicine-med. oncology, 1985. Intern internal medicine Beth Israel Med. Ctr., NYC, 1978—79, resident internal medicine, 1979—81; fellow hematology NYU Med. Ctr., 1981—84; prof. medicine Robert Wood Johnson Med. Sch., NJ, assoc. dir. divsn. hematology NJ, chief divsn. hematology NJ; with Robert Wood Johnson Univ. Hospital, New Brunswick, NJ. Office: Robert Wood Johnson University Hospital One Robert Wood Johnson Place New Brunswick NJ 08901 Office Phone: 732-828-3000.

PHILIPP, SEBASTIAN, cardiologist; m. Andrea Philipp; children: Marie, Anna, Marie; children: Anna, Lilly. MD, PhD, Free U. Berlin, 1995. Cert. cardiologist Bd. Germany, 2007. Resident Charité Berlin-Buch, 1988—2003; staff cardiologist West-German Heart Ctr., Essen, 2005—; dir. dept. cardiology Elbe Klinikum Stade, 2009. Dir. Cardiovasc. Rsch. Ctr., Essen, 2005. Fellow: European Soc. Cardiology. Office: West-German Heart Ctr Essen Hufelandstr 55 Essen 45122 Germany also: Elbe Klinikum Stade Bremer Voerder St 111 21682 Stade Germany Home: Ave der Werft 13 21680 Stade Germany Office Phone: 494141971451. Business E-Mail: sebastian.philipp@uk-essen.de.

PHILIPP, THOMAS, physician, educator; b. Königsberg, Germany, Apr. 30, 1942; s. Wolfgang Georg and Katja Olga Philipp; m. Ulrike Maria Luise Woescher, July 2, 1941; children: Sebastian Alexander, Anna-Kathrin Lauterbach, Tobias Peter, Christoph Michael. Abitur, Athenaeum, Stade, Germany, 1948—61. Staatsexamen U. Mainz, Germany, 1968. MD U. Mainz, 1969—71, prof. internal medicine, 1978—81; prof. internal medicine and nephrology Free U., Berlin, 1981—87; head dept. int. med. Klinikum, Karlsruhe, Germany, 1987—88; head dept. int. med. and nephrology U. Clinic, Essen, Germany, 1988—, ärztlicher direktor, 1998—2001. Senate mem. Deutsche Forschungsgemeinschaft (DFG), Bonn, Germany, 1990—96. Author: (more than 400 scientific publications) Pathogenesis And Treatment Of Hypertension (Franz Gross Preis: German Soc. Hypertension, 1994). Oberstabsarzt (res.) med. svc., 1968—74. Recipient Boehringer Ingelheim Prize, 1978. Mem.: Rotary Essen Nord (pres. 1995—96). Achievements include research in hypertension, nephrology, transplantation, immunology, and cardiology. Home: Elsass Str 31 Essen 45259 Germany Office: U Clinic Dept Int Medicine Hufeland Str 55 Essen 45122 Germany Personal E-mail: thomas.philipp@uni-essen.de.

PHILIPP, THOMAS, gynecologist; b. Vienna, Apr. 27, 1965; D, U. Vienna, 1989. Cons. Danube Hosp. Vienna, 1998—. Asst. prof. U. Vienna, 2005—11. Recipient Lindemann prize, German Soc. Endoscopy, Establishe Clinician award, European Soc. Human Reproduction. Avocation: skiing. Office: Langobardenstrasse 122 Vienna 1220 Austria Business E-Mail: thomas.philipp@wienkav.at.

PHILIPPON, MARC JOSEPH, orthopaedic surgeon; b. Quebec City, Can., May 9, 1965; arrived in U.S., 1990; s. Pontien Aderville and Micheline (Lortie) P.; m. Senenne Catalina Reid, Mar. 25, 1995; children: Michèle, Marc-Christophe, Mia-Véronique. BA with honors, Fla. Atlantic U., 1987; MD, McMaster U., Hamilton, Ont., Can., 1990. Lic. physician, Fla., Pa.; diplomate Am. Bd. Orthopaedic Surgery. Orthop. surgery resident U. Miami, Jackson Meml. Hosp., 1995; orthopaedic surgeon Holy Cross Hosp., Ft. Lauderdale, Fla., 1995, chief orthopaedic surgery, 2000-01; chief orthopaedic surgeon humanitarian mission to Ukraine Kiev Orthopaedic Inst., 1997; orthopaedic surgeon Broward Gen. Hosp., Ft. Lauderdale, 1998—2002; dir. sports medicine/hip disorders dept. orthopaedic surgery U. Pitts. Med. Ctr.; dir. fellowship program U. Pitts. Med. Ctr. for Sports Medicine, dir. hip arthroscopy fellowship, dir. golf medicine program, dir. Fla. site; orthop. surgeon, ptnr. Steadman-Hawkins Clinic, Vail, Colo., 2005—. Cons. Howmedica Inc., Rutherford, N.J., 1996-97, Smith & Nephew Inc., Memphis, 1998-99, Zimmer (Bristol-Myers Squibb),, NHL, NFL, NBA and MLB profl. teams and has treated PGA golfers; clin. adv. bd. Oratec Interventions, Inc., Menlo Park, Calif., 1998-2002; clin. asst. prof., U. Pitts. Med. Ctr.; med. cons. Ctr. for Sports Medicine; orthop. surgeon Nat. Hockey League Players Assn.; lectr. in field. Contbr. chapters to books, articles to profl. jours. Bd. dirs. Svc. Agy. for Sr. Citizens, Ft. Lauderdale, 1996-2000. Farquharson scholar Can. Med. Rsch. Coun., 1989. Fellow Internat. Coll. Surgeons, Am. Acad. Orthop. Surgeons; mem. AMA, Fla. Med. Assn., Am. Orthop. Soc. for Sports Medicine, Arthroscopy Assn. N.Am. (master instr.), Herodicus Soc., Phi Kappa Phi. Roman Catholic. Achievements include invention of orthopaedic surgery instrument and devices. Avocations: skiing, tennis, sailing, hockey, soccer, golf. Office: Steadman Hawkins Clinic 181 W Meadow Dr Ste 400 Vail CO 81657 Office Phone: 970-476-1100.

PHILIPPOU, ATHINEOS, retired medical educator, pharmacologist; b. Athens, Greece, Sept. 22, 1931; s. Ioannis and Andromachi Philippou; m. Gesine Freiin von Medem, July 29, 1976. MD, U. Athens, Greece, 1959. Cert. dozent U. Frankfurt, Germany, 1965. Alexander von Humboldt Stiftung fellow Dept. Physiology U. Cologne, Germany, 1959—60, Dept. Pharmacology U. Frankfurt, 1959—62; dozent and asst. prof. Dept. Pharmacology Med. Sch. Essen, 1965—70; prof. and head of divsn. Dept. Pharmacology and Toxicology U. Wuerzburg, 1970—82; prof. and head dept. Dept. Pharmacology and Toxicology U. Innsbruck, Austria, 1982—99; prof. dr. med. & dr. H.C. Vis. prof. Mill Hill Inst. Med. Rsch., London, 1968, Coll. de France, Paris, 1973, CDRI, Lucknow, India, 1978. Contbr. chapters to books, articles to profl. jours.; mem. editl. bd. Naunyn-Schmiedeberg's Archives of Pharmacology, 1972—82, 1992—2000; co-editor: Naunyn-Schmiedeberg's Archives of Pharmacology, 1982—92; mem. editl. bd. Clin. and Exptl. Hypertension, 1978—86, Jour. Autonomic Pharmacology, 1981—2001, European Jour. Pharmacology, 1967—93; author: New Aspects of the Role of Adrenoceptors in the Cardiovascular System, 1986, History and Achievements of the Departments of Pharmacology, Clinical Pharmacology and Toxicology in the German Speaking Countries, Vol. 1, 2004, Vol. II, 2007, Vol. III, 2011, Geschichte und Wirken der Pharmakologischen, klinisch Pharmakologischen Und Toxikologischen Institute Im deutschsprachigen Raum. Home: Hoehenstrasse 106 Tirol Innsbruck 6020 Austria Office: Dept Pharmacology and Toxicology Peter-Mayr-Strasse 1 Tirol Innsbruck 6020 Austria Office Phone: 0043512280489. Home Fax: 0043512292468. Business E-Mail: athineos.philippou@uibk.ac.at.

PHILLIPS, ANTHONY GEORGE, neurobiology researcher; b. Barrow, Cumbria, Eng., Jan. 30, 1943; came to Can., 1953; s. George William and Mabel Lilian (Wood) P. BA, U. Western Ont., London, Can., 1966, MA, 1967, PhD, 1970. Asst. prof. psychobiology U. B.C., Vancouver, Canada, 1970-75, assoc. prof., 1975-80, prof., 1980—, head dept. psychology, 1994-99, prof. dept. psychiatry, 1999—, founding dir. U. B.C. Inst. Mental Health. Founder Quadra Logic Tech., Inc., Vancouver. Contbr. numerous papers to sci. jours. Chair inst. adv. bd. CIHR Inst. for Neurosci. Mental Health & Addiction, 2001—; bd. dirs. Tibetian Refuge Aid Soc., 1980—; chmn. Can.-India Village Aid, Vancouver, 1981—86, 2003—05. Recipient Killam Rsch. prize Can. Coun., 1977, D.O. Hebb award Can. Psychol. Assn.; Steacie fellow Nat. Scis. and Engring. Rsch. Coun. Can., 1980. Fellow Royal Soc. Can.; mem. Soc. Neurosci., Can. Soc. for Neurosci., Can. Coll. Neuropsychopharmacology. Office: U BC Dept Psych 2255 Wesbrook Mall Vancouver BC Canada V6T 1Z3 Office Phone: 604-822-4624. Business E-Mail: aphillips@psych.ubc.ca.

PHILLIPS, CHANDLER ALLEN, biomedical engineer, human factors engineer; b. LA, Dec. 21, 1942; s. Chandler A. and Ann P.; m. Jane Draper, Feb. 14, 1980. AB in Biol. Scis., Stanford U., 1965; MD, U. So. Calif., 1969; AB in Classical Langs., Wright State U., 1982; PhD (hon.), U. Human Studies, Las Vegas, 1985. Registered profl. engr., Ohio, Calif. Rsch. physician U. Dayton, Ohio, 1972-74; asst. prof. physiology Wright State U., Dayton, 1975-79, assoc. prof. biomed. engring., 1979-84, prof. biomed. engring., 1984-91, prof. biomed. and human factors engring., 1991—99, prof. biomed. indsl. and human factors engring., 1999—, Brage Golding disting. prof. rsch., 2007—. Author: Functional Electrical Rehabilitation, 1991, Human Factors Engineering, 2000; sr. editor: Mechanics of Skeletal and Cardiac Muscle, 1983, Effective Extremity Prostheses, 1989; regional editor Auto Medica, 1997-03; mem. editl. bd. Jour. Biomechanics, 1984-87, Jour. Clin. Engring., 1984-98, Auto Medica, 1988-97, Prosthetics-Orthotics Engring., 1995-98. Amateur radio operator W6SWV. Capt. USAF, 1970—72. Fellow: IEEE (life Harry Rowe Mimno award 1984), Ohio Acad. Sci., Aerospace Med. Assn. (John Paul Stapp award 2002), Am. Inst. Med. and Biol. Engring., Am. Acad. Neurologic Orthopedic Surgeons (hon.). Avocations: commercial-instrument pilot, fishing, classical philology. Office: Dept Biomed Indsl Human Factors Engring Wright State U Dayton OH 45435 Office Phone: 937-775-5044.

PHILLIPS, CHARLES DAVID, gerontologist, health services researcher, public health professional; b. Abilene, Tex., Nov. 3, 1948; s. Willie Everette and Mary Charlene Phillips; m. Catherine Hawes, June 2, 1978; 1 child, Anna Michelle Tankersley. BA, Tarleton State U., Stephenville, Tex., 1971; MPH, U. NC, Chapel Hill, 1987; PhD, U. Tex., Austin, Tex., 1979. Asst. prof., dept. polit. sci. U. N.C., Chapel Hill, 1980—87, rsch. scientist RTI Internat., Rsch. Triangle Park, NC, 1988—96, dir. Myers Rsch. Inst., Beachwood, Ohio, 1996—2000; regents prof. dept. health policy and mgmt. Sch. Rural Pub. Health, Coll. Sta., Tex., dir. health svcs. rsch. program, 2000—, head doctoral studies, 2001—07. Mem. grad. faculty Tex. A&M U., 2000—. Mem. editl. bd.: The Gerontologist, 2000—09. Recipient Pub. Svc. award, Nat. Citizens Coalition Nursing Home Reform, 2005, Alumni Academic Forum honoree, Tarleton State U., 2006, Regents Prof. award, TAMU Sys. Bd. Regents, 2008; named Gerontologist of Yr., U. Tex., Houston Ctr. Aging, 2001; named to Rschr. Honor Roll, Nat. Citizens Coalition Nursing Home Reform, 2000, ISI Highly Cited Authors Social Scis. Fellow: Gerontol. Soc. Am., interRAI; mem.: APHA, Nat. Pub. Health Honor Soc., Academy-Health, Delta Omega. Democrat. Office: Sch Rural Pub Health TAMUSHSC 1266 Tamu College Station TX 77843 Business E-Mail: phillipscd@srph.tamhsc.edu.

PHILLIPS, GERALD B., internal medicine scientist, educator; b. Bethlehem, Pa., Mar. 20, 1925; s. Abel H. and Cecilia P.; m. Maria Bonzi Lewis, July 15, 1970; children: Abigail, Elizabeth. AB, Princeton U., 1946; MD, Harvard Medical Sch., 1948. Diplomate Am. Bd. Internal Medicine. Intern Presbyn. Hosp., NYC, 1948-50; rsch. fellow Thorndike Meml. Lab., Med. Sch. Harvard U., Boston, 1950-53; vis. fellow biochemistry Columbia U. Coll. Physicians and Surgeons, NYC, 1954-56, from assoc. in medicine to assoc. prof., 1956-73, prof., 1973—. Sr. attending physician St. Lukes-Roosevelt Hosp.; attending physician NY-Presbyn. Hosp. Sr. asst. surgeon USPHS, 1952-54. Mem.: Am. Soc. for Biochemistry and Molecular Biology, Am. Soc. for Clin. Investigation, Alpha Omega Alpha. Home: 196 E 75th St New York NY 10021-3257 Business E-Mail: gbp1@columbia.edu. *

PHILLIPS, GRETCHEN, retired social worker; b. Erie, Pa., July 14, 1941; life ptnr. Beverly Campbell, June 10, 1989. BA, Mercyhurst Coll., 1966; MSW, Yeshiva U., 1972; postgrad., Advanced Ctr. Psychotherapy, 1972-73, Washington Sq. Inst., 1973-77. LMSW NY, ACSW. Psychiat. social worker, forensic social worker Creedmoor Psychiat. Ctr., Queens Village, NY, 1972-80; med. social worker Bellevue Hosp. Ctr., NYC, 1980-83; probation officer NYC Probation, Bklyn., 1983—2009. Home: 125 Radford St Apt 3C Yonkers NY 10705

PHILLIPS, HOLLY L., internist, medical reporter; b. Jan. 19, 1971; BA cum laude in English Lit., Williams Coll.; MD, Columbia U., 2000. Resident Lenox Hill Hosp., NYC, pvt. practice, tchr. Dept. Internal Medicine; medical reporter WCBS-TV, 2007—11. Contbr., medical expert NBC News, ABC News, CNN, MSNBC, CNBC, Fox News. Contbr. (health columns) Vogue, Town and Country, Cosmo, Gotham; contbr. articles to med. jours. Vol. Park Ave. Women's Shelter. Office: Lenox Hill Hosp 120 E 87th St #P20A New York NY 10128 *

PHILLIPS, JOHN P(AUL), retired neurosurgeon; b. Danville, Ark., Oct. 14, 1932; s. Brewer William Ashley and Wave Audrey (Page) P.; m. June Helen Dunbar, Dec. 14, 1963; children: Todd Eustace, Timothy John Colin, Tyler William Ashley. AB cum laude, Hendrix Coll., 1953; MD with honors, U. Tenn., 1956. Diplomate Am. Bd. Neurol. Surgeons. Intern Charity Hosp. La., New Orleans, 1957; resident surgery U. Tenn. Hosps., 1958; resident neurol. surgery U. Tenn. Med. Units, 1958-62; practice medicine, specializing in neurol. surgery Salinas, Calif., 1962-93; ret., 1993. Chief of staff, chief of surgery Salinas Valley Meml. Hosp.; mem. staffs Community Hosp. Monterey Peninsula, U. Calif. Hosp., San Francisco; asst. clin. prof. U. Calif., 1962—. Commd. Ky. col. Mem. AMA, ACS, Internat. Coll. Surgery, Harvey Cushing Soc., Congress Neurol. Surgery, Western Neurosurg. Assn., San Francisco Neurol. Soc., Pan Pacific Surg. Assn., Stanford U. Faculty Club (emeritus), Alpha Omega Alpha, Phi Chi, Alpha Chi. Personal E-mail: john674514@gmail.com.

PHILLIPS, KATHARINE ANNE, psychiatrist; b. Bronxville, NY, Apr. 17, 1955; d. Harry Scott and Mary (Bryan) P. AB summa cum laude, Dartmouth Coll., 1977, MD, 1987. Lic. med. doctor. Dep. editor Harvard Rev. of Psychiatry, Belmont, Mass., 1991—94; prof. psychiatry Brown U. Sch. Medicine, Providence, 2003—. Recipient Outstanding Resident award NIMH, 1989;, Outstanding Psychiatrist award for clin. psychiatry Mass. Psychiat. Soc., 1994, one of Best Drs. in America, Nat Edit., 2001-03, 2005-. Mem. AMA, Am. Psychiat. Assn. (disting. fellow, spl. presdl. commendation award 2004), Phi Beta Kappa, Alpha Omega Alpha. Business E-Mail: katharine_phillips@brown.edu.

PHILLIPS, M. IAN, physiologist, educator; b. London, July 30, 1938; arrived in US, 1967; s. Robert Leonard and Winifred Maud Phillips; m. Blanca Aguiar, Nov. 29, 2004; m. Kate Phillips (div.). BSc with honors, U. Exeter, Eng., 1962; PhD, U. Birmingham, Eng., 1967, DSc, 1985. Vis. asst. prof. U. Mich., Ann Arbor, 1967—69; fellow Calif. Inst. Tech., Pasadena, 1969—70; prof. U. Iowa, Iowa City, 1970—80; chmn., prof. U. Fla., Gainesville, 1980—2003; v.p. rsch. U. South Fla., Tampa, 2003—06; Norris prof. Keck Grad. Inst., Claremont, Calif., 2006—. Program dir. neuro. NSF, Washington, 1990; chmn. cardiovascular study sect. NIH, Washington, 1992—94; dir. Ctr. Rare Disease Therapies, 2008—. Editor: Regulatory Peptides, 1990—2006, Gene Therapy, 2002, Antisense Therapeutics 2d edit., 2005; co-author: Principles of Hormone & Behavior, 2005; author: (plays) Rembrandt, 12 books, 300 papers. Bd. dirs. Moffit Cancer Ctr., Tampa, Fla., 2003—06. Recipient Lucian award, McGill U., Can., 1989, Frank Annunzio award, Christopher Columbus Found., 2002, Merit award, NIH, 1995—2006; named Norris Prof. Life Scis., 2007. Fellow: Am. Assn. Adv. Sci., Am. Heart Assn. Achievements include discovery of brain peptides in hypertension; research in gene therapy for hypertension, stem cell rsch. on heart failure. Office: Keck Grad Inst 535 Watson Dr Claremont CA 91711 Home: 616 McKenna St Claremont CA 91711 Home Phone: 727-507-1190; Office Phone: 909-607-7487.

PHILLIPS, PETER C., child neurologist; MD, U. Conn., 1978. Prof. pediat. dept. Sch. Medicine Univ. Pa., 2000—; sect. chief Ctr. for Childhood Cancer Rsch.; attending physician; prof. neurology dept. Children's Hosp. of Phila., 2000—, dir. Pediat. Neuro Oncology Program, resident child neurology dept. Assoc. prof. neurology dept. Children's Hosp. of Phila., 1995—2000; asst. prof. neurology dept. Sch. Medicine Univ. Pa., 1991—95, asst. prof. pediat. dept. Sch. Medicine, 1991—95, assoc. prof. pediat. dept. Sch. Medicine, 1995—2000. Co-author: (publs.) Sexual partners for the stressed: facultative outcrossing in the self-fertilizing nematode Caenorhabditis elegans, 2009, Evolutionary rates and centrality in the yeast gene regulatory network, 2009, Purging deleterious mutations under self fertilization: paradoxical recovery in fitness with increasing mutation rate in Caenorhabditis elegans, 2010, Retinal nerve fiber layer thickness in children with optic pathway gliomas, 2011, and numerous others. Named one of the Top Doctors, Phila. Mag., 2011. Office: Children's Hospital of Philadelphia 324 S 34th St Philadelphia PA 19104 Office Phone: 215-590-4142. Office Fax: 215-590-5120.

PHILLIPS, RACHEL RHODES, radiologist, consultant; b. Bebington, Cheshire, England, Oct. 31, 1959; d. John Bevan and Rachel Barnetson Phillips; m. Robin Patrick Choudhury, June 7, 1997, children: Benjamin Tibor Choudhury, Sophia Este Choudhury, Maya Simone Choudhury. MB ChB, Leeds U., 1982. Lic. physician. Fellow in paediatric radiology Brit. Columbia's Children's Hosp., Vancouver, British Columbia, Canada, 1991—93; sr. registrar in radiology St Bartholomew's Hosp., London, 1993—94, rsch. fellow in mri, 1994—95; cons. radiologist The Whittington Hosp., London, 1995—2001; rsch. scholar Med. Ctr. Mri Dept. NYU, NYC, 1999—2001; cons. radiologist The Churchill Hosp., Oxford, Oxfordshire, England, 2002—. Sr. lectr. U. Coll. Med. Sch., London, 1997—2001. Contbr. chapters to books. Scholar, The King's Fund travelling scholar, 1999; Mouat Jones scholar, U. Leeds, 1981, The King's Fund travelling scholar, 1990, travelling fellow, Brit. Inst. Radiology, Amersham, 1999. Fellow: Royal Coll. Radiologists; mem.: Assn. U. Radiologists, Brit. Inst. Radiologists, Royal Coll. Physicians (manpower adv. panel 1987—90, standing com. of members 1987—90). Office: Churchill Hosp Radiology Dept Old Road OX3 7LJ Oxford England Office Fax: +(44) 1865 225946. Personal E-mail: rachelrp@aol.com. E-mail: rachel.phillips@orh.nhs.uk.

PHILLIPS, S. MICHAEL, allergist, medical educator, immunologist; MD, U. Wis. Intern Hosp. of Univ. Pa., resident, fellow, Harvard Univ.; dir. allergy programs U. Pa. Health System; prof. medicine and neurology U. Pa. Sch. Medicine; dir. clin. allergy and immunology svcs. Presbyterian Med. Ctr.- UPHS. Co-author: (publs.) Differential cytokine and chemokine production characterizes experimental autoimmune meningitis and experimental autoimmune encephalomyelitis, 2000, Elimination of Granuloma but not Splenic Lymphocytes by Fas-Fas Ligand Mediated Apoptosis in S. Mansoni Infected Mice-Am., 2001, Dependence of Obstructive Airway Disease on CD40L igand, 2001. Named one of Top Docs, Phila Mag., 2011. Mem.: ACP, Am. Fedn. of Clin. Rsch., Am. Coll. of Allergy, Asthma and Immunology, Clin. Immunology Soc., Am. Acad. of Allergy, Asthma, and Immunology. Office: Presbyterian Medical Center Mutch Bldg, 5th Fl 51 N 39th St Philadelphia PA 19104 Home Phone: 215-662-2775. Office Fax: 215-615-5055.

PHILLIPS, SIDNEY FREDERICK, gastroenterologist, educator; b. Melbourne, Australia, Sept. 4, 1933; s. Clifford and Eileen Frances (Fitch) P.; m. Decima Honora Jones, Mar. 29, 1957; children: Penelope Jane, Nichola Margaret, David Sidney. M.B.BS, U. Melbourne, 1956, MD, 1961. Resident med. officer Royal Melbourne Hosp., 1957-61, asst. sub-dean clin. sch., 1961-62; research asso. Central Middlesex Hosp., London, 1962-63; rsch. assoc. Mayo Clinic, Rochester, Minn., 1963-66, cons. in gastroenterology, 1966-2000; prof. medicine Mayo Med. Sch., 1976-2000, prof. medicine emeritus, 2000—, dir. gastroenterology rsch. unit, 1977-94; program dir. Mayo Gen. Clin. Rsch. Ctr., 1974-87; dir. Mayo Digestive Diseases Core Ctr., 1984-90; Karl F. and Marjory Hasselman prof. rsch., 1994-2000. Editor: Digestive Diseases and Sciences, 1977-82, Gastroenterology International, 1990-95; sr. assoc. editor: Gastroenterology, 1991-96; contbr. chpts. to books, articles to profl. jours. Fellow ACP, Royal Coll. Physicians, Royal Australian Coll. Physicians; mem. Am. Motility Soc. (pres. 1994-96), Am. Soc. Clin. Investigation (emeritus), Gastroenterology Soc. Australia (hon.), Am. Gastroenterology Assn. Assn. Am. Physicians, Brit. Soc. Gastroenterology (hon.). Office: St Mary's Hosp Gastroenterology Unit 200 1st St SW Rochester MN 55905-0001 Home: Dakota on the Park 209 8th St E #411 Saint Paul MN 55101-3389 Personal E-mail: decimasidney@aol.com.

PHILLIPS, WALTER MILLS, III, psychologist, educator; b. NYC, Sept. 29, 1947; s. Walter Mills and Grace Mary (Mullen) P.; m. Anne Marie Boyle, July 3, 1971; children: Jonathan, Elizabeth. BS, Fordham U., 1970; MA, U. S.D., 1973, PhD, 1975. Lic. clin. psychologist, Conn.; diplomate Am. Coll. Forensic Examiners, Am. Bd. Disability Evaluators, Am. Bd. Disability Analysts; cert. sr. disability analyst. Adolescent resident counselor Hawthorne (N.Y.) Cedar Knolls Sch., 1970—71; NIMH tng. fellow, 1971—75; clin. psychology intern Inst. of Living, Hartford, Conn., 1974—75, clin. staff psychologist, 1975—79, sr. staff psychologist, 1979—82, asst. dir. dept. clin. psychology, 1980—82, dir. clin. psychology tng., 1980—82; co-dir. outpatient psychiatry U. Conn., Farmington, 1982—88; asst. prof. psychiatry, dir. psychiatry evaluation svc. U. Conn. Health Ctr., 1982—88, dir. Anxiety Rsch. and Treatment Ctr., 1985—88; pvt. practice psychotherapy Hartford, 1976—; dir. adolescent/young adult svc. Grandview Psychiat. Resource Ctr., Waterbury, Conn., 1988—90; dir. psychology Waterbury Hosp., 1990—98; pvt. practice clin. psychology Waterbury and Middlebury, Conn., 1990—. Asst. clin. prof. psychiatry Sch. Medicine Yale U., New Haven, Conn., 1988-2006; ret. psychiatry faculty, 2007-; mem. psychology exec. com. Sch. Medicine Yale U., New Haven, 1990-98. Contbr. articles to profl. jours. Mem. APA, Am. Psychotherapy Assn. (diplomate), Conn. Psychol. Assn., Soc. Psychotherapy Rsch., Soc. Personality Assessment, Conn. Hosp. Assn. (chmn., dir. psychology conf. 1992-96), N.Y. Acad. Scis., Sigma Xi. Office: 86 Strathmore Rd Middlebury CT 06762 Office Phone: 203-758-8333. Business E-Mail: phillips.walter@comcast.net.

PHILLIPS, WINFRED MARSHALL, academic administrator, professor, mechanical engineer; b. Richmond, Va., Oct. 7, 1940; s. Claude Marshall and Gladys Marian (Barden) P.; children: Stephen, Sean. BSME, Va. Poly. Inst., 1963; MA in Engring., U. Va., 1966, DSc, 1968. Mech. engr. U.S. Naval Weapons Lab., Dahlgren, Va., 1963; NSF trainee, tchg. and rsch. asst. dept. aerospace engring. U. Va., Charlottesville, 1963—67, rsch. scientist, 1966—67; asst. prof. dept. aerospace engring. Pa. State U., University Park, 1968-74, from assoc. prof. to prof., 1974—80, assoc. dean rsch. Coll. Engring., 1979—80; head Sch. Mech. Engring. Purdue U., West Lafayette, Ind., 1980-88; dean Coll. Engring. U. Fla., Gainesville, 1988-99, assoc. v.p. engring., 1989—99, v.p. rsch. and Don and Ruth Eckis prof. biomed. engring., 1999—. Bd. dir. Wells Fargo Bank, Gainesville; vis. prof. U. Paris, 1976—77; adv. com. Nimbus Corp., 1985—90, Hong Kong U. Sci. and Tech., 1990—93, AvMed Inc.; co-founder, v.p. CEO Inc., 1990—; acad. adv. coun. Indsl. Rsch. Inst., 1990—93; exec. com. Accreditation Bd. on Engring. and Tech., 1991—96; sci. adv. com. Electric Power Rsch. Inst., 1994—99; vice-chmn. Southeastern Coalition for Minorities in Engring., 1995—, chmn., 2001—04; internat. revs. for univs. in Saudi Arabia, Russia, Netherlands, Kuwait, Mexico, China, France Accreditation Bd. on Engring. and Tech., 1995—; bd. dirs Oak Ridge Associated Univs., 2002—, chair coun., mem. exec. com., 2002—, chmn. bd., 2009—; mem. US Pres.'s Commn. on Nat. Medal of Sci., 2003—08. Sect. editor Am. Soc. Artificial Internal Organs Jour., 1985-99; contbr. over 175 articles to profl. jours., chpts. to books. Mem. Ind. Boiler and Pressure Vessel Code Bd., 1981—88; bd. dirs. Ctrl. Pa. Heart Assn., 1974—80, U. Fla. Found., 1989—91, 1995—2001. Recipient Career Rsch. award, NIH, 1974—78, NIH Surgery and Bioengring. Study sect., 1988—91, Fla. High Tech. and Industry Coun., 1990—94, Nat. Engring. award, Am. Assn. Engr. Socs., 2000, Linton Grinter award, 2000, Global Messenger award, Southeastern Consortium for Minorities in Engring., 2003; named Disting. Hoosier Ind., 1987, Sagamore of the Wabash, 1988. Fellow AAAS, AIAA, ASEE (vice chair 2001-02, chmn. bd. 2002—, Lamme award 2003), ASME (hon. sr. v.p. edn. 1986-88, bd. dirs. 1995-2000, pres. 1998-99, Dedicated Svc. award 2001, Ralph Coates Roe medal 2005), Biomed. Engring. Soc.(fellow, 2005, 2005), NY Acad. Scis., Am. Astron. Soc., Am. Inst. Med. and Biol. Engring. (founding fellow, chair coll. fellows 1994-95, pres. 1996-97), Am. Soc. Engring. Edn. (past chmn. long range planning soc. awards 1990-92, vice chmn. engring. deans coun. 1991-93, chair 1993—, bd. dirs. 1994-98, 1st v.p. 1994-95, pres. 1996-97), Royal Soc. Arts, Am. Soc. Artificial Internal Organs (trustee 1982-90, sec.-treas. 1986-87, pres. 1988-89, adv. bd. 1998—), ABET (pres. 1996-97); mem. Nat. Assn. State Univs. and Land-Grant Colls. (com. quality of engring. edn.), Univ. Programs in Computer-Aided Engring., Design and Mfg. (bd. dirs. 1985-91), Wash. Accord (chair 2007-11), IEA (chair 2010-11), Am. Phys. Soc., Internat. Soc. Biotheology, Fla. Engring. Soc., Cosmos Club, Fla. Blue Key, Rotary (pres. Lafayette 1987-88), Sigma Xi, Phi Kappa Phi, Phi Tau Sigma, Sigma Gamma Tau, Tau Beta Pi (eminent engr.). Achievements include research in artificial heart pumps; reentry aerodynamics; blood rheology; modeling blood flow; fluid dynamics of artificial hearts; use of smooth blood contacting surface; prosthetic valve fluid dynamics; laser Doppler studies of unsteady biofluid dynamics. Home: 4140 NW 44th Ave Gainesville FL 32606-4518 Office: U Fla Rsch and Grad Programs 223 Grinter Hall Gainesville FL 32611 Office Phone: 352-392-9271.

PHILLIS, JOHN WHITFIELD, physiologist, educator; b. Port of Spain, Trinidad, Apr. 1, 1936; came to U.S., 1981; s. Ernest and Sarah Anne (Glover) P.; m. Pamela Julie Popple, 1958 (div. 1968); children: David, Simon, Susan; m. Shane Beverly Wright, Jan. 24, 1969. B in Vet. Sci., Sydney U., Australia, 1958, D in Vet. Sci., 1976; PhD, Australian Nat. U., 1961; DSc, Monash U., Australia, 1970. Sr. lectr. Monash U., 1963-69; vis. prof. Ind. U., Indpls., 1969; prof. physiology, assoc. dean rsch. U. Man., Winnipeg, Canada, 1970-73; prof., chmn. dept. physiology U. Sask., Saskatoon, Canada, 1973-81, asst. dean rsch., 1973-75; prof. physiology Wayne State U., Detroit, 1981—2004, prof. emeritus, 2004—, chmn. dept. physiology, 1981-97; courtesy prof. U. Fla., Gainsville, 2004—. Mem. scholarship and grants com. Can. Med. Rsch. Coun., Ottawa, Ont., 1973-79, rsch. prof., 1980; mem. sci. adv. bd. Dystonia Med. Rsch. Found., Beverly Hills, Calif., 1980-85, Curtis Rsch. Inst., Risingsun, Ohio, 1998-2000; mem. sci. adv. panel World Soc. for Protection of Animals, 1982-98; Wellcome vis. prof. Tulane U., 1986; mem. acad. scholars Wayne State U., 1995. Author: Pharmacology of Synapses, 1970; editor: Veterinary Physiology, 1976, Physiology and Pharmacology of Adenosine Derivatives, 1983, Adenosine and Adenine Nucleotides as Regulators of Cellular Function, 1991, The Regulation of Cerebral

Blood Flow, 1993, Novel Therapies for CNS Injuries: Rationales and Results, 1996; editor Can. Jour. Physiology and Pharmacology, 1978-81, Progress in Neurobiology, 1973-97. Mem. grants com. Am. Heart Assn. of Mich., 1985-90, mem. rsch. coun., 1991-92, mem. rsch. forum com., 1991-96, chair, 1992-93; mem. Brain/Stroke Consortium Study Group, Am. Heart Assn., 1998. Wellcome fellow London, 1961-62; Can. Med. Rsch. Coun. grantee, 1970-81; NIH grantee, 1983-2000. Mem. Brit. Pharmacol. Soc., Am. Physiol. Soc., Soc. Neurosci., Internat. Brain Rsch. Orgn. Office: Wayne State U Sch Medicine Dept Physiology 540 E Canfield Ave Detroit MI 48201-1928 Personal E-mail: jphillis@med.wayne.edu.

PHOON, COLIN KIT-LUN, pediatric cardiologist, medical educator, biomedical researcher; b. London, Dec. 7, 1963; came to U.S., 1968; s. Wai Wor and Alice Phoon; m. Janet Rose. BA in Biophysics, Johns Hopkins U., 1985; MPhil in Pharmacology, Cambridge U., Eng., 1986; MD, U. Pa., 1990. Diplomate in pediatrics and pediatric cardiology Am. Bd. Pediatrics. Intern, then resident in gen. pediatrics Johns Hopkins Hosp., Balt., 1990-93; fellow in pediatric cardiology U. Calif. Med. Ctr., San Francisco, 1993-96; asst. prof. pediat./pediatric cardiology NYU Sch. Medicine, NYC, 1996—2003, assoc. prof., 2003—; attending physician NYU Med. Ctr./Bellevue Hosp. Ctr., NYC, 1996—, NYU Downtown Hosp., NYC, 1998—2001, NYU Hosp. Joint Diseases, NYC, 1999—; dir. pediatric echocard. lab. NYU Hosps. Ctr., 2002—. Cons. Charles B. Wang Cmty. Health Ctr., N.Y.C., 1998—. Author: Guide to Pediatric Cardiovascular Physical Examination or How to Survive an Outreach Clinic, 1998; contbr. chapters to books, articles to profl. jours. Mem. Johns Hopkins Nat. Alumni Schs. Com. Recipient Dr. A.O.J. Kelly prize U. Pa., 1990, Francis Schwentker award Johns Hopkins Hosp., 1993, Clin Sci. Devel. award NIH/NHLBI, 2001—06; Winston Churchill Found. scholar, 1985-86; Am. Heart Assn. fellow, 1995-96, J.T. Tai and Co. Found. fellow, 2006-07; Rsch. Career grant NIH, 2001-06. Fellow: Am. Soc. Echocardiography (mem. Echo Challenge Champion Team 2001, Echo Investigator award 2006—07), Am. Acad. Pediatrics (2d prize Young Investigator award competition 1998, Young Investigator Basic Sci. award sect. cardiology 1999), Am. Coll. Cardiology; mem.: Soc. Pediatric Rsch., N.Y. Pediatric Echocardiography Soc. (steering com. 1997, sec. 1999—), Am. Heart Assn. (mem. coun. basic cardiovascular scis. 1984—, mem. coun. on cardiovasc. disease in the young 1991—, program com. Coun. on Cardiovascular Disease in the Young 2002—05, grant rev. com., clinically applied rsch. 2004—06, grant rev. com., cardiac devel. 2008—11, Scientist Devel. grantee 2000—01, grant-in-aid 2006—10, grant 2010, Barth Syndrome Found. grant 2001—), Alpha Omega Alpha, Phi Beta Kappa, Churchill Scholars Soc. Avocations: reading, music, lacrosse, singing. Office: NYU Pediat Cardiology Program Pediat Echo Lab 160 E 32nd St 2d Fl New York NY 10016-6402 Office Phone: 212-263-5940.

PHUNG, NGUYEN DINH, medical educator; b. Ninh Binh, Vietnam, Sept. 25, 1950; came to U.S., 1975; s. Thu Dinh Nguyen and Minh Tuyet Le; m. Thuy Thanh Tran, Sept. 25, 1974; children: The-Ngoc, Khoi-Nguyen, Thien Huong. MD, Saigon Med. Sch., 1973. Diplomate Am. Bd. Internal Medicine, Am. Bd. Allergy and Immunology. Clin. instr. medicine, staff physician U. Okla. Health Scis. Ctr. & Vets. Hosp., Oklahoma City, 1982-84; clin. asst. prof. medicine U. Tex. Med. Sch., Houston, 1989—. Co-author: Practical Allergy & Immunology, 1983; contbr. articles to profl. jours. Mem. ACP, Am. Acad. Allergy and Immunology. Avocations: writing, music. Office: Allergy and Asthma Clinic 2905 Milam St Houston TX 77006-3609

PI, EDMOND HSIN-TUNG, psychiatry educator; MD, Cath. U. Coll. Medicine, 1972. Cert. in subspecialty psychosomatic medicine, Am. Bd. Psychiatry and Neurology. Chief resident U. Ky. Med. Ctr., Lexington, 1977-78; instr. psychiatry U. So. Calif. Sch. Medicine, LA, 1978-80, asst. prof., 1980-83; assoc. prof. Med. Coll. Pa., Phila., 1983-85, U. So. Calif. Sch. Medicine, 1985-88, prof. clin. psychiatry, 1988—98; prof. Charles R. Drew U. Medicine and Sci., 1998—2003; clin. prof. psychiatry Sch. Medicine, UCLA, 1999—2005; prof. clin. psychiatry Sch. Medicine, U. So. Calif., 2005—, assoc. chair for clin. affairs, dept. psychiatry, 2006—. Asst. dir. psychopharmacology U. So. Calif. Sch. Medicine, 1978-80; asst. dir. adult psychiat. clinic L.A. County and U. So. Calif. Med. Ctr., 1980-83; dir. adult psychiat. clinic Med. Coll. Pa., Phila., 1983-85; dir. Adult Psychiat. Inpatient Svcs., L.A. County and U. So. Calif. Med. Ctr., 1985-91, dir. Adult Psychiat. Outpatient Svcs., 1995-97; dir. transcultural psychiatry U. So. Calif. Sch. Medicine, 1991-98; med. dir. State of Calif. Dept. Mental Health, 1997-98; dir. Consultation and Liaison Svcs., L.A. County and U. So. Calif. Med. Ctr., 1998; exec. vice-chmn., assoc. ctr. dir. Augustus F. Hawkins Mental Health Ctr., Martin Luther King. Jr./Charles R. Drew U. Med. Ctr., 1998-2003; dir. psychiat. inpatient svc. Harbor/UCLA Med. Ctr., 2003-05; dir. psychiat. consultation and liaison svcs. L.A. (Calif.) County and U. So. Calif. Med. Ctr., 2005—, assoc. chair clin. affairs, 2006—. Author: Reactions to Psychotropic Medications, 1987, (book chpts.) Transcultural Psychiatry, Clinical Psychopharmacology, 1985—; contbr. articles to profl. jours. Mem. Calif. Gov.'s Com. Employment Disabled Persons, Sacramento, 1993—2007; bd. dirs. Chinese Bus. Assn., LA, 1990—92, Com. of 100, NYC, 1993—98, San Gabriel chpt. ARC, Calif., 1994—97, Mental Health Assn., LA County, Calif., 1995—97, 1998—2001. Vis. scholar Com. on Scholarly Comm. with People's Republic of China U.S. Nat. Acad. Scis., Washington, 1987-88; Treval fellow Am. Coll. Neuropsychopharmacology, 1982. Fellow Am. Psychiat. Assn. (chair com. Asian-Am. psychiatrists 1998-2000), Am. Soc. Social Psychiatry, Pacific Rim Coll. Psychiatry (treas. 1991-97), Am. Coll. Psychiatrists; mem. Soc. Study Psychiatry and Culture, Pacific Rim Assn. Clin. Pharmogenetics, Assn. Chinese Am. Psychiatrists (pres. 1995—). Avocations: photography, writing, travel, tennis, media communications. Office: LAC & USC Med Ctr Dept Psychiatry 2010 Zonal Ave # 1P1 Los Angeles CA 90033 Office Phone: 323-226-7975. Business E-Mail: ehpi@usc.edu.

PIACENTINI GÓMEZ, ENRIQUE ARIEL, emergency physician; b. Buenos Aires, Nov. 25, 1971; MD, U. Buenos Aires, 1996; PhD, U. Aútonoma de Barcelona, 2011. Physician Hosp. U. Mutua Terrassa, 2003—. Mem.: Soc. Catalana de Medicina Intensiva i Crítica. Office: Pl Dr Robert 5 Terrassa Barcelona 08221 Spain Personal E-mail: enpiache@yahoo.com.ar.

PIACITELLI, JOHN JOSEPH, retired county official, pediatrician, educator; b. Providence, Sept. 1, 1936; s. Joseph A. and Elsie (Mignacca) P.; m. Carol Ann Keirn, Aug. 19, 1961; 1 child, James. BS, U. R.I., 1958; MA, SUNY, Buffalo, 1963; MD, Creighton U., 1964. Diplomate Am. Bd. Pediatrics. Intern Buffalo Gen. Hosp., 1964-65; pediatric resident Children's Hosp. of Buffalo, 1965-67; pediatrician East Nassau Med. Group, North Babylon, N.Y., 1969-79; dir. Charlotte County Health Dept., Punta Gorda, Fla., 1980—2003; ret., 2003. Asst. clin. instr. SUNY, Buffalo, 1965-67, instr. in clin. pediatrics, L.I., 1972-79, asst. prof. pediatrics, 1979. Contbr. articles to profl. jours. Mem. health adv. com. Charlotte County Sch., 1981-96; mem. local planning orgn. adv. com., Charlotte County, Fla., 1986-87; mem. Indigent Health Care Adv. Bd., Charlotte County, 1988-2003; chmn. Charlotte County AIDS Task Force, 1988-91; chmn. adv. com. Head Start Health Svcs., 1991-94. Maj. M.C., U.S. Army, 1967-69, emeritus fellow, Am. Acad. Pediat. (cert.) Mem. Charlotte County Med. Soc.

PIANKA, GEORGE, orthopedic surgeon; arrived in US, 1964; s. Antoni and Aleksandra Pianka; m. Audrone Julia Raskys, Aug. 16, 1986; children: George, John Paul, Mark, Matthew. BA, Cornell U., Ithaca, NY, 1980; MD, U. Conn., Farmington, 1984. Intern Lenox Hill Hosp., NYC, 1984, resident orthopedics, 1985—89, attending physician orthopedics, 1990, chief hand surgery; fellow hand surgery Hosp. for Joint Diseases, NYC, 1989—90; attending physician orthopedics Phelps Meml. Hosp., Sleepy Hollow, NY, 1995. Contbr. chapters to books. Recipient Resident Tchg. award, Lenox Hill Orthopedic Dept., 1995, 2000. Fellow: Am. Soc. for Surgery of Hand, Am. Acad. Orthopedic Surgeons; mem.: NY Soc. for Surgery of Hand. Avocations: tennis, fishing, skiing. Office: Hudson Valley Bone and Joint Surgeons 24 Saw Mill River Rd Hawthorne NY 10532 also: 73 E 71st St New York NY 10021 Office Phone: 914-631-7777, 212-472-5899. Personal E-mail: aidadrpianka@hotmail.com.

PIANOWSKI, LUIZ FRANCISCO, pharmacist, biochemist; b. Castro, Brazil, May 25, 1957; s. Francisco and Eugênia Harmel Pianowski; m. Isanira Fortes Pianowski, Apr. 28, 1979; children: Melissa, Luiz Francisco Pianowski Filho, Giselle. Pharmaceutics and Biochemistry, Ponta Grossa State U., 1974—79. Doctorship Porto Pharm. U. - Portugal, 2001. Chemistry and biology tchr. Christian Inst., Castro, Brazil, 1979—85; owner and dir. Pianowski Lab. of Clin. Analysis, Castro, Brazil, 1985—93. Indsl. dir. Hebron SA, Caruaru, Brazil, 1994—2001; r&d/ phytomedicines dir. Aché Pharm. Laboratories SA, Guarulhos, Brazil, 2001—02; cons. Several industries, 2002—; mem. and pres. Aché's Sci. Coun., Guarulhos, Brazil, 2001—. Recipient Citizen of Castro City who Shines, 2000. Mem.: Am. Assn. of Pharm. Scientists. Christian. Achievements include discovery of natural giardicid and amebicid made of mentha spicata; patents for; research and development of six new medicines; first to stabilize the formula of male contraception made of gossypol. Avocations: movies, reading, travel. Office: Pianowski & Pianowski S/C Ltda - ME Avenida Campinas 120 São Paulo Atibaia 12947-150 Brazil E-mail: luiz@pianowski.com.br.

PIARULLI, FRANCESCO, cardiologist; s. Raffaele Piarulli and Teresa Videtta; m. Sabrina Spolladore, Feb. 24, 2001; 1 child, Marta. Degree, U. Padova, 1983, degree in geriatric medicine, 1987, degree in cardiology, 1994; degree in angiology, U. Catania, 1990. Physician Inst. Internal Medicine, Padova, Italy, 1983—89; with Operative Unit Geriatric Medicine, Porto Viro, Rovigo, Italy, 1989—99; leading pjysician Complex Operative Unit Diabetology, Padova, 1999—; with Simple Operative Unit Angiology and Vascular Diagnosis, 2001—. Office: Diabetes Clinic Via dei Colli 4 Padua 35100 Italy Office Fax: 049/8216838. Business E-Mail: francesco.piarulli@unipd.it.

PIAZZINI, ADA, neuropsychologist, therapist; b. Milan, Apr. 26, 1960; d. Ernesto Piazzini, Giovanna Alfieri; m. Maurizio Ferrera; 1 child, Giulia Ferrera. Degree in Psychology, U. Milan, 1984; Grad. Degree, U. Pavia, Italy, 1988. Rschr. clin. psychology U. Milan, 1988—90; cons. neuropsychology Epilepsy Ctr., San Paolo Hosp., U. Milan, 1991—. Vis. scholar U. Calif. Grad. Sch. Edn., Berkeley, 1990; vis. rschr. Montreal (Can.) Neurol. Inst., 1997; prof. clin. psychology U. Milan, 1997—2000; mem. Commn. on Neuropsychology, Internat. League Against Epilepsy, West Hartford, 1998—. Contbr. articles to profl. jours. Mem. UNICEF, Milan, 1998—2002. Grantee, European Cmty., 1998, 1999, 2000. Mem.: Italian Psychologist Register. Home: Via Lamarmora 22 20122 Milan Italy Office: Epilepsy Ctr San Paolo Hosp Via A Di Rudini 8 20142 Milan Italy Home Phone: 0039 02 5513955; Office Phone: 0039 02 81844200.

PICARD, FREDERIC JEAN, orthopedic surgeon, consultant, researcher; b. Besancon, France, May 13, 1961; s. Guy and Marie-France (Drefuss) P.; children: Roxane, Guillaume, Mathis and Ludovic (twins), Perle; m. Lalao Hanitra Rakotoarivelo, July 18, 1998. MD, U. Besancon, 1987; Degree in Gen. Surgery, U. Grenoble, France, 1990; M in Biomechanics/Anatomy, U. Lyon and Grenoble, France, 1991; Degree in Hand and Upper Limb Surgery, U. Paris, 1993. Cert. hosp. practitioner. Resident Univ. Hosps., Grenoble/Lyon, 1987-93; hosp. asst. Univ. Hosp., Grenoble, 1993-96; lectr. anatomy U. Grenoble, 1993-96; responsible for application devel. computer assisted surgery Aesculap/B. Braun Co., France and Germany, 1997. Vis. scholar Northwestern U. and Northwestern Orthopedic Inst., Chgo., 1998; project engr., sys. developer Ctr. Orthopedic Rsch./Carnegie Mellon U., Pitts., 1999-2001; cons. in field. Contbr. articles to profl. jours. Mem. Am. Acad. Orthopaedic Surgeons (internat. affiliate), French Coll. Orthopaedic and Trauma Surgeons, Computer Assisted Orthop. Surgery Soc., Golden Jubilee Nat. Hosp. (Eng.) (cons. orthop. surgeon, founder, rsch. unit). Achievements include patents in field. Avocations: swimming, reading, music. Office: Golden Jubilee Nat Hosp Beardmore Street G81 4HX Clydebank Glasgow Scotland Office Phone: 0141 951 5567. Business E-Mail: frederic.picard@gjnh.scot.nhs.uk.

PICARDI, ANTONIO, internal medicine educator; b. Casoria, Italy, June 1, 1961; s. Mariano Picardi and Maria Teresa Iazzetta. MD, U. Federico II, 1987; PhD, U. Navarra, 1995. Intern Inst. Med. Pathology, U. Federico II, Naples, Italy, 1984—87; young investigator S. Raffaele Hosp., Milan, 1987—89; resident internal medicine and hepatology U. Navarra, Pamplona, Spain, 1989—94; vice head chief internal medicine area U. Campus Bio-Medico, Rome, 1994—2000, prof. internal medicine, 2000—, chief Hepatology Unit, 2002—09, chair clin. medicine-hepatology, 2009—; prof. specialty sch. internal medicine, allergology and clin. immunology, endocrinology, gastroenterology, oncology, clin. pathology, infectious diseases. Mem.: Endocrine Soc., Coll. of Tchrs. of Internal Medicine, Italian Soc. Internal Medicine, European Assn. for Study of Diabetes, Am. Diabetes Assn., Italian Assn. Study of Liver, European Assn. Study of Liver. Home: via b1 Trigoria 60B Rome 100128 Italy Office: Univ Campus Bio-Medico of Rome Via Alvaro del Portillo 200 Rome RM 00128 Italy Office Phone: 3906225411207. Office Fax: 390622541456. Business E-Mail: a.picardi@unicampus.it.

PICARELLI, ANTONIO, gastroenterologist; b. Cosenza, Italy, Dec. 16, 1956; s. Osvaldo Picarelli and Giannina Vadalà; m. Giuseppina Patera, July 28, 1984; children: Giovanna, Mattia. MD, U. Rome, 1982; degree in Gastroent., U. Rome La Sapienza, 1987. Diplomate. Rschr. U. Rome, 1990—, lectr. medicine, surgery and diet. Regional sci. cons. Italian Celiac Assn., 1998—2002, nat. sci. cons., 2002—; head Lazio Celiac Support Ctr. Contbr. scientific papers to profl. pubs. Achievements include research in celiac disease. Office Fax: +390649970524; Home Fax: +39065002520. Personal E-mail: awtovio.picarelli@uniroma1.it.

PICCALUGA, PIER-PAOLO, hematologist, researcher; b. Bologna, Italy, Feb. 5, 1973; s. Alessandro Piccaluga and Patrizia Tommasina. MD, U. of Bologna, 1997, Splty. in Hematology, 2001, PhD, 2005. Board Certified Diplomate Order of the Med. Doctors of Bologna, Italy, 1998. Hematology fellow Inst. of Hematology, Bologna, Italy, 1997—2003; postdoctoral rsch. fellow Inst. for Cancer Genetics, Columbia U., NYC, 2003—04; rsch. fellow Inst. of Hematology Seragnoli, U. of Bologna, 2005—. Contbr. articles to profl. jours. Recipient Luigi Casati, Accademia dei Lincei, 1998, Francesco Schiassi, Order of the Med. Doctors of Bologna, 2002; Rotary Found. Academic-Year Ambassadorial scholar, Rotary Internat., 2003, Vanda Vanini e Sandro Cavagnino, Associazione Cristina Bassi, 2003, Leonino Fontana e Maria Lionello, AIRC, 2005. Mem.: European Hematology Assn. (assoc.), Italian Assn. of Exptl. Hematology (assoc.), Italian Assn. of Hematology (assoc.), Am. Soc. of Clin. Oncology (assoc.). Achievements include research in original findings in lymphoma biology. Office: Inst of Hematology Seragnoli Via Massarenti 9 Italy Bologna 40138 Italy Office Fax: 00390516364037; Home Fax: 00390516364037. Business E-Mail: ppicca@med.unibo.it.

PICCIANO, ANNE, physician, educator; Grad., U. Pa., Philadelphia, 1987. Diplomate Am. Bd. Family Medicine, cert. adolescent medicine. Resident family medicine West Jersey Health Sys., 1988—90; physician JFK Med. Ctr., Edison. Asst. clin. prof. family medicine Univ. Medicine and Denstistry of NJ. Office: JFK Medical Center 65 James St Edison NJ 08820 Office Phone: 732-321-7487. Office Fax: 732-906-4927.

PICCOLI, BRUNO GIDIETTO, occupational physician; b. Milan, May 16, 1948; s. Augusto Piccoli and Maria Vittorina Valdevit; m. Deborah Ann Elliott; children: Jennifer Karen, Daisy Claire, Rupert Daryl. Degree in med. and surgery, U. Milan, 1976. Intern U. Milan, 1976—82; med. officer Tchg. Hosp. ICP, Milan, 1981—. Com. sec. Internat. Commn. on Occupl. Health, 1985—87, com. chmn., 1987—; cons., Rome, 1998—. Contbr. scientific papers. Avocations: physical training, billiards. Office: Tchg Hosp U Milan Via San Barnaba 8 20122 Milan MI Italy E-mail: bpiccoli@unimi.it.

PICHARD, AUGUSTO D., cardiologist, medical educator; b. Santiago, Chile, Sept. 26, 1945; came to U.S., 1971; s. Roberto M. Pichard and Eliana Merino Descalzi; m. Nancy L. Prendergast, June 29, 1973; children: Nicole, Dominique, Alicia, Robert. Grad., Cath. U. Chile, MD, 1969. Cert. Am. Bd. Internal Med., 1975, Am. Bd. Internal Med., Cardiovascular Disease, 1977, Am. Bd. Internal Med., Interventional Cardiology, 1999. Intern Catholic Univ. Chile, 1968—69, resident, 1969—70, resident in cardiology, 1970—71; fellow Cleveland Clinic, 1971—73, assoc. mem. staff, 1973-75; lab. dir. Mt. Sinai Hosp., NYC, 1975-81; assoc. prof. medicine Mt. Sinai Med. Sch., NYC, 1978-81, Cath. Univ. Chile, 1981-82; cardiologist, dir. cardiac catheterization lab. Washington Hosp. Ctr., Washington, 1983—; prof. medicine George Washington U., Washington, 1983-89, clin. prof. medicine, 1990—; cardiologist Washington Cardiology Ctr. Mem. med. bd. Washington Hosp. Ctr., 1997, 99; chmn. bd. Medlantic Rsch. Inst., Washington, 1998—. Mem editl. bd. Am. Jour. Cardiology, 1992-98. Named Hon. Mem. Faculty Cath. U. Chile, 1994. Fellow ACP, Am. Coll. Cardiology, Am. Heart Assn., Soc. Cardiac Angio and Intervention. Roman Catholic. Avocations: tennis, ski, yoga. Office: Washington Cardiology Ctr 110 Irving St NW Washington DC 20010-2976 Office Phone: 202-877-5975. Office Fax: 202-877-3339.

PICK, EDGAR, immunologist, biochemist; b. Lugoj, Romania, Feb. 15, 1938; s. Erwin and Barbara (Gal) P.; m. Leora Syrkin, Mar. 21, 1965; children: Anat, Dan. MD, Hebrew U., 1965; PhD, U. London, 1970. Rsch. fellow Scripps Rsch. Found., La Jolla, Calif., 1965-67; rsch. assoc. Inst. Dermatology, London, 1967-70; from sr. lectr. to prof. Tel Aviv U. Med. Sch., 1970—2008, Roberts-Guthman chair in immunopharmacology, 1989—2008. Dir. Miverva-Cohnheim Ctr. Phagocyte Rsch., 1994-2008, head Sackler Inst. Molecular Med., 1997-2000; head Kodesz Inst. of Host Def. Against Infectious Diseases, 1999—2008. Mem. editl. bd. Immunobiology, 1980-2005, Internat. Jour. Immunopharmacology, 1985-2000, J. Leukocyte Biology, 1996-2001, FASEB Jour., 2006—. Fellow Am. Assn. Immunologists, Soc. for Leukocyte Biol., Am. Soc. Biochem. and Molecular Biol. Jewish. Avocations: literature, architecture, art history, philosophy, science history. Home: 75 Einstein St 69102 Tel Aviv Israel Office: Tel Aviv U 69978 Tel Aviv Israel Office Phone: 972-3-640-7872. Business E-Mail: epick@post.tau.ac.il.

PICKERING, LARRY KENNETH, pediatrician, researcher; m. Margaret Jane Thompson, July 8, 1967; children: Margaret Anne, Andrew Michael. MD, W.Va. U. Sch. Medicine, 1970. Diplomate Am. Bd. Pediat. in Pediats., Nat. Bd. Med. Examiners. Intern pediat. svc. St. Louis Children's Hosp., 1970-71, resident pediat. svc., 1971-72; fellow pediat. infectious diseases St. Louis Children's Hosp. and Washington U. Sch. Medicine, 1972-74; asst. prof. pediat. U. Tex. Med. Sch., Houston, 1974-77, assoc. prof. pediat., 1977-82, prof. pediat. dept. pediat. divsn. infectious diseases, 1982-92, prof. program in immunology, 1982-92. Cons. M.D. Anderson Hosp. and Tumor Inst., Houston, 1974-78, St. Joseph Hosp., Houston, 1975-89, Meml. Hosp. Sys., Houston, 1977-92, AMA; assoc. prof. pediat. M.D. Anderson Hosp. and Tumor Inst., U. Tex. Cancer Ctr., 1978-83, prof. pediat., 1983-92; infection control med. advisor Speech and Hearing Inst., U. Tex. Health Sci. Ctr., Houston, 1978-87, prof. Grad. Sch. Biomed. Scis., 1982-89; adj. prof. pharmaceutics dept. pharmaceutics Coll. Pharmacy, U. Houston, 1983-92; dir. Ctr. for Pediat. Rsch., Ea. Va. Med. Sch., Children's Hosp. of The King's Daus., Norfolk, 1992-2001; David R. Park prof. pediat., 1989-92, dir. divsn. infectious diseases dept. pediat., 1975-1992; prof., CHKD chair in pediatric rsch. Ea. Va. Med. Sch., Norfolk, 1992-2001; prof. pediats. dept. pediats. Emory U. Sch. Medicine, Atlanta, 2001-; external examiner and reviewer dept. pediat. U. Jordan, Amman, 1984; mem. subboard pediat. infectious diseases Am. Bd. Pediat., 1991-96; mem. planning com. First Internat. Pediat. Infectious Diseases Conf., Monterey, Calif., 1995; mem. sci. com. First World Congress of Pediat. Infectious Diseases, 1995; mem. steering com. E. Mead Johnson Award for Rsch. in Pediat., 1996-99; presenter in field; assoc. dir. spl. projects, Nat. Immunization Program, Ctrs. Disease Control & Prevention, Atlanta, 2000-01, sr. advisor to dir. Nat. Ctr. for Immunization and Respiratory Diseases, 2001-, exec. sec. Adv. Comm. Immmir Practices Ctr. Disease Ctrl. & Prevention, Atlanta, 2005-. Author: (with H.L. DuPont) Infections of the Gastrointestinal Tract, 1980, Infectious Diseases of Children and Adults; editor: (with R.R. Howell and F.H. Morriss) Human Milk in Infant Nutrition and Health, 1986, (with M.T. Osterholm, J.O. Klein and S.S. Aronson) Infectious Diseases in Child Day Care: Management and Prevention, 1987, Infections in Day Care Centers Seminars in Pediatric Infectious Diseases, 1990, Diarrheal Disease, 1994, (with S. Long and C. Prober) Principles and Practice of Pediatric Infectious Diseases, 1997, 3rd edit., 2008; contbg. editor: Infectious Disease Clinics in North America, 1992; editor-in-chief Pediat. Infectious Diseases: Clin. Updates, Nat. Found. for Infectious Diseases, 1994-2000; mem. editl. bd. Infectious Diseases Newsletter, 1985-89, Infection, 1988, Pediat., 1990-93, Report on Pediat. Infectious Diseases, 1990-95, co-editor, 1993-95, Pediatric. Infectious Disease Jour., 1987-96, 2001--, Seminars in Pediat. Infectious Diseases, 1997—2001, Vaccine Bull., 1997-2001, Infectious Diseases in Children, 1997-09; editor; contbr. articles to profl. jours. Med. adv. com. Met. Houston chpt. March of Dimes, 1974-76, bd. dirs., 1975-80, chmn. profl. adv. com., 1977-79; mem. rsch. com. Nat. March of Dimes, 1999-2004. Named Disting. Alumnus, W.Va. U. Sch. Medicine, Morgantown, 1995, Edward J. van Liere Rsch. award. Fellow Infectious Diseases Soc. Am. (exec. com. Emerging Infections Network 1997-2000, mem. coun. 2003--06); mem. AAAS, Am. Acad. Pediats., Intersci. Conf. on Antimicrobiol Agts. and Chemotherapy, Internat. Soc. for Rsch. in Human Milk and Lactation, Am. Soc. for Clin. Pharmacology and Therapeutics, Am. Soc. for Tropical Medicine and Hygiene, Am. Pediat. Soc., Am. Soc. Microbiology, Am. Acad. Pediat. (com. on infectious diseases 1990-96, assoc. editor RedBook 1990-97, editor 1997-, exec. com. sect. breastfeeding 2001—03), Am. Fedn. for Clin. Rsch., Nat. Found. of Infectious Diseases (bd. dirs. and treas. 1997—, chair continuing med. edn. com. 1999—2003), Va. Pediat. Soc., Tex. Pediat. Soc., Tex. Med. Assn., Tex. Infectious Diseases Soc. (coun. mem. 1982-84), Harris County Pediat. Soc. (edn. com. 1975-79), Harris County Med. Soc., Houston Acad. Medicine, Houston Pediat. Soc. (constn. and by-laws com. 1978-82), So. Soc. for Pediat. Rsch. (coun. mem. 1981-83, Founder's award 1994), Soc. for Pediat. Rsch. (chair infectious diseases subspecialty sect. 1995, co-chair seminar Epidemiology 1995), Pediat. Infectious Diseases Soc. (pres.-elect 1993-95, pres. 1995-97, Disting. Physician award, 2007), The Milk Club (exec. com. 1995-99), ICAAC (program com. 1997-2002), AAP (chair rsch. com. and exec. com. sect. on breastfeeding), Infectious Diseases Soc. Am. (coun. mem. 2003-06, sci. program com., 2007-10, chair panel on immunization guideline devel., 2008-09). Avocations: tennis, biking, reading. Office: CDC and Prevention Nat Ctr Immunization Respiratory Disease 1600 Clifton Rd NE # MsE05 Atlanta GA 30333 Office Phone: 404-639-8562. Office Fax: 404-639-8626. Business E-Mail: LPickering@cdc.gov.

PICKETT, CECIL BRUCE, retired medical products executive; b. Canton, Ill., Oct. 5, 1945; married; two children. BS in Biology, Calif. State U., Hayward, 1971; PhD in Cell Biology, UCLA, 1976. Sr. rsch. and devel. positions Merck & Co., Inc. (formerly Schering-Plough Corp.); fellow, cell biology UCLA, 1976—78; with Merck Sharp & Dohme Rsch. Labs., 1978—93; exec. v.p., discovery rsch. Schering-Plough Rsch. Inst., Kenilworth, NJ, 1993—2002, pres., 2002; sr. v.p. Schering Corp., 2004; pres. SPRI, 2004; exec. dir. Biogen Idec, Inc., pres., Rsch and Devel., 2006—09. Macy scholar Marine Biol. Lab, Woods Hole, Mass., 1978; vis. asst. prof. Coll. Medicine Howard U., Washington, 1978-83; adj. assoc. prof. N.J. Sch. Medicine & Dentistry, 1985-88; assoc. prof. U. Montreal, 1989; adj. prof. McGill U., 1990; disting. lecturer, Jonsson Comprehensive Cancer Ctr., UCLA, 1995; mem. sci. adv. bd. FDA; member, mem. GM Adv. Council, Cancer Rsch. Found., 2004. Contbr. articles to profl. jours.; various editl bds.: med. jours. and rsch. orgns. Bd. visitors Columbia U. Med. Ctr.; mem. sci. adv. bd. FDA; mem., adv. com. NIH; mem. The Nat. Acad. of Sciences Inst. of Medicine; mem. vol. bd. dir. NJ Performing Arts Ctr. Recipient Robert A. Scala Award and Lectureship in Toxicology, Rutgers U. & U. Medicine & Dentistry of NJ, 1993, Founders award, CIIT Centers for Health Research, 2001. Mem. AAAS, IOM, NAS, Am. Soc. Biochemistry & Molecular Biology, Am. Assn. Cancer Rsch., Am. Soc. Cell Biology, Am. Assn. Advancement Sci.; mem. adv. com. to dir. NIH. Office: Zimmer Holdings Inc 345 East Main St Warsaw IN 46580 Office Phone: 574-267-6131. Office Fax: 574-372-4988. Personal E-mail: cecil.pickett@zimmer.com. *

PICKHARDT, PERRY J., radiology educator, researcher; BS in Physics, U. Wis., Madison, 1991; MD, U. Mich. Med. Sch., 1995. Resident, diagnostic radiology Mallinckrodt Inst. Radiology, Wash. U., St. Louis, 1995—99; dept. head, radiology US Naval Hosp., Guantanamo Bay, Cuba, 1999—2000; head, GI-GU imaging Nat. Naval Med. Ctr., Bethesda, Mich., 2000—03; asst. prof., radiology Uniformed Svcs. U. Health Scis., Bethesda, Md.; assoc. prof., radiology U. Wis. Med. Sch., Madison, Wis., 2003, assoc. prof., abdominal imaging. Co-editor textbook on body CT; pub. a number of scientific papers; contbr. chapters to books. Figley Fellowship, AJR Editl. Office, Winston-Salem, NC, 2002. Office: U Wis Sch Medicine and Pub Health E3/366 Clinical Sciences Ctr 600 Highland Ave Madison WI 53792-3252 Office Phone: 608-263-9028. Business E-Mail: ppickhardt2@uwhealth.org.

PICKLE, LINDA WILLIAMS, biostatistician; b. Hampton, Va., July 19, 1948; d. Howard Taft and Kathryn Lee (Riggin) Williams; m. James B. Pearson, Jr., Oct. 14, 1984; 1 child from previous marriage, Diane Marie. BA, Johns Hopkins U., 1974, PhD in Biostats., 1977; postgrad., George Washington U., 1986—87. Computer programmer Comml. Credit Computer Corp., Balt., 1966-69; systems analyst, computer programmer Greater Balt. Med. Ctr., 1969-72; grad. tchg. asst. biostats. Johns Hopkins U., Balt., 1974-77; adj. asst. prof. divsn. biostats. and epidemiology Georgetown U. Med. Sch., Washington, 1983—88, assoc. prof., 1988-91, dir. biostats. unit V.T. Lombardi Cancer Rsch. Ctr., 1988-91; biostatistician Nat. Cancer Inst. NIH, Bethesda, Md., 1977-88, sr. math statistician divsn. cancer control/population scis., 1999—2007; math. statistician office rsch. methodology Nat. Ctr. Health Stats., Hyattsville, Md., 1991-99; chief statistician StatNet Consulting LLC, Gaithersburg, Md., 2007—; adj. prof. dept. geography and pub. health scis. Pa. State U., 2008—. Author: Atlas of U.S. Cancer Mortality Among Whites: 1950-80, 1987, Atlas of U.S. Cancer Mortality Among Nonwhites: 1950-1980, 1990, Atlas of United States Mortality, 1996, U.S. Predicted Cancer Incidence, 2003; contbr. articles to profl. jours.; co-author: Visualizing Data Patterns with Micromaps, 2010. Recipient Hammer award, US Govt., 2000. Fellow: Am. Statis. Assn.; mem.: Biometric Soc., Sigma Xi, Phi Beta Kappa. Achievements include research in statistical methods in epidemiology, mapping health statistics.

PIEGARI, JAMES A., psychologist; b. Bklyn., Aug. 4, 1951; s. Vincent and Olympia Piegari. BS in Psychology, Georgetown U., 1972; MA in Clin. Psychology, St. John's U., 1975; MA in Psychology, Rutgers U., 1995, New Sch. Social Rsch., 1995; PhD in Psychology, Saybrook Grad. Sch. and Rsch. Ctr., 1999. Lic. psychologist NY, cert. sch. psychologist NY, Cornell U., Dispute Resolution Cert. Program, 2000, in mind body meditation and healing Columbia U., Coll. Physicians and Surgeons, Health Sci. Divsn., 2001, in Rational Emotive Behavior Theory and Techniques Albert Ellis Inst., Primary and Advanced Tng., 2004, Albert Ellis Inst., Primary and Advanced Tng., 2006. Ops. rsch. analyst USPHS Hosp., SI, NY, 1976—78; applied behavioral scis. specialist United Cerebral Palsy Assns. NY State, SI, 1978—80, Terence Cardinal Cooke Health Care Ctr., NYC, 1980—2001, psychologist, 2002—; pvt. practice psychologist SI, 2002—. Mem. publs. com. Flower Hosp., NYC, 1980—81; cons. Vietnamese refugee program Mission of Immaculate Virgin, Mt. Loretto, SI, 1986—96; assoc. prof. Mercy Coll., Arthur Kill Correctional Facility, SI, 1989—90; supt. provider psychol. svcs. NYC Dept. Edn., 2002—; cert. mediator S.I. Cmty. Dispute Resolution Ctr.; mem. alumni admissions program Georgetown U. Contbr. articles to profl. jour., chapters to books. Mem. Health and Hosps. Com. NYC Cmty. Bd., SI, NY, 1979—80; charter mem. Friends of South Beach Psychiat. Ctr., SI, NY, 1980—81, bd. dirs., 1980—81, chmn. mental health symposium com., 1980—81; mem. appellate divsn. panel mental health profl. psychologist Supreme Ct., NY. Recipient Employee Recognition award, Terence Cardinal Cooke Health Care Ctr., 2001. Mem.: APA, NY State Psychol. Assn. Avocations: Civil War artifacts, photography, travel, motorcycle touring. Home and Office: 7 Azalea Ct Staten Island NY 10309

PIEL, ANTHONY, retired lawyer; b. NY, May 26, 1936; BA, Princeton U., 1958; LLD, Harvard Law Sch., 1963. Dir. cabinet & gen. legal counsel WHO, 1972—96. Bd. dirs., cons. WHO Collaborating Ctr. Ulm U., 1996—. Mem.: UN Assn. Home: PO Box 332 286 Gay St Rt 41 Sharon CT 06069 Personal E-mail: apiel01@snet.net.

PIEN, HOWARD H., pharmaceutical executive; b. 1958; BS, MIT; MBA, Carnegie Mellon U. With Abbott Laboratory, Inc.; various sales, market rsch., licensing & product mgmt. positions Merck & Co., Inc. (formerly Schering Plough Corp.); dir., new product devel. SmithKline Beecham, 1991—92, v.p., 1991—95, dir., product mktg., 1992—93, dir., mktg., 1993—95, mng. dir., sr. v.p. England, 1995—97, sr. v.p., dir., North Asia, 1997; various exec. positions, including pres., pharm. internat. GlaxoSmithKline plc, 2000—03; pres., CEO Chiron Corp. (acquired by by Novartis AG), Emeryville, Calif., 2003—07, chmn., 2004—07; pres., CEO & chmn. Medarex, Inc. (acquired by Bristol Myers Squibb Co.), Princeton, NJ, 2007—09; chmn. Vanda Pharmaceuticals, Inc., 2010—. Bd. dirs. ViroPharma, Inc., Vanda Pharmaceuticals, Inc., ImmunoGen, Inc., 2007. Office: Vanda Pharmaceuticals Inc 9605 Medical Ctr Dr Ste 300 Rockville MD 20850 Office Phone: 240-599-4500. Office Fax: 301-294-1900. Business E-Mail: howard.pien@vandapharma.com. *

PIEPGRAS, DAVID G., neurosurgeon, educator; b. Luverne, Minn., 1940; MD, U. Minn., 1965. Diplomate Am. Bd. Neurol. Surgery. Intern Mary Hitchcock Hosp., Hanover, Minn., 1965—66; resident in surgery Hennepin County Gen. Hosp., Mpls., 1969—70; resident in neurol. surgery Mayo Grad. Sch. Medicine, Rochester, 1970—74; staff St. Mary's Hosp., Rochester, 1974—, Rochester Meth. Hosp., 1974—; staff cons. dept. neurosurgery Mayo Clinic, Rochester, 1974—, prof. neurol. surgery. Bd. dirs. Am. Bd. Neurol. Surgery, 2002—. Fellow: ACS; mem.: AMA, Congress of Neurol. Surgeons, Am. Acad. Neurol. Surgeons. Office: Mayo Clinic Dept Neurol Surgery Rochester MN 55905-0001

PIEPHO, ROBERT WALTER, pharmacy educator, researcher; b. Chgo., July 31, 1942; s. Walter August and Irene Elizabeth (Huybrecht) Apfel; m. Mary Lee Wilson, Dec. 10, 1981. BS in Pharmacy, U. Ill.-Chgo., 1965; PhD in Pharmacology, Loyola U., Maywood, Ill., 1972. Registered pharmacist, Ill., Mo. Assoc. prof. U. Nebr. Med. Ctr., Omaha, 1970-78; prof. pharmacy, assoc. dean Sch. Pharmacy U. Colo., Denver, 1978-86; prof. pharmacol., dean U. Mo. Sch. Pharmacy, Kansas City, 1986—2010, prof., 2010—. Contbr. articles to profl. jours., chpts. to books. Pres. Club Monaco Homeowners Assn., Denver, 1980-82. Named Outstanding Tchr. U. Nebr. Coll. Pharmacy, 1975; recipient Arthur Hassan Colo. Pharmacal Assn., 1983, Excellence in Teaching U. Colo. Med. Sch., 1983, Mo. Bowl Hygeia award, 2010. Fellow Am. Coll. Clin. Pharmacology (regent 1983-88, 91-96, pres. 1998-2000); mem. Am. Soc. Hosp. Pharmacists, Am. Soc. Pharmacology and Exptl. Therapeutics, Rho Chi Roman Catholic. Office: U Mo Sch Pharmacy 2464 Charlotte St Kansas City MO 64108-2718 Office Phone: 816-235-2404. Business E-Mail: piephor@umkc.edu.

PIEPMEIER, JOSEPH MASSA, neurosurgeon, educator; MD, U. Tenn., 1975. Diplomate Am. Bd. Neurol. Surgery. Resident Yale-New Haven Hosp., fellow, 1977—82, with; dir. surg. neuro-oncology Yale Sch. of Medicine, sect. chief neuro-oncology, vice chmn. clin. affairs neurosurgery, prof. neurosurgery, mem. Yale med. group. Office: Yale-New Haven Hospital 800 Howard Ave 3rd Fl New Haven CT 06519 Office Phone: 203-785-2791. Office Fax: 203-785-6916.

PIERCE, CHESTER MIDDLEBROOK, retired psychiatrist, educator; b. Glen Cove, NY, Mar. 4, 1927; s. Samuel Riley and Hettie Elenor (Armstrong) P.; m. Jocelyn Patricia Blanchet, June 15, 1949; children: Diane Blanchet, Deirdre Anona. AB, Harvard U., 1948, MD, 1952; ScD (hon.), Westfield Coll., 1977, Tufts U., 1984; D in Engring. Tech. (hon.), Wentworth Inst. Tech., 1997. Instr. psychiatry U. Cin., 1957-60; asst. prof. psychiatry U. Okla., 1960-62, prof., 1965-69; prof. edn. and psychiatry Harvard U., 1969—; pres. Am. Bd. Psychiatry and Neurology, 1977-78; ret., 1997. Mem. Polar Rsch. Bd.; cons. USAF. Author publs. on sleep disturbances, media, polar medicine, sports medicine, racism; mem. editl. bds. Advisor Children's TV Workshop; chmn. Child Devel. Assn. Consortium; bd. dirs. Action Children's TV. With M.C. USNR, 1953-55. Fellow: Brit. Royal Coll. Psychiatrists (hon.), Royal Australian and New Zealand Coll. Psychiatrists (hon.); mem.: Am. Acad. Arts and Scis., Am. Orthopsychiat. Assn. (pres. 1983—84), Black Psychiatrists Am. (chmn.), Inst. Medicine of NAS. Democrat. Home: 17 Prince St Jamaica Plain MA 02130-2725

PIERCE, DONALD SHELTON, retired orthopedic surgeon, educator; b. Castine, Maine, May 21, 1930; s. Frederick Ernest and Jeannie (Emmet) P.; m. Janet Ten Broeck, Dec. 29, 1956; children: Donald Shelton, Stanton ten Broeck, Frederick Ernest, Jennifer Emmet. AB cum laude, Harvard U., 1953, MD, 1957. Diplomate Am. Bd. Spine Surgery, Am. Bd. Orthop. Surgery; lic. lay eucharistic minister Episcopal Ch., 2004. Intern U. Hosp., Cleve., 1957-58, resident, 1958-62; rsch. assoc. biomechanics lab. U. Calif., San Francisco, 1962-64; practice medicine specializing in orthopedic surgery San Francisco, 1962-64; instr. orthopedic surgery U. Calif. Med. Sch., San Francisco, 1962-64, Harvard Med. Sch., 1964-66; clin. and rsch. assoc. J.P. Kennedy Jr. Meml. Hosp., Brighton, Mass., 1964-66; clin. assoc. in orthopedics Harvard Med. Sch., 1966-67, clin. asst. prof. orthopaedic surgery, 1979-87, clin. assoc. prof., 1987-2000; ret., 2000; sr. orthopedic surgeon Mass. Gen. Hosp., Boston. Chief dept. rehab. medicine Mass. Gen. Hosp., Boston, 1965-72, assoc. orthopedic surgeon, 1969—, vis. orthopedic surgeon, 1969—; lectr. dept. mech. engring. MIT, 1970-72. Co-author: Amputees and Their Porstheses, 1971; author: The Total Care of Spinal Cord Injuries, 1977; contbr. articles in field to profl. jours. Pres. Wellesley (Mass.) Friendly Aid Assn., 1965-67, dir., 1967-70; dir. Family Svc. Counseling Region West, Wellesley, 1965-67; mem. exec. com., task force chmn. Mass. Rehab. Planning Commn., 1966-68; pres. Maine Ret. Skippers Race, 2003-05; co-chmn. capital campaign com. Trinity Espic. Ch., Maine. With USAF, 1951-52. Fellow ACS, Am. Acad. Orthopedic Surgeons, Royal Soc. Health, Pan Am. Med. Assn., Soc. Internat. Chirurgerie, Ortopaedie et Traumatologie; mem. NAS (mem. skeletal com. 1965-68, mem. subcom. basic projects, mem. com. prosthetics R & D 1966-68), NRC (musculoskeletal com., mem. subcom. basic projects, mem. com. prosthetics R & D), Othopedic Rsch. Soc., Am. Orthopaedic Assn., Cervical Spine Rsch. Soc. (pres. 1986), Fedn. Spine Assns. (pres. 1987), N.E. Med. Assn. (pres.), Ezekiel Hersey Coun., Harvard Med. Sch. (mem. Dean's Coun.). Personal E-mail: treetops-1@comcast.net.

PIERCE, JAMES CLARENCE, surgeon, educator; b. Huron, SD, Aug. 5, 1929; s. Henry Montraville and Carrie Bernice (Matson) P.; m. Carol Sue Wilson, 1967; children: Henry MacDonald, Richard Matson, Elizabeth Gail. BA, Carleton Coll., 1951; MD, Harvard U., 1955; MS, U. Minn., 1963, PhD in Surgery, 1966. Diplomate Am. Bd. Surgery. Surg. intern Peter Bent Brigham Hosp., Boston, 1955-56; surg. fellow U. Minn., 1959-66; instr. surgery Med. Coll. Va., Richmond, 1966, prof. surgery and microbiology, 1972-75; dir. Tissue Typing Lab., 1969-75; attending surgeon, dir. surg. research, dir. transplantation service St. Luke's Hosp. Center, NYC, 1975-78; prof. surgery Columbia U., 1976, Ailsa Mellon Bruce prof. surgery, 1977-78; clin. prof. surgery Pa. State U. and, 1979-88; chmn. dept. surgery Geisinger Med. Center, Danville, Pa., 1979-90, chmn. emeritus, 1990—93. Clin. prof. surgery Jefferson U., 1990—. Contbr. articles to profl. jours. Elder Presbyn. Ch. With M.C., USAF, 1957-59. NIH fellow, 1963-65; Royal Soc. Medicine Found. travelling fellow, 1971; James IV Assn. Surg. traveller, 1978 Mem. ACS (pres. Ctrl. Pa. chpt. 1981-82), Transplant Soc., Am. Soc. Transplant Surgeons, Ea. Surg. Soc., JCP Soc., Soc. Univ. Surgeons, Sigma Xi. Republican. Home: 114 Maple St Danville PA 17821-8415

PIERCE, JOHN RANDALL, medical inspector, pediatrician; b. Nashville, May 9, 1947; MD, U. Tenn., 1971. Cert. Pediatrics, 1977, Neonatal-Perinatal Medicine, 1981. Chief Dept. Pediatrics, residency program dir. U.S. Army Med. Corps.; dep. comdr. clin. svcs., dir. med. edn. Walter Reed Army Med. Ctr.; cons. pediatrics US Surgeon Gen.; dep. med. inspector Veterans Health Adminstrn., US Dept. Veterans Affairs, Washington, 2002—04, med. inspector, 2004—. Asst. prof. pediatrics Uniformed Svcs. U. of Health Scis.; historian Walter Reed Soc. Co-author: Yellow Jack: How Yellow Fever Ravaged America and Walter Reed Discovered Its Deadly Secrets, 2005; contbr. articles to profl. jours. Col. med. corps US Army. Decorated Legion of Merit, Meritorious Svc. Medal, Joint Svc. Commendation Medal, Army Commendation Medal, Army Achievement Medal, Order of Mil. Med. Merit Surgeon Gen. Fellow: Am. Acad. Pediatrics. Office: US Dept Veterans Affairs Vets Health Adminstrn 810 Vermont Ave NW Washington DC 20420 Office Phone: 202-461-4094. E-mail: john.pierce@va.gov. *

PIERCE, MICHAEL NORMAN, internist; b. NYC, May 1, 1955; s. Samuel and Ingeborg Pierce. BA in Biology, SUNY, Binghamton, 1977; MD, U. Vt., 1982. Diplomate Am. Bd. Internal Medicine, 2007, cert. internal medicine specialist, HIV specialist AAHIVS. Intern, gen. surg. resident L.A. County/U. So. Calif. Med. Ctr., LA, 1982—84; intern, resident in internal medicine Calif.-Pacific Med. Ctr., San Francisco, 1985—88; attending physician St. Francis Meml. Hosp., San Francisco, 1989—96, Montefiore Med. Ctr., East Elmhurst, NY, 1997—98, St. Barnabas Hosp./CHS/HHC, East Elmhurst, 1998—2001; asst. attending physician St. Luke's Roosevelt Hosp. Ctr., NYC, 2002—05, assoc. attending physician, 2005; dir. HIV medicine All Med Med. and Rehab. NY, 2006—, dir. internal medicine attending, 2006—. Chair Spring conf. St. Luke's Roosevelt Hosp. Ctr., 2003; judge, mem. abstract rev. bd. for resident's poster competition NY Downstate ACP-ASIM sci. meetings, 1997—; mem. CME med. bd. com. St. Luke's Roosevelt Hosp. Ctr., NYC, 2002—05, key faculty, internal medicine residency program; asst. clin. prof. medicine Columbia U. Coll. Physicians and Surgeons, NYC, 2002—05; active HIV mgmt. preceptorship program Johns Hopkins U. Sch. Medicine, Balt., 2001; mem. Infectious Disease Soc. Am., Infectious Disease Soc. Am. HIV Med. Assn.; HIV med. specialist State of NY; prin. investigator Pfizer clin. trial of Maravaroc; dir., internal medicine, HIV medicine; founder Suboxone Program, All Med. & Rehabilitation NY, Bronx, 2008—. Co-author: International HIV Controllers Study-Ragon Institute of MGH, MIT & Harvard, 2010; mem. editl. bd. Johns Hopkins U. Sch. Medicine Advanced Studies in Medicine, 2002—05; contbr. articles to profl. publs. Recipient Physician's Recognition award, AMA, 1991—;

Pharm. Mfrs. Assn. grantee, 1979. Fellow: ACP (com. on med. students 2001—05), Soc. Gen. Internal Medicine; mem.: AMA, Soc. Gen. Internal Medicine, ACPE, Am. Coll. Occupl. and Environ. Medicine, N.Y. County Med. Soc., Med. Soc. State N.Y. (surveyor-reviewer hosp. CME programs 1998—, mem. com. on edn.). Office Phone: 718-292-0100. Business E-Mail: mpierce@mail.allmed.net.

PIERCE, NATHANIEL FIELD, medical researcher, educator; b. Rudyard, Mich., July 27, 1934; s. Warren David and Mabel Field Pierce; m. Diane June Baxter; children: Shanti, Christopher, Matthew. MD, U. Mich., 1958. Staff physician Pu-Li Christian Hosp., Taiwan, 1960—61; resident coord. Johns Hopkins Internat. Ctr. for Med. Rsch. and Tng., Calcutta, India, 1966—68; asst. prof. medicine Johns Hopkins U. Sch. Medicine, Balt., 1968—72, assoc. prof. medicine, 1972—79, prof. medicine, 1979—2005; prof. internat. health Johns Hopkins U. Bloomberg Sch. Pub. Health, 1995—2005, prof. emeritus Bloomberg Sch. Pub. Health, 2005—. Dir. divsn. infectious diseases Balt. City Hosp., 1970—85, chmn. exec. comm. human rsch., 2003—05; short term cons. multiple assignments WHO, Geneva, 1971—82, chair sci. working group on bacterial enteric infections, 1983—85, rsch. coord. program for control of diarrhoeal diseases, 1985—90, sr. tech. advisor divsn. diarrhoeal and acute respiratory disease control, 1990—96; mem. cholera adv. com. Nat. Inst. Allergy and Infectious Diseases, NIH, Bethesda, Md., 1971—73, mem. U.S. cholera panel U.S.-Japan Med. Sci. Program, 1972—76, chmn. U.S. cholera panel, US-Japan Med. Sci. Program, 1977—84; rsch. assoc. Sir William Dunn Sch. Pathology, Oxford (Eng.) U., 1973—74; mem. adv. com. on health, biomed. R&D commn. on internat. rels. NAS, Washington, 1981—83; chair steering com. for the trial of pneumococcal conjugate vaccine in The Gambia Med. Rsch. Coun. Labs., Fajara, 1998—2005; chair internat. adv. com. for trial of pneumococcal conjugate vaccine in South Africa, South African Inst. Med. Rsch., Johannesburg, 1998—2001; mem., bd. dir. Child Health Found., 2007—. Contbr. chapters to books, articles to profl. jours. Recipient Pollin prize, Pediat. Rsch., 2002, Disting. Svc. award, U. Mich. Med. Coll. Alumni Soc., 2010. Mem.: Am. Soc. for Clin. Investigation, Infectious Diseases Soc. Am. (life). Episcopalian. Avocations: cabinet making, gardening. Personal E-mail: natepierce@earthlink.net.

PIERCE, WILLIAM SCHULER, cardiac surgeon; b. Wilkes-Barre, Pa., Jan. 12, 1937; s. William Harold and Doris Louis (Schuler) P.; m. Peggy Jayne Stone, June 12, 1965; children: William Stone, Jonathan Drew. BS, Lehigh U., 1958; MD, U. Pa., 1962. Intern U. Pa., 1962—63; resident in surgery Hosp. U. Pa., 1963—70; asst. prof. M.S. Hershey Med. Ctr., Pa. State U. Coll. Medicine, Hershey, 1970—73, assoc. prof., 1973—77, prof. surgery, 1977—, chief divsn. cardiothoracic surgery, 1991—95; assoc. chmn. dept. surgery, dir. rsch., dept. surgery, 1995—97. Contbr. over 300 articles to profl. jours. With USPHS, 1965—67. Fellow: ACS; mem.: AAAS, AMA, Soc. Clin. Surgery., Am. Surg. Assn., Soc. Univ. Surgeons, So. Pa. Assn. Thoracic Surgery, Inst. Medicine, Assn. Acad. Surgery, Am. Heart Assn., Soc. Vascular Surgery, Am. Soc. Artificial Internal Organs, Internat. Cardiovascular Soc. Achievements include invention of inventor cardiac valve, blood pump. Office: Milton S Hershey Med Ctr PO Box 850 Hershey PA 17033-0850 Office Phone: 717-531-8328. Business E-Mail: wpierce@hmc.psu.edu.

PIERI, ROBERTO, general practice physician; b. Cesena, Italy, Nov. 16, 1954; s. Romano and Eda (Rondoni) P. Degree in Medicine, U. Bologna, Italy, 1978, specialization in nephrology, 1981. First aid physician Nat. Health Svc., Cesenatico, Italy, 1979-85, community pediatrician, 1982-99, prof. Nursing Sch. Cesena, 1979-96; pvt. practice Cesena, 1981—; med. educator Third Age Univ., 1992—2006. Head pediatric accident rsch., Cesena, 1983-99. Author: La Stampa Cesenate nel Periodo Giolittiano, 1982; editor, co-author: Children and Environmental Risks, 1991, Guidelines of Hyperlipemia, 1999. Mem. Nat. Geographic, AAAS. Avocations: photography, art, travel. Office: Galleria OIR 16/E 47023 Cesena Italy Home: Via Pescheria 38 47521 Cesena FC Italy Office Phone: 0039-0547-29510, 337613196. E-mail: hrgpi@tin.it.

PIERONI, ROBERT EDWARD, internist, educator, military officer; b. Portland, Maine, June 20, 1937; s. Ansel Kirby and Agnes Mary (Dumais) P.; m. Dorothy Louise McDonnell, Oct. 3, 1970; children: Michelle Kirby, Robert Francis. BS, Boston Coll., 1959; MD, Pa. State U., 1971. Diplomate Am. Bd. Internal Medicine, Am. Bd. Family Practice, Am. Bd. Allergy and Immunology, Am. Bd. Quality Assurance, Am. Bd. Geriatric Medicine. Chemist Mass. Dept. Pub. Health, Boston, 1962-71, sr. bacteriologist, 1971-74; asst. prof. internal medicine U. Ala., Tuscaloosa, 1974-76, assoc. prof. dept. internal medicine and family practice, 1976-81, prof. internal medicine and family practice, 1981—; enlisted U.S. Army, 1961, advanced through grades to col., 1981. Prior cons. VA Hosp., Tuscaloosa, T. Hardin Med. Facility and Partlow State Hosp., Tuscaloosa, 1974—; cons. FDA, Dept. Def. Contbr. articles to profl. jours., chapters to books. Decorated Bronze Star, 1991, Commendation for Valor; recipient Golden Stethoscope award, 1982, Faculty Recognition award, 1986, Ala. Golden Eagle Humanitarian award Ala. Sr. Citizens Hall of Fame, 1988 and Physicians award, 1998, Wright A. Garner scientist award Ala. Acad. Sci., 1997, Designator A Proficiency award Army Surgeon Gen., 2001. Mem. AMA, ACP, Am. Coll. Allergy, Asthma and Immunology, Am. Geriatric Soc., Gerontol. Soc. Am., Am. Acad. Family Physicians, Physicians for Human Rights, VFW, Am. Legion. Democrat. Roman Catholic. Avocations: mountain trekking, scuba diving, studying medical and military history, reading. Home: 398 Riverdale Dr Tuscaloosa AL 35406-1814 Office: U Ala Dept Internal Medicine PO Box 870326 Tuscaloosa AL 35487-0001 Office Phone: 205-348-1287. Personal E-mail: dp398@comcast.net.

PIERSCIONEK, BARBARA KRYSTYNA, optics scientist; b. London, Oct. 20, 1960; d. Jan and Alfreda (Fatyga) F.; 1 child, Tomasz John. BS in Optometry, U. Melbourne, 1982, PhD, 1988; MBA, U. Bradford, 2000; diploma in Law, Leeds Met. U., 2001, diploma in legal practice, 2002, LLM, 2004. Rsch. officer U. Melbourne (Australia), 1988-91; lectr. La Trobe U., Melbourne, 1992—, supr., 1993—96; sr. lectr. U. Bradford (Eng.), 1997—2000, sr. rsch. fellow, 2000—04; prof. U. Ulster, Ireland, 2004—. Optometrist pvt. practice, Melbourne, 1983—; cons. optical properties of sunglasses, U. Melbourne 1984-85; cons. cleaning system contact lenses, Invetech. Pty. Ltd., Melbourne, 1989—; organizer sch. com. Australian Soc. Med. Rsch., Melbourne, 1995—; res. mem. Ombudsman's com. La Trobe U., 1994—, Rsch. & Grad. Studies com., 1996—; panel assessors Nat. Health & Med. Rsch. Coun. Australia; panel assessors Australian Rsch. Coun., referee panel Health Rsch. Coun. New Zealand; speaker in field; justice of peace, Magistrites Ct., 2004— Contbr. articles to profl. jours. Register of women Office of Status of Women, Dept. Prime Min. and Cabinet, Australia, 1995—; friend Royal Acad. Arts. Project grantee Nat. Health and Med. RSch. Coun., 1992-94; Schultz fellow Nat. Vision Rsch. Inst., Melbourne, 1991-92, R.D. Wright fellow, 1992-95, Nat. Health and Med. Rsch. Coun. fellow, 1996. Mem. Internat. Women in Optics, Australian Optometrical Assn., Australian Sci. Communicators (founding mem.), Biomed. Optics Soc. Avocations: art history, theater, opera, piano, writing. Office: Univ Ulster Dept Biomed Sci Cromore Rd Coleraine BT52 1SA Northern Ireland Home Phone: 44 1943603836; Office Phone: 44 2870323293. Business E-Mail: b.pierscionek@ulster.ac.uk.

PIERSON, RICHARD NORRIS, JR., medical educator; b. NYC, Sept. 22, 1929; s. Richard Norris and Dorothy (Stewart) Pierson; m. Alice Roberts, Aug. 26, 1974; children from previous marriage: Richard N., Olivia Tiffany, Alexandra de Forest, Cordelia S.C. stepchildren: Alice W. Dunn, Eric C.W. Dunn. BA, Princeton U., 1951; MD, Columbia U., 1955. Diplomate Am. Bd. Internal Medicine, Am. Bd. Nuclear Medicine. Resident St. Luke's Roosevelt Hosp., NYC, 1955—61, assoc. dir., 1961—65, dir. div. nuclear medicine, 1965—89, dir. body composition unit, 1965—2003, attending physician, 1975—; prof. clin. medicine Columbia U., 1980—; dir. medicine Hackensack Hosp., 1973—74; staff assoc. Brookhaven Nat. Lab., 1970—2002; rsch. scholar Lawrence Radiation Lab., Berkeley, Calif., 1970—71. Bioengring. inst. Columbia U., 1976—, chmn., 1989—94. Editor: Quantitative Radiocardiography, 1975; contbr. 153 articles to profl. jours. Warden St. Paul's Ch., 1980—82; bd. dirs. Englewood Health Dept., NJ, 1966—74, Empire Blue Cross/Blue Shield, NY, 1978—91, v.p. NY, 1990—91. NIH grantee, 1973—76, 1986—2003, John A. Hartford grantee, 1967—70. Fellow: ACP, NY Acad. Medicine; mem.: AAAS, Nat. Physicians Alliance, NY County Med. Soc. (pres. 1978—79), Soc. Nuclear Medicine (greater NY area pres. 1982—83, del. to AMA 1991—2001, trustee 1991—, Berson-Yalow award 1995), Alliance for Continuing Med. Edn. (pres. 1987—89), Am. Med. Rev. Rsch. Ctr. (AMA del. NY State 1978—90, chmn. 1984—89), Am. Bur. Med. Advancement in China (pres. 1979—87), NY County Health Svc. Rev. Orgn. (chmn. 1980—82), Am. Inst. Nutrition, Am. Physiol. Soc., Physicians for a Nat. Health Program, NY Metro Chpt. (bd. mem., spkr. 2003—), Century Assn., P&S Alumni Assn. (pres. 1989—91), Englewood Field Club. Home: 60 Lincoln St Englewood NJ 07631-3117 Office: St Lukes Roosevelt Hosp Ctr 1111 Amsterdam Ave New York NY 10025-1716 Home Phone: 201-569-3562; Office Phone: 212-523-3385. Business E-Mail: RNP1@columbia.edu.

PIESSENS, JAN HENDRIK, cardiologist, educator; b. Ruisbroek, Antwerpen, Belgium, July 25, 1941; s. Benedikt and Irene (Gottfried) P.; m. Maria Christine Lepoutre, Aug. 3, 1968; children: Mark, Peter, Kristin. MD, Cath. U., Leuven, Belgium, 1965, Cardiologist, 1970. Resident in internal medicine and cardiology Univ. Hosp., Leuven, 1965-69; invasive cardiology fellow Cleve. Clinic, 1969-70; prof. medicine Cath. U., Leuven, 1979; prof. emeritus, 2006. Fellow Am. Coll. Cardiology, Soc. of Cardiac Angiography; mem. Belgian Soc. Cardiology. Home: Galgebergstraat 45 Leuven Belgium 3000 E-mail: riale9@mac.com.

PIETROFESA, JOHN JOSEPH, psychologist, educator; b. NYC, Sept. 12, 1940; s. Louis John and Margaret P.; m. Cathy Marks, June 22, 1985; children: John, Paul, Maria, Dolores. EdB cum laude, U. Miami, 1961; MEd, 1963, Ed.D., 1967. Diplomate Am. Bd. Sexology; cert. cognitive behavior therapist, forensic counselor, sex therapist; lic. psychologist, social worker. Counselor Dade County (Fla.) pub. schs., 1965-67; prof. edn. Wayne State U., Detroit, 1967—; div. head theoret. and behavioral founds., 1977-83; dept. chair counselor edn., 1999—. Cons. Nat. Football League, 2003—; cons. to various schs., hosps. and univs. Author: The Authentic Counselor, 1971, 2nd edit., 1980, School Counselor as Professional, 1971, Counseling and Guidance in the Twentieth Century, 1971, Elementary School Guidance and Counseling, 1973, Career Development, 1975, Career Education, 1976, College Student Development, 1977, Counseling: Theory Research and Practice, 1978, Guidance: An Introduction, 1980, Counseling: An Introduction, 1984; mem. editl. bd. Counseling and Values, 1972-75. 1st lt. Mil. Police Corps, AUS, 1963-65. Mem. APA, ACA, Mich. Counseling ASsn., Assn. Counselor Edn. and Supervision, Phi Delta Kappa. Home: PO Box 99 Bloomfield Hills MI 48303-0099 Office: Wayne State U 321 Education Detroit MI 48202 Home Phone: 248-646-0821; Office Phone: 248-642-6066.

PIETRUSKI, JOHN MICHAEL, JR., pharmaceutical executive; b. Sayreville, NJ, Mar. 12, 1933; m. Roberta Jeanne Talbot, July 3, 1954; children: Glenn David, Clifford John, Susan Jane. BS with honors, Rutgers U., 1954; LLD (hon.), Concordia Coll., 1993. With Proctor and Gamble Co., 1954-63; pres. med. products div. C.R. Bard, Inc., 1963-77; with Sterling Drug, Inc., NYC, 1977-88; pres. Pharm. Group, 1977-81, corp. exec. v.p., 1981-83, pres., COO, 1983-85, chmn., CEO, 1985-88; pres. Dansara Cons., 1988—; chmn. Encysive Pharms., Inc., 1990—2008. Bd. dirs. Xylos Corp., Trial Card Inc. 1st lt. US Army, 1955—57. Mem.: Union League Club (N.Y.C.), Phi Beta Kappa. Office: One Penn Plaza Ste 3408 New York NY 10119 Home: 27 E Corsica Ct Farmingdale NJ 07727-4312 Office Phone: 212-268-5510. Personal E-mail: jmpco4@aol.com.

PIFFARETTI, GABRIELE, surgeon; b. Como, Miss., June 5, 1974; MD, U. Insubria Sch. Medicine, PhD, 2000, degree in Vascular Surgery, 2006. Staff surgeon Varese U. Hosp., 2008—. Recipient Rocco Docimo award, 2001. Mem.: Italian Soc. Vascular and Endovascular Surgery, European Soc. Cardiovasc. Surgery, European Soc. Vascular Surgery. Avocation: football. Office: Via Guicciardini 9 Varese Lombardia 21100 Italy Office Fax: 390332278581. Business E-Mail: gabriele.piffaretti@uninsubria.it.

PIGOTT, MELISSA ANN, social psychologist; b. Ft. Myers, Fla., Jan. 28, 1958; d. Park Trammell and Leola Ann (Wright) P.; m. David H. Fauss, Jan. 1, 1988. BA in Psychology, Fla. Internat. U., Miami, 1979; MS in Social Psychology, Fla. State U., 1982, PhD in Social Psychology, 1984. Rsch. asst. Fla. Internat. U., 1978-79, Fla. State U., Tallahassee, 1980-84; dir. mktg. rsch. Bapt. Med. Ctr., Jacksonville, Fla., 1984-89; rsch. assoc. Litigation Scis., Inc., Atlanta, 1989-91; sr. litigation psychologist Trial Cons., Inc., Miami, 1991-93; dir. rsch. Magnus Rsch. Cons. Inc., Ft. Lauderdale, 1993—. Adj. prof. psychology U. North Fla., Jacksonville, 1985-89, Nova Southeastern U., Ft. Lauderdale, 1995—. Author: Social Psychology: Study Guide, 1990, Social Psychology: Instructors Manual, 1990; contbr. articles to profl. jours. Mem. ACLU, Am. Psychol. Assn., Am. Psychol. Law Soc., Amnesty Internat., Civitan Internat., Southeastern Psychol. Assn., Soc. for Psychol. Study of Social Issues, Soc. Personality and Social Psychology, Greenpeace, Psi Chi. Democrat. Avocations: concerts, playing piano, going to the beach, bass guitar. Office: Magnus Rsch Cons Inc 1305 NE 23rd Ave Ste 1 Pompano Beach FL 33062-3748

PIHLAJA, T. KALEVI, retired chemistry professor; b. Aura, Finland, Feb. 13, 1940; MSc, U. Turku, 1964, PhD, 1967; PhD in Pharm. Chemistry (hon.), Szeged, Hungary, 1989; PhD in Philosophy (hon.), Abo Acad., Turku, Finland. Tchg. asst. U. Turku, 1964—69, assoc. prof. organic chemistry, 1971—77, prof. phys. chemistry specialized structural and phys. organic chemistry, 1978—95, prof. phys. chemistry specialized natural products and environ. chemistry, 1995—2008, emeritus prof., 2008—; hon. prof. St. Petersburg, Russia. Jr. rsch. fellow Acad. Finland, 1969—70, sr. rsch. fellow, 1970—71, rschr., 1973, 77, 1987—91, 1998—99. Fellow: Royal Soc. Chemistry; mem.: Finnish Acad. Scis., Finnish Peatland Soc., Turku Sirkkala Rotary Club, Assn. Finnish Peat Industries (hon.), Finnish Chem. Soc., Am. Chem. Soc. Avocations: travel, fishing, winemaking. Home: Untolantie 2b as 5 Littoinen 20660 Finland Office Phone: 358505532470. Personal E-mail: kpihlaja@utu.fi.

PIKDOKEN, LEVENT, periodontist, educator; b. Adana, Oct. 21, 1964; DDS, Istanbul U., Turkey, 1988; PhD, Gulhane Mil. Med. Acad., Ctr. Dental Scis., 1997. Postdoc. fellow Gulhane Mil. Med. Acad., Haydarpasa Tng. Hosp., Dept. Dentistry, Sect. Periodontology, asst. prof., 2001—11, assoc. prof., 2011—. Vis. assoc. scientist Columbia U., Coll. Dental Medicine, Dept. Periodontology, NY, 2004—05. Office: Tibbiye Cad Istanbul Uskudar 34668 Turkey E-mail: ml_pikdoken@yahoo.com.

PIKOVSKAYA, IRINA, pharmacist, consultant; d. Rafail and Sima Plotkin; 1 child, Olga. PharmD, LI U., Bklyn., 2001. Lic. pharmacist NY. Cons. Irina & Olga Rsch., NYC, 2000—02; sr. mgr., licensing & devel. Pfizer, Inc, NYC, 2002—. Treas. LI U., Bklyn., 2002—04. Fellow, Pfizer, Inc., 2000; scholar, Jewish Found. for Edn. Women, 1998—2001; Dean's scholar, LI U., 1996—2001. Mem.: Am. Assn. of Health-System Pharmacists (licentiate), Am. Pharmacist's Assn. (licentiate), Am. Soc. of Cons. Pharmacists (corr.), Jewish Found. for Edn. Women (assoc.). Avocations: jogging, skiing, music, drawing, accordion. Office: Pfizer Inc 235 E 42nd St New York NY 10017 Business E-Mail: irina.pikovskaya@pfizer.com.

PILCHER, ELIZABETH STEFFENS, dentist; b. Ft. Wayne, Ind., Aug. 21, 1956; BS, Coll. Charleston, 1977; DMD, MUSC Coll. Dental Medicine, 1981. Prof., dentistry Med. U. SC, 1989—2010, asst. dean, instl. effectiveness, 2010—. Bd. dirs. Charleston County Disabilities Bd., 1997—. Office: 173 Ashley Ave Charleston SC 29425 Office Fax: 843-792-1593. Business E-Mail: pilchees@musc.edu.

PILCZ, MALETA, psychotherapist, consultant; b. Poland, June 5, 1945; arrived in US, 1949; s. Victor and Hana P. BA in Psychology, Bklyn. Coll., 1967; MA in Social Work, U. Chgo., 1969. Diplomate Am. Bd. Examiners Clin. Social Work, diplomate in clin. social work; cert, lic. social worker, N.Y. Psychotherapist Scholarship and Guidance Assn., Chgo., 1969-71; family therapist, supr. Northwestern Meml. Hosp., Chgo., 1972-75; pvt. practice, psychotherapist, cons. Chgo., 1974-80, NYC, 1980—; cons. to med. group practices, small law firms and family bus.'s, 1990—. Field work instr. U. Chgo. Sch. of Social Svcs., 1974-75; instr. dept. psychiatry Northwestern U. Med. Sch., 1973-75; cons. faculty Ctr. for Family Studies, Family Inst. Chgo., 1978-80; assoc. staff Ackerman Inst. Family Therapy, N.Y.C., 1983-88; part-time instr. Hunter Coll. Sch. of Social Work, N.Y.C., 1985-88; cons. N.Y.C. Bd. Edn., 1988-2004. Author: Understanding the Survivor Family; thematic cons. documentary film The Legacy, 1979 (Cigne Gold Eagle, Red Ribbon Am. Film Festival, 1980). Fellow Am. Orthopsychiat. Assn.; mem. NASW (diplomate clin. social work), Am. Group Psychotherapy Assn., Acad. Cert. Social Workers. Avocations: world travel, hiking, theater, the arts. Office: 330 E 46th St Apt 12D New York NY 10017-3076

PILGERAM, LAURENCE OSCAR, biochemist; b. Great Falls, Mont., June 23, 1924; s. John Rudolph and Bertha Roslyn (Phillips) P.; m. Cynthia Ann Moore, Apr. 16, 1971; children: Karl Erich, Kurt John. AA, U. Calif., Berkeley, 1948, BA, 1949, PhD, 1953. Instr. dept. physiology U. Ill. Profl. Coll., Chgo., 1954-55; asst. prof. dept. biochemistry Stanford (Calif.) U. Sch. Medicine, 1955-57; dir. arteriosclerosis rsch. lab. U. Minn. Sch. Medicine, Mpls., 1957-65, Santa Barbara, Calif., 1965-71; dir. coagulation lab., assoc. dir. Cerebrovascular Rsch. Ctr., Baylor Coll. Medicine, Tex. Med. Ctr., Houston, 1971-75; dir. Thrombosis Control Labs., Palo Alto, Calif., 1975-79, Santa Barbara, 1979—; prof. dept. molecular biology U. Calif., Santa Barbara, 2004—. Cons. NIH, Bio-Sci. Labs., FDA; del. Coun. on Thrombosis and Coun. on Strokes, Am. Heart Assn. Assembly. Co-editor: Nutrition and Thrombosis for the Nat. Dairy Coun., 1973; contbr. sci. articles to profl. jours. Recipient CIBA award, London, 1958, Karl Thomae award, Germany, 1973; NIH grantee, 1954-75; Life Ins. Med. Rsch. Fund fellow, 1952-54. Mem. Am. Soc. for Biochemistry and Molecular Biology. Office: PO Box 1583 Goleta PO Santa Barbara CA 93116 Office Phone: 805-967-5994.

PILLAI, ANAND KRISHNA, orthopedist; b. Trivandrum, Kerala, India, May 29, 1972; s. Krishna Pillai and Lakshmy Vishwanath. MS in Orthop., Kasturba Med. Coll., Mangalore, 1999; MBBS, Govt. Med. Coll., Trivandrum, 1996. Specialist registrar NHS Glasgow & Clyde, Scotland, 2004—; cons. orthops. & trauma surgery Nine Wells Hosp., Dundee, Scotland; lead foot & ankle svc. clin. lectr. U. Adelaide. Mem. Lereno Font Svc. Fellow: RCS (orthop. mem.).

PILLER, LAURENCE WILLIAM, clinical technologist, consultant; b. Plymouth, Devon, Eng., Mar. 9, 1927; s. James William and Helen (Martin) P.; m. Jane Rosemary Cousins, Feb. 8, 1959; children: Richard Gordon, Linda Jane (dec. 1990). Diploma in Clin. Tech.-Cardiology, Assoc. Soc. Cardiol. Techs., 1953. Registered clin. technologist, S.A. Med. & Dental Coun. Technician Nat. Heart Hosp., London, 1950-54; tech. advisor New Electronic Products, London, 1954-56; technologist Groote Schuur Hosp., Cape Town, S. Africa, 1956—, ret., part-time, 1992—. Lectr. U. Cape Town, South Africa, 1965-83; mem. study group of circulation of giraffe, South Africa, 1956; presenter in field. Author: (book) Manual of Cardio-Pulmonary Technology, 1964, Essential Cardiac Technology, 1996; contbr. over 20 articles to profl. jours. Com. mem. St. Lukes Hospice, Cape Town, 1995—. 2d lt. Brit. Army Royal Signals, 1946-49, U.K. and Germany.

Named Most Disting. technologist U. Cape Town, 1992. Fellow South African Cardiac Soc. Soc. Cardiological Technicians U.K. (fellowship 1958); mem. South African Soc. Clin. Technologists (fellowship 1987), South African Med. & Dental Coun. (profl. bd. 1982), Am. Soc. Cardiovascular Profls., B. Tech, 1997, Durban Technikon, (hon.). Democrat. Methodist. Avocations: electronics, hospice bereavement counsellor, fund raiser, history wwii.

PILLER, SABINE CHRISTINE, virologist, medical research scientist; b. Vienna, Jan. 8, 1970; d. Kurt Johannes and Ingrid Ludmilla Piller; m. Michael John Smith, Sept. 15, 1994; children: Christopher Michael, Karissa Marie. BS, U. Vienna, 1991; MS, U. Ala., Birmingham, 1993; PhD, Australian Nat. U., Canberra, 1998. Rsch. assoc. U. of Vienna, Vienna, 1993—94; postdoctoral fellow U. Ala., Birmingham, 1998—2000; sr. rsch. officer/ group head Ctr. for Immunology, Sydney, NSW, Australia, 2000—03; vis. fellow Australian Nat. U., Canberra, Australia, 2000—02; adj. sr. lectr. U. of NSW, Sydney, NSW, Australia, 2002—; sr. rsch. officer/ group head Westmead Millennium Inst., Westmead, NSW, Australia, 2003—. Contbr. articles to profl. jours. Participated in video histories of Australian scientists Australian Acad. Scis., Canberra, 2001—01. Recipient Travel Award, Australian Acad. Scis., 2001, Conf. scholarship to attend first IAS Conf. in Buenos Aires, Argentina, Internat. AIDS Soc., 2001, Young Investigator Career award, Centre for Immunology, 2000—03; Project grantee, Nat. Health and Med. Rsch. Coun., 2003—. E-mail: sabine_piller@wmi.usyd.edu.au.

PILLIOD, JAMES P., state legislator; b. NYC, Aug. 9, 1930; s. James J. and Mary Alice (Phillips) Pillod; m. Judith Bean; children: Charly, David, Jay, Linda, Mary, Sharon, Susan. BA, Yale U., 1952; MD, Duke U., 1960. Diplomate American Bd. Pediatrics. Staff physician Midland Mich. Gen. Hosp. and U. Hosp., 1960—64, Lake Regional Gen. Hosp., 1964; physician pvt. practice, 1964—96; mem. Belknap, Dist. 05 NH House of Reps., Concord, 1996—. Lt. (j.g.) USN. Diplomate Acad. of Pediatrics; mem. AMA (past del.), NH Med. Soc. (past pres.), NH Hosp. Assn. (Physician Staff Mem. of Yr. 1988), NH Pediat. Soc. (Pub. Servant of Yr. 1997). Republican. Home: 504 Province Rd Belmont NH 03220-3723 Office: State House 107 N Main St Concord NH 03301 Office Phone: 603-271-2548. Home Fax: 603-528-1935. E-mail: jimp3047@metrocast.net.

PILLSBURY, HAROLD CROCKETT, III, otolaryngologist; b. Balt., Dec. 5, 1947; m. Carol Higgins Pillsbury; children: Matthew, Benjamin, Thomas. BA, George Washington U., Washington, 1970, MD, 1972. Diplomate Nat. Bd. Med. Examiners, Am. Bd. Otolaryngology; lic. Conn., N.C. Resident gen. surgery U. N.C., Chapel Hill, 1972-73, resident otolaryngology, 1973-76; fellow Kantonsspital, Zurich, Switzerland, 1977; asst. prof. otolaryngology Yale U., New Haven, Conn., 1977-81, assoc. prof. otolayngology, 1981-82; assoc. prof. surgery, otolayngology, head and neck surgery U. N.C. Sch. Medicine, Chapel Hill, 1982-86, prof. surgery, otolaryngology, head and neck surgery, 1986—, Thomas J. Dark Disting. Prof., 1991—. Civilian cons. USAF Surgeon Gen. for Otolaryngology-Head and Neck Surgery, 1993; hon. guest lectr. Alpha Omega Alpha Induction Ceremonies, U. N.C., Chapel Hill, 1990, 91, Sch. of Medicine Commencement Ceremony, U. N.C., 1990., Whitehead lectr. Whitehead Med. Soc., U. N.C., 1994. Countbr. numerous articles to profl. jours. Recipient John A Kirchner Tchg. award, 1980, Disting. Alumni Achievement award George Washington U., 2006. Mem. Am. Acad. Otolarygology-Head and Neck Surgery (past pres. 1998-99, Honor award 1985, Disting. Svc. award 1994, Harris Mosher award 1986), Am. Bd. Otolaryngology (pres. 2004-06), Am. Laryngol., Rhinol. and Otol. Soc. (pres. 2007), Am. Laryngol. Assn. (past pres. 2000-01), Soc. Univ. Otolaryngologists (past pres. 1997-98), Alpha Omega Alpha, Triological Soc. (pres. 2008). Office: Univ NC Dept Otolaryngology Head & Neck Surgery G125 Physicians Office Bldg 170 Manning Dr Chapel Hill NC 27599-7070 Office Phone: 919-966-3342.

PILOUS, BETTY SCHEIBEL, medical/surgical nurse; b. Cleve., July 30, 1948; d. Raymond W. and Dorothy E. (Groth) S.; m. Lee Alan Pilous, Sept. 11, 1970; 1 child. Diploma in nursing, Huron Rd. Hosp., Cleve., 1970; BSBA, St. Joseph's Coll., 1989, MHSA, 1996. RN, Ohio; CPHQ. Nurse Huron Rd. Hosp., Cleve., 1970-71, Hillcrest Hosp., Cleve., 1974-77; head nurse, relief supr. Oak Park Hosp., Oakwood, Ohio, 1977-81; head nurse med.-surg. Bedford Hosp., Ohio, 1981-87; dir. inpatient svcs. Meridia Euclid Hosp., Euclid, Ohio, 1987-93. Coord. hosp. info. system for nursing, chair nurse practice com., los com. nursing liaison; DON, Manor Care, Willoughby, Ohio; team leader referral/assessment Hospice Western Res.; dir. clin. svcs. Total Health, 1998, dir. HCQIP, Ohio, 1999, dir. Post Acute Svcs., 2001-; dir. cmty.based svcs. Ohio KePRO, 2005-08, dir. quality Kindred Hosp., Cleve, 2008-10, Wellcare Ohio, 2011-. Former instr. ARC; chair nurse practice com. Am. Heart Assn.; mem. nursing standards com. Cmty. Hosp. of Bedford; mem. health and safety com. Twinsburg Schs., Ohio, 1984, mem. curriculum com., 1981-83; chairperson standards com. Cmty. Hosp. of Bedford; former counselor jr. high youth 1st Congl. Ch., Twinsburg; past chair adv. bd. chairperson Brecksville Rainbown Assembly for Girls, 1992; mem. Twinsburg Libr. Levy Com., 1991; mem. Gov.'s Task Force on Compassionate Care, 2003-04. Recipient Paradiam award, 1991. Mem. Ohio Citizen League Nursing Nurse Execs. Network (former sec.), Ohio Hosp. Assn., Ohio Orgn. Nurse Execs., Ohio Directors of Nursing Assocs. Long Term Care, Nat. League Nursing, Southeast Cleve. Mid Mgrs. Ohio Orgn. Nurse Exec., Acad. Med.-Surg. Nursing (charter mem.), Networking Group Nurse Mgrs. (initiated), Order Eastern Star, Sigma Theta Tau, Iota Psi. Avocations: hiking, helping children. Office Phone: 216-447-9604. Personal E-mail: bpilous@aol.com.

PIMENTEL-FILHO, FERNANDO RODRIGUES, academic administrator, endocrinologist; b. Goiânia, Goiás, Brazil, May 20, 1965; s. Fernando Rodrigues and Maria Dinair de Almeida Pimentel; m. Elizete Guimarães Rocha Rocha; children: Aline Rocha Pimentel, Denise Rocha Pimentel. MD with honors, U. Fed. Goiás, 1989; MS, U. de São Paulo, 1996, PhD, 1999. Resident Hosp. Heliópolis, São Paulo, 1991; resident in endocrinology and metabolism Hosp. Brigadeiro, São Paulo, 1992—94; asst. dr. Brigadeiro Hosp., São Paulo, 1993—98, Clin. Hosp., U. São Paulo, 1996—98; supr. dr. hormone sect. Brigadeiro Hosp. Lab., 1997—98; chief clin. dept. Unoeste Med. Sch., São Paulo, 1999—2000, dir. med. sch., 2002—. Prof. endocrinology and metabolism Unoeste Med. Sch., São Paulo, 1998—. Contbr. articles to profl. jours. Mem.: Endocrine Soc., Soc. Brasileira Endocrinologia Metabologia (assoc.). Home: Av Irineu Sesti 149 Resid Damha I São Paulo Presidente Prudente 19053-360 Brazil Office: Hosp U Av José Bongiovani 1297 Jd Bongiov São Paulo Presidente Prudente 19050-680 Brazil Office Fax: 55-18-229-1571; Home Fax: 55-18-223-2244. Personal E-mail: pimentel@stetnet.com.br.

PIMPARKAR, BHALCHANDRA DATTATRAYA, gastroenterologist, educator; b. Vairag, India, June 30, 1923; s. Dattatraya Narhar and Laxmi (Diwakar) P.; m. Deshmukh Kusum Vinayak, June 15, 1947; children: Vivek, Sandhya, Aruna, Neeta. MB, BChir, Seth G.S. Med. Coll., Bombay, 1950; DSc, U. Pa., 1960. House physician TN Med. Coll., Bombay, India, 1950; resident Freedmen's Hosp., Howard U., Washington, 1954-57; instr. U. Pa., Phila., 1957-60; hon. asst. prof. Seth G.S. Med. Coll., Bombay, 1963-70, prof. medicine, 1970-81, prof. emeritus, 1981—. Hon. physician Bombay Hosp., 1965-81, hon. dir., 1978-81; hon. physician Nanawati (India) Hosp., 1961—; hon. physician to gov. Govt. of Maharashtra, Bombay, 1977—. Contbg. author Gastroenterology, 1964, 3d edit., 1984. World Congress of Gastroenterology fellow, Copenhagen, 1972. Fellow Nat. Acad. Med. Sci. (India), Indian Coll. Physicians, Am. Coll. Gastroenterology; mem. Indian Soc. Gastroenterology (pres. 1981). Avocations: farming, gardening, reading. Office: Laud Mansion M Karve Rd Mumbai 400004 India Home: Cumballa Crest Peddar Rd 400 026 Mumbai India Home Phone: 91 22 23513252; Office Phone: 91 22 23853387. Personal E-mail: vivekpimparkar@hotmail.com.

PIÑA, ILEANA L., cardiologist, medical educator; arrived in US, 1954; d. Luis and Josefina Garcia; 1 child, Victoria. AA, Miami Dade Cmty. Coll., 1969; BS in Chemistry, magna cum laude, U. Miami, Coral Gables, 1972; MD, U. Miami Sch. Medicine, 1976. Diplomate Nat. Bd. Med. Examiners, Am. Bd. Internal Medicine, Am. Bd. Clin. Pharmacology, cert. in cardiovasc. disease, lic. Fla., Pa., Ohio. Asst. prof. divsn. cardiology U. Miami Hosp. & Clinics, 1972—76, 1982—87, intern gen. surgery, 1976—77; staff physician Clearwater Cmty. Hosp., Fla., 1977—78; resident internal medicine U. South Fla., Tampa, 1978—80, chief resident internal medicine, 1980; cardiology fellow U. Miami Sch. Medicine, 1980—82; attending physician, dir. exercise lab. Jackson Meml. Hosp., Miami, 1982—87; assoc. prof. medicine, dir. heart failure & cardiac rehab. Hahnemann U., Phila., 1987—91; assoc. prof. medicine Temple U., Phila., 1991—98, prof. medicine, 1998—99; prof. medicine, divsn. cardiology, dir. heart failure & cardiac transplantation Case Western Res. U., Cleve., 1999—. Attending physician, dir. cardiac fitness ctr. Hahnemann U. Hosp., 1987—89; mem. heart failure team, coord. cardiopulmonary exercise lab. Temple U., 1991, dir. cardiomyopathy, 93; staff physician Temple U. Hosp., 1991—94, dir. heart failure, co-dir. heart failure/transplant, 1993—94, attending physician, dir. cardiac rehab., 1994—99; attending physician, VA quality scholar Lewis Stokes Vets Affairs Med. Ctr., Cleve., 2003—; past mem. cardio-renal adv. com. FDA; past chair coun. on cardiovasc. rehab. & secondary prevention World Heart Fedn. Mem. editl. bd.: Am. Jour. Cardiology, Jour. Cardiac Rehab., Jour. Cardiac Failure; contbr. articles to profl. jours. Founder scholarship for med. students Miami Dade Cmty. Coll., 1987. Recipient Cmty. Svc. award, Cuban Lions Club, 1982, Alumna award, Miami Dade Cmty. Coll., 1984, Floridana award, Cuban Women's Club, 1984, Trail Blazer award, Women's Com. of 100, 1984; grantee, Joseph Collins Found., 1976, Kynett Meml. Found., 1988. Fellow: Am. Coll. Cardiology, Am. Heart Assn. (chair eart ailure & transplantation, Coun. Clin. Cardiology, vice chair heart failure com.); mem.: Heart Failure Soc. America (mem. exec. coun., mem. care standards com.). *

PINALS, ROBERT STANTON, physician; b. Elizabeth, NJ, Aug. 23, 1931; s. Herman and Goldie (Kotler) P.; m. Emanuella DiAssisi, June 20, 1953; children: Deborah, David, Stephen. BA, Cornell U., 1952; MD, U. Rochester, 1956. Diplomate in internal medicine and rheumatology Am. Bd. Internal Medicine. Chief rheumatology Lemuel Shattuck Hosp., Boston, 1961—63; from instr. to asst. prof. medicine Tufts U. Sch. Medicine, Boston, 1963—69; from assoc. prof. to prof. medicine SUNY, Syracuse, 1969—79; prof. medicine U. Tenn., Memphis, 1978—84, U. Med. Dentistry N.J.-Robert Wood Johnson Med. Sch., Piscataway, 1984—2008; clin. assoc. dept. medicine Mass. Gen. Hosp., Boston, 2010—. Mem., cons. arthritis adv. com. FDA, Washington, 1985-93, chmn., 1986-89; mem. rheumatology subsplty. com. Am. Bd. Internal Medicine, 1988-95; vice chmn. dept. medicine U. Med. Dentistry N.J., 1997—2008; chmn. dept. medicine Princeton Med. Ctr., 1984-97 Contbr. numerous chpts. to books, more than 130 articles to profl. jours. Bd. dirs. Ctrl. N.Y. chpt. Arthritis Found., 1969-78, pres., 1976-77. Capt. USAF, 1957-59. Rheumatology fellow, Mass. Gen. Hosp., Boston, 1961—63. Master: Am. Coll. Rheumatology; fellow: ACP. Office: MGH Rheumatology Assocs Yawkey 2100 55 Fruit St Boston MA 02114 Personal E-mail: bob@pinals.com. *

PINAULT, DIDIER, medical researcher; b. La Charite-sur-Loire, Nievre, France, Oct. 23, 1955; PhD in Neurosci., U. P & M Curie, Paris, 1990; degree, U. Strasbourg, 2001. Prof. Inserm, U. Strasbourg, 1997—, prin. investigator, 1997. Mem.: French, European & Am. Socs. Neuroscis. Achievements include research in models of CNS diseases, the underlying cell-to-network mechanisms. Office: Inserm Universite de Strasbourg Strasbourg Alsace 67085 France Business E-Mail: pinault@unistra.fr.

PINCKNEY, NEAL T., psychologist, retired educator; b. NYC, July 26, 1935; s. Leo Allen and Jean P.; children: Andrew Allen, Jennifer Elizabeth, Matthew Ian. Cert. polit. social and hist. issues, King's Coll., U. Durham, 1957; AB, U. So. Calif., 1958, postgrad., 1958—61; PhD, Oxford U., 1966; postgrad., U. Vienna, U. Hiroshima, Stanford U. Mem. Pub. Welfare Commn., LA County, 1958—60; tchr. pub. schs., LA, 1960—61; tchr., counselor Las Vegas, 1961—62; admnistr. therapist psychiat. clinic, 1962—63; educator, dir. guidance svc. Dept. Def. Overseas Dep. Schs., Eng. and Japan, 1963—67; pvt. practice clin. psychology, 1967—87; lectr. Calif. State U., Sacramento, 1967—68, asst. prof., 1968—71, assoc. prof., 1971—77, prof. psychology and edn., 1977—87, prof. emeritus, 1987—, chmn. dept. behavioral scis., 1980—82, prof. counseling psychology, coord. grad. studies, dept. adminstrn., counseling and policy studies, 1992—; founder, clin. dir. Healing Heart Found., 1993—. Vis. prof. U. Calif.-Davis, 1979—; psychologist, instr. enforcement psychology and human rels. Calif. Hwy. Patrol, 1967-80; dir. Univ. Software Evaluation Project, 1987; tech. cons., adv. Ministry Edn. and Culture, Govt. Brazil, Brasilia, 1974-76; cons. psychologist Calif. Med. Facility, Vacaville, various law enforcement agys.; prof. U. Hawaii, lectr. U. Hawaii, Leeward CC, 1992-93; mem. profl. treatment team Preventive Medicine Rsch. Inst.-Ornish Residential Retreat for Reversing Heart Disease, 1996; sponsor, builder Makaha Chartres Labyrinth; webmaster Healing Heart Website, moderator, sponsor internet discussion group; dir. Judge Rotenberg Ednl. Ctr., 2004-06. Author: Healthy Heart Handbook, 1994, Law and Ethics in Counseling and Psychotherapy, A Casebook, 1961, 86; pub. USER, a Software Report Card, 1987; editor: Incite Newsletter of Hawaii Portable Computer Users Assn., 1987-88; editor: Ency. of Psychology, 2d edit. Served with 3d Armored Divsn. U.S. Army, 1954-55. Queen's scholar Eng., 1956-57; scholar Dept. State Fgn. Svc. Inst., 1974; fellow Ford Found., 1960-61. Mem. APA, Brit. Psychol. Assn., Japanese Psychol. Assn., Brazilian Psychol. Assn., Am. Ednl. Rsch. Assn., Am. Assn. Counseling and Devel., Am. Radio Relay League (life), Hawaii Personal Computer Users Group (pres. 1989-91, sys. operator Electronic Bulletin Bd. Svc.), Quarter Century Wireless Assn. (life), Vegetarian Soc. of Hawaii (bd. dirs.), No. Calif. DX Club, Hawaii DX Assn., Phi Delta Kappa, Delta Phi Epsilon, Commonwealth Club San Francisco, Oxonian Club Tokyo, Toastmasters (area gov. 1962-63), Mason Home: Ste 1601 1650 Ala Moana Blvd Honolulu HI 96815-1411 Personal E-mail: amigenic@email.com.

PINCUS, THEODORE, microbiologist, rheumatologist, educator; AB, Columbia U., 1961; MD, Harvard U., 1966. Assoc. Sloan-Kettering Inst., NYC, 1973-75; asst. prof. medicine/immunology, dir. clin. immunology lab. Stanford (Calif.) U., 1975-76; prof. Wistar Inst., Phila., 1976-80; adj. assoc. prof. medicine-rheumatology U. Pa., Phila., 1976-80; prof. medicine and microbiology Vanderbilt U., Nashville, 1980—. Fellow ACP, Am. Rheumatism Assn., Am. Soc. Microbiology. Achievements include description of morbidity and mortility of rheumatoid arthritis; analyses of host genetic and psychosocial variables in chronic diseases; description of host genetic control of experimental retrovirus infection; description of psychological and economic consequences of chronic disease; analysis of "mind body" explanations of associations between socioeconomic status and chronic disease. Office: Vanderbilt U Divsn Rheumatology & Immunology 203 Oxford House Nashville TN 37232-0001 *

PINEDA, ALBERT ANTHONY, obstetrician, gynecologist, educator; b. NYC, Feb. 15, 1937; MD, N.Y. Med. Coll., 1963. Diplomate Am. Bd. Ob-gyn. Intern St. Vincents Hosp., NYC, 1963-64; resident in ob-gyn. Flower-Fifth Ave Hosp.-N.Y. Med. Coll., NYC, 1964-68; fellow in gynecol. oncology Met. Hosp., NYC, 1968-69; med. staff St. Joseph's Hosp. Med. Ctr., Paterson, N.J.; clin. assoc. prof. N.Y. Med. Coll., 1976, Seton Hall U. Grad. Sch. Med. Edn., 1991—2010; clin. prof. St. George's U. Sch. Medicine, 1995—2010; pvt. practice Clifton, N.J. Cons. ZEG Epidemology Ctr., Berlin. Mem. ACOG, Soc. Gynecol. Oncology, N.J. Med. Soc., Passaic County Med. Soc. *

PINEDA, CARLOS EDUARDO, surgeon; b. Guatemala City, Feb. 2, 1981; MD, U. San Carlos Guatemala, 2006. Postdoc. fellow Dept. Surgery, Stanford U. Sch. Medicine, 2006—08, surgery resident, 2008—. Cons. Engring. Mega-Project, U. del Valle, Guatemala, 2005—06. Mem.: Resident and Assoc. Soc. ACS. Avocations: piano, guitar. Home: 397 College Ave #C Palo Alto CA 94306 Personal E-mail: ccpineda@gmail.com.

PINEDA, JOSE, pediatrician, educator; b. Guatemala City, Mar. 27, 1967; MD, Francisco Marroquin U. Sch. Medicine, 1993; MS in Clin. Investigation, Wash. U., St. Louis, 2009. Asst. tchr. physiology Francisco Marroquin U., 1992; asst. prof., pediatric critical care medicine, dept. pediat. U. Fla., Gainesville, 2001—05; assoc. dir., ctr. traumatic brain injury studies McKnight Brain Inst. U. Fla., Gainesville, 2002—05; med. dir., respiratory care St. Louis Children's Hosp., 2006—08; asst. prof. pediat. and neurology, dir., pediatric neurocritical care program, divsn. critical care medicine Wash. U. Sch. Medicine, St. Louis, 2005—. Med. adv. panel, infrared imaging medicine program US Army CECOM Night Vision & Electronics Sensors Directorate, 1999—2001; adv. bd. Safe Kids Coalition, Gainesville, 2004—05; sci. adv. bd. Banyan Diagnostics, 2004—05; spkrs. bur. Integra Neuroscis., 2007; question writer Am. Bd. Pediatric Neurol. Surgery, 2009. Recipient Outstanding Divsn. Tchg. award, Dept. Pediat., Wash. U. Sch. Medicine, New Faculty Start Up award, Howard Hughes Med. Inst. Biomedical Rsch. Support Program, Fall award, Children's Miracle Network. Mem.: Nat. Neurosurgical Soc. (Chile). Office: St Louis Children's Hosp Campus Saint Louis MO 63110 Business E-Mail: hossenlopp_t@kids.wustl.edu.

PINHEIRO, LESLIE, physician; b. Kochi, India, Aug. 9, 1962; MBBS, St. John's Med. Coll. Hosp., India, 1986, MD, 1992. SHO registrar Nat. Health Svc., 1993—98; registrar Tan Tock Seng Hosp., Singapore, 2001—03, physician, 2001—, assoc. cons., 2003—05, cons., 2005—11. Recipient Courage Star award, Nat. Healthcare Group, 2003, Silver medal, EXSA, Spring Singapore, 2005, Gold medal, 2006. Mem.: RCP (UK), Assn. Physicians India (life). Avocations: reading, tennis, movies. Home: SAVIOS PO Palliport Ernakulam Dist Kochi Kerala 683515 India Personal E-mail: l.pinheiro@mailcity.com.

PINHEIRO, SIMONE NAKAO, psychiatrist; b. Dourados, Mar. 27, 1973; PhD, U. São Paulo, 2008; student in Law, UNIGRAN, 2008—. Physician U. Fed. do Triângulo Mineiro, 1997. Field rschr. Faculdade Medicina Ribeirão Preto, U. São Paulo, 2001—07; psychiatrist Pvt. Clinic, 2008—. Contbr. articles to profl. jour. Avocation: travel. Office: Rua Monte Alegre 1793 Dourados Mato Grosso do Sul 79825-070 Brazil E-mail: pinheirosnp@yahoo.com.

PINILLA, ANA RITA, neuropsychologist, researcher; b. NYC, May 20, 1957; d. Louis and Luz Maria (Diaz) P.; children: Jorge Javier, Juan Carlos, Ana Mari. BS magna cum laude, U. P.R., Rio Piedras, 1978; MS, Caribbean Ctr., San Juan, PR, 1980, PhD, 1988. Lic. psychologist, P.R. Prof. psychology Inter-Am. U., San Juan, 1980—91; neuropsychologist Neuropsychol. Svcs. to Devel. Deficiencies Children, Bayamon, PR, 1987—88; asst. dir. Gov.'s Prevention Program, San Juan, 1988—90; exec. dir. Learning Disability Ctr., San Juan, 1990—94; external evaluator prevention program Roberto Clemente Sports City, Carolina, PR, 1990—95. Cons. ednl. programs Gov.'s Office; adviser, evaluator drug prevention programs, 1994-96; clin. dir. Options, P.R., 1996-97; med. subdir. Learning Ctr.-Hosp. Interamericano de Medicine Avanzada; cons. in field; pres. Alternative Psychol. Svcs., 2000-01; assoc. prof. Pontificia Cath. U.,P.R., 2000—, dir., 2004— Author: Analysis of Wisc-R, 1988, Managing the Divorce Crisis: An Integrated Model, 1999, Cognition and Affect, 2008; contbr. articles to profl. publs. Mem. Internat. Neuropsychol. Soc.,

Nat. Acad. Neuropsychology. Achievements include development of program of services to learning disabled children using neuropsychological approach, development of tests for measurement character traits. Home Phone: 787-635-2514. Business E-Mail: apinilla@libertypr.net, apinilla@email.pucpr.edu.

PINJIA, MENG, science educator; b. Liaoning, Mar. 12, 1955; D, Shenyang Pharm. U., 2000. Prof. Chinese People's Pub. Security U., Beijing, 1999—. Office: Chinese People's Pub Security University Dept Forensic Sci Nanli 1# Muxidi Xicheng Dist Beijing 100038 China Office Fax: 86-10-83903375. Business E-Mail: mengpinjia@163.com.

PINKAS-GOROV, LENA, nuclear medicine physician; b. Sofia, Bulgaria, Sept. 14, 1950; d. Avram and Nora Pinkas; m. Todor Gorov, June 16, 1942; children: Maxim Gorov, Robert Gorov. MD, Bulgarian Med. Acad., Sofia, 1974. Bd. cert. nuc. medicine Israel, 1994, bd. cert. anesthesiology Bulgarian Med. Acad., 1979, bd. cert. nuc. medicine Bulgarian Med. Acad., 1987. Chief physician Assaf Harofeh Med. Ctr., Zerifin, Israel, 1995—2001; head Nuc. Medicine Inst. Kaplan Med. Ctr., Rehovot, Israel, 2001—. Mem.: Soc. Nuc. Medicine, Israeli Soc. Nuc. Medicine. Office: Kaplan Med Ctr 76100 Rehovot Israel Office Fax: 972-8-9441380. Personal E-mail: lena_p@clalit.org.il.

PINKEL, DONALD PAUL, pediatrician; b. Buffalo, Sept. 7, 1926; s. Lawrence William and Ann (Richardson) P.; m. Marita Donovan, Dec. 26, 1949 (div. 1981); children: Rebecca, Nancy, Christopher, Mary, Thomas, Anne, Sara, John, Ruth; m. Cathryn Barbara Howarth, May 16, 1981; 1 child, Michael. BS, Canisius Coll., 1947; MD, U. Buffalo, 1951. Diplomate Am. Bd. Pediatrics, Pediatric Hematology and Oncology, Nat. Bd. Med. Examiners. From intern to resident to chief resident Children's Hosp., Buffalo, 1951-54; research fellow Children's Hosp. Med. Ctr., Boston, 1955-56; chief. of pediatrics Roswell Park Meml. Inst., Buffalo, 1956-61; founding dir. St. Jude Children's Rsch. Hosp., Memphis, 1961-73; chmn. pediatrics Med. Coll. Wis., Milw., 1974-78; pediatrician-in-chief Milw. Children's Hosp., 1974-78; founding dir. Midwest Children's Cancer Ctr., Milw., 1974; chief. of pediatrics City of Hope Med. Ctr., Duarte, Calif., 1978-82; chmn. pediatrics Temple U. Sch. Medicine, Phila., 1982-85; prof., Kana Rsch. chair, dir. pediatric leukemia program M.D. Anderson Cancer Ctr. U. Tex., Houston, 1985-93; prof. pediat. U. Tex. Med. Sch., Houston, 1985-99; prof. emeritus U. Tex.-M.D. Anderson Cancer Ctr., Houston, 1994—. Clin. prof. pediats. U. So. Calif., LA, 2002—; adj. prof. biol. scis. Calif. Polytechnic State U., San Luis Obispo, Calif., 2001—. Contbr. articles to profl. jours. Bd. dirs. Lee County Coop. Clinic, Mariana, Ark., 1972-74. Served with USN, 1944-45, served to 1st lt. U.S. Army, 1954-55. Recipient Albert Lasker award for Med. Rsch., Lasker Found., 1972, Windermere Lectureship Brit. Pediatric Assn., 1974, David Karnofsky award Am. Soc. Clin. Oncology, 1978, Zimmerman prize for Cancer Rsch. Zimmerman Found., 1979, Charles Kettering prize Gen. Motors Cancer Rsch., 1986, Clin. Rsch. award Am. Cancer Soc., 1988, Return of the Child award Leukemia Soc. Am., 1992, Pollin prize in pediat. rsch. N.Y. Presbyn. Hosp., 2003. Mem. Am. Soc. Clin. Oncology, Am. Pediat. Soc., Am. Assn. Cancer Rsch., Soc. Exptl. Biology and Medicine, Am. Soc. Hematology. Democrat. Roman Catholic. Avocations: swimming, sailing. Home: 275 Marlene Dr San Luis Obispo CA 93405 E-mail: donpinkel@gmail.com.

PINKER, STEVEN ARTHUR, psychology professor; b. Montreal, Que., Can., Sept. 18, 1954; arrived in US, 1976; s. Harry and Roslyn (Wiesenfeld) P.; m. Rebecca Goldstein BA in Exptl. Psychology, McGill U., Montreal, 1976; PhD, Harvard U., 1979; DSc (hon.), McGill U., 1999; DPhil (hon.), Tel Aviv. U., 2003, U. Newcastle, 2005; DUniv (hon.), U. Surrey, 2003. Postdoctoral fellow Center for Cognitive Sci., MIT; asst. prof. psychology Harvard U., Cambridge, Mass., 1980-81, Stanford U., Palo Alto, Calif., 1981-82, MIT, Cambridge, 1982—85, assoc. prof. brain & cognitive sci., 1985—89, prof., 1989—, co-dir. Center for Cognitive Sci., 1985—94, dir. McDonnell-Pew Center for Cognitive Neuroscience, 1994—99, Peter de Florez prof., 2000—03; Johnstone Family prof. psychology Harvard U., 2003—. Cons. Cognitive and Instructional Sis. Group, Xerox Corp. Palo Alto Rsch. Centers, 1981—82; vis. scholar, dept. of psychology Harvard Univ., 1987—88; vis. scholar, cognitive devel. unit Med. Rsch Coun., London, 1988; vis. scholar, dept. of psychology and linguistics Univ. Calif., Santa Barbara, 1995—96; hon. vis. prof., dept. of psychology Univ. of Auckland, New Zealand, 2001—04; inst. advisor Allen Inst. for Brain Sci., Seattle; spkr. in field. Author: Language Learnability and Language Development, 1984, Learnability and Cognition, 1989, The Language Instinct, 1994, How the Mind Works, 1997 (LA Times Science Book Prize, 1998, finalist for Pullitzer prize, 1998), Words and Rules: The Ingredients of Language, 1999, The Blank Slate: The Modern Denial of Human Nature, 2002 (finalist for Pulitzer prize, 2003), The Stuff of Thought: Language As a Window Into Human Nature, 2007; assoc. editor Cognition, 1984—; advisor, Am. Heritage Dictionary; serves on several advisory and editorial bds., contbr. articles to sci. jours. and chapters in books. Recipient Troland Rsch. award NAS, 1993, Golden Plate award, Am. Acad. of Achievement, 1999, Henry Dale prize Royal Instn. Gt. Britain, 2004, Henry Dale prize Royal Instn. of Gt. Britain, 2004; named Humanist Laureate Internat. Acad. Humanism, 2001, Humanist of Yr., Am. Humanist Assn., 2006. Fellow AAAS, APA (Disting. Early Career award 1984, Boyd McCandless award 1986, William James Book prize 1995, 99, 2003, Eleanor Maccoby Book prize 2003), Am. Acad. Arts and Scis., Linguistics Soc. Am. (Linguistics, Lang. and Pub. Svcs. award 1997), Am. Psychol. Soc. Office: Dept Psychology Harvard Univ William James Hall 970 33 Kirkland St Cambridge MA 02138 Office Phone: 617-495-0831. Office Fax: 617-495-3278. Business E-Mail: pinker@wjh.harvard.edu.

PINKERTON, JOANN V., obstetrician, gynecologist, educator, academic administrator; b. Laurel, Miss., Nov. 3, 1954; B, U. Va.; MD, Med. Coll. Va., Richmond, 1981. Resident, ob-gyn. U. Va., Charlottesville, 1981—85, chief resident; med. dir. Midlife Health Ctr.; prof. ob-gyn. U. Va., Charlottesville, vice-chair, academic affairs. Bd. dirs. Nat. Women's Health Women Resource Ctr.; planning mem. Va. Govt. Women's Health Initiative annual conf.; developed and moderated U. Va. Women's Health Festival; invited internat. spkr. on women's health issues. Author: Understanding Midlife Health (ALA award). Named Best Doctors in America, 2007—08. Fellow: Am. Coll. Obstetricians and Gynecologists; mem.: Am. Med. Women's Assn., Va. Obstetrics and Gynecology Soc., N.Am. Menopause Soc. (pres. bd. trustees 2008—09, scientific chair, 2008 annual meeting, past pres. profl. edn. com.). Office: U Va Dept Obstetrics and Gynecology Md-Obgy Ob & Gyn Admin PO Box 801104 Norhtridge Ste 104 Charlottesville VA 22908 Office Phone: 434-243-4727, 434-243-4720. Office Fax: 434-243-4706. Business E-Mail: jvp9u@virginia.edu. E-mail: jvp9u@hscmail.mcc.virginia.edu, jvpinkerton@virginia.edu.

PINN, VIVIAN W., federal agency administrator, pathologist; b. Halifax, Va., 1941; BA, Wellesley Coll., Mass., 1963; MD, U. Va. Sch. Medicine, 1967. Intern pathology Mass. Gen. Hosp., Boston, 1967-68, rsch. fellow, 1968-70; asst. pathologist Tufts U. New Eng. Med. Ctr. Hosp., Boston, 1970-77, pathologist, 1977-82; asst. to assoc. prof. pathology Tufts U. Sch. Medicine, 1971-82, asst. dean student affairs, 1974-82; prof., dept. chair pathology Howard U. Coll. Medicine, Washington, 1982-91; dir. Office Rsch. on Women's Health (ORWH), NIH, Bethesda, Md., 1991—, assoc. dir. rsch. women's health, ORWH, 1994—. Pres. Nat. Med. Assn., 1989—90; co-chair NIH Working Group Women in Biomed. Careers. Recipient Disting. Alumna award, U. Va. Sch. Medicine, 1992, Walter Reed Alumni Achievement award, 2007, Walter Ridley Trailblazer award, 2007, Alumni Achievement award, Wellesley Coll., 1993, Excellence in Leadership award, Dominion Resources Svcs., Inc., 2008, James D. Bruce Meml. award, ACP, Catherine McFarland award for disting. svc. in women's health, Med. Coll. Pa., Women in Medicine Leadership Devel. award, Assn. Am. Med. Colleges, Margaret E. Mahoney award for outstanding svc. in advancing the quality of health care for women, Commonwealth Fund, Pres.'s Achievement award, Am. Med. Women's Assn., Lifetime Achievement award, Jacobs Inst.; named an Alumni Luminary, U. Va. Sch. Medicine, 1998. Fellow: Am. Acad. Arts & Scis. Office: NIH OWHR 6707 Democracy Blvd Ste 400 Bethesda MD 20892 Office Phone: 301-402-1770. Office Fax: 301-402-1798. Business E-Mail: vivian.pinn@nih.gov. *

PINNA, ANTONIO, ophthalmologist, educator; b. Sassari, Italy, July 12, 1963; s. Gianni Paolo Pinna and Cesira Casu; m. Vittoria Sanna, Apr. 24, 1999; children: Beatrice, Pietro Paolo. Degree in Medicine and Surgery, U. Sassari, 1990. Cert. in ophthalmology U. Sassari, 1994. Sr. registrar Eye Clinic, Nuoro, Sardinia, Italy, 1998—99; asst. prof. ophthalmology U. Sassari, 2000—. Contbr. scientific papers to profl. jours. Recipient Best Poster award, EVER congress, 2007; grantee, U. Sassari, 1990—94, Consorzio Interuniversitario per i Trapianti d'Organo, Rome, 1994—97, Ministero per l'Università e la Ricerca Scientifica, Rome, 1998—2000. Mem.: European Assn. Retina Specialists, European Assn. Vision and Eye Rsch., Med. Contact Lens and Ocular Surface Assn., Am. Acad. Ophthalmology. Office: University Sassari Inst Ophthalmology Viale San Pietro 43A Sassari Sardinia 07100 Italy Office Fax: 39079228484. Business E-Mail: apinna@uniss.it.

PINSON, CHARLES WRIGHT, surgeon, educator, academic administrator; b. Albuquerque, May 29, 1952; s. Ernest Alexander and Jean Elizabeth Pinson. Student, Miami U., Oxford, Ohio, 1970-72; BA, U. Colo., Boulder, 1974, MBA, 1976; MD, Vanderbilt U., 1980. Diplomate Am. Bd. Surgery, Am. Bd. Surg. Critical Care, Nat. Bd. Med. Examiners. Resident in gen. surgery Oreg. Health Sci. U., Portland, 1980-86; fellow gastrointestinal surgery Lahey Clinic, Burlington, Mass., 1986-87; fellow transplant surgery Harvard U., Boston, 1987-88; dir. liver transplant program VA Western region, Portland, 1989-90, Oreg. Health Sci. U., Portland, 1988-90; interim chmn. dept. surgery Vanderbilt U., Nashville, 1993-95, chief divsn. hepatobiliary surgery and liver transplantation, 1990—2004, vice-chmn. dept. surgery, 1995-2001; dir. Vanderbilt Transplant Ctr., Nashville, 1993—; chmn. med. bd. Vanderbilt U. Med. Ctr., Nashville, 1997-99; chief of staff Vanderbilt U. Hosp., Nashville, 1997—2004; H. William Scott prof., chmn. dept. surgery Vanderbilt U., Nashville, 2001—04; chief med. officer, assoc. vice chancellor for clin. affairs Vanderbilt U. Med. Ctr., Nashville, 2004—09; dep. vice chancellor health affairs CEO Vanderbilt Hosp. & Clinics; pres. Vanderbilt Health Svc.; sr. assoc. dean Vanderbilt Med. Ctr. Adv. bd. Pacific N.W. Transplant Bank, Portland, 1989—90, Tenn. Donor Svcs., Nashville, 1991—, sec., 2003—05. Mem. editl. bd. Annals Surgery, Jour. Gastrointestinal Surgery, Liver Transplantation, HPB; contbr. articles to profl. jours., chapters to books. Chair liver and intestine allocation com. United Network Organ Sharing, 2003—05; bd. dirs. ARC, Nashville, 1992—94, Am. Liver Found., 1992—96, Ronald McDonald House, 2002—, United Network Organ Sharing, 2000—02, Hosp. Hospitality House, Nashville, 2005—. Fellow, Am. Heart Assn., 1983—84. Mem.: Internat. Hepatopancreatobiliary Assn. (mem. sci. com. 2000—03, mem. exec. com. 2003—, treas. 2004—08, pres. elect. 2008—), Internat. Liver Transplantation Soc., Soc. Surgery Alimentary Tract, Assn. Acad. Surgery, N. Pacific Surg. Assn. (mem. sci. program 1990—92), Western Surg. Assn., So. Surg. Assn., Am. Surg. Assn., So. Med. Assn. (chmn. sect. surgery 1997—2001), Am. Physiologic Soc., Am. Hepatopancreatobiliary Assn. (mem. exec. com. 1997—, treas. 1999—2003, pres. elect 2001—03, pres. 2003—05), Am. Gastroent. Assn., Am. Soc. Study Liver Diseases, Am. Soc. Transplant Surgeons, Soc. Surg. Oncology, Halsted Soc., Soc. Univ. Surgeons, Phi Beta Kappa, Sigma Xi, Alpha Omega Alpha. Office: Vanderbilt U Med Ctr D3300 MCN Nashville TN 37232-5545

PINSON, LARRY LEE, pharmacist, state agency administrator; b. Van Nuys, Calif., Dec. 5, 1947; s. Leland J. and Audrey M. (Frett) Pinson; m. Margaret K. Pinson, Mar. 18, 1972; children: Scott C., Kelly E. Degree, U. Calif., Davis, 1969; AA, Am. River Coll., Sacramento, 1968; PharmD, U. Calif., San Francisco, 1973. Lic. pharmacist Calif., Nev. Staff pharmacist/asst. dir. pharm. svcs. St. Mary's Hosp., Reno, 1973-77; chief pharmacist May Ang Base USAF, 1973-77; owner & mng. pharmacist Silverda Pharmacy, 1979—2001; mng. pharmacist Scolari's Food & Drug, Reno, 2001—05; exec. sec. Nev. State Bd. Pharmacy, 2005—, pres., 1996—2004, exec. sec., 2005—; pharm., therapeutics com. State Nev., 2004—06. Cons. pharmacist Physicians Hosp., 1974—93, Reno Med. Plz., 1973—2001, Rural Calif. Hosp. Assn., 1973—74, Ford Ctr. Foot Surgery, 1980—2007; pharmacy coord. Intensive Pharm. Svcs., 1986—87; cons. Calif. Dept. Health & Corrections, Susanville, 1975—76, Nev. Med. Care Adv. Bd., Carson City, 1984—87; provider, reviewer Nev. State Bd. Pharmacy, Reno, 1975—84; instr. Nev. CC, 1974—76; adj. prof. Idaho State U., Pocatello, 1989—, ND State U., 2006—. Co-author: Care of Hickman Catheter, 1984. Softball coach Reno/Sparks Recreation Dept., 1973—92; bd. dirs. Am. Cancer Soc., 1986—90; mem. State of Nev. Pharmaceutics and Therapy Com., 2004—05, Nev. Arthritis Found.; cubmaster Pack 153 Boy Scouts Am., Verdi, Nev., scoutmaster com. chmn. Reno troop 1, 1988—92. Recipient Bowl of Hygeia award, Nev. Pharmacists Assn. and A. H. Robbins Co., 1984; named Pharmacist of the Yr., Nev. Pharm. Alliance, 1999. Mem.: U. Calif. San Francisco Alumni Assn. (pres. 2009—), Greater Nev. Heatlh Sys. Agy., Nev. Profl. Stds. Rev. Orgn., Nev. Pharmacists Assn. (pres. 1981—82), Am. Pharm. Assn., Nat. Assn. Bds. Pharmacy, Kappa Psi. Avocations: skiing, fishing, backpacking, softball, golf. Home: PO Box 478 Verdi NV 89439-0478 Office: 431 W Plumb Ln Reno NV 89509 Office Phone: 775-850-1440. Personal E-mail: Rx2005@aol.com.

PINTER, GABRIEL GEORGE, retired physiology educator; b. Bekes, Hungary, June 23, 1925; came to U.S., 1958; s. Lajos and Regina (Szilagyi-Farkas) Pinter; m. Berit Helgesen, Dec. 19, 1958 (dec. May 1980); children: Renee Astrid, Eva Ingelill; m. Vera Lederer Dallos, May 24, 1984. MD, U. Sch. Medicine, Budapest, Hungary, 1951. Asst. prof. U. Sch. Medicine, Budapest, Hungary, 1951-56; rsch. assoc. U. Inst. Med. Rsch., Oslo, Norway, 1957-58; asst. prof. U. Tenn., Memphis, 1958-61; from asst. prof. to prof. U. Md., Balt., 1961-92; retired. Vis. prof. King's Coll., London, 1990-94. Contbr. articles to profl. jours.; translator (with wife) philos. and lit. works into Hungarian. Recipient A.V. Humboldt prize, Germany, 1980; Swedish Royal Med. Soc. fellow, Uppsala, 1972. Mem. Am. Physiol. Soc., Physiol. Soc. Gt. Brit., Scandinavian Physiol. Soc., European Soc. Microcirculation.

PINTO, HARLAN A., oncologist, educator; b. NYC; AB, Brown U., 1979; MA, Yale U., 1983. Assoc. prof. Stanford U. Sch. Medicine, 1991—. Mem.: Am. Soc. Clin. Oncology. Office: Stanford Cancer Ctr 875 Blake Wilbur Dr Stanford CA 94305 Office Fax: 650-849-1213. Business E-Mail: harlan@stanford.edu.

PINTO, NICANOR RODRIGUES DA SILVA, physician; b. Venceslau, Sao Paulo, Feb. 24, 1958; MD, Escola Paulista Medicina, 1982; PhD, U. Sao Paulo, 2009. Pub. health physician U. Fed. São Paulo, 1985—. Mem.: São Paulo Pub. Health Assn., Brazilian Colective Health Assn. Office: Rua Botucatu 740 Vila Clementino São Paulo 04123-062 Brazil Business E-Mail: nrspinto@unifesp.br.

PINTO-MARTIN, JENNIFER ANNE, epidemiologist, educator; b. Colma, Calif., Mar. 17, 1957; d. Douglas Wellman Pinto and Elizabeth Kathleen (O'Hara) Hazard; m. Muscoe Burnett Martin, Aug. 17, 1986; children: Emily Grace Martin, Nora Mills Martin, Charlotte Elizabeth Martin, Muscoe (Jack) Burnett Martin. BS, Stanford U., 1974—78; MPH, U. Calif., Berkeley, 1980—82, PhD, 1982—84. Asst. prof. Columbia U., NYC, 1984—90, U. Pa., Phila., 1990—97, assoc. prof., 1998—2005, prof., 2005—, dir., Masters in Pub. Health Program, 2007—. Dir., Ctr. for Autism and Develop. Disabilities Rsch. and Epidemiology U. Pa.; cons., Interagency Autism Coordinating Com. NIH; mem. scientific review com. Nat. Inst. Neurological Diseases and Stroke, Am. Pub. Health Assn., Soc. for Epidemiological Rsch.; mentor and advisor to numerous grad. and undergraduate students. Mem. editl. bd. Pediatric and Perinatal Research. Grantee Ctr. for Autism Rsch., CDC, 2001. Mem.: Soc. for Pediat. Epidemiologic Rsch. (former pres.), Internat. Soc. for Autism Rsch. (sec.). Office: Univ Pennsylvania Sch Nursing 418 Curie Blvd Philadelphia PA 19104-4217 Business E-Mail: pinto@nursing.upenn.edu.

PINTO NETO, LAURO FERREIRA DA SILVA, medical educator; b. Vitoria, Sept. 21, 1955; MD, Fed. U. Espirito Santo, 1979, MS, 1999. Assoc. prof. Med. Sch. Santa Casa de Vitoria, 1981—; pres. Med. Regional Coun. Espirito santo, 1993—95; mem. immunization technic com. Brazil Health Ministry, 2009, cons. aids brazilian guidelines, 2009. Mem.: Brazilian Soc. Immunizations, Brazilian Soc. Tropical Diseases, Brazilian Soc. Infectology. Avocations: jogging, reading. Office: Rio Branco St 310 Santa Lucia Vitoria Es 29055-640 Brazil Office Fax: 55 27 32035050. E-mail: lauro.neto@emescam.br.

PIOMBINO, NICHOLAS, psychotherapist; b. NYC, Oct. 5, 1942; s. Nicholas Bruce and Ruth Mary (Rothbart) P. BA with honors, CCNY, 1964; MSW, Fordham U., 1971; cert. in adult psychoanalysis and psychotherapy, Postgrad. Ctr. Mental Health, NYC, 1982. Diplomate in clin. social work; cert. psychotherapist, social worker, N.Y. Social worker Manhattan State Hosp., NYC, 1971-73; pvt. practice psychotherapy NYC, 1976—; sch. social worker N.Y.C. Bd. Edn., 1974—2001; staff psychotherapist Postgrad. Ctr. Mental Health, 1978-86; supr., mem. faculty Psychoanalytic Inst. N.Y. Counseling and Guidance Svc., NYC, 1987—. Author: Poems, 1988, Light Street, 1996, Theoretical Objects, 1999, Fait Accompli, 2007, Free Fall, 2007, (essays) The Boundary of Blur, 1993, The Boundary of Theory, 2000, Hegelian Honeymoon, 2004, (book) Contradicta: Aphorisms, 2008, numerous poems; contbr. articles to profl. jours.; Exhibited in group shows at Maryann Boesky Gallery, 2001, Harvard Dudley House, 2005, PS 122, 2006; editor: (poetry anthology) OCHO 14, 2007. Mem. Postgrad. Psychoanalytic Soc., Soc. Clin. Social Work Psychotherapists. Office: 680 W End Ave New York NY 10025-6815 Home: 44 Prospect Park W Apt F2 Brooklyn NY 11215-2344 Office Phone: 212-316-1871. E-mail: hpiombino@earthlink.net.

PIOMBONI, PAOLA, medical educator; b. Siena, Italy, Apr. 6, 1962; Degree in Biol. Scis., U. Siena, 1987, PhD, 1995. ART lab. dir. hosp. U. Siena, 2005, assoc. prof. faculty medicine, 2007—. Mem.: ESHRE. Avocation: volleyball. Office: Viale Bracci 14 Siena 53100 Italy Business E-Mail: paolapiomboni@unisi.edu.

PIOT, PETER (BARON), global health professor; b. Leuven, Belgium, Feb. 17, 1949; MD, U. Ghent, 1974; PhD in Microbiology, U. Antwerp, 1981, PhD (hon.), 1997, Free U., 1995; DSc (hon.), U. West Indies, 2005, Clark U., 2007, U. Liege, 2008, U. Ghent, 2010. Sr. fellow microbiology and infectious diseases U. Washington, 1978—79; prof. microbiology Inst. Tropical Medicine, 1980—92; prof. pub. health Free U., Brussels, 1989—94; assoc. dir. Global Program AIDS/WHO, Geneva, 1995; exec. dir. Joint UN Program on HIV/AIDS, Geneva, 1995—2008; under sec.-gen. UN, 2002—08; prof. global health, dir. Imperial Coll., London, 2009—10; sr. fellow Gates Found., Seatle, 2009; scholar in residence Ford Found., 2009; prof. Coll. France, Paris, 2009—10; dir. London Sch Hygiene & Tropical Medicine, 2010—; global health prof. CMG. Dir. Project SIDA, Kinshasa; assoc. prof. U. Nairobi, STD/AIDS Project, Kenya; co-discoverer Ebola virus; Socrates chair, European Acad., Yuste, Spain, 2004; pres., King Boudouin Found., Terrence Higgins Trust, London, Vlerick Sch. Mgmt., Ghent, Belgium. Editor: (with others) Chlamydial Infection, 1982, (with J.M. Mann) AIDS and HIV Infection in the Tropics, 1988, (with P. Lamptey) Handbook on AIDS Prevention in Africa, 1990, 2d edit. 1991, (with others) Basic Laboratory Procedures in Clinical Bacteriology, 1991; co-author:

AIDS in Africa: A Handbook for Physicians, 1992, Reproductive Tract Infections in Women, 1992, (with K.K. Holmes)Sexually Transmitted Diseases, 1999, 2008 (with M. Carael) L'Epidemie de Sida et la Mondialisation des Risques, 2005. Knighted baron King Albert II, 1995; decorated officier l'Ordre Nat. du Léopard (Zaïre), comdr. l'Ordre du Lion (Sénégal), Nat. Order Burkina Faso Mali and Madagascar; NATO fellow, 1978-79; recipient Kerkheer prize Medicine, 1989, Health award Flemish Cmty., 1990, AMICOM award Medicine, 1991, H. Breurs prize, 1992, A. Jaunioux prize, 1992, van Thiel award, 1993, Glaxo award infectious diseases, 1995, Nelson Mandela award, 2001, Gold medal Royal Acad. Arts and Scis., Belgium, 2002, E. Calderone medal Columbia U., 2003, Vlerick award, Belgium, 2004, Congl. Achievement award, Philippines, 2005, Grand Ofcl. Order Infante Don Enrique, Portugal, 2005, Acad. Alliance Found. Global Health Leadership award, NY, 2005; named Outstanding Physician, AMA, Chgo., 2004, CMG UK, 2010 Fellow Royal Coll. Physicians (London), Acad. Medicine, Sci.; mem. Royal Acad. Medicine, Royal Acad. Overseas Scis., Internat. AIDS Soc. (pres. 1992), Inst. Medicine, US Nat. Acad. Scis., other European, US, and African socs. Achievements include co-discovering the Ebola virus. Office: London Sch Hygiene & Tropical Medicine Keppel St London WC1E 7HT England Business E-Mail: peter.piot@lshtm.ac.uk.

PIOTROWSKI, WOJCIECH JERZY, physician, educator; b. Lódz, Poland, Aug. 14, 1962; MD, Med. U. Lódz, 1986, PhD, 1992. Asst. Dept. Pneumology and Allergy, Med. U. Lódz, 1986—92, asst. prof., 1992—2000, sr. lectr., 2000—. Recipient 2nd Degree award, Polish Soc. Internal Medicine. Mem.: Polish Soc. Allergology, European Respiratory Soc., Polish Soc. Respiratory Diseases. Avocations: skiing, music. Office: Kopcinskiego 22 Lódz 90-153 Poland Office Fax: 4842 678 2129. Business E-Mail: piotrow@toya.net.pl.

PIOU-BREWER, MAGALIE, psychotherapist, educator, small business owner; b. Arthabaska, Que., Can., Apr. 26, 1971; d. Edouard Louis and Jacqueline Dorcal Piou; m. Michael Alexander Brewer, July 21, 2003; children: Anya Lilly Brewer, Jasmine Rosa Brewer. Student, Cath. U., Leuven, Belgium, 1991—92; BA in Comm., Loyola Coll., Balt., 1993, MS in Pastoral Counseling, 2000, PhD in Clinical Psychology, George Washington U., 2004. Lic. counselor. Assoc. dir. admissions Loyola Coll., Balt., 1994—2001; child psychotherapist Stevenson Psychol. Svcs., Columbia, Md., 2001—03; clin. dir. Bridgeway Counseling Svcs., Columbia, 2004—; exec. dir. MPB Group, Inc., Columbia, 2004—. Adj. asst. prof. Loyola Coll. Grad. Ctr., Columbia, 2005—; spkr. in field. Acad. fellow, George Washington U., 2000—03, Maternal/Child Health grant, Kennedy Kreiger Inst., Balt., 2003. Mem.: APA, Am. Counselors Assn., Am. Mental Health Counselors Assn. Avocations: reading, travel. Office: MPB Group Inc 9650 Santiago Rd Ste 11 Columbia MD 21045 Office Phone: 410-730-2385.

PIPCHICK, MARGARET HOPKINS, advance practice psychiatric nurse, marriage and family therapist; m. Robert Pipchick; children: Christine, Kevin. BSN, Seton Hall U., 1968; MA, NYU, 1974; grad., Blanton Peale Grad. Inst., NYC, 1981; PhD, The Union Inst., 2001. Cert. disaster crisis counselor NJ. Various staff positions hosps., NY, NJ; teaching asst. Seton Hall U., South Orange, NJ, 1971-72; staff therapist, faculty Blanton-Peale Counseling Ctr., Cranford, NJ, 1974-90; pvt. practice individual, couple and family therapy Cranford, 1981—. Adj. faculty Fairleigh Dickenson U., Teaneck, NJ, 1989-93, Kean Coll., 1994, 95. Drew U., 2003. Contbr. chpt. to Founds. Psychiat. Mental Health Nursing. Mem. ANA, NJ State Nurses Assn., Am. Assn. Marriage and Family Therapists, Soc. Advanced Practice Psychiatric Nurses, Sigma Theta Tau. Office Phone: 908-272-9088.

PIRAINO, BETH, medical educator; b. Gary, Ind., Mar. 3, 1949; d. Carl Albert and Dorothy Hans Holley; m. Paul M. Piraino; children: Matthew, Lisa. BS, U. Pitts., 1970, MD, Med. Coll. Pa., 1977. Bd. cert. medicine and nephrology. From asst. prof. to prof. U. Pitts. Sch. Medicine, 1982-95, prof. medicine, 1995—. Office: U Pitts 3504 5th Ave Ste 200 Pittsburgh PA 15213 Office Phone: 412-383-4899.

PIRHONEN, JOUKO, obstetrician, educator; b. Siilinjärvi, Finland, Mar. 29, 1957; s. Teuvo and Elna Pirhonen; m. Tiina Sassi; children: Laura Elina, Antti. MD, U. Kuopio, Finland, 1981; PhD in Ob-Gyn., U. Turku, Finland, 1990. Cert. perinatal medicine subspecialist U. Turku, 1993. Physician Open Care Ctr., Kouvola, Finland, 1982—84; resident ob-gyn. Lahti Ctrl. Hosp., Finland, 1984—87, intern surgery, 1987—88; resident ob-gyn. U. Turku, 1988—90, maternal fetal fellow, dept. ob-gyn., 1990—93, assoc. prof. ob-gyn., 1996; vis. prof., divsn. maternal fetal medicine, dept. ob-gyn. Yale U., New Haven, 1993—94; sr. cons., dept. ob-gyn. U. Lund, Malmö, Sweden, 1994—97, assoc. prof. ob-gyn., 1996; chief physician, divsn. maternal fetal medicine, dept. ob-gyn. U. Bergen, Norway, 1997—2000; prof., divsn. maternal fetal medicine, dept. ob-gyn. U. Oslo, 2000—, head and dir., 2000—. Leading scientist Dir. Health and Social Affairs, Oslo, 2005—. 2nd lietenant Inf. Recipient Ulla-Maija Mäkilä award, Finnish Gynecol. Assn., 1991, Seth Wichmann award, 1996. Mem.: Norwegian Ultrasound Assn. Avocations: running, travel. Office: Univ Oslo Kirkeveien 166 Oslo 0407 Norway Home: Sikgatan 36 262 57 Angelholm Sweden Personal E-mail: tj.pirhonen@gmail.com. Business E-Mail: jouko.pirhonen@medisin.uio.no.

PIRNAY, STEPHANE OLIVIER, toxicologist, consultant; b. Paris, Oct. 25, 1974; s. Henri Charles Raoul and Jeanine Pirnay; m. Aurelie Manela, Apr. 6, 2008. PharmD, Faculté de Pharmacie, Paris, 2001; PhD, Faculté de Pharmacie, 2004. Cert. toxicologist Ecole doctorale du médicament, 2004. Toxicologist Schering Plough, Levallois Perret, Ile de France, France, 2001—04, Lab. de toxicologie de la préfecture de police, Paris, 1999—2004; attaché en toxicologie U. René Descartes Paris V, 2006—08; cons. Jb Consulting, Villeneuve La Garenne; vis. fellow Nida - Nih, Balt., 2005—06. Contbr. scientific papers to profl. publs. Recipient award, U. Paris, 2006, Nat. Acad. Pharmacy, 2005. Office: Jb Consulting 233 Quai D'Asnieres Villeneuve La Garenne Ile De France 92390 France Personal E-mail: pirnaystephane@yahoo.com.

PIRODSKY, DONALD MAX, psychiatrist, educator; b. Freeport, NY, Feb. 2, 1945; s. Max and Doris Geilhard (Biedermann) P.; m. Gail Giufre Pallotta, Jan. 4, 1997; children: Laura Anne, Jason Donald. BA, Hofstra U., Hempstead, NY, 1966; MD, SUNY, Syracuse, 1970. Diplomate Am. Bd. Psychiatry and Neurology, Nat. Bd. Med. Examiners. Intern Northwestern U. Med. Ctr., Chgo., 1970-71; resident in psychiatry Strong Meml. Hosp., Rochester, NY, 1973-74, U. Ariz. Med. Ctr., Tucson, 1974-76; instr. psychiatry SUNY Health Sci. Ctr., Syracuse, 1976-78, attending psychiatrist, 1976-91, asst. prof. psychiatry, 1978-85, mem. exec. com. of med. coll. assembly, 1979-82, clin. assoc. prof., 1985—2006, adj. attending psychiatrist, 1991—2006; pvt. practice Syracuse and Fayetteville, NY, 1976—2006, Canastota, NY, 2006—; staff psychiatrist, dir. consultation/liaison svc. Syracuse VA Med. Ctr., 1976-87, chmn. pharmacy rev. and therapeutic agts. com., 1980-86. Psychiat. cons. Ariz. Sch. Deaf and Blind, Tucson, 1975-76, Syracuse Devel. Ctr., 1977-2006, Rochester Sch. Deaf, 1978-81; ex-officio mem. Family Counseling Agy., Tucson, 1975-76; adj. attending psychiatrist SUNY Health Sci. Ctr., Syracuse, 1991-2006. Author: Primer of Clinical Psychopharmacology: A Practical Guide, 1981, (with Jerry S. Cohn) Clinical Primer of Psychopharmacology: A Practical Guide, 2d edit., 1992; contbr. articles to profl. jours., chpts. to med. books. Lt. comdr. USPHS, 1971-73. Fellow Am. Psychiat. Assn. (Disting., mem. cen. NY dist. br.); mem. Am. Psychosomatic Soc., Am. Assn. Mental Retardation, Med. Soc. State of NY, NY State Psychiat. Assn., Onondaga County Med. Soc. Episcopalian. Avocations: sports, collecting baseball cards and other sports memorabilia. Home and Office: 5393 Cambiago St Sarasota FL 34238-4771 Office Phone: 315-247-9681.

PIROLA, LUCIANO, research scientist; b. Bergamo, Italy, Aug. 8, 1968; D in Biol. Scis., U. Milan, 1995; PhD in Biochemistry, U. Fribourg, 2000. Postdoc. rsch. assoc. French Nat. Inst. Health and Med. Rsch., 2000—04, rsch. technician, 2001—03, rschr., 2005—08, 2010—. Vis. scientist BakerIDI, Heart and Diabetes Inst., Melbourne, 2008—10. Fellow fellowship, French Found. Med. Rsch., 2003—04; grant, fellowship, French Nat. Inst. Health and Med. Rsch./NHMRC Australia, 2008. Mem.: French Diabetes Soc., European Assn. Study Diabetes. Avocation: bicycling. Office: French Nat Inst Health and Med Rsch U1060 South Lyon Med Faculty 165 Chemin du Grand Revoyet Oullins 69921 France

PIRRO, ALFRED ANTHONY, JR., emergency physician; b. Stamford, Conn., May 17, 1961; s. Alfred Anthony, Sr. and Frances (Battaglia) Pirro. BA in Natural Scis., Johns Hopkins U., Balt., 1983; MD, U. Conn., Storrs, 1987. Diplomate Am. Bd. Anesthesiology, Am. Bd. Critical Care Medicine. Resident in surgery Hosp. of St. Raphael, New Haven, 1987-90; fellow in neurosurgery Hartford Hosp., Conn., 1991-92, resident in anesthesiology, 1992-95, critical care fellow, 1995-97, staff anesthesiologist, 1997-99, emergency medicine physician Windham Hosp., Willamantic, Conn., 1991—; instr. anesthesiology John Dempsey Hosp.-U. Conn. Sch. Medicine, Hartford, 1997-99; owner Hosp. Physician Specialists, Elkton, Md., 2006—08; med. dir. hospitalist program Union Hosp. Cecil County, Elkton, 2004—, chmn. dept. hospitalist medicine, 2007—, med. dir. ICU. Chmn. critical care, chmn. med. records com. Union Hosp. Cecil County, 2002—, mem. med. exec. com., 2007—, sec., treas. med. staff, 2007—09, v.p. med. staff, 2010—, med. dir. Calvert Manor Nursing and Rehab Ctr., Rising Sun, Mo., 2007—; sec., treas. & med. staff U. Hosp., 2008—. Advisor Lally for Congress campaign, Mineola, NY, 1994. Scholar, Pitney Bowes, 1979; Beneficial-Hodson scholar, Johns Hopkins U., 1979. Mem.: AMA, Soc. Critical Care Medicine, Md. State Med. Soc. Republican. Office Phone: 443-350-4544. Personal E-mail: aapjrmd@aol.com.

PISANO, ETTA D., radiologist, educator; AB cum laude, Dartmouth Coll., 1979; MD, Duke U. Cert. Diagnostic Radiology Am. Bd. Radiology, 1988. Radiology resident Beth Israel Hosp., Boston, 1984—88, chief resident, 1986—87, dir. mammography, 1988—89; med. dir. Carolina Screening Mammography, 1989—93; residency program dir. Dept. Radiology U. NC Sch. Medicine, 1992—96, section chief Breast Imaging Sect., 1989—2005, program dir. Post-grad. Continuing Med. Edn. Course in Breast Imaging, 1989—2005, Kenan prof. radiology and biomedical engring., dir. Biomed. Rsch. Imaging Ctr., 2003—, vice dean academic affairs, 2006—. Contbr. articles to profl. jours. Recipient Francis W. Gramlich Philosophy Prize, 1979, Health Breakthrough award, Ladies' Home Jour., 2006; named one of 20 Most Influential People in Radiology, Diagnostic Imaging, 2002, America's Best Breast Cancer Doctors, Redbook, 2001. Fellow: Soc. Breast Imaging; mem.: Inst. Medicine, Assn. Profl. Women in Medicine and Sci. (mem. Nominating and Salary Equity Com. 1994—), Assn. Univ. Radiologists, Am. Coll. Radiology, Am. Assn. Women's Radiologists, Am. Med. Women's Assn. (Women in Sci. Award 2005), Radiological Soc. North Am., Internat. Digital Mammography Devel. Group (chair 1996—, pres. pro tem 2001—), Am. Roentgen Ray Soc. Office: U NC Chapel Hill Sch Medicine 503 Old Infimary Chapel Hill NC 27599-7510 Home: 1319 Cove Ave Sullivans Island SC 29482-9769 Home Phone: 919-942-1166; Office Phone: 919-966-4397. E-mail: etpisano@med.unc.edu.

PISARSKA, MARGARETA, gynecologist; b. NYC, Feb. 5, 1966; MD, SUNY Upstate Med. U., 1992. Dir. divsn. reproductive endocrinology & infertility, dept. ob-gyn. Cedars-Sinai Med. Ctr., 2004—, co-dir. ctr. androgen-related rsch. and discovery, 2010—. Asst. prof. dept. ob-gyn. UCLA, 2004—11; bd. mem. divsn. reproductive endocrinology and infertility Am. Bd. Ob-gyn., 2011—. Recipient REAP award, Office of Rsch. on Women's Health; named Woman of Yr., Am. Biog. Inst. Bd. Internat. Rsch., 2009; Academic Tng. fellowship, Am. Coll. Obstetricians and Gynecologists, Ortho-McNeil, grant, Women's Fund for Health Edn. and Rsch. Mem.: Pacific Coast Reproductive Soc., Soc. Gynecologic Investigation, Endocrine Soc., Soc. Reproductive Endocrinology and Infertility, Am. Soc. Reproductive Medicine. Office: 8635 W 3rd St #160W Los Angeles CA 90048 Business E-Mail: pisarskam@cshs.org.

PISCIOTTA, VIVIAN VIRGINIA, retired psychotherapist; b. Chgo., Dec. 7, 1929; d. Vito and Mary Lamia; m. Vincent Diago Pisciotta, Apr. 1, 1951; children: E. Christopher, Vittorio, V. Charles, Mary A. Pisciotta Higley, Thomas Sansone BA Clin. Psychology, Antioch U., 1974; MSW, George Williams Coll., 1984; postgrad., Erickson Inst. No. Ill., 1990. Lic. clin. social worker, Ill.; diplomate in clin. social work. Short-term therapist Woman Line, Dayton, Ohio, 1976—79; psychotherapist Cicero Family Svcs., Ill., 1982—83, Maywood - Proviso Family Svcs., Ill., 1983—84, Maple Ave. Med. Ctr., Brookfield, Ill., 1985—88, Met. Med. Clinic, Naperville, Ill., 1986—88; allied staff Riveredge Psychiat. Hosp., Forest Park, Ill., 1986—97; psychotherapist, pvt. practice Oakbrook, Ill., 1988—96; psychotherapist, co-founder Archer Austin Counseling Ctr., Chgo., 1988—89; founder Archer Counseling Ctr., Chgo., 1989—97; psychotherapist Columbia Hospitals' Columbia Riveredge Hosp., Forest Park, 1997; allied staff Linden Oaks Psychiat. Hosp., Naperville, 1990—97; founder Archer Ctr., Ariz., 1997—99; psychotherapist pvt. practice, 1988—2004; ret., 2004. Substitute tchr. Chgo. Pub. H.S., 1981; instr. Ariz. State U. Livelong Learning Acad., 2002-03; cons. psychotherapy, 2005— Author treatment prog., workshops in field Co-founder Co-op Nursery Sch., Rockford, Ill., 1956; leader Great Books of the Western World series, Piqua, Ohio, 1977, Rockford, 1960-65; leader Girl Scouts U.S., St. Bridget Sch., Rockford, 1968-71 Mem. Assn. Labor-Mgmt. and Cons. on Alcoholism, Soc. Clin. Exptl. Hypnosis, NASW, Acad. Cert. Social Workers, Nat. Social Work Register (cert.), Antioch U. Alumnus Assn., Rockford Coll. Alumnae Orgn. (newsletter contbr. 1972-73), Soc. for Clin. and Exptl. Hypnosis (assoc.), Internat. Soc. for Clin. and Exptl. Hypnosis (assoc.) Republican. Roman Catholic. Avocations: reading, travel, study/research, music, religion. Personal E-mail: vivmaryann@aol.com.

PI-SIQUES, FELIP, surgeon, educator; b. Banyoles, Girona, Spain, Dec. 5, 1947; D, U. Barcelona, 1977, PhD, 1990. Chief Inst. Catalan de la Salud, 1996—. Prof. Barcelona U., 1995. Grant, Albeert Einstein MC. Avocation: sports. Home: Via Layetana 51 2 2 Barcelona 08003 Spain Business E-Mail: fpi@ub.edu.

PISTOLE, THOMAS GORDON, microbiology professor; b. Detroit, Sept. 17, 1942; s. Leotis Merton Pistole and Lillian Nell (Bosley) Besser; m. Donna Dulcie Straw, Sept. 11, 1965; children: James Alexander, Jennifer Katharine. PhB, Wayne State U., 1964, MS, 1966; PhD, U. Utah, 1969. Postdoctoral fellow U.S. Army, Frederick, Md., 1969-70; research assoc. U. Minn., Mpls., 1970-71; asst. prof. U. NH, Durham, 1971-77, assoc. prof., 1977-83, prof., 1983—, chmn., 1983-92, dist. prof., 2006, co-dir. discovery program undergrad. edn., 2007—08, dir., 2008—09. Vis. scientist Weizmann Inst., Rehovot, Israel, 1979; vis. prof. U. Edinburgh, Scotland, 1986; faculty fellow Office of V.P. for Acad. Affairs U. NH, 1996-99, 2011-; mem. ad hoc study sect. U.S. Dept. Agr., 2002, grad. asst. Areas Nat. Need Review Panel, US Dept.Edn., 2010. Co-editor: Biomedical Application of the Horseshoe Crab, 1979; mem. editl bd.: Jour. Invertebrate Pathology, 1988—90. NRC fellow, 1969-70; NIH sr. internat. fellow, 1986; grantee NIH, 1975-77, 89-93, 96-2006, NSF, 1981-84. Mem.: Am. Assn. Advancement Sci., Am. Assn. Immunologists, Am. Soc. Microbiology. Avocations: singing, collecting old sheet music, walking, cooking. Office: U NH Rudman Hall Dept Molecular Cellular & Biomed Scis 46 College Rd Durham NH 03824-2618 Home Phone: 603-868-5766; Office Phone: 603-862-0111. Business E-Mail: thomas.pistole@unh.edu.

PI-SUNYER, F. XAVIER, physician, educator; b. Barcelona, Catalonia, Spain, Dec. 3, 1933; came to U.S., 1945; s. James and Mercedes (Diaz) Pi-S.; m. Penelope Wheeler; children: Andrea, Olivia, Joanna. BA, Oberlin Coll., Ohio, 1955; MD, Columbia U., NYC, 1959; MPH, Harvard U., Boston, 1963; D in Honoris Causa (hon.), U. Barcelona, 2003; D in Honris Causa (hon.), U. Roma Tor Vergata, 2007. Jr. registrar in medicine St. Batholomew's Hosp. and Med. Sch., London, 1961—62, rsch. fellow Harvard Sch. Pub. Health, Ibadan, Nigeria, 1963—64; endocrine-metabolism resident, fellow medicine Thorndike Lab. & Boston City Hosp., 1964—65, intern, resident medicine St. Luke's Hosp., NYC, 1959—61, asst. to assoc. attending physician, 1965—75, asst. dir. medicine, 1965—67, chief, metabolism sect., 1972—77; jr., to sr. attending physician St. Luke's-Roosevelt Hosp. Ctr., NYC, 1975, chief, divsn. endocrinology, diabetes & nutrition, 1977, dir., joslin ctr. diabetes, 1985—2002, dir., van itallie ctr. weight loss & maintenance, 1993—2002, endocrinology fellowship program dir., 1977—; assoc. to sr. attending physician Presbyn. Hosp., NYC, 1978—2006; assoc. dir. to dir. NY Obesity Rsch. Ctr., NYC, 1981—; vis. physician Rockefeller U., NYC, 1985—2002; instr., assoc. medicine Columbia U., NYC, 1965—70, fellow clin. nutrition, 1965—66, asst. to assoc. prof. clin. medicine, 1970—78, prof. clin. medicine, 1985—91, prof. medicine, 1991—; affiliate staff Joslin Diabetes Ctr., Boston, 1993—99. Mem. adj. faculty Rockefeller U., 1984—; vis. physician Rockefeller U. Hosp., 1984—; attending physician Presbyn. Hosp., 1985—; sr. investigator N.Y. Heart Assn., 1968-73; Hsien Wu investigator St. Luke's-Roosevelt Hosp., 1982-90; Sigma Xi lectr. Pa. State U., 1989; Howard Heinz vis. prof. Med. Coll. Pa., 1987; Pfizer vis. prof. in diabetes Boston U./Tufts U./Harvard U., 1995, U. Md., 1997; mem. C study sect. NIDDKD, 1988-92, mem. task force on obesity, 1990—, mem. nutrition study sect., 1983-87; v.p. Am. Bd. Nutrition, 1987-88; chmn. task force obesity treatment and prevention Nat. Heart, Lung and Blood Inst., 1995—; mem. sci. bd. FDA, 2004—; mem. expert adv. com. U.S. Dietary Guidelines, 1995; mem. U.S. dietary guidelines adv. com. USDA/HHS, 2004-05. Editor-in-chief Obesity Rsch. Jour., 1997-2002; assoc. editor: Internat. Jour. Obesity, 1994-; contbr. numerous articles to profl. jours. Active NY State Rsch. Coun., Albany, 1986—2001; mem., pres. Am. Diabetes Assn., Alexandria, Va., 1978—93; active NY Acad. Medicine, NYC, 1981; mem. bd. dirs. Am. Bd. Nutrition, Washington, 1983—97; pres. Am. Soc. Clin. Nutrition, Washington, 1989—90; mem. various task forces Inst. Medicine, NAS, Washington, 1991—2002; pres. N.Am. Assn. Study Obesity, Washington, 1994—95; bd. trustees Oberlin Coll., 1998—2005; com. mem. US Dietary Guidelines Adv. Comm, Washington, 2003—05, US Dietary Guidelines, Washington, 2008. Fogarty Internat. fellow, NIH, 1979—80. Mem. USDA/HHS (mem. U.S. dietary guidelines adv. com. 2004-10), Am. Soc. for Clin. Nutrition (coun. 1987-90, pres. 1989-90), Am. Diabetes Assn. (exec. com. 1990-93, pres. 1992-93), N.Am. Assn. Study Obesity (v.p. 1992-93, pres. 1994-95, Stunkard award 2003), N.Y. State Health Rsch. Coun., N.Y. Acad. Medicine (com. on pub. health 1983-96), Inst. of Medicine (food and nutrition bd., task force on dietary reference intakes 1999-2002), NAS (mem. task force on opportunities in nutrition and food sci. 1992-93, task force on dietary reference intakes 1999-2002). Liberal. Achievements include research in diabetes and obesity. Avocations: skiing, theater, art, music. Office: St Luke's-Roosevelt Hosp Ctr 1111 Amsterdam Ave New York NY 10025 Office Phone: 212-523-4161. Office Fax: 212-523-4830. Business E-Mail: fxp1@columbia.edu.

PITCHAI, DAISY, biology professor; b. Tiruchirappalli, Tamil Nadu, India, Oct. 13, 1958; MSc, Bharathidasan U., MPhil, 1986, PhD, 1998. Lectr. zoology Holy Cross Coll., 1980—98, reader zoology, 1998—2002, vice prin., 1998—2001, assoc. prof., zoology & coord. biotechnology, 2002—. Mem.: Indian Assn. Biomedical Scientists, Soc. Biotechnologists, Soc. Reproductive Biology and Comparative Endocrinology. Avocation: music. Office: Holy Cross Coll Tepakulum Tiruchirappalli Tamilnadu 620002 India Office Phone: 94438 36695. Personal E-mail: daisylesslie@yahoo.com.

PITCHUMONI, CAPECOMORIN SANKAR, gastroenterologist, educator; b. Madura, India, Jan. 20, 1938; came to U.S., 1967; s. Sankara and Jaya (Lekshmi) Iyer; m. Prema Iyer, Nov. 11, 1964; children: Sheila, Shoba, Suresh. Student, St. Xavier Coll., India, 1953-55; MB BS, Trivandrum Med. Coll., India, 1959, MD, 1965. Intern Med. Coll., Trivandurm, India, 1961-63; resident in gastroenterology Yale U., 1967-69; N.Y. Med. Coll., 1969-72; practice medicine specializing in gastroenterology NYC, 1972—; asst. prof. medicine Kottayam Med. Coll., India, 1967, N.Y. Med. Coll., 1972-75, assoc. prof., 1975-80, prof. clin. medicine, 1980-85, prof. medicine, 1985—, assoc. prof. preventive and social medicine, 1975-86, prof. community and preventive medicine, 1986—; chief sect. gastroenterology Our Lady of Mercy Med. Ctr., NYC, 1980—, assoc. dir. medicine, 1985—, program dir. internal medicine, 1987—, dir. medicine, 1992, chmn. emeritus dept. medicine, 2002—; chief divsn. gastroenterology St. Peters U. Hosp., New Brunswick, NJ, 2002—. Contbg. author med. textbooks; contbr. articles to profl. jours. Recipient Om Prakash award Indian Soc. Gastroenterology, 1976, Outstanding Scientist of Yr. award MV Spltys., Madras, 1994, Oration award Thangavelu Endowment, 1994. Master ACP, Am. Coll. Gastroenterology (gov. 1996-2000), ACP; fellow Royal Coll. Physicians and Surgeons Can., Am. Coll. Nutrition, Am. Gastroent. Assn.; mem. Assn. Physicians India, India Soc. Gastroenterology (life), Am. Inst. Nutrition, Gastrointestinal Endoscopy, Am. Soc. for Clin. Nutrition. Hindu. Home: 1 Nevius Pl Somerset NJ 08873 Office: St Peters U Hosp New Brunswick NJ Personal E-mail: drpitchumoni@gmail.com. *

PITCOCK, JAMES ALLISON, retired pathologist; b. Little Rock, Sept. 13, 1929; s. Radford Bolling and Anne (Whitelaw) P.; m. Cynthia Jean Dehaven, June 18, 1954; children: Allison P. Fentress, James Dehaven. BS, MIT, 1951; MD, Washington U., 1955. Diplomate Am. Bd. Pathology. Intern Vanderbilt U., Nashville, 1955-56; resident Barnes Hosp., St. Louis, 1956-59, 61-62; asst. pathologist St. Vincents Hosp., Little Rock, 1963, Bapt. Meml. Hosp., Memphis, 1964-75, asst. dir. labs., 1975-87, dir. labs., 1987-95; ret. Vol. faculty U. Tenn. Med. Sch., Memphis, 1965-96, acting chair pathology, 1986-89; com. chair, mem. Am. Heart Assn., Memphis, 1976-84, exec. com., 1983-87, pres., 1985-86. Contbr. chpts. to books and articles to profl. jours. Capt. USAF, 1959-61. Mem. Alpha Omega Alpha, Sigma Xi. Episcopalian. Achievements include experimental and scholarly work in experimental hypertension and surgical pathology.

PITISUTTITHUM, PUNNEE, medical educator, researcher; b. Nakornsrithammaraj, Thailand, Aug. 24, 1957; d. Keakmin Sailee and Nongluck Sailoa; m. Punnee Iamsom Pitisuttithum, Sept. 16, 1984; children: Panyavee, Onsiri, Napasprom. Premed. sci., Mahidol U., Bangkok, 1978, MB, BS, 1982, diploma in tropical medicine and hygiene, 1984. Diplomate Thai Bd. Internal Medicine, Thai Medicine Coun. Lectr. faculty tropical medicine Mahidol U., Bangkok, 1985—90, asst. prof. faculty tropical medicine, 1990—95, assoc. prof. faculty tropical medicine, 1995—2004, prof. faculty tropical medicine, 2004—, asst. dir. Hosp. for Tropical Diseases, 1993—96, dep. head dept. clin. tropical medicine, 1998—, prin. investigator HIV Vaccine Trial Ctr. faculty tropical medicine, 1998, chief clin. infectious disease unit, 2000. Mem. adv. com. on prevention and control of infectious preventable by vaccine disease Min. Pub. Health, 2000—01; mem. task force on rsch. and devel. Global Alliance for Vaccines and Immunization, Switzerland, 2001—04. Contbr. articles to profl. jours. Mem. Adhoc Com. Clin. Trials capacity working group, Global HIV Vaccine Enterprise. Mem.: Internat. Infectious Disease Soc., Internat. AIDS Soc., Thai Med. Soc. for the Study of Sexually Transmitted Diseases, Thai Med. Women's Assn., Parasitology and Tropical Medicine Assn. Thailand, Thai Med. Coun., Med. Assn. Thailand, Royal Coll. Physicians Thailand. Achievements include involved in setting up the first HIV-1 vaccine efficacy trial in developing country. Office: Clin Infectious Disease Unit 420/6 Rajvithi Rd Rajthevee Bangkok 10400 Thailand Home: 233/460 Muban Nantawan 10270 Samut Prakan Samut Prakan Thailand

PITKIN, ROY MACBETH, retired obstetrician, educator; b. Anthon, Iowa, May 24, 1934; s. Roy and Pauline Allie (McBeath) Pitkin; m. Marcia Alice Jenkins, Aug. 17, 1957; children: Barbara, Robert Macbeth, Kathryn, William Charles. BA with highest distinction, U. Iowa, 1956, MD, 1959. Diplomate Am. Bd. Ob-Gyn. Intern King County Hosp., Seattle, 1959—60; resident in ob-gyn U. Iowa Hosps. and Clinics, Iowa City, 1960—63; asst. prof. ob-gyn U. Ill., 1965—68; assoc. prof. ob-gyn U. Iowa, Iowa City, 1968—72, prof., 1972—87, head dept. ob-gyn, 1977—87; prof. UCLA, 1987—97, head dept. ob-gyn., 1987—95, prof. emeritus, 1997—. Mem. residency rev. com. ob-gyn., 1981—87; chmn., 1985—87. Author: The Green Journal 50 Years On, 2003, Whom the Gods Love Die Young: A Modern Medical Perspective on Illness that Caused the Early Death of Famous People, 2008; co-editor: The Best of After Office Hours, 2003; editor-in-chief Year Book of Obstetrics and Gynecology, 1975—86, Clinical Obstetrics and Gynecology, 1979—2000; editor: Obstetrics and Gynecology, 1985—2001; editor emeritus Obstetrics and Gynecology, 2001; contbr. articles to med. jours. Served to lt. comdr. M.C. USNR, 1963—65. Recipient NIH career awardee, 1972—77, Disting. Alumni Achievement award, U. Iowa, 2002. Fellow: Royal Ob-Gyn. (ad eundem); mem.: Coun. Sci. Editors (Dist. Svc. award 2002), Inst. Medicine, NAS, Soc. Perinatal Obstetricians (pres. 1978—79), Soc. Gynecol. Investigation (pres. 1985—86), German Soc. Gyn-Ob. (hon.), Ctrl. Asn. Ob-Gyn., Am. Gyn-Ob. Soc. (pres. 1994—95), Am. Coll. Ob-Gyns., AMA (Goldberger award in clin. nutrition 1982). Presbyterian. Home: 78900 Rancho La Quinta Dr La Quinta CA 92253-6252 Personal E-mail: r.pitkin@earthlink.net.

PITMAN, ANDREW P., pulmonologist; MD, SUNY. Diplomate Am. Bd. Internal Medicine, 1983, Am. Bd. Internal Medicine-sleep medicine, Am. Bd. Internal Medicine-critical care medicine, 1987, cert. pulmonary/critical care 1986. Resident NYC Hosp.; fellow Sch. of Medicine Univ. of Md.; co-chief critical care medicine sec. Jefferson Health system, chief pulmonary and critical care medicine; dir. ICU Bryn Mawr Hosp. Pulmonary cons. athletic dept. Villanova Univ.; med. & pulmonary physician World Team Tennis Phila. Freedoms; chmn. critical care com. Bryn Mawr Hosp., chmn. ICU quality/resource utilization com., physician's adv. com. quality assurance & utilization review. Co-author (with D. Peterson): (publs.) Apnea Syndrome, 1996; co-author: (with R. Vender) Pulmonary Diseases. Mem.: AMA, The Laennec Soc. of Pulmonary Specialists, The Philip A. Drinker Soc. for Critical Care, Soc. of Critical Care Medicine, Am. Thoracic Soc. Office: Bryn Mawr Hospital MOB North Ste 101 830 Old Lancaster Rd Bryn Mawr PA 19010 Office Phone: 866-225-5654.

PITMAN, GERALD H., plastic surgeon; AB, Williams Coll.; MD, U. Pa. Diplomate Am. Bd. Plastic Surgery. Resident in surgery Columbia divsn. NY Presbyn. Hosp., NYC; resident in plastic surgery NYU Med. Ctr., fellow in microsurgery, attending plastic surgeon, Tisch Hosp./Manhattan Eye, Ear and Throat Hosp. Clin. prof. surgery NYU Sch. Medicine; lectr. in field. Author: Liposuction and Aesthetic Surgery, 1993; contbr. numerous articles to profl. jours. Fellow: ACS, NY Acad. Medicine; mem.: Am. Soc. Plastic and Reconstructive Surgeons, NY State and County Med. Socs., NY Regional Soc. Plastic and Reconstructive Surgeons, NE Soc. Plastic Surgeons, Am. Soc. Aesthetic Plastic Surgery, Am. Soc. Plastic Surgeons. Achievements include pioneering the use of power-assisted liposuction and considered one the best in the world for this procedure. Avocations: boating, fishing, skiing, triathlons. Office: 170 E 73rd St New York NY 10021 Office Phone: 212-517-2600. Office Fax: 212-628-0774. Business E-Mail: info@drpitman.com, drpitman@drpitman.com.

PITOT, HENRY CLEMENT, III, pathologist, educator; b. NYC, May 12, 1930; s. Henry Clement and Bertha (Lowe) Pitot; m. Julie S. Schutten, July 29, 1954; children: Bertha(dec.), Anita, Jeanne, Catherine, Henry, Michelle, Lisa, Patrice. BS in Chemistry, Va. Mil. Inst., 1951; MD, Tulane U., 1955, PhD in Biochemistry, 1959, DSc (hon.), 1995. Diplomate Am. Coll. Pathology, 1960. Instr. pathology Med. Sch. Tulane U., New Orleans, 1955-59; postdoctoral fellow McArdle Lab. U. Wis., Madison, 1959-60, mem. faculty Med. Sch., 1960—, prof. pathology and oncology, 1966-99, prof. emeritus, 1999—, chmn. dept. pathology, 1968-71, acting dean Med. Sch., 1971-73, dir. McArdle Lab., 1973-91. Recipient Borden Undergrad. Rsch. award, 1955, Leaderle Faculty award, 1962, Career Devel. award, Nat. Cancer Inst., NIH, 1965, Parke-Davis award, 1968, Noble Found. Rsch. award, 1984, Esther Langer award, U. Chgo., 1984, Hilldale award, U. Wis., 1991, Founders award, Chem. Industry Inst. Toxicology, 1993, Midwest Regional chpt. Soc. Toxicology award, 1996, Emeritus Faculty award, U. Wis. Med. Sch., 2001, Disting. Lifetime Toxicology award, Soc. Toxicology, 2003, Gold-headed Cane award, Am. Soc. Investigative Pathology, 2005, Lifetime Disting. Alumnus award, Tulane Med. Sch., 2005, Disting. Svc. award, Assn. Pathology Chairs, 2005. Fellow: AAAS, N.Y. Acad. Scis.; mem.: Soc. Toxicologic Pathologists, Soc. Toxicology, Soc. Surg. Oncology (Lucy J. Wortham award 1981), Soc. Exptl. Biology and Medicine (pres. 1991—93), Am. Soc. Investigative Pathology (pres. 1976—77), Am. Cancer Soc. (life), Japanese Cancer Soc. (hon.), Am. Chem. Soc., Am. Soc. Biochemistry and Molecular Biology, Am. Assn. Cancer Rsch., Am. Soc. Cell Biology. Roman Catholic. Home: 314 Robin Pkwy Madison WI 53705-4931 Office: U Wis McArdle Lab Cancer Rsch 1400 University Ave Madison WI 53706-1599 Office Phone: 608-262-3247. Business E-Mail: pitot@oncology.wisc.edu.

PITT, BERTRAM, cardiologist, educator, consultant; b. Kew Gardens, NY, Apr. 27, 1932; s. David and Shirley (Blum) P., m. Elaine Liberstein, Aug. 10, 1962; children: Geoffrey, Jessica, Jillian BA, Cornell U., 1953; MD, U. Basel, Switzerland, 1959. Diplomate Am. Bd. Internal Medicine, Am. Bd. Cardiology. Intern Beth Israel Hosp., NYC, 1959-60, resident Boston, 1960-63; fellow in cardiology Johns Hopkins U., Balt., 1966-67, from instr. to assoc. prof., 1967-77; prof. medicine, dir. div. cardiology U. Mich., Ann Arbor, 1977-91, prof. medicine Sch. Medicine, 1991—2005, prof. medicine emeritus Sch. Medicine, 2005—; chmn., steering com. NHLBI TOPCAT Trial, 2008—. Author: Atlas of Cardiovascular Nuclear Medicine, 1977; editor: Cardiovascular Nuclear Medicine, 1974; co-editor: Clinical Trials in Cardiology, 1997, Current Controlled Trials in Cardiovascular Medicine, 1999—. Served to capt. U.S. Army, 1963-65. Mem. ACP, Am. Coll. Cardiology, Am. Soc. Clin. Investigation, Assn. Am. Physicians, Am. Physiol. Soc., Am. Heart Assn. (James. B. Herrick award 2005), Assn. Univ. Cardiologists, Am. Coll. Chest Physicians, Johns Hopkins U. Soc. Scholars. Home: 24 Ridgeway St Ann Arbor MI 48104-1739 Office: U Mich Divsn Cardiology 1500 E Medical Center Dr Ann Arbor MI 48109-0005 Business E-Mail: bpitt@umich.edu.

PITT, HENRY ANTHONY, surgeon, researcher, medical educator; b. Elizabeth, NJ, Mar. 23, 1945; m. Elizabeth Jane Chambliss, June 21, 1969; children: Laura Elizabeth Teufel, David Andrew, Susan Clare. AB, Cornell U., 1967, MD, 1971. Diplomate Am. Bd. Surgery. Resident Johns Hopkins Hosp., Balt., 1971—73, 1975—78; asst. prof. surgery U. Calif., LA, 1979—85; prof. surgery Johns Hopkins U., Balt., 1985—97, Med. Coll. Wis., Milw., 1997—2004, Ind. U., Indpls., 2004—. Coach Little League Baseball, Pacific Palisades, Calif., 1980—84. Lt. comdr. USN, 1973—75. Recipient Letter in Baseball, Cornell U., 1967, Shipley award, So. Surg. Assn., 1989; named Aprahamian Tchr. of Yr., Med. Coll. Wis., Surgery, 2002, Hon. Prof., Tongi Med. Coll., Wuhan, China, 2006, 2nd Military Med. Coll./ Shanghai, 2008. Fellow: Royal Coll. Surgeons, Edinburgh (hon.); mem.: Internat. Hepato-Pancreato-Biliary Assn. (life; pres. 2004—06), Soc. Surgery Alimentary Tract (life; v.p. 2004—05), Am. Surg. Assn. (life; fellowship com. 2001—07), Am. Hepato-Pancreato-Biliary Assn. (life; pres. 1999—2001), Soc. Clin. Surgery (life; pres. 1998—2000), Soc. U. Surgeons (life; sec. 1985—86), Alpha Omega Alpha (life; pres. 1970—71). Achievements include research in gallstone pathogenesis and the role of obesity in pancreatic cancer. Avocation: golf. Office: Indiana University 535 Barnhill Drive RT 130D Indianapolis IN 46202 Office Fax: 317-274-4554. Business E-Mail: hapitt@iupui.edu. *

PITT, WILLIAM ALEXANDER, cardiologist; b. July 17, 1942; came to U.S., 1970; s. Reginald William and Una Sylvia (Alexander) P.; children: William Matthew, Joanne Katharine. MD, U. B.C., Vancouver, 1967. Diplomate Royal Coll. Physicians Can. Intern Mercy Hosp., San Diego, 1967-68, resident, 1970-71, assoc. dir. cardiology, 1972-92; resident Vancouver Gen. Hosp., 1968-70, U. Calif., San Diego, 1971-72; with So. Calif. Cardiology Med. Group, San Diego, 1984—; pvt. practice Clin. Cons. Cardiology. Bd. trustees San Diego Found. for Med. Care, 1983-89, 91—, pres., chmn. bd. trustees, 1986-88, med. dir., 1991-96; trustee Pacific Found. for Med. Care, 1996—, med. dir., 1996—; bd. dirs. Mut. Assn. for Profl. Services, Phila., 1984-92; pres. Alternet Med. Svcs., Inc., 1992-95; pres. and med. dir. San Diego IPA, 1995-2005. Fellow Royal Coll. Physicians Can., Am. Coll. Cardiology (assoc.); mem. AMA, Am. Heart Assn., Calif. Med. Assn., San Diego County Med. Soc., San Diego County Heart Assn. (bd. dirs. 1982-88). Episcopalian. Office: So Calif Cardiology Med Group 6386 Alvarado Ct Ste 101 San Diego CA 92120-4906 Home Phone: 619-596-0894; Office Phone: 619-265-1237. Personal E-mail: wmapitt@sbcglobal.net.

PITTALUGA, PAUL, vascular surgeon; b. Nice, Riviera, France, Oct. 5, 1965; s. Jean-Marie and Evelyne Walker-Rouze P.; m. Helene Thevenin, July 4, 1987 (div. Jan. 1995); 1 child, Thomas; m. Barbara Falkowski, Feb. 3, 1996; children, Charles, Theodora. BS, U. Nice, 1984, MD, 1995, cert. vascular surgery, 1995. Resident surgery Nice U. Hosp., 1990-95; vascular surgeon Nontes (France) U. Hosp., 1995-96, Nice U. Hosp., 1996-97, cons. vascular surgery, 1997-98, Riviera Veine Inst., 1998—. Contbr. articles to profl. jours. Home: 36 CHemin Oes Travails Cagnes Sur Mer France Office: Riviera Veine Inst 6 Rue Gounod 06000 Nice France Office Phone: 0033493856171.

PITTMAN, CONSTANCE SHEN, endocrinologist, educator; b. Nanking, China, Jan. 2, 1929; arrived in US, 1946; d. Leo F.-Z. and Pao Kong (Yang) Shen; m. James Allen Pittman, Jr., Feb. 19, 1955; children: James Clinton, John Merrill. AB in Chemistry, Wellesley Coll., 1951; MD, Harvard U., 1955. Diplomate Am. Bd. Internal Medicine, sub-bd. Endocrinology. Intern Baltimore City Hosp., 1955-56; resident U. Ala., Birmingham, 1956-57; instr. in medicine U. Ala. Med. Ctr., Birmingham, 1957—59, fellow dept. pharmacology, 1957-59, from asst. prof. to assoc. prof., 1959-70, prof., 1970—. Prof. medicine Georgetown U., Washington, 1972—73; mem. diabetes and metabolism tng. com. NIH, Bethesda, Md., 1972—76, mem. nat. arthritis, metabolism and digestive disease coun., 1975—78, mem. gen. clin. rsch. ctrs. com., 1979—83, 1987—90; bd. dirs., mem., exec. dir. Internat. Coun. for Control of Iodine Deficiency Diseases, 1994—; mem. Iodine Deficiency Disorders Elimination Steering Com. Kiwanis Internat., 2002—. Interim editor: ICCIDD Newsletter, 2004—06. Master ACP; mem. Assn. Am. Physicians, Am. Soc. for Clin. Investigation, Endocrine Soc. (coun., 1978-79, pres. women's caucus 1978-79), Am. Thyroid Assn. (pres. 1990-91), Kiwanis (mem. iodine deficiency disorders steering com.). Achievements include research in activation and metabolism of thyroid hormone; kinetics of thyroxine conversion to triiodothyrine in health and disease states; control of iodine deficiency disorders. Emails. Office: UAB Div Endocrinology/Metab Lab Med Ctr Birmingham AL 35294-0001 Office Phone: 205-934-0800. Business E-Mail: cpittman@uab.edu.

PITTMAN, JACQUELYN, retired mental health nurse, nursing educator; b. Pensacola, Fla., Dec. 22, 1932; d. Edward Corry Sr. and Hettie Oean (Wilson) P. BS in Nursing Edn., Fla. State U., 1958; MA, Columbia U., 1959, EdD, 1974. Physician asst. Med. Ctr. Clinic, Pensacola, 1953-55; clin. instr., asst. dir. nursing svc. Sacred Heart Hosp., Pensacola, 1955-56; instr. psychiat. nurse Fla. State Hosp., Chattahoochee, 1958; instr. psychiat. nursing Pensacola Jr. Coll., 1959-60, 62-63; chmn. div. nursing Gulf Coast C.C., Panama City, Fla., 1963-66; asst. prof. U. Tex., Austin, 1970-72, assoc. prof., 1972-80; prof. nursing, coord. curriculum and tchg. grad. program La. State U. Med. Ctr., New Orleans, 1980-99, rep. faculty senate, 1997-99; pres.-elect faculty assembly Sch. Nursing La. State U. Med. Ctr. Sch. Nursing, New Orleans, 1997-98, pres., 1998-99; ret., 1999. Curriculum cons. Nicholls State U., Thibodaux, La., 1982, Our Lady of Lake Sch. Nursing, Baton Rouge, 1983; rsch. liaison So. Bapt. Hosp., New Orleans, 1987-89, Med. Ctr. La., 1992-99; mem. adv. bd. Sister Henrietta Guyot Professorship; mem. planning com. Nichols State U./La. State U. Med. Ctr. Partnership, 1996-99. Mem. ethics com., trustee Hotel Dieu Hosp., New Orleans, 1987—91; judge Internat. Sci. and Engring. Fair Assn., 1990, 1992; del. La. State Nurses' Assn. State Conv., 1992, 1994; assoc. Libr. of Congress, Smithonian Instn.; mem. Dem. Nat. Comm., Presdl. Task Force, 1992, Ctr. for Study of Presidency; tchr. Christian edn. program for mentally retarded St. Ignatius Martyr Ch., 1979—80; tchr. initiation team Rite of Christian Initiation of Adults, Our Lady of the Lake Cath. Ch., Mandeville, La., 1983—86; v.p., bd. dirs. St. Tammany Guidance Ctr., Inc., Mandeville, 1987—91; mem. parish outreach meals-on-wheels program St. Tammany, Covington, La., 2001—02. Mem. ANA, LWV, Am. Assn. Adv. Sci. Directory, N.Y. Acad. Scis., Acad. Polit. Sci., Libr. of Congress Assocs., Nat. Trust for Hist. Preservation, La. Endowment for Humanities, La. Nurses Assn. (archivist 1987-99, state task force com. to preserve hist. documents 1987-99), So. Nursing Rsch. Soc., Nat. League Nursing, Boston U. Nursing Archives, Women's Inner Cir. Achievement N.Am. Cmtys., Internat. Order of Merit, World Found. Successful Women, Wilson Ctr. Assocs., Kappa Delta Pi, Sigma Theta Tau. Democrat. Roman Catholic. Avocations: swimming, golf, travel, reading, louisiana history. Address: 204 Woodridge Blvd Mandeville LA 70471-2604 Personal E-mail: jpit204@att.net.

PITTMAN, JAMES ALLEN, JR., endocrinologist, educator; b. Orlando, Fla., Apr. 12, 1927; s. James Allen and Jean C. (Garretson) Pittman; m. Constance Ming-Chung Shen, Feb. 19, 1955; children: James Clinton, John Merrill. BS, Davidson Coll., 1948, DSc (hon.), 1981; MD, Harvard, 1952; DSc (hon.), U. Ala., Birmingham, 1984, Chung Shan Med U., Taichung, Taiwan, 2005. Intern, asst. resident medicine Mass. Gen. Hosp., Boston, 1952—54; tchg. fellow medicine Harvard U., 1953—54; clin. assoc. NIH, Bethesda, Md., 1954—56; instr. medicine George Washington U., 1955—56; chief resident U. Ala. Med. Ctr., Birmingham, 1956—58, instr. medicine, 1956—59, asst. prof., 1959—62, assoc. prof., 1962—64, prof. medicine, 1964—92, dir. endocrinology and metabolism divsn., 1962—71, co-chmn. dept. medicine, 1969—71, also prof., physiology and biophysics, 1967—92, dean, 1973—92, Disting. prof., 1992—. Mem. endocrinology study sect. NIH, 1963—67; mem. nat. adv. rsch. resources coun. NIH, 1991—95; asst. chief med. dir. rsch. and edn. in medicine U.S. VA, 1971—73; prof. medicine Georgetown U. Med. Sch., Washington, 1971—73; mem. grad. med. edn. nat. adv. com. HEW, 1976—78; mem. HHS Coun. on Grad. Med. Edn., 1986—90; hon. prof. Chung Shan Med. and Dental Coll., Taiwan, 1994; sr. advisor Internat. Coun. on Ctrl. of Iodine Deficiency Diseases, 1994—96. Author: Diagnosis and Treatment of Thyroid Diseases, 1963; contbr. articles in field to profl. jours. Master: Am. Coll. Endocrinology; fellow: AAAS; mem.: ACP, Stearman Restorers Assn., Hist. Sci. Soc., Am. Soc. for the History of Medicine, So. Soc. Clin. Investigation (Founder's medal 1993), Am. Fedn. Clin. Rsch. (pres. So. sect., nat. coun. 1962—66), Am. Chem. Soc., Am. Diabetes Assn., Am. Ornithologists Union (life), NY Acad. Scis. (life), Endocrine Soc. Ecuador (hon.), Soc. Nuc. Medicine, Am. Thyroid Assn., Am. Assn. Clin. Endocrinologists, Endocrine Soc., Assn. Am. Physicians, Inst. Medicine of NAS, Harvard U. Med. Alumni Assn. (pres. 1986—88), Wilson Ornithol. Club (life), Alpha Omega Alpha, Phi

Beta Kappa, Omicron Delta Kappa. Office: U Ala Sch Med Pittman CAMS 1924 7th Ave S Birmingham AL 35294-0007 Personal E-mail: japdoc@msn.com. Business E-Mail: japdoc@uab.edu.

PITTMAN, ROY CLINTON, JR., neurosurgeon, theologian, lawyer, philosopher; b. Florence, SC, Oct. 12, 1931; s. Roy Clinton and Edna Hester (Altman) P.; m. Therese Huguette Lamarche Pittman, Apr. 1958 (div. May 1976); 1 stepdaughter, Michele Lois Young; children: Charlotte Elisabeth, Clinton Christopher, Russell Roy; m. Jeanne Elmore Waters Pittman, Oct. 10, 1976. BS magna cum laude, Wofford Coll., Spartanburg, SC, 1952; MD, Med. U. S.C., Charleston, 1956; JD, Washburn U. Coll. Law, Topeka, Kans., 1991; MDiv with honors, Emory U. Candler Sch. Theology, Atlanta, 1995; DSc (hon.), The London Inst., 1973. Diplomate Am. Bd. Neurol. and Orthopedic Surgery; ordained to ministry Ea. Orthodox Ch., 2000; bar: Fla. 1992, U.S. Dist. Ct. (mid. dist.) Fla. 1992. Intern U.S. Naval Hosp., Newport, RI, 1956-57; resident in neurology U.S. Naval Hosp.-Nat. Naval Med. Ctr., Bethesda, Md., 1957-58; neurologist East Coast Neuropsychiat. Ctr.-U.S. Naval Hosp., Phila., 1958-59, head neurology br., 1959; resident in neurosurgery Jefferson Med. Coll. Hosp., Phila., 1959-61, chief resident, 1961-62; resident in gen. surgery Hahnemann Med. Coll. Hosp., Phila., 1962-63; pvt. practice neurol. surgery Morton Plant and Mease Hosps., Clearwater-Dunedin, Fla., 1963-82, Cmty. Hosp. of New Port Richey, New Port Richey, Fla., 1978-88; pvt. practice legal medicine, med. jurisprudence & bioethics Pittman Profl. Assn., Clearwater, Fla., 1995-98, Tarpon Springs, Fla., 1995-98; pres., gen. counsel The Quintessential Corp., Tarpon Springs, 1998-2000; founder, prior Trinity House Retreat, Greek Orthodox Monastery of the Holy Trinity, 2001—. Protestant chaplain Morton Plant/Mease Countryside Hosp., Clearwater, Fla., 1997-98. Contbr. articles to profl. jours. Pres. St. Petersburg (Fla.) Coll. Alumni Assn., 1973-75. Lt. MC, USN, 1956-59, lt. comdr., 1962. Recipient Top Paper Bioethics and The Law award Washburn U. Coll. Law, Topeka, Kans., 1990, Top paper Comparative Civil Law award Cumberland Sch. Law and U. Heidelberg Germany Faculty of Law, 1990; endowed Jeanne Pittman ann. Bioethics and the Law Top Paper award Washburn U. Coll. Law, Topeka, 1995. Fellow Internat. Coll. Angiology, Royal Soc. Health, Internat. Coll. Surgeons, Am. Coll. Legal Medicine; mem. AMA, Congress Neurol. Surgeons, Fla. Med. Assn., Fla. Bar, Phi Beta Kappa, Phi Delta Phi. Jeffersonian Democrat. Avocations: stamp collecting/philately, anthropology, travel.

PIVEN, JOSEPH, psychiatrist, educator; BS in Psychology, U. Md., MD. Intern Good Samaritan Hosp., Phoenix; resident in psychiatry Johns Hopkins Hosp., fellow in child & adolescent psychiatry; fellow in psychiatric genetics Johns Hopkins U. Sch. Medicine; prof. psychiatry UNC Sch. Medicine. Office: 101 Manning Dr Chapel Hill NC 27514 Office Phone: 919-843-8641. E-mail: jpiven@med.unc.edu.

PIVER, M. STEVEN, gynecologic oncologist; b. Washington, Sept. 29, 1934; s. Harry Samuel and Sonia (Bard) P.; m. Susan Myers, June 25, 1958; children: Debra Ellen, Carolyn Jan, Kenneth Stuart. BS, Gettysburg Coll., 1957; MD, Temple U., 1961. Diplomate Am. Bd. Ob-Gyn, Am. Coll. Surgeons. Intern Nazareth Hosp., Phila., 1961—62; resident Johns Hopkins U. Hosp., Balt., 1962; resident ob-gyn. Pa. Hosp. U. Pa., Phila., 1965—68; fellow gynecologic oncology Hosp. Tumor Inst. U. Tex., Houston, 1968—70; asst. prof. gynecologic oncology UNC Sch. Medicine, 1970—71; assoc. chief gynecologic oncology Roswell Park Cancer Inst., Buffalo, 1972—83, founder, dir. Gilda Radner Familial Ovarian Cancer Registry, 1981—, chief gynecologic oncology, 1984—97; clin. prof., dir. divsn. gynecologic oncology SUNY, Buffalo, 1986—87, prof. gynecology, 1998—, chair emeritus gynecologic oncology, 1998—. Cons., editor Yearbook of Cancer, 1972-88; assoc. editor Nat. Cancer Inst., PDQ, 1984—; mem. editl. bd. The Female Patient, 1989—, Oncology Reports, 1993—; author: Ovarian Malignancies: Clinical Care of Adults and Adolescents, 1983, Gilda's Disease: Sharing Personal Experiences and a Medical Perspective on Ovarian Cancer, 1996, Myths and Facts About Ovarian Cancer, 1997; editor: Ovarian Malignancies: Diagnostic and Therapeutic Advances, 1987, Manual of Gynecologic Oncology/Gynecology, 1989, Conversations About Cancer, 1990, Handbook of Gynecologic Oncology, 1995; contbr. more than 300 articles to profl. jours. Bd. dirs. United Way Buffalo Erie County, 1986-91; chmn. bd. trustees D'Youville Coll., Buffalo, 1989—; pres. Friends Night People, Buffalo, 1988-97. Capt. USAF, 1962-64. Hon. fellow Phi Beta Kappa, Gettysburg Coll., 1956, Tex. Assn. Obstetricians Gynecologists, 1983, Alpha Omega Alpha, Temple U. Sch. Medicine, 1995; named Citizen Yr., Buffalo News, 1989; recipient YMCA Leadership award Buffalo YMCA, 1990, Brotherhood/Sisterhood Award Medicine (Western NY Region), NCCJ, 1991, St. Marguerite D'Youville Coll. Cmty. Svc. award, 1992. Fellow ACS, Am. Coll. Obstetricians and Gynecologists; mem. Am. Soc. Clin. Oncology, Soc. Gynecologic Oncologists, Soc. Surg. Oncology, Am. Radium Soc., Phi Beta Kappa, Alpha Omega Alpha. Achievements include documentation of hydroxyurea as a radiation sensitizer in cervix cancer that significantly improves cure rate and that ovarian cancer can be inherited; patent for method of enhancing the efficacy of anti-tumor agents. Home: 315 Lincoln Pky Buffalo NY 14216-3127 Office: Sisters Hosp 2157 Main St Buffalo NY 14214-2692 Business E-Mail: mpiver@chsbuffalo.org.

PIZZA, COSIMO, chemist, researcher, nutritionist; s. Paolo Pizza and Carmela Nigro; m. Sonia Piacente, Sept. 26, 1998; life ptnr. Elisa Gionti (div.); children: Irene, Chiara, Alessandra, Silvia, Paolo. Laurea in Farmacia, U. Naples, Italy, 1972. Assoc. prof. U. Naples Federico II, 1985—94; prof. U. Messina, Messina, Italy, 1994—96, U. Salerno, Fisciano, Salerno, Italy, 1996—. Dir. Dept. Pharm. Scis., Fisciano, 2000—06; vice dean Faculty Pharmacy U. Salerno, Fisciano, 2006—. Master: Italian Soc. Phyto-Chemical (pres. 2005—). Achievements include research in chemistry and biological activity of medicinal and food plants. Home: Via XXIV Maggio 3 Eboli (SA) Salerno 84025 Italy Office: Dipartimento di Scienze Farmaceutiche Via Ponte Don Melillo 84084 Fisciano Salerno Italy Office Fax: 39 089969602. Business E-Mail: pizza@unisa.it.

PIZZI, ANTONIO, chemist; b. Rome, May 15, 1946; s. Dino and Luisa Sara (Folena) P.; m. Nellie Edith Napier, Feb. 24, 1973; children: Romain, Michelle, Alexis, Dominique. D of Chemistry, U. Rome, 1969; PhD Chemistry, U. of the Orange Free State, S. Africa, 1978; DSc, U. Stellenbosch, S. Africa, 1985. Rschr. Sentrachem, Johannesburg, 1970; works chemist Pretoria Portland Cement, Port Elizabeth, South Africa, 1970-71; rschr. Novoboard, Port Elizabeth, 1971-76; dir. Nat. Timber Rsch. Inst., Pretoria, South Africa, 1977-89; prof., chmn. polymer chemistry U. Witwatersrand, Johannesburg, S. Africa, 1989-95; prof., chmn. indsl. wood chemistry Enstib U. de Nancy, Epinal, France, 1994—; exterior prof. U. Laval, Que., Canada, 2008—. Vis. prof. Tsukuba U., Japan, 1997, Nanjing Forestry U., 1995, U. Florence, Italy, 1998, 99; Scuola Normale di Pisa, Italy, 2000; dir., tech. Burmah Adhesives and Sealants, Johannesburg, 1983-84; assessor FAIR programme European Commn., Brussels, 1997, chmn., COST action on Adhesives European Commn., Brussels, 1999, 2000, 2001, 2002. Editor, author: Wood Adhesives, Vol. 1, 1983, Vol. 2, 1989, Handbook of Adhesive Technology, 1994, 2d edit., 2003, Adhesion Promotion Techniques for Advanced Materials, 1999; author: Advanced Wood Adhesives Technology, 1994; mem. editl. bd. profl. and sci. jours.; contbr. articles to profl. jours. Decorated chevalier Palmes Academiques; recipient Bark award Forest Products Soc., Boston, 1980, Markwardt Woodbright award, Orlando, 1985, Sci. Achievement award Internat. Union For Rsch. Orgns., Montreal, Can., 1990, finalist Rene Descartes prize European Commn., Brussels, 2000 05; named Millennium Acad. lectr., U.S., 2000, Schweighofer prize for Innovation in Wood Sci., Vienna, Austria, 2005, Swiss Tech. Innovation award, Baden, Switzerland, 2006. Mem. Internat. Acad. Wood Sci. (sec. 1992-95, acad. lectr. 2000; Josef Umdasch Rsch. prize, Vienna, 2008). Office: Enstib U de Nancy 1 27 Rue Philippe Seguin Epinal 88000 France Office Phone: +33-329-29-6117. Business E-Mail: antonio.pizzi@enstib.uhp-nancy.fr.

PIZZI, ROMAIN, veterinarian, consultant; b. Port Elizabeth, South Africa, Nov. 5, 1974; s. Antonio Pizzi and Nellie Napier. B in Vet. Medicine, U. Pretoria, 1999; MSc in Wild Animal Health, U. London, 2000. Diplomate in Zoological Medicine Royal Coll. of Vet. Surgeons, 2005, cert. in Small Animal Surgery Australian Coll. of Vet. Scientists, 2005, recognized specialist Royal Coll. Vet. Surgeons, 2006. Vet. surgeon Mere Vet. Surgery, Blackpool, England, 2000—02; vet. rschr. Bombay Natural History Soc. and Inst. of Zoology, Pinjore, India, 2002—03; sr. clin. scholar Edinburgh U. and Royal Zool. Soc. of Scotland, 2003—05; head of vet. pathology Zool. Soc. of London, London Zoo, 2005—06; dir. Zool. Medicine Ltd., Roslin, Scotland, 2006—; specialist vet. surgeon Inglis Vet. Ctr., Dunfermline, Scotland, 2006—10, Royal Zool. Soc. Scotland, Edinburgh Zoo, 2009—. Cons. clin. pathologist Nationwide Lab., Poulton, Lancashire, 2001—06, Greendale Vet. Laboratories, Woking, Surrey, 2005—07; presenter Creature Clinic, BBC, 2006; presenter Vet on the Loose Discovery's Animal Planet TV Channel. Contbr. articles to profl. jours., chapters to books. Fellow: Royal Entomol. Soc.; mem.: Brit. Vet. Zool. Soc. (BVZS) (mem.governing coun. 2004—08, public relations officer). Roman Catholic. Achievements include research in penguin diseases; invertebrate conservation medicine, wildlife pathology; wildlife and zoo animal medicine and surgery; exotic animal surgery; comparative endoscopic surgery; zoo animal surgery; rabbit surgery. Avocations: double-bass, Karate (black belt), tango. Office: Zoo Medicine Ltd Pitcorthie Sch House Aberdour Rd Dunfermline KY11 4QY Scotland Business E-Mail: romain@zoologicalmedicine.org.

PIZZO, PHILIP A., dean, pediatrician, educator; b. NYC, Dec. 6, 1944; BA, Fordham U., 1966; MD, U. Rochester, 1970. Diplomate Am. Bd. Pediat., Am. Bd. Hematology/Oncology. Intern Children's Hosp. Med. Ctr., Boston, 1970-71, jr. asst. resident, 1971-72, sr resident, 1972-73; clin. assoc. Pediatric Oncology Br. of Nat. Cancer Inst., 1973-75, investigator, 1975-76, sr. investigator, 1976-80; head infectious disease sect. Pediatric Br. of Nat. Cancer Inst., 1980-96, chief pediat., 1982-96; sci. dir. divsn. clin. scis. Nat. Cancer Inst., 1994-96, prof. pediat. Sch. Medicine, Uniformed Svcs. U. Health Sci., 1987-96, Thomas Morgan Rotch prof., chmn. dept. pediat. Harvard U. Sch. Medicine, Boston, 1996—2001; dean Stanford U. Sch. Medicine, 2001—. Bd. dirs. Elizabeth Glaser Pediatric AIDS Found., 1996—2006, vice chmn. bd. dirs., 2002—06; bd. dirs. Calif. Health Care Institutes, 2003, Found. for NIH, 2003—; bd. trustees U. Rochester, 2009—; bd. govs. Koc U., Turkey, 2010—. Fellow: Infectious Disease Soc. America (publications com. 1987—90, mem. com. on Aids 1988—94, counselor, bd. dirs. 1996—99); mem.: American Assn. Med. Colleges (adminstrv. bd., coun. deans 2004, exec. com. 2006—08, chmn.-elect, coun. deans 2009, bd. dirs. 2009), Assn. Academic Health Centers (bd. dirs. 2006—, chmn.-elect bd. dirs. 2008—09, chmn. bd. dirs. 2009—), Inst. Medicine of Nat. Acad. Sciences (mem. health sci. policy bd. 1999—2002, chmn. health sci. policy bd. 2002—05, coun. mem. 2006—), Internat. Immunocompromised Host Soc. (program com. 1983—84, 1985—86, v.p. 1994—96, pres.-elect 1996—98, pres. 1998—2000), American Soc. Clin. Oncology (program com. 1983—84, membership com. 1984—88, edn. com. 1986—, local arrangement com. 1990—, awards com. 1992—95, chmn. nomination com. 1992—95, bd. dirs. 1996—99). Office: Stanford U Sch Med 300 Pasteur Dr, Ste M121 Palo Alto CA 94305 also: 730 Welch Rd Palo Alto CA 94304 Office Phone: 650-724-5688. Office Fax: 650-725-8040. E-mail: philip.pizzo@stanford.edu. *

PIZZO, SALVATORE VINCENT, pathologist; b. Phila., June 22, 1944; s. George J. Pizzo and Aida (Alcaro) Lepore; m. Carol Ann Kurkowski, Dec. 28, 1968 (dec. 2009); children: Steven, David, Susan. PhD, Duke U., 1972; BS, St. Joseph's Coll., 1966; MD, Duke U., 1973. Asst. prof. Duke U. Med. Ctr., Durham, NC, 1976-80, assoc. prof., 1980-85, prof., 1985—, disting. prof. pathology, 2006—, dir. med. scientist tng. program, 1987—2007, chmn., 1991—. Mem., chmn. program rev. com. NIH, Bethesda, Md., 1986-90; vice chmn. Gordon Conf. Proteases, Holderness, N.H., 1990, chmn., 1992-96; cons. in field, 1980—; mem. Cellular and Molecular Basis of Disease Rev. Com., 1990-96. Contbr. articles to profl. jours. Grantee NIH, 1976—, Am. Cancer Soc., 1976—; Disting. Faculty award, Duke U., 2004, Dean's award for excellence in mentoring, 2004; named one of the top 150 cited authors for jours. in the life sciences. Fellow AAAS; mem. Am. Heart Assn. (exec. com. Thrombosis coun. 1990, 92), Am. Chem. Soc., Am. Assn. Pathologists (program com. 1985-88, long range planning com. 1990-92), Am. Soc. Biological Chemists, Alpha Sigma Nu, Phi Beta Kappa, Alpha Omega Alpha, Sigma Xi. Achievements include patents in field; research in lipoproteins in coagulation and fibronolysis, a link to atherosclerosis, anticoagulation drug development; identification of ATP synthase as the target for Angiostatin action. Office: Duke U Med Ctr PO Box 3712 Durham NC 27710-0001 Office Phone: 919-684-3528, 919-421-3058. Business E-Mail: pizzo001@mc.duke.edu.

PIZZOLI, ANDREA LUDOVICO, orthopedist; b. Verona, Oct. 2, 1969; Degree in Medicine, Verona U., 1994, degree in Orthops. and Traumatology, 1999. Trauma surgeon Pub. Hosp. Mantua, 1999—. Master: Italian Soc. Orthop. and Traumatology. Avocations: stamp collecting/philately, bicycling. Home: Via Rovereto Verona Veneto 37100 Italy Home Fax: 390376201059. Personal E-mail: andreapizzoli@hotmail.com.

PIZZOLITTO, STEFANO, pathologist; b. Udine, Italy, July 30, 1954; s. Vittorino and Liliana (Cossio) P.; m. Gloria Allegretto, Sept. 6, 1986; children: Marco, Francesca. Degree in medicine and surgery, U. Trieste, 1979. Asst. pathologist Pordenone Hosp., Italy, 1980—83, Udine Hosp., Italy, 1983—88, sr. pathologist, 1991, sr. pathologist, cons., 1991—. Cons. pathologist Hosp., San Vito Al Tagliamento, Italy, 1983-2000; cons. forensic medicine Law-Ct., Udine, 1988—; head unit of electron microscopy dept. pathology U. Udine, 1994-99; chief dept. anatomic pathology Hosp. Santa Maria della Misericordia, Udine, 1999-. Co-author: Tumors of the Thyroid Gland, 1992, Physiopathology of the Cervical Plexus, 1995, Am. Jour. Pathology, Cancer, CID, Nephron; contbr. articles to profl. jours. Mem. Rotary (sec. 1991—, pres. 2000). Avocations: modern art, history medicine, skiing. Home: Via Strassoldo 25 33100 Udine Italy Office: Hosp Santa Maria della Misericordia Udine Dept Pathology 33100 Udine Italy Office Phone: 00390432552821. Business E-Mail: pizzolitto.stefano@aoud.sanita.fvg.it.

PIZZUTILLO, PETER D., surgeon; b. Camden, NJ, July 9, 1944; s. Costello W. and Ida Pizzutillo; m. Barbara Pizzutillo, June 13, 1981; children: Lara, Peter, Amy, Julie, Alex. BS, St. Joseph's Coll., 1966; MD, Jefferson Med. Coll., 1970. Diplomate Am. Bd. Orthop. Surgery. Intern Thomas Jefferson Univ. Hosp., 1970—71, resident in orthop. surgery, 1971—75; orthop. surgeon USAF, Lakenheath, England, 1975—78; attending surgeon Alfred I. DuPont Inst., Wilmington, Del., 1978—86; dir. pediat. orthop. Thomas Jefferson U., Phila., 1986—95, St. Christopher's Hosp. for Children, Phila., 1995—, bd. dirs., 2000—; prof. orthop. surgery and pediat. Drexel U. Coll. Medicine, Phila., 1995—. Editor: Pediatric Orthopaedics in Primary Care, 1997, Jour. Pediat. Orthop., 1995—; reviewer Jour. Bone and Joint Surgery, 1985—. Asst. scoutmaster Radnor Boys Scouts, Pa., 2002—. Maj. USAF, 1975—78. Fellow: Am. Acad. Orthop. Surgeons; mem.: Am. Orthop. Assn., Pediat. Orthop. Soc. N.Am. Roman Catholic. Avocations: reading, tennis, jogging, sailing. Office: St Christopher's Hosp for Children Front St at Erie Ave Philadelphia PA 19134 Home Phone: 610-667-2572; Office Phone: 215-427-3423, 215-427-3131, 215-427-3422. Personal E-mail: peter.pizzutillo@tenethealth.com.

PLAA, GABRIEL LEON, toxicologist, educator; b. San Francisco, May 15, 1930; arrived in Can., 1968; s. Jean and Lucienne (Chalopin) P.; m. Colleen Neva Brasefield, May 19, 1951; children: Ernest (dec.), Steven, Kenneth, Gregory, Andrew, John, Denise, David. BS, U. Calif., Berkeley, 1952; PhD, U. Calif., San Francisco, 1958. Diplomate Am. Bd. Toxicology. Asst. toxicologist City/County San Francisco, 1954-58; asst. prof. Sch. Medicine Tulane U., New Orleans, 1958-61; assoc. prof. U. Iowa, Iowa City, 1961-68; prof. U. Montreal, 1968-95, chmn. dept. pharmacology, 1968-80, vice-dean Faculty Medicine, 1982-89, dir. Interuniv. Ctr. Rsch. in Toxicology, 1991-95; ret., 1995; prof. emeritus, 1996. Dorothy Snider disting. lectr. U. Ark., 1995; chmn. Can. Coun. Animal Care, Ottawa, Ont., Can., 1985-86. Editor Toxicology and Applied Pharmacology, 1972-80; contbr. over 200 articles to profl. jours. 1st lt. U.S. Army, 1952-53, Korea. Recipient Thienes award Am. Acad. Clin. Toxicology, 1977, Founders' award Chem. Industry Inst. Toxicology, 1998, Excellence award PhRMA Found, 2001. Fellow Acad. Toxicol. Scis.; mem. Am. Soc. Pharmacology, Soc. Toxicology Can. (pres. 1981-83, Henderson award 1969, award of distinction 1994), Pharm. Soc. Can. (pres. 1973-74), Soc. Toxicology (pres. 1983-84, Achievement award 1967, Lehman award 1977, Edn. award 1987, Amb. award 1987, Merit award 1996). Roman Catholic. Home: 236 Meredith Ave Dorval PQ Canada H9S 2Y7 Office: U Montreal Dept Pharm PO Box 6128 Sta Centre-Ville Montreal PQ Canada H3C 3J7 Business E-Mail: plaag@magellan.umontreal.ca.

PLACIK, OTTO JOSEPH, plastic surgeon; b. June 26, 1962; BS in Medicine, Northwestern U., 1985, MD with distinction, 1987. Cert. Nat. Bd. Med. Examiners, 1988, diplomate Am. Bd. Plastic Surgery. Resident in gen. surgery Northwestern U., 1987—90, resident in plastic surgery, 1990—93; adj. staff Evanston Hosp. Corp., Glenview, Ill., 1991—92, 1994, locum tenens staff, 1995, attending staff, 1996—; fellow Shriners Hosp. for Crippled Children, 1992, consulting staff, 1995—; fellow in aesthetic reconstruction, surgical house officer St. Joseph Hosp., Chgo., 1993; fellow microvascular and hand surgery Davies Med. Ctr., U. Calif., San Francisco, 1994; non-voting attending staff Northwest Cmty. Hosp., Arlington Heights, Ill., 1995—; courtesy staff Meth. Hosp., Chgo., 1995—; plastic surgeon MD Aesthetics Skin Care Ctr., Arlington Heights, Ill., 1995—; courtesy staff Holy Family Hosp., Des Plaines, Ill., 1996—2003; asst. prof. clin. surgery Northwestern U., 1997—; vice chief Sect. Plastic Surgery, Northwest Cmty. Hosp., 1998, 1999, chief, 2000, 2001; consulting staff St. Elisabeth Hosp., Chgo., 1999—. ASPRS resident del. Coun. Med. Splty. Socs., 1993, mem. resident task force, 93; mem. interdisciplinary cancer com. Northwest Cmty. Hosp., 1995, mem. emergency care com., 98; mem. ISMIE Plastic Surgery Subcommittee, 2000; treas. plastic surgery edn. rsch. Northwestern U., 2002; mem. Enhance Ednl. Found. Scholarship Com., 2006—. Assoc. editor Chicago Health Mag., Chicago Image, 2003—. Named to Consumers' Guide to Top Doctors, 2002, 2005—07, America's Cosmetic Doctors and Dentists, 2003, The Best of the US, 2007. Mem.: Soc. Laparoendoscopic Surgeons, Am. Soc. Aesthetic Plastic Surgery, Am. Acad. Facial Plastic and Reconstructive Surgery, Lipoplasty Soc., Ill. State Med. Soc., AMA (Physician's Recognition award 1996—99), Chgo. Soc. Plastic Surgery, Midwest Assn. Plastic Surgeons, Alpha Omega Alpha (co-pres. 1986, Honor Med. Soc. 2005). Office: Assoc Plastic Surgeons SC MD Aesthetics Skin Care Ctr 880 W Central Rd Ste 3100 Arlington Heights IL 60005-2467 also: 680 N Lake Shore Dr Ste 830 Chicago IL 60611-2201 also: MD Aesthetics LLC 845 N Michigan Ave Ste 923E Chicago IL 60611 also: Northwestern U Montgomery Ward Meml Bldg 303 E Chicago Ave Evanston IL 60208 Office Phone: 847-398-1660, 312-787-5313, 312-335-2070. Office Fax: 847-398-1784. Business E-Mail: bodysculptor@asprsdial.org, o-placik@northwestern.edu.

PLANTE, IANIK, radiobiologist; s. Ludovic Plante and Michelle Lemay. BSc in Physics, U. Sherbrooke, Qué., Can., 1995, MD, 2002, MSc in Radiobiology, 2005, PhD in Radiobiology, 2009. Lectr. Dept. Physics, U. Sherbrooke, 2007; rsch. scientist NASA Johnson Space Ctr., Houston, 2007—. Mem.: Biophys. Soc., Radiation Rsch. Soc.

Achievements include development of space radiation simulation program RITRACKS. Office: NASA Johnson Space Ctr 2101 NASA Pky Mail Code SK Bldg 37 Houston TX 77058 Office Phone: 281-244-6426. Business E-Mail: ianik.plante-1@nasa.gov.

PLASSCHAERT, ALPHONS JOHANNES MARIE, dental educator, academic administrator, foundation administrator; b. Helmond, Netherlands, Jan. 3, 1942; s. Arthur Prudent and Francisca Alida (van Schijndel) P.; m. Pauline Louise van Lommel, June 4, 1966; children: Véronique, Alain, Sabine, Nicole. DDS, U. Utrecht, The Netherlands, 1966; PhD, U. Nijmegen, The Netherlands, 1972. Clin. instr. U. Nijmegen, 1967-69, sr. lectr., 1969-76, prof., chmn. dept. cariology, 1976—89, 1995—2004, dean Dental Sch., 1986-89, vice-chancellor, 1990-94; pres. Found. for Blind, Theofaan, The Netherlands, 1992-2000, Found. Edward Schillebeeckx, 1994—2002. Chmn. dental sect. Orgn. Cooperating Dutch Univs., Utrecht, 1986-89; pres. Justitia et Pax Commn., The Netherlands, 1999-2009. Author: Preventieve Maatregelen, 1972; editor: Ergonomie in de Tandheelkunde, 1981, Cariology and Endodontology, 1976-86, 1989; asst. editor Jour. Caries Rsch., 1983-89; pres. Found. Dutch Dental Jour., Amsterdam, 1987-2006; contbr. articles to profl. jours. Concertmaster Symphony Orch. Nijmegen, 1981—2007; leader Animato String Quartet, Nijmegen, 1981-93, Valkhof String Quartet, Nijmegen, 1993—. Fulbright scholar, 1984, 1994. Mem. Internat. Assn. Dental Rsch., Acad. Operative Dentistry (pres. European sect. 2000-02), Assn. Dental Edn. Europe (pres. 2003-05), Thijmgenootschap (v.p. 1999-2004, pres. 2004-09), Radboud U. & Acad. Hosp. Nijmegen (bd. gov. 2008-). Roman Catholic. Avocations: violin playing and making, tennis, running. Home: Witsenburgselaan 56 6524 TL Nijmegen Netherlands E-mail: plasschaert@hetnet.com.

PLASSMANN, JUERGEN, radiologist, educator; s. Juergen and Margret Plassmann; m. Margit Maier, June 13, 1992; children: Linus, Cilly Coco. MD, U. Witten/Herdecke, Germany, 1989. Asst. physician Muelheim (Germany) Radiol. Inst., 1989—91, sr. physician, cons., 1995—; asst. physician, lectr. U. Saarland, Homburg/Saar, Germany, 1992—94; sr. physician, cons. St. Marien Hosp., Muelheim, 1995—. Lectr. U. Witten/Herdecke, 1995—. Translator (co-author): Interventional Computed Tomogaphy. Mem.: German Radiol. Soc., Soc. Interventional Radiology, Assn. Interventional Outpatient Radiology, Cardiovasc. and Interventional Radiol. Soc. of Europe, Vascular Access Soc. Office: Muelheim Radiol Inst Schulstrasse 10 Northrhine-Westfalia Muelheim D-45468 Germany Office Fax: +49-208-992099. Business E-Mail: plassmann@mri.de.

PLATKOV, EFIM, research scientist; b. Minsk, Belarus, June 3, 1937; s. Michael Platkov and Liza Schneider; children: Marina, Valeria. MD, Med. Inst., Minsk, 1960, PhD, 1973; DSc, Inst. Immunology, Moscow, 1986. Prof. Hosp. Village, Radoshkovichy, Belarus, 1960—63; physician Mcpl. Hosp., Minsk, Belarus, 1963—80; head Dept. Allergic Diseases Regional Gen. Hosp., Minsk, 1980—85; asst. reader prof. Postgrad. Med. Inst., Minsk, 1985—91, prof., 1991; sr. sci., head Dept. Occupation Environment Health Sanz Med. Ctr. Laniado Hosp., Netanya, Israel, 1995—. Cons. Ctr. Occupation and Allergic Diseases, Minsk, 1985—91, Sanz Med. Ctr., Netanya, Israel, 2000—05. Author: (book) Differential Diagnosis of Asthma Forms; contbr. articles pub. to profl. jour. Mem.: Israel Pain Assn., Israel Soc. Occupl. Diseases, Israel Med. Assn. Avocation: travel. Home: Hasida 4/7 Hadera 38000 Israel Office: Sanz Med Ctr Laniado Kiryat Sanz Netanya Israel Business E-Mail: plat@laniado.org.il.

PLATSOUCAS, CHRIS DIMITRIOS, immunologist; b. Athens, Greece, Apr. 17, 1951; came to U.S., 1973; s. Dimitrios Evagelos and Maria (Tsonidis) P.; m. Emilia L. Oleszak, Oct. 18, 1985. BS, Patras U., Greece, 1973; postgrad., Purdue U., 1974; PhD, MIT, 1978. Rsch. fellow/assoc. Meml. Sloan-Kettering Cancer Ctr., NYC, 1978—81, asst. mem., 1982—85, asst. prof., 1981-85, head lab. biol. response modifiers, 1981-85; assoc. prof. dept. immunology M.D. Anderson Cancer Ctr., Houston, 1985-89, prof., dep. chmn., 1989-93, Ashbel Smith professorship, 1991-92, H.L. and O. Stringer professorship in cancer rsch., 1992-93; L.H. Carnell prof. dept. microbiology, immunology Temple U. Sch. Medicine, Phila., 1993—2007, chmn. dept. microbiology and immunology, 1993—2006; acting dean Coll. Sci. and Tech. Temple U., Phila., 1998-2000, dean Coll. Sci. and Tech., 2000—04, Old Dominion U., Norfolk, Va., 2007—; dean Coll. Sci.; dir. Ctr. Mol. Medicine; prof. Biol Sci. Biotech. cons., sci. reviewer study sects. NIH, Bethesda, Md., 1982—. Contbr. numerous articles to profl. jours. Nat. Rsch. Svc. award NIH, 1978-79; grantee NIH, Am. Cancer Soc., State of Tex., many others. Mem. Am. Assn. Immunologists, Am. Soc. Hematology, Am. Assn. Biochem & Molecular Biology, Soc. Investigative Pathology, Am. Assn. Cancer Rsch. Greek Orthodox. Achievements include patents in field; research on human T cell immunology, on T-cell antigen receptors, on tumor-infiltrating lymphocytes in malignant melanoma and ovarian carcinoma, on organ transplantation, on chronic rejection, on AIDS, on multiple sclerosis, schlerodema, osteoarthritis, and other autoimmune diseases. Office: Old Dominion Univ Office of Dean, Coll Sci 4600 Elkhorn Ave OCNPS Rm 143 Norfolk VA 23529 Office Phone: 757-683-3277. Business E-Mail: cplatsoucas@odu.edu, cplatsoucas@cox.edu.

PLATT, JEFFREY LOUIS, experimental surgeon, immunologist, pediatric nephrologist, educator; b. New Rochelle, NY, Mar. 21, 1949; s. Charles Alfred and Paula Platt. BA in Politics with honors, NYU, 1971; postgrad., Columbia U., 1971-73; MD, U. Southern Calif., 1977. Diplomate Am. Bd. Pediatrics, Nat. Bd. Med. Examiners. Pediatrics intern Children's Hosp. LA, 1977-78, resident, 1978-79, Della M. Mudd resident, 1979-80; med. fellow in pediatric nephrology U. Minn., Mpls., 1980-85, instr. dept. pediatrics, 1985-86, asst. prof., 1986-88, assoc. prof. pediatrics and cell biology and neuroanatomy, 1988-92; prof. surgery, pediatrics and immunology depts. Duke U., Durham, NC, 1992—98, Dorothy W. and Joseph W. Beard prof. exptl. surgery, 1994—98; prof. surgery immunology and pediatrics Mayo Clinic, Rochester, Minn., 1998—2008, dir. transplantation biology, 2006—08; prof. surgery U. Mich., 2008—, prof. microbiology and immunology, 2008—. Mem. editl. bd.: Transplantation, Transplant Immunology, Xenotransplantation, Jour. Immunology, Cellular Immunology; mem. editl. bd. Human Immunology, editor Innate Immunity; contbr. over 500 articles to med. jours.; author: 4 books. Recipient Clinician-Scientist award Am. Heart Assn., 1983-88, Established Investigator award Am. Heart Assn., 1988-93, Inst. Medicine of NAS. Mem. AAAS, NIH (Merit award), Assn. Am. Physicians, Fellow Am. Heart Assn (coun. kidney in cardiovasc. disease, coun. basic sci.), Internat. Soc. Nephrology, Am. Assn. Immunologists, Am. Fedn. Clin. Rsch., Am. Soc. Nephrology, Am. Assn. Pathologists, Soc. for Devel. Biology, Clin. Immunology Soc., Soc. Pediatric Rsch., Soc. Glycobiology, Soc. Exptl. Biology and Medicine, Alpha Omega Alpha. Office: Dept Surgery Univ Mich Biomedical Sciences Res Bldg 109 Zina Pitcher Pl Ann Arbor MI 48109 Office Phone: 734-615-6819. Business E-Mail: plattjl@umich.edu.

PLATTS, ALZINETE (ALZI) DE OLIVEIRA, dentist, translator; b. João Pessoa, Paraíba, Brazil, May 18, 1947; d. Antonino Cavalcanti and Elizete Ferreira de Oliveira; m. James Edward Platts, June 4, 1975; children: Jeffrey, Derek. DDS, Fed. U. Paraíba, João Pessoa, Brazil, 1966—69, cert. English Studies, 1967—68, cert. German Studies, 1968—69. Dentist pvt. practice, João Pessoa, Campina Grande, Paraíba, Brazil, 1970—71, Rural Worker Social Security and Welfare Fund, Alagoa Nova, Paraíba, Brazil, 1971—74, Nat. Inst. Social Security Industry Social Svcs., Campina Grande, Paraíba, Brazil, 1971—74; founder, translator, editor Sci-Tech Translations, East Hartford, Conn., 1985—; project mgr. US Human Health Divsn. Merck and Co. Inc., Rahway, NJ, 1988—94, translator and editor English, Spanish, Portuguese, 1988—94; translator U.S. Govt. Joint Publications Rsch. Svcs., Reston, Va., 1988—93; translator, interpreter, transcriptionist INS, Hartford, Conn., 1988—90; med. translator, healthcare divsn. US Congl. Office Tech. Assessment, Washington, 1992; founder, translator, editor MD Translations, Hartford, Conn., 2003—. Freelance journalist: Brazilian Times, Boston USA; translator: Drug Labeling in Developing Countries, 1993. Dentist Rondon Project (Brazilian Peace Corps.), Porto Murtinho Mato Grosso do Sul, Brazil, 1968—69, João Pessoa, Paraíba, 1968—69; event prodr., promoter Brazilian arts and culture cmty. events Ganza Entertainment, Hartford, 1997—; mem. Alumni Assn. Superior War Coll., João Pessoa, Paraíba, Brazil, 1970—74. Recipient Cert. Distinction as Portuguese Translator, US Joint Publications Rsch. Svcs., 1990. Mem.: World Assn. Med. Editors (assoc.), Am. Med. Writers Assn. (assoc.), Am. Assn. Dental Editors (assoc.), Am. Translators Assn. (assoc.; founding mem. Portuguese Lang. Divsn.). Avocations: Brazilian music, dance, jazz, yoga, travel. Office: MD Translations 1 Gold St 20G Hartford CT 06103 E-mail: info@mdtranslations.com.

PLATTS-MILLS, THOMAS ALEXANDER EVELYN, immunologist, educator, researcher; b. Colchester, Essex, Eng., Nov. 22, 1941; arrived in US, 1982; s. John Faithful and Janet Katherine (Cree) Platts-Mills; m. Roberta Rosenstock, Apr. 9, 1970; children: Eliza, Timothy, James, Oliver. BA in Animal Physiology, Balliol Coll., Eng., 1963; PhD, London U., 1982. Fellow in medicine Johns Hopkins U., Balt., 1971-74; staff mem. Med. Rsch. Coun., England, 1975—79; hon. cons. physician Northwick Park Hosp., London, 1978-82; Oscar Swineford, Jr. prof. medicine & microbiology, head divsn. allergy & immunology U. Va., Charlottesville, 1982—, dir. Asthma & Allergic Diseases Ctr., 1993—. Mem. immunological scis. study sect. NIH, 1988—92. Mem. editl. bd. Am. Jour. Respiratory Critical Care Medicine, Clin. & Exptl. Immunology, Clin. Allergy, Jour. Immunological Methods; contbr. articles to profl. jours. Fellow: Royal Soc. London, Royal Coll. Physicians; mem.: Southeastern Allergy Assn. (pres. 1987—88, Hal Davidson award 1986), Brit. Soc. Allergy & Clin. Immunology, Am. Acad. Allergy, Asthma & Immunology (v.p. 2004—05, pres.-elect 2005—06, pres. 2006—07), Assn. Am. Physicians. Office: U Va Med Sch PO Box 801335 Charlottesville VA 22908-0225 Office Phone: 434-924-2209. Office Fax: 434-924-5779. E-mail: tap2z@virginia.edu.

PLAUCHE, NANCY CAROLINE, retired counselor; b. Lima, Ohio, Oct. 31, 1938; d. Willis Sylvanis and Mabel Louise (Neiswander) Siferd; m. Jack Plauche (div. 1979); children: Michel, Jacqueline, Jon. BFA, Ohio U., 1960; MS, Nova U., Ft. Lauderdale, Fla., 1984; PhD, The Union Inst., Cin., 1989. Counselor Pinellas county Schs., St. Petersburg, Fla., 1980—2002; smoke stopper's instr. Nat. Ctr. for Health Promotion/Morton Plant Hosp., Clearwater, Fla., 1986-92; ret., 2002. Co-dir. Counseling & Profl. Cons. Svcs., St. Petersburg, 1984-88. Co-author: All About Me, 1985, Safer Parenting, 1985; contbr. articles to profl. jours. Mem. Dem. Exec. Com., Wood City W.Va., 1977-79; sustainor Jr. League St. Petersburg. Mem. APA, So. Assn. Coll. Counselors, Am. Psychol. Soc., Am. Arbitration Assn., People to People Internat., Fla. Counseling Assn., Fla. Sch. Counselors Assn., Clearwater Area Panhellenic Assn. Democrat. Avocations: painting, drawing, travel, cultural exchange.

PLAVSIC, BRANKO MILENKO, radiologist, educator; b. Zagreb, Yugoslavia, Croatia, Feb. 14, 1947; came to U.S., 1989; s. Milenko and Nevenka P. MD, U. Zagreb, 1972, MS, 1974, PhD, 1975. Asst. prof. U. Zagreb, 1986, prof. radiology, chief abdominal radiology, 1988; prof. radiology, vice-chmn., dir. abdominal radiol./rsch. Tulane U., New Orleans, 1991—2006; dir. abdominal radiology and rsch. dept. radiology Health Scis. Ctr. Tex. Tech U., El Paso, 2006—. Co-author: (with A.E. Robinson, R.B. Jeffrey) Gastrointestinal Radiology: A Concise Text, 1992; contbr. articles to profl. jours. Avocations: poetry, music. Office: Tex Tech U Health Scis Ctr Dept Radiology El Paso TX 79905

PLESKOW, DOUGLAS, medical educator, director; b. Buffalo, Nov. 12, 1956; BA, U. Rochester, 1978; MD, U. Buffalo, 1982. Assoc. clin. prof., medicine, co-dir., endoscopy Harvard Med. Sch. Beth Israel Deaconess Med. Ctr., 1987—. Named Man of Yr., Nat. Pancreas Found. Fellow: Am. Soc. Gastrointestinal Endoscopy, Am. Gastroenterology Assn.; mem.: Am. Coll. Gastroenterology. Office: 110 Francis St Boston MA 02215 Business E-Mail: dpleskow@bidmc.harvard.edu.

PLESNICAR, STOJAN JOSIP, oncologist, educator, consultant; b. Gorica, Feb. 5, 1925; arrived in Slovenia, 1934; s. Josip and Luisa (Martelanc) P.; m. Ljudmila Mila Gec, 1956 (div. 1988); children: Andrew, Tadeusz. MD, U. Ljubljana, Slovenia, 1954. Intern Gen. Hosp., Koper, 1955-57; resident The Inst. Oncology, Ljubljana, 1958-63; asst. prof. The Faculty of Medicine, Ljubljana, 1964-72; rsch. fellow Karolinska Sjukhuset, Stockholm, 1973—96; prof. oncology U. Ljubljana, 1976—, chmn., chair oncology, 1982—96, head dept. tumor biology, 1986-95; lectr. European Sch. Oncology, Milan, 1985—93; prof. emeritus Polytechnic, Nova Gorica, Slovenia, 2005—. Vis. prof. U. Nebr. Med. Sch., Omaha, 1981, 82; dir. The Inst. of Oncology, Ljubljana, 1982-86; lectr. Sch. Environ. Scis., Nova Gorica, Slovenia, 1997-, mem. Senate, U. Politecnic, Nova Gorica, Slovenia; mem. Acad. Coun., chair oncology and radiotherapy Faculty of Medicine, U. Maribor, Slovenia. Author: Cancer--A Preventable Disease, 1990 (honorable mention, 1994); co-founder, editor-in-chief, mem. editl. bd.: Radiology and Oncology, 1990 (recognition of merits Federative Cancer Soc., 1990); editor: ESO Challenge newsletter; mem. editl. bd.: Cancer Letters, Seminars in Oncology, Oncology, Archiw fuer Geschwulstforschung, Libri Oncologici, Zdravstveni Vestnik, Croatian Med. Jour., Cahiers de Cancerologie, guest editor: Seminars in Oncology, 2001. Mem. The Djerba Group, 1995. Recipient Golden medal Slovenian Cancer Soc., 1992. Mem. Am. Assn. for Cancer Rsch., N.Y. Acad. Scis., Cancer Rsch. Found. (co-founder 1993), Acad. Assn. for Third U. in Slovenia (pres.), Lion's Club Ljubljana (gov. 1998-99). Avocation: history. Home: Tesarska St No 6 1000 Ljubljana Slovenia E-mail: stojan.plesnicar@mf.uni-lj.si.

PLESS, HEDWIGA See SCHWARTZ, HEDWIGA

PLESS, JORGEN EMIL, plastic surgery consultant; b. Apr. 13, 1934; s. Villy Emanuel and Gerda Frederikke (Bork) P.; m. Eva Festersen, May 21, 1961; children: Thomas, Torsten. MD, Copenhagen U., 1960; DDS, Copenhagen Dental Sch., 1969. Intern Sundby Hosp., 1960-61, Odense U. Hosp., Denmark, 1961, Svendborg Hosp., 1961-62, resident, 1963, asst. registrar surg. dept., 1962-65; registrar Rigshospitalet Copenhagen, 1965-67; sr. registrar Finsen Inst., Copenhagen, 1969-73, Odense U. Hosp., 1973-76, cons. plastic surgery dept., 1976-98, vice-chmn. med. com., 1982-85, chmn. med. com., 1985-89; com. mem. Inst. Exptl. Surgery, Copenhagen, 1970-73; chmn. med. adv. ethics com. Mermaid Clinic Ebeltoft, 1989-95; founder, chmn. TVT Svendborg, 2004. Ednl. insp. Danish Nat. Bd. Health, 1996—2000; comml. mentor, 2002—04. Contbr. articles to profl. jours. Councillor Coun. Fyn, Denmark, 2001—04, Region So. Denmark, 2005—, mem. vision healthcare policies com., 2009, mem. com. hosp. structure, 2009—; coun. mem. City of Svendburg, 2005—10; founder, vice-chmn. Ind. Citizens Party Funen, Svendborg, 1999—. Mem. Danish Soc. Plastic Reconstructive Surgery (pres. 1986-89), Danish Orgn. Plastic Surgery (chmn. 1994-98), Danish Soc. Head Neck Oncology (sec. 1974-85), Danish Soc. Microsurgery (founder, pres. 1974-78), Scandinavian Assn. Plastic Surgeons (pres. 1986-88), Rotary (Paul Harris fellow 1988). Home and Office: Liljevej 4 DK5700 Svendborg Denmark Office Phone: 004570721186. Personal E-mail: jorgen.pless@tegronsyddanmark.dk, jorgenpless@gmail.com.

PLESTINA-BORJAN, IVNA, ophthalmologist, surgeon; m. Zarko Borjan, July 27, 1985; 1 child, Ivan Borjan. MD, U. Zagreb, 1982, degree in Ophthalmology, 1989, MS in Ophthalmology, 1995. Lic. in ophthalmology U. Zagreb, 1989, cert. in PHACO surgery Winteracademy, Schruns, Austria, 2001. Gen. practioner Health Ctr. Split, Split, 1982—85; resident in ophthalmology Clinic for Eye Diseases, Faculty Medicine, U. Zagreb, 1985—89, ophthalmologist, surgeon, 1989—91; ophthalmologist, vitreoretinal and cataract surgeon Clin. Hosp. Split, 1991—. Lectr. ultrasonography in ophthalmology Faculty Medicine, U. Split, 2005—. Contbr. chapters to books, numerous scientific papers in field of ophthalmology. Named one of Best Posters, Hellen Keller Found., 2006. Mem.: European Soc. Contactology, Cath. Assn. Croatian Physicians (assoc.), Assn. Vitreoretinal Surgeons (assoc.), European Soc. Cataract and Refractive Surgery (assoc.), Croatian Soc. Ophthalmology (assoc.). Roman Catholic. Avocations: travel, reading, skiing, swimming. Home: Zgon 14 Solin 21210 Croatia Office: Clin Hosp Split Spinciceva 2 Split 21000 Croatia Office Phone: 00385 21 556402. Office Fax: 00385 21 556407. Business E-Mail: iplestina@krizine.kbsplit.hr.

PLETSCH, MARIE ELEANOR, plastic surgeon; b. Walkerton, Ont., Can., May 3, 1938; came to U.S. 1962; d. Ernest John and Olive Wilhemina (Hossfeld) P.; m. Ludwig Philip Breiling, Aug. 25, 1967; children: John, Michael, Anne. MD, U. Toronto, 1962. Diplomate Am. Bd. Plastic Surgery. Intern Cook County Hosp., Chgo., 1962-63, resident, gen. surgery, 1963-64, St. Mary's Hosp., San Francisco, 1964-66; resident in plastic surgery St. Francis Hosp., San Francisco, 1966-69; practice med. specializing in plastic surgery Santa Cruz, Calif., 1969—; Monterey, Calif., 1990—; adminstr. Plasticenter, Inc., Santa Cruz, 1976-88, med. dir., 1987-88. Mem. AMA, Am. Soc. Plastic and Reconstructive Surgeons, Calif. Soc. Plastic Surgeons (mem. coun. 1986-89, sec. 1989-93, v.p. 1994-95, pres. elect 1995-96, pres. 1996-97), Am. Soc. Aesthetic Plastic Surgeons, Calif. Med. Assn., Assn. Calif. Surgery Ctrs. (pres. 1988-92), Santa Cruz County Med. Soc. (bd. govs. 1983-88, 1992-94), Santa Cruz Surgery Ctr. (bd. dirs. 1988-93, 2004—). Roman Catholic.: 24571 Silver Cloud Ct Monterey CA 93940 Office: Santa Cruz Can Am Medical 223A Mount Hermon Rd Scotts Valley CA 95066- Office Phone: 831-462-1000. Personal E-mail: drpletsch@sbcglobal.net.

PLEVA, JESSICA CARMEN, psychologist; b. Hamburg, Germany, July 20, 1979; BS in Psychology, Flinders U., South Australia, 2001, PhD in Clin. Psychology, 2006. Registered psychologist South Australian Psychol. Bd., 2006, cert. MAPS Australian Psychol. Soc., 2006, clin psychologist Australian Psychol. Soc., Coll. Clin. Psychologists, 2007. Contbr. articles to psychol. jours. Recipient medal, Flinders U., 2001. Mem.: Psychologists Assn. (South Australian Br.), Australian Assn. Cognitive Behavioural Therapy, Australian Psychol. Soc. (Psychology prize 2001). Office: Anxiety Disorders & Trauma Clinic 83 Currie St Adelaide South Australia 5000 Australia

PLIAKOS, IOANNIS, surgeon; b. Thessaloniki, Greece, Nov. 28, 1973; MD, 1999. Physician AHEPA U. Hosp., 2009—. Office: St Kyriakidi 1 Thessaloniki 54645 Greece Personal E-mail: plliakos@hotmail.com.

PLIANBANGCHANG, SAMLEE, international organization official; b. Samutprakarn, Thailand, June 6, 1940; s. Boonta and Boonreon Plianbangchang; m. Duangratana Intakanok, Aug. 7, 1970; children: Pinyupa, Kraitos. MD, U. Med. Scis., Bangkok, 1965; MPH, Tulane U., New Orleans, 1970, DPH, 1972; cert. in comprehensive health planning, Johns Hopkins U., Balt., 1972; DPH (hon.), Mahidol U., Bangkok, 2004, Chulalongkorn U., 2007. Cert. in internat. pub. health American Bd. Preventive Medicine, in preventive & social medicine Thai Med. Coun. Med. officer Ministry Pub. Health, Bangkok, 1965-74, dir. tech. divsn., Dept. Med. Svcs., 1974-81, dir. Office Nat. Adv. Bd. Disease Prevention & Control, 1981-84; cons. WHO, New Delhi, 1984-85, regional planning officer, 1985-94, dir. prevention & control diseases, 1994—96, dep. regional dir., dir. programme mgmt., 1996—2000, regional dir. South East Asia, 2004—; sr. specialist pub. health Chulalongkorn U., 2000—01, dean Coll. Pub. Health, 2001—04. Fellow: APHA, American Coll. Preventive Medicine; mem.: Thai Health Assn., Thai Med. Coun., Delta Omega. Buddhist. Avocations: reading, gardening, boating, driving, fishing. Office: WHO Regional Office South East Asia World Health House Indraprastha Estate Mahatama Gandhi Marg New Delhi 110002 India Home Phone: 662-2391-1547; Office Phone: 91-11-2334-0804. Business E-Mail: samleep@neayo.who.int. *

PLICHT, BJÖRN, cardiologist, researcher; b. Oberhausen, North Rhine Westphalia, Germany, Oct. 30, 1976; s. Horst-Günter and Barbara Plicht. Degree, Med. Sch., U. Essen, Germany, 2003. Cert. A Levels Exam. Freiherr-vom-Stein-Gymnasium, Oberhausen, Germany, 1996. Attending West-German Heart Ctr., Cardiology Clinic, U. Essen, 2004—. Alternative civilian svc. in geriatric care Elly-Heuss-Knapp-Stiftung, Oberhausen, Germany, 1996—97. Rsch. grant, IFORES, Duisburg-Essen Med. Sch., 2001, Travel grant European Assn. Echocardiography and IEEE, 2006. Mem.: Paul-Ehrlich Soc., Paul-Ehrlich-Gesellschaft für Chemotherapie, Internat. Soc. Cardiovasc. Infectious Diseases, European Assn. Echocardiography (corr.), German Soc. Cardiology (corr.), European Soc. Cardiology (corr.). Office: West German Heart Ctr Hufelandstrasse 55 Essen NRW 45122 Germany Business E-Mail: bjoern.plicht@uk-essen.de.

PLIMACK, ELIZABETH R., oncologist; MD, NYU Sch. Medicine, 2002; MS in Patient Based Biologic Rsch., U. Tex. Grad. Sch. Biomedical Sci., 2008. Cert. Am. Bd. Internal Medicine. Intern & resident NYU Med. Ctr.; fellow in med. oncology U. Tex. MD Anderson Cancer Ctr.; attending physician dept. medical oncology Fox Chase Cancer Ctr. Mem.: Am. Soc. Clinical Oncology, Am. Assn. for Cancer Rsch. Office: Fox Chase Cancer Center 333 Cottman Ave Philadelphia PA 19111-2497 Office Phone: 215-728-2570.

PLON, SHARON E., clinical geneticist, educator; BS, MIT, 1980; MD, Harvard Med. Sch., 1987; PhD, Harvard U., 1987. Cert. Am. Bd. Med. Genetics, 2006. Resident internal medicine Univ. Wash., 1987—88; fellow molecular genetics Nat. Cancer Inst., 1988—90; fellow med. genetics Fred Hutchinson Cancer Rsch. Ctr., 1990—93; assoc. prof. pediat. and molecular and human genetics Baylor Coll.; chief cancer genetics clinic Tex. Children's Hospital. Mem.: Am. Coll. Med. Genetics, Am. Soc. Human Genetics. Office: Texas Children's Hospital Clinical Care Center 6701 Fannin St 14th Fl Houston TX 77030 Office Phone: 832 822-3334. Office Fax: 832-825-4276.

PLOTKIN, STANLEY ALAN, virologist; b. NYC, May 12, 1932; s. Joseph and Lee (Fishbein) P.; m. Susan Lannon, Nov. 24, 1979; children: Michael, Alec. BA, NYU, 1952; MD, SUNY, NYC, 1956; MA (hon.), U. Pa., 1974; D (hon.), U. Rouen, 2006, Complutense U. Madrid, 2009. Diplomate Am. Bd. Pediat., Am. Acad. Pediat. Intern Cleve. Met. Gen. Hosp., 1956-57; resident pediat. Phila. Children's Hosp., 1961—62, dir. divsn. infectious diseases, sr. physician, 1969—90; registrar Hosp. for Sick Children, London, 1962-63; assoc. mem. Wistar Inst., Phila., 1963-74, prof. virology, 1974—; asst. prof. pediat. U. Pa., Phila., 1966-71, assoc. prof., 1971-74, prof., 1974-91; prof. emeritus, 1991—, assoc. chmn. dept. pediat. U. Pa., Phila., 1986-88; med. and sci. dir. Pasteur-Mérieux-Connaught Labs. (now Sanofi-Pasteur), Marnes-la-Coquette, France, 1991-97; advisor to pres. Sanofi Pasteur, Swiftwater, Pa., 1997—2009. Adj. prof. internat. health Johns Hopkins U., Balt., 2000—; lectr. Pediat. Acad. Soc. DNA Vaccine Soc. Advanced Vaccinology Course; chair Pediat. Infections Diseases Children Hosp. Phila. Assoc. editor: Am. Jour. Epidemiology, 1967-87, Proc. Soc. Exptl. Biology and Medicine, 1968-85, Pediatric Infectious Disease jour., 1982-87, Vaccine jour., 1983—, Biologicals, 2000—, Human Vaccines, 2005—, Clin. Vaccine Immunology, 2006—, Clin. Infectious Diseases, 2007—. Served as med. officer USPHS, 1957-60, bd. mem. Rostropovich Found. Decorated Legion of Honor (France); recipient Bruce medal, ACP, 1987, Clin. Virology award, Pan Am. Group Rapid Viral Diagnosis, 1995, Gold medal, Sabin Found., 2002, Children's Hosp., Phila., 2006, Fleming award, Infectious Diseases Soc. Am., 2004, Marshall award, European Soc. Pediat. Infectious Diseases, 2006, medal, Fondation Mérieux, Finland award, Nat. Found. Infectious Diseases, 2009, Hilleman prize, Am. Soc. Microbiology, 2009; named Disting. Physician, Pediat. Infectious Diseases Soc., 1993, Disting. Alumnus, Children's Hosp., Phila., 2001, Prof. chair, Childrens Hosp. Phila; grantee, Joseph P. Kennedy Found., 1964—66, Hartford Found., 1971—73, NIH, 1973—. Fellow: AAAS; mem.: NAS (Inst. of Medicine), Rostropovich Found. (bd. mem.), U. Complutense (Madrid) (hon. doc.), U. Rouen (France) (hon. doc.), French Acad. Medicine (foreign mem.), World Soc. Pediat. Infectious Diseases (pres. 2003—06), Am. Acad. Pediat. (chmn. infectious diseases com. 1987—90), Am. Soc. Microbiology, Am. Epidemiology Soc., Am. Pediat. Soc., Soc. Pediat. Rsch., Hungarian Soc. Microbiology (hon.). Achievements include pioneering work on vaccine strains for protection against polio, rabies, rubella, rotavirus and cytomegalovirus. Office Phone: 215-297-9321. Personal E-mail: stanley.plotkin@vaxconsult.com.

PLOTZ, CHARLES MINDELL, physician, educator; b. NYC, Dec. 6, 1921; s. Isaac and Rose (Bluestone) P.; m. Lucille Weckstein, Aug. 5, 1945; children: Richard, Thomas, Robert. BA, Columbia U., 1941, D.Sc., 1951; MD, L.I. Coll. Medicine, 1944. Diplomate: Am. Bd. Internal Medicine. Intern New Haven Hosp., 1944-45; resident internal medicine Kings County Hosp., 1945-46, Maimonides Hosp., 1948-49; postdoctoral research fellow USPHS, Columbia Coll. Phys. and Surgs., 1949-50; practice medicine, specializing in internal medicine Bklyn., 1950—; chief Arthritis Clinic, attending physician Kings County Hosp. Center, 1950-85; chief L.I. Coll. Hosp. (Arthritis Clinic), 1950-65; asst. attending physician Mt. Sinai Hosp., 1955—; chief Mt. Sinai Hosp. (Arthritis Clinic), 1955-65, Arthritis Clinic, State U., Hosp., 1967-85; asst. physician Columbia-Presbyn. Med. Center, 1949-71; attending physician Bklyn. State Hosp.; dir. ambulatory care Bklyn. Hosp.Ctr., 1991-93; emeritus prof. medicine SUNY, 1991—; professorial lectr. Mt. Sinai Sch. Medicine, 1992—; emeritus prof. in medicine SUNY, 1991—. Cons. physician Peninsula Gen. Hosp., Jamaica Hosp.; cons. on rheumatology VA Hosp., Bklyn., L.I. Coll. Hosp.; cons. family practice Luth. Med. Ctr.; vis. cons. internal medicine Jewish Gen. Hosp., Mont., Que., Can., 1965; cons. internal medicine Avicenna Hosp. and Wazir Akbar Hosp., Kabul, Afganistan, 1965; prof. medicine, dir. continuing edn., chmn. dept. family practice SUNY Downstate Med. Ctr., 1967-91, prof. emeritus medicine and family practice, 1991—; Fulbright lectr. U. Paris, 1984, 91; professorial lectr. Mt. Sinai Sch. Medicine, 1992—. Editorial adv. bd.: Pakistan Med. Forum; editor-in-chief: Clin. Rheumatology in Practice, 1981—; editor-in-chief: Advances in Rheumatology, 1986—, Rheuma21st.com, 1998—. Mem. nat. bd. govs. Arthritis Found., 1964-82, bd. govs. N.Y. chpt., 1965—, v.p., 1971-83, trustee, 1977-82, N.Y. chpt. sr. v.p., 1977-82, vice chmn. bd. trustees, 1983-85, 87—, pres., 1985-87; trustee Leo N. Levi Meml. Nat. Arthritis Hosp., Alumni Fund-Alumni Assn. SUNY Downstate Med. Center, Bklyn. Inst. Arts and Scis., Bklyn. Bot. Garden; mem. adv. bd. MEDICO, corp. mem., 1977—; treas. Internat. League Against Rheumatism, 1981-89; trustee Internat. League Against Rheumatism Trust, 1981-89. Served to capt. AUS, 1946-48. WHO fellow U. Negev, 1974; master Am. Coll. Rheumatology, 1991—; recipient Gold medal Am. Coll. Rheumatology, 1992. Master Am. Coll. Rheumatology (Gold medal 1992), fellow ACP, Am. Acad. Family Physicians (charter), N.Y. Acad. Medicine (chmn. edn. com. 1976-78); mem. AMA, (N.Y. chpt.), AAUP, Internat. Soc. for Rheumatic Therapy (chmn. 1987-89), Am. Fedn. Clin. Rsch., Am. Rheumatism Assn. (past sec.-treas.), N.Y. Rheumatism Assn. (past pres., exec. com.), Harvey Soc., (N.Y. chpt.), Kings County med. socs., Bklyn. socs. internal medicine, Soc. Tchrs. Family Medicine, N.Y. State Acads. Family Physicians, Soc. Urban Physicians, Mystery Writers Am., Sigma Xi, Alpha Omega Alpha; hon. mem. Rheumatology Soc. France, Rheumatology Soc. Japan, Rheumatology Soc. Mex., Rheumatology Soc. Brazil, Rheumatology Soc. Yugoslavia, Rheumatology Soc. Norway, Rheumatology Soc. Egypt, Med. Soc. Czechoslovakia, Cosmos Club, Heights Casino Club. Home: 184 Columbia Hts Brooklyn NY 11201-2105 also: 450 Clarkson Ave Brooklyn NY 11203-2056 E-mail: rheuma21st@aol.com. *

PLOUVIER, STÉPHANE RENÉ, retired biologist; b. Steenwerck, France, Apr. 19, 1934; s. Henri Louis and Marie Louise (Leman) P.; m. Geneviève Tetard, July 2, 1960; children: Fabienne, Grégoire (dec.), Bruno, Laurence, Marc. Physician, Ecole de Sante Navale, Bordeaux, France, 1960; Cert. Virology, Bacteriology, Serology, Inst. Pasteur, Paris, 1969; Cert. in Gen. Chemistry and Pathology, U. Marseille, France, 1973; Cert. in Hematology, U. Bordeaux, France, 1978. Physician Army Health Svc., Biskra, Algeria, 1962, asst. physician hosps. Tananarive, Madagascar, 1963-65, Bordeaux, 1966-68, Strasbourg, France, 1970-72, Frejus, France, 1973-74; dir. dept. parasitic diseases Orgn. Coop. Lutte Contre les Grandes Endemies, Bobo Dioulasso, Burkina Faso, 1974-75; dir. Pvt. Lab. Biology, Bordeaux, 1975-78, Libourne, France, 1980-94; ret., 1995. Asst. tchr. Inst. U. Tech., La Rochelle, France, 1979-80. Contbr. articles to profl. jours. Decorated medaille AFN Ordre Nat. du Merite (France). Fellow Royal Soc. Medicine; mem. AAAS. Roman Catholic. Achievements include research on impedance of the human body, blood, microbial metallogeny; study of an immunofluorescent antibody against Setaria labiatopapillosa in patients suffering from Onchocerciasis and/or filariosis; epidemiologic model of hyperendemic Onchocerciasis; diagnosis test of Bilharziosis by combining filtration of urines and lugol staining; RAMAN spectroscopy and microanalysis applied to microbial metallogeny; relationship between circulating organometallic chromophore complexes and carcinogenesis, thrombogenesis and bacterial L. forms; role of lesions of red cells in thrombogenesis, Nycthemeral variation of urinar free radical scavenger effect observed by means of di-phenyl-picryl-hydrazyl hydrate, patent for kinetics of blood clot retraction (thromboscopy); microanalysis in leprosy and Alzheimer's disease; the pathogenic role in Leprosy of L.forms of bacillus cereus type 1. Home: 38 Rue du Village du Chateau 33320 Le Taillan Medoc France Home Phone: 05-56-35-35-94. Personal E-mail: stephane.plouvier@orange.fr

PLUMMER, CHRIS, neurologist, educator; b. Toowoomba, Queensland, Australia, Apr. 28, 1970; s. Earle and Anne Plummer; m. Kim Rees, Sept. 8, 2001; children: Polly, Annabel, Phoebe. BmedSci, U. Queensland, Brisbane, 1993, MBBS, 1995; PhD, U. Melbourne, Victoria, Australia, 2008. Med. registrar Royal Brisbane Hosp., 1999—2001; neurology registrar Austin and St. Vincent's Hosp., Melbourne, 2002—04, cons. neurologist, 2005—, co-investigator, epilepsy and multiple sclerosis clin. trials, 2005 ; clin. lectr. U. Melbourne, 2005—, rschr., 2005—, lectr., 2005—, examiner, 2005—. Editl. adv. bd. mem. Virtual Med. Ctr. Neurology, Melbourne, 2006—. Contbr. articles to profl. jours. Fellow: RACP, mem.: Epilepsy Soc. Australia, Australian Assn. Neurologists. Achievements include research in electroencephalographic source localization in focal epilepsy. Office: St Vincent's Neurology 35 Victoria Parade Fitzroy 3065 Melbourne VIC Australia Office Phone: 0392882211. Office Fax: 0392883350. Personal E-mail: chrisplummer@ozemail.com.au. Business E-Mail: chris.plummer@svhm.org.au.

PLUMMER, ORA BEATRICE, nursing educator, consultant; b. Mexia, Tex., May 25, 1940; d. Macie Idella (Echols); children: Kimberly, Kevin, Cheryl. BSN, U. N.Mex., 1961; MS in Nursing Edn., UCLA, 1966. Nurse's aide Bataan Meml. Meth. Hosp., Albuquerque, 1958—60, staff nurse, 1961—62, 1967—68; staff nurse, charge nurse, relief supr. Hollywood Cmty. Hosp., Calif., 1962—64; instr. U. N.Mex. Coll. Nursing, Albuquerque, 1968—69; sr. instr. U. Colo. Sch. Nursing, Denver, 1971—74, asst. prof., 1974—76; staff assoc. III We. Interstate Commn. for Higher Edn., Boulder, Colo., 1976—78; DON Garden Manor Nursing Home, Lakewood, Colo., 1978—79, nurse surveyor, cons., 1979—87; ednl. coord. Colo. Dept. Health, Denver, 1987—96. Active in faculty devel. Colo. Cluster of Schs.; bd. dirs. Domestic Violence Initiative, Aurora Mental Health Ctr., 2008. Contbr. articles to profl. jours. Mem. adv. bd. Affiliated Children's and Family Svcs., 1977; mem. Colo. Instnl. Child Abuse and Neglect Adv. Com., 1984-92; trustee Colo. Acad., 1990-96; mem. planning com. State Wide Conf. on Black Health Concerns, 1977; mem. staff devel. com. Western Interstate Commn. for Higher Edn., 1978, mem. minority affairs com., 1978, mem. coordinating com. for baccalaureate program, 1971-76; active in minority affairs, U. Colo. Med. Ctr., 1971-72; mem. ednl. resources com., pub. rels. com., rev. com. for reappointment, promotion and tenure U. Colo. Sch. Nursing, 1971-76, mem. regulatory tng. com., 1989-93; mem. gerontol. adv. com. Met. State Coll., 1989-94; mem. expert panel long term care tng. manual Health Care Financing Adminstrn., Balt., 1989; mem. employee diversity com. Colo. Dept. Health, 1989-96; mem. Nurse Del. to Cuba, 2000, People to People Peace Initiative to Egypt, 2008; bd. dir., Aurora Mental Health Ctr., Colo., 2008-, program & planning com. bd. dir., 2009-. Nominee Nightingale award, Colo., 2003. Avocations: public speaking, teaching, coaching mentoring, consultation. Office: 4300 Cherry Creek South Dr Denver CO 80246-1523 Office Phone: 303-692-2890.

PLUNKETT, J. JERILL, anesthesiologist; b. Charleston, W.Va., Oct. 3, 1958; BS, Coll. William and Mary, 1980; MD, U. Cin., 1986. Asst. physician chief The Permanente Med. Group, 2006—. Assoc. prof. U. Calif., San Francisco, 1989—2008. Mem.: Soc. Cardiovasc. Anesthesiologists, Internat. Anesthesia Rsch. Soc., Am. Soc. Anesthesiologists, Alpha Omega Alpha. Avocations: skiing, cooking, travel. Office: The Permanente Med Group Administration 7300 N Fresno St Fresno CA 93720 Office Fax: 559-892-0707. Business E-Mail: jj.plunkett@kp.org.

PNEUMAN, LINDA JACKSON, retired physician; b. Memphis, July 9, 1938; d. John Thomas Jackson, Jr. and Winnie Griffin Jackson; m. Gerald Warnick Pneuman, June 16, 1978 (dec.); m. Terry Robert Cobb, Nov. 8, 1957 (div. 1974); children: Kimberly Winn Kirby, Elizabeth Lankford Fredricksmeyer. BS magna cum laude, U. Memphis, 1961; MD, Meharry Med. Coll., Nashville, 1976. Tchr. chemistry and biology St Mary's Episcopal Sch., Memphis, 1960—62; rsch. asst. Vanderbilt U. Psychopharmacology Rsch. Ctr., Nashville, 1966—67; intern, resident St. Joseph's Hosp., Denver, 1976—77; physician Denver U. Student Health Svc., Denver, 1977—81, US Dept. Def., Bad Aibling, Bavaria, Germany, 1978—79, U. Colo. Student Health Svc., Boulder, 1981—88, Calif. State U., Chico, Calif., 1988—2002; ret. Chair quality assurance U. Colo. Student Health Svc., Boulder, 1985—88; chair human subjects com. U. Colo., Boulder, 1986—88; chair quality assurace Calif. State U., Chico Student Health Svc., 1988—97, acting dir., 2000—01; chief clin. medicine Calif. State U. Chico, 1997—2001. Vol. naturalist City of Boulder Open Space and Mountain Parks, 2005—06; bd. mem. Boulder Valley Women's Clinic, 1986—88; fund raiser Friendship Bridge, Evergreen, Colo., 2005—10. Named Ark. Master Naturalist, 2010—11; Outstanding Student scholar, Hill Family Found., 1974, 1975. Mem.: Alpha Omega Alpha (life). Democrat. Episcopalian. Home: 5413 S Grandview Little Rock AR 72207 Personal E-mail: lpneuman@csuchico.edu.

POBER, BARBARA R., geneticist, educator; b. Jan. 29, 1951; BA, Yale Coll., 1973; MD, Yale Sch. Medicine, 1978. Geneticist, instr., pediat. Children's Hosp. Harvard Med. Sch., 1987—91; geneticist, assoc. prof., genetics Yale U. Sch. Medicine, 1991—2003; geneticist, prof., pediat. Mass. Gen. Hosp. Harvard Med. Sch., 2003—. Mem., rsch. and med. adv. bd. Williams Syndrome Assn., 1991—2011. Recipient Lifetime Svc. award, Williams Syndrome Assn., 2010; named one of Best Dr. in Boston, Boston Mag., 2009, 2010. Fellow: Am. Coll. Med. Genetics; mem.: Am. Soc. Human Genetics. Office: Simches Rsch Bldg 185 Cambridge Boston MA 02114 Office Fax: 617-726-1566. Business E-Mail: pober.barbara@mgh.harvard.edu.

POBLANO, ADRIAN, physician, researcher; b. Xochimilco, Federal District, Mexico, Mar. 5, 1960; s. Juan Poblano and Jovita Luna; m. Socorro Alcala, Mar. 19, 1967; children: Roman, Adriana Poblano Alcala. MD, Met. U. Xochimilco, 1982, MSc, 1990; PhD, Met. U. Iztapalapa, 2003. Assoc. rschr. Inst. Comm. Disorders, Mexico City, Federal District, 1987—90, head rschr., 1991—2000, Nat. Ctr. for Rehab., 2000—; prof. Nat. Inst. Perinatology, 1993—2004, Met. U. Xochimilco. Editor: Basic Issues In Audiology, Early Detection And Treatment Of Neurological Damage. Recipient Aaron Saenz Mexican Acad. Pediat. award, 2001. Mem.: Group Studies Birth Defects. Office: Nat Ctr Rehab Mexico-Xochimilco 289 Mexico City 14389 Mexico Home: Channel of Recodo Bo San Jose 253 16034 Xochimilco Mexico E-mail: drdyslexia@starmedia.com.

POCCHIARI, MAURIZIO, neuroscientist; b. Rome, June 25, 1953; s. Francesco and Giuliana (Tommasi) P.; m. Silvia Graziano, Sept. 13, 2007; children: Eleonora, Lorenza, Gineura, Carolina. MD, Cath. U., Rome, 1977, specialist in neurology, 1981. Postdoctoral fellow Nat. Rsch. Coun., Rome, 1978-80; asst. prof. neurology Cath. U., Rome, 1980-87; assoc. prof. microbiology U. Lecce, Italy, 1987-91; assoc. prof. gen. pathology U. Aquila, Italy, 1991; head rsch. lab. Dept. Cell Biology and Neuroscis. Inst. Superiore di Sanitá, Rome, 1992—. Vis. fellow NIH, Bethesda, Md., 1980-83; chief Nat. Registry Creutzfeldt-Jakob Disease, Rome, 1993—. Contbr. articles to profl. jours. Mem. Am. Soc. for Microbiology, Am. Soc. for. Virology. Achievements include scientific work in the field of spongiform encephalopathies. Home: Lungotevere Portuense 150 00153 Rome Italy Office: Inst Superiore di Sanitá Viale Regina Elena 299 00161 Rome Italy E-mail: pocchia@iss.it.

POCHAPIN, MARK BENNETT, gastroenterologist, educator; MD, Cornell U., 1988. Diplomate Am. Bd. Internal Medicine, Am. Bd. Internal Medicine-gastroenterology. Intern Cornell Med. Ctr., NYC, resident internal medicine, 1989—91; fellow gastroenterology Montefiore Med. Ctr., 1991—93; assoc. prof. medicine Cornell Univ.; attending physician NY-Presbyn. Hosp. Office: New York-Presbyterian Hospital Ground Level 1315 York Ave New York NY 10021 Office Phone: 212-746-4014. Office Fax: 212-746-5845.

POCHETTINO, ALBERTO, thoracic surgeon, educator; MD, Northwestern U. Chgo., 1987. Lic. NY, 1993, Pa., 1994, Ill., 2002, diplomate Am. Bd. Surgery, 1995, Am. Bd. Thoracic Surgery, 1997. Intern gen. surgery SUNY, 1988; resident gen. surgery SUNY-Upstate Med. Ctr., 1992; resident cardiothoracic surgery Hosp. Univ. Pa., 1994; assoc. prof. surgery; dir. lung transplantation program Pa. Hosp., assoc. dir. thoracic aortic surgery program, assoc. surg. dir. adult congenital heart disease program. Named one of America's Top Doctors, 2007—08, 2010, Top Doctors, Phila. Mag., 2007—. Mem.: Internat. Soc. for Heart and Lung Transplantation, Am. Heart Assn., Soc. of Gastro-intestinal Endoscopic Surgeons, ACS, Am. Assn. for the Advancement of Sci. Office: Pennsylvania Hospital Garfield Duncan Bldg Ste 305 700 Spruce St Philadelphia PA 19106 Office Phone: 800-789-7366.

POCHI, PETER ERNEST, physician; b. Boston, Mar. 8, 1929; s. Anesti and Alice (Peterson) P.; m. Barbara Orlob, June 11, 1955; children: Alan, Rena. AB cum laude, Harvard Coll., 1950; MD, Boston U., 1955. Diplomate Am. Bd. Dermatology. Intern Boston City Hosp., 1955-56, vis. dermatologist, 1978-91, assoc. dir., 1967-74, 78-84, acting chief dermatology, 1984-85; resident in dermatology Boston U. Hosp., 1958-61, vis. dermatologist, 1977-91, acting chief dermatology, 1984-85; assoc. in medicine Peter Bent Brigham Hosp., Boston, 1972-78; sr. cons. in dermatology Lemuel Shattuck Hosp., Boston, 1975-91; Herbert Mescon prof. dermatology Sch. Medicine, Boston U., 1988-91, prof. emeritus, 1991—, interim chmn. dept. dermatology, 1984-85. Cons. med. service in dermatology Boston VA Hosp., 1978-82; lectr. dermatology Sch. Medicine, Tufts U., 1980-91; assoc. staff New Eng. Med. Ctr. Hosp., 1981-91. Assoc. editor Jour. Investigative Dermatology, 1968-73; contbg. editor Year Book of Dermatology, 1983-90; mem. editl. bd. Archives of Dermatology, 1979-84, Jour. Am. Acad. Dermatology, 1981-90; hon. editor Acta Dermatovenerologica Albanica, 2004—; contbr. articles to med. jours

Bd. dirs. Cmty. Music Ctr., 1973-77, 97-2003, corp. mem., 1994-97, 2005—; governing bd. Boston Musical Theater, 2000-03. With USN, 1956-58. USPHS fellow, 1960-62, 62-63; USPHS grantee, 1965-84 Fellow Am. Acad. Dermatology (bd. dirs. 1981-85); mem. Am. Fedn. Clin. Rsch., AMA, Boston Dermatol. Club (sec.-treas. 1967-69), Boston U. Sch. Medicine Alumni Assn. (pres. 1979-80), Boston U. Nat. Alumni Coun., Dermatology Found., Evans Med. Found. (dir., sec.), Internat. Soc. Dermatology, Mass. Acad. Dermatology, Mass. Med. Soc. (chmn. sect. dermatology 1977-78), New Eng. Dermatol. Soc., Soc. Investigative Dermatology (bd. dirs. 1976-81, v.p. 1986-87), Am. Acne and Rosacea Soc. Home: 333 Commonwealth Ave Apt #9 Boston MA 02115-1933 Personal E-mail: pepderm@bu.edu.

POCHI, SUBBARAYAN RAMALINGAM, biomedical researcher; b. New Delhi, May 19, 1965; arrived in U.S., 1999; s. Ramalingam Kumaraswamy and Sundary Pochi; m. Malancha Sarkar, Sept. 2, 1994; children: ShuvamBharathy Subbarayan, Bhargavi Subbarayan. BS in Zoology, U. Madras, India, 1986, MS in Biomedical Genetics, 1988; PhD, Banaras Hindu U., Varanasi, India, 1994. Rschr. Nat. Inst. Genetics, Mishima, Shizuoka Ken, Japan, 1997—98; asst. scientist U. Miami (Fla.) Sch. Medicine, 2002—; mem. faculty in biology U. Miami and Miami Dade Coll., 2005—. Recipient Young Scientist award, Internat. Union Biochemistry and Molecular Biology, 1994, Japanese Govt. Rsch. Awards for Fgn. Specialist, Sci. and Tech. Agy., Japan., 1995; fellow, Sci. and Tech. Agy., Govt. Japan, 1995—96. Mem.: Soc. Biol. Chemists India (life). Office: Univ Miami Sch Medicine 1550 NW 10th Ave Fox 431A (D8-4) Miami FL 33136 Business E-Mail: spochi@med.miami.edu.

POCOSKI, DAVID JOHN, cardiologist; b. Waterbury, Conn., July 15, 1945; s. Edward J. and Stella E. (Kolpa) Pocoski; m. Madelyn M. Pocoski, Sept. 25, 1971; 1 child, Sarah C. BS, U. Conn., Storrs, 1967; MD magna cum laude, Upstate Med. Ctr., Syracuse, NY, 1971. From intern to fellow in cardiology U. Rochester, NY; founder, pres. Osler Clinic of Medicine, Melbourne, Fla.; chief of staff, dir. cardiac rehab. Sea Pines Rehab. Hosp.; chmn. dept. cardiology Holmes Regional Med. Ctr., Melbourne. Commr. Holy Name Jesus Cath. Ch. Maj. USAF, 1974-76. Recipient Outstanding Scientist of the 20th Century award. Fellow Am. Coll. Cardiology; mem. AMA, Alpha Omega Alpha, Phi Beta Kappa. Republican. Roman Catholic. Avocations: music, art, running, community service. Home: 930 S Harbor City Blvd Melbourne FL 32901-1963 Office: Chmn Dept Cardiology Holmes Regional Med Ctr Melbourne FL 32901 Office Phone: 321-725-5050. Personal E-mail: fdhp93a@aol.com.

PODBIELSKI, SUE, insurance company executive; BS in Fin., U. Louisville, Ky. Various positions Health Net Inc., Humana, Inc.; v.p., ops. Ingenix; COO, consumer solutions Uniprise; v.p., product devel. UnitedHealthcare, v.p., sales & account mgmt. Ky.; various positions, v.p. UnitedHealth Group, Inc., 2002—05; gen. mgr., large group bus. unit UniCare, 2005—07; v.p. WellPoint Inc., 2005—07; pres., gen. mgr. Midwest CIGNA HealthCare, 2007—. Office: CIGNA Healthcare 525 W Monroe St Chicago IL 60661-3633 Business E-Mail: sue.podbielski@cigna.com. *

PODBOY, JOHN WATTS, psychologist; b. York, Pa., Sept. 27, 1943; s. August John and Harriett Virginia (Watts) Podboy; 1 child, Matthew John. BA, Dickinson Coll., 1966; MS, San Diego State Coll., 1971; PhD, U. Ariz., 1973. Dir. Vets. Counseling Ctr., U. Ariz., Tucson, 1972—73; project dir. San Mateo County, Human Relations Dept., Redwood City, Calif., 1974; cons. clin. psychologist Comprehensive Care Corp., Newport Beach, Calif., 1974—75; staff psychologist Sonoma State Hosp., Eldridge, Calif., 1975—81; cons. clin. psychologist Sonoma County Probation Dept., Calif., 1976—88; asst. prof. Sonoma State U., 1977—81; dir. Sonoma Diagnostic & Remedial Ctr., 1979—82; pvt. practice Kenwood, Calif., 1982—; cons. Calif. Superior Cts., 1983—85. Chmn. San Mateo County Diabetes Assn., 1975. Served to lt. USNR, 1966—69. Fellow: Am. Bd. Med. Psychotherapists, Am. Coll. Forensic Psychology; mem.: APA, Nat. Rehab. Assn., Nat. Coun. Alcoholism, Redwood Psychol. Assn. (pres. 1983), Western Psychol. Assn. Home: PO Box 488 Kenwood CA 95452-0488 Office Phone: 707-833-6023. Personal E-mail: ikpod@yahoo.com.

PODDAR, NISHANT, physician; b. Jamshedpur, India, Dec. 29, 1973; MB, Veer Surendra Sai Med. Coll. & U. Hosp., India, BChir, 1998, MBBS, MD in Internal Medicine, 2003, Brookdale U. Hosp. and Med. Ctr., Bklyn., 2009. Pres., jr. physician assn. Veer Surendra Sai Med. Coll. & U. Hosp., 2001—02, chief, house staff, 2001—02, Safdarjung U. Hosp. Dept. Interventional Cardiology, 2004—05, Brookdale U. Hosp. and Med. Ctr., 2008—09, physician, hematology and oncology, 2009—, chief fellow, hematology and oncology, 2011—. Mem.: ACP, Delhi Med. Coun. (India), Orissa Med. Coun. (India), Am. Soc. Hematology, Am. Soc. Clin. Oncology. Avocations: tennis, golf. Home: 7 Hegeman Ave Apt 15F Brooklyn NY 11212 Personal E-mail: drnpoddar@yahoo.com.

PODGORNY, GEORGE, emergency physician; b. Tehran, Iran, Mar. 17, 1934; arrived in US, 1954, naturalized, 1973; s. Emanuel and Helen (Parsian) Podgorny; m. Ernestine Koury, Oct. 20, 1962; children: Adele, Emanuel II, George, Gregory. BS, Maryville Coll., 1958; postgrad., Bowman Gray Sch. Medicine, 1958; MD, Wake Forest U., 1962. Intern surgery NC Bapt. Hosp., Winston-Salem, 1962—63, chief resident gen. surgery, 1966—67, with, cardiothoracic surgery, 1967—69; sec.-treas. Forsyth Emergency Svcs., Winston-Salem, 1970—80; sr. med. examiner Forsyth County, NC, 1972—; dir. dept. emergency medicine Forsyth Meml. Hosp., Winston-Salem, 1974—80; chmn. residency rev. com. emergency medicine East Carolina U. Sch. Medicine, Greenville, 1980—88, clin. prof. emergency medicine, 1984—; mem. Accreditation Coun. Grad. Med. Edn. Contbr. articles to profl. publs.; editl. bd. mem. Anns. Emergency Medicine, Med. Meetings. Chmn. bd. trustees Emergency Medicine Found.; chmn. residency rev. com. emergency medicine Accreditation Coun. Grad. Med. Edn.; founder Western Piedmont Emergency Med. Svcs. Coun., 1973; trustee Forsyth County Hosp., Authority, 1974—75; bd. dirs. Medic Alert Found. Internat., NC Health Coordinating Coun., 1975—82, Piedmont Health Systems Agy., 1975—84; dir. Emergency Med. Svcs. Project Region II NC, 1975—; mem. NC Emergency Med. Svcs. Adv. Coun., 1976—81; assoc. prof. clin. surgery Bowman Gray Sch. Medicine, Wake Forest U., Winston-Salem, 1979—. Fellow: Southeastern Surg. Congress, Royal Soc. Medicine, Royal Soc. Health (Great Britain), Internat. Coll. Angiology, Internat. Coll. Surgeons; mem.: AMA (chmn. coun. sect. emergency medicine 1978—90), Am. Bd. Emergency Medicine (pres. 1976—81), Am. Coll. Emergency Physicians (charter, pres. 1978—79, alt. del. 1990—). Home and Office: 2115 Georgia Ave Winston Salem NC 27104-1917 Office Phone: 336-727-1161.

PODRAZA, JEFFERY THOMAS, physical therapist, educator; b. Buffalo, Apr. 8, 1977; Degree in Phys. Therapy, Daemen Coll., 2000; PhD student in Biomechanics & Physiology, U. Buffalo. Cert. orthop. specialist Am. Bd. Phys. Therapy Specialties. Staff phys. therapist Prog. Phys. Therapy, 2000—06; per diem phys. therapist Cath. Health Sys. Buffalo Ptnrs. Rehab., 2003—; staff phys. therapist Kenneth Kurtz Phys. Therapy and Assocs., 2006—, ctr. coord., clin. edn., 2010—. Adj. prof., phys. therapy Daemen Coll., 2005—, clin. instr., Villa Marie Coll., 2010—; course contbr., doctoral studies dept. rehab. & exercise scis. U. Buffalo, 2009—; Ad hoc manuscript peer reviewer Peer Reviewed Jour. The Knee, 2010—. Recipient Carlton Myers award, U. Buffalo Sch. Pub. Health and Health Related Professions, 2010. Mem.: APTA, AOSSM. Avocations: fly fishing, gardening. Home: 101 Angelacrest Ln West Seneca NY 14224 Personal E-mail: jefferypodraza@yahoo.com.

PODSHIBYAKIN, DMITRY VASILYEVICH, research scientist; b. Saratov, Russia, Aug. 11, 1984; MS, N.G. Chernyshevsky Saratov State U., 2006; PhD, Saratov State Tech. U., 2010. Jr. rsch. scientist Saratov Rsch. Vet. Inst. RAAS, 2009—. Office: 53 Strelkovoi divizii 6 Saratov 410028 Russia Office Fax: 7(8452)20-08-30. Business E-Mail: podshibyakin@list.ru.

POEHLING, KATHERINE, pediatrician; d. Gary Poehling; m. Timothy Peters, May 4, 1996; children: Jennifer Peters children: Robert Peters. MD, Wake Forest Sch. of Medicine, Winston-Salem, NC, 1995; MPH, Vanderbilt U. Sch. of Medicine, Nashville, Tenn., 2001. Lic. NC Med. Bd., 2007, cert. Bd. Am. Acad. Pediat., 1998. Fellow Vanderbilt U., Nashville, 1999—2002, asst. prof. of pediat., 2002—07; assoc. prof. pediats. Wake Forest Sch. Medicine, Winston-Salem, NC, 2007—. Mem. NC Med. Bd., 2007. Fellow: Am. Acad. Pediat.; mem.: Soc. Pediatric Rsch., Acad. Pediat. Assn., Infectious Disease Soc. Am., Alpha Omega Alpha. Achievements include research in Clin. rsch. on pediat. respiratory infections. *

POGGI, GUIDO, oncologist, consultant; b. Pavia, Italy, Oct. 1, 1964; s. Giorgio Poggi and Carla Rossi; m. Ilaria Vietti, June 29, 1996; children: Francesco, Mariasole, Glorgio. MD, U. Pavia, 1990. Cert. in Hematology 1994, in Ultrasonography 1996, in gastroenterology 2004, in senology 2008; in molecular oncology 2010. Asst. physician, dept. med. oncology Maugeri Found., Pavia, Italy, 1993—99, staff hepatologist, 2002—. Asst. physician Dept. Emergency Medicine, Alessandria, Italy, 1999—2000. Mem.: SIUMB (assoc.). Office: Salvatore Maugeri Found via Ferrata 8 Pavia 27100 Italy Home: via Folla Di Sotto 74 Pavia Italy E-mail: guido.poggi@fsm.it.

POGLIAGHI, SILVIA, medical researcher; b. Verbania, Italy, Jan. 18, 1968; MD, U. Brescia, 1992; PhD, U. Milan, 2002. Rsch. asst. prof. U. Verona, 2005—. Mem.: Am. Coll. Sports Medicine. Home: via Cantarane 9 Colognola ai Colli Verona 37030 Italy Business E-Mail: silvia.pogliaghi@univr.it.

POGO, GUSTAVE JAVIER, cardiothoracic surgeon, educator; b. Buenos Aires, Feb. 7, 1957; came to US, 1964; s. Angel Oscar and Beatriz (Garcia-Tuñon) P.; m. Janis Teitler, Feb. 17, 1983; children: Michael Tyler, Katherine Elizabeth. BA cum laude, NYU, 1979, MD, 1983. Cert. Am. Bd. Surgery, Am. Bd. Thoracic Surgery. Intern gen. surgery North Shore Univ. Hosp., Manhasset, NY, 1983—84, resident gen. surgery, 1984—88, mem. provisional surg. staff, 1991—94, asst. attending surgeon to sr. attending surgeon, 1994—; resident cardiothoracic surgery Mt. Sinai Med. Ctr., NYC, 1988—91; adj. assoc. prof. surgery NYU Sch. Medicine. Contbr. articles to profl. jours. Fellow ACS, Am. Coll. Chest Physicians, Am. Coll. Cardiology; mem. Soc. Thoracic Surgery. Office: North Shore Univ Hosp 300 Community Dr Manhasset NY 11030-3801 Office Phone: 516-562-4970. Office Fax: 516-562-3787.

POGUE, JOHN MARSHALL, physician; b. Washington, Sept. 21, 1945; s. L(loyd) Welch and Mary Ellen (Edgerton) P. AB with honors, Princeton U.; MD, Georgetown U. Diplomate Nat. Bd. Med. Examiners. Intern, resident Georgetown U. Hosp., Washington; editor, author Bradford Jour., 1983—; historian Gov. William Bradford Compact, 1996—, surgeon, 1999—; v.p., 2005—08, pres., 2008—. Spkr. and lectr. in field of cardiology. Author: Herbert Martin Giffin, M.D., A Role Model Physician and a Doctor's Doctor: From Princeton to Johns Hopkins, Mayo Clinic, USN, and Yater Clinic, 2000, Sir William Osler, M.D., The Preeminent Physician: From McGill to the University of Pennsylvania, Johns Hopkins, and Oxford, 2004, Caldwell Blakeman Esselstyn, Jr., M.D. of the Cleveland Clinic, Defeater of Coronary Artery Heart Disease Through Low-Fat, Plant-Based Nutrition, 2008; designer Ofcl. Gov. William Bradford Flag, 1987 (New Constellation award Nat. Flag Found., 1996), Ofcl. Order of Descs. of Colonial Physicians and Chirurgiens Flag, 2005; editor, contbr.: Pogue/Pollock/Polk Genealogy as Mirrored in History, From Scotland to Northern Ireland/Ulster, Ohio, and Westward, 1990 (recipient 5 First Pl. Genealogy awards, recipient 2 Meritorious History awards), assoc. editor: Hereditary Soc. Blue Book, 1997, 1998, 1999, 2000; dir.(of film): Hugo Victor Rizzoli, Preeminent Neurosurgeon, A.B. and M.D., Johns Hopkins, Neurosurg. Tng. at Johns Hopkins Hosp., 2005; contbr. articles on cardiology to med. jours. Fellow Royal Soc. Medicine, Royal Microscopical Soc. Oxford, Royal Statis. Soc., Royal Geog. Soc., Royal Soc. Arts, Internat. Soc. Holter and Noninvasive Electrocardiology; mem. British Cardiovascular Soc., Premium Profl., Silver Heart, Am. Heart Assn. (coun. clin. cardiology, coun. arteriosclerosis, thrombosis & vascular biology, coun. basic cardiovasc. scis.), AMA, Royal Soc. Medicine (cardiology sect., cardiothoracic sect.), European Soc. Cardiology, Laennec Cardiovasc. Sound Soc., Brit. Soc. Echocardiography, Am. Soc. Echocardiography (coun. cardiac sonography, coun. intraoperative echocardiography, coun. pediat. & congenital heart disease, coun. Vascular Ultrasound), Internat. Soc. Cardiovasc. Ultrasound, Internat. Cardiac Doppler Soc., Internat. Soc. Electrocardiology (Glasgow U., Scotland), Internat. Soc. Holter and Noninvasive Electrocardiology, Internat. Acad. Cardiovasc. Scis., Can., British Soc. Cardiovascular Magnetic Resonance, Soc. Cardiovasc. Magnetic Resonance, Internat. Atherosclerosis Soc. Coun., Capital Area Heart Failure Soc. (founding mem. 2002), British Soc. for Heart Failure, Heart Failure Soc. Am., Heart Valve Soc. Am. (cardiac imaging coun.), Internat. Soc. Cardiovasc. Pharmacotherapy, Switzerland, British Soc. for Cardiovascular Rsch., Internat. Soc. Heart Rsch., Can. (cardiac metabolism sect. mem., stem cell & gene therapy sect. mem., Ischemia, cardioprotection & Mitochondria sect. mem.), Cardiac Muscle Soc., World Heart Fedn., Switzerland, European Assn. Cardiovasc. Prevention and Rehab., European Microscopy Soc. (Netherlands), Friends Nat. Libr. Medicine (founding mem. 1988), Friends McGill U. Osler Med. Libr., Friends Oxford U. Mus. History Sci., Ashmolean Natural History Soc. Oxford, Oxford Hist. Soc., Internat. Shakespeare Assn. (Stratford-upon-Avon), Princeton U. Alumni Assn., Princeton Tigertones Alumni, DC Soc. Mayflower Descs. (surgeon 1998-), Order Descs. Colonial Physicians and Chirurgiens (surgeon gen. 1994-2000, 2006-, chmn. hon. membership com. 1994-, v.p. gen. 2000-03, pres. gen. 2003-06, hon. pres. gen. life, 2006—), Nat. Gavel Soc., Hereditary Order of Descs. of Colonial Govs. (rec. sec. gen. 2005-, surgeon gen. 2011-), Dutch Colonial Soc. (Colonial mem. 2010), Provincial Families Md., Kenwood Citizens Assn., Royal Soc. Medicine Club, London, Royal Soc. Medicine Med. Art Soc., RSM Music Soc., Royal Soc. Medicine Music Club, Royal Soc. Medicine Book Club, Princeton U. Club, Washington, Oxford Bibliographical Soc. Oxford U. Bodleian Libr. Avocations: classical music, reading. Home and Office: 5204 Kenwood Ave Chevy Chase MD 20815-6604

POHLY, JOHANNES PAUL, physician, scientist; b. Berlin, Aug. 13, 1956; s. Kurt and Eleonore Fischer; m. Gabriele Pohly, Oct. 15, 1993; children: Devendra, Nadine, Emanuel, Celine. Grad., Med. Sch., Berlin, 1988; Doctorate, Free U., Berlin, 1998. Rsch. asst. Inst. Clin. Pharmacology, Berlin, 1989-90; scientist Acad. Sci. and Tech., Berlin, 1990-93; ward doctor Bürger Hosp., Berlin, 1993; trainee health care mgr. Assn. Internat. Mgmt., Berlin, 1994-95; med. expert Fed. Inst. for Drugs and Med. Devices Pharmacovigilance dept., Bonn, Germany, 1995—2001; med. expert, head diagnostics unit Fed. Inst. for Drugs and Med. Devices, 2002—. Contbr. articles to profl. jours. Mem. Internat. Soc. Pharmacovigilance, European Agency for the Evaluation of Med. Products (nominated expert). Achievements include research on preclinical and first clinical tests of the choline esterase inhibitor galanthamine in the treatment of Alzheimers disease. Office: Bundesinstitut Arzneimittel Kurt-Georg-Kiesinger-Allee 3 D-53175 Bonn Germany Business E-Mail: pohly@bfarm.de.

POHODENKO-CHUDAKOVA, IRINA, oral surgeon, researcher; b. Perm, Russia, Feb. 2, 1968; d. Oleg and Tamara Chudakov; m. Dmitri Pokhodenko, Jan. 19, 2000; children: Nikolay Pohodenko, Nikita Pohodenko. Diploma in cranio-maxillofacial surgery, Minsk State Med. Inst., Belarus, 1990, candidate of medicine, 1993; D in acupuncture, State Med. Inst., Minsk, 1991; MD, Russian Inst., Moscow, 2005. Head sci. lab. for people stomatological assistance Belarussian State Med. U., Minsk, 1993—2000, tchr., 2000—03, assoc. prof. stomatological dept., 2003—05, assoc. prof. Cranio-Maxillofacial Dept., 2005—06, prof. Cranio-Maxillofacial Dept., 2006—. Cons in acupuncture Republic Ctr. Cranio-maxillofacial and Plastic Surgery, Minsk, 1996—. Author: Manual for Traditional Ways of Acupuncture Application in Maxillofacial Areas. Mem.: Belarussian Assn. for Cranio-maxillofacial Surgeons, Belarussian Assn. Stomatologists, European Assn. for Cranio-maxillofacial Surgery (assoc.). Achievements include patents for acupuncture needle. Avocations: literature, art, architecture, embroidery, cooking. Office: Belarussian State Med Univ Dzerzhinskogo Prospekt 83 AV 220116 Minsk Minskiy Belarus Office Fax: +375 17 2724497. Business E-Mail: ip-c@yandex.ru.

POINDEXTER, BYRON D., plastic surgeon; b. Beech Grove, Ind., Apr. 2, 1966; married. BA in Chemistry, Psychology summa cum laude, phi beta kappa hon. soc., Ind. U., 1984—88, MD summa cum laude, alpha omega alpha hon. soc., 1988—92. Diplomate Am. Bd. Plastic Surgery. Resident gen. surgery Univ. of Fla., 1992—96; fellow plastic surgery Univ. of Ala., 1996—98; staff surgeon Austin-Weston Ctr. for Cosmetic Surgery. Co-author: (publs.) Selection of Patients for Renal Artery Repair Using Captopril Testing, 1995, A Simple Method of Lower Extremity Arteriography in the Laboratory Rat, 1998, Microvascular Surgery Utilizing the Endoscope as the Sole Source of Visual Assistance, 1998, The Present Status of Endoscopy, 1998, Rejuvenation of the Aged Face, 2000, Surgical Treatment of the Aged Mouth, 2003, Lip Recontouring, 2005. Recipient Ray Bierstedt Memorial award, Univ. of Ala., Distinguished Alumni Svc. award, Ind. Univ. Mem.: Va. Soc. of Plastic Surgeons, Nat. Capital Soc. of Plastic Surgeons (pres.), Am. Bd. of Plastic Surgery. Achievements include research in Histopathyology of Specimens from Elective Breast Reductions; Anatomy of the Malar Fat Pads and Central Third of the Face; General and Local Anesthesia in Strabismus Surgery; C14 Labeled Leucine Uptake in the Ovine Fetus: Fed and Fasting Models of Neonatal Nutrition. Office: Austin-Weston Center for Cosmetic Surgery 1825 Samuel Morse Dr Reston VA 20190 Office Phone: 703-893-6168.

POIRIER, LOUIS JOSEPH, neurology educator; b. Montreal, Que., Can., Dec. 30, 1918; s. Gustave Joseph and Calixta (Brault) P.; m. Liliane Archambault, June 11, 1947; children: Guy, Michel, Louise, Esther. BSc, U. Montreal, 1942, MD, 1947; PhD, U. Mich., 1950; D (hon.), U. Rennes, France, 1973. Asst. prof. U. Montreal, 1950-55, assoc. prof., 1955-58, prof. faculty of medicine, 1958-65; chmn. dept. anatomy Faculty of Medicine, Laval U., Cité Universitaire, Que., 1970-78, prof. exptl. neurology, 1970-83; dir. Centre de Rsch. in Neurobiology, Laval U. and Hosp. de l'Enfant-Jesus, 1977-85, prof. emeritus, 1985—. Editor: Advances in Neurology, vol. 24, 1979; contbr. articles to profl. jours. Pres. Que. Health Scis. Research Council, 1978-81. Decorated officer Order of Can.; recipient Que. sci. award, 1975; Killam commemorative scholar, 1977, 78 Mem. AAAS, Royal Soc. Belgium (hon.), Neurol. Soc. France (hon.), Am. Assn. Anatomists, Am. Physiol. Soc., Soc. for Neuroscis., Internat. Brain Research Orgn., Can. Med. Assn. (emeritus). Address: 603 Chemin Caron Lac Simon Montpellier PQ Canada J0V 1M0

POITOUT, DOMINIQUE GILBERT M., orthopedic surgeon, educator; b. Paris, Dec. 1, 1946; s. Pierre Augustin M. and Helene Marie J. (Baudrais) P.; m. Isabelle Badorc, 1998; children: Pierre-Brice R., Jean-Roch D. (dec.), Marie-Elodie A., Jade A. MD, U. Paris, 1973; M in Human Biology, U. Marseille, 1976; M in Biomechanics, U. Montpellier, 1976; M in Anthropology, 1976, M in Neuroanatomy, 1977, M in Gen. Anatomy, 1977, DEA in Geology and Anthropology, 1978. Extern hosp., Paris, 1967-70; intern hosp., 1970-71, Marseille, France, 1971-76; asst. in anatomy, 1973-76; chief of clinic, 1976-82; prof. orthopedic surgery exceptional class U. Hosp. Ctr. U. Aix-Marseille, 1982—; chief of svc., chmn. orthopedic dept. Univ. Hosp. Ctr. of U. Aix-Marseilles, 1986—; dir. surg. orthopedic rsch. lab. Faculty of Medicine, Marseille, 1991—; chief operative dept. U.

Hosp. North, 2001; invited permanent prof. U. Shanghai, China, 2002; internat. cons. Cath. Pontifica Santiago Chile, 2009. Nat. dir. D.E.A. for orthopedic biomechanics, Diploma Surg. Scis. for Biomechanics and Biomaterials, 1986—; mem. bd. Coll. Orthopaedic and Traumatologic Surgeons, 1999-2007; orthopedic and traumatologic med. expert Prefecture des Bouches du Rhone; expert Ins. Socs., Social Security; expert commn. Nat. Med. Accident; Visitor High Authority Health, Med. Expert High Authority Health, French Aging Sanitary Security, French Agy. Normalination, others; dir. surg. orthopedic rsch. lab. Faculty of Medicine, U. Marseille, 1991—, dir. redaction and med. com., 1984—; dir. diploma orthopedic oncology, 1991—; dir. Interuniversity Diploma Surgical Tech. and Reconstruction, 2007-;mem. infectious disease com., Commn. Tropical Medicine Hosp., 1999, graft and transplantation com., 1999; mem. Medico Surgical Comm. Hosps. Mamuthe; organizer profl. confs.; internat. expert in health care and social programs; v.p. NOA-HumaniTerra Internat., 2011 Author: Locomotor System Allografts, 1986, Orthopedic Biomechanic, 1987, Atlas of Orthopedic and Traumatologic Surgery of the Knee, 1992, Atlante Di Tecnica E Chirurgica del Ginocchio, 1994, Atlas of Open Knee Surgery, 1995, Expertise in Orthopedic Traumatologie and Medical Responsibility, 1999, 2004, 08, Bone Metastasis, 2001, Rheumatology and Orthopedic for Internat., 2003, 2011, Biomechanics and Biomaterials in Orthopaedics, 2004, Mini Invasive Surgery of the Hip, 2011; editor: Orthopedic and Traumatologic Letter; co-editor-in-chief: European Jour. Orthop. Surgery, European Jour. Orthop. and Traumatologic Surgery; mem. editl. bd. Orthopedic and Traumatologie Rev., Hip Internat., Tissue Banking, Revue D'Afrique Noire; contbr. articles and papers to numerous profl. jours. Councillor of the Townhall of Marseille, 1983-88, v.p. of the commn. of social action, 1983-88; pres. Perspectives for Health Futures in France, Perspectives for Health Futures in Europe, 1992; mem. transplantation and graft commn., infection commn. U. Hosp. Marseille; mem. fedns. polytraumatology and oncology/sarcomas U. Hosp. Ctr. Marseille North. Recipient High French Com. for Civil Def. Mem. Nat. Acad. Surgery (bd. dirs., pres. comm. internat. relationships), Nat. Acad. Medicine (mem. com. relationships, mem. com. surgery, mem. com. oncology), Internat. Soc. Orthopedic Surgery, Internat. Soc. Rsch. in Orthopedics and Traumatology, European Soc. Biomechanics, European Soc. Biomaterials, Belgian Orthopedic Surgery Soc., Chilean Orthopedic Surgery Soc. (spl. advisor), N.Y. Acad. Scis., French Soc. Orthopedic Surgery, Surg. Soc. Marseille (pres. 2004—2008), Ortho Nare Nostrum Soc. (oncology referent 2002), Orthopedic and Traumatologic Soc. Great South (pres. 2005), French Coll. Orthopedic and Neurologic Surgeons (bd. dirs.), Human itena Internat. (med. councilor), Rsch. Group Locomotor Sys. (pres.), Rsch. Assn. Intraosseous Circulation, French Tissue Assn. (treas.), Rsch. Group Biomaterials and Grafts (pres.), AO France Assn. (past pres., trustee), AO Alumni Assn., Freedom and Family Club Assn. (pres.), Tastevin Club (officer, comdr.), Rotary Club of Aix en Provence, Lions Club Marseille Vieux Port (past pres.), Knight of St. Jean of Jerusalem, Rhodos and Malta., Knight Honour Legion., Hospitalis Nare Nostrum (pres. 2011) Achievements include research pelvic hip and knee arthroplaty, traumatology, allografts of bone, cartilage and ligaments and orthopedic oncology. Office: Centre Hosp U Chemin des Bourrely 13015 Marseilles France Office Phone: 0033 (0) 49 1968694. Personal E-mail: dominique.poitout@ap-hm.fr.

POL, SAE SATISH, medical educator; b. Satara, Maharashtra, India, Nov. 16, 1968; MSc in Microbiology, Pune U., India, 1991, PhD in Medical Microbiology, 2005. Asst. prof. B. J. Medical Coll., Pune, 1993—. Contbr. articles to profl. jours. Avocation: mountain climbing. Home: 63 United Western Society 'Adiparna'apar Pune Maharashtra 411052 India Home Fax: 020 25110776. Personal E-mail: aparnapol@rediffmail.com.

POLAND, GREGORY A., medical professor, researcher; b. Quantico, Va., Aug. 16, 1955; s. James Poland; m. Jean Marie Poland; children: Caroline Marie, Eric Gregory, Matthew Gregory. BA in Biology, magna cum laude, Ill. Wesleyan U., Bloomington, 1977; MD, So. Ill. U., Springfield, 1980. Diplomate Am. Bd. Internal Medicine. Chief resident, instr. internal medicine Abbott-Northwestern Hosp., Mpls., 1984-85; asst. prof. internal medicine East Tenn. State U., Johnson City, 1985-87, VA Med. Ctr., Mpls., 1987-88; asst. prof. medicine Mayo Clinic Coll. Medicine, Rochester, Minn., 1988-93, assoc. prof. medicine, 1993-97, prof. medicine, infectious diseases, molecular pharmacology and experimental therapeutics, 1997—, Mary Lowell Leary prof. medicine, 2004; assoc. chair rsch., dept. medicine Mayo Clinic & Found., 1999—, dir. Vaccine Rsch. Group, Immunization Clinic and Prog. in Translational Immunovirology & Biodefense. Vis. prof. Capital Med. Coll., Beijing, 1994, Mich. State U., East Lansing, 1995, Santa Clara Valley Hosp, Stanford U., San Jose, Calif., 1995, U. Wis., Milw., 1997, So. Ill. U., 1997; mem. exec. com., chmn. Nat. Coalition Adult Immunization; bd. dirs. Nat. Found. Infectious Diseases, 1997—; mem. steering com. Nat. Network Immunization Info. Am. editor (med. jour.) Vaccine, 2000—; contbr. articles to profl. jours., chapters to books. Recipient US Surgeon Gen. award, Ctrs. Disease Control & Prevention and Health Care Fin. Adminstrn., 1998, Outstanding Pub. Svc. Medal, US Sec. Defense, 2003; named Outstanding Clin. Investigator of Yr., Mayo Clinic & Found., 1997; grantee Nat. Fund Med. Edn., 1988. Fellow: ACP; mem.: AMA, Internat. Soc. Vaccines (pres.), Infectious Diseases Soc. of America, Am. Soc. Clin. Pharmacology & Therapeutics, Internat. Soc. Travel Medicine, Am. Soc. Microbiology, Am. Fedn. Med. Rsch., Assn. Prog. Dirs. Internal Medicine, Minn. Med. Assn. Office: Mayo Clinic Dept Internal Medicine 200 First St SW 611 B Guggenheim Bldg St SW Rochester MN 55905-0001 Office Phone: 507-284-9039. Business E-Mail: poland.gregory@mayo.edu.

POLAT, ONUR, medical educator; b. Ankara, Turkey, July 3, 1971; MD, Hacettepe U., 1995. Asst. prof. Ankara U., 2005—. Office: Sihhiye Opera Ankara 06100 Turkey Office Fax: 903125083032. Personal E-mail: onurpolat1971@yahoo.com.

POLFLIET, SARAH JEAN, physician; b. Austin, Minn., July 4, 1975; d. Richard John and Charlotte Bertha Polfliet. BS in Physiology, U. Calif., Santa Barbara, 1998; MD, U. Va., Charlottesville, 2002; MD in Psychiat., Law, U. Calif., San Francisco, 2006. DEA Certification Med. Bd. of Calif., 2003, lic. MD Med. Bd. of Calif., 2003, cert. Am. Bd. Psychiatry & Nuerology, 2008. Sec. in cmty. rels. U. Calif., 1997—98, asst. instr. of biology lab., 1998, resident physician San Francisco, 2002—06; physician Schuman-Liles Cmty. Psychiatry Clinic, Oakland, Calif., 2003—06; pvt. practice in psychiat. and psychopharmacology, San Francisco, 2006—; chief resident intensive svcs. Langley Ptnr. Psychiat. Inst., 2006. Psychiatry physician, women's high-risk obstetric clinic San Francisco Gen. Hosp., 2004—05. Recipient Julius R. Krevans award for Clin. Excellence, U. Calif., San Francisco, 2003, Pathology Honors, U. Va., Sch. of Medicine, 1999—2000, Edwin Alston award, U. Calif. San Francisco Psychiatric Residency Program, 2006; Bowman's scholarship, U. Va., Sch. of Medicine, 1999—2000, Forensic Fellow, U. Calif. San Francisco, Psychiatry and Law Program, 2006—07. Fellow: Am. Psychiat. Assn. (hon.); mem.: Am. Assn. Psychiat. and Law, U. Calif., Santa Barbara, Alumni Assn. (hon.), Alpha Omega Alpha (hon.), Assn. Women Psychiatrists (hon.), No. Calif. Psychiat. Assn. (hon.), U. Va., Sch. of Medicine, Alumni Assn. (hon.). Achievements include research in evaluating training of psychiatry residents about neuroleptic medications; rural suicide outreach programs in Virginia, including composition of suicide outreach survey and meta-analysis of data to further assist tele-psychiatry program. Office: 369 pine St Ste 218 San Francisco CA 94104 Home: 912 Cole St 381 San Francisco CA 94117

POLICHETTI, GIULIANO, pharmacist; b. Sarno, Salerno, Italy, Mar. 24, 1977; Degree in Chemistry and Pharm. Tech., U. Naples, Italy, 2003, postgrad. in Pharmacology, 2007. Cert. pharmacist U. Naples, 2004, in chemistry 2004. Pvt. practice, Roccapiemonte, Salerno, 2005—07; rschr. U. Naples, 2008—; adj. tchr. pharmacology, 2008—. Avocations: bicycling, skiing, travel, running. Office: University Naples Federico II Via S Pansini 5 Naples 80131 Italy Home: Viale della Pace 60 84086 Roccapiemonte SA Italy Office Phone: 393286152481. Personal E-mail: giulianopolichetti@email.it.

POLIDO, WILFREDO TRIÑO, surgeon, educator; b. Iloilo City, Philippines, Jan. 20, 1971; BS in Biology, U. Philippines, 1992; MD, Far Ea. U., Nicanor Reyes Med. Found., 1996. Surg. fellow Asian Ctr. Liver Diseases and Transplantation, Gleneagles Hosp., Singapore, 2005—06; cons. physician dept. surgery St. Luke's Med. Ctr., Manila, Philippines, 2004—11, head liver transplantation, dept. surgery, 2006—11; asst. prof. dept. surgery Inst. Medicine, Far Ea. U., Nicanor Reyes Med. Found., Quezon City, 2006—11. Fellow: Philippine Coll. Surgeons; mem.: Quezon City Med. Soc., Philippine Assn. Laparoscopic and Endoscopic Surgeons, Philippine Med. Assn. Office: Gleneagles Hosp Annexe Block #02-37 Singapore 258500 Singapore Personal E-mail: wpolido@yahoo.com.

POLIN, RICHARD A., neonatal-perinatal doctor, educator; BA, Temple U., 1966, MD, 1970. Diplomate Am. Bd. Pediatrics, Am. Bd. Pediatrics-neonatal-perinatal medicine. Intern Children's Meml. Hosp., Ill., pediat. resident Ill., 1970—72; sr. resident pediat. Babies and Children's Hosp.- Columbia Presbyn. Med. Ctr., NY, 1972—73; chief resident in pediat. Babies Hosp.- Columbia Presbyn. Med. Ctr., 1974—75, fellow in neonatal-perinatal medicine, 1973—74, 1975—77; dir. divsn. of neonatology Columbia Univ. Med. Ctr., prof. of pediat., attending. Co-author various publs. Recipient Outstanding Pediatric Attending Babies Hosp., Children's Hosp. in Phila., 1978—79, 1982—83, Nat. Neonatal Educ. award, 2006, Outstanding Alumnus, Temple U. Office: Columbia University Medical Center Department of Neonatology 3959 Broadway Room CHC 1 115 New York NY 10032 Office Phone: 212-305-5827. Office Fax: 212-305-7086.

POLK, DAVID BRENT, pediatrician, educator; BS in Chemistry and Biology summa cum laude, Ouachita U., 1980, MD, U. Ark., Little Rock, 1984. Diplomate Am. Bd. of Pediat., 1999. Prof. & chair, dept. pediat.; prof. biochem. & molecular biology; v.p. acad. affairs CHLA, vice dean clin. affairs; dir. Sabn Inst. Child & Adolescent Health Rsch., U. South Calif. & Childrens Hosp., LA. Office: 4650 Sunset Blvd MS#71 Los Angeles CA 90027 Office Fax: 323-361-3719. Business E-Mail: dbpolk@chla.usc.edu. *

POLK, HIRAM CAREY, JR., surgeon, educator; b. Jackson, Miss., Mar. 23, 1936; s. Hiram Carey and Dorris (Hemby) P.; m. Susan Galandiuk; children: Susan Elizabeth, Hiram Cary. BS, Millsaps Coll., 1956; MD, Harvard U., 1960. Intern Barnes Hosp., St. Louis, 1960-61, resident, 1961-65; instr. in surgery Washington U., St. Louis, 1964-65; asst. prof. surgery U. Miami, Fla., 1965-69, assoc. prof., 1969-71; prof. chmn. dept. surgery U. Louisville, 1971—; pres., chmn. bd. U. Surg. Assocs., PSC, 1971—2005; chmn. bd. Clin. Services Assn., Inc. Mem. merit rev. bd. for surgery VA, 1983—85. Author: (with H.H. Stone) Contemporary Burn Management, 1971, Hospital-Acquired Infections in Surgery, 1977; (with B. Gardner, H.H. Stone and W.L. Sugg) Basic Surgery, 1978; (with H.H. Stone and B. Gardner) 2d edit., 1983, 3d edit., 1987, 4th edit., 1992, 5th edit., 1995; (with D.C. Carter) Trauma, 1982; (with J.E. Conte Jr. and L.S. Jacob) Antibiotic Prophylaxis in Surgery: A Comprehensive Review, 1984; (with J.D. Richardson and L.M. Flint Jr.) Trauma: Clinical Care and Pathophysiology, 1987; contbr. articles to profl. jours.; mem. editl. bd. So. Med. Jour., 1970-72, Jour. Surg. Rsch., 1970-72, 75-77, 78-80, Current Problems in Surgery, 1973—, Surgery, 1975-85, Current Surgery, 1977—, Current Surg. Techniques, 1977—, Emergency Surgery: A Weekly Update, 1977—, Collected Letters in Surgery, 1978—, Brit. Jour. Surgery, 1981-94; chief editor Am. Jour. Surgery, 1986-2004. Fellow Royal Coll. Surgeons Edinburgh (hon.); mem. ACS (gov. 1972-80), AMA, Allen O. Whipple Soc. (exec. coun. 1977-80), Am. Assn. Cancer Edn. (exec. coun. 1968-72), Am. Assn. Surgery of Trauma, Am. Burn Assn., Am. Cancer Soc. (pres. Ky. div. 1989-90, nat. del. dir. 1989-92, 93-95), Am. Surg. Assn. (sec. 1984-89, pres. 2005), Acad. Surgery (pres. 1975-76), Cen. Surg. Assn., Assn. Am. Med. Colls. (chmn. ad hoc com. on Medicare and Medicaid 1978-79), Collegium Internat. Chirurgiae Digestivae (sec.-treas. 1981-86, pres. 1986-87), Coun. on Public Higher Edn. (task group on health scis.), Halsted Soc., Jefferson County Med. Soc., Ky. Med. Assn., Ky. Surg. Soc. (pres. 1982-83), Louisville Surg. Soc. (pres. 1989-90), Residency Rev. Com. for Surgery (vice chmn. 1981-83, chmn. 1983-85), Soc. Internat. de Chirurgie, Soc. Surgery Alimentary Tract (treas. 1975-78, pres. 1985-86), Soc. Clin. Surgery, Soc. Surg. Chairmen, Soc. Surg. Oncology (pres. 1984-85), Soc. Univ. Surgeons (treas. 1971-74, pres. 1979-80), James IV Assn. Surgeons (v.p. 2002—), Southeastern Surg. Congress (exec. coun. for Ky. 1985-86, pres. 1994-95), So. Med. Assn. (vice chmn. sect. on surgery 1969-70, chmn. sect. 1972-73, sec. 1970-72, exec. coun. for Ky. 1971-77, 89-90), So. Surg. Assn. (pres. 1988-89), Alpha Omega Alpha. Home: 5609 River Knoll Dr Louisville KY 40222-5846 Office: U Louisville Dept Surgery Louisville KY 40292-0001 Office Phone: 502-852-1897. Business E-Mail: hcpolk01@gwise.louisville.edu.

POLLACK, IAN FREDRIC, physician, researcher; b. Holliswood, NY, Aug. 26, 1960; s. Jonah and Roberta Minnie (Wainick) P.; m. Constance Shenk, Aug. 15, 1982; children: Benjamin Nathan, Andrew Maxwell. BS magna cum laude, Emory U., 1980; MD, Johns Hopkins U., 1984. Intern in surgery U. Pitts., 1984-85, resident in neurosurgery, 1985-91, postgrad. fellow dept. neurobiology, 1988-90, asst. prof. dept. neurosurgery, 1990-96, assoc. prof., 1996—99, prof., 1999—, Walter Dandy prof., 2001—, co-dir. Brain Tumor Ctr., 1996—. Chmn. brain tumor strategy group. Contbr. articles to New Eng. Jour. Medicine, Cancer Rsch., Exptl. Neurology, Jour. Neurosurgery, Cancer, Jour. Neurosurgery Rsch., Neurosurgery, Brain Rsch., others. Van Wagenen fellow Am. Assn. Neurol. Surgeons, 1991; recipient Resident Rsch. award ACS, 1990, Pitts. Neurosci. Soc., 1989, Preuss award Am. Assn. Neurol. Surgeons and Congress Neurological Surgeons Joint Sect. on Tumors, 1989, Young Clinician Investigator award Am. Assn. Neurol. Surgeons, 1992. Mem. AAAS, Congress of Neurol. Surgeons, Phi Beta Kappa, Alpha Omega Alpha. Achievements include research in the growth factor response properties of human brain tumor cells in culture, the role of selective inhibitors on tumor growth in culture, molecular markers of brain tumor prognosis and immunotherapeutic strategies for brain tumors. Office: U Pitts Dept Neurosurgery 9402 Presbyn Univ Hosp 230 Lothrop St Pittsburgh PA 15213-2536 also: Children Hosp Pgh UPMC Neuosurg Faculty Pavilion 4fl Childrens Hosp Dr 45th and Penn Pittsburgh PA 15224 also: Childrens Hosp Pitts Dept Neurosurgery 4401 Penn Ave Pittsburgh PA 15224 Office Phone: 412-692-5881. E-mail: ian.pollack@chp.edu.

POLLACK, IRWIN WILLIAM, psychiatrist, educator; b. Phila., Aug. 14, 1927; s. Nathan and Rose (Bergman) P.; m. Barbara Jean Callaway, Oct. 9, 1988; children from previous marriage: Nathaniel Edward, Joshua Frank, Jonathan Daniel AB, Temple U., 1950; MA, Columbia U., 1951; student, U. Pa., 1951—52; MD, U. Vt., 1956. Diplomate: Am. Bd. Psychiatry and Neurology. Intern Grad. Hosp. U. Pa., 1956—57; asst. resident psychiatry Henry Phipps Psychiat. Clinic (John Hopkins Hosp.), 1957—60; chief resident psychiatry Johns Hopkins Hosp., 1960—61, adminstr. psychosomatic clinic, psychiat. liaison svc., 1961—64; psychiatrist-in-chief Sinai Hosp., Balt., 1964—69; mem. faculty psychiatry Coll. Medicine and Dentistry N.J. (Rutgers Med. Sch.), 1968—87, 1987—, clin. prof. psychiatry, 1998. Assoc. prof. psychiatry, 1968-70, prof. psychiatry, 1979-99, emeritus prof. psychiatry 1999-, chmn. dept. Univ. Medicine and Dentistry N.J.; prof. neurology, dir. Ctr. for Cognitive Rehab.; exec. dir. Coll. Medicine and Dentistry (Cmty. Mental Health Ctr.), 1970-77 Served with USNR, 1945-46 Fellow Am. Psychiat. Assn. (life); mem. N.J. Psychiat. Assn., Am. Psychosomatic Soc., Am. Congress Rehab. Medicine, Alpha Omega Alpha Achievements include spl. research or problems of time and space perception, psychology of phys. disability, doctor-patient relationships, cognitive retraining of brain-injured persons.

POLLACK, MARK HARRIS, psychiatrist; b. Bklyn., Oct. 29, 1957; MD, N.J. Med. Sch., Newark, 1982. Diplomate American Bd. Psychiatry & Neurology 1987. Intern Waltham (Mass.) Hosp., 1982—83; resident Mass. Gen. Hosp. Dept. Psychiatry, fellow, dir. Ctr. for Anxiety & Traumatic Stress Related Disorders Boston, 1990—2011, prof. psychiatry Harvard Medical Sch., Boston, Grainger prof., chmn. dept. psychiatry Rush Medical Coll., Chgo., 2011—. Mem.: Anxiety Disorders Assn. America. Office: Rush University Medical College 2150 W Harrison St Chicago IL 60612 Office Phone: 312-942-5372. Office Fax: 312-942-6216. *

POLLACK, MURRAY MICHAEL, pediatrician, medical association administrator; b. Bklyn., Nov. 1, 1947; s. Louis R. and Shirley Pollack; children: Seth, Haley. BA in Biology, U. Rochester, 1970; MD, Albert Einstein Sch. Medicine, 1974. Diplomate Am. Bd. Pediat., Am. Bd. Pediatric Critical Care. Intern, then resident in pediat. Children's Nat. Med. Ctr., Washington, 1974-77, intensivist, 1978-96, dir. health svcs. and clin. rsch., 1990-96, sect. head critical care medicine, 1995—2006; exec. dir. Ctr. for Hosp. Bases Svcs., 1999—2006; chief. med., acad. officer VPMA Phoenix Children's Med. Hosp., 2007—. Chief, critical care medicine, prof. anesthesiology and pediatrics George Washington U. Med. Sch., 1988-2007; dir. Ctr. Health Svcs. Rsch., Children's Rsch. Inst.; dir. Pediat. ICU Evaluations, 1994-2007; exec. chair Hosp. Based Ctr. of Excellence, 1999-2006; chief med. and acad. officer Phoenix Children's Hosp., 2007-; chair, prof. U. Ariz. Coll. Medicine, Phoenix, 2011-. Mem. editl. bd. Critical Care Medicine; contbr. articles to profl. jours. Recipient Disting. Career award, Am. Acad. Pediat., 2001, Disting. Investigator award, Am. Coll. Critical Care Medicine, 2002, Douglas K. Richardson Lifetime Achievement award, Soc. Pediatric Rsch., 2003; grantee, PHHS, 1989—, Robert Wood Johnson Found., 1986—89. Fellow Coll.Critical Care Medicine (faculty, reviewer, moderator 1987—), Nat. Assn. Children's Hosps. (quality com. 1991-95), Am. Bd. Pediat. (sub-bd. critical care 1991-95). Achievements include research in quantifying the relationship between physiologic instability and mortality risk, reduced risk of death associated with pediatric intensive care, creation of pediatric risk of mortality score. Personal E-mail: genpollack@comcast.net. Business E-Mail: mpollack@phoenixchildrens.com.

POLLACK, RICHARD J., epidemiologist, educator; b. Cin., Feb. 4, 1957; BS, Cornell U., 1979; PhD, U. Pa., 1988. Rsch. assoc. Harvard Sch. Pub. Health, 1988; vis. scientist Mass. Inst. Tech., 1989—90; adj. asst. prof. Tufts U., 2009; rsch. assoc. prof. Boston U., 2010—. Commr. Norfolk county mosquito control project Mass. Dept Agrl. Resources, 2002, chair mosquito adv. group, 06; chair sci. & tech. com. Am. Mosquito Control Assn., 2008—10; pres., chief sci. officer Identify US LLC, 2010. Contbr. to profl. publs. Recipient Stauber award, Am. Soc. Parasitologists. Home: 32 Crescent Rd Needham MA 02494 Business E-Mail: rpollack@hsph.harvard.edu.

POLLACK, ROBERT ELLIOT, biologist, educator, writer; b. Bklyn., Sept. 2, 1940; s. Ephraim Hyman and Molly (Pollack) P.; m. Amy Louise Steinberg, Dec. 23, 1961; 1 child, Marya BA in Physics, Columbia U., 1961; PhD in Biology, Brandeis U., 1966. Asst. prof. pathology Med. Sch. NYU, NYC, 1969-70; sr. scientist Cold Spring Harbor Lab., NY, 1971-75; prof. microbiology Med. Sch., SUNY-Stony Brook, 1975-78; prof. biol. sci. Columbia U., NYC, 1978—; dean Columbia Coll., NYC, 1982-89. Bd. dirs., chmn. sci. adv. bd. Tapestry Pharms., 1994-; instr. Pratt Archtl. Sch., Bklyn., 1970; lectr. psychiatry Ctr. for Psychoanalytic Tng., Columbia U., 1999—, dir. Ctr. for the Study of Sci. and Religion, 1999—; vis. prof. pharmacology Albert Einstein Coll. Medicine, Bronx, N.Y., 1977-92; dean's disting. lectr. in Humanities, Columbia Med. Sch., 2000; lectr. Rosenthal Colloquium, March of Dimes, 1989; McGregory lectr. Colgate U., 1979; du Vigneaud lectr. Med. Sch., Cornell U., 1983.

Co-editor: Readings in Mammalian Cell Culture, 1973, 3d rev. edit., 1981, Signs of Life, 1984 (translations in 7 langs., Lionel Trilling award 1995), The Missing Moment, 1999, The Faith of Biology and the Biology of Faith, 2000; mng. editor BBA Revs. on Cancer, 1980-86; contbr. numerous rsch. articles on molecular cell biology to profl. jours. Trustee N.Y. Found., 1988-96, Brandeis U., 1989-94, Solomon Schechter Sch. of N.Y.C., 1996-98; fellow World Econ. Forum, 1995—; bd. overseers List Coll. of the Jewish theol. Sem. of Am., 1996-99; pres. Jewish Campus Life Fund, Columbia U., 1997-2001. Recipient Rsch. Career Devel. award NIH, 1974, Alexander Hamilton medal, 1989, Lionel Trilling award Columbia U., 1995; NIH spl. fellow Weizmann Inst., Rehovot, Israel, 1970-71; grantee Nat. Cancer Inst., NIH, 1968-92, Am. Cancer Soc., 1985-94; John Simon Guggenheim fellow, 1993. Fellow AAAS; mem. N.Y. Acad. Scis., Am. Soc. Microbiology. Office: Columbia U Fairchild Hall 1212 Amsterdam Ave # Mc2419 New York NY 10027-7003 Office Phone: 212-854-2409. Business E-Mail: pollack@columbia.edu.

POLLACK, ROBERT HARVEY, psychology professor; b. NYC, June 26, 1927; s. Solomon and Bertha (Levy) P.; m. Martha Dee Katz, Aug. 20, 1948; children: Jonathan Keith, Lance Michael, Scott Evan. BS, CCNY, 1948; MS, Clark U., Worcester, Mass., 1950, PhD, 1953. Lectr. U. Sydney, Australia, 1953-61; spl. rsch. fellow Columbia U., NYC, 1960-61; chief div. congitive devel. Inst. Juvenile Rsch., Chgo., 1961-63, dep. dir. rsch., 1963-69; from clin. asst. prof. to clin. assoc. prof. rsch. U. Ill. Coll. Medicine, Chgo., 1962-67; prof. psychology U. Ga., Athens, 1969-96, chair grad. program. exptl. psychology, 1970-78, chair grad. study com., 1978-86; prof. emeritus, 1996—; chair grad. program in life-span psychology U. Ga., Athens, 1988-96. Editor: The Experimental Psychology of Alfred Binet, 1969; contbr. over 100 articles and chpts. to profl. publs. Cpl. U.S. Army, 1945-46. Grantee Nat. Inst. Child Health and Human Devel., 1965, 67, 72, 78. Fellow AAAS, Am. Psychol. Assn.; mem. Am. Assn. Sex Edn., Counsellors and Therapists, Gerontol. Soc. Am., Australian Psychol. Soc., Soc. for Researching Child Devel., Soc. for Sci. Study Sex, Sigma Xi. Democrat. Avocations: travel, stamp collecting/philately, opera, military history. Office: U Ga Dept Psychology Athens GA 30602 Office Phone: 706-542-3084. Business E-Mail: bpollack@uga.edu.

POLLACK, RONALD FRANK, healthcare organization executive, lawyer; b. NYC, Feb. 21, 1944; s. Max Louis and Hanna Esther (Borchardt) Pollack Baruch; m. Rebecca Lucy Bolling, Jan. 8, 1972; children: Sarah Shoshana, Abraham Max, Martin Landrum. BA, Queens Coll., 1965; JD, NYU, 1968. Bar: N.Y. 1968, D.C. 1978, U.S. Ct. Appeals (D.C. cir) 1970, U.S. Ct. Appeals (5th cir.) 1971, U.S. Ct. Appeals (6th cir.) 1974, U.S. Supreme Ct. 1973. Atty. Ctr. on Social Welfare Policy and Law, NYC, 1968-73; founder, exec. dir. Food Research and Action Ctr., NYC, 1970-80; dean Antioch Sch. Law, Washington, 1980-83; exec. dir. Families U.S.A., Washington, 1983—. Sec. treas., bd. dirs. Food Research and Action Ctr., Washington, 1980—; mem. civil legal services D.C. Jud. Conf. Com., 1980-83; appointee Pres.'s Adv. Commn. on Consumer Protection and Quality in the Health Care Industry, 1997-98. Author: If We Had Ham, We Could Have Ham and Eggs...If We Had Eggs: A Study of the National School Breakfast Program, 1972, Out to Lunch: A Study of USDA's Child Care Feeding and Summer Feeding Programs, 1974; co-author: On the Other Side of Easy Street: Myths and Facts About the Economics of Old Age, 1987. Treas. Jewish Fund for Justice, 1985-88, bd. dirs., 1985-93; bd. dirs. Am. Jewish World Service, Self-Help Community Services, 1974-77; mem. domestic adv. bd., project rev. bd. U.S.A. for Africa/Hands Across Am., 1986-88; v.p. of bd. dirs. Burgundy Farm Country Day Sch., 1988-90, pres. 1990-91; bd. dirs. Americans for Health, 1986-91. Arthur Garfield Hays Civil Liberties fellow, 1967-68; research fellow Legal Services Corp., Washington, 1978-80 Office: Families USA 1201 New York Ave Washington DC 20005

POLLARD, HARVEY B., medical educator, neuroscientist; b. San Antonio, May 26, 1943; BA in Biology, Rice U., 1964; MS in Biochemistry, U. Chgo., 1969, MD, 1969, PhD, 1973. Rsch. assoc. NIH-Nat. Inst. Arthritis and Metabolic Diseases, Bethesda, Md., 1969-71, sr. investigator, 1972-74, 1977-79, sect. chief, 1979-81; lab. chief Nat. Inst. Diabetes, Digestive and Kidney Diseases, Bethesda, 1981-96; prof., chair dept. anatomy, physiology and genetics Uniformed Svcs. U. Sch. Medicine, Bethesda, 1997—. Contbr. over 275 articles to profl. jours. With USPHS, 1969-96. Recipient Commendation medal USPHS, 1982, Alumni award for Disting. Svc., U. Chigo. Alumni Assn., 1989, NIH Inventor's award, 1991. Mem. Biophys. Soc., Soc. for Neurosci., Am. Soc. for Pharmacology and Exptl. Therapeutics, Soc. for Cell Biology, Endocrine Soc., Am. Coll. Psychoneuropharmacology, Am. Soc. for Biochemistry and Molecular Biology, Am. Assn. Anatomists., Am. Physiol. Soc., Institute of Medicine of Washington, D.C. *

POLLARD, THOMAS DEAN, cell biologist, educator; b. Pasadena, Calif., July 7, 1942; s. Dean Randall and Florence Alma (Dierker) Pollard; m. Patricia Elizabeth Snowden, Feb. 7, 1964; children: Katherine, Daniel. BA cum laude, Pomona Coll., Claremont, Calif., 1964; MD cum laude, Harvard Med. Sch., 1968. Intern Mass. Gen. Hosp., Boston, 1968—69; staff assoc. lab. biochemistry Nat. Heart and Lung Inst., Bethesda, Md., 1969—72; asst. prof. anatomy Harvard Med. Sch., Boston, 1972—75, assoc. prof., 1975—78; Bayard Halsted prof., dir. dept. cell biology and anatomy Johns Hopkins U. Sch. Medicine, Balt., 1977—96; pres. Salk Inst. Biol. Studies, La Jolla, Calif., 1996—2000, prof., 1996—2001, U. Calif., San Diego, 1996—2001; Eugene Higgins prof. molecular, cellular and devel. biology and cell biology Yale U., New Haven, 2001—06, prof. cell biology, 2002—, prof. molecular biophysics and biochemistry, 2003—, Sterling prof. molecular, cellular and devel. biology and cell biology, 2006—; dean Grad. Sch. Arts & Scis., 2010—. Vis. scientist Med. Rsch. Coun. Lab. Molecular Biology, Cambridge, England, 1984; mem. NRC Commn. Life Sci., 1990—97, chair, 1993—97; mem. coun. NIH Nat. Inst. Gen. Med. Sci.; adj. prof. biology, bioengineering and chemistry and biochemistry U. Calif., San Diego, 1997—2001; chair dept. molecular, cellular and devel. biology Yale U., 2004—. Contbr. articles to profl. jours.; mem. editl. bd.: Cell Biology - Internat. Reports, 1976—81, Jour. Cell Biology, 1977—82, Jour. Submicroscopic Cytology, 1978—82, Cell Motility and the Cytoskeleton, 1980—94, Jour. Muscle Rsch. and Cell Motility, 1980—88, Microscopy Rsch. and Technique, 1981—93, Current Opinion in Cell Biology, 1988—, Current Biology, 1991—, Protein Profile, 1994—97, Trends in Biochemical Scis., 1995—, Procs. NAS, 1996—98, assoc. editor: Molecular Biology of the Cell, 1991—. Recipient Rsch. Career Devel. award, US Pub. Health Svc., 1974—78, MERIT award, Nat. Inst. Gen. Med. Sci., 1988—98; co-recipient Lewis S. Rosentiel Disting. Work in Basic Med. Rsch. award, Brandeis U., 1996, Gairdner Found. Internat. award, 2006; Winston Churchill Overseas fellowship, Churchill Coll., UK, 1984, Guggenheim fellowship, 1994. Fellow: Am. Acad. Microbiol., AAAS (bd. dirs. 2006—), Inst. Medicine, Biophys. Soc. (mem. coun. 1977—80, pres. 1992—93, Pub. Svc. award 1997), NAS, Am. Acad. Arts & Scis.; mem.: Am. Soc. Biochemistry and Molecular Biology, Marine Biol. Lab. (trustee 1991—97), Am. Soc. Cell Biology (mem. exec. com. 1976—77, mem. coun. 1976—79, pres. 1987—88, K.R. Porter lectr. 1989, E.B. Wilson medal 2004). Achievements include patents in field. Office: Dept Molecular Cellular and Devel Biology Yale U PO Box 208103 New Haven CT 06520-8103 E-mail: thomas.pollard@yale.edu. *

POLLEY, RICHARD DONALD, microbiologist, chemist; b. Bklyn., Feb. 23, 1937; s. George Weston and Evelyn (Tuttle) P.; m. Linda R. Radford, Sept. 21, 1991; children from previous marriage: Gordon MacHeath, Jennifer Elizabeth, Tabitha Isabelle, Sean Sullivan. Student, Trinity Coll., 1954-57; BS, Hofstra U., 1960. Lic. nuclear radiation tech. U.S. Govt., 2003. Asst. advt. mgr. tech. Sun Chem. Corp., 1961-63; tech. advt. mgr. Celanese Plastics Co., Newark, 1963-67; account dir. McCann Indsl. Tech. Sci. Mktg., NYC, 1967-68, v.p., gen. mgr. Miami, 1968-70; pres. Intercapital Belgium S.A., Brussels, Nassau, Bahamas, Panama City, Panama, 1970-72; cons. Nuclear Regulatory Commn., Atomic City, Idaho, 1975—76; founder, pres., tech. dir. Iodinamics Corp., Lancaster, Pa., El Paso, Tex., El Paso, Tex., 1973-76; founder, CEO, COO, tech. dir., bd. dirs., chmn. Hydrodine Corp., Miami, 1976—2002, chmn., CEO, tech. dir., 1986—2002, also bd. dirs. Founder, chmn. CEO, COO, tech. dir. Polymorphic Polymers Corp., Miami, 1978—90; founder, COO, tech. dir., CEO, bd. dirs. Omnidine Corp., Miami, 1980—98, bd. dirs.; pres., tech. dir. Skin Care Labs., Inc., Miami, Fla., 1979—90; tech. dir. Hydrodine Biotech (Far East) Ltd., Bangkok, Thailand, Hong Kong, Singapore and Kuala Lumpur, 1989—98; CEO, tech. dir. Polllabs., Sao Paulo, Brazil, 1990—2000; tech. dir. Ecology Tech. do Brasil, Sao Paulo, 1993—2000; tech. dir., environ. and agrl. mgr. Environ. Tech. do Brasil, Sao Paulo, 1995—; chief internat. tech. dir. environ. microbiology Gen. Environ. Sci. Corp., Solon, Ohio, 1993—2000; chmn., co-founder Peer Group Influencers Ltd., London, Miami, 1988—98; v.p., bd. dirs. Internat. Airlines, Long Beach, Calif., 1984—2000; COO, tech. dir. Swiver Corp., Miami, 1994—2002; tech. dir. chief scientist Infinity Techs., Ltd., Panama City, 1996—98; founder, bd. dirs., CEO, pres., tech. dir. PolleyTech Corp., Pembroke Pines, Fla., 1998—; overseas dir. field Iodine Deficiency Disease med. demonstration projects Beth Israel Hosp., Harvard U. Med. Sch., 1977—88; lectr. Harvard Bus. Sch., 1980; cons. water disinfection control, water environments Pan Am. Health Orgn., others; med. and tech. dir. Enzymes Brasil, Ltd., Sao Paulo, 2001—, med. mgr., tech. dir., Guayaquil, Ecuador, 2001—; chmn. med./sci. adv. bd., found. tech. dir. RAH Med. Rsch. Found., Napa Valley, Calif., 2001—; cons. IGFA Wetlands Project, 2001—; founder, CEO, COO, chmn. bd. dirs. Xurex Nano-Coatings Corp., Davie, Fla., 2005—. Mem. editl. adv. bd. Chem. Week, 1988; contbr. articles to profl. jours.; patentee. Mem. cmty. bd. Am. Heart Assn., Am. Stroke Assn., Broward County, PR. Recipient R. Buckminster Fuller Home of the Future award for paints and water system, 1976. Mem. AAAS, NRA, Am. Concrete Inst., N.Y. Acad. Scis., Internat. Iodine Inst. (chmn. bd. and tech. dir. 1976—), Associaçao de Ciencia e Tecnologia Ambiental (bd. dirs. Sao Paulo 1993—), The Nature Conservancy, World Wildlife Fund, Sierra Club, Audubon Soc., Wilderness Soc., Defenders of Wildlife, Environ. Defense Org., Fla. Wildlife Fedn., Internat. Game Fish Assn., others. Achievements include patents for farm, industrial, commercial, medical, environmental and household protective coatings and water treatment devices, nuclear industries; fields of medicine, environmental protection, agriculture and enzymes soil road building, asphalt and soil enzymes roads, lagoons, aquaculture, ponds; drinking water reservoirs, hazardous waste containment area soil reservoirs; soil aircraft landing strips; coinventor, foundational nano-molecular protective coatings. Office: Xurex Nano-Coatings Corp 531 Gallatin Place NW Albuquerque NM 87121 E-mail: rpolley@xurex.com.

POLLICK, HOWARD FRANKLIN, dentist, educator; b. Manchester, Eng., Apr. 21, 1945; BDS, U. Manchester, 1967; MPH, UC Berkeley, 1980. Health sci. clin. prof. U. Calif. San Francisco, 1981—. Cons. Calif. Dept. Pub. Health, 2007—. Recipient Grand Marshall award, Sch. Dentistry UCSF, 2003, Excellence Clin. Tchg. award, 2004, Fluoridation Spl. Merit award, Assn. State and Territorial Dental Dirs., 2010, Disting. Faculty Mem. award, Am. Coll. Dentists Northern Calif. Sect., 2011. Mem.: APHA, ADA, Internat. Assn. Dental Rsch., Calif. Dental Assn., Omicron Kappa Upsilon (Rho Rho chpt.). Avocation: golf. Office: 707 Parnassus Ave Box 0758 San Francisco CA 94143-0758 Business E-Mail: howard.pollick@ucsf.edu.

POLLIN, TONI I., endocrinologist, educator; MS in Molecular, Cellular & Devel. Biology, U. Minn., 1997; PhD in Human Genetics, U. Md., 2004. Diplomate Am. Bd. Genetic Counseling, 1999. Asst. prof. divsn. endocrinology, diabetes & nutrition U. Md. Sch. Medicine. Office: 660 W Redwood St Rm 445C Baltimore MD 21201 Office Phone: 410-706-1630. Office Fax: 410-706-1622. E-mail: tpollin@medicine.umaryland.edu.

POLLOCK, AVRUM N., radiologist, educator; b. Winnipeg, May 4, 1963; MD, U. Man., 1988. Dir. pediatric radiology residency chop Children's Hosp. Phila., 2002—. Asst. prof. radiology U. Pitts. Sch. Medicine, 1996—2002, U. Pa. Sch. Medicine, 2002—10, clin. assoc. prof. radiology, 2010—. Fellow: Royal Coll. Physicians & Surgeons Can.; mem.: Am. Soc. Neuroradiology, Soc. Pediatric Radiology, Am. Roentgen Ray Soc., Radiol. Soc. N.America. Avocations: piano, singing, photography, genealogy. Office: 3400 Civic Ctr Blvd Philadelphia PA 19104 Business E-Mail: pollocka@email.chop.edu.

POLONSKY, KENNETH S., dean; b. Johannesburg, Feb. 9, 1951; came to U.S., 1976; m. Lydia Polonsky; children: Tamar, Daniel, Jonathan. MD, U. Witwatersrand, Johannesburg, South Africa, 1973. Diplomate Am. Bd. Internal Medicine. Resident sect. endocrinology dept. Internal medicine U. Chgo., 1976-78, fellow, 1978-80, rsch. assoc., 1980-81, asst. prof., 1981-87, assoc. prof., 1987-90, prof., chief sect. endocrinology, 1990-99, exec. v.p. med. affairs, dean divsn. biol. sciences, dean Pritzker Sch. Medicine, Richard T. Crane disting. svc. prof. medicine, 2010—; Adolphus Busch prof. medicine, chmn. dept. Washington U. Sch. Medicine, St. Louis, 1999—2010, prof. cell biology and physiology, 2000—10. David Pyke vis. prof. Kinbgs Diabetes Ctr., Kings Coll. Hosp., London, 1998; Harold Rifkin vis. prof. Montefiore Med. Ctr. and Albet Einstein Coll. Medicine, Bronx, N.Y., 1998; Kroc lectr. U. Ala., Birmingham, 1999, U. Pa. Sch. Medicine, Phila., 2000; Priscilla White lectr. Joslin Diabetes Ctr., Brigham and Women's Hosp., Boston, 2001. Mem. editl. bd. Diabetes Care, Jour. Clin. Endocrinology and Metabolism, Diabetes, Endocrine Revs., Am. Jour. Physiology, Endocrinology and Metabolism; mem. editl. bd., cons. editor Jour. Clin. Investigation; contbr. over 190 articles to med. jours., including Diabetes, Am. Jour. Physiology, Endocrinology and Metabolism, Nat. Genetics, Metabolism, Jour. Clin. Endocrinology and Metabolism. Recipient career devel. award Schweppe Found., 1983-86, merit award NIH, 1997; grantee NIH, 1981—; fellow Juvemile Diabetes Found., 1979-81, rsch. grantee, 1981-83, 84-86, 88-90. Mem. Am. Diabetes Asn. (Solomon A. Berson rsch. career devel. award 1981-83, pilot and feasibility grantee 1988-90, mentor-based fellow 1996-99), Am. Fedn. for Clin. Rsch., Am. Physiol. Soc., Am. Soc. for Clin. Investigation, Assn. Am. Physicians, Endocrin Soc., Ctr. Soc. for Clin. Rsch. Office: University Chgo Med Ctr 5841 S Md Ave MC 1000 Chicago IL 60637 Office Phone: 773-702-3004. Office Fax: 773-702-1897. Business E-Mail: polonsky@bsd.uchicago.edu. *

POLSKY, MORRIS BRIAN, physician; b. Charleston, W.Va., Jan. 7, 1969; MD, USC Som, 1995. Ptnr. OACM, 2001—. Home: 12601 Holtz Ln Reisterstown MD 21136 Personal E-mail: mpolsky99@yahoo.com.

POLUNINA, ANNA GENNADIEVNA, neurologist, researcher; b. Moscow, Dec. 25, 1971; d. Gennadiy Serafimovich Polunin and Larisa Nikolaevna Polunina; m. Alexey Viktorovich Begachev; children: Andrey Begachev, Antonina Begacheva, Gennadiy Begachev. MD in Neurology, Moscow Med. Acad., 1997, PhD, 1997. Rschr. Moscow Rsch. Practical Ctr. Narcology, 1997—, neurologist, 1967—, Mcpl. Clin. Hosp., Moscow, 1998—2007, Bakulev's Sci. Ctr. Cardiac-vascular Surgery, Moscow, rschr., 2000—; practitioner, neurology Mcpl. Ambulatory Clinic, Moscow, 2008—. Contbr. articles to numerous profl. jours. Achievements include research in effects of chronic heroin consumption on brain structure and function, etiology and prevention of neurological complication of on-pump surgery. Office: Moscow RP Ctr Narcology Ul Lublinskaya 37/1 Moscow Russia Home: Leninsky Prt 156-368 119571 Moscow Russia Home Fax: 7 495 4387624. Personal E-mail: anpolunina@mail.ru.

POLVERINI, PETER J., dean, dental educator; m. Carol Polverini. BS in Biology, Marquette U., Milw., 1969, DDS, 1973; DMS, Harvard Med. Sch., 1977. Diplomate American Bd. Oral and Maxillofacial Pathology. Asst. prof. dept. diagnostic & surg. scis, U. Pitts. Sch. Dental Medicine, 1977—81; assoc. prof. pathology, dir. Lab. Diagnostic Oral & Maxillofacial Pathology Northwestern U. Med. & Dental Sch., Chgo., 1981—92; prof. dentistry, chief oral & maxillofacial pathology U. Mich. Sch. Dentistry, Ann Arbor, 1992—95, chair dept. oral medicine, pathology & surgery, 1995—96, chair dept. oral medicine, pathology & oncology, 1996—2000, Donald A. Kerr endowed collegiate prof., 1996—2000, prof., dean, 2003—; dean U. Minn. Sch. Dentistry, Mpls., 2000—03. Assoc. editor Angiogenesis, mem. editl. bd. Jour. Oral Pathology & Medicine, Lab. Investigation; contbr. articles to profl. jours., chapters to books. Fellow: AAAS, American Coll. Dentists; mem.: Internat. Assn. Dental Rsch. (Disting. Scientist award), Inst. Medicine. Address: U Mich Sch Dentistry 1011 N Univ Ave Ann Arbor MI 48109-1078 Office Phone: 734-763-3311. Office Fax: 734-763-5142. Business E-Mail: neovas@umich.edu. *

POLYAK, KORNELIA, oncologist, researcher; MD, Albert Szent-Gyorgyi Med. U., Hungary, 1991; PhD, Cornell U., 1995. Fellow Johns Hopkins Oncology Ctr.; assoc. prof. dept. med. oncology Harvard Med. Sch.; researcher Dana Farber Cancer Inst. Recipient Scholar award, V Found., 2001. Mem.: Am. Assn. Cancer Rsch. Office: Dana-Farber Cancer Institute 44 Binney St Dana 740C Boston MA 02115 Office Phone: 617-632-2106. Office Fax: 617-580-8490. E-mail: kornelia_polyak@dfci.harvard.edu.

POLYAKOV, VALERIY, physician cosmonaut; b. Apr. 27, 1942; married; 1 child. Grad., First I. M. Sechenov's Moscow Med. Inst., 1965; D in Med. Sciences, 1997. Rsch. dr. Soyuz TM-6 / MIR-3 / MIR-4 / Soyuz TM-7, 1988—89; dr. cosmonaut Soyuz TM-18 / MIR-15 / MIR-16 / MIR-17 / Soyuz TM-20, 1994—95. Dep. dir. IMBP, 1989—97; prof. Internat. Academy of Astonautics. Office: c/o Russian Federal Space Agency Schepkina St 42 Moscow Russia Office Fax: 4956889063, 4999754467. *

POLYMEROS, DIMITRIOS, gastroenterologist; b. Athens, July 2, 1967; Degree, U. Athens, 1991. Cons. gastroenterologist Attikon U. Hosp., 2003—. Home: 73 Perikleous St Athens Attiki 15232 Greece Personal E-mail: dimpolymeros@yahoo.com.

POMAHAC, BOHDAN, plastic surgeon, educator; b. Mar. 8, 1971; MD, Palacky U. Sch. Medicine, Czech Republic, 1996. Diplomate Am. Bd. Plastic Surgery. Intern gen. surgery Brigham & Women's Hosp., Boston, 1996—99, resident gen. surgery, 1999—2001, resident plastic surgery, 2001—03, chief resident plastic surgery, 2004, assoc. dir. BWH Burn Ctr., 2004—; asst. prof. Harvard Med. Sch. Contbr. articles to profl. jours. Grantee Greenwall Found. Mem.: Am. Soc. Reconstructive Transplantation (founding mem.), Plastic Surgery Rsch. Coun., Am. Burn Assn., Am. Soc. Reconstructive Microsurgery, Am. Soc. Plastic Surgery. Achievements include leading 35-member medical team that performed the second facial transplant surgery operation in the US on April 9, 2009, a 17 hour procedure in which doctors donated their time while the hospital donated the other costs related to the operation. Office: Brigham & Womens Hosp Divsn Plastic Surgery 75 Francis St Boston MA 02115 Office Phone: 617-732-7796. Office Fax: 617-732-6387. Business E-Mail: bpomahac@partners.org.

POMERANTZ, MARVIN, thoracic surgeon; b. Suffern, NY, June 16, 1934; s. Julius and Sophie (Luksin) Pomerantz; m. Margaret Twigg, Feb. 26, 1966; children: Ben, Julie. AB, Colgate U., 1955; MD, U. Rochester, 1959. Diplomate Nat. Bd. Med. Examiners, Am. Bd. Surgery, Am. Bd. Thoracic Surgery (bd. dirs. 1989-95). Intern Duke U. Med. Ctr., Durham, NC, 1959—60, resident, 1960—61, instr. surgery, 1966—67; asst. prof. surgery U. Colo. Med. Sch., Denver, 1967—71, assoc. prof. surgery, 1971—74, assoc. clin. prof. surgery, 1974—93, prof. surgery, chief gen. thoracic surgery, 1992—; chief thoracic and cardiovascular surgery Denver Gen. Hosp., 1967—73, asst. dir. surgery, 1967—70, assoc.dir. surgery, 1970—73; pvt. practice Arapahoe CV Assocs., Denver, 1974—92; prof., chief gen. thoracic surgery sect. U. Colo. Health Sci. Ctr., 1992—; resident Duke U. Med. Ctr., Durham, NC, 1963—67. Clin. assoc. surgery br. NCI, 1961—63; mem. staff Univ. Hosp., Denver, Denver Gen. Hosp., Rose Med. Ctr., Denver, Denver VA Med. Ctr., Children's Hosp., Denver, U. Coll. Health Sci. Ctr., 1992—, bd. dirs., 1990—96; vice chmn. Am. Bd. Thoracic Surgery, 1995—97, chmn., 1997—99. Guest editor Chest Surgery Clinics N.Am., 1993; contbr. numerous articles to profl. publs., chapters to books. Master: AMA; fellow: ACS, Am. Coll. Chest Surgeons; mem.: Soc. Vascular Surgeons, Soc. Thoracic Surgeons (nomenclature/coding com. 1991—95, standards and ethics com., govt. rels. com., chmn. program com. 1994—95), Rocky Mtgn. Traumatologic Soc., rgery Soc., Internat. Cardiovascular Soc., Denver Acad. Surgery (pres. 1980), Colo. Med. Soc., Am. Heart Assn. (bd. dirs. Colo. chpt. 1993), Am. Assn. Thoracic Surgeons (program com. 1991), Western Thoracic Surg. Assn. (v.p. 1992, pres. 1993—94, counselor-at-large 1988—90). Office: UCHSC Divsn CTS 4200 E 9th Ave # C310 Denver CO 80262-0001 Business E-Mail: marvin.pomerantz@uchsc.edu.

POMERANTZ, RHONDA J., dermatologist; BS, U. Pa., 1985; MD, NYU, 1989. Intern NYU Med. Ctr., NYC, resident in internal medicine; resident in dermatology SYNY Health Sci. Ctr., Bklyn.; attending physician NYU Med. Ctr., NYC, 1995—. Mem.: Women's Dermatologic Soc., Am. Acad. Dermatology. Office: 35 E 35th St New York NY 10016 Office Phone: 212-684-6140. Office Fax: 212-689-5748.

POMEROY, CLAIRE, dean, academic administrator, medical educator; m. William Preston Robertson. MD, U. Mich. Coll. Medicine; MBA, U. Ky. Resident in internal medicine and infectious disease U. Minn., fellow internal medicine and infectious diseases, faculty mem., established HIV clinic at Mpls. Veterans' Adminstrn. Med. Ctr.; chief divsn. infectious diseases U. Ky. Coll. Medicine, asst. dean clin. affairs, assoc. dean rsch. informatics, prof.; exec. assoc. dean U. Calif. Davis Sch. Medicine, 2003, prof. infectious diseases and microbiology and immunology, vice chancellor human health sciences, 2005—, dean, 2005—. Faculty senate coun. U. Ky.; reviewer Nat. Institutes of Health, Dept. Veterans' Affairs. Bd. trustee U. Ky. Office: Office of Dean UC Davis Health Sys 2315 Stockton Blvd Sacramento CA 95817 Office Phone: 916-734-3578. E-mail: cpomeroy@ucdavis.edu. *

POMEROY, JOHN C., child and adolescent psychiatrist, educator; MD, St. George's Hosp. Med. Sch., England, 1973. Diplomate Am. Bd. Psychiatry and Neurology-adult psychiatry, Am. Bd. Psychiatry and Neurology-child and adolescent psychiatry. Resident in psychiatry St. Mary's Hosp., London, 1975—79; fellow in child and adolescent psychiatry Univ. Iowa Hosp., 1979—81; assoc. prof. psychiatry SUNY, Stony Brook, NY; founding dir. Matt and Debra Cody Ctr. for Autism and Devel. Disabilities; child and adolescent psychiatrist Stony Brook Univ. Med. Ctr. Office: Stony Brook University Medical Center East loop Rd Stony Brook NY 11794 Office Phone: 631-444-4000.

POMEROY, KENT LYTLE, physical medicine and rehabilitation physician; b. Phoenix, Ariz., Apr. 21, 1935; s. Benjamin Kent and Laverne (Hamblin) Pomeroy; m. Karen Jodelle Thomas (dec. Dec. 1962); 1 child, Charlotte Ann; m. Margo Delilah Tuttle, Mar. 27, 1964 (div. Jan. 1990); children: Benjamin Kent II, Janel Elise, Jonathan Barrett, Kimberly Eve, Kathryn M.; m. Kellie Sue Mahan, Dec. 22, 2007; m. Brenda Pauline North (dec. Sept. 15, 2005). BS in Phys. Sci., Ariz. State U., 1960; MD, U. Utah, 1963. Diplomate Am. Bd. Phys. Medicine and Rehab., Am. Bd. Pain Medicine, lic. homeopathic medicine Ariz., diploma Brit. Inst. Homeopathy, lic. in allopathic medicine Ariz. Rotating intern Good Samaritan Hosp., Phoenix, 1963-64, resident in phys. medicine and rehab., 1966-69, asst. tng. dir. Inst. Rehab. Medicine, 1970 74, dir. residency tng., 1974-76, asst. med. dir., 1973-76; dir. Phoenix Phys. Medicine Ctr., 1980-85, Ariz. Found. on Study Pain, Phoenix, 1980-85; pvt. practice Phoenix, 1976—. Lectr. in field. Contbr. Leader Grand Canyon Coun.,Boy Scouts Am.; ret. mem. exec. posse Maricopa County Sheriff's Office, Phoenix, 1981—2003, posse comdr., 1992—94, qualified armed posseman; mem. med. adv. bd. Grand Canyon-Saguaro chpt. Nat. Found. March of Dimes, 1970—78, missionary, 1955—57. Recipient Scouter's Tng. award, Grand Canyon Coun., Boy Scouts America, 1984, Scouter's Woodbadge, 1985; named one of Am. Top Physicians, Consumer Rsch. Coun. of Am., 2003. Fellow: Am. Coll. Pain Mgmt. & Sclerotherapy; mem.: AMA, Ariz. Homeopathic and Integrative Med. Assn. (pres. 2001—04), Am. Assn. Orthopedic Medicine (co-founder, past pres., mem. emeritus, lifetime acnievement award 2003), Law Enforcement Alliance of Am., Nat. Sheriff's Assn., Ariz. Med. Assn., Ariz. Soc. Phys. Medicine (pres. 1977—78), Nat. Eagle Scout Assn., Am. Acad. Pain Medicine, Prolotheraphy Assn. (pres. 1981—83). Mem. Lds Ch. Avocations: camping, drawing, painting, writing, music. Office: 3610 N 44th St #210 Phoenix AZ 85018 Office Phone: 602-912-4996. Personal E-mail: kentpomeroy@qwestoffice.net.

POMFRET, DAVID B., medical educator, internist; b. Somerset, Mass., Nov. 22, 1937; s. David B. Pomfret and Rhea Chouinard; m. Anna Rafferty, Mar. 31, 1964; children: Mark, Bruce, Scott, Heidi. BS, Stonehill Coll., 1959; MD, Univ. Coll., Dublin, Ireland, 1964. Diplomate Am. Bd. Internal Medicine. Chief medicine Leonard Morse Hosp., Natick, Mass., 1968—71, chief staff, 1976—80; clin. prof. Tufts U., Boston, 1976—; prof. medicine Tumaini U., Moshi, Tanzania, 1996—2000. Author: Computer Science, 1998, Dispatches From Kilimanjaro, 2006. Recipient Gold medal in surgery, UCD Sch. Medicine, 1964, Silver medal in medicine, 1964; named Outstanding Alumnus, Stonehill Coll., 2003. Fellow: ACP. Republican. Roman Catholic. Avocations: skiing, sailing, offshore racing. Home and Office: 20 Grey Gull Rd Jamestown RI 02835-2808 Office: 15 Rolling Ridge Box 48 Bartlett NH 03812-0048 Office Phone: 603-374-2705. Personal E-mail: pomfret1@cox.net.

POMMIER, YVES GEORGES, medical researcher; b. Caen, Calvados, France, Apr. 1, 1951; came to U.S., 1988; s. Roger Pommier and Marie-Therese Blais; m. Françoise Champey, Jan. 4, 1988; children: Gabriel, Elie. MS in Pharmacology, U. Paris, 1978, MD cum laude, 1981, PhD, 1986. Cert. radiation safety authorized user NIH. Resident Paris Hosps., 1978-81; pharmacology asst. U. Paris., 1979-81; vis. fellow Nat. Cancer Inst., NIH, Bethesda, Md., 1981-84, vis. scientist, 1984-95, prin. investigator, 1995—, chief Lab. Molecular Pharmacology, Ctr. Cancer Rsch., 1997—, head DNA Topoisomerase / Integrase Group. Organizer internat. conf. HIV-1 Integrase Inhibitors, 1996; lectr. in field. Mem. editl. bd. Cancer Rsch., Molecular Pharmacology, Anticancer Drug Design, others; contbr. articles to med. jours.; patentee in field. Recipient Impact Medicine Med. Dr. for Yr. 2000, 1992, Fed. Tech. Transfer award, 1994; competitive tng. grantee French Found. for Biol. Rsch., 1981, NIH intramural grantee AIDS Targeted Antiviral Program of Office of Dir., 1993-94, 95-96, 97-98. Mem. French Soc. Pharmacology, Am. Fedn. for Clin. Rsch., Am. Assn. for Cancer Rsch. (program com. 1996-99, chmn. CaiN award 1998), N.Y. Acad. Scis., NIH Apoptosis Interest Group. Democrat. Avocations: painting, tennis, coaching soccer team. Office: Ctr Cancer Rsch Lab Molecular Pharmacology Bldg 37 Rm 5068 37 Convent Dr Bethesda MD 20892-4255 Office Phone: 301-496-5944. Office Fax: 301-402-0752. E-mail: pommier@nih.gov. *

POMYJE, JIRI, hematologist, researcher; b. Trinec, Moravia, Czech Republic, June 26, 1972; s. Jirí Pomyje and Dagmar Pomyjová; m. Jitka Neprasová, Nov. 22, 1971; 1 child, Adam Jirí. MD, Charles U., 1996, PhD, 2003. Postdoctoral fellow Vascular Biology and Thrombosis dept. U. Vienna, 2003—; asst. prof. Patho-physiology dept. Charles U., Prague, Czech Republic, 1999—; physician Charles U. Gen. Hosp., Prague, 1996—2003. Grantee Congenital defects of hematopoiesis, Internal Grant Agy. of the Czech Ministry of Health, 2001—03. Mem.: European Network Trainees in Ob-Gyn., European Study Group for Cell Proliferation, Internat. Soc. Exptl. Hematology. Achievements include research in Blood vessels growth in physiological and pathological situations, tumor angiogenesis.

PONAUSUIA, SEIULI ELIZABETH, public health service officer; Cert. in Capital Budgeting, USDA Grad. Sch., 1992, cert. in Cost Acctg., 1995; AS in Bus. Mgmt., American Samoa CC, 1996, AS in Acctg., 1998; B in Pub. Mgmt., Golden Gate U., San Francisco, 1999, MPA, 2001. With Nat. Pacific Ins. Ltd., Hartford Fire Ins. Co.; fin. mgr. American Samoa Dept. Health, Pago Pago, 1987, acting dir., 2010—11, dir., 2011—. Office: American Samoa Department of Health Territory of American Samoa Pago Pago AS 96799 Office Phone: 684-633-4606. Office Fax: 684-633-5379. *

PONDER, BRUCE ANTHONY JOHN, cancer geneticist; b. Haywards Heath, Sussex, Eng., Apr. 25, 1944; s. Anthony West and Dorothy Mary (Peachey) P.; m. Margaret Ann Hickinbotham, Aug. 2, 1969; children: Jane, Katherine, Rosamund, William. BA, Cambridge U., 1965, MB, BChir, 1968, MA, 1972; PhD, London U., 1977. Clin. rsch. fellow Imperial Cancer Rsch. Fund, London, 1973-77; fellow cancer rsch. campaign Dana Farber Cancer Ctr., Harvard Med. Sch., Cambridge, Mass., 1977-78; sr. registrar and ICRF fellow St. Bartholomew's Hosp., London, 1978-80; fellow cancer rsch. campaign Inst. of Cancer Rsch., London, 1980—86, section head human cancer genetics, 1987-89; reader in human cancer genetics U. London, 1987-89; dir. cancer rsch. campaign Human Cancer Genetics Rsch. Group, Cambridge (Eng.) U., England, 1989—; cons. physician Addenbrooke's Hosp., Cambridge, England, 1989—; co-dir. Wellbeing Ovarian Cancer Rsch. Ctr., Cambridge, England, 1996-2000, Strangeways Rsch. Lab., Cambridge, England, 1997—, Hutchison/MRC Rsch. Ctr., 2001—; dir. Cancer Rsch. Eng./Cambridge Rsch. Inst., 2004—. Mem. rsch. adv. com. Cancer Rsch. Campaign, London, 1987 05; co-chmn. gene mapping task force Nat. Neurofibromatosis Found., N.Y., 1987-92; mem. sci. rsch. adv. bd. European Orgn. for Rsch. and Treatment of Cancer, 1989-93; mem. human genetics commn., U.K., 1999-01; UK rep., chmn. sci. coun. World Health Orgn. Internat. Agy. Rsch. in Cancer, Lyon, 2005. Co-editor: (book) Biology of Carcinogenesis, 1987; contbr. articls to profl. jours. Recipient Merck prize European Thyroid Assn., 1996, Hamilton Fairley award European Soc. Med. Oncology, 2004, Bertner award M.D. Anderson Hosp., 2007; Named Open Scholar, Cambridge U., 1962, Travelling Fellow, Nuffield Found., Pakistan, 1968, Hon. Cons. Physician, Royal Marsden Hosp., and Guys Hosp., London, 1980, Life Fellow, Cancer Rsch. Campaign, 1989. Fellow Jesus Coll. Cambridge U., Royal Coll. Physicians (Croonian lectr. 1998), Royal Coll. Pathologists, Royal Soc., Acad Med. Scis.; mem. Brit. Assn. Cancer Rsch. (treas. 1983-86), Brit. Soc. Devel. Biology, Am. Soc. Human Genetics, Royal West Norfolk Golf Club Avocations: gardening, golf, travel. Office: Cancer Rsch Ctr Cambridge Rsch Inst Robinson Way Cambridge CB2 0RE England Office Phone: 44 1223 404124. Business E-Mail: bruce.ponder@cancer.org.uk.

PONDER, CATHERINE, clergywoman; b. Hartsville, SC, Feb. 14, 1927; d. Roy Charles and Kathleen (Parrish) Cook; 1 child, Richard. Student, Worth Bus. Coll., 1948; BS in Edn., Unity Ministerial Sch., 1956; doctorate (hon.), Unity Sch., 1976. Ordained to ministry Unity Sch. Christianity, 1958. Min. Unity Ch., Birmingham, Ala., 1958-61, founder, min. Austin, Tex., 1961-69, San Antonio, 1969-73, Palm Desert, Calif., 1973—. Author: (books) The Dynamic Laws of Prosperity, 1962, The Prosperity Secret of the Ages, 1964, The Dynamic Laws of Healing, 1966, The Healing Secret of the Ages, 1967, Pray and Grow Rich, 1968, The Millionaires of Genesis, 1976, The Millionaire Moses, 1977, The Millionaire Joshua, 1978, The Millionaire from Nazareth, 1979, The Secret of Unlimited Prosperity, 1981, Open Your Mind To Receive, 1983, Dare To Prosper!: The Prospering Power of Prayer, 1983, The Prospering Power of Love, 1984, Open Your Mind to Prosperity, 1984, The Dynamic Laws of Prayer, 1987, (memoir) Prosperity Love Story, From Rags to Enrichment, 2003. Office: 73-669 US Hwy 111 Palm Desert CA 92260-4033

PONGIYA, UMA DEVI, healthcare educator; b. Udumalpet, May 25, 1969; MSc, PSG Coll. Arts and Sci., Coimbatore, 1992; PhD, Bharathiar U., Coimbatore, 2007. Sr. lectr. Periyar U., Salem, 1993—2000, chair person, bd. studies, 1997—2000; head dept. Vivekanandha Coll., Tiruchengodu, 2000—04; asst. prof. NGP Coll. Arts and Sci., 2004—08; asst. prof. SG Karunya U., Coimbatore, 2008—, coord., cmty. health svc. Chair-person, bd. studies Bharathiar U., 2000—08, squad mem., bd. examination. Mem. Indian Soc. Tech. Edn., New Delhi. Recipient Tamil Nadu Young Women Scientist award, Ministry of Higher Edn., Govt. of Tamilnadu. Mem.: Schizophrenia Rsch. Found. (Chennai). Home: B4D Martin Residency Bharathiar Rd S Coimbatore Tamil Nadu 641 006 India Personal E-mail: umadevipongiya@rediffmail.com.

PONOMAREVA, NATALYA VASILYEVNA, neurologist, neurophysiologist; d. Vasily Maximovich Ponomarev and Nina Ivanovna Nevzorova; m. Vitaly Fedorovich Fokin. Degree Medicine (hon.), 2nd Moscow State Med. Inst., 1981; PhD in Neurophysiology, First State Med. Inst., 1986, MD in Neurology, 1986. Cert. neurologist First State Med. Inst., 1983. Group leader aging neurophysiology Rsch. Ctr. Neurology RAMS, Moscow, 2004—. Author (with Vitaly Fokin): (book) Neuroenergetics Brain Physiology; contbr. articles to profl. jours. Grant, Regional Pub. Fund Assistance, Nat. Medicine, 2005—06, Russian Found. Basic Rsch., 2008. Mem.: Russian Soc. Neurologists, Russian Physiol. Soc. Achievements include invention of method of assessment of cerebral energy metabolism by electrophysiological technique; research in neurophysiological alterations in non-demented individuals related to apolipoprotein E genotype and to risk of Alzheimer's disease,EEG predictors of effect of glutamatergic and cholinergic therapy in Alzheimer's disease. Office: Rsch Ctr Neurology RAMS Obucha-by-st 5 Moscow 105064 Russia Office Phone: 7 495 917 07 65. Business E-Mail: ponomare@yandex.ru.

PONSKY, JEFFREY LAWRENCE, surgeon; b. Cleve., Sept. 23, 1946; s. Howard and Esther P.; m. Jacqueline Goldberg; children: Lee, Todd, Zac, Kimberly. BA, Miami U., 1967; MD, Case Western Res. U., 1971, MBA, 1990. Diplomate Am. Bd. Med. Examiners, Am. Bd. Surgery; lic. physician, Ohio. Gen. surgery intern Univ. Hosps. of Cleve., 1971-72, gen. surgery resident, 1972-76; pvt. practice gen. surgery Cleve., 1976—; asst. surgeon Univ. Hosps. Cleve., 1976—97, dir. surgical Endoscopy, 1977—79; dir., dept. Surgery Mt. Sinai Med. Ctr., Cleve., 1979—97; dir., Endoscopic Surgery Cleve. Clinic Found., 1997—2004, exec. dir., Minimally Invasive Surgery Ctr., 1998—2000, dir. Grad. Med. Ed., 1999—2004; chmn. dept. surgery U. Hosps. Cleve., 2005—; prof., vice chmn. dept surgery Case Western Reserve U. Sch. Medicine, Oliver H. Payne Prof., chmn. dept surgery, 2005—. Sr. instr. surgery Case Western Res. U., 1976-77, asst. prof. surgery, 1977-84, assoc. prof., 1984-91, prof. surgery, 1991-; lectr. in field. Contbr. numerous articles to profl. jours.; abstract reviewer Gastrointestinal Endoscopy, 1983-89; contbg. editor Endoscopy Rev., 1988; editorial bd. Am. Jour. Gastroenterology, 1989—, Surg. Laparoscopy and Endoscopy Jour., 1990—; guest editor Am. Jour. Surgery,1 991, World Jour. Surgery, 1991 Capt. USAR, 1972-78. Fellow ACS; mem. AMA, Am. Bd. Surgery (pres. 2005-06), Cleve. Acad. Medicine, Ohio Med. Assn., Cleve. Surg. Soc., Am. Gastroenterol. Assn., Soc. for Surgery of Alimentary Tract, Am. Coll. Gastroenterology, Am. Soc. Gastrointestinal Endoscopy, Collegium Internationale Chirurgia Digestivae, Soc. Am. Gastrointestinal Endoscopic Surgeons, Ctrl. Surg. Assn., Soc. Univ. Surgeons, Am. Soc. Parenteral and Enteral Nutrition, Assn. for Acad. Surgery, Am. Surg. Assn., N.E. Ohio Soc. Gastrointestinal Endoscopy, Phi Sigma. Office: U Hosps Cleveland 11100 Euclid Ave Cleveland OH 44106

PONTAGA, INESE, education educator, physician, researcher; b. Kraslava, Latvia, July 28, 1965; d. Voldemars Pontags and Karija Pontaga. MD (hon.), Latvian Med. Acad., Riga, Latvia, 1983—89; PhD, Inst.Clin. and Exptl. Medicine, Latvian State U., 1997. Lab. asst. Latvian Sci. Institite of Traumatology and Orthopaedics, Riga, Latvia, 1987—89; post-graduate student Latvian Sci. Inst. of Traumatology and Orthopaedics, Riga, Latvia, 1990—92, rsch. asst., 1992—94; rschr. Lab. of Biomechanics of Latvian Med. Acad., Riga, Latvia, 1994—96; physician Dept. of Internal Diseases of the Riga Hosp. No.2, Riga, Latvia, 1990—2000; docent, tchg. physiology Latvian Acad. Sports Edn., Riga, Latvia, 1998—2003, assoc. prof., tchg. physiology, 2003—09, prof. tchg. psysiology, 2009—. Head dept. anatomy, physiology, biochemistry and hygiene Latvian Acad. Sports Edn., Riga, 2001—. Contbr. articles pub. to profl. jour. Mem. Latvian Union of Scientists, Riga, Latvia, 2005—. Grantee Rsch. Grant No.01.0036 Leader, Latvian Coun. of Sci., 1999 - 2003. Mem.: Latvian Soc. of Internal Medicine (assoc.), Latvian Assn. of Sports Medicine (assoc.), European Soc. of Biomechanics (assoc. young scientists travel grant to the ESB Conf. in Leuven, Belgium 1996). Christian. Avocations: gardening, drawing, classical music, travel. Office: Latvian Acad Sports Edn Brivibas Gatve 333 1006 Riga Latvia Office Phone: 371 67543449. Office Fax: 371 67557953. Personal E-mail: inesep65@hotmail.com. Business E-Mail: inese.pontaga@lspa.lv.

PONTE, EURO, physician; b. Trieste, Italy, Mar. 21, 1942; MD, PhD, Padua, Italy, 1966. Cert. in internal medicine 1971, in radiology 1974, in cardiology 1980. Prof. angiology, history of medicine U. Trieste, 2009. Vis. prof. U. Beograd. Mem.: Italian Red Cross, Paulescu Diabetes Soc. Bucharest. Home: via Guglielmo Marconi 18 viale C ELISI60 Trieste 34100 Italy Business E-Mail: ponte@units.it.

PONTIUS, ANNELIESE ALMA, retired psychiatrist; b. Chemnitz, Saxony, Germany, May 19, 1921; arrived in US, 1957; d. Karl Gottfried and Clara Alma Mueller; m. Dieter Johann Jakob Pontius, July 7, 1951. MD, Johann Wolfgang Goethe U., Frankfurt, Germany, 1950; Grad., Munich Analytic Inst., Germany, 1953. Diplomate Am. Bd. Psychiatry and Neurology, 1963. Intern Univ. Hosps., Frankfurt, 1950—51, Munich, 1951—53, Hamburg, Germany, 1953—54; resident McGill U., Montreal, Que., Canada, 1955—57, Auspices Mass. Tng. Faculty, Worcester, Mass., 1957—59; rsch. assoc. child psychiatry Lenox Hill Hosp., NYC, 1962—64; pvt. practice NYC, 1966—99. Vis. neuro-psychiatrist NYU Med. Ctr., NYC, 1969—76, clin. asst. prof., 1972—76; vis. scientist NIMH, Rockville, Md., 1971—72; vis. prof. dept. neurology U. Heidelberg, 1973, 75, 77, 80; asst. psychiatrist McLean Hosp., Belmont, Mass., 1977—84, lectr. psychiatry, 1977—81, asst. clin. prof., 1981—86; assoc. clin. prof. Harvard Med. Sch., 1986—2001; ret.; clin. assoc. psychiatrist Mass. Gen. Hosp., Boston, 1984—2001; associateship Behavioral and Brain Scis., 1992—. Contbr. articles to profl. jours. Med. expert U.S. HHS, 1968—99. Fellow: NY Acad. Medicine, Explorers Club; mem.: AAAS (organizer, spkr. 6 symposia), Neurowissenschaftliche Gesellschaft, Am. Acad. Psychiatry and Law, NY Acad. Scis. (mem. conf. rev. panel 1993—99), Am. Psychiat. Assn. Achievements include proposal new subtype of partial seizures: limbic psychotic trigger reaction with primate model; visuo-spatial tests, used in testing of hunter gatherers on four continents, culture fair Kohs block design modifications and Draw-a-Person-With-Face-in-Front Test. Avocations: travel, swimming, sewing, photography. Address: Waldschmidt Str 6 60316 Frankfurt Germany E-mail: anneliese_pontius@hms.harvard.edu.

PONTO, JULIE ANN, oncological nurse, educator; b. Mpls., Dec. 25, 1961; MSN, U. Calif., San Francisco, 1994; PhD, U. Utah, 2008. Oncology clin. nurse specialist Mercy Healthcare Sacramento, 1994—96; clin. nurse specialist, women's cancer program Mayo Clinic, 1996—2009; prof. Winona State U., 2004—. Pres. Oncology Nursing Certification Corp., 2003—05; grad. faculty counselor Sigma Theta Tau Internat.-Kappa Mu, 2008—10; pres.-elect Oncology Nursing Soc., 2010—11. Named Advanced Oncology Cert. Nurse of Yr., Oncology Nursing Cert. Corp., New Vol. of Yr., Am. Cancer Soc.,

Sacramento chpt. Mem.: ONS (SE Minn. chpt), Nat. Assn. Clin. Nurse Specialists, Oncology Nursing Soc., Sigma Theta Tau Internat. Avocations: hiking, golf, travel. Office: 859 30th Ave SE Rochester MN 55904 Business E-Mail: jponto@winona.edu.

PONTONE, STEFANO, medical researcher; b. Rome, Mar. 13, 1974; MD, Sapienza U. Rome, PhD, 2000, degree in Gen. Surgery, 2008. Rsch. scientist Sapienza U. Rome, 2009—. Mem.: Italian Soc. Digestive Endoscopy, European Soc. Gastrointestinal Endoscopy. Office: Vle Regina Elena 324 Rome 00161 Italy Business E-Mail: stefano.pontone@uniroma1.it.

PONTRELLI, GIUSEPPE, pediatrician; b. Bari, Aug. 28, 1976; Degree in Medicine, U. Pisa, 2002; degree in Pub. Health, U. Rome Tor Vergata, 2006. Physician Clin. Trial Ctr., Ospedale Pediat. Bambino Gesù, 2010—. Expert European Medicines Agy., 2007. Office: Piazza Sant'Onofrio 4 Rome 00165 Italy Business E-Mail: giuseppe.pontrelli@opbg.net.

PONTZER, RAYMOND E., internist; MD, Hahnemann Drexel U., Phila. Diplomate Am. Bd. Internal Medicine, Am. Bd. Internal Medicine-infectious disease. Resident Med. Coll. Pa., Phila., fellow; hosp. affiliations include Univ. Pitts. Med. Ctr. Passavant, Univ. Pitts. Med. Ctr. St. Margaret. Office: Romano And Pontzer Limited 105 Braunlich Dr Pittsburgh PA 15237 Office Phone: 412-348-0330.

POOLE, ANDREW EDWARD, pediatric dentist, human geneticist, educator; b. Burton-on-Trent, Staffordshire, Eng., Aug. 4, 1935; came to US, 1962; s. Reginald Leslie and Eunice Winifred (Salt) P.; m. Deirdre-Anne Farnan, Dec., 1962; children: Nichola Ruth, Timothy Sean, Amelia Anne. BDS, London Hosp. Dental Sch., 1960; MS in Pediatric Dentistry, U. Rochester, 1965, PhD, 1970. Instr. London Hosp., 1961-62, U.Rochester, NY, 1965-70; asst. prof. U. Conn. Health Ctr., Farmington, 1970-74, assoc. prof., 1974-85, prof. pediat. dentistry, 1985-96, prof. emeritur pediatric dentistry, 1996; dir. craniofacial disorders team Conn. Children's Med. Ctr., 1996—2000. Co-dir. U. Conn. Craniofacial Disorders Team, 1981-84, dir. 1985-96. Guest editor Dental Clinics N.Am., 1975; contbr. articles to profl. publ., chpt. to books. Fellow Eastman Dental Dispensary, 1962-65, U. Rochester, 1965-70; NIH grantee, 1970—. Mem. Royal Coll. Surgeons, Internat. Assn. Dental Rsch., Am. Acad. Pedodontics, Am. Assn. Human Genetics, AAAS, Soc. Craniofacial Genetics (sec.-treas. 1984-92, pres. 1992-93), Am. Coll. Med. Genetics, Sigma Xi. Home: 26 Howland Lane Wellfleet MA 02667 Office: U Conn Health Ctr Farmington Ave Farmington CT 06030-0001 also: Conn Childrens Med Ctr 282 Washington St Hartford CT 06106-3322 Personal E-mail: andrewdeirdre.poole@verizon.net.

POON, CHRISTINE A., dean, business educator, retired pharmaceutical company executive; b. Cin., June 23, 1952; d. James and Virginaia Poon; m. Mike Tweedle. BS in Biology, Northwestern U., 1973; MS in Biology & Biochemistry, St. Louis U., 1973; MBA in Fin., Boston U., 1982. Various mgmt. positions Bristol-Myers Squibb Co., 1985—2000, v.p., sr. v.p. for Can. & Latin America pharm. ops., pres., gen. mgr. Squibb Diagnostics' Can. operation, 1994, pres. Med. Devices, 1997—98, pres. internat. medicines, 1998—2000; co. group chmn. pharm. group Johnson & Johnson, New Brunswick, NJ, 2000—01, worldwide chmn. pharms. group, 2001—03, worldwide chmn. medicines and nutritionals, 2003—09, vice chmn., mem. exec. com., 2005—09; dean, John W. Berry Sr. Chair in Bus. Max M. Fisher Coll. Bus., Ohio State U., Columbus, Ohio, 2009—. Bd. dirs. Johnson & Johnson, 2005—09, Prudential Financial, Inc., 2006—, Regeneron Pharmaceuticals, Inc., 2010—; mem. supervisory bd. Royal Philips Electronics, 2009—; mem. advisory bd. Healthcare Businesswomen's Assn. Bd. dirs. Fox Chase Cancer Ctr., Phila. Named Woman of Yr., Healthcare Businesswomen's Assn., 2004, Bus. Leader of the Future, CNBC/ The Wall St. Jour., 2005; named one of 50 Women to Watch, Wall St. Jour., 2005, 2006, The 100 Most Powerful Women, Forbes mag., 2005, 2007, 2008, The 10 Most Powerful Women in NJ Bus., Star-Ledger, 2006, The 50 Most Powerful Women in Bus., Fortune mag., 2006, 2007. Office: Ohio State U Fisher Coll Bus 201 Fisher Hall 2100 Neil Avenue Columbus OH 43210 Office Phone: 614-292-2666. E-mail: poon.36@osu.edu.

POON, ERIC G., internist, educator; BSEE, Cornell U., Ithaca, NY, 1993; MD, Harvard Med. Sch., Boston, 1998; MPH, Harvard Sch. Pub. Health, 2003. Resident physician Brigham & Women's Hosp., Boston, 1998—2001, assoc. physician, 2001—, dir. clin. informatics, 2007—; asst. prof. Harvard Med. Sch., 2006—. Cons. AHRQ HIT Nat. Resource Ctr., Rockville, Md., 2004—06; LMR clin. content product mgr. Partners Healthcare, Boston, 2005—07. Contbr. articles to profl. jours. Achievements include research in the use of health information technology to improve the quality of care and patient safety in both the ambulatory and hospital settings. Office: Brigham & Womens Hosp Divsn Gen Medicine 3F 1620 Tremont St Boston MA 02120 Office Phone: 781-416-9336. Office Fax: 617-732-7072. Business E-Mail: epoon@partners.org. *

POON, ERIC SIN-KAM F., pediatrician, educator; Attended, U. La Salle Mexican Sch. Medicine, 1982. Diplomate Am. Bd. Pediatrics. Resident in pediat. LI Coll. Hosp., Bklyn., 1983—86; fellow in pediatric cardiology NY Hosp. Cornell Ctr., NY, 1986—88; asst. clin. pediat. Cornell Univ.-Weill Med. Coll.; with NY Presbyn. Hosp. / Weill Cornell; pediatrician NY Downtown Hosp. Office: New York Downtown Hospital 170 William St - Pediatrics New York NY 10038 Office Phone: 212-312-5350.

POON, MICHAEL, cardiologist, educator; Med. degree, Mt. Sinai Sch. Medicine, NY, 1987. Diplomate Am. Bd. Internal Medicine, Am. Bd. Cardiology-cardiovascular disease. Resident in internal medicine Mt. Sinai Med. Ctr., NY, 1988—91, fellow in cardiovascular disease, 1991—93, with; prof. SUNY Stony Brook, 2008; dir. advanced cardiac imaging Stony Brook Univ. Med. Ctr., 2008. Immediate past pres. Soc. Cardiovascular Computed Tomography. Recipient Clin. Scientist award, Am. Heart Assn., 2008, Young Investigator award, 2008; named to NY Mag.'s Best Dr. Listing, 2004, 2010. Achievements include research in Quantitative assessment of coronary CTA correlating with QCA, IVUS and FFR; The role of coronary CTA in the assessment of acute chest pain; Novel role of computed aided diagnosis in the triage of coronary artery disease following coronary CTA; One-stop evaluation of ischemic heart disease using cardiac MRI. Office: Stony Brook University Medical Center Nicolas Rd Stony Brook NY 11794-8460 Office Phone: 631-638-2121. Office Fax: 631-444-7538.

POON, TAK LUN, orthopedic surgeon, photographer; b. Hong Kong; Grad., Munsang/Coll.Kings Coll., Hong Kong, 1975; BS, MB, U. Hong Kong, 1982. Resident Princess Margaret Hosp./United Christian Hosp., 1983; med. officer Queen Elizabeth Hosp., Hong Kong, 1984-85, Kowloon Hosp., Hong Kong, 1986-87, Princess Margaret Hosp., Hong Kong, 1988, Queen Elizabeth Hosp., Hong Kong, 1989; sr. med. officer Queen Mary Hosp., Hong Kong, 1990-97—, cons., 1997—; hon. assoc. prof. Hong Kong U., 1997—. Med. officer Hong Kong br. Brit. Red Cross Soc., 1984—; cons. med. officer Hong Kong Red Cross br. Chinese Red Cross Soc., 1997—. Author: (poetry collection) Chu-Ju-Ji I, 1982, Chu-Ju-Ji II, 1984. Fellow Royal Coll. Physicians and Surgeons (Glasgow); mem. Govt. Doctors Assn. Hong Kong (sec. 1990-91), Hong Kong Pub. Doctors Assn. (pres. 1996-99), Hong Kong Med. Assn. (coun. 2002—), Hong Kong Aviation Club, Eddy's Magic Club Hong Kong. Avocations: photography, aviation, magic. Home: F15 Block 6 Site 9 Whampoa Garden Kowloon Hong Kong Office: Rm 1329 Ctrl Bldg Pedder St Hong Kong SAR China Home Phone: 852-61002234; Office Phone: 852-31677310. Personal E-mail: poontl@gmail.com.

POORAN, NAKECHAND R., gastroenterologist, educator; b. Berbice, Guyana, Jan. 6, 1970; MD, St. George's U., 1997. Assoc. prof. Penn State Milton S. Hershey Med. Ctr., 2005—. Fellow: Am. Coll. Gastroenterology; mem.: Am. Soc. Gastrointestinal Endoscopy, ACP, Am. Gastrointestinal Assn. Office: Penn State Milton S Hershey Med Ctr Hershey PA 17033 E-mail: boraalan@aol.com.

POPAT, SAURIN RAJNIKANT, oncologist, surgeon; b. Kampala, Uganda, Aug. 19, 1969; s. Rajnikant Nagi and Bharti Rajnikant Popat; m. Katharine Elizabeth Herbert, Sept. 11, 1999; children: Alexander Shivam, Evan Kavi, Carys Meera Rose. BA, Queen's U., Kingston, Ont. Can., 1990, MBA, 2010, Cornell U., Ithaca, NY, 2010; MD, U. Western Ont., 1992. Asst. prof. surgery U. Rochester, NY, 2000—04, asst. prof. otolarynology, 2004—06; asst. prof. surg. oncology Roswell Park Cancer Inst., Buffalo, 2006—09. Dir. head and neck surg. oncology U. Rochester Med. Ctr., 2000—06; bd. dir. Univera Health, Buffalo, 2007—; self-employed med. legal cons., Rochester, 2002—06, Buffalo, 2006—; clin. asst. prof. HNS, 2009—. Contbr. scientific papers to profl. jours., chapters to books. Vo. physician med. aid mission U. Toronto, Thailand, 1996. Recipient Roundtree prize, U. Western Ont., 1990. Fellow: Am. Bd. Otolaryngology - Head & Neck Surgery, Am. Head and Neck Soc., Royal Coll Physicians and Surgeons Can., Am. Coll. Surgeons, Royal Coll. Surgeons Can., Royal Coll. Physicians. Avocations: hockey, golf, sailing. Office: Dept Head & Neck Plastic & Reconstructive Surgery Prie County Med Ctr 462 Grider St Buffalo NY 14215 Office Phone: 716-882-1023. Business E-Mail: delawaremedicalgroup@yahoo.com.

POPE, ANDREW M., health science association administrator; PhD in Physiology and Biochemistry. Acting dir., sr. program officer, Neuroscience and Behavioral Health Bd. Inst. of Medicine-Nat. Academies, 1998-99, dir., Health Sciences Policy Bd., 1999—, acting dir., Neuroscience and Behavioral Health Bd., 2003—. Office: Inst Medicine 500 5th St, NW Washington DC 20418-0007

POPE, C. ARDEN, III, economics professor; b. Logan, Utah, Sept. 30, 1955; s. Clive Arden Pope Jr. and Vivian Harper Pope; m. Ronda Lou Gneiting, Aug. 5, 1977; children: Jaren Clive, Devin Garret, Weston Arden, Nolan Gneiting, Bryson Ron, Dallin Kimball, Collin Harper. BS, Brigham Young U., Provo, Utah, 1978; MS, PhD, Iowa State U., Ames, 1981. Rsch. assoc., staff economist Iowa State U., 1980—82; asst. prof. Tex. A&M U., College Station, 1982—84; asst. to assoc. prof. Brigham Young U., 1984—94, prof. econs., 1994—. Vis. scientist Harvard Sch. Pub. Health, Boston, 1992—93. Author: (book chapter) Acute respiratory effects of particulate air pollution, Epidemiology of acute health effects, Epidemiology of chronic health effects, Outdoor Air: Particles, Epidemiology of Particle Effects, Effects of particulate air pollution exposures, Epidemiological evidence of relationship between particle exposure and cardiovascular outcomes, Air Pollution: Coronary Heart Disease Epidemiology; contbr. articles to numerous profl. jours. Recipient Creative Achievement award, Brigham Young U., 1986, Karl G. Maeser, Excellence in Rsch. and Creative Arts award, 1995, Karl G. Maeser Disting. Faculty Lectr., 2006, Mary Lou Fulton Professorship, 2005-, Clarence Olds Sappington Meml. Lectr., Am. Coll. Occupl. and Environ. Medicine, 1997, Lectr. award, Sigma Xi, 2000, Thomas T. Mercer Joint prize, Am. Assn. Aerosol Rsch. and the Internat. Soc. Aerosols in Medicine, 2001, Governor's medal Sci. & Tech., Utah Governor's Office, 2004; fellow Interdisciplinary Programs in Health, Harvard U., 1992-1993, Honorary, Am. Coll. Chest Physicians, 2008. Fellow: Am. Coll. Chest Physicians (hon.). Avocations: running, backpacking, community and church youth leader. Office: Brigham Young Univ 130 Fob Provo UT 84602 E-mail: cap3@byu.edu.

POPE, HARRISON GRAHAM, JR., psychiatrist, educator; b. Lynn, Mass., Dec. 26, 1947; s. H. Graham and Alice (Rider) P.; m. Mary M. Quinn, June 7, 1974; children: Kimberly, Hilary, Courtney. AB summa cum laude, Harvard U., 1969, MPH, 1972, MD, 1974. Diplomate Am. Bd. Psychiatry and Neurology. Resident in psychiatry McLean Hosp., Belmont, Mass., 1974-77, clin. rsch. fellow Mailman Rsch. Ctr., 1977-79, asst. psychiatrist, 1979-84, assoc. psychiatrist, 1984-92, psychiatrist, 1992—, chief biol. psychiatry lab., 1984—; Dupont-Warren rsch. fellow Harvard Med. Sch., Boston, 1976-77. Instr. psychiatry Harvard Med. Sch., Boston, 1977-82, asst. prof., 1982-85, assoc. prof., 1985-99, prof. 1999—; staff psychiatrist Hampstead (N.H.) Hosp., 1976-80; vis. fellow The Maudsley Hosp., London, 1977, Hôpital. Ste. Anne, Paris, 1977; mem. Am. Psychiat. Assn., 1976-80, adv. com. on schizophrenic, paranoid and affective disorders, 1979, adv. com. on preparation of DSM-III-R, 1984, task force on nomenclature and stats., 1979, 84. Author: Voices from the Drug Culture, 1971, The Road East, 1974, (with J.I. Hudson) New Hope for Binge Eaters: Advances in the Understanding and Treatment of Bulimia, 1984; co-editor: The Psychobiology of Bulimia, 1987, Use of Anticonvulsants in Psychiatry: Recent Advances, 1988, Psychology Astray: Fallacies in Studies of "Repressed Memory" and Childhood Trauma, 1997; The Adonis Complex: The Secret Crisis of Male Body Obsession, 2000; mem. editl. bd. European Psychiatry, Paris, 1984—, Internat. Jour. of Eating Disorders, 1984—, Jour. Clin. Psychiatry, 1993-; contbr. numerous articles to profl. jours. Named one of Outstanding Americans under 40 Esquire mag., 1984; fellow Scottish Rite Schizophrenia Program, No. Masonic Jurisdiction, 1977-81, Charles A. King Trust, Boston, 1977-79. Avocation: weightlifting. Office: McLean Hosp 115 Mill St Belmont MA 02478-1048

POPELAR, JIRI, neuroscientist; b. Jaromer, Czech Republic, Dec. 10, 1949; s. Jan Popelar and Jirina Popelarova; m. Miroslava Dolezelova, June 25, 1952; children: Jan, Hana Popelarova, Ivana Popelarova. Degree, Charles U., Prague, 1973, PhD, 1981. Scientist in tng. Acad. Scis., Prague, Czech Republic, 1973—81, rschr., 1981—. Grantee, Grant Agy. of the Czech Republic, 1998—2006. Mem.: Czech Neurosci. Soc. Avocations: travel, bicycling, gardening. Office: Inst Exptl Medicine AS CR Videnska 1083 Prague 14220 Czech Republic Office Fax: +420 241062787. E-mail: jpopelar@biomed.cas.cz.

POPESCU, IRINEL PETRE, surgeon; b. Filiasi, Romania, Apr. 22, 1953; s. Petre Gheorghe and Elena Dumitru Popescu; m. Liliana Gheorghe Niculescu, Oct. 20, 2000. BA, Lycee Fratii Buzesti, Craiova, Romania, 1971; MD, U. Bucharest, Romania, 1977. Asst. prof. faculty medicine U. Bucharest, Bucharest, 1980—93, lectr., 1993—96, asst. prof., 1996—99, prof. surgery, 1999—; rsch. asst. U. Pitts., 1992, Mt. Sinai Hosp., NYC, 1992—94. Med. dir. Fundeni Hosp., Bucharest, 1995—97; dir. Inst. Postgrad. Tng., Romania, 1998—99; sec. of state Ministry of Health, Romania, 1999—2000. Co-editor CD-Rom of laproscopic surgery. Mem. Romanian Senate, 2007—. Lt. Romanian armed forces, 1978—79. Mem.: Romanian Acad. Scientists, Romanian Acad. Med. Scis., Romanian Assn. Laproscopic Surgery, Romtransplant (pres. 1997—), Internat. Assn. Surgeons and Gastroenterologists (treas. 2001—). Conservative. Greek Orthodox. Avocations: chess, lecturing, classical music, travel. Office: Fundeni Hosp 258 Sos Fundeni Bucharest Romania Home: Strada Semilunei 8 20797 Bucharest Romania Office Phone: 21-3180417. Fax: 40-1-2403248. Business E-Mail: irinel.popescu@icfundeni.ro.

POPIELA, TADEUSZ, surgeon, educator; b. Nowy Sacz, Poland, May 23, 1933; s. Jan and Bronisława (Chełmecka) P.; m. Mieczysława Werner, Oct. 28, 1955; children: Anna, Tadeusz. Diploma, Jagiellonian U., Kraków, Poland, 1955, doctor's degree, 1961, habilitation, 1965, prof.'s degree, 1972; degree (hon.), Pomeranian Med. Acad., Szczecin, 2002, Wrocław Med. U., 2003, Med. Acad., Warsaw, 2005. Specialization in gen. surgery I, specialization in gen. surgery II. Rsch. asst. dept. surgery III dept. Gen. Surgery Jagiellonian U., Kraków, 1955-65, prof. asst., 1965-71, head surg. unit gastroenterology, 1971-76, head 1st dept. gen. and GI surgery, 1976—2003, rector med. acad., 1972-81, head intraoperative radiotherapy and chemotherapy, 1st dept. gen. and gastrointestinal surgery, 2003—. Head clin. and basic sci. State Com. Sci. Rsch., 1991-2005; vis. prof. U. Ill., Chgo., 1975, 81, U. Chir. Klinik Wurzburg, 1974, 79, Loyola U. Med. Ctr., 1988, 93, U. Erlangen, 1983, Med. Hochschule, Hanover, 1993, 94, Stanford U. Sch. Medicine, 2002, others; presenter in field. Contbr. more than 450 articles to profl. publs., several monographs. Recipient Pres. Best Poster prize World Congress CICD, Jerusalem, 1986, 2 1st prizes Internat. Gastric Cancer Congress, Kyoto, 1995; First Prize 3rd, 1999, 4th, 2000, 8th, 2004, annual meeting of European Soc. Surgery; award City of Cracow, 2002. Mem.: ACS, Polish Oncological Union (head sci. coun. 2004—, pres.-elect 2008), Internat. Soc. Surgery, European Soc. Endocrine Surgeons, Internat. Soc. Digestive Diseases (nat. del.), Soc. Laparoscopic Surgeons, European Digestive Surgery, Internat. Assn. Pancreatology, Internat. Coll. Surgeons, Polish Acad. Scis., Polish Acad. Arts and Scis., World Assn. Hepato-Pancreato-Biliary Surgery, Internat. Gastro-Surg. Club, Internat. Gastric Cancer Assn. (head Sci. Coun. 2001—, coun. mem. 2003—), Am. Gastroent. Assn., Midgerman Soc. Gastroenterology (hon.), Polish Soc. Ultrasonography (hon.), Polish Soc. Surg. Oncology (hon.), J.E. Purkyne Czech Soc. Surgeons (hon.), Polish Cybernetical Soc. (hon.), German Soc. Surgery (hon.), Soc. Polish Surgeons (hon.; pres. 1987—89), Polish Gastroent. Assn. (hon.), Polish Order Merit (officer grand cross 2001, Laur Jagiellonski medal 2001, Merentibus medal 2003). Home: 47 Walerego Goetla St 30-065 Cracow Poland Office: 1st Dept Gen and GI Surgery Jagiellonian U 40 Kopernika St 31-501 Cracow Poland Office Phone: 48 12 4213583. E-mail: mspopiel@cyf-kr.edu.pl.

POPOVA, EKATERINA, neurologist; b. Kiev, Ukraine, Mar. 8, 1980; Degree in Neurology, Moscow Med. Acad., 2003, student in Med. Scis., 2009. Neurologist Moscow City Hosp. Ctr. Multiple Sclerosis, 2009—. Avocation: swimming. Office: Dvintzev Moscow 127018 Russia Office Fax: 74956890281. E-mail: epopova1980@yandex.ru.

POPOVENIUC, GEANINA, endocrinologist; b. Romania, Apr. 11, 1981; MD, U. de Medicine si Farmacine Carol Davila, Bucharest, 2006. Internal medicine resident, Wash. Hosp. Ctr. Georgetown U. Hosp., 2008—11, endocrinology fellow, 2011—. Avocations: tennis, skiing. Home: 6331 Eight St Alexandria VA 22312 Personal E-mail: geanina.popoveniuc@medstar.net.

POPOVIC, TANJA, physician, research scientist; b. Zagreb, Croatia, June 2, 1956; came to U.S., 1989; d. Bosko and Ivana (Poljanac) P.; m. Boris Uroic, Aug. 11, 1979; children: Igor, Iva. MD, U. Zagreb Sch. Medicine, 1979, MS, 1983, PhD, 1986. Resident in clin. microbiology U. Zagreb Hosp. Infectious Disease, 1980-83, clin. microbiologist, 1983-89; asst./assoc. prof. microbiology U. Zagreb Sch. Medicine, 1985-89; Fulbright postdoctoral fellow Ctr. Disease Control and Prevention, Atlanta, 1989-90, mem. Cholera Task Force, 1991-94, chief Diphtheria Lab., prin. investigator Diphtheria rsch., 1995-97, chief Epidemiol. Investigation Lab., 1997, assoc. dir. science, 2004—06, chief sci. officer, 2006—10, dep. assoc. dir. sci., 2010—. Prin. investigator various internat. projects; cons. WHO, 1997, Russian State Com. Sanitary and Epidemiol. Surveillance, 1994, Inst. de Salud Carlos III, Madrid, 1994; organizer and chair 8 nat. and internat. meetings, confs. and workshops; invited lectr. over 20 internat. meetings and confs.; reviewer internat. scientific projects, including Third World Acad. Scis., Trieste, Italy, Wellcome Trust, London; cons. Nat. Immunization Program in diphtheria surveillance studies in U.S.; WHO cons. meningitis in Africa. Contbr. chpts. to books, articles to numerous profl. jours. and conf. procs., including Jour. Infectious Diseases, Jour. Food Microbiology, Jour. Clin. Microbiology, European Jour. Infectious Disease and Clin. Microbiology, others; reviewer Jour. Tropical Medicine and Hygiene, Jour. Clin. Microbiology, Jour. Pediat., Jour. Infectious Diseases. Brit. Coun. scholar, Worcester (Eng.) Royal Infirmary, 1987, 88. Mem. Am. Soc. Microbiology, WHO Diphtheria Working Group, Pasteur Inst. Molecular Subtyping Database Group (Paris). Office: Ctrs Disease Control Prevention 1600 Clifton Rd Atlanta GA 30333 *

POPOVIC-GRLE, SANJA, pulmologist educator; b. Zagreb, Croatia, Mar. 2, 1960; MD, Med. Sch., U. Zagreb, 1983, PhD, 1995. Chief outpatients dept. U. Hosp. Ctr. Zagreb, Clinic Lung Diseases Jordanovac, 2004—. Asst. prof. Med. Sch., U. Zagreb, 2008—. Mem.: European Acad. Allergy and Clin. Immunology. Avocation: gardening. Office: Jordanovac 104 Zagreb 10000 Croatia Office Fax: 3851232-55-06. Business E-Mail: sanja.grle@kbc-zagreb.lu.

POPOVICH, JOHN, JR., internist, medical association administrator; MD, U. Mich. Residency Henry Ford Hosp., Detroit, dir., Medical Intensive Care Unit, div. head, Pulmonary and Critical Care, 1989—99, chair, dept. of Internal Medicine, 1999—. Recipient Laureate Award, Mich. Chpt., Am. Col. of Physicians. Fellow: Henry Ford Hosp., Pulmonary disease, Critical Care med.; mem.: Am. Bd. of Internal Medicine (chair 2005—06), Am. Coll. of Chest Physicians, Am. Thoracic Society, Am. Soc. of Internal Medicine (vice chair 2007), Am. Coll. of Physicians. Office: c/o Henry Ford Health System 2799 W Grand Blvd Detroit MI 48202 Office Phone: 800-436-7936.

POPPAS, DIX PHILLIP, pediatric urologist, researcher, consultant; b. Richmond, Va., Oct. 30, 1957; s. Phillip Henry and Virginia Lee Poppas; m. Dorothy Poppas, May 24, 1984; children: Nicole, Elena, Phillip. BS in Biology, Va. Commonwealth U., 1982; MD, Ea. Va. Med. Sch., 1990. Resident N.Y. Hosp., NYC, 1990-94, chief pediatric urology, 1996—; sr. clin. assoc. in urology Cornell U. Med. Ctr., NYC, 1993-94, assoc. prof., 1996—; fellow Harvard Med. Sch., Boston, 1994-96; dir. lab. N.Y. Presbyn. Hosp., NYC, 1997—, assoc. prof. urology, 1997—. Vis. fellow in urology Cornell U. Med. Ctr., N.Y.C., 1994-96; pres. Futurescope Ind., LLC, N.Y.C., 1994—; chmn., exec. v.p., chief med. officer Promethean Surg. Devices, Del., N.Y., 1999—. Rsch. scholar Nat. Kidney Found., 1994, Valentine scholar N.Y. Acad. Medicine, 1994-95; Edwin Beer fellow N.Y. Acad. Medicine, 2001—. Fellow Am. Coll. Surgeons; mem. Am. Urologic Assn., Soc. Fetal Urology, Am. Acad. Pediat. Am. Soc. Laser Medicine and Surgery, Larchmont Yacht Club. Greek Orthodox. Achievements include invention of Laser Tissue Welding Control System, Protein Solder Composition Method for Use, Modified Solder for Delivery of Bioactive Substances and Method of Use. Office: NY Presbyn Hosp Box 94 525 E 68th St New York NY 10021-4870 Office Phone: 212-746-5337. E-mail: dpoppas@PSDLLC.com.

POPPERS, PAUL JULES, anesthesiologist, educator; b. Enschede, Netherlands, June 30, 1929; arrived in USA, 1958, naturalized, 1963; s. Meyer and Minca (Ginsburg) P.; m. Ann Feinberg, June 3, 1969; children: David Matthew, Jeremy Samuel. MD, U. Amsterdam, 1955. Diplomate Am. Bd. Anesthesiology. Instr. anesthesiology Columbia U., NYC, 1962 63, assoc., 1963 65, asst. prof. anesthesiology, 1965-71, assoc. prof. anesthesiology, 1971-74; prof., vice chmn. dept. anesthesiology NYU, 1974-79; prof., chmn. dept. anesthesiology Stony Brook U., NY, 1979—97, disting. prof., chmn. dept anesthesiology, 1997—2000, disting. prof. emeritus, 2000—. Cons. Brookdale Med Ctr. Bklyn, 1975-2000, VA Med. Ctr. Northport, N.Y., 1979-2000, The N.Y. Hosp. Med. Ctr. of Queens (formerly Booth Meml. Hosp.), Flushing, N.Y., 1979-98, L.I. Jewish Med. Ctr., New Hyde Park, N.Y., 1980-98, Ea. L.I. Hosp., Greenport, N.Y., 1995-99, Am. Hosp. Paris, 1989-93; cons., lectr. USN, 1968-83 Author: Regional Anesthesia, 1977; editor: Beta Blockade and Anaesthesia, 1979; sect. editor Jour. Clin. Anesthesia, 1990-2000, mem. editl. bd. Internat. Jour. Clin. Monitoring and Computing, 1990-2000, Anaesthesiology Digest, 1991-94, Gynecologic and Obstetric Investigation, 1996-2001; contbr. over 200 articles to profl. jours. Rsch. fellow NIH, 1961; recipient medal Polish Acad. Scis., Poland, 1987, Univ. medal Jagiellonian U., Krakow, Poland, 1987, 1st Sci. award Post-grad. Assembly in Anesthesiology, named Hon. Prof. Anesthesiology, U. Leiden, The Netherlands, 1977. Fellow Am. Coll. Anesthesiology, Am. Coll. Ob-gyns., Royal Soc. Medicine, Post-grad. Assembly in Anesthesiology (hon. chmn. 1989-2005); mem. Am. Soc. Anesthesiologists, Assn. Univ. Anesthesiologists, Internat. Anesthesia Rsch. Soc., Soc. Obstetric Anesthesia and Perinatology, Am. Soc. Regional Anesthesia, Jerusalem Acad. Medicine, Am. Soc. Pharmacology and Exptl. Therapeutics, Fedn. Am. Soc. Exptl. Biology, Sigma Xi. Home Phone: 212-396-9026. Personal E-mail: paulpoppers@hotmail.com.

POPTSOVA, MARIA, research scientist; b. Annaba, Algeria, Oct. 19, 1972; PhD, Moscow State U., 2005. Rsch. fellow U. Conn., 2005—10, Weill Cornell Med. Coll., 2010—. Dir. Janussys, Ltd., 2002—. Home: 465 Main St Apt 11C New York NY 10044 Personal E-mail: maria.poptsova@gmail.com.

PORAYKO, MICHAEL K., internist, educator; s. Peter Porayko and Anne Haley; m. Karen Manoukian, June 13, 1987; children: Chris, Caitlyn. MD, U. Ill., Rockford, 1981. Diplomate Am. Bd. Internal Medicine, cert. Am. Bd. Internal Medicine-Transplant Hepatology, Am. Bd. Internal Medicine-Gastroenterology. Intern Mich. State Univ. Associated Hospitals, 1982, resident, 1984; fellow, hepatobilary medicine Lahey Clinic Med. Ctr. and New England Deaconess Hosp., 1987; fellow Mayo Clinic, Rochester, Minn., 1988; assoc. prof. medicine, med. dir. liver transplantation Vanderbilt U., Nashville, 2002—. Designer exam. for hepatologists Am. Bd. Internal Medicine, Phila., 2004—06. Mem.: ACP (bd. dirs. 2004—06, Rsch.award 1985). Achievements include research in nutrition in Cirrhotic patients. Office Phone: 615-322-0128.

POREMBA, CHRISTOPHER, pathologist, educator; MD, Westfalische Wilhelms-U., Munster, 1994, PhD, 1995. Bd. cert. pathologist Arztekammer Westfalen-Lippe, 2000. Prof., vice chmn. Heinrich-Heine-U., Dusseldorf, Germany, 2002—08; chmn. Ctr. Histology, Cytology and Molecular Pathology Rsch. Park, Trier, Germany, 2008—. Recipient various awards and prizes, 1997—. Mem.: German Assn. Pathologists, Am. Assn. Cancer Rsch. Office: Dir Zentrum fur Histologie Zytologie und Molekulare Diagnostik ZHZMD Max-Planck Strasse 18-20 D-54296 Trier Germany Office Phone: 49-651-99258320. Office Fax: 49-(0)651-99-258383. Business E-Mail: poremba@patho-trier.de.

PORIES, WALTER JULIUS, surgeon, educator; b. Munich, Jan. 18, 1930; s. Theodore Francis and Frances (Lowin) P.; m. Muriel Helen Aronson, Aug. 18, 1951; children: Susan E., Mary Jane, Carolyn A., Kathy G.; m. Mary Ann Rose McCarthy, June 4, 1977; children: Mary Lisa, Michael McCarthy. BA, Wesleyan U., Middletown, Conn., 1952; MD with honors, U. Rochester, 1955. Diplomate Am. Bd. Surgery, Am. Bd. Thoracic Surgery. Intern Strong Meml. Hosp., Rochester, NY, 1955—56, resident, 1958—62; chmn. dept. surgery Wright-Patterson AFB, Ohio, 1952—67; asst. prof. surgery and oncology U. Rochester, 1967—69; prof. surgery and assoc. chmn. dept. surgery Case Western Res. U., 1969—77; prof. surgery, biochemistry, exercise and sport medicine East Carolina U., Greenville, NC, 1977—, chmn. dept. surgery, 1977—96, dir. Metabolic Inst., 2005—08; chief surgery Pitt County Meml. Hosp., 1977—96, prof. surgery U. Health Scis. of Uniformed Svcs., 1982—; founder, assoc. dir. Rochester Cancer Ctr., 1967—69; founder, dir. Cleve. Cancer Ctr., 1972—77, Hospice of Cleve., 1975; founder, chmn. bd. Hospice of Greenville, 1981; med. dir. Home Health Care of Greenville, 1978—83; pres. Surg. Rev. Corp., Raleigh, 2003—. Founder, chmn. bd. Ctr. for Creative Living, 1985-91; pres., chmn. Echo Mgmt. Orgn., 1994—; vis. scholar NIH, 1996; sec. treas., pres. N.C. Med. Bd., 1997-2003. Author: Clinical Applications of Zinc Metabolism, 1974; editor: Operative Surgery series, vols. 1-4, 1979-83, Office Surgery for Family Physicians, 1985; editor in chief Current Surgery, 1990-2005; editor Nat. Curriculum for Residency in Surgery, 4th edit., 1988—. Bd. dirs. Boy Scouts Am., Cleve., 1974-77, Greenville Arts Mus., 1980-82; pres. Sequoiah, Inc., 1999—; bd. dirs. East Carolina U. Found., United Meth. Homes, 2003-. Maj. USAF, 1955-67; col. USAR, 1979-91, comdr. USAF Hosp., Durham, N.C.; activated Desert Shield, 1990. Decorated Legion of Merit; Thorndyke scholar, 1948-51; recipient McLester award USAF, 1966, Miss. Magnolia Cross, 1989, Presdl. citation for Desert Shield, 1994; named to Hon. Order of Ky. Cols., 1965. Fellow ACS, Am. Coll. Cardiology, Am. Coll. Chest Physicians; mem. Soc. for Vascular Surgery, Soc. Surg. Oncology, Soc. Univ. Surgeons, Am. Surg. Assn., Soc. Environ. Geochemistry (past pres.), Residency Rev. Com. for Surgery (vice-chair 1992-98), So. Surg. Assn., Soc. for Thoracic Surgery, Ea. Carolina Health Orgn. (pres., chmn. bd. 1994-99), Assn. Programs Dirs. in Surgery (pres. 1995-96), N.C. Surg. Assn. (pres. 1995-96), Am. Soc. Bariatic Surgery (pres. 2002), Sigma Xi (O. Max Gardner prize), Phi Kappa Phi. Home: Deep Sun Farm 7464 NC 43 N Macclesfield NC 27852 Office: East Carolina U Dept Surgery Greenville NC 27858 Office Phone: 252-744-3290. Business E-Mail: pories@ecu.edu. *

PORKERT, MANFRED (BRUNO), medical sciences educator, author; b. Decin, Czech Repub., Aug. 16, 1933; arrived in West Germany, 1945; s. Bruno and Elfriede (Walter) P.; m. Elisabeth Friederike Herrmann, 1974 (div. 1978); 1 child, Christine Franka; m. Helga Hartung, 1997. PhD, Universite de Paris, 1957. Rsch. fellow Centre Nat. de la Rechereche Sci., Paris, 1955-57, Deutsche Forschungsgemeinschaft, Munich and Bonn, Fed. Republic Germany, 1959 69; dozent Universitat Munich, 1970-75, prof., 1975-78, prof. extraordinary, 1978-95, prof. emeritus, 1996—. Editor, pub.: Acta Medicinae Sinensis, 1980-85; cons. editor Chinesische Medizin, 1986-92; exec. editor-in-chief Internat. Normative Dictionary of Chinese Medicine, 1989—; contbr. numerous articles to profl. jours. Mem. interdisciplinary lectures com. U. Munich, 1975-79, mem. univ. coun., 1977-79, sec. philos. faculty, 1975-77. Mem. Internat. Chinese Medicine Soc. (founder, pres. Munich chpt. 1978-85), Internat. Sci. Chinese Med. Assn. (co-founder 1999—). Avocation: photography. Home Phone: +33 5 4922 6336; Office Phone: +33 5 4922 6336. Office Fax: +33 5 4922 3322.

PORKODI, RAMANATHAN, rheumatologist, consultant; b. Chennai, India, June 14, 1952; d. Palanivelu K N and Shyamala. MD in Gen. Medicine, 1980, D.M. in Rheumatology, 1995. Registered Med. Paractioner Tamilnadu Med. Coun. Rheumatology tutor Madras Med. Coll., Chennai, India, 1982—96, asst. prof. rheumatology, 1996—2008, prof. and head rheumatology, 2008—10; ret., 2010. Author: Manual Of Rheumatology, 1999; assoc. editor: Jour. Indian Rheumatology Assn., 1996—98; author: Rheumatology Principles and Practice. Mem.: Indian Rheumatology Assn. (exec. com. mem. 1991—95). Avocations: reading, watching tv. Home: 11/4 Peters Ln Kannagi St E Tam Tamilnadu Chennai 600059 India Office Phone: 98411-29281. E-mail: drporkodi rheum@yahoo.com.

PORT, JOHN D., radiologist, educator; b. Chgo., Aug. 26, 1964; s. Curtis D. and Janice M. Port; m. Dolores M. Arellano, Sept. 3, 1989; children: Cristina A., Jenna M. BS, MIT, Cambridge, 1986; PhD, U. Ill. Chgo., 1992, MD, 1994. Cert. neuroradiologist Am. Bd. Radiology, 2001. Staff radiologist Dept. Radiology, Mayo Clinic, Rochester, Minn., 2000—, assoc. prof. radiology, 2008—, rsch. chair, 2008—, asst. prof. psychiatry, 2010. Contbr. scientific papers. Mem.: Am. Soc. Neuroradiology, Internat. Soc. Magnetic Resonance Medicine (ann. meeting planning com. 2005—08). Avocations: exercise, sailing, theater. Office: Mayo Clinic 200 First St Southwest Rochester MN 55905 Business E-Mail: port.john@mayo.edu.

PORTER, ANDREW CALVIN, dean, psychologist, educator; b. Huntington, Pa., July 10, 1942; s. Rutherford and Grace (Johnson) P.; children: Matthew, Anna, John, Joe, Kate. BS, Ind. State U., 1963; MS, U. Wis., 1965, PhD, 1967. Vis. asst. prof. Ind. State U., 1967; asst. prof. ednl. psychology Mich. State U., East Lansing, 1967—70, dir. office rsch. consultation, 1967—73, assoc. prof. ednl. psychology, 1970—74; vis. scholar Nat. Inst. Edn., Washington, 1973—74, chief measurement and methodology divsn., 1974—75; prof. ednl. psychology Mich. State U., East Lansing, 1974—88; assoc. dir. basic skills group Nat. Inst. Edn., Washington, 1975—76; dir. Sch. Advanced Studies Coll. Edn. Mich. State U., East Lansing, 1979—81, assoc. dean rsch. and grad. study Coll. Edn., 1981—85; Anderson-Bascom prof. edn., prof. ednl. psychology U. Wis., Madison, 1988—2003, dir. Wis. Ctr. Edn. Rsch., 1988—2003; Patricia and Rodes Hart prof. ednl. leadership and policy Vanderbilt U., Nashville, 2003—07, dir. Learning Scis. Inst., 2003—07; dean Grad. Sch. Edn., U. Pa., 2007—. Mem adv. com. What Works Clearinghouse Inst. Edn. Scis., 2002-, steering com. math./sci. partnerships, Nat. Acad. Sci., 2003-2005, nat. assessment governing bd., 2004-; chmn. adv. coun. on edn. stats., U.S. Dept. Edn., 1994-2001; chair bd. Internat. Studies, Nat. Acad. Sci., Nat. Rsch. Coun., 1998-2001 Editor: (with A. Gamoran) Methodological Advances in Cross-National Surveys of Educational Achievement, 2002; mem. editl. bd. Tchrs. Coll. Record, 1995—, Am. Ednl. Rsch. Jour., 2004—. Bd. dirs. Madison Urban League, 1992-96. Recipient Disting. Alumni award, Ind. State U., 1994, Sch. Edn. Dean's Club Faculty Disting. Achievement Award, U. Wis.-Madison, 1996, Crystal Apple Award, Mich. State U., 2000, Alumni Achievement award, U. Wis., Madison, 2005. Mem. Am. Ednl. Rsch. Assn. (pres. 2001, Outstanding Reviewer award 2003), Nat. Coun. Edn. Measurement, Nat. Coun. Tchrs. Math., Nat. Acads. (lifetime nat. mem.), Nat. Acad. Edn. (v.p. 2005), Phi Delta Kappa (life). Office: U Pa Grad Sch Edn 3700 Walnut St Philadelphia PA 19104 Office Phone: 215-898-7014. E-mail: andyp@gse.upenn.edu.

PORTER, GEORGE HOMER, III, physician, medical foundation executive; b. Charlotte, NC, Sept. 7, 1933; s. George Homer Jr. and Sallie Mapp (Jacob) P.; m. Virginia Pillow, Apr. 5, 1958; 1 child, Virginia Mapp (dec.). AB magna cum laude, Duke U., 1954, MD with honors, 1958. Diplomate Am. Bd. Internal Medicine, Am. Bd. Hematology, Am. Bd. Med. Oncology. Intern internal medicine Duke U. Med. Ctr., Durham, NC, 1958-59; asst. resident medicine, instr. medicine Barnes Hosp., Washington U. Sch. Medicine, St. Louis, 1959-60; sr. resident physician The Peter Bent Brigham Hosp., Boston, 1960-61; clin. assoc. medicine, fellow hematology NIH, Bethesda, Md., 1961-64; staff hematologist-oncologist Ochsner Clinic, New Orleans, 1964—; chmn. emeritus, dept. hematology/oncology Ochsner Health Sys., New Orleans; trustee, mem. exec. com. Alton Ochsner Med. Found., New Orleans, 1973—, pres., chief exec. officer, 1980—2001; pres. Ochsner Clinic Found., New Orleans, 2001—. Prin. investigator Southeastern Cancer Study Group, 1973-78; bd. dirs. Eye, Ear, Nose and Throat Hosp., New Orleans, 1986—, Hibernia Corp., Hiberna Nat. Bank, New Orleans, 1980-92. Bd. dirs. Am. Cancer Soc., New Orleans, 1978-89, La. Cancer and Lung Trust Fund, 1980—, Leukemia Soc. Am., 1968-72, The Chamber, New Orleans, 1984-88, Bus. Task Force on Edn., New Orleans, 1985—, Bur. Govtl. Rsch., New Orleans, 1988—, Metrovision Partnership, New Orleans, 1990—. Named Tchr. of Yr., Alton Ochsner Med. Found., 1967. Fellow ACP (life), Internat. Soc. Hematology; mem. AMA, ABA (mem. sect. on med. schs.), AAAS, Internat. Assn. for Study Lung Cancer (founding), Am. Fedn. Clin. Rsch., Am. Hosp. Assn., Am. Assn. Clin. Oncology, Am. Assn. Hematology, Am. Soc. Internal Medicine, Internat. AIDS Soc., La. Med. Soc., Am. Cancer Soc., Orleans Med. Soc. Soc. Surg. Oncology, Am. Coll. Legal Medicine (assoc.-in-medicine, bd. trustees NO/AIDS Task Force, bd. dirs. Acad. Med. Ctr. Consortium), Internat. Soc. for AIDS Edn., Assn. for Health Care Rsch., Mensa, SAR, Royal Soc. St. George, Milton Soc., Confrerie chevaliers du Tastevin, New Orleans Country Club, Boston Club, Century Assn. (N.Y.C.), Pickwick Club, Phi Beta Kappa. Office: Ochsner Clinic Found 1516 Jefferson Hwy New Orleans LA 70121-2429 *

PORTER, JOHN EDWARD, lobbyist, lawyer, former congressman; b. Evanston, Ill., June 1, 1935; s. Harry H. and Beatrice V.P. Porter; 5 children. BSBA, Northwestern U., 1957; JD with distinction, U. Mich., 1961; LLD (hon.), Northwestern U., Tufts U., Mt. Sinai Sch. Medicine, Oreg. Health Scis. U., Howard U., Rush U. Bar: Ill. 1961, DC 2005, US Supreme Ct. 1968, US Ct. Fed. Claims. Honor law grad. atty. Appellate Divsn. US Dept. Justice, Washington; mem. Ill. House of Reps., 1973 79, US Congress from 10th Ill. Dist., 1980—2001; ptnr. Hogan Lovells LLP (formerly Hogan & Hartson), Washington, 2001—. Founder, co-chmn. Congl. Human Rights Caucus; chmn. PBS, Research! America; vice chair Found. for NIH; trustee Brookings Inst.; mem. Coun. on Fgn. Rels., Inst. Medicine, Bretton Woods Com.; bd. mem. Nat. Space Biomedical Rsch. Inst.; former bd. mem. RAND Corp., Population Resource Ctr. Trustee emeritus John F. Kennedy Ctr. for Performing Arts. Recipient Anatoly Scharansky Freedom Award, Chgo. Action for Soviet Jewry, Henry M. Jackson Leadership Award, Union of Couns. for Soviet Jewry, Outstanding Congl. Leadership Award, Nat. Family Planning and Reproductive Health Assn., Lorax Award, Global Tomorrow Coalition, Beacon Award, Am. Soc. Assn. Execs., Pub. Health Continuum Award for Disting. Congl. Svc., Coalition for Health Funding, Morris K. Udall Pub. Svc. Award, Michael J. Fox Found., Dr. Nathan Davis Award, Am. Med. Assn., Lifetime Achievement Award, Am. Psychiatric Assn. and the Academic Consortium, Decade of the Brain Award, Soc. for Neuroscience, Lifetime Achievement Award, Juvenile Diabetes Found., Paul G. Rogers Award, Assn. Academic Health Ctrs., Award for Pub. Svc. Excellence, Assn. Am. Med. Colls., Disting. Pub. Svc. Award, Am. Soc. Microbiology, Svc. Award, Am. Soc. for Cell Biology, Public Service Award, Fedn. Am. Socs. for Experimental Biology, Edwin C. Whitehead Award, Research! America, Mary Wood Lasker Award for Pub. Svc., Albert and Mary Lasker Found.; named one of 50 Top Lobbyists, Washingtonian mag., 2007. Mem.: Inst. Medicine, Inter Am. Dialogue, Coun. Fgn. Rels. Republican. Office: Hogan Lovells US LLP Columbia Square 555 Thirteenth St, NW Washington DC 20004 Home Phone: 708-684-0890; Office Phone: 202-637-5695. Office Fax: 202-637-5910. E-mail: john.porter@hoganlovells.com.

PORTER, JOHN WESTON, counselor, consultant, administrator; b. Fostoria, Ohio, Dec. 26, 1939; s. William Thomas and Ida Elizabeth (Carter) Porter. Student, U. Cin., 1958; BA, Heidelberg U., 1961; MA in Cmty. Psychology, U. DC, 1973, MA in Counseling, 1975; postgrad., Antioch Coll., Yellow Springs, Ohio, 1974, Frostburg U., Md., 1970, George Washington U., Washington, DC, 1968. Cert. Nat. Bd. Cert. Counselors, DC. Claims rep. Social Security Adminstrn., Cleve. and Akron, Ohio, 1961-62; office mgr. Phoenix Cos., Washington and LA, 1966-70; rschr. Frostburg U., U. DC, 1970-73; edn. and career devel. specialist DC Pub. Schs., 1973-79, career edn. unit, 1979-83, Career Assessment Ctr., 1983-85, asst. dir. guidance and counseling, 1985-95; mem. cmty. adv. coun. Washington Hosp. Ctr., 1987—. Counseling mentor DC Pub. Schs., 1998—2003; dir. Westport Consulting, 2001—10; cons. DC Pub. Sch. HiScip program, New Couns. Mentor, 2001—02. Contbr. articles to profl. jours. Vice chmn. adv. coun. Group Health Assn., Washington, 1977—79, 1981—83; sec. Md.-DC Am. Coll. Testing Coun., 1987—88, vice chair, 1988—90, chair, 1990—91, mem. exec. com., 1991—2005; mem. adv. com. Children's Edn. Found., 1989—93, mem. fund raising com., 1989—, exec. bd., 1992—2005, asst. treas., 1992—93, treas., 1993—95; pres. N.E. Hill Found., 1990—92; mem. com. DC Career and Tech. Edn. Task Force, 2000; team chmn. Wilson HS, 2002, mem. student mgmt. task force, 2002—03, grant rev. panelist, 1998, 2002—03; mem. planning com. Friends of Turkey Thicket Rec. Ctr., 2005, cons., 2005—; treas. Tues. Evening Square Dance Group, 2006—08, exec. com. mem., 2008—10. Lt. (j.g.) USN, 1962—66, lt. USNR. Recipient award, Ohio Acad. Sci., 1954—57, Cleve. Plain Dealer Operation Demonstrate, 1956, Svc. award, Heidleberg U. Publs., 1961, Recognition cert., DC Assn. Career Devel., 1975, 1976, DC City Coun., 1982, Children's Edn. Found., 1990, Recognition award Outstanding Contbn. to Guidance and Counseling, 1987, Commn. Svc. award, Advisory Neighborhood Commn., 2004, 2005. Mem.: ACA (counselor adv.-legis.), Medallion Club, Heritage Soc., Heidelberg U., RECOG, Am Assn. Career Edn., Heidelberg U., 6/Class Legacy Fund Com., Coun. Accreditation Counseling and Related Ednl. Programs (site visit team 1989—), Assn. Counselor Edn. and Supervision, DC Career Devel. Assn. (treas. 1983—86, exec. bd. 1983—90), DC Sch. Counselors Assn. (Outstanding Leadership award 1994), Nat. Career Devel. Assn. (assembly del. 1984, master career coun. 2003), Am. Sch. Counselors Assn. (chair rsch. com. 1990—91, career guidance com., leadership recognition cert. 1987), Am. Counseling Assn. (chmn. govt. rels. N. Atlantic region 1980—81, cert. Outstanding Contbn. in Govt. Rels. 1982, Recognition award 1987), DC Counseling Assn. (treas. 1975—77, exec. bd. 1975—80, sec. 1977—78, pres. 1979—80, trustee 1989—92, treas. 1991—92, trustee 2003—04, exec. bd. mem. 2008—, trustee 2008—, counselor adv.-legis., Mem. of the Yr. 1980, Outstanding Leadership award 1980), Phi Delta Kappa (George Washington U. chpt.) (edn. found. rep. 1993—95, v.p. membership 1995—96, pres. 1996—97, MACI project adv. coun. Hosp. Sick Children 1997—98, rev. panel DC vocat. edn. grants 1998, sec., lic. profl. counselor, DC 1995—2011). Home: 821 Taylor St NE Washington DC 20017-2009 Personal E-mail: jw.wb.porter@erols.com. *

PORTER, ROGER JOHN, research and development company executive, neurologist, pharmacologist; b. Pitts., Apr. 4, 1942; s. John Keaggy and Margaret (Parker) P.; m. Candace Marie Leland, Feb. 17, 1968; children: David, Stacey. BS, Eckerd Coll., 1964; MD, Duke U., 1968; DSc (hon.), Eckerd Coll., 2008. Diplomate Nat. Bd. Med. Examiners, Am. Bd. Neurology, Am. Bd. Electroencephalography. Intern U. Calif., San Diego, 1968-69; resident in neurology U. Calif., San Francisco, 1971-74; fellow rsch. tng. program Duke U., Durham, NC, 1966-67; staff assoc. sect. epilepsy Nat. Inst. Neurol. Diseases and Stroke, NIH, Bethesda, Md., 1969-71; investigator U. Calif., San Francisco, 1972-73; sr. rsch. assoc. epilepsy br. neurol. disorders program Nat. Inst. Neurol. and Communicative Disorders and Stroke, NIH, Bethesda, 1974-78, asst. chief epilepsy br., 1977-79, acting chief, 1979-80, acting chief clin. epilepsy sect., IRP, 1979-84, chief epilepsy br. neurol. disorders program, 1980-84, chief med. neurology br. and clin. epilepsy sect. IRP, 1984-87; dep. dir. Nat. Inst. Neurol. Disorders and Stroke, NIH, Bethesda, 1987-92; v.p., clin. pharmacology Wyeth-Ayerst Rsch., Radnor, Pa., 1992-97, v.p. clin. rsch., 1997—99, v.p., dep. head clin. rsch., 1999—2002; cons., 2002—. Adj. prof. neurology U. Pa., 1993—; prof. neurology Uniformed Svcs. U. Health Scis., Bethesda, 1980-93, adj. prof. pharmacology, 1982—; cons.-lectr. neurology Nat. Naval Med. Ctr., Bethesda, 1978-93; chmn. White House Subcom. on Brain and Behavioral Scis., 1990-92; scholar-in-residence Assn. Am. Med. Colls., Washington, 1989-90; mem. NIMH/Nat. Inst. Neurol. Disorders and Stroke Coun. of Assembly of Scientists, 1983-86, pres., 1985-86; mem. pharmacy and therapeutics com. NIH, 1977-86, chmn., 1978; mem. instnl. rev. bd. human subjects Nat. Inst. Neurol. Disorders and Stroke, 1984-87, chmn., 1986-87. Mem. editl. bd. Acta Neurologica Scandanavica, 1991-97, Annals of Neurology, 1987-92, Epilepsia, 1982-86; contbr. articles to profl. jours., chpts. to books; author 13 books, writer, contbr. 5 motion pictures, 1 exhibit. Bd. trustees Eckerd Coll., 1994—97; commd. officer USPHS, 1969—92. Recipient MacArthur Outstanding Alumnus award Eckerd Coll., 1977, Fulbright Disting. Prof. award, 1985, Disting. Alumnus award Duke Duke U. Med. Ctr., 1989, USPHS Dist. Svc. Medal, 1991, USUHS Commendable Svc. Award, 2001. Fellow Coll. Physicians Phila. (trustee 2006—, sec. 2008-), Am. Acad. Neurology, Am. Neurol. Assn.; mem. Am. Electroencephalographic Soc., Am. Epilepsy Soc. (pres. 1989-90), Soc. Neurosci., Am. Soc. Clin. Pharmacology and Therapeutics, Am. Soc. Exptl. Neurol. Therapeutics (pres. 2008-10, past pres. 2010-), Internat. League Against Epilepsy (sec. gen. 1989-93), Am. Soc. Pharmacology and Exptl. Therapeutics. Home and Office: 461 Timber Ln Devon PA 19333-1232 Office Phone: 610-989-3767. Business E-Mail: rjportermd@aol.com.

PORTER, VERNA R., neurologist, educator; m. Dr. William G. Buxton; children: William Buxton, John Buxton, Andrew Buxton. MD, UCLA, 1994. Diplomate Am. Bd. of Psychiatry and Neurology, 2000. Chief neurology divsn. Santa Monica/UCLA Med. Ctr., 2002—; assoc. clin. prof. dept. neurology UCLA, 2002—. Contbr. articles to profl. jours. Named one of America's Top Physicians, Consumer Rsch. Coun. of Am., 2004—05, 2006—07, 2008—; named to, Southern Calif. Super Doctors Publ. Mem.: Am. Acad. Neurology (life). Achievements include research in Dementia and Alzheimer's disease. Office: UCLA/Santa Monica Neurological Assoc 1328 16th St 2nd Fl Santa Monica CA 90404 Office Fax: 310-319-4552.

PORTER, WAYNE RANDOLPH, dermatologist; b. Washington, Jan. 10, 1948; s. James Randolph and Betty Rose (Burgess) P. BS, MIT, 1970; MD, Duke U., 1973. Diplomate Am. Bd. Internal Medicine, Am. Bd. Dermatology. Intern U. Miami (Fla.) Affiliated Hosps., 1973-74; resident in internal medicine U. Miami Sch. Medicine, 1973-76, resident in dermatology, 1976-78, clin. instr., then asst. prof. dermatology (vol.), 1978-85, assoc. prof. (vol.), 1985—2005, prof., 2005—. Adj. prof. Barry U. Sch. Grad. Medicine, 2000—; practice medicine specializing in dermatology, North Miami Beach, 1978—; mem. staff U. Miami-Jackson Meml. Hosp. Mem. med. adv. bd. Dade-Broward chpt. Lupus Found. Am. Fellow Internat. Soc. for Dermatologic Surgery, Am. Acad. Dermatology, Am. Assn. Dermatologic Surgeons; mem. AMA, ACP, Internat. Soc. Pediat. Dermatology, Fla. Med. Assn., Fla. Dermatology Soc., Miami Dermatol. Soc. (pres.), Dade County Med. Assn., So. Med. Assn., Bath Club (Miami Beach), Coral Reef Yacht Club. Office: 909 N Miami Beach Blvd Miami FL 33162-3712 Home Phone: 305-285-8983; Office Phone: 305-949-4223. E-mail: wrpmd@bellsouth.net.

PORTES, ARLINDO JOSE FREIRE, ophthalmologist, director; b. Rio de Janeiro, Aug. 29, 1965; MD, UFRJ, 1989, PhD, 2001. Ophthalmologist Hosp. Souza Aguiar, 1992—2000; dir. Portes Eye Clinic, 1998—. Adj. prof. Estacio de Sá U., UNESA, 2001—. Recipient award, Essilor. Mem.: Brazilian Coun. Ophthalmology (mem. commn. blindness prevention 2010—11), Brazilian Soc. Ophthalmology (bd. dirs. 2009—, chief editor 2011—), Am. Acad. Ophthalmology. Avocations: chess, reading, movies. Office: Ave N S Copacabana 195/409-412 Rio de Janeiro 22020-002 Brazil Office Fax: 0552125414532. Business E-Mail: portes@uol.com.br.

PORTEUS, MATTHEW H., pediatric hematologist, oncologist; b. Pomona, Calif., Aug. 15, 1964; AB magna cum laude, Harvard U., 1986; MD, PhD, Stanford U. Sch. Medicine, 1994. Diplomate Am. Bd. Pediat., cert. in pediatric hematology-oncology. Pediatric internship Children's Hosp., Boston, 1994—95, pediatric residency, sr. asst. resident, 1995—96; pediatric hematology/oncology fellow Dana Farber Cancer Inst., Boston, 1996—99; postdoc. scholar Calif. Inst. Tech., 1999—2003; asst. prof. pediat. and biochemistry U. Tex. Southwestern Med. Ctr. Contbr. articles to profl. jours. Recipient Burroughs Wellcome Fund Career Devel. award, 2003; grantee Howard Hughes Med. Inst. Postdoc. Rsch. Fellowship for Physicians, 2002. Office: U Tex Southwestern Med Ctr Porteud Lab 5323 Harry Hines Blvd Dallas TX 75390 also: Childrens Med Ctr 1935 Medical District Dr Dallas TX 75235 Office Fax: 214-648-3896, 214-648-3122. E-mail: matthew.porteus@utsouthwestern.edu. *

PORTIER, CHRISTOPHER JUDE, public health service officer, research scientist; b. Houma, La., Apr. 3, 1956; life ptnr. Meike Mevissen; children: Katherine Mary, Margaret Claire. BS, Nicholls State U., Thibodaux, LA, 1977; MS, U. NC, Chapel Hill, 1979; PhD, U. NC, 1981. Math. statistician NIEHS, Research Triangle Park, NC, 1978—90, head risk methodology sect., 1990—93, chief lab. computational biology and risk analysis, 1993—2005, prin. investigator, environ. sys. biology, 1993—2010, assoc. dir. risk assessment, 1996—2000, dir. environ. toxicology program, 2000—06, assoc. dir. nat. toxicology program, 2000—06, dir. office risk assessment rsch., 2006—09, assoc. dir., 2006—09, sr. advisor to the dir., 2009—10; dir. Agency Toxic Substances and Disease Registry Dept. Health and Human Services, 2010—; dir. Nat. Ctr. Environ. Health Centers for Disease Control and Prevention, Atlanta, 2010—. Com. chmn. Internat. Agy. for Rsch. Cancer, Lyon, France, 1995—2008, WHO, Geneva, 1995—2008, sci. advisor, 2006—08; mem. EPA FIFRA Sci. Adv. Panel, Washington, 1998—2004; co-chmn. health and environ. sub com. President's Nat. Com. Sci. and Tech., Washington, 2003—05, chmn. toxics and risk sub com., 2005—. Recipient James E. Grizzle Disting. Alumnus award, Dept. BioStatistics, U. NC, 1991, Spiegelman award, Am. Pub. Health Assn., 1995, Disting. Achievement award, Am. Statis. Assn., 1995, Outstanding Risk Practitioner award, Internat. Soc. Risk Analysis, 2000, Best Paper award, Soc. Toxicology, 1995, Risk Assessment Splty. Sect. Paper of Yr., 2005, 2006. Fellow: Internat. Statis. Inst., Am. Statis. Assn., World Innovation Found.; mem.: Russian Nat. Academy Natural Sci. (Foreign Corr. 1992). Office: Centers Disease Control and Prevention 1600 Clifton Rd Atlanta GA 30333 *

PORTNOF, JASON E., dentist, educator; b. May 29, 1976; DMD, Nova Southeastern U. Coll. Dental Medicine, 2002; MD, Cornell Med. Coll., 2006. Asst. prof. Albert Einstein Coll. Medicine, 2009—11. Mem.: AAOMS. Office: 447 Rt 10 Ste 5 Randolph NJ 07869 Office Fax: 973-328-3405. Business E-Mail: jap9016@med.cornell.edu.

PORTO, ANA LUCIA FIGUEIREDO, biochemist, educator; b. Ipojuca, Pernambuco, Brazil, Dec. 20, 1957; Degree in Chemistry, U. Rural Fed. Pernambuco, 1976; PhD in Engring. Chemistry, U. Campinas, 1998. Assoc. prof. U. Rural Fed. Pernambuco, 1991—. Mem.: Soc. Brazilian Biochemistry and Molecular Biology. Office: RDom MAnoel de Medeiros Dois Irmãos Recife Pernambuco 52171900 Brazil Office Fax: 00 55 81 33206057. E-mail: analuporto@yahoo.com.br.

POSER, ERNEST GEORGE, psychologist, educator; b. Vienna, Mar. 2, 1921; emigrated to Can., 1942, naturalized, 1946; s. Paul and Blanche (Furst) P.; m. Maria Jutta Cahn, July 3, 1953; children: Yvonne, Carol, Michael. BA, Queen's U., Kingston, Ont., 1946, MA, 1949; PhD, U. London, 1952. Diplomate: Am. Bd. Profl. Psychologists; registered psychologist, B.C. Asst. prof. U. N.B., 1946-48; chief psychologist N.B. Dept. Health, 1952-54; prof. psychology McGill U., Montreal, 1954-83, assoc. prof. psychiatry Faculty Medicine, 1963-83; dir. behavior therapy unit Douglas Hosp. Center, Montreal, 1966-83; adj. prof. dept. psychology U. BC, 1984-95, clin. prof. dept. psychiatry, 1984—88. Author: Adaptive Learning: Behavior Modification with Children, 1973, Behavior Therapy in Clinical Practice, 1977. Chair World Views Collaborative, Vancouver, BC, 2004—. Hon. fellow Middlesex Hosp., London, 1964 Fellow Canadian Psychol. Assn., Am. Psychol. Assn. Home Phone: 604-222-4748. Personal E-mail: erjuposer@shaw.ca.

POST, MARTIN ROGER, cardiologist; b. Bklyn, NY, Apr. 11, 1943; BA, Univ. Pa., 1963; MD, SUNY, Syracuse, 1967. Diplomate Am. Bd. Internal Med., 1974, Am. Bd. Internal Med., Cardiovascular Disease, 1974. Intern Ohio State Univ. Hosp., 1967—68, resident in cardiology, 1968—70; fellow NY Hosp. Cornell Med. Ctr., 1970—72; clinical asst. prof. med. NY Hosp. Cornell Univ. Med. Ctr., 1976—; ptnr., cardiologist NY Cardiology Associates; attending physician NY Presbyterian Hosp. Cardiologist World Wrestling Entertainment Wellness Program, 2006. Contbr. articles to profl. jours. Named one of America's Top Doctors, Castle Connolly. Fellow: Am. Coll. Cardiology, Am. Heart Assoc. (Scientific Council). Office: NY Cardiology Associates 425 E 61st St New York NY 10021 Office Phone: 212-734-3545. Office Fax: 212-752-3281.

POST-GORDEN, JOAN CAROLYN, retired psychology educator; b. Oak Park, Ill., July 3, 1932; d. DeWitt T. and Mary Jane (Lewellen) Post; children: Gregrey Wayne, Jeffrey Scott, Kayle Lynn, Tamara Anne. BS, Manchester Coll., Ind., 1964; MS, U. Ga., 1967, PhD, 1970. Lic. psychologist, Colo. Tchr. Clarke County Schs., Athens, Ga., 1964-65; part-time asst. prof. Tex. Tech U., Lubbock, 1968-69; instr. So. Colo. State Coll., Pueblo, 1970-71; asst. prof. U. So. Colo., Pueblo, 1971-76, assoc. prof., 1976-81, prof., 1981—99, chmn. dept., 1991—99, ret., 1999, prof. emeritus, 1999—. Asst. to city mgr., Champaign, Ill., 1980-81; psychologist So. Ctrl. Ill. Devel. Dist., Flora, 1979-80; dir. scholarly and creative activities U. So. Colo., 1988-91 Contbr. chpt. to book and articles to profl. jours. NDEA fellow, 1964-66, Danforth teaching fellow, 1978, faculty fellow Colo. State Div. Mental Health, 1986-87. Mem. APA, Soc. for Rsch. in Child Devel., Rocky Mountain Psychol. Assn., Colo. Psychol. Assn., Psi Chi, Sigma Xi, Alpha Omicron Pi. Avocation: scuba diving. Home: 24 Cactus Dr Key West FL 33040-5632

POSTIER, RUSSELL GLEN, surgeon; b. Cushing, Okla., Nov. 21, 1949; s. Cecil Glen and Myrtle Ann Postier; m. Ruthann Fortner, Sept. 24, 1977; 1 child, Lee Allen. MD, U. Okla., 1975. Diplomate Am. Bd. Surgery, 1982. Resident in surgery Johns Hopkins U., Balt., 1975—80, asst. chief surgery svc., 1980—81; faculty mem. dept. surgery U. Okla., Oklahoma City, 1981—, chmn. dept. surgery, 1997—. Pres. Southwestern Surg. Congress, Chgo., 2001—02. Fellow: Am. Coll. Surgeons (pres.), Am. Surg. Assn., So. Surg. Assn., Soc. U. Surgeons; mem.: American Bd. Surgery (dir. 2001—, pres. 2008—09). Office: Dept Surgery Univ Okla PO Box 26910 WP 2140 Oklahoma City OK 73190

POSTON, GRAEME JOHN, surgeon, director; b. Oldham, Eng., Aug. 6, 1955; MBBS, U. London, 1979, MS, 1988. Cons. surgeon Royal Liverpool U. Hosp., 1990—2004; dir., surgery Aintree U. Hosp., Liverpool, 2004—. Pres. Brit. Assn. Surg. Oncology, 2005—07; chair Colorectal Cancer Guideline Devel. Group, Nat. Inst. Clin. Excellence, 2009—; pres. elect European Soc. Surg. Oncology, 2010—. Contbr. articles to numerous profl. jours. Recipient Kilroe medal, Christie Hosp., Manchester, N. K. Misra medal, Indian Assn. Surg. Oncology. Fellow: RCS (Edinburgh), RCS (Eng.) (chair, Cancer Svcs. Com. 2005—07, Stanford Cade medal), Assn. Upper Gastrointestinal Surgeons Gt. Britain and Ireland (pres. 2010—), Assn. Surgeons India, Coll. Surgeons Sri Lanka. Avocations: mountain climbing, travel, scuba diving. Office: Aintree University Hosp Longmoor Ln Liverpool Merseyside L23 6TJ England Office Fax: 44151 529 8547. Business E-Mail: graeme.poston@aintree.nhs.uk.

POSTON, WALKER SEWARD CARLOS, II, medical educator, researcher; b. Oakland, Calif., May 27, 1961; s. Walker Seward Poston and Donna Casey Davidson; m. Sabra Lynn Archuleta-Poston, Aug. 11, 1984; children: Diego Jean-Pierre, Olivia Magdellena. BA in Biol. Scis., U. Calif., Davis, 1983; PhD in Psychology, U. Calif., Santa Barbara, 1990; MPH, U. Tex., Houston, Health Sci. Ctr. Clin. psychology resident USAF Med. Ctr., Wright-PAtterson AFB, Ohio, 1989-90; dir. psychology svcs., asst. chief mental health svcs. 9th Med. Group, Beale AFB, 1990-92; fellow in behavioral medicine Wilford Hall Med. Ctr., 1992-93; chief health and rehab. psychology svc. Malcolm Grow Med. Ctr., 1993-95, faculty, 1993-95; clin. asst. prof. dept. med. and clin. psychology F. Edward Herbert Sch. Medicine, Bethesda, Md., 1993-95; asst. prof. medicine Baylor Coll. Medicine, Houston, 1995-99; asst. prof. Clin. Health Psychology Program U. Mo., Kansas City, 1999—2003, assoc. prof., 2003—, asst. prof. medicine, 2002—03, assoc. prof., 2003—, assoc. chair Dept. Psychology, 2002—04, dir. grants and contracts Ctr. for Study of Health Outcomes Rsch. and Edn., Mid America Heart Inst., St. Luke's Hosp. and Children's Mercy Hosp., 2004—. Rsch. exchange. scientist Karolinska Inst., Stockholm, 1997, Stockholm, 98. Contbr. articles to profl. jours. Recipient Minority Scientist Devel. award, Am. Heart Assn., 1995, Nat. Merit scholar, 1979—80; U. Calif. Doctoral scholars fellow, 1984—85, 1985—86, 1986—87, 1988—89, Clin. fellow, Wilford Hall Med. Ctr., Lackland AFB, 1992—93. Fellow: N.Am. Assn. for Study of Obesity, Am. Heart Assn. Coun. on Nutrition, Physical Activity and Metabolism & Coun. on Epidemiology and Prevention; mem.: Soc. Air Force Clin. Psychologists, Soc. Rsch. on Nicotine and Tobacco, Soc. Behavioral Medicine, Internat. Soc. Nutrition Rsch., Am. Soc. Nutritional Scis., Am. Coll. Epidemiology. Office: U Mo Kansas City 4825 Troost, Ste 124 Kansas City MO 64110 Office Phone: 816-235-1381. Office Fax: 816-235-5581. E-mail: postonwa@umkc.edu.

POSWAL, ARVIND, surgeon, director; b. Delhi, India, Dec. 19, 1968; MBBS, AFMC, 1991. Chmn. and mng. dir. Dr. A's Clinic, 1997—. Recipient Top Drs. Healthcare Excellence awards, Big Brand Rsch., 2010, Internat. Gold Star Millennium award, Citizens Integration Peace Soc. Mem.: Indian Pub. Health Assn., Nat. Soc. Cosmetic Physicians, Indian Soc. Cosmetic Chemist, European Soc. Hair Restoration Surgery, Internat. Soc. Hair Restoration Surgery. Avocations: chess, reading, writing, travel. Office: A-9 First Fl CR Pk New Delhi Delhi 110019 India Office Fax: 011-26274368.

POTEMPA, KATHLEEN M., dean, nursing educator; b. Oct. 3, 1948; Diploma in Nursing, Providence Hosp. Sch. Nursing, Southfield, Mich., 1970; BA in Psychology summa cum laude, U. Detroit, 1974; MS in Nursing, Rush U., 1978, D in Nursing Sci., 1986. Charge nurse coronary ICU Holy Cross Hosp., Ft. Lauderdale, Fla., 1970-71; staff nurse, charge nurse cardiovasc. ICU Henry Ford Hosp., Detroit, 1971-74; nurse practitioner Rush-Presbyn.-St. Luke's Med. Ctr., Chgo., 1974-75; nursing edn. coord. dept. nursing Michael Reese Hosp. and Med. Ctr., Chgo., 1975-77, nursing supr., 1977-78; asst. unit leader dept. gerontol. nursing Rush U. Coll. Nursing, Chgo., 1978-79, asst. chmn., 1979-80, assoc. chmn., asst. prof. gerontol. nursing, 1980-85, asst. prof. gerontol. nursing, 1985-86; asst. prof. nursing, dept. internal medicine, practitioner Rush Med. Coll., Rush U., 1987-88; asst. then assoc. prof. dept. med.-surg. nursing Coll. Nursing, U. Ill., Chgo., 1988—96, dir. tng., pre and postdoctoral fellowship instnl. rsch., 1992—94, exec. assoc. dean Coll. Nursing, 1994-95, interim dean Coll. Nursing, 1995-96; prof., dean Sch. Nursing Oreg. Health Scis. U., Portland, 1996—2006, v.p., 2002—06; dean, prof. nursing, Sch. Nursing U. Mich., Ann Arbor, 2006—. Rsch. assoc. Robert Wood Johnson Tchg. Nursing Home Project, VA Edward Hines Jr. Hosp., Hines, Ill., 1985-86, co-dir. Exercise Rsch. Lab., 1985-86; dir. nursing Johnston R. Bowman Health Ctr. for Elderly, Rush Presbyn. St. Luke's Med. Ctr., Chgo., 1980-85. Contbr. articles to profl. jours. Recipient Oreg. Med. Rsch. Found. Mentor award, 2002, Disting. Alumni award, Rush U., 2003. Fellow Am. Acad. Nursing; mem. ANA (coun. nurse rschrs.), Am. Soc. Hypertension, Gerontol. Soc. Am., Midwest Nursing Rsch. Soc., Heart Assn. Met. Chgo., Am. Heart Assn. Oreg., Ill. Coun. Nurse Rschrs., Am. Heart Assn. (coun. cardiovasc. nursing, coun. hypertension, coun. on strokes), Am. Assn. Coll. Nursing Bd. (sec. 2004), Sigma Theta Tau. Office: U Mich Sch Nursing 400 N Ingalls Rm 1320 Ann Arbor MI 48109 Office Phone: 734-764-7185. Office Fax: 734-764-7186.

POTHAKOS, KONSTANTINOS, medical researcher; b. Thessaloniki, Greece, 1965; PhD, SUNY, Stony Brook, 2005. Rsch. fellow Thomas Jefferson U., 2010—. Mem.: Soc. Neurosci., SIgma Xi. Avocation: reading. Office: 1020 Locust St Rm 521 Philadelphia PA 19107 E-mail: pothakos@gmail.com.

POTHARAJU, NAGABHUSHANA RAO, retired neurophysician; s. Venkata Subba Rao and Lalitha Annapurneswari Potharaju; m. Kamala Devi Surabhi, Dec. 7, 1978; children: Anil Kumar, Rahul. BSc, Osmania U., Hyderabad, India, 1969, MBBS, 1976, DM in Neurology, 1991; DCH, Gandhi Med. Coll., Hyderabad, 1979, MD in Pediat., 1981. Cert. Deutsche Akademie Entwicklungs-Rehab., E.V., Munich, 1987. Civil asst. surgeon Dist. Hosp., Govt. Andhra Pradesh, Nalgonda, 1982—83; asst. prof. pediat. Gandhi Med. Coll. Hosp., Hyderabad, 1983—88; prof. and head dept. neurology and chief neurologist Kurnool Med. Coll. and Govt. Gen. Hosp., India, 1994; prof. neurology and chief pediatric neurologist Osmania Med. Coll. and Niloufer Hosp., 1994—2001, prof. and head dept. neurology & chief pediatric neurologist, 2001—05; tutor neurology and civil asst. surgeon Osmania Med. Coll., Gen. Hosp., Hyderabad, 1990—91, asst. prof. neurology, asst. neurologist, 1991—94, prof. and head dept. neurology, chief neurologist, 2005—06. Nat. expert Japanese encephalitis Govt. India, New Delhi, 1999—2009; short term cons. WHO, Kathmandu, Nepal, 2006—08; advisor Japanese encephalitis Govt. Andhra Pradesh, Hyderabad, 1991—; cons. Japanese encephalitis PATH, 2000—; chmn. Nat. Expert Com. Mgmt. Japanese

Encephalitis, Govt. of India, 2006—09; faculty WHO, PATH; hon. mem. Regional Asia Pacific Bd. Experts Japanese Encephalitis. Contbr. scientific papers to profl. jours. & books. Recipient First prize in All India Inter-Medical Competitions in Instrumental Music, Govt. Med. Coll., Berhumpur, Orissa, India, 1975, Acharya Sushruta Sadbhavana Puraskar, 2009. Mem.: Neuroped, Indian Pediat. Neurologist's Assn. (sec. 1995—), Indian Acad. Neurology, Indian Acad. Pediat. Achievements include discovery of a new killer disease entitled epidemic brain attack and its treatment; first to reduce case fatality rate in Japanese encephalitis in India & Nepal. Avocations: swimming, chess, music, computers. Home: 10-3-185 Saint John's Rd Secunderabad 500025 India Home Phone: 91 40 27821210. Personal E-mail: nagabhushanarao@gmail.com, neuropedindia@hotmail.com.

POTSIC, WILLIAM PAUL, otolaryngologist, educator; b. Berwyn, Ill., May 22, 1943; s. Andrew M. and Estella (Buschak) P.; m. Roberta I. Kite; children: Amie, Jordan. BS, U. Ill., 1965; MD cum laude, Emory U., 1969; postgrad., U. Pa.; M in Med. Mgmt., Tulane U., 1998. Intern, resident U. Chgo., 1969-74; practice medicine specializing in pediatric otolaryngology Phila., 1974—; staff Presbyn. Hosp., U. Pa. Hosp., Phila., Children's Seashore House, Phila.; prof. otorhinolaryngology and human comm. U. Pa., Phila., 1974—, E. Mortimer Newlin prof., 1994—2008; dir. div. otorhinolaryngology and human comm. Children's Hosp., Phila., 1975—2007, med. staff, 1982-84, med. dir. Cochlear Implant Program, 1991—, vice-chmn. clin. affairs dept. surgery, 1995—, dir. ambulatory surg. svcs., 1997—, med. dir. ctr. for childhood comm., 1999—2008. Author: Surgical Pediatric Otolaryngology, 1997; contbr. articles to profl. jours. Recipient 1st prize for clin. rsch. Am. Acad. Ophthalmology and Otolaryngology, 1977, Sylvan E. Stool award for outstanding lifetime contbns. in ear nose and throat advances in children, Presdl. award Soc. Otorhinolaryngology and Head and Neck Nurses, 2002; NIH grantee Mem. AMA, Am. Acad. Otolaryngology Head and Neck Surgery, Am. Laryngology, Otolgy and Rhinology Soc., Am. Coll. Physician Execs., Internat. Acad. Cosmetic Surgery, Pa. Med. Soc., Phila. Coll. Physicians, Phila. County Med. Soc., Phila. Laryngol. Soc. (treas. 1983), Phila. Pediatric Soc., Am. Laryngol. Assn. (Gabriel Tucker award 2005), Phila Laryngol. Soc. (pres. 1984), Phila. Soc. Facial Plastic Surgeons, Politzer Soc., Soc. Ear, Nose and Throat Advances in Children (pres. 1983), Am. Soc. Pediatric Otolaryngology (pres. 1991, Potsic Ann. award for basic sci. rsch.), Soc. Univ. Otolaryngologists, Am. Acad. Pediat., Alpha Omega Alpha, Phi Chi. Home: 1057 Beaumont Rd Berwyn PA 19312-2007 Office: Children's Hosp Phila 34th And Civic Center Blvd Philadelphia PA 19104 Office Phone: 215-590-3440. E-mail: potsic@email.chop.edu.

POTTASH, A. CARTER, psychiatrist, hospital executive; b. Phila., Nov. 30, 1948; s. R. Robert and Elizabeth (Braunschweig) P. BS with high honors, Trinity Coll., Hartford, Conn., 1970; MD, Yale U., 1974. Intern Tufts U. Sch. Medicine, Springfield, Mass., 1974-75; clin. fellow Yale-New Haven Hosp., 1977-78; fellow Yale U., New Haven, 1975-78; med. dir. Psychiatric Diagnostic Labs. Am., Summit, NJ, 1979-83. Lectr., cons. in field; vis. prof. St. Elizabeth Med. Ctr., Northeastern Ohio U. Coll Medicine, 1979; clin. prof. NYU, 1989—; pres. Fla. Consultation Svcs., P.A., West Palm Beach, 1992—, Psychiatric Assocs. N.J., P.A., Summit, N.J., 1970-93, Met. Med. Group P.C., N.Y.C., 1981-92, So. Fla. Med. Group P.A., Delray Beach, 1984-93, Stony Lodge Hosp., Inc. and Stony Lodge Med. Group P.C., Briarcliff Manor, N.Y., 1985—, Hampton Med. Group, P.A., Rancocas and Summit, N.J., 1986-95; exec. med. dir. Fair Oaks Hosp., Summit, 1978-92, The Regent Hosp., N.Y.C., 1981-92, Lake Hosp of the Palm Beaches, Lake Worth, Fla., 1984-92, Fair Oaks Hosp. at Boca/Delray, Fla., 1984-92, Hampton Hosp., Rancocas, N.J., 1986-95—; chmn. Stony Lodge Hosp., Briarcliff Manor, N.Y., 1985—. Editor Psychiatry Letter, 1980-91; mem. editl. bd. Internat. Jour. Psychiatry in Medicine, 1978-87, The Psychiatric Hosp., 1982—, Jour. Nat. Assn. Pvt. Psychiatric Hosps., 1980-81, Fla. Psychiatry Newsletter, 1992—; reviewer Jour. Nervous and Mental Disorders, Alcoholism, Clin. and Exptl. Rsch., JAMA, Hosp. and Cmty. Psychiatry; contbr. articles to profl. jours. Mem. adv. bd. Mothers for More Halfway Houses, N.Y.C., 1986—; cons. com. on women and alcoholism Jr. League of N.Y.C., 1987; bd. dirs. Met. Soc. Arts, N.Y.C., 1984-87, South Fla. Sci. Mus. Fellow Am. Coll. Clin. Pharmacology, Assn. Clin. Scientists, Nat. Acad. Clin. Biochemistry, Am. Psychiat. Assn. (disting. life fellow), The Acad. Medicine N.J.; mem. AMA, Soc. Neurosci., Nat. Acad. Clin. Biochemistry, Palm Beach County Med. Soc., Am. Acad. Clin. Psychiatrists, Brit. Brain Rsch. Assn. (hon.), European Brain and Behavioral Soc. (hon.), Am. Soc. Addiction Medicine, Am. Academy of Addiction Psychiatry (founding mem. 1987), Fla. Med. Soc., Palm Beach County Psychiat. Soc., Med. Soc. State N.Y., Med. Soc. N.J., Union County Med. Soc., N.Y. Athletic Club, Canoe Brook Country Club, Beacon Hill Club, Phi Beta Kappa, Delta Phi Alpha. Office: PO Box 381 Palm Beach FL 33480-0381 Office Phone: 561-837-2215.

POTTEBAUM, SHARON MITCHELL, farm manager, retired health educator; b. Champaign, Ill., Jan. 7, 1948; d. Robert D. and Louise M. (Straits) Mitchell; m. Joseph R. Pottebaum; children: Pamela, Nicholas. BS in Secondary Health Edn., Ohio State U., 1969, MA in Health Edn., 1978. Cert. occupl. hearing conservationist 1984, health edn. 7-12 Ohio Dept. Edn., 1969, health edn. K-12 Ohio Dept. Edn., 1978. Health edn. supr. Ctr. Sci. and Industry, Columbus, Ohio, 1970—72; jr. h.s. health tchr., dist. health coord. Scioto-Darby City Bd. Edn., Hilliard, Ohio, 1972—74; Drug, Alcohol, Tobacco & Human Behavior Project coord. Ohio State U., Columbus, 1974—75, instr. health edn., 1975—76; pub. health edn. cons. child health unit Ohio Dept. Health, Columbus, 1978—79; dir. edn. and tng. Family Hosp., Milw., 1980—85; instr. health edn. U. Wis.-Whitewater, 2000—03; CEO Mitchell-Pottebaum Farms LP, 2003—. Health edn. cons., tchrs. aide Hillside Elem. Sch., Brookfield, Wis., 1988—97; ind. sales rep. World Book-Childcraft, Brookfield, 1985—88; Head Start tng. tech. assistance project cons. Westinghouse Health Systems, 1979—82; profl. continuing edn. coord. Gtr. Milw. Assn. Hosp. Staff Devel. Dirs. and Wis. Soc. Health Edn. and Tng., 1980—85; adv. mem. geriatric edn. planning com. and indsl. medicine task force coms. Family Hosp., Milw., 1981—84. Co-author: (textbook) Teaching Health Science in Middle and Secondary Schools, 1981, Toward A Healthy Lifestyle Through Elementary Health Education, 1980; editor: (monthly newsletter) The Post Graduate, 1990—92 (Wisconsin's "Nellie Bly" First Place Award for Outstanding Branch Newsletter, category of 100+ members, 1992). Recipient cert. of leadership, YWCA Gtr. Milw., 1984. Mem.: AAUW (editor bull. West Suburban-Milw. br. 1990—92, fundraiser 1990—, treas. 1992—94, pres.-elect 1995—96, pres. 1996—97, chair travel group 1997—2000, state historian Wis. chpt. 1998—2000, bd. dirs. Wis. chpt. 1998—2000, br. historian 1999—2001, chair Women's History Month 1999—2001, co-v.p. program 2006—08, named scholarship honoree, 5-star br. award 1997), Champaign County Farm Bur. Avocations: travel, photography, painting, scrapbooks. Home: 2815 Almesbury Ave Brookfield WI 53045 Home Phone: 262-784-0270. Personal E-mail: s_pottebaum@hotmail.com.

POTTER, ANDREW ROBERT, ophthalmologist; s. Geoffrey and Constance Potter. MA, MBBchir, U. Cambridge, 1975; DO, U. Dublin, 1984; diploma in Tropical Medicine, Liverpool U., Eng., 1989. Med. officer Galmi Hosp., Niger, 1978—79; resident in anaesthesia Royal Berkshire Hosp., Reading, England, 1979—80; med. officer Bembereke, Benin, 1981—82; resident in ophthalmology Kent and Sussex Hosp., Tunbridge Wells, England, 1982—84; ophthalmologist Christian Blind Mission, Central African Republic, 1984—89, Abomey, Benin, 1990—96, Boko Hosp., Parakou, Benin, 1996—2005; dir. of hosp. St. Andre de Tinre, Parakou, Benin, 2006—. Vis. ophthalmologist in field. Contbr. articles to profl. jours. Mem.: Royal Coll. Gen. Practioners, Royal Coll. Ophthalmologists, Order Brit. Empire. Achievements include first to establish largest surgical eye service in Republic of Benin. Avocations: running, writing, reading obituaries. Home: B P 924 Parakou Benin Office: Christian Blind Mission Oakington Milton Cambridge England E-mail: arpotter@doctors.org.uk.

POTTER, JOHN FRANCIS, oncologist, surgeon; b. NYC, July 26, 1925; s. John Albert and Isabelle Cecelia (Sullivan) P.; m. Tanya Agnes Kristof, Nov. 19, 1955; children: Tanya Jean, Miriam Isabelle, John Mark. MD, Georgetown Med. Sch., 1949. Intern Grasslands Hosp., Valhalla, NY, 1949-50, resident in surgery, 1949-50, Georgetown U. Hosp., Washington, 1953-56; sr. investigator Nat. Cancer Inst., Bethesda, Md., 1957-60; chief divsn. surg. oncology Georgetown Med. Ctr., Washington, 1960-85; instr, asst.prof., then assoc. prof. surgery Georgetown U. Sch. Medicine, 1957-64, prof., 1969—2000; dir. Vincent T. Lombardi Cancer Rsch. Ctr., Washington, 1967-87, U.S. Mil. Cancer Inst., Bethesda, Md., 2000—. Mem. presdl. apptd. mem. bd. regents Uniformed Svcs. U. of the Health Scis., 1999. Hon. prof. Universidad Cayetano Heredia, Lima, Peru, 1980. Lt. (j.g.) USNR, 1951-53. Recipient Pres.'s medal Georgetown U., 1991. Mem. Soc. Surg. Oncology (rep. adv. bd.), ACS, Assn. Am. Cancer Insts. (v.p. 1985-86, pres. 1986-87, bd. dirs. 1982, chmn. bd. dirs. 1987-88), So. Surg. Assn., Peruvian Cancer Soc. (hon.). Office: US Mil Cancer Inst Walter Reed Army Med Ctr Bldg # A109 6900 Georgia Ave NW Washington DC 20307 *

POTTER, JULIA MUIR, pathologist, educator; b. Perth, Western Australia, Australia, Dec. 11, 1946; B in Med. Sci., U. Western Australia, 1971; MBBS, Australian Nat. U., PhD, 1975. Lectr. sr. lectr. dept. pharmacology U. Western Australia, 1975—88; sr. lectr. U. Queensland, Dept. Medicine, 1988—95; dir. chem. pathology Prince Charles Hosp., Brisbane, 1997—2002, Queensland Health Pathology Svc., 2002—03; prof. pathology & exec. dir. Australian Nat. U. Med. Sch. & ACT Health, 2003—. Fellow: Royal Australasian Coll. Pathologists. Office: ACT Pathology Canberra Hosp Canberra Australian Capital Territory 2606 Australia Office Fax: 61 02 6244 2912. Business E-Mail: julia.potter@act.gov.au.

POTTS, ANTHONY VINCENT, optometrist, orthokeratologist; b. Detroit, Aug. 10, 1945; m. Susan Claire, July 1, 1967, 1 child, Anthony Christian. Student, Henry Ford Community Coll., 1964—65, Eastern Mich. U., 1965—66; OD, So. Coll. Optometry, 1970; MS in Health Svcs. Mgmt., LaSalle U., 1995. Practice orthokeratology and contact lenses, Troy, Mich., 1975—; divsn. chief Def. Med. Standardization Bd., Fort Detrick, Md. Lectr., author orthokeratology, medically necessary contact lenses and astigmatism; adj. prof. NYCO Bethesda Naval Hosp. Comdr. MSC, USN, 1992—2010. Fellow Internat. Orthokeratology Soc. (membership chmn. 1976-83, bd. dirs. local chpt. 1976-83, chmn. Internat. Eye Rsch. Found. sect. 1981-83, bd. dirs. nat. chpt. 1985—, adminstv. dir. nat. chpt. 1985—, chmn. nat. chpt. 1987-1992), Fellow Am. Acad. Optometry, Am. Optometric Assn.; mem. Am. Assn. Healthcare Execs., Armed Forces Optometric Soc., Nat. Eye Rsch. Found., Naval Order Am., Assn. of Mil. Surgeons of U.S., Am. Coll. Healthcare Execs. Roman Catholic. Office: Med Sq Troy 1575 W Big Beaver Rd Ste 11C Troy MI 48084-3525 Personal E-mail: drspotts@sbcglobal.net.

POTTS, DAVID MALCOLM, family planning specialist, educator; b. Sunderland, Durham, England, Jan. 8, 1935; came to the U.S., 1978; s. Ronald Windle and Kathleen Annie (Cole) P.; m. Marcia Jaffe (dec.); children: Oliver, Henry; m. Martha Madison Campbell, Mar. 25, 1995. MA, Cambridge U., Eng., 1960, MB, BChir, 1962, PhD, 1965. Med. dir. Internat. Planned Parenthood Fedn., London, 1969-78; pres., CEO Family Health Internat., Research Triangle Park, N.C., 1978-90; Bixby prof. population and family planning U. Calif. Sch. Pub. Health, Berkeley, 1990—. Fellow and dir. med. studies Sidney Sussex Coll. U. Cambridge., Cambridge, England; Cosgrove lectr. Am. Coll. Ob-gyn, 2005. Author: Textbook of Contraceptive Practice, 1967, 2nd edit., 1983, Abortion, 1977, Victoria's Gene: Haemophilia & the Royal Family, 1997, Ever Since Adam and Eve: The Evolution of Human Sexuality, 1999, Sex and War: how Biology Explains Warfare & Terrorism and offers a Path to a Safer World, 2008. Recipient Hugh Moore award Population Action Internat., Washington, 1972, Citizen award The Ind., Durham, N.C., 1987, Charles Schultz Lifetime Achievement award. Fellow AAAS, Royal Coll. Ob-gyn.; mem. Internat. Union Study Population, Population Assn. Am. Achievements include developments in contraception condoms, spermicides and manual vacuum aspiration; studies in breastfeeding, maternal mortality and contraceptive safety. Office: Sch Pub Health Warren Hall Univ Calif Hl Berkeley CA 94720-0001 Office Phone: 510-642-6915. Business E-Mail: potts@berkeley.edu.

POULOS, CLARA JEAN, retired nutritionist; b. LA, Jan. 1, 1941; d. James P. and Clara Georgie (Creighton) Hill; m. Themis Poulos, Jan. 31, 1960. PhD in Biol., Fla. State Christian U., 1974; PhD in Nutrition, Lafayette U., 1984; D in Nutritional Medicine, Hearts of Jesus and Mary Coll., 1986. Registered nutritionist, cert. hypnotherapist, clin. densitometry technician, diabetes edn. Dir. rsch. Leapou Lab., Aptos, Calif., 1973—76, Monterey Bay Rsch. Inst., Santa Cruz, Calif., 1976—2001; nutrition specialist Santa Cruz, 1975—2001; dir. nutritional svcs., health enhancement, lifestyle planning, 1983—97; chief tech. and rsch. Osteoporosis Diagnostic Ctr., Santa Cruz, 2000—04; chief tech. rsch. Osteoporosis Care Ctr., San Jose, 2001—07. Instr. Stoddard Assocs. Seminars; cons. Biol-Med. Lab., Chgo., Nutra-Med Rsch. Corp., NY, Akorn-Miller Pharmacal, Chgo.; cons. Threshold Lab. Monterey Bay Aquaculture Farms, Calif.; cons. Resurrection Lab., Calif. Author: Alcoholism-Stress-Hypoglycemia, 1976, The Relationship of Stress to Alcoholism and Hypoglycemia, 1979; assoc. editor: Internat. Jour. Bio-Social Research, Health Promotion Features; editor: Nutrition and Dietary Consultant Jour.; columnist: The Connection Newspaper; contbr. articles to profl. jours. Recipient Najulander Internat. Rsch. award, 1971, Wainwright Found. award, 1979, various state and local awards. Fellow: Internat. Acad. Nutritional Consultants, Am. Nutritionist Assn., Internat. Coll. Applied Nutrition; mem.: AAAS, Internat. Fishery Assn. (health assoc.), Calif. Acad. Sci., Am. Public Health Assn., Am. Heart Assn. (pres. Santa Cruz br. 1990—91), Internat. Platform Soc., Am. Diabetes Assn. (profl., pres. Santa Cruz chpt., editor newsletter The Daily Balance Santa Cruz chpt., sec. No. Calif. chpt.), MUSE-Computer Users Group, Am. Women's Bowling Assn., Quota, Toastmistress. Business E-Mail: cjp1918@netscape.net.

POULOS, JAMES THOMAS, endocrinologist, educator; b. Lynn, Mass., Apr. 11, 1938; s. Thomas Dimitrios and Christine Julia (Zorzy) Poulos; m. Mary Margaret White, June 22, 1963; 1 child, Christopher Kreag. BS, Tufts U., 1959, MD, 1963. Diplomate Am. Bd. Internal Medicine, Am. Bd. Endocrinology and Metabolism. Intern New Eng. Med. Ctr., Boston, 1963—64, resident, 1964—65; resident and fellow in endocrinology U. Chgo., 1967—70; practice medicine specializing in endocrinology Lafayette, Ind., 1970—2004. Adj. prof. clin. pharmacology Purdue U., West Lafayette, Ind., 1976—95, mem. pres.'s coun., 1995—, mem. cmty. adv. com. Sch. Liberal Arts, 2008—; chmn. therapeutics com. Ind. Dept. Medicaid, 2002—; clin. faculty Ind. U. Sch. Medicine, mem. dean's search com., 1998; with Friend Convocation Purdue, 1970—; mem. therapeutics com. Ind. U. Sch. Medicine, 2002—04; dir., pres. med. staff Lafayette Home Hosp., 1978—79; pres. Arnett HMO, 1986—97; bd. dirs. North Ctrl. Health Svc.; chmn. therapeutics com. State of Ind. Family and Social Svc. Adminstrn., 2002—; dir. regional diabetes ctr. Sisters of St. Francis Health Systems Inc., 1985—, Greater Lafayette Health Svc., 1985—, mem. mission com., 2005—08; bd. dirs. GLHS Inc., 2005; mem. mission com. Sisters St. Francis Health Sys.; pres. Whitecroft Farms, 2011. Co-author: The Metabolic Influence of Progestins Advances in Metabolis Disorders, 1971; contbr. articles to profl. publ. Mem. Nat. Rep. Senatorial Com., Nat. Rep. Congrl. Com.; bd. dirs., co-dir. Coalition Living Well After 50, 2007—. With M.C., US Army, 1965-67. Fellow ACP (councilor-at-large Ind. chpt.), Am. Coll. Endocrinology, Am. Assn. Clin. Endocrinologists; mem. AMA, Am. Diabetes Assn. (dir. Ind. chpt. 1980—, pres. 1986-88, 96-98, bd. dirs., com. profl. practice 1987-88, pres. 1994—), Endocrine Soc., Internat. Diabetes Fedn., Am. Lung Assn. (pres. West Ctrl. Ind. 1982-83), Lafayette C. of C, Nat. Lipid Assn., Ind. Endocrine Soc., Ind. Lipid Working Group, John Purdue Club. Home and Office: 1000 Windwood Ln West Lafayette IN 47906-4737 Office Phone: 765-743-1741.

POULOS, STANLEY, plastic surgeon; BA in Chemistry, So. Meth. Univ., Dallas, Tex., 1970; MD, Univ. Tex., San Antonio, 1974. Cert. Am. Bd. Plastic Surgery, 1982. Intern in gen. surgery Univ. Calif., San Francisco, 1974—75, resident in gen. surgery, 1974—77, fellow in plastic surgery St. Francis Meml. Hosp. Plastic and Reconstructive Surgery Ctr., 1977—80, clin. prof., divsn. plastic surgery Greenbrae Surgery Ctr., Calif., 2004; co-dir., chief Plastic Surgery Ctr. Marin, Calif.; clin. prof., former asst. chmn., past chief., divsn. plastic surgery Marin Gen. Hosp., Greenbrae; former chief surgery and plastic surgery Ross Gen. Hosp., Calif.; co-founder Plastic Surgery Specialists, Greenbrae. Mem.: Marin Med. Soc., Am. Soc. Plastic Surgeons, Calif. Soc. Plastic Surgeons, Calif. Med. Assn. Office: Plastic Surgery Specialists 350 Bon Air Rd Ste 300 Greenbrae CA 94904 Office Fax: 866-398-4480.

POULTON, ROBERTA DORIS, nurse, consultant; b. Balt., Oct. 19, 1943; d. Charles Robert and Mary Doris (Guercio) P. Nursing diploma, Md. Gen. Hosp., 1964. Staff nurse Md. Gen. Hosp., 1964-67, Project Hope, Colombia, 1967, Tunisia, 1969-70, St. Agnes Hosp., Balt., 1968-69, team leader, 1972-83, staff nurse-preceptor, 1983-88, nurse mgr. pediatric emergency rm./ambulatory svcs., 1988-93, pediat. hemophilia coord., 1993—2003; sch. nurse Mother Seton Acad., Balt., 2004—. Pediat. ambulatory specialty clin. nurse; hemophilia nurse Johns Hopkins Med. Instn., Balt., 1998-2003; cons. in field. Democrat. Baptist. Personal E-mail: rpoulton43@aol.com.

POURCELOT, LEANDRE GEORGES, nuclear medicine specialist, medical educator; b. Orchamps-Vennes, France, Sept. 7, 1940; s. Paul René P. and Genevieve Adele Vivot; m Daniele Elise Cailler, Dec. 27, 1962; children: Philippe, Alain. Grad. elec. engring., Nat. Inst. Applied Scis., Lyon, France, 1963; D in Engring., Faculty of Scis., Lyon, 1967; MD, Faculty of Medicine, Tours, France, 1978, specialist in nuc. medicine, 1980. Rschr. INSA, Lyon, 1963-67; asst. prof. Faculty of Medicine, Tours, France, 1968-79, prof., 1979—2006; head dept. nuc. medicine and ultrasound U. Hosp., Tours, 1982—2006. Dir. INSERM Unit 316, Tours, 1988-2003, GIP Ultrasons, Tours, 1990—2006. Author 2 books; co-author 3 books; editor 1 book; contbr. over 300 articles and presentations to internat. jours. and meetings. Recipient Judith Resnik award IEEE Biomed. Engring., 1995, Ian Donald Gold medal, 2003. Fellow Am. Inst. Ultrasound in Medicine (hon.); mem. French Soc. Ultrasound in Medicine (pres., co-founder), Ordre Nat. du Mérite (France), Légion d'Honneur (France), Christian Doppler Soc. (hon.), French Doppler Club (pres., founder). Achievements include inventor first European ultrasonic doppler system, real-time doppler flow imaging; research interests include ultrasonic captors for medical echography, space medicine and technology. E-mail: leandre.pourcelot@aliceadsl.fr.

POURNARAS, SPYRIDON, medical educator, researcher; b. Larissa, Greece, Nov. 4, 1969; s. Antonios Pournaras and Dorothea Pournara; m. Alexandra Polyzou, Dec. 26, 1994; children: Dorothea Pournara, Vissarion, Antonios. MD, Aristotelian U. Thessaloniki, Greece, 1993, PhD, 2000. Cert. in microbiology AHEPA U. Hosp., Thessaloniki, 1999. Lectr. Med. Sch., U. Thessaly, Larissa, Greece, 2002—07, asst. prof., 2007—. Dir. Dept. Clin. Chemistry, U. Hosp. Larissa, Greece, 2009—. Contbr. articles to profl. jours. Grant, European Soc. Clin. Microbiology and Infectious Diseases, 2008. Achievements include research in antimicrobial chemotherapy. Office: University Hosp Larissa Biopolis Larissa 41110 Greece Office Fax: 30 2413 501570. Business E-Mail: pournaras@med.uth.gr.

POUSSAINT, ALVIN FRANCIS, psychiatrist, educator; b. NYC, May 15, 1934; s. Christopher Thomas and Harriet (Johnston) P. BA, Columbia U., 1956; MD, Cornell U., 1960; MS, UCLA, 1964. Intern UCLA Ctr. for Health Sci., 1960-61, resident in psychiatry Neuropsychiat. Inst., 1961-64, chief resident, 1964-65; So. field dir. Med. Com. Human Rights, Jackson, Miss., 1965-66; asst. prof. psychiatry Tufts U. Med. Sch., 1966-69; assoc. prof. psychiatry, assoc. dean students Harvard Med. Sch., 1969-75, 78—, prof. psychiatry, 1993—, dean students, 1975-78. Cons. HEW, 1969-73. Author numerous articles in field. Nat. treas. Black Acad. Arts and Letters, 1969-70, Med. Com. Human Rights, 1966—. Recipient Michael Schwerner award, 1968, Am. Black Achievement award in Bus. and the Professions Johnson Pub. Co., Inc., 1986, John Jay award for Disting. Profl. Achievement Columbia Coll., N.Y., 1987, Medgar Evers Medal of Honor Beverly Hills/Hollywood chpt. NAACP, Hollywood, Calif., 1988, and numerous hon. degrees. Fellow AAAS, Am. Orthopsychiatric Assn., Am. Psychiat. Assn. (mem. com. on Black Psychiatrists 1970-75); mem. Nat. Med. Assn., Am. Acad. of Child Psychiatry, Children's Longwood. Office: Judge Baker Ctr 53 Parker Hill Ave Boston MA 02120-3225

POWELL, BAYARD LOWERY, oncologist, educator; b. Raleigh, NC, June 22, 1954; MD, U. N.C., 1980. Diplomate Am. Bd. Internal Medicine, Am. Bd. Med. Oncology. Intern, then resident in internal medicine N.C. Bapt. Hosp., Winston-Salem, 1980-83, mem. staff; fellow hematologic oncology Bowman Gray Sch. Medicine, Winston-Salem, 1983-86, prof. hematologic oncology, sect. chief hematologic oncology, dir. leukemia svc. Named one of NC's Best Doctors, Bus. NC mag., 2002. Mem. ACP, Am. Assn. for Cancer Rsch., Am. Soc. Hematology, Am. Soc. Clin. Oncology. Office: Cancer Ctr Wake Forest Univ Sch Med Med Ctr Blvd Winston Salem NC 27157-0001 also: 2707 Buena Vista RD Winston Salem NC 27106 Office Phone: 336-713-5440, 336-716-4354. Business E-Mail: bpowell@wfubmc.edu.

POWELL, DAVID REED, medical association administrator; b. Syracuse, NY, Apr. 13, 1951; BA, Rutgers U., 1973; MD, UMDNJ, 1977. Prof. pediat. Tex. Children's Hosp., Baylor Coll. Medicine, 1986—2000; sr. v.p., metabolism rsch. Lexicon Pharms., Inc., 2000—. Mem.: Am. Soc. Nephrology, Am. Soc. Pediatric Nephrology, Endocrine Soc., NAASO, Am. Diabetes Assn. Home: 5327 Stillbrooke Rd Houston TX 77096 Personal E-mail: dpowell@lexpharma.com.

POWELL, DEBORAH ELIZABETH, academic administrator, pathologist; b. Lynn, Mass., Nov. 28, 1939; MD, Tufts U., 1965. Diplomate Am. Bd. Pathology. Intern Georgetown Med. Ctr., Washington, 1965-66; resident in pathology NIH, Bethesda, Md., 1966-69; exec. dean, vice-chancellor clin. affairs U. Kans. Sch. Medicine, Kansas City, 1997—2002; dean, asst. v.p. for clin. scis. U. Minn. Med. Sch., Mpls., 2002—09, dean emeritus, 2009—; assoc. v.p. new med. edn. programs U. Minn. Academic Health Ctr., 2009—. Past pres. U.S. & Can. Acad. Pathology, Inc.; trustee Am. Bd. Pathology. Mem.: Assn. American Med. Colleges (chair 2009—10), Am. Soc. Investigative Pathologists, Inst. Medicine, Coll. Am. Pathologists. Office: University Minn Med Sch 420 Delaware St SE Minneapolis MN 55455 Home Phone: 952-546-1215. Business E-Mail: dpowell@umn.edu. *

POWELL, DON WATSON, gastroenterologist, educator; b. Gadsden, Ala., Aug. 29, 1938; s. Gordon C. and Ruth (Bennett) P.; m. Frances N. Rourke; children: Mary Paige, Drew Watson, Shawnne Margaret. BS with honors, Auburn U., 1960; MD with highest honors, Med. Coll. Ala., Birmingham, 1963. Diplomate Am. Bd. Internal Medicine, Am. Bd. Gastroenterology. Intern, resident P.B. Brigham Hosp., Boston, 1963-65; resident Yale U. Sch. Med., New Haven, 1968-69, spl. NIH fellow in physiology, 1969-71; asst. prof. medicine U. N.C., Chapel Hill, 1971-74, assoc. prof., 1974-78, prof., 1978-91; mem. external adv. bd., v.p. for rsch. U. Tex. Health Sci. Ctr., San Antonio, 2005—07; external advisor Hispanic Health Disparities Ctr., U. Tex., El Paso, 2005—07, Rehab. Rsch. Career Devel. Ctr., U. Tex. Med. Br., 2008—, Tex. Med. Ctr. Digestive Diseases Ctr., 2009—. Chief divsn. digestive diseases U. NC, 1977-91, dir. Ctr. Gastrointestinal Biol. Diseases, 1985-91, assoc. chmn. clin. affairs dept. medicine, 1989-91; mem. merit rev. bd. VA, 1977-80; cons. WHO, Geneva, 1980-82, Burroughs-Wellcome, Inc., Research Triangle Pk., N.C., 1981-82, Hoffman-LaRoche, Inc., Nutley, NJ, 1982-93, Glaxo Smith Kline, Harlow, Eng., 2004-05, Lexicon Genetics, The Woodlands, Tex., 2005-06; mem. gen. medicine A-2 study sect. NIH, 1985-89; Edward Randall and Edward Randall, Jr. Disting. chmn. U. Tex. Med. Br., Galveston, 1991-02, prof. internal medicine, neurosci. and cell biology, 1991—, assoc. dean rsch., Sch. Medicine, 2002-06, Bassel and Frances Blanton disting. prof. in internal medicine, 2008-; mem. Nat. Inst. Diabetes Digestive and Kidney Diseases Adv. Coun., 1994-97; coun., bd. rep. adv. com. to dir. NIH, 1996-97; program dir. Gen. Clin. Rsch. Ctr., 2003-09, interim dir. gastroenterology, 2006-; dir. Inst. for Translational Scis. Clin. Rsch. Ctr., 2009-; assoc. editor Prin. Clin. Gastroenterology, 2005. Assoc. editor: Textbook of Gastroenterology, 5th edit., 2009, Atlas of Gastroenterology, 4th edit. 2009, Cecil Textbook of Medicine, 22d edit., 2004; mem. editl. bd. Am. Jour. Physiology, Gastrointestinal and Liver Physiology, 1979-97, Am. Jour. Med. Sci., 1984-92, Regulatory Peptide Letter, 1990-2008, Annals of Internal Medicine, 1993-96, Current Treatment Options in Gastro, 1998-2005; contbr. over 200 articles to profl. jours. Capt. M.C., U.S. Army, 1965-68. Recipient Rsch. Career Devel. award NIH, 1973-78, Merit award, 1987, Outstanding Physician of Yr. award Gulf Coast chpt. Crohn's Colitis Found. Am., 1994, John P. McGovern MD award in Oslerian Medicine, 2002, others. Master ACP (mem. med. knowledge self-assessment program VII gastroenterology com. 1983-85), ACS (Tex. chpt.) (Best Drs. in America, 1996-2010), Am. Gastroentrol. Assn. Inst. (Don W. Powell lectr., UTMB 2007); fellow AAAS, mem. Am. Physiol. Soc., Am. Gastroenterol. Assn. (v.p. 1991-92, pres. 1993-94, coun. acad. rep. 1999—, Julius Friedenwald medal 2001, Mentored Rsch. award 2005, fellow 2006), Gastroenterology Rsch. Group (chmn. 1988-89), So. Soc. Clin. Investigation, Federated Socs. Gastroenterology and Hepatology (chmn. 1996-98, Assn. Am. Physicians, Am. Clin. and Climatol. Assn., Alpha Omega Alpha (bd. dirs. 2000—). Avocation: singing. Office: U Tex Med Br 4 106 McCullough 301 Univ Blvd Galveston TX 77555-0764 Office Phone: 409-772-5607. Business E-Mail: dpowell@utmb.edu.

POWELL, DONALD ASHMORE, clinical research psychologist; b. Spartanburg, SC, Oct. 29, 1938; s. Russell Kermit Powell and Mignon Kathlene Cox; m. Palmyra Langston, 1961 (div. 1972); children: Donald Langston, Donetta Plamyra, Ashley Preston, Stephanie Anne; m. Shirley L. Buchanan, Aug. 17, 1992 (dec. June 1998); m. Trisha Pope, May 18, 2002. BS, U. S.C., 1960, MA, 1962; PhD, Fla. State U., 1967. Rsch. psychologist Dorn VA Med. Ctr., Columbia, S.C., 1969—, acting dir. R&D, 1996-2000; prof. U. S.C. Sch. Medicine, Columbia, 1979—. Adj. prof. U. S.C., Columbia, 1969—; cons. U.S. Heart, Lung and Blood Inst., Bethesda, 1986—; program specialist VA Mental Health and Behavioral Scis., Washington, 1984-88. Author: (with others) Eyeblink Conditioning, 1999. Rsch. fellowship NIH, 1967-69; vis. scholar NIH, 1974; recipient Merit Rsch. award Dept. of Vet. Affairs, 1996—. Mem. Soc. for Neurosci., Am. Psychol. Soc., Pavlovian Soc. (Pavlovian Rsch. award 1991), Soc. for Neurosci. (pres. S.C. chpt. 1980-81, councilor 1982-85). Democrat. Avocations: running, reading. Office: Dorn VA Med Ctr 6439 Garners Ferry Rd Columbia SC 29209-1638 Office Phone: 803-695-6821. Business E-Mail: donnie.powell@med.va.gov.

POWELL, GRAHAM EDWARD, psychologist, author; b. Portsmouth, Hampshire, Eng., Dec. 12, 1949; s. Victor Andrew and Alice Ellen (Stone) Powell; m. Penelope Jill Dalton Powell, June 28, 1970; children: Charlotte Clare, Sophie Katherine. BSc, U. Coll. London, 1971; M.Phil., Inst. Psychiatry, London, 1973, PhD, 1976. Lectr. U. London, 1973—79, sr. lectr., 1979—84; dir. clin. psychology U. Surrey, Eng., 1984—; chmn. Headway, Guildford, 1985—; hon. top grade clin. psychologist South West Thames Regional Health Authority, 1985—. Author: Person Perception; Brain and Personality, 1979, Brain Function Therapy, 1981; contbr. articles to profl. jours. Mem.: Ch. of Eng., Brit. Psychol. Soc. (clin. divsn., pres. 2005—06). Office: Psychology Dept Univ Surrey Guildford GU2 5XH England

POWELL, JAMES BOBBITT, health facility administrator, pathologist; b. Burlington, NC, Aug. 28, 1938; s. Thomas Edward and Sophia (Sharpe) P.; m. Pamela Oughton, Sept. 12, 1969 (div. Sept. 1979); 1 child, Daphne P. Markcrow; m. Anne Ellington, Oct. 20, 1984; children: James Bobbitt (dec.), John Banks, James Rosser, Helen Bobbitt. BA, Va. Mil. Inst., 1960; MD, Duke U., 1964. Diplomate Am. Bd. Pathology. Intern Duke U. Med. Ctr., Durham, NC, 1964-65; resident Cornell Med. Ctr., NYC, 1965-67, Englewood (N.J.) Hosp., 1967-69; founder Biomed Labs, Burlington, NC, 1969—; pres. Roche Biomed. Labs., 1982-95; pres., CEO Lab. Corp. Am. Holdings, 1995-97; CEO Tripath Imaging, Burlington, NC, 1997—2000. Bd. dirs. Mid-Carolina Bank; bd. dirs. Vis. Internat. Faculty. Contbr. articles to sci. pubs. Trustee Elon U., NC, 1979—; bd. dirs. Alamance Found. Maj. M.C. US Army, 1969—72. Mem. Alamance Country Club. Republican. Methodist. Avocations: tennis, US military history. Office: 1573 York Pl Burlington NC 27215-3355

POWELL, JEFFREY SCOTT, endocrinologist; s. Norman Emory and Barbara Ellen Powell; m. Ellen Lynn Rothbaum, June 11, 1995; children: Abigail, Ryan. BA cum laude in Biology, Harvard U., Cambridge, Mass., 1991; MD, Albert Einstein Coll., Bronx, NY, 1995. Diplomate Am. Bd. Internal Medicine. Intern to resident in internal medicine Columbia Med. Ctr., NYC, 1995—98; fellow in endocrinology Colubmia U., Coll. Physicians and Surgeons, NYC, 1998—2001; endocrinologist Mt. Kisco (N.Y.) Med. Group, 2001—. Chief divsn. endocrinology No. Westchester Hosp., Mt. Kisco, 2006—. Contbr. articles to profl. jours. Fellow: Am. Coll. Endocrinology; mem.: Am. Assn. Clin. Endocrinology, Alpha Omega Alpha. Office: Mt Kisco Med Group 90 S Bedford Rd Mount Kisco NY 10549 Office Phone: 914-241-1050. Office Fax: 914-242-2915. *

POWELL, LAWRIE WILLIAM, physician, educator; m. Margaret Emily Ingram, Jan. 5, 1958; children: Elizabeth Ellen, Mark Ingram. MD, Brisbane State High Sch., Queensland, Australia, 1952. Cert. medicine prof. Med. Bd. Queensland, 1958. Prof. medicine U. Queensland, Brisbane, 1974—88. Contbr. articles to profl. jours. Fellow: RACP, RCP. Office: Royal Brisbane & Women's Hosp Butterfield St 4029 Brisbane QLD Australia

POWELL, LISA M., science educator, researcher; b. Toronto, Can., Apr. 1, 1966; PhD, Queen's U., 1995. Assoc. prof. Queen's U., 1994—2003; rsch. prof., sr. rsch. scientist U. Ill., Chgo., 2001—. Fellow: Sch. Policy Studies, Queen's U.; mem.: Am. Soc. Health Economists, Internat. Health Economics Assn. Office: 1747 W Roosevelt Rd M/C 275 Chicago IL 60608 Business E-Mail: powelll@uic.edu.

POWELL, RICE, medical products executive; Various positions Baxter Internat., Inc., Biogen, Inc., Ergo Sciences, Inc., 1978—96; joined Fresenius Med. Care AG & Co., 1997—, mem. mgmt. bd., 2004—; co-CEO Fresenius Med. Care North America, 2004—, pres. & CEO, Renal Therapy Group. Office: Fresenius Med Care North America Reservoir Woods 920 Winter St Waltham MA 02451-1457 Office Phone: 781-699-9000.

POWELL, THOMAS EDWARD, III, biological supply company executive, physician; b. Elon College, NC, Aug. 1, 1936; s. Thomas Edward and Sophia Maude (Sharpe) Powell; m. Betty Durham Yeager, June 19, 1965; children: Frances Powell Barnes, Thomas Edward IV, Caroline Powell Rogers. AB in Biology, Va. Mil. Inst., 1957; MD, Duke U., 1961; MA, Harvard U., 1966. Surgeon USPHS, 1966—68; co-founder Biomed. Reference Labs., Inc., Burlington, NC, 1969, exec. v.p., 1969—75, chmn. exec. com., 1979—82, dir.; exec. v.p. Carolina Biol. Supply Co., Burlington, 1968—80, chmn., 1977—80, 1994—, pres., 1980—94, Wolfe Sales Corp., Burlington, 1980—84, Waubun Labs. Inc., Schriever, La., 1980—, Bobbitt Labs., Inc., Burlington, 1983—94, bd. mgrs. Wachovia Bank and Trust Co. N.A., Burlington. Contbr. articles to profl. jours. Bd. dirs. United Way Alamance County, Burlington, 1968—, Elon Coll., NC, 1968—, sec., 1975—; bd. dirs. Am. Cancer Soc., Burlington, 1971—81, Burlington Day Sch., 1973—, pres., 1974—78, 1980—84; bd. dirs. NC Citizens for Bus. and Industry, Raleigh, 1983—87, Nat. Found. for Study of Religion and Econs., Greensboro, 1984—88, Blue Ridge Sch., Dyke, Va., 1985—90. Served to capt. USAR, 1957—66. Recipient Citizens Svc. award, Elon Coll. Alumni Assn., 1980. Mem.: Newcomen Soc., Assn. Venture Founders, NC Med. Soc., Alamance-Caswell Med. Soc., NC Acad. Sci., Assn. Biology Lab. Edn., Greensboro City Club, Hope Valley Country Club (Durham, NC), NC Country Club (Pinehurst), Congl. Country Club (Washington), Capital City Club (Raleigh), Alamance Country Club (Burlington). Democrat. Mem. Christian Ch.

POWER, A. KATHRYN, federal agency administrator; m. Brian Power; children: Matthew, Brendan. EdB, St. Joseph's Coll., Emmitsburg, Md.; MEd, Western Md. Coll. Tchr. various pub. schs.; computer sys. analyst US Dept. Def.; exec. dir. RI Coun. Cmty. Mental Health Centers, 1985—90; dir. RI Anti Drug Coalition, Governor's Drug Policy Office, RI, RI Dept. Mental Health, Retardation & Hospitals, 1993—2003; dir. Ctr. Mental Health Services, Substance Abuse & Mental Health Services Adminstrn. (SAMHSA), US Dept. Health & Human Services, Rockville, Md., 2003—, dir. Ctr. Substance Abuse Prevention, 2010—11. Pres. Nat. Assn. State Mental Health Program Directors, 1997. Capt. USNR. Recipient Secretary's award for disting. svc., HHS, 2004, 2005, 2006; fellow Toll fellow, Coun. State Legislators, 1991. Office: Substance Abuse & Mental Health Services Administration 1 Choke Cherry Rd Rockville MD 20857 *

POWERS, JAMES S., medical educator; b. Erie, Pa., Aug. 23, 1951; MD, U. Rochester, NY, 1977. Assoc. prof. Vanderbilt U. Sch. Medicine, 1983—. Assoc. clin. dir. Tenn. Valley Geriat. Rsch. Edn. & Clin. Ctr., 1990. Recipient F. Tremaine Billings Tchg. award, Vanderbilt U. Sch. Medicine, Marsha Goodwin-Beck VA Interdisciplinary award, Vets. Adminstrn., 2009. Fellow: ACP, Gerontologic Soc. America, Am. Geriat. Soc., Am. Coll. Nutrition. Avocation: music. Office: 7159 Vanderbilt Med Ctr E Nashville TN 37146 Office Fax: 615-936-3156.

POWLES, TREVOR JAMES, physician, oncologist; b. London, Mar. 8, 1938; s. Leonard William David and Florence Irene (Conolly) P.; m. Penelope Margaret Meyers, July 27, 1968; children: James Watson, Thomas Bartholomew, Lucy Alexandra. BSc, St. Bartholomews Med. Coll., London, 1961, MB, BS, 1964; PhD, Inst. Cancer Rsch., London, 1975. House physician, registrar Royal Postgrad. Med. Sch., London, 1967-68; registrar St. Bartholomews Hosp., London, 1969-70; rsch. fellow Med. Rsch. Coun., London, 1971-72; sr. lectr. Inst. Cancer Rsch., London, 1973-75; cons. physician Royal Marsden Hosp., London, 1975—2003; head of breast cancer unit, 1993—2003; prof. breast oncology Inst. Cancer Rsch., London, 1998—; cons. breast oncologist St. Anthony's Hosp., London, 2002—, Parkside Hosp., London, 2002—, The Liste Hosp., London, 2002—. Vis. prof. MD Anderson Cancer Ctr., Houston, 1993, Dana Farber Cancer Ctr., Harvard, Boston, 1996, Tom Baker Cancer Ctr., Calgary, Can., 1998; dir. Advance Cytometrix Inc., San Francisco, 1993-96, Oncotech Inc., Irvine, 1996—2008, Intact Med. Inc., Dublin, Ohio, 1998—. Co-author, editor: (books) Breast Cancer Management, 1981, Prostaglandins and Cancer, 1982, Medical Management of Breast Cancer, 1991; contbr. articles to profl. jours. Recipient All Parties Parliamentary award for outstanding achievement in Breast Cancer, 2003, Brinker award, Susan G. Komen Found., 2005. Mem. Internat. Assn. Cancer Prevention (v.p. 1995—), Breast Cancer Rsch. Trust (trustee 1975—), U.K. Breast Cancer Coordinating Com. Avocations: horse riding, skiing, reading. Office: The Parkside Oncology Clinic 49 Parkside Wimbledon London Sw19 5NB England

POWSNER, EDWARD RAPHAEL, physician; b. NYC, Mar. 17, 1926; m. Rhoda Lee Moscovitz, June 8, 1950; children: Seth, Rachel, Ethan, David. SB in Elec. Engring., MIT, 1948, SM in Biology, 1949; MD, Yale U., 1953; MS in Internal Medicine, Wayne State U., 1957; MHSA, U. Mich. Diplomate Am. Bd. Nuclear Medicine, Am. Bd. Pathology in clin. pathology and anatomic pathology, Am. Bd. Internal Medicine; lic. physician, Mich. Intern Wayne County Gen. Hosp., Eloise, Mich., 1953-54, resident internal medicine, 1954-55, Detroit Receiving Hosp., 1955-56; fellow in hematology Wayne State U. and Detroit Receiving Hosp., 1957-58; clin. investigator VA Hosp., Allen Park, Mich., 1958-61, chief nuclear medicine svc., 1961-78; dir. clin. labs. Mich. State U., East Lansing, 1978-81; staff pathologist Ingham Med. Ctr., Lansing, Mich., 1978-81; dir. nuclear medicine St. John Hosp., Detroit, 1982-95. Rsch. asst. biology MIT, 1948-49, 50; asst. instr. medicine Wayne State U. Coll. Medicine, 1954-56, instr., 1959-61; assoc. prof. pathology Wayne State U. Sch. Medicine, 1961-68, assoc. medicine, 1961, prof. pathology, 1968-78; prof. pathology Mich. State U., 1978-81, assoc. chairperson, 1980-81, clin. prof., 1981-82; chief clin. labs. Detroit Gen. Hosp., 1969-73; chief lab. svcs. Health Care Inst., Wayne State U., 1976-78; mem. adv. coun. Nuclear Medicine Tech. Cert. Bd., 1990-91. Bd. editors Am. Jour. Clin. Pathology, 1963-76, 83-88; author 2 textbooks, 11 chpts., 50 peer reviewed papers, 17 abstracts and other publs. With U.S. Army, 1944-47. Mem. AMA (sect. coun. on pathology), Am. Soc. Clin. Pathologists (rep. 1987-89, 93-2000, govt. rels. com. 1993-95, mem. coun. nuclear medicine 1978-82, chmn. 1982-84), Am. Coll. Nuclear Physicians, Am. Soc. Nuclear Cardiology, Coll. Am. Pathologists, Detroit Acad. Medicine, Mich. Soc. Pathologists, Mich. State Med. Soc., Soc. Nuclear Medicine, Washtenaw County Med. Soc., Sigma Xi, Tau Beta Pi.

POZDNYAKOVA, NADEGDA, cardiologist; b. Golovingino, Penza, Jan. 27, 1964; MD, Sarotov State Med. U., 1987; D (hon.), Russian Fedn. Cardiologist Penza Inst. Postgrad. Med. Edn., 2000—. Office: Stasova 8a Penza 440060 Russia Business E-Mail: pozdnyakova-n-v@rambler.ru.

POZNANSKI, ANDREW KAROL, pediatric radiologist; b. Czestochowa, Poland, Oct. 11, 1931; came to U.S., 1957, naturalized, 1964; s. Edmund Maurycy and Hanna Maria (Ceranka) P.; children: Diana Jean, Suzanne Christine. BSc, McGill U., 1952, MD CM, 1956. Diplomate: Am. Bd. Radiology, Royal Coll. Physicians and Surgeons Can. Intern Montreal (Que., Can.) Hosp., 1956-57; resident Henry Ford Hosp., Detroit, 1957-60, staff radiologist, 1960-68, U. Mich. Med. Center, Ann Arbor, 1968-79, co-dir. pediatric radiology C.S. Mott Children's Hosp., Ann Arbor, 1971-79; radiologist-in-chief Children's Meml. Hosp., Chgo., 1979-99; prof. radiology U. Mich., 1971-79, Northwestern U. Med. Sch., 1979—. Bd. dirs. Nat. Coun. on Radiation Protection, 1983-90; mem. Internat. Commn. on Radiologic Protection, 1981-89; mem. adv. panel on radiologic devices FDA, 1975-77, chmn., 1976-77; trustee Am. Bd. Radiology, 1993-2003. Author: The Hand in Radiologic Diagnosis, 1974, 2d edit., 1983, Practical Approaches to Pediatric Radiology, 1976; co-author: Bone Displasias, An Atlas of Genetic Disorders of Skeletal Development, 2002 bd. editors: Skeletal Radiology, 1975-95, Radiographics, 1980-84, Pediatric Radiology, 1986-91. Mem.: AMA, Internat. Skeletal Soc. (founder, pres. 1992—94), John Caffey Soc., Radiol. Soc. N.Am., Soc. Pediatric Radiology (pres. 1980—81), Am. Roentgen Ray Soc. (pres. 1993—94), Polish Radiol. Soc. (hon.), Can. Assn. Radiologists (hon.), European Soc. Radiology (hon.), Alpha Omega Alpha. Office: Childrens Meml Hosp 2300 N Childrens Plz Chicago IL 60614-3394 Office Phone: 773-880-3521. Business E-Mail: apoznanski@ameritech.net.

POZNER, JASON N., plastic surgeon; Grad. with distinction in rsch., Mt. Sinai Med. Sch. Diplomate Am. Bd. of Plastic Surgery, lic. Fla., NY. Resident gen. surgery Mt. Sinai Med. Ctr., NY; resident plastic surgery NY Downstate Med. Ctr.; fellow in microsurgery Montefiore Med. Ctr.; fellow in aesthetic and endoscopic plastic surgery Md.; fellow Am. Coll. of Surgeons; asst. prof. plastic surgery John's Hopkins Med. Ctr.; founder Sanctuary Plastic Surgery; co-owner Sanctuary Med. Aesthetic Ctr., Boca Raton, Fla. Adjunct clin. faculty dept. of plastic surgery Cleve. Clinic, Fla. Mem.: Am. Soc. for Lasers in Medicine and Surgery, Am. Soc. of Aesthetic Plastic Surgery, Am. Soc. of plastic Surgeons. Office: Sanctuary Medical Aesthetic Center Suite C101 4800 North Federal Highway Boca Raton FL 33431 Office Phone: 800-407-4319. Office Fax: 561-886-0981.

POZZI, GINO, medical educator, researcher; s. Franco Pozzi and Miranda L. Dal Lago. MD, Cath. U. Sacred Heart, Rome, 1986. Diplomate Italian Ministry U. and Rsch., 1986. Med. officer Italian Navy, Rome, 1987—88; rschr. Cath. U. Sacred Heart, 1998—, asst. prof. Achievements include research in substance abuse, anxiety disorders, occupational psychiatry. Office: Catholic Univ Sacred Heart 1 largo Francesco Vito Rome 00168 Italy Home: Viale Tito Livio 112 Rome 00136 Italy Office Phone: 39.339.3799078. Personal E-mail: ginopoz@tin.it. Business E-Mail: gpozzi@rm.unicatt.it.

PRABAHAR, MURUGESAN RAM, nephrologist, educator; married, Aug. 27, 2006. MBBS, Tirunelveli Med. Coll., India, 1998; MD, Madras Med. Coll., Tamilnadu, India, 2002, DM, 2006. Cert. in nephrology Nat. Bd. Exams., New Delhi, 2006. Asst. prof. Sri Ramachandra U., Chennai, 2006—. Cons. nephrologist Sri Ramachandra Med. Ctr., 2006—. Office: Sri Ramachandra Med Coll 1 Ramachandra Nagar Chennai Tamilnadu 600116 India Personal E-mail: prabahar76@yahoo.co.in.

PRABHAKARA MURTY, POTHARAJU VENKATA SAI, industrial hygienist, researcher; b. Bhimavaram, Andhrapradesh, India, Sept. 2, 1962; m. Sunitha Prabhakar Nandivada, Feb. 27, 1994; children: Potharaju Kiranmayi, Potharaju Sai Surya Jayanth. PhD in Chemistry, Andhra U., 1992. Indsl. hygienist Occupl. Health Svcs., Visakhapatnam Steel Plant, Andhrapradesh, India, 1992—. Contbr. articles to profl. jours. Recipient Internat. Travel award, Nat. Safety Coun., Orlando, Fla., 2005; fellow, Indian Nat. Sci. Acad., Coun. of Sci. and Indsl. Rsch., India, 2004, scholar, European Edn. Program Epidemiology, Italy, 2005, HELP course organizers, Japan, 2003. Mem.: Soc. Risk Analysis (assoc.). Achievements include research in Assessment of risk at workplace; Occupational noise exposure studies in Visakhapatnam steel plant; Biological monitoring of benzol plant employees. Office: Steel Plant Occupational Health Services Andhra-pradesh Visakhapatnam 530031 India Office Fax: 0091 891 251 8631. Personal E-mail: pvspmurty@hotmail.com.

PRABHAKARAN, LATHY, nurse; b. Singapore, Mar. 2, 1964; B in Nursing, U. Sydney, 1997; M in Clin. Nursing, Flinders U. South Australia, 2004. Sr. nurse clinician Tan Tock Seng Hosp., 2003—. Avocation: reading. Office: Tan Tock Seng Hosp 11 Jalan Tan Toc Singapore 308433 Singapore Office Fax: (65) 6357-8022. Business E-Mail: lathy@singnet.com.sg.

PRABHAKARAN, P. S., hospital administrator; Prof., bd. dirs. Kidwai Meml. Inst. Oncology, India, 1998—; vice chancellor Rajiv Gandhi U. Health Sci., India, 2005—. Office: Rajiv Gandhi University 4th T Block Jaya Nagar Bangalore 560 041 India Office Phone: 011918026961934. *

PRABHU, SHIVANANDA, medical educator, surgeon, consultant; b. Mangalore, India, Sept. 12, 1968; s. Vishwanath and Lillybai Prabhu; m. Mamatha Prabhu, Apr. 1, 1998; children: Samarth, Samhita. MB, BChir, Mysore Med. Coll., 1991; MS in Gen. Surgery, Seth G.s. Med. Coll., Mumbai, 1996. Asst. prof. Kasturba Med. Coll., Mangalore, India, 1997—2002, assoc. prof., 2002—. Cons. surgeon Kasturba Med. Coll. Hosp., Mangalore, 1997—. Author: The Art of History Taking, 2003; contbr. articles to local newspapers. Mem.: Indian Med. Assn., Assn. Surgeons India. Avocations: TV, reading, music. Office: Kasturba Med Coll Attavar Mangalore 575001 India Home: Shivaniketan Haleangadi 574 146 Mangalore India Office Phone: 0824-2445858 ext. 5360. Personal E-mail: shivanadaprabhu@yahoo.com.

PRABHUDESAI, MUKUND M., physician, educator, health facility and academic administrator, researcher; b. Lolyem, Goa, India, Mar. 17, 1942; came to U.S., 1967; s. Madhav R. and Kusum M. Prabhudesai; m. Sarita Mukund Usha, Feb. 1, 1972; 1 child, Nitin M. MB, BS (MD), G.S. Med., Bombay, 1967, postgrad., 1973-75. Diplomate Am. Bd. Pathology. Asst. pathologist Fordham Hosp., Bronx, NY, 1973-74, assoc. pathologist, 1974-76; assoc. dir. clin. pathology Lincoln Med., Bronx 1976, dep. dir. pathology, 1977-79; chief pathology and lab. medicine svc., coord. R&D Illiana Med. Ctr., Danville, Ill., 1979—, dir. electron microscopy lab., 1987—. Senator U. Ill. Chgo.; co-investigator U. Ill. Coll. Medicine, Urbana-Champaign, clin. prof. pathology and internal medicine, 1982—. Contbr. articles to Am. Jour. Clin. Nutrition, Jour. AMA, Am. Jour. Clin. Pathology. Member Gifted Student Adv. Bd., Danville, 1984-86; v.p. Am. Cancer Soc. Vermilion County chpt., 1982, pres., 1986-88. VA rsch. grantee, 1980-82, 82-85, 83. Fellow Coll. Am. Pathology (inspector 1981-, Ill. state del. to C.A.P. Ho. Dels. 1992-, mem. reference com. 1993, chair, standard and integration com., 2000-); mem. AAAS, Am. Coll. Physician Execs., Ill. State Soc. Pathologists (bd. dirs. 1990-2011, health and wealth cons., chmn. membership com. 1990-). Achievements include development of cancer of bladder following portocarval shunting; research in adverse effects of alcohol on lung structure and metabolism; on effects of soy and bran on cholesterol, fish and coronary artery disease, endocrine response to soy protein, in induction and reversibility of atherosclerosis in trout, effects of ethanol on Vitamin A, lymphatics in atherosclerosis, iron in atherosclerosis, development of dermofluorometer for detection of P.V.D. Office: PO Box 3583 Placida FL 33946 Personal E-mail: mdesaih@aol.com. E-mail: sarita@soltec.net.

PRADHAN, SURESH CHANDRA, pharmacologist, educator; b. Bamur, Orissa, India, Apr. 3, 1951; s. Achyuta Nanda and Rasabati P.; m. Nirupama Pradhan, May 23, 1981; children: Pritam, Prita. BS, Buxi Jagabandhu Bidyadhar Coll., Bhubeneswar, India, 1970; MBBS, Maharaja Krushna Chandra Gajapati Med. Coll., Berhampur, India, 1975; MD in Pharmacology, Inst. Med. Scis., Banaras Hindu U., Varanasi, India, 1980. Cert. of registration Orissa Coun. Med. Registration. House physician Shambhu Nath Pandit Hosp., Calcutta, 1976-77; jr. resident Inst. Med. Scis., Banaras Hindu U., Varanasi, India, 1977-78, sr. resident, 1978-81; lectr. Mahatma Gandhi Inst. Med. Scis., Sewagram, India, 1981-84; asst. prof. Jawaharlal Inst. Post-Grad. Med. Edn. and Rsch., Pondicherry, India, 1984-88, assoc. prof., 1988-92, prof., 1992—2007, dir. prof., 2007—. PhD guide Pondicherry (India) U., 1991—. Assoc. editor Indian Jour. Pharmacology, 1992-94, cons. editor, 1994-98; contbr. articles to profl. jours. Recipient Uvnas prize Indian Pharmacol. Soc., 1990. Fellow Indian Coll. Allergy and Applied Immunology, WHO (regional office S.E. Asia); mem. Indian Assn. Med. Jour. Editors, Indian Med. Assn. (Pondicherry br.), Internat. Soc. Infectious Diseases, N.Y. Acad. Scis., Indian Acad. Tropical Parasitology (life), Indian Pharm. Soc. (v.p. 2003, conf. southern regional joint orgn. sec., 2008). Hindu. Avocations: reading, writing, travel, coin collecting/numismatics. Office: JIPMER Dept Pharmacology 605 006 Pondicherry India Home Phone: 0413-2271164; Office Phone: 0413-2272380 ext. 3333. E-mail: scpradham@jipmer.edu.

PRADO, MARCELO PIRES, orthopedist; b. Sao Paulo, Brazil, Oct. 6, 1966; s. Carlos Eduardo and Virginia Pires Prado; m. Ana Paula Mariotto Prado, June 21, 1991; children: Laura Mariotto, Julia Mariotto. MD, Faculdade Medicina U., Sao Paulo, 1991, MS in Medicine, 2001. Asst. physician., foot and ankle group Inst. Ortopedia Traumatologia HC FMUSP, Sao Paulo, 2006—09; foot and ankle specialist Hosp. Israelita Albert Einstein, Sao Paulo, 1998—. Physician foot & ankle specialist Hosp. Coração, Sao Paulo, 1998—. Recipient APM Sao Paulo Med. Assn. award, Godoy Moreira, 1994, Prof. Manlio Nápoli award, 10th Brazilian Congress Foot and Ankle Surgery., 2001. Mem.: Am. Orthopaedic Foot and Ankle Soc., Federaciόm Latinoamericana Medicina y Cirurgia Del pie y la pierna, Brazilian Foot and Ankle Soc., Brazilian Orthop. and Trauma Soc. Avocations: travel, music. Office: Hospital Israelita Albert Einstein Office 320 Av Albert Einstein 627 A1 Block 3rd Fl Sao Paulo SP CEP 05651-901 Brazil Home: Avenida Padre Pereira de Andrade 430 05469-000 Sao Paulo SP Brazil Office Phone: 55 11 37473204, 551199312623. Office Fax: 55 11 21519376. Business E-Mail: mpprado@einstein.br.

PRADO, WILLIAM MANUEL, retired psychologist, educator; b. NYC, Oct. 20, 1927; s. Manuel Fernando and Amor Maria (Bango) P.; m. Elizabeth Ann Avery, Aug. 16, 1953; children: Cheryl, Stuart, Mark. BA, Johns Hopkins U., 1950; MA, U. Ala., 1953; PhD, U. Okla., 1958. Staff psychologist VA Hosp., Little Rock, 1958-85, asst. chief psychologist svcs., 1961-82; asst., assoc. and adj. prof. psychology Philander Smith Coll., Little Rock, 1967-85; instr. Little Rock U., 1959-69, U. Ark. Grad. Ctr., Little Rock, 1963—67, St. Johns Sem., Little Rock, 1963—67; clin. psychologist in pvt. practice Little Rock, 1961—2003. Cons. in field. Contbr. articles to profl. jours. Served with U.S. Army, 1946-47. Recipient Math and Sci. Gold medal Rensselaer Poly. Inst., 1944. Mem. Am. Psychol. Assn., Ark. Assn. Profl. Psychologists, Ark. Psychol. Assn. Democrat. Roman Catholic. Avocations: music, art, movies, travel.

PRADO MONTES DE OCA, ERNESTO, medical researcher; b. Guadalajara, Mex., Oct. 14, 1978; BSc in Biology, U. de Guadalajara, 2002, PhD in Human Genetics, 2007. Rsch. scientist Nat. Coun. Sci. and Tech., 2008—. Molecular diagnostics dept. head NIDIAC SA, 2007—08. Recipient Rsch. award, Mexican Inst. Social Ins., 2006, Rsch. grant, Fed. Funds Mexican Govt. Mem.: Nat. Rschrs. Sys. Achievements include design of HIV-1 viral load molecular assay; design and validation of four molecular assays for DEFB1 gene SNPs as disease markers for atopic dermatitis and lepromatous leprosy. Avocations: sports, literature, movies. Office: Ave Normalistas 800 Guadalajara Jalisco 44270 Mexico Office Fax: 52-33-3345-5200 ext. 1001. E-mail: ernestoprado@hotmail.com.

PRAGASAM, VISWANATHAN, biomedical researcher, educator; b. Vellore, June 5, 1975; PhD, U. Madras, 2005. Assoc. prof. VIT U., 2008—, divsn. leader, 2010—. Recipient Young Investigator award, Dept. Sci. & Tech., Govt of India. Avocation: cricket. Office: Room No 103 Renal Research Lab SBST V Vellore Tamilnadu 632 014 India Business E-Mail: pvishvanath@yahoo.com.

PRAGER, KENNETH MICHAEL, pulmonologist, educator; b. Bklyn., Jan. 3, 1943; s. Max and Hilda Prager; m. Regene Eleanore Gronich, June 25, 1967; children: Karen Rachel Kramer, Joshua Harris, Tamar Anne, Benjamin Dov. BA, Columbia U., 1964; MD, Harvard U., 1968. Cert. ME in internal med. Am. Bd. Internal Med. Intern Columbia Presbyn. Med. Ctr., NYC, 1968—69, resident, 1971—72; chief med. resident Billings Hosp. U. of Chgo., 1972—73; from assoc. in medicine to clin. prof. Columbia Coll. of Physicians and Surgeons, NYC, 1973—99, clin. prof. of medicine, 1999—2007, prof. clin. medicine, 2007—. Dir. of clin. ethics Columbia Presbyn. Med. Ctr., 1998—, chmn. of med. ethics com., 1994—. Co-author: Medical Ethics Issues in the Elderly, 2003; contbr. articles to profl. jours. and newspapers. Bd. dirs. Am. Coun. on Sci. and Health, NYC, 2001—10; fellow NY Acad. Medicine, 2010—; mem. Bd. of Health, Englewood, NJ, 1989—92; chmn. bd. dirs. Moriah Sch., Englewood, NJ, 1983—85. Asst. surgeon, acting med. dir. USPHS Indian Health Svc., 1969—71. Recipient Med. Housestaff Tchg. award, NY Presbyn. Hosp., Dept. Medicine, 1999—2000, Physician of Yr. award, Dept. Nursing, Columbia Presbyn. Med. Ctr., 2003, Alfred Markowitz Svc. award, NY Presbyn. Hosp., Soc. Practitioners, 2006, Leonard Tow Humanism in Medicine award, Columbia U. Coll. Physicians and Surgeons, 2006, EWIG Clin. Edn. award, Dept. Medicine, Columbia U. Medical ctr, 2007—08. Fellow: ACP; mem.: AMA, Am. soc. for bioethics and Humanities, Med. Soc. of the State of N.Y., Am. Coll. of Chest Physicians. Jewish. Home: 231 South Dwight Place Englewood NJ 07631 Office: Columbia University Medical Center 161 Fort Washington Avenue New York NY 10032 Personal E-mail: pragerk@gmail.com.

PRAGER, MARTINA, geneticist, researcher; b. Bielefeld, North Rhine Westphalia, Germany, Nov. 28, 1957; d. Gerhard and Karin Prager. B in Sci., U. Mainz, Germany, 1990. Lab. supr. Inst. Legal Medicine and Forensic Sci., Mainz, 1980—94; group mgr. devel. diagnostics Biotest, Dreieich, Hesse, Germany, 1994—2002; head prodn. molecular genetic diagnostics BAG Health Care GmbH, Lich, Hesse, 2002—. Contbr. articles to profl. jours. Achievements include development of test kits for molecular genetic blood group typing. Office: BAG Health Care GmbH Amtsgerichtsstr. 1-5 35423 Hesse Lich Germany Office Phone: 49 0 6404 925 222. Office Fax: 49 0 6404 925 33 222. Business E-Mail: prager.martina@bag-healthcare.com.

PRAGER, RICHARD L., cardiologist, educator; b. Bklyn., Aug. 22, 1945; MD, SUNY, 1971. Asst. prof. surgery Vanderbilt Med. Ctr., 1978—83; prof. surgery St. Joseph Mercy Hosp., 1984—99, U. Mich., 1999—. Cardiovasc. ctr. dir. U. Mich., 2003—11, thoracic surgery residency program dir., 2009—11. Mem.: Am. Heart Assn., Am. Surg. Assn., Am. Coll. Cardiology, Southern Thoracic Surg. Assn., Mich. Soc. Thoracic & Cardiovasc. Surgeons, Soc. Thoracic Surgeons. Avocations: tennis, running. Office: 5144 Cardiovascular Ctr 1500 E Medical Center Dr Ann Arbor MI 48109 Office Fax: 734-764-2255. Business E-Mail: rprager@med.umich.edu.

PRAKASH, ANAND, biology educator; b. Muzaffarnaga, India, Aug. 20, 1942; s. Dal Chandra and Ram Katori. BSc, Agra U., India, 1960, MSc, 1962, PhD, 1967, MBBS in Alternative Medicine, 2003, postgrad. diploma in Hosp. Mgmt., 2005; postdoc., U. Salford, Eng., 1991. Lectr. DAV (P.G.) Coll., India, 1962-67, assoc. prof., 1967—97, prin., 1998-2000, ret., 2000. Dir. Lab. Fisheries Biology, India, 1976—; North India rep. Fishing Chimes, India, 1992—; freelance journalist, 1976—. Author: Introduction to Paleontology; designer apparatus to measure rate of water expultion in crabs, 1980; contbr. articles to profl. publs. Maj. Nat. Cadet Corps, 1964—94; mem. State and Dist. Environ. Com. India, 1996—; v.p. Nature Conservators, Muzaffarnager, 1984—; advisor Fish Farmers Assn., India, 1985—. Grantee rsch. project fisheries Univ. Grants Commn., 1976-82, 87-90, State Coun. of Sci. and Tech., 1978-80. Mem. Zool. Soc. India (life), Ichthyological Soc. India (life). Avocations: reading, mysticism, shooting. Home: 153 Brahampuri Muzaffarnagar 251 001 India Office Phone: 09411815978.

PRAKASH, ELAPULLI SANKARANARAYANAN, physiologist; b. Nagercoil, India, Sept. 15, 1977; s. E. S. Sankaranarayanan and Vanaja Sankar. MBBS, U. Chennai, 2001; BS, Jawaharlal Inst., 2004; MD, Pondicherry U., 2004. Sr. resident Dept. Physiology Jawaharlal Inst. Postgraduate Med. Edn. and Rsch., Pondicherry, India, 2004—. Contbr. articles to profl. jours. (Best Case Report award Jipmer Sci. Soc., 2004). Mem.: Am. Stroke Assn., Am. Heart Assn., The Am. Physiol. Soc., Assn. Physiologists and Pharmacologists India (life). Achievements include discovery of deep breathing at 6 breaths per minute considerably reduces the frequency of premature ventricular complexes (PVC) in a subset of patients with frequent unifocal PVC. Home: Plot No 14 Sivakripa First Main Rd Tamil Nadu 600044 India Personal E-mail: drsprakash@yahoo.com, dresprakash@gmail.com.

PRAKASH, JYOTI, psychiatrist, researcher; b. Muzaffarpur, Bihar, India, June 1, 1971; s. Santosh Kumar and Bina Ghosh; m. Suparna Das, Apr. 17, 1998; children: Jyotsana Jeevantika, Srijan Saswat. MBBS, Armed Forces Med. Coll., Pune, India, 1995, MD in Psychiatry, 2002; postgrad. in Human Resource and Pers. Mgmt., Indian Institute Modern Mgmt., Pune, India, 2007; postgrad. in Computer Application, Inst. Advanced Study in Edn., Rajsthan, 2009. Registered med. practitioner Med. Coun. India, 1995, psychiatrist Med. Coun. India, 2003. Intern Armed Forced Med. Coll., Pune, India, 1995—96, resident, 1999—2002; asst. prof. psychiatry Base Hosp., New Delhi, 2002—05; postdoctoral fellow in child psychiatry NIMH and Neuroscis., Bangalore, India, 2005; mil. psychiatrist Indian Level III Hosp., UN, Goma, Democratic Republic of Congo, 2006—07; psychiatrist Mil. Hosp., Pathankot, 2007—09; reader psychiatry Armed Forces Med. Coll., Pune, 2009—. Contbr. articles to profl. jours. Adolescents trainers Sch. Mental Health Program, New Delhi, 2004—05. Fellow: Indian Assn. Geriatric Mental Health (life), Indian Assn. Pain Rsch. and Therapy (life), Indian Assn. Child and Adolescent Psychiatry (life); mem.: Pune Psychiat. Assn. (exec. coun. mem. 2009—), Delhi Psychiat. Soc. (joint sec. 2004—, Ravi Pandey Meml. Young Scientist award 2003), Assn. Indsl. Psychiatrists India (life), Indial Psychiat. Soc. (life). Avocations: rafting, running, theater. Home: Jagdishpuri Bihar Muzaffarpur 842002 India Office: Armed Forces Med Coll Sholapur Rd Wanavadi 110 40 Pune India Personal E-mail: drjyotiprakashpsy@yahoo.com.

PRANDINI, MIRTO NELSO, neurosurgeon, educator; b. São Paulo, Brazil, Aug. 24, 1944; s. Mirto and Diva Prandini; m. Maria Estela Melega, Nov. 10, 1973; children: Nelson Henrique, Thais Melega, Maria. D, Fed. U. São Paulo, 1967. Diplomate São Paulo Brazil, 1967. Jr. registar Edinburgh U., 1971—73; assoc. prof. Fed. U. São Paulo, Brazil, 1987—, chmn. neurosurgical dept., 2000—; presdtl. bd. mem. Hosp. Santacruz. Patients asst. Hosp. Santa Cruz, São Paulo, 1974—2009, pres. bd. support to presdl. directory. Home: Rua Dos Crisantemos 117 São Paulo 04049 020 Brazil Office: Federal Univ São Paulo Rua Botucatu 591 Cj 103 São Paulo 04023 062 Brazil Office Fax: 551155497109; Home Fax: 551150713774. Business E-Mail: mnprandini@uol.com.br.

PRANEVICIUS, OSVALDAS, physician; b. Lithuania, Sept. 27, 1966; MD, Kaunas Med. U., 1989, PhD, 1992. Attending physician NY Hosp. Queens, 2005—. Home: 300 Albany St 6E New York NY 10280 Business E-Mail: opranevicius@aol.com.

PRANGE, ARTHUR JERGEN, JR., psychology and psychiatry professor, neuroscientist; b. Grand Rapids, Mich., Sept. 19, 1926; s. Arthur Jergen and Martha Frances (Elliott) P.; m. Sarah Elizabeth Bowen, Feb. 4, 1950; children— Christine Anne, Martha Louise, Laura Beth, David Elliott. BS, U. Mich., 1947, MD, 1950. Intern Wayne County Gen. Hosp., Eloise, Mich., 1950-51; resident in psychiatry U. NC, Chapel Hill, 1954-57, instr., 1957-60, asst. prof., 1960-64, asso. prof., 1964-68, prof. psychiatry, 1968-83, Boshamer prof. psychiatry, 1983—, acting chmn. dept. psychiatry, 1983-85, dir. NIMH Clin. Rsch. Ctr., 1979—. Vis. scientist Med. Rsch. Coun. Unit, Epson, Surrey, Eng., 1968-69; chmn. clin. projects rsch. rev. com. HEW, NIMH, 1975-76, chmn. bd. sci. counselors, 1986-87; mem. psychopharmacologic drugs adv. com. HEW, FDA, 1979-82. Editor: The Thyroid Axis, Drugs and Behavior, 74; Contbr. articles to med. jours. Recipient NIMH Career Devel. award 1961-69, Career Scientist award, 1969-95, Gold Medal award Soc. of Biol. Psychiatry, 1992, Exemplary Psychiatrist award Nat. Alliance for the Mentally Ill, 1997, Selo prize Nat. Alliance for Rsch. in Schizophrenia and Affective Disorders, 1997. Fellow Am. Psychiat. Assn. (life, Rsch. in Psychiatry award 1996), Am. Coll. Neuropsychopharmacology (life, pres. 1987,

Hoch award 1995); mem. Internat. Soc. Psychoneuroendocrinology (founding mem.), NC Neuropsychiat. Assn., Collegium Internationale Neuropsychopharmacologicum, Royal Coll. Psychiatrists (London). Home: 6503 Meadowview Rd Hillsborough NC 27278-8314 Office: Univ NC Sch Medicine Dept Psychiatry Chapel Hill NC 27599-0001

PRANGE, HILMAR WALTER, neurology educator; b. Reichenbach, Germany, Aug. 4, 1944; s. Georg Friedrich Reinhold and Gertrud Wilhelmine (Mueller) P.; m. Carin Juliane Schroeter, Mar. 14, 1970; children: Klaus Richard, Juliane. MD, U. Rostock, Germany, 1969, lic. specialist neurology and psychiatry, 1974; Habilitation, Georg-August U., Goettingen, Germany, 1982. Medical diplomate; lic. in intensive care medicine, 1997. Med. resident Regional Hosp., Stralsund, Germany, 1969-71; med. asst. then psychiatrist Univ. Hosp., Rostock, 1971-75; asst. med. dir. Ev. Johannes Hosp., Bielefeld, Germany, 1975-76; head neurologic out-patient clinic Univ. Hosp., Goettingen, Germany, 1976-78, asst. med. dir. dept. neurology, 1979—87, dir. neurol. intensive care unit, 1987—2007. Mem. expert group German Ministry of Health. Author: Neurosyphilis, 1987, Infectious Diseases of the Central Nervous System, 1995; editor: CNS Barriers and Modern CSF Diagnostics, 1993, Systemic Infections Causing Bacterial CNS Diseases, 1997, Infectious Diseases of the Central Nervous System, 2001, Emergencies in Neurology, 2002, Neurological Intensive Medicine, 2004; contbr. articles to profl. jours.; author: Recommendations to Diagnostics and Therapy of Shock 2005 and 2010. Grantee German Forschungsgemeinschaft, German Tech. Cooperation, German MS Soc. Mem.: EMEA, German Med. Assn. (mem. commn. drug security), European Neurol. Soc., Neurol. Soc. Cyprus (hon.). Lutheran. Avocations: history, sports, swimming. Office Phone: 0049 551 392740. Office Fax: 0049-551-398405. Business E-Mail: hprange@gwdg.de, hilmarprange@gmx.de.

PRASAD, ANANDA SHIVA, medical educator; b. Buxar, Bihar, India, Jan. 1, 1928; came to U.S., 1952, naturalized, 1968. s. Radha Krishna and Mahesha (Kaur) Lall; m. Aryabala Ray, Jan. 6, 1952; children: Rita, Sheila, Ashok, Audrey. BSc, Patna Sci. Coll., India, 1946, MB, BChir, 1951; PhD, U. Minn., 1957; doctorate honoris causa, U. Claude Bernard of Lyon, 1999. Intern Patna Med. Coll. Hosp., 1951-52; resident St. Paul's Hosp., Dallas, 1952-53, U. Minn., 1953-56, VA Hosp., Mpls., 1956; instr. dept. medicine Univ. Hosp., U. Minn., Mpls., 1957-58; vis. assoc. prof. medicine Shiraz Med. Faculty, Nemazee Hosp., Shiraz, Iran, 1958—60; prof. medicine chair Shiraz Med. Faculty Nemaee Hosp., 1960—61; asst. prof. medicine and nutrition Vanderbilt U., 1961-63; mem. faculty, dir. div. hematology dept. medicine Wayne State U., Detroit, 1963-84, assoc. prof., 1964-68, prof., 1968-2000, dir. research dept. medicine, 1984-97, disting. prof., 2000—. Mem. staff Harper-Grace Hosp., VA Hosp., Allen Park, Mich.; mem. trace elements subcom. Food and Nutrition Bd., NRC-Nat. Acad. Scis., 1965-68; chmn. trace elements com. Internat. Union Nutritional Scis.; mem. Am. Bd. Nutrition; pres. Am. Coll. Nutrition, 1991-93. Author: Zinc Metabolism, 1966, Trace Elements in Human Health and Disease, 1976, Trace Elements and Iron in Human Metabolism, 1978, Zinc in Human Nutrition, 1979, Biochemistry of Zinc, 1993; editor: Clinical, Biochemical and Nutritional Aspects of Trace Elements, 1982, Am. Jour. Hematology, Jour. Trace Elements in Exptl. Medicine; editor: Zinc Metabolism, Current Aspects in Health and Disease, 1977; co-editor: Clinical Applications of Recent Advances in Zinc Metabolism, 1982, Zinc Deficiency in Human Subjects, 1983, Essential and Toxic Trace Elements in Human Health and Disease, 1988, Essential and Toxic Trace Elements in Human Health and Disease: An Update, 1993; Jour. Am. Coll. Nutrition; contbr. articles to profl. jours., also reviewer. Trustee Detroit Internat. Inst., Detroit Gen. Hosp. Rsch. Corp., 1969—72. Recipient Rsch. Recognition award Wayne State U., 1964, award Am. Coll. Nutrition, 1976, Disting. Faculty Fellowship award Wayne State U., 1986, Medal of Honor, City of Lyon, France, 1989, Pioneer in Sickle Cell Disease Rsch. award Nat. Heart Lung Blood Inst./NIH, 1997; Pfizer scholar, 1955-56, WCMS Spl. Recognition award for Profl. Ach., 1998, Klaus Schwartz medal Internat. Assn. Bioinorganic Scientists, 2001, Spl. Recognition award Am. Assn. Physicians India, 2001, Mahidol award, Bangkok, 2010; inducted Heritage Hall Fame, Mich., 2003, Asian Acad. Hall Fame, 2007. Master ACP (Outstanding Rsch. Related to Medicine award 2007), Am. Coll. Nutrition; fellow AAAS, Am. Inst. Nutrition (trace elements panel), Internat. Soc. Hematology; mem. AMA (Goldberger award 1975), Internat. Soc. Trace Element Rsch. in Humans (pres. 1986-92, chmn. steering com. 1985-86, Raulin award 1989), Am. Soc. Clin. Nutrition (awards com. 1969-70), Am. Fedn. Clin. Rsch. (pres. Mich. 1969-70), Am. Physiol. Soc., Am. Soc. Clin. Investigation, Am. Soc. Hematology (Disting. Emeritus mem.), Assn. Am. Physicians, European Acad. Scis., Arts and Humanities (corr.), Ctrl. Soc. Clin. Rsch., Soc. Exptl. Biology and Medicine (councillor Mich. 1967-71), Wayne State U. Acad. Scholars (pres.-elect 1997-98, pres. 1998-99), Wayne County Med. Soc., Internat. Soc. Internal Medicine, Am. Soc. Clin. Nutrition (Robert H. Herman award 1984), Nutrition Soc. India (Gopalan oration award 1988), Nat. Heart, Lung, Blood Inst. NIH (mem. coun. 2002-2004), Cosmos Club (Washington), Sigma Xi. Home: 4710 Cove Rd Orchard Lake MI 48323-3604 Office: Univ Health Ctr 5-C 4201 Saint Antoine St Detroit MI 48201-2153 Office Phone: 313-577-1597. Business E-Mail: prasada@karmanos.org.

PRASAD, NARAYAN, nephrologist, educator; b. Madhubani, Bihar, July 10, 1968; DM, Sanjay Gandhi Postgrad. Inst. Med. Scis., Lucknow, 1983, MD, DNB, Sanjay Gandhi Postgrad. Inst. Med. Scis., Lucknow, MNAMS in Nephrology, 2003. Assoc. prof. Sanjay Gandhi Postgrad. Inst. Med. Scis., Lucknow, 2009—, mem., governing body, 2010. Exec. mem. Indian Soc. Organ Transplant, 2004—06; sec. Peritoneal Dialysis Soc. India, 2009. Recipient Young Investigator award, Japan Kidney, 2005, Muthoot M George Meml. and Kerala Kidney Rsch. award, Tanker Found., Chennai, 2010. Mem.: Indian Soc. Nephrology (treas. 2004—09), Internat. Soc. Peritoneal Dialysis, Internat. Soc. Nephrology (Bansal Oration award, Jansen Cilag award), ERA-EDTA, Am. Soc. Nephrology. Avocations: swimming, bicycling. Office: Sanjay Gandhi Postgrad Inst Med Scis Campus Rae Bareli Rd Lucknow Uttar Pradesh 226014 India Office Fax: 91-522-2668017.

PRASAD, SHIV, medical educator; b. Fatehpur, India, Apr. 8, 1961; B in Vet. Sci., Govind B in Vet. Sci., M in Vet. Sci., Govind Ballabh Pant U. Agr. & Tech., Pantnagar, PhD, 1984. Tchr., rschr. Govind Ballabh Pant U. Agr. & Tech., Pantnagar, 1987, prof., vet. gynaecology, 2005—. Recipient Swaminath Iyar award, Indian Vet. Assn., 1998. Avocation: badminton. Home: I/43-A Lal Bagh Pantnagar Pantnagar Uttarakhand 263145 India Home Fax: 05944-233473. Personal E-mail: shivp2003@yahoo.co.uk.

PRASAD, SUYASH, pediatrician; s. Birendra and Manjula Prasad. MBBS, U. Newcastle-upon-Tyne, Eng., 1993. Resident med. officer pediat. Alder Hey Children's Hosp., Liverpool, England, 1996—97, Royal Alexander Hosp. for Children, Sydney, 1997—2002; pediatrician Cromwell Hosp., London, 2002—; pediatrician, clin. rsch. physician Eli Lilly and Co, England, 2002—06; med. dir. Genzyme Therapeutics, 2006—10, Bio Marc. Pharm., 2010—. Contbr. articles to profl. jours. Mem.: Faculty of Pharm. Physicians, Royal Coll. Physicians, Royal Coll. Paediatrics and Child Health.

PRASAD, VINOD, nephrologist, healthcare educator; m. Salini R. MD, Med. Coll., Trivandrum, India, 1999; MPH, U. Md., College Park, 2002. Diplomate Am. Bd. Internal Medicine, 2005, lic. Ednl. Commn. Fgn. Med. Grads., 2002. Resident, internal medicine Drexel U., Phila., 2002—05; fellow, nephrology Westchester Med. Ctr., NY Med. Coll., Valhalla, 2005—. Rsch. fellow U. Md., College Park, 2001—02. Scholar, George Wash. U., 2000. Mem.: NY Med. Soc. (assoc.), Renal Physician Assn. (assoc.), Am. Soc. Nephrology (assoc.). Achievements include research in unmasking iron deficiency in chronic kidney disease patients on erythropoietin; correction of hemoglobin and outcomes in renal disease study; gene exercise research study; pentoxifylline in Erythropoietin resistant anemia.

PRASARTRITHA, THAVAT, retired cardiologist; b. Bangkok, June 12, 1951; BS, Mahidol U., Bangkok, 1973, MD, 1975. Dep. dir. Ctr. Excellence in Orthop., Lerdsin Gen. Hosp., 1979—. Mem.: Med. Coun., Orthop. Assn. Avocations: golf, computers. Office: Lerdsin Gen Hosp 190 Silom Rd Bangkok 10500 Thailand Office Fax: 66-2-3539836. E-mail: geennikul@gmail.com.

PRASHANTH, K., biotechnologist, educator; b. Bengaluru, July 14, 1970; MSc, Manasagangothri, 1994; PhD, JIPMER, 2002. Prin. investigator Ctr. DNA fingerprinting and Diagnostics, 2002—06; asst. prof. Pondicherry U., 2006—. Grant, Fedn. European Microbiol. Soc. Mem.: Biotech Rsch. Soc. India, Indian Assn. Med. Microbiologists. Avocations: painting, photography. Office: Pondicherry University Dept Biotechnology Pondicherry 6050 014 India E-mail: prashi2k@yahoo.com.

PRATHER, DONNA LYNN, psychiatrist; b. Charlotte, NC, Nov. 4, 1946; d. James Boyd and Ann (Joyner) P. BA, Queens Coll., Charlotte, 1968; MD, U. N.C., 1978. Supr. Meckenburg County Dept. Social Svcs., Charlotte, 1971-74; family practice intern Charlotte Meml. Hosp., 1978-79, resident in family practice, 1979-81; fellow in family medicine U. N.C., Chapel Hill, 1981-82; resident in psychiatry N.C. Meml. Hosp., Chapel Hill, 1982-85; pvt. practice psychiatry Chapel Hill, NC, 1985—. Psychiatrist Person Counceling Ctr., Roxboro, N.C., 1983-92; med. dir. Orange-person-Chatam Mental Health Ctr., Chapel Hill, 1992—; clin. assoc. prof. U. N.C., Chapel Hill, 1985—. Mem. N.C. Psychiat. Assn., N.C. Med. Soc., Am. Psychiat. Assn., N.C. Psychiat. Assn. (chmn., com. for women 1990-91, ethics com. 1997-99). Avocation: music. Office: 200 N Greensboro St Ste D-7 Carrboro NC 27510 Office Phone: 919-929-6519.

PRATI, LAURA, chemistry professor; b. Milan, Nov. 9, 1959; PhD, U. Milan, 1982. Prof. U. Degli Studi Milan, 2000—. Office: Via Venezian 21 Milan 20133 Italy Business E-Mail: laura.prato@unimi.it.

PRATIBHA, ANKOLA A., pediatrician, educator; d. Harendra B. and Sarojini H. Naik; m. Arun D. Ankola, May 12, 1981; children: Anuja A. Ankola children: Ashish A. Ankola. MD in Pediat., Seth G.S Med. Coll., Mumbai, DCH, 1980. Diplomate Am. Bd. Pediat., 1987. Dir. neonatology Met. Hosp. Ctr., NYC, 1994—; prof. clin. pediat. NY Med. coll., Valhalla, 2008—. Same as above. Recipient Tchg. Award, Dept. Pediat., Met. Hosp. Ctr., 1995, 1998. Fellow: Am. Acad. Pediat. Achievements include research in neonatology. Office: Met Hosp Ctr 1903 First Ave New York NY 10029

PRATT, DONALD GEORGE, physician; b. Higgins, Tex., Oct. 19, 1946; s. George Horace and Esta Vici (Barker) P. BS in Biomed. Sci., West Tex. State U., 1970; MD, U. Tex., Galveston, 1974. Diplomate Am. Bd. Family Practice, Am. Bd. Radiology (Radiation Oncology). Intern Scott & White Meml. Hosp., Temple, Tex., 1974-75, resident in gen. surgery and pathology, 1975-77, physician, 1979—83; resident in family practice McLennan County Med. Edn. and Rsch. Found., Waco, Tex., 1977-79; physician Family Practice Assocs., El Paso, Tex., 1983; owner, pvt. contractor Minor Emergency Ctrs., Amarillo, Tex., 1983-85; resident in radiation therapy U. Tex., Galveston, 1985-88; ptnr. Cons. in Radiation Oncology, P.A., Amarillo, 1988—2003, pres., 1994—2003, Cons. in Radiation Oncology, 1994—2003; dir. dept. radiation oncology Harrington Cancer Ctr., Amarillo, 1994—2003, pres. staff, bd. dirs., 1995-99; prin. investigator Radiation Oncology Group, 1988-95; pres. of staff Harrington Cancer Ctr., 1995—99; ptnr. Cons. in Radiation Oncology, P.A., Amarillo, 1988—2003, pres., 1994—2003; cons. in radiation oncology, 1994—2003. Dir. Dept. Radiation Oncology Harrington Cancer Ctr., Amarillo, Tex., 1994—2003. Mem. AMA, Am. Soc. Therapeutic Radiology and Oncology, Tex. Med. Assn., Potter/Randall County Med. Soc., Tex. Radiol. Soc. Home: 261 S Timbercreek Dr Amarillo TX 79118-3751

PRATT, GEORGE JANES, JR., psychologist, author; b. Mpls., May 3, 1948; s. George Janes and Sally Elvina (Hanson) P.; m. Vonda Pratt; 1 child, Whitney Beth. BA cum laude, U. Minn., 1970, MA, 1973; PhD with spl. commendation, Calif. Sch. Profl. Psychology, San Diego, 1976. Diplomate Am. Acad. Pain Mgmt., Assn. Comprehensive Energy Psychology; lic. psychologist, Calif., 1976. Psychology trainee Ctr. for Behavior Modification, Mpls., 1971—72, U.Minn. Student Counseling Bur., 1972—73; predoctoral clin. psychology intern San Bernardino County Mental Health Svcs., Calif., 1973—74, San Diego County Mental Health Services, 1974—76; mem. staff San Louis Rey Hosp., 1977—78; postdoctoral clin. psychology intern Mesa Vista Hosp., San Diego, 1976; clin psychologist, dir. Psychology and Cons. Assocs. of San Diego, 1976—90; chmn. Psychology and Cons. Assocs. Press, 1977—94. Bd. dirs. Optimax, Inc., 1985-94; pres. George Pratt Ph.D., Psychol. Corp., 1979—; chmn. Pratt, Korn & Assocs., Inc., 1984-94; mem. staff Scripps Meml. Hosp., La Jolla, Calif., 1986—, chmn. psychology, 1993-95, 2000—; founder La Jolla Profl. Workshops, 1977-81; clin. psychologist El Camino Psychology Ctr., San Clemente, Calif., 1977-78; grad. teaching asst. U. Minn. Psychology and Family Studies divsn., 1971; teaching assoc. U. Minn. Psychology and Family Studies divsn., Mpls., 1972-73; instr. U. Minn. Extension divsn., Mpls., 1971-73; faculty Calif. Sch. Profl. Psychology, 1974-83, San Diego Evening Coll., 1975-77, Nat. U., 1978-79, Chapman Coll., 1978, San Diego State U., 1979-80; vis. prof. Pepperdine U., L.A., 1976-78; cons. U. Calif. at San Diego Med. Sch., 1976-78, also instr. univ., 1978—; psychology chmn. Workshops in Clin. Hypnosis, 1980-84; cons. Calif. Health Dept., 1974, Naval Regional Med. Ctr., 1978-82, ABC-TV; also speaker. Author: Sensory/Progressive Relaxation, 1979, Effective Stress Management, 1979, Clinical Hypnosis: Techniques and Applications, 1985, Rx for Stress, 1994; co-author: A Clinical Hypnosis Primer, 1984, 88, 2009, HyperPerformance, 1987, 2009, Release Your Business Potential, 1988, Instant Emotional Healing, 2000, Emotional Self-Management, 2000; contbr.: Hypnosis: Questions and Answers, 1986, Handbook for Hypnotic Suggestions and Metaphors, 1990, Imagery in Sports and Physical Performance, 1994. With USAR, 1970-76. Fellow Am. Soc. Clin. Hypnosis (cert., approved cons.); mem. APA, Nat. Register of Health Svc. Providers in Psychology, San Diego Soc. Sex. Therapy and Edn. (past pres.), San Diego Soc. Clin. Hypnosis (past pres.), San Diego Psychol. Assn., Grammys (voting mem.), U. Minn. Alumni Assn., Beta Theta Pi. Office: Scripps Meml Hosp Campus 9834 Genesee Ave Ste 321 La Jolla CA 92037-1216 Home: 1127 Muirlands Vista Way La Jolla CA 92037-6210 Office Phone: 858-457-3900.

PRATT, HARRY DAVIS, retired entomologist; b. North Adams, Mass., Apr. 13, 1915; s. Harry Edward and Ethel Mae (Davis) P.; m. Caroline Georgine Kreiss, Apr. 13, 1944 (dec. May 1951); children: Harry Davis Jr., Katherine Maria Pratt Garrison, George Kreiss; m. Dora Belle Ford, Nov. 29, 1952 (dec. July 1998). BS, Mass. State Coll., 1936, MS, 1938; PhD, U. Minn., St. Paul, 1941. Registered profl. entomologist. Asst. entomologist USPHS Malaria Control War Areas, San Juan, 1942-46; chief med. entomol. lab. USPHS Communicable Disease Ctr., Atlanta, 1946-53, chief insect rodent tr., 1953-63, chief Aedes aegypti control tng., 1964-68; chief insect rodent control tng. Environ. Control Agy., Atlanta, 1968-72; cons., tchr., writer Atlanta, 1972—. Spl. cons. Econ. Coop. Administrn., Saigon, Vietnam, 1950, WHO, Geneva, 1966, Kuala Lumpur, Malaysia, 1969. United meth. South Carolina, 2003—08. Fellow Entomol. Soc. Am. (life); mem. Am. Mosquito Control Assn. (pres. 1967), Entol. Soc. Washington, Ga. Entomol. Soc. Mem. Christian Ch. (Disciples Of Christ). Home: 104 So Almond Dr Simpsonville SC 29681

PRATT, ROBERT JOHN, nursing educator; b. Eau Claire, Wis., June 27, 1941; s. Mary Jane Elizabeth Stubbs and Leonard William Paulson. Diploma in nursing, U. London, 1976, MS in Health Edn., 1984. V.p. Riverside Coll. Health Studies, London, 1986—94; prof. nursing Thames Valley U., London, 1994—2011; emeritus prof. nursing U. West London, 2010. Dir. Richard Wells Rsch. Ctr. Thames Valley U., London, 1994—2010; assoc. dean rsch. U. West London, 2010—. With USN, 1959—63. Decorated comdr. Order Brit. Empire. Fellow: Higher Edn. Acad., Royal Soc. for the Encouragement of Arts, Manufactures and Commerce, Royal Coll. Nursing. Office: University West London Paragon Campus Boston Manor Rd TW8 9GA Brentford Middlesex England Business E-Mail: robert.pratt@uwl.ac.uk.

PRAVEEN KUMAR, GIDEON, medical researcher, consultant; b. Chennai, Jan. 29, 1982; PhD, VIT U., 2010. Cons. Ruby Physiotherapy, 2003—05; rsch. engr. VIT U., 2007—08; industry analyst Frost & Sullivan, 2008—, healthcare cons., 2008—. Recipient Best Project award, Lemelson Recognition & Mentoring Programme. Mem.: IEEE, BMES, SBAOI. Avocations: music, cricket, politics. Office: 7th Fl Karumuttu Ctr 498 Anna Chennai Tamil Nadu 600035 India Personal E-mail: gideonpraveenkumar@gmail.com.

PRECH, MAREK, cardiologist; b. Gniezno, Poland, Sept. 14, 1968; MD, Poznan U. Med. Scis., 1993, PhD, 2004. Physician, rsch. scientist Poznan U. Med. Scis., 1994; head Dept. Invasive Cardiology, 2007—. Mem.: ESC, EHRA, EAPCI, Polish Cardiac Soc. Avocation: jogging. Office: Kiepury 45 Leszno Wielkopolska 64-100 Poland Business E-Mail: mmprech@wp.pl.

PREDA, DAN, radiologist; b. Sibiu, Romania, Mar. 6, 1956; s. Nicolae and Olimpia Preda. Degree, U. Medicine and Pharmacy, 1982. Cert. Romania Min. of Health, 1994. Med. intern Clin. Children Hosp., Cluj-Napoca, 1982—85; pediat. County Hosp., Bistrita-Nasaud County, 1985—88; resident, asst. tchr. U. of Medicine and Pharmacy, Radiology Dept., 1988—94; radiologist, 1994—; advanced MRI specl. stages U. Aarhus, Mr-Ctr., Aarhus, Denmark, 1995—99; radiologist, MRI subspecialty Radiology Dept. U. Aarhus, Aarhus, Denmark, 1999—2002, County Clin. Hosp. of Cluj County, 2002—. Mem.: Internat. Soc. for Magnetic Resonance in Medicine, European Soc. Resonance Magnetic and Biology, European Congress Radiology, Radiological Soc. N.Am. Avocations: travel, reading, tennis, cars. Office: Spitalul Clinic Judetean Cluj STR Clinicilor 1-3 400006 Cluj Napoca Romania Home: Strada Donath M3X, Ap. 4 400290 Cluj-Napoca Romania

PREETA, KUTTY, epidemiologist; b. Kuwait, Apr. 2, 1971; MPH, Sch. Pub. Health, Boston U., 2005; MBBS, Kasturba Med. Coll., 1998, MD. Epidemiologist Ctrs. Disease Control & Prevention, 2007—. Home: 1326 Briarhill Ln Atlanta GA 30324 Business E-Mail: pkutty@cdc.gov.

PREISS, THOMAS, molecular biologist, researcher; b. Marburg, Hessen, Germany, July 21, 1965; s. Helmut Heinz and Ingrid (Fanta) P. Diploma in chemistry, Philipps U., Marburg, Germany, 1991; PhD, U. Newcastle, Newcastle-upon-Tyne, Eng., 1995; habilitation in biochemistry, U. Heidelberg, Germany, 2001. Rschr. European Molecular Biology Lab., Heidelberg, 1995—. Contbr. articles to profl. jours. including Nature, Molecular Cell and Current Opinion Genetics Devel. Recipient Erasmus prize European Union, 1989-90; European Molecular Biology Orgn. fellow, 1995-97, fellow G. Daimler K. Benz Found. Mem. Soc. for Biochemistry and Molecular Biology. Avocations: skiing, record collecting. Office: European Molecular Biol Lab Meyerhofstrasse 1 69117 Heidelberg Germany E-mail: preiss@embl-heidelberg.de.

PREMACK, DAVID, psychologist; b. Aberdeen, SD, Oct. 26, 1925; s. Leonard B. and Sonja (Liese) P.; m. Ann M. James, Oct. 26, 1951; children: Ben, Lisa, Timothy. BA magna cum laude, U. Minn., 1949, PhD, 1955. Rsch. assoc. Yerkes Labs. Primate Biology, Orange Park, Fla., 1955; rsch. assoc., asst. prof. psychology U. Mo., Columbia, 1956-58, assoc. prof., 1959-62, prof., 1963-64, U. Calif., Santa Barbara, 1965-75; vis. prof. Harvard U., 1970-71; prof. U. Pa.,

1975—. Artist-in-residence Yaddo, Saratoga Springs, N.Y., 1955; fellow Van Leer Jerusalem Inst., 1980, Inst. for Advanced Study, Berlin, 1985-86; vis. scientist Japan Soc. for Promotion Sci., 1980; univ. rsch. lectr. U. Calif., Santa Barbara, 1973; mem. sci. gov. bd. Fyssen Found., Paris, 1989—; assoc. neurosci. rsch. program, La. Jolla, Calif., 1991—. Author: Intelligence in Ape and Man, 1976, (with Ann James Premack) The Mind of an Ape, 1983, Gavagai! Or the Future History of the Animal Language Controversy, 1986 (with Dan Sperber and Ann James Premack) Causal Cognition: A Multidisciplinary Debate, 1995, (with Ann James Premack) Original Intelligence: Unlocking the Mystery of Who We Are, 2003, French translation, 2003, Japanese translation, 2005; mem. editl. bd. Jour. Exptl. Psychology: Animal Processes, 1976—, Cognition, 1977—, Brain and Behavior Sci., 1978—, Jour. Cognitive Neurosci. Served with U.S. Army, 1943-46. Ford Found. tchg. intern, 1954; USPHS postdoctoral fellow, 1956-59; Social Sci. Rsch. Coun. fellow, summer 1963; Ctr. for Advanced Study in Behavioral Scis. fellow, 1972-73; Guggenheim fellow, 1979-80; grantee NSF, 1961—, USPHS, 1960-80; recipient Kenneth Craik Resch. award St. John's Coll.-Cambridge U., 1987, Internat. Sci. prize Fyssen Found., Paris, 1987. Fellow AAAS; mem. Am. Psychol. Soc. (William James fellow 2005), Soc. Exptl. Psychologists. Personal E-mail: davidpremack@msn.com.

PREMINGER, BETH AVIVA, plastic surgeon; d. Ben Israel and Susan Ruth Preminger; m. David Henry Hiltzik, Aug. 16, 2001; children: Stella Rose Hiltzik, Nathan Alexander Hiltzik. BA magna cum laude, Harvard U., 1999; MD, Cornell U., 2003; MPH, Columbia U., 2007. Resident dept. gen. surgery NY Presbyn. Hosp., Weill Cornell Med. Coll., NYC, 2003—06, ethics fellow, 2007—; clin. rsch. fellow divsn. plastic surgery Meml. Sloan-Kettering Cancer Ctr., NYC, 2006—07; fellow divsn. plastic surgery NY Presbyn. Hosp., Columbia and Cornell U., NYC, 2007—. Recipient Janet M. Glasgow Meml. Achievement Citation, Weill Med. Coll., Cornell U., 2003; grantee, Meml. Sloan Kettering Aging and Cancer Inst., 2006; fellow, Mt. Sinai Grad. Sch., 1998, Cornell Med. Coll., 2000; Max Kade fellowship, Am. Austrian Found., 2003. Mem.: Am. Osler Soc. (William B. Bean Rsch. award 2000), Am. Soc. Plastic Surgeons, Alpha Omega Alpha (pres. Cornell chpt. 2002—03). Avocations: scuba diving, swimming, travel. Office: Beth Aviva Preminger MD PLLC 325 E 79th St New York NY 10075-0954 Office Phone: 212-706-1900.

PREMMANISAKUL, SUMAIT, physician, consultant; b. Phitsanulok, Thailand, Sept. 14, 1966; s. Hansraj Arora and Chitta Premmanisakul; m. Nilarat Narula, June 1, 1993; 1 child, Natasha. MBBS, Indhira Gandhi Med. Coll., Simla, India, 1992. Cert. in aviation medicine Otago U., New Zealand, 2005, in aeromedical evacuation Otago U., 2005. Med. dir. Global Doctor Clinic, Bangkok, 2001—. Med. cons. Samitivej Hosp., Bangkok, 2004—. Designated med. examiner Civil Aviation Safety Authority, Australia, 2004—. Mem.: Australian Soc. Aerospace Medicine, Internat. Soc. Travel Medicine, Aerospace Med. Assn. Business E-Mail: sumait@globaldoctorclinic.com.

PRENDERGAST, BRIAN, psychologist, educator; BA in Psychology, Williams Coll., 1993; PhD in Psychology, U. Calif., Berkeley, 1998. Fellow Johns Hopkins U., Ohio State U.; assoc. prof. psychology U. Chgo., mem. Inst. for Mind & Biology. Office: University of Chicago Dept of Psychology 5848 S University Ave Chicago IL 60637 Office Phone: 773-702-2895. Office Fax: 773-702-6898.

PRENDERGAST, ROBERT ANTHONY, pathologist educator; b. Bklyn., Nov. 6, 1931; BA, Columbia U., 1953; MD, Boston U., 1957. Intern Bellevue Hosp., 1957-58; resident Boston City Hosp., 1958-59, Meml. Sloan-Kettering Hosp., 1959-61; vis. physician Rockefeller U., 1963-65, asst. prof., 1965-70, assoc. prof. opthamology, 1970-99; prof. ophthalmology and pathology Johns Hopkins U. Sch. Medicine, 1999—, prof. emeritus, 2002. Bd. dirs. Marine Biol. Lab., Woods Hole, Mass., 2001—08, adj. sr. scientist, 2006 . Mem. Am. Assn. Immunology, Am. Soc. Exp. Pathology, H.G. Kunkel Soc., Assn. Vision & Ophthal., Pluto Club. Achievements include research in cellular immunology, ontogeny of the immune response, transplantation immunology, viral immunopathology, immunopathology of ocular inflammatory diseases. Office: Marine Biol Lab Woods Hole MA 02543 Home Phone: 508-457-1375. Business E-Mail: rprender@mbl.edu.

PRENGLER, MARA, pediatrician; b. Buenos Aires, 1963; arrived in England, 1996; MD with honors, U. Buenos Aires, 1988; PhD in Child Health, U. Coll. London, 2005. Registered med. practitioner, cert. prof. cert. Gen. Med. Coun. U.K., specialist in pediats. Ministry of Health, Buenos Aires. Pediat. resident Children's Hosp. Dr. R. Gutierrez, U. Buenos Aires, 1989—93; practitioner in neurology Gen. Hosp. Dr. Ramos Mejia, U. Buenos Aires, 1993—94; practitioner child neurology Children's Hosp. Dr. R. Gutierrez, U. Buenos Aires, 1994—96; rsch. fellow in pediat. neurology Inst. Child Health and Great Ormond St., London, 1996—2006. Rsch. fellow in pediat. neurology dept. pediats. collaborative study Aristotle U. Thessaloniki, Greece, 2002; fellow Beth Israel Ctr., NYC, 2001. Co-author: Genetics of Stroke, 2003; contbr. articles to profl. jours., chapters to books; author: Stroke and Cerebrovascular Disease in Childhood, 2011. Recipient scholarships/grants, Ian Karten Charitable Trust, 1996—98, B'nai B'rith Leo Baeck Lodge, 1996—2002, Inst. Child Health, Friends of the Wolfson Ctr., 2003, K. Horemis prize, Greek Pediat. Soc., 2003. Fellow: Royal Soc. Medicine; mem.: Brit. Med. Assn., Argentine Soc. Pediats. (assoc.), Brit. Pediat. Neurology Soc. Avocations: films, arts, literature, theater, music. Address: 9 Brooklands Ct 14-16 Surbiton Rd Kingston-upon-Thames Surrey KT1 2HE England Personal E-mail: mprengler@hotmail.com.

PRENSKY, ARTHUR LAWRENCE, pediatric neurologist, educator; b. NYC, Aug. 31, 1930; s. Herman and Pearl (Newman) P.; m. Sheila Carr, Nov. 13, 1969. AB, Cornell U., 1951; MD, N.Y. U., 1955. Diplomate: Am. Bd. Psychiatry and Neurology. Intern Barnes Hosp., St. Louis, 1955-56; resident and research fellow in neurology Harvard U., Mass. Gen. Hosp., Boston, 1959-66; instr. neurology Harvard Med. Sch., 1966-67; mem. faculty Washington U. Sch. Medicine, St. Louis, 1967—, prof. pediatrics and neurology, to 1975, Allen P. and Josephine B. Green prof. pediatric neurology, 1975-2000, prof. emeritus of neurology, 2000—; pediatrician St. Louis Children's Hosp.; neurologist Barnes and Allied Hosps., Jewish Hosp., St. Louis. Vis. prof. Royal Children's Hosp., Melbourne, Australia, 2010. Author: (with others) Nutrition and the Developing Nervous System, 1975; editor: (with others) Neurological Pathophysiology, 2d edit, 1978, Advances in Neurology, 1976; mem. editorial bd. Pediatric Neurology, 1984-90, Jour. Child Neurology, 1985—. Served with USAF, 1957-59. Fellow Am. Acad. Neurology; mem. Am. Neurol. Assn., Am. Soc. Neurochemistry (mem. council 1973-77), Central Soc. Neurol. Rsch. (pres. 1977-78), Child Neurology Soc. (pres. 1979-80, Hower award 2000), Am. Pediatric Soc., Internat. Child Neurology Assn., Japanese Soc. Child Neurology, Profs. Child Neurology (pres. 1984-86) Office: 1 Children's Pl Saint Louis MO 63110-1014 Home: 1215 Moorland Woods Ct Saint Louis MO 63146 Office Phone: 314-454-6120, 314-780-0790. Business E-Mail: prenskya@neuro.wustl.edu.

PRESCOTT, JOHN E., medical association administrator, former dean; m. Charlotte Dillis; children: Katie, Amy, Allison. BS, MD, Georgetown U. Cert. emergency medicine. Faculty mem. W.Va. U., Morgantown, W.Va., 1990; pres. and CEO W.Va. U. Health Assoc., Morgantown, W.Va., 1999; chmn. dept. of emergency medicine W.Va. U., Morgantown, W.Va.; sr. assoc. dean W.Va. U. Sch. Medicine, Morgantown, W.Va., dean, 2004—08; chief academic officer Assn. American Med. Colleges, 2008—. Intern in emergency medicine Brooke Army Med. Ctr., San Antonio; founding chmn. W.Va. U. Dept. Emergency Medicine; founding dir. W.Va. U. Ctr. for Rural Emergency Medicine; bd. mem. comm. on the future of emergency care in the U.S. Inst. of Medicine, 1998—; mem. bd. dirs. Critical Illness and Trauma Found. Recipient Presdl. Heroism award, W.Va. U. Fellow: Am. Coll. of Emergency Medicine. Office: Assn American Med Colleges 2450 N St NW Washington DC 20037 Office Phone: 202-828-0533. Business E-Mail: jprescott@aamc.org. *

PRESCOTT, LAURIE FRANCIS, clinical pharmacology educator, physician; b. London, May 13, 1934; s. Frederick and Jessica (Raison) P.; m. Josephine Anne Carpentieri, Dec. 12, 1957; children: Nicholas, Katherine, Caroline, Christina; m. Jennifer Ann Gorvin, Sept. 6, 1980. MA, U. Cambridge, Eng., 1957, MB, BChir, 1960, MD, 1968. Resident medicine Boston City Hosp., 1962-63; rsch. fellow Johns Hopkins Hosp., Balt., 1963-65; lectr. dept. therapeutics U. Aberdeen, 1965-69; sr. lectr., reader dept. clin. pharmacology U. Edinburgh, Scotland, 1969-85, prof. clin. pharmacology, 1985-97, emeritus prof., 1997—. Cons. physician The Royal Infirmary, Edinburgh, 1969-95. Author: Paracetamol (Acetaminophen): A Critical Bibliographic Review, 1996, 2d edit., 2001; editor: Drug Absorption, 1979, Handbook of Clinical Pharmacokinetics, 1983, Rate Control in Drug Therapy, 1985, Novel Drug Delivery, 1989. With RAF, 1954-57. Fellow Royal Coll. Physicians Edinburgh, Royal Soc. Edinburgh, Royal Coll. Physicians (London), Faculty Pharm. Physicians. Avocations: music, gardening, sailing. Home: Redfern 24 Colinton Rd Edinburgh EH10 5EQ Scotland

PRESTI, SALVATORE, pediatric cardiologist, educator; MD, Facolta Di Medicina, Rome, 1978. Diplomate Am. Bd. Pediatrics, 1984, Am. Bd. Pediatrics pediatric cardiology, 2003. Resident pediat. Univ. Hosp. Brooklyn-SUNY Med. Ctr., 1979—80, Lenox Hill Hosp., NYC, 1980—82; fellow pediatric cardiology NYU Langone Med. Ctr., 1982—84; assoc. clin. prof. NYU Sch. Medicine. Co-author: (articles) Digoxin toxicity in a premature infant: treatment with Fab fragments of digoxin-specific antibodies, 1985, Cardiac Disease in Children with Human Immunodeficiency Virus (HIV) Infection (Abstract), 1989, Congenital fistulous tract between aorta and right atrium presenting as heart failure in a newborn, 1989, The disappearing pulmonary artery band, 1990, Results of urgent or emergency repair for symptomatic infants under one year of age with single or multiple ventricular septal defect, 1992, The intermittent ductus revisited: echocardiographic evidence and successful coil occlusion: a case report and review of literature, 1998. Office: New York University Langone Medical Center 110 E 59th St New York NY 10022 Office Phone: 212-832-9880. Office Fax: 212-644-8666.

PRESTON, ANDREW JOSEPH, pharmacist, drug company executive; b. Bklyn., Apr. 19, 1922; s. Charles A. and Josephine (Rizzutto) Pumo; m. Martha Jeanne Happ, Oct. 10, 1953; children: Andrew Joseph Jr., Charles Richard, Carolyn Louise, Frank Arthur, Joanne Marie, Barbara Jeanne. BSc, St. John's U., 1943. Cert. bus. intermediary Internat. Bus. Brokers Assn. Mgr. Press Club, Bklyn. Nat. League Baseball Club, 1941-42; purchasing agt. Drug and Pharm. divsn. Intrassind, Inc., 1947; chief pharmacist Hendershot Pharmacy, Newton, NJ, 1949; agt. Bur. of Narcotics, U.S. Treasury Dept., 1948-49; owner Preston Drug & Surg. Co., Boonton, NJ, 1949-86; CEO Preston Pharmaceutics, Inc., Butler, NJ, 1970-80, Preston Bus. Cons., Inc., Kinnelon, NJ, 1987—. Commr. NJ State Bd. Pharmacy, 1970—72, pres., 1973; organizer State of NJ Drug Abuse Spkrs. Program, 1970—76; chmn. Morris County Drug Abuse Coun., 1969—70; lectr. drug abuse and narcotic addition various cmty. orgns., 1968—78; mem. adv. bd. Nat. Cmty. Bank, Boonton, 1973. Contbr. editls. to profl. jours. Chmn. bldg. fund com. Riverside Hosp., Boonton, 1963; mem. exec. com. Gov. Tom Kean Ann. Ball, 1985—86; chmn. Pharmacists of NJ for election of Pres. Ford, 1976, Pharmacists for Gov. Tom Kean, 1981—84, NJ Pharmacists for Reagan/Bush, 1984; mem. exec. com. Morris County Overall Econ. Devel. Com., 1976—82; chmn. Pharmacists for Fenwick, 1982; v.p. Kinnelon (NJ) Rep. Club, 1980; Rep. com. Kinnelon, 1990; mem. adv. com. to Congressman Dean Gallo on Pres. Clinton's Health Security Plan, 1994; mem. Morris County (NJ) Rep. Fin. Com., 1972; pres. Ronald Reagan NJ Re-Election Adv. Bd., 1984. Lt. (j.g.) USNR, 1943—46. Recipient Bowl Hygeia award, Robbins Co., 1969, Pres.'s award, E.R. Squibb, 1968, Square Club award, NJ Pharm., 1969, Andrew J. Preston award for Polit. Action established in his honor, 1999, Spl. NJ Pharmacists award for loyal svc., NJ Pharm. Assn., NJ Polit. Action Com., 2002. Mem.: VFW, Morris-Sussex Pharmacists Soc., Morris County Pharm. Assn., NJ Pub. Health Assn., Pharmacists Guild NJ, Pharmacists Guild Am. (pres. NY divsn. 1946—47), Inst. Bus. Appraisers, Internat. Bus. Brokers Assn., NJ Narcotic Enforcement Officers Assn., Internat. Narcotic Enforcement Officers Assn., Nat. Cmty. Pharmacists Assn., NJ Pharm. Assn. (econs. com. 1960—65, pres. 1967—68, Oscar Singer Meml. award 1987, William H. McNeil award 1994, Presdl. Citation award 2000, Spl. NJ Pharmacists award 2002), Am. Pharm. Assn., St. John's Alumni Assn., NJ Assn. Realtors, Nat. Assn. Realtors, Morris County Bd. Realtors, Am. Legion, Smoke Rise Club, KC (4th Degree 2005), Elks. Roman Catholic. Home and Office: 507 Pepperidge Tree Ln Kinnelon NJ 07405-2223 Home Phone: 973-838-4873; Office Phone: 973-838-5342.

PRESTON, ELIZABETH A., psychologist; b. Missoula, Mont., May 9, 1957; d. Jay William and Elizabeth (Cummings) P.; children, Katherine Jennifer Lee, Jayson Douglas Lee. BA summa cum laude, U. Minn., 1979; PhD, Princeton U., 1984; Postdoctoral Cert., Calif. Sch. Profl. Psychology, 1988; student, Pacific Sch. Religion, Berkeley, 2009—10. Postdoctoral intern El Dorado County, Placerville, Calif., 1984-85, San Mateo (Calif.) County, 1985-87; adj. faculty Calif. Sch. Profl. Psychology, Berkeley, 1987; postdoctoral intern Kaiser Permanent, Santa Rosa, Calif., 1988-89; therapist Waldenhouse, Inc., San Francisco, 1989; clin. dir. Alinda Youth Svcs., Fairfield, Calif., 1990; therapist Kairos Unltd., Oakland, Calif.; pvt. practice Oakland, Calif., 1994—2011. Named Woman of Yr. in Medicine & Healthcare Am. Biog. Inst., 2010; NSF fellow, 1980-83; U. Mont. scholar, 1975-76, 77-78. Mem. Am. Psychol. Assn., Phi Beta Kappa, Phi Kappa Phi. Office: 4100-10 Redwood Rd 126 Oakland CA 94619 Office Phone: 510-482-5344. Business E-Mail: bethpreston@sbcglobal.net.

PRETELL-MAZZINI, JUAN ABELARDO AUGUSTO, pediatrician; b. Lima, Peru, June 23, 1976; MD, Alberto Hurtado Sch. Medicine, 2003. Cert. pediat. orthop. surgeon Children's Hosp. Phila., 2011. Pediat. orthop. fellow Children's Hosp. Phila., 2010—. Fellow, AO Switzerland. Mem.: AO Alumni, SOMACOT, SECOT, SICOT. Avocations: bowling, weightlifting, movies. Mailing: 212 Shoreline Dr Berwyn PA 19312 Personal E-mail: el_giova23@yahoo.com.

PRETI, ANTONIO, psychiatrist, researcher, educator; b. Cagliari, Italy, Apr. 23, 1958; s. Franco and Elena (Onnis) P.; m. Paola Miotto, Aug. 31, 1998. Degree in medicine, U. Cagliari, 1986; qualification in psychiatry, U. Padua, Italy, 1992. Med. diplomate. Intern Dept. Pharmacology, Cagliari, 1983-86, Dept. Psychiatry, Cagliari, 1987-88; asst. psychiatry br. Dept. Emergency, Padua, 1991-92; cons. CMG Health Ctr., Cagliari, 1995—; adj. prof. U. Chieti, Italy, 2006—07. Cons. jud. ct., Cagliari, 1995—; sr. lectr. dept. psychology U. Cagliari, 2000, adj. prof. clin. psychology, 2001—, child and adolescent neuropsychiatry, 2003-2005, biol. basis of behavior, U. Chieti, 2006-07; coun. mem. healthcare advisors Gerson Lehrman Group, 2004, sci. advisor and cons. Mental Health Dept., Milan, 2008-. Co-author: L'Aggressivita Carocci, Roma, 2002, Paranoia in the "Normal" Positions, Hauppauge, NY, 2011; contbr. articles to profl. jours. Mem. Italian Soc. Psychiatry, Soc. for Neurosci., European Soc. Clin. Neuropharmacology, N.Y. Acad. Sci., World Psychiat. Assn. (mem. psychotherapy sect. 2005-, co-chmn., 2008-). Avocations: photography, writing novels, music composition. Office: Genneruxi Med Ctr Via Costantinopoli 42 9129 Cagliari CA Italy E-mail: apreti@tin.it.

PRETORIUS, HESTER GERTIE, medical association administrator; b. South Africa, Aug. 7, 1959; BA, Rand Afrikaans U., 1979, DLitt et Phil in Psychology, 1989. Prof. psychology, coord. Rand Afrikaans U., 2001—02, prof., dep. chairperson, dept. psychology, coord., 2002—05; prof., acting chairperson, dept. psychology, coord. U. Johannesburg, 2005, dir., Inst. Child & Adult Guidance, 2005—08, dir., Psychol. Svcs. & Career Devel. Ctr., 2008 . Mem. senate U. Johannesburg, 2002—; vice chairperson, profl. bd. Psychology of Health Professions Coun. South Africa; rschr. Nat. Rsch. Found. Mem.: Internat. Family Therapy Assn., Health Professions Coun. South Africa (Counselling & Rsch. Psychologist). Avocations: reading, birdwatching. Office: PO Box 524 PsyCaD APK Auckland Pk Johannesburg Gauteng 2006 South Africa Business E-Mail: hgpretorius@uj.ac.za.

PREVIC, FRED HENRY, psychologist, educator; b. Pitts., Dec. 13, 1952; BA, Dartmouth Coll., 1974; PhD, U. NC, Greensboro, 1982. Rsch. physiologist Air Force Rsch. Lab., 1986—99; sr. human factors rschr. Northrop Grumman Info. Tech., 1999—2006; staff scientist SW Rsch. Inst., 2006—07; sci. tchr. Eleanor Kolitz Acad., 2008—09; lectr. Tex. A&M, San Antonio, 2010—. Cons. Wyle, Inc., 2010—. Author: (book) Spatial Disorientation in Aviation, 2004, The Dopaminergic Mind in Human Evolution and History, 2009. Named Civilian of Yr., Air Force Rsch. Lab. Mem.: Mind Sci. Found. Avocations: gardening, jogging, music. Home: 10906 Whispering Wind San Antonio TX 78230

PREVOR, RUTH CLAIRE, psychologist; b. NYC, June 20, 1944; d. Gustav and Greta (Dreifuss) Strauss; m. Sydney Joseph P., July 4, 1963; children: Joy, Grant, Jed. BA, U. P.R., 1966; PhD, Caribbean Ctr. of Postgrad., Studies, San Juan, 1988. Cert. forensic psychologist, critical incident stress debriefing. Asst. dean Caribbean Ctr. of Postgrad. Studies, 1986-87; dir. prenatal edn. Ashford Meml. Hosp., San Juan, 1987; pvt. practice San Juan, 1984—; advisor, field faculty Vt. Coll., Norwich U., 1990-91. V.p. bd. trustees Carlos Albizu U., San Juan and Miami campuses, 2001—09, bd. trustees, 2009-. Bd. dirs. Jewish Cmth. Ctr., Miramar, P.R., 1986—, pre-sch., 1990-98; pres. Home and Sch./St. John's Prep., San Juan, 1980-81, P.R. chpt. Hadassah Sch., 1972-74; presdl. adv. com., 1990-92. Mem. Am. Psychol. Assn., Assn. of Psychology of P.R. (hon. award 1984), Caribbean Counselors Assn., Nat. Assn. Children with Learning Disabilities, Nat. Register Health Svc. Providers in Psychology. Office: Ashford Med Ctr 29 Washington St Ste 300 San Juan PR 00907-2125 Office Phone: 787-722-0768.

PRIBAZ, JULIAN JOSEPH, plastic surgeon, medical educator; b. Trieste, Italy, June 3, 1948; MD, U. Melbourne, Australia, 1972. Diplomate Am. Bd. Plastic Surgery, 1986, registered in Medicine Mass., 1987, cert. added qualification in hand surgery 1990. Intern in gen. surgery St. Vincent's Hosp., Melbourne, 1973, resident in gen. surgery, 1974—76; resident in plastic surgery Southern Ill. U., Spingfield, 1980—82; resident in surgery Geelong Hosp.; resident in gen. surgery Salisbury Gen. Infirmary; clinical instr. plastic surgery U. Melbourne, 1982—87; clinical instr. surgery Harvard Med. Sch., Boston, 1987—89, asst. prof. surgery, 1989—94, assoc. prof. surgery, 1994—2002, prof. surgery, 2002—; with Children's Hosp. Boston, Brigham and Women's Hosp., Boston, 1987—, dir. Harvard plastic surgery residency tng. program, 1999—. Reviewer editl. bd. Microsurgery, 1987—, Jour. Reconstructive Microsurgery, 1992—, Annals of Plastic Surgery, 1992—; vis. prof. Plastic Surgery Ednl. Found.; BK rank traveling prof. Royal Australian Coll. Surgeons, 2000. Recipient Faculty Tchg. award, Harvard/Brigham/Children's, 1994, 1996, Faculty award, Harvard Med. Sch. Mem.: Assn. Academic Chmn. Plastic Surgery, Plastic Surgery Rsch. Coun., New England Soc. Plastic and Reconstructive Surgeons, Mass. Soc. Plastic Surgery, Mass. Med. Soc., Boston Hand Soc., Am. Soc. Plastic and Reconstructive Surgery, Am. Soc. Reconstructive Microsurgery (chmn. sci. program com.), Am. Soc. Surgery of Hand, AMA, Am. Assn. Hand Surgery (mem. sci. program com.). Office: Brigham and Womens

Hosp Divsn Plastic Surgery 75 Francis St Boston MA 02115 Office Phone: 617-732-6390. Office Fax: 617-732-6387. Business E-Mail: jjpribaz@bics.bwh.harvard.edu, jpribaz@partners.org.

PRIBITKIN, EDMUND A., medical educator; b. Sao Jose dos Campos, Brazil, May 14, 1960; BA, John Hopkins U., 1982; MD, U. Pa., 1986. Prof., vice chmn. Thomas Jefferson U., 1992—. Fellow: Am. Acad. Facial Plastic & Reconstructive Surgery, Am. Acad. Otolaryngology-Head & Neck Surgery. Avocations: basketball, gardening, travel. Office: Dept Otolaryngology-Head & Neck Surgery Philadelphia PA 19107 Office Fax: 267-200-0820. Business E-Mail: edmund.pribitkin@jefferson.edu.

PRICE, ANDY, health facility company executive, accountant; B in Acctg., Fla. State U., 1984. CPA. Sr. audit mgr. BDO Seidman, Atlanta, 1989—96; sr. v.p., corp. contr. Centennial HealthCare Corp., 1996—2004; v.p. ops. acctg. HealthSouth Corp., 2004—09, chief acctg. officer, 2009—. Office: HealthSouth Corp 3660 Grandview Pky Ste 200 Birmingham AL 35243 Office Phone: 205-967-7116. Office Fax: 205-969-3543. Business E-Mail: andy.price@healthsouth.com. *

PRICE, DOUGLAS ARMSTRONG, chiropractor; b. Pitts., Feb. 17, 1950; s. Walter Coachman and Janet (Armstrong) P.; m. Ann Georgette Martino, Jan. 31, 1989; 4 children. BA, Brown U., 1972; D Chiropractic, Life Chiropractic Coll., Atlanta, 1983. Diplomate Am. Bd. Chiropractic Examiners; cert. rehab. doctor; life extension physician; ind. med. examiner, Fla., in whiplash and brain injury traumatology. Owner, CEO Applied Biomech. and Musculoskeletal Rehab., Tampa, 1989—, All Am. Chiropractic Clinic; pvt. practice Tampa, 1984—, Manalapan, Fla., 1994-96; clin. dir. Camber Clinics, South Tampa, Haines City, Fla., 1999—2001, Fla. Pain, Trauma, and Injury Clinics, Tampa, 2001—. Dir. Myofascial Therapy Found. Author: Protocols for Practioners Utilizing Myofascial Trigger Point Treatment, 1998; prodr. therapeutic exercise video for cervical and lumbar rehab.; contbr. articles to profl. jours. Magnetic Resonance Imaging fellow; named to Brown U. Athletic Hall of Fame; Southeastern Masters Champion Shotput, Discus, 1990-91. Fellow: Am. Gerontology Assn., Chiropractic Rehab. Assn., Am. Coll. Sports Medicine; mem.: APHA, Hillsborough County Chiropractic Soc. (bd. dirs. 1990—93, pres. 1992—93), Fla. Chiropractic Assn., Am. Chiropractic Assn., KC (trustee). Democrat. Roman Catholic. Achievements include research in Russian stimulation applications in low back rehabilitation; application of micro and interferential currents with utilization of manual travel myofascial release techniques, use of micro and interferential currents with manual treatment of myofascial pain syndromes. Home: 90 W Davis Blvd Tampa FL 33606-3535 Office Phone: 813-849-2459. Personal E-mail: douglasmyodoc@aol.com.

PRICE, ELY, dermatologist; b. NYC, Aug. 9, 1932; s. Jacob and Mary P.; m. Joan Savitt, Jan. 18, 2009; children from previous marriage: Jeremy, Andrew. BS cum laude, CCNY, 1953; AM, Ind. U., 1956; MD, U. Lausanne, Switzerland, 1964. Diplomate Am. Bd. Dermatology. Intern Brookdale Hosp. Med. Ctr., Bklyn., 1964-65, resident internal medicine, 1965-66; fellow Mt. Sinai Hosp., NYC, 1965-66; resident in dermatology Kings County Hosp., Bklyn., 1966-69; practice dermatology Bay Ridge Skin and Cancer Dermatology, P.C., Bklyn., 1969—; attending-in-charge, head dermatology Maimonides Med. Ctr., Bklyn., 1985—; clin. assoc. prof. dermatology SUNY Sci. Ctr., Bklyn., 1985—. Cons. in medicine Luth. Med. Ctr., Bklyn., 1988—; cons. in dermatology Victory Med. Hosp., Bklyn., 1989—. Fellow ACP, Am. Acad. Dermatology, Am. Soc. Dermatol. Surgery, N.Y. Acad. Medicine. Avocation: golf. Office: Bay Ridge Skin & Cancer Dermatology PC 9921 4th Ave Brooklyn NY 11209-8347 Home: 5598 Vista Del Mando S Unit B Laguna Woods CA 92637-6923

PRICE, JUDITH HOLM, educational psychologist; b. Milw., Nov. 6, 1937; d. Paul James and Dorothy Ruth (Munton) Holm; m. Thomas Munro Price, Aug. 8, 1959; children: Scott Michael, Andrea Lynn. BA, Carroll Coll., 1959; MA, U. Iowa, 1973; PhD, U. Wyo., 1980. Nat. cert. sch. psychologist. Tchr. Waukesha Pub. Sch., Wis., 1959, Madison Pub. Sch., 1959-63; preschool assessment specialist Grant Wood Area Edn. Agy. 10, Cedar Rapids, Iowa, 1976-78; Ednl. Resource Ctr. facilitator Albany County Sch. Dist. 1, Laramie, Wyo., 1980-89, dir. spl. svc., 1989—93; acad. dean Brush Ranch Sch., Tererro, N.Mex., 1993—96; hist. home renovator Yerington, Nev., 1997—. Substitute tchr. Melbourne (Australia) Sch., 1978; temporary prof. U. Wyo., Laramie, 1981, 84; mem. computer conf. com. Wyo. Dept. Edn., Casper, 1984-85, com. for devel. spl. edn. database, 1987, task force cert. standards for early childhood spl. edn. tchr., 1988; speaker Wyo. Fedn. CEC, Riverton, 1986, task force on specific learning disability criteria, 1988; conf. mem. Council for Exceptional Children Software Conf., Washington, 1986; provider state-wide inservice Specific Learning Disability Criteria, 1988. Spl. edn. rules and regulations task force Wyo. Dept. Edn., 1990—92; mem. Wyo. gov. Early Intervention Coun., 1990—93; governing bd. pres. South Lyon Health Ctr., Inc., 2003—07, dir., 2001—; chmn. South Lyon Healthcare Found., Inc., 2007—. Mem. Nat. Assn. Sch. Psychologists (alt. del. 1983), Wyo. Sch. Psychoednl. Assn., Council for Exceptional Children (com. specific learning disability 1987-88, speaker 1988, pres. Frontier chpt. 1989), Assn. Curriculum Devel., N.Mex. Assn. Non-Pub. Sch., Rotary Internat. Yerington Club (co-pres. 2008-09), Phi Kappa Phi, Phi Delta Kappa, 2003. Avocations: computers, skiing, camping, travel. Office: The Nordyke House 727 State Route 339 Yerington NV 89447-9553

PRICE, MAX RODNEY, academic administrator, medical educator; b. Johannesburg, Oct. 6, 1955; s. Alan Price and Ellen Katzenstein; m. Deborah Posel, Sept. 25, 1988; children: Jessica Posel, Ilan Shaun Posel. MB BCh, U. Witwatersrand, Johannesburg, 1979; BA (PPE), Oxford U., United Kingdom, 1980—83; MSc (Cmty. Health), London Sch. of Hygiene and Tropical Medicine, London, 1985—86; Diploma in Occupaitonal Health, U. of Witwatersrand, Johannesburg, 1991—92. Med. intern Baragwanath Hosp., Soweto, South Africa, 1980; sr. ho. officer Johannesburg Hosp., 1984; med. rsch. officer health sys. devel. unit Tintswalo Hosp., Acornhoek, Gazankulu, South Africa, 1985; rsch. fellow London Sch. Hygiene and Tropical Medicine, 1986—87; from sr. rschr. to dir. Ctr. for Health Policy U. Witwatersrand, Johannesburg, 1988—95, dean Faculty Health Scis., 1996—2006; vice-chancellor designate U. Cape Town, 2007—08, vice-chancellor, 2008—. Chair bd. dirs. Wits Health Consortium, Johannesburg, 1998—; dir. Wits Donald Gordon Med. Centre, Johannesburg, 2002—; mem. Med. and Dental Professions Bd., Pretoria, South Africa, 1999—; chmn. Undergraduate Edn. and Tng. Com. ofMed. and Dental Professions Bd., Pretoria, 2004—. Contbr. articles to profl. jours. Mem. exec. com. Nat. Med. and Dental Assn., South Africa, 1984—93; mem. South African Bd. Jewish Edn., 2000—03. Hon. fellow, Colls. Medicine South Africa, 2004. Jewish. Office: Univ Cape Town Private Bag X3 Rondebosch 7701 South Africa Home: 74 Kilkenny Rd 2193 Johannesburg 2193 South Africa Office Fax: 27-11-6423533. Personal E-mail: max.price@uct.ac.za.

PRICE, ROBERT ALAN, physicist, researcher; b. Liverpool, Merseyside, Eng., Aug. 27, 1959; s. William George and Iris Price; m. Gillian Kay Clark, Dec. 23, 1995. BSc, Open U., Eng.; MS in Med. Physics, Surrey U., Eng., 1993; PhD, Imperial Coll., London U., 1997. Registered clinical scientist Health Professions Coun., 2005. Rsch. scientist Mod, London, 1980—86, Ferranti PLC, Weymouth, 1986—87; sr. cons. Theta Systems and Analysis, Aldershot, 1990—92; lectr. MoD, London, 1993—94; rsch. scientist Imperial Coll., U. London, 1997—98; principle physicist Clatterbridge Ctr. Oncology, NHS Trust, Wirral, Merseyside, 1998—2004; assoc. dean rsch., rsch. dir. City U., London, 2004—. Rsch. dir. City U., London, 2004—, chmn. ethics com., 2005—. Achievements include development of First 4 dimensional QA system for Intensity modulated Radiotherapy; linear Metal Oxide Field Effect Transistor Array for intracavitary Radiation Dosimetry; research in Fundimental limits of dose measurement using semicoductor devices. Office: City U Inst Health Sci Northampton Sq London EC1V OHB England Office Fax: +44 20 7040 5690. Personal E-mail: rprice1495@aol.com. E-mail: r.price@city.ac.uk.

PRICE, THEODORA HADZISTELIOU, mental health services professional; b. Athens, Greece, Oct. 1, 1938; arrived in U.S., 1967; d. Ioannis and Evangelia (Emmanuel) Hadzisteliou; m. David C. Long Price, Dec. 26, 1966 (div. 1989); children: Morgan N., Alkes D. L. Diploma in piano tchg., Nat. Conservatory, Athens, 1958; BA in History/Archaeology, U. Athens, 1961; DPhil, U. Oxford, Eng., 1966; MA in Clin. Social Work, U. Chgo., 1988. LCSW. Mus. asst., resident tutor U. Sydney, 1966-67; instr. anthropology Adelphi U., NYC, 1967-68; archaeologist Hebrew Union Coll., Gezer, Israel, 1968; asst. prof. classical archaeology/art U. Chgo., 1968-70; jr. rsch. fellow Harvard Ctr. Hellenic Studies, Washington, 1970-71; clin. social worker Harbor Light Ctr., Salvation Army, Chgo., 1988-89; therapist Inst. Motivational Devel., Lombard, Ill., 1989-90; caseworker & therapist Jewish Family & Cmty. Svc., Chgo., 1989—90; staff therapist Family Svc. Ctrs. of South Cook County, Chicago Heights, 1990-91; pvt. practice child, adolescent, family therapy Bolingbrook, Ill., 1990—; dir. counseling svcs., clin. supr., psychotherapist Family Link, Inc., Chgo., 1993; staff therapist Cen. Bapt. Family Svcs., Gracell Rehab., Chgo., 1991, 91-92; casework supr., counselor Epilepsy Found. Greater Chgo., Chgo., 1992-93; therapist children, adolescents and families dept. foster care Cath. Charities, Chgo., 1993-94; individual and family therapist South Ctrl. Cmty. Svcs. Individual-Family Counseling Svcs., Chgo. Heights, 1994-97. Bd. dirs., counselor Naperville Sch. Gifted and Talented, 1982—84; lectr. in field. Author: (monograph) Kourotrophos, Cults and Representations of the Greek Nursing Deities, 1978; contbr. articles to profl. jours. Eleutherios Venizelos scholar, 1962—65, Meyerstein Traveling grantee, Oxford, Eng., 1963, 1964. Mem.: NASW, Bd. Cert. Diplomate, Am. Bd. Clin. Soc. Workers, Ill. Clin. Social Workers, Nat. Acad. Clin. Social Workers. Avocations: piano, Byzantine chanting, writing. Home and Office: 10 Pebble Ct Bolingbrook IL 60440-1557 Office Phone: 630-378-1187.

PRICE, TREVOR ROBERT PRYCE, psychiatrist, educator; b. Concord, NH, Nov. 29, 1943; BA, Yale U., 1965; MD, Columbia U., 1969. Diplomate Am. Bd. Psychiatry and Neurology (sr. examiner l985—), with Geriatric Psychiatry, Am. Bd. Internal Medicine, Nat. Bd. Med. Examiners. Intern in medicine Med. Ctr. U. Calif., San Francisco, 1969-70; resident in internal medicine Med. Ctr. of U. Calif., San Francisco, 1972-74; resident in psychiatry Dartmouth Med. Sch., Hanover, N.H., 1974-77, asst. prof., assoc. prof. psychiatry and medicine, 1977-85; assoc. prof., prof. psychiatry U. Pa. Sch. Medicine, Phila., 1985—88; dir. psychiat. in-patient svcs. Hosp. of U. Pa., 1985-88; prof. psychiatry Med. Coll. Pa., Pitts., 1989-90, prof. psychiatry and medicine, 1991-95, 1993—2002; chmn. dept. psychiatry Med. Coll. Pa. and Hahnemann U., Pitts., 1989-95, sr. assoc. dean, 1993-95; pres., CEO Allegheny Neuropsychiat. Inst., Pitts., 1994—98, exec. dir., 1994—; chmn. dept. psychiatry Med. Coll. Pa. Hahnemann Sch. Medicine, Phila., 1995—2002; prof. psychiatry and med. Drexel U. Coll. Med., Phila., 2002—03, chmn. dept. psychiatry, 2002; pvt. practice Bryn Mawr, Pa., 2002—; pres., treas. Price & Price Practices Psychiatry, PC, Bryn Mawr, 2003—. Bd. dirs. Coll. Health Consortium, Inc., Phila., Highland Dr. Rsch. and Edn. Found., Yale Club Pitts., Pitts. Psychoanalytic Found., Med. Coll. Pa. Hosp.; mem. blue ribbon bd. Alzheimer's Disease Alliance, Western Pa., 1989-97; mem. governing bd. Med. Coll. of Pa. Hosp., 1999-2002. Mem. editl. bd. Convulsive Therapy, 1984-94, Jour. Neuropsychiatry and Clin. Neurosci., 1992—, Allegheny Gen. Hosp. Jour. Neurosci., 1992-98, Seminars in Neuropsychiatry, 1995—; editl. reviewer 15 psychiat. and med. jours., 1978; contbr. chpts. to books and articles in profl. jours. Mem. N.H. Commn. on Laws Effecting Mental Health, 1974-75; bd. dirs. Advanced Studies Program, Friends of St. Paul's Sch., Concord, N.H., 1983-87. Recipient William C. Menninger award Ctrl. Neuropsychiat. Assn., 1977, Faculty Teaching award dept. psychiatry Dartmouth Med. Sch., 1984, Pres. award for Exceptional Achievement AHERF, 1994, numerous grants. Fellow: Am. Coll. Psychiatrists, Am. Neuropsychiat. Assn. (bd. dirs. 1993—95, exec. dir. 1995), Am. Psychiat. Assn. (disting. life fellow); mem.: Assn. Medicine and Psychiatry, Assn. Convulsive Therapy, Assn. Acad. Psychiatry, Am. Assn. Dirs. Psychiat. Residency Tng., Assn. for Acad. Psychiatry, Soc. Biol. Psychiatry, Am. Assn. Chairmen of Depts. Psychiatry, Pa. Psychiat. Assn., Columbia Club of Phila., Yale Club Phila., H-Y-P Club Pitts., Yale Club Pitts. Avocations: fly fishing, tennis, reading, piano, kayaking. Office: 950 Haverford Rd Ste 302 Bryn Mawr PA 19010 Office Phone: 610-527-5926. Personal E-mail: myTwins2@verizon.net.

PRICKETT, DAVID CLINTON, physician; b. Fairmont, W.Va., Nov. 26, 1918; s. Clinton Everett and Mary Anna (Gottschalk) Prickett; m. Mary Ellen Holt, June 29, 1940 (dec. Feb. 1987); children: David C., Rebecca Ellen, William Radcliffe, Mary Anne, James Thomas, Sara Elizabeth; m. Pamela S. Blackstone, Nov. 17, 1991 (dec. Mar. 2002). Student, Fairmont State Coll., 1940—42; AB, W.Va. U., 1944; MD, U. Louisville, 1946; MPH, U. Pitts., 1955. Pres. Prickett Chem. Co., 1938-43; acct. W.Va. Conservation Commn. and Fed. Works Agy., 1941, 42; lab. asst., instr. chemistry W.Va. U., 1943; intern Louisville Gen. Hosp., 1947; surg. resident St. Joseph's Hosp., Parkersburg, W.Va., 1948-49; gen. practice W.Va., 1948-50, 55-61; mem. staff Fairmont (W.Va.) Gen. Hosp., 1955-60, Fairmont Emergency Hosp., 1955-60; physician USAF, N.Mex. and Calif., 1961-62, U.S. Army, Fort Ord, Calif., 1963-64; resident physician San Luis Obispo County Hosp., 1965-66; pvt. practice LA, 1967—; mem. staff St. Francis Hosp., LA, 1970-71; physician So. Calif. Edison Co., 1981-84. Physician Bethlehem Mines Corp., Idamay, W.Va., 1956; resident physician Sedgwick County Hosp., Wichita, Kans., 1964-65; med. dir. South Gate auto assembly plant GM, 1969-71; staff physician City of LA, 1971-76; relief med. practice Appalachia summer seasons, W.Va. and Ky., 1977, 86, 88-97. Author: The Newer Epidemiology, 1962, rev., 1990, Public Health, A Science Resolvable by Mathematics, 1965; contbr. articles to profl. jours. Sr. counsellor, US Commercial Travelers, Fairmont, W.Va., 1939-40; med. officer USPHS, Navajo Indian Reservation, Tohatchi (N.Mex.) Health Ctr., 1953-55, surgeon, res. officer, 1957-59; pres. W.Va. Pub. Health Assn., 1951-52; sec. indsl. and pub. health sect. W.Va. Med. Assn., 1956; W.Va. dist. 4 health officer; health officer Marion County, W.Va., 1951-53; dist. health officer Allegheny County, Pa., 1957; officer Aux. Civil Def. Police, W.Va., 1942; med. advisor Boy Scouts Am., W.Va., 1956-57, N.Mex., 1954; mem. Med. Rsv. Corps of LA, 2005—. 2d lt. AUS, 1943-46. Dr. Thomas Parran fellow U. Pitts. Sch. Pub. Health, 1955; named to Hon. Order Ky. Cols. Fellow APHA; mem. AMA, Am. Occupl. Med. Assn., Am. Acad. Family Physicians, Western Occupl. Med. Assn., Calif. Med. Assn., Los Angeles County Med. Assn., SR, W.Va., Am. Legion, Elks, Sierra Club Calif., Rio Hondo Symphony Guild, Phi Chi. Avocations: photography, amateur radio, square and round dancing, history, church choir. Address: PO Box 4032 Whittier CA 90607-4032 Office Phone: 626-330-4106.

PRIDHAM, THOMAS GRENVILLE, retired microbiologist; b. Chgo., Oct. 10, 1920; s. Grenville and Gladys Etheral (Sloss) P.; m. Phyllis Sue Hokamp, July 1, 1943 (dec. Feb. 1994); children: Pamela Sue, Thomas Foster, Grenville Thomas, Rolf Thomas, Montgomery Thomas; m. Edna Lee Boudreaux, Mar. 6, 1995 (dec. Apr. 2006). BS Chemistry, U. Ill., 1943, PhD Bacteriology, 1949. Instr. bacteriology U. Ill., Champaign-Urbana, 1947; rsch. microbiologist No. Regional Rsch. Lab., USDA, Peoria, Ill., 1948—51, No. Regional Rsch. Lab. USDA, Peoria, 1953—65, U.S. Indsl. Chem., Balt., 1951—52; supr. tech. ops. Acme Vitamins, Inc., Joliet, Ill., 1952—53; sr. rsch. biologist U.S. Borax Rsch. Corp., Anaheim, Calif., 1965—67; supervisory rsch. microbiologist No. Regional Rsch. Ctr. USDA, Peoria, 1967—81, head agrl. rsch. culture collection No. Regional Rsch. Lab., 1967—81; ret., 1981. Cons. Mycogen Corp., San Diego, 1985-87; U.S. sr. scientist Germany, Darmstadt, 1977 Contbg. author: Actinomycetales: The Boundary Microorganisms, 1974, Bergey's Manual of Determinative Bacteriology, 1974, Synopsis and Classification of Living Organisms, 1982; mem. editl. bd. Jour. Antibiotics, 1969-81; contbr. articles to Jour. Bacteriology, Applied Microbiology, Phytopathology, Actinomycetes, Mycologia, Devel. Indsl. Microbiology, Jour. Antibiotics, Internat. Bull. Bacteriological Nomenclature Taxonomy, Antibiotics Ann., Antimicrobial Agts., Chemotherapy, also others With USNR, 1943-45, with Rsch. Res., 1948-54, lt. ret. Fulbright scholar, Italy, 1952; grantee Soc. Am. Bacteriologists, 1957 Fellow: Am. Acad. Microbiology; mem.: Alexander von Humboldt Assn. Episcopalian. Achievements include patents in fermentative production of riboflavin and of antibiotics; research in microbial culture collection technology and management, systematics of streptomycetes, industrial microbiology. Home: Rancho Del Rey Mobile Home Estates 208 PO Box 1098 Sunset Beach CA 90742

PRIEGO, VICTOR M., oncologist, hematologist, educator; MD, Autonomous U. Guadalajara. Diplomate Am. Bd. Internal Medicine, Am. Bd. Internal Medicine-med. oncology. Resident in internal medicine Providence Hosp., DC; fellow in hematology and oncology Howard Univ. Hosp., Georgetown Univ. Med. Ctr.; fellow in hematology and oncology Lombardi Cancer Rsch. Ctr. Georgetown Univ.; prin. investigator eastern coop. oncology group Suburban Hosp.; clin. asst. prof. medicine Georgetown Univ.; co-founder Ctr. for Cancer and Blood Disorders, Md., hematologist/oncologist, 1995—. Named one of Top Oncologists and Hematologists, Wash. Mag., 2005—. Mem.: Pan Am. Med. Soc. (pres., Wash. met. area 2010), Am. Soc. Hematology, Am. Soc. Clin. Oncology, Am. Coll. Physicians. Office: Center for Cancer and Blood Disorders 6420 Rockledge Dr Bethesda MD 20817 Office Phone: 301-571-0019. Office Fax: 301-571-0988.

PRIMACK, BRIAN ADAM, physician; b. NYC, Apr. 22, 1969; s. Aron and Karen (Margolis) Primack; m. Jennifer Hope Engel. BA magna cum laude in English and Math with distinction in English, Yale U., New Haven, 1991; EdM, Harvard U., Cambridge, Mass., 1993; MD summa cum laude, Emory U., Atlanta, 1999; MS in Methodology, U. Pitts., 2008. Lic. physician Pa., 2001, diplomate Am. Bd. Family Practice. Counselor Yale U., New Haven, 1986—87; tchr. Am. Sch. of Niamey, Niamey, West Africa, Niger, 1991—92; instr. math. U. Md., College Park, 1993—95; resident dir. Emory U., Atlanta, 1995—97; dean of students Exploration Summer Program, Wellesley, Mass., 2000; family practice resident UPMC St. Margaret Hosp., Pitts., 1999—2002; asst. prof. sch. medicine U. Pitts., Pitts., 2002—. Actor: Gemini Theater Comedy Improvisation Troupe, 1999—2003, Cloak and Dagger Dinner Theater, 2000, Murder Upon Request Theater Group, 1997, Romeo and Juliet, 1995. Pres., bd. dirs. American Cancer Soc., 2010—; v.p. bd. dirs. Am. Cancer Soc., 2008—10. Recipient Gaston Cmty. Svc. award, Emory U. Sch. Medicine, 1997, Saybrook Fellows prize, Yale U., 1991, Am. Cancer Soc. award, 2003, Innovation in Edn. award, U. Pa., 2005, Bronze Telly award, 2006, New Investigator award, Soc. Adolescent Health and Medicine, 2006, Junior Faculty Scholar award, U. Pitts. Cancer Inst., 2010, Early Career Investigator award, Soc. Behavioral Medicine, 2010; named Niger Nat. Champion, Jeux Mathematique Math. Competition, 1992; Robert W. Woodruff fellow, Emory U., 1995, Robert Wood Johnson Physician Faculty scholar, 2006. Mem.: Nat. Assn. Media Literacy Edn., Soc. Behavioral Medicine, Soc. Adolescent Medicine (New Investigator award 2006). Avocations: guitar, harmonica, piano. Personal E-mail: bprimack@pitt.edu.

PRIMM, RICHARD KIRBY, physician; b. Thomasville, NC, May 23, 1944; s. Richard Wesley and Gertrude (Berrier) P.; m. Sharon Kay Lucas, Dec. 28, 1968; children: Heather, Lucas. BA, Duke U., 1966; postgrad., Baylor U., 1966-67; MD, U. N.C., 1970. Intern internal medicine Vanderbilt U. Hosp., Nashville, 1970-71, resident in internal medicine, 1973-75, chief resident, 1975-76; fellow cardiovascular diseases U. Ala., Birmingham, 1976-78, chief fellow, instr. medicine,

1978-79; asst. prof. medicine Vanderbilt U. Sch. Medicine, Nashville, 1979-84; staff cardiologist Wenatchee Valley Med. Ctr., 1984—. Clin. asst. prof. medicine U. Wash., Seattle, 1985-91, clin. assoc. prof. medicine, 1991-2003, clin. prof. medicine, 2003—; adminstrv. lead dept. cardiology Wenatchee Valley Clinic, 1987-91, 1997-2006. Contbr. articles to profl. jours. Capt. U.S. Army, 1971-73. Recipient Heusner Pupil award U. N.C., 1969, Hillman Teaching Excellence award Vanderbilt U., 1976. Fellow: Am. Coll. Cardiology (gov. Wash. chpt. 2002—05); mem.: AHA, Wash. Heart Assn. (trustee 1990—94), North Pacific Soc. Internal Medicine (pres. 2007), Physicians for Social Responsibility, Alpha Omega Alpha. Avocations: backpacking, skiing. Office: Wenatchee Valley Med Ctr 820 N Chelan Ave Wenatchee WA 98801-2028 Home Phone: 509-662-3789; Office Phone: 509-663-8711. Business E-Mail: rprimm@wvmedical.com.

PRIMUS, WENDELL, legislative staff member; b. Eldora, Iowa; BA, Iowa State U., Ames, PhD in Econs. Asst. prof. econs. Georgetown U., Washington; subcom. on human resources staff dir., ways and means com. US House of Reps., Washington, chief economist, ways and means com., minority staff dir., joint econ. com., 2003—05, sr. policy advisor budget and health, Rep. Nancy Pelosi, 2005—; dep. asst. sec. human services policy US Dept. Health and Human Services, Washington, 1993—97; dir. income and security Ctr. on Budget and Policy Priorities, Washington, 1997—2003. Vis. prof. law and pub. policy U. Md. Democrat. Office: 235 Cannon House Office Bldg Washington DC 20515 Office Phone: 202-225-4965. Office Fax: 202-225-8259.

PRINCETON, JOY CAROL, retired nursing educator; b. St. Paul, Dec. 8, 1935; d. Eugene Russell Princeton and Margaret Edna Ehlers Princeton; children: Todd A. Myers, Michael D. Myers, Sarah C. Mooney. BSN, U. Colo., 1969, MSN, 1970, MA in Anthropology, 1975, PhD in Anthropology, 1977. RN Minn., Colo., N.C., Utah. Head nurse, obstetrics Abbott Hosp., Mpls., 1958—65; supr. obstetrics Boulder Meml. Hosp., Colo., 1965—68; asst. prof. U. Co. Sch. Nursing, Denver, 1970—73; assoc. prof. Duke U. Sch. Nursing, Durham, NC, 1978—81; prof. U. Utah Coll. Nursing, Salt Lake City, 1982—95; assoc. dir. U. Hosp., Salt Lake City, 1987—91. Mem. White House Com. on Children & Youth, Colo. Chpt., Denver, 1970—73; expert panel mem. Am. Acad. Nursing, Culturally Competent and Sensitive Health Care, Washington, 1991—93; cons. U. N.C. Med. Sch., Chapel Hill, NC, 1984—85, U. Rochester Sch. of Nursing, NY, 1988, NIH, Nat. Ctr. Nursing Rsch., 1988, U. Capetown Sch. Medicine, South Africa, 1990—91, HHS, PHS Divsn. Nursing, Rockville, Md., 1987—88, 1990—91, St. Louis U. Med. Ctr., 1990—91, Regis Coll. Sch. of Nursing, Denver, 1990—91; adv. Utah State Dept. Health, Salt Lake City, 1991—92; cons. in field, grad. student mentor, 1995—. Author: Maternity Nursing Today, 1973—77 (Am. Nurses Assn. Book of Yr., Parent/Child Nursing, 1973); mem. editl. bd.: Health Care for Women, 1984—94, Medical Anthro Quar., 1984—88, 1993—94, Scholarly Inquiry for Nursing Practice, 1985—90, Jour. Profl. Nursing, 1985—91, 1994—97, Jour. Nursing Edn., 1991—94, Nursing Outlook Jour., 1993—94; contbr. articles to profl. jours.; review panel mem. profl. jours., 1995—2006. Named Nurse of Yr., NC Nurses Assn., 1980; grantee, Dept. Health and Human Svcs., 1982—95, Ednl. grants, Dept. Health, Edn. and Welfare, U. Colo. Programs, 1970—73, grants for master's and doctoral edn., U.S. Pub. Health Svc., 1982—95. Fellow: Soc. Applied Anthropology, Am. Acad. Nursing. Democrat. Avocations: library work, hiking, camping, travel. Home: 2720 14th St Boulder CO 80304 Office Phone: 303-444-8163.

PRINCIPI, ANTHONY JOSEPH, information technology executive; b. NYC, Apr. 16, 1944; s. Antonio Joseph and Theresa (Principotta) P.; m. Elizabeth Ann Ahlering, June 26, 1971; children: Anthony Jr., Ryan, John BS, U.S. Naval Acad., 1967; JD, Seton Hall U., 1975. Commd. 2d lt. U.S. Navy, 1967, advanced through grades to comdr., 1984, line officer Washington, 1967-72; atty. JAGC, San Diego, 1975-80; counsel Com. on Armed Service U.S. Senate, Washington, 1980-83, staff dir. Com. on Vet.'s Affairs, 1984—88; dep. adminstr. congl. & pub. affairs VA, Washington, 1983-84; dep. sec. US Dept. Veterans Affairs, Washington, 1989-90, acting sec., 1992—93; ptnr. Luce, Forward, Hamilton & Scripps, San Diego, 1990-95; sr. v.p., CEO Lockheed Martin IMS Integrated Solutions Co., Santa Clara, Calif., 1995-2001; pres. QTC Medical Services, Inc., 2001; sec. US Dept. Veterans Affairs, Washington, 2001—05; chmn. QTC Management, Inc., Alexandria, Va., 2005—; v.p., govt. rels. Pfizer, Inc., 2005—, sr. v.p. Chmn. Base Realignment & Closure (BRAC) Commn., 2005—; bd. dirs. Perot Sys. Corp., 2005—, Mut. of Omaha Ins. Co., 2005—. Decorated Bronze Star with combat "V", Vietnamese Cross of Gallantry, Navy Commendation medal with combat "V" (3); recipient Meritorious Service medal VA, 1983 Mem. ABA (chmn. subcom. gen. practice sect. 1985—) Republican. Roman Catholic. Avocations: gardening, skiing. Mailing: QTC Management Inc PO Box 5679 Diamond Bar CA 91765 Home Fax: 909-859-2101. Business E-Mail: aprincipi@qtcm.com. *

PRINGLE, KEVIN CRAIG, pediatric surgeon, medical researcher; s. George William and Valerie Mary Pringle; m. Carol Ann Pringle; children: Julie Anne Kitchen, Fiona Mary, Craig William. MB, ChB, U. Otago, Dunedin, New Zealand, 1970. Surg. registrar Dunedin Hosp., Dunedin, Otago, New Zealand, 1973—75; pediat. surg. registrar Royal Children's Hosp., Melbourne, Victoria, Australia, 1975—77; pediat. surgery fellow U. Chgo., 1977—78; asst. prof. pediat. surgery U. Ill., 1978—81; from asst. prof. to assoc. prof. pediat. surgery U. Iowa, Iowa City, 1981—87; sr. lectr. pediat. surgery Wellington Sch. Medicine, Wellington, New Zealand, 1987—90, assoc. prof. pediat. surgery, 1990—2000; prof. pediat. surgery, head dept. ob-gyn. Sch. Medicine and Health Scis. U. Otago, New Zealand, 2000—02, prof. pediat. surgery, head dept. surgery and anaesthesia and ob-gyn., 2002—06, prof. pediat. surgery, head dept. ob-gyn, 2006—. Founding co-editor in chief Fetal Diagnosis and Therapy, Basel, Switzerland, 1986—. Contbr. articles to profl. jours. Fellow: Royal Australasian Coll. Surgeons; mem.: Pacific Assn. Pediatric Surgeons (pres. 2006—07), Internat. Fetal Medicine & Surgery Soc. (pres. 1989—90). Achievements include research in lung devel. in diaphragmatic hernia and into renal devel. in obstructive uropathy. Office: Wellington Sch Medicine & Health Sci Dept Obs & Gyn P O Box 7343 Newtown 6242 Wellington New Zealand Office Fax: 64 4 389-5318. E-mail: kevin.pringle@otago.ac.nz. *

PRINN, RONALD G., atmospheric science educator; b. Hamilton, New Zealand, June 11, 1945; BSc, U. Auckland, New Zealand, 1967, MSc with 1st honors, 1968; ScD, MIT, 1971. Asst. prof. MIT, Cambridge, Mass., 1971-76, assoc. prof., 1976-82, prof., 1982-93, Tokyo Electric Power Co. prof., 1993—, head dept. earth, atmospheric and planetary scis., 1998—2003. Chair com. on earth sci. NAS, Washington, 1982-84; chair Internat. Global Atmospheric Chemistry Project, Stockholm, 1988-95. Recipient Vernadsky Meml. lectr. Russian Acad. Sci., Moscow, 1984. Fellow Am. Geophys. Union (Macelwane medal 1981), AAAS (chmn. atmospheric and hydrospheric scis. 1999). Office: MIT Bldg 54-1312 Cambridge MA 02139 Business E-Mail: rprinn@mit.edu.

PRINZ, RICHARD ALLEN, surgeon; b. Chgo., Ill., May 13, 1946; MD, Loyola U., Chgo., 1972. Diplomate Am. Bd. Surgery, bd. dirs., 1994—. Intern Barnes Hosp., St. Louis, 1972-73, resident in surgery, 1973-74, Loyola U., Chgo., 1974-77, attending surgeon, 1980-93; staff Rush Presbyn.-St. Luke's Med. Ctr., Chgo., 1993—; Helen Shedd Keith prof., chmn. dept. gen. surgery Rush U., Chgo., 1993—. Mem. Am. Surg. Assn., Am. Assn. Endocrine Surgeons (pres. 1996), Midwest Surg. Assn. (pres. 1997), Western Surg. Assn. (treas. 1993-97, pres. 2002-), Chgo. Surg. Soc. (pres.-elect 2002-, pres. 2003). Office: Rush U 818 Profl Bldg 1725 W Harrison St Chicago IL 60612-3828 Office Phone: 312-942-6511. Business E-Mail: rprinz@rush.edu.

PRIOLEAU, PHILIP G., dermatologist; Studied, Med. U. SC. Diplomate Am. Bd. Pathology-anatomic pathology, Am. Bd. Dermatology, Am. Bd. Dermatology-dermapathology. Intern Univ. of Va. Med. Ctr.; resident Duke Univ. Med. Ctr., NC; fellow NY Univ. Med. Ctr., Mt. Sinai Med. Ctr., Wash. Univ. Med. Sch. Office: New York-Presbyterian Hospital/Weil Cornell Ste C 1035 5th Ave New York NY 10028 Office Phone: 212-794-3548. Office Fax: 212-794-2203.

PRIORI, ALBERTO, medical educator; b. Torino, Italy, Nov. 19, 1962; PhD, La Sapienza U., Rome, 1995. Clin. rsch. fellow Human Movement and Balance Unit Nat. Hosp., London, 1991; attending physician neurology Fondazione IRCCS Cà Granda-Ospedale Maggiore Policlinico, Milan, 1998—2011, dir. clin. ctr. neurostimulation, neurotech. and movement disorders, 2009—11; prof. clin. neurology and neurophysiology U. Milan Med. Sch., IRCCS Ospedale Maggiore Policlinico, 2002—. Assoc. prof. dept. neurol. scis. U. Milan, 2002—11. Mem.: Com. Parkinson Disease in Lombardy, Ct. Appeal in Juvenile Ct. (Brescia) (hon.). Home: Fondazione IRCCS Cà Granda-Ospedale Milan 20122 Italy Personal E-mail: scgr.neurostimolazione@unimi.it.

PRISANT, LOUIS MICHAEL, cardiologist, educator, researcher, author; b. Albany, Ga., Dec. 25, 1949; s. Bennie Martin and Mozelle Cosper Prisant; m. Rose Corinth Trincher, June 28, 1975 (dec. Nov. 7, 2008); children: Michelle Elizabeth Underwood, Louis Michael. BA, Emory U., Atlanta, 1971; MD, Med. Coll. Ga., Augusta, 1977. Diplomate Nat. Bd. Med. Examiners, 1978, Am. Bd. Internal Medicine, 1980, in cardiovascular diseases 1983, cert. in geriat. medicine 1990, diplomate Am. Bd. Clin. Pharmacology, 1991, Am. Bd. Forensic Examiners, 1996, Am. Bd. Forensic Medicine, 1996, cert. specialist in clin. hypertension Am. Soc. Hypertension, 1999, diplomate Am. Bd. Clin. Lipidology, 2005. Internship: straight medicine Med. Coll. Ga., Augusta, Ga., 1977—78, residency: internal medicine, 1978—80, cardiology fellow, 1980—82, instr. medicine, 1982—83, asst. prof. medicine, 1983—89, tenure assoc. prof. medicine, 1989—94, prof. medicine, 1994—, dir. hypertension & clin. pharmacology unit, 2002—09, emeritus prof. medicine, 2010—; chpt. pres. Am. Coll. Clin. Pharmacology Ahlquist Soc., 1992—95; dir. cardiology fellowship tng. program, 1996—2001; nominating com. Am. Soc. Hypertension, NYC, 2001—04, CME com., 2007—; co-chmn., Sphygmomanometer Com. Assn. Advancement Med. Instrumentation, Arlington, Va., 2001—07, chief med. resident, 1979—80. Editl. bd. mem. Heart Disease, 1999—2004, Blood Pressure Monitoring, 1995—; sect. editor Jour. Clin. Hypertension, 1999—; editl. bd. mem. Jour. Clin. Pharmacology, 2003—, Am. Jour. Therapeutics, 2000—, Jour. Clin. Lipidology, 2006—; chief med. resident Current Hypertention Reviews, 1979—80. Editor: (textbook) Hypertension in the Elderly; contbr. articles to profl. jours. Recipient Disting. Faculty award, Med. Coll. Ga., 2006; named one of America's Top Cardiologists, 2008—09. Fellow: Am. Coll. Cardiology; mem.: ACP, AMA (Physicians Recognition award 1982—), Sydenstricker Soc., Am. Heart Assn., Coun. on High Blood Pressure Rsch., Am. Coll. Forensic Examiners, Coun. on Geriat. Cardiology, Am. Coll. Chest Physicians, Am. Assn. U. Profs., Southeast Lipid Assn., Nat. Lipid Assn., Am. Soc. Echocardiography, Am. Coll. Clin. Pharmacology, Am. Soc. Hypertension (pres. Carolinas & Ga. chpt. 2005—07). Jewish. Avocations: science fiction, computers, scuba diving. Home: 617 Brae Burn Martinez GA 30907 Office: Med Coll Ga 1467 Harper St Augusta GA 30912 Home Fax: 706-868-8434. Personal E-mail: lprisant@comcast.net.

PRISCO, DOUGLAS LOUIS, physician; b. NYC, Nov. 30, 1945; s. Frank James and Isabel (Gaetano) P.; m. Marianne Paula Mangano, Jan. 8, 1972; children: Jennifer Leigh, Douglas Louis, Dana Lauren, Andrew Michael. AB, Georgetown U., 1967; postgrad., N.Y. U., 1967-68; MD, U. Rome, 1974. Diplomate Am. Bd. Internal Medicine, sub-bd. Pulmonary Diseases. Intern Mt. Sinai Svcs., Elmhurst, NY, 1974-75, resident in medicine, 1975-77, pulmonary medicine fellow, 1977-79; practice medicine specializing in pulmonary medicine New Hyde Park, NY, 1979—; clin. asst. in medicine Bklyn. Hosp., Bklyn., 1979-81; pulmonary cons. and admitting physician Booth Meml. Hosp. (now N.Y. Hosp. Med. Ctr. of Queens); admitting physician L.I. Jewish Hosp., New Hyde Park, Mt. Sinai of Queens, 1999—; chief pulmonary medicine Deepdale Gen. Hosp., 1980-93; clin. asst. Mt. Sinai Sch. Medicine, NYC, 1977-79; physician adviser St. Barnabas Hosp., 1981-82; pres. Met. Pulmonary Assocs., P.C., 1980—, Met. Pulmonary P.C., 1985—; v.p. network devel. Parkway Hosp., 1997; admitting physician North Shore Forest Hills., NY. Physician adv. to Queens County Profl. Stds. Rev. Orgn., 1979-85; co-chmn. quality assurance com. downstate region Island Peer Rev. Orgn., 1990-96, mem., 2010-, vice chmn. pro-tem regional quality assurance com., NY, 1993-96; chief pulmonary diseases Little Neck Cmty. Hosp. (formerly Deepdale Gen. Hosp.), 1980-96, pulmonary chief, med. dir., 1993-96; pres. Med. Staff Soc., 1992-96, med. bd.; cons. Queens divsn. Island Peer Rev. Orgn., 1985-96, Astoria (NY) Med. Group, dir. pulmonary svcs., 1999—. Mem. Rep. Senatorial Inner Cir., 1990. Fellow Am. Coll. Chest Physicians; mem. ACP, Am. Lung Assn. Queens (bd. dirs. 1988—, honoree 1997), Queens County Med. Soc., Port Washington Yacht Club (former chmn. jr. activities 1987-88, fleet surgeon 1991-93, 95-97, bd.d irs. 1995-97), Capitol Hill Club, Integrated Delivery Systems of N.Y. (vice chmn., chmn. 1995—). Roman Catholic. Address: Ste 201 3003 New Hyde Park Rd New Hyde Park NY 11042-1214 Office Phone: 516-488-2880. Personal E-mail: dlpmd@aol.com.

PRISCO, FRANK J., psychotherapist; b. NYC; s. Frank J. and Isabel (Gatano) P.; m. August Frances; children: Frank, Christian, Meredith. BS in History, NYU, 1964, MA in History and Psychology, 1972, PsyD in Psychoanalysis, 1980. Diplomate Am. Psychotherapy Assn., Am. Bd. Psychol. Specialties of Am. Coll. Forensic Examiners; cert. psychoanalyst, cert. med. hypnotherapist. Cons., staff therapist Creedmore Psychiat. Ctr.; faculty Psychanalytic Inst., LI; pvt. practice Ctr. for Modern Psychoanalytic Studies; instr. psychology N.Y.C. Bd. Edn. Trainer of trainers Conflict Mgrs. Program, N.Y.C.; discussion leader Gt. Books Found. Eucharistic min. Cath. Ch.; group leader Great Books Found. Recipient Soc. of Emil award, 1980. Mem. AAAS, Am. Psychol. Soc., Am. Assn. Guidance and Counseling, N.Y. Acad. Scis., Nat. Assn. Advancement Psychoanalysis, Am. Poetry Assn. (Poet Merit award 1988-90), Soc. Modern Psychoanalysis. Home: 14710 22ND Ave Whitestone NY 11357-3512 Office Phone: 718-445-5596.

PRISCO, MARCO, biology professor; b. Bari, Italy, May 11, 1961; D in Biol. Scis., U. Bari, Italy, 1992; PhD, U. Siena, Italy, 2006. Asst. prof., dept. stem cells biology, regenerative medicine Thomas Jefferson U., 2009—. Adj. asst. prof., dept. biology Sbarro Inst., Temple U., Coll. Sci. & Tech., 2011; editl. mem. Am. Jour. Pathology. Office: 10th & Locust St BLSB 933 Philadelphia PA 19107 Business E-Mail: marco.prisco@jefferson.edu.

PRISELAC, THOMAS M., hospital executive, educator; BA in Biology, Washington & Jefferson Coll.; MPH Health Svcs. Adminstrn. and Planning, U. Pitts. Asst. adminstr. Cedars-Sinai Med. Ctr., LA, 1979—81, assoc. adminstr., 1981—82, sr. assoc. adminstr., 1982—83, v.p. adminstrn., 1983—85, sr. v.p. ops., 1985—91, exec. v.p., COO, 1988—94, pres., CEO, 1994—. Adj. prof. UCLA Sch. Pub. Health; tchr., principles of orgn. leadership Master of Pub. Health for Health Professionals; past chmn. Coun. of Teaching Hosp. of Assn. of Am. Med. Coll.; chmn. Calif. Healthcare Assn., Healthcare Assn. of Southern Calif.; trustee Am. Hosp. Assn., chmn., 2009; bd. dirs. VHA, Inc., Nat. Com. for Quality Healthcare, Calif. Healthcare Found.; lectr. in field. Bd. dirs. Blue Cross Calif. Office: Cedars Sinai Med Ctr 8700 Beverly Blvd Rm 2628 Los Angeles CA 90048 Address: UCLA Sch Pub Health Dept Health Services Box 951772 Los Angeles CA 90095-1772 Office Phone: 310-423-5711, 310-206-3435. Office Fax: 310-423-0120, 310-206-4722. Business E-Mail: tmp@cshs.org. *

PRITZ, MICHAEL BURTON, neurological surgeon; b. New Brunswick, NJ, Oct. 8, 1947; s. John Ernest and Helen Violet (Rockoff) P.; m. Edmay Marie Gregorcy, Feb. 18, 1973; children: Edmond Louis, Benjamin David. BS, U. Ill., 1969; PhD, Case Western Res. U., 1973, MD, 1975. Diplomate Am. Bd. Neurol. Surgery. Asst. prof. neurol. surgery U. Calif. Irvine Med. Ctr., Orange, 1981-85, assoc. prof., 1985-93, prof., 1993, U. Calif. Irvine Med. Ctr., Orange, 1993—; prof. sect. neurol. surgery Ind. U. Sch. Medicine, Indpls., 1993—, prof. neurol. surgery, 1993—. Contbr. articles to profl. jours. Recipient Herbert S. Steuer award Case Western Res. U., Cleve., 1975; NSF fellow, 1968; Edmund J. James scholar U. Ill., Champaign, 1968-69. Mem. Soc. Neurosci., Am. Assn. Anatomists, Am. Assn. Neurol. Surgeons, Congress Neurol. Surgeons, Soc. Neurol. Surgeons of Orange County (pres. 1985-86, sec.-treas. 1984-85), Ind. State Neurosurg. Soc. (pres. 1996-98). Office Phone: 317-274-5728. Business E-Mail: mpritz@iupui.edu.

PRIVRATSKY, JAMIE R., physician scientist; b. Dickinson, ND, Sept. 26, 1980; PhD in Pharmacology, Med. Coll. Wis., 2010. Med. scientist tng. program fellow Med. Coll. Wis., 2004—. Predoc. fellowship, Am. Heart Assn. Mem.: Alpha Omega Alpha. Avocations: golf, reading. Home: 4609 W Morgan Ave Greenfield WI 53220 Business E-Mail: jprivrat@mcw.edu.

PROCCI, WARREN R., psychiatrist; b. S.I., NY, Jan. 19, 1947; s. Waddie R. and Anita M. (Veen) P.; m. Linda L. Kautza, June 4, 1972. BS, Wagner Coll., 1968; MD, U. Wis., 1972; PhD, So. Calif. Psychoanalytic Inst., 1984. Diplomate Am. Bd. Psychiatry and Neurology. Intern Univ. Hosps., Madison, Wis., 1972-73, resident, 1971-74; asst. prof., then assoc. prof. psychiatry Sch. Medicine U. So. Calif., LA, 1975-82; assoc. prof., dir. residency edn. in psychiatry Harbor-UCLA Med. Ctr., Torrance, 1982-88, assoc. clin. prof., 1988-97, clin. prof., 1997—. Bd. trustees Wagner Coll., 1999—, vice chmn., 2009—. Mem. Am. Psychoanalytic Assn. (councilor at large 1997-2001, treas. 2002-08, pres. 2010-), So. Calif. Psychoanalytic Inst. (pres. 1994-96, tng./supervising psychoanalyst 1991—, dean tng. sch. 1996-2001). Office: 230 S San Rafael Ave Pasadena CA 91105-1525 Office Phone: 626-793-7957. Personal E-mail: wrprocci@sbcglobal.net. *

PROCIDANO, MARY ELIZABETH, psychologist, educator; b. New Rochelle, NY, Apr. 1, 1954; d. John D'Arge and Dorothy Diane (Utter) Procidano; m. Stephen Anthony Buglione, Aug. 9, 1986; children: Daniel Stephen, Katherine Mary, Anne Elizabeth. BS (hon.), Fordham U., Bronx, NY, 1976; PhD in Psychology, Ind. U., 1981. Lic. psychologist, NY. Assoc. instr. Ind. U., Bloomington, Ind., 1979—80; intern in clin. psychology Inst. of Living, Hartford, Conn., 1980—81; asst. prof. Fordham U., Bronx, NY, 1981—90, asst. chair psychology dept., 1984—87, chair inst. rev. bd. protection human subjects, 1986—94, mem. faculty senate, 1990—, chair, faculty senate student life com., 2008—11, mem. coll. coun. and various com., advisor, chair psychology dept., 1996—2002, assoc. prof., 1990—, assoc. chair undergrad. studies, 2005—; pvt. practice, clin. psychology Scarsdale, NY, 1992—96, 2009—; staff psychologist CHE Sr. Psychol. Assocs., 2005—06, Sr. Citizens Care Group, 2006—08. Assoc. dean Fordham U. Grad. Sch. of Art's and Sci., 1996. Cons. editor Jour. of Personality and Social Psychology, 1989-92; contbg. articles and chapters to profl. and scholarly journals and books. Mem. APA, Am. Phys. Soc., STAR, Phi Beta Kappa, Sigma Xi, Psi Chi. Roman Catholic. Avocations: gardening, hiking, cooking. Office: Fordham U Dept Psychology Bronx NY 10458 Office Phone: 718-817-0925. Business E-Mail: procidano@fordham.edu.

PROCKOP, DARWIN JOHNSON, biochemist, medical educator; b. Palmerton, Pa., Aug. 31, 1929; s. John and Sophie (Gurski) Prockop; m. Elinor Sacks, Apr. 15, 1961; children: Susan Elizabeth, David John. AB, Haverford Coll., 1951; MA, Oxford U., 1953; MD, U. Pa., 1956; PhD, George Washington U., 1962; DSc (hon.) (hon.), U. Oulu, Finland, 1983, U. So. Fla., 1993. Investigator NIH,

1957—61; assoc., asst. prof., asso. prof., prof. medicine and biochemistry U. Pa., Phila., 1961—72; prof., chmn. dept. biochemistry U. Medicine and Dentistry of N.J. (Rutgers Med. Sch.), Piscataway, NJ, 1972—86; prof., chmn. dept. biochemistry and molecular biology Jefferson Med. Coll., Phila., 1986—96, dir. Jefferson Inst. Molecular Medicine, 1986—96; prof., dir. Ctr. for Gene Therapy, MCP/Hahnemann Med. Coll., Phila., 1996—2000; prof., dir. Ctr. Gene Therapy Tulane U. Med. Ctr., New Orleans, 2000—08; dir. Tex. A & M Health Sci. Ctr. Inst. Regenerative Med., Scott & White Temple, 2008—. Contbr. Served with USPHS, 1958—61. Recipient Disting. Alumnus award, George Washington U., 1991, U. Pa., 1994, Hopkins Meml. medal., Brit. Biochem. Soc, 1998; named hon. companion, U. Manchester, 1999; grantee, NIH, 1961—; fellow Fulbright Found., 1951—53. Mem.: NAS, Am. Assn. Physicians, Am. Soc. Clin. Investigation, Am. Soc. Biol. Chemists, Acad. Finland, Inst. Medicine, Alpha Omega Alpha, Phi Beta Kappa. Achievements include research in on collagen and gene therapy. Home: 291 Locust St Philadelphia PA 19106-3913 Office: Ctr Gene Therapy Tulane U Med Ctr 1430 Tulane Ave New Orleans LA 70112-2699 E-mail: dprocko@tulane.edu.

PROCTOR, CONRAD ARNOLD, physician; b. Ann Arbor, Mich., July 14, 1934; s. Bruce and Luena Marie (Crawford) P.; m. Phyllis Darlene Anderson, June 23, 1956; children: Sharon Heimbach Pins, Barbara Jan Brown, David Conrad, Todd Bruce. MD, U. Mich., 1959, MS, 1964. Cert. Am. Bd. Otolaryngology. Intern St. Joseph Mercy Hosp., Ann Arbor, 1959-60; jr. clin. instr. Univ. Hosp., Ann Arbor, 1961-63, sr. clin. instr., 1963-65; chief dept. otolaryngology Munson Army Hosp., Ft. Leavenworth, Kans., 1965-67; mem. attending staff William Beaumont Hosp., Royal Oak, Mich., 1967—. Instr. Am. Acad. Otolaryngology, Washington, 1968-82, guest examiner, Chgo., 1978-79. Author: Current Therapy in Otolaryngology, 1984-85; (booklet) Dietary Treatment of Meniere's Syndrome, 1983, Hyperinsulinemia and Tinnitus, 1988; (manual) Hereditary Sensorineural Hearing Loss, 1978, Etiology, Treatment of Fluid Retention in Meniere's Syndrome, 1992; (med. jour.) Abnormal Insulin Levels and Vertigo, 1981. Mem. US 5th Army Basketball, Tennis teams, 1965-67; dir. Christian edn. Bloomfield Hills (Mich.) Bapt. Ch., 1969-72, fin. chmn., 1975-78, Sunday sch. tchr., 1967—. Served to capt. U.S. Army, 1965-67. Chief otolaryngology Munson Army Hosp., 1965—67. Recipient Commdg. Gen.'s Acheivement award Ft. Leavenworth, Kans., 1967, Merit award Am. Acad. Otolaryngology, 1978, USA 1st Pl. Med. Rsch. award, SAMA, 1959; holder 9 world and 4 state of Mich. records Internat. Game Fish Assn., 7 world records Nat. Fresh Water Fishing Hall Fame. Mem. AMA, Mich. State Med. Assn., Oakland County Med. Assn., Am. Bd. Otolaryngology, ACS, Triological Soc., Otosclerosis Study Group, Internat. Game Fish Assn. (Nat. Fresh Water Fishing Hall of Fame), Am. Legion, U.S. Tennis Assn., Victors and Presidents Club (Ann Arbor), Phi Eta Sigma, Phi Kappa Phi, Phi Beta Kappa, Am. Rhinol. Soc., Am. Legion. Republican. Avocations: Arctic exploration, fishing, baseball. Office: 2251 Squirrel Rd Ste 105 Auburn Hills MI 48326-4601 Office Phone: 248-288-2137.

PROCTOR, DEBORAH A., hospital administrator; children: Britt, Gregory, Jessica, Greg. BSN, 1973; MSN, UCLA, 1976. Cons. Hay Group; in various leadership positions Voluntary Hosps. America, Dallas, Ascencion Health, St. Louis, chief adminstrv. officer, sr. v.p.; in various leadership positions St. Joseph Health System, Orange, Calif., ICU nurse St. Joseph Hosp., nurse St. Joseph Hosp., assoc. prof., pres., 2006—, CEO, 2006—. Contbr. articles to profl. publs. Recipient Disting. Alumna award, Coll. Health and Human Svcs., Bishop Tod D. Brown award, 2008; named one of Top 25 Women in Healthcare, Modern Healthcare Mag., 2011. Mem.: Cath. Healthcare Alliance (past. bd. dirs.), Cath. Healthcare Assn. (past. bd. dirs.). Avocations: travel, golf, reading. Office: St Joseph Health System 500 S Main St Ste 1000 Orange CA 92868 Office Phone: 714-347-7500.

PROCTOR, MARK ROBERT, pediatric neurosurgeon; b. NYC, Oct. 22, 1964; s. Seymour and Roslyn Proctor; m. Charlotte McKee, Apr. 14, 1991; children: Maxwell children: Kenneth. BA, Dartmouth Coll., 1986; MD, Columbia U., 1990. Cert. Am. Bd. Neurol. Surgery, 2001, Am. Bd. Pediatric Neurosurgery, 2002. Intern Columbia Presbyn. Hosp., 1990; resident Georgetown U., 1991—97; fellow in pediat. neurosurgery Children's Hosp., Boston, 1997—98, pediat. neurosurgeon, 1997—. Office: Children's Hosp 300 Longwood Ave Boston MA 02115 E-mail: mark.proctor@childrens.harvard.edu.

PROCTOR, RICHARD A., medical educator; b. Detroit, July 6, 1945; MD, U. Mich., 1970. Emeritus prof. U. Wis. Sch. Medicine & Pub. Health, 1976—. Pvt. practice, 2010. Recipient Alexander von Humboldt Disting. Rschr. award, Alexander von Humboldt-Stiftung. Fellow: Infectious Diseases Soc. America. Office: 835 Asa Gray Ann Arbor MI 48105 Business E-Mail: rap@facstaff.wisc.edu.

PROCZKO-MARKUSZEWSKA, MONIKA, surgeon; b. Gdansk, Poland, Mar. 30, 1971; PhD in Gen. Surgery, Med. U. Gdansk, 1998. Specialist in gen. surgery 2007. Resident U. Hosp. Gdansk, 2000; specialist in gen. surgery, dept. gen., endocrine and transplant surgery Med. U. Gdansk, 2007—. Lectr. European Program for Pomeranian Region for Med. Professions Promedicine, 2009. Mem.: Polish Assn. Gastroenterology, Endocrinological Sect. Polish Surgeons Soc., European Assn. Endoscopic Surgery, Polish Surgeons Soc. Avocations: golf, art, cooking. Office: Debinki 7 Gdansk Pomeranian Region 80-952 Poland Office Fax: 48583492410.

PROFFIT, WILLIAM ROBERT, orthodontics educator; b. Harnett County, NC, Apr. 19, 1936; s. Glenn Theodore and Edna Marie (Queener) P.; m. Sara Thomas, Sept. 20, 1953; children: Lola Ann, Edward Thomas, Glenn Theodore. BS, U. N.C., 1956, DDS, 1959; student, Campbell Coll., Buies Creek, NC, 1952-53; PhD, Med. Coll. Va., 1962; MS, U. Wash., 1963; FDS, Royal Coll. Surgeons, 1990. Cert. Am. Bd. Orthodontics. Investigator Nat. Inst. Dental Research, Bethesda, Md., 1963-65; asst. prof. orthodontics U. Ky., Lexington, 1965-68, assoc. prof., 1968-71; prof. U.Ky., Lexington, 1971-73; prof. orthodontics U. Fla., Gainesville, 1973-75; prof., chmn. dept. orthodontics U. NC, Chapel Hill, 1975—, Kenan prof., 1992. Cons. NIH, Bethesda, 1974, 76— Author: Contemporary Orthodontics, 1986, 4th edit., 2006; co-author: Surgical Correction of Dentofacial Deformity, 1980, Surgical-Orthodontic Treatment, 1990, Contemporary Treatment of Dentofacial Deformity, 2003; contbr. articles to sci. jours. Served to lt. comdr. USPHS, 1963-65. Fulbright research scholar U. Adelaide, Australia, 1972 Mem. ADA, Am. Assn. Orthodontists, Internat. Assn. Dental Rsch., Phi Beta Kappa. Democrat. Presbyterian. Office: UNC Sch Dentistry Dept Orthodontics Chapel Hill NC 27599-7450 Home: 750 Weaver Dairy Rd # 229 Chapel Hill NC 27514-1468 E-mail: william_proffit@dentistry.unc.edu.

PROFFITT, DENNIS R., psychology professor, department chairman; BS in Psychology, Pa. State U., 1970, MS in Psychology, 1973, PhD in Psychology, 1976. Asst. prof. psychology Wesleyan U., Middletown, Conn., 1976—79, U. Va., Charlottesville, 1979—85, assoc. prof. psychology, 1985—91, prof. psychology, 1991—, founding dir. cognitive sci. program, 1992—, Cavalier disting. tchg. prof., 1999—2001, Commonwealth prof. psychology, 2004—, chmn. dept. psychology. Cons. editor: Perception & Psychophysics, 1983—93, Jour. Exptl. Psychology: Human Perception and Performance, 1988—99, Psychol. Rev., 1990—96, Psychol. Sci., 2003—, Perception, 2003—; contbr. articles to profl. jours. Recipient James McKean Cattell Sabbatical award, 1988—89; grantee, NSF, 2005—09, NIH, 2007—, US Army, 2007—08. Fellow: Am. Psychol. Soc. Office: Dept Psychology Univ Va PO Box 400400 Charlottesville VA 22904-4400 Office Phone: 434-924-0655. Business E-Mail: drp@virginia.edu.

PROIETTI, LUCA, medical educator; b. Rome, July 21, 1974; MD, Med. Sch. Cath. U. Rome, 1999. Asst. prof. Cath. U. Rome, 2006—. Office: Largo A Gemelli 8 Rome 00168 Italy Office Fax: 39063051161. Personal E-mail: proiettil@yahoo.it.

PRONOVOST, PETER J., anesthesiologist, medical educator; b. Waterbury, Conn., Feb. 22, 1965; s. Henry and Ann Pronovost; m. Marlene Rosemary Miller, Oct. 5, 1996; children: Ethan, Emma. BS in Biology & Philosophy, Fairfield U., Conn., 1987; MD, Johns Hopkins U., Balt., 1991; PhD, Johns Hopkins Sch. Hygiene & Pub. Health, 1999. Diplomate Am. Bd. Anesthesiology, lic. Md. Intern emergency medicine John Hopkins Hosp., Balt., 1991—92, resident anesthesiology & critical care medicine, 1992—95, fellow critical care medicine, 1994—96; instr. dept. surgery, dept. anesthesiology & critical care medicine Johns Hopkins U. Sch. Medicine, 1997—98, asst. prof., 1998—2001, assoc. prof., 2001—05, prof., 2005—. Cons. Vol. Hosps. of America, Irving, Tex., 2000—; med. advisor Leapfrog Group, Washington, 2000—; med. dir. Ctr. Innovations & Quality Care, Balt., 2001—; chair adv. panel ICU core measures Joint Commn. Accreditation of Healthcare Organizations, Oakbrook Terrace, Ill., 2002—; chair strategic planning com. Soc. of Critical Care Medicine, Chgo., 2002—; presenter Internat. AIDS Conf. Co-author: Safe Patients, Smart Hospitals: How One Doctor's Checklist Can Help Us Change Health Care from the Inside Out, 2010; mem. editl. bd. Jour. Clin. Outcomes Mgmt.; contbr. articles pub. profl. jours. Recipient John Eisenberg Patient Safety Rsch. award, 2004; named a MacArthur Fellow, John D. & Catherine T. MacArthur Found., 2008; named one of 100 Most Influential People in the World, TIME mag., 2008. Fellow: Am. Coll. Critical Care Medicine; mem.: AMA (assoc.), Assn. Univ. Anesthesiologists, Internat. Anesthesia Rsch. Soc., Anesthesia Rsch. Soc. (assoc.), Am. Soc. Anesthesiologists (assoc.), Am. Soc. Critical Care Anesthesiologists (assoc.), Assn. Health Svcs. Rsch. (assoc.), Soc. Critical Care Medicine (founding mem., bd. trustees Patient Safety Found., Presdl. citation 2002, Rsch. award 2001), Delta Omega, Alpha Epsilon Delta, Alpha Sigma Nu. Achievements include research in the fields of patient safety, patient care in the intensive care unit (ICU), quality health care, evidence-based medicine, and the measurement and evaluation of safety efforts. Office: Johns Hopkins U Sch Medicine 600 N Wolfe St Meyer 295 Baltimore MD 21287-7294 Office Fax: 410-502-3235. E-mail: ppronovo@jhmi.edu. *

PROPST, CATHERINE LAMB, biotechnology and pharmaceutical company executive; b. Charlotte, NC, Mar. 10, 1946; d. James Pinckney and Eliza M. Propst. BA magna cum laude, Vanderbilt U., 1967; M of Philosophy, Yale U., 1970, PhD, 1973. Head microbiology div. GTE Labs., Waltham, Mass., 1974-77; various sr. mgmt. positions Abbott Labs., North Chicago, Ill., 1977-80; v.p. rsch. and devel. Ayerst (Wyeth) Labs., Plainview, NY, 1980-83; v.p. rsch. and devel. worldwide Flow Gen. Inc., McLean, Va., 1983-85; pres., CEO Affiliated Sci. Inc., Ingleside, Ill., 1985-97; pres., chmn., CEO Tex. Biotech. Found., Hempstead, Tex., 1997—. Vis. prof. genetics U. Ill., Chgo., 1989—90; founder, exec. dir. Ctr. for Biotech., Northwestern U., 1990—95; pres. Ill. Biotech. Ctr., 1995—97; bd. dirs. several cos.; bd. dirs., mem. sci. adv. bd. Keystone Symposia on Molecular and Cellular Biology, 1997—2002. Author, editor Computer-Aided Drug Design, 1989, Nucleic Acid Targeted Drug Design, 1992; contbr. articles to profl. jours. Recipient many sci. and bus. awards; named to Outstanding Working Women in the U.S., 1982. Fellow: Soc. Indsl. Microbiology (bd. dirs. 1990—93), Nat. Coun. Biotech Ctrs. (bd. dirs. 1995—97); mem.: AAAS, Nat. Wildlife Fedn., Consortium for Plant Biotech. Rsch. (bd. dirs. 1994—99), Phi Beta Kappa, Sigma Xi. Episcopalian. Avocations: horseback riding, skiing, raising Black Angus and Black Brangus cattle. Office: Texas Biotech Found PO Box 17 Hempstead TX 77445-0017 Office Phone: 979-826-3075. Office Fax: 979-826-9710.

PROSE, NEIL STUART, pediatric dermatologist; b. NYC, 1949; MD, NYU, 1975. Cert. Am. Bd. Dermatology, 1983. Intern in pediat. San Francisco Gen. Hosp., 1975—76; resident in dermatology SUNY, 1980—83, asst. prof. pediat., 1983—84; dermatologist Duke U. Med. Ctr., Durham, NC, assoc. prof. medicine. Office: Duke U Med Ctr PO Box 3252 Durham NC 27710 Office Phone: 919-684-5146. Office Fax: 919-681-8073. Business E-Mail: prose001@mc.duke.edu.

PROSNITZ, ROBERT G., radiation oncologist educator; BA in Economics and Polit. Sci. (cum laude), Yale U., 1991; MD, Duke U., 1996; MPH in Clin. Effectiveness, Harvard Univ. Sch. of Pub. Health, 2000. Diplomate Am. Bd. Radiology-radiation oncology, 2001. Intern Beth Israel Hosp., Boston; resident Harvard Univ.; asst. prof. radiation oncology Univ. of Pa. Health System. Named one of Top Docs, Phila. Mag., 2011. Mem.: Am. Soc. for Clin. Oncology, Am. Soc. for Radiation Oncology. Mailing: Perelman Center for Advanced Medicine Concourse Level 3400 Civic Center Blvd Philadelphia PA 19104 Office: Hospital of the University of PA Department of Radiation Oncology 2 Donner Bldg 3400 Spruce St Philadelphia PA 19104 Office Phone: 800-789-7366, 215-614-0083. Office Fax: 215-349-5455. Business E-Mail: robert.prosnitz@uphs.upenn.edu.

PROSPERI, CARLOS HUGO, biologist, educator, researcher; b. Cordoba, Argentina, Nov. 29, 1954; s. Rinaldo Alberto and Elsa Angela (Sitano) P.; children: Mariana Elizabeth, Gabriela Mercedes. Bachelor, Monserrat Coll., 1972; Lic. in Philosophy, U. Cordoba, 1978, PhD in Biology, 1984. Rschr. Anctarctic Inst., Buenos Aires, 1978-79, Inst. Phylosophyc Anthropology, 1980-91, Autonomous U. Madrid, 1990-92; prof. U. Cordoba, 1988—, U. Blas Pascal, 2002. Vis. prof. Queen's U., Kingston, Can., 1987; v.p. Can. Cultural Ctr., Cordoba, 1988—; rschr. Nat. Coun. Rsch., 1981—; vice head Dept. Botany, 1988-90; coord. nat. net for the early alert of cyanatoxical water blooms, Min. Pub. Health, 2006; dir. Hydric Resources Nat. Sec. Environment and Sustainable Devel.; cons. internat. jour. Contbr. articles to profl. jours. Recipient Tchg. award U. Cordoba, 1993, 95. Mem. Argetinian Soc. Botany, Internat. Phycological Soc., N.Y. Acad. Scis. Roman Catholic. Avocations: scuba diving, classical music, militaria collections. Home: Velez Sarsfield 272 5000 Cordoba Argentina Office: Univ Cordoba Velez Sarsfield 299 5000 Cordoba Argentina Home Phone: 54-11-4212883, (+54-351) 4212883; Office Phone: 54351155059884. Personal E-mail: cprosperi@yahoo.com.ar.

PROTAS, ELIZABETH J., physical therapist, academic administrator; m. Eugene D. Protas, Mar. 6, 1950; 1 child, Mark Jason. PhD, SUNY, Buffalo, 1974—80. Cert. phys. therapist Tex., 1980. Assoc. dean, sch. phys. therapy Tex. Woman's U., Houston, 1980—2002; chair, dept. phys. therapy U. Tex. Med. Br., Galveston, 2002—06, interim dean, 2006—08, dean, 2008—. Bd. trustees Am. Coll. Sports Medicine, Indpls., 2002—04. Recipient Joseph Valley Gerontologica Profl. of Yr. award, U. Tex. Health Sci. Ctr., 2000; grantee Support Rsch. and Tng. Grad. Students, Dept. of Veterans; fellow Founding Fellow, Am. Assn. Cardiovasc. and Pulmonary Rehab. Mem.: Am. Phys. Therapy Assn. (Worthingham fellow 2008). Achievements include research in Rehabilitation outcomes for persons with chronic disabilities. Office: U Tex Med Branch 301 U Blvd Galveston TX 77555-1144

PROUDMAN, SUSANNA MARGARET, rheumatologist, researcher; b. Adelaide, South Australia, Australia, Oct. 11, 1963; d. Rodney Henry and Jean Campbell Wicks; m. Timothy William Proudman; children: Rebecca Christine, Charlotte Jean, William Rodney. MBBS with honors, U. Adelaide, 1986. Physician trainee Royal Adelaide Hosp., 1987—91, Rheumatology and Rehab. Rsch. Unit, Leeds Gen. Infirmary, North Yorshire, England, 1996—97; vis. cons. rheumatologist Royal Adelaide Hosp., 1998—; consulting rheumatologist Wakefield Ho., Adelaide, 1998—; Nat. Health and Med. Rsch. Coun. postgrad. scholar U. Adelaide, 1992—95, sr. lectr., 1998—. Chief med. resident Royal Adelaide Hosp., 1991, mem., 2000—04, coord.; coun. mem. Fed. Com. Australian Rheumatology Assn., 2002—05; mem. Rheumatology Advanced Tng. Royal Australasian Coll. Physicians, 2004, Therapeutics Com. Australian Rheumatology Assn.; doctors tng. rep. Australian Med. Assn. South Australian Br. Coun., Adelaide, 1991—93; chair Rheumatology Advanced Tng. Selection Com., Adelaide, 2006—07, Australian Scleroderma Interest Group; mem. Pulmonary Interstitial Vascular, Orgnl. Taskforce, Australia, U. Adelaide, U. Adelaide, Musculoskeletal Rev. Com., Med. Sch.; advanced trainee rep. Royal Australian Coll. Physicians South Australian State Com., Adelaide, 1992—94; mem. Royal Adelaide Hosp., 1991, Med IV Musculoskeletal Clin. Scis. Com., 1998—2005, Australian Rheumatology Assn., Adelaide, 1998—2000, co-convenor, South Australian br., 1993, convenor organising com., co-convenor ann. sci. meeting, South Australian br., 2001, Adelaide, 08, sec., 2002—03, pres., south australian br., 2005—06; mem. Arthritis Rsch. Trust, Australia, 2008, mem. grant com., 10. Contbr. 50 articles to profl. jours. Chair events com. fundraising Wilderness Sch., Adelaide, 2006, mem. events com. fund-raising, 2003—, coun. governors, 2007—. Recipient Kabi Pharmacia Young Investigator award, Australian Rheumatology Assn., 1992, Sanofi-Winthrop Travel award, 1994, Kabi Pharmacia Young Investigator award, 1995, Student award, Australasian Soc. Exptl. Pathology, 1994, Best Presentation prize, Royal Australasian Coll. Physicians, 1994, Keith Sheridan prize, U. Adelaide, 1985, Elder prize, 1981, Christopher & John Campbell prize, 1982, Charles Gosse medal, 1984, Thornber Bursary award, 1981, Ian Furler Meml. prize, 1985, Frank S. Hone Meml. prize, 1986, H.K. Fry Meml. prize, 1986; grantee, Arthritis and Rheumatism Coun., 1997, Royal Adelaide Hosp. SPF, 1998, Arthritis Found. Australia, 2000, Royal Adelaide Hosp. and Arthritis Found. Australia Grant-in-Aid, 2003, Nat. Med. and Rsch. Coun., 2003—05, RAH, IMVS Rsch. Com., 2005, Dept. Health and Ageing, 2006; Michael Mason Travelling fellow, Arthritis Found. Australia, 1996, Unrestricted Ednl. grant, Actelion Australia Pharmaceuticals, 2006, Equipment grant, Rebecca Cooper Found., 2007, grant, NHMRC, 2010—. Mem.: Med. Bd. South Australia. Office: Rheumatology Unit Royal Adelaide Hosp North Tle Adelaide 5000 Australia Business E-Mail: sproudman@tpg.com.au.

PROUGH, RUSSELL ALLEN, biochemistry professor, academic administrator; b. Twin Falls, Idaho, Nov. 5, 1943; s. Elza Leroy and Beulah Elsie (Huddleston) P.; M. Betty Marie Ehlers, Dec. 26, 1965; children: Jennifer Sally, Kimberly Marie. BS in Chemistry, Coll. of Idaho, 1965; PhD in Biochemistry and Biophysics, Oreg. State U., 1969. Postdoctoral fellow VA Hosp., Kansas City, Mo., 1969-72; instr. biochemistry U. Tex. Southwestern Med. Sch., Dallas, 1972-73, asst. prof. biochemistry, 1973-77, assoc. prof. biochemistry, 1977-82, prof. biochemistry, 1982-86, U. Louisville Sch. Med., 1986—, chmn. dept., 1986—99, 2007—08, vice dean rsch., assoc. v.p. rsch., 1998—2003, 2008—, Preston Pope Joyes endowed chair biochemical rsch., 2003. Mem. NIH Toxicology Study Sect., 1984-88, State of Nebr. Smoking Disease and Cancer Rsch. Program, 1984-91, Nat. Insts. Environ. Health Scis. rsch. com., 1999-2003. Assoc. editor Drug Metabolism and Disposition, 1994—, Drug Metabolism Rev., 2002—, Pharmacology and Therapeutics, 2005—. Recipient Rsch. Career Devel. award USPHS. Mem. Am. Soc. Biochemistry and Molecular Biology, Am. Soc. Pharmacology and Exptl. Therapeutics, Internat. Soc. for Study of Xenobiotics, Sigma Xi. Lutheran. Office: U Louisville Dept Biochemistry and Molecular Biology Louisville KY 40292-0001 Office Phone: 502-852-7249. Business E-Mail: russ.prough@louisville.edu.

PROUT, CURTIS, internist, educator; b. Swampscott, Mass., Oct. 13, 1915; s. Henry Byrd and Eloise (Willett) P.; m. Daphne Brooks, June 27, 1939 (div. 1985); children: Diana P. Cherot, Daphne P. Cook, Rosamond P. Warren, Phyllis P.; m. Diane Neal Emmons, Dec. 7, 1985. AB, Harvard U., 1937, MD, 1941. Diplomate Am. Bd. Internal Medicine. Intern Peter Bent Brigham Hosp., Boston, 1942; resident in internal medicine Johns Hopkins Hosp., Balt., 1943; research fellow Mass. Gen. Hosp., Boston, 1944—45; practice medicine specializing in internal medicine, 1945—; asst. dir. Univ. Health Services Harvard U., Cambridge, Mass., 1961-72; dir. prison health project Office of Econ. Opportunity, 1972-74; asst. dean Harvard Med. Sch., Boston, 1980-94, asst. clin. prof. medicine, 1975-82. Trustee Humane Soc. Mass., Boston, 1975-2005, pres., 2004; bd. dirs. Nat. Commn. on

Correctional Health Care, 1980-98, chmn., 1990; dir., treas. The Med. Found., Boston, 1980-98. Chmn. Bd. Health, Dover, Mass., 1960-75. Fellow ACP, Mass. Med. Soc.; mem. AMA, Am. Clin. and Climatol. Assn., Tavern Club of Boston (pres. 1980-82). Avocations: sailing, writing. Home and Office: 115 School St Manchester MA 01944-1232 Personal E-mail: dr.curtisprout@adelphia.net.

PROUT, GEORGE RUSSELL, JR., medical educator, urologist; b. Boston, July 23, 1924; s. George Russell and Marion (Snow) P.; m. Loa Katherine Wheatley, Oct. 17, 1950; children: George Russell III, Elizabeth Louise. Student, Union Coll., 1943, DSc (hon.), 1990; MD, Albany Med. Coll., 1947, DSc (hon.), 1988; MA (hon.), Harvard U., 1969. Intern Grasslands Hosp., Valhalla, NY, 1947-48; asst. resident in surgery, 1948-50; surg. resident Grasslands Hosp., Valhalla, NY, 1948-50; resident N.Y. Hosp., NYC, 1952-56; fellow in surgery Meml. Ctr. Cancer & Allied Diseases, 1954—55; asst. attending physician Meml. Ctr. for Cancer and Allied Disease, NYC, 1956-57; asst. clinician in surgery James Ewing Hosp., NYC, 1956-57; assoc. prof., chmn. div. urology U. Miami, 1957-60; prof., chmn. div. urology Med. Coll. Va., 1960-69; chief urol. svc. Mass. Gen. Hosp., Boston, 1969-89; prof. surgery Harvard Med. Sch., 1969-89, emeritus prof. surgery Boston, 1989—; hon. urologist Mass. Gen. Hosp., Boston, 1989—. Chmn. Adjuvants in Surg. Treatment of Bladder Cancer; mem. adv. task force Nat. Cancer Inst., 1968—, cons., 1990—; expert cons. divsn. surveillance, 1991—; Finland coop. ATBC study, 1991—; chmn. Nat. Bladder Cancer Group, 1973—86. Editor-in-chief: Urologic Oncology, 1994—2000. With USNR, 1950-52. Fellow ACS, Acad. Medicine Toronto (corr.); mem. AMA, AAUP, Am. Urol. Assn., Can. Urol. Assn., Japanese Urol. Soc. (hon.), Am. Cancer Soc., Soc. Surg. Oncology, Soc. Univ. Urologists, Dallas So. Clin. Soc. (hon.), Am. Assn. Genitourinary Surgeons, Soc. Pediat. Urology, Soc. Urol. Oncology, Soc. Internat. Urologists, Soc. Basic Urol. Rsch., Alpha Omega Alpha. Home (Winter): 224 Corsair Rd Duck Key FL 33050 Home and Office: 1800 River Watch Ave Annapolis MD 21401 Home Phone: 305-289-0770. Personal E-mail: drurocsal@aol.com.

PROVAZNIKOVA, DANA, medical researcher; b. Praha, Apr. 24, 1979; MSc, Charles U., 2003. Rsch. scientist Inst. Hematology and Blood Transfusion, 2003—. Mem.: Czech Union Biochemistry and Molecular Biology. Home: Horni 383 Ricany Praha 128 20 Czech Republic Personal E-mail: d.provaz@centrum.cz.

PROVDA, LOIS M., psychologist, educator; BS in Social Studies, Boston U., BS in English, 1962; MA in Spl. Edn., NYU, 1964, PhD in Ednl. Psychology, 1983. Cert. marriage, family and child counselor, learning handicapped specialist, reading specialist, advanced study in edn. 1976. Ednl. dir. Payne Whitney Psychiat. Clinic NY Hosp., NYC, 1964—68; dir. reading Buckingham Sch., Bklyn., 1968—73; instr. CUNY, Bklyn., 1973—76, UCLA, 1996—2003; ednl. psychologist LA, 1976—. Ednl. cons. NY Assn. Blind, NYC, 1974—76; ednl. specialist psychol. svcs. dept. Bur. Jewish Edn., LA, 1982—; with Northern LA Select Blue Ribbon Com. on Autism, 2009—; bd. dirs Kol Hanearim, Inglewood; inventor Pencil Grip Inc., Inglewood, Calif. Fellow: Orthopsychiatric Assn.; mem.: NY Acad. Sci., Internat. Reading Assn., Am. Assn. Sch. Psychology, Assn. Ednl. Therapists. Home and Office: 9911 W Pico Blvd Ste 675 Los Angeles CA 90035 Office Phone: 310-277-5551. Personal E-mail: lprovda@aol.com.

PROVINE, ROBERT RAYMOND, neuroscientist, psychology professor; b. Tulsa, May 11, 1943; s. Robert William and Thelma Fern (Morgan) Provine; m. Helen R. Weems; children: Kimberly, Robert. BS in Psychology, Okla. State U., 1965; PhD in Psychology, Washington U., St. Louis, 1971. Rsch. assoc. Washington U., 1971-72, rsch. asst. prof., 1972—74; asst. prof. psychology U. Md. Balt. County, 1974—76, assoc. prof., 1976—83, prof., 1983—. Author: Laughter: A Scientific Investigation, 2000; contbr. articles to profl. jours., chapters to books. Fellow: Assn. Psychol. Sci.; mem.: AAAS, Psychonomic Soc., Soc. Neurosci., Psi Chi, Sigma Xi. Achievements include research in neurobehavioral development and evolution of the nervous system to include human laughter, yawning, language and social behavior. Office: Dept Psychology U Md Baltimore County Baltimore MD 21250-0001 *

PRUDIL, LUKAS, law educator; m. Zdenka Konickova, Sept. 23, 2000; 1 child, Simon Martin. M, Masaryk U., Brno, Czech Republic, 1997, PhD, 2002. Bar: Czech Bar Assn. 2000. Lectr. med. faculty Masaryk U., Brno, Czech Republic, 1997—2002, sr. lectr. med faculty, 2002—; atty., 2000—. Editor: Jour. Zdravotnicke Pravo U Praxi, 2003—06. Mem. ethics com. Ministry of Health, Czech Med. Chamber; mem. ethics com. med. faculty Masaryk U. Mem.: World Assn. Med. Law, Czech Med. Assn. J.E. Purkyne. Office: Med Faculty Masaryk U Komenskeho nam 2 Brno 602 00 Czech Republic Office Fax: 420 542 210 593. Business E-Mail: info@prudil.cz.

PRUETT, BRANDON SCOTT, neurologist, researcher; b. Shelby, NC, Dec. 7, 1983; BA, Northwestern State U., 2006; PhD student, La. State U. Health, Shreveport, 2006—. Physician, rsch. fellow La. State U. Health, 2006—. Mem.: Soc. Neurosci. (Shreveport chpt.) (student rep. 2009—10, sec. 2010—11). Avocation: running. Office: 1501 Kings Hwy Shreveport LA 71103 Business E-Mail: bpruet@lsuhsc.edu.

PRUITT, BASIL ARTHUR, JR., surgeon, retired military officer; b. Nyack, NY, Aug. 21, 1930; s. Basil Arthur and Myrtle Flo (Knowles) P.; m. Mary Sessions Gibson, Sept. 4, 1954; children: Scott Knowles, Laura Sessions, Jeffrey Hamilton. AB, Harvard U., 1952, postgrad., 1952—53; MD, Tufts U., 1957. Diplomate Am. Bd. Surgery. Intern Boston City Hosp., 1957—58, resident surgery, 1958—59, 1961—62; commd. capt., M.C. U.S. Army, 1959, advanced through grades to col., 1972; resident Brooke Gen. Hosp., Ft. Sam Houston, Tex., 1962—64; chief clin. divsn. Inst. Surg. Rsch., Ft. Sam Houston, 1965—67; chief profl. svcs. 12th Evacuation Hosp., Vietnam, 1967—68; comdr., dir. U.S. Army Inst. Surg. Rsch., Brooke Army Med. Ctr., Ft. Sam Houston, 1968—95, ret., 1995; clin. prof. gen. surgery U. Tex. Health Sci. Ctr., San Antonio, 1975—, Dr. Ferdinand P. Herff chair surgery, 2009—; prof. surgery Uniformed Svcs. U. Health Scis., Bethesda, Md., 1978—. Mem. surgery, anaesthesiology and trauma study sect. NIH, 1978—82; mem. Shriners Burns Adv. Bd., 1985—92, Shriners Med. Adv. Bd., 1992—95, Shriners Rsch. Adv. Bd., 1996—2006, Shriners Clin. Outcomes Studies Adv. Bd., 1999—2007; merit rev. bd. for surgery VA, 1990—93; bd. dirs. Am. Bd. Surgery, 1982—88, sr. mem., 1989—. Author med. books; contbr. chpts. to textbooks, articles to profl. jours.; mem. editl. bd. Jour. Trauma, 1975-94, editor, 1995—; mem. edit. bd.: Archives Surgery, 1981-93, Consultations in Surgery, Correspondence Society of Surgeons, Collected Letters, 1978-2000, Circulatory Shock, 1985-93, Jour. Burn Care and Rehab., 1984-87, Jour. Investigative Surgery, 1987-97, Shock, 1993—, Current Opinion in Surg. Infections, 1993-2001, Sepsis, 1996-2002, Injury, 1998-2003, Turkish Jour. Trauma, 2002—, English edit. Chinese Jour. Traumatology, 1998—, Med. Jour. Chinese People's Liberation Army, 2005—. Decorated Bronze Star, Legion of Merit, DSM; recipient ISS/SIC Danis prize, 1995, G. Whitaker Internat. Burns prize, 2000, US Army Med. Rsch. and Materiel Command Lifetime Achievement award, 2002, Tanner-Vandeput-Boswick Burn prize, 2006, Roswell Park medal, 2007, Disting. Alumni award, 2007, King Faisal Internat. prize, 2008. Fellow: ACS (pre and postoperative care com. 1969—79, vice chmn. 1973—75, gov. 1973—79, com. on trauma 1974—84, internat. rels. com. 1983—93, chmn. 1987—89), Am. Coll. Critical Care Medicine (Disting. Investigator award 2000); mem.: We. Trauma Assn., Ea. Assn. Surgery Trauma, N.Am. Burn Soc. (pres. 1993—94), Shock Soc. (clin. counselor 1995—98, pres. 2007—08, chmn. 2005 program com.), Internat. Surg. Group, Surg. Infection Soc. (recorder 1980—84, pres. 1985—86), Assn. Acad. Surgery, Internat. Soc. Surgery, Surg. Biol. Club III, Am. Assn. Surgery Trauma (recorder 1976—80, bd. mgr. 1976—80, pres. 1982—83, bd. mgr. 1982—86, 1995—), Halsted Soc. (pres. 1985—86), So. Surg. Assn. (pres. 2004—05), We. Surg. Assn. (dist. rep. 1984—88, pres. 1993—94), Tex. Surg. Assn., Am. Surg. Assn. (2d v.p. 1980—81, pres. 1999—2000, Medallion 1998), Soc. Univ. Surgeons (Lifetime Achievement award 2007), Am. Trauma Soc. (pres. Tex. divsn. 1974—75, dir. 1974—, sec. 1986—88, v.p. 1988—90, pres.-elect 1990—92, pres. 1992—94), Am. Burn Assn. (life; program com. chmn. 1971—73, bd. trustees 1974—79, pres. 1975—76, chmn. archives com. 1991—, hon. mem. 2002, Lifetime Achievement award 2010), Internat. Soc. Burn Injuries (hon.; nat. rep. 1974—82, co-chmn. disaster planning com. 1982—86, pres.-elect 1990—94, pres. 1994—98, life mem. 2002), Smoke Burn and Fire Assn. (adv. coun. 1976—2008), Surgeons' Travel Club (pres. 2002—03), Mediterranean Club Burns and Fire Disasters (life; regional rep. Ams. 1999—). Home: 402 Tidecrest Dr San Antonio TX 78239-2517 Office: U Tex Health Sci Ctr Dept Surgery 7703 Floyd Curl Dr San Antonio TX 78229-3900 also: Editl Office Jour Trauma 7330 San Pedro Ste 654 San Antonio TX 78216-6236 Home Phone: 210-655-4769; Office Phone: 210-342-7903. Business E-Mail: pruitt@uthscsa.edu.

PRUITT, DEAN GARNER, psychologist, educator; b. Phila., Dec. 26, 1930; s. Dudley McConnell and Grace (Garner) P.; m. France Juliard, Dec. 27, 1959; children: Andre Juliard, Paul Dudley, Charles Alexandre. AB, Oberlin Coll., 1952, MS, Yale U., 1954, PhD, 1957. Postdoctoral fellow U. Mich., 1957-59; rsch. assoc. Northwestern U., 1959-61; asst. prof., then assoc. prof. U. Del., 1961-66; assoc. prof. to prof. SUNY, Buffalo, 1966—96, disting. prof., 1996—2001, disting. prof. emeritus, 2001—, dir. grad. program in social psychology, 1969—73, 1976—77, 1985—88, 1998—2001; disting. scholar in residence George Mason U., 2001—. Author: Negotiation Behavior, 1981, (with J. Z. Rubin and S.H. Kim) Social Conflict, 1986, 94, 2004, (with P.J. Carnevale) Negotiation in Social Conflict, 1993; editor: (with R.C. Snyder) Theory and Research on the Causes of War, 1969, (with K. Kressel) Mediation Research, 1989. Grantee Office Naval Rsch., 1965, NIMH, 1969, NSF, 1969, 74, 76, 80, 83, 86, 88, 93, Guggenheim Found., 1978-79. Fellow APA, Am. Psychol. Soc., Soc. for Psychol. Study Social Issues; mem. Internat. Assn. for Conflict Mgmt. (pres. 1990-92, Lifetime Achievement award 1997), Internat. Soc. Polit. Psychology (v.p. 1984-85, Harold D. Lasswell award 1992), Phi Beta Kappa, Sigma Xi. Home: 9006 Friars Rd Bethesda MD 20817-3320 Office: George Mason U Sch Conflict Analysis and Resolution Fairfax VA 22030-4444 E-mail: deangpruitt@gmail.com.

PRUSINER, STANLEY BEN, neurologist, biochemist, educator; b. Des Moines, May 28, 1942; s. Lawrence Albert and Miriam (Spigel) Prusiner; children: Helen Chloe, Leah Anne. AB cum laude, U. Pa., Phila., 1964, MD, 1968, DSc (hon.), 1998, Dartmouth Coll., Hanover, NH, 1999, U. Liege, Belgium, 2000, Pa. State U., 2001; PhD (hon.), Hebrew U., Jerusalem, 1995, René Descartes U., Paris, 1996, Claremont Grad. U., Calif., 2007; MD (hon.), U. Bologna, Italy, 2000. Diplomate Am. Bd. Neurology. Intern medicine U. Calif., San Francisco, 1968—69, resident neurology, 1972—74, asst. prof. neurology, 1974—80, assoc. prof., 1980—84, prof., 1984—, prof. biochemistry, 1988—2008, dir. Inst. Neurodegenerative Diseases, 1999—. Mem. neurology rev. com. Nat. Inst. Neurodegenerative Diseases (NIND), NIH, Bethesda, Md., 1982—86, Bethesda, 1990—92; mem. sci. adv. bd. French Found., LA, 1985—, chmn. sci. adv. bd., 1996—; mem. sci. rev. com. Alzheimer's Disease Diagnostic Ctr. & Rsch Grant Program, Calif., 1985—89; chmn. sci. adv. bd. Am. Health Assistance Found., Rockville, Md., 1986—2000, hon. mem. bd. dirs., 2001—; mem. adv. bd. Alzheimer's Disease and Related Disorders Found., San Francisco, 1985—91; mem. spongiform encephalopathy adv. com. FDA, 1997—2001; bd. govs. Found. Biomed. Rsch., Washington, 2002—; bd. dirs. Fromm Inst. Lifelong Learning, San Francisco, 2002—, Internat. Longevity Ctr., NYC, 2003—; chmn. bd. dirs. InPro Biotech. Inc., San Francisco, 2001—08; dir. Inst. Neurodegenerative Diseases, Imperial Coll., London, 2007—08. Editor: The Enzymes of Glutamine Metabolism, 1973, Slow Transmissible Diseases of the Nervous System, 2 vols., 1979, Prions--Novel Infectious Pathogens Causing Scrapie and CJD, 1987, Prion Diseases of Humans and Animals, 1992, Prions Prions Prions, 1996, Molecular and Genetic Basis of Neurologic Disease, 3d edit., 2003, Prion Biology and Diseases, 2d edit., 2004; contbr. articles to profl. jours. Trustee Congregation Sherith Israel, San Francisco, 1999—2002, U. Pa., 2000—05. Lt. comdr. USPHS, 1969—72. Recipient Potamkin prize for Alzheimer's Disease rsch., NIH, 1991, Disting. Med. Grad. award, U. Pa. Sch. Medicine, 1991, Med. Rsch. award, Met. Life Found., 1992, Christopher Columbus Discovery award, NIH/Med. Soc. Genoa, Italy, 1992, Charles A. Dana award, 1992, Dickson prize, U. Pitts., 1992, Max Planck Rsch. award, Alexander von Humboldt Found./Max Planck Soc., 1992, Gairdner Found. Internat. award, 1993, Albert Lasker award for basic med. rsch., 1994, Caledonian Rsch. Found. prize, Royal Soc. Edinburgh, 1995, Paul Ehrlich & Ludwig Darmstaedter award, Germany, 1995, Paul Hoch award, Am. Psychopath. Assn., 1995, Wolf Found. prize in medicine, Israel, 1996, ICN Virology prize, 1996, Victor & Clara Soriano award, World Fedn. Neurology, 1996, Pasarow Found. prize, 1996, Charles Leopole Mayer prize, French Acad. Scis., 1996, Keio Internat. prize, 1996, Baxter award, Am. Assn. Med. Colleges, 1996, Louisa Gross Horwitz prize, Columbia U., 1997, Nobel prize in physiology/medicine, 1997, K.J. Zulch prize, Gertrude Reemtsma Found., 1997, Benjamin Franklin medal, Franklin Inst., 1998, Jubilee medal, Swedish Med. Soc., 1998, Sir Hans Krebs medal, Fedn. European Biochem. Socs., 1999, Ellen Browning Scripps medal, 2000, Disting. Alumni award, U. Pa. Coll. Arts & Scis., 2003, Commonwealth award, 2004, William Beaumont medal, 2005, Nat. Medal Sci., The White House, 2010; grantee, Howard Hughes Med. Inst., 1976—81; Alfred P. Sloan Rsch. fellow, U. Calif., 1976—78. Fellow: AAAS, Royal Coll. Physicians, Am. Acad. Arts & Scis., Am. Soc. Microbiology; mem.: NAS (coun. mem. 2007—10, Inst. Medicine, Richard Lounsbery award extraordinary achievements biology and medicine 1993), NRC (governing bd. mem. 2008—), World Jewish Acad. Scis., Serbian Acad. Scis., Protein Soc. (Amgen award 1997), Royal Soc. London, Am. Philos. Soc., Am. Soc. Molecular Biol. & Biochemistry, Am. Soc. Cellular Biology, Am. Soc. Cell Biology, Genetics Soc. Am., Am. Soc. Human Genetics, Soc. Neurosci., Am. Chem. Soc., Am. Soc. Biochemistry & Molecular Biology, Am. Soc. Clin. Investigation, Am. Neurol. Assn., Am. Soc. Virology, Am. Soc. Neurochemistry, Am. Assn. Physicians, Am. Acad. Neurology (George Cotzias award outstanding rsch. 1987, Presdl. award 1993, Disting. Achievement award 1998), Bohemian Club, Concordia Argonaut Club (bd. dirs. 1997—2005). Office: U Calif Inst Neurodegenerative Diseases 513 Parnassus Ave HSE 774 San Francisco CA 94143-0518 Office Phone: 415-476-4482. Business E-Mail: stanley@ind.ucsf.edu. *

PRUZAN-CLAIN, DEBRA, dermatologist; Attended, Brown U., 1982, U. Pa., 1986. Diplomate Am. Bd. Dermatology. Intern internal medicine dept. Mt. Sinai Med. Ctr., NYC, 1987; resident dermatology dept. SUNY Health Sci. Ctr., Brooklyn, 1990; diplomate Ma. Acad. of Dermatology; hosp. affiliations include Stamford Hosp. Recipient Castle Connolly Top Doctor: New York Metro Area; named one of Castle Connolly Am.'s Top Doctor, Top Doctor Greenwich, Westport; named to Top Doctors, New York Magazine, 2011. Mem.: Fairfield County Med. Assn., Conn. State Med. Soc. Office: Dermatology Center of Stamford LLC 1290 Summer St Stamford CT 06905-5325 Office Phone: 203-325-3576. Office Fax: 203-325-4280.

PRYMULA, ROMAN, epidemiologist, department chairman; b. Pardubice, Czech Republic, Feb. 4, 1964; s. Adolf Prymula and Marie Prymulova; m. Ruslana Rudikova, July 19, 1986; children: Karolina Prymulova, Albert. MD, Sch. Medicine, Charles U., Hradec Kralove, 1988; PhD, Mil. Med. Acad., Hradec Kralove, 1994. Specialist in epidemiology Czech Republic, 1995, specialist in public health Sch. Pub. Health, Czech Republic, 1998, specialist in microbiology Czech Republic, 2003, cert. in internat. hosp. mgmt. HSMC, U. Birmingham, 1995, prof. hygiene, epidemiology and preventive medicine Pres. of Czech Republic, 2007. Asst. prof., dept. epidemiology Mil. Med. Acad., Hradec Kralove, Czech Republic, 1990—97, chair, dept. mgmt. and mil. pharmacy, 1998—2002, rector, 2002—04; dean Faculty Mil. Health Scis. U. Def., Hradec Kralove, Czech Republic, 2004—09, chair, dept. epidemiology, 2006—09; dir. U. Hosp., 2009—. Contbr. articles to profl. jours. Col. Med. Corps., 2005—08, Hradec Kralove. Decorated medal of Czech Republic Army III Min. Def., medal; recipient Rsch. grants, Ministry Health, 2000, Kredba prize, 2007; grantee Rsch. grants, Ministry Health, 1998; fellow Internat. Hosp. Mgmt. program, Brit. Coun., 1994; Rsch. grants, Ministry Health, 1996. Home: E Benese 1554 Hradec Králové 500 12 Czech Republic Office: University Hosp Hradec Kralove 500 05 Czech Republic Office Fax: 420-495-833-800. Personal E-mail: prymula@pmfhk.cz, prymula@seznam.cz.

PRYOR, CAROL GRAHAM, retired obstetrician, gynecologist; b. Savannah, Ga. m. Louis O.J. Manganiello, June 11, 1950; children: Carol Helen, Victoria Manganiello Mudano. AB, Ga. Coll., 1939; MD, Med. Coll. Ga., 1947. Rotating intern City Hosps., Balt., 1947-48; asst. resident pathology Baroness Erlanger Hosp., Chattanooga, 1948; intern. obstetrics City Colls., Balt., 1949; coll. physician Ga. State Coll. for Women, Milledgeville, Ga., 1949-50; resident obstetrics City Hosps., Balt., 1950-51; asst. resident gynecology Univ. Hosp., Balt., 1951-52, sr. resident ob-gyn. Augusta, Ga., 1952; pvt. practice ob-gyn. Augusta, 1952—2008; chmn. ob-gyn. St. Joseph Hosp., Augusta, 1998; ret., 2008. Chair ob-gyn. dept. St. Joseph Hosp., Augusta. Mem., former pres. Iris Garden Club, Augusta; mem. coun. on maternal and infant health State of Ga., Atlanta, 1981-90; mem. edn. found. AAUW, 1961-63, state v.p., state pres., 1963-65. Recipient Cert. of Achievement-Community Leadersip, Ga. div. AAUW, 1982; named Med. Woman of Yr., Ga. br. 51 Am. Med. Women's Assn., 1961; Heritage award Ga. Coll. and State U., 2001, Achievement award, Ga. Coll. U., 1982. Fellow ACS (1st woman mem. Ga. chpt.); mem. ACOG, AMA, Richmond County Med. Soc., So. Med. Assn., So. Surg. Congress, Delta Kappa Gamma. Democrat. Methodist. Personal E-mail: cpryor@bellsouth.net.

PRYOR, DAVID BRAM, health science association administrator; b. Charleston, SC, Oct. 18, 1951; s. Sydney and Grace Prystowsky; m. Christin Marie Kennedy; children: Rebecca Whitaker, Rachel Celia, Grace Eileen. Attended, U. Mich., Ann Arbor, 1969—72; MD, U. Mich. Med. Sch., 1972—76. Cert. Am. Bd. Internal Medicine, 1979, bd. cert. cardiovascular diseases 1983, lic. Pa., 1976, NC, 1979, Mass., 1994, Minn., 1996, Mo., 2004. Intern in medicine Pa. Hosp., Phila., 1976—77, resident in medicine, 1977—79; fellow in cardiology Duke U. Med. Ctr., Durham, NC, 1979—81, asst. prof. medicine, 1983—89, assoc. prof. medicine, 1989—94; sr. staff mem. cardiovascular divsn. Duke U., Durham, NC, 1981—94, dir. section clinical epidemiology and biostatistics, 1984—89, dir. clinical program devel., 1993—94; pres. New England Med. Ctr. Hosp., Boston, 1994—95; prof. medicine Tufts U. Sch. Medicine, 1994—97; sr. v.p./chief info. officer Allina Health Sys., Mpls., 1995—2001; chief med. officer Ascension Health, St. Louis, 2001—. Program com. and biometry track chair 11th Symposium on Computer Applications in Med. Care, 1987; bd. dir. Clinical Rsch. Internat., Inc., 1989—90, PatientKeeper (Virtmed) Inc., 2001—06; chmn. task force reducing med. uncertainty Joint Commn. Accreditation Healthcare Orgn., 1989—91, adv. coun. performance measurement, 1995—2005, chmn. adv. coun. performance measurement, 1998—2003, mem. performance measurement coord. com., 1998—2000; chmn. epidemiology and prevention track Am. Coll. Cardiology Sci. Session Com., 1991—92, chmn. health svc. delivery track, 1991—92; mem. exec. com. and steering com. Health Care Financing Adminstrn., Coop. Cardiovascular Project, 1992—94; chmn. ops. com. Acad. Med. Ctr. Consortium, 1992—94; mem. sci. session program com. Am. Heart Assn., 1994—96; chmn. bd. dir. Strategicare, Inc., 1996—99; bd. gov. Bioengineering Inst., U. Minn., Mpls., 1996—2002; mem. 2000 Spring Congress Sci. Program com. Am. Med. Informatics Assn. (AMIA), 1999—2000; mem. IT expert adv. panel Nat. Quality Forum (NQF) Nat. Forum for Health Care

Quality Measurement and Reporting, 2001—02; mem. adv. bd. Ctr. Info. Tech. Leadership (CITL), 2001—10; cons. prof. Cardiovascular Inst., Favaloro Found., Buenos Aires, 1994—97; cons. assoc. prof. medicine Duke U. Med. Ctr., 1994—; adj. prof. epidemiology U. Minn. Sch. Pub. Health, Mpls., 1996—2002; pres. New England Med. Ctr., Boston, 1994—95; adj. prof. St. Louis U. Sch. Pub. Health; numerous positions with Allina Health Sys., Mpls., 1995—2001; reviewer numerous jour. and rsch. grants; presenter in field; mem. numerous nat. and internat. com.; cons. in field. Contbr. articles to jour., chapters to books. Recipient Innovations in IT awards, 2nd place, HIMMS and Deloitte and Touche (Allina Health Sys.), 1998, Tng. for Future, 3rd place, Allina Health Sys., 1998, Quest for Best award, 2000, Silver award, 2001, 50 Most Powerful Physician Execs., Modern Healthcare, 2008, CareScience Exec. Leadership award, 2006; named Laureate, Computerworld Smithsonian award, Allina Health Sys., 1999, Lifetime Scholar, Barton Haynes Soc., Duke U., 2005; named one of 100 Most Powerful People in Healthcare, Modern Healthcare, 2002, 2005, 50 Most Powerful Physician Execs., Modern Physician, 2005, Modern Healthcare, 2006; fellow, Am. Coll. Med. Informatics, 1986, Am. Soc. Clinical Investigation, 1992. Fellow: Am. Coll. Med. Informatics, Am. Coll. Physicians, Am. Coll. Cardiology; mem.: Am. Med. Informatics Assn., Am. Heart Assn. (fellow coun. on clinical cardiology), Am. Soc. Clinical Investigation, Am. Fedn. Clinical Rsch. Office: Ascension Health 4600 Edmundson Rd Saint Louis MO 63134 Office Phone: 314-733-8192, 314-733-8196. Business E-Mail: dpryor@ascensionhealth.org.

PRYPCHAN, LIDA D., psychiatrist; b. Caracas, Venezuela, July 8, 1960; arrived in USA, 1989; d. Roman Orestes Prypchan Hryculak and Edel Sayagues Sanchez. MD, U. Carabobo, Venezuela, 1986. Cert. physician Ednl. Commn. Fgn. Med. Grads., USA, Venezuela, adult psychiatrist U. Ctrl. Venezuela, Venezuelan Psychiatric Assn. Physician Clinica Residencia Carabobo, Valencia, Venezuela, 1986—89; rsch. assoc., the Schizophrenia Project at We. Psychiatric Inst. and Clinic U. Pitts. Med. Ctr., 1989—90, rsch. assoc., the Anxiety Disorders Project at Pitts. Adolescent Alcohol Rsch. Ctr., 1990—92, sr. rsch. assoc. World Psychiatric Assn., 1990—94; adult psychiatric resident Hosp. U. Caracas, U. Ctrl. de Venezuela, 1996—99, Elmhurst Hosp. Ctr., NY, 2001—05; fellow Child and Adolescent Psychiatry Elmhurst Hosp. Ctr., Mt. Sinai Sch. Medicine, 2005—07; attending adult, child and adolescent psychiatrist Wyo. Behavioral Inst., 2007—. Sr. rsch. assoc. Elmhurst Hosp. Ctr./World Psychiatric Assn., 2003—05; founder ppplusa.org, 2008. Contbr. articles to profl. jours. Active mem. Soka Gakkai Internat.-USA, 1989—. Recipient Nat. Sci. Journalism award, Venezuela, 1987, 1988, 1989. Mem.: AMA, Nat. Assn. Mental Illness, Wyo. Psychiatric Assn., Wyo. Med. Assn., Acad. Child and Adolescent Psychiatry, Am. Psychiatric Assn. Democrat. Buddhist. Avocations: movies, theater, travel, walking, reading. Home: 2661 East 15th St Unit 204 Casper WY 82609 Office: Wyo Behavioral Inst 2417 East 15th St Casper WY 82609 Office Phone: 307-237-7444. Personal E-mail: lidaprypchan@hotmail.com.

PRYZDIA, MICHAEL RAYMOND, language educator; b. Chgo., June 3, 1963; BA, Lewis U., 1986; PhD, Bowling Green State U., 1994. Lectr. Ariz. State U., 2004—. Cons. Life Design, Inc., 1994—2004. Mem.: Assn. Integrated Studies. Avocation: yoga. Office: 411 N Ctrl Ave Phoenix AZ 85004 Office Fax: 602-496-0655. Business E-Mail: michael.pryzdia@asu.edu.

PRZYBYLSKI, SANDRA MARIE, speech pathologist; b. Berwyn, Ill. d. Raymond and Julie Marie (Vocelka) Hammers; m. James Przybylski; children: Eric, Sara. BS, U. Iowa, 1968; MA, U. Ill., 1971. Cert. clin. speech pathologist; speech/lang., educable mentally retarded education, learning disabilites and elem. tchr., life, Mo. Speech, lang. pathologist LaPlata Sch. Dist., Mo., 1974—87, Maysville Sch. Dist., Mo., 1990—92, Bucklin Sch. Dist., Mo., 1992—2005; speech therapist Ability Network, Sainte Genevieve, Mo., 2002—, Schuyler County Sch. Dist., Mo., 2005—09. Named to Disting. Svc. Registry-Speech and Hearing, 1990. Mem. Am. Speech, Lang., Hearing Assn., Autism Soc. Am., Mo. State Tchrs. Assn., Mo. Speech, Lang. and Hearing Assn. Personal E-mail: sprzy02@yahoo.com.

PSENÁK, OSKAR, internist, researcher, educator; b. Nové Zámky, Czechoslovakia, Sept. 30, 1973; s. Judita Psenáková and Karol Psenák. MD, Charles U., Prague, 1998, PhD, 2003. Resident internist Gen. U. Hosp., Prague, 1999—2003, Paracelsus Tchg. U. Hosp., Salzburg, Austria, 2004—08, specialist internal medicine, 2008—; asst. prof. Charles U., 1st Med. Sch., Prague, 2003—04. Contbr. articles to profl. jours. Recipient Mayor's prize for clin. cancer rsch., Nové Zámky, 2005. Mem.: Austrian Med. Assn. Roman Catholic. Avocations: classical music, history, languages, movies, piano. Home: Rudolf-Biebl Str 2/Top 39 Salzburg 5020 Austria Office: Paracelsus Univ Hosp Dept Internal Medicine III Mullner Hauptstr 48 Salzburg 5020 Austria Business E-Mail: psenak@europe.com.

PTACEK, LOUIS JOHN, medical educator, medical researcher; b. Madison, Wis., May 14, 1961; married. BS in Math., U. Wis., Madison, 1982, MD, 1986. Lic. Utah, 1987, cert. Am. Bd. Neurology and Psychiatry, 1993, lic. Calif., 2005. Intern in medicine U. Wash., 1986—87; resident in neurology U. Utah, 1987—90, chief neurology resident, 1989—90, Muscular Dystrophy Assn. neuromuscular fellow, 1990—91, postdoc in molecular biology, 1991—94, instr. neurology, 1990—92, asst. prof. neurology, 1992—96, assoc. prof. neurology and human genetics, 1996—2002, dir. neurogenetics divsn., 2000—03, prof. neurology and human genetics, 2002—03; prof. neurology U. Calif., San Francisco, 2003—, dir. neurogenetics divsn., 2003—, John C. Coleman disting. prof. neurogenerative diseases, 2004—. Assoc. investigator Howard Hughes Med. Inst., 1997—2003, investigator, 2003—. Assoc. editor Annals of Neurology, 1997—, Neurogenetics, 1997—, Neuromuscular Disorders, 2000—04, Jour. Neuroscience, 2005—. Fellow: Am. Acad. Arts and Sciences, Am. Soc. for Clin. Investigation; mem.: Am. Acad. Neurology, NAS Inst. Medicine. Office: U Calif San Francisco Fu & Ptacek Labs 1550 4th St San Francisco CA 94158-2324 Office Phone: 415-502-5614. Office Fax: 415-502-5641. E-mail: ljp@ucsf.edu.

PTAK, JEFFREY J., plastic surgeon; BA, Stanford U., 1972; MD, Mich. State U., 1980. Diplomate Am. Bd. Plastic Surgery, 1989. Chief resident gen. surgery Maricopa Med. Ctr., Phoenix, 1985; intern plastic surgery Univ. of NC, Chapel Hill, 1987; instr. plastic surgery Mayo Med. Sch., Scottsdale, Ariz.; lectr. plastic surgery topics & sci. technologies. Fellow: Am. Coll. of Surgeons; mem.: Ariz. Med. Assn., Am. Soc. of Aesthetic Plastic Surgeons, Ariz. Plastic & Reconstructive Surgeons, Am. Soc. of Plastic Surgeons. Office: 9431 E Ironwood Square Dr Scottsdale AZ 85258 Office Phone: 480-451-9220. Office Fax: 480-451-9226.

PTASHNE, MARK STEVEN, molecular biology professor; b. Chgo., June 5, 1940; s. Fred and Mildred P.; m. Lucy Gordon, 1994. BA, Reed Coll., 1961; PhD, Harvard U., 1968. Lectr. biochemistry Harvard U., Cambridge, Mass., 1968-71, prof., 1971—73, chmn. dept. biochemistry and molecular biology, 1980-83, Herchel Smith prof. of molecular biology, 1993-97; Ludwig prof. molecular biology Sloan Kettering Cancer Rsch. Ctr., NYC, 1997—. Feodor Lynen lectr. U. Miami, Fla., 1988. Author: A Genetic Switch, 1986; contbr. numerous articles to sci. jours. Recipient Eli Lilly award, 1975, prix. Charles-Leopold Mayer Acad. des Scis., Inst. de France, 1977, Louisa Gross Horwitz prize Bd. Trustees Columbia U., 1985, Gairdner Found. Internat. award, 1985, Albert Lasker award for Basic Med. Rsch., Lasker Found., 1997; co-recipient Ledle award Harvard U., 1986, GM Sloan prize, 1990. Fellow N.Y. Acad. Sci., Am. Acad. Sci.; mem. NAS, Fedn. Am. Scis. (bd. sponsors 1981). Avocations: opera, classical music, violin. Office: Sloan Kettering Cancer Rsch Ctr 1275 York Ave # New York NY 10021-6094 Office Phone: 212-639-2297. Office Fax: 212-717-3627. Business E-Mail: m-ptashne@mskcc.org. *

PUANGSUVAN, SOMPORN, surgeon, consultant; b. Rajburi, Thailand, 1941; arrived in US, 1967; s. Boon and Sanguan P.; m. Chintana Chanvitayapongs, Mar. 18, 1978; children: Nick, Neesann. MD, Chiengmai U., Thailand, 1966. Diplomate Am. Bd. Surgery. Intern St. Clares Hosp., NYC, 1967—68; resident Aultman Hosp., Canton, Ohio, 1968—69, Tuskegee VA Hosp., Ala., 1969—73; pvt. practice Caruthersville, Mo., 1979—. Attending physician Pemiscot County Meml. Hosp., Hayti, Mo., chief surgery 1994, surg. cons. 1979—. Fellow ACS. Office: Doctors Clinic PO Box 201 Caruthersville MO 63830-0201 Office Phone: 573-333-1124.

PUCCI, ALDO RAYMOND, behavior management specialist; b. East Liverpool, Ohio, Nov. 4, 1963; s. Dominic Thomas Jr. and Maria Pia (Rossi) P.; m. Sandra Lea Hough, June 15, 1985; 1 child, Aldo Raymond Jr. BA in Psychology, West Liberty State Coll., 1985; MA in Clin. Psychology, Radford U., 1987. Psychologist Cumberland Mountain Community Svcs., Cedar Bluff, Va., 1987-89, dir. of evaluation, 1989-90; behavior mgmt. specialist Hancock-Brooke Mental Health Svcs., Weirton, W.Va., 1990; now pres. Rational Living Therapy Inst., Weirton, W.Va. Mem. adj. faculty SE Va. CC, Richlands, 1987-90. Mem.: Nat. Assn. Cognitive-Behavioral Therapists (pres.). Avocations: electronics, computer science, body building. Office: Rational Living Therapy Inst 102 Gilson Ave Weirton WV 26062 Office Phone: 304-723-3980. Business E-Mail: aldo@rational-living-therapy.org. *

PUCCIONI-SOHLER, MARZIA, neurologist, researcher, educator; d. Ettore and Zelia Nunes (Puccioni) P.; 2 children. Med. diplomate, Fluminense Fed. U., Niteroi, Rio de Janeiro, 1984; MS in Neurology, 1991; specialist in neurology, Pontificia U. Católica, Rio de Janeiro, 1987; PhD, Georg August U., Goettingen, Germany, 1995. Neurologist, med. resident in internal medicine and neurology Fed. U. Rio de Janeiro, 1985—88; mem. staff neurology svc. Clementino Fraga Filho U. Hosp./Fed. U. Rio de Janeiro, 1988—2000, responsible Cerebrospinal Fluid Lab. clin. pathology dept., 1999—, coord. rsch. com., 2002—; postdoctoral Neuro-Immunology br. NIH, Bethesda, Md., 2002. Cons. Cerebrospinal Fluid Lab (Neurolife), Rio de Janeiro, 1995—; adj. prof. neurology Sch. Medicine and Surgery, U. Rio de Janeiro, 2002—. Contbr. articles to profl. jours. Grantee Deutscher Akademischer Autauschdienst (DAAD), 1991-94, Conselho Nacional de Pesquisa, 1994, 2000, 2004 rsch. grantee Funcação Universitária José Bonifácio, 1998-2000, 2004—, travel grantee Fundação de Amparo e Pesquisa Rio de Janeiro, 2000, 04. Mem. Brazilian Acad. Neurology (coord. Brazilian cerebrospinal fluid group 2000-2004), Internat. Soc. Neurovirology. Office: Fed U Rio de Janeiro Rio de Janeiro RJ Brazil Home: Praia do Flamengo 66 - 219. Sala - 220 22210-903 Rio de Janeiro RJ Brazil Office Phone: 55 21 25622494. Business E-Mail: mpuccioni@hucff.ufrj.br.

PUDDU, PAOLO EMILIO, cardiologist, educator, researcher; b. Rome, Oct. 7, 1952; s. Claudio Puddu and Maria Antonietta Dantoni; m. Isabella del Balzo di Presenzano, Nov. 29, 1979 (dec. Nov. 18, 2008); children: Antonio Raimondo, Gian Lorenzo (dec.), Pier Ludovico, Francesco Simone. MD, Univ. La Sapienza, Rome, 1976, diploma in cardiology, 1979; diploma in hemodynamics, U. Montreal, Can., 1980; Diploma in Exptl. Surgery, U. Marseilles, France, 1983. Rsch. fellow U. Montreal, 1979-80, U. Marseilles, 1980-84; asst. prof. U. Rome, 1984-90; prof. pharmacology Cardiology Sch., Rome, 1990—2006, prof. cardiovasc. medicine, 2007—; dir. lab. cardiovascular pharmacology U. Rome Sch. Medicine, 1991—. Contbr. articles to profl. jours. Lt. Italian Air Force, 1978. Fellow: European Soc. Cardiology, Am. Coll. Cardiology; mem.: Assn. Cardiovasc. Rsch. (Rome) (v.p. 2006—), French Soc. Pharmacology (corr.), Italian Soc. Cardiovasc. Rsch. (founding), French Soc. Cardiology. Avocations: heraldry, pope history, enthomology. Office: Inst Cardiac Surgery Viale del Policlinico 161 Rome RM Italy Office Phone: 3964997-2659. E-mail: puddu.pe@iol.it.

PUDDU, PIETRO, dermatologist, hospital administrator; s. Giovanni Raffaelle and Elena Emilia. MBBChir, State U. Milan, Italy, 1985; specialization in Allergy and Immunology, U. Rome La Sapienza, 1997; B in Medicine and Surgery, U. Milan, 1985. Cert. specialist dermatology Cath. U. Sacro Cuore, 1989, specialist in rheumatology U. Siena, Italy, 1997. Asst. dermatologist Inst. Dermopatico Dell'immacolata, Rome, 1985—86; hosp. chief Missionary San Michele Noen, Cameroon, 1987—89; cons. dermatologist 5th Divsn., 1993—; health svc. coord. and scientific dir. and missionary hosp. and outpatient clinics Zojaekeschillit Temire, Tiran, Albania, 1995—99; dir. immunodermatology Inst. Dermopatico Dell'immacolata, Rome, 1998—2004; mem. Sr. Counsel Italian Healthcare. Sci. dir. Inst. Dermopatico Dell'immacolata, Rome, 1998—2004, dir. immunodermatology, 1999—2004; advisor to pres. IDI Healthcare Group, 1999—2004. Co-author (with A.R. Buffo): Dermatologia, 1999; author (with Ciminelli, Gianetti and Rebora): Manuale di Dermatologia Medica E Chirurgica: Autoimmune System of the Skin, 2004; contbr. chapters to books, articles to 159 profl. jours. Mem. scientific-tech. safety com. Winter Olympic Games, Turin, Italy, 2006. Comdr. Italian Army, 1997. Named Commendatore of Italian Republic, 1997, Order Malta, Sovereign Mil. Hospitaller Order St. Johns Jerusalem Rhodes Malta, 1997. Mem.: Internat. Soc. Tropical, Geographical & Ecol. Dermatology, Internat. Soc. Dermatology Tropical, Geographical and Ecological, European Soc. Dematol. Rsch., Italian Soc. Dermatology Venerology. Roman Catholic. Avocations: sailing, model electric trains. Office: Inst Dermopatico Dell immacolata Via Dei Monti di Creta 104 00167 Rome RM Italy Office Phone: 0039 06 6646 4427. Office Fax: 0039 06 6646 4496, 06 66464227.

PUENTE, RAUL, gynecologic oncologist, researcher; b. La Unión, Chile, May 28, 1946; s. Raúl Puente and Clemencia Piccardo; m. María Antonieta Guerrero, Dec. 18, 1973; children: Andrea, María Fernanda, Fabián. Licence in medicine, Sch. of Medicine U. de Concepción, Chile, 1971; MD, Faculty of Medicine U. de Chile, 1972; MD in gynecologic oncology, Dept. OB-GYN U. Austral, Chile, 1978. Specialist in OB-GYN Faculty of Medicine U. Austral de Chile, 1975. Attendant gynecologist Dept. OB-GYN, Hosp. Regional U. Austral, Valdivia, Chile, 1972—75, asst. prof., 1984—97, chief of gynecology, 1982—, chief of gynecologic oncology, 1985—, assoc. prof., 1997—2002, full prof., 2002—. Mem. adv. bd. of tumors. Hosp. Regional U. Austral, Valdivia, Chile, 1980—, mem. adv. bd. gynecologic oncology, 1986—; pres. Sociedad Austral de Obstetricia y Ginecologia, Valdivia, Chile, 1989—91; dir. Dept. OB-GYN, Hosp. Regional U. Austral, 1997—2004; mem. sci. bd. Virtual Acad. of Medicine Help.Net, Basilea, Switzerland, 2000—; sec. pre-congress course Internat. Gynecologic Cancer Soc., Buenos Aires, 2000, mem. internat. sci. com., Louisville, 00; pres. Gynecologic Oncology First Mtg. Chile-Argentina, Valdivia, Chile, 2001; mem. nat. adv. bd. post grad. fellowship, ob-gyn Chilean Assn. Faculties of Medicine, Santiago, Chile, 2001—; founding pres. Chilean Soc. Gynecologic Oncology, Santiago, Chile, 2001—; reviewer cons. Critical Reviews in Oncology/Hematology. Elsevier B.V., Genolier, Switzerland, 2002, European Jour. of OB-GYN and Reproductive Biology. Elsevier B.V., Amsterdam, 2003—; mem. editl. bd. Elsevier Publishers B.V., Amsterdam, 2005—; reviewer cons. Internat. Gynecologic Cancer Soc., Louisville, 2005. Contbr. articles various profl. jours. Recipient Fgn. Hon. Mem., Asociación Argentina de Ginecología Oncológica, 2003, Pres., Chilean Soc. of Gynecologic Oncology, 2004. Fellow: ACS (assoc.); mem.: Sociedad Chilena de Ginecología Oncológica (assoc.), NY Acad. of Scis. (assoc.), Asociación Argentina de Ginecología Oncológica (assoc.), European Soc. of Gynecol. Oncology (assoc.), Internat. Gynecologic Cancer Soc. (assoc.), Sociedad Chilena de Colposcopia y Patología del Tracto Genital Inferior (assoc.), Sociedad Austral de Obstetricia y Ginecología (assoc.), Sociedad Chilena de Obstetricia y Ginecología (assoc.). Roman Catholic. Avocations: driving, travel, gastronomy, movies, lyrics. Office: Hosp RegionalU Austral Simpson 850 5 Piso Valdivia Casilla 567 Chile Home: Carlos Anwandter 400 567 Valdivia Chile Office Fax: 56.63. 221693; Home Fax: 56.63.221693. E-mail: rpuente@uach.cl.

PUESCHEL, SIEGFRIED M., pediatrician, educator; b. Waldenburg, Germany, July 28, 1931; came to U.S., 1961; naturalized, 1971; widowed. Student, Braunschweig Coll., Germany, 1953-55, Leibniz Coll., Tubingen, Germany, 1955-56, U. Tubingen, Germany, 1955-57, Free U., Berlin, 1957-58, U. Freiburg, Germany, 1958; MD summa cum laude, Med. Acad., Dusseldorf, Germany, 1960; MPH, Harvard U., 1967; PhD, U. R.I., 1985; JD, So. New Eng. Sch. Law, 1996. Diplomate Am. Bd. Pediatrics, Am. Bd. Med. Genetics. Intern Mercer Hosp., Trenton, NJ, 1961-62; jr. resident in pediatrics Children's Hosp., Honolulu, 1962-63; asst. resident in pediatrics Children's Hosp. Med. Ctr., Boston, 1963-64, asst. in mental retardation, 1967-68, assoc. in mental retardation, 1968-75, dir. Down Syndrome Program, 1970-75, dir. PKU Clinic, 1972-75; sr. resident in pediatrics Montreal Children's Hosp., 1964-65, fellow in biochemical genetics/metabolism, 1965-66; assoc. physician R.I. Hosp., Providence, 1975-79, dir. child devel. ctr., 1975-94, dir. PKU and Amino Acid Program, 1975—, dir. Down Syndrome Program, 1978—, physician, 1979—. Instr. pediatrics Harvard U., Cambridge, Mass., 1968-74, asst. prof. in pediatrics, 1974-75, lectr. in pediatrics, 1975—; asst. prof. in pediatrics Brown U., Providence, 1975-77, assoc. prof. in pediatrics, 1977-85, prof. in pediatrics, 1985—; consulting pediatrician Waltham (Mass.) Hosp., 1968-75; cons. in genetics Lying in Hosp., Boston, 1969-75, Women and Infants Hosp., Providence, 1975—; cons. Devel. Evaluation Clinic Children's Hosp. Med. Ctr., Boston, 1975—; mem. prevention of mental retardation com. Internat. League of Socs. for Persons with Mental Handicaps; mem. rsch., prevention and program svc. com. Assn. for Retarded Citizens U.S.; mem. nat. conf. on rsch. perspectives in down syndrome Nat. Inst. Child Health and Rehab. Svcs.; mem. state-of-the-art conf. on down syndrome Office Spl. Edn. and Rehab. Svcs. U.S. Dept. Edn.; mem. nat. adv. child health and human devel. coun. NIH, Washington; mem. sub-com. on tng., edn. and quality assurance-tech. assistance Devel. Disabilities Coun., R.I.; mem. med. adv. com. Spl. Olympics. Author chpts. to books; mem. editl. bd. Down Syndrome Papers and Abstracts for Profls., Exceptional Parents, Down's Syndrome: Rsch. and Practice; reviewer numerous jours.; contbr. articles to profl. jours. Grantee Mass. Dept. Health, 1968, Vigneron Meml. Fund, 1984-85, Charlotte Taylor Fund, 1985-86, Dept. Health and Human Svcs., 1982-86, March of Dimes Nat. Found., 1987-89, Sigma-Tau Pharm., Inc., 1990-93; recipient Recongnition award March of Dimes, 1976, Recognition award Blackstone Valley chpt. R.I. Assn. for Retarded Citizens, 1979, Fogarty Founders award, 1988, Edn. award Muscular Dystrophy Assn., 1985, 86, Muscular Dystrophy Tchg. award, 1988, Recognition award Devel. Ctr. for Handicapped Personsn-Utah State U., 1986, Down Syndrome Assn. of Greater Cin. award, 1986, Colegion John Langdown Down award Mexico City, 1987, Disting. Rsch. award Assn. for Retarded Citizens of U.S., 1990, Conn. Down Syndrome Assn. award, 1991, Sindrome de Down award Asociación Down de Monterrey (Mexico), 1994. Fellow Am. Acad. Pediatrics, Am. Coll. Med. Genetics (founder); mem. AAAS, Am. Assn. Mental Retardation (Profl. Contbn. award 1991), Am. Acad. Cerebral Palsy and Devel. Medicine, Am. Pediatric Soc., Am. Soc. Human Genetics, Nat. Down Syndrome Congress (past pres., Recognition for Disting. Svc. award 1980, Mid-Hudson Valley award 1983, Achievement in Rsch. award 1988, Outstanding Physician award 1991), N.Y. Acad. Sci., R.I. Med. Soc., New Eng. Regional Genetics Group, Soc. Inherited Metabolic Disorders, Down Syndrome Soc. R.I. (award 1985), Assn. for Children with Down Syndrome (bd. dirs.). Office: RI Hosp Child Devel Ctr 593 Eddy St Providence RI 02903-4923 Office Phone: 401-444-8477.

PUFFER, JAMES C., sports medicine physician, educator, medical association administrator; married. BS, UCLA, MD, 1976. Prof., chief, divsn. family medicine UCLA; prof., family medicine Univ. Ky., Lexington; exec. dir., sec. Am. Bd. Family Medicine, Lexington,

Ky., 2003—05, pres., CEO, 2005—. Physician US Winter Olympic Team, Sarajevo, 1984; head team physician US Summer Olympic Team, Seoul, 1988; mem., sports medicine, sports sci. coun. US Olympic Com., 1985—92; com. mem. NCAA Com. on Competitive Safeguards and Med. Aspects of Sports, 1983—90; cons. Pres. Coun. on Physical Fitness and Sports, 1988—90. Assoc. editor Medicine and Science in Sports and Exercise, 1989—98, editor-in-chief Sports Medicine Digest, 1992—, editl. bd. mem., peer reviewer numerous profl. jours. Recipient Duke Paoa Kahanamoku award, USA Water Polo, 2004. Fellow: Am. Coll. Sports Medicine; mem.: US Olympic Sports Medicine Soc. (bd. dir. 1993—96), Am. Med. Soc. for Sports Medicine (pres. 1996—97, founding mem.), Am. Bd. Family Medicine (bd. dir. 1989—94, exec. com. mem.-at-large 1993—94, v.p. bd. dir. 1993—94). Avocation: water polo. Office: American Board of Family Med Ste 550 1648 Mcgrathiana PKWY Lexington KY 40511-1342 Office Phone: 859-269-5626. Business E-Mail: jpuffer@theabfm.org. *

PUGH WILLIAMS, SALLY, physician; b. St. Athan, Vale of Glamorgan, Wales, Mar. 24, 1955; children: Dafydd, Wiliam. MB BCh, Welsh Nat. Sch. Medicine, Cardiff, 1978. Sr. house officer in cardiology Riyadh Armed Forces Hosp., Riyadh, Saudi Arabia, 1979—80; tng. internal medicine South Wales Hosps., 1980—83; prin. in gen. practice Wokingham, England, 1989—90; med. advisor INCO Europe, Swansea, Wales, 1992—95, occupl. health svcs. mgr., 1995—2004; dir. Health and Environment Nickel Inst., 1996—2004; chief med. officer Inco Ltd., Toronto, Ont., Canada, 2004—06; regional med. officer Tata Steel, Wales, 2006—; med. advisor Brit. Steel Pensions Funds, 2009. Chair sci. adv. com. Nickel Producers Environ. Rsch. Assn., Durham, NC, 1996—2000; chair health adv. group Eurometaux, Brussels, 1997—2000. Contbr. chpt. to med. books. Named Welsh Woman of Yr., Western Mail and Echo, 2002; fellowship, RCP, 1998. Home: 3 Cwrt Llanfair Saint Mary Ch Cowbridge CF71 7PH Wales Personal E-mail: sal24pw@hotmail.com.

PUGLIESE, AGOSTINO GIORGIO ANGELO, microbiologist; b. Turin, Italy, May 23, 1948; MD, U. Turin, 1973. Lic. MD Italy, 1973, postdoc. in microbiology Turin, 1976, postdoc. in hygiene and preventive medicine Parma, 1979, postdoc. in infectious diseases Turin, 1984. Prof. medicine U. Turin, 1977—2007, ret., 2007, collaborator. Contbr. articles to profl. jours., chapters to books. Mem.: Italian Soc. Virol, Italian Soc. Allergol & Clin Immunol, NY Acad. Scis., European Soc. Clin. Microbiol. & Infectious Disease, Lions Club (assoc.). Achievements include research in clinical microbiology & in viral emergent infections & autoimmune diseases. Office Phone: 039 011 4393865. Office Fax: 039 011 4393882. Business E-Mail: agostino.pugliese@nethouse.it.

PUGLISI, FILADELFIO, engineer; b. Florence, Italy, Nov. 5, 1943; s. Alfio and Maria (Gulisano) P.; m. Giovanna Michi, Jan. 29, 1975; children: Alfio Timothy, Annalena. Doctorate, U. Pisa, Italy, 1970. Dir. aux. svcs. S. Cabrini Hosp., Montreal, Can., 1972-74; design engr. Montreal Engring. Co., Can., 1974-77; rsch. assoc. U. Montreal, 1977-81; prof. Tech. Inst. L. DaVinci, Florence, Italy, 1981—, U. Florence, 2002—; head bioengring. unit F.P.J., Florence, 1980—. Author: (book) The Renaissance Flutes of Italy, 1995, Biomeccanica, 2007; contbg. author: Electrophysiological Kinesiology, 1993, Respiratory and Critical Care Medicine, 1996, Ear Acupuncture Diagnosis, 2010. Lt. Italian artillery, 1970-72. Mem. European Soc. Biomechanics, Am. Soc. Automotive Engring. Roman Catholic. Avocation: early music. Home: Via Pilastri 34 I-50121 Florence Italy Office: Tech Inst L Da Vinci via Del Terzolle 91 Firenze 50127 Italy Business E-Mail: filadelfio.puglisi@tin.it.

PUISEUX-DAO, SIMONE, retired biology professor; b. Paris, Sept. 5, 1930; d. Toai Ngoc Dao and Emilie Chambon; m. Gérard Puiseux; children: Dominique Puiseux, Pascale Puiseux. Ecole Normale Superieure, Faculty Sci. Paris, 1949—53, Agregation, 1953, DSc, 1960. Rschr. Nat. Ctr. Sci. Rsch., Paris, 1953—56; asst. in botany Faculty Sci., Paris, 1956—59, chief botany, 1959—65; prof. cell biology and environ. toxicology Faculty Sci., then U. Paris 7, 1965—99; prof. emeritus U. Paris 7, 1999—. Head associated unit Nat. Ctr. Sci. Rsch., Paris, 1974—86; head unit Nat. Inst. Health and Med. Rsch., Villefranche/Mer, France, 1985—93. Author: (book) Acetabularia and Cell Biology, 1970; editor: Molecular Biology of Nucleocytoplasmic Relationships, 1975; co-editor: (book collection) Rencontres en Toxinologie, 2001; co-editor: (founding) Plant Sci. Letters (now Plant Sci.), 1973; author: (films) Intracellular Streaming in Acetabularia Mediterranea, 1977 (Internat. prize for sci. film Venice, 1977, 1st French prize Toulouse, 1978). Named Knight, Order of Merit, 1975, Officer, 1981, Knight, Palmes Académiques, 1977, Officer, 1986, Comdr., 1998. Mem.: French Soc. Study Toxins (founding pres.), Assn. Rsch. Toxicology (founding pres.). Avocations: music, travel, cooking. Office: Nat Mus Natural History 12 rue Buffon Paris 75005 France Home Phone: 33 (0)1 45 66 80 68; Office Phone: 33 (0)1 40 79 31 83. Office Fax: 33 (0)1 40 79 35 94. Business E-Mail: spdao@mnhn.fr.

PUKEL, CLIFFORD STUART, physician; b. Bronx, NY, Nov. 15, 1955; s. Bayas William and Pearl (Buchholtz) P.; children: Zachariah, Jacob. BA in Biology, Queens Coll. CUNY, 1979; MD, U. Miami, 1991. Rsch. technician Sloan-Kettering Inst. for Cancer Rsch., NYC, 1980-83, rsch. asst., 1983-85; rsch. assoc. dept. medicine U. Miami, Fla., 1985-87; resident dept. internal medicine U. W.Va., Charleston, 1991-94; fellow hematology, oncology, instr. medicine Dartmouth-Hitchcock Med. Ctr., Lebanon, NH, 1994-97; pvt. practice Wichita, 1998—2000, Eau Claire, Wis., 2000—02, Vince Lombardi Cancer Clinic, Green Bay, Wis., 2002—07, Aurora Bay Care Med. Ctr., Green Bay, 2002—07; asst. prof. clin. medicine U. Kans. Sch. Medicine, Wichita, 1998-99, U. Wis. Sch. Medicine, Madison, 2000—; CEO Cancer Vaccine Inst., Cancer Immunotherapy Inst., 2009—; asst. prof. SMG hematology-oncology clinic SW Washington Med. Ctr., Vancouver, 2009—. Vis. scientist Escola Paulista de Medicina, Sao Paulo, Brazil, 1984. Author: Cancer and the Human Condition, 2010; contbr. articles to profl. jours. Free Sons of Israel scholar, 1974, N.Y. State Regents scholar, 1974, U. Miami Med. Sch. scholar, 1990. Jewish. Achievements include patent for Method for Detecting the Presence of GD3 Ganglioside; notable findings on role of gangliosides in human cancer, on role of cytokines in diabetes mellitus. Home: 2824 Timber Ln Green Bay WI 54313-5842 Business E-Mail: drpukel@aol.com.

PUKROP, RALF, psychotherapist, psychologist, researcher; b. Dortmund, Germany, Jan. 1, 1967; s. Ingo Pukrop and Edelgard Sachsenröder; m. Gabriele Führich-Pukrop; 1 child, Joana; children: Josefine children: Joshua Cremer. PhD, U. Cologne, 1997, SciMD, 2003. Lic. Psychotherapist Bezirksregierung Köln, 2003. Head of sect. for exptl. and clin. psychology Dept. of Psychiatry and Psychotherapy, U. of Cologne, Cologne, Germany, 1996—; prof. U. Cologne, Germany, 2004—. Mem. of editl. bd. Jour. of Personality Disorders (Guilford Press), New York, NY, 2003—. Mem. editl. bd.: Jour. Personality Disorders, European Jour. Personality; contbr. articles to profl. jours. Mem.: Internat. Soc. for the Study of Personality Disorders.

PULCRANO, MELANIA, endocrinologist, researcher; b. Pomigliano D'Arco, Naples, Italy, May 5, 1973; d. Salvatore Pulcrano and Giovanna Panico; m. Vincenzo Scialo', May 30, 2002; 1 child, Elena Floranne Scialo'. Med. degree, Second U., Naples, 1998. Bd. cert. diplomate in endocrinology U. Federico II, Naples, 2003, diplomate U. Paris Sud, France, 2005. Physician dept. clin. endocrinology and oncology U. Federico II, 1999—. Fellowship, U. Federico II, 2008. Mem.: Italian Soc. Endocrinology, European Soc. Endocrinology. Achievements include research in clinical outcome in patients with thyroid cancer. Office: Ariz Poli Univ Federico II Via Sergio Pansini 5 80131 Naples NA Italy Personal E-mail: mpulcrano@libero.it.

PULIAFITO, CARMEN ANTHONY, dean, ophthalmologist, healthcare executive; b. Buffalo, Jan. 5, 1951; s. Dominic F. and Marie A. (Nigro) P.; m. Janet H. Pine, May 19, 1979 AB cum laude, Harvard Coll., 1973, MD magna cum laude, 1978; MBA, U. Pa., 1997. Diplomate Am. Bd. Ophthalmology. Intern Faulkner Hosp., Tufts U. Sch. Medicine, 1978-79; resident Mass. Eye and Ear Infirmary, Boston, 1979-82, retina fellow, 1982-83; instr. Harvard Med. Sch., Boston, 1983-85, asst. prof., 1985-89, assoc. prof., 1989-91, dir. divsn. continuing edn. dept. ophthalmology, 1989-91; dir. Bascon Palmer Eye Inst., Miami, 2001—07; dean Keck Sch. Medicine, U. So. Calif., LA, 2007—. Vis. scientist MIT Regional Laser Ctr., Cambridge, 1982—, asst. prof. health scis. and tech. program, 1987-89, assoc. prof., 1989-91; mem. staff Mass. Eye and Ear Infirmary, Boston, 1983; dir. Morse Laser Ctr., Mass. Eye and Ear Infirmary, 1986-91, dir. New Eng. Eye Ctr., 1991-2001; prof., chmn. dept. ophthalmology Tufts U. Sch. Medicine, 1991-2001, prof. ophthalmology and health mgmt., 1997-2001; adj. prof. biomed. engring. Tufts U., 1991—; chmn. med. bd. New Eng. Med. Ctr. Hosps., 1994-95, ophthalmologist in chief, 1991-2001; assoc. examiner Am. Bd. Ophthalmology, 1990—; sr. v.p. for network devel. Lifespan, 1997-2001; prof., chmn. dept. ophthalmology U. Miami Sch. Medicine, 2001—, med. dir. Anne Bates Leach Eye Hosp., 2001—. Author: (with D. Albert) Foundations of Ophthalmic Pathology, 1979, (with R. Steinert) Principles and Practice of Ophthalmic YAG Laser Surgery, 1984, Lasers in Surgery and Medicine: Principles and Practice, 1996, (with M.R. Hee, J.S. Schuman and J.G. Fujimoto) Optical Coherence Tomography of Ocular Diseases, 1996, (with E. Reichel) Atlas of Indocyanine Green Angiography, 1996; editor-in-chief Lasers in Surgery and Medicine, 1987-95, Ophthalmic Surgery and Lasers, 1995—; contbr. about 120 articles to profl. jours. Pres. Am. Soc. for Laser Medicine and Surgery, 1994-95; v.p. Mass. Soc. Eye Physicians and Surgeons, 1994-96; assoc. examiner Am. Bd. Ophthalmology, 1990—; retina trustee Assn. Rsch. in Vision and Ophthalmology, 1995-99, pres., 2000-01. Recipient Richard and Hinda Rosenthal award in visual scis., 1994, Man of Vision award Boston Aid to the Blind, 1993, Leon Goldman award Biomed. Optics Soc., 1993, I Migliori award Pirandello Lyceum of Mass., 1994. Fellow Am. Acad. Ophthalmology, Am. Soc. for Laser Medicine and Surgery (pres. 1994-95); mem. Assn. Rsch. in Vision and Ophthalmology (pres. elect 1998-99, pres. 1999-2000, immediate past pres. 2000-2001), Mass. Soc. Eye Physicians and Surgeons (v.p. 1994-96). Roman Catholic. Office: Keck Sch Medicine U So Calif 1975 Zonal Ave Los Angeles CA 90033 Office Phone: 323-442-1900. Office Fax: 323-442-2724. Business E-Mail: deanksom@usc.edu, cpuliafito@usc.edu.

PULIDO, JOSE S., physician; b. Apr. 29, 1956; BA with hons., U. Chgo., 1976, MS, 1977; MD, Tulane U., New Orleans, 1981; MBA, U. Iowa, 1993; MPH, U. Ill., 2005. Diplomate Am. Bd. Ophthalmology. Intern Tulane Affil. Hosps.-Charity Hosp., New Orleans, 1981-82; resident in ophthalmology U. Ill., Chgo., 1982-85, chief resident in ophthalmology, 1985-86; fellow vitreoretinal surgery Bascome Palmer Eye Inst./U. Miami Sch. Medicine, 1986-87, fellow retina rsch., 1987; fellow ocular oncology Wills Eye Hosp./Thomas Jefferson U. Sch. Medicine, Phila., 1998; head and prof. dept. ophthalmology and visual scis. U. Ill., Chgo., 1998—. Instr. organic chemistry U. Chgo., 1976-77; asst. prof. ophthalmology Coll. of Medicine, U. Iowa, Iowa City, 1987-92, assoc. prof., 1992-97, prof. 1997-98; prof. and chmn. U. Ill., 1998-2004; prof. Mayo Clinic, 2005. Reviewer numerous jours., including: Archives of Ophthalmology, 1985—, Ophthalmology, 1987—, Am. Jour. of Ophthalmology, 1992—, others; abstract editor: Diabetes 2000 Newsletter, 1992—, Ophthalmology World News, 1994-96, others; editor: Evidence-Based Eye Care, 1998—; contbr. articles to profl. jours. Mem. Am. Diabetes Assn. (del.), Am. Acad. Ophthalmology, Pan-Am. Acad. Ophthalmology, Retina Soc., Vitreous Soc., Fluorescein Reading and Macular Evaluation, Assn. for Rsch. in Vision and Ophthalmology, Am. Coll. Surgeons, Schepens Internat. Soc., Am. Ophthal. Soc., Macula Soc. Office: Mayo Clinic 200 First St SW Rochester MN 55905 *

PULLEN, TIMOTHY L., corporate financial executive; BS, Rochester Inst. Tech.; MBA, Seattle U. Positions through v.p., fin. Hillhaven Corp., 1983—95; v.p. Tenet Healthcare Corp., Dallas, 1995—99, controller, 1995—2003, sr. v.p., 1999—2003, exec. v.p., chief acctg. officer, 2003—, interim CFO, 2005. Office: Tenet Healthcare Corp Ste 100 13737 Noel Rd Dallas TX 75240

PULLIAM PLUMMER, JOYCE, medical technician; Lab. tech., Brook Army Med. Army Sch., 1972—73. Lab. tech. quality control Technicon Corp., Middletown, Va., 1980—82; tech./limited x-ray Selma Med. Assoc., Winchester, Va., 1982—. Author poetry. With US Army, 1972—80. Mem.: Am. Soc. for Clin. Lab. Sci. Avocations: poetry, painting, gardening, crafts. Home: PO Box 372 Stephens City VA 22655 Office: Selma Med Assoc Inc 104 Selma Dr Winchester VA 22601

PULLMAN, SETH L., neurologist, educator; b. White Plains, NY, Aug. 31, 1953; BSc, McGill U., 1975; MD, McGill Sch. Medicine, 1979. Med. staff fellow NIH, 1984—86; prof. Columbia U. Med. Ctr., 1986—; pres. emeritus Ralph's U. & Grill. Founder, dir. Clin. Motor Physiology Lab., 1990—; sci. adv. bd., musicians Dystonia Med. Rsch. Found., 2000—; Sea Otter Tremor cons. Movement Disorders Group, 2004—. Fellow: Am. Acad. Neurology. Office: The Neurological Inst NY New York NY 10032-3702 Office Fax: 212-305-0743. Business E-Mail: sp31@columbia.edu.

PUMAIN, RENÉ, science educator, researcher; s. Emmanuel and Suzanne Pumain; m. Denise Roger, Sept. 21, 1968; 1 child, Olivier. PhD, U. Pierre et Marie Curie, Paris, 1970. Prof. U. Pierre et Marie Curie, 1972—. Rsch. team leader Inserm, Paris, 1976—. Pres. Promotion Neuroscis. Européennes, Paris, 2006, AWSB IdF, Paris, 2008. Grant, FFRE, 2006. Achievements include patents for antiepileptic drug. Office: Inserm 2ter Rue d'Alésia Paris 75014 France Business E-Mail: rene.pumain@inserm.fr.

PUMARIEGA, ANDRES JULIO, medical administrator, educator, researcher; b. Matanzas, Cuba, Jan. 25, 1953; came to U.S., 1962; s. Andrès Augustin and America Maria (Mechoso) P.; m. JoAnne Buttacavoli, Dec. 26, 1975; children: Christina Marie, Nicole Marie. BS, U. Miami, Coral Gables, Fla., 1973; MD, U. Miami, Fla., 1976. Resident in psychiatry Duke U., Durham, N.C., 1976-78, fellow in child psychiatry, 1978-80; dir. child psychiatry consultation/liaison svc. Vanderbilt U., Nashville, 1980-83; clin. asst. prof. psychol. Meharry Coll. Med., 1981—89; dir. pediat. psychiatry consultation/liaison svc. Tex. Children's Hosp. Baylor Coll. Medicine, Houston, 1983-86; dir. divsn. child adolescent psychiatry U. Tex. Med. Bd., Galveston, 1986-91, dir. residency program, 1987-92; prof. neuropsychiatry and behavioral scis. U. S.C., Columbia, 1992-96, dir. divsn. child and adolescent psychiatry, 1992-96, vice-chmn. dept. neuropsychiatry and behavior sci., 1994-96; assoc. dir. William S. Hall Psychiat. Inst., Columbia, 1992-96; prof. psychiatry and behavioral scis. East Tenn. State U., Johnson City, 1996—2006, chmn. dept. psychiatry and behavioral scis., 1996-2001, dir. divsn. child and adolescent psychiatry, 1996—2006, dir. Ctr. of Excellence Children in Custody, 2002—06; chmn. dept. psychiatry Reading Hosp. and Med. Ctr., Pa., 2006—10; prof. psychiatry Temple U., Phila., 2006—11, chief, child & adolescent psychiatry, 2010—11; clin. prof. psychiatry U. Medicine and Dentistry NJ, Camden, 2006—, Phila. Coll. Osteopathic Medicare, 2007—; chair dept. psych. Cooper U. Hospital, 2011—; prof., chair dept. psychiatry Cooper Sch. Medicine Rowan U. Examiner in child psychiatry and gen. psychiatry Am. Bd. Psychiatry and Neurology, Chgo., 1983—; co-investigator, mem. exec. com. Ctr. Cross-Cultural Rsch., Galveston, 1989-91; chmn. rsch. com. and exec. bd. S.C. Pub. Acad. Mental Health Consortium, 1994-96; chair Nat. Latino Behavioral Health Work Group, 1995—2000; chair Hispanic panel managed care initiative Ctr. for Mental Health Svcs. Substance Abuse and Mental Health Adminstrn., 1996—2000; cons. Ctr. for Substance Abuse Treatment USPHS, 1995-96; mem. nat. adv. coun. Ctr. Mental Health Svcs., Substance Abuse and Mental Health Adminstrn. U.S. Dept. HHS, 1997-2001. Editor: (with H. Vance) Clinical Assessment of Child and Adolescent Behavior, 2001; (with N. Winters) Handbook of Child and Adolescent Systems of Care: The New Community Psychiatry, 2003; japanese translation, Y. Ono, 2007, Chinese Translation, 2008; editor Psychline Jour. Hispanic Am. Psychiatry, 2005-06; assoc. editor Jour. Child and Family Studies, 1996-2002, Am. Jour. Orthopsychiatry, 2005-; contbr over 160 articles, chpts., monographs, and over 190 abstracts to profl. jours. Bd. dirs. Tex. Network for Children, Austin, 1986-88, Ctrl. Hispanic David Torres, Reading, Pa., 2007—; mem. adv. coun. Ptnrs. Advocacy Network, 1990-92. Recipient Exemplary Psychiatrist award, Nat. Alliance for Mentally Ill, 1993, 1997, cert. of merit for beneficiary svc., Health Care Fin. Adminstrn., U.S. Dept. HHS, 1996, Jasper Chen See MD Healthcare Profl. award, Caron Found., 2009, Cmty. Svc. award, Regional Coun. Child & Adult Psychiatry SE-Pa., 2009; named to Alumni Hall of Fame, U. Miami Sch. Medicine, 1999; grantee, Ctr. for Cross-Cultural Rsch., NIMH, Bethesda, Md., 1988—92, Fullerton Found., 1993—95; Minority Child Psychiatrist Tng. grant, NIMH, 1988—92, site coord., grantee, Nat. Assn. State Mental Health Dir. Rsch. Fellowship, 1993—, Forest Pharm., 2000. Fellow: Coll. Physicians Phila., Am. Orthopsychiat. Assn. (bd. dir. 2004—, pres. elect 2007—09, pres. 2010—11), Tenn. Coun. Child and Adolescent Psychiatry (pres. 2001—06), Am. Coll. Psychiatrists, Am. Acad. Child Psychiatry (chmn. work group on sys. of care 1994—2001, chmn. cmty. psych. com. 2001—07, chmn. diversity and culture com. 2007—, Outstanding Mentor award 1994, Catchers in the Rye award 2001, Jeanne Spurlock Diversity and Culture award and lectr. 2007), Am. Acad. Pediat., Acad. Psychosomatic Medicine, Am. Psychiat. Assn. (chair Hispanic com. 2006—09, disting. fellow, Simon Bolivar award 2004, Silver award outstanding svcs. 2004); mem.: Am. Assn. Social Psychiatry (bd. mem. 2009—11, v.p. 2011—), S.C. Soc. Child and Adolescent Psychiatry (founding pres. 1996—97), Tex. Mental Health Assn. (mem. children's adv. com. 1991—92), Tenn. Soc. Child Psychiatry (sec. 1982—83, pres. 2001—06), Bay Area Pediat. Soc. (pres. 1990—91), Soc. Profs. of Child Psychiatry, Am. Assn. Cmty. Psychiatrists (bd. dir. 1996—2006, Ethics in Pub. Managed Care award 2000), Nat. Mental Health Assn. (bd. dir. 1999). Roman Catholic. Avocations: swimming, political history, public affairs. Home: 27 Linree Ave Reading PA 19606-9075 Office: Cooper Univ Hospital Dept Psych Educ & Rsch Bldg 401 Haddon Ave Camden NJ 08103

PUMPER, ROBERT WILLIAM, microbiologist, educator; b. Clinton, Iowa, Sept. 12, 1921; s. William R. and Kathrine M. (Anderson) P.; m. Ruth J. Larkin, June 24, 1951; 1 son, Mark. BA, U. Iowa, 1951, MS, 1953, PhD, 1955. Diplomate: Am. Soc. Microbiology. Asst. prof. Hahnemann Med. Coll., Phila., 1955-57; prof. microbiology U. Ill. Med. Sch., Chgo., 1957-92, prof. emeritus, 1992—, Raymond B. Allen Med. lectr., 1970, 74, 76, 87. Co-author: Essentials of Medical Virology; contbr. articles to profl. jours. Served with USAAF, 1942-46. Recipient Chancellors' award U. Ill., Bombeck award, 1992 Mem. Tissue Culture Assn., Sigma Xi, Phi Rho Sigma. Lutheran. Home: 18417 Argyle Ave Homewood IL 60430-3007

PUNNOOSE, A. JOHN, hospital administrator; BSc in Chemistry, Dehli U., New Dehli, 1989; MBA, Nagpur U., India, 1991; MPhil in Health & Health Sys. Mgmt., Birla Inst. Tech. and Scis., Pilani, India, 1997; attended, Indian Inst. Mgmt., Ahmedabad, India, 2007. CEO Advanced Medicare & Rsch. Inst., Apollo Hosps. Enterprises Ltd., India, 2003—05, Madras Med. Mission, India, 2005—07; healthcare advisor Kapico Holding Co., Kuwait, 2007; CEO Royale Hayat Hosp., Kuwait; sr. gen. mgr., ops. Indian Hosps. Corp. Ltd.; mng. ptnr., prin. cons. Oyster Internat. Healthcare Consulting, India. Grantee Ctr. Social Innovation fellowship, Stanford U. Grad. Sch. Bus., 2007. Office: Oyster International Healthcare Consulting 22

College Rd Nungambakam Chennai 600006 India Office Phone: 914428258877. Personal E-mail: john@johnpunnoose.com. Business E-Mail: john@oysterhealthcare.org.

PUNWANEY, JUANITA, dermatologist; d. Bhagwan Sitaldas and Lavina B. Punwaney. BA summa cum laude, Columbia U., NYC, 1987; MD in Parasitology, Nutrition and Biostats. with honors, Columbia Coll. Physicians and Surgeons, NYC, 1991. Diplomate Am. Bd. Dermatology, Nat. Bd. Med. Examiners. Intern Columbia Presbyn. Med. Ctr., NYC, 1991—92; resident in dermatology Wayne State U./Detroit Med. Ctr., 1992—95; dermatologist Allied Dermatology Svcs., PC, Detroit, 1995—96, Midwest Health Ctr., PC, Dearborn, Mich., 1997—98, Advanced Dermatology, PC, Fresh Meadows, NY, 1998—99, DOCS Physicians Affiliated with Beth Israel Med. Ctr., Valhalla, NY, 2001—03, ProHEALTH Care Assocs., LLP, Lake Success, NY, 2004—06, North Shore-Long Island Jewish Health Sys., Lake Success, 2006—07, Manhattan's Physician Group, 2011—. Cons. in field. Fellow: Am. Acad. Dermatology; mem.: Met. Mus. Art, Young Patrons Soc. Lincoln Ctr., NY Delta Phi Beta Kappa. Avocations: walking, jogging, swimming, travel. Office: Manhattan's Physician Group 590 Fifth Ave New York NY 10036

PURCELL, ANN RUSHING, state legislator, human services manager; b. Reidsville, Ga., May 12, 1945; d. William Robert and Katie (Dasher) Rushing; m. Dent Wiley Purcell, May 26, 1966; children: Edwin Wiley, Mieke Ann, Mikki Marie. BS in Edn., Ga. So. Coll., 1966; degree (hon.), Ga. Future Farmers Am., 1999. Cert. secondary tchr. Tchr. math. Evans H.S., Ga., 1966-68; tchr. math., earth and sci. Beaumont Jr. H.S., Lexington, Ky., 1969-70; substitute tchr. Tallahassee, 1970's; agt. Noblin Realty, Tallahassee, 1970's; office mgr. Radiation Therapy Assocs., PC, Savannah, Ga., 1979—2008, Chatham Radiation Oncology, PC, 2008—; state rep. Ga. House of Reps., Atlanta, 1991—2005, state rep. Dist. 159, 2009—. Author: Purcells of South Georgia and Other Related Families, 1976, Purcell Family History 1777-2006. Bd. dirs. Med. Assn. Ga. Polit. Action Com., Atlanta, 1988-89, Girl Scout Coun. Savannah, 1991-93, Effingham YMCA, 1999-; Effingham County fin. chmn. State YMCA, 1991-05, vice chmn. steering com., 1999, bd. dirs., 1999; trustee Ga. So. U. Found., 1992-2009, Armstrong Atlantic U. Found., 2004-05, 06, 07, 08, sec., 2005, 06, 07, Vice Chmn. Bd., 2007, 08, chmn. bd. 2008-09; mem. adv. com. Effingham County Extension Svc., 1992-2006; chmn. steering com. Effingham YMCA Bd., 2004, 05, 06, 07, chmn. fin. devel., 2005-07; mem. adv. com. Treutlin Home, 1999-04; bd. adv. Claxton Youth Detention Ctr. Hon. comdr. 165th Ga. Air Guard Airlift, 1997-04; hon. mem. Civil Air Patrol, 2001-05, Ga. State Patrol, 2001; hon. mem. Civil Air Patrol, 2010-; state bd. mem. Ga. Dept. Tech. and Adult Edn., Tech. Coll. Sys. Ga., 2005-09; co-chmn. Ga. Edn. Joint Edn. Com., 2006, 07, 08, 09; Effingham Campus of Savannah Tech. Coll., 2007, 2008, 09; mem. adv. bd. Ga. Pacific, 2006-09; bd. dirs. New Ebenezer Retreat Ctr., 2006-09, chmn. bd. trustees Armstrono Atlantic, 2008-09. Decorated WA-PO-HE award Ga. Nat. Air Guard, Minuteman award, Dept. Def. Commendation medal, Charles Dick award Nat. Guard Assn. US; recipient Friend of Medicine award, Med. Assn. Ga., 1991, 1993, 1994, 1996, Ga. Vet. award, 2003, Guardian of Small Bus. award, Nat. Fedn. Ind. Bus., 1992, 1994, 1996, Commendation cert., Ga. Emergency Mgmt. Agy., 1995, Vol. of Yr. award, Effingham 4-H, 1998, Nat. Am. hon. degree, Future Farmers Am., 1999, Friend of State 4-H award, 1999, Svc. award, Effingham Recreation Dept., 2000, Cmty. Svc. award, Guyton Masonic Lodge, 2000, Hon. Family Consumer Cmty. Leaders of Ga. award, 2001, Ga. Pub. Health award, 2003, Effingham Jr. Adv. Family Connection award, 2003, 2004, Environ. Leadership award, Ga. Conservation Voters, 2003, 2004, Pub. Rels. award, Ga. Ext. Assn. of Family and Consumer Scis., 2003, Leadership award, Ga. Water Coalition, 2003, 2004, City of Pembroke award, 2004, Bryan County Svc. award, 2004, Friend of Effingham 4-H award, 2005, Friends award, Ga. Med. Soc., 2005, Vol. Yr., Coastal Ga. YMCA, 2007, Med. Ctr. award, Meml. Health U., 2010, Ga. Nat. Guard award, 2010, award, City Rincon, 2010; named Ga.'s Legislator of Yr., Ga. Sch. Counselors Assn., 1996, Ga. Legislator of Yr., Coastal Conservation Assn. Ga., 1998, Vol. of Yr., Effingham YMCA, 2006; named to Hon. Ga. State Patrol, 2001. Mem. Aux. to the Med. Assn. Ga. (pres. 1985), Aux. to the Ga. Med. Soc. (pres. 1981-82), Ga. Salzburger Soc. (bd. dirs. 2005, 10, v.p. 2005, 06, 07, pres., 2007—09), Effingham County Pub. Ofcls. Assn., Rotary Internat. (Effingham bd. dirs., 2007-08, 2008-09, Paul Harris fellow 2003), Ga. Peace Officers Assn. (hon.), Am. Legion, (Post 322, Ga.), Rincon Noon Lions Club, Exch. Club, Salzburger Vereine V. (Berlin) (hon.). Republican. Methodist. Avocations: painting, genealogy, fishing. Office: Ga Gen Assembly 504 Coverdell Legis Office Bldg Atlanta GA 30334 Office Phone: 404-656-0188.

PURCELL, KAREN BARLAR, naturopathic physician, nutritionist, opera singer, writer; b. Miami, Fla. d. Raymond and Elita Barlar; m. John A. Purcell, June 11, 1977 (div. Dec. 1986); 1 child, Carl; m. Roy Gene Autry, Dec. 31, 1987 (dec. Mar. 2003). MusB, U. Cin., 1969; MusM, New Eng. Conservatory Music, Boston, 1971; postgrad., Bastyr U., Seattle, 1997-98; D in Naturopathy, Natural Health Acad. Healing Arts, Tenafly, NJ, 1991. Diplomate Am. Bd. Naturopathic Physicians, 1997, cert. master herbalist, Dallas; ordained to mininstry Progressive Universal Life Ch., 1998. Assoc. prof. U. Miami, 1974-77, Dade County Jr. Coll., Miami, 1974—77; pvt. practice, NYC, 1990—. Assoc. prof. NYU, 1988-92, Strasberg Theater Inst., NYC, 1988-92, UN Internat. Sch., NYC, 1992-96; dist. mgr. Nature's Sunshine Products; spkr. in field Author: Simplified Nutritional Handbook, 1996, How to Survive a Nuclear Disaster, 2002, Fearless Aging; opera singer, 1970—. Founder WINS Found. for Moderate to Severe Brain Disorders, 1999—. Mem. Am. Naturopathic Med. Assn., Internat. and Am. Assn. Clin. Nutritionists, Internat. and Am. Assn. Counselors and Therapists, Nat. Spkrs. Assn. Avocations: botany, cooking, travel. Personal E-mail: kbpurcell@aol.com.

PURCELL, ROBERT HARRY, virologist, researcher; b. Keokuk, Iowa, Dec. 19, 1935; s. Edward Harold and Elsie Thelma (Melzl) P.; children: David Edward, John Leslie. BA in Chemistry, Okla. State U., 1957; MS Biochemistry, Baylor U., 1960; MD, Duke U., 1962. Intern in pediatrics Duke U. Hosp., Durham, NC, 1962-63; officer USPHS, 1963; with Epidemic Intelligence Svc., Communicable Disease Ctr. Atlanta; assigned to vaccine br. Nat. Inst. Allergy and Infectious Diseases, Bethesda, Md., 1963-65; sr. surgeon Lab. Infectious Diseases, NIH, Bethesda, Md., 1965-69, med. officer, 1969-72, med. dir., 1972-74, head hepatitis viruses sect., 1974-2001, co-chief, 2001—; dist. investigator NIH, 2007. Organizer, invited participant, speaker numerous nat. and internat. symposia, confs., workshops, meetings; temporary advisor WHO, 1967—; expert cons. in hepatitis U.S.—China, U.S.—Taiwan, U.S.—Japan, U.S.—Russia, U.S.—India, U.S.—Pakistan Bilateral Sci. Agreements; lectr. various virology classes. Reviewer numerous sci. jours.; contbr. 700 articles to profl. jours., chpts. to books; 40 patents in field. Recipient Superior Svc. award USPHS, 1972, Meritorious Svc. medal USPHS, 1974, Gorgas medal, 1977, Disting. Svc. medal USPHS, 1978, Disting. Alumni award Duke U. Sch. Medicine, 1978, Eppinger prize 5th Internat. FALK Symposium on Virus and Liver, Switzerland, 1979, Medal of City of Turin, Italy, 1983, Gold medal Can. Liver Found., 1984, Nat. Acad. Scis., 1988, King Faisal Internat. prize for Medicine, 1998, Rsch. Sci. award Hepatitis Found. Internats., 1999; named to Alumni Hall of Fame East Okla. State Coll., 1996, Dist. Alumni award Okla State U., 2009 Fellow AAAS, Washington Acad. Scis., Am. Acad. Microbiology, Molecular Medicine Soc., Ind. Nat. Sci. Acad.; mem. Am. Epidemiology Soc., Am. Soc. Microbiology, Am. Soc. Virology, Soc. Epidemiol. Rsch., Infectious Diseases Soc. Am. (Squibb award 1980), N.Y. Acad. Scis., Am. Soc. Clin. Investigation, Assn. Am. Physicians, Am. Coll. Epidemiology, Am. Assn. Study of Liver Diseases (Disting. Achievement award 2000), Internat. Assn. Study and Prevention Virus Associated Cancers, Internat. Assn. Biol. Standardization, Internat. Assn. Study Liver, Soc. Exptl. Biology and Medicine (Disting. Scientist award 1986), Nat. Acad. Scis. (Washington chpt. 1988). Office: NIH Lab Infectious Diseases 50 S Dr MSC 8009 Rm 6523 Bethesda MD 20892-8009 Office Phone: 301-496-5090. Business E-Mail: rpurcell@niaid.nih.gov.

PURCHASE-OWENS, FRANCENA, marketing professional, consultant, educator, scholar; b. Milw., Nov. 14, 1960; d. Johnny Purchase Sr. and Arlene (Roberts) Pleas Brown. Student, Grand Rapids CC, Mich., 1978—79, Ga. State U., Atlanta, 1980; degree, Patricia Stevens Coll., Atlanta, 1980; student, Milw. Area Tech. Coll., 1982; AA cum laude, Bryant Stratton Coll., 1982; student, Cardinal Stritch Coll., Milw., 1982—83, Mount Mary Coll., 1984, U. Wis., 1987—88, Grand Valley state U., Grand Rapids, 1996; BS in Applied Liberal Studies, Western Mich. U., Kalamazoo, 1997, M in Ednl. Leadership cum laude, 2004; student, U. Phoenix, Grand Rapids, Mich., 2006—, Capella U., Grand Rapids, 2006—, Fla. Internat. U., Miami, 2009—. Cert. Mich. Profl. Sch. Modeling, 1980, adminstr. cert. State Mich., State Bd. Edn. & Dept. Edn. Various office, clerical positions, 1972—84; sec. internat. mktg. dept. Am. Seating, Grand Rapids, 1980—81; adminstrv. asst. to Elizabeth Kubler-Ross Ga. State U., 1980; investment mgmt. sec. M&I Bank, Milw., 1984-85; cons. United Devel. Corp., Milw., 1986-88; sales Weathermasters Industries, Milw., 1989; paraprofessional Grand Rapids Pub. Schs., Mich., 1990-92; temp. helper Dayton Hudson, Grand Rapids, 1990; customer svc. rep. Kent County Conv. and Visitors Bur., Grand Rapids, 1995; customer svc. rep. children's dept. Meijers, Inc., 1995; mktg. rschr. Wirthlin Worldwide, Grand Rapids, 1996-98; pres. Creative Works, Grand Rapids, 1988—, Francena Purchase Internat. Honors & Awards Soc., Grand Rapids, 1999—, Francena Purchase Internat. Applied Liberal Studies Soc., 1999—, Francena Purchase Internat. Applied Profl. Studies Soc., 2000—, Purchase Bus. Inst., Grand Rapids, 1999—; rsch. specialist Directions in Rsch., Grand Rapids, 2004—05, 2008—; mktg. rschr. Francena Purchase Cons. Svcs., Grand Rapids, 2006—; asst. Health Program Grand Rapids Cmty. Coll., 1993. Sec. Mich. Nat. Bank, Grand Rapids, 1980-81, spkr. Bryant Stratton Coll., Milw., Wis., 1982, Volt. Tech. Svcs., Milw, 1980, United Devel. Corp. Access, Milw., 1988; asst. to pres. Alissia Cosmetics, Miss Black Pageant, 1980; legal sec. to atty. David Clowers, Milw., 1980; asst. exec. sec. Manpower Internat. Inc., Milw., 1982-84; human resource asst., computer programmer, sec., Patricia Stevens Coll., Milw., 1985-86; sales First Home Fin., Grand Rapids, 1998; activities asst. Olds Manor Grand Rapids, Mich., 1998; grad. student adv. bd. Western Mich. U., 1999, 2001; commencement spkr. Bryant & Stratton Coll., Milw., 1982; cons. in field. Co-editor: Smoke Signal, 1975; contbr. articles to profl. jours. Miss J. fashion bd. Jacobson's Dept. Store, East Grand Rapids, Mich., 1979, mem. pub. com., refreshment com., model; bd. mem. adminstrv. profls. Bryant & Stratton Coll., Milw., 1981-82; tutor Kent County Literacy Coun., Grand Rapids, 1988; host Grad. Rapids Cmty. Media Ctr., 2007-, adv. bd. ITT Tech. Inst, Wyoming, Mich., 2010; intake asst. Baxter Cmty. Ctr., Grand Rapids, 1989; bus. adv. bd. mem. ITT Tech. Inst., Wyo., Mich., 2010-11; vol. Jerry's Kids, Jerry Lewis Muscular Dystrophy Telethon, Patricia Stevens Coll., 1985-86, Grand Valley State U., United Way, Grand Rapids, 1990, co-chair, 2006-, TV fundraiser vol., chair cmty. investment coun., 2006—09, basic needs investment com., 2006-, agy. impact com., United Way, Grand Rapids, 2007—10, United Way, Edn. Coun., Grand Rapids, 2009-11, United Way Agency Impact Com., 2007-; reading condr. SE Neighborhood Assn., Grand Rapids, 1990, reading program asst. 1993, mem. exec. bd. dirs, 2006; rehab. asst. Kent Comty. Hosp. Complex, Grand Rapids, 1991; mem. literacy coun. Kent County Literacy Coun., Grand Rapids, 1991—; vol. Kent Cmty. Hosp., Grand Rapids, 1992, Metro Health (formerly Met. Hosp.), Grand Rapids, 1992; mem. task force First Call Help United Way, Grand Rapids, 1992, Herkimer Apt. Projects, Weston Apts. Dwelling Place, Grand Rapids, 1999; facilitator trainer Employers Coalition for Healing Racism, Grand Rapids, 1997, Citizens Cirs. Resource Ctr., Grand Rapids, 1998, Ptnrs. in Pub. Edn., Grand Rapids, 1999, United Way Champions of Diversity, 1999; bd. dirs.program and quality com., pers. com., fin. com., Adhoc Com., Touchstone Innovaré Mental Health, Grand Rapids, 1999-2007, consumer adv. bd., Grand Rapids, 2000—, mem. nominating com., 2000-01, Kent County Cmty. Mental Health, 1999—; com. mem. Cherry St. Health Svcs., Grand Rapids, 2003; cons. Children King Day Care Ctr., Together Faith Ministries, Grand Rapids, 1998; asst. sec. First Missionary Bapt. Ch., Grand Rapids, 2005—07, fin. asst., 2005-07, program com., 2005-07, exec. bd. dirs., 2006-07; pastors asst. First Missionary Bapt. Ch., Grand Rapids, 2005—, adult usher bd., kitchen com., 2007; program com. First Vol. Cancer Soc., bus. program adv. com. mem. ITT Tech. Inst., 2010- Finalist Miss Black Milw. Pageant, 1981, Internat. Faces, Milw., 1985, Internat. Theatre Arts, Milw., 1986; recipient Typist award Edn. Assn., 1981, Leadership award Milw. Area Tech. Coll. Office Edn. Assn., 1977, 78, MATC Times, 1981, The Zephyr Mag., 1981, 1st Pl. extemporaneous speaking, 1979, 1st Pl. extemporaneous speaking with Letter of Recognition from Wis. Sen. Berger, 1981, Shorthand awards Bryant Stratton Coll., 1981-82, Machine Transcription award, 1981, Century award, 1982, cert. recognition, Kiwanis Club Internat., 1978, Letter of Recognition, Western Mich. U., Honors Coll., 1989, Am. Soc. Training & devel., 2002, Kent County Literacy Coun, 1991, Kent County Literacy Coun., 1991, Personal Svc. and Sales Accomplishment cert. Manpower, Inc., 1982, Appreciation cert. Touchstone Innovare Bd. Mem., Grand Rapids, 1998-2007, United Way, Grand Rapids, Mich., 2010-11, SE End Neighborhood Assn., Grand Rapids, 1993, 2006-07, Recognition Appreciation Cert., 2007; Leadership Recognition, Profl. Bus. Leaders, Milw., 1981-82, Recognition Appreciation cert. United Way, Impact Com., Grand Rapids, 2007-09, Mark Kistler's Summer Art Camp, Grand Rapids, 2006, SE End Neighborhood Assn., 2006, 07, Appreciation Cert., United Way, 2006-11, recognition appreciation cert. Mpls. & Minn. Cmty. Spotlight recognition, Capella U., 2006-07, Young Alumni Student Spotlight recognition Western Mich. U., Kalamazoo, 2002, 06-07, Bryant and Stratton Coll., 2007, other honors and awards; Phillip Morris scholar Alverno Coll., 1981, Thurgood Marshall Assistantship scholar Western Mich. U., 1989, 1998, Nontraditional Student grantee 1994, 2000, Thurgood Marshall Tuition grantee, 2000, Typing awards, Bryant & Stratton Coll., Milw., 1982; Internat. Cert. of Recognition, Phi Delta Kappa, 2011; named Mem. of Yr., Princeton Global Network, 2010. Mem.: Ednl. Leadership Assn., Am. Soc. Curriculum Devel., West Mich. Postal Customer Coun., Office Edn Assn., Profl. Bus. Leaders, Econ. Club Grand Rapids, Internat. Econ. Assn., Cmty. Media Ctr. (scholarships com.), Soc. Human Resource Mgmt., Am. Mgmt. Assn., Am. Soc. Tng. and Devel. (Cert. Recognition 1991), Parkinson's Assn., Alzheimer's Assn., Rotary Internat. (spkr., Grand Rapids, Mich. 1979), Western Mich. U. Alumni, Paraprofessional Assn., Internat. Jaycees, Networking and Leads (mem. networking and leads com., com.), Phi Beta Kappa, Phi Beta Lambda (sec. elect 1981—82), Phi Lambda Theta (Cert. Recognition 2002—). Avocations: modern dancing, reading, tennis, writing. Address: PO Box 88304 Kentwood MI 49518 Personal E-mail: francenapurchase@comcast.net.

PURDY, ALAN HARRIS, biomedical engineer; b. Mt. Clemens, Mich., Dec. 13, 1923; s. Harry Martin and Elinor (Harris) P.; m. Anna Elizabeth Sohn, Aug. 16, 1968 (dec.); children: Catherine, Charles, Susan, Harry; m. Margaret Josephine Kelley, Mar. 5, 1997. BSME, U. Miami, 1954; MS in Physiology, UCLA, 1967; PhD in Engring., U. Mo., 1970. Cert. clin. engr., Washington. Project engr. in acoustics Arvin Industries, Columbus, Ind., 1954-56, AC Spark Plug Co., Flint, Mich., 1956-60; asst. prof. engring. Calif. Poly. U., Pomona, 1960-62; assoc. dir. biomed. engring. U. Mo., Columbia, 1967-71; dep. assoc. dir., assoc. dir. Nat. Inst. for Occupational Safety and Health, Rockville, Md., 1971-81, scientist, biomed. engr. Cin., 1983-86; asst. dir. Fla. Inst. Oceanography, St. Petersburg, 1981-83; pres. Alpha Beta R & D Corp., San Marcos, Calif., 1986—. Cons. Smithy Muffler Corp., L.A., 1961-62, Statham Instruments, L.A., 1966; cons. faculty, Tex. Tech. U., Lubbock, 1972-73; lectr. U. Cin., 1980. Patentee in diving, acoustical and occupational safety fields. Pilot CG Aux., 1989-98. With USAF, 1942-43. Nat. Heart Inst. spl. fellow, 1963-67; Fulbright scholar, Yugoslavia, 1984. Mem. Acoustical Soc. Am., Biomed. Engring. Soc., Am. Inst. Physics, Exptl. Aircraft Assn., DAV, FAA (Inspection Authorization 1983, Designated airaworthiness Rep., 2003). Democrat. Home and Office: 941 Cycad Dr San Marcos CA 92078-5013 E-mail: alan87941@nethere.com.

PURDY, JAMES AARON, medical physics professor; b. Tyler, Tex., July 16, 1941; s. Walter Bethel and Florence (Hardy) P.; m. Marilyn Janette Coers, Jan. 29, 1965; children: Katherine, Laura. BS, Lamar U., 1967; MA, U. Tex., 1968, PhD, 1971. Cert. ABMP 1999, 2000, 2005, 2010. Asst. rsch. scientist U. Tex., Austin, 1969-71; rsch. asst. M.D. Anderson Hosp. and Tumor Inst., Houston, 1968-69, fellow in med. physics, 1972-73; from instr. physics to prof. Sch. of Medicine, Washington U., St. Louis, 1973—83, chief physics sect., 1976—2004, prof., 1983—2004, assoc. dir. Radiation Oncology Ctr., 1987—2004; prof., vice chmn. Med. Ctr. Dept. Radiology Oncology U. Calif., Davis, 2004—. Mem. NIH Radiaton Study sect. Divsn. Rsch. Grantes, 1991-95; Landauer lectr., Oakland, Calif., 1991. Editor: Three Dimensional Treatment Planning, 1991, Advances in Radiation Oncology, 1992, 3D Radiation Treatment Planning and Conformal Therapy, 1995, A Practical Guide to 3D Planning and Conformal Radiation Therapy, 1999, 3-D Conformal and Intensity Modulated Radiation Therapy: Physics and Clinical Applications, 2001, Technical Basis of Radiation Therapy, 2006; sr. physics editor: Internat. Jour. Radiation Oncology, Biology, and Physics, 1996—2003. With USMC, 1961-64. Fellow Am. Assn. Physicists in Medicine (pres. 1985, William D. Coolidge award 1997), Am. Coll. Radiology (ACR Gold Medal 2002), Am. Coll. Med. Physics (chmn. bd. chancellors 1990, Marvin M.D. Williams award 1996); mem. Am. Bd. Med. Physics (vice chmn. 1988-92), Am. Bd. Radiology, Am. Soc. Therapeutic Radiology and Oncology (ASTRO Gold medal 2000). Methodist. Avocation: travel. Home: 918 Eucalyptus St Davis CA 95616 Office: Univ Calif Davis Med Ctr Dept Rad Oncology 4501 X St Ste G140 Sacramento CA 95817 Home Phone: 530-758-9149; Office Phone: 916-734-3932. Business E-Mail: james.purdy@ucdmc.ucdavis.edu.

PURI, MAN MOHAN, pulmonologist; b. Delhi, India, Oct. 28, 1961; s. Jodh Parkash and Prem Lata Puri; m. Poonam Ahuja Puri, Feb. 26, 1987; 1 child, Gaurav. MBBS, Maulana Azad med. Coll., Delhi, 1982; D in Anesthesia, Maulana Azad Med. Coll., Delhi, 1986; MD in Respiratory Diseases & Tuberculosis, Vallabbhai Patel Chest Inst., Delhi, 1990. Med. officer CGHS, Delhi, 1986—88, LRS Inst. Tb and Respiratory Diseases, Delhi, 1990—91, chest physician, 1991—, head dept. Tb and respiratory diseases, 2002—05, head Dhanvantari critical care respiratory unit, 2002—05. Mem. editl. bd. Indian Jour. Tuberculosis. Mem.: Tuberculosis Assn. India (mem. exec. coun.), Indian Med. Assn. (v.p. 2001), Assn. Physicians India, Nat. Coll. Chest Physician (life). Office: LRS Inst Tb & Respiratory Diseases Sri Aurbindo Marg New Delhi 110005 India Home: ST 6 Nirmal Deep House No 2 110 021 New Delhi India Home Phone: 91-011-24112268; Office Phone: 91-011-9212701933. Personal E-mail: purimmpuri@yahoo.com, mmpuri@rediffmail.com.

PURKAYASTHA, SUKALYAN, radiologist, consultant; b. Silchar, India, Jan. 8, 1972; s. Sudhangshu Ranjan and Sakti Purkayastha; m. Papiya Choudhury, Dec. 9, 2002; 1 child, Saanvi. MBBS, Silchar Med. Coll., India, 1997; MD in Radiodiagnosis, Assam Med. Coll., 2000; DM in Neuroradiology, Sree Chitra Med. Inst. Med. Scis. and Tech., 2003. Registered Assu Coun. Med. Registration, 1995, gen. med. registration UK, registered in clin. radiology. Jr. resident radiology Silchar (India) Med. Coll., 1995—97; cons. radiology Sree Chitra Tirunal Inst., Trivandrum, India, 2004—. Contbr. articles to profl. jours. Hindu. Achievements include research in neuroradiology. Avocations: travel, badminton, reading. Office: Sree Chitra Tirunal Institute Medical College Trivandrum 695011 India Home: Link Road 788 006 Silchar India Personal E-mail: sukalyanp@yahoo.co.in.

PURKERSON, MABEL LOUISE, physician, physiologist, educator; b. Goldville, SC, Apr. 3, 1931; d. James Clifton and Louise (Smith) P. AB, Erskine Coll., 1951; MD, M.U.S.C., Charleston, 1956. Diplomate Am. Bd. Pediat. Instr. pediat. Washington U. Sch. Medicine, St. Louis, 1961-67, instr. medicine, 1966-67, asst. prof. pediat., 1967-98, asst. prof. medicine, 1967-76, assoc. prof. medicine, 1976-89, prof., 1989-98, prof. emerita, 1998—, assoc. dean curriculum, 1976-94, assoc. dean acad. projects, 1994-98. Cons. in field. Editl. bd. Am. Jour. Kidney Diseases, 1981-87; contbr. articles to profl. jours. Mem. bd. counselors Erskine Coll., 1971—87, trustee, 2000—06, The Mabel Dorn Reeder Found., 2007—; historian St. Louis Symphony Orch., trustee; bd. dir. St. Louis Symphony Orchesta, 1999—2008, hon. trustee, 2008—; bd. dirs. Trailnet, 2008—, St. Louis Acad. Sci., 2008—, Erskine Coll. Alumni Assn., 2008—11, Opera Theatre, St. Louis, 2009—, Mo. History Mus., 2009—, The Explorers Club, 2010—; emeritus trustee Mo. Botanical Garden, St. Louis, 2010—. USPHS spl. fellow, 1971-72. Mem. Am. Heart Assn. Coun. on the Kidney (exec. com. 1973-81), Am. Physiol. Soc., Am. Soc. Nephrology, Internat. Soc. Nephrology, Ctrl. Soc. Clin. Rsch., Am. Soc. Renal Biochemistry and Metabolism, Internat. Assn. History Nephrology, Am. Osler Soc., Explorer's Club (chair St. Louis chpt., 2005-10bd. dirs, 2010, Sweeney medal 2010, Disting. Svc. award, Alumni Assn. Washington U. Sch. Medicine 2011), Sigma Xi (chpt. sec. 1974-76), Alpha Omega Alpha. Home: 20 Haven View Dr Saint Louis MO 63141-7902 Home Phone: 314-994-1649. Business E-Mail: purkerm@wustl.edu.

PUROHIT, DEVANG B., medical researcher; b. Vadodara, Gujarat, May 12, 1980; B in Pharmacy; M in Pharmacy, U. Baroda, 2002. Rsch. scientist Ranbaxy Labs. Ltd., 2008—. Office: Ranbaxy Lab Ltd R & D 1 Plot 20 Gurgaon Haryana 122001 India Business E-Mail: devang.purohit@ranbaxy.com.

PUROHIT, RAMESH CHANDRA, pathologist; b. Jodhpur, India, Nov. 5, 1944; MBBS, S. P. Med. Coll., Bikaner, 1966; MD, S. M. S. Med. Coll., Jaipur, 1971. Specialist pathologist Ministry of Health, Papua New Guinea, 1979—82; cons. pathologist R. P. Diagnostic Ctr., 1984—. Fellow: Indian Coll. Pathology; mem.: Indian Assn. Pathologists and Microbiologists. Avocation: gardening. Office: Hakim Baag Opp Sardar Children Sch Jodhpur Rajasthan 342001 India E-mail: dr.rameshpurohit@gmail.com.

PURVES, WILLIAM KIRKWOOD, biologist, educator; b. Sacramento, Oct. 28, 1934; s. William Kirkwood and Dorothy (Brandenburger) P.; m. Jean McCauley, June 9, 1959; 1 son, David William. BS, Calif. Inst. Tech., 1956; MS, Yale U., 1957, PhD, 1959. NSF postdoctoral fellow U. Tubingen, Germany, 1959-60; Nat. Cancer Inst. postdoctoral fellow UCLA, 1960-61; asst. prof. botany U. Calif., Santa Barbara, 1961-65, assoc. prof. biochemistry, 1965-70, prof. biology, 1970-73, chmn. dept. biol. scis., 1972-73; prof. biology, head biol. sci. group U. Conn., Storrs, 1973-77; Stuart Mudd prof. biology Harvey Mudd Coll., Claremont, Calif., 1977-95, prof. emeritus, 1996—, chmn. dept. biol., 1985-95, chmn. dept. computer sci., 1985-90; adj. prof. plant physiology U. Calif., Riverside, 1979-85. V.p., sci. dir. The Mona Group LLC, 1996-2004. Author: Life, the Science of Biology, 1983, 8th edit., 2007. NSF sr. postdoctoral fellow U. London, 1967, Harvard U., 1968; vis. fellow computer sci. Yale U., 1983-84; vis. scholar Northwestern U., 1991; NSF rsch. grantee, 1962-83, 97-2001. Fellow AAAS; mem. Sigma Xi. E-mail: Bill_Purves@hmc.edu.

PURVEZ, AKHTAR, interventional pain medicine physician, speaker, pain policy advocate, author; b. Srinagar, India, Apr. 1, 1958; s. Muzaffar Aazim and Padshah (Jan) Mir; m. Mudhasir Bashir; children: Ana Mir, Sama Mir. MB, BS, Govt. Med. Coll., India, 1981. Diplomate and cert. in pain medicine Am. Bd. Anesthesiology, Am. Bd. Pain Medicine, Am. Bd. Disability Analysts. Content review bd. mem. CNN Profl. TV Network; resident anesthesiology Govt. Med. Coll., 1998—2001, fellow in pain mgmt., 2002; med. dir. Ctr. for Pain Mgmt., Charlottesville, Va., 2002—; clin. adj. profl. Lincoln Meml. U., Harrogate. Avocations: literature, mountain climbing, charities, metaphysics, metacommunication. Home Phone: 834-825-2481. E-mail: apurvez@hotmail.com.

PURVIN, JACK MITCHELL, physician; b. Bklyn., May 27, 1953; s. Saul and Sylvia (Masey) P. BA in Psychology, U. Denver, 1975; postgrad., U. Autonoma de Guadalajara, Mex., 1978-81; MD, Dominica Sch. of Medicine, 1983. Pres. P.E.C. Inc., Del. Developer diabetic food products, pmlis sys. Patentee in field. Owner Jack M. Purvin Found. Mem. Am. Diabetes Assn., Montana Hist. Soc. Avocations: chess, coin collecting/numismatics, philatelic collections, rare documents, sports. Home: 1901 84th St Apt 4A Brooklyn NY 11214-3032 Office: PEC Inc PO Box 140028 Brooklyn NY 11214-0028 Home Phone: 718-759-7335. Personal E-mail: jackpurvin@aol.com.

PUSHPALATHA, K., medical researcher; b. Davanagere, Karnataka, India, Jan. 24, 1973; MBBS, J. J. M. Med. Coll., Davangere, 1995, MS, 2002. Lectr. St John's Med. Coll., Bangalore, Karnataka, 2003—04; sr. resident Kidwai Meml. Inst. Oncology, Bangalore, 2005—07; jr. cons. Kailash Hosp. and Rsch. Ctr., Noida, Uttar Pradesh, 2007; sr. rsch. fellow Dr. B. R. Ambedkar Inst. Cancer, All Inst. Med. Scis., New Delhi, 2007—08; sr. rsch. assoc. All India Inst. Med. Scis., 2008—. Exec. mem. organizing com. nat. CME ob-gyn., expert spkr. teleconf. Indira Gandhi Nat. Open U. All India Inst. Med. Scis., 2010. Fgn. Travel grant, Coun. Sci. and Indsl. Rsch., Travel grant, Dept. Sci. and Tech., Fin. grants, CCSTDS, 2010. Fellow: Internat. Med. Sciis. Acad.; mem.: Assn. Gynaecologic Oncologists India, Am. Soc. Clin. Oncology (assoc.), FOGSI. Avocations: swimming, cooking. Office: All India Inst Med Scis Dept Obstetrics and Gynaecology New Delhi Delhi NCR 110029 India

PUTHAVATHANA, PILAIPAN, virologist; b. Bangkok, July 28, 1950; PhD, Mahidol U., 1978. Prof. Mahidol U., 1973—. Office: Faculty Medicine Siriraj Hospital 2 Bangkoknoi Bangkok 10700 Thailand Office Phone: 66-2419-7059. Office Fax: 66-2418-2663. Business E-Mail: siput@mahidol.ac.th.

PUTNEY, JEFFREY G., cosmetic dentist; Grad., Marquette U., 1982. Pvt. practice Jeffrey G. Putney DDS, Wis. Named one of Top Five Dentists, Milw. Mag., 2009. Mem.: Wis. Dental Assn., ADA, Seattle Study Club, Milw. Study Club. Office: Jeffrey G Putney DDS 12320 W Oklahoma Ave West Allis WI 53227 Office Phone: 414-321-6890. Office Fax: 414-321-6890.

PUTTERMAN, ALLEN MICHAEL, surgeon, oculofacial plastic surgeon; b. Beloit, Wis., May 19, 1938; s. Mayer Leon and Mollie (Tankel) P.; m. Jacqueline Orner, Dec. 23, 1962 (div. 1978); 1 child, Jill Tracy; m. Lynett Solomon, Sept. 24, 1983. BS, U. Wis., 1960, MD, 1963. Cert. zumba tchr., blackbelt NIA instr. Intern Cook County Hosp., Chgo., 1963-64; resident in ophthalmology Michael Reese Hosp., Chgo., 1966-69, dir. oculoplastic surgery, 1970—, chief ophthalmology, 1996—2008; fellow in oculoplastic surgery Manhattan Eye, Ear and Throat Hosp., NYC, 1969-70; pvt. practice, Chgo., 1970—; prof. ophthalmology, co chief oculoplastic surgery U. Ill., Coll. Medicine, Chgo., 1970—. Editor: Cosmetic Oculoplastic Surgery, 1983, 3d edit., 1999; contbr. articles to med. jours., chpts. to textbooks. Capt., M.C., USAF, 1964-66. Named one of America's Top Drs., 2003, 2006, 2007, 2008, 2009, 350 Top Doctors, Chgo. Mag., 2004, 2006; named to Best Doctors in America. Fellow ACS, Am. Soc. Ophthalmic Plastic and Reconstructive Surgery (pres. 1982, Wendell Hughes lectr. 1984, Baylis Lifetime Achievement in Cosmetic Plastic Surgery award, 2005), Am. Acad. Ophthalmology (sr. honor award), Chgo. Ophthal. Soc. (v.p. 1991, pres.-elect 1992, pres. 1993). Avocations: skiing, bicycling, aerobics, yoga, Nia & Zumba. Home: 161 E Chicago Ave Apt 43B Chicago IL 60611-6678 Office: 111 N Wabash Ave Ste 1722 Chicago IL 60602-2007 Office Phone: 312-372-2256. Office Fax: 312-372-1762. E-mail: puttermanmd@hotmail.com.

PUTTERMAN, CHAIM, rheumatologist, researcher; b. Elizabeth, NJ; MD, Technion-Israel Inst. Tech., Haifa, 1985. Diplomate rheumatology Am. Bd. Internal Medicine. Int. Ramban Med. Ctr., Haifa, Israel, 1985; res. Hadassah Hosp., Ein-Kerem, Jerusalem, 1990—93; chief rheumatology divsn. Albert Einstein Coll. of Medicine, 2004—; chief Rheumatology Divsn. Montefiore Med. Ctr., 2004—; prof. medicine and microbiol Albert Einstine Coll. Medicine. Dir. rheumatology tng. program Montefiore Med. Ctr., 2004—11. Recipient Physician-Scientist Career Devel. award, Arthritis Found., 1994—97, Robert Wood Johnson Charitable Trust SLE Young Scholar award, 1997—2000, Hulda Irene Duggan Arthritis Investigator award, 2000—05, Rsch. Steps to a Cure Leadership award, 2002, Clin. Scientist award, NIH, 1997—2002, Lupus Rsch. Inst. Novel Rsch. Project in Lupus award, SLE Found., 2001—04. Fellow: Am. Coll. Rheumatology; mem.: Am. Soc. Clin Investigation, Am. Assn. Immunologists. Achievements include research in the renal pathogenicity of anti-DNA antibodies and lupus nephritis. Office: Albert Einstein Coll Medicine Div RheumatolForscheimer 701 AE Com 1300 Morris Park Ave Bronx NY 10461

PUTTLITZ, DONALD HERBERT, microbiologist; b. Kingston, NY, Apr. 21, 1938; s. Adalbert Siegfried and Elizabeth Ann (Barthel) P.; m. Barbara Ann Dingman, July 19, 1969; children: Michelle, Brian, Laura. BS with distinction, SUNY, New Paltz, 1959; MS, SUNY, Albany, 1961; PhD, Cornell U., 1965. Diplomate emeritus Am. Bd. Med. Microbiology. Assoc. microbiologist Beth Israel Med. Ctr., NYC, 1967-85; supr. microbiology Jamaica (N.Y.) Hosp., 1985-92; instr. physician asst. program Touro Coll., NYC, 1986-88; supr. microbiology Sound Shore Med. Ctr. of Westchester, New Rochelle, NY, 1993-97. Mem. faculty Mt. Sinai Coll. Medicine, 1972-85. Mem. N.Y.C. Bd. Edn., 1997-2007. Predoctoral traineeship fellow NIH, 1964-65, postdoctoral traineeship fellow USPHS, 1965-67. Mem. AAAS, Am. Soc. Microbiology, N.Y.C. Soc. Microbiology, Northeastern Asn. Microbiology & Infectious Diseases. Roman Catholic. Home: 116 Horace Harding Blvd Great Neck NY 11020-1107

PUTUKIAN, MARGOT, sports medicine physician; b. Newton, Mass., Aug. 15, 1962, d. John Harry and Elissa Ann (Bedrosian) P. BS in Biology, Yale U., 1984; MD, Boston U., 1989. Cert. internal medicine; cert. additional qualifications sports medicine. Intern Strong Meml. Hosp. Primary Care, Rochester, N.Y., 1989-92, fellow in internal medicine Mich. State U., East Lansing, 1992-93, fellow in sports medicine, 1992-93; dir. athletic medicine, assoc. clin. prof. Robert Wood Johnson UMDNJ; head team physician dir. athletic med. U. Princerton, 2004—; assoc. clin. prof. Robert Wood Johnson Woat Project UMDNJ, 2004—, asst. prof. orthop. rehab., 1993—2004; dir. Primary Care Sports Medicine Pa. State U., 1998—2004; team physician Pa. State U., 1993—2004, US Lacrosse; chair Sports Sci. Safety Com. Asst. prof. orthopedic rehab. Hershey (Pa.) Med. Ctr., 1993-2004. Head, neck, spine com. NFL; chair, sports sci., safety com. US Lacrosse, team physician. Fellow Am. Coll. Sports Medicine; mem. Am. Med. Soc. Sports Medicine (bd. dirs. 1996—2005, pres. 2004-05), Team Physician US Soccer, ACP. Democrat. Office: Princeton University Health Services Washington Rd Princeton NJ 08544 Business E-Mail: putukian@princeton.edu.

PUUSEPP-BENAZZOUZ, HELEN, medical researcher, physician; b. Tallinn, Estonia, Feb. 21, 1981; arrived in Australia, 2008; d. Vello and Viivi Puusepp; m. Ben Benazzouz, July 26, 2008. MD, U. Tartu, Estonia, 2005, D in Medicine, 2009. Ambulance physician Tartu Kiirabi, Tartu, 2006—08; hosp. scientist PaLMS, Royal North Shore Hosp., Sydney, 2008—11; physician St. George Hosp., Sydney, 2011—. Personal E-mail: helenpuusepp@gmail.com.

PUYAU, FRANCIS ALBERT, retired radiology educator, physician; b. New Orleans, Dec. 1, 1928; s. Frank Albert and Rose Sue (Jones) P.; m. Geraldine Sally diBenedetto, June 6, 1951; children: Michael, Stephen, Jeanne Marie, Julie, Melissa. BS, Notre Dame U., 1948; MD, La. State U., 1952. Diplomate Am. Bd. Pediat., Am. Bd. Pediat. Cardiology, Am. Bd. Radiology. Intern Charity Hosp., New Orleans, 1952-53, resident in pediat., 1955-57; from instr. pediat. to prof. radiology and pediat. La. State U. Sch. Medicine, New Orleans, 1957-74, acting head dept. radiology, 1971-72, head dept., 1972-74; asst. prof. pediat. Vanderbilt U., 1961-68; fellow dept. diagnostic radiology Charity Hosp., New Orleans, 1968-70; prof. radiology and pediat. Tulane U. Sch. Medicine, New Orleans, 1974-97, prof. medicine, 1974-95, acting chmn. dept. pediat., 1976-78; cons. St. Tammany Hosps., Covington, La., 1968-81; dir. cardiac catherization lab. dept. cardiology Charity Hosp., New Orleans, 1970-85; staff radiologist Our Lady of the Lake Regional Med. Ctr., Baton Rouge, 1986-93, ret., 1997. Mem. staff Hotel Dieu, New Orleans, 1973-80; head x-ray dept. Children's Hosp. of New Orleans, 1976-82. Contbr. articles to profl. jours. With USPHS, 1953-55. Fellow Am. Coll. Cardiology, Am. Coll. Radiology; mem. East Baton Rouge Med. Soc., So. Soc. Pediatric Research, Am. Coll. Radiology, La. Radiology Soc., New Orleans Radiology Soc. (pres. 1985), New Orleans Pediatric Soc., Soc. Chmn. Acad. Radiology Depts., Radiol. Soc. N.Am., Am. Roentgen Ray Soc., Assn. Univ. Radiologists, Southern Yacht Club (New Orleans), Alpha Omega Alpha. Roman Catholic. Home: 458 Shady Lake Pkwy Baton Rouge LA 70810-4322

PWEE, KENG HO, public health physician; MBBS, Nat. U. Singapore, 1991, MMed in Pub. Health, 1999. Cert. specialist accreditation and registration in public health medicine Singapore Med. Coun., Singapore, 2002. Med. officer Ministry of Health, Singapore, 1992—97, asst. dir., 1997—2007, dep. dir., 2007—. Capt. NS, med. corps Singapore Armed Forces, 1995—; assoc. editor Singapore Med. Jour., 2004—; mem., editl. bd. Internat. Jour. Tech. Assessment Healthcare, Singapore, 2007—; chair, internat. sci. program com. 6th Health Tech. Assessment Internat. Annual Meeting, 2009. Editor: Ministry of Health Clinical Practice Guidelines. Fellow: Acad. Medicine Singapore (Chpt. Pub. Health and Occupl. Physicians) (hon. sec. 2004—05); mem.: Guidelines Internat. Network (bd. trustees 2010—), Health Tech. Assessment Internat. (bd. dirs. 2010—). Office: Ministry Health 16 Coll Rd Singapore 169854 Singapore Office Phone: 65 63259251. Office Fax: 65 63257859. Business E-Mail: pwee_keng_ho@moh.gov.sg.

PYATIBRATOV, MIKHAIL G., research scientist; b. Kyzylorda, Kazakhstan, May 4, 1963; BS, St. Petersburg State U., Russia, MS, 1986; PhD in Molecular Biology, Moscow State U., 1996. Rsch. scientist Inst. Protein Rsch., Russian Acad. Sciences, Pushchino, Russia, 1996—; postdoc. fellow Dept. Microbiology, U. Hawaii, Honolulu, 1999—2001; postdoc. fellow, dept. neurosci. and cell biology U. Medicine and Dentistry NJ, Robert Wood Johnson Med. Sch., Piscataway, NJ, 2009. Fellowship, EMBO, EMBL, Heidelberg, Germany, FEBS, Rsch. grant, Russian Found. Basic Rsch., FEMS. Mem.: Russian Biochem. Soc. Avocations: reading, travel, sports. Office: Institutskaya St 4 Pushchino Moscow Region 142290 Russia Office Fax: 7(4967)318435.

PYERITZ, REED EDWIN, geneticist, educator, medical researcher; b. Pitts., Nov. 2, 1947; s. Paul L. and Ida Mae (Meier) P.; m. Jane Ellen Tumpson, May 28, 1972; 2 children. SB in Chemistry, U. Del., 1968; AM, Harvard U., 1971, PhD in Biochemistry, 1972, MD, 1975. Diplomate Am. Bd. Internal Medicine, Am. Bd. Med. Genetics. Intern Peter Bent Brigham Hosp., Boston, 1975-76; resident Peter Bent Bingham Hosp., Boston, 1976-77, Johns Hopkins Hosp., Balt., 1977-78; from instr. to prof. medicine and pediatrics Sch. Medicine, John Hopkins Hosp., Balt., 1977-93, chair dept. human genetics, 1994-00, prof. human genetics, medicine and pediatrics, 1994-01, MCP Hahnemann Sch. Medicine, 1993-00, prof. medicine and genetics U. Pa. Sch. Medicine, Phila., 2001—, chief divsn. med. genetics, 2001—, vice chair, dept. med., 2008—, chair com. on appointments and promotions, 2004—08, mem. faculty senate exec. comm., 2006—; dir. Penn Ctr. Integration Genetic Healthcare Tech., 2007—, chair, senate com. faculty, 2009—. Dir. Inst. Genetics, Allegheny U. Health Sci., 1993-99; dir. Ctr. for Med. Genetics, Allegheny Gen. Hosp., 1995-00; chief physician Md. Athletic Commn., Balt., 1978-93; med. adv. bd. Nat. Marfan Found., N.Y.C., 1982—, chmn. 1982-93, clin. care adv. bd., Nat. Neurofibromatosis Found., 1985—; med. adviser Alliance of Genetic Support Groups, 1994-01; mem. rsch. adv. bd. Nat. Orgn. Rare Disorders, 1989-00; mem. rsch. adv. com. Am. Heart Assn., 1996-98; mem. genetic adv. bd. Nat. Cancer Inst., 1996-99; mem. med. adv. bd. Can. Marfan Assn., 1999-, chmn., 2003-; mem. sci. adv. bd. Hereditary Hemorrhagic Telangiectasia Found., 2003—, chair med. adv. bd., Canadian Marfan Assn., 2003-08, Can. Inst. Health Rsch., 2005-, sci. adv. bd., Coriell Inst. Med. Res., 2008-. Co-editor Principles and Practice of Medical Genetics, 1992-; mem. editl. bd. New Eng. Jour. Medicine, 1993-96, JAMA, 1997-2001, Circulation, 2002—; contbr. over 300 articles to profl. publs. Lt. col. USAR Med. Corp., 1981—91. NIH grantee. Fellow: ACP, Am. Coll. Med. Genetics (dir. 1992—94, pres.-elect 1995—96, founding fellow, pres. 1997—99, past pres. 1999—2000); mem.: AAAS (coun. 2009—), AMA, Human Med. Genetics (assoc. prof., councilor 1998—2004, pres. 2000—02), Am. Coll. Med. Genetics Fedn. (sec. treas. 2001—), Coll. Physicians Phila., Am. Med. Accred. Program (spl. adv. com. 1998—2000), Assn. Profs. Human Med. Genetics (pres. elect 1998—99, pres. 2000—02), Assn. Am. Physicians, Am. Soc. Clin. Investigation, Am. Fedn. Med. Rsch., Physician Consortium for Performance Improvement, Am. Heart Assn., Am. Soc. Human Genetics (chmn. program com. 1994—95, bd. dirs. 2005—07). Office: Divsn Med Genetics Maloney 538 U Pa Sch Medicine 3400 Spruce St Philadelphia PA 19104-4283 Office Phone: 215-662-4740. Business E-Mail: reed.pyeritz@uphs.upenn.edu.

PYERS, JENNIE E., developmental psychologist; AB in Art Hist., Smith Coll., Northampton, Mass., 1995; PhD in Psychology, U. Calif., Berkeley, 2004. Vis. rschr. Max Planck Inst. Psycholinguistics, Nijmegen, Netherlands, 2001—02; postdoc. fellow Ctr. Rsch. in Lang. U. Calif., San Diego, 2004—06; asst. prof. psychology Lab. Lang. & Cognitive Devel., Wellesley Coll., Mass. Marion Cabot Putnam Meml. fellow devel. psychology Radcliffe Inst. Advanced Study, Harvard U., 2009—10. Contbr. articles to profl. jours. Office: Wellesley Coll Psychology Dept 106 Central St Wellesley Hills MA 02481 Office Phone: 781-283-3736. Office Fax: 781-283-3730. Business E-Mail: jpyers@wellesley.edu. *

PYNOOS, ROBERT S., psychiatrist, educator; b. Calif., Jan. 15, 1947; BA, Harvard U., 1968; MD, Columbia U., 1973. Diplomate Am. Bd. Psychiatry and Neurology, 1980. Prof., psychiatrist UCLA Semel Inst., 1980—. Prof. in residence European Soc. for Child & Adolescent Psychiatry. Recipient Rsch. Contbn. award, 2007. Mem.: Internat. Soc. for Traumatic Stress Studies (Lifetime Achievement award 2001). Office: 11150 W Olympic Blvd Ste 650 Los Angeles CA 90064 Office Fax: 310-235-2612. Business E-Mail: rpynoos@mednet.ucla.edu.

PYO, SUHKNEUNG, medical educator; b. Seoul, Korea, July 24, 1953; m. Weasook Shin, Jan. 5, 1983; children: Jinhee, Hyunjoon. PhD, U. S.C., 1991. Cert. pharmacist. Rsch. assoc. NYU, NYC, 1991-93; from asst. prof. to assoc. prof. Sungkyunkwan U., Suwon, Korea, 1993-2000, prof., 2001—. Editl. bd. mem. Cancer Letters, 2007—, Toxicology Letters, 2008—, Blue Biotech. Jour., 2011—. Mem. Soc. Investigate Pathology, Soc. Leukocyte Biology Home: Yangchun-gu Shinjung-dong Seoul 178-133 Republic of Korea Office: Sungkyunkwan Univ Jangan-gu Chunchun-dong 300 Suwon 440-746 Republic of Korea Fax: 82-31-292-8800. Business E-Mail: snpyo@skku.edu.

PYOTT, DAVID EDMUND IAN, pharmaceutical executive; b. London, Eng., Oct. 13, 1953; married; 4 children. MA, U. Edinburgh, 1975; diploma in German and European Law, U. Amsterdam, 1976; MBA, London Bus. Sch., 1980. Numerous positions Sandoz Nutrition, Barcelona, 1980-90, gen. mgr., 1990-92; pres., CEO Sandoz Nutrition Corp., Mpls., 1992-95; head divsn. nutrition Sandoz Internat. AG, 1995—97; mem., exec. com. Novartis AG (merger Sandoz and Ciba), 1995—97; pres. Allergan, Inc., Irvine, Calif., 1998—2006, 2011—, CEO, 1998—, chmn., 2001—. Bd. dirs. PhRMA, Avery Dennison Corp., Edwards Lifescis. Corp., Advanced Med. Optics, Inc.; chmn. Calif. Healthcare Inst.; mem. bd. dirs. U. Calif. (Irvine) Grad. Sch. Mgmt.; mem.LA Bus. Advisors; vice-chair Chief Exec. Roundtable for UCI Bd. dirs. Internat. Coun. of Ophthalmology Found., Eyecare Am.; pres. Pan-Am. Ophthalmological Found. Mem. Pharm. Rsch. and Mfrs. Am. (bd. dirs., Allergan rep.), Pan Am. Assn. Ophthalmology (bd. dirs.), L.A. Bus. Advisors. Achievements include transforming Botox, an obsure treatment for rare muscular diseases, into a cultural and medical phenomenon. Office: Allergan Inc 2525 Dupont Dr Irvine CA 92612-1531 Address: Allergan Inc PO Box 19534 Irvine CA 92623 *

PYSH, JOSEPH JOHN, neurologist, neuroanatomist; b. Olyphant, Pa., Nov. 14, 1935; s. John Andrew and Anna Mary (Marusin) P.; m. Deborah Ann Prass, Dec. 15, 1991. BA in Biology, Wayne State U., 1958; DO, Midwestern U. Chgo. Coll. Osteo. Medicine, 1962; PhD in Neuroanatomy, Northwestern U., Chgo., 1967. From instr. to assoc. prof. anatomy Northwestern U., Chgo., 1966-86, acting chmn. cell biology and anatomy, 1978-81, resident physician in neurology, 1983-86; assoc. prof. neurology Mich. State U., East Lansing, 1986-95, prof. neurology, 1995—, founding mem. dept. neurology, 2000—, emeritus prof. neurology, 2008—, founding dir. neurology residency program, 2001—03. Grant referee NSF, Washington, 1974—; frequent CME neurology speaker in field. Contbr. numerous articles to profl. jours; manuscript reviewer various orgns., Washington and N.Y.C. Recipient Tchg. award Northwestern U.; NIH grantee, 1969-82. Fellow Am. Coll. Neuropsychiatrists; mem. AAAS (life), AMA, NIH (mem. rsch. grant neurology study sect. 1976-77), Am. Acad. Neurology, Am. Soc. Cell Biology, Am. Assn. Anatomists, Soc. Neurosci., Sigma Xi. Achievements include research in synaptic transmission and brain development. Avocations: rare book collecting, sailing. Office: Mich State U Coll Osteo Medicine Dept Neurology 138 Service Rd A217 Clin East Lansing MI 48824 Office Phone: 517-432-9277. Business E-Mail: pysh@msu.edu.

PYUN, BOK YANG, pediatrician, educator; d. Yong Ho Pyun and Jung Mook Choi. MD, Ewha Womans U. Seoul, 1978, Hanyang U., Seoul, PhD, 1987. Prof. Soonchunhyang U. Hosp., Seoul, 1983—; pres. The Korean Acad. Pediat. Allergy & Respiratory Disease, 2011. Treas. Korean Pediatric Soc., Seoul, 2009—. Editor in chief Korean Acad. Pediat. Allergy & Respiratory Diseases, Seoul, 1995—2004, dir. legislation com., 2009; pres. Com. Pediat. Atopic Dermatitis, Seoul, 2001; sec. gen. Korean Pediat. Soc., Seoul, 2006—09, Korean Asthma & Allergy Found., Seoul, 2005. Recipient Best Poster award, Korean Acad. Pediat. Allergy & Respiratory Diseases, 2006, Best Article award, 2007, Rsch. Award, 2007, 2009, Paper award, 2007, Best Rsch. award, Korean Pediat. Soc., 2008, Best Article award, 2008.

PYUN, YOUNG DON, psychiatrist, director; b. Seoul, Republic Of Korea, Feb. 9, 1956; s. Yong Neu Hyun; m. Nam Hee Won, Jan. 3, 1996; 1 child, Seok Beom Byeon. MD, Seoul Nat. U., 1980, MA, 1991, PhD, 1998. Cert. psychiatrist Govt. of Korea, 1987, Am. Bd. Med. Hypnosis, 1990. Intern Seoul Nat. U. Hosp., 1980—81, psychiat. resident, 1984—87; chief, dept. psychiatry Seoul Eulji Hosp., 1987—89; vis. lectr. psychiatry Harvard U., Cambridge, Mass., 1989—90; vis. scholar psychiatry Stanford U. Sch. Medicine, Calif., 2007—08; dir. Pyun Neuropsychiat. Clinic, Seoul, 1990—. Pres. Korean Soc. Clin. Hypnosis, Seoul, 1989—. Author: (book) Introduction to Medical Hypnosis; contbr. articles to profl. jours. Master: Korean Soc. Clin. Hypnosis; mem.: Korean Neuropsychiat. Assn. Roman Catholic. Home: Tower Palace D-3603 Dogogdong Gangnamgu Seoul 135-534 Republic of Korea Office: Pyun Neuropsychiat Clinic 628-10 Yoksamdong Gangnamgu Seoul 135-080 Republic of Korea Office Fax: 02-564-7585. E-mail: pyunyd@naver.com.

QAZI, MUJTABA A., ophthalmologist; b. Karachi, Pakistan, Jan. 5, 1971; arrived in US, 1975; s. Asghar H. and Rehana Qazi; m. Erum Qazi, Aug. 3, 1995; children: Amaan, Rida, Ameen. BA, NYU, 1993, MD, 1997. Diplomate Am. Bd. Ophthalmology. Intern St. Vincent's Hosp., NYC, 1997—98; resident dept. ophthalmology Boston U. Med. Ctr., 1998—2001; chief resident dept. ophthalmology Boston VA Med. Ctr., 2000; fellow in corneal, anterior segment and refractive surgery Pepose Vision Inst., Chesterfield, Mo., 2001—02. Dir. clin. studies Pepose Vision Inst.; clin. instr. Washington U. Sch. Medicine, St. Louis. Author: Pupil Assessment for Refractive IOLS, 2008, Tonometry and Biomechanical Analysis, 2008; reviewer Am. Jour. Ophthalmology, Jour. of Refractive Surgery. Bd. mem. Midwest Cornea Rsch. Found. Named Best Dr's in St. Louis, 2008. Mem.: Internat. Soc. Refractive Surgeons, Am. Soc. Cataract & Refractive Surgery, Am. Acad. Ophthalmology. Office: Pepose Vision Inst PC 1815 Clarkson Rd Chesterfield MO 63017 Office Phone: 636-728-0111. E-mail: mqazi@peposevision.com.

QI, XIAO-SHI, surgeon, medical association administrator; s. Ansheng Qi and Cheng-lin Li. MD, Tianjin Med. U., China, 1982. Cert. USMLE ECFMG, 1998, gen. surgeon U. Paris, 1987, cardiothoracic vascular surgeon 1991, pediat. cardiologist 1992. Surgeon U. Paris, 1985—96; rsch. faculty Northwestern U., Med Sch., Chgo., 1997—98; fellow U. Mass., Worcester, Miami, 1998—99; pres. US Med. Edn. & Med. Consultation China, Chengdu, China, 2007—. Author: (textbook) Complication of Lung and Heart Transplantation. Pres. US Med. Edn. & Med. Consultation, Beijing, ChengDu, 2007—. Recipient Alexnder D. Longmuir award, CDC, 2003. Mem.: Cardio Thoracic Surgery Net (Phila.). Office: US Med Edn Med Consultation 95 New 37-3-HuaYu Rd ChengHua Dist Chengdu Province Sichuan China Personal E-mail: xiaoshiqi.md@gmail.com.

QI, ZHONGQUAN, surgeon, consultant; b. Harbin, China, Oct. 4, 1960; s. Diansheng Qi and Xiulian Guo; m. Weishu Wang; children: Anna Zuguang, Julia Zulin. MD, Harbin Med. U., 1984; PhD, Lund U., Sweden, 1999. Resident surgeon Harbin Med. U., 1985—90, surgeon-in charge, lectr., 1991—93, prof., 2001—; rschr., physician Lund U., Malmo, Sweden, 1993—. Cons., dir. Qi-Med, Malmo, Sweden, 2003—; PhD supr. Harbin Med. U., 2003—; hon. prof. Guangxi Med. U., Nanning, 2005—. Coord. Assn. Promoting Peace and Unification in China, Malmo, 2004—05; pres., founder Sweden Malmö Chinese-Swedish Friendship and Culture Ctr., 1999—2005; chmn. Sweden Malmö Chinese Vis. Scholars Assn., 1995—2005. Recipient 1st prize Sci. and Tech. Progress award, Heilongjiang Provincial Govt., 1989, 1993. Achievements include patents pending for Mouch Heart and Small Intestine Transplant model. Avocations: music, cooking. Office: Dept Exptl Rsch Ing 137 UMAS SE-205 02 Malmö Sweden Office Fax: 46-40-336207. Personal E-mail: zhongquan_qi@hotmail.com. E-mail: zhongquan.qi@med.mas.lu.se.

QIAN, CHAO-NAN (MILES QIAN), medical educator, director; b. Indonesia, Sept. 7, 1966; MD, Sun Yat-sen U., 1992, PhD, 1999. Prof., asst. dir. Sun Yat-sen U. Cancer Ctr., 2007—. Med. expert Nat. Plan Healthy China 2020 Health Ministry of China; dep. dir. NCCS-VARI Translational Rsch. Lab. Nat. Cancer Ctr. Singapore, 2007—09; assoc. editor Chinese Jour. Cancer, 2009—. Avocation: stamp collecting/philately. Office: 651 Dongfeng E Rd Guangzhou Guangdong 510060 China Business E-Mail: qianchn@sysu.edu.cn.

QIAN, SHENGYOU, engineering educator, director; b. Yongzhou, Oct. 2, 1965; PhD, Shanghai Jiaotong U., 1997. Prof., dir. dept. electronic info. sci. Hunan Normal U., 2003—, mem. academic com., 2010. Recipient Siemens prize, Sienmens Ltd., China, award, Hunan Normal U., Excellent Sci. Rschr. award, Coll. Physics & Info. Sci., Hunan Normal U., Excellent Paper award, Hunan Provincial Sci. & Tech. Dept. Mem.: Chinese Soc. Biomed. Engring. Avocation: swimming. Office: Hunan Normal University Changsha Hunan 410081 China Business E-Mail: syqian@foxmail.com.

QIAN, XIAOMING, dean; b. Hubei Province, Oct. 2, 1964; PhD, Hong Kong Poly. U., 2005. Dean Tianjin Poly. U., 2007—. Office: Chenglindao 63 Tianjin 300160 China Office Fax: 022-24528287. Business E-Mail: cnhmq@126.com.

QIAN, YUN, medical association administrator; b. Jiangsu, Mar. 25, 1972; MS, Nanjing Med. U., 2001, PhD. Assoc. chief preventive medicine Wuxi Ctr. Disease Control & Prevention, 2009—. Recipient Outstanding Performance award, Wuxi Health Bur. Master: Wuxi Profl. Com. Non-communicable Disease Prevention & Control. Avocation: piano. Office: 499 Jincheng Rd Wuxi Jiangsu 214023 China E-mail: wxqianyun111@sina.com.

QIANG, JI, thoracic surgeon; b. Sichuan, Oct. 1, 1977; MD, Tongji U., 2004. With, dept. cardiac surgery Tongji Hosp., 2001—. Office: 389 Xincun Rd Shanghai 200065 China Office Fax: 081-021-56377580. Personal E-mail: jiqiang1977@yahoo.com.cn.

QIANG, YA-WEI, medical educator; b. China, June 27, 1960; MD, Chiba U. Sch. Medicine, PhD, 1999. Asst. prof. Myeloma Inst. Rsch. and Therapy UAMS, 2005—. Sr. Rsch. grant, Multiple Myeloma Rsch. Found., Rsch. fellowship, NIH, scholarship, Japanese Internat. Edn. Found. Mem.: Internat. Bone and Mineral Soc., Am. Soc. Bone and Mineral Rsch., Am. Assn. Cancer Rsch., Am. Soc. Hematology. Office: 4301 West Markham St Little Rock AR 72205 Business E-Mail: yqiang@uams.edu.

QIAO, JIAN-HUA, pathologist, researcher; b. Shanghai, Sept. 17, 1960; m. Mei-Qian Guan, Sept. 27, 1985; children: Mona G., George S. Qiao-Guan. MD, Shanghai Med. U., 1984. Diplomate Am. Bd. Pathology, 2003. Resident diagnostic radiology Children's Hosp., Shanghai Med. U., 1984—90, chief resident diagnostic radiology, 1988—90; rsch. fellow cardiology Cedars-Sinai Med. Ctr., LA, 1990—91, resident pathology, 1997—2002; asst. rschr. cardiologist UCLA Med. Ctr., 1991—97, fellow cardiac and pulmonary pathology, 2002—03, clin. instr., 2003—04; staff attending pathologist Mercy Hosp., Bakersfield, Calif., 2004—06, Cath. Healthcare West, 2004—, Calif. Hosp. Med. Ctr., 2006—. Contbr. articles to profl. jours. Recipient Physician Recognition award, AMA, 2001—07, Nathan B. Friedman, M.D. prize for rsch., Cedars-Sinai Med. Ctr., 2002, 1st prize, Shanghai Life Sci. Young Investigator Forum, 1998; named Am. Top Physicians, Consumer's Rsch. Coun. Am., 2007—08. Fellow: Coll. Am. Pathologists; mem.: L.A. Soc. Pathologists (bd. dirs.), US and Can. Acad. Pathology. Achievements include research in size of atherosclerotic plaque in coronary arteries in patients who died from acute myocardial infarction; rejection in cardiac transplantation; mouse models for athersclerosis; discovery of define genetic determination of arterial calcification; heart disease and HIV infection; describe cartilage cells in artery wall in human calcified diabetic peripheral vascular disease; research in imaging studies of pulmonary hypertension in Chinese children with congenital heart disease; gated MRI in diagnosis of congenital heart disease in children in Shanghai. Avocations: swimming, bicycling, stamp collecting/philately, photography. Office: Calif Hosp Med Ctr Dept Pathology 1401 S Grand Ave Los Angeles CA 90015 Office Phone: 213-742-5791. Personal E-mail: jianhuaqiao@yahoo.com. Business E-mail: jian-hua.qiao@chw.edu.

QIN, DANIAN, medical educator; b. Nangchang, China, Nov. 18, 1959; PhD, U. Hong Kong, 1996. Prof. Shantou U. Med. Coll., 2003. Office: 22 Xinling Rd Shantou Guangdong 515031 China Business E-Mail: dnqin@stu.edu.cn.

QIN, HAN, physician; b. Lianyungang, June 10, 1977; MD, Fourth Mil. Med. U., 2008. Attending physician First People's Hosp. Lianyungang City, 2008—. Office: #182 Tongguan Rd Lianyungang Jiangsu 222002 China E-mail: lygsy2003@163.com.

QIN, XIAOFA, medical educator, research scientist; b. Botou, Hebei, China, June 1, 1963, s. Hai-Quan Qin and Xiu-Qin Ma, m. Shuqin Zheng, June 19, 1991; children: Jason Zhe, Ryan. MD in Pub. Health, Beijing Med. U., 1986, MS in Toxicology, 1989, PhD in Toxicology, 1992. Lectr. Beijing Med. U., 1992—94, assoc. prof., 1994—96; postdoctoral asst. La. State U. LSU Med. Ctr., Shreveport, 1996; postdoctoral fellow U. Cin. Coll. Medicine, 1996—2004, rsch. instr., 2004—06; asst. prof. U. Medicine Dentistry NJ, Newark, 2006—. Temp. advisor WHO, Manila, 1995; com. mem. Chinese Soc. Indsl. Toxicology, 1994—96. Contbr. articles to profl. jours. Recipient 3d Advance in Scis. & Tech. award, Ministry of Health China, 1996. Achievements include research in finding the possible causative role of digestive proteases and dietary chemicals in inflammatory bowel disease; the possible cause of the mysterious bilirubin or biliverdin predominance in animals etc. Home: 918 Willow Grove Rd Westfield NJ 07090-3522 Personal E-mail: xiaofa_qin@yahoo.com.

QIN, YUFEN, immunologist, researcher; m. Yiping Zhang. MD (hon.), Harbin Med. U., China, 1977, MD in Immunology, 1982; PhD summa cum laude (hon.), U. Würzburg, Germany, 1990. Resident First Tchg. Hosp., Harbin Med. U., 1982—85; rsch. fellow Dept. Neurology U. Calif., Irvine, 1990—93; rsch. scientist Inst. Pathology, U. Würzburg, 1993—95, Dept. Virology, U. Quebec Inst. Armand-Frappier, Laval, 1995—96, Montreal Nuerol. Inst. Hosp., McGill U., 1996—99; asst. rschr. Dept. Neurology, U. Calif., Irvine, 1999—2003, asst. prof., 2003—. Contbr. articles to profl. jours. Recipient Rsch. award, Max-Planck Soc., 1986—90, Deutsche Forschungsgemeinschaft, 1993—95, van den Noort award, U. Calif., Dept. Neurology, 2005; grantee, Nat. Multiple Sclerosis Soc., 2000—03, NIH, 2001—06; fellow, U. Calif., 1990—93. Mem.: AAAS (assoc.), NY Acad. Sci. (assoc.), Am. Acad. Neurology (assoc.; multiple sclerosis sect.). Peace Party. Achievements include discovery of multiple sclerosis being considered as a neural and axonal autoimmune disease; glycolytic enzymes glyceraldehyde-3-phosphate dehydrogenase (GAPDH) and triosephosphate isomerase (TPI) being identified as target antigens in MS; antobodies in MS brains attack glycolytic enzymes in neuron and axon of a majoriey of MS patients; patents for B cell-mediated immune response in MS, in particular the patents at early stages of clinically isolated syndromes for the early diagnosis and treatment; patents pending for development of diagnosis kits for early detect glycolytic enzyme autoimmunoty in patients with MS and patients with other diseases. Avocations: philosophy, writing, travel, logical argumentation, photography. Office: U Calif 100 Irvine Hall Irvine CA 92697-4275 Business E-Mail: qiny@uci.edu.

QIN, ZHANG, medical educator; b. Shanghai, Nov. 17, 1963; MD, Jiao Tong U., 1987. Prof. Burn Ctr. Ruijin Hosp., 2005—. Mem.: Chinese Burn Assn. Office: 197 Ruijin Er Rd Shanghai 200025 China

QIN, ZHENG-HONG, neuroscientist, pharmacologist; b. Suzhou, China, Mar. 10, 1955; s. Jin-Dao and Yun-Bao Qin; m. Yumei Wang, Oct. 3, 1980; 1 child, Tao. MD, Suzhou Med. Coll., China, 1980, MS, 1985; PhD, Med. Coll. Pa., 1995. Lectr. Suzhou (China) Med. Coll., 1985—88; post doctoral rschr. NIH, Bethesda, Md., 1995—99; instr. Med. Sch. Harvard U., Boston, 1999—2003; prof. Sch. Medicine Soochow U., Suzhou, 2003—. Instr. Mass. Gen. Hosp., Boston, 1999—2003, vis. asst. prof., 2003—, Harvard U., 2003—. Contbr. articles to profl. jours. Recipient Grad. Student Recognition award, Grad. Sch. Biol. Sci., Med. Coll. Pa., 1994, Most Outstanding Thesis award, 1994, Zhou's Rsch. award, Soochow U. and Zhou's Found., 2005. Mem.: Soc. Neurosci. China, Soc. Pharmacology, Soc. Neurosci. USA. Achievements include patents in field; patents pending for. Avocation: ping pong/table tennis. Home: Hu pan Hua Yuan Bldg 8 Unit 1502 Suzhou 215006 China Office: Dept Pharmacology Soochow Univ Sch Medicine Suzhou China

QING, FENG, physician; b. China, July 22, 1962; MD, China Med. U., 1986; PhD, U. London, 1999. Physician William Beaumont Hosps., 2006—. Prof. Oakland U. William Beaumont Sch. Medicine, 2010. Mem.: Am. Coll. Nuc. Medicine, Soc. Nuc. Medicine. Avocation: swimming. Office: 44201 Dequindre Rd Troy MI 48085 Office Fax: 248-964-4848. Business E-Mail: fqing@beaumont.edu.

QINGGUO, QI, endodontist; b. Laiwu, Jan. 21, 1972; DDS, Med. U. West China, PhD, 2004. Dir. Sch. Dentistry Shandong U., 2005—. Mem.: ASM, IADR. Avocations: travel, sports. Office: 44-1 Wenhuaxi Rd Jinan Shandong 250012 China Business E-Mail: qqg@sdu.edu.cn.

QINYING, WANG, otolaryngologist; b. Hubei, Mar. 21, 1976; MD, Zhejiang U., 2000. Physician Zhejian U., 2004. Office: 79# Qingchun Rd Hangzhou Zhejiang 310003 China E-mail: huxl324@163.com.

QIU, XUQIANG, sports medicine physician; b. Hongjiang City, Hunan, China, Oct. 14, 1965; B, Hunan Mmed. U., 1989; PhD, South Ctr. U., 2006. Assoc. chief physician, dept. sports medicine Xiangya Hosp., 2000. Mem.: Ctr. Sports Medicine. Avocations: Go, chess, badminton. Office: 87 Xiangya Rd Changsha Hunan 410008 China Business E-Mail: qxqyd@sina.com.

QIU, YUNPING, medical researcher; b. Jiangxi, China, July 26, 1979; BSc, China Pharm. U., 2001; PhD, Shanghai Jiao Tong U., 2008. Postdoc. rsch. fellow U. NC, Greensboro, 2009—11, rsch. scientist, 2011—. Mem.: AAAS. Avocation: swimming. Office: 500 Laureate Way Kannapolis NC 28081 Business E-Mail: y_qiu@uncg.edu, qyp29@163.com.

QU, ZHIJUN, physician; b. Pingxiang, Jiangxi, China, Oct. 18, 1971; BSc, Jiangxi Medicine Coll., 1994; MD, Huazhong Sci. and Tech. U., 2005. Assoc. chief physician Longgang Dist. Ctrl. Hosp. Shenzhen, 2005—. Evaluation expert Govt. Procurement Ctr. Shenzhen, 2006—. Mem.: Guangdong Soc. Hepatology. Avocation: travel. Office: 1228 Shenhui Rd Shenzhen Guangdong 518116 China Business E-Mail: 334635323@qq.com.

QUACKENBUSH, MARGERY CLOUSER, psychoanalyst, researcher; b. Reading, Pa., Apr. 30, 1938; d. Carl Brumbach and Katherine Elvina (Althouse) Clouser; m. Robert Mead Quackenbush, July 3, 1971; 1 child, Piet Robert. BFA, Pratt Inst., 1960; MA, Calif. Grad. Inst., 1982; PhD in Psychoanalysis, Internat. U. Grad. Studies, NYC, 2001. Cert. in psychoanalysis Ctr. for Modern Psychoanalytic Studies, 1992. Instr. Pratt Inst., Bklyn., 1978-79, Fashion Inst. of Tech., NYC, 1980-81; counselor Wiltwyck, Bronx Ctr., 1981-82; exec. dir. Nat. Assn. for Advancement of Psychoanalysis, NYC, 1982—; pvt. practice in psychoanalysis NYC, 1980—. Adj. prof. Union Inst., 2007. Mem. Lenox Hill Dem. Club, N.Y.C., 1993-95; spkr. various cmty. groups, 1991—. Recipient Maison Blanche award, 1959, Miriam Berkman Spotnitz award, 1992, Am. Bd. Accreditation Profl. Svc. award, 2000-04. Mem. Nat. Assn. for Advancement of Psychoanalysis, Nat. Soc. DAR, Alumni Assn. of the Ctr. for Modern Psych. Studies (sec. 1992-94, Alumni Assn. program dir., v.p. 1995-98), Soc. Modern Psychoanalysts. Democrat. Avocations: reading, writing, golf, horseback riding. Home: 460 E 79th St Apt 14E New York NY 10075-1447 Office: Nat Assn Advancement Psychoanalysis 80 8th Ave # 1501 New York NY 10011-5126 Office Phone: 212-741-0515. Personal E-mail: margeryquackenbush@yahoo.com. Business E-Mail: mq@naap.org.

QUADAGNO, JILL, sociology professor; BA, Pa. State U., 1964; MA in Sociology, U. Calif., Berkeley, 1966; PhD in Sociology, U. Kans., 1976. Fellow Nat. Insti. Mental Health, 1965—66; asst. prof. dept. sociology U. Kans., 1977—81, assoc. prof., 1981—85, prof., 1985—87; Mildred & Claude Pepper Eminent scholar in social serontology, prof. sociology Fla. State U., 1987—. NSF vis. prof. Harvard U., 1988; sr. policy advisor President's Bi-Partisan Commn. Entitlement & Tax Reform, 1994. Author: Color of Welfare: How Raism Undermined the War on Poverty, 1994, One Nation, Uninsured: Why the US Has No National Health Insurance, 2005; assoc. editor Jour. Health &Social Behavior, 2007—, mem. editl. bd. American Sociol. Rev., 2005—07, consulting editor Jour. Gerontology, 2005—; contbr. articles to profl. jours. Named to Kans. Women's Hall of Fame, 1984; fellow, John Simon Guggenheim Meml. Found., 1994—95. Fellow: Gerontological Soc. America (pres. 1997—98); mem.: Inst. Medicine, Nat. Acad. Social Ins. (bd. dirs. 2007—), Sociol. Rsch. Assn., American Sociol. Assn. (Disting. Scholar award 1994). Office: Pepper Institute on Aging and Public Policy Florida State univ Tallahassee FL 32306 Office Phone: 850-644-8827. Office Fax: 850-644-2304. E-mail: jquadagno@fsu.edu. *

QUAEGEBEUR, JAN MODEST, pediatric thoracic surgeon; b. 1945; MS, U. Notre Dame, Namur, Belgum, 1965; MD, Catholic U. Leiden, Leuven, Belgum, 1969; PhD cum laude, State U.Leiden, Netherlands, 1986. Diplomate Am. Bd. Surgery. Resident gen. surgery St. Michel Clin., Brussels, 1969—73; fellowship cardiovasc. surgery Baylor U. Coll. Medicine, Houston, 1973—74; fellowship cardiopulmonary surgery U. Hosp. Leiden, 1974—78, staff surgeon, chief dept. thoracic surgery, 1978—86; prof. pediat. cardiac surgery Erasmus U., Rotterdam, Netherlands, 1986—90; asst. attending surgeon NY-Presbyn. Hosp./Columbia U. Med. Ctr., NYC, 1990—91, assoc. attending surgeon, 1991—98, attending surgeon, 1990—, dir. pediat. cardiac surgery, 1991—; asst. prof. surgery Columbia U. Coll. Physicians & Surgeons, NYC, 1990—91, assoc. prof. surgery, 1991—98, prof. surgery, 1998—. Spl. fellow cardiac surgery U. Ala., Birmingham, 1977, Harvard Med. Sch., Boston, 1978; pres. Surgeons of Hope Found., 2007—. Contbr. articles to profl. jours. Named one of America's Top Dr.'s, Castle Connolly Med. LTD; named to NY Mag. Best Dr.'s. Mem.: Dutch Assn. Thoracic Surgery, European Assn. Cardio-Pulmonary Surgery, NY Med. Soc., NY Soc. Thoracic Surgery, Congenital Heart Surgeons Soc., Soc. Thoracic Surgeons, Internat. Soc. Heart and Lung Transplanation, Am. Assn. Thoracic Surgery. Avocations: golf, skiing, tennis. Mailing: NY Presbyn Babies & Childrens Hosp N Rm 276 3959 Broadway New York NY 10032 Office Phone: 212-305-5975. Office Fax: 212-305-4408.

QUAH, HAK-MIEN, surgeon; b. Singapore, Feb. 26, 1971; MBChB, U. Bristol, 1997; M in Med. Surgery, Nat. U. Singapore, 2002. Cons. surgeon Singapore Gen. Hosp., 2008—. Dir. Singapore Polyposis Registry. Fellow. Acad. Medicine (Singapore), Royal Coll. Surgeons (Edinburgh). Office: Dept Colorectal Surgery Singapore Singapore 169608 Singapore Office Fax: 65-62262009. Business E-Mail: quah.hak.mien@sgh.com.sg.

QUAINI, FEDERICO, oncologist, educator; b. Cremona, July 4, 1948, MD, U. Parma, 1974, degree in Hematology, U. Modena, 1977. Assoc. prof. oncology U. Parma, 1985—; dir. U. Ctr. CISTAC, 2005. Expert mgr. regenerative medicine U.-Hosp. Parma, 2008. Mem.: Am. Heart Assn. Avocations: skiing, tennis, motorcycling. Office: via Gramsci 14 Parma 43126 Italy Office Fax: 390521033271. Business E-Mail: federico.quaini@unipr.it.

QUAM, LOIS, federal agency administrator; b. June 12, 1961; m. Matt Entenza; children: Ben, Steve. BA magna cum laude, Macalaster Coll., Minn., 1983; MA in Philos., Politics, and Economics, U. Oxford, 1985. Chair Minn. Health Care Access Commn., 1989; dir. rsch. and eval. UnitedHealth Group, 1989-93, v.p. pub. sector svcs., 1993, CEO AARP/United divsn. Mpls., 1996-98, exec. v.p., CEO Ovations, 2002—06, exec. v.p., pres. pub. & sr. markets group, 2006—07, pres., CEO pub. & sr. markets, 2007; head of strategic investments green economy and health Piper Jaffray & Co., Mpls., 2007—09; founder, chmn. Tysvar, LLC, Minn., 2009—11; exec. dir., Global Health Initiative US Dept. State, Washington, 2011—. Bd. dirs. General Mills, 2007—11, Coun. Fgn. Rels.; bd. trustees George C. Marshall Found., Nat. Wildlife Found.; adv. com. American Democracy Inst.; sr. fellow Ctr. for American Progress; sr. adv. on rural health issues White House Task Force Nat. Health Care Reform, 1993—96. Mem. editl. bd.: British Med. Jour.; contbr. articles to profl. jours. Bd. trustees Macalester Coll. Recipient America-Norway Heritage Fund award, Nordmann-Forbundett Norway-American Assn., Macalester Coll. Disting Alumni award; named one of The Next 20 Female CEOs, Pink Mag. & Forté Found., 2006, The 50 Most Powerful Women in Bus., Fortune mag., 2006, The Top 25 Women in Healthcare, Modern Healthcare mag., 2011; Rhodes Scholar. Mem.: Phi Beta Kappa. Office: US Dept State c/o Global Health Initiative 2201 C St NW Washington DC 20520 *

QUAN, STUART FUN, researcher, educator; b. San Francisco, Calif., May 16, 1949; s. Stuart Fun and Mabel (Wing) Q.; m. Diana Lee, Dec. 18, 1971; children: Jason Stuart, Jeremy Ryan-Stuart. MD, U. of Calif., San Francisco, San Francisco, CA, 1970—74; AB, U. of Calif., Berkeley, Berkeley, CA, 1967—70. Diplomate Am. Bd. Internal Medicine, Am. Bd. Pulmonary Diseases, Am. Bd. Critical Care Medicine, Am. Bd. Sleep Medicine. Intern in internal medicine U. of Wis., Madison, Wis., 1974—75; prof. of medicine U. of Ariz., Tucson, Ariz., 1992—2006, prof. of anesthesiology, 1992—2006, prof. of pub. health, 2002—06, prof. emeritus of medicine, 2006—; vis. prof. of medicine Harvard Med. Sch., Boston, Mass., 2006—08, lectr. in medicine, 2009—; resident in internal medicine U. of Wis., Madison, Wis., 1975—77; fellow in critical care medicine U. of Calif., San Francisco, San Francisco, Calif., 1977—78, fellow in emergency medicine, 1978—79; fellow in pulmonary medicine U. of Ariz., Tucson, Ariz., 1979—80, instr. in medicine, 1980—81, asst. prof. of medicine, 1981—86, assoc. prof. of medicine, 1986—92, assoc. prof. of anesthesiology, 1987—92. Chmn. and cons. adv. panel on anesthesia and respiratory devices FDA, 1987-89; vis. prof. medicine Harvard Med. Sch., 2007-; mem. Am. Bd. Sleep Medicine, 1991-96; mem. adv. bd. Nat. Ctr. Sleep Disorder Rsch., 2002—; mem. rev. com. internal medicine Accreditation Council on Graduate Med. Edn., 2005—; chmn. test writing com. sleep medicine Am. Bd. Internal Medicine, 2006-. Co-author: Respiratory Diseases--A Pathophysiological Approach, 1984; editor-in-chief Jour. Clinical Sleep Medicine, 2005-; editor Harvard Sleep Health and Edn. Program; contbd. chpts. to various books; contbr. numerous articles to med. jours. Pres. Gymnastics Support Orgn., Tucson, 1985-87. Recipient Phi Beta Kappa, U. of Calif., Berkeley, 1970, Alpha Omega Alpha, U. of Calif., San Francisco, 1973, Helmut S. Schmidt Award, Am. Bd. of Sleep Medicine, 1995, Nathaniel Kleitman Award, Am. Acad. of Sleep Medicine, 2005; scholar Regents Scholar, U. of Californa, San Francisco, 1972. Fellow Am. Coll. Chest Physicians, Am. Acad. Sleep Medicine (chmn. accreditation com. 1995-96, pres. 1999-2000, bd. dirs. 1996-2005); mem. Am. Thoracic Soc., Am. Fedn. Clin. Rsch., Nat. Assn. Med. Dirs. Respiratory Care, Soc. for Critical Care Medicine, Phi Beta Kappa, Alpha Omega Alpha. Avocations: skiing, hiking, swimming. Office: Div Sleep Medicine Harvard Med School 401 Park Dr 2nd Floor East Boston MA 02215 Home Phone: 617-670-0725; Office Phone: 617-998-8842. Office Fax: 617-998-8823. E-mail: squan@arc.arizona.edu.

QUASTEL, MICHAEL REUBEN, nuclear medicine physician, educator; b. Cardiff, U.K., June 30, 1933; s. Juda Hirsch and Henrietta (Jungman) Q.; m. Eva C.R. Torngren, June 27, 1962; children: Jonas, Daniel, Aaron, Benjamin. BS with honors, McGill U., Montreal, Can., 1953, MD, CM, 1957; PhD, U. Ottawa, Can., 1971. Diplomate Am. Bd. Nuclear Medicine, Israel Bd. of Nuclear Medicine, Am. Bd. Allergy and Clin. Immunology, Nat. Bd. Med. Examiners. Intern Charity Hosp. La., New Orleans, 1957-58; rsch. fellow Def. Rsch. Bd. of Can., Royal Cancer Hosp., London, 1958-59; resident in nuc. medicine UCLA Med. Ctr., 1959-61; rsch. assoc. Pasadena (Calif.) Found. for Med. Rsch., 1961-62; rsch. fellow, resident depts. oncology and physiology Hadassah Hosp. Hebrew Univ., Jerusalem, 1962-65; head biology sect., radiation protection divsn. Health and Welfare Can., Ottawa, 1965-70, head environ. mutagenic sect., environ. health divsn., 1970-74; from physician to head Soroka Med. Ctr. Inst. Nuc. Medicine, Beersheva, Israel, 1974-98; from assoc. prof. to prof. faculties of natural and health scis. Ben Gurion U. of The Negev, Beersheva, Israel, 1974—98, emeritus prof., 1998—; head nuc. medicine MAR Diagnostic Ctr., Beersheva, 1998—2008. Chmn. 12th Internat. Leucocyte Culture Conf., 1978; co-chmn. Internat. Conf. in Radiation and Health, 1996; chmn. Chernobyl com. fac. of health scis. Ben Gurion U. of the Negev, Beersheva, 1991—94. Editor: Cell Biology and Immunology of Leukocyte Function, 1979, Radiation and Human Health, 1997; contbr. numerous articles to profl. jours. Chmn. Light Opera Group of the Negev, Beersheva, 1988—89, 1998—99. Recipient fellowship Harvard Med. Sch. and Mass. Gen. Hosp., Boston, 1980-81, Eleanor Roosevelt fellowship U. British Columbia, Vancouver, 1987-88, grant Med. Rsch. Coun. Can., grant War Against Cancer, Israel, grant Leukemia Rsch. Found., Israel, grant Israel U.S. Binational Sci. Found., grant Israel Acad. Scis. Mem. European Soc. Nuclear Medicine, Soc. Nuclear Medicine, Israel Soc. Nuclear Medicine. Avocations: light opera, choral music. Home: 7 Rehov Shaked 84965 Omer Israel Business E-Mail: maay100@bgu.ac.il.

QUATTRONE-CARROLL, DIANE ROSE, clinical social worker; b. NYC, July 18, 1949; d. Mario Anthony and Filomena (Serpico) Quattrone; m. Rene Eugene Carroll Jr., June 7, 1980; children: Jenna Cristine, Jonathan Rene. BA cum laude, Bklyn. Coll., 1971; MSW, Rutgers U., 1974. Lic. marriage and family counselor, lic. clin. social worker, N.J., bd. cert. diplomate in clin. social work. Clin. social worker, field instr. Essex County Guidance Ctr., East Orange, N.J., 1974-82; exec. dir. Psychotherapy Info. and Referral Svc., Madison, N.J., 1982-87; pvt. practice Sparta, N.J., 1982—. Nat. Assn. Social Workers. Avocation: travel. Office Phone: 973-729-2442.

QUDEIMAT, MUAWIA A., dental educator; b. Kuwait, Feb. 20, 1969, BDSc, Jordan U. Sci. and Tech., 1992, MDSc, Leeds Dental Inst., 1996. Asst. prof. Jordan U. Sci. and Tech., 1997—2004; cons., pediat. dentistry Ministry of Health KSA, 1999—2000; assoc. prof. Kuwait U., 2009—. Founding mem. Jordanian Soc. Pediat. Dentistry, 1999; mem., examiner Jordanian Dental Accreditation Coun., 2002—05, Jordanian Dental Specialty Bd. Coun., 2003—05, local rep. Orgn. Safety, Asepsis and Prevention, 2006—09. Fellow: Royal Coll. Dentists Can.; mem.: Internat. Assn. Dental Rsch., Arab Soc. Pediat. Dentistry, Internat. Assn. Pediat. Dentistry, European Acad. Pediat. Dentistry. Avocations: reading, hiking, travel. Office: Faculty Dentistry PO Box 24923 Safat Kuwait City 13110 Kuwait Business E-Mail: mqudeimat@hsc.edu.kw.

QU DONG, YIN, orthopedist, educator; b. Pengan County, Sichuan, Jan. 15, 1965; Degree, Suzhou Med. Coll., 1988, PhD, 2002. Dir., orthop. dept. Wuxi No 9 Hosp., 2005—. Adj. prof. Nanjing Traditional Chinese Medicine U., 2003—. Recipient award, China Nat. Nuc. Corp., 2nd prize, Jiangsu Province. Avocations: travel, sports, fishing. Office: Liang Xi Rd 999 Wuxi City Jiangsu Province 214061 China Business E-Mail: yinqudong@sina.com.cn.

QUEEN, ROBIN MARIE, lab administrator; b. Nashville, Jan. 16, 1978; BS, U. NC, Chapel Hill, 2000, PhD, 2004. Dir., Michael W. Krzyzewski human performance lab. Duke U. Med. Ctr., 2004—. Cons. HipKnee Ark. Found., 2010. Rsch. grant, Orthopaedic Rsch. and Edn. Found., Am. Orthop. Foot and Ankle Soc., Piedmont Rsch. Found., DonJoy Orthop. Mem.: Internat. Soc. Biomechanics, Am. Soc. Biomechanics, Am. Coll. Sports Medicine, Am. Acad. Orthop. Surgeons. Avocations: running, hiking, skiing. Office: 102 Finch Yeager Bldg DUMC 3435 Durham NC 27710 Office Fax: 919-681-7067. Business E-Mail: robin.queen@duke.edu.

QUE HEE, SHANE STEPHEN, environmental health educator; b. Sydney, Oct. 11, 1946; came to U.S., 1978; s. Robert and Beris (Byers) Que Hee. BS, U. Queensland, Brisbane, Australia, 1968, MS, 1971; PhD, U. Saskatchewan, Can., 1976. Registered profl. indsl. hygienist. Asst. prof. U. Cin., 1978-84, assoc. prof., 1984-89, U. Calif., LA, 1989-94, vice chair, 1992—94, prof. LA, 1994—; dist. prof. Nat. Taiwan U., 2009—; dir. UCLA Ind. Hygiene Program, 2009—. Mem. Hazardous Materials Data Bank Nat. Libr. Med., 1984—89; mem. biol. monitoring com. Am. Indsl. Hygiene Assn., 1993—; mem. com. on methods for water and waste water Am. Water Works Assn., Am. Pub. Health Assn., 1993—, mem. biol. environ. expt. level com., 2007—; mem. bd. sci. counsellors NIOSH, 2001—04; mem. Nat. Toxicol Program Rsch. on Carcinogens, 2006—. Author: The Phenoxyalkanoic Acids: Chemistry, Analysis and Environmental Pollution, 1981, Biological Monitoring: An Introduction, 1993, Hazardous Waste Analysis, 1999, Biological Monitoring Guide, 2004; contbr. more than 180 articles to profl. jours. and book chpts. Sec. Lesbian Gay Acad. U., Cin., 1978-87, pres. 1988-89, facilitator Gay/Lesbian March Activists, Cin., 1987-89; pres. Lesbian Gay Health and Health Policy Found., L.A., 1994—2011. Postdoctoral fellow McMaster U., Hamilton, Ont., Can., 1976-78. Fellow Am. Inst. Chemists, Am. Indsl. Hygiene Assn. (chmn. biol. environ exposure level project team 2008-09); mem. AAAS, Am. Indsl. Hygiene Assn. Biological Monitoring Com. (sec. 2006, vice-chmn. 2007, chmn. 2008), Am. Coll. Toxicology, Am. Indsl. Hygiene Assn., Am. Chem. Soc., Am. Conf. Indsl. Govt. Hygienists, Am. Pub. Health Assn., N.Y. Acad. Scis. Avocations: civil rights, piano, writing, tennis, bridge, chess. Home: 923 Levering Ave Unit 102 Los Angeles CA 90024-6612 Office: UCLA Sch Pub Health Dept Environ Health Sci 650 Charles Young Dr S Los Angeles CA 90095-1772 Office Phone: 310-206-7388. Business E-Mail: squehee@ucla.edu. *

QUENCER, ROBERT M., neuroradiologist, researcher; b. Jersey City, Nov. 14, 1937; s. Arthur Bauer and Isabell (Moore) Quencer; m. Christine F. Thomas, Sept. 16, 1972; children: Kevin, Keith. BS, Cornell U., 1959, MS, 1963; MD, SUNY, Syracuse, 1967. Diplomate Am. Bd. Radiology, Nat. Bd. Med. Examiners; cert. of added qualifications in neuroradiology. Intern Jackson Meml. Hosp., Miami, Fla., 1967-68; resident in radiology Columbia U., NYC, 1968-71, fellow in neuroradiology, 1971-72; asst. prof. Downstate Med. Ctr., Bklyn., 1972-76; assoc. prof. U. Miami, 1976-79, prof., 1979-92, chmn., prof., 1992—, chief sect. neuroradiology, 1976-86, dir. divsn. magnetic resonance imaging, 1986-92, Robert Shapiro MD prof. radiology, chmn. dept. radiology. Vis. prof. U. Tenn. Coll. Medicine, Memphis, 1982, Downstate Med. Ctr. Coll. Medicine, Bklyn., 1992, U. Vt. Coll. Medicine, Burlington, 1983, NY Med. Coll., Valhalla, 1984, U. Va. Sch. Medicine, Charlottesville, 1984, U. Ky. Sch. Medicine, Lexington, 1985, Yale U. Sch. Medicine, New Haven, 1986, 2000, Columbia U. Sch. Medicine, NYC, 1986, The Mayo Clinic & Found., Rochester, Minn., 1987, Med. Coll. Va., Richmond, 1988, U. Pa. Sch. Medicine, Phila., 1988, Harvard U. Sch. Medicine/Mass. Gen. Hosp., Boston, 1989, U. Conn., Farmington, 1990, Kumamoto, Japan, 1993, U. Man., Can., 1992, Mich. State U., 1996, Mt. Sinai Med. Ctr., 1997, Cornell U. Sch. Medicine, 1998, U. Minn., 2001, U. Ky., 2002; UTMB Galveston, 2003; Dartmouth Hitchcock Med. Sch., 2003, Duke Univ. Sch. of Med., 2003, U. Calif., San Francisco, 2005, U. Mass., 2006; guest lectr. Asian Oceanic Soc. Neuroradiology, 2001, Internat. Med. Soc. Paraplegic, Lucerne, Switzerland, 2001; Phaler lectr. Phila. Roentgen Soc., 1995; dir. programs in dept. radiology U. Miami Sch. Medicine, 1984, 86, Med. Coll. Wis., 1990, 92, Kauai, Hawaii, 1991, Whistler, B.C., 1990; guest lectr. at ASEAN Congress of Radiology, Malaysia, 1992, Royal Australia Radiology Soc., Brisbane, 1993, Brazilian Congress Neurology, 1996, NY Roentgen Soc., 1997, Somerset MR course, Torquay, UK, 1998, Republic of China, 1999, Yale U., 2000, U. Minn., 2001, U. Tex., 2003, Duke U., 2003, U. Calif., San Francisco, 2005, Downstate Med. Ctr., 2007; adv. cons. NIH, 1987, 90; sci. merit reviewer V.A., 1987; presenter, lectr. in field. Author: Neurosonography, 1988; dep. editor Am. Jour. Neuroradiology, 1984-96, editor-in-chief, 1998—; assoc. editor for neuroimaging Yearbook of Neurology and Neurosurgery, 1991—; manuscript reviewer Am. Jour. Neuroradiology, 1984—, Paraplegia, 1989—, Radiographics, 1991—, Pediatrics, 1993—, Radiology, 1994—; mem. editl. bd. Jour. Clin. Neuro-Ophthalmology, 1980-90; contbr. articles to profl. jours. Pres. Am. Soc. Neuroadiology, 1994-95; prin. investigator NIH Grant on imaging/pathology of spinal cord injury; chmn. Commn. Neuroradiological Socs. World Fedn. Neuroradiology Soc., 2003-, Neuroradiology Sci. Program Com. Radiological Soc. North Am., Scientific RSNA Program, 2008-, dir. for neuroradiology, 2004-; Lt. (j.g.) USN, 1959-61. Fellow Am. Coll. Radiology, Am. Soc. Neuroradiology (pres. 1994-95, program com. 1985-89, 92, editl. com. 1984—, publs. com. 1984—, Gold medal 2007); mem. AMA, Fla. Radiology Soc. (Gold medal 2008-), Radiol. Soc. N.Am. (program subcom. on neuroradiology 1990-94, chmn. neuroradiology program 2004—, sci. program dir. 2008—), Southeastern Neuroradiol. Soc. (founder, pres. 1980-81, examiner for bd. certification in radiology and neuroradiology), Fla. Radiol. Soc. (magnetic resonance com. 1991-92, gold medal award, 2008), Alpha Omega Alpha. Avocations: golf, travel. Business E-Mail: rquencer@med.miami.edu.

QUERLEUX, BERNARD, cosmetics executive; b. Chaumont, July 3, 1957; PhD, Grenoble U., 1987; habil in Biophysics, Paris XII U., 1995. Rsch. group leader L'OREAL Rsch. & Innovation, 1990, sr. rsch. assoc., 2010. Sci. chmn. Internat. Soc. Biophysics & Imaging Skin, 2005; hon. prof. Franche Comté U., 2010. Avocation: musician. Office: 1 Ave Eugene SCHUELLER Aulnay Sous Bois 93600 France Business E-Mail: bquerleux@rd.loreal.com.

QUEST, DONALD O., bank executive; b. St. Louis, Nov. 20, 1939; s. Oliver Harry and Elaine Elsie (Henderson) Q.; m. Ilona Maris, July 20, 1969; children: Wendy Elaine, Amy Ilona, Susan Elissa. BS, U. Ill., 1961; MD, Columbia U., 1970. Diplomate Am. Bd. Neurol. Surgery. Intern Mass. Gen. Hosp., Boston, 1970—71, resident, 1971—72, Neurol. Inst. N.Y., NYC, 1972—76; attending neurosurgeon Downstate Med. Coll., Bklyn., 1976—78; attending physician The Valley Hosp., 1978, Columbia-Presbyterian Med. Ctr., 1978; asst. dean, Student Affairs Columbia University, attending neurosurgeon NYC, 1978—; chmn. Am. Bd. Neurological Surgery, Houston; prof. Columbia University, 1989. Bd. dirs. Hudson City Bancorp, Inc., 1983—. Mem. Neurosurgical Assocs., NY; pres. Am. Assn. of Neurological Surgeons, Am. Acad. of Neurological Surgeons, Congress of Neurological Surgeons, 1986—87; chmn., sec. Am. Bd. of Neurological Surgery, 1996. Lt. USN, 1961—66. Mem. Neurol. Soc. Am., Am. Acad. Neurol. Surgery, Am. Assn. Neurol. Surgery, Congress Neurol. Surgeons, Soc. Neurol. Surgeons. Avocations: literature, music. Office: Hudson City Bancorp Inc Bd Directors W 80 Century Rd Paramus NJ 07652 also: Neurol Inst NY 710 W 168th St New York NY 10032-2603 Office Phone: 201-967-1900. Office Fax: 201-967-0332. E-mail: dquest@hcsbnj.com. *

QUEVEDO, JOAO, neurologist; b. Passo Fundo, Brazil, May 30, 1974; s. Joao Abrev and Lucia Helena Q. MD, U. Fed. RGS, Porto Alegre, Brazil, 1998. Jr. asst. rschr. dept. biochemistry U. Fed. RGS, 1994—. Mem. Soc. Neurosci., N.Y. Acad. Sci. Office: UFRGS Centro de Memolria Rua Ramiro Banceros 2600 90035003 Porto Allegre RS Brazil

QUICK, JONATHAN DICKINSON, health organization executive; b. Albany, NY, June 5, 1951; s. James F. and Olva F. (Faust) Q.; m. Tina L. Burdick, May 1, 1982; children: Janneke C., Katrina F., Kimberly C. AB magna cum laude, Harvard U., 1974; MPH, MD, U. Rochester, 1979. Diplomate Am. Bd. Family Practice, Am. Bd. Preventive Medicine. Resident/chief resident family medicine Duke U., Durham, NC, 1982; chief of staff USPHS Hosp., Talihina, Okla., 1982-84; dir. drug mgmt. program Mgmt. Scis. for Health, Boston, 1984-89, health svcs. advisor Peshawar, Pakistan, 1989-91; health planner Min. of Health, Nairobi, Kenya, 1991-94; med. officer WHO, Geneva, 1995-96, dir. essential drugs, 1996-98, dir. essential drugs and medicines policy, 1999—2004; pres., CEO Mgmt Scis. For

Health, Boston, 2004—. Adj. assoc. prof. Boston U. Sch. Pub. Health, 1990—; cons. Aga Khan Health Scis., Tanzania, 1982-83. Editor: Managing Drug Supply, 1997; co-editor: Preventive Stress Management in Organizations, 1997; co-author: Stress and Challenge at the Top, 1990, Rhinos in the Rough: A Golfer's Guide to Kenya, 1993, Financial Times Guide to executive Health, 2002; editl. bd. Jour. Occupl. Health Psychology, 1995—. Mem. worship team Hope Christian Ch., Ferney-Voltaine, France, 1996—. Lt. USPHS, 1982-84. Fellow Royal Soc. Medicine, Am. Coll. Preventive Medicine; mem. Am. Acad. Family Physicians, Rotary Interant. (com. mem. 1992-94). Avocations: jazz and rock 'n roll drumming, jogging, skiing, writing. Office: Mgmt Scis Health 165 Allandale Rd Boston MA 02130 Office Phone: 617-250-9396.

QUICK, ROGER, recruitment company executive; Spokesman, chief lobbyist Ill. Hosp. Assn., exec. v.p.; pres. Ill. Hospital's Rsch. and Ednl. Found.; mng. ptnr. healthcare Korn/Ferry Internat.; head healthcare practice Norman Broadbent; co-founder, pres., CEO Quick, Leonard Kieffer, Chgo. Chmn. Smoke Free Chgo., 2005, Smoke Free Ill., 2006; bd. trustees Columbus-Cabrini Med. Ctr., Chgo.; vice chmn. bd. trustees North Ctrl. Coll. Mem.: Nat. Alzheimer's Assn. (former mem. bd. dirs.), American Cancer Soc. (former Ill. state chmn., mem. nat. bd. dirs., mem. polit. action com., St. George's award). Office: Quick Leonard Kieffer 555 W Jackson Blvd Fl 2 Chicago IL 60661 Office Phone: 312-876-9800. Office Fax: 312-876-9264. *

QUIE, PAUL GERHARDT, pediatrician, educator; b. Dennison, Minn., Feb. 3, 1925; s. Albert Knute and Nettie Marie (Jacobson) Quie; m. Elizabeth Holmes, Aug. 10, 1951; children: Katie, Bill, Paul, David. BA, St. Olaf Coll., 1949; MD, Yale U., 1953; PhD (hon.), U. Lund, 1993. Diplomate Am. Bd. Pediat., Nat. Bd. Med. Examiners (mem.). Intern Hennepin County Hosp., 1953—54; pediatric resident U. Minn. Hosps., 1957—59; mem. faculty U. Minn. Med. Sch., 1959—, prof. pediat., 1968—99, prof. microbiology, 1974—99, assoc. dean of students, 1992—, Am. Legion meml. heart rsch. prof., 1974—91, Regents prof., 1991; Regent's prof. emeritus, 1999—; interim dir. Ctr. for Biomed. Ethics U. Minn. Med. Sch., 1985—86; attending physician Hennepin County Hosp., 1959—91. Cons. U. Minn. Nursery Sch., 1959—91; chief of staff U. Minn. Hosp., 1979—84; vis. physician Radcliffe Infirmary, Oxford, England, 1971—72; mem. Adv. Allergy and Infectious Disease Coun., 1976—80; mem. pediat. com. NRC, 1978; mem. bd. sci. counselors Gamble Inst., 1985—90; vis. prof. U. Bergen, 1991; hon. prof. U. Hong Kong Med. Sch., 1995; vis. prof. pediat. Chubu Hosp., Nagasaki, Japan, 1996; co-dir. internat. med. edn. and rsch. prog. U. Minn. Med. Sch., 1998—. Editl. bd. Pediat., 1970—76, Rev. Infectious Diseases, 1989—92. Pres. Fairview Found., 1998—2007; bd. dirs. Ctr. for Victims of Torture, Elizabeth Glaser Pediat. AIDS Found., 1998—2005. Med. officer USNR, 1954—57. Recipient E. Mead-Johnson award, Am. Acad. Pediat., 1971, Shotwell award, Hennipen Med. Soc., 2001, Gold Headed Cane award in Pediat., 2005; fellow Guggenheim, 1971—72, Alexander von Humboldt, 1986; scholar John and Mary R. Markle, 1960—65. Mem.: Minn. Acad. Medicine (pres. 1993—94), Assn. Am. Physicians, Am. Acad. Pediat., Minn. Acad. Pediat., Am. Soc. Clin. Investigation, Am. Pediatric Soc. (coun. 1976—83, pres. 1987—88), Soc. Pediatric Rsch., Infectious Diseases Soc. Am. (coun. 1977—82, pres. 1985, Bristol award 1994), Am. Soc. Microbiology, Am. Fedn. Clin. Rsch., Minn. Med. Found. (pres. 1986—88), N.W. Pediat. Soc., Inst. Medicine of NAS. Achievements include research in function of human leukocytes and internat. med. ed. and rsch. Home: 2154 Commonwealth Ave Saint Paul MN 55108 Office: PO Box 293 Minneapolis MN 55455-0374 Office Phone: 612-626-2558. Business E-Mail: quiex001@umn.edu.

QUIGLEY, HARRY ALAN, ophthalmologist, medical professor; b. St. Louis, Sept. 17, 1945; children: David, Erica. AB with honors, Harvard Coll., Cambridge, Mass., 1967; MD, Johns Hopkins U. Sch. Medicine, Balt., 1971. Diplomate Am. Bd. Ophthalmology. Intern ophthalmology Mt. Zion Hosp., San Francisco, 1971—72; resident ophthalmology/glaucoma Wilmer Opthal. Inst., Johns Hopkins U., 1972—75; fellowship Bascom Palmer Eye Inst., U. Miami, Fla., 1975—77; asst. prof. Johns Hopkins U. Sch. Medicine, 1977—80, assoc. prof., 1980—85, prof., 1985—94, A. Edward Maumenee prof. ophthalmology, 1994—. Dir. Dana Ctr. Preventive Ophthalmology, Wilmer Inst. Glaucoma Svc.; organizer WHO-sponsored meeting Worldwide Glaucoma 2000. Editor-in-chief (med. jour.) Investigative Ophthalmology & Visual Sci., 1993—97; contbr. articles to profl jours. Recipient Prix Jules Francois, European Soc. Ophthalmology, Mackenzie Medal, Ophthal. Soc. Scotland, Gregg Medal, Australian Soc. Ophthalmology, Mooney Medal, Irish Ophthal. Soc., Doyne Medal, Oxford Ophthal. Congress, Lewis Rudin prize, NY Acad. Scis.; named Best Tchr., Chgo. Ophthal. Soc.; named one of America's Top Doctors, Castle Connolly Med. Ltd., 2002—07. Mem.: Am. Glaucoma Soc. (founding mem.), Assn. Rsch. Vision & Ophthalmology (chmn. glaucoma sect. 1984—84, sec.-treas. 1987—92, trustee 1987—97, Friedenwald award 2004). Achievements include research in progenitor cells derived from adult eyes; the epidemiology of eye disease and glaucoma in American, African, Asian, and Hispanic populations; first to report long-term success with laser iridotomy. Office: Johns Hopkins Hosp Wilmer 122 600 N WolfeSt Baltimore MD 21287 Office Fax: 410-955-2542.

QUIGLEY, ROBERT LAWRENCE, cardiothoracic surgeon, educator; b. Halifax, NS, Can., Dec. 16, 1957; came to U.S., 1988; s. John Howden and Gloria Lorraine (Monseur) Q.; m. Debra Kristine Crumb, Sept. 4, 1993. BS, Dalhousie U., Halifax, 1978; MD, U. Toronto, Ont., Can., 1982; DPhil, Oxford U., Eng., 1988. Diplomate Am. Bd. Surgery, Am. Bd. Critical Care, Am. Bd. Thoracic Surgery. Intern U. Toronto, 1982-83, resident in surgery, 1983-85; rsch. fellow Oxford U., 1985-88; resident in Surgery Duke U. Med. Ctr., Durham, N.C., 1988-90, fellow in cardiothoracic surgery, 1990-92; asst. prof. surgery Northwestern U.-Evanston (Ill.) Hosp., 1992-95, dir. Surg. Rsch. Lab., 1994-95; assoc. cardiothoracic surgery Guthrie Clinic, Sayre, Pa., 1995—. Recipient rsch. award Med. Rsch. Coun. Can., 1986-88, Golden Apple award med. students Duke U. Med. Ctr., 1990; faculty fellow ACS, 1994-96. Fellow Am. Coll. Surgeons, Am. Coll. Chest Physicians; mem. Soc. Critical Care Medicine, Alpha Omega Alpha. Avocations: running, sailing, water and snow skiing, swimming. Home: 316 Drive C Strathmont Pk Elmira NY 14905 Office: Guthrie Clinic Dept Surgery Guthrie Sq Sayre PA 18840 *

QUILLIAN, WARREN WILSON, II, pediatrician, educator; b. Miami, Fla., Jan. 21, 1936; s. Warren Wilson and Rosabel (Brown) Q.; m. Sallie Ruth Creel, July 26, 1958; children: Rutledge, Ruth, Warren C., Frances. MD, Emory U., 1961. Diplomate Am. Bd. Pediat. (examiner 1966—, bd. dirs. 1974-80, 1992-98, treas. 1978, v.p. 1979, pres. 1980). Intern in pediat. Vandertilt U., Nashville, 1961-62; resident Children's Hosp. Med. Ctr., Harvard U., Boston, 1962-63; chief resident Grady Meml. Hosp., Emory U., Atlanta, 1963-64; pvt. practice Coral Gables, Fla., 1966. Instr., asst. clin. prof., assoc. clin. prof., now clin. prof. pediat. U. Miami Med. Sch., 1966—; emeritus staff, bd. dirs. Miami Children's Hosp.; emeritus staff Jackson Meml. Hosp.; past chief pediat. Doctors' Hosp.; mem. hon. staff Mercy Hosp., Bapt. Hosp., South Miami Hosp.; chmn. health adv. com. Dade County Schs.; bd. dirs., v.p. Am. Bd. Pediat. Found., 1991-98; mem. adv. bd. McGlannon Sch.; cons. Fla. Divsn. Med. Svcs.; bd. dirs. Bank Coral Gables. Contbr. articles to med. jours. Hon. bd. dirs. Soc. Abused Children of Children's Home Soc., Miami, 1980-84; mem. Coral Gables Code Enforcement Bd., 1986-88; team-sch. physician Coral Gables Sr. H.G., 1980-88; bd. dirs. Dade County March of Dimes, Miami, 1968-72; bd. advisors Dade County Assn. Retarded Children, 1968-76; trustee Emory U., 1991-97; mem. coun. ministries, youth coord., mem. fin. com., Sunday Sch. tchr. United Meth. Ch. Coral Gables, 1966—; chair staff parish rels. com.; mem. bd. advisors The Growing Place; mem. Citizens Bd. U. Miami, 1997—; v.p. bd. Good Hope Equestrian Tng. Ctr. for the Handicapped, 1999-. Capt. M.C., U.S. Army, 1964-66. Recipient citation of merit Emory U., 1980, Alumni Commendation, Miami Children's Hosp., 1983, Tchg. award U. Miami Sch. Medicine, 1995, 2002, 06, Winston Churchhill medal, 1999, Commendation Key to City, City of Coral Gables, 2007, named Citizen of Yr., 2005, Lifetime Achievement award Miami Children's Hosp., 2007; named to CGHS Athletic Hall of Fame, 1996, Wisdom Hall of Fame, 1998. Fellow Am. Acad. Pediat.; mem. AMA, Fla. Med. Assn. (sch. health com.), Fla. Pediat. Soc. (past chmn. sch. health com.), So. Med. Assn., Dade County Med. Assn. (sch. health com., continuing edn. com.), Empirical Soc. (past pres.), Soc. for Pediat. Rsch., So. Perinatal Soc., Greater Miami Pediat. Soc. (past pres., chmn. legis. and sch. health com., Hall of Fame), Miami Med. Forum (past pres., Haverfield Cup 1985, Mansfield Trophy 1983, 88, 98), Sr. Soc. Emory U., Biscayne Bay Yacht Club (commodore, bd. govs.), DVS Sr. Honor Soc., Alpha Omega Alpha, Omicron Delta Kappa, Alpha Epsilon Upsilon, Phi Delta Theta. Democrat. Avocations: fishing, golf, boating.

QUILLIGAN, EDWARD JAMES, retired obstetrician, gynecologist, educator; b. Cleve., June 18, 1925; s. James Joseph and Maude Elvira (Ryan) Q.; m. Betty Jane Cleaton, Dec. 14, 1946; children: Bruce, Jay, Carol, Christopher, Linda, Ted. BA, MD, Ohio State U., 1951; MA (hon.), Yale, 1967. Intern Ohio State U. Hosp., 1951-52, resident, 1952-54, Western Res. U. Hosps., 1954-56; asst. prof. obstetrics and gynecology Western Res. U., 1957-63, prof., 1963-65; prof. obstetrics and gynecology UCLA, 1965-66; prof., chmn. dept. Ob-Gyn Yale U., 1966-69, U. So. Calif., 1969-78, asso. v.p. med. affairs, 1978-79; prof. Ob-Gyn. U. Calif., Irvine, 1980-83, vice chancellor health affairs, dean Sch. Medicine, 1987-89; prof., chmn. ob.-gyn. dept. U. Wis., 1983-85; prof., chmn. Ob-Gyn Davis Med. Ctr. U. Calif., Sacramento, 1985-87, vice chancellor Health Scis., dean Coll. Med. Irvine, 1987-89, prof. ob-gyn, 1987-94, prof. emeritus ob-gyn., 1994; exec. dir. med. edn. Long Beach (Calif.) Meml. Health Svcs., 1995—2005; ret., 2005. Contbr. articles to med. jours.; editor-in-chief emeritus: Am. Jour. Obstetrics and Gynecology. Served to 2d lt. AUS, 1944—46. Recipient Centennial award Ohio State U., 1970 Mem. Soc. Gynecologic Investigation, Am. Gynecol. Soc., Am. Coll. Ob-Gyn., Sigma Xi. Home: 1 Goldenglow Irvine CA 92612-4077 E-mail: equilligan@cox.net.

QUINCHE, FLORENCE, communications educator; b. Lausanne, Switzerland, Feb. 17, 1973; Diploma, Paris U., 2000; Phd, Lausanne U., 2004. Rsch. fellow Sorbonne Nouvelle, UFR Communication, 2001—02; asst. Lausanne U., Ethics Dept., 2002—06; maître de conférences Nancy U., Communication Dept., 2006—10. Editing bd. mem. Le champ éthique, Labor et Fides ed. Contbr. articles to profl. jours. Mem.: Ethique et santé. Avocation: photography. Home: 21 av de Cour Lausanne 1007 Switzerland Personal E-mail: florencequinche@yahoo.fr.

QUINN, DONAL, diagnostic equipment company executive; BS in Econs., Cork U., Ireland. Exec. positions with Mallinckrodt Med., Abbott Labs.; group pres. Biology products divsn. Dade Behring, Deerfield, Ill., 1998-99, pres. Europe, Mid. East and Africa divsn., 1999—2000, pres. internat., 2000—02, pres. global customer mgmt., 2002—07, COO, 2007; exec. v.p., chief customer officer Siemens Healthcare Diagnostics, 2007—08, CEO, 2008—. Fellow: Inst. Chartered Mgmt. Accountants. Office: Siemens Healthcare Diagnostics 1717 Deerfield Rd Deerfield IL 60015-0778

QUINN, JOSEPH FRANCIS, neurologist, educator; b. Islip, NY, May 14, 1962; s. Gerard Augustine and Ellen Mary Quinn; m. Joan Ellen Blankenship, Sept. 14, 1991; children: Charles Patrick, Rose Philomena, Lucia Rose. BA in Biochemistry, Harvard U., 1985; MD, U. So. Calif., 1990. Diplomate Am. Bd. Psychiatry and Neurology, 1997. Intern in internal medicine LA County-U. So. Calif. Med. Ctr., LA, 1990—91; resident in neurology Oreg. Health Scis. U., Portland, 1991—94, fellow in dementia/geriatric neurology, 1996—98, sr. instr., dir. gen. neurology, 1994—96; staff neurologist Portland (Oreg.) VA Med. Ctr., 1994—; asst. prof. neurology dept. neurology Oreg. Health Scis. U., Portland, 1997—. Lectr. in field; cons. Oreg. Mus. Sci. and Industry. Author: (chpt.) Neurodegenerative Dementias, 1999, Handbook of Dementing Illnesses, 2002; assoc. editor: Jour. Alzheimer's Disease, 2003—, ad hoc reviewer: Archives of Neurology, Jour. Gerontology, Am. Jour. Clin. Nutrition, Neurosci. Letters, Jour. Am. Geriatric Soc.; contbr. over 50 articles to profl. jours. Rsch. Career Devel. grantee, Dept. VA, 1999—2002, Advanced Rsch. Career Devel. grantee, 2002—, Clin. Hypotheses in Neuroscience grantee, Dana Found., 1999—2001. Mem.: Soc. Neurosci., Am. Acad. Neurology. Democrat. Roman Catholic. Office: OHSU Neurology CR-131 3181 SW Sam Jackson Pk Rd Portland OR 97201 E-mail: quinnj@ohsu.edu.

QUINN, KATHERINE SARAH, psychologist; d. George and Esther Blank; m. Ed Quinn (div. 1994); children: Adam(dec.), Molly Quinn Panepinto. BA in Psychology, U. Nev., 1982, MA in Psychology, 1987; PhD in Psychology (hon.), Calif. Sch. Profl. Psychology, 1999. Intern Children's Behavioral Svcs., Las Vegas, 1980—83, child devel. specialist, 1984—85; rsch. devel. coord. San Diego County Mental Health, 1988—97; intern Southwood Hosp., San Diego, 1991—92; therapist Child Sexual Abuse Treatment Ctr., San Diego, 1992—93; post-doctoral intern Neuropsychological Assessment and Psychotherapy, Solana Beach, Calif., 1999—2002; pvt. practice Solana Beach, 2002—04, Del Mar, Calif., 2004—. Mem.: APA, San Diego Psychol. Assn. Roman Catholic. Avocations: reading, music, opera, theater, hiking. Home: 721 Genter St La Jolla CA 92037 Office: 240 9th St Del Mar CA 92014 Office Phone: 858-720-0682. Business E-Mail: quinnphd@san.rr.com.

QUINN, LOIS MARIE, health service innovator; b. Boston, Sept. 8, 1933; d. Charles Edward and Grace Marie (Lowder) Seabrook; m. Richard Edward Quinn (div.); children: Deborah Marie, Christopher Edward, Erin Elizabeth, Patrick Richard. RN, Boston City Hosp.; BA, Glassboro State Coll., 1977; MA, Ctrl. Mich. U., 1982. Pediatric staff nurse Boston City Hosp.; staff nurse, coronary care nurse, supr., patient edn. coord.dir. nursing svc. Rancocas Valley Hosp., Willingboro, NJ, 1967—78; nursing mgmt. cons. Am. Medicorp., Bala Cynwyd, Pa., 1977-78; asst. adminstr. Washington Meml. Hosp., Turnersville, N.J., 1978-80; pres. Lois Quinn Assocs. Nursing Mgmt. Cons., Willingboro, 1980—83; mgr. nursing svcs. Universal Health Svcs., Inc., King of Prussia, Pa., 1983-84, dir. mgmt. svcs. and profl. stds., 1984-90; dir. profl. svcs. Am. Healthcare Mgmt. Inc., 1990-93, v.p. profl. affairs, 1993-94; sr. v.p. profl. affairs Primary Health Sys., Inc., 1994-97; founder Touch Ministry Compassionate Massage, Devon, Pa., 1998—2010. Mem. Assoc. Bodywork and Massage Profls., Common Cause, Amnesty Internat., Green America, Bread for World, Surrey Svc. Srs, Sigma Iota Epsilon. Roman Catholic. Address: 3962 Lansdale Rd University Heights OH 44118-3122

QUINN, RICHERT EDWARD, retired surgeon; b. Evanston, Ill., Apr. 18, 1941; BS, St. Louis U., 1963; MD, U. Mo., 1968. V.p. risk management COPIC, 1994—2009. Gen. surgeon Greeley Med. Clinic, 1973—94. Fellow: AMA, ACS, Colo. Med. Soc. Avocations: golf, fly fishing. Home: 6524 24th St Rd Greeley CO 80634 Personal E-mail: rquinn@copic.com.

QUINNAN, GERALD VINCENT, JR., medical educator; b. Boston, Sept. 7, 1947; s. Gerald Vincent and Mary (Lally) Q.; children: Kevin, Kylie, Kathleen, John, Gerald; m. Leigh A. Sawyer. AB in Chemistry, Coll. Holy Cross, 1969; MD cum laude, St. Louis U., 1973. Diplomate Am. Bd. Internal Medicine. Intern, resident, fellow Boston U. Med. Ctr., 1973-77; med. officer Bur. Biologics, USPHS, Bethesda, Md., 1977; advanced through grades to asst. surgeon gen. RADM USPHS, 1992; dir. herpes virus br., dep. dir. div. virology Bur. Biologics, Bethesda, 1980-81; dir. div. virology Ctr. for Drugs and Biologics, Bethesda, 1981-88; dep. dir. Ctr. Biologics Evaluation and Rsch., Bethesda, 1988-93, acting dir., 1990-92; prof. Uniformed Svcs. U. Health Scis., Bethesda, 1993—, chair preventive medicine, 2002—. Contbr. chpts. to books, numerous articles to profl. jours.; editl. bd./reviewer several jours. Fellow Infectious Diseases Soc. Am.; mem. AAAS, Am. Soc. for Microbiology, Am. Soc. for Clin. Investigation, Sigma Xi, Alpha Omega Alpha. Roman Catholic. Office: Uniformed Svcs U Hlth Scis Dept Preventive Medicine & Biometrics 4301 Jones Bridge Rd Bethesda MD 20814-4712 Home Phone: 301-460-6625; Office Phone: 301-295-3173. Business E-Mail: gquinnan@usuhs.mil.

QUIÑONES-HINOJOSA, ALFREDO, neurosurgeon, educator; b. Mexico, Mexico, Jan. 2, 1968; m. Anna Quiñones; children: Gabriella, David, Olivia. BA, Escuela Normal Urbana Fed. Fronteriza, Mexicali, Mexico, 1986; Transfer core curriculum to the U. Calif., San Joaquin Delta Cmty. Coll., Stockton, Calif., 1991; BA in Psychology (highest honors), U. Calif., Berkeley, 1994; MD (cum laude), Harvard Med. Sch., Boston, 1999. Basic Life Support Calif., 1999, Advanced Cardiac Life Support Cert. Calif., 1999, Advanced Trauma Life Support Cert. Calif., 1999, lic. Calif., 2001, Md., 2005. Migrant worker San Joaquin Valley, Frenso, Calif., 1987—88; crew leader Calif. Railcar Repair, Stockton, Calif., 1988—91, 1990—91; statistics tutor, Tutor Learning Ctr. San Joaquin Delta Coll., Stockton, Calif., 1990—91; calculus & physics asst. profl. develop. program U. Calif., Berkeley, 1992—94, lab. asst., neuroscience dept., 1994, intern, gen. surgery San Francisco, 2000, tng. in clin. rsch., dept. epidemiology and biostatistics, 2003, NIH postdoctoral fellowship, dept. develop. and stem cell biology, 2004, resident, neurosurgery, 2005; house officer, internal medicine St. Francis Hosp., San Francisco, 2002—04; asst. prof. neurosurgery & oncology John Hopkins U. Sch. Medicine and Sidney Kimmel Comprehensive Cancer Ctr., 2005—07; asst. prof., cellular and molecular medicine John Hopkins U. Sch. Medicine, 2007—, assoc. prof. neurosurgery, 2007—; clin. dir., Brain Tumor Surgery Program John Hopkins Bayview Hosp., 2005—; attending neurosurgeon John Hopkins Hosp., 2005—, John Hopkins Bayview Hosp., 2005—. Invited spkr. in field; cons. Revolution Health Group, 2006—; Alpha Omega Alpha vis. prof. Mt. Sinai Sch. Medicine, 2008; vis. prof. U. Utah, Dept. Neurosurgery, 2008. Editl. bd. mem. Self Assessment in Neurosurgery, Topic Editor, Cerbrovascar, 2004, Journal Neurosurgery, 2004—, Journal Neursurgery: Neurosurgical Focus. Topic Editor, Stem cells opportunities in Neursurgery, 2005—, Journal Neurosurgery Clinics of NAm., 2007—, jour. peer review activities Neurosurgery, 2004—, ad hoc reviewer Cancer Research Journal, 2007—, Journal National Cancer Institute, 2007—, Journal Neurology, 2007—, Journal Experimental Neurology, 2007—, Stem Cells Journal, 2007—, Journal Neurology (India), 2007—, Journal Comparative Neurology, 2007—, Journal Neurosurgicall Review, 2007—, Journal Rejuvenation Research, 2007—, Journal Neuro-Oncology, 2007—; contbr. chapters to books, several articles to profl. jours. Mem. adv. bd. Cord Found., 2007—, Angels of the Operating Room Organization, 2007—; bd. dirs. Hispanic Scholarship Fund, 2007—. Recipient San Francisco Police Dept. Commendation award, 2003, City of San Francisco Appreciation award, 2003, Edwin Boldrey Sci. award, 55th Ann. Meeting San Francisco Neurological Soc., 2003, 57th Ann, Meeting San Francisco Neurological Soc., 2005, Howard Hughes Med. Inst. Physician-Scientist Career award, 2006, Herbert W. Nickens award, Assn. Am. Med. Colleges, 2006, Robert Wood Johnson Found. award, 2007, Popular Sci. Mag. Brilliant 10 Scientists award, 2007, Internat. Hispanics award Sol Azteca, 2008, Merage Found. Nat. Leadership in Sci. and Medicine award, 2008; named one of Balt. Mag. US Top Docs, 2007, Hispanic Bus. Jour. Top 100 Most Influential Hispanics in the US, 2007; grantee Robert Wood Johnson Found., 2008—, NIH/NINDS, 2006—. Mem.: AMA, Am. Soc. for Clin. Oncology (Found. Career Develop. award 2006), Am. Brain Tumor Assn., Am. Assn. for Cancer Rsch., ACS (First Pl., Region IX Resident Paper Competition 2003, Franklin Martin Faculty Rsch. award 2006), Congress of Neurological Surgeons (Blue Ribbon award for Poster Presentation 2002), Am. Assn. Neurological Surgeons (Ronald Bittner award 2004, Jour. Neurooncology award 2004, Lorenz Surgical Young Clinician Investigator award 2006), Soc. for Exptl. Biology and Medicine, AAAS, Assn. for Ethnic Diversity in the Neurosciences, Boston Area Neuroscience Group, Mass. Med. Soc., Pfeiffer Fellow, Hinton-Wright Soc., Harvard Med. Sch., Soc. for the Advancement of Chicanos and Native Americans in Sci., Soc. for Neuroscience, Am. Assn. Neurological (mem. exec. com. 2007—), Nat. Chicano Health Organization and Latin American Student Assn., Harvard Med. Sch., Sigma Xi (Honorable mention award 1999). Office: Dept Neurosurgery Cancer Research Bldg II 1550 Orleans St Rm 247 Baltimore MD 21231-1044 Address: John Hopkins Bayview Medical Ctr Dept Neurosurgery 4940 Eastern Ave B-121 Baltimore MD 21224-2780 Office Phone: 410-502-2906, 410-550-3367. Office Fax: 410-502-7995, 410-550-0748. Business E-Mail: aquinon2@jhmi.edu.

QUINTANILLA, ANTONIO PAULET, retired physician, educator; b. Feb. 8, 1927; came to U.S., 1963, naturalized, 1974; s. Leandro Marino and Edel Paulet Quintanilla; m. Mary Parker Rodriguez, May 2, 1958; children: Antonio Paulet, Angela, Francis, Cecilia, John. PhD, San Marcos U., 1948, MD, 1957. Assoc. prof. physiology U. Arequipa, Peru, 1960-63; assoc. in physiology Cornell U., N.Y., 1963-64; prof. physiology U. Arequipa, 1964-68; assoc. prof. medicine Northwestern U., 1969-80, prof., 1980-2000; ret., 2000. Chief renal sect. VA Lakeside Hosp., 1976-90; cons. nephrologist Northwestern Meml. Hosp., Evanston Hosp., 1990-98, sr. attending emeritus; lectr. nat. Ctr. Advanced Med. Edn., Chgo.; mem. adv. bd. Am. Fedn. Clin. Rsch. Contbr. articles on renal disease to med. jours.; author books in English, French and Spanish, poetry, short stories. Fellow ACP; mem. Ctrl. Soc. Clin. Rsch., Internat. Soc. Nephrology, Am. Soc. Nephrology, Am. Physiol. Soc. Home: 820 Graceland Ave #303 Des Plaines IL 60016 Personal E-mail: aqpaulet@gmail.com.

QUINTELLA-LUNDEMAN, CLAUDIA BARBOSA, medical researcher, educator; d. Sergio Medina Quintella; m. John Lundeman. PhD, Bauru Dental Sch., U. São Paulo, 2007. Contbr. scientific papers.

QUIRK, PHILLIP L., pharmacologist, researcher; b. Milw., Sept. 23, 1966; BA, U. Wis., Milw., 1991; PhD, Colo. State U., 1998. NRSA postdoctoral fellow Case Western Res. Sch. Medicine, Cleve., 1999—. Recipient Nat. Rsch. Svc. award, Nat. Inst. Mental Health, 2001—. Mem.: Soc. for Neurosci. Office: Ind Univ Dept Psychology Bloomington IN 47405

QUIROS-TEJEIRA, RUBEN ELOY, pediatrician, educator, researcher; b. Panama, July 5, 1962; s. Felix A. Quiros and Olimpia Tejeira de Quiros; m. Nubia Noemi Navarrete, Nov. 12, 1994; children: Ruben Eloy Quiros Jr., Jonathan Elias Quiros, Jacob Eli Quiros. MD, Nat. U. Panama, 1986. Cert. Am. Bd. Pediat., 1995, diplomate Am. Bd. Hosp. Physicians, 2005, Am. Coll. Ethical Physicians, 2005. Resident Children's Hosp. Panama, 1988—91; sci. rschr. duPont Hosp. Children, Thomas Jefferson U., Wilmington, Del., 1992; resident Thomas Jefferson U., Phila., 1993—95; asst. prof. pediat. U. Rochester, NY, 2000—01, dir. pediatric hepatology, 2000—01; asst. prof. pediat. and surgery Baylor Coll. Medicine, Houston, 2001—04, med. dir. pediatric liver transplantation, 2001—04; assoc. prof. pediat. and surgery U. Tex., 2004—09, med. dir. pediatric liver, intestinal transplantation, 2004—09, dir. pediatric hepatology, 2004—09, assoc. prof. pediat. U.T. M.D. Anderson Cancer Ctr., Houston, 2005—09, prof. pediat. surgery U. Nebr. Med. Ctr., 2009—, chief pediat. GI hepatologyg & nutrition, 2009—, med. dir., 2009—, fellow, program dir., 2009—; med. dir. GI Hepatolog & Nutrition Childrens Hosp & Med. Ctr., 2009—; prof. pediat. Creighton U., 2010—. Chmn. med. adv. com. Am. Liver Found., South Tex. Chpt., Houston, 2004—09, bd. dirs.; reviewer peer rev. jour. Am. Jour. Transplantation, Edmonton, Canada, 2004—, Jour. Pediatric Gastroent. and Nutrition, Denver, 2004—, Archives Med. Rsch., Mexico D.F., 2003—, Bone Marrow Transplantation Jour., London, 2002—, Jour. Pediat., Cin., 2004—; med. adv. bd. mem. Life Gift Organ Donation Ctr., Houston, 2002—09, Alagille Syndrome Alliance, Tualatin, Oreg., 2004—, Hepatitis Mag., Houston, 2005—07, Liver Health Mag., Houston, 2007—10; chmn. internat. com. N.Am. Soc. Pediatric Gastroent., Hepatology and Nutrition, Flourtown, Pa., 2007—09. Contbr. articles to profl. jours. Mem. focus group Tex. Gulf Digestive Disease Ctr., 2004—09. Recipient Herman Roseblum award, Thomas jefferson U., 1994—95; grantee, NIH; fellow, UCLA, 1995—98, 1998—2000. Fellow: AMA (assoc.), Am. Acad. Pediatric (assoc.); mem.: AAAS (assoc.), Assn. Med. Students U. Panama (hon.), Nat. Med. Assn. Panama (hon.), Panamanian Pediatric Soc. (hon.), Internat. Liver Transplantation Soc. (assoc.), Am. Gastroent. Assn. (assoc.), Am. Assn. Study Liver Disease (assoc.), Am. Soc. Transplantation (assoc.; mem. diversity and minority affairs com. 2006—09), N.Am. Soc. Pediatric Gastroent., Hepatology and Nutrition (assoc.), Internat. Pediatric Transplant Assn. (assoc.), Am. Liver Found. (assoc.), Jefferson Med. Coll. Alumni Assn. (hon.). Mem. Christian Ch. Office: Univ Nebraska 985160 Nebraska Medical Ctr Omaha NE 68198-5160

QUITTELL, LYNNE M., pediatrician, pulmonologist; MD, Sackler Sch. of Medicine, 1981. Diplomate pediatric pulmonology, Am. Bd. of Pediatrics. Resident Long Island Jewish Med. Ctr., 1984; fellow St Christophers Hosp. for Children; with NY Presbyn. / Columbia. Office: Morgan Stanley Children's Hospital of NewYork-Presbyterian 3959 Broadway 166th St New York NY 10032 Office Phone: 212-305-5122.

QUITTERER, URSULA MARIA, pharmacologist, educator; d. Johann and Rosa Quitterer. PhD, U. Mainz, Germany, 1994. Cert. in pharmaceutical scis. State Bavaria, Germany, 1990, habilitation pharmacology and toxicology U. Wuerzburg, Germany, 2001. Vis. scientist Roche Pharma Inc., Palo Alto, Calif., 1995—96; C1 sci. asst. U. Wuerzburg, 1997—2001, C2 prof., 2002—05; full prof. molecular pharmacology Swiss Fed. Inst. Tech., Zurich, Switzerland, 2005—, Med. Faculty, U. Zurich, 2007—. Head, molecular pharmacology unit Swiss Fed. Inst. Tech., Zurich, Switzerland, 2006—, dep. dir., 2009—10, inst. dir., 2010—. Contbr. articles to profl. jours. Recipient Rsch. award, State of Bavaria, 1999; grantee, Swiss NSF, Switzerland, 2007. Mem.: German Soc. Pharmacology and Toxicology, Pfizer AG (adv. bd. pharmacology). Achievements include discovery of relevance of G-protein-coupled receptor dimerization for human disease. Office: Swiss Fed Inst Tech Winterthurerstrasse 190 Y17m70 8057 Zurich Switzerland

QUON, WANDA ANN, plastic surgeon; b. Los Angeles, Mar. 2, 1967; d. Bill Jack and So Fa (Ng) Q. BS, Univ. Southern Calif., 1989; DO, Univ. Health Scis., 1996. Pvt. practice in cosmetic laser surgery. Mem. Am. Osteopathic Assn., Am. Coll. General Practitioners, Am. Coll. Osteopathic Family Physicians, Mo. Assn. Osteopathic Physicians, Phi Sigma Soc. Avocations: piano, tennis, swimming, model building, carving. Office: 808 N Hill St Los Angeles CA 90012-2321 also: 300 E Main St Alhambra CA 91801 also: 201 W Garvey Ave Monterey Park CA 91754-1602

QURESHI, BASHIR AHMAD, physician; b. India, Sept. 25, 1935; s. Haji Nazir and Hajan Khatoon Qureshi; children: Shehnaz Parveen, Salma Zareen, Nasira Shaheen, Naheed Yasmin, Riaz Massod. MB BChir, Nishtar Med. Coll., Multan, Pakistan, 1961. Gen. practitioner, Hounslow, England, 1969—. Lectr. in field. Author: (book) Transcultural Medicine - Dealing with Patients from Different Cultures, Religions, and Ethnicities, 1989, 1994; editor: London Medicine, 1984—85; guest broadcaster various TV and radio shows; contbr. articles to profl. jours. and newspapers. V.p. Conservative Assn. of Feltham and Heston, London, 1995—. Fellow, Royal Coll. Pediats. and Child Health., 2006, Faculty Sexual & Reproductive Health, Royal Coll. Ob/gyns, 2006; Assoc., Faculty Occupl. Medicine Royal Coll. Physicians, 1978. Fellow: Royal Coll. Gen. Practitioners (mem. coun. 1990—93, 1994—97, 2003—06), Royal Soc. Medicine (hon. mem. gen. practice sect. 1998, pres. gen. practice sect. 2000—01); mem.: Coll. St. Georges Windsor Castle, NHS Trust Assn., UK (chmn. 2006), Med. Journalists Assn., Soc. Apothecaries (licentiate), MAPHA (hon.), Royal Soc. Pub. Health (hon.; emeritus v.p.), Royal Coll. Physicians Edinburgh and Glasgow (licentiate), Media Medics, Assn. Broadcasting Drs., Gen. Med. Coun., Soc. of Friends of St. George's and Descendants of Knights of the Garter. Conservative. Muslim. Achievements include first to transcultural medicine. Avocations: travel, films, dance, concerts, dining out. Personal E-mail: drbashirqureshi@hotmail.com.

QURESHI, WAQAR A., medical educator; MD, Royal Free Hosp. Sch. Medicine, London, 1983. Diplomate in med. U. London, 1984, Am. Bd. Internal Medicine, 1990, in gastroenterology 1993. Chief endoscopy Baylor Coll. Medicine, Houston, 1997—, assoc. prof. medicine, 2002—, prof. medicine, 2009—. Fellow: ACP, Royal Coll. Physicians(UK), Am. Soc. Gastrointestinal Endoscopy (mem. stds. practice guidelines), Am. Coll. Gastroenterology (mem. edn. com.). Office: Baylor Coll Medicine 1709 Dryden St Ste 800 Houston TX 77030 Office Phone: 713-798-0964. Office Fax: 713-798-0951.

QVIST, JESPER, physician, consultant; b. Copenhagen, Feb. 18, 1941; s. Ejnar and Ulla Qvist; m. Dorte Mortensen, Dec. 9, 1943; children: Thomas, Tavs, Jens Adam. MD, Copenhagen U., 1966. Bd. cert. anesthesiologist Bd. Health, Denmark, 1976, lic. physician Mass., 1994. Intern medicine and surgery Copenhagen Municipality, 1966—68; residency anesthesia Copenhagen U. Hosp., 1968—71; clin. and rsch. fellow Harvard Med. Sch., Boston, 1971—71; head ICU Copenhagen County Hosp., Herlev, Denmark, 1978—90; cons. intensive care King Faisal Specialist Hosp., Riyadh, Saudi Arabia, 1991—94; assoc. prof. anesthesia Harvard Med Sch., Mass. Gen. Hosp., Boston, 1995—96, dir. infectious disease ICU care Rigs Hosp., Copenhagen, 1996—2000, dir. neuro-intensive care unit, 2000—02, head Respiratory Ctr. East, 2002—07; cons. neuro intensive care unit, 2007—. Rsch. fellow NSF for Polar Rsch., McMurdo, Antarctica, 1974—83, Harvard Med Sch., Boston, 1987—88; rsch. fellow/cons. Kantonspital, Basel, Switzerland, 1982—83. Contbr. chapters to books, articles to profl. jours. Mem. ctrl. sci.-ethical com. for human rsch. under the Ministry of Health, Copenhagen, 1988—89. Lt. Danish Mil., 1967—68. Recipient Antarctica Svc. medal for valuable contributions to Sci. in Antarctica, Nat. Found. for Polar Rsch., 1974—83; Fulbright scholar, Danish-Am. Soc., 1971—74. Achievements include research in seal and human diving research in Antarctica and Korea. Avocation: birdwatching. Office: The Rigshospital Blegdamsvej 9 2100 Copenhagen Denmark Office Fax: 45 3545 2479. Business E-Mail: qvist@rh.dk.

QWARNSTROM, EVA ELISABET, biology professor; b. Lund, Sweden, Apr. 29, 1951; DDS, U. Lund, Sweden, 1975; PhD, U. Lund NIH Bethesda; MD, 1984. Prof., cell biology U. Sheffield, 2001—. Office: Sch Medicine & Biol Scis Sheffield Yorkshire S10 2RX England Office Fax: 44-0-114-271-1863. Business E-Mail: e.qwarnstrom@sheffield.ac.uk.

RAABE, GERHARD KARL, epidemiologist; b. Flushing, NY, Feb. 24, 1948; s. Oscar Albert and Eugenie; m. Barbara Irene Douglas, Nov. 27, 1969; children: Andrew John, Emily Jean. BA in Biology, Hofstra U., 1969; MS in Computer Sci., Pratt Inst., 1971; DrPH, Columbia U., 1987. Sr. rsch. scientist N.Y. State Dept. Mental Hygiene, NYC, 1970-77; med. systems analyst Mobil Oil Corp., NYC, 1977-79, indsl. med. advisor, 1979-81, mgr. epidemiology and med. info. svcs., 1982-89, dir. epidemiology and med. info. svcs. Princeton, N.J., 1990-97; dir. med. info. and health risk assessment Global Med. Svcs., Mobil Bus. Resources Corp., 1997-99; pres., prin. scientist occupl. and environ. health Health Risk Scis., Inc., New Hope, Pa., 1999—. Cons. spl. studies Cornell U. Med. Ctr., NYC, 1973-77; cons. NYC Health Systems Agy., 1976; chmn. occupational health com. Fla. Phosphate Coun., Lakeland, 1979-85; reviewer profl. jours.; expert panelist WHO, IARC, U.S. EPA. Contbr. articles to profl. jours., chpts. to books. Fellow Am. Coll. Epidemiology; mem. AAAS, Soc. for Epidemiologic Rsch., Internat. Soc. for Environ. Epidemiology, Am. Petroleum Inst. (chmn. epidemiology 1985-88, chmn. health and product stewardship 1996-2000), NY Acad. Scis., Soc. for Risk Analysis, Indsl. Epidemiology Forum (chmn. 1991), Internat. Commn. on Occupl. Health. Republican. Lutheran. Avocations: science fiction, tennis. Home: 2215 Aquetong Rd New Hope PA 18938-1149 Office: Health Risk Scis Inc PO Box 189 New Hope PA 18938-0189 Office Phone: 215-862-5718. Personal E-mail: gkraabe@cs.com.

RAAF, JOHN HART, retired surgeon, educator, health facility administrator; b. Portland, Oreg., Aug. 10, 1941; s. John E. and Lorene (Rardin) R.; m. Heather Neilson, June 15, 1965; children—Jennifer, John, Sabrina AB magna cum laude, Harvard U., 1963, MD cum laude, 1970; D.Phil., Oxford U., 1966. Diplomate Am. Bd. Surgery. Intern Mass. Gen. Hosp., Boston, 1970-71, resident in surgery, 1971-73, 75-77; research fellow Sloan-Kettering Inst., NYC, 1973-75; fellow in immunology Meml. Hosp., NYC, 1973-74; faculty assoc. in surgery M.D. Anderson Hosp. and Tumor Inst., Houston, 1977-78, asst. prof. surgery, 1978-79, Cornell U. Med. Coll., NYC, 1979-81; assoc. prof. surgery Meml. Sloan-Kettering Cancer Ctr., NYC, 1981-85; dir. Cleve. Clinic Cancer Ctr., 1985-90; chmn. dept. surgery Meridia Huron Hosp., Cleve., 1991-94; chief surg. svc. VA Med. Ctr. Cleve., 1994-2001; prof. surgery Case Western Res. U., 1994—2001, vice chmn. dept. surgery, 1994-2001. Mem. selection coms. for Rhodes scholarships, Vt., 1969-71, New Eng., 1969-71, La., 1977, Tex., 1978, Ohio, 1989-94; mem. soft tissue sarcoma discussion group Nat. Cancer Inst., 1980; mem. clin. trials com. Nat. Cancer Inst., NIH, 1984-88 Co-author Meml. Sloan-Kettering Cancer Ctr. publs., 1980; also numerous articles, chpts., abstracts, letters, short papers, movies, med. photographs; editor: Diagnosis and Treatment of Soft Tissue Sarcomas, 1993; editor-in-chief Primary Care and Cancer, 1981-92; mem. editorial bd. Meml. Sloan-Kettering Cancer Ctr. Clin. Bull., 1979-82; assoc. editor Oncology mag., 1987-92; mem. editorial com. Cleve Clinic Jour. Medicine, 1987-90. Rhodes scholar Oxford U., Eng., 1963; nat. scholar Harvard U. Med. Sch., 1966-70; Am. Cancer Soc. postdoctoral scholar Harvard U. Med. Sch., 1969-70; ACS scholar Mass. Gen. Hosp., Boston, 1975-77; Am. Cancer Soc. jr. faculty clin. fellow, 1980-83. Fellow ACS; mem. Am. Assn. Cancer Research, Am. Assn. Endocrine Surgeons, Am. Soc. Clin. Oncology, Assn. Acad. Surgery, Assn. Am. Rhodes Scholars, Cen. Surg. Assn., Soc. Surg. Oncology (publs. com. 1981-84, working group on edn. 1982, membership com. 2000), Meml. Hosp. Alumni Soc. (chmn. program com. 1982), River Place Athletic Club, Charaka Club (N.Y.C.). Home: 225 SW Montgomery St #5 Portland OR 97201

RAB, GEORGE T., pediatric orthopedic surgeon; b. Cleve., Nov. 11, 1946; s. Thomas P. and Patricia S. Rab; m. Wendy Andereson Rab, Aug. 31, 1968; children: Geoffrey W., Nicholas A. BS, Northwestern U., Chgo., 1968; MD, Northwestern U., 1970; MS, U. Minn., Mpls., 1975. Lic. physician Calif., diplomate Am. Bd. Orthop. Surgery, Nat. Bd. Med. Examiners. Intern in surgery Chgo. Wesley Meml. Hosp., 1970—71; resident in orthop surgery Mayo Clinic, Rochester, Minn., 1971—75; resident in pediat. orthop. surgery Gillette Children's Hosp., St. Paul, 1974; asst. prof. dept. orthop. surgery Sch. Medicine, U. Calif., Davis, 1977—82, assoc. prof. dept. orthop. surgery, 1982—88, prof. dept. orthop., 1988—, Ben Ali chair in pediat. orthop., 1998—, chair dept. orthop. surgery, 2000—06. Guest lectr. Shriners Hosp. for Crippled Children and Sch. Medicine Oreg. Health Scis. U., Portland, 1985, Duncan Seminar Children's Orthop. Hosp. and Med. Ctr., Seattle, 1987; vis. prof., guest lectr. dept. orthop. Children's Hosp. Med. Ctr., Cin., 1986; vis. prof., guest lectr. Carrie Tingley Hosp. Annual Meeting, Albuquerque, 1992; vis. prof., guest lectr., Robert Samilson lectr., San Francisco, 96; vis. prof. U. Calif., Irvine, 1998, U. Colo., 1999, New Eng. Med. Ctr., 1999, Children's Hosp. Med. Ctr. of Akron, Ohio, 2001; Arthur A. Thibodeau vis. prof. Tufts U. Sch. Medicine, 1999; John M. Roberts vis. prof. Children's Hosp. of New Orleans, 2000; vis. prof., Leslie Meyers lectr. Shriners Hosp., Greenville, SC, 2001; Charles LeRoy Lowman vis. prof. Orthop. Hosp., LA, 2002; orthop. surgeon, med. dir. motion analysis lab. Shriners Hosp. for Children, 1993—, pediat. orthop. specialist Sutter Cmty. Hosps., Sacramento, 1987—; vis. assoc. prof. dept. orthop. Harvard Med. Sch., Boston, 1983—84; rsch. fellow gait lab. Children's Hosp., Boston, 1983—84; editl. cons. Am. Jour. Diseases of Children, 1990—93; cons., rev. com. Orthop. Rsch. and Edn. Found., 1994—99; civilian cons. med. specialist in pediat. orthop. surgery Oakland Naval Hosp., Calif., 1990—95; pediat. orthop. cons. Kaiser Permanente Hosp., Sacramento, 1977—98. Mem. editl. bd. Gait and Posture, 1992—97, bd. editors Jour. Pediat. Orthopedics, 1992—, Jour. Children's Orthopedics, 2006—. Bd. dirs. Sacramento Make-A-Wish Found., Inc., 1988—92. Maj. US Army, 1975—77. Recipient Goldsmith Intern Humanitarian award, Chgo. Wesley Meml. Hosp., 1971, Frank Stitchfield award, Hip Soc., 1976, annual award for excellence in tchg. clin. scis., Kaiser Found. Hosp., 1978, Best Poster award, Gait and Clin. Analysis Soc. Meeting, 2000, named Outstanding Clin. Instr., U. Calif. Davis Sch. Medicine, 1980, Outstanding Tchr. of Yr. in Orthop. Surgery, 1991, 1996; named one of Best Drs. in Am., 2005—06; Berg-Sloat Traveling fellow, 1977. Fellow: Am. Acad. Pediat., Am. Acad. Orthop. Surgeons (com. on biomed. engring. 1980—82, com. on psychomotor skills 1980—87, com. ednl. content 1981—82, sec. com. on biomed. engring. 1982—85, subcom. on pediat. of com. on exams. and evaluations 1985—91, chmn. com. on biomed. engring. 1986—87); mem.: Sierra Sacramento Valley Med. Soc., Sacramento Pediat. Soc., Paul R. Lipscomb Soc., West Coast Gait Lab. Group, Western Orthop. Assn., Calif. Med. Assn., Am. Orthop. Assn., Pediat. Orthop. Soc. N.Am. (com. on computer applications in pediat. orthop. 1985—90), Orthop. Rsch. Soc., Internat. Soc. Electrophysiol. Kinesiology, Internat. Pediat. Orthop. Think Tank (site selection com. 1998—2000), Gait and Clin. Movement Analysis Soc. (awards com. 2001—02), Am. Soc. Biomechanics (arrangements com. annual meeting 1987, pres.-elect 1989—90, exec. com. 1989—93, pres. 1990—91), Am. Bd. Orthop. Surgery (certifying examiner 1984—92), Am. Acad. Cerebral Palsy and Devel. Medicine (nominating com. 1990—94). Avocations: bicycling, sailing, hiking, cooking. Office: Dept Orthop Surgery U Calif-Davis 4860 Y St # 3800 Sacramento CA 95817 Office Phone: 916-734-5770. Office Fax: 916-734-7904. E-mail: george.rab@ucdmc.ucdavis.edu. *

RABAGO, LUIS RAMON, physician; b. Santander, Aug. 31, 1954; MD, U. Autonoma De Madrid, 1977, PhD, 2006. Physician FEA-Imsalud, Madrid, 1987—. Recipient award, Baxter España, Fundación Española Del Aparato Digestivo, 2010. Mem.: Assn. Española De Endoscopias, ASGE, Assn. Española De Digestivo. Avocations: bicycling, music, sports. Home: Palmeras 4 P10 B°1 Alcorcon Madrid 28922 Spain Personal E-mail: lrabagot@gmail.com.

RABB, HAMID, nephrologist, educator; b. Dhaka, Bangladesh, June 22, 1962; s. Abdur Rabb and Aishah Farhat; m. Nausheen Rabb, Apr. 10, 1987; children: Adam, Samy, Neil. MD, McGill U., 1985. Resident in medicine UCLA, 1985-88; fellow in nephrology Harvard U., Boston, 1988-91; scientist McGill U., Montreal, Que., Can., 1991-92; chief renal lab. U. South Fla., Tampa, 1992-98; assoc. prof. U. Minn., Mpls., 1998—; dir. Minn. Med. Rsch. Found. kidney lab. Hennepin County Med. Ctr., Mpls., 1998; assoc. prof. Johns Hopkins Univ. Med. Sch., Balt. Reviewer FDA, Rockville, Md., 1994. Contbr. chpts. to books, over 60 articles to profl. jours. Recipient Physician Leadership award AMA, 1990, Clin. Scientist award Nat. Kidney Found., NYC, 1999. Fellow ACP; mem. Am. Soc. Nephrology, Am. Soc. Advancement of Sci., Am. Soc. Transplantation (sci. adv. com. 1999—; Roche Clin. Sci. Investigator award (assoc. prof. level), 2007).

RABB, HARRIET SCHAFFER, academic administrator, lawyer; b. Houston, Sept. 12, 1941; d. Samuel S. and Helen G. Schaffer; m. Bruce Rabb, Jan. 4, 1970; children: Alexander, Katherine. BA in Govt., Barnard Coll., 1963; JD, Columbia U., 1966. Bar: N.Y. 1966, U.S. Supreme Ct. 1969, D.C. 1970. Instr. seminar on constl. litig. Rutgers Law Sch., 1966-67; staff atty. Ctr. for Constl. Rights, 1966-69; spl. counsel to commr. consumer affairs NYC Dept. Consumer Affairs, 1969-70; sr. staff atty. Stern Cmty. Law Firm, Washington, 1970-71; asst. dean urban affairs Law Sch., Columbia U., NYC, 1971-84, prof. law, dir. clin. edn., 1984-99, George M. Jaffen prof. law and social responsibility, 1991-99, vice dean, 1992-93; gen. counsel Dept. Health and Human Svcs., Washington, 1993—2001; v.p., gen. counsel Rockefeller U., NYC, 2001—. Mem. faculty employment and tng. policy Harvard Summer Inst., Cambridge, Mass., 1975-79. Author: (with Agid, Cooper and Rubin) Fair Employment Litigation Manual, 1975, (with Cooper and Rubin) Fair Employment Litigation, 1975. Bd. dirs. Ford Found., 1977-89, NY Civil Liberties Union, 1972-83, Lawyers Com. for Civil Rights Under Law, 1978-86, Legal Def. Fund NAACP, 1978-93, Mex. Am. Legal Def. and Edn. Fund, 1986-90, Legal Aid Soc., 1990-93, The Hastings Ctr., 2004-, mem. exec. com.; mem. exec. com. Human Rights Watch, 1991-93; trustee Trinity Episcopal Sch. Corp., 1991-93; mem. external adv. bd. Columbia U. Ctr. Bioethics, 2002-; mem. adv. bd. Howard Hughes Med. Inst. Bioethics, 2007—10. Mem.: NAS (com. on sci., tech. and law 2007—). Office: Rockefeller University 1230 York Ave New York NY 10065 Office Phone: 212-327-8070. Business E-Mail: hrabb@rockefeller.edu.

RABER, WOLFGANG, physician, researcher, educator; b. Graz, Austria, 1966; s. Fritz and Sighild Raber; m. Elisabeth M. Raber; children: Katharina F., Sebastian P. Student, U. Vienna, 1993. Bd. cert. physician Vienna, 2004. Sr. resident dept. medicine, endocrinology and metabolism U. Vienna, 1994—, prof. medicine. Musician: (violinist) various string quartet CD recordings. Avocations: music, swimming. Office: Univ Vienna Dept Medicine III Waehringer Guertel 18-20 1090 Vienna Austria Office Fax: +43-1-40593234; Home Fax: +43-1-9135216. Personal E-mail: wolfgang.raber@meduniwien.ac.at. Business E-Mail: wolfgang.raber@gmx.at.

RABI, SUGANTHY, medical educator; b. Nagercoil, July 29, 1966; MBBS, Tirunelveli Med. Coll., 1989; MS DipNB, Christian Med. Coll., 2001. Asst. prof. anatomy Christian Med. Coll., 2001—06, assoc. prof., 2006—10, prof., 2010—. Sr. Tng. fellowship, Friends Vellore, 2007. Mem.: Assn. Anatomists, Tamil Nadu, Anat. Soc. India. Avocations: reading, music. Office: CMC Campus Bagayam Vellore Tamil Nadu 632002 India Office Fax: 0091-416-2262788. Business E-Mail: suganthyrabi@cmcvellore.ac.in.

RABIE, MENAN ABD-EL-MAKSOUD, psychiatrist, educator; b. Cairo, Jan. 1, 1974; MBBH, Ain Shams U., MSc, 1997, MD in Neuropsychiatry, 2005. Asst. lectr. Dept. Neuropsychiatry, Inst. Psychiatry, Faculty Medicine, Ain Shams U., 2001—06, lectr., 2006—11, asst. prof., 2011—; assoc. mem. Internat. Fedn. Psychiat. Epidemiology, 2009—11. Cons. psychiatry Fakhry Hosp., Al-Khobar, San Marino, 2007—09; peer reviewer Jour. Schizophrenia Rsch., 2010—11. Contbr. scientific papers to profl. jours. Travel fellowship, 13th Conf., Internat. Fedn. Psychiat. Epidemiology, Taiwan. Mem.: Egyptian Psychiat. Assn., Internat. Fedn. Psychiat. Epidemiology (assoc.). Avocations: reading, travel. Home: 3 Elsafa st Mekka st Elnozha Elgedida Cairo Heliopolis 1234 Egypt Home Fax: 226836379. Personal E-mail: menan74@yahoo.com.

RABIE, WILLEM JACOBUS, physician, educator; b. Worcester, South Africa, Sept. 16, 1957; s. Theunis Johannes and Louisa Helena Rabie; m. Sophia Fredrieka Rabie; children: Willem Jacobus, Anria. MBChB, U. Free State, Bloemfontein, 1984; M.Family Medicine, U. Free State, 1990. Intern Dept. Health, Free State, 1985; med. officer Dept. Family Medicine, Univ. Free State, 1986—90, sr. med. officer, cons., 1991—92, sr. specialist, sr. cons. and sr. lectr., 1993—. Advanced trauma life support instr. Trauma Soc. South Africa, 1996—; lectr. in field; assessor investigation, specialist witness Health Professions Coun. of South Africa; judge various sci. expos for schs. Univ. of the Free State; mem. interdisciplinary panel of reviewers Health SA Gesondheid Interdisciplinary Rsch. Jour. Contbr. articles to profl. jours. Recipient Award for Exceptional Svc., Pelonomi Hosp., 2001. Mem.: Health Professions Coun. of South Africa. Achievements include research into various drugs and drug reactions. Avocations: gardening, running. Home: Sergeant St 16 Bloemfontein 9301 South Africa Office: Univ Free State Dept Family Medicine 9301 Bloemfontein South Africa Office Phone: 082 8006492, 2782 8006492. Office Fax: 051 4039610. Business E-Mail: rabiew@fshealth.gov.za.

RABIJEWSKI, MICHAK S., physician; b. Zakopane, Poland, Aug. 9, 1969; MD, PhD, Med. U. Warsaw, 1994. Physician dept. endocrinology Med. Ctr. Postgrad. Edn., 1994—. Mem.: Internat. Soc. Study Aging Male. Office: Ceglowska 80 Warsaw 01-809 Poland Office Fax: 48 22 8343131. Business E-Mail: mirab@cmkp.edu.pl.

RABIN, JILL MAURA, obstetrician, gynecologist, educator; d. Gilbert and Zita Rabin; life ptnr. Barbara Friedlander; 1 child, Aaron. BA, Hofstra U., Hempstead, NY, 1975; MD, SUNY, Downstate Med. Ctr., Bklyn., 1981. Diplomate NY State Dept. Edn., Office of Profls., 1983, Am. Bd. Ob-gyn., Dallas, 1987. Site dir., med. student tchg. program, ob-gyn. Albert Einstein Coll. Medicine, Bronx, NY, 1993—, assoc. prof. clin. ob-gyn. and women's health, 1997—; assoc. investigator, clin. track Feinstein Inst. Med. Rsch., Manhasset, NY; chief, divsn. ambulatory care, dept. ob-gyn. LI Jewish Med. Ctr., NSLIJHS, New Hyde Pk., NY, 1989—, head urogynecology, 1992—, site dir., ob-gyn., glen cove family practice residency program Hempstead, 2000—, chair, libr. and informatics com.; chair, women's leadership coun. profile enhancement subcom. and mem., women's leadership coun. Hofstra U. Med. Sch. Partnership with North Shore-LIJ Health Sys., 2009—; prof. ob-gyn. Hofstra Northshore LIJ Sch. Medicine, 2011—. Cons. Nat. Assn. Continence, Charleston, SC, 1995—; mem. NY Obstet. Soc., NYC, 2005—, LI Ctr. Bus. and Profl. Women, Manhasset, 2002—; mem., nat. sci. adv. bd., women's health Eli Lilly, Indpls., 2002—03; cons. HDIS, Olivette, Mo., 2009—. Author: (book) Mind Over Bladder, You're Never Too Old to Have Fun, What Girls Have and Guys Don't-Wouldn't You Like to Know; guest editor (book) Manual of Obstetrics, Little Brown; contbr. articles to med. jours., chapters to books. Mem. Children's Hearing, Edn. and Rsch., Inc., Yonkers, NY, 1972—82; student cantor Congregation Adath Israel, Newtown, Conn., 1997—2010; mem. NYS Office of Profl. Med. Conduct, Troy, NY, 1999—2010, bd. mem., 1999—2010. Recipient Excellence in Tchg. award, Assn. Profs. Ob-gyn., 1997, Nat. Faculty award, Coun. Resident Edn. Ob-gyn., 2005; grantee, NY State Dept. Health, 2004—10, UJA Fedn., 2004—10; Galloway fellowship, Meml. Sloan Kettering Cancer Ctr., 1984, Queens Hosp.'s Adolescent Pregnancy Prevention Program grant, Office of Population Affairs, HHS, 1990—2000. Fellow: Am. Coll. Obstetricians and Gynecologists; mem.: Internat. Continence Soc., Assn. Women Surgeons, Hofstra U. Women in Leadership Coun., Am. Urologic Assn., Am. Urogynecologic Soc., Nat. League Am. Pen Women, Inc. Achievements include patents pending for confidence-building incontinence pad; pessary for treating vaginal prolapse; finger protector for surgeons; digital retractor; apparatus for monitoring detrusor pressure exerted by a bladder; research in computerized voiding diary; estrogen receptor variant structure and action. Avocations: writing, swimming, music. Office: LIJ Med Ctr NS-LIJ Health Sys 270-05 76th Ave MH-G069 New Hyde Park NY 11040 Office Fax: 718-962-6739. Business E-Mail: jrabine@nshs.edu.

RABIN, MONROE STEPHEN ZANE, physicist; b. Bklyn., Dec. 19, 1939; s. Louis and Helen (Haspel) R.; m. Joan Greenblatt, Feb. 27, 1965; children: Elaine Judith, Carolyn Sandra. AB, Columbia Coll., 1961; PhD, Rutgers U., 1967. Physicist Lawrence Berkeley (Calif.) Lab., 1967-72; assoc. prof. physics U. Mass., Amherst, 1972-81, prof. physics, 1981—; vis. physicist Stanford Linear Accelerator Ctr., Palo Alto, Calif., 1979-80; vis. scholar Physics Dept. Harvard U., Cambridge, Mass., 1986-87; Soriano scholar in radiol. physics, radiation therapy dept. Mass. Gen. Hosp., Boston, 1986-87. Mem. oversight panel Proton Therapy Med. Facility, Mass. Gen. Hosp., Boston, 1991-96. Contbr. articles to Physical Rev., Physical Rev. Letters, Physics Letters, Nuclear Instruments and Methods. Mem. Am. Phys. Soc., Sigma Xi. Achievements include research in experimental particle physics, medical physics, cancer therapy using accelerated protons, ductal carcinoma in situ and heavy-ion physics. Home: 21 Atwater Cir Amherst MA 01002-3205 Office: U Mass Dept Physics Amherst MA 01003 Office Phone: 413-545-0424. Business E-Mail: rabin@physics.umass.edu.

RABINOFF, MICHAEL DAVID, psychiatrist; b. Milw., Mar. 23, 1950; DO, U. New Eng., 1997; PhD, Calif. Inst. Integral Studies, 1993. Diplomate Am. Bd. Psychiatry and Neurology. CEO Biogenesys, Inc., 1993—; asst. rsch. psychiatrist UCLA Dept. Psychiatry, 2003—; adult psychiatrist, sr. ptnr. Kaiser Permanente, 2003—. Grant, Stanley Med. Rsch. Inst., UCLA Ctr. Aging, Psychiatry fellowship, Eli Lilly, fellowship, NIMH Instl. Tng. Grant. Mem.: Am. Osteo. Assn., Soc. Rsch. Nicotine and Tobacco, Am. Soc. Nutrition. Office: Kaiser Permanente Adult Psychiatry 5755 San Jose CA 95123 Office Phone: 408-972-3288. Office Fax: 408-972-3242. Business E-Mail: mrabinoff@mednet.ucla.edu.

RABINOVICH, C. EGLA, pediatrician, rheumatologist; d. Sergio and Nelly Rabinovich; m. Kenneth Wayne Jordan, May 3, 1986; children: Danielle Jordan, Nicholas Jordan, Kyle Jordan. BS, U. Ill., Champaign-Urbana, 1981; MD, So. Ill. U., 1985; MPH, U. NC, Chapel Hill, 1991. Cert. in pediat. rheumatology Am. Bd. Pediats., 2006. Assoc. pediat. Duke U., Durham, NC, 1991—93, asst. prof., 2002—10, assoc. prof., 2010—; asst. prof. U. Chgo., 1993—2001. Mem.: Am. Coll. Rheumatology (pediatric exec. com. 1992—2006, Amgen/REF Vis. Professorship 2006). Office: Duke U Med Ctr Box 3212 Durham NC 27710 Office Phone: 919-684-6475. Office Fax: 919-684-6616. *

RABINOVICH, REGINA, pediatrician, epidemiologist, director; married; 3 children. MD, Southern Ill. U.; MPH, U. NC, Chapel Hill. Pediat. intern U. NC, chief resident; fellow epidemiology tng. program Nat. Inst. Allergy and Infectious Diseases, 1988—91, various positions including chief clin. and regulatory affairs divsn. microbiology and infectious diseases, 1991—99; dir. malaria vaccine initiative Program for Appropriate Tech. in Health; dir. infectious diseases program Bill & Melinda Gates Found., 2003—. Mem. vaccine adv. com. Nat. Vaccine Program Office, Am. Acad. Pediat., Inst. Medicine, WHO. Recipient Merit award, NIH, 1993, Dir.'s award, 1995. Office: Bill and Melinda Gates Found PO Box 23350 Seattle WA 98102 Office Phone: 206-709-3100.

RABINOWITZ, HOWARD K., physician, educator; b. Pitts., Sept. 25, 1946; s. Mac and Anne (Morgan) R.; m. Carol A. Gelles, Feb. 4, 1968; children: Elyse, Daniel J. Student, Rutgers U., 1964-67; MD, U. Pitts., 1971. Diplomate Am. Bd. Family Practice, Am. Bd. Pediatrics. From instr. to assoc. prof. Dept. Family Medicine Jefferson Med. Coll., Phila., 1976-90, vice chmn., 1990-95, prof., 1990—; dir. Physician Shortage Area Program (PSAP), Phila. Bd. dirs. Am. Bd. Family Practice, Lexington, Ky., pres., 1992-93. Contbr. articles to profl. jours; author: Caring for the Country: Family Doctors in Small Rural Towns, 2004. With USPHS, 1972-74. RWJ Health Policy fellow, 1993-94. Fellow Phila. Coll. Physicians; mem. AMA, Soc. Tchrs. Family Medicine, Am. Acad. Family Physicians, Inst. Medicine. Office: Jefferson Med Coll Dept Family Medicine Ste 401 1015 Walnut St Philadelphia PA 19107-5005 Office Phone: 215-955-7416. Office Fax: 215-955-0640. E-mail: Howard.Rabinowitz@jefferson.edu.

RABINOWITZ, JACK GRANT, radiologist, educator; b. Monticello, NY, July 9, 1927; s. Abraham and Bessie (Sussman) R.; m. Rica Gedalia Arnon, Oct. 19, 1972; children— Antoine, Anne, Pierre, Yaron, Tal. BA, UCLA, 1949; MD, U. Berne, Switzerland, 1955. Diplomate: Am. Bd. Radiology. Intern Kings County Hosp., Bklyn., 1955-56, resident, 1956-59; instr. radiology Downstate Med. Center, Bklyn., 1960-61, assoc. prof. radiology, 1967-70, prof. radiology, 1970-73; asst. radiologist Mt. Sinai Sch. Medicine, NYC, 1962-65, asst. prof. radiology, 1965-66, asso. prof. radiology, 1966-67, prof., chmn. dept. radiology, 1978-95, prof., 1995—. Asso. attending radiologist Mt. Sinai Hosp., N.Y.C., 1965-67, dir. radiology, 1978—; radiologist-in-chief Bklyn.-Cumberland Med. Center, Bklyn., 1967-70; dir. diagnostic radiology Kings County Hosp. Center, Bklyn., 1970-73; prof., chmn. dept. diagnostic radiology U. Tenn., Memphis, 1973-78; cons. in radiology VA Hosp., Bronx, N.Y. Author: Pediatric Radiology, 1978, Radiology for the Primary and Emergency Care of Physicians, 1981. Fellow Am. Coll. Radiology; mem. Radiol. Soc. N. Am., Am. Roentgen Ray Soc., Assn. Univ. Radiologists, AMA, Soc. Chmn. Acad. Radiology Depts. Office: Mt Sinai Hosp 1 Gustave L Levy Pl New York NY 10029-6500 Home Phone: 201-501-8190. Business E-Mail: jack-rabinowitz@msnyu.health.org.

RABINOWITZ, YARON GIL, psychologist, educator, military officer; b. Memphis, Dec. 21, 1973; s. Jack Grant and Rica Rabinowitz; m. Bethany Lee Washington, June 7, 2008; 1 child, Mia Jaden. AB in Govt., Harvard U., Cambridge, Mass., 1996; MA in History, Stanford U., Calif., 2000; PhD in Clin. Psychology, Pacific Grad. Sch. Psychology, Palo Alto, Calif., 2005. Cert. psychologist Ala. History tchr. Blair Acad., Blairstown, NJ, 1996—98; clin. rschr. Stanford U. Sch. Medicine, 2000—04; commd. 2d lt. US Army, 2004, advanced through grades to capt., 2004; clin. psychology resident Walter Reed Army Med. Ctr., Washington, 2004—05; dep. command psychologist JFK Spl. Warfare Ctr. and Sch., Fort Bragg, NC, 2005—06; command psychologist Spl. Forces Assessment and Selection Program, JFK Spl. Warfare Ctr. and Sch., Fort Bragg, NC, 2006—; asst. prof. psychology Tex. A&M U., Corpus Christi. Contbr. articles to profl. publs. Decorated Nat. Svc. ribbon, Army Parachutist badge, Army Commendation medal, Global War on Terrorism ribbon; recipient Student Award for Excellence in Alzheimer's Rsch., California-Nevada Alzheimer's Assn., 2004, STAR award for achievement, Palo Alto VA Health Care Sys., 2004; Health Profession scholar, US Army Med. Dept., 2002—04, Jared and Mae Tincklenberg fellow, Pacific Grad. Sch. Psychology, 2002—03, Rabbi Stephen S. Pearce fellow, 2003—04. Mem.: APA (chmn. grad. students 2004—05, chmn. advocacy coord. team 2003—04), Divsn. Mil. Psychology. Avocations: triathlons, wrestling, music, travel, accordion. Office: Dept of Psychology Tex 16M Univ 6300 Ocean Dr Corpus Christi TX 78412 Office Phone: 361-825-2719, 361-825-2350. Personal E-mail: rubes0509@gmail.com.

RABKIN, MITCHELL THORNTON, physician, educator, hospital administrator; b. Boston, Nov. 27, 1930; s. Morris Aaron and Esther (Quint) Rabkin; m. Adrienne M. Najarian, June 24, 1956; children: Julia Margaret, David Gregory. AB magna cum laude, Harvard U., 1951, MD cum laude, 1955; DSc (hon.), Brandeis U., 1983; DPharm (hon.), Mass. Coll. Pharmacy, 1983; DSc (hon.), Curry Coll., 1989, Northeastern U., 1994; DHumLet (hon.), Salem State Coll., Mass., 1995. Cert. Am. Bd. Internal Medicine. Intern Mass. Gen. Hosp., Boston, 1955—56, resident in internal medicine, 1956—57, 1959—60, chief resident, 1962, mem. staff, 1963—72, bd. consultation, 1972—80, hon. physician, 1981—; clin. fellow NIH, Bethesda, Md., 1957—59; gen. dir. Beth Israel Hosp., Boston, 1966—80, pres., 1980—96; CEO CareGroup, Boston, 1996—98; now disting. inst. scholar Carl J. Shapiro Inst. for Edn. and Rsch. Harvard Med. Sch. and Beth Israel Deaconess Med. Ctr., Boston, 1996—; dir. Washington Adv. Group LECG, 1999—. Asst. prof. medicine Harvard U., 1969—70, assoc. prof., 1971—83, prof., 1983—, pres. med. alumni coun., 2002—03; chmn. Albert Schweitzer Fellowship, 2005—, chair. bd. dirs., 2007—08. With USPHS, 1957—59. Fellow: AAAS, ACP, Am. Acad. Arts and Scis.; mem.: Inst. Medicine of NAS, Assn. Am. Med. Colls. (chmn. 1996—97), Soc. Med. Adminstrs., Mass. Med. Soc., Tavern Club Boston, Harvard Club of Boston. Jewish. Office: Beth Israel Deaconess Med Ctr/Harvard U Shapiro Inst Edn and Rsch 330 Brookline Ave Boston MA 02215-5400 Office Phone: 617-667-9400. Personal E-mail: mtrabkin@mindspring.com. Business E-Mail: mrabkin@theadvisorygroup.com.

RABUN, JOHN BREWTON, JR., criminal justice agency administrator; b. Augusta, Ga., Nov. 16, 1946; s. John Brewton and Alsie Imor (Bateman) R.; m. Anna Betsy Park, Dec. 27, 1967; children: Kerry Kristin, John Candler. BA, Mercer U., 1967; postgrad., So. Bapt. Theol. Sem., 1967—70; MSW, U. Louisville, 1971. Cert. social worker Ky., DC. Exec. dir. Ky. Civil Liberties Union, Louisville, 1971—72; dir. Cmty. Residential Treatment Svcs., Louisville, 1973—78; program mgr. Field Svcs., Louisville, 1978—80, Exploited and Missing Child Unit, Louisville, 1980—84; exec. v.p., COO Nat. Ctr. for Missing and Exploited Children, Washington, 1984—2006, COO, 1984—, exec. v.p., 2006—. Mem. Alderman's Task Force on Social Svcs., Louisville, 1982, Mayor's City Youth Commn., Louisville, 1983-84; trainer and/or cons. to numerous agys. in U.S., U.K., Can., Mex., Belgium, Germany, Austria, Netherlands. Author: (book) Healthcare Guideslines Infant Abduction, 2009; contbr. articles to profl. jours., chapters to books. Recipient Key to City of Louisville, 1983, Disting. Alumnus award U. Louisville, 1985, 2003, Russell L. Colling Lit. award Internat. Assn. for Healthcare Security and Safety, 1991; named hon. chief of police City of Louisville, 1982; Alumni fellow U. Louisville, 1999. Mem. ACLU, NASW, Nat. Sheriff's Assn., Internat. Juvenile Officers Assn., Acad. Cert. Social Workers, Internat. Assn. Healthcare Safety and Security, Am. Soc. Indsl. Security, Internat. Assn. Chiefs of Police. Baptist (deacon). Avocations: photography, hunting, fishing, internet. Office: Nat Ctr for Missing and Exploited Children 699 Prince St Alexandria VA 22314-3117 Office Phone: 571-259-2112. Business E-Mail: jrabun@ncmec.org.

RACE, GEORGE JUSTICE, pathology educator; b. Everman, Tex., Mar. 2, 1926; s. Claude Ernest and Lila Eunice (Bunch) R.; m. Annette Isabelle Rinker, Dec. 21, 1946; children: George William Daryl, Jonathan Clark, Mark Christopher, Jennifer Anne (dec.), Elizabeth Margaret Rinker. MD, U. Tex., Southwestern Med. Sch., 1947; MS in Pub. Health, U. N.C., 1953; PhD in Ultrastructural Anatomy and Microbiology, Baylor U., 1969. Intern Duke Hosp., 1947-48, asst. resident pathology, 1951-53; intern Boston City Hosp., 1948-49; asst. pathologist Peter Bent Brigham Hosp., Boston, 1953-54; pathologist St. Anthony's Hosp., St. Petersburg, Fla., 1954-55; staff pathologist Children's Med. Center, Dallas, 1955-59; dir. labs. Baylor U. Med. Center, Dallas, 1959-86, chief dept. pathology, 1959-86, vice chmn. exec. com. med. bd., 1970-72; cons. pathologist VA Hosp., Dallas, 1955-71; adj. prof. anthropology and biology So. Meth. U., Dallas, 1969; instr. pathology Duke, 1951-53, Harvard Med. Sch., 1953-54; asst. prof. pathology U. Tex. Southwestern Med. Sch., 1955-58, clin. assoc. prof., 1958-64, clin. prof., 1964-72, prof., 1973-94, prof. emeritus, 1994—, dir. Cancer Center, 1973-76, assoc. dean for continuing edn., 1973-94, emeritus assoc. dean, 1994—. Pathologist-in-chief Baylor U. Med. Ctr., 1959-86, prof. biomed. studies Baylor Grad. sch., 1989-94; chmn. Baylor Rsch. Found., 1986-89; prof. microbiology Baylor Coll. Dentistry, 1962-68, prof. pathology, 1964-68, prof., chmn. dept. pathology 1969-73, dean A. Webb Roberts Continuing Edn., 1973-94; spl. advisor on human and animal diseases to gov. State of Tex., 1979-83. Editor: Laboratory Medicine (4 vols.), 1973, 10th edit., 1983; Contbr. articles to profl. jours., chpts. to textbooks. Pres., Tex. div. Am. Cancer Soc., 1970; chmn. Gov.'s Task Force on Higher Edn., 1981. Served with AUS, 1944-46; flight surgeon USAF, 1948-51, Korea. Decorated Air medal. Fellow AAAS, Coll. Am. Pathologists, Am. Soc. Clin. Pathologists; mem. AMA (chmn. multiple discipline research forum 1969), Am. Assn. Pathologists, Internat. Acad. Pathology, Am. Assn. Med. Colls., Explorers Club (dir., v.p. 1993-2000), Sigma Xi, Alpha Omega Alpha. Office Phone: 214-528-7501. Office Fax: 214-526-8607. Personal E-mail: georgejrace@yahoo.com.

RACE, TIM, editor; BA, Miami U., 1978; MA, Bowling Green State U., 1980; MS in journalism, Am. U., 1983. Editor CMP Publications; exec. editor Comm. Week; editor, Bus. World sect. New York Times Co., 1989—91, info. tech. & media editor, 1991—97, founding editor, Circuits sect., 1997—98, editor, Monday Bus. sect., 1998—2004, tech. & health care editor, 2004—. Mem.: Assn. Healthcare Journalists. Office: New York Times 620 8th Ave New York NY 10018 Office Phone: 212-556-1526. Office Fax: 212-556-1448. Business E-Mail: timrace@nytimes.com. *

RACHANOW, GERALD MARVIN, lawyer, pharmacist; b. Balt., Aug. 7, 1942; s. Louis and Lillyan (Binstock) R.; m. Sally Davis, July 26, 1964; children: Mindy, Shelly, Gary. BS in Pharmacy, U. Md., 1965; JD, U. Balt., 1972. Bar: Md. 1973, U.S. Dist. Ct. Md. 1977, U.S. Supreme Ct. 1977. Consumer safety officer FDA, Rockville, Md., 1973-96, dep. dir. divsn. OTC drug evaluation, 1978-96, regulatory counsel divsn. OTC drug products, 1996—2005, regulatory counsel office nonprescription products, 2005—08; ptnr. Rachanow & Wolfson, Owings Mills, Eldersburg, Md., 1975—; cons. OTC Drug Product Law, 2009—. Contbr. fed. drug law exam. Nat. Assn. Bds. Pharmacy, 1985. Contbr. articles to profl. jours. Fellow Am. Soc. Pharmacy Law; mem. ABA, Soc. FDA Pharmacists, Heuisler Honor Soc. Avocations: chess, stamp and coin collecting, sports. Home and Office: 6700 Sweet Clover Ct Eldersburg MD 21784-6385 Home Phone: 410-549-7713; Office Phone: 410-549-7714.

RACHEL, JOHN DAVID, surgeon; b. Elmira, NY, Jan. 13, 1969; BS, Mich. State U., 1991; MD, Wayne State U., 1995. V.p. Met. MD, 2001—. Bd. dirs. Am. Bd. Cosmetic Surgery, 2010. Recipient John Orlando Roe award, Am. Acad. Facial Plastic and Reconstructive Surgery. Fellow: ACS. Office: 2350 Ravine Way Ste 400 Glenview IL 60025 Office Fax: 847-832-9430. E-mail: jdrachel@gmail.com.

RACHELEFSKY, GARY STUART, medical educator; b. NYC, 1942; BS, Columbia Coll., 1963. Intern Bellevue Hosp. Ctr., NYC, 1967-68; resident in pediatrics Johns Hopkins Hosp., 1968-70, Ctr. Disease Control, 1970-72; fellow UCLA Med. Ctr., 1972-74; prof. allergy and immunology, dir. exec. care UCLA, Ctr. Asthma, Allergy and Immunology. Fellow Am. Acad. Allergy, Asthma and Immunology (bd. dirs., past pres.). Mailing: 14933 Alva Dr Pacific Palisades CA 90272 Personal E-mail: rachruss@ix.netcom.com. Business E-Mail: grachelefsky@mednet.ucla.edu.

RACKOW, ERIC C., health care company executive; Grad., Franklin and Marshall Coll.; MD, SUNY, Downstate Med. Ctr., Brooklyn, 1971. Bd. cert. internal medicine, cardiovasc. diseases, critical care medicine, internal medicine, 1975, cardiology, 1977, critical care, 1987. Residency Kings County Hosp. Ctr., 1970—72, chief residency, 1972—73, clin. fellow, 1973—75; dir. clin. trials NYU Hosp. Ctr.; prof. heath care mgmt. NYU Med. Ctr., Sch. Medicine; sr. v.p., chief med. officer NYU Hosp. Ctr., NYC, 2000—04, pres., 2004—07; pres., CEO SeniorBridge, NYC, 2007—. Adj. prof. medicine NY Med. Coll.; chmn. emeritus St. Vincent's Hosp. & Med. Ctr. of NY, Dept. Medicine; hon. role, Physician-in-Chief Inst. Critical Care Medicine; past pres. Soc. Critical Care Medicine; past chair Am. Bd. Internal Medicine, Critical Care Medicine Subspecialty Bd. Contbr. articles to profl. jours. Office: 845 Third Ave New York NY 10022 Office Phone: 212-263-2606, 212-994-6100. Business E-Mail: eric.rackow@nyumc.org.

RADAFY, EMILIEN, surgeon, consultant; b. Madagascar, South Africa, July 9, 1958; MD, Madagascar U., 1985. Cert. ENT specialist Nantes U., France, 1990. Sr. cons. Nantes U. Hosp., France, 1991—; head, dept. and ref. ctr. cochlear implantation Centre Hosp. Mangot-Vulcin, Martinique, France, 2011—. Assoc. prof. UFR Santé, Faculté de Médecine, École d'Orthophonie, Nantes, 1995—2010. Mem.: AFOP, Societe Internationale d'Otologie et Otoneurochirurgie de Langue Francaise, Societe Francaise d'ORL, Société Française d'ORL Pédiatrique, French Nat. ENT Soc. Avocations: motorcycling, diving. Office: 1 Pl Ricordeau Nantes Pays de Loire 44000 France Business E-Mail: emiradafy@gmail.com.

RADCLIFFE, PETER J., medical researcher, educator; Attended, Gonville and Caius Coll., Cambridge, Eng.; MD, 1978. Med. tng. Cambridge and St. Bartholomew's Hosp., London; tng. in renal medicine Oxford U.; sr. fellow Wellcome Trust; head oxygen sensing group Weatherall Inst. Molecular Medicine, Henry Wellcome Bldg. Genomic Medicine and Henry Wellcome Bldg. Molecular Physiology at Oxford U.; univ. lectr. Oxford U., 1992—96, titular prof., 1996—2003, Nuffield prof. medicine, 2003—, head dept. medicine, 2004—. Contbr. articles to profl. jours. Recipient Milne-Muerke Found. award, 1991, Graham Bull prize, 1998, Internat. Soc. Blood Purification award, 2002, Louis-Jeantet prize for Medicine, 2009, Gairdner Internat. award, Gairdner Found., Can., 2010. Fellow: EMBO, Acad. Med. Sciences, Royal Soc.; mem.: American Acad. Arts & Sciences (hon.). Office: Nuffield Dept Clin Medicine University Oxford Henry Wellcome Bldg Old Road Campus Headington Oxford OX3 7BN England Business E-Mail: pjr@well.ox.ac.uk. *

RADEL, EVA, pediatrician, hematologist; b. Vienna, Apr. 10, 1934; came to U.S., 1939; d. Ernest O. and Marian (Feiks) Grossman; m. Stanley Robert Radel, May 31, 1954; children: Carol, Laura. AB, N.Y. U., 1954, MD, 1958. Pediatric intern, resident Bronx Mcpl. Hosp. Ctr., 1958-61; pediatric hematology rsch. fellow Albert Einstein Coll. Medicine, Bronx, 1961-63; pediatrician, head pediatric hematology Morrisania city Hosp., Bronx, 1963-76; assoc. dir. pediatrics North Cen. Bronx Hosp., 1978-82; attending physician pediatric hemetology out patients Montefiore Med. Ctr., Bronx, 1965-79, svc. head pediatric hematology-oncology, 1979—2004; head pediatric hematology North Cen. Bronx Hosp., 1976-97. Responsible investigator Children's Cancer Study Group, 1980-2001; dir. pediatric hematology-oncology Albert Einstein Coll. Medicine, Bronx, 1980-2004; prin. investigator Children's Oncology Group, 2001-05 Fellow Am. Acad Pediatrics; mem. Am. Soc. Hematology, Am. Soc. Pediatric Hematology-Oncology, Soc. for the Study of Blood. Office: Childrens Hosp at Montefiore Sect Pediat Hematology-Oncology 3415 Bainbridge Ave Bronx NY 10467-2401 Office Phone: 718-741-2342. Business E-Mail: eradel@montefiore.org.

RADEMACHER, DANA ELLIS, urologist; b. Denver, Sept. 25, 1964; s. James Dennis and Barbara Jane Rademacher; m. Jonella Gross, Sept. 5, 1987; children: Ryan John, Erin Janelle, Connor Jacob. MD, U. Colo., Denver, 1992. Diplomate Wis., Minn., 1998, cert. bd. cert. urologist Am. Bd. Urology, 2003. Intern in gen. surgery U. Calif. Davis Med. Ctr., Sacramento, 1992—94, resident in urology, 1994—98; urologist FranciscanSkemp Mayo Healthcare, LaCrosse, Wis., 1998—. Chmn. fin. com. FranciscanSkemp Mayo Healthcare, 2001—07. Recipient Am. Outstanding Dr. award, 2006; named Americas Outstanding Drs., 2006—08, Americas Outstanding Urologist, 2008, Am. Top Dr., 2006—, Am. Top Urologist, 2009—, Am. Outstanding Surgeons, 2010. Mem.: N.Ctrl. Cancer Treatment Grp. (assoc.), N.Ctrl. Urol. Assn. (assoc.), Am. Urol. Assn. (assoc.). Office: FranciscanSkemp Mayo Healthcare 800 West Ave S La Crosse WI 54601

RADER, DANIEL J., cardiologist, educator; BA, Lehigh U., 1981; MD, Pa. Med. Coll., 1984. Intern Yale-New Haven Hosp., resident; fellow NIH; prof. dept. medicine, pharmacology & pathology U. Pa. Sch. Medicine; dir. Preventive Cardiovascular Medicine & Lipid Clinic Penn Heart & Vascular Ctr. Office: University of Pennsylvania 654 Biomedical Rsch Bldg 421 Curie Blvd Philadelphia PA 19104-6160 Office Phone: 215-573-4176. Office Fax: 215-573-8606. E-mail: rader@mail.med.upenn.edu.

RADFORD, DOROTHY JANE, cardiologist; b. Nambour, Queensland, Australia, Jan. 10, 1943; d. John Wesley Radford and Joyce Cameron Burnett. MBBS, U. Queensland, Brisbane, 1966, MD, 1990. Resident med. officer Princess Alexandra Hosp., Brisbane, 1967—69, med. registrar, 1967—69, Chermside Chest Hosp., Brisbane, 1970; sr. house officer Nat. Heart Hosp., London, 1971—72; registrar cardiology & gen. medicine Royal Infirmary Edinburgh, 1972—74; cardiology fellow Hosp. Sick Children, Toronto, Ontario, Canada, 1974—76, staff cardiologist, 1976—77; paediat. cardiologist, Prince Charles Hosp. TPCH, Brisbane, 1977—2007, dir., Adult Congenital Heart Unit, 2008—. Contbr. scientific papers. Fellow: Cardiac Soc. Australia & New Zealand, RACP Australia & New Zealand, RCP (Edinburgh); mem.: Order Australia (AM 1998). Office: Prince Charles Hosp Rode Rd 4032 Chermside QLD Australia Office Fax: 617 3139 4715.

RADHAKRISHNAN, NERUKAV, physician; s. Krishnan and Parvathy Warrier; m. Shoba Madhavan, Jan. 16, 1979; children: Kavita Krishnan, Madhu Krishnan. MBBS, Calicut Med. Coll., Kerala, India, 1973. Cert. independent practitioner in gastro-intestinal physiological measuremen Assn. of Gastro-intestinal Physiology, UK, 2004, specialist in gastroenterology and gen. med. Postgraduate Med. Edn. Bd., UK, 2007, FRCP London. Pre-registration house officer Calicut Med. Coll., 1972—73, sr. house officer, medicine, 1973—75; resident gen. duty med. officer Ministry of Health, Tabriz, Iran, 1975—76, med. specialist, gen. medicine and gastroenterology Dammam, Saudi Arabia, 1984—87; gen. duty med. officer Govt. Health Svcs., Kerala, 1976—79; sr. med. officer, gen. medicine and gastroenterology Nat. Health Svc., Greater Manchester, England, 1979—82; registrar, gastroenterology Dist. Gen. Hosp., Bury, England, 1983—84; staff physician, gen. medicine and gastroenterology Birch Hill Hosp., Rochdale, England, 1990—94; assoc. specialist, internal medicine and gastroenterology The Pennine Acute Hosp. NHS Trust, Rochdale, England, 1994—. Contbr. scientific papers to profl. jours. Mem.: British Soc. Gastroenterology. Achievements include research in antiseptic spary with antibiotic in percutaneous endoscopic gastrostomy patients; described a novel technique, Quill technique for managing buried bumper syndrome in patients with percutaneous endoscopic gastrostomy. Home: 7 Woodcock Close Rochdale OL11 5QA England Office: Pennine Acute Hosp NHS Trust Whitchall St Rochdale OL12 0NB England Office Fax: 44 0 1706 517992. Personal E-mail: nerukavr@gmail.com. Business E-Mail: nerukav.radhakrishnan@pat.nhs.uk.

RADIGAN, FRANK XAVIER, retired pharmaceutical executive; b. Paterson, NJ, Apr. 13, 1933; s. John Joseph and Susan Clair (Brett) R.; m. Julia Lou Smith, Aug. 27, 1960 (div. Nov. 1988); children: Francis Gregory, Patricia Louise, Brett Frasier; m. Carol E. Berkley, June 26, 1992; children: Dana, Traci. AB in Sociology, Seton Hall U., 1955; MBA Mktg., U. Hartford, 1968. Asst. mgr. Beneficial Fin. Co., Newark, 1955-57; hosp. rep. Becton-Dickinson Co., Rutherford, 1957—58; dist. mgr. Merck Human Health Divsn., West Point, Pa., 1958-98; ret., 1998; sales rep. Merck Human Health Divsn., 1958—68, dist. mgr., 1968—98; hon. pres. Md. Pharmacist Assn., 1999—2000; ret., 1998; hon. pres. Bow Air CC. Horse breeder, 1976—86. Active Greater Balt. SCORE; hon. pres. Md. Pharmacist Assn., 1977—2000, Balt. Met. Pharmacists Assn., 1984; elected to Passaic County Dem. Com., 1955—56; chmn. St. John the Baptist Social Justice Com., New Freedom, Pa., 1981—85. Capt. USAR. Mem.: Am. Pharm. Assn., Saton Hall Prep Alumni Assn., U. Hartford Alumni Assn., Saton Hall U. Alumni Assn., Pleasant Valley Golf Club, Elks. Roman Catholic. Home: 12236 Roundwood Rd Apt 108 Lutherville MD 21093

RADULESCU, ELENA, hematologist, immunocytochemist, researcher; b. Rosiorii-de-Vede, Teleorman, Romania, May 14, 1927; d. Gheorghe A. and Voica Gh. (Popescu) Radulescu; m. Alexandru A. Matusan, Sept. 2, 1952 (div. Mar. 1969); 1 child, Mircea Radu Matusan. Degree in Medicine, Faculty Gen. Medicine, Cluj, Romania, 1953; MD, PhD in Med. Scis., U. Medicine and Pharmacy, Cluj-Napoca, Romania, 1977; postgrad., Royal Post Grad. Med. Sch., London, 1983, 87, 90, Royal Marsden Hosp., York U., 2000. Cert. Univ. Prof. Romanian Med. Scis. Acad., 1999. Lab. physician Oradea Hosp., Romania, 1953-57; lab. specialist CFR Hosp., 1957-66; rschr. dept. hematology Oncol. Inst., Ion Chiricuta, Cluj, 1966-91; sr. rschr. Cluj-N. br.Biotehnos S.A., Bucharest, 1991-93, 2d Pediatric Clinic, Cluj, 1993—2002; sr. specialist clin. lab. Pvt. Polyclinic, 2002—05; sr. specialist clin. lab., Synevo Lab. Cluj-Napoca Medicover, 2006—10. Rschr. in hematology Oncological Inst., Cluj, 1966-78, sr. rschr., 1978-91, 91-96; chmn. Internat. Congress of Histochemistry and Cytochemistry, Helsinki, 1984, Washington, 1988, Paris, 1991, others; pres. Oncological Union, Cluj-Napoca, 1980-82; hon. mem. prof.'s coun. U. Medicine and Pharmacy, Cluj-Napoca, mem. 14th congress European Hematology Soc. Co-author: Cancer Malignant Haemopathies, 1982; contbr. articles to profl. jours. Grantee York U.,2000, Internat. Congress of Histochemistry and Cytochemistry, 2000, Internat. Soc. for Analytical Molecular Morphology, 2000, others, 1983, 87, 90, Order of Internat. fellowship, 2010-; recipient Excellence award IBC, Cambridge, 2004, Internat. Peace prize Am. Biog. Inst., 2006-07, World Lifetime Achievement award, Gold medal, ABI, 2007; named Internat. Scientist of Yr., 2005, World Wide Honors List, 2005, Great Women of 21st Cen. ABI, 2007, Woman of Yr., 2009, 10, Legion of Honor, 2010, ABI, 2011, IBC, Am. Medal of Honor, 2009, Presdl. Seal of Honor, 2009, Woman of Yr., 2011, Cambridge Cert. Outstanding Med. Achievement, IBC, 2011; name one of Top 100 Health Profl. IBC, 2009, Gold Medal, ABI, 2007-11, Woman of Yr. award, 2011, Outstanding Med. Achievement award, Cambridge Cert., IBC, 2011, Role of Honor award, IBC, 2011, award, World Who Women, Internat. Hippocrates award, IBC, 2011, Tesga award, 2011, Recognition award, World Congress Arts, Sci. & Commn., 2011, Dir. Gen. Leadership award, 2011. Mem. Internat. Fedn. Rschrs. for Sci. and Tech. (Gt. Britain), World Soc. Cellular and Molecular Biology N.Y., Internat. Soc. Hematology (European and African divsn.), European Hematology Assn. Mem. Romanian Social Democrat Party. Orthodox. Avocations: art, music, travel. Home: Henry Coanda Unirii No 1 et III AP 16 400417 Cluj-Napoca 400417 Romania E-mail: elena.radulescu@personal.ro.

RADVAN, MARTIN, physician; b. Trebic, Czech Republic, Mar. 23, 1981; MD, Masaryk U. Brno, 2005. Physician Hosp. Trebic, 2005—. Office: Purkynovo Sq Trebic Vysocina 67401 Czech Republic Business E-Mail: martinrad@post.cz.

RAFEYAN, ROUEEN, psychiatrist, educator; b. Tehran, Iran, Oct. 1, 1961; came to U.S., 1979; s. Majid Rafeyan and Nezhat Babanoury; m. Helena Linda Hernandez, Feb. 15, 1991; 1 child, Ryan Michael. BA, Knox Coll., 1981; MD, U. Istanbul, Turkey, 1989. Cert. Am. Bd. Psychiatry & Neurology, 2001; Am. Bd. Psychiatry and Neurology. Resident U. Ill. Chgo., 1996; dir. outpatient clin. svcs., dir. med. student edn. Michael Reese Hosp., Chgo., 1996-99; med. dir. Rush Presbyn., Chgo., 1997—; asst. clin. prof. psychiatry U. Ill., Chgo., 1996—; asst. prof psychiatry Rush U., 2005—. Cons. Threshold Cmty. Mental Health Ctr., Chgo., 1996—. Mem. AMA, Am. Psychiatric Assn., Ill. Psychiatric Soc., Chgo. Med. Soc. Avocations: tennis, music, world history. Office Phone: 773-536-2700. Personal E-mail: roueen@msn.com.

RAFFAELE, POPOLO, psychiatrist; b. Rome, June 23, 1966; Degree in Medicine & Surgery, U. Cattolica del Sacro Cuore Rome, 1992, degree in Psychiatry& Psychotherapy, 1997. Psychiatrist, psychotherapist Terzo Centro Psicoterapia Cognitiva, Rome, 2000—11; psychiatrist SPDC, 1998—2001; psychiatrist ASL RM/F Mental Health Svc., 2001—06, psychiatrist ASL RM/E, 2007—. Trainer Assn. Psicologia Cognitiva, 2005—10, Scuola Psicoterapia Cognitiva, 2005—10, Soc. Italiana Terapia Comportamentale e Cognitiva, 2008—11, Studi Cognitivi, 2010—11; prof. Techniques Psychiat. Rehab.in II facoltà Sapienza U. Roma (formerly La Sapienza), 2010—11. Office: Via Gasparri 21 Rome 00168 Italy Office Fax: 00390668354252. Business E-Mail: popolo.r@libero.it.

RAFFERTY, JANICE F., colon and rectal surgeon, educator; BA, Miami U., Ohio, 1984; MD, Ohio State U., Columbus, 1988. Diplomate Am. Bd. Surgery, 1996, Am. Bd. Surgery, 2004, Am. Bd. Colon and Rectal Surgery, 1997, Am. Bd. Colon and Rectal Surgery, 2006. Resident in gen. surgery Univ. Cin. Hosp., Ohio, 1988—94, chief resident in surgery, 1994—95; rsch. fellow Univ. Cin., 1990—92; ECMO fellow Children's Hosp. Med. Ctr., 1991—92; fellow in colon and rectal surgery Barnes Jewish Hosp., St. Louis, 1995—96; hosp. affiliations include Univ. Hosp., Christ Hosp.; assoc. prof. surgery Univ. Cin., chief divsn. colon and rectal surgery. Reviewer Annals of Surgery, Diseases of Colon and Rectum, Internat. Jour. Urogynecology, Jour. Surgical Oncology, World Jour. of Surgery. Mem. Crohn's & Colitis Found. of America. Fellow: Am. Soc. of Colon and Rectal Surgeons, ACS; mem.: AMA, Ohio Valley Soc. Colon and Rectal Surgeons, Cin. Surgical Soc., Cin. Acad. Medicine, Assn. Women Surgeons. Office: University of Cincinnati Cancer Institute 234 Goodman St Cincinnati OH 45219 Office Phone: 513-929-0104. Business E-Mail: janice.rafferty@uc.edu.

RAFFIN, THOMAS ALFRED, physician, educator, academic venture capitalist; b. San Francisco, Jan. 25, 1947; s. Bennett L. and Caroline M. Raffin; m. Michele Raffin, June 19, 1987; children: Ross Daniel, Jason Bennett, Nicholas Ethan; m. Margaret Raffin, June 23, 1969; 1 child, Elizabeth S. AB in Biol. Sci., Stanford Med. Sch., 1968, MD, 1973. Cert. Am. Bd. Internal Medicine, diplomate Am. Bd. Pulmonary Medicine, Am. Bd. Critical Care Medicine. Med. resident Peter Bent Brigham Hosp., 1973-75; fellow in respiratory medicine sch. medicine Stanford U., Stanford, Calif., 1975-78, med. fiberoptic bronchoscopy service dir. med. ctr., 1978—, acting asst. prof. sch. medicine, 1978-80, assoc. dir. med. ctr. intensive care units, med. dir. dept. respiratory therapy hosp., 1978—, assoc. prof. medicine sch. medicine, 1986-95, chief divsn. pulmonary and critical care, 1990—2004, prof. medicine sch. of medicine, 1995—, Colleen and Robert Haas emeritus prof. medicine/biomed. ethics, 1999—; dir. emeritus Stanford U. Ctr. for Biomed. Ethics, 1989—; co-founder Rigel Pharms., Inc. Co-founder, gen. ptnr. Telegraph Hill Ptnrs., San Francisco, 2002—; bd. dirs. New Link Genetics, AngioScore, Pneum Rx, LDR Holding, Freedom Innovations Apprise Bio. Author: Intensive Care: Facing the Critical Choices, 1988; contbr. articles to profl. jours.; watercolor show, Thomas Reynolds Gallery, San Fransisco, 2009. V.p. lung cancer com. No. Calif. Oncology Group, 1983—85; com. mem. NIH Workshop, 1984; pres. Raffin Family Found., San Francisco. Recipient award, Henry J. Kaiser Found., 1981, 1984, 1988, 1997, Arthur L. Bloomfield award, 1981. Fellow: ACP (rep. coun. subspecialty socs. 1986), Am. Coll. Chest Physicians (program com. mem. 1985—86); mem.: AAAS, Calif. Thoracic Soc., Soc. Critical Care Medicine, Calif. Med. Assn. (chmn. sect. chest diseases 1984—85), Santa Clara County Med. Soc., Santa Clara County Lung Assn., Am. Thoracic Soc., Am. Fedn. Clin. Rsch. Independent. Jewish. Avocations: painting, gardening, raising miniature donkeys, Nigerian dwarf goats. Office: Telegraph Hill Ptnrs 360 Post Ste 601 San Francisco CA 94108 also: Ctr Biomed Ethics Stanford U 701 Welch Rd Ste A1105 Palo Alto CA 94304-1709 Office Phone: 415-765-6980. Business E-Mail: tar@stanford.edu.

RAFI, MOSTAFA, ophthalmologist; b. Oujda, Morocco, May 20, 1947; s. Miloud Rafi and Fatna (Hemri) R.; m. Amina Samir Rafi, Aug. 5, 1973; children: Fedoua, Nada. PhD in Medicine, U. Rabat, 1974; diploma in Ophthalmology, U. Paris, 1976. Cert. ophthalmologist Paris. Asst. prof., Sale, 1976; prof. Auicenne's Hosp., Rabat, 1980-86, Specialty Hosp., Rabat, 1986-97; head dept., 1990—; pvt. practice Clinique d'Ophtalmologie, Rabat. Dir. Sale's Hosp., 1983-85; head of OTO-Neuro-Ophthalmology Dept., 1990—; pres. 1982-85, v.p., 1986-89, Moroccan Ophthalmological Soc., pres. Qualification's Commn. in Ophthalmology, 1987-93. Mem. Direction of the Social Assn. Anjoad, 1983—; pres. Assn. Against Blindness, 1993—. Recipient Gov.'s award, Oujda, 1989, Settat, 1995, Honor award Moroccan Soc. of Ophthalmology, 2004. Avocations: golf, hunting, tennis. Home: 252 rue Beni Garfat Rabat Morocco Office: Specialty Hosp Afdal Rabat Morocco Home Phone: 21237751805; Office Phone: 212 37660389/90.

RAFNSSON, SNORRI BJORN, epidemiologist, researcher; b. Akureyri, Iceland, June 18, 1974; s. Rafn Heidar Thorsteinsson and Birna Astridur Bjornsdottir; m. Efrosyni Argyri, July 14, 2007. BSc in Nursing, U. Akureyri, Iceland, 2000; MSc in Epidemiology, U. Edinburgh, Scotland, 2002, PhD in Epidemiology, 2007. Rsch. assoc. in epidemiology U. Edinburgh Med. Sch., 2006—07, rsch. fellow epidemiology, 2007—. Vis. lectr. U. Akureyri Sch. Health Scis., 2004—. Mem.: Icelandic Epidemiology Assn., European Young Epidemiologists Assn., Internat. Soc. Vascular Behavioural and Cognitive Disorders. Lutheran. Avocations: sports, music, drums, travel, photography. Home: 11 12 Valleyfield St Edinburgh EH3 9LP Scotland Office: Univ Edinburgh Med Sch Teviot Place EH8 9AG Edinburgh EH8 9AG Scotland Business E-Mail: s.b.rafnsson@ed.ac.uk.

RAGAVAN, MUNISAMI, physician; b. Krishnagiri, Feb. 20, 1978; MBBS, TVMC, 1999; MS, AII MS, MRCS, AIIMS, MCh, 2007. Physician MIOT Hosp., 2010—. Head dept. pediat. surgery, 2008—. Recipient Gold medal. Master: Indian Med. Coun. Avocations: cricket, dance. Office: Mt Poonamalie Rd Manpakkam Chennai Tamil Nadu 600089 India Business E-Mail: dr_ragavan_2001@rediffmail.com.

RAGGIO, CATHLEEN L., orthopedist; MD, Cornell Med. Coll., 1978. Diplomate Am. Bd. Orthop. Surgery. Asst. orthop. surgeon, dept. pediat., adolescent orthop. & spine disorders Hosp. Spl. Surgery, NYC, 1995—. Office: Hosp for Special Surgery 535 E 70th St New York NY 10021 Office Fax: 516-222-7980.

RAGHAVAN, DEREK, oncologist, medical researcher, educator; b. Aug. 11, 1949; came to U.S., 1991; divorced; 2 children. MB, BS with honors, Sydney U., 1974; PhD, London U., 1984. Cert. Royal Australian Coll. Physicians, Fgn. Lic. Exam Coun., Ednl. Coun. Fgn. Med. Grads., Gen. Med. Coun. (U.K.), NSW Med. Bd. (Australia). Resident, registrar Royal Prince Alfred Hosp., Sydney, 1974-77; lectr., sr. registrar Royal Marsden Hosp., London, 1978-80; rsch. fellow Ludwig Inst. Cancer Rsch., London, 1978-80; med. rsch. specialist U. Minn., Mpls., 1980-81; sr. specialist med. oncology Royal Prince Alfred Hosp., Sydney, 1981-91; prof., chief solid tumor oncology and investigational therapeutics Roswell Park Cancer Inst. and SUNY, Buffalo, 1991-97; prof. medicine and urology U. So. Calif., LA, 1997—2003, chief divsn. med. oncology, 1997—2003, assoc. dir. Norris Cancer Ctr., 1997—2004; prof., dir. Cleve. Clinic Taussig Cancer Ctr., 2004—10; prof., clin. medicine U. NC, 2011. Pres. med. staff Roswell Park Cancer Inst., Buffalo, 1995—96; mem. oncology drug adv. com. FDA, 1996—2000; mem., cancer ctrs. support rev. com. Nat. Cancer Inst., 2000—05; prof. medicine SUNY, Buffalo, 1991—97, prof. urology, 1996—97; assoc. dir. U. So. Calif.-Norris Cancer Ctr. U. So. Calif., 1997—2003; mem. sci. adv. bd. Southwest Oncology Group, 1998—2005, bd. govs., 1998—2004, vice chair genitournairy com., 1998—2006; vice chair genitouring cancer com. Radiation Therapy Oncology Group, 1995—97; mem. sci. adv. com. European Orgn. Rsch. and Treatment Cancer, 2000—, mem., external sci. audit com., 2001—07; mem. external adv. bd. Comprehensive Cancer Ctr. U. Ala., Birmingham, 2002—04; mem. external adv. bd. Ohio State U. James Comprehensive Cancer Ctr., 2002—09; mem. clin. trials and awards adv. com. Cancer Rsch. UK, 2002—06; mem. NCI Clin. Oncology Study Sect., 2007—10; mem. clin. oncology study sect. Nat. Cancer Inst., 2007—; pres. Levine Ctr. Inst. Editor: The Management of Bladder Cancer, 1988, Textbook of Uncommon Cancer, 1988, 3d edit. 2006, Principles and Practice of Genitourinary Oncology, 1997, ACS Atlas of Clinical Oncology-Germ Cell Tumors, 2002, Fast Facts: Bladder Cancer, 2006, Bladder Cancer: A Guide for Patients and Families, 2008; assoc. editor Urologic Oncology, 1995—, Clin. Cancer Rsch., 1996—; mem. editl. bd. Jour. Clin. Oncology, 1990-94, 2006-2009, European Jour. Cancer, The Prostate, The Breast, Prostate Cancer, Advances in Oncology, Abstracts in Hematology and Oncology, 1998-2000, Oncology, Brit. Jour. Urology; bd. cons. Jour. Urology, 1996-2006; contbr. articles to profl. jours. Rsch. grantee Nat. Health amd Med. Rsch. Coun., Australia, 1983-90; traveling fellow NSW Cancer Coun., Sydney, 1978; named Hospice Physician of Yr., Hospice of Buffalo, 1994. Fellow: AAAS, ACP (MKSAP XI com. 1997—98, sci. program com. 2000), Royal Australian Coll. Physicians (chair specialist adv. com. in med. oncology 1988—90); mem.: Sydney U. Med. Soc. (pres. 1974), Med. Oncology Group Australia (chmn. 1988—90), Soc. Urologic Oncology, Am. Assn. Cancer Rsch., Am. Soc. Clin. Oncology (liaison Am. joint com. on cancer 1995—2000, AJCC liaison 1995—2000, chair cancer comms. com. 1998—2000, 1998—2000, program com. 1999—2000, mem. pub. issues com. 2000—02, chair Diversity Working Party 2006—09, assoc. editor People Living With Cancer Website). Avocations: tennis, squash. Office: Levine Cancer Inst Carolinas HealthCare Sys PO Box 32861 Charlotte NC 28232-2861 Office Phone: 704-355-3512. Business E-Mail: derek.raghavan@carolinashealthcare.org.

RAGHUNATHAN, SHRIRAM, biomedical researcher; b. Chennai, India, June 28, 1984; PhD, Purdue U., 2010. Grad. rsch. asst., dept. biomedical engring. Purdue U., 2006—10, postdoc. rsch. scientist, ctr. implantable devices, 2010—11; sr. rsch. scientist Cyberonics Inc., 2011—. Co-founder Vocordys LLC, 2009—10. Recipient Excellence Circuit Design award, AMD Corp., Excellence Neural Engring. award, NSF. Mem.: IEEE, Am. Epilepsy Soc. Avocation: music. Office: 206 S Martin Jischke Dr MJIS 2083 West Lafayette IN 47907 Business E-Mail: sraghun@purdue.edu.

RAGHUVEER, GEETHA, pediatrician, educator; b. Mysore, India, Dec. 11, 1959; MBBS, Mysore U., India, 1983. Cert. Pediat., Pediat. Cardiology. Intern pediat. Govt. Med. Coll., Mysore, India, 1981—92; residency pediat. Montefiore Med. Ctr., Albert Einstein Coll. Medicine, NY, 1995—97; fellow pediat. cardiology U. Iowa Hospitals and Clinics; assoc. prof. pediat. U. Mo.-Kansas City Sch. Medicine. Office: Children's Mercy Hosp and Clinics KCM05 2401 Gillham Rd Kansas City MO 64108

RAGINS, HERZL, retired surgeon; b. Tel Aviv, July 27, 1929; arrived in US, 1929; s. Aaron and Ida (Kraus) R.; m. Karen Anderson, Sept. 16, 1979; 1 child, Jonathan Daly. BS, U. Ill., 1949; MS, MD, U. Ill., Chgo., 1951; PhD, U. Chgo., 1956. Intern Cook County Hosp., Chgo., 1951-52; surg. resident U. Chgo. Clinics, 1952-53, 55-60; gastrointestinal endoscopy fellowship Beth Israel Hosp., NYC, 1972-73; clin. prof. surgery A. Einstein Coll. Medicine, Bronx, NY, 1973—2007, ret., 2007. Contbr. articles to profl. jours. Capt. USAF, 1953-55, Korea. Mem. ACS, Am. Soc. Gastrointestinal Endoscopy, Am. Gastroent. Assn., Am. Physiol. Soc., Soc. Surgery Alimentary Tract, Soc. Am. Gastrointestinal Endoscopic Surgeons, Am. Soc. Colorectal Surgeons. Avocations: gardening, tennis. Personal E-mail: herzl.ragins@gmil.com. *

RAGNARSSON, KRISTJAN TOMAS, physiatrist; b. Reykjavik, Iceland, Nov. 15, 1943; s. Ragnar T. and Vigdis (Schram) Arnason; m. Hrafnhildur Agustsdottir; children: Hildur Schmidt, Vigdis Boulton, Thorunn Zimmermann, Kristin. BA, U. of Iceland, Reykjavik, 1963; MD, U. Iceland, Reykjavik, 1966. Diplomate Am. Bd. Phys. Medicine and Rehab. 1976. Gen. practitioner Dist. Pub. Health, Reykjavik, Iceland, 1969—70; instr. NYU, New York, 1973—79; lectr. rehab. medicine U. Iceland, Reykjavik, Iceland, 1976; instr. NYU Med. Ctr., New York, 1973—79, asst. prof. rehab. medicine, 1976—82, assoc. prof., 1982—86; Lucy G. Moses prof., chmn. dept. rehab. medicine Mt. Sinai Sch. Medicine, New York, 1986—. Bd. dirs. World Rehab. Fund, NYC, 1993—; pres. Med. Bd. Mt. Sinai Hosp., 1995—97; chair, Bd. Govs. Faculty Practice Assn. Mt. Sinai Sch. Medicine, 1997—2003; chmn. NIH Consensus Devel. Conf. Panel on Rehab. of Persons with Traumatic Brain Injury, 1997—99. Contbr. articles to profl. jours., chpts. to books. Pres. bd. trustees Am. Scandinavian Found., NYC, 2000—03; bd. dirs. Icelandic Am. Soc. N.Y., NYC, 1977—85. Decorated Knights Cross of the Icelandic Order of the Falcon Pres. of Iceland; recipient Dr. Howard A. Rusk Humanitarian award, World Rehab. Fund, 1995, Outstanding Faculty award, Com. of 1000 Mt. Sinai Med. Ctr., 1997, The Jacobi Medallion, Alumni Ass. of Mt. Sinai Hosp., 1998, Lifetime Achievement award, ASIA, 2002, Excellence in Tchg. award, N.J. Med. Sch., 2002, Ellis Island medal of honor, 2004; grantee Mt. Sinai Spinal Cord Injury Model System grantee, Nat. Inst. on Disability and Rehab. Rsch., 1990—. Mem.: Am. Acad. Phys. Medicine and Rehab. (chmn. mktg. task force 1995—98), Assn. of Acad. Physiatrists (chmn. legis. affairs com. 1995—2003, sec. 2003), Am. Paraplegia Soc. (bd. dirs. 1997—99), Am. Spinal Injury Assn. (pres. 1993—95, Disting. Svc. award 1995), Am. Congress of Rehab. Medicine (Disting. Mem. Svc. award 1993), Icelandic Am. C. of C. (N.Y.C.), Am. Scandinavian Soc. N.Y. Office: Mt Sinai Med Ctr Box 1240 1425 Madison Ave New York NY 10029 Office Phone: 212-659-9340.

RAGO, THOMAS A., orthopedist, surgeon; Attended, Columbia U., 1977. Diplomate Am. Bd. of Orthopaedic Surgery, Am. Bd. of Orthopaedic Surgery-hand surgery. Intern surgery Roosevelt Hosp., 1978—79; resident orthopaedic surgery Presbyn. Hosp., 1979—82; fellow hand surgery Columbia-Presbyn. Med. Ctr., 1982—83; with St. Vincent's Med. Ctr., Bridgeport Hosp. Mailing: Connecticut Hand & Upper Extremity Center 3101 Main St Bridgeport CT 06606 Office Phone: 203-374-5892. Office Fax: 203-374-5822.

RAGUENAUD, MARIE-EVE, medical doctor, epidemiologist; d. Jean-Pierre Raguenaud and Suzy Van Rymenant; 2 children. BSc in Biology, McGill U., Montreal, Can., 1990; MD, McGill Med. Sch., Montreal, 1994; diploma, Inst. Tropical Medicine, Antwerp, 1997; MSc in Epidemiology, London Sch. Hygiene & Tropical Medicine, 2004. Program coord. Action Against Hunger, Chibia, Huila, Angola, 1994—95; physician Hôsp. Nivelles, Belgium, 1995—96, Médecins Sans Frontières, Abyei, North Kordofan, Sudan, Burundi, Azerbaijan, Indonesia, 1997—2002, med. advisor, tuberculosis & neglected tropical diseases, 2002—07, med. epidemiologist Phnom Penh, Cambodia, 2007—09, French Inst. Pub. Health Surveillance, 2009—. Contbr. articles to sci. jours.; author (editor): (book) Saudade, 2011. Recipient Nobel Peace prize, Médecins Sans Frontières, 1999.

RAH, UEON WOO, physician, director; d. Gong Kun Rah and Chun Soon Kim; m. Young Hyuk Lee, Mar. 28, 1981; 1 child, Sungi Il Lee. MD, Yonsei U. Coll. Medicine, Seoul, Republic of Korea, 1980, Yonsei U., 1984, PhD, 1992. Cert. Korea Ministry Heatlth & Welfare, 1980, physiatrist 1984. With Korean Acad. Rehab. Medicine, Seoul, 2000—; chmn. & dir. Dept. Phys. Med. & Rehabil, Ajou U. Med. Sch., Suwon, Kyunggi-do, Republic of Korea, 2003—11; chairperson publ. com. 4th World Congress of ISPRM, Seoul, Republic of Korea, 2005—07; dir. med. com. Korean Sports Assn. Disabled, Seoul, 2007—09; with Korean Soc. Neuro Rehabilitation, Seoul, 2007—11, Korean Assn. Med. Jour. Editors, Seoul, 2008—; pres. Korean Assn. Pain Medicine, Seoul, 2008—09; academic duties Korean Med. Women's Assn., Seoul, 2008—10; pres. Korean Soc. Neurorhabilitation, 2011—. Cons. Nat. Pension Svc., Seoul, 2000—; mem. distbn. com. Korea Global United Way, Kyunggi Divsn., Suwon, Kyunggi-do, 2006—. Deaconess Presbyn. Ch. Joint, Anseong, Kyunggi-do, 2009—; med. classifier Korean Paralympic Com., Seoul, 1994—. Recipient Maj. Citation award, Uiwang City, 2002, Presdl. Citation award, Ministry Govt. Adminstrn. & Home Affairs, 2003, Achievement awards, Ajou Med. Ctr., 2006—, Ministry Culture, Sports & Tourism, 2008. Office: Ajou Med Ctr San 5 Wonchon-Dong Youngtong-Gu 442-721 Suwon Kyunggi-do Republic of Korea Office Fax: 82-31-219-5799. Business E-Mail: uwrah@hanmail.net.

RAHIMI, SAUM A., medical educator; b. Lansing, Mich., Sept. 29, 1975; MD, St. George's U., 2002. Asst. prof. surgery Robert Wood Johnson Med. Sch., 2009—. Mem.: ACS. Office: One Robert Wood Johnson Pl MEB-541 New Brunswick NJ 08903 Office Fax: 732-235-8538. Personal E-mail: saum.rahimi@gmail.com.

RAHKO, PETER SAMUEL, medical educator; b. Toledo, Oct. 20, 1952; MD, Minn., 1979. Prof., medicine U. Wis. Sch. Medicine and Pub. Health, 1985—. Fellow: ACP, Am. Soc. Echocardiography, Am. Heart Assn., Am. Coll. Cardiology; mem.: Heart Failure Soc. America. Office: G7/343 CSC Mail Code 3248 600 Highland Madison WI 53792-3248 Office Fax: 6058-263-0405. Business E-Mail: psr@medicine.wisc.edu.

RAHMAN, RAFIQ UR, oncologist, educator; b. Mirali, Pakistan, Mar. 3, 1957; came to U.S., 1985; s. Rakhman and Bibi (Sana) Gul; m. Shamim Ara Bangash; children: Maryam, Hassan, Haider. BS, MB, U. Peshawar, Pakistan, 1980. Bd. cert. internal medicine, med. oncology, hematology; lic. physician Pa., Ala., Ky. House officer in internal medicine Khyber Tchg. Hosp.-U. Peshawar, 1980-81, house officer in gen. surgery, 1981, jr. registrar med. ICU, 1983-84; jr. registrar internal medicine Khyber Tchg. Hosp., 1981-82; sr. registrar internal medicine Khyber Tchg. Hosp.-Lady Reading Hosp. & Postgrad. Inst., Peshawar, 1984-85; Audrey Meyer Mars fellow in med. oncology Roswell Park Cancer Inst., Buffalo, 1985-86; resident in internal medicine SUNY-Buffalo Gen. Hosp.-Erie County Med. Ctr.-VA Med. Ctr., 1986-88; chief resident in internal medicine SUNY-Buffalo-Erie County Med. Ctr., 1988; fellow in hematology and med. oncology SUNY-Buffalo-Roswell Park Cancer Inst., 1989-90; hematologist, med. oncologist Daniel Boone Clinic and Harlan A.R.H., 1991-92; clin. asst. prof. medicine U. Ky., 1991—; attending physician, hematology, med. oncologist Hardin Meml. Hosp., Elizabethtown, Ky., 1993—, chief medicine, 1996, pres.-elect med. staff, 2001—02, pres. med. staff, 2002—03. Tchr. med. students Med. Sch., SUNY; participant CALGB protocol studies Roswell Park Cancer Inst., investigator. Editor English sect. Cenna mag.; contbr. articles to profl. jours. Founder Cmty. Uplift Program, Pakistan; founding dir. Pakistan Human Devel. Fund, Pakistan Am. Leadership Ctr., Washington. Mem.: Assn. Pakistan Physicians Ky. and Ind. (pres. 2002—03), Ky. Med. Assn. Avocations: travel, aeromodeling, swimming, studying political science and history. Home: 400 Briarwood Cir Elizabethtown KY 42701-6915 Office: 1107 Woodland Dr Ste 105 Elizabethtown KY 42701-2789 Home Phone: 270-769-2003; Office Phone: 270-769-6665. Personal E-mail: rahmanrafiq@hotmail.com.

RAHMAN, SHAFIQUR, neuropharmacologist, scientist, professor, editor, consultant; b. Faridgonj, Chandpur, Bangladesh, Jan. 1, 1963; d. Mohammad Ali and Momotaj Begum; m. Moursheda Rahman, May 24, 1993; 2 children, Zarin and Kashfia. BSc with honors, Dhaka U., Bangladesh, 1985, MSc, 1987; PhD, Meml. U., Newfoundland, Can., 1995. Lectr. Jahangirnagar U., Dhaka, 1988—93, asst. prof., 1993—97, assoc. prof., 1997—98; rsch. assoc. Ind. U. Sch. Medicine, Indpls., 1998—2001; scientist Ctr. Addiction Mental Health, 2001—04; asst. prof. dept. psychiatry and neurosci. U. Toronto, Canada, 2002—04; sr. rsch. sci. Ctr. Drug Abuse Rsch. Translation, U. Ky., 2005—07; assoc. prof. Coll. Pharmacy, SD State U., Brookings, SD, 2008—, disting. rschr. 2009. Cons. Inst. Psychiat. Rsch., Indpls., 1998—; rschr., investigator in field. Editor Neurosci. Pharmacology Jours., Jour. Drug Discovery Therapeutics, Jour. CNS Neurol. Disorder, Drug Targets, Progress in Molecular Biology & Translational Science, 2009-; editor Brain As A Drug Target. Contbr. articles to profl. jours.; investigator, rschr. for profl. jour. articles. Active Lions Club Dhaka Topekhana, 1984-88, ADHUNIK, Dhaka, 1989-98. Recipient Chancellor and Pres. Bangladesh, Dhaka, 1987, rsch. grant, Ctr. Drug Addiction and Mental Health, Toronto, Can., 2001, U. Toronto, Can., 2001, Nat. Inst. on Drug Abuse, US, 2002, Canadian Inst. Health Rsch., 2003, Nat. Inst. on Alcoholism & Alcohol Abuse, US, 2008, Am. Found. Pharm. Edn., US, 2008; vis. scientist rsch. grantee Ind. U. Sch. Medicine, 1998; Meml. Rsch. fellow Meml. U., Newfoundland, 1990, Clark Found. Postdoctoral fellow Clarke Inst. Psychiatry, U. Toronto, Can., 1995. Mem. Internat. Brain Rsch. Orgn., Soc. for Neurosci., Am. Soc. Pharmacology Expert Therpeutics, Soc. Rsch. Nicotine and Tobacco, Canadian Ctr. of Substance Abuse, Am. ASSO Coll. Pharmacy, Am. ASSO Pharmacist Scientist, Am. Soc. Neurochemistry. Avocations: writing, reading, travel. Office: SD State Univ Coll Pharmacy Dept Pharm Scis Avera Health & Sci Ctr. SAV265 Box 2202C Brookings SD 57007 Office Phone: 605-688-4239. Business E-Mail: shafiqur.rahman@sdstate.edu.

RAHMAN, YUEH-ERH, biologist; b. Kwangtung, China, June 10, 1928; came to U.S., 1960; d. Khon and Kwei-Phan (Chan) Li; m. Aneesur Rahman, Nov. 3, 1956; 1 dau., Aneesa. BS, U. Paris, 1950; MD magna cum laude, U. Louvain, Belgium, 1956. Clin. and postdoctoral research fellow Louvain U., 1956-60; mem. staff Argonne (Ill.) Nat. Lab., 1960-72, biologist, 1972-81, sr. biologist, 1981-85; prof. pharmaceutics Coll. Pharmacy, U. Minn., Mpls., 1985—2002, prof. emeritus, 2002—, dir. grad. studies, pharmaceutics, 1989-92, head dept. pharmaceutics, 1991-96, 97-98. Vis. scientist State U. Utrecht, Netherlands, 1968-69; adj. prof. No. Ill. U., DeKalb, 1971-85; cons. NIH.; Mem. com. of rev. group, div. research grants NIH, 1979-83 Author; patentee in field. Recipient IR-100 award, 1976; grantee Nat. Cancer Inst., Nat. Inst. Arthritis, Metabolic and Digestive Diseases. Fellow Am. Assn. Pharm. Scientists; mem. AAAS, Am. Soc. Cell Biology, N.Y. Acad. Scis., Radiation Rsch. Soc., Assn. for Women in Sci. (1st pres. Chgo. area chpt. 1978-79). Unitarian Universalist. Home: 939 Coast Blvd Unit 6G La Jolla CA 92037-4115

RAHME, RALPH, neurosurgeon, researcher; b. Bsharreh, Lebanon, June 28, 1979; MD, St. Joseph U., Beirut, 2001, degree in Neurosurgery, 2009. Resident, intern, surgery U. Medicine and Dentistry, Newark, 2002—03; resident, neurosurgery Thomas Jefferson U., Phila., 2003—04; St. Joseph U., Beirut, 2005—08; resident, fellow, neurosurgery U. Montreal, Montreal, Canada, 2008—10; fellow, vascular and endovascular neurosurgery U. Cin., 2010—. Newsletter editor and webmaster World Assn. Lebanese Neurosurgeons, 2005; invited ad hoc reviewer Clin. Anatomy, 2008, Child's Nervous Sys., 2010; invited reviewer Jour. Pediatric Neuroradiology, 2011. Mem.: World Assn. Lebanese Neurosurgeons, Soc. NeuroInterventional Surgery, AANS/CNS Cerebrovascular Sect., Congress Neurol. Surgeons, Am. Assn. Neurol. Surgeons. Avocations: philosophy, politics, chess, soccer. Office: 260 Stetson St Ste 2200 Cincinnati OH 45219 Business E-Mail: rrahme@waln.org.

RAI, RAVISHANKAR VITTAL, biology professor; b. India, June 9, 1957; MSc, U. Mysore, Karnataka, India, 1980, PhD, 1990. Prof. dept. microbiology studies U. Mysore, 2007—. Office: University Mysore Dept Microbiology Studies Mysore Karanatka 570006 India Office Fax: 918212340361. Personal E-mail: raivittal@gmail.com.

RAIBLEY, PARVIN RUDOLPH, retired dentist; b. Boonville, Ind., Nov. 19, 1926; s. Otto Sr. and Hallie Marie (Hedges) R.; m. Mary Helen Holder, Aug. 31, 1946; children: Bruce D. (dec.), Brian L., Brent A. Degree, Purdue U., 1945; student, U. Evansville, 1946—50; BS in Dentistry, Ind. U., 1951, DDS, 1954. Practice gen. dentistry, Evansville, Ind. 1954—2008. Counselor Boy Scouts Am. With U.S. Army, 1944-45. Named Dentist of Yr. Ind. Acad. Gen. Dentistry, 1992. Fellow Acad. Gen. Dentistry, Internat. Coll. Dentists; mem. ADA, First Dist. Dental Soc., Ind. Dental Assn. (Disting. Svc. award 2010-), Ind. Acad. Gen. Dentistry, S.W. Ind. Oral Health Found. (disbursement com.), Masons. Republican. Methodist. Avocations: farming, forestry, fishing, poetry, gardening. Home: 7100 Olive St Evansville IN 47715-3625 Home Phone: 812-477-0486.

RAIFORD, DAVID S., medical association administrator; BS in Biology, MIT, 1981; MD, John Hopkins U., 1985. Assoc. vice chancellor, health affairs Vanderbilt U. Med. Ctr., 2009—. Prof., medicine Vanderbilt U. Sch. Medicine, 2003, prof., med. edn. & adminstrn., 06, sr. assoc. dean, faculty affairs, 08. Fellow: Am. Coll. Gastroenterology, Am. Coll. Physician; mem.: Am. Assn. Study of Liver Diseases, Assn. Am. Med. Colls. Office: Vanderbilt University Med Ctr 320 Light Hall Nashville TN 37232-0260

RAIJMAN, ISAAC, gastroenterologist, educator; b. Empalme, Sonora, Mex., July 6, 1959; arrived in US, 1985, naturalized, 2000; s. Jose and Amalia (Langsam) R. MD, Nat. Autonomous U., Mexico City, 1985; postgrad., U. Wis., Milw., 1985—89, U. Tex., Houston, 1989—92. Diplomate Am. Bd. Internal Medicine, Am. Bd. Gastroenterology. Resident in medicine Mt. Sinai Hosp., Milw., 1986-88, chief resident, 1989; fellow in therapeutic endoscopy Wellesley Hosp., U. Toronto, 1992—93; rsch. fellow in gastroenterology U. Tex., Houston, 1989-90, clin. fellow, 1990-92, asst. prof. medicine, 1993-97, dir. therapeutic endoscopy, 1993-97, asst. prof. M.D. Anderson Cancer Ctr., 1993—2000, dir. ann. therapeutic endoscopy course, 1995-97, dir. therapeutic endoscopy, 2002—, assoc. prof. Houston, 2002—, Baylor Coll. Medicine, Houston, 2005—, U. Houston, 2005—. Chair Ann. Therapeutic Endoscopy Meeting; chair gastroenterology and endoscopy sub. com., GI subcom. on endoscopic credentialing and quality assurance Hermann Hosp., Houston. Author: Pancreas, 1993, Bockus Textbook of Gastroenterology, 1993; also numerous articles; reviewer jours. in field. Fellow Am. Gastroenterology Assn.; mem. Am. Coll. Gastroenterology, Internat. Assn. Pancreatology, Am. Soc. Gastrointestinal Endoscopy, Am. Soc. Internal Medicine. Jewish. Avocation: painting. Office: 6620 Main Ste 1510 Houston TX 77030 Office Phone: 713-795-4444. Personal E-mail: raijman.i@gmail.com.

RAIKOU, VAIA DIMITRIOU, medical researcher, consultant; b. Greece, Sept. 25, 1959; PhD, Aristotelio U., 1995. Rschr., cons. Nat. and Kapodistrian U. Athens, 1995—. Office: Agiou Thoma 17 Athens Goudi 11527 Greece Business E-Mail: vraikou@med.uoa.gr.

RAIMER, BEN G., pediatrician, public health service officer; b. Woodville, Tex., Dec. 23, 1946; s. Abner Martin and Ollie Odom Raimer; m. Sharon Smith Smith, May 22, 1976; children: Anna Elizabeth, David William, Lauren Allison. BS, East Tex. Bapt. Coll., Marshall, 1969; MA in Human Genetics, U. Tex., Galveston, 1970, MD, 1974. Cert. Am. Bd. Pediat., 1979. Pediatrician, mng. ptnr. Galveston County Pediat. Assocs., Tex. City, 1977—93; v.p. and CEO cmty. health svcs. U. Tex. Med. Br., Galveston, 1993—2007. Chmn. Tex. Statewide Health Coordinating Coun., Austin, 1997—2007, Tex. Correctional Manage Health Care Com., Huntsville, 1998—2003; mem. Tex. Health Inst., Austin, 1998—2007; vice chmn. Galveston Bd. Health. Author: (medicine) Various. Dir. emeritus Communities Joined in Action, Tampa, Fla., 2007; presdl. elector Rep. Party, Austin, 1988; chmn. Rep. Party Galveston County, 1984—94; chmn. bd. dirs. Galveston C. of C., 2007—. Recipient Ray Helfer Award (Child Abuse Prevention), Am. Acad. of Pediat., 1998, Martin Luther King Jr Humanitarian Award, Kingfest Galveston Com., 2007, Disting. Alumnus Award, Grad. Sch. of Biomedical Sciences, UTMD, 2004, J. Wesley Smith Achievement Award, East Tex. Bapt. U., 1999, Ashbel Smith Disting. Alumnus Award, UTMB Sch. of Medicine, 2004, Best Doctors in Am., Best Doctors in Am., 2003-2004, 2005-2006, 2007-2008, Nicholas and Katherine Leone Award, Adminstrv. Excellence, U. of Tex. Med. Br., 1998, Sealy Soc. Mustard Seed Award, UTMB Sealy Soc., 1996, Thinking Positively for Health, Tex. Pub. Health Assn., 2006. Fellow: Am. Acad. Pediat.; mem.: AMA, Am. Correctional Health Profls., Am. Telemedicine Assn., Tex. Pediat. Soc. (life), Tex. Rural Health Assn., Soc. for Pediat. Dermatology, Arty. Club (life; pres. 1997—98). Conservative. Baptist. Avocations: travel, photography, reading, hiking, camping. Office: U Tex Med Br 301 University Blvd Adminstrn Ste 5118 Galveston TX 77550 Office Fax: 409-772-9935. Business E-Mail: bgraimer@utmb.edu.

RAINA, AMRESH, cardiologist; b. Srinagar, India, Nov. 22, 1976; BA, Harvard U., 1999; MD, Columbia U., 2003. Resident internal medicine NY Presbyn. Hosp., Columbia U. Med. Ctr., 2003—06; fellow cardiovasc. disease Hosp. U. Pa., 2007—11; attending physician heart failure/transplant cardiology Allegheny Gen. Hosp., 2011—. Mem.: Am. Coll. Cardiology, Am. Heart Assn. Home: 1649 Shady Ave Pittsburgh PA 15217 Business E-Mail: amresh.raina@uphs.upenn.edu, araina@wpahs.org.

RAINE, CEDRIC STUART, retired medical educator; b. Eastbourne, Eng., May 11, 1940; BSc in Zoology with honors, U. Durham, 1962; PhD, U. Newcastle, Tyne, DSc in Medicine, 1967. Prof., pathology, neurology, neurosci. Albert Einstein Coll. Medicine, 1968—2008, rsch. dir., soc. pres., lab. chief, 1968—2008. Recipient Redway award, NY State Med. Soc., Dystel award, Am. Acad. Neurology Nat. MS Soc., 1996, Lifetime Achievement award, Consortium MS Ctrs., 2005; Javitts grant, NIH, 1985—92. Fellow: Royal Coll. Pathologists; mem.: Am. Neurol. Assn., Am. Acad. Neurology, Am. Assn. Neuropathologists (Weil award 1969, 1975), Brit. Soc. Neuropathology. Avocations: sailing, gardening. Office: 1300 Morris Pk Ave Rm F140 Bronx NY 10461 Office Fax: 718-430-3710. Business E-Mail: cedric.raine@einstein.yu.edu.

RAINER, WILLIAM GERALD, cardiac surgeon; b. Gordo, Ala., Nov. 13, 1927; s. Jamie Flournoy and Lula (Davis) R.; m. Lois Sayre, Oct. 7, 1950; children: Vickie, Bill, Julia, Leslie. Student, Emory U., Atlanta, Ga., 1943-44, U. Ala., 1944-45; MD, U. Tenn., Memphis, 1948; MS in Surgery, U. Colo., Denver, 1958. Diplomate Am. Bd. Surgery, Am. Bd. Thoracic Surgery. Intern Wesley Hosp., Chgo., 1949; gen. practice medicine Blue Island, Ill., 1950-52; resident Denver VA Hosp., 1954-59; practice medicine specializing in cardiac surgery Denver, 1960—. Bd. dirs. St. Joseph Hosp. Found., Denver; disting. clin. prof. surgery U. Colo. Health Sci. Ctr. Contbr. articles to profl. jours. Active Colo. Symphony Assn.; dir. emeritus St. Joseph Hosp. Found. Bd. Lt. U.S. Army, 1952-54. Decorated Bronze Star; recipient Disting. Alumnus award U. Tenn. Health Sci. Ctr., 1992, Florence Sabin award U. Colo. Health Sci. Ctr., 1998, Disting. Svc. award U. Colo., 2004, Outstanding Clin. Vol., U. Colo. Health Sci. Ctr., 2006, Disting. Svc. award, Western Thoracic Surg. Assn., 2006. Mem. Soc. Thoracic Surgeons (sec. 1980-85, pres. 1989, historian 1992—, Disting. Svc. award 1998), Colo. Med. Soc. (pres. 1984-85), Denver Med. Soc. (pres. 1984), Denver Clin. and Pathology Soc. (pres. 1997), Am. Coll. Chest Physicians (pres. 1984), Am. Bd. Thoracic Surgeons (bd. dirs. 1982-88), Am. Surg. Assn., Am. Assn. Thoracic Surgery, Societé Internationale de Chirugie, Cactus Club. Avocations: photography, travel. Office: 2552 E Alameda 48 Denver CO 80209 Office Phone: 303-601-0532. Personal E-mail: wrainer@qwest.net.

RAINES, C. FAY, medical association administrator, dean; BS & MS in Nursing, U. Va.; PhD in Nursing, U. Md. Assoc. dean for acad. programs U. Va. Sch. Nursing, interim dean; assoc. provost for inst. effectiveness U. Ala. Coll. Nursing, dean & prof., 1990—. Ed. bd. Jour. Profl. Edn. Mem.: Am. Assn. Colleges Nursing (pres.). Office: One Dupont Cir NW Ste 530 Washington DC 20036 Office Phone: 202-463-6930. Office Fax: 202-785-8320.

RAINES, DEBORAH A., neonatal/perinatal nurse specialist, educator, nursing researcher, consultant; BSN, Syracuse U., NY, 1978; MSN, U. Pa., Phila., 1982; PhD, Med. Coll. Va. at Va. Commonwealth U., Richmond, 1992. Disting. practitioner, Nat. Acads. Practice, 2004. Nursing edn. coord., perinatal nurse specialist George Wash. U. Med. Ctr., Washington, 1984—89; nurse, maternal infant nurse Med. Coll. Va. Hosps., Richmond, 1992—98; asst. to assoc. prof. Va. Commonwealth U., Richmond, 1992—2000; prof. Fla. Atlantic U., Boca Raton, Fla., 2000—. Cmty. svc. assoc. Va. Commonwealth U., 1997—99; online tchg. liaision Fla. Atlantic U., 2001—04, dir., principle investigator, 2003—06, dir. accelerated second degree program, 2003—06, freshman reading program leader, 2007—, dir. scholarship tchg., 2009—; cons. Palm Healthcare Found., West Palm Beach, Fla., 2004—. Editor: (book) Perinatal Secrets, 2004; author: The Quick Study for Nursing, 2007; contbr. articles to profl. jours. Bd. mem. Karen Slattery Early Edn. Devel. Rsch. Ctr., Boca Raton, Fla., 2003—07. Recipient Excellence in Edn. award, Soc. Pediat. Nurses, 2002, Disting. Tchr. the Yr., Fla. Atlantic U., 2004, Excellence in Undergraduate Tchg. award, 2005, Cmty. Ptnr. award, Palm Health Care Found., 2006, Excellence in Online Tchg. award, e-College Internat., 2007, Faculty Svc. award, TIAA/CREF, 2007, Outstanding Alumni award, Med. Coll. Va., 2007. Mem.: Nat. League for Nursing, Assn. Women's Health Obstet. and Neonatal Nurses (Medallion of Excellence 2000), Sigma Theta Tau (Evidence Based Practice award 2007). Avocations: travel, reading, theater, music. Office: Fla Atlantic Univ 777 Glades Rd Boca Raton FL 33431 Business E-Mail: draines@fau.edu.

RAINES, JEFF, biomedical scientist, medical research director; b. NYC, Sept. 5, 1943; s. Otis J. and Mildred C. (Wetzler) Raines; children: Gretchen Christena, Victoria Jean. BSME, Clemson U., 1965; MME, U. Fla., 1967; PhD in Biomed. Engring., MIT, 1972. Mem. staff MIT, Cambridge, 1968—70; biophysicist dept. surgery Mass. Gen. Hosp., Boston, 1972—77, dir. Vascular Lab., 1972—77; instr. surgery Harvard Med. Sch., Boston, 1973—77; preceptor Harvard/MIT Sch. Health Scis., 1976—77; rsch. dir., dir. Vascular Lab. Miami (Fla.) Heart Inst., Miami Beach, 1977—88; adj. prof. bioengring. U. Miami, Coral Gables, 1977—; prof. surgery U. Miami (Fla.) Sch. Medicine, 1977—; with Miami Vein Ctr., 2004—. Prin. investigator series NIH programs and pharm. firms, 1977—; Harvard Travelling fellow lectr. in Europe, 1975. Contbr. numerous articles on biomechanics, cardiovasc. diagnosis, dynamics and instrumentation to sci. jours. Recipient Apollo Achievement award, NASA, 1969; fellow, NIH, 1972. Fellow: Am. Assn. Physicists in Medicine, Am. Coll. Radiology, Am. Coll. Cardiology; mem.: ASME, AAAS, Cardiovasc. Sys. Dynamics Soc. (founding mem., editor 1976—, pres. 1980—82), Internat. Cardiovasc. Soc., Instrument Soc. Am., Biomed. Engring. Soc., New Eng. Cardiovasc. Soc., Am. Heart Assn., MIT Club, Harvard Club, Coral Gables Club, Kiwanis, Sigma Xi, Tau Beta Pi. Republican. Presbyterian. Achievements include patents for medical devices; development of mathematical models of arterial hemodynamics and clinical use of autotransfusion. Home Phone: 305-246-0333; Office Phone: 305-987-0922. Personal E-mail: drjraines@yahoo.com.

RAINSFORD, KIM DRUMMOND, biomedical researcher, educator; b. Adelaide, Australia, Apr. 2, 1941; s. Keith Carr and Ruth Alice (Drummond) R.; m. Marion Jago, June 30, 1968 (div. 1981); children: Miriam Ann Estelle, Andrea Louise Reece; m. Veronica Koechli, Aug. 20, 1983; children: Alexander Keith, William Lawrence. BSc, Australian Nat. U., 1968; PhD, U. London, 1970; D (hon.), Pecs U. Medicine, 1997. Chartered scientist 05. Sr. lectr. U. Tasmania, Hobart, 1972-79; vis. sr. scientist Lilly Rsch. Ctr., Windlesham, England, 1980-81; reader U. Zimbabwe, Harare, 1981-82; Wellcome sr. scientist, sr. assoc. & head anti-infl. res. group Strangeways Res. Lab. U. Cambridge, England, 1982—88; prof. McMaster U., Hamilton, Ont., Canada, 1988-92; prof., chmn. biomed. scis. Sheffield Hallam U., England, 1992—2006, emeritus prof. biomed. scis., 2006—. Guest prof. U. Basel, Switzerland, 1979-80; past chmn. Heads Univ. Ctrs. Biomed. Sci., London, 2000-03, cons. in fields Editor-in-chief: Internat. Jour. Inflammapharmacology, 1999—; assoc. editor, mem. editl. bd. Jour. Pharmacy & Pharmacology, 1987—, Inflammation Rsch., 1977—, Internat. Jour. Immunopathology, Pharmacology, 1994—2009; author 25 books and more than 200 articles in field of inflammatory diseases and their therapy, including Ibuprofen. A Critical Bibliographic Review, 1999, Aspirin and Related Drugs, 2004, Nimesulide: Actions, Uses and Safety, 2005. Mem. parish coun. St. Anne's Ch., Baslow, 1993-2006, St. Peter's Ch., Edensor, Chatsworth, Derbyshire, 2008-, founder, dir. Bioronica Ltd., biotech. & clin. phamacology cons. Fellow Royal Coll. Pathologists, Royal Soc. Chemistry, Royal Coll. Physicians (Edinburgh), Royal Soc. Medicine, Soc. Biology (former Inst. Biology), New Zealand Inst. Chemistry, Inst. Biomed. Sci.; mem. Australian Coll. Edn., Hungarian Gastroenterology Soc.(hon), World Wide Hungarian Med Acad., Hungarian Experntl. & Clin. Pharmacoligical Soc. Avocations: horticulture, classical music. Office: Sheffield Hallam U Howard St Sheffield S1 1WB England Office Phone: 44-114-225-3006. Business E-Mail: k.d.rainsford@shu.ac.uk.

RAISON, CHARLES LOUIS, psychiatrist, educator; Graduated with honors, Stanford U.; Masters in English, U. Denver; MD, Wash. U. Sch. Medicine, St. Louis, Mo. Resident UCLA Neuropsychiatric Inst. and Hosp., LA; jr. faculty mem., dir., emergency psychiatric services and assoc. dir., consultation and evaluation services UCLA; asst. prof. psychiatry and behavioral sciences Emory U. Sch. Medicine, Atlanta, 1999—, clin. dir., Mind-Body Program, 1999—, co-dir., Collaborative for Contemplative Studies, 1999—. Lectr. in field. Mental health expert CNN, appears frequently in broadcast and print media on topics related to stress, sickness and depression. Mem.: Alpha Omega Alpha. Achievements include being internationally known for expertise in the diagnosis and treatment of interferon-alpha-induced depression and anxiety. Office: 1639 Pierce Dr Ste 4000 Atlanta GA 30322 Office Phone: 404-712-8800. Business E-Mail: craison@emory.edu.

RAJ, A. JESU AROCKIA, research scientist; b. June 11, 1975; PhD, Manonmaniam Sundaranar U., India, 2004. Postdoc. rsch. fellow U. Malaya, Malaysia, 2010—. Lab mgr. Divsn. Genetics & Molecular Biology, 2010. Recipient Young Scientist award, Dept. Sci. & Tech., Govt. of India, New Delhi. Mem.: Soc. Aquaculture Profls. Avocations: reading, travel, music. Home: Plot 97A Apt 97A/1 Senthil Perungudi Chennai Tamil Nadu 600096 India Personal E-mail: jesuaraj@yahoo.com.

RAJ, DOMINIC S., nephrologist; b. Nagercoil, India, July 7, 1954; MBBS, Madurai Med. Coll., 1982; MD, Stanley Med. Coll., 1986. Chief, dept. nephrology St. Johns Med. Coll., Bangalore, 1993—95; prof., medicine U. N.Mex, 2007—09; chief, divsn. renal diseases and hypertension George Wash. U., 2009—. Dir., nocturnal dialysis program Da Vita, 2010. Recipient Young Investigator award, Nat. Kidney Found., GCRC Rsch. award, U. N.Mex; Rsch. grant, NIH. Mem.: Nat. Kidney Found., Internat. Soc. Nephrology, Am. Soc. Nephrology (abstract com. chair 2009, ASN week end chair 2010). Avocations: travel, history, running. Office: 2150 Pennsylvania Ave NW Washington DC 20037 Office Fax: 202-741-2285. Business E-Mail: draj@mfa.gwu.edu.

RAJA, BALAJI, medical educator; b. Vellore, Tamil Nadu, India, June 21, 1984; PhD, SRM U., 2011. Asst. prof. SRM U., 2007—10, Nat. Inst. Tech., 2010—. Contbr. articles to profl. jours. Recipient Best Oral Presenter award, Vit U. Mem.: Soc. Biotech. India, Indian Soc. Tech. Edn. Avocation: reading. Home: 27/5a P S M St Velapadi Vellore Tamilnadu 632001 India Personal E-mail: balajiraja_vlr@yahoo.com.

RAJA, SHAHZAD G., thoracic surgeon, researcher; b. Lahore, Punjab, Pakistan, Jan. 17, 1972; s. Shahbaz Munir Raja and Shamim Akhtar; m. Irfana Abdullah, Sept. 26, 2004; 1 child, Roheen Shahzad. BSc, U. Punjab, Lahore, Pakistan, 1993; MBBS, King Edward Med. Coll., Lahore, Pakistan, 1995. Resident dept. surgery Mayo Hosp., Lahore, Pakistan, 1998—2000, resident dept. cardiovascular surgery, 2000—01; resident dept. cardiac surgery U. Hosp. Wales, Cardiff, 2001—02, Harefield Hosp., London, 2002—03; sr. resident dept. cardiac surgery Alder Hey Hosp., Liverpool, 2003—04, Royal Hosp. Sick Children, Glasgow, Scotland, 2004—. Reviewer Annals of Thoracic Surgery, Am. Jour. Cardiology. Contbr. scientific papers to profl. jours. Organizer Little Heart Matters, Glasgow. Named Best All Round Grad., King Edward Med. Coll., Pakistan, 1995—96. Mem.: Royal Coll.Surgeons Edinburgh (life). Achievements include research in novel indications of sildenafil (Viagra). Office: Royal Hosp Sick Children Dalnair St Lanarkshire Glasgow G3 8SJ Scotland Home: Facultat de Psicologia Flat 2/2 24 Nairn St G3 8SF Glasgow Scotland Office Fax: +44(0)1412019204; Home Fax: +44(0)1412019204. Personal E-mail: drrajashahzad@hotmail.com. E-mail: shhzdri@yahoo.co.uk.

RAJAH, JAISHEN, pediatrician; b. Durban, South Africa, Dec. 29, 1961; s. Devrajh Sundorajh Rajah and Krishnathavee Rajah; m. Subashnie Devkaran, Aug. 17, 2002; 1 child, Nikira. MBBCh, South African Med. Coun., 1988, Fcpeds, 1994, Critical Care in Pediat., 1998, DA, 2000; BA, U. South Africa, 1994. Pediatric cons. Chris Hani Baragwanath Hosp., Johannesburg, 1994—96, critical care cons. pediat., 1997—2000; sr. pediatric cons. Sheikh Khalifa Med. City, Abu Dhabi, United Arab Emirates, 2001—, sr. cons., 2001—, dir. pediatric advanced life support, 2004—. Childrens magician (theodaora foundation) TRUSTEE, magician and lecturer (magic shows for sick children) Magic, Humour And Medicine, IBM (Lectr. At The Hague, FISM World Championship Of Magic, 2003), contbr. scientific papers to profl. jours. Recipient Best On Web:Acid Base Balance: Finding Common Ground:, Am. Thoracic Soc., 2001. Mem.: Ludwig Von Mises Inst., Internat. Brotherhood Of Magicians. Office: Sheikh Khalifa Med City Dept Pediat PO Box 51900 Abu Dhabi United Arab Emirates Office Fax: 00971 2 6104962. Business E-Mail: rajjai741@skmc.gov.ae.

RAJAN, SANKAR, nutritionist; b. Srivilliputhur, Tamil Nadu, India, May 11, 1953; MBBS, Kilpauk Med. Coll., 1976; MD, U. Bombay, 1984. Ret. col. Army Med. Corp, Ministry of Def., India, 1977—2001; regional tech. advisor Micronutrient Initiative, Regional Office, 2001—04; project officer UNICEF India Country Office, 2004—06; spl. advisor, regional rep. Global Alliance Improved Nutrition, 2006—. Clin. work, rsch., tchg., 1977—2011. Recipient Sir Sriram Meml. award, Nat. Acad. Med. Scis., India, Sivanthi Adityan Gold medal, Assn. Physicians India. Fellow: Indian Coll. Physicians; mem.: Nat. Acad. Med. Scis. (India). Avocations: tennis, golf, music, music, reading. Home: 104 Mall Apt Mall Rd New Delhi 110054 India Home Fax: 011-43147579. Business E-Mail: rsankar@gainhealth.org.

RAJANDRAM, RAMA KRSNA, physician; b. Malaysia, Dec. 18, 1979; DDS, Nat. U. Malaysia, 2004; MDS in Oral and Maxillofacial Surgery, U. Hong Kong, MFDS RCS (Ed), 2010. Physician Nat. U. Malaysia, 2005—. Clin. specialist, lectr. Nat. U. Malaysia, 2005. Mem.: Royal Coll. Surgeons Edinburgh. Avocation: reading. Office: Oral & Maxillofacial Dept Fac Kuala Lumpur 50300 Malaysia Personal E-mail: decruze79@yahoo.com.

RAJENDRAN, BABU, ophthalmologist, director; b. Vizag, India, Oct. 12, 1945; MBBS, KMC, Mangalore, 1971; MS in Ophthalmology, KMC, Manipal, 1975. Med. dir. Eye Rsch. Found., 1983—. Pres. All India Ophthal. Soc., 2009—10. Recipient Lifetime Achievement Award, Tamil Nadu Ophthalmic Assn. Fellow: ACS; mem.: Am. Acad. Ophthalmology. Office: Eye Rsch Foundation 180 Arcot R Chennai Tamil Nadu 600026 India Business E-Mail: drbabu@eth.net.

RAJIAH, PRABHAKAR, radiologist; s. Rajiah Samuel and Shantha Rajiah. MBBS, Madras Med. Coll., India, 1996, MD in Radiology, 2000. Cert. CCT Post Grad. Med. Edn. & Tng. Bd., 2005. Sr. fellow & acting instr. U. Wash., Seattle, 2007—08; clin. fellow cardiovasc. imaging Cleve. Clinic Found., 2008—. Recipient Rsch. award, RSNA, 2007; Roentgen fellowship, 2008. Fellow: Royal Coll. Radiologists; mem.: Soc. Cardiovasc. Computed Tomography, Soc. Cardiovasc. MRI, Am. Roentgen Ray Soc., Radiol. Soc. N.Am. E-mail: rprabhakar73@hotmail.com.

RAJKOWSKA, GRAZYNA, biology professor; b. Warsaw, Mar. 15, 1955; MSc, Warsaw U., 1979; PhD, Nencki Inst. Exptl. Biology, 1986. Prof. U. Miss. Med. Ctr., 1994—. Rsch. grant, NIMH. Mem.: Collegium Internat. Neuropsychopharmacology, Am. Coll. Neuropsychopharmacology, Soc. Neurosci., Soc. Biol. Psychiatry. Avocations: languages, hiking, swimming, bicycling. Home: 311 Pinewood Ln Ridgeland MS 39157 E-mail: grajkowska@umc.edu.

RAJSHEKHAR, VEDANTAM, neurosurgeon, educator; b. Madras, India, Apr. 15, 1959; s. Krishnamohan and Padmavathy Vedantam; m. Rupa Nambiar, May 22, 1983; 1 child, Aditya. MBBS, Christian Med. Coll., Vellore, India, 1981, MCh in Neurosurgery, 1987. Cert. neurosurgeon. Resident CMC Hosp., Vellore, 1982-87, lectr., 1987-92, assoc. prof., 1992-96, prof., 1996—, head neurosurgery unit, 1996—. Author: Solitary Cysticercus Granuloma, 1999; contbr. chpts. to books, articles to profl. jours. Mem. Indian Soc. for Stereotactic and Functional Neurosurgery (sec.-treas. 1994-2000, pres. 2005—), Congress of Neurol. Surgeons, Neurol. Soc. India (Madurai Neuro award 1986). Avocations: swimming, badminton. Office: Christian Med Coll Hosp Dept Neurol Scis 632004 Vellore India Office Phone: 091 416 2282767.

RAJU, MINNIE M., clinical nurse informaticist, critical care nurse; arrived in U.S., 1974; d. Pazhavilla I. and Mary Raju. BS in Biology, Albany State U., 1994; ADN, Rockland CC, Suffern, NY, 1997; BSN, U. Md., 2003, MS in Nursing Informatics, 2005. RN N.Y., Md., DC. Clin. nurse Nyack Hosp., NY, 1997—99, Washington Hosp. Ctr., 1999—, clin. mgr., 2004—05; applications devel. mgr. Computer Scis. Corp., 2005—08; clin. nurse informaticist NIH, 2008—; MD Wash. Hosp. Ctr., 1999—2011. Mem.: Am. Assn. Critical Care Nurses, Health Info. Mgmt. Sys. Soc., Greater Washington Area Chamber Am. Assn. Critical Care Nurses, Sigma Theta Tau. Seventh Day Adventist.

RAJU, RAMANATHAN, hospital administrator; m. Samanthi Raju. MD, MS, Madras Med. Coll.; MBA, U. Tenn., 2000. Resident, fellow vascular surgery Luth. Med. Ctr., Bklyn., sr. v.p., dir. med. edn., dir. gen. surgery, dir. trauma; chief med. officer Coney Island Hosp., COO, 2005; exec. v.p. med. and profl. affairs, COO NYC Health and Hospitals Corp.; CEO Cook County Health and Hospitals Sys., Chgo., 2011—. Office: Cook County Health & Hospitals System 1900 W Polk St Chicago IL 60612 Office Phone: 312-864-1111. *

RAKIC, PASKO, neuroscientist, educator; b. Ruma, Yugoslavia, May 15, 1933; came to U.S., 1969; m. Patricia Goldman, 1969. MD, U. Belgrade, 1959, PhD in Devel. Biology and Genetics, 1969. With inst. path. physiology Med. Sch. U. Belgrade, 1959-61, resident in neurosurgery, 1961-62; NIH research fellow neuropathology Harvard Med. Sch., Boston, 1962-66; asst. prof. Inst. Biol. Rsch., Belgrade, 1967-68; from asst. prof. to assoc. prof. neuropathology and neuroscience Harvard Med. Sch., 1969-77; prof. neurosci. Yale Med. Sch., New Haven, 1977-78, Dorys McConnell Duberg prof. neurosci., 1978—, also chmn. neurobiology dept. Author of 300 sci. papers and gen. books on brain orgn. and devel. Co-recipient Kavli prize for neurosci., Norwegian Acad. Sci. and Letters in partnership with the Kavli Found. and the Norwegian Ministry of Edn. and Rsch., 2008. Mem.: AAAS, NAS, Inst. Med., Am. Phys. Soc. (Lashley award, Fyssen Internat. Sci. prize, Gerard prize, Pasarw award, Henry Gray award, Bristol Myers Squibb award), Soc. Neurosci. (pres. 1996). Office: Yale U Neurosci Program L200 SHM PO Box 208074 New Haven CT 06520 Office Phone: 203-785-4330.

RAKOWSKI, THOMAS JOHN, medical oncologist; Attended, Cornell U., Ithaca; MD, SUNY, Syracuse, 1976. Diplomate Am. Bd. Internal Medicine, Am. Bd. Internal Medicine-med. oncology, Am. Bd. Internal Medicine-hematology, Subspecialty Bd. Oncology, lic. NJ, 1981. Fellow Columbia-Presbyn. Med. Ctr., NY; resident in internal medicine SUNY Med. Ctr., Syracuse, 1979; resident in hematology NY Presbyn. Hosp., 1981; hosp. affiliation includes Valley Hosp. Named one of Best Doctors, NY Mag., 2010. Office: Valley Hospital Luckow Pavilion 1 Valley Health Plz Paramus NJ 07652 Office Phone: 201-634-5578.

RALL, WILFRID, neuroscientist, researcher, artist; b. LA, Aug. 29, 1922; s. Udo and Doris (Keiser) R.; m. Ava Lou Freed, 1946 (dec.); children: Sarah E., Madelyn Rall Badger; m. Mary Ellen Condon, 1983. BS summa cum laude, Yale U., 1943; MS, U. Chgo., 1948; PhD, U. N.Z., 1953. Jr. physicist Manhattan Project U. Chgo., 1943-46, biophysics fellow, 1946-48; lectr., sr. lectr. physiology, biophysics U. Otago, Dunedin, N.Z., 1949-56; head biophysics divsn. Naval Med. Rsch. Inst., Bethesda, Md., 1956-57; biophysicist, office math. rsch. Nat. Inst. Arthritis and Metabolic Diseases, Bethesda, 1957-67; sr. rsch. physicist math. rsch. br. Nat. Inst. Diabetes and Digestive and Kidney Diseases, 1967-94; scientist emeritus Nat. Insts. Health, 1994—. Mem. NRC Com. on Brain Scis., 1968-73. Contbr. articles to profl. jours. Fellow: Am. Acad. Arts and Sciences; mem.: Soc. Neurosci. (Swartz prize 2008). Achievements include being an amateur sculptor.

RALLI, MASSIMO, otolaryngologist; b. Rome, Jan. 20, 1982; MD, U. Roma La Sapienza, 2006—06. Cert. in otolaryngology U. Cattolica del Sacro Cuore, Milan, 2011. With Inst. otolaryngology U. Cattolica del Sacro Cuore, 2007—. Pres. bd. dirs. DomainsBot Srl, 2005, CEO, 2005—09; adj. prof. SUNY, Buffalo, 2009; pres., CEO Roma Tld Srl, 2009. Recipient Politzer prize, Politzer Soc., Internat. Soc. Otologic Surgery and Sci. Mem.: Italian Assn. Otolaryngology, Soc. Neurosci., Assn. Rsch. Otolaryngology. Home: Via Polibio 52 Rome 00136 Italy Business E-Mail: massimoralli@mac.com.

RALPH, LARS JOEL, dentist, researcher; b. Gothenburg, Sweden, Feb. 20, 1950; s. Joel and Kerstin (Börjesson) R.; m. Maria (Larsson) de Val, July 1, 1978 (div. Sept. 1983); children: Lillie, Björn; m. Maud Hartelius, Sept. 30, 1983 (div. Apr. 1998); children: Carl, Max, Oscar. B of Odontology, U. Gothenburg, Sweden, 1970, DDS, 1975. Pub. dental health officer Kristianstad County Coun., Sweden, 1975—76, Children's Clin., Gothenburg, 1976—79; pvt. practice Gothenburg, Sweden, 1977—91; asst. faculty odontology U. Lund, Malmö, Sweden, 1986; pub. dental health officer Västra Götaland Region, Sweden, 2000; rschr. Swedish Sch. Libr. and Info. Sci. U. Borås, Sweden, 1996—99; pub. dental health officer Norrbotten County Coun., Sweden, 2001—. Cons. dentist Mutomo Hosp., Kenya, 2000; lectr. in field. Contbr. articles to profl. jours. Bd. dirs. Soc. of Friends of Röhss Mus. Applied Art & Design, Gothenburg, 1981-90. Lt. j.g. Royal Swedish Navy Dental Corps., 1978. Grantee U. Lund, 1986, 87, 89, Dental Soc. Gothenburg, 1990, Wilhelm & Martina Lundberg Found, Malmö, 1990, Hultén Rsch. Fund, Malmö, 1987, Crafoord Found., Lund, 1986, 88, 89; travel grantee Knut & Alice Wallenberg Found., 1988; Swedish Med. Rsch. Coun., 1986, 88, 91. Mem. Swedish Dental Assn., Swedish Soc. Medicine, Rotary Club (pres. 2006-07), Norrbotten Soc. Dentistry (vice chmn. 2007-, lay judge Lulea dist. ct., 2011-). Achievements include research in MRI on masticatory muscles. Home: S 933 33 Storgatan 55 A Arvidsjaur Sweden Office Phone: 46960-57691.

RALPH, ROBERT ALAN, ophthalmologist, educator; b. New Haven, Jan. 29, 1941; s. Joseph S. and Elsie S. Ralph; m. Jan Eden; children: Alison, Stephanie. AB, Harvard U., Cambridge, Mass., 1961; MD, Tufts U., Boston, 1965. Diplomate Am. Bd. Ophthalmology. Intern, then resident in surgery Yale Med. Ctr., New Haven, 1965—67; clin. assoc. Nat. Cancer Inst., Bethesda, Md., 1967—69; resident in ophthalmology Georgetown U., Washington, 1969—72, clin. prof. ophthalmology, 1995—2007; fellow in cornea rsch. Mass. Eye and Ear Infirmary, Boston, 1972—74; pvt. practice ophthalmology Washington, Rockville, Md., 1974—2010; asst. prof. ophthalmology Wilmer Eye Inst., Johns Hopkins U., Balt., 1995—2008. Cluster constructions photography and wood. With USPHS, 1967—69. Recipient L. Harrell Pierce, MD Wilmer Tchg. award, 1999, Allan D. Jensen award, Johns Hopkins U. Med. Sch., 2004; named Tchr. of Yr., Georgetown U., Dept. Ophthalmology, 1976. Fellow: ACS, Am. Acad. Ophthalmology; mem.: Photographic Soc. Am., Cosmos Club. Avocations: photography, art, creative writing. Home and Office: 11400 Grundy Ct Potomac MD 20854

RAM, CHITTA VENKATA, physician; b. Machilipatnam, India, Oct. 24, 1948; s. Chitta M. Row and Chitta (Cheruvu) Sarojini; m. Ashalata Ram, Feb. 17, 1979; children: Gita, Radha. B.Sci, Marathwada U., Aurangabad, India, 1966; MD, Osmania U., Hyderabad, India, 1972. Diplomate Am. Bd. Internal Medicine. Resident in internal medicine Brown U., R.I. Hosp., Providence, 1974-76; fellow in hypertension Hosp. U. Pa., Phila., 1976-77; faculty assoc. U. Tex. Southwestern Med. Ctr., Dallas, 1977-78, asst. prof., 1978-83, assoc. prof., 1983-89, prof. internal medicine, 1989—. Dir. Tex. Blood Pressure Inst., Dallas; dir. rsch. and edn. Dallas Nephrology Assocs.; hypertension unit St. Paul Med. Ctr., Dallas, dir. continuing med. edn. dept., 1996-98, chmn. instnl. rev. com., 1996-98, pres. med. staff, 1997-98; dir. Tex. Blood Pressure Inst., Dallas. Contbr. numerous articles to profl. jours. and chpts. to textbooks; editl. cons., reviewer numerous nat. and internat. jours. and pubs. Pres. Tex. IndoAm. Physician Soc., Dallas, 1988; trustee Dallas/Ft. Worth Hindu Temple Soc., Dallas, 1988. Named Outstanding Tchr. St. Paul Med. Ctr., 1982; recipient Mother of India award, 1992. Master ACP; fellow Am. Coll. Cardiology, Am. Coll. Chest Physicians (regent), Am. Coll. Clin. Pharmacology; mem. Am. Assn. Physicians from India (pres.-elect 1994-95, pres. 1995-96), Tex. Indo-Am. Physicians Soc. Home: 1420 Viceroy Dr Dallas TX 75235 Office Phone: 214-358-2300. E-mail: ramv@dneph.com.

RAMACHANDRAN, C. P., retired medical educator; b. Kuala Lumpur, Malaysia, June 3, 1936; MSc, U. London, Liverpool, 1959; DMS, U. Tokyo, 1967. Chief Filariasis rsch. and control WHO, Geneva, 1978—96. Asst. prof. faculty medicine U. Malaya, 1963—67; chief Filariasis rsch. and control Inst. Med. Rsch., Kuala Lumpur, 1967—70; prof. and dean Sch. Biol. Scis. U. Sains Malaysia, 1970—92. Recipient Mary Kingsley medal, U. Liverpool Sch. Tropical Medicine, Sandhosham Gold medal, Malaysian Soc. Tropical Medicine. Fellow: Inst. Biology London, World Acad. Scis., Liverpool Sch. Tropical Medicine, Acad. Medicine Malaysia, Acad. Scis. Malaysia, Malaysian Soc. Tropical Medicine (hon.), Australasian Coll. Tropical Medicine (hon.), Royal Soc. Tropical Medicine London (hon.). Avocation: squash. Home: Blvd 1/63 Off Jalan Tunku. Bukit Tunku Kuala Lumpur Wilayah 50480 Malaysia Home Fax: 603-26986152. Personal E-mail: ramacp@hotmail.com.

RAMACHANDRAN, MEENAKSHISUNDARAM, finance company executive; b. Rajapalayam, Tamilnadu, India, May 31, 1982; s. Ramachandran and Amirthavalli. MBBS, Madras Med. Coll., 2007. Cert. physician Tamilnadu Med. Coun. Contbr. articles to numerous med. jours. Recipient Block Lock Meml. Gold Medal, Madras Med. Coll., India. Fellow: Am. Endocrine Soc.; mem.: Indian Med. Coun., Tamilnadu Med. Coun. Home: 104/1/1 Ponnagaram Krnagar Post 626 108 Rajapalayam India Home Phone: 91-4563-236506. Personal E-mail: rmsundar_chandran@yahoo.co.in.

RAMADAN, MOHAMED HAFEZ, neurosurgeon, educator; b. Cairo, Mar. 4, 1961; m. Marwa AbdelRahim Abdallah, May 9, 1991; children: Alia, Lamia, Dana, Ahmed. CM, Cairo U., 1982; Ednl. Commn. for Fgn. Grads., Cairo Egypt, 1982; MSc in Gen. Surgery, Cairo U., 1986. Prof. of neurosurgery Cairo U., 2001—; adj. prof. of neurosurgery U. of Pitts. Sch. of Medicine, Pitts., 2005—. Chief neurosurgery cons. North Am. Rsch. Unit (NAMRU) in Cairo, 2000—, UN High Commr. for Refugees (UNHCR) relief agencies, Cairo, 2002—; neurosurgery cons. CARITAS, Cairo, 2003—; chief neurosurgery cons. Palestinian Authority, Cairo, 2001—; neurosurgery cons. Maj. Pvt. Hospitals, Cairo, 1999—; lectr. of neurosurgery Cairo U., 1991—96, assoc. prof. of neurosurgery, 1996—2001. Recipient award, Palestinian Authority, 2002, Hon. distinction in duty, Egyptian Syndicate, 2002; grant, Japanese Internat. Cooperation Agy., 1990, scholarship, Mainz U. Germany, 1991. Master: Mid. East Neurosurgical Soc. (assoc.; advisor 2000—05); mem.: Am. Assn. of Neurosurgery (assoc.; internat. mem. 2004—05), Internat. Soc. for Pediatric Neurosurgery (assoc.). Achievements include design of a nonlinear biomechanical model for evaluation of cerebrospinal fluid shunt systems. Home: 32 Hassan Ibrahim Hassan Str Cairo 11371 Egypt Office: Cairo Univ Sch Medicine 1 26th July Str Cairo 11111 Egypt Home Fax: 5889880. Personal E-mail: dindinosi@hotmail.com.

RAMALLE-GOMARA, ENRIQUE, epidemiologist; b. Rincon de Soto, La Rioja, Spain, Aug. 13, 1960; BSc in Anthropology, U. Murcia, Spain, 1999; PhD in Medicine, U. Valladolid, Spain, 2004. Chief epidemiology Dept. Pub. Health, 1999—. Adj. prof. U. Nat. Edn. a Distancia, 2005—11. Mem.: Spanish Soc. Epidemiology. Home: General Espartero 5-11 A Logrono La Rioja 26003 Spain Business E-Mail: enrique.ramalle@larioja.org.

RAMAMOORTHY, SONIA L., colon and rectal surgeon, educator; MD, Boston U., Mass. Diplomate Am. Bd. Surgery, 2002, Am. Bd. Colon and Rectal Surgery, 2005. Resident in gen. surgery Univ. Calif. San Diego, 1996—2001, rsch. fellow, 2005—06, assoc. prof.; fellow in colon and rectal surgery Barnes Jewish Hosp., St. Louis, 2001—02; hosp. affiliations include Univ. Calif. San Diego Thornton Hosp., La Jolla; hosp. affiliations include Moores Cancer Ctr. Univ. Calif. San Diego Med. Ctr., Hillcrest. Author: Detection of multiple human papillomavirus genotypes in anal carcinoma, Transrectal endoscopic retrorectal access (TERA): a novel NOTES approach to the peritoneal cavity, The inflammatory response in transgastric surgery: gastric content leak leads, The impact of proton-pump inhibitors on intraperitoneal sepsis: a word of caution for transgastric NOTES procedures. Office: University of California San Diego Medical Center Moores Cancer Center 3855 Health Sciences Dr La Jolla CA 92093 Office Phone: 800-926-8273.

RAMAN, SHANKAR, surgeon; b. Thirukoilur, India, Apr. 2, 1977; s. Lakshminarayanan and Vidya Raman; m. Nivedita Krishnan, May 28, 2007; 1 child, Sahaana. MBBS, JIPMER, Pondicherry, India, 2000; MS, JIPMER, Pondicherry U., India, 2003; DNB, Nat. Bd. Examiners, New Delhi, 2003; MD, ECFMG, Phila., 2006. Diplomate Nat. Bd. Med. Examiners, New Delhi, 2003. Sr. resident surgery Jipmer, 2003—04; resident surgery Bronx Lebanon Hosp. ctr., NY, 2006—11; registrar surgery Kent & Canterbury Hosp., England, 2006; sr. ho. officer William Harvey Hosp., Ashford, England, 2005—06; jr. resident surgery JIPMER, 2000—03; fellow colon and rectal surgery Henry Ford Hosp., Detroit. Contbr. chapters to books. Recipient MOH Hassan Kuthoos Maricar Endowment prize, JIPMER, 2000, Dr SC Mitra award, 2004, SB SEN award, Pondicherry U., 2004. Mem.: Am. Soc. Metabolic and Bariatric Surgery, Am. Tamil Med. assn., JIPMER Alumni Assn., Med. Soc. NY, Royal Coll. Surgeons Edinburgh, ACS, SAGES. Achievements include research in helicobacter pylori and association to erosive gastroduodenitis, venous ulcers; REM sleep deprivation and its association with hypothalamic self stimulation; analgesia and single incision laparoscopic surgery, endolumenal revision of obesity surgery. Office: Bronx Lebanon Hosp Ctr Selwyn Ave Bronx NY 10457 Personal E-mail: shankarrraman@gmail.com.

RAMANAN, SUNDARAM V., internist, hematologist, oncologist; s. Tarakad Appadoraier Sundaram. MD, MS, Vellore Christian Med. Coll., India, 1959. Prof. medicine U. Conn., Farmington, 1976—; emeritus attending physician St. Francis Hosp., Hartford, Conn., 1993—; assoc. prof. medicine West Va. U. Fellow: ACP (corr.), Royal Soc. Medicine (London), Royal Coll. Physicians (Edinburgh). Office: St Francis Hosp 1000 Asylum Ave Ste # 1004 Hartford CT 06105 Office Phone: 860-714-4152. *

RAMANATHAN, RANGASAMY, pediatrician; arrived in US, 1982; s. Rangaswamy Naidu and Gunavathi Rangaswamy; m. Prema Naidu, July 12, 1978; children: Anusha, Vinitha. MBBS, Stanley Med. Coll., Chennai, India, 1975; D, Madras Med. Coll., Chennai, India, 1978, MD in Pediat., 1981, NY Med. Coll., NY, 1984. Diplomate Am. Bd. Pediat., 1987, neonatal-perinatal medicine Am. Bd. Pediat., 1987. Intern Lincoln Med. Ctr., NY, 1982—83, resident, 1983—84; clin. instr. pediat. U. So. Calif., LA, 1984—86; rsch. fellow Harbor U. Calif. Med. Ctr., LA, 1987—88; asst. prof. pediat. sch. medicine Olive View med. ctr. U. Calif., Sylmar, Calif., 1988; asst. prof. of pediat. Keck sch. medicine U. So. Calif., LA, 1988—98, assoc. prof. of pediat. Keck sch. medicine, 1998—2002, prof. pediat. Keck sch. medicine, 2003—, assoc. divsn. chief divsn. neonatology Keck sch. medicine, 2003—. Program dir, neonatal-perinatal medicine fellowship Keck sch. medicine U. So. Calif., 2002—; med. dir. newborn icu Women's and Chlidren's Hosp., LA, 1988—; sect. head divsn. neonatology Women's and Children's Hosp., 2001—, med. dir. respiratory therapy dept., 1991—; assoc. med. dir. Good Smaritan Hosp., LA, 1989—; dir. high risk infant follow-up program Good Samaritan Hosp., 1990—, chief neonatolgy sect., 2003—; lectr. in field. Contbr. articles to profl. jours. Recipient Outstanding Tchr. award, Dept. Pediat., U. So. Calif., 2004, Richard H. Paul Disting. Tchg. award, U. So. Calif., 2005; named Physician of Yr., Good Samaritan Hosp., LA, 2004; named one of Best Doctors in Am., Best Doctors, Inc., Boston, 2005. Mem.: Am. Acad. Pediat. (regional trainer 1991—). Achievements include research in molecular basis of lung injury and oxgen radical mediated disorders in newborn infants. Avocation: travel. Office: Women's & Children's Hosp LAC+USC 1240 North Mission Rd Room L-919 Los Angeles CA 90033 Office Phone: 323-226-3406. Business E-Mail: ramanath@usc.edu.

RAMEH, CHARBEL ELIAS, surgeon, educator; b. Kfar Matta, Aley, Lebanon, Feb. 13, 1979; Specialist in Otolaryngology, Head and Neck Surgery, Am. U. Beirut Med. Sch., 2008; degree in Otology and Neurotology, U. Marseille, France, 2009. Asst. prof. otolaryngology, head and neck surgery St. Georges Hosp. U. Med. Ctr., Mt. Lebanon Hosp., 2010—. Mem.: Politzer Soc., Alpha Omega Alpha. Avocations: ballroom dancing, tennis. Office: Mount Lebanon Hosp Camille Chamoun Beirut 1 Lebanon Personal E-mail: charbelrameh@hotmail.com.

RAMESH, NARAYANAPERUMAL, medical researcher; b. Nagercoil, Tamilnadu, India, Mar. 29, 1972; s. Ramaiah Nadar Narayanaperumal and Muthia Nadar Pushpavalli; m. Sundaresan Ajithakumari, May 22, 2005; 1 child, R. A. Sakthia. BSc, Manonmaniam Sundaranar U., Tirunelveli, 1993, PhD, 2000; MSc, Bharathiar U., Coimbatore, 1995. Rsch. officer Grd Ednl. Trust, Coimbatore, 2001—02; sr. lectr. Ponniah Ramajayam Coll., Thanjavoor, Tamilnadu, 2002—03; rsch. coord. Centre Medicinal Plants Rsch., Sri Kaliswari Coll., Sivakasi, 2003—. Cons., advisor in medicinal plants Sri Kaliswari Coll., Sivakasi, Tamil Nadu, India, 2003. Author: Herbal Drugs and Biotechnology, 2004, Ethnobotany of the Kamis, 2006; contbr. articles to profl. jours. Trainer, medicinal plants and mushroom cultivation, processing and utilization Grd Ednl. Trust, Coimbatore, 2001—02. Grantee, Sri Kaliswari Trust, 2004. Hindu. Achievements include invention of antimicrobial activity of luteoforol; two new plant varities; ethnomedicinal plants uses; rediscovery of three extinct species. Avocations: reading, writing, music. Home: 18/110c Balasubramaniapuram Tamil Nadu Kanniyakumari 629 702 India Office: Sri Kaliswari Coll Meenashipuram 626 130 Sivakasi 626 130 India Personal E-mail: nprg@rediffmail.com.

RAMET, JOSE, pediatrician, educator; b. Antwerp, Belgium; m. Francoise Lallemand; children: David, Philippe. MD, PhD, Vrije Universiteit, Brussels Belgium, 1973—80. Pediatrics Vub Belgium, 1985. Prof. of pediat. Picu Az Vub, Brussels, 2001—05; prof. Antwerp U. Hosp, chmn. Belgium, 2005—, Queen Paola Children's Hosp., 2005—. Secretary-general cesp CESP, Brussels. Pres. Belgian Soc. Pediatrics, 2007—; vice-president u. hosp. VUB, Belgium, 2002. Mem.: Belgium Soc. Pediatrics (pres. 2007—). Achievements include research in Clinical Research Pediatrics. Office: Univ Hosp Antwerp UZA Pediatrics Wilmarsstraat 10 2030 Antwerp Belgium Office Fax: 00 32 3 8214300. Business E-Mail: jose.ramet@uza.be.

RAMINENI, SATHEESH K., orthopedist; b. India, Feb. 18, 1976; MD, Gandhi Med. Coll., 2000. Rsch. assoc. U. Toledo Med. Ctr., 2007—08, orthop. trauma fellow, 2008—09; orthop. foot and ankle surgery fellow Pa. Hosp., U. of Pa., 2009—10; orthop. adult reconstructive surgery fellow NY U. Hosp. Joint Diseases, 2010—; staff orthop. surgeon Okla. City VA Med. Ctr., 2011—. Recipient V. S. Ratnakar award, NTR U. Health Scis., Vijayawada, Andhra Pradesh India. Fellow: Am. Orthop. Foot and Ankle Soc. Home: 14317 84th Ave Apt 2 Briarwood NY 11435

RAMIREZ, AMELIE G., health facility administrator, director; b. Laredo, Tex., Oct. 17, 1951; m. David Gutierrez. MPH, U. Tex., Houston; DPH, U. Tex. Asst. dir. adminstrn. and cmty. health promotion S.Tex. Health Rsch. Ctr., U. Tex. Health Sci. Ctr., San Antonio, 1989—94, assoc. dir. cmty. health promotion, 1994—97; assoc. dir., Ctr. Cancer Control Rsch. Baylor Coll. Medicine, Houston, 1997—99, dep. dir., Chronic Disease Prevention and Control Rsch. Ctr., 1999—2006; dir., Inst. Health Promotion Rsch. U. Tex. Health Sci. Ctr., 2006—, prof. epidemiology and biostatistics, Dielmann chair in health disparities and cmty. outreach rsch. Mem. Lance Armstrong Found., Austin, Tex., 2007; mem. selection com. Am. Cancer Soc., 2004; mem. external adv. com. to NIH grant Sch. Pub. Health, U. Medicine and Dentistry of NJ, 2005; mem. Nat. Childrens Study Adv. Com., Md., 2006; chair Social Mktg. and Cancer Genetics Among Hispanics, Tex., 2007; mem. Susan G. Komen Sci. Adv. Bd., Tex., 2007, Inst. Medicine and Divsn. Earth and Life Studies Roundtable on Translating Genomic Based Rsch. Health, Tex., 2007—; adv. bd. mem. Avon Found. Breast Cancer Crusade, Tex., 2007—; chair fed. adv. bd. Cervical Cancer Early Detection Program, Ctrs. Disease Control, Tex., 2007—. Recipient First Pl. award, Women in Comm., 1997, Bronze Telly award, Nat. Hispanic/Latino Cancer Network, 2002, Silver, Platinum and Bronze Quill award, 2005, Prof. Survivorship award, Susan G. Komen for Cure, 2007. Mem.: APHA, Inst. Medicine Nat. Academies, Internat. Union Health Promotion Edn., Soc. Pub. Edn., Soc. Behavioral Medicine, Am. Acad. Health Behavior, Am. Soc. Preventive Oncology. Office: Univ Tex Health Sci Ctr 8207 Callaghan Rd Ste 353 San Antonio TX 78230

RAMÍREZ, ANA SOFÍA, veterinarian, educator; b. Las Palmas de Gran Canaria, Spain, Oct. 10, 1971; Degree in Pharmacy, U. Complutense Madrid, 1994; MS in Pub. Health, U. Las Palmas de Gran Canaria, PhD in Vet., 2000. Sr. lectr. U. Las Palmas de Gran Canaria, 2000—11, dep. head. dept., 2009—, assoc. prof., 2011—. Named Hon. Rsch. fellowship, U. Liverpool, Eng. Mem.: Internat. Orgn. Mycoplasmology. Achievements include research in mycoplasmology. Avocations: piano, yoga, reading. Office: Trasmontaña Arucas Las Palmas 35413 Spain Office Fax: 34 928 451142. Business E-Mail: aramirez@dpat.ulpgc.es.

RAMIREZ, MARCELLUS FRANCIS LIM, cardiologist, b. Zamboanga City, Philippines, Aug. 18, 1972; s. Manuel Ong and Lydia Lim Ramirez. BS in Med. Tech. magna cum laude, U. Santo Tomas, Manila, 1992; MD cum laude, U. Santo Tomas, Espana, Manila, Philippines, 1996. Cert. in internal medicine Philippine Coll. Physicians, diplomate Philippine Coll. Cardiology/ Philippine Heart Assn. Chief resident dept. medicine U. Santo Tomas, Manila, 2000—01, chief fellow sect. cardiology, 2004; fellow clin. electrophysiology and cardiac pacing Nat. Heart Ctr., Singapore, 2005—. Cons. U. Santo Tomas, 2005, Healthway Med. Clinics, Makati, Metro Manila, 2005, presenter in field. Contbr. articles to profl. publs. Scholar, U. Santo Tomas, 1992—96; Asia Brewery Med. Splty. scholar, Tan Yan Kee Found., 2005—. Fellow: Philippine Coll. Cardiology (Most Outstanding Fellow in Cardiology 2005), Philippine Coll. Physicians (Most Outstanding Resident in Medicine 2002); mem.: Filipino Chinese Med. Soc. Inc., UST Med. Alumni Assn. Office: U Santo Tomas Hosp Espana St Sampaloc Manila Philippines Personal E-mail: mightyramirez@yahoo.com.

RAMÍREZ-BARBA, ECTOR JAIME, public health service officer, surgeon, educator; b. León, Guanajuato, Mexico, Dec. 1, 1956; s. Rigoberto Ramírez-Díaz and Ma. de Jesús Barba-Barba; m. Elvia Rodríguez-Villalobos, Oct. 31, 1981; children: Ector Ramírez-Rodríguez, Jaime Ramírez-Rodríguez. MD, Universidad de Guanajuato, León, Mex., 1978; degree in gen. surgery, Universidad de Guadalajara, Jalisco, Mex., 1984; M in Adminstrn., U. Guanajuato, Mex., 1990; PhD, Pacific Western U., 1994. Dir. gen. hosp. Instituto de Seguridad y Servicios Sociales de los Trabajadores del Estado, León, 1988—89; chmn. Sch. Medicine Universidad de Guanajuato, León, 1990—97, sr. rschr., prof., 1994—; gen. sec. U. Guanajuato, 1999—2000; assoc. rschr. Secretaría de Salud, Guanajuato, 2002—; sec. health Gobierno del Estado de Guanajuato, 2000—. Advisor Consejo Mexicano de Cirugía Gen., México City, 1993—95; pres. Colegio de Médicos Especialistas en Cirugía Gen. de Guanajuato, León, 1996—97; sec. Colegio Médico del Estado de Guanajuato, León, 1996—98; nat. pres. Mex. Assn. Gen. Surgery, 1997—98; mem. Asociación de Facultades y Escuelas de Medicina, México, 1999; pres. Sociedad de Gastroenterología del Estado de Guanajuato, León, 2000—02. Fellow: ACS, Academia Mexicana de Cirugía General (sr.). Office: Secretaría de Salud de Guanajuato Tamazuca 4 Guanajuato 36000 Mexico Office Fax: 01152-473-732-5193; Home Fax: 01152-477-781-1853. Personal E-mail: ramirezbarba@hotmail.com. E-mail: ramirezbarba@guanajuato.gob.mx.

RAMÍREZ-CAMACHO, RAFAEL, medical educator; b. Jaén, Spain, Apr. 9, 1947; s. Antonio Ramírez and Mercedes Camacho; m. Carmen Amorim Gaudencio. Degree in Medicin, U. Complutense, Madrid, 1964; PhD, U. Autónoma, Madrid, 1980. Residency Centro Nal Especialidades Quirurgicas, Madrid, 1973—76; med. asst. Serv ENT Hosp. Ramón y Cajal, Madrid, 1976—86; med. cons. ENT. Hosp. U. Puerta de Hierro, Madrid, 1986—2006, prof. chief; titular prof. Medicine Faculty, U. Autónoma, Spain, 2005—; chief prof. Ear Rsch. Group. Office: Hosp Univ Puerta de Hierro- Joaquín Rodrigo 2 Majadahonda Madrid 28922 Spain

RAMIREZ DIAZ, SANTIAGO PAULINO, geriatrician, researcher; b. Mexico City, Sept. 15, 1971; s. Jose Manuel Ramirez Isunza; m. Sandra Patricia De Alba Pérez Maldonado. MD, U. Autonoma Aguascalientes, Mexico, 1995; PhD in Geriatrics, U. Complutense Madrid, 2005; post grad., Harvard U., Cambridge, Mass. Diplomate rsch. U. Complutense Madrid, 2002, geriatric specialist Hosp. Clinico San Carlos de Madrid, 2005, Alzheimer's disease sub-specialist Hosp. Clinico San Carlos de Madrid, 2005, cert. Mexican Coun. Geriatrics, 2006. Coord. pvt. sect. Hosp. Miguel Hidalgo, Aguascalientes, Mexico, 1997—98, geriatrician, 2005—; geriatrician and rschr. geriatric dept. Hosp. Clinico San Carlos de Madrid, 2000—05; prof. and rschr. U. Autónoma de Aguascalientes, 2005—. Rschr. European Alzhemer's Disease Consortium, Madrid, 2002; coord. memory clinic Hosp. Miguel Hidalgo, Aguascalientes, Mexico, 2005—. Author: La familia: el actor no protegido., Protocolo diagnóstico de demencias, Cómo Optimizar el Diagnóstico y el Tratamiento en las Alteraciones de Conducta en el Anciano, La Enfermedad de Alzheimer día a día con el enfermo.; med. editor: abstract sect. Geriatrics Mag. (Spanish edit.); contbr. chapters to books, articles to profl. jours. Recipient Nicolas Kaufer award, Am. Brit. Med. Ctr., 1999, Premio Pañella Casas, 2002; fellow, Found. Fernández-Cruz, 2003; Janssen-Cilag fellow, 2003. Mem.: Mexican Assn. Geriatrics and Gerontology, European Alzheimer's Disease Consortium, Spanish Soc. Geriatrics and Gerontology. Achievements include research in Alzheimer's disease and related disorders; aging. Avocations: travel, golf, fishing, photography. Office: Centro Geriátrico Sierra Nevada 219 Fracc Los Bosques Aguascalientes 20120 Mexico E-mail: ramirezdiazsp@gmail.com.

RAMIREZ-RIVERA, JOSE, physician; b. Mayaguez, PR, June 26, 1929; s. Jesus Ramirez and Nieves Rivera; m. Leila Suner, May 14, 1971; children: Frederico, Steven, Sally, Juliette, Natasha, Leila. BA, Johns Hopkins U., 1949; MD, Yale U., 1953. Diplomate Am Bd Internal Med, re-certified 1974. Intern U. Md. Hosp., 1953-54; resident in medicine Univ. Hosp., Balt., 1954-55, fellow in hematology, 1958-59, resident, 1959; staff physician VA Hosp., Balt., 1960-67, assoc. chief of staff, 1962-68; asst. in medicine Johns Hopkins U., 1960-67, instr. in medicine, 1967-68; asst. prof. medicine U. Md., 1961-68; assoc. prof. Duke U., Durham, NC, 1968-70; dir. med. edn. and clin. investigation Western Region P.R., 1970-80; chief medicine Mayaguez (P.R.) Med. Ctr., 1971-82; chief Pulmonary Disease Sect., Va. Hosp., Durham, 1968—70. Prof med Univ PR, San Juan, 1974—, dir univ med servs Med Sci Campus, 1982—86; prof med Univ Cent del Caribe, 1998—; dir Rincon Rural Health Project, 1975—82; assoc chief staff educ VA Med Ctr, San Juan, 1990—92; dir clin investigation La Concepcion Hosp, San German, 1996—. Author: A Todo Pulmon A Gun Region Eaters, 2011; contbr. articles to med. jours.;, author books of Puerto Rican Legends. Bd dirs Soc Educ Suroeste. With USPHS, 1955—57. Decorated Comendador Imperial Orden Hispanica de Carlos V; named Man of Yr., PR Med. Soc. Western Sect., 1975, 1981. Master. ACP (pres. PR chpt. 1986—88, Blaine Brower Travelling Scholar 1967, Laureate award 2005); fellow: Coll. Chest Physicians, Royal Soc. Med (London); mem.: Imperial Orden Hispanica de Carlos V (Abelardo Diaz Alfaro prize 2010), Puerto Rican Fedn. Bioethics (bd. dirs. 1999—2002, pres. 2002—10), Soc. Autores Puertorriguenos, PR Lung Assn. (bd. dirs. 1975—80), Casa Espana (bd. dirs. 1998—2005), Alliance Francaise PR (v.p. 1993—96, pres. 1996—2000, bd. dirs. 2006—09), PEN Club. Roman Catholic. Achievements include creating a technique of lung lavage for alveolar proteinosis. Avocations: classical music, literature. Office Phone: 787-793-6576. Personal E-mail: ramirez.r629@gmail.com.

RAMJEE, GITA, medical researcher; b. Uganda, Apr. 8, 1956; m. Pravin Ramjee; children: Shaniel, Rushil. BSc with honors, U. Natal, 1980, MSc, 1990, PhD, 1994. Chief specialist scientist Med. Rsch. Coun., Durban, Kwazulu-Natal, South Africa, 2001—, dir. HIV prevention rsch., 2002—; prof. Tamil Nabu Med. U., India, 2006; dir. HIV/AIDS lead program Tamil Nabu Med. U., 2006. Head South African Microbicide Rsch. Initiative; co-chair Microbicide Devel. Programme; mem. task force Dept. Health; mem. sci. adv. com. Reproductive Health Rsch. Unit, mem. ethics com.; mem. tech. com. NIH Clin. Trials Unit, 2007—. Grantee, NIH, 2000—05, HIV Prevention Trials Network, 2000—, Microbicide Devel. Programme grantee, Dept. for Internat. Devel., 2001—, Gates Found., 2003—. Mem.: Internat. AIDS Soc., South African Med. and Dental Coun. Office: Hormeyer Rd 3630 Durban 3630 South Africa Office Fax: 27-31-2423806. Business E-Mail: nadine.landsmann@mrc.ac.za, ramjeeg@mrc.ac.za.

RAMLI, MUSA, psychiatrist, educator; b. Malaysia, Mar. 8, 1973; MBBS, UKM, 1998, MMed in Psychiatry, 2006. Assoc. prof. Internat. Islamic U. Malaysi, Indera Mahkota, 2006—. Mem.: Malaysian Psychiat. Assn. Office: Internat Islamic University Malaysia Kuantan Pahang 25200 Malaysia Office Fax: 609-5145866. Personal E-mail: ramlidr@yahoo.com.

RAM-LIEBIG, GOUYA, urologist, researcher; d. Emad and Felor Ram; m. Soeren Liebig, Apr. 22, 1995; children: Andian Roman Liebig, Batis Liebig. MD, Johann Wolfgang U., Frankfurt, 1994. Approbation Regierungspraesidium Dresden, Germany, 1998. Rsch. fellow UCLA, 1996—97; physician, rschr. Tech. U. Dresden, 2001—. Contbr. articles to profl. jours. Recipient 2d prize in exptl. urology, Germany, 2004. Mem.: European Assn. Urology, German Urology Soc. Achievements include patents for in vitro engineering of urinary bladder constructs. Home: Goethe allee 9 01309 Dresden Germany Office: Budapester Strasse 3 01069 Dresden Germany Office Fax: 49-351-484 3135; Home Fax: 49-351-3125405. Personal E-mail: raliebig@web.de. E-mail: info@urotec.de.

RAMM, DOUGLAS ROBERT, psychologist; b. New Haven, Dec. 11, 1949; s. Robert Frederick and Gladys (Torgrimson) R.; m. Barbara Stephens, Aug. 10, 1974; children: Jennifer, Jessica. BA, Ithaca Coll., 1972; MA, Duquesne U., 1974, PhD, 1979. Diplomate Am. Bd. Profl. Psychology; bd. cert. clin. psychologist Am. Bd. Profl. Psychology. Staff psychologist Westmoreland Hosp., Greensburg, Pa., 1976-79, chief clin. psychologist, dir. child & adolescent psychiat., 1979-82; pvt. practice Greensburg, Pa., 1980—. Pres. Ethics, Inc., Ctr. for Sci. Study of Values and Morality, 1995-98; cons. U. Pitts., Pa. Bur. Vocat. Rehab., Westmoreland County Ct. of Common Pleas; past pres. Mental Health Assn. Westmoreland County. Author: Clinically Formulated Principles of Morality, 1996, Consider the Scientific Study of Morality, 1998, The Formula for Happiness, 2004, Principles for Achieving Emotional Well-Being, 2005, Motivating Juvenile Offenders Toward Making Responsible Revision in Daily Life, 2009. Mem. APA, ASCD, Am. Philos. Assn., Pa. Psychol. Assn., Acad. Clin. Psychology, Soc. Personality Assessment, Nat. Acad. Neuropsychologists, Nat. Register Health Svc. Providers in Psychology, Am. Coll. Forensic Examiners (diplomate), Soc. Bus. Ethics, Rotary Club. Methodist. Office: 225 Humphrey Rd Ste 4 Greensburg PA 15601-4571 Office Phone: 724-832-9096. Personal E-mail: rammpsychsvcs@aol.com.

RAMNANAN, CHRISTOPHER J., physiologist, educator; b. Montreal, Que., Can., Aug. 7, 1979; BSc in Biochemistry with honors, Carleton U., 2002, PhD, 2006. Rsch. and tchg. faculty Vanderbilt U. Sch. Medicine, 2006—. Postdoc. fellowship, Vanderbilt U. Diabetes Rsch. and Tng. Ctr., 2010. Mem.: Am. Assn. Anatomists, European Assn. Study of Diabetes (Travel grant 2010), Am. Diabetes Assn. (fellowship 2006—10). Office: Vanderbilt University Dept Molecular Physiology Nashville TN 37232 Business E-Mail: chris.ramnanan@vanderbilt.edu.

RAMNATH, NITHYA, physician, educator; b. India, Sept. 23, 1964; MBBS, Jawaharlal Inst. Post-Grad. Med. Edn. and Rsch., 1987. Rsch. fellow Wayne State U., 1996; assoc. prof. U. Mich., 2008—. Mem.: ASCO. Office: 1500 E Med Ctr Dr Ann Arbor MI 48109 Personal E-mail: nithyaramnath@hotmail.com.

RAMOS, LEONARDO ADDEO, physician; b. Jan. 2, 1975; PhD, UNIFESP, 2009. Physician UNIFESP, 2004—. Office: Sabara 566 CJ 194 Sao Paulo 01244001 Brazil Personal E-mail: leo_ramos@hotmail.com.

RAMOS-DURAN, LUIS RAUL, physician, director; b. Mex. City, Sept. 9, 1973; MD, UACH Mex., 1998; degree in Radiology, UNAM, 2002—02. Radiology and MRI house staff Am. Brit. Cowdray Med. Ctr. Nat. Autonomous U. Mex. Mex. City, 1999—2003, prof. and program dir. clin. fellow MRI and advanced MRI techniques, 2004—06; staff radiologist Hosp. Angeles de las Lomas. Huixquilucan, Estado de Mex. Mex., 2003—06; clin. dir. MRI and diagnostic neuroradiology, vis. prof. radiology Tex. Tech U. Health Scis. Ctr. and Paul L. Foster Sch. Medicine, El Paso, 2006—07, clin. dir. MRI and diagnostic neuroradiology, asst. prof. radiology, 2009—; cardiovasc. imaging house staff, vis. prof. radiology Dept. Radiology and Radiol. Sci. Med. U. SC, Charleston, 2008—09. Recipient First Pl., Harvard Med. Sch. Mem.: AMA, Mexican Soc. Radiology & Imaging (First Pl.), Mexican Fedn. Radiology, Radiol. Soc. N.Am. (First Pl.), Internat. Soc. Magnetic Resonance Medicine. Avocations: mountain climbing, deep sea fishing. Home: 6321 Franklin Vista El Paso TX 79912 Business E-Mail: luis.ramosduran@ttuhsc.edu.

RAMOS-MARTÍNEZ, ERNESTO, pathologist; b. Chihuahua, Mex., Feb. 7, 1948; s. Ernesto and Fabiola (Martinez-Fourzán) Ramos-Avilés; m. Ana Maria Torres-Moye, Aug. 9, 1973; 1 child, Ernest David. MD, Chihuahua U., 1972; degree in anatomic pathology, Mex. U., 1976. Intern Nat. Med. Ctr. Hosps. Mex. Social Security, Mexico City, 1973-74, resident in anatomic pathology, 1974-77; prof. pathology Mex. U., 1975-85; anatomic pathologist Mex. Social Security, Mexico City, 1977-85, Chihuahua, 1985-92, U. Hosp., Chihuahua, 1992—2007, prof. histology Chihuahua U., 1986-99, prof. pathology, 1999—2007. Assoc. researcher Mex. Social Security, 1983-85, chief postgrad. sch. Med. U. Chihuahua, 1986-88, sec. rsch. and postgrad. studies, 1988-92. Contbr. articles to profl. publs. Pres. Chihuahua U. Found., 1995-99. Recipient Best Proffered Paper award, Soc. Gastroenterology, 1985, Chihuahua prize in biology area, Govt. Chihuahua State, 1999, Excellency prize in med. sci., Pfizer Med. Humanities Inst., 2006. Fellow Mex. Soc. Pathologists, Lat. Am. Soc. Hepatology Argentina, Lat. Am. Soc. Pathology, Med. Coll. Chihuahua (pres. 1991-93), Lat. Am. Fedn. Socs. Ob-Gyn; mem. Nat. Acad. Medicine, Chihuahua Soc. Pathology (pres. 1996-97). Roman Catholic. Avocations: reading, jogging, movies, golf. Office: Gomez Farias Valentin 115 31000 Chihuahua CHIH Mexico Office Phone: 52 614 4 16 51 99. Personal E-mail: eramos48@prodigy.net.mx.

RAMPAUL, RAJENDRA S., surgeon; b. London, June 24, 1971; s. Ramjas Rampaul and Golsin D. Teelucksingh; m. Rachel J. Laquis, June 16, 2006. MB, MD, U. Nottingham. Cert. MRCS Royal Coll. of Surgeons, Edinburgh, 2003. Surgeon specialist Nottingham Breast Unit, England, 1999—. Mem.: GMC, Royal Coll. Surgeons. Office: University Nottingham Nottingham NG1 5PB England Personal E-mail: mszrsr@nottingham.ac.uk.

RAMSAY, DAVID LESLIE, physician, dermatologist, educator; b. Rochester, NY, Apr. 25, 1943; s. Joseph Walter and Jean (Eastwood) R. AB in English with honors, Ind. U., 1965, MD, 1969; MEd, U. Ill., 1973. Diplomate Am. Bd. Dermatology. Assoc. faculty mem. Ind. U., Indpls., 1965-69; intern in medicine George Washington U. Med. Ctr., 1969-70; resident in dermatology NYU Med. Ctr., 1970-73; dir. dermatology residency tng. Nat. Naval Med. Ctr., Bethesda, Md., 1973-75; asst. prof. medicine Georgetown U., Washington, 1974-75; asst. prof. dermatology NYU, 1974-78, assoc. prof. dermatology, 1978-95, prof. dermatology, 1995—2003, clin. prof. dermatology, 2003—, NYU senator, 1986-94, pres. faculty coun., 1988-90, dir. ednl. affairs dermatology, 1975—2002, dir. cutaneous lymphoma sect., 1975—. Author: Simulations in Dermatology, 1974; contbg. author: Adolescent Dermatology, Basic Mechanisms of Physiologic and Aberrant Lymphoproliferation in the Skin, Hematology and Oncology Clinics in North America; sr. editor: Jour. of Drugs in Dermatology, 2003-; contbr. more than 25 articles to profl. jours. Pres., bd. dirs. One Fifth Ave. Apt. Corp., N.Y.C., 1978-80; trustee Bklyn. Acad. Music, 1989—, chmn. visual arts com., chmn. edn. com; bd. dirs. Cutaneous Lymphoma Found., 2003—. Lt. comdr. USN, 1973-75. NIH fellow U. Ill., 1972-73. Fellow ACP, Internat. Soc. Cutaneous Lymphomas, Am. Acad. Dermatology; mem. Am. Dermatologic Assn. Roman Catholic. Avocations: collecting visual art, swimming, reading. Home: One Fifth Ave New York NY 10003 Office: NYU Med Ctr 530 5th Ave New York NY 10036-5101 E-mail: DRamsay1@nuc.rr.com.

RAMSEY, DAVID SELMER, retired health facility administrator; b. Mpls., Feb. 19, 1931; s. Selmer A. and Esther D. (Dahl) R.; m. Betty Seiler, May 15, 1953; children— Scott, Stewart, Thomas BS, U. Mich., 1953, MS in Microbiology, 1954, M.H.A., 1962. Research asst. Detroit Inst. Cancer Research, 1954-60; asst. adminstr. Harper Hosp., Detroit, 1962-68, assoc. adminstr., 1968-72; exec. v.p. Iowa Meth. Med. Ctr., Des Moines, 1972-83, pres., 1983-93, Iowa Health Sys., 1993-95, Fine Wood Designs, 1996—. Avocations: golf, tennis, photography. Home: 18710 Poco Rio Dr Rio Verde AZ 85263-7108

RAMSEY, NANCY LOCKWOOD, retired nursing educator; b. LA, Jan. 26, 1943; d. Jack Thanke and Virginia Lee (Slaughter) Lockwood; m. Gordon S. Ramsey, June 24, 1972; children: Douglas Lockwood, Kathryn Anne. BSN, Loma Linda U., Calif., 1966; MSN, Duke U., Durham, NC, 1969; postgrad., Calif. State U., LA, 1974. Cert. clin. nurse specialist. Staff nurse various hosps., 1966—82, 1991—92, 1999; clin. instr. Azusa-Pacific U., Calif., 1984, 1991; instr. U. N.C., Chapel Hill, 1968—70, Calif. State U., LA, 1970—74; acting dir. nursing edn. Children's Hosp. L.A., 1974—75; prof. nursing L.A. City Coll., 1974—87, East L.A. Coll., Monterey Park, Calif., 1987—99; instr. lead tchr. Garden Grove, Calif., 2001; staff nurse Hospice Care Calif., 2001—03. Instr. pediatric nursing State Bd. Rev. Classes, L.A. and San Francisco, 1975-82; instr. statewide nursing program Calif. State U., Dominguez Hills, 1983-84 Author, editor: Child and Family Concepts of Nursing Practice, 1982, 87; contbr. articles to profl. jours. Home: 8840 Arroyo Azul St Las Vegas NV 89131-3902 Personal E-mail: nrrn@cox.net.

RAMSEY, PAUL GLENN, dean, internist; b. Pitts., 1949; MD, Harvard U., 1975. Diplomate Am. Bd. Internal Medicine. Intern Cambridge Hosp., 1975-76; resident in medicine Mass. Gen. Hosp., Boston, 1976-78, Univ. Wash., Seattle, 1980-81, fellow infectious diseases, 1978-80, prof., 1991—, chmn. dept. medicine, 1992-97, dean Sch. Med., 1997—; physician-in-chief Univ. Wash. Medicine, 1992-97, 1997—2006, CEO, exec. v.p. med. affairs, 2006—. Mem.: Inst. Medicine, AAAS, Assn. Am. Physicians, Am. Fedn. Clin. Rsch., ACP. Office: U Wash Sch Medicine PO Box 356350 Seattle WA 98195-6350 *

RAMSEY-GOLDMAN, ROSALIND, physician; b. NYC, Mar. 22, 1954; d. Abraham L. and Miriam (Colen) Goldman; m. Glenn Ramsey, June 29,1 975; children: Ethan Ramsey, Caitlin Ramsey. BA, Case We. Res. U., 1975, MD, 1978; MPH, U. Pitts., 1988, DPH, 1992. Med. resident U. Rochester, NY, 1978—81; chief resident Rochester Gen. Hosp., 1981—82; staff physician U. Health Svc., Rochester, 1982—83; rheumatology fellow U. Pitts., 1983—86, instr. medicine, 1986—87, asst. prof., 1987—91, co-dir. Lupus Treatment and Diagnostic Ctr., 1987—91; asst. prof. medicine Northwestern U., Chgo., 1991—96, assoc. prof. medicine, 1996—2001, prof. medicine, 2001—; soc. rsch. prof. Solovy Arthritis Rsch. Dir. Chgo. Lupus Registry, Northwestern U., Chgo., 1991—, chairperson Systemic Lupus Internat. Collaborating Clinics Group, 2003-08; program dir. Gen. Clin. Rsch. Ctr. at NCRR/NIH, 2005-08; dir. Clin. Rsch. Unit, NUCATS, NCRR/NIH, 2008- Contbr. rsch. articles to profl. jours. Recipient Finkelstein award Hershey (Pa.) Med. Ctr., 1986. Fellow ACP, Am. Coll. Rheumatology; mem. Soc. for Epidemiologic Rsch., Ctrl. Soc. Clin. Rsch. Office: Northwestern U Feinberg Sch Medicine McGaw Pavilion 240 E Huron Ste M-300 Chicago IL 60611 Office Phone: 312-503-8003. Business E-Mail: rgramsey@northwestern.edu.

RAMSHAW, BRUCE JOHN, surgeon; b. Hollywood, Fla., Feb. 22, 1963; s. John Gorton and Lynn Cecilia (Homeyer) R.; m. Linda Sue Mele, Nov. 2, 1996; 3 children. BS, U. Fla., 1985, MD, 1989. Intern, resident Ga. Bapt. Med. Ctr., Atlanta, 1989-94; attending surgeon Letton & Mason Surg. Group, Atlanta, 1994—. Mem. AMA, ACS, Soc. Gastrointestinal Endoscopic Surgeons, Soc. Critical Care Medicine, Southeastern Surg. Congress. Home: 1364 Clifton Rd NE # 124 Atlanta GA 30322-1059

RAN, TAO, orthopedist; b. China, Mar. 31, 1969; BS, Sun-Yet-San U. Med. Sci., 1993. Mem. Chinese Med. Assn., 1995—. Avocations: bridge, badminton. Office: 20 Xisi Rd Nantong Jiangsu 226001 China E-mail: nigetr007@yahoo.com.cn.

RANA, ANIL, pharmacist, researcher; b. Chandigarh, India, Mar. 14, 1979; PharmB, SBS PG Inst. Biomed. Scis. & Rsch., Dehradoon, India, 2001; PharmM, U. Inst. Pharm. Scis., Panjab U., Chandigarh, 2004. Rsch. assoc. Ranbaxy Labs. Ltd, R & D Ctr., Gurgaon, India, 2004—06, rsch. scientist, 2006—08, sr. rsch. scientist, 2008—. Recipient Global Appreciate award, Ranbaxy Labs. Ltd. Mem.: Almuni-SBS PG Inst. Biomed. Scis. & Rsch., Almuni-U. Inst. Pharm. Scis., Panjab U. Avocations: swimming, reading. Office: Ranbaxy Labs Ltd PDR Dept Gurgaon Haryana 122001 India E-mail: anilrana14@rediffmail.com.

RAND, A. BARRY (ADDISON BARRY RAND), retirement association executive; b. Washington, Nov. 5, 1944; s. Addison Penrod and Helen (Matthews) Rand; m. Donna Rand, 1990; 1 child, Allison 1 stepchild, Christopher. Attended, Rutgers U., NJ; BS in Mktg., Am. U., Washington, 1968; MBA, Stanford U., Calif., 1972, MA in Mgmt. Sci., 1973. Sales rep. Xerox Corp., 1968—70, regional sales rep., 1970—80, corp. dir. major account mktg., 1980—81, v.p. major account mktg. ops., 1981—82, v.p. field ops., 1983—84, v.p. Ea. ops., 1984—85, corp. v.p., 1985—86, sr. v.p., v.p. US mktg. group, 1986—92, exec. v.p. worldwide ops., 1992—99; chmn., CEO Avis Group Holdings, Inc., Garden City, NY, 1999—2001; non-exec. chmn. Aspect Comm., 2001—03; chmn., CEO Equitant Corp., 2003—05; CEO American Association Retired Persons (AARP), Washington, 2009—. Bd. dirs. Agilent Technologies Inc., 2000—, AT&T Wireless, 2001—03, Campbell Soup Co., 2005—. Bd. trustee Howard U., Washington. Recipient NAACP Image award, 1993; named to Nat. Sales Hall of Fame, 1993. Democrat. Office: AARP 601 E St NW Washington DC 20049 *

RAND, JOELLA MAE, retired nursing educator, counselor; b. Akron, Ohio, July 9, 1932; d. Harry S. and Elizabeth May (Miller) Halberg; m. Martin Rand (dec.); children: Craig, Debbi Stark. BSN, U. Akron, 1961, MEd in Guidance, 1968; PhD in Higher Edn. Adminstrn., Syracuse U., 1981. Lic. mental health counselor 2006. Staff nurse Akron Gen. Hosp., 1953-54; staff-head nurse-instr. Summit County Receiving, Cuyahoga Falls, Ohio, 1954-56; head nurse psychiat. unit Akron Gen. Hosp., 1956-57; instr. psychiatric nursing Summit County Receiving, Cuyahoga Falls, 1957-61; head nurse, in-service instr. Willard (N.Y.) State Hosp., 1961-62; asst. prof. Alfred (N.Y.) U., 1962-76, assoc. prof., assoc. dean, 1976-78, acting dean, 1978-79, dean, 1979-90, dean coll. profl. studies, 1990-91, prof. counseling, 1991-2000; ret., 2000. Cons. N.Y. State Regents Program for Non-Collegiate Sponsored Instrn., 1984; cons. collegiate programs N.Y. State Dept. Edn., 1985, Elmira Coll., 1991, U. Rochester, 1992-93; accreditation visitor Nat. League for Nursing, 1984-92; ednl. cons. Willard Psychiat. Hosp., 1992-93; mem. profl. practice exam. subcom. Regents Coll., 1990-95. Vol. Willard Drug Treatment Ctr., 1997—; bd. dirs. Williard Drug Treatment Ctr., Romulus Zoning Bd., 2002—; vol. Red Cross, 2003—, co-capt. disaster team, 2004—05; bd. dirs. Five Point Correctional Facility, Willard Drug Treatment Ctr. Recipient Tchg. Excellence award Alfred U., 1977, Mary E. Gladwin Outstanding Alumni award Akron U. Coll. Nursing, 1983, Alfred Alumni Friends award, 1989, Grand Marshall commencement Alfred U., 1993, Vol. of Yr. award Willard Drug Treatment Ctr., 1999, Named Outstanding Vol. WDTC, 2007-09, Cert. Appreciation, Seneca County Cmty. Svcs. Bd., 2005. Mem.: ACA (NAR rep. 2000—04, co-capt. disaster team Red Cross-Finger Lakes chpt. 2003—05, pres. NYCA 2005, Seneca County Med. Reserve Corps. 2005—), Genesee Valley Edn. Com. (chair 1984—86), Western N.Y. League Nursing (bd. dirs. 1991—93), Genesee Regional Consortium (v.p.), N.Y. State Coun. of Deans (treas. 1984—88), N.Y. State Counseling Assn. (v.p.-elect profl. svcs. 1995—96, v.p. profl. svcs. 1996—98, 1999—2000, pres. 2005—06), Sigma Theta Tau (treas. Alfred chpt. 1984—85). Avocations: boating, fishing, public speaking in areas of family and child abuse. Personal E-mail: drand@rochester.rr.com.

RAND, RHONDA, dermatologist; Grad., U. Calif., Harvard Med. Sch. Intern. Mt. Sinai Hosp., NY; resident Harvard Med. Sch.; asst. clin. prof. UCLA (Univ. of Calif. at LA); chief dermatology Cedars-Sinai Med. Ctr., 2005—08. Contbr. numerous published papers, articles for books on diseases of the skin, hair and nails. Mem. Dermatology Found. Named one of Best Doctors, LA Mag., LA Times. Mem.: LA Met. Dermatol. Soc., Am. Acad. of Dermatology, Am. Soc. of Dermatologic Surgery. Office: Laser and Skin Surgery Center Cosmetic and Medical Dermatology 436 N Roxbury Drive No 212 Beverly Hills CA 90210 Office Phone: 310-273-0467.

RAND, RICHARD PIERCE, plastic surgeon; b. San Diego, Mar. 25, 1955; AB, Stanford U.; MD, U. Mich., 1981. Cert. Am. Bd. Plastic Surgery, Am. Bd. Surgery, Nat. Bd. Med. Examiners. Resident in surgery Tufts-New Eng. Med. Ctr., Boston, 1981—86; resident in plastic reconstructive surgery Emory U., 1986—89; fellow in craniofacial surgery fellow U. Miami, 1989; chief of plastic surgery U. Wash. Med. Ctr., 1990—2000; owner, dir. Northwest Ctr. Aesthetic Plastic Surgery, Bellevue, Wash. Examiner Am. Bd. Plastic Surgery. Recipient Sr. Resident Chmn.'s award in Gen. Surgery, Tufts-New Eng. Med. Ctr.; named one of Top100 Golf Doctors in Am., Golf Digest, 2006; named to Best Doctors in America, Seattle's Best Doctors, America's Top Doctors, America's Top Surgeons, America's Top Physicians, America 's Top Cosmetic Doctors and Dentists. Fellow: Am. Coll. Surgeons; mem.: Wash. State Med. Assn., Ralph A. Deterling Surg. Soc., Maurice J. Jurkiewicz Soc., King County Med. Soc., Royal & Ancient Assn. Plastic Surgeons, Seattle Surg. Soc., Wash. Soc. Plastic Surgeons (Golden Hands/Golden Scalpel award), Northwest Soc. Plastic Surgeons, Am. Soc. Maxillofacial Surgeons, Am. Soc. Plastic Surgeons, Am. Soc. Aesthetic Plastic Surgery, Am. Soc. Plastic Surgeons, Phi Beta Kappa. Office: Northwest Ctr for Aesthetic Plastic Surgery Ste 630 1135 116th Ave NE Bellevue WA 98004 Office Phone: 866-616-6183. Office Fax: 425-455-0921.

RANDALL, LESLIE MICHELLE, medical educator; b. Kty., Feb. 14, 1974; MD, U. Louisville Sch. Medicine, 2001, degree in Ob-gyn, 2005. Diplomate Nat. Bd. Med. Examiners. Gynecologist oncologist, asst. prof. UCI Med. Ctr., 2005—. Office: Dept Ob-Gyn Divsn Gynecologic Oncology University Calif Irvine UCI Med Ctr 101 The City Dr Blog 56 Ste 260 Orange CA 92868 Office Phone: 714-456-7356. Office Fax: 714-456-6632. Business E-Mail: irandall@uci.edu.

RANDALL, NEIL WARREN, gastroenterologist; b. White Plains, NY, Mar. 24, 1957; s. Leroy Bruce and Libby Cynthia (Brandt) R.; m. Linda Ilene Zell, Oct. 31, 1992. BA, U. Va., 1978; MD, U. Md., 1983. Diplomate Am. Bd. Internal Medicine with subspecialty in gastroenterology, geriat. Resident in internal medicine Ochsner Clinic, New Orleans, 1983-86; fellow in gastroenterology Tufts U., Boston, 1986-88; staff gastroenterologist Cleve. Clinic Fla., Fort Lauderdale, 1988-92, Geisinger Clinic, Danville, Pa., 1992-97, Pa. State Geisinger Health Sys., Danville, 1997-98; med. dir. gastrointestinal endoscopy Geisinger Health Sys., 1999-2000; gastroenterologist Gastroenterology Group of Naples, 2001—. Fellow ACP, Am. Coll. Gastroenterology; mem. Am. Soc for Gastroent. Endoscopy. Avocations: theater, travel, wine. Office: Gasterenterology Group of Naples 1064 Goodlette-Frank Rd Naples FL 34102-5449 Office Phone: 239-649-1186.

RANDALL, PETER, retired plastic surgeon; b. Phila., Mar. 29, 1923; s. Alexander and Edith Tilghman (Kneedler) R.; m. Rose Gordon Johnson, May 1, 1948; children: Deborah K., Peter G., Julia B., Susanna T. BA, Princeton U., 1944; MD, Johns Hopkins U., 1946; MS (hon.), U. Pa., 1969. Diplomate Am. Bd. Plastic Surgery. Intern Union Meml. Hosp., Balt., 1946—47; asst. resident in surgery Hosp. of U. of Pa., Phila., 1949—50; fellow in plastic surgery Barnes Hosp.-St. Louis Childrens Hosp., 1950—52, resident in plastic surgery, 1952—53; asst. instr. plastic surgery Washington U., St. Louis, 1950—53; from asst. prof. to assoc. prof. plastic surgery U. Pa. Hosp., Phila., 1953—69, prof. plastic surgery, 1969—, emeritus prof. plastic surgery; chief div. plastic surgery sch. medicine U. Pa., Phila., 1979—87; ret., 1994. Sr. surgeon Children's Hosp. Phila., 1965—. Contbr. articles to profl. jours. Pres. Plastic Surgery Edn. Found., 1972-73. Lt. (j.g.) USNR, 1947-49. Fellow: ACS (bd. govs., chmn. 1982—84, 1st v.p. 1985—86), Am. Assn. Plastic Surgeons (hon. Clinician of Yr. award 1987, disting. fellow 1994); mem.: AMA, Am. Cleft Palate Assn. (pres. 1965—66, Honors award 1986), Plastic Surgery Rsch. Coun. (founder, chmn. 1964—65), Phila. Acad. Surgery, Phila. County Med. Soc., Northea. Soc. Plastic Surgery (founder), Am. Surg. Assn., Coll. Physicians of Phila., Am. Soc. Plastic Surgeons (pres. 1978—79, Spl. Achievement award 1987), Am. Bd. Plastic Surgery (vice-chmn. 1976—77), Am. Cleft Palate Ednl. Found. (founder, pres. 1972—73), Robert H. Ivy Soc. (founder, pres. 1966—67), Halsted Soc., Sigma Xi.

RANDAZZO, MARISA R., psychologist; d. Hilary Phillip and Susan Hilborn Reddy; m. Robert Salvatore Randazzo, May 15, 2004. BA in Psychology and Religion, Williams Coll., 1989; MA in Psychology, Princeton U., 1993, PhD in Psychology, 1995. Chief rsch. psychologist US Secret Svc., Washington, 1996—2004; sr. expert Bus. Intelligence Advisors, Boston, 2004—06; pres. Threat Assessment Resources Internat., Reno, 2006—; mng. ptnr. Sigma Threat Mgmt. Assoc., 2010—. Editl. bd. Jour. Threat Assessment, 2001—. Contbr. articles. Recipient Recognition award, US Secret Svc., 1998—2004, Bicentennial Medal Recipient, Williams Coll., 2005; fellow, Soc. Psychol. Study Social Issues, Washington, 1995—96. Mem.: APA, Am. Psychology-Law Soc. (program chair 1998—2000). Achievements include research in American school shooters; preventing violence in schools; co-authoring a federal model of school threat assessment credited in the media and law enforcement with preventing school attacks. Office Fax: 775-424-6687. Business E-Mail: mrr@threatresources.com.

RANDOLPH, LINDA A., medical association administrator; b. Washington, Mar. 3, 1941; d. Oscar Horace Randolph and Marie Louise Fernandez. BS in zoology, Howard U., 1962, MD, 1967; MPH in maternal and child health, U. Calif., Berkeley, 1971; DHL (hon.), SUNY, Albany, 2009. Intern in internal medicine and pediat. Harlem Hosp. Ctr., NYC, 1967—78, resident in pediat., 1968—70; dir. health services, Project Head Start Dept. Health and Human Services, Washington, 1972—79; assoc. state health commr. for NYC affairs NY State Dept. Health, 1980—83, dir. office of pub. health, 1983—91; faculty SUNY Albany Sch. Pub. Health; exec. dir. Task Force on Meeting the Needs of Young Children Carnegie Corp. of NY, 1991—94; clin. prof. cmty. medicine, pediat. and psychiatry Mt. Sinai Sch. Medicine, NYC, 1991; dir. Nat. Women's Resource Ctr. Substance Abuse and Mental Health, 1995—99; co-chief exec. officer DC Developing Families Ctr., Washington, 1999—2002, pres. and CEO, 2003—. Recipient Haven Emerson award for Disting. Svc., Pub. Health Assn. NYC, 1983, Leadership award, Westchester Black Women's Polit. Caucus, 1987, Disting. Svc. award, NY State Fedn. Profl. Health Educators, 1988, Cmty. Svc. award, Greater Harlem C. of C., 1994, Martha May Eliot award for Exceptional Health Services to Mothers and Children, Am. Pub. Health Assn., 2001. Mem.: Inst. Medicine, NY Acad. Medicine, Alpha Omega Alpha. Office: DC Developing Families Ctr 801 17th St NE Washington DC 20002-7200 Office Phone: 202-398-2007. Office Fax: 202-398-2027.

RANE, ANDERS JAN, pharmacologist, educator; b. Stockholm, July 4, 1943; s. Torsten B. and May B.M. (Ohlsson) R.; m. Kristina A. Erichs, Apr. 26, 1945; children: Fredrik, Mattias, Johanna. BMed, Karolinska Inst., Stockholm, 1964, Lic. Medicine, 1969, MD, 1973. Cert. specialist in clin. pharmacology. Dep. head clin. pharmacology Karolinska Univ. Hosp., Karolinska Inst., Stockholm, 1976-85; prof., head pharmacotherapeutic unit, divsn. drugs Nat. Bd. Health & Welfare, 1985-90; prof. clin. pharmacology Uppsala U., 1990-98; head dept. clin. pharmacology Univ. Hosp., Uppsala, 1990-98; prof. clin. pharmacology Karolinska Inst., Stockholm, 1998—; chmn. dept. clin. pharmacology Karolinska Univ. Hosp., Sweden, 1999—2010. USPHS internat. postdoctoral rsch. fellow Vanderbilt U., Nashville, 1975-76; vis. prof. Children's Hosp., Columbus, Ohio, 1984, Case Western Res. U., Cleve., 1987; rsch. guest Molecular Pharmacology Group, Imperial Cancer Rsch. Fund, Edinburgh UK, 1992; mem. WHO Expert Adv. Panel on Cancer; mem. Coun. of the Swedish Cancer Soc.; chmn. of sect. on drugs Swedish Assn. of Med. Scis., 1982-84. Contbr. articles to profl. jours. Recipient Poulsson medal, Norwegian Soc. Pharmacol. Toxicology, 2002. Fellow: Swedish Assn. Med. Scis. (Trafvenfelts award 1978); mem.: European Assn. Clin. Pharmacology and Therapeutics (councillor 1999—2007), Swedish Assn. Clin. Pharmacology (chmn. 1996—99), Internat. Union Pharmacology (councillor divsn. clin. pharmacology 1989—92, treas. 1992—2000), European Soc. Devel. Pharmacology (sec. gen. 2001—04, pres. 2004—06, bd. dirs.). Avocations: ornithology, music. Office: Karolinska Inst Karolinska U Hosp Dept Clin Pharmacology SE-14186 Stockholm Sweden Office Phone: 46 8 58581051. Business E-Mail: anders.rane@ki.se.

RANGARAJ, DHARANIPATHY, medical physicist clinician scientist entertainer educator; b. Erode, Tamilnadu, India, Mar. 7, 1980; Degree in Nuc. Engring., Med. Physics, U. Mo., Columbia, 2004; MBA, Wash. U., St. Louis, 2011. Diplomate Am. Bd. Radiology, 2009. Grad. rsch. asst. U. Mo., 2001—04, adj. asst. prof., 2009; lectr., radiation oncology Ind. U., 2004—05; med. physics resident Wash. U., 2005—07, med. physicist, instr. radiation oncology, 2008—; asst. prof. radiation oncology U. Tex. Southwestern, Dallas, 2007—08. Bd. dir. rep. Am. Assn. Med. Physicist, 2009—. Rsch. grant, Varian Med. Sys. Mem.: Am. Coll. Med. Physicist, Am. Assn. Med. Dosimetrist, Am. Assn. Therapeutic Radiology, Am. Assn. Physics Medicine. Avocations: tennis, chess, cricket. Office: 4921 Parkview Plz Campus Box 8224 Saint Louis MO 63043 Business E-Mail: drangaraj@radonc.wustl.edu.

RANGARAJAN, SUNAD, physician; b. Bangalore, Karnataka, India, May 26, 1978; s. Rangarajan Ramaswami and Vani Rangarajan; m. Ramya Hulikul Ramachandra Rao, Apr. 23, 2006. MBBS, Kempegowda Inst. Med. Scis., Bangalore, 2002; MD in Internal Medicine, St. John's Med. Coll. Hosp., Bangalore, 2005. Diplomate in internal medicine Nat. Bd. Examinations, New Delhi, India, 2006. Postgrad. rschr. internal medicine St. John's Med. Coll. Hosp., 2002—05, lectr. med. ICU, 2006, lectr. divsn. respiratory diseases, dept. medicine, 2006—08; resident, internal medicine Maimonides Med. Ctr., Brooklyn, NY, 2008—. Recipient Elio Lugaresi award for Sleep Rsch., World Assn. Sleep Medicine, 2007. Mem.: Assn. Physicians India (life). Hindu. Avocations: music, chess, philosophy. Home: 1016 50th St Apt 3K Brooklyn NY 11219 Office: Maimonides Med Ctr 4802 Tenth Ave Brooklyn NY 11219 Personal E-mail: sunadil@yahoo.com. Business E-Mail: srangarajan@maimonidesmed.org.

RANGNEKAR, VIVEK MANGESH, molecular biologist, researcher; b. Bombay, Dec. 17, 1955; s. Mangesh Vithal and Sanjivani (Dewoolkar) R.; m. Vidya Vivek Varsha Kulkarni, May 15, 1981; children: Vidyuta, Viraj. MSc, U. Bombay, 1979, PhD, 1983. Postdoctoral fellow U. Chgo., 1983-86, asst. prof., 1988-91; rsch. assoc. Rush Med. Ctr., Chgo., 1986-87; asst. prof. U. Ky., Lexington, 1992-96, assoc. prof., 1996-99, prof., 1999—2004, assoc. dir., Markey Cancer Ctr., 2004—, Alfred Cohen endowed chair oncology rsch., 2005—. Cons. NIH/NCI and Dept. of Def. Contbr. articles to profl. jours. Mem. AAAS, Am. Soc. Microbiology. Achievements include identification of Par-4 gene that causes cell death; development of a cancer resistant mouse. Office: U Ky 800 Rose St Lexington KY 40536-0001 Business E-Mail: vmrang01@email.uky.edu.

RANHEIM, ERIK A., pathologist, educator; b. Minn., Oct. 10, 1966; BA, U. Pa., 1984; MD, U. Minn., PhD, 1996. Clin. instr. Stanford U. Sch. Medicine, 1999—2003; assoc. prof. U. Wis. Sch. Medicine and Pub. Health, 2003—. Office: 600 Highland Ave K4/432 CSC Madison WI 53792-8550 Business E-Mail: earanheim@wisc.edu.

RANIOLO, ROBERT JOHN, surgeon, educator; MD, Univ. Autonoma de Guadalajara, 1981. Diplomate Am. Bd. Surgery. Intern Misericordia Hosp.; chief resident in gen. surgery Lincoln Hosp. and Mental Ctr., 1983—88; fellow Internat. Coll. Surgeons; asst. attendant dept. surgery Dobbs Ferry Hosp.; asst. prof. dept. gen. surgery NY Med. Coll.; chief dept. gen. surgery Phelps Meml. Hosp. Ctr. Fellow: ACS; mem.: Soc. of Breast Surgeons, NY Met. Breast Cancer Group Inc., Westchester Surgical Soc, Med. Soc. of the State of NY, Surgical Soc. of the NY Med. Coll., Soc. of Am. Gastrointestinal Endoscopic Surgeons. Office: Phelps Memorial Hospital 701 N Broadway Tarrytown NY 10591 Office Phone: 914-366-3000. Office Fax: 914-366-1314.

RANJAN, MANISH, neurosurgeon, educator; b. India, May 5, 1976; MBBS, Patna Med. Coll., 2000; MCh, NIMHANS, 2007. Chief resident NIMHANS, 2007—08, asst. prof. neurosurgery, 2008—. Recipient Dr. J. Mishra Gold medal, Patna Med. Coll.; Nat. Merit scholarship, State Govt., Neurosurgeon Traveling fellowship, World Fedn. Neurosurg. Socs. Mem.: Congress Neurol. Surgeons, Indian Soc. Stereotactic & Functional Neurosurgery, Bangalore Neurol. Soc., Neurol. Soc. India. Office: Dept Neurosurgery NIMHANS Hosp Bangalore Karnataka 560029 India E-mail: drmanishranjan@gmail.com.

RANNEY, RICHARD RAYMOND, periodontist educator, researcher, dean; b. Atlanta, July 11, 1939; s. Russell Ballou and Maureen Joan (Bannon) R.; m. Beverly Anne Toton, June 10, 1961 (div.); children: Christine Marie, Kathleen Anne; m. Patricia Marie DeNoto, Feb. 22, 1969; children: Maureen Frances, Russell Christopher. DDS, U. Iowa, 1963; MS, U. Rochester, 1969; D (hon.), U. Buenos Aires, 1995. Asst. prof. periodontology U. Oreg., 1969-72; assoc. prof. periodontics Va. Commonwealth U., Richmond, Va., 1972-78, prof., 1978-86, dir. grad. periodontics, 1972-76, chmn. dept. periodontics, 1974-77, asst. dean rsch. and grad. affairs, 1977-84, asst. dean rsch., 1984-86; dir. Clin. Rsch. Ctr. Periodontal Diseases, Richmond, 1978-86; prof. Sch. Dentistry U. Ala., Birmingham, 1986-91, dean, 1986-89; prof. U. Md., Balt., 1991—2005, prof. emeritus, 2005, dean, 1991—2002; Sr. Policy fellow Am. Dental Edn. Assn., 2003—04, Gies Edn. fellow, 2004—05; dir. Eastman Dental Ctr. Found., Inc., 2005—; sr. cons. Acad. for Academic Leadership, 2006—. Contbr. chpts. to books, articles to profl. jours. With USPHS, 1963-66. Nat. Inst. Dental Rsch. grantee, 1970-86. Fellow: AAAS, Am. Coll. Dentists, Internat. Coll. Dentists; mem.: ADA, Am. Dental Edn. Assn. (Presdl. citation 2005), Am. Assn. Dental Rsch. (pres. 1990—91), Internat. Assn. Dental Rsch. (pres. 1995—96, basic rsch. periodontology award 1985), Am. Acad. Periodontology, Omicron Kappa Upsilon, Sigma Xi. Home Phone: 410-923-1049. Personal E-mail: pranney3@comcast.net.

RANTANEN, TAPIO T., dermatologist; b. Tampere, Finland, Dec. 28, 1946; s. Lasse Aulis Rantanen and Hilkka Tellervo Pennanen; MD, U. Bern, 1973. Lic. specialist in dermatology and venereology Nat. Health Adminstrn., Finland, 1980. Physician Health Ctr. Hämeenkyrö; resident Helsinki U. Ctrl. Hosp.; clin. instr. Tampere U., 1979—80; chief physician Itä-Savo Hosp. Dist., Savonlinna, Finland, 1981—93, Päijät Häme Hosp. Dist., Lahti, Finland, 1993—2010. Bd. dir. Infoderm Oy, Tampere, Finland. Author: (computer application) Infoderm. Recipient 1st class Knight decoration, Order of Finland's Lion, 2004. Mem.: European Acad. Dermatology and Venereology (bd. dirs. 2007—), European Bd. Dermatology-Venereology (treas. 2000—05, bd. dirs. 1996—2007), Finnish Dermatol. Soc. (treas. 1991—2003, pres. 2003—06). Office: Ihopiste Hämeenkatu 25B Tampere 33200 Finland Office Fax: 358 3 222 8012. Business E-Mail: tapio.rantanen@fimnet.fi.

RANU, HARCHARAN SINGH, biomedical scientist, administrator, orthopaedic biomechanics educator; b. Lyallpur, India; came to U.S., 1976; s. Jodh Singh and Harnam Kaur R. BSc, De Montfort U., Eng., 1963; MSc, U. Surrey, Guilford, Eng., 1967, Cambridge U., Eng., 1972; PhD, Middlesex Hosp. Med. Sch. and U. Westminster, London, 1975; diploma, MIT, 1984. Chartered engr., scientist, Eng. Med. scientist Nat. Inst. Med. Rsch. of the Med. Rsch. Coun., London, 1967-70; rsch. fellow Middlesex Hosp. Med. Sch. and Poly. of Cen. London, 1971-76; rsch. scientist Plastics Rsch. Assn. of Great Britain, Shawbury, Eng., 1977; asst. prof. Wayne State U., Detroit, 1977-81; prof. biomed. engring./orthopaedic biomechanics biomaterials La. Tech. U., Ruston, 1982—; prof., chmn. dept. biomechanics N.Y. Coll. Osteo. Medicine, Old Westbury, 1989-93; dir. tng. Rehab. R&D Ctr., 1983-85; mem. La. Tech. U. Libr. Com., 1983-85; chmn. design competition Assn. Biomed. Engrs.; mem. steering com. So. Biomed. Engring. Confs., 1983—; chmn. tech. in health care conf. U. Cambridge, 1985; chmn. Internat. Symposium on Bioengring., Calcutta, India, 1985; dir. orthopaedic biomechanics rsch. labs., staff Nassau County Med. Ctr., Long Island, 1989—; prof., exec. asst. to pres., and dir. doctoral program Life U., Marietta, Ga., 1993—; pres. Am. Orthop. Biomechanics Rsch. Inst., Atlanta, 1997—; prof. Coll. Applied Med. Scis., King Saud U., Riyadh; cons. orthop. dept. Coll. Medicine. Biomed. engring. faculty com. La. Tech. U., faculty com., rsch. awards com., grad. studies com., grad. faculty, acad. bd. dirs; vis. scientist Dryburn Hosp., Durham, Eng., 1985-87, cons., 1988—; vis. prof. U. Istanbul, 1982, Lab. de Recherch Orthopediques, Paris, 1985—, Kings Coll. Med. Sch. U. London, 1989—, Indian Inst. Tech., New Delhi, Postgrad Inst. Med. Edn. and Rsch., Chandigarh, India, 1989—, Polytech. Ctrl. London, 1991—, U. Buenos Aires, Pontific Cath. U. Chile, Fed. U. Rio de Janeiro; adj. prof. Coll. Physicians and Surgeons Columbia U., NYC, 1988—, Inst. Biol. Physics USSR Acad. Sci., Moscow, 1990, NY Coll. Podiatric Medicine, 1991—, CUNY, 1992—; cons. Lincoln Gen. Hosp., Ruston, La., 1982-85, La. State U. Med. Ctr., Shreveport, 1982—, St. Luke's and Roosevelt Hosp. Ctr., NY, 1988—, Foot Clinics N., 1991—, Vets. Affairs Med. Ctr., NY, 1992—, others; media resource svc. Inst. Pub. Info., NY, 1989—; med. scientist, cons. NATO, 1982—; presenter, lectr. in field; external examiner for doctoral candidates All India Inst. Med. Scis., New Delhi, Indian Inst. Tech., New Delhi, Banaras Hindu U., Varanasi, India, 1994; prof. U. Surrey, 2009; pres. Am. Orthop. Biomechanics Rsch. Inst., Atlanta, 1997; rsch. award com. mem. Am. Coll. Sports Medicine. Author: Rheological Behavior of Articular Cartiliage Under Tensile Loads, 1967, Effects of Ionizing Radiation on the Mechanical Properties of Skin, 1975, Effects of Fractionated Doses of X-irradiation on the Mechanical Properties of Skin--A Long Term Study, 1980, Effects of Ionizing Radiation on the Structure & Physical Properties of the Skin, 1983, 3-D Model of Vertebra for Spinal Surgery, 1985, Application of Carbon Fibers in Orthopaedic Surgery, 1985, Relation Between Metal Corrision & Electrical Polarization, 1989, The Distribution of Stresses in the Human Lumbar Spine, 1989, Medical Devices & Orthopaedic Implants in the United States, 1989, Spinal Surgery by Modeling, 1989, Multipoint Determination of Pressure-Volume Curves in Human Intervertebral Discs, 1993, Evaluation of Volume-Pressure Relationship in Lumbar Discs Using Model and Experimental Studies, 1994, A Mechanism of Laser Nuclectomy, 1994, Microminiaturization in Laser Surgery in Vivo Intradiscal Pressure Measurements in Lumbar Intervertebral Discs, 1994, An Experimental and Mathematical Simulation of Fracture of Human Bone Due to Jumping, 1994; editor The Lower Extremity, 1993—; guest editor IEEE Engring. in Medicine & Biology, 1991; mem. editl. bd. Med. Instrumentation, 1988—, Jour. Biomed. Instrumentation & Tech., 1988—, Jour. Med. Engring. & Tech., 1989—, Jour. Med. Design & Material, 1990—, Jour. Long-Term Effects Med. Implants, 1991—, Biomed. Sci. & Tech., 1991—, Health & Fittness, 2007, rsch. award com. Am. Coll. Sports Medicine, 2009; reviewer Jour. Biomechanics, 1981—, Clin. Biomechanics, 1984—, Jour. Biomed. Engring., 1981, Phys. Therapy, 1990—, IEEE Biomed. Transactions, 1991—, Jour. Engring. in Medicine, 1989—; contbr. articles to profl. jours. Faculty advisor India Students Assn. Wayne State U., 1980. Recipient Edwin Tate award U. Surrey, 1968, Third Internat. Olympic Com. World Congress On Sprots Scis. award, Atlanta, 1995; numerous rsch. grants. Fellow ASME (bioengring. com. 1990—, award L.I. chpt. 1991, peer reviewer 2010), Biol. Engring. Soc. (London, President's prize 1984), Instn. Mech. Engrs. (chmn. revv. bd. for corp. memberships, James Clayton awards 1974-76), Inst. Physics and Engring. in Medicine; mem. AAAS, Am. Soc. Biomechanics (edn. com. 1990—), Orthopaedic Rsch. Soc., Am. Coll. Sports Medicine, Biomed. Engring. Soc., India Assn., India Assn. North La., Sci. Coun. Eng. (chartered scientist). Sikh. Achievements include research in microfracture simulation of human vertebrae under compressive loading, laserectomy of the human nucleus pulposus and its effect on the intradiscal pressure, pressure-volume relation in human intervertebral discs, in vitro and in vivo intradiscal pressure measurements before and after laserectomy of the human nucleus pulposus, gait analysis of a diabetic foot, bioengineering in the millennium, bioengineering-building the future of biology and medicine, bioengineering the cutting edge of biology and medicine in the millennium, in vivo micro-fracture simulation in Indian Olympic field hockey players, relief from low-back pain in sports by infusion of saline into the human nucleus pulposus and establishing the pressure-volume relationship, clinical applications of bioinstrumentation for better health, fifth IOC World Congress on sports sciences, micro-fracture simulation in tennis players, human gait analysis normal and pathological, simulation of micro-fracture injury in female gymnasts-an in vivo study, pattern recognition in human gait, identification of ethnicity from human gait; micro-fracture injury simulation in pole vaulting and female gymnasts; 3-D simulation of drop in intradiscal pressure in spinal discs due to laserectomy; Ranu's principle and laserectomy to relieve low back pain; Ranu's cumulative gait effect phenomenon, invivo micro-fracture simulation in skiers; 3-D foot pressure measurements in normal and diabetic persons; normal and abnormal gait of successive steps with miniature triaxial load cells; gait analysis of amputees initally and one month later for successive steps; stress-fracture simulationi n ski jumpers, the effect of ovariectomy on antioxidant system of bone, micro-fracture simulation in vivo in human bone, amputees gait analyses for sucssessive steps, viscoelastic properties of the human spinal disc, normal and prevention of pedal sequelae in diabetic patients a 3D pattern analysis, ovariec tomy and its antioxidative effects on bone. Office: Life Univ Sch Grad Studies Marietta GA 30060 Personal E-mail: profranu@yahoo.com.

RAO, AKKINEPALLI BADRI NARAYAN, physician, educator; b. Hyderabad, India, Oct. 7, 1923; arrived in Australia, 1973; s. Sita Ram and Rama Chudamma (Rangaraju) R.; m. Norah Janet Gardner, Mar. 22, 1958; children: Priti, Nandita. FSc, Osmania U., 1942, B Medicine B Surgery, 1947. House surgeon medicine, surgery and obstetrics, Hyderabad, 1948; house surgeon ear nose and throat Royal Nat. Ear Nose and Throat Hosp., London, 1951-52; registrar ear nose and throat Birmingham and Midland Ear Nose and Throat Hosp., 1952-54; ear nose and throat surgeon Osmania Gen. Hosp. and Med. Coll., Hyderabad, 1954-67, prof. ear nose and throat, 1958-73; cons. ear nose and throat surgeon Birmingham Regional Hosp., Eng., 1967-69; sr. ear, nose and throat surgeon Royal Darwin (Australia) Hosp., 1973-97, emeritus ear, nose and throat cons.; emeritus prof. ear, nose and throat Osmania Med. Coll., Hyderabad, India. Fgn. collaborant Acta Otolaryngologica, Stockholm; vis. ear, nose and throat specialist Mackay Base Hosp., Queensland, 1997—; lectr., presenter in field. Contbr. articles to profl. publs., chpts. to books. Recipient Citizen of Australia award Australian Day Coun., 1996, Order of Australia, 1997; fellow Internat. Coll. Surgeons, 1957-67. Fellow Royal Soc. Medicine; mem. Royal Commonwealth Soc. Australia (life), Australian Med. Assn. (mem. exec. coun. N.T. sect.), Neuro Equilibriomatic Soc., Prosper Meniere Soc., Assn. Otolaryngologists of India (life), Otolaryngol. Soc. Australia. Avocations: travel, teaching. Home: 57 Pamela St Mount Waverley VIC 3149 Australia Office: Royal Darwin Hosp Casuarina Darwin 0811 Australia Office Phone: 61 3 9560 8595.

RAO, DABEERU C. (D.C. RAO), epidemiologist, educator; b. Apr. 6, 1946; came to U.S., 1972; naturalized. s. Ramarao Patnaik and Venkataratnam (Raghupatruni) R.; m. Sarada Patnaik, 1974; children: Ravi, Lakshmi. BS in Stats., Indian Statis. Inst., Calcutta, 1967, MS, 1968, PhD, 1971. Rsch. fellow U. Sheffield, England, 1971-72; asst. geneticist U. Hawaii, Honolulu, 1972-78, assoc. geneticist, 1978-80; dir. divsn. biostats. Washington U. Med. Sch., 1980—, assoc. prof. St. Louis, 1980-82, prof. depts. biostats., psychiatry and genetics, 1982—. Adj. prof. math., 1982—. Author: A Source Book for Linkage in Man, 1979, Methods in Genetic Epidemiology, 1983, Genetic Epidemiology of Coronary Heart Disease, 1984; editor-in-chief Genetic Epidemiology jour., 1984-91; contbr. over 400 articles to profl. jours. Grantee NIH, 1978—; Telugu Assn. N.Am., 1995 Mem. Am. Statis. Assn., Am. Soc. Human Genetics, Internat. Genetic Epidemiology Soc. (pres. 1996), Behavior Genetics Assn., Soc. Epidemiol. Rsch., Biomed. soc. Office: Washington U Sch Medicine Divsn Biostats Box 8067 660 S Euclid Ave Saint Louis MO 63110-1010 E-mail: rao@wubios.wustl.edu.

RAO, KIRAN V., medical educator; b. Warren, Mich., Dec. 1, 1973; MD, J.S.S. Med. Coll., 2003. Asst. prof. UMDNJ U. Hosp., 2009—. Fellow: ACG. Home: 2004 Deerfield Dr Edison NJ 08820 Personal E-mail: kye73@yahoo.com.

RAO, KUMAR PRASANNA, dentist; b. Mangalore, May 8, 1973; BDS, Karnataka U., 1998; MDS, Rajiv Gandhi U. Health Scis., 2005. Dentist Yenepoya U., 1998—, oral and maxillofacial radiologist, 2005—. Mem.: Indian Dental Assn. Avocation: music. Office: University Rd Deralakatte Mangalore Karnataka 575018 India E-mail: drjpkrao@gmail.com.

RAO, K.V.R. MOHAN See KOTTAMASU, MOHAN

RAO, NAREN P., psychiatrist; b. Kolar, India, Apr. 30, 1981; MBBS, Sri Devaraj Urs Med. Coll., Kolar, 2004; MD in Psychiatry, NIMH and Neurosci., Bangalore, 2008. Sr. resident, psychiatry NIMH and Neurosci., 2008—. Rsch. scientist Cognitive Neurobiology Lab. NIMHANS, Bangalore, 2008—11. Contbr. articles to profl. jours. Recipient Aristotle's Rsch. award, Internat. Soc. Brain and Behaviour, Internat. Young Investigator award, Internat. Congress Schizophrenia Rsch., Tilak Venkoba Rao Oration award, Indian Psychiat. Soc., Young Scientists award, World Fedn. Socs. Biol. Psychiatry; Young Investigator Travel fellowship, Schizophrenia Internat. Rsch. Soc. Mem.: Indian Psychiat. Soc. Avocations: travel, theater. Office: Dept Psychiatry NIMHANS Hosur Rd Bangalore Karnataka 560029 India Personal E-mail: docnaren@gmail.com.

RAO, NARSING A., ophthalmologist, pathologist, educator; arrived in U.S., 1968; MD, Osmania U., Hyderabad, India, 1967. Cert. Am. Bd. Ophthalmology, Am. Bd. Pathology. Prof. ophthalmology and pathology U. So. Calif., LA, 1983—; dir. uveitis and ophthalmic pathology Doheny Eye Inst., LA, 1983—. Contbr. articles to profl. jours. Pres. Internat. Uveitis Soc., Bethesda, Md., 2000—05. Recipient Zimmerman Gold (Bietti) medal, Am. Acad. Ophthalmology, 2003; grantee, NIH, 1985—2008. Mem.: Am. Ophthal. Soc. Achievements include research in free radical biology. Office: Doheny Eye Inst 1450 San Pablo St Los Angeles CA 90033 Office Fax: 323-442-6634. Business E-Mail: nrao@usc.edu.

RAO, PRABAKAR KUMAR, ophthalmologist, educator; b. India, Feb. 28, 1968; BA, UCSD, 1991; MD, USC, 1995. Assoc. prof. Wash. U., St. Louis, 2006—. Fellow: Am. Acad. Ophthalmology. Office: Campus Box 8096 660 South Euclid Ave Saint Louis MO 63110 Business E-Mail: rao@vision.wustl.edu.

RAO, PULIVARTHI, medical educator; b. Ongole, Andhra Pradesh, India, July 5, 1958; PhD, Nagarjuna U., 1987. Sr. rsch. scientist Meml. Sloan Ketterin Cancer Ctr., 1998—99; asst. prof. Baylor Coll. Medicine, 1999—2008, assoc. prof., 2008—. Recipient Rsch. award, Multiple Myeloma Rsch. Found. Mem.: Am. Assn. Cancer Rsch., Am. Assn. Advancement Sci., Am. Soc. Human Genetics. Avocation: stamp collecting/philately. Home: 2308 Bending Spring Dr Pearland TX 77584 Business E-Mail: phrao@txccc.org.

RAO, RAMISETTI NAGESWARA, research scientist; b. Machilipatnam, Jan. 15, 1955; MSc, Osmania U., 1983, PhD, 1990. Scientist Indian Inst. Chem. Tech., 1978—. Recipient Rsch. award, Indian Drug Manufacture Assn., 1987, Best Publ. award, IICT, 1990, 1992, 1994, Husain Zaheer Meml. award, Indian Inst. Chem. Tech.; German Academic Exch. fellowship, DAAD. Mem.: Oil Tech. Assn. India, Indian Soc. Analytical Scientists, A.P. Pollution Control Bd. Office: IICT Tarnaka Hyderabad Andhra Pradesh 500007 India Business E-Mail: rnrao@iict.res.in.

RAO, SESHU, physician; b. India, Apr. 20, 1979; MBBS, Adichunchanagiri Inst. Med. Scis., 2003; MD, U. Mo. Kans. City, 2006. Cardiovasc. disease fellow U. Mo. Kans. City, 2009—. Recipient Excellence award, U. Mo. Kans. City; named Internal Medicine Cons. of Yr., 2008. Mem.: ACP, Heart Rhythm Soc., Am. Heart Assn., Am. Coll. Cardiology, Alpha Omega Alpha. Avocations: tennis, golf. Home: 21601 W 53rd Ter Shawnee KS 66226 Personal E-mail: chepseshu@gmail.com.

RAO, SHIVA KUMAR, surgeon, educator; b. Poona, India, Feb. 15, 1948; MD, Karnatak Med. Coll., Hubli, India, 1973; MS, U. Bombay, 1978. Intern Karnatak Med. Coll. Hosp., Hubli, 1973-74; fellow gen. surgery Mt. Sinai Hosp., Hartford, 1982-83; resident surgery Bronx Lebanon Hosp. Ctr., 1984-90; surgeon Halifax Meml. Hosp., Roanoke Rapids, NC, 1995. Clin. asst. prof. U. N.C., Chapel Hill. Recipient Leadership award (Internat. Med. Grad. Physician), AMA Assn., 2005. Fellow ACS, Internat. Coll. Surgeons, Royal Coll. Surgeons Eng.; mem. AMA, Soc. Am. Gastrointestinal Endoscopic Surgeons. Home: 511 Holly Rd Roanoke Rapids NC 27870-2270 Office: Shiva K Rao 40 Anna Louise Ln Roanoke Rapids NC 27870-8648

RAO, SUNIL V., cardiologist, educator; MD, Ohio State U. Coll. Medicine, 1996. Resident Duke U. Med. Ctr., 1996—99, fellow, 1999—2004, cardiologist, asst. prof. medicine. Office: 508 Fulton St 111A Durham NC 27705 Office Phone: 919-286-0411 ext. 2352. Office Fax: 919-286-6821.

RAO, UMA N.M., pathologist; U.S. citizen; MBBS, Govt. Med. Coll., Mysore, India, 1968. Cert. bd. cert. anatomic pathology, diplomate in anat. pathology Am. Bd. Pathology. Faculty Roswell Park Cancer Inst., 1973—92; prof. pathology dept. pathology U. Pitts. Sch. Medicine, U. Pitts. Med. Ctr., 1992—. Guest lectr. in field. Contbr. articles to profl. jours., abstracts, chpts. to books. Fellow: Coll. Am. Pathologists; mem.: Am. Soc. Investigative Pathology, U.S./Can. Acad. Pathology. Office: U Pitts Med Ctr Presbyn Shady Side Univ Hosp Rm No 2 9WG 5230 Centre Ave Pittsburgh PA 15232

RAO, VIJAY MADAN, diagnostic radiologist; MD, All India Inst. of Med. Sciences, 1973. Diplomate Am. Bd. of Radiology-diagnostic radiology, Am. Bd. of Radiology-neuroradiology. Intern internal medicine Albert Einstein Med. Ctr., 1975; resident diagnostic radiology Jefferson Hosp., 1978, chair dept. of radiology. Named top dr., Phila. Mag., 2007, 2010. Office: Thomas Jefferson University Hospital Radiology Department 132 S 10th St 1087 Main Bldg Philadelphia PA 19107 Office Phone: 215-955-7264.

RAO, VISHAL U.S., otolaryngologist; b. Mumbai, Oct. 9, 1978; MS, Jawaharlal Nehru Med. Coll., 2001. Cons. oncologist, head and neck surgeon Fortis Hosp., 2009—; postdoc. fellow Tata Meml. Hosp., 2008. Nat. exec. mem. Fedn. Head & Neck Oncology; convener Tobacco Free Bangalore. Recipient Gold medal, Rajiv Gandhi U. Health Scis., Assn. Otolaryngologists India, Best Video award, Maharastra Br. Mem.: Karnataka Med. Coun. Avocation: music. Home: K 301 Kasba Block Raj Lakeview 3761 Bangalore Karnataka 560076 India Office Phone: 06-91-9739774949. Personal E-mail: drvishalrao@yahoo.com.

RAO, ZIHE, academic administrator, biophysicist; b. Nanjing, Jiangsu, China, Sept. 6, 1950; Grad., U. Sci. and Tech. China, 1977; M, Chinese Acad. Scis., 1982; PhD, Melbourne U., 1989. Rschr. lab. molecular biophysics Oxford U., 1989—96; dir. Nat. Lab. Biomacro-molecules; prof. Tsinghua U., 1997—2006, vice dean sch. life sci. and medicine; pres. Nankai U., 2006—; prof., dir. gen. Chinese Acad. Scis. Inst. Biophysics, Beijing. Contbr. articles to sci. jours. Recipient Qiushi Outstanding Scientist prize, Hong Kong, 1999, Yangtze River Disting. Scholar prize, Ministry of Edn., 2000, He Liang Heli Found. Sci. and Tech. prize, 2003, Tan Kah Kee Sci. award, 2006. Fellow: Third World Acad. Scis. (Trieste Sci. prize in Medical Sciences 2006); mem.: Chinese Crystallography Soc. (pres.), Chinese Biophysics Assn., Internat. Orgn. Biol. Crystallography (v.p.), Chinese Acad. Scis. Office: Chinese Acad Scis Inst Biophysics 15 Datun Rd Chaoyang Dist Beijing 100101 China E-mail: raozh@sun5.ibp.ac.cn, raozh@xtal.tsinghua.edu.cn. *

RAPAPORT, DAVID P., plastic surgeon, educator; Grad., Boston U.; MD, Tel Aviv U., Israel. Diplomate Am. Bd. Surgery, Am. Bd. Plastic Surgery. Chief resident gen. surgery Beth Israel Hosp., 1985—90; chief resident plastic surgery NYU Med. Ctr., 1990—92, fellow microsurgery NY, 1992—93; asst. prof. divsn. of plastic and recon-structive surgery Univ. South Fla., 1993—97; plastic surgeon NY, 1998—; founder, dir. USF Residnets' Cosmetic Surgery Clinic. Co-author: (publs.) Phase I/II Trial for the treatment of cutaneous and subcutaneous tumors using electrochemotherapy, 1996, Intraoperative radiolymphoscintigraphy improves sentinel lymph node identification for patients with melanoma, 1996, Residency training in aesthetic surgery: maximizing the resident' experience, 1998, Parotid Selective Lymphadenectomoy in Malignant Melanoma, Annals of Plastic Sur-gery, 1999, numerous publs. Fellow: ACS; mem.: Am. Soc. for Aesthetic Plastic Surgery, Am. Soc. of Plastic and Reconstructive Surgeons, Plastic Surgery Rsch. Coun. Office: 905 5th Ave New York NY 10021 Office Phone: 212-249-9955. Business E-Mail: info@drrapaport.com.

RAPAPORT, ROBERT, pediatric endocrinologist; b. Romania, Feb. 23, 1949; MD, SUNY Downstate Med. Ctr., Bklyn., 1974. Cert. in pediat. 1980, in pediatric endocrinology 1983. Internship in pediat. LI Jewish Med. Ctr., Glen Oaks, NY, 1974—75, residency in pediatric endocrinology, 1974—77; fellowship in pediatric endocrinology St. Christopher's Hosp. Children, Phila., 1977—78, NY Hosp. Cornell Med. Ctr., NYC, 1978—80; hosp. appointment Children's Hosp., Newark; assoc. prof., dept. pediat. U. Medicine & Dentistry NJ, Newark; prof. pediat. Mt. Sinai Sch. Medicine, NYC, Emma Eliza-beth Sullivan prof. pediatric endocrinology and diabetes, chief, divsn. pediatric endocrinology and diabetes, dir., Hall Family Ctr. Pediatric Endocrinology and Diabetes. Contbr. articles to profl. jours. Office: Mt Sinai One Gustave L Levy Pl New York NY 10029 Office Phone: 212-241-6936. Office Fax: 212-876-4395. Business E-Mail: robert.rapaport@mssm.edu.

RAPAPORT, SAMUEL I., educator, physician; b. Los Angeles, Nov. 19, 1921; s. Hyman and Bertha (Krupnick) R.; m. Joyce Mildred Cooperman, Oct. 3, 1951; children: Susan Rapaport Braunwald, Sally Rapaport Hartinian, Mark Hyman, Bruce Allen. Student, UCLA; MD, U. So. Calif., 1945. Diplomate: Am. Bd. Internal Medicine (mem. bd. 1973-80, bd. govs. 1976-80, sec.-treas., chmn. hematology subcom. 1978-80). Intern Los Angeles County Hosp., 1945; resident medicine VA Hosp., Long Beach, Calif., 1948-50, chief hematology sect., 1950-57; asso. prof. medicine U. Calif. at Los Angeles Med. Center, 1957-58; mem. faculty U. So. Calif. Sch. Medicine, 1958-74, head hematology div. dept. medicine, 1958-74, prof. medicine, 1964-74; head hematology div. Los Angeles County-U. So. Calif. Med. Center, 1958-74; chief med. service San Diego VA Hosp., 1974-78; prof. medicine U. Calif., San Diego 1974-96; prof. emeritus, 1996—; vice chmn. dept. medicine U. Calif., 1974-78, co-head hematology-oncology div., 1978-87, prof. pathology, 1980-93; dir. Hematology Lab., U. Calif.-San Diego Med. Ctr., 1980-87. Cons. hematology tng. grants study sect. Nat. Inst. Arthritis and Metabolic Diseases, 1968-71; mem. med. adv. coun. Nat. Hemophilia Found., 1970, 77—; chmn. adv. com., div. blood diseases and resources Nat. Heart, Lung and Blood Inst., 1980-82, mem. adv. coun., 1989-93; mem. hematology study sect. NIH, 1984-88, chmn. study sect., 1977-88. Author: Introduction to Hematology, 1971, 2d edit., 1987; also papers in field. Chmn. coun. on thrombosis Am. Heart Assn., 1995-97. Served with USAAF, 1946-48. Spl. fellow Nat. Heart Inst., U. Oslo, 1964-65; Fulbright research scholar U. Oslo, 1953-54; fellow Sackler Inst. for Advanced Study, Tel Aviv U., 1983; recipient Disting. Sci. Achieve-ment award Coun. on Arteriosclerosis, Thrombosis, and Vascular Biology Am. Heart Assn., 2001. Master ACP (John Phillips Meml. award for outstanding work on clin. medicine 1996); fellow Am. Acad. Arts and Sciences; mem. Assn. Am. Physicians, Am. Soc. Hematology (pres. 1977), Western Soc. Clin. Rsch. (pres. 1966), Am. Fedn. Clin. Rsch. (chmn. Western sect. 1960), Am. Soc. Clin. Investigation, Western Assn. Physicians (pres. 1973) Home: 7887 Lookout Dr La Jolla CA 92037-3951

RAPHAEL, CAROL, health care association administrator; b. NYC, Apr. 21, 1942; BA, CUNY, 1962; MEd, Boston U., 1965; MPA, Harvard U., 1979. Dir. EDP planning & contract mgmt. NYC Human Resources Adminstrn., 1979-82, asst. dep. adminstr., Office Home Care Svcs., 1982-84, dep. commr. med. assistance program, 1984-88, exec. dep. commr. income & med. assistance adminstrn., 1988-89; dir. ops. mgmt. Mount Sinai Med. Ctr., NYC, 1989; pres., CEO Vis. Nurse Svc. NY, 1989—. Bd. dirs. AARP (Am. Assn. Retired Persons), 2010—, Lifetime Healthcare Cos. Bd. dirs. Am. Found. Blind, Pace U., NYC. Named one of The 100 Most Influential Women in NYC Bus., Crain's NY Bus., 2007, The 50 Most Powerful Women in NY, 2009. Office: Vis Nurse Svc NY 107 E 70th St New York NY 10021-5003 E-mail: craphael@visitingnurseservice.org, carol.raphael@vnsny.org.

RAPINI, RONALD PETER, dermatology educator; b. Akron, Ohio, Feb. 15, 1954; s. Vincent Thomas and Joann Irene (Tufexis) R.; m. Mary Jo Beigel, June 16, 1979; children: Brianna Marie, Sarina Elizabeth. BS in Biology, U. Akron, 1975; MD, Ohio State U., 1978. Diplomate Am. Bd. Dermatology (bd. dirs. 1996-2004, pres. 2004), Am. Bd. Dermatopathology. Assoc. prof. U. Tex. Med. Sch., Houston,

1983-93; prof. and chair dermatology dept. Tex. Tech. U., Lubbock, 1994—2002; prof., chair dept. dermatology U. Tex. Med. Sch., 2002—, MD Anderson Cancer Ctr., Houston, 2002—. Author (with K.G. Gross and H.K. Steinman): Mohs Surgery, 1999; author: (with J. Bolognia and J. Jorizzo) Dermatology, 2007; author: Practical Der-matopathology, 2005, of over 150 other publications. Fellow Am. Acad. Dermatology (bd. dir. 2010-), Am. Soc. Dermatol. Surgery (bd. dir. 1995-98), Soc. Investigative Dermatology; mem. AMA, Am. Soc. Dermatopathology (pres. 1998-99), Am. Soc. Mohs Surgery (pres. 2003), Internat. Soc. Dermatopathology, Tex. Dermatol. Soc. (pres. 2006—07). Avocations: tennis, entomology, piano. Office: U TEx Med Sch 6655 Travis St 980 Houston TX 77030-0001 Office Phone: 713-745-1113.

RAPOPORT, JUDITH, psychiatrist; b. NYC, July 12, 1933; d. Louis and Minna (Enteen) Livant; m. Stanley Rapoport, June 25, 1961; children: Stuart, Erik. BA, Swarthmore Coll., 1955; MD, Harvard U., 1959. Lic. psychiatrist. Cons., child psychiatrist NIMH/St. Elizabeth's Hosp., Washington, 1969—72; clin. asst. prof. Georgetown U. Med. Sch., Washington, 1972—82, clin. assoc. prof., 1982—85, clin. prof. psychiat., 1985—; med. officer biol. psychiatry br. NIMH, Bethesda, Md., 1979—82, chief, child psychiatry lab. of clin. scis., 1982—84, chief, child psychiatry div. intramural rsch. programs, 1984—; prof. psychiatry George Washington U. Sch. Med., Washington, 1979—; prof. pediat. Georgetown U., Washington, 1985—. Cons. in field. Author: (non-fiction) The Boy Who Couldn't Stop Washing, 1989 (best seller literary guild selection, 1989), Childhood Obsessive Compulsive Disorder, 1989. Recipient Scolnick award, MIT, 2005. Fellow: Am. Acad. Arts & Sci., Am. Acad. Child Psychiatry, Am. Psychiat. Assn.; mem.: Inst. Medicine, D.C. Psychiat. Assn. Home: 3010 44th Pl NW Washington DC 20016-3557 Office: NIMH Rm 3N202 10 Center Dr Bldg 10 Bethesda MD 20892-0001 Office Phone: 301-496-6081. Business E-Mail: rapoport@helix.nih.gov.

RAPOSEIRAS-ROUBIN, SERGIO, cardiologist; b. Santiago De Compostela, Spain, Nov. 26, 1983; Degree in Medicine, Santiago Compostela, 2007. Physician dept. cardiology, 2008. Office: Travesía da Choupana s/n Santiago De Compostela Coruña 15000 Spain Personal E-mail: raposeiras26@hotmail.com.

RAPOSO DO AMARAL, CASSIO E., plastic surgeon; b. Sao Paulo, Brazil, Dec. 12; s. Cassio M. Raposo do Amaral and Raposo do Amaral A. Vera Lucia. MD, San Francisco Sch. Medicine, Sao Paulo, 2000. Cert. Brazilian Soc. Plastic Surgery, 2006. V.p. Sobrapar, Campinas, Sao Paulo, 2006—08, dir. plastic surgery divsn., 2007—08. Mem.: Brazilian Soc. Plastic Surgery (Ivo Pintanguy award 2006). Home: R Alameda das Palmeiras 25 Campinas Sao Paulo 31094-776 Brazil Office: Sobrapar Avenida Adopho Lutz 100 13083-880 Campinas SP Brazil Office Phone: 551937499701, 55 19 32547378. Office Fax: 55-19-32895380; Home Fax: 55-19-32547378. Personal E-mail: cassioradoso@hotmail.com. Business E-Mail: cassioeduardo@sobrapar.org.br.

RAPPAPORT, MARGARET MARY WILLIAMS EWING, psy-chologist, physician, writer, pilot, consultant; b. Nov. 16, 1947; d. Leo J. and Marie L. (Rischle) Williams; m. Herbert Rappaport (div.); children: Amanda, Alexander. BA, U. Buffalo; MA, SUNY; PhD, MD, U. Colo. Zone Perfect cert. instr. Prof., rschr. U. Dar es Salaam, Tanzania; with Rappaport Assocs., Phila., 1974-94; exec. dir. Inst. for Parent/Child Svcs., Phila., 1978-94; pres., CEO Diabetes Edn. Ctr. Cape Cod, 2002—03. Mem. adj. faculty Temple U., Phila., 1974—94; aviation safety counselor FAA; cons., spkr. in field.; pres. Reach New Heights, Inc., 1994—2005; founder Fit to Fly. Mem. AAUP, Nat. Profl. Spkrs. Assn., Cosmopolitan Club, Orleans Yacht Club. Home: PO Box 1845 Orleans MA 02653-1845 Office Phone: 508-255-9570. Personal E-mail: rappaportmm@yahoo.com.

RAPPAPORT, MARTIN PAUL, internist, nephrologist, educator; b. Bronx, NY, Apr. 25, 1935; s. Joseph and Anne (Kramer) R.; m. Bethany Ann Mitchell; children: Karen, Steven; stepchildren: Aaron Cole, Kevin Cole. BS, Tulane U., 1957, MD, 1960; diploma, Tulane Med. Sch., New Orleans, 2010. Diplomate Am. Bd. Internal Medi-cine, Nat. Bd. Med. Examiners. Intern Charity Hosp. of La., New Orleans, 1960-61, resident in internal medicine, 1961-64; pvt. practice internal medicine and nephrology, Seabrook, Tex., 1968-72, Webster, Tex., 1972-98; internist Univ. Med. Group, Houston, 1998; mem. courtesy staff Mainland Ctr. Hosp. (formerly Galveston County Meml. Hosp.), Texas City, 1968-96, Bapt. Meml. System, 1969-72, 88-98; mem. staff Clear Lake Regional Med. Ctr., 1972-98; cons. staff St Mary's Hosp., 1973-79; cons. nephrology St. John's Hosp., Nassau Bay, Tex.; fellow in nephrology Northwestern U. Med. Sch., Chgo., 1967—68; clin. asst. prof. in medicine and nephrology U. Tex., Galveston, 1969—2009; part-time physician dept. family medicine outpatient clinics U. Tex. Med. Br., Galveston, 2000; locum tenens, 2000—06; ret., 2005. Lectr. emergency med. technician cours e, 1974-76; adviser on respiratory therapy program Alvin (Tex.) Jr. Coll., 1976-82; cons. nephrology USPHS, 1979-80. Served to capt. M.C. U.S. Army, 1961-67. Fellow ACP, Am. Coll. Chest Physicians; mem. Internat., Am. Socs. Nephrology, So. Med. Assn., Tex. Med. Assn., Tex. Soc. Internal Medicine (bd. govs. 1994-96), Am. Soc. Artificial Internal Organs, Tex. Acad. Internal Medicine, Harris County Med. Soc., Am. Geriatrics Soc., Bay Area Heart Assn. (bd. govs. 1969-75), Clear Lake C. of C., Conroe Rotary Club, Rotary, Phi Delta Epsilon, Alpha Epsilon Pi, Tulane Alumni Assn. (50 Yr. diploma 1960-2010), Tex. Med. Assn. Home: 15913 Malibu W Willis TX 77318-6784

RAPPAPORT, NORMAN HARVEY, plastic surgeon; b. Phila., Apr. 23, 1947; s. Herbert and Ruth Rappaport; m. Deborah Ann Finn, Oct. 2, 1982; children: Jonathan David, Betsy, William. BA, LaSalle Coll., 1969; DDS, Temple U., 1972; MD, Hahnemann Med. Coll., 1975. Diplomate Am. Bd. Plastic Surgery. Resident in gen. surgery Abington (Pa.) Meml. Hosp., 1975-78; fellow in hand surgery U. Pa., Phila., 1978; resident in plastic surgery Baylor Coll. Medicine, Houston, 1978-80; clin. assoc. prof. surgery Baylor Coll. Surgery, Houston, 1994—. Contbr. articles to profl. jours. Fellow: ACS; mem.: AMA, Houston Surg. Soc. (pres. 2001), Tex. Soc. Plastic Surgeons, Tex. Med. Assn., N.Am. Burn Soc., Houston Soc. Plastic Surgeons (pres. 2002), Harris County Med. Soc., Am. Assn. Hand Surgeons, Am. Assn. Plastic Surgeons, Am. Soc. for Aesthetic Plastic Surgery, Am. Soc. Plastic Surgeons (bd. dirs. 1998—2000), Plastic Surgery Ednl.

Found. (bd. dirs. 1994—2000), Am. Soc. Maxillofacial Surgeons (pres. 2000), Omicron Kappa Upsilon. Office: 6560 Fannin St Ste 1812 Houston TX 77030-2775 Office Phone: 713-790-4500. E-mail: nhr@hcps.cc.

RAPPAPORT, RAPHAEL, medical educator; b. Leipsig, Germany, June 5, 1932; arrived in France, 1933; s. David and Helen (Rus-niewsky) R.; m. Georgette Andrée Rathenau, June 19, 1959; children: Alain Thierry, Nathalie, Delphine. MD, U. Paris, 1959. Intern, resident Hosp. Enfants Malades, Paris, 1954-60; prof. pediat. U. Paris, 1970-83, prof. devel. biology, 1983—98; dir. rsch. lab. Inserm, Paris, 1984-95; head pediatric endocrinology unit Hosp. Enfants Malades, Paris, 1970-98, chmn. pediat. dept., 1987-96, dir. rsch. inst., 1997-2000, prof. emeritus, 2001—; cons., 1998—2001. Vis. prof. Johns Hopkins U., Balt., 1973; prof. emeritus Faculty Necker, Paris; advisor for edn. ministry Univ. France, 1976—79, Inserm, 1986—98; lectr. Rui-Jin Shanghai Med. U., 2000—. Editor: Pediatric Endocrinology, 1993, 2007, Developmental Endocrinology, 2001, site editl. dir., Endocrinologic Expert.net. Rsch. fellow Johns Hopkins Hosp., Balt., 1960. Mem. European Soc. for Pediat. Endocrinology (sec.-elect 1976-86, pres. elect 1985, chmn. sci. program com. 1992-98, Andrea Prader prize 1990), Pediat. Endocrinology Soc., Endocrine Soc. USA, Bd. the Found. Motrice. Avocations: mountain climbing, music. Home: 17 Rue de L'Yvette 75016 Paris France Office: Hosp Enfants Malades 149 Rue de Sevres 75015 Paris France Personal E-mail: raphael.rappaport@wanadoo.fr. E-mail: rappaport@necker.fr.

RAPPLEY, MARSHA D., dean, physician, educator; BS in Nursing, U. Mich., 1980; MD, Mich. State U. Coll. Human Medicine, 1984. Cert. in gen. pediatrics and devel. & behavioral pediatrics Am. Bd. Pediatrics. Resident in pediatrics Mich. State U. Coll. Human Medi-cine, faculty mem., 1988—, interim assoc. dean acad. affairs, 2002, interim chair Dept. Pediatrics & Human Devel., 2001—03, divsn. dir. gen. pediatrics and dir. gen. pediatric clinics, 1991—2001, assoc. dean acad. affairs, 2003—, prof. Dept. Pediatrics and Human Devel., acting dean, 2005—06, dean, 2006—, divsn. dir. Devel. and Behavioral Pediatrics, dir. Collaborative Devel. Clinic. Office: Office of Dean Univ Mich Coll Human Medicine A118-E Fee Hall East Lansing MI 48824-1316 Office Phone: 517-353-4998. E-mail: rappley@msu.edu.

RAPTIS, GEORGE, medical oncologist, educator; MBA, NYU; MD, Mt. Sinai Sch. of Medicine, 1987. Diplomate Am. Bd. Internal Medicine-med. oncology, registered NY, 1989. Intern Mt. Sinai Hosp., 1988, resident in internal medicine, 1990; fellow in oncology-hematology Meml. Sloan-Kettering Cancer Ctr., 1993, hosp. affilia-tions include, Mercy Med. Ctr., NY Presbyn. Hosp., Mt. Sinai Med. Ctr.; assoc. prof. medicine, hematology and med. oncology Mt. Sinai Sch. of Medicine, NY, assoc. prof. obstetrics, gynecology and reproductive sci., assoc. chief divsn. hematology and med. oncology. Author: (articles) Translation, please, 2007, Pilot study of acupuncture for the treatment of joint symptoms related to adjuvant aromatase inhibitor therapy in postmenopausal breast cancer patients, 2007, Effect of pretreatment distress on daily fatigue after chemotherapy for breast cancer, 2008, Conducting Molecular Epidemiological Research in the Age of HIPAA: A Multi-Institutional Case-Control Study of Breast Cancer in African-American and European-American Women, 2009, Highlights of the Chemotherapy Foundation Symposium XX-VII: therapeutic options for breast cancer, 2010. Named one of Best Doctors, NY Mag., 2009—10. Office: Mount Sinai Medical Center 1 Gustave L. Levy Pl New York NY 10029-6574 Office Phone: 212-639-5441.

RASALKAR, DARSHANA DATTATRAY, radiologist; b. India, July 17, 1976; MBBS, KJ Somaiya Med. Coll., 1998; DMRD, King Edward Meml. Hosp., Mumbai, DNB, 2007. Radiologist King Ed-ward Meml. Hosp., Prince Wales Hosp., CUHK, Hong Kong, 2001—11; cons. radiologist, dept. radiology Kokilaben Dhirubhai Ambani Hosp., Mumbai, 2011—. Fellow: Royal Coll. Radiologists (London). Office: Kokilaben Dhirubhai Ambani Hosp Dept Radiology 4 Bunglow Andheri West Mumbai 400053 India Office Phone: 26321189. Office Fax: 26487269.

RASCHKA, CHRISTOPH JOSEF, sports physician, internist, an-thropologist; b. Fulda, Hessen, Germany, Jan. 8, 1961; s. Herbert Helmut and Marga Rosa Elisabeth (Herget) Raschka; m. Sonja Raschka; children: Jonas, Paula. MD cum laude, Justus-Liebig U., 1987; PhD magna cum laude, Johannes-Gutenberg U., 1988; DSc Sports cum laude, Ruhr U., 1994; Habil, Goethe U., 2001; habil in Sports Medicine, Maximilians U. Wuezburg, 2010. Cert. in sports medicine, acupuncture, chiropractic, homeopathy, tropotherapy, natur-opathy, prevention of radiation, emergency medicine, diving medi-cine, traditional Chinese med., electroacupuncture and health care mgmt. Asst. Inst. Anthropology, Mainz, 1987—88; resident social medicine, psychosomatics and internal medicine Frankenklinik, Bad Neustadt/Saale, Germany, 1988—89; resident internal medicine and gastroenterology St. Markus-Krankenhaus, Frankfurt-Main, 1989; resident internal medicine rehab. and cardiology KVB-Klinik, Koenigstein/Taunus, 1989; resident cardiology, gastroenterology, nephrology, oncology, emergency medicine, intensive care medicine, endoscopy, dialysis, infectious disease Klinikum Fulda, 1990—98; asst. prof. sports medicine and sci. of sports Johann-Wolfgang Goethe U., Frankfurt-Main, 1998—2003; resident surgery and emergency medicine Helios St. Elizabeth Klinik, Hünfeld, 2003—04, resident gen. medicine and family medicine Praxis Langenbieber, Rhön, 2004—05, sr. physician dept. internal medicine and intensive care, 2005—08; gen. and internal medical practise Huenfeld, 2008—; pvt. dozent sports medicine. Lectr. Acad. for Sch. Nurses, Fulda, 1992-93; lectr. social pedagogy U. Applied Scis. Fulda, 1999-2003; tchr. Sch. for Nurses of Klinikum Fulda, 1991-98; lectr. anthropology Fulda, 1992-93; mem. mng. com. Hesse's Fedn. Sports Medicine, Fulda Acad. Interdisciplinary Emergency Medicine. Author: Ein Beitrag zur Medizinalgeschichte Fuldas unter spezieller Beruecksichtigung der Inneren Medizin, 1996, Sports Anthropology, 2006, Herzsport, 2010, Doping, 2011; book reviewer Jour. Comparative Human Biology, 1995—, Jour. Naturarzt, 1995—, Chinese Jour. Physiology, 2011, Clinics, 2011, others; reviewer Sportorthopädie-Sporttraumatologie, 2005—, Brit. Jour. Sports Medicine, 2006—, Applied Physiology, Nutrition and Metabolism, 2006—, Jour. Sports Sci. and Medicine, 2007—, Internat. Jour. Sports Medicine, 2008-, reviewer Wilderness and Environmental Medicine, 2008, Medicine Sportiva, 2008-, Euro-pean Jour. Clin. Investigation, 2008; contbr. over 500 articles to profl. jours. Johannes-Gutenberg U. scholar, 1987. Mem. German Soc. Sports Physicians, German Soc. Physicians Acupuncture, German Soc. Physicians Naturopathy, German Soc. Internal Medicine, Soc.

German Internists, Gesellschaft Orthopädische Traumatologische Sportmedizin. Roman Catholic. Avocations: weightlifting, jogging, volleyball, cross country skiing, Aikido. Home: Edith-Stein-Strasse 34 36100 Petersberg Hessen Germany Office: lm Igelstueck 31 Huenfeld D36088 Germany also: Julius Maximilians Universität inst Sports Sa Judenbuchlweg 11 Würzburg Bavaria 97082 Germany

RASENICK, MARK MITCHELL, neuroscientist; b. Chgo., Sept. 5, 1949; s. Maurice Milton and Eleanore Ruth (Fox) R.; m. Helene Joy Shambelan, Sept. 1, 1974; children: Elliot S., Matthew M., Emily A. BA, Case Western Res., 1971; PhD, Wesleyan U., Middletown, Conn., 1977; postdoctoral fellow, Yale U., 1977—81. Assoc. rsch. scientist Yale U., New Haven, 1981—83; various edn. positions to prof., dept. physiology and biophysics and psychiatry U. Ill./Chgo. Coll. Medicine, 1983—93, dir. grad. studies, 1990—96, prof., 1993—, dir. biomed. neurosci. tng. program, 1995—, prof. psychiatry, 1997—, disting. u. prof., 2008; Robert Wood Johnson Health Policy fellow Sen. Com. on Health Edn., Labor and Pensions E.M Kennedy D-MA, 1999—2000. Mem. cellular neurosci. panel NSF, Washington, 1988—, spl. study sections NIH, 1990-, cell biology panels breast cancer, 1998-; expert witness neuropharmacology, 1987—; cons. various pharm. cos., 1987—; founder Pax Neurosci., 2010; sect. editor BMC Neurosci., 2011, global health ambassador Paul Rogers Soc., 2009 Mem. editl. bd. Neuropsychopharmacology, 2003—, Biochem. Biophysica Acta, 2005—, Psychopharmacology, 2006-, Translational Research, 2007-, Open Psychiatry, 2008-, Open Pharmacology, 2009-; contbr. articles to profl. jours., book chpts. to profl. publs. Sci. cons. Sch. Dist. 37, Wilmette, Ill., 1989—; coach Jr. Football, Wilmette, 1989—; active Commn. on Social Action of Reform Judaism, 1998-2004. Recipient Outstanding Young Faculty award Chgo. Cmty. Trust, 1984-86, Rsch. Scientist Devel. award NIMH, Bethesda, 1987—; grantee NIMH, 1984—, NSF, Washington, 1987—, Am. Heart Assn., Dallas, 1989—, NIA, 1997—, NIDA, 2005-; Univ. scholar U. Ill., Urbana/Chgo., 1989—. Mem. AAAS (elected fellow 2011), Am. Soc. Biol. Chemistry and Molecular Biology(pub. affairs adv. com., 2008-), Am. Coll. Neuropsychopharmacology (liasonn com. 2005-08, adv. com., 2008-), Am. Soc. for Cell Biology, Soc. for Neurosci. (pres. Chgo. chpt. 1994, gov. pub. affairs com., internat. affairs com.), Union of Concerned Scientists, UIC Colloquium for Signal Transduction (pres. 1990—), Sigma Xi. Jewish. Avocations: bicycling, sailing, squash, light verse. Office: Dept Physiol and Biophys Coll Med Univ Ill 835 S Wolcott M/C 901 Chicago IL 60612 Home Phone: 847-998-6883; Office Phone: 312-996-7370. Business E-Mail: raz@uic.edu.

RASETTI-ESCARGUEIL, CHRISTINE INES, pharmacist; d. Enrico Luciano Rasetti and Jacqueline Madeleine Krall; m. Renaud Stephane Escargueil, June 3, 1995; children: Romain Luciano Pierre Escargueil, Antoine Jean-Enzo Escargueil. Degree in Pharm. Scis. (hon.), Paris, 1990; PhD in Pharmacology, U. Rene-Descartes, Paris, 1995. Postdoc. engr. Atomic Energy Commissariat, Orsay, Essonnes, France, 1996—2000; sci. writer Clin. Rsch. Orgn., Paris, 2001—05; rsch. assoc. Sch. Pharmacy, Cardiff U., Wales, 2005—06; sr. scientist NIBSC, HPA, Potters Bar, Hertfordshire, England, 2006 . Editor Nova Pubs., NYC, 2009—. Sci. Rsch. grant, Found. pour la Rsch. Med., Home Office, MRC. Mem.: Royal Soc. Medicine.

RASHID, KAMAL A., university administrator, research educator; b. Sulaimania, Kurdistan, Iraq, Sept. 11, 1944; came to U.S., 1972; s. Ahmad Rashid and Habiba M. Muhiedin; m. Afifa B. Sabir, May 23, 1970; children: Niaz K., Neian K., Suzanne K. BS, U. Baghdad, Iraq, 1965; MS, Pa. State U., 1974, PhD, 1978. Lab. instr. U. Baghdad, Iraq, 1966-72, mem. faculty U. Basrah, Iraq, 1978-80, U. Sulaimania, Iraq, 1980-83; sr. rsch. assoc., vis. prof. Pa. State U., University Park, 1983-86, rsch. assoc. prof. dept. biochemistry and molecular biology, 1992-2000, assoc. dir., prof. biotechnology ctr. Utah State U., Logan, 2000— Dir Biotech. Tng. Program program Pa. State U., 1989-2000, dir. summer symposium molecular biology, 1991-92; v.p. Cogenic Inc., State College, Pa., 1989-90; cons., spkr. biotech. tng. program developer. Contbr. articles to profl. jours. Iraqi Ministry Higher Edn. scholar. Mem. AAAS, Soc. for Indsl. Microbiology, Am. Soc. Microbiology, Am. Chem. Soc., Environ. Mutagen Soc., Rotary. Avocations: travel, swimming, reading. Home: 2835 N 2050 E Logan UT 84341-8327 E-mail: krashid@cc.usu.edu.

RASKA, KAREL FRANTISEK JULIAN, JR., pathologist, virologist, educator; b. Prague, Czech Republic, May 26, 1939; arrived in U.S., 1965; s. Karel Raska and Helena (Heller) Raskova; m. Jana Dostalova, Feb. 18, 1960; children: Karel III, Francis. MD, Charles U., Prague, 1962; PhD in Biochemistry, Czechoslovak Acad. Scis., Prague, 1965. Diplomate Am. Bd. Pathology (anatomic and clin., immunopathology). Fellow Yale U. Sch. Medicine, New Haven, 1965—66; assoc. Waksman Inst. Microbiology, New Brunswick, NJ, 1966—67; scientist Czech Acad. Sci., Prague, 1967—68; prof. microbiology and pathology Rutgers Med. Sch., Piscataway, NJ, 1968—82; profl. pathology, lab. medicine, microbiology U. Medicine and Dentistry-Robert Wood Johnson Med. Sch., New Brunswick, 1982—; prof., chmn. dept. lab medicine and pathology U. Medicine and Dentistry NJ Med. Sch., Newark, 1989—92; chmn. dept. lab medicine and pathology St. Peter's U. Hosp., New Brunswick, 1992—. Cons. Newark Beth Israel Med. Ctr., Newark, 1991—2001, E. Orange (NJ) VA Med. Ctr., 1991—; vis. prof. Charles U. Med. Sch., Prague, 1993—94; prof. path. and lab. medicine Drexel U., Coll. Medicine, Phila., 2005—. Contbr. articles to profl. jours., chapters to books. Trustee N.J. Organ Sharing Network, Springfield, 1991—2000; pres. Czechoslovak Soc. for Arts and Scis. in Am., 2006—; mem. exec. bd. Slavic Heritage Inst., 2007—. Lt. Czechoslovak Air Force, 1962—63. Recipient Silver medal, Senate of Czech Republic, 2010, Medal of Merit, 1st grade, Pres. of Czech Republic, 2010; grantee, NIH, 1975—93, Damon Runyon-Walter Winchell Cancer Rsch. Fund, 1975, NJ Commn. Cancer Rsch., 1985—86, 1994—95. Mem.: Learned Soc. of the Czech. Republic, Am. Soc. Cell Biologists, Am. Soc. Virology, NJ Soc. Pathology, Assn. Univ. Pathologists, Internat. Acad. Pathology, Am. Assn. Cancer Rsch., Am. Soc. Clin. Immunology, Am. Assn. Immunology, Am. Soc. Investigative Pathology. Avocations: skiing, boating. Office: St Peters Univ Hosp Dept Lab Medicine & Pathology 254 Easton Ave New Brunswick NJ 08901 Personal E-mail: jkraskamd@aol.com.

RASKE, KENNETH E., medical association administrator; b. July 5, 1947; Rsch. assoc. AMA; study dir. Am. Hosp. Assn.; sr. v.p., dep. dir. Mich. Hosp. Assn.; pres., CEO Greater NY Hosp. Assn., 1984—. Lectr. and commentator in field; creator Health Econs. and Outcomes Rsch. Inst. Named to Who's Who in DC, Crain's NY Bus., 2009. Office: Greater NY Hosp Assn 555 W 57th St 15th Fl New York NY 10019 Office Phone: 212-506-5401. Business E-Mail: raske@gnyha.org. *

RASKIN, BERNARD, dermatologist; B in Physics, UCLA; grad., Calif. Irvine Med. Sch. Diplomate Am. Bd. Dermatology, Am. Bd. Internal Medicine. Resident UCLA (Univ. of Calif. LA), asst. clin. prof. dept. medicine divsn. of dermatology; founder Mohs Micrographic Surgery Ctr. of America. Mem. adv. com. cancer devel. biology Calif. State Univ. Northridge. Fellow: Am. Soc. of Dermatologic Surgery, Am. Acad. of Dermatology; mem.: L.A. County and Calif. Med. Assns., Am. Soc. of Dermatology, Am. Acad. of Cosmetic Surgery, Am. Soc. for Mohs Surgery, Am. Soc. of Laser Medicine and Surgery. Office: Advanced Dermatology and Cosmetic Care 23861 McBean Parkway Suite E21 Valencia CA 91355 Office Phone: 661-254-3686. Office Fax: 661-254-5671.

RASKIN, JEFFREY B., medical educator; s. James M. and Devy Raskin; m. Bobbie C. Campbell; children: Scott E., Tracy A., Lori A. MD, U. Miami Sch. Medicine, 1965. Prof. medicine U Miami Sch.Medicine, 2002—; prof., Cye Mandel chair gastroenterology U. Miami Sch. Medicine, 2002—. Contbr. articles to profl. jours. Mem., dist. athletic adv. com. Miami-Dade Sch. Dist., 1989—2005. Capt. USAF, 1966—68, Smyrna, Tenn. Recipient Disting. Svc. award, Fla. Gastroenterologic Soc., 2002, Disting. Alumnus award, U. Miami Sch. Medicine, 2004. Fellow: ACP, AGA, ASGE, Am. Coll. Gastroentology. Office: U Miami Jackson Meml Med Ctr 1611 NW 12 th Ave Rm SW 220 Miami FL 33136 Office Phone: 305-243-8644. Office Fax: 305-325-9476. Business E-Mail: jraskin@med.miami.edu.

RASKIN, MICHAEL NEIL, psychologist, writer; b. Jersey City, Sept. 16, 1945; s. Max and Ruth Shapiro Raskin. BA, Fairleigh Dickinson U., 1968, MA, 1969; PhD, U.S. Internat. U., 1975. Lic. psychologist Maine, 1976. Staff psychologist Greystone Park Psychiat. Hosp., NJ, 1972—73; dir. psychol. svcs. Tri-County Mental Health Svcs., Lewiston, Maine, 1976—2000; pvt. practice Lisbon Falls, Maine, 2000—. Instr. psychology Fairleigh Dickinson U., Teaneck, NJ, Union Coll., Elizabeth and Cranford, NJ, County Coll. Morris, Dover, NJ, U. Maine, Topsham, Lewiston and Arburn, Maine; past pres. Etc-Mfg. Inc, Lisbon Falls, Maine; owner Dr. Mikes Madness The Cafe. Author: (textbook) Islands of Certainty in an Ocean of Fear, 2002, (novels) JUD.US, 2005, JUD.US.TOO, 2006, SNAFU, 2008, A Funny Thing Happened on My Way to Hereafter, 2007. Mem.: Maine Soc. Forensic Psychologists, Maine Psychol. Assn. Avocations: writing, poetry. Home: 752 Newell Brook Rd Durham ME 04222 Office: Michael N Raskin PhD PA 8 Main St Lisbon Falls ME 04252 Office Phone: 207-353-7254.

RASKIN, PHILIP, physician, educator; b. Pitts., Dec. 31, 1940; BA, Wash. and Jefferson Coll., 1962; MD, U. Pitts., 1966. Prof., medicine U. Tex. Southwestern Med. Ctr. Dallas, 1970—. Recipient Alumni award, Wash. & Jefferson Coll., 2007, Hench award, U. Pitts., 2011; Owens fellowship. Office: 5323 Harry Hines Blvd Ste G05238 Dallas TX 75390-8858 Office Fax: 214-648-4854. Business E-Mail: philip.raskin@utsouthwestern.edu.

RASMASON, FREDERICK CHARLES, III, emergency nurse, director; b. Evergreen Park, Ill., May 10, 1958; s. Frederick C. Jr. and Kathleen M. R.; m. Concepcion A. Rasmason, Nov. 14, 1981; children: F. Charlie IV, Randy. Diploma, Clin. Specialist Sch., 1977; BSN, Chgo. State U., 1988; MS in Human Svc. Adminstrn., Spertus Coll., 1997. RN, Ill.; CEN; cert. TNS, TNCC, ACLS, PALS, PHTLS, emergency dept. nursing. Staff nurse Holy Family Hosp., Des Plaines, Ill., Mt. Sinai Med. Ctr., Chgo., King Drew Med. Ctr., Calif., emergency dept. staff Provident Hosp. Cook County, Chgo., dir. nurses, mgr. clin. svcs., 2007—. Sgt. U.S. Army, 1976-82, 86-88. Named Nightingale Soc. Honors Mem.; recipient U.S. Achievement Acad. Scholastic All-Am. award, U.S. Achievement Acad. Nat. Collegiate Nursing award. Mem. AACN, Emergency Nurses Assn., Ill. Nurses Assn., Calif. Nurses Assn. Mailing: 2738 B Rt 34 #118 Apt Oswego IL 60543-8301 Office: Comprehensive Medical Staffing 555 W Madison St Apt 4607 Chicago IL 60661-2533 E-mail: frasmason@aol.com.

RASMUSSEN, ALICE CALL, retired nursing educator; b. Grand Rapids, Mich., Dec. 16, 1947; d. Amon Burton and Jessie Pearl (Dann) Call; m. Charles P. Rasmussen, Apr. 16, 1972. BSN, Andrews U., 1971; MSN, Med. Coll. Ga., 1977; postgrad., Ferris State U., 1990. Staff nurse Lockwood-MacDonald Hosp., Petoskey, Mich., 1971—72; instr. Lake Michigan Coll., Benton Harbor, Mich., 1973—87; nursing coord. and health sci. dept. chair Lake Mich. Coll., Benton Harbor, Mich., 1986—2003; ret., 2003. Vice chair Mich. Bd. Nursing, 1998-2000; bd. trustees Watervliet Cmty. Hosp., 2002- Mem. AAUW, NAFE, Mich. League for Nursing, Mich. Coun. Nursing Edn. Adminstrs., Nat. Ordn. ADN, S.W. Mich. Nurse Educator Network, Sigma Theta Tau. Home: 9088 4th St Berrien Springs MI 49103-1637

RASMUSSEN, CAREN NANCY, health facility administrator; b. Ft. Riley, Kans., July 7, 1950; d. Stanley Junior and Katherina Wilhelmina R. AAS, Grand Rapids Jr. Coll., 1970; BS, U. Md., 1977; MS, Johns Hopkins U., 1997. Cert. profl. contracts mgr. Contract specialist Kadena Air Base, Okinawa, 1979-81; med. sec. Walter Reed Army Med. Ctr., Washington, 1970-72, sec. procurement, 1972-76, contract specialist, 1976-79, 81-84, procurement analyst, 1984—, sr. contracting specialist, 1988—2001, Nat. Cancer Inst., 2001—. Fellow NAFE; mem. Nat. Contract Mgmt. Assn. Democrat. Avocations: photography, stamp collecting/philately, gardening, travel. Home: 18632 Clovercrest Cir Olney MD 20832-3057 Office: Nat Cancer Inst Rsch Contracts br Rockville MD 20852 Business E-Mail: cnrasmussen@jhu.edu.

RASMUSSEN, KATHLEEN MAHER, nutritional sciences educator; b. Dayton, Ohio, Mar. 1, 1948; AB, Brown U., Providence, 1970; MSc, Harvard U., Cambridge, Mass., 1975, ScD, 1978. Registered dietitian. Tchr. sci. Cape Hatteras Elem. Sch., Buxton, NC, 1971-72; analytical chemist Berkley Machine Works, Foundry Co., Norfolk, Va., 1972-73; rsch. assoc. dept. nutrition Harvard U., Boston, 1978; instr. div. nutritional scis. Cornell U., Ithaca, N.Y., 1981-83, asst. prof., 1983-88, assoc. prof., 1988-96, com. chair, 2007—09, assoc. dir. grad. affairs Ithaca, N.Y., 1992-95, prof., 1996—, assoc. dean, sec. Univ. Faculty, 1997-2000. Com. mem. NAS, Washington, 1988-96; Pew faculty scholar in nutrition Nat. Ctr. Sci. Rsch., Meudon-Bellevue, France, 1989-90; com. chair IOM, Washington, 2007-09, 2011-. Trustee Cornell U., 2004—08. NIH trainee, 1974-80; NIH grantee, 1984-90, 87—, 93—, 2001—, various other grants and awards, 1982-85, 88-89, 89-92, 92-94, 93-96, 97-99, 2001—. Mem.: Internat. Soc. Rsch. in Human Milk and Lactation (pres. 2002—03), Brit. Nutrition Soc., Am. Soc. Clin. Nutrition, Am. Soc. Nutrition Scis. (sec. 1999—2002, pres. 2004—05). Office: Cornell U Div Nutritional Sci 111 Savage Hall Ithaca NY 14853-6301 Office Phone: 607-255-2290. Business E-Mail: kathleen.rasmussen@cornell.edu.

RASMUSSEN, LUCINDA ANN, social worker; b. St. Anthony, Idaho, Jan. 22, 1950; M in Social Work, U. Utah, 1981, PhD, 1995. Foster care worker Dept. Social Svcs., Family Svcs., 1981—83; social worker Utah State Prison, 1983—84; clin. social worker Primary Children's Med. Ctr., Salt Lake City, 1984—95; assoc. prof. San Diego State U. Sch. Social Work, 1995—. Bd. dirs. Calif. Coalition Sexual Offending, 2007—. Recipient Outstanding Grad. Faculty, San Diego State U. Coll. Health & Human Svcs., 2008, 2011. Mem.: NASW, Assn. Treatment Sexual Abusers. Avocations: travel, golf. Office: 5500 Campanile Dr San Diego CA 92182-4119 Business E-Mail: lucindarasmussen@cox.net.

RASMUSSEN, STEN GROTTRUP, radiology physician; b. Copenhagen, Mar. 12, 1943; s. Hans Peter and Lilly (Grottrup) R.; m. Kristin Lange, June 7, 1993; chldren Asger, Signe. MD, U. Copenhagen, 1970; postgrad in Ayurvedic Medicine, 1983—92; DSc in Creative Intelligence (hon.), Maharishi Vedic U., 1993. Cert. Gen. Practitioner, Nat. Bd. Health, Denmark, 1974, Diagnostic Radiology, Nat. Bd. Health, 1981. Trainee, surgery, psychiatry, internal medicine, radiology, 1971—81; clin. lectr., radiology U. Copenhagen, Gentofte Hosp., 1977—80; cons. radiologist Aarhus U. Hosp., Denmark, 1993—96; chief staff x-ray dept. Odder Hosp., Denmark, 1996—2003. Mem. various adv. bds., 1997—2003., cons. radiologist, Aarhus U. Hosp., 2003-06, Horsens, Braedstrup and Odder Regional Hosp., 2007-08. Bd. dir. Rörvig Folk H.S., 1999—2009. Mem. Danish Soc. Radiology. Avocations: meditation, epistemology. Personal E-mail: stenraz@gmail.com.

RASMUSSEN, VALAIRE N., biologist; b. Daly City, Calif., Dec. 6, 1966; BS in Economics, Calif. Poly. State U., San Luis Obispo, 1990. Cost analyst Air Force Flight Test Ctr., 1990—93; procurement analyst TRW Space and Def. Sector, 1993—2001; rsch. scientist Stanford U. Sch. Medicine, 2001—09; biostatistics cons., 2009—. Recipient Outstanding Achievement award, Calif. Poly. State U., Sch. Bus., Superior Performance award, Air Force Flight Test Ctr., US Air Force, Outstanding Performance award, TRW Space and Def. Sector. Mem.: Nat. Assn. of Profl. Women. Avocations: photography, travel. Home: 101 Dover Ct San Bruno CA 94066 Personal E-mail: valaire@earthlink.net.

RASOOL, SHEIKH AJAZ, microbiologist, educator, researcher; b. Talwan Jallandhar, India, Feb. 28, 1947; s. Sheihk Ziker Muhammad and Alam Bibi; m. Sadiya Ajaz, May 21, 1977; children: Muhammad Adil, Munazza, Muhammad Rabi. BS, D.J. Govt. Sci. Coll., Karachi, Pakistan, 1966; MS in Microbiology, U. Karachi, 1968; PhD, Moscow State U., 1976. Asst. lectr. U. Karachi, 1968-71, lectr., 1971-77, asst. prof., 1977-85, assoc. prof., 1985-89, prof. microbiology, 1989—, chmn. microbiology, 1996—2000, meritorious prof., 2004—, dean faculty sci., 2006—07, adj. prof., 2009—; eminent scientist & rschr. HEC, 2007—09. Vis. prof. microbiology Shah A. Latif U., Khairpur, Pakistan, 1980-81, 86, 88, registered rsch. supr., 1988—; vis. prof. Sindh U., 1998-2000; postdoctoral fellow biology U. Essex, Colchester, Eng., 1990; DSc (HC) The Open Intern U. for Complementary Medicine, Colombo, Sri Lanka, 1996. Author: Genetic Damages and Their Repair, 1987, Bacteriocins: The Protein Antibiotics, 1992, Manual of Microbiology for the Students of Medicine, 1995, Bacterial Viruses: basic and applied concepts, 2002; mem. editl. bd. World Applied Sci. Jour. Recipient Best Rschr. award, Kar. U., 1996, HEC Best Univ. Tchr. award, 2003, Lifetime Achievement award, 2004, Presdl. Acad. Excellence award, Aizaz_e_Kamal, 2007; rsch. grantee Karachi U., 1981—, U. Grants Commn., Pakistan, 1987, 90, 93, Pakistan Sci. Found., 1990-92, 94-97, 2000-03, 09-, Third World Acad. Scis., Italy, 1989, 93, Pakistan Atomic Energy Commn., 1994-97, Pakistan Agrl. Rsch. Coun., 2003-06, ONR USA Project, 1998-2000, WWF-Pak Water Project, 2006-08, HEC-Pak Project, 2006-08. Mem. Pakistan Microbiology Soc. (life), Pakistan Bot. Soc. (life), Pakistan Pharmacol. Soc. (life), NY Acad. Sci, Unikarians (life), Djarians (life). Muslim. Avocations: writing, chess, cricket, ping pong/table tennis, reading. Office: U Karachi Dept Microbiology Karachi Sindh 75270 Pakistan Home: A54/A Kar UnivHousing Sch 33 Sector 18A Karachi 75280 Pakistan Office Phone: 922199261111. Personal E-mail: rasoolajaz@yahoo.com.

RASSMAN, WILLIAM R., plastic surgeon; BS in Biology, L.I. U., 1962; MD, Med. Coll. Va., 1966. Diplomate Am. Bd. Surgery, lic. Calif., Fla., N.Y., Hawaii, Va., Pa., Ill., Nev., Ga., N.C., Wash., Colo., Md., N.J. Intern U. Minn., 1966—67; fellow in cardiovascular surgery Cornell Med. Ctr., 1968—69, resident in orthop. surgery, 1967—69; resident in gen. vascular surgery Dartmouth Med. Ctr., 1971—73; founder, mng. ptnr. N.E. Kingdom Surg. Assocs., 1973—79; staff surgeon, bus. advisor Hilo Med. Group, 1979—83; pres. Bosley Med. Group, 1988—90; CEO IntelliMED Corp., 1984—; pres., founder RW2 Med. Group, 2001—; founder, pres. Maven Technologies, 2001—, New Hair Inst. Med. Group, LA, 1991—. Cons. IBM, Hosp. Corp. Am., Control Data Corp., E.I. DuPont; lectr. in field. Achievements include patents for hair transplant harvesting device and method for its use; development of and design of heart valves, intra-aortic balloon pump and balloon technology, safety chamber for intra-aortic balloon; and design pulsatile assistance device; design of sophisticated commercial point of transaction clinical information systems for surgery; software scheduling system with application in real time. Office: 2080 Century Park E STE 607 Los Angeles CA 90067-2009

RÅSTAM, LENNART, physician, educator; b. Kristinehamn, Värmland, Sweden, Mar. 8, 1945; s. Åke and Kerstin Råstam; m. Ann Sofi Gemfeldt, May 14, 1967; children: Jacob, Johanna Rydergren, Maria. MD, Gothenburg U., 1972, PhD, 1983. Prof. pub. health and medicine Lund U., Malmö, Sweden, 1995—, chmn. dept. cmty. medicine, 1998—2004, chmn. dept. clin. scis., 2005—. Fellow: Am. Heart Assn. E-mail: lennart.rastam@med.lu.se.

RASTOGI, ANIL KUMAR, health products executive; b. India, July 13, 1942; came to U.S., 1969, naturalized, 1978; s. R.S. and K.V. Rastogi; m. Anjali Capur, Mar. 18, 1970; children: Priya, Sonya. BS with honors, Lucknow U., 1963, MS, 1964; PhD in Polymer Sci.,

McGill U., 1969. From staff to dir. corp. diversification portfolio Owens-Corning Tech. Ctr., Granville, Ohio, 1969—87; v.p. Mead Imaging, Miamisburg, Ohio, 1987-89; pres. Mead Cycolor Divsn., Dayton, Ohio, 1989-92; v.p., gen. mgr.infusion systems div. Pharmacia Deltec, Inc., St. Paul, 1992-93, exec. v.p., 1993-94; COO SIMS Deltec, Inc., St. Paul, 1994-95; pres., COO Sabratek Corp., Niles, Ill., 1995—98; pres., CEO NOMOS Corp., Sewickley, Pa., 1998—2002; v.p. entrepeneurship and tech. commercialization Drexel U., Phila., 2002—05; pvt. investor Reston, Va., 2005—. Mem. adv. bd. Central Ohio Tech. Coll.; lectr., cons. in field. Author of 15 bus. and tech. publs.; patentee in field. Bd. dirs. Licking County Family Services Assn.; bd. dirs. Tech. Alliance of Central Ohio; v.p. local United Way; bd. dirs. and treas. Columbus Bus. Tech. Ctr.; mem. Overview Adv. Com. Strategic Hwy. Research Program. Fellow NRC Can., 1966-69 Mem. AAAS, Am. Mgmt. Assn., Am. Chem. Soc., Soc. Plastics Engrs., Comml. Devel. Assn., Med. Alley (bd. dirs.), Health Ind. Mfrs. Assn., Nat. Infusion Therapy Alliance (bd. dirs.), Toastmasters (past pres.), Rotary, Sigma Xi. Home and Office: 704 Applehill Ct Gibsonia PA 15044

RASTOGI, RAJUL, radiologist; b. Ajmer, Rajasthan, Sept. 17, 1975; MBBS, Jawahar Lal Nehru Med. Coll., Ajmer, 2000; MD in Radio-Diagnosis, Sardar Patel Med. Coll., Bikaner, Rajasthan, 2003. Cons., head radiologist Yash Hosp. and Rsch. Hosp., 2006—. Contbr. articles to sci. profl. jours. Recipient Gold & Silver medal, Jawahar Lal Nehru Med. Coll., Utkrashtha Sewa Samman award, Prerna Manch, Moradabad. Mem.: Indian Med. Assn., Indian Coll. Radiology and Imaging, Indian Radiol. and Imaging Assn. (Dr. V.P. Lakhanpal Gold medal, Dr. K.M. Rai Oration award), Nat. Acad. Med. Scis., Internat. Med. Scis. Acad. Office: Civil Lines Kanth Rd Moradabad Uttar Pradesh 244001 India

RATH, BARBARA ANGELIKA, pediatrician; MD, Friedrich-Alexander-U., Erlangen, Germany; Dr. med., U. Basel, Switzerland. Lic. Ministry Health, Munich/Bavaria, 1998, cert. ECFMG Phila., 2000, lic. US med. LSBME, New Orleans, 2003. Intern AiP infectious diseases Depts. Virology and Internal Medicine, Ludwig Maximilans U., Munich, 1996—98; postdoc. rsch. fellow, infectious diseases Stanford U., Palo Alto, 1998—2001; resident, pediat. Duke U. Med. Ctr., Durham, 2001—03; clin. fellow, pediatric infectious diseases Tulane U., New Orleans, 2003—06; rsch. assoc. U. Children's Hosp., Basel, Switzerland, 2006—07; fellow, pediatric intensive care Dept. Pediat., Med. U. Vienna, 2008—. Prin. investigator, pediatric HIV trial Hosp. del Nino, Lima, Peru, 2005—; gen. coord., Brighton Collaboration U. Children's Hosp., Basel, 2006—07; founder, co-chair, Internat. Implementation Working Group Brighton Collaboration, 2007—, leader, bell's palsy working group, 2007—08; founder Vienna Vaccine Safety Initiative Med. U. Vienna, 2008—. Contbr. articles to numerous profl. jours. Mem. Bring New Orleans Back Health and Social Svcs. Com., New Orleans, 2005. Recipient Second Pl. Award, 4th Fellow/Resident Rsch. Symposium, Duke Pediat., 2002, Poster award, 42nd Ann. Meeting of IDSA, Pediatric Infectious Disease Soc., 2004, Travel award, 42nd Ann. Meeting IDSA, 2004; grantee Matching Funds, U. Children's Hosp. Basel, 2006, Brighton Collaboration WHO Proposal, 2007, Brighton Collaboration Proposal, European Ctr. Disease Prevention and Control, 2007; scholar Rsch. Award, SE Europe Soc. (DAAD), 1994, ERASMUS, European Union, 1995, Individual stipend for rsch. elective in Lima, Peru, Bloomberg Sch. Pub. Health, 2005; Fed. scholarship for Particularly Gifted Graduates, State of Bavaria, Germany, 1989—96, Travel grants, Deutscher Akademischer Austausch Dienst, 1995, Stanford Postdoctoral fellowship (AIDS Tng. Grant), Stanford U., 1998—2001. Mem.: AMA, Austrian Med. Assn., European Soc. for Pediatric Infectious Diseases, Pediatric Infectious Diseases Soc., Infectious Diseases Soc. Am., Am. Acad. Pediat., Medicus Mundi, Bavarian Med. Assn. Personal E-mail: barbara.rath@gmail.com.

RATH, LINDA LORRAINE, nurse; b. Conneaut, Ohio, Jan. 9, 1953; d. Charles Virgil and Alva Lorraine (Borowoky) R. BS, Lynchburg Coll., 1979; MS in Nursing, Vanderbilt U., 1983. Cert. neonatal nurse practitioner. Staff nurse Va. Bapt. Hosp., Lynchburg, 1974-76, charge nurse, supr., 1976-79; nursing instr. Lynchburg Gen. Hosp., 1979-80; asst. head nurse Duke U., Durham, N.C., 1980-81; staff nurse Nashville Gen. Hosp., 1982-83; neonatal nurse practitioner U. Tenn. Med. Ctr., Nashville, 1983-85, transport coordinator, nursing supr., flight nurse, 1985—; emergency med. technician Knoxville, Tenn., 1988—. Mem. neonatal adv. com. subcom. on transp., Tenn., 1985—; mem. Tenn. Emergency Med. Technician Helicopter Safety Task Force, 1987. Vanderbilt U. Coll. Nursing vis. scholar-grantee, Nashville, 1982. Mem. Nat. Flight Nurses Assn., Nat. Assn. Neonatal Nurses (standards of practice com. 1988—), Sigma Theta Tau. Republican. Office: U Tenn Med Ctr 1924 Alcoa Hwy # 113D Knoxville TN 37920-1511

RATH, MAURICE MONROE, retired physician; b. Newark, Oct. 2, 1914; s. Sigmund and Lena (Marenus) R.; m. Lydia Harke, Nov. 17, 1940; 1 child, Roger. AB, Ind. U., 1936, MD, 1943; MS, NYU, 1941; PhD, U. Md., Balt., 1942. Diplomate Am. Bd. Family Practice. Pvt. practice, Short Hills, NJ, 1946-63; with FDA, Washington, 1963-65; med. dir. Carter-Wallace Pharm. Co., Cranbury, NJ, 1965-70; dir. restoration ctr. VA Hosp., East Orange, NJ, 1970-73; med. staff physician VA Hosps., Tampa, St. Petersburg, Fla., 1973-80. Assoc. prof. clin. pharmacology Med. Coll. U. NJ, Newark, 1970-75; assoc. prof. medicine U. South Fla. Med. Sch., Tampa, 1973-80; rschr. in field. With USPHS, 1943-46. Fellow Am. Coll. Cardiology, Stroke Coun., Am. Heart Assn., Am. Coll. Therapeutics and Clin. Pharmacology; mem. Phi Beta Kappa, Alpha Omega Alpha. Home: 641 Via Milano Circle Apopka FL 32712

RATHI, MANOHAR LAL, pediatrician, neonatologist; b. Beawar, Rajasthan, India, Dec. 25, 1933; came to U.S. 1969, naturalized; s. Bagtawarmal and Sitadevi (Laddha) R.; m. Kamla Jajoo, Feb. 21, 1960; children: Sanjeev A., Rajeev. MBBS, Rajasthan U., 1961. Diplomate Am. Bd. Pediats., sub-bd. Neonatal Perinatal Medicine; lic. physician, N.Y., Ill., Calif. Resident house physician internal medicine Meml. Hosp., Darlington, U.K., 1963-64; resident sr. house physician pediatrics Gen. Hosp., Oldham, U.K., 1964-65; dir. perinatal medicine Christ Hosp. Perinatal Ctr., Oak Lawn, Ill., 1974-98, attending physician, 1974—2002; assoc. prof. pediatrics Rush Med. Coll., Chgo., 1979—; cons. obstetrician Christ Hosp., Oak Lawn, 1974—2000; cons. neonatologist Little Company of Mary Hosp., Evergreen Park, Ill., 1972—2002, Palos Cmty. Hosp., Palos Heights, Ill., 1978—2002; chmn. Midwest Neoped Assocs., Oak Brook, Ill., 1997—2009. Cons./lectr. in field. Contbr. articles to profl. jours.; editor: Clinical Aspects of Perinatal Medicine, 1984, Vol. I, 1985, Vol. II, 1986, Current Perinatology, 1989, Vol. II, 1990; editor with others: Perinatal Medicine Vol. I, 1978, Vol. I, 1980, Vol. II, 1982. Hummell Found. grantee, 1976-77, WyethLab grantee, 1977-78; recipient Physicians Recognition award AMA, 1971-74, 91-92, Outstanding New Citizen's award State of Ill., 1978, Asian Human Svcs. of Chgo., 1988, Nitric Oxide Study by Ohmeda, 1994-95. Fellow Am. Acad. Pediats. (perinatal sect., Ill. chpt. treas. 1994-96); mem. AMA, Chgo. Med. Soc., Ill. Med. Soc., Chgo. Pediat. Soc., Med. Soc. County of Kings Bklyn., N.Y. Acad. Scis., Am. Thoracic Soc., Soc. Critical Care Medicine. Republican. Hindu. Office Phone: 630-325-8847. Personal E-mail: mrathi33@gmail.com.

RATHOD, DINESH, pathologist; b. Ahmedabad, India, Nov. 24, 1974; MD in Pathology, M. P. Shah Med. Coll., 2002. Pathologist Superreligare Diagnostics, Ahmedabad, 2002—. Mem.: GAPM. Home: D-502 Supath-2 Apt Old Vadaj Ahmedabad Gujarat 380013 India Personal E-mail: rathod_pathology@rediffmail.com.

RATNAKAR, KAMARAJU SUGUNA, pathologist, educator; b. Guntur, Nov. 30, 1944; MBBS, Guntur Med. Coll., 1968; MD, All India Inst. Med. Scis., 1972. Head ocular pathology All India Inst. Med. Scis., 1973—79; prof., head pathology M R Med. Coll., Gulbarga, Karnataka, 1979—86; dean, prof. pathology Nizams Inst. Med. Scis., Hyderabad, Andhra Pradesh, India, 1986—2004; prof. Global Med. Edn. & Rsch., Global Hosps., Hyderabad, 2005—. Dean NIMS, 1993—98. Recipient Prof Govinda Reddy Gold medal, NTR Health U. Fellow: Indian Coll. Pathologists, Internat. Coll. Surgeons; mem.: Indian Assn. Pathologists and Microbiologists (BK Aikat Oration Gold medal). Avocations: reading, writing. Home: 1-216/159 St Ln 2 Karthikeyan Hyderabad Andhra Pradesh 500076 India Personal E-mail: kamaraju.ratnakar@gmail.com.

RATNER, BUDDY DENNIS, biomedical engineer, educator; b. Bklyn., Jan. 19, 1947; s. Philip and Ruth Ratner; m. Cheryl Cromer; 1 child, Daniel Martin. BS in Chemistry, Bklyn. Coll., 1967; PhD in Polymer Chemistry, Bklyn. Poly. U., 1972. From fellow to prof. U. Wash., Seattle, 1972—86, prof., 1986—, Darland prof. bioengring., 2005—. Dir. U. Wash. Engineered Biomaterials Engring. Ctr.; founder Asemblon, Inc., Healionics, Inc. Editor: Surface Characterization of Biomaterials, 1989, Plasmas and Polymers, 1994-99, Biomaterials Science: An Introduction to Materials in Medicine, 2d edit., 2004, Characterization of Polymeric Biomaterials, 1997; mem. editl. bds. 9 jours. and book series; editor Jour. Undergrad. Rsch. in Bioengring., 1998—; contbr. over 400 articles to profl. jours. Recipient Faculty Achievement/Outstanding Rsch. award, 1990, Perkin Elmer Phys. Electronics award for excellence in surface sci., Acta Biomaterialia Gold medal, 2009. Fellow AAAS, Internat. Acad. Med. and Biol. Engring., Am. Inst. Med. Biol. Engring. (founder, pres. 2002-03), AVS Sci. Technol. Soc. (Medard Welsh medal 2002); mem. AIChE (C.M.A. Stine award 1998), Nat. Acad. Engring., Am. Chem. Soc., Internat. Soc. Contact Lens Rsch., Materials Rsch. Soc., Soc. for Biomaterials (pres. 1991-92, Clemson award 1989, fellow 1994, Founders award 2004, C.W. Hall award 2006), Biomed. Engring. Soc. Achievements include patents in field. Home Phone: 206-286-0969; Office Phone: 206-685-1005. E-mail: ratner@uweb.engr.washington.edu.

RATTAN, SURESH INDER SINGH, gerontologist, researcher, philosopher; b. Amritsar, Punjab, India, May 20, 1955; s. Mohinder Singh and Kamal Jit Rattan; m. Anita Doodani, July 23, 1979; 1 child, Anuresh Rishabh. BSc with honors, Guru Nanak Dev U., Amritsar, 1976, MSc with honors, 1977; MPh, Jawaharlal Nehru U., New Delhi, 1979; PhD, Nat. Inst. Med. Rsch., London, 1982; DSc, Aarhus U., Denmark, 1995. Pool officer Jawaharlal Nehru U., New Delhi, 1983-84; assoc. prof. Aarhus U., Denmark, 1984—2001, prof. biogerontology, 2001—. Cons. Senetek Biotech. Co., London, 1986-2006. Editor: (spl. issue) Mutation Research on Aging, 1991, 12 books; mem. editl. bd. BioEssays Jour., 1985-90, Mutation Rsch.: DNAging, 1989-95, Jour. Bioscis., 1991-94; chief editor Biogerontology, series editor of a five volume books on biology of aging; inventor patent for certain anti-aging formulae of kinetin; originator of concept of virtual genes for aging called virtual gerontogenes and vitagenes; contbr. over 180 sci., psychol. and lit. articles to internat. jours., mags. and newspapers. Brit. Coun. fellow, 1979-82. Avocations: tabla drums, literary writing. Office: Aarhus U Dept Molecular Biology Aarhus DK-8000 Denmark Office Phone: 45-89-42-5034. Personal E-mail: sureshrattan@hotmail.com.

RATTNER, DAVID W., surgeon; MD, Johns Hopkins U. Sch. Medicine, 1978. Diplomate Am. Bd. of Surgery, 1986. Intern, surgery Mass. Gen. Hosp., Boston, 1978—79, resident, surgery, 1979—85, chief gen. and gastrointestinal surgery divsn., 1999—; prof. surgery Harvard Med. Sch., Boston. Contbr. articles to profl. jours. Mem.: ACS, Am. Surgical Assn., Soc. for Surgery Alimentary Tract, Soc. Surgical Oncology, Soc. Am. Gastrointestinal and Endoscopic Surgeons (pres. 2004—05). Office: Mass Gen Hosp Divsn Gen Surgery 15 Parkmans St WANG (WACC) 460 Boston MA 02114 Office Fax: 617-724-0355. Business E-Mail: drattner@partners.org. *

RAU, BETTINA M., surgeon, researcher; b. Memmingen/Allgaeu, Germany, Feb. 22, 1966; Abitur (Coll.), Kolleg der Schulbrueder, Illertissen/Germany, 1976—85. Bd. cert. surgeon Aerztekammer Baden-Wuerttemberg, Germany, 2002. Resident in gen. surgery Dep. of Surgery, U. of Ulm, Ulm, Germany, 1994—2002; chief resident in gen. surgery Dep. of Surgery, U. Saarland, Homburg/Saar, Germany, 2002—03, attending surgeon, 2004—. Med. cons. selfstanding, Homburg/Saar, Germany, 2004—. Editor (asst.): (professional scientific periodical) Langenbeck's Archives of Surgery; contbr. scientific papers 25 reviews, articles numerous pub. to profl. jour., chapters to books. Recipient Abraham-Vater Clin. Pancreatology prize, German Pancreatic Club, 2003, Best Clin. Paper award, 19th World Congress Internat. Soc. Digestive Surgery, 2004; grantee, German Fed. Ministery of Edn. and Rsch., 1996—98, European Pancreatic Club, 1997—99, German Rsch. Coun., 1998—2001, 2001—04, Am. Pancreatic Assn., 2000, U. Saarland, 2005. Mem.: Internat. Assn. of Pancreatology (corr.), European Hepato Pancreato Biliary Assn. (assoc.), German Soc. of Visceral Surgery (assoc.), German Soc. of Surgery (assoc.), European Digestive Surgery (assoc.). Office: Univ Saarland Bldg 57 Kirrberger Strasse 72076 Homburg 66421 Germany Office Fax: 0049-6841-16 23132.

RAU, MAGDA, ophthalmologist; b. Zlin, Czechoslovakia, Aug. 31, 1952; arrived in Germany, 1982; d. Jaromir Broul and Vera Broulova; m. Cestmir Mican, Dec. 20, 1975 (div. 1992); 1 child, Cestmir Mican; m. Björn Rau, Dec. 23, 1996. Degree, Coll., Frydlant, Czechoslovakia, 1970; med. diploma, Palacky U., Olomouc, 1976; ophthalmologist diploma, Prag, Czechoslovakia, 1980, Munich, 1984. Intern Residency Hosp., Frydek-Mistek, Czech Republic, 1976—82; ophthalmologist Prof. Dr. Dausch Eye Dept., Amberg, Germany, 1983—85; practice owner Furth Im Wald, 1985—; day clinic owner Augenklinik, Cham, 1995—; chief ophthalmologist Hosp., 1995—; pvt. clinic owner Privatklinik Rau, 2000—. Contbr. articles to opththalmological jours.; author: (interactive CD-ROM) ICRS (Intrastromal Corneal Ring Segments), 1999, 2001; co-author: (book) Multifocal IOLS, 2008; author: Lasek-Viscodissection for Multicokale Ols, Mikro Koaxizle Thacoemulsifikation; contbr. articles to profl. jours.; co-author: Lasek Lasek Viscodissection Multinationale IOLs MCP. Mem. Albert Schweizer Stiftung Lambarene, 1996. Mem.: European Soc. Cataract and Refractice Surgery, Internat. Soc. Refractive Surgery. Roman Catholic. Avocations: tennis, horseback riding, skiing, skating. Home: Aepflet 24 93437 Furth im Wald Germany Office: Ophtalmologist Practice Von Mueller Str 12 93437 Furth im Wald Germany Office Phone: 00499973-801242.

RAU, ROLF, retired rheumatologist, human services manager; b. Kolmar, Posen, Germany, Nov. 7, 1933; s. Paul and Hildegard (Guse) R. MD, Med. Clinic, Giessen, Germany, 1960, asst. prof. medicine, 1981, prof. medicine, 1989. Med. asst. Med. Clinic, Gießen, 1961-69, Rheumatism Clin. Universitätsspital, Zürich, Switzerland, 1969—71; sr. physician Rheumatism Clin. Stadtspital Triemli, Zürich, 1971-78; head dept. rheumatology Evang. Fachkrankenhaus, Ratingen, Germany, 1978-98. Contbr. numerous articles to profl. jours. on rheumatism and its treatment, radiology of rheumatoid arthritin, chpts. to textbooks on rheumatology; author (books) Treatment with Gold, MTX, Biologics, Imaging Methods in RA, Atlas on Scoring Methods. Master Am. Coll. Rheumatology, Swiss Assn. Rheumatology, German Assn. Rheumatology (hon.), German Internal Medicine Assn., Austrian Assn. Rheumatology. Avocations: hiking, tennis, piano, theater. Home: Irisweg 5 D-40489 Düsseldorf Germany Office Phone: 49 203 740441. E-mail: rau.herborn@t-online.de.

RAUCHER, HAROLD S., pediatrician, educator; MD, Mt. Sinai Sch. Medicine, 1978. Diplomate Am. Bd. Pediatrics, Am. Bd. Pediatrics-pediatric infectious disease. Assoc. clin. prof. pediat. Mt. Sinai Sch. Medicine; intern in pediat. Mt. Sinai Med. Ctr., resident in pediat., 1978—80, fellow in pediatric infectious disease, 1980—82, pediatrician; with Lenox Hill Hosp. Office: Mount Sinai Medical Center 1125 Pk Ave New York NY 10128 Office Phone: 212-289-1400. Office Fax: 212-289-5714.

RAUDONE BUMBLAUSKIENE, LINA, research scientist, educator; b. Kaunas, Lithuania, June 10, 1983; PhD, Lithuanian U. Health Scis., 2006. Asst. prof. Lithuanian U. Health Scis., 2006—, rsch. scientist, 2010—. Avocations: literature, photography, swimming. Office: Mickeviciaus 9 Kaunas 44307 Lithuania Personal E-mail: lina3b@yahoo.com, raudone.lina@gmail.com.

RAUGALIENE, RASA, cardiologist; b. Lithuania, Nov. 14, 1953; MD, Kaunas Inst. Medicine, 1977, PhD. Sr. rschr. Kaunas Inst. Cardiology, 1977—2010; physician Kaunas Clin. Hosp., 2004—. Assoc. prof. Kaunas Acad. Phys. Edn., 2005. Mem.: European Soc. Cardiology. Avocations: travel, gardening, skiing. Home: Vijokliu 43 2 Kacergine Kauno Raj LT 53446 Lithuania Home Fax: 370 37263694. Personal E-mail: rasarau@gmail.com, rasara@takas.lt.

RAUSHER, DAVID BENJAMIN, internist, gastroenterologist; b. Bklyn., Sept. 15, 1952; s. Herbert and Shirley Ruth R.; m. Judy A. Steinlauf, Aug. 8, 1976; children: Scott, Michael, Steven. BA, Hamilton Coll., 1973; MD, SUNY, Bklyn., 1977. Diplomate Am. Bd. Internal Medicine, Am. Bd. Gastroenterology. Resident Emory U. Hosps., Atlanta, 1977-80, fellow in gastroenterology, 1980-82; pres. Atlanta Ctr. for Gastroenterology, Decatur, Ga., 1982—; med. dir. Atlanta Endoscopy Ctr., Decatur, 1994—. Chmn. diagnostic treatment ctr. DeKalb Med. Ctr., Decatur, Ga., 1985—, co-chief gastroenterology, 1995-97, chief sect. gastroenterology, 1998—. Fellow: Am. Gastroenterology Assn., Am. Coll. Gastroenterology. Office Phone: 404-296-1986.

RAVDIN, PETER MARCUS, internist, educator, oncologist; b. June 3, 1949; MD, U. Miami Sch. Med., 1981; PhD in Neurobiology, Cornell U. Cert. Internal Medicine, Med. Oncology. Resident U. Wis., Madison, 1981—84, fellow, 1984—87; asst. prof. to clin. prof. med. oncology U. Tex. Health Sci. Ctr., San Antonio; rsch. prof. biostatistics U. Tex. MD Anderson Cancer Ctr., San Antonio; exec. officer Southwest Oncology Group. Spkr. in field. Prin. author (computer program) Adjuvant!; contbr. several articles to profl. jours.

RAVÉ, GUILLAUME, physical education educator; b. Mayenne, France, Apr. 8, 1984; MS, UFR Montpellier, France, 2007. Phys. trainer Profl. Sports Ltd. Co., Stade Lavallois Mayenne Football Club, 2007. Home: 58 Bis rue Sainte Catherine Laval Pays de la Loire 53000 France Business E-Mail: rave.gui@voila.fr.

RAVEH, JORAM, retired otolaryngologist, craniomaxillofacial surgeon; s. Deborah Rosenstrauch-Berniker and Siegfried Rosenstrauch; m. Heidi Roth, Oct. 26, 1966; 1 child, Shirley. Dr. in Dental Medicine, U. Berne, 1967; Dr. in Medicine, U. Tel-Aviv, 1972. Cert. in otolaryngology, head neck surgery U. Berne, 1980. Craniomaxillofacial surgeon U. Tel-Aviv, 1967—71, 1973—80, 1985—2005; assoc. prof. U. Berne, 1980—85, developed unique dept. including otolaryngology, craniomaxillofacial, skull base aspects, 1985—2005, head, assoc. prof., full prof. Invited speaker, course director craniofacial/skull base congress meetings, 1983—2005. Contbr. chapters to books, articles to med. jours. Fellowship dir. Am. Acad. Facial Plastic/Reconstructive Surgery, 1992—2005, del. war injuries reconstruction Croatia, 1993; sr. mem. Acad. Facial Plastic and Reconstructive Surgery. First lt. Air Force, 1958—60, Israel, Army Military Svc. Recipient Edn. Courses award, Am. Acad. Otolaryngology, Head/Neck, 1997, award, N.Am. Skull Base Soc., 2005. Mem.: European Skull Base Bd. (exec. mem. 2001—05), Am. Acad. Facial Plastic. Achievements include innovative methods concerning Craniomaxillofacial and Skull Base Surgery, Titanium, Plates, Rigid Screw Fixation, Lower Jaw joint Prosthesis, Subcranial approach for management Skull Base Tumors, Anomalies, Injuries; these methods were adopted by the specialties worldwide. Home: Koenizberg St 76 3097 Berne 3097 Switzerland Office Phone: 0041319722829. Home Fax: 0041319726129. Personal E-mail: j.raveh@bluewin.ch.

RAVEN, BERTRAM H(ERBERT), psychology professor; b. Youngstown, Ohio, Sept. 26, 1926; s. Morris and Lillian R.; m. Celia Cutler, Jan. 21, 1961; children: Michelle G., Jonathan H. BA in psychology summa cum laude with great distinction, Ohio State U., 1949, MA in psychology, 1950; PhD in social psychology, U. Mich., 1953. Rsch. assoc. Rsch. Ctr. for Group Dynamics, Ann Arbor, Mich., 1952-54; lectr. psychology U. Mich., Ann Arbor, 1953-54; vis. prof. U. Nijmegen, U. Utrecht, Netherlands, 1954-55; psychologist RAND Corp., Santa Monica, Calif., 1955-56; prof. UCLA, 1956—, chair dept. psychology, 1983-88, prof. emeritus, 1991—. Vis. prof. Hebrew U., Jerusalem, 1962-63, U. Wash., Seattle, 1965, U. Hawaii, Honolulu, 1968, London Sch. Econs. and Polit. Sci., 1969-70; external examiner U. of the W.I., Trinidad and Jamaica, 1980—, rsch. assoc. Psychol. Rsch. Ctr., 1993—; participant Internat. Expert Conf. on Health Psychology, Tilburg, Netherlands, 1986; cons., expert witness in field, 1979—; mem. internat. adv. bd. Acad. Freedom, Bar-Ilan U., 2005—; mem. sci. bd. Kurt Lewin Ctr. Psychol. Rsch. Kazimierza Wielkiego U., Poland; affiliate prof. U. Haifa, 2006—. Author: (with others) People in Groups, 1976, Discovering Psychology, 1977, Social Psychology, 1983, Social Psychology: People in Groups (Chinese edit.), 1994; editor: (with others) Contemporary Health Services, 1982, Policy Studies Rev. Ann., 1980; editor: (with others) Lewinian Psychology, 2006; editor: Jour. Social Issues, 1969-74; mem. editl. bd. Jour. of Criminology and Social Psychology, 2001-, Revista de Psicologia de la Salud, 1995-; mem. adv. bd. Jour. Entrepreneurship, 2004-; contbr. articles to profl. jours. Co-dir. Tng. Program in Health Psychology, UCLA, 1979-88; cons. WHO, Manila, 1985-86; cons., expert witness various Calif. cts., 1978—; mem. bd. dir., UCLA Emeriti Assn., 2007-. Guggenheim fellow, Israel, 1962-63; Fulbright scholar Netherlands, 1954-55, Israel, 1962-63, Britain, 1969-70; recipient Citation from L.A. City Coun., 1966, 2006, Rsch. on Soc. power by Calif. Sch. of profl. psychology, L.A., 1991; NATO sr. fellow, Italy, 1989. Fellow APA (chair bd. social and ethical responsibility 1978-82, ethics com. 2003-06), Assn. Psychol. Sci., Soc. for Psychol. Study of Social Issues (pres. 1973-74, coun. 1995-97, Kurt Lewin award 1998), Soc. for Personality and Social Psychology; mem. AAAS, Am. Sociol. Assn., Internat. Assn. Applied Psychology, Soc. Exptl. Social Psychology, Assn. Advancement of Psychology (founding, bd. dirs. 1974-81), Internat. Soc. Polit. Psychology (governing coun. 1996-98), Interam. Psychol. Soc., Am. Psychology-Law Soc. Democrat. Jewish. Avocations: guitar, travel, international studies. Home: 2212 Camden Ave Los Angeles CA 90064-1906 Office: UCLA Dept Psychology Los Angeles CA 90095-1563 Business E-Mail: raven@ucla.edu.

RAVENHOLT, REIMERT THOROLF, epidemiologist, researcher; b. Milltown, Wis., Mar. 9, 1925; s. Ansgar Benedikt and Kristine Henriette (Petersen) R.; divorced; children: Janna, Mark, Lisa, Dane; m. Betty Butler Howell, Sept. 26, 1981. BS, U. Minn., 1948, MB, 1951, MD, 1952; MPH, U. Calif., Berkeley, 1956. Bd. cert. preventive medicine. Intern USPHS Hosp., San Francisco, 1951-52; epidemic intelligence service officer USPHS Communicable Disease Ctr., Atlanta, 1952-54; dir. epidemiology and communicable disease div. Seattle-King County Health Dept., 1954-61; epidemiology cons. European area USPHS, Paris, 1961-63; assoc. prof. preventive medicine U. Wash. Med. Sch., Seattle, 1963-66; dir. Office of Population, AID, Washington, 1966-79, World Health Surveys, Ctrs. for Disease Control, 1980-82; asst. dir. epidemiology and research Nat. Inst. Drug Abuse, Rockville, Md., 1982-84; chief epidemiology br. FDA, Rockville, Md., 1984-87; dir. World Health Surveys, Inc., Seattle, 1987-93; pres. Population Health Imperatives, Seattle, 1993—. Author/designer website Adventures in Epidemiology. Served with USPHS, 1951-54, 61-63. Recipient Disting Honor award AID, 1973, Hugh Moore Meml. award IPPF and Population Crisis Com., 1974. Fellow Am. Coll. Epidemiology, APHA (Carl Schultz award 1978), mem. Am. Coun. on Sci. and Health (bd. dirs.); mem. Cosmos Club (Washington). Independent. Achievements include discovery of cause of Meriwether Lewis' death of progressive neurosyphilis and benguineu fronklinedire illness from second stage syphodis; malinquont cellular evolution, the loucet, and originator world Fertility survey. Home: 3156 E Laurelhurst Dr NE Seattle WA 98105-5333

RAVETCH, JEFFREY VICTOR, molecular biologist, immunologist, educator; s. Sylvia and Paul H. Ravetch; m. Wendy Evans Joseph, Oct. 27, 2001. Grad., Yale U., New Haven; PhD in Genetics, Rockefeller U.; MD, Cornell U. Postdoctoral rschr. NIH; mem. faculty Meml. Sloan-Kettering Cancer Ctr. and Cornell Med. Coll., 1982; guest investigator lab. cellular physiology and immunology Rockefeller U., NYC, 1984, prof., 1996—, Theresa and Eugene M. Lang prof., 1997—, head of Leonard Wagner lab. molecular genetics and immunology. Mem. sci. adv. bd. Cancer Rsch. Inst., Irvington Inst. Med. Rsch., Damon Runyon Found.; co-founder, former dir. MacroGenics, Rockville, Md., 2000. Contbr. articles to profl. jours. Recipient Burroughs Wellcome Fund award in molecular parasitology, 1986, Willam B. Coley award, Cancer Rsch. Inst., 2007; named a Pew Scholar, 1985. Fellow: Am. Acad. Arts and Sciences, NAS; mem.: NAS Inst. Medicine, Am. Assn. Immunologists (Lee J. Howley Jr. award 2004, Huang Found. Meritorious Career award 2005). Office: Leonard Wagner Lab Molecular Genetics and Immunology Rockefeller U 1230 York Ave New York NY 10021 E-mail: ravetch@rockefeller.edu.

RAVIKUMAR, THANJAVUR SUBRAMANIAM, surgical oncologist; b. Madras, India, Mar. 12, 1950; came to U.S., 1976; s. P. and Rajamani Subramaniam; m. Srikala Kandaswamy, Sept. 8, 1975; 1 child, Shruti. MS, Madras Med. Coll., 1976; MD, U. Edinburgh, Scotland, 1978. Diplomate Am. Bd. Surgery. Surg. resident Maimonides Med. Ctr., Maimonides Hosp., Bklyn., 1976-80; surg. oncology fellow U. Minn. Hosps., Mpls., 1980-82; rsch. fellow Harvard Med. SCh., Boston, 1982-84, asst. prof. surgery, 1986-89, assoc. prof. surgery, 1989-90; asst. prof. surgery SUNY Downstate Med. Ctr., Bklyn., 1984-85; assoc. prof., chief surg. oncology Yale U. Sch. Medicine, New Haven, 1990—. Chmn. cancer com. Yale New Haven Hosp., 1991—; cancer program dir. Yale-China Assn., New Haven, 1992—; prof. surgery and molecular genetics Robert Wood Johnson Med. Sch., N.J., 1993-98; chief surgery, assoc. dir. Cancer Inst. of N.J., 1993-98; prof., chmn. dept. surgery Albert Einstein Coll. of Medicine, Montefiore Med. Ctr., N.Y., 1998—. Contbr. articles to profl. jours. Mandelberg traveling fellow Maimonides Med. Ctr., Bklyn., 1978. Fellow Royal Coll. Surgeons, Am. Coll. Cryosurgery; mem. Soc. Surg. Oncology (clin. trials and govt. rels. com. 1991—, James Ewing Found. award 1983), Soc. Univ. Surgeons, Am. Assn. Cancer Rsch. Achievements include first human clin. trial of isolated hepatic perfusion chemotherapy using a novel double balloon catheter for treating liver cancers, new approaches to treat tumors spread into liver with cryosurgery and laser surgery. Home: 239 E 79th St Apt 15B New York NY 10021-0816 Office: Albert Einstein Coll Medicine Montefiore Med Ctr 3400 Bainbridge Ave Fl 4 Bronx NY 10467-2404 E-mail: travikum@montefiore.org.

RAVINDRANATH, DIVY, psychiatrist; MS, U. Calif., Berkeley, 2003; MD, U. Calif., San Francisco, 2005. Staff psychiatrist Vets. Affairs Health Sys., 2010—. Recipient Laughlin fellowship, Am. Coll. Psychiatrists. Mem.: Assn. Academic Psychiatry, Acad. Psychosomatic Medicine, Am. Psychiat. Assn. Office: Ann Arbor VAMC 2215 Fuller Rd Ann Arbor MI 48105 Business E-Mail: divyr@med.umich.edu.

RAVINET, EMILIE CATHERINE MARIE, ophthalmologist, consultant; b. Boulogne, France, Apr. 28, 1966; d. Antoine Denarie and Andree Leport; m. Philippe Jacques Marie Ravinet, July 4, 1986; children: Alban, Marguerite, Thibault. MBBCh cum laude, Wits Med. Sch., S.Africa, 1990, degree in ophthalmology, 1996; doctorate, U. Lausanne, Switzerland, 2002. Cons. Wits U., 1998; fellow glaucome Hosp. Jules Gonin, Lausanne, Switzerland, 1998—2001, cons., 2001—. Contbr. articles and reviews to profl. jours., chapters to books. Mem.: French Opthal. Soc., South African Med. and Dental Coun., Swiss Ophthal. Soc. Home: Chemin des Geais 3 1066 Epalinges Switzerland E-mail: ravinet.emilie@bluewin.ch.

RAVNSKOV, UFFE, retired internist, nephrologist and researcher; b. Copenhagen, Oct. 12, 1934; s. Knud Erik and Birgitte (Germer) R.; m. Kirsten Ravnskov, 1959; children: Søren, Pernille, Lars; m. Bodil Thordarson, June 6, 1992. MD, U. Copenhagen, 1962; PhD, U. Lund, Sweden, 1973. Intern dept. surgery Hosp. Hudiksvall, Sweden, 1962-63; intern dept. medicine Hosp. Skellefteå, Sweden, 1963-64; resident dept. medicine Hosp. Sandviken, Sweden, 1964-68; rsch. fellow dept. nephrology U. Hosp. Lund, Sweden, 1968-71, rsch. fellow dept. clin. chemistry, 1971-72, asst. prof. dept. nephrology, 1972-79; pvt. practitioner, ind. rschr. Lund, 1979-2000; ret., 2000. Mem. editl. bd. Cholesterol and of Jour. Lipids. Author: The Cholesterol Myth, (Swedish edit.), 1991, (Finnish edit.), 1992, (Am. edit.), 2000, Fat & Cholesterol are Good for You, 2009, Swedish edit., 2010, Danish edit., 2010, Polish edit., 2010, Dutch edit., 2011, Ignore The Awkward, 2010, Danish and Swedish edit., 2010; contbr. articles to profl. jours. Recipient Skrabanek award The Skrabanek Found. Trinity Coll., 1998, Leo Huss-Walin award Goteborg U., 2007. Mem. Internat. Sci. Oversight Bd.(head Internat. Network Cholesterol Skeptics) Home: Magle Stora Kyrkogata 9 S-22350 Lund Sweden

RAWANDALE-PATIL, ASHISH, urologist, professor, researcher; b. Sheffield, Eng., July 31, 1971; MBBS, Pune, 1994, MS in Gen. Surgery, 1998; MCh in Urology, Bombay Hosp. Inst. Med. Scis., 2001. Dir. Tejnaksh Healthcare Pvt. Ltd. Urologist Inst. Urology, 2003. Named Guinness World Records. Mem.: Indian Urology Assn., European Urology Assn., Am. Urology Assn. Achievements include patents in field. Office: Inst Urology Sakri Rd Dhule Maharashtra 424001 India Personal E-mail: instituteofurology@gmail.com.

RAWITCH, ALLEN BARRY, medical educator, academic administrator; b. Chgo., Dec. 29, 1940; s. Sam and Jean Rawitch; m. Patricia Nan Karlan, July 21, 1962; children: Bruce, David. BS in Chemistry, UCLA, 1963, PhD in Biol. Chemistry, 1967. Rsch. fellow U. Ill., Urbana, 1967-69; asst. prof. Kent (Ohio) State U., 1969-73, assoc. prof., 1973-75, U. Kans. Med. Ctr., Kansas City, 1975-80, prof., 1980—, asst. dean student affairs, 1999-2000, vice chancellor acad. affairs, dean grad. studies, 2000—, chmn. biochemistry and molecular biology, 2002—03. Vice chair biochemistry U. Kans. Med. Ctr., 1977-95, chair edn. coun., 1995-99 Editor Med. Biochemistry Question Bank, 1985-94; contbr. articles to profl. jours. Res. police officer capt. Overland Park Police Dept., 1979—. Rsch. grant NIH, 1971-2000, NSF, 1970, Am. Heart Assn., 1998-2002. Mem. Am. Soc. for Biochemistry and Molecular Biology, The Protein Soc., Am. Thyroid Assn., Sigma Xi. Avocations: amateur radio, woodworking, target shooting. Office: Office Acad Affairs U Kans Med Ctr 3901 Rainbow Blvd Mail Stop 1040 Kansas City KS 66160-0001 Office Phone: 913-588-1258. Business E-Mail: arawitch@kumc.edu.

RAWLINGS, DOUGLAS ERIC, microbiology educator; b. East London, South Africa, Nov. 11, 1950; s. Herbert Edward and Dorothy Grace (Immelman) R.; m. Janet Lesley Asbury, Dec. 15, 1973; children: Barry, Kim, Sarah-Jane. BS with honors, Rhodes U., S. Africa, 1972, PhD, 1976. Rsch. officer Leather Industries Rsch. Inst., Grahamstown, 1976-77; lectr. U. of the Witwatersrand, Johannesburg, 1978-81; sr. lectr. U. Cape Town, 1982-87, prof., 1988-98; prof., chmn. dept. microbiology U. Stellenbosch, South Africa, 1998—, deputy dean, 2000—06, 2009—, dean, 2007—08. Cons. Sasol, Secunda, 1979-81. Contbr. articles to profl. jours., books and publs. Capt. S. African Def. Force/Army, 1970-81. Fellow U. Cape Town, 1990; named A-Rated Scientist, Found. for Rsch. Devel., S. Africa, 1992, 96, 2001, 2006; recipient PanLabs award Soc. Indsl. Microbiology, 1997, Rectors award U. Stellenbosch, 2005. Fellow Royal Soc. of S. Africa (gen. sec. 1997-2003, pres. 2004—); mem. South Africa Acad. Scis. (Havenga prize, 2011), South Africa Soc. Microbiology (Silver medalist 1992), SA Acad. Sci. & Arts (Havenga prize 2011). Assembly of God. Avocations: bicycling, orchid collecting. Office: Dept Microbiology Univ Stellenbosch 7600 Stellenbosch South Africa Office Fax: 27-21-808 5846. Personal E-mail: der@sun.ac.za.

RAWLINS, JEREMY MARK, plastic surgeon, educator; b. Aldershot, England, Feb. 19, 1974; s. Christopher John and Mary Joan Rawlins; m. Hazel Ruth Shurmer, Sept. 21, 2002; children: Anna Charlotte, Madeline Lucy, Edward Samuel, Isabelle Kate. MD with honors, U. Leeds, England, 1997; MPhil in Life Scis., U. Bradford, England, 2004; MRCS, Royal Coll. Surgeons, UK, 2002. Lic. plastic surgeon RCS, 2002. Surg. intern Leeds Gen. Infirmary, England, 1997—98; resident surg. officer Hervey Bay Hosp., Queensland, Australia, 1998—99; surg. residency St. James U. Hosp., Leeds, 2001—02; specialist plastic surgeon Yorkshire Deanery, Leeds, 2004—; plastic surgery and burns sr. fellow U. Western Australia, Royal Perth Hosp., 2009—; cons. plastic surgeon Mid-Yorkshire Hosps., 2010. Lectr. Plastic Surgery and Burns Rsch. Unit U. Bradford, 2002—. Contbr. articles to profl. jours. Fellow: RCS; mem.: Brit. Burn Assn., Brit. Assn. Plastic, Reconstructive, and Aesthetic Surgeons. Achievements include research in basic science, clinical, and epidemiological burns research; microsurgery; skin cancer; plastic surgery. Avocations: bicycling, running, swimming, sailing, photography. Personal E-mail: jeremy_rawlins@hotmail.com. Business E-Mail: j.m.rawlins@bradford.ac.uk.

RAWNSLEY, HOWARD MELODY, pathologist, educator; b. Long Branch, NJ, Nov. 20, 1925; s. Walter A. and Elizabeth (Melody) R.; m. B. Eileen Fiddes, Sept. 5, 1967; children: Virgilia Ingram, Elizabeth Sue. AB, Haverford Coll., Pa., 1949; MD, U. Pa., Phila., 1952. Diplomate Am. Bd. Pathology (trustee 1988-96). Intern Hosp. U. Pa., 1952-53, resident, 1953-57; practice medicine, specializing in pathology Phila., 1957-75; mem. Wm. Pepper Lab., U. Pa., 1957-75, asst. dir., 1960-68, dir., 1968-75; assoc. dir. Clin. Research Ctr., 1962-67, acting dir., 1969— 70, asst. prof. pathology and medicine, 1960-65, assoc. prof., 1965-69, prof., 1969—75; prof. pathology Dartmouth Hitchcock Med. Ctr., Hanover, NH, 1975-95, chmn. dept., 1980-87, sr. v.p. med. affairs, 1987-94. Cons. VA Hosp.; mem. exec. com. Am. Bd. Med. Spltys., 1998-2001. Chmn. bd. dirs. New Eng. Blood Svcs. ARC, 1996—2000, 2002—05. With US Army, 1944—46. Woodward fellow in chemistry, 1953-55 Mem. AMA, ARC (biomed. svcs. com. 1990-92), Pathology Soc. Phila. (pres.), Coll. Am. Pathologists (bd. govs. 1985-93), Coll. Am. Pathologists Found. (bd. dirs. 2003-08), Am. Soc. Clin. Pathology (Disting. Svc. award 1995).

RAY, ALBERT, physician, educator; b. NYC, Aug. 8, 1948; s. Herman and Stella (Meritz) R.; m. Cheryl Antecol, Oct. 8, 1977; children: Heather, Erin, Samantha. BA, Bklyn. Coll., 1969; MD, Cath. U. Louvain, Belgium, 1976. Diplomate Am. Bd. Family Practice, Can. Coll. Family Physicians, cert. profl. coder AAPC. Intern Meml. U. of Nfld., St. John's, Can., 1976; resident McGill U., Montreal, 1978; family physician SCPMG, San Diego, 1978—. Clin. prof. U. Calif., San Diego, 1978—; cmty. faculty UCLA, USD, U. Calif., Davis, USC; clerkship cmty. adv. bd. U. Calif., San Diego, 1995—; pres. profl. staff Kaiser Found. Hosp.; bd. dirs. So. Calif. Permanente Med Group; asst. chief family medicine Kaiser Permanente, San Diego; physician dir, patient edn. & health promotion Kaiser Permanente, regional asst., med. dir bus. mgmt, physician dir. doc. choice wellness ctr. Author: Lecons d'Histologie, 1973; contbr. to profl. jours. Program chair adult edn. Congregation Beth Israel, 1995; bd. dirs. Temple Emanuel, San Diego, 1990, Agy. for Jewish Edn.; expert reviewer Med. Bd. Calif., 1995; spl. med. cons. Calif. Dept. of Corps., 1996; hon. chmn. physician's adv. bd. Nat. Rep. Congl. Com. Named Family Physician of Yr., Calif. Acad. Family Physicians, 2002. Fellow: Am. Acad. Family Physicians; mem.: Calif. Acad. Family Physicians, San Diego Acad. Family Physicians, San Diego County Med. Soc. (councilor 2002—03, treas. 2004—06, pres.-elect 2006—07, pres. 2007—08), Calif. Med. Assn. (trustee), AMA (vice chair Calif. delegation). Avocations: golf, tennis, travel, antiques, gardening. Office: 7035 Convoy Ct San Diego CA 92111 Office Phone: 619-516-7446.

RAY, CHARLES DEAN, neurosurgeon, spine surgeon, bioengineer, inventor; b. Americus, Ga., Aug. 1, 1927; s. Oliver Tinsley and Katherine (Broadfield) Ray; children: Bruce, Marlene. AB, Emory U., Atlanta, 1950; MS, U. Miami, Coral Gables, 1952; MD, Med. Coll. Ga., 1956. Diplomate Am. Bd. Neurol. Surgery, Am. Bd. Spine Surgery, Internat. Cert. Commn. Cert. Clin. Engr. Intern Bapt. Meml. Hosp., Memphis, 1956-57; resident, rsch. assoc. neurosurgery U. Tenn. Hosp., Memphis, 1957-62; fellow, rsch. asst. Mayo Clinic and Found., Rochester, Minn., 1962-64; asst. prof. neurosurgery, lectr. bioengring. Johns Hopkins U. Med. Sch., Balt., 1964-68; chief dept. engring. F. Hoffmann-LaRoche, Basel, Switzerland, 1968-73; clin. assoc. prof. medicine U. Minn., Mpls., 1973—83; practice medicine specializing in spinal neurosurgery Mpls., 1982—96, Norfolk, Williamsburg, Va., 1996—2000. Lectr. U. Basel, Switzerland, 1968—73; dir. emeritus Inst. Low Back and Neck Care, 1982—96; med. dir. The Spine Fellowship Program Ea. Va. Med. Sch., Norfolk, Va.; pres. Am. Coll. Spine Surgery; mem. staff Sentara Hosps., Norfolk, Abbott-Northwestern Hosp., Mpls.; chmn. bd. pres. Cedar Devel. Corp., Cedar Surg., Inc., 1985—92; v.p. med. rsch. Medtronic, Inc., Mpls., 1972—79; bd. dirs. Herman Miller, Inc., 1987—97; chmn. emeritus, med. dir. Raymedica, Inc., Mpls.; cons. in field; adj. prof. orthopedics Ain Shams U., Cairo, 2002—, U. Colo., Denver, 2002—04; pres. N.Am. Spine Soc., Internat. Spine Arthroplasty Soc.; vis. prof. Ain Shams U., Cairo. Author: Principles of Engineering Applied to Medicine, 1964, Medical Engineering, 1974, Lumbar Spine Surgery, 1988; contbr. over 360 articles to profl. publs. Chmn. com. materials and devices World Fedn. Neurosurg. Socs., 1977—, Cosmos Club, 1976—; vestry St. Martin's Episcopal Ch., Wayzata, Minn., 1976-79. With USN, 1945-49. Named Disting. Alumnus, Med. Coll. Ga., 1999; recipient Gold award for Best Med. Device Design of Yr. R&D 100, 2000, Leon Wiltse award for Contbns. to Spine Science and Mgmt., 1999. Fellow: ACS, Royal Soc. Health, Am. Coll. Spine Surgery (pres.); mem.: ASTM, AMA (sr.), IEEE (sr.), Internat. Spine Arthroplasty Soc. (pres.), N.Am. Spine Soc. (past pres., chmn., Wiltse award 1999), Internat. Orgn. Standardization, Pan-Am. Med. Assn. (life), Am. Assn. Neurol. Surgeons (sr.), Internat. Soc. Stereotaxic and Functional Neurosurgery, Internat. Fedn. Med. Biol. Engring., West Germany Armed Forces Med. Soc., Congress Neurol. Surgeons, Mpls. Club, Sigma Xi. Achievements include over 54 US patents and over 100 foreign patents. Home and Office: 3463 State Street #535 Santa Barbara CA 93105 Office Phone: 805-964-7026. Personal E-mail: inveray@gmail.com.

RAY, MARILYN ANNE, nursing educator, researcher; b. Hamilton, Ont., Can., Jan. 24, 1938; d. Arthur William Anthony and Elvera Caroline (Montag) Ray; m. James L. Droesbeke, Aug. 18, 1979 (dec. Nov. 2001). Diploma, St. Joseph's Hosp. Sch. Nursing, Hamilton, 1958; BSN, U. Colo. Denver, 1968, MSN, 1969; MA in Anthropology, McMaster U, 1978; PhD of Nursing, U. Utah, 1981; HD (hon.), Nev. State Coll., 2005. RN Fla., cert. transcultural nurse, CTN-A. Instr. sch. nursing U. San Francisco, 1970—72; asst. prof. sch. nursing McMaster U., 1973—76; asst. prof. U. Colo., 1984—89; Christine E. Lynn eminent scholar Coll. Nursing Fla. Atlantic U., Boca Raton, 1989—94, prof. Coll. Nursing, 1995—2004, adj. prof., 2004—05, prof. emeritus, 2006—. Vis. prof. U. Colo., 1989—2004; Yingling vis. scholar Va. Commonwealth U., Richmond, 1994—95; vis. prof. Alta. Heritage Found., U. Alberta, 2005. Author: Transcultural Caring Dynamics in Nursing & Healthcare, Nursing, Caring & Completely Science: For Human Environment Wellbeing, (book) A Study of Caring Within an Institutional Culture: The Discovery of the Theory of Bureaucratic Caring, 2010; contbr. articles to profl. jours. Col. USAF, 1967—99. Recipient Leininger award, 1989, Disting. Alumni award, U. Utah Coll. Nursing, 2007; Transcultural Nursing scholar, 2005. Fellow: Soc. Applied Anthropology; mem.: ANA, Soc. Med. Anthropology, Soc. Applied Anthropology, Internat. Assn. Human Caring (charter), Space Nursing Soc. (charter), Aerospace Human Factors Assn. (charter), Coll. Nurses Ont., Transcultural Nursing Soc. (cert., mem. editl. bd. jour., bd. mem. qualitative health rsch., Tranculturral Nursing award), Am. Anthrop. Assn., Sigma Theta Tau. Avocations: travel, music. Home Phone: 561-470-8109. Business E-Mail: mray@fau.edu.

RAY, ROSABELL HARRIET See BATTIN, R.

RAY, SWAPAN KUMAR, molecular biologist; b. Chakdaha, India, June 17, 1957; arrived in U.S., 1990; s. Somendra Chandra and Sefali Rani (Bhowmick) R. BS with honors, U. Calcutta, India, 1978, MS, 1980, PhD, 1989. Postdoctoral rsch. assoc. Brookhaven Nat. Lab., Upton, 1990-92; postdoctoral fellow Med. U. S.C., Charleston, 1993, instr. medicine, 1994-95, rsch. scientist, 1997-98; instr. medicine Emory U., Atlanta, 1995-96; asst. prof. neurology Med. U. S.C., Charleston, SC, 1998—2004; assoc. prof. neurology Med. U. SC., 2004—07, prof., pathology, microbiology and immunology, 2008—. Reviewer: 68 biomed. jours.; contbr. over 150 articles to profl. jours. Recipient Postdoctoral award, NIH, 1990—92, 1993, Co-investigator award, 1997, Investigator award, 2003, 2006, Spinal Cord Injury Rsch. Fund SC, 2003—11, Co-investigator award, Am. Health Assistance Found., 1998. Mem. Soc. for Neurosci., N.Y. Acad. Sci., Am. Soc. for Biochemistry and Molecular Biology, Am. Assn. for Cancer Rsch., Am. Soc. Neurochemistry, Internat. Soc. Neurochemistry, Internat. Brain Rsch. Orgn., Hollings Cancer Ctr., S.C. Cancer Alliance. Achievements include research revealing that chemotherapeutic drugs (Ara-C, Mitoxantrone and Taxol) cause internucleosomal DNA fragmentation in leukemic cells; Bcl-xS expression induces differentiation in CML K562 cells; retinoids downregulate telomerase activity in AML and glioblastoma cells; some plant-derived pure compounds are capable of inducing apoptosis in neuroblastoma and Ewing's sarcoma cells; calpain is activated and involved in apoptosis in Alzheimer's disease, Parkinson's disease, cerebral ischemia, epilepsy, traumatic brain injury, spinal cord injury and EAE. Avocations: bird watching, classical music, gardening. Office: Univ SC Sch Medicine Pathology Microbiology and Immunology 6439 Garners Ferry Rd Columbia SC 29209 Business E-Mail: swapan.ray@uscmed.sc.edu.

RAY, WAYNE ALLEN, epidemiologist, educator; b. Yakima, Wash., July 2, 1949; s. Allen and Patsy (McKay) R.; m. Janine Elise Thorson, June 11, 1972; children: Lily Amelia, Lea Camille. BS, U. Washington, 1971; MS, Vanderbilt U., 1974, PhD, 1981. Research assoc. Vanderbilt U. Sch. Medicine, Nashville, 1974-75, research instr., 1975-78, research asst. prof., 1979-83, asst. prof., 1984-85, dir. div. pharmacoepidemiology, 1984—, assoc. prof., 1985-90, prof., 1991—. Contbr. articles to profl. jours. Recipient Burroughs Wellcome scholar in Pharmacoepidemiology Am. Coll. Preventive Medicine, 1984. Mem. Am. Statis. Assn., Assn. Computing Machinery, Computer Soc. of IEEE, Soc. Epidemiologic Research, Am. Pub. Health Assn., Phi Beta Kappa. Avocation: gardening. Office: Vanderbilt U A-1124 Medical Ctr N 1211 22d Ave S Nashville TN 37232-2637

RAY, WILLIAM JACKSON, psychologist; b. Birmingham, Ala., Sept. 3, 1945; s. William J. and Mary K. Ray; m. Judith Mebane, Aug. 22, 1987; children from previous marriage: Adam, Lauren. BA, Eckerd Coll., 1967; MA, Vanderbilt U., 1969, PhD, 1971; Fellow in med. psychology, Langley Porter Neuropsychiat. Inst., U. Calif. Med. Center, San Francisco, 1971-72. Prof., dir. clin. psychology tng. program Pa. State U., 1972—, dir. clin. trng., 1991-97, dir. scan program specialization cognitive & effective neurosci., 2007—. Author: (with R.M. Stern) Biofeedback, 1977, (with others) Evaluation of Clinical Biofeedback, 1979, (with R.M. Stern and C.M. Davis) Psychophysiological Recording, 1980, 2d edit. (with R.M. Stern and K. Quigley), 2000, Methods Toward a Science of Behavior and Experience, 1981, 10th edit., 2011, (with E. Susman & L. Feajous) Emotion, Cognition, Health and Development in Children and Adolescents, 1992, (with L. Michelson) Handbook of Dissociation, 1996 (Cornelia Wilbur award ISSD); series editor: Plenum Series in Behavioral Psychophysiology and Medicine. Recipient Nat. Media award Am. Psychol. Found., 1976, 78, Rsch. award Best Empirical Paper, Soc. Clin. Experimental Hypnosis. Mem. AAAS, APA, APS, Soc. Psychophysiol. Rsch. Office: Dept Psychology Pa State U University Park PA 16802 Home Phone: 814-234-3402; Office Phone: 814-863-1726. Business E-Mail: wjr@psu.edu.

RAYA, AFRODITI CHR., nursing educator; b. Polygyros, Halkidiki, Greece, Mar. 23, 1928; d. Christos N. and Chryssoula Chr. (Kioroglou). BSN magna cum laude, Boston U., 1965; MA, Columbia U., NYC, 1966, MEd, 1974, EdD, 1975. Staff nurse Evangelismos Hosp., Athens, 1957-61, tchr. Higher Sch. Nursing, 1961-66, dir. nursing studies, 1966-86. Adj. assoc. and prof. dept. nursing, U. Athens, 1981-97, emeritus prof., 1997—; mem. ministry exam. com. Mental Health Nursing Specialty Cert., Athens, 1984—, Thessaloniki, Greece, 1992—, Ioannina, Greece, 1996; mem. adv. com. Technol. U. Cyprus, Lemessos, Greece, 2006-. Author: (books) The Nurse: The Grandeur of Her Profession, 1972, Psychiatric Nursing: A Conceptual Approach, 1975, Psychiatric Nursing - Fundamental Principles, 1978, Basic Nursing, 1987, Mental Health and Psychiatric Nursing, 2009, Basic Nursing - Theoretical and Deontological Principles, 2002, 6th edit., 2005; co-editor: Collaborative Research in Nursing, 1981, Quality in Nursing-Realities and Visions, 1996; mem. editl. bd. Nursing Ethics, Jour. Psychiat. and Mental Health Nursing. Nursing adv. com. Tech. U. Cyprus. Recipient scholarship Greek State Scholarship Inst., Athens, 1963-66. Mem. Hellenic Nat. Grad. Nurses' Assn., Greek Soc. Nursing Studies, Greek Anti-Cancer Soc., Greek Gerontol. Soc., Internat. Coun. Nurses (bank of experts). Greek Christian Orthodox. Avocations: reading, writing, travel. Home: Frangokklisias 12 151 25 Athens Greece Office Phone: 0030-210-6198619. Office Fax: 0030-210-6198619.

RAYBECK, MICHAEL JOSEPH, surgeon; b. Danbury, Conn., Oct. 5, 1945; s. Michael Thomas and Edythe Caroline (Tomaino) R. BS, Mt. St. Mary's Coll., Emmitsburg, Md., 1967; MD, Tulane U., 1971. Diplomate Am. Bd. Surgery, Am. Bd. Quality Assurance Utilization Rev. Physicians; cert. physician exec. Intern in surgery St. Vincent's Hosp. and Med. Ctr., NYC, 1971-72; resident in gen. and vascular surgery Ochsner Found. Hosp., New Orleans, 1974-78; ptnr. Lauderdale Surg. Group, P.A., Ft. Lauderdale, 1978—2004; med. dir. Cigna Health Care, Chattanooga, 2004—. Med. adv. com. Dept. Profl. Regulation, State of Fla., 1991-98; pres. med. staff Holy Cross Hosp., 1995, vice chmn. PHO, v.p. med. affairs, 1997—2002. Bd. dirs. Am. Heart Assn., Ft. Lauderdale, 1988-91. Fellow ACS, Soc. Am. Gastrointestinal Endoscopic Surgeons; mem. Am. Soc. Colon-Rectal Surgeons. Republican. Roman Catholic. Avocations: swimming, travel, languages. Home: 622 Georgia Ave Apt 307 Chattanooga TN 37402-1406 Home Phone: 954-600-6963; Office Phone: 423-321-4422. Personal E-mail: mjjrmd@comcast.net.

RAYBURN, CAROLE ANN (MARY AIDA), psychologist, researcher, writer, consultant; b. Washington, Feb. 14, 1938; d. Carl Frederick and Mary Helen (Milkie) Miller; m. Ronald Allen Rayburn (dec. Apr. 1970). BA in Psychology, Am. U., 1961; MA in Clin. Psychology, George Washington U., 1965; PhD in Ednl. Psychology, Cath. U. Am., 1969; MDiv in Ministry, Andrews U., 1980. Lic. psychologist, Md. Psychometrician Columbian Prep. Sch., Washington, 1963; clin. psychologist Spring Grove State Hosp., Catonsville, Md., 1966—68; pvt. practice, 1969, 1971—; staff clin. psychologist Instl. Care Svcs. Divsn. D.C. Children's Ctr., Laurel, Md., 1970—78; psychologist Md. Dept. Vocat. Rehab., 1973—74; psychometrician Montgomery County Pub. Schs., 1981—85. Lectr. Strayer Coll., Washington, 1969-70; forensic psychology expert witness, 1973—; guest lectr. Andrews U., Berrien Springs, Mich., 1979, Hood Coll, Frederick, Md., 1986-88; instr. Johns Hopkins U., 1986, 88-89; adj. faculty Profl. Sch. Psychology Studies, San Diego, 1987; adj. asst. prof. Loyola Coll., Columbia, Md., 1987; cons. Julia Brown Montessori Schs., 1972, 78, 82—, VA Ctr., 1978, 91-93; adv. grad. psychol. students Cardinal Stritch U., Milw., 2005-. Author (copyrighted inventories); Religious Occupational and Stress Questionnaire, 1986, Organizational Relationships Survey, 1987, Attitudes Toward Children Inventory, 1987, State-Trait Morality Inventory, 1987, Body Awareness and Sexual Intimacy Comfort Scale (BASICS), 1993, Inventory on Religiousness, 1997, Inventory on Spirituality (IS), 1996, Sports, Exercise, Leadership and Friendship Questionnaire, 1997, Peacefulness Inventory, Life Choices Inventory, 1998, Inventory on the Supreme and Work, 1999, Children's and Adolescents' Peace Inventory, 2002, Inventory on Well-Being, 2004, TEACH: Traumatic Experiences and Children's and Adolescents' Health, 2005, Creative Personality Inventory, 2005, Intuition Inventory, 2005, Health and Traumatic Experiences in Adults, 2005, Inventory on Religiousness, Children's Version, 2005, (with Lee Richmond) Killers of the Spirit, Restores of the Soul, 2010; Co-editor: (with M.J. Meadow) A Time to Weep and a Time to Sing, 1985, (with Violet Franks) Springer Pub Focus on Women Series Co-ed, 2005, (with Lillian Comas-Diaz) Woman Soul: Inner Life of Women's Spirituality, 2008, (with Violet Franks) Women & Psychology Series: Women of Vision is in this Series, 2010, (with Violet Franks) Psychology of Women Series, 2008, (with E. Gavin, A. Clamar, M.A. Siderits) Women of Vision, 2007; contbg. author: Montessori: Her Method and the Movement (What You Need to Know), 1973, Drugs, Alcohol and Women: A National Forum Source Book, 1975, The Other Side of the Couch: Faith of the Psychotherapist, 1981, Clinical Handbook of Pastoral Counseling, 1985, An Encyclopedic Dictionary of Pastoral Care and Counseling, 1990, Religion Personality and Mental Health, 1993, (Lee Richmond) Killers of the Spirit Restorers of the Soul, 2010; co-editor (with Violet Franks) Springer Focus on Women Series, Handbook for Women Mentors: Transcending Barriers of Stereotype, Race, and Ethnicity, 2009, (with Florence Denmark's Mary Reuder and Asuncion Austria); cons. editor Profl. Psychology, 1980-83; assoc. editor: Jour. Pastoral Counseling, 1985-90, guest editor, 1988; co-proposer: (with Lee Richmond) The Theory and Field of Theobiology: interfacing of theology and the sciences, 1998; proposer: Creative Personality Theory, 2011, author; mem. editl. bd.: Internat. Jour. Ethics (Nova Sci.), 2004—; contbr. numerous articles to profl. jours. Bd. dirs. Psychologists Ethical Treatment of Animals, 1998-2000; spkrs. Task Force Mont County NOW, 2002-07, treas., 2005-07, chair Task Force Women's Spirituality, pres., 2007-09. Recipient Svc. award Coun. for Advancement Psychol. Professions and Scis., 1975, cert. D.C. Dept. Human Resources, 1975, 76, cert. recognition D.C. Psychol. Assn., 1976, 1985; AAUW rsch. grantee, 1983. Fellow: APA (editl. bd. Jour. Child Clin. Psychology 1978—82, divsn. psychology women chair task force on women and religion 1980—81, chair equal opportunity affirmative action divsn. clin. psychology 1980—82, clin. psychology women's sect. 1984—86, divsn. psychology issues in grad. edn. and clin. tng. 1988—, program chair 1991—94, pres. divsn. psychology of religion 1995—96, gen. psych. divsn. liaison to comm. internat. rels. 2004—, fellow com. mem. clin. psychology divsn. 2006, fellows chair, clin. psychology divsn. 2007—09, fellow, divsn. on internat. psychology, divsn. psychology of religion, psychology of women, clin. psychology, cons. psychology, gen. psychology, psychotherapy, state assn. affairs, divsn. media psychology, divsn. family psychology, study sci. social issues, div. child youth & family svcs., health psychology divsn., theoretical & philol. psychology, trauma psychology, psychology ethnic minority affairs, ednl. psychology, Mentoring award divsn. clin. psychology, sect. of clin. psychology of women 1997, divsn. psychology of religion 1997, William C. Bier rsch. award divsn. psychology of religion 2000), APA Soc. Clin. Psychology (chair 2005—09), Md. Psychol. Assn. (editor newsletter 1975—76, chair ins. com. 1981—83, pres. 1984—85, exec. adv. com. 1985—, chpt. recognition 1978), Am. Assn. Applied & Preventive Psychology (sec. 1992—93, chair fellows com. 1992—93), Am. Orthopsychiat. Assn.; mem.: Montgomery County NOW (treas. 2005—07, pres. 2007—09), Soc. Psychol. Study Social Issues (mem. com. on internat. rels. in psychology), Md. Assn. Counseling and Devel., Md. Asn. Measurement and Evaluation (pres. 2005—07), Balt. Assn. Cons. Psychologists (pres. 1991—92), Assn. Practicing Psychologists Montgomery-Prince George's Counties (pres. 1986—88, editor newsletter 1990—, treas. 1996—98), Internat. Soc. Polit. Psychology, Psi Chi (hon.). Achievements include research in stress in religious professionals, women and stress, women and religion, pastoral counseling, state-trait morality inventory, leadership, mentoring, clergy stress, psychotherapy, children, body image; intimacy, peacefulness, spirituality, life choices, religiousness, well-being, work, traumatic experiences and health, creative personality, intuition. Address: 1200 Morningside Dr Silver Spring MD 20904-3149

RAYBURN, WILLIAM FRAZIER, obstetrician, gynecologist, educator; b. Lexington, Ky., Aug. 19, 1950; s. Charles Calvin and Charlotte Elizabeth (Ballard) R.; m. Pamela Rae Gilleland, Nov. 27, 1976; children: Lindsay Ann, Britany Beth, Drake Tanner. BS, Hampden Sydney Coll., 1971; MD, U. Ky., 1975; MBA in Healthcare Bus. Adminstrn., U. Tex., 2007. Diplomate Nat. Bd. Med. Examiners, Am. Bd. Ob.-Gyn. (examiner), Divsn. Maternal-Fetal Medicine. Intern family medicine U. Iowa Hosps. and Clinics, Iowa City, Iowa, 1975-76; resident ob.-gyn. U. Ky. Med. Ctr., Lexington, 1976-79; fellow in maternal-fetal medicine dept. ob.-gyn. Ohio State U. Hosps., Columbus, 1979-81; asst. prof. ob.-gyn. U. Mich. Med. Sch., Ann Arbor, 1981-83, assoc. prof. ob.-gyn., 1983-86; assoc. prof. dept. ob.-gyn. and pharmacology U. Nebr. Coll. of Medicine, Omaha, 1985-88, prof. dept. ob-gyn. and pharmacology, 1988-92, U. Okla. Coll. Medicine, Oklahoma City, 1992-98, John W. Records endowed chair, 1992-98; prof. dept. ob/gyn U. N.Mex. Sch. Medicine, Albuquerque, 1998—, chair dept. ob/gyn, 1998—. Prof., chair dept. ob-gyn. U. N.Mex. Sch. Medicine, Albuquerque, 1998—, Randolph V. Seligman endowed prof., 1999—; chief obstetrics U. Okla. Coll. Medicine, Oklahoma City, 1992-98; dir. maternal fetal medicine dept. ob-gyn. U. Mich. Med. Ctr., 1981-85; reviewer for various jours.; mem. staff U. Nebr. Med. Ctr., 1985-92, U. Okla. Health Sci. Ctr., 1992-98, Presbyn. Hosp., Oklahoma City, 1992-98, Univ. Hosp., Albuquerque, 1998—; chief staff U. N.Mex. Hosps., 2006-08, bd. regents U. N.Mex., 2006-; bd. trustees U. N.Mex. Hosp., 2006-. Author: Obstetrics/Gynecology: Pre Test Self Assessment and Review, 1982; (with others) Every Woman's Pharmacy: A Guide to Safe Drug Use, 1983, Obstetrics for the House Officer, 1984, 2d rev. edit., 1988, Every Woman's Pharmacy, 1984, The Women's Health and Drug Reference, 1993, Oklahoma Notes: Obstetrics and Gynecology, 1994, 2d rev. edit., 1996, Obstetrics and Gynecology for the House Officer, 1996, 2d rev. edit., 2001; editor: (with F.P. Zuspan) Drug Therapy in Obstetrics and Gynecology, 1982, 3d rev. edit., 1992, Changing Landscape of Academic Womens Health Care, Ob-Gyn., 2011; symposia editor Diagnosis and Management of the Malformed Fetus, Jour. Reprod. Medicine, 1982, Operative Obstetrics, Clinics in Perinatology, 1983, Controversies in Fetal Drug Therapy, Clin. Obstetrics and Gynecology, 1991, Drugs in Pregnancy, Clinical Obstetrics and Gynecology, 2002, Substance Use Disorders in Women, 2003; editor-in-chief Jour. Reproductive Medicine, 2002-03, The Obstetrician Gynecologist Workforce the US Facts, Figures and Impleasers, 2011; editor, Obstet Gynae Cl No Am, 2004-; contbr. more than 50 chpts. to books, more than 250 articles to profl. jours., delivered more than 200 abstract papers at sci. meetings. Dir. maternal and infant care programs U. Nebr. Med. Ctr., Omaha, 1986-92; U.S. Pharmacopeia Conv. field reviewer, 1983—. Recipient Residents' prize paper award Ky. Ob.-Gyn. Soc., 1978, 79, Faculty Teaching award for Excellence, 1993, 94, 96, 03-10, Rsch. Excellence award Soc. Perinatal Obstetricians, 1998, Nat. Tchg. award Assn. Profs. in Gynecology & Obstetrics, 2005, Disting. Alumnus award, U. Ky. Coll. Medicine, 2005. Fellow Am. Coll. Ob-Gyn. (Ephraim McDowell prize paper award 2d pl. 1978, 1st pl. 1979, Searle-Donald F. Richardson Prize Paper award 1980, Best Doctors in Am., 1998, 2000); mem. Am. Gynecol. and Obstet. Soc., Coun. Univ. Chairs in Ob-Gyn., Soc. Maternal Fetal Medicine, Assn. Profs. in Gynecology and Obstetrics (Faculty Excellence in Tchg 2005), Soc. for Gynecol. Investigation, Teratology Soc. Achievements include contributions to the knowledge of drug effcts on developing fetus and of principals about induction of labor and to the influence he has had on peers not only through teaching and patient care but through his extensive writing. Office: U New Mex Health Sci Ctr 2211 Lomas Blvd NE # Acc-4 Albuquerque NM 87106-2745 Business E-Mail: wrayburn@salud.unm.edu.

RAYCHAUDHURI, SUBHADIP, engineering educator; b. Kolkata, India, Sept. 14, 1972; PhD, U. Rochester, 2002. Asst. prof. U. Calif. Davis, 2004—. Office: 451 Health Sciences Dr Davis CA 95616 Business E-Mail: raychaudhuri@ucdavis.edu.

RAYMENT, CARY, retired pharmaceutical executive; BA in Edn., Univ. Wash.; MBA, Univ. Kans., Lawrence; grad., Harvard Program for Mgmt. Devel. Various sales, mktg. positions Kendall Co., 1974—83; dir., sales, mktg. to v.p. mktg. CooperVision IOL (acquired by Alcon), 1983—89; v.p. mktg., surgical products Alcon Inc., Fort Worth, 1989—91, v.p., gen. mgr. surgical products, 1991—95, v.p., gen. mgr., managed care, 1996—97, v.p., internat. mktg., 1997—2000, v.p., gen. mgr., surgical divsn., 2000—01, sr. v.p., US, 2001—04, CEO, 2004—09, chmn., 2005—09, non-exec. chmn., 2009—10, vice chmn., 2010—. Bd. dir. Am. Soc. Cataract, Refractive Surgery Found., Nat. Alliance Eye Vision Rsch., Found. Am. Acad. Ophthalmology, Adv. Med. Tech. Assn. Bd. dir. United Way Met. Tarrant County. Office: Alcon Inc 6201 S Freeway Fort Worth TX 76134 *

RAYMOND, BRUCE ALLEN, retired surgeon, medical association administrator; b. Aberdeen, SD, Dec. 8, 1924; s. Samuel A. and Pearl (Blackstone) R.; m. Virginia Stratton, Apr. 2, 1948 (div. 1969); children: Judith Ann, Jaqueline Marie, Bruce Allen Jr., Brian Andrew; m. Jane Molnar, Nov. 15, 1969; children: Douglas A., Andrew D., Colin K. BS, Leland Stanford U., U. S.D., 1945; MD, Washington U., St. Louis, 1949. Diplomate Am. Bd. Surgery, Am. Bd. Thoracic Surgery. Intern U. Ored. Med. Sch. Hosps., Portland, 1949-50; resident Walter Reed Gen. Hosp., Washington, 1953—60, asst. chief thoracic surgery, 1959-60; chief thoracic and cardiovascular surgery Letterman Gen. Hosp., San Francisco, 1960-64, Fitzsimmons Gen. Hosp., Denver, 1967-69, chief dept. surgery, 1969-71; pvt. practice surgery Warwick, RI, 1975-86; sr. med. dir. various insurance co.; med. dir. The Health Plan of the Upper Ohio Valley, 1996—2003. Asst. clin. prof. U. Colo., 1967-71; assoc. clin. prof. surgery Northwestern U., Chgo., 1973-80; mem. staff Kent County Med. Mem. Hosp., Warwick, 1975-86, Miriam hosp., Providence, 1975-86; cons. in field. Contbr. articles to profl. jours. Col. MC US Army, 1949—72. Decorated Legion of Merit. Fellow ACS, Am. Coll. Cardiology, Am. Coll. Chest Physicians; mem. Soc. Thoracic Surgeons. Avocation: skiing. Home: 218 Salem Dr Upper Saint Clair PA 15241-2226 Personal E-mail: braymond66@adelphia.net.

RAYNER, VICTORIA LEIGH, medical educator, consultant; b. Sacramento, Mar. 6, 1954; d. Harold Edward Rayner and Angela Jane Allitore; m. Vallucci Rayner, July 20, 1997. BA, Coll. of Marin, 1974; AA in Bus. Studies, Highline CC, Seattle, 1976. Lic. post-secondary instr. Calif., 1995, continuing edn. instr. Calif. Bd. of Registered Nursing, 1996. Founder and pres. Bay Area Skin Assn., San Francisco, 1981; founder and dir. Ctr. Appearance and Esteem, 1987; founder Camouflage Therapy Clinic, dept. dermatology San Francisco Gen. Hosp., 1987, clin. assoc. Camouflage Therapy Clinic, 1986—; clin. assoc. Alta Bates Hosp., Berkeley; founder Rayner Inst. Career Advancement, Washington; owner Creative Career Bldg. Inst. Contbg. mem. and presenter U. Calif. Arts and Lectrs., San Francisco, 1988—; adv. bd. Dermascope, Sunnyvale, Tex., 1990—, Les Nouvelle Esthetique, Coral Gables, Fla., 1990—; adv. com. rsch. divsn. Almay

Cosmetics, Oxford, NC, 1992—93; cons. and rep. Nat. Assn. Women in Bus., mem. public rels. com., 1993—95; founder Women's Forum for Discussion Group, San Francisco, 1996; spokesperson Fibroid Ctr. Wash. Med. Ctr.; lectr. on med. esthetics; presenter in field. Author: Clin. Cosmetology; A Med. Approach to Aesthetic Procedures, 1993, A Survival Guide for Today's Career Woman, 1994; columnist Skin Inc. Mag.; contbr. articles to profl. jours., chapters to books. Hon. chmn. Bus. Adv. Coun., Washington, 2005; leader medical esthetics trng. and care Task Force Legis. Reform of Patients' Rights, Sacramento, 1993—95; bd. dirs. Alissa Ann Ruch Burn Found., San Francisco, 1991—93. Recipient For Those Who Care Vol. award, KRON-TV, 1989, Merit award, Commn. on Status of Women of City and County of San Francisco, 1993, Contribn. to Cosmetology, Internat. Congress of Esthetics, 2003. Mem.: NAFE, Am. Med. Women Assn. (author online distance edn. course 2006), Nat. Cosmetology Esthetic Assn., Am. Soc. Plastic Surgery Skin Care Specialists, Dermatology Nursing Assn. Independent. Roman Catholic. Achievements include development of long distance learning programs in esthetic procedures; women over forty, reentry career devel. programs; four outpatient cosmetic rehabilitation clinics for women and children. Avocations: interior design, cooking, reading, painting.

RAYNOR, RICHARD BENJAMIN, neurosurgeon, educator; b. NYC, Aug. 16, 1928; s. Murray and Mildred (Pitt) R.; m. Barbara Golob; children: Geoffrey, Michele. BSME, U. Mich., 1950; MD, U. Vt., 1955. Diplomate Am. Bd. Neurol. Surgery. Intern Mt. Sinai, NYC, 1955-56; residency Neurol. Inst. Presbyn. Hosp., NYC, 1956-57, Nat. Hosp., London, 1957; residency neurosurgery Neurol. Inst. Presbyn. Hosp., 1958-62; assoc. in neurosurgery Coll. Physicians and Surgeons Columbia U., NYC, 1965-77; clin. assoc. prof. NYU, NYC, 1977-2000, clin. prof., 1984—. Pvt. practice neurosurgery, N.Y.C., 1965—. Cons. editor Spine; contbr. over 50 articles to profl. jours., chpts. to books. Served as capt. U.S. Army, 1962-64. Fellow Am. Coll. Surgeons; mem. Cervical Spine Research Soc. (pres. 1986-87), Am. Assn. Neurol. Surgeons, Congress Neurol. Surgeons. Clubs: University (N.Y.C.). Avocation: skiing. Office: 870 United Nation Plaza New York NY 10017 Office Phone: 212-317-9309, 917-301-0214.

RAYSHOUNY, SAMI, cardiologist, internist; BSc in Biology, U. Toledo, Toledo, Ohio, USA, 1971—75; MB, BChir, Ain Shams U., Cairo, Egypt; diploma in Modern Asthma Mgmt., Aarhus U. Hosp., Denmark; postgrad. in Cardiology, Med. Coll. Cert. in Occupl. Medicine Lebanese Order of Physicians. Resident cardiologist cardiology dept. Berbir Med. Ctr.; warden USA Embassy, 1996—. V.p. Assn. Lebanese Human Rights, Lebanon, 1998; mem. Lebanese Red Cross, Lebanon, 2004. Recipient Dar Al Nadwa and Lebanese Health Assn. award, 1997, Nat. Com. for The Lebanese Child award, 1999, Lebanese Red Cross award, 2004, Trad Med. Hosp. award, 2004, Pub. Ambulatory System award, 2005, Al Montada Al Kaomi Al Arabi award, 2005, Nabatieh Nat. Traders Assn., 2005, Trad. Med. Ctr. award, 2005. Mem.: Lebanese Soc. of Gen. Practice (award recieved 2004), The UN Assn. of Lebanon (mem. trustees 1998—2007), The Lebanese Health Assn. (pres. 1996—, award recieved 1996), The Am. Alumni Assn. of Lebanon (pres. 2005—06, award recieved 2004), The Right of Health Com. (pres. 1990), Lebanese Order of Physicians (v.p. 1992, mem. disciplinary com. 1996, award recieved 1996), The Najjar Med. Com. (gen. sec. 1993), The Lebanese Grad. From Republic of Egypt Universities (founder, pres.). Office: Trad Medical Center PO Box 113-6431 53 Mexique St Beirut Lebanon also: Blue Tower Medical Center PO Box 11-7588 Beirut Lebanon Office Phone: 9611369494, 9611737135. Office Fax: 9611361663. *

RAYSON, GLENDON ENNES, internist, preventive medicine specialist, writer; b. Oak Park, Ill., Dec. 2, 1915; s. Ennes Charles and Beatrice Margaret (Rowland) R.; m. Sarah Weida. AB, U. Rochester, NY, 1939; MD, U. Ill., Chgo., 1948; MPH, Johns Hopkins U., Balt., 1965; MA, Northwestern U., Evanston, Ill., 1965. Diplomate Am. Bd. Internal Medicine, Am. Bd. Preventive Medicine, Am. Bd. Forensic Medicine, Am. Bd. Forensic Examiners. Resident in internal medicine Presbyn.-St. Luke's Hosp., Chgo., 1953-56; physician-in-charge Contagious Disease Hosp., Chgo., 1956-58, asst. med. supt., 1958-64; rsch. assoc. Sch. Hygiene and Pub. Health Johns Hopkins U., Balt., 1966-71; internist Johns Hopkins Hosp., 1971-82, Columbia Free State Health Plan, Balt., 1984-91; pvt. practice Balt., 1984—; with Neurodiagnostics Assocs., 1990—2001. Attending internist emergency rm. South Balt. Gen. Hosp., 1982-84; asst. prof. health sci. U. Ill., Chgo., 1958-64; fellow in gastroenterology and endocrinology Presbyn.-St. Luke's Hosp., 1956-58. Contbr. articles to med. jours., chpt. to book. Vol. physician, Vietnam, 1968, 71, 72, 73; mem. Citizens Amb. Program Delegation to Vietnam, 1993. Capt. M.C., USAF, 1951-53. Master: Am. Acad. Cardiology; fellow: Am. Coll. Forensic Examiners Inst., Am. Geriatrics Soc., Am. Col. Preventive Medicine; mem.: APHA, ACP-Am. Soc. Internal Medicine, AMA. Avocations: poetry, writing, composing songs. Home: 2485 N Pk Rd W240 Hollywood FL 33021

RAZA, ASIM, psychiatrist; b. Rawalpindi, Pakistan, Apr. 27, 1958; s. Kamal and Sughra Raza. FSc, Sir Syed Sch. and Coll., Rawalpindi, 1975; BSc, B Medicine and Surgery, Rawalpindi Med. Coll., 1983. Diplomate Am. Bd. Psychiatry and Neurology. Intern dept. medicine Rawalpindi Gen. Hosp., 1983; med. officer dept. medicine Cantonment Gen. Hosp., Rawalpindi, 1984—91, med. officer outpatient dept., 1991—92; resident dept. psychiatry U. Mo. Sch. Medicine, Kansas City, 1993—97, chief resident dept. psychiatry, 1996—97; mem. staff Counseling Assocs., Inc., Conway, Ark., 1998—. Cons. in field; mem. spkrs. bur. Pfizer Inc., Wyeth Pharms., Sanofi-Aventis Pharms., Novartis, Sepracor Inc.; adv., cons. Pfizer Inc. Treas. Residents Assn. Western Mo., Kansas City, 1994—95, v.p., 1995—96, pres., 1996—97. Recipient Psychiatry Resident of Yr. award, Pfizer, 1997; fellow, Eli Lilly, 1994. Fellow: Am. Psychiat. Assn. (Wyeth Ayerst Resident Reporter 1996, mem.-in-tng. rep. Western Mo. br. 1996—97); mem.: Ark. Psychiat. Soc. Home: 1801 Champlin Dr 112 Little Rock AR 72223 Office Phone: 501-336-8300. Business E-Mail: araza@caiinc.org.

RAZDAN, SANJAY, urologist; b. Rugby, Northern Ireland, Apr. 24, 1962; s. Jawahar Lal and Shanti Razdan; m. Shashi Khosa; 1 child, Shirin. MD, Ganesh Shankar Vidyarthi Meml. Med. Coll., Kanpur, India, 1985; MCh (Master of Chirurgical), SMS Med. Sch., Jaipur, India, 1993. Diplomate Am. Bd. Urology. Sr. registrar urology SMS Med. Schools & Hospitals, 1990—93; intern urology Univ. Medicine & Dentistry NJ, Newark, 1995—96; fellow female urology & neurourology Boston U. Med. Ctr., 1996—98; resident surgery U. Miami./Jackson Meml. Hosp., Fla., 1996—99, resident urology, 1999—2003; advanced fellowship in endourology & minimally-invasive urologic oncology Thomas Jefferson U. Hosp., Phila., 2003—04; chmn. dept. surgery, dir. Urology Ctr. Excellence Jackson South Cmty. Hosp., Miami, dir. Internat. Robotic Prostatectomy Inst. Dir. Comprehensive Kidney Stone Ctr., Miami. Co-author: Manual of Urology, 1999, Operative Urology/Surgical Skills, 2000, Clinical Urogynecology, 2000; contbr. articles to profl. jours. Physician Doctors Without Boundaries, Miami, 1996—2001. Recipient Pfizer award for outstanding contbn. to field of urology, 2004, Outstanding Laparoscopic Surgeon award, Soc. Laparoscopic Surgeons. Mem.: Endourology Soc., Am. Urol. Assn. Achievements include performing minimally-invasive robotic prostatectomy on patients with prostate cancer in less than 90 minutes resulting with minimal or no blood loss. Avocations: swimming, tennis, golf. Office: Urology Ctr Excellence S Fla Deering Med Plz 9380 SW 150th St Ste 200 Miami FL 33176 Office Phone: 305-251-8650. Personal E-mail: urodoc96@aol.com. *

RAZIN, AHARON, biochemist, educator; b. Tel Aviv, Apr. 6, 1935; s. Yehezkiel and Matilda (Golante) Rosenberg; m. Varda Wittenberg; children: Gilad, Dalit. MSc, Hebrew U., Jerusalem, 1962, PhD, 1967. Lectr. Hebrew U., 1967-71, sr. lectr., 1971-76, assoc. prof., 1976-82, prof., 1982—, head dept. cellular biochemistry, 1980—84, Jacob Grunbaum prof. med. scis. Postdoc. fellow NIH, 1968; rsch. fellow Calif. Inst. Tech., 1969—70. Editor: Biochemistry of DNA Methylation, 1994, Biochemistry and Biology of DNA Methylation, 1995; contbr. articles to profl. jours. Recipient Gairdner Internat. award, Gairdner Found., Can., 2011; co-recipient Wolf Prize in Medicine, Wolf Found., 2008; Fogarty scholar, 1984. Mem.: European Molecular Biology Orgn., Am. Assn. Cancer Rsch., Human Genome Orgn. Office: Hebrew U Med Sch Hadassah Medical Center Ein Karem 91999 Jerusalem Israel *

RAZZAQ, QUAISAR MAHMOOD, emergency physician; b. Daska, Pakistan, Dec. 6, 1961; s. Abdul and Ghulam Sughra Razzaq; m. Shagufta Quaisar Nazeer, Dec. 22, 1985; 1 child, Dawud Ali. MB, BChir, Aberdeen Med. Sch., Scotland, 1985. Trainee surgeon, 1985—91; trainee heart surgeon and emergency medicine, 1991—94; trainee emergency medicine South Africa, 1994—97; cons. emergency physician, 1997—99; cons. emergency physician, emergency dept. head Tawam Hosp., Al Ain, United Arab Emirates, 1999—. Organizer disaster response sys. Gen. Authority Health Affairs, Abu Dhabi, United Arab Emirates, 2006—. Fellow: Coll. Emergency Medicine UK, Royal Coll. Surgeons Edinburgh, Royal Coll. Physicians and Surgeons Glasgow. Avocation: gardening. Home: 67 Longspring Watford WD24 6QA England Office: Emergency Dept Tawam Hosp PO Box 15258 Al Ain United Arab Emirates Personal E-mail: qmrazzaq@hotmail.com.

RAZZOUK, ANEES JACOB, surgeon; s. Yacoub and Mona Razzouk; m. Teri Thompson; children: Jacob, Gabrielle. BA, Mid. East Coll., 1975; MA, Andrews U., 1977; MD, Loma Linda U., 1982. Medical Examiner Nat. Bd. of Med. Examiners, General Surgery Am. Bd. of Surgery, Thoracic Surgery Am. Bd. of Surgery, Surgical Critical Care Am. Bd. of Surgery, Md State of Calif. Lectr. of math. Loma Linda U., Calif., 1978; asst. prof. of surgery Loma Linda U., Sch. of Medicine, 1990—99, prof. of surgery, 2000—, dir. of thoracic surgery residency program, 2001—, chief, divsn. of cardiothoracic surgery, 2002—, chmn. dept. cardiovascular and thoracic surgery, 2007—. Fellowship Hosp. for Sick Children, Toronto, Canada, 1990—91. Recipient Humanitarian award, Hosp. for Sick Children, Toronto Can., 2000; Albert Starr scholar, 1990. Fellow: ACS, Am. Coll. of Cardiology; mem.: The Western Thoracic Surg. Assn., Internat. Soc. for Heart & Lung Transplantation, Soc. of Thoracic Surgeons, Congenital Heart Surgeons' Soc., Internat. Soc. for Minimally Invasive Cardiac Surgery, Western Soc. for Pediatric Rsch., Pacific Coast Surg. Assn., Am. Assn. for Thoracic Surgery, Calif. Soc. of Thoracic Surgeons, Am. Soc. for Artificial Internal Organs, The Nat. Honor Med. Soc. (life), The Nat. Honor Math. Soc. (life), Alpha Omega Alpha (life), Pi Mu Epsilon (life). Office: Loma Linda U Med Ctr 11175 Campus St Ste 21121 Loma Linda CA 92354 E-mail: arazzouk@llu.edu. *

RE, LAMBERTO MARIA, neuropharmacology educator, researcher; b. Ancona, AN, Italy, Sept. 24, 1950; s. Rinaldo and Adele (Beccacece) R.; m. Elia Cavalieri, Mar. 8, 1974; children: Alessandro, Francesco, Simone. MD, U. Ancona, Italy, 1983. Rschr. U. Ancona, 1989—. Reviewer Archives of Med. Rsch., Mex., 1994—. With Italian Army, 1972-73. Mem. Italian Soc. Pharmacology, N.Y. Acad. Scis. Home: Via Togliatti 65 60131 Ancona Italy Office: Univ Ancona Ranieri 2 60131 Ancona Italy

READ, IAN C., pharmaceutical executive; b. 1953; BSChemE, London U. Imperial Coll., 1974. Cert. Inst. Chartered Accts. Eng. & Wales, 1978. Operational auditor Pfizer, Inc., 1978, CFO Mexico, country mgr. Brazil, pres. Internat. Pharmaceuticals Group Latin America/Canada, 1996, exec. v.p. Europe/Can., 2000, v.p., 2001—06, exec. v.p. Africa/Middle East, 2004, exec. v.p. Latin America, 2006, sr. v.p., pres. worldwide pharm. ops. NYC, 2006—10, CEO, 2010—. Bd. dirs. Kimberly-Clark Corp., 2007—, Pfizer Inc., 2010—; bd. mem. US Coun. for Internat. Bus., European Fedn. Pharmaceutical Industries & Associations. Named a Power Player, Advt. Age, 2008. Office: Pfizer Inc 235 E 42nd St New York NY 10017 Office Phone: 212-573-2323. Business E-Mail: ian.c.read@pfizer.com. *

READ, VIRGINIA HALL, retired biochemistry professor; b. Louisville, Miss., Oct. 15, 1937; d. Angus R. and Hassie (Bowie) Hall; m. Dale Gilbert Read Sr., Mar. 5, 1960; children: Laura Read Sprabery, Dale Gilbert Jr., Eva Read Warden. BS, U. Miss., 1959; MS, U. Miss., Jackson, 1962, PhD, 1964. Instr. biochemistry U. Miss., Jackson, 1965-66, asst. prof. biochemistry, 1966-68, 70-74, assoc. prof. biochemistry, 1974-2000, assoc prof. pathology, 1979-2000; asst. prof. medicine U. Ala., Birmingham, 1968-70. Contbr. articles to Jour. Clin. Investigation, Jour. Clin. Endocrinology and Metabolism, Nature, Biochem. Pharmacology. Grantee U.S. Pub. Health Svc., 1960-62, fellow, 1968-70. Mem. Am. Assn. Clin. Chemistry, Acad. Clin. Biochemistry, Endocrine Soc., Sigma Xi. United Methodist. Home Phone: 601-992-1890. Personal E-mail: vh44424@bellsouth.net.

READE, MICHAEL CHARLES, critical care physician; b. London, Eng., Sept. 8, 1970; BSc in Medicine, U. Sydney, Australia, 1992, MBBS with honors, 1995; DPhil, U. Oxford, 2003; MPH, U. Pitts., 2007. Diplomate Royal Coll. Surgeons, 1991. Critical Care Resident Royal North Shore Hosp., Sydney, Australia, 1996—97, Anaesthetic / Critical Care Registrar, 1998—99; Clin. Rsch. Fellow U. Oxford, Oxford, Oxfordshire, England, 2000—02; specialist registrar John Radcliffe Hosp., Oxford, England, 2002—03; sr. registrar intensive care Austin Hosp., Melbourne, Australia, 2004—05; fellow critical care medicine U. Pitts. Med. Ctr., Pitts., 2005—06, instr. critical care medicine, 2006—. Med. officer Royal Australian Army Med. Corps, London and Sydney, NSW, Australia, 1989—. Travelling fellowship, Royal Australian Coll. Physicians, 2005. Fellow: Coll. Chest Physicians, Coll. Intensive Care Medicine, Australian and New Zealand Coll. Anaesthetists; mem.: Soc. Critical Care Medicine, Assn. Mil. Surgeons US, Australian Mil. Medicine Assn. Office: Austin Hospital ICU Studley Rd Heidelberg VIC 3084 Australia Business E-Mail: Michael.reade@austin.org.au.

READING, ANTHONY JOHN, retired psychiatrist, educator; b. Sydney, Sept. 10, 1933; s. Abe Stanley and Esma Daisy R.; m. Elisabeth Ann Hoffman, July 27, 1975; children— Wendy Virginia Elisabeth, Sarah Alexandra Jane. MBBS, U. Sydney, 1956; MPH, Johns Hopkins U., Balt., 1961, DSc, 1964. Intern Sydney Hosp., 1957-58; resident in psychiatry Johns Hopkins Hosp., Balt., 1965-68; asst. prof. psychiatry and medicine Johns Hopkins U. Sch. Medicine, Balt., 1968-73, assoc. prof. psychiatry, 1973-75, dir. psychiat. liaison service, 1974-75; dir. comprehensive alcoholism program Johns Hopkins Hosp., 1972-75; prof. U. South Fla. Coll. Medicine, 1975—2006, chmn. dept. psychiatry and behavioral medicine, 1975—2002, assoc. dean, 1993-96; med. dir. Bay Med. Behavioral Health Ctr., Panama City, Fla., 2004—05; ret., 2006. Mem.: AAAS.

REAGAN, JANET THOMPSON, psychologist, educator; b. Sept. 15, 1945; d. Virgil Joe and Carrie (Alexander) Thompson; children: Natalia Alexandria, Robert Barry. BA in Psychology, Berea Coll., 1967; PhD in Psychology, Vanderbilt U., 1972. Mgr. rsch. and eval. Nashville Mental Health Ctr., 1971-72; mgr. eval. Family Health Found., New Orleans, 1973-74; asst. prof. dept. health systems mgmt. Tulane U., New Orleans, 1974-77; dir. eval. Project Heavy West, LA, 1977-78; asst. prof. health adminstrn. Calif. State U.-Northridge, 1978-83; assoc. prof., dir. health adminstrn., 1983-87; prof., dir. health adminstrn., 1987—. Cons. in field. Contbr. articles to profl. jours., chpts. to books; mem. editl. bd. Jour. Long Term Care Adminstrn., Healthcare Papers. Mem. Am. Pub. Health Assn., Am. Coll. Health Care Adminstrn., Am. Coll. Health Care Execs. (com. on higher edn. 1987, chmn. 1991), Assn. Univ. Programs in Health Adminstrn. (task force on undergrad. edn. 1985-90, chmn. 1988-90, mem. bd. dirs. 1995, chmn. bd. dirs. 1998-99), Psi Chi, Phi Kappa Phi. Office: Calif State U Dept Health Sci Northridge CA 91330-0001 Business E-Mail: janet.reagan@csun.edu.

REAMAN, GREGORY HAROLD, pediatric hematologist, oncologist; b. Akron, Ohio, Sept. 9, 1947; s. Harold J. and Margaret U. (D'Alfonso) R.; m. Susan J. Pristo, Sept. 7, 1974; children: Emily Margaret, Sarah Elizabeth. BS in Biology, U. Detroit, 1969; MD, Loyola U., Chgo., 1973. Diplomate Nat. Bd. Med. Examiners, Am. Bd. Pediats. with subspecialty in pediat. hematology and oncology. Pediatric intern Loyola U. Med. Ctr., 1973-74; resident in pediatrics Montreal Children's Hosp., McGill U., 1974-76; clin. assoc. pediatric oncology br. Nat. Cancer Inst., NIH, Bethesda, Md., 1976-78, investigator pediatric oncology br., 1978-79; assoc. dept. hematology/oncology, attending physician Children's Nat. Med. Ctr., Washington, 1979—, chmn. dept. hematology/oncology, 1985—2003, dir. med. spl. svcs., 1995—99, exec. dir. Ctr. for Cancer and Blood Disorders, 1999—2002; asst. prof. pediats. Sch. Medicine and Health Scis. George Washington U., 1979—82, assoc. prof. pediats., 1982—87, prof. pediats., 1987—. Assoc. chmn. Children's Cancer Group; strategic planning com. Children's Oncology Svcs. of Met. Washington; exec. v.p. for sci. and med. affairs Nat. Childhood Cancer Found./Children's Oncology Group, first group chmn.; mem. oncologic drugs adv. com., FDA, 2002-06; chmn. Pediat. sub-com., bd. dir. Am. Soc. Clin. Oncology. Mem. editl. bd. Cancer Data Query, Nat. Cancer Inst., Jour. Clin. Oncology, Am. Jour. Pediat. Hematology Oncology, Cancer, Pediatric Blood and Cancer, Leukemia and Lymphoma, The Oncologist; reviewer Blood, Jour. Clin. Oncology; assoc. editor: Cancer, 1990-2000; contbr. articles to profl. publs. Trustee Nat. Childhood Cancer Found., Arcadia, Calif.; bd. dirs. Am. Cancer Soc., Atlanta; trustee, chmn. patient care and profl. edn. coms. Leukemia Soc. Am. Lt. comdr. USPHS, 1976-79, Res., 1979—. With US Pub. Health Svc., 1976—80, with active reserves, 1980—99. Folger Summer scholar Am. Cancer Soc.; recipient Spl. Fellowship Rsch. award Leukemia Soc. Am., 1980-82, Tree of Life award, Leukemia and Lymphoma Soc.; grantee DHHS, Nat. Cancer Inst., 1987—. Mem. Soc. Pediat. Rsch., Am. Soc. Hematology, Am. Pediat. Soc., Am. Fedn. Clin. Rsch., Am. Soc. Clin. Oncology, Am. Assn. Cancer Rsch., Am. Soc. Pediat. Hematology/Oncology, Children's Oncology Group, Washington Blood Club, Alpha Omega Alpha. Democrat. Roman Catholic. Home: 7306 Brennon Ln Chevy Chase MD 20815-4064 Office: Children's Nat Med Ctr 111 Michigan Ave NW Washington DC 20010-2916 Office Phone: 240-235-2220. Business E-Mail: greaman@childrensoncologygroup.org. *

REAU, NANCY, medical educator; b. Ohio, Dec. 15, 1969; MD, Ohio State U., 2001. Assoc. prof. medicine U. Chgo., 2006—. Office: University Chgo 5841 S Maryland MC7120 Chicago IL 60637 Office Fax: 773-834-1288. Business E-Mail: nreau@medicine.bsd.uchicago.edu.

REBAR, ROBERT WILLIAM, medical association administrator, obstetrician, gynecologist, educator; b. Stillwater, Okla., Apr. 22, 1947; s. John and Blanche (Fried) R.; m. Margo Storm Freeborn, July 7, 1969; children: Bryan Matthew, Jeannette Heather, Darren Wade. BS, U. Mich., 1969, MD, 1972. Diplomate Am. Bd. Ob-Gyn, cert. spl. competence in reproductive endocrinology. Intern Parkland Meml. Hosp., Dallas, 1972-73, resident in ob-gyn, 1973-74; sr. resident in ob-gyn U. Calif. San Diego Med. Ctr., 1976-78; asst. prof. dept. reproductive medicine U. Calif., San Diego, 1978-82, assoc. prof. div. reproductive endocrinology, dept. reproductive medicine, 1982-84; prof., head sect. reproductive endocrinology and infertility, dept. ob-gyn Northwestern U., Chgo., 1984-88; George B. Riley prof. dept. ob-gyn U. Cin., 1988—99, chmn. dept., 1988—99; assoc exec. dir. Am. Soc. Reproductive Medicine, Birmingham, Ala., 2000—02, exec. dir., 2002—. Clin. assoc. physician, NIH, 1974-76, mem. reproductive endocrinology study sect., 1986-89; mem. NIH population rsch. com., 1992-96; vol. clin. prof., dept. OB-GYN U. Ala. Birmingham. Co-editor: Principles and Practice of Endocrinology and Metabolism, 1990, Gynecology and Obstetrics: A Longitudinal Approach, 1992; co-editor: Infertility, Evaluation and Treatment, 1995; mem. editorial bd. Jour. Clin. Endocrinology and Metabolism, 1985-88, Obstetrics and Gynecology, 1993-96. Asst. surgeon USPHS, 1974-76. Fellow Am. Coll. Obstetrics and Gynecology; mem. Endocrine Soc., Am. Soc. Reprodn. Medicine (program com. 1989-91), Am. Gynecol. Obstetric Soc., Soc. Gynecol. Investigation, Pacific Coast Fertility Soc. (Wyeth award 1972, 82), Phi Beta Kappa, Alpha Omega Alpha. Office: ASRM 1209 Montgomery Hwy Birmingham AL 35216-2809 Business E-Mail: rrebar@asrm.org. *

REBARBER, ANDREI, obstetrician, gynecologist, educator; b. Bucharest, Romania, Sept. 9, 1966; arrived in U.S., 1972; s. Sergiu and Antoinette Rebarber; m. Leslie Binder, July 3, 1995; children: Sarah, Emma. BS cum laude, CCNY, 1989; MD cum laude, SUNY, Syracuse, 1991. Cert. Am. Bd. Ob-gyn., maternal-fetal medicine. Intern and resident dept. ob-gyn. Beth Israel Med. Ctr., NYC, 1991—95; fellow maternal-fetal medicine dept. ob-gyn. Yale U. Sch. Medicine, New Haven, 1995—97; assoc. prof. divsn. maternal-fetal medicine dept. ob-gyn. NYU Sch. Medicine, NYC, 1997—2005; med. dir. Bellevue Hosp. Birth Ctr., NYC, 1999—2002, MFM Assocs., NYC, 2005—; assoc. prof. divsn. maternal-fetal medicine dept. ob-gyn. Mt. Sinai Sch. Medicine, NYC, 2005—. Asst. attending Bellevue Hosp. Ctr., NYC, 1997—2005, NYU Med. Ctr., NYC, 1997—; cons. Chilton Meml. Hosp., Pompton Plains, NJ, 1999—2001, Valley Hosp., Ridgewood, NJ, 1997—; presenter in field. Contbr. articles to profl. jours. Grantee, Haemonetics Rsch., 1997, Ross Products/Abbott Labs., 2001, 2002, Woodside Biomed., Inc., 2002. Fellow: ACOG, Bellevue Ob-gyn. Soc.; mem.: AMA (Physician Recognition award 1999—2002), N.Y. Obstet. Soc., Internat. Soc. Ultrasound in Ob-gyn., Am. Inst. Ultrasound in Medicine, Soc. Maternal-Featl Medicine. Avocation: tennis. Office Phone: 212-722-7409.

REBELLO, MARLENE MUNSON, speech pathologist, consultant; b. San Jose, Calif., Oct. 15, 1948; d. Alfred Vernon and Rose Zita (Pereira) Nunes; m. Steven Del Munson, Mar. 21, 1970 (div. 1982); m. William Wayne Rebello, Dec. 5, 1992. BA, San Jose State U., 1970, MA, 1971; MS in Counseling, U. LaVerne, 1990. Speech pathologist Newark Unified Sch. Dist., Calif., 1971—2005, Washington Hosp., Fremont, Calif., 1980-89; pvt. practice Fremont and Pleasanton, Calif., 1980—. Cons. in field. Recipient Bank of Am. award, 1966, Cabrillo scholarship, Nat. Merit scholarship, 1966, Maria Leonard award Outstanding Sr. Grade Point Average, 1970; fellow VA, 1970. Mem. Calif. Speech and Hearing Assn., Pleasanton Sister City Assn. (v.p. 1996-2002, pres. 2003, mem. pres. 2005-, fundraising chair 2005-), Newark Tchrs. Assn. (treas. 1971), Save Our Sunol Found., Calif. Tchrs. Assn., Arthur & Elena Court Conservation Soc., Pleasanton North Rotary (Paul Harris fellow). Avocations: antiques, decorating, gourmet cooking. Home and Office: 10579 Foothill Rd Sunol CA 94586-9464 Personal E-mail: marspot@aol.com.

REBHUN, JOSEPH, allergist, immunologist, medical educator; b. Przemysl, Poland, Oct. 7, 1921; came to U.S., 1950; s. Baruch and Serel R.; m. Maria Birkenhejm, Aug. 10, 1945; children: Lillian Friedland, Richard B.R., Donald. MD, U. Innsbruck, Austria, 1950; MS in Medicine, Northwestern U., 1954. Diplomate Am. Bd. Allergy and Immunology. Intern Barnert Meml. Hosp., Patterson, NJ; resident in internal medicine Tompkins County Meml. Hosp. and Cornell U., NY, 1951-52; fellow in allergy Northwestern U. Med. Sch./Chidlren's Meml. Hosp., Chgo., 1952-54; fellow instr. Northwestern U. Med. Sch., 1954; asst. clin. prof. medicine Loma Linda U., 1957-93; clin. prof. medicine U. So. Calif., LA, 1965-91, ret., 1998. Chief allergy Chgo. Eye, Ear, Nose and Throat Hosp., 1953-55; cons. Pacific State Hosp., Spadra Pomona Valley Cmty. Hosp., Pomona Casa Colina Hosp. Author: SOS, 1946, The Cry of Democracy for Help, God and Man in Two Worlds, 1985, The Embers of Michael, 1993, Crisis of Morality and Reaction to the Holocaust, 1998, Leap to Life: Triumph Over Nazi Evil, 2000, Why Me?, 2004, A Bridge to the Generations, 2009; contbr. numerous articles to med. jours. Pres. Am. Congress Jews from Poland, 1969—70. Capt. U.S. Mil., San Francisco, capt. med. reserve corps., L.A. Recipient honors City and County of L.A., L.A. Office Dist. Atty., Senate of State of Calif., all 1985. Fellow Am. Acad. Allergy (rsch. coun. 1960-65), Am. Coll. Allergy, Assn. Clin. Allergy and Immunology; mem. West Coast Allergy Soc., Calif. Allergy Assn., L.A. Soc. Allergy, L.A. Med. Assn., Calif. Med. Assn, Pomona Valley (head of Med. Reserve Corp). Office Phone: 909-624-1792. Personal E-mail: joerebhun@yahoo.com.

REBOK, DOUGLAS E., insurance company executive, accountant; m. Barb Rebok; 2 children. BA in Acctg., Loma Linda U., Calif.; MBA, U. So. Calif., LA. CPA Oreg. Budget and reimbursement specialist Adventist Med. Ctr., Portland, Oreg., 1976, contr., v.p. fin.; sr. v.p., CFO Adventist Health, Roseville, Calif., 1983—. Mem.: Healthcare Fin. Mgmt. Assn., American Inst. CPA. Office: Adventist Health 2100 Douglas Blvd Roseville CA 95661 Office Phone: 916-781-2000. Office Fax: 916-783-9146. *

RECCHIA, FRANCESCO, oncologist, researcher; b. Rome, May 27, 1946; s. Amedeo and Cornelia (Sudano) R.; m. Mildred del Rosario Estrada, Dec. 16, 1982; children: Cornelia Ortensia Carla, Francesca Mildred. MD cum laude, U. Rome, 1970, degree in oncology cum laude, 1984. Surgical asst. Civil Hosp., Avezzano, Italy, 1970-76; fellow in cardiovascular surgery Tex. Heart Inst., Houston, 1976-77; staff physician Civil Hosp., 1978-84; fellow med. oncology MD Anderson Hosp., Houston, 1985; chief med. oncology Civil Hosp., 1986—. Cons. physician Fondazione Carlo Ferri Monterotondo, Rome, 1993. Served in Italian army, 1972-73. Mem. Am. Soc. Clin. Oncology, Am. Assn. Cancer Rsch. Avocations: photography, computers. Home: Via Del Castagveto 15 67056 Luco Dei Marsi Italy Office: Civil Hosp Localita 3 Conche I-67051 Avezzano Italy Home Phone: +39-0863-52119; Office Phone: +39-086-3499250. Business E-Mail: frecchia1946@libero.it.

RECEK, CESTMIR, retired surgeon; b. Ostrava, Czech Rep., Nov. 21, 1927; s. Josef Recek and Marta Reckova; m. Marie Novotna, Oct. 6, 1956 (div.); m. Iva Krivkova, May 2, 1976; children: Lenka, Martin, Milos. MD, Charles U., Prague, Czech Rep., 1952. Vascular - cardiovasc. surgeon U. Hosp., Hradec Kralove, Czech Republic, 1955—84; cardiovasc. surgeon Landeskrankenhaus, Klagenfurt, Austria, 1984—90. Cons. Deusch-Ordens-Spital, Friesach, Austria, 1990—99. Contbr. articles to profl. jours. Achievements include research in venous hemodynamics on calf muscle venous pump called as ambulatory pressure gradient which triggers reflux in varicose vein disease; definition of basic hemodynamic terms, such as physiological decrease in pressure, ambulatory venous hypertension, ambulatory pressure gradient, rebuttal of the theory of incompetent calf perforators. Home: Mantlergasse 24 Vienna A-1130 Austria Personal E-mail: recek@aon.at.

RECHT, MICHAEL P., medical educator, department chairman; b. Pitts., June 6, 1958; MD, U. Pa., 1983. Louis Marx prof., chair NYU Langone Med. Ctr., 2008. Office: 550 First Ave IRM 229 New York NY 10016 Business E-Mail: dagosm01@nyumc.org.

RECHTER, LESLEY, physician, educator; Grad., NY Med Coll., 1976. Diplomate Am. Bd. Family Medicine. Resident family medicine Nassau County Med Ctr., East Meadow, 1977—79; physician Stony Brook Univ. Med. Ctr. Assoc. clin. prof. family medicine SUNY. Office: Stony Brook University Medical Center 54 Birchwood Pk Dr Jericho NY 11753-2202 Office Phone: 516-933-6850.

RECK, MARTIN, oncologist; b. Ahrensburg, Germany, July 17, 1965; s. Ewald and Anneliese Reck; m. Andrea Koy, June 4, 1990; children: Lara Maria, Matthis Leonhardt, Linus Manuel. PhD, U. Hamburg, 1995. Diplomate State Med. Bd. Registration, Schleswig Holstein, 1993, in pulmonology 2002, in internal medicine State Med. Bd. Registration, Hamburg, 2001. Asst. med. dir. Hosp. Grosshansdorf, Schleswig Holstein, Germany, 2003—; head dept. clin. trials Hosp. Grosshansdorf, Dept. Thoracic Oncology, 2004—, head dept. thoracic oncology, 2011—. Mem. esmo faculty group chest tumors ESMO, Lugano, Switzerland; mem. iaslc membership com. IASLC, Aurora, Colo., 2007—. Recipient AIO-Wissenschaftspreis, Arbeitsgemeinschaft Internistische Onkologie, 2004; named Professorship, U. Lübeck, 2008. Mem.: Internat. Assn. for the Study of Lung Cancer, European Soc. of Med. Oncology, Am. Society Clin. Oncology. Office: Hosp Grosshansdorf Wöhrendamm 80 Grosshansdorf Schleswig Holstein 22927 Germany Office Fax: 0049 4102 691317.

RECTOR, M. EUGENE, retired community pharmacist; b. Sequin, Tex., Aug. 16, 1950; m. Marcia A. Rector, May 15, 1982. AA, Blinn Coll., 1970; BS in Pharmacy, U. Tex., Austin, 1972; BA in Philosophy, U. Tex., Dallas, 1982, MS in Mgmt. and Adminstrn. Scis., 1985; PharmD, Broadmore U., Belize City, Belize, 1998. Staff pharmacist Baylor U. Med. Ctr., Dallas, 1973-81, Presbyn. Hosp., Dallas, 1981-86; dir. pharmacy Madison St. Joseph Health Ctr., Madisonville, Tex., 1986—2001; pharmacist Walgreens #4999, 2001—10, Walmart, 2010—. Fellow Am. Coll. Apothecaries; mem. Am. Soc. Health-Sys. Pharmacists, Tex. Soc. Health-Sys. Pharmacists, Lions Club, Masons (Vickery Lodge 1351, Rogers Prairie Lodge 540 past master), Shriners. Republican. Methodist. Avocations: hunting, ranching. Home: 16584 Fm 3 S Normangee TX 77871-3511 Home Phone: 936-855-2898. Personal E-mail: rattlinr@windstream.net.

REDBERG, RITA FRAN, cardiologist; b. NYC, 1956; BA, Cornell Univ.; MD, Univ. Pa. Sch. Med., 1982; MSc, London Sch. Economics, 1980. Diplomate Am. Bd. Internal Medicine, 1985, Am. Bd. Internal Medicine, Cardiovascular Diseases, 1989. Intern Columbia-Presbyn. Med. Ctr., NYC, 1982-83, resident, 1983-85, fellow in cardiol. internal medicine, 1985-88; fellow in non-invasive cardiology Mt. Sinai Med. Ctr., NYC, 1988—90; staff mem., asst. prof. through prof. of med., and dir. Women's Cardiovascular Services Univ. Calif. San Francisco Med. Ctr., 1990—. Author: You Can Be a Woman Cardiologist, Heart Healthy: The Step-by-Step Guide to Preventing and Healing Heart Disease, Coronary Disease in Women: Evidence-based Diagnosis and Treatment. Thouron Fellowship, Robert Woods Johnson Fellow in health policy. Mem. AMA (founding mem. Women in Cardiology com., 1994), ACP, Am. Coll. Cardiology (mem. advocacy com.), Am. Heart Assn. (chair Sci. Adv. Bd. for Choose to Move program, chair Communications com., mem. sci. publications com.), Am. Soc. Echocardiology. Office: U Calif San Francisco Med Ctr 505 Parnassus Ave # M314D San Francisco CA 94122-2722 Office Phone: 415-476-6874. Office Fax: 415-502-8627. Business E-Mail: redberg@medicine.ucsf.edu.

REDBURN, AMBER LYNNE, nursing educator; b. West Plains, Mo., Jan. 4, 1963; d. Norris Bert and Chlora Ivene (Brickey) Cozort; m. Timothy Mark Redburn, Apr. 26, 1997; 1 child, Corby Lee. BSN, Rockhurst Coll. and Rsch. Coll. of Nursing, Kansas City, Mo., 1985. RN Mo. Psychiat. staff nurse Cox Med. Ctr. North, Springfield, Mo., 1985; psychiat. technician Park Cen. Hosp., Springfield, 1985-86; orthop. staff nurse St. John's Regional Health Ctr., Springfield, 1986-97; comprehensive care nurse Ozarks Med. Ctr., West Plains, 1997-98, nurse educator, 1998, also former instr. BLS, 1998; short term BLS instr. South Ctrl. Area Vocat.-Tech. Sch., West Plains, 1998; para profl. West Plains HS, 2005—11, West Plains Elem. Sch., 2011—. Mem. com. St. John's Med. Explorer Post 339, 1989-90, pres., 1990-91; mem. Greene County Rep. Party-TARGET, 1993-97; mem. Rep. Nat. Com., 1995-98; mem. com. S.W. Mo. Nurses Recognition Dinner, 1992-97, chair, 1994-97; mem. West Plains Adult Day Svcs., 1997; reading vol. West Plaine Elem. Sch., 2004-2005. Mem. Mo. State Tchrs. Assn., 2006-, Mo. Nurses Assn. (corr. sec., past bd. dirs., 4th dist., mem. nominating com., med.-surg. spl. interest group 1993-98, sec. 1996-98, regional dir. region F 1994-96, mem. nominating com. 2004—08, Mo. Nurses Assn.-PAC com. 1996-2007, comm. com. 1995-99, state bd. dirs. 1997-99, membership and mktg. com. 1997-99, nursing practice com. 1999, regional dir. region F 2002-2004), Nat. Assn. Orthopedic Nurses, Sigma Theta Tau, 2007-.

REDDICK, DEIRDRE SHADEIA, physician assistant; b. Bklyn., Sept. 22, 1967; d. Thomas Boykin and Frances Reddick. BS in Chemistry, cum laude, Claflin U., 1989; BS Physician Asst., CUNY, 2002. Social worker, case mgr. King's County Hosp. Ctr., Bklyn., 1993—99; physician asst. Lyndon Baines Johnson Health Complex, Bklyn., 2002—06, Bedford Stuyvesant Family Health Ctr., Bkln., NY, 2007—. Mem. Christian Cultural Ctr. Mem.: N.Y. State Soc. Physician Assts. (pres.'s award 2001), Am. Acad. Physician Assts., Bklyn.-Tech. HS Alumni Assn., Claflin U. Alumni Assn., CUNY Alumni Assn. Avocations: reading, dance. Home: 134-20 87th Ave 4C Kew Gardens NY 11418

REDDY, ASHOK KUMAR, microbiologist; b. Alluru, Andhra Pradesh, India, May 15, 1975; MSc in Med. Microbiology, Kasturba Med. Coll., 2000; PhD, Nizams Inst. Med. Scis., 2006. Microbiologist L.V. Prasad Eye Inst., 2007—10; cons. microbiologist GHR Micro Diagnostics, 2010—. Recipient Iamm Silver Jubly prize, Indian Assn. Med. Microbiologists; Sci. and Tech. Rsch. grant. Mem.: Indian Assn. Med. Microbiologists, Am. Soc. Microbiology. Avocation: music. Office: 2nd Fl 145 Dwarakapuri Colony Punjagutta Hyderabad Andhra Pradesh 500082 India Personal E-mail: ashokreddyg999@yahoo.com.

REDDY, BAKTHA NELLCORE BABU, physician, medical educator, consultant, researcher; b. Vadanellore, India, Apr. 4, 1938; s. Babu Reddy and Janaki Ammall Nellore; m. Bharathi Baktha Reddy, May 13, 1965; children: N. B. Chalakanth, N. B. Saravathy, N.B. K. Kumaran. MBBS, Stanley Med. Coll., Madras, Tamil Nadu, 1962; diploma in Dermatology, Madras Med. Coll., Madras, Tamil Nadu, 1972, MD, 1979; diploma in Med. Edn., Univ. Dundee, UK, 1990. Registered Dermatologist Tamil Nadu Med. Coun. Med. officer Hemerijcky Leprosy Ctr., Polambakkam, 1963—76; asst. prof. Madras Med. Coll., Madras, 1977—79; assoc. prof. Stanley Med. Coll., Madras, 1979—81; cons. dermatologist/lepersy Kaduna State, Nigeria, South Africa, 1981—85; dir. tng. All Africa Leprosy Tng., Ethiopia, 1985—92; cons. World Health Orgn. Ctr., Khartoum, 1992—93; pres. Clinrx Lab., Madras, 1997—. Dir. Damien Found., Brussels, 1993—96; dir. tng. Scheilfleim Leprosy Ctr., Vellore, India, 1998—2000; cons. prof. emeritus med. univ. MGR Med. Univ., Madras, 1999—. Author: (7 booklets) Self Learning Materials on Leprosy. Cmty. devel. program Grama Mempttu Sangam, 1994—, Integrated Devel. Program, Vadanellore, 1995—. Mem.: Am. Acad. of Dermatology. Achievements include research in herbal medicines successfully done on psoriasis technology; transdermal drug delivery-first human study on insulin Human Growth Hormone. Avocations: yoga, educational technology activies, community development. Office: Praveena Hosp Vandalur Rd Kelambakkam 603103 India Home: Vandalur Rd E 1 Mahajyothi Nilayam 603 103 Kelambakkam India Office Phone: +98404 24146. Personal E-mail: baktha_reddy@yahoo.com.

REDDY, BALAJI MALAPALLI, radiologist; b. Bangalore, India, Sept. 4, 1967; MBBS, Bangalore Med. Coll., 1992; MD in Radiology, Kasturba Med. Coll., 1995. Radiologist Medinova Diagnostics, 1995—97, Mallige Med. Ctr., 1997—99; chief radiologist Global Hosps., Hyderabad, 1999—2005; radiologist, mng. ptnr. Focu Diagnostics, 2005—. Cons., mng. ptnr. Sri Venkata Sai Health Care, 2005. Mem.: Indian Radiol. and Imaging Assn. Avocations: travel, reading. Office: Focus Diagnostics Sai Baba Temple Ln Hyderabad Andhra-pradesh 500082 India Office Fax: 914023351124. Personal E-mail: mcbalaji@hotmail.com.

REDDY, CHANDRASEKARA G., research scientist; b. Hyderabad, Andhra Pradesh, India, Jan. 1, 1948; s. Anki G. and Lakshminarayanamma Reddy; m. ThulasiDevi Reddy; children: Venkatrama G., Madhuri G. PhD, U. Delhi, India, 1976. Cert. D.A.M U. Bombay, 1981. Head, lancaster synthesis Clariant India Ltd., Chennai, Tamilnadu, India, 1998—2003; rsch. coord. Vittal Mallya Sci. Rsch. Found., Bangalore, Karnataka, India, 2004—. Vol. Vedantha Samiti, Delhi, 1972—76. Rsch. fellow, Coun. Sci. and Indsl. Rsch., 2005—09. Mem.: Am. Chem. Soc. Achievements include patents for anticancer compounds, synthesis of active pharmaceutical ingredients by non-infringing processes, isolation of new antibiotics. Home: 53/19 Theertha Apts 4th Main Rd Malleswaram Bangalore Karnataka 560055 India Office: Vittal Mallya Sci Rsch Found 94/3 23rd Cross 29th Main BTM IInd Stage Bangalore Karnataka 560076 India Business E-Mail: gcreddy@vmsrf.org.

REDDY, DANIEL JOSEPH, vascular surgeon; b. Jackson, Mich., June 2, 1947; s. Martin Joseph and Phyllis Watson Reddy; m. Diane Marie D'Angelo; children: Caitlin Marie, Daniel Martin. BS, Georgetown U., 1969; MD, U. Mich., 1973. Diplomate in gen. surgery and vascular surgery Am. Bd. Surgery. Sr. staff vascular surgeon Henry Ford Hosp., Detroit, 1979—, chief of vascular surgery, 1997—, dir. vascular surgery fellowship tng. program, 1997—, d. emerick szilagyi chair in vascular surgery, 2002—. Mem. bd. govs. Henry Ford Med. Group, Detroit, 1995—2002; prof. surgery Wayne State U.; staff surgeon John D. Dingell VA Med. Ctr., Detroit. Author numerous papers, exhibits, movies, abstracts. Bd. mem. Christus Medicus, Metro Detroit, 1999—. Ignatius Academic scholar, Georgetown U., 1965—69, Traveling Pub. Health fellow to Yugoslavia, Am. Assn. Med. Colls., 1973. Fellow: ACS (Fredrick Coller award 1975); mem.: Parents Club West Point Mich. Chpt., Friends of Boston U. Varsity Women's Ice Hockey, Midwestern Vascular Surgery Soc., Ctrl. Surg. Assn., Western Surg. Assn., Soc. Vascular Surgery. Independent. Roman Catholic. Achievements include patents for Reddy Treadle Asssessing Arterial Systems. Avocation: ice hockey.

REDDY, GUNDAM CHANDRASEKHARA, endocrinologist, consultant; s. Gundam Venkata and Gundam Balamma Reddy; m. Gundam Lakshmi Devi, June 1, 1954; children: Gundam Ramesh, Sirisha Gundam, Gundam Sucharitha. BBS, Kurnool Med. Coll., S.V. Univ., India, 1966—77, MB, MD in Internal Medicine. DM in Endocrinology Banaras Hindu U., Varanasi, Up, India, 1987. Asst. prof. medicine GMC & KMC Coll. & Hosp., Kurnool&Guntur, Ap, India, 1978—85; prof. endocrinology Osmania Gen. Hospital & Osmania Med. Coll., Hyderabad, 1993—. Cons. endocrinologist Aditya Nursing Home, Hyderabad, India, 1988—. Contbr. articles in Lay Press, Ty and Radio (BEST Dr.& RASHTRIA RATTAN AWARD, 2003). Diet exhbns., free Diabetic screening/counselling; med. cons. to politicians Ap State, Hyderabad, Andhra Pradesh, 1993—2003. Recipient Examiner To Dm Endocrinology, Banaras Hindu U., 2003, Rashtria Rattan award for Medical Excellence. Mem.: EASD, RSSDI, many others, Internat. Endocrine Soc., Endocrine Soc. of India (v.p. 1997—98), Assn. of Physicians of India (life). Achievements include research in endocrinological disorders.

REDDY, LAKKIREDDY HARIVARDHAN, medical researcher; b. India, Aug. 19, 1975; Degree in Pharmacy, RGUHS Bangalore, 1998; PhD in Pharm. Scis., MS U. Baroda, 2005. Rsch. exec. Sun Pharm. Industries Ltd., Baroda, India, 2004—05; scientist CNRS, U. Paris, 2005—08; head Sanofi-Aventis, 2009. Co-editor (with L. Harivardhan Reddy, Patrick Couvreur): Macromolecular Anticancer Therapeutics, Cancer Drug Discovery and Development Series; contbr. articles to sci. profl. publs. Mem.: European Assn. Cancer Rsch. Office: Pharmaceutical Scis Dept Sanofi-Aventis 13 Quai Jules Guesdes Vitry-sur-Seine 94403 France Business E-Mail: harivardhanr@gmail.com.

REDDY, MALLIKARJUNA DADITHOTA, physician; Studied, Gandhi Medical Coll., 1982. Diplomate Am. Bd. Family Medicine. Resident family medicine Cath. Med. Ctr., 1987—90; with St. Josephs Hosp. Yonkers, Svcmc-Cath. Med. Ctr., Flushing Primary Care

Assocs. LLP; physician NY Hosp. Queens. Office: New York Hospital Queens 7218 164th St Fresh Meadows NY 11365 Office Phone: 718-969-6640. Office Fax: 718-969-1050.

REDDY, PREETHA, hospital administrator; b. Hyderabad, India, 1957; d. P.C. Reddy. BS in Chemistry, U. Madras; MA, Annamalai U. Joint mng. dir. Apollo Hosps., Chennai, India, 1991—93; mng. dir. Apollo Hosps. Enterprise Ltd., Chennai, India, 1989—. Advisor on healthcare to Govt. of India; mem. Nat. Quality Coun.; bd. dirs. Apollo Hosps. Internat. Ltd., PCR Investments Ltd., Apollo Sindoori Hotels Ltd., A B Med. Ctrs. Ltd., Apollo Mumbai Hosps. Ltd., Lanka Hosps. Corp. Ltd., Samudra Healthcare Enterprises Ltd., Imperial Cancer Hosp. and Rsch. Ctr. Ltd.; alt. dir. Lanka Hosp. Corp. Ltd. Named one of 50 Most Powerful Internat. Women in Bus., Fortune mag., 2009, 2010, 150 Women Who Shake the World, Newsweek, 2011. Office: Apollo Hospitals 21 Greams Lane Off Greams Road 600 006 Chennai India *

REDDY, SATISH, pharmaceutical executive; b. India, June 9, 1967; BSChemE, Osmania U., Hyderabad, Andhra Pradesh, India, 1988; MS in Medicinal Chemistry, Purdue U., West Lafayette, Ind., 1991. Exec. dir. mfg. & new product devel. Dr. Reddy Labs., Ltd., Hyderabad, 1993—97, mng. dir., COO, 1997—. Co. rep. to Indian Pharm. Assn. Recipient India Corp. Citizen of Yr. award, India Bus. Leader Awards, 2005, Disting. Alumni award, Purdue U., 2009; named a Young Global Leader, World Economic Forum, 2007. Mem.: Confederation Indian Industry (chmn. Andhra Pradesh chpt. 2003—04, nat. coun. 2004—), Young Presidents' Orgn., Young Entrepreneurs' Orgn. (founding mem. Hyderabad chpt.). Mailing: Dr Reddy Laboratories 8 2 337 Road No 3 Banjara Hills Hyderabad 500034 Andhra Pradesh India

REDDY, TUNGA TRISHUL, physician; b. India, Jan. 16, 1978; MD, Kasturba Med. Coll., Manipal, 2003. Chief resident physician East Tenn. State U., 2009—, instr., Internat. Med. Grad. Inst., 2009—. Recipient Outstanding Resident award, Caduceus Club and Quillen Coll. Medicine Orgn.; fellowships, U. Miami. Mem.: Am. Assn. Physicians of Indian Origin, Rural Health Assn. Tex., TNAFP, Am. Assn. Family Physicians. Avocations: photography, yoga, basketball. Home: 1185 W Mt View Rd Apt #1322 Johnson City TN 37604-2530 Personal E-mail: drtrishul@gmail.com.

REDDY, VENKATA RAMI, research scientist, director; b. Khammam, Andhra Pradesh, Sept. 4, 1957; MSc, 1980, PhD, 1984. Rsch. scientist, cons. NIRRH, ICMR, 1994, dep. dir., sr. grade, 2009—. Recipient Best Scientist award, NIRRH, Swarnakantha Dingley award, ICMR. Master: Chem. Purchase Com., NIRRH; mem.: NIRRH, Translational Rsch. Com. Avocations: reading, cricket. Office: NIRRH JM St RGThadani Marg P Mumbai Maharastra 400012 India Office Fax: 91-24139412. Business E-Mail: reddyk@nirrh.res.in.

REDDY, VENKATA RAMI, medical researcher; b. Khammam, Andhrapradesh, India, Sept. 15, 1956; MSc, 1980, PhD, 1984. Rsch. scientist Nat. Inst. Rsch. in Reproductive Health, ICMR, 1994—, dep. dir., 2009—. Recipient Swarnakantha Dingley award, ICMR. Master: NIRRH (mem. translational rsch. com., Best Scientist). Avocations: reading, cricket. Home: NIRRH JM St RG Thadani Marg Mumbai Maharastra 400012 India Home Fax: 91-24139412. Personal E-mail: shrichi@rediffmail.com.

REDDY KANDAKURE, PRAMOD, cardiologist; b. Aurangabad, India, Feb. 14, 1973; MS in Surgery, DNB in Surgery, Seth GS Med. Coll., Parel, Mumbai, MBBS, 1996; MCH, B. J. Med. Coll., Pune, India, DNB, 2005. Cons. cardiac surgeon Apollo Hosp., Hyderabad, India, 2005—07, Innova Hosp., Hyderabad, 2007—. Contbr. articles to profl. jours. Fellow: Rural Health Soc.; mem.: Mem. Internat. Homeo. Medicine Soc., Paediat. Cardiol. Soc. India, Indian Assn. Cardiothoracic Surgeon. Avocations: music, cricket, reading. Home: ARCA Vivek Residency Flat 202 Ahobh Hyderabad Andhra Pradesh 00007 India Personal E-mail: drpramodreddy@yahoo.com.

REDLICH, CARRIE A., pulmonologist, educator; MD, Yale U., New Haven, Conn., 1982, MPH, 1988. Diplomate Am. Bd. Internal Medicine, 1986, Am. Bd. Internal Medicine-occupl. medicine, 1990, Am. Bd. Internal Medicine-pulmonary disease, 2002. Intern Yale Univ. Sch. Medicine, New Haven, 1983, resident in internal medicine, 1984—86, resident in occupl. medicine, 1986—87, fellow, 1987, Univ. Wash., Seattle, 1987—89; prof. medicine Yale Sch. Medicine; dir. occupl. and environ. medicine program Yale Med. Group. Office: Yale New Haven Hospital 135 College St 3rd Fl New Haven CT 06510 Office Phone: 203-785-4197. Office Fax: 203-785-7391.

REDMAN, BARBARA KLUG, nursing educator; b. Mitchell, SD; d. Harlan Lyle and Darlien Grace (Bock) Klug; m. Robert S. Redman, Sept. 14, 1958; 1 child, Melissa Darlien. BS, S.D. State U., 1958; MEd, U. Minn., 1959, PhD, 1964; LHD (hon.), Georgetown U., 1988; DSc (hon.), U. Colo., 1991; M in Bioethics, U. Pa., 2004, MBE, 2004. RN. Asst. prof. U. Wash., Seattle, 1964-69; assoc. dean U. Minn., Mpls., 1969-75; dean Sch. Nursing U. Colo., Denver, 1975-78; VA scholar VA Cen. Office, Washington, 1978-81; postdoctoral fellow Johns Hopkins U., Balt., 1982-83; exec. dir. Am. Assn. Colls. Nursing, Washington, 1983-89, ANA, Washington, 1989-93; prof. nursing Johns Hopkins U., Balt., 1993-95; dean, prof. Sch. Nursing U. Conn., Storrs, 1995-98; dean Coll. Nursing Wayne State U., Detroit. Vis. fellow Kennedy Inst. Ethics, Georgetown U., 1993-94; fellow in med. ethics Harvard Med. Sch., 1994-95. 2004—; sr. fellow U. Pa. Ctr. for Bioethics, 2004—. Author: Practice of Patient Education, 1968—; contbr. articles to profl. jours. Bd. dirs. Friends of Nat. Libr. of Medicine, Washington, 1987—. Recipient Disting. Alumnus award S.D. State U., 1975, Outstanding Achievement award U. Minn., 1989; sr. fellow, U. Pa. Ctr., 2004-. Fellow Am. Acad. Nursing. Home: 12425 Bobbink Ct Potomac MD 20854-3005 Office: Wayne State U 5557 Cass Ave Detroit MI 48202-3615

REDMAN, ROBERT SHELTON, pathologist, dentist; b. Fargo, ND, Aug. 1, 1935; s. Kenneth and Elizabeth Francis (McMillan) R.; m. Barbara Darlien Klug, Sept. 14, 1958; 1 child, Melissa Darlien Redman Johnson. Student, S.D. State U., 1953-55; BS, DDS, U. Minn., 1959, MSD, 1963; PhD, U. Wash., 1969. Cert. Am. Bd. Oral and Maxillofacial Pathology. Clin. asst. prof. sch. dentistry U. Minn., Mpls., 1963-64, assoc. prof., 1969-75; assoc. prof. sch. dentistry U. Colo., Denver, 1975-78; staff dentist, chief oral pathology rsch. lab. Dept. VA Med. Ctr., Denver, 1975-78, Washington, 1978—. Clin. assoc. prof. Balt. Coll. Dental Surgery U. Md., 1989-2007, deans faculty adj. prof., 2007-; cons. Children's Orthop. Hosp., Seattle, 1966-69; program specialist in oral biology Dept. VA, Washington, 1982-86; adj. scientist Nat. Inst. Dental and Craniofacial Rsch., NIH, 1997—. Contbr. 14 chpts. to books, over 120 articles to profl. jours.; mem. editl. bd. Jour. Dental Rsch., 1995-98, Biotech. and Histochemistry, 2000—; bd. reviewers Anatomical Record, 2004—. Mem. Biol. Stain Commn., 1999—, bd. trustees, 2002-2005. Capt. U.S. Army, 1959-61. Recipient Carl A. Schlack award Assn. Mil. Surgeons US, 1997. Fellow Am. Acad. Oral and Maxillofacial Pathology; mem. ADA, Am. Assn. Anatomists, Internat. Assn. Dental Rsch. (program chmn. salivary rsch. group 1982-86, sec.-treas. 1995-2001, Salivary Rschr. of Yr., Salivary Rsch. Group 2001, William J. Gies award, 2009), Soc. In Vitro Biology, Omicron Kappa Upsilon. Presbyterian. Achievements include discovery and naming of an unique minor salivary gland in the rat; documentation of the relationship between weaning and maturation of salivary glands, of mitotic division of well-differentiated salivary gland cells of all types, including acinar, ductal and myoepithelial cells, of constant cell cycle length and very low rate of apoptosis in salivary glands during development and into maturity; determination of mode of inheritance of benign migratory glossitis, co-developer method to maintain salivary gland acinar cells in culture and several cell lines of these cells, documentation of head and neck cancer in smad 4 deficient mice. Office: Dept VA Med Ctr (151-I) Oral Pathology Rsch Lab 50 Irving St NW Washington DC 20422-0001 Personal E-mail: robert.redman@med.va.gov.

REDMOND, DONALD EUGENE, JR., neuroscientist, educator; b. San Antonio, June 17, 1939; s. Donald Eugene and Viola (Kellum) R.; m. Patricia Welder (Robinson), Dec. 22, 1972; one child Andy J. BA, So. Meth. U., 1961; MD, Baylor U., 1968; MAH, Yale U., 1987. Diplomate Am. Bd. Psychiatry and Neurology. With Lab. of Clin. Sci., NIMH, Bethesda, Md., 1973-74; asst. prof. psychiatry Yale U., New Haven, 1974-77; assoc. chief clin. neurol. sci. unit Conn. Mental Health Ctr., New Haven, 1974-87; assoc. prof. psychiatry Yale U., New Haven, 1978-87; pres. St. Kitts Bio Med. Rsch. Found., St. Kitts, West Indies, 1983—, Axion Rsch. Found., Hamden, Conn., 1985—; prof. psychiatry, dir. neurol. behavior lab. Yale U., New Haven, 1987—, dir. neurol. transplant program for neurol. diseases, 1987—; prof. neurol. surgery, 1993—; with Yale Univ., New Haven, 1993. Contbr. articles to profl. jour.; patentee in field. With USPHS, 1972-74. Recipient Rsch. Scientist Award NIMH, 1980-2001; Found. Fund Prize, Am. Psychiatric Assoc., 1981, Bernard Sanberg Rsch. award Am. Soc. Nuerol. Transplantation & Repair., 2011; grantee NIMH, 1974-91; Nat. Inst. Neurol. Diseases and Stroke, 1986—; others. Mem.: Internat. Soc. Motor Disturbances, Am. Soc. Neural Transplantation and Repair (coun. mem. 1994—98, pres. 2002), Am. Coll. Neuropsychopharmacology (fellow 2002—03). Office: Yale Sch Medicine 300 George St 9th Fl Ste 32 New Haven CT 06511-6624 Office Phone: 203-785-4432.

REDONDO-FIGUERO, CARLOS GODOFREDO, pediatrician, educator; b. Lérida, Spain, May 21, 1953; MD, U. Valladolid, 1976; PhD, U. Leioa, 2000. Dr. Servicio Cántabro de Salud, 1981—. Adj. prof. pediat., faculty medicin U. Cantabria, 1995—2011. Mem.: Soc. Española de Pediatría. Office: Vargas 57 Cantabria Santander 39010 Spain Business E-Mail: carlos.redondo@unican.es.

REDPATH, JOHN LESLIE, medical researcher, educator; b. Wooler, Eng., Dec. 10, 1942; BSc in Chemistry & Physics with honors, U. Newcastle-upon-Tyne, 1965, PhD in Radiation Chemistry, 1968. Prof. radiation oncology U. Calif. Irvine, 1977—. Instl. Rsch. grant, Am. Cancer Soc. Mem.: Am. Assn. Cancer Rsch., Radiation Rsch. Soc. (pres. 2000—01). Avocations: hiking, birdwatching, photography. Office: University Newcastle-upon-Tyne Dept Radiation Oncology Irvine CA 92697 Business E-Mail: jlredpat@uci.edu.

REECE, E. ALBERT, dean, obstetrician, gynecologist, perinatologist; b. Spanishtown, Jamaica, Jan. 3, 1950; came to U.S., 1969; s. Wilfred Anderson Reece and Daisy Lucinda (Price) Reece Batten; m. Sharon Andrea Blake, July 28, 1974; children: Kelie, Brynne, Sharon-Andrea II. BS with honors, L.I. U., 1973; MD, NYU, 1978; PhD in Biochemistry, U. West Indies; MBA, Fox Sch. Bus. Mgmt., Temple U.; ob/gyn specialty diploma, Columbia U., 1982; maternal-fetal subspecialty diploma, Yale U., 1984. Diplomate Am. Bd. Ob-Gyn.; bd. cert. maternal-fetal medicine. Intern, resident Columbia U., Presbyn. Med. Ctr., NYC, 1978-82; materal-fetal medicine fellow Yale U. Sch. Medicine, 1982-84, asst. prof. ob-gyn New Haven, 1984-87, assoc. prof. ob-gyn, 1987-90; Abraham Roth prof., chmn. obstetrics, Gynecology and reproductive sciences Temple U. Sch. Medicine, Phila., 1991—2001; vice chancellor, dean, v.p. for med. sciences U. of Arkansas for Med. Sciences, Coll. of Med., Little Rock, 2002—06; John Z. and Akiko K. Bowers disting. prof., dean U. Md. Sch. of Medicine, 2006—; v.p. med. affairs U. Md., 2006—. Elected IOM (chair pediatrics, obstetrics & gynecology, 2003-), NAS, 1998. Co-editor Diabetes Mellitus in Pregnancy: Principles and Practice, 1st edit., 1988, 2nd edit., 1995, Medicine of the Fetus and Mother, 1992, 2nd edit., 1999, A Study Guide for Medicine of the Fetus and Mother, 1992, A Handbook of Medicine of the Fetus and Mother, 1995; co-author: Fundamentals in Obstetric and Gynecologic Ultrasonography, 1993; contbr. articles, abstract to profl. jours. in excess of 400. Mem. sci. adv. com. March of Dimes, 1993—; mem. sci. adv. bd. NIH-DC Infant Mortality Initiative, 1993—; mem. adv. com. Nat. Inst. Child Health and Human Diseases, NIH, 1994—; trustee Reading Rehab. Hosp., 1992—; mem. bioeffects com. AIUM, 1992-95. Grantee March of Dimes, 1985-87, Friedman Found., 1990-92, William Penn Found., 1989-93, Am. Diabetes Assn., 1991-93, NIH, 1992—; named one of Top 100 Black Physicians in Am., Black Enterprise Mag., 2001. Fellow Am. Coll. Ob-Gyn., Coll. Physicians Phila.; mem. Am. Diabetes Assn. (coun. on diabetes in pregnancy), Am. Inst. Ultrasound in Medicine, Hellenic Perinatal Soc. Greece (hon.), Nat. Med. Assn. (exec. com. 1987-88, chmn. ob-gyn. sect. 1991-93), NAS Inst. Medicine ((in conjunction with NRC) mem. adv. com., Human Embryonic Stem Cell Rsch., 2006-), New Haven Obstet. Soc., Soc. for Gynecol. Investigation, Soc. Perinatal Obstetricians (leader diabetes spl. interest 1992-94, bd. mem. 1995—), Phila. Perinatal Soc. (program chair 1993—), Phila. Obstet. Soc. (mem. coun. 1992-94). Seventh-Day Adventist. Office: U Md Sch Medicine 14-029, Bressler Rsch Bldg 655 W Baltimore St Baltimore MD 21201-1559 Office Phone: 410-706-7410. Office Fax: 410-706-0235. E-mail: deanmed@som.umaryland.edu. *

REED, CAROLYN E., thoracic surgeon; b. Farmington, Maine, 1950; BA in Chemistry, U. Maine, 1972; MD, U. Rochester, 1977. Cert. Am. Bd. Surgery, 1983, Thoracic Surgery, 1986. Intern surgery NY Hosp. Cornell Medical Ctr., 1977—78, resident surgery, 1978—81, chief resident surgery, 1981—82, asst. surgeon, 1977—81, surgeon, 1981—82, instr. surgery (thoracic), 1983—85; fellowship surgical oncology Meml. Sloan-Kettering Cancer Ctr., 1982—83; asst. prof. surgery Medical U. SC, 1985—89, assoc. prof. surgery, 1989—93, assoc. prof. surgery with tenure, 1993—96, prof. surgery, 1997—, assoc. program dir. Cardiothoracic Surgery Residency Program, 1996—2000, Alice Ruth Reeves Folk Endowed Chair of Clinical Oncology, 1999; chief thoracic surgery Veterans Adminstrn. Hosp., 1985—98; assoc. dir. clinical affairs Hollings Cancer Ctr., 1998—2000, dir., 2000—04, deputy dir. clinical affairs, 2004—; section chief gen. thoracic surgery Medical U. SC, 2004—. Mem.: Women in Thoracic Surgery, Soc. Thoracic Surg., Am. Assoc. Thoracic Surgery, Am. Bd. Thoracic Surgery. Office: MUSC Ashley River Tower Ste 7018 MSC 295 25 Courtenay Dr Charleston SC 29425

REED, DIANE MARIE, retired psychologist; b. Joplin, Mo., Jan. 11, 1934; d. William Marion and Olive Francis (Smith) Kinney; m. William J. Shotton; children: Wendy Robison, Douglas Funkhouser. Student, Art Ctr. Col., LA, 1951-54; BS, U. Oreg., 1976, MS, 1977, PhD, 1981. Lic. psychologist. Illustrator J.L. Hudson Co., Detroit, 1954-56; designer, stylist NYC, 1960-70; designer, owner Decor To You, Inc., Stamford, Conn., 1970-76; founder, exec. dir. Alcohol Counseling and Edn. Svcs., Inc., Eugene, Oreg., 1981-86, clin. supr., 1986, Christian Family Svcs., Eugene, 1986-87; pvt. practice Eugene, 1985—94; co-founder Reed Consulting, Bend, Oreg., 1995—2000; pvt. practice Bend, Oreg., 2000—04; ret., 2005. Evaluator Vocat. Rehab. Div., Eugene, 1982—; alcohol and drug evaluator and commitment examiner Oreg. Mental Health Div., 1981—86. Named Disting. Alumnus, Ctrl. Oreg. region U. Oreg. Coll. Edn., 2003. Mem.: AAUW, APA, Ctr. Ore. Psychological Assn. (pres. elect), Lane County Psychol. Assn. (pres. 1989—90), Oreg. Psychol. Assn., U. Oreg. Nat. Alumni, Ctrl. Oreg. Llama Assn. (pres. 1999—2000), Bend C. of C., Sunriver Area C. of C. (bd. dirs. 1997—98), Sunriver Women's Club (comm. chair), Toastmasters Internat., Rotary (pres. 1997—98, Rotarian Yr. 1996—97, 1997—98). Avocations: photography, skiing, hiking, backpacking.

REED, GEORGE ELLIOTT, surgeon, educator, dean; b. NYC, Aug. 4, 1923; m. Anne Miller Moore, 1995; children from previous marriage: Elizabeth E., George E. Jr. DVM, Cornell U., 1944; MD, NYU, 1951. Diplomate Am. Bd. Surgery, Bd. Thoracic Surgery. Successively intern, resident, chief resident NYU Bellevue Med. Ctr., NYC, 1951-56, Berg fellow in cardiovascular surgery, 1956 59; from asst. prof. to assoc. prof. surgery NYU, NYC, 1959-69, prof., 1969-78; prof. surgery, chief cardiothoracic surgery NY Med. Coll., Valhalla, 1978—2004, vice dean, 1996—2004; pres. med. staff Westchester County Med. Ctr., Valhalla, NY, 1989-93, med. dir., 1992—2004; dir. George E. Reed Heart Ctr. Westchester County Med. Ctr. Westchester Med. Ctr., Valhalla, 1994—2002; pres. Med. Faculty Health Alliance, Valhalla, 1994—2004, chief cardiovascular surgery, 1960—65; dir. Residency Program NYU, 1965—77, prof. emeritus surgery, 2005—. Cons. surgery N.Y. State Dept. Health, Albany, 1963—90, VA, NYC, 1969—78, Lenox Hill Hosp., NYC, 1971—91, Kingston (N.Y.) Hosp., 1971—90, pres. Federated Faculty Practice Plan, 1996—99; adv. bd. Asian Cardiovasc. Thoracic Annals; presenter in field; med. adv. bd. Columbia Meml. Hosp., Hudson, NY, 2002—; pres. Eastview Found., 1992—. Sect. editor: Heart Disease, mem. editl. bd.: Heart and Health Reports; contbr. articles to profl. jours., chapters to books. Fellow: ACS, Am. Coll. Cardiology; mem.: Internat. Soc. Artificial Internal Organs, Am. Soc. Artificial Internal Organs, Heart Rhythm Soc., Internat. Assn. Cardiac Biol. Implants, Am. Trauma Soc., Soc. Thoracic Surgeons, Am. Assn. Thoracic Surgery, Harvey Soc., Am. Trudeau Soc., Alpha Omega Alpha (faculty). Avocations: woodworking, landscape design. Office: 4993 Route 9G Germantown NY 12526 Personal E-mail: georgereed23@hotmail.com.

REED, JAMES WHITFIELD, internist, educator, endocrinologist; b. Pahokee, Fla., Nov. 1, 1935; s. Thomas Reed and Chineater (Grey) Whitfield; married; children: David M., Robert A., Mary I., Katherine E. BS summa cum laude, W.Va. State Coll., Institute, 1954; MD, Howard U., Washington, DC, 1963. Diplomate Am. Bd. Internal Medicine, Am. Bd. Endocrinology and Metabolism; cert. specialist in clin hypertension, Am. Soc. Hypertension. Commd. US Army, 1963, advanced through grades to col., 1981; postdoctoral rsch. fellow U. Calif. Med. Ctr., San Francisco, 1969—71; resident in internal medicine Madigan Army Med. Ctr., Tacoma, 1966—69, chief endocrinology and metabolism, 1971—76, chief dept. clin. rsch., 1976—78; chief dept. medicine Eisenhower Army Med. Ctr., Augusta, Ga., 1978-81; assoc. prof. internal medicine edn. for FP program U. Tex., Dallas, 1981—84; prof. medicine Morehouse Sch. Medicine, Atlanta, 1985—, chmn. dept., 1985—92, chmn. grad. med. edn., 1992—96, activity chmn., 1986—88, dir. internal medicine residency, 1992—98, dir. Clin. Rsch. Ctr., 1998—2000, assoc. chair and prof. medicine, 1992—, chief endocrinology, 1992—, chief of medicine svc. at Grady. Dir. endocrinology, fellowship Madigan Army Med. Ctr., 1976-78; dir., chief medicine and program dir. internal medicine residency program Eisenhower Army Med. Ctr., 1978-81, chmn. directorate of clin. investigation, 1978-81, dir. endocrinology fellowship program; med. cons. Tuskegee VA Hosp., Ala., 1985—; mem. nat. high blood pressure edn. com. NHLBI/NIH, Nat. Diabetes Mellitus Adv. Coun., Nat. Diabetes Adv. Bd., NHLBI working Com. on Hypertension and Diabetes; chmn. Sub Com. Special Population and Situations, chmn. subcom., exec. com. Joint Nat. Commn. Detection Evaluation and Treatment of High Blood Pressure; diabetes epidemic action coun. Am. Diabetes Assn; mem. IOM/NAS Com. Med. Evaluation Vets. Disability Compensation, 2006-08. Author: Black Man's Guide to Good Health, 1994, rev. edit., 2011, High Blood Pressure: The Black Man and Woman's Guide to Living with Hypertension, 2002, Living with Diabetes: A Guide for Patients and Parents, 2005, 2nd edit., 2011; contbr. articles to profl. jours. Med. advisor, chmn. March of Dimes, Pierce County, Tacoma, 1976-78; pres. Charles Drew Sickle Cell and Health Bd., Tacoma, 1976-78; task force on cardiovascular risk reduction Am. Heart Assn. Decorated Legion of Merit, Meritorious Svc. medal; recipient Disting. Alumni award Nat. Assn. for Equal Opportunity in Higher Edn., 1988, Nat. Alumnus of Yr. award W.Va. State Coll., 1987; named to ROTC Hall of Fame, W.Va. State Coll., 1987. Master ACP; fellow Am. Coll. Clin. Endocrinologists; mem. Assn. Profs. Medicine, Endocrine Soc., Internat. Soc. Hypertension in Blacks (v.p. 1986-92, pres. 1992—2001, Lifetime Achievement award), Assn. Program Dirs. in Internal Medicine, Am. Heart Assn. (task force on cardiovasc. risk), Alpha Phi

Alpha, Alpha Omega Alpha Med. Honor Soc. Democrat. Avocations: bowling, skiing. Office: Morehouse Sch Medicine 720 Westview Dr SW Atlanta GA 30310-1495 Office Phone: 404-756-5788. Business E-Mail: jreed@msm.edu.

REED, JAMIE LYNN, medical researcher; b. Ind., Aug. 19, 1980; PhD, Vanderbilt U., Nashville, 2009. Rsch. assoc. Vanderbilt U., 2010—. Recipient Ruth L. Kirschstein Nat. Rsch. Svc. award, NIH, Nat. Inst. Neurol. Disorders and Stroke; rsch. grant, NIH. Mem.: Soc. Neurosci. Avocations: jogging, writing. Office: Vanderbilt University Dept Psychology 301 Wilson Hall 111 21st Ave S Nashville TN 37240 Business E-Mail: jamie.l.reed@vanderbilt.edu.

REED, KANDALL, dean, medical educator, surgeon; DO, Kans. City U. Coll, Medicine and Biomedical Sciences, 1974; B, Midwestern U., Wichita Falls, Tex. Cert. Am. Bd. Surgery, Am. Bd. Osteopathic Surgery. Gen. surgery resident Brooke Army Med. Ctr. Fort Sam Houston, 1974—79; staff surgeon Ft. Knox, Ky., 1979—81; chief surgeon Brooke Army Med. Ctr., 1983—86; prof. surgery Des Moines U., 1983—, chmn. dept. surgery, 1990—2003, dean Coll. Osteopathic Medicine, 2003—; dir. med. edn., Gen. Surgery Residency Program Mercy Med. Ctr. Med. dir. Mercy Surgical Affiliates, Katzman Breast Ctr. Mercy Med. Ctr.; bd. dirs. Mercy Clinic Sys. Contbg. author (textbooks) Carcinoid Tumors and the Carcinoid Syndrome, Surgical Management of Radiation Injury to the Gastrointestinal Tract. Ret. as Colonel USAR. Fellowship in surgical oncology, U. Minn., 1981—83. Fellow: Am. Coll. Osteopathic Surgeons (pres. 2002—03), Am. Coll. Surgeons; mem.: Iowa Oncology Rsch. Associates, Iowa Acad. Surgery, Am. Osteopathic Assn., Soc. Surgical Oncology, Am. Assn. Univ. Professors, Assn. of Surgical Edn., Phi Sigma Alpha. Office: Dean of Coll Osteopathic Medicine Des Moines Univ 3200 Grand Ave Des Moines IA 50312-4198 Office Phone: 515-271-1513. Office Fax: 515-271-1521. E-mail: kendall.reed@dmu.edu. *

REED, KATHLYN LOUISE, occupational therapist, retired educator; b. Detroit, June 2, 1940; d. Herbert C. and Jessie R. (Krehbiel) R. BS in Occupl. Therapy, U. Kans., 1964; MA, Western Mich. U., 1966; PhD, U. Wash., 1973; MLIS, U. Okla., 1987. Occupl. therapist in psychiatry Kans. U. Med. Ctr., Kansas City, 1964-65; instr. occupl. therapy U. Wash., Seattle, 1967-70; assoc. prof. dept. occupl. therapy U. Okla. Health Scis. Ctr., Oklahoma City, 1973-77, prof., 1978-85, chmn. dept. occupl. therapy, 1973-85; libr. edn. info. svcs. Houston Acad. Medicine Tex. Med. Ctr. Libr., 1988-97; assoc. prof. Texas Woman's U., Houston, 2006—10, assoc. prof. emeritus, 2010—. Cons. Okla. State Dept. Health, 1976-77, Children's Convalescent Ctr., Oklahoma City, 1977-80, Oklahoma City Pub. Schs., 1980-81; vis. scholars program Tex. Woman's U., 1991-94, adj. prof. Sch. Occupl. Therapy, 1992-97, vis. prof., 1997-2006. Author: (with Sharon Sanderson) Concepts of Occupational Therapy, 1980, 4th edit., 1999, Models of Practice in Occupational Therapy, 1983, Quick Reference to Occupational Therapy, 1991, 2d edit., 2000, (with Julie Pauls) Quick Reference to Physical Therapy, 1996, 2d edit., 2004; (with S. Cunningham) Internet Guide for Rehabilitation Professionals, 1997; (with Sally Pore) Quick Reference to Speech-Language Pathology, 1999. Vol. crisis counselor Open Door Clinic, Seattle, 1968-72; mem. exec. bd. Seattle Mental Health Inst., 1971-72; Mem. Citizen Participation Liaison Coun., Seattle, 1970-72. Recipient Award of Merit, Can. Assn. Occupl. Therapists, 1988, Svc. award 2010. Fellow: Am. Occupl. Therapy Assn. (chmn. ethics commn. 2008—10, Merit award 1983, Slagle lectr. award 1985, Svc. award 1985, 2001); mem.: Am. Hippotherapy Assn., Soc. for the Study of Occupations, Am. Occupl. Therapy Found., Med. Libr. Assn. (Rittenhouse award 1987, Acad. Health Info. Professions), Tex. Occupl. Therapy Assn. (Roster of Merit award 2002, Disting. Svc. award 2004), Tex. Occupl. Therapy Found. (hon.; pres. 1999—2010), Okla. Occupl. Therapy Assn. (pres. 1974—76), Coun. Exceptional Children, World Fedn. Occupl. Therapists, N.Am. Riding for Handicapped Assn., Sigma Kappa (Colby award 1994), Pi Theta Epsilon. Democrat. Home: 6699 De Moss Dr Houston TX 77074-5003 Personal E-mail: klreed3@juno.com.

REED, KEVEN CHARLES, optometrist; b. Fairfield, Calif., Feb. 5, 1951; BA, Ind. U., 1973, OD, 1977. Cert. examiner Fla. State Bd. Optometric physoician Orange Pk. Eye Ctr., 2007—. Hosp. dir. Naval Hosp. Okinawa, Japan, 1994—98, splty. leader to US navy surgeon gen., 2001—04. Decorated Def. Meritorious Svc. medal Hon. Donald Rumsfeld Sec. Def. Fellow: Am. Acad. Optometry. Office: 905 Pk Ave Ste 100 Orange Park FL 32073 Office Phone: 904-264-1206. Office Fax: 904-264-3685. Personal E-mail: reedkc@comcast.net.

REED, LAWRENCE SAMUEL, plastic surgeon, medical educator; b. Upland, Pa., Mar. 8, 1943; MD, SUNY Downstate, 1969. Diplomate Am. Bd. Plastic Surgery. Intern in surgery Bronx Mcpl. Hosp.-Einstein, 1969—70; resident in plastic surgery Einstein Affiliated Hosps., 1970—72; resident in gen. surgery U. Pa. Grad. Hosp., 1972—75; resident in plastic surgery NY Hosp./Cornell Med. Ctr., 1975—77; fellow Meml. Sloan-Kettering, 1976; consulting med. staff Southampton Hosp., 1986—; asst. attending surgeon plastic surgery NY-Presbyn. Hosp., Weill Divsn., 1993—; clinical asst. prof. plastic surgery Weill Med. Coll., Cornell U., 1993—; asst. attending plastic surgeon Manhattan Eye, Ear and Throat Hosp., 1996—; pvt. practice Reed Ctr. for Plastic Surgery, NYC. Mem. editl. bd. NewBeauty Mag. Fellow: ACS; mem.: Internat. Coll. Surgeons, NY Met. Breast Cancer Soc., NY State Med. Soc., NY Regional Soc. Plastic and Reconstruction Surgeons, Am. Assn. Accreditation Ambulatory Surgery Facilities (mem. strategic planning com., mem. audit com., mem. disciplinary/investigative review com., chmn. accreditation com., chmn. standards com., treas. exec. bd., sec. bd. dirs.), Northeastern Soc. Plastic Surgeons, Med. Soc. County and State of NY, Am. Soc. Aesthetic Plastic Surgery, Inc. (mem. internet steering com., spokesperson non-surg. procedure com., mem. membership com., vice chmn. corp. sponsorship/fin. com., chmn. bylaws com., mem. bd. dirs.), Am. Soc. Plastic Surgeons. Office: Reed Ctr for Plastic Surgery 45 E 85th St New York NY 10028 Office Phone: 212-772-8300. Office Fax: 212-517-6832. Business E-Mail: info@thereedcenter.com.

REED, MICHAEL JOHN, dentist, dean, educator; b. Wednesbury, Eng., Dec. 25, 1940; came to U.S., 1967, naturalized, 1972; s. Harry Ernest and Ida Veva (Heywood) R.; m. Pamela Twycross, July 4, 1965 (div. Feb. 1976); children: Justine Marianne, Helena Clare; m. Ingrid Liepins, Sept. 8, 1978; children: Kathryn Anne, Matthew Harrison. BS with honors, U. Durham, Eng., 1963; B in Dental Surgery, U. Newcastle-Upon-Tyne, Eng., 1967; PhD, SUNY, Buffalo, 1971. Lic. dentist U.K., N.Y., Miss. Instr. oral biology SUNY, Buffalo, 1971-72, asst. prof. oral biology, 1972-77, assoc. prof., 1977-79; asst. dean Sch. Dentistry, U. Miss., Jackson, 1980-85, assoc. dean, 1985; dean, prof. oral biology Sch. Dentistry, U. Mo., Kansas City, 1985—. Cons. Nat. Inst. Dental Rsch., Washington, 1975-85. Contbr. numerous articles to profl. jours. Recipient rsch. career devel. award NIH, 1975-80. Fellow Acad. Dentistry Internat., Internat. Coll. Dentists, Am. Coll. Dentists; mem. ADA (cons. 1982—, joint com. on nat. dental exam., 1988-93, chair 1992-93), Am. Assn. Dental Schs. (sect. chair 1985-86. chmn. schs. coun. of deans, 1992-93, pres. 1997-98), Am. Assn. Dental Rsch. (councillor 1974-76), Fedn. Dentaire Internat., Am. Assn. for Microbiology, Mid-Am. Masters Club, Omicron Kappa Upsilon. Episcopalian. Avocations: running, European current affairs. Office: U Mo-Kansas City Sch Dentistry 650 E 25th St Kansas City MO 64108-2716 Office Phone: 816-235-2010. Office Fax: 816-235-2157. Business E-Mail: reedm@umkc.edu.

REED, ROBERT LAYTON, health care administrator; b. Dover, Del., Aug. 27, 1937; s. Charles Henry and Nellie Pearl (Ryan) R.; m. Diane Elizabeth McAneny, Sept. 15, 1968 (div. 1974); 1 child, Nathaniel. BS, U. Del., 1959. Dep. adminstr. State of Del., 1962-66, health care adminstr., 1967-68; dir. ops. Retirement Living, Wilmington, Del., 1969-76, v.p., 1977—; sr. v.p. Retirement Living-Forum Group, Inc., Wilmington, Del., 1977—90. Pres., owner Healthcare Placement Svcs. Del., 1990-95; cons. State of Del., 1999. Pres. Greenville (Del.) Retirement Community, 1983—, pres., bd. dirs. Del. Music Sch., vice chair, bd. dirs. DEl. Health Resources. Mem. Am. Healthcare Assn. (bd. dirs. 1986, 88, 89), (care and retirement living cons. 1990-), Del. Health Care Facilities Assn. (pres. 1980, 83, 86), Kiwanis (local treas. 1968-69, pres., chmn.), Univ. and Whist Club (Wilmington). Methodist. Office: Le Concorde Vista 9 Mc Cormick Dr Hockessin DE 19707

REEDY, ANITA M., oncological nurse; b. Va., Mar. 7, 1949; AA, Harford CC, 1977; MSN, Johns Hopkins U., 1998. Clin. nurse specialist Johns Hopkins Hosp., 1998—2000, nurse mgr., 2000—. Vol. Leukemia & Lymphoma Soc., 2005—11. Mem.: Oncology Nursing Soc., Sigma Theta Tau. Avocations: reading, gardening. Home: 1324 Harford Sq Dr Edgewood MD 21040 Home Fax: 410-955-8914.

REEFER, JOHN, internist; MD, U. Pitts., Pa., 1977. Diplomate Am. Bd. Internal Medicine, Am. Bd. Internal Medicine-geriatric medicine. Intern Presbyn. Univ. Hosp., Pitts., 1978, resident, 1980; internal medicine physician Butler Meml. Hosp., Pa. Office: Butler Medical Associates 111 Woody Dr Butler PA 16001 Office Phone: 724-285-0870.

REES, MICHAEL A., urologist; MD, U. Mich., Ann Arbor; PhD, U. Cambridge. Resident in urology U. Va., Charlottesville; fellow in transplantation U. Cambridge, England; assoc. prof. urology U. Toledo Med. Ctr., med. dir. Paired Kidney Donation Prog., 2004—; founder Alliance for Paired Donation. Office: U Toledo Med Ctr 3000 Arlington Ave Toledo OH 43614 Office Phone: 419-383-7025. Office Fax: 419-383-3153.

REES, MYRDDIN, surgeon; b. Carmarthen, Wales, May 29, 1950; s. Harold Haydn and Sally Meirwen Rees; children: Tom, Victoria. MBBS, Westminster Med. Sch., 1973; MS, London U., 1983. Dir. endoscopy unit North Hampshire Hosp., 1986—2000, undergrad. surg. tutor, 1986—95; with postgrad. med. & conf. ctr. The ARK, 1995—; cons. surgeon North Hampshire Hosps., England. Co-author: Complications of Colon and Rectal Surgery, 1985, Shock: The Reversible Step Towards Death, 1986, General Surgery: Treatment and Prognosis, 1986, Principles and Practices of Surgical Laparoscopy, 1994, Clinical Challenges in Hepatobiliary and Pancreatic Surgery, 2002, Surgery of the Liver, Bile Ducts and Pancreas in Children, 2002; contbr. articles to profl. jours. Recipient Arthur Evans Meml. award, Westminster Med. Sch., 1974, Alan Edwards Meml. award, Royal Soc. Medicine, 1979, Travel award, Royal Coll. Surgeons Eng., 1980, Video prize, Assn. Surgeons of Eng. & Ireland, 2000, Ethicon prize, Royal Soc. Medicine; scholar, 1980. Fellow: Royal Coll. Surgeons Edinburgh; mem.: Internat. Hepato-Pancreato-Biliary Assn., Royal Soc. Medicine (coun. mem. sect. surgery 1988—90, sec. sect. surgery 1990—92, v.p. sect. surgery 1992—96, pres. sect. surgery 1999—2000), Assn. Upper Gastrointestinal Surgeons Gt. Brit. & Ireland (pres. 2006—08), Assn. Surgeons Gt. Britain & Ireland, Alton Achsner Surg. Soc. Home: North Hampshire Hosp Aldermaston Road RG24 9NA Basingstoke England

REESE, HAYNE WARING, psychologist, educator; b. Comanche, Tex., Jan. 14, 1931; s. Tom F. and Marion (Waring) R.; m. Patsy Atwood, Aug. 24, 1957 (div. Apr. 1967); children: Anne, William, Margaret; m. Nancy Mann, Dec. 16, 1967; 1 child, Bradley. Student, So. Meth. U., 1949-50; BA, U. Tex., 1953, MA, 1955; PhD, U. Iowa, 1958. Asst. prof. U. Buffalo, 1958-62; assoc. prof. SUNY-Buffalo, 1962-66, prof., 1966-67, U. Kans., Lawrence, 1967-70; Centennial prof. psychology W.Va. U., Morgantown, 1970-2000, dir. grad. tng. in life-span devel. psychology, 1973-2000, Centennial prof. emeritus, 2000—. Mem. initial rev. groups div. research grants NIH, Washington, 1969-71, 74-78, 79-84; vis. prof. SUNY, Buffalo, 1970, U. Iowa, 1972, U. Hawaii, 1975, S.W. China Normal U., 1997, 2000. Author: Perception of Stimulus Relations, 1968, Basic Learning Processes in Childhood, 1976; co-author: Experimental Child Psychology, 1970, Life-Span Developmental Psychology, 1977, 1988, Child Development, 1979; editor: Advances in Child Development and Behavior, 26 vols., 1969-2001; co-editor: Life-Span Developmental Psychology, 8 vols., 1973-97, Behaviour Science, 1986, Varieties of Scientific Contextualism, 1993; assoc. editor: Jour. Exptl. Child Psychology, 1975-83, editor, 1983-97, mem. editl. bd. 1965-74, 98-2000. Served with U.S. Army, 1954. Fellow AAAS; mem. Soc. for Rsch. in Child Devel., Assn. for Behavior Analysis Home Phone: 817-346-2865. Personal E-mail: haynereese@aol.com.

REESE, JEFF, pediatrician, educator; b. Kans. City, Mo., Nov. 16, 1960; BA, U. Kans., 1982, MD, 1987. Assoc. prof. Vanderbilt U. Med. Ctr., 2002—. Office: 1135 Light Hall/MRB IV Bldg 2215 B Garland Ave Nashville TN 37232 Business E-Mail: jeff.reese@vanderbilt.edu.

REEVES, GRAFTON DULANY, pediatric endocrinologist; s. William Handy and Eleanor Fotterall Reeves; m. Diana Burke Reeves, July 6, 1968; children: Pamela Reeves Gilmartin, Dulany Reeves Dent. MD, Temple U., Phila., 1973; BA, Yale U., 1967. Cert. in pediat. 1978, ped. endo. 1978. Resident in pediat. Med. Ctr. Daleware, 1973—76; fellow in pediat. endocrinology U. Va., 1976—78; pvt. practise, 1978—96; chief divsn. pediatric endocrinology duPont Hosp. for Children, Wilmington, Del., 1996—; clin. prof. pediat.rics Thomas Jefferson U. Fellow: Am. Bd. Pediat., Am. Acad. Pediat. (life). Office: duPont Hosp for Children 1600 Rockland Rd Wilmington DE 19803 Home: 5 Brandywine Falls Rd Wilmington DE 19806 Business E-Mail: greeves@nemours.org.

REEVY-MANNING, GRETCHEN MARIA, psychologist, educator; b. Cortland, NY, Oct. 17, 1964; d. William Robert and Carole May Reevy; m. Todd Royal Manning. AB in Psychology, U. N.C., 1986; PhD in Psychology, U. Calif., Berkeley, 1994. Lectr. psychology dept. Dominican Coll., San Rafael, Calif., 1993—98; lectr. U. Calif., Davis, 1994, Profl. Sch. Psychology, San Francisco, 1995; lectr. psychology dept. Calif. State U., East Bay, 1994—. Co-editor: The Praeger Handbook on Stress and Coping, 2007; author: Encylopedia of Emotion, 2010; co-editor: Personality, Stress and Coping: Implications for Education, 2011. Grantee, Rand Corp., 1993. Mem.: APA, Soc. for Psychological Study of Social Issues, Assn. Psychol. Sci., Western Psychol. Assn., Phi Beta Kappa, Psi Chi. Avocations: swimming, reading, running. Office: Calif State Univ Psychology Dept Hayward CA 94542 Office Phone: 510-885-3421. Business E-Mail: gretchen.reevy@csueastbay.edu.

REFAAT, MAGED MOHAMED, medical educator; b. Ismalia, Egypt, Dec. 1, 1959; MBBCh, Ain Shams U., 1983, MD in Internal Medicine, 1991. Prof., faculy medicine Ain Shams U., 1985—. Mem.: ASOAACI, ESOCI, WAO, ESOC, EAACI. Avocation: music. Office: 8 Mayo Bldg Nasr Cairo 11354 Egypt Office Fax: 0020222725919. Personal E-mail: dr_maged_refaat@hotmail.com.

REFAAT, MARWAN, Lebanon cardiology fellow; b. Pa., Jan. 1979; MD, Am. U. Beirut, NYC, 2003. Lic. Commonwealth Mass., 2006, Commonwealth Pa., 2007, diplomate Am. Bd. Internal Medicine, 2007. Resident internal medicine Mass. Gen. Hosp., Harvard Med. Sch., Boston, 2004—07, med. rsch. fellow, 2000; clin. fellow medicine Harvard Med. Sch., 2004—07; fellow, cardiovasc. diseases U. Pitts. Med. Ctr., 2007—. Contbr. scientific papers. Prevention cardiovasc. diseases, 2004—08. Recipient Carolyn L. Kuckein Rsch. award, Alpha Omega Alpha, 2002, Physicians Recognition award, AMA, 2005, Dept. Medicine award, Mass. Gen. Hosp., 2007, Am. Heart Assn. Rsch. award, 2008, Heart Rhythm Soc., 2008; grantee Med. Rsch., Mass. Gen. Hosp., 2000. Mem.: AMA, ACP (Rsch. award 2004), Mass. Med. Soc. (resident fellow sect. 2005—07, Rsch. award 2007), Am. Coll. Cardiology. Achievements include research in more than 25 citations of my research work. Home: Apt B308 2133 Stockton St San Francisco CA 94133-2040

REFEIDI, ABDULLAH, dean, consultant; MD, SCHS, Saudi Arabia, 2000. Bd. cert. general surgent Saudi Commn. Health Specialties, 2000. Asst. prof. coll. medicine King Khalid U., Abha, Aseer, Saudi Arabia, 2002—, dean, coll. dentistry, 2006—; cons. laparoscopic surgeon Aseer Ctrl. Hosp., Abha, 2003—. Pres., regional southern tng. com. gen. surgery program Saudi Health Commn., Riyadh, Saudi Arabia, 2007—. Contbr. articles to profl. jours. Laparoscopy fellowship, Heidelberg U, Germany, 2001—03.

REFINETTI, ROBERTO, biopsychologist; b. Sao Paulo, Brazil, Nov. 19, 1957; came to U.S., 1988; s. Renato and Maria Stella (Barroso) R.; m. Kathleen Diane Zylan, Mar. 5, 1988 (div. Aug. 1991); 1 child, Lauren Lynne; m. Theresa Kaye Tolleson, Aug. 11, 2000. BA in Philosophy, Pontifical Cath. U., Sao Paulo, 1981; BS in Psychology, U. Sao Paulo, 1981, MA in Psychology, 1983; PhD in Psychology, U. Calif., Santa Barbara, 1987. Asst. prof. U. Sao Paulo, 1986-88; fellow U. Calif., Santa Barbara, 1988-89, U. Ill., Champaign, 1989-90, U. Va., Charlottesville, 1990-92; asst. prof. Coll. William and Mary, Williamsburg, Va., 1992-97; mgr. profl. publs. Montage Media Corp., Mahwah, NJ, 1997-98; pvt. practice Birmingham, Ala., 1998-99; asst. prof. U. SC, Salkehatchie, 1999—2005, prof., 2005—, academic dean, 2006—. Author: Circadian Physiology, 1999, 2d edit., 2005; editor-in-chief Jour. Circadian Rhythms, 2003-, Sexuality & Culture, 2010-; contbr. over 180 articles to profl. jours Area grantee NIH, 1996, 2002; recipient Nat. Rsch. Svc. Individual award NIMH, 1991, Career award NSF, 1995, 2004. Mem. Am. Physiol. Soc., Am. Psychol. Soc., Soc. Neuroscience, Soc. Rsch. on Biol. Rhythms. Office: Circadian Rhythm Lab Univ SC 807 Hampton St Walterboro SC 29488 Office Phone: 843-549-6314. E-mail: refinetti@sc.edu.

REFSUM, HELGE, medical professor; b. Oslo, Sept. 16, 1947; s. Sigvald B. and Sigrid E. (Dahlstrøm) R.; children: Helge Haakon, Ingvild, Erle. MD, U. Oslo, 1973, dr. med., 1976. Rsch. fellow inst. pharmacology U. Oslo, 1974-77; assoc. prof. depts. physiology and pharmacology U. Tromsø, Norway, 1978-82, chief dept. clin. pharmacology, 1983-84, prof. dept. med. physiology, 1984-93; mgr. R&D Nycomed, Oslo, 1993-99; prof., chief dept. psychopharmacology Diakonhjemmet Hosp., 2000—. Vis. rsch. assoc. cardiovascular rsch. inst. U. Calif., San Francisco, 1979-80; vis. prof. dept. medicine U. Calgary, Canada, 1985-86. Author: Electrophysiological and Mechanical Effects of Calcium on Cardiac Muscle, 1976, Myocardial Ischaemia and Protection, 1983, Alpha-Adrenoceptor Blockers in Cardiovascular Disease, 1985, Heart and Brain: Brain and Heart, 1989, Cold Physiology and Cold Injuries, 1991; contbr. articles to profl. jours. Recipient AC Houen award, 1978, Fogarty Internat. award, 1979, Alberta Heritage Found. for Med. Rsch. award, 1985, awards Norwegian Coun. on Cardiovascular Diseases, Norwegian Rsch. Coun. for Sci. and Humanities. Mem.: Internat. Union Pharmacologists, Internat. Union Physiol. Scis. Avocations: outdoor sports, skiing, rowing (former norwegian champion). Office: Diakonhjemmet Hosp PO Box 85 Vinderen N-0319 Oslo Norway Home: Lokkalia 5 783 Oslo Norway Business E-Mail: helge.refsum@diakonsyk.no.

REGADAS, FRANCISCO SERGIO PINHEIRO, medical association administrator; b. Fortaleza, Ceara, Brazil, May 20, 1949; s. Francisco Neves and Rosa Maildes Pinheiro Regadas; m. Sthela Maria Murad Regadas, Aug. 29, 1997; children: Carolina Murad, Marina Murad. Grad. in Medicine, Medicine. Fed. U. Cear, Fortaleza -, 1975; PhD, Sch. Medicine USP, Sao paolo,Brazil, 1990. Cert. Fed. U. Ceara, 1975. Head dept. surgery Sch. Medicine. U.F.C, Fortaleza, Ceara, Brazil, 1996—2000. Titular prof. Sch. Medicine. U.F.C., 2002—. Prodr.: (development surgical technique) TRREMS procedure (Best presentation. Dept. Surgery. Sch. Medicine Fed. U. Ceara, 2006). Vice-president brazilian soc. coloproctology. Recipient Premio Boticario Ferreira., Prefeitura de Fortaleza, 1990, Premio Raoul Palmer, Brazilian Soc. Laparoscopic Surgery, 1991, Cidadão da cidade de Milhã, Prefeitura Mcpl. de Milhã, 1993. Mem.: Brazilian Coll. of

Surgeons, Brazilian Coll. Digestive Surgery, Brazilian Soc. Coloproctology. Achievements include first to surgical devices. Home: Av Edilson Brasil Soares 1892 Fortaleza Ceara 60834220 Brazil Office: Hospital Sao Carlos Avenida Pontes Vieira 2551 60130-241 Fortaleza CE Brazil Home Fax: 55-85-3257.7728. Business E-Mail: sregadas@hospitalsaocarlos.com.br.

REGALO, SIMONE CECILIO HALLAK, dentist, educator; b. Ribeirão Preto, São Paulo, Brazil, Feb. 15, 1965; d. Rubens Issa and Leana Cecilio Hallak; m. Carlos Alberto Regalo, Jan. 9, 1988; children: Henrique Hallak, Eduardo Hallak, Isabela Hallak. Degree in Dentristry, U. Estadual Londrina, 1988. Assoc. prof. São Paulo U., Ribeirão Preto, 2002—. Ethics com. mem. CONEP, Brasília, 2007—08. Home: Rua Casemiro De Abreu 435 Apto 102 Ribeirão Preto São Paulo 14020060 Brazil Office: Univ De São Paulo Avenida Do Café Ribeirão Preto São Paulo 14040-904 Brazil Office Phone: 55-16-36024015. Office Fax: 55-16-36330999. Business E-Mail: schregalo@forp.usp.br.

REGAN, DAVID, neuroscientist; b. Scarborough, Eng., May 5, 1935; arrived in Can., 1976; m. Marian Pauline Marsh, Aug. 15, 1959; children: Douglas Lawrence, Howard Michael BSc, London U., 1957, MSc, 1958, PhD, 1964, DSc, 1974. Lectr. physics London U., 1960-65; reader neurosci. Keele U., England, 1965-75; prof. psychology Dalhousie U., Canada, 1976-80, prof. physiology, 1980-84, assoc. prof. medicine, 1978-84, prof. medicine, 1984-87, prof. ophthalmology, 1980-87, prof. otolaryngology, 1980-84, Killam rsch. prof., 1978-82; prof. engring. Rutgers U., 1985-86; prof. psychology York U., 1987—2003, prof. biology; prof. ophthalmology U. Toronto, Ont., Canada, 1987—. Retained inventor Wilkinson-Graviner Group, Eng., 1970-75; cons. Westinghouse, Pitts., 1980-86; co-dir. human performance in space lab. Inst. for Space and Terrestrial Sci., York U., 1989-2002, disting. rsch. prof., 1991-93, emeritus, 1993—; indsl. rsch. chair aviation vision Natural Sci. and Engring. Rsch. Coun. Can./Can. Aviation Electronics, 1993-2003; Spinoza profl. U. Amsterdam, The Netherlands, 1999. Author: Human Evoked Potentials, 1972, Human Brain Electrophysiology, 1989, Human Perception of Objects, 2000; editor: Spatial Vision, 1989, Binocular Vision, 1989, Vision Research, 1992; contbr. over 250 articles to profl. jours.; holder 8 patents. Recipient Forman prize for med. rsch., 1983, Prentice medal, 1990, Sir J.W. Dawson Medal, Royal Soc. Can., 1997, award of excellence Nat. Sci. and Engring. Rsch. Coun. Can., 2000, Proctor medal, 2000, Queen Elizabeth II medal, 2002, Hebb medal, 2003; rsch. grantee NIH, NRC, Air Force Office Sci. Rsch., Nat. Scis. and Engring. Rsch. Coun. Can., Med. Rsch. Coun.; mem. Order of Can., 2001; Killam fellow, 1990. Fellow: Optical Soc. Am., Royal Soc. Can.; mem.: Netherlands Royal Acad. (fgn.), Am. Acad. Optometry, Royal Coll. Sci. (London) (assoc.), Assn. Rsch. in Vision and Ophthalmology, Soc. Clin. Electroretinography, Exptl. Psychology Soc. Avocations: cricket, walking, modern european history. Office: York U Dept Psychology 4700 Keele St North York ON Canada M3J 1P3 Business E-Mail: dregan@yorku.ca.

REGAN, PETER FRANCIS, III, physician, medical educator; b. Bklyn., Nov. 11, 1924; s. Peter Francis Jr. and Veronica (Tierney) R.; m. Laurette Patricia O'Connor, June 18, 1949; children: Peter, Stephen, William, Elizabeth, John, Carol. MD, Cornell U., Ithaca, NY, 1949. Diplomate Am. Bd. Psychiatry and Neurology, Nat. Bd. Med. Examiners. Intern in medicine N.Y. Hosp., 1949-50; asst. resident psychiatry Payne Whitney Psychiat. Clinic, 1950, 53-54, resident, 1954-56; asst. prof. psychiatry Cornell U. Med. Coll., 1956-58; prof., head dept. psychiatry U. Fla. Coll. Medicine, chief psychiat. svc. Univ. Teaching Hosp., 1958-64; prof. psychiatry SUNY, Buffalo, 1964-84, v.p. health affairs, 1964-67, exec. v.p. univ., 1967-69, exec. v.p., acting pres. univ., 1969-70, vice chancellor acad. programs, 1970-71; assoc. chief staff for edn. Buffalo VA Med. Ctr., 1979-84; prof. psychiatry U. Tex. Health Sci. Ctr., San Antonio, 1984-87, assoc. dean Sch. Medicine, 1986-87; assoc. chief staff for edn. San Antonio VA Med. Ctr., 1984-86, chief staff, 1986-87; dep. assoc. chief med. dir. for acad. affairs VA Cen. Office, Washington, 1987-88, assoc. chief med. dir. for acad. affairs, 1988-92; prof. emeritus / sen. cons. dept. psychiatry SUNY, Buffalo, 1992—; interim chair dept. psychiatry Med. U. S.C., 2001—02. Project dir. Ctr. for Ednl. Rsch. and Innovation, OECD, 1972-74. Author: (with F. Flach) Chemotherapy in Emotional Disorders, 1960, (With E. Pattishall) Behavioral Science Contributions to Psychiatry; contbr. articles to profl. jours. Capt. M.C. AUS, 1951-52. Fellow Am. Psychiat. Assn., Am. Coll. Psychiatrists (bd. regents 1986-95, 2d v.p. 1988, 1st v.p. 1989, pres.-elect 1990, pres. 1991); mem. AMA, Alpha Omega Alpha.

REGENSBURG, NORA IRENE, ophthalmologist; b. Rotterdam, ZH, Netherlands, Apr. 8, 1945; d. Aron Regensburg and Gretha Vogelaar; m. Harry G. M. Laagland; children: Suzanne Renting, Nicole Laagland, Saskia de Rooy, Deirdre de Rooij, Joachim de Rooij. MD, U. Leiden, Netherlands, 1971. Cert. in ophthalmology MSRC, Utrecht, Netherlands, 1975. Ophthalmologist Hosp. Boxmeer, Netherlands, 1975—82, Hosps. Venray, St. Anna Hosp., Oss, Netherlands, 1982—98; assoc. prof. ophthalmology Academic Med. Ctr., Amsterdam, 1998—. Bd. mem. Nat. Assn. Med. Specialists, Utrecht, 1990—94, Nat. Coun. Pub. Health, Utrecht, 1993—96, Royal Dutch Med. Assn., Utrecht, 1993—98; cons. profl. interest Dutch Assn. Ophthalmologists, Utrecht, 1992—98. Mem.: Chamber Academic Med. Specialists (bd. mem. 2002—). Avocations: travel, sailing, skiing, art. Office: Academic Med Ctr Meibergdreef 9 1105 AZ Amsterdam Netherlands Business E-Mail: n.i.regensburg@amc.uva.nl.

REGIS, DARIO, orthopaedic surgeon; b. Verona, Italy, Nov. 12, 1959; s. Enzo Regis and Italia Lamon. Diplomate U. Verona, orthopaedics specialization U. Verona, sports medicine specialization U. Verona. Asst. orthopaedics Inst Clin. Orthopedics and Traumatology-Policlinico G.B. Rossi, U. Verona Faculty Medicine and Surgery, 1994—2001, asst. prof. orthopaedics, 2002—. Mem. sci. com. Incontro Italo-Polacco Orthopedics and Traumatology, Verona, 1996. Contbr. articles to profl. jours. Recipient Scoliosis grant, Cassa di Risparmio di Verona, Vicenza, Belluno e Ancona, 1988—93, Orthopaedic fellowship, Germany, 1997. Mem.: Societa Italiana di Ortopedia e Traumatologia, Am. Acad. Orthopedic Surgeons, Sports Medicine Italian Fedn. (assoc.). Office: Clinica Ortopedica e Traumatologica Piazza LA Scuro 10 Verona 37134 Italy Home: Via Campofiore 57 37129 Verona VR Italy Office Phone: 045-8124369. Office Fax: 0458027470. Business E-Mail: regisdario@siot.it.

REGISTER, MITZI LYONS, medical technician; b. Winter Garden, Fla., Nov. 11, 1955; AS, Tallahassee CC, 1977. Mgr. diagnostic radiology Radiology Assoc. Tallahassee, Pa., 1986—2005, dir. mktg., 2005—08, mgr. front office asst., 2008—. Mem.: ARRT, ASRT. Avocations: water sports, camping, travel. Office: 1600 Phillips Rd Tallahassee FL 32308 Office Fax: 850-878-9729. Business E-Mail: mregister@radassociates.com.

REH, THOMAS EDWARD, radiologist, educator; b. St. Louis, Sept. 12, 1943; s. Edward Paul and Ceil Anne (Golden) Reh; m. Benedette Texada Gieselman, June 22, 1968; children: Matthew J., Benedette T., Elizabeth W. BA, St. Louis U., 1965, MD, 1969. Diplomate Am. Bd. Radiology, Nat. Bd. Med. Examiners. Intern St. John's Mercy Med. Ctr., St. Louis, 1969—70; resident St. Louis VA Hosp., 1970—73; fellow in vascular radiology Beth Israel Hosp., Boston, 1973—74; radiologist St. Mary's Health Ctr., St. Louis, 1974—, chmn. dept. radiology, 1986—2009; clin. assoc. prof. radiology, 1989—; clin. prof. radiology, 1996—, St. Louis U. Sch. Medicine, 1996—, mem. Fellow: Am. Coll. Radiology; mem.: St. Louis Met. Med. Soc., Radiol. Soc. N.Am., Confrerie des Chevaliers du Tastevin Club, St. Louis Club, Delta Sigma Phi, Alpha Sigma Nu, Alpha Omega Alpha. Republican. Roman Catholic. Home: 9850 Waterbury Dr Saint Louis MO 63124-1046

REHM, PATRICE KOCH, radiologist, educator; b. DeSoto, Mo., Nov. 23, 1954; d. James Clarence and Eleanor (Koch) R. BA in Chemistry, U. Mo., 1977; MD, Yale U., 1981. Diplomate Am. Bd. Radiology, Am. Bd. Nuc. Medicine. Intern in medicine Waterbury (Conn.) Hosp., 1981-82; resident in radiology Yale New Haven Hosp., 1982-83, 84-85, fellow in neuroradiology, 1985-86, fellow in nuclear medicine, 1986-87; resident in radiology SUNY Upstate Med. Ctr., Syracuse, 1983-84; clin. assoc. Cleve. Clinic, 1987-88, staff physician, 1988-89, Presbyn. Hosp., Charlotte, N.C., 1989-91, Georgetown U. Med. Ctr., Washington, 1992—2000; assoc. prof. radiology, dir. nuc. medicine U. Va. Health Sys., Charlottesville, Va., 2000—10, dir. nuc. medicine, program dir. nuc. radiology, 2000—, prof. radiology, 2010—. Fellow Am. Coll. Radiology, Radiologic Soc. N.Am., Soc. Nuc. Medicine. Office: U Va Health Sys PO Box 800170 Charlottesville VA 22908

REHMANI, RIFAT, emergency physician, consultant, epidemiologist; s. Sharafatullah Khan and (Late) Mahbuba (Enver) Rehmani; m. Uzma Rifat Rehmani, Mar. 11, 1996; children: Rameesha Rifat, Muhammad Moiz. MBBS, Sindh Med. Coll., Karachi, 1983; MSc, Dalhousie U., Halifax, Can., 2004. Resident in internal medicine Jinnah Postgrad. Med. Centre, Karachi, 1986—89, Aga Khan U., Karachi, 1989—92, 1993—98, head sect. emergency medicine, 1999—2005, epidemiologist, 2002—05; cons. in emergency medicine King Abdul Aziz N.G. Hosp., Al-Ahsa, Saudi Arabia, 2005—, epidemiologist, 2005. Dir. emergency medicine residency program Aga Khan U., 2000—05, chair residency com. King Abdul Aziz N.G. Hosp., 2005—; mem. task force road safety Govt. Sindh, Karachi; mem. faculty Pre-Hosp. Care, England. Editor: Trauma Manual, Evidence Based Protocols for Paramedics Developed by the Divsn. Emergency Svcs., Dept. Emergency Medicine, Dalhousie U., 2003, Med. Policy, Protocols, and Procedure Manual Emergency Medical Svcs. Recipient Honors in internal medicine in final profession, Karachi U., 1983, Chief Resident award, Aga Khan U., 1992, Hosp. Devel. award, 1998; Intra mural Rsch. grants, 1999, 2001, Internat. Devel. scholar, Aga Khan Found., Can., 2002—04. Mem.: Brit. Assn. Accident and Emergency Medicine, Am. Coll. Emergency Physicians. Office: King Abdul Aziz NG Hosp Po Box 2477 31982 Al-Hasa Saudi Arabia Office Fax: 966-3-591-0000 ext. 3347. Personal E-mail: rifatrehmani@hotmail.com.

REIBER, HANSOTTO, retired neurochemistry professor; b. Stuttgart, Mar. 6, 1940; Diploma in Biochemistry, U. Tubingen, 1970; Dr. rer. nat. in Phys. Chemistry, U. Braunschweig, 1974. Dept. prof. Dr. M. Eigen Max Planck Inst. Biophys. Chemistry, Gottingen, 1971—74; rsch. fellow, dept. neurochemistry Max Planck Inst. Exptl. Medicine, 1974—78; head, neurochemistry lab., dept. neurology U. Gottingen, 1978—2005, prof. neurochemistry, 1988—2005; supr., organizer CSF Survey, INSTAND, 1991—. Prof. invitado U. de Ciencias Medicas de la Habana; guest lectr., rsch. fellow clin. neurochem. & CSF diagnosis Rsch. Coop. Physics Faculty Habana, 2000—. Editor text books; contbr. sci. articles to profl. jours. and text books. Recipient Habilitation, 1984, Marlene de Luca award, 1988, award, El Pleno de la Acad. de Ciencias de Cuba, 2006. Mem.: Cerebrospinal Fluid Rsch Group World Fedn. Neurology, German Soc. CSF Diagnosis and Clin. Neurochemistry (spkr. 1992—96, 1999—2003), Soc. Cubana de Immunologia (hon.). Achievements include research in CSF analysis, theory of blood-CSF barrier function and CSF flow; dynamics of brain and blood derived-proteins in CSF; aqueous humor for diagnosis of eye diseases; neuroimmunology and basic research in chronic neurological diseases; nonlinear dynamics of biological processes, self organization concepts in biological and medical sciences; applications of complexity sciences, epigenesis vs epigenetics, brain-mind discussion. Office: CSF and Complexity Studies Muehlenstr 8 Rostock D-18055 Germany Office Phone: 49 381 8575039. Business E-Mail: ho@horeiber.de.

REICH, STANLEY BENJAMIN, retired radiologist, medical educator; b. NYC, Feb. 20, 1921; s. Harry Max Reich and Bessie Bangel; m. Adele Axelrod, Dec. 15, 1944; children: Linda, James, Judi. AB, Cornell U., 1941; MD, NYU, 1944. Diplomate Am. Bd. Radiology, Am. Bd. Nuclear Medicine. Intern Bellevue Hosp., NYC, 1944-45, resident in radiology, 1946-49; asst. prof. NYU/Bellevue Hosp., NYC, 1949-50; clin. prof. radiology U. Calif., San Francisco, 1952-72, 77—; prof. radiology U. Colo., Denver, 1972-77, U. Calif. Davis, Sacramento, 1977—2008; ret.; chief radiology No. Calif. VA Clinics, Martinez, 1979-98. Contbr. articles to profl. jours. Pres. Concordia-Argonaut Club, San Francisco, 1963-65; cons. Travis AFB, Fairfield, Calif., 1977—, Exec. Svc. Corps., San Francisco, 1997-2002. Lt. (sr.) USN, 1944-47, 50-52. Fellow Am. Coll. Radiology; mem. Am. Soc. Thoracic Radiology (sec. 1967), Am. Radium Soc. Avocations: travel, photography. Home: 2 Abbott Way Piedmont CA 94618-2610 Personal E-mail: asreia@att.net.

REICHEL, MARTIN, dermatologist, educator; b. NYC, June 4, 1961; s. Joseph and Geraldine Reichel; m. Laura Reichel, July 15, 1990; children: Andrew Berkeley, Julia Frederica, Theodora Rainier, Violet Wawona. AB, Harvard U., Cambridge, Mass., 1983; MD with distinction in microbiology and immunology, Albert Einstein Coll. Medicine, NYC, 1988. Diplomate Am. Bd. Dermatology, Am. Bd. Dermatopathology, Am. Bd. Clin. and Lab. Dermatol. Immunology. Intern Montefiore Med. Ctr., Bronx, NY, 1988—89; resident & chief resident U. Calif., Davis, 1989—92; fellow dermatopathology NYU Med. Ctr., 1992—93, fellow clin. and lab. dermatol. immunology, 1993—94; asst. prof. clin. dermatology Coll. Physicians and Surgeons, Columbia U., NYC, 1994—, assoc. clin. prof. dermatology, 2009. Author: Histologic Diagnosis of Inflammatory Skin Diseases, 1997. Recipient Dermatologist Investigator award, Dermatology Found., 1996, Clin. Career Devel. award, 1997; scholar, Psoriasis Rsch. Assn., 1996. Fellow: Internat. Soc. Dermatopathology, Am. Soc. Dermatopathology, Am. Acad. Dermatology. Avocation: photography. Home: 8 Masterton Rd Bronxville NY 10708 Office: 161 Ft Washington Ave New York NY 10032

REICHENEDER, CLAUDIA ANNA, medical educator, researcher; d. Ludwig and Anna Reicheneder. Degree, 1991; degree in Orthodontics, U. Regensburg, Bavaria, Germany, 1999; DDS, PhD, U. Munich, Germany, 1992. Cert. World Fedn. Orthodontists, 2001. Orthodontist U. Regensburg, 1999—, sr. instr. orthodontist, prof. and postdoc. lectr., 2010—. Contbr. articles to sci. jours. Roman Catholic. Achievements include research in orthodontics. Office: Univ Regensburg Orthodontics Franz-Josef-Strauss Allee 11 Regensburg Bavaria D-93053 Germany Office Phone: 499419446090. Business E-Mail: claudia.reicheneder@gmx.net.

REICHERT, LEO EDMUND, JR., biochemist, department chairman, endocrinologist; b. NYC, Jan. 9, 1932; s. Leo and Anne (Holsten) R.; m. Gerda Sihler, July 20, 1957; children: Leo, Christine, Linda, Andrew. BS, Manhattan Coll., NYC, 1955; PhD, Loyola U., Chgo., 1960. Asst. prof. biochemistry Emory U. Med. Sch., Atlanta, 1960-66, assoc. prof., 1966-72, prof., 1972-79; prof., chmn. dept. biochemistry Albany (N.Y.) Med. Coll., 1979-88, prof. biochemistry and molecular biology, 1988-99; dir. Tucker Endocrine Rsch. Inst., LLC, Atlanta, 2000—08. Dir. human and animal hormone isolation lab. (NIH), Emory U. Med. Sch., 1960-75; mem. med. adv. bd. Nat. Pituitary Agy., 1971-74; com. on glycoprotein hormones Nat. Hormone and Pituitary Program, 1968-86; mem. reproductive biology study sect. NIH, 1971-75; mem. adv. panel on cellular physiology NSF, 1983-86, divsn. of integrative and neuro biology, 1992; mem. WHO Expert Adv. Panel on Biol. Standardization, 1984-2006, Nat. Bd. Med. Examiners, Part I, 1989-91. Mem. editl. bd. Endocrinology, 1967-75, Molecular and Cellular Endocrinology, 1977-83, 90-94, charter mem. Biology of Reproduction, 1968-70, 86-90, Andrology, 1983-86, Molecular Andrology, 1989-99; contbr. more than 275 articles to profl. jours., patentee in field. With USMC, 1949—52. Listed among 75 endocrinologists, 1000 scientists most cited, 1965-78. Mem.: Soc. for Study of Reprodn., Andrology Soc. (coun. 1983—87), Endocrine Soc. (ethics adv. com. 2000—01, Ayerst award 1970), Am. Soc. Biol. Chemists. Home: 1974 Mountain Creek Dr Stone Mountain GA 30087-1018 Personal E-mail: lerjr@aol.com.

REICHGOTT, MICHAEL JOEL, medical educator, physician; b. Newark, July 26, 1940; s. Leo and Gertrude (Millman) R.; m. Lynn Gay Haar, Dec. 22, 1962; children: Jay Howard, Seth Alan, Douglas Jordan. AB, Gettysburg Coll., Pa., 1961; MD, Albert Einstein Coll. Medicine, 1965; PhD, U. Calif., San Francisco, 1973. Diplomate Am. Bd. Internal Medicine. Fellow in clin. pharmacology U. Calif., 1969-72; asst. prof. medicine U. Pa., Phila., 1973-81, assoc. prof., 1981-84, Albert Einstein Coll. Medicine, Bronx, NY, 1984—94, prof., 1994—, assoc. dean students and grad. med. edn., 1989—99, assoc. dean clin. affairs and grad. med. edn., 1999—2010, dir. for conflict of interest and human subjects protection, 2010—; med. dir. Bronx Mcpl. Hosp. Ctr., 1984-89. Mem. Liaison Com. on Med. Edn., 2002, chmn. 2008-09, Field Sec., 2010-, NY State Bd. Profl. Med. Conduct, 2009-; presenter in field. Contbr. articles to profl. jours. V.p. Larchmont Temple, NY, 1990-92, pres., 1992-94. Maj. M.C., US Army, 1967-69, Vietnam. Fellow ACP (com.); mem. Assn. Am. Med. Colls. (com. 1990—), NY Acad. Medicine, Phila. Acad. Medicine, Soc. for Gen. Internal Medicine (com.), AMA (sect. med. schs., chair 2003-04, del. 2007-10), Assoc. Med. Schs. NY(chair edn. com., 2006-) Avocations: camping, gardening, print collector. Office: Albert Einstein Coll of Medicine 1300 Morris Park Ave Bronx NY 10461-1926 Office Phone: 718-430-4082. Business E-Mail: michael.reichgott@einstein.yu.edu.

REICHLIN, SEYMOUR, endocrinologist, educator; b. NYC, May 31, 1924; s. Henry and Celia (Rosen) R.; m. Elinor Thurman Dameshek, June 24, 1951 (dec. Mar. 7, 2011); children: Seth David, Douglas James, Ann Elise. Student, CCNY, 1940-41; AB, Antioch Coll., 1945; MD, Washington U., St. Louis, 1948; PhD, U. London, 1954. Intern N.Y. Hosp., 1948-49; asst. resident Barnes Hosp., St. Louis, 1949-50, N.Y. Hosp., 1950-51; chief resident Barnes Hosp., 1951-52; research fellow physiology dept. Maudsley Hosp., London, Eng., 1952-54; instr. psychiatry Washington U., 1954-55, asst. prof. psychiatry and medicine, 1955-60; asso. prof. medicine U. Rochester, 1960-66, prof., 1966-69; prof., head dept. med. and pediatric spltys. Sch. Medicine U. Conn., 1969-71, prof., head dept. physiology, 1971-72; prof. medicine Tufts U., 1972-97, prof. emeritus, 1997—; rsch. prof. U. Ariz., 1994-2000. Sr. physician New Eng. Med. Ctr., 1972-93, sr. endocrinologist, 1993-96; mem. endocrinology study sect. NIH, 1966-70; mem. adv. panel FDA, 1977-79; mem. coun. Nat. Inst. Kidney, Diabetes, Digestive Diseases, 1987-90. Mem. editl. bd. Endocrinology, 1969-74, New Eng. Jour. Medicine, 1976-79, Jour. Psychoneuroendocrinology, 1979-83, Brain, Behavior and Immunity, 1990—; contbr. articles to profl. jours. Bd. dirs. Founds. Fund, New Haven, 1968-70; med. adv. bd. Med. Found., Boston, adv. bd. MacArthur Found., 1988. Served with AUS, 1943-44. Recipient Berthold medal, German Endocrine Soc., 1983, Disting. Alumnus award, Washington U. Sch. Medicine, 1993, Recipient Rebecca Rice award, Antioch Coll., 1995, Horace Mann Alumni award; Commonwealth Fund fellow, Inst. Psychiatry, U. London, 1952—54, Lowell M. Palmer Med. Rsch. fellow, 1954—56. Master ACP-Am. Soc. Internal Medicine (award 2002); fellow AAAS, Am. Acad. Arts and Scis., Acad. Arts and Scis. U. Bologna (fgn.); mem. Ctrl. Soc. Clin. Rsch., Am. Soc. Clin. Investigation, Assn. Am. Physicians, Am. Physiol. Soc., Endocrine Soc. (Eli Lilly award 1972, Disting. Leadership award 1986, pres. 1975-76), Brit. Soc. Endocrinology, Am. Psychosomatic Soc., Am. Thyroid Assn., Internat. Brain Orgn., Assn. for Rsch. in Nervous and Mental Disease (pres. 1976-79), Pituitary Soc. (pres. 1994-95, Disting. Leadership award 1995), Sociedad Mexicana de Nutricion y Endocrinologia (hon.), Sigma Xi, Alpha Omega Alpha. Home: 685 S La Posada Cir GH 3402 Green Valley AZ 85614 Personal E-mail: reichlin@laposadagv.net.

REICHMAN, LEE BRODERSOHN, physician; b. NYC, June 25, 1938; s. Theodore and Elinore (Brodersohn) R.; m. Rose Ehrinpreis, Oct. 9, 1965; children: Daniel Mark, Deborah Gar. AB, Oberlin Coll., Ohio, 1960; MD, NYU, 1964; MPH, Johns Hopkins U., Balt., 1971. Intern Bellevue Hosp., I Med. Divsn., NYC, 1964-65, resident, 1967-68, Harlem Hosp. Ctr., NYC, 1968-69, fellow in pulmonary medicine, 1969-70; dir. Bur. Tb, Bur. Chronic Disease, N.Y.C. Health Dept., 1971-73, asst. commr. health, 1973-74; assoc. prof. medicine U. Medicine and Dentistry N.J. Med. Sch., Newark, 1974-78; prof. medicine N.J. Med. Sch., Newark, 1978—, prof. preventive medicine, cmty. health, 1993—; dir. pulmonary div. U. Medicine and Dentistry N.J.-N.J. Med. Sch. Univ. Hosp., 1974-92; founding exec. dir. N.J. Med. Sch. Nat. Tb Ctr., 1993—2006, N.J. Med. Sch. Global Tuberculosis Inst., 2006—. Cons. CDC, Atlanta, 1970—; prin. investigator pulmonary complications of HIV infection NHLBI, 1987—95; prin. investigator Model Tb Ctr. CDC, 1993—2003, prin. investigator Nat. Tb Trials Consortium, 1994—99, adv. coun. for elimination of Tb, 2002—; prin. investigator Regional Tng. & Med. Conv. Ctr. CDC, 2003—; sr. advisor WHO Stop TB Partnership, Geneva, 2007—. Editor: Tuberculosis-A Comprehensive International Approach,1st edit, 1993, 2d edit., 2000; author: Timebomb-The Global Epidemic of Multi-Drug Resistant Tuberculosis, 2002; contbr. articles to profl. jours. Bd. dirs. Art Ctr. No. N.J., 1979-86; chmn. N.J. Commn. on Smoking of Health, 1986-87; mem. N.J. TB Adv. Coun., 1976—, chmn. 1991—; chair Nat. Coalition for Elimination of Tb, 1992—2004; mem. N.J. Clean Air Coun., 1987. With USPHS, 1965-67. Recipient Nat. Heart Lung and Blood Inst., Pulmonary Acad. career award, 1975-80, Preventive Pulmonary Acad. career award, 1987-92, Tb Acad. career award, 1993—98, 1st prize trade category Am. Med. Writers Assn., 2002, Solomon A. Berson Med. Alumni Achievement award NYU, 2003. Fellow ACP, Am. Coll. Chest Physicians (gov. 1984-90, pres. NJ chpt. 1982-84, Simon Rodbard Meml. lectr. 2000); mem. Am. Thoracic Soc. (hon. life 1999-), Internat. Union Against Tb and Lung Disease (exec. com. 1982-92, vice chair exec. com. 1989-91, N.Am. Region Disting. Svc. award 2001), Am. Lung Assn. (hon. life 1999-, nat. bd. dirs. 1980-94, pres. elect 1991-92, pres. 1992-93, past pres. 1993-94, Will Ross medalist 1999), NJ Thoracic Soc. (pres. 1982-84), Am. Lung Assn. NJ (hon. life 1996-, bd. dirs. 1976—86, pres. 1984-86), Global Alliance for Tb Drug Devel. Stakeholders Assn. (pres., 2004-05, bd. dirs., 2006-10), Paul G. Rogers Soc. (amb. 2009-). Office: Global Tuberculosis Inst PO Box 1709 225 Warren St Newark NJ 07101-1709 Home Phone: 201-541-4020; Office Phone: 973-972-3270. E-mail: reichmlb@umdnj.edu.

REICHMAN, O. HOWARD, retired neurosurgeon; b. Washington, Oct. 1, 1932; s. Owen Gustav Reichman and Stella May Cheshire; m. Nancy Lou Topping; children: Howard Reed, Kathleen Ericksen, Owen Stanley, Russell Wayne, Shirley Anne Ence, Mark Vernon children: Douglas James. BA in Math., U. Utah, Salt Lake City, 1952, MD, 1956. Diplomate neurol. surgeon Am. Bd. Neurol. Surgery, 1966. Chmn., dept. neurol. surgery Loyola U. Med. Ctr., Maywood, Ill., 1973—97, prof. emeritus, 1997—. Contbr. articles to profl. publs. Leader and innovator neurol. surgery, Maywood, Ill., 1964—2010. Maj. army res. Med. Corp, 1956—64, Salt Lake City, NYC, Denver. Mem.: Am. Assn. Neurol. Surgeons. Republican. Achievements include development of microneurosurgical skills. Avocations: hiking, skiing, violin, music. Home: 241 West Woodside Dr Provo UT 84604-4422 Office: Loyola University Med Ctr 2160 South First Ave Maywood IL 60153 Office Fax: 708-216-4948; Home Fax: 801-375-2968. Personal E-mail: nancy@reichmanfam.net. Business E-Mail: vprabhu@lumc.edu.

REID, HELEN VERONICA, provost; b. Reading, Eng., Sept. 25, 1956; d. Alan A. and Teresa H. (Thatcher) Ware; m. Gary B. Reid, May 29, 1976; children: Robert, Jennifer, Kristen. BA in Biology, U. Tex., 1976; BSN, U. Tex., Arlington, 1978; MSN, Tex. Women's U., 1983; EdD, U. North Tex., 2000. CCRN, 1980, cert. CPR instr. Asst. nurse coord., staff nurse, float pool nurse Parkland Meml. Hosp., Dallas, 1979—83, float pool nurse, 1987—93; instr. Trinity Valley CC, Kaufman, Tex., 1983—86, leader freshman team, 1986—90, dean health occupations, 1990—2006; provost Health Sci. Ctr., 2007—. Mem.: Tex. Assn. Deans and Dirs. for Profl. Nursing Programs (treas. 2005—), Tex. C.C. Tchrs. Assn., Nat. Orgn. ADN (pub. rels. dir. 1998—2002, treas. 2006—), Tex. Orgn. for ADN (sec. 1988—92, nominating com. chair 1995—96, pres.-elect 2002—03, pres. 2003—05, past pres. 2005—06), Tex. Assn. Vocat. Nurse Educators, Phi Kappa Phi, Sigma Theta Tau. Office Phone: 972-932-4309. Business E-Mail: reid@tvcc.edu.

REID, JOHN LOW, pharmacologist, educator; b. Glasgow, Scotland, Oct. 1, 1943; s. James and Irene Margaret (Dale) R.; m. Randa Pharaon, May 2, 1964; children: James, Rebecca Louise. MA, Oxford U., 1965, BM BCh, 1967, DM, 1973. Rsch. fellow Royal Postgraduate Med. Sch., London, 1970—73, reader, 1975—78; vis. fellow Med. Rsch. Coun., Bethesda, Md., 1973—74; vis. scientist USPHS/NIMH, Bethesda, 1974—75; prof. U. Glasgow, Scotland, 1978—2009, emeritus prof. Author: Lecture Notes in Clinical Pharmacology, 1981, 7th edit., 2006 Fellow Royal Coll. Physicians London, Royal Coll. Physicians Glasgow, Royal Coll. Physicians Ireland, Royal Soc. Edinburgh; mem. European Soc. Hypertension (pres. 1991-93), Brit. Hypertension Soc. (pres. 1989-91). Avocations: gardening, outdoors, opera, rugby. Home: Reid Maryland Black Bull Ln Fencott Oxfordshire OX5 2RD England Personal E-mail: johnlreid@btinternet.com.

REID, JOHN MITCHELL (JACK REID), biomedical engineer, researcher, consultant; b. Mpls., June 8, 1926; s. Robert Sherman and Meryl (Mitchell) R.; m. Virginia Montgomery, Dec. 31, 1949 (div.); children: Donald, Kathryn, Richard; m. Shadi Wang, June 30, 1983; 1 child Xuang-Xuang Hu. BS, U. Minn., 1950, MS, 1957; PhD, U. Pa., 1965. Engring. assoc. U. Minn., Mpls., 1950-54; rsch. engr. St. Barnabas Hosp., Mpls., 1954-57; assoc. U. Pa., Phila., 1957-66; rsch. asst. prof. U. Wash., Seattle, 1966-72; rsch. engr. Providence Hosp., 1972-74; dir. bioengring. Inst. of Applied Physiology & Medicine, 1973-81; Calhoun prof. Drexel U., Phila., 1981-94, prof. emeritus, rsch. prof., 1994—. Adj. prof. radiology Thomas Jefferson Med. Sch., Phila., 1982—; affiliate prof. U. Washington, 1995—; cons. Inst. Applied Physiology and Medicine, Seattle. Contbr. numerous articles to profl. jours.; 5 U.S. patents on devel. of ultrasonic med. imaging. Scoutmaster Boy Scouts Am., Mpls., 1955-57, Phila., 1960-65, cub and scoutmaster, Seattle, 1965-70. With USN, 1944—46. Recipient Pioneer award Soc. Vascular Technologists, 1994, Outstanding Alumni award U. Minn., 2010; grantee NIH; Professorship in his named established at Drexel U. Sch. Biomed. Engring. and Health Sys., Phila., 2004. Fellow IEEE, Am. Inst. Ultrasound in Medicine (bd. govs., Pioneer award), Acoustical Soc. Am., IEEE Engring. in Medicine and Biology Soc. (Lifetime Achievement award 1993), Am. Inst. Med. and Biol. Engrs.; mem. World Fedn. Ultrasound in Medicine and Biology (hon.). Home: 16711 254th Ave SE Issaquah WA 98027-6973 Business E-Mail: jmreid@u.washington.edu.

REID, ROBERT ALFRED, physician; b. Milan, June 8, 1939; BA in English Lit., U. Colo., 1961, MD, 1965. Intern U. Colo. Med. Ctr., 1965-66, resident, 1968-71; dir. med. affairs Santa Barbara Cottage Hosp., Calif., 1992—2009, med. staff cons. Calif., 2009—. Mem. AMA, Am. Coll. Ob-gyn., Calif. Med. Assn. (pres. 1998). Personal E-mail: rreid@gmail.com. *

REID, ROBERT TILDEN, medical association administrator, internist; b. Dallas, Feb. 20, 1931; s. Robert Tilden and Gldays Tressy (King) R.; divorced; children: Robert Tilden, Richard Thomas, Annette Marie, Randolph Young. BS, So. Meth. U., Dallas, 1957; MD, U. Tex.-Southwestern, Dallas, 1959. Diplomate Am. Bd. Internal Medicine, Am. Bd. Rheumatology, Am. Bd. Allergy and Immunology. Intern Parkland Meml. Hosp., Dallas, 1959-60, resident, 1960-63; with Scripps Clinic and Rsch., La Jollla, Calif., 1963-70; pvt. practice La Jollla, Calif., 1970—; chief staff Scripps Meml. Hosp., La Jollla, Calif., 1976-78; scientific dir. Erik and Ese Banck Clinical Rsch. Ctr., San Diego, 1994—. Mem. San Diego County Med. Soc. (pres. 1991), Calif. Med. Assn. (trustee 1992-95). Office: 8716 Production Ave San Diego CA 92121 Home Phone: 858-481-2910; Office Phone: 858-271-0049. Personal E-mail: banckcrc@pacbell.net.

REID-ANDERSON, JAMES, amusement park company executive; BS in Commerce with honors, U. Birmingham, Eng.; MBA, Rutgers U. Exec. level positions with Pepsico Inc., Grand Met. PLC, Mobil Oil Corp.; COO, chief adminstrv. officer Wilson Sporting Goods, Chgo., 1994-96; exec. v.p., CFO Dade Behring, Deerfield, Ill., 1996-97, exec. v.p., CFO, chief adminstrv. officer, 1997-99, pres., COO, 1999—2000, pres., CEO, 2000—02, chmn., pres., CEO, 2002—07; CEO Siemens Healthcare Diagnostics, 2007—08; mem. mng. bd. Siemens AG, 2008, CEO, healthcare sector, 2008, adv. to mng. bd., 2008—10; adv. Apollo Mgmt. L.P., 2008—10; chmn., pres., CEO Six Flags Entertainment Corp., Dallas, 2010—. Bd. dirs. Stericycle Inc., 2009—, Brightpoint, Inc., 2010—, Six Flags Entertainment Corp, 2010—. Fellow Chartered Assn. Cert. Accts. Office: Six Flags Entertainment Corp 924 Ave J East Grand Prairie TX 75050

REIDENBERG, MARCUS MILTON, physician, educator; b. Phila., Jan. 3, 1934; m. June Wilson, July 14, 1957; children: Bruce, Joel, Julie. Student, Cornell U., 1951-54; MD, Temple U., 1958. Diplomate Am. Bd. Internal Medicine. Intern Community Gen. Hosp., Reading, Pa., 1958-59; resident Temple U. Hosp., Phila., 1962-65; from instr. to assoc. prof. Temple U. Med. Sch., Phila., 1962-75; assoc. prof. Cornell U. Med. Coll., NYC, 1975-76, prof. pharmacology, head div. clin. pharmacology, 1976—, prof. medicine, 1980—, prof. pub. health, 2002—, acting assoc. dean, 1981-82, asst. dean, 1988—; attending physician N.Y. Hosp., 1980—2006. Vis. physician Rockefeller U. Hosp., NYC, 1980—99; mem. project adv. group FDA, Rockville, Md., 1977-82; vice chmn. Joint Commn. on Prescription Drug Use, Washington, 1977-80; mem. study sect. NIH, Bethesda, Md., 1980-86; del. US Pharmacopeal Conv., 1975-80. Author: Renal Function and Drug Action, 1971; editor: various books, Clin. Pharmacology and Therapeutics, 1985—2001; contbr. articles to profl. jours. Served to lt. M.C., USNR, 1960-62. Recipient Research Career Devel. award NIH, 1970, Julius Sturmer award Phila. Coll. Pharmacy and Sci., 1982, Oscar B. Hunter award Am. Soc. Clin. Pharmacology and Therapeutics, 2008. Fellow ACP; mem. Am. Soc. Clin. Investigations, Assn. Am. Physicians, Am. Soc. Clin. Pharmacology and Therapeutics (pres. 1984-85, Rawls Palmer award 1981), Am. Soc. Pharmacology and Exptl. Therapeutics (award 1983, Harry Gold award 1999, Torald Sollmann award 2011), Internat. Union Pharmacology (vice chmn. sect. clin. pharmacology 1984-87, chmn. 1987-89), World Health Organization Expert Com. on the Selection and Use of Essential Drugs (vice chmn. essential drugs com. 2003, 05, chmn. essential medicine com. 2007, 2009). Office: Cornell U Med Coll Dept Clin Pharmacology 1300 York Ave New York NY 10021-4805 Office Phone: 212-746-6227.

REIFF, JAMES STANLEY, osteopathic physician, addictions and psychiatric physician, surgeon; b. Mar. 17, 1935; s. Nathan Edgar and Freda Matilda (Imhoff) R.; m. Sharon Ann Kraybill, June 9, 1956 (div. April 1970); children: Gregory James, James Stanley II, Cynthia Diane, Jeffery Cameron. BA in Chemistry, Goshen Coll., 1957; DO, Chgo. Coll. Osteo Medicine, 1961. Biochemist Miles/Ames Pharm. Co., Elkhart, Ind., 1955-57; pvt. practice Mich. City, Ind., 1962-69; addictions physician Oaklawn Psychiat. Ctr., Elkhart, 1974-84; med. dir. Life Recovery Ctr., Elkhart, 1987-90, Substance Abuse Coun., St. Joe County, Mich., 1990-95, Am. Plasma Mgmt., Inc., various, Mich., Ind, 1991-97; mem. staff Cmty. Mental Health Svcs., St. Joe County, 1993-97; vol. svc. with Lakeland Prison, Mich. Dept. Corrections, 2001—. Bd. dirs. Home for Runaway Kids - Victory House, Elkhart, Ind., 1974-76, 12 Step House Meth. Ch.-Halfway House, Elkhart, 1974-77; bd. dirs., treas. Caldwell Home Corp.-Social Rehab. Ctr. for Alcoholism, Elkhart, 1984-87; bd. dirs. Hope House, Jonesville, Mich.; vol. Dept. Corrections, 2001—. Organist First Presbyn. Ch., Sturgis, Mich., 1993-97. Mem. AMA, Am. Osteopathic Assn., Am. Soc. Addiction Medicine (com. on addiction medicine in correctional facilities 1993—), Mich. State Med. Soc., St. Joe County Med. Soc. Avocation: piano. Home and Office: 28275 E Congress St Sturgis MI 49091-9181 Office Phone: 269-659-4706.

REIFFEL, JAMES, cardiologist, educator; b. NYC, Sept. 20, 1943; s. Martin Lawrence and Roslyn (Siskind) R.; m. Bonnie Geffen, Mar. 18, 1967; children: Gabrielle, Jamie. BA, Duke U., 1965; MD, Columbia U., 1969. Diplomate NASPE, Am. Bd. Internal Medicine, subsplty. bd. Cardiovascular Disease, subsplty. bd. Clin. Cardiovascular Electrophysiology; cert. Nat. Bd. Examiners. Intern Presbyn. Hosp., NYC, 1969-70, resident, 1970-72, asst. physician, 1974-76, asst. attending physician, 1976-80, assoc. attending physician, 1980-88, attending physician, 1988—, assoc. dir. electrophysiology lab., 1979-91; dir. electrophysiology programs Coll. Physicians & Surgeons, Columbia U., NYC, 1991-99, dir. electrocardiography lab., 1999—, assoc. in clin. medicine NYC, 1974-76, asst. prof. clin. medicine, 1976-80, assoc. prof. clin. medicine, 1980-88, prof. clin. medicine, 1988—. Pres. Soc. Practitioners Columbia Presbyn. Med. Ctr., 2003—05. Contbr. articles to profl. jours. With USAR, 1970—76. Fellow Cardiology, Presbyn. Hosp., 1972—74. Fellow ACP, Am. Heart Assn., Coun. Clin. Cardiology, Am. Coll. Cardiology, N.Y. Cardiol. Soc.; mem. N.Y. Heart Assn., Med. Soc. County of N.Y., Med. Soc. State of N.Y., Am. Fedn. Clin. Rsch., Cardiac Electrophysiologic Soc., N.Am. Soc. Pacing and Electrophysiology, Am. Coll. Medicine, Health Physicists Soc. Office: 161 Ft Washington Ave New York NY 10032-3713

REIJONSAARI, KARITA HANNELE, research director; b. Finland, July 17, 1978; MS in Economics, Helsinki Sch. Economics, 2004; Licentiate in Tech., Aalto U., 2007. Rsch. dir. Aalto U., HEMA Inst., 2007—, sr. rschr. Office: Otaniementie 17 Espoo 00076 Finland E-mail: karita.reijonsaari@aalto.fi.

REIJO PERA, RENEE A., reproductive science director, educator; BS in Biology, U. Wis., 1983; PhD in Molecular and Cell Biology, Cornell U., 1993. Damon-Runyan/Walter Winchell postdoctoral fellow Whitehead Inst. for Biomedical Rsch. Lab., 1993—97; instr., human genetics, dept. biology MIT, 1995; asst. prof. in residence, dept. ob-gyn. & reproductive scis., physiology & urology, programs in human & cancer genetics, develop. & stem cell biology U. Calif., San Francisco, 1997—2003, assoc. prof. in residence dept. ob-gyn. & reproductive scis., physiology & urology, programs in human & cancer genetics, develop. & stem cell biology, 2003—, co-dir., program in human stem cell biology, 2004—, assoc. dir., Ctr. for Reproductive Scis., 2004—. Invited participant, chair German Am. Frontiers of Sci., NAS, 2000—03. Contbr. several articles to profl. jours. Scholar Searle Found., 1998—2001; DuPont Tchg. Fellow, 1989, US Army Biotechnology Grad. Fellowship, 1991—93. Office: U Calif Dept Obstetrics Gynecology & Reproductive Sciences 513 Parnassus Ave Rm HSE 1634 Box 0556 San Francisco CA 94143-0556 Office Phone: 415-476-3178. Office Fax: 415-476-3121. Business E-Mail: reijoperar@obgyn.ucsf.edu.

REILING, RICHARD BERNARD, physician; b. Dayton, Ohio, June 29, 1941; s. Walter Anthony Sr. and E. Dorothy (Unger) R.; m. Elizabeth Castellini, June 20, 1964; children: Maureen Elizabeth, Richard Bernard Jr. BS, U. Dayton, 1963; MD cum laude, Harvard U., 1967. Diplomate Nat. Bd. Med. Examiners. Intern, then residentin surgery Boston City Hosp., 1967-73; fellow in surgery Lahey Clinic Found., Boston, 1970; practice medicine specializing in surgery Kettering, Ohio, 1975; v.p. cancer svcs. OhioHealth, Columbus, 2000—02; med. dir. Presbyn. Cancer Ctr., Charlotte, NC, 2003—; staff mem. Presbyn. Hosp., Presbyn. Matthews Hosp. Instr. surgery Harvard Med. Sch., 1968-73; assoc. clin. prof. surgery Wright State U., 1979-81, assoc. prof. surgery, 1991-2000, clin. prof. surgery, 2000—; chief of staff Kettering Med. Ctr., Ohio, 1982-83. Contbr. articles to profl. jours. Scoutmaster Boy Scouts Am., Kettering, 1982-85; past pres. Assn. Cmty. Cancer Ctrs., 2006. Served to maj. USAF, 1973-75, v.p., vice-chair The Am. Coll. of Surgeons, 2008-09, vice-chair, ACCME, 2010- Fellow ACS (past pres. Ohio chpt. 1986-87, Disting. Svc. award 2004, v.p. 2008-09, vice chair 2006-); mem. AMA (mem. Coun. Med. Edn.), Ohio Med. Assn., Montgomery County Med. Soc., Societe Internationale de Churgerie, Assn. Cmty. Cancer Ctrs. (past pres. 2007). Avocations: sailing, flying, golf. Office: Presbyterian Cancer Ctr 200 Hawthorne Lane PO Box 33549 Charlotte NC 28233 Home Phone: 704-373-0133; Office Phone: 704-384-9955. Office Fax: 704-385-5679. E-mail: rbreiling@novanthealth.org.

REILLY, ANN ELIZABETH, internist; MD, Thomas Jefferson U., 1978. Diplomate Am. Bd. Internal Medicine, 1981. Intern Main Line Hosp. Lankenau, 1979, resident, 1981; hosp. affiliation includes Paoli Meml. Hosp.; attending physician. Named one of the Top Doctor, Phila. Mag., 2011. Mem.: AMA, ACP, Chester County Med. Soc., Pa. Med. Soc. Office: Lankenau Hospital Ste E 500 Chesterbrook Blvd Wayne PA 19087 Office Phone: 610-296-0222. Office Fax: 610-296-3255.

REILLY, JOAN, retired nursing educator; b. Johnson, Wash., May 2, 1931; d. Jacob and Vernice Althea (Marine) Steiner; m. Robert Joseph Reilly, June 20, 1960; children: Sean Michael, Patrick Joseph, Bridget Colleen. BSN, Wash. State U., 1953; MSN, St. Louis U., 1970; EdD, Seattle U., 1989. RN. Staff nurse VA Hosp., Spokane, 1953—55, 1962—63; office nurse pediatrician's office Spokane, 1955—56; nursing supr. Bakersfield Meml. Hosp. (Calif.), 1956—58; instr. St. Luke's Sch. Nursing, Spokane, 1958—60; staff nurse Ireland Army Hosp., Ft. Knox., Ky., 1961—62; instr. St. Joseph Sch. Nursing, Tacoma, 1964—65, 1966—67; nursing svc. staff asst. St. Joseph Hosp., Tacoma, 1970; charge nurse St. Peter Hosp., Olympia, Wash., 1973—74; vis. nurse Tacoma Gen. Hosp., 1974—77; instr. Tacoma CC, 1977—92; with Wash. State Nursing Commn., 1992—99; ret., 1999. Unit svc. chmn. ACS, Tacoma, 1977; mem. corp. Hospice

Tacoma, 1981—; vol. ARC, Karlsruhe, Germany, 1971; mem. Tacoma Zool. Soc., 1983, Friends of Libr., Steilacoom, Wash., 1983, Steilacoom Hist. Mus. Soc., 1983; key person United Way, Tacoma, 1983—84; parish nurse St. Luke's Episc. Ch., 2004—; group facilitator Good Grief Ctr., 2004—; chmn. Christian Edn. Com., 2006—; ch. vestry mem., 2005—08; cancer care vol., 2011—. Vol. Cancer Care New, 2011—. Named to Sigma Theta Tau Internat., 1998. Mem.: Tacoma Musical Playhouse (bd. mem. 1997—2000), Irish Cultural (pub. com. Tacoma 1982—83), Ft. Steilacoom Running, Alcoholism Profl. Staff Soc. Wash., NW Nurses Soc. on Chem. Dependency, Nat. Assn. Alcohol and Drug Abuse Counselors, Wash. State Nurses' Assn. (chmn. Ways and Means Com. 1982—83, bd. dirs. 1981—84), Phi Kappa Phi. Home: 1521 Willow Pl Wenatchee WA 98801-8005 *

REILLY, JOHN J., JR., pulmonologist, educator; Attended, Harvard Coll., Boston. Diplomate Am. Bd. Internal Medicine, Am. Bd. Internal Medicine-pulmonary disease. Resident Brigham & Women's Hosp., Boston, fellow; prof., vice chair pulmonary, allergy and critical care medicine divsn. Univ. of Pitts. Med. Ctr. Co-author: (publs.) Computed tomographic-based quantification of emphysema and correlation to pulmonary function and mechanics., 2008, Physiologic and Computed Tomographic Predictors of Outcome from Lung Volume Reduction Surgery, 2009, Airway Wall Attenuation: A Biomarker of Airway Disease in Subjects with COPD, 2009, Pulmonary hypertension and computed tomography measurement of small pulmonary vessels in severe emphysema., 2010, and numerous others. Mailing: University of Pittsburgh Medical Center Comprehensive Lung Center 3601 Fifth Ave 4th Fl Pittsburgh PA 15213 Office: University of Pittsburgh Medical Center 1220 Scaife Hall 3550 Terrace St Pittsburgh PA 15261 Office Phone: 412-648-6161, 412-648-9641. Office Fax: 412-648-2117. Business E-Mail: reillyj@pitt.edu.

REILLY, JOHN P., orthopedist, surgeon; b. NY, USA, Nov. 1955; BS, Poly. Inst. of NY, 1977; MD, SUNY, 1981. Diplomate Am. Bd. Orthopaedic Surgery, 2001. Intern SI Hosp., 1982; asst. resident orthopaedic surgery Children's Hosp., 1983; resident orthopaedic surgery Lenox Hill Hosp., 1986; fellow Md. Inst. for Emergency Med. Svcs. Sys., 1987; team physician SI Yankees, Wagner Coll. Football, Poly Prep High Sch., Monsignor Farrell High Sch., St. Joseph by the Sea, Port Richmond, SI Tech, Moore Cath.; with SI Univ. Hosp. Office: Staten Island University Hospital 3311 Hylan Blvd Staten Island NY 10308 Office Phone: 718-667-7500.

REILLY, PATRICK GERARD, pulmonologist; MD, Royal Coll. of Surgeons, 1987. Diplomate Am. Bd. of Internal Medicine critical care medicine, Am. Bd. of Internal Medicine-pulmonary disease. Intern Mercy Hosp. of Pitts., 1988, resident, 1990; fellow Univ. of Pitts. Med. Ctr., 1993; physician St. Clair Hosp. Office: St Clair Hospital 1050 Bower Hill Rd Ste 101 Pittsburgh PA 15243 Office Phone: 412-942-5620.

REIM, MARTIN, retired ophthalmology educator; b. Klein-Döbbern, Germany, Feb. 26, 1931; Med. exam., U. Marburg, Fed. Republic Germany, 1957, D of Medicine, 1958. Intern Univ. Hosp., Marburg, 1957-59; resident in ophthalmology Univ. Eye Clinic, Marburg, 1961-66, sr. physician, 1966-67, 68-72, provisional dir., 1972-73; asst. Inst. Biochemistry U. Marburg, 1959-61, assoc. prof. ophthalmology, 1971; sr. rsch. fellow Retina Found., Boston, 1967-68; dir. eye clinic Tech. U. Aachen, Germany, 1973-96. Dean student affairs faculty of medicine Tech. U. Aachen, 1974-81; med. dir. Univ. Hosp., Aachen, 1981-84. Author: Augenheilkunde, 1985, 5th edit., 1996; author: (with S. Wolf and B. Kirchhof) Diagnosen am Augenhintergrund, 2003; author: The Ocular Fundus, 2005; author: (with S. Wolf and B. Kirchof) Examen de Fondo de Ojo, 2005; contbr. articles to profl. publs., books. Bd. dirs. Aachen Ctr. of Tech. Transfer in Ophthalmology, 1997; chmn. ethics com. Faculty of Medicine, 2002—07. Rsch. grantee Deutsche Forschungsgemeinschaft, 1961-96; recipient Alcon Rsch. award Alcon Labs., Ft. Worth, 1989, von-Graefe award, 2006. Mem. European Coun. Ophthalmology, Societas Europaea Opthalmologica, Deutsche Ophthal. Gesellschaft (hon.; pres. 1985-86), Assn. Eye Rsch. (London, gen. sec. 1976-90), European Vision and Eye Rsch. Assn., Assn. Rsch. in Vision and Ophthalmology, Internat. Soc. Eye Rsch., Acad. Ophthalmology, Rotary. E-mail: martin.reim@post.rwth-aachen.de.

REIMERS, HERMAN ALLAN, physician; b. Lakeside, Mich., Apr. 12, 1947; s. Herman Benjamin and Josephine Estella (Edwards) Reimers; m. Helga Silvia Markgraf, Nov. 28, 1981; 1 child, Oliver Mark. BS, Carthage Coll., 1971; MD, U. Karl-Francis, Graz, Austria, 1985; diploma, Styrian Acad. Gen. Practice, 1998. Orderly St. Joseph Meml. Hosp., Mich., 1963-65; nurse Waukegan Meml. Hosp., Ill., 1968-71; resident State Hosp., Feldbach, Austria, 1986—89; pvt. practice physician St. Oswald, Austria, 1990—. Cons. in field. Vol. emergency dr. ASB Ambulance Svc., Hitzendorf, Austria; chief physician, bd. dirs., vol. ASB Emergency Svc., 1999—2006. Fellow: Kiwanis; mem.: Children's Diabetes Soc., Van Switen Soc. Vienna, Styrian Acad. Gen Practitioners, Austrian Soc. Cancer. Avocations: model trains, stamp collecting/philately, coin collecting/numismatics, skiing. Home: 8113 PLW 159 Saint Oswald Austria Office Phone: 0043 312 322 440. Personal E-mail: areimers@gmx.net.

REIMOLD, ANDREAS, medical educator; b. Boston, Sept. 25, 1961; AB, Harvard U., 1980; MD, Columbia U. Asst. prof. U. Tex. Southwestern Med. Ctr., 2000—. Office: 5323 Harry Hines Blvd Dallas TX 75390-8884 Business E-Mail: andreas.reimold@utsouthwestern.edu.

REIN, SUSANNE, surgeon, researcher; b. Chemnitz, Sachsen, Germany, Sept. 9, 1977; d. Johannes and Ilona Rein. Student of Medicine, Humboldt U., Berlin, 1996—2003, Faculté Médecine Marseille - U. Méditerranée, Marseille, 2003; DrMed, Germany, 2004. Intern Trauma Ctr., U. Tübingen, Dept. Plastic, Hand, Reconstructive and Burn Surgery, Tübingen, Baden-Würrtemberg, Germany, 2004, Carl Gustav Carus U. Hosp., Dept. Trauma and Reconstructive Surgery, Dresden, Germany, 2004—, Dept. Orthop., Trauma, Hand, Visceral and Minimal Invasive Surgery, Crailsheim, Germany, 2008—. Contbr. articles to rsch. jours. Recipient Hans-von-Seemen, Deutsche Gesellschaft für Plastische und Wiederherstellungschirurgie, 2008; fellow, Assn. Osteosynthesis, 2007. Mem.: Deutsche Gesellschaft für Plastische, Rekonstruktive und Ästhetische Chirurgie, Deutsche Gesellschaft für Musikphysiologie und Musikermedizin. Office: Carl Gustav Carus Univ Hosp Fetscherstr 74 Dresden Sachsen 01307 Germany Home: Falkenauer Str. 8 9573 OT Grünberg Augustusburg 09573 Germany Office Fax: 49-351-458-4307. Business E-Mail: susanne.rein@web.de, susanne.rein@uniklinikum-dresden.de.

REINA, CARRILLO JOSÉ GABRIEL, physician, surgery educator; b. Caqueza, Cundinamarca, Colombia, May 15, 1937; s. Hernández Santos Reina and Reina Evidalia Carrillo; m. Uriz María Encarnación Rivas, Dec. 12, 1958; 1 child, Rivas María Teresa. MD, Universidad Javeriana, 1965. Attending vascular surgeon Caprecom, Bogotá, 1970—75; instr. gen. surgery Universidad del Rosario, Bogotá, Colombia, 1973—76, prof. gen. surgery, 1977—78; chief gen. surgery Hosp. Ctrl. de la Policia Nacional, Bogotá, 1975—77; chief dept. surgery Clínica Hosp. Juan N. Corpas, Bogotá, 1977—2005. Author: (book) Nociones de Cirugía General, Nutrición Parenteral. Recipient Medalla al Mérito, Policía Nacional, 1996. Fellow: ACS, Sociedad Colombiana de Cirugía Vascular, Sociedad Colombiana de Gastroenterología, Colegio Colombiano de Cirujanos, Real Colegio Español de Médicos, Internat. Soc. Surgeons. Católica. Avocation: magic. Home: Calle 61 No 9 - 38 Apt 902 Cundinamarca Bogota Colombia Office: Fundación Universitaria Juan N Corpas Cra 111 No 157 - 45 Cundinamarca Bogota Colombia Business E-Mail: gabriel.reina@juanncorpas.edu.co.

REINECKE, MANFRED, medical educator; b. Hamm, Germany, Aug. 11, 1944; s. Werner and Ilse Reinecke; m. Veronika Reinecke; children: Robert, Marie. PhD, U. Munster, Germany, 1974. Assoc. prof. U. Heidelberg, Germany, 1984—88; vis. scientist Karolinska Inst., Stockholm, 1989—90; prof. Inst. Anatomy, U. Zurich, Switzerland, 1990—, dir., 2007—. Office: Univ Zurich Winterthurerstrasse Zurich Switzerland Business E-Mail: reinecke@anatom.uzh.ch.

REINER, SCOTT, insurance company executive; m. Margo Reiner; children: Christian, Alixandria. BSN, Pacific Union Coll., Angwin; M in Health Adminstrn., Calif. State U., Northridge. Pres., CEO, COO Glendale Adventist Med. Ctr., Calif.; v.p. specialty ops., v.p. for devel. and managed care Tenn. Christian Med. Ctr., Nashville; sr. v.p. strategic ops. Gen. Health System, Baton Rouge; CEO largest hosp. Adventist Health, sr. v.p., 2007—11, exec. v.p., COO, 2011—. Chair Feather River Hosp., Calif., Howard Meml. Hosp., Ukiah Valley Med. Ctr., Adventist Med. Ctr., Hanford, Ctrl. Valley Gen. Hosp., Selma Cmty. Hosp., San Joaquin Cmty. Hosp., Bakersfield, Simi Valley Hosp., St. Helena Hosp., Napa Valley, Clear Lake. Mem.: Hosp. Assn. Southern Calif. (exec. com.). Office: Adventist Health 2100 Douglas Blvd Roseville CA 95661 Office Phone: 916-781-2000.

REINER, ZELJKO, cardiologist, director; b. Zagreb, Croatia, May 28, 1953; MD, U. Zagreb, 1976, PhD, 1982—82. Head divsn. clin. rsch., dept. pahophysiology U. Hosp. Ctr. Zagreb, 1986—95, head divsn. metabolic diseases, 2003, head dept. internal medicine, 1995—2003, dir., 2004—. Assoc. prof. Sch. Medicine, U. Zagreb, 1986—88, prof., 1988, tenure prof. internal medicine, 97. Recipient Ladislav Rakovac award, Croatian Med. Assn., City of Zagreb Award, City Zagreb Coun.; named Hon. Citzen of Korcula, Korcula City Coun. Master: Croatian Acad. Med. Scis., Croatian Nat. Acad. Sci. and Arts; fellow: Am. Coll. Cardiology, European Soc. Cardiology, Royal Coll. Physicians London. Avocations: poetry, skiing. Office: Kispaticeva 21 Zagreb 10000 Croatia Office Fax: 38512379922. Business E-Mail: zreiner@kbc-zagreb.hr.

REINHARDT, UWE ERNST, economist, educator; b. Osnabrueck, Germany, Sept. 24, 1937; came to U.S., 1964; s. Wilhelm and Edeltraut (Kehne) R.; m. Tsung mei Cheng, May 25, 1968; children Dirk, Kara, Mark B.Commerce with honors, U. Sask., Saskatoon, Can., 1964; MA in Economics, Yale U., 1965, M.Ph. in Economics, 1967, PhD, 1970; DSc (hon.), Med. Coll. of Pa., 1987, CUNY, 1994, SUNY, 1998. Asst. prof., economics and pub. affairs Princeton University, NJ, 1968—74, assoc. prof., 1974-79, prof., 1979, James Madison prof., polit. economy, prof., economics NJ, 1984—. Bd. dirs. McAllister Holdings, Amerigroup Corp.; trustee Tchrs. Ins. and Annuity Assn., 1978-93, H&Q Health Fund; cons. Urban Inst., Washington, 1971-75, HEW, 1974—, HHS, Math., Inc., Princeton, 1970-80, AT&T, Basking Ridge, N.J., 1976-82, Nat. Westminster Bank USA, N.Y.C., 1979—, mem. Nat. Leadership Commn. Health Care, 1986—; mem. spl. adv. bd. VA, 1981-85; mem. U.S. Physicians' Payment Rev. Commn., U.S. Congress, 1986—; pres. Assn. for Health Svcs. Rsch., 1989-90, Found. Health Svcs. Rsch., 1990-91; mem. bd. advisors Nat. Inst. Healthcare Mgmt., 1993—, Pew Health Professions Commn., 1997—; mem. Coun. Econ. Impact Health Reform, 1994—; mem. external adv. panel health and nutrition World Bank, 1997—; chair coordinating com. Commonwealth Fund Internat. Program Health Policy, 1998—; commr. Kaiser Commn. Medicaid and Uninsured; trustee Duke U. Health Sys., Triad Hosps., Inc., Medcast/WebMD. Author: Physician Productivity and the Demand for Health Manpower, 1975; mem. editorial bd. Health Affairs, 1982—, New Eng. Jour. Medicine, 1989-92, Health Mgmt. Quar., Health Policy and Edn., Milbank Meml. Quar., Jour. AMA, 1991—; assoc. editor Jour. Health Econs., 1980-85, mem. editorial bd., 1981-83; contbr. articles to profl. jours. Bd. dirs. Nat. Acad. Aging, 1993—. Mem. Nat. Inst. Health Care Mgmt., Inst. Medicine Nat. Acad. Scis. (gov. council 1979-82) Office: Amerigroup Corp Bd Directors 4425 Corporation Ln Virginia Beach VA 23462 also: Princeton U 351 Wallace Hall Princeton NJ 08544 Office Phone: 757-490-6900, 609-258-4781. Office Fax: 757-518-3600, 609-258-5974. Business E-Mail: reinhard@princeton.edu. *

REINHART, JOHN BELVIN, retired child and adolescent psychiatrist, educator; b. Merrill, Wis., Dec. 22, 1917; s. Dabney Belvin and Ann (Toomey) R.; m. Helen Elsen Reinhart, Jan. 3, 1949; children: Peter, Catherine, Ann, John, Frederick, Andrew. BA, Duke U., 1939; MD, Bowman Gray Sch. Medicine, Winston-Salem, NC, 1943. Diplomate Am. Bd. Pediatrics, Am. Bd. Psychiatry in child and adolescent psychiatry. Instr. pediatrics Bowman Gray Sch. Medicine, Winston-Salem, 1950-52; asst. prof., assoc. prof., prof. pediatrics and psychiatry U. Pitts. Sch. Medicine, 1956-83, emeritus prof. pediatrics, 1983—; clin. prof. psychiatry Bowman Gray Sch. Medicine, Winston-Salem, 1986-99, ret., 1999—. Co-Author: A Baby's First Year, 1956. Capt. M.C. AUS, 1946-48. Roman Catholic. Avocations: reading, golf, tennis, travel. Home: 600 Carolina Village Rd Apt 1415 Hendersonville NC 28792-2803

REINHART, MARY ANN, medical board executive; b. Jackson, Mich., Aug. 14, 1942; d. Herbert Martin and Josephine Marie (Keyes) Conway; m. David Lee Reinhart, Dec. 28, 1963; children: Stephen Paul, Michael David. MA, Mich. State U., 1983, PhD, 1985. Rsch. asst. Mich. State U., East Lansing, 1979-82, 85, teaching asst. dept psychology, 1982-84, asst. prof. Office Med. Edn. R&D, Coll. Human Medicine, 1985-88, chairperson collegewide evaluation com., Coll. Human Medicine, 1985—88, adj. asst. prof. Office Med. Edn. R&D, Coll. Human Medicine, 1988—; cons. Am. Bd. Emergency Medicine, East Lansing, 1985—88, assoc. exec. dir., 1988-95, dep. exec. dir., 1995-2000, exec. dir., 2000—10. Reviewer Annals of Emergency Medicine, 1987-95, Acad. Emergency Medicine, 1995-99. Bd. dirs. Neahtawanta Rsch. and Edn. Ctr., Traverse City, Mich., 1991—. Mem. APA (divsn. indsl./orgnl. psychology, health psychology), Phi Kappa Phi. Achievements include application of chart stimulated recall method of assessment in a national medical recertification examination; development and implementation of national longitudinal study of emergency medicine residents and emergency physicians and implementation of a national maintenance of certification system for emergency physicians.

REINHERZ, HELEN ZARSKY, social worker, researcher; b. Boston, Aug. 4, 1923; d. Zachary and Anna (Cohen) Zarsky; m. Samuel E. Reinherz, Aug. 29, 1943; 1 son, Ellis. AB magna cum laude, Wheaton Coll., 1944; MS, Simmons Coll., 1946; S.M., Harvard U., 1962, Sc.D., 1965. Social worker Newton Family Service, Mass., 1946-49, Mass. Gen. Hosp., Boston, 1949-51; supr. psychiat. social work State Hosp., Waltham, Mass., 1958-61; faculty mem. Simmons Coll., Boston, 1965—2010, prof. methods rsch., 1972—2010, dir. research Sch. Social Work, 1968-93, dir. PhD program, 1993-96, prof. emeritus, 2010. Prin. investigator Identifying Children at Risk, 1976—84, Adaption in Adolescence, 1987—93, Adult Rsch. Project, 1998—2001, Early Adulthood Rsch. Project, 1993—97, Simmons Longitudinal Study, 2001—10, Study Adolescent Drug Abuse, 1971—73; rsch. cons. Dept. Mental Health, 1970—80; chmn. Gov.'s Adv. Coun. on Mental Health and Retardation, 1972; mem. adv. com. Mental Health Manpower fo Fed. Govt., 1980—82. Author (with H. Wechler, D. Dobbins): Social Work Research in the Human Services, 1976; author: (with M. Heywood, J. Camp) A Community Response to Drug Abuse, 1976; cons., assoc. editor: Jour. Prevention, 1980—91, mem. fed. adv. com.: Rsch. in Prevention Rev., 1984—87, editl. bd.: Jour. Early Adolescence, cons. editor: NASW Jour.; contbr. articles to profl. jours. Recipient Maida H. Solomon award, Simmons Coll. Alumni, 1961, Disting. Career award, Soc. Social Work and Rsch., 2005, Rsch. Achievement award, NASW, 2005; grantee, Grant Found., 1963, Med. Found., 1967—69, NIMH, 1975—84, 1987—2007; NIH tng. fellow, 1961—65. Fellow Am. Orthopyschiat. Assn.; mem. Acad. Cert. Social Workers, Am. Pub. Health Assn., Coun. Social Work Edn., Harvard Sch. Pub. Health Alumni Assn. (sec.-treas. 1965-68), Phi Beta Kappa, Delta Omega. Office: Simmons Sch Social Work 300 The Fenway Boston MA 02115 Home: 1010 Waltham St Apt 453 Lexington MA 02421-8066 Business E-Mail: helen.reinherz@simmons.edu, reinherz@simmons.edu.

REININGER, HARRY, anesthesiologist, composer; b. Galatz, Roumania, Feb. 1, 1923; s. Jaques and Ida (Lieber) R.; m. Nina Scribanu, Mar. 20, 1961 (div. 1964); m. Miriam Mezei, Mar. 29, 1984. Specialist in Pulmonary Diseases, U. Bucharest, Roumania, 1949; Specialist in Anesthesiology, U. Tel Aviv, 1973. Med. doctor diplomate. Sr. doctor Filaret Hosp., Bucharest, Roumania, 1949-61; sr. doctor Anesthesiology Dept. Asaf Harofe Hosp., Israel, 1962-90; med. cons. Maccabee Pvt. Clinic, 1969—. Chief editor radio and TV, Bucharest, Roumania, 1949-59; musical cons. Jewish State Theater, Bucharest, 1949-61; conductor Chamber Music Orch., Bucharest, 1949-53. Contbr. numerous articles to profl. med. jours.; author musical plays in Roumanian and Iddish langs. and light music for radio and TV. Dir. Creative Activity in Theater, Israel, 1961—. Recipient Abraham Goldfaden prize, 1992. Mem. N.Y. Acad. Scis., Union of Composers in Roumania, Israeli Soc. of Composers. Avocation: writing music for theater. Home: 2 Herzog Str 62915 Tel Aviv Israel

REIS, STEVEN E., cardiologist; MD, Harvard Med. Sch., Boston, MA, 1987. Diplomate Am. Bd. Internal Medicine, lic. to practice Pa., 1994, cert. cardiovasc. disease. Intern Johns Hopkins Univ. Sch. of Medicine, Balt., 1994; hosp. affiliation includes Univ. of Pitts. Med. Ctr. Office: University of Pittsburgh Medical Center Presbyterian 200 Lothrop St Pittsburgh PA 15213-2582 Office Phone: 412-647-2345.

REISBERG, BARRY, geriatric psychiatrist, neuropsychopharmacologist; b. Bklyn., Dec. 3, 1947; s. Harry and Claire (Cohen) R.; m. Rosalie DePaola, Feb. 23, 1974 (dec. Oct. 1975); m. Nancy A. Minich, May 7, 1988. BA, CUNY, Bklyn., 1968; MD, N.Y. Med. Coll., 1972. Diplomate Am. Bd. Psychiatry and Neurology, Am. Bd. Geriatric Psychiatry. Intern NY Med. Coll./Met. Hosp., NYC, 1972—73, resident in psychiatry, 1972-75; fellow dept. psychiatry Middlesex Hosp. Med. Sch. U. London, 1975; staff psychiatrist Franklin D. Roosevelt VA Hosp., Montrose, NY, 1975-78; staff psychiatrist Neuropsychopharmacology Rsch. Unit NYU Med. Ctr., NYC, 1978-80, asst. attending psychiatrist, 1978—2001, clin. dir. Silberstein Aging and Dementia Clin. Rsch. Ctr., 1978—, attending psychiatrist, 2002—. Adj. prof. Ctr. for Studies in Aging McGill U., Montreal, Que., 1993—; clin. instr. dept. psychiatry N.Y. Med. Coll., Valhalla, 1975—78; asst. prof. NYU Sch. Medicine, NYC, 1978—84, assoc. prof., 1984—90, prof., 1990—; rsch. collaborator, vis. clinician Brookhaven Nat. Labs., Upton, NY, 1979—90; dir. clin. core NIMH Clin. Rsch. Ctr., 1989—93, Nat. Inst. Aging Alzheimer's Disease Ctr., 1990—; dir. Zachary and Elizabeth M. Fisher Alzheimer's Disease Edn. and Resources Program NYU Sch. Medicine, 1995—; med. and sci. adv. bd. Alzheimer's Assn., Chgo., 1993—97; med. and sci. panel Alzheimer's Disease Internat., 1997—; chmn. Prevention Work Group Alzheimer's Disease Internat., 2008—; cons. psychiatrist N.Y. VA Hosp., 1980—89; chmn. work group WHO, Copenhagen, 1984; mem. aging sect. NIH, 1986—90; vis. prof. Palmerston North

Postgrad. Med. Soc., New Zealand, 1991; rsch. adv. bd. WHO Project on Alzheimer's Disease, 1995; Bayer vis. prof. St. Louis U. Sch. Medicine, 1999; vis. prof. Georgetown U. Med. Ctr., 2004; vis. prof. in geriatrics Stony Brook U. Health Scis. Ctr., 2005, Zachary & Elizabeth M. Fisher Med. Found., 1995—98, Fisher Ctr. Alaheimers Rsch. Found., 1299—2010, Leonard Litwin Fund Alzheimers Disease Rsch., 2004—09, Woodbourne Found., 2008—, Hagedorn Fund, 2006—11, Louis J. Kay & June E. Kay Found., 2011, Stringer Found., 2011. Author: Brain Failure, 1981; editor: Alzheimer's Disease, 1983; editor: (with others) Diagnosis and Treatment of Senile Dementia, 1989; guest editor Drug Devel. Rsch., Internat. Psychogeriat., mem. editl. bd. Jour. Am. Aging Assn., 1985—2004, Alzheimer's Disease and Associated Disorders, 1985—2004, Jour. Geriat. Psychiatry and Neurology, 1986—, Am. Jour. Alzheimer's Disease, 1986—, Internat. Psychogeriat., 1989—96, Am. Jour. Geriat. Psychiatry, 1992—2001, Rsch. and Practice in Alzheimer's Disease, 1999—, Middle East Jour. of Age and Aging, 2004—, Polish Jour. Geriatric Psychiatry, 2005—, Middle Eastern Jour. Psychiatry & Alzheimer's, 2010—, assoc. editor Psychiat. Quar., 2007—; contbr. over 275 articles to med. and sci. jours. and books. Recipient Home Care award Vis. Nurse Svc. NY, 1985, Disting. Svc. award, Internat. Psychogeriatric Assn., 2001, Ann. Barry Reisberg Lectr. award Hearthstone Alzheimer's Family Found., 2002-, Lifetime Achievement award Alzheimer's Assn. and 9th Internat. Conf. on Alzheimer's Disease and Related Disorders, 2004, Disting. Scientist award, Am. Assn. Geriat. Psychiatry, 2011; fellow NSF, 1963, Coun. on Internat. Ednl. Exch.-Japan Soc., Tokyo, 1968; grantee NIH, 1979-85, 87-2003, 90-95, NIMH, 1983-85, Adminstrn. on Aging, 1998-2007. Fellow: Am. Aging Assn. (bd. dris. 1990—92), Am. Psychiat. Assn. (life); mem.: Am. Coll. Neuropsychopharmacology, Am. Assn. Geriat. Psychiatry (sec. 1991—92, bd. dirs. 1992—96, Disting. Scientist award 2011), Alzheimer's and Related Disorders Soc. India (hon.), Internat. Psychogeriat. Assn. (bd. dirs. 1985—93, treas. 1993—95, pres.-elect 1995—97, pres. 1997—99, Disting. Svc. award 2001). Achievements include patents for assessment of dementia; patents in field; Alzheimer's medications. Office: NYU Sch Medicine Silbersteln Aging and Dementia Clin Rsch Ctr 145 E 32nd St New York NY 10016 Office Phone: 212-263-8550. Business E-Mail: barry.reisberg@nyumc.org.

REISCHAUER, ROBERT D., think-tank executive; AB, Harvard U., 1963; MIA, Columbia U., 1966, PhD, 1971. Spl. asst. to dir., dep. dir., asst. dir. human resources and cmty. devel. Congl. Budget Office (CBO), Washington, 1975-81, dir., 1989-95; sr. v.p. The Urban Inst., 1981-86, pres., 2000—; chmn. bd. trustees MDRC (formerly Manpower Devel. Rsch. Corp.), 1999—2000; vice chair payment adv. commn. Medicare, 2001—08. Author: (with Henry J. Aaron) Countdown to Reform: The Great Social Security Debate, 2001 (revised and updated); editor: Setting National Priorities: Budget Choices for the Next Century, 1997; co-editor: Medicare: Preparing for the Challenges of the 21st Century, 1998, Setting National Priorities: The 2000 Election and Beyond, 1999; contbr. articles to profl. jours., chpts. to books. Sr. Fellow econ. studies Brookings Inst., 1970-75, 86-89, 95-2000. Office: Urban Inst 2100 M St NW Washington DC 20037 Office Phone: 202-261-5400. Business E-Mail: rreischauer@urban.org.

REISDORFF, EARL J., medical association administrator; m. Jane Reisdorff; children: Rebecca, Hannah. MD, U. Cin., 1984. Residency in emergency medicine Mich. State U.; emergency physician Ingham Regional Med. Ctr., Lansing, Mich., dir. med. edn.; assoc. prof. emergency medicine Mich. State U. Emergency Medicine Residency Program, former program dir.; exec. dir. American Bd. Emergency Medicine, 2010—. Lectr. Assn. Hosp. Med. Edn., Washington; sec. to the Coun. on Grad. Med. Edn. US Dept. Health and Human Services, 2003. Editor: Emergency Medicine Clinics of North America; coeditor: Pediatric Emergency Medicine, Emergency Radiology; peer reviewer: sci. specialty jours.; contbr. articles to profl. jours., chapters to books. Mem.: Mich. Coll. Emergency Physicians (bd. dirs. 1998—2003, pres. 2004—05), American Bd. Emergency Medicine (oral bd. cert. examiner 1994, item write for qualifying exam 1999—2009, sr. case writer oral cert. exam), Alpha Omega Alpha. Office: American Bd Emergency Medicine 3000 Coolidge Rd East Lansing MI 48823-6319 Office Phone: 517-332-4800. Office Fax: 517-332-2234. *

REISH, ORIT, medical geneticist; b. Petach Tikva, Israel, Mar. 8, 1956; d. Joseph and Rina Soffer; m. Giora Reish, June 3, 1981; children: Ron, Offer. MD, Ben Gurion U., Ber Sheva, Israel, 1982. Cert. in med. genetics Am. Bd., 1996. Resident in pediats. Tel Aviv U., 1985—91, Hashron Hosp., Petach Tikva, 1985—91, staff physician neonatal intensive care, 1991—92; fellow in genetics U. Minn., Mpls., 1992—95; med. geneticist Meir Med. Ctr., Kfar Saba, Israel, 1995—99; head genetics inst. Assaf Harofe Med. Ctr., Zerifin, Israel, 1999—; sci. adv. bd. chief Isreal scientist; sr. lectr. pediat. Sockler Sch. Medicine, U. Tel Aviv. Mem. med. rev. bd., mem. pregnancy termination com. Assaf Harofe Med. Ctr. Contbr. articles to med. jours. With Israeli mil. svcs., 1974—76. Mem.: Israeli Med. Assn., Israeli Bd. Med. Genetics, Am. Bd. Med. Genetics. Avocations: travel, piano. Home: 11 Faglin St NEVE OZ 49777 Petach Tikva Israel Office: Assaf Harofeh Med Ctr Genetics Inst 70300 Zerifin Israel Office Phone: 972 8 9779617, 972-8-9778211. Office Fax: 972 8 9778212. Personal E-mail: oreish@post.tau.ac.il. Business E-Mail: reish@asaf.health.gov.il.

REISMAN, ROBERT E., allergist, educator; b. Buffalo, Nov. 1, 1932; s. Harry S and Jessie (Goldberg) Reisman; m. Rena Estry, Sept. 5, 1954; children: Jeanne, Linda, Nancy, David. MD, SUNY-Buffalo, 1956; Dr.h.c., U. Montpellier, France, 1982. Diplomate Am. Bd. Internal Medicine, Am. Bd. Allergy and Clin. Immunology. Intern Buffalo Gen. Hosp., 1956-57, resident in medicine, 1957-59; practice medicine specializing in allergy and clin. immunology Buffalo, 1961—; co-dir. Allergy Rsch. Lab., Buffalo Gen. Hosp., 1970—90; clin. prof. pediatrics and medicine SUNY, Buffalo, 1978—. Mem. panel allergenic extracts Bur. Biologists FDA; bd. dirs. Am. Bd. Internal Medicine, 1984—86, Am. Bd. Allergy and Clin. Immunology, 1981—86, chmn., 1985. With US Army, 1968—69. Master: ACP; fellow: Am. Acad. Allergy (pres 1980—81). Home: 113 Carriage Cir Buffalo NY 14221-2163 Office: 295 Essjay Rd Williamsville NY 14221-8216 also: 85 High St Buffalo NY 14203-1149 Office Phone: 716-630-1130. Business E-Mail: rreisman@buffalomedicalgroup.com.

REISNER, ANDREW DOUGLAS, psychologist; b. Ithaca, NY, Dec. 28, 1955; s. Gerald Seymour and Estelle Ruth (Siegel) R.; m. Deborah Kay Dermen, Aug. 1, 1981; children: David Aaron, Alyssa Danielle. BA, Allegheny Coll., Meadville, Pa., 1977; MA, Edinboro U., Pa., 1978; D of Psychology, Baylor U., Waco, Tex., 1987. Lic. psychologist, Ohio. Psychology asst. Tiffin Devel. Mental Health Ctr., 1979—80, Cmty. Counseling Svcs., Galion, Ohio, 1980—83, chief clin. officer, 1990—99; pvt. practice, 1996—99; intern in clin. psychology Mich. State U., East Lansing, 1986—87; postdoctoral tng. in clin. psychology Harding Hosp., Worthington, Ohio, 1987—88; psychologist Ctr. for Individual Family Svcs., Mansfield, Ohio, 1988—90, Appalachian Behavorial Healthcare, Cambridge, Ohio, 1999—2008, Athens, Ohio, 2008—10. Cons. MedCtrl. Crestline Hosp., Ohio, 1989-99, Forensic Diagnostic Ctr., Byesville, Ohio, 1999—; exec. dir. Forensic Diagnostic Ctr., 2010-; mem. adj. faculty Ashland U., 1993-96. Contbr. chpt. to book, articles to profl. jours. Mem. APA. Office: Forensic Diagnostic Ctr Dist Nine PO Box 126 60788 Southgate Rd Byesville OH 43723-0126 Office Phone: 740-439-4136. Personal E-mail: fdcd9@frontier.com.

REISNER, STEVEN J., psychologist; b. Bklyn., 1954; AB in Psych., Princeton U., NJ, 1976; MS in Clin. Psych., Columbia U., NYC, 1986, MPhil in Clin. Psych., 1987, PhD in Clin. Psych., 1989. Lic. Clin. Psychologist NY. Intern clin. psych. Yale U. Dept. Psychiatry, New Haven, 1986—87; rsch. fellow clin. psych. SUNY Health Sci. Ctr., Bklyn., 1987—89; pvt. practice individual/couple's treatment NYC, 1993—. Adj. asst. prof. Bklyn. Coll., 1980—81; adj. prof. Columbia U., 1989—; faculty, supr. internat. trauma studies prog. NYU, 1999—; faculty NYU Psychoanalytic Inst., 2002—; clin. asst. prof. NYU Med. Sch., 2006—. Editl. assoc. Jour. Am. Psychoanalytic Assn., 2002—04, editl. bd. Studies in Gender and Sexuality, 2003—; contbr. articles to profl. jours. Dir. trauma/arts prog. REFUGE, NY, 1999—2003; cons. psychosocial/trauma response in Kosovo Internat. Orgn. Migrations, Geneva, 2000—02; cons. trauma treatment Heartland Alliance Human Rights & Human Needs, 2005—06; cons. staff-stress response UN. Recipient Obie award, 1981, Freud Meml. award, Columbia U. Tchrs. Coll., 1990. Mem.: Am. Psychol. Assn. (Doctoral Dissertation award 1989). Office: Steven J Reisner PhD 225 W 15th St Ste C New York NY 10011 Office Phone: 212-633-8391. Personal E-mail: drreisner@gmail.com.

REISS, BETTI, biological and medical researcher, writer, editor; b. Denver, May 23, 1944; d. Louis A. and Edna Eda R. BS, CUNY, 1965; MS, NYU, 1971, PhD, 1974. Rsch. assoc. Pub. Health Rsch. Inst., NYC, 1974-75; assoc. Am. Health Found., Valhalla, N.Y., 1976-87, 91-92, Westchester Med. Ctr., Valhalla, 1988-90; med. writer, sci. comms. Purdue Frederick Co., Norwalk, Conn., 1992-95. Author: Experimental Colon Carcinogenesis, 1982; author, editor: Advances in Modern Environmental Toxicology, 1985; contbr. articles to profl. jours. NSF fellow 1967. Achievements include development of organ culture system for study of carcinogenesis, cell culture methodology for study of asbestos toxicology and carcinogenicity. Home and Office: 12 Wascussue Ct New Canaan CT 06840

REISS, GEORGE RUSSELL, JR., retired pediatrician; b. Phila., Dec. 25, 1928; s. G. Russell Sr. and Mary Ellen (Brogan) R.; m. Rosemarie Theresa Curcillo, Sept. 19, 1959; children: Mary Elizabeth, Stephanie, G. Russell III, Charlene. BA, LaSalle U., 1953; MD, Temple U., 1957. Diplomate Am. Bd. Pediatrics. Intern Misericordia Hosp., Phila., 1957-58; resident pediatrics St. Christopher Hosp. for Children, Phila., 1958-60; pvt. practice Glenside, Pa., 1960—2010; pediatrician emeritus Abington Meml. Hosp, Pa., 2010—. With USCG, 1946-49. Mem. Montgomery County Med. Soc., Pa. Med. Soc., Am. Acad. Pediatrics, AMA, Am. Assn. Pro-Life Pediatricians. Roman Catholic. Personal E-mail: grcreissjr@aol.com.

REISS, MICHAEL, medical oncologist, researcher; b. Addis Ababa, Ethiopia, Sept. 22, 1950; came to U.S., 1982; s. Willy and Lies (Gerzon) R.; m. Elisabeth Meta Souget, Mar. 15, 1977; children: Kim, Daniel J. Student, U. Amsterdam Med. Sch., The Netherlands, 1968-73; MD, U. Amsterdam, 1976, Yale U. Sch. Medicine. Cert. Bd. Internal Medicine, The Netherlands; fed. licensing exam.; lic. physician Conn. Clk., subintern U. Amsterdam Hosps. and Affiliated Hosps., 1974-76; rsch. assoc. Cen. Lab. Netherlands Red Cross Blood Trans. Lab. for Immunology, U. Amsterdam, 1976-77; intern in internal medicine Med. Coll. Ohio, Toledo, 1977-78; resident in internal medicine U. Hosp. Binnengasthuis, Amsterdam, 1978-82; rotation in med. oncology Netherlands Cancer Inst., Amsterdam, 1980; postdoctoral fellow in med. oncology Yale U. Sch. Medicine, 1982-85, instr. in med. oncology, 1985-87, asst. prof. dept. internal medicine Yale Comp. Cancer Ctr., 1987-91, assoc. prof. dept. internal medicine Yale Comp. Cancer Ctr., 1991—2001; attending physician Yale New Haven Hosp., 1985—2001; med. oncologist Yale Comprehensive Breast Care Ctr., 1989—2001, co-dir., 1992—2001; dir. breast cancer rsch. program Yale Cancer Ctr., 1995—2001; prof., molecular genetics, microbiology & immunology Cancer Inst. NJ, 2001—, prof., internal medicine, 2001—. Chmn. rsch. com. sect. med. oncology Yale U. Sch. Medicine, 1986—, fellowship com. sect. med. oncology, 1986—, cancer edn. com. Yale Comprehensive Cancer Ctr., 1989—, funds and fellowships com., 1991-95; mem. instnl. grant rev. com. Am. Cancer Soc., 1988-94; invited mem. Sec.'s Spl. Conf. on Breast Cancer, NIH, 1993; reviewer Netherlands Cancer Found. Rsch. Grants. Reviewer: Cancer Rsch., Blood, Jour. Cell Physiology, Cancer Comms., European Jour. Cancer Clin. Oncology; contbr. articles to profl. jours. 2d lt. Dutch Army, 1975-77. Recipient Swebilius Cancer Rsch. award, 1985-86; clin. fellow Queen Wilhelmina Cancer Found., Amsterdam, 1982-84; rsch. grantee numerous orgns. Mem. AAAS, Am. Assn. for Cancer Rsch., Am. Soc. Clin. Oncology, Am. Soc. Cell Biology, Am. Fedn. for Clin. Rsch. Avocations: complexity theory, computers, fishing, bicycling, music. Office: Univ Medicine Dentistry NJ-Robert Wood Johnson Med Sch Cancer Inst NJ 195 Little Albany St New Brunswick NJ 08903-2681 Office Phone: 732-235-6031. Office Fax: 732-235-6267. Business E-Mail: michael.reiss@umdnj.edu.

REISS, ROBERT FRANCIS, physician; b. Watertown, NY, Dec. 11, 1938; s. Ernest Paul and Elizabeth Munk (Clark) R.; m. Giovanna Dora Bassi, Mar. 18, 1964; children: Carroll, Christian, Mark, Dylan. AB, Syracuse U., 1959; MD, U. Bologna, Italy, 1965. Diplomate Am. Bd. Pathology (hematology, transfusion medicine). Dir. lab. hematology and blood bank State U. Hosp., Bklyn., 1975-77; asst. prof. pathology SUNY Downstate Med. Ctr., Bklyn., 1975-77; dir. Hudson Valley Blood Svc., Valhalla, NY, 1978-85; assoc. prof. pathology and medicine N.Y. Med. Coll., Valhalla, 1978-88; med. dir. N.Y. Blood Ctr., NYC, 1985-88; dir. lab. hematology and transfusion medicine Columbia-Presbyn. Med. Ctr., NYC, 1988-98; prof. clin. pathology and clin. medicine Columbia U. Coll. Physicians and Surgeons, NYC, 1988—; v.p., chief med. officer N.Y. Blood Ctr., NYC, 1998—2001, 2006—09. Chmn. steering com. Hudson Valley Blood Resources Assn., Valhalla, 1981-85; chief examiner blood banking N.Y.C. Dept. Health, 1980-86, mem. adv. com. on blood banking, 1988-90; mem. instnl. rev. bd. N.Y. Blood Ctr., N.Y.C., 1991-2001. Editor, co-author: Clinical Laboratory Medicine, 1992; contbr. more than 50 articles to med. jours., chpts. to books. Bd. mgrs. camping plus N.Y.C. Mission Soc., 1975-78; scout leader Boy Scouts Am., N.Y.C., 1975-80. Col. U.S. Army, 1966-69, USAR, 1988—2005. Fellow Assn. Clin. Scientists (vice chair sect. on hematology and transfusion medicine, 1999—); mem. Am. Assn. Blood Banks (dist. advisor 1982-88, mem. editl. bd. Ann. Clin. Labs. Sci. 1999—), Coun. Hosp. Blood Bank Dirs. Greater N.Y. (bd. dirs. 1989-98), Am. Soc. Hematology. Avocations: travel, running, stamps. Office Phone: 718-446-2739. Business E-Mail: rfr1@columbia.edu. *

REITAN, RALPH MELDAHL, clinical neuropsychologist, former educator; b. Beresford, SD, Aug. 29, 1922; s. John O. and Anna (Meldahl) Reitan; m. Lucille Ann Kirsch, Feb. 14, 1952 (dec. July 1985); children: Ellen, Jon, Ann, Richard, Erik. BA, Ctrl. YMCA Coll., Chgo., 1944; PhD, U. Chgo., 1950. Cert. in clin. psychology and clin. neuropsychology Am. Bd. Profl. Psychology. Instr. U. Chgo., 1948-51; asst. prof. Roosevelt U., Chgo., 1950-51; from asst. prof. to prof. Ind. U. Med. Sch., Indpls., 1951-70; prof. U. Wash., Seattle, 1970-77, U. Ariz., Tucson, 1977-86; pres. Reitan Neuropsychology Labs., Tucson, 1981—. Cons. NIH, Bethesda, Md., 1960—71, VA, Washington, 1955—84, NASA, Washington, 1964—66. Author: Traumatic Brain Injury, 1985, Neuropsychological Evaluation of Older Children, 1992, The Halstead-Reitan Neuropsychological Test Battery, 1993, Detection of Malingering and Invalid Test Results, 1998, Mild Head Injury: Intellectual, Cognitive and Emotional Consequences, 2000, 15 others; contbr. more than 300 articles to profl. jours. Trustee Easter Seal Rsch. Found., Chgo., 1974—83. With US Army, 1942—43. Fellow: APA, Nat. Acad. Neuropsychology; mem.: Reitan Soc., Coalition Clin. Neuropsychology Practitioners, Am. Acad. Neurology (affiliate), Am. Neurol. Assn. (Lifetime Svc. awards, Father of Field Clin. Neuropsychology). Avocations: walking, birdwatching. Home: 4831 N Via Serenidad Tucson AZ 85718-5715 Office: Reitan Neuropsychology Labs PO Box 66080 Tucson AZ 85728-6080 Personal E-mail: reitanlabs@aol.com.

REITH, MAARTEN EDUARD A., neurochemist; b. Utrecht, Netherlands, Dec. 29, 1946; arrived in US, 1978; s. Jan Franciscus and Katherina (Poelmann) Reith; m. Irma Araujo, Apr. 26, 1980; 1 child, Catherina. BS, U. Utrecht, 1968, MS, 1971, PhD, 1975. Rsch. scientist Rudolf Magnus Inst. Pharmacology, Utrecht, 1971—74; sr. rsch. scientist Inst. Molecular Biology, Utrecht, 1974—78; rsch. scientist Ctr. Neurochemistry, NYC, 1978—80, sr. rsch. scientist, 1980—81; assoc. prof. pharmacology Coll. Medicine U. Ill., Peoria, 1991—95, prof., 1995—2003; prof. psychiatry Sch. Medicine NYU, 2003—. Adj. prof. biol. sci. Ill. State U., Normal, 1996—; consulting mem. study sect. Nat. Inst. Drug Abuse, Rockville, Md., 1987—, NIH, Washington, 1998-; invited panelist Winter Conf. Brain Rsch., 1988, 91, 93-95, 97, 2001. Editor: Neurotransmitter Transporters, 1996, 2d edit., 2002, Cerebral Signal Transduction, From First to Fourth Messengers, 2000, Dopamine and Glutamate in Psychiatric Disorders, 2005; mem. editl. bd. Jour. Neurosci. Methods, 2001—, Neurochem. Rsch., 2004—; editl. cons. European Jour. Pharmacology, 2002-. Grantee, NIH, 1983—. Fellow European Brain Behavior Soc., 1971; mem. Am. Soc. Biochemistry and Molecular Biology, Internat. Soc. Neurochemistry, Soc. Neurosci., Am. Soc. Pharmacol. Exptl. Therapy, NY Acad. Sci. Achievements include first characterization of receptors for cocaine, assessment of allosteric modulation of sodium channels by cocaine congeners, first description of regulation of dopamine transport by arachidonic acid, elucidation of factors determining dopamine interaction with its transporter, discovery of precise binding site for tricyclic and SSRI antidepressant in crystal homologue of monoamine transporters. Office: NYU Sch Medicine Dept Psychiatry Rm MHL-HN518 423 E 23rd St # 15 New York NY 10010-5011 Home Phone: 212-842-0827; Office Phone: 212-263-8267. Business E-Mail: maarten.reith@med.nyu.edu.

REITZ, BRUCE ARNOLD, cardiac surgeon, educator; b. Seattle, Sept. 14, 1944; BS, Stanford U., 1966; MD, Yale U., 1970. Diplomate: Am. Bd. Surgery, Am. Bd. Thoracic Surgery. Intern Johns Hopkins Hosp., Balt., 1970-71, cardiac surgeon-in-charge, 1982-92; resident Stanford U. Hosp., Calif., 1971-72, 74-78; clin. assoc. Nat. Heart Lung Blood Inst., NIH, Bethesda, Md., 1972-74; asst. prof. Stanford U. Sch. Medicine, 1977-81, assoc. prof., 1981-82; prof. surgery Johns Hopkins U. Sch. Medicine, Balt., 1982-92; prof., chmn. Sch Medicine Stanford (Calif.) U., 1992—2005; prof. Stanford U. Sch. Medicine, 2005—10, prof. emeritus, 2010—. Developer heart-lung transplant technique, 1981. Office: Stanford U Sch Medicine Dept Cardiothoracic Surgery Stanford CA 94305-5407 Office Phone: 650-725-4497. Business E-Mail: breitz@stanford.edu.

REITZ, JOANNE BELLAM, health information executive; b. Rochester, NY, Dec. 26, 1950; d. Ernest Wilson and Anne (Hasenhnor) Bellam; 1 child, Stephen Ernest Reitz. AS in Applied Scis., Monroe C.C., Rochester, NY, 1971; BS in Bus. Mgmt. and Econs., Health Care Adminstrn., SUNY, Rochester, 1993. Registered health info. technician, info. adminstr. Med. records technician Genesee Meml. Hosp., Batavia, N.Y., 1971-76, St. Jerome Hosp., Batavia, 1976-79; dir. med. records and health info. mgmt. LeRoy Village Green Nursing Home, NYC, 1979-94; health info. mgr., 1995; cons. health info., med. records Scottsville, N.Y., 1996—. Cons. Livingston County Skilled Nursing Home, Geneseo, N.Y., 1987—,

Norloch Nursing Home, Rochester, 1991—, Brae Loche Nursing Home, Rochester, 1991—, LivingstonCounty Health Related Facility, Mt. Morris, N.Y., 1992—, Rochester Rehab. Ctr., 1995—; instr. Bryant and Stratton Coll. for Med. Programs, Highlands Living Ctr., 1996-97, neonatal ICU U. Rochester, Strong Meml. Hosp., 1997—; dir. health info. mgmt./medical recs. code and compliance officer Anthony L. Jordan Health Corp., 2000-07, Seneca Nat. Indian Dept. Health Manager Health Info., 2007-. Mem. Am. Health Info. Mgmt. Assn., N.Y. State Health Info. Mgmt. Assn., Rochester Health Info. Mgmt. Assn., greater Rochester chpt. Assn. Records Mgrs. and Adminstrs. Home and Office: 949 Scotts Mumford Rd Scottsville NY 14546 Personal E-mail: kesha44@msn.com.

REJENT, MARIAN MAGDALEN, retired pediatrician; b. Toledo, Aug. 12, 1920; d. Casimir Stanley and Magdalen (Szymanowski) R. BS, Mary Manse Coll., 1943; MD, Marquette U., 1946; MPH, U. Mich., 1960. Diplomate Am. Bd. Pediatrics. Intern St. Vincent Med. Ctr., Toledo, 1946-47; resident communicable diseases City Hosp., Cleve., 1947-48; resident pediatrics Childrens Hosp., Akron, Ohio, 1948-50; pvt. practice Toledo, 1950-54; chief div. maternal child health Toledo Bd. Health, 1953-64; dir. pediatrics Maumee Valley Hosp., Toledo, 1964-69; assoc. prof. pediatrics Med. Coll. Ohio, Toledo, 1969-76; med. dir. State Crippled Childrens Program, Columbus, Ohio, 1976-78; attendant pediatrician St. Vincent Med. Ctr., Toledo, 1978-80, 87-99; chief pediatric svcs. Wake County Health Dept., Raleigh, NC, 1980-87; ret. clin. prof. pediatrics Med. Coll. Ohio, 1998; ret., 1999. Exec. com. March of Dimes, 1988-92. Mem. AMA, APHA, Am. Acad. Pediatrics, Am. Med. Women's Assn., Ohio PHA, Ohio State Med. Assn., NW Ohio Pediatric Assn., Acad. Medicine Toledo, Alpha Omega Alpha. Republican. Roman Catholic. Avocations: travel, photography, painting. Home: Woodlands Apt 304 4030 Indian Rd Toledo OH 43606

REKATE, HAROLD LOUIS, neurosurgeon; b. Annapolis, Md., Nov. 1, 1944; m. Mary Warren, Feb. 3, 1967; children: Jason Warren, Sarah Connell Rekate Cahalane. BS, Duke U., 1966; MD, Med. Coll. Va., Richmond, Va., 1970. Diplomate Am. Bd. Neurol. Surgery, Am. Bd. Pediat. Neurol. Surgery; lic. Ohio, Ariz. Intern U. Hospitals Cleve., Ohio, 1970—71, resident, gen. surgery Ohio, 1971—72, resident, neurol. surgery Ohio, 1972, Ohio, 1974—78, asst. neurosurgeon Ohio, 1978—84, dir., pediat. neurosurgery Ohio, 1978—84; asst. prof. neurosurgery Case Western Res. U. Sch. Medicine, Cleve., 1978-84, asst. prof. surgery, pediatrics, 1979—84; chief pediat. neurosurgery Barrow Neurol. Inst., Phoenix, 1985—, chmn., pediatric neurosciences, 2001—, dir., hypothalamic hamartoma program; chief, pediatric neurosurgery St. Joseph's Hosp. and Med. Ctr., Ariz.; chief, sect. neurosurgery Phoenix Children's Hosp., 1987—91. Mem. academic adv. coun., Case Western Reserve U. Sch. Medicine, 1980-84, chmn. search com. for chief divsn. pediat. neurology, 1981; mem. child protection team, U. Hospitals Cleve., 1978-84, Birth Defects Ctr., 1978-84, dir. Child's Brain Ctr., 1980-84; mem.trauma and critical care task force, Rainbow Babies and Children's Hosp., 1980-82, mem. planning and priorities bd., 1982-84; clin. prof. dept. surgery, sect. neurosurgery U. Ariz. Sch. Medicine, Tucson, 1985-; adj. assoc. prof. sys. engring. 1985-91; hosp. affiliation Phoenix Children's Hosp., 1985-2001; sec.-treas., Children's Rehabilitative Svcs. IPA, 1992, mem. pediat. adv. task force, Children's Health Ctr., St. Joseph's Hosp. and Med. Ctr., Phoenix, Ariz., 1992; bd. dirs. Mercy Healthcare Ariz. 1997-2001; invited lectr. in field. Contbr. several articles to profl. jours.; mem. editl. bd. Clin. Neurosurgery, 1984—87, Pediatric Neurosurgery, Child's Nervous System and Jour. Neurosurgery, Pediatrics, guest editor Neurosurgical Focus-Occipital Plagiocephaly, 1997, Neurosurgical Focus-Hydrocephalus, 2007, ad hoc reviewer Neurology, Neurosurgery, & Cancer. Maj., Med. Corps US Army, 1972—74, Fort Benning, Ga. Recipient award for outstanding edn. and treatment of Spina Bifida, Spina Bifida Assn. So. Ariz., 1986—88, Pudenz award for Excellence in Rsch. in Cerebrospinal Fluid Physiology, 1992, Anthony J. Raimondi, MD Medalist, Outstanding Contbn. in Pediat. Neurology-Oncology, 1999. Mem.: Cleve. Acad. Medicine Trauma Com., Acad. Medicine Cleve., Ohio State Neurosurgical Soc., Northeast Ohio Neurosurgical Soc., European Soc. Pediat. Neurosurgery (permanent vis. faculty 1988—), World Fedn. Neurosurgical Societies (mem. scientific program com., World Congress Neurosurgery 1999), Am. Soc. Pediatric Neurosurgeons (treas. 1996—98, sec. 1998—2000, pres.-elect 1999—2000, pres. 2000), Internat. Soc. Pediat. Neurosurgery (mem. by-laws com. 1986, mem. com. edn. 1986—87, mem. liaison com., rep. N.Am. 1987, chmn., scientific program com. 1994—98, pres. 1999—2000), Congress Neurol. Surgeons (chmn., video libr. com. 1982, chmn., sergeant-at-arms com. 1983, chmn., scientific session IV 1984, chmn., spl. courses 1985), Am. Assn. Neurol. Surgeons (chmn. ad hoc com. joint status pediat. sect. 1985—88, chmn., membership com. pediat. sect. 1986—88, chmn. by-laws com. 1988—90, sec., pediat. sect. 1991—94), Pediat. Oncology Group (edn. com. mem. 1997—2001). Office: Barrow Neurol Inst Barrow Neurol Assocs 500 W Thomas Rd Ste 400 Phoenix AZ 85013 Office Phone: 602-406-3632. Office Fax: 602-406-6126. Business E-Mail: Harold.rekate@chw.edu.

RELKIN, NORMAN R., neurologist, educator; MS, Yeshiva U., 1984, MD, PhD, Yeshiva U., 1987. Diplomate Am. Bd. Neurology, lic. NY. Resident neurology NY Hosp., 1988—91, fellow behavioral neurology, 1991—92; assoc. prof. neurology Cornell Univ.; physician NY Presbyn. Hosp., 1987—, dir. cornell med. ctr., 1993—. Office: New York- Presbyterian Hospital 428 E 72nd St Ste 500 New York NY 10021 Office Phone: 212-746-2441. Office Fax: 212-746-5584.

RELL, M. JODI (MARY JODI RELL), former Governor of Connecticut; b. Norfolk, Va., June 16, 1946; m. Lou Rell, 1967; children: Meredith, Michael. Attended, Old Dominion U., Norfolk, Western Conn. State U.; LLD (hon.), U. Hartford, 2001; D (hon.), U. New Haven, 2004. Mem. Dist. 107, dep. minority leader Conn. House of Reps., Brookfield, 1985—95; lt. gov. State of Conn., 1995—2004, gov., 2004—11. Appt. chair Hartford Econ. Devel. Adv. Group, 1998. Trustee YMCA Western Conn.; past vice chmn. Brookfield Rep. Town Com. Recipient Impact award, Conn. Tech. Coun., 2001, Nathan Davis award for outstanding govt. svc., AMA, 2008, Leadership award, Nat. Order Women Legislators (NOWL), First Kids 2001 Policy Leadership award, Conn. Voices for Children, Arnold Markle Pub. Svc. award; named a Melvin Jones fellow, Lions Club Internat. Found., 2003. Mem.: Women Execs. in State Govt., Nat. Order Women Legislators (past v.p. & nat. pres.), Brookfield Bus. & Profl. Women's Club, Brookfield Rep. Women's Club (past pres.). Republican. Office Fax: 860-524-7395. E-mail: Governor.Rell@po.state.ct.us. *

RELLE, ATTILA TIBOR, dentist, geriatrics services professional; b. Columbus, Ohio, Aug. 31, 1959; s. Ferenc Matyas and Trudi (Tubach) Relle; m. Kim Ann McDonald, Apr. 26, 1986; 1 child, Ilona. DDS, Case We. Res. U., 1985; BS, Ohio State U., 1985, postgrad., 1985—88, postgrad., 1993, Wright State U. Sch. Medicine, 1988-93, NYU, 2003—04; DMD, Case We. Reserve U., 2004—. Dentist Mobile Care Corp., Dublin, Ohio, 1985; assoc. dentist Richard P. Deeds, DDS and Assocs., Columbus, 1985-86; dentist Family Dental and Denture Ctr. II, Dayton, Ohio, 1986-87; gen. dentist Midwest Mobile Dental Care, Inc., Hamilton, Ohio, 1988-91, Mobile Dental Care, Inc., Hamilton, Ohio, 1991-92; gen. dentist, owner Attila T. Relle, DDS & Assocs., Columbus, 1985—2007, Hilliard, 1995—, Attila T. Relle, DMD & Assocs., Upper Arlington, Ohio, 2004—; dentist Jerry Owens, D.D.S. and Assocs., Lancaster, Ohio, 1989-92; state dir. Ohio Residentcare dental geriatric program Meridian Svc. Care Corp. of Ohio, 1992-94, gen. dentist, 1992-94; dentist Mercy Meml. Hosp., 2002—, Meml. Hosp. of Union County, 2003—06. Co-chmn. Ohio Dental Careers Day, Columbus, 1980—81; regional dir. Midwest Mobile Dental Care, Inc., 1988—89; mem. adv. com. N.Am. Health Corp., 1989—92; sci. judge Ohio Acad. Sci., Delaware, 1985—92. Mem. Columbus Maennerchor, 1986—88, Hungarian Cultural Assn., Hungarian Reformed Ch., 1999—; benefactor Columbus Zoo and Aquarium, 1998—2000, mem., 1996—, Franklin Count Farm Bur., 1999—, Brookwood Presbyn. Ch., 1974—. Recipient Americas Top Dentist award, Consumers Rsch. Coun. America, 2010. Mem.: ADA, AMA, Am. Acad. Implant Dentistry, Hoverclub of Am., Inc., U.S. Figure Skating Assn., Columbus Dental Soc., Ohio Dental Assn., Am. Student Dental Assn., U.S. Tennis Assn. (Midwest/Ohio Valley), Ohio State U. Alumni Assn. (life), Hungarian Assn. Magyar Tarsasag Hungarian Congress Arpad Acad., Alumni Case Western Res. Univ. Sch. Dentistry, Civitan Internat. (pres. Ea. Columbus club 1986—87). Presbyterian. Avocations: tennis, skiing, boating, hovercraft, ice skating. Home and Office: Attila T Relle DMD & Assocs 2818 Swansea Rd Upper Arlington OH 43221-1754 Office: Ste 100 4984A Scioto Darby Rd Hilliard OH 43026-1550 Office Phone: 614-270-2389. Business E-Mail: relle.core@core.com.

RELLING, MARY V., pharmaceutical researcher, professor; BS, U. Ariz. Coll. Pharmacy, Tucson, 1982; PharmD, U. Utah Coll. Pharmacy, Salt Lake City, 1985. Lic. Nat. Assn. Boards Pharmacy, cert. in pharmacotherapy. Pharmacist, internal medicine/coronary care unit Vets. Adminstrn. Med. Ctr., Tuscon, 1982—83; resident clin. pharmacy U. Utah Health Scis. Ctr., 1983—85; rsch. fellowship pharm. divsn. St. Jude Children's Rsch. Hosp., Memphis, 1985—87; rsch. fellowship dept. pharmacology U. Basel, Switzerland, 1987—88; asst. prof. U. Tenn. Coll. Pharmacy, Memphis, 1988—94, assoc. prof. dept. clin. pharmacy & pharm scis., 1994—99, prof. dept. clin. pharmacy & pharm scis., 1999—. Asst. mem. pharm. dept. St. Jude Children's Rsch. Hosp., 1988—95, assoc. mem., 1995—2001, mem., 2001—, chair pharm. dept., 2003—, dir. pharmacokinetics shared resource St. Jude Children's Rsch. Hosp. Cancer Ctr., 1990—2006; Gerhard Levy disting. lectr. SUNY Buffalo, 2002; mem. clin. pharmacology subcom. FDA Ctr. Drug Evaluation & Rsch., 2002 ; prof. dept. pediat. U. Tenn., 2002—. Mem. editl. bd. Pharmacotherapy, 1993—2007, Clin. Pharmacology & Therapeutics, 1996—2008, Leukemia, 1999—, Pharmacogenetics, 2001—, Pharm. Rsch., 2001—, Jour. Clin. Oncology, 2004—06, Blood, 2004—09; contbr. articles to profl. jours. Recipient Roland T. Lakey award, Wayne State U., Detroit, 2006, Jack R. Cole Disting. Alumnus award, U. Ariz., 2007. Mem.: Am. Soc. Human Genetics, Am. Soc. Hematology, Am. Soc. Clin. Oncology (Pediatric Oncology award 2009), Am. Assn. Cancer Rsch., Am. Coll. Clin. Pharmacy (Russell R. Miller award 2002), Am. Soc. Clin. Pharmacology & Therapeutics (bd. dirs. 1999—2002, v.p. 2000—01, Leon I. Goldberg Young Investigator award 1998), Am. Assn. Colleges of Pharmacy. Office: St Jude Childrens Rsch Hosp Pharm Dept 262 Danny Thomas Pl MS 313 Memphis TN 38105 Office Phone: 901-595-3663. Office Fax: 901-595-8869. E-mail: mary.relling@stjude.org. *

RELMAN, ARNOLD SEYMOUR, physician, editor, educator; b. NYC, June 17, 1923; s. Simon and Rose (Mallach) Relman; m. Harriet Morse Vitkin, June 26, 1953; children: David Arnold, John Peter, Margaret Rose. AB, Cornell U., 1943; MD, Columbia U., 1946; LLD (hon.), U. Pa.; ScD (hon.), Med. Coll. Wis., Union U., Med. Coll. Ohio, CUNY; DMSc (hon.), Brown U.; DLH (hon.), SUNY; LittD (hon.), Temple U. Diplomate Am. Bd. Internal Medicine. House officer New Haven Hosp., Yale, 1946—49; NRC fellow Evans Meml., Mass. Meml. hosps., 1949—50; practice medicine, specializing in internal medicine Boston, 1950—68, Phila., 1968—77; asst. prof., prof. medicine Boston U. Sch. Medicine, 1950—68; dir. Boston U. Med. Services, Boston City Hosp., 1967—68; prof. medicine, chmn. dept. medicine U. Pa.; chief med. services Hosp. of U. Pa., 1968—77; editor New Eng. Jour. Medicine, Boston, 1977—91, editor emeritus, 1991—; sr. physician Brigham and Women's Hosp., Boston, 1977—; prof. medicine and social medicine Harvard Med. Sch., 1977—93, prof. medicine and social medicine emeritus, 1993—95, prof. emeritus, 1995—. Cons. NIH, USPHS; mem. bd. registration in medicine Commonwealth of Mass., 1995—2001. Author: A Second Opinion, 2007; editor: Jour. Clin. Investigation, 1962—67; editor: (with F.J. Ingelfinger and M. Finland) Controversy in Internal Medicine, Vol. 1, 1966, Controversy in Internal Medicine, Vol. 2, 1974; contbr. articles to profl. jours. Trustee Columbia U., 1990—96; bd. dirs. Hastings Ctr., 1981—83. Recipient Columbia Alumni Gold medal, 1980, Disting. Svc. award, Am. Coll. Cardiology, 1987, McGovern award, Cosmos Club Washington, 1991, John Peters award, Am. Soc. Nephrology, 1992, George Polk award in journalism, 2003. Master: ACP (John Phillips medal 1985); fellow: Am. Acad. Arts and Scis.; mem.: AMA, Am. Fedn. Clin. Rsch. (past pres.), Am. Soc. Clin. Investigation (past pres.), Inst. of Medicine of NAS (coun. 1979—82), Mass. Med. Soc., Am. Physiol. Soc., Assn. Am. Physicians (coun., pres. 1983—84, Kober medal 1993), Alpha Omega Alpha, Phi Beta Kappa (senator 1991—98). Office: Brigham and Women's Hosp Dept Medicine 181 Longwood Ave Fl 5 Boston MA 02115-5804

REMAKUS, BERNARD LEO, physician, medical educator, writer, medical journalist; b. Wilkes-Barre, Pa., Oct. 28, 1948; s. Leo W. and Adel Bertha (Macho) R.; m. Charlotte M. Amorebello, Aug. 17, 1974; children: Christopher B., Alexandra T., Matthew B. BS, King's Coll., 1970; MEd, E. Stroudsburg State Coll., 1972; MD, Temple U., 1978. Diplomate Nat. Bd. Med. Examiners, Am. Bd. Internal Medicine. Resident Abington Meml. Hosp., 1978-81; pvt. practice Hallstead, Pa., 1981—; instr. SUNY, Binghamton, N.Y., 1981—; clin. asst. prof. Temple U. Sch. Medicine, 2004—. Chief of staff, dir. emergency medicine, chmn. ethics com. Barnes-Kasson County Hosp., Susquehanna, Pa.; med. journalist Internal Medicine World Report, Old Bridge, N.J., 1991—; lectr. Discovery Internat., Deerfield, Ill., 1994—; spkr. in field. Author: The Malpractice Epidemic, 1990, 2nd edit. 2004, Cassidy's Solution, 1995, Medicine from the Heart, 2002, Medicine Between the Lines, 2004, (novel) Mia, 2011, (screenplay), 2008; mem. editl. adv. panel Internal Medicine World Report, 1998—; pub. 221 East Pub.; contbr. over 200 articles to profl. jours. Recipient Physicians Recognition award, AMA, 1981, 1984, 1987, 1990, 1993, 1996, 1999, 2002, 2005, 2008, 2011, SUNY Health Sci. Ctr. Tchg. award, 1997, Am.'s Top Physicians award, 2003—. Roman Catholic. Office: Rd 2 PO Box 367 Hallstead PA 18822-0367 Office Phone: 570-879-4800.

REMBAR, JAMES CARLSON, psychologist; b. NYC, May 4, 1949; s. Charles Isaiah and Billie Ann (Olsson) R.; m. Jill Bailin, June 4, 1988; 1 child, Lilianna. BA, Sarah Lawrence Coll., 1972; MA, U. Mich., 1976, PhD, 1978. Lic. psychologist, psychoanalyst, N.Y. Clin. psychologist U. Mich. Med. Ctr., Ann Arbor, 1978-80; instr. psychology in psychiatry N.Y. Hosp. Cornell U. Med. Coll., White Plains, 1980-84, clin. asst. prof., 1984—2002, coord. child and adolescent psychology Westchester div., 1982-87; pvt. practice clin. psychologist Irvington, White Plains, NY, 1981—. Mem. faculty, supervisor Westchester Ctr. for Study of Psychoanalysis and Psychotherapy, 1989—, dir. continuing edn., 1992-95, dir. child and adolescent psychotherapy tng. program, 1998-2004, dir. curriculum. 2007—; cons. Andrus Children's Home, Yonkers, N.Y., 1987-97. Contbr. articles to profl. jours., chpt. in book. Mem. N.Y. State Psychol. Assn., Westchester County Psychol. Assn., Psychoanalytic Assn. Westchester Ctr. Avocations: tennis, music. Office: 510 N Broadway White Plains NY 10603-3217 Home: 91 Main St Dobbs Ferry NY 10522 Office Phone: 914-949-1980. Personal E-mail: jsixo@aol.com.

REMBIELAK, AGATA IZABELA, radiation oncologist, medical physicist, researcher; b. Zabrze, Poland, Oct. 18, 1972; d. Piotr Eugeniusz and Grazyna Danuta Rembielak; m. Zbigniew Tur, Aug. 22, 2005; 1 child, Paula Alexandra Tur. MD, Silesian Med. Acad., 1997; BSc in Med. Phys., Silesian U., 1998; PhD, Silesian Med. Acad., 2003; MD, Manchester U., 2010. Bd. cert. radiation oncologist Poland, 2007. Staff physician Ctr. Oncology Inst., Gliwice, Poland, 2002—07; staff physician academic dept. radiation oncology U. Manchester, England, 2007—09; staff physician clin. oncology dept. Christie Hosp., Manchester, 2009—. Author: HDR Brachytherapy; contbr. articles to various med. pubs. Mem.: Polish Soc. Radiation Oncology (assoc.), Polish Oncological Assn. (assoc.), European Soc. Therapeutic Radiology and Oncology (assoc.). Office: Christie at Oldham Rochdale Rd Oldham OL1 2JH England

REMBOS, STEVEN, podiatrist; Cert. Am. Bd. Foot and Ankle Surgery, Endoscopic Techniques Foot and Ankle, Advanced Ankle Arthroscopy Techniques, Holmium LASER Ankle Arthroscopy Technique. Podiatric med. dir. Ambulatory Surg. Ctr; podiatrist Hosp Plaza Foot and Ankle Inst., 1988—. Lectr. on foot and ankle pathologies; tchr. of advanced podiatric surg. techniques of foot and ankle pathologies. Mem. Physicians Adv. Bd., Washington. Fellow: Internat. Soc. Podiatric Laser Surgeons, Am. Coll. Foot and Ankle Surgeons; mem.: Ill. Podiatric Med. Assn., Am. Podiatric Med. Assn. Office: Hosp Plz Foot and Ankle Inst Ste 103 3800 Highland Ave Downers Grove IL 60515 E-mail: drrembos@thefootspecialists.com.

REMBUSCH, JOSEPH JOHN, retired psychologist, management consulting executive; b. Joliet, Ill., June 29, 1939; s. Joseph Earl and Agnes Cecilia (Heinen) R. AA, Joliet Jr. Coll., 1959; BS in Psychology, U. Ill., 1962; MA in Tchg., Rockford Coll., Ill., 1970; postgrad., No. Ill. U., DeKalb, 1961—66, postgrad., 1970—73; attending, No. Ill. U., DeKalb, 2007—10; postgrad., Western Colo. U., Grand Junction, 1973—75; MLA in Ancient Asian Studies, U. Chgo., 2005; MA in Am. History, NI U. Dekalb, 2010. Registered psychologist, Ill. Sci. tchr. Crete-Monee Sch. Dist., Crete, Ill., 1963-64; clin. caseworker Ill. State Sch. Boys, St. Charles, 1964-65; dir. guidance Hiawatha Unit Dist. #426, Kirkland, Ill., 1966-69; registrar Kishwaukee Community Coll., Malta, Ill., 1969-81; spl. rep., dist. mgr., regional mgr. George S. May Internat., Park Ridge, Ill., 1982-86, 89-01, divisional sales mgr., 1986-89, coord. client svcs., 2001—02, maj. account exec., 2002—03; ret., 2003. Pvt. practice psychology DeKalb, Ill., 1971-80; cons. psychologist Ill. Div. Vocat. Rehab., DeKalb, 1971-79, lectr., Col. Elmer Ellsworth & Abraham Lincoln. Recipient Advisor of Yr. award, Delta Upsilon Internat. Fraternity, 2010. Mem. Illini Great Dane Club, Delta Upsilon (chpt. advisor, Northern Ill. U., Internat. Advisor. of Yr., 2010), Phi Delta Kappa. Republican. Roman Catholic. Home: 1616 Margaret Ln Dekalb IL 60115

REMICK, SCOT CLIFTON, oncologist, clinical investigator, educator; b. New Rochelle, NY, Oct. 16, 1956; s. Robert Merrick and Marjorie Allis (Stamm) R. BA, SUNY, Oswego, 1978; MD, N.Y. Med. Coll., Valhalla, 1982. Resident Johns Hopkins Hosp., Balt., 1982-85; fellow Clin. Cancer Ctr. U. Wis. Clin. Cancer Ctr., Madison, 1985-88; assoc. prof. Dept. Medicine Albany (N.Y.) Med. Coll., 1988-96; with Case Western Res. U., Cleve., 1996—, assoc. prof. dept. medicine, dir. devel. therapeutics divsn. hematology/oncology, prof. medicine. Prin. investigator numerous oncology and HIV/AIDS clin. trials, Albany, 1988—, dir., prof. Medicine Mary Babb Randolph Cancer Ctr., W.Va. U. Sch. Medicine, 07-. Contbr. over 130 papers, textbook chpts. and abstracts. Active Am. Cancer Soc. (Career Devel. award 1991), Albany. Fellow Am. Coll. Physicians; mem. Am. Assn. for Cancer Rsch., Am. Soc. Clin. Oncology, Alpha Omega Alpha. Office: West Virginia Unviersity MBR Cancer Ctr 1801 RCB HSC South PO Box 9300 Morgantown WV 26506 Business E-Mail: sremick@hsc.wvu.edu.

REMKUS, CONNIE ELAINE, nutritional consultant; d. Charles Edward and Phyllis Mary Remkus. BSBA in Acctg., San Francisco State U., 1986. Registered nutritional cons. Sch. Nutritional Sci., San Jose, Calif. Flight attendant United Air Lines, Chgo., 1966—2002; self-employed property and investment mgr. Chgo., 1973—2003; tax preparer David Nitz & Assocs., San Mateo, Calif., 1975; nutritional cons., ind. distbr. Diamite Corp., San Carlos, Calif., 1988—95; field v.p. Symmetry Direct, Chgo., 1995—. Mem. Clippeo Wings Chgo. Chapt., 2010—, South Loop Neighbors, Chgo., 2001—05; vol. SPCA, San Mateo, 1984—87. Recipient United Airlines award of Merit, 1987. Mem.: Clipped Wings Chgo., Airline Flight Attendants Union (membership chair grievance com. 1967—70), Bus. Networking Internat. (sec. 2001—03, asst. dir., amb. 2002—03). Avocations: travel, real estate, health and wellness, dance. Personal E-mail: remkus@att.net.

REMLEY, KAREN, state agency administrator, public health service officer; married. MD, U. Mo., Kansas City, 1980; MBA Health Services Mgmt. Cert., Duke U., Durham. Cert. Am. Bd. Med. Examiners, Am Bd. Pediat. and Pediatric Emergency Medicine. Attending physician Children's Hosp. of the King's Daughters, Norfolk, Va.; cmty. faculty, sch. pub. health Eastern Va. Med. Sch., asst. prof. pediat.; assoc. med. dir. Trigon, 1998—2000; chief med. officer Operation Smile, Inc., 2000—01; CEO Physicians for Peace, 2001—03; med. dir. external quality Anthem Blue Cross Blue Shield, Va., 2004—06; v.p. med. affairs Sentara Leigh Hosp., Norfolk, 2006—08; commr. Va. Dept. Health, 2008—. At-large bd. mem. Virginians Improving Patient Care and Safety. Mem.: Am. Acad. Pediat. Office: Va Dept Health 109 Governor St PO Box 2448 Richmond VA 23218-2448

REMMES, KARL MARIA UDO, radiologist, photographer; b. Tübingen, Germany, July 2, 1954; s. Karl August and Trude (Köppeler) R.; m. Alexandra Maria Magdalena Nix, Aug. 18, 1988; 1 child, Undine Carla Alexandra. Grad., U. Tübingen, Germany, 1986, PhD cum laude, 1986. With Saaletalklinik, Neustadt, Germany, 1986-87; asst. St. Vinzenz, Düsseldorf, Germany, 1988-90, Bethesda, Duisburg, Germany, 1990-93; freelancer several radiol. insts., Germany, 1994. Cons. practice in radiology and nuc. medicine, Hansa. Contbr. articles to profl. jours. Fellow: European Soc. Radiology, Royal Soc. Arts, Royal Photog. Soc. (sr. imaging scientist), Royal Soc. Medicine; mem.: Radiological Soc. North America. Avocations: art, music. Office Phone: 49.173.2642678. Personal E-mail: udo@remmes.com. Business E-Mail: u.remmes@mac.com.

REMZI, FEZA H., colon and rectal surgeon, department chairman; MD, Hacettepe U., Turkey, 1989. Diplomate Am. Bd. Surgery, 2006, Am. Bd. Colon and Rectal Surgery, 2007. Intern Cleve. Clinic, Ohio, 1991, resident in surgery, 1996, fellow in colorectal surgery, 1997, surgeon, dir. Ctr. for Internat. Med. Edn., chmn. colorectal surgery dept. Co-author: Transmural inflammation is not pathognomonic for Crohn's disease of the pouch, 2011, Gender of the patient may influence perioperative and long term complications after IPAA, 2011, Prevalence and Clinical Implications of Positive Serum Anti-Microsomal Antibodies in Symptomatic Patients with Ileal Pouches, 2011, Elevated Serum IgG4 is Associated with Chronic Antibiotic-Refractory Pouchitis, 2011, Pelvic abscess associated with anastomotic leak in patients with ileal pouch-anal anastomosis (IPAA): transanastomotic or CT-guided drainage?, 2011, various others. Named one of Best Doctors, Cleve. Mag., 2007—, numerous others. Fellow: Annual Nat. Surgical Congress (hon.); mem.: Am. Gastroenterology Assn., Am. Soc. of Colon and Rectal Surgeons, ACS. Office: Cleveland Clinic 9500 Euclid Ave Cleveland OH 44195 Office Phone: 216-444-7000.

REN, KAWAGUCHI, cardiologist, director; b. Mito, Ibaraki, Japan, Feb. 10, 1971; s. Masahiro and Etsuko Kawaguchi; m. Kawaguchi Yukie, May 9, 1999. MD, Teikyo U. Medicine, Tokyo, 1995. Dir. cardiology Gunma Prefectural Cardiovasc. Ctr., Maebashi, Japan, 2008—. Fellow: Japanese Soc. Interventional Cardiology (sr.), Soc. Interventional Cardiology (sr.). Office: Gunma Prefectural Cardiovasc Ctr 3-12 Kameizumi-machi Maebashi 371-0004 Japan Office Fax: 81-27-269-1492.

REN, XIAOPING, medical researcher; b. Harbin, July 27, 1961; MD, Harbin Med. U., 1984. Asst. prof. U. Cin., 2005—. Microsurgeon Harbin Fist Hosp. & U. Louisville, 1984—2000. Mem.: Am. Heart Assn., Am. Assn. Hand Surgery. Achievements include a clinical feasible protocol to induce tolerance to limb allografts using mixed allogeneic chimerism. Avocations: swimming, bicycling, travel. Home: 7963 Hedgewood Cir Mason OH 45040 E-mail: renxg@uc.edu.

REN, XING JIAN, physician; b. Shanghai, June 27, 1961; s. Yun Feng Ren and Xin Yi Zhang; m. Bei Xie, June 27, 1990; 1 child, Oriana Leigh. MD, Shanghai First Med. Coll., 1984. Diplomate internal medicine and geriatric medicine Am. Bd. Internal Medicine. Resident in surgery Shanghai Ruhui Hosp., China, 1984-85; resident Ft. Wayne (Ind.) Med. Edn. Program, 1993-94; resident, intern in medicine Loyola U. of Chgo., Maywood, Ill., 1994-97; fellow in medicine Harvard Med. Sch., Boston, 1997-99; staff physician Scripps Clinic Found., La Jolla, Calif., 1999—; asst. clin. prof. medicine U. Calif. Sch. Medicine, 2003—, assoc. clin prof., 2009—. Bd. dirs. Scripps Clinic Med. Group, 2006—09, asst. v.p., 2007—09. Co-author: Virology, 1986; contbr. articles to profl. jours. Fellow Harvard Med. Sch., 1998; recipient 1st prize Nat. Med. Student Competition for Knowledge of Med. Lit., 1983, grad. student scholarship U. N.C., Chapel Hill, scholarship Carolina Biotechnolgoy Ctr., others. Fellow ACP; mem. AMA, Mass. Med. Soc., Am. Geriatrics Soc., Fell. Am. Coll. Physician. Home Phone: 858-794-9284; Office Phone: 619-245-2830. Business E-Mail: ren.xing@scrippshealth.org.

RENARD, RONALD LEE, allergist; b. Chgo., July 31, 1949; s. Robert James and Dorothy Mae (Fruik) R.; m. Maureen Ann Gilmore, Aug. 5, 1972 (div. Mar. 1992); children: Jeffrey, Stephen, Justin, Leigh Ellen; m. Catherine L. Walker, Apr. 1, 1992; children: Morgan, Michal, Luke. Degrees in Lang., U. de Montepellier, France, 1970; BS in French, U. San Francisco, 1971; MD, Creighton U., 1976. Dir. med. ICU, lt. U.S. Army Hosp., Ft. Leonard Wood, Md., 1980-81; dir. respiratory therapy, asst. chief allergy svc. Walter Reed Med. Ctr., Washington, 1981-84; staff allergist Chico (Calif.) Med. Group, 1984-86; allergist pvt. practice Redding, Calif., 1986—. Dir. ACLS program Enloe Hosp., Chico, 1988-91; bd. dirs. Am. Lung Assn. Calif., 1989-91, med. dir. asthma camp, Chico, Redding, 1986-95; asst. prof. medicine USPHS, Bethesda, Md., 1982-84; asst. prof. family medicine U. Calif. Davis Med. Sch., Redding, 1990-94; Shasta County Planning Commr., 1994-95. Contbr. articles to profl. jours. Fellow Am. Acad. Allergy and Immunology, Am. Coll. Allergists; mem. Assn. Mil. Allergists, Calif. Thoracic Soc., Alpha Omega Alpha. Republican. Roman Catholic. Avocations: hunting, biking. Office: 1505 Victor Ave Redding CA 96003 Office Fax: 530-246-8856. Personal E-mail: rrenard@juno.com.

RENNER, ANDREW IHOR, surgeon; b. Buenos Aires, Aug. 1, 1951; came to U.S., 1956; s. Vladimir and Emelia R.; m. Cristina Sasyk, Apr. 17, 1982. MD, Albert Einstein Coll. Medicine, 1975. Diplomate Am. Bd. Surgery. Pvt. practice gen. surgery, Burbank, Calif.; chief of staff Providence-St. Joseph Med. Ctr., 2005, 2006; chief of quality assurance Providence St. Joseph Hosp., 2007—08; chief of surgery Encino Hosp, 2009—11. Chmn. dept. surgery St. Joseph Hosp., Burbank, 1995-97, vice chief of staff Providence St. Joseph Med. Ctr., Burbank, 2003-04, chief of staff, 2005-06. Fellow ACS, Internat. Coll. Surgeons; mem. Am. Soc. Gen. Surgeons, L.A. Surg. Soc. Office: 2701 W Alameda Ave Ste 300 Burbank CA 91505-4408 Office Phone: 818-843-1492. Office Fax: 818-843-5283. *

RENNERT, OWEN MURRAY, pediatrician, geneticist, educator; b. NYC, Aug. 8, 1938; s. David Rennert and Frieda (Weinsteiner) Sommer; m. Sandra Serota, Mar. 22, 1964; children: Laura, Rachel, Ian. BS, BA, U. Chgo., 1957, MD, 1961, MS in Biochemistry, 1963. Diplomate Am. Bd. Pediatrics, Am. Bd. Genetics, Am. Bd. Med. Genetics. Assoc. prof. pediatrics U. Fla. Coll. Medicine, Gainesville, 1968—70, assoc. prof. biochemistry, 1970—71, head instl. divsn. genetics, endocrinology and metabolism, 1970—78, prof. pediatrics, biochemistry and neurosci., 1971-78; prof. biochemistry, prof. and head dept. pediatrics U. Okla., Oklahoma City, 1977-88; chief pediatrics svc. and head genetics, sect. endocrinology and metabolism Okla. Children's Mem. Hosp., Oklahoma City, 1977-88; prof., chmn. dept. pediatrics Georgetown U. Sch. Medicine, Washington, 1988-98, prof. dept. biochemistry and molecular biology, 1995—98, prof. emeritus, 1998—2000; spl. asst. to dir. ctr. rsch. mothers and children Nat. Inst. Child Health Human Devel., NIH, Bethesda, Md., 1998—2000, dir. Ctr. Rsch. Mothers and Children, 2000, sci. dir. divsn. intramural rsch., 2000—. Co-author: Metabolism of Trace Metals in Man: Developmental Biology and Genetic Implications (2 vols.), 1984; contbr. articles to profl. jours. Bd. dirs. Children's Med. Rsch., Oklahoma City, 1984-88. Served to sr. surgeon USPHS, 1964-66. Named Clin. Scientist of Yr., Am. Assn. Clin. Scientists, 1978. Mem. Am. Pediatric Soc., Am. Acad. Pediatrics, Soc. Pediatric Research, Am. Coll. Clin. Nutrition, Biochem. Soc., Am. Soc. Molecular Biology and Biochemistry, Am. Coll. Med. Genetics, Am. Soc. Human Genetics. Office: NICHD/NIH Divsn Intramural Rsch 31 Center Dr Bldg 31 Rm 2A46 Bethesda MD 20892-2425 Home Phone: 301-299-6174; Office Phone: 301-594-5984. Business E-Mail: rennerto@mail.nih.gov.

RENNO, TOUFIC, medical researcher, director; b. Lebanon, Jan. 31, 1960; s. Antoine Renno and Najla Henoud; m. Brigitte Henoud, July 27, 1985; 1 child, Tatiana. PhD, U. McGill, Montreal, Canada, 1993. Postdoc. fellow Ludwig Inst. Cancer Rsch., Lausanne, Switzerland, 1994—98; staff scientist Centre d'Immunologie Pierre Fabre, Saint-Julien, France, 1998—2001; sr. scientist Schering-Plough Rsch. Inst., Dardilly, France, 2001—04; rsch. dir. Inst. Nat. de la Sante et de la Recherche Medicale, Lyon, France; founder and CSO GenSilence, Lyon, 2004—. Cons., rheumatoid arthritis rsch. Hôpital Rangeil, Toulouse, France. Centennial fellowship, Med. Rsch. Coun. Can., 1995—98, BQR grant, U. Lyon, 2005—06, grant, Ligue Nationale Contre le Cancer, 2006—08, Agence Nat. de Recherche, 2007—, Canceropole Rhone Alpes, 2008—. Achievements include patents for cancer therapy. Office: CNRS UMR5201 Ctr Leon Berard 28 rue Laennec Lyon 69373 France Office Fax: 33469166660, 33 472 543037. Business E-Mail: renno@lyon.fnclcc.fr.

RENOUX, ANDRÉ, retired physicist researcher; b. Courbevoie, France, Oct. 27, 1937; s. Robert and Jeanne (Noël) R.; divorced; children: Vincent, Nathalie. Lic. Sci., Faculty Scis. Paris, 1958, D 3d cycle, 1961, D, 1965. Asst. Faculty Scis., Paris, 1959—61, master asst., 1961—66; prof. faculty scis. U. Tunis, Tunisia, 1966—69, U. Brest, France, 1969—80; prof. U. Paris, 1980—2003, dir. lab. phys. aérosols et transfert des contaminations, 1980—2008, dir. DESS (3d cycle) sci. des aerosols-génie de l'Aérocontamination, 1981—2003, prof. emeritus, 2003—. Gen. chmn. European Aerosol Conf., Blois, France, 1994; del. Internat. Coun. for Engring. and Tech., UNESCO, 2000-; adminstr. Maisons Maternelles, 2005-, pres., Commn. Air Pollution Communaute Urbaine De BREST, 1974-80, Com. Nucleation IAMAP IUGG, 1975-83, Com. Nat. Pour l'Enseignement et La Recherche, 1976-80, admintr., Sci. Coun. Inst. Nat. Physique Physique Des Particules Physique Nucleaire, 1976-1981, v.p., Soc. France Nuclear Energy BRETAGNE, 1977-81, adminstr., Soc. France Radioprotection, 1978-85, pres., Sci. Com. ICCCS Meeting Paris, 1982, mem., French del., Internat., Radiation Protection Agy., Meeting Berlin, 1984, administr., Asssn. Preventive Atmospheric Pollution, 1985-2002, mem., Sci. Com. Nat. Inst. Rsch. & Safety, 1987-2002, chmn., Aerosol Divsn. Fine Particle Soc., 1989-1992, guest editor FPS, 1991-1992, administr., French Meterol. Soc., 1992-96, dir., Com. ERASMUS Program Air Pollution Tech., 1993-98, dir., Internat. Program Com. Global Warming, 1996-2003. Author: (with D. Boulaud, Lavoisier, Ed.) Les Aérosols, Physique et Métrologie, 1998; mem. editl. bd. Idojaras, 1979—, Pollution Atmospherique, 1979-2003, Aerosol Sci. & Tech., 1992-2000, Revue Salles Propres, 2000-02; contbr. over 300 articles to profl. jours. Gen. sec. Syndicat d'initiative, Brest, 1973-77; mem. Cons. Com. Univs., France, 1973-77. Recipient Legion Banner award, United Cultural Conv., 2007, award, Internat. Jury Internat. Aerosol Rsch. Assembly, 1999—2003. Mem. Am Assn. Advancement Rsch., N.Y. Acad. Scis., Com. Regional Anti-Pollution Brest (pres. 1973-80), Soc. France for Nuclear Energy idFNE (pres. 1987-91), Am. Assn. Aerosol Rsch., Gesellschaft Aerosolforschung, Hungarian Meteorol. soc. (hon.), French Aerosol. Rsch. Assn. (pres. 1983-2000, hon. pres. 2000—), European Aerosol Assembly (co-founder, pres. 1998-2000), Office Professionnel de qualification des Entreprises de l'Ultrapropreté (pres. 1995—), Chevalier des Dames du vin et de la Table, Ordre de l'Echarpe. Avocations: tennis, opera, photography. Home: 11 Sq de L'eau Vive 94000 Creteil France Business E-Mail: renoux.andre@numericable.fr.

REN-PATTERSON, RENEE FENG, neuropathologist, neuroscientist; m. James Reid Patterson. MD, Fourth Mil. Med. U. Xian, P.R. China, 1976; MSc, 1989; PhD, U. Hong Kong, Sch. Medicine, 1994. Physician-in-charge clin. pathologist Xijing Hosp., Dept. Pathology, Xian, 1976—89; rsch. assoc. Dept. Anatomy and Cell Biology, Faculty Medicine, U. Hong Kong, 1989—94; vis. fellow Nat. Cancer Inst., Bethesda, Md., 1994—98; sr. postdoc. rschr. Georgetown U., Washington, 1998—2000; sr. rsch. scientist NIMH, Bethesda, 2000—. Mem.: Soc. Neuroscience. Citizens. Achievements include research in a double-mutant mouse model that should prove valuable in studying gene-gene interactions; innovative strategies to acquire genotype-phenotype associations from skin fibroblast cells by targeting risk genes for schizophrenia. Avocations: music, ballet, reading, travel.

RENSHAW, CHARLES LUCIUS, retired surgeon; b. Ft. Worth, Tex., Apr. 2, 1935; s. Horace Stephen and Carol Jim Renshaw; m. Sally Marie Tull, June 22, 1957; children: Stephen Vance, Lisa Carol, Lucius Scott, Julie Kay. BA, Tex. Christian, Ft. Worth, 1957; MD, Johns Hopkins, Balt., 1961; Degree in Ranch Mgmt., Tex. Christian, 1989. Diplomate Tex. Bd. Med. Examiners, 1961, Am. Bd. Orthop. Surgery, 1969. Orthop. surgeon US Army, Ft. Ord, Calif., 1967—69; pvt. practice orthop. surgeon All Saints Hosp., Ft. Worth, 1969—89; stock farmer Wise County, Tex., 1989—. Chief med. staff All Saints Hosp., 1983—85. Maj. US Army, 1967—69, Ft. Ord. Mem.: Alpha Omega Alpha, Phi Beta Kappa. Avocation: sport shooting. Personal E-mail: lrfarms@aol.com.

RENTOS, PETER GEORGE, medical educator; b. Reading, Pa., Aug. 21, 1929; s. George John and Stavroula (Blamblas) R.; m. Margaret Perados, Jan. 22, 1956; children: George, Michael. BA, Albright Coll., 1959; MPH, U. Mich., 1964; PhD, U. Iowa, 1970. Indsl. hygienist Pa. Dept. Health, Harrisburg, 1960—66; health svcs. officer USPHS, Salt Lake City, 1966—68, scientist Cin., 1970—71, sr. scientist, 1971—77, scientist dir., 1977—92; assoc. prof. U. South Fla., Tampa, 1992—. Rsch. grant adminstr. Nat. Inst. for Occupl. Safety and Health, Cin., 1971-76. Editor: Evaluation and Control of the Occupational Environment, 1992, Occupational Safety Research/Personal Protection, 1975, Shift Work and Health, 1976. Chmn. Health and Safety Com., Boy Scouts Am., Pitts., 1962; sec. Jr. C. of C., Meadville, Pa., 1965; pres. Met. Area Religious Coalition, Cin., 1988. Col. USPHS, 1966-92. Recipient Spoke award Boy Scouts Am., 1963. Mem. Am. Indsl. Hygiene Assn., Am. Soc. Safety Engrs., Fla. Fedn. for Safety. Greek Orthodox. Avocations: photography, fishing, bicycling, walking. Home: 3951 Brightside Ln Palm Harbor FL 34685-2630 Office: U South Fla Col Pub Health MDC56 13201 Bruce B Downs Blvd Tampa FL 33612-3805 Office Phone: 813-974-6661. Business E-Mail: prentos@health.usf.edu.

RENTOUMIS, ANN MASTROIANNI, psychotherapist; b. New Haven, Apr. 27, 1928; d. Luigi Mastroianni and Marion Dallas; m. George Rentoumis, June 27, 1959; children: Michael, Mary, Anne. BA in Psychology, Vassar Coll., 1949; postgrad., Boston U. Med. Sch., 1949-50; MS in Social Work, Columbia U., 1952. Diplomate Am. Bd. Social Work, Am. Psychotherapy Assn.; lic. cert. social worker; lic. marriage and family therapist. Child and adolescent therapist Bklyn. Psychiat., 1952-55; family therapist Community Svc. Soc., NYC, 1955-58; psychotherapist Bleuler Psychotherapy Ctr., LI, N.Y., 1958-60, Adolescent Psychiat. Clinic, Tex. Children's Hosp., Houston, 1975-76; pvt. practice Houston, 1976-77, Lauderdale Psychiat. Group, Ft. Lauderdale, Fla., 1978-90, Pompano Beach, Fla., 1990-93, Ft. Lauderdale, 1993—. Bd. dirs. Envirodyne, Inc., 1989—2000. Pres. Pine Crest Sch. Mothers Club, 1985-86; v.p. Opera Soc., 1987-88, bd. dirs., 1998—, parliamentarian 2000-02, parlimentarian, 2006-07; bd. govs., v.p. exec. bd. Fla. Philharm Orch., 1988-91, bd. dirs., 1990-2003; pres. Ft. Lauderdale Philharm. Soc., 1988-90; bd. dirs. Goodwill Ambassadors, 2003-2006, Symphony of Am. Soc., 2005-08. Recipient Golden Rule award J.C. Penney Co., 1990; named Woman of Yr., Am. Cancer Soc., 1989, Woman of Style and Substance, Ft. Lauderdale Philharm. Soc., 1998, Diva award Fla. Grand Opera, 2009, Bd. Opera Soc. 2000-. Fellow Am. Psychotherapy Assn., Am. Orthopsychiat. Assn.; mem. Am. Assn. Marriage and Family Therapists, Am. Group Therapy Assn., Royal Dames of Cancer Rsch., Inc. (trustee 2006—, bd. mem. 2011-), Thousand Plus Club, Harbor Beach Surf Club (v.p. 1986-90). Avocations: piano, tennis, swimming. Home: 2200 S Ocean Ln Ph 6 Fort Lauderdale FL 33316-3836 Office: 1326 SE 3d Ave Fort Lauderdale FL 33316-1260 Office Phone: 954-767-0048.

RENWANZ BOYLE, ANDREA, nursing educator; b. Somerville, Sept. 30, 1948; DNSc, U. Calif. San Francisco, 1988. Assoc. prof. San Francisco State U., 1989—. Recipient Disting. Faculty award, SFSU Academic Senate. Home: 821 Spring Dr Mill Valley CA 94941 Home Fax: 415-338-0555. Business E-Mail: aboyle@sfsu.edu.

REPENSHEK, MARK F., healthcare ethicist; b. Sheboygan, Wis., July 5, 1973; BS, U. Wis., 1996; PhD, St. Louis U., 2005. Healthcare ethicist Columbia St. Mary's Health Sys., 2002—. Bd. dirs. ethics com. CHRISTUS Health, 2008; bd. dirs. Milw. Cath. Home, 2010; chairperson-theologian and ethicist com. Cath. Health Assn., 2010. Recipient Tomorrow's Leaders award, Cath. Health Assn. Mem.: Cath. Theol. Soc. America, Soc. Christian Ethics, Am. Soc. Bioethics & Humanities. Avocations: bicycling, writing. Office: 2320 N Lake Dr Ste 1621 Milwaukee WI 53211 Business E-Mail: mrepensh@columbia-stmarys.org.

REPLOGLE, ROBERT LEE, cardiovascular and thoracic surgeon; b. Ottumwa, Iowa, Sept. 30, 1931; s. Ralph Ruby and Edith Dorothy (Swartz) R.; m. Carol A. Heeschen, Aug. 24, 1958; children: Robert E., Jennifer Bremer, Edith Sheffer. MD cum laude, Harvard U., 1960; DSc (hon.), Cornell Coll., 1972. Diplomate Am. Bd. Surgery, Am. Bd. Thoracic Surgery, Am. Bd. Pediat. Surgery. Intern in surgery U. Minn. Hosp., 1960-61; asst. resident in surgery Peter Bent Brigham Hosp.,

Boston, 1961-63, Mass. Gen. Hosp., Boston, 1965-66; sr. resident in surgery Children's Hosp. Med. Ctr., Boston, 1966; asst. in surgery Children's Hosp. Med. Ctr. and Harvard Med. Sch., Boston, 1966-67; asst. prof. surgery Pritzker Sch. Medicine U. Chgo., 1967-70, assoc. prof. surgery and head, sect. pediat. surgery, 1970-73, prof. surgery and head, sect. pediat. surgery, 1973-74, prof. surgery and head, sect. cardiac surgery, 1973-80, prof. surgery, sect. cardiac surgery, 1973-90; med. dir. cardiac surgery unit Ingalls Meml. Hosp., 1989-98; chief divsn. cardiac surgery Columbus Hosp., Chgo., 1987-97; pres. CTS Net Inc., Chgo., 1998—. Vis. prof. Albany Med. Coll., 1974, Dalhousie Sch. of Medicine, Halifax, 1975, Walter Reed Army Med. Ctr., 1978, U. Miami Med. Sch., 1992, Philippine Heart Ctr. for Asia March, 1979, Health Inst. Japan, Tokyo, 1982, Creighton Med. Sch., 1988, Brooke Army Med. Ctr., 1993, U. Heidelberg, 1995, Kerkoff Clinic/Max Planct Inst., Bad Nanheim, Germany, 1995, German Heart Ctr., Munich, 1995, Peter Bent Brigham Hosp. Harvard Med. Sch., 1996; mem. surgery and bioengring. study sect. HHS, NIH, 1979-83; mem. ad hoc adv. com. bypass angioplasty revascularization investigation, NIH, 1993-94; mem. subcom. on quality N.Y. State Dept. Health, 1989-96, mem. subcom. on resources and facilities, 1993—, mem. cardiac adv. com., 1989—; pres. Ctsnet.org, Inc., 1999—. Author: (with others) Microcirculation, Perfusion, and Transplantation of Organs, 1970, The Critically Ill Child, 1972, Surgical Clinics in North America, 1976, Biprosthetic Cardiac Valves, 1979, Year Book of Nuclear Medicine, 1981, among others; mem. editl. bd. Jour. Cardiac Surgery, 1982-99; contbr. more than 125 articles to profl. jours. With USN, 1951-54. Recipient Merit award Philippine Heart ctr. for Asia, Manila, 1985, Friendship award Shanghai Chest Hosp., 1987; fellowship U. Chgo., MacLean Ctr. Clin. Ethics. Mem. AMA (diagnostic and therapeutic tech. assessment panel 1995—, ho. of dels. 1992—, joint rev. com. on ednl. programs for physicians assts. 1979-84), ACS (com. on allied health pers. 1979-84, chmn. 1983-84, com. on med. motion pictures 1979-85, com. on membership 1988—, residency rev. com. for thoracic surgery of the accreditation com. for grad. med. edn. 1992-95, 96—), Ill. State Med. Soc., Chgo. Med. Soc., Am. Surg. Assn., European Assn. for Cardiothoracic Surgery, Soc. for Acad. Surgery, Am. Heart Assn. (adv. coun. cardiovasc. surgery 1968-71), Soc. Univ. Surgeons, Internat. Cardiovasc. Soc., Societe Internationale de Chirurgie (N.Am. chpt.), Am. Assn. for Thoracic Surgery (del. AMA 1992—, com. on soc. responsibility 1991—), Soc. Thoracic Surgeons (program com. 1978-81, chmn. 1981, com. on medico-legal affairs, chmn. 1985-88, ad hoc fin. adv. com. 1987-89, ad hoc exhibitors adv. com. 1988-89, ad hoc com. on social responsibility 1992-95, ad hoc database liaison com. 1993-94, database liaison com. 1994—, ad hoc com. on physician-specific mortality for cardiac surgery 1993-96, stds. and ethics com. 1984-88, treas. 1986-92, exec. com. 1986—, pres.-elect. 1995-96, pres. 1996-97, rep. to the coun. of med. specialty socs. 1990—, annals of thoracic surgery liaision com. 1992—, com. on grad. edn. in thoracic surgery 1992—, com. on major issues in thoracic surgery 1993, chmn. 1994, 95, pres.-elect coun. med. splty. socs. 1997-98, pres. coun. med. specialty socs. 1998-99), Coun. of Med. Specialty Socs., German Cardiac Surgery Soc. (hon. mem.). Avocations: wine collecting, photography, travel. Address: CTS Net Inc 1160 E 56th St Chicago IL 60637-1541 Business E-Mail: bob@replogle.org.

REPPUCCI, NICHOLAS DICKON, psychologist, educator; b. Boston, May 1, 1941; s. Nicholas Ralph and Bertha Elizabeth (Williams) R.; m. Christine Marlow Onufrock, Sept. 10, 1967; children: Nicholas Jason, Jonathan Dickon, Anna Jin Marlow Chapman. BA with honors, U. N.C., 1962; MA, Harvard U., 1964, PhD, 1968. Lectr., rsch. assoc. Harvard U., Cambridge, Mass., 1967-68; from asst. prof. to assoc prof. Yale U., New Haven, 1968-76; prof. psychology U. Va., Charlottesville, 1976—, dir. cmty. psychology tng. program, 1976—, dir. grad. studies in psychology, 1984-95, 97-98. Originator biennial conf. on community rsch. and action, 1986. Author: (with J. Haugaard) Sexual Abuse of Children, 1988; (with P. Britner and J. Woolard) Preventing Child Abuse and Neglect Through Parent Education, 1997; editor: (with J. Haugaard) Prevention in Community Mental Health Practice; (with E. Mulvey, L. Weithorn and J. Monahan) Mental Health, Law and Children, 1984; assoc. editor Law and Human Behavior, 1986-96, mem. editl. bd., 1996-2005; mem. editl. bd. Am. Jour. Cmty. Psychology, 1974-83, 88-91, New Psychology & Pub. Policy, 2008-; contbr. articles to profl. jours., chpts. in books. Adv. bd. on prevention Va. Dept. Mental Health, Mental Retardation and Substance Abuse Svcs., Richmond, 1986-92. Recipient Disting. Scholar in psychology award Va. Assn. Social Sci., 1991, Outstanding Psychology Tchg. award, U. Va., 2005, Mentoring and Tchg. award Am. Psychology and Law Soc., 2007. Fellow APA (chmn. task force on pub. policy 1980-84), Am. Psychol. Soc., Soc. for Cmty. Rsch. and Action (pres. 1986, Disting. Contbn. award in theory and rsch. 1998, Inaugural award for ednl. mentoring 1999), Phi Beta Kappa. Office: U Va Dept Psychology PO Box 400400 Charlottesville VA 22904-4400 Office Phone: 434-924-0662. E-mail: ndr@virginia.edu. *

REQUARDT, HERMANN, health products executive; b. Engern, Germany, Feb. 11, 1955; B; student in physics, Technical U., Darmstadt, Germany; dipl.-phys., Dr. phil. nat., U. Frankfurt, Germany. Academic asst. Frankfurt U., 1979—82; rsch. asst. Inst. Aviation Medicine, Germany, 1982—84; rschr. med. engring. group, sectional imaging divsn. Siemens AG, Germany, 1984—89, head devel., magnetic resonance divsn., 1989—91, head project mgr., magnetic resonance divsn., 1991—92, head high-field systems devel., 1992—93, head surface coils pilot project, 1993—95, head magnetic resonance divsn., 1995—2001, mem. exec. mgmt., med. solutions group, 2001—06, head corp. tech. dept., 2006—, CEO healthcare sector, 2008—. Mem. mng. bd. Siemens AG, 2006—; hon. prof. Johann Wolfgang Goethe U., Frankfurt, Germany, 2006. Office: Siemens AG Wittelsbacherplatz 2 80333 Munich Germany *

RERAT, ALAIN ANDRE, nutrition researcher, consultant; b. Nancy, France, July 16, 1926; s. Armand Philippe and Lucienne Victorine (Vautrin) R.; m. Kirsten Halsteen, Apr. 20, 1957; children: Elisabeth, Karin. BS, Lycee Lakanal, Sceaux, France, 1943; DVM, Nat. Vet. Sch., Alfort, France, 1949; MS, Sorbonne U., Paris, 1956, DSc, 1960. Rsch. asst. Nat. Inst. Agrl. Rsch., Paris, 1952-57, sr. rschr., 1957-62, prin. sci. officer, 1962-63, sr. prin. sci. officer, 1963-91, dir. rsch. emeritus, 1991—. Dir. pig breeding sta. Nat. Inst. Agrl. Rsch., Jouy-en-Josas, France, 1961-72, head nat. ctr. for animal prodn., 1970-72, head dept. nutrition, 1972-84, dir. nutrition physiology lab., 1972-91; dir. nutrition rsch. ctr. Nat. Ctr. Sci. Rsch., Paris, 1972-82. Author, co-editor: Digestive Physiology in the Pig, 1982, The Pig and Its Breeding, 1986; author: Nutrition, Food and the Environment, 1994; contbr. over 500 articles to profl. jours. Lt. France-Germany Vet. Svcs., 1949-50; vet. capt., res., 1960-76. Recipient Haupt prize Henneberg-Lehmann, Gottingen U., Germany, 1979, Physiology award Acad. Scis., Paris, 1980, Internat. award of animal nutrition Roche Firm, Basel, Switzerland, 1988, European Nutrition award, 1995; named Officer de la Legion d'Honneur, Officier du Merite National, Commandeur du Merite Agricole. Mem. Vet. Acad. France (pres. 1992), Agr. Acad. France (pres. 2006), Nat. Acad. Medicine, Spanish Royal Acad. Vet. Scis., French Assn. Nutrition (pres. 1978-84, 86-92), European Assn. Animal Prodn. (pres. commn. pig prodn. 1972-78), Fedn. European Nutrition Socs. (sec. gen. 1983-91), Internat. Union Nutritional Scis. (v.p. 1989-97). Avocations: tennis, skiing, dive-hunting, music. Home: 9 rue d'Ardenay 91120 Palaiseau France E-mail: kial-rerat@club-internet.fr.

RESCH, MÁRIA, psychiatrist, researcher; b. Mosonmagyaróvár, Gyor-Moson-Sopron, Hungary, Sept. 20, 1967; d. István Resch and Mária Tóth; life ptnr. Tamás Bella. Degree in Medicine, Semmelweis U., 1995; degree in Med.-Jurisprudence, Eötvös Lóránd U., 1999; degree in Psychiatry, Semmelweis U., 1999, degree in Psychotherapy, 2003, PhD, 2004, degree in Addictology, 2007. Psychiatrist Jahn Ferenc Dél-Pesti Hosp., Budapest, Hungary, 1995—99, Erzsébet Hosp., Sopron, Hungary, 2000—06; head physician Petz Aladár County Tchg. Hosp., Gyor, Hungary, 2006—. Chief med. officer State Pub. Health & Med. Officer Svc., Gyor-Moson-Sopron County, 2006—. Contbr. scientific papers. Mem.: Hungarian Acad. Scis., Hungarian Psychiatry Assn., Internat. Coll. Psychosomatic Medicine. Achievements include research in gynaecological psychosomatics of eating disorders, eating disorders in sport, role of personality in politics, political psychology. Avocations: music, travel, sports. Home: Kazinczy tér 10 Sopron Gyor-Moson-Sopron County 9400 Hungary Office: Petz County Tchg Hosp Zrínyi u 13 Gyor 9024 Hungary Personal E-mail: reschm@freemail.hu. Business E-Mail: resch.maria7@upcmail.hu.

RESCHE, FRANÇOIS, medical educator, former academic administrator; Prof. and researcher, neurosurgery Univ. de Nantes, France, v.p., pres., 2002—07. Pres., bd. dir. House of Social Sci. Guépin Angel (public interest group). Office: l'Universite de Nantes 1 quai de Tourville 44000 Nantes France Business E-Mail: francois.resche@presidence.univ-nantes.fr.

RESCORLA, ROBERT ARTHUR, psychology professor; b. Pitts., May 9, 1940; s. Arthur R. and Mildred J. (Jenkins) Rescorla; m. Shirley Steele, children: Eric, Michael. BA, Swarthmore Coll., 1962; PhD, U. Pa., 1966, MA, Yale U., 1974, PhD (hon.), Ghent U., Belgium, 2006. Successively asst. prof., assoc. prof., prof. Yale U., New Haven, 1966—80; prof. psychology U. Pa., Phila., 1981—, James Skinner prof. sci., 1986—2000, Christopher H. Browne disting. prof. psychology, 2000—, dean of coll. Sch. Arts and Scis., 1994—97. Author: Pavlovian Second Order Conditioning, 1980; editor: Animal Learning and Behavior, 1995—97; contbr. articles to profl. jours. Recipient Ira Abrams Tchg. award, 1999, Horsley Grant award, Pavlovian Soc., 2005. Fellow: Am. Acad. Arts and Sciences; mem.: AAAS (pres. sect. J, psychology 1988—89), APA (pres. divsn. 3 1985, Disting. Sci.Contbn. award 1986), NAS, Psychonomic Soc. (mem. governing bd. 1979—85, chmn. publ. bd. 1985—86), Ea. Psychol. Assn. (bd. dirs. 1983—86, pres. 1986—87, Warren medal 1991), Soc. Exptl. Psychologists, Am. Psychol. Soc. (William James fellow). Office: U Pa Dept Psychology 3720 Walnut St Philadelphia PA 19104-3604

RESENDE JÚNIOR, JOÃO CHRYSOSTOMO, medical educator; b. Entre Rios de Minas, Minas Gerais, Dec. 18, 1964; Degree in Vet., U. Fed. Minas Gerais, 1988; DSc, U. Fed. Lavras, Minas Gerais. Assoc. prof. U. Fed. Lavras, 1996—, coord. vet. medicine course, 2004—08, dean, 2008—; Sandwich fellowship Wageningen U., Netherlands, 2003. Mem.: Am. Dairy Sci. Assn. Avocations: soccer, travel. Office: University Federal Lavras Caixa Postal 3037 Campus da DMV Lavras Minas Gerais 37200-000 Brazil Office Fax: 55 35 38291113. Business E-Mail: joaocrj@dmv.ufla.br.

RESMAN-TARGOFF, BETH HOLLY, pharmacist, educator; d. Norman M. and Rowena Resman; m. Ira N. Targoff, June 14, 1981; 1 child, Deborah Judith Targoff. BS in Pharmacy, SUNY, Buffalo, 1973, PharmD, 1976. Registered pharmacist NY, 1974, Okla., 1991. Clin. coord., asst. dir. pharmacy The Buffalo Gen. Hosp., 1976—81; clin. instr. SUNY, 1976—81; clin. prof. U. Okla., Oklahoma City, 1981—. Mem. adv. bd. Annals Pharmacotherapy, 1989—. Contbr. chapters to books. Fellow: Am. Coll. Clin. Pharmacy; mem.: Okla. Soc. Health-Sys. Pharmacists (Pharmacist of Yr. 2011), Am. Assn. Colls. Pharmacy, Am. Pharmacists Assn., Okla. Soc. Health-Sys. Pharmacists, Am. Soc. Health-Sys. Pharmacists, Phi Kappa Phi, Rho Chi (region VI councilor 2008—, Outstanding Faculty Mem., U. Okla. Chpt. 1992—2006, 2008—11). Avocations: travel, photography. Office: Univ Okla Coll Pharm 1110 N Stonewall Oklahoma City OK 73117

RESNICK, ADRIENNE JO, clinical social worker, psychotherapist; b. NYC, July 19, 1954; d. Martin and Molly Starkman; m. Paul Resnick, Sept. 30, 1978; 1 child, Elana. BA, NYU, 1975, MSW, 1981. Psychothcrapist Stamford Child Guidance Clinic, Conn., 1981—83; group facilitator YWCA, White Plains, NY; psychotherapist pvt. practice, Sleepy Hollow, 1983—. Author: Sometimes I Feel Blue, 2002, Food Play, 2002. Recipient Founders Day award, NYU, N.Y.C., 1975. Mem.: NASW (diplomate), Am. Soc. Trial Cons., Acad. Cert. Social Workers, Soc. Clin. Social Work. Avocations: writing, travel, yoga. Office: 239 N Broadway Sleepy Hollow NY 10591 Office Phone: 914-633-3389. Personal E-mail: agres719@aol.com.

RESNICK, ELAINE BETTE, psychotherapist, licensed clinical social worker; b. Orlando, Fla., Apr. 2, 1944; d. Julius Milton and Annette (Chusid) Bernstein; m. Peter Schuyten (div. 1973); m. Richard B. Resnick, May 21, 1975; children: Demian, Jesse, Nora; 1 stepchild, Deborah. BA with honors, NYU, 1966; MSW, CUNY, 1971; postgrad., NYU, 1992—. Cert. Inst. for Study Psychotherapy, 1979, comprehensive tng. program with chronically and terminally ill patients, 2002; lic. clin. social worker, N.Y.; cert. in hypnosis tng. and supervision Columbia U., 1978; bd. cert. and diplomate in clin. social work. Field work supr. NYU, NYC, 1973-82; rsch. assoc. N.Y. Med. Coll., NYC, 1973—82; clin. dir. divsn. drug abuse rsch treatment NY Med. Coll., NYC, 1977—83; field work supr. York Coll., NYC, 1976-77, Wurzweiler Sch. of Social Work, Yeshiva U., 1991—; clin. instr. N.Y. Med. Coll., NYC, 1982-83; pvt. practice NYC, 1973—; lectr. Marymount Manhattan Coll., 1974—75; clin. dir. Psychiatry & Family Therapy, NYC, 1986—. Psychiat. social worker, Divsn. Biol. Psychiat. Met. Hosp., 1971-1973 N.Y. State Psychiat. Inst., 1970-71, Columbia U. Sch. Medicine; social worker Intensive Family Counseling Unit N.Y.C. Dept. Social Svcs., 1969-70; psychiat. social worker, St. Vincent's Hosp., 1970; adj. asst. prof. NYU Grad. Sch. Social Work, 1977-82. Contbr. articles to profl. jours.; responsible for numerous presentations in field. Fellow Soc. Clin. Social Work Psychotherapists; mem. NASW, Nat. Registry Health Care Providers in Clin. Social Work. Office Phone: 212-678-6949. Office Fax: 212-678-6949. E-mail: elaine02@mac.com.

RESNICK, JEFFREY I., plastic surgeon; b. Jersey City, Mar. 2, 1954; s. Victor and Regina (Bistritz) R.; m. Michele Gail Zinger, July 12, 1981; children: Andrew Gregory, Daniel Zachary. BS, Yale U., 1975; MD, U. Pa., 1980. Diplomate Am. Bd. Surgery, Am. Bd. Plastic Surgery. Resident in surgery Mass. Gen. Hosp., Boston, 1980—85, resident in plastic surgery, 1985—87; asst. clin. prof. plastic surgery UCLA, 1987—, fellow in craniofacial surgery, 1987—88; asst. prof. clin. surgery U. So. Calif, Santa Monica, 1998—. Contbr. articles to profl. jours. Surgeon Interplast, Vietnam, Nepal, Myanmar. Mem. Am. Assn. Plastic Surgeons., Am. Soc. Plastic Surgeons, Am. Soc. Maxillofacial Surgeons, Am. Cleft Palate-Craniofacial Assn., Plastic Surgery Ednl. Found., Sigma Xi, Alpha Omega Alpha. Office: PO Box 572426 Tarzana CA 91357-2426 Office Phone: 310-315-0222. Personal E-mail: resnick.jeffrey@gmail.com. *

RESNICK, MICHAEL B., pediatrician; b. Chgo., Sept. 27, 1942; BSED, U. Fla., 1965, EdD, 1972. Prof. pediats. U. Fla Coll. Med., 1974—, dir. maternal child health Edn. Data Rsch. Ctr., 1976—2005. Recipient Rsch. Achievement award, U. Fla. Mem.: APA. Avocations: sports, gardening, hiking. Home: 700 SW 29th Pl Gainesville FL 32601 Home Fax: 352-334-1361. Business E-Mail: mresnick@ufl.edu.

RESNICK, RHODA BRODOWSKY, psychotherapist; b. Mar. 22, 1930, d. Isador and Rose (Wasserman) Brodowsky; m. Jack H. Resnick, May 21, 1950; children: Steven E., Caryn B. BS, CCNY, 1951; MS, Queens Coll., 1973; postgrad., Hunter Coll. Tchr. N.Y.C. Bd. Edn., 1960—80, guidance counselor, 1980—; psychotherapist L.I. Cons. Ctr., 1973—77; pvt. practice psychotherapy, 1975—. Fellow, L.I. Inst. Mental Health, 1975. Mem.: PGA, United Fedn. Tchrs., Am. Pers. and Guidance Assn., PGA Hole in One Club, Am. Contract Bridge League (Bronze life). Home: 340 E 64th St New York NY 10065 Office Phone: 212-355-0002. E-mail: xrojac@hotmail.com.

RESNICK, STEVEN DAVID, pediatric dermatologist, educator; b. NYC, Mar. 18, 1956; AB, Brown U., Providence, 1978; MD, Yale U. Sch. Medicine, New Haven, 1982. Diplomate Am. Bd. Dermatology, lic. Pediat. Dermatology. Intern pediat. U. Wash./Children's Hosp. Med. Ctr., Seattle, 1982-83; resident dermatology U. Calif. San Francisco, 1983-86, fellowship pediat. dermatology, 1986—87; staff NC Meml. Hosp., 1988—95; asst. prof. dermatology and pediatrics U. NC, Chapel Hill, 1994-95; assoc. clin. prof. dermatology and pediatrics Columbia U. Coll. Physicians & Surgeons, Chapel Hill, 1995—; divsn. chief dermatology Mary Imogene Bassett Hosp., Cooperstown, NY, 1995—. Contbr. articles to profl. jours. Named one of Best Dr.'s in America, Best Dr.'s Inc. Fellow: Soc. Pediat. Dermatology, Am. Acad. Dermatology, Am. Acad. Pediat. (exec. com. mem.). Office: Bassett Healthcare Divsn Dermatology 1 Atwell Rd Cooperstown NY 13326-1301 Office Phone: 607-547-3300. Office Fax: 607-547-4648.

RESNIK, DAVID BENJAMIN, medical humanities educator, researcher; b. Boston, Nov. 30, 1962; s. Michael David and Janet Depping Resnik; m. Susan Preston, Aug. 6, 1988; children: Peter Benjamin, Michael Thomas. BA, Davidson Coll., 1985; MA, U. N.C., 1987, PhD, 1990; JD, Concord U., 2003. Asst. prof. U. Wyo., Laramie, 1990-95, assoc. prof., dir. Ctr. for Advancement Ethics, 1995-98; prof. dept. med. humanities Brody Sch. Medicine East Carolina U., Greenville, NC, 1998—2004. Assoc. dir. Bioethics Ctr., Univ. Health Sys., Greenville, 1998—2004, biolethicist Nat. Inst. Environ. Health Sci., 2004-. Author: The Ethics of Science, 1998, Germline Gene Therapy, 1999, Responsible Conduct of Research, 2003, Owning the Genome, 2004, Dying Declarations, 2005, The Price of Truth, 2007, Playing Politics With Science, 2009. Grantee Gen. Elec., 1991, NSF, 1996, 2005. Mem. AAAS Baptist. Office: Nat Inst Environ Health Sci PO Box 12233 Research Triangle Park NC 27709 Office Phone: 919-541-5658. E-mail: resnikd@niens.nih.gov.

RESNIK, ROBERT, medical educator; b. New Haven, Dec. 7, 1938; s. Nathan Alfred and Elsie (Hershman) R.; m. Lauren Brahms, Oct. 29, 1966; children: Andrew Scott, Jamie Layne. BA, Yale U., 1960; MD, Case Western Res. U., 1965. Intern in internal medicine Mt. Sinai Hosp., Cleve., 1965-66; resident in ob-gyn. Yale U. Sch. Medicine, 1966-70; asst. prof. Sch. Medicine U. Calif., San Diego, 1974-78, assoc. prof., 1978-82, prof. reproductive medicine, 1982—, chmn. dept., 1982-95, dean clin. affairs, 1988-90, dean admissions, 1995—2003. Cons. Nat. Heart, Lung and Blood Inst. NIH, Washington, 1987; mem. exec. com. Coun. Residency Edn. Ob-Gyn, Washington, 1988-94, residency rev. com., 1988-94. Editor: (textbook) Maternal-Fetal Medicine: Principles and Practice, 1984, 5th edit., 2004; contbr. numerous articles to profl. jours. Major U.S. Army, 1970-72. Recipient Lifetime Achievement award, Soc. Maternal Fetal Medicine, 2004, Mentor of Yr., U. Calif. San Diego, 2005; Rsch. grantee, Nat. Found., NIH. Fellow: Royal Coll. Obstet. Gynecologists (ad eundem), N.W. Obstet. Gynecological Soc., Pacific Coast Obstet. and Gynecol. Soc., Am. Coll. Ob-Gyn. (vice chmn. obs. practice com. 1998—2000), New England Obstet. Gynecological Soc.; mem.: San Diego Gynecol. Soc. (pres. 1982), Am. Gynecologic and Obstet. Soc. (pres. 2009—), Perinatal Rsch. Soc. (pres. 1985), Soc. Gynecologic

Investigation (coun. 1983—88), Yale Club, Am. Gynecol. Club (pres. 2002—03). Office: UCSD Med Ctr 200 W Arbor Dr 8433 San Diego CA 92103-8433 Business E-Mail: rresnik@ucsd.edu.

RESSLER, KERRY, psychiatrist, educator; BS in Molecular Biology, MIT; MD, PhD, Harvard Sch. Medicine. Resident Emory U. Sch. Medicine, asst. prof. psychiatry & behavioral sciences; co-dir. Grady Meml. Hosp. Post-traumatic Stress Disorders Clinic; investigator Howard Hughes Med. Inst. Office: Department of Psychiatry and Behavioral Sciences 954 Gatewood Rd Atlanta GA 30329 Office Phone: 404-727-7739. Office Fax: 404-727-8070. E-mail: kressle@emory.edu.

RESTIVO, ANGELO, surgeon; b. Cagliari, Italy, Sept. 2, 1973; MD, U. Cagliari, 2004. Gastrointestinal surgeon dept. surgery U. Cagliari, 2009—. Mem.: Italian Soc. Surg. Oncology, European Soc. Surg. Oncology, Italian Soc. Colorectal Surgery. Office: Policlinico Universitario Monserrato Cagliari 09100 Italy Business E-Mail: angelorestivo@tiscali.it.

RESWICK, JAMES BIGELOW, former government official, biomedical engineer; b. Ellwood City, Pa., Apr. 16, 1922; s. Maurice and Katherine (Parker) R.; children: James Bigelow, David Parker (dec.), Pamela Reswick; m. Irmtraud Orthlies Hoelzerkopf, Dec., 27, 1973. SBME, MIT, 1943, SM, 1948, ScD, 1952; DEng (hon.), Rose Poly. Inst., 1968. Asst. prof., then assoc. prof., head machine design and graphics div. MIT, 1948-59; Leonard Case prof. engring., dir. Engring. Design Ctr., Case Western Res. U., 1959-70; prof. biomed. engring. and orthopaedics U. So. Calif., also dir. of rsch. dept. orthopaedics, 1970-80; assoc. dir. tech. Nat. Inst. Handicapped Rsch., U.S. Dept. Edn.; dir. VA Rehab. R & D Evaluation Unit VA Med. Ctr., Washington, 1984-88; dir. rsch. scis. Nat. Inst. on Disability and Rehab. Rsch. U.S. Dept. Edn., Washington, 1989—94; ret., 1994; acting dir. Nat. Inst. Disability and Rehab. Rsch., Washington, 1989-91. Engring. cons. on automatic control, product devel., automation and bio-med. engring. Mem. com. prosthetics R & D Nat. Acad. Scis., 1962-; chmn. design and devel. com.; mem. bd. rev. Army R & D Office, 1965-; mem. applied physiology and biomed. engring. study sect. NIH, 1972-. Author: (with C.K. Taft) Introduction to Dynamic Systems, 1967; also articles.; Editor: (with F.T. Hambrecht) Functional Electrical Stimulation, 1977; series on engring. design, 1963-; inventor, patentee in field. Chmn. Mayor's Commn. for Urban Transp., Cleve., 1969. Served to lt. (j.g.) USNR, 1943-46, PTO. Decorated officer Yugoslav Flag with golden wreath medal (Yugoslavia), 1990; recipient Product Engring. Master Designer award, 1969, Isabelle and Leonard H. Goldenson award United Cerebral Palsy Assn., 1973; NSR sr. postdoctoral fellow Imperial Coll., London, 1957. Fellow IEEE, Am. Inst. Med. and Biological Engring. (founder); mem. ASME (honor award for best paper 1956, sr. mem.), Am. Soc. Engring. Edn., Instrument Soc. Am., Biomed. Engring. Soc. (sr. mem., pres. 1973, dir.), Am. Acad. Orthopedic Surgeons (assoc.), Inst. Medicine of NAS, NAE, Internat. Soc. Orthotics and Prosthetics, Orthopaedics Rsch. Soc., Rehab. Engring. Soc. N.Am. (founding pres.), Sigma XI. Home: 1834 Calf Mountain Rd PO Box 549 Crozet VA 22932 Home Phone: 434-987-8040. Personal E-mail: jbreswick@yahoo.com.

RETSCH-BOGART, GEORGE Z., pediatric pulmonologist, surgeon; b. 1952; MD, U. Cin., 1978. Diplomate Am. Bd. Pediat., cert. in Pediat. Pulmonology. Resident pediat. U. Minn., Mpls., 1978—81; fellowship pediat. pulmonary U. NC Sch. Medicine, Chapel Hill, 1986—89, assoc. prof. divsn. pediat. pulmonology, dir. Cystic Fibrosis Ctr.; clin. staff NC Children's Hosp. Contbr. articles to profl. jours. Mem.: Cystic Fibrosis Found., Am. Acad. Pediat. Achievements include research in complex airway disorders in children. Mailing: UNC Dept Pediat, CB #7217 130 Mason Farm Rd Chapel Hill NC 27516 Office Phone: 919-966-4131. Office Fax: 919-966-6049.

RETTERSTOL, NILS, retired psychiatrist; b. Oslo, Oct. 3, 1924; s. Kittel and Kathrine (Steen) R.; m. Kirsten Christensen, Aug. 16, 1958; children: Trine Lise, Kjetil, Lars Jorgen. MS, U. Oslo, 1950, Dr.Med., 1966. Med. officer Dikemark Hosp., Ulleval Hosp., Oslo, 1952-56, Runwell Hosp., Eng., 1956-57; resident Ulleval Hosp., Oslo, 1957-58; assoc. prof., dep. dir. U. Psychiat. Clinic, Oslo, 1959-68; prof. psychiatry U. Bergen; head dir. Neevengarden Hosp., Bergen, 1969-73; prof. psychiatry U. Oslo, 1973-94; head dir. Gaustad Hosp., Oslo, 1973-94; retired, 1995. Head Norwegian Bank Narcotic Problems; chmn. Norwegian Commn. Forensic Psychiatry, 1983—97; cons. in field. Author: (49 books including) Paranoid and Paranoiac Psychoses, 1966; author: (with A. Sund) Drug Dependence, 1967, Suicide, 1970, Suicide, 5th edit., 1995, Prognosis in Paranoid Psychoses, 1970; author: (with Eitinger and A.A. Dahl) Crisis and Neuroses, 5th edit., 1990; author: (with L. Eitinger) Forensic Psychiatry, 4th edit., 1990; author: (with Eitinger and U. Malt) Psychoses, 4th edit., 1984, Suicide A European Perspective, 1993; author: (with A.A. Dahl, L. Eitinger and U. Malt) Textbook of Psychiatry, 1994, Labyrinths of the Human Mind, 1998; author: (with T. Moe and M. Sorensen) Physical Activity-A Resource in Psychiatric Treatment, 1998; author: (with O. Ekeberg and L. Mehlum) Suicide, 2002; author: (with U. Malt and A.A. Dahl) Textbook of Psychiatry, 2003; author: (with J.K. Jorgensen) In Borderline: From the Life of a Psychiatrist, 2003; author: Great Thoughts, Unquiet Mind: 21 Psychiatric Profiles, 2004; editor: Scand. Med. Yearbook, 1972—94, Eur. Archives of Psychiatry and Neurological Sics., 1975—89, Norwegian Jour. Suicidology, 1996—2002; European editor: Jour. Drug Issues, 1980—97; co-editor: Psychopathology, 1983. Capt. Norwegian Army. Decorated comdr. Royal Order St. Olav; recipient gold medal for psychiat. rsch., H.M. The King of Norway, rsch. prize Norwegian Coun. Humanities and Sci., 1978. Mem.: Internat. Acad. Suicide Rsch., French Assn. Psychiatry, Norwegian Psychiat. Soc., Norwegian Med. Soc., Finnish Assn. Psychiatry, German Assn. Neurology and Psychiatry, Internat. Assn. Suicide Prevention and Crisis Intervention (hon.; pres. 1989—91, hon. prize 2000), Assn. European Psychiatrists (hon.), Swedish Psychiat. Assn. (hon.), Norwegian Acad. Sci. (hon.). Office: Gaustad Hosp Boks 24 Gaustad 320 Oslo 3 Norway

RETTIG, MICHAEL E., orthopedist, surgeon, educator; Attended, SUNY, 1982—86. Diplomate Am. Bd. of Orthopaedic Surgery, Am. Bd. of Orthopaedic Surgery-hand surgery, 1994. Intern gen. surgery NY Univ. Med. Ctr., 1986—87, resident orthopaedic surgery, 1987—91; clin. fellow orthopaedic hand surgery Mayo Clinic, 1991—92; clin. fellow shoulder surgery Hennepin County Med. Ctr., 1992—93; asst. prof. orthopaedic surgery NY Univ. Sch. of Medicine; with NY Univ. Hosp. for Joint Diseases, NY Univ. Langone Med. Ctr. Co-author: (publs.) Newest advances in the operative treatment of basal joint arthritis, 2007, Outcome Following Acute Primary Distal Ulna Resection for Comminuted Distal Ulna Fractures at the Time of Operative Fixation of Unstable Fractures of the Distal Radius, 2009, Avulsion injuries of the flexor digitorum profundus tendon, 2011, and numerous other publications. Office: New York University Langone Medical Center 3rd Fl 317 E 34th St New York NY 10016-4974 Office Phone: 212-263-4263.

REULAND, PETER, nuclear medicine physician, researcher; b. Gürzenich, Nordrhein-Westfalen, Germany, Oct. 3, 1953; s. Heinz Jakob and Hanni (Müller) R.; m. Marietta Antonia Anspach, Sept. 29, 1977; children: Anna-Kristina, Milena, Irina. MD, Tech. H.S., Aachen, Ger., 1984; PhD, Eberhard-Karls U., Tübingen, Ger., 1991. Physicist Inst. Theor. Physics Tech. H.S., Aachen, Ger., 1977-79, physiologist Inst. Cardiac Physiology, 1979-84; fellow dept. nuclear medicine Eberhard-Karls U., Tübingen, Ger., 1985-89, resident dept. nuclear medicine, 1989-91; tech. dir. Inst. Nuclear Medicine, Freiburg, Germany, 1992—; prof. U. Tubingen, 1992—2002, U. Freiburg, 2002—. Dir. Euro-PET Ctr., Freiburg, 1995—; prof. U. Tübingen, 1992—, Eberhard-Karls U., 1991; head PET Group. Author: Skeletal Scintigraphy, 1989; contbr. articles to profl. jours. Mem. So. W. Ger. Soc. Nuclear Medicine (v.p. 1993—), Soc. Nuclear Medicine, Soc. European Nuclear Medicine, Assn. German Nuclear Physicians (head 1995—). Avocations: fine arts, classical music, swimming, ethnology. Office: Schwabentorplatz 6 79098 Freiburg Baden-Württemberg Germany Office Phone: 004 9761 3633011. Personal E-mail: preuland@gux.de. Business E-Mail: reuland@nuklearmedizin-Freiburg.de.

REUS, MANUEL PINTADO, radiologist; b. Murcia, Spain, Sept. 17, 1947; s. Manuel García Reus and María Pintado Pintado; m. Carmen Mellado Martínez, Oct. 7, 1973; children: Patricia Reus, Manuel Reus. Cert. radiologist U. Murcia, 1977. Assoc. med. vascular and intervencional radiology Hosp. U. Virgen la Arrixaca, Murcia, 1978—88, assoc. med. divsn. ultrasound, 1989—2000, chief divsn. ultrasound, 2000—06, chmn. dept. radiology, 2006—08; assoc. prof. U. Murcia. Author: (book) Excellence in Service Diagnostic Imaging; contbr. articles to profl. jours. Recipient Nat. awards, Royal Acad. Medicine, 1996, award, Ministry Sci. and Innovation. Madrid, 2007. Mem.: Spanish Soc. Ultrasound, European Assn. Radiology, Spanish Soc. Radiology, SERAM. Roman Catholic. Avocation: bicycling. Home: Avd Reino Murcia Altorreal 23 Molina de Segura Murcia 30509 Spain Office: HU Virgen La Arrixaca El Palmar Murcia Spain Personal E-mail: mreus@um.es. Business E-Mail: m.reus@carm.es.

REUS, WERNER ALOIS, physician; b. Darmstadt, Germany, Oct. 14, 1951; s. Luitpold A. and Gertrud K. (Jarisch) R.; m. Maria E. Nagler, Oct. 31, 1980 (div.). MD, Heidelberg U., Germany, 1978. Asst. physician U. Heidelberg, 1978-79, Frauenklinik Stuttgart, Germany, 1979-81, U. Tübingen, Germany, 1981-87; cons. Frauenklinik Ingolstadt, Germany, 1987-88, U. Zürich, Switzerland, 1988-89, Free Univ., Berlin, 1990-93, Panorama Health Ctr., Scheidegg im Allgäu, Germany, 1996-98; pvt. practice in ob-gyn., psychotherapy, couples therapy Tübingen, Germany, 1999—; hon. prof., 2003; Plettenberg lectr., 2008—. Contbr. articles on perinatal physiology and ultrasound and psychotherapy. Mem. Internat. Soc. Ultrasound in Ob-Gyn. (founding mem.), Internat. Soc. Gynecol. Endocrinology, NY Acad. Scis., Sigmund Freud Soc., German Soc. Ultrasound in Medicine, German Soc. Perinatal Medicine. Roman Catholic. Avocations: history, archaeology. Office: Dobler str 10 D-72074 Tübingen Germany Office Phone: 49 7071 51500. Personal E-mail: empedokles1@me.com.

REUTER, HARALD, pharmacologist; b. Düsseldorf, Germany, Mar. 25, 1934; s. Rudolf and Else (Koerfer) R.; m. Lieselotte Speckmann, Aug. 10, 1960; children: Kirsten, Andreas, Sabine. Diploma, U. Freiburg, Germany, 1959; MD, U. Mainz, Germany, 1960; Dr.h.c. (hon.), U. Basel, 2010. Asst. dept. pharmacology U. Mainz, 1960-65, privatdozent, 1965-69; prof. pharmacology U. Bern, Switzerland, 1969-99, dean med. faculty, 1983-85, chmn. dept. pharmacology, 1971-99, prof. emeritus, 1999—. Vis. prof. various univs. in Eng., Israel, U.S., Japan and China. Co-author: Calcium Movement in Excitable Cells, 1975; editor: Sodium-Calcium Exchange, 1989; mem. editorial bd. numerous sci. jours.; contbr. over 140 articles to internat. jours. Recipient Outstanding Rsch. award Internat. Soc. Heart Rsch., 1984, Ciba-Geigy-Drew award Drew U., 1984, Marcel-Benoist prize Swiss Govt., 1985, Schmiedeberg-Plakette award German Pharmacology Soc., 1987, K.S. Cole award Biophys. Soc., 1993, Ernst-Jung medal for medicine in gold, 2002, Dr. H.C. U. Basel award, 2010. Mem. NAS, Academia Europaea, Deutsche Akademie der Naturforscher Leopoldina, Swiss Acad. Med. Scis., Acad. Royale Médecine Belgique. Avocations: reading, music, hiking, skiing, art. Home: Hofenstrasse 125 CH 3032 Hinterkappelen Switzerland E-mail: reuter@pki.unibe.ch.

REUTER, STEWART RALSTON, retired radiologist; b. Detroit, Feb. 14, 1934; s. Carl H. and Grace M. R.; m. Marianne (Ahfeldt), June 6, 1966. BA, Ohio Wesleyan U., 1955; MD, Case Western Res. U., 1959; JD, U. San Francisco, 1980. Diplomate: Am. Bd. Radiology, Am. Bd. Legal Medicine. Bar: Tex., 1981. Intern U. Calif., San Francisco, 1959—60, resident in radiology, 1960—63; instr. radiology Stanford U., Calif., 1963—64; asst. prof. U. Mich., Ann Arbor, 1966—69; assoc. prof. U. Calif., San Diego, 1969—72; prof. U. Mich., Ann Arbor, 1972—76, U. Calif., San Francisco and Davis, 1976—80; prof., chmn. dept. radiology Health Sci. Ctr., U. Tex., San Antonio, 1980—2001, prof. emeritus, 2001. Co-author: Gastrointestinal Radiology, 3d edit., 1986; mem. editorial bd. Am. Jour. Roentgenology, 1975-91, Iatrogenics, 1990-93; contbr. articles to profl. journals. Picker Fellow, 1964-66. Fellow: Soc. Interventional Radiologists (pres. 1978, Gold medal 2004), Am. Coll. Legal Medicine (bd. gov. 1985—91, 1992—94, sec. 1994, pres. elect 1995, pres. 1996), Am. Heart Assn., Am. Coll. Radiology (councillor 1996—99, fellow emeritus 2000); mem.: Am. Roentgen Ray Soc., Assn., Soc. Gastrointestinal Radiologists, Tex. Radiol. Assn. (trustee 1989—92, pres. 1994, trustee 1995—98, Gold medal 2000), Assn. Univ. Radiologists, Am. Bd. Legal Medicine, Tex. Bar Assn. Office: U Tex Health Sci Ctr Dept Radiology 7703 Floyd Curl Dr San Antonio TX 78284-6200 Home: 1115 Calle Catolina Santa Fe NM 87501 Business E-Mail: reuter@uthscsa.edu.

REVAI, KRYSTAL, medical educator; b. NYC, July 28, 1969; MD, Semmlweis U., 1995; MPH, U. Tex., Houston, 2002. Asst. prof., clin. head, divsn. gen. pediat. and adolescent medicine U. Ill., 2009—. Breastfeeding coord. Ill. Chpt. Am. Acad. Pediat., 2009—11. Fellow: AAP; mem.: ABM. Office: 840 S Wood St Chicago IL 60612 Business E-Mail: revai@uic.edu.

RÉVAI, TAMÁS, nephrologist; b. Budapest, Hungary, Oct. 13, 1962; s. R. István and Istvánné (König Éva) R.; m. Andrea Földes, July 13, 1986; 1 child, Peter, Ristvan. MD, Med. U., Budapest, 1988; med. diploma in internal diseases, 1994, PhD, 2008. Physician Hosp. Ujpest, Budapest, 1988-93; dialysis physician Hosp. SZT László, Budapest, 1993; head outpatient dept. nephrology Hosp. SZT János, Budapest, 1996—. Cons. nephrologist Hosp. SZT Imre, Budapest, 1996—; cons. nephrologist, dir. nephrol. dept. Hosp. of Police Force, Budapest, 1997—; lectr. in field. Mem. European Dialysis and Transplant Assn.-European Renal Assn., Hungarian Soc. for Hypertension. Avocations: golf, swimming, excursions, collecting books and stamps. Home: Jókai UTCA 26 1066 Budapest Hungary Office: SZT János Hosp Diósárok u 1 1125 Budapest Hungary E-mail: dnt@t-online.law.

REVAK, BERNADETTE BERNIE, nursing administrator; b. Calif., Jan. 17, 1957; BSN, Calif. State U., Domininguez Hills, 2003, MSN, 2006. Chargemaster coord. ValleyCare Health Sys., 2000—03, mgr. pub. health svcs., 2003—08, dir. infection control, outpatient clinics, pub. health, 2008—; adj. faculty pediat. Chabot CC, 2001—05. Steering com. mem. Chabot-Las Positas CC Dist., 2003—05; mentor catheter associated urinary tract infections BEACON Patient Safety Collaborative, 2010; mentor, advisor catheter associated urinary tract infections Inst. Healthcare Improvement, 2011. Mem.: Cert. Bd. Infection Control and Epidemiology, Assn. Profls. in Infection Control and Epidemiology, Inc. Avocations: travel, sewing. Office: 5555 West Las Positas Blvd Pleasanton CA 94588 Business E-Mail: brevak@valleycare.com.

REVEL, JEAN-PAUL, biology professor; b. Strasbourg, France, Dec. 7, 1930; arrived in U.S., 1953; s. Gaston Benjamin and Suzanne (Neher) Revel; m. Helen Ruth Bowser, July 27, 1957 (div. 1986); children: David, Daniel Neher, Steven Robert; m. Galina Avdeeva Moller, Dec. 24, 1986 (dec. 2004); 1 stepchild, Karen (dec.). BS, U. Strasbourg, 1949; PhD, Harvard U., 1957. Rsch. fellow Cornell U. Med. Sch., NYC, 1958-59; from instr. to prof. Harvard Med. Sch., Boston, 1959-71; prof. Calif. Inst. Tech., Pasadena, 1971—, emeritus, 2006—, AB Ruddock chair in biology, 1978—2006, dean of students, 1996—2005, emeritus, 2006—. Mem. sch. advisors bd. Nat. Insts. Aging, Balt., 1977-80; mem. ad hoc adv. biology NSF, Washington, 1982-83; mem. Nat. High Voltage Microscopy Adv. Group, Bethesda, Md., 1983, Nat. Rsch. Resources Adv. Coun., 1986-90. Author: (with E.D. Hay) Fine Structure of Developing Avian Cornea, 1969, over 150 publs., 1952-99; editor: Cell Shape and Surface Architecture, 1977, Science of Biological Specimen Preparation, 1986; mem. editl. bd. Jour. Cell Biology, 1969-72, Internat. Rev. Cytology, 1970, Cell and Tissue Rsch., 1979—, Molecular and Cell Biology, 1983-91; editor in chief Jour. Microscopy Soc. Am., 1994-96. Fellow AAAS (leader biol. scis. sect. 1991-92, Gordon conf. cell adhesion); mem. Am. Soc. Cell Biology (pres. 1972-73), Electron Micros. Soc. Am. (pres. 1988, Disting. Scientist award 1993), Soc. Devel. Biology. Avocations: watercolors, photography. Office: Calif Inst Tech # 114-96 Pasadena CA 91125-0001 Home Phone: 626-796-0701; Office Phone: 626-395-4986. Business E-Mail: revelj@caltech.edu.

REVER, GEORGE WRIGHT, psychiatrist, health facility administrator; b. Balt., May 18, 1928; s. William Benjamin and Amy Blanche (Wright) R.; m. Bridget Valerie Hanley, 1961 (dec. 1988); children: Kurt, Maeve Rever Raedle; m. Ann Roe, Feb. 4, 1994. BS, U. Md., 1950; MD, U. Md., Balt., 1957. Rotating intern Mercy Hosp., Balt., 1957-58; resident psychiatry and neurology VA Hosp., Boston, 1958-60; fellow Harvard Med. Sch., Cambridge, Mass., 1960-64, clin. instr. psychiatry, 1964—2004; psychiatrist divsn. legal medicine Cambridge Ct., 1960-71; psychiatrist Cambridge Ct. Clinic Divsn. of Legal Medicine, Mass., 1960-71; pvt. practice Cohasset, Mass., 1963-90, Easton, Md., 1990-93; psychiatric cons. Travelers Aid Soc., Boston, 1966-74; psychiatrist Eunice Kennedy Shriver Ctr., Waltham, Mass., 1967-90; fellow child psychiatry Mass. Gen. Hosp., Boston, 1960-61, 62-63, fellow community mental health, 1963-64, staff psychiatrist, 1964-90, dir. child psychiatry tng. program neuropsychiatry devel. disabilities sect., 1967-90, asst. pediatrician, 1969-71, psychiat. cons. social svc. dept., 1970-74, psychiatrist Chelsea Health Ctr., 1974-77, hon. psychiatrist, 1991—2004; med. dir. Brockton Family and Community Rsch., Mass., 1979-90; psychiatric cons. Benedictine Sch., Ridgely, Md., 1990—; child and adolescent psychiatrist Wicomico County Health Dept., Salisbury, Md., 1990-91, Queen Anne County Mental Health, Centreville, Md., 1990-92, Talbot County Mental Health, Easton, 1990-92, med. dir., 1992—2002, Regional Mid-Shore Mental Health Svcs., 1998—2005, Caroline County Mental Health Clinic, 2005—, Bay Hundred Behavioral Health Svcs./Choptank Cmty. Health Svcs., 2005—08, Eastern Shore Psychological Svcs., Easton, Md., 2007—. Part-time fellow child psychiatry Mass. Gen. Hosp., Boston, 1961-62, James Jackson Putnam Children's Ctr., Roxbury, Mass., 1961-62; cons. Am. Heritage Dictionaries, 1992; fleet surgeon Miles River Yacht Club, 2000—04. Editl. cons. The Am. Jour. of Child and Adolescent Psychiatry, 1994—. Sgt. U.S. Army, 1950-52, Korea. Decorated Bronze Star medal; Recipient Talbot County Assn. Retarded Citizens award, 1993. Fellow: Am. Psychiat. Assn. (life Disting.), Am. Coll. Forensic Examiners (life); mem.: AMA, Am. Soc. Clin. Psychopharmacology, Soc. Biol. Psychiatry, Assn. Child Psychology and Psychiatry, Am. Neuropsychiat. Assn., Talbot County Med. Soc., Med. and Chururg. Faculty Md., Md. Psychiat. Soc., Am. Assn. Mental Retardation, Am.

Assn. Cmty. Psychiatrists, Am. Acad. Child and Adolscent Psychiatry. Home: 8627 North Bend Cir Easton MD 21601-7327 Office Phone: 410-822-5007. Business E-Mail: rever@shore.intercom.net.

REVERE, VIRGINIA LEHR, psychologist; b. Long Branch, NJ; d. Joseph and Essie Lehr; m. Robert B. Revere; children: Elspeth, Andrew, Lisa, Robert Jr. PhB, U. Chgo., 1949, MA, 1959, PhD, 1971. Lic. cons. clin. psychologist, Va. Intern, staff psychologist Ea. Mental Health Reception Ctr., Phila., 1959-61; instr. Trenton (N.J.) State Coll., 1962-63; psychologist Trenton State Hosp., 1964-65, Bucks County Psychiat. Ctr., Phila., 1965-67; assoc. prof. Mansfield (Pa.) State U., 1967-77; clin. rsch. psychologist St. Elizabeth Hosp., Washington, 1977-81, tng. psychology coord., 1981-83, psychologist, 1985-91; child psychologist Cmty. Mental Health Ctr., Washington, 1983-85; pvt. practice Alexandria, Va., 1980—. Cons., lectr. in field. Author: Applied Psychology for Criminal Justice Professionals, 1982; contbr. articles to profl. jours. Recipient Group Merit award St. Elizabeth's Hosp., 1983, Community Svc. award D.C. Psychol. Assn., 1978, Outstanding Educator award, 1972; traineeship NIH, USPHS, Chgo., 1963-65; fellow Family Svcs. Assn., 1958-59. Mem. APA, No. Va. Soc. Clin. Psychologists, Va. Acad. Clin. Psychologists. Office Phone: 703-780-4872. Personal E-mail: rrevere923@aol.com.

REVERTE, MARIA (DEL PERPETUO SOCORRO), pharmacologist; b. Caracas, Venezuela, May 24, 1953; arrived in Spain, 1972; d. Isidoro Reverte and María Bernal; m. Juan Antonio García Iglesias; children: Juan Antonio, Rosa María, Carmen. MD, U. Complutense Madrid, Spain; PhD in Medicine, U. Salamanca, 1989. Cooperator in edn. U. Complutense, Madrid, 1980-81; mem. med. dept. Glaxo Lab., Madrid, 1982-83; clin. trials monitor Hoechst Iberia, Barcelona, 1983-84; lectr. pharmacology U. Salamanca, 1985-92, assoc. prof. pharmacology, 1992—2004, prof. pharmacology, 2005—; hon. prof. Albert Schweitzer Internat. U. Collaborator Inst. Reina Sofia Investigation Nefrologia, Salamanca, 1994—2000, Inst. Neuroscis. Castilla and Leon, Instituto Universitario de Ciencias de la Educación, 2001—. Contbr. articles to books and profl. jours. Recipient Travel award Am. Soc. for Biochemistry and Molecular Biology, 2000, Legion of Honor award, United Cultural Convention, 2005; named Dame Internat. World Order in Sci. Edn. and Culture. Mem.: Internat. Woman's Review (founder mem.), Bibliotheque World Wide, Amigos de Naciones Unidas, Internat. Acad. Sci. (academician), Colegio Médicos Salamanca, London Diplomatic Acad., N.Y. Acad. Sci., French Soc. Pharmacology and Spanish Soc. Pharmacology, Assn. Española de Medicina de la Industria Farmaceutica. Roman Catholic. Office: U Salamanca Fac Medicine Dept Fisiologia y Farmalologia Avalfonsox El Sabio 37007 Salamanca Spain Business E-Mail: socorro@usal.es.

REVES, JOSEPH GERALD (JERRY REVES), anesthesiology educator, dean; b. Charleston, SC, Aug. 14, 1943; s. George Everett and Frances (Masterson) R.; m. Virginia Cathcart, Jan. 05, 1945; children: Virginia Masterson, Christine Frances, Elizabeth Cathcart. BA, Vanderbilt U., 1965; MD, Medical Coll. S.C., 1969; MS, U. Ala., Birmingham, 1973. Lic. anesthesiologist S.C., Ala., Md., N.C.; Diplomate Am. Coll. Anesthesiology, Am. Bd. Anesthesiology. Rsch. asst., dept. pharmacology Med. Coll. SC, 1965, 1966, intern U. Ala. Hosp. and Clinics, Birmingham, Ala., 1969-70, resident in anesthesiology, 1970-72; post-doctoral, dept. anesthesia and physiology U. Ala. Med. Sch., 1972; instr., dept anesthesiology U. Ala. Hosp. and Clinics, 1973; dept. tng. staff, anesthesiology Nat. Naval Med. Ctr., Bethesda, Md., 1973-75; clin. instr., dept. anesthesiology George Washington U. Sch. Med., Washington, 1973-75; assoc. prof., dept. anesthesiology U. Ala. Hosp. and Clinics, 1975-78; dir., div. anesthesiology rsch. U. Ala., 1977-84, prof. anesthesiology, 1978-84; clin. anesthesia coord. UAB Cardiac Transplant Program, Birmingham, 1982-84; prof. anesthesiology, dir. cardiothoracic anesthesia Duke U. Med. Ctr., Durham, NC, 1984-1991; dir. Duke Heart Ctr., Duke Med. Ctr., Durham, NC, 1987-97; interim chmn., dept. anesthesiology Duke U. Med. Ctr., 1990-91, prof. and chmn., dept. anesthesiology, 1991—2001; dean, v.p. for med. affairs Med. U. SC Coll. Medicine, Charleston, 2001—. Cons. Hoffman-LaRoche, Somatogen, Abbott/Oximetric. Contbr. to numerous profl. jours., refereed jours., chpts. in books, published scientific reviews, selected abstracts, editorials, films, audio visual presentations, letters, positions and background papers; author: Acute Revascularization of the Infracted Heart, 1987, Common Problems in Cardiac Anesthesia, 1987, Intravenous Anesthesia and Analgesia, 1988, Anesthesiology Clinics of North America, 1988, Anesthesia, 1990, International Anesthesiology Clinics, 1991; Cardiac Anesthesis, Privileges and Practice, 1994; editor: Anesthesia and Analgesia, 1984—, cardiovascular sect. editor 1991—; editorial bd. Society Cardiovascular Anesthesia Monograph Series (chmn. 1986-89), Current Opinion in Anaesthesia 1987—, American Antec Newsletter 1989—; co-editor in chief: Current Opinion in Anaesthesiology 1990—. Dir. Clairmont Ave Hist. Preservation Com. 1976-78; Am. Heart Assn. (Durham chpt. pres. 1988-90, com. mem. anesthesiology, radiology and surgery rsch. study com. 1988-91). Grantee NIH 1991—, Janssen Pharmaceutica 1991-93, Anaquest 1989-92, Diprivan Ednl. grant ICI Pharmaceuticals Group 1991-92. Fellow Am. Coll. Cardiology; mem. AMA, Durham County Medical Soc., Internat. Soc. on Oxygen Transport to Tissue, N.C. Soc. Anesthesiologist (edn. com. 1992—), N.C. State Medical Soc., Birmingham Vanderbilt Club (bd. dirs. 1975-80, 1st v.p. 1979, pres. 1980), Southern Med. Assn. (chmn. elect. anesthesiology sect. 1976-77, chmn. 1977-78, chmn. 1988-89), Southern Soc. Anesthesiologists (v.p. 1978-79, pres. elect 1979-80, pres. 1980-81), Soc. Cardiovascular Anesthesiologists (pres. 1979-80), Assn. Univ. Anesthetists (elected to mem. 1980), Assn. Cardiac Anesthesiologists (elected to mem. 1982, pres. 1990), Soc. for Neuroleptanalgesia (bd. dirs. 1988), U. Ala. Birmingham Nat. Alumni Soc. (dist. dir., bd. dirs. 1991-93), Internat. Anesthesia Rsch. Soc. (bd. Trustees 1992—), Am. Soc. Anesthesiologists (com. sub-specialty representation 1980—, subcommittee on clin. circulation 1992—, com. geriatric anesthesia 1992—), Sigma Xi, Alpha Omega Alpha. Achievements include research on effects of age on neurologic response to cardiopulmonary bypass; cerebral blood flow and metabolism during cardiac surgery; automated delivery system of intravenous anesthetic drugs; pathophysiology of cardiopulmonary bypass; redesign of medical education. Office: Med U SC PO Box 250617 96 Jonathan Lucas St Ste 601 Charleston SC 29425 Office Phone: 843-792-2842. Business E-Mail: revesj@musc.edu.

REVICH, BORIS ALEX, environmentalist; b. Moscow, Dec. 21, 1944; Degree, Moscow Medicine Inst., 1968. Head, dept. Inst. Forecasting Russian Acad. Sci., 1992—. Recipient Nobel Peace prize, IPCC. Mem.: Internat. Soc. Environ. Epidemiology. Office: Nachimovsky Av 47 Moscow 117418 Russia Office Fax: 7 495 718 97 71. Business E-Mail: revich@ecfor.ra.

REVISHVILI, AMIRAN, health facility administrator; b. Feb. 11, 1956; Pres. Pan-Russian Scientific Soc. of Clin. Electrophysiology; founding pres. Ctr. of Surg. and Interventional Arrhythmology, Ministry of Health of the Russian Fed.; exec. dir. dept. of tachiarrhytmias Bakulev Scientific Ctr. of Cardiovasc. Surgery. Mailing: c/o Ministry of Health Russian Federation 3 Rakhmanovsky Pereulok Moscow Russia Office Phone: 4956284453. Office Fax: 4956272944. *

REW, ROBERT SHERRARD, pharmacologist; b. Pendleton, Oreg., Aug. 14, 1943; s. Ronald Royal and Patricia (Sherrard) Rew; m. Nora Eileen Kozan, Nov. 1, 1974; 1 child, Keenan Jay. BS, Whitman Coll., Walla Walla, Wash., 1966; MS, Wash. State U., Pullman, 1968; ScD, Johns Hopkins Med. Insts., Balt., 1974. Rsch. assoc. Notre Dame U., South Bend, Ind., 1972-76; lab. chief USDA, Beltsville, Md., 1976-82; sr. rsch. fellow Merck Inst., Rahway, NJ, 1982-85; vis. scientist CSIRO, Sydney, 1985-86; mng. parasitology rschr. Smith Kline Beecham, West Chester, Pa., 1986-90; assoc. dir. product devel. Pfizer Inc., NYC, 1990-96, mgr. tech. svcs. Exton, Pa., 1996—2001; pres. Rsch. Consulting, West Chester, Pa., 2001—. Adj. prof. U. Pa., Phila., 1987-03, NY Med. Coll., 1984-86, U. Md., College Park, 1980-82; pres. Rew Ranches, Inc., Pendleton, Oreg., 1993-; USPHS tchg. asst. Washington State U., 1966-68; USPHS rsch. asst. Johns Hopkins U., 1968-72; NIH postdoctoral fellow Notre Dame U., 1972-77; dir., malaria rschr. Drs. for Life, South Africa, 2003-04. Author: Agriculture Chemicals of the Future, 1984, Antimicrobial Therapy in Veterinary Medicine, 1993, 2000; author, editor: Chemotherapy of Parasite Diseases, 1986, Macrocyclic Lactones in Antiparasitic Therapy, 2003. Bd. dirs. House of His Creation, Gap, Pa., 1997-2005, Encuentro Ministries, 2005—, Ancient of Days, 2000-2006. Mem. Am. Assn. Vet. Parasitologists (pres.-elect 1998-99, pres. 1999-2000), Am. Soc. Parasitologists (industry com. 1994-98), Helminthol. Soc. of Wash, World Assn. for Advancement of Vet. Parasitologists. Avocations: skiing, fishing, coaching. Office: Rewsearch Consulting 400 N Wawaset Rd West Chester PA 19382

REWCASTLE, NEILL BARRY, neuropathologist; b. Sunderland, Eng., Dec. 12, 1931; arrived in Can., 1955; s. William and Eva R.; m. Eleanor Elizabeth Barton Boyd, Sept. 27, 1958 (dec. Jan. 1999); 4 children. MB, ChB cum laude, U. St. Andrews, Scotland, 1955; MA, U. Toronto, 1962. Licentiate Med. Coun. Can., 1957; cert. in gen. pathology, 1962, cert. in neuropathology, 1968. Rotating intern Vancouver Gen. Hosp., 1955-56; resident in pathology Shaughnessy Hosp., Vancouver, 1956-57, St. Michaels & Toronto Gen. Hosp., Ont., Canada, 1957-60; demonstrator dept. pathology U. Toronto, 1964-65, lectr., acting head divsn. neuropathology dept. pathology, 1965—69, assoc. prof., 1969-70, prof., head divsn. neuropathology, 1970—81; fellow, pathology Med. Rsch. Coun. Can., U. Toronto & Deutsche Forschungsantalt fur psychiatrie, Munich, 1960-64; prof. & head dept. pathology U. Calgary, 1981-91, prof., 1991—2000, prof. emeritus pathology, lab. medicine, clin. neuroscis., 2000—, mem. neurosci. rsch. group, 1982—2003, sr. pathologist Toronto Gen. Hosp., 1970—81. Dir. dept. histopathology Foothills Hosp., Calgary, 1981-91, pathologist, 1981—2003, cons. neuropathology, 1981-2003; spl. acad. adv. to dean faculty medicine U. Calgary, 1995-97; presenter in field. Contbr. over 146 articles to profl. jour., chpts. to books. Recipient Queen Elizabeth Silver Jubilee medal, 1977. Fellow: Royal Coll. Physicians & Surgeons Can.; mem. Can. Assn. Neuropathologists (ret. mem., sec. 1965-69, pres. 1976-79), Am. Assn. Neuropathologists (sr.), Sunshine Coast Power and Sail Squadron (comdr. 2007-09, past comdr. 2009-), Gibsons Curling Club (bd. dirs. 2006-09) Sunshine Coast Golf and Country Club. Avocations: gardening, philately, golf, curling, sailing. Personal E-mail: rewcastb@telus.net.

REX, DOUGLAS KEVIN, gastroenterologist, educator; b. Ft. Wayne, Ind., Aug. 21, 1954; Grad. with highest distinction (summa cum laude), Harvard Coll., 1976; MD, Ind. U. Sch. Medicine, 1980. Cert. Internal Medicine, 1985, Pediatric Gastroenterology, 1987. Intern, internal medicine Ind. U. Med. Ctr., Indpls., 1980—81, resident, internal medicine, 1981—82, fellow, 1982—84; chief med. resident, gastroenterology Ind. U. Hosp., Indpls., 1984—85, clin. gastroenterologist, dir., endoscopy; joined Ind. U. Sch. Medicine, Indpls., 1985, hosp. appt., medicine, prof., dept. medicine, divsn. gastroenterology and hepatology, chancellor's prof. Chmn. US Multisociety. Task Force on Colorectal Cancer, 1999—2006. Contbr. articles to profl. jours., chapters to books; assoc. editor Jour. Watch Gastroenterology, Reviews on Gastroenterological Disorders, mem. editl. bd. Clin. Gastroenterology and Hepatology, Jour. Clin. Gastroenterology, World Jour. Gastroenterology, Gastroenterology and Hepatology. Mem.: Am. Coll. Gastroenterology (rep. to Nat. Colorectal Cancer Round, chmn. bd. govs., past sec., past treas., past pres.). Office: Ind U Dept Medicine 550 University Blvd Rm 4100 Indianapolis IN 46202-5149 Office Phone: 317-274-0912. Office Fax: 317-274-5449. Business E-Mail: drex@iupui.edu.

REY, FERNANDO GONZÁLEZ, psychologist, educator; b. Havana, Cuba, June 27, 1949; Brasil; s. Fernando Cristobal González and Concepción Rey; m. Albertina Mitjáns, Dec. 29, 1983; 1 child, Fernando Luis González 1 stepchild, Miguel Angel Sirés; m. Patricia Arenas Bavtista, Nov. 18, 1972 (div. Nov. 1982); children: Zochil González Arenas, Boris González Arenas. Diploma in psychology, U. Havana, 1973; PhD in Psychology, Inst. Gen. and Pedagogical Psychology, Moscow, 1979; ScD, Inst. of Psychology, Acad. of Scis., Moscow, 1987. Asst. prof. psychology U. Havana, 1977—80, assoc. prof. psychology, 1980—85, full prof. psychology, 1985—95; full vis. prof. psychology U. Brasilia, Brazil, 1995—99; prof. Inst. Higher Edn. of Brasilia, Brazil, 1999—2004; assoc. prof. Sch. Medicine, Fed. U. Cear Fortineza, 2002—04; prof. Ponthifiscal Cath. U. Campinos, Sao Paulo, Brazil, 2004—07, Brazilian U. Ctr., 2008—. Vis. prof. doctoral program health psychology Autonomous U. of Madrid, 1996, vis. prof., 2005—; head dept. gen. psychology Sch. of Psychology, U. Havana, 1977—79, 1978—87, dean, 1988—91, vice rector, 1991—95. Author: Epistemological Problems of Psychology, 1993 (Nat. Prize of Cultural Critique, 1997), Qualitative Epistemology and Subjectivity, 1997, Qualitative Research in Psychology: Directions and Challenges, 1999; co-author: Personality: Its Education and Development, 1989 (Nat. Prize of Cultural Critique, 1990); contbr. articles to profl. pubs., chapters to books. Mem Communistic Party of Cuba, 1984—95. Recipient Interam. prize of psychology, Interam. Soc. of Psychology, Costa Rica, 1991. Mem.: Interam. Soc. Psychology (1985 1985, Interamerican Prize of Psychology 1991). Avocations: swimming, literature. Office: Pontifical Cath Univ Campinas Campus II Av Joh Boyd Dunlop 13059-900 Campinas Brazil Mailing: Sqs Quadra 407 Bloco R - Apt 206 70256-180 Brasilia DF Brazil Office Phone: 55-19-37298534. Personal E-mail: gonzalez_rey49@hotmail.com. Business E-Mail: gonzalezrey@terra.com.br.

REYES, RAUL GREGORIO, surgeon; b. Tegucigalpa, Morazan, Honduras, June 18, 1928; came to U.S., 1939; s. Julio Gregorio and Mercedes Ofelia (Mazzoni) Reyes-Zelaya; m. Mildred Dane Smith, 1951 (dec. May 1990); children: Tyra, Kimberly; stepchildren: Javier, Christian; m. Blanca Lidia Milla, Apr. 2, 1993. BS, Georgetown U., 1945; MD, George Washington U., 1950. Diplomate Nat. Bd. Med. Examiners, Am. Bd. Surgery. Intern Charity Hosp., New Orleans, 1950-51; resident Emergency Hosp./George Washington U., Washington, 1951, Charity Hosp., New Orleans, 1952-55; chief thoracic surgery San Felipe Hosp., Tegucigalpa, 1955-56; assoc. to ptnr. Browne-McHardy Clinic, New Orleans, 1955-60, 60-73; med. dir. New Orleans Indsl. Clinic, 1956-58; chief of surgery and orthopedics Lallie Kemp Regional Hosp., Independence, La., 1987-89, med. dirs., 1988-89; owner, pres. Raul G. Reyes, A Med. Corp., New Orleans, 1973—. Owner, pres. Internat. Maritime Med. Svcs., New Orleans, 1978—, Catracho Enterprises, New Orleans, 1975—, Phys. Therapy Svcs. of New Orleans, 1975—; faculty La. State Univ. Sch. Medicine, 1953—, others. Inventor in field; contbr. articles to profl. jours. Chmn. Rep. Hispanic Assembly, New Orleans, 1983; pre-cand. Nat. Party, Honduras, 1985; founder Literacy Ctrs. of Honduras, 1991; presdl. candidate Christian Dem. Party of Honduras, 1994. Named to Hon. Consul of Honduras, Hon. Citizen, City of New Orleans. Mem. ACS, AMA, So. Med. Assn., La. State Med. Soc., Orleans Parish Med. Soc., Colegio Medico de Honduras. Roman Catholic. Avocations: tennis, reading, writing, social progs. Office: PO Box 15379 New Orleans LA 70175-5379 Office Phone: 504-904-0961. Personal E-mail: raulgreyesm.d@aol.com.

REY-GIRAUD, AGNÈS, health products executive; m. Chris Rey Giraud; children: Charlotte, Julie. MBA, U. Chgo.; M in Engring., Ecole Nationale d'Ingenieurs de Saint-Etienne, France; M of Ops. Mgmt., ESC, Lyon, France. Various mgmt. positions in mktg., gen. mgmt., ops., sales, fin. and info. systems in US and Europe Xerox; v.p., gen. mgr. eBusiness Express Scripts, Inc., Md. Heights, Mo., 2000—02, sr. v.p. prog. devel., 2002—03, sr. v.p. product mgmt., 2003—06, sr. v.p. strategy and bus. devel., 2006—, sr. v.p. supply chain orgn., 2006—07, exec. v.p. trade rels. & develop. markets, 2007—08, pres. internat. ops., 2008—. Office: Express Scripts Inc 14000 Riverport Dr Maryland Heights MO 63043-4805 Office Phone: 314-770-1666. *

REYNOLDS, ERNEST WEST, retired internist, educator; b. Bristow, Okla., May 11, 1920; s. Ernest West and Florence (Brown) R. BS, U. Okla., 1942, MD, 1946, MS, 1952. Diplomate: Am. Bd. Internal Medicine. Intern Boston City Hosp., 1946-47; resident Grady Meml. Hosp., Atlanta, 1949-50; practice medicine Tulsa, Okla., 1953-54; prof. medicine U Mich., 1965-72; prof. medicine, dir. cardiology U. Wis., 1972-90, prof. emeritus, 1991—. Dir. Kellogg Found. Comprehensive Coronary Care Project, 1967-72; chmn. NIH Cardiovascular Study Sect. A, 1972-73 Mem. editorial bd.: Am. Heart Jour; Contbr. articles to profl. jours. Served to capt. AUS, 1947-49. Mem. Am. Heart Assn. (fellow coun. clin. cardiology), Ctrl. Soc. Clin. Rsch. Home: 17 Red Maple Trl Madison WI 53717-1515 Personal E-mail: ernest_reynolds@yahoo.com.

REYNOLDS, HARMONY R., cardiologist, educator; b. May 20, 1973; MD, NYU Sch. Medicine, 1997. Asst. prof. medicine, assoc. dir., cardiovasc. clin. rsch. ctr. NYU Langone Med. Ctr., 2004—. Fellow: Am. Soc. Echocardiography, Am. Coll. Cardiology; mem.: ACP, AHA Go Red Women Com., Am. Heart Assn. (Young Heart award). Office: 530 1st Ave Skirball 9R New York NY 10016 Business E-Mail: harmony.reynolds@nyumc.org.

REYNOLDS, HERBERT YOUNG, internist; b. Richmond, Va., Aug. 20, 1939; s. George Audney and Pearle Maupin (Young) R.; m. Anne Browning Leavell, July 11, 1964; children: Nancy, George, William Stuart. BA in English, U. Va., 1961, MD, 1965; MA (hon.), Yale U., 1979. Diplomate Am. Bd. Internal Medicine, Am. Bd. Allergy and Immunology. Intern NY Hosp., Cornell Med. Ctr., NYC, 1965—66, asst. physician, fellow in medicine, 1966—67; clin. assoc., lab. clin. investigation Nat. Inst. Allergy, Infectious Diseases, NIH, Bethesda, Md., 1967—70, chief clin. assoc., lab. clin. investigation, 1968—69; chief resident, instr. medicine U. Hosp. U. Wash., Seattle, 1970—71; sr. investigator, lab. clin. investigation Nat. Inst. Allergy, Infectious Diseases, NIH, Bethesda, 1971—76; assoc. prof. internal medicine Yale U. Sch. Medicine, New Haven, 1976—79, prof., 1979—88, head pulmonary divsn.; J. Lloyd Huck prof. medicine, chmn. dept. Pa. State U., Milton S. Hershey Med. Ctr., 1988—2002; assoc. chmn. divsn. medicine Pa. State Geisinger Health Sys., 1997—2000, chief medicine ops. Hershey Med. Ctr. Region, 1997—2000; med. officer Lung Biology and Disease br., divsn. lung diseases NHLBI/NIH, Bethesda, 2002—11; prof. medicine emeritus Pa. State U. Coll. Medicine, 2002—. Adj. prof. medicine Uniformed Svcs. U. Health Scis., Bethesda, 2003—; mem. exec. com. Coll. Medicine Pa. State U.-Hershey Med. Ctr., 1988-2002, exec. bd. U. Hosp., 1988-2002, fin. bd. acad. enrichment fun, 1988-95, dean's adv. com., 1988-97, diversity task force, 1995-2002, physicians faculty practice plan exec. com. 1996-97, human resources team leader, 2000-02; dept. chair rep. Milton S. Hershey Med. Ctr. Bd., 2000-2002; cons. in infectious diseases Nat. Naval Med. Ctr., NIH, Bethesda, 1971-76, clin. rsch. com., 1971-76, chmn., 1974-76, pulmonary disease adv. com. divsn. of lung diseases NHLBI, 1978-82, sci. counselors bd., 1984-88, data and safety monitoring bd. registry of patients with deficiency of Alpha-1 Antitrypsin, 1989-96. Mem. editl. bd. Lung, 1978-2005, Am. Jour. Medicine, 1979-89, Jour. Clin. Investigation, 1980-86, Am. Rev. Respiratory Diseases, 1980-87, Jour. Applied Physiology, 1981-89, Resident Physician, 1981-95; contbr. 326 articles to profl. jours. and med. textbooks. Parent com. Troop 1 Boy Scouts Am., Madison, 1979-82; bd. dirs. Neighborhood Music Sch., Guilford, Conn., 1978-87; Music at Gretna, 1994-2002; bd. dirs. Harrisburg Symphony, 1996-2000; active All Saints Episc. Ch., Hershey; pulmonary infections com. Cystic Fibrosis Found., Bethesda, 1980-86; mem. coun. sci. advisors Parker B. Francis Found., Kansas City, Kans., 1983-87; internat. com. World Orgn. for Sarcoidosis and other Granulomatous Disorders, 1987-95; bd. dirs., mem. coun. Am. Lung Assn., 1989-93, bd. govs. 1990-93, com. mem., 1990-93; coach Guilford Soccer League, 1985-88; vol. Mercy Health Clinic, Gaithersburg, Md., 2003—. Surgeon USPHS, 1967-70. John Edward Nobel fellow, 1961-65; named Outstanding Med. Specialist in USA, Town and Country Mag., 1989, 97, The Best Med. Specialists, Town & Country mag., 1995, One of 400 Best Drs. in U.S. Good Housekeeping Mag., 1991, Best Drs. in Am., 1992-; recipient Nat. Inst. Health award of Merit, 2006, Nat. Inst. Health Dir. award, 2007, 09, 11. Fellow ACP (coun. subsplty. socs. 1989-2000, gov. Pa. Ea. Region 1, 2000-02), Am. Coll. Chest Physicians (program com. 1978-84), Infectious Disease Soc. Am., Coll. Physicians Phila.; mem. Am. Thoracic Soc. (sec.-treas. 1987-88, bd. dirs. 1989-93, v.p. 1988-89, pres. 1991-92), Am. Soc. Clin. Investigation, Assn. Am. Physicians, Am. Assn. Immunologists, Am. Fedn. Clin. Rsch., Am. Clin. and Climatol. Assoc. (v.p. 2001-02, pres. 2002-03), Acad. Medicine Wash., Interurban Clin. Club (emeritus 1989), Hershey Country Club, Farmington Country Club, Raven Soc., Phi Beta Kappa, Alpha Omega Alpha, Omicron Delta Kappa. Avocations: tennis, violin. Home: 226 E Caracas Ave Hershey PA 17033-1309

REYNOLDS, JAMES, management consultant; s. Richard James and Esther (Nikander) R.; m. Joanne M.J. BA in Econs., NYU, 1965, postgrad., 1965-66. Cons. to pres. Rothrock, Reynolds & Reynolds Inc., NYC, 1966-70; sr. v.p. health, med. div. Booz, Allen & Hamilton, NYC, 1970-80; pres. Reynolds & Co. (mgmt. cons.), San Francisco, NYC, Washington, 1981—. Developer Combining Pay for Performance with Gain Sharing to align incentives, Leap Frog Group, 2007, developer, HAC Focused Gain Sharing Program, 2008; bd. dirs. Booz, Allen & Hamilton, 1977-79; chmn. bd. J.X. Reynolds Fine Arts, Ltd., 1979—; lectr. Harvard Sch. Pub. Health; faculty mem. Am. Coll. of Healthcare Execs.; bd. dirs. Health Ctr. Mgmt. Inst., Richmond, Va., 1977; mem. health adv. bd. Hunter Coll., 1980—. Mem. editl. bd. Physicians Fin. News. Recipient NYU Founders award, 1965 Mem. Am. Pub. Health Assn., Am. Mgmt. Assn., Assn. Am. Med. Colls., Am. Hosp. Assn., Hosp. Mgmt. Systems Soc., Hosp. Fin. Mgmt. Assn., Asia Soc., China Inst., Phi Beta Kappa, Guggenheim Mus., Mus. Modern Art, Met. Mus. Art, Met. Opera Guild (NYC) Episcopalian. Home and Office: Reynolds & Co 333 E 51st St New York NY 10022-6702 Home: 333 E 51st St New York NY 10022-6702 Office Phone: 212-826-1818. Business E-Mail: jreynolds@jxreynolds.com.

REYNOLDS, JUDITH AMY, nutritionist, animal scientist, consultant, educator; d. Jacob Alen and Mary Emeline Lundgren; m. Rodney Roger Reynolds, Aug. 28, 1971; children: Andrea Mary Rickards, James Christopher. AA summa cum laude, Anoka Ramsey CC, 1988; BS summa cum laude, St. Cloud State U., 1990; MS, Tex. A&M U., 1993, PhD, 1997. Cert. Profl. Animal Scientist Am. Registry Profl. Animal Scientists, 1995. Co-owner, mgr. Reynolds Quarter Horses, Palmyra, Mo., 1978—; grad. asst. rschr. Tex. A&M U., College Station, 1990—91, grad. asst. tchr., 1991—95; long term substitute tchr. biology, anatomy physiology, chemistry Princeton and Elk River Pub. Sch. Sys., Minn., 1997—98; divisional equine tech. specialist Archer Daniels Midland Animal Health Nutrition and MoorMan's Inc., Quincy, Ill., 1998—2001; equine nutritionist Archer Daniels Midland Alliance Nutrition Inc., Quincy, 2001—, equine product and tech. mgr., 2007—. Asst. prof. William Woods U., Fulton, Mo., 1995—97; assoc. faculty John Woods CC, Quincy, Ill., 2004—; spkr. in field; ofcl. reviewer Nat. Rsch. Coun., Nutrient Requirements of Horses, 2007; mem. Equine Sci. Soc. Nutrition Com., 2006—. Author: (online source) Equine Nutrition in the 21st Century (1st Pl. Online Svc. To Reader, 2003); contbr. articles in to profl. jours. Vol. Princeton Pub. Schools, Princeton, Minn., 1983—90; vol. leader; horse sci., horse bowl, horse advancement, vet. sci. Isanti County 4-H, Minn., 1983—90; vol. leader horse judging, market steers, poultry Bryan HS Future Farmers of Am., Tex., 1992—94; vol. horse judge Brazos County, College Station, Tex., 1991—94, Tex. A&M U., College Station, 1991—95; vol. horse bowl team coach Mo. State 4-H, 1996—97; vol. 4-H horse judge Audrain and Calloway Counties, Fulton, Mo., 1996—97. Recipient High Point All Around Horse, Minn. Quarter Horse Assn., 1980, Two Register of Merit Horses, Am. Quarter Horse Assn., 1980, 1982, Four High-Point and Res. Performance Gelding awards, Five State Champions, Five Res. State Champions, Minn. Quarter Horse Assn., 1980-1983, One Performance Horse Qualified, Outstanding Horses of World, World Equine Rsch. Inst., 1983; Mensa scholarship, Am. Mensa, 1987, Alliss scholarships, Alliss, 1987-1990, Academic scholarships, Anoka Ramsey CC, 1987-1988, St. Cloud State U., 1988-1990. Mem.: Am. Registry Profl. Animal Scientists, Equine Sci. Soc. (nutrition com. 2006—), Am. Quarter Horse Assn., Nat. Reining Horse Assn., Phi Kappa Phi, Psi Chi, Kappa Delta Pi, Phi Theta Kappa, Gamma Sigma Delta. Achievements include development of equine feeds and supplements, SENIORGLO, MOORGLO, PRO-VITA-MIN 20 supplement tubs, FORAGE FIRST Horse Rewards, MOORGLO Canadian formula, GROSTRONG QuadBLOCK Canadian formula; Stay STRONG Metabolic Mineral Pellets, JUNIORGLO, HEALTHY GLO Nuggets, HEALTHY GLO Meal, PRIMEGLO. Avocations: horses, reading, writing, cooking. Office: ADM Alliance Nutrition 1000 N 30th St Quincy IL 62305 Office Fax: 217-222-9060. Business E-Mail: judy.reynolds@adm.com.

REYNOLDS, LOUISE MAXINE KRUSE, retired school nurse; b. Waynesboro, Va., May 28, 1935; d. Emil Herman and Cora Lee (Hammer) Kruse; m. Elbert B. Reynolds Jr., June 13, 1964; children: David Emil, Jane Marie. Diploma, Rockingham Meml. Hosp., 1956; student, Madison Coll., Tex. Tech U. RN, Tex., Va, cert. sch. nurse. Head nurse orthopedic, opthalmology dept. surgery Duke U., Durham, N.C., 1961-62; head nurse surg. fl. Waynesboro (Va.) Hosp., 1962-64; sch. nurse Lubbock (Tex.) Ind. Sch. Dist., 1974-94, ret., 1994. Pres. Vol. Network Luth. Home, Lubbock, Tex., 1996-2000; sec. Luth. Student Coun., Tex. Tech., Lubbock, 1999-2000. Recipient recognition for contbn. to ch. and cmty., Aid Assn. for Luths. Mem. DAR (sec. Nancy Anderson chpt. 2000-02, chpt. chaplain 2002-04, chpt. treas. 2006-08), Va. Nurses Assn. (dist. sec., chair), Tex. Assn. Sch. Nurses (sec., treas. dist. 17, program chair 1989 state conv., records dir. Thrivent Lubbock area chpt. band 2006—10). Personal E-mail: lmkreynolds@yahoo.com.

REYNOLDS, MARJORIE LAVERS, nutritionist, educator; b. Collingwood, Ont., Can., Jan. 10, 1931; d. Henry James and Laura (Wilson) Lavers; m. John Horace Reynolds, Aug. 17, 1963; children: Steven, Mark. BA, U. Toronto, 1953; MS, U. Minn., 1957; PhD, U. Wis., 1964; AS, State Tech. Inst. Knoxville, 1982. Registered dietitian. Rsch. dietitian Mayo Clinic, Rochester, Minn., 1957-59; rsch. dietitian Cleve. Met. Gen. Hosp., 1959-60; rsch. assoc. U. Tenn., Knoxville, 1963-66; instr. Ft. Sanders Sch. Nursing, Knoxville, 1967-76, State Tech. Inst., Knoxville, 1982-88; substitute secondary sch. tchr. Knox County Schs., Knoxville, 1989-93. Contbr. articles to biochem. and nutrition jours.; newsletter editor Juvenile Diabetes Found., Knoxville, 1985-93. Sec. Midway Rehab. Ctr., Knoxville, 1987—2001. Mem.: LWV, Knoxville Dist. Dietetic Assn. (pres. 1971—72, Outstanding Dietitian 1973—74), Tenn. Dietetic Assn. (pres. 1973—74, Outstanding Dietitian 1973—74), Omicron Nu. Democrat. Presbyterian. Avocations: reading, sports. Home: 7112 Stockton Dr Knoxville TN 37909-2534

REYNOLDS, ROBERT GREGORY, toxicologist, management consultant; b. July 29, 1952; s. Robert G. and Loys Delle (Kever) R.; m. Phyllis Thurrell, May 1983. BS in Nutrition and Food Sci., MIT, 1973, postgrad. in toxicology, 1973—78; postgrad. in mgmt., Sloan Sch. Mgmt., 1977—78. Cert. AM.APMP. Mng. editor The Grad. Mag. MIT, Cambridge, 1975-78; v.p. Internat. Contact Bur., Ft. Lauderdale, Fla., 1977—. Staff toxicologist, asst. to v.p. mktg. Enviro Control, Inc., Rockville, Md., 1978-79; dir. tech. resources Borriston Rsch. Labs., Inc., Temple Hills, Md., 1979-80; dir. mktg. Northrop Svcs., Inc., Rsch. Triangle Park, N.C., 1980-88, mgr. bus. devel., NSI Tech. Svcs.Corp., 1988-89; mgr. proposal mgmt. Roy F. Weston, Inc., West Chester, Pa., 1989-90; project dir. Human Health Scis., 1990-91; pres. Spectrum Mgmt. Assocs., Loveland, Ohio, 1991—; mgmt. cons., 1981—; dir. bus. devel. Groundwater Tech., Inc., Chadds Ford, Pa., 1992-93; v.p. fed. programs ETG Environ. Inc., Blue Bell, Pa., 1993-94; dir. govt. bus. devel. OHM Corp., Findlay, Ohio, 1994-97; toxicol. cons. Energy Resources Co., Inc., Cambridge, 1976-77. Contbr. chpts. in textbook, lab. manual, sci. jours. and govt. publs. Bd. dirs. Ossipee Lake Alliance. NSF fellow, 1973. Mem. Assn. Proposal Mgmt. Profls., Nat. Def. Indsl. Assn., Soc. Am. Mil. Engrs.

REZAI, ALI, neurosurgeon, educator; MD, U. Southern Calif. Cert. neurological surgery. Intern NYU Med. Ctr., resident, fellow, dir. ctr. functional & restorative neurosurgery; fellow U. Toronto, Karolinska Inst., Stockholm; dir. ctr. for neurological restoration Cleveland Clinic, prof. neurosurgery. Editorial bd. Neurosurgery Jour. Editor: Textbook of Neuromodulation. Recipient Innovation award, NorTech, 2005, Innovator of Yr., Cleveland Clinic, 2007; named one of the Best Doctors in America, Guide to America's Top Doctors, 2001—08. Fellow: Inst. of Physics, Congress Neurological Surgeons (exec. bd. mem.); mem.: Soc. U. Neurosurgeons, Soc. for Neuroscience, Am. Soc. Stereotactic & Functional Neurosurgery (sec. & treas.), North Am. Neuromodulation Soc., Am. Assn. Neurological Surgeons (Investigator award 1998), Alpha Omega Alpha. Office: Cleveland Clinic Main Campus 9500 Euclid Ave MC-S31 Cleveland OH 44195 Office Phone: 216-444-4720.

REZNICK, RICHARD HOWARD, pediatrician; b. Chgo., Oct. 31, 1939; s. Louis and Mae Reznick; m. Barbara Ann Glantz, June 20, 1965; children: Steven L., Alicia T., Scott M., Stacey R. BS, U. Ill., 1961; MD, Loyola U., Chgo., 1965. Diplomate Am. Bd. Pediatrics. Resident in pediat. Michael Reese Hosp., Chgo., 1966-68; pediatrician USAF, Homestead AFB, Fla., 1968-70; pediatrician pvt. practice Winnetka, Ill., 1970—71, Scottsdale, Ariz., 1971—. Pres. med. staff Phoenix Children's Hosp., 1990-93, bd. dirs. 1990-94. Capt. USAF, 1968-70. Fellow Am. Acad. Pediatrics (treas. Ariz. chpt. 1982-84); mem. Ariz. Med. Assn., Phoenix Pediatric Soc. (treas. 1976-77), Maricopa County Med. Soc. Avocations: music, bicycling, gardening, stamp collecting/philately. Office: Papago Buttes Pediatric Ctr 8573 E San Alberto Ste E100 Scottsdale AZ 85258-4318 Office Phone: 480-778-1732.

REZNICK, STEVEN MICHAEL, orthopedic surgeon, educator; b. Washington, 1954; 3 children. BS, U. Md., 1975; MD, George Washington U., 1979; MBA, Columbia U., 2000. Diplomate Am. Bd. Orthopedic Surgery. Resident in gen. surgery George Washington U., 1979-81; resident in orthop. surgery U. Mich., Ann Arbor, 1981-84; clin. instr. orthopedic surgery UCLA Sch. Medicine, 1988-94. Sr. aviation med. examiner FAA, 1985-87; talk show host KGIL-Radio, L.A., 1987-90. Mem. Calif. Rep. Party, Calif. Rep. Assembly, bd. dirs. Palm Springs chpt., 1996-98. Fellow Internat. Coll. Surgeons, Am. Coll. Surgeons, Am. Acad. Orthopedic Surgeons, Beta Gamma Sigma Honor Soc. Avocation: aviation. Home: PO Box 101 Somers NY 10589 E-mail: smr50@columbia.edu.

REZNIKOV, ALEXANDER GRIGORIEVICH, endocrinologist, physiologist, pharmacologist; b. Odessa, Ukraine, Nov. 12, 1939; s. Grigoriy A. and Anna I. (Ghimelfarb) R.; m. Liudmila Alexieevna Largina, July 25, 1940; 1 child, Vladislav. MD, Med. Inst. Odessa, 1962; PhD, Med. Inst. Kiev, 1965; dr. med. sci., Bogomoletz Inst. Physiology, Kiev, 1974. Physician Hosp., Sukhoi Yelanetz, Ukraine, 1962-65; rschr. Inst. Endocrinology and Metabolism, Kiev, 1965-73, chief dept., 1973—. Vis. prof. U. Tex., Dallas, 1990, U. Toronto, 1995—96, Lawson Rsch. Inst., London, Canada, 1995; prof. biology U. Kyiv Moghyla, Kiev, 1997—98; cons., lectr. Schering AG, Kiev, 1996—2007, Medial AG, Kiev, 1996—2001, Bayer HealthCare, 2007—. Author: Sex Hormones and Brain Differentiation, 1982, Inhibitors of Adrenal Cortex, 1972, Methods of Hormone Analysis, 1980, Antiandrogens, 1988, Hormone-Neurotransmitter Imprinting of Neuroendocrine Control of Reproduction, 1994, Endocrine Therapy of Prostate Cancer, 1999, Androgen Deprivation Strategy in Prostate Cancer, 2001, Prenatal Stress and Neuroendocrine Pathology, 2004. V.p. Pathophysiol. Soc. Ukraine, Kiev, 1995—. Recipient State Prize for Scientific Achievements Ukraine Govt., 1976. Mem.: N.Y. Acad. Sci., Internat. Fedn. Neuroendocrinology, Nat. Acad. Med. Sci. Ukraine, Nat. Acad. Sci. Ukraine. Avocations: painting, music, reading. Home: 10 Klovsky Spusk Apt 61 01021 Kiev Ukraine Office: Inst Endocrinol & Metabol 69 Vyshgorodskaya Str 04114 Kiev Ukraine Home Phone: 380-44-2888818; Office Phone: 380-44-4328655. Personal E-mail: reznikov39@gmail.com.

RHA, JOUNG-HO, neurologist, educator; b. Seoul, Republic of Korea, Oct. 24, 1962; MD, Seoul Nat. U. Med. Coll., 1987, PhD, 1998. Prof., neurology Inha U. Med. Coll., 1997—. Vis. scholar UCLA Stroke Ctr., 2001—03. Mem.: Korean Neurol. Assn., Am. Acad. Neurology, Korean Stroke Assn., Am. Stroke Assn., World Stroke Orgn. Office: Inha University Hosp Neurology Choo Incheon 400-103 Republic of Korea Office Fax: 82-32-890-3864. Business E-Mail: jhrha@inha.ac.kr.

RHA, SEUNG WOON, cardiologist, physician; b. Seoul, Republic of Korea, June 17, 1965; s. Euy Seob and Kyung Soon (Kim) Rha; m. Yeon Kyung Lee, Aug. 10, 1991; children: Hee Won, Ji Won. BS, Korea U., 1993, MS, 1997, PhD, 2003. Diplomate Bd. Internal Medicine, 1998, Bd. Cardiology, 2004. Clin. fellow in cardiology Korea U. Anam Hosp., Seoul, 2002—03; rsch. fellow in interventional cardiology Washington Hosp. Ctr., 2003—04; clin. prof. cardiology Korea U. Guro Hosp., Seoul, 2004—05, asst. prof. cardiology Cardiovasc. Ctr., 2005—. Contbr. scientific papers in field. Med. svc. dir Migrant Worker's Hosp., Seoul, 2004—05. Recipient Best Intern award, Korea U. Hosp., 1994; named Best Resident internal medicine, 1995, Best Pub. Med. Dr., Korean Ministry Health and Welfare, 2000. Fellow: European Soc. Cardiology, Soc. Cardiovasc. Angiography and Interventions, Am. Heart Assn., Am. Coll. Cardiology. Baptist. Avocations: piano, basketball, tennis, music. Home: Gubanpo Apt 108-202 Seoul 137-049 Republic of Korea Office: Cardiovasc Ctr Korea U Guro Hosp 80 Guro-dong Guro-gu Seoul 152-703 Republic of Korea Office Phone: 82-2-2626-3020. Personal E-mail: swrha617@yahoo.co.kr.

RHEA, DEBORAH, healthcare educator; b. Dallas, Aug. 27, 1957; EdD, U. Houston, 1995. Assoc. dean, prof. Harris Coll. Nursing & Health Scis., Tex. Christian U., 1999—. Owner, phys. edn. curriculum writer, trainer Froglessons, 2005—11. Recipient Health Care Hero award, Dallas Bus. Jour., 2007, Tchg. award, Tex. Christian U., 2008, Outstanding Alumna award, U. Houston, Coll. Edn.; Phys. Edn. Program grant, Carol M White Fed. grant. Fellow: Am. Alliance Health, Phys. Edn., Recreation & Dance; mem.: Tex. Assn. Health, Phys. Edn., Recreation, & Dance, Assn. Applied Sport Psychology. Avocations: travel, gardening. Office: 3005 Stadium Dr Rickel 172P Fort Worth TX 76129 Business E-Mail: d.rhea@tcu.edu.

RHEA, MATTHEW R., exercise scientist, researcher; b. Logan, Utah, June 5, 1973; s. Ken and Virginia Rhea; m. Kellie Rhea, Oct. 11, 1995. BSc, So. Utah U., Cedar City, 1998; MSc, Ariz. State U., Tempe, 2001, PhD, 2004. Dir. rsch. Firefighter Health and Fitness Rsch. Inst., 2003—05; dir. condition Elite Sports Conditioning, 2004—06; dir. human movement Still U., 2006—. Cons. Phoeniz Fire Dept, 2002—04; health and exercise cons. Mesa Fire Acad., 2002—04. Contbr. articles to profl. jours. Founder Fire Fighter Health and Fitness Inst., Phoenix, 2003. Pedrick scholar, Ariz. State U. Mem.: Acad. of Sports Medicine, Am. Coll. Sports Medicine, Nat. Strength and Conditioning Assn. Avocations: sports, outdoor recreation. Home: 5850 E Still Cir Mesa AZ 85206

RHEE, DONG-KWON, researcher, microbiology educator, pharmacist; b. Poo Yeo, Chung Nam, Korea, Mar. 28, 1953; s. Man-Seok and Mok-Ja (Do) R.; m. Myoung Ran Park, Mar. 28, 1982; children: Eun-Jung, Kyoung-Min, June-Hyeok. BS, Sung Kyun Kwan U., Seoul, Korea, 1977; MS, Korea Adv. Inst. Sci. & Tech., Seoul, Korea, 1979; PhD, U. Ill., Chgo., 1988. Cert. pharmacist, Korea. Rsch. scientist Korea Ginseng, Tobacco Rsch. Inst., Seoul, 1979-82; rsch. asst. U. Ill., Chgo., 1982-87, rsch. fellow, 1987-88; from asst. to prof. Sung Kyun Kwan U., Su Won, Republic of Korea, 1988—. Acting chmn. dept. pharmacy Sung Kyun Kwan U., Su-Won, Korea, 1989-92; advisor Nat. Inst. Safety Rsch., Seoul, 1990-92, 2008-; mem. Ministry Pub. Health Drug Safety Review Bd., Seoul, 1991—; editor-in-chief J. Ginseng Rsch., 2008-10, v.p., Korean Soc. Ginseng, 2011-, commr., Microbiol. Soc. Korea, 2011, head, World Class U. Lab., 2008-; fellow Yale U., Dept. Pharmacology, New Haven, Conn., 1993-94. Recipient fellowship Sung Kyun Kwan U., Seoul, 1973-75, Korean Govt., Korea Advanced Inst. Sci. and Tech., Seoul, 1977-79, U. Ill., Chgo., 1987-88. Mem. Biochem Soc. of Korea (coun. 1992—), Pharm. Soc. Korea (sec.-gen., 1997-98, Pharmicist Assn. Seoul (chmn. bd. sci. com. 1992), Pharmicist Assn. Korea (bd. dirs. sci. com. 1992). Buddhist. Office: Sung Kyun Kwan U Sch Pharm 300 Chunchun-dong 440-746 Su-Won Kyongido Republic of Korea Office Phone: 82-31-290-7707. Fax: 82-31-290-7727. Business E-Mail: dkrhee@skku.ac.kr.

RHEE, EUN-JUNG, medical educator; b. Seoul, Republic of Korea, Aug. 17, 1972; d. Kyung-Ui Rhee and Hie-Lan Kim; m. Hyung-Geun Oh, June 10, 2000; 1 child, Youn-Jin Oh. MD, Ewha Women's U., 1997; M in Medicine, Cath. U., 2004. Cert. in Internal Medicine Korean Assn. Internal Medicine, 2003. Intern Ewha Women's U. Hosp., Seoul, Republic of Korea, 1997—98; resident in internal medicine Kangbuk Samsung Hosp., Sungkyunkwan U. Sch. Medicine, 1999—2003, fellow in endocrinology, 2003—05, instr., dept. endocrinology, 2005—07, asst. prof. dept. endocrinology, 2007—. Author: Metabolism, Clinical Endocrinology; contbr. articles to profl. jours. in field. Recipient Fall Academic award, Korean Diabetes Assn., 2003, Spring Academic award, 2004, Fall Excellent Rsch. Publ. award, Korean Endocrine Soc., 2005, Korean Soc. Bone Metabolism, 2005; Hyo-suk Rsch. grant, Kangbuk Samsung Hosp., 2004, Rsch. grant, Ewha Women's Med. Sch. Alumni Assn., 2005. Mem.: Am. Soc. Bone and Mineral Rsch., Endocrine Soc. (Clin. Investigator Trainees Travel grant 2005), Am. Diabetes Assn. Office: Kangbuk Samsung Hosp Endocrinology 108 Jongro ku Pyung dong Seoul 110746 Republic of Korea Office Fax: 82-2-2001-2049. Business E-Mail: hongsiri@hanmail.net.

RHEE, HEE SOON, health facility administrator; Asst. med. dir. Winfield Hosp., 1974—78; resident in medicine Trenton Pyschiat. Hosp., 1978—82, physician, 1982—87; med. dir. Seoul Fgn. Clinic, Republic of Korea, 1987—2009; dir. internat. clinic Korea Univ. Anam Hosp. Office: Korea University Medical Center 126-1 5Ka Anam-Dong Sungbuk-Ku Seoul 136-705 Republic of Korea Office Phone: 029205677. *

RHEE, KA-YOUNG, anesthesiologist, researcher; d. Ho-Kyung and Moon-Ja (Han) Rhee. MD, Seoul Nat. U., 1992, PhD, 1998. Lic. physician Ministry of Health, South Korea, 1992, anesthesiologist Ministry of Health, South Korea, 1997. Clin. prof. Seoul Nat. U., 2002—05; asst. prof. Konkuk U. Sch. Medicine, Seoul, 2005—08; assoc. prof. Konkok U. Sch. Medicine, 2009—; adj. prof. Seoul Nat. U., Republic of Korea, 2009—. Mem.: Internat. Anesthesia Rsch. Soc., Korean Soc. Anesthesiologists. Roman Catholic. Avocations: gardening, marine zoology. Office: Konkuk Univ Sch Medicine 1 Hwayangtong Gwangjinku Seoul 143-701 Republic of Korea Office Phone: 82-2-2030-5446. Office Fax: 82-2-2030-5449. Business E-Mail: rheeky@kuh.ac.kr.

RHEE, PETER MEONG, surgeon, medical educator; b. Seoul, South Korea, Sept. 18, 1961; m. Emily Rhee; children: Michael, Anna. BS in Health Systems Engring., Ga. Inst. Tech., 1983; MD, Uniformed Svcs. Univ. Health Scis., F. Edward Hebert Sch. Medicine, Bethesda, Md., 1987; MPH, U. Wash., Seattle, 1994; diploma in med. care of catastrophes, Soc. Apothecaries, London, 1999. Diplomate American Bd. Surgery, cert. in surg. critical care. Intern gen. surgery Balboa Naval Hosp., San Diego, 1987—88; resident gen. surgery/trauma U. Calif. Irvine Med. Ctr., 1988—92; fellow trauma & critical care Harborview Med. Ctr., Seattle, 1993—95; asst. prof. Uniformed Svcs. Univ. Health Scis., 1993—99, assoc. prof., 1999—2003, prof. surgery & molecular cellular biology, 2003—07, dir. Trauma Readiness & Rsch. Inst. Surgery; prof. surgery, med. dir. trauma & critical care U. Ariz., Tuscon, 2007—, chief divsn. trauma, critical care & emergency surgery, Univ. Med. Ctr. Personal surgeon to Pres. Bill Clinton, China, 1998; dir. Navy Trauma Training Ctr., LA County U. So. Calif. Med. Ctr., 2002—07; cons. Office Naval Rsch., Arlington, Va., Marine Corps Commandants War Fighting Lab., Quantico, Va. Contbr. articles to profl. jours., chapters to books. Served as battlefield casualty physician/surgeon USN. Decorated Legion of Merit, Def. Meritorious Svc. Medal, Navy Commendation Medal. Fellow: ACS, American Coll. Critical Care Medicine. Achievements include in 2001, becoming one of the first American military surgeons to be deployed in Afghanistan at Camp Rhino; established the first surgical unit in Ramadi, Iraq in 2005; in Jan. 2011, gaining national media attention as the attending trauma physician for US Rep. Gabrielle Giffords who had been shot in the head near Tucson, holding press conferences to update the public on her condition. Office: U Ariz Med Ctr PO Box 245066 1501 N Campbell Ave 5th Fl Tucson AZ 85724 Office Phone: 520-694-6144. Office Fax: 520-626-6101. E-mail: prhee@surgery.arizona.edu. *

RHEE, POONG-LYUL, gastroenterologist; b. Seoul, Republic of Korea, May 11, 1961; MS in Med. Sci., Seoul Nat. U., 1989, PhD in Med. Sci., 1992. Staff physician Seoul Boramae City Hosp., 1992—94; staff gastroenterologist Samsung Med. Ctr., 1994—. Asst. prof. Dept. Medicine, Sungkyunkwan U. Sch. Medicine, 1997—2001, assoc. prof., 2001—07, vice dean, 2003—09, prof., 2007. Mem.: Korean Soc. Gastrointestinal Endoscopy, Korean Soc. Gastroenterology (Dr. Paul Janssen award), Korean Assn. Internal Medicine, Korean Med. Assn., Am. Gastroenterology Assn. Avocations: mountain climbing, hiking, travel. Office: 50 Irwon-dong Gangnam-gu Seoul 135-710 Republic of Korea Office Fax: 82-3-3410-3849. E-mail: plrhee@gmail.com.

RHEE, YANG-KEUN, internist; b. Chollabuk-do, Republic of Korea, Feb. 10, 1947; Degree in Medicine, Chonbuk Nat. U., Republic of Korea, 1986, M in Internal Medicine, 1986, MD, 1986. Intern Chonbuk Nat. U. Hosp., Chonju, Republic of Korea, 1977-78, resident, 1982-88, pres., 1997—2000; prof. Chonbuk Nat. U., Chonju, 1982—, dir., 1997—, dean grad. sch., 2006—. Pres. Korean Acad. Asthma, Allergy and Clin. Immunology, 2001, v.p., 2006—, Korean Soc. Allergology, 2006; pres. Korean Acad. Tuberculosis and Respiratory Diseases, 2005. Office: 634-18 Gumam 2dong Dukjin-gu Junju-shi Jeollabuk Republic of Korea Office Phone: 82-63-250-1678. Business E-Mail: ryk@chonbuk.ac.kr.

RHEINSTEIN, PETER HOWARD, healthcare company executive, physician, lawyer; b. Cleve., Sept. 7, 1943; s. Franz Joseph Rheinstein and Hede Henrietta (Neheimer) Rheinstein Lerner; m. Miriam Ruth Weissman, Feb. 22, 1969; 1 child, Jason Edward. BA with high honors, Mich. State U., 1963, MS, 1964; MD, Johns Hopkins U., 1967; JD, U. Md., 1973. Bar: Md. 1973, DC 1980, US Supreme Ct. 2000; cert. Am. Bd. Family Medicine, 1977, 1983, 1989, 1995, 2001, 2008, added qualifications in Geriatrics 1996, 2006, lic. Md., 1967, Calif., 1968, DC, 1975. Intern USPHS Hosp., San Francisco, 1967-68; resident in internal medicine USPHS Hosp. (now Homewood Hosp. Ctr.), Balt., 1968-70, lt., 1967—68, lt. comdr., 1968—70; instr. internal medicine and physician U. Md., Balt., 1970-73; med. dir. extended care facilities CHC Corp., Balt., 1972-74; dir. drug advt. and labeling divsn. FDA, Rockville, Md., 1974-82, acting dep. dir. Office Drugs, 1982-83, acting dir. Office Drugs, 1983-84, dir. Office Drug Stds., 1984-90, dir. medicine staff Office Health Affairs, 1990-99; sr. v.p. for med. and clin. affairs Cell Works, Inc., Balt., 1999—2004; pres. Severn Health Solutions, 2000—. Bd. dirs. Marnac, Inc., Dallas, 2003-09; chmn. FDA Bur. Drugs Com. on Advanced Sci. Edn., 1978-86, Rsch. in Human Subjects Com., 1990-92; adj. prof. forensic medicine George Washington U., 1974-76; WHO cons. on drug regulation Nat. Inst. for Control Pharm. and Biol. Products, China, 1981-90; advisor on essential drugs WHO, 1985-90; FDA del. to US Pharmacopeial Conv., 1985-90, coord. com. for assessment and transfer of tech. NIH, 1990-99, mem. health care fin. adminstrn. tech. adv. com., 1990-98, Nat. Adv. Coun. on Healthcare Policy, Rsch. and Evaluation, 1990-99, Healthy People 2000/2010 Steering Com., 1990-99, US Preventive Svcs. Task Force, 1990-96, CDC Nat. Task Force on Cmty. Preventive Svcs., 1996-99, Nat. Task Force on CME Industry/Provider Collaboration, 1992—, ann. meeting chmn., 2003, mem. com. chmn., 2002-05, US Adopted Names Coun. Rev. Bd., 2004-05, US Adopted Names Coun., 2006—; cons. in legal medicine and regulatory affairs, 1999—; mem. adv. bd. Nat. Commn. for Cert. of CME Profls., 2006- Co-author: Human Organ Transplantation, 1987; spl. editl. advisor Good Housekeeping Guide to Medicine and Drugs, 1977-80; mem. editl. bd. Legal Aspects Med. Practice, 1981-89, Drug Info. Jour., 1982-86, 91-95; pub. Discovery Medicine, 2001-; contbr. articles to profl. jours. V.p. Intercultural Friends Found., 1998—. Recipient Commendable Svc. award, FDA, 1981, Group award of merit, 1983, 1988, Group Commendable Svc. award, 1989, 1992—93, 1995, 1999, Commr.'s Spl. citation, 1993; NIH Nat. Cancer Inst. SBIR grant, 2001. Fellow: Am. Acad. Family Physicians, Am. Coll. Legal Medicine (bd. govs. 1983—93, chmn. fin. com. 1985—88, treas. 1985—88, chmn. publs. com. 1988—93, chmn. fin. com. 1990—91, treas. 1990—91, jud. coun. 1993—95, bd. govs. 2011—, Pres.'s awards 1985, 1986, 1989—91, 1993, Gold medal 2003); mem.: APHA, AMA (life; ho. of dels. 2002—), ABA, Assn. Clin. Rsch. Profls., Acad. Medicine Wash., Math. Assn. Am., Md. Bar Assn., Johns Hopkins Med. and Surg. Assn., Nat. Assn. Ret. Fed. Employees (life), Soc. Indsl. and Applied Math. (life), Balt. City Med. Soc., Md. State Med. Soc. (del. to US Pharmacopeial Convention 2008—), Fed. Bar Assn. (chmn. food and drug com. 1976—79, Disting. Svc. award 1977), Drug Info. Assn. (bd. dirs. 1982—90, pres. 1984—85, v.p. 1986—87, pres. 1988—89, chmn. ann. meeting 1991, steering com. Ams. 1991—2004, chmn. ann. meeting 1994, Outstanding Svc. award 1990), Am. Bd. Legal Medicine (treas. 2003—11, chmn. 2011—), Acad. Pharm. Physicians and Investigators (trustee 1999—2003, pres. Washington-Balt. chpt. 1999—2003, v.p. AMA rels. 1999—, sec./treas. 2008—09, pres. 2010—11), Mich. State U. Honors Coll. Alumni Assn. (bd. dirs. 1998—2001, pres. 2000—01), Fed. Exec. Inst. Alumni Assn. (life), Mensa (life), U. Md. Alumni Assn. (life), Johns Hopkins U. Alumni Assn. (life), FDA Alumni Assn. (life), Mich. State U. Alumni Assn. (life), John Hopkins Club, Annapolis Yacht Club, Chartwell Golf and Country Club, Delta Theta Phi (life). Achievements include finalizing regulations and development of guidance and precedents to ensure accuracy and fair balance in prescription drug promotion; implemented Drug Price Competition and Patent Term Restoration Act of 1984, authored medication goals for Healthy People 2000 and 2010. Avocations: boating, exercise, real estate. Home and Office: 621 Holly Ridge Rd Severna Park MD 21146-3520 Home Phone: 410-647-9501; Office Phone: 410-647-9500. Office Fax: 410-647-6135. Personal E-mail: phr@jhu.edu.

RHEUBAN, KAREN SCHULDER, pediatric cardiologist, educator; b. Jamaica, NY, 1949; married; 3 children. MD summa cum laude, Ohio State U. Coll. Medicine, 1974. Diplomate Am. Bd. Pediat., Am. Bd. Pediat. Cardiology. Intern pediat. U. Va., Charlottesville, 1974—75, resident pediat. cardiology, 1975—78, fellowship, 1978—80, prof. pediat. cardiology, 1980—, assoc. dean continuing med. edn., 1990—, med. dir. office of telemedicine. Contbr. articles to profl. jours. Recipient Elizabeth Zintl Leadership award, U. Va. Women's Ctr., 2005; named one of Best Dr.'s in America, Best Dr.'s Inc., named to Nat. Libr. Med. tribute to women physicians, 2003. Fellow: Am. Coll. Cardiology, Am. Acad. Pediat.; mem.: Am. Telemedicine Assn. Achievements include research in congenital heart disease; telemedicine applied to rural health care; tele-echocardiography. Mailing: UVA Main Hosp PO Box 800707 Charlottesville VA 22908 Office Phone: 434-924-2481. Business E-Mail: ksr5g@virginia.edu.

RHEW, PERRY JAMES, federal judge; BS in Psychology/Biology, Southeast Mo. State U., Cape Girardeau, 1980; JD, UMKC Sch. Law, Kansas City, 1983. Lic. Mo., 1983. Pub. defender State of Mo., Kennett, 1983-84; asst. prosecuting atty. Dunklin County, Kennett, Mo., 1985-86; prosecuting atty., 1986-90; adjunct prof. Bus. Law Southeast Mo. State U., Cape Girardeau, 1987-89; assoc. circuit judge 35th Judicial Circuit, Kennett, Mo., 1990; US adminstrv. law judge Social Security Adminstrn., Cleve., 1997—2005; mng. adminstrv. law judge Office of Medicare Hearings and Appeals, US Dept. Health & Human Services, Cleve., 2005, acting chief adminstrv. law judge, 2005—06, chief U.S. adminstrv. law judge, 2006—. Bd. dirs. Family Counseling Ctr., Kennett, Mo., 1986-90, Stapleton Detoxification Ctr., Kennett, Mo., 1986-90, Ctr. for Family Resources, Malden, Mo., 1986-90, Cmty. Caring Counsel, Kennett, Mo., 1993-2005. Author: eight published plays. Elected prosecuting atty., 1986, elected assoc. circuit judge, Dunklin Co. Mo., Kennett, 1990, 94. Recipient Young Alumni Merit award Southeast Mo. State U., Cape Girardeau, Mo., 1993, Denman Dist. Evangelism award United Meth. Ch., 1993. Mem. Mo. Bar Assn., Dunklin County Bar, Lions Club Internat. Mem. United Meth. Ch. Avocations: writing, composer, singing, cooking. Office Phone: 216-615-4000. Office Fax: 216-615-4115.

RHIE, GI-EUN, microbiologist; d. Dong Sung Rhie and Eun Jung Kwon; m. Jungchan Park, June 10, 1991; 1 child, Young-Joon Park. BS in Microbiology, Seoul Nat. U., Republic of Korea, 1987, MS in Microbiology, 1989; PhD in Biochemistry, Brown U., Providence, 1994. Postdoc. rsch. fellow Brown U., 1994—95, Seoul Nat. U., 1996—98, Korea Nat. Inst. Health, 1989—99; rsch. fellow Seoul Nat. U. Hosp., 1999—2001, Harvard Med. Sch., Boston, 2002—04; sr. rsch. scientist Korea Nat. Inst. Health, Seoul, 2004—. Mem. editl. bd.: Korean Jour. Microbiology; contbr. articles to profl. jours. Recipient Honor prize, Seoul Nat. U., 1985; grantee Rsch. fellowship, Brown U., 1993; fellow, Korea Rsch. Found., 1997;, Brown U., 1989—90, Postdoc. fellowship, Internat. Vaccine Inst., 2002—03. Achievements include patents for anthrax conjugate vaccine and antibodies against bacilli and anthrax toxins. Avocation: painting. Office: Korea National Institute of Health 187 Osongsaengmyeong2-ro Cheongwon-gun Chungbuk 363-951 Republic of Korea Office Phone: 82 43 719 8270. Business E-Mail: gerhie@nih.go.kr.

RHIE, JONG WON, plastic surgeon, educator; b. Seoul, Republic Of Korea, Jan. 23, 1956; s. Jinhwan Rhie and Byunghee Choi; m. Ok-Joo Kang, Apr. 20, 1959; children: Sang-Woo, Sang-Hun. MD., Cath. U. Korea, Seoul, PhD, 1993. Cert. plastic surgeon Korea, 1989. Dir. Plastic Surgery, Kangnam St. Mary's Hosp., Seoul, 2004—; chief Dept. Plastic Surgery, Cath. U. Korea, Seoul, 2005—, prof. Chief sci. program com. Korean Soc. Plastic and Reconstructive Surgeons, Seoul, 2008—. Recipient award, Korea Soc. Plastic And Econstructive Surgery. Office: Dept Plastic Surgery Cath Univ 505 Banpo-dong Seocho-gu Seoul 137-701 Republic of Korea Office Fax: 82-2-594-7230. Business E-Mail: rhie@catholic.ac.kr.

RHIM, HYUNCHUL, radiologist, educator; s. Hong-Gyu and Yeon-Soo Rhim; m. Kyoung-Suk Kim; children: Jun-Ha, Jun-Won. BS, Hanyang U., Seoul, Republic of Korea, 1985, MS, 1987, PhD, 1993. Instr. Hanyang U. Hosp., Seoul, 1993—95, asst. prof., 1995—97, 1999—2000, assoc. prof., 2000—; rsch. fellow U. Tex. Health Sci. Ctr., San Antonio, 1997—98, asst. prof., 1998—99. Presenter in field. Contbr. articles to profl. jours. Capt. Chooncheon Mil. Hosp., 1990—92, Korea. Grantee, Korean Ministry Health and Welfare, 2002—. Mem.: Korean Med. Assn., Korean Soc. Ultrasound in Medicine (assoc.), Korean Soc. Radiology (assoc.), Soc. Gastrointestinal Radiologist (assoc.), Radiol. Soc. N.Am. (assoc.). Achievements include patents pending for radiofrequency stent for transluminal ablation; first to radiofrequency ablation of benign cystic lesion; research in intrahepatic portal flow modulation during RF ablation. Office: Hanyang Univ Hosp 17 Haengdang-Dong Sungdong-Gu Seoul 133-792 Republic of Korea

RHO, SAE HEUN, ophthalmologist; b. Busan, Republic Of Korea, July 7, 1950; s. Zae Myon Rho and Suk Eui Chung; m. Young Sil Chung, Oct. 3, 1977; children: Seung Soo, Seung Yoon. MD, Yonsei U. Coll. Medicine, Seoul, Republic of Korea. Cert. ophthalmologist Korean Ophthal. Soc., 1983. Dir. Korean Ophthal. Soc., 2003—04; insp. Korean Glaucoma Soc.; head dir., dept. ophthalmology Inje U. Paik Hosp., Busan, Dong-a U. Med. Ctr., Busan. Com. mem. Christian Broadcasting Sys., Busan; correctional com. mem. Ministry Justice; mem. Special Edn. Bd., Busan. Capt. Army, 1975—78, Korea. Recipient Achievement award, Ministry Justice, Mayor Busan Met. City; ARVO Traveler grant, Assn. Rsch. Vision and Ophthalmology, 2008. Mem.: Korean Ophthal. Soc., Am. Acad. Ophthalmology. Office: Dong-a Univ Med Ctr 3/1 Dongdaesin-dong Seo-gu Busan 602-715 Republic of Korea Office Fax: 82-51-254-1987. Business E-Mail: shrho@dau.ac.kr.

RHOADS, JON MARC, pediatric gastroenterologist, educator; b. Nov. 7, 1953; BA, Johns Hopkins U., Balt.; MD, Johns Hopkins Med. Sch., 1980. Diplomate Am. Bd. Pediat., Am. Bd. Pediat. Gastroenterology. Resident UCLA Hosp. & Clinic; fellowship Hosp. for Sick Children, Toronto, Ontario, Canada; prof. pediat. gastroenterology & nutrition U. Tex Med. Sch., Houston, 2006—. Contbr. articles to profl. jours. Mem.: N. Am. Soc. Pediat. Gastroenterology, Hepatology & Nutrition. Mailing: U Tex Med Sch 6431 Fannin St MSB 3137 Houston TX 77030 Office Fax: 713-500-5750. Business E-Mail: j.marc.rhoads@uth.tmc.edu.

RHODE, EDWARD ALBERT, veterinary medicine educator, veterinary cardiologist; b. Amsterdam, NY, July 25, 1926; s. Edward A. and Katherine (Webb) R.; m. Dolores Bangert, 1955; children: David E., Peter R., Paul W., Robert M., Catherine E. DVM, Cornell U., 1947. Diplomate Am. Coll. Veterinary Internal Medicine. Prof. emeritus vet. medicine U. Calif., Davis, 1964—, chmn. dept. vet. medicine, 1968-71; assoc. dean instrn. U. Calif. Sch. Vet. Medicine, Davis, 1971-81, dean, 1982-91. Mem. AAAS, Nat. Acad. Practices, Am. Coll. Vet. Internal Medicine, Am. Vet. Medicine Assn., Basic Sci. Coun., Am. Heart Assn., Am. Acad. Vet. Cardiology, Am. Physiol. Soc., Calif. Vet. Medicine Assn. Office: U Calif Sch Vet Med Davis CA 95616 E-mail: earhode@ucdavis.edu.

RHODES, JOHN RICHARD, immunologist, pharmaceutical executive; b. Bradford, Eng., Nov. 27, 1947; s. Norman Frederick and Lorna Mary Rhodes; m. Heather Margaret Rafferty, Dec. 29, 1972; children: Chloe Elizabeth, Leonie Alexandre. BSc, U. Coll., London, 1969, PhD, 1972. Vis. fellow Nat. Inst. of Allergy and Infectious Diseases, Bethesda, Md., 1972—74; Beit meml. fellow U. Cambridge, England, 1974—77, sr. rsch. assoc. dept. pathology, 1977—82; sr. rsch. scientist Wellcome Rsch. Labs., Beckenham, England, 1982—95; prin. scientist Glaxo Wellcome, Stevenage, England, 1995—2001; dir. disease strategy Glaxo Smith Kline, Stevenage, England, 2001—. Recipient Yamagiwa Yoshida Internat. Cancer Study award, U. Tex. Med. Br., 1982. Fellow: Royal Coll. of Pathologists, London. Achievements include discovery of intercellular covalent chemical events in immune induction and their manipulation by covalently reactive, Schiff base-forming drugs. Office: Glaxo Smith Kline R & D Gunnels Wood Road SG1 2NY Stevenage England Office Fax: 44 1438 768091. E-mail: john.r.rhodes@gsk.com.

RHODES, LINDA JANE, psychiatrist; b. San Antonio, May 23, 1950; d. George Vernon and Lucy Agnes (O'Dowd) R. BA, Trinity U., 1972; MD, U. Tex. Med. Br., 1975. Diplomate Am. Bd. Pediat.; bd. certified, Am. Bd. Psychiatry and Neurology. Resident in pediat. U. Tex. Med. Br., Galveston, 1975-78; fellow in ambulatory pediat. U. Tex. Health Sci. Ctr., Houston, 1978-80, resident in psychiatry San Antonio, 1990-92, child and adolescent psychiatrist, fellow in biol. psychiatry, 1992-95, asst. prof. psychiatry, 1995—2004; pediatrician Kelsey Seybold Clinic, P.A., Houston, 1980-95. Pediat. rep. Tex. Lay Midwifery Bd. Tex. Dept. Health, Austin, 1994-95. Active San Antonio Conservation Soc., Nat. Trust for Hist. Preservation, San Antonio Mus. Assn., Trinity U. Assocs., 1992-95; mem. McNay Art Inst.; bd. dirs. Mind. Sci. Found., 1995-2000., Tex. Found. Psychiatric Edn. & Rsch., 1997—, sec., 1998-99, treas., 1999-2004; chair, asst. league Tex. Found. Psychiat. Edn. and Rsch., 2007-09. Fellow Am. Acad. Pediat.; mem. Am. Psychiat. Assn., Am. Acad. Child and Adolescent Psychiatry (past gifts and endowments com., child abuse and neglect com.), Ambulatory Pediat. Assn., Tex. Pediat. Soc., Tex. Soc. Psychiat. Physicians, Tex. Acad. Child and Adolescent Psychiatry, Am. Med. Women's Assn., Am. Soc. Clin. Psychopharmacology, Tex. Med. Assn. (com. on child and adolescent health), AMA, Bexar County Psychait. Soc. (sec. 2000-01, pres. 2002-2003, past pres. 2003-2004), Baxter County Med. Soc.

RHOMBERG, WALTER U., retired radiologist, oncologist; b. Feldkirch, Austria, Jan. 1, 1941; s. Hermann and Eleonore (Müller) Rhomberg; m. Michaela Rhomberg, Oct. 21, 1989; children: Eva-Maria, Thomas, Claudia. MD, U. Innsbruck, Austria, 1965, U. Zurich, Switzerland, 1968. Head dept. radiooncology Acad. Tchg. Hosp., Feldkirch, 1980—2006; ret., 2006. Fellow hemato-oncology Roswell Pk. Meml. Inst., Buffalo, 1970—71; prof. clin. oncology Hannover U.

Med. Sch., Germany, 1994; lectr. in field. Contbr. articles to profl. jours. Recipient Johann Georg Zimmermann award, Hannover Med. Sch., 1976, Leopold Freund medal, Austrian Soc. Radiooncology, 2006; Hans Meyer scholar, Radiol. Soc. Lower Saxony, 1973. Mem.: Radiol. Soc. Lower Saxony, Austria Soc. Surgical Oncology, European Soc. Therapeutic Radiooncology, Austrian Soc. Radiooncology. Roman Catholic. Avocations: mountain climbing, literature, music, science. Home: Unterfeldstrasse 32 A-6700 Bludenz Austria Office Phone: 43 664 3943043. Personal E-mail: walter.rhomberg@gmx.at.

RHOTON, ALBERT LOREN, JR., neurosurgeon, educator; b. Nov. 18, 1932; s. Albert Loren and Hazel Arnette (Van Cleve) R.; m. Joyce L. Moldenhauer, June 23, 1957; children: Eric L., Albert J., Alice S., Laural A. BS, Ohio State U., 1954; MD cum laude, Washington U., St. Louis, 1959. Diplomate Am. Bd. Neurol. Surgery (bd dirs. 1985-91, vice-chmn. 1991). Intern Columbia Presbyn. Med. Ctr., NYC, 1959; resident in neurol. surgery Barnes Hosp., St. Louis, 1961-65; cons. neurol. surgery Mayo Clinic, Rochester, Minn., 1965-72; chief divsn. neurol. surgery U. Fla., Gainesville, 1972-80, R.D. Keene prof., 1980—, chmn. dept. neurol. surgery, 1980-2000, chmn. emeritus, 2000—. Developer microsurg. tng. ctr.; hon. v.p. World Congress of Neurosurgery, 2005-; hon. prof. Beijing (China) Capital U., 2005—; lectr. in field. Author: The Orbit and Sellar Region: Microsurgical Anatomy and Operative Approaches, 1996, Anatomy and Surgical Approaches to the Temporal Bone, Cranial Anatomy and Surgical Approaches, Chinese and English edits., 2003, Anatomy and Surgery Approaches to the Temporal Bone; mem. editl. bd. Neurosurgery, Jour. Microsurgery, Surg. Neurology, Jour. Fla. Med. Assn., Am. Jour. Otology, Skull Base Surgery; contbr. articles to profl. jours. Hon. pres. World Congress Endoscopic Skull Base Surgery, 2009; bd. dirs. Neurosurgery Edn. and Rsch. Found. Recipient Disting. Faculty award, U. Fla., 1981, Alumni Achievement award, Washington U. Sch. Medicine, 1985, Jones award for outstanding spl. med. exhibit of yr., Am. Assn. med. Illustrators, 1969, Jameison medal, Neurosurg. soc. Australasia, 1997, Outstanding Achievement award, World Congress of Skull Base Surgery, 2000, medal of honor, World Fedn. Neurosurg. Socs., 2001, medal, Neurosurg. Soc. Am., 2001, endowed professorship named in his honor, U. Fla., Lifetime Achievement award, Wall of Fame Honoree, Honorary Alumnus award, 2001, medal of honor, Neurosurg. Soc. of Am., 2001, Bucy award, U. Chgo., 2002, Golden Neuron award, World Acad. Neurosurgery, 2009, Disting. Svc. award, Southern Surg. Soc., 2010; named Neurosurgeon of Yr., World Neurosurgery Jour., 2011; grantee NIH, VA, Am. Heart Assn. Mem. ACS (bd. govs. 1978-84), AMA (Billings Bronze medal 1969), Fla. Brain Tumor Assn. and Moffitt Cancer Ctr. (Lifetime Achievement award, 2008), Congress Neurol. Surgeons (pres. 1978, Exceptional and Disting. Svc. award 2004, honored guest 1993, Founders Laurel award 2006), Nat. Found. Brain Rsch. (bd. dirs. 1990-94), Nat. Coalition for Rsch. in Neurol. Disorders (bd. dirs. 1990-94), Neurol. Soc. Am. (medal 2001), Internat. Congress Meningiomas (hon. pres. 2000), Neurosurg. Soc. Brazil (hon., honored guest 2004), Neurosurg. Soc. Japan (hon., Honored guest 2002), Neurosurg. Soc. Mex. (hon.), Neurosurg. Soc. Can. (hon.), Neurosurg. Soc. Uruguay (hon.), Neurosurg. Soc. Venezuela (hon.), Neurosurg. Soc. Turkey (hon.), Korean Neurol. Soc. (hon.), Neurosurg. Soc. Tex. (hon.), Neurosurg. Soc. Okla. (hon.), Neurosurg. Soc. Wis. (hon.), Neurosurg. Soc. Ga. (hon.), Neurosurg. Soc. Rocky Mountain (hon.), Neurosurg. Soc. China (hon.), Neurosurg Soc. Argentina (hon.), Latin Am. Neurosurg. Soc. (hon.), Neurosurg. Soc. Chili (hon.), Fla. Neurosurg. Soc. (pres. 1978), Am. Assn. Neurol. Surgeons (chmn. vascular sect., treas. 1983-86, v.p. 1987-88, pres. 1989-90, exec. com. 1993, Cushing medal 1998), Soc. Neurol. Surgeons (treas. 1975-81, pres. 1993), So. Neurol. Soc. (v.p. 1976), Alachua County Med. Soc. (exec. com. 1978), Fla. Med. Assn., Am. Surg. Assn., Soc. Univ. Neurosurgeons, Am. Heart Assn. (stroke coun., Outstanding Achievement award 1971), N.Am. Skull Base Soc. (pres. 1993-94, honored guest 2001, Lifetime Achievement award 2005), Am. Acad. Neurol. Surgery, Acoustic Neuroma Assn. (med. adv. bd. 1983-2000, chmn. 1992-2001, chmn. emeritus 2001—), Trigeminal Neurol. Assn. (med. advisor bd. 1992—), Hemifacial Spasm Assn. (med. adv. bd. 2002—), Internat. Interdisciplinary Congress on Craniofacial and Skull Base Surgery (pres. 1996-97), Internat. Soc. Neurosurg. Tech. and Instrument Invention (pres. 1997—), Japanese Skull Base Soc. (hon. pres. 2000), Internat. Soc. for Microsurgery Anatomy (hon. pres. 2002, 2004-), World Fedn. Neurosurg. Soc. (hon. v.p. 2005—), World Congress Endoscopic Surgery Brain, Skull Base & Spine (hon. guest), Internat. Levantine Forum, (Turkey) (hon. pres., 2008-), Congress World Fed. SROH Base Socs., Vancouver, BC (honored guest 2008), European Skull Base Soc.(Rotterdam)(hon. mem.), Columbian Neurosurg. Soc., European Skill Base Soc.(hon.) Achievements include design of more than 200 microsurgery instruments; fundraising for 11 endowed chairs at University of Florida. Home: 2505 NW 22d Ave Gainesville FL 32605-3819 Office: U Fla Dept Neurosurgery PO Box 100265 100 S Newell Dr Gainesville FL 32610 Office Phone: 352-273-7788, 352-273-9000. Business E-Mail: rhoton@neurosurgery.ufl.edu.

RHUDY, JAMIE L., psychology professor; b. Sherman, Tex., July 4, 1971; BA, Austin Coll., 1993; PhD, Tex. A&M U., 2002. Assoc. prof. U. Tulsa, 2003—. Recipient Faculty Tchg. award, U. Tulsa, Excellence in Tchg. award, Henry Kendell Coll. Arts & Sci., Disting. Early Career award, Okla. Psychol. Assn.; grant, NIH, NIAMS. Mem.: Soc. Neurosci., Soc. Psychophysiological Rsch., Internat. Assn. Study Pain, Am. Pain Soc. Office: University Tulsa Dept Psychology Tulsa OK 74104 Personal E-mail: j.l.rhudy@gmail.com.

RHYOU, IN HYEOK, hospital administrator; b. Milyang, July 4, 1966; MD, Seoul Nat. U., 1992. V.p. Pohang Semyeong Christianity Hosp., 1992—2010, pres., 2010—. Mem.: Korean Microsurgery Soc. (dir. 2006—, Achievement award), Korean Hand Soc. (dir. 1996—2010, editl. mem. 2010—), Korean Shoulder & Elbow Soc. (editl. mem. 2010—). Avocations: reading, golf, tennis, mountain climbing. Office: Nam Gu Daedo Dong 94-5 Pohang Kyoengbuk 790-822 Republic of Korea Office Fax: 82-054-289-1766. Personal E-mail: inhyeok_r@yahoo.co.kr.

RHYU, KEE HYUNG, orthopedist, educator; b. Seoul, Republic Of Korea, Mar. 1, 1968; s. Hyung Rae Rhyu and Chong Wha Chung; m. Yoo Kyoung Lee, Apr. 27, 2002; children: Jinyoung, Jimin. MD, Seoul Nat. U., 1992, MS, 2002, PhD, 2008. Cert. Ministry Health, Bd. Orthopedic Surgery, 1997. Clin. fellow Seoul Nat. U. Hosp., 2000—01; asst. prof. Kangwon Nat. U., Chuncheon, Kangwon-Do, Republic of Korea, 2002—07; clin. assoc. prof. Kyung Hee U. East-West Neo Med. Ctr., Seoul, Republic of Korea, 2007—09, assoc. prof., 2010—. Com. mem. Asia Pacific Orthopedic Assn., Seoul, 2006; cons. surgeon Nat. Labor Welfare Corp., Chuncheon, Kangwon-Do, 2006—09; active mem. SICOT, Brussels, 2005—. Contbr. articles to profl. jours. Capt. Air Force, 1997—2000, Osan, Korea. Grant, Asian Pacific Orthop. Assn., 2006, Nat. Health Ins. Rev. & Assessment, 2008. Mem.: Korean Arthroscopy Soc. (academic bd. mem. 2010—), Korean Human Tissue Bank (med. dir. 2010—), Korean Soc. Computer Assisted Orthop. Surgery (bd. mem. 2010—), Korean Soc. Hip Arthroscopy, SICOT, Orthopaedic Rsch. Soc., Korean Orthopaedic Assn. (mem. exam. bd. 2009—), Korean Hip Soc. (editl. bd. mem. 2007—, mng. editor 2009—, academic bd. mem. 2010—). Office: Kyung Hee University Hosp Gangdong 149 Sangil-dong Gangdong-Ku Seoul 134-727 Republic of Korea Office Fax: 82-2-440-6296. E-mail: khrhyu@gmail.com.

RHYU, PAUL HOSANG, physician; b. Seoul, Republic of Korea, Aug. 16, 1967; DC, ND, OMD, Nat. U. Health Scis., PhD, 1994. Pres. Internat. Certification Commn. Acupuncture & Oriental Medicine, 2003—. Pres. World Assn. Dr., 2005—. Recipient Harvey award, Internat. Certification Commn. Acupuncture & Oriental Medicine. Mem.: MENSA. Avocation: fencing. Office: 10090 Main St Suite 103 Fairfax VA 22031 Business E-Mail: phrphd@yahoo.co.kr.

RIA, ROBERTO, oncologist, researcher; b. Taranto, Italy, July 29, 1967; s. Paolo Ria and Maria Carallo; life ptnr. Michela Dibenedetto. MD, U. Bari, Italy, 1993. Cert. oncologist. Rschr. sect. gen. pathology U. Brescia (Italy) Med. Sch., 1992—93, U. Bari Med. Sch., 1993—; med. asst. dept. hematology and stem cell transplantation U. Perugia (Italy) Med. Sch., Perugia, 2002—03; med. asst. internal medicine unit Umberto I Gen. Hosp., Corato, Bari, Italy. Oncology adviser, Terlizzi, Bari, Italy, 2005—. With Italian Army, 1993—94. Rsch. grantee, 1998—2001. Mem.: European Hematology Assn. (assoc.), Italian Soc. Immunology (assoc.), Italian Soc. Internal Medicine (assoc.). Office: DIMO Sect Internal Medicine Piazza Giulio Cesare 11 Bari I-70124 Italy Home: Via Firenze 74 76123 Andria BT Italy Office Fax: +39.080.5478859. Personal E-mail: robria@libero.it.

RIBAK, CHARLES ERIC, neuroscientist, educator; b. July 19, 1950; s. Marcus and Adele (Blank) R.; m. Julia Marianne Wendruck, Jan. 2, 1977; children: Marc Aaron, William Michael. BS, SUNY, Albany, 1971; PhD, Boston U., 1975. Assoc. rsch. scientist City of Hope Med. Ctr., Duarte, Calif., 1975-78; from asst. prof. to full prof. U. Calif., Irvine, 1978-90, prof., 1990—. NIH NLS-2 Study Sect., 1989-92. Assoc. editor Jour. Neurocytology, London, 1984-88, Epilepsy Rsch., 1986-2006, Brain Rsch., 1988-2010, Jour. Mind and Behavior, 1988-2010, Anatomy and Embryology, 1992-96, Jour. Hirnforschung, 1993-99, Archives of Med. Rsch., 1993-, Epilepsia, 1995-2004, Hippocampus, 2000-, Acta Histochemica et Cytochemica, 2005-2011; contbr. over 175 articles on brain rsch. to profl. jours. Recipient Michael prize, 1987, Citation Classic award, 1987, Javits award, 1990; NSF grantee, Washington, 1981-84, 87-91, 96-98, rsch. grantee NIH, 1979, 83, 86, 90, 99, 2005; Klingenstein fellow, 1983. Fellow AAAS; mem. Soc. Neurosci., Internat. Brain Rsch. Orgn., Cajal Club (pres. 2000-02). Office: U Calif Dept Of Anatomy Neurob Irvine CA 92697-1275 Home Phone: 949-388-7090; Office Phone: 949-824-5494. E-mail: ribak@uci.edu.

RIBBANS, WILLIAM JOHN, orthopaedic surgeon, consultant; b. Northampton, Eng., Nov. 28, 1954; s. Maurice Arthur and Sheila Beryl (Brightwell) R.; m. Sian Elizabeth William, Sept. 10, 1983; children: Rebecca Elizabeth, Hannah Alexandra, Abigail Victoria. BSc with honors, Royal Free U., London, 1977, MB, BS, 1980; MCh. Orthop., U. Liverpool, 1990; PhD, U. Glamorgan, 2003. Registrar in surgery Windsor, Northwick Park, Eng., 1984-86; clin. fellow Harvard U., Boston, 1986-87; sr. registrar Middlesex Hosp., London, 1987-90; clin. fellow Sheffield, Eng., 1990; cons. surgeon Royal Free Hosp., London, 1991-96, Northampton, Eng., 1996—. Hon. sr. lectr. Royal Free Sch Medicine, London, 1996—2000; mem. ct. examiners Royal Coll. of Surgeons of Eng., 2003—; tutor in field; vis. prof. U. Northampton, 2005—. Guest editor Clin. Orthops. and Related Rsch., 1997—. Fellow Royal Coll. Surgeons England and Edinburgh (Brit. Orthop. Assn. (rsch. grant Wishbone Appeal 1995); mem. PTO, World Hemophilia Fedn. (sec. 1996-2000, musculo-skeletal com. 1994—), Brit. Med. Assn. Anglican. Avocations: rugby football, athletics, stamp collecting/philately, music, fell walking, sports memorabilia. Office: Northampton Gen Hosp Cliftonville Northampton NN1 5BD England Home: Chartlands Cherry Tree Ln NN4 7AT Great Houghton England Office Phone: 01604-662888. Business E-Mail: wjribbans@uk-consultants.co.uk.

RIBBLE, JOHN CHARLES, medical educator; b. Paris, Tex., July 26, 1931; s. Elbert Alfred and Dorothy (Pyeatt) R.; m. Anne Blythe Hoerner; 1 stepchild Helen Blythe Strate Kielty. MD, U. Tex., 1955. Diplomate Am. Bd. Internal Medicine. Asst. prof. medicine Cornell U., NYC, 1962-66, assoc. prof. pediatrics, 1966-78, assoc. dean, 1974-78, Med. Sch., U. Tex., Houston, 1978-86, dean, 1986-95; vis. scholar The Health Inst. New Eng. Med. Ctr., Boston, 1995-96; prof. medicine U. Tex., Houston, 1996—. Mem. Nat. Adv. Coun. Gen. Med. Scis. NIH, Bethesda, Md., 1988-91. Episcopalian. Home: 6200 Willers Way Houston TX 77057-2808 Office: U Tex Med Sch 6431 Fannin St Houston TX 77030-1501 Office Phone: 713-500-6709. E-mail: johnribble@comcast.net.

RIBBLE, RONALD GEORGE, psychologist, educator, writer, behavioral consultant; b. West Reading, Pa., May 7, 1937; s. Jeremiah George and Mildred Sarah (Folk) Ribble; m. Catalina Valenzuela Torres, Sept. 30, 1961; children: Christina, Timothy, Kenneth. BSEE cum laude, U. Mo., 1968, MSEE, 1969, MA, 1985, PhD, 1986. Bd. cert. forensic examiner, diplomate in behavioral sci. Am. Bd. Psychol. Spltys., Am. Coll. Forensic Examiners; cert. in homeland security, bd. cert. forensics examiner BCFE, Am. Soc. Law, Medicine & Ethics Psychologist & Elec. Engr. Enlisted USAF, 1956-60, advance through grades to lt. col., 1976—81; rsch. dir. Coping Resources, Inc., Columbia, Mo., 1986; pres., co-owner Towers and Rushing Ltd. (Pubs. and Psychol. Cons., Troubadour 1997-2001), San Antonio, 1986—; referral devel. Laughlin Pavilion Psychiat. Hosp., Kirksville, Mo., 1987; program dir. Psychiat. Insts. of Am., Iowa Falls, Iowa, 1987-88; lead psychotherapist Gasconade County Counseling Ctr., Hermann, Mo., 1988; sr. lectr. U. Tex., San Antonio, 1989—2002; lectr. Trinity U., San Antonio, 1995-96; assessment clinician Afton Oaks Psychiat. Hosp., San Antonio, 1989-91; ret. from tchg., 2002. Faculty cons. Edn. Testing Svc., 1997; psychologist Olmos Psychol. Svcs., Inc., San Antonio, 1991—93; vol. assessor Holmgreen Children's Shelter, San Antonio, 1992—93; founder Ruth Bohn Weissman Scholarship in Creative Writing U. Tex., San Antonio, 1994—2004; co-sponor Lyric Recovery Festival, Carnegie Hall, 2000; condr. seminars, revs. for maj. publs.; founding mem. U. Mo.-Columbia Bd. Psychology Leaders, 2007. Author: (book) Apples, Weeds, and Doggie Poo, 1995, Dont' Eat the Snake!, 1999; contbr. essays to psychol. refernce books, poetry to anthologies periodicals, lyrics to popular music; interviewer: celebrities in performing and lit. arts, 1995—, columnist: Feelings, 1993—97; pub. access TV appearances, 1991—. Founding cabinet mem. World Peace and Diplomacy Forum; vol. announcer pub. radio sta., Colombia, 1993; vol. Cath. Family and Children's Svc., San Antonio, 1989—91; chpt. advisor Rational Recovery Program for Alcoholics, San Antonio, 1991—92; mem. Pres. Leadership Cir., 1994—2002; contbg. mem. Dem. Nat. Com., 1983—, Presdl. Congl. Task Force, 1994; del. Boone County Dem. Conv., Mo., 1984. Recipient Roberts Meml. prize, Lyric Poetry Jour., 1995, Internat. Peace prize, United Cultural Conv., U.S.A., 2002, DaVinci Diamond award, Internat. Biographical Ctr., 2004, Am. Medal Hon. award, Am. Biographical Inst., 2004; named Legion of Honour, Internat. Biog. Ctr., 2008. Fellow: Am. Coll. Forensic Examiners; mem.: ACLU, Am. Soc. Law, Medicine & Ethics, USN Inst., Internat. Found. for Protection Officers, Internat. Soc. Genetic Genealogists, MENSA, Assn. Psychol. Sci., London Diplomatic Acad., Academic Coun., Internat. Soc. Polit. Psychology, Acad. Polit. Sci., Soc. for the Psychol. Study of Social Issues, The Jefferson Coun. (founder, dir. 2002), Physicians for Social Responsibility (leadership cir.), So. Poverty Law Ctr. (leadership coun. for tchg. tolerance), Soc. Profl. Journalists, Interfaith Alliance, Mil. Officers Assn., Air Force Assn., Internat. Platform Assn. (Poetry award 1995). Independent. Deist. Avocations: running and fitness, poetry, singing, public speaking. Home: 14023 N Hills Village Dr San Antonio TX 78249-2534 Address: Towers and Rushing Ltd San Antonio TX 78249 Office Phone: 210-558-1393. Personal E-mail: rribble@earthlink.net.

RIBEIRO, CRISTIANO HOSSRI, medical association administrator; b. Sao Jose Dos Campos, Jan. 1, 1975; PhD, Santa Casa De Sao Paulo, 2000. Dir. Ortoclinica, 2010—. Office: Av 9 De Julho 1017 Sao jose dos Campos Sao Paulo 12240280 Brazil Personal E-mail: alelorenti@yahoo.com.br.

RIBEIRO, JERRI LUIZ, educational association administrator; b. Canoas, Brazil, Feb. 2, 1971; D, Fed. U. Rio Grande do Sul, 2007. Coord. Meth. U. Ctr., 2002—. Home: Rua Itaboraí 1342/802 Porto Alegre RS 90670-030 Brazil Personal E-mail: jerriribeiro@yahoo.com.br.

RIBEIRO, JOAQUIM ALEXANDRE, medical researcher, medical educator; b. Vila Fernando, Guarda, Portugal, Aug. 9, 1941; s. Antonio Alexandre and Joaquina (Purificacao) Ribeiro; m. Isabel Maria Perdigao, Dec. 28, 1962 (div. Feb. 1992); children: Patricia, Filipa, Tiago; m. Ana Sousa Sebastiao, June 21, 1993; children: Francisco, Joaquim. MD, U. Lisbon, Portugal, 1966; PhD, U. Edinburgh, Scotland, 1982. Asst. Gulbenkian Inst. Sci., Oeiras, Portugal, 1970—74, asst. investigator, 1974—82, investigator, 1982—88, sr. investigator, 1988—97; dir. Lab. Neuroscis., Faculty Medicine U. Lisbon, 1997—. Prof. U. Lisbon, Portugal. Contbr. articles to profl. jours. Tenent Health Corps, Mozambique, 1967-70. Mem. Brit. Pharm. Soc., Internat. Soc. Neurochemistry. Office: U Lisbon Lab Neuroscis Fac Medicine Avenida Egas Moniz 1649-028 Lisbon Portugal Office Phone: 00351 21 798 51 83. Business E-Mail: jaribeiro@fm.ul.pt.

RIBEIRO, JOYCE BENZAQUEM, chemist; b. Rio de Janeiro, Apr. 23, 1977; MSc, U. Fed. Rio de Janeiro, 2003, DSc, 2007, attending. Rsch. U. Fed. do Rio de Janeiro, 2002—. Home: Cambui 134 ap 204 Rio de Janeiro 21911-130 Brazil Personal E-mail: joyce_benzaquem@yahoo.com.br.

RIBEIRO, JULIO STEDILE, plastic surgeon, director; MD, U. Fed. Medicine Pelotas, Rio Grande Do Sul, Brazil, 1984. Dir. Clinica Stedile Ltd., Porto Alegre, Rio Grande Do Sul, 1990—. Mem., sci. pubs. editl. bd. Brzilian Jour. Otorhinolaringology, Sao Paulo, 2003—. Contbr. scientific papers (1st Pl., U. Miami Sch. Medicine, 1997, 1st Pl., 7th L.Am. Otolaryn. and Facial Plastic Surgery Congress, 1997). Recipient Dr. Osvaldo Cruz Hon. medal, 1998, Spl. Nat. Citizen award, 1999, Golden Scalpel award, Top Brazilian Plastic Surgeon, 2001; named Top Quality in Medicine award, Brazil, 1999—2000. Mem.: Internat. Fedn. Facial Plastic Surgery Socs. (Alexandria, Va.) (bd. dirs. 1997—2004, Commemorative Cert., 10th Anniversary Tribute Fedn. 2008), Brazilian Acad. Facial Plastic Surgery (Sao Paulo) (founding mem. 1997—2008, dir. 2004—06, mem. sci. com. 2004—06). Achievements include development of needle-holder, scissors with reduced terminal; scissors with needle point for septo-nasal perforation microsurgery; shaver for rhinoplasty. Home: Ave Palmeiras 365 Apt 201 Porto Alegre Rio Grande Do Sul 90470-300 Brazil Office: Clinica Stedile Ltd Ave Nilo Peçanha 2825 CJ 1403 Porto Alegre Rio Grande Do Sul 91330-001 Brazil Office Fax: 51-21111017; Home Fax: 51-32079789. Business E-Mail: clinica@stedile.med.br.

RIBEIRO, LUCIANA ABEID, research scientist; b. Ribeirão Preto, Jan. 24, 1986; MSc, U. Fed. São Paulo, 2007. Rschr. U. Fed. de São Paulo, 2007. Avocations: cooking, jogging, reading. Home: Guilherme Fantacini 248 Batatais São Paulo 143000000 Brazil Personal E-mail: lu_abeid@hotmail.com.

RIBEIRO, MARCELO LIMA, medical educator; b. Sao Paulo, Brazil, May 13, 1976; PhD, UNICAMP, 2004. Prof. Universidade Sao Francisco, 2001. Office: Av Sao Francisco de Assis 218 Braganca Paulista Sao Paulo 12916900 Brazil Business E-Mail: marcelo.ribeiro@saofrancisco.edu.br.

RIBEIRO, SERGIO CONTI, gynecologist; b. São Paulo, Brazil, Aug. 22, 1968; Degree in Med., FMUSP, 1991, PhD, 2001. Head laparoscopic gynecologic surgery group Hosp. Das Clínicas Da FMUSP, 2007—. Bd. dirs. SOBENGE, 2004—08, SOPEGI, 2005—09. Recipient Hon. Mention award, Internat. Jour. Obstetrics Gynecology, Medicine award, BEST, 2004. Mem.: SOGIA, SOGESP, FEBRASGO, AAGL. Office: Rua Joaquim Floriano 466 Conjunto 708 São Paulo 04534-002 Brazil Business E-Mail: sergiocontiribeiro@terra.com.br.

RIBEIRO, VINICIUS BUCCELLI, research scientist; b. São Paulo, Brazil, July 22, 1983; B in Biol. Scis., Mackenzie U., 2005; PhD student, U. São Paulo. Rsch. scientist U. São Paulo, 2003—07, 2009—; biotech. cons. Gehaka Biotech. Co., 2007—09. Reviewer Foodborne Pathogens Disease, 2009, Brazilian Jour. Microbiology, 2010, Jour. Microbiology and Antimicrobials, 2011; head dir., health clinic Beta Corpus, 2010. Recipient Sci. Merit award, Head Mems. Brazilian Soc. Microbiology, 2005, 2007. Fellow: Fundação de Amparo a Pesquisa do Estado de São Paulo; mem.: Internat. Assn. Food Protection, Brazilian Soc. Microbiology. Avocations: sports, travel. Office: 580 Lineu Prestes Ave São Paulo 05508-000 Brazil Personal E-mail: viniciusbuccelli@yahoo.com.br.

RIBEIRO-PAES, JOÃO TADEU, medical educator; b. São Paulo, Brazil, Dec. 12, 1958; MD, U. São Paulo, 1993, PhD, 1995. Assoc. prof. U. São Paulo, 1995—. Contbr. scientific papers. Avocation: football. Office: University São Paulo Ave Dom Antonio 2100 Assis São Paulo 19806-900 Brazil Business E-Mail: jtrpaes@yahoo.com.br.

RICARD, JACQUES LOUIS, microbiologist; b. Neuilly, Seine, France, May 23, 1926; arrived in Sweden, 1968; s. Joseph Honoré and Suzanne (Chalon) R.; m. Odette Cadart, 1948 (div. 1970); children: Suzanne, Michele; m. Suoma Kanerva Leinonen, June 19, 1971; 1 child, Thomas. Diploma, Institut Agricole, Fribourg, Switzerland, 1945; AB with honors, U. Calif., Davis, 1955, MA, 1961; PhD, Oreg. State U., 1966. Cert. secondary tchr., Calif. Bacteriologist Campbell Soup Co., Sacramento, 1948-60; rsch. asst. U. Calif., Davis, 1960-61; instr. Sacramento City Coll., 1961-63; rsch. asst. Oreg. State U., Corvallis, 1963-66, asst. prof., 1966-68; vis. scientist Skogshögskolan, Stockholm, 1968-69; mgr. IC Lab., Incentive AB, Stockholm, 1969-72; pres. BINAB Bio-Innovation AB, Älgarås, Sweden, 1972-98, tech. adviser, 1998—2008. With French infantry, 1944-45. Roman Catholic. Achievements include patents for biofungicides. Avocation: aquaculture. Office: BINAB Bio-Innovation AB Pjungserud Bredholmen 12 545 92 Algaras Sweden

RICARDO, CUÉLLAR, orthopedist; b. Madrid, June 22, 1955; MD, Osakidetza, PhD student, 1978—. Orthop. surgeon Traumatología y Ortopedia. Master: AE Artroscopia, SECOT. Avocation: flying. Office: Plz Easo 6 2° San Sebastián Guipuzcoa 20006 Spain Business E-Mail: ricuellar@telefonica.net.

RICCI, WILLIAM, orthopedist, educator; b. Syosset, NY, Mar. 20, 1964; MD, Duke U., 1992. Prof., orthop. surgery Wash. U. Sch. Medicine, 1998—. Chair, program com. Orthop. Trauma Assn., 2006—10, bd. dirs., exec. com., 2006—11, chair, edn. com., 2011—. Mem.: St. Louis Orthop. Soc., Orthop. Trauma Assn., Am. Acad. Orthop. Surgery. Office: 1 Barnes Hosp Plz Saint Louis MO 63110 Business E-Mail: ricciw@wustl.edu.

RICCIONI, MARIA ELENA, medical researcher; b. Rome, Nov. 14, 1961; MD, Cath. U. Rome, 1986; degree in Gen. Surgery, U. La Sapienza, Rome, 1991. Rschr. Catholica U. Rome, 2002—. Mem.: Italian Soc. Endoscopy. Office: Largo Agostino Gemelli 8 Rome 00168 Italy Office Fax: 39-06-30156581. Business E-Mail: melena.riccioni@rm.unicatt.it.

RICE, CHARLES LANE, surgeon, educator; b. Atlanta, May 22, 1945; s. Marion Jennings and Molly Black R.; children: Aaron Nicholas, Patrick Marion. AB, U. Ga., 1964; MD, Med. Coll. Ga., 1968. Commd. ensign USN, 1966, advanced through grades to comdr., 1976, ret., 1977; intern Bowman Gray Sch. Medicine, Winston-Salem, NC, 1968-69; resident Nat. Naval Med. Ctr., Bethesda, Md., 1969-73; asst. prof. surgery U. Chgo., 1977-80, assoc. prof. surgery, 1980-84; dir. intensive care unit Michael Reese Hosp., Chgo., 1977-84; prof., vice chmn. dept. surgery U. Wash., Seattle, 1985-92; surgeon-in-chief Harborview Med. Ctr., Seattle, 1985-92; Dr. Lee Hudson- Robert R. Penn prof., chmn., divsn. gen. surgery U. Tex. Southwestern Med. Ctr., Dallas, 1992-93; prof. surgery U. Ill., Chgo., 1993—2005, prof. physiology and biophysics, 1996—2005, vice dean Coll. Medicine, 1994-99, vice chancellor health affairs, 1999—2004; prof. surgery, pres. Uniformed Svcs. U. of Health Scis., Bethesda, Md., 2005—. Robert Wood Johnson Health Policy fellow, 1991-92; legis. asst. to U.S. senator Tom Daschle, 1991-92, acting asst. sec. Def. for Health Affairs, 2010. Assoc. editor Jour. of Surg. Rsch., 1983-90; contbr. articles to profl. jours. Rep. Accrediting Coun. Grad. Med. Edn., chair elect, 2001—02, chair, 2002—04. Capt. USNR, 1989—2003. Decorated Legion of Merit. Fellow ACS (gov. 1992-98, vice chmn. com. on trauma 1992-93), Am. Surg. Assn., Am. Assn. for Surgery of Trauma (com. chair 1989-91); mem. Soc. Univ. Surgeons, Am. Physiol. Soc., Shock Soc. (pres. 1991-92), Ctrl. Surg. Assn., Pacific Coast Surg. Assn., So. Surg. Assn., Nat. Libr. Medicine (mem. bd. regents 2005-). Democrat. Episcopalian. Office: Uniformed Svcs U Health Sci Office of Pres 4301 Jones Bridge Rd Bethesda MD 20814-4799 Office Phone: 301-295-3013. Business E-Mail: crice@usuhs.edu.

RICE, DERICA W., pharmaceutical executive; b. Decatur, Ala., 1965; m. Robin Rice; 3 children. BSEE, Kettering U. (formerly GMI Engring. and Mgmt. Inst.), Flint, Mich., 1988; MBA, Ind. U., 1990. Internat. treasury assoc. Eli Lilly & Co., 1990—92, various positions including sales rep., mgr. global fin. planning and analysis for med. devices divsn., global planning mgr. pharms., fin. dir., CFO Can., 1995—97, exec. dir., CFO European ops. London, 1997—2000, gen. mgr. England, 2000—03, Ireland, 2000—03, mem. Diversity Leadership Coun., v.p., contr., 2003—06, sr. v.p., CFO, 2006—10, exec. v.p., global services, CFO, 2010—. Bd. dirs. Clarian Health North, Target Corp., 2007—. Bd. govs. Indpls. Mus. Art. Named Most Powerful Executives in Corporate America, Black Enterprise Mag., 2009, Top 100 Under 50 Executives, Diversity MBA Mag. Office: Eli Lilly and Co Lilly Corp Ctr 893 S Delaware Indianapolis IN 46285 Office Phone: 317-276-2000. Office Fax: 317-276-4878. *

RICE, DONALD BLESSING, corporate executive, former federal official; b. Frederick, Md., June 4, 1939; s. Donald Blessing and Mary Celia (Santangelo) R.; m. Susan Fitzgerald, Aug. 25, 1962; children: Donald Blessing III, Joseph John, Matthew Fitzgerald. BSChemE, U. Notre Dame, 1961, DEng (hon.), 1975; MS in Indsl. Mgmt., Purdue U., 1962, PhD in Econs., 1965, D (hon.) in Mgmt., 1985; LLD (hon.), Pepperdine U., 1989; LHD (hon.), West Coast U., 1993; D in Pub. Policy (hon.), Rand Grad. Sch., 1995. Dir. cost analysis US Dept. Def., Washington, 1967-69, dep. asst. sec. for resource analysis, 1969-70; asst. dir. Office Mgmt. and Budget, Exec. Office of the Pres., Washington, 1970-72; pres., CEO The Rand Corp., Calif., 1972-89; sec. USAF, Washington, 1989-93; pres., COO Teledyne, Inc., LA, 1993-96; chmn. Scios, Inc., Sunnyvale, Calif., 1998—2003; pres., CEO Agensys, Inc., Santa Monica, Calif., 1996—, chmn., 2002—07. Bd. dirs. Vulcan Materials Co., Wells Fargo & Co., Chevron Corp.; mem. nat. adv. com. oceans and atmosphere Dept. Commerce, 1972-75; mem. Nat. Sci. Bd., 1974-86; mem. adv. coun. Coll. Engring., U. Notre Dame, 1974-88; chmn. Nat. Commn. Supplies and Shortages, 1975-77; mem. adv. panel Office Tech. Assessment, 1976-79; mem. Def. Sci. Bd., 1977-83, sr. cons., 1984-88; dir. for sec. def. and Pres. Def. Resource Mgmt. Study, 1977-79; mem. U.S. Commn. Nat. Security/21st Century, 1998-2001; trustee RAND, 2001-, chmn. grad. sch. bd. govs., 1999—. Author articles. Served to capt. AUS, 1965-67. Recipient Sec. Def. Meritorious Civilian Svc. medal, 1970, Def. Exceptional Civilian Svc. medal, 1993, Forrestal award, 1992; Ford Found. fellow, 1962-65. Fellow AAAS, Nat. Acad. of Pub. Adminstrn.; mem. Inst. Mgmt. Scis. (past pres.), Tau Beta Pi. Office Phone: 310-820-8029 ext. 210. Business E-Mail: drice@agensys.com.

RICE, DOROTHY PECHMAN, medical economist; b. Bklyn., June 11, 1922; d. Gershon and Lena (Schiff) Pechman; m. John Donald Rice, Apr. 3, 1943; children: Kenneth D., Donald B., Thomas H. Student, Bklyn. Coll., 1938—39; BA, U. Wis., 1941; DSc (hon.), Coll. Medicine and Dentistry N.J., 1979. With hosp., and med. facilities USPHS, Washington, 1960—61; med. econs. studies Social Security Adminstrn., 1962—63; health econs. br. Community Health Svc., USPHS, 1964—65; chief health ins. rsch. br. Social Security Adminstrn., 1966—72, dep. asst. commr. for rsch. and statistics, 1972—75; dir. Nat. Ctr. for Health Stats., Rockville, Md., 1976—82; prof. Inst. Health & Aging U. Calif., San Francisco, 1982—94, prof. emeritus, 1994—. Developer, mgr. nationwide health info. svcs.; expert on aging, health care costs, disability, and cost-of-illness. Contbr. articles to profl. jours. Recipient Social Security Adminstrn. citation, 1968, DSM, HEW, 1974, Jack C. Massey Found. award, 1978, UCSF medal, 2002. Fellow: Am. Statis. Assn.; mem.: LWV, APHA (domestic award for excellence 1978, Sedgwick Meml. medal 1988), Assn. Health Svc. Rsch. (President's award 1988), Inst. Medicine. Office: Univ Calif Sch Nursing 3333 California St Ste 340 San Francisco CA 94118 Office Phone: 415-476-5685. Personal E-mail: dorothy.rice@comcast.net. Business E-Mail: dorothy.rice@ucsf.edu.

RICE, FRANCES MAE, physician; b. Oakland, Calif., Apr. 19, 1931; d. George Henry and Clara Evelyn (Youngman) Rice. AB in Psychology cum laude, U. Calif., Berkeley, 1953; MPH in Epidemiology, U. Calif., Sch. Pub. Health, Berkeley, 1964; MD, U. Calif., San Francisco, 1957. Intern U. Calif. Hosp., San Francisco, 1957-58; pediatric resident U. Calif., San Francisco, 1959-61; pediatric and family physician HMO, Hanford, Calif., 1974-75; clin. pediatrician Kern County Health Dept., Bakersfield, Calif., 1975-76, physician, 1989, Kern Med. Group, Inc., Bakersfield, 1976-83; pvt. practice Shafter, Calif., 1983-89; physician Mercy Medicenter, Bakersfield, 1990-91, K.C.E.O.C. Family Health Clinic, Bakersfield, 1993-98, Berkeley Women's Health Ctr., 1999—. USPHS fellow, 1963—64. Fellow: Royal Soc. Medicine; mem.: N.Y. Acad. Sci. Avocations: music, literature. Home: 6103 Majestic Ave Oakland CA 94605

RICE, JERRY MERCER, toxicologist, pathologist; b. Washington, Oct. 3, 1940; s. John Earle Rice and Leona (Mercer) Greiner; m. Mary Jane Janocha, Jan. 10, 1978; children: Stacey Lynn, Stephen Mark. BA, Wesleyan U., 1962; PhD, Harvard U., 1966. Commd. officer USPHS, 1966, ret., 1996; rsch. scientist Nat Cancer Inst., Bethesda, Md., 1966-81, chief Lab. of Comparative Carcinogenesis Frederick, Md., 1981-94, 96, assoc. dir. Frederick Cancer Rsch. and Devel. Ctr., 1994-95, acting dir. divsn. cancer etiology, 1994-95, ret., 1996; sr. scientist WHO, 1996—2002, ret., 2002; chief unit of carcinogen identification and evaluation Internat. Agy. for Rsch. on Cancer, Lyons, France, 1996—2002, cons. in toxicology, 2003—; disting. prof., dept. oncology Lombardi Comprehensive Cancer Ctr., Georgetown U., Washington, 2003—. Editor: Perinatal Carcinogenesis, 1979; co-editor: Organ and Species Specificity in Chemical Carcinogenesis, 1983, Perinatal and Multigeneration Carcinogenesis, 1989, The Use of Short and Medium Term Tests for Carcinogens and Data on Genetic Effects in Carcinogenic Hazard Evaluation, 1999, Species Differences in Thyroid, Kidney and Urinary Bladder Carcinogenesis, 1999, Mech. of Carcinogenesis-contributions of molecular epidemiology, 2004,; contbr. rsch. articles and revs. in mechanisms of chem. carcinogenesis to profl. jours.; dir. emeritus IARC monographs on the evaluation of carcinogenic risks to humans. Recipient Outstanding Svc. medal, US Pub. Health Svc., 1990, Meritorious Svc. medal, 1996, George Scott Meml. award, Toxicology Forum, 1997. Mem. James Smithson Soc., Smithsonian Instn., Internat. Soc. Differentiation (emeritus), Am. Assn. Cancer Rsch. (emeritus), Phi Beta Kappa, Sigma Xi, Soc. Toxicology. Avocations: viticulture, tropical orchids, wild mushrooms. Home: 3213 Coquelin Ter Bethesda MD 20815-4840 Personal E-mail: jmricewas@aol.com. Business E-Mail: jr332@georgetown.edu.

RICE, JOY KATHARINE, psychologist, education educator; d. Joseph Theodore and Margaret Sophia (Bednarik) Straka; m. David Gordon Rice, Sept. 1, 1962; children: Scott Alan, Andrew David. BFA with high honors, U. Ill., 1960; MS, U. Wis., 1962, MS, 1964, PhD, 1967. Lic. clin. psychologist. USPHS predoctoral fellow dept. psychiatry Med. Sch. U. Wis., Madison, 1964-65, asst. dir. Counseling Ctr., 1966-74, dir. Office Continuing Edn. Svcs., 1972-78, prof. ednl. policy studies and women's studies, 1974-95, clin. prof. psychiatry, 1995—; pvt. practice psychology Psychiat. Svcs., S.C., Madison, 1967—. Mem. State Wis. Ednl. Approval Bd., Madison, 1972—73; mem. Adult Edn. Commn. U.S. Office Career Edn., Washington, 1978; co-chmn. Wis. Lt. Gov.'s Task Force on Women and Depression, 2005—. Author: Living Through Divorce, A Developmental Approach to Divorce Therapy, 1985, 2d edit., 1989, Transforming Leaderships Diverse Visions and Women's Voices, 2007; mem. editl. bd. Lifelong Learning, 1979—86; cons. editor: Psychology Women Quar., 1986—88, assoc. editor:, 1989—94, cons. editor: Handbook of Adult and Continuing Education, 1989, Encyclopedia of Women and Gender, 2001, Handbook of Girls' and Women's Psychological Health, 2005, Handbook of Couple Therapy, 2005, Handbook of Feminism & Women's Rights Worldwide, 2010; contbr. articles to profl. jours. Pres. Big Sisters Dane County, 2002, bd. dirs.; co-chair Wis. Lt. Gov.'s Task Force on Women and Depression, 2005—06. Recipient Disting. Achievement award, Ednl. Press Assn. Am., 1992, John Fritschler Jr. award for Disting. Achievement, 2004; Knapp fellow, U. Wis., Madison, 1960—62, Tchg. fellow, 1962—63. Fellow: APA (exec. bd. psychology women divsn. 1994—, internat. psychology divsn. 1998—, exec. bd. 1998—, chair internat. com. women 2000—02, chair com. internat. rels. psychology 2005, divsn. pres. 2006, Disting. Leadership award 2000—02, Woman of Yr. award, Sect. for Advancement of Women in Counseling Psychology 2007, Denmark Reuder award Internat. Contbr. Women & Gender 2011); mem.: Family Svc. Madison (bd. dirs. 2005—09, v.p. 2010, pres. 2011), Am. Assn. Continuing and Adult Edn. (Meritorious Svc. award 1978—80, 1982), Internat. Coun. Psychologists (bd. dir. 1998—2001, sec. 2002—04, bd. dir. 2004—), Nat. Assn. Women Edn. (editl. bd. jour. 1984—88, cons. editor Initiatives 1988—91), TEMPO Internat. (bd. dir., sec. 2000—03, 2006—, pres. elect 2009, pres. 2010), Rotary, Phi Delta Kappa. Avocations: interior decorating, painting, gardening, travel. Home: 4230 Waban Hl Madison WI 53711-3711 Office: 2727 Marshall Ct Madison WI 53705-2255 Office Phone: 608-238-9354.

RICE, KENNER CRALLE, medicinal chemist; s. Kenner Cralle Jr. and Annie Grace Rice. BS, Va. Mil. Inst., 1961; PhD, Ga. Inst. Tech., 1966. Sr. scientist Ciba-Geigy Corp., Summit, 1969—72; sr. staff fellow NIH, Bethesda, Md., 1972—76, rsch. chemist, 1977—86; chief sect. drug design and synthesis Nat. Inst. Diabetes, Digestive and Kidney Diseases, Bethesda, Md., 1987—88; chief lab. medicinal chemistry NIDDK, NIH, Bethesda, Md., 1989—2006; chief chem. biology rsch. br. Nat. Inst. on Drug Abuse, 2006—. Adj. prof. pharmacology U. Md., Balt., 1985—; mem. Fed. Sr. Exec. Svc., Bethesda, 1989—98, Fed. Sr. Biomed. Rsch. Svc., 1998—; affiliate prof. Va. Commonwealth U., Richmond, 1995—; vis. prof. pharmacology U. Ill., Peoria, 1995—; adj. prof. medicinal chemistry Comprehensive Drug Rsch. Ctr. U. Miami, 1995—. Author (with others): Pharmacological Reviews, 1987; editor: NIDA Research Monograph 96, 1990; contbr. more than 600 rsch. papers to profl. jours. Capt. US Army, 1966—68. Recipient Internat. Sato Meml. award, Japanese Pharm. Soc., 1983, Rsch. Achievement award, Am. Pharm. Assn., 1987, Hillebrand prize, Chem. Soc. Washington, 1986, Divsn. Medicinal Chemistry award, Am. Chem. Soc., 1996, Rsch. Achievement award, Am. Assn. Pharm. Scientists, 1998, Chem. Pioneer award, Am. Inst. Chemists, 2000, Nathan B. Eddy award, Coll. Problems of Drug Dependence, 2001, Bristol-Myers Squibb Smissman award, Am. Chem. Soc. Divsn. Medicinal Chemistry, 2007; named to Medicinal Chemistry Hall of Fame, 2007. Fellow: Coll. on Problems of Drug Dependence (bd. dirs. 1988—92, 1997—2001); mem.: Am. Coll. Neuropsychopharmacology, Cosmos Club. Achievements include 42 patents in organic chemical synthesis and pharmacology of drugs of abuse; development of NIH opiate total synthesis as first practical synthesis of opium alkaloids and derivatives as narcotics and narcotic antagonists. Office: NIH NIDA Chem Biology Rsch Br 5625 Fishers Ln Rm 4N 03 Mail Stop 9415 Rockville MD 20852 Business E-Mail: kr21f@nih.gov.

RICE, LAWRENCE, hematologist, educator; b. Bklyn., Mar. 27, 1949; m. Laura Rice; children: Jennifer Webb, Michael. MD, Emory U., 1974; BS in Zoology, U. Fla., 1970. Diplomate Am. Bd. Hematology. Intern, resident in medicine Baylor Coll. Medicine, Houston, 1974—77, clin. and rsch. fellow in hematology, 1977—79, asst. prof. medicine, 1979—86, assoc. prof., 1986—99, prof. medicine, prof. thrombosis rsch., 1999—2007, adj. prof. medicine, 2007—; chief hematology The Meth. Hosp., Weill Cornell Med. Coll., 2007—; prof. medicine Weill Cornell Med. Coll., 2008—. Contbr. articles to profl. jours. Named to Baylor Outstanding Faculty Educator Hall of Fame, Dept. Medicine, 2003. Office: Methodist Hosp Cornell Univ Dept Medicine 6550 Fannin Ste 1001 Houston TX 77030 Business E-Mail: lrice@tmhs.org.

RICE, PATRICIA A., hospital and healthcare company executive; Adminstr. Lakeview Rehab. Hosp. Continental Med. Sys., Inc., 1987, various mgmt. positions, 1987—96, sr. v.p. clin. ops., 1994—96, exec. v.p. hosp. ops. divsn., 1996—97; sr. v.p. hosp. ops. Select Med. Holdings Corp., 1997—99, exec. v.p. ops., 1999—2002, COO, 2002—, pres., 2005—. Named one of Top 25 Women in Healthcare, Modern Healthcare mag., 2011. Office: Select Medical Holdings Corp 4716 Old Gettysburg Rd Mechanicsburg PA 17055 Office Phone: 717-972-1100. Office Fax: 717-972-1042. *

RICE, RONALD JAMES, retired hospital administrator; b. Springfield, Mo., Feb. 5, 1944; s. Glen Elwood and Alice Jeanett (Robinson) R. BSBA, Cen. Mo. State U., 1966, MABA, 1969, Specialist, 1972. Lic. nursing home adminstr.; lic. risk mgr. Unit mgr. Bapt. Med. Ctr., Kansas City, Mo., 1970-71; dir. unit mgmt. Ind. Health Ctr., Independence, Mo., 1971-72; adminstrv. officer Meth. Hosp., Jacksonville, Fla., 1972-73, dir. personnel, 1973-74; assoc. adminstr. Humana Hosp. Orange Park (Fla.), 1974-77; adminstr. Cathedral Rehab. Hosp., Jacksonville, 1977-79, Marion County Gen. Hosp., Hamilton, Ala., 1979-80, Nassau Gen. Hosp., Fernandina Beach, Fla., 1980-85, Reception Med. Ctr., Lake Butler, Fla., 1985-91; regional adminstr. health svcs. Dept. Corrections, Gainesville, Fla., 1991—; sr. health svc. adminstr. Columbia Correctional Instn., 1999—2006; ret., 2010. Cons. Clay Meml. Hosp., Green Cove Springs, Fla., 1976-77, Allied Health Care, Jacksonville, 1989. Mem. Polit. Action Com., Fla. Hosp. Assn., 1990, Coun. on Crime and Delinquency, Gainesville, 1990,

Human Resources Com., Orlando, 1991; active Orange Park Presbyn. Ch. With U.S. Army, 1967-69. Decorated Army Commendation medal. Fellow Am. Coll. Health Care Execs.; mem. Am. acad. Med. Adminstrs., Am. Coll. Health Care Adminstrs., Am. Soc. Personnel Adminstrs., Fla. Hosp. Assn., Rotary (pres. 1984-86). Democrat. Avocations: boating, collecting model cars, reading. Home: 1744 Horton Dr Orange Park FL 32073-2757 Personal E-mail: ricerjq45@aol.com.

RICE, STEPHEN GARY, pediatrician, sports medicine physician, educator; b. Bklyn., Dec. 21, 1945; s. Abraham S. Rice and Anne (Shelling) Rice-Brown; m. Hilary Jo Turett, May 10, 1987; children: Adam, Bryan. AB, Columbia Coll., 1967; MD, PhD, NYU, 1974; MPH, U. Wash., 1983. Diplomate in pediat. and sports medicine Am. Bd. Pediat. Intern, resident Children's Hosp. and U. Wash., Seattle, 1974-77; faculty mem. sports medicine U. Wash., Seattle, 1977-96; program dir. primary care sports medicine fellowship Jersey Shore Univ. Med. Ctr., Neptune, NJ, 1996—; clin. prof. pediat., Robert Wood Johnson Med. Sch. U. Medicine and Dentistry NJ, New Brunswick, 2011—. Team physician U. Wash., 1977-81, Georgian Ct. U., 1997-; developer, dir. Athletic Health Care Sys., 1978—; dir. Jersey Shore Sports Medicine Ctr., 1997-; med. cons., NJ Youth Soccer Olympic Devel. Program, 2002-; cons. in field; bd. dirs. NJ PCORE, 2008-, chmn. NJ Student Athlete Cardiac Screening Task Force, 2010-11. Author: Athletic Health Care System, 1988. Mem. Alumni Representative Com., Columbia Coll., 1974-, Concussion in Sports Steering Com., Brain Injury Assn. NJ, 2005-. Recipient Commendation award, Washington State Interscholastic Activities Assn., 1981, 1995, Vol. Faculty Tchg. award, UMDNJ-Robert Wood Johnson Med. Sch., 2000, Silvio O. Conte award, Brain Injury Assn. NJ, 2006; named one of Top Drs. in Sports Medicine, NJ Mag., 2001, 2003, 2005, 2010, 2011, Top Drs. in Greater NY Metro. Area, Castle Connelly, 2002—11. Fellow: Am. Coll. Sports Medicine (chmn. health and sci. policy com. 2000—, mem. bd. trustees 2007—10), Am. Acad. Pediat. (chmn. sports medicine com. NJ chpt. 1999—2011, chmn. govt. affairs com. NJ chpt. 2000—06, sec.-editor NJ chpt. 2002—04, exec. com. sports medicine and fitness coun. 2003—09, treas. NJ chpt. 2004—06, v.p.-elect NJ chpt. 2006—08, v.p. NJ chpt. 2008—10, pres. NJ chpt. 2010—); mem.: AAHPERD, Med. Soc. NJ, Am. Med. Soc. Sports Medicine, Nat. Strength and Conditioning Assn. Avocations: sports, cooking, gardening, gilbert & sullivan, chess. Home: 6 Wildflower Ct Manalapan NJ 07726-2861 Office: Jersey Shore Univ Med Ctr Dept Pediat PO Box 397 Neptune NJ 07754-0397 Office Phone: 732-776-2384. Business E-Mail: srice@meridianhealth.com.

RICE, THOMAS HOWARD, healthcare educator; b. Washington, Apr. 21, 1954; s. John Donald and Dorothy Pechman R.; m. Katherine Anne Desmond, Oct. 21, 1953; children: Clara, Daniel. BA, U. N.C., 1976; MA, U. Calif., Berkeley, 1979, PhD, 1982. Sr. health economist SRI Internat., Menlo Park, Calif., 1979—83; assoc. prof. U.N.C. Sch. Pub. Health, Chapel Hill, 1983—91; prof. UCLA Sch. Pub. Health, 1991—, vice chancellor for academic personnel, 2006—11. Chmn. bd. dir. Acad. Health, Washington, 2005—06; editor Med. Care Rsch. and Rev., Thousand Oaks, Calif., 1994—2000; chair Dept. Health Svcs., UCLA Sch. of Pub. Health, 1996—2000. Author: Economics of Health Reconsidered, 2009; editor: Changing the U.S. Health Care System, 2006. Recipient Young Investigator of the Yr. award, Assn. Health Svcs. Rsch., 1988, Thompson prize, Assn. U. Programs in Health Adminstrn., 1992, Article of the Yr. award, Assn. Health Svcs. Rsch., 1998. Mem.: Inst. of Medicine. Office: 2138 Murphy Hall Los Angeles CA 90095-1405 Office Phone: 310-206-9345. Business E-Mail: trice@conet.ucla.edu. *

RICH, J. RONALD, neurosurgeon; s. Jesse J. and Dexter Cheatham Rich; m. Linda Christy Johnson, Aug. 26, 1976; children: Scott, Brian, Colin. AA, Phoenix Coll., 1957; BS in Chemistry, Ariz. State U., Tempe, 1961; MD, U. Utah, Salt Lake City, 1964. Diplomate Am. Bd. Neurol. Surgery, lic. physician Calif., 1965, Ariz., 1965. Intern in surgery UCLA Sch. Medicine, 1964—65, resident in surgery, 1965—66, resident in neurosurgery, 1966—71, chief resident in neurosurgery, 1970—71; postdoctoral fellow NIH, 1969—70, spl. postdoctoral fellow in tumor immunology, 1972—74; chief neurosurgery svc. Harbor-UCLA Med. Ctr., Torrance, Calif., 1971—72; attending physician Wadsworth VA Hosp., LA, 1974—76; staff surgeon Daniel Brotman Meml. Hosp., Culver City, Calif., 1974—82, Daniel Freeman Marina Hosp., Marina Del Rey, Calif., 1974—90, Kaiser Found. Hosp., LA, 1975—77; sr. staff surgeon Santa Monica-UCLA Med. Ctr., 1974—, Saint John's Hosp. and Health Ctr., Santa Monica, 1976—; attending staff UCLA Ctr. Health Scis., 1994—. Acting asst. prof. surgery/neurosurgery UCLA Sch. Medicine, 1970—71, adj. asst. prof. surgery/neurosurgery, 1971—75; asst. vis. surgeon UCLA Ctr. for Health Scis., 1971—72; chmn. sect. neurosurgery Santa Monica-UCLA Med. Ctr., 1979—2003, mem. exec. bd., 1984—86, chmn. dept. surgery, 1985—86, chief of staff, 1986; chmn. sect. neurosurgery Saint John's Hosp. and Health Ctr., 1990—; del. Joint Coun. State Neurosurg. Socs., 1996—99; lectr. in field. Contbr. articles to profl. jours., chapters to books. Maj. USAR, 1965—71. Named one of LA's Best Drs., LA Mag., 1996, Best in the West, Pacific Coast Physicians, Physicians Mag., 1996, Best Drs. in America, 1996, Best Drs. in Am., Pacific Region, Woodward and Smith, 1997, America's Top Surgeons, Consumers Rsch. Coun., 2007. Mem.: ACS, Calif. Assn. Neurol. Surgeons (dir. 1993—96, 1st v.p. 2001—02, pres.-elect 2002—03, pres. 2003—04, cons. bd. 2005—), Congress Neurol. Surgeons, Bay Surg. Soc. (exec. bd. 1982—89, sec.-treas. 1984, v.p. 1985, pres. 1986), Am. Assn. Neurol. Surgeons, So. Calif. Neurosurg. Soc., Fedn. Western Neurol. Socs. Avocations: wine, food, travel. Business E-Mail: bayneurosurg@aol.com.

RICH, MICHAEL OGDEN, pediatrician, educator, filmmaker, researcher; b. Washington; children: Desta, Erik, Jason, Ian. BA, Pomona Coll., Claremont. Calif., 1977; MD, Harvard Med. Sch., Boston, Mass., 1991; MPH, Harvard Sch. Pub. Health, Boston, Mass., 1997. Diplomate Am. Bd. Pediat., sub-bd. Gen. Pedia, Nat. Bd. Med. Examiners, Am. Bd. Pediat., Gen. Pediat., Am. Bd. Pediat., Sub-board in Adolescent Medicine, cert. Am. Bd. Pediat., Sub-board in Adolescent Medicine, lic. Commonwealth of Mass. Bd. Registration in Medicine. Intern, pediat. Children's Hosp. Boston, 1991—92, resident, pediat., 1991—94, fellow, adolescent medicine, 1994—96, asst. in medicine, 1996—; dir., prin. investigator, Video/Intervention Prevention Assessment (VIA) Children's Hosp. Boston/Harvard Med. Sch., 1994—, dir., founder, Ctr. on Media and Child Health, 2002—; staff physician Bentley Coll., Waltham, Mass., 1996—; clin. fellow, pediat. Harvard Med. Sch., 1994—96, instr., pediat., 1996—2000, asst. prof. pediat., 2000—; instr., pub. health practice Harvard Sch. Pub. Health, 1997—2003, asst. prof. soc., human develop. and health, 2003—. Quality improvement, adolescent/young adult clinic com. mem. Children's Hosp. Boston, 1994—99; med. dir., v.p. Health Act, Boston, 1996—99; bd. dirs. Asthma and Allergy Found. America (New. Eng. Chpt.), 1998—; risk reduction/health comm. rsch. mem. Dana Farber/Harvard Comprehensive Cancer Ctr., 1999—; mem. Workgroup on Comm. and HIV/STD Prevention, Nat. Inst. Mental Health, 1999, Roundtable on the Impact of the Media on Adolescent Sexual Attitudes and Behaviors, Ctrs. for Disease Control and Prevention, 2004; vis. prof. U. Vt. Sch. Medicine, 1999, Hosp. for Sick Children/U. Toronto, 2000, U. Medicine and Dentistry NJ, 2000, Royal Children's Hosp., Melbourne, Australia, 2001; Morris Blum Meml. vis. prof. U. Minn., 2002; scholar The Academy, Harvard Med. Sch., 2002—; Am. Acad. Pediat. CATCH vis. prof. Schneider Children's Hosp. and LI Jewish Hosp., 2003; mem. bd. visitors Menninger Clinic Baylor Coll. Medicine, Methodist Hosp. Found., 2005—; adv. bd. mem. Children's Digital Media Ctr., Georgetown U., Washington, 2005—, PBS Kids, 2006—, Candie's Found., 2006—; mem. bd. advisors Parents Mag., 2007—; Rutherford B. Pohill vis. prof. U. Ala., 2007; invited presenter in field. Mem. editl. bd. PREP Audio, 2006—, Pediatrics, 2002—05; co-editor: Adolescent Medicine, State of the Art Reviews, 2003—; Ad-Hoc Reviewer for several publications, —, written chapters for Children and Television: 50 Years of Research. Discussant, co-ordinator, asthma edn. radio talk show Enough is Enough, WJMN 94.5FM, Waltham, Mass., 1997; presenter (with Jackie Joyner-Kersee), Don't Let Asthma Keep You from Going for the Gold Dimock Cmty. Health Ctr., Roxbury, Mass., 1997; mem. exec. bd., Flashpoint, Media Literacy Initiative Office of the Eastern Dist. Atty., Salem, 1998—; columnist News in Sch. Health, Divsn. of Sch. Health, Mass. Dept. Health, 1998; cons. physician WINGS Program/Winsor Sch., Boston, 1999; presenter, VIA: The Illness Experience of Children and Adolescents Inst. of Contemporary Art., Boston, 2003, presenter, discussant, Patient-Doctor Relationships, 2003. Fellow: Soc. for Adolescent Medicine (Nat.) (spl. interest group leader 1996—), Am. Acad. Pediat. (Holroyd-Sherry award 2005); mem.: Internat. Comm. Assn., Soc. for Pediat. Rsch., Am. Pub. Health Assn., Soc. for Adolescent Medicine (New Eng. Chpt.) (Finalist, New Investigator award 1997, New Investigator award 1998), AMA, Mass. Med. Soc., Physicians for Social Responsibility, Physicians for Human Rights. Avocations: scuba diving, aficionado of opera, fine wine and theater. Office: Division Adolescent/Young Adult Medicine Children's Hosp Boston 300 Longwood Ave 1 Autumn-5 Boston MA 02115 Office Phone: 617-355-5420. Office Fax: 617-730-0004. Business E-Mail: michael.rich@childrens.harvard.edu.

RICH, PRESTON BERKELEY, surgeon; b. Balt., Aug. 14, 1967; MD, Med. Coll. Va., 1993; MBA, U. NC Kenan-Flagler Bus. Sch., 2010. Chief trauma, critical care, and emergency surgery U. NC Health Care Sys., 2004—. V.p., chief med. officer Entegrion, 2008; chief med. officer Bioshape Solutions, 2009. Recipient Outsanding Cmty. Svc. award, U. NC at Chapel Hill. Fellow: ACS; mem.: AMA, Am. Coll. Healthcare Execs., Soc. U. Surgeons, Am. Assn. Surgery Trauma, Phi Beta Kappa, Alpha Omega Alpha, Beta Gamma Sigma. Avocations: running, sailing. Office: University NC Sch Medicine 4008 Burnett Womack Bldg Chapel Hill NC 27599 Office Fax: 919-966-0369. Business E-Mail: prich@med.unc.edu.

RICH, TYVIN ANDREW, radiation therapist; b. Trenton, NJ, Feb. 6, 1948; s. Jospeh Anthony and Mary Virginia R.; m. Christine Schmiel, June 5, 1977; children: Andrew, Karina, Alexander, Austin. BA, Rutgers U., 1969; MD, U. Va., 1973. Instr. Joint Ctr., Boston, 1979-82; asst. prof. Harvard Med. Sch., Boston, 1982-84, M.D. Anderson Cancer Ctr., Houston, 1984-85, assoc. prof., 1986-92, dir. clinics, 1988-90, prof., 1992—; chmn. dept. radiation oncology U. Va. Health Scis. Ctr., prof. dept. radiation oncology. Chmn. GI com. Radiation Therapy Oncology Group, Phila., 1990—; mem. editl. bd. Jour. Infusional Chemotherapy, Ontario, Can., 1991—, M.D. Anderson Cancer Ctr., Oncology, Houston, 1990—, Internat. Jour. GI Cancer, London, 1991—. Recipient Nat. Rsch. Svc. award Nat. Cancer Inst., 1978. Mem. AMA, Am. Coll. Radiology, Am. Soc. Clin. Oncology, Soc. for Surgical Oncology, Am. Radium Soc., Am. Soc. for Therapeutic Radiology and Oncology, New Eng. Cancer Soc., Tex. Radiol. Soc. Office: U Va Health Cancer Ctr Dept Radiation Oncology Box 800383 Jefferson Park Ave Charlottesville VA 22908

RICHARD, FINKEL S., child neurologist; BA in Chemistry, Wash. and Jefferson Coll., 1974; MD, Wash. U., 1978. Diplomate Am. Bd. Pediat., 1984, Am. Bd. Electrodiagnostic Med., 1999, Am. Bd. Psychiatry and Neurology-child neurology, 1986, Am. Bd. Psychiatry and Neurology-neuromuscular medicine, 2008. Peditrics prof. neurology dept. Univ. Pa.; fellow Children's Hosp. Boston, pediatrics resident, 1978—80; hosp. affiliation includes Bringham and Womens Hosp., Beth Israel Hosp. Co-author: (publs.) An expanded version of the Hammersmith Functional Motor Scale for SMA II and III patients, 2007, Consensus statement for standard of care in spinal muscular atrophy. Journal of child neurology, 2007, A teenager with focal weakness, 2008, Umbilical cord blood transplantation for juvenile metachromatic leukodystrophy, 2008, and numerous others. Named one of the Top Doctors, Phila. Mag., 2011. Office: The Children's Hospital of Philadelphia Neurology Division 34th St Civic Center Blvd Philadelphia PA 19104 Office Phone: 215-590-2763. Office Fax: 215-590-2223. E-mail: finkel@email.chop.edu.

RICHARD, ROBERT CARTER, psychological consultant; b. Waterloo, Iowa, Apr. 4, 1938; s. Quentin Leroy and Adeline Pauline (Halverson) R.; m. Shirley Ruth Jones, Aug. 25, 1962 (div. Mar. 1999); children: David, John; m. Jacqueline J. Mendes, Feb. 19, 2000; stepchildren: Julianne Mendes, Katherine Mendes. BA Wheaton (Ill.) Coll., 1960; BD, Fuller Theol. Sem., 1963, PhD, 1973; STM, Andover Newton Theol. Sch., 1964. Ordained to ministry Am. Bapt. Conv., 1963; lic. psychologist, Calif. Pastor Peninsula Bapt. Ch., Gig Harbor, Wash., 1965-68; marriage, family counselor Glendale Family Svc., Calif., 1970-71; psychol. asst. Oakland and Pleasant Hill, Calif., 1972—73; psychologist Rafa Counseling Ctr., Pleasant HIll, 1974—2006; ret., 2006. Mem. faculty John F. Kennedy U., Orinda, Calif., 1975-78; adj. faculty mem. New Coll., Berkeley, Calif, 1986; mem. dean's nat. adv. coun. Sch. Psychology, Fuller Theol. Sem., 2005—; co-founder, bd. dirs. New Directions Counseling Ctr., 1974-81; rschr. assertiveness tng., lay counselor tng., psychotherapy and religious experience, treatment of adults abused as children; bd. dirs. Fuller Psychological and Family Svc., 2008-. Author: (with Deacon Anderson) The Way Back: A Christian's Journey to Mental Wholeness, 1989; contbr. articles to profl. publs. Recipient Integration of Psychology and Theology award, 1973. Mem.: APA. Republican. Avocations: boating, astronomy, photography. Personal E-mail: starryrobert@aol.com.

RICHARDS, ANN ADAIR, psychologist; b. Tulsa, Jan. 28, 1949; d. William Jenkins and Virginia Ann (Daniels) Richards; 1 child, Desiree Ann Perkins. BS in bus. edn., U. Okla., 1970; BA in theatre arts, U. No. Colo., 1983, MA in agy. counseling, 1985, EdS, 2002. Nationally Certified School Psychologist, lic. Professional Counselor Colo. Regulatory Bd. Workshop coord. Rocky Mtn. Planned Parenthood, Denver, 1977—79; para prof., remedial reading Denver Pub. Schools, 1979—80; generalist clinician Centennial Mental Health Ctr., 1986—95; children and family therapist No. Range Behavior Health, Greely, Colo., 1995—99; pvt. practice Greely, 1999—2000; sch. psychologist intern Northeast Bd. Cooperative Ednl. Svcs., Haxton, Colo., 2000—01; sch. psychologist East Ctrl. Bd. Cooperative Ednl. Svcs., Limon, Colo., 2001—. Chair and vice chair Logan County Sexual Assault Team, Sterling, Colo., 1989—95; co-dir. drama club play Woodlin Sch., 2000, participant reading challenge, 06, 07; crisis response coord. East Ctrl. Bd. Cooperative Ednl. Svcs., 2001—09, autism coord., 2005—08, rti coord., 2005—07, supr. sch. psychologists, interns, practicum students, 2006, supr. sch. psychologists, interns, practicum students neuropsych.spec, 08; mem. crisis response team Colo. Soc. Sch. Psychologists, 2004—09. Spl. olympics vol. Sterling H.S., 1992—94; bd. mem. Yuma Cmty. Resource Ctr., Yuma, Colo., 1986—88, Help for Abused Ptnrs., Sterling, Colo., 1989—95, sec., 1989—95; com. mem. Arts Picnic, Greeley, Colo., 1983. Recipient Women of the Yr., Beta Sigma Phi Social Svc. Sorority, 2000, Scholarship, Am. Assn. of U. Women; Circle Key Alumni grant, Kappa Kappa Gamma Found., 1994, 1995, Mildred Guch Scholarship, U. No. Colo., 1984—85. Mem.: Colo. Soc. Sch. Psychologists, Nat. Assn. Sch. Psychologist. Democrat. Lutheran. Avocations: weightlifting, aerobics, movies, reading, interior decorating. Office: East Ctrl Bd Ednl Svcs 820 2d St Limon CO 80828 Home: 836 Rumford Ln Fort Collins CO 80525-4296

RICHARDS, CECILE, healthcare network executive; b. 1957; d. David and Ann Richards; 3 children. BA in History, Brown U., 1980. Labor organizer, La., Calif., Tex., 1980—95; founder Texas Freedom Network, 1995—2002; dep. chief of staff to Rep. Nancy Pelosi US Congress, Washington, 2002—03; founder, pres. America Votes, Washington, 2003—06; pres. Planned Parenthood Fedn. America, Inc., NYC, 2006—. Bd. dirs. NARAL Pro-Choice Am., Planned Parenthood Action Fund; founder, bd. dirs. Tex. Freedom Network, 1995. Democrat. Office: Planned Parenthood Fedn Am Inc 434 W 33rd St New York NY 10001-2601 Office Phone: 212-541-7800. Office Fax: 212-245-1845.

RICHARDS, PAUL GRANSTON, seismologist, geophysics educator; b. Cirencester, Eng., Mar. 31, 1943; arrived in US, 1965; naturalized, 1980; s. Albert George and Kathleen Margaret (Harding) R.; m. Jody Margaret Porterfield, June 1, 1968; children: Mark, Jessica, Gillian. BA, Cambridge U., Eng., 1965; MS, Calif. Inst. Tech., Pasadena, 1966, PhD, 1970. Asst. prof. geology Columbia U., NYC, 1971—76, chmn. geol. scis., 1980-83, assoc. prof. geol. scis., 1976—79, prof. geol. scis., 1979—96; Mellon prof. natural scis. Columbia. U., NYC, 1987—2008; prof. earth and environ. scis. Columbia U., NYC, 1996—2008; assoc. dir. Lamont-Doherty Geol. Obs., Columbia U., Palisades, 1980—83, mem. adminstrv. com., 1987—90, 1994—98. Seismic rev. panel USAF Tactical Applications Ctr., 1985—; mem. Coun. Fgn. Rels., 1992—. Co-author: Quantitative Seismology, 2 vols., 1980, 2nd edit., 2002; bd. editors Wave Motion, 1985-92, Jour. Computational Acoustics, 1991-97. Recipient Leo Szilard lectureship award, Am. Phys. Soc., 2006; Sloan Found. rsch. fellow, 1973-77, Guggenheim Found. fellow, 1977-78, MacArthur Found. fellow, 1981-86, fellow Royal Norwegian Coun. Scientific and Indsl. Rsch., 1989; William C. Foster fellow and vis. scholar, US Arms Control and Disarmament Agy., 1984-85, 1993-94; vis. scholar Los Alamos Nat. Lab., 1997, Phi Beta Kappa vis. scholar, 2000-01. Fellow AAAS, Royal Astron. Soc., Am. Acad. Arts and Scis., Am. Geophys. Union (mem. coun. 1990-94, pres. seismology sect., 1992-96; Macelwane award 1976); mem. Inc. Rsch. Institutions for Seismology (chmn. presdl. search com., 1985, 1990, exec. com., 1987-90, vice-chmn. bd. dirs., 1988-90, standing com. data mgmt. ctr., 1996-99, nominating com., 2003-04), Seismological Soc. America (bd. dirs. 2002-09, Reid medalist 2009), Soc. Exploration Geophysicists, Arms Control Assn. Episcopalian. Office: Lamont-Doherty Earth Obs 61 Rte 9W Palisades NY 10964 E-mail: richards@ldeo.columbia.edu.

RICHARDS, PRISCILLA ANN, medical/surgical nurse; b. Providence, Nov. 10, 1949; d. Frank L. Thornton and Dorothy A. Maker; children: Tanya Rene, Jason Edward. Assoc. Degree Nursing, Lincoln Land C.C., Springfield, Ill., 1980. RN Ill., 1980, R.I., 1997. Cert. nursing asst. Meml. Med. Ctr., Springfield, 1971—73, lic. practical nurse, 1973—80, RN, 1980—97, South County Nursing and Subacute Ctr., North Kingstown, RI, 1997—2000, Elmhurst Extended Care, Providence, 2000—05, Maxim Health Care, Providence, 2005—. Sgt. USAF, 1968—71. Baptist. Avocations: reading, swimming, yard work. Home: 71 Wells Ave Warwick RI 02889 Personal E-mail: prissy200959@aol.com.

RICHARDSON, BRENT EARL, otolaryngologist; BA in Biology and Anthropology, Washington U., St. Louis, 1986; MD with honors, U. Wash., Seattle, 1990; MS in Otolaryngology, U. Minn., Mpls., 1996. Cert. Am. Bd. Otolaryngology, 1997. Fellow, laryngology and voice Loyola U. Med. Ctr., Maywood, Ill., 1996—97; intern, dept. surgery Hennepin County Med. Ctr., Minneapolis, Minn., 1990—91, resident, dept. surgery, 1991—92; resident, dept. otolaryngology U.

Minn., Minneapolis, 1992—96; attending physician, surgical svc., divsn. otolaryngology Hines VA Med. Ctr., Ill., 1997—2002; attending physician Foster McGaw Hosp., Loyola U. Med. Ctr., Maywood, Ill., 1997—2003; asst. prof., otolaryngology Stritch Sch. Medicine, Loyola U. Chgo., Maywood, Ill., 1997—2003; attending physician Advocate Good Samaritan Hosp., Downers Grove, Ill., 2003—; laryngologist Bastian Voice Inst., Downers Grove, Ill., 2003—. Cons., surgical svc., divsn. otolaryngology Hines VA Med. Ctr., Ill., 2002—03; invited presenter in the field. Contbr. articles to profl. jours. Named to Guide to America's Top Physicians, Consumers' Research Coun. Am., 2003. Mem.: Nat. Assn. Teachers of Singing, Am. Speech-Language-Hearing Assn., Dysphagia Rsch. Soc., Christian Soc. Otolaryngology/Head and Neck Surgery, Christian Med. Assn., Chgo. Laryngological and Otological Soc., Am. Acad. Otolaryngology/Head and Neck Surgery, Am. Acad. Med. Ethics, Phi Kappa Phi, Alpha Omega Alpha. Office: Bastian Voice Inst 3010 Highland Pkwy Ste 550 Downers Grove IL 60515 Office Phone: 630-724-1100. Office Fax: 630-724-0084.

RICHARDSON, DAVID WALTHALL, cardiologist, educator, consultant; b. Nanking, China, Mar. 22, 1925; s. Donald William and Virginia (McIlwaine) R.; m. Frances Lee Wingfield, June 12, 1948; children: Donald, Sarah, David. BS, Davidson Coll., 1947; MD, Harvard U., 1951. Diplomate Am. Bd. Internal Medicine, Am. Bd. Cardiology. Intern, resident Yale New Haven Hosp., 1951-53; resident, fellow Med. Coll. Va., Richmond, 1953-56, assoc. prof. to prof. medicine, 1962-95, prof. emeritus, 1995—2007, prof. medicine, 2007—. Chmn. divsn. cardiology, 1972-87; interim chmn. dept. medicine, 1973-74; chief cardiology, assoc. chief staff for rsch. VA Hosp., Richmond, 1956-61, dir. cardiology tng. program, 1990-95, prof. medicine Health Sci. Disease Va. Commonwealth U., 1995-; vis. scientist Oxford U., Eng., 1961-62; vis. prof. U. Milan, Italy, 1972-73. Contbr. articles to profl. jours. Moderator Hanover Presybery, Presbyn. Ch. U.S., Richmond, 1970; chmn. events com., NHLBI Cardiac Arrhythmia Suppression Trial, 1983-92, NHLBI Anti-Arrhythmics versus Implantable Defibrillators Trial, 1993-97. Served with USN, 1944-46. Fellow Am. Coll. Cardiology (gov. VA 1970-72), Am. Heart Assn. (coun. clin. cardiology and high blood pressure rsch.); mem. Am. Soc. Clin. Investigation, Am. Clin. and Climatol. Assn. Democrat. Presbyterian. Home: 1500 Westbrook Ct CYA 1105 Richmond VA 23227-3366 Office Phone: 804-200-1256. Personal E-mail: dwr1@wcrichmond.org, davidr1925@gmail.com.

RICHARDSON, DEAN WHEELER, equine surgeon, veterinary educator; b. Aug. 30, 1953; married; 1 child. BS, Dartmouth Coll., Hanover, NH, 1974; DVM, Ohio State U., Coll. Vet. Medicine, 1975—79. Internship surgical residency training prog., U. Pa., 1979; with New Bolton Ctr., U. Pa. Sch. Vet. Medicine, Kennett Sq., Pa., 1979—, Charles W. Raker prof. equine surgery, chief of Large Animal Surgery. Mem. editl. bd. Specialty Mag. in the Sci. Biol. Chemicals, mem. adv. editl. bd. Zeitschrift für Metallkunde. Recipient Norden Disting. Teaching award, Disting. Alumni award, Coll. Vet. Medicine, Ohio State U., 2005. Mem.: Osteosynthesis Soc., Grayson-Jockey Club (mem. scientific adv. bd.). Achievements include recognized for teaching AO Veterinary in North America and Switzerland; leading authority in orthopedic surgery and long bone fractures in horses; renown for performing life saving surgery on Kentucy Derby winner Barbaro, 2006. Avocations: horseback riding, basketball, golf, birdwatching. Office: U Pa New Bolton Ctr 382 W St Rd Kennett Square PA 19348 Office Phone: 610-925-6264. Office Fax: 610-925-8120. E-mail: dwr@vet.upenn.edu.

RICHARDSON, DONALD EDWARD, neurosurgery educator; b. Vicksburg, Miss., Oct. 5, 1931; s. Edward K. and Ina Mae (Cooper) R.; children: Donna Richardson Boas, Scott, David, W. Jeffrey, Cooper E.H. BS in Chemistry, Millsaps Coll., Jackson, Miss., 1953; MD, Tulane U., New Orleans, 1957. Diplomate Am. Bd. Neurol. Surgery. Intern in surgery Charity Hosp., New Orleans, 1957-58, resident in neurosurgery, 1961-62, Ochsner Found. Hosp., New Orleans, 1958-60, VA Hosp., New Orleans, 1960-61; instr. Dept. Neurosurgery, Tulane U., 1962-64, asst. prof., 1964-67, assoc. prof., 1967-74, prof., chmn., 1980—, program dir. residence-tng. program, 1980, adj. prof. dept. biomed. engring., 1984—; clin. assoc. prof. dept. neurosurgery La. State U., New Orleans, 1974-80. Dir. Pain Treatment Ctr. Hotel Dieu Hosp., New Orleans, 1978-93, mem.-at-large exec. com., 1978-84, chmn. spl. procedures com., 1984-93; chief neurosurgery sect. Charity Hosp. La. New Orleans, 1980—, VA Hosp. New Orleans, 1980—; mem. neurosurgery staff, Toure Infirmary, So. Bapt. Hosp., Pendelton Meml. Meth. Hosp., St. Jude Med. Ctr.; chmn. Neurosurgery dept. Tulane U. Med. Ctr. Hosp., 1980—, oper. rm. and exec. coms., 1980—; invited presenter in field; lectr. and expert in field. Contbr. articles to profl. jours.; featured on Miracle Workers, ABC, 2006. Fellow ACS; mem. AAAS, AMA, Am. Assn. Neurol. Surgeons, Am. Pain Soc., Am. Soc. for Stereotactic and Functional Neurosurgery, Assn. for Acad. Surgery, Congress Neurol. Surgeons, Internat. Assn. for Study Pain, Internat. Neurosurg. Soc., La. Neurol. Soc. (pres. 1979), La. State Med. Soc., Neuroelectric Soc., N.Y. Acad. Sci., Orleans Parish Med. Soc., Research Soc. Neurol. Surgeons, Royal Soc. Medicine, Soc. for Neurosci., So. Med. Assn., So. Neurosurg. Assn., Oscar Creek Surg. Soc., Midwest Pain Soc., Can. Neurosurg. Soc., Am. Acad. Pain Medicine, Alton Ochsner Med. Found. Soc., Soc. Neurol. Surgeons, La. Med. Rev. Found., Am. Acad. Clin. Neurophysiology, Alpha Omega Alpha. Lodges: Rotary. Achievements include first to pioneer in the field of brain stimulation for the treatment of chronic pain; performed the first deep brain stimulation for Parkinson's disease in the state of Louisiana; performed the first deep brain stimulation for Tourette's Syndrome in Louisiana, which was the second one performed in the US. Avocations: boating, travel, collecting art. Office: Tulane U Sch of Medicine Dept of Neurosurgery 1430 Tulane Ave New Orleans LA 70112-2699 also: Tulane U Hosp and Clinic 1415 Tulane Ave New Orleans LA 70112 Address: Lakeview Regional Med Ctr 95 E Fairway Dr Covington LA 70433 Office Phone: 504-988-5565. Business E-Mail: der@tulane.edu.

RICHARDSON, JAMES DAVID, surgeon; b. Morehead, Ky., 1945; MD, U. Ky., 1970. Diplomate Am. Bd. Surgeons, Am. Bd. Vascular Surgery, Am. Bd. Thoracic Surgery, Am. Bd. SCC. Intern U. Ky. Med. Ctr., Lexington, 1970, resident, 1971-72, U. Tex., San Antonio, 1972-76; surgeon Norton Hosp., Louisville, 1977—; prof. surgery U. Louisville, 1979—; pres. Am. Bd. Surgery, 1998-99. Past pres. So. Surg. Assn., Western Surg. Assn. Editor: (jour.) Am. Surgeon, 2005—. Fellow ACS (bd. regents); mem. AMA, Am. Assn. Surgery of Trauma, Soc. Surgery Alimentary Tract, Alpha Omega Alpha. Office: U Louisville Dept Surgery 550 S Jackson St Louisville KY 40202-1622 Office Phone: 502-583-8303, 502-852-5452.

RICHARDSON, JOSEPH HILL, physician, medical educator; b. Rensselaer, Ind., June 16, 1928; s. William Clark and Vera (Hill) R.; m. Joan Grace Meininger, July 8, 1950; children: Lois N., Ellen M., James K. MS in Medicine, Northwestern U., 1950, MD, 1953. Diplomate Am. Bd. Internal Medicine. Intern U.S. Naval Hosp., Great Lakes, Ill., 1953-54; physician internal medicine, hematology pvt. practice, Marion, Ind., 1959-67, Ft. Wayne, Ind., 1967—. Assoc. clin. prof. medicine Ind. U. Sch. Medicine, 1993—; founding mem. The Reviewing Physician Group, 2001—08. Contbr. articles to profl. jours. Fellow in medicine Cleve. Clinic, 1956-59. Fellow: AAAS, ACP; mem.: AMA, Masons. Home and Office: 8726 Fortuna Way Fort Wayne IN 46815-5725 Office Phone: 260-485-1391.

RICHARDSON, MARK A., otolaryngologist, dean; b. Cleve., Sept. 22, 1949; m. Ellen Richardson; 2 children. MD, Med. U. S.C., 1975. Diplomate Am. Bd. Otolaryngology. Intern U. South Fla., Tampa, 1975-76; resident in otolaryngology Med. U. Hosp., Charleston, S.C., 1976-79; fellow in pediatric otolaryngology Children's Hosp. Med. Ctr., Cin., 1979-80, mem. staff Seattle, 1980-94; prof. U. Wash., Seattle, 1980-94; prof. dept. otolaryngology/head and neck surgery Johns Hopkins U., Balt., 1995-2001; prof. and chmn. dept. otolaryngology/head and neck surgery Oreg. Health Scis. U., Portland, 2001—; interim dean Oreg. Health & Sci. U. Sch. Medicine, 2006—07, dean, 2007—. Fellow ACS, Am. Soc. Head and Neck Surgery; mem. Am. Acad. Otolaryngology/Hea dnd Neck Surgery, Am. Acad. Pediatrics, Am. Broncho-Esophogeal Assn., Triologic Soc. Office: OHSU Sch of Medicine Office of the Dean, L102 3181 SW Sam Jackson Park Rd Portland OR 97239 Office Phone: 503-494-8220. *

RICHARDSON, MARTHA (MARCIE) KIRK, obstetrician, gynecologist; b. Peterborough, NH, Sept. 12, 1949; Grad., Radcliffe Coll.; MD, U. Calif. San Diego Sch. Medicine, 1974. Intern, ob-gyn. Cambridge Hosp., 1974—75; resident & dept. gen. obstetrics & gynecology Beth Israel Deaconess Hosp., Mass., 1975—79; dir. menopause consultation svc. Harvard Vanguard Med. Assocs., asst. med. dir. dept. obstetrics & gynecology; clinical instr. obstetrics & gynecology Harvard Med. Sch., 1980—. Adv. bd. Harvard Women's Health Watch. Editorial adv. Our Bodies, Ourselves: Menopause, 2006. Mem.: North Am. Menopause Soc. (bd. trustees, former chmn. edn. com.). Office: 165 Dartmouth St Boston MA 02116-3502 Office Phone: 617-859-5250. Office Fax: 617-859-5051.

RICHARDSON, MARY L., psychotherapist; b. Topeka, Oct. 4, 1953; d. Darrell and Beverly Nutter; m. Kenneth T. Richardson Jr. children: Shad Martin, Cheralyn Pasbrig, Kenneth T. Richardson III, Russ Richardson. BS in Addictions Counseling, Westbrook U., W.Va., 2001, MPhil in Transpersonal Psychology. Lic. ind. substance abuse counselor, Ariz. State Behavioral Health, cert. Ariz. Bd. Cert. Addictions Counselors, IRQC, cert. Internat. Addictions Counselor, cert. addictions counselor, Hawaii. Counselor The Meadows Treatment Ctr., Phoenix, 1986-88; co-founder Co-Dependents Anonymous, 1986—; co-founder, adminstr. The Orion Found., 1988—90, Richardson Consulting & Counselling Assocs., 1988—; co-owner Phoenix Cons. & Counseling Assocs., Ariz., 1988—; lectr. workshop presenter Las Vegas Recovery Ctr., Nev. Founder, adminstr. The Orion Found., Ariz.; project mem. The Hutoomkhum Com. and Support Program, Hopi Reservation, Ariz.; cons. Baywood Hosp., 1988-89; faculty instr. The Recovery Source, 1989-90; chair Nat. Conv. Women, 1992; facilitator Your Healing Journey Workshop, 2002-. Author: Women's Acts of Power, 1991-93, Relationship Recover, 1992—, Women's Empowerment, 1992—, Body, Mind & Spirit, 1994—. Mem. Nat. Assn. Alcoholism & Drug Abuse Counselors, Nat. Reciprocity Consortium. Avocations: writing, sculpting, dance, herbology. Office: 15020 N Hayden Rd 204 Scottsdale AZ 85260 Office Phone: 602-230-8994.

RICHARDSON, PETER ANTHONY, gynecologist, educator; b. Perth, Western Australia, Jan. 23, 1939; Degree in Med., U. West Australia, 1963. Cons., reproductive medicine Pivet Med. Ctr., 1983—2010; adj. prof. Cairns Fertity Ctr., 2009—, Ctrl. Queensland U., Rockhamton, 2010. Recipient Queen Elizabeth Jubilee medal, Australian Govt. Fellow: RANZCOG (Melbourne), RCOG (London). Avocations: opera, music, trumpet, jazz. Home: 54 Cinderella St Machans Beach Queensland 4878 Australia Home Fax: 61740550020. Personal E-mail: ozzappa@bigpond.com.

RICHARDSON, SALLY KEADLE, academic administrator; b. Mar. 2, 1933; d. Okey P. and Viola Miriam (Graybeal) Keadle; m. Don Rule Richardson, Dec. 15, 1961; children: Miriam Paige, Ruth Evan. AB, Vassar Coll., 1954. Regional pub. info. rep. Columbia Gas Sys., Charleston, W.Va., 1958-62; dir. Children's Mus., Charleston, 1963; coord. space-related sci. project Kanawha County Schs., Charleston, 1967-68; vol. dir. Rockefeller for Gov. Campaign, Charleston, 1972, program dir., 1976, 80; dir. admissions W.Va. Wesleyan Coll., Buckhannon, 1974-75; spl. asst. Office of Gov. State of W.Va., 1977, dep. commr. dept. welfare, 1978-79, dep. dir. dept. health, 1979-83; chmn. W.Va. Health Care Cost Rev. Authority, Charleston, 1983-85. Health care cons., Charleston, 1985-89; dir. W.Va. Pub. Employees Ins. Agy., Charleston, 1989-93; vice-chmn. W.Va. Health Care Planning Task Force, 1992-93; mem. White House Health Care Reform Task Force, Washington, 1993; dir. Medicaid Bur., Health Care Financing Adminstrn., U.S. DHHS, Balt., 1993-96; acting dep. adminstr. HCFA, U.S. DHHS, Washington, 1996-97; dir. HCFA Ctr. for Medicaid and State Ops., 1997-99; mem. U.S. DHHS Governing Coun. on Children and Youth, 1993-97, co-chmn. U.S. DHHS Children's Health Initiative, 1997-99; co-chmn. U.S. DHHS Home and Cmty. Based Svcs. Task Force, 1996-99; mem. U.S. DHHS Pub. Health Coun.'s D.C. Task Force, 1994-99; mem. Nat. Adv. Com. on Rural Health, DHHS, 2000-04; bd. dirs. Molina Healthcare, Inc. W.Va. rep. Task Force on So. Children, So. Growth Policies Bd., 1978-79; co-chmn. exec. com. W.Va. Internat. Yr. of Child, 1979; staff mem. Com. on Human Resources Nat. Gov. Assn., 1983-85; trustee U. Charleston, 1994-; bd. dirs. Children's Home Soc., Charleston, 1999—. Mem. Acad. Health, Nat. Rural Health Assn. Democrat. Office: WVa U Inst Health Policy Rsch 3110 Maccorkle Ave SE Rm 3015 Charleston WV 25304-1210

RICHARDSON, SAMANTHA JANE, biochemist, researcher; b. Melbourne, Australia, Apr. 12, 1967; d. John Graham Richardson and Lynette Faye Damman. BS with honors, U. Melbourne, 1990, PhD, 1995. Rsch. officer U. Melbourne, 1996—97; postdoctoral fellow Australian Rsch. Coun., 1998—2000, rsch. fellow, 2001—05; assoc. prof. Mus. Natural History, Paris, 2006—07; sr. rsch. fellow RMIT U., Melbourne, Australia, 2007—10, sr. lectr., 2010—. Contbg. author: Platypus and Echidnas, 1992, Recent Developments in Comparative Endocrinology and Neurobiology, 1999, The Blood-Cerebiospinal Fluid Barrier, 2005; mem. editl. bd. Physio Biochem Zool, The Australian Biochemist, Biochem Journal., Current Proteomics, The Open Evolution; contbr. articles to profl. jours.; reviewer in field; contbr.; editor: (book) Recent Advances in Transthyretin Evolution, Structures & Biological Functions (Springer), 2009; contbr. articles to profl. publs.; contbg. author: The Neurology of Australian Marsopiolsy, 2010. Recipient Tech. Diffusion Program award for young rschr. to attend symposium on Australia's sci. future, Australian Acad. Sci., 2000, Edgeworth David medal, Royal Soc. NSW, 2001, Young Rschr. award, European-Australian Sci. and Tech. Conf., 2001; Student Travel grantee, Australian Acad. Sci., 1993. Mem.: European Soc. Comparative Endocrinology, Australian and New Zealand Soc. Comparative Physiology and Biochemistry (Student Presentation award 1992), Australian Soc. Biochemistry and Molecular Biology (Victorian state rep. 2002—04, Postdoctoral Travel fellow 1996). Avocation: violin. Office: RMIT Univ Sch Med Scis Po Box 71 Bundoora Victoria 3083 Australia Office Phone: 61399257897, 61399257897. Business E-Mail: samantha.richardson@rmit.edu.au.

RICHARDSON, STEPHEN GILES, biotechnologist, research and development company executive, writer; b. Mpls., Sept. 17, 1951; s. Richard Giles and Constance Bernice (Krieg) R. BA in English and Chemistry, cum laude, Wartburg Coll., 1972; MS in Chemistry, U. Iowa, Iowa City, 1974, PhD in Organic Chemistry, 1981; postdoctoral, Duke U., Durham, NC, 1982—84. Cert. project mgmt. profl. Project Mgmt. Inst. Ter. mgr. Wyeth Labs., Phila., 1974-76; rsch. asst. U. Iowa, Iowa City, 1976-82; rsch. assoc. Duke, Durham, NC, 1982-84; scientist Becton Dickinson Rsch. Ctr., Research Triangle Park, NC, 1984-86; devel. group leader Dade Diagnostics divsn. Baxter Healthcare, Miami, Fla., 1986; rsch. group leader Organon Teknika Corp divsn., Akzo Nobel N.V, Durham, NC, 1987-89, R & D sect. head, internat. R & D area mgr., 1989-90, program mgr., 1990-94, assoc. dir., head product devel., 1994-96, project mgmt. dir., microbiology bus. area R & D, 1997—2001; program dir. global mktg. and strategic devel. bioMerieux, Inc., Durham, NC, 2001—04; pres. Adamantane Corp., 2004—. Pres., and chair Serv-Quik Foods, Inc. Contbr. articles to profl. jours.; patentee in field; bd. readers IVD Technology Mag. Co-founder Libertarian Party Minn., Mpls., 1972, del. nat. conv., 1998; exec. sec. Iowa Coun. to Repeal Conscription, Waterloo, 1971. Mem. Am. Soc. Microbiology, Am. Chem. Soc., Royal Soc. Chemistry UK, NY Acad. Scis., Electronic Frontier Found., Triangle Stamp Club (pres. Chapel Hill, 1997-98, 2008-09), Friends Lake Orange Civic Ass. (v.p., dir.), Orange County Voice (dir.), Sigma Xi. Libertarian. Achievements include discovery of transient neutral heteroaryl radicals as viable organic synthetic intermediates, such as, to halopurine nucleosides; MDA-180 hemostasis analyzer system, BacT/ALERT 3D blood culture system family. Office Phone: 919-643-3021. Office Fax: 919-640-1344. Business E-Mail: adamantanc@embarqmail.com.

RICHARDSON, WILLIAM, surgeon, educator; b. Portsmouth, Va., Jan. 7, 1952; MD, EVMS, 1977; MS CLN, Duke U., 2002. Prof. surgery, assoc. cmo Duke U., 1987—, assoc. cmo quality, safety, 2010—. Mem.: AOA. Avocations: fly fishing, magic. Office: 3077 DUMC Trent Dr Durham NC 27710 Office Fax: 919-681-7366. Business E-Mail: richa015@mc.duke.edu.

RICHARDSON, WILLIE FORREST, JR., physician, consultant; s. Willie Forrest Richardson. BS in Biology (hon.), Pembroke State U., 1996; MD, East Carolina U., 2000. Diplomate Am. Bd. Dermatology, lic. dermatologist N.Mex., Fla. Intern in internal medicine Med. U. S.C., Charleston, 2000—01; resident indermatology U. N.Mex. Health Scis. Ctr., Albuquerque, 2001—04; staff dermatologist Gallup Indian Med. Ctr., N.Mex., 2003—06; dermatologist Presbyn. Med. Group-Kaseman Dermatology, Albuquerque, 2004—05; staff dermatologist Broward Gen. Med. Ctr., Ft. Lauderdale, Fla., 2005—; dermatologist Las Olas Dermatology, Ft. Lauderdale, Fla., 2005—08; founder Natura Dermatology & Cosmetics, 2006—. Author: (textbook) Native American Skin Disease, 2005; contbr. articles to profl. jours. Recipient Indian Health Svc. scholarship, U.S. Dept. HHS, 1994—96, Premedical scholarship, Indian Health Svc., 1993-1996, Outstanding Clin. Excellence award, Gallup Indian Svc. Divsn., 2003. Fellow: Am. Soc. Mohs Surgery; mem.: AMA, Broward County Dermatology Soc., Broward County Med. Assn., Am. Acad. Dermatology, Alpha Chi. Achievements include research in Native American skin disease. Office: Natura Dermatology & Cosmetics 1120 Bayview Drive Fort Lauderdale FL 33304 Personal E-mail: nativehealer@aol.com.

RICHERSON, HAL BATES, retired internist, allergist, immunologist, educator; b. Phoenix, Feb. 16, 1929; s. George Edward and Eva Louise (Steere) R.; m. Julia Suzanne Bradley (dec. 1996), Sept. 5, 1953; children: Anne, George, Miriam, Julia, Susan. BS with distinction, U. Ariz., 1950; MD, Northwestern U., 1954. Diplomate Am. Bd. Internal Medicine, Am. Bd. Allergy and Immunology, Bd. Diagnostic Lab. Immunology; lic. physician, Iowa. Intern Kansas City (Mo.) Gen. Hosp., 1954-55; resident in pathology St. Luke's Hosp., Kansas City, 1955-56; trainee in neuropsychiatry Brooke Army Hosp., San Antonio, 1956; resident in medicine U. Iowa Hosps., Iowa City, 1961-64, fellow in allergy and immunology, 1964-66; fellow in immunology Mass. Gen. Hosp., Boston, 1968-69; instr. internal medicine U. Iowa Coll. Medicine, Iowa City, 1964-66, asst. prof., 1966-70, assoc. prof., 1970-74, prof., 1974-98, ret., 1998, prof.

emeritus, 1998—; acting dir. divsn. allergy/applied immunology U. Iowa Hosps. and Clinics, Iowa City, 1970-72, dir. allergy and clin. immunology sect., 1972-78, dir. divsn. allergy and immunology, 1978-91; gen. practice, asst. to Gen. Surgeon Ukiah, Calif., 1958; gen. practice medicine Holbrook, Ariz., 1958-61. Vis. lectr. medicine Harvard U. Sch. Medicine, Boston, 1968-69; vis. prof., rsch. scientist U. London and Brompton Hosp., 1984; prin. investigator Nat. Heart, Lung and Blood Inst., 1971-94, mem. pulmonary diseases adv. com., 1983-87; prin. investigator Nat. Inst. Allergy and Infectious Diseases, 1983-94; dir. Nat. Inst. Allergy and Infectious Diseases' Asthma and Allergic Diseases Ctr., U. Iowa, 1983-94; mem. VA Merit Rev. Bd. in Respiration, 1981-84; mem. com. NIH Gen. Clin. Rsch. Ctrs., 1989-93; mem. rev. reserve NIH, 1993-98; mem. bd. sci. advisors Merck Inst., 1990-94; presenter lectures, seminars, continuing edn. courses; mem. numerous univ., coll. and hosp. coms., 1970—; cons. Merck Manual, 1982, 87, 92, 96-97. Contbr. numerous articles and revs. to profl. jours., chpts. to books; reviewer Sci., Jour. Immunology, Jour. Allergy and Clin. Immunology, Am. Rev. Respiratory Disease, New Eng. Jour. Medicine, Ann. Internal Medicine. Served to capt. U.S. Army, 1956-58. NIH fellow 1968-69. Fellow ACP (Laureate award 1996), Am. Acad. Allergy Asthma & Immunology (Disting. Clinician award 1998); mem. AMA (mem. residency and rev. com. for allergy and immunology; mem. accreditation coun. for grad. med. edn. 1980-85, vice-chmn. 1984-85), AAAS, Iowa Med. Soc., Iowa Thoracic Soc. (chmn. program com. 1964-65, 69-71, pres. 1972-73, mem. exec. com. 1972-74), Am. Thoracic Soc. (bd. dirs. 1981-82, councilor assembly on allergy and immunology 1980-81, mem. nominating com. 1988-90), Iowa Clin. Med. Soc., Am. Fedn. Clin. Rsch., Am. Assn. Immunologists, Ctrl. Soc. Clin. Rsch. (chmn. sect. on allergy-immunology 1980-81, mem. coun. 1981-84), Alpha Omega Alpha. Avocations: reading, trombonist, swimming, scuba diving. Home: 31 Lucon Dr Iowa City IA 52246 Personal E-mail: richersonh@mchsi.com. *

RICHERT, JOHN ROLIN, neuroimmunologist, educator; b. Boston, June 9, 1945; s. Daniel Arnold and Esther (Beamer) Richert; m. Nancy Dembeck, July 5, 1969. BA, Cornell U., 1966; MD, U. Rochester, 1970. Diplomate Am. Bd. Med. Examiners, Am. Bd. Psychiatry and Neurology. Intern, resident in medicine Strong Meml. Hosp. U. Rochester, NY, 1970-72; resident in neurology Mayo Clinic, Rochester, Minn., 1974-77; fellow Nat. Multiple Sclerosis Soc. NIH, Bethesda, Md., 1977-80; rsch. asst. prof. neurology Georgetown U. Med. Ctr., Washington, 1980-83, asst. prof. neurology, 1983-89, assoc. prof. neurology, 1989-93, prof. neurology, 1993—2005, prof., chair dept. microbiology and immunology, 1997—2005; v.p. rsch. and clin. programs Nat. Multiple Sclerosis Soc., NYC, 2005—07, exec. v.p. rsch. and clin. programs, 2007—10; v.p. sr. neurology fellow Biogen Idec Inc., 2010—; mem. data and safety monitoring bd. Acorda Therapeutics, Hawthorne, NY, 2005—07, Novartis, Basel, Switzerland, 2005—06; mem. data and safety monitoring com. Biogen Idec, Cambridge, 2007—10. Mem. physician adv. bd. Biogen Inc., Cambridge, Mass., 1994-2000; cons. Immunex, Inc., Seattle, 1998-2000; external adv. com. VA Multiple Sclerosis Ctr. of Excellence, U. Md. Multiple Sclerosis Ctr., Balt., 2003-2005; sci. adv. bd. TolerGenics, Inc., Rockville, Md., 2001-2005; cons. Health Sci. Ctr. for Continuing med. Edn., NY, 2003; mem. med. adv. com. Multiple Sclerosis Soc. Can., 2006—10, sci. rev. com. mem. World Congress On Treatment and Rsch. Multiple Sclerosis, 2007-08, rsch. ref. group mem. MS Internat. Fedn., 2007-10, sci. adv. bd. BioMS European Biomaker Gr., 2008-; mem. MS Rsch. Australia Rsch. Rev. Bd., 2009-; bd. dirs. Georgetown U. Hosp., 2000-05. Mem. editl. bd.: Neurotherapeutics, 2002—. Mem. immunol. scis. study sect. NIH, 1989, mem. mental health AIDS and immunology rsch. study sect., 1992, mem. neurol. disorders program project com., 2003, Brain Disorders and Clin. Neuroscience spl. emphasis panel, 2003-2004; pub policy com. mem. Assn. Med. Sch. Microbiology and Immunology Chairs, 2002-05, chair, 2004-05. Maj. USAF, 1972-74. Recipient Honoree award, Musical Moments MS, NJ Performing Arts Ctr., 2011. Fellow Am. Acad. Neurology; mem. Internat. Soc. Neuroimmunology, Nat. Multiple Sclerosis Soc. (med. adv. bd. 1988-91, 93-96, profl. adv. com. 1988-2005, sci. peer rev. com. 1993-98), Am. Neurol. Assn., Am. Assn. Immunologists, Am. Soc. for Biochemistry and Molecular Biology, Am. Soc. for Exptl. Neurotherapeutics (pub. com. 2006—), Alpha Omega Alpha, BioMS European Biomarker Group Proteomic Based Biomarker Study (sci. adv. bd. 2008-) Avocations: tennis, golf, skiing. Office: Biogen Idec Inc 14 Cambridge Ctr Cambridge MA 02142 Home Phone: 301-654-6293; Office Phone: 617-679-3678. Business E-Mail: john.richert@biogenidec.com.

RICHES, VIVIENNE CATHERINE, psychologist, researcher, educator; b. Sydney, June 8, 1949; d. Henry Eric Hughes and Bettie Shiela Miller; m. Rodger Barry Riches, June 3, 1977; children: Tanya Nicole, Kieran Barry. BA, U. NSW, 1968, diploma in Edn., 1969; MA with honors, Macquarie U., 1978, PhD, 1997. Cert. in ministry Internat. Inst. Creative Ministries, 1987, advanced cert. in ministry Internat. Inst. Creative Ministries, 1988; cert. tchr. NSW Dept. Edn., 1971, registered psychologist NSW Psychologists Registration Bd., 1991, cert. in assessment and workplace tng. The Assn. S.E. Asian Nations Tng. and Edn. Svcs., 2002. Grad. tchr. NSW Dept. Edn., 1970—74; rsch. asst. Macquarie U., Sydney, NSW, 1976, sr. rsch. asst., 1977—81, sr. rsch. fellow, 1989—97; clin. psychologist Commonwealth Rehab. Svc., Sydney, 1983—89; sr. rsch. fellow, psychologist Ctr. Disability Studies, Sydney, 1998—; pvt. practice psychologist Hillsong Health Centre, Sydney, 1996—2006; coord. and lectr. pastoral counselling Hillsong Internat. Leadership Coll., Sydney, 1985—99; clin. sr. lectr. U. Sydney, 1996—, sr. rsch. fellow, 2002—05; clin. psychologist Royal Rehab. Ctr., Sydney, 1999—. Invited mem. NSW Inter-departmental Com. Transition, Sydney, 1989—95; rep. bd. studies spl. edn. reference panel Disability Coun. of NSW, Sydney, 1993—94; editl. cons. Australian Jour. Rehab. Counselling, 1994—99; chairperson for external rev. panel Basic Skills Tng. Divsn. Australian Com. Tng. Curriculum, 1995; mgmt. com. mem. Regional Disability Liason Officer Project, Sydney, 1995—97; supr. intern psychologists, 1996—; bd. studies & external curriculum adv. mem. Hillsong Leadership Coll., Sydney, 1996—97; mem. bd. reference OZFAME Inst., Sydney, 1997—; mem. case classification expert panel for case based funding Fed. Dept. Family and Cmty. Services, 2001. Author: Communicating Everyday Teaching Interaction Skills to Persons with Developmental Disabilities, Standards of Work Performance; A Functional Assessment and Training Manual for Training People with Disabilities for Employment, Everyday Social Interaction: A Program for People with Disabilities, (tng. programs) Social Development Training Program; author: (with Lwellyn, Parmenter, Hindmarsh and Chan) I-CAN: An Instrument to Assess and Classify the Support Needs of People with Disabilities, 2005; author: Anger Wise: A Problem Solving Approach to Handling Anger Wisely, 2006. Mem. adv. bd. Choice Solutions, Sydney, 1994—99; cons. on disability issues Anglican Adoption Agy., Sydney, 1995—2005; mem. kidz in change Hillsong Ch., Sydney, 1995—97; adv. bd. mem. Hillsong Ch. Sexual Abuse Programs, Sydney, 2005—; curriculum developer -counseling and recovery programs Hillsong Ch., Sydney, 1996—2006, facilitator, group leader, trainer counseling and recovery programs in anger mgmt., depression, self esteem, 1996—2005. Recipient Queens Guide award, Girl Guides, 1965; grantee with Parmenteretal, Orgn. Econ. Co-operation and Devel. Ctr. Ednl. Rsch. and Innovation, 1995, Fed. Dept. Human Services and Health, 1995; scholar Rsch. in Devel. Disabilities, Australian Inst. Inclusive Communities, 1997; Rsch. Seeding Grant, Macquarie U., 1994, Nat. Profl. Devel. Project Grant, Dept. Edn., Employment, Tng. & Youth Affairs, 1994—95, Australian Rsch. Coun. Linkage Grant (with Llewellyn et al), 2002-2004. Mem.: Psychologists in Devel. Disability, Internat. Assn. Sci. Study Intellectual Disability, Australasian Soc. Study Intellectual Disability, Australian Psychol. Soc., Health Care in Christ, Cavalier King Charles Spaniel Club (NSW), Cavalier King Charles Spaniel Club UK, Canine Coun. NSW. Achievements include research in I-CAN instrument to assess and classify support needs of people with disabilities. Avocation: dog breeding and showing. Office: Ctr Disability Studies PO Box 6 Nsw Ryde 1680 Australia Office Fax: 61298077503. Business E-Mail: vriches@med.usyd.edu.au.

RICHESON, JAMES GRADY, JR., dentist; m. Nancy Richeson; 1 child, Suzanne. DDS, Georgetown U. Dentist, Washington. Recipient Disting. Svc. award, Georgetown Dental Alumni, 2003. Fellow: Pierre Fauchard Acad., Am. Coll. Dentists, Acad. Gen. Dentistry (pres.-elect 2001—02, pres. 2002—03, v.p., treas., bd. trustee, budget and fin. com., regional dir., Found. bd. dirs.); mem.: ADA (alt. del. 2001—, del. 2004), DC Dental Soc. (The Sterling V. Meade Disting. Svc. award 2004), DC Acad. Gen. Dentistry (past pres.), Georgetown U. Alumni Club of Met. Washington (past pres.). Office: 4400 Jenifer St NW Ste 340 Washington DC 20015-2113 Office Phone: 202-364-5246. Business E-Mail: jim@yourdentaldr.com.

RICHEY, DONALD, dermatologist; Grad., U. Oregon Medical Sch. Diplomate Am. Bd. Dermatology, cert. histopathology. Intern Milwaukee County Hosp., Milwaukee; resident U. Southern Calif.; family practice physician US pub. health svc. dept. Indian Health, lt. comdr. US pub. health svc. gen. med. office, 1965; staff Enloe Med.Ctr., Chico, Calif. Pres. North Valley Dermatology Soc., Sacramento Dermatologic So. Recipient American Academy of Dermatology Members Making a Difference award, 2007, American Academy of Dermatology "Member Making a Difference" and Service award, Public Service award. Mem.: North Valley Dermatology Society, Sacramento Dermatologic Soc., Am. Acad. of Dermatology Surgery, Am. Soc. for Laser Medicine and Surgery, Am. Soc. of Cosmetic and Aesthetic Surgery, Butte Glenn Med. Soc., Calif. Med. Assn., Calif. Dermatology Soc., Fellow Am. Acad. of Dermatology. Office: North Valley Dermatology Center 251 Cohasset Rd 2nd Fl Chico CA 95926 Office Phone: 530-342-3686.

RICHHEIMER, MICHAEL STEVEN, allergist, immunologist, educator; MD, St. George U., 1985. Registered NY, 1988, diplomate Am. Bd. Allergy and Immunology, 2006. Intern St. Joseph Hosp., 1986, resident in internal medicine, 1988; fellow in allergy and immunology Stony Brook Univ. Med. Ctr., 1990; assoc. clin. prof. allergy and immunology SUNY; hosp. affiliations include South Nassau Cmtys. Hosp., Stony Brook Univ. Med. Ctr. Named one of Best Doctors, NY Mag., 2010. Office: Stony Brook University Medical Center 1855 Union Blvd Bay Shore NY 11706 Office Phone: 631-665-6363. Office Fax: 631-665-5162.

RICHIE, RODNEY CHARLES, critical care and pulmonary medicine physician; b. Big Springs, Tex., Aug. 17, 1946; s. Howard Mouzon and Gloria (Hollingshead) R.; m. Sara Lee Dilley, July 13, 1968; children: Megan Kathryn, Paul Nathan. BA in Chemistry, So. Meth. U., 1968; MD cum laude, Baylor Coll., 1972. Diplomate in Internal Medicine, Pulmonary, Ins. Medicine. Resident in medicine Baylor Affiliated Hosps., Houston, 1973-75, chief med. resident, 1975, fellow in pulmonary medicine, 1976-77; pres. Waco Lung Assocs., Tex., 1977—2007; assoc. clin. prof. cmty. medicine Heart of Tex. Cmty. Health Ctr./U. Tex. SW Med. Sch., 2004—. Med. dir. Tex. Life Ins., Waco, 1985—, Cmty. Hospice of Waco, 1996—, EMSI, Waco, Tex., 1997—. Chmn. med. staff Hillcrest Bapt. Med. Ctr., Waco, 1993; chmn. bd. dirs. GH Pape Found., Waco, 1993. Fellow: ACP, Am. Coll. Chest Physicians; mem.: AMA, Am. Thoracic Soc., Am. Acad. Internal Medicine (del. to AMA), Tex. Club Internists. Episcopalian. Avocations: skiing, writing, reading. Home: 3509 Lake Heights Dr Waco TX 76708-1005 Office: 7003 Woodway Dr Ste 311 Waco TX 76712 Office Phone: 254-741-1688. Personal E-mail: rodney.richie@gmail.com.

RICHMAN, DANIEL I., pain medicine physician, anesthesiologist, educator; MD, U. Medicine and Dentistry of NJ, 1980. Diplomate Am. Bd. Anesthesiology, 1991, Am. Bd. Pain Medicine, 1994, lic. NY. Resident anesthesiology Hartford Hosp., Conn., 1987—90; fellow in pain medicine Hosp. for Spl. Surgery, 1990—91, attending anesthesiologist; clin. asst. prof. of anesthesiology Weill Cornell Med. Coll. Named one of Top Doctors in Pain Mgmt., Castle Connolly, Best Doctors in NY, NY Mag., 2009—11. Mem.: Am. Soc. of Anesthesiology, The Hosp. Graduate's Soc., Am. Pain Soc., Internat. Anesthesia Rsch. Soc., Internat. Assn. for the Study of Pain, NY State Soc. of Anesthesiologists, Am. Soc. of Anesthesiologists. Office: Hospital for Special Surgery 535 East 70th St New York NY 10021 Office Phone: 212-606-1000.

RICHMAN, DAVID PAUL, neurologist, educator, researcher; b. Boston, June 9, 1943; s. Harry S. and Anne (Goodkin) R.; m. Carol Mae von Bastian, Aug. 31, 1969; children: Sarah Ann, Jacob Charles. AB, Princeton U., 1965; MD, Johns Hopkins U., 1969. Diplomate Am. Bd. Psychiatry and Neurology. Intern, then asst. resident in medicine Albert Einstein Coll. Medicine, NYC, 1969-71; resident in neurology Mass. Gen. Hosp., Boston, 1971-73, chief resident, 1973-74; instr. neurology Harvard U. Med. Sch., Boston, 1975-76; asst. prof. neurology U. Chgo., 1976-80, assoc. prof., 1981-85, prof., 1985-91, Straus prof. neurol. Scis., 1988-91; prof. neurology U. Calif., Davis, 1991—, chmn. dept., 1991-97. Mem. com. Nat. Inst. Aging, NIH, 1984-85, mem. immunogical scis. study sect., 1986-90. Mem. AAAS, Am. Assn. Immunologists, Am. Acad. Neurology, Am. Neurol. Assn., Phi Beta Kappa, Sigma Xi. Office: U Calif Davis Dept Neurology 1515 Newton Ct Davis CA 95616-4859 Office Phone: 530-754-5020. Business E-Mail: dprichman@ucdavis.edu.

RICHMAN, DOUGLAS DANIEL, medical virologist, educator, internist; b. NYC, Feb. 15, 1943; s. Daniel Powell and Louise Kohnstamm (Woolf) R.; m. Eva Acquino, June 21, 1965; children: Sara, Matthew. AB cum laude, Dartmouth Coll., 1965; MD, Stanford U., 1970. Diplomate Am. Bd. Internal Medicine, Am. Bd. Infectious Diseases, Am. Bd. Med. Examiners. Intern Stanford Med. Sch., Calif., 1970—71, resident, 1971—72; rsch. assoc. LID/NIAID NIH, Bethesda, Md., 1972—75; fellow Beth Israel and Children's Hosps., Harvard Med. Ctr., Boston, 1975—76; asst. prof. depts. pathology and medicine U. Calif., San Diego, 1976—82, assoc. prof., 1982—88, prof., 1988—, Florence Seeley Riford chair in AIDS rsch., 2004—. Vis. prof. Hubei Med. Coll., Wuhan, People's Republic of China, 1987, Tokyo Med. and Dental U., Kumamoto U. Sch. Medicine, Inst. for Virus Rsch. at Kyoto U., St. Marianna U., Tokyo, Inst. Med. Rsch., Tokyo, Fukishima Prefecture Med. Sch., Japan, 1990; vis. fellow Clare Hall, U. Cambridge, 1984-85; mem. U. Calif. Pres.'s Cancer Rsch. Coord. Com., 1984-89, NIH AIDS Rsch. Rev. Com., 1987-90; cons. FDA Ctr. for Drugs and Biologics, 1986-89; dir. U. Calif.-San Diego Ctr. for AIDS Rsch., AIDS Rsch. Inst. Co-editor: Clin. Virology, —; mem. editl. bd.: Antimicrobial Agts. and Chemotherapy, 1987—, Jour. of AIDS, 1988—, Antiviral Agts., 1988—, AIDS, 1990—, AIDS Alert, 1990—, Antiviral Drug Resistance, 1996—, Virology, 1997—, others; contbr. more than 550 articles to profl. jours. Recipient Lowell Rantz award in infectious diseases, 1970, AMA Physicians Recgonition award, 1976, 79, 82, 85, 88, William S. Middleton award Dept. Vet. Affairs, 2002; John Simon Guggenheim fellow, 1984. Fellow: ACP, AAAS, We. Assn. Physicians, Am. Assn. Physicians, Infectious Diseases Soc. Am.; mem.: Am. Clin. and Climatologic Assn., VA Soc. for Physicians in Infectious Diseases, Internat. AIDS Soc., Internat. Soc. Antiviral Rsch., Am. Soc. for Virology, Am. Fedn. for Clin. Rsch., Am. Soc. for Microbiology. Office: U Calif San Diego Dept Pathology & Medicine 9500 Gilman Dr La Jolla CA 92093-0679

RICHMAN, JOSEPH HERBERT, retired public health officer; b. Balt., Aug. 13, 1941; s. Samuel and Beatrice Richman. BS, Howard U., 1962, MD, 1966; MPH, Johns Hopkins U., 1974. Intern Maimonides Med. Ctr., Bklyn., 1966-67; resident in pediat. Sinai Hosp. of Balt., 1967-69; chief sch. health P.G. Health Dept. of Md., Cheverly, Md., 1972-75; dir. area health svcs. Montgomery County Health Dept., Bethesda, Md., 1975-82; county chief pub. health physician State of Del., Dover, 1982-99; ret., 2000; med. cons. Ariz. Med. Bd., 2009—. Capt. USAF, 1969—71. Recipient Outstanding Svc. award, Delaware Health and Soc. Svc., 1999. Fellow Am. Acad. Pediatrics (emeritus), Am. Coll. Preventive Medicine, Am. Coll. Physician Exec., Am. P.H. Assn.; mem. AMA, Masons, Phi Beta Kappa. Democrat. Jewish. Avocations: golf, photography. Home: PO Box 880852 Boca Raton FL 33488-0852 Home Phone: 561-482-3154. Personal E-mail: joefortsedgwick@aol.com.

RICHMAN, MARC HERBERT, engineer, forensic specialist, educator; b. Boston, Oct. 14, 1936; s. Samuel and Janet (Gordon) R.; m. Ann Raeshel Yoffa, Aug. 31, 1963. BS, MIT, 1957, ScD, 1963; MA, Brown U., 1967. Registered profl. engr., Conn., Mass., R.I.; cert. forensic examiner. Cons. engr., 1957—; engr. shipbldg. div. Bethlehem Steel Corp., Quincy, Mass., 1957; instr. metallurgy MIT, Cambridge, 1957-60, research asst. dept. metallurgy, 1960-63; instr. metallurgy div. univ. extension Commonwealth of Mass., 1958-62; asst. prof. engring. Brown U., Providence, 1963-67, assoc. prof., 1967-70, prof., 1970-98, dir. central electron microscopy facility Materials Research program, 1971-86, dir. undergrad. program in engring., 1991-98; prof. emeritus, 1998—; pres. Ednl. Aids of Newton Inc., Providence, 1968-71, Marc H. Richman Inc., Providence, 1981—. Guest scientist Franklin Inst., Phila., 1959; vis. prof. U. R.I., Kingston, 1970-71; biophysicist dept. medicine Miriam Hosp., Providence, 1974-87; biogengr. dept. orthopaedics R.I. Hosp., 1979-93; prof. emeritus Brown U., Providence, 1998—. Author: Introduction to Science of Metals, 1967; also articles; editor Soviet Physics: Crystallography, 1970-94; mem. editl. adv. bd. Materials Characterization, 1970—98, Jour. Forensic Engring., 1985-88. Served to maj. Ordnance Corps, U.S. Army, 1963. Recipient Engr. of Yr. award R.I. Soc. Profl. Engrs., 1993. Fellow Nat. Acad. Forensic Engrs. (cert.), Am. Coll. Forensic Examiners (cert.), Am. Inst. Chemists, Inst. Materials (U.K.); mem. ASCE, AIME, NSPE, ASEE (Outstanding Young Faculty award 1969), NAFE (bd. cert. diplomate in forensic engring.), Am. Soc. Metals (sec.-treas. 1965-68, chmn. R.I. chpt. 1968-69, Albert Sauveur Meml. award 1968, 69), Providence Engring. Soc. (pres. 1991-92, Freeman award for engring. achievement 1989), B'nai B'rith, Sigma Xi, Tau Beta Pi. Home: 291 Cole Ave Providence RI 02906-3452 Office Phone: 401-751-9656. Personal E-mail: mhrichman@aol.com.

RICHMAN, MICHAEL F., thoracic surgeon, consultant; b. Chgo., Ill., June 1, 1965; MD, Georgetown U., 1991. Diplomate Am. Bd. Surgery, Am. Bd. Thoracic Surgery. Intern, surgery U. Southern Calif. Med. Ctr., LA, 1991—92, resident, suregery, 1992—96; fellow in cardiothoracic & vascular surgery U. Miami Jackson Meml. Hosp., 1997; clin. instr. surgery U. Southern Calif. Sch. Medicine, LA, 1996; founder Ctr. for Cholesterol Mgmt., 2005—, Elite Laser Vein Ctr., 2006—. Cholesterol expert WebMD; editorial bd. Clinical Jour. Lipidology. Fellow: Nat. Lipid Assn., Am. Coll. Chest Physicians, ACS. Office: Ctr for Cholesterol Management 1950 Sawtelle Blvd Los Angeles CA 90025 Office Phone: 310-481-3939. Office Fax: 310-481-3949.

RICHMOND, JOHN C., surgeon, educator; b. Boston, Jan. 17, 1950; BA, U. Pa., 1972; MD, Tufts U. Sch. Medicine, 1976. Prof. orthop. surgery Tufts U. Sch. Medicine, 2001—. Chmn., orthop. surgery New Eng. Bapt. Hosp., 2004. Recipient Disting. Svc. award, Tufts U. Alumni Assn. Fellow: AAOS; mem.: AOA, AOSSM (O'donahue Clin. Rsch. award, Cabaud Basic Sci. award), AANA. Office: 830 Boylston St Chestnut Hill MA 02467 Office Fax: 617-264-1101. Business E-Mail: jrichmon@nebh.org.

RICHTER, BRANKO BRANIMIR, retired parasitologist; b. Zagreb, Croatia, Jan. 10, 1920; s. Franjo and Vjera (Marakovic) R.; m. Željka Vodopija, Jan. 10, 1953; children: Jasna, Darko, Davor. MD, U. Zagreb, 1943, PhD, 1978. Diplomate Bd. Tropical Medicine. Epidemiologist Antimalaria Unit, Yugoslav Nat. Army, 1947-49; coord. antimalaria campaign Fed. Com. Health, Belgrade, Yugoslavia, 1949-50; parasitologist Pub. Health Inst. Croatia, Zagreb, 1950-60; head dept. microbiology, parasitology U. Zagreb, 1960-86, prof. microbiology, 1965-86; vice dean Zagreb med. Sch., 1981-85; ret., 1986. Malaria experts panel WHO, Geneva, 1955-95. Author: Medicinska Parasitologija, 6th edit., 2002; contbr. articles to profl. jours. Mem. Croatian Med. Assn., Croatian Acad. med. Sci. (v.p. 1993-2000, Laudatio 1995), German Soc. Tropical Medicine. Avocation: casting and collecting tin soldiers. Home: Gajeva Ulica 36 10-000 Zagreb Croatia E-mail: amzh@zg.hinet.hr.

RICHTER, DARKO, pediatrician; b. Zagreb, Croatia, Aug. 3, 1955; s. Branimir and Zeljka Richter; m. Sandra Krizaj, Nov. 27, 1993; children: Tanja, Maja, Iva. MD, Med. Faculty, U. Zagreb, Zagreb, 1979. Asst. dir. U. Hosp. Ctr., Zagreb, Croatia, 1993—2000, chief pediat. allergy and immunology, 1994—2003; chief critical care, allergy and immunology Pediat. Respiratory Disease, Zagreb, 2003—; intern Gen. Hosp. "Holy Ghost", Zagreb, Croatia, 1979—80; resident U. Hosp. Ctr., Dept Pediat., Zagreb, 1980—86. Cons. in field. Translator: (chpt.) Harrisons Principles of Internal Medicine 13th ed.; contbr. articles to profl. jours. Chief coord. humanitarian aid U. Hosp. Ctr., Zagreb, 1991—95. Recipient Gold And Silver Sponsorships, European Respiratory Soc., 2001—03; fellow, French Govt., 1985—86. Mem.: Croatian Soc. Pediat. Pulmonology (v.p. 1998—), Croatian Med. Assn., European Acad. Allergy and Clin. Immunology, European Soc. Immunodeficiencies, European Respiratory Soc. Roman Catholic. Achievements include research in quantitative weight-corrected methacholine bronchial challenge testing in pediatrics; development of non-invasive mechanical ventilation for children; research in genomic analysis in primary immunodeficiency. Home: Gajeva 36 Zagreb 10000 Croatia Office: Pediat Respiratory Hosp Srebrnjak 100 Zagreb 10000 Croatia Office Fax: +385 - 1 - 244-1885. Personal E-mail: darko.richter@zg.htnet.hr. E-mail: darkorichter@hotmail.com.

RICHTER, EDWIN F., physiatrist, educator; MD, NYU, 1987. Diplomate Am. Bd. Physical Medicine and Rehab., 1992. Resident physical medicine & rehab. Rusk Inst. of Rehab. Medicine NYU Langone Med. Ctr., 1988—91; asst. clin. prof. physical medicine and rehab. NYU Sch. of Medicine; attending physician Stamford Hosp., Conn. Office: Stamford Hospital Jeanne S Rich Professional Office Bldg 166 West Broad St Stamford CT 06902 Office Phone: 203 276 4220. Office Fax: 203-276-4240.

RICHTER, JOEL, gastroenterologist, educator; BS, Tex. A&M U.; MD, U. Tex. Diplomate Am Bd. Internal Medicine, gastroenterology Am Bd. Internal Medicine. Intern Nat. Naval Med. Ctr., Bethesda, Md., 1976, resident, 1978, fellow gastrointestinal, 1980; prof. Sch. of Medicine Temple Univ., Richard L. Evans chair medicine dept.; hosp. affiliation includes Temple Univ. Hosp. Author: Effect of Helicobacter Pylori Eradication On The Treatment of Gastro-Esophageal Reflux Disease, 2004; co-author: Laryngeal Signs And Symptoms And Gastroesophageal Reflux disease (GERD): A Critical Assessment Of Cause And Effect Association, 2003, Predictors of Outcome of Pneumatic Dilation In Achalasia, 2004, Erythromycin In The Short- And Long-Term Control of Dyspepsia Symptoms in Patients With Gastroparesis, 2004, Complexities of Managing Achalasia At A Tertiary Referral Center: Use of Pneumatic Dilatation, Heller Myotomy, And Botulinum Toxin Injection, 2004, various publs. Named Recognized Dr., HealthGrades. Mem.: AMA, ACP, Am. Soc. of Gastrointestinal Endoscopy, Am. Gastroent. Assn., Am. Coll. Gastroenterology. Office: Temple University Hospital 3401 N Broad St Philadelphia PA 19140 Office Phone: 800-836-7536. Business E-Mail: jrichter@temple.edu.

RICHTON, SAMUEL M., pediatric endocrinologist; b. Pittsfield, Mass., Aug. 17, 1948; m. Marsha Lee Richton, May 25, 1975; children: Jonathan, Joshua, Jeanette, Simcha, Jesse. BS, U. Mass., 1970; MS, Yale U., New Haven, 1972; MD, Albert Einstein Coll. Medicine, Bronx, NY, 1975. Diplomate Am. Bd. Pediat., Am. Bd. Pediat. Endocrinology. Resident pediat. Rainbow Babies & Children's Hosp., Cleve., 1975-77; fellow pediat. endocrinology and metabolism U. Md., Balt., 1977-78; fellow pediat. Harvard Med. Sch., Boston; rsch. fellow Juvenile Diabetes Found. Children's Hosp., Boston, 1978-80; physician Diabetes Med. Group, LA, 1980-81; asst. prof. U. Ill. Coll. Medicine, Chgo., 1981-84, Chgo. Med. Sch., 1984-87; dir. endocrinology Cook County Children's Hosp., Chgo., 1984-87; dir. divsn. pediat. endocrinology Miami Children's Hosp., 1987—. Med. dir. South Fla. Diabetes Camp, Miami, 1987—. Contbr. articles to profl jours. Fellow: Am. Acad. Pediat.; mem.: Lawson Wilkens Pediat. Endocrine Soc., Internat. Diabetes Fedn., Am. Diabetes Assn. Office: Miami Childrens Hosp 3100 SW 62nd Ave # 122 Miami FL 33155-3009 Office Phone: 305-662-8398. Office Fax: 305-663-8581.

RICIERI, DENISE DA VINHA, physical therapist, educator; b. São Paulo, Brazil, Apr. 29, 1965; PhD, Fed. U. Paraná, 2008. Phys. therapist State U. Londrina, 1985. Adj. prof. Fed. U. Paraná, 2006—. Assoc. rschr. Fed. Technol. U. Paraná, 2009. Office: Rua Coração Maria 92 Curitiba Paraná 80215-370 Brazil Business E-Mail: denise.ricieri@ufpr.br.

RICKEL, ANNETTE URSO, psychology and psychiatry researcher, educator; b. Phila. d. Ralph Francis and Marguerite (Calcaterra) Urso; 1 child, John Ralph Rickel. BA, Mich. State U., 1969; PhD, MD, U. Mich., 1972. Lic. psychologist, Mich., marriage & family therapist, NY. Faculty early childhood edn. Merrill-Palmer Inst., Detroit, 1967-69; adj. faculty U. Mich., Ann Arbor, 1969-75; asst. dir. N.E. Guidance Ctr., Detroit, 1972-75; asst. prof. psychology Wayne State U., Detroit, 1975-81; vis. assoc. prof. Columbia U., NYC, 1982-83; assoc. prof. psychology Wayne State U., 1981-87, asst. provost, 1989-91, prof. psychology, 1987-95; Am. Coun. on Edn. fellow Princeton and Rutgers Univs., 1990-91; clin. prof. dept. psychiatry Georgetown U., Washington, 1995—2000; program officer Rockefeller Found., 2000—03; pres. Annette Urso Rickel Found., 2003—; prof. Weill Cornell Med. Coll., 2005—, NY Presbyn. Hosp., 2010—. AAAS and APA Congl. Sci. fellow on Senate Fin. Subcom. on Health and Pres.'s Nat. Health Care Reform Task Force, 1992—93. Cons. editor Jour. of Cmty. Psychology, Jour. Primary Prevention; co-author: Social and Psychological Problems of Women, 1984, Preventing Maladjustment..., 1987; author: Teenage Pregnancy and Parenting, 1989, Keeping Children From Harm's Way, 1997, High Risk Sexual Behavior, 1998, Understanding Managed Care, 2000, Attention Deficit Hyperactivity Disorder in Children and Adults, 2006, Chronic Illness in Children and Adolescents, 2007; contbr. articles to profl. jours. Mem. Pres.'s Task Force on Nat. Health Care Reform, 1993; bd. dirs. Children's Ctr. of Wayne County, Mich., 1989—, The Epilepsy Ctr. of Mich., 1984-92, Nat. Symphony Orch., 1997—, Reading is Fundamental, 2000—, v.p., Chamber Music Soc. of Lincoln Ctr., 2002—, The Kellogg Found., 1996-97, The John D. and Catherine T. MacArthur Found., 1998-99; pres., Soc. Meml. Sloan Kettering Cancer Ctr., 2002-11. Grantee NIMH, 1976-86, Eloise and Richard Webber Found., 1977-80, McGregor Fund, 1977-78, 82, David M. Whitney Fund, 1982, Katherine Tuck Fund, 1985-90, NIH, 2000; recipient Career Devel. Chair award, 1985-86. Fellow APA (div. pres. 1984-85); mem. Internat. Women's Forum, Soc. for Rsch. in Child Devel., Soc. for Rsch. in Child and Adolescent Psychopathology, Internat. Assn. of Applied Psychologists, Sigma Xi, Psi Chi. Roman Catholic. Office Phone: 212-710-1040. Personal E-mail: rickelau@aol.com.

RICKELS, KARL, psychiatrist, educator; b. Wilhelmshaven, Germany, Aug. 17, 1924; came to U.S., 1954, naturalized, 1960; s. Karl E. and Stephanie (Roehrhoff) R.; m. Rosalind Wilson, June 27, 1964; children: Laurence Arthur, PhD, Stephen W., Michael R. MD, U. Muenster, 1951. Intern Dortmund (Germany) City Hosp., 1951-52; postgrad. tng. U. Erlangen, U. Frankfurt, City Hosp. Kassel, 1952-54; resident in psychiatry Mental Health Inst., Cherokee, Iowa, 1954-55, Hosp. U. Pa., Phila., 1955 57; from instr. to assoc. prof. U. Pa., Phila., 1957-69, prof. psychiatry, 1969—, prof. pharmacology, 1976-98, Stuart and Emily B.H. Mudd prof. human behavior, 1977—, chief mood and anxiety disorders program, 1964—2010, chmn. com. on studies involving human beings, 1985-98. Chief psychiatry Phila. Gen. Hosp., 1975-77. Editor, author 10 books; contbr. over 570 articles to profl. publs. Fellow Am. Coll. Neuropsychopharmacology (life; charter), Am. Psychiat. Assn. (life), Coll. Physicians Phila., Collegium Internat. Neuro-Psychopharmacologicum, Psychiat. Rsch. Soc., European Coll. Neuropsychopharmacology (corr.). Home: 1324 Youngsford Rd Gladwyne PA 19035 Home Phone: 610 649 1838; Office Phone: 215-746-6417. Business E-Mail: krickels@mail.med.upenn.edu.

RICKETSON, GEORGE MANNING, III, retired surgeon; b. Atlanta, Ga., 1937; MD, U. Fla., 1966. Diplomate Am. Bd. Surgery. Intern Bethesda Naval Hosp, Md., 1966-67; resident in surgery USN Hosp., Portsmouth, Va., 1967-71; pvt. practice Sacred Heart Hosp., Pensacola, Fla.; pvt. practice, group partnership McMahon Ricketson Stockamp, Pensacola, Fla.; ret., 2002. Fellow: ACS; mem.: Southeastern Surg. Congress. Office: McMahon Ricketson Stockamp 5014 Barranca Lora Pensacola FL 32514 Home Phone: 850-477-5146. Personal E-mail: pricketson@cox.net. *

RICKETTS, SUSAN AUSTIN, retired demographer; b. Mass., May 7, 1945; BA, Wellesley Coll., 1967; MA, U. Pa., PhD, 1973. Honorarium faculty U. Colo., Denver, 1973, lectr., internat. seminar series population, Med. Ctr., 1974—77; dir., region VIII family planning data sys. US Dept. Health, Edn., and Welfare, 1974—76; demographer CC Fin. Study, Edn. Commn. States, 1980—81; maternal and child health demographer Colo. Dept. Pub. Health and Environment, 1976—2011. Mem.: APHA, Population Assn. America, Colo. Pub. Health Assn.

RICORDI, CAMILLO, surgeon, researcher; b. NYC, Apr. 1, 1957; m. Valerie A. Grace, Aug. 8, 1986; children: M. Caterina, Eliana G., Carlo A. MD, Milan U., Italy, 1982. Trainee in gen. surgery San Raffaele Inst., Milan, 1982-85; NIH trainee Washington U. Sch. Medicine, St. Louis, 1985-88; attending surgeon San Raffaele Inst., Milan, 1988-89; asst. prof. to assoc. prof. surgery U. Pitts., Pa., 1989-93; disting. prof. medicine, prof. biomed. engring., microbiology and immunology, chief divsn. cellular transpl., dir. cell transplantation ctr. Diabetes Rsch. Inst., U. Miami, Fla., 1993—, sci. dir., chief acad. officer Fla., 1996—, Stacy Joy Goodman chair in Diabetes Rsch., 1998—. Reviewer of applications for grants Can. and Am. Diabetes Assns., Juvenile Diabetes Found., NIH; chmn. First and Third Internat. Congresses of Cell Transplant Soc., Pitts., 1992, Miami, 1996, 5th Internat. Congress on Pancreas and Islet Transplantation, Miami, 1995, others; mem. editl. bd. Transplantation, Cell Transplantation, Transplantation Procs., Jour. Tissue Engring. Editor: Pancreatic Islet Cell Transplantation, 1992, Methods in Cell Transplantaion, 1995; co-editor-in-chief Cell Transplantation, Graft; assoc. editor Am. Jour. Transplantation, 2003—; contbr. numerous chpts. to books and articles to jours. including Immunology Today, Jour. Clin. Investigation, New Eng. Jour. Medicine, Hepatology, Diabetes, Transplantation, Endocrinology, Procs. NAS, USA, Am. Jour. Physiology, Surgery, Nature, Nature Genetics, Lancet, Nature Immunology Rev. Grantee Juvenile Diabetes Found. Internat., 1988—, NIH, 1993—, Galileo Lectr., EASD, Rome, 2008; recipient Nessim Habif World prize of surgery, 2001. Mem. AAAS, Cell Transplant Soc. (founder, pres. 1992-94), Am. Soc. Transplant Surgeons, Internat. Pancreas and Islet Transplant Assn. (v.p. 1979-99, pres. 1999-2001), The Transplantation Soc., Am. Diabetes Assn. (councillor, 2003-, Outstanding Sci. Achievement award 2002). Achievements include patents in cellular biotechnologies. Office: U Miami Diabetes Rsch Inst PO Box 016960 Miami FL 33101 Business E-Mail: ricordi@miami.edu.

RIDDER, GERD JUERGEN, otolaryngologist; b. Bad Driburg, Nordrhein-Westfalen, Germany, Nov. 15, 1969; s. Werner Antonius and Brigitte Johanna Ridder; m. Anna-Maria Weygoldt, May 5, 2000 (div.); children: Johannes Nikolaus children: Charlotte Antonia. MD, Hannover Med. Sch., 1996. Cert. physician 1996. Resident Dept. Otorhinolaryngology-Head and Neck Surgery U. Freiburg, Freiburg, Germany, 1997—2001, specialist Dept. Otorhinolaryngology-Head and Neck Surgery, 2002—03, sr. registrar, 2004—06, COO, 2006—, prof. otolaryngology-head and neck surgery, 2006; resident Inst. Molecular Medicine and Cell Rsch. Albert-Ludwigs-U., Freiburg, 2001. Vis. physician Bnai Zion Med. Ctr. Dept. Otolaryngology Israel Inst. Tech., Haifa, Israel, 1998. Contbr. articles to profl. jours. Recipient Award of the Assn. for Promotion of Rsch. and Theory in the Field of Gen. Surgery, 1994. Mem.: German Soc. for Ultrasound in Medicine, German Soc. of Otorhinolaryngology-Head and Neck Surgery (Poster award 2003, 2004). Office: Univ Freiburg Killianstr. 5 79106 Freiburg 79106 Germany Office Fax: +49-761-270-4111. Business E-Mail: ridder@hno.ukl.uni-freiburg.de.

RIDDICK, DANIEL HOWISON, obstetrician, gynecologist, priest; b. Lynchburg, Va., Dec. 12, 1941; s. Joseph Henry and Nancy Eloise (Gordon) R.; m. Louisa McIntosh Spruill, June 9, 1963; children: Ellen, Daniel. BA, Duke U., 1963, MD, 1967, PhD in Physiology, 1969. Diplomate Am. Bd. Ob-Gyn, Am. Bd. Reproductive Endocrinology; ordained priest Episc. Ch., 1969. Asst. prof. physiology Duke U., Durham, NC, 1973-74; asst. prof. ob-gyn U. Conn. Sch. Medicine, Farmington, 1974-76, dir. reproductive endocrinology and infertility, 1974-85, assoc. prof. ob-gyn, 1976-81, prof. ob-gyn, 1981-85; prof., chmn. ob-gyn dept. U. Vt., Burlington, 1985-97, assoc. dean grad. med. edn., 1987-88. Editor: Reproductive Endocrinology in Clinical Practice, 1987; editor: (with others) Pathology of Infertility, 1987. Mem. ACOG, Am. Fertility Soc. (pres. 1992-93), Am. Gynecol. and Obstet. Soc. Avocation: sheep-raising. Home: 680 Mayo Rd Huntington VT 05462-9410 Office: Fletcher Allen Health Care Dept of Obstetrics & Gynecology 111 Colchester Ave Burlington VT 05401-1416 Office Phone: 802-847-1400. E-mail: dan.riddick@vtmednet.org.

RIDDICK, FRANK ADAMS, JR., physician, healthcare administrator; b. Memphis, June 14, 1929; s. Frank Adams and Falba (Crawford) Riddick; m. Mary Belle Alston, June 15, 1952; children: Laura Elizabeth Dufresne, Frank Adams III, John Alston. BA cum laude, Vanderbilt U., 1951, MD, 1954. Diplomate Am. Bd. Internal Medicine. Intern Barnes Hosp., St. Louis, 1954—55, resident in medicine, 1957—60; fellow in metabolic diseases Washington U., St. Louis, 1960—61; staff Ochsner Clinic (Ochsner Found. Hosp.), New Orleans, 1961—, head sect. endocrinology and metabolic disease, 1976—83, asst. med. dir., 1968—72, assoc. med. dir., 1972—75, med. dir., 1975—92; CEO Alton Ochsner Med. Found., New Orleans, 1992—2001; CEO emeritus Ochsner Clinic Found., 2001—. Bd. govs. Am. Bd. Internal Medicine, 1973—80; clin. prof. Tulane U., New Orleans, 1977—; trustee Alton Ochsner Med. Found., 1973—, CEO, 1991—, chmn. bd. Ochsner Health Plan, 1983—92, pres. Orleans Svc. Corp., 1976—80, South La. Med. Assocs., New Orleans, 1978—; dir. Brent House Corp., New Orleans, 1980—; chmn. Accreditation Coun. on Grad. Med. Edn., 1986—87, v.p. nat. resident matching program, 1986—90, mem. accreditation coun. on med. edn., 1988—90. Bd. govs. Isidore Newman Sch., New Orleans, 1987—93; trustee St. Martin's Protestant Episc. Sch., Metairie, La., 1970—84. Recipient Tchg. award, Alton Ochsner Med. Found., 1969, Disting. Alumnus award, Castle Heights Mil. Acad., 1979, Physician Exec. award, Am. Coll. Med. Group Adminstrs., 1984, Disting. Alumnus award, Vanderbilt U. Sch. Medicine, 1988. Master: ACP; fellow: Am. Coll. Physician Execs. (pres. 1987—88); mem.: NAS Inst. Medicine, AMA (ho. dels. 1971—92, chmn. coun. on med. edn. 1983—85, coun. on jud. and ethical affairs 1995—2002, chair 2001—02, Disting. Service award 2003), Am. Group Practice Assn. (pres. 1992—94), Soc. Med. Adminstrs. (pres. 1995—), Am. Diabetes Assn., Endocrine Soc., Am. Soc. Internal Medicine (trustee 1970—76, Disting. Internist award), Cosmos Club, New Orleans Country Club, Boston Club. Office: Ochsner Clinic 1516 Jefferson Hwy New Orleans LA 70121-2429 Home: 150 Broadway 709 New Orleans LA 70118-7610 Office Phone: 504-842-4019. Business E-Mail: friddick@ochsner.org.

RIDER, LISA G, pediatric rheumatologist, researcher; b. Newark; MD, Duke U. Sch. of Medicine, 1983—87. Pediatric Rheumatologist Am. Bd. Pediat. Med. officer and staff scientist Ctr. for Biologics Evaluation and Rsch., FDA, Bethesa, Md., 1993—2001; dep. chief Environ. Autoimmunity Group, Nat. Inst. Environ. Health Scis. NIH, Bethesda, Md., 2001—. Med. adv. bd. mem., chri rsch. com. The Myositis Assn., Washington, 1996—2009; spl. govt. employee FDA, Rockville, Md., 2001—03; adv. coun. Pediatric Rheumatology Collaborative Study Group, Cincinnati, Ohio, 1998—. Editor: Myositis and You; contbr. articles to profl. jours., chapters to books. Vol. Garrett Pk. Elem. Sch., Md., 2002—06. Capt. US Pub. Health Svc., 1991—, Bethesda, MD. Fellow, PhRMA, 1985—86; Eugene Stead Rsch. fellow, Duke U., 1985—86. Fellow: Am. Acad. Pediat., Am. Coll. Rheumatology (exec. coun. pediatric rheumatology sect. 2003—08); mem.: Phi Beta Kappa. Achievements include research in juvenile myositis, rheumatic disease, environmental risk factors, autoantibodies, immunogenetics, outcome measures. Office: NIEHS NIH CRC 4-2352 MSC 1301 10 Center Dr Bethesda MD 20892-1301 Business E-Mail: riderl@mail.nih.gov.

RIDGEWAY, SHARON MARILYN, psychologist, researcher, mental health services professional; b. Bromley, Kent, Eng., Aug. 27, 1959; d. Lawrence Donald and Greta (Polchar) R.; m. Noel Thomas Traynor. Student, Solihull Tech. Coll., Eng., 1976-77; BA in Psychology/Sociology with honors, Sunderland U., Eng., 1983; MSc in Applied Social Sci., U. London, 1987; D in Psychology, Mental Health and Deafness, U. Manchester, Eng., 1992-98, PhD in Psychology, 1998. Chartered psychologist; cert. qualification in social work, psychodynamic approaches to practice. Social work asst. with deaf people Cumbria Deaf Assn., 1983-85; team leader social svc. London Borough of Barnet, 1988-90; rsch. psychologist, head counseling svcs. Nat. Ctr. Mental Health and Deafness, Manchester, Eng., 1990—. Dir., designer tutor counseling skills, personal growth courses, U. Manchester, 1983—, dir. bd. studies counseling skills deaf people, 1992-96, designer, coord. nat. cert. course in mental health and deafness, 1994; mem. adv. group deaf issues and social work diploma Open U., mem. diploma social work course team, 1989-91; tng. com. Alliance Deaf Svc. Users and Providers, 1989-92; mem. working group Keep Deaf Children Safe, 1989-92; mgmt. com. exec. Manchester Disability Group, 1991-93; designer media programme for mental health awareness, deaf cmty. programme; presenter in field; coord. Expert Mental Health, World Federation Deaf, 2009-. Author: The Deaf Alliance (Counselling and Deaf People), 1994; editor: (newsletter) Spl. Interest Group Psychologists in Deafness, 1992-94, Progress Through Equality, 1995; contbr. articles to profl. jours. Mgmt. com. exec. Manchester Disability Group, 1991-93; gov. local edn. authority Newbrook Sch., W. Didsbury, Manchester, 1993—; trustee Deafway, Preston, Lancashire, 1998-2000. Hon. fellow U. Manchester; recipient Leo Baeck award Leo Baeck Coll., 1984, 85. Mem. Deaf Profls. in Mental Health Care (founder, sec. 1991-96, chair 1998—), European Deaf Profls. in Mental Health Care (pres. 1994-96, Brit. Deaf Assn. rep. 1994—), Brit. Soc. Mental Health and Deafness (rep. Brit Deaf Assn. 1993—, v.p. 1996, chmn. 2000—), Brit. Assn. Social Workers, Brit. Assn. Psychologists, European Soc. Mental Health and Deafness Coun. Socialist. Jewish. Avocations: debates on deaf issues, reading, painting. Office: Nat Ctr Mental Health & Deafness MH Svc Salford Bury New Rd Prestwich M25 3BL England Home: 28 Milton Crescent SK8 1NU Cheadle England Office Phone: 07770 587172. Personal E-mail: daisystables@aol.com. Business E-Mail: sharon.psychology@talktalk.net.

RIDKER, PAUL M., cardiologist, medical educator; b. St. Louis, Oct. 2, 1959; BS, Brown U., Providence, 1981; MD, Harvard Med. Sch., 1986; MPH, Harvard Sch. Pub. Health, 1992. Diplomate Am. Bd. Internal Medicine, cert. in Cardiovasc. Disease. Intern Brigham & Women's Hosp./Harvard Med. Sch., Boston, 1986—87, resident internal medicine/cardiology, 1987—89, fellow cardiology, 1989—91, assoc. physician, dir. Ctr. Cardiovasc. Disease Prevention, 1991—; also co-dir. Leducq Ctr. Cardiovasc. Rsch. Brigham & Women's Hosp.; co-dir. Reynolds Ctr. Cardiovasc. Rsch. Harvard Med. Sch., 2003—, Eugene Braunwald prof. medicine. Chief med. resident Vets. Adminstrn. Boston Health Care, 1989; Simon Dack vis. prof. Mt. Sinai Med. Ctr., 2000; cons. cardiologist So. Jamaica Plain Health Ctr., Boston. Consulting editor: Circulation jour.; contbr. articles to profl. jours., chapters to books. Recipient Clinician Scientist award, Am. Heart Assn., 1992—97, Established Investigator award, 1997—2002, SmithKline Beecham Faculty Devel. award, 1997—99, Disting. Clin. Scientist award, Doris Duke Charitable Found., 2000, Linus Pauling Lecture & Prevention award, Am. Coll. Advancement Medicine, 2000; named one of America's Ten Best Rschrs. in Sci. & Medicine, TIME mag., 2001, 100 Most Influential People, 2004. Fellow: Am. Coll. Cardiology; mem.: Am. Assn. Physicians, Am. Soc. Clin. Investigation, Am. Epidemiol. Soc. Achievements include research in arterial inflammation, an immune-system reaction that is the most powerful contributor after cholesterol to heart attacks; design of federal guidelines advocating CRP evaluation as a new method for cardiovascular disease detection; patents in field. Office: Brigham & Womens Hosp Divsn Preventive Medicine 900 Commonwealth Ave E 3rd Fl Boston MA 02215 Office Phone: 617-278-0869. E-mail: pridker@partners.org.

RIDRUEJO, PEDRO, psychiatrist, educator; b. Soria, Spain, Feb. 26, 1931; s. Emiliano Ridruejo and Maria Eusebia Alonso. JD, U. Complutense, Madrid, 1953, MS in polit. and econ. scis., 1963, PhD, 1964; BS in ednl. scis., U. Barcelona, 1965; BS in psychology, U. Complutense, Madrid, 1971; BS in biol. scis., U. Valencia, 1976; PharmD, U. Complutense, Madrid, 1977; MD, U. Pais Vasco, Bilbao, Spain, 1980. Specialist in Psychiatry Sch. Psychiatry. U. Complutense, Madrid, 1978, Specialist in Endocrinology Sch. Endocrinology. U. Complutense, Madrid, 1979; Diplomate in Applied Psychology Sch. Psychology, U. Madrid, 1961, Diplomate in Sociology Sch. Sociology., U. Madrid, 1980. Fellow U. Paris, 1957—58, Harvard U., 1961, Munich U., 1962; asst. prof. philosophy U. Complutense, Madrid, 1959; full prof. philosophy H.S. Teruel, Spain, 1960; dir. Guadalupe Residence, Madrid, 1960—62; full prof. psychology Sch. Tchrs., Alava, Spain, 1963, Sch. Publicity, Madrid, 1964; dir. Inst. Applied Psychology, Albacete, Spain, 1964—67; aggregate prof. U. Complutense, Madrid, 1967—68; dir. U. Coll. Toledo, Spain, 1969—70; full prof., chmn. U. Valencia, Spain, 1972—75, U. Autonoma of Madrid, 1975—78; psychiatrist in clin. social security Social Security, Leganes. Moratalaz, Spain, 1978—83; cons., tchr. Crownsville Hosp. Ctr., Annapolis, Md., 1980; dir., rsch. group FONAS, Madrid, 1981; pvt. cons. psychoneuroendocrinology Madrid, 1982—85; full prof. and chmn. in psychiatry, sch. medicine U. Autonoma de Madrid, 1986—2002; dir. dept. psychiatry U. Autonoma Madrid, 1995—2002; pres., chmn. med. psychology Spanish Soc. Psychiatry, Madrid, 1998—2002; prof. emeritus psychiatry U. Autonoma Madrid, 2002—. Psychiatry cons. Nat. Inst. Social Security, Madrid, 1978—83; cons. tchr. Crownsville Hosp. Ctr., Md., 1980; chmn. Univs. Murcia, Valencia, Automoma de Madrid, dir., dean, 1980—81; spanish del. Conf. Health Ministers Latin Am., Madrid, 1981; dir. master in psychotherapy U. Autonoma Madrid, 1998—2002; spkr. in field; sci. com. mem. Wold Assn. Psychiatry. Contbr. articles to various profl. scientific jours. Recipient scholarship, Rockefeller Found., 1957—58, Harvard U., 1962, Medall Cross Isabel La Catolica, Min. Fgn. Affairs, 1960, Min. Edn., 1965, 1968. Mem.: World Assn. Psychiatry, Spanish Soc. Psychosomatic Medicine, Spanish Soc. Gerontopsychiatry, Spanish Soc. Legal Psychaitry, Spanish Soc. Psychogeriatry, Spanish Soc. Biol. Psychiatry, Internat. Psychogeriatric Assn., Am. Psychiat. Assn., Spanish Soc. Psychiatry. Roman Catholic. Achievements include research in risk factors in dementia pathology; the areas of environmental psychiatry, psychogeriatics, and psychomedical/psychosomatic problematics. Avocations: swimming, travel, music. Office: Sch Medicine Univ Autonoma Arzobispo Morcillo s/n Madrid 28029 Spain Home: Calle Vegafria 1 28035 Madrid Spain Home Fax: +34-913737173. E-mail: pedro.ridruejo@uam.es.

RIED, STEPHANIE, physiatrist, educator; BS in Speech Pathology and Audiology, Howard U., Washington, 1973; MA in Speech Pathology, Western Mich. U., Kalamazoo, 1974; postgrad in Phys. Medicine and Rehab., U. Mich., Ann Arbor, 1989—92, MD, 1986. Diplomate Am. Bd. Physical Medicine and Rehab., Am. Bd. Pediatrics, Nat. Bd. Medical Examiners, cert. clin. competence in speech pathology. Resident Baylor Coll. of Medicine, Houston, 1986—89; chief resident dept. of phys. medicine and rehab. Univ. of Mich. Med. Ctr., Ann Arbor, 1991—92; pediatric physiatrist Children's Seashore House, Phila., 1992—97; med. staff. mem. Children's Hospital of Phila., 1992—97; pediatric physiatrist Driscoll Children's Hosp., Corpus Christi, Tex., 1997—2002; clin. dir. nat. ctr. for children's rehab. Nat. Rehab. Hosp., Washington, 2003—04; asst. prof. sch. of medicine Temple Univ., Phila.; med. dir. Spina Bifida program Children's Nat. Med. Ctr., Washington; pediatric physiatrist Shriners Hosps. for Children, Phila., 2002—04, med. dir. for rehab., 2004—. Office: Shriners Hospitals for Children 2900 Rocky Point Dr Tampa FL 33607 Office Phone: 813-281-0300.

RIEDEL, RICHARD F., oncologist, educator; b. White Plains, NY, Mar. 2, 1972; BA, Colgate U., 1994; MD, Thomas Jefferson U., 2000. Asst. prof. Duke U. Med. Ctr., 2007—, assoc. program dir., hematology-oncology fellowship program, 2008—, med. dir., solid tumor inpatient svc., 2008—, assoc. dir., Duke Sarcoma program, clin. and translational rsch., 2010—, Duke Cancer Inst. Mem.: Connective Tissue Oncology Soc., Am. Soc. Clin. Oncology. Home: 6 Shadow Moss Pl Durham NC 27705

RIEGEL, BYRON WILLIAM, ophthalmologist; b. Evanston, Ill., Jan. 19, 1938; s. Byron and Belle Mae (Huot) Riegel; m. Marilyn Hills, May 18, 1968; children: Marc William, Ryan Marie, Andrea Elizabeth. BS, Stanford U., 1960; MD, Cornell U., 1964. Diplomate Nat Bd Med Examiners, Am Bd Ophthalmology 2007. Intern King County Hosp., Seattle, 1964-65; asst. resident in surgery U. Wash., Seattle, 1965; resident in ophthalmology U. Fla., Fla., 1968-71; pvt. practice medicine specializing in ophthalmology Sierra Eye Med. Group, Inc., Visalia, Calif., 1972—2007, cons., 2008—. Chief staff Kaweah Delta Dist Hosp, 1978—79, bd dirs, asst secy, 1983—90; asst. med. dir. Sierra Ambulatory Surg Ctr, Visalia, Calif., 2000—07. Flight surgeon USN, 1966—68. Co-recipient Fight-for-Sight Citation for rsch. in retinal dystrophy, 1970. Fellow: ACS, Am. Acad. Ophthalmology; mem.: Am. Soc. Cataract and Refractive Surgery, Calif. Acad. Ophthalmology (v.p. 3d party liaison 1994—96, dir. 1996—98), Tulare County Med Asn, Calif. Med. Assn. (del. 1978—79), Rotary. Roman Catholic. Home: 3027 Keogh Ct Visalia CA 93291-4228 Personal E-mail: briegel@pacbell.net.

RIEGER, GEBHARD, physician, researcher, medical educator; b. Vienna, Mar. 10, 1940; s. Herwigh and Marianne (Kerschbaum) R.; m. Irmgard Strasser, June 18, 1966; children: Reingard, Herwig, Wolfgang, Bernhard. Degree, Secondary Sch., Linz, 1959. Med. dr. Med. Sch. U., Vienna, 1966; asst. I. U. Eye Clinic, Vienna, 1966-72, eye specialist, 1972; lectr. U. Eye Clinic, Innsbruck, Austria, 1998, u. prof., 2003; emeritus head dept. ophthalmology Paracelsus Inst., Bad Hall, Austria, 2008. Grantee Dr. Heinz and Helen Adam, Frankfurt, 1990; Decoration of Merit in Gold for Svcs. to Upper Austria, 2007, Austrian Cross of Honour for Sci. & Art I Class, 2009. Mem. Austrian Opthal. Soc., Vienna Opthal. Soc., German Opthal. Soc., N.Y. Acad. Scis., Soc. Free Radical Rsch., Austrian Soc. Balneology and Med. Climatology, Assn. Austrian Cure Physicians, Paracelsus Soc. Balneology and Iodine Rsch., Med. Soc. Upper Austria, Van Swieten Soc. Vienna. Avocations: mountain climbing, hiking, editing of a cultural review. Home: Eduardshoehe 19 A-4540 Bad Hall Upper Austria Austria Office: Paracelsus Soc Kurpromenade A-4540 Bad Hall Austria Office Phone: 0043 7258 2193. Office Fax: 0043 7258 2193.

RIENHOFF, HUGH, venture capitalist, physician, geneticist; m. Lisa Hane, 1998; 3 children. BA in Biology and English Lit., Williams Coll.; MD, Johns Hopkins U. Genetics researcher Fred Hutchinson Cancer Rsch. Ctr., Seattle; ptnr. biotechnology investing New Enterprise Associates, Menlo Park, Calif.; dir. Abingworth Mgmt. Ltd., London; founder, chmn., CEO DNA Sciences (formerly Kiva Genetics), 1998—2001; gen ptnr. Vanguard Ventures, 2002; joined bd. dirs. GeneEd, 2004—, chmn. Faculty mem., dept. molecular biology and genetics John Hopkins U. Sch. Medicine; founder MyDaughtersDna.org, 2007—.

RIEUX-LAUCAT, FRÉDÉRIC, medical researcher; b. Paris, June 2, 1965; PhD, U. Paris, 1993. Prin. investigator INSERM, 2006—. Cons. Txcell. Mem.: French Soc. Immunology (Jacques Oudin award). Office: Hopital Necker 149 rue de sèvres Paris 75015 France Office Fax: 33142730640. Business E-Mail: frederic.rieux-laucat@inserm.fr.

RIEW, K. DANIEL, cervical spine surgeon; b. Seoul, Republic of Korea, July 28, 1958; arrived in U.S., 1966; s. C. Keith and H. Kim Riew; m. Mary Kahng, Sept. 12, 1992. MD, Case Western Res. U., 1984. Diplomate Am. Bd. of Orthopaedic Surgery. Asst. attending physician, instr. medicine Cornell U. Med. Ctr., NYC, 1987—89; resident gen. surgery Beth Israel Med. Ctr., NYC, 1989—90; resident orthop. surgery George Washington U. Hosp., Washington, 1990—94; fellow spine surgery U. Hosps. Cleve./Case We. Res. U.; from asst. prof. to prof. Washington U. Sch. Medicine, St. Louis, 1995—2005, Mildred B. Simon disting. prof. orthop. surgery, prof. neurol. surgery, 2006—, chief cervical spine surgery, dir. Orthopedic-Rehab. Inst. for Cervical Spine Surgery. Contbr. articles to profl. jours. (Cervical Spine Rsch. Soc. Outanding Basic Sci. Rsch. award, 2000, Mayfield award for basic sci. Am. Assn. of Neurol. Surgeons, 2000, North Am. Spine Soc. Outstanding Paper award, 2000, Russell S. Hibbs Basic Sci. award Scoliosis Rsch. Soc., 2000). Recipient C. Richard Bowman award, N.Y. Hosp., Cornell Med. Ctr., 1987, Caring Spirit award, Barnes-Jewish Hosp., 2001, Best Paper award, Am. Soc. Spine Radiology, 2005, Mentor award, 2006, Excellence in Tchg. award, 2007; grantee, Orthopaedic Rsch. and Edn. Found., 2002—05. Fellow: Am. Acad. Orthop. Surgeons; mem.: Mo. State Orthop. Assn., Mid. Am. Orthop. Assn., Am. Orthop. Assn., Scoliosis Rsch. Soc., Orthop. Rsch. Soc., N.Am. Spine Soc. (CME com. and surg. care com. 2000, Outstanding Paper award 2003), Cervical Spine Rsch. Soc. (clin. outcomes com. 2001, Outstanding Clin. Rsch. award 2004, Clin. Poster award 2005, Outstanding Clin. Rsch. award 2006, Outstanding Clin. Poster award 2006). Avocations: skiing, golf. Office: Washington U Sch of Medicine ste 11300 One Barnes-Jewish Hosp Plz Saint Louis MO 63110

RIFFEE, WILLIAM H., dean, pharmacy educator; BS in Pharmacy, W.Va. U., 1967; PhD in Pharmacology, Ohio State U., 1975. Clin. pharmacy officer divsn. hosps. USPHS Commd. Corps, 1967—70; prof. divsn. pharmacology/toxicology U. Tex. Coll. Pharmacy, Austin, 1975—96; prof. dept. pharmacodynamics, dean U. Fla. Coll. Pharmacy, Gainesville, 1996—. Achievements include research in the area of educational technology and its utility in the classroom; innovation in the area of teaching and the use of television and computer-based presentation technology as well as the use of the computer as a learning tool; design of electronic classrooms that incorporate video with computer workstations for student's use. Office: U Fla Coll Pharmacy PO Box 100484 Gainesville FL 32610 Office Phone: 352-392-9714. Office Fax: 352-392-3480. Business E-Mail: riffee@cop.ufl.edu.

RIFFENBURGH, ROBERT HARRY, biostatistician, researcher; b. Christiansburg, Va., June 19, 1931; s. Harry Buchholz and Ada Swallow Riffenburgh; m. Gerrye Harlow, Nov. 22, 1952; children: Robin, Scott, Marc, Karen, Douglas. BS, Coll. William and Mary, Richmond, Va., 1951, MS, 1953; PhD, Va. Poly. Inst., Blacksburg, 1957. Asst. prof. math. Va. Poly. Inst., Blacksburg, 1955—57, U. Hawaii, Honolulu, 1957—61; prof., head dept. stats. U. Conn., Storrs, 1962—70; prof. stats. San Diego State U., 1968—74, 1979—82, 1990—93, 2006—; head, biomedical program Naval Undersea Ctr., San Diego, 1970—73; scientist Naval Facility, Brawdy, Wales, 1974—77; math. statistician Naval Ocean Systems Ctr., San Diego, 1977—82; leader, naval ops. rsch. NATO SHAPE Tech. Centre, The Hague, Netherlands, 1982—86; head, ops. rsch. NATO Undersea Rsch. Centre, La Spezia, Italy, 1986—90; chief biostats. Naval Med. Ctr. San Diego, San Diego, 1991—. Pres. and ceo Gen. Systems Analysis Co., Storrs, Conn., 1963—70. Author: Statistics in Medicine; contbr. articles to profl. jours. Capt. NATO, 1982—89. Decorated Navy Commendation Medal; Predoctoral fellow, NIH, 1954-1956. Fellow: Royal Statis. Soc. (life), Am. Statis. Assoc. (life); mem.: Internat. Biometrics Soc., Phi Kappa Phi, Sigma Xi. Home: 3069 Award Row San Diego CA 92122 Office: Naval Med Ctr San Diego 34800 Bob Wilson Dr San Diego CA 92134 Home Phone: 858-453-4334; Office Phone: 619-532-9414. Office Fax: 619-532-8137. Personal E-mail: riff@sdsu.edu. Business E-Mail: robert.riffenburgh@med.navy.mil.

RIFKIN, BARRY R., dean, dental educator, researcher; b. Trenton, NJ, Mar. 30, 1940; s. Samuel H. and Ida M. Rifkin; m. Harriet Smith, Mar. 1960 (div. Sept. 1981); children: Avery, Carl; m. Linda Ruth Rosenberg, Nov. 1993; 1 child, Hannah. BS, Ohio State U., 1961; MS, U. Ill., 1964; DDS, Temple U., 1968; PhD, U. Rochester, 1974. Andrew Mellon fellow U. Rochester Med. Ctr., 1974; assoc. pathologist Strong Meml. Hosp., 1974—80; assoc. prof. NYU, NYC, 1980—84, chmn. dept. oral medicine, 1980—87, prof., 1984—91, chmn. dept. oral medicine and pathology, 1987—91, head divsn. basic scis., 1991—98, prof. emeritus, 1998—; prof. oral biology and pathology, dean SUNY Stony Brook Health Sciences Ctr. Sch. Dental Medicine, 1998—. Rschr. in field; bd. mem. Friends of the Nat. Inst. of Dental and Craniofacial Rsch., 2005—. Sr. editor Biology and Physiology of the Osteoclast, 1992; mem. editl. bd.: Jour. Dental Rsch.; contbr. articles and abstracts to profl. jours. Fellow: Am. Coll. Dentists; mem.: AAAS, Am. Soc. Bone and Mineral Rsch., Internat. Assn. Dental Rsch., Am. Soc. Cell Biology, N.Y. Acad. Scis., Am. Assn. Oral Biologists (pres. 1992—93), Sigma Xi, Omicron Kappa Upsilon. Office: Stony Brook Univ Sch Dental Medicine 160 Rockland Hall Stony Brook NY 11794-8700 Office Phone: 631-632-8950. Office Fax: 631-632-9105. E-mail: barry.rifkin@stonybrook.edu.

RIFKIN, LAURENCE R., cosmetic dentist; DDS, U. SC, 1976. Cosmetic dentist, Beverly Hills, Calif.; internat. lectr.; faculty in dentistry Univ. Southern Calif., UCLA. Profl. artist and sculptor Rifkin Sculptor. Mem.: Am. Acad. of Cosmetic Surgery, Acad. of Microscope Enhanced Dentistry. Office: Private Practice 414 North Camden Drive Suite 1280 Beverly Hills CA 90210 Office Phone: 310-273-0200. Office Fax: 310-205-0718.

RIFKIN, MATTHEW D., radiologist; b. NYC, Mar. 26, 1949; m. Susan Greenberg, 1971; children: Adam, Jason. BA, Brandeis U., 1971; MD, Albert Einstein Coll., 1974. Intern in medicine Montefiore Hosp. and Med. Ctr., Bronx, NY, 1974—75, resident in diagnostic radiology, 1975—78; fellow in ultrasound/CT Johns Hopkins Hops. and Med. Ctr., Balt., 1978—79; instr. radiology Johns Hopkins Hosp. and Med. Sch., Balt., 1978—79; clin. asst. prof. radiology U. Miami Sch. Medicine, Fla., 1979—81, Jefferson Med. Coll., Thomas Jefferson U., Phila., 1981—83, asst. prof. radiology, 1983—85, assoc. prof. radiology, 1983—86, prof. urology, 1985—91, prof., assoc. chair dept. radiology, 1986—91; clin. prof. Coll. Allied Health Sci., Thomas Jefferson U., Phila., 1984—91, 1991; chair dept. radiology Albany Med. Coll., 1991—98, prof. radiology, 1991—98, prof. surgery, 1995—99; prof., vice chmn., chief diagnostic radiology SUNY Sch. Medicine, Stony Brook, 1999—2003, prof. urology, 1999—2003, prof. radiology, 2009—; chmn. radiology Good Samaritan Hosp., West Islip, NY, 2002—10; dir. radiology St. Catherine of Siena Hosp., Smithtown, NY, 2004—10, St. Charles Hosp., Port Jefferson, NY, 2005—10, Mather Hosp., Port Jefferson, 2007—10; dir. Mother Hosp., Port Jefferson, NY, 2007—10; adj. prof. radiology SUNY Sch Medicine, Stony Brook, 2009—; prof. radiology NY Coll. Osteo. Medicine, 2004—; exec. v.p. Physician Integration Atlantic Health Solution, Tampa, Fla., 2010—, Babylon, NY, 2010—. Cons. radiology VA, Perry Point, Md., 1978—79; staff radiologist Johns Hopkins Hosp., Balt., 1978—79, Plantation Gen. Hosp., Fla., 1979—80, St. Mary's Hosp., West Palm Beach, Fla., 1980—81; med. and ednl. dir. med. sonography St. Mary's Hosp. Sch. Diagnostic, West Palm Beach, 1980—81; staff radiology Thomas Jefferson Univ. Hosp., Phila., 1981—91; dir. radiology rsch. Jefferson Med. Coll., Thomas Jefferson U. Hosp., 1986—91, dir. divsn. magnetic resonance imaging, 1986—91; med. svc. dir. dept. radiology Albany Med. Ctr. Hosp., 1996—98, chief radiologist, 1991—98; vice chair, chief diagnostic radiology, chief clin. ops., chief abdominal radiology SUNY Health Sci. Ctr., Stony Brook, 1999—2003; dir. Mather Meml. Hosp., 2007—; presenter in field. Contbr. scientific papers and articles to profl. jours.; author: Diagnostic Imaging of the Lower Genitourinary Tract, 1985, Handbook of Normal Ultrasound Anatomy, 1985; author: (editor) Intraoperative and Endoscopic Ultrasound, 1987; author: Ultrasound of the Prostate, 1988, 1997, Ultrasound, 1991; editor: Ultrasound of the Urinary Tract, 1991; co-editor: Interventional

Radiology of the Genitourinary Tract, 1993; co-author: Pocket Atlas of Normal Ultrasound Anatomy, 2001, Diagnostic Imaging of the Scrotum and External Male Genitalia, 2002. Fellow: Phila. Coll. Physicians, Am. Coll. Radiology, Am. Inst. Ultrasound Medicine; mem.: Atlanta Health Mgmt., Soc. Uroradiology. Personal E-mail: mdrifkin@usa.net.

RIFKIND, ARLEEN B., pharmacologist, researcher, educator; b. NYC, June 29, 1938; d. Michael C. and Regina (Gottlieb) Brenner; m. Robert S. Rifkind, Dec. 24, 1961; children: Amy, Nina. BA, Bryn Mawr Coll., 1960; MD, NYU, 1964. Resident Bellevue Hosp., NYC, 1965; clin. assoc. Endocrine br. Nat. Cancer Inst., 1965—68; rsch. assoc., asst. resident physician Rockefeller U., 1968—71; from asst. prof. to assoc. prof Weill Med. Coll. Cornell U., NYC, 1971—83, prof. pharmacology Weill Med. Coll., 1983—, chmn. Gen. Faculty Coun. Weill Med. Coll., 1984—86. Mem. Nat. Inst. Environ. Health Scis. Rev. Com., 1981-85, chmn., 1985-86; mem. toxicology study sect. NIH, 1989-91, chmn., 1991-93; bd. sci. counselors USPHS Agy. for Toxic Substances and Disease Registry, 1991-95; adv. com. FDA, Spl. Studies Relating to the Possible Long-Term Health Effects of Phenoxy Herbicides and Contaminents, 1995-99; external adv. bd. Environ. Health Scis. Ctr., Wayne State U., 1999—. Assoc. editor Drug Metabolism and Disposition, 1997-2005; mem. editl. bd. Toxicology and Applied Pharmacology, 1996-2002, Biochem. Pharmacology, 1996—2003; contbr. articles to profl. jours. Chair Friends of Libr., Jewish Theol. Sem. Am., 1984-86; trustee Dalton Sch., 1986-92; bd. govs. Am. Jewish Com., 1999—; bd. dirs. N.Y. chpt. Am. Jewish Com. Recipient Andrew W. Mellon Tchr.-Scientist award, 1976-78, Excellence in Tchg. award Weill Med. Coll. Cornell U., 2004 Mem. AAAS, Internat. Soc. Study Xenobiotics, Am. Soc. Clin. Investigation, Am. Soc. Pharmacology and Exptl. Therapeutics, Endocrine Soc., Soc. Toxicology. Office: Cornell U Med Coll Dept Pharmacology 1300 York Ave New York NY 10021-4805 Business E-Mail: arifkind@med.cornell.edu.

RIGATELLI, GIANLUCA, invasive cardiologist; b. Embu, Kenya, Oct. 12, 1971; s. Giorgio Giuseppe Rigatelli and Loredana Cappellari; m. Elisa Zuliani, Sept. 5, 1998; children: Emanuele, Linda. MD, U. Padua, Italy, 1996, cardiologist, 2000; PhD, U. Verona, 2010. Cert. European Bd. Internat. Radiology, 2010. Resident, cardiology catheterization lab. Legnago Tchg. Hosp., Verona, Italy, 1996—98; fellow interventional cardiology unit Cittadella Tchg. Hosp., Padua, Italy, 1998—2000, attending physician, rschr., 2000—01, attending physician interventional cardiology unit intensive coronary carei, 2001—; attending physician interventional cardiology unit Rovigo Gen. Hosp., 2003. Dir. Internat. Symposium on Bio-Cardiac Assist and Repair. Contbr. articles and revs. to profl. jours., chapters to books; mem. editl. bd. Jour. Geriatric Cardiology and Multiorgan Failure, reviewer Jour. Cardiovascular Medicine, Internat. Jour. Cardiology, Chest, Cardiovasc. Internat. Radiology Jour., Circulation, Heart and Vessels, European Jour. Cardiothoracic Surgery, Circulation. Mem. CUAMM Internat. Coll. for Health Cooperation in Developing Countries, Padua, Italy, 1990—2002. Fellow: ACP, Cardiovasc. Intervention Radiology Soc. Europe, Am. Coll. Cardiology, European Soc. Cardiology, European Assn. Pediatric Cardiology, Nat. Assn. Hosp. Cardiology, Soc. Cardiac Angrography and Interventions. Roman Catholic. Achievements include research in congenital heart diseases interventions and peripheral vascular disease, endovascular management. Avocations: Karate, modelism. Office: EndoCardioVascular Therapy Rsch Via Wolfgang Amadeus Mozart 9 37045 Verona VR Italy Personal E-mail: jackyheart@hotmail.com. Business E-Mail: jackyheart@libero.in.

RIGEL, DARRELL SPENCER, dermatologist, educator, skin cancer researcher; b. Montclair, NJ, June 20, 1950; s. Geldon and Gertrude (Kochansky) R.; m. Beth Carol Hollander, Aug. 4, 1974; children: Ethan, Adam, Ashlee. SB, MIT, 1972, SM, 1974; MD, George Washington U., 1978. Diplomate Am. Bd. Dermatology. Intern N.Y. Hosp.-Cornell Med. Ctr., NYC, 1978-79; resident in dermatology NYU Med. Ctr., 1979-82, dermatologic surgery and oncology fellow, 1982; chief resident NYU Hosp., Bellevue Hosp., Manhattan VA Hosp., 1981-82; pvt. practice NYC, 1982—; dir. dermatology PMI Strang Clinic, NYC, 1982-90. Attending physician NYU Hosp., NYC, 1983—, Bellevue Hosp. Ctr., NYC, 1983—; clin. instr. dermatology NYU Med. Ctr., 1983-86, clin. asst. prof., 1986-90, clin. assoc. prof., 1991-97, clin. prof., 1997—; sci. cons. to numerous cos. and orgns.; pres., chief exec. officer Iris, Inc., NYC, 1987—. Author, editor: Pigmentated Lesions, 1985, Cancer of the Skin, 2005; contbr. numerous articles to profl. jours. Bd. dirs. Am. Cancer Soc., NYC, 1985—. Recipient nat. citation Am. Cancer Soc., 1987. Fellow Am. Acad. Dermatology (nat. sec.-treas., 1997-99, bd. dirs., chmn. pres. 1999-2000, presdl. comm. on melanoma and skin cancer, chmn. on computer tech. 1985-89, Presdl. citation 1985, pres., 1999-2000); mem. AMA, Am. Dermatologic Assn. (sec., treas. 2001-07, pres. 2007-08), Dermatologic Soc. Greater N.Y. (v.p. 1988, pres. 1989), Iris Golf Club (pres. 1987-89). Avocations: golf, fishing, chess, sailing. Office: 35 E 35th St Ste 208 New York NY 10016-3814

RIGG, CHARLES ANDREW, pediatrician; b. Hamilton, Victoria, Australia, Oct. 18, 1926; arrived in U.S., 1963; s. Arthur Oscar and Mary Eileen (Wingrove) Rigg. B Medicine, Surgery with honors, Sydney U., 1951. Registrar pediat. unit St. Mary's Hosp., London, 1956, 1958; registrar professorial unit Children's Hosp., Sydney, 1954—56; fellow adolescent medicine Boston Children's Hosp., 1963—64, staff adolescent medicine, 1964—65; asst. prof. pediat. Georgetown U. Med. Sch., 1965—67; chief dept. adolescent medicine Children's Nat. Med. Ctr., Washington, 1967—80, Boston City Hosp., 1981—83; med. dir. Outer Cape Health, Provincetown, Mass., 1983—88; pediatrician, med. dir. Medicenter Five, Harwich, Mass., 1988—95, pediatrician, 1995—97; cons. pediatrician May Ctr. Child Devel., Chatham, Mass., 1990—; pediatrician Harwich Town Pub. Sch. Sys., 1997—. Cons. Nat. Naval Med. Ctr., Bethesda, Md., 1973—80, Walter Reed Army Med. Ctr., Washington, 1973—80; courtesy staff medicine Children's Hosp., Boston, 1983—2005, emeritus mem. courtesy staff, 2005—; vis. prof. Philippine Pediat. Soc., 1978, 9th Congress Brazilian Med. Assn., 1979, 16th Internat. Congress Pediat., Barcelona, 1980; from asst. prof. to assoc. prof. child health George Washington U. Med. Sch., 1967—80; assoc. prof. pediat. Boston U., 1981—83. Editor: Adolescent Medicine Present and Future Concepts, 1980; contbr. articles to profl. jours. Mem. Shakespeare Libr., Washington, Nat. Trust Hist. Preservation, Nat. Trust Australia, Tasmania, Royal Oak Soc. Maj. M.C. Royal Australian Army, 1951—60, lt. col. USAR, 1985—91. Model Tng. Program Adolescent Medicine grantee, Maternal and Child Health Svcs.-U.S. Govt., 1967—80, Comprehensive health Svcs. Adolescent Ctr. grantee, Mass. Dept. Pub. Health, 1981—83. Fellow: Royal Australasian Coll. Physicians, Am. Acad. Pediatrics (life); mem.: Soc. Adolescent Medicine (Washington, DC chpt. pres. 1974—76, New Eng. chpt. pres. 1982—84, charter, treas., chmn., legis. com.), Folger Shakespeare Libr., Royal Sydney Golf Club. Episcopalian. Avocations: historic preservation, gardening, theater, music, walking. Office Phone: 508-945-1147.

RIGGS, ARTHUR D., health facility administrator, research scientist; b. Modesto, Calif., Aug. 8, 1939; s. John Arlis and Nelly Laura Riggs; m. Jane Merill, June 12, 1960; children: Karen, Lynelle, Derrick. AB in Chemistry, U. Calif., Riverside, 1961; PhD in Biochemistry, Calif. Inst. Tech., Pasadena, 1966. Predoctoral fellow biology dept. Calif. Inst. Tech., 1961—66; postdoctoral fellow Salk Inst. for Biol. Studies, La Jolla, Calif., 1966—69; assoc. rsch. scientist dept. molecular biology City of Hope Nat. Med. Ctr., Duarte, Calif., 1969—74, sr. rsch. scientist, 1974—83, assoc. chmn. divsn. biology, 1979—81, chmn. divsn. biology, 1981—83, assoc. dir. rsch., 1998—99; adj. prof. U. So. Calif., Los Angeles, 1978—; assoc. dir. for lab. rsch. City of Hope Cancer Ctr., 1981—87, dir. shared resources, 1993—95; chmn. divsn. biology Beckman Rsch. Inst. City of Hope, 1983—87, 1994—2000, dir., 1999—, 2000—; founding dean City of Hope Grad. Sch., Duarte, 1994—98. Contbr. articles to profl. jours. Recipient Rsch. award, Juvenile Diabetes Found., 1979, Disting. Alumnus award, U. Calif., Riverside, 1988, Tech. Leadership award, 2004. Mem.: NAS. Achievements include first human protein produced in bacteria; first man-designed and man-made gene; discovery of new type of genetics. Avocations: hiking, kayaking, mountain biking. Office: Beckman Rsch Inst City of Hope 1450 E Duarte Rd Duarte CA 91010

RIGGS, BYRON LAWRENCE, JR., physician, educator; b. Hot Springs, Ark., Mar. 24, 1931; s. Byron Lawrence and Elizabeth Ann (Patching) R.; m. Janet Templeton Brewer, June 24, 1955; children: Byron Kent, Ann Templeton. BS, U. Ark., 1953, BS in Medicine, 1955, MD, 1955; MS in Medicine, U. Minn., 1962. Diplomate Am. Bd. Internal Medicine, Am. Bd. Endocrinology. Intern Letterman Army Hosp., San Francisco, 1955-56; resident in internal medicine Mayo Grad. Sch. Medicine Hosp., Rochester, Minn., 1958-61; asst. to staff Mayo Clinic and Found., Rochester, 1961, mem. staff internal medicine and metabolism, 1962—; faculty U. Minn. Med. Sch., Rochester, 1962—74, assoc. prof., 1970-72, prof., 1972—; Purvis and Roberta Tabor prof. med. rsch. Mayo Clinic Coll. Medicine Sch., Rochester, 1974—2003, chmn. divsn. endocrinology and metabolism, 1974—84, prof. emeritus, 2003—; mem. gen. medicine B study sect. NIH, 1979-82. Nat. adv. bd. NIAMS/NIH, 1987-91, disting. investigator Mayo Found., 1991-2003 Contbr. articles to profl. jours. Dist. investigator Mayo Found., 1991—. Served with M.C. AUS, 1956-58. Recipient Postgrad. Travel award Mayo Found., 1961, Kappa Delta award Am. Acad. Orthopedic Surgery, 1972, Disting. Alumni award U. Ark., 1998, Mayo Found., 2000, Cable Disting. Svc. award AACE, 2002; Traveling fellow Royal Soc. Medicine, 1973 Master ACP; mem. AMA, AAAS, Am. Coll. Endocrinology, Assn. Am. Physicians, Am. Soc. Clin. Investigation, Endocrine Soc. (Rorer Clin. Investigator award 1989), Am. Fedn. Clin. Rsch. (councillor Midwest sect. 1969-71), Am. Soc. for Bone and Mineral Rsch. (pres. 1985-86, Bartter Clin. Investigation award 1990, Career Recognition award, Newman Disting. Svc. award 2002, Outstanding Mentorship Rodam award 2005), Ctrl. Soc. Clin. Rsch. (councillor, Nat. Osteoperoisis Found. (Legands In Osteoperoisis award 2009). Office: Mayo Clinic 200 1st St SW Rochester MN 55905-0002 Home: 801 Pleasant Valley Dr Unit 22 Little Rock AR 72227-2163

RIGUCCI, SILVIA, physician; b. Rome, Aug. 11, 1983; MD, 2007. Physician Sant'andrea Hosp., 2008—. Office: Via Di Grottarossa 1035-1039 Rome 00189 Italy Personal E-mail: s.rigucci@hotmail.com.

RIGUEIRA, JOSE LUIS DE M. ROCHA, surgeon; b. Figueira da Foz, Portugal, Feb. 5, 1938; s. João Gomes Rigueira and Maria Dagmar Rocha; m. Maria Odette Moura, Aug. 5, 1961; children: Luis Miguel, Filipe Nuno. Med. diploma, Med. Sch., Lisbon and Coimbra, Portugal, 1961; cert., U. Laval, Que., Can., 1970. Cert. gen. surgery specialist Lisbon. Resident Hosp. du St. Sacrament, Quebec, Canada, 1966—70; fellow U. Laval, 1970; specialist in surgery Hosp. Geral, Coimbra, 1973, surg. cons., 1976. Bd. dirs. Portuguese Coll. Surgeons, Coimbra; mem. adv. bd. Portuguese Surg. Rev.; assoc. prof. Coimbra U., 1976—80. Contbr. articles to profl. jours. Lt. Health Svc., 1962—65, Angola. Fellow: Portuguese Surg. Soc., Royal Coll. Physicians. Roman Catholic. Avocation: painting. Office: 65-1 David Sousa 3080 Figueira Portugal Home: 72-1D Sotto Mayor 3080 Figueira Portugal Office Phone: 233423732. Personal E-mail: jlrigueira@sapo.pt.

RIIKONEN, CHARLENE BOOTHE, international health administrator; b. Washington, June 10, 1942; d. John Edward and Frances Elizabeth (Jett) Boothe; m. Esko Riikonen, 1989; children: Cynthia Lee, Anthony John, Jennifer Elizabeth. AA with high honors, Howard C.C., 1977; BA magna cum laude, U. Md., 1979. Asst. dir. univ. rels., alumni dir. U. Md., Catonsville, 1977-81, assoc. dir. univ. rels. and devel. College Park, 1982-83; sr. devel. officer Internat. Ctr. Diarrheal Disease Rsch., Dhaka, Bangladesh, 1984-86; exec. v.p. Child Health Found. (formerly Internat. Child Health Found.), Columbia, Md., 1985-97; pres. Cera Products, LL., Jessup, Md., 1997—, mng. dir., CEO. Cons. to organize symposium oral rehydration therapy Nat. Coun. Internat. Health, Washington, 1987; organizer internat. symposium on food-based oral rehydration therapy Aga Khan U., Pakistan, 1989; organizer consensus conf. cereal-based oral rehydration therapy, Columbia, Md., 1993. Author: (tng. manual) Prevention and Treatment of Childhood Diarrhea with Oral Rehydration Therapy, Nutrition and Breastfeeding, 1992; editor procs. Oral Rehydration Therapy Symposia, 1987, 89, 93, 94; editor Child Health News, 1993—; contbr. articles to profl. jours. Pub. affairs chmn. United Way, Washington Capital Area, Prince Georges County, 1981-83; v.p. Waterfowl Assn.; pres. Windstream Assn., 1988-89; v.p. Waterfowl Terrace Assn., 1994—; mem. pub. rels. com. Md., Del. Cable TV Assn., Balt., 1981-83. Mem. APHA (internat. maternal-child health com.), AAUW, Nat. Coun. Internat. Health Assn., U. Md. Balt. County Alumni Assn. (bd. dirs. 1979-83), Women's Internat. Pub. Health Network. Clubs: Columbia Assn. Athletic (Md.) (capt. women's traveling racquetball team 1979-83). Democrat. Avocations: racquetball, windsurfing, skiing, painting. Office: Cera Products Inc 55 Mathewish Dr # 220 Conway SC 29526 Office Phone: 893-892-2600. Business E-Mail: customerservice@ceraproducts.us.

RIIS, POVL, physician, educator, editor; b. Copenhagen, Dec. 28, 1925; s. Lars O. and Eva E. (Erdmann) R.; m. Else Harne, May 1, 1954; children: Eva, Karen, Mette, Jakob. MD, U. Copenhagen, 1952, Dr.Med. Sci., 1959; Dr.Med.Sci. (hon.), U. Odense, 1996, Nord U. Gothenburg, 1998. Physician-in-chief med. dept. B. Gentofte Hosp., Copenhagen, 1963-76; physician-in-chief med.-gastroent. dept. C. Herlev U. Hosp., Copenhagen, 1976-96; working chmn., editor-in-chief AgeForum, 1997—. Prof. medicine Copenhagen U., 1974-96; mem. sci. Danish Nat. Ency. Author: Medical Science and the Advancement of World Health, 1985, Ethical Issues in Preventive Medicine, 1985, Ethical Dilemmas in Health Promotion, 1987; author, co-author: Scientific Dishonesty, 1992, Research Involving Human Subjects, 1989, Bearing and Perspective, 1988, Face Death, 1989, Medical Ethics, 1985, Biobanks, 1996, Sport and Ethics, 1997, Ethics and Clinical Medicine, 1998, Aging and Frailty, 1999, The Ethics of Research Related to Health Care in Developing Countries, 2002, The History of the Danish Council of Ethics, 2007, Ethics and Clinical Pain, 2006, 09; editor Danish Med. Bull., 1968-91, Bibliothek for Laeger, 1965-91, Nordic Medicine, 1982-91; editor-in-chief Jour. Danish Med. Assn., 1957-91; mem. editl. bd. JAMA, 1994—. Chmn. Nordic Coop. Bd. for Med. Sci., 1970-72, Nordic Publ. Bd. for Medicine, 1970-72, Danish Med. Rsch. Coun., 1972-74; v.p. European Sci. Found., 1974-77, exec. coun., 1978-83; mem. Danish Helsinki Com. Human Rights, 1985-90; chmn. nat. med. com. Danish Red Cross, 1985-93, exec. coun. 1983-93, chmn. Com. First Aid and Health Promotion, 1991-93; chmn. Nat. Sci. Ethical Com. for Medicine, 1979-98; chmn. Age Forum, 1996—; evaluator European Union, 1999; founding mem. Dan. Min. Inst. and Health Newly Set Up Com. Health Aging, 2011; mem. Coun. of Europe, CDBI, 1997; mem. Nuffield Found. Bioethics, 1999-01, Found. Psychiatry, 1996; mem. epidemiology coun. U. Aarhus, 2005. Recipient Alfred Benzon prize, 1964, August Krogh prize, 1974, Christenson-Ceson prize, 1974, Klein prize, 1981, Barfred-Pedersen prize, 1981, Hagedorn prize, 1983, Nordic Gastro prize 1983, Jacobsen prize, 1995, Thorvald Madsen prize, 1995, Danish Hon. prize in rsch. ethics, 2002, AstraZeneca Hon. prize in Gastroenterology, 2004, Islandic Med. Hist. medal, 2005, Islandic Falcon Order, 2010, Lauritzen prize, 2005, prize Jour Norw. Med. Assn. Internet Editors, 2010 Mem. Internat. Orgn. for Study Inflammatory Bowel Diseases, Vancouver Group Internat. Med. Jour. Editors, Royal Coll. Physicians (hon.), Icelandic Med. Assn. (hon.), Swedish Med. Assn., Finnish Med. Assn., Danish Dental Assn. (ethical com. 2000-10). Office Phone: 45-72423990.

RIKKERS, LAYTON FREDERICK, surgeon; b. Fond du Lac, Wis., Jan. 31, 1944; s. Judson John and Dorothy (Layton) R.; m. Diane Lynn Foster, Aug. 20, 1966; children: Steven, Kristin. BS, U. Wis., 1966; MD, Stanford U. Sch. Medicine, 1970. Diplomate Nat. Bd. Med. Examiners, Am. Bd. Surgery. Intern U. Utah Sch. Medicine, Salt Lake City, 1970-71, surgical residency, 1971-76; instr. surgery Emory U. Sch. Medicine, Atlanta, 1976-77; from asst. prof. surgery to acting chmn. div. gen. surgery U. Utah Sch. Medicine, Salt Lake City, 1977-84; prof., chmn. dept. surgery U. Nebr. Med. Ctr., Omaha, 1984-96, U. Wis., Madison, 1996—, prof. surgery, 2009—. Interim dean Coll. Medicine, U. Nebr. Coll. Medicine, 1991-93, M.M. Musselman prof. surgery, 1990—; cons. Omaha Vet. Adminstrv. Ctr., 1984-86, NIH, 1992, Gov.'s Blue Ribbon Coalition on Health Care, Nebr., 1993-94. Editor: Surgical Clinics of North America, 1990; editor-in-chief Annals of Surgery, 1996—; contbr. articles to profl. jours. Mem. Am. Surgical Assn., Am. Coll. Surgeons (com. chair 1993-95), Am. Bd. Surgery (clin. chmn. 1994-95), Soc. Clin. Surgery (pres. 1994-95), Soc. Surgery Alimentary Tract (pres. 2000), Halsted Soc. (pres. 2000). Episcopalian. Avocations: hiking, reading, skiing, travel. Office: U Wis H4/710 Clin Sci Ctr 600 Highland Ave Madison WI 53792-3284

RILEY, LAURA E., obstetrician, gynecologist; MD, U. Pitts. Sch. Medicine. Cert. maternal & fetal medicine Am. Bd. Obstetrics & Gynecology. Resident U. Pitts. Med. Ctr.; dir. labor, delivery & infectious disease Mass. Gen. Hosp. Spokeswoman Soc. for Maternal Fetal Medicine. Office: Mass General Hospital Vincent OB/GYN Service 55 Fruit St YAW 4 Boston MA 02114 Office Phone: 617-724-2229. Office Fax: 617-724-3498.

RILEY, WILLIAM JOHN, neurologist; b. Seattle, Oct. 24, 1930; s. William John and Virginia (McCarthy) R.; m. Joan Marie Weismann, 1956 (div. 1976); children: Sean, Kevan, Megan, Janeen, Michael; m. Margit Mary Winstrom, 1976; children: Britta, Shane, Timothy. MS in Anatomy, U. Chgo., 1958, MD, 1960; PhD, U. Minn., 1965. Intern Mpls. Gen. Hosp., 1961-62; resident U. Minn. Hosps., 1962-65; asst. chief neurology Mpls. Gen. Hosp., 1965-69; chief neurology St. Luke's Episcopal Hosp., Houston, 1970-85; pres., CEO Tex. Neurol. Clinic Assn., Houston, 1969—. Staff sgt. USAF, 1951-55. Recipient Disting. Tchg. award Minn. Med. Found., Mpls., 1969. Fellow: ACP, Tex. Neurol. Soc. (pres. 2002—, Lifetime Achievement award 2005), Am. Acad. Neurology; mem.: Alpha Omega Alpha, Tex. Med. Assn. (pres. 9th dist. 1991), Sigma Xi. Roman Catholic. Avocation: ranching. Office: Tex Neurological Clinic Assn 4126 SW Freeway # 1130 Houston TX 77027-7306 Office Phone: 713-621-9291. Personal E-mail: wjrileymd@aol.com.

RILLING, DAVID CARL, surgeon; b. Phila., Oct. 10, 1940; s. Carl Adam and Elizabeth Barbara (Young) R.; m. Karina Sturman, Mar. 25, 1972; children: Jonathan David, Alexander Valentine, Claudia Carla. BS with honors in Biology, Dickinson Coll., Carlisle, pa., 1962; MD, Hahnemann U., 1966. Diplomate Am. Bd. Surgery. Intern Hosp. of U. Pa., Phila., 1966-67; resident Abington (Pa.) Meml. Hosp., 1967-68, 70-73; surgeon Pennridge Surg Assocs., Sellersville, Pa., 1973—.

Active staff Grand View Hosp., Sellersville, Pa., chmn. dept. surgery, 1985-89, pres. med. staff, 1995. Lt. col. U.S. Army, 1968-70, Vietnam, USARMC. Decorated Bronze Star medal, Nat. Def. Svc. medal, Vietnam Svc. medal. Fellow Am. Coll. Surgeons; mem. AMA, Soc. Clin. Vascular Surgery, Pa. Med. Soc., Bucks County Med. Soc., Vietnam Vascular Registry. Achievements include one of the first surgeons to successfully re-attach a completely severed upper arm in 1974. Avocations: paleontology, tennis, skiing. Office: Pennridge Surg Assocs 915 Lawn Ave Sellersville PA 18960-1571 Office Phone: 215-257-3697.

RIM, HAN-JONG, medical educator; b. Seoul, Republic of Korea, Dec. 25, 1931; MD, Seoul Nat. U., 1957, PhD, 1963. Prof. Coll. Medicine Korea U., 1973—97, prof. emeritus, 1997—. Contbr. articles to profl. publs. Recipient Civil Order merit. Home: 1145 Hwagok 6 Dong Gangseo-Gu 102-1301 Ujangsan Lotte Castle Apt Seoul 157-734 Republic of Korea Business E-Mail: hjrim@korea.ac.kr.

RÍMAN, JOSEF, biology professor; b. Horni Suchá, Karviná, Czechoslovakia, Jan. 30, 1925; s. Alois and Hilda (Glaserová) Říman; m. Věra Tomková, July 16, 1950. MD, Charles U., Prague, Czechoslovakia, 1950; PhD, Czechoslovak Acad Sci., Prague, 1955, DSc in Chemistry, 1966; DSc in Biology (hon.), J.E. Purkyně U., Brno, Czechoslovakia, 1987. Rsch. physician 1st Clinic Pediatrics Charles U., Prague, 1950-51, prof. med. faculty, 1967-72; sr. scientist Inst. Organic Chemistry Czechoslovak Acad. Sci., Prague, 1951-74, founder, dir. Inst. Molecular Genetics, 1976—91, sci. sec., 1978-81, v.p., 1981-86, pres., 1986-90; vis. prof. Duke U., Durham, NC, 1968; acad. rep. UNESCO, 1980-86; Czechoslovak nat. rep. Internat. Coun. Sci. Unions, 1982-84. Dep. Ho. Nations Fed. Assembly, Prague, 1986—89; chmn. commn. INTERKOSMOS, 1986—90; founder Czechosclovak Biochemistry Retroviruses Inst. Molecular Genetics, Prague; participant UNESCO Symposium Sci. and Culture 21st Century, Vancouver, Canada, 1989. Mem. editl. bd. Neoplasma Slovak Acad. Scis., 1967, Acta Virologica, 1970, Biologica, 1982, Cancer Biochemistry and Biophysics, 1985; chmn., chief editor: Czechoslovak Encyclopaedia, 1986—90; contbr. articles to profl. jours. Recipient State prize, Govt. of Czechoslovakia, 1969, 1977, J. E. Purkeyne medal, 1979, Order of Labor, 1983, J. E. Purkyne Silver medal, Czechoslovak Med. Soc., 1986, Gold medal, Slovak Acad. Sci., 1989, State prize, USSR, 1978, Gold G. Dimitrov medal, Govt. of Bulgaria, 1986, Gold Einstein-Russel Pugwash medal, Pugwash Conf., 1987, Hippocrates medal, Kyoto U. Med. Sch., 1988, J. E. Fogarty medal, NIH, 1988, Gold medal, Nagoya U. Med. Sch., 1990, Kunio Yagi Gold Meml. medal, 1990. Fellow: Indian Nat. Sci. Acad. (fgn.); mem.: Academician, Ctrl. European Acad. Sci., Art and Letters (Paris) (v.p. 2009), G. W. Liebniz Soc., German Soc. Biol. Chemistry (fgn.), Czechoslovak Soc. Immunology (hon.), Hungarian Acad. Sci. (hon.), Slovak Soc. Biochemistry (hon.), Bulgarian Acad. Sci. (fgn.), German Acad. Scis. (fgn.), Czechoslovak Acad. Sci. (chief editor Folia Biologica 1975, G. J. Mendel Gold plaque 1975, Gold pin G. W. Leibniz 2005, medal of Honor, numerous others), Russian Acad. Sci. (fgn., M. L. Lomonosov Gold medal 1987). Avocation: history of science. Office: Acad Sci Inst Molecular Genetics Fleming Square 2 166 37 Prague Czech Republic Office Phone: 420 2 3333 09 71. E-mail: riman@img.cas.cz.

RIMEL, REBECCA WEBSTER, foundation administrator; b. 1951; BS, U. Va., 1973; MBA, James Madison U., 1983. Head nurse, emergency dept. U. Va. Hosp., Charlottesville, 1973-74, coord. med. out-patient dept., 1974-75, nurse practitioner dept. neurosurgery, 1975-77, instr. in neurosurgery, 1975-80, asst. prof., 1981-83; program mgr. health Pew Charitable Trusts, Phila., 1983-84; asst. v.p. Glenmede Trust Co., Pew Charitable Trusts, Phila., 1984-85; v.p. for programs Pew Charitable Trusts, Phila., 1985-88, exec. dir., 1988-94, pres., CEO, 1994—. Mem. Coun. on Founds., Washington; prin. investigator dept. neurosurgery U. Va., 1981—83; adv. com. Boxing U.S. Olympics, 1983—86; adv. coun. Nat. Inst. of Neurol. Disorders and Strokes, 1988—91, bd. dirs., Thomas Jefferson Meml. Found., Deutsche Banc Flag Investors Fund, VIASYS Healthcare Inc., 2007—, CardioNet, Inc., 2009—. Contbr. chpts. in books, articles and abstracts to profl. jours. Recipient Disting. Nursing Alumni award, U. Va., 1988; fellow Kellogg Nat. fellow, 1992. Mem.: APHA, ANA, Va. State Nurses Assn. (membership and credentials com. 1982—86), Emergency Dept. Nurses Assn., Am. Assn. Neurosurg. Nurses, Am. Acad. Nursing. Address: The Pew Charitable Trusts 2005 Market St Ste 1700 Philadelphia PA 19103-7017

RIMER, BARBARA K., dean, healthcare educator; b. Wilkes Barre, Pa., Jan. 14, 1949; BA in English, U. Mich., 1970, MPH in Med. Care Adminstrn. and Health Edn., 1973; PhD in Health Edn., Johns Hopkins Sch. of Hygiene and Public Health, 1981. Instr. Wayne State U. Sch. Medicine, Detroit, 1973-75; program dir. Nat. Cancer Inst., Bethesda, Md., 1975-77; intervention coord. Johns Hopkins Oncology Ctr., Balt., 1977-79; rsch. assoc. Johns Hopkins Sch. Hygiene and Public Health, Balt., 1977-79; sr. health educator Fox Chase Cancer Ctr., Phila., 1981-87, dir. health comms. rsch., 1981-87, dir. behavioral rsch., 1987-91, dir. population sci. for behavioral rsch., 1990-91; dir. cancer prevention, detection and ctrl. rsch. Duke Comprehensive Cancer Ctr., Durham, NC, 1991-97; sr. fellow Aging Ctr. Duke U. Med. Ctr., Durham, NC, 1991-97, assoc. prof. in cmty. and family medicine, 1991-93, prof. cmty. and family medicine, 1993-97; acting dep. dir. Duke Comprehensive Cancer Ctr., Durham, NC, 1995-96; dir. cancer ctrl. and population scis. Nat. Cancer Inst., Rockville, Md., 1997—2002; dep. dir. population scis. Lineberger Cancer Ctr. University of North Carolina, Chapel Hill, 2003—05, alumni disting. prof. Dept. Health Behavior & Health Edn., 2003—, dean Sch. Pub. Health, 2005—. Adj. assoc. prof. dept. health behavior and health edn. U. N.C. Sch. of Public Health, Chapel Hill, NC, 1992-97; adj. mem. Fox Chase Cancer Ctr., Phila., 1992-97; preceptor, lectr. Temple U., 1983-91; guest lectr. Duke U. Med. Ctr., 1991-97, U. N.C. Sch. Public Health, 1991-93; Judith P. Schlager vis. prof. Dana-Farber Cancer Inst., 1995; disting. vis. lectr. Harvard U., 1998; mem. institutional review bd. Fox Chase Cancer Ctr., 1983-88, vice chair, 1988-91; proposal review, site visitor Nat. Cancer Inst., 1985-95; chairperson tech. advisory com. Am. Lung Assn., 1987; external advisory com. Vermont Regional Cancer Ctr., 1988-89; advisory com. Brown U., U. R.I. Cancer Prevention Rsch. unit, 1988-95; mem. Am. Assn. Retired Persons task force on smoking, 1989-91, Health Promotion adv. bd. Wesley Found., 1990-91, program com. annual mtg. Am. Soc. Preventive Oncology, 1990-93, chair, 1993 mtg., expert adv. com. AMC Cancer Rsch. Ctr./Ctrs. for Disease Ctrl. Coop. Agreement, 1991, adult edn. subcom. and tobacco materials review group Am. Cancer Soc., 1991; mem. Nat. Task Force on Breast Cancer Ctrl. Am. Cancer Soc., 1992, chair Nat. and State (NC) Task Force on Breast Cancer Ctrl., 1992; mem. Pub. Edn. subcom. on Adult Edn. Am. Cancer Soc., 1992; mem. adv. bd. Office of Cancer Comms., NCI, 1992; mem. Clin. Cancer com. Duke U. Med. Ctr., 1992-95; mem. Cancer Ctrs.' Support com. NCI, 1993-94, Recruitment and Adherence com. Office of Women's Health NIH, 1993, Report com. Internat. Workshop on Screening for breast cancer NCI, 1993, Detection and Treatment subcom. on Breast Cancer Am. Cancer Soc., 1993, 94, Nominating com. Soc. Behavioral Medicine, 1993-96, adv. com. on cancer coordination and ctrl. State of NC, 1993-97; invited participant and com. chair Frontiers of Behavioral Medicine mtg., Chantilly, Va., 1993; invited co-chair Sec. Shalala's Mtg. to develop nat. strategic plan for breast cancer, Bethesda, Md., 1993; chair, mem. Nat. Cancer Adv. Bd. (presdl. appointment), 1994-97; bd. dirs. Am. Family Life Assurance Corp., 1995—; fellowship selection com. Am. Assn. Cancer Rsch., 1996; mem. exec. com. Acad. Behavioral Medicine Rsch., 1998, Charles S. Mott Selection com. of Gen. Motors Cancer Rsch. Found., 1999, Inst. Medicine com. effective health comm. and behavior change strategies for diverse populations, 2000. Editor: special cancer issue Health Education Research, 1998-89; editl. bd. Health Education Quarterly, 1985-87, guest editl. bd. 1983; editl. bd. Jour. of Compliance in Health Care, 1989-90, Health Edn. Rsch., 1990-98, Cancer Prevention, Epidemiology and Biomarkers, 1990—, Patient Edn. and Counseling, 1994—, Breast Diseases, 1998—, Cancer Causes and Control, 1998—, Effective Clin. Practice, 2000—; assoc. editor: Preventive Medicine, 1990—; reviewer Am. Jour. Preventive Medicine, Am. Jour. Public Health, Annals of Internal Medicine, Health Edn. Quarterly, Health Services Research, Jour. of Am. Med. Assn., Jour. Nat. Cancer Inst., Milbank Quarterly, Women's Health, 1986—; contbr. numerous articles, papers to profl. pubs. Fellow Johns Hopkins Sch. of Hygiene and Public Health, 1979-81, Soc. of Behavioral Medicine, 1997; recipient Mayhew Derryberry award Am. Public Health Assn., 1992, Best Visual Presentation of Session award Soc. of Behavioral Medicine, San Diego, 1995, Citation award Soc. Behavioral Medicine, 1996, Disting. Achievement award Am. Soc. Preventive Oncology, 1997, Herbert J. Block Leadership award Ohio State U., 1997, John P. McGovern award in Health Promotion U. Tex. Sch. Public Health, 1999. Mem.: Inst. Medicine. Office: Sch Public Health Univ North Carolina 170 Rosenau Hall Campus Box 7400 Chapel Hill NC 27599-7400 Office Phone: 919-966-3215. Office Fax: 919-966-7678. E-mail: brimer@unc.edu. *

RIMM, ERIC B., medical educator, researcher; b. Buffalo; BS, U. Wis., Madison, 1985; DSc in Epidemiology, Harvard Sch. Pub. Health, Boston, 1991. Rsch. asst. dept. preventive medicine U. Wis. Med. Sch., Madison, 1985—86; tchg. fellow epidemiology Harvard Sch. Pub. Health, 1988—91, rsch. fellow nutrition & epidemiology, 0191—1992, rsch. asoc. epidemiology, 1992—94, asst. prof. epidemiology & nutrition, 1994—98, assoc. prof. epidemiology & nutrition, 1998—; asst. prof. medicine Channing Lab., Harvard Med. Sch., 1996—2005, assoc. prof. medicine, 2005—, dir. program cardiovasc. epidemiology, 2007—. Mem. spl. rev. bd., epidemiology unit Can. Nat. Cancer Inst., Toronto, 1996; mem. exec. com. Boston Obesity Nutrition Rsc.h Ctr., 2002; mem. USDA 2010 Dietary Guidelines Adv. Com., 2008—. Tech. editor New Eng. Jour. Medicine, 1996—2000, assoc. editor Am. Jour. Epidemiology, 1998—, Obesity Rsch., 2002—05, Am. Jour. Clin. Nutrition, 2007—, guest editor Circulation, 2006—; contbr. articles to profl. jours. Recipient Nat. Rsch. Svc. award, Nat. Inst. Environ. Health Scis., 1986—91. Mem.: Am. Soc. Nutrition, N.Am. Assn. Study of Obesity, Soc. Epidemiologic Rsch. (Student Workshop award 1989), Am. Heart Assn. Office: Harvard Sch Pub Health 655 Huntington Ave Bldg II Rm 373a Boston MA 02115 Office Phone: 617-432-1843. Business E-Mail: eric.rimm@channing.harvard.edu, erimm@hsph.harvard.edu. *

RIMOIN, DAVID LAWRENCE, medical geneticist; b. Montreal, Nov. 9, 1936; s. Michael and Fay (Lecker) Rimoin; m. Mary Ann Singleton, 1962 (div. 1979); 1 child, Anne; m. Ann Piilani Garber, July 27, 1980; children: Michael, Lauren. BSc, McGill U., Montreal, 1957, MSc, MD, CM, 1961; PhD, Johns Hopkins U., 1967; LHD (hon.), Finch U., 1997. Asst. prof. medicine, pediat. Washington U., St. Louis, 1967—70; assoc. prof. UCLA, 1970—73, prof., 1973—, chief med. genetics, Harbor-UCLA Med. Ctr., 1970—86; chair dept. pediat., dir. Med. Genetics and Birth Defects Ctr. Cedars-Sinai Med. Ctr., LA, 1986—2004, Steven Spielberg chair, 1989—, dir. Med. Genetics Inst., 2004—. Chmn. coun. Med. Genetics Orgn., 1993. Co-editor: Emory and Rimoin's Principles and Practice of Medical Genetics, 1983, 5th edit., 2007; contbr. chapters to books, articles to profl. jours. Recipient E. Mead Johnson award, Am. Acad. Pediat., 1976, Col. Harland Saunders award, March of Dimes, 1997, Pioneer in Medicine award, Cedars Sinai Med. Ctr., 2001, Extraordinary Merit award, UCLA Med. Alumni Assn., 2005, Legends Harbor award, LA Biomed. Found., 2006, Leadership award, Am. Soc. Human Genetics, 2006, Lifetime Achievement award, Coll. Med. Genetics, 2010. Fellow: Am. Coll. Med. Genetics (pres. 1991—96, bd. dirs. 1996—2000), AAAS, ACP; mem.: Inst. of Medicine, Assn. Am. Physicians, Am. Pediat. Soc., Am. Soc. Human Genetics (pres. 1984, Leadership award 2006), Am. Bd. Med. Genetics (pres. 1979—83), Western Soc. Pediat. Rsch. (pres. 1995, Ross Outstanding Young Investigator award 1976), Western Soc. Clin. Rsch. (pres. 1978), Am. Fedn. Clin. Rsch. (sec.-treas. 1972—75), Am. Coll. Med. Genetics Found. (pres. 1999—2002, bd. dirs. 2002—), Johns Hopkins Soc. Scholars. Office: Cedars Sinai Med Ctr 8700 Beverly Blvd Los Angeles CA 90048-1865 Office Phone: 310-423-4461. Business E-Mail: david.rimoin@cshs.org.

RIMPLER, HORST, biology educator; b. Berlin, Sept. 22, 1935; s. Carl-Friedrich and Margarete (Jurk) R.; m. Brigitte Kirchner, Aug. 17, 1962; children: Stephan, Andreas. Grad., Freie Univ., Berlin, 1960, PhD, 1964, Habilitation, 1969. Prof. biology Freie Univ., Berlin, 1971-76; prof. Inst. Pharm. Biology, U. Freiburg (Germany), 1976-2000, prof. emeritus Inst. Pharm. Biology, 2000—. Co-author: Pharmazeutische Biologie, 2009; editor: Biogene Arzneistoffe, 1999; co-editor: Hagers Handbuch der Pharmazeutischen Praxis, 1992-94; contbr. articles to profl. jours. Mem. Soc. for Medicinal Plant Rsch. Home: Burgunder Str 32 D 79104 Freiburg Germany

RINALDI, PETER, dental educator; Lectr.; clin. instr. Las Vegas Inst., Univ. Ky.; clin. dir. aesthetic advantage Hands-on continuums NYU, Baylor Coll of Dentistry, Palm Beach CC, Eastman Dental Sch., London; dentist Washington Ctr. for Dentistry. Advisor Brasseler Dental, Kerr Dental, Ivoclar Dental, 3M Dental, Zenith Dental. Named one of Top Dentists, Consumer's Coun. of America. Fellow: Internat. Congress of Osseous Integration; mem.: Am. Acad. of Cosmetic Dentistry. Office: Washington Center For Dentistry 8th Fl 1430 K St NW Washington DC 20005 Office Phone: 202-223-6630.

RINALDI, RENEE ZAIRA, physician; b. NYC, Dec. 10, 1949; d. John James and Concetta Rinaldi; m. Kenneth Robert Ballard, June 16, 1977; children: Claudia Michele, Celeste Noelle, Christopher Charles. BA, Barnard Coll., Columbia U., 1971; EdM, Harvard U., 1973; MD, NY Med. Coll., 1976. Diplomate Am. Bd. Internal Medicine and Rheumatology. Intern Met. Hosp., NYC, 1976—77; resident in medicine San Fernando program UCLA, Sepulveda Campus, 1977—79; staff internist Olive View Hosp., Van Nuys, Calif., 1979—80; fellow rheumatology UCLA, 1980—82; practice medicine specializing in rheumatology LA, 1983—; asst. clin. prof. medicine ULCA, 1983—; clin. chief rheumatology Cedars Sinai Med. Ctr., LA, 1996—2000. Jane Wyman Clin. fellow, 1981. Mem. So. Calif. Rheumatology Soc., LA County Women's Med. Assn., Am. Coll. Rheumatology Office: 150 N Robertson Blvd Ste 224 Beverly Hills CA 90211 Office Phone: 310-659-5905.

RINDFLEISCH, J. ADAM, medical educator; b. Arco, Idaho, June 19, 1971; BA, Coll. Idaho, 1993; MD, Johns Hopkins U., 2000. Asst. prof. U. Wis., 2006—. Mem.: Am. Bd. Holistic Integrative Medicine, Am. Acad. Family Physicians. Avocations: gardening, travel, writing. Office: 5618 Odana Rd Madison WI 53719 Office Fax: 608-274-0310. Personal E-mail: adamrindfleisch@gmail.com.

RINDONE, JOSEPH PATRICK, clinical pharmacist, educator; b. Santa Fe, Oct. 4, 1954; s. Guido Salvatore and Elizabeth Ann (Murphy) R.; m. Diane Marie Rollins, June 23, 1991; children: Jacqueline, Alexandra. BS, U. Nebr., 1977; PharmD, Creighton U., 1978. Lic. pharmacist, Nebr., Calif. Staff pharmacist Bergan Mercy Hosp., Omaha, 1978, Phoenix (Ariz.) VA Med. Ctr., 1978-81, clin. resident, 1981; clin. pharmacist Tucson VA Med. Ctr., 1982-93; assoc. prof. U. Ariz., Tucson, 1982—; clin. pharmacist Prescott (Ariz.) VA Med. Ctr., 1993—, rsch. coord., 1994—. Author: Therapeutic Monitoring of Antibiotics, 1991; contbr. articles to Arch. Internal Medicine, Pharmacotherapy, Clin. Therapeutics, Am. Jour. Cardiology, Am. Jour. Therapeutics, Chest, West Jour. Medicine, Am. Jour. Health Sys. Pharm., Federal Practioner, Jour. AMA, Jour. Pharm. Practice, British Jour. Cli9n. Pharm. Regents scholar U. Nebr., 1976. Mem.: Clin. Pharm Therapy. Avocations: sports, photography, bridge, astronomy. E-mail: JosephRindone@med.va.gov.

RING, ALICE RUTH BISHOP, retired preventive medicine physician; b. Ft. Collins, Colo., Oct. 11, 1931; d. Ernest Otto and Mary Frances Bishop; m. Wallace Harold Ring, 1956 (div. 1969); children: Rebecca, Eric, Mark; m. Robert Charles Diefenbach, Sept. 10, 1977. BS, Colo. State U., 1953; MD, U. Colo., 1956; MPH, U. Calif., Berkeley, 1971. Diplomate Am. Bd. Preventive Medicine. Physician cons. Utah State Divsn. Health, Salt Lake City, 1960—65; med. dir., project head start Salt Lake City Cmty. Action Program, 1965—70; resident Utah State Divsn. Health, 1969—71; asst. assoc. regional health dir. USPHS, San Francisco, 1971—75, med. cons. Atlanta, 1975—77, dir. primary care, 1977—84; dir. divsn. diabetes control Ctrs. Disease Control, Atlanta, 1984—88; dir. WHO Collabor Ctr., Atlanta, 1986—91; dir. preventive medicine residency Ctrs. Disease Control, Atlanta, 1988—93; exec. dir. Am. Bd. Preventive Medicine, 1993—98. Trustee Am. Bd. Preventive Medicine, 1990—92; lectr. Emory U. Sch. Pub. Health, 1988—94; bd. dirs. Redwood Coast Med. Svcs., v.p., 1994—2004; mem. adv. com. Shamli Hospice, Gualala, Calif.; mem. adv. coun. Sonoma County Area Agy. on Aging, Santa Rosa, Calif., 2001—07, sec., 2004—06, v.p., 2006—07; bd. dirs. Alliance Rural Cmty. Health, Calif., 2002—04. Co-author: Clinical Diabetes, 1991; author: History of the American Board of Preventive Medicine, 2002. Bd. dirs. Diabetes Assn. Atlanta, 1985—90. Recipient Disting. Svc. award, Am. Bd. Med. Splties, 2004. Fellow: Am. Coll. Preventive Medicine (bd. dirs. 1990—94, Spl. Recognition award 1998); mem.: AMA (grad. med. edn. adv. com. 1993—97), Steering Com. Environ. Commons, Am. Bd. Med. Specialists (Disting. Svc. award 2004), Am. Acad. Pediat., Assn. Tchrs. Preventive Medicine. Office: PO Box 364 Gualala CA 95445-0364 Business E-Mail: ard@mcn.org.

RING, ALVIN MANUEL, pathologist, educator; s. Julius and Helen (Krolik) R.; m. Cynthia Joan Jacobson, Sept. 29, 1963; children—Jeffrey, Melinda, Heather. BS, Wayne State U., 1954; MD, U. Mich., 1958. Intern Mt. Carmel Hosp., Detroit, 1958-59; resident in pathology Michael Reese Hosp., Chgo., 1960-62; asst. pathologist Kings County Hosp., Bklyn., 1962-63; assoc. pathologist El Camino Hosp., Mountain View, Calif., 1963-65; chief pathologist, dir. labs. St. Elizabeth's Hosp., Chgo., 1965-72, Holy Cross Hosp., Chgo., 1972-87, Silver Cross Hosp., Joliet, Ill., 1990—. Instr. SUNY, 1962-63, Stanford U., 1963-65; asst. prof. pathology U. Ill., Chgo., 1966-69, assoc. prof., 1969-78, prof., 1978—; adj. clin. prof. No. Ill. U., 1981-87; adj. prof. med. edn. U. Ill. Coll. Medicine, 1988—; chmn. histotech. Nat. Accrediting Agy. for Clin. Lab Scis., 1977-81; mem. spl. adv. com. Health Manpower, 1966-71; pres. Spear Computer Users Group, 1981-82; mem. adv. com. Mid-Am. chpt. ARC, 1979-85; pres. Pathology and Lab Cons., Inc., 1985—; adj. prof., med. dir. Med. Tech., Moraine Valley CC, 1994—; originator, coord. pathology, med. decision-making courses Nat. Ctr. for Advanced Med. Edn., 1981—, others; co-coord. computer courses Midwest Clin. Conf., 2000—; pathology adv. bd., Genentech, 2007-, Clarient, 2010-. Author: Laboratory Correlation Manual, 1968, 82, 86, Laboratory Assistant Examination Review Book, 1971, Review Book in Pathology, Anatomic, 1986, Review Book in Pathology, Clinical, 1986; mem. editorial bd. Lab. Medicine, 1975-87; contbr. articles to med.

jours. Fellow: Am. Soc. Clin. Pathology, Coll. Am. Pathology (insp. 1973—, ins. com. 2002—06, membership com. 2005—06, PathPac bd. dirs. 2007—, mem. House of Delegates 2007—, found. bd. mem. 2010—, adv. com. on health care delivery); mem.: AMA, Assn. Brain Tumor Rsch. (cons.), Am. Assn. Blood Banks, Chgo. Pathol. Soc. (censor 1980—88, exec. com. 1985—89, program com. 1987—), Ill. Pathol. Soc. (trustee 1997—), Chgo. Med. Soc. (alt. councilor 1980—85), Ill. Med. Soc., Exec. Svc. Corps (exec. cons. 1988—), Phi Lambda Kappa (chpt. pres.). Home: 100 Graymoor Ln Olympia Fields IL 60461-1213 Office: Silver Cross Hosp 1200 Maple Rd Joliet IL 60432-1497

RING, BONNIE, psychologist, consultant, episcopal priest; b. NYC, Apr. 22, 1940; Attended, Vassar Coll., 1957—59; BA, NYU, 1962; EdM, Boston U., 1964, EdD, 1972. Lic. psychologist Calif., 1974. Tchg. fellow Boston U. Sch. Mgmt.; fellow Ctr. Applied Behavioral Scis., Boston U., 1963—65; tng. specialist Econ. & Youth Opportunities Program, LA, 1966; rsch. asst. UCLA, 1966—67; tng. assoc., coord. intern program U. Calif., Statewise Ext., 1967—68; counseling psychologist U. Calif., Santa Cruz, 1969—73, assoc. dir. clin. svcs. Irvine, 1973—75; assoc. dean Calif. Coll. Podiatr. Medicine, San Francisco, 1975—77; pres. Bonnie Ring, EdD, A Psychol. Corp., San Francisco, 1977—86; psychologist pvt. practice, 1986—; mem. tng. staff Exec. Effectiveness Seminar Am. Mgmt. Assn., 1978—82; host daily psychol. call-in talk show Sta. KSFO, San Francisco, 1980—81; cons. AT & T Western Region, 1982—86. Ordained Episcopal priest, 1992; dir. elder ministry St. Johns Episcopal Ch., Oakland, 2004—05. Mem.: Spiritual Dirs. Internat., Eye Movement Desensitization & Regroceesing Internat. Assn., Nat. Register Health Svc. Providers, Calif. Psychol. Assn., Pi Lambda Theta. Democrat. Office: 2305 Asbby Ave Berkeley CA 94705 Office Phone: 650-728-0555.

RING, TIMOTHY MICHAEL, pharmaceutical executive; b. Buffalo, Sept. 30, 1957; s. Roger Michael and Leone Ann (Reitmeier) R.; m. Kathryn L. Gleason; 4 Children. BS in Indsl. Labor Relations, Cornell Univ., 1979. Coll. grad. in tng. GM, Detroit, 1979-80, labor relations rep., 1980, salaried personnel rep., 1980-81, sr. salaried personnel rep., 1981-82, sr. labor relations rep., 1982-83; div. personnel mgr. Abbott Laboratory, Inc., North Chicago, Ill., 1983-84, regional personnel mgr., 1984-86, dir. personnel Pacific, Asian and African ters., 1986-87, dir. personnel Pacific, Asian, African and European ters., 1987—92; corp. v.p., human resources CR Bard, Inc., NJ, 1992—93, group v.p.-internat., 1993—97, group pres.-coronary vascular products, 1997—99, group pres.-electrophysiology, peripheral vascular products, 1999—2003, chmn, CEO, 2003—. Mem. Delta Upsilon. Republican. Roman Catholic. Avocations: real estate investments, tennis, golf, sailing. Office: CR Bard 730 Central Ave Murray Hill NJ 07974 Office Phone: 908-277-8000. *

RING, W(ILLIAM) STEVES, thoracic and cardiovascular surgeon; b. Patterson, NJ, Aug. 12, 1945; s. William Steves and Nancy J. (Gettings) R.; m. Denise B. Passmore, 1969; children: William Steves III, Ashley Brinton. BA, Brown U., 1967, MMS, 1969; MD, Harvard U., 1971. Diplomate Am. Bd. Surgery, 2001, Am. Bd. Thoracic Surgery, 2004; cert. Nat. Bd. Med. Examiners, 1972, Tex. State Bd. Med. Examiners. Intern, then resident in surgery, fellow Duke U., Durham, NC, 1971-73, 75-77, resident in surgery, fellow, 1977-82; instr. surgery U. Minn., Mpls., 1983-85, asst. prof., 1985-87, dir. cardiac transplantation, 1984-87; prof., chmn. divsn. thoracic surgery U. Tex. Southwestern Med. Ctr., Dallas, 1988—2000, Frank M. Ryburn, Jr. disting. chair cardiothoracic surgery, 1989—, chmn. dept. cardiovascular thoracic surgery, 2000—; chief thoracic and cardiovascular surgery Parkland Meml. Hosp., Dallas, 1988—, Zale Lipshy Univ. Hosp., Dallas, 1988—; dir. cardiac transplantation St. Paul Med. Ctr., Dallas, 1988—. William D. Seybold lectr. in surgery U. Tex. Southwestern Med. Ctr., 1988, presenter, president's lecture series, 2007. Mem. editl. bd. Clin. Transplantation; contbr. articles to profl. jours. Mem. exec. com. Dallas affiliate Am. Heart Assn., 1988—, pres., 1992-93; mem. exec. com. S.W. Organ Bank, 1988—. Maj. USAF, 1973-75. Recipient Nat. Rsch. Svc. award NIH, 1978-79, Gladys Faschena award Dallas affiliate Am. Heart Assn., 1990. Fellow ACS, Am. Coll. Cardiology, Am. Coll. Chest Physicians; mem. Am. Soc. Transplant Surgeons (mem. membership com. 1991—), Internat. Soc. Heart and Lung Transplantation, Am. Assn. Thoracic Surgery, Transplant Soc, World Soc. Pediatric and Congenital Heart Surgery, Southern Thoracic Surg. Assn. (councilor 2004, Kent Trinkle edn. lectr. 2002) Home: 3501 Euclid Ave Dallas TX 75205-3213 Office: U Tex Southwestern Med Ctr 5323 Harry Hines Blvd Dallas TX 75390-7208

RINGER, STEVEN ALAN, physician; b. Hingham, Mass., Mar. 24, 1952; MD, CWRU, PhD, 1982. Chief newbron medicine Brigham and Women's Hosp., 1988—. Office: 75 Francis St Boston MA 02115 Business E-Mail: sringer@partners.org.

RINK, LAWRENCE DONALD, cardiologist; b. Indpls., Oct. 14, 1940; s. Joe Donald and Mary Ellen (Rand) R.; m. Eleanor Jane Zimmerly, Aug. 10, 1963; children: Scott, Virginia. BS, DePauw U., 1962; MD, Ind. U., 1966. Diplomate Am. Bd. Internal Medicine, Am. Bd. Cardiology, Critical Care Medicine. Clin. asst. prof. Ind. U. Med. Sch., Indpls., 1973-79, clin. assoc. prof., 1979-85, clin. prof. medicine, 1985—; cardiologist IMA, Inc., Bloomington, Ind., 1974—; med. dir. Ind. U. Human Performance Lab., 1994—; dir. cardiac rehab. Bloomington Hosp., 1976—, dir. cardiology, 1983—; CEO, chmn. bd. dirs. IMA Inc., 1995—. Physician Ind. U. Basketball Team, 1979—; dir. med. edn. Bloomington Hosp., 1976—; med. dir. Track and Field Pan Am. Games, 1987; U.S. Olympic Physician Olympic Sports Festival, 1989, World Univ. Games, 1990, Olympic Games, Barcelona, 1992, World Univ. Games, Daegu, Korea, 1993, Fukuoka, Japan, 1995, Korea, 1997, Majorca, Spain, 1999, Beijing, 2001, Korea, 2003, Innsbruck, 2005; N.Am. continent rep. Fed. Internat. Student Univ. Sports, pres., 2004—, pres. med. commn. Bd. dirs. J.O. Ritchie Soc., Ind. U. Med. Sch. Bd. dirs., dean's coun. Ind. U. Med. Sch., 1992—. Recipient Quality of Life award Major Bloomington, 1978; named Most Outstanding Flight Surgeon, USN, 1968, Most Outstanding Alumnus, Ind. U. Med. Sch., 1998. Fellow Am. Coll. Cardiology, Am. Heart Assn. (Corvitae award 2003), Am. Soc. Critical Care, Am. Coll. Sports Medicine; mem. AMA, Ind. U. Med. Alumnae Assn. (pres. 1986-87, exec. alumna coun.). Avocations: reading, writing, golf, tennis. Office: IMA Inc 550 Landmark Ave Bloomington IN 47403 E-mail: lrink@ima-md.com. *

RINK, THOMAS, nuclear medicine physician; b. Hanau, Hessen, Germany, May 20, 1963; s. Karl-Heinz and Gisela (Goebel) R. MD, U. Frankfurt, 1989. Physician in-tng. Nuc. Medicine Mcpl. Hosp., Hanau, affiliated to Johann-Wolfgang-Goethe-U., Frankfurt/Main, 1989—90; asst. physician Nuc. Medicine Mcpl. Hosp., Wiesbaden affiliated to Johannes-Gutenberg-U., Mainz, 1991—93; asst. physician surgery St. Vinzenz Hosp., Hanau, 1993—94; asst. physician nuc. medicine U. Frankfurt, 1995—96; chief dept. nuc. medicine Mcpl. Hosp., Hanau affiliated to Johann-Wolfgang-Goethe-U., Frankfurt/Main, 1996—. Contbr. articles to profl. jours. Mem. Soc. of Nuc. Medicine, European Assn. of Nuc. Medicine, Rotary Internat. Home: Röntgenstr 36 63454 Hanau Germany Office: Mcpl Hosp Dept Nuclear Med Leimenstr 20 D-63450 Hanau Germany Office Fax: 01149-6181-23368. Business E-Mail: rink@em.uni-frankfurt.de.

RINSCH, MARYANN ELIZABETH, occupational therapist; b. LA, Aug. 8, 1939; d. Harry William and Thora Analine (Langlie) Hitchcock; m. Charles Emil Rinsch, June 18, 1964; children: Christopher, Daniel, Carl. BS, U. Minn., 1961. Registered occupational therapist Calif., lic. Calif., 2003. Staff occupl. therapist Hastings State Hosp., Minn., 1961-62, Neuropsychiat. Inst., LA, 1962-64; staff and sr. occupl. therapist Calif. Children's Svcs., LA, 1964-66, head occupl. therapist, 1966-68; rschr. A. Jean Ayres, U. So. Calif., LA, 1968-69; pvt. practice neurodevel. and sensory integraton Tarzana, Calif., 1969-74; pediat. occupl. therapist neurodevel. & sensory integration St. Johns Hosp., Santa Monica, Calif., 1991-95; pvt. practice, cons. Santa Monica-Malibu Unified Sch. Dist., 1994-2001; pvt. practice, 2001—10. Mem. alliance bd. Natural History Mus., LA County, 1983-2009; cub scouts den mother Boy Souts Am., Sherman Oaks, Calif., 1986-88, advancement chair Boy Scout Troop 474, 1989-92; mem. Vol. League San Fernando Valley, Van Nuys, Calif., 1985-93; trustee Viewpoint Sch., Calabasas, Calif., 1987-90; bd. dirs. Valley Women's Ctr., 1990-91. Mem. Am. Occupl. Therapy Assn., Calif. Occupl. Therapy Assn. Personal E-mail: merinsch@yahoo.com.

RIORDAN, MICHAEL C., hospital administrator; b. NJ, 1959; BA in Liberal Arts and English, Columbia U., 1980, MA in Edn. and Psychology, 1981; M in Health Sys., Ga. Inst. Tech., 1986. Various positions Crawford Long Hosp., Atlanta, COO, sr. assoc. adminstr. Emory U. Hosp. Sys., Atlanta, 1995—2000; exec. v.p. and COO U. Chgo. Hospitals, 2000—01, pres. and CEO, 2001—06; pres., CEO Greenville Hosp. Sys., 2006—. With USMC, 1981—85. Office: Greenville Hosp Sys 701 Grove Rd Greenville SC 29605 *

RIOS-DALENZ, JAIME LUIS, pathologist, educator; b. Cochabamba, Bolivia, Nov. 13, 1933; s. Humberto Rios-Zambrana and Carmen H. Dalenz; m. Haydee M. Ismael, Apr. 18, 1960; children: Mauricio, Maria Eugenia. B of Humanities, La Salle Coll., La Paz, Bolivia, 1951; med. degree, San Simon U., Cochabamba, 1960. Cert. in anatomical pathology and clin. pathology Am. Bd. Pathology. Resident in pathol. anatomy Del Valle U., Cali, Colombia, 1960-61; resident in clin. pathology Ball Meml. Hosp., Muncie, Ind., 1961-64; resident in pathol. anatomy Temple U. Hosp., Phila., 1965-66; pathologist Hosp. # 1 CNS, La Paz, 1969-93, chief pathology dept., 1993-96; from asst. prof. pathology to assoc. prof. pathology San Andres U., La Paz, 1968-85, prof. pathology, 1985-87, prof. emeritus, 1989—, chief of dept. pathology, 1987-94. Dir. La Paz Cancer Registry, 1988—; pres. Bolivian Commn. on Smoking, La Paz, 1983-99; coord. Bolivian Network on Health Info., La Paz, 1988—2002; lectr. U. Liverpool, U.K. Editor: Cancer in La Paz, pathology textbook, Bdinion Archiving Medical History Salud Boliviana Sources; contbr. articles to sci. publs. Recipient Gold medal WHO, 1992, Profl. Merit award Bolivian Med. Assn., 1996. Mem. Bolivian divsn. Internat. Acad. Pathology (pres. 1986-10), Bolivian Acad. Medicine (pres. 1999—2002), Latin Am. Soc. Pathology (pres. 1979-81), Bolivian Med. Editors Assn. (pres. 1997—2002), Bolivian Chpt. Internat. Med. Geology Assn.(pres., 2009-10) Avocation: travel. Address: PO Box 490 La Paz Bolivia Home: Calle del Aviador # 100 La Paz Bolivia Office: Hosp Metodista Dept Pathology La Paz Bolivia

RIOUX, PIERRE AUGUST, psychiatrist; b. Hartford, Conn., Sept. 2, 1953; s. Berchmans and Mary (Sauter) R. BA, Concordia Coll., 1975; MD, U. N.D., 1981. Diplomate Am. Bd. Psychiatry and Neurology. Intern U. Mich., 1981-82, resident, 1982-85; asst. prof. dept. psychiatry Emory U., Atlanta, 1985-86; attending physician VA Med. Ctr., Atlanta, 1985-86; staff physician UniMed Med. Ctr., Minot, ND, 1986-87, med. dir. adult partial hospitalization program, 1988-98, dir. behavioral health svcs., 1990—2001; med. dir. North Ctrl. Human Svc. Ctr., Minot, 1987-98; med. dir. stress unit Austin Med. Ctr., 2001—; med. dir. behavioral health Mayo Health Sys., Austin, 2003—06, med. dir. dept. psychiatry and psychology, 2006—; instr. Mayo Med. Sch., 2003—. Cons. North Ctrl. Human Svc. Ctr., 1986—2001; mem. chem. dependency unit UniMed Med. Ctr, 1986—; mem. adv. bd. UniMed Med. Ctr., 1998—2001; clin. prof. neurosci. U. N.D. Sch. Medicine, 1986—96; mem. family practice residence adv. bd. com. U. N.D., 1987—95; physician advisor N.D. Health Care Rev., Inc., 1987—2001; dir. psychiat. svcs. Dakota Boys Ranch, Minot, 1990—94; med. dir. Rural Mental Health Consortium, 1999—2001; instr. Mayo Med. Sch., 2003—. Bd. Am. Coll. of Heraldry, 2003; comsumer rsch. coun. America's Top Psychiatrists, 2002—. Recipient Nat. Alliance for the Mentally Ill Exemplary Psychiatrist award, 1993, Top Psychiatrists in Am. award Consumers Rsch. Coun. Am., 2003. Fellow Am. Coll. Forensic Examiners (life); mem. AMA, Am. Psychiat. Assn. (pres. N.D. dist. br. 1993-96, dep. rep. area IV coun. 1993-98, mem. psychiat. svcs. achievement awards bd. 1996-97, chmn. 1998, fellowship award 1996, disting. fellowship award 2003), Assn. Am. Physicians and Surgeons, Am. Soc. Clin. Psychopharmacology, N.D. Psychiat. Assn. (dist. br. exec. coun. 1997-2001), N.D. Med. Assn. (mem. commn. on socio-econ. affairs 1997-2001), Internat. Soc. for Philos. Enquiry (pres.2002-05) Avocation: art. Office: PO Box 188 Austin MN 55912-0188

RIPA, RINALDO, endocrinologist, educator; s. Alfred Ripa and Mary Benvenuti; m. Anne Mary Belardinelli, May 27, 1967; children: Sara, Phillip, Mary Clair, Lucy. MD, Bologna U., Italy, 1959, degree in State Abilitation Med. Activity, 1960; degree in Med. Semeiology, Italian Ministry of U., Rome, 1968, degree in Med. Pathology, 1969, degree in Endocrinology, 1971. Sports medicine specialist Chieti U. Italy, 1974, specialist in cardiology U. Turin, 1961, specialistin endocrinology U. Florence Italy, 1963, specialist in geriatry & gerontology 1964, specialist in infectious diseases U. Modena Italy, 1965, specialist in isotopic techniques U. Bologna, 1967, specialist in internal medicine 1973, specialist in med. nephrology U. Parma Italy, 1971. Head internal medicine Civic Hosp. G. Marconi, Cesenatico, Forlì-Cesena, Italy, 1970—80, Hosp. S. Maria delle Croci, Ravenna, Italy, 1980—82, Casa di Cura Villa Maria, Rimini, Italy, 1982—; prof. gen. physiology U. Ferrara, Italy, 1968—69, prof. endocrinology, 1969—76. Med. cons. Casa di Cura S. Lorenzino, Cesena, Italy, 1982—94. Editor: (med. book) Renin-Angiotensin System (1st award, A. Azzi Ferrara Italy, 1968); contbr. articles to numerous sci. jours. Mem. Carim Fin. Bank, Rimini, 1989—; econ.-fin. expert Cassa Risparmio Rimini, 1989—2010. Master: European Inst. Oncology (Milan) (no-smoking expert, master 2001—10); fellow: AAAS; mem.: Rotary Club Internat. (Rimini) (pres. 1995—96). Achievements include research in hormonal laboratory techniques. Office: Casa Di Cura Villa Maria v Matteotti 24 Rimini 47921 Italy Personal E-mail: rinaldoripa@libero.it.

RIPLEY, DAVID L., physician, educator; b. Ky., Feb. 10, 1900; BA, Emory U., 1985; MD, Med. Coll. Ga., 1996. Med. dir. brain injury rsch. Shepherd Ctr., 2001—04, Craig Hosp., 2004—. Asst. prof. dept. rehab. medicine Emory U. Sch. Medicine, 2000—04; asst. prof. dept. phys. medicine and rehab. U. Colo. Sch. Medicine, 2004; med. dir. Rocky Mountain Regional Brain Injury Model Sys., 2004; bd. dirs. Brain Injury Assn. Colo., 2008. Recipient Silver award, Nat. Health Info. Awards, Herman J Flax Resident Edn. and Leadership award, Med. Coll. Va., Most Innovative Program award, Williamsburg Traumatic Brain Injury Conf. Fellow: Am. Acad. Phys. Medicine and Rehab. (Pres.'s Rsch. Citation); mem.: Colo. Med. Soc., Am. Congress Rehab. Medicine. Avocations: skiing, bicycling, music. Office: CNS Med Group 3425 S Clarkson Englewood CO 80113 Business E-Mail: dripley@craighospital.org.

RIPSIN, CYNTHIA MARIE, physician, director; b. Mpls., Mar. 27, 1956; MS, U. Minn., MPH, 1992; MD, Eastern Va. Sch. Medicine, 1997. Rsch. scientist dept. family medicine U. Minn., 1990—92; owner, sole propr. Boykins Family Practice, Va., 2001—07; asst. prof. family medicine U. Tex. Med. Br., 2007—10; assoc. dir. UTSW Austin Family Medicine Residency Program, 2010—. Adj. prof. Eastern Va. Med. Sch., 2003—07, mem., instl. rev. bd., com. protection human subjects rsch., 2005—06, Seton Family Hosp., 2010—; med. dir. 3-Share Ins. Option Small Employees, 2008—10. Finalist Jeremiah Stamler award, Am. Heart Assn., Sect. Cardiovasc. Epidemiology. Mem.: Soc. Tchr.'s Family Medicine, Am. Acad. Family Medicine. Avocation: woodworking. Office: 1313 Red River St Ste 100 Austin TX 78701 Business E-Mail: cmripsin@seton.org.

RISCH, NEIL J., geneticist, epidemiologist; b. LA, Feb. 25, 1951; s. Frank and Sonya Risch. BS in Math., Calif. Tech. Inst., Pasadena, 1972; MS in Math., U. Ill., Urbana, 1973; PhD in Biomathematics, UCLA, 1979; MA (hon.), Yale U., 1993. Tchg. asst. math. U. Ill., 1972—73, med. statistician Brentwood LA Vets. Adminstrn. Hosp., 1973—76; rsch. scientist dept. med. genetics NY State Psychiat. Inst., 1979—82; asst. prof. biostatistics Columbia U., NYC, 1981-84; asst. prof. biostatistics and genetics Yale U. Sch. Medicine, New Haven, 1984-87, assoc. prof., 1987-92, prof., 1992—94; prof. genetics Stanford U. Sch. Medicine, Calif., 1995—2004, prof. statistics, 1997—2004; prof. epidemiology and biostatistics, Lamond Family Found. disting. prof. human genetics U. Calif., San Francisco, 2005—. Contbr. articles to profl. jours. Recipient NIH Rsch. Career Devel. award, 1987, Rsch. award, American Mental Health Fund, 1987. Mem.: AAAS, Biometrics Soc., American Soc. Human Genetics (Curt Stern award 2004), Inst. Medicine. Office: UCSF Box 0794 San Francisco CA 94143 Office Phone: 415-476-1127. E-mail: rischn@humgen.ucsf.edu. *

RISHER, WILLIAM HENRY, cardiothoracic surgeon, educator; b. New Orleans, Oct. 3, 1958; m. Michele Helene Van Kuren, July 11, 1981; children: Amelia Alexandra, Jordan Prescott, Olivia Leigh. Student, U. New Orleans, 1981; BS in Biomed. Engring., Tulane U., 1981; MD, La. State U., 1985. Diplomate Am. Bd. Surgery, Am. Bd. Thoracic Surgery; lic. surgeon, NY, Pa., Ga., La.; cert. ACLS, advanced trauma life support, pediatric advanced life support provider, basic life support provider. Resident in gen. surgery Alton Ochsner Med. Found., New Orleans, 1985-90, chief resident, 1989-90, resident and fellow in cardiovascular surgery, 1990-92, chief resident, 1991-92; flight care physician Ochsner Flight Care, 1986-92; assoc. prof. cardiothoracic surgery Med. Ctr. U. Rochester, NY, 1992—2002; chief St. Luke's Regional Heart Program, Bethlehem, Pa., 2002—10; chief cardiothoracic surgery La. State U. Med. Ctr., New Orleans, 2010—. Presenter in field. Contbr. over 20 articles to med. and sci. jours. T.H. Harris scholar Tulane U, 1977-79, full scholar, 1979-81. Fellow ACS, Am. Coll. Cardiology (assoc.); mem. AMA, Am. Coll. Chest Physicians, Soc. Thoracic Surgeons, Internat. Soc. Heart and Lung Transplantation, S.E. Surg. Congress, So. Med. Assn., Med. Soc. County Monroe, Rochester Acad. Medicine, Rochester Cardiovascular Soc., Upstate Soc. Thoracic Surgeons, Rochester Surg. Soc., Assn. for Advancement of Med. Instrumentation, Alton Ochsner Med. Soc., Tau Beta Pi, Alpha Omega Alpha. Home: 4 Sonia Pl Jefferson LA 70121 Office Phone: 504-568-4752. Personal E-mail: mbajo5@aol.com. Business E-Mail: wrishe@lsuhsc.edu.

RISS, ERIC, psychologist; m. Miriam Barbara Schoen; children: Arthur, Suzanne, Wendy. BA, Bklyn. Coll., 1950; PhD, NYU, 1958. Diplomate Am. Bd. Psychotherapy. Pvt. practice psychotherapy, family therapy and marriage counseling, NYC, 1952; sr. psychologist N.Y.C. Diagnostic Ctr., 1954-57; with Marriage and Family Life Inst., NYC, 1956-92, cons., 1956-58, dir. pub. edn., 1960-73, chmn. bd. dirs., 1961-73, dir., 1973-92; mem. attending staff, supr. psychotherapy and family therapy Payne Whitney Psychiat. Clinic, N.Y. Hosp., NYC, 1971-78; clin. instr. psychology and psychiatry Cornell U. Med. Coll., 1971-72, clin. asst. prof., 1973-78; dir. Inst. for Exploration of Marriage, 1976-84; chief psychologist Artists, Writers and Performers Psychotherapy Ctr., 1978-92. Sr. psychologist N.Y.C.

Diagnostic Center, 1954-57; with Marriage and Family Life Inst., N.Y.C., 1956-92; cons., 1956-58, dir. pub. edn., 1960-73, chmn. bd. dirs., 1961-73, dir., 1973-92; mem. attending staff, supr. psychotherapy and family therapy Payne Whitney Psychiat. Clinic, N.Y. Hosp., N.Y.C., 1971-78; clin. instr. psychology and psychiatry Cornell U. Med. Coll., 1971-72, clin. asst. prof., 1973-78; dir. Inst. for Exploration of Marriage, 1976-84; chief psychologist Artists, Writers and Performers Psychotherapy Center, 1978-92; lectr. Bklyn. Coll., 1955-62; cons. Fordham Hosp., 1956-68; psychotherapist N.Y. Neuropsychiat. Center, 1958-60; psychotherapist Community Guidance Service, N.Y.C., 1958-61; founder, head Natural Psychotherapy Internat., 1999—; webmaster www.naturalpsychotherapy.com. Contbr. numerous articles to profl. jours. Mem. APA, N.Y. State Psychol. Assn., Am. Acad. Psychotherapy, N.Y. State Marriage, Family and Child Counseling Assn. (pres. 1971-72), Acad. Family Psychology. Office: 174 E 73rd St New York NY 10021-4352 Office Phone: 212-988-4700. Business E-Mail: eriss@naturalpsychotherapy.info. E-mail: eriss@naturalpsychotherapy.com, eriss@npsy.com. *

RISSE, GUENTER BERNHARD, physician, historian, educator; b. Buenos Aires, Apr. 28, 1932; s. Francisco B. and Kaete A. R.; m. Alexandra G. Paradzinski, Oct. 14, 1961; children— Heidi, Monica, Alisa. MD, U. Buenos Aires, 1958; PhD, U. Chgo., 1971. Intern Mercy Hosp., Buffalo, 1958-59; resident in medicine Henry Ford Hosp., Detroit, 1960-61, Mt. Carmel Hosp., Columbus, Ohio, 1962-63; asst. dept. medicine U. Chgo., 1963-67; asst. prof. dept. history of medicine U. Minn., 1969-71; asso. prof. dept. history of medicine and dept. history of sci. U. Wis., Madison, 1971-76, prof., 1976-85, chmn. dept. history of medicine, 1971-77; prof. dept. history health scis. U. Calif., San Francisco, 1985-99, prof. dept. anthropology, history and social medicine, 1999-2001, prof. emeritus, 2001—, dept. chair, 1985—99; affiliate prof. dept. bioethics and humanities U. Wash. Sch. Medicine, Seattle, 2002—. Author: Paleopathology of Ancient Egypt, 1964, Hospital Life in Enlightenment Scotland, 1986, Mending Bodies-Saving Souls: A History of Hospitals, 1999, New Medical Challenges During the Scottish Enlightenment, 2005; editor: Modern China and Traditional Chinese Medicine, 1973, History of Physiology, 1973, Medicine Without Doctors, 1977, AIDS and the Historian, 1991, Culture, Knowledge and Healing, Historical Perspectives of Homeopathic Medicine in Europe and North America, 1998; mem. editl. bd. Jour. History of Medicine, 1971-74, 90-93, Clio Medica, 1973-88, Bull. History of Medicine, 1980-94, Medizinhistorisches Jour., 1981—, Med. History, 1989-95, NTM Internat. Jour. of History, Ethics, Medicine, 1992—, History of Philos. Life Scis., 1993—, Asclepio, 1995—, Health and History, 1998—. With Argentine Armed Forces, 1955. Recipient NIH grants, 1971-73, 82-84, WHO grant, NIH grant San Francisco's Plague: The View from Chinatown, 2007-09, fellowship History & L.Am. Med. Sys., 1979; named Logan Campbell Disting. Lectr., New Zealand, 1994, Karl Sudhoff Meml. Lectr., Germany, 2000. Mem. Am. Assn. History of Medicine (pres. 1988-90, William H. Welch medal 1988, Lifetime Achievement award 2005), History Sci. Soc., Deutsche Gesellschaft fur Geschichte der Medizin, European Assn. History of Medicine and Health, Internat. Network for History of Pub. Health, Mex. Soc. History and Philosophy of Medicine, Peruvian Assn. Med. Ethnology and History, Brit. Soc. for Social History of Medicine, Argentine Ateneo de Historia de la Medicina, AIDS History Group (co-chair 1988-94), Internat. Network for History of Hosps. (convenor 1995—), Bay Area Med. Hist. Club (pres. 1994-96). Home: 2612 SW 167th St Burien WA 98166-3228 Business E-Mail: risseg@u.washington.edu.

RISTICH, MIODRAG, psychiatrist; b. Belgrade, Yugoslavia, July 19, 1938; arrived in US, 1967; s. Teodosije and Gordana (Isailovic) Ristich; m. Yvonne Muriel Cunliffe, May 6, 1967; children: Katharine Alexandra, Elizabeth Victoria. MD, U. Belgrade, 1962. Resident psychiatry Manhattan Psychiat. Ctr., NYU, 1980-83; med. dir. Cambridge (Minn.) State Hosp., 1967-72; dir. Willowbrook State Sch., Staten Island, NY, 1972-74; med. dir. DeWitt Rehab. Nursing Ctr., NYC, 1976—; clin. asst. prof. psychiatry NYU Med. Sch., 1996—. Pvt. practice psychiatry, NYC, 1973—. Mem.: AMA, Royal Coll. Psychiatrists, Am. Assn. Geriatric Psychiatry, Am. Psychiat. Assn. Republican. Avocation: tennis. Home: 37 Sunrise Ln Upper Saddle River NJ 07458-1631 Office: 201 E 79th St Apt 7J New York NY 10075-0835 Home Phone: 201-934-5513; Office Phone: 212-737-6990. Personal E-mail: mristich@yahoo.com.

RISTOW, BRUNNO, plastic surgeon; b. Brusque, Brazil, Oct. 18, 1940; s. Arno and Ally Odette (von Bruettner) Ristow; m. Urannia Carrasquilla Gutierrez, Nov. 10, 1979; children from previous marriage: Christian Kilian, Trevor Roland. Student, Coll. Sinodal, Brazil, 1956—57; MD magna cum laude, U. Brazil, 1966. Diplomate Am. Bd. Plastic and Reconstructive Surgery. Intern in surgery Hosp. dos Estrangeiros, Rio de Janeiro, 1965, Hosp. Estuadual Miguel Couto, Brazil, 1965—66, Instituto Aposentadoria Pensao Comerciarios Hosp. for Gen. Surgery, 1966; resident in plastic and reconstructive surgery Dr. Ivo PItanguy Hosp. Santa Casa de Misericordia, Rio de Janeiro, 1967; fellow Inst. Reconstructive Plastic Surgery NYU Med. Ctr., NYC, 1967—68, jr. resident, 1971—72, sr. and chief resident, 1972—73; practice medicine specializing in plastic surgery Rio de Janeiro, 1967, NYC, 1968—73, San Francisco, 1973—; asst. surgeon NY Hosp., Cornell Med. Ctr., NYC, 1968—71. Clin. instr. surgery NYU Sch. Medicine, 1972—73; chmn. plastic and reconstructive surgery divsn. Presbyn. Hosp., Pacific Med. Ctr., San Francisco, 1974—92, chmn. emeritus, 1992—. Contbg. author: Cancer of the Hand, 1975, Current Therapy in Plastic and Reconstructive Surgery, 1988, Male Aesthetic Surgery, 1989, How They Do It: Procedures in Plastic and Reconstructive Surgery, 1990, Middle Crus: The Missing Link in Alar Cratilage Anatomy, 1991, Surgical Technology International, 1992, Aesthetic Plastic Surgery, 1993, Mastery of Surgery: Plastic and Reconstructive Surgery, 1993, Reoperative Aesthetic Plastic Surgery of the Face and Breast, 1994; contbr. articles to profl. jours. With M.C. Brazilian Army Res., 1959—70. Decorated knight Venerable Order of St. Hubertus, Knight Order St. John of Jerusalem; fellow in surgery, Cornell Med. Sch., 1968—71. Fellow: ACS, Internat.Coll. Surgeons; mem.: AMA (Physician's Recognition award 1971—83), San Francisco Med. Assn., Calif. Med. Assn., Calif. Soc. Plastic Surgeons, Internat. Soc. Aesthetic Plastic Surgeons, Am. Soc. Plastic and Reconstructive Surgeons, Am. Soc. Aesthetic Plastic Surgery (chmn. edn.), San Francisco Olympic Club. Republican. Evangelical. Office: Calif Pacific Med Ctr 2100 Webster St Ste 501 San Francisco CA 94115-2373 Office Phone: 415-202-1507. Office Fax: 415-202-0131. Personal E-mail: info@brunnoristow.com.

RISTOW, GEORGE EDWARD, neurologist, educator; b. Albion, Mich., Dec. 15, 1943; s. George Julius and Margaret (Beattie) R.; 1 child, George Andrew Martin. BA, Albion Coll., 1965; DO, Coll. Osteo. Medicine/Surgery, Des Moines, 1969. Diplomate Am. Bd. Psychiatry and Neurology. Intern Garden City Hosp., 1969-70; resident Wayne State U., 1970-74; fellow U. Newcastle Upon Tyne, 1974-75; asst. prof. dept. neurology Wayne State U., Detroit, 1975-77; assoc. prof. Mich. State U., East Lansing, 1977-83, prof., 1983-84, 95—, prof., chmn., 1984-95, prof. emeritus, 2001—. Fellow Am. Acad. Neurology, Royal Soc. Medicine; mem. AMA, Am. Osteo. Assn., Pan Am. Med. Assn., World Fedn. Neurology, Am. Coll. Neuropsychiatrists (sr.). Home: 19534 Gulf Blvd Apt 102 Indian Shores FL 33785

RITCH, ROBERT HARRY, ophthalmologist, educator; b. New Haven, May 14, 1942; s. Edward Lewis and Minerva (Grosberg) R. BA cum laude, Harvard U., 1965, MA, 1967; postgrad., Rice U., 1967—68; MD, Albert Einstein Coll. Medicine, 1972. Diplomate Am. Bd. Ophthalmology, Am. Bd. Laser Surgery. Intern St. Vincent's Med. Ctr., NYC, 1972-73; resident in ophthalmology Mt. Sinai Sch. Medicine, NYC, 1973-75, chief resident, 1975-76, Heed Ophthalmic Found. fellow, 1976-77, NIH-Nat. Rsch. Svc. fellow, 1976-78, asst. clin. ophthalmologist, 1976-77, instr., 1977-78, asst. prof., 1978-80, assoc. prof., 1980-82; attending ophthalmologist Beth Israel Med. Ctr., NYC, 1978—; chief Glaucoma Svc. NY Eye and Ear Infirmary, NYC, 1983—, surgeon dir., 1991—; Shelley and Steven Einhorn Disting. chair in ophthalmology, 2007—. Cons. ophthalmologist VA Hosp., Bronx, 1978—82, Manhattan Eye, Ear & Throat Hosp., 1989—; dir. glaucoma svc. Elmhurst Hosp., 1978—82, acting dir. dept. ophthalmology, 1979—82; chief glaucoma svc. NY Eye and Ear Infirmary, NYC, 1983—, surgeon dir., 1991—; adj. sr. scientist Singapore Eye Rsch. Inst., 1997; adj. prof. Mt. Sinai Sch. Medicine, 2005—; prof. clin. ophthalmology NY Med. Coll., Valhalla, 1983—2008, prof. ophthalmology, 2008—; Arthur Bedell Meml. lectr. Wills Eye Hosp., Phila., 1995; John Edwin Brown Meml. lectr. Ohio State U., Columbus, 1996; Schoenburg Meml. lectr. Ill. Eye and Ear Infirmary, Chgo., 1996; Schlaegel lectr. U. Ind., Indpls., 1996; Gerasimos Frenimopoulos Meml. lectr. Duke U., 1997, Joseph M. Bryan Meml. lectr., 97; Roger P. Mason Meml. lectr. Howard U., 1997; Abraham S. Ticho lectr., Jerusalem, 98; Anagnostakis-Trantus lectr., Athens, 98; Sanford Gifford Meml. lectr., Chgo., 98; Annie Wong lectr. Chinese U., Hong Kong, 1999; Arthur Lim lectr., Hong Kong, 2001; Am. Glaucoma Soc. Subspecialty Day lectr. Am. Acad. Ophthalmology, New Orleans, 2001; King Khaled Meml. lectr., Riyadh, 03; Chew Sek-Jin Meml. lectr., Hong Kong, 03; Irving Leopold Meml. lectr., Irvine, Calif., 04; Francis Proctor Meml. lectr., San Francisco, 05; Julius Silver Meml. lectr., NY, 06; Irving Leopold Meml. lectr., NY, 06; Robert Shaffer lectr. Am. Acad. Opthalmology, 2007; program chmn. East Coast Glaucoma Symposium, NY, 2000; cons. Sukhumvit Hosp., Bangkok, 1994; pres. Internat. Eye Cons., Ltd., 1995—, NY Glaucoma Rsch. Inst., 1996; mem. adv. bd. Dr. to Dr., Berkeley, Calif., 1995—; sec., treas., chmn. sci. adv. bd. Glaucoma Found., 1984—; med. dir., chmn., grant rev. com.; med. dir. Children's Right to Sight, prin. investigator Collaborative Initial Glaucoma Treatment Study, 1993—2003; mem. adv. bd. Sturge-Weber Found., 1996; mem. glaucoma adv. com. Nat. Soc. to Prevent Blindness, 1986—; organizing chmn. Bangkok Ophthal. Congress, 1985—93, Optic Nerve Rescue & Restoration Think Tank, NY, 1994—2003, First Internat. Think Tank on Exfoliation Syndrome, NY, 1999, Myanmar Internat. Ophthal. Congress, 1997, 99, 2003; internat. sci. com. Internat. Congress of Ophthalmology, Sydney, 2002; sci. organizing com. mem. 4th Internat. Glaucoma Congress, Barcelona, 2003; external assessor U. Malaya, 1988—96; cons. Tun Hussein Onn Nat. Eye Hosp., Kuala Lumpur, Malaysia, 1996—; internat. adv. bd. 4th Internat. Symposium of Ophthalmology, Shantou, China, 2002; mem. steering com. Assn. Internat. Glaucoma Soc., 2002—; internat. advisor Tianjin Med. Ctr., China, 2002—; hon. pres. Chinese Internat. Glaucoma Congress, Beijing, 2004; mem. sci. organizing com. 5th Internat. Glaucoma Congress, Capetown, South Africa, 2005; chmn. sci. organizing com. glaucoma sect. World Congress Ophthalmology, Sao Paulo, Brazil, 2006; organizing chmn. Kazakhstan Ophthalmological Congress, Almaty, 2006, ARVO/AAO Symposium on Nanotech., Am. Acad. Ophthalmology, 2007; organizing com. World Glaucoma Congress, Singapore, 2007; bd. dirs. Helen Keller Internat.; hon. prof., dept. anatomy Hong Kong U., 2008—; lectr. in field; Robert Herbst lectr., 2008; Tkc Liv meml. lectr., 08; Huang-Uhan meml. lectr., 08; hon. lectr. Optometric Glaucoma Soc., 2008; lectr. 17th Am. Glaucoma Soc., 2008; spl. lectr. APAO, 2009; organizing chmn. Glaucoma Sect. World Ophthlmology Congress, Hong Kong, 2008; co-chmn. & organizer First Annual World Glaucoma Day, 2008; program chmn. Glaucoma Asia-Pacific Acad. Ophthalmology, Bali, 2009; organizing chmn. Hong Kong Nenotech. Symposium, 2009, Internat. Update Eye Disease, Lima, Peru, 2009; lectr. Prevention Blindness Shield, Riyadh, 2010; organising chmn. Glaucoma Sec. World Ophthal. Congress, Berlin, 2010; program chmn. Glaucoma Asia Pacific Academy Ophthal., Beijing, 2010. Author (with M.B. Shields): The Secondary Glaucomas, 1982, The Glaucomas, 1988, 1996; author: (with R. Caronia) Classic Papers in Glaucoma, 2000; spl. sect. editor: Jour. Glaucoma, 1991—98, mem. editl. bd.: Sight-saving, 1981—86, Opthalmic Laser Therapy, 1984—88, Ophthalmic Resident, 1992—95, Ophthalmic Surgery and Lasers, 1995—, Microsurgery, 1994—2004, Ophthalmology Times, 1996—2001, Jour. Glaucoma, 1998—, Internat. Glaucoma Rev., 1999—, Archives Ophthalmology, 2004—08, BMC Ophthalmology, 2005—, Expert Rev. Ophthalmology, 2005—, Asian Jour. Ophthalmology, 2006—, contbg. editor: Ophthalmic Practice, 1993—2005; contbg. editor Jour. Ocular Biology, Diseases, and Informatics, 2007—, advisory panel US Ophthalmic Review, 2007—; contbr. to films on laser therapy, over 1400 articles and abstracts in field. Bd. dirs. Dooley Found./Intermed. USA, 1991—, UN, Southeastern Nigeria Eye Care Outreach Coll. Med. Scis. U. Calabar, Nigeria, 1996—; vol. Devel. Coun., 1991-93; chmn. bd. dirs. I-Med. Devel Corp., 1991-94; sci. adv. bd. Singapore Eye Rsch. Inst.; bd. govs. Internat. Soc. for Imaging of the Eye, 2002—; adv. com. Internat. Coun. Ophthalmology, 2002—, chmn., adv. com. to bd. dirs., 2009-, Jeddah Tchg. Mission, Saudi Arabia, 2011, convener Glaucoma Program APAO, Sydney, 2011 Hon. scholar, Harvard U., 1965, NSF fellow, 1966-67, Harvard Traveling fellow, Rice U., 1967-68; recipient Acad. Investigator award, NIH, 1978-81, Disting. Svc. award, Internat. Ctr. NY, 1981, Exec. Dirs. award, 1985, Founders award, Nat. Exhibits by Blind Artists, 1985, Gold medal of Merit and Honor, Greek Glaucoma Soc., 1998, Ophthalmology Times Achievement in Ophthalmology award, 1998, Louis Rudin award for rsch. in glaucoma, 1999, Dean's Disting. Rsch. award NY Med. Coll., 2008, Decorated comdr. Grace Sovereign Order of Orthodox Knights Hospitalier of St. John of Jerusalem; named spl. honoree, Helen Keller Found., 2000, Glaucoma Found., 2000; Jesse H. Neal award for editl. achievement, 2000, John Kearny Rodgers Physician of Yr. award, NY Eye and Ear Infirmary, 2005; Albion O. Bernstein award, Med. Soc. State of NY, Dean's Disting. Rsch award, NY Med. Coll., 2007, TKC Liu Meml. award for Leadership in Ophthalmology, Hong Kong 2008, Glaucoma Found. award for Innovation and Excellence in Glaucoma 2008, Ronald F. Lowe Medal of the Australia-New Zealand Ophthalmol Soc., 2008, Dominick Purpura Disting. Alumnus Annual award, Albert Einstein Coll. of Medicine 2009., Jose Rizal Internat. medal APAO, Sydney, 2011 Fellow Am. Acad. Ophthalmology (edn. distbn. subcom. 1994-97, book/jour. link subcom. 1994-97, distbn. adv. subcom. 1997-2000, chmn. subcom., 2001-, Honor award, 1985, sr. honor award 1995, Lifetime Achievement Honor award 2007, Leaders in Edn. Ophthalmology award 2007), Heed Ophthalmic Found. (ophthalmologist of Yr. 1996), Am. Ophthalmol. Soc. (program com. 2002-2004), NY Acad. Medicine, Royal Coll. Ophthalmologists (UK), ACS, Internat. Coll. Surgeons, Am. Soc. Laser Surgery Medicine (chmn. ophthalmology sect. 1991-92, moderator and program chmn. joint sci. symposium on glaucoma 1991), NY Acad. Medicine (sec. sect. on ophthalmology 1991-92, chmn. 1993-94, Charles May Meml. Lectr. 1991, bd. trustees 2003—); mem. AMA, AAAS, NY State Med. Soc., NY County Med. Soc., Assn. Rsch. in Vision and Ophthalmology (program com., glaucoma sect. 1991-93, program chmn. 1993-94, internat. com. 2003-, bd. trustees 2003-08, v.p. 2007-08, Disting. Svc. award 2009, Gold fellow 2009), Am. Assn. Ophthalmology, Ophthal. Soc. UK, Internat. Assn. Ocular surgeons, Internat. Congress Ophthalmology (glaucoma com. 1994-), NY Intra-Ocular Lens Implant Soc., Manhattan Ophthal. Soc., Assn. Internat. Glaucoma Soc., Internat. Soc. Eye Rsch., Soc. Clin. Trials, Pan-Pacific Anterior Segment Soc. (v.p. 1985-88), Internat. Coun. Ophthalmology (adv. com.), NY Acad. Sci., Ophthalmic Laser Surgery Soc. (sec.-treas. 1982-98, 2000-, pres. 1998-2000), NY Soc. Clin. Ophthalmology (rec. sec. 1988-90, program chmn. 1990-91, pres. 1991-92), NY Glaucoma Rsch. Inst. (pres. 1996-), Am. Soc. Cell Biology, Am. Telemed Assn., Internat. Soc. On-Line Ophthalmologists (mem. orgn. com., chmn. glaucoma sect. 1995—), Internat. Fedn. Cell Biologists, Philippine Soc. Ophthalmology (hon.), Thailand Ophthal. Soc. (hon.), Italian Assn. for Study of Glaucoma (hon.), La.-Miss. Ophthal. and Otolarygol. Soc. (hon.), Can. Implant Soc. (hon.). Home: 455 E 57th St # 14D New York NY 10022-3065 Office: NY Eye and Ear Infirmary 310 E 14th St New York NY 10003-4201 Home Phone: 212-980-7187; Office Phone: 212-477-7540. Personal E-mail: ritchmd@earthlink.net.

RITCHEY, A. KIM, pediatric hematologist-oncologist, educator; MD, U. Cin., 1972. Cert. nat. bd. med. examiners, diplomate Am. Bd. Pediatrics, Am. Bd. Pediatrics-pediatric hematology/oncology. Resident Johns Hopkins Hosp., 1975; fellow Yale Univ., 1980; prof. pediatrics Univ. of Pitts. Recipient Professional Research Consultants (PRC) Four Star Customer Service award, 2005; named one of Best Doctors in America, 2005, Top Doctors, 2005. Mem.: Am. Soc. of Clin. Oncology, Am. Soc. of Pediatric Hematology/Oncology, Children's Oncology Group. Office: Childrens Hospital of Pittsburgh of UPMC 4401 Penn Ave Fl 9 Pittsburgh PA 15224 Office Phone: 412-692-5055. Office Fax: 412-692-7693. E-mail: kim.ritchey@chp.edu.

RITCHEY, KENNETH WILLIAM, human services administrator; b. Washington, June 7, 1947; s. Conrad Monroe and Katherine Costance (Sheris) (dec. 2004) R.; m. Nancy Jayne Kirk, Aug. 22, 1970; children: Kirk Damon, Erin Kathryn (dec. Apr. 1988). BS in Edn., Shippensburg U., 1969; MEd in Spl. Edn., U. Va., 1972; MS in Ednl. Adminstrn., U. Dayton, 1980; D, U. Dayton, Leadership Dayton, 1991; grad. sr. execs. in state & local govt. program, Harvard U., 1992. Spl. edn. tchr. Shippensburg Area Sch. Dist., Pa., 1969-71; head cross country and track coach Shippensburg U., 1970-74; master tchr., coord. work experience program Lincoln Intermediate Unit, New Oxford, Pa., 1971-76; adult edn. tchr. Franklin County Prison, Chambersburg, Pa., 1972-76; asst. supt. mgmt. svcs. Montgomery County Bd. Mental Retardation & Devel. Disabilities, Dayton, Ohio, 1977-83, supt. bd., 1983-99; dir. Ohio Dept. Mental Retardation and Devel. Disabilities, Columbus, 1999—2007; asst. commr. divsn. devel. disabilities NJ Dept. Human Svcs., 2007—11. Mem. part-time faculty edn. dept. U. Dayton, 1983-97; mem., vice-chair cmty. and mil. adv. com. ARC, 1986-95, needs and priorities com. Human Svcs. Levy Coun., 1982-84, 87-99; trustee Ohio Polit. Action Com., Brighter Tomorrow Found., 1990-2000, County Corp., 1992-98. Former editor statewide newsletter for tchrs. and profls. in Work Experience. Vol. mem. cmty. and agys. resources coun. United Way, 1986—98; v.p. HelpLink Bd., pres.; mem. Gov.'s Vision Com., Ill., 1997—2000, Gov.'s Cabinet; bd. dirs. Ohio Pub. Images, Inc., past pres. Recipient Harold Hilty Humanitarian award, United Cerebral Palsy Rehab. Svcs., 1994, Robert Weaver Disting. Svc. award, Montgomery County Bd. Mental Retardation and Devel. Disabilities, 1999, Svc. award, Profl. Assn. on Retardation, 2002, Chair's Recognition award, Wright State U. Dept. Psychiatry, 2005, Cmty. Star award, Franklin County, 2006, Ray Ferguson Advocacy award, ARC, Ohio, 2007; honored by, Ohio Assn. County Bds., 2005. Mem.: Ohio Self Determination Assn. (Catalyst award 2003), Nat. Assn. State Dirs. Devel. Disabilities Svcs. (chair nat. policy work group 2002, bd. trustees 2004, sec.-treas. 2005—, pres. 2009—11), Supts. Assn. (exec. com.), Ohio Supts. County Bds. Mental Retardation (v.p., pres.), Phi Beta Kappa. Democrat. Methodist. Home: 86 Lochatong Rd Ewing NJ 08628 Personal E-mail: k1ritchey@aol.com. *

RITCHIE, MARGARET RENWICK, education educator, researcher; b. Scotland; m. Sandy Ritchie; children: Sandy, Tiffany, Alisdair, Dominique, Tanya, Danielle. PhD, U. St. Andrews, Scotland, BSc with honors, 1980. Practitioner of complementary medicine

Glasgow SWchool of Complementary Medicine, Glasgow, Glasgow, Scotland; tchr. of chemistry Harris Acad., Dundee, Dundee, Scotland. Cons. Ximed Group, Oxford, England. Author: Nutritional Therapy; editor. Fellow Rsch. Fellowship, Melville Trust; scholar Travel, Royal Soc. Mem.: Sci. adv. panel Inst. of Optimum Nutrition, Sci. adv. com. Nutritional Therapy Coun. Achievements include first to First researcher in the world to identify and validate biomarkers of phyto-oestrogen intake; First researcher in the world to construct and validate a phyto-oestrogen database; First researcher to analyse breast tumours for phyto-oestrogens. Office Fax: 44(0)1334463482; Home Fax: 44(0)1382530699. Personal E-mail: mrr3@tesco.net. E-mail: mrr3@st-andrews.ac.uk.

RITCHIE, ROBERT IAN, emergency physician, consultant; b. Newport, Wales, Sept. 16, 1963; s. E. M. Ritchie; m. Petriana Gordon-Ritchie, July 27, 1991; children: Lincoln, Stefan. MBBS, U. W.I., Jamaica, 1988; fgn. med. grad. in med. scis., 1990; diploma in Mgmt., Leceister U., Eng., 2004. Cert. in advanced life support 2008, provider in pediatric advanced life support 2008, provider in advanced trauma life support Mass. Gen. Hosp., Boston, 2001, Syracuse Hosp., 2006, provider in pedatric emergency trauma advanced life support 1998, in major incident med. mgmt. and support 1998, spl. situation in major incident med. mgmt. 1998, specialist in accident and emergency medicine 2003, in European pediatric advanced life support 2004. Med. intern in gen. medicine, gen. surgery, child health/pediat. and ob-gyn., Kingston, Jamaica, 1988; med. intern in casualty/emergency medicine, orthopedics, pub. health and anat. pathology, 1990; resident in ob-gyn. Victoria Jubilee Hosp., Kingston, West Indies, 1990—91; resident in orthopedics U. Hosp. WI, St. Andrew, Jamaica, 1991—92; house officer, acute internal medicine and elderly geriatric medicine Medway Maritime Hosp., Gillingham, England, 1992—93; sr. house officer, resident in emergency medicine Medway Maritime Hosp., 1993—94, sr. house officer trainee in gen. surgery, orthop. and urology, 1994—96, emergency medicine registrar trainee, 1996, emergency medicine registrar trainee, registrar in emergency medicine and internal medicine, 1996—99, registrar in child health/pediat., 1999—2000, registrar in critical care medicine, intensive care, cardiology and anesthetics, 2001; registrar trainee in emergency medicine Kings Coll. Hosp., London, 1999—2000, Greenwich Dist. Gen. Hosp., London, 2000—01, U. Hosp. Lewisham, London, 2001—03, resident in ophthalmology, psychiatry and ear, nose and throat, 2002—03; cons. in accident and emergency medicine Southend Hosp. NHS Trust, South-on-Sea, England, 2003—06, cons. in emergency medicine, 2003—06; with Accident Ctr. Medway Maritime NHS Trust, Gillingham, 2006—. Presenter in field; cons. in field. Recipient IWL award, 2009. Fellow: Royal Coll. Surgeons, Faculty Accident and Emergency Medicine (presenter meeting 1997, 2001, 2000), Royal Coll. Physicians and Surgeons Glasgow; mem. Am. Coll. Emergency Physicians (presenter meeting 2005). Office: Medway Maritime NHS Trust Emergency Dept Windmill Rd Gillingham Kent ME7 5NY England Office Phone: 44 (0) 1634 833911, 44 (0) 1634 833974. Business E-Mail: robert.ritchie@aol.com.

RITCHIE, WALLACE PARKS, JR., retired surgeon, educator; b. St. Paul, Nov. 4, 1935; s. Wallace Parks and Alice Ransome (Otis) R.; m. Barbara Carey Jewell, Aug. 10, 1960; children: Stephanie, David, Jessica. BA, Yale U., 1957; MD, Johns Hopkins U., 1961; PhD, U. Minn., 1971. Diplomate Am. Bd. Surgery. Intern, resident in surgery Yale U., New Haven, 1961-63; resident in surgery U. Minn. Hosps., Mpls., 1963-69, instr. in surgery, 1969-70; from asst. prof. to prof. surgery U. Va. Sch. Medicine, Charlottesville, 1973-83; prof., chmn. dept. surgery Temple U. Sch. Medicine, Phila., 1983-93; exec. dir. Am. Bd. Surgery, Phila., 1994—2002; ret. Editor textbook: Essentials of Surgery, 1994; contbr. over 160 sci. articles to profl. jours. Lt. col. M.C., U.S. Army, 1970-73. USPHS grantee, 1974-85. Office: Am Bd Surgery Inc 1617 John F Kennedy Blvd Philadelphia PA 19103-1821 Personal E-mail: wallace.ritchie@verizon.net.

RITTENBERGER, JON, emergency physician, educator; b. Johnstown, Pa., Mar. 17, 1976; MD, U. Pitts., 2002, MS, 2007. Asst. prof. emergency medicine U. Pitts., 2007—. Fellow: Am. Coll. Emergency Physicians. Office: 3600 Forbes Ave Ste 400A Pittsburgh PA 15261 Office Fax: 412-364-7873. Business E-Mail: rittjc@upmc.edu.

RITTER, DALE WILLIAM, obstetrician, gynecologist; b. Jersey Shore, Pa., June 17, 1919; s. Lyman W. and Weltha B. (Packard) Ritter; m. Winnie Mae Bryant, Nov. 13, 1976; children: Eric, Lyman, Michael, Gwendolyn, Daniel. AB, UCLA, 1942; MD, U. So. Calif., 1946. Diplomate Am. Bd. Ob-Gyn. Intern LA County Hosp., 1945—46, resident, 1948—52, admitting room resident, 1948—52; pvt. practice Chico, Calif., 1952—98; founder, mem. staff, past chmn. bd. dirs. Chico Cmty. Meml. Hosp. Guest lectr. Chico State Coll., 1956—; staff Enole Hosp., Chico, 1952—, Glenn Gen. Hosp., Willows, Calif., 1953-98, Gridley Meml. Hosp., Calif., 1953-80; spl. cons. obs. Calif. Dept. Pub. Health, No. Calif., 1958-70. Contbr. articles to profl. jours. Bd. dirs. No. dist. Children's Home Soc., Chico, 1954-70. With AUS, 1943-45, M.C., AUS, 1946-48. Recipient Pro-Life award, Calif. KC, Citizenship award, SAR, Good Citizenship medal. Fellow ACS, Am. Coll. Ob-Gyn; mem. AMA, AAAS, DAV, Calif. Med. Assn., Internat. Soc. Hypnosis, Am. Soc. Clin. Hypnosis, Am. Fertility Soc., Pacific Coast Fertility Soc., Assn. Am. Physicians and Surgeons, Pvt. Drs. Am., Butte-Glenn County Med. Soc. (past pres.), Am. Cancer Soc. (past bd. dirs. Butte County), Christian Med. Soc., Am. Assn. Pro-life Obstetricians and Gynecologists, Butte-Glenn County Tumor Bd., Anthrop. Assn. Am., Archaeol. Inst. Am., Soc. Calif. Archaeology, Oreg. Archaeology Soc., Archeol. Survey Assn., Southwestern Anthrop. Soc., Am. Rock Art Rsch. Assn. (Pioneer award), Calif. Hist. Soc., Calif. Oreg. Trails Assn., Australian Rock Art Rsch. Assn., Internat. Assn. for Study of Prehistoric and Ethnologic Religions, Fretted Instrument Guild Am. (dir. Banjo Kats 'n Jammers), North Valley Banjo Band, Am. Philatelic Soc., Am. Horse Coun., Peruvian Paso Horse Registry of N.Am., Assn. Owners Breeders Peruvian Paso Horses, Sons of Am. Revolution, Am. Legion, named Sons Am. Revolution, Citizenship award, WWII, Rotary (Paul Harris fellow), Gideons Internat., Phi Chi, Lambda Sigma, Zeta Beta Sigma, Am. Vets. Republican. Home: PMB 156 975 East Ave Chico CA 95926-1308

RITTER, TOBIAS, chemistry professor; b. Lubeck, Germany, Jan. 10, 1975; MS, TU Braunschweig, Germany, 1999; PhD, ETH Zurich, 2004. Assoc. prof. Harvard U., 2006—. CTO SciFluor, 2011. Mem.: Am. Chem. Soc. Office: Harvard University 12 Oxford St Cambridge MA a2138 Business E-Mail: ritter@chemistry.harvard.edu.

RITTERBAND, ARNOLD B., internist; b. NYC, July 21, 1926; s. Max Ritterband and Sara Abelson; m. Phyllis Rosenthal Ritterband, Aug. 3, 1957; children: Alan, Vicki, David. AB, Columbia Coll., NYC, 1945; MD, Columbia Coll. Physicians and Surgeons, NYC, 1950. Cert. Am. Bd. Internal Medicine. Intern Mt. Sinai Hosp., NYC, 1950—51; asst. resident medicine Inst. Columbia Presbyn. Med. Ch., 1951—52; asst. res. medicine Mt. Sinai Hosp., 1952—53; asst. resident neurology Neurol. Inst. Columbia-Presbyn. Med. Ctr., NYC, 1951—52; fellow rheumatology NYU Divsn. Goldwater Meml. Hosp., NYC, 1955—56; fellow epidemiology Columbia U. Sch. Pub. Health, NYC, 1956—61; med. dir. St. Clare's Hosp., Schenectady, 1959—60; pvt. practice Schenectady, 1959—2004; co-med. dir. Schenectady Free Clinic, 2003—; fellow pathology, 1953—54; fellow pathology asst. res. medicine Mt. Smith Hosp., 1954—55. Clin. prof. medicine Albany Med. Sch., NY, 2007—. Contbr. articles to profl. jours. Founder, chmn. Schenectady County Commn. Health Care Issues, 1986. With USNR, 1945—46, PTO. Recipient Sen. Edward J. Speno award, NY State Fedn. Profl. Health Educators, 1998. Democrat. Jewish. Achievements include research in coronary heart disease. Office: Schenectady Free Health Clinic 600 Franklin St Schenectady NY 12305 Home: 915 Northumberland Dr Schenectady NY 12309

RITVO, JONATHAN I., psychiatrist, educator; AB cum laude, Harvard Coll., Cambridge, Mass., 1969, MD, 1973. Lic. Calif., 1975, diplomate Am. Bd. Psychiatry and Neurology-psychiatry, 1980, Am. Bd. Psychiatry and Neurology-addiction psychiatry, 2002. Resident internal medicine Beth Israel Deaconess Med. Ctr., Boston, 1973—74; resident psychiatry Univ. Colo. Health Sci. Ctr., 1975—78, tng. dir. addiction psychiatry residency program, 1995—2008; clin. assoc. medicine Med. Sch. Harvard Coll., Cambridge, Mass., 1973—74; emergency room physician Morton Hosp., Taunton, Mass., 1974, Anna Jaques Hosp., Newburyport, Mass., 1974—75; instr. psychiatry Sch. Medicine Univ. Colo., 1978—79, asst. prof. psychiatry Sch. Medicine, 1979—88, clin. assoc. prof. psychiatry Sch. Medicine, 1988—2007, clin. affiliate Sch. Profl. Psychology, 1991—94, clin. prof. psychiatry Sch. Medicine, 2007—; psychiatrist I Denver Gen. Hosp., 1978—82, ward chief adult psychiat. inpatient svc. 4-west, 1978—84, psychiatrist II, 1982—92, dir. psychiat. emergency and consultation svc., 1984—89; attending psychiat. consultation svc. Denver Gen. Hosp./Denver Health Med. Ctr., 1989—98, med. dir. inpatient addiction psychiatry svc. 4-East, 1989, advanced physician specialist, 1992—2007; med. dir. substance use disorders svc. outpatient behavioral health svcs. Denver Health Med. Ctr., 1998—2007; med. dir. ctr. for dependence, addiction and rehab. Univ. Colo. Hosp., 2007—. Temp. gen. med. officer Indian Health Svc., Sacaton, Ariz., 1974, Fort Yates, ND, 74. Co-author: (publs.) Staffing Patterns and the Weekly Cycle of Community Meetings on an Adult Inpatient Unit, 1982, Charcoal Stercolith with Intestinal Perforation in a Patient Treated for Amitriptyline Ingestion, 1994, A Survey of Addiction Training Programming in Psychiatry Residencies, 2002, Tramadol Dependence: Treatment with Buprenorphine/Naloxone, 2007, The Psychiatric Management of Patients with Alcohol Dependence, 2007. Named one of Denver's Top Doctors, Addiction Psychiatry, 5280 Denver's Mile High Mag., 2004, 2007—09. Office: University of Colorado Hospital 12401 East 17th Ave Aurora CO 80045 Office Phone: 720-848-0000.

RIVARA, FREDERICK PETER, pediatrician, educator; b. Far Rockaway, NY, May 17, 1949; s. Frederick P. and Mary Lillian (Caparelli) R.; m. J'May Bertrand, May 17, 1975; children: Matthew, Maggie. BA, Holy Cross Coll., 1970; MD, U. Pa., 1974; MPH, U. Wash., 1980. Diplomate Am. Bd. Pediatrics. Intern Children's Hosp. and Med. Ctr., Boston, 1974-75, resident, 1975-76, Seattle, 1978-80; RWJ clin. scholar U. Wash., Seattle, 1978-80, assoc. prof. pediatrics, 1984-89, prof. pediatrics, head divsn. gen. pediatrics, 1994—; mem. staff Nat. Health Svc. Corps, Hazard, Ky., 1976-78; asst. prof. pediatrics U. Tenn., Memphis, 1981-84. Editor Archives of Pedatrics and Adolescent Medicine. Fellow Am. Acad. Pediatrics; mem. Ambulatory Pediatrics Assn., SPR, Am. Pediat. Soc., Internat. Assn. Child, Adolescent and Injury Prevention (pres. 1993-2000), Inst. Medicine (Washington), Acad. Sci. Office: Harborview Med Ctr 325 9th Ave PO Box 359960 Seattle WA 98195-9960 Business E-Mail: fpr@uwashington.edu.

RIVENES, SHANNON MARIE, pediatric cardiologist; b. Calgary, Alberta, Canada, Dec. 3, 1966; d. Steven Bryce Holmgren and Gayle Marie Cooper; m. Scott Richardson Rivenes, Oct. 7, 1995; children: Bradley S., Bailey M. BA, BS, So. Meth. U., Dallas, 1989; MD, U. Ariz., Tucson, 1993. Diplomate in pediat. Am. Acad. Pediat., 1996, in pediat. cardiology 2000. Pediatric cardiologist Tex. Children's Hosp., Houston, 1999—; asst. prof. pediat. Baylor Coll. Medicine, Houston, 1999—. Dir. Tex. Children's Health Ctrs. Cardiology Clinics, Houston, 2006—09. Contbr. articles to profl. jours. Com. mem. Am. Heart Assn. Operation Heartbeat, Houston, 2002—04; bd. mem. Am. Heart Assn., Sugar Land, Tex., 2001—06, Health Edn. Adv. Coun., Ft. Bend ISD, Sugar Land, 2003—07. Recipient Merck Manual award, U. Ariz., 1993; grantee We. Fedn. Clin. Rsch., 1991. Fellow: Am. Acad. Pediat.; mem.: Soc. Pediat. Echocardiography, Am. Soc. Echocardiography, Am. Coll. Cardiology, Am. Heart Assn., Alpha Omega Alpha. Office: Texas Children's Hosp Cardiology 6621 Fannin MC 19345-C Houston TX 77030 Office Fax: 832-825-5630. Business E-Mail: smrivene@texaschildrenshospital.org.

RIVERA, PAUL W., neurologist; b. Sioux City, Iowa, Feb. 26, 1943; s. Julian and Mary Rivera; m. Jackie Rivera; children: Paul Jr., Beth, John. BS in Biology, UCLA, 1965, MD, 1969. Lic. CPR Iowa, 1970, cert. in neurology Iowa, 1973. Neurologist Univ. of Iowa Hosp., 1979—90, neurology dept. head, 1991—2000; adj. prof. Univ. of Iowa, 2000—; chief neurologist Meriks Medicine, Coralville, Iowa, 2003—. Intern Univ. of Iowa Hosp., 1970—73, neurological resident, 1973—78. Contbr. articles to profl. med. jours. Mem.: AMA (dist. rep. 2001—03, Most Active Dist. Rep. 2002). Democrat. Roman Catholic. Avocations: accordion, aquariums, yodelling. Office: Meriks Medicine 1490 Coralville Coralville IA 52241-1013

RIVERA-NUNEZ, ZORIMAR, research scientist; PhD, U. Mich., 2009. Rsch. assoc. Armed Forces Inst. Pathology, 2002—03; rsch. asst. U. Mich., 2004—08; rsch. assoc. NRC, 2009—. Reviewer Elsevier, 2010. Mem.: APHA, Soc. Epidemiology Rsch., Soc. Pediatric & Perinatal Epidemiologic Rsch., Internat. Soc. Environ. Epidemiology. Avocation: cooking. Office: 26W Martin Luther King (MS-4110) Cincinnati OH 45268 Home Fax: 513-569-7916. Personal E-mail: zoryma@hotmail.com. Business E-Mail: rivera-nunez.zorimar@apa.gov.

RIVERA-SINCLAIR, ELSA, psychologist, consultant, researcher; b. Lima, Peru, Dec. 2, 1927; came to U.S. 1954; d. Jorge Maximo Rivera Bodero and Hortencia Resurreccion Vega Alvarado; m. Walter Ward Sinclair, Oct. 30, 1957; children: Harold Anthony, Thomas Edgar (dec.), Ian Paul. AA in Gen. Edn., Montgomery Coll., Takoma Park, Md., 1976; BA in Psychology, U. Md., Coll. Pk., 1979; MA in Clin. Psychology, U. Md., Balt. County, 1982; PhD in Counseling Psychology, U. Md., Coll. Pk., 1988. Diplomate in clin. psychology Am. Bd. Psychol. Spltys., 1998. Psychology extern Spring Grove Hosp., Catonsville, Md., 1980—81; psychology intern Veterans Administrn. Med. Ctr., Washington, 1985—86; clin. psychologist PHS evaluation facility/inpatient care St. Elizabeths Hosp. Immigration/Naturalization, Washington, 1989; clin. psychologist acute care St. Elizabeths Hosp., Washington, 1989; clin. psychologist DC Dept. Mental Health, Washington, 1996—2003. Bd. dirs. Mayor of D.C. Multicultural Task Force, 1992-94, CMHS, Dept. Human Svcs. Contbr. article to a profl. jour. Recipient Vol. award Andromeda Transcultural Hispano Mental Health Ctr., 1998; fellow APA, 1982. Mem. APA, DC Psychol. Assn., Md. Psychol. Assn., Phi Kappa Phi. Avocations: travel, painting, reading, poetry, classic music. Home: 116 Fleetwood Ter Silver Spring MD 20910 Personal E-mail: universe@morishe.com.

RIVIERE, JIM EDMOND, pharmacologist, toxicologist, educator; b. New Bedford, Mass., Mar. 3, 1953; s. Raymond R. Riviere and Gertrude E. Pelletier-Riviere; m. Nancy Ann Monteiro-Riviere, May 31, 1976; children: Christopher, Brian, Jessica. BS, MS, Boston Coll., 1976; DVM, PhD, Purdue U., 1980, DSc (hon.), 2007. Lic. vet. medicine; diplomate Am. Bd. Forensic Medicine, Acad. Toxicological Sci. From asst. prof. to assoc. prof. NC State U., Raleigh, 1981-88, prof., 1988-92, Burroughs-Wellcome disting. prof. pharmacology, 1992—, dir. Ctr. Chem. Toxicology Rsch. and Pharmacokinetics, 1989—, dir. Biomath. Prog., 2005—07, alumni disting. grad. prof., 2010—. Cons. for govt. and pharm. cos.; mem. sci. bd. FDA. Author, editor 10 books, author over 477 rsch. manuscripts. Recipient Ebert prize Am. Pharm. Assn., 1991, Disting. Alumni award Purdue U., 1991, Outstanding Rsch. award NC State U. Alumni Assn., 1993, Harvey Wiley medal, 1997, J.F. Davis award, 2011, FDA Commrs. Spl. citation, 1997, O. Max Gardner award U. NC Sys., 1999; numerous rsch. grants. Fellow Am. Acad. Vet. Pharmacology and Therapeutics (editor 1989-92, 99—, First Rsch. award 1998, Disting. fellow), Inst. Medicine Nat. Academies (elected); mem. Am. Assn. Pharm. Scientist, Soc. Toxicology, Am. Vet. Med. Assn., Am. Coll. Forensic Examiners, Bd. of Sci. Coun. Nat. Toxicology Prog. Achievements include 6 patents in field. Avocations: baseball, boating, beachcombing. Office: NC State U 4700 Hillsborough St Raleigh NC 27606-1428 Home Phone: 919-881-9219. Business E-Mail: Jim_Riviere@ncsu.edu.

RIVKIN, MICHAEL J., neurologist, director; b. Washington, Jan. 22, 1956; AB, Brown U., 1977; MD, U. Va., 1984. Dir., cerebrovascular disorders and stroke program, neurology in-patient svc. chief, dept. neurology Chidlren's Hosp. Boston, 1992—. Assoc. prof., neurology Harvard Med. Sch., 2003. Mem.: Am. Acad. Neurology, Child Neurology Soc. Office: Childrens Hosp Boston St Pavilion 154 Dept Neurology Boston MA 02115 Business E-Mail: michael.rivkin@childrens.harvard.edu.

RIVOIRE, WALDEMAR AUGUSTO, medical educator; b. Caxias do Sul, RS, Brazil, June 2, 1941; s. Wolmar and Antonietta Pippino Rivoire; m. Lenira Franchini Rivoire, Dec. 26, 1945; children: Daniela, Tiago. Degree in Medicine, Faculdade De Medicina, Porto Alegre, 1965, MD magna lauda, 2006; PhD magna lauda, Faculdade De Medicina. Post grad. tchr. methodology Edu. Sch., Porto Alegra, 1972; post grad. tchr. gyn. Med. Sch., Porto Alegre, 1966—69, concurso publico prof. & avxiliar, 1974, concurso publico prof. & asst., 1978, concurso interno prof. adj., 1988, concurso interno prof. assoc., 2006—; ex mem. editl. bd. Internat. Fedn. Cenvical Pathology & Colposcopy. Dir. Div. Gyn. Oncology Hosp. De Clinicas, Porto Alegre, 1974—. Author: (book) Rotinas Em Gynecologia, 2006—10; contbr. articles to profl. jours. Recipient Cirv & Bia Oncologia award, Colposcopia Rio De Janiene. Mem.: Brazilian Soc. Colposcopy (past pres., Premio De Rene Cartier award 1990), Am. Soc. Cervical Pathology & Colposcopy (past liason), Latin Am. Fedn. Low Genital Tract Pathology & Colposcopy (past pres.), Large Internat. Fed. Carvical Pathology and Colposcopy, Nomination Federa Latino Am. De Patologia Do Tracto Genital Inferior E Coldoscopia. Avocations: magic, movies, music. Home: Rua Disnard 72 90850-030 Porto Alegre RS Brazil

RIX, HERVÉ HENRI FERNAND, biomedical engineer, educator; b. Phnom-Penh, Cambodia, Nov. 10, 1944; B, Lycée Masséna, Nice, 1962; Doctorat d'Etat ès Sciences, U. Nice, 1980, M in Signal Processing and Control. Lectr., sr. lectr. U. Nice-Sophia Antipolis, 1969—88, prof., 1988—2010, emeritus prof., 2010—. Head biomed. signal processing team Lab. Signaux et Sys. de Sophia Antipolis, UMR, UNS-CNRS, 1980—2008; coord. stochatic processes modulus Doctoral Sch. Info. and Communication Scis., U. Nice-Sophia Antipolis, 1985—2003; French project coord. rsch. programs biomed. signal processing and analysis Lab. I3S Sophia Antipolis and Inst. Biocybernetics and Biomed. Engring., Warsaw, 1997—2008, CNRS, France, PAS, Poland; mem. sci. coun. Internat. Ctr. Biocybernetics, Polish Acad. Scis., 2002—. Mem.: IEEE, Soc. Française de Chronobiologie, Soc. Française de Génie Bioméd. Achievements include research in high resolution ECG. Home: 42 Ave Saint-Barthélemy Nice Paca 06100 France Personal E-mail: rix@i3s.unice.fr.

RIYAZ, NAJEEBA, dermatologist, educator; d. Mohamed Thypparambil and Amina Mohamed; m. Riyaz Riyaz, Sept. 14, 1978; children: Faiz Riyaz Arakkal, Roshin Riyaz Arakkal. MBBS, Govt. Med. Coll., Calicut, India, 1978, MD in Dermatology, 1986, diploma in Venereology and Dermatology, 1985. Diplomate Nat. Bd. Dermatology New Delhi, 1986. Asst. ins. med. officer Kerala Health Svcs., 1981—83; lectr. in dermatology Govt. Med. Coll., Calicut, 1983—94, from asst. to assoc. prof. dermatology, 1994—2002, prof. and head dermatology and venereology, 2002—. Dean faculty modern medicine Kannur U., Kerala; mem. rsch. coun. Calicut U., Kerala, mem. faculty bd. health scis.; asst. ins. med. officer Kerala Health Svs.; lectr. in dermatology; asst. prof. dermatology; assoc. prof. in dermatology; prof. head dermatology. Author: Dermatology Digest - MCQS, 2004; co-author: Sisurogangalum Prathividhikalum (Malayalam lang.), 1999, Pediatrics & Medicine Made Easy, 2000, Textbook of Pediatric Gastroenterology and Hepatology, 2002. Fellow: Am. Acad. Dermatology; mem.: Kerala Med. Coll. Tchrs. Assn. (life), Indian Med. Assn. - Assn. Med. Specialties (life), Indian Assn. Dermatologists, Venereologists and Leprologists (life Appreciation award for best br. sec. 1996), Assn. Cutaneous Surgeons India (life), Indian Med. Assn. (life). Avocations: attending free medical camps for poor, travel, reading. Office: Govt Medical College Kovoor Kerala Calicut 673 008 India Home: Chalappuram Road 673 002 Calicut 673 002 India Personal E-mail: najeeba_riyaz@rediffmail.com.

RIZK, MAGED, cardiologist, researcher; b. Cairo, Apr. 12, 1961; s. Mostafa Rizk; m. Magda Rashad, May 25, 1992; children: Ahmed, Rahma. MD, Ain Shams U., 1985; PhD in Pharmacology and Toxicology, U. Medicine and Dentistry NJ, 1992. Cert. Am. Bd. Internal Medicine, 1996, ABIM Bd. Cert. in Cardiology 2000, Bd. Cert. in Echocardiography 2001. Instr., dept. medicine NY Med. Coll., Valhalla, NY, 1995—97, cardiology fellow, 1997—2000; asst. prof. cardiology St. Louis U., 2000—01; cardiology cons. Cardiovascular Cons., PC, Sterling Heights, Mich., 2001; dir. noninvasive cardiology St. John Macomb Hosp., 2006. Pres. Grad. Student Assn. UMDNJ, Newark, 1990—91; instr. of medicine NY Med. Coll., Valhalla, 1995—96; pres., CEO Medcom Am. Inc., Elmsford, NY, 1995—97; dir. Cardiology So. Ill., Herrin, 2000—01. Doctorate fellowship, UMDNJ, 1987. Mem.: ACP, Am. Soc. Nuc. Cardiology, Am. Soc. Echocardiography, Am. Heart Assn., Am. Assn. Univ. Profs., Am. Coll. Cardiology. Achievements include patents for Anticoagulant effect of aspirin and salicylamide, 1992. Avocation: tennis. Home: 2221 Custer Dr Troy MI 48085-6728 Office Phone: 586-274-2450. Personal E-mail: maged@sbcglobal.net.

RIZZI GILLESPIE, TERESA MARIE, bilingual speech-language pathologist; b. Denver, Aug. 8, 1964; d. Theophilus Marcus and Maudie Marie (Pitts) R.; m. Eric W. Gillespie, December 12, 2003; 1 child: Brice. BA in Speech Pathology & Audiology, U. Denver, 1986, BA in Spanish, 1986; MS in Speech Pathology, Vanderbilt U., 1988. Pediatric speech-lang. pathologist Rose Med. Ctr., Denver, 1988—90; pvt. practice Denver, 1990—2002; owner, operator Talk of The Town Speech-Lang. Pathologists, Denver, 1990—2002, Niños De Colo., Denver, 1995—2005; Spanish tchr. Jewish Cmty. Ctr., Denver, 1991—92, Temple Emanual, Denver, 1992—95; bilingual pediatric speech-lang. pathologist Children's Hosp., Denver, 1994—98; bilingual speech-lang. pathologist Denver Pub. Schs., 2002—. Spanish tutor and interpreter, Denver, 1988—; bilingual pediatric speech-lang. pathologist United Cerebral Palsy Assn., Denver, 1998-99, Rocky Mountain SER Head Start, Denver, 2008-2009; bilingual speech-lang. pathologist Colo. Dept. Edn. English Lang. Learners Exceptional Needs Project, Denver, 2004-2006; presenter in field at state and nat. levels; rschr. in field. G'arin grantee Ctrl. Agy. Jewish Edn., 1993, grantee U. No. Colo. Grad. Sch., 1994. Mem. Am. Speech-Lang. Hearing Assn. (Continuing Edn. award 1991), Phi Sigma Iota. Achievements include research in use of mild gain amplifier in articulation therapy. Avocations: computers, chess, reading. Office Phone: 720-423-8286. Business E-Mail: teresa_gillespie@dpsk12.org.

RIZZO, LENIO, psychiatrist, educator; b. Abano, Italy, July 12, 1948; s. Enrico and Olga (Albertin) Rizzo; m. Annalisa Girardis, July 21, 1972; children: Valerio, Rossella. MD, U. Medicine, Padua, Italy, 1973. Specialist in pediats. U. Medicine, Padua, 1975—77; specialist in neuropsychiatry of children U. Pisa, Italy, 1977, specialist in psychiatry, 1988; dr. asst. Unit Child Neuropsychiatry, Asolo, 1995—97, chief dr. Camposam, 1997—2001, Treviso, 2001—; prof. child psychopathology U. Medicine, Padua, 2002; prof. child psychiatry U. Psychology, Padua, 2003. Vis. prof. U. Paris 5, U. Paris 7, rschr. dept. psychology. Editor: Borderline Disorder Child, 1996, Anorexia Bulimia, 2006, Foetal Psychiatria, 2007. Office: Unit Child Neuropsychology Hosp Piazza Ospedale 4 31-100 Padua Italy Home: Via Ospedale Civile 6 35121 Padua PD Italy

ROACH, CHRISSY, marketing executive; b. Fort Worth, Tex., Feb. 11, 1979; Degree in Mktg., Ariz. State U., 2001. Ops. mgr. Morrison Vein Inst., 2003—. Bd. dirs. Amigos de Salud, 2002. Avocations: running, reading. Office: 8575 E Princess Dr #223 Scottsdale AZ 85255 Office Phone: 480-860-6455. Business E-Mail: chrissy@morrisonveininstitute.com.

ROARK, H. MICHAEL, plastic surgeon; b. Natick, Mass. married. AA, Grossmont CC, 1964; BS, Oreg. State U., 1966; MD, U. Calgary, 1975. Diplomate Am. Bd. Surgery, 1981, Am. Bd. Plastic Surgery, 1984, lic. Can., 1975, gen. lic. physician and surgeon Fedn. Licensing Exam./Ont. Can., 1982, Calif., 1983. Intern straight surg. Mt. Sinai Hosp., Toronto, Ont., Canada, 1975—76; resident gen. surgery Ottawa Civic Hosp. and Ottawa Gen. Hosp., Ont., Canada, 1976, Univ. of Toronto Gaille Program in Postgrad. Surgery, Toronto, Ont., Canada, 1977—80, resident plastic surgery, 1980—82; clin. fellow plastic surgery divsn. Sunnybrook Med. Ctr. Univ. of Toronto, 1982—83; hosp. staff appointments include Grossmont Hosp., La Mesa, Calif., 1983—2006, Sharp Meml. Hosp., San Diego, 1985—2005, Scripps Meml. Hosp., La Jolla, Calif., 1983—; immediate past med. dir. La Jolla Cosmetic Surgery Ctr., Calif., cosmetic, plastic and reconstructive surgeon Calif.; founder and former med. dir. Alvarado Inst. of Plastic & Reconstructive Surgery; med. dir. Alvarado Wellness Anti-Aging & Longevity Ctr. Mem.: Am. Soc. of Plastic Surgeons Lipoplasty Soc., Am. Soc. for Aesthetic Plastic Surgery, Calif. Soc. of Plastic Surgery, San Diego Plastic Surgery Soc. (v.p. 1997, pres. 1998), Calif. Med. Soc., San Diego County Med. Soc., Am. Soc. of Plastic Surgeons. Office: La Jolla Cosmetic Surgery Center 9850 Genesee Ave Ste 480 La Jolla CA 92037 Office Phone: 858-452-2066. Office Fax: 858-452-9910. Business E-Mail: drroark@ljcsc.com.

ROARKE, MICHAEL CHARLES, medical educator, nuclear medicine physician; b. Albany, NY, May 8, 1959; s. Charles Augustus and Joan Ann Roarke; m. Maria Giuliani, June 25, 1988; 1 child, Michael Andrew. BS, SUNY, Albany, 1981, MS, 1982; MD, U. Rochester Sch. Medicine, NYC, 1990. Cert. Am. Bd. Radiology, 1995, Am. Bd. Nuc. Medicine, 1996. Chemistry tchr. Albany Acad. Boys, NY, 1982—86; intern internal medicine St. Mary's Hosp., Rochester, 1990—91; resident diagnostic radiology Mallinckrodt Inst. Radiology, St. Louis, 1991—95, fellow nuc. medicine, 1995—96; asst. prof. radiology U. Tex. Med. Ctr., Houston, 1996—97, Mayo Med. Sch., Scottdale, 1997—. Sect. head nuc. radiology Mayo Clinic Ariz., Scottsdale, Ariz., 1997—2007, med. dir. nuc. radiology, 1997—2007. Recipient Best Intern award, St. Mary's Hosp. Internal Medicine Program, 1991, Tchr. Recognition award, White House Commn. on Presdl. Scholars, 1985; named one of Best Doctors in Am., 2003—08, America's Top Physicians, Consumer's Rsch. Coun., 2005—08; Klingenstein Summer Tchg. fellow, Columbia U., 1983. Mem.: AAAS, Am. Roentgen Ray Soc., Acad. Molecular Imaging (assoc.), Soc. Nuc. Medicine (assoc.), Radiol. Soc. N.Am. (assoc.), Beta Beta Beta, Alpha Omega Alpha (life). Avocations: music, composing, mineral photography, coin collecting/numismatics. Office: Mayo Clinic Ariz 13400 East Shea Blvd Scottsdale AZ 85259 Personal E-mail: mroarke@aol.com.

ROBB, GEOFFREY LAWRENCE, plastic surgeon; b. El Paso, Tex., May 28, 1946; s. Giles Anthony and Mary Jo (Lawrence) R.; m. Cathy Jean Cross, May 31, 1974; children: Tiffany, Kimberly, Courtney, Carly, Melaney, Mary. BS, U. Miami, 1969, MD, 1974. Diplomate Am. Bd. Otolaryngology. Commd. ensign USNR, 1970-92; advanced through grades to capt., 1989; resident in otalaryngology, mem. staff US Naval Hosp., San Diego, 1974-79, otolaryngologist Orlando, Fla., 1979-83; plastic surgeon USN Sponsorship at U. Pitts., 1983-85, microvascular surgeon, 1985; plastic surgeon U.S. Naval Hosp., Portsmouth, Va., 1985-88; ret., 1992; chief plastic surgery U.S. Naval Hosp., Portsmouth, Va., 1988-92; vice chmn. plastic surgery M.D. Anderson Cancer Ctr., Houston, 1992-97, chmn. plastic surgery, 1997—, dep. chmn. divsn. surgery, 1994—, dir. postgrad. med. edn., 1992—, med. dir. plastic surgery clinic, 1992—, assoc. med. dir. skin cancer ctr., 1996. Contbg. author: Reconstructive Plastic Surgery for Cancer, 1995, Endoscopic Plastic Surgery, 1995, Advanced Skin Cancer of Head and Neck, 1995; contbr. articles to profl. jours. Fellow ACS, Am. Soc. Plastic Reconstructive Surgeons, Am. Soc. Reconstructive Microsurgeons, Am. Assn. Plastic Surgeons; mem. Internat. Soc. Reconstructive Microsurgery, Tex. Soc. Plastic Surgeons, Houston Soc. Plastic Surgeons, KC. Avocations: physical fitness, weightlifting, tennis, running. Office: MD Anderson Cancer Ctr 1515 Holcombe Blvd # 443 Houston TX 77030-4009 E-mail: grobb@mdanderson.org.

ROBB, PAUL A., reproductive endocrinologist; b. Can., July 20, 1963; MSc, U. Toronto, 1992, MD, 1996. OB/Gyn resident U. Toronto, 2001; physician Med. Coll. Wis., 2004—; fellowship REI, Cincinnati, Ohio, 2004. Named one of Best Drs. in Am. Fellow: Royal Coll. Physicians and Surgeons, Am. Bd. Ob-Gyn. Avocations: Cycling, running, tennis. Office: Med Coll Wis Dept Ob-Gyn 9200 W Wisconsin Ave Milwaukee WI 53226 Business E-Mail: probb@mcw.edu.

ROBB, PETER JOHN, consultant surgeon otorhinolaryngology; b. Dundee, Scotland, Apr. 27, 1956; s. Allan John and Margaret Steven Robb; m. Josephine Ann Lord; children: Sophie Jane, Georgina Lindsay. BSc Psychology 1st Class Honours, London University, The Royal London Hospital, 1975—78; MBBS, London U., 1981. Intern profl. surg. unit Royal London Hosp., 1981—82; resident Addenbrookes Hosp., Cambridge, England, 1982—83; hon. cons. otolaryngologist Royal Surrey County Hosp., Guildford, 2001—; resident otolaryngology Guy's Hosp., London, 1984—91; rsch. fellow U. Wash., Seattle, 1986—87; fellow pediat. laryngology Queen Alexandra Hosp. for Children, Sydney, 1989—90; pres. elect Royal Soc. Medicine Sect. Lekyugology & Rhinology. Clin. dir. surgery Epsom (Surrey, Eng.) Gen. Hosp., 1996—99; chmn. Intercollegiate Bd. Otolaryngology, 2008—11. Mem. editl. bd.: CME Bull. Otorhinolaryngology - Head & Neck Surgery, 1996; contbr. articles to profl. publs., 2001. Fellow: Royal Coll. Surgeons Edinburgh, Royal Coll. Surgeons Eng. (mem. ct. examiners), Royal Soc. Medicine (coun. mem. sect. laryngology and rhinology 2000—03, hon. treas. and coun. mem.); mem.: ENT UK Coun., NHS Modernization Agy., Nat. Inst. for Clin. Excellence (chmn., guidelines review panel 2004—11), Examiners Intercollegiate Bd. in Otolaryngology, Court of Examiners, Brit. Assn. Pediat. Otorhinolaryngology (sec. 1999—2002, pres. 2006—08, hon. sec.), Brit. Med. Assn. Avocations: travel, writing. Office: Epsom and St Helier Univ Hosps NHS Trust Epsom Surrey KT18 7EG England Home Phone: 01372 275161; Office Phone: 01372 735226. Personal E-mail: peter.robb@esth.nhs.uk.

ROBBERSTAD, MAGNUS KNUTSON, neurology consultant; b. Oslo, May 20, 1932; s. Knut and Eldrid (Fjalestad) R.; m. Aslaug Goderstad, Sept. 29, 1956, (dec.) Oct. 12, 2007; children: Eldrid Gro, Tonje Solveig, Ingunn Kristin MD, U. Oslo, 1956; examinee, Govt. Health Adminstrn. Sch., Oslo, 1964; specialist phys. medicine and rehab., U. Oslo, 1975, specialist neurology, 1978, specialist social adminstrn., 1983. Intern Porsgrunn Hosp. Group, 1957—58; staff mem. Oslo Mcpl. Hosp. Group, 1969—73, Oslo U. Hosp. Group, 1973—80; staff Tromsoe U. Hosp., 1981; med. cons. neurology Nat. Ins. Adminstrn., Oslo, 1982—84, chief med. cons., 1984—2002, sr. med. cons., 2002—04; pvt. practice neurology, 2004—. Fed. health officer, Nord-Odal, 1959-61, Leirfjord, 1961-69 Co-author: (ency.) Norsk Allkunnebok, 1958-64, (textbooks) Medisinsk journalskriving, 1979, rev., 1987, Nevrologi fra barn til voksen, 1997, (nonfiction) Målreising, 1967; author: (textbook) Rettleiing i journalskriving, 1956 Mem. County Parliament, Leirfjord, 1963-69, Nesodden, 1971-75; chmn. Ednl. Bd., Leirfjord, 1963-69; mem., vice-chmn. Bd. Energy, Nesodden County, 1988-2000. 1st lt. Royal Norwegian Air Force, 1958-59 Grantee Storebrand Ins. Co., 1972 Mem. Norwegian Soc. Neurology, Norwegian Soc. Phys. Medicine, Acad. Norwegian Lang. (bd. dirs., pres. 1979-2000), Medisinsk Mällag (direction bd., pres. 1954—) Lutheran. Avocations: languages, camping, politics. Home Phone: 47-66912795; Office Phone: 47-90034477. Personal E-mail: magnuskr@online.no.

ROBBINS, DARRYL ANDREW, pediatrician; b. Modesto, Calif., Sept. 16, 1945; s. Jerome and Grace (Bass) Robbins; m. Harriette Lee Eisenberg, June 12, 1971; children: Jennifer Lynn, Julie Ellen, Allison Beth. BS, Dickinson Coll., 1967; DO, Phila. Coll. Osteo. Medicine, 1971. Diplomate Am. Bd. Pediat. Intern Doctor's Hosp., Columbus, Ohio, 1971-72; resident in pediatrics Children's Hosp. Med. Ctr., Cin., 1972-75; pvt. practice specializing in pediat. Columbus, 1975—. Mem. genetics svcs. adv. com. Ohio Dept. Health, 1978—86; bd. dirs. Diocesan Child Guidance Ctr., Columbus, 1983—88, vice-chmn., 1986; pres. med. staff Columbus Children's Hosp., 1996; with Ohio Pediat. Psychiatry Decision Support Network Ohio Dept. Mental Health, 2009—. Trustee Nationwide Children's Hosp., Columbus, 2001—; bd. dirs. Children's Practicing Pediatricians, Columbus, 1991—94, 1998—, pres., 2001—. Recipient Samuel Dalinsky Meml. award for Outstanding Graduating Resident, Cin. Children's Hosp., 1975, Lifetime Achievement award, Ohio State Coll. Medicine, 2004, Career Contbn. award, Columbus Children's Hosp., 2004; named Pediatrician of the Yr., 1982, 1990. Fellow: Am. Acad. Pediat.; mem.: Columbus Med. Forum (treas. 2011), Ctrl. Ohio Pediatric Soc. (pres. elect 1988, pres. 1989—90). Jewish. Office: 453 Waterbury Ct Gahanna OH 43230-5309 Home: 6388 Portrait Cir Westerville OH 43081 Home Phone: 614-245-8542; Office Phone: 614-471-0652. Personal E-mail: drobbinshome@att.net.

ROBBINS, ELIZABETH, pediatric hematologist, oncologist; b. Palo Alto, Calif., 1951; Attended, Stanford U., Calif.; BA in English, U. Calif. Berkely; MD, U. Calif. Davis, 1978. Diplomate Am. Bd. Pediat., Am. Bd. Pediat. Hematology-Oncology. Intern pediat. Boston City Hosp., 1978—79; resident pediat. Mass. Gen. Hosp., Boston, 1979—80, resident hematologic oncology, 1980—81, fellowship, 1981—83, staff, 1986—92; rsch. fellow Inst. Maladies du Sang Hosp., Paris; staff U. Calif. San Francisco Children's Cancer and Blood Disorder Prog., 1992—; assoc. clin. prof. pediat. U. Calif. San Francisco. Contbr. articles to profl. jours. Mem.: Children's Oncology Grp., Am. Soc. Hematology. Mailing: U Calif Hosp 400 Parnassus Ave San Francisco CA 94143 Office Phone: 415-476-3831. Office Fax: 415-502-4372. Business E-Mail: robbinse@peds.ucsf.edu.

ROBBINS, JOHN BENNETT, medical researcher; b. Bklyn., Dec. 1, 1932; BA, NYU, 1956; MD (hon.), U. Goteborg, Sweden, 1959. Intern, resident Children's Med. Svc. Mass. Gen. Hosp., Boston, 1959—60; rsch. fellow dept. pediat. U. Fla., 1961—64; guest scientist dept. chem. immunology Weizmann Inst. Sci., Rehovot, Israel, 1965—66; asst. prof. pediat. and microbiology U. Fla., Gainesville, 1964—67; from asst. prof. to assoc. prof. pediat. Albert Einstein Coll. Medicine, 1967—70; clin. dir. Nat. Inst. Child Health and Human Devel. NIH, 1970—72; chief devel. immunology br. NIH, 1971—74; dir. divsn. bacterial products FDA, 1974—83; former chief lab. devel. and molecular immunity Nat. Inst. Child Health and Human Devel. NIH, sr. investigator sect. on bacterial disease, pathogenesis & immunity. Henry Bale Meml. lectr. Nat. Inst. Biol. Stds. and Control, 1979; Erwin Neter Meml. lectr. U. Buffalo, 1984; Henry L. Barnett lectr. Albert Einstein Coll. Medicine, 1985; Maxwell Finland lectr. Infectious Disease Soc. Am., 1989; Louis Weinstein lectr. Tufts U., 1989. Recipient E. Mead Johnson award, Am. Acad. Pediat., 1975, Albert Lasker Clin. Med. Rsch. award, Albert and Mary Lasker Found., 1996. Fellow: Am. Acad. Microbiology; mem.: NAS, Am. Philos. Soc., Nat. Inst. Medicine, Am. Assn. Immunologists, Assn. Am. Physicians, Am. Soc. Clin. Investigation, Soc. Infectious Disease, Soc. Pediatric Rsch. Achievements include development of first effective typhoid fever vaccine for children. Office: Eunice Kennedy Shriver Nat Inst Child Health & Human Devel 6 Center Dr Rm 2A04 Bethesda MD 20892 Office Phone: 301-496-0850. Office Fax: 301-402-9108. Business E-Mail: robbinsjo@mail.nih.gov. *

ROBBINS, MEREDITH TURNBACH, medical educator; b. Tuscaloosa, Ala., Dec. 31, 1974; BS, Tulane U., 1997; Ph., U. Ala., Birmingham, 2002. Asst. prof. U. Ala., 2007—. Rsch. grant, NIH. Mem.: Jr. League Birmingham, Am. Pain Soc., Internat. Assn. Study Pain, Soc. Neurosci. Office: 901 19th St S BMR2 Rm 202 Birmingham AL 35294 Business E-Mail: met@uab.edu.

ROBBINS, RICHARD JAMES, endocrinologist, researcher; b. Danbury, Conn., Sept. 21, 1948; s. James Bernard and Ann Patricia Robbins; m. Anne Kathleen Schmiesing, Aug. 29, 1970; children: Andrew Richard, Heather Kathleen Kollar. MD, Creighton U., Omaha, Nebr., 1975. Cert. internal medicine and endocrinology Am. Bd. Internal Medicine, 1978. Dir. neuroendocrine unit Yale Med. Sch., New Haven, 1985—94; chief, endocrine svc. Meml. Sloan-Kettering Cancer Ctr., NYC, 1994—2005; prof., chmn. dept. medicine Meth. Hosp., Houston, 2005—. Recipient Alpha Omega Alpha, Creighton U., 1975, Henry Christian award, Am. Fedn. Clin. Rsch., 1993, Disting. Svc. award, Pituitary Soc., 1995, William Lees Lectureship, Johns Hopkins U., 2004, Best Doctors in NYC, 2005, Top Doctors in Cancer, Castel Connolly Med., Ltd., 2005—07, Charles and Anne Duncan Disting. Chair, Meth. Hosp., 2006, Best Doctors in Am., 2007. Fellow: ACP. Achievements include research in the synthesis of neuropeptides in mammalian cerebral cortex; first human to human neural transplantation for Parkinson's Disease; discovery of selective loss of inhibitory somatostatin interneurons in human epilepsy; use of recombinant human TSH for treatment of thyroid cancer; prognostic value of PET scanning in metastatic thyroid cancer.

ROBBINS, ROBERT CLAYTON, surgeon; b. Laurel, Miss., Nov. 20, 1957; AA in Chemistry, Jones Jr. Coll., Ellisville, Miss., 1977; BS in Chemistry, Millsaps Coll., Jackson, Miss., 1979; MD, U. Miss. Med. Ctr., Jackson, Miss., 1983. Cert. cardiothoracic surgery Am. Bd. Thoracic Surgery, gen. surgery Am. Bd. Surgery. Intern, gen. surgery U. Miss. Med. Ctr., Jackson, 1983—84, resident, gen. surgery,

1984—85, chief resident, gen. surgery, 1988—89; postdoctoral fellow, cardiothoracic transplantation, dept. surgery Columbia-Presbyn. Med. Ctr., 1986; clin. assoc., cardiothoracic surgery, surgery br., Nat. Heart Lung Blood Inst. NIH, Bethesda, Md., 1986—88; resident, cardiothoracic surgery Stanford U. Hosp., Calif., 1989—91, chief resident, cardiothoracic surgery Calif., 1991—92, co-dir., Cardiac Clin. Ctr. Calif., 2002—, dir., Stanford Inst. for Cardiovascular Medicine Calif., 2004; pediat. fellow, congenital heart surgery Emory U. Sch. Medicine, Atlanta, 1992, Royal Children's Hosp., Melbourne, Australia, 1993; dir., cardiothoracic transplantation lab. Stanford U. Sch. Medicine, 1993—, acting asst. prof., cardiothoracic surgery, 1993—95, asst. prof., cardiothoracic surgery, 1995—2001, dir., heart, heart-lung, and lung transplant program, 1998—, assoc. prof., cardiothoracic surgery, 2001—05, chmn., dept. cardiothoracic surgery, 2005, prof., cardiothoracic surgery, 2005—. Dir., clin. cardiothoracic surgery tchg. conf., 1993—2006; mem. expert panel on minimally invasive surgery Health Tech. Ctr., 2001; bd. dirs. Calif. Transplant Donor Network, 1997—2005, Cohesion Technologies, Palo Alto, 2000—; mem. scientific adv. bd. Cardica, Inc., Menlo Park, Calif., 1997—, bd. dirs., 2000—; mem. scientific adv. bd. Cytograft Tissue Engring. Inc., Novato, Calif., 2000—, bd. dirs., 2003—; mem. scientific adv. bd. Transvascular, Inc., Menlo Park, Calif., 1995—2000, Embol-X, Inc., Sunnyvale, Calif., 1995—98, ArthroCare, Corp., Sunnyvale, Calif., 1997—2000, Cardio Vention, Inc., Palo Alto, 1997—99, A-med, Inc., Sacramento, 1997—2000, Microheart, Inc., Sunnyvale, Calif., 1999—2001, Radiant Med., Redwood City, Calif., 2000—, Curis, Inc., Cambridge, Mass., 2001—, Paracor Surgical, Inc., Sunnyvale, Calif., 2001—; mem. clin. adv. bd. Xoma, LLC, Berkeley, Calif., 2002—, Afmedica, Inc., Kalamazoo, 2005, Theregen, Corp., San Francisco, 2005—; mem. physician adv. panel Cardiac Surgery Technologies, Medtronic, Inc., Mpls., 2001—. Ad hoc reviewer Nat. Inst. Neurological Disorders and Stroke Study Sect., NIH, 1996, manuscript reviewer Jour. Thoracic and Cardiovascular Surgery, 1996—, mem. editl. bd., 2001—, manuscript reviewer Annals Thoracic Surgery, 1995—, New Eng. Jour. Medicine, 1996—, abstract reviewer Internat. Soc. Heart and Lung Transplantation, 1996—, mem. editl. bd. Cardiac Surgery Digest, 2001—, Jour. Heart and Lung Transplantation, 2003—, Innovations, 2005—, guest editor, surgical supplement Circulation, 2002—05; contbr. several articles to peer-reviewed jours. Mem. Thoracic Organ Transplantation Com. United Network for Organ Sharing, 1999—2002, Region 5 Thoracic Organ Rep. and Review Bd. Chamn., 1999—2002; rsch. com. mem. Thoracic Surgery Found. for Rsch. and Edn., 2000—; mem. Calif. Transplant Donor Network Med. Affairs Com., 1996—. Fellow: Am. Coll. Cardiology, Am. Heart Assn. (Vivien Thomas Young Investigator award selection com. 1997—, mem. exec. com., coun. on cardiothoracic and vascular surgery 1997—, mem. program com. 1999—), ACS; mem.: Bay Area Soc. Thoracic Surgeons (founding mem.) (pres. 2006, bd. dirs. 2000—), Soc. U. Surgeons, Am. Soc. Transplantation, Am. Soc. Transplant Surgeons, 21st Century Cardiac Surgical Soc., Transplantation Soc., AAAS, Internat. Soc. Heart and Lung Transplantation (co-chair, ventricular assist device coun. 2000—02, bd. dirs. 2000—, program chair 2001—02, mem. program com. 2003, pres. 2006), San Francisco Surgical Soc., Assn. Academic Surgeons (vice-chair, cardiovascular surgery and anesthesia coun. 2005—, mem. strategic planning com. 2006), Soc. Thoracic Surgeons (mem. workforce on clin. edn. 2004—, workforce on surgical treatment end-stage cardiopulmonary disease 2004—), Western Thoracic Surgical Assn., Am. Assn. Thoracic Surgery (membership com. 2003—06, mem. edn. com. 2003—, chair membership com. 2005—06), Cardiothoracic Surgery Network, James D. Hardy Soc., Andrew G. Morrow Soc., Alpha Omega Alpha (Resident award 1989). Achievements include patents in field. Office: Dept Cardiothoracic Surgery Falk Cardiovasc Rsch Ctr Stanford U Sch Medicine 300 Pasteur Dr CVRB MC 5407 Stanford CA 94305-5407 Office Phone: 650-725-3828, 650-723-5771. Fax: 650-725-3846. E-mail: robbins@stanford.edu.

ROBBINS, SUSAN PAULA, social work educator; b. Bklyn., Aug. 15, 1948; d. Harold Jess and Rose (Bernstein) R. AA, Manhattan C.C., 1972; BA summa cum laude, Hamline U., 1974; MSW, U. Minn., 1976; PhD, Tulane U., 1979. Adj. instr. dept. sociology and social work Augsburg Coll., Mpls., 1975-76; part-time instr. women's studies program U. Minn., Mpls., 1976; rsch. and grant cons. Seminole Tribe of Fla., Hollywood, 1978-79, child and adolescent caseworker, program planning cons., 1979-80; coord. criminal justice/corrections program St. Mary's Dominican Coll., New Orleans, 1979-80; asst. prof. social work New Orleans Consortium, 1978-80, U. Houston, 1980-86, assoc. prof., 1986—, assoc. dean acad. affairs, 1998-2000. Cons. ABA Multi Door Program, Houston, Cmty. Svc. Option Program, Houston; mediator Dispute Resolution Ctrs., Houston, 1982—; trainer Tex. Dept. Protective Svcs. Tng. Inst., 1995—. Author (with others): Encyclopedia of Social Work, Social Workers' Desk Reference; contbr. articles and book chpts. to profl. jours. Women's Club of Mpls. fellow, 1975, Nat. Inst. of Mental Health fellow, 1976-78; recipient Nat. Faculty Excellence award Univ. Continuing Edn. Assn., 1998. Mem. NASW, Coun. on Social Work Edn., Social Welfare Action Alliance, Assn. for Cmty. Orgn. and Social Adminstrn., So. Sociol. Soc., Phi Kappa Phi (sec. Houston chpt. 1984—). Democrat. Jewish. Office: University Houston Grad Coll Social Work 110HA Social Work Bldg Houston TX 77204-4013 Office Phone: 713-743-8103. Business E-Mail: srobbins@uh.edu.

ROBBOY, STANLEY J., pathologist, educator; s. John and Sarah (Shapiro) R.; m. Anita Wyzanski, July 21, 1968 (div. 1981); children: Elizabeth, Caroline; m. Marion Meyer, June 14, 1990. Student, U. Mich., 1958-61, MD, 1965. Diplomate Am. Bd. Pathology, Am. Bd. Med. Mgmt. Intern Mt. Sinai Hosp, Cleve., 1965-66; resident to chief in pathology Mass. Gen. Hosp., 1966-70, asst. in pathology, 1972-73, asst. pathologist, 1973-76, assoc. pathologist, 1976-84; resident in pathology Boston Hosp. for Women, 1970; instr. Tufts Med. Sch., 1968-69; asst. prof. pathology Harvard Med. Sch., Boston, 1972-76, assoc. prof., 1976-84; prof. pathology U. Medicine and Dentistry N.J.-N.J. Med. Sch., Newark, 1984—92, chmn. dept., 1984-89, prof. ob-gyn, 1990—92, pathologist-in-chief, 1984-89, dir. faculty practice service, 1985-89; prof., vice chmn. dept. pathology Duke U., 1992—, prof. ob-gyn., 1993—. Cons. pathologist St. Joseph Hosp., Paterson, NJ, 1985—92, St. Barnabas Hosp., Livingston, NJ, 1985—92, Beth Israel Hosp., Newark, 1985—92, VA Med. Ctr., Durham, 1992-2011, Durham Reg. Hosp., 2003-11, Raleigh Com. Hosp., 2003-11; pathologist (DES) Registry Rsch. Transplacental Hormonal Carcinogenesis (formerly Clear-Cell Adenocarcinoma Registry), 1972-83; pathologist, prin. investigator Nat. Collaborative Diethylstilbestrol project, 1974-82; vis. scientist New Eng. Primate Ctr., 1973-84; vis. prof. U. Shiraz Med. Sch., Iran, 1976; commr. NJ Commn. on Cancer Rsch., 1987-92; sr. advisor East Asia Cons. Group, Boston, LA and Tokyo, 1984-85; reference panel for diagnostic and therapeutic tech. AMA, 1982—99; mem. nat. med. com. Planned Parenthood Fedn. Am., 1990-93, vice chmn. com. on oncology, 1993; mem. DES steering com. Nat. Cancer Inst., 1995—; mem. exec. editl. bd. Arch Path Lab Med, 2005-; bd. dir. Pamet Sys. Inc., 1991-09. Mem. editl. bd. Human Pathology, 1980-90, Cervix and the Low Female Genital Tract, 1983-94, Internat. Jour. Gynecologic Pathology, 1985-; editor: Informatics in Pathology, 1985-88, Pathology Rsch. and Practice, 1990-2000, Gynecologic Oncology, 1997-2004, InsScight, 1998-; sect. editor Functional Biomarkers in Disease, 2005-; editor-in-chief, Pathology the Female Reproductive Tract, edits. 1 & 2; contbr. articles to profl. jours. Trustee Am. Pathology Found., 1984—86; NJ commn. Cancer Rsch., 1987—92; co-pres. Chapel Hill Kehillah, 2005—08, Triangle Jewish Film Festival, 2007—08; pres. Coll. Am. Pathologists, 2011—; chair Triangle Jewish Film Festival, 2007—08. Maj. US Army, 1970—72. Recipient Jr. Faculty award Am. Cancer Soc., 1972-75, Found. prize Am. Coll. Ob-Gyn, 1975, Coll. Am. Pathologist Pres. award, 2005; Sara & Mutt Evans Outstanding Cmty. Svc. award, Durham-Chapel Hill, 2005; Pardee fellow U. Mich., 1961, Lederle Lab. fellow, 1962, Eliza Howell fellow, 1964, Ford Found. fellow, 1964-65; clin. fellow Am. Cancer Soc., 1967-68. Fellow Am. Soc. Clin. Pathologists (chmn. pathology telecommunications network com. 1983, task force on computers 1980-83, council on med. informatics 1983-84, planning and scope com. 1983-84, co-chmn. pathology communication network 1983-87, coun. anat. pathology, 1995-2001, future directions, 1995-98), Coll. Am. Pathologists (alt. Mass. del. to house dels. 1981-84, co-chmn. pathology comm. network 1983-85, alt. NJ del. to house dels. 1985-92, exec. com. and advisor nomenclature and classification of disease 1975-80, editl. bd. Systematized Nomenclature Medicine 1976-80, gov. 1999-2005, mem. reimbursement com., 1992-94, profl. and econ. affairs com., 1995-97, outcomes com., 1999-2000, vice chmn. coun. on pub. affairs 1999-2005, coun. of govt. prof. affairs, 2000-2004, credentials com., 2000-04, spokesperson, 2001—, performance measurement com. 2000, nat. meeting planning com. 2003—08, vice chmn. election oversight com. 2006-09, leadership devel. com. 2006-08, strategic planning com., 2008-11, pres. elect 2009-11, pres. 2011-, chair transformation program office steering com.), Soc. Gynecologic Oncologists Assocs.; mem. Arthur Purdy Stout Soc. Surg. Pathology (membership com. 1980-86, treas. 1993-2001, pres.-elect 2001-03, pres. 2003-05), Internat. Acad. Cytology, Internat. Acad. Pathology (edn. com. 1979-83), Internat. Soc. Gynecologic Pathologists (chmn. membership com. 1982-84), Mass. Soc. Pathology (3d party relations 1978-84, chmn. computer com. 1981-84), NC Med. Soc., NC Soc. Pathology, NJ Med. Soc., NJ Soc. Pathology (edn. and profl. rels. coms. 1984-92, exec. com. 1985-92), Chapel Hill Kehillah (co-pres. 2004—08). Jewish. Office: Duke U Med Ctr PO Box 3712 Durham NC 27710-0001 Office Phone: 919-684-3656. Business E-Mail: stanley.robboy@duke.edu.

ROBERT, HARPER G., medical educator; b. Oakland, Calif., Jan. 1, 1944; AB, U. Calif., Berkeley, 1966; PhD in Clin. Psychology, U. Tex., Austin, 1971. Assoc. prof. Menninger Dept. Psychiatry and Behavioral Scis. Baylor Coll. Medicine, 1979—. Office: 1977 Butler Blvd Ste E4400 Houston TX 77030 Office Fax: 713-798-3465. Business E-Mail: rharper@bcm.edu.

ROBERT, LESLIE (LADISLAS), research center administrator, consultant; b. Budapest, Hungary, Oct. 24, 1924; s. Louis and Elizabeth (Bardos) Robert; m. Barbara Klinger, Nov. 19, 1949 (dec.); children: Marianne, Catherine, Elisabeth; m. Jacqueline Labat, Dec. 20, 1976. Student, U. Szeged, Budapest, Hungary, 1944—48; MD, U. Paris, 1953; PhD, U. Lille, France, 1977; MD (hon.), Med. U. Budapest, 1991. Mem. med. faculty dept. biochemistry U. Paris, 1949-59; postdoctoral rsch. fellow dept. biochemistry Sch. Medicine U. Ill., Chgo., 1959—60; postdoctoral rsch. assoc., spl. fellow biochem. & ophthal. res. Columbia U., NYC, 1960—61, postdoctoral rsch. assoc., spl. fellow, 1962—67; dir. biochemistry lab. Inst. for Immunobiology INSERM/CNRS, Broussais Hosp., Paris, 1962-66; founder 1st rsch. ctr. on connective tissue biochemistry CNRS, U. Paris XII, Créteil, France, 1966-94; adminstr. connective tissue unit Cell Biology Lab. U. Paris VII, 1995-97; rsch. dir. French Nat. Rsch. Ctr., Paris, 1974-94, hon. rsch. dir., 1995—; founder rsch. ctr. for clin. and biol. rsch. on aging Charles Foix-Jean Rostand Hosp., Ivry, France, 1993-2001; med. faculty Lab. Immunology U. Paris VI, 1997-98; mem. staff ophthalm. rsch. lab. Hotel Dieu Hosp., Paris, 1998—2009; dir. rsch. lab. in exptl. gerontology Hosp. Emile Roux, Limeil-Brevannes, France, 2001—07. Founder French Soc. Connective Tissue Rsch., 1963, Fedn. European Soc. Connective Tissue Rsch., 1967; cons. several pharm firms; mem Sci Coun Arteriosclerosis Research Inst, Univ Munster, Germany, 1970—96. Author: 9 books on biology of aging including, Time in Biology, 2002, Bio-Logics of Aging, 2004, Secrets of Longevity, 2006; mem editl. bd.: several sci. jours.; author: (monograph series) Frontiers of Matrix Biology, 11 vols.; contbr. over 1000 articles to profl. jours. Recipient Spl. Sci. prize, Sci. Writers, Paris, 1966, Reiss prize in Ophthalmology, 1970, Novartis Prize Gerontol. Rsch., Internat. Assn. Gerontology, 1997, Verzar medal for gerontol. rsch., U. Vienna, Austria, 1994; named Scientist of Yr., Soc. Antioxy Rsch. France, 2009. Mem.: Hungarian Acad. Sci., French Atherosclerosis Soc. (pres 1993—98), Acad. Sci. Nord/Rhein-Westphalie (Germany) (corr.). Home: 7 Rue Jean Baptiste Lully 94440 Santeny France Home Phone: 33-1-43860240. Personal E-mail: lrobert5@wanadoo.fr.

ROBERTS, ALAN SILVERMAN, orthopedic surgeon; b. Apr. 20, 1939; s. Joseph William and Fannie (Margolies) S.; children: Michael Eric, Daniel Ian. BA, Conn. Wesleyan U., Middletown, 1960; MD, Jefferson Med. Coll., Phila., 1966. Rotating intern Lankenau Hosp., Phila., 1966—67; resident in orthop. Tulane U. Med. Coll., 1967—71; pvt. practice specializing in orthop. and hand surgery LA, 1971—. Clin. faculty UCLA Med. Coll., LA, 1971—76. Contbr. articles to profl. jours. With AUS, 1961. Recipient. Canadian Boys 1st Under Single Champion award, 1953, US Boys 1st Under Singles Champions, 1954, US Jr. Boys 18 Under Singles Champions, 1957, Riordan Hand fellow, 1969, Boyes Hand fellow, 1971. Mem. AMA, ACS, Am. Acad. Orthop. Surgeons, Calif. Med. Assn., LA County Med. Assn., We. Orthop. Assn., Riordan Hand Soc. Republican. Jewish. Avocation: tennis. Office Phone: 310-652-6242.

ROBERTS, ANDREW B., vascular surgeon; MD, U. Minn., 1975. Diplomate Am. Bd. Surgery-vascular surgery, Am. Bd. Surgery-gen. surgery. Intern Mass. Gen. Hosp., Boston, 1976, resident gen. surgery; resident Flinders Med. Ctr., Adelaide, Australia; fellow Mass. Inst. of Tech., 1981; fellow vascular surgery St. Thomas Hosp., Nashville, 1984; prof. surgery Sch. of Medicine Temple Univ. Named one of the Top Doctor, Phila Mag., 2011. Office: Temple University Hospital Department of Surgery 3401 N Broad St Philadelphia PA 19140 Office Phone: 215-707-9850. Office Fax: 215-707-5901.

ROBERTS, ANNE CHRISTINE, interventional radiologist, educator; b. Boston, Feb. 20, 1951; d. John D. and Edith Mary (Johnson) R.; m. John Edward Arnold, Feb. 25, 1989. BA, UCLA, 1972, MA, 1973; MD, U. Calif. San Diego, La Jolla, 1982. Diplomate Am. Bd. Radiology, cert. of added qualification interventional radiology, 1994. Clin. fellow radiology Harvard Med. Sch., Boston, 1983-87; asst. prof. radiology U. Calif. San Diego, La Jolla, 1987-93, assoc. prof., 1993-98, prof., 1998—; intern. ob-gyn. Cedar-Sinai Med. Ctr., LA, 1982—83; diagnostic radiology resident Mass. Gen. Hosp., Boston, 1983—86, fellow vascular interventional radiology, 1986—87; bd. chancellors Am. Coll. Radiology, 2009—, sec., treas, 2010—. Chief vascular radiology VA Med. Ctr., La Jolla, 1990-93, acting chief of radiology, 1992-93; chief of radiology Thornton Hosp., 1993-96; chief vascular and interventional radiology U. Calif. San Diego Med. Ctr., La Jolla, 1996—. Author: (with others) Current Practice of Interventional Radiology, 1991, Vascular Diseases: Surgical and Interventional Therapy, 1994, Abram's Angiography, 1996; contbr. articles to profl. jours. Fellow Am. Heart Assn. (mem. exec. coun. cardiovascular coun.), Am. Coll. Radiology, Soc. Cardiovasc. and Interventional Radiology (sec.-treas. 1994-95, program dir. 1994, coun. chair exec. com. 1995-96, pres. 1996-97); mem. Western Angiographic and Interventional Radiology Soc. (sec.-treas. 1994-95, program dir. 1994, pres. 1995-96), Radiol. Soc. N.Am., Roentgen Ray Soc., ACGME Radiology Residency Rev. Com (vice chair, 2009-). Office: Thornton Hosp/UCSD Med Ctr 9300 Campus Point Dr La Jolla CA 92037-1300

ROBERTS, HYMAN JACOB, internist, researcher, author, historian, publisher; b. Boston, May 29, 1924, s. Benjamin and Eva (Sherman) R.; m. Carol Antonia Klein, Aug. 9, 1953; children: David, Jonathan, Mark, Stephen, Scott, Pamela. MD cum laude, Tufts U., 1947. Diplomate Am. Bd. Internal Medicine. Intern, resident Boston City Hosp., 1947-49, resident Mcpl. Hosp., Washington, 1949-50; rsch. fellow, instr. medicine Tufts Med. Sch., Boston, 1948-49; Georgetown Med. Sch., Washington, 1949-50; fellow in medicine Lahey Clinic, Boston, 1950-51; mem. staff Good Samaritan and St. Mary's Hosps., West Palm Beach, Fla., 1955—; dir. Palm Beach Inst. Med. Rsch., West Palm Beach, 1964—; pres. Sunshine Sentinel Press, Inc. Lectr. two day seminar on The New Frontiers in Legal Medicine, Seminar on Def. Against Alzheimer's Disease; U.S. rep. Coun. of Europe for Driving Stds., 1972. Author: Difficult Diagnosis, Spanish and Italian edits., 1958, The Causes, Ecology and Prevention of Traffic Accidents, 1971, Is Vasectomy Safe?, 1979, Aspartame (NutraSweet): Is It Safe?, 1989, Sweet'ner Dearest, 1992, Is Vasectomy Worth the Risk?, 1993, Mega Vitamin E: Is It Safe?, 1994, The Spirit of Modern Taiwan, 1994, West Palm Beach: Centennial Reflections, 1994, A Guide to Personal Peace, 1994, Defense Against Alzheimer's Disease, 1995, Health and Wealth, Palm Beach Style, 1997, The CACOF Conspiracy: Lessons of the New Millennium, 1998, Princess Diana, The House of Windsor and Palm Beach, 1998, Ignored Health Hazards for Pilots and Drivers, 1998, Breast Implants or Aspartame Disease?, 1999, Aspartame Disease: An Ignored Epidemic, 2001, Useful Insights for Diagnosis, Treatment and Public Health, 2002, Protecting Mankind: One Physician's Quest, 2007, Morning Masterpieces: A Photographic Giverny, 2007, A Manifesto for American Medicine, 2009, Cracks in the Level Playing Field of Medicine, 2011; (play) My Wife, The Politician; assoc. editor: Tufts Med. Alumni Bull, Boston, 1978-87, Nutrition Health Rev.; contbr. sci. and med. articles to profl. and theol. jours. Pres. Cmty. Day Sch., West Palm Beach, Fla., 1974; founder Fla. Atlantic U., 1968; founder, dir. Jewish Fedn. Palm Beach County, West Palm Beach, 1960-72. Served to lt., USNR, 1951-54. Outstanding Young Man Jr. C. of C. Fla., 1958; hon. Ky. col.; grantee Norton Art Gallery, U. Fla. Art Mus., U. Ga. Art Mus., Armory Art Ctr. and Mus., West Palm Beach, Fla., A & M U., Tufts Med. Schs., (Roberts Core Libr.), Presidents Club Benefactors, U. Ga., Ringling Art Mus., Northwood U., recipient Gold Share cert. and silver certs. Inst. Agr. and Food Scis., U. Fla., 1974-78; Paul Harris fellow Rotary Found., 1980; named Grand Founder, U. Miami, 2005. Fellow ACP, Am. Coll. Chest Physicians, Am. Coll. Physicians, Am. Acad. Neurology, Endocrine Soc., Am. Fedn. Clin. Rsch., Am. Coll. Angiology (gov. 1981), Pan Am. Med. Assn. (chmn. endocrinology 1982), So. Med. Assn., N.Y. Acad. Scis., U. Miami Soc. Univ. Founders (grand founder), U. Miami Ibis Soc., Governors Club West Palm Beach (a founder), Executive Club (founder), Rotary (pres.), B'nai B'rith, Order St. George (knight of magistral grace 1992), Alpha Omega Alpha, Sigma Xi. Achievements include research in medical diagnosis, diabetes, hypoglycemia, postvasectomy state, Vitamin E metabolism, pentachlorophenol, heavy metal toxicity, narcolepsy, traffic accidents, thrombophlebitis, aspartame, Alzheimer's disease, brain tumors, health care, nutrition and bioethics. Home: 6708 Pamela Ln West Palm Beach FL 33405-4175 also: Sunshine Sentinel Press Inc PO Box 17799 West Palm Beach FL 33416-7799 Office Phone: 561-588-7628. Personal E-mail: hjrobertsmd@aol.com.

ROBERTS, J. SCOTT, psychologist, educator; BA in English, Duke U., 1992; MA in Clinical Psychology, U. Mich., 1996, PhD in Clinical Psychology, 1999. Lic. clinical psychologist, cert. geropsychology. Fellow Ann Arbor VA Health Svcs. Rsch. & Devel. Ctr., Harvard Med. Sch. Dept. Psychiatry; asst. prof. dept. neurology Boston U. Sch. Medicine; co-dir. edn. core Boston U. Alzheimer's Disease Ctr.; asst. prof. health behavior & edn. U. Mich. Sch. Pub. Health. Mem.: Nat. Coalition for Health Profl. Edn. in Genetics, Gerontological Soc. America, Am. Soc. Bioethics & Humanities, Am. Pub. Health Assn.,

Am. Psychological Assn. Office: 1420 Washington Heights Rm M5065 Ann Arbor MI 48109 Office Phone: 734-369-3283. Office Fax: 734-763-7379. E-mail: jscottr@umich.edu.

ROBERTS, JAMES ALLEN, retired urologist, educator; b. Beach, ND, May 31, 1934; s. Earl Fernando and Maria Ellen Roberts; m. Hilda Peachy Roberts, Nov. 29, 1986; children from previous marriage: Jennifer Lou Roberts Walsh, Mary Ellen Roberts Wargo, Thomas Jay. MD, U. Chgo., 1959. Diplomate: Am. Bd. Urology. Intern U. Chgo. Sch. Medicine, 1959-60, resident in urology, 1961-65; from mem. faculty to prof. Tulane U. Med. Sch., New Orleans, 1971-99, prof. urology, 1999—, assoc. chmn., 1986—99; sr. research scientist, head dept. urology Tulane Regional Primate Research Center, Covington, 1972-99; prof. emeritus, 1999—; fellow Fogarty Sr. Internat. NIH, 1984; ret., 2005. Mem. editorial bd. Am. Jour. Kidney Diseases and Urol. Rsch.; contbr. articles to profl. jours. Bd. dirs. Highland Park Hosp., 1985-87. With USN, 1965—67. Recipient grants NIH, Original Rsch. award Southern Med. Assn., 1990, Cert. Achievement Am. Urological Assn., 1997; Fulbright Sr. scholar, 1999-2000. Fellow ACS; mem. St. Tammany Parish Med. Soc. (pres. 1979), Soc. Rsch. on Calculous Kinetics, La. Urol. Soc., Am. Urol. Assn., Soc. Univ. Urologists, Nat. Kidney Found., Soc. Exptl. Biology and Medicine, Nat. Inst. Health (SAT study sect. 1995-99), Sigma Xi. Office: 83 Towne Place Dr Hendersonville NC 28792 Personal E-mail: jamroberts83@gmail.com.

ROBERTS, JEANETTE C., dean, pharmacy educator; BS in Biochemistry, Albright Coll., Reading, Pa., 1979; PhD in Medicinal Chemistry, U. Minn., Mpls., 1986; MPH, U. Utah, 2001. Quality control chemist Warner-Lambert Co., Rockford, Ill., 1979; chemist minerals divsn. Dept. Natural Resources, St. Paul, 1980—81; rsch. fellow isotope/nuc. chemistry divsn. Los Alamos Nat. Lab., N.Mex., 1986—88; asst. prof. medicinal chemistry U. Utah Coll. Pharmacy, Salt Lake City, 1988—94, assoc. prof., 1994—2001, prof., 2001—03, adj. prof., 2003—, adj. asst. prof. pharmacology/toxicology, 1992—94, adj. assoc. prof., 1994—2001, adj. prof., 2001—, interim chair dept. medicinal chemistry, 1995—96, adj. assoc. prof. foods/nutrition, 2000—01, adj. prof., 2003—, assoc. dean academic affairs, 2000—03; prof. divsn. pharm. scis., dean U. Wis. Sch. Pharmacy, Madison, 2003—. Vis. prof. dept. pediat. U. Vienna, 1998; cons. Jean Brown Assoc., Salt Lake City, 1999, Utah Health Informatics, Salt Lake City, 1999—2000, Protein Solutions, Inc., Salt Lake City, 1999—2000. Co-author: Drugs and Justice, 2005. Recipient Disting. Tchg. award, U. Utah Coll. Pharmacy, 1995, 2003. Mem.: AAAS, Utah Pub. Health Assn., Mountain West Region Soc. Toxicology, Am. Soc. Pharmacognosy, Am. Assn. Cancer Rsch., Am. Chem. Soc. (sec. 1990—92), Am. Assn. Colleges of Pharmacy, Delta Omega, Phi Kappa Phi, Rho Chi. Achievements include patents in field. Office: U Utah Coll Pharmacy Rennebohm Hall 1126B 777 Highland Ave Madison WI 53705 Office Phone: 608-262-1414. Office Fax: 608-262-3397. Business E-Mail: jroberts@pharmacy.wisc.edu.

ROBERTS, JOHN ROBERT, cardiothoracic surgeon, consultant; b. Athens, Tenn., Apr. 5, 1959; s. Doyle Ford and Frankie Howard Roberts; children: Amanda, Timothy, John Anthony, Thomas. AB summa cum laude, Duke U., 1981; MD with honors, Yale U., 1985; MBA, Auburn U., 2003. Bd. cert. gen. surgery Am. Bd. Surgery, bd. cert. thoracic surgery Am. Bd. Thoracic Surgery, lic. med. practice Tenn. Resident surgeon Johns Hopkins Hosp., Balt., 1986—92, fellow in surg. oncology, 1992—93; fellow in thoracic surgery Brigham and Women's Hosp., Boston, 1993—95; asst. prof. U. Pa., Phila., 1995—97; chief gen. thoracic surgery Vanderbilt U., Nashville, 1997—2003; thoracic surgeon The Surg. Clinic, Nashville, 2003—; with Southeastern Rsch. Assocs., 2008—. Ingram Prof. Cancer Rsch. Vanderbilt U., 1997—2009; Richard Wilson vis. prof. surg. oncology Harvard Med. Sch.; lectr. in field. Reviewer: jours. CHEST, Annals of Thoracic Surgery, Jour. Thoracic and Cardiovasc. Surgery; contbr. articles to profl. jours. Capt. USAR, 1999—2003. Recipient Resident Rsch. award, Johns Hopkins Hosp., 1986, grants in field. Master: Am. Coll. Chest Physicians (Alfred Soffler award); fellow: ACS (mem., com. on applicants 2006—, scholarship for health policy 2003—); mem.: Workforce on Health Policy, Reform and Advocacy, So. Thoracic Surg. Assn., Soc. Thoracic Surgeons, Am. Soc. Clin. Oncology, So. Assn. for Oncology, Soc. Cell and Tissue Kinetics, Alpha Omega Alpha, Phi Kappa Phi. Achievements include mentoring the winner of the Alfred Soffler Award from the American College of Chest Physicians in 2008; patents pending for directional suction catheter; combined stapler-dissector. Avocation: Tae Kwon Do. Office: The Surg Clinic #356 24th Ave Nashville TN 37203 Office Phone: 615-342-7345. Personal E-mail: johnbob999@msn.com, robertshame@comcast.net. Business E-Mail: jroberts@tsclinic.com.

ROBERTS, JONATHAN C., pharmaceutical executive; Grad., Sch. Pharmacy Va. Commonwealth Univ. Area v.p. stores CVS Pharmacy Inc., 1997—2002, sr. v.p. store ops., 2002—05; sr. v.p., CIO CVS Caremark Corp., 2006—09, exec. v.p. Rx purchasing pricing & network rels., 2009—10, exec. v.p., COO PBM divsn., 2010—. Mem. SureScripts Exec. Adv. Coun., eHealth Initiatives Leadership Coun. Bd. dir. ALS Therapy Alliances. Office: CVS Caremark Corp 1 CVS Dr Woonsocket RI 02895 *

ROBERTS, KENNETH B., radiation oncologist, educator; BS, MIT, 1979; MD, Duke U., 1984, student, 1994. Cert. med. oncology 1989, diplomate Am. Bd Internal Medicine, 1987, Am. Bd. Radiation-radiation oncology, 1995. Resident in internal medicine Ohio Sate Univ. Hosps., 1985—87; fellow in hematology and oncology Duke Univ. Med. Ctr., 1987—89, resident in radiation oncolgy, 1989—92; assoc. prof. of therapeutic radiology Yale-New Haven Hosp., med. dir. Office: Yale- New Haven Hospital 20 York St New Haven CT 06510 Office Phone: 203-688-4242. Office Fax: 203-688-6937.

ROBERTS, KENNETH BARRY, pediatrician; b. Macon, Ga., Feb. 27, 1944; MD, Johns Hopkins U., Baltimore, 1969. Cert. in pediat. Am. Bd. Med. Specialties. Intern in pediat. Johns Hopkins Hosp., 1969—70, resident in pediat., 1970—71, resident, 1973—76; dir. pediat. tchg. programs Moses H. Cone Meml. Hosp., Greensboro, NC; prof. pediat. U. NC, Chapel Hill. Mem.: Fedn. Pediat. Orgns. Office: Moses H Cone Meml Hosp 1200 N Elm St Greensboro NC 27401 Office Phone: 336-832-8064. Office Fax: 336-832-7893. Business E-Mail: kenneth.roberts@mosescone.com.

ROBERTS, KENNETH BOYETT, pharmacy educator, former dean; b. Sharon, Tenn., Nov. 7, 1944; s. James Russell and Blanche (Boyett) Roberts; m. Kittye Louise Rice, Oct. 20, 1968; children: Millicent Boyett, LouAnne Rice. BS in Pharmacy, U. Tenn., Memphis, 1964-67; MBA in Mktg., U. Tenn., Knoxville, 1973; PhD in Health Care Adminstrn., U. Miss., Oxford, 1975. Tchg. asst. U. Miss. Sch. Pharmacy, Oxford, 1973-75, prof., dean, 1989—2000; asst. prof. U. Tex., Austin, 1975-77; exec. dir. Mo. Found. Pharm. Care, St. Louis, 1977-79; prof. pharmacy U. Tenn., Memphis, 1979-89, assoc. dean, 1984-89; exec. dir. Am. Coll. Apothecaries, Memphis, 1981-85; dean U. Ky. Coll. Pharmacy, 2000—09, dean emeritus, 2009—. Cons. Chapman Drug Co., 1985—92, Cardinal Health, 1992—96; pres. West Tenn. Health Edn. Ctr., Memphis, 1987—88. Author: Establishing a Professional Pharmacy Practice, 1980, Managing Support Personnel in Community Pharmacy, 1982, Guidelines for Marketing a Pharmacy Practice, 1983, Guidelines for Pharmacy Management by Self Study, 1984, Guidelines for Establishing Pharmacy Services for Hospice, 1987. Asst. dir. pharmacy US Naval Hosp., Great Lakes, Ill., dir. pharmacy Taipei, Taiwan; mem. Ky. Pharmacy Leadership Coun.; appt. mem. Ky. Innovations Commn., 2000. Recipient Profl. Promotions award, Ky. Pharmacists Assn., 2002, Disting. Svc. award, 2011, Pres.'s award, Ky. Soc. Hosp. Pharmacists, 2003, Outstanding Dean award, Am. Pharmacists Assn. Student Acad., 2009; named a Charles R. Walgreen Meml. fellow, Am. Found. Pharm. Edn., 1974—75. Fellow: Am. Coll. Apothecaries (Dean's Recognition award 1998); mem.: Am. Soc. Health Sys. Pharmacists., Kty. Pharm. Assn., Rsch. & Edn. Found. (bd. dirs.), Profl. Pharma. Fraternity Rsch. & Edn. Found. (bd. dirs.), Tenn. Pharmacists Assn., Am. Assn. Colleges of Pharmacy (bd. dirs. 1997—99), Am. Soc. Hosp. Pharmacists, Am. Pharm. Assn., Internat. Fedn. Pharmacists, Am. Assn. Pharm. Scientists, Phi Lambda Sigma, Phi Kappa Phi, Rho Chi, Kappa Psi (nat. pres. 1987—89, Citation of Appreciation 1989), Pi Kappa Alpha, Sigma Xi, Kappa Psi (dir.). Address: 701 The Grange Ln Lexington KY 40511-9577 Office: University Ky Coll Pharmacy 789 South Limestone St Rm 251 Lexington KY 40536-0596 Office Phone: 859-323-7148. E-mail: krobe2@email.uky.edu.

ROBERTS, LARRY SPURGEON, biological science educator, zoologist; b. Texon, Tex., June 30, 1935; s. E. Fowler and Frances Wray (Huggins) R.; m. Maria Elek, Feb. 7, 1962; children: Gregory Lorinc, Bruce Tibor, Teresa Margit, Eric Miklos. BS, So. Meth. U., Dallas, 1956; MS, U. Ill., Urbana, 1958; DSc, Johns Hopkins U., Balt., 1961. Cert. scuba instr. Nat. Assn. Underwater Instrs. From asst. prof. to prof. zoology U. Mass., Amherst, 1963-79; prof. biol. scis. Tex. Tech U., Lubbock, 1979-90, chmn. dept., 1979-84. Adj. prof. biol. scis. U. Miami, 1990-99, Fla. Internat. U., 1990-93, 99—2010, adj. prof., molecular microbiology & infectious diseases, 2008-10. Author (with others): Foundations of Parasitology, 1977, 8th edit., 2009; author: Integrated Principles of Zoology, 1979, 14th edit., 2008, Biology of Animals, 1982, 7th edit., 1998, The Underwater World of Sport Diving, 1991, Animal Diversity, 5th edit., 2009. Mem. Amherst Dem. Town Com., 1968-79, vice chmn., 1972-76; mem. Amherst Town Meeting, 1966-76; mem. Amherst Zoning Bd. Appeals, 1972-75, vice chmn., 1972-75; recorder West Tex. Dems., 1985-86; mem. Dade County Dem. Exec. Com., 1991-2011. NIH postdoctoral trainee, 1961-63; NSF fellow, 1958, NIH fellow, 1969-70; recipient Disting. Svc. cert. Mass. Tchrs. Assn., 1979. Mem. AAAS, ACLU (vice chmn. Hampshire County chpt. 1966-68, bd. dirs. Lubbock chpt. 1985-89, vice chmn. 1988-89, bd. dirs. Miami, Fla. chpt. 1991-2010, 1st v.p. 1998-00, treas. 2000-06, Fla. State bd. dirs., treas. 2006-09), Am. Soc. Parasitologists (Henry Baldwin Ward medal 1971, coun. mem. at large 1980-83, v.p. 1984-85, 96-97, pres. 1998-99), Am. Micros. Soc. (v.p. 1974-75, exec. com. 1978-81), Mass. Soc. Profs. (pres. 1977-78), Soc. Protozoologists, Am. Soc. Tropical Medicine and Hygiene, Southwestern Assn. Parasitologists (v.p. 1982, pres. 1983), Southeastern Soc. Parasitologists (pres.-elect 1993, pres. 1994), Internat. Soc. Reef Studies, Crustacean Soc., Am. Acad. Underwater Scis., Sigma Xi. Home: 437 Fellowship Cir Gaithersburg MD 20877 Personal E-mail: lroberts1@compuserve.com.

ROBERTS, LEIGH MILTON, psychiatrist; b. Jacksonville, Ill., June 9, 1925; s. Victor Harold and Ruby Harriet (Kelsey) R.; m. Marilyn Edith Kadow, 1946 (dec. 1995); m. Ellen Rabenhorst, 2003; children: David, Carol Troxell, Paul, Nancy Mills. BS, U. Ill., 1945, MD, 1947. Diplomate Am. Bd. Psychiatry and Neurology. Intern St. Francis Hosp., Peoria, Ill., 1947-48; gen. practice medicine Macomb, Ill., 1948-50; resident in psychiatry U. Wis. Hosps., Madison, 1953-56; staff psychiatrist Mendota (Wis.) State Hosp., 1956-58; mem. faculty U. Wis. Med. Sch., Madison, 1959-89, prof. psychiatry, 1971-89, acting chmn. dept., 1972-75. Cons. in psychiatry, 1989-; mem. spl. rev. bd. Wis. Parole Bd. Sex Crimes Law, 1962-88, forensic cons., 1988—; mem. Dane County Devel. Disabilities Bd., 1962-66, Wis. Planning Com. Mental Health, 1963-65, Wis. Planning Com. Health, 1969-71, Wis. Planning Com. Vocat. Rehab., 1966-68, Wis. Planning Com. Health Centers, 1967-71, Wis. Mental Health Adv. Com., 1973-78; bd. dirs. Methodist Hosp., Madison, Dane County Rehab. House, Dane County Assn. Mental Health; cons. in field. Editor: Community Psychiatry, 1966, Comprehensive Mental Health, 1968; contbr. articles profl. jours. Pres. Wis. Coun. Chs., 1976-78; bd. dirs. Madison Campus Ministry, St. Benedict Center; trustee North Central Coll., Naperville, Ill. Served with USNR, 1943-45, 50-53. Decorated Bronze Stars, Purple Heart. Fellow Am. Psychiat. Assn. (trustee 1981-84), Wis. Psychiat. Assn. (pres. 1967) Methodist. Home and Office: 33 S Midvale Blvd Madison WI 53705 Business E-Mail: lmroberts21@tds.net.

ROBERTS, LYNNE J., physician; b. St. Louis, 1952; d. H. Clarke and Dorothy R.; m. Richard Beadle Jr., July 18, 1981; 2 children. BA with distinction, Ind. U., Bloomington, 1974; MD, Ind. U., 1978. Diplomate Am. Bd. Dermatology, Am. Bd. Pediatrics, Am. Bd. Laser Surgery. Intern in pediats. Children's Med. Ctr., Dallas, 1978-79, resident in pediats., 1979-80; resident in dermatology U. Tex. Southwestern Med. Ctr., Dallas, 1980-83, chief resident in dermatology, 1982-83, asst. instr. dermatology and pediatrics, 1983-84, asst. prof., 1984-90, assoc. prof., 1990-99; prof., 1999—; physician Cons. Dermatol. Specialists, Dallas, 1990-93; pres. Lynne J. Roberts, MD, PA, Dallas, 1993—. Dir. dermatology Children's Med. Ctr., Dallas, 1986-2000; dermatology sect. chief Med. City Dallas Hosp., 1994-95, 95-97. Contbr. articles to profl. jours., chpts. to books. Recipient Scholastic Achievement Citation Am. Med. Women's Assn., 1978. Fellow Am. Acad. Dermatology, Am. Soc. Laser Medicine and Surgery (bd. dirs. 1994-97); mem. Soc. Pediatric Dermatology, Am. Soc. Dermatologic Surgery, Tex. Med. Assn., Kappa Alpha Theta, Alpha Omega Alpha. Avocations: horseback riding, reading, fishing, swimming, camping. Office: Ste 360 8144 Walnut Hill Ln Dallas TX 75231 Home Phone: 214-340-4522; Office Phone: 469-232-9300.

ROBERTS, MELVILLE PARKER, neurosurgeon, educator; b. Phila., Oct. 15, 1931; s. Melville Parker and Marguerite Louise (Reiman) R.; m. Sigrid Marianne Magnusson, Mar. 27, 1954; children: Melville Parker III, Julia Pell, Erik Emerson. BS, Washington and Lee U., 1953; MD, Yale U., 1957. Diplomate: Am. Bd. Neurol. Surgery. Intern Yale Med. Ctr., 1957, neurosurgical resident, 1958-60, 62-64, Am. Cancer Soc. fellow in neurosurgery, 1962-64, instr., 1964; asst. prof. surgery Sch. Medicine U. Va., Charlottesville, 1965-69; practice medicine specializing in neurol. surgery Hartford, Conn., 1970-1998; mem. staff Hartford Hosp.; asst. prof. surgery Sch. Medicine U. Conn., Farmington, 1970-71, assoc. prof., 1972-75, assoc. prof. neurology, 1974-77, chmn. divsn. neurosurgery, 1971-84, prof. surgery, 1975—, acting chmn. dept. neurology, 1973-77, acting chmn. dept. surgery, 1974-77, William Beecher Scoville prof. neurosurgery, 1976-98, first endowed professorial chair, prof. emeritus, 1998—; instr. Yale Sch. Medicine, 1963—64. James Hudson Brown rsch. fellow Yale U., 1957. Author: Atlas of the Human Brain in Section, 1970, 2d edit., 1987, The Brain Atlas, 1998; mem. editl. bd.: Conn. Medicine, 1973-98; contbr. articles to profl. jours. Capt. MC, US Army Reserve, Okinwawa, 1960-61 Fellow Royal Soc. Medicine London (life); mem. Am. Assn. Neurol. Surgeons, Soc. Neurol. Surgeons, Congress Neurol. Surgeons (bd. dirs. joint spinal sect. with Am. Assn. Neurol. Surgeons, chmn. ann. meeting 1987, sci. program chmn. ann. meeting 1988), Assn. for Rsch. in Nervous and Mental Diseases, New Eng. Neurosurg. Soc. (bd. dirs. 1976-79, pres. 1989-91), Yale Surg. Soc., Sigma Xi (hon.), Lambda Chi Alpha, Soc. Brit. Neurol. Surgeons, Rsch. Soc. Neurol. Surgeons, Soc. Rsch. into Hydrocephalus and Spina Bifida, Conn. Acad. Arts and Sci., Vereingung Schweizer Neurochirugen, Mory's Assn., Beaumont Med. Club (pres. 1988, New Haven), Yale Club NY, Sloane Club (London). Episcopalian.

ROBERTS, NANCY S., physician, educator, obstetrician, gynecologist; MD., Jefferson Med. Coll. Diplomate Am. Bd. Ob-Gyn, 1982, cert. maternal-fetal medicine 1984. Intern Abington Meml. Hosp.; resident Thomas Jefferson Univ. Hosp.; fellow Pa. Hosp.; hosp. affiliations include Paoli Hosp., 1990—, Riddle Hosp., 1993, Bryn Mawr Hosp., 1994; with Main Line Perinatal Inc.; asst. prof. dept. of ob-gyn. Jefferson Medical Coll.; hosp. affiliations include Lankenau Med. Ctr., 1984—, attending physician and system chmn. Bd. mem. Lankenau Inst. for Med. Rsch.; ob-gyn. edn. com. mem. Lankenau Hosp., med. ops. com. mem.; bd. mem. Obstet. Soc. of Phil. Found. Co-author: (publ.) A Randomized Controlled Trial of Misoprostol Versus Oxytocin in Preventing Postpartum Blood Loss, Objective Measurement of Blood Loss at Delivery, Monoamniotic Twins. Recipient Nat. Faculty award, Coun. on Resident Edn. in Ob-gyn., 2000; named one of the Best Doctors, Main Line Today Mag., 2002, the Top Doctors, Phila. Mag., 1991, 1994, 1996, 1999, 2000, 2002, 2005, 2006, 2011. Mem.: Bd. of Maternity Care Coalition, Soc. of Maternal-Fetal Medicine Specialists, Pa. Perinatal Soc., Pa. Med. Soc., Am. Coll. of Ob-Gyn. Office: Lankenau Medical Center MOB E Ste 353 100 Lancaster Ave Wynnewood PA 19096 Office Phone: 610-649-9021. Office Fax: 610-649-8058.

ROBERTS, RICHARD JOHN, molecular biologist, biochemist; b. Derby, Eng., Sept. 6, 1943; arrived in US, 1969; s. John Walter and Edna Wilhelmina (Allsop) Roberts; m. Elizabeth Dyson, Sept. 21, 1965 (dec.); children: Alison, Andrew; m. Jean E. Tagliabue; children: Christopher, Amanda. BS in Chemistry, U. Sheffield, 1965, PhD in Organic Chemistry, 1968. Rsch. fellow Harvard U., Cambridge, Mass., 1969—70, rsch. assoc., 1971—72; sr. staff investigator Cold Spring Harbor Lab., NY, 1972—87, asst. dir., 1987—92; cons. New Eng. Biolabs., Ipswich, Mass., 1974—92, chief sci. officer, 1992—. Mem. sci. adv. bd. Genex, Rockville, Md., 1977—85. Contbr. articles to profl. jours. Recipient Nobel prize in physiology/medicine, Nobel Found., 1993; fellow, John Simon Guggenheim Meml. Found., 1979. Fellow: Royal Soc.; mem.: Am. Soc. Microbiology. Achievements include discovery of introns in eukaryotic DNA and the mechanism of gene-splicing. Office: New Eng Biolabs 240 County Rd Ipswich MA 01938-2723 Office Phone: 978-380-7405. E-mail: roberts@neb.com. *

ROBERTS, VICTOR LAWRENCE, endocrinologist, educator; m. Lucy Duque-Roberts; children: Mara Isabelle, Allan Joshua, Daniel Alexander. MD, Autonomous U., Guadalajara, Mexico, 1979; MBA, Crummer Grad. Sch. Bus., Rollins Coll, Winter Pk., Fla., 1995. Diplomate in endocrinology, diabetes and metabolism Am. Bd. Internal Medicine, 1987, in internal medicine Am. Bd. Internal Medicine, 1984, Am. Bd. Quality Assurance and Utilization Review Physicians, Am. Coll. Physician Executive Physicians, cert. diabetes educator, healthcare quality manager ABQAURP. Consulting endocrinologist Endocrine and Diabetes Assoc. Tex., Dallas, 1985—88; pres., c.e.o., and consulting endocrinologist Endocrine Assoc. Fla., PA, Lake Mary, 1988—. Prof. internal medicine U. Ctrl. Fla. Coll. Medicine, Orlando, 2008—; clin. prof. medicine U. Fla. Coll. Medicine, Gainesville, 2001—; clin. prof. pharmacy practice U. Fla. Coll. Pharmacy, 2006—; clin. prof. clin. scis. Fla. State U. Coll. Medicine, Tallahassee, 2006—; deans Aesculapian Soc. UCF Coll. Medicine, 2010—. Contbr. articles to profl. medical publications in English and Spanish. Mem., ctrl. Fla. med. Res. corps Fla. Dept. Health, Orlando, 2008—; pres. Orange County Med. Soc., 2001. Recipient Academic and Leadership Achievement award, Nat. Honor Soc., 1970, Governor's Appointment Diabetes Adv. Coun. award, Fla. Governor's Office, 2000—04. Fellow: Am. Inst. Healthcare Quality, Am. Coll. Endocrinology, Am. Coll. Physicians; mem.: Am. Diabetes Assn. (nat. bd. 1997—2000), Best Dr. and Top Dr., Orlando Mag., Am. Assn. Clinical Endocrinologists (nat. bd. 2004—10), Best Dr. America.

Avocations: spending time with my family, travel, reading biographies and novels, golf. Office: Lake Emma Professional Ctr Suite 2060 766 N Sun Dr Lake Mary FL 32746 Office Phone: 407-331-1117. Personal E-mail: victorlrobertsmd@gmail.com.

ROBERTS, WENDY EILEEN, dermatologist; BA, Sarah Lawrence Coll., 1980; MD, Stanford U. Sch. of Medicine, 1984. Lic. Hawaii Medical License, 1989, California Medical License, 2009, diplomate Am. Bd. of Dermatology, 1992, Am. Bd. of Dermapathology, 1993. Intern gen. surgery Highland Gen. Hosp., 1984—85, resident surgery, 1985—86; resident dermatology LA County/King Drew Med. Ctr., 1988—91; fellow dermatopathology NY Univ. Med. Ctr., 1991—92; hosp. affiliation/s Jerry L. Pettis V.A. Hosp., 1992—96, Loma Linda Univ. Med. Ctr., 1992—96; founding dir. dermapathology divsn. Loma Linda Univ. Med. Sch., 1992—96, asst. clin. prof. dermatology and internal medicine, 1998—2008. Reviewer Jour. of the Am. Acad. of Dermatology, 1992—95; dermapathology cons. Calif. Tumor Tissue Registry, 1992—95; John L. Kenney symposium guest lectr. Nat. Med. Assn., 1997—98; reserve mem. Am. Acad. of Dermatology, 1992—2000, mem. com. on physician pratice, 2001—04, mem. healthcare delivery com., 2001—04, mem. needs assessment com., 2004—07, mem.orgnl. structure com., 2004—07, mem. nominating com., 2006—08, mem. melanoma and skin cancer screening com., 2008—11; mem. med. alumnae bd. Stanford Univ., 2004—. Recipient The Annual Installation and awards of Excellence, The Rancho Mirage C. of C., 1998, Dermatology Found., Leaders Society, 2000, Model State award, 2005, Am. Acad. of Dermatology, 2004, Volunteerism award, 2005, Golden Triangle award, Am Acad. of Dermatology, 2005, Am. Acad. of Dermatology, 2009, Breaking the glass ceiling award, Women's Leadership Forum, 2008; named Top Doctor, Palm Springs Life, 2005, 2006, 2007, 2008; nominee The Desert Cities Athena award, 1997, 1998, 1999. Office: Desert Dermatology Skin Institute 72-301 Country Club Dr Suite 101 Rancho Mirage CA 92270 Office Phone: 760-346-4262. Office Fax: 760-340-9892. E-mail: Drwerderm@aol.com.

ROBERTS, WILBUR EUGENE, dental educator, research scientist, wine importer; b. Lubbock, Tex., Nov. 16, 1942; s. Wilbur Eugene Roberts and Elva Etna (Chance) Turnwall; m. Cheryl Ann Jones, June 6, 1967; children: Jeffery Alan, Carrie Jean. DDS, Creighton U., 1967; PhD in Anatomy, U. Utah, 1969; cert. in orthodontics, U. Conn., 1974; DHC in Medicine (hon.), Lille U., France, 1996. Diplomate Am. Bd. Orthodontics. Rsch. fellow U. Utah, Salt Lake City, 1967—69; postdoctoral fellow U. Conn., Farmington, 1971—74; from asst. prof. to prof. dentistry U. Pacific, San Francisco, 1974—88; prof. chmn. dept. orthodontics Ind. U., Indpls., 1988—93, chmn. dept. oral and facial devel., 1993—97, prof. physiology and biophysics Sch. Medicine, 1988—2000, dir. grad. orthodontics program Sch. Dentistry, 1988—, head orthodontics sect., 1997—2008, prof. emeritus, 2008—; mem. steering com. Biomechs. and Biomaterials Rsch. Ctr. Ind. U.-Purdue U., Indpls., 1990—96; NRC sr. rsch. assoc. NASA Ames Rsch. Ctr. Moffett Field, Calif., 1982—83; Jarabak prof. orthodontics Ind. U., Indpls., 1997—2008; CEO, sec.-treas. VinElite Imports, Inc., Indpls., 1999—2005. Dir. Bone Rsch. Lab. U. Pacific, 1980—88, dir. Oral Devel. Clinic, 1980—86, Dr. Fred West Meml. lectr., 1989, 97; rsch. cons. Neodontics Corp., Laguna Nigel, Calif., 1982—85, Denar Corp., Anaheim, Calif., 1985—87, Nobelpharma AG, Goteborg, Sweden, 1988, Dental Implant Clin. Rsch. Group, Ann Arbor, Mich., 1991—, Align Tech., Mountain View, Calif., Oral Medicine and Biology Study sect. NIH, 1992—96, Rsch. Coun. ADA, 1992, accreditation cons. in orthodontics ADA Coun. on Dental Accreditation, 1996—2002; task force on faculty recruitment Am. Assn. of Orthodontics, 1998—2002; adj. prof. mech. engring. Purdue U., Indpls., 1990—; assoc. prof. implantology, maxillofacial surgery U. Lille, France, 1987—; guest prof. U. Western Ont., Canada, 1987; Dr. George Grieve Meml. lectr. Can. Dental Assn., 1993; mem. internat. affairs com. Ind. U.-Purdue U., Indpls., 1995—2005; sci. cons. Align Tech. Corp.; vis. prof. U. Melbourne, Australia, U. Frankfurt, Germany, Lomalinda U., Calif.; U.S. importer Mud House Wine Co. Ltd., Marlbourgh, New Zealand, Oakridge Vineyards, Ltd., Australia, Rymill Wines, Coonawarra, Australia; ptnr. Vinters of Zuperb Zinfandel, Paso Robles, Calif.; owner Roberts' Renner Rd. and Castle Vineyards, New Zealand; keynote lectr. Moyers Symposium, U. Mich., 2004; Hine meml. lectr. Ind. U., 2006; pres. Roberts Orthodontics, PC, 2006—; owner Jawbone Winery and Vineyards LLC, Healdsburg. Contbr. sci. articles to profl. jours. Rep. campaign worker, Contra Costa County, Calif., 1980-82; ch. sch. supt. San Ramon Valley Meth. Ch., Alamo, Calif., 1979-81; adult ministries council San Ramon Valley Meth. Ch., Danville, Calif., 1984-86; sci. cons. St. Isadore Sch. and San Ramon Valley High Sch., Danville, 1978-86; chmn. bldg. com. Sunrise at Geist United Meth. Ch., Indpls.; mem. planning bd. Vols. in Medicine, Indpls., 2000-2001. Lt. comdr. USN, 1969-71, Vietnam. Decorated Navy Commendation medal; recipient Cosmos Achievement award, NASA, 1981, 1988, 1992, medal, City of Paris, 1989, City of Rouen, France, 1991, Rsch. award, Ind. U. Sch. Dentistry, 1993, Gold Medallion award, U. of Pacific Sch. Dentistry, 2001, Isaac Lew award, Am. Acad. Implant Dentistry, 2002, Jarabak award, Am. Assn. Orthodontists, 2003, Dale B. award, Am. Bd. Orthodontics; named Eminent scholar, Okla. U., 1995. Fellow: Am. Coll. Dentists, Internat. Coll. Dentists; mem.: Pacific Dental Rsch. Found. (pres. 1976—80), Am. Assn. Dental Rsch., Med. Dental Guild Calif. (pres. 1982—83, Gold Key award 1985), Conf. of the Co. of Wine Tasters of Normandy (pres. Ind. med. chpt. 1992—97, Master of the Cave 1997—2001, Baron of Honor 1999, Master of Embassies 2001—05), Omicron Kappa Upsilon. Avocations: fishing, skiing. Home: 8260 Skipjack Dr Indianapolis IN 46236-8429 Office: Ind U Sch Dentistry Sch Dentistry Sect Orthodontics 1121 W Michigan St Indianapolis IN 46202-5211 E-mail: werobert@iupui.edu. *

ROBERTS-BROWN, ARLENE MARIA, executive assistant; b. East St. Louis, Ill., May 30, 1939; d. Joe Roberts and Elizabeth Smith; children: Johnny Purchase Jr., Francena Purchase-Owens, Darlene Pleas-McLemore, Regenia Pleas, Rodney Brown. Student, Jordan Coll., Grand Rapids, Mich., 1987—89. Cert. long-term care facility nurse aid, State of Mich. Dept. Pub. Health, 1990. Nurse aide Raybrook Nursing Home, Grand Rapids, 1990—91; asst. Grand Rapids Pub. Schs., 1994—95; tchg. asst. New Branches Sch., Grand Rapids, 1992—93; exec. asst. Francena Purchase Consulting Svcs., Grand Rapids, 2004—; pastoral asst. First Missionary Baptist Ch., Grand Rapids, Mich. TV appearance, Grand Rapids Cmty. Media TV, 2007; contbr. articles to profl. jours. Mem. Rev. Popov Ministries, Grand Rapids, 1994—; choir bd. mem. East Paris Christians Reformed Ch., Grand Rapids, 2008—. Recipient cert. of recognition, Grand Rapids Pub. Schs., 1994, Francena Purchase Consulting Svcs., 2006—11, Cert. of Recognition, Francena Purchase Consulting Svcs., Grand Rapids, Mich., 2006—11, Francena Purchase Consulting Svcs., Kentwood, Mich., 2006—11. Mem.: West Mich. Postal Customer Coun. Avocation: reading. Home: PO Box 88304 Kentwood MI 49518

ROBERTSON, ABEL L., JR., pathologist; b. St. Andrews, Argentina, July 21, 1926; came to U.S., 1952, naturalized, 1957; s. Abel Alfred Lazzarini and Margaret Theresa G. (Anderson) R.; m. Irene Kirmayr Mauch, Dec. 26, 1958; children: Margaret Anne, Abel Martin, Andrew Duncan, Malcolm Alexander. BS, Coll. D.F. Sarmiento, Buenos Aires, Argentina, 1946; MD suma cum laude, U. Buenos Aires, 1951; PhD, Cornell U., 1959. Fellow tissue culture div. Inst. Histology and Embryology, Sch. Medicine Inst. Histology and Embryology, 1947-49; surg. intern Hosp. Ramos Mejia, Buenos Aires, 1948-50; fellow in tissue culture research Ministry of Health, Buenos Aires, 1950-51; resident Hosp. Nacional de Clinicas, Buenos Aires, 1950-51; head blood vessel bank and organ transplants Research Ctr. Ministry of Health, Buenos Aires, 1951-53; fellow dept. surgery and pathology Sch. Medicine Cornell U., NYC, 1953-55; asst. vis. surgery U. Hosp. N.Y., NYC, 1955-60; asst. prof. research surgery Postgrad. Med. Sch. NYU, NYC, 1955-56; asst. vis. surgeon Bellevue Hosp., NYC, 1955-60; assoc. prof. research surgery NYU, 1956-60, assoc. prof. pathology Sch. Medicine and Postgrad Med. Sch., 1960-63; staff mem. div. research Cleve. Clinic Found., 1963-73, prof. research, 1972-73; assoc. clin. prof. pathology Case Western Res. U. Sch. Medicine, Cleve., 1968-72, prof. pathology, 1973-82, dir. interdisciplinary cardiovascular research, 1975-82; exec. head dept. pathology Coll. Medicine, U. Ill., Chgo., 1982-88; prof. pathology Coll. Medicine U. Ill., 1982-93, prof. emeritus, 1993—; vis. prof. emeritus cardiovascular med. Core Analysis Lab., Stanford U. Coll. Medicine, 1995—, cardiac pathologist, 2000—. Rsch. fellow N.Y. Soc. Cardiovasc. Surgery, 1957-58; mem. rsch. study subcom. of heart com. N.E. Ohio Regional Med. Program, 1969—. Mem. internat. editl. bd. Atherosclerosis, Jour. Exptl. and Molecular Pathology, 1964—, Lab. Investigation, 1989—, Acta Pathologica Japonica, 1991—; contbr. articles to profl. jours. Recipient Rsch. Devel. award NIH, 1961-63, Disting. Alumnus award Grad. Sch. Med. Sci. Cornell U., 2003. Fellow AAAS, Am. Heart Assn., Am. Coll. Cardiology, Am. Coll. Clin. Pharmacology, Am. Heart Assn. (established investigator 1956-61, nominating com. coun. on arteriosclerosis 1972), Royal Microscopical Soc., Royal Soc. Promotion Health (Gt. Britain), Am. Geriat. Soc., N.Y. Acad. Scis., Cleve. Med. Library Assn.; mem. AMA, AAUP, Am. Soc. for Investigative Pathology, Am. Inst. Biol. Scis., Am. Judicature Soc., Am. Soc. Cell Biology, Am. Soc. Pathologists, Am. Soc. Nephrology, Assn. Am. Physicians and Surgeons, Assn. Computing Machinery, Electron Microscopy Soc. Am., Assn. Pathology Chmn., Internat. Acad. Pathology, Soc. Cardiovasc. Pathology, Internat. Cardiovasc. Soc., Internat. Soc. Cardiology (sci. council on arteriosclerosis and ischemic heart disease), Internat. Fed. on Genetic Engring. and Biotechnology, Internat. Soc. for Heart Rsch., Internat. Soc. Nephrology, Internat. Soc. Stereology, Pan Am. Med. Assn. (life, councillor in angiology 1966), Ill. Registry Anatomical Pathology (treas. 1985-87), Chgo. Pathology Soc., Reticuloendothelial Soc. Leucocyte Biology, Soc. Cryobiology, Tissue Culture Assn., Ohio Soc. Pathologists, Electron Microscopy Soc. Northeastern Ohio (pres., trustee 11966-68), Heart Assn. Northeastern Ohio, N.Y. Soc. Cardiovasc. Surgery, N.Y. Soc. Electron Microscopists, Cuyahoga County Med. Soc., Cleve. Soc. Pathologists, The Oxygen Soc., Sigma Xi. Home: PO Box 3125 Half Moon Bay CA 94019 Office Phone: 650 712-0657. Office Fax: 650-712-0357. Personal E-mail: abelrobertsonmd@yahoo.com.

ROBERTSON, CLAUDIA S., physician, educator; b. Ft. Worth, June 6, 1950; BS, Baylor U., 1972; MD, Baylor Coll. Medicine, 1975. Prof. Baylor Coll. Medicine, 1982—. Grant, NIH-NINDS, Dept. Def. Fellow: Am. Coll. Critical Care Medicine; mem.: ACP, Nat. Neurotrauma Soc., Soc. Critical Care Medicine. Office: One Baylor Plz Houston TX 77030 Business E-Mail: claudiar@bcm.tmc.edu.

ROBERTSON, DAVID, physician, pharmacologist, educator; b. Sylvia, Tenn., May 23, 1947; s. David Herlie and Lucille Luther (Bowen) R.; m. Rose Marie Stevens, Oct. 30, 1976; 1 child, Rose. BA, Vanderbilt U., 1969, MD, 1973. Diplomate Am. Bd. Internal. Medicine, Am. Bd. Clin. Pharmacology. Intern Johns Hopkins U., Balt., 1973-74, asst. resident, 1974-75, asst. chief svc. in medicine, 1977-78; fellow in clin. pharmacology Vanderbilt U., Nashville, 1975-77, asst. prof. medicine and pharmacology, 1978-82, assoc. prof., 1982-86, prof., 1986—, prof. neurology, 1991—, Elton Yates prof. autonomic disorders, 1998—, dir. clin. rsch. ctr., 1987—; dir. Ctr. Space Physiology and Medicine, 1989—, Med. Sci. Tng. Program, 1993—2003; mem. staff Vanderbilt Hosp., Burroughs Wellcome scholar in clin. pharmacology, 1985-91; prin. investigator Autonomic Rare Diseases Clin. Rsch. Consortium, 2009—. Author: (with B.M. Greene and G.J. Taylor) Problems in Internal Medicine, 1980, (with C.R. Smith) Manual of Clinical Pharmacology, 1981, (with Italo Biaggioni) Disorders of the Autonomic Nervous System, 1995, (with Italo Biaggioni, Geoffrey Burnstock, Phillip A. Low and Julian F.R. Paton) Primer on the Autonomic Nervous System, 1996, 3rd edit., 2011, Robertson's Autonomic Neuroscience, Japanese, 2007, (with Gordon H. Williams) Clinical and Translational Science: Principles of Human Research, 2009; editor: APOR Newsletter, 2004-08, Spotlight on Rare Diseases, 2010-; editor-in-chief: Drug Therapy, 1991-94; assoc. editor, Jour. Pharmacol. Exptl. Therapy, 1998—; assoc. editor: Jour. Chinese Med. Assn., 1995-; mem. editl. bd. Am. Jour. Medicine, Autonomic Neuroscience, Clin. Pharm. and Therapeutics, Clin. Autonomic Rsch., Am. Jour. Med. Sci., Current Topics in Pharmacology, Rambam-Maimonides Med. Jour., 2009-. Logan Clendening fellow, Reykjavik, Iceland, 1969; Adolph-Morsbach grantee Bonn, Germany, 1968; recipient Rsch. Career Devel. award NIH, 1981, Grant W. Liddle award for leadership in rsch., 1991, 1995-99 NASA Neurolab prin. investigator, Tchg. award Nat. Program Dir.'s Assn., 2003, Rschr. of Yr. award Nat. Dysautomia Rsch. Found., 2001, PhRMA award for Excellence in Pharmacology, Earl Sutherland prize, 2007. Fellow Am. Heart Assn. Coun. Hypertension and Circulation, ACP (tchg. and rsch. scholar 1978-81), Am. Autonomic Soc. (founding pres. 1992-94); mem. Am. Acad. Neurology, Soc. Neurosci., Am. Inst. Aeronautics and Astronautics, U.S. Pharmacopeial Conv., Nat. Bd. Med. Examiners, Aerospace Med. Assn. (space sta. sci. and applications com.), NASA (microgravity human rsch. com.), FDA Com. on Rare Disorders, Am. Fedn. Med. Rsch., Am. Soc. Clin. Investigation, Assn. Am. Physicians, Assn. Patient-Oriented Rsch. (bd. dirs., founding pres. 1998-99), So. Soc. Clin. Investigation, Am. Soc. Clin. Pharmacology and Therapeutics, Automatic Disorders Clin. Rsch. Consortium (prin. investigator, 2009-), Phi Beta Kappa, Alpha Omega Alpha (hon., bd. dirs. 1995-2004. William Darby award 2000). Baptist. Home: 4003 Newman Pl Nashville TN 37204-4308 Office: Vanderbilt U Clin Rsch Ctr 21st Ave S Nashville TN 37232-2195 Business E-Mail: david.robertson@vanderbilt.edu.

ROBERTSON, EDWIN MALCOLM, psychology educator; s. Ronald and Elizabeth Robertson. BA, U. Cambridge, UK, 1994; DPhil, U. Oxford, UK, 1998; BM BCh, House Physician & House Surgeon, Oxford Med. Sch., 2001. Rsch. fellow Harvard Med. Sch., 2001—03, instr., 2003—05, asst. prof., 2005—10, assoc. prof., 2010—. Editor PLoS ONE, San Fransisco, 2006—. Contbr. multiple rsch. articles to profl. jours. Recipient R01, NIH, 2005—; grant, NSF, 2009—. Mem.: NSF (divisn. behavioral & cognitive scis.). Office: Harvard Med Sch 330 Brookline Ave Boston MA 02215

ROBERTSON, JOSEPH E., JR., academic administrator, ophthalmologist, educator; b. Jackson County, Ind., July 24, 1952; s. Joseph E. and Virginia Faye (Baxter) R.; children: Kathryn Faye, Charles Joseph. BS in Neuroscience, cum laude, Yale U., 1974; MD, Ind. U., 1978; MBA, U. Oreg., 1997. Diplomate Am. Bd. Ophthalmology. Intern Bapt. Med. Ctr., Birmingham, Ala., 1978-79; resident Oreg. Health Sci. U., Portland, 1979-82; pvt. practice Vancouver, Wash., 1982-83; fellow Oreg. Health Sci. U./Devers Hosp./Good Samaritan Hosp., Portland, 1983-84; vitreous surgery fellow Steve Charles, M.D., Memphis, 1984-85; asst. prof. Oreg. Health Sci. U., Portland, 1985-92, assoc. prof., 1992-97, prof., chmn. dept. ophthalmology, 1997—, dir. Casey Eye Inst., 1998—2003, interim dean, 2001—02, dean Sch. Medicine, 2003—06, pres., 2006—. Contbr. articles to profl. jours., chpts. to books; editor videotapes. Apptd. mem. Oreg. Commn. for the Blind, 1988-94. Mem. Am. Acad. Ophthalmology (Oreg. rep. to coun. 1992-95, COVE com. 1988-93, skills transfer adv. com. 1994-98, nat. chair and state coord. Diabetes 2000), Oreg. Acad. Ophthalmology (pres. 1990-91), Univ. Med. Group (exec. com. 1997—, v.p. 1998—), Oreg. Med. Assn. Democrat. Presbyterian. Avocations: skiing, windsurfing, snowboarding, hiking, jogging. Office: OHSU Office of Pres 3181 SW Sam Jackson Park Rd Portland OR 97239-3098 also: Casey Eye Inst OHSU 3375 SW Terwilliger Blvd Portland OR 97239 Office Phone: 503-494-3056.

ROBERTSON, NED, dentist; b. Rumford, Maine, Mar. 3, 1950; s. Edward Norris and Edith Louise (Kirk) Robertson; m. Susan Elizabeth Valentine, July 21, 2001; 1 child, Olivia; children: Christie Portia, Juliet Melissa(dec.), Jenni Celia, Edward Noah, Jessica Edith. BS in Biology, Antioch Coll., Yellow Springs, Ohio, 1973; MS in Epidemiology, Ohio State U., 1977; DDS, Case Western Res. U., 1983, DMD, 2004. Faculty adv. to med. students Ohio State U., Columbus, 1975-77; rsch. cons. Ohio Dept. Health, Columbus, 1976-77; rsch. assoc. UCLA, 1977; epidemiologic/statis. cons. LA, 1977; medic J & L Steel Corp., Cleve., 1979-84; pvt. practice Cleveland Heights, Ohio, 1983-91, Lyndhurst, Ohio, 1995-2000. Mem. adj. faculty Cuyahoga C.C., Cleve., 1986-88; assoc. prof. Sch. Dentistry Case Western Res. U., 1991-96; asst. prof. Case Western Res. U. Sch. Dentistry, Cleve., 1997-2003; pvt. contractor Indian Health Svc. Dental Clinic, Pine Ridge, S.D., 1999-2000; clin. instr. U. Md. Dental Sch., 1999-00. Pres. Robertson Family Assn. of N.Am., 1986-88. Recipient numerous rsch. grants; named one of Best Dentists in Am., No. Ohio Live mag., 2007. Mem.: ADA, Internat. Congress Oral Implantologists, Am. Acad. Craniofacial Pain, Internat. Assn. for Study of Pain, Greater Cleve. Dental Soc., Ohio Dental Assn., Acad. Gen. Dentistry, Midwest Pain Soc., Acad. Laser Surgery, U.S. Dental Inst., Am. Chronic Pain Assn., Ohio Acad. Gen. Dentistry, Am. Pain Soc., Am. Acad. Pain Mgmt. Avocations: scuba diving, cross country skiing, camping, canoeing, bicycling. Office: 24755 Chagrin Blvd Ste 145 Beachwood OH 44122-5692 Office Phone: 216-468-0041. Business E-Mail: dentalned@aol.com.

ROBERTSON, ROSE MARIE, cardiologist, educator; b. Detroit, May 15, 1945; d. Joseph Michael and Rose Marie (Pink) Stevens; m. David Robertson, Oct. 31, 1978; 1 child, Rose Marie. BA, Manhattanville Coll., 1966; MD, Harvard Med. Sch., 1970. Diplomate Nat. Bd. Medicine, 1971, Am. Bd. Internal Medicine, 1974, Cardiovascular Medicine, 1975. Intern in medicine Mass. Gen. Hosp., Boston, 1970-71, resident in medicine, 1970-72; fellow in cardiovasc. medicine Johns Hopkins Med. Sch., Balt., 1973-75, asst. prof. medicine, 1976—77, Vanderbilt U. Med. Ctr., Nashville, 1975-82, assoc. prof. medicine, 1982-89, dir. cardiovasc. tng. program, 1990—2000, assoc. dir. cardiology, 1987—2000, prof. medicine, 1989—. Mem. adv. bd. Robert Wood Johnson Found., AMFDP, 1990-, chair, 2003-; mem. bd. Assn. for Patient-Oriented Rsch.; mem. cardiovasc. study sect. NIH, Bethesda, Md., 1993-97; invited spkr., lectr. Contbr. articles to profl. jours., chpts. to books. Fellow Am. Coll. Cardiology, Am. Heart Assn. (pres. 2000-01, chief sci. officer 2003-), Am. Autonomic Soc., Am. Fedn. for Clin. Rsch., Am. Soc. Clin. Investigation, Am. Clin. and Climatol. Assn., Assn. Univ. Cardiologists. Home: 4003 Newman Pl Nashville TN 37204-4308 Office: 7272 Greenville Ave Dallas TX 75231 Office Phone: 214-706-1295. E-mail: rosemarie.robertson@heart.org.

ROBERTSON, RUSSELL G., physician, dean; b. Ypsilanti, Mich., Nov. 7, 1952; s. Lyle R. and Harriet L. Robertson; m. Sandra K. Lorts, Aug. 9, 1975; children: Judd L., Amelia K. MD, Wayne State U., 1982. Lic. physician Wis., 1985. Resident in family medicine Mich. State U., Grand Rapids, 1982—85; asst. dir. St. Michael Family Practice, Milw., 1985—87; program dir. family practice residence Columbia Hosp., Milw., 1987—99; assoc. dean faculty affairs Med. Coll. Wis., Milw., 2001—05; prof., chair dept. family medicine Feinberg Sch. Medicine, Northwestern U., Chgo., 2005—11; v.p. med. affairs, dean med. sch. Rosalind Franklin U. Medicine and Sci.,

Chgo., 2011—. Author: (TV series) The Doctor Is In. Mem. Coun. Grad. Med. Edn., Washington, 2002—05. Grantee, Healthier Wis., 2005. Mem.: Med. Soc. Milwaukee County (pres.-elect 2004—05), Wis. Acad. Family Physicians (assoc.; second v.p. 2004—05). Avocations: writing, travel, automobile care. Office: Rosalind Franklin University Medicine and Sci 3333 Green Bay Rd North Chicago IL 60064 Office Phone: 847-578-3301. Business E-Mail: russell.robertson@rosalindfranklin.edu. *

ROBERTSON, WILLIAM WRIGHT, JR., orthopedist, educator; b. Mayfield, Ky., Dec. 26, 1946; m. Karel Virginia Dierks, Jan. 26, 1974. BA, Rhodes Coll., 1968; MD, Vanderbilt U., 1972; MBA, Geo Washington U., 2000. Intern U. Calif., San Diego, 1972-73, resident in orthop. surgery, 1975-76, Vanderbilt U., Nashville, 1976-79; asst. prof. orthop. Tex. Tech U., Lubbock, 1979-86; assoc. prof. U. Pa., Phila., 1986-90; prof. orthop. surgery George Washington U., Washington, 1990-2000; chmn. pediat. orthop. Children's Nat. Med. Ctr., Washington, 1990-99. Field rep. accreditation coun. grad. med. edn. Fellow Am. Acad. Orthop. Surgeons, Am. Orthop. Assn., Pediat. Orthop. Soc. (bd. dirs. 1993-96—). Avocations: gardening, music. Office: Accreditation Coun Grad Med Edn 515 N State St Chicago IL 60610 Home Phone: 301-718-7867. Business E-Mail: wrobertson@acgme.org.

ROBILLARD, JEAN EUGENE, academic administrator; b. Montreal, 1943; m. Renee Robillard. BA, U. Montreal, 1964, MD, 1968. Pediat. residency Saint Justine Hosp., Montreal, 1969—72; pediat. nephrology fellowship UCLA Med. Ctr., Los Angeles, 1972—73, U. Iowa Med. Ctr., Iowa City, 1973—74; asst. prof., dept. pediat. U. Montreal Coll. Med., 1975—76; asst. prof. Dept. Pediat., Coll. Med., U. Iowa, 1974—75, 1976—78, assoc. prof., 1978—82, dir. nephrology div., 1976—96, prof., 1982—96, vice chmn.; chief pediat. U. Mich., Ann Arbor, 1996—2003; physician-in-chief C.S. Mott Children's Hosp., 1996—2003; dean Roy J. and Lucille A. Carver Coll Medicine, U. Iowa, 2003—08; v.p. med. affairs U. Iowa, 2007—. Editl. bd. Jour. Pediat., 2001—; bd. dirs. Am. Bd. Pediat., 2001—, chmn. bd. dirs., 2006—07. Author of over 220 sci. papers. Recipient Disting. Alumni Award for Achievement, U. Iowa, 2002. Fellow: Coun. for High Blood Pressure Rsch., Am. Heart Assn., Royal Coll. Physicians & Surgeons; mem.: Iowa Bus. Coun., Climatologically Assoc., Am. Clin., Nat. Med. Assoc., Am. Soc. Transplant Physicians, The Perinatal Rsch. Soc, Soc. for Gynecologic Investigation, Am. Physiol. Soc., Am. Assn. for Advancement Sci. (fellow 1999), Am. Soc. Pediat. Nephrology (pres. 1994—95), Soc. Pediat. Rsch., Am. Heart Assn., Am. Soc. Nephrology, Internat. Soc. Nephrology, Internat. Pediat. Nephrology Assn., Midwest Soc. Pediat. Rsch. (Founder's Award 2002), Am. Acad. Pediat., Am Pediat. Soc. Office: Roy J & Lucille A Carver Coll Med 312 CMAB Iowa City IA 52242

ROBINS, PERRY, dermatologist, educator, foundation administrator; MD, U. Heidelberg, 1961. Intern Orange Meml. Hosp., 1961—62; resident in dermatology, syphilology Bronx VA Med. Ctr., 1962—64; clin. fellow in dermatology, syphilology NYU Med. Ctr., 1965—67, prof. emeritus dermatology, clin. prof., chief, Mohs micrographic surgery unit; founder, pres. Internat. Soc. Dermatologic Surgery, The Skin Cancer Found. Author: Sun Sense: A Guide to the Prevention and Early Detection of Skin Cancer, Understanding Basal Cell Carcinoma: What You Need to Know, Understanding Squamous Cell Carcinoma: What You Need to Know, Play it Safe in the Sun; co-author (with M. Perez): Understanding Melanoma: What You Need to Know; contbr. articles to profl. jours. Recipient Presdl. Citation, Internat. Soc. Dermatologic Surgery. Fellow: Am. Acad. Dematology (hon. Award Excellence in Edn., Golden Triangle award, Presdl. Citation); mem.: Am. Soc. Dermatol. Surgery (past pres.), Am. Coll. Mohs Micrographic Surgery (founder, past pres.). Office: 345 E 37th St Ste 209 New York NY 10016 also: Skin Cancer Found 149 Madison Ave Ste 901 New York NY 10016 Office Phone: 212-263-7222. Office Fax: 212-686-5842. *

ROBINSON, ADAM MAYFIELD, JR., career military officer, surgeon; b. Louisville, Nov. 9, 1950; s. Adam Mayfield and Addie Hilda (Brown) Robinson; m. Judith Schevtchuk, Dec. 29, 1973 (div. Aug. 1982); m. Yuko Sakurai, Aug. 30, 1984. AB in Polit. Sci., Ind. U., 1972; MD, Ind. U. Sch. Medicine, Indpls., 1976; MBA, U. South Fla., 1994. Diplomate Am. Bd. Surgery, Am. Bd. Colon & Rectal Surgery. Commd. ensign USN Med. Corps, 1977, advanced through grades to capt., 1990, then vice adm., gen. med. officer Ponce, PR, 1977-78, gen. surgery resident Bethesda Naval Hosp. Md., 1978-82, staff gen. surgeon Yokosuka Naval Hosp. Japan, 1982-84, ship's surgeon USS Midway Yokosuka, 1982-84, head divisn. colon-rectal surgery Bethesda Naval Hosp., 1985-90, asst. head gen. surgery, 1987-90, chmn. dept. gen. surgery Portsmouth Naval Hosp. Va., 1990—95, acting med. dir., 1994—95, force surgeon, comdr. Naval Surface Force, US Atlantic Fleet Norfolk, Va., 1995—97, exec. officer Naval Hosp. Jacksonville, Fla., 1997—99, dir. readiness Bur. Medicine & Surgery, 1999—2000, prin. dir. clin. & prog. policy, acting dep. asst. sec. of def. for health affairs, 2000—01, cmdg. officer Naval Hosp. Yokosuka, 2001—04, acting chief Med. Corps, dep. chief med. support ops. Bur. Medicine & Surgery, 2004, comdr. Nat. Naval Med. Ctr. Bethesda, 2004—05, comdr. Navy Medicine Nat. Capital Area Region, 2005—07, surgeon gen., chief Bur. Medicine & Surgery, 2007—. Fellow colon-rectal surgery Carle Clinic, U. Ill., Champaign, 1984—85. Contbr. articles to profl. jours. Fellow: ACS, Am. Soc. Colon & Rectal Surgeons; mem.: AMA, Assn. Program Dirs. in Surgery (bd. dirs. 1990), Assn. Mil. Surgeons US, Nat. Med. Assn., Beta Gamma Sigma. Avocations: ballroom dancing, golf, singing. Office: USN Navy Pentagon Washington DC 20503 *

ROBINSON, ALEXANDER JACOB, retired psychologist; b. St. John, Kans., Nov. 7, 1920; s. Oscar Frank and Lydia May (Beitler) R.; m. Elsie Louise Riggs, July 29, 1942; children: Madelyn K., Alicia A., David J., Charles A., Paul S., Marietta J., Stephen N. BA in Psychology, Ft. Hays State U., Kans., 1942, MS in Clin. Psychology, 1942; postgrad., U. Ill., 1942-44. Cert. psychologist, sch. psychologist. Chief psychologist Larned State Hosp., Kans., 1948-53, with employee selection, outpatient services, 1953-55; sch. psychologist County Schs., Modesto, Calif., 1955-61, Pratt Jr. Coll., Kans., 1961-66; fed. grantee, writer assoc. dir. Exemplary Federally Funded Program for Spl. Edn., Pratt, 1966-70; dir. spl. edn., rschr. Stafford County Schs., St. John, 1970-81, ret., 1981. Supr. testing and data Incidence of Exceptional Children in Kansas, Kans. State U., Ft. Hays, 1946; writer, asst. dir. Best Exemplary Federally Funded Program on Spl. Edn., Pratt, 1966-70; fed. grantee, rschr., writer, study dir. Edn. for the High-Performance Child, St. John, 1970—, Psychogenesis of the Sociopathic Personality. Minister, The Ch. of Jesus Christ. Served to 2d lt. U.S. Army, 1944-46, PTO. Mem. NY Acad. Scis., Libr. of Congress. Lodges: Lions (program chmn. St. John 1974-76). Achievements include research in normal children with a learning disability and their specific developmental requirement. Avocations: history, ethnology, anthropology, music, literature. Home and Office: 402 E 1st Saint John KS 67576 Office Phone: 620-549-3373.

ROBINSON, AMANDA R., research scientist; b. Findlay, Ohio, Dec. 16, 1983; Degree in Microbiology, Ohio Wesleyan U., 2006; PhD in Cellular & Molecular Biology, U. Wis., Madison, 2011. Rsch. assoc. U. Wis., 2006—. Cancer Biology Tng. grant, NIH. Office: 1400 University Ave McArdle 613 Madison WI 53706 Business E-Mail: arrobinson@wisc.edu.

ROBINSON, DANIEL N., psychology and philosophy professor; b. NYC, Mar. 9, 1937; s. Henry S. and Margaret R.; children: Tracey, Kimberly; m. Francine Malasko, 1967. BA, Colgate U., 1958; MA, Hofstra U., 1960; PhD, CUNY, 1965. Rsch. psychologist, electronics rsch. labs. Columbia U., 1960-65, asst. dir. sci. honors program, 1964-68, sr. rsch. psychologist, electronics rsch. labs., 1965-68, asst. dir. of life scis. electronics rsch. labs., 1967-68; asst. prof. dept. psychology Amherst Coll., 1968-70, assoc. prof., 1970-71; dir. grad. program dept. psychology Georgetown Univ., 1981-83, chmn. dept. psychology, 1973-76, 85-91, assoc. prof., 1971-74, prof., 1974—, adj. prof. philosophy Washington, 1996—97, disting. rsch. prof. and prof. psychology, 1998—2001, disting. prof. emeritus, 2002—. Vis. lectr. psychology Princeton U., 1965-68; vis. prof. Folger Shakespeare Inst., 1977; vis. prof., BYU, 1988-2000, adj. prof., Inst. Psychol. Scis., 2003-, bd. scholars, Princeton James Madison Program, 2001-,vis. sr. mem. Linacre Coll., vis. lectr. philosophy Oxford (Eng.) U., 1991—, faculty fellow, 1999—, philos. faculty, 2002—; vis. prof. Princeton U., 2001; adj. prof. Columbia U., 2002-2005; cons. NIH, 1967-70, NSF, 1965-75, PBS, 1978-84, 1985-88, MacArthur Found., 1985, Atty. Gen's. Task Force on Crime, 1980, HHS, NIH, 1988. Author: Psychology: A Study of Its Origins and Principles, 1972, The Enlightened Machine: An Anlytical Introduction to Neuropsychology, 1973, 80, Psychology: Traditions and Perspectives, 1976, An Intellectual History of Psychology, 1976, The Mind Unfolded: Essay's on Psychology's Historic Texts, 1978, Systems of Modern Psychology: A Critical Sketch, 1979, Psychology and Law: Can Justice Survive the Social Sciences?, 1980, An Intellectual History of Psychology-Revised Edition, 1981, 3rd edit., 1995, Toward A Science of Human Nature: Essays on the Psychologies of Hegel, Mill, Wundt, and James, 1982, Philosophy of Psychology, 1985, Aristotle's Psychology, 1989, (with William R. Uttal) Foundations of Psychobiology, 1983, (with Sir John Eccles) The Wonder of Being Human: Our Mind and Our Brain, 1984; editor Heredity and Achievement, 1970, Readings in the Origins and Principles of Psychology, 1972, Significant Contributions to the History of Psychology, 1977-78, Annals of Theoretical Psychology, 1990, Social Discourse and Moral Judgment, 1992, Wild Beasts and Idle Humours: Legal Insanity from Antiquity to the Present, 1996, Consciousness and Mental Life, 2008; editor Jour. Theoretical and Philosophical Psychology, 1997-2002; contbr. chpts. to books, reference books, articles to profl. jours. Recipient Inst. for Advanced Study in the Humanities fellow, U. Edinburgh, 1986-87; Pres's. medal Colgate U., 1986, Pub. Svc. award Gen. Svcs. Adminstrn., 1986. Fellow APA (past pres. divsns. 24 and 26, Lifetime Achievement award Divsn. History of Psychology 2001, Disting. Contbn. award Divsn. Theoretical and Philos. Psychology 2001), Witherspoon Inst. (Sr.); mem. Sigma Xi, Psi Chi. Home: 300 E Main St Middletown MD 21769 Office Phone: 301-676-0015, 202-337-1969. Personal E-mail: dnmrobinson@msn.com. Business E-Mail: dan.robinson@philosophy.ox.ac.uk.

ROBINSON, GAIL PATRICIA, retired mental health counselor; b. Medford, Oreg., Dec. 31, 1936; d. Ivan T. and Evelyn H. (Hamilton) Skyrman; m. Douglas L. Smith; children: Shauna J., James D. BS in Edn., Oreg. State U., 1958, PhD in Counseling, 1978; MS in Counseling, Western Oreg. State Coll., 1974. Tchr. Monterey (Calif.) Pub. Schs., 1958-59, Corvallis (Oreg.) Pub. Schs., 1959-62, 69-75, counselor, 1977-81; pvt. practice Corvallis, 1977-95. Vol. therapist Children's Svcs. divsn., Linn and Benton Counties, 1982-83; asst. prof. Western Oreg. State coll., 1977, counselor, 1982-83; mem. grad. faculty Oreg. State U., Corvallis, 1978-95; presenter workshops, lectr. in field. Contbr. articles to profl. jours. Mem. Benton County Mental Health Citizens Adv. Bd., 1979-85, chair, 1982-83; trustee WCTU Children's Farm Home, 1978-84, chair child welfare com., 1982-83, pres., 1984; adv. bd. Old Mill Sch., 1979-85, chair, 1979-81; bd. dirs. Cmty. Outreach, 1979-83; mem. Benton Com. for Prevention of Child Abuse, 1979-85, v.p., 1982; mem. Oreg. Bd. Lic. Profl. Counselors and Therapists, 1989-95, chair, 1989-90, Aurora Colony Hist. Soc., vol., 2000-, bd. dirs., 2005-10, sec., 2006—08, pres. 2008-10. Mem. ACA (govt. rels. com. 1988-91, professionalization com. 1988-92, pres. 1996-97), Am. Mental Health Counselors Assn. (chair consumer and pub. rels. com. 1988-91, bd. dirs. Western region 1989-91, chair strategic planning com. 1994-95, pres. 1992-93), Oreg. Counseling Assn. (chair licensure liaison com. 1985-91, exec. bd. 1985-88, steering com. 1986-87, register editorial com. 1985-86, Disting. Svc. award 1985, 87, Leona Tyler award 1989), Oreg. Mental Health Counselors Assn. Personal E-mail: robinsgp@comcast.net.

ROBINSON, HERBERT HENRY, III, psychotherapist, educator; b. Leavenworth, Wash., Mar. 31, 1933; s. Herbert Henry II and Alberta (Sperber) R.; m. Georgia Murial Jones, Nov. 24, 1954 (div. 1974); children: Cheri Dean Asbury, David Keith, Peri Elizabeth Layton, Tanda Rene Graff, Gaila Daire. Grad. of Theology, Bapt. Bible Coll., 1959; BA in Philosophy/Greek, Whitworth Coll., 1968; MA in Coll. Teaching, Ea. Wash. U., 1976; PhD, Gonzaga U., 2002. Cert. psychotherapist, perpetrator treatment program supervision; nat. bd. cert. counselor. Choir dir. Twin City Bapt. Temple, Mishawaka, Ind., 1959-61; min. Inland Empire Bapt. Ch., Spokane, Wash., 1961-73; tchr. philosophy Spokane C.C., 1969-72; dir. Alternatives to Violence, Women in Crisis, Fairbanks, Alaska, 1985-87; tchr. pub. rels. U. Alaska, Fairbanks, 1986-87; dir. Alternatives to Violence Men Inc., Juneau, 1988-89; tchr. leadership mgmt. U. Alaska S.E., Juneau, 1988-89; min. Sci. of Mind Ctr., Sandpoint, Idaho, 1989-92; dir., therapist Tapio Counseling Ctr., Spokane, 1991—2011; cert. psychotherapist, supr. perpetrator treatment program Wash. Cons. Lilac Blind/Alpha Inc./Marshall Coll., Spokane, 1975-85, Alaska Placer Mining Co., Fairbanks, 1987; tchr. Spokane Falls C.C., Spokane, 1979-85; seminar, presenter Human Resource Devel., Spokane and Seattle, Wash., Pa., 1980; guest trainer United Way/Kellogg Found. Inst. for Volunteerism, Spokane, 1983. 1st trombone San Diego Marine Band, 1953-56, Spokane Symphony, 1961; bd. dirs. Tanani Learning Ctr., Fairbanks, 1987; mem. consensus bldg. team Sci. of Mind Ctr., Sandpoint, 1989-92. Cpl. USMC, 1953-56. Mem. ACA, Assn. for Humanistic Edn. and Devel., Assn. for Religious Values in Counseling, Internat. Assn. Addictions and Offender Counselors, Internat. Assn. Marriage and Family Counselors, Am. Assn. Profl. Hypnotherapists, Masterson Inst. Office: Tapio Counseling 722 E 5th Ave Spokane WA 99202-2302 Home Phone: 509-927-9825; Office Phone: 509-534-5028. E-mail: peace@herb-robinson.com.

ROBINSON, HURLEY, surgeon; b. LA, Feb. 25, 1925; s. Edgar Ray and Nina Madge (Hurley) R.; m. Mary Anne Rusche, Mar. 14, 1953; children: Kathleen Ann Robinson Petschke, Mary Elizabeth, Lynda Jean Robinson Lamb, William Hurley, Patricia Kay Robinson Hardy, Paul Edgar. Student, U. Calif., Berkeley, 1943, U. Calif., Santa Barbara, 1946—48; BS, Northwestern U., 1950, MD, 1952. Diplomate Am. Bd. Surgery. Intern Wesley Meml. Hosp., Chgo., 1952-53; resident in gen. surgery Milw. County Hosp., 1953-57; surgeon Abbott Med. Group, Ontario, Calif., 1957-59; pvt. practice Upland, Calif., 1959-64; ptnr. Robinson & Schechter Surg. Med. Group, Upland, 1964-92; part-time pvt. practice, 1993—2007. Instr. dept. surgery San Bernardino County Med. Ctr., San Bernardino, Calif., 1959-79; sr. surg. staff San Antonio Cmty. Hosp., Upland, 1958—, trustee, 1979-81, pres. med. staff, 1980; mem. staff Pomona (Calif.) Valley Med. Ctr.; exec. com. San Bernardino County Med. Ctr., 1974, adv. bd., 1974; clin. asst. vascular surgery The London Hosp., Eng., 1973; cons. in field. Contbr. article to Wis. Med. Jour. Chmn. troop com., camp dr. Boy Scouts Am., Upland, 1970-72. With U.S. Army, 1943-46. Fellow: ACS, Am. Coll. Angiology, Am. Coll. Chest Physicians; mem.: AMA, European Soc. Vascular Surgery, L.A. Surg. Soc., Soc. Clin. Vascular Surgery, Pan-Pacific Surg. Assn., Tri-County Surg. Soc. So. Calif. (pres.), San Bernardino County Med. Soc., Calif. Med. Assn., Am. Med. Soc. Republican. Presbyterian. Office: 124 Garnet Ave Newport Beach CA 92662-1009 Office Phone: 949-673-1183. Personal E-mail: hurleyrobinson@sbcglobal.net.

ROBINSON, JAMES CAREY, neurosurgeon; b. Camden, NJ, Oct. 12, 1964; BS in Premed. Scis., Ea. Coll., 1987; MD, Med. Coll. Pa., 1990. Pres., neurosurgeon Atlanta Brain & Spine Care, 2001—; pres. Spectrum Spine LLC, 2011—; cranial neurosurgery specialist Brain-Expert.com, 2011—. Med. dir., gamma knife unit Piedmont Hosp., Atlanta, 2005—. Mem.: Soc. Neuro-Oncology, AANS Sect. Tumors, Sigma Zeta Nat. Sci. Honor Soc., Am. Assn. Neurol. Surgeons, Alpha Omega Alpha. Avocations: fishing, photography. Home and Office: 3045 Paces Lake Ct Atlanta GA 30339 Personal E-mail: jim@brainexpert.com. Business E-Mail: jim@spectrumspine.com.

ROBINSON, JANE JENIFER ANN, nurse researcher, educator; b. Birmingham, Eng., Nov. 6, 1935; d. Reginald Milton and Florence (Troop) London; m. Anthony David Robinson, Feb. 6, 1959; children: Ann Louise Robinson Sutcliffe, Felicity Jane Robinson Wood, Kathryn Mary Robinson Roodner MA, U. Keele, Eng., 1980, PhD, 1986. Theatre sister Winford Orthop. Hosp., 1957—58; staff nurse Bristol Homeopathic Hosp., Bristol, England, 1959, North Staffs Royal Infirmary, 1968—69; health visitor Staffs County Coun., 1970—74; nursing officer Mid-Staffs Health Authority, 1974—77, health visitor, 1977—79; lectr. Wolverhampton Poly., 1980—81, 1983—84; rsch. officer Sandwell Health Authority, 1981—83; dir. nursing policy studies ctr. U. Warwick, 1985—89; prof., head dept. U. Nottingham, England, 1989—97, emeritus prof., 1997—. Advisor WHO, 1985-97, Internat. Coun. Nurses, 1999, mem. North Staffs Local Rsch. Ethics, 2003- Author: The NHS Under New Management, 1990, Nurses Manage, 1995, Health Needs Assessment: Theory and Practice, 1996, Interdisciplinary Perspectives on Health Policy and Practice, 1999; editor Jour. Advanced Nursing, 1997-2001, editor-in-chief, 2001-02; editor Internat. Nursing Rev., 2002—; contbg. author conf. procs Fulbright sr. rsch. scholar, 1996-97 Fellow Royal Coll. Nursing (health and social policy com. 1991-92, chair women's issues subcom. 1995-99, rsch. com. 1997-99, rep. workgroup European Nurse Rschrs. 1998—); mem. Chartered Inst. Pers. and Devel., Social Policy Assn. (women's nat. commn. 1995-98), Univ. Women's Club Avocation: travel. Office: Blackwell Publishing 9600 Garsington Rd Oxford OX4 2DQ England also: Internat Coun of Nurses 3 Place Jean Marteau CH 1201 Geneva Switzerland

ROBINSON, JOE SAM, neurosurgeon, educator; b. Atlanta, July 21, 1945; s. Joe Sam and Nell (Mixon) R.; m. Elizabeth Ann Moate, Apr. 3, 1982; children: Joe Sam III, Edward Richard, Thomas McRae. AB cum laude, Harvard Coll., 1967; MD, U. Va., 1971; MS, Northwestern U., 1975. Surg. intern Emory U., 1971-72, resident in surgery, 1972-73; resident in neurosurgery Northwestern U., 1973-78; instr. U. Ill., 1978-79, Yale U., 1979-81; pres. Ga. Neurosurg. Inst. P.A., Macon, 1981—. Prof., chief neurosurgery Mercer U. Sch. Medicine, Macon, 1986; chief surgery Med. Ctr. Ctrl. Ga., Macon, 1989—, vice chmn. surgery, 1991-97, chmn. dept. surgery, 1996—; vis. neurosurgeon China, 1992, Konaus Acad. Neurosurgery Inst., Lithuania, 1992; clin. prof. Med. Coll. Ga., 2002; chmn. Ga. Bd. Physicians Workforce, 2007, physician Trauma Rep. Ga. Trauma Commn. Lt. col. USANG, 1972-95. Fellow Internat. Coll. Surgeons (vice regent 1983-93); mem. Am. Assn. Neurol. Surgeons, Congress Neurol. Surgeons, AAAS, Ga. Neurosurg. Soc., Alpha Omega Alpha. Republican. Methodist. Office: Ga Neurosurg Inst PA 840 Pine St Ste 880 Macon GA 31201-7525 Business E-Mail: vickie@ganeurosurg.org.

ROBINSON, JUNE KERSWELL, dermatologist, educator; b. Phila., Jan. 26, 1950; d. George and Helen S. (Kerswell) R.; m. William T. Barker, Jan. 31, 1981. BA cum laude, U. Pa., 1970; MD, U. Md., 1974. Diplomate Am. Bd. Dermatology, Nat. Bd. Med.

Examiners, Am. Bd. Mohs Micrographic Surgery and Cutaneous Oncology. Intern Greater Balt. Med. Ctr., Hanover, NH, 1974, resident in medicine, 1974—75; resident in dermatology Dartmouth-Hitchcock Med. Ctr., Hanover, 1975—78, chief resident, clin. instr., 1977—78, instr. in dermatology, 1978; fellow Mohs; chemosurgery and dermatologic surgery NYU Skin and Cancer Clinic, NYC, 1978—79; instr. in dermatology NYU, NYC, 1979; asst. prof. dermatology Northwestern U. Med. Sch., Chgo., 1979, asst. prof. surgery, 1980—85, assoc. prof. dermatology and surgery, 1985—91, prof. dermatology and surgery, 1991—98; prof. medicine and pathology, dir. divsn. dermatology Cardinal Bernardin Cancer Ctr., Loyola U. Med. Ctr., 1998—2004, program leader skin cancer clin. program, 1998—2004; prof. medicine Med. Sch. Dartmouth U., 2004—05, chief Dermatology Sect. Hitchcock Med. Ctr., 2004—05; prof. clin. dermatology, Feinberg Sch. Medicine Northwestern U., Chgo., 2006—11, prof. dermatology, 2011. Mem. consensus devel. conf. NIH, 1992; mem. panel on use of sunscreens Internat. Agy. for Rsch. on Cancer, WHO, 2000; lectr. in field. Author: Fundamentals of Skin Biopsy, 1985, also audiovisual materials; editor: (textbooks) Atlas of Cutaneous Surgery, 1996, Cutaneous Medicine and Surgery: An Integrated Program in Dermatology, 1996, Surgery of the Skin, 2005, 2010; editor (with Rigel DS, Ross M, Friedman RJ, Cockerell CJ, Lim HW, Stockfeeth E, Kirkwood JM)Canver of The Skin, 2011; mem. editl. bd. Archives of Dermatology, 1988-97; sect. editor The Cutting Edge: Challenges in Med. and Surg. Therapeutics, 1989-97, editor, 2004—; contbg. editor Jour. Dermatol. Surgery and Oncology, 1985-88; mem. editl. com. 18th World Congress of Dermatology, 1982; contbr. numerous articles, abstracts to profl. publs., chpts. to books. Bd. dirs. Northwestern Med. Faculty Found., 1982-84, chmn. com. on benefits and leaves, 1984, nominating com. 1988. Grantee Nat. Cancer Inst., 1985-91, 2004—09, 2011-, Am. Cancer Soc., 1986-89, Skin Cancer Found., 1984-85, Dermatology Found., 1981-83, Northwestern U. Biomed. Rsch., 1981, Syntex, 1984. Fellow: Am. Coll. Mohs Chemosurgery (chmn. sci. program ann. meeting 1983, chmn. publs. com. 1986—87, chmn. task force on ednl. needs 1989—90, co-editor bull. 1984—87, Frederic E. Mohs Career Achievement award 2008); mem.: Chgo. Dermatol. Soc., Women's Dermatol. Soc. (pres. 1990—92, Wilma Bergeld, MD Visionary and Leadership award 2002), Soc. Investigative Dermatology, Am. Soc. Dermatol. Surgery (pres. 1994—95, Samuel J. Stegman award disting. svc. 2006), Dermatology Found. (trustee 1995—98), Am. Acad. Dermatology (asst. sec.-treas. 1995—98, sec.-treas. 1998 2001, bd. dirs. 1993—95, Stephen Rothman Lectr. award 1992, Presdl. citation 1992, 2000), Am. Dermatol. Assn., Am. Cancer Soc. (pres. Ill. divsn. 1996—98, St. George Disting. Svc. medal 2004). Office: Northwestern U Feinberg Sch Med Dept Dermatology 132 E Delaware Pl #5806 Chicago IL 60611 E-mail: wtbjkr@rcn.com.

ROBINSON, KAREN VAJDA, dietician; BS in Home Econs., Montclair State Coll., 1980; MS in Health Scis./Dietetics, James Madison U., 1992. Cert. food svc. sanitation mgr., N.J. 1984. Dietician Roosevelt Hosp., Edison, NJ, 1980-85; asst. mgr. UVA (U. Va.) Dining Svcs., Charlottesville, 1985-86; temp. sales sec., mem. banquet prep. staff Boar's Head Inn, Charlottesville, 1986 88; head diet counselor Diet Ctr., Charlottesville, 1986-90; dietetic intern VA Med. Ctr., Hampton, Va., 1991; pub. health nutritionist Ctrl. Shenandoah Health Dist., Waynesboro Health Dept., Va., 1993-97. Grad. dietetic intern mentor, 1993—97; cons. dietitian Hebrew Hosp. Home, Bronx, NY, 1998, food svc. mgr. Sodexho Marriott Svcs., Morningside House Nursing Home, Bronx, 1998—99; clin. dietitian Yonkers (NY) Gen. Hosp., 1999—2001; cmty. svcs. instr. Westchester C.C., Valhalla, NY, 2001; outpatient dietitian Pk. Care Pavilion (formerly Yonkers Gen. Hosp.), 2001—10, inpatient dietitian, 2001—; clin. dietitian St. John's Riverside Hosp., Yonkers, 2002—, mentor student dietetics, 2006, 2010 11; outpatient dietitian St. John's Riverside, Valentine Lane Family Practice, Yonkers, 2005, 2007—08; pulmonary rehab. dietitian St. John's Riverside, 2010—. Contbr. articles to local newspapers. Mem. Charlottesville Health Promotion Coalition, 1993-97. Mem.: Dietitians in Nutrition Support Dietetic Practice Group, Westchester Rockland Dietetic Assn. (health fairs chair 1998—2001, scholarship com. mem. 2000, pub. rels. co-chair 2000—01, sec. 2001—08, chmn. nominating com. 2003—04, health fairs com. 2005—07, scholarship com. mem. 2006, mem. com. 2008—10, scholarship com. mem. 2009, nominating com. 2010, grantee 2000), Va. Dietetic Assn. (exec. bd. 1996—97), Blue Ridge Dietetics Assn. (nat. nutrition month coord. 1993—95, editor newsletter 1993—96, mem. exec. bd. 1993—97, pres.-elect 1995—96, scholarship com. 1996, pres. 1996—97), Va. Pub. Health Assn. (sec. 1995, awards chair 1996—97), Healthy Aging Practice Group (dietritians nutrition support), Am. Dietetic Assn. (registered). Home: 102 Hunter Ln Ossining NY 10562 Office Phone: 914-964-4216. Personal E-mail: kvrobinson@aol.com.

ROBINSON, MARY JO, pathologist; b. Spokane, Wash., May 26, 1954; d. Jerry Lee and Ann (Brodie) R. BS in Biology, Gonzaga U., 1976; DO, Des Moines U., 1987. Diplomate Nat. Bd. Osteo. Med. Examiners, Am. Osteo. Bd. Pathology; cert. anatomic pathology, lab. medicine and dermatopathology. Med. technologist Whitman Cmty. Hosp., Colfax, Wash., 1977—81, Madigan Army Med. Ctr., Ft. Lewis, Wash., 1981—83; intern Des Moines Gen. Hosp., 1987—88; resident in pathology Kennedy Meml. Hosp., Stratford, NJ, 1988—92; asst. prof. pathology Sch. Medicine U. Medicine & Dentistry NJ, Stratford, 1992—2008; staff pathologist Kennedy Meml. Hosp., Cherry Hill, NJ, 1995—2008; fellow in dermatopathology Jefferson Med. Coll., Phila., 1994—95; assoc. pathologist Pacific NW Pathology Assoc., Kent, Wash., 2008—10; assoc. prof. pathology Pacific NW U. Health Scis., 2009—. Fellow Coll. Am. Pathologists; mem. AMA, Am. Osteo. Assn., Am. Soc. Clin. Pathologists, Am. Osteo. Coll. Pathologists (pres. 2003-04, 1st prize resident paper 1992), N.J. Assn. Osteo. Physicians and Surgeons, Am. Osteo. Bd. Pathologists (chmn. 2003-09). Avocations: astronomy, antiques, science fiction. Office: 200 University Pky Yakima WA 98901 Personal E-mail: mrobin7403@aol.com. Business E-Mail: mrobinson@pnwu.org.

ROBINSON, NATHANIEL DAVID, JR., physician, consultant; b. Kans. City, Mar. 6, 1941; s. Nathaniel David Robinson and Dorothy Mae McLaughlin; m. Joanne Marie Kaleida, July 7, 1979; children: Donelle, Nathaniel David Robinson III. BSEE, U. RI, 1963; MD, U. Bologna, 1975. Cert. bd. cert. ins. medicine. Intern Roger Williams Gen. Hosp. Brown U., Providence, 1975—76; resident St. Francis Hosp. and Med. Ctr. U. Conn., Hartford, 1976—77; resident Hamot Med. Ctr., Erie, Pa., 1977—79, Mt. Sinai Med. Ctr., Miami Beach, Fla., 1981—82; med. officer USPHS Hosp., Seattle, 1979—81, VA, Nashville, 1982—85; med. dir. CNA, Nashville, 1985—95, v.p., med. dir., 1997—2004; asst. med. dir. Am. United Life, Indpls., 1995—97; med. cons. AIG Am. Gen., Nashville, 2005—. Cons. in field. Contbr. articles to profl. jours. Mem.: IEEE, AMA, Fla. Med. Assn., Midwest Med. Dirs. Assn., Providence Engring. Soc., Nashville Acad. Medicine, Tenn. Med. Assn., Am. Acad. Ins. Medicine, Am. Radio Relay League. Avocation: amateur radio. Home: 1304 Choctaw Trail Brentwood TN 37027-7422 Office: AIG Am Gen American General Ctr Nashville TN 37250-0001 Office Phone: 615-749-1171. Personal E-mail: djdrobinson@comcast.net. Business E-Mail: k1ant@ieee.org.

ROBINSON, NEWELL BRUCE, cardiothoracic surgeon; b. Columbus, Miss., Mar. 31, 1951; s. Jo Newell and Virginia (Henderson) Robinson; m. Victoria Margaret Genovese, Apr. 27, 1986; children: Ruth, Sarah, Bryce, Hunter. BS, Davidson Coll., Charlotte, NC, 1973; MD, U. Miss. Sch. Med., 1977. Diplomate Am. Bd. Surgery, Am. Bd. Thoracic Surgery, lic. physician, Miss., NY, Wash. Intern surgery NY Hosp., Cornell U. Med. Ctr., 1971—79, resident surgery, 1978-79, 81-83, chief resident surgery, 1983-84, resident, chief resident cardiothoracic surgery, 1984-86; trauma fellow burn/trauma rsch. Harborview Med. Ctr., U. Wash., 1979-81; sr. resident surg. oncology Meml. Sloan Kettering Cancer Ctr., 1982-84, fellow thoracic surg. oncology, 1984; asst. attending cardiothoracic surgery St. Francis Hosp., Roslyn, N.Y., 1986—. Instr. dept. surgery NY Hosp., Cornell U. Med. Ctr. Contbr. articles to profl. jours. Recipient NIH rsch. award, Harborview Med. Ctr., U. Wash., 1979—81. Fellow: ACS, Internat. Coll. Surgeons, Am. Coll. Cardiology, Coll. Chest Physician; mem.: AMA, Soc. Thoracic Surgeons., NY Thoracic Surg. Soc., Nassau County Med. Soc., NY Acad. Scis., Nassau County Med. Soc., Am. Burn Assn. Avocations: computer science, sailing, skiing, tennis, weight and aerobic training. Office: Cardiothoracic Surgery PC 100 Port Washington Blvd Roslyn NY 11576-1353 Office Phone: 516-627-2173. Office Fax: 516-365-5813.

ROBINSON, PETER GLENN, dentist, researcher; b. North Ferriby, Yorkshire, UK, July 24, 1957; s. Peter and Sheila Robinson; m. Julie Claire Weeks, Oct. 2, 2005; children: Ted, Wilkie, Elsa. BS in Dental Surgery, Guy's Hosp. Dental Sch., London, 1981, MSc, U. London, 1992, PhD, 1996; FRACDS, Sydney, 1998; FHEA, 2007; FDSRCS, London, 2007. Dental public health specialist Gen. Dental Coun., 2002; cert. FFPH London, 2009. Dental surgeon, London, 1981—86; clin. asst. Mortimer Market Dental Clinic, London, 1986—95; clin. rsch. fellow United Med. and Dental Schs., London, 1992—97; clin. sr. lectr. King's Coll., London, 1997 2002; prof. U. Sheffield, 2002—, dep. dean U. Sheffield, Dental Sch., 2007 . Editor Brit. Soc. Dental Rsch., 2007—; chair Dirs. Sch. Dental Hygiene and Therapy, 2007—. Contbr. scientific papers to profl. jours. Mem.: Brit. Assn. Study Cmty. Dentistry. Office: Univ Sheffield Dental Sch Claremont Cresent S10 2TA South Yorkshire England Office Fax: +44 (0)114 271 7843. Business E-Mail: peter.g.robinson@sheffield.ac.uk.

ROBINSON, PETER J., retired dean, periodontal educator, pathologist; b. St. Louis, May 31, 1941; s. Hamilton Burrows-Greaves and Katherine (Long) R.; m. Letticia Schumacher, July 18, 1964; children: Elizabeth Haskins Vance, Emily Hamilton. BA, Drake U., Des Moines, 1963; DDS, U. Mo., Kansas City, 1966; PhD, U. Pa., Phila., 1972. Dental intern U.S. Army, Washington, 1966-67; asst. prof. U. Pa., Phila., 1973-75; prof., chmn. periodontics Northwestern U., Chgo., 1975-88, chmn. stomatology, 1988-97; dean, prof. periodontology U. Conn. Sch. Dental Medicine, 1997—2006, dean emeritus, 2007, prof. emeritus, 2009; sr. policy fellow Am. Dental Edn. Assn., 2007—. Co-author: Transplantation for Dental Specialties, 1980. Pres. Dist. 38 Sch. Bd., Kenilworth, Ill., 1985-87. Capt. U.S. Army, 1966-69. Recipient Procter & Gamble Guest Scientist award Am. Dental Assn. Rsch. Inst., Chgo., 1983, Fogarty award NIH, Washington, 1984. Mem. ADA (sr. scientist Rsch. Inst.), Internat. Assn. Dental Rsch. (pres. periodontal rsch. group 1990-92), Midwest Soc. Periodontology (pres. 1986-87), Ill. Soc. Periodontology (pres. 1985-86). Achievements include patent on Northwestern periodontal probe.

ROBINSON, REBECCA LYNNE, medical researcher; b. Evansville, Ind., Dec. 9, 1967; d. Sherman Joseph and Joyce Jeane Black; m. Robert Wayne Robinson, Aug. 8, 1992; children: Calder Luke, Mary Helen Ellie. BA, U. So. Ind., 1990; MS, Purdue U., 1995. Tchg. asst. Ind. U.-Purdue U., 1990—92; rsch. asst. Osgood Lab. for Cross-Cultural Rsch., Indpls., 1990—93; rsch. analyst Regenstrief Inst./Bowen Rsch. at Ind. U. Sch. Medicine, Indpls., 1993—98; rsch. scientist St. Vincent Hosp., Indpls., 1996—98; health outcomes rsch. adv. Eli Lilly and Co., Indpls., 1998—. Cons. Osgood Lab. for Cross-Cultural Rsch., 1993—98, Ind. Hand Ctr., Indpls., 1996—98, Ind. State Dept. Health, Indpls., 1996—98; presenter in field. Contbr. articles to profl. jours. Facilitator, team leader, participant Ministry of Moms, Nativity Ch., Indpls., 2001—05. Recipient Outstanding Grad. Student award, Purdue U., 1992, Best Author Presentation award, 17th World Congress on Psychosomatic Medicine, 2003, Rsch. award, Marketscan, 2005; grantee Agy. for Health Care Policy and Rsch., 1990—95. Mem.: DAR. Home: 3828 Senour Rd Indianapolis IN 46239 Office Fax: 317-277-7444. E-mail: rlrobinson@lilly.com.

ROBINSON, THOMAS CHRISTOPHER, health science educator; b. Buffalo, Oct. 16, 1944; s. Christopher Sidney and Eleanor Florence (Martin) R.; m. Rena H. Robinson; children: Diane Robinson Dunn, Kristen O'Melia. BA, SUNY, Buffalo, 1966, EdM, 1968, PhD, 1971; grad. mgmt. devel. program, Harvard U., Cambridge, Mass., 1989. Admissions officer, office of admissions and records SUNY, Buffalo, 1966-72, assoc. dean Sch. Health Related Professions, 1975-78; asst. dir. Erie County Lab., Buffalo, 1972-75; assoc. dean Coll. Allied Health Professions, U. Ky., Lexington, 1978-84, dean Coll. Health Scis., 1984—2004, prof., 1984—2008, dean emeritus, 2005—, prof. emeritus, 2008—; wine educator Tamber Bey Vineyards, Oaku, Calif. Cons. MDS Labs., Hamilton, Ont., Can., 1973-75, Joint US-Arabian Commn. on Econ. Cooperation, 1986-87, West Sussex Inst. Higher Edn., Bogner Regis, U.K., 1987, U. Wis. Sys. Ctrs. of Excellence Program, 1988, Pub. Health Svc. Health Resources Adminstrn., 1983, 90-91; mem. exec. com. Nat. Practitioner Data Bank, 1992-94, cons. 1994-95; hon. mem. faculty Khabarovsk (Russia) Med. Inst., 1996; bd. dirs. Health Ky. Contbr. articles to profl. jours. Mem. Health Sys. Agy. Coun., Buffalo, 1977-78, Western NY Hemophilia Soc. Bd. Buffalo, 1977-78, Lexington-Fayette County Bd. Health, Lexington, 1987-91, program excellence project Ohio Bd. Regents, United Way of Bluegrass Healthcare Devel. Bd., 1991; cons. La. Bd. Regents, 1995, 98, 2001, 04, 06, 07, 10, Univ. Wolverhampton fellow, UK, 1991; bd. dirs. Ky. HealthCare Improvement Authority, 2006—; mem. leadership coun. Am. Diabetes Assn., Lexington, 2007-09. Sgt. NY Army N.G., 1968-74. Guard Staff Sgt. New York State US Army, 1968—74. Recipient Svc. award, Jour. Allied Health, 1986; Internat fellow, Hatfield Coll., Un. Durham, Eng., 2005. Mem. Assn. Schs. Allied Health Professions (bd. dirs. 1985-87, Svc. award 1987, Fellow award 1988, pres. 1991-94, past pres. 1994-95, Outstanding Mem. award 1995), Ky. Allied Health Consortium (bd. dirs. 1985-93, chair 1995-96), So. Assn. Allied Health Deans (sec. 1986-88, chmn. 1988-90), Assn. Schs. Allied Health Professions (pres. 1991-94), Ky. Hosp. Assn., Ky. Assn. Healthcare Facilities, So. Assn. Colls. and Schs. (chair and accreditation evaluator), Sigma Phi Epsilon. Avocations: travel, genealogy, gardening. Business E-Mail: tcrobi01@uky.edu.

ROBINSON, TONYA WEBSTER, pediatrician, educator; b. Richmond, Ind., Feb. 23, 1959; BS, Purdue U., 1981; MD, Ind. U., 1985. Neonatologist, dept. pediat. U. Louisville, 1991, assoc. prof., 1991—. Fellow: Am. Acad. Pediat. Office: 571 South Floyd St Louisville KY 40202 Business E-Mail: twrobi01@louisville.edu.

ROBINSON, WILLIAM ANDREW, retired health service executive, physician; b. Phila., Pa., Jan. 31, 1943; s. Colonial Washington and Lillian Dorothy Robinson; m. Jacqueline Ellen Garcia, Mar. 28, 1980; 1 child, David Alan; 1 child by previous marriage, William Andrew Jr. BA, Hampton U., 1964; MD, Meharry Med. Coll., 1971; MPH, Johns Hopkins U., 1973. Diplomate Nat. Bd. Med. Examiners; lic. physician, Md. Rotating intern George W. Hubbard Hosp., Nashville, 1971-72, emergency room physician, 1972; med. officer gastrointestinal drug sect., bur. drugs FDA USPHS, HEW, Rockville, Md., 1973-75; dep. dir. office health resources opportunity USPHS, HHS, Rockville, Md., 1975-80, dep. dir. bur. health professions health resources adminstrn., 1980-87, chief med. officer health resources and svcs. adminstn., 1987 89, dep. asst. sec. minority health, dir. office minority health Washington, 1989-91, acting adminstr. health resources and svc. adminstrn. Rockville, Md., 1993-94, chief med. officer health resources and svc. adminstrn., 1991—2007, dir. Office Pub. Health Affairs, 1996-97, dir. Ctr. for Quality, 1997—2006, dir office Min. Health and Health Disparities, 2006—07. Chmn. sr. execs. performance rev. bd. Office of Asst. Sec. for Health, 1990-91; pub. health svc. rep. 2d Internat. Conf. on Health Promotion, Adelaide, South Australia; health cons. com. on interior and insular affairs U.S. Ho. of Reps., Washington, 1982-83; appointed field faculty dept. family and comty. health Meharry Med. Coll., 1979; U.S. rep. to WHO Primary Health Care Conf., Alma Ata, Kazahkstan. Mem. nat. editl. bd. Jour. Health Care for the Poor and Underserved, 1991. Capt. U.S. Army, 1964-67. Recipient Nat. Urban Coalition Comty. Health Svc. award, 1972, Letter of Appreciation, Chmn. Congl. Black Caucus Health Braintrust, U.S. Ho. of Reps., 1988. Mem. AMA, APHA, Am. Acad. Family Physicians, Blacks in Govt., Fed. Physicians Assn., Nat. Med. Assn., Sr. Execs. Assn., Delta Omega (Alpha chpt., pres., 2005-07). *

ROBISON, RON, pharmaceutical executive; married; 4 children. BA, Oreg. State Univ.; M in Med. Informatics, Univ. Utah; MD cum laude, Oreg. Health Sci. Univ. Assoc. dir., clin. rsch. Mallinckrodt Med., Inc.; v.p., clin. rsch., med. affairs, chief med. officer Nycomed, Inc. (formerly Sanofi-Sterling Winthrop); various positions to sr. v.p., rsch. devel., worldwide med. dir. Amersham Health, UK; sr. v.p. rsch. devel., chief med. officer Solvay Pharm. Inc., Marietta, Ga., 2002—06, sr. v.p., head global and regulatory affairs, 2006—. Mem.: Drug Info. Assn., Soc. Med. Decision Making, Am. Med. Informatics Assn., Am. Inst. Ultrasound in Medicine, Internat. Soc. Magnetic Resonance in Medicine, Radiological Soc. N. Am., Alpha Omega Alpha. Office: Solvay Pharm Inc 901 Sawyer Rd Marietta GA 30062 Office Phone: 770-578-9000. Office Fax: 770-578-5597.

ROBLES, PABLO, cardiologist, consultant; b. Madrid, Sept. 1, 1966; s. Dionisio and Antonia (Velasco) Robles; m. Maria Luisa Rodriguez, Apr. 11, 1992; children: Marisa, Marta. Degree in Medicine, Complutense U., 1991; degree in Cardiology, Hosp. La Paz, Madrid, 1996. Diplomate in echocardiography Spanish Soc. Cardiology, 2004, in transthoracic echocardiography European Soc. Cardiology, 2005, in transesophageal echocardiography European Soc. Cardiology, 2005. Cons. cardiologist Hosp. Joan XXIII, Tarragona, Spain, 1997, Hosp. Principe Asturias, Alcalá de Henares, 1997—98, Fundación Hosp. Alcorcón, 1998—. Contbr. articles to profl. jours. Fellow: European Soc. Cardiology; mem.: Am. Soc. Echocardiography (assoc.), Spanish Soc. Cardiology (assoc.), European Soc. Echocardiography (assoc.). Home: C/Doña Maquita la Música 34 Getafe 28903 Spain Office: Fundación Hosp Alcorcón C/Budapest n° 1 Alcorcón Spain Personal E-mail: problesve@yahoo.es. Business E-Mail: probles@fhalcorcon.es.

ROBMAN, LIUBOV DANIELEVNA (LUBA), biomedical researcher, ophthalmologist; b. East Kazakhstan, Soviet Union, June 18, 1948; arrived in Australia, 1992; d. Daniel Semionovich Robman and Esfir Aronovna Feldman; m. Yakov Lazarevich Gershenzon, Aug. 30, 1975; children: Alexander Yakovlevich Gershenzon, Esther Rachel Gershenzon. MD, City of Alma-Ata State Med. Inst., Kazakhstan, 1972; PhD in Ophthalmic Surgery, City of Odessa Academician V.P. Filatov Eye Rsch. Inst., Ukraine, 1984; PhD in Ophthalmic Epidemiology, U. Melbourne, Australia, 2000. Cert. ophthalmologist Kazakhstan Eye Rsch. Inst., Alma-Ata, 1973. Head cornea clinic Kazakhstan Eye Rsch. Inst., 1980—81, ophthalmic rsch. fellow, 1982—84, cons. ophthalmologist, 1982—86, head rsch. & mgmt. unit, 1984—86; sr. lectr., dept. ophthalmology Alma-Ata State Inst. Further Tng. Med. Drs., 1986—92; cons. ophthalmologist Mcpl. Hosp. No 12, Neurol. Ward, 1986—92, Hosp. Disabled after WW2, Alma-Ata, 1988—92; rsch. fellow dept. ophthalmology U. Melbourne, Ctr. Eye Rsch. Australia, Victoria, 1994—2007, sr. rsch. fellow, 2007—. Rsch. grants, Perpetual Trustees, 2001, 2006, ANZ Trustees, 2001, Ophthalmic Rsch. Inst. Australia, 2004, 2007, 2008, 2009, 2010, Am. Health Assistance Found., 2005, 2008—09, Wagstaff fellowship, Royal Victorian Eye and Ear Hosp., 2007—08. Mem.: Internat. Epidemiol. Assn., Internat. Soc. Geog. and Epidemiol. Ophthalmology, Pub. Health Assn. Australia, Australian Epidemiol. Assn., Assn. Rsch. and Vision Ophthalmology. Office: Ctr Eye Rsch Australia 32 Gisborne St East Melbourne VIC 3002 Australia Office Fax: 61 3 9662 3859. E-mail: liubov@unimelb.edu.au.

ROBOZ, GAIL J., medical association administrator, educator; b. NYC, Sept. 29, 1968; BA, Yale U., 1990; MD, Mt. Sinai Sch. Medicine, 1994. Clin. assoc. Weill Med. Coll. Cornell U., 1995—97, instr. medicine, 2000—01, asst. prof. medicine, 2001—08, mem., protocol rev. com., divsn. hematology & oncology, 2005, dir., leukemia program, 2007—, assoc. prof. medicine, 2008—. Mem. Leukemia Svc. Length-of-Stay Task Force, 2006—09; reviewer Clin. & Translational Sci. Ctr. Cornell U., 2009—. Recipient New Innovator award, Co-Investigator, NIH, ?We Care? award, Weill Cornell Physician Orgn.; Rsch. grant, Katherine John Murphy Found., Myeloproliferative Disorders Found., Lupin Found. Mem.: Am. Soc. Clin. Oncology, Am. Soc. Hematology. Office: Weill Med Coll Cornell University New York NY 10021 Business E-Mail: gar2001@med.cornell.edu.

ROCCA, WALTER AMERICO, medical researcher; b. Castiglione Tinella, Cuneo Province, Italy, Feb. 13, 1956; s. Giovanni Augusto Rocca, Anna Ernesta Bella; m. Liliana Gazzuola; 1 child, Giulia. MD, U. Padua, Italy, 1980; MPH, Johns Hopkins U. Sch. Hygiene and Pub. Health, 1983. Cert. neurology Italy. Cons. neuroepidemiologist Italian Multicentre Study Dementia, Centro SMID, Florence, Italy, 1986—93; rschr. Italian Nat. Rsch. Coun., Targeted Project on Aging, Florence, Italy, 1992—93; sr. assoc. cons. Mayo Clinic, Rochester, Minn., 1993—97, cons., 1997—. Assoc. prof. epidemiology and neurology Mayo Med. Sch., Rochester, Minn., 1993—2000, prof. epidemiology and neurology, 2000—. Author several books; contbr. chapters to books, articles to numerous profl. jours. Recipient Luigi Amaducci award, Italian Soc. Neurology, 2000; grantee, NIH. Mem.: AMA, Am. Neurol. Assn., Am. Epidemiol. Soc., Soc. Epidemiol. Rsch., Am. Acad. Neurology (chair Schoenberg award subcom. 1995—2001), Delta Omega. Avocations: literature, travel, swimming. Office: Mayo Clinic Divsn Epidemiology 200 First St SW Rochester MN 55905 Home Phone: 507-252-5617; Office Phone: 507-284-3568. Office Fax: 507-284-1516. Business E-Mail: rocca@mayo.edu.

ROCCHI, STEPHANE, medical researcher; b. Nice, France, Oct. 31, 1968; PhD, Nice U., 1998. Rschr. INSERM u895, 1998—. Office: University Hosp av de Ginestiere Nice 06204 France Business E-Mail: srocchi@unice.fr.

ROCCHIETTI MARCH, MASSIMILIANO, endocrinologist; b. Florence, Italy, Nov. 16, 1967; Degree in Medicine, U. Rome Sapienza, 1992, PhD in Andrological Scis., 2001, MS in Andrology, 2009. Physician, internal medicine unit Sant'Andrea Hosp., 2001—. Adj. prof. U. Rome Sapienza, 2004—11. Office: via Grottarossa 1035 Rome 00189 Italy Office Phone: 00390633775969. Business E-Mail: massimiliano.rocchietti@uniroma1.it.

ROCCO, VINCENZO, medical association administrator; b. Caracas, Venezuela, Dec. 24, 1958; s. Gabriele Rocco and Adele Alma Rodriguez; life ptnr. Sylvie Alice Geraldine Huck; 1 child, Virgile. Degree in Biology, U. Naples, Italy, 1989. Contract rschr. U. Paris XI - Paris VII, 1990—98; pharm. dir. Ce.M.O.N. s.r.l., Naples, 1998—2007; adminstr. LUIMO, Naples, 2007—. Bd. mem. Radical Party, Naples, 1979—84. Libertarian. Avocations: singing, reading, travel. Office: LUIMO Viale Antonio Gramsci 18 80122 Napoli NA Italy Office Fax: 00390817613665. Business E-Mail: v.rocco@luimo.org.

ROCH, LEWIS MARSHALL, II, ophthalmic surgeon, medical entrepreneur; b. Mineola, Tex., Aug. 13, 1934; s. Lewis Marshall and Gladys Irene (Hoover) R.; m. Lois Afton Price; children: Lewis Marshall Roch III, Katrina Ann Seitz. BA, U. Tex., Austin, 1955; MD, U. Tex. Southwestern, Dallas, 1959. Diplomate Am. Bd. Ophthalmology. Intern USPHS Hosp., Boston, 1959-60, resident in ophthalmology New Orleans, 1960-63, dep. chief ophthalmology, 1963-64, chief opthalmology Seattle, 1964-67; attending ophthalmic surgeon Ball Meml. Hosp., Muncie, Ind., 1967—, chmn. dept. surgery, chmn. clin. staff, 1975, chmn. exec. com., 1984—87, bd. dirs., 1984—90, mem. fin. com., 1984—87; founder, CEO, med. dir. The Eye Ctr. Group, Muncie, 1985—, The Surgi Ctr. Group, Muncie, 1985—. Mem. exec. com. Ind. Acad. Ophthalmology, 1978-82; bd. dirs. Cardinal Health Ventures, Paragent, LLC, Cardinal Ethanol, LLC, Cardinal Health Found., Inc., 1999-, Ball Meml. Found., 1998-; clin. asst. prof. Ind. U. Sch. Medicine, 1978—. Chmn. Muncie-Delaware Devel., 2000-03; active Ball State U. Bus. Forecasting Roundtable, 2000—; exec. v.p. Muncie-Delaware Econ. Devel., 2000-02; trustee Minnetrista Cultural Ctr., 2002—; bd. dirs. United Way Delaware County, 2003-06. Fellow ACS, Am. Acad. Ophthalmology; mem. AMA, Ind. State Med. Assn., Muncie Acad. Medicine (pres. 1981-82), Am. Soc. Cataract and Refractive Surgeons, Am. Coll. Physician Execs., Muncie-Delaware C. of C. (bd. dirs. 1999-2003), Rotary. Republican. Achievements include first to work in outpatient ambulatory surgery; innovation in intraocular lens implantation in cataract surgery; integration of physician's practices with hospital health care delivery systems. Office: 2006 N Robinwood Dr Muncie IN 47304-2857 also: The Eye Ctr Group LLC 200 N Tillotson Ave Muncie IN 47304-3988 E-mail: lmroch@comcast.net.

ROCHA, GUILHERME, physician; b. Salvador, Bahia, Brazil, Apr. 8, 1974; MD, EBMSP, 2007. Physician Hosp. Olhos do Parana, 2003. Office: Av Anita Garibaldi 4669 Curitiba Parana 82220000 Brazil E-mail: guigojnmr@hotmail.com.

ROCHA, RAQUEL, nutritionist, educator; b. Feira de Santana, Bahia, Oct. 19, 1974; D, Sch. Medicine, 2009. Adj. prof. & coord., clin. nutrition gastroenterology Sch. Nutrition, Fed. U. Bahia, 2007. Office: Av Araujo Pinho 32 Salvador Bahia 40110-150 Brazil

ROCHE, GILLES, pharmaceutical company executive; b. Grenoble, France, Dec. 25, 1949; s. Marcel François and Janine (Fossemagne) R.; m. Anne-Marie Gatel, June 23, 1973; children: Caroline, Julien, Benjamine. MS in Biostatistics, 1973, MS in Pharmacology, 1981; MS in Microbiology, Nancy U., France, 1981; MD, Paris Med. U., 1974. Cert. in pediat. and internal medicine. Resident Nancy U. Hosp., 1973-79, hosp. asst., chief of clinic, 1979-83; rsch. mgr. Sanofi, France, 1983-87; med. dir. Pharmuka (RP), France, 1987-92; sr. dir. Rhône Poulenc Rorer, Antony, 1992-97, v.p., 1997—, dir., 1987—. Contbr. over 120 articles to profl. jours.; patentee in field. Mem. Am. Soc. Microbiology, French Internal Medicine Soc. Avocations: sports, reading, stamp collecting/philately. Home: 246 rue de Charenton 75012 Paris France Office: Rhône-Poulenc Rorer 20 Ave Raymond Aron 92165 Antony France E-mail: gilles.roche@aventis.com.

ROCHE, JAMES RICHARD, pediatric dentist, university dean; b. Fortville, Ind., July 17, 1924; s. George Joseph and Nelle (Kinnaman) R.; m. Viola Marie Morris, May 15, 1949; 1 child, Ann Marie Roche Potter. DDS, Ind. U., 1947, MS in Dentistry, 1983. Diplomate Am. Bd. Pediat. Dentistry, 1959. Prof. Ind. U. Sch. Dentistry, Indpls., 1968—88, chmn. divsn. grad. pediat. dentistry, 1969-76, asst. dean faculty devel., 1976-80, assoc. dean faculty devel., 1980-87, assoc. dean for acad. affairs, 1987-88, prof. emeritus, 1988—. Cons. Coun. Dental Edn., Hosp. Dental Svc. and Commn. Accreditation, Am. Dental Assn., Chgo., 1977-1983; pres. Coll. Diplomates, Am. Bd. Pediat. Dentistry, 1968; chmn. Am. Bd. Pediat. Dentistry, 1980-81, exec. sec.-treas., 1982-2002. Pfc US Army, 1943-44, capt., 1952-54. Recipient Disting. Teaching Recognition award Ind. U., 1976, Experience Excellence Recognition award Ind. U., Purdue U., Indpls., 1984, Outstanding Svc. award Ind. Optometric Assn., 1989. Fellow Internat. Coll. Dentists, Am. Coll. Dentists (named Fund Recipient, 2007, Ind. Sect. Ethics award, 2009), Am. Acad. Pediat. Dentistry (bd. dirs. 1967-70), Pierre Fauchard Acad.; mem. ADA (cons. Bur. Dental Health Edn. 1977-87, Coun. Dental Edn., Hosp. Dental Svc. and Commn. Accreditation, chgo., 1977-83), Am. Soc. Dentistry for Children (award of excellence 1993), Ind. Dental Assn. (v.p. 1973-74, chmn. legis. com. 1968-77, lobbyist 1970-77, honor dentist 2008), Indpls. Dist. Dental Assn. (pres. 1967-68), Ind. U.-Purdue U. Indpls. Sr. Acad. (charter), Masons, Scottish Rite, Omicron Kappa Upsilon (pres. Theta Theta chpt., 1967), Psi Omega Fraternity (mem. Omega chpt. 1946), Ind. U. Sch. Dentistry Alumni Assn. (Disting. Alumnus award, 2003), Ind. U. Pediat. Dentistry Alumni Assn. (Disting. Alumnus award 2005). Home and Office: 1193 Woodgate Dr Carmel IN 46033-9232 Office Phone: 317-574-9769.

ROCHE, NICOLAS, respiratory medicine professor; b. Paris, July 13, 1964; MD, U. Paris, 1994, PhD, 2003. Sr. lectr. Hôtel-Dieu, Asst. Publique Hôpitaux de Paris, U. Paris Descartes, 2004—08, prof. respiratory medicine, 2008—. Mem.: Soc. de Pneumologie de Langue Française, European Respiratory Soc., Am. Thoracic Soc. Office: Pneumologie et Réanimation Hôtel-Dieu Paris 75004 France Office Fax: 33-1-42-34-84-48. Business E-Mail: nicolas.roche@htd.aphp.fr.

ROCK, JOHN AUBREY, gynecologist, obstetrician, educator, administrator, emeritus chancellor; b. Corpus Christi, Tex., Oct. 21, 1946; s. William A. and Burta (Wheeler) R.; children: John Aubrey Jr., Deborah Ellen, Daniel Authur; m. Martha Miller. BS in Zoology, La. State U., Baton Rouge, 1968; MD, La. State U., New Orleans, 1972; MS in Healthcare Mgmt., Harvard U., 2003. From asst. prof. to prof. ob-gyn. Sch. Medicine Johns Hopkins U., Balt., 1978-80, prof. pediatrics Sch. Medicine, 1988-92, dir. reproductive endocrinology Sch. Medicine, 1979-91, dep. dir. Sch. Medicine, 1985-88; chmn. Union Meml. Hosp., Balt., 1991-92; James Robert McCord prof., chmn. dept. ob-gyn. Emory U. Sch. Medicine, Atlanta, 1992—2002; chancellor La. State U. Health Scis. Ctr., New Orleans, 2002—06, chancellor emeritus, prof. ob-gyn., pediat. and pub. health, 2002—07; sr. v.p. health affairs Fla. Internat. U., Miami, 2007—. Cons. Dept. Army, Washington, 1982-93, NASA, Houston, 1988—; chmn. ad hoc com. on in vitro fertilization State of Md., 1985. Author: Reparative and Constructive Surgery of the Female Generative Tract, 1983, Endometriosis, 1988, TeLinde's Operative Gynecology, 1991, 9th edit., 2003, Reproductive Endocrinology, Surgery and Technology, 1995; mem. editl. bd. Fertility and Sterility jour., 1986-94, Gynecology Surgery, 1989—. Fellow ACOG; mem. Am. Gynecol. and Obstet. Soc., Soc. Gynecol. Surgeons (pres. 1998-99), Am. Soc. for Reproductive Medicine (pres. 1996-97), Soc. Gynecologic Investigation, Soc. Reproductive Surgeons (pres. 1986), World Endometriosis Soc. (pres. 2000-02), Rotary, Phi Kappa Phi, Alpha Omega Alpha. Methodist. Office Phone: 305-348-0570. Business E-Mail: rockj@fiu.edu.

ROCKEY, SARAH JEAN (SALLY ROCKEY), federal agency administrator; PhD in Entomology, Ohio State U., 1985. Postdoc. fellow U. Wis.; prog. officer Coop. State Rsch. Edn. & Extension Svc. (CSREES), US Dept. Agr., 1986, dep. adminstr. competitive rsch. grants & award Mgmt. unit, then chief info. officer CSREES, 2002—05; dep. dir. Office Extramural Rsch. NIH, Bethesda, Md., 2002—08, acting dep. dir. extramural rsch., 2008—10, dep. dir. extramural rsch., 2010—. Recipient Presdl. Rank award, 2004. Office: NIH Office Extramural Rsch Bldg 1 Shannon Bldg 144 1 Ctr Dr Mail Stop 0155 Bethesda MD 20892 Office Phone: 301-496-1096. Business E-Mail: sally.rockey@nih.gov. *

ROCKLAND, LAWRENCE HOWARD, psychiatrist, consultant; b. NYC, Apr. 13, 1932; s. Milton and Bess Sherry Rockland; m. Charlotte Francis Roberts, June 29, 1957; children: Nancy, Thomas, Peter. BS, Union Coll., 1952; MD, Albany Med. Ctr., 1956. Diplomate Am. Bd. Psychiatry and Neurology. Rsch. psychiatrist NIMH, Bethesda, Md., 1959—61; pvt. practice Scarsdale, Larchmont, NY, 1961—; instr. psychiatry Georgetown Med. Coll., Washington, 1961—63; asst. prof. psychiatry Albert Einstein Coll. Medicine, NYC, 1967—76; assoc. prof. clin. psychiatry Cornell U. Med. Coll., NYC, 1982—99; assoc. prof. psychiatry emeritus Weill/Cornell Med. Coll., NYC, 1999—; assoc. prof. clin. psychiatry U. Mass. Med. Coll., Worcester, 1999—2002; psychiatric cons. Synergy Montceud, NY. Cons. Montgomery County Child Clinic, Rockville, Md., 1962—66, US Peace Corps, Washington, 1963—66, Carson Adult Family Clinic, Westfield, Mass., 1999—2002. Contbr. articles to profl. jours., chapters to books; author: Supportive Therapy, 1989, Supportive Therapy for Borderlines, 1992, La Terapia di Sostegno, 1994. Surgeon USPHS, 1959—2005. Fellow: Am. Psychoanalytic Assn. (exec. coun. 1976—79, 1985—2005), Am. Psychiat. Assn. (disting. life fellow); mem.: Group for Advancement Psychiatry, Sigma Xi, Phi Beta Kappa, Alpha Omega Alpha. Avocations: music, hiking, physical exercise, reading. Home and Office: 7 East Drive Larchmont NY 10538 Office Phone: 914-834-7601.

ROCKOFF, MARK ALAN, pediatric anesthesiologist; b. Jersey City, Apr. 13, 1948; s. Aaron and Rose Rockoff; m. Elizabeth Sceery, Aug. 6, 1978; children: Benjamin, Jillian, Michael. BS, MIT, 1969; MD, Johns Hopkins U., 1973. Diplomate Am. Bd. Pediatrics, Am. Bd. Anesthesiology. Pediatric intern and resident Mass. Gen. Hosp., Boston, 1973-75, anesthesia resident, 1975-77, assoc. dir. pediatric ICU, 1979-81; neuroanesthesia fellow U. Calif., San Diego, 1978-79; assoc. dir. ICU Children's Hosp., Boston, 1981-89, assoc. anesthesiologist-in-chief, 1988—; med. dir. operating rm., 1992-99; prof. anaesthesia Harvard Med. Sch., Boston, 1999—. Editor jours. Survey of Anesthesiology, 1984-94, Jour. Neurosurg. Anesthesiology, 1994-98. Fellow: Soc. Critical Care Medicine, Am. Acad. Pediats., Am. Soc. Anesthesiologists; mem.: Soc. Pediat. Anesthesia (pres. 1996—98), Am. Bd. Anesthesiology (dir. 2000—). Office: Children's Hosp 300 Longwood Ave Boston MA 02115-5737

ROCKOFF, S. DAVID, radiologist, physician, educator; b. Utica, NY, July 21, 1931; s. Samuel and Sarah (Rattinger) R.; m. Jacqueline Garsh; children— Lisa E., Todd E., Kevin D. AB, Syracuse U., 1951; MD, Albany Med. Coll., 1955; M.Sc. in Medicine, U. Pa., 1961. Diplomate: Am. Bd. Radiology. Intern U.S. Naval Hosp., Bethesda, Md., 1955-56; resident and fellow in radiology, USPHS trainee dept. radiology p. of U. Pa., Phila., 1958-61; staff radiologist NIH, Bethesda, Md., 1961-65; asst. prof. radiology Yale U. Sch. Medicine, New Haven, 1965-68, assoc. prof., 1968; asst. attending radiologist Yale-New Haven Med. Center, 1965-68; assoc. prof. radiology Washington U. Sch. Medicine, St. Louis, 1968-71; asst. radiologist Barnes and Allied Hosps., St. Louis, 1969-71; cons. radiologist VA Hosp., St. Louis, 1969-71, Homer G. Phillips Hosp., St. Louis, 1968-71; prof. radiology George Washington U. Sch. Medicine, Washington, 1971—, chmn. dept. radiology, 1971-77, head pulmonary radiology, 1978—, interim chmn. dept. radiology, 1989-90, prof. emeritus radiology, 1993—. Cons. NIH, 1972—; vis. prof. Hadassah U., Beersheba U., Rambam Hosp., Israel, 1977; cons. in radiology VA Hosp., Washington, 1972-77, U.S. Naval Med. Center, Bethesda, 1973-77; mem. diagnostic radiology adv. com. NIH, 1973-76; mem. Cancer Research Manpower Rev. Com., NIH, 1978 Editor-in-chief: Investigative Radiology, 1965-76; editor-in-chief emeritus, 1976—; editor Jour. Thoracic Imaging, 1985; reviewer Jour. Computed Tomography, 1997—; contbr. articles to profl. jours. Served with USN, 1955-58; Served with USPHS, 1961-63. Recipient numerous USPHS grants. Fellow Am. Coll. Radiology (pres.-elect DC chpt. 1976), Am. Coll. Chest Physicians; mem. Am. Fedn. Clin. Rsch., DC Med. Soc. (med.-legal com. 1975-78), AMA, Radiol. Soc. N.Am. (roster of disting. sci. advisors Rsch. and Edn. Found. 1999), Assn. Univ. Radiologists, Soc. Thoracic Radiology (pres. 1983-84, exec. dir. 1984-87, Gold medal 2007). Home: PO Box 675650 Rancho Santa Fe CA 92067-5650 Personal E-mail: drockoff@cox.net.

RODABAUGH, KERRY J., gynecologist, educator; b. Ottumwa, Iowa, Dec. 3, 1962; BSBC, East Carolina U., 1985; MD, Duke U., 1990. Asst. prof. U. Mo., 1997—2001; assoc. prof., oncology Roswell Pk. Cancer Inst., 2001—08; assoc. prof. U. Nebr. Med. Ctr., 2008—. Mem., nat. med. dirs. adv. bd. Nat. Med. Legal Partnership Ctr., 2008—. Mem.: Soc. Gynecologic Oncology. Office: 983255 Nebr Med Ctr Omaha NE 68198 Office Fax: 402-559-3133. Business E-Mail: krodabaugh@unmc.edu.

RODALLEC, MATHIEU HENRI, physician; b. France, Apr. 20, 1974; Diploma in Radioanatomy, U. Paris V, 1999, diploma in Anatomy, Imagining, Morphogenesis, 2001; MD, U. Paris VI, 2002. Diplomate U. Paris VI, 2002. Fellow Beaujon Hosp., Clichy, 2002—04; cons. Found. Hosp. St. Joseph, Paris, 2004—. Author: (encyclopedia) Diagnostic Imaging; contbr. articles to profl. jours. Recipient Silver Medal, U. Paris VI, 2002. Mem.: French Soc. Neuroradiology, French Soc. Radiology, N. Am. Radiol. Soc. Avocations: travel, music, films. Office: Fond Hosp St Joseph 185 Rue Raymond Losserand Paris 75014 France Office Fax: 0144123850.

RODEN, MICHAEL W., endocrinologist; b. Vienna, Feb. 11, 1961; s. Othmar and Erika (Dostal) Roden; m. Agnes E. Kasseroler, Jan. 3, 1992; 1 child, Daniel. MD, U. Vienna, 1986. Diplomate Austrian Bd. Internal Medicine. Rsch. fellow pharmacology U. Vienna Med. Sch., 1986-88, asst. physician in internal medicine, 1988-94, assoc. prof. endocrinology, 1995—2003; Max Kade Found. rsch. fellow Yale U. Med. Sch., New Haven, 1994-95; head 1st med. dept. Hanusch Hosp., Vienna; dir. German Diabetes Ctr. Leibniz Ctr. Diabetes Rsch., Germany, 2008—; dir. dept. metabolic diseases U. Dusseldorf, 2008—; prof. internal medicine, 2008—. Contbr. articles to profl. jours. Recipient J. Skoda award, Austrian Soc. Internal Medicine, 1996, F. Wewalka prize, Austrian Soc. Gastroenterology, 1992, Ferdinand Bertram award, German Diabetes Assn., 2001, Internat. Novartis award, 2004, Minkowski prize, 2006; grantee, Austrian Nat. Bank, 1994, Austrian Sci. Found., 1995, European Found. Study Diabetes, 2002. Mem.: European Assn. F. T. Study Diabetes, Endocrine Soc., Am. Diabetes Assn., European Assn. Study Diabetes (coun. mem. 2002—), European Soc. Clin. Investigation (v.p. 1996—2002, award 2006). Roman Catholic. Office: Inst Clinical Diabetology Aufm Hennekamp 65 Düsseldorf D-40225 Germany

RODENBERG, HOWARD DAVID, emergency physician, former state agency administrator; b. Chgo., Oct. 18, 1962; s. Joseph Harris and Harriet Ann (Burgheim) R. BA in Biology with distinction, MD, U. Mo., Kansas City, 1986. Diplomate Am. Bd. Emergency Medicine, Nat. Bd. Med. Examiners; cert. ACLS instr. and affiliate faculty, advanced trauma life support, pediatric advanced life support, basic trauma life support; cert. flight surgeon NASA. Resident in emergency medicine Truman Med. Ctr., Kansas City, 1986-89; assoc. prof., chief sect. prehosp. care U. Fla. Coll. Medicine, Gainesville, 1989-95, dir. med. student edn. div. emergency medicine, 1989-91, clin. resource faculty social-ethical issues med. practice; med. dir. air flight program Shands Teaching Hosp.-U. Fla., Gainesville; med. dir. EMS prog. Ctrl. Fla. Cmty. Coll.; EMS med. dir. Volusia County, Fla.; dir. Volusia County Health Dept., Daytona Beach, Fla., 2003—05; emergency physician Halifax Med. Ctr., Daytona Beach, Fla.; dir. div. health Kans. Dept. Health & Environment, Topeka, 2005—08. Sys. med. dir. Alachua County Dept. Fire and Rescue Svcs., Gainesville; cons. Emergency Health Svc., Med. Rescue Internat., Johannesburg, South Africa, 1995-96; rsch. assoc. NASA Kennedy Space Ctr., Fla., 1989; mem. guest faculty Brit. Assn. for Immediate Care, Cambridge, Eng., 1992, 94, 95; vis. cons. in accident and emergency medicine Addenbrooke's Hosp. and Cambridge U. Sch. Clin. Medicine, 1992, 95; vis. lectr. in disaster mgmt. and prehosp. care Ptnrs. of Ams., Colombia, 1992, lectr. Australia, Eng., Scotland, Italy, South Africa; bd. dirs., mem. planning com. North Ctrl. Fla. Trauma Agy., 1990, co-chmn. med. adv. panel, 1991; others; cons. emergency health svcs. Medical Rescue Internat. Johannesburg; field physician during Rwandan refugee crisis, Medical Rescue Internat. Editor: (with I. Blumen) Air Medical Physician's Handbook, 1993, 94, (with T. Martin) Aeromedical Transportation: A Clinical Guide; mem. editl. bd. Air Medicine jour., 1993—; contbr. articles to med. jours., chpts. to books. Mem. emergency med. svc. programs adv. bd. Santa Fe C.C., 1991; mem. emergency med. svcs. adv. coun., Alachua County, 1991; mem. North Ctrl. Fla. adv. bd. ACLS, 1991. Fellow Am. Coll. Emergency Physicians; mem. Air Med. Physicians Assn. (founding, bd. dirs. 1992—, liaison to Aerospace Med. Assn., 1992—), Fla. Assn. Emergency Med. Svcs. Med. Dirs. (bd. dirs. 1990-91, sec.-treas. 1991-92, v.p. 1993-94, pres. 1994-95, N.E. Fla. regional med. advisor 1991-95), Fla.-Colombian Ptnrs. (bd. trustees 1994—), Omicron Delta Kappa, Pi Kappa Phi. Avocations: flying, travel.

RODGERS, BRADLEY MORELAND, pediatric, thoracic surgeon; b. Montclair, NJ, Jan. 16, 1942; BA, Dartmouth Coll., Hanover, NH, 1963, BS, 1964; MD, Johns Hopkins U., Balt., 1966. Diplomate Am. Bd. Surgery, Am. Bd. Pediat. Surgery, Am. Bd. Thoracic Surgery. Intern Duke U., Durham, NC, 1966-67, resident cardiovasc. surgery, 1967-68, resident thoracic surgery, 1970-73; fellowship Nat. Inst. Health, 1968-70; chief resident pediat. surgery Montreal Children's Hosp., 1973-74; asst. prof. pediat. & surgery U. Fla., Gainesville, 1974-81; prof. surgery & pediat., chief div. pediatric surgery U. Va., Charlottesville, 1981—. Contbr. articles to profl. jours. Mem.: So. Thoracic Surg. Assn. (chmn. 1993, Osler Abbott award 1989), Am. Acad. Pediat., Am. Pediat. Surgical Assn. (pres. 2002). Mailing: U Va Dept Pediat Surgery PO Box 800709 Charlottesville VA 22908 Office Fax: 434-924-2656. Business E-Mail: bmr@virginia.edu.

RODGERS, CARIE S., psychologist, educator; b. Kans., Feb. 4, 1970, BA, U. Kans., 1992; PhD, U. Oreg., 2000. Cert. in clin. psychology Am. Bd. Profl. Psychology. Postdoc. fellow VA San Diego Healthcare Sys., 2000—03, staff psychologist, 2003—05, dir., mil. sexual trauma program, 2005—08; assoc. dir., edn. & dissemination VA Ctr. Excellence Stress & Mental Health, 2007—. Clin. instr. U. Calif., San Diego, 2003—06, asst. clin. prof., 2006—, assoc. clin. prof., 2011. Fellow: Am. Acad. Clin. Psychology; mem.: APA, Internat. Soc. Traumatic Stress Studies, Assn. Behavioral & Cognitive Therapies, Assn. VA Psychologist Leaders. Office: 3350 La Jolla Village Dr San Diego CA 92161 Business E-Mail: carie.rodgers@va.gov.

RODGERS, GRIFFIN PLATT, federal agency administrator, researcher; b. New Orleans, Nov. 4, 1954; BS, Brown U., Providence, 1976, MD, 1979, MBA, Johns Hopkins U., Balt., 2005. Cert. Internal Medicine, Emergency Medicine, Hematology. Intern Barnes Hosp., Wash. U. Sch. Medicine, St. Louis, resident internal medicine; fellowship hematology/oncology George Washington U. and Washington Vets. Adminstrn. Med. Ctr.; dep. dir. Nat. Inst. Diabetes and Digestive and Kidney Diseases (NIDDK), NIH, Bethesda, Md., 2001—07, acting dir., 2006—07, dir., 2007—. Gov. Am. Coll. Physicians, 1994—97; chair Hematology Subspecialty Bd.; bd. dirs. Am. Bd. Internal Medicine. Contbr. articles to profl. jours., chapters to books. Recipient Richard & Hinda Rosenthal Found. award, 1998, Arthur S. Fleming award, 2000, Legacy of Leadership Award, 2002. Mem.: Assn. Am. Physicians, Am. Soc. Clin. Investigation, Am. Soc. Hematology. Office: NIDDK Bldg 31 Rm 9A52 31 Ctr Dr MSC 2560 Bethesda MD 20892-2560 Office Phone: 301-496-5741. Business E-Mail: griffin.rodgers@nih.gov. *

RODGERS, LAWRENCE RODNEY, internist, educator; b. Clovis, N.Mex., Mar. 9, 1920; s. Samuel Frank and Lillian (O'Connor) R.; m. Ivy Lorna Piper, Aug. 6, 1943; children: Lawrence Rodney (dec.), Ivy Elizabeth, George Piper. BS, West Tex. State U., 1940; MD, U. Tex., 1943. Diplomate Am. Bd. Internal Medicine. Intern Phila. Gen. Hosp., 1943-44, resident in medicine, 1946-49; assoc. internist Tumor Inst., U. Tex. M.D. Anderson Hosp., Houston, 1949—; chmn. dept. medicine Hermann Hosp., Houston, 1966-71; assoc. prof. clin. medicine Baylor U., 1949—; prof. clin. medicine U. Tex., 1972—. Editor: Harris County Physician, 1976-80. Bd. dirs. Tex. Med. Found.; trustee Houston Mus. Med. Sci., 1981. Maj. M.C. AUS, 1944-46. Decorated Bronze Star with two oak leaf clusters; recipient Ashbel Smith Disting. Alumnus award U. Tex. Med. Br.-Galveston, 1993, Mastership award Am. Coll. Physicians, 1996. Fellow ACP (gov. for Tex. 1979-83, Laureate Internist Tex. award 1994); mem. AMA (del. 1975-94), Tex. Med. Assn. (elected emeritus), Harris County Med. Soc. (exec. bd. 1978-82, v.p. 1984), Am. Heart Assn., Houston Soc. Internal Medicine (pres. 1974), Houston Acad. Medicine (pres. 1981), Houston Philos. Soc. (pres. 1993-94), Doctor's Club Houston (bd. govs. 1984-88, pres. 1986). Personal E-mail: rod3920@aol.com.

RODGERS, STEPHEN JOHN, lawyer, physician, consultant; b. Phila., July 10, 1943; s. Harry Edward Rodgers and Antoinette Julia Muckenfuss; m. Roberta Elaine Rhine, Sept. 21, 1974; children: Abigail Elizabeth, Rebecca Elizabeth. MD, Hahnemann U., 1969; JD, Widener U., 1989. Bar: Pa. 1990, N.J. 1990; med. lic., Pa., Del., N.J. Pvt. practice in family practice and emergency medicine Del. Pain Clinic, Wilmington, 1975-89, asst. dir., 1989-92; pvt. practice as medicolegal cons. Wilmington, 1992—. Mem. Med. Assistance and Health Svcs. Adv. Bd., NJ, 1996-98; chair Task Force on Ind. Med. Exam., Dept. Labor and Industry, Commonwealth of Pa., 1996-98, mem. Delaware Med. Res. Corps. Comdr. USN, 1968-75; capt. USNR, 1975—; surgeon gen. N.J. Naval Militia Joint Command. Fellow Am. Acad. Family Physicians, Am. Acad. Disability Evaluating Physicians, Am. Acad. Emergency Medicine, Am. Coll. Legal Medicine; mem. Aerospace Med. Assn., Pa. Bar Assn. (health care com. 1991—), Del. Acad. Medicine, NJ Acad. Family Physicians (ho. of dels. 1989-91), Vietnam Vets. America, Del. Med. Res. Corps., Pa. Occupl. & Environ. Med. Soc. (bd. dirs.). Republican. Roman Catholic. Avocations: equestrian, pro bono veterans and disability advocate. Home: PO Box 54 Alloway NJ 08001-0054 Office: Ste 14 1701 Augustine Wilmington DE 19803

RODGERS, SUZANNE HOOKER, physiologist, ergonomics consultant; b. Rochester, NY, Dec. 26, 1939; d. John Ashmead and Priscilla May (Bodman) Rodgers AB, Vassar Coll., 1961; PhD, U. Rochester Med. Ctr., 1967. Postdoctoral fellow USPHS Middlesex Hosp., London, 1966—68; ergonomist Eastman Kodak Co., Rochester, 1968—82; ind. cons. in ergonomics Rochester, 1982—2010. Author: Working With Backache, 1985; tech. editor, prin. author Ergonomic Design for People at Work, 1983, 86, co-editor, contr. Kodak's Ergonomic Design for People at Work 2d edit., 2003 Bd. dirs., chmn. com., v.p. Rochester Philharm. Orch. Inc., 1969-75; bd. dirs. Opera Theatre Rochester, 1969-75; bd. dirs., chmn. com., pres. Monroe County Bd. Health, Rochester, 1979-88, bd. dirs. Literacy Vols. Rochester, 2010-. Avocations: photography, gardening, reading, silent films. Home and Office: 169 Huntington Hls Rochester NY 14622-1121 Office Phone: 585-544-3587. Personal E-mail: shrodgers@aol.com.

RODIER, GUÉNAËL ROMARIC, public health service officer; b. Dakar, Senegal, Apr. 1, 1956; s. Michel Louis Rodier and Noëlle Marie Blandin de Chalain; m. Hélène Françoise Duquesne, Aug. 7, 1981; children: Clémence Maric, Solène Véronique, Louis Guénaël, François Pierre. MD, U. Paris V, 1983; MSc in Clin. Tropical Medicine, London Sch. Hygiene and Tropical Medicine, 1990. Cert. pub. health specialist Conseil Nat. de l'Ordre des Médecins, France. Pvt. practice, Djibouti, 1983—88; rsch. assoc. Internat. Health Program, U. Md., Balt., 1990—94; investigative officer US Naval Med. Rsch. Unit No.3, Cairo, 1990—94; coord. epidemic alert and response WHO, Geneva, 1995—2000, dir. communicable disease surveillance and response, 2000—05, dir. internat. health regulations coord. program, 2006—, spl. adviser communicable diseases to regional dir., Regional Office for Europe Copenhagen, 2005—06 Recipient Frederick Murgatroyd award, London Sch. of Hygiene and Tropical Medicine, 1990, Louis Weisntein award, Infectious Diseases Soc. Am., 1993. Home: Marly 71420 Marly sur Arroux France Office: WHO 20 Ave Appia 1211 27 Geneva Switzerland Office Fax: 4122 791 4666. E-mail: rodiorg@who.int.

RODIN, HOWARD ALAN, periodontist; b. Bronx, NY, Oct. 21, 1942; s. David and Edna (Fialkow) R.; m. Gail Sandra Stein, July 8, 1967; children: Dennis, Stephanie. BS, Fairleigh Dickinson U., 1964, MS in Physiology, 1966; DDS, Howard U., 1970; cert. in periodontics, Columbia U., 1973. Intern Sydenham Hosp., NYC, 1970-71; staff dept. virology Mt. Sinai Hosp., 1964-66; postdoctoral fellow Fairleigh Dickinson U., Teaneck, NJ, 1971; pvt. practice Babylon, 1973-82, Smithtown, 1978—; staff dept. spl. surgery St. John's Hosp., 1979-81, 85 91. Cons. NYU Med. Ctr./Goldwater Meml. Hosp., 1995-97; planning com. Greater L.I. Dental Meeting, 1973-97, gen. chmn., 1985; asst. clin. prof. periodontics Columbia U., 1986-88; pres. L.I. Acad. Periodontists, 1986-90; mass disaster forensic identification team TWA Flight 800; mem. forensic identification team World Trade Ctr., 2001. Contbr. articles to profl. jours. Fellow Am. Coll. Dentists (chmn. NY sect. 2002), Am. Soc. Forensic Odontology, Internat. Coll. Dentists, Pierre Fauchand Acad., Acad. Dentistry Internat., NY Acad. Dentistry (Humanitarian award, 2002), Suffolk Acad. Medicine (pres. 1992-93, trustee 1990-95), Am. Acad. Osseointegration, Am. Acad. Forensic Scis.; mem. ADA (del., alt. del. 1989-2001), Internat. Assn. Dental Rsch. (periodontal rsch. com. 1984—2008, implantology rsch. com. 1995—2008, Hatton award competition 1968), Am. Acad. Periodontology, Suffolk County Dental Soc. (bd. dels. 1981—, pres. 1991, Robert Raskin Meml. award 2007), NY State Soc. Periodontists (bd. dirs.), NY Acad. Scis., Suffolk Soc. Forensic Dentistry (exec. com. 1995-2004), Columbia U. Periodontal Alumni Assn. (trustee 1996—2008, Disting. Alumnus award), Nat. Acads. Practice, Sigma Xi, Alpha Omega (pres. 1985-87), Omicron Kappa Upsilon. Office Phone: 631-360-0090. *

RODIN, JUDITH SEITZ, foundation administrator, former academic administrator; b. Phila., Sept. 9, 1944; d. Morris and Sally R. (Wilson) Seitz; m. Paul R. Verkuil; 3 children. AB in Psychology, U. Pa., Phila., 1966; PhD in Psychology, Columbia U., NYC, 1970. Asst. prof. psychology NYU, 1970—72, Yale U., New Haven, 1972—75, assoc. prof. psychology, 1975—79, prof. psychology, 1979—83, Philip R. Allen prof. psychology, 1984—94, prof. medicine & psychiatry, 1985—94, dir. Health Psychology Training Prog., 1982—89, chmn. dept. psychology, 1989—91, dean Grad. Sch. Arts & Scis., 1991—92, provost, 1992—94; pres. U. Pa., Phila., 1994—2004, pres. emerita, 2004—, prof. psychology, medicine & psychiatry, 1994—2007, Fox leadership prof., 2000—07; pres. Rockefeller Found., NYC, 2005—. Chair rsch. network on determinants & consequences of health-promoting & health-damaging behavior John D. & Catherine T. MacArthur Found., 1983—93; mem. ind. panel rev. safety procedures, The White House, Washington, 1994—95; chair adv. com. Robert Wood Johnson Found., 1994—; mem. Coun. Competitiveness, 1997—; bd. dirs. Aetna Inc., 1995—2004, AMR Corp., 1997—, Comcast Corp., 2002—, Citigroup Inc., 2004—. Author: Body Traps: Breaking the Binds That Keep You from Feeling Good About Your Body, 1993, The University & Urban Renewal: Out of the Ivory Tower and Into the Streets, 2007; co-author: Obese Humans and Rats, 1974, A Distinctive Approach To Psychological Research: The Influence of Stanley Schachter, 1987, Self Directedness: Cause and Effects Throughout the Life Course, 1990, The Weight Maintenance Survival Guide, 1990, Women and New Reproductive Technologies: Medical, Psychosocial, Legal, and Ethical Dilemmas, 1991, Eating, Body Weight, and Performance in Athletes: Disorders of Modern Society, 1992, Public Discourse in America: Conversation and Community in the Twenty-First Century, 2003; editor: Appetite Jour., 1979—92; contbr. articles to profl. jours., chapters to books. Mem. Pa. Task Force Higher Edn. Funding, 1994; bd. dirs. Catalyst, NYC, 1994—; trustee Brookings Inst., Washington, 1995—; pres. steering com. America Reads, 1997—2000. Recipient Wilbur Lucius Cross medal, Yale Grad. Sch. Alumni Assn., 1992, Golden Plate award, Am. Acad. Achievement, 1994, Woman of Inspiration award, Am. Anorexia Bulimia Assn., 1995, Glass Ceiling award, ARC, 1995, Sara Lee Frontrunner award, 1999, Disting. Daughters of Pa. award, 2000, Beacon award, Trustees Coun. of Penn Women, 2001, Phila. award, 2003; named one of Pa.'s Most Politically Powerful Women, PoliticsPA.com, 2003, The 100 Most Influential Women in NYC Bus., Crain's NY Bus., 2007, The 50 Most Powerful Women in NY, 2009, America's Best Leaders, US News & World Report, 2009; grantee NSF, 1973—82, NIH, 1981—; fellow John Simon Guggenheim Meml. Found., 1986—87; Woodrow Wilson fellow, 1966—67, Columbia U. Disting. Faculty fellow, 1967—70, Yale U. Jr. Faculty fellow, 1974—75. Fellow: APA (bd. sci. affairs 1979-82, Disting. Sci. award 1977, Outstanding Contbn. award 1980, Lifetime Achievement award 2005), AAAS, Acad. Behavioral Medicine Rsch., Soc. Behavioral Medicine; mem.: Am. Philosophical Soc., Conn. Acad. Sci. & Engring., Am. Psychosomatic Soc., Soc. Experimental Social Psychology, NY Acad. Scis., Inst. Medicine, Am. Acad. Arts & Scis., Sigma Xi (pres. Yale chpt. 1986-87), Phi Beta Kappa. Achievements include becoming the first women to be named president of an Ivy League institution, 1993. Office: Rockefeller Found 420 Fifth Ave New York NY 10018 Office Phone: 212-869-8500. Office Fax: 212-764-3468. Business E-Mail: president@rockfound.org. *

RODNING, CHARLES BERNARD, surgeon; b. Pipestone, Minn., Aug. 4, 1943; s. Selmer Bernard and Ida Amanda (Selness) R.; m. Mary Elizabeth Lipke, June 15, 1968; children: Christopher Bernard, Soren Piers, Kai Johannes. BS, Gustavus Adolphus Coll., St. Peter, Minn., 1965; MD, U. Rochester, 1970; PhD, U. Minn., 1979. Diplomate Am. Bd. Med. Examiners, Am. Bd. Surgery. Intern, asst. resident dept. surgery U. Rochester Sch. Medicine and Dentistry, 1970-72; assoc. resident to chief resident, med. fellow dept. surgery U. Minn. Health Scis. Ctr., Mpls., 1972-79; prof. dept cell biology and neurosci. U. South Ala., Mobile, 1981—, prof. dept. surgery, 1981—, vice chmn. dept. surgery, 1981—2006, chmn. dept. surgery, 2006—, dir. gen. surgery, 1996—; pres. Med. Soc., County Mobile, 2010—; pres. ala. chpt. ACS, 2010—. Field liaison physician Commn. on Cancer-ACS, Chgo., 1984—; mem. med. adv. bd. Ala. Organ & Tissue Ctr., Birmingham, 1988—; mem. Bd. Health County of Mobile, pres., 2007, counsellor, Med. Assn. State Ala., 2011. Author: Elan Vital, 1988, Wode and Ston, 1988, Sorrowful Wheel, 1989, Ponderings, 1990, The Sea Rises in the West, 1991, Stepping Stones, 1991, Snowbound Below the Firn Line, 1991, Love Knot, 1994, Papering Dreams, 1994, Carry Onward, 1996, Swaying Grass, 1998, Tradition of Excellence: Pictorial History of Surgical Education at the Mobile General Hospital and University of South Alabama College of Medicine and Medical Center, 1999; reviewer: Jour. Histochem. Cytochem., 1988—; contbr. (articles) Clin. Anatomy, Surg. Endoscopy, Pharos, Jours. Thoracic Cardiovasc. Surgery, So. Med. Jour., others. Bd. dirs. Mobile Mental Health Ctr., Mental Health Found. of South Ala., Mobile Med. Mus., Christian Med. Ministry of South Ala., bd. trustees; sec.-treas. bd. censors Med. Soc. Mobile County, 2006. Comdr. USN, 1974-81. Recipient Physicians Recognition award AMA, 1980, 85, 88, 91, 95, 99, 02, Bacaner Rsch. award Minn. Med. Found., 1979, Humanism in Medicine award Arnold P. Gold Found., Healthcare Found. N.J., 2002, Howard L. Holley award Med. Assn. State Ala., 2002, Disting. Svc. award Alumni Assn., South Ala., 2010 Fellow ACS (mem, exec. coun.), Internat. Coll. Surgeons (vice regent Ala. chpt. 1989—), mem. Iota Delta Gamma, Alpha Omega Alpha, Phi Kappa Phi, Gold Humanism Honor Soc, Med. Soc. County Mobile, (sec.-treas. 2007, mem. bd. censors, 2006, 08, v.p. 2008, pres.-elect 2009, pres. 2010), Ala. Chapter Am. Coll. Surgeons (sec., treas., 2008, pres.-elect 2009, pres. 2010). Office: U South Ala Coll Med Allied Health Professions Mobile AL 36617-2293 Office Phone: 251-471-7034. Business E-Mail: crodning@usouthal.edu.

RODOSKY, MARK W., orthopedic surgeon; MD, CUNY, 1987. Cert. orthopaedic surgery. Resident Univ. Pitts.; fellow Columbia Univ. Hosp., NY; hosp. affiliations include Univ. Pitts. Med. Ctr. St. Margaret, Pa., Univ. Pitts. Med. Ctr. Mercy, Univ. Pitts. Med. Ctr. Presbyn., Univ. Pitts. Med. Ctr. Mercy South Side Surgery Ctr. Office: University of Pittsburgh Medical Center Center for Sports Medicine 3200 S Water St Pittsburgh PA 15203 Office Phone: 412-432-3600.

RODRIGUES, PAULO, urologist; b. Bauru, Oct. 7, 1963; MD, U. São Paulo, 1987, PhD, 1991. Dir., urology Hosp. 9 Julho São Paulo, 2008—. Named one of Best Drs. Brazil, AMB. Master: Brazilian Urol. Soc.; mem.: Soc. Urodynamics and Female Urology, Am. Urol. Assn. Office: Rua Teixeira da Silva 34 São Paulo 04002-020 Brazil Office Fax: 55 11 32666455. Business E-Mail: paulortrodrigues@uol.com.br.

RODRIGUEZ, AGUSTIN ANTONIO, surgeon; b. Hato Rey, P.R., Aug. 20, 1961; s. Agustin and Esther Rodriguez (Gonzalez) R.; m. Liana Esther Lopez, 1993; children: Agustin Andrés, Claudia Sofía, Alvaro Agustin, Alejandro Agustin. AB in Biology, Harvard Coll., 1982; MD, U. P.R., San Juan, 1986. Diplomate Nat. Bd. Med. Examiners, Am. Bd. Surgery, Am. Bd. Gen. and Vascular Surgery. Intern Boston U. Med. Ctr., 1986-87, resident in surgery, 1988-93, acad. trainee surgery; vascular fellow Tufts U., New England Med. Ctr., 1993-95; asst. prof. surgery Tufts U. Sch. Medicine, Boston, 1995—. Assoc. prof. surgery Sch. Medicine U. P.R., San Juan, 1996-2004, prof. surgery. 2004—, also chief vascular surgery sect. Contbr. articles to profl. jours. Fellow ACS, Am. Soc. Angiology; mem. AMA, Am. Numismatic Soc., Am. Numismatic Assn., Mass. Med. Soc., N.Y. Acad. Scis., European Soc. Vascular Surgery (assoc.), Am. Venous Forum, Interam. Coll. Physicians and Surgeons, Am. Soc. Clin. Vascular Surgery, Assn. Acad. Surgery, Soc. Am. Gastrointestinal and Endoscopic Surgeons, Coll. Med. Surgeons P.R., Cirujanos Vasculares de Habla Hispana, Alpha Omega Alpha. Republican. Home: 1924 Calle Sauco Rio Piedras PR 00927-6718 Office: U PR Sch Medicine Dept Surgery San Juan PR 00936-5067 Office Phone: 787-763-2440, 787-765-1630. Personal E-mail: drgusrodriguez@aol.com.

RODRIGUEZ, ALFONSO J., medical researcher; b. Caracas, Venezuela, Nov. 13, 1975; s. Alfonso J. and Aurora Delcarmen (Morales) R. BS, Los Arcos, Caracas, 1992. Assoc. rschr. Western U., Puerto La Cruz, Venezuela, 1993-96; student prof. microbiology Jose Maria Vargas Med. Sch., Caracas, 1997-98; invited prof. microbiology

Faculty of Dentistry, Caracas, 1997-2000; faculty assembly rep. Ctrl. U. Venezuela, Caracas, 1998-99. Contbr. articles to profl. jours.; peer reviewer Can. Family Physician Jour. Fellow Royal Soc. Tropical Medicine and Hygiene; mem. Am. Soc. Microbiology, Am. Soc. for Clin. Pathology, Internat. Soc. for Anaerobic Bacteria, Internat. Soc. Infectious Diseases, Internat. AIDS Soc., Sci. Soc. Med. Students Ctrl. U. Venezuela (v.p., pres. 1999-2001), Venezuelan Sci. Soc. Med. Students (gen. sec. 2001—), Venezuelan Soc. for Microbiology, L.Am. Fedn. Med. Students Sci. Soc. (regional councillor 2000-01), Alliance for Prudent Use of Antibiotics, Anaerobe Soc. Ams. Roman Catholic. Avocations: photography, piano, tennis. Home: C R LA T-2 10-2 Sec Pque Cigarral Urb La Boyera 1083 Caracas Miranda Venezuela Office: Res Guararute Piso 7 Apt 71 Av Paez Chacao Caracas Mirnada 1083 Venezuela Fax: 58-2-943-25-73. E-mail: bacteroides79@hotmail.com, venvirology98@hotmail.com.

RODRIGUEZ, ALFREDO EDUARDO, cardiologist; b. Cordoba, Argentina, Oct. 3, 1950; s. Alfredo and Clotilde (Garcia Basabilvaso) R.; m. Marta Maria Biagioni; children: Alfredo Matias, Gaston Alfredo, Agustina, Tomas Moises, Clara Maria. MD, Cordoba Sch. Medicine, 1974. Bd. cert. in clinical cardiology, 1981. Resident in internal medicine Air Force Hosp., Cordoba, Argentina, 1974; resident in cardiology Favaloro Found., Buenos Aires, Argentina, 1975-78; fellow St. Marys Hosp., San Francisco, 1980-81; asst. dir. Catheterization Lab., Buenos Aires, 1984-88; head interventional cardiology Aescitorenia Hosp., Buenos Aires, 1988-99, Otamendi Hosp., Buenos Aires, 1994—. Prof. sch. medicine Barcel Univ., 1999; dir. cardiology Adrogue Clinic, 1999—; cons. Interventional cardiology Spanish Hosp., 1993—, Argerich Hosp., 1990. Editor: Current Tendencys in Cardiology, 1987, Coronary Angioplasty, 1985; contbr. more than 300 articles to profl. jours. Recipient Ethica award Erasmus Ctr., Rotterdal Netherlands, 1997, B Luis Sivori Buenos Aires Sch. Medicine, 1990, Solaci, Latin Am. Interventional Soc., 1997; Nat. Acad. Medicine, 1981, 2001, Iberoam. Soc. Cardiology, 2000, Arpentine Soc. Cardiology, 1993. Fellow Am. Coll. Cardiology, Anders Gruenzig Cardiovascular Soc.; mem. Latin Am. Soc. Interventional Cardiology. Roman Catholic. Avocations: biking, golf, paddle, music, books of history. Home: Av Callao 1441-4 Fl B Buenos Aires Argentina Office: Otamendi Hosp Calle Gral M de Azcuenaga 880 C1115AAB Buenos Aires Argentina Office Phone: (54 11) 4813-5532. E-mail: centroceci@sion.com, rodrigueza@sanatorio-otamendi.com.ar.

RODRIGUEZ, JORGE JACINTO, psychiatrist; b. Moron, Ciego de Avila, Cuba, Jan. 28, 1950; s. Nicolas Mercedes Rodriguez and Fela Julia Sánchez; m. Miriam L. de León, Apr. 0, 2005; 1 child, Elisabet. MD, U. Camaguey, Cuba, 1972; PhD, U. Havana, Cuba, 1991. Cert. psychiatry Ministry Health Cuba, 1978. Prof. psychiatry U. Camaguey, 1973—88; head psychiatry dept. U. Hosp. Calixto Garcia, Havana, 1988—97, prof., 1973—88; temp. internat. advisor mental health Pan Am. Health Orgn., Regional Office WHO, 1996—2004, mental health advisor Guatemala, 1997—2004, mental health advisor ctrl. Am. countries Panamá, 2004—06, mental health program coord. Washington, 2006—. Mental health coord. Ministry Health, Havana, 1989—97, psychiatrist and mental health advisor, Sao Tome, 1980—81, several mgr. and academic posts, Camaguey and Havana, 1973—96; coord. academic bd. social psychiat. ms course Med. U. Havana, 1994—97, chmn., 1994—97. Contbr. articles to numerous profl. jours. Master: Assn. Psiquiátrica Guatemalteca (hon.). Home: 2501 Q St NW Apt 223 Washington DC 20007 Business E-Mail: rodrigjo@paho.org.

RODRIGUEZ, RENÉ F., orthopedic surgeon; MD, Salamanca Univ., Spain; postgrad study, NY Polyclin. Hosp., Queens Hosp. Ctr., Jewish Cronic Diseases Hosp., Health Policy Inst. at George Washington Univ. Cert. Am. Bd. Orthopedic Surg. Chief Veterans Adminstrn. Med. Ctr., Miami; and orthopedic staff Jackson Meml. Med. Ctr., Cedars Med. Ctr., Univ. Miami Sch. Med. Bd. sci. counselors, Nat. Ctr. for Health Statistics CDC, Atlanta, 2003—. Founder, editor-in-chief Medico Interamericano, Medico Familia. Co-founder, co-chmn. Nat. Hispanic Youth Initiative. Recipient Officer of the Cross, Spain, Knight of the Order of Jerusalem, Knight of Malta, Freddie award in recognition of pub. svc. as an Adv. to the underserved in Am., MediMedia USA, 2004. Fellow: Soc. Med. Cons. to Armed Forces, Cuban Orthopaedic Soc. in Exile, Am. Coll. internat. Physicians, Internat. Coll. Surgeons, Am. Fracture Assn., Am. Coll. Surgeons, Am. Trauma Soc. (founding mem.), NY Acad. Medicine.; mem.: Nat. Confederation of Hispanic-Am. Med. Assns. (founder, chmn.), Interamerican Coll. Physicians and Surgeons (pres.). Office: Orthoped Surg Sect VA Med Ctr 1201 NW 16th St Miami FL 33125 E-mail: rrr@icps.org. *

RODRIGUEZ-AGIRRETXE, IÑAKI, ophthalmologist; b. San Sebastian, Spain, May 13, 1969; MD, U. Navarra, 1993. Physician Osakidetza and ICQO, 1999—. Home: Alcalde Jose Elosegui 199 B San Sebastian Guipuzcoa 20015 Spain Business E-Mail: ira@icqo.org.

RODRIGUEZ-ALCANTARA, FELIPE, epidemiologist, director; b. Palencia, Spain, Dec. 16, 1958; MD, Complutense U. Madrid, 1982; PhD, Autonomous U. Madrid, 1989. Med. adviser SmithKline & Beecham, 1997—2002; infectious disease area mgr. GlaxoSmithKline, 2002—09; med. dir. ViiV Healthcare, 2009—. Mem.: Spanish Soc. Primary Caare. Avocations: diving, bicycling, mountain climbing, music, photography. Home: C/ Castilla 5 Las Rozas de Madrid Madrid 28290 Spain Business E-Mail: felipe.rodriguez-alcantara@viivhealthcare.com.

RODRIGUEZ ARROYO, JESUS, gynecologic oncologist; b. Arecibo, PR, Jan. 11, 1948; s. Jesus Rodriguez and Blanca Arroyo; m. Annie Arsuaga, June 3, 1972; children: Ivan, Patricia. BS, U. P.R., San Juan, 1968, MD, 1972, postgrad., 1976. Diplomate Am. Bd. Ob-Gyn; bd. cert. in gynecologic oncology. Assoc. dir. gynecologic oncology Oncology Hosp., Rio Piedras, PR, 1978-83; assoc. prof. ob-gyn, dir. gynecologic oncology U. Hosp. Sch. Medicine, Rio Piedras, 1978-85, AuxiLio Mutuo Hosp., Rio Piedras, 1979—2011; arch. U. Hosp. Sch. Medicine, San Juan, 2001—09, prof. ob-gyn., 2001—09. Instr. ob-gyn. U. PR Sch. Medicine, 1976-78, asst. prof., 1978-83, assoc. prof., 1984, Sch. Medicine Cath. U., 2000-2009. Contbr. articles to med. jours. Mem. Citizen Ambassador Cancer Mgmt. Del. to USSR, 1990. Mem. AAAS, Am. Coll. Surgeons, NY Acad. Scis., PR Med. Assn. (jud. ethical coun. 1990-91), Internat. Gynecologic Cancer Soc., Soc. Gynecologic Oncologists, Dorado Beach Hotel, Caparra Country Club. Home: 1910 Pasionaria St Urban Santa Maria San Juan PR 00927 Office: Caribbean Oncology & Gyn Assn PO Box 194557 San Juan PR 00919-4557 Home Phone: 787-767-3801; Office Phone: 787-250-0276. Business E-Mail: caribbeanoncology@gmail.com.

RODRIGUEZ-CRUZ, EDWIN, pediatrician, internist, educator; b. San German, PR, Dec. 18, 1967; MD, San Juan Bautista Sch. Medicine, 1992; degree in Interventional Pediat. Cardiology, Children's Hosp. Mich., 2000. Assoc. prof. pediat. San Juan Bautista Sch. Medicine, 2008—. Dir., divsn. cardiology San Jorge Children's Hosp., 2008—; bd. dirs. Dr. Garcia Rinaldi's Found., 2009. Recipient Dr.'s Choice awards, PR, 2011, Best Attending's Tchg. award, San Juan Bautista Sch. Medicine Graduating Class, 2007. Mem.: Am. Acad. Pediat., PR's Med. Assn., Soc. Cardiac Angiography and Interventions, PR's Pediat. Soc., Am. Coll. Cardiology. Office: 270 Convento St Ste # 1 Santurce PR 00912 Office Fax: 787-294-9707. E-mail: cardiopeds@onelinkpr.net.

RODRIGUEZ-GONZALEZ, MANUEL, gynecologist; b. Vila-real, Spain, Mar. 15, 1968; s. Manuel Rodriguez and Carmen Gonzalez; m. Rosana Fuster, Mar. 10, 1967; children: Anna Rodriguez, Carlos Rodriguez. Dr., U. Sch. of Medicine, Valencia, 1992. Doctor U. of Valencia, 2002. Gynecologist Instituto Valenciano de Infertilidad, Valencia, Spain, 1998—2001. Dir. Instituto Valenciano de Infertilidad, Castellon, Spain, 2001—03. Mem.: SEGO and SEF (assoc.). Office: Instituto Valenciano de Infertilidad Avd Capuchinos 63 Castellon 12003 Spain Office Fax: 964-26-12-20. E-mail: ivicastellon@ivi.es.

RODRIGUEZ-JIMENEZ, ROBERTO, psychiatrist; b. Madrid, June 11, 1970; s. Oscar Rodriguez-Caumel and Concepcion Jimenez-Parra; m. Marisol Martin-Lopez; children: Laura Rodriguez-Martin, Roberto Rodriguez-Martin, Silvia Rodriguez-Martin. MD, U. Autonoma, Madrid, 1994, MA in Psychotherapy, 2001, PhD in Psychiatry, 2004; BA in Psychology, U. Española de Edn.a Distancia, Madrid, 2000. Lectr. U. Autonoma, Madrid, 1995—96; psychiat. day hosp. coord. Complejo Hosp., Ciudad Real, Spain, 2000—02; cons. psychiatrist San Blas Mental Health Svc. IMSALUD, Madrid, 2002—03, Hosp. Univ. 12 de Octubre, Madrid, 2003—; assoc. prof. U. Complutense, Madrid, 2005—. Rschr. Fondo de Investigacion Sanitaria (FIS). Instituto de Salud Carlos III. Ministerio de Sanidad y Consumo, Madrid, 2001—, FIS & Ctr. Investigation Biomed. Red Mental Health Inst., CPBERSAM. Contbr. scientific paper and books. Achievements include research in field. Avocations: reading, music, mountain climbing. Office: Hosp Univ 12 de Octubre Avda Andalucia s/n Madrid 28041 Spain Office Fax: 34 91 390 85 34. Business E-Mail: roberto.rodriguez.jimenez@gmail.com.

RODRIGUEZ-LARRAIN P. JORGE, retired internist, cardiologist, consultant; b. Lima, Peru, June 12, 1924; s. Emilio Rodriguez-Larrain and Isabel Pendergast; m. Lucila Echecopar, Feb. 16, 1952; children: Lucila Rodriguez-Larrain, Patricia Rodriguez-Larrain, Monica Rodriguez-Larrain, Ana Maria Rodriguez-Larrain, Jorge Rodriguez-Larrain, Rocio Rodriguez-Larrain, German Rodriguez-Larrain, Lorena Rodriguez-Larrain. MD, Univ. Nacional Mayor de San Marcos, Lima, 1950; Electrogardiography Specialist, Inst. de Cardiología de Mex., 1953; Adminstrn., IPAE, Lima, 1971; Hosp. Adminstrn., ESAE, Lima, 1972; Inspectory, Inspectoria Gen. del Ejercito, Lima, 1973. Med. intern Hosp. Ctrl. de Sanidad de las Fuerzas Policiales, Lima, 1948—50, med. asst., 1950—52, mem. staff cardiovasc. dept., 1954—66, chief cardiovasc. dept., 1967—70; dir. Hosp. Ctrl. de la Sanidad de las Fuerzas Policiales, Lima, 1974—75; fellow in cardiology Michael Reese Hosp., Chgo., 1952—53; mem. hon. staff cardiovasc. dept. Hosp. Dos de Mayo, Lima, 1954—62; prof. asst. U. Mayor de San Marcos, Lima, 1956—60; gen. insp. Sanidad de las Fuerzas Policiales, Lima, 1973—74, gen. dir., 1976—78; med. dir. Clinica El Golf de San Isidro, Lima, 1995—96; sub dir. Hosp. Ctrl. de Sanidad de las Fuerzas Policiales, Lima; ret. Pres. Peruvian Cardiovasc. Assn., Lima, 1971—73; founder, gen. sec. Cardiovasc. Andean Sec., Lima, 1972—74; pres. South Am. Union Cardiovasc. Assns., Lima, 1975—77, Andean Med. Coun., Lima, 1991—92. Contbr. proyecto de ley nacional, sector salud, proyecto de ley, sector salud, proyector de ley, proyecto de ley, elaboracion de proyecto, plan de emergencia, sector salud. Directive coun. del. Confedacion de Profesionales Universitarios Liberales del Peru, Lima, 1966; dist. maj. Mcpl. Govt. of Miraflores, 1981—83; vocal Consejo Regional III del Colegio Medico del Peru, Lima, 1970—71; dean Peruvian Med. Sch., Lima, 1990—91. Gen. Sanidad de las Fuerzas Policiales, 1948—78, Lima. Decorated Orden al Merito de la Guardia Civil del Peru, Grado de Gran Oficial Guardia Civil del Peru, Orden al Merito de la Guardia Republicana del Peru, Grado de Gran Oficial Guardia Republicana del Peru, Orden al Merito de la Policia de Investigaciones del Peru, Grado de Gran Oficial, Insignis de Honor de la Sanidad de las Fuerzas Policiales del Peru, Primer Grado; recipient Huesped Ilustre de la Ciudad de Arequipa, entrega de las Llaves de la Ciudad, Mcpl. Govt. of Province of Arequipa, 1972, Orden del Sol del Peru, Grado de Gran Oficial, Peruvian Govt., 1975, Huesped Ilustre de la Ciudad de Piura, Mcpl. Govt. of Province of Piura, 1981, Orden Daniel Alcides Carrion, Grado de Gran Oficial, Peruvian Govt., 1981, Orden de Rio Branco de la Republica Do Brasil, Grado de Comendador, Brazilian Govt., 1981, Extraordinary Merit medal, Colegio Medico del Peru, 1992, Civic medal, Mcpl. Govt. of Miraflores, 1993, Honors Plate, South Am. Union Cardiovasc. Assns., 1993. Fellow: Am. Coll. Cardiology (emeritus, honors plate); mem.: Peruvian Med. Fedn., Uruguayan Soc. Cardiology (corr.), Chilean Soc. Cardiology (corr.), Argentinean Soc. Cardiology (hon.), Armed Police Health Acad. (assoc.), Peruvian Health Acad. (assoc.), Nat. Med. Assn. (assoc.), Peruvian Soc. Cardiology (assoc.; hon. pres. 2005), Club de Regatas Lima (life). Roman Catholic.

RODRIGUEZ-MOJICA, WILMA, radiologist, educator; b. Mayaguez, PR, Mar. 23, 1946; d. Manuel and Rosa (Mojica) Rodriguez; divorced; 1 child, Rebecca Rodriguez-Rodriguez. BS, U. P.R., Mayaguez, 1966; MD, U. P.R., San Juan, 1970. Diplomate Am. Bd. Radiology. Intern U. P.R. Dist. Hosp., 1970-71, resident in diagnostic radiology, 1971-75; radiologist Auxilio Mutuo Hosp., Rio Piedras, P.R., 1976-79; radiologist ptnr. Advanced Radiology Group, Hato Rey, P.R., 1979—. Assoc. prof. radiology dept. radiol. scis. U. P.R. Sch. Medicine, Rio Piedras, 1986—; dir. ultrasound Univ. Hosp. Med. Scis. Campus U. P.R., 1980—, proctor radiology electives for med. students, 1975—. Recipient Disting. Citizen award Jaycees Club, 1979, Lions Club, 1987, Mcp. Assembly Women's Week, 1993. Mem. Am. Coll. Radiology (P.R. chpt., treas. 1982-84, counselor 1992, 94), Radiol. Soc. N.Am., Am. Inst. Ultrasound in Medicine, Am. Assn. Women Radiologists, Soc. Radiologists in Ultrasound. Democrat. Roman Catholic. Avocations: reading, drawing. Home: Parque de las Fuentes Apt 2403 Hato Rey PR 00918 *

RODRIGUEZ NORIEGA, EDUARDO, epidemiologist; b. Colima, Mexico, June 27, 1942; MD, U. Guadalajara, 1966, PhD, 2005. Chief, infectious diseases divsn. Hosp. Civil de Guadalajara, Fray Antonio Alcalde, 1999—; prof. medicine U. Guadalajara, 1978. Recipient Diplomate, Am. Bd. Internal Medicine. Mem.: Infectious Disease Soc. of Am. Office: Justo Sierra 2350 1 Piso Colonia Ladr Jalisco Guadalajara 44280 Mexico Home Phone: ernern1@hotmail.com; Office Phone: 3338095379. Office Fax: 3336850501.

RODRÍGUEZ-ROMO, LAURA, pediatrician; b. Monterrey, Nuevo Leon, Méx., Jan. 8, 1975; MD, U. Autonoma de Nuevo Leon, 1998. With pediatric hematology Svc. de Hematología Hosp. U. UANL, 2008—; founder, rsch. group pediat. stem cell transplant Mexico; collaborator Unidos por el Arte contra el Cancer Infantil. Adj. prof. Pediatric Hematology Svc. UANL, 2008—11, Sch. Medicine Inst. Tecnológico y de Estudios Superiores de Monterrey, prof., hematology, 2009—11; med. dir. Twining Program Cook Children Hosp. Svc. de Hematología Hosp. U., 2010—11. Mem.: Nat. Rsch. Sys. Mex., Assn. Mexicana de Hematología. Home: Ave San Jemo 500 Monterrey Nuevo Leon 64630 Mexico Personal E-mail: wawwis@yahoo.com, lauranrodriguezromo@gmail.com.

RODRIGUEZ Y BAENA, RUGGERO, oral surgeon, educator; b. Milan, Jan. 8, 1957; s. Ferdinando and Velia (Vergano) R. y B.; m. Cinzia Codebó, Feb. 29, 1992; children: Alessandra, Arianna. MD, DDS, U. Pavia, Italy, 1981, specialist in dentistry and oral surgery, 1985. Pvt. practice gen. dentistry and oral surgery, Pavia and Milan, 1982—; assoc. prof. oral pathology U. Pavia, 2000. Vis prof. dept. oral surgery U. Pavia, 1988—. Author: Implant Prostheses, 1996, Minor Pre-Prosthetic Surgery, 1998; (CD-Rom) Implant Dentistry, 1998, Introduction to Biomechanics in Implant Dentistry, 2002, Atlas of Oral Radiology, 2006 With Italian Air Force, 1978-79. Mem. Am. Acad. Osseointegration, Italian Soc. Osseointegration (treas. 1999, bd. dirs. 2005), European Assn. Osseointegration. Avocations: gymnastics, tennis, flying, computers. Home: Via Vasto 1 20121 Milan Italy Office: Via Colombo 1 27100 Pavia Italy Home Phone: +390236511174; Office Phone: +39038220062. E-mail: ruggero.rodriguez@unipv.it.

ROE, THOMAS LEROY WILLIS, retired pediatrician; b. Bend, Oreg., Sept. 1, 1936; MD, U. Oregon Health Scis. U., Portland, 1961. Diplomate Am. Bd. Pediatrics. Intern U. Calif., San Francisco, 1961-62, resident, 1962-64; physician Sacred Heart Med. Ctr., Eugene, Oreg.; pvt. practice Peace Health Med. Group, Eugene, 1969—2006; clin prof. pediatrics U. Oreg., Portland, 1985—2006; ret., 2006. Fellow Am. Acad. Pediatricians; mem. AMA, North Pacific Pediatrics Soc. Office: Peace Health Med Clinic 1162 Willamette St Eugene OR 97401-3568 Office Phone: 541-687-6061. Business E-Mail: troe@peacehealth.org.

ROEDER, ROBERT GAYLE, biochemist, molecular biologist, educator; b. Boonville, Ind., June 3, 1942; s. Frederick John and Helene (Bredenkamp) Roeder; m. Suzanne Himsel, July 11, 1964 (div. 1981); children: Kimberly, Michael; m. Cun Jing Hong, June 2, 1990; 1 child, Maxine. BA summa cum laude (Gilbert scholar), Wabash Coll., 1964, DSc (hon.), 1990; MS, U. Ill., 1965; PhD (USPHS fellow), U. Wash., 1969; DSc (hon.), Washington U., 2005. Am. Cancer Soc. fellow dept. embryology Carnegie Instn. Washington, Balt., 1969-71; asst. prof. biol. chemistry Washington U., St. Louis, 1971-75, assoc. prof., 1975-76, prof., 1976-82, prof. genetics, 1978-82, James S. McDonnell prof. biochem. genetics, 1979-82; prof. lab. biochemistry and molecular biology Rockefeller U., NYC, 1982—, Arnold O. and Mabel S. Beckmann prof. molecular biology and biochemistry, 1985—. Cons. USPHS, 1975-79, Am. Cancer Soc., 1983-86. Recipient Dreyfus Tchr.-Scholar award Dreyfus Found., 1976, molecular biology award NAS-U.S. Steel Found., 1986, outstanding investigator award Nat. Cancer Inst., 1986-2002, Dickson prize in medicine, 2001, Albert Lasker award for Basic Med. Rsch., Lasker Found., 2003, Salk Inst. medal for Rsch. Excellence, 2010; co-recipient Lewis S. Rosenstiel award for disting. work in basic med. scis. Brandeis U., 1995, Passano award Passano Found., Inc., 1995, Alfred P. Sloan prize GM Cancer Rsch. Found., 1999, Louisa Gross Horowitz award Columbia U., 1999, Gairdner Found. Internat. award, 2000, ASBMB-Merck Award, 2002; grantee NIH, 1972-, NSF, 1975-79, Am. Cancer Soc., 1979-85. Fellow AAAS, Am. Acad. Arts and Scis., Am. Acad. Microbiology, NY Acad. Scis.; mem. NAS, Am. Chem. Soc. (Eli Lilly award 1977), Am. Soc. Biol. Chemists, Am. Soc. Microbiologists, Am. Soc. Immunologists, Am. Diabetes Assn., European Molecular Biology Orgn. (assoc.), Harvey Soc. (pres. 1994), Phi Beta Kappa. Office: Rockefeller U 1230 York Ave New York NY 10065-6399 Business E-Mail: roeder@rockefeller.edu. *

ROEDIGER, PAUL MARGERUM, internal medicine consultant; b. Princeton, NJ, June 30, 1932; s. Paul Otto and Helen Mae (Margerum) R.; m. Janice Ann Balint, Aug. 18, 1956, (dec. 14th Jan., 2010); children: Pamela, Matthew, Joan. AB, Princeton U., 1954; MD, Jefferson Med. Coll., 1958. Dir. med. edn. Abington (Pa.) Meml. Hosp., 1965—2005, chief divsn. gen. internal medicine, 1972-2000. Vestry mem. St. Ann's Episcopal Ch., Abington, 1965—. Fellow ACP, Coll. Physicians of Phila. Home: 1250 Greenwood Ave Jenkintown PA 19046 Office: 1200 York Rd Dixon Bldg Abington PA 19001-3800 Office Phone: 215-481-2603. Business E-Mail: amhgme@amh.org.

ROEHRIG, JOHN T., immunologist, educator; BS in Microbiology, U. Ill., 1973; PhD in Microbiology, U. Mo.-Columbia, 1977. Rsch. microbiologist divsn. vector-borne infectious diseases Ctr. Disease Control and Prevention, Fort Collins, Colo., 1981-84, supervisory rsch. microbiologist, 1984—, chief immunochemistry br./sect., 1985-98; chief arbovirus diseases br. Colo. State U., Fort Collins, 1981—, biosafety com. mem., 1981—, affiliate faculty mem. dept. microbiology, 1981—. Presenter in field. Ad hoc reviewer Am. Jour. of Tropical Medicine and Hygiene, Archives of Virology, Infectio and Immunity, Jour. of Gen. Virology, Jour. of Infectious Diseases, Jour. of Med. Virology, Jour. of Virology, Virology and Virus Rsch.; contbr. chpts. to books and numerous articles to profl. jours. Grantee U.S. Army, 1987-90, NATO, 1987-90, WHO, 1989-91. Mem. AAAS, Am. Soc. for Virology, Am. Soc. for Microbiology, Am. Com. for Arthropod-Bone Viruses, Protein Soc., Am. Peptide Soc., Am. Soc. for Tropical Medicine and Hygiene, U. Ill. Alumni Assn., U. Mo. Alumni Assn., Sigma Xi. Office: Divsn Vector Borne Infectious Diseases Ctrs Disease Control PO Box 2087 Fort Collins CO 80522-2087 *

ROENIGK, RANDALL K., dermatologist, health science association administrator; BA in Biology and Psychology, Northwestern U., MD. Resident U. Minn. Medical Sch.; prof. dermatology Mayo Clinic. Mem.: American Bd. Medical Specialists (bd. dirs. 2009—), American Bd. Dermatology (pres. elect 2008, pres. 2009). Office: Mayo Clinic 200 First St SW Rochester MN 55905 Business E-Mail: roenigk.randall@mayo.edu.

ROEPENACK, DWIGHT ELMER, public health service officer; b. Chgo., May 23, 1947; s. Elmer Henry and Hazel Ethel Roepenack; m. Carol Ann Jasica, Oct. 11, 1980. AA, Wilbur Wright Jr. City Coll., Chgo., 1968; BS in Biology, Northland Coll., Ashland, Wis., 1970; postgrad. in Pub. Policy and Adminstrn., Northwestern U., Chgo., 2009. Lic. environ. health specialist 1981, cert. swimming pool operator 1984, lic. environ. health practitioner 1976, cert. scuba diver, lic. amateur radio, cert. emergency preparedness FEMA, 2002, hazardous materials awareness Ill, 2002, emergency repsonse tng. cert. 2004. Quality assurance auditor Wyler Foods, Northbrook, Ill., 1971—72; engr. product supr. NPC Pronto Foods, Inc., Chgo., 1972—75; with Baxter Travenol Lab., 1975—76; dept. head sanitation salerno Megownen Biscuit Co., Niles, Ill., 1976—78; plant sanitarian Revere Sugar Corp., Chgo., 1978—82; health dept. inspector Evanston North Shore Health Dept., Ill., 1983—88; health and lic. officer Village Niles, 1988—. Self employed contract sanitarian pest control, 1982—89. Weather spotter Nat. Weather Svc., 1992—; mem. zoning bd. appeals, planning commr. Villiage Morton Grove, Ill., 1993—; water safety instr. ARC, first air instr.; mem. Morton Grove Traffic Safety Commn., Morton Grove, Ill., 1984—92; theatre adv. bd. Loyola U., 1992—93. Mem.: Nat. Orgn. Am. Radio Relay League, Chgo. Art Inst., Chgo. Field Mus., Interlochen Nat. Music Camp, Nat. Environ. Health Assn., Ill. Environ. Health Assn. Independent. Lutheran. Office: Village Niles Cmty Devel 1000 Civic Center Dr Niles IL 60714 Business E-Mail: der@vniles.com.

ROERDINK, JOS B.T.M., science educator; PhD, U. Utrecht, Netherlands, 1983. Prof. computer sci. U. Groningen, Netherlands, 1992—. Office: Univ Groningen Nijenborgh 9 Groningen 9747 AG Netherlands Office Fax: 31-50-3633800.

ROGACHEFSKY, ARLENE SANDRA, dermatologist; b. Rochester, NY, June 29, 1970; d. Hymen Rogachefsky and Deanna Rogachefsky Luntz; m. David Black, Oct. 27, 2001; children: Mitchell Harris Black, Ellie Rachel Black. BA with honors, Brown U., Providence, 1992; MD magna cum laude, SUNY, Buffalo, 1996. Diplomate Am. Bd. Dermatology, cert. Am. Coll. Mohs Micrographic Surgery and Cutaneous Oncology. Intern in internal medicine Cleve. Clinic Found., 1996—97, resident in dermatology, 1997—2000; fellow Mohs and cosmetic laser surgery Office of Dr. David Goldberg, Westwood, NJ, 2000—01; assoc. Skin Laser and Surgery Specialists NY and NJ, Hackensack and Westwood, NJ, 2001—03, Affiliated Dermatologists and Dermatol. Surgeons, Morristown, NJ, 2005—. Program dir. procedural dermatology fellowship Affiliated Dermatologists and Dermatol. Surgeons, 2006—. Contbr. articles to profl. jours. Home: 160 Myrtle Ave Millburn NJ 07041 Office: Affiliated Dermatologists and Dermatologic Surgeons 182 S St Ste 1 Morristown NJ 07960 Office Phone: 973-267-0300. E-mail: arogachefsky@hotmail.com.

ROGAL, GARY JEFFREY, cardiologist; b. Newark, Nov. 20, 1952; s. David and Bert Shane Rogal; m. Camille Elizabeth Rogal, Oct. 18, 1981; children: David, Jennifer, Sarah. BA, George Washington U., 1974, MD, 1978. Diplomate Am. Bd. Internal Medicine, Am. Bd. Cardiovasc. Disease. Resident in internal medicine L.I. Jewish-Hillside Med. Ctr., 1978-81; resident in cardiology U. Rochester-Strong Meml. Hosp., 1981-84; asst. prof. medicine Albany Med. Coll., NY, 1984-86; chief cardiology St. Barnabas Med. Ctr., Livingston, NJ, 1998—, dir. cardial rehab.; pvt. practice gen. and invasive cardiology, spl. interest complementary medicine and cardiology, 1986—. Fellow Am. Coll. Cardiology; mem. Am. Heart Assn. (bd. dirs.), Hertiage Affiliation (bd. dirs.), Phi Beta Kappa Avocations: photography, skiing, resistance/aerobic training. Office: Diagnostic & Clinical Cardiology 375 Mount Pleasant Ave West Orange NJ 07052-2724 Office Phone: 973-731-9442. E-mail: grogal@sbhcs.com.

ROGALSKI, CAROL JEAN, clinical psychologist, educator; b. Chgo., Sept. 25, 1937; d. Casimir Joseph and Lillian Valentine Rogalski. BS, Loyola U., Chgo., 1961; PhD, NYU, 1968; cert. in psychoanalysis, Postgrad. Ctr. Mental Health, 1973. Lic. clin. psychologist, N.Y., Ill. Rsch. assoc. William Alanson White Inst., NYC, 1961-66; rsch. asst., intern Hillside Hosp., Glen Oaks, N.Y., 1966-68; cons. Mt. Sinai Hosp., NYC, 1968-73; staff psychologist Jesse Brown VA Hosp., Chgo., 1974—; clin. asst. prof. psychiatry Med. Sch. U. Ill., 1996—. Instr. technique and history of illuminated manuscripts Morton Arboretum, Lisle, Ill. Mem. editorial bd. Internat. Jour. Addictions, 1994-98; contbr. articles to profl. publs. Mem.: Guild of Natural Sci. Illustrators, Nature Artists' Guild, Chgo. Soc. for Psychotherapy Rsch. (chair 1988—91), Communal Studies Assn., Parker Libr., Corpus Christi Coll. Cambridge, Eng. Avocations: watercolors, illuminated manuscripts. Office: Jesse Brown VA Hosp 820 S Damen Ave Chicago IL 60612-3728 Office Phone: 312-569-7490.

ROGALSKI, LOIS ANN, speech and language pathologist; b. Bklyn. d. Louis J. and Filomena Evelyn (Maro) Giordano; m. Stephen James Rogalski, Jun e 27, 1970; children: Keri Anne, Stefan Louis, Christopher James, Rebecca Blair, Gregory Alexander. BA, Bklyn. Coll., 1968; MA, U. Mass., 1969; PhD., NYU, 1975. Lic. speech and lang. pathologist, N.Y.; cert. Nat. Acad. Sports Medicine; cert Powerhouse Pilates; cert. for yoga, profl. trainer Yogafit, Nat. Acad. Sports Medicine, yoga instr., pilates fitness instr., 2003-, cert. silver sneakers instr., 2005-; cert. 500 hr. yoga instr., Westchester Inst. Yoga, zumba fitness instr. Speech, lang. and voice pathologist Rehab. Ctr. of So. Fairfield County, Stamford, Conn., 1969, Sch. Health Program-P.A. 481, Stamford, 1969-72, pvt. practice speech, lang. and voice pathology Scarsdale, NY, 1972—. Cons. Bd. Coop. Ednl. Svcs., 1976-79, Handicapped Program for Preschoolers for Alcott Montessori Sch., Ardsley, N.Y., 1978—; rsch. methodologist Burke Rehab. Ctr., 1977. Mem. profl. adv. bd. Found. for Children with Learning Disabilities, 1978—; bd. dirs. United Way of Scarsdale-Edgemont, 1988-89; instr. religious instr. CCD Immaculate Heart of Mary Ch., Scarsdale, 1991—; bd. dirs. Scarsdale Teen Ctr., Inc., 1998—. Fellow Rehab. Svcs. Adminstrn., 1968-69; N.Y. Med. Coll., 1972-75. Mem. N.Y. Speech & Hearing Assn., Westchester Speech & Hearing Assn., Am. Speech, Hearing & Lang. Assn. (cert. clin. competence), Coun. for Exceptional Children, Assn. on Mental Deficiency, Am. Acad. Pvt. Practice in Speech Pathology & Audiology (bd. dirs., treas. 1983-87, pres. 1987-89), Internat. Assn. Logopedics & Phoniatrics, Sigma Alpha Eta. Avocations: yoga, pilates. Office Phone: 914-723-6721.

ROGAN, ELEANOR GRONIGER, oncologist, educator; b. Nov. 25, 1942; d. Louis Martin and Esther (Levinson) G.; m. William John Robert Rogan, June 12, 1965 (div. 1970); 1 child, Elizabeth Rebecca. AB, Mt. Holyoke Coll., 1963; PhD, Johns Hopkins U., 1968. Lectr. Goucher Coll., Towson, Md., 1968-69; rsch. assoc. U. Tenn., Knoxville, 1969-73, U. Nebr. Med. Ctr., Omaha, 1973-76, asst. prof., 1976-80, assoc. prof. Eppley Inst., dept. pharm. scis., 1980-90, prof. dept. pharm. scis. and dept. biochem. & molecular biol, 1990—2007, chair, dept. environ. agrl. and occupl. health, 2007—. Contbr. articles to profl. jours. Predoctoral fellow USPHS, Johns Hopkins U., 1965-68; recipient Linus Pauling Functional Medicine award, 2006, UNMC Disting. Scientist award, 2007. Mem. AAAS, Am. Assn. Cancer Rsch., Soc. Toxicology. Democrat. Roman Catholic. Home: 8210 Bowie Dr Omaha NE 68114-1526 Office: U Nebr Med Ctr Eppley Inst 986805 Nebr Med Ctr Omaha NE 68198-6805 Home Phone: 402-397-7342; Office Phone: 402-559-4095. Business E-Mail: egrogan@unmc.edu.

ROGATZ, PETER, retired physician; b. NYC, Aug. 5, 1926; s. Julian and Sally (Levy) Rogatz; m. Marjorie Plaut, June 10, 1949; children: Peggy Joy, William Peter. BA, Columbia Coll., 1945; MD, Cornell U., 1949; M.P.H., Columbia U., 1956. Cert. Am. Bd. Preventive Medicine 1958. Intern Lenox Hill Hosp., NYC, 1949-50, resident, 1950-51, VA Hosp., Bronx, NY, 1951-52, N.Y. Hosp., NYC, 1952-53; dep. dir. Montefiore Hosp., NYC, 1960-63; dir. L.I. Jewish Med. Center, 1964-68, Univ. Hosp., SUNY, Stony Brook, 1968-71; sr. v.p. Blue Cross/Blue Shield of Greater N.Y., 1971-76; prin., founding ptnr. RMR Health and Hosp. Mgmt. Cons., Inc., Roslyn Heights, NY, 1976-84; v.p. med. affairs Vis. Nurse Service, NY, 1984-91; med. dir. Staff Builders, Inc., 1992-98. Prof. cmty. medicine SUNY, Stony Brook, 1968—94; mem. N.Y.C. Mayor's Commn. on Delivery of Health Svcs., 1967; v.p. Health and Welfare Coun. of Nassau County, 1968—72; bd. dirs. Cmty. Coun. Greater N.Y., 1974—77; mem. Task Force on N.Y.C. Crisis, 1976—81; chmn. bd. dirs. Cmty. Health Program affiliated with L.I. Jewish Med. Ctr., 1989—94; chmn. bd. dirs. Managed Health Inc., 1990—94. Author: Organized Home Medical Care in New York City, 1956; co-author (with Eli Ginzberg): Planning for Better Hospital Care, 1961; mem. edit. bd. Preventive Medicine, 1975—81; contbr. articles to profl. jours. Bd. dirs. Choice in Dying, 1994—2000, Compassion and Choices of N.Y., 1998—. Recipient Dean Conley award, Am. Coll. Hosp. Adminstrs., 1975; fellow, Commonwealth Fund, 1955. Fellow: ACP, Am. Coll. Preventive Medicine, N.Y. Acad. Medicine, APHA; mem.: N.Y. County Med. Soc., N.Y. State Med. Soc., N.Y. Pub. Health Assn., Am. Hosp. Assn., AMA. Home and Office: 299 E Overlook Port Washington NY 11050 Home Phone: 516-767-0189; Office Phone: 516-767-0189. Personal E-mail: rogatz2@aol.com.

ROGERS, DONALD ROBERT, retired pathologist; b. Tacoma, Apr. 7, 1932; s. John Robert and Thelma Ethel (Neely) Rogers; m. Georgia Lee Miller, June 9, 1956; children: Steven, Julie. BS, U. Puget Sound, 1954; MD, U. Wash., 1958. Diplomate Am. Bd. Pathology. Intern Mpls. Gen. Hosp., 1958-59; resident U. Wash., Seattle, 1963-66; pathologist Alaska Regional Hosp., Anchorage, 1967-94; ret., 1994. Med. examiner State of Alaska, 1967—94; cons. forensic pathology. Contbr. articles to profl. jours. Nat. del. dir. Am. Cancer Soc., Alaska, 1983—84, bd. dirs. Alaska, 1967—94. Lt. comdr. USN, 1959—62. Fellow: Coll. Am. Pathologists; mem.: ACS (mem. Anchorage unit 1967—94), Nat. Assn. Med. Examiners, Anchorage Med. Soc. (pres. 1972), Ala. State Med. Assn. (pres. 1989—91), Rotary. Republican. Home and Office: 921 Old Klatt Rd Anchorage AK 99515-3254

ROGERS, ELIZABETH LONDON, retired geriatrics services professional; BA, Mt. Holyoke Coll., St. Hadley, Mass., 1967; MD, Jefferson Med. Sch., Phila., 1971. Lic. internal medicine, gastroenterology, and geriatrics Am. Bd. of Internal Medicine. Chief of staff Balt. VA Med. Ctr., 1982—93; prof. dept. of medicine U. of Md. Med. Sch., Baltimore, 1990—93; assoc. dean for clin. medicine Duke U. Med. Sch., Durham, NC, 1993—96; acting chief of staff VA Healthcare Sys., New Haven, 1996—2002; chief ambulatory and primary care Yale New Haven VA Med. Ctr., 1996—2002; ret., 2002. Pres. Bradmer Biotech, Miami, 2002—05; dir. Cardiome Pharma, Vancouver, B.C., Canada, 2003—04; assoc. prof. med. sch. Yale U., 1996—2002. Chmn., pres. London Charitable Found., Miami, Fla. Recipient Geriat. scholarship, Hartford Found., 1984—85. Fellow: ACP.

ROGERS, FRED BAKER, medical educator; b. Hamilton, NJ, Aug. 25, 1926; s. Lawrence H. and Eliza C. (Thropp) R. AA, Princeton U., 1947; MD, Temple U., 1948; MS in Medicine, U. Pa., 1954; MPH, Columbia U., 1957; spl. student, Johns Hopkins U., 1962. Diplomate: Am. Bd. Preventive Medicine. Intern Temple U. Hosp., Phila., 1948-49, chief resident physician, 1953-54; USPHS fellow Temple U. Sch. Medicine, 1954-55, asst. prof. preventive medicine, 1956-58, assoc. prof., 1958-60, prof., 1960-90, prof. emeritus, 1991—, chmn. dept., 1970-77. Lectr. epidemiology Columbia U. Sch. Pub. Health, 1957-68, Sch. Nursing, U. Pa., 1964-67; cons. USN Hosp., Phila., 1964-73 Author: A Syllabus of Medical History, 1958, Help-Bringers: Versatile Physicians of N.J, 1960, Epidemiology and Communicable Disease Control, 1963, Studies in Epidemiology, 1965, (with A.R. Sayre) The Healing Art, 1966, (with M.E. Cashel) Your Body is Wonderfully Made, 1974; mem. editorial bd. Am. Jour. Pub. Health, 1967-73; contbr. articles to profl. jours. With M.C. USNR, 1950-53, Korea, capt. (ret.) USNR. Recipient Chapel of Four Chaplains award, 1982. Fellow ACP; mem. AMA (past chmn. sect. preventive medicine), Am. Pub. Health Assn., Royal Soc. Medicine of London (hon.), Sigma Xi, Alpha Omega Alpha, Phi Rho Sigma. Clubs: Campus (Princeton); Franklin Inn (Phila.); Charaka (N.Y.C.); Osler (London). Home: 333 W State St Apt 6K Trenton NJ 08618-5722 Office: Temple U Sch Med Philadelphia PA 19140

ROGERS, JAMES N., anesthesiologist, educator; MD, U. Ariz., 1987. Diplomate Am. bd. Anesthesiology, 1993, Am. bd. Anesthesiology-pain medicine, 1994. Intern Tucson Med. Ctr., 1988; resident Bexar County Hosp., 1991, fellow, 1992; attending physician Audie L. Murphy Veterans Hosp., 1991—, chief anesthesia svcs, 2009—; attending physician faculty Univ. Hosp., San Antonio, 1991—; active med. staff dept. of anesthesiology St. Luke's Baptist Hosp., Houston, 1995—; assoc. prof. orthopaedics Univ. Tex. Health Sci. Ctr., San Antonio, 1995—, assoc. prof. anesthesiology, 2000—, dir. of residency program, 2009—. Office: University Hospital 4502 Medical Drive San Antonio TX 78229-4493 Office Phone: 210-358-4000. E-mail: rogersjn@uthscsa.edu.

ROGERS, LEE FRANK, radiologist; b. Colchester, Vt., Sept. 24, 1934; s. Watson Frank and Marguerite Mortimer (Cole) R.; m. Donna Mae Brinker, June 20, 1956; children: Michelle, Cynthia, Christopher, Matthew. BS, Northwestern U., 1956, MD, 1959. Commd. 2d lt. U.S. Army, 1959, advanced through grades to maj., 1967; rotating intern Walter Reed Gen. Hosp., 1959-60; resident radiology Fitzsimons Gen. Hosp., 1960-63; ret., 1967; radiologist Bapt. Meml. Hosp., San Antonio, 1967-68, U. Tex. Med. Sch., San Antonio, 1968-71, dir. residency tng., radiologist Houston, 1972-74; prof., chmn. dept. radiology Northwestern U. Med. Sch., Chgo., 1974-95; editor-in-chief Am. Jour. Roentgenology, Winston-Salem, NC, 1995—2003; prof. radiology U. Ariz. Health Scis. Ctr., 2003—. Fellow Am. Coll. Radiology (past pres.), Am. Roentgen Ray Soc. (past pres.); mem. Assn. Univ. Radiologists (past pres.), Radiol. Soc. N.Am., Am. Bd. Radiology (past pres.), Alpha Omega Alpha. Episcopalian. Home: 8235 N Fairway View Dr Tucson AZ 85742 Home Phone: 520-544-0807, Office Phone: 520-626-6794. Personal E-mail: lfrogers@comcast.net.

ROGERS, MEGAN ELIZABETH, clinical psychologist; b. Bradford, Pa. d. James Russell and Martha Ann (Spencer) R.; m. Thomas J. Sarac, Oct. 17, 1992; children: Isaac W. Sarac, Rhianna A. Sarac. BA in Psychology with deptl. honors., Coll. of Wooster, 1985; MA in Psychology, U. Chgo., 1991; D in Clin. Psychology, Minn. Sch. Profl. Psychology, 2001. Lic. clin. psychologist. Social worker Selfhelp Cmty. Svcs., NYC, 1985-87; tchg. asst. U. Chgo., 1988-89; rsch. asst. U. Chgo. Hosp., 1988-90, mental health therapist Counseling and Personal Devel., Phillips, Wis., 1991-94; intern in clin. psychology Battle Creek VA Med. Ctr., 1998-99; prof. psychology Inver Hills C.C., Minn., 2001—02, Centery C. C., Minn., 2002—07; clin. psychologist So. Ctrl. Human Rels. Ctr., Owatonna, Minn., 2008—. Contbr. articles to profl. jours. Coord. soup and bread program, Wooster, 1982-85. U. Chgo. fellow, 1989. Mem. APA, Phi Beta Kappa. Democrat. Presbyterian. Home: 438 Cherry St Owatonna MN 55060 Home Phone: 507-446-1214; Office Phone: 507-413-0582. Personal E-mail: doctormeganrogers@gmail.com.

ROGERS, MICHAEL BRUCE, orthodontist; b. Augusta, Ga., Oct. 25, 1945; s. Bruce Lattimer and Dorothy (Baird) R.; m. Elizabeth Bennett, Dec. 21, 1968; children: Bruce, Kay, Alison, Lisa. Student, Emory U., 1963-65, DDS, 1969; cert. in orthodontics, Med. Coll. Ga., 1973. Diplomate Am. Bd. Orthodontists, 1980. Pvt. practice orthodontics, Augusta, 1973—; orthodontic resident Ga. Health Scis. U. Asst. clin. prof. Sch. Dentistry, Med. Coll. Ga., Augusta, 1973—. Decorated Army Commendation medal; named John F. Mac Meritorous Svc. award, Emory Dental Alumni Assn., 2009. Fellow: Ga. Acad. Dental Practice, Internat. Coll. Dentists, Pierre Fauchard Acad., Am. Coll. Dentists, Ga. Dental Assn. (hon.; spkr. ho. of dels. 1999—2004, v.p. 2004—05, pres.-elect 2005—06, pres. 2006—07, gen. chn. 1993 ann. meeting); mem.: Augusta Dental Soc. (pres. 1985—86), Med. Coll. Ga. New Dental Sch. (mem. dental sch. steering. com.), Ea. Dist. Dental Soc. (pres. 1982—83), Med. Coll. Ga. Orthodontic Alumni Assn. (pres. 1981—83), Ga. Assn. Orthodontists (v.p. 1983—84, pres. 1984—85, Exemplary Svc. award 1991, 2006), So. Assn. Orthodontists (spokesperson, sec.-treas. 1993—95, dir. 1995—97, pres. 1999—2000, Disting. Svc. award 2002), Am. Assn. Orthodontists (Ga. del., chmn. mem., ethics and jud. concerns, spkr. of house 1995—97, trustee 2002—10, chmn. investment com. 2008—09, chmn. budget adv. com. 2008—09, mem. exec. com. 2008—11, sec., treas. 2009—10, pres. 2011—), ADA (del. 1992—99, 2003—06), Omicron Kappa Upsilon, Psi Omega (pres. 1967—68, Fraternal Achievement award 1969). Roman Catholic. Home: 3214 Candace Dr Augusta GA 30909-3259 Office: 3545 Wheeler Rd Augusta GA 30909-6517

ROGERS, MICHAEL E., exercise physiology educator, researcher; b. Seneca Falls, NY; s. Philip W. and Martha A. Rogers; m. Nicole L. Beardsley. BS in Sports Medicine, Mt. Union Coll., Alliance, Ohio, 1991; PhD, Kent State U., 1996. Cert. strength and conditioning specialist Nat. Strength and Conditioning Assn., 2000. Rsch. assoc. Brooks AFB, San Antonio, 1996—98; prof. Wichita (Kans.) State U., 1998—. Dir. Ctr. for Phys. Activity and Aging Wichita State U., 1999—, chair, dept. human performance studies. Contbr. articles to profl. jours. Mem.: Am. Coll. Sports Medicine (pres. regional chpt. 2002—03). Achievements include development of low cost, safe, and effective physical activity programs to improve strength and balance in older adults. Office: Wichita State Univ 106G Heskett Ctr Wichita KS 67260-0016 Office Phone: 316-978-5959. Business E-Mail: michael.rogers@wichita.edu.

ROGERS, NICOLA J., biochemist; b. Eng., Sept. 9, 1971; BSc in Chemistry, King's Coll. London, 1992, PhD in Microbiology, 1996. Rsch. scientist Unilever Rsch. Port Sunlight Labs., 1998—2000; sr.

rsch. scientist CSIRO Land and Water, 2001—. Mem.: Soc. Environ. Toxicology and Chemistry. Office: CSIRO Land and Water Lucas Heights Research Labs Lucas Heights NSW 2234 Australia Business E-Mail: nicola.rogers@csiro.au.

ROGERS, RITA DORIS LUCK, family nurse practitioner; b. Lincoln County, Kans., Feb. 6, 1948; d. Ernest F. and Rea N. (Nelson) Luck; m. Eugene W. Rogers, Mar. 15, 1969; children: R. Michelle, Sara J (dec.), Brandon G. Diploma, Wesley Sch. Nursing, 1969; BSN cum laude, Ft. Hays State U., 1992, MSN, 1996. RN, ARNP, Kans., Mo., Nebr.; cert. family nurse practitioner ANCC, AANP. Float, relief charge nurse Wesley Med. Ctr., Wichita, 1969-71; charge nurse Mitchell County Hosp., Beloit, Kans., 1971-72; dir. PHN III Jewell County Health Dept., Mankato, Kans., 1973-74; office nurse Dr. A.T. Llana, Superior, Nebr., 1975-76; head nurse, evening supr. Jewell County Hosp., 1977-97; family nurse practitioner Dr. Judith Butler, Superior, 1997—98; interim dir. nursing Sterling (Kans.) Presbyn. Manor, 1998-99, Kansas City Presbyn. Manor, 1999, Wichita Presbyn. Manor, 2004; nurse cons. Presbyn. Manors Mid-Am., Wichita, Kans., 1999—2003; interim nurse practitioner Statcare Minor Emergency Ctr., Salina, Kans., 2000; clin. edn. spec. Presbyn. Manors Mid-Am, Wichita, Kans., 2003—05; dir. health svcs. Asbury Park, Inc., Newton, 2005—08; family nurse practitioner Larned State Hosp., 2008—. Allied health adj. faculty Cloud C.C., Concordia, Kans., 1988-2000, Perkins grant coord. North Ctrl. Kans. Area Vo-Tech., Beloit, 1988; county chair Am. Cancer Soc., Mankato, 1972-74; sec. Jewell County Mental Health Assn., 1973-75; parliamentarian Dist. XII Kans. State Nurses Assn., Topeka, 1975-79; infection control com., med. staff mem. Brodstone Meml. Hosp., Superior, Nebr., 1997-98; mem. nursing standards com. and products specifications com. Prebyn. Manors of Mid-Am., 1998-2005, ind. contractor, Nation's Care Link, 2003-; cert. leader for Arthritis Found. Aquatics Program, 2004-06; mem., ethics com. & infection control com. med. staff Larned State Hosp. Columnist Rap with Rita, 1973-74. County and club leader 4-H, Jewell County, 1977-91, Mitchell County, 2000—; tchr. Sunday sch. Luth. Ch., Mankato, 1979-82. Scholar Kans. Health Found., 1993, Midwest Organ Bank, 1994, Ft. Hays State U., 1994, Dane G. Hansen Found., 1994, Kans. Nurses' Found. Wesley Alumni, 1995. Mem. Am. Acad. Nurse Practitioners, Sigma Theta Tau, Kans. Med. Soc. Avocations: gardening, crocheting, computers. Home: 309 N Columbus St Jewell KS 66949-9582 Office: 1301 ks HWY 264 Larned KS 67550 Home Fax: 785-428-7929. Business E-Mail: rita.rogers@lsh.ks.gov, rdrnp96@att.net.

ROGERS, ROBERT ERNEST, medical educator; s. Jessie H. and Willie L. (Bahr) Rogers; m. Barbara Ann Hill, May 16, 1950; children: Robert E., Jr., Stephanie Ann Thompson, Cheri Lee Heck. BS in Biology, John B. Stetson U., 1949; MD, U. Miami, 1957. Diplomate Am. Bd. Ob-Gyn. Commd. 1st lt. M.C., U.S. Army, 1952, advanced through grades to col., 1971—74; ret. U.S. Army, 1974; intern Brooke Gen. Hosp., San Antonio, 1957-58, chief resident ob-gyn, 1960-61; resident in ob-gyn Jackson Meml. Hosp., Miami, Fla., 1958-60; fellow gynecology M.D. Anderson Hosp., Houston, 1965-66; asst. chief ob-gyn Tripler Army Med. Ctr., Honolulu, 1966-69; chmn. ob-gyn Walter Reed Med. Ctr., Washington, 1969-70, Madigan Army Med. Ctr., Tacoma, 1970-74; prof. Ind. U. Sch. Medicine, Indpls., 1974—, also chief gynecol. div., 1974—; chief ob-gyn svd. Wishard Meml. Hosp., Indpls., 1983-87. Contbr. articles to profl. jours.; editl. bd. Jour. Am. Coll. Surgeons, 2003—. Bd. dirs. Lake Stonebridge Homeowner's Assn., 2000—03, sec., 2000—03. Recipient Army Commendation medal, 1969, Army Meritorious Service Medal, 1971, Army Legion of Merit, 1974, Army Surgeon General's "A" Prefix for Profl. Excellence, 1974. Mem.: ACS, ACOG (chmn. gynecol. practice com., commr. practice, Sci. Exhibit award Armed Forces dist. 1971, Zimmerman Cons. award Armed Forces dist.), AMA (Certificate Merit for Sci. Exhibit 1971), Felix Rutledge Soc. (pres. 1981, historian), Internat. Soc. Advancement Humanistic Studies Medicine (pres. 1997—98), Soc. Gynecol. Oncologists, Soc. Gynecol. Surgeons (pres. 1983—84). Avocations: gardening, photography. Office: Ind U Sch Medicine 550 University Blvd Indianapolis IN 46202-5149 Personal E-mail: boberogers@hotmail.com. Business E-Mail: reroger@iupui.edu.

ROGERS, ROY STEELE, III, dermatologist, educator, dean; b. Hillsboro, Ohio, Mar. 3, 1940; s. Roy S. Jr. and Anna Mary (Murray) R.; m. Susan Camille Hudson, Aug. 22, 1964; children: Roy Steele IV, Katherine Hudson. BA, Denison U., 1962; MD, Ohio State U., 1966; MS, U. Minn., 1974. Cert. dermatologist, dermatopathologist and immunodermatologist. Intern Strong Meml. Hosp., Rochester, NY, 1966—67; resident Duke U. Med. Ctr., Durham, NC, 1969—71, Mayo Clinic, Rochester, Minn., 1972—73, cons., 1973—, prof. dermatology, 1983—, dean Sch. Health Related Scis., 1991—99. Adv. coun. Rochester Community Coll., 1991-2000; citation of appreciation Internat. League Dermatologic Soc., 2007. Contbr. over 250 sci. articles to publs. Mem. Rochester Planning and Zoning Comm., 1980—88; bd. dir. Casabella Assn., 2006—08. Capt., flight surgeon USAF, 1967—69. Recipient Alumni Achievement award Ohio State U. Coll. Medicine, 1991, Alumni citation Denison U., 1993, Faculty Svc. award Mayo Med. Sch., 1993, Gold medal 2d Med. Sch., Charles U., Prague, 2002; named Disting. Educator, Mayo Clinic, 2004, Paul A. O'Leary Lectureship, 2005. Mem. Am. Acad. Dermatology (hon., bd. dirs. 1987-91, v.p. 1999, Everett C. Fox lectureship 2005, Gold Triangle award 2004, Thomas G. Pearson Meml. Edn. award 2004), Am. Soc. Dermatologic Allergy and Immunology (sec.-treas. 1988-2000), Am. Dermatologic Assn. (v.p. 2002-03), Soc. Investigative Dermatology, Assn. Schs. Allied Health Professions, Dermatology Found. (Annenberg Circle 2002, Lifetime Career Educator award, 2011), Brit. Soc. Oral Medicine. Avocations: travel, reading, walking. Office: Mayo Clinic 200 1st St SW Rochester MN 55905-0002 Home: 4555 E Mayo Blvd Apt 3417 Phoenix AZ 85050 Office Phone: 507-284-2555. Business E-Mail: rogers.roy@mayo.edu.

ROGERS, WILLIAM RAYMOND, retired academic administrator, psychologist, educator; b. Oswego, NY, June 20, 1932; s. William Raymond and A. Elizabeth (Hollis) R.; m. Beverley Claire Partington, Aug. 14, 1954; children: John Partington, Susan Elizabeth Apple, Nancy Claire Glassman. BA magna cum laude, Kalamazoo Coll., 1954; BD, U. Chgo. and Chgo. Theol. Sem., 1958; PhD, U. Chgo., 1965; MA (hon.), Harvard U., 1970. Cons., staff counselor Counseling and Psychotherapy Rsch. Ctr., U. Chgo., 1960-62; tchg. fellow, counselor to students Chgo. Theol. Sem., 1961-62; asst. prof. psychology and religion, dir. student counseling Earlham Coll., Richmond, Ind., 1962-68, assoc. prof. psychology and religion, assoc. dean of Coll., 1968-70; vis. lectr. pastoral counseling Harvard U. Div. Sch., Cambridge, Mass., 1969-70, prof. religion and psychology Div. and Edn. Schs., 1970-80, faculty chmn. clin. psychology and pub. practice, 1970-72, chmn. counseling and cons. psychology, 1979-80; prof. psychology and religious studies Guilford Coll., Greensboro, NC, 1980—, pres., 1980-96, pres. emeritus, 1996—. Bd. dirs. Moses Cone Health Sys., 1984-96, Moses Cone-Wesley Long Cmty. Health Found., 1996-2002, chmn. 1996-2002; bd. dirs. BB&T, Kendal Corp., chmn. 2005-09. Author: The Alienated Student, 1969, Project Listening, 1974, Nourishing the Humanistic in Medicine, 1979; Contbr. articles to profl. jours. Bd. dirs. Greensboro Symphony Soc.; mem. Cemala Found, Mary Reynolds Babcock Found. Danforth Found. fellow, Blatchford Traveling fellow U. Chgo. and Chgo. Theol. Sem. Mem.: Islesboro Hist. Soc. (pres. 1999—2002), So. Assn. Colls. and Schs., Nat. Assn. Ind. Colls. and Univs., Friends Com. on Nat. Legislation (mem. policy com.), Friends Assn. Higher Edn., Soc. Values in Higher Edn., Tarratine Club of Dark Harbor (bd. govs.), Rotary (past pres.). Mem. Soc. Of Friends. Home: 4212 B Trillium Ln Greensboro NC 27410-8871

ROGGERO, MARIA PIA, psychologist, director; b. Milan, Jan. 16, 1949; Degree in Psychology, 1975; PhD, Italian Soc. Relational Psychoanalysis, 1985. Prof., bd. dirs. Italian Soc. Relational Psychoanalysis, 1990—2011, v.p., 2006—08, co-dir., 2008—. Mem.: IFPS, IARPP. Avocations: music, mountain climbing. Office: Via De Amicis 48 Milan 20123 Italy Office Fax: 3902861938. E-mail: mproggero@tiscalinet.it.

ROGHANI, ALI, neuroscientist, educator; b. Esfahan, Iran, 1956; BA, U. Kans., Lawrence, 1979; PhD, U. Ill., Urbana, 1986. Rsch. staff assoc. UCLA, 1990—95; assoc. prof. pharmacology and neuroscience Tex. Tech U. Health Scis. Ctr., 1995—. Adj. assoc. prof. Tex. Tech U. Inst. Environ. and Human Health, 2003—. Mem.: NY Acad. Scis., Am. Physiol. Soc., Am. Soc. Pharmacology and Exptl. Therapeutics, Am. Soc. Biochmistry and Molecular Biology, Soc. Neurosci., Phi Beta Upsilon, Phi Beta Kappa. Avocations: reading, sports. Office: 3601 4th St Lubbock TX 79430 Office Phone: 806-743-2425 ext 258. Business E-Mail: ali.roghani@ttuhsc.edu.

ROGIDO, MARTA RAQUEL, medical educator; b. Villa Elisa, Entre Rios, Argentina, Aug. 13, 1957; d. Juan Rogido and Irma Dora Joannaz; MD, U. Buenos Aires, 1981. Lic. in pediatrics Am. Bd. Pediat., 1998, in neonatal perinatal medicine Am. Bd. Pediat., 1999. Pediat. resident Hosp. Ninos, Buenos Aires, 1982—85; neonatal fellowship, 1985—87; asst. prof. pediat. U. Buenos Aires, 1987—91; clin. instr. pediat. U. Calif., San Francisco, 1995—97, asst. prof. pediat., 1999—2001, Emory U., Atlanta, 2001—05, assoc. prof. pediat., 2005—06; assoc. prof. neurology U. Medicine and Dentistry NJ, Newark, 2006—. Nat. dir. resuscitation program Argentinian Acad. Pediat., Buenos Aires, 1990—91. Grantee Rsch. grant, William Tooley Meml. Fund, 1993, Wyeth Pediatric Rsch. Fund, 1994, Emory Egleston Children's Rsch. Ctr., 2002—03, United Cerebral Palsy Found., 2004—06. Fellow: Am. Acad. Pediat.; mem.: SIBEN Neonatal Ibero-Am. Soc., European Soc. Pediatric Rsch., Soc. Pediatric Rsch. Office: Morristown Meml Hosp 100 Madison Ave Morristown NJ 07960 Office Fax: 973-290-7175. Business E-Mail: marta.rogido@atlantichealth.org.

ROGOFF, JEROME HOWARD, psychiatrist, psychoanalyst, forensic expert; b. Detroit, Dec. 21, 1938; s. Abraham Solomon and Sarah Riva (Epstein) R.; (div. 1983); m. Erika Kathleen Keller, Sept. 25, 1983. BA cum laude, Harvard Coll., Cambridge, Mass., 1960; MD, Case Western Res. U., Cleve., 1965. Diplomate Am. Bd. Psychiatry and Neurology. Physician Peace Corps USPHS, Kathmandu, Nepal, 1966-68; clin. fellow psychiatry Harvard Med. Sch., Boston, 1975-79; staff psychiatrist Westwood (Mass.) Lodge Hosp., 1972-74; assoc. clin. prof. psychiatry Tufts Med. Sch., Boston, 1977-86; assoc. chief, psychiatry and dir., inpatient Psychiatry, day hosp. Faulkner Hosp., Boston, 1975-94; pvt. practice psychiatry, psychoanalysis and forensic psychiatry, 1994—. Cons. psychiatrist Mass. Parole Bd. Probate Ct. Plymouth County, Mass., LEAA, Washington, 1971-78; med. psychiat. dir. ct. diversion program Boston TASC-A, 1974-75; treas. Guild for Continuing Edn., Boston, 1981-95; founding dir. Law and Psychiatry Resource Ctr., Boston, 1983-2005; adj. prof. Simmons Sch. Social Work, Boston, 1981-85; lectr. psychiatry Harvard Med. Sch., Boston, 1986-94, 2001-. Chmn. psychiatry team Combined Jewish Philanthropies, Boston, 1978—83, assoc. chmn. med. team, 1984—87, social planning and allocations com., 1991—98, cmty. svcs. com., 1998—2007, chmn. chronic mental illness com., 1999—2000, disabilities com., 2000—04; bd. dirs. Jewish Vocat. Svc., Boston, 1987—91. Fellow: Am. Psychiat. Assn. (life; Disting., pub. affairs rep. 1988—94, budget com. 1996—2002, assembly rep. 2000—07, chmn. corr. com. on confidentiality 2003—07, task force to revise code of ethics 2005—, area dep. rep. 2007—09, mem. assembly exec. com. 2007—, area rep. 2009—); mem.: APA, AMA, Am. Assn. Pvt. Practice Psychiatrists, Am. Acad. Psychiatry and Law, Mass. Psychiat. Soc. (chair pub. affairs com. 1988—92, councillor 1988—94, chair nominating com. 1990, chair pub. affairs com. 1993—94, pres.-elect 1998—99, pres. 1999—2000, chair nominating com. 2000, Mass. rep. to Assembly 2000—07). Democrat. Avocations: cabinetry, carpentry, cooking, classical music, languages. Home and Office: 659 Chestnut St Waban MA 02468-2035 Office Phone: 617-964-1805.

ROGOL, ALAN DAVID, pediatric endocrinologist; b. New Haven, Mar. 9, 1941; s. Oscar and Bess (Halperin) R.; m. Joanne Schoderbek, Nov. 2,1968; children: Ian, Babette. BS, MIT, 1963; PhD, MD, Duke U., 1970. Diplomate Am. Bd. Pediat., 1975, pediat. sub-bd. endocrinology. Prof. U. Va., Charlottesville, 1975—, prof. clin. pediatrics, 2002—; clin. prof. internal medicine Med. Coll. Va., Richmond; pres. ODR Consulting, Charlottesville, Va., 2002—. Prin. clin. scientist INSMED Pharmaceuticals, Inc., 1999—2001. Lt. comdr. USPHS, 1972-74. Fellow Am. Coll. Sports Medicine, Am. Acad. Pediats.; mem. Lawson Wilkins Pediatric Endocrine Soc. (sec. 2004—), Endocrine Soc., Am. Pediat. Soc. Office: U Va Health Sys Dept Pediat PO Box 800386 Charlottesville VA 22908-0386 Business E-Mail: arogol@estone.net. E-mail: adr@virginia.edu.

ROH, JONG YUL, research scientist; b. Seoul, Republic of Korea, Dec. 7, 1972; PhD, Seoul Nat. U., 2003. Postdoc. fellow Seoul Nat. U., 2003—04, Ohio State U., 2004—06, Seoul Nat. U., 2006—10; staff scientist Korea Ctrs. Disease Control & Prevention, 2010—. Mem.: Entomol. Soc. Korea, Korean Soc. Applied Entomology. Office: 187 Osongsaengmyeong2-ro Gangoe-myeon Cheongwon-gun Chungbuk 363-951 Republic of Korea Office Fax: 82-43-719-8589.

ROH, MEE SOOK, medical educator, pathologist; b. Daegu, Republic of Korea, July 23, 1966; d. Sang-Yoon Roh and Myung-Soon Lee. PhD, Dong-A U., Busan, Republic of Korea, 1997. Cert. Korea Bd. Anatomical Pathology Korean Soc. of Pathologists. Intern Dong-A U. Med. Ctr., Busan, 1991—92, resident dept. pathology, 1992—96, fellow dept. pathology, 1998—2001; chief dept. pathology Moon Hwa Hosp., Busan, 1997—98; lectr. Dong-A U. Coll. of Medicine, Busan, 2001—03, asst. prof., 2003—07, assoc. prof., 2007—. Vis. doctor Dept. Pathology Baylor Coll. Medicine, Houston, 1996; vis. scholar Coll. Medicine Kyoto U., 2003; vis. scholar Meml. Sloan Kettering Cancer Ctr., 2006—07. Contbr. articles to profl. jours. Grantee, Korea Rsch. Found., 2001, Korea Sci. and Engring. Found., 2004, 2005, 2006, 2007, 2008, 2009—10, 2010—11. Mem.: Pulmonary Pathology Soc., Korean Soc. Cytopathology, Korean Med. Assn., Internat. Acad. Pathology, Korean Assn. Study of Lung Cancer, Korean Soc. Pathologists. Home: GS XIT APT 305-1104 Yongho-dong Nam-gu Busan 608-790 Republic of Korea Office: Dong-A U Coll Medicine 1-3 ga Dongdaeshin-dong Seo-gu Pusan 602-714 Republic of Korea Office Fax: 82-51-243-7396. Business E-Mail: msroh@dau.ac.kr.

ROH, MICHAEL HOWARD, medical educator; b. Republic of Korea, Nov. 27, 1976; MD, U. Mich. Med. Sch., PhD, 2005. Asst. prof. U. Mich. Med. Sch., 2009—. Avocation: piano. Office: University Mich Dept Pathology Ann Arbor MI 48109-5054 Personal E-mail: michaelhroh@gmail.com.

ROH, YOUNG JUNG, ophthalmologist; b. Seoul, Mar. 7, 1970; MD, Cath. U. Korea, 1995. Asst. prof. St. Mary's Hosp., 2003—. Mem.: Am. Soc. Retina Specialist. Office: #62 Yoido-Dong Youngdeungpo-Gu Seoul 150-713 Republic of Korea Office Phone: 82-2-37791848. Business E-Mail: youngjungroh@hanmail.net. E-mail: himeridian@yahoo.co.kr.

ROHACK, JOHN JAMES, cardiologist; b. Rochester, NY, Aug. 22, 1954; s. John Joseph and Margaret Elizabeth (McLaughlin) R.; m. Charlotte (Charli)McCown, Dec. 7, 1980; 1 child, Elisha Monique Feigle. BS with highest honors, U. Tex., El Paso, 1976; MD with honors, U. Tex. Med. Branch, Galveston, 1980. Diplomate Am. Bd. Internal Medicine. Intern U. Tex. Med. Br. Hosps., Galveston, 1980—81, resident internal medicine, 1981-83, chief resident internal medicine, 1983-84, fellow cardiology, 1984-86; instr. medicine U. Tex. Med. Br., Galveston, 1983-86; asst. prof. medicine to assoc. prof. Tex. A&M Coll. Medicine, College Station, 1986—2002, prof., 2002—, sect. chief cardiology, 1989-97, prof., 2002—. Assoc. med. dir. Scott and White Health Plan Bryan Coll. Sta., 1995-97; assoc. med. dir. for med. ops. Scott and White Clinic, Temple, Tex., 1997-2000, med. dir. Health Plan, 2000-04, med. dir. sys. improvement, 2004-, dir. healthcare policy, 2004-, sr. staff cardiologist; bd. dirs. Health for All Clinic, v.p., 1994-96; mem. Accreditation Coun. on Continuing Med. Edn., 1995-99, Liaison Com. on Med. Edn., 1999-2001; med. dir. Fitlife Ctr. Tex. A&M U., College Station, 1990-97; mem. bd. commrs. Joint Commn. on Accreditation of Healthcare Orgns., 2002—2008. Bd. dirs. Am. Heart Assn., Brazos Valley College Station, 1987-97, Tex. affiliate Austin, 1991-98, 1st v.p., 1994-95, pres.-elect, 1995-96, pres., 1996-97. Named Disting. Alumnus, U. Tex., El Paso, U. Tex., Galveston; named one of 50 Most Powerful Physician Executives in Healthcare, Modern Healthcare and Modern Physician, 2009. Fellow ACP, Am. Coll. Cardiology (bd. dirs. Tex. chpt. 1992-97); mem. AMA (alt. del. house of dels. 1984-93, del. 1993-2001, coun. on med. edn. 1995-2001, chair elect 1996-97, chair 1997-98, bd. trustee 2001-11, pres.-elect 2008-, exec. com. 2003-06, chair 2004-05, pres.-elect 2008-2009, pres. 2009-10, immediate past. pres., 2010-11), Tex. Med. Assn. (exec. coun. med. student sect. 1981-82, chair, coun. on med. edn., house of dels. 1982—, trustee 1994-2002, pres.-elect 1999-2000, pres. 2000-2001). Avocations: golf, gardening, reading, ranching. Office: Scott and White Clinic 2401 S 31st St Temple TX 76508-0001 *

ROHAN, THOMAS E., epidemiologist, educator; MD, U. Adelaide, Australia, 1975, PhD in Epidemiology, 1986; M.Sc in Epidemiology, U. London, 1981, M.Sc. in Med. Statistics, 1996. Intern Broken Hill Hosp., Australia, 1976—77; resident Flinders Med. Ctr., Australia, 1977; rsch. fellow U. Melbourne, 1979—80, CSIRO Divsn. Human Nutrition, 1981—86; sr. lectr. dept. environ. & preventive medicine St. Bartholomew's Hosp., 1986—87; epidemiologist MRC Epidemiology & Med. Care Unit, London, 1987—88; asst. prof. dept. preventive medicine & biostatistics U. Toronto, 1989—90, assoc. prof. dept. preventive medicine & biostatistics, 1990—97, dir. NCIC Epidemiology Unit, 1995—96, prof. dept. pub. health sciences, 1997—2000; adj. prof. dept. oncology McGill U., 1996—; prof. & chmn. dept. epidemiology & population health Albert Einstein Coll. Medicine, 2000—, assoc. dir. population rsch., 2000—. Recipient Terry Fox Cancer Rsch. Scientist award, Nat. Cancer Inst. Canada, 1996. Fellow: Australasian Faculty of Pub. Health Medicine, Am. Coll. Epidemiology, Royal Australian Coll. General Practitioners; mem.: Am. Assn. Cancer Rsch., Soc. Epidemiologic Rsch. Office: Albert Einstein College of Medicine Belfer Bldg Rm 1301 1300 Morris Park Ave Bronx NY 10461 Office Phone: 718-430-3355. Office Fax: 718-430-8653. E-mail: rohan@aecom.yu.edu.

ROHATGI, SHASHANK, pharmaceutical executive, researcher; s. Sher and Prabha Singh; m. Prapti Rohatgi, Apr. 30, 1997; 1 child, Shlok. B in Pharmacy, Birla Inst. Tech., Pilani, Rajasthan, India, 1991; PhD, U. Fla., 1995; MBA, St Joseph's U., Phila., 2000. Sr. pharmacokineticist Somerset Pharms., Tampa, Fla., 1995—96; disting. scientist Aventis, Bridgewater, NJ, 1996—. Adj. faculty U. Fla., Gainesville, 2002—03. Fellow, Am. Coll. Clin. Pharmacology. Achievements include research in PK/PD of inhaled Drugs. Office:

Aventis 1041 Rt 202-206N Bridgewater NJ 08807 Home: 399 Thornall St Ste 11 Edison NJ 08837-2240

ROHDE, RODNEY E., medical educator; b. Smithville, Tex., June 29, 1967; BS, Tex. State U., 1990, MS, 1992, PhD, 2010. Pub. health microbiologist, molecular epidemiologist Tex. Dept. State Health Svcs. Bur. Labs., 1992—2002; assoc. prof., assoc. rsch. dean Tex. State U., 2002—. Healthcare adv. bd. mem., healthcare acquired infections Johnson & Johnson ASP, 2010. Recipient Presdl. award, Tex. State U. Coll. Health Professions, Charles C. Shepard Sci. Assessment and Epidemiology award, CDC. Mem.: Am. Soc. Virology, Pan Am. Soc. Clin. Virology, Tex. Soc. CLS, Am. Soc. Clin. Pathology, Am. Soc. Clin. Lab. Sci. (Key to Future award, Sci. Rsch. award), Omicron Sigma. Avocations: reading, sports. Office: 601 University Dr HPB 361 San Marcos TX 78666 Business E-Mail: rrohde@txstate.edu.

ROHLF, F. JAMES, biologist, educator; b. Blythe, Calif., Oct. 24, 1936; BS, San Diego State Coll., 1958; PhD in Entomology, U. Kans., 1962. Asst. prof. biology U. Calif., Santa Barbara, 1962-65; assoc. prof. statis. biology U. Kans., 1965-69; assoc. prof. biology SUNY, Stony Brook, 1969-72, prof., 1972—2004, chmn. dept. ecology and evolution, 1975—80, 1990—91, disting. prof., 2004—10, grad. program dir., 2005—06, John S. Tall prof., 2011—. Statis. cons. NY Pub. Svc. Commn., 1975-78, IBM, 1977-81, US EPA, 1978-80, TMT, 2006-; vis. scientist IBM, Yorktown Heights, NY, 1976-77, 80-81; vis. prof. U. Rome, 1997, 99; guest prof. U. Vienna, 2004. Recipient Hamilton award, NIOSH, 2010. Fellow: Am. Acad. Arts and Scis., AAAS; mem.: Internat. Fedn. Classification Socs. (coun. 2005—07), Classification Soc. N.Am. (pres. 1975—78, editl. bd. 1984—, bd. dirs. 1994—97, fin. com. 2004—06, rep. to coun. 2004—07, election com. 2006—07, bd. dirs. 2006—), Soc. Systematic Biologists, Biometric Soc. Achievements include research and development of statistical methods and software for geometric morphometrics and applications of multivariate analysis to systematics and population biology. Office: Stony Brook U Dept Ecology And Evolution Stony Brook NY 11794-5245

ROHN, REUBEN DAVID, medical educator, director; arrived in US, 1947, naturalized, 1954; s. Aryeh and Rachel (Brenner) R.; m. Judith Semel, Sept. 6, 1971; 1 child, Karen. BA cum laude, Bklyn. Coll., 1967; MD, N.Y. Med. Coll., 1971. Diplomate Am. Bd. Pediat., Am. Bd. Pediatric Endocrinology, Am. Bd. Pediatrics-Adolescent Medicine, 2009. Intern in pediat. Montefiore Hosp., Bronx, N.Y., 1971-72, resident in pediat., 1972-74; fellow in adolescent medicine U. Md. Hosp., Balt., 1974-76; preceptor in pediat. Johns Hopkins U. Sch. Health Svcs., Balt., 1975-76; asst. prof. dept. pediat. Ea. Va. Med. Sch., Norfolk, 1976-82; coord. pediat. clerkship Ea. Va. Med. Sch., Children's Hosp. of King's Daus., Norfolk, 1977-90; prof. dept. pediat. Ea. Va. Med. Sch., Norfolk, 1989—; adj. prof. chemistry Old Dominion U., Norfolk, 1984—; dir. adolescent medicine, endocrinology Children's Hosp. of King's Daus., Norfolk, 1976—2008, dir. endocrinology, 2008—. Mem. curriculum com. Ea. Va. Med. Sch., 1977-79, clerkship coords. com. 1977-90, genetics com., 1978-80, evaluation com. 1979-91, chmn. selectives com., 1981-82, ad hoc com. on consultation, 1982-83, student progress com., 1983-85, student health com., 1985-87, LCME com. on curriculum, 1990-92; mem. child abuse com. mem. promotions com, 2009-2010, Children's Hosp. of King's Daus., 1976-80, chmn. adolescent adv. com., 1976-80, patient care com. 1980-94, nutrition com. 1980-94, utilization rev. com., 1980-82, med. records com., 1987-89, gen. med./surg. task force com., 1987-88, chmn. dept. promotions com., 1990—; bd. dirs. Pediat. Faculty Assocs., 1994-98, mgmt. com. Children's Specialty Group, 1998-2000; spkr. in field. Reviewer Jour. Adolescent Health Care, 1986—, mem. editl. bd., 1989-92; contbr. articles to profl. jours. Mem. Norfolk Sch. Health Coun., 1977—93, mem. ad hoc com. infant screening program for hypothroidism Commonwealth of Va., 1977-79, cons., 1979—; mem. cmty. adv. bd. Norfolk Adolescent Pregnancy Prevention Svc. Project, 1981-83; bd. dirs. Elizabeth River chpt. Am. Diabetes Assn., 1982-85, South Hampton Roads chpt. 1985-93; mem. adv. com. Norfolk-Virginia Beach Jr. League, 1987-88; judge ann. Health Edn. Fair, Norfolk Pub. schs., 1980-94; pres. VA/Carolines chpt. Soc. Adolescent Medicine, 1998-2000. Recipient grant Bressler Rsch. Fund, 1975-76, Biomed. Rsch. Devel. grant Ea. Va. Med. Sch., 1978, 78-79, 79-80. 81-82, 83-84, Children's Health Found. grant, 1988-89. Fellow: Am. Acad. Pediat. (youth and adolescence com. Va. chpt. 1978—2000); mem.: Am. Diabetes Assn., Lawson Wilkins Pediat. Endocrine Soc., Soc. Adolescent Medicine (abstract reviewer 1984—91), Sigma Xi. Avocations: photography, folk dancing, astronomy. Office: Childrens Hosp Kings Daus 601 Childrens Ln Norfolk VA 23507-1910 Office Phone: 757-668-7237. Business E-Mail: rohnrd@chkd.org.

ROHNER, THOMAS JOHN, JR., urologist; b. Trenton, NJ, Jan. 1, 1936; s. Thomas J. and Julia (Kanyo) R.; m. Jessie Rohner; children: Christopher, James. BA, Yale U., 1957; MD, U. Pa., 1961. Diplomate Am. Bd. Urology. Intern Hosp. U. Pa., Phila., 1961-62, resident in gen. surgery, 1962-64, resident in urology, 1964-67; asst. prof. surgery M.S. Hersey Med. Ctr., Pa. State U., Hershey, 1970-71, assoc. prof., 1971-75, prof., 1975—2007, emeritus prof., 2007—, chief urol. divsn. Hershey, 1970-2000; assoc. dean for clin. affairs M.S. Hershey Med. Ctr., Pa. State U., Hershey, 1996-99, interim chair dept. surgery, 1998-99, chief of med. staff, 1999-2000. Corp. mem. Pa. Blue Shield, 1991—; bd. dirs. Highmark, Inc., 2003-08, bd. dirs. Highmark Medicare Svc., 2008- Contbr. articles to profl. jours. Served to maj. M.C., U.S. Army, 1967-69. USPHS fellow, 1969-70; grantee HEW, 1971-76, USPHS, 1971-76 Fellow ACS (pres. ctrl. Pa. chpt. 1983-84, bd. govs. 1991-97); mem. Am. Urol. Assn. (pres. mid-Atlantic sect. 1986-87, bd. dirs. 2006-), Urol. Assn. Pa., Phila. Urol. Soc. (pres. 1980-81), Assn. Acad. Surgeons, Am. Bd. Urology (trustee 1995-2001), Pa. Med. Soc., Dauphin County Med. Soc., Soc. Pediat. Urology, Soc. Univ. Urologists (pres. 1990-91), Nat. Urol. Assn. (bd. dirs. 2006), Societe Internationale d'Urologie, Transamerican Urol. Rschrs. Home: 2907 Mt Gretna Rd Elizabethtown PA 17022-9689 Home Phone: 717-367-0404. Business E-Mail: trohner@psu.edu.

ROHR, ALBERT SCHUMM, allergist, immunologist; MD, U. Tex., 1977. Diplomate Am. Bd. Internal Medicine, 1980, Am. Bd. Allergy and Immunology, 1983. Intern Presbyn. Hosp.-Univ. Pa., resident; fellow Univ. Calif., LA, clin. assoc. prof.; clin. asst. prof. Univ. Pa.; pvt. practice Rohr and Columbo Asthma Allergy and Immunology Specialists, 1983—; hosp. affiliations include Bryn Mawr Hosp., 1991—, Paoli Hosp., 1992—, Lankenau Med. Ctr., 2006—. Named one of Top Doc, Phila. Mag., 2004, 2005. Fellow: Am. Coll. of Chest Physicians. Office: Rohr and Columbo Asthma Allergy and Immunology Specialists Ste 101 209 W Lancaster Ave Paoli PA 19301 also: Bryn Mawr Hospital Ste 107 875 County Line Rd Bryn Mawr PA 19010 Office Phone: 610-527-2000. Office Fax: 610-525-6772.

ROHREN, BRENDA MARIE ANDERSON, therapist, educator; b. Kansas City, Mo., Apr. 18, 1959; d. Wilbur Dean and Katheryn Elizabeth (Albright) Anderson; m. Lathan Edward Rohren, May 10, 1985; 1 child, Amanda Jessica. BS in Psychology, Colo. State U., 1983; MA in Psychology, Cath. U. Am., 1986; M in Forensic Scis., Nebraska Wesleyan U., 2007. Lic. mental health practitioner, independent mental health practitioner, alcohol/drug counselor 2009, master addiction counselor 2009, CARF Surveyor 2009. Mental health therapist, sr. case mgr. Rappahannock Area Community Svcs. Bd., Fredericksburg, Va., 1986-88, mental health therapist, case mgmt. supr., 1988; rsch. assoc. Inst. Medicine, NAS, Washington, 1988-89; supr. adult psychiat. program Lincoln (Nebr.) Gen. Hosp., 1989, program supr. mental health svcs., 1989-91; adj. instr. S.E. Community Coll., Lincoln, 1990—2008; assessment and referral specialist Rivendell Psychiat. Ctr., Seward, Nebr., 1993-95; therapist Lincoln Day Treatment Ctr., Lincoln, Nebr., 1993-95; mental health, substance abuse therapist Cmty. Mental Health Ctr., Lincoln, 2004—; pres. Behavioral Health Resources LLC, 2011—. Adj. instr. Coll. of St. Mary, 1994—2001; therapist Rape/Spouse Abuse Crisis Ctr., Lincoln, 1996—2002; substance abuse counselor Independence Ctr., Lincoln, 2002—08; computer cons. Syscon Corp., Washington, 1983—84; domestic abuse therapist Bryan LGH Med. Ctr., Lincoln, Nebr., 2004—07; asst. coord. Lancaster County Behavioral Health Coalition, 2005—06. Author: (report) Bottom Line Benefits: Building Economic Success Through Stronger Families; editor: (newsletter) Alliance for Mentally Ill, Lincoln, 1993-2002. Active Nat. Alliance for the Mentally Ill-Lincoln, Nebr. Domestic Violence/Sexual Assault Coalition; asst. coord. Lancaster County Behavioral Health Coalition, 2005-06. Mem. APA (assoc.), ACA, Nat. Assn. Alcohol and Drug Abuse Counselors, Nebr. Psychol. Assn. (assoc.), Nebr. Counseling Assn., EMDRIA. Democrat. Roman Catholic. Avocations: interior decorating, reading, landscaping, camping. Home: 3821 S 33rd St Lincoln NE 68506-3806 Office: Cmty Mental Health Ctr 2201 S 17th St Lincoln NE 68502 Office Phone: 402-441-6619. Personal E-mail: brenda@neb.rr.com.

ROHRER, HEINRICH, physicist; b. Buchs, Switzerland, June 6, 1933; m. Rose-Marie Egger, 1961; children: Doris, Ellen. Diploma in Physics, Swiss Fed. Inst. Tech. (ETH), Zurich, 1955, PhD in Physics, 1960; DSc (hon.), Rutgers U., NJ, 1987, Marseilles U., France, 1988, Madrid U., 1988, Tsukuba U., Japan, 1994, Frankfurt U., Germany, 1996, Tohoku U., Japan, 2000. Rsch. asst. Swiss Fed. Inst. Tech., 1960-61; postdoc. rschr. Rutgers U., New Brunswick, NJ, 1961-63; staff Zurich Rsch. Lab. IBM, Switzerland, 1963-97, mgr. phys. scis. dept., 1986—88, ret., 1997; rschr. Materials Sci. Inst. Madrid(CSIC), 1997-2000, RIKEN, Waco, Japan, 1998, Tohoku U., Sendai, Japan, 1998—99. Rschr. rschr. Materials Sci. Inst. (CSIC) Madrid, 1997—2000, RIKEN Corp., Japan, 1998—2000; vis. scholar U. Calif., Santa Barbara. Recipient King Faisal Internat. prize for sci., 1984, Hewlett Packard Europhysics prize, 1984, Nobel prize for physics, 1986, Cresson medal, Franklin Inst., Phila., 1987; named to Nat. Inventors Hall of Fame, 1994; IBM fellow, 1986. Fellow: Royal Microscopical Soc. (hon.); mem.: NAS (fgn. hon.), Swiss Acad. Tech. Scis., Zurich Phys. Soc. (hon.), Swiss Assn. Engring. & Architecture (hon.), Swiss Phys. Soc. (hon.). Achievements include invention of the first scanning tunneling microscope (STM) that allowed for the first images of individual atoms on the surface of materials. E-mail: h.rohrer@gmx.net.

ROHRICH, ROD(NEY) JAMES, plastic surgeon, educator; b. Eureka, SD, Aug. 5, 1953; s. Claude and Katie (Schumacher) R.; m. Diane Louise Gibby, July 3, 1990; children: Taylor Rodney, Rachel Nicole. BA summa cum laude, ND State U., 1975; MD with honors, Baylor Coll., 1979; LittD (hon.), U. ND, 2006. Diplomate Am. Bd. Plastic Surgery, Nat. Bd. Med. Examiners. Instr. surgery Harvard Med. Sch. Mass. Gen. Hosp., Boston, 1985-86; asst. prof. U. Tex. Southwestern Med. Ctr., Dallas, 1986-89, assoc. prof., 1989-91, prof., chmn. dept. plastic surgery, 1991—, Betty and Warren Woodward chair in plastic surgery, 1999; chief plastic surgery Parkland/Zale Univ. Med. Ctr., Dallas, 1989-99. Pres., faculty senate U. Tex., crystal charity ball disting. chair in plastic surgery. Mem. editl. bd. Selected Readings in Plastic Surgery, The Cleft Palate and Craniofacial Jour.; editor Plastic and Reconstructive Surgery, 2005—; contbr. articles to med. jours. Bd. dirs. Save-the-Children Found., Dallas, March of Dimes, Dallas, Dallas for Children; class mem. Leadership Dallas, 1989-90; mem. Adopt-A-Sch., Dallas Summer Mus. Guild, Dallas Mus. Art, Dallas Symphony Assn., Tex. Health Found., Youth Leadership Dallas. Grantee Urban Rsch. Fund, 1982, United Kingdom Ltd. Ednl. Rsch. Fund, 1983, Oxford Cleft Palate Found., 1983, Am. Assn. Plastic Surgeons, 1985, Plastic Surgery Ednl. Found., 1985, 89, 90, U. Tex. Health Sci. Ctr. Dept. Surgery, 1986, Howmedica, 1989, ConvaTec-Squibb, 1989, 91, ConvaTec, 1991; recipient Disting Svc. award Plastic Surg. Ednl. Found., 1997, Alumni Achievement award, N.D. State U., 1997. Mem. AAAS, AMA (Thomas Cronin award 1988, 90, Clifford C. Snyder award 1990), fellow, ACS, Am. Assn. Hand Surgery, Am. Burn Assn., Am. Cleft Palate Assn., Am. Soc. Law and Medicine, Am. Soc. Maxillofacial Surgeons, Am. Soc. for Surgery the Hand, Am. Soc. Plastic and Reconstructive Surgeons, Am. Trauma Soc., British Med. Assn., Nat. Vascular Malformations Found. Inc. (med. and sci. adv. bd.) Tex. Med. Assn., Tex. Soc. Plastic Surgeons, Mass. Gen. Hosp. Hand Club, Dallas County Med. Soc., Assn. Acad. Chmn. Plastic Surgery (pres.), Dallas Soc. Plastic Surgeons, Harvard Med. Sch. Alumni Assn., Inst. for Study of Profl. Risk, Plastic Surgery Rsch. Coun., Reed O. Dingman Soc. Plastic Surgeons, So. Med. Assn., Am. Soc. Plastic Surgeons (pres. 2004), Assn. Academic Chairmen Plastic Surgery (pres. 2008). Republican. Roman Catholic. Office: UT Southwestern Med Ctr Dept Plastic Surgery 5323 Harry Hines Blvd Dallas TX 75390-9132 Office Phone: 214-645-3119. Business E-Mail: rod.rohrich@utsouthwestern.edu.

ROIZEN, MICHAEL FREDRIC, anesthesiologist, medical educator, writer; b. NY, Jan. 7, 1946; m. Nancy J. Roizen; children: Jeffery, Jennifer. AB in Chemistry, with honors, Williams Coll., Williamstown, Mass., 1967; MD, U. Calif. Sch. Medicine, San Francisco, 1971. Diplomate Am. Bd. Internal Medicine, Am. Bd. Anesthesiology. Intern internal medicine Beth Israel Hosp., Boston, 1971—72, resident anesthesia, 1972—73; pharmacology rsch. assoc. NIH, Bethesda, Md., 1973-75; resident anesthesia U. Calif., San Francisco, 1975—77, asst. prof., 1977-81, assoc. prof., 1981-85; prof. internal medicine U. Chgo., 1985—2001, prof. & chair dept. anesthesia and critical care, 1985—2001; prof. anesthesiology, v.p. biomed. scis. & dean SUNY Upstate Med. U., Syracuse; CEO Biotechnology Rsch. Corp. Ctrl. NY; chief wellness officer, chmn. divsn. anesthesiology, critical care medicine & comprehensive pain mgmt. Cleve. Clinic, 2005—, chief wellness officer, chair Wellness Inst., 2007—. Co-founder, chair RealAge, Inc., 1998, mem. sci. adv. bd.; panel mem., past chair adv. com. FDA. Author: Essence of Anesthesia Practice, 1997, RealAge: Are You As Young as You Can Be?, 1999 (Books for Better Life awards Best Wellness Book, 1999, #1 NY Times bestseller), The RealAge Makeover: Take Years off Your Looks and Add Them to Your Life, 2004; co-author (with John La Puma): The RealAge Diet: Make Yourself Younger With What You Eat, 2002 (NY Times bestseller), Cooking the RealAge Way: Turn Back Your Biological Clock with More than 80 Delicious and Easy Recipes, 2003; co-author: (with Tracy Hafen) The RealAge Workout: Maximum Health, Minimum Work, 2006; co-author: (with Mehmet Oz) YOU: The Owner's Manual: An Insider's Guide to the Body that Will Make You Healthier and Younger, 2005 (#1 NY Times bestseller), YOU: On A Diet: The Owner's Manual for Waist Management, 2006 (#1 NY Times bestseller), YOU: The Smart Patient: An Insider's Handbook for Getting the Best Treatment, 2006 (NY Times bestseller), YOU: Staying Young: The Owner's Manual for Extending Your Warranty, 2007 (#1 NY Times bestseller), YOU: Being Beautiful: The Owner's Manual to Inner and Outer Beauty, 2008, That Will Make You Healthier and Younger (revised and expanded edition), 2008, YOU: Having a Baby: The Owner's Manual to a Happy and Healthy Pregnancy, 2009, YOU: On a Diet- The Owner's Manual for Waist Management (revised0, 2009, YOU: The Owner's Manual for Teens-A Guide to a Healthy Body and Happy Life, 2011; author: (compact disc) YOU: On a Walk, 2007, YOU: Breathing Easy: Meditation and Breathing Techniques to Help You Relax, Refresh and Revitalize, 2008; contbr. numerous articles to profl. peer-reviewed jours., chapters to books; columnist Reader's Digest, Every Woman mag., host (terrestrial radio show) YOU The Owner's Manual Radio Show, TV appearances include Oprah Winfrey Show, Today, 20/20, CNN, CBS, Good Morning America, Montel Williams Show, Larry King Live, others. Mem.: Soc. Cardiovasc. Anesthesiologists (pres. 1995—97), Am. Soc. Anesthesiologists, Phi Beta Kappa, Am. Bd. Internal Medicine (assoc.), Am. Bd. Anesthesiology (assoc.), Alpha Omega Alpha. Achievements include 13 US and many fgn. patents. Avocation: squash. Office: Cleve Clinic Main Campus Mail Code TR2 01 9500 Euclid Ave Cleveland OH 44195 also: RealAge Inc 5375 Mira Sorrento Pl Ste 250 San Diego CA 92121 also: RealAge Inc 555 Fifth Ave 14th Fl New York NY 10017 Office Phone: 216-444-2595. *

ROIZMAN, BERNARD, virologist, educator; b. Chisinau, Rumania, Apr. 17, 1929; arrived in US, 1947, naturalized, 1954, s. Abram and Liudmilla (Seinberg) Roizman; m. Betty Cohen, Aug. 26, 1950; children: Arthur, Niels. BA, Temple U., Phila., 1952, MS, 1954; ScD in Microbiology, Johns Hopkins U., Balt., 1956; DHL (hon.), Gov.'s State U., 1984, MD (hon.), U. Ferrara, Italy, 1991; DSc (hon.), U. Paris, 1997, U. Valladolid, Spain, 2001. From instr. microbiology to asst. prof. Johns Hopkins Med. Sch., 1956—65; from mem. faculty Divsn. Biol. Scis. to prof. U. Chgo., 1965—69, prof., 1969—, chmn. dept. molecular genetics and cell biology, 1985—88, Joseph Regenstein Disting. Svc. prof., 1984—. Co-founder Aviron, Inc., 1992; convener herpes virus workshop, Cold Spring Harbor, NY, 72; lectr. Am. Found. for Microbiology, 1974—75; mem. spl. virus cancer program devel. rsch. working group Nat. Cancer Inst., 1967—71; mem. steering com. human cell biology program NSF, 1971—74; mem. adv. com. cell biology and virology Am. Cancer Soc., 1970—74; chmn. herpes virus study group Internat. Commn. Taxonomy of Viruses, 1971—73; mem. Internat. Microbiol. Genetics Commn. Internat. Assn. Microbiol. Scis., 1974—81; mem. sci. adv. coun. NY Cancer Inst., 1971—88; mem. adv. bd. Leukemia Rsch. Found., 1972—77; mem. herpes-virus working team WHO/FDA, 1978—81; mem. bd. sci. cons. Sloan Kettering Inst., NYC, 1975—81; mem. study sect. exptl. virology NIH, 1976—80; mem. task force on virology Nat. Inst. Allergy and Infectious Disease, 1976—77; mem. com. to establish vaccine priorities Nat. Inst. Medicine, 1983—85; chmn. sci. adv. bd. Tampa Bay Rsch. Inst., 1983—, chmn. bd. trustees, 1991—97; mem recombinant adv. com. NIH, 2008—; cons. in field. Editor: (book) Herpes Viruses, Vol. 1, 1982, Herpes Viruses, Vol. 2, 1983, Herpes Viruses, Vols. 3 and 4, 1985, The Human Herpesviruses, 1993, Infectious Diseases in an Age of Change, 1995; editor-in-chief: Jour. Infectious Agts. and Disease, 1992—96, mem. editl. bd.: Infectious Diseases, 1965—69, Jour. Virology, 1970—, Jour. Intervirology, 1972—85, Archives of Virology, 1975—81, Virology, 1976—78, Microbiologica, 1978—, Cell, 1979—80, Virology, 1983—, Jour. Hygiene, 1985—91, Gene Therapy, 1994, Wiley Encyclopedia of Molecular Medicine, 2002; contbr. scientific papers, chapters to books. Trustee Goodwin Inst. Cancer Rsch., 1977—2004. Recipient Lederle Med. Faculty award, 1960—61, Career Devel. award, USPHS, 1963—65, Pasteur award, Ill. Soc. Microbiology, 1972, Esther Langer award for Achievement in Cancer Rsch., 1974, Outstanding Alumnus in Pub. Health award, Johns Hopkins U., 1984, ICN Internat. prize in Virology, 1988, J. Allyn Taylor Internat. prize in Medicine, 1997, Bristol-Myers Squibb award for Disting. Infectious Disease Rsch., 1998, Abbott-ASM lifetime achievement award, 2008; named hon. prof., Shandong Acad. Med. Scis., China, 1985; grantee Facutly Rsch. Assoc., Am. Cancer Soc., 1966—71, USPHS/NIH, 1958—, Am. Cancer Soc., 1962—90, NSF, 1962—79; fellow Travelling, Internat. Agy. Rsch. Against Cancer, Karolinska Inst., Stockholm, 1970; scholar Am. Cancer Soc., Pasteur Inst. Paris, 1961—62. Fellow: AAAS, Japanese Soc. for Promotion of Sci., Am. Acad. Arts and Scis.; mem.: NAS, Inst. Medicine, Johns Hopkins U. Soc. Scholars, Chinese Acad. Engring. (fgn.), Hungarian Acad. Scis. (fgn.), Brit. Soc. Gen. Microbiology, Hong Kong Biotech. Assn. (hon.), Am. Soc. Molecular Biology and Biochemistry, Am. Soc. Virology, Am.

Soc. Microbiology, Am. Assn. Immunologists, Am. Acad. Microbiology, Inst. Medicine, Quadrangle Club (Chgo.). Home: 5555 S Everett Ave Chicago IL 60637-1968 Office Phone: 773-702-1898. Business E-Mail: bernard.roizman@bsd.uchicago.edu.

ROJANAPITHAYAKORN, WIWAT, biomedical researcher; b. Chonburi, Thailand, Oct. 25, 1950; s. Sia Cheng Bae and Sew Hiang Tae; m. Pachira Thitivora, May 2, 1980; children: Nonthida, Pachara, Naruepon. MD, Mahidol U., 1976, MPH, 1983. Cert. in preventive medicine Thai Med. Coun., 1984, in field epidemiology Ministry Pub. Health, 1982. Intern Ramathibodi Hosp., Mahidol U., Bangkok, 1976—77; dir. AIDS programme Ministry Pub. Health, 1987—89, dir. regional office of communicable disease control Ratchaburi, Thailand, 1989—92, sr. expert Bangkok, 1992—99; team leader UNAIDS Asia Pacific Intercountry Team, Bangkok, 1999—2001; med. officer WHO Mongolia, Ulaanbaatar, Mongolia, 2002—04; HIIV/AIDS team leader WHO China, Beijing, 2005—08; WHO rep. Mongolia, 2009—. Prof. Health Sci. U., Mongolia, 2004. Editor over 10 public health jours.; contbr. over 100 articles to profl. jours. Recipient Prince Mahidol award, 2009. Mem.: The Thai Med. Soc. Study Sexually Transmitted Infections (assoc.; pres. 1998—2000). Achievements include development of the 100% condom use program which has been recognized as one of the most successful HIV/AIDS prevention measures. Home: Apartment 2703 MegaHall He Yuan Street Beijing Chaoyang district 100028 China Office: WHO Mongolia 3rd Fl Ministry Health Building Olympic St Ulaanbaatar 13 Mongolia Home: Apt 7 Building 417 Chingeltei Distict Ulaanbaatar Mongolia Office Fax: 97611324683. Personal E-mail: wiwatroj@yahoo.com. Business E-Mail: wiwatr@wpro.who.int.

ROJAS, JIMENA, ophthalmologist; b. Argentina, Feb. 21, 1973; MD, U. de Buenos Aires, 1997; PhD, U. de Valladolid, 2008. Surgeon trainee Italian Hosp., Buenos Aires, 1998—99; ophthalmologist trainee Hosp. Durand, Buenos Aires, 1999—2004; ophthalmologist, retinologist Inst. Applied Ophthalmobiology, 2005—. Ad-honorem prof. U. de Buenos Aires, 1995—98; fellow retina U. de Valladolid, 2004—05, assoc. prof., 2009—. Mem.: Spanish Vitreo-Retinal Soc. Office: Calle de Belen 17 Valladolid 47011 Spain E-mail: rojasjimena@yahoo.com.

ROJAS-REYNA, GUILLERMO ALFONSO, general and vascular surgeon, medical educator; b. Mex. City, Mex., June 26, 1954; s. Guillermo Alfonso Rojas and Concepcion Reyna; m. Georgina Echeverria, Aug. 5, 2000; children: Alejandra Rojas, Guillermo Rojas, Marcus Rojas. BSc, Colegio Columbia, 1973; MD, Universidad Nacional Autonoma de Mexico, 1979, diploma in adminstrn. and fin. direction of hosps., 2004. Diplomate Am. Bd. Surgery, Am. Bd. Med. Quality Assurance. Gen. surgeon Washington (DC) Hosp. Ctr., 1979—85; vascular surgeon Newark Beth Israel Med. Ctr., 1985—87; chief vascular surgery ABC Med. Ctr., Inst. de Asistencia Privada, Mexico City, 1988—; prof. surgery Faculty Medicine, Universidad Nacional Autonoma de Mexico, 1996—; chief surgery ABC Med. Ctr. Recipient Ernest Alva Gould MD Surg. Ho. Officer award, Washington Hosp. Ctr., 1985, Nat. award, Mex. Soc. Angiology, 1986, Amistad award, Soc. Mil. Vascular Surgeons, Washington, 1992, Altruism award, Consejo de Vocales de La Junta de Asistencia Privada Para el D.F., Mexico City, 1998. Fellow: ACS; mem.: Mex. Acad. Surgery. Home: Ave Desierto de los Leones 1323-5 01700 Mexico City Mexico Office: ABC Med Ctr IAP Sur 136 # 210-508 1120 Mexico City Mexico Home Phone: 5255 5585 1254; Office Phone: 5255 5272 3410. Office Fax: 5255 5516 9970. Personal E-mail: mdrrojas@hotmail.com.

ROKER, CHRISTOPHER A., microbiologist, photographer; arrived in US, 1986; s. John A. T. and LueElla Roker; m. Elizabeth Moxey, Apr. 14, 1984; children: Krislar, Kwame, Kofi. BS in Med. Tech., LI U., 1996, post graduate, 2003—; student, NY Inst. Photography, 1975—78; student in Commercial Photography, Germain Sch. Photography, 1980—82. Cert. clin. lab. scientist Nat. Certify Agy. Lab. Profls. Profl. photographer, studio owner Esquire Photography Studio, Nassau, The Bahamas, 1983—88; photographic retoucher Color Wheel Inc., NYC, 1986—95; microbiologist Shield Med. Lab., Bklyn., 1995—99, Sherman-Abrams Med. Lab, Bklyn., 1999—2006, Analytical Diagnostic Labs Inc., Bklyn., 1999—. Photographer (exhibitions), NYC, Nassau, Bahamas, Down by the Sea, Body Works, New York After Dark. Mem.: Am. Soc. Clin. Lab. Sci., Am. Soc. Microbiology (mem. sub-com. 2002—). Avocations: sports, poetry, writing, jazz. Office: Analytical Diagnostic Labs Inc 2115 Ave X Brooklyn NY 11235 Home and Studio: 6119 Braidwood Lane NW Acworth GA 30101 Office Phone: 718-646-6000. Office Fax: 718-646-0820. Business E-Mail: carokers@msn.com.

ROKEY, ROXANN, cardiologist; b. Concordia, Kans., Feb. 21, 1953; d. Ned W. and Lou (Stine) Rokey; m. Loren A. Rolak, 1977; children: Kelley, Stacey. BA, Ariz. State U., 1975; MD, U. Ariz., 1978. Diplomate Am. Bd. Internal Medicine, Am. Bd. Cardiovascular Disease. Intern Baylor Coll. Medicine, Houston, 1978-79, resident, 1979-81, fellow in cardiology, 1981-84, instr. medicine, 1984-85, asst. prof. medicine, 1985-92, asst. prof. pediatrics, 1987-92, assoc. prof. medicine, 1992-94; staff cardiologist Marshfield (Wis.) Clinic, 1994—. Dir. noninvasive cardiology lab. Ben Taub Gen. Hosp., Houston, 1984-92, dir. high risk obstetrical cardiology clinic, 1984-94; dir. clin. cardiac NMR imaging The Meth. Hosp., Houston, 1984-94; dir. adult congenital heart disease clinic Tex. Children's Hosp., Houston, 1992-94. Co-editor: Coronary and Cerebrovascular Disease, 1990; contbr. articles to profl. jours. Mem. Women's Heart Inst., Am. Heart Assn., Houston, 1993-94, mem. editl. bd., 1990-94, mem. advanced imaging coun., Dallas, 1993—. NIH grantee, 1987-93. Fellow ACP, Am. Coll. Cardiology, Am. Coll. Chest Physicians; mem. AMA, Mortar Bd., Phi Beta Kappa. Achievements include research in integrated computerized catheterization lab database and report generator, integrated computerized echocardiography lab database and report generator, time-varying filter electrocardiography gating device to reduce NMR induced gradient artifacts. Office: Marshfield Clinic 1000 N Oak Ave Marshfield WI 54449-5702

ROKKAS, THEODORE, gastroenterologist; b. Trikala, Thessaly, Greece, May 15, 1953; s. Apostolos and Adroniki Rokkas; m. Christine Kingsbury, Apr. 28, 1984; children: Constantine-Robert, Nicki. MD, Med. Sch. Aristotelian U., Thessalinoki, Greece, 1977. Head, gastroenterology dept. Henry Dunant Hosp., Athens, Greece, 2000—. Fellow: European Bd. Gastroenterology, Am. Gastroent. Assn., Am. Coll. Gastroenterology. Achievements include research in intestinal adaptation after enterectomy; significance of helicobacter pylori in upper GI pathology. Office: Henry Dunant Hosp 107 Messogion Ave Athens 11526 Greece

ROKOSZ, GREGORY JOSEPH, emergency medicine physician, lawyer, educator; b. Passaic, NJ, Mar. 27, 1955; s. Ferdinand and Stella D. (Wirkowski) R.; m. Christine M. Muller, Oct. 1, 1983; 1 child, Stefanie Lee. BA in Biol. Scis. with honors, Rutgers U., 1977; DO, Des Moines U., 1980; JD magna cum laude, Seton Hall U., 1999. Diplomate Am. Bd. Osteo. Emergency Medicine, Am. Osteo. Bd. Family Physicians. Intern Met. Hosp., Phila., 1980-81; resident in family practice Union (N.J.) Hosp., 1981-82, emergency dept. physician, 1982-94, 98, dir. med. edn., 1993-2001, v.p. med. affairs, 1994-2000, sr. v.p. med. and acad. affairs, 2001—; v.p. med. edn. St. Barnabas Health Care Sys., 2000—; dir. transitional yr. residency program St. Barnabas Med. Ctr., 2000—02; med. dir. N.J. Paramedic Registry Exam., 1990-94; mobile ICU insp. N.J. Dept. Health, Office EMS, Newark, 1990-94; med. dir. St. Barnabas Outpatient Ctrs., 2003—; assoc. dean Mt. Sinai Sch. Medicine for St. Barnabas Health Care Sys., 2003—08, U. Medicine and Dentistry NJ-NJ Med. Sch., 2008—, assoc. clin. prof. emergency medicine, 2008—. Mem. N.J. Bd. Med. Examiners, Trenton, 1994—2005, v.p., 1997—99, pres., 1999—2001; clin. instr. dept. emergency medicine U. Medicine and Dentistry Sch. Osteo. Medicine, Stratford, 1992—93, asst. clin. prof., 1993—94; asst. prof. emergency medicine N.Y. Coll. Osteo. Medicine/N.Y. Inst. Tech., Old Westbury, 1994—96, assoc. prof., 1996—, clin. asst. dean, 1997—; assoc. prof. dept. emergency medicine St. George's U. Sch. Medicine, 2001—08; dir. emergency medicine residency program Newark (N.J.) Beth Israel Med. Ctr., 1998—99; expert witness in emergency medicine; vice-chmn. N.Y. Coll. Osteo. Medicine Ednl. Consortium, 1999—; mem. accreditation rev. com. Accreditation Coun. Continuing Med. Edn., 2000—05, chair, 2004—05; mem. Physician Exec. Constituency Group N.J. Hosp. Assn., 2001—, chair Physician Exec. Constituency Group, 2003—. Contbg. author Continuous Quality Improvement for Emergency Departments, 1994, mem. Seton Hall Law Rev., 1997—99. Fellow Am. Coll. Emergency Physicians, Am. Coll. Osteo. Emergency Physicians; mem. ABA, Am. Osteo. Assn., Am. Coll. Osteo. Family Physicians, Assn. Osteo. Dirs. and Med. Educators, Am. Coll. Physician Execs., Assn. for Hosp. Med. Edn., Grad. Med. Edn. Coun. N.J. (mem. adv. bd. 1997-2005). Republican. Roman Catholic. Avocations: skiing, sports, cultural events, music. Home: 8 Wildlife Run Boonton NJ 07005-9043 Office: St Barnabas Med Ctr 95 Old Short Hills Rd Livingston NJ 07039 Office Phone: 973-322-5733. Personal E-mail: grokosz@sbhcs.com.

ROKYTA, RICHARD, physiologist, physician, educator; b. Užhorod, Czech Republic, Jan. 19, 1938; s. Richard and Ružena (Laštuvková) R.; m. Věra Vinklářová, July 8, 1961; children: Richard, Pavel. MD, Charles U., Plzeň, Czech Republic, 1961, CSc, 1969, DrSc, DSc, 1991. Sr. lectr. dept. pathophysiology med. faculty Charles U., Plzeň, 1961-82, asst. prof. dept. physiology/pathophysiology Prague, 1982-91, prof., 1991—, vice dean 3rd med. faculty, 1990-97. Editor, author: Lecture Notes on Physiology and Pathophysiology, 1969, 81, 87, 93, 95, 96; translator textbook: Memorix, 1993, Textbook of Physiology, 1995, 2005, Douleur (Pain), Somatology I, II, 2002, 2006, Pathophysiology, 2003, Structure and Function of the Human Body, 2002, Pain, 2006; contbr. over 430 articles to profl. jours., chpts. to books. Decorated knight Acad. Palmes French Govt.; recipient Gold medal City of Grenoble, 1988, Bronze and Gold medal of 3d Med. Faculty, Charles U., 1988-98, The Prize of Paul Janssen Found., 2003, 2005; recipient Gold medal, Charles U., Prague, 2008, Gold medal, Inst. Exptl. Medicine Acad. Scis., 2008; Gold Purkyne medal, Czech Med. Soc., 2008. Fellow Physiol. Soc. UK; mem. Czech Physiol. Soc. (v.p. 1982—), The Physiological Soc., NY Acad. Sci., Internat. Union Physiological Scis., Internat. Brain Rsch. Orgn., Fed. European Physiological Socs., Collegium Internat. Activitatis Nervosae Superioris, Czech Med. Ass. (hon.), Czech Physiol. Soc. (hon.), Soc. de Physiologie, France (sec.), Football Club Slavia (pres. 1961—), Tennis Sport Club Slavia (pres. 1971-75), Czech Med. Soc. (hon., Laufberger medal 1993), Soc. Physiologie (sci. sec. 1980—). Avocations: football, tennis, skiing, literature. Home: Polní 50 307 07 Plzeň Czech Republic Office: 3d Med Fac Dept Physiology Ke Karlovu 4 120 00 Prague 2 Czech Republic Office Phone: 420 224 923 824. Fax: 420 224923827. Business E-Mail: richard.rokyta@lf3.cuni.cz.

ROLAND, J. THOMAS, surgeon, researcher; b. Lancaster, Pa., May 14, 1957; s. John and Geraldine Roland; m. Betsy Pfeffer, June 15, 1985; children: Jillian, Allison, Stephen. MD, Temple U. Sch. Medicine, Phila., 1983. Cert. Am. Bd. Otolaryngology, 1993. Assoc. prof. NYU Sch. Medicine, 2003—, prof. otolaryngology and neurosurgery, dir. otology, neurotology, 2004—, co-dir. cochlear implant ctr., chmn. otolaryngology, 2010. Editor: (text book) Cochlear Implants. Lt cmdr USPHS, 1986—88, Fort Yuma PHS Indian Hosp. Fellow: Am. Acad. Otolaryngology (com. memberships 2006—08). Independent. Luthern. Achievements include development of multiple cochlear implant electrodes. Avocations: skiing, tennis, travel. Office: NYU Sch Medicine 550 First Ave Ste 7N New York NY 10016 Office Fax: 212-263-2019; Home Fax: 212-263-2019. Business E-Mail: john.roland@nyumc.org.

ROLAND, JOHN THOMAS, JR., otolaryngologist, medical educator; b. Lancaster, Pa., May 14, 1957; MD, Temple U., 1983. Resident gen. surgery NYU Med. Ctr., 1983—85, resident otolaryngology, 1988—92, clin. fellowship neurotology, 1992—93; chmn. Dept. Otolaryngology-Head and Neck Surgery NYU Langone Med. Ctr., prof., chair, Mendik Found. assoc. prof. otology Dept. Otolaryngology; co-dir. NYU Cochlear Implant Ctr. Lt. comdr. US Pub. Health Svc., clin. dir. Fort Yuma PHS Indian Hosp., 1986—88. Contbr. articles to med. jours. Office: NYU Langone Medical Center 550 First Ave, Suite 7Q New York NY 10016 Office Phone: 212-263-5565. Office Fax: 212-263-2019. *

ROLAND, KENNETH LYNN, microbiologist, educator; b. Birmingham, Ala., Feb. 17, 1954; BS, Auburn U., 1976; PhD, U. Ala., Birmingham, 1987. Sr. scientist Megan Health, Inc., 1994—2000; assoc. dir. Avant Immunotherapeutics, 2000—07; rsch. assoc. prof. Ariz. State U., 2007—. Mem.: AAAP, Am. Assn. Avian Pathologists (P.P. Levine award), Am. Soc. Microbiology. Avocations: piano, guitar. Office: The Biodesign Inst 1001 S McAllist Ave Tempe AZ 85287 Business E-Mail: kenneth.roland@asu.edu.

ROLAND, WILLIAM, internist, educator; b. Oct. 13, 1960; MD, U. Mo., Columbia, 1989. Prof., clin. internal medicine U. Mo., Columbia Sch. Medicine, 1994—2011. Office: 5 Hospital Dr Columbia MO 65212 Business E-Mail: rolandw@health.missouri.edu.

ROLDAN-VALADEZ, ERNESTO, diagnostic radiologist, clinical researcher; s. Graciela and Alejandro Roldan-Valadez. MD magna cum laude, Autonomous U. Guerrero, Acapulco City, Mexico, 1996; diploma, U. Nat. Autonoma Mex., Mexico City, 2005, MS in Med. Scis., 2008. Cert. Mexican Nat. Coll. of Gen. Med., 2003, diplomate Diagnostic Radiology Mexican Bd. of Radiology, 2006, lic. Gen. Med. Mexico, 2006. Res., diagnostic radiology Medica Sur Hosp., Mexico City, 2003—06, jr. staff mem., dept. radiol., 2006, fellowship, PET-CT unit, dept. radiol., 2006—07; diagnostic radiologist, magnetic resonance unit Medica Sur Hosp. & Clin. Found., Mexico City, 2007—. Contbr. articles to profl. jours. Recipient Honor Mention, Mex. Autonomous U. of Guerrero, Med. Sch. of Acapulco City, 1990—96, 3rd Pl. Painting Contest, Mexican Nat. Inst. Med. Sciences and Nutrition. Mex. City., 1994, 2nd Pl., Mexican Ann. Mtg. of Radiology., 2004, 3rd. Pl. Rsch. Study, 1st Internat. Congress in Magnetic Resonance, 2005. Mem.: Mexican Soc. of Radiology (1st pl. for best radiology rsch. study 2008), European Sch. Magnetic Resonance in Medicine and Biology (assoc.), Radiol. Soc. of N.Am. (assoc.), Am. Roentgen Ray Soc (assoc.). Avocations: sports, jogging, movies, hiking, photography. Office: Medica Sur Hospital & Clin Found Puente de Piedra # 150 14050 Mexico City DF Mexico Office Fax: (52-55) 5424-4429. Personal E-mail: ernest.roldan@usa.net.

ROLETT, ELLIS LAWRENCE, cardiologist, educator; b. NYC, July 10, 1930; s. Daniel Meyer and Mary Elaine (Warshaw) R.; m. Virginia Ann Vladimir, Mar. 25, 1956; children: Roderic Lawrence, Barry Vladimir, Daniel Alfred. BS, Yale U., 1952; MD cum laude, Harvard U., 1955. Diplomate: Am. Bd. Internal Medicine, Am. Bd. Cardiovas. Disease. Intern, resident in medicine Mass. Gen. Hosp., Boston, 1955-56, 59-61; asst. resident N.Y. Hosp.-Cornell U. Med. Ctr., NYC, 1956-57; Am. Heart Assn. research fellow Peter Bent Brigham Hosp., Boston, 1961-63; mem. faculty U. N.C., Chapel Hill, 1963-74, then prof., 1971-74; prof. UCLA, 1974-77; chief cardiology VA Wadsworth Hosp., LA, 1974-77, Dartmouth-Hitchcock Med. Ctr., Hanover, NH, 1977—87; prof. Dartmouth Med. Sch., Hanover, 1977-97, prof. medicine active emeritus, 1997—. Vis. scientist August Krogh Inst., Copenhagen, 1984; mem. merit rev. bd. Cardiovasc. studies VA, 1976-79, chmn., 1978-79; mem. regional rsch. rev. com. New Eng. Am. Heart Assn., 1978-83; mem. sci. bd. Stanley J. Sarnoff Endowment for Cardiovasc. Sci., 1992-97, chmn., 1994-95, bd. dirs., 1997-2000; mem. lit. sect. rev. com. Nat. Libr. Medicine, 1995-99, chmn., 1998-99; dir. Vt.-Karelia (Russia) Med. Project, St. Petersburg Univ. Global Fund. Bd. dirs. N.H. affiliate Am. Heart Assn., 1978-85; pres. N.H. affiliate Am. Heart Assn., 1983-85. Served to capt. M.C. USAF, 1957-59. Recipient Lederle Med. Faculty award, 1965-68, USPHS Career Devel. award, 1967-72; grantee USPHS/NIH, 1964-76, VA Merit Rev. Rsch. Program, 1975-77, Mathers Found., 1984-86, 93-96, Am. Heart Assn., 1989-91. Mem. AAAS, Am. Physiol. Soc., Internat. Soc. Heart Rsch., Phi Beta Kappa, Alpha Omega Alpha Office: Dartmouth Med Sch Hanover NH 03755 Home: 80 Lyme Rd Apt 221 Hanover NH 03755-1231 Office Phone: 603-650-1360. Business E-Mail: ellis.rolett@dartmouth.edu. *

ROLFE, RIAL DEWITT, microbiologist; b. Mo., Feb. 25, 1952; PhD, U. Mo., 1978; MBA, Tex. Tech. U., 2002. Prof., dept. microbiology & immunology Tex. Tech. U. Health Scis. Ctr., 2001—, chair, dept. health orgn. mgmt. sch. medicine, 2002—05, assoc. v.p. academic svcs., 2005—06, v.p. academic affairs, 2006—08, sr. v.p. academic affairs, 2009—. Bd. councilors Soc. Intestinal Microbial Ecology & Disease, 1987—91; bd. dirs. El Paso Inst. Cmty. Health, 1991—96; treas. Soc. Microbial Ecology & Disease, 1991—97, 2001—06; health related institutions vaue added task force chair Tex. Higher Edn. Coord. Bd., 2009—10. Recipient Prof. Extraordinaire award, Autonomous U. Guadalajara, Mex., 1986, Faculty Recognition award, Tex. Tech U. Health Scis. Ctr., 2009. Mem.: AAAS, Soc. Coll. & U. Planning, Anaerobe Soc. Americas (Charter mem.), Am. Soc. Intestinal Microbial Ecology & Disease (Charter mem.), Am. Soc. Microbiology. Office: 3601 4th St STOP 6298 Lubbock TX 79430 E-mail: rial.rolfe@ttuhsc.edu.

ROLLER, RICHARD JOHN, biology professor; b. Oak Pk., Ill., Dec. 27, 1958; BA, Lawrence U., 1980; PhD, Harvard U., 1988. Postdoc. fellow U. Chgo., 1988—94; prof. U. Iowa, 1994—. Mem.: Am. Soc. Microbiology. Avocations: piano, singing. Office: 3-432 BSB University Iowa Iowa City IA 52242 Office Fax: 319-335-9958. Business E-Mail: richard-roller@uiowa.edu.

ROLLINS, DIANN ELIZABETH, retired occupational health nurse, primary school educator, activist and advocator; b. Newark, Dec. 13, 1943; d. Lewis Paul and Letitia Lavinia Rollins. RN, Meth. Hosp. Sch. Nursing, Phila., 1964; postgrad., Howard U., 1966, Milton Coll., 1969—72, West Chester State Coll., 1972—79; cert. bldg. maintenance, John F. Kennedy Vocat. Tech., 1992; BSN, Thomas Jefferson U., 2000. RN Pa., N.J.; cert. religious sci. practitioner United Ch. Religious Sci., 2003. Nurse Meth. Hosp., Phila., 1964—66, 1967—69, Mercy Hosp., Janesville, Wis., 1969—72, Chester County Hosp., West Chester, Pa., 1972—74, Cheyney U., Pa., 1974—75, Embreeville State Hosp., coatesville, 1976—78; agy. nurse Norristown, Phila., 1978—86, Medox, Olsten, Kimberly, Phila., 1985-86; RN supr. New Ralston House, Phila., 1986-87, 88-89; agy. nurse Kimberly, Quality Care, Olsten, Medox, others, Phila., 1987-89; info. and referral specialist Nat. Mental Health Consumer Self Help Clearing House, Phila., 1992-93; intern ACT NOW Southeastern Mental Health Program, Phila., 1993-94; nursery sch. tchr. Bambino Gesu Child Devel. Ctr., Phila., 1994-99; primary instr. nursing assts.

ARC, 2000—01, Clin. Pathways Educators Ins., 2001—02; supplemental staff nurse Breslin Learning Ctr., 2002—05, LPN instr., 2003—05; staff nurse Bayada Nurses, 2002—06; postal nurse (occupl. health nurse) US Post Office, 2003—07. Spkr. in field. Vol. instr. program Franklin Inst., Phila., 1973-74; vol. multimedia first aide instr. ARC, Wilmington, Del., 1975-83; vol. plan II nurse blood mobiles ARC, S.E. Pa., 1982-85, 2009. Recipient Stella M. Mummert maternal/child care award, Meth. Hosp., 1964. Mem. Alumnae Meth. Hosp. Sch. Nursing, Four Chaplains Legion of Honor. Avocations: reading, writing, walking, singing. Home Phone: 215-220-0389; Office Phone: 215-600-7667.

ROLLINS, JONATHAN D., medical researcher; b. Charleston, SC, Aug. 4, 1984; BS, Clemson U., 2007. Rsch. asst. Greenwood Genetic Ctr., 2008—. Peer reviewer Acta Paediat., 2010. Avocations: tennis, photography, fishing. Home: 7 Huckleberry Ct Aiken SC 29803 Personal E-mail: jrollins.sc@gmail.com.

ROLLO, F. DAVID, healthcare company executive, cardiologist; b. Endicott, NY, Apr. 15, 1939; s. Frank C. and Augustine L. (Dumont) R.; m. Linda Wood, June 1, 1991; children: Mindee, Alex. BA, Harpur Coll., 1959; MS, U. Miami, 1965; PhD, Johns Hopkins U., 1968; MD, Upstate Med. Ctr., Syracuse, NY, 1972. Diplomate Am. Bd. Nuc. Medicine. Asst. chief nuc. medicine svcs. VA Hosp., San Francisco, 1974-77, chief nuc. medicine Nashville, 1977-79; sr. v.p. med. affairs Humana Inc., Louisville, 1980-92; dir. nuc. medicine div. Vanderbilt U. Med. Ctr., Nashville, 1977-81; prof. radiology Vanderbilt U., Nashville, 1979—; pres., CEO Metricor Inc., Louisville, 1992-95; sr. v.p. med. affairs HCIA, Louisville, 1995-96; sr. v.p. med. affairs, med. dir. Raytel Med. Corp., San Mateo, Calif., 1996-99; chief med. officer ADAC Labs., Milpitas, Calif., 1999—2002; internat. chief med. officer Philips Med. Sys., 2003—. Mem. med. adv. com. IBT, Washington, 1984—; mem. pvt. sector liaison panel Inst. of Medicine, Washington, 1983—; bd. dirs. ADAC Labs. Editor: Nuclear Medicine Physics, Instruments and Agents, 1977; co-editor: Physical Basis of Medical Imaging, 1980, Digital Radiology: Focus on Clinical Utility, 1982, Nuclear Medicine Resonance Imaging, 1983; mem. editorial adv. bd. ECRI, 1981—. Pres. bd. dirs. Youth Performing Arts Coun., Louisville, 1984-85; bd. dirs. Louisville-Jefferson County Youth Orch., 1983-85; sr. v.p., exec. com. USA Internat. Harp Competition, 1992-, chmn., 1994-. Fellow Am. Coll. Cardiology, Am. Coll. Nuc. Physicians (profl. Am. Coll. Radiology com. 1982-84, chmn. 1984), mem. AMA, Soc. Nuc. Medicine (trustee 1979-83, 84—, Cassen Meml. lectr. western region 1980, 84), Radiol. Soc. N.Am., NEMA (chmn. nuc. medicine sect., 2002-, bd. mem., 2002-, testimony medicine expert, 2003-), Am. Coll. Radiology, Ky. Sci. Tech. Coun. (exec. bd. 1987—), Advancement Med. Instrumentation (bd. dirs. 1986—), Louisville C. of C. (chmn. MIC com. 1987—). Avocations: racquetball, squash, golf. Home: 15735 Peach Hill Rd Saratoga CA 95070-6447

ROLLS, BARBARA JEAN, nutritionist, educator, director; b. Washington, Jan. 5, 1945; d. Howard Julian and Patricia Jane Simons; m. Edmund Thomson Rolls, Sept. 6, 1969 (div. Jan. 1983); children: Melissa May, Juliet Helen. BA, U. Pa., 1966; PhD, Cambridge U., Eng., 1970; MA (hon.), Oxford U., Eng., 1970. Mary Somerville rsch. fellow Oxford U., 1969—72, IBM rsch. fellow, 1972—74, jr. rsch. fellow Wolfson Coll., 1974—75, E.P. Abraham rsch. fellow Green Coll., 1979—82, fellow in nutrition, 1983—84; assoc. prof. psychiatry Johns Hopkins U. Sch. Medicine, Balt., 1984-91, prof., 1991-92; Jean Phillips Shibley prof. biobehavioral health Pa. State U., State College, 1992-94, prof., nutritional scis. Helen A. Guthrie chair nutrition, 1994—; dir. lab Study Human Ingestive Behaviour, 1992—. Mem. Nat. Diabetes and Digestive and Kidney Diseases Adv. Coun., 1994—98; cons. in field. Author: Thirst, 1982, Carbohydrates and Weight Management, 1998, Volumetrics: Feel Full on Fewer Calories, 2000, The Volumetrics Eating Plan, 2005; mem. editl. bd. Am. Jour. Physiology, 1985—99, Trends Food Sci. and Tech., 1991—93, Am. Jour. Clin. Nutrition, 1992—98, Obesity, 1992—2002, Nutrition Rev., 1993—97, Appetite, 1981—; contbr. articles to profl. jours. Recipient Merit award, NIH, 1997, Internat. award for Modern Nutrition, 2001; grantee, NIH, 1997—2010, Med. Rsch. Coun. U.K., 1969—84; Thouron scholar, Cambridge U., 1966—69. Fellow: AAAS; mem.: Am. Soc. Nutrition (W.O. Atwater lectr. 2007, fellow 2011, award in human nutrition 1995, Centrum Ctr. Nutrition Sci. award 2008, Geo. A. Bray Founders award 2010), Obesity Soc. (coun. 1991—93, v.p. 1994—95, pres.-elect 1995—96, pres. 1996—97), Soc. Study Ingestive Behavior (bd. dirs. 1986—90, pres.-elect 1990—91, pres. 1991—92), Am. Physiol. Soc., Am. Dietetic Assn. (hon.), Golden Key (hon.; Atwater lectr. 2007, Centrum Ctr. Nutrition Sci. award 2008). Office: Pa State University 226 Henderson Bldg University Park PA 16802-6501 Business E-Mail: bjr4@psu.edu.

ROLSTON, KENNETH VIJAYKUMAR ISAAC, medical educator; b. India, Apr. 23, 1951; MBBS, Christian Med. Coll., Ludhiana, India, 1973. Infectious diseases fellow Hahnemann U., Phila., 1983; dir., clin. trials, ambulatory and supportive care oncology rsch. program UT MD Anderson Cancer Ctr., 1992—98, chief, sect. infectious diseases, 1994—2005, prof., medicine, 1995—, dep. chmn., dept. infectious diseases, infection control and employee health, 2006—10. Adj. prof., dept. clin. scis. Coll. Pharmacy U. Houston, 2001—11; adj. prof., dept. medicine Sect. Infectious Diseases Baylor Coll. Medicine, 2009—11. Fellow: ACP, Infectious Diseases Soc. America; mem.: AMA, Multinational Assn. Supportive Care in Cancer, Am. Soc. Clin. Oncology. Avocations: cricket, cooking, gardening. Office: MD Anderson Cancer Ctr 1515 Holcombe Blvd Unit 362 Houston TX 77030 Office Phone: 713-792-7303. Business E-Mail: krolston@mdanderson.org.

ROMANELLI, PANTALEO, neurosurgeon, researcher; b. Novi Velia, Italy, Sept. 28, 1969; m. Rosa Pace, Jan. 16, 1999; children: Francesco, Giulio, Rosalia, Pietro. MD, Second U. Naples, 1994. Clin. instr. dept. neurosurgery Stanford U., Calif., 2002—03, cons. prof. neurosurgery, 2008—; chief, functional neurosurgery IRCCS Neuromed, Pozzilli, Italy, 2004—. Guest scientist Brookhaven Nat. Lab., Upton, NY, 2005—07; sci. dir. Cyberknife dept., Iatropolis Clinic, Athens, Greece, 2007; vis. scientist European Synchrotron Radiation Facility, Grenoble, France, 2008—. Contbr. scientific papers (Cyberknife Soc. Intracranial award, 2003, Dean's fellowship, Stanford U., 2001, AANS-CNS Novalis Cmty. award, 2008). Achievements include first to treat optic nerve sheat meningiomas with image guided robotic staged radiosurgery; development of new radiosurgery device able to use submillimetric beams; image-guided volumetric reconstruction of basal ganglia and thalamic structures. Office: IRCCS Neuromed Via Atinense 18 Pozzilli 86077 Italy Home: Via Boschetto 2 86077 Pozzilli IS Italy Office Fax: 00390865929276; Home Fax: 00390865925351. Personal E-mail: radiosurgery2000@yahoo.com.

ROMANI, JOHN HENRY, educator; b. Milan, Mar. 6, 1925; s. Henry Arthur and Hazel (Pettengill) R.; m. Barbara A. Anderson; children: David John, Paul Nichols, Theresa A. Anderson. BA, U. NH, MA, 1949; PhD, U. Mich., 1955. Instr. U. NH, 1950, U. Mich., Ann Arbor, 1954—55, prof., asst. to assoc. dean Sch. Pub. Health, 1961—69, assoc. v.p., 1971—75, chmn. health planning and adminstrn., 1975—80, prof., 1971-93, prof. emeritus pub. health adminstrn., 1993—, faculty assoc. program on environment, 2004—; interim chair Pub. Health Policy and Adminstrn., 1991—92; faculty assoc. ERB Inst., 2008—. Asst. prof. W. Mich. U., 1956-57; assoc. dir. Cleve. Met. Svcs. Commn., 1957-59; assoc. prof. U. Pitts., 1959-61; vice chancellor, prof. U. Wis.-Milw., 1969-71; rsch. fellow Brookings Instn., 1955-56; mem. task force Nat. Commn. on Orgn. Cmty. Health Svcs., 1963-66; dir. staff Sec.'s Com. on Orgn. Health Activities, HEW, 1965-66; dir. Govtl. Affairs Inst., 1969-75, chmn., 1970-72; trustee Pub. Adminstrn. Svc., 1969-75, chmn., 1973-75; mem. Delta Dental Plan Mich., 1972-78, bd. dirs. 1972-78, chmn. consumers' adv. coun., 1975-77; bd. dirs. Ctr. for Population Activities, 1975-81, chmn., 1975-81; lifetime vis. prof. Capital U. Economics and Bus., Beijing, 1996—; vis. rschr. Human Scis. Rsch. Coun., Pretoria, South Africa, 1999—. Author: The Philippine Presidency, 1956; editor: Changing Dimensions in Public Administration, 1962; contbr. articles to profl. jours. Trustee Congregational Summer Assembly, 1982-85; commr. Accrediting Commn. on Edn. for Health Svcs. Adminstrn., 1989-95. Served with AUS, 1943-46, ETO. With US Army, 1943—46. Fellow Am. Pub. Health Assn. (chmn. program devel. bd. 1975-77, exec. bd. 1975-80, governing coun. 1975—, pres. 1979, chmn. publs. bd. 1984-88), Royal Soc. Health (hon.), Am. Polit. Sci. Assn. (life); mem. ASPA (past mem. coun.), Population Assn. Am., Phi Kappa Phi, Pi Sigma Alpha, Pi Gamma Mu, Delta Omega. Home and Office: 2125 Nature Cove Ct Apt 108 Ann Arbor MI 48104 *

ROMANO, CORRADO, pediatrician, medical geneticist; b. Avola, Siracusa, Italy, Nov. 22, 1957; s. Felice and Raffaela Romano; m. Pinella Failla; children: Felice, Giuseppe. MD, Cath. U., Rome, 1982; postgrad. in pediatrics, U. Catania, Italy, 1989, postgrad. in med. genetics, 1993. Registrar Oasi Inst. Rsch. Mental Retardation, Troina, Italy, 1988-90, sr. registrar, 1990-92, dep. head dept. pediat., 1992-2000, head unit of pediat., 2000—03, head unit of pediat. and med. genetics, 2003—. Contbr. articles to profl. jours., chpt. to book. Mem. Assn. Amici dell'Oasi di Troina (chmn. 1993-), Italian Soc. Human Genetics (exec. bd. mem., 2006—). Roman Catholic. Office: Oasi Inst Rsch Via Conte Ruggero 73 94018 Troina Italy Home Phone: +39 0935 650165; Office Phone: +39 0935 936285. Business E-Mail: cromano@oasi.en.it.

ROMANO, JOHN FRANCIS, dermatologist; b. SI, NY, July 4, 1948; BS, St. Peter's Coll., 1969; MD, Cornell U., 1973. Diplomate Am. Bd. Dermatology. Intern Einstein Hosps., NYC, 1973—74; resident in medicine St. Vincent's Hosp., NYC, 1974—76; resident in dermatology N.Y. Hosp., NYC, 1976—78; pvt. practice dermatology NYC, 1979—; attending physician St. Vincent's Hosp., NYC, 1979—; clin. asst. prof. dermatology Weill Hosp. Cornell U., 1979—; also asst. attending dermatologist N.Y. Presbyterian Hosp. Mem.: N.Y. State Dermatologic Soc., Am. Soc. for Laser Medicine and Surgery, Am. Soc. for Dermatologic Surgery, Am. Acad. Dermatology. Avocation: sailing. Office: 36 7th Ave New York NY 10011-6609 Office Phone: 212-242-5815. Business E-Mail: info@westvillagedermatology.com.

ROMANO, JOSEPH ANTHONY, healthcare education and marketing consultant; b. Bklyn., Sept. 5, 1946; s. Anthony Wilbur and Anne R.; m. Linda Rose Giacalone, Sept. 23, 1972; children: Nicholas Joseph, Christine Dianne. Student, Villanova U., 1964-66; BS Pharm. Sci., Columbia U., 1970, D Pharmacy, 1972. Clin. resident Lenox Hill Hosp., NYC, 1970-72; asst. dean, asst. prof. Columbia U., NYC, 1972-76, SUNY, Buffalo, 1976-78; assoc. dean, assoc. prof. U. Wash., Seattle, 1978-83; assoc. dir. medicine Pfizer Labs., NYC, 1983-85, product mgr., 1985, asst. to pres., 1985-87; sr. v.p., group dir. Hill & Knowlton, Inc., NYC, 1987-88; exec. dir. external affairs Sandoz (Novartis), NYC, 1988-89; pres., COO, Med. Mktg., NYC, 1989-92; vice chair Nelson Communications, Inc. Worldwide (divsn. Publicis), NYC, 1992—2002; chmn., CEO, SCIENS Worldwide Healthcare Comms., 1996—2002; co-chmn. Nelson Prof. Sales, 1998-2000; prin. May Flower Consulting, 2002—. Mem. U.S. Nat. Adv. Com. Health Profls., Washington, 1980-86. Co-author: Clinical Pharmacology, Pharmacy State Board Reviews, 1976, 78, 85, The Vitamin Book, 1985, 2000; contbr. articles to profl. jours. Fellow Royal Soc. Health London; mem. Am. Pharm. Assn., Am. Soc. Healthcare Pharmacists, Am. Assoc. Study Headaches, U.S. Golf Assn., Rho Chi. Avocations: photography, stamp collecting/philately, golf, music, cooking. Office Phone: 908-625-0014. Personal E-mail: jromano103@gmail.com.

ROMANOS, GEORGE EVANGELOS, dentist; b. Athens, Sept. 24, 1964; arrived in Germany, 1987; s. Evangelos and Rallou (Joannidou) R.; 1 child, Eva-Maria. DDS, Athens U., 1987; dr.med.dent., U. Berlin, 1990, cert. Periodontics, 1990; cert. Prosthodontics, U. Freiburg, Germany, 1993; cert. Oral Surgery, U. Frankfurt, Germany, 1993. Asst. prof. U. Berlin, 1987-90, U. Freiburg, 1990-93, U. Frankfurt, 1993—. Vis. prof. U. Malaysia, 1992; vis. asst. prof. U. Utah, 1998. Contbr. articles to profl. publs. Fellow Am. Soc. Lasers in Medicine and Surgery, Wound Healing Soc., German Assn. for Lasers in Dentistry (bd. dirs.). Avocation: photography. Office: Dental Sch Frankfurt Theodor Stern Kai 7 60590 Frankfurt Germany

ROMANOWSKI, CHARLES ANTHONY JOZEF, neuroradiologist; s. Hieronim J. and Amelia Romanowski; m. Sarah Theresa Susan Moor Allen, Aug. 20, 1988; children: Matthew L. A., Anthony S. T., David S. J., Hannah L. D. BSc (hon.), U. Manchester, Eng., 1983, MB, 1986. European Qualification in Neuroradiology European Bd. of Neuroradiology, 2006. Sr. registrar in neuroradiology Manchester Royal Infirmary, 1994—95; radiology registrar Royal Hallamshire Hosp., Sheffield, England, 1989—94, cons. neuroradiologist, 1995—. Contbr. scientific papers to profl. jours. Recipient Nycomed scholarship, Brit. Inst. of Radiology, 1993, Kodak scholarship, Royal Coll. of Radiologists, U.K., 1995. Fellow: Royal Coll. Radiologists; mem.: World Fed. Neuroradiological Soc., Royal Coll. Physicians Glasgow, European Soc. Neuroradiology (U.K. nat. del. 2004—07), British Soc. Neuroradiologists (com. mem. 2004—07, ESNR and WFNRS del., faculty mem. ECNR & Erasmus MRI course, chmn. exam. com., ESNR). Avocations: music, Polish history and culture, travel, photography. Office: Royal Hallamshire Hosp Royal Hallamshire Hospital Glossop Road S10 2JF Sheffield England

ROMANOWSKI, ERIC GERALD, medical researcher; b. Ligonier, Pa., Aug. 31, 1959; BS, Duquesne U., 1981, MS, 1983. Rsch. dir. Charles T. Campbell ophthalmic microbiology lab. U. Pitts., 1984—. Editl. bd. mem. Cornea, 2004; cons. Alcon Labs., 2005—11, Inspire Pharms., 2008—11; editl. bd. mem. Interdisciplinary Perspectives on Infectious Diseases, 2011; cons. Allergan, Inc., 2007—09. Mem.: European Assn. Vision and Eye Rsch., Ocular Microbiology and Immunology Group, Internat. Soc. Antiviral Rsch., Am. Soc. Microbiology, Assn. Rsch. in Vision and Ophthalmology, Phi Kappa Phi. Avocations: golf, baseball. Office: Eye & Ear Inst 203 Lothrop St Pittsburgh PA 15213 Office Fax: 412-647-5880. Business E-Mail: romanowskieg@upmc.edu.

ROMANS, JUANITA F., hospital administrator; BS in Biology, U. Detoit, 1978; MS in Nursing, Wayne State U., 1987. RN Detroit Medical Center, dir. clin. care and nursing sys., 1984—88; sr. assoc. adminstr. Henry Ford Hosp., 1988—94; exec. dir. Promedica Health Sys., Children's Med. Ctr. of N.W. Ohio, 1994—95; v.p. patient care svcs. Toledo Hosp., Ohio, 1994—97; sr. v.p. hosp. and clinics Evanston Northwestern Healthcare, Ill., 1997; sr. v.p. Meml. Hermann Healthcare Sys., 2001—03; COO Meml. Hermann Hosp., 2001—03; CEO Memorial Hermann - Texas Medical Centers, 2003—. Bd. dirs. Newfield and Ptnrs., Newfield Exploration Co., 2005—. Mem.: Tex. Hosp. Assn., Tex. Exec. Women, Tex. Assn. Pub. and Non-profit Hosp., Greater Houston Partnership, Am. Coll. Healthcare Execs., South Maine Ctr. Assn., Save Our ERs (bd. dirs.). Office: Memorial Hermann Healthcare System 7737 Southwest Fwy Ste 200 Houston TX 77074 Office Phone: 713-448-5555. Office Fax: 713-448-5665. *

ROMBEAU, JOHN LEE, surgeon, educator; b. LA, May 8, 1939; s. Lee Payne and Dora Georgina (Hobbs) R.; m. Maureen Elizabeth Parker, Sept. 7, 1970; children: Suzanne, Charles. BA, LaSierra Coll., 1962; MD, Loma Linda U., 1967. Intern L.A. County U. So. Calif. Med. Ctr., 1967-68, resident in gen. surgery, 1971-74, chief resident in gen. surgery, 1974-75; resident in gen. surgery Good Samaritan Hosp., LA, 1970-71; spl. fellow in colon and rectal surgery Cleve. Clinic, 1975-76, rsch. surg. fellow, 1976; asst. prof. surgery U. Calif., Davis, 1976-79, Hosp. of U. Pa. Sch. Medicine, Phila., 1979-86, assoc. prof. surgery, 1987-94, prof. surgery, 1994—. Rsch. fellow in nutrition and metabolism Joslin Diabetes Ctr., Brigham and Women's Hosp., Harvard Med. Sch., 1984. Co-author: Nutritional and Metabolic Care of the Hospitalized Patient, 1986; co-editor: Atlas of Nutritional Support Techniques, 1989, Clinical Nutrition: Enteral and Tube Feeding, 1984, 2d edit., 1990, 3rd edit., 1996, Clinical Nutrition: Parenteral Nutrition, 1986, 2d edit., 1993, Physiologic and Clinical Aspects of Short-Chain Fatty Acids, 1995. Capt. U.S. Army, 1968-70, Vietnam. Recipient Vol. Achievement award Crohn's and Colitis Found., 1992. Fellow ACS (mem. pre and postoperative care com. 1982-92), Am. Soc. Colon and Rectal Surgeons, Pa. Soc. Colon and Rectal Surgeons; mem. Am. Surg. Assoc., Am. Soc. for Parenteral and Enteral Nutrition (pres. 1988, assoc. editor jour. 1978-90, editor-in-chief elect jour. 1990, editor-in-chief jour. 1991—), Alpha Omega Alpha. Achievements include development of specialized gastrostomy-jejunal feeding tube. Office: Hosp of U Pa 4 Silverstein 3400 Spruce St Philadelphia PA 19104-4206

ROMEO, ANTHONY ALBERT, orthopedic surgeon; b. Walnut Creek, Calif., Nov. 8, 1961; s. Sam J.W. and Patricia Ann (DeFilippo) Romeo; children: Brianna, Alyssa, Danielle, Christin, Sabrina. BS, U. Notre Dame, Ind., 1983; MD, St. Louis U. Sch. Medicine, 1987. Diplomate Am. Bd. Orthopedic Surgery, Nat. Bd. Med. Examiners, lic. Ill. Intern dept. gen. surgery Cleve. Clin. Found., 1987-88, resident dept. orthopaedic surgery, 1988-92; fellow shoulder/elbow svc., dept. orthopedic surgery U. Wash., Seattle, 1992-93; assoc. prof. dept. orthopaedics Rush Med. Coll., Chgo., 1993—; med. staff Rush-Presbyn.-St. Luke's Med. Ctr., 1993—, Oak Park Hosp., Ill., 1994—. Staff surgeon Univ. Hosp./Vet.'s Adminstrn Hosp./Harborview Med. Ctr./Children's Hosp. & Med. Ctr., Seattle, 1992—93. Contbr. articles to profl. jours. Recipient Disting. Alumni award, St. Louis U. Sch. Medicine, 1987; named a Top Doc, Chgo. Mag., 1997; named one of Best Doctors in America, Best Doctors, Inc., 1998. Fellow: Am. Acad. Orthopaedic Surgeons; mem.: AMA, St. Louis U. Med. Sch. Alumni Assn., Mid-America Orthopaedic Assn., Ill. State Med. Soc., Chgo. Med. Soc., Am. Shoulder & Elbow Soc. (assoc.), Ill. Orthopaedic Assn., Notre Dame Orthopaedic Soc., Am. Orthopaedic Soc. Sports Medicine, Arthroscopy Assn. N.Am., Alpha Sigma Nu, Alpha Omega Alpha (founder, pres.). Office: Rush Univ Med Ctr 1725 W Harrison St Ste 1063 Chicago IL 60612-3836 Office Phone: 312-243-4244, 312-432-2342.

ROMEO, MARCO, plastic surgeon; b. Catania, Italy, May 4, 1981; MD, Catania U., 2005. Cert. secialist in plasti surgery Messina U., 2010. Rsch. fellow Canniesburn Plastic Surgery Unit, Glasgow, 2008—10; plastic surgery cons. Clinica U. Pamplona, 2010—. Avocations: motorcycling, skiing. Home: Via Nuovaluce 48 Tremestieri Etneo Catania Sicily 95030 Italy Personal E-mail: marcosicily@interfree.it.

ROMER, DANIEL, university official, psychologist, educator; b. Caracas, Venezuela, Apr. 19, 1947; arrived in U.S., 1948; s. Adolf and Eleanor (Rittermann) R.; m. Lauren B. Alloy, Jan. 4, 1985; 1 child, Adrienne. AB, Dartmouth Coll., 1969; PhD, U. Ill., Chgo., 1974. Rsch. fellow Dept Mental Health, Chgo., 1976-79; vis. asst. prof. Northwestern U., Evanston, Ill., 1979-81; adj. assoc. prof. U. Ill., 1981-89; assoc. rsch. dir. Leo Burnett Co., Chgo., 1982-89; sr. rschr.

Annenberg Sch. for Comm., U. Pa., Phila., 1990—2000, sr. fellow Ctr. for Cmty. Partnerships, 1996—, rsch. dir. Inst. for Adolescent Risk Comm., 2001—. Mem. nat. expert panel on adolescent STD prevention Ctr. for Disease Control and Prevention, Atlanta, 2000-01; mem. rev. panels NIH, Washington, 1994-97, 98—. Mem. editl. bd. Jour. Exptl. Social Psychology, 1988-91, Youth and Society, 2001—; contbr. over 125 articles to psychol. and pub. health jours., chpts. to books, edited books. Grantee NIMH, 1992—, Ford Found., 1994. Mem. APS, APHA, SPR. Office: Annenberg Pub Policy Ctr 202 S 36th St Philadelphia PA 19104 Business E-Mail: dromer@asc.upenn.edu.

ROMERO, JORGE ANTONIO, neurologist, educator; b. Bayamon, PR, Apr. 15, 1948; s. Calixto Antonio Romero-Barcelo and Antonia (de Juan) R.; m. Helen Mella, June 20, 1970 (div. 1983); children: Sofia, Jorge, Alfredo, Isabel; m. Cheryl Raps, Aug. 1994; 1 child, Jessica. SB, MIT, 1968; MD, Harvard U., 1972. Diplomate Am. Bd. Psychiatry and Neurology. Intern U. Chgo. Hosp. and Clinics, 1972-73; resident Mass. Gen. Hosp., Boston, 1975-78; rsch. fellow in pharmacology NIMH, Bethesda, Md., 1973-75; asst. prof. neurology Harvard Med. Sch., Boston, 1979-92; mem. staff VA Med. Ctr., Brockton, Mass., 1979-92; assoc. physician Brigham and Women's Hosp., Boston, 1980-92; chmn. dept. neurology Ochsner Clin. Baton Rouge, 1993-97; assoc. clin. prof. neurology La. State U. Sch. Medicine, 1996-97; attending physician Baylor U. Med. Ctr., Dallas, 2002—. Cons. Mass. Mental Health Ctr., Boston, 1987-92. With USPHS, 1973-75. Recipient Career Devel. award VA, 1979. Mem. Am. Acad. Neurology. Office: Barnett Tower Ste 901 3600 Gaston Ave Dallas TX 75246 Office Phone: 214-827-5525. Personal E-mail: rneurology@sbcglobal.net.

ROMERO, RICARDO VICENTE, gastroenterologist; b. Ponce, PR, Mar. 5, 1972; s. Vicente Romero and Ana Rosa Soler; m. Susana Lauraelena Dipp, June 23, 2001; 1 child, Sofia Gabriela. MD, Ponce Sch. of Medicine, Ponce, PR, 1999. Diplomate Am. Bd. Internal Medicine, 2002, Am. Bd. Internal Medicine Gastroenterology, 2005. Gastroenterology staff, clin. educator Baystate Med. Ctr., Springfield, Mass., 2005—; asst. prof. medicine Tufts U. Md. Sch. Dir. endoscopy Baystate Med. Ctr., 2005—. Recipient Samuel Floch award, Norwalk Hosp. Affiliated with Yale U., 2002. Mem.: ACP, Am. Soc. for Gastrointestinal Endoscopy, Am. Coll. Gastroenterology. Roman Catholic. Avocations: travel, painting, music. Office: Baystate Med Ctr 759 Chestnut St Springfield MA 01199 E-mail: ricardo.romero@bhs.org.

ROMERO, ROBERTO J., perinatologist, educator; b. Maracaibo, Venezuela, Sept. 19, 1951; MD magna cum laude, U. Nat. Zulia, Maracaibo, 1974. Cert. Ob-Gyn., 1984, Maternal-Fetal Medicine, 1987. Intern in ob-gyn. Hosp. Gen. del Sur, Maracaibo, Venezuela, 1975—76; resident in maternal fetal medicine Yale U., 1976—79, chief resident, 1978—79, fellow in gynecol. oncology, 1980—82, asst. prof., 1982; prof. ob-gyn. Wayne State U. Sch. Medicine, Detroit, 1992—; dir. perinatology rsch. br. NIH Nat. Inst. Child Health and Human Devel., Detroit, 1992—, prog. dir. for obstetrics and perinatology. Mem.: Inst. Medicine. Office: Nat Inst Child Health and Human Devel 4704 St Antoine Blvd Detroit MI 48201 Office Phone: 313-993-2700. Office Fax: 313-993-2694. E-mail: romeror@mail.nih.gov.

ROMERO-GONZÁLEZ, MAURICIO, psychiatrist, educator, consultant; b. Santafe de Bogota, Colombia, Nov. 15, 1960; arrived in U.S., 2000; s. Carlos Guillermo Romero and Dora Cecillia Gonzalez. MD, Colegio Mayor del Rosario, Bogota, 1989, cert. in ednl. resources, 1984; Specialist in Psychiatry, U. Rosario, Bogota, 1989; MPH, U. Conn., Storrs, 2005. Med. intern Hosp. Univ. del Valle, Cali, 1983-84, Med. Social Svc./Primary Attention Unit, Planadas, 1985; emergency room med. coord. Hosp. San Blas, Bogota, 1986-87; med. resident in psychiatry Hosp. San Jose, Bogota, 1986-89; med. cons. in psychiatry Hosp. San Blas, Bogota, 1989-93; chief human rights dept. Mil. U., Bogota, 1995-97; psychotherapist Connection Inc., New Haven, 2009—. Neurophysiology instr. K. Lorenz U., Bogota, 1988—89; mental health prof. Colegio Mayor del Rosario, Bogota, 1990—2002; mental health cons. Ministry of Health, Bogota, 1990—91; nat. health advisor for mental health, addiction behavior and HIV/SIDA program Ombudsman Office, Bogota, 1992—97; chief divsn. mental health Ministry of Health, 1997—2000; dir. of course; Human Rights Colegio Mayor del Rosario, dir. of course: HIV/AIDS, 1997—2000; invited asst. prof. psychiatry Yale U., New Haven, 2000—02, study coord. Dept. Psychiatry develop. medication against cocaine addiction, 2007—08; clin. sr. psychologist The Connection Counseling Ctr., New Haven, 2009—; psychotherapist advisor mental health program Hispanos Unidos Inc., New Haven, 2002—06; participant World Health Conf. UCLA, 1998; founder, pres. CT Latino P.FLAG Inc., 2002—; pres. bd. dirs. Mapiripana Yurupari of New Eng. Inc., 2002—. Author: Psychotherapy, 1994, Special Mental Health Assistant in Special Case of Masacre de Trujillo-Valle, 1995, Nat. Policy of Mental Health of Colombia, 1997, Risk Reduction in Addiction Behavior, 1997; contbr. articles to profl. jours. including Rev. Colegio Mayor del Rosario. Mem Colombian Liberal Party; tech. dir. Fundacion Connaccion, Bogota, 1987—88, exec. Rafael Pombo scholarship, Colegio Mayor del Rosario, 1970—72, Hon. scholar, 1973—77. Mem.: Soc. Colombiana de Psiquiatria, Asociacion Medica Rosarista (hon.). Liberal. Jewish. Avocations: music, beach volleyball, art. Personal E-mail: ganimedeszues@yahoo.com, maoct@yahoo.com. Business E-Mail: mauricio.romero-gonzalez@emayu.org.

ROMICS, IMRE, urologist, educator; b. Erd, Hungary, May 16, 1947; s. Istvan and Katalin (Berenyi) R.; m. Eva Gorbe, May 1, 1953; children: Katalin, Miklos. MD, Semmelweis Med. U., Budapest, Hungary, 1971. Asst. prof. Inst. Pathophysiology, Semmelweis U., Budapest, 1971—74, 1974—89, sr. fellow, 1989—92; assoc. prof. dept. urology Semmelweis U., Budapest, 1992—95, prof., chmn. dept. urology, 1997—; head dept. urology Nat. Inst. Rheumatol. Physiotherapy, Budapest, 1995—97. Pres. Coll. Hungarian Bd. Urology, Budapest, Hungary, 2000—04; bd. mem. European Sch. Urology; parliamentarian mem. Hungarian Sci. Acad. Contbr. to books and articles to profl. jours. Mem. Hungarian Urology Soc. (sec. 1988—, exec. com. 1990—, pres. bd. urology 2000—), German Urology Soc., Am. Urology Assn. (pres. bd.), N.Y. Acad. Scis., European Assn. Urology (mem. scholarship and hist. coms.). Avocations: 20th century history, languages. Office: Semmelweis Univ Dept Urology Ullöi út 78/B 1082 Budapest Hungary Home: Tarogato u 52 1021 Budapest Hungary Office Phone: 3612100796. Business E-Mail: romimre@urol.sote.hu.

ROMITA, MAURO CHARLES, plastic surgeon; b. NYC, Jan. 16, 1947; MD, U. Miami, 1973. Diplomate Am. Bd. Surgery, Am. Bd. Plastic Surgery. Resident, fellow NYU Med. Ctr., 1974—81; pvt. practice plastic surgery NYC, 1999—; founder, med. dir. Ajune Ctr. for Beauty Synergy, NYC. Attending physician St. Vincent Hosp. Med. Ctr., NYC; asst. clin. prof. surgery NY Med. Coll. Contbr. articles to numerous profl. jours. Mem. Boys Town of Italy; bd. govs. Sound Shore Med. Ctr. Mem.: Am. Bd. Plastic Surgery (diplomate), Am. Soc. Plastic Surgeons. Office: 853 5th Ave New York NY 10021-5802 also: Ajune 1294 Third Ave at 74th St New York NY 10021 Office Phone: 212-628-0044.

ROMMER, JAMES ANDREW, physician; b. Newark, Aug. 22, 1952; s. Thomas Colman and Hortense (Marsh) R.; m. Linda Joan Anderson, Oct. 7, 1979; children: Elizabeth Anne, Nicole Marie. BS, Haverford Coll., 1974; MD, Cornell U., 1978. Diplomate Am. Bd. Internal Medicine. Intern N.Y. Hosp., Cornell Med. Ctr., NYC, 1978-79, resident in internal medicine, 1978-81; fellow in internal medicine Johns Hopkins Med. Sch., Balt., 1981-82; pvt. practice Livingston, N.J., 1982—. Attending physician St. Barnabas Med. Ctr., Livingston, 1984—, exec. com., 1990, 94, 96, v.p. med. staff, 2001; co-chief divsn. of internal medicine, 1996-99, clin. chief dept. medicine, 1996-98; asst. clin. prof. Mt. Sinai Sch. Medicine, N.Y.C., 1998. Fellow ACP; mem. AMA, Am. Soc. Internal Medicine, Alpha Omega Alpha. Avocations: tennis, reading, jogging. Office: 349 E Northfield Rd Livingston NJ 07039-4802 Office Phone: 973-992-2227. Personal E-mail: jrommer176@aol.com, jrommer176@gmail.com.

ROMOFF, JEFFREY ALAN, healthcare executive; b. NYC, Nov. 30, 1945; s. Richard Warren and Evelyn (Alter) Romoff; m. Vivian Irene Goodman, Aug. 25, 1966 (dec. June 1983); children: Jennifer Ann, Rebecca Lynn; m. Stefania Ferrarese, Dec. 2002. BS magna cum laude in Social Scis., CCNY, 1967; M.Phil. in Polit. Scis., Yale U., 1971; Doctor Pub. Svc. (hon.), Chatham Coll., 2005. Teaching fellow Yale U., 1969-70, teaching assoc., 1970-71; exec. dir. Central Naugatuck Valley Mental Health Council, Waterbury, Conn., 1971-73; regional programing dir. Western Psychiat. Inst. and Clinic (U. Pitts.), 1973-74, assoc. dir. div. edn. and research, 1974-75; assoc. dir. Western Psychiat. Inst. and Clinic, 1975—86; adj. asst. prof. pub. health U. Pitts., 1981—, instr. psychiatry, 1982—, assoc. v.p. health scis., 1984-86, vice chancellor health scis., 1986-92, sr. vice chancellor for Health Adminstrn., 1992—96; exec. v.p. U. Pitts. Med. Ctr., 1986-92, pres., CEO, 1992—. N.Y.C. Regents scholar CCNY, 1963-67 Mem. Am. Hosp. Assn. (governing coun. sect. for mental health and psychiat. scvs. 1986-89), Am. Psychiat. Assn. (chmn. joint com. with Am. Hosp. Assn. 1983-84), Hosp. Assn. Pa., Coun. Psychiat. Svc. Providers (exec. com. 1981-84) Jewish. Home: 3208 Fox Run Rd Allison Park PA 15101-1506 Office: U Pitts Med Ctr Forbes Tower 200 Lothrop St Ste 11045 Pittsburgh PA 15213-2546 *

RONAN, LAURENCE JOSEPH, internist, pediatrician; b. Evanston, Ill., Jan. 11, 1954; MD, Harvard U., 1987. Intern, internal medicine Mass. Gen. Hosp., 1987, resident, 1988, staff physician; staff physician, Team 2 Internal Medicine Assocs. Team internist Boston Red Sox; internal medicine rep. Med. Alliance for Iraq. Vol. Project Hope. Named one of Best Doctors, Boston Mag., 2007. Office: Internal Medicine Assocs 15 Parkman St WAC 605 Boston MA 02114-3117

RONCELLA, SILVIO, biologist, researcher; b. Orvieto, Tr, Italy, Jan. 24, 1952; s. Agostino Roncella and Luisa Poggi; m. Teresa Delfino; 1 child, Claudia. PhD, U. Pisa, 1977. Registered Profl. Italian Order Biologist, 1980. Rsch. group coord. clin. immunology lab. Nat. Inst. Cancer Rsch., Genova, Italy, 1982—98; chief molecular biology lab. Presidio Ospedaliero Sant'Andrea, La Spezia, Italy, 1998—. Prof. temp. appointment medicine U. Genova, 1995—99. Contbr. articles to numerous profl. jours. Sgt. Marine Mil., 1978—79, Italy. Mem.: Società Italiana di Ematologia Sperimentale. Avocations: chess, photography, reading, travel. Office: Ospedale Sant'Andrea Via Mario Asso n°2 Sp La Spezia 19124 Italy Home: Largo Venticinque Aprile n— 8 54033 Carrara MS Italy Home Phone: 39058570924; Office Phone: 39 0187 604560. Business E-Mail: silvio.roncella@asl5.liguria.it.

RONDELLI, DAMIANO, hematologist, educator; b. Faenza, Italy, Jan. 13, 1963; MD, U. Bologna, Italy, 1990; specialization in Hematology, U. Bologna, 1994. Asst. prof. U. Bologna, 1995—2002; assoc. prof. medicine U. Ill., Chgo., 2002—11, prof. medicine, 2011—, dir., stem cell transplant program, 2002—. Editor: Storia delle Discipline Medicine history of medical Disciplines, 1999, 2003. Recipient Commendatore dell' Ordine della Stella della Solidarieta' Italiana, Pres. Italian Republic. Mem.: Am. Soc. Blood & Marrow Transplantation, Am. Soc. Hematology. Avocation: history. Office: 909 S Wolcott MC734 Chicago IL 60612 Office Fax: 312-413-7963. Business E-Mail: drond@uic.edu.

RONG, SHU, nephrologist; b. Nanjing, Jiangsu, China, Oct. 1, 1972; BS, Second Mil. Med. U., 1996, MD, 2007. Assoc. chief physician Dept. Nephrology, Changzheng Hosp., 2009—. Recipient Mil. Med. Achievement prize, Gen. Logistics Dept., China. Mem.: ISN. Office: 415 Fengyang Rd Shanghai 200003 China Business E-Mail: jingweisy@126.com.

RONG, SONG MEI, agricultural studies educator; b. Huixian city, China, Mar. 18, 1977; PhD, Chinese Acad. Scis., 2007. Prof. Henan Agrl. U., 2007—. Office: Cultural Rd 95 Zhengzhou Henan 450002 China Personal E-mail: smr770505@yahoo.com.cn.

RØNNE, MOGENS, retired cytogeneticist, researcher; b. Rønne, Denmark, Nov. 6, 1941; s. Harry and Manna (Rønne) Pedersen; m. Elisabeth Andersen; Feb. 26, 1965; children: Annette My, Mark. BS in Biology, U. Copenhagen, 1968, MS in Biology, 1971, PhD in Genetics, 1973, DSc, 1998. Postdoctoral Copenhagen U., 1973—75; asst. prof. Odense (Denmark) U., 1975—77, sr. rsch. scientist, 1977—85, assoc. prof., 1985—91; sci. cons. Odense Rsch. Park, 1992—93; sr. rsch. scientist Aarhus (Denmark) U., 1993—94; environ. mgr. Nordisk Tekstil A/S, 1996—2000; ret., 2000. Vis. prof. Notre Dame U., South Bend, Ind., 1985, Purdue U., Lafayette, Ind., 1987, Hokkaido (Japan) U., 1988, M.D. Anderson Cancer Ctr., Houston, 1989; mem. various chromosome standardization coms. Mem. editl. bd. In Vivo, 1989—; referee Hereditas, 1990—, Anticancer Rsch., 1987—, Genet. Sel. Evol., 1988—, Cytogenetic Cell Genetics, 1997, Biotechnology, 1998; contbr. over 100 articles to profl. jours. Served to sgt. Denmark Infantry, 1960-62. Recipient Rsch. grant Odense U., 1977-83, grant Danish Med. Rsch. Coun., 1983-85, grant Danish Cancer Soc., 1986-91, grant Sasakava Found., Japan, 1988. Mem. Danish Soc. Med. Genetics. Home: Skovvej 20 DK-5462 Morud Denmark Office Phone: +45 65964218. Personal E-mail: mogensronne@gmail.com.

RONNEVI, LARS-OLOF H., physician; b. Stockholm, May 21, 1948; MD, Karolinska Inst., 1979, PhD, 1976. Dir. head ops. Karolinska U. Hosp., 1999—. Assoc. prof. anatomy Karolinska Inst., 1978—84, assoc. prof. neurology, 1988—. Avocation: yachting. Office: Karolinska University Hosp Stockholm S-171 76 Sweden Business E-Mail: lars-olof.ronnevi@karolinska.se.

ROOK, ALAIN, dermatologist, educator; Attended, U. Mich. Diplomate Am. Bd. Dermatology, Am. Bd. Internal Medicine, Am. Bd. Allergy and Immunology, Am. Dietetic Assn.-renal, cert. nephrology. Intern McGill Hosp.; resident Hosp. Univ. of Pa.; fellow Nat. Institutes of Health; dir. photopheresis program Univ. of Pa. Health System, prof. dermatology. Named one of Top Docs, Phila. Mag., 2004—, Best Doctors in America, 2005—10, America's Top Doctors, 2007—08, 2010. Office: Perelman Center for Advanced Medicine S Pavilion 1st Fl 3400 Civic Center Blvd Philadelphia PA 19104 Office Phone: 800-789-7366.

ROOKLIN, ANTHONY R., immunologist, allergist; BS, Muhlenberg Coll.; MD, Thomas Jefferson U.; MPH, U. Calif. Diplomate Am. Bd. Allergy and Immunology, Am. Bd. Pediatrics. Intern pediat. Georgetown Univ. Hosp., Washington, resident pediat.; chief resident pediat. Children's Hosp. Med. Ctr., Oakland, Calif.; fellow allergy and clin. immunology Thomas Jefferson Univ.; clin. assoc. prof. pediat. Thomas Jefferson Univ, Phila.; fellow pediat. pulmonary disease The Children's Hosp., Phila.; pvt. practice Asthma and Allergy Assocs., Chester, Pa.; co-chief, divsn. allergy and immunology Crozer-Chester Med. Ctr. Co-author: (book) iving with Asthma, 2005. Fellow: Am. Coll. of Allergy, Asthma and Immunology, Am. Acad.of Allergy, Asthma and Immunology, Am. Acad. of Pediat. Office: Crozer-Chester Medical Center One Medical Ctr Blvd Chester PA 19013 Office Phone: 610-447-2000. Office Fax: 610-447-2262.

ROONGPISUTHIPONG, CHULAPORN, medical educator; b. Bangkok, Bangkok, Apr. 18, 1952; d. Anan and Sunee (Loiduanshai) Thuntanapornchai; m. Anuvat Roongpisuthipong, Nov. 8, 1979; 3 children. BS, Mahidol U., Bangkok, 1975; MD, Mahidol U., 1977, Grad. Diploma in Clin. Sci., 1979. Diplomate Thai Bd. Internal Medicine, Am. Bd. Nutrition. Clin. instr. Faculty of Medicine, Ramathibodi Hosp./Mahidol U., Bangkok, 1982—83, asst. prof., 1983—88, assoc. prof., 1988—95, prof. medicine, 1995—. Bd. dirs. Sunghee Hosp., Bangkok, 1995—; advisor Grad. Program in Nutrition, Kasetsart U., Bangkok, 1988—, maj. advisor, 1996—; mem. com. of examination bd. Royal Coll. Physicians of Thailand, Bangkok, 1988—; bd. dirs. cardiac rehab. Ramathibodi Hosp., Bangkok, 1995. Editl. adv. bd. Nutrition: The Internat. Jour. of Applied and Basic Nutritional Sci., 2001—, editor-in-chief Thai Jour. of Parenteral and Enteral Nutrition, 1992—, reviewer Songklanakarind Med. Jour., 1993; editor (reviewer): European Jour. Clin. Nutrition, 1996; author: (book) Slim Fast, 2001, Diabetes Mellitus, 1985, Clinical in Chest Medicine, 1986, Emergency Medicine, 1988, Medical Management of the Surgical Patient, 1988, Manual of Total Parenteral Nutrition, 1990, Manual of Medical Food, 1991, Nutrition Step for Health, 1991, Manual of Food Exchange, 1991, Enteral and Parenteral Nutrition, 1993, Thai Elderly, 1994, Ambulatory Care in Medicine, 1994, Advance in Medicine, 1995. Recipient Comdr. (3d class), Most Noble Order of the Crown of Thailand, 1987, Knight Comdr. (2d class), 1989, Most Noble Order of the White Elephant, 1993, Knight Grand Cross (1st class), Most Noble Order of the Crown of Thailand, 1997, KnighGrand Cross (1st cross), Most Exalted Order of the White Elephant, 1999. Mem.: Nat. Rsch. Inst., Med. Assn. Thailand, Soc. of Parenteral and Enteral Nutrition of Thailand (bd. dirs. 1991—), Nutrition Assn. of Thailand, Royal Coll. Physicians of Thailand, Women's Med. Assn. Thailand, Fedn. Assn. of Socs. Exptl. Biology, Am. Soc. Clin. Nutrition, Am. Inst. Nutrition. Achievements include research in in hyperlipidemia, thiamine, obesity, diabetes mellitus, renal diseas and totall parenteral nutrition. Avocation: drawing. Home: 99 Moo 11 Krisdanakorn 20 Bangkok 10170 Thailand Home Phone: 662 4414666. Personal E-mail: racrp@mahidol.ac.th.

ROOS, RAYMOND PHILIP, medical educator; Bd. cert. Am. Bd. Psychiatry and Neurology, 1976. Marjorie and Robert E. Straus prof. in neurol. sci. U. Chgo., 1986—. Recipient Matthew T. Moore award, Am. Assn. Neuropathologists, 1971, Career Devel. award, Schweppe Found., 1978—81, Sr. Fellowship award, Nat. MS Soc., 1988—89, Donald W. Mulder award, ALS Assn., 2004, Nat. Rsch. Svc. award, NIH, 1988—89. Fellow: AAAS, Am. Acad. Neurology (mem. sci. com.); mem.: Nat. MS Soc. (chmn. 2007—, rsch. program adv. com. 2002—), Am. Soc. Virology, Am. Neurol. Assn. (assoc.), Soc. Neuroscience, Johns Hopkins Soc. Scholars. Achievements include research in Neurovirology. Office: U Chgo Dept Neurology MC2030 5841 S Maryland Ave Chicago IL 60637

ROOSE, STEVEN PAUL, physician; b. May 24, 1948; BA, Harvard U., 1970; MD, Mt. Sinai, 1974. Prof. Columbia U., 1978. Office: 1051 Riverside Dr New York NY 10032 Office Fax: 212-543-6100. Business E-Mail: spr2@columbia.edu.

ROOSEVELT, JAMES, JR., insurance company executive, lawyer; b. LA, Nov. 9, 1945; s. James and Romelle (Schneider) R.; m. Ann M. Conlon, June 15, 1968; children: Kathy, Tracy, Maura. AB in Govt.

with honors, Harvard U., 1968, JD, 1971; completed Advance Mgmt. Program, Harvard Bus. Sch. Bar. Mass. 1971, DC 1973, US Ct. Appeals (DC cir.) 1973, US Ct. Appeals (1st cir.) 1976, US Supreme Ct. 1975. Assoc. Winthrop, Stimson, Putnam & Roberts, NYC, 1971, Herrick & Smith, Boston, 1975-80, ptnr., 1981-86, Nutter, McClennen & Fish, Boston, 1986-88, Choate, Hall & Stewart, Boston, 1988-98; assoc. commr. for retirement policy Social Security Adminstrn., Washington, 1998-99, co-chair, Tufts Health Care Inst.; sr. v.p., gen. counsel Tufts Health Plan, Waltham, Mass., 1999—2005, pres., CEO, 2005—. Bd. dirs. Kenneth B. Schwartz Ctr., RI Quality Inst.; chmn. Mass. Assn. of Health Plans. Mem. Dem. Nat. Com., Washington, 1980—, Dem. State Com., Boston, 1980—; trustee Emmanuel Coll., Boston, 1982-92, 95—2011; trustee Care Group, Inc., Boston, 1996-00, Mt. Auburn Hosp., Cambridge, Mass., 1984-2000, chmn., 1988-92, chmn. bd. overseers, 2000—06. Lt. JAGC, USN, 1972-75. Mem. ABA, Boston Bar Assn., Mass. Bar Assn., American Health Lawyers Assn. (pres. 2002-03), Mass. Hosp. Assn. (trustee 1987-99, chmn. 1996-97), Harvard Club. Roman Catholic. Avocation: public policy. Office: Tufts Health Plan 705 Mount Auburn St Watertown MA 02472 Office Phone: 617-972-9400. Business E-Mail: james_roosevelt@tufts-health.com. *

ROOT, ALLEN WILLIAM, pediatrician, educator; b. Phila., Sept. 24, 1933; s. Morris Jacob and Priscilla R.; m. Janet Greenberg, June 15, 1958; children: Jonathan, Jennifer, Michael. AB, Dartmouth Coll., 1955, postgrad. Med. Sch., 1954-56; MD, Harvard U., 1958. Diplomate Am. Bd. Pediatrics (mem. bd. 1985—), Am. Bd. Pediatric Endocrinology (mem. bd. 1985-90, chmn. 1990). Intern Strong Meml. Hosp., Rochester, NY, 1958-60; resident in pediatrics Hosp. U. Pa., Phila., 1960-62; fellow in pediatric endocrinology Children's Hosp. of Phila., 1962-65; assoc. physician in pediatrics U. Pa. Sch. Medicine, 1964-66, asst. prof. pediatrics, 1966-69; assoc. prof. pediatrics Temple U. Sch. Medicine, Phila., 1969-73, prof., 1973; asst. physician in endocrinology Children's Hosp. Phila., 1965-69; chmn. divsn. pediatrics Albert Einstein Med. Center., Phila., 1969-73; prof. pediatrics U. South Fla. Coll. Medicine, Tampa, 1973—, prof. biochemistry, 1987—2007, assoc. chmn. dept. pediatrics, 1974-99, dir. sect. pediatric endocrinology, 1973-96. Dir. univ. tchg. svcs. All Children's Hosp., St. Petersburg, 1973-89; mem. Fla. Infant Screening Adv. Coun., 1979-06, chmn., 1994-06; mem. Hillsborough County Thyroid Adv. Com., 1980; mem. med. adv. com. Nat. Pituitary Agy., 1974-78, mem. growth hormone subcom., 1972-79, 81-85; chmn. Fla. Legis. Infant Screening Task Force, 2002. Author: Human Pituitary Growth Hormone, 1972; co-editor: (with C. La Cauza) Problems in Pediatric Endocrinology, 1980; mem. editl. bd. Jour. Pediats., 1973-81, Jour. Adolescent Health Care, 1979-95, Jour. Pediat. Endocrinology and Metabolism, 1985-, Jour. Clin. Endocrinology and Metabolism, 1993-96, 2001-04, Growth, Genetics and Hormones, 1993-, Pediat. in Rev., 1995-2001; assoc. editor Adolescent and Pediat. Gynecology, 1992-95, Current Opinion in Pediats., sect. editor, Endocrine and Metabolism, 1993-, mem. editl. bd. 2006-, Internat. Jour. Pediatric Endocrinology, 2009-. USPHS grantee, Birth Defects Found. grantee. Mem. AAAS, Am. Pediatric Soc., Soc. Pediatric Rsch., Lawson Wilkins Pediatric Endocrine Soc. (treas. 1979-88, pres. 1988-89), Endocrine Soc., Am. Acad. Pediatrics, Am. Fedn. Clin. Rsch., Soc. Exptl. Biology and Medicine, Soc. Nuclear Medicine, N.Y. Acad. Sci., Phila. Coll. Physicians, Phila. Endocrine Soc. (bd. dirs. 1971-72, treas. 1973), Dartmouth Coll. Alumni Coun., Dartmouth Club. Office: 600 5th Ave S Saint Petersburg FL 33701-4816 Business E-Mail: roota@allkids.org. *

ROOT-BERNSTEIN, ROBERT SCOTT, biologist, educator; b. Washington, Aug. 7, 1953; s. Morton Ira and Maurine (Berkstresser) Bernstein; m. Michèle Marie Root-Bernstein, Sept. 2, 1978; children: Meredith Marie, Brian Robert. AB, Princeton U., 1975, PhD, 1980. Postdoctoral fellow Salk Inst. for Biol. Studies, La Jolla, Calif., 1981-82, rsch. assoc., 1983-84; from asst. to assoc. prof. Mich. State U., East Lansing, 1987-96, prof., 1996—. Cons. Parke-Davis Pharm. Rsch. Divsn., Ann Arbor, 1990-96, Chiron Corp., 1992-96; mem. adv. bd. Soc. for Advancement Gifted Edn., Chgo., 1987-92; Sigma Xi nat. lectr., 1994-96. Author: Discovering, 1989, Rethinking AIDS, 1993, Honey, Mud, Maggots and Other Medical Marvels, 1997, Sparks of Genius, 1999; columnist The Scis. mag., 1989-92, The Leonardo mag., 2004—; contbr. numerous articles to profl. jours. MacArthur Found. fellow, 1981-86; recipient D.J. Ingle Meml. Writing prize, 1988. Mem. Phi Beta Kappa (hon.), Sigma Xi. Avocations: painting, photography, cello, drawing, model building. Office: Mich State U Dept Physiology Biomed & Phys Scis Bldg East Lansing MI 48824 Office Phone: 517-355-6475 ext. 1101. Business E-Mail: rootbern@msu.edu.

ROPER, WILLIAM LEE, dean, preventive medicine physician, administrator; b. Birmingham, Ala., July 6, 1948; s. Richard Barnard and Jean (Fyfe) R.; m. Maryann Roper, Jan. 14, 1978 AA, Fla. Coll., 1968; BS, U. Ala, 1970, MD, 1974, M.P.H., 1981. Diplomate Am. Bd. Pediatrics, Am. Bd. Preventive Medicine. Intern, resident in pediatrics U. Colo. Med. Ctr., Denver, 1974-77; health officer Jefferson County Dept. Health, Birmingham, 1977-82, 83; White House fellow Washington, 1982-83; spl. asst. to Pres. for health policy, 1983-86; adminstr., Health Care Finance Adminstrn. HHS, Washington, 1986-89; dep. asst. to pres. for domestic policy The White House, Washington, 1989-90; adminstr. Agy. for Toxic Substances and Disease Registry and dir. Ctrs. for Disease Control and Prevention, Atlanta, 1990-93; sr. v.p. Prudential Health Care, Roseland, NJ, 1994-97; pres. Prudential Ctr. for Health Care Rsch., Atlanta, 1993-95; dean, sch. pub. health, prof. medicine and health policy U. NC, Chapel Hill, 1997—2004, dean Sch. Medicine, 2004—, vice chancellor med. affairs, 2004—, CEO U. NC Health Care, 2004—. Mem. Inst. Medicine, Phi Beta Kappa, Alpha Omega Alpha Republican. Office: Office of Dean U NC Med School 125 MacNider Bldg CB #7000 Chapel Hill NC 27599 Office Phone: 919-966-4161. *

RORKE-ADAMS, LUCY BALIAN, neuropathologist, pathologist, educator; b. St. Paul, June 22, 1929; d. Aram Haji and Karzouhy (Ousdigian) Balian; m. Robert Radcliffe Rorke, June 4, 1960 (dec. Mar. 31, 2002); m. Boyce M. Adams, Apr. 16, 2004 (dec. June 21, 2006). AB, U. Minn., Mpls., 1951, MA, 1952, BS, 1955, MD, 1957. Diplomate Am. Bd. Pathology. Intern Phila. Gen. Hosp., 1957-58, resident anat. pathology and neuropathology, 1958-62, asst. neuropathologist, 1963-67, chief pediat. pathologist, 1967-68, chief neuropathologist, 1968-69, chmn. dept. anat. pathology and chief neuropathologist, 1969-73, chmn. dept. pathology, 1973-77, pres. med. staff, 1973-75; neuropathologist Children's Hosp., Phila., 1965—, pres. med. staff, 1986-88, acting pathologist-in-chief, 1995-2000. Cons. neuropathologist Wyeth Rsch. Labs., Radnor, Pa., 1961—87, Wistar Inst. Anatomy and Biology, Phila., 1967—93; assoc. prof. pathology U. Pa. Sch. Medicine, Phila., 1970—, prof. pathology, 1973—, clin. prof. neurology, 1979—, clin. prof. pediat., 1997—; forensic neuropathologist Office Med. Examiner, Phila., 1977—2004. Author: Myelinization of the Brain in the Newborn, 1969, Pathology of Perinatal Brain Injury, 1982; mem. editl. bd. Jours. Neuropathology Exptl. Neurology, 1980—85, 1993—98, Pediat. Neurosurgery, 1984—2002, Child's Nervous Sys., 1984—88, Brain Pathology, 1990—95; contbr. articles to profl. jours. Lucy Balian Rorke-Adams chair Neuropathology Children's Hosp. Phila. Recipient Provost's award for excellence in tchg., U. Pa., 2003; NIH fellow, 1961—62, NIH grantee, 1963—68. Fellow: Coll. Am. Pathologists; mem.: AMA, Phila. Coll. Physicians (trustee 2002—04, treas. 2004—08, trustee 2009—), Burlington County Med. Soc., Am. Neurol. Soc., Am. Soc. Neuroradiology (hon.), Am. Assn. Neuropathologists (exec. coun. 1976—85, v.p. 1979—80, pres. 1981—82, Meritorious Svc. award 1999), Phila. Neurol. Soc. (v.p. 1971—72, editor transactions 1973, pres. 1975—76, Richard D. Wood Disting. Alumina award 2007). Office: Childrens Hosp Phila 324 S 34th St Philadelphia PA 19104-4399 Home: 316 E Maple Ave Moorestown NJ 08057-2014 Business E-Mail: Rorke@email.chop.edu.

ROS, EMILIO, physician, consultant; b. Girona, Spain, Feb. 6, 1945; MD, Barcelona Sch. Medicine, 1969, PhD, 1990. Cons. Inst. U. Dexeus, 1989, Hosp. Clínic Barcelona, 1978—2002, sr. cons., 2003—. Contbr. articles to profl. jours., chapters to books. Grant, Spanish Ministry Health. Mem.: Internat. Atherosclerosis Soc., European Atherosclerosis Soc., Soc. Española de Arteriosclerosis. Avocations: reading, skiing, walking. Home: Ravella 15 2-1 Barcelona 08021 Spain Home Fax: 34 93 4537829. Business E-Mail: eros@clinic.ub.es.

ROSA, ANTONIA MARIA, nursing educator; b. Mato Grosso do Sul, Feb. 6, 1970; Degree in Nursing, Fed. U. Mato Grosso do Sul, 1999; MPH, Fed. U. Mato Grosso, 2008. Nurse Regional Hosp. Cáceres, 2001, mgr., 2009; asst. prof. State U. Mato Grosso, 2006—. Mem.: Brazilian Assn. Pediatric Nurses. Avocation: reading. Office: Avenida Getúlio Vargas 2335 Caceres Mato Grosso 78200 000 Brazil Office Fax: 55(65)3221-0500. Business E-Mail: antonia-mr@unemat.br.

ROSALES, OSCAR R., cardiologist; b. Barranquilla, Colombia, Mar. 17, 1959; s. Oscar and Grace (Cepeda) R.; m. Marguerite F. Miranne, Jan. 11, 1960; children: Andrew Daniel, Sophie Marguerite. MD, Javeriana U., Bogota, Colombia, 1982. Diplomate Am. Bd. Internal Medicine. Intern, chief med. resident Tulane U., New Orleans, 1984-88; fellow in cardiology Yale U., New Haven, 1988-91, asst. prof. medicine, 1993-96; fellow in interventional cardiology U. Tex., Houston, 1991-92, assoc. prof. medicine, dir. critical care quality assurance program West Haven VA Med. Ctr., 1993-96; dir. coronary care unit Ochsner Clinic, New Orleans, 1996-97; dir. cath lab., pres. med. staff Meml. Hermann Hosp., Houston. Author: Hemodynamic Forces and Vascular Cell Biology, 1993. Recipient Humanism in Medicine award, Arnold P. Gold Found., NJ, 2002, tchg. award, Alpha Omega Alpha, 2006, Tulane U., Ochsner Clinic and U. Tex. Med. Sch., Houston. Fellow Am. Coll. Cardiology, Soc. Cardiovas. Angiography and Interventions; mem. Am. Heart Assn. Roman Catholic. Avocations: tennis, reading, jogging. Office: Med Ctr Heart Cons 6400 Fannin St #2220 Houston TX 77030 Home Phone: 713-838-0224; Office Phone: 713-796-2220. E-mail: orosales@mcheart.net.

ROSALES-ARZU, FEDERICO, plastic surgeon; b. Antigua, Guatemala, Aug. 1, 1943; s. Federico and Adelina (Arzu) Rosales; m. Ana Moreno, Apr. 26, 1969; children: Federico, Carolina, Diego. MD, San Carlos U., 1969; MD in Plastic Surgery, Baylor Coll. Medicine, Houston, Tex., 1977. Resident in gen. surgery St. Vincent's Hosp., 1973-75; resident in plastic surgery Baylor Coll. Medicine, Houston, 1975-77; chief svc. plastic surgery Roosevelt Hosp., Guatamala City, 1978-93; plast. surgeon Med. Ctr. Hosp., Guatemala City, 1980—. Plastic surgeon Orthopedic & Rehab. Hosp., Guatemala City, 1981-95. Mem. Internat. Confedn. Plastic Reconstructive & Aesthetic Surgery, Iberolatin Am. Plastic Surgery Fedn., Guatemalan Coll. Physicians & Surgeons. Roman Catholic. Avocations: softball, tennis, squash, photography. Mailing: Sect 378/Gua 7801 NW 37th St Doral FL 33166-6503 Office: Edificio Centro Medico IIEdificio Centro 6a. Avenida 3-22 Zona 10 Ofc 402 1010 Guatemala City Guatemala Guatemala Personal E-mail: rosmorfam@citel.com.gt.

ROSALION, ALEXANDER, cardiothoracic surgeon; b. Melbourne, Victoria, Australia, Feb. 11, 1951; s. Valery and Valentina (Andrussen) R.; m. Ruth Margaret Freeman, May 19, 1973; children: Catherine Louise, Richard Alexander, David Anthony. MB, BS, U. Melbourne, 1975, B Med. Sci., 1975. Intern Royal Melbourne Hosp., 1976-78, surg. registrar, 1979-82; cardiothoracic surg. registrar St. Vincents Hosp., Melbourne, 1983-84; fellow cardiac surgery Johns Hopkins Hosp., Balt., 1985, Case We. Res. U. Hosp., Cleve., 1985-87; surgeon cardiac and thoracic Austin Hosp., Melbourne, 1987—. Cardiothoracic surgeon St. Vincents Hosp., Melbourne, 1992—; thoracic surgeon We. Hosp., Melbourne, 1988-94, Maroondah Hosp., Melbourne, 1994—, Box Hill Hosp., 2004—; clin. instr. U. Melbourne, 1988—; presenter in field. Contbr. articles to profl. jours. Fellow Royal Australasian Coll. Surgeons; mem. AAS, AMA, Cardiac Soc., Thoracic Soc., Thoracic Surgeons, Australasian Soc. Cardiac and Thoracic Surgeons, Assn. Thoracic and Cardiovascular Surgeons of Asia. Russian Orthodox. Avocation: photography. Home: 77 Greythorn Rd Balwyn North 3104 Australia Office: 18 Martin St Heidelberg 3084 Australia Office Phone: 61 3 9457 1837. Personal E-mail: alex@rosalion.net.

ROSALSKY, BARBARA ELLEN, artist, community health nurse; b. NYC, Nov. 16, 1948; d. Ellis M. Rosalsky and Claire (Schwartz) Rosalsky Shapiro; m. Dennis Robinson (div.). BA, SUNY, Plattsburgh, 1970. Sales girl Cambridge Artist Art Supply Store, Mass., 1970—71; artist Pillar of Fire mag., Zarephath, NJ, 1977; home health aide CMR, Bound Brook, NJ, 1978—; designer New Brunswick Tomorrow, NJ, 1980—93; art therapist Middlesex Hosp., New Brunswick, 1981—83; vol. office Robert Wood Johnson Hosp., 1995—2008. One-woman shows include The Bird and Me, 1980, Highland Pk. Libr., N.J., The City, 2003, exhibited in group shows at Other Artists Other Art, Robeson Newark Gallery, N.J., 1983, Greeter State Theatre, 2007—11. Mem. Cultural Arts Commn., Piscataway, N.J., 1993-2007; mem. Ams. for the Arts Action Fund, 2006-10. SUNY Plattsburgh scholar, 1970. Mem.: Women's Caucus Art, Quality Inn Swim Club. Democrat. Avocations: piano, swimming, dance, print making. Home: 114 Woodland Rd Piscataway NJ 08854-4222

ROSARIO, LUIS BRAS, cardiologist; b. Lisbon, Portugal, Nov. 21, 1964; s. Antonio and Maria (Bras) R. MD, Lisbon U., 1988; PhD, U. Lisbon Med. Sch., 2005. Cert. cardiologist Health Ministry and Med. Order; cert. Am. Soc. Echocardiography, Am. Soc. Nuclear Cardiology. Intern Hosp. Santa Maria, Lisbon, 1989-91; resident Hosp. Santa Marta, Lisbon, 1991-92, fellow, 1992-95, cardiologist, 1996—97, 2009—; fellow cardiovascular divsn. Brigham & Women's Hosp., 1995—96; cardiologist Hosp. Garcia de Orta, 1998—2005; asst. physiology dept., asst. Molecular Medicine Inst. Lisbon U., 2002—05, cons. masters program, 2003—; cardiologist Hosp. Santa Cruz, Lisbon, 2005—, Ctr. Hospitalar Lisboa Norte, 2009—. Physiology monitor Lisbon U. Med. Sch., 1986-91; fellow Univ. Coll., London, 1995, Harvard Med. Sch., Boston, 1995 96; cardiologist Hosp. Santa Marta, Lisbon, Portugal; head heart failure unit Hosp. Garcia Orta, Lisbon, vis. physician Brigham & Womens Hosp., 1998; rschr. Molecular Medicine Inst., Lisbon U., 2006.; cons. masters program Lisbon Tech. U., 2003—; ind. postdoctoral Gulbenkian Sci. Inst., 2007-; cons. masters program biomed. scis. U. Algarve, vis. prof. biomedicine masters program, 2008-. Recipient Rsch. award Portuguese Health Ministry, 1996. Fellow: European Soc. Cardiology (European Cardiologist Diploma 2005); mem.: Portuguese Soc. Cardiology (bd. dirs. 2000, Independent Post Doctoral Inst. Gulbenkian Ciencia). Avocations: music, painting, tennis, mountain biking, sailing. Office: Av Cinco de Outubro 75-3 1050-049 Lisbon Portugal Home: Rua Quinta Grande 8 R/C 2780-156 Oeiras Portugal Office Phone: 351213159507. Personal E-mail: lbr@net.vodafone.pt.

ROSARIO, NELSON AUGUSTO, medical educator; b. Londrina, Parana, Brazil, Feb. 7, 1949; m. Teresa Rosario, Sept. 6, 1973. MD, U. Parana, Curitiba, 1972; PhD, Unicamp, Campinas, 1994. Prof. pediat. U. Parana, Curitiba, 1980—. Dir. allergy divsn. UFPR, Curitiba, 1985—. Sci. dir. Allergy Soc., Sao Paulo, Brazil, 2000—. Office: Univ Parana Rua General Carneiro 181 80060-900 Curitiba PR Brazil Office Fax: 5541 3339 Ext. 7043.

ROSARIO-GUARDIOLA, REINALDO, dermatologist; b. Santurce, PR, Sept. 17, 1948; s. Tomas and Aurea (Guardiola) Rosario; m. Fe Milagros Rivera, Aug. 19, 1972; children: Amarillis, Reinaldo, Gadiel. BS, U. P.R., 1968, MD, 1972. Rsch. fellow photobiology Harvard Med. Sch., Boston, 1976-77; chief, dermatology sect. San Juan VA Hosp., Rio Piedras, 1979—2008; pvt. practice, 2008—. Bd. dirs. Wesleyan Acad. Guaynabo, P.R., 1990-99. Grantee Dermatology Found., 1978. Fellow Am. Acad. Dermatology; mem. P.R. Dermatol. Soc. (pres. scientific com. 1978-79, pres.-elect 1999-2000, pres. 2000-01), Harvard-MGH House Officers Club, Alpha Omega Alpha. Office: 652 Munoz Rivera Ave Ste 3170 San Juan PR 00918-4293 Home Phone: 787-731-1773; Office Phone: 787-765-2305. Personal E-mail: reinaldo_rsr@yahoo.com. Business E-Mail: rrosario@icepr.com.

ROSBE, KRISTINA W., pediatric otolaryngologist, surgeon; BA magna cum laude, Wellesley Coll., Mass., 1989; MD, Dartmouth Med. Sch., Hanover, NH, 1993. Diplomate Am. Bd. Otolaryngology-Head and Neck Surgery, lic. Calif. Resident gen. surgery U. NC Hosp., Chapel Hill, 1993—94, resident otolaryngology, 1994—98; fellowship pediat. otolaryngology Children's Hosp., Boston, 1998—2000; assoc. prof. U. Calif. San Francisco, dir. divsn. pediat otolaryngology, 2002—. Contbr. articles to profl. jours. Mem.: Am. Acad. Pediat., Soc. Ear, Nose, & Throat Advances in Children, Am. Soc. Pediat. Otolaryngology, Am. Acad. Otolaryngology— Head & Neck Surgery. Achievements include research in the association between neonatal upper airway symptoms and laryngopharyngeal reflux; sinus disease and hearing loss in patients with cystic fibrosis. Mailing: U Calif Pediat Otolaryngology 1300 S Eliseo Dr Ste 204 Greenbrae CA 94904 Office Phone: 415-353-2757. Business E-Mail: krosbe@ohns.ucsf.edu.

ROSCH, PAUL JOHN, internist, educator; b. Yonkers, NY, June 30, 1927; s. Samuel Joseph and Mary (Gang) R.; m. Lorraine Marie Hunt, June 27, 1951; children: David Carl, Jonathan Hunt, Jane Ellen, Michael Edward, Richard Joseph, Donna Marie; m. Marguerite Delamater, Sept. 12, 1972. AB, Brown U., NYU, 1948, MA, 1950; MD, Albany Med. Coll., 1954. Diplomate Am. Bd. Internal Medicine. Fellow Inst. Exptl. Medicine and Surgery, U. Montreal, Que., Canada, 1951-52; intern, asst. resident in medicine Johns Hopkins Hosp., 1954-56; resident in medicine, then chief dept. metabolism Walter Reed Med. Ctr., 1956-58; physician-in-charge nuclear medicine St. John's Riverside Hosp., Yonkers, 1959-67, dir. endocrine clinic, sr. attending physician, 1959-96, vice chief of staff, 1977; chief endocrine clinic St. Joseph's Hosp., 1959, sr. cons. in medicine, 1980—; pres. Am. Inst. Stress, Yonkers, 1978—, sr. cons. in medicine, 1980—; clin. prof. medicine and psychiatry N.Y. Med. Coll., 1980—. Asst. clin. prof. medicine Mt. Sinai Hosp. Sch. Medicine, 1963-67; former adj. prof. medicine in psychiatry U. Md. Sch. Medicine. From asst. to assoc. editor Health Comm. and Informatics; editor-in-chief Stress Medicine, 1990—; mem. editorial bd. AMA Archives Internal Medicine, Folia Clinica Internat, Jour. Human Stress, Internat. Jour. Psychosomatics, Am. Jour. Health Promotion, Cardiovascular Revs. & Reports, Internat. Jour. Stress Mgmt., Comprehensive Therapy, Jour. Human Behavior; contbg. editor Creative Living; contbr. articles to profl. jours. Bd. govs. Jewish Community Ctr.; bd. dirs. Family Svc. Soc., Mensana Clinic, 1980—; chmn. bd. Internat. Found. Biosocial Devel. and Human Health, 1980—; mem. adv. bd. Image Inst., 1980—. Capt. AUS, 1956-58. Fellow ACP, Internat. Stress Mgmt.

Assn. (hon. v.p. 1991—), Am. Coll. Cardiology, Internat. Acad. Medicine, Am. Coll. Angiology, NY Diabetes Assn.; mem. Westchester Diabetes Assn. (pres. 1968), Internat. Law Enforcement Stress Assn. (adv. bd. 1980—), Yonkers Acad. Medicine (bd. govs., pres. 1971), NY Cardiology Soc., Acad. Psychosomatic Medicine, Soc. Behavioral Medicine, NY Acad. Scis., Endocrine Soc., Am. Diabetes Assn., Westchester Soc. Internat. Medicine (past pres.), Stress Mgmt. Assn. (hon. v.p.), NY State Soc. Internal Medicine (pres. 1974), Soc. Nuclear Medicine (bd. dirs.), Am. Fedn. Clin. Rsch., Am. Soc. Internal Medicine, Am. Geriatrics Soc., Elmwood Country Club, Atlantis Golf Club, Breakers Golf Club, St. Andrews Golf Club. Home: 10 Old Jackson Ave Hastings On Hudson NY 10706-3203 Office Phone: 914-963-1200. Personal E-mail: stress124@optonline.net.

ROSE, ARON D., ophthalmologist, educator; b. Norwalk, Conn., Sept. 23, 1958; s. Gilbert and Anne Rose; m. Stacey L. Miller; children: Jenna, Lauren, Hannah. BA (hon.), Brown U., Providence, 1980; MD, NY Med. Coll., Valhalla, 1985; degree in ophthalmology, Mt. Sinai Sch. of Medicine, NYC, 1989. Fellow Am. Bd. Ophthalmology, 1989. Assoc. clin. prof. Yale U. Sch. Medicine, New Haven, 1989—, Yale U. Sch. Nursing, New Haven, 1996—. Dir., residency tng. Yale U. Dept. Ophthalmology and Visual Scis., New Haven, 1992—94; cons. Advanced Med. Optics, Santa Ana, Calif., 2003—; sect. editor Techniques in Ophthalmology, 2007—; found. co-dir. Eye Team Worldwide, 2010—. Composer: Quartet for Clarinet & Strings, 1980; contbr. articles various profl. jours. Advisor JusticeWorks Med. Humanitarian Assn., Newtown, Pa., 1994—99; bd. mem. New Haven Med. Assn., 1995—2004; strategic oversight New Haven Hunger & Relief, 1997—2006; invited faculty Project Orbis Internat., NYC, 1992—2006; advisor Yale China Health Adv. Com. Recipient Brand Music Premium for Excellence in Musical Composition, Brown U., 1980, Departmental Honors, 1980; named one of Best Drs. in America, 2010—. Fellow: Am. Acad. Ophthalmology (life); mem.: European Soc. Cataract and Refractive Surgeons, Conn. Soc. Eye Physicians, Conn. Glaucoma Soc., New Eng. Ophthal. Soc., Conn. State Med. Soc., Am. Soc. Cataract and Refractive Surgeons. Office: Stony Creek Med Ctr Business Park Dr Branford CT 06405 *

ROSE, DAVID, surgeon, educator; MD, Columbia U. Diplomate Am. Bd. Surgery-gen. surgery, Am. Bd. Surgery-breast surgery. Intern Cornell Univ., NY, resident NY; fellow Meml. Sloan-Kettering Cancer Ctr.; hosp. affiliations include Bryn Mawr Hosp., 1983, Lankenau Med. Ctr., 1994, Paoli Hosp., 1997; clin. assoc. prof. surgery Thomas Jefferson Univ. Hosp.; clin. assoc. prof. surgery Sch. of Medicine Drexel Univ.; chief gen. surgery; attending physician. Author: (publs.) Ten Year Results of Immediate Reconstruction following Mastectomy for Carcinoma of the Breast, 1995, Results of Laparoscopic Inguinal Herniorraphy compared to Conventional Repair. Poster Presentation, 1996, Laparoscopic Inguinal Hernia Repair- 900 cases in a single practice, 2000. Founding mem. Radnor Ednl. Found.; bd. mem. Bryn Mawr Hosp. Found. Recipient Radnor Volunteer of the Year award, 1995, AMA Physician Recognition award, 1998, Bryn Mawr Hosp. Staff Med. Milestones award, 2005; named Top Doctor, Doctors Across Am., 2003—04; named one of the Top Doctor, Phila. Mag., 1996, 1999, 2002, 2004—05, 2011, Am.'s Top Doctors, 2004. Mem.: ACS, Nat. Surg. Adjuvant Breast Project, Phila. Acad. of Surgeons, Soc. Laparoendoscopic Surgeons, Montgomery County Med. Soc., Pa. Med. Soc. Office: Bryn Mawr Hospital MOB N Ste 306 830 Old Lancaster Rd Bryn Mawr PA 19010 Office Phone: 610-527-1185. Office Fax: 610-527-1940.

ROSE, ERIC ALLEN, pharmaceutical executive; b. Bronx, NY, Jan. 25, 1951; s. Herb and Myra (Morgenstern) Rose; m. Ellise Delphin; children: Adam, Sydney, Zachary, Gabriel. BA summa cum laude, Columbia Coll., NYC, 1971; MD, Columbia U., NYC, 1975. Diplomate Am. Bd. Thoracic Surgery, Am. Bd.Surgery. Exec. v.p., Life Sciences MacAndrews & Forbes Holdings Inc.; surg. rsch. fellow NIH, 1977; dir., cardiac transplantation svc. Columbia Presbyn. Med Ctr., 1982—93, dir., surgical cardiac intensive care unit, 1982—86, dir., clin. perfusion svc., 1986—95, chief cardiothoracic surg. svc., 1990—96; asst. prof., surgery Coll. Physicians & Surgeons Columbia U., 1982—88, assoc. prof., 1988—93, prof., 1993—; intern surgery NY Presbyn. Hosp., 1975—76, resident surgery, 1976—79, resident thoracic surgery, 1980—81, asst. attending surgeon, 1982—86, assoc. attending surgeon, 1982—93, attending surgeon, 1993—, chmn., Surgery, surgeon-in-chief, Columbia Presbyn. Ctr., 1994—2007; dir., cardiothoracic svc. St. Michael's Med. Ctr., Newark, 1997—2001; prof., surgery Johnson & Johnson, 1999—; chief surgeon Columbia U. Med. Ctr., 1994—, assoc. dean, translational rsch., 2004—05; interim CEO SIGA Technologies Inc., 2001, chmn., CEO, 2007—; chmn., Dept. of Health Mt. Sinai Sch. of Med., 2008. Bd. dirs. NY Regional Transplant Program. Contbr. articles to profl. jours.; author: (book) Management of End-Stage Heart Disease, 1998, Second Opinion: The Columbia Presbyterian Guide to Surgery, 2000; editl. bd. Jour. Heart Transplantation, 1982—86, Jour. Thoracic Cardiovascular Surgery, 1993—. Mem., Heart Transplantation Com. United Network for Organ Sharing. Recipient William Cumming Meml. award in Experimental Psychology, Robert Loeb Meml. award in Internal Med., Allen O. Whipple Meml. award in Surgery. Fellow: Am. Coll. Cardiology; mem.: AMA, ACS, Soc. U. Surgeons, Soc. U. Surgeons, Soc. Thoracic Surgeons, NY Soc. Thoracic Surgery, NY Heart Assn., NY County Med. Soc., Internat. Soc. Heart & Lung Transplantation (bd. councilors, pres. 1993), Am. Surgical Assn., Am. Soc. Transplant Surgeons (com. on heart transplantation), Am. Heart Assn. (exec. com. of coun. cardiovascular surgery), Am. Coll. Physician Inventors, Am. Assn. Thoracic Surgery, Alpha Omega Alpha, Phi Beta Kappa. Achievements include research in mechanical alternatives to transplantation. Office: SIGA Technologies Inc 35 E 62nd St New York NY 10065 also: NY Presbyn Hosp Columbia Milstein Bldg Rm 7435 177 Fort Wash Ave New York NY 10032 also: Columbia U 622 W 168th St New York NY 10032 Office Phone: 212-305-9600, 212-672-9100. Office Fax: 212-305-3100, 212-672-3130. Business E-Mail: erose@mafgrp.com. E-mail: erose@siga.com. *

ROSE, JESSICA, medical educator; d. Menko and Marjorie DeWitt Rose; children: Will Jackson Agramonte, Thomas Grant Agramonte. BS in Zoology, U. C. Davis, Calif., 1980; PhD in Physiology, Stanford U., Calif., 1991. Sr. rsch. scientist, dept orthop. Surgery Stanford U., 1994—2003, asst. prof., dept orthop. Surgery, 2003—10, assoc. prof., dept. orthop. surgery, 2010—; dir., motion & gait analysis lab Lucile Packard Childrens Hosp., Palo Alto, 1989—. Taskforce mem. Nat. Ctr. Med. Rehab. Rsch., 1998—99; adv. bd. botulinum toxin b Elan Pharms, San Francisco, 2000—02; faculty adv. bd. Clayman Inst. Studies Gender, Stanford U., 2003—08; editl. reviewer Archives Phys. Medicine & Rehab., 2006—07; sci. rsch. reviewer NSF, 2007—08; taskforce mem. NIH, Pediats Motor Disorders, 2001—; course dir., anatomy movement Stanford U., 2004—; editl. reviewer Devel. Medicine & Child Neurology Jour., London, 2005—, Jour. Applied Biomechanics, 2009—; primary investigator Nat. Rsch. Network Artificial Walking Cerebral Palsy, 2008—; rsch. com. mem. Am. Acad. Cerebral Palsy & Devel. Medicine, 2010—. Editor: (book) Human Walking. Bd. mem. Com. Green Foothills, Palo Alto, 1999—2006. Recipient Harman Neuroscis. Clin. Endowment award, Stanford U., 2005—07; Dean's Postdoc. fellowship, Stanford U. Sch. Medicine, 1992, Ednl. fellowship, Am. Lung Assn., 1986—87. Fellow: Am. Acad. Cerebral Palsy and Devel. Medicine (rsch. com. mem.). Achievements include research in neonatal brain and motor deficits in preterm children and neuromuscular mechanisms of cerebral palsy. Office: Dept Orthopedic Surgery Stanford Univ 770 Welch Rd Ste 400 Palo Alto CA 94304 Office Phone: 650-497-8084. Office Fax: 650-498-7521. Business E-Mail: jessica.rose@stanford.edu.

ROSE, JOAN BRAY, water microbiologist, researcher, educator; b. San Bernardino, Calif., Mar. 5, 1954; d. Raymond Taylor and Betty (Soukup) Bray; m. Tom J. Rose, Dec. 3, 1976; children: Rachel Lynn, Jared Kevin. MS in Microbiology, U. Wyo., 1980; PhD in Microbiology, U. Ariz., 1985. Rsch. assoc. dept. microbiology, immunology, nutrition U. Ariz., Tucson, 1986-89; asst. prof. dept. environ. and occupl. health U. South Fla. Coll. Pub. Health, Tampa, Fla., 1989—94, assoc. prof. dept. marine sci., 1994—97, prof. coll. marine sci., 1998—2002; Homer Nowlin endowed chair water rsch. Mich. State U., East Lansing, 2003—, co-dir. ctr. water sci., 2005—, co-dir. ctr. advancing microbial risk assessment, 2005—. Bd. dirs. sci. adv. EPA subcom. Coliert Testing. Editor Internat. Jour. Environ. Health Rsch., 1991; contbr. articles to profl. jours. Spkr. Earth Day, Pasco County, 1990. Fellow AAAS; mem. NAE, NAS, Nat. Acad. Engring., Am. Soc. Microbiology (com. mem. 1990-93), Am. Water Works Assn. (chmn. 1987—). Achievements include development of methods for and recognition of Waterborne Cryptosporidium. Office: Mich State University Dept Fisheries Wildlife Crops Soil Sci 13 Natural Resources Bldg East Lansing MI 48824 Office Phone: 517-432-4412. Office Fax: 517-432-1699. Business E-Mail: rosejo@msu.edu. *

ROSE, JOHN CHARLES, internist, educator; b. NYC, Dec. 13, 1924; s. Hugh Stanley and Marie-Louise (Delury) R.; m. Dorothy Anne Donnelly, June 26, 1948; children— Nancy, Ellen, John Charles, Richard, Christopher. BS, Fordham U., 1946; MD magna cum laude, Georgetown U., 1950, D.Sc. (hon.), 1973; D.C.L. (hon.), Mt. St. Mary's Coll., 1973. Diplomate: Am. Bd. Internal Medicine, Am. Bd. Family Practice. Intern Walter Reed Army Hosp., 1950-51; resident, research fellow Georgetown U., VA hosps., Washington, 1950-54; established investigator Am. Heart Assn., 1954-57; instr., asst. prof. medicine Georgetown U., 1954-57, coord. med. edn., 1957-58, assoc. prof. physiology and biophysics, 1958-60, prof., 1960-91, chmn. dept. physiology and biophysics, 1958-63, dean Sch. Medicine, 1963-73, 78-79, prof. medicine, 1973-91, prof. emeritus, 1991—, vice chancellor Med. Ctr., 1984-87. Assoc. editor Am. Family Physician, 1955-62, chief med. editor, 1962-88; assoc. editor Acad. Medicine, 1992-95; contbr. articles to sci. publs. Trustee Charles E. Culpeper Found., 1986-96. Served to 2d lt. USAAF, 1943-45. Decorated Air medal. Master ACP; mem. Am. Physiol. Soc., Soc. Exptl. Biology and Medicine (nat. councillor 1962-63), Am. Heart Assn. (fellow sect. circulation). Clubs: Cosmos (Washington). Home: 5710 Surrey St Chevy Chase MD 20815-5520 *

ROSE, MICHAEL ROBERTSON, evolutionary biology educator, consultant; b. Iserlohn, Germany; s. James Barry and Charlotte Julia Rose; children: Darius, Caitlin, Liam, Muireann. BS, Queen's U., Kingston, Ont., Can., 1975, MS, 1976; PhD, U. Sussex, Eng., 1979. NATO sci. fellow U. Wis., Madison, 1979-81; asst. prof. Dalhousie U., Halifax, N.S., Canada, 1981-85, assoc. prof., 1985-87; assoc. prof. evolutionary biology U. Calif., Irvine, 1987-90, prof., 1990—, dir. Intercampus Rsch. Program Exptl. Evolution, 2004—05, dir. Network Exptl. Rsch. Evolution, 2006—. Author: Evolutionary Biology of Aging, 1991, Adaptation, 1996, Darwin's Spectre, 1998, Methuselah Flies, 2004, The Long Tomorrow, 2005, Evolution and Ecology of the Organism, 2006, Experimental Evolution, 2009. Recipient President's prize Am. Soc. Naturalists, 1992, Busse award World Congress Gerontology, Adelaide, Australia, 1997. Mem. AAAS, Soc. for Study Evolution. Avocation: music. Office Phone: 949-824-8121. E-mail: mrrose@uci.edu.

ROSE, NOEL RICHARD, immunologist, microbiologist, educator; b. Stamford, Conn., Dec. 3, 1927; s. Samuel Allison and Helen (Richard) R.; m. Deborah S. Harber, June 14, 1951; children: Alison, David, Bethany, Jonathan. BS, Yale U., 1948; MA, U. Pa., 1949, PhD, 1951; MD, SUNY, Buffalo, 1964; MD (hon.), U. Cagliari, Italy, 1990; ScD (hon.), U. Sassari, Italy, 1992; Order of the First Class (hon.), Ctrl. U. Venezuela, 1997. From instr. to prof. microbiology SUNY Sch. Medicine, Buffalo, 1951-73, dir. Center for Immunology, 1970-73, dir. Erie County Labs., 1964-70; dir. WHO Collaborating Center for Autoimmune Disorders, 1968—; prof. immunology and microbiology, chmn. dept. immunology and microbiology Wayne State U. Sch. Medicine, 1973— 82; prof., chmn. dept. immunology and infectious diseases Johns Hopkins U. Sch. Hygiene and Pub. Health, Balt., 1982-93, prof. medicine and environ. health scis., 1982—, prof. molecular microbiology and immunology, 1993—; prof. pathology Johns Hopkins U. Sch. Medicine, 1994—; dir. Johns Hopkins Autoimmune Disease Rsch. Ctr., 1998; chmn. NIP Auto-Immune Diseases Coordinating Com., 2004—06. Cons. in field. Editor: (with others) International Convocation on Immunology, 1969, Methods in Immunodiagnosis, 1973, 3d, 4th rev. edit., 1986, The Autoimmune Diseases, 1986, 2d edit., 1992, 3d edit., 1998, 4th edit., 2007, Microbiology, Basic Principles and Clinical Applications, 1983 Principles of Immunology, 1973, 2d rev. edit., 1979, Specific Receptors of Antibodies, Antigens and Cells, 1973, Manual of Clinical Laboratory Immunology, 1976, 6th edit., 2002, Genetic Control of Autoimmune Disease, 1978, Recent Advances in Clinical Immunology, 1983, Clinical Immunotoxicology, 1992, Manual of Human Immunology, 1997; editor in chief Clin. Immunology and Immunopathology, 1988-98; contbr. articles to profl. jours. Recipient award Sigma Xi, 1952, award Alpha Omega Alpha, 1976, Lamp award, 1975, Faculty Recognition award Wayne State U. Bd. Govs., 1979, Pres.'s award for excellence in teaching, 1979, Disting. Service award Wayne State U. Sch. Medicine, 1982, U. Pisa medal, 1986, U. Venezuela medal, 1998, AESKU Lifetime Achievement award, 2004, Keystone Lifetime Achievement award, 2006, Nicolaus Copernicus medal 2009; named to Acad. Scholars Wayne State U., 1981; Josiah Macy fellow, 1979. Fellow AAAS (coun. 2004—), APHA, Am. Acad. Allergy and Immunology, Am. Acad. Microbiology, Assn. Med. Lab Immunologists; mem. Acad. Clin. Lab. Physicians and Scientists, Am. Assn. Immunologists, Am. Soc. Investigative Pathology, Am. Soc. Clin. Pathologists, Am. Soc. Microbiology (hon.; Abbott Lab. Clin. and Diagnostic Immunology award 1993, Profl. Achievement award 2003), Brit. Soc. Immunology, Coll. Am. Pathologists, Sociètè Française d'Immunologie, Can. Soc. Immunology, Polish Acad. Sci. (fgn. mem.), Soc. Exptl. Biology and Medicine Coun., Clin. Immunology Soc. (sec., treas., pres. 1993), Austrian Immunology Soc. (hon. mem.), Sigma Xi (pres. Johns Hopkins U. chpt. 1988), Alpha Omega Alpha, Delta Omega. Office: Johns Hopkins U 615 N Wolfe St Baltimore MD 21205-2103

ROSE, NORMA LOUISE, retired human services manager; d. Elzie Mars and Hattie Mae Rose. MBA, Chapman U., Orange County, Calif., 1979. With Hewlett-Packard Co., San Diego, 1959—98, prodn. worker, 1959—78, order processing clk., prodn. supr., pers. rep., coll. recruiting mgr., human resources mgr.; ret., 1998. Mem. Smithsonian Inst. Mem.: Nat. Com. Preserve Social Security & Medicare, Friends Smithsonian, Hon. Citizen George Wash. Mt. Vernon, Nat. Geographic, AARP, Commanders Club, Hewlett Packard Retiree Club. Home: 24218 Via Llano Murrieta CA 92562-5581 Personal E-mail: normar15@verizon.net.

ROSE, STEPHEN, medical researcher; Chief rsch. officer Found. Fighting Blindness. Office: 11435 Cronhill Dr Owings Mills MD 21117-2220 Office Phone: 410-568-0150. E-mail: info@FightBlindness.org.

ROSEBROUGH, WALTER M., JR., medical products executive; b. Enid, Okla., Mar. 27, 1954; s. Walter M. and Mary Lou (Allman) R.; m. Carol Sue Waldron, Oct. 5, 1974; children: J. Benjamin, Elizabeth Erin. B in Indsl. Engring., Gen. Motors Inst., 1977; MBA, Stanford U., 1979. From coop. student to gen. foreman GM, Kansas City, Kans., 1972—79, staff analyst, 1979—80, sr. staff analyst, 1980—81, staff asst. to group v.p., 1982; v.p., mktg. Support Sys. Internat. aka SSI Med. Svcs., Inc., Charleston, SC, 1987—88, pres., CEO, 1988—94; dir., strategic planning Hill-Rom Co., Inc. (divsn. of Hillenbrand Industries), Batesville, Ind., 1982—83, v.p., strategic planning, bus. devel., 1983—87, pres., Sales, Svc., Internat., 1994—95, pres., CEO, 1995—2000; exec. v.p., spl. adv. to CEO Hillenbrand Industries, Inc., 1999—2000; pres., CEO Vasocor, Inc., 2000—02, Coast Hydraulics, Inc., 2005—07; pres., CEO & bd. dirs. STERIS Corp., Mentor, Ohio, 2007—. Bd. dirs. Joerns Healthcare. Bd. dirs. Margaret Mary Hosp., Batesville, 1983-87, Charleston Symphony Orch., 1992-93; mem. adv. bd. Charleston So. U., 1991-92, bd. visitors, 1992—; mem. pres. adv. bd. Med. U. SC Mem. Health Industries Mfg. Assn. (chmn. health fin. com. 1988), Gen. Motors Inst. Alumni Assn. (bd. dirs. 1986-88), Sigma Chi. Methodist. Office: STERIS Corp 5960 Heisley Rd Mentor OH 44060-1834 Office Phone: 440-354-2600. Office Fax: 440-392-8972. Business E-Mail: walter_rosebrough@steris.com. *

ROSEEUW, DIANE ISABELLE, dermatologist; b. Ostend, Belgium, Jan. 14, 1947; d. Jean and Isabelle (Teygeman) R.; children: Benoit De Vigne, Nathalie De Vigne. Student, Free U. Brussels, 1972, MD in Sport, 1973, PhD, 1983. Sports physician Free U. Brussels, 1972-73, dermatologist, 1973-76, chief dept. dermatology, 1981—; physician Free U. Brussels Hosp., 1977-79; fellow U. Mich., Ann Arbor, 1979-81. Contbr. articles to profl. jours. Mem. Royal Belgian Soc. Dermatology (mem. commn. 1976—, v.p. 1991-93, pres. 1995-99), European Acad. Dermatology (pres. Brussels chpt. 1995, treas. 1995-2001), Recognition Dermatology Com. (pres. 2007-) Avocation: sports. Office: Free U Brussels Dept Dermatology Laarbeeklaan 101 1090 Brussels Belgium Business E-Mail: carine.vleminckx@uzbrussel.be.

ROSEFSKY, JONATHAN BENENSOHN, pediatrician; b. Johnson City, NY, June 28, 1939; s. I. J. and Elsie S. Rosefsky; m. Sue Perel, 1964 (div. 2005); children: Katherine, Douglas, Matthew. AB, Cornell U., 1960; B in Med. Sci., Dartmouth U., 1962; MD, Harvard U., 1964. Diplomate Am. Bd. Pediat., lic. Pa., Va. Intern in surgery Vanderbilt Univ. Hosp., Nashville, 1964-65; resident in pediatrics Children's Hosp. Med. Ctr., Boston, 1965-67; pediatrician USAF Med. Corps, Langley AFB, Va., 1967-69; dir. neonatal ICU United Health Svcs. Hosp., Johnson City, NY, 1969-74; pvt. practice Binghamton, NY, 1969-86; pres. Notation Systems, Inc., Binghamton, 1981-89; asst. dir. clin. devel. McNeil Consumer Products Co., Ft. Washington, Pa., 1986-89; dir. med. svcs., sr. dir. med. affairs Wyeth-Ayerst Labs., St. David's, Pa., 1989—99; pres. Fluidmotive, Inc., Haverford, Pa., 2000—, HydroCoil Power, Inc., Wynnewood, Pa., 2006—08, chmn., CTO, 2009—; cons., primary clin. leader Mature Products, Johnson & Johnson PRD, 2008—09. Cons. pediat. N.Y. State Dept. Social Svcs., Albany, 1976—86; FDA adv. com. Gen. Hosp. and Personal Use Devices, Rockville, Md., 1986; industry rep. FDA Adv. Com. on Immunology Devices, Rockville, 1987—93; asst. prof. Pediat. Jefferson Med. Sch., Phila., 1987—2008; chmn. com. on ethics in clin. trials Pharm. Rsch. & Mfrs. Assn., 1998; pharm. device cons. Rapid Pathogen Screening Corp., 2004—08. Contbr. articles to profl. jours. Chmn. Citizen's Adv. Com. to Mayor of Binghamton, NY, 1971. Capt. USAF, 1967—69. Recipient Physician's Recognition award, AMA, 2007. Fellow: Am. Coll. Nutrition, Am. Acad. Pediat.; mem.: Mainline YMCA (bd. dirs. 2005—08), Harvard Club NYC. Achievements include invention of back wedge, mole marker, DecTRR electronic camouflage, ribbon drive: propulsion, pump, hydrocoil low head hydroelectric turbine. Avocations: skiing, swimming, photography, languages, travel. Home: 1359 Arbordale Rd Wynnewood PA 19096 Office Phone: 877-790-7972. Business E-Mail: hydrocoilpower.inc@att.net.

ROSEL, JESÚS, psychology professor; Degree in psychology, Universidad de Barcelona, Spain, 1974; D in psychology, Universidad de Salamanca, Spain, 1984. Expert in Data Analysis Universidad Jaume I, 1991. Psychologist, Svc. for the Handicapped, Salamanca, Spain, 1976—84; lectr. Universidad de Málaga, Málaga, Spain, 1984—91, Universidad Jaume I, Castellón, Spain, 1991—99, prof., 1999—. Contbr. articles various profl. jours. Rsch. on the Handicapped grantee, European Coun., 1980, Rsch. Project grantee, DGICYT (Ministerio de Educación y Ciencia), 1994—96, FIS (Ministerio de Sanidad), 1997—99, Rsch. Project grant, Fundación BANCAJA, 2000—06, Generalitat Valenciana, 2003—06. Mem.: European Assn. of Methodology (assoc.). Achievements include research in verbalism in blind that is not a psychopathological trait, but rather a positive means of adapting to social environment; Box-Jenkins time-series model, the mean and the constant have different values; qualification of the children are a function of the parents-teachers relation; longitudinal data analysis with structural equations, and binge administration of ecstasy impairs the survival of neural precursors. Office: Univ Jaume I Dept Psychology E S Métodos Castellón 12080 Spain Office Fax: 964 72 92 62. Business E-Mail: rosel@psi.uji.es.

ROSEN, ALLEN DAVID, plastic surgeon; b. Bklyn., Mar. 5, 1957; MD, SUNY-Buffalo, 1983. Diplomate with subspecialty in hand surgery Am. Bd. Plastic Surgery, cert. advanced edn. in cosmetic surgery Am. Soc. Aesthetic Plastic Surgery, diplomate Nat. Bd. Med. Examiners. Intern Columbia-Presbyn. Med. Ctr., NYC, 1983—84, resident in surgery, 1984—86, resident in plastic surgery, 1986—88, fellow in hand surgery, 1987; pvt. practice plastic surgery, 1987—; founding ptnr., med. dir. The Plastic Surgery Group, Montclair, NJ, 1995—; med. dir. North Fullerton Surgery Ctr., Montclair. Attending plastic surgeon, former chief divsn. plastic surgery Gen. Hosp. Ctr. Passaic, NJ; attending plastic surgeon, former chief dept. plastic surgery Mountainside Hosp., Montclair, NJ; attending plastic surgeon St. Barnabas Med. Ctr.; clin. asst. prof. U. Medicine and Dentistry NJ, Newark; spokesperson Am. Soc. Plastic and Reconstructive Surgery, 1990—. Active IRAQ STAR, Inc.; mem. grant com. Found. Diabetes Rsch. Recipient Sergio award, Healing the Children, Nat. Leadership award, Physician Adv. Bd. Fellow: ACS; mem.: NJ Soc. Plastic and Reconstructive Surgery, Am. Cancer Soc. (past pres.), Alpha Omega Alpha. Office: Plastic Surgery Group 37 N Fullerton Ave Montclair NJ 07042 Office Fax: 973-233-1933, 973-233-1934.

ROSEN, BRUCE R., diagnostic radiologist, educator; AB in Astronomy, Harvard U., Cambridge, Mass., 1977; MS in Physics, MIT, 1980, PhD in Physics, 1984; MD, Hahnemann Med. Coll. & Hosp., Phila., 1982. Diplomate American Bd. Radiology, Nat. Bd. Med. Examiners. Clin. fellow dept. radiology Mass. Gen. Hosp., Boston, 1983—87, dir. clin. NMR (nuc. magnetic resonance), 1987—91, co-dir. Athinoula A. Martinos Ctr. Biomedical Imaging (formerly MGH-NMR Ctr.), 1991—98, dir. Martinos Ctr., 1998—; instr. radiology Harvard Med. Sch., 1987—88, asst. prof. radiology, 1988—91, assoc. prof., 1991—98, prof., 1999—, prof. health scis. & tech., 2007—. Vis. scientist dept. nuc. engring. Whitaker Coll. Health Scis. & Tech., MIT, 1985—92, dir. radiol. scis. divsn., dept. nuc. engring., 1992—99. Contbr. articles to profl. jours. Fellow: Internat. Soc. Magnetic Resonance in Medicine (Gold Medal 1997); mem.: Inst. Medicine, Phi Beta Kappa, Sigma Xi. Office: Martinos Center Biomedical Imaging 149 Thirteenth St Ste 2301 Charlestown MA 02129 Office Phone: 617-726-5122. E-mail: Bruce@nmr.mgh.harvard.edu. *

ROSEN, CLARK ALAN, physician; b. San Jose, Calif., June 12, 1962; BA, U. Calif., 1989; MD, Rush U., 1984. Diplomate Am. Bd. Otolaryngology. Intern in gen. surgery Oreg. Health Sci. U., Portland, Oreg., 1989-94; fellow in laryngolog, upper airway physiology U. Tenn., Memphis, 1994-95; asst. prof. otolaryngology U. Pitts., 1995—, dir. voice ctr., 1995—, asst. prof. sch. health rehab. sci., comm. sci. disorders, 1999—. Med. cons. Laryngeal Papillomatosis Adv. Project, 1994—, WQED, 1995—; advisor Voice Found. India Internat., 1996—; adv. coun. Internat. Scientific Com., 1997—; scientific adv. bd. Voice Found., 1999; presenter in field. Author: (chpt.) Comprehensive Management of Swallowing Disorders, 1998; co-author: Dynamic Assessment Using Flexible Endoscopy Videotape, 1998, (chpt.) Pdeiatric Emergency Procedures, 1997, Otolaryngology for the Internist, 1998; editor: E Medicine Online Textbook, 1999; content editor Phonoscope, Head Neck Pathology/Disorders, 1995—; reviewer Am. Jour. Otolaryngology, 1995—, Annals Otolaryngology, Rhinology, Laryngology, 1995—, Otolaryngology Jour. Club Jour., 1996—, Otolaryngology-Head Neck Surgery, 1996—; contbr. articles to profl. jours. Mem. Duquesne com. Pitts. Opera Ctr., 1997—. Mem. AMA, ACS, Am. Acad. Otolaryngology (speech voice swallowing disorders com. 1996—), Am. Acad. Facial Plastic Reconstructive Surgery, Oreg. Med. Assn., Pa. Med. Soc., Allegheny County Med. Soc., Multnomah County Med. Soc., Pitts. Otological Soc. Home: 210 Saint Charles Pl Pittsburgh PA 15215-1463 Office: Eye and Ear Inst 200 Lothrop St Ste 500 Pittsburgh PA 15213-2546 Fax: 412-647-2080. E-mail: crosen@vms.cis.pitt.edu.

ROSEN, JULES, geriatric psychiatrist, educator; MD, U. Cin., 1978. Diplomate Am. Bd. Psychiatry and Neurology, 1984, Am. Bd. Psychiatry and Neurology-geriatric psychiatry, 2003, lic. Pa., 1985. Intern Univ. Mich. Med. Ctr., 1979, resident psychiatry, 1979—82; chief geriatric psychiatry svcs. Univ. Pitts. Med. Ctr., dir. geriatric psychiatry fellowship program; prof. psychiatry Univ. Pitts. Named Educator of the Year, Am. Assn. of Geriatric Psychiatry, 2003. Office: University of Pittsburg Medical Center 200 Lothrop St Pittsburgh PA 15213-2582 Office Phone: 412-647-8762. Fax: 412-586-9300. E-mail: rosenji@upmc.edu.

ROSEN, MARK A., anesthesiologist, educator; MD, U. Calif., San Francisco, 1977. Diplomate Am. Bd. Anesthesiology. Prof. U. Calif., San Francisco, 1981—. Office: U Calif San Francisco 513 Parnassus Ave San Francisco CA 94143 Business E-Mail: rosenm@anesthesia.ucsf.edu.

ROSEN, MICHEL, retired prosthodontist; b. Mulhouse, France, Jan. 25, 1936; came to U.S., 1970; s. Jean-James and Suzanne (Mulstein) R.; m. Naomi Schultz, May 20, 1965; 1 child, Robert. DDS, U. Louis Pasteur, Stasbourg, France, 1962; MSc in Dentistry, Boston U., 1973, DSc in Biology, 1974. Lic. dentist, Mass. Hosp. prin. French Air Force, Dakar, Senegal, 1963—64; pvt. practice Belfort and Antibes, France, 1964—70, various, Mass., 1974—91, Switzerland, 1991—92; ret., 1992; consul gen. Senegal, West Africa, Boston, 1994—2004. Asst. clin. prof., asst. dir. overseas affairs Boston U., 1971-74; asst. clin. prof. Tufts U., Boston, 1980-81; instr. Harvard U., Boston, 1990-91; internat. cons. West Africa. Contbr. articles to profl. jours. Lt. French Air Force, 1985-94; maj. Mass. Mil. Res. Recipient Gold medal City of Nice, France, 1981, Bronze Eagle award City of Nice, France, 1982, Officier de l'ordre du merite award Rep. of Senegal, 1998, Comdr. de l'ordre du Lion Senegal, 2000. Mem. Assn. Mil. Surgeons of U.S., Rabboni Lodge AF and AM, Nat. Sojourners, Assn. of First Corps. of Cadets, Ancient and Hon. Artillery Co. Avocations: diplomacy, travel, reading. Home and Office: 708 Pineside Ln Naples FL 34108-2777 Home Fax: 239-596-5925. Personal E-mail: naomi.michel@comcast.net.

ROSEN, PAUL PETER, retired pathologist; b. Bklyn., Aug. 16, 1938; s. George and Beate (Caspari) R.; m. Mary Sue, Aug. 7, 1994; children: Susan Deborah, Jonathan Daniel. BS, Swarthmore Coll., 1960; MD, Columbia U., 1964. Asst. attending pathologist Meml. Hosp., NYC, 1970-73; asst. prof. pathology Cornell U. Med. Sch., NYC, 1972-78; assoc. attending pathologist Meml. Hosp., NYC, 1973-78, attending pathologist, 1978-98; assoc. prof. pathology Cornell U. Med. Sch., NYC, 1978-84, prof. pathology, 1984—2010, emeritus prof., 2010—; assoc. mem. Sloan Kettering Inst., NYC, 1980-84; mem. tenure title Meml. Sloan-Kettering Cancer Ctr., NYC, 1984-98; sr. cons. pathologist Dickstein Cancer Treatment Ctr., White Plains, NY, 1998-99; attending pathologist, chief of breast pathology NY Presbyn. Hosp., NYC, 1999—2009, sr. cons. breast pathology, 2009; emeritus prof. pathology, 2010—. Adj. prof. pathology N.Y. Med. Coll., Valhalla, N.Y., 1996-99. Author: Rosen's Breast Pathology, 1996, 2d edit., 2001, 3rd edit., 2009, Breast Pathology: Diagnosis by Needle Core Biopsy, 1999, 3rd edit., 2010; co-author: 2d edit., 2005; co-author: Tumors of the Mammary Gland, 1993; co-editor Pathology Annual, 1977—95, Revs. Pathology, 1996—98; contbr. more than 300 articles to profl. jours.

ROSEN, RHODA, obstetrician, gynecologist; b. Trenton, NJ, Jan. 17, 1933; d. Max and Gussie (Thierman) R.; m. Seymour Kanter, Aug. 19, 1956; children: Cynthia, Gregg Kanter, Larry Kanter, Brad. BA, U. Pa., 1954, MD, 1958. Diplomate Am. Bd. Obstetrics and Gynecology. Intern Albert Einstein Phila. Med. Ctr., 1958-59, resident, 1959-62, assoc. staff gynecology exec. com.; clin. prof. ob-gyn. Temple U. Med. Sch., Phila.; attending physician Rolling Hill Hosp., Elkins Park, Pa.; pvt. practice ob-gyn. Phila., 1962—. Chmn. gynpathology com. Albert Einstein Med. Ctr., Phila.; arbitrator N.Y. Stock Exch. Bd. dirs. Joseph J. Peters Inst.; docent Barnes Found., Merion, Pa. Fellow ACOG, ACS; mem. AMA, Nat. Assn. for Arbitrators for N.Y. Stock Exchange, Pa. Med. Soc., Phila. Colposcopy Soc. (past pres.), Ex-Residents Assn. (past pres. Albert Einstein Med. Ctr.), Philadelphia County Med. Soc. (com.), Phila. Bar Assn. (com.), Jewish. Avocations: bicycling, art, swimming, music. Home: 1420 Locust St Apt 35K Philadelphia PA 19102

ROSEN, RITCHARD, surgeon; b. Bklyn., Mar. 29, 1958; DPM, Temple U. Coll. Podiatric Medicine, 1984. Chief, podiat. surgery Holy Name Med. Ctr., 1994—. Faculty UMDNJ- Newark Campus, 1993. Fellow: Am. Coll. Foot and Ankle Surgeons; mem.: Am. Podiat. Med. Assn., NJ Pediat. Med. Soc. Avocations: baseball, golf. Office: 142 Engle St Englewood NJ 07631 Office Fax: 201-568-9891. Business E-Mail: r-rosen@mail.holyname.org.

ROSEN, ROBERT J., vascular and interventional radiologist; BS, Temple U., 1972; MD, MCP Hahnemann U., 1976. Diplomate Am. Bd. Radiology-diagnostic radiology. Intern Hahnemann Med. Coll., Phila., 1976—77, resident radiology, 1977—79; fellow vascular and interventional radiology Hosp. of Univ. of Pa., 1979—80; instr. radiology Univ. of Pa., 1979—80; cons. vascular and interventional radiology Manhattan Veterans adminstrn. Hosp., NY, 1980—; attending physician, dept. radiology Bellevue Hosp., NY, 1980; dir., fellowship tng., vascular and interventional radiology NYU Med. Ctr., 1980—; asst. prof. radiology NYU, 1980—85, assoc. prof. radiology, 1985—; cons. interventional radiology Cardiothoracic Ctr., Monte Carlo, Monaco, St. Vincent's Hosp. and Med. Ctr. NY, 1983—96; cons. vascular and interventional radiology Escorts Heart Inst., New Delhi, 1990; jr. asst. attending radiology St. Lukes-Roosevelt Hosp., 1993—95; chief, interventional vascular oncology and embolization Lenox Hill Heart and Vascular Inst., NY, co-dir., divsn. peripheral and endovascular intervention. Recipient Alpha Omega Alpha, 1975, Diagnostic Radiology prize, Hahnemann Med. Coll. and Hosp., 1976, Merck award for Academic Excellence, 1976; fellow Soc. of Cardiovasc. and Interventional Radiology, 1984. Office: Lenox Hill Heart and Vascular Institute 9th Fl 130 E 77th St New York NY 10021 Office Phone: 212-434-2606. Office Fax: 212-434-2610.

ROSEN, STEVEN TERRY, medical professor, oncologist, hematologist; b. Bklyn., Feb. 18, 1952; MB, Northwestern U. Med. Sch., Evanston, Ill., 1972, MD, 1976. Diplomate Am. Bd. Internal Medicine, cert. in med. oncology, hematology. Resident internal medicine McGaw Med. Ctr./Northwestern U., 1976—79; fellow med. oncology Nat. Cancer Inst., NIH, 1979—81; Genevieve Teuton prof. medicine, divsn. hematology/oncology Northwestern U. Feinberg Sch. Medicine, 1989—, dir. Robert H. Lurie Comprehensive Cancer Ctr., 1989—. Dir. clin. programs Northwestern Meml. Hosp., 1989—. Editor: Contemporary Oncology, 1990—95, Cancer Treatment & Rsch., 1995—, In Touch, 1998—2002; contbr. articles to profl. jours. Recipient Alumni Achievement award, Northwestern U. Med. Sch., 1994, Martin Luther King Humanitarian award, Northwestern Meml. Hosp., 1995, Marv Samuel award, Chgo. Baseball Cancer Charities, 1996. Mem.: AMA, ACP, AAAS, Ctrl. Soc. Clin. Rsch., Am. Soc. Clin. Oncology, Am. Soc. Hematology. Office: Northwestern University Divsn Hematology/Oncology 303 E Superior Lurie 3-125 Chicago IL 60611-3093 Office Phone: 312-908-5250. Business E-Mail: s-rosen@northwestern.edu. *

ROSEN, THEODORE, dermatologist; b. Chgo., Sept. 20, 1949; MD, U. Mich., 1974. Asst. prof. dermatology U. Tex. Med. Sch. at Houston, 1978—81; chief dermatology Michael E DeBakey VA Med. Ctr., 1981; prof. dermatology Baylor Coll. Medicine, 1981—. Chmn., vice-chair, sec.-treas. dermatology sect. Southern Med. Assn., 1992—98; pres. Houston Dermatol. Soc., 1998—99; bd. dirs. Noah Worcester Dermatol. Soc., 2011—. Fellow: Am. Acad. Dermatology (bd. dirs. 2007—11); mem.: Am. Dermatol. Assn., Tex. Med. Assn., Am. Soc. Laser Medicine, Tex. Dermatol. Soc. (v.p. 2007—08). Avocations: coin collecting/numismatics, films. Home: 2815 Plumb Houston TX 77005 Office Phone: 713-798-6131. Personal E-mail: vampireted@aol.com.

ROSENBAUM, DAN, critical care physician; b. Paris, Apr. 30, 1954; s. Benjamin Rosenbaum and Meri Rivilis; m. Christiane Belin; children: Mathieu, Thomas, Pierre. MD, France, 1980. Cert. in anesthesiology France, 1982, in critical care France, 1986, in emergency medicine France, 1987, in disaster medicine France, 1988. Physician Gen. Hosp., Saint Nazaire, France, 1983—92, chief emergency dept. and critical care unit Nevers, 1992—94, chief critical care unit Vannes, 1994, head med. bd., 1995—97; sr. cons. ALTAO, Lille, France, 1998—. Achievements include working as a senior consultant with the firm ALTAO whose aim is advice and audit for hospital organization and managing. Office: Ctr Hosp Bretagne-Atlantique boulevard General Maurice Guillaudot 56000 Vannes France Office Phone: 32 297 014141. Office Fax: 0033297014227. Personal E-mail: dan.rosenbaum@wanadoo.fr. Business E-Mail: dan.rosenbaum@ch-bretagne-atlantique.fr.

ROSENBAUM, DAVID MARK, engineering executive, consultant, educator; b. Boston, Feb. 11, 1935; s. Frederick and Elizabeth (Gelman) R.; m. Karen Jeanne Smith, Dec. 27, 1964; children: Benjamin Micah, Shoshana Elizabeth. BSc, Brown U., 1956; MS, Renessaler Poly. Inst., 1958; PhD, Brandeis U., 1964. Asst. rsch. prof. Boston U., 1964-65; assoc. prof. Poly. U., Bklyn., 1969-70; pres. Network Analysis Corp., Glen Cove, NY, 1970-72; asst. dir. Office of Nat. Narcotics Intelligence, Washington, 1973-74; cons. to comptr. gen. GAO, Washington, 1975-78; dir. Office of Radiation Programs EPA, Washington, 1978-81; pres. Tech. Analysis Corp., McLean, Va., 1981—. Cons. Dir. of Licensing, AEC, Washington, 1972-73. Author: Super Hilbert Space and the Quantum Time Operator, 1969, Liquefield Energy Gases Safety, 1978, A Statistical Procedure for Testing Pacemakers, 1978, Health Effects of Low-Level Radiation, 1981, A Statistical Procedure for Cluster Recognition with Application to Atlanta Leukemia Data, 1983. Mem. IEEE (sr.), Am. Phys. Soc. Office: Tech Analysts Corp # 202 6723 Whittier Ave Mc Lean VA 22101-4533 Personal E-mail: dmrose@radix.net.

ROSENBAUM, JERROLD FRANK, psychiatrist; b. Feb. 1, 1947; MD, Yale U., 1973. Psychiatrist-in-chief Mass. Gen. Hosp., 2000—. Office: 55 Fruit St Bulfinch 351 Boston MA 02114 Office Fax: 617-726-2688. Business E-Mail: jrosenbaum@partners.org.

ROSENBAUM, KENNETH N., clinical geneticist; BS, U. Louisville, Ky., 1968; MD, U. Louisville, 1971. Diplomate Am. Bd. Pediatrics, cert. Am. Bd. Med. Genetics. Intern Children's Nat. Med. Ctr., 1971—72, resident, 1972—74, hosp. affiliation include; fellow pediatric genetics Johns Hopkins Hosp., 1976—77. Co-author: (jour. articles) Acampomelic campomelic dysplasia: further radiographic variations, 1997, Otologic manifestations of Wolf-Hirschhorn syndrome, 1998, Exclusion of the branchio-oto-renal syndrome locus (EYA1) from patients with branchio-oculo-facial syndroime, 2000, Scanning for telomeric deletions and duplications and uniparental disomy using genetic markers in 120 children with malformations, 2001, Prolyl 3-hydroxylase 1 deficiency causes a recessive metabolic bone disorder resembling lethal/severe osteogenesis imperfecta, 2007, and numerous others. Recipient Pediatrician of the Yr., Montgomery-Prince George's, 1994, Sauber award, Children's Nat. Med. Ctr., 2009; named one of America's Top Doctors, Castle-Connelly, 2004—06. Mem.: Am. Acad. Pediat. Achievements include as a world-renowned expert in dysmorphology and syndromic conditions. Office: Children's National Medical Center 111 Michigan Ave NW Washington DC 20010 Office Phone: 202-476-5000.

ROSENBAUM, MARLON S., cardiologist, educator; Undergraduate in Chemistry, Vassar Coll., 1972—76; attended, NYU Sch. Medicine, 1976—80; postgrad. in Cardiology, 1983—85, postgrad. in Electrophysiology, 1985—87. Diplomate Am. Bd. Internal Medicine, Am. Bd. Cardiology-cardiovascular diseases. Assoc. clin. prof. Columbia Univ. Med. Ctr., dir. Schneeweiss Adult Congenital Heart ctr.; intern in internal medicine NY Presbyn. Med. Ctr., 1980—81, resident in internal medicine, 1981—83, cardiologist. Co-author: (publs.) Progressive tricuspid valve disease in patients with congenitally corrected transposition of the great arteries, 1998, Validation of SPECT equilibrium radionuclide angiographic right ventricular parameters, 2001, You Gotta Have Heart: A Parent's Guide to Congenital Heart Defects, 2001, Congenital Heart Disease in the Adult, 2002. Office: New York Presbyterian Medical Center 161 Ft WA Ave Ste 5 New York NY 10032 Office Phone: 212-305-6936. Office Fax: 212-305-0490.

ROSENBAUM, MICHAEL A., pediatrician, educator; b. NYC, Dec. 7, 1956; s. Salo Rosenbaum and Vivian Fromberg; m. Nina J. Chertoff, Oct. 16, 1983; children: Matthew, Amanda. BA in Neuroscience, Amherst Coll., 1978; MD, Cornell U., 1982. Diplomate Am. Bd. Pediatrics, Am. Bd. Pediatric Endocrinology. Intern in pediat. Columbia Presbyn. Hosp., NYC, 1982—83, resident in pediat., 1983—85; fellow in pediatric endocrinology NY Hosp., NYC, 1985-88; rsch. assoc. Rockefeller U., NYC, 1988-92, asst. prof., 1993—97; ptnr. W. End Pediat., NYC, 1989—; assoc. prof. clin. pediat. and medicine Columbia Presbyn. Med. Ctr., NYC, 1997—; attending physician NY Presbyn. Hosp., NYC, 1997—. Recipient Ethan Sims Young Investigator award N.Am. Assn. Study Obesity, 1987; named to America's Top Doctors, 2006, NY Mag. Best Doctors, 2006; John Woodruff Simpson fellow Amherst Coll., 1978, Norman and Rosita Winston fellow Cornell U., 1982-85; Amparo Rugarcia scholar Rockefeller U., 1981-91. Fellow Am. Acad. Pediat.; mem. AMA, Am. Diabetes Assn., Nat. Obesity and Weight Coun. Inst. (advisor 1993—), NY County Med. Soc. Avocations: reading, theater. Office:

Columbia Presbyn Med Ctr 1150 Saint Nicholas Ave New York NY 10032-3822 also: West End Pediatrics 450 W End Ave New York NY 10024 Office Phone: 212-305-9949, 212-469-3070. Office Fax: 212-851-5306. E-mail: mr475@columbia.edu.

ROSENBERG, AARON GLEN, orthopedist, educator; BS, Rensselaer Polytechnic Inst., 1974; MD, Albany Med. Coll. Union Univ., 1978. Diplomate Am. Bd. Orthopedic Surgeons, 1986, cert. in Orthopaedic Surgery 1995. Instr., orthopedic surgery Harvard Med. Sch., 1983—84, Rush Univ. Med. Ctr., Chgo., 1979—83, adj. attending in orthopedic surgery, 1981—83, clin. instr., 1983—85, asst. attending in orthopedic surgery, 1983—92, asst. prof., dept. orthopedic surgery, 1985—92, assoc. prof., 1992—96, sr. attending in orthopedic surgery, 1996—, prof., 1996—. Mem. adv. bd. Zimmer Inst.; bd. dirs. Am. Acad. Orthopaedic Surgeons, dir., instr., Orthopaedic Learning Ctr. Editor: (instructional CD-ROM) The Arthritic Knee; co-editor: (textbook) The Adult Hip-Lippincott, 2000, The Adult Knee-Lippincott, 2002; contbr. articles to numerous profl. jours. Fellow: Am. Acad. Orthopedic Surgeons; mem.: The Hip Soc., The Knee Soc., The Internat. Hip Soc. Achievements include design of several joint replacement devices including the VerSys Hip System, Nex Gen Knee System, and ZMR Revision Hip System. Office: Rush Univ Med Ctr Profl Bldg Ste 1063 1725 W Harrison St Chicago IL 60612

ROSENBERG, CHARLES ERNEST, historian, educator; b. NYC, Nov. 11, 1936; s. Bernard and Marion (Roberts) R.; m. Carroll Ann Smith, June 22, 1961 (div. 1977); 1 child, Leah; m. Drew Gilpin Faust, June 7, 1980; 1 child, Jessica. BA, U. Wis., 1956, DHL, 1997; MA, Columbia U., 1957, PhD, 1961. Fellow Johns Hopkins U., Balt., 1960-61; asst. prof. U. Wis., 1961-63; assoc. prof. U. Pa., Phila., 1965-68, prof. history, 1968—, chmn. dept., 1974—75, 1979—83, 1991—95; prof. history of sci. Harvard U., 2001—, chmn. dept. history of sci., 2003—04. Author: The Cholera Years: The United States in 1832, 1849 and 1866, 1962, The Trial of the Assassin Guiteau: Psychiatry and Law in the Gilded Age, 1968, No Other Gods: On Science and Social Thought in America, 1976, The Care of Strangers: The Rise of America's Hospital System, 1987, Explaining Epidemics and Other Studies in the History of Medicine, 1992, Our Present Complaint: American Medicine Then and Now, 2007; editor Isis, 1986-89. Bd. dirs. Mental Health Assn. Southea. Pa., 1973—76, Libr. Co. of Phila., 1980—2010, Ctr. Advanced Study Behavioral Scis., 1999—2005. Nat. Inst. Health Research grantee, 1964-70; Guggenheim Found. fellow, 1965-66, 89-90; Nat. Endowment Humanities fellow, 1972-73; Rockefeller Found. humanities fellow, 1975-76; fellow Inst. Advanced Study, 1979-80, Ctr. Advanced Study in Behavioral Scis., 1982-83. Fellow: Am. Philos. Soc. (coun. 2006—), Am. Acad. Arts and Scis.; mem.: Orgn. Am. Historians (exec. bd. 1985—88), Soc. Social History of Medicine (pres. 1981), History of Sci. Soc. (coun. 1972—75, George Sarton medal 1995), Am. Assn. History Medicine (coun. 1974—76, pres. 1992—94, William H. Welch medal 1969, Lifetime Achievement award 2010), Inst. Medicine of NAS. Office: Harvard U Dept History of Sci Cambridge MA 02138 Home: 33 Elmwood Cambridge MA 02138 Office Phone: 617-495-9953. Business E-Mail: rosenb3@fas.harvard.edu.

ROSENBERG, DAVID BRENT, facial plastic and reconstructive surgeon, otolaryngology-head and neck surgeon; BS, Cornell U., 1989; MD, Cornell U. Med. Coll., 1993. Cert. Am. Bd. of Facial Plastic and Reconstructive Surgery, fellow Am. Bd. of Facial Plastic and Reconstructive Surgery, cert. Am. Bd. of Otolaryngology-Head and Neck Surgery, fellow Am. Acad. of Otolaryngology-Head and Neck Surgery. Intern gen. surgery Lenox Hill Hosp., 1993—95; resident otolaryngology-head and neck surgery Manhattan Eye, Ear and Throat Hosp., 1995—99; fellowship facial plastic surgery Robert-Wood Johnson U. Hosp., 1999; attending surgeon Manhattan Eye, Ear and Throat Hosp., Lenox Hill Hosp. Invited presenter in the field. Contbr. of articles to several profl. jours.; featured in the press Elle Mag., French Edition, 2006, Plastic Surgery Products, 2007, Forbes Life: Executive Women, 2008, Elle Mag., 2008, Vogue, 2008, New York Mag., 2008, Town & Country, 2009, 2010. Chmn. Young Face of Giving-Facial Plastic Surgeons at Their Best. Mem.: NY Soc. of Facial Plastic Surgery, Am. Rhinologic Soc., AMA, Am. Acad. of Facial Plastic and Reconstructive Surgery. Office: 115 E 61st St New York NY 10065 Office Phone: 212-832-8595. Office Fax: 212-421-0176. *

ROSENBERG, DAVID R., psychiatrist, educator; b. NYC, Jan. 17, 1963; BS in Biomedical Sci., U. Mich., 1984, MD, 1988. Assoc. prof. Dept. Psychiatry & Behavioral Neuroscis., Wayne State U., 1996—2000, prof., 2000; Miriam L. Hamburger endowed chair, child psychiatrist Children's Hosp. Mich. Wayne State U. Sch. Medicine, 2000—. Mem.: Soc. Biol. Psychiatry (A.E. Bennett award 1977), Am. Psychiat. Assn., Am. Coll. Neuropsychopharmacology, Am. Acad. Child and Adolescent Psychiatry. Avocations: tennis, reading. Office: University Health Ctr 9B 4201 St Antoine 5C Detroit MI 48201 Office Fax: 313-577-5900. Business E-Mail: drosen@med.wayne.edu.

ROSENBERG, KENNETH PAUL, addiction psychiatrist; MD, Yeshiva U., 1983. Diplomate Am. Bd. Psychiatry and Neurology, Am. Bd. Psychiatry and Neurology-addiction psychiatry. Resident in psychiatry NY-Presbyn. Hosp./ Weill Cornell Med. Ctr., 1988, fellow in addiction psychiatry, 1991, fellow, 1992, hosp. affiliation includes. Named one of Best Doctors, NY Mag., 2010. Office: New York-Presbyterian Hospital Weill Cornell Medical Center 100 E 71st ST New York NY 10021 Office Phone: 212-861-8807, 212-861-4688.

ROSENBERG, LUCILLE GLICKLICH, retired physician, child psychiatrist; b. Fond du Lac, Wis., Jan. 10, 1926; d. Peter and Freda (Pevnick) Barash; m. Marvin Glicklich, Sept. 12, 1948 (div. Apr. 1983); children: Daniel, Anne, Peter, Lynn, Barry; m. John A. Rosenberg, Aug. 12, 1984. BA, U. Wis., 1947, MD, 1950. Diplomate Am. Bd. Pediats., Am. Bd. Psychiatry and Neurology, Am. Bd. Child Psychiatry. Intern Youngstown Hosp. Assn., Ohio, 1950—51; intern, pediats. Milw. Children's Hosp., 1951—53, dir. liaison psychiatry, 1975—85, hosp. staff appointments, Milw. Psychiatric Hosp., Milw. County Med. Comples, Mt. Sinai Med. Ctr.; med. dir. children's divsn. Curative Workshop, Milw., 1959—63, Easter Seals Child Devel. Program, 1963—67; chief med. cons. Milw. Pub. Schs., 1964—67; asst. prof. pediats. Med. Coll. U. Wis., Milw., 1965—85, prof. psychiatry, 1971—85, clin. prof., 1985—, prof. psychiatry, 1995—; physician, medicine, psychiatry Marquette Med. Sch. Associated, Wis., 1967—69; child psychiatry fellow Marquette and Milw. Childrens Hosp., 1969—71; dir. Child-Family Psychiatry Program; assoc. prof., vice chmn. dept. psychiatry U. Wis. Med. Sch., Milw. Clin. Campus, 1985—; med. dir. child and adol. psychiat. clinic Sinai Samaritan, 1985—; lectr. various colls. and univs. Cons. in field. Contbr. articles to profl. publs. Bd. trustees Youth Commn., 1971—77, Congl. Beth Israel, 1975—77; bd. dir. Milw. Bd. Jewish Edn. Bd., 1971—78, pres., 1974—76, Milw. Jewish Fedn., 1977—84, Cong. Shir Hadash, 2010; active mem. N'Shei group aJewish Parenting, Communication 80's, Jewish Fedn. Women's Divsn., Milw. Children's Hosp. Jr. Aux. Target M.D. Program U. Wis., 1981; congl. Emmanuel Yom Hashoah, 1982, Milw. Neonatal Nursing Consortium, Marquette U. Panel Survivors Holocaust, 1984; mem. Kesher Jewish Woman's Network; mem., task force teen pregnancies Planned Parenthood, 1984; bd. dirs. Wis. State Med. Soc. Found., 1996—, Milw. Jewish Coun. Cmty. Rels., 1997—; mem. edn. com. Congregation Shir Hadash, 2010, bd. dirs., 2010—. Recipient Disting Svc, Lifetime Achievement award, Wis. Coun. Child & Adolesent Psychiat., 2009. Fellow: Am. Acad. Pediats. (Wis. Br.), Am. Psychiat. Assn., Am. Acad. Child and Adolescent Psychiatry (mem. com. 1988—); mem.: AMA, Wis. Soc. Jewish Learning, Art At Large (adv. bd. mem. 2008—), Strengthening Wis. Families (legis. coun. com. mem. 2008—), Wis. Psychiat. Assn. (pres.-elect 1993—95, pres. 1995—97, coun. mem. 1989—), Wis. Coun. Child and Adolescent Psychiatry (sec. 1981—82, pres.-elect 1982—83, pres. 1983—85, 1984—86), Women Medicine Wis. (bd. dirs. 1979—82, pres. 1979—80), Am. Med. Women's Assn. (Southeastern Wis. chpt. vice-dir. 1977—79), Milw. County Med. Soc. (sec. treas. 1981, pres.-elect 1984, pres. 1985), Wis. State Med. Soc. (del. 1978—, bd. dirs. 1985—, reference com. 1982—), Soc. Adolescent Medicine, Milw. Pediat. Soc., Am. Acad. Child and Adolescent Psychology (alt. regional assembly del. 1989—), Am. Orthopsychiatric Assn., Wis. Coun. Adolescent and Child Psychiatry, Am. Soc. Adolescent Psychiatry. Jewish. Avocations: travel, bicycling, tennis, walking, reading. Home: 3431 N Lake Dr Milwaukee WI 53211-2919 Personal E-mail: lucyrose@sbcglobal.net.

ROSENBERG, RICHARD F., physician, radiologist; b. NYC, June 13, 1942; s. Henry J. and Sylvia (Harris) R.; m. Judith Wolf, May 5, 1985; 1 child, Glen. BA, Colgate U., 1964; MD, N.Y. Med. Coll., 1968. Diplomate Am. Bd. Radiology. Intern Met. Hosp., NYC, 1968-69; resident Montefiore Hosp. and Med. Ctr., Bronx, NY, 1969-70, 72-74, chief resident, 1974; radiologist Lipsay & Rosenberg, Great Neck, NY, 1974-78; dir. gastrointestinal radiology North Shore U. Hosp., Manhasset, NY, 1978-82; radiologist, owner Great Neck Radiologists, 1982—. Mem. adv. bd. Bank of Great Neck, 1990-94. Contbr. articles to profl. jours. Lt. comdr. USN, 1970-72. Fellow Am. Coll. Gastroenterology; mem. Am. Coll. Radiology, Alpha Omega Alpha. Republican. Office: Great Neck Radiologists 935 Northern Blvd Great Neck NY 11021-5309 Office Phone: 516-829-4414. *

ROSENBERG, ROBERT ALLEN, psychology professor; b. Phila., July 31, 1935; s. Theodore Samuel and Dorothy (Bailes) R.; m. Geraldine Bella Tishler, Sept. 3, 1961; children: Lawrence David, Ronald Joseph. BA, Temple U., 1957, MA, 1964; BS, Pa. Coll. Optometry, 1960, OD, 1961. Lic. optometrist, psychologist, Pa. Instr. Pa. Coll. Optometry, Phila., 1962-65, asst. prof., 1965-67; asst. prof. psychology Community Coll. Phila., 1967-76, assoc. prof., 1976—. Pvt. practice optometry, Roslyn, Pa., 1965-95; assoc. in practice optometry, Huntingdon Valley, Pa., 1995-98. Contbr. articles to profl. jours. Named Humanitarian Chapel of Four Chaplains Bapt. Temple, 1980. Fellow Am. Acad. Optometry; mem. Am. Optometric Assn., Pa. Optometric Assn., Bucks-Montgomery Optometric Assn., Alumni Assn. Pa. Coll. Optometry (v.p. 1992-98, sec. 1991-2006, bd. mem. 2006—). Avocations: singing, acting, photography, writing, public speaking. Home: 970 Corn Crib Dr Huntingdon Valley PA 19006-3304 Office: Community Coll Phila 1700 Spring Garden St Philadelphia PA 19130-3991 Business E-Mail: rrosenberg@ccp.edu.

ROSENBERG, ROGER NEWMAN, neurologist, educator, department chair; b. Milw., Mar. 3, 1939; s. Sol J. and Cora D. (Newman) R.; m. Adrienne Turick, June 24, 1962; children: Jennifer, Lara Degree, Tufts U., 1957-60; BS, Northwestern U., 1961, MD with distinction, 1964. Diplomate Am. Bd. Psychiatry and Neurology. Intern Harvard Med. Service, Beth Israel Hosp., Boston, 1964-65; resident in neurology Neurol. Inst., Columbia U., NYC, 1965-67, instr. neurology, 1967-68; research assoc. Lab. of Biochem. Genetics, NIH, Bethesda, Md., 1968-70; clin. instr. Howard U. Med. Sch., Washington, 1969-70; asst. prof. neuroscis. Sch. Medicine, U. Calif.-San Diego, 1970-71; assoc. prof. neuroscis. and pediatrics, attending neurologist Univ. Hosp., U. Calif.-La Jolla, 1971-74; prof., chmn. dept. neurology U. Tex. Southwestern Med. Ctr., Dallas, 1973-91, prof. physiology, 1976—, Zale Disting. chair, prof. neurology, 1990—, dir. Alzheimer's Disease Rsch. Ctr., 1989—. Attending neurologist Parkland Meml. Hosp. and Children's Med. Ctr., Dallas, 1974—, Zale Lipshy Univ. Hosp., 1990—; mem. staff Presbyn. Hosp., Dallas, 1974—, St. Paul's Hosp., Dallas, 1974—; cons. staff VA Hosp., Dallas, 1974—; mem. nat. med. adv. bd. Nat. Ataxia Found., Mpls., 1971—, Myasthenia Gravis Found., 1973; chmn. med. adv. bd., dir. med. sci. research Internat. Joseph Diseases Found., Livermore, Calif., 1977—; lectr. Japanese Soc. Neurology, 1987, 94, 2010, Chinese Neurol. Soc., 1987, Spanish Neurol. Soc., 1992; chmn. bd. sci. councilors NINDS/NIH, 1984-86; pres. (hon.), Intl. French Soc. of Neurology Charcot Centenary Symposium, 1993. Editor Jour. Neurogenetics; mem. editl. bd. Neurology, 1977-82, 91-97, Trends in Neurosci., 1980-86, Current Opinion in Neurology & Neurosurgery, 1990—, Jour. of AMA, 1997—; chief editor Archives of Neurology, 1997—; contbr. articles to profl. jours. Bd. dirs. Winston Sch., Dallas, 1974-80; trustee World Fedn. Neurology, 2005. 1st Woody Guthrie scholar, 1971; USPHS grantee; recipient Disting. Alumnus award Neurol. Inst., N.Y., 1994, Nancy R. McCune Alzheimer's Rsch. award Alzheimer's Ass., 2005, Lifetime Achievement award Tex. Neurol. Soc., 2005, 1st medal World Congress Neurology, Bangkok, 2009. Fellow AAAS; mem. Am. Neurol. Assn. (hon.), Am. Acad. Neurology (chmn. sci. program com. nat. meetings 1979-84, elected councillor exec. bd. 1984-89, pres. 1991-93), Am. Neurochem. Soc., Tissue Culture Soc., Soc. Neurosci., Am. Fedn. Clin. Rsch., Soc. Pediat. Rsch., Internat. Child Neurology Assn., Am. Neurol. Assn. (hon., 1st v.p. 1987), Ctrl. Soc. Neurol. Rsch., Can. Congress Neurol. Scis. (hon.), Spanish Neurol. Soc. (hon.), Sigma Xi, Alpha Omega Alpha (Merit award Northwestern U. Alumni Assn. 1986). Home: 4425 Wildwood Rd Dallas TX 75209-2801 Office: U Tex Southwestern Med Ctr Dallas TX 75235 Business E-Mail: roger.rosenberg@utsouthwestern.edu.

ROSENBERG, SAUL ALLEN, oncologist, educator; b. Cleve., Aug. 2, 1927; BS, Western Res. U., 1948, MD, 1953. Diplomate Am. Bd. Internal Medicine, Am. Bd. Oncology. Intern Univ. Hosp., Cleve., 1953—54; resident in internal medicine Peter Bent Brigham Hosp., Boston, 1954—61; research asst. toxicology AEC Med. Research Project, Western Res. U., 1948—53; asst. prof. medicine and radiology Stanford (Calif.) U., 1961—65, assoc. prof., 1965—79, chief divsn. oncology, 1965—93, prof., 1970—95; prof. emeritus, 1995—; Am. Cancer Soc. prof. Stanford (Calif.) U., 1983—89, assoc. dean, 1989—92. Chmn. bd. No. Calif. Cancer Program, 1974—80. Contbr. articles to profl. jours. Served to lt. M.C. USNR, 1954—56. Master: ACP; fellow: Am. Coll. Radiology (hon.); mem.: Western Assn. Physicians, Western Soc. Clin. Rsch., Radiation Rsch. Soc., Calif. Acad. Medicine, Assn. Am. Physicians, Am. Soc. Clin. Oncology (pres. 1982—83), Inst. Medicine NAS, Am. Assn. Cancer Rsch., Am. Soc. Therapeutic Radiotherapy Oncology (hon.). Office: Stanford U Sch Medicine Div Oncology 269 Campus Dr Stanford CA 94305

ROSENBERG, SEYMOUR, psychologist, educator; b. Newark, Sept. 7, 1926; s. Morris and Celia (Weiss) R.; children: Harold Stanley, Michael Seth. BS, The Citadel, 1948; MA, Ind. U., 1951, PhD, 1952. Rsch. psychologist USAF, San Antonio, 1952-58, U. Kans., Lawrence, 1958-59, Bell Tel. Labs., Murray Hill, NJ, 1959-65; vis. prof. psychology Columbia U., NYC, 1965-66; prof. psychology Rutgers U., New Brunswick, NJ, 1966—2000, chmn. dept. psychology, 1981-83, 94-95, prof. emeritus psychology, 2001—. Adj. prof. Rutgers U. Med. Sch., 1974—2000; vis. scholar U. Leuven, Belgium, 1983, Belgium, 92, Univ. de Provence, France, 1990; panel mem. NSF, 1970—72. Cons. editor Jours. Personality Social Psychology, 1968-69; assoc. editor, 1970-73; contbr. articles to profl. jours. With USN, 1945—46. Grantee, NSF, 1965—90, NIMH, 1966—68; Rsch. scientist grantee, 1968—73, Social Sci. Rsch. Coun. fellow, 1973—74. Fellow APA; mem. Soc. Exptl. Social Psychology, Psychometric Soc., Classification Soc., NY Acad. Sci., Ea. Psychol. Assn. Home and Office: 689 Canal Rd Somerset NJ 08873-7327

ROSENBERG, STEVEN AARON, surgeon, medical researcher; b. NYC, Aug. 2, 1940; s. Abraham and Harriet (Wendroff) Rosenberg; m. Alice Ruth O'Connell, Sept. 15, 1968; children: Beth, Rachel, Naomi. BA, Johns Hopkins U., 1960, MD, 1963; PhD, Harvard U., 1968. Resident in surgery Peter Bent Brigham Hosp., Boston, 1963—64, 1968—69, 1972—74; resident fellow in immunology Harvard U. Med. Sch., Boston, 1969—70; clin. assoc. Immunology Br. Nat. Cancer Inst., NIH, Bethesda, Md., 1970—72, chief Surgery Br., 1974—, head tumor immunology sect. Mem. U.S.-USSR Coop. Immunotherapy Program, 1974—, U.S.-Japan Coop. Immunotherapy Program, 1975—; clin. assoc. prof. surgery George Washington U. Med. Ctr., 1976—; prof. surgery Uniformed Svcs. U. Health Scis. Author: The Transformed Cell: Unlocking the Mysteries of Cancer, 1992; editor-in-chief: Jour. Immunotherapy; contbr. articles to profl. jours. Served with USPHS, 1970-72 Recipient Meritorious Svc. medal, US Pub. Health Svc., 1981, 1986, Armand Hammer Cancer prize, 1988, Friedrich Sasse prize, U. West Berlin, 1986, Nils Alwell prize, Stockholm, Sweden, 1987, Disting. Alumnus award, Johns Hopkins U., 1987, Simon Shubitz prize, U. Chgo. Cancer Rsch. Ctr., 1988, Griffuel prize, French Assn. Rsch. on Cancer, 1988, Cancer award, Milken Family Found., 1988, Ellis Island medal of honor, 1998, Heath Meml. award, MD Anderson Cancer Ctr., 2002, Richard V. Smalley, MD, Meml. award, Internat. Soc. Biological Therapy of Cancer, 2005; co-recipient Armand Hammer Cancer prize, 1985; named Scientist of Yr., R&D mag., 1990. Mem.: Inst. Medicine, Am. Soc. Clin. Oncology (bd. dirs., Karnofsky prize 1991, John Wayne award for clin. rsch. 1995), Am. Assn. Cancer Rsch., Am. Assn. Immunologists, Transplantation Soc., Halsted Soc., Surg. Biology Club II, Soc. Surg. Oncology, Am. Surg. Assn. (Flance-Karl award 2002), Soc. Univ. Surgeons, Alpha Omega Alpha, Phi Beta Kappa. Office: Nat Cancer Inst Bldg 10 Rm 3-3940 10 Center Dr MSC 1201 Bethesda MD 20892 Office Phone: 301-402-4164. Office Fax: 301-402-1738. E-mail: sar@nih.gov. *

ROSENBLATT, ALICE F., healthcare insurance company executive; With The New Eng., William M. Mercer, Inc., Mut. of NY; chief actuary, sr. v.p. HMO and grp. svcs. Blue Cross of Calif., 1987—89; sr. v.p., chief actuary Blue Cross/Blue Shield Mass., 1989—93; prin. health and welfare grp. Coopers & Lybrand, Boston; positions through chief actuary, exec. v.p. integration planning and implementation Wellpoint Health Networks, Inc., 1996—2004; exec. v.p. integration planning/implementation, chief actuary WellPoint, Inc., Indpls., 2004—07, exec. v.p., integration & info. mgmt. officer, chief actuary, 2007—08. Commr. Medicare Payment Adv. Commn. Fellow: Soc. Actuaries (bd. dirs.); mem.: Am. Acad. Actuaries (bd. dirs.).

ROSENBLATT, MICHAEL, pharmaceutical executive, internist; b. Lund, Sweden, Nov. 27, 1947; s. Arthur Rosenblatt and Jean (Strosberg) Bialer; m. Patricia Ellen Regenbogen, Aug. 23, 1969; children: Anna Miriam, Adam Richard. AB summa cum laude, Columbia U., NYC, 1969; MD magna cum laude, Harvard U., Cambridge, Mass., 1973. Diplomate Am. Bd. Internal Medicine. Intern to resident Mass. Gen. Hosp., Boston, 1973-75, clin. rsch. fellow endocrinology and metabolism, 1975-77, chief endocrine unit, 1981-84; instr. medicine Harvard University, Boston, 1976-78, asst. prof. medicine, 1978-82, assoc. prof. medicine, 1982-85; v.p. for biol. rsch. Merck Sharp & Dohme Rsch. Labs., 1984-87, v.p. for biol. rsch. and molecular biology, 1987-89, sr. v.p. rsch., 1989-92; dir. divsn. health sci. and tech. Harvard-MIT, 1992-98; Ebert prof. molecular medicine Harvard Med. Sch., Boston, 1992-98; chief divsn. bone and mineral metabolism Beth Israel Hosp., Boston, 1992—2000, 2002—03; dean, prof. physiology and medicine Tufts U. Sch. Medicine, Boston, 2003—09; exec. v.p., chief medical officer Merck & Co., Inc., Whitehouse

Station, NJ, 2009—. Faculty dean acad. programs Beth Israel Deaconess Med. Ctr., Harvard Med., 1996—2000, George R. Minot prof. med., 1996—2003; exec. dir. Carl J. Shapiro Inst. Edn. and Rsch. at Harvard Med. Sch. and Beth Israel Deaconess Med. Ctr., 1996—2000, pres., 1999—2001. Editor: Atrial Natriuretic Factor Endocrinology and Metabolism Clinics of N.Am., 1987; contbr. numerous sci. articles on parathyroid hormone and calcium metabolism to leading sci. jours. Recipient Vincent du Vigneaud award Gordon Confs., Kingston, R.I., 1986, Fuller Albright award Am. Soc. for Bone and Mineral Rsch., 1986, citation Japan Endocrine Soc., Tokyo, Taiwanese Osteoporosis Soc., Tainan. Fellow AAAS, Am. Coll. Physicians; mem. The Endocrine Soc., Am. Soc. for Biochemistry and Molecular Biology, Am. Soc. for Clin. Investigation, Am. Soc. Bone and Mineral Rsch. (pres. 1997-98), Assn. Am. Physicians, Inter-Urban Clin. Club (pres. 1997-98). Office: Merck & Co 1 Merck Dr PO Box 100 Whitehouse Station NJ 08889-1000 *

ROSENBLOOM, ARLAN LEE, pediatrician, educator; s. Harris Phillip and Esther (Schneider) R.; m. Edith Kathleen Peterson, Sept. 14, 1958; children: Eric David, Maliah Jo, Disa Lynn, Harris Phillip. BA, U. Wis., 1955, MD, 1958. Diplomate Am. Bd. Pediatrics, Am. Bd. Pediatric Endocrinology, Am. Coll. Epidemiology. Intern Los Angeles County Gen. Hosp., 1958-59; resident in gen. practice Ventura County Hosp., Ventura, Calif., 1959-60; physician-in-chief Medico Hosp., Kratie, Cambodia, 1960-61; med. officer Pahang, Malaysia, 1961-62; resident in pediatrics U. Wis. Hosp., Madison, 1962-63, 64-65, fellow in pediatric endocrinology, 1963-64, 65-66; asst. prof. pediatrics U. Fla., Gainesville, 1968-71, assoc. prof., 1971-74, prof., 1974-96, disting. svc. prof. emeritus, 1996—2004, adj. disting. svc. prof. emeritus, 2004—, founder, chief div. endocrinology, 1977-94, dir. Office for Internat. Health Programs, 1995-99, mem. Ctr. for African Studies, mem. Ctr. for Latin Am. Studies. Assoc. dir. Clin. Rsch. Ctr., 1969-74, dir., 1974-80; dir. Nat. Found. March of Dimes Birth Defects Ctr., 1969-73; med. dir. Gainesville Youth Clinic, 1972-74; mem. adv. com. Nat. Disease and Therapy Index; mem. Fla. Com. Children and Youth, 1972; data work group chmn. Nat. Diabetes Commn., 1975; mem. epidemiology and disease control study sect. NIH, 1978-82; vis. prof. McMaster U. Med. Centre, 1974-75, hon. prof. Ctrl. U. Quito, Ecuador, 2001; cons. epidemiologist Boston U. Health Policy Inst., West Africa, 1983-84; mem. affiliate faculty dept. clin. psychology U. Fla., 1984—; pres., dir. Fla. Camp for Children and Youth with Diabetes, 1970-90; dir. N. Fla. Regional Diabetes Program Children and Youth, 1974-88; dir. U. Fla. Diabetes Rsch. Edn. and Treatment Ctr., 1977-90, clin. and sci. adv. bd. Children's Diabetes Found., Denver, 1978-86; dir. N. Fla. Regional Diabetes and Endocrine Program for Children and Youth, 1988-96; asst. med. dir. Children's Med. Svcs., Dist. 3/13, 1986-2000, med. dir., 2001-04; med. dir. Med. Foster Care Prgm., 1995-2000; mem. nat. diabetes adv. bd. NIH, 1990-94, internat. dir. Inst. for Endocrinology, Metabolism and Reprodn., Quito, 1990-99; mem. panel on devices FDA, 1999—2003, mem. editl. bd. Internat. Jour. Pediat. Endocrinology 2009-, eMedicine 2002-, UpToDate 2006-. Editor Acta Paediatrica Belgica, 1979-82, Today in Medicine (Diabetes), 1989—; mem. editl. bd. European Jour. Pediat., 1987-02, Jour. Pediat. Endocrinology and Metabolism, 1983-09, Clin. Pediat., 1989-2002, Diabetes Care, 1992-95, Jour. Clin. Endocrinology and Metabolism, 1995-2000, Clin. Diabetes, 1996-99, Pediatric Diabetes, 1999—; contbr. over 360 articles to profl. jours. & chpts. to books. Epidemiologist smallpox eradication program USPHS, Yaounde, Cameroon, 1966-68, comdr. inactive Res., 1968-69, capt. inactive Res., 1987-, assoc. recruiter, 2005-. sr. surgeon, comdr. med. epidemiologist, advisor West African Smallpox Eradication, Measles Control Program, Yaounde, Cameroon, 1966, 68, Inactive Res., 1969, 79, capt. Inactive Res. 1979, 2010; assoc. recruiter 2005-10; active duty, St Bernard Parish LA, USPHS Clinic, 2006. Recipient Faculty Rsch. prize U. Fla. Coll. Medicine, 1994, U. Wis. Med. Alumni Citation, 1995, U. Fla. Blue Key Disting. Faculty award, 1995, Hon. Prof. Ctrl. U. Quito Ecuador 2001, Disting. Physician award Endocrine Soc., 2003, Internat. Soc. Pediat. and Adolescent Diabetes, Prize for Achievement in Sci., Edn., & Advocacy on Behalf of Young People with Diabetes, 2004, Lilly Life Profl. hero award, 2006. Mem. Am. Acad. Pediatrics (sect. on endocrinology, sr. sect.), Am. Diabetes Assn. (bd. dirs. 1986-90), Brit. Diabetic Assn., Fla. Diabetes Assn. (dir.), Alachua County Med. Soc., Internat. Soc. Pediatric Adolescent Diabetes, Endocrine Soc., Pediatric Endocrine Soc., Am. Pediatric Soc., Soc. Pediatric Rsch., Commissioned Officers Assn. Democrat. Avocations: photography, art. Home: 2902 SW 1st Ave Gainesville FL 32607-3002 Office: Children's Med Svcs Ctr 1701 SW 16th Ave Gainesville FL 32608-1153 Home: 9333 Old A1A St Saint Augustine FL 32086-8580 Office Phone: 352-334-1393. Business E-Mail: rosenal@peds.ufl.edu. *

ROSENBLOOM, MICHAEL, thoracic surgeon, educator; MD, NYU, 1981. Diplomate Am. Bd. Surgery, Am. Bd. Thoracic Surgery, lic. Fla., 1996, NJ, 2007. Resident gen. surgery NYU Med. Ctr., 1986; fellow cardiothoracic surgery Barnes Jewish Hosp., 1987, resident cardiothoracic surgery, 1989; assoc. prof. surgery; head dept. cardiothoracic surgery Cooper Univ. Hosp., physician. Named Top Physician, South Jersey Mag., 2010; named one of Top Doctors, Phila. Mag., 2010—, Inside Jersey Mag. Fellow: Am. Coll. of Chest Physicians, Am. Coll. of Cardiology, ACS; mem.: Southern Thoracic Surg. Assn., Soc. of Thoracic Surgeons, Fla. Soc. of Thoracic and Cardiovascular Surgeons, AMA, Am. Heart Assn., 21st Century Cardiothoracic Surg. Soc. Office: Cooper University Hospital Bldg Two Ste G 900 Centennial Blvd Voorhees NJ 08043 Office Phone: 856-342-2141.

ROSENBLUM, JAY ALAN, neurologist; b. Newark, June 12, 1933; s. Irving and Peggy (Carpenter) R.; m. Judith Grandes, Sept. 1958 (div. 1965); children: Melissa, Shepherd, Todd; m. Sue Goldman Rosenblum, June 13, 1971; 1 child, Steven. AB with honors, U. Pa., 1954; MD, Wake Forest Med., 1958; GM, U. Pa., 1965. DIplomate Am. Acad. of Pain Mgmt., Am. Bd. Forensic Medicine; cert. neurorehabilitation physician. Dir. neurology Madison Ave Hosp., NYC, 1980, N.Y. Infirmary Hosp., NYC, 1980; clin. cons. in neurology N.Y. State Dept of Health, NYC, 1985; instr. in neurology N.Y. Med. Coll., 1985; clin. asst. prof. neurology NYU Med. Sch., 1965, 1970—. Asst. vis. neurologist Bellevue Hosp., NYC; bd. dirs. Am. Bd. Forensic Medicine, Spingifield, Mo., bd. adv. for profl. standing; dir. indsl. medicine seminar Coll. of Ins., NYC, 1988-89; moderator diagnosis and treatment back disorders Acad. of Medicine, NYC, 1991; lectr. in field; pres. med. bd. NY Infirmary-Beekman Downtown Hosp., 1982; mem. NY State Bd. for Profl. Med. Conduct, 2004. Contbr. articles to profl. publs. Task force of handicap vehicles Dept. Health, City of N.Y., 1985; impartial specialist-neurology U.S. Dept. Labor, 1985. Capt. U.S. Army, 1959-62. Fellow Am. Soc. Indsl. Medicine (pres. 1993), Am. Acad. of Infared Imaging (pres. 1995); mem. Am. Back Soc. (dir. neurothemograhy workshop 1989), NY County Med. Soc. (bd. dirs., chmn. bd. censors 2002). Office: 65 E 76th St New York NY 10021-1844 Office Phone: 212-249-7867. Personal E-mail: ps206@aol.com.

ROSENBLUM, MARC K., pathologist, educator; MD, U. Miami, Coral Gables, Fla., 1979. Diplomate Am. Bd. Pathology-anatomic pathology, Am. Bd. Pathology-neuropathology. Resident in anatomic pathology Mt. Sinai Med. Ctr., NY, 1983—84; fellow in neurol. pathology Bellevue NYU Med. Ctr., 1985—87; prof. pathology Weill coll. Cornell Univ.; fellow in pathology Meml. Sloan-Kettering Cancer Ctr., NY, 1983—85, chief neuropathology and autopsy svc., acting chief cytology svc., founder's chair. Office: Memorial Sloan-Kettering Cancer Center 1275 York Ave New York NY 10065 Office Phone: 212-639-3844.

ROSENBLUM, MARTIN JEROME, ophthalmologist; b. NYC, Apr. 7, 1948; s. Philip and Rita (Steppel) R.; m. Zina Zarin, May 31, 1975; children: Steven David, Richard James. BS, Bklyn. Coll., 1968; MD, U. Ariz., 1973; postgrad., Columbia U., 1977. Diplomate Am. Bd. Ophthalmology, Nat. Bd. Med. Examiners. Intern Cornell U., NYC, 1973-74; resident N.Y. Med. Coll., 1975-78, instr., 1978-79; practice medicine specializing in eye surgery St. Petersburg, Fla., 1979—. Asst. clin. prof. ophthalmology, U. So. Fla.; attending surgeon St. Anthony's Bayfront Med. Ctr., Am. Soc. for Cataract and Refractive Surgery, Ctr. Spl. Surgery; med. dir. Suncoast Eye Clinic, Pa. Fellow ACS, Am. Acad. Ophthalmology; mem. AMA, Am. Soc. Ophthalmic Plastic and Reconstructive Surgery, Fla. Med. Assn., Fla. Soc. Ophthalmology, Pinellas County Med. Soc., Bayou Country Club. Republican. Jewish. Avocations: tennis, golf, travel, skiing. Office: 2200 16th St N Saint Petersburg FL 33704-3106 Home: 7676 Hunter Lane Pinellas Park FL 33782 Office Phone: 727-822-4729. E-mail: mjreye@aol.com.

ROSENBLUM, NORMAN G., gynecologic oncologist, educator; BA, Villanova U., 1969, MS in Biology, 1971; attended, Thomas Jefferson U., 1975, MD, 1978. Diplomate Am. Bd. Ob-Gyn, Am. Bd. Ob-Gyn-gynecologic oncology. Intern Hosp. of the Univ. of Pa., resident ob-gyn, 1982, fellow gynecologic oncology, 1984; former chief gynecologic oncology dept. of surg. oncology Fox Chase Cancer Ctr.; chief gynecologic oncology dept. of ob-gyn Main Line Health Hosp.; dir. divsn. of gynecologic oncology dept. of ob-gyn Thomas Jefferson Univ. Hosp; clin. prof. ob-gyn. Thomas Jefferson Med. Coll. Office: Thomas Jefferson University Hospital - Center City Campus 111 S 11th St Philadelphia PA 19107 Office Phone: 215-955-6000.

ROSENBLUM, STUART B., chemist; PhD, SUNY, Stony Brook, 1987. Rsch. fellow Schering Plough Rsch. Inst., Kenilworth, NJ, 1987—2009, Merck Rsch. Labs, 2009—. Recipient Thomas Alva Edison Patent award, R&D Council NJ, 2002; named a Hero of Chemistry, Am. Chem. Soc., 2004; named an Inventor of the Yr., Intellectual Property Owners Assn., 2005. Achievements include invention of Zetia cholesterol reducing drug. Office: Merck Rsch Labs 2015 Galloping Hill Rd Bldg K15-1545 Kenilworth NJ 07033 Business E-Mail: stuart.rosenblum@spcorp.com.

ROSENBLUTH, LUCILLE MAXINE, health research facility administrator; b. NYC, Sept. 18, 1931; d. David and Rhea (Farber) Moses; m. Sol Rosenbluth, June 8, 1952, children: Shelly Kratzer, Martin. BA in Polit. Sci., Bklyn. Coll., 1952; M in Pub. Adminstrn., NYU, 1953. Intern N.Y. State Adminstrn. Internship Program, 1953-54; rsch. aide N.Y. State Workmen's Compensation Bd., 1954-55; personnel asst. Dept. Personnel, NYC, 1955-57; lectr. Bklyn. Coll., 1958, 59; rsch. asst. Temporary State Commn. on Operation N.Y.C. Govt., 1959-60; cons. Dept. Health, NYC, 1960-61; rschr. study of profl., tech. and managerial manpower needs City of N.Y. Brookings Instn., 1961-63; cons. personnel utilization Dept. Health, NYC, 1963-64; chief rschr. Med. and Health Rsch. Assn. N.Y.C., Inc., 1964-67, project coord., work com. chmn. systems study of sch. health records, 1967-70, project dir., policy com. chmn. N.Y.C. infant day care study, 1970-75, exec. v.p., 1975-86, pres., 1986—. Cons. Commonwealth of Mass., 1982; mem. adj. faculty grad. sch. program in pub. health, dept. environ. and community medicine Rutger Med. Sch. U. Medicine and Dentistry N.J., 1984-86; mem. maternal and child health steering com. Sch. Pub. Health Columbia U., 1983—, lectr. pub. health, 1986—. Author: (with others) Caring Prescriptions: Comprehensive Health Care Strategies for Young Children in Poverty, 1993; contbr. articles to profl. jours. Fellow N.Y. Acad. Medicine (assoc., exec. com. on pub. health); mem. APHA (chair breastfeeding com. 1985, 86, 87), Family Planning Couns. Am. (chair grantee adv. com. Region II 1987, 88), N.Y. State Family Planning Advocates, N.Y. State Pub. Health Assn. (co-chmn. legis. com., bd. dirs. 1986—), Pub. Health Assn. N.Y.C., Soc. Rsch. Adminstrs., Health Care Execs. Forum (pres. 1988, 89), Hermann Biggs Soc., Women's City Club N.Y. (chair com. pub. health 1982-84). Office: Medical Health Rsch Assn of NYC 40 Worth St Rm 720 New York NY 10013-2988 *

ROSENBLUTH, MORTON, retired periodontist educator; b. NYC, Sept. 28, 1924; s. Jacob and Eva (Bigeleissen) R.; m. Sylvia Fradin, July 2, 1946; children: Cheryl Bonnie, Hal Glen. BA, NYU, 1943, grad. program in periodontia, oral medicine, 1946, DDS, 1946. Diplomate Am. Bd. Periodontology. Intern Bellevue Hosp., NYC, 1946-47, resident, 1947; individual practice dentistry NYC, 1947-59; individual practice periodontia North Miami Beach, Fla., 1960—; individual practice periodontia, TMJ, implantology Bay Harbor Islands, Fla., 1995—2010. Periodontist Mt. Sinai Hosp., N.Y., Polyclinic Hosp. and Med. Sch. N.Y., Mt. Sinai Hosp., Miami Beach, Fla., Parkway Gen. Hosp.; chief dental dept. North Miami Gen. Hosp.; chmn. periodontia sect. Dade County Rsch. Ctr.; clin. assoc. prof. divsn. oral and maxillofacial surgery U. Miami Sch. Medicine; assoc. clin. prof. Southeastern U. Health Scis.; assoc. prof. Nova Southeastern U. Coll. Dental Medicine; lectr. throughout U.S.A., Israel, Mexico, Rome, Teheran, Bangkok, Hong Kong, Tokyo, Honolulu, Jamaica, Paris, London, Sicily, Budapest, Berlin, Luxembourg, South Africa and others; vis. lectr. U. Tenn. Dental Coll., NYU Dental Coll.; cons. VA Hosp., Miami. Contbr. articles to profl. jours. Mem. adv. bd. U. Fla. Coll. Dentistry; mem. profl. adv. bd. North Dade Children's Ctr., Hope Sch. Mentally Retarded Children; mem. sci. adv. com. United Health Found.; chmn. Dental divsn. United Fund of Dade County, Combined Jewish Appeal; nat. chmn. Hebrew U. Sch. Dental Medicine; bd. dirs. Health Planning Coun. South Fla.; pres. Condominium Assn.; bd. dirs. and bd. overseers Am. Friends of Hebrew U.; mem. med. adv. bd. Dade-Broward Lupus Found.; trustee Jewish Congregation, 1961-64. With AUS, 1943-44, as capt. USAF, 1951-52. Recipient Maimonides award State of Israel, 1979. Fellow Am. Coll. Dentists, Internat. Coll. Dentists; mem. ADA, Am. Acad. Periodontology, Am. Assn. Hosp. Dental Chiefs, Am. Acad. Dental Medicine, Am. Soc. Advancement Gen. Anesthesia in Dentistry, Am. Soc. Periodontists, Fla. Soc. Periodontists, Northeastern Soc. Periodontists, Fla. Dental Soc. (chmn. coun. on legislation), Miami Dental Soc., Miami Beach Dental Soc., East Coast Dental Soc. (sec.-treas. 1968, pres. 1971-72), North Dade Dental Soc. (pres. 1963-64), Fedn. Dentaire Internat., Fla. Acad. Dental Practice Adminstrn., Alpha Omega (pres. 1978-78, internat. regent 1973-75, internat. editor 1975-77, internat. pres.-elect 1977-78, internat. pres. 1979, chmn. bd. Alpha Omega Found. 1985-90), Am. Dental Interfrat. Coun. (pres. 1981-82), Nocoma Club (pres. 1958-60), NYU Century Club (local chmn.), Jockey Club (bd. govs.), KP, Masons, Kiwanis (bd. dirs. 1965), Chaine Des Rotisseurs (Miami Beach charge de missions). Home: 20281 E Country Club Dr Apt # 1001 Aventura FL 33180 Personal E-mail: periomort@aol.com.

ROSENCRANTZ, MAGNUS NILS, radiologist; b. Kalmar, Sweden, Jan. 31, 1932; s. Erik Magnus and Elsie Ingegerd (Malmstroem) R.; m. Anita Eivor Davidsson, Apr. 20, 1957; children: Gunilla, Ulrika, Henrik. MB, U. Gothenburg, 1954, MD, 1959, PhD, 1975. Fellow in radiology U. Gothenburg, Sweden, 1959-64, assoc. prof. radiology, 1964-77; prof. and head dept. radiology U. Oerebro, Sweden, 1977-78; head radiology dept. Vaenersborgs Hosp., 1979-82, 84-89; assoc. prof. radiology Kantonsspital Bruderholz, Switzerland, 1989-97; cons. radiologist Carlander Hosp., Gothenburg, 1998—2003, Lundby Hosp., Gothenburg, 2003—05, Kungsbacka Hosp., 2005—, West Froelunda Specialist Hosp., 2007—. Vis. prof. radiology UCLA, 1978-79, 82-84. Mem. Swedish Soc. Med. Radiology, Radiology Soc. Sweden, Swedish Med. Assn. Avocations: photography, sailing. Personal E-mail: m.rosencrantz@hotmail.com.

ROSENDAHL, CLIFF OMER, physician; b. New Zealand, Feb. 14, 1951; MBBS, U. NSW, 1974. V.p. Skin Cancer Coll. Australia and New Zealand, 2010—. Fellowship, Skin Cancer Coll. Australia and New Zealand. Avocation: history. Office: 5 Larbonya Crescent Capalaba Brisbane Queensland 4157 Australia Office Fax: 61732453022. Business E-Mail: cliffrosendahl@bigpond.com.

ROSENDAHL, LENE, psychologist; b. Borås, Sweden, Jan. 30, 1963; PhD, Linköping U., 2010. Physician, dept. clin. physiology Lund U., 1990—. Office: Clin Physiology Länssjukhuset Ryhov Jönköping 55185 Sweden Business E-Mail: lene.rosendahl@lj.se.

ROSENFELD, ISADORE, cardiologist, educator; b. Sept. 7, 1926; arrived in U.S., 1950, s. Morris and Vera (Friedman) Rosenfeld; m. Camilla Master, Aug. 19, 1956; children: Arthur, Stephen, Hildi, Herbert. BS, McGill U., 1947, M.D.C.M., 1951, diploma in internal medicine, 1956, DSc (hon.), 1999; PhD (hon.), Tel Aviv U. Intern Royal Victoria Hosp., Montreal; resident Balt. City Hosp.; clin. asst. prof. medicine NY Hosp. Weil Cornell Med. Ctr., NYC, 1964—71, clin. assoc. prof., 1971—79, clin. prof., 1979—. Now hon. fellow; attending physician NY Hosp., NYC, 1989—, Meml. Sloan Kettering Cancer Ctr.; juror Lasker Sci. Awards, 1974—90; dir. Rsch. Am., 1990; Rossi Disting prof. clin. medicine NY Hosp. Weil Cornell Med. Ctr., 1993—; vis. prof. Baylor U. Coll. Medicine, 1982; mem. practicing physicians adv. coun. to U.S. Sec Health and Human Svcs., practicing physician, 1992—96; bd. overseers Cornell U. Med. Coll., 1980—; bd. vistors U. Calif. Sch. Medicine, Davis, 1983—; cons. NIH; invited lectr. Am. Coll. Physicians; lectr. in field; TV commentator in field; dr. Philosophiae Honoris Causa Tel Aviv U., 2002; trustee Nat. Health Mus., Washington, 2003; mem., Adv. Coun. Paul G. Rogers Soc. for Global health Research, 2006; mem. Lehman Coll. Sci. Faculty Adv. Com., 2006; chmn., bd. of trustee Sackler Sch. of Medicine, NYC, 2007. Author: EKG and X-Ray in Diseases of the Heart, 1963, The Complete Medical Exam, 1978, Second Opinion, 1981, Modern Prevention, 1986, Symptoms, 1988, The Best Treatment, 1991, Doctor, What Should I Eat?, 1995, Dr. Rosenfeld's Guide to Alternative Medicine, 1997, Love Now-Age Later, 1999, Power to the Patient: The Treatment to Insist on When You're Sick, 2002, Dr. Isadore Rosenfeld's Breakthrough Medicine, 2004, Healing Breakthroughs, 2004, Dr. Isadore Rosenfeld's Breakthrough Health, 2005; med. cons.: Vogue mag., 1993—97, FOX News Channel, 1996—; contbg. editor: Parade mag., 1997—; health editor:, 1998—. Pres. Rosenfeld Heart Found., NYC, 1974—; bd. dirs. N.Y. Heart Assn., 1979—82; mem. nat. adv. com. Harriman Inst. Advanced Study of Soviet Union, 1982—; mem. nat. adv. comm. increasing physical activity program Robert Wood Johnson Found. Recipient Vera award, The Voice Found., 1981, Inaugural award, N.Y. Heart Assn., Silver award for patient edn. and info., Nat. Health Info. Rsch. Chr., 1996, Citizen of the World award, U.N., 1999, Siver award, Nat. Health Info., 1999, Gold Triangle award, Am. Acad. Dermatology, Silver award, Nat. Mature Media awards, Dist. Med. Svc. award, Am. Physicians Fellowship, Merit award, Consumer Health Pub. Assn., Am. Consumer Publ. Assn. and Am. Consumer Publ. Corp, 2000, Advocacy award for impact on pub. opinion through the Media, Rsch. Am., 2001, Lifetime Achievement award, Found. Biomed. Rsch., Gold Triangle award, Am. Acad. of Dermatology, 2002, Silver award, Nat. Health Info. Rsch. Ctr., 2002, NPI Excellence in Immunization award, 2003, Maurice R. Greenberg Disting. Svc. award, NY Presbyn. Hosp., Well Cornell Med. Ctr., 2006. Fellow: Am. Physician's Fellowship for Israel (hon. nat. pres. 1975—), N.Y. County Med. Soc. (bd. censors 1979—83, v.p. 1983—84, pres. 1984—85, bd. trustees 1985—), Royal Coll. Physicians Can., Am. Coll. Chest Physicians,

ACP, Cornell Alumni Assn. (hon.). Jewish. Achievements include research in hypertension; angina pectoris; sudden cardiac death; arteriosclerosis. Office: 125 E 72nd St New York NY 10021-4250 *

ROSENFELD, JEFFREY VICTOR, neurosurgeon; b. Melbourne, Victoria, Australia, Nov. 19, 1952; s. Joseph Rosenfeld and Lorraine Behrend; m. Deborah Sarah Kipen, Oct. 23, 1988; children Hannah Elizabeth, Alexander Oscar, Gabriella Rebecca. MB, BS, U. Melbourne, Australia, 1976, MS, 1992, MD, 2006. Commd. lt. Royal Australian Army M.C., 1984, advanced through grades to maj. gen., 2009, sr. med. officer 4th Brigade, 2001—; registrar in neurosurgery Royal Melbourne Hosp., Parkville, Australia, 1985-88, asst. neurosurgeon, 1988-91, dep. dir. dept. neurosurgery, 1996—2000; registrar in neurosurgery Radcliffe Infirmary, Oxford, Eng., 1987; chief resident in neurosurgery Cleve. Clinic Found., 1987-88; head dept. neurosurgery Monash Med. Ctr., Clayton, Victoria, Australia, 1990-92; dir. dept. neurosurgery Royal Children's Hosp., Melbourne, 1993—; assoc. prof. pediat. and surgery U. Melbourne, 1997—; prof. neurosurgery U. Papua New Guinea, 2000—; staff officer grade 1 health adminstrn. Regional Health Support Agy., 1998; prof., dir. neurosurgery The Alfred Hosp. and Monash U., 2001—06; policy advisor to dir. gen. of Def. Health Svcs., Australian Def. Force, 2003—; dir. health res. Australian Army, 2005—06; prof., head dept. surgery Ctrl. Clin. Sch., 2006. Vis. rsch. fellow dept. surgery U. Melbourne, Parkville, 1981-91; vis. prof. Singapore Children's Hosp., 2002, Radcliffe Infirmary, Oxford, Eng., 2002, Sally Harrington Goldwater Meml. Barrow Neurol. Inst., Phoenix, 2003, others; adj. prof. Ctr. for Mil. and Vets. Health, U. Queensland, 2006—; hon. prof. dept. neurosurgery Capital Med. Scis. U., Beijing, China, 2006—. Author (with D.A.K. Watters): Neurosurgery in the Tropics, 2000; mem. editl. bd.: Jour. Clin. Neuroscience, Australian Def. Force Health Svcs. Jour., Am. Jour. Disaster Medicine; contbr. more than 170 articles to profl. jours. Corps surgeon St. John Ambulance, 1967—; commr. St. John Ambulance (Victoria), 2001—05. With Australian Mil. Decorated comdr. Order of St. John, Commendation medal USAF; recipient Geoffrey Harkness medal, RAAMC, 2001, medal, Centenary of Fedn., 2003, Michael E. DeBakey Internat. award, 2009; named Victorian of the Yr., 2002. Fellow: ACS, Royal Coll. Surgeons (Edinburgh) (Syme medal and Syme professorship 1991, King James IV professorship 2002), Australasian Coll. Tropical Medicine, Royal Australasian Coll. Surgeons (neurosurg. 1984—, Victoria road trauma com. 1991—, trauma com. 1993—, mem. bd. neurosurgery 1999—, Victorian state govt. trauma com. 2000—, gen. surg., John Mitchell Crouch Rsch. Fellowship award 2004); mem.: World Fedn. Neuro Socs. (mem. ethics com. 2006—), World Soc. Functional and Stereotactic Neurosurgery (pres. UN Assn. Australia, Victorian divsn. 2001—, v.p. UN Assn. Australia 2001—), Australasian Assn. Mil. Medicine, Internat. Soc. Pediat. Neurosurgery, Am. Assn. Neurol. Surgeons, Congress Neurol. Surgeons (USA), Neurosurg. Soc. Australasia (exec. com. 1999—, chmn. trauma com. 2001—), UN Assn. Australia (pres. Victorian divsn. 2001—04, nat. v.p. 2001—04). Avocations: music, wind instrumental performance. Office: Ste 5 4th Flr 517 St Kilda Rd Melbourne VIC 3004 Australia Business E-Mail: j.rosenfeld@alfred.org.au.

ROSENFELD, RICHARD M., pediatric otolaryngologist, educator; MD, SUNY, 1984. Diplomate Am. Bd. Otolaryngology. Resident otolaryngology Mt. Sinai Med. Ctr., NYC, 1984—89; fellow pediatric otolaryngology Children's Hosp. of Pitts., 1989—91; chmn. otolaryngology LI Coll. Hosp.; prof. and chmn. otolaryngology SUNY Downstate Med. Ctr., pediatric otolaryngology. Recipient Excellence in Pediatric Otolaryngology, Robert Ruben Award; named one of Best Doctors in America, NY Mag., Best Doctors in NY, 1996. Mem.: Otolaryngology-Head and Neck Surgery (editor-in-chief), Auditory-Oral Sch. of Brooklyn (bd. dirs), Am. Soc. of Pediatric Otolaryngology (bd. dirs), Am. Acad. of Otolaryngology-Head and Neck Surgey (bd. dirs). Office: State University of New York Downstate Medical Center 450 Clarkson Ave Brooklyn NY 11203 Office Phone: 718-270-1000.

ROSENFELD, STEVEN IRA, ophthalmologist; b. NYC, Nov. 18, 1954; s. Frederick and Pearl (Stern) R.; m. Lisa Allyson Klar, June 24, 1978; children: Michael, Julie. BA, Johns Hopkins U., 1976; MD, Yale U., 1980. Diplomate Am. Bd. Ophthalmology, Nat. Bd. Med. Examiners. Intern Yale-New Haven Hosp., 1980-81; resident Barnes Hosp., St. Louis, 1981-84; fellow Bascom Palmer Eye Inst., Miami, Fla., 1984-85; ptnr. in pvt. practice Delray Eye Assocs., Delray Beach, Fla., 1985—. Clin. instr. Bascom Palmer Eye Inst., 1985-90, asst. clin. prof., 1990-96, assoc. clin. prof., 1996—2009, clin. prof., 2010-; assoc. examiner Am. Bd. Ophthalmology, Phila., 1993—. Author: The Eye in Systemic Disease, 1990, Lens and Cataract, 1996; contbr. articles to profl. jours. Recipient Harry Rosenbaum Rsch. award Washington U. Sch. Medicine, 1984; named one of Best Doctors in Am., 1996—; Heed Ophthalmic Found. fellow, 1984. Fellow ACS, Am. Acad. Ophthalmology (chmn. B.C.S.C. section Lens and Cataract Surgery 2002-06, BCSC sect. Refractive Surgery 2006-, Honor award 1999, Sr. Achievement award 2007, Secretariat award 2007), Soc. Heed Fellows; mem. Castroviejo Corneal Soc., Eye Bank Assn. Am., Fla. Med. Assn., Fla. Soc. Ophthalmology, Assn. for Rsch. in Vision and Ophthalmology, Ocular Microbiology and Immunology Group, Phi Beta Kappa, Alpha Omega Alpha. Avocations: tennis, golf, fly fishing, lacrosse. Office: Delray Eye Assocs 16201 South Military Trail Delray Beach FL 33484-6503 Office Phone: 561-498-8100.

ROSENFELD, SUZANNE, pediatrician; b. NYC; d. Lester and Carol Rosenfeld; m. Henry Pollack, Aug. 24, 1986. BA, Sarah Lawrence Coll., Bronxville, NY, 1975; MD, Columbia U., NYC, 1980. Cert. in pediat. Am. Bd. Med. Specialties, 1986. Intern in pediat. Mt. Sinai Hosp, NYC, 1980—81; resident in pediat. Columbia U., 1981—83; resident Babies & Children Hosp. of NY; fellow Cornell U.-NY Hosp., 1983—84; clinical instr. pediat., asst. attending pediatrician NY-Presbyn. Hosp. Named to America's Top Doctors, 2006, NY Mag. Best Doctors, 2006. Office: 450 W End Ave New York NY 10024 also: 2 Fifth Ave New York NY 10021 Office Phone: 212-769-3070. Office Fax: 212-769-4703.

ROSENFELD, WILLIAM E., physician; b. NYC, Mar. 16, 1952; MD, Tex. Tech., 1979. Dir. Comprehensive Epilepsy Care Ctr. Children and Adults, 1991—. Mem.: ANA, AES. Avocations: running, walking. Office: 222 S Woods Mill Rd Ste 610N Chesterfield MO 63017 Office Fax: 314-453-0163. Personal E-mail: werosenfeld@msn.com.

ROSENFIELD, LORNE KING, plastic surgeon; b. Winnipeg, Man., Can., Jan. 24, 1956; children: Lauren, Ian, Michael. BS in Medicine, U. Man., Winnipeg, 1976; MD, U. Man., 1980. Diplomate Am. Bd. Surgery, Am. Bd. Plastic Surgery. Resident in gen. surgery St. Mary's Hosp., San Francisco, 1985-87; intern. Mt. Zion, San Francisco; fellow in plastic surgery Baylor Coll. Medicine, 1987; tchr. U. Calif. San Francisco Med. Ctr., Stanford U. Hosps.; chmn. dept. plastic surgery Mills-Peninsula Hosp., Burlingame, Calif., 1995—, vice chmn. dept. surgery, 1997—. Past chmn. St. Mary's Hosp., San Francisco, 1992-95; expert cons. Med. Bd. Calif., 1997—. Mem. Burlingame/San Mateo C. of C. Fellow Am. Coll. Surgeons; mem. San Francisco Med. Soc. (mem. ethics com. bd. 1990-95), Rotary. Avocations: writing, photography, cooking. Office: Peninsula Plastic Surgery Inc 1750 El Camino Real Ste 405 Burlingame CA 94010-3217 Office Phone: 650-692-0467. Office Fax: 650-692-0110.

ROSENGART, TODD KENNETH, cardiothoracic surgeon, researcher, neurosurgeon, consultant; b. Bklyn., Jan. 24, 1960; s. Martin Rosengart and Barbara Kodish; m. Debra Helen Rosengart, June 15, 1989; children: Michael, Eric. BS with distinction, Northwestern U., Evanston, Ill., 1981; MD with distinction, Northwestern U., Chgo., 1983. Diplomate Am. Bd. Surgery, Am. Bd. Thoracic Surgery. Intern in gen. surgery NYU Med. Ctr., NYC, 1983-84, resident in gen. surgery, 1984-85, resident and chief resident in gen. surgery, 1987-89; med. staff fellow NIH, Bethesda, Md., 1985-87; asst. thoracic surgeon N.Y. Hosp., 1989-90, thoracic surgeon, 1990-91; instr. Cornell U. Med. Coll., NYC, 1989-90, asst. prof. surgery, 1991-93, asst. prof. cardiothoracic surgery, 1993-97, assoc. prof. cardiothoracic surgeery, 1997—; assoc. prof. cardiothoracic surgery Weill Med. Coll. Cornell U., NYC, 1998—; assoc. attending cardiothoracic surgeon N.Y. Presbyn. Hosp., NYC, 1997-99; chief cardiothoracic surg. Evanston (Ill.) Hosp., 1999—; prof. surgery Northwestern U. Med. Sch., 1999—2006; head CT surgery Stony Brook U., SUNY, Stony Brook, NY, 2007—. Sr. registrar Hosp. for Sick Children, London, 1991; asst. Harley St. Clinic, London, 1991; tchg. asst. NYU Med. Ctr., 1988-89; asst. attending surgeon Jamaica Hosp., 1993-96; United Hosp. Med. Ctr., 1994—; attending physician N.Y. Hosp. Med. Ctr. of Queens, 1995—; mem. Ctr. for Vascular Biology, 1996—; assoc. attending cardiothoracic surgeon N.Y. Hosp., 1997, N.Y. Presbyn. Hosp., 1998—; vis. assoc. prof. surgery Columbia U., 1997—; vis. assoc. attending surgeon Presbyn. Hosp., 1997—; manuscript reviewer, presenter, cons. in field. Editl. bd. Cardiac and Vascular Regeneration: Angiogenesis and Myogenesis, Basic th Therapeutic, 1999—; contbr. numerous articles to profl. publs., chpts. to books; patentee gene transfer therapy delivery devide and method, perfusion and occlusion device and method. Nat. Merit scholar, 1977; recipient rsch. award A.G. Morrow Soc., 1987, 97; grantee miles Labs., 1992—, N.Y. Heart Assn., 1994-97, Datascope Corp., 1995—, AccuLase, Inc., 1995—, St. Jude Med., 1996—, Picower Found., 1996—, U.S. Surg. Corp., 1996—, Thoracic Surgery Found. Rsch. and Edn. 1997-99, OrthoBiotech, 1997—, Baxter Healthcare Corp., 1998—, NIH, 1998—. Fellow ACS, Am. Coll. Cardiology (Ill. chpt. alternate councilor 2002—), Am. Coll. Chest Physicians; mem. AAAS, Am. Fedn. Clin. Rsch., Am. Heart Assn. (sci. coun. on cardiothoracic and vascular surgery, met. Chgo. bd. dirs. 2002—, coun. cardiovascular surgery and anesthesia exec. com. 2002—, coun. cardiovascular surgery and anesthesia chmn. memership and comm. com. 2003—, coun. cardiovascular surgery and anesthesia program 2003—, mem., mktg. and comm. com. 2004—), Am. Soc. Gene Therapy (cardiovascular scientific com. 2003—), Nat. Assn. for Bloodless Medicine and Surgery (bd. dirs. 1997—), Andrew Morrow Soc. Cardiac Surgeons, N.Y. Soc. Thoracic Surgery (membership com. 1994-97, chmn. membership com. 1998—, program com. 1994—, chmn. program com. 1997-99), Soc. Thoracic Surgeons, Soc. Univ. Surgeons, N.Y. Acad. Scis., 21st Century Cardiac Surg. Soc. (pres. 1998-2000, membership chmn. 1995-96, v.p. 1996-98), N.Y. Soc. Thoracic Surgery (chmn., membership com. 2001-2002, workforse health policy, reform and advocacy 20003—), Chgo. Cardiac Surgery Soc. (chmn. orgn. com. 2002, pres. 2003-2004), Spencer Soc. Surgeons, Alpha Omega Alpha, Phi Rho Sigma. Office: Stony Brook Univ Med Ctr T19-030 Stony Brook NY 11794

ROSENMAN, KENNETH D., medical educator; b. NYC, Feb. 25, 1951; AB, Cornell U., 1972; MD, NY Med. Coll., 1975. Bd. cert. internal medicine; bd. cert. occupational and preventive medicine. Asst. prof. U. Mass., Amherst, 1979-81; dir. occupational and environ. health N.J. Dept. Health, Trenton, 1981-86; pvt. practice Plainsboro, NJ, 1986-88; assoc. prof. Mich. State U., East Lansing, 1988-93, prof., 1993—. Office: Mich State U 117 W Fee Hall East Lansing MI 48824-1316 Office Phone: 517-353-1846. E-mail: rosenman@msu.edu.

ROSENSCHEIN, GUY RAOUL, pediatric and visceral surgeon, airline pilot; b. July 28, 1953; s. Maurice and Caroline (Meller) R. MD, Lariboisiere-St. Louis, Paris, 1977. Qualified airline transport pilot; FAA-approved aviation med. examiner, flight instr. Intern Hosp. St.-Louis, 1973-74, Hosp. Lariboisière, 1975-76; resident Hosp. de Paris, 1977-80, Hosp. Bretonneau, 1977-78, Hosp. Lariboisière, 1979-80, Hosp. de Monaco, Monte Carlo, 1980-81, Hosp. St. Vincent de Paul, Paris, 1981-82, attache, 1982-84, asst., 1984-86, asst. prof. pediat. surgery; chef de clinique U. Paris, 1984-86; attache Hosp. de Villeneuve St. Georges, 1987-94, C.H.S. Saine Anne, Paris, 1982-94; maitre de stage hospitalier Faculty Med. de Creteil, 1987-92; profl. transport instr., 1993; attending pediat. surgery Maimonides Med. Ctr., 1994-97, S.I. Univ. Hosp., 1994-2000, St. John's Regional Health Ctr., Springfield, Mo., 2000, N.W. Med. Ctr., Springdale, Ark., 2001—10, Wash. Region Med. Ctr., Fayetteville, Ark., 2010—. Pilot, 1981; asst. clin. prof. of surger UAMS, U. Ark., 2003, assoc. clin. prof. surgery U. Mo., Columbia, founder, ceo, instr. NY Helicopter Flight Svcs., Springdale, 2006. Author: Pancreatite non traumatique et non infectieuse de l'enfant, 1982. Capt., M.C., French Armed Forces, 1977. Mem. Nat. Assn. Flight Instrs., TE Flying Club (chief flight instr. 1995-2000). Home: PO Box 395 Springdale AR 72765-0395 Office: Minimal Access Surgery Clinic 5230 Willow Creek Dr Springdale AR 72762 Office Phone: 479-927-3100. Business E-Mail: guy.rosenschein@gmail.com.

ROSENSTEIN, ROGER G., hand surgeon; b. NYC, July 28, 1949; BA, Columbia U., 1971, MD, 1975. Diplomate Am. Bd. Orthopedic Surgery with qualifications in surgery of hand. Intern, surg. resident The Roosevelt Hosp., NYC, 1975-77; resident in orthopedic surgery Columbia Presbyn. Med. Ctr., NYC, 1977-80; fellow in hand surgery Thomas Jefferson U., Phila., 1980-81; hand surgeon in pvt. practice Paramus, N.J., 1981—. Asst. clin. prof. orthopedic surgery U. Medicine and Dentistry N.J., Newark, 1986—; chief hand surgery sect. Hackensack (N.J.) U. Med. Ctr., 1989—. Contbr. articles to profl. jours. Fellow Am. Acad. Orthopedic Surgery; mem. Am. Soc. Surgery of the Hand, N.Y. Soc. Surgery of the Hand. Office: 22 Madison Ave Paramus NJ 07652-2721 Office Phone: 201-587-7767.

ROSENSTOCK, ARTHUR RICHARD, plastic surgeon, educator; b. NYC, Feb. 4, 1947; MD, U. Libre de Bruxelles, 1976. Intern, gen. surgery Metro Hosp.-NY Med. Coll., NY, 1976—77; resident gen. surgery NY Med. Coll., Valhalla, NY, 1977—81; fellow plastic & reconstructive surgery Med. Coll. Va., Richmond, Va., 1981—83; hosp. appointment, surgery, admitting privileges Stamford Cmty. Hosp., 1983—; clin. instr. Columbia Presbyn. Coll. Physicians and Surgeons, NYC, 2005—; private practice Stamford, Conn., 1983—. Mem.: Am. Soc. Plastic Surgeons, Am. Soc. for Aesthetic Plastic Surgery. Avocations: painting, photography, architectural design, fly fishing. Office: 1290 Summer St Ste 3100 Stamford CT 06905 Office Phone: 203-359-1959. Office Fax: 203-359-9344. E-mail: arosenstockmd@aol.com, arr52@columbia.edu.

ROSENSTOCK, LINDA, dean, medical educator; b. NYC, Dec. 20, 1950; m. Lee Bailey; children: Adam Lee, Matthew Lynn. AB in Psychology, Brandeis U., 1971; student, U. B.C., Vancouver, Can., 1971-72; MD, MPH, Johns Hopkins U., 1977. Diplomate Am. Bd. Internal Medicine, Am. Bd. Preventive Medicine; lic. physician and surgeon, Wash. Med. resident then chief resident U. Wash., Seattle, 1977-80, resident in preventive medicine, instr. medicine, 1980-82, asst. prof., 1982-83, 83-87, lectr. environ. health, 1982-83, adj. asst. prof., 1983-86, mem. grad. sch. faculty, 1985—, assoc. prof., 1987-93, prof. medicine and environ. health, 1993—94, also dir. programs, 1994; dir. Nat. Inst. Occupational Safety and Health, Washington, 1994—2000; dean UCLA Sch. of Pub. Health, 2000—, prof. environ. health sciences, 2000—; prof. medicine UCLA Sch. Medicine, 2000—. Dir. Harborview Med. Ctr., Seattle, 1981-87, acting sect. head, 1992-94; dir. Nat. Inst. Occupational Safety and Health, Washington, 1994—. Assoc. editor Internat. Jour. Occupational Medicine and Toxicology, 1991—; mem. editorial bd. Am. Jour. Indsl. Medicine, 1985-94, Jour. Gen. Internal Medicine, 1987-90, Environ. Rsch., 1987—, Western Jour. Medicine, 1990—; bd. dirs. PacifiCare Health Systems, 2003-05, Skilled Healthcare Group, Inc., 2009-; contbr. numerous articles to profl. jours. Mem. exec. bd. Physicians for Human Rights, 1990—; mem. occupl. health adv. bd. United Auto Workers GM, 1990-94, chair, 1993-94; mem. task force on pneumoconioses Am. Coll. Radiology, 1991-94; mem. external adv. panel Agrl. Health and Safety Ctr., 1992-93; mem. adv. com. Ctrs. for Disease Control, 1992-94; mem. com. to survey health effects of mustard gas and lewisite Inst. Medicine, 1992, mem. bd. health promotion and disease prevention, 1993-94; mem. bd. sci. counselors HHS, 1993-94, mem. exec. com. nat. toxicology program, 1994—; mem. med. adv. bd. Teamsters Internat., 1993-94. Recipient Upjohn Achievement award Harborview Med. Ctr., 1978, Jean Spencer Felton MD award Western Occupational Med. Assn., 1988, Environ. and Occupational Medicine award Nat. Inst. Environ. Health Scis., 1991-94; Robert Wood Johnson scholar, 1980-82, Henry J. Kaiser scholar, 1984-89. Fellow ACP (health promotion subcom. 1989-90, clin. practice subcom. 1990-91), Collegium Ramazzini; mem. APHA (chair membership com. 1983-85, chairperson occupational helath and safety sect. 1985-86, gov. coun. 1986-88), Am. Coll. Occupational Medicine (mem. jud. com. 1989-94), Am. Thoracic Soc. (com. health care policy and clin. practice 1990-93), Internat. Commn. Occupational Health (sci. com. epidemiology in occupational health 1989—), Soc. Gen. Internal Medicine (program planning com. 1987, Glaser award com. 1993-94), Western Assn. Physicians, Pacific Interurban Clin. Club. Office: UCLA Sch Pub Health 16-035 Ctr for Health Sciences Box 951772 Los Angeles CA 90095

ROSENSTRAUCH, DOREEN, physician, scientist, nurse, educator; RN, Humboldt U. of Berlin, Germany, 1991; MD, Guericke U., Germany, 1997; PhD magna cum laude, U. Tex. Health Sci. Ctr.; PhD, Humboldt U. Physician U. Otto-von-Guericke, Magdeburg, Germany, 1997—98; rsch. fellow Tex. Heart Inst./St. Lukes Hosp, Houston, 1998—2000, rsch. scientist, 2000—; instr. U. Tex. HSC, Houston, 2001—02, asst. prof. medicine, 2003—. Dir. internat. coop., bd. mem., vis. prof. Tanzania Heart Inst., 1997—; hon. prof. Asociacion Mexicana dela los Animals de Laboratorio (AMCAL), Mexico, 2001—; adj. prof. U. Houston, 2004—, Rice U., 2004—. Contbr. articles to profl. jours. Mem. Friend of Houston-Leipzig Sister City Assn., Houston, 1998—, Friend of the German-Am. C. of C., Houston, 1998—2002, Internat. Alliance, Houston, 2002—. Recipient Rsch. award, Tex. Heart Inst., 2000; grantee NIH grantee, 2004—; Roderick Duncan MacDonald Rsch. Fund grantee, St. Luke's Episcopal Hosp., 2003—, NSF grantee, 2003—. Fellow: AHA (inaugural fellow 2002—); mem.: Assn. Women Faculty, Evaluation and Promotion Med. Students, Tanzania Heart Inst. (dir. internat. coop., mem. bd. 1997—), Ctr. Biology Chronic Disease, Gerson Lehrman Group's Coun. Healthcare Advisors, Internat. Soc. Heart and Lung Transplantation (invited mem. 2000—). Office: 3014 Cliffdale Ave Houston TX 77091

ROSENSTREICH, DAVID LEON, medical educator, immunologist, allergist; b. NYC, Nov. 16, 1942; s. Joseph S. and Gertrude (Tankenbaum) R.; m. Victoria Abokrek, June 13, 1965; children: Jonathan, Peter, Rebecca. BS in Chemistry, CCNY, 1963; MD, NYU, 1967. Intern, resident Bronx (N.Y.) Mcpl. Hosp. Ctr., 1967-69; clin. assoc. NIAID, NIH, Bethesda, Md., 1969-72; sr. investigator NIDR, NIH, Bethesda, 1972-78; vis. assoc. prof. Rockefeller U., NYC, 1978-80; prof. medicine Albert Einstein Coll. Medicine, NYC,

1980—, dir. div. allergy and immunology, 1980—. Dir. Bronx Asthma Project. Editor: Mitogens in Immunobiology, 1975, Cellular Functions in Immunity and Inflamation, 1980; assoc. editor Clin. Revs. in Allergy, 1987—, Annals of Allergy, 1994—. Comdr. USPHS, 1969-78. Fellow Am. Soc. Clin. Investigation, Am. Acad. Allergy and Immunology, Am. Coll. Allergy, Am. Assn. Physicians. Avocation: winemaking. Office: Albert Einstein Coll Med 1635a Poplar St Bronx NY 10461-1926 Office Phone: 718-405-8075.

ROSEN-SUPNICK, ELAINE RENEE, physical therapist; b. NYC, May 7, 1951; d. Oscar Arthur and Sydell (Zimmerman) R.;m. Jed Supnick, Apr. 21, 1985. BS, CUNY, 1973; MS, L.I. U., Bklyn., 1977; D of Health Sci., U. St. Augustine, 1998. Cert. orthop. specialist/Am. Bd. Phys. Therapy Specialists. Phys. therapy cons. Lenox Hill Hosp. Home Care, NYC, 1977-83, Group Health Ins., Queens, N.Y., 1977-83, Vis. Nurse Assn., Bklyn., 1977-83; sr. phys. therapist Bird S. Coler Hosp., Roosevelt Island, N.Y., 1973-77; prof. CUNY-Hunter Coll., 1977—; ptnr. Queens Phys. Therapy Assocs., Forest Hills, N.Y., 1982—. Fellow Am. Acad. of Orthop. Manual Phys. Therapists; mem. Am. Phys. Therapy Assn. (bd. cert. orthop. specialist, cert. phys. ther Democrat. Jewish. Office: Queens Phys Therapy Assocs 6940 108th St Flushing NY 11375-3851 E-mail: elaine.rosen@hunter.cuny.edu.

ROSENTHAL, ALBERT LESTER, dermatologist, educator; b. New Bedford, Mass., July 25, 1926; s. Myer and Ruth Naomi (Gourse) R.; m. Carol Ash, July 30, 1969; children: Robert, Jill, Bruce. BA magna cum laude, Tufts U., 1946, MD, 1951. Diplomate Am. Bd. Dermatology. Intern RI Hosp., Providence, 1951-52, asst. resident surgery, 1952-53; asst. resident dermatology Mass. Gen. Hosp., Boston, 1955-56; asst. in dermatology NYU, 1958-60; practice medicine specializing in dermatology Trenton, NJ, 1958—; attending dermatologist Mercer Hosp., 1958—, chief dermatologist, 1958-93; chief dermatology Helene Euld Hosp., 1973-85; assoc. in dermatology U. Pa., Phila., 1969-73; assoc. prof. dermatology Hahnemann Med. Coll., Phila., 1973-87, clin. prof. dermatology, 1987—; mem. staff Grad. Hosp. Pa., 1969-73, Hamilton Hosp., chief dermatologist, 1972-76. Contbr. articles to profl. jours. Trustee Friend of the NJ State Mus., 1972—, chmn. bd. trustees, 1980-82, v.p. fine arts, 1978-80; gov. appointee adv. coun. NJ State Mus., 1994-2000, exec. com., 2001-; adv. bd. Princeton Sr. Resource Ctr., 1997—, exec. com.; adv. bd. Am. Art Newark Mus., 1998 2002; mem. Mercer County Cultural and Heritage Commn., 1982-2000, chmn., 1984-2000; mem. Mercer County Open Space Preservation Commn., 1992-2000; founding mem. Leader's Soc. Dermatology Found., 1988; gov. appointee Bd. Trustees NJ State Mus., 2000—, exec. com. sec. 2002—. Served to capt., M.C., USAF, 1953-55. Mem. Am. Acad. Dermatology, Pa. Acad. Dermatology, Noah Worcester Dermatology Soc., Phila. Dermatology Soc. (pres. 1984-85), NJ Dermatology Soc., NJ Med. Soc., Mercer Med. Soc., AMA. Jewish. Office: 74 Franklin Corner Rd Lawrenceville NJ 08648-2102 E-mail: carosentha@aol.com.

ROSENTHAL, AMNON, pediatric cardiologist; b. Gedera, Israel, July 14, 1934; came to U.S., 1949, naturalized, 1959; s. Joseph and Rivka Rosenthal; m. Prudence Lloyd, July 22, 1962; children: Jonathan, Eben, Nathaniel. MD, Albany Med. Coll., 1959. Intern Buffalo Children's Hosp., 1959-60; resident in pediatrics Children's Hosp. Med. Center, Boston, 1960-62, resident in pediatric cardiology, 1965 68; asso. prof. pediatrics Children's Hosp. Med. Center and Harvard U. Med. Sch., Boston, 1975-77, prof. pediatrics C.S. Mott Children's Hosp., U. Mich., Ann Arbor, 1977—2006, assoc. dir. dept. pediatrics, 1989-92, dir. pediatric cardiology, 1977-97, prof. emeritus pediatrics, 2006—. Served to capt. M.C. USAF, 1962-65. Recipient Outstanding Clinician award (Pediat.), U. Mich., 2002, Disting. Svc. award, 2003, Founders award, Am. Acad. Pediat., 2003, Humanitarian award, Jewish Fedn., 2007, Meritorious Achievement award, AHA, 2008; Amnon Rosenthal endowed professorship, U. Mich., 1994. Mem. Am. Acad. Pediatrics, Soc. for Pediatric Rsch., Am. Pediatric Soc., Am. Heart Assn., Am. Coll. Cardiology, Am. Bd. Pediatrics, Am. Bd. Pediatric Cardiology (chmn. 1987-88). Office: CS Mott Children's Hosp Ann Arbor MI 48109-0204 Business E-Mail: amnonr@umich.edu.

ROSENTHAL, ELIZABETH ROBBINS, physician; b. Bklyn., Feb. 10, 1943; d. Marc and Ruth Jackson (Oginz) Robbins; m. Samuel Leonard Rosenthal; children: Thomas, Benjamin, Marc. AB, Smith Coll., 1963; MD, NYU, 1967. Diplomate Am. Bd. of Dermatology. Intern in pediatrics Upstate Med. Ctr., Syracuse, NY, 1967-68; resident in dermatology Henry Ford Hosp., Detroit, 1968-69, Roosevelt Hosp., NYC, 1969-70, Boston U. Med. Ctr., 1972-74; pvt. practice Mamaroneck, NY, 1976—; attending United Hosp., Pt. Chester, NY, 1994—2004; bd. mem. Physicians Nat. Health Program NY Chpt., 2008—. Asst. clin. prof. Albert Einstein Coll. Medicine, Bronx, 1978—. Bd. dirs. Community Counseling Ctr., Mamaroneck, N.Y., 1982—. Fellow Am. Acad. Dermatology; mem. N.Y. State Med. Soc., NOW, Westchester County Med. Soc., Am. Med. Women's Assn. Office: 1600 Harrison Ave Mamaroneck NY 10543-3145 Office Phone: 914-698-2190. E-mail: drelizrose@optonline.net. *

ROSENTHAL, HOWARD GARY, psychotherapist, educator, author; b. St. Louis; s. Merle Lewis and Shirley (Partegyl) R.; m. Patricia Rosenthal, June 7, 1987. AA, Florissant Valley Coll., 1972; BA in Psychology, U. Mo., St. Louis, 1974, MEd in Counseling, 1976; EdD in Counseling, St. Louis U., 1981. Psychotherapist Mid-West Stress Ctr., St. Charles, Mo., 1987—. Psychotherapist Gen. Guidance Group, St. Louis, 1976—; prof., program dir. human svcs. St. Louis C.C., Florissant Valley, 1987—, founding mem., Bd. Cert. Human Svcs. Profl., 2010. Author: Not With My Life I Don't, 1988, Before Your See Your First Client, 1997, Favorite Counseling and Therapy Homework Techniques, 2001, 2010, 2nd edit., 2011, Human Services Dictionary, 2003, Therapy's Best, 2006; (audio tapes) Audio Study Guide for Counselor Licensure, 1990, 2005; (video) Suicide Prevention Techniques That Work, 1991, The Encyclopedia of Counseling, 1993, 2002, Vital Information And Review Questions For The NCE, CPCE and State Counseling Exams, Spl. 15th Anniversary edit., 2007, Spl. 15th Anniversary edit. Audio CDs, 2009; editor: Favorite Counseling & Therapy Techniques, 1997, 2011; contbr. articles to profl. jours. Recipient Mo. Juvenile Justice award, 1987, Emerson Excellence Tchg. award, 1998; named to Hall of Fame St. Louis C.C., 1988, Commemorative Award, Founding Human Services Bd. Cert. Practitioner, 2010. E-mail: drhowardr@juno.com.

ROSENTHAL, J. THOMAS, hospital administrator, medical educator; b. Richmond, 1949; BA, Johns Hopkins U.; MD, Duke U., 1974. Intern Johns Hopkins U., Balt., 1970; resident U. Va. Hosp., Charlottesville, Va., 1976, Lahey Clinic Found., Boston, 1980; exec. vice chmn. dept. surgery UCLA Sch. Medicine, 1991, prof. surgery/urology, 1993—, assoc. vice chancellor, 2003—; dir., vice provost UCLA Med. Group, 1996—; chief med. officer UCLA Health Sys., 1999—; vice provost UCLA Med. Group Affairs. Office: UCLA Urology/David Geffen Sch Medicine Box 951731 14-214R CHS Los Angeles CA 90095-1731 Office Phone: 310-825-4686. *

ROSENTHAL, RICHARD JAY, psychiatrist; b. NYC, Jan. 12, 1939; s. Sam and Yvette Loraine (Kapelov) Rosenthal; m. Strawn Rosenthal, Nov. 10, 1984. BA, Cornell U., 1960; MD, Albert Einstein Coll. of Medicine, 1964. Diplomate Nat. Bd. Med. Examiners, Am. Bd. Psychiatry and Neurology. Resident in psychiatry Mt. Sinai Hosp., NYC, 1968; clin. assoc. L.A. Psychoanalytic Inst., 1980; pvt. practice Los Angeles, 1970—; asst. clin. prof. psychiatry UCLA, 1971—2005, clin. prof. psychiatry, 2006—; faculty L.A. Psychoanalytic Inst., 1984—; dir. inpatient gambling treatment program Westwood Hosp., 1990—93; chief of psychiatry CPC Westwood Hosp., LA, 1992—93; supr. attending Cedars Sinai Med. Ctr., LA, 1982—; co-dir. UCLA Gambling Studies Program, 2003—. Founder/pres. Calif. Coun. on Problem Gambling, 1986—99; com. on impulse disorders APA Task Force on DSM IV, 1988—93; com. on social and econ. impact of path. gambling Nat. Acad. Sci., 1998—99; vis. prof. psychiatry UCLA, 2005—06. Contbr. chapters to books, articles to jours. Beit T'Shuvah Residential Treatment Ctr. L.A., 1992—94; adv. com. Little Hoover Commn. on Gambling in Calif., 1997; trustee Mus. Photog. Arts, San Diego. Lt. comdr. USN, 1968—70. Recipient Rsch. award, Nat. Coun. on Problem Gambling, 1993, Herman Goldman award, 1995, Robert Custer award, 2004. Fellow: Am. Psychiat. Assn. (life disting.); mem.: Internat. Dostoevsky Soc., So. Calif. Psychiat. Soc. (ethics com. 1992), Inst. for the Study of Gambling and Comml. Gaming (adv. bd. 1993—), Am. Acad. Psychiatrists in Alcoholism and Addictions. Achievements include first controlled study of repetitive self mutilation(demonstrated progression and role of dissociation); author of current diagnostic criteria for pathological gambling; co-investigator on first genetic study of pathological gambling (demonstrating physiological predisposition); research establishing the legitimacy of the disorder; founding of California council on problem gaming, started first inpatient treatment program on the west coast, began UCLA gambling studies program, mentored researchers and clinicans. Avocations: photography, fly fishing. Office: 435 N Roxbury Dr Beverly Hills CA 90210 Office Phone. 310-278-3746.

ROSENTHAL, ROBERT, psychology professor; b. Giessen, Germany, Mar. 2, 1933; came to U.S., 1940, naturalized, 1946. s. Julius and Hermine (Kahn) R.; m. Mary Lu Clayton, Apr. 20, 1951; children: Roberta, David C., Virginia. AB, UCLA, 1953, PhD, 1956; PhD (hon.), U. Giessen, 2003. Diplomate clin. psychology Am. Bd. Examiners Profl. Psychology. Clin. psychology trainee Los Angeles Area VA, 1954-57; lectr. U. So. Calif., 1956-57, acting instr. UCLA, 1957; from asst. to assoc. prof., coordinator clin. tng. U. N.D., 1957-62; vis. assoc. prof. Ohio State U., 1960-61, lectr. Boston U., 1965-66; lectr. clin. psychology Harvard U., Cambridge, Mass., 1962-67, prof. social psychology, 1967-95, chmn. dept. psychology, 1992-95, Edgar Pierce prof. psychology, 1995-99, Edgar Pierce prof. emeritus, 1999—; disting. prof. U. Calif., Riverside, 1999—, univ. prof. sys. wide, 2008—. Author: Experimenter Effects in Behavioral Research, 1966, enlarged edit., 1976; (with Lenore Jacobson) Pygmalion in the Classroom, 1968, expanded edit., 1992, Meta-analytic Procedures for Social Research, 1984, rev. edit., 1991, Judgment Studies, 1987; (with others) New Directions in Psychology 4, 1970, Sensitivity to Nonverbal Communication: The Pons Test, 1979; (with Ralph L. Rosnow) The Volunteer Subject, 1975, Primer of Methods for the Behavioral Sciences, 1975, Essentials of Behavioral Research, 1984, 3d edit., 2008, Understanding Behavioral Science, 1984, Contrast Analysis, 1985, Beginning Behavioral Research, 1993, 6th edit., 2008, People Studying People: Artifact and Ethics in Behavioral Research, 1997, (with Ralph L. Rosnow and Donald B. Rubin) Contrasts and Effect Sizes in Behavioral Research: A Correlational Approach, 2000; (with Brian Mullen) BASIC Meta-analysis, 1985; editor: (with Ralph L. Rosnow) Artifact in Behavioral Research, 1969, Skill in Nonverbal Communication, 1979, Quantitative Assessment of Research Domains, 1980, (with Thomas A. Sebeok) The Clever Hans Phenomenon: Communication With Horses, Whales, Apes and People, 1981, (with Blanck and Buck) Nonverbal Communication in the Clinical Context, 1986, (with Gheorghiu, Netter and Eysenck) Suggestion and Suggestibility: Theory and Research, 1989, (with Harrigan and Scherer) The New Handbook of Methods in Nonverbal Behavior Research, 2005. Recipient Donald Campbell award Soc. for Personality and Social Psychology, 1988, James McKeen Cattell Sabbatical award, 1995-96; co-recipient Golden Anniversary Monograph award Speech Comm. Assn., 1996; named Watson lectr. U. N.H., Lanzetta Meml. lectr. Dartmouth Coll., Bayer lectr. Yale Sch. Medicine, Foa lectr. Temple U., Disting. Alumni lectr. UCLA, Marschak lectr. UCLA; Guggenheim fellow, 1973-74, fellow Ctr. for Advanced Study in Behavioral Scis., 1988-89; sr. Fulbright scholar, 1972; recipient Gold Medal for Life Achievement in Sci. of Psychology Am. Psychol. Found., 2003. Fellow AAAS (co-recipient Sociopsychol. prize 1960, co-recipient Behavioral Sci. Rsch. prize 1993), Am. Acad. Arts & Scis., APA (divsn. evaluation, measurement, and stats., co-recipient Cattell Fund award 1967, co-chmn. Task Force on Statis. Inference, Disting. Sci. award for applications of psychology, 2002, Disting. Sci. Contbns. award, 2002, divsn. evaluation, measurement and stats., others), Am. Psychol. Soc. (charter, James McKeen Cattell award 2001); mem. Soc. Exptl. Social Psychology (Disting. Scientist award 1996), Ea. Psychol. Assn. (Disting. lectr. 1989), Mid-we. Psychol. Assn., Western Psychol. Assn. (Lifetime Achievement award, 2009), Mass. Psychol. Assn. (Disting. Career Contbn. award 1979), Soc. Projective Techniques (past treas.), Phi Beta Kappa, Sigma Xi. Office: Univ Calif Psychology Bldg Riverside CA 92521-0001 Office Phone: 951-827-4503.

ROSENWAKS, ZEV, obstetrician, gynecologist, educator, reproductive endocrinologist; b. Rehovot, Israel, Oct. 9, 1946; s. Ira and Esther Rosenwaks; m. Stacy Rosenwaks; children: David, Gaelin. BA, CUNY, Bklyn., 1968; MD, SUNY Downstate Med. Ctr., Bklyn., 1972. Lic. med. doctor N.Y., 1972, Md., 1976, Va., 1983, diplomate Am. Bd. Obstetrics and Gynecology, 1978, Am. Bd. Obstetrics and Gynecology Divsn. Reprod. Endocrinology, 1981. Resident, dept. obstetrics and gynecology Long Island Jewish-Hillside Med. Ctr., NYC, 1972—76; postdoctoral fellow, reproductive endocrinology Johns Hopkins Hosp., Balt., 1976—78; dir. divsn. reprod. endocrinology SUNY, Stony Brook, 1978—83, asst. prof. dept. obstetrics and gynecology, 1978—82; attending obstetrician-gynecologist Long Island Jewish-Hillside Med. Ctr., NY, 1978—83; physician-in-charge, divsn. reprod. endocrinology Queens Hosp. Ctr., NY, 1978—83; assoc. prof. dept. obstetrics and gynecology SUNY, Stony Brook, 1982—83; prof. dept. obstetrics and gynecology Ea. Va. Med. Sch., Va., 1984—88; attending obstetrician-gynecologist Norfolk Gen. Hosp., Va., 1983—88; dir. divsn. reprod. medicine, dept. obstetrics and gynecology Ea. Va. Med. Sch., Va., 1983—88, dir. Howard and Georgeanna Jones Inst. for Reproductive Medicine Va., 1983—88, dir. IVF program, 1983—88, dir. reproductive endocrine lab., 1983—88; attending obstetrician-gynecologist N.Y. Presbyn. Hosp., NY, 1988—; prof. dept. obstetrics and gynecology Weill Med. Coll. Cornell U., NY, 1988—; dir. Ctr. for Reproductive Medicine and Infertility N.Y. Presbyn Hosp.-Weill Cornell, 1988—; Revlon disting. prof. of reproductive medicine in obstetrics and gynecology Weill Med. Coll. Cornell U., 1994—, prof. reproductive medicine Inst. for Reproductive Medicine, 2000—; dir. Inst. Reproductive Medicine N.Y. Presbyn. Hosp.-Weill Cornell, 2000—. Cons. Smithtown Gen. Hosp., 1979—83; rsch. cons. NIH Spl. Study Sect. Reproductive Disorders, 1982, NIH U. Fla. Sch. Medicine, 1982, March of Dimes, 1983, NIH Site Visit, Dept. Pediatrics Adrenal Hyperplasia Program, Cornell Med. Ctr., 1984, NIH Rsch. Grant Review, 1996; grant rev. The Wellcome Trust, 1997; endometriosis expert advisory bd. Amgen/Praecis, 1999; scientific adv. bd. mem. FF-MAS Adv. bd., 1999, Cetrotride ASTA Med. Bd., 2000; spkr. in field. Internat. editl. bd. mem. Israel Jour. Obstetrics and Gynecology, editl. bd. mem. Assisted Reproduction Reviews; editor: Jour. Assisted Reproductive Technology/Andrology; assoc. editor Jour. Assisted Reproduction and Genetics, section editor Current Opinion in Obstetrics and Gynecology, 1990; editor: Reproductive Endocrinology, Surgery and Technology; editl. advisory bd. Weill Med. Coll. Encyclopedia of Health and Healing, editl. bd. mem. Seminars in Reproductive Endocrinology, reviewer Am. Jour. Obstetrics and Gynecology, Archives of Internal Medicine, Endocrinology, Fertility and Sterility, Human Reproduction/Molecular Human Reproduction, Internat. Jour. Gynecology and Obstetrics, Internat. Jour. Andrology, Jour. of Clin. Endocrinology and Metabolism, Jour. Am. Med. Assn., Jour. Assisted Reproduction and Genetics, New England Jour. Medicine, Obstetrics and Gynecology, Obstetrics and Gynecological Survey, Today's Woman; contbr. articles to profl. jours. Pres. Soc. Reproductive Endocrinology, 1987—88, Soc. Assisted Reproductive Tech., 1991—92; mem. bd. of overseers Weill Med. Coll. Cornell U., 2002—. Grantee, Johns Hopkins U. Inst. Rsch. Grant, 1977—78, Syntex Corp., 1976—78, Eli Lilly Corp., 1979—81, Nat. Inst. Mental Health, 1982—85, Ortho Pharmaceutical Corp., 1986, Roussel-Uclaff, 1986, Ortho-Pharmaceutical Corp., 1986—88, Agy. for Internat. Devel., 1986—88, Akzo Nobel-Organon Org., 1997—98, Serono Labs., 1998—99, Dept. Health and Human Svcs., 1999—2000, Serono Labs., 1999—2000, Weill-Cornell Gen. Clin. Rsch. Ctr., 1999—2002, Akzo Nobel-Organon, 2001—02. Office: Ctr for Reproductive Medicine and Infertility 505 E 70th St Ste 340 New York NY 10021

ROSENWASSER, MELVIN P., orthopedist, surgeon, educator; Attended, Columbia U., 1976. Diplomate Am. Bd. of Orthopaedic Surgery, Am. Bd. of Orthopaedic Surgery-hand surgery. Intern St. Luke's-Roosevelt Hosp. Ctr., 1977—79; resident NY-Presbyn. Hosp., 1979—82; fellow NY Orthopaedic Hosp., 1982—83; prof. orthopaedic surgery Columbia Univ.; with NY-Presbyn. Hosp. Office: NewYork-Presbyterian Hospital 161 Fort Washington Ave New York NY 10032 Office Phone: 212-305-4565.

ROSENWASSER, ROBERT H., neurosurgeon, educator; MD, La. State U. Med. Ctr., New Orleans, 1979. Diplomate Am. Bd. Neurol. Surgery, lic. Pa., 1980, registered NY, 1992, lic. NJ, 2005. Intern in gen. surgery Temple Univ. Hosp., 1980, resident in neurosurgery, 1984; fellow in vascular surgery London Health Sciences Centre, 1984; fellow in neurology NYU Med. Ctr., 1993; chair neurol. surgery Thomas Jefferson Univ. Hosp. Named one of Top Doctors, Phila. Mag., 2007, 2010. Fellow: Am. Coll. of Surgeons; mem.: Congress of Neurol. Surgeons, Am. Assn. of Neurol. Surgeons. Office: Thomas Jefferson University Hospital 2nd Fl 909 Walnut St Philadelphia PA 19107 Office Phone: 215-955-7000. Office Fax: 215-503-7038.

ROSHAL, LEONID, pediatrician; b. Livni, Russia, Apr. 27, 1933; Grad. Pediatrician, 2nd State Moscow Med. Inst., 1951—57; studied Clin. Ordinature, State Mcpl. Pediatric Hosp., 1959—61. Dist. pediatrician Pediatric Municipal Polyclinics, 1957; with Clin. and Scientific Rsch. Inst., 1961—81; head emergency surgery and trauma dept. Ctr. of Childrens health of Russian Acad. of Med. Sciences., 1981, prof., 1982; exec. dir. & chief Moscow Clin. and Rsch. Inst. of Emergency Childrens Surgery and Trauma, 2003. Team head soviet childrens doctors, Mongolia, 1980; team head childrens doctors, Armenia, 88, Chelyabinsk, Russia, 89; chief orgn. group Armenian Healthcare Ministry, 1988; organiser med. aid to children, Iran, 90; with med. aid and liberation of children Yugoslavia War, 1991; chmn. Coordination Med. Coun. of defenders of White House, Moscow, 1991; hon mem. Assn. of Pediatric Surgeons of Russia, 1995; hon. prof. Inst. for Advanced Med. Tng., Georgia, 2002; hon. dr. Armenian Acad. of Sciences, 2003; hon. mem. Asian Assn. of Physicians (AMDA), 2004, UN Internat. Royal Acad., 2005, Kazakh Nat. Med. Univ., 2006, Med. Chamber of Armenia, 2007; mem. bd. World Assn. of Disaster and Emergency Medicine, 2007; pres. Nat. Med. Chamber, 2010; chmn. med. section Civil Chamber of Russian Fed., 2005—08. Hon. pres. Samu Social Internat., Moscow, 2004. Decorated Medal for svcs. to Moscow, Medal for svcs. to Russian Healthcare System, civil medal "Golden Star"; recipient State Medal (Defeder of Free Russia), Russia, 1992, State Order of Courage award, 2002, State Order of

Armenia "Mkhitar Heratzi", 2004, Mongolian State "Order of the Polar Star", 2006, "Medal of Great Leader", Pres. of Pakistan, 2007, State Order of the Republic of North Ossetia-Alanija "To the Glory of Ossetia" award, 2008, Russian State Order for "Great svcs. for the Motherland", 2008, Civil Order "for the Rebirth of Russia" award, 2003, Civil Order "for the sacrificial svc. to Russia", 2003, Civil Order of Peter the Great, the 1st Rank, 2004, Ludvig Nobel prize, 2010; named Childrens Doctor of the World, 1996, Nat. Hero of Russia, 2002, Pride of Russia, 2002, Man of the Year, 2002, Person of the Year, 2002, European of the Year, Readers Digest, 2005, Star of Europe, Business Week, 2005; nominee Childrens Dr. of the Year, Union of Pediatricians of Russia, 2005. Mem.: Russian Presdl. Coun. for Promoting Civil Soc. Devel. and Human Rights, Lion's Club Intercontinental, Moscow (Pres. 1994), Platform "Eurasian Dialogue" (Turkey), British Assn. of Pediatric Surgeons. Office: International Charitable Fund for Children in Disasters and Wars 20 Bolshaya Polynka 119180 Moscow Russia Office Phone: 74959592779. Office Fax: 74959590080. *

ROSHEL, JOHN ALBERT, JR., orthodontist; b. Terre Haute, Ind., Apr. 7, 1941; s. John Albert and Mary M. (Griglione) R.; m. Kathy Roshel; children: John Albert III, James Livingston, Angela Kay. BS, Ind. State U., 1963; DDS, Ind. U., 1966; MS, U. Mich., 1968. Individual practice dentistry specializing in orthodontics, Terre Haute, 1968—. Mem. ADA, Am. Assn. Orthodontists, Terre Haute C. of C., Terre Haute Country Club, Lions, Elks, KC, Lambda Chi Alpha, Delta Sigma Delta, Omicron Kappa Upsilon. Roman Catholic. Home: 15 E Wedgeway Dr Terre Haute IN 47802-4983 Office: 4241 S 7th St Terre Haute IN 47802-4367 Office Phone: 812-238-2451.

ROSIN, DANNY, surgeon; b. Israel, Apr. 26, 1963; MD, Sackler Sch. Medicine (formerly Tel Aviv University's Med. Sch.), 1990. Attending surgeon Sheba Med. Ctr., 1998—. Sr. lectr. Sackler Sch. Medicine, 2009. Mem.: Internat. Soc. Surgery, Soc. Am. Gastrointestinal and Endoscopic Surgeons, European Soc. Endoscopic Surgery, Israeli Soc. Surgery (mem. Soc. Internat. Chirurgie). Home: PO Box 56014 Tel Aviv 61560 Israel Home Fax: 972-3-5283283. Business E-Mail: drosin@mac.com.

ROSINSKI, EDWIN FRANCIS, medical educator; b. Buffalo, June 25, 1928; s. Theodore Joseph and Josephine M. (Wolski) R.; m. Jeanne C. Hueniger, Oct. 27, 1951; children: John T., Mary E., Sarah J. BS, SUNY, Buffalo, 1950; EdM, U. Buffalo, 1957, EdD, 1959. Prof. health scis. Med. Coll. Va., Richmond, 1959-66; dep. asst. sec. HEW, Washington, 1966-68; exec. vice chancellor U. Calif., San Francisco, 1968-72, prof., 1972-94; prof. emeritus medicine & pharmacy, 1994—. Adv. Rockefeller Found., N.Y.C., 1962-67, WHO, Geneva, 1962-78, Imperial Com. Health, Tehran, Iran, 1974-77; cons. Stanford Research Inst., Menlo Park, Calif., 1975-79. Author: The Assistant Medical Officer, 1965; contbr. over 100 articles to profl. jours. Served with USAF, 1950-54. Recipient spl. citation HEW, 1968, Merrell Flair award, 1991; named disting. prof. Australian Vice Chancellors Office, 1974, disting. vis. prof. Tulane U., New Orleans, 1983, Alumni of Yr. SUNY, Buffalo, 2006. Fellow AAAS; mem. Assn. Am. Med. Colls. (Merrel Flair award), Am. Ednl. Research Assn., Soc. Health and Human Values (founding mem.), Calif. Pharmacists Assn. (hon.), Phi Delta Kappa. Roman Catholic. Avocation: physical fitness. Home: 80 Sotelo Ave San Francisco CA 94116-1423

RØSKAFT, EIVIN, evolutionary biologist, scientist; b. Namsos, Norway, Feb. 16, 1951; s. Odd and Aase (Olsen) R.; m. Berit Solberg, May 31, 1969; children: Tove, Hanna. BS, U. Trondheim, Norway, 1976, MS, 1978, PhD in Zoology, 1984. Postdoctoral U. Wash., Seattle, 1984-85; assoc. prof. U. Trondheim, 1988-91, dean faculty sci., 1989-91, dir. Ctr. Envir. and Devel., 1991-93, prof., 1993-99; dir. Norwegian Inst. Nature Rsch., Trondheim, 1993-99; prof. evolutionary biology dept. zoology Norwegian U. Sci. and Tech., Trondheim, 1999—, head dept. biology, 2002—. Lt. Norwegian Infantry, 1978-96. Recipient Sci. award Royal Norwegian Sci. Soc. Mem. N.Y. Acad. Scis. Home: Boks 156 7566 Vikhamar Norway Office: Norwegian U Sci and Tech N-7491 Trondheim Norway Office Phone: 47 735 96291. Business E-Mail: roskaft@bio.ntnu.no.

RÖSLER, NORBERT FELIX, neurologist, neuroscientist; b. Lörrach, Germany, Mar. 19, 1962; MD, Freiburg U., Germany, 1989; Dr. med. habil., postdoc. lectr. qualification, Magdeburg U., 2002. Lic. MD Germany, 1989; cert. postdoc. lectr. Magdeburg U., 2002. Sci. asst. dept. neurology Marburg U., Germany, 1989-94; sci. asst. dept. psychiatry Freiburg U., Germany, 1995-97; neuroscientist Ludwig Boltzmann Inst. Clin. Neurobiology, Vienna, 1994—95, 1998—2001; asst. med. dir. dept. neurorehabilitation Hosp. Rodach, Coburg, Germany, 1997-98. Neurol. sociomed. cons., Magdeburg, Saxony-Anhalt, Germany, 2001—05, Berlin, 2005—; lectr., privatdozent Magdeburg U., 2002—. Contbr. articles to profl. jours. and books. Mem. German Socs. Neurology, Clin. Neurophysiology, Psychiatry and Psychotherapy, CSF Rsch. Group, World Fedn. Neurology, European Soc. Clin. Neuropharmacology Business E-Mail: norbert.roesler@med.ovgu.de.

ROSLI, ROZITA, science educator, researcher; b. Batu Gajah, Malaysia, Mar. 12, 1960; d. Rosli Dato' Bendahara and Rasimah Hj Darimi; m. Ajmal M Abdul Razak Al-Aidrus, Nov. 20, 1984; children: Mohamed Shafiq Ajmal, Mohamed Shabyl Ajmal. B in biology, Ind. U., Purdue U., 1980—83; M in biology, Ball State U., 1984—86, D in molecular biology, 1988—93. Rsch. assoc. Ind. U. Sch. Medicine, Indpls., 1994—96; lectr. U. Malaya, 1996—97; lectr., assoc. prof. U. Putra Malaysia, 1998—. Coord. pharmacogenomics interim lab. Nat. Inst. for Pharmaceuticals and Nutraceuticals, Serdang, Selangor, Malaysia, 2001—; chmn. tech. panel (health sector) for rsch. grants U. Putra Malaysia, Serdang, 2000—, dep. dean rsch. and postgrad. studies, 2004—. Contbr. articles to profl. jours. Recipient Travel grant, UNESCO, 1998; Travel award, Fogarty Internat., 1996, Rsch. grants, Ministry of Sci. and the Environment, Malaysia, 1998, 2000, 2002, 2003, scholarship, Harvard U., 2006. Mem.: Genetics Soc. of Malaysia (treas. 2003), Malaysian Soc. for Molecular Biology and Biochemistry (life). Achievements include development of cholera DNA vaccine; research in pharmacogenomics of breast cancer in Malaysian patients; anti-cancer drug discovery from natural products. Avocations: gardening, cooking, travel, music. Home: D501 Puteri Palma Condominium 101 Resort Putrajaya 62502 Malaysia Office: Universiti Putra Malaysia Faculty Medicine & Health Sciences 43400 Serdang Malaysia Office Fax: 603-8942 6957. Personal E-mail: r_rosli@yahoo.com. Business E-Mail: rozita@medic.upm.edu.my.

ROSLIN, MITCHELL STEVEN, bariatric surgeon; b. Bklyn., Dec. 19, 1962; Grad., U. Pa.; MD, NYU, 1987. Diplomate Am. Bd. Surgery. Resident gen. medicine Maimonides Med. Ctr., Bklyn., 1988—93, dir. bariatric surgery, 1996; chief obesity surgery Lenox Hill Hosp., NYC, 2000—. Clin. assoc. prof. SUNY Health Sci. Ctr., Bklyn. Contbr. articles to profl. jours. Named one of NY's Best Minimally Invasive Surgeons, NY Mag., 2000—. Fellow: ACS; mem.: AMA, Soc. Am. Gastrointestinal & Endoscopic Surgeons, Am. Soc. Bariatric Surgery. Office: Lenox Hill Hosp Manhattan Minimally Invasive & Bariatric Surgery 186 E 76th St 1st Fl New York NY 10021 *

ROSMAN, HOWARD S., cardiologist, educator; b. Detroit, Aug. 29, 1947; s. Carl and Mae S. Rosman; m. Sarine John-Rosman, Aug. 21, 1999; m. Nancy R Rosenhaus, Aug. 4, 1974 (div. Apr. 17, 1997); 1 stepchild, Akash D. Patel children: Sarah Z., Benjamin J., David A., John M. BA, Harvard Coll., Cambridge, Mass., 1969; MD, U. Mich., Ann Arbor, 1975. Resident in internal medicine Emory U., Ga., 1978; vis. fellow cardiology Royal Postgraduate Med. Sch., London, 1979; fellowship in cardiovascular disease Emory U., Ga., 1981; sr. staff physican Henry Ford Health Sys., Detroit, 1982—99; sr. staff physician St John Hosp. and Med. Ctr., Detroit, 1999—. Clin. asst. prof. of medicine U. of Mich., Ann Arbor, Mich., 1983—88; assoc. chief divsn. of cardiology Henry Ford Health Sys., Detroit, 1987—99; clin. assoc. prof. of medicine U. of Mich., Ann Arbor, Mich., 1989—94; program dir. cardiology fellowship Henry Ford Hosp., Detroit, 1987—99, dir. of undergraduate med. edn., 1992—99; prof. of internal medicine Case Western Res. U., Cleveland, Ohio, 1995—99; mem. bd. of governors Henry Ford Health Sys., Detroit, 1997—99; councilor Am. Coll. of Cardology, Mich. Chpt., Mich., 1999—2005; cardiology program dir. St John Hosp. and Med. Ctr., Detroit, 1999—; prof. of medicine Wayne State U., Detroit, 1999—. Pres. Am. Heart Assn., Metro Detroit, 2004—06. Recipient Outstanding Faculty Tchr., U. Mich. Med. Students, 1982 - 1994 (11 awards), Henry Ford Hosp. Residents, 1983 - 1999 (6 awards), Instr. of the Yr., St John Hosp. Cardiology Fellows, 1999 - 2005 (3 awards), Dept. of Internal Medicine Tchg. award, Wayne State U. Med. Sch., Medicine Faculty, 2003. Fellow: Am. Heart Assn., Am. Coll. Cardiology (pres. Mich. chpt. 2008—, gov. 2008—). Office: 22101 Moross Rd 2nd Fl Vep Cardiology Grosse Pointe MI 48236 E-mail: howard.rosman@stjohn.org. *

ROSMAN, SAMANTHA L., pediatrician, emergency physician; m. David A. Rosman. BA magna cum laude, Bryn Mawr Coll.; MD with honors, Columbia U., 2004. Resident pediat. Children's Hosp. Boston.; fellow pediat. emergency medicine Boston Med. Ctr. Mem.: AMA (bd. trustees 2005—09, chair Task Force on Health Sys. Reform), Med. Soc. of State of NY (former mem. House of Del.), Mass. Med. Soc., Am. Coll. Emergency Physicians, Am. Acad. Pediat. Office: Boston Med Ctr One Boston Medical Center Place Boston MA 02118 *

ROSNER, DAVID, history and public health professor; b. NYC, Mar. 13, 1947; s. Alex and Sophie (Gordon) Rosner; m. Kathlyn Conway, July 28, 1979; children: Zachary, Molly. BA, CCNY, 1968; MPH, U. Mass., 1972; PhD, Harvard U., 1978. Asst. prof. Baruch Coll., CUNY, 1978—80, disting. prof. history, 1996—98; prof. history Columbia U., NYC, 1998—, Ronald H. Lauterstein prof. sociomedical scis., Mailman Sch. Pub. Health, 2007—, co-dir. Ctr. History & Ethics of Pub. Health NYC. Adj. prof. cmty. medicine Mt. Sinai Sch. Medicine, NYC. Author: A Once Charitable Enterprise: Hospitals and Health Care in Brooklyn and New York 1885-1915, 1982; co-author (with Gerald Markowitz): Slaves of the Depression: Workers' Letters About Life on the Job, 1987, Children, Race, and Power: Kenneth and Mamie Clark's Northside Center, 1996, Deceit and Denial: The Deadly Politics of Industrial Pollution, 2002, Are We Ready? Public Health since 911, 2006; editor: Hives of Sickness: Public Health and Epidemics in New York City, 1996; co-editor: Health Care in America: Essays in Social History, 1979, The Contested Boundaries of American Public Health, 2008; mem. editl. bd. Jour. Pub. Health Policy, 1999—, contbg. editor Pub. Health Reports, 2002—; contbr. articles to profl. jours. Recipient Robert Wood Johnson Investigator award, 2002—05, Upton Sinclair award, American Indsl. Hygiene Assn., 2005, Disting. Alumnus award, U. Mass.; fellow John Simon Guggenheim Meml. Found., 1987—88; NEH fellow, 1983—84. Mem.: APHA (mem. governing coun. 1994—96, Arthur Viseltear award 2000), Inst. Medicine, Sigma Xi. Achievements include recognition as a specialist in occupational and environmental health history and in the history of public health. Office: Mailman Sch Pub Health Dept Sociomedical Scis Columbia Univ 722 W 168th St Ste 934 New York NY 10032 Office Phone: 212-305-1727. Business E-Mail: dr289@columbia.edu. *

ROSNER, HOWARD L., medical association administrator; b. Miami Beach, Fla., Dec. 7, 1956; BS, U. Miami, 1977; MD, U. Miami Sch. Medicine, 1980. Dir. pain mgmt. Weill-Cornell Med. Coll., 1989—2002; med. dir., pain ctr. Cedars-Sinai Med. Ctr., 2002—. Office: 444 S San Vicente Blvd Suite 1101 Los Angeles CA 90046 Office Fax: 310-423-9610. Business E-Mail: howard.rosner@cshs.org.

ROSNER, INGRID K., pediatric allergist; b. 1947; MD, Wayne State U. Sch. Med., Detroit, 1972. Diplomate Am. Bd. Pediat., Am. Bd. Allergy & Immunology, lic. NY. Resident Boston Med. Ctr.; resident pediat. Boston City Hosp., 1973—77, Children's Hosp. Boston, 1977—78, fellowship, 1978—79; attending physician NY Presbyn./Weill Cornell Med. Ctr.; pvt. practice allergist, immunologist, 1991—. Contbr. articles to profl. jours. Mailing: Ingrid Rosner MD 301 E 66th St New York NY 10021 Office Phone: 212-650-9000.

ROSNOW, RALPH LEON, psychologist, educator; b. Balt., Jan. 10, 1936; s. Irvin and Rebecca (Faber) R.; m. Mimi Quin Medinger, Aug. 12, 1963. BS, U. Md., 1957; MA, George Washington U., 1958; PhD, Am. U., 1962. Asst. prof. Boston U., 1963-67; assoc. prof. Temple U., Phila., 1967-70, full prof., 1970-2001; vis. prof. London Sch. Econs., 1973, Harvard U., Cambridge, Mass., 1978, 1988-89; Thaddeus Bolton prof. Temple U., 1982—2001, Thaddeus Bolton prof. emeritus, 2002—, dir. social and orgnl. psychology divsn. psychology, 1988-2000. Cons. editor jours. and encys. in psychology and comm.; cons. on rsch. methods and data analysis, 1976—. Author: Paradigms in Transition, 1981; author: (with Robert Rosenthal) The Volunteer Subject, 1975; editor: Artifacts in Behavioural Research:Rosenthal & Rosnow's Classic Books, 2009; author: Essentials of Behavioral Research, 3d edit., 2008, Contrast Analysis, 1985, Beginning Behavioral Research, 6th edit., 2008, People Studying People, 1997, Contrasts and Effect Sizes in Behavioral Research, 2000; author: Understanding Behavioral Science, 1984; author: (with Gary Fine) Rumor and Gossip, 1976; author: (with Mimi Rosnow) Writing Papers in Psychology, 8th edit., 2009; author: Primer of Methods for the Behavioral Science, 1975; editor (with Robert Rosenthal): Artifact in Behavioral Research, 1969; author (with Robert E. Lana): Introduction to Contemporary Psychology, 1971; author: (with Mary Gergen & al) Psychology:A Beginning, 1989; editor (with Marianthi Georgoudi): Contextualism and Understanding in Behavioral Science; editor: (with E. J. Robinson) Experiments in Persaasion, 1967. Recipient George A. Miller award Soc. Gen. Psychology, 1999. Fellow: APA, AAAS, Am. Psychol. Soc.; mem.: Soc. Exptl. Social Psychology. Home: 177 Biddulph Rd Radnor PA 19087-4506

ROSOF, EDWARD, pediatrician; married. B in Chemistry, Lafayette Coll., 1967; MD, Thomas Jefferson U. Med. Coll., 1971. Diplomate Am. Bd. Pediatrics, lic. to practice NJ, 1972, Pa., 1973. Intern pediat. Children's Hosp. Phila., 1972, resident pediat., 1974, fellow endocrinology, diabetes and metabolism, 1975; hosp. affiliations include Children's Hosp. Pa., Virtua Hosp. Voorhees, Virtua Meml. Hosp., Virtua West Jersey Hosp., Marlton, Berlin, Virtua duPont Pediatric Program; with Advocare Marlton Pediat. Named Top Doc, Phila. Mag., 2010, South Jersey mag.; named one of the Top Doctors, NJ Monthly, 2005. Fellow: Am. Acad. Pediat. Avocations: bicycling, travel, spending time at the Jersey shore. Office: Virtua 401 Rt 73 N Lake Center Bldg 50 Ste 401 Marlton NJ 08053 Office Phone: 856-355-6000.

ROSOL, GERI, medical association administrator; b. Salisbury, Md., July 28, 1949; BS in Med. Tech., U. Md., 1977; MS in Healthcare Adminstrn., U. Phoenix, 2006, degree summa cum laude. Clin. lab. mgr. Lifetime Health, 2002—05; practice adminstr. John R. McClean & Assocs. Cardiology, 2006—07; program dir. Wound Care Ctr., Atlantic Gen. Hosp., 2007—. Tchr., dept. head Calvary Chapel Christian HS, 1999—2002; adj. prof. SUNY, 2002—04. Recipient Robert A. Warriner award, Diversified Clin. Svcs., award. Mem.: Colo. Assn. Continuing Med. Lab. Edn., SUNY Med. Tech. Adv. Com., Clin. Lab. Mgrs. Assn., Eastern Shore Med. Mgrs. Assn. Avocations: travel, cooking, jogging. Office: 10231 Old Ocean City Blvd Berlin MD 21811 Office Fax: 410-629-6869. Business E-Mail: grosol@diversifiedcs.com.

ROSS, ALLEN GUY, healthcare educator, department chairman; b. Antigonish, Nova Scotia, Can., Dec. 14, 1964; PhD, U. Queensland, 1998, MD, 2010. Prof., chair, pub. health Griffith U., 2008—. Dir., population health rsch. Griffith Health Inst., 2009—. Mem.: Australasian Faculty Pub. Health Medicine. Avocations: travel, reading. Office: Griffith University University Dr Meadowbrook Queensland 4131 Australia Office Fax: 61-7-33821034. Business E-Mail: a.ross@griffith.edu.au.

ROSS, EDWARD, cardiologist; b. Fairfield, Ala., Oct. 10, 1937; s. Horace and Carrie Lee (Griggs) R.; m. Catherine I. Webster, Jan. 19, 1974; children: Edward, Ronald, Cheryl, Anthony. BS, Clark Coll., 1959; MD, Ind. U., 1963. Diplomate Am. Bd. Internal Medicine; cert. specialist in clin. hypertension Am. Soc. Hypertension. Intern Marion County Gen. Hosp., Indpls., 1963; resident in internal medicine Ind. U., 1964-66, 68, cardiology rsch. fellow, 1968-70, clin. asst. prof. medicine, 1970; cardiologist Capitol Med. Assn., Indpls., 1970-74; pvt. practice medicine, specializing in cardiology Indpls., 1974—. Staff cardiologist Winona Meml. Hosp., Indpls., chief cardiovascular disease, 2000-04, med. dir. cardiovascular svcs., 2000-04, med. dir. cardiac cath lab, 2000-04, chief interventional cardiology, 2000-04; staff Meth. Hosp., Indpls., chmn. cardiovasc. sect., 1989-96; chmn. cardiovasc. sect., dir. cardiovasc. ctr. Meth. Hosp., 1990-92; bd. dirs. Meth. Hosp. Heart-Lung Ctr., med. dir. cardiovasc. svcs., 1991-98; med. dir. cardiovascular svcs. Methodist Hosp., Indpls., Ind., 2000-06, cardiac catheterization lab., 2000-06, cardiovascular programs, Clarian Health Indpls., 2000—, cardiovascular svcs., Cardicac Cath. Lab., cardiovascular programs, Clarian Health Ptnrs., 2000-06, sr. cardiologist, Methodist Cardiology Physician, 2006-. Assoc. editor Angiology, Jour. Vascular Disease; sr. editor Jour. Vascular Medicine, 1983—. Mem. Ctrl. Ind. Health Planning Coun., 1972-73; bd. dirs. Ind. chpt. Am. Heart Assn., 1973-74, multiphasic screening East Side Clinic, Flanner Ho. of Indpls., 1968-71; med. dir. Nat. Ctr. for Health Svc. R&D, HEW, 1970; consumer rep. radiologic device panel health FDA, 1988-92; dir. hypertensive screening State of Ind., 1974; J.B. Johnson Cardiovasc. lectr. Nat. Med. Assn., 1991. Capt. MC, USAF, 1966-68. Recipient Lifetime Achievement award, Ctr. Leadership Devel., 2003, Leadership award, Indpls. Police Dept., 2005; scholar, Nat. Found. Health, 1955, Gorges Found., 1956; Woodrow Wilson fellow, 1959. Fellow Royal Soc. Promotion of Health (Eng.), Am. Coll. Angiology (v.p. fgn. affairs, sec. 1993—), Internat. Coll. Angiology, Am. Soc. of Angiology, Am. Coll. Cardiology, Assn. Black Cardiologists (mem. bd. dirs. 1990-94); mem. NAACP, AMA, Am. Soc. Contemporary Medicine and Surgery, Nat. Med. Assn. (coun. sci. assembly 1985-89), Ind. Med. Soc., Marion County Med. Soc., Am. Coll. Physicians, Am. Heart Assn., Ind. Soc. Internal Medicine (pres. 1987-89), Ind. State Med. Assn. (chmn. internal medicine sect. 1987-89), Ind. Med. Soc., Aesculapean Med. Soc., Hoosier State Med. Assn. (pres. 1980-84, 90-95), Urban League, Alpha Omega Alpha, Alpha Kappa Mu, Beta Kappa Chi, Omega Psi Phi. Methodist. Office: 1801 N Senate Blvd #310 Indianapolis IN 46202 Home Phone: 317-966-4848; Office Phone: 317-962-2500. Business E-Mail: eross@iuhealth.org.

ROSS, ELEANOR, retired medical association administrator; M.Nursing, U. Toronto, Ont., Can. RN Ont., Can. Chief nursing practice Women's Coll. Hosp., Toronto, Ont.; asst. prof. U. Toronto

Sch. Nursing; dir. Internat. Coun. Nurses, Geneva, 1997—2005; ret. Mem.: Can. Nurses Respiratory Assn. (pres. 1984—85), Registered Nurses Assn. of Ont. (pres. 1987—89), Can. Nurses Assn. (pres. 1994—96). Office: Internat Council Nurses 3 Pl Jean Marteau 1201 Geneva Switzerland Home: 858 Metler Rd Fenwick ON L0S 1C0 Canada Office Phone: 41-22-908-01-00.

ROSS, GERALD HARVEY, family practice and environmental medicine physician; s. Henry Warburton and Norine Hazel (Bishop) Ross; m. Heather M. Pollett, Aug. 15, 1970; children: Graham D.P., Andrew W.J. BSc, Dalhousie U., Halifax, Can., 1969, MD, 1974. Diplomate Internat. Bd. Environ. Medicine, Am. Bd. Environ. Medicine, cert. Coll. Family Physicians Can., 1979, Family Medicine Can. Family medicine practice, New Minas, Nova Scotia, Canada, 1974—87; med. fellow Environ. Health Ctr., Dallas, 1987—89, med. staff, 1989—99; med. dir. N.S. Environ. Medicine Clinic, Halifax, Canada, 1990—94; rschr. Gerald H. Ross, M.D., P.L.L.C., Bountiful, Utah, 1999—; med. dir. Utah Meth. Cops Project, 2007—. Mem. adv. com. Environ. Hypersensitivites Ont. Dept. Health, Toronto, 1989—94; rsch. fellow Breakspeare Hosp. for Environ. Medicine, Kings Langley, Hertfordshire, England, 1988—89. Co-author reports to Ont. Ministry of Health; contbr. chapters to books, articles to profl. jours., 30 sci. papers; mem. editl. bd. Internat. Jour. Hygiene and Environ. Health, 2001—03, Environ. Epidemiology and Toxicology, 1998—2001, mem. East Coast adv. com. The Med. Post, Toronto, 1978—94. Many leadership positions, 1988—99. Grantee, Innovations in Edn. Utah, 2003; Internat. Fellow in environ. medicine, NS Dept. Health, 1987—89. Fellow: Royal Soc. Medicine (UK), Am. Acad. Environ. Medicine (chair rsch. com. 1991—94, bd. dirs. 1993—98, pres. 1995—97, Appreciation award 1998—, Herbert Rinkel award for excellence in tchg. the principles of environ. medicine 2005, Jonathan Forman Award for outstanding contribution to the field of environ. med. 2010); mem.: AMA, Assn. Am. Physicians and Surgeons, Am. Coll. Nutrition, Can. Soc. Environ. Medicine, Coll. Family Physicians Can., Am. Bd. Environ. Medicine (bd. govs. 1993—), Chem. Sensitivity Found. (bd. dirs.), Can. Med. Assn., Tex. Med. Assn. Mem. Lds Ch. Avocations: reading, movies.

ROSS, IAN BEAUDOIN, neurosurgeon, educator; b. Montreal, Que., Can., Feb. 29, 1960; came to the U.S., 2000; s. Ian Cathcart and Jacqueline Joan Ross; m. Catherine Sylvia Pitfield, June 1, 1985; children: Felicia Lillian, William Leopold. BSc, McGill U., Montreal, 1981; MD, Queen's U., Kingston, Can., 1985; MSc, U. Toronto, Can., 1992. Asst. prof. U. Man., Winnipeg, Can., 1993-99, assoc. prof., 1999-2000, U. Miss., Jackson, 2000—05, prof., 2005—; vis. assoc. biology Calif. Inst. Tech., 2008—. Vis. fellow Fondation Rothschild, Paris, 1998-99. Contbr. articles to profl. jours. Recipient Penfield McNaughton award Montreal Neurol. Inst., 1992; fellow Fund award Health Sci. Ctr., Winnipeg, 1998. Fellow ACS, Royal Coll. Surgeons Can. (Clin. Traineeship award 1999); mem. Am. Assn. Neurol. Surgeons, Can. Neurosurg. Soc. (provincial rep. 1998-99). Avocations: reading, skiing, tennis, opera. Home: 1605 Pegfair Estates Dr Pasadena CA 91103 Office: 630 S Raymond Ave Ste 330 Pasadena CA 91105 Office Phone: 626-793-8194. E-mail: ianrossmd@aol.com.

ROSS, IVAN ALFRED, biologist; b. Guyana, Mar. 31, 1953; MS, U. Md., 1986. Biologist US FDA, 1987—. Author: Medicinal Plants of the World Volumes 1, 2 and 3, 1998—2005. Avocations: farming, writing, boating. Office: 8301 Muirkirk Rd Laurel MD 20708 E-mail: rossivan@msn.com.

ROSS, JIM W., gynecologist, director; b. King City, Calif., Oct. 1, 1942; BS, Baylor U., 1965; MD, UCLA, PhD, 1972. Dir. Ctr. Female Continence & Urogynecology, 1976—. Clin. prof., dept. ob-gyn. UCLA, 1996—2008. Contbr. articles to sci. profl. publs. Mem.: SGS, ICS, IUGA, AUGS, AAGL. Achievements include development of advanced laparoscopy in female pelvic floor surgery. Avocations: photography, travel. Office: 335 Katherine Ave Salinas CA 93901 Business E-Mail: ctrreprodmed@sbcglobal.net.

ROSS, JOHN, JR., cardiologist, educator; b. NYC, Dec. 1, 1928; s. John and Janet (Moulder) R.; children: Sydnie, John, Duncan; m. Lola Romanucci, Aug. 26, 1972; children: Adan, Deborah Lee. AB, Dartmouth Coll., 1951; MD, Cornell U., 1955. Intern Johns Hopkins Hosp., 1955—56; resident Columbia-Presbyn. Med. Center, NYC, 1960—61, NY. Hosp.-Cornell U. Med. center, 1961—62; chief sect. cardiovascular diagnosis cardiology br. Nat. Heart Inst., Bethesda, Md., 1962—68; prof. medicine U. Calif., San Diego, 1968—2000, also dir. cardiovascular div., 1968—91, rsch. prof. medicine, 2000—, disting. prof. medicine, 2003—; prof. cardiovascular research Am. Heart Assn. Western States Affiliate, 1984—99. Mem. cardiology adv. com. Nat. Heart, Lung and Blood Inst., 1975-78, task force on arteriosclerosis, 1978-80, adv. council, 1980-84; bd. dirs. San Diego Heart Assn.; vis. prof. Brit. Heart Assn., 1990. Author: Mechanisms of Contraction of the Normal and Failing Heart, 1968, 76, Understanding the Heart and Its Diseases, 1976; mem. editorial bd. Circulation, 1967-75, 80-88, editor in chief 1988-93, Circulation Research, 1971-75, Am. Jour. Physiology, 1968-73, Annals of Internal Medicine, 1974-78, Am. Jour. Cardiology, 1974-79, 83-88, Jour. Clin. Investigation, 1992-97, Italian Heart Jour., 1998-99, Jour. Cardiac Failure, 2000-05, Circulation Jour. Japan, 2000—; cons. editor Circulation, 1993-03; contbr. chpts. to books, sci. articles to profl. jours. Served as surgeon USPHS, 1956—63. Decorated grande ufficiale Order of Merit of Republic of Italy, 1998; recipient Ing. Enzo Ferrari prize for Enzo Ferrari, Modena, Italy, 1989, James B. Herrick award Coun. Clin. Cardiology Am. Heart Assn., 1990, Academic Mentorship award Am. Heart Assn., 2004; Distinction award Weill Cornell Med. Coll. Alumni Assn., 2009. Master Am. Coll. Cardiology (v.p. trustee, pres. 1986-87, Disting. Scientist award 1990); fellow ACP; mem. Am. Soc. Clin. Investigation (councillor), Am. Physiol. Soc., Assn. Am. Physicians, Cardiac Muscle Soc., Assn. Univ. Cardiologists, Assn. West. Physicians (councillor), Japanese Circulation Soc. (hon.). Achievements include development of and application of transseptal left heart catherization for the diagnosis of heart disease; conceptualized "afterload mismatch" in the left ventricle of the heart and its application in the diagnosis and treatment of valvular heart disease and heart failure; demonstrated experimentally that reperfusion of a coronary artery after prolonged occlusion salvages heart muscle and partially restores heart function. Home: 8599 Prestwick Dr La Jolla CA 92037 Office: U Calif Dept Med M # 0613B San Diego CA 92093

ROSS, JUNE ROSA PITT, biologist, educator; b. Taree, NSW, Australia, May 2, 1931; came to U.S., 1957; d. Bernard and Adeline Phillips; m. Charles Alexander, June 27, 1959. BSc with honors, U. Sydney, New S. Wales, Australia, 1953, PhD, 1959, DSc, 1974. Rsch. assoc. Yale U., New Haven, 1959—60, U. Ill., Urbana, 1960—65, Western Wash. U., Bellingham, 1965—67, assoc. prof., 1967—70, prof. biology, 1970—2003, prof. emeritus, 2004—, chair dept. biology, 1989—90. Pres. Western Wash. U. Faculty Senate, Bellingham, 1984-85; conf. host Internat. Bryozoology Assn., 1986. Author (with others): A Textbook of Entomology, 1982, Geology of Coal, 1984; editor (assoc.): Palaios, 1985—89; contbr. 166 articles to profl. jours. Recipient J. Wolfensohn Award of Excellence Sydney U. Grad. Union of N.Am., 1995, P. and R. Olscamp Outstanding Rsch. award Western Wash. U., 1986; NSF grantee. Mem.: Internat. Bryozoology Assn. (pres. 1992—95), The Paleontol. Soc. (councillor 1984—86, treas. 1987—93), Australian Marine Scis. Assn., U.K. Marine Biol. Assn. (life). Avocations: hiking, classical music. Office: Western Wash U Dept Biology Bellingham WA 98225-9160 Office Phone: 360-650-3634. E-mail: ross@fire.biol.wwu.edu.

ROSS, LEONARD LESTER, retired academic administrator; b. NYC, Sept. 11, 1927; s. Aaron Theodore and Shirley (Smolen) R.; m. Marcella Gamel, June 23, 1951 (dec. Aug. 1995); children: Jane, Jill; m. Frances Robb, Nov. 12, 1998; 1 chld, Jennifer. AB, NYU, 1946, PhD, 1954. Asst. prof. U. Ala. Med. Coll., 1954-57; assoc. prof. Cornell U. Med. Coll., 1957-69, prof., 1969-73; vis. prof. Cambridge U., 1967-68; prof., chmn. dept. anatomy Med. Coll. Pa., Phila., 1973-89, exec. v.p., Annenberg dean, 1989-93, pres. and Annenberg dean, 1993-94, provost and Annenberg dean Phila., 1993-96; provost Allegheny U., Phila., 1996-98. Exec. v.p. Allegheny Health, Edn. and Rsch. Found. Assoc. editor: Anat. Record, 1976. Served with M.C., U.S. Army, 1946-47. Recipient Lindback award for teaching, 1976; NIH sr. research fellow, 1967-68 Mem. Am. Assn. Anatomists (exec. com. 1984-88), Soc. Neurosci., Soc. Cell Biology, N.Y. Soc. Electron Microscopists (pres. 1975-76), Assn. Anatomy Chairmen (pres. 1983-84), AAUP (nat. council 1974-77), Sigma Xi. Personal E-mail: rossll63@netscape.net.

ROSS, MALCOLM, minerals consultant; b. Washington, Aug. 22, 1929; s. Clarence Samuel and Helen Hall (Frederick) R.; m. Daphne Dee Virginia Riska, Sept. 1, 1956; children: Christopher A., Alexander MacC. BS in Zoology, Utah State U., 1951; MS in Chemistry, U. Md., 1959; PhD in Geology, Harvard U., 1962. Rsch. mineralogist U.S. Geol. Survey, Washington, 1954-5, 61-74, Reston, Va., 1974-95, scientist emeritus, 1996—; minerals and health cons., 1999—. Prin. investigator lunar sci. program NASA, 1969—74. Author: Asbestos and Other Fibrous Minerals, 1988; contbr. over 100 articles to profl. jours. First lt. US Army, 1952—54. Recipient Disting. Svc. award, U.S. Dept. Interior, 1986; grantee Fulbright Commn., Cyprus, 2000. Fellow Mineral. Soc. Am., Geol. Soc. Am., AAAS; mem. Am. Geophys. Union, Clay Minerals Soc., Can. Mineral Assn., Mineral Soc. Am. (bd. dirs. treas. 1976-80, v.p. 1990, pres. 1991, Pub. Svc. award, 1990). Republican. Congregationalist. Achievements include research in on asbestos and asbestos-related disease. Avocations: long distance bicycling, photography. Home: 1608 44th St NW Washington DC 20007-2025 Personal E-mail: mrdrr@earthlink.net.

ROSS, MICHAEL WALLIS, public health educator; b. Palmerston North, New Zealand, Nov. 17, 1951; arrived in U.S., 1993; s. Wallis Malcolm and Lois Verrell (Stewart) R. BA with honors, Massey U., New Zealand, 1974; BS in Sociology, SUNY, 1976; MA in Social-Clin. Psychology, Victoria U. Wellington, New Zealand, 1975; diploma in Tertiary Edn., U. New Eng., Australia, 1984; PhD, U. Melbourne, Australia, 1980; MPH, U. Adelaide, Australia, 1989; M in Health Pers. Edn., U. NSW, Australia, 1991; diploma in STDs, Prince of Songkla U., Thailand, 1992, diploma in Applied Criminology, 2003; MSt in Criminology, U. Cambridge, 2004; DrMed, U. Malmö, Sweden, 2006. Mem. Secular Franciscan Order. Postdoctoral fellow U. Helsinki, Finland, 1979; sr. demonstrator psychiatry Flinders U., Adelaide, 1979-85; dir. STD/HIV Epidemiology and Rsch. South Australian Health Commn., Adelaide, 1985-89; assoc. prof. Sch. Cmty. Medicine U. NSW, Sydney, 1989-93; prof. Sch. Pub. Health, U. Tex., Houston, 1993—. Bd. dirs. Kolbe House, Houston, 1994-2005; chmn. bd. Saving Lives Through Alternate Options, Houston, 2000-08. Author: The Married Homosexual Man: A Psychological Study, 1983, Psychovenereology: Personality and Lifestyle Factors in Sexually Transmitted Diseases in Homosexual Men, 1986; (with L.C. Channon-Little) Discussing Sexuality: A Guide for Health Practitioners, 1991; (with L.A. Lewis) A Select Body: The Gay Dance Party Subculture and the HIV/AIDS Pandemic, 1995; (with L. Nilsson Schönnesson) Coping With HIV Infection: Psychological and Existential Responses in Gay Men, 1999; (with L.C. Channon-Little and B.R.S. Rosser) Sexual Health Concerns: Interviewing and History Taking for Health Practitioners, 1999; editor: Homosexuality and Social Sex Roles, 1983, Homosexuality, Masculinity and Femininity, 1985, The Treatment of Homosexuals with Mental Health Disorders, 1988, Psychopathology and Psychotherapy in Homosexuality, HIV/AIDS and Sexuality, 1995; (with W.A.W. Walters) Transsexualism and Sex Reassignment, 1986; (with L. Bennett and D. Miller) Health Workers and AIDS: Rsch., Intervention and Current Issues in Burnout and Response, 1995; co-sci. editor: Surgeon-General's Call to Action on Sexual Health and Responsible Sexual Behavior, 2001; contbr. articles to profl. jour. Recipient U.S. Surgeon Gen.'s Exemplary Svc. medal, 2002, Kinsey award, 2003. Fellow APA, Brit. Psychol. Soc., Royal Soc. Health, Royal Soc. Arts, New Zealand Psychol. Soc., Soc. for the Sci. Study of Sexuality (pres. 2000-01, Disting. Sci. Achievement award 2005), Soc. Antiquaries Scotland., Royal Australian Coll. Physicians (hon.), Commander Order St. Lazaurs. Roman Catholic. Avocations: aerobatic flying, reading. Home: 401 Anita St Apt 34 Houston TX 77006-3434 Office: Sch Pub Health U Tex PO Box 20036 Houston TX 77225-0186 Office Phone: 713-500-9652. Business E-Mail: michael.w.ross@uth.tmc.edu.

ROSS, NICK (NICHOLAS ROSS), broadcaster, journalist; b. London, Aug. 7, 1947; s. John Caryl and Joy Dorothy (Richmond) Ross; m. Sarah Caplin, Mar. 1, 1985; children: Adam Michael, Sam Max, Jack Felix. BA in Psychol. with honors, Queen's U. Belfast, 1971, D (hon.), 2002. Conf. moderator blue chip cos.; presenter radio and TV BBC, London, 1971—. Vis. prof. U. Coll. London, 2002—. Prodr. TV series; prodr.: (radio shows); dir.(writer): (radio & TV shows). Bd. mem. UK Govt. Bds., 1984—2004; trustee UK Stem Cell Found.; chmn. Wales Cancer Bank Adv. Bd.; adv. bd. mem. UK Cancer Tissue Bank; ex bd. mem. Health Quality Svc.; ex mem. Com. Ethics Gene Therapy; gene therapy adv. com. Nuffield Com. Bioethics; with Health Nation Wider Working Group, NHS Review Team, Health Care Relations Action Group, Kings Fund Consensos Panel Breast Cancer Treatment. Named Radio Broadcaster of Yr., 1997. Fellow: Royal Soc. Medicine; mem.: RCP (mem. com. ethical issues & medicine). Office: c/o Sarah Caplin PO Box 999 London W2 4XT England Office Phone: 020 7243 1325. Office Fax: 44 (0)20 7792 9200. E-mail: nick@nickross.com.

ROSS, PATTI JAYNE, obstetrics and gynecology educator; b. Nov. 17, 1946; d. James J. and Mary N. Ross; m. Allan Robert Katz, May 23, 1976. BS, DePauw U., 1968; MD, Tulane U., 1972. Diplomate Am. Bd. Ob-Gyn. Asst. prof. U. Tex. Med. Sch., Houston, 1976—82, assoc. prof., 1982—98, prof., 1998—2004, dir. adolescent ob-gyn., 1976—, dir. student edn., dir. devel. dept. ob-gyn.; adv. bd. Teva Bayer, Meck Pharm. Cons. in field; spkr. in field; appeared on Lifetime TV network. Contbr. articles to profl. jours. Mem. Rape Coun.; vol. Children's Miracle Network/Hermann's Children's Hosp.; Olympic torch relay carrier, 1996; founder Women's Med. Rsch. Fund, U. Tex. Med. Sch., Houston; bd. dirs. Am. Diabetes Assn., 1982—, Susan Komen Found. Recipient Patti Jayne Ross Professorship, 2004. Mem.: Profl. Women Execs., Orgn. Women in Sci., Am. Women's Med. Assn., AAAS, Soc. Adolescent Medicine, Assn. Profs. Ob-Gyn., Houston Ob-Gyn. Soc., Harris County Med. Soc., Tex. Med. Assn., River Oak Breakfast Club, Sigma Xi. Roman Catholic. Office: 6431 Fannin St 3278 Houston TX 77030-1501 Office Phone: 713-500-6431. Business E-Mail: patti.j.ross@uth.tmc.edu.

ROSS, R. DALE, retired medical products executive; b. 1942; Sales mgmt. positions Am. McGaw Laboratories; founder, pres., CEO HMSS Inc., 1982—90; chmn., CEO Am. Oncology Resources, Houston, 1992—99, US Oncology, Houston, 1999—2008, exec. chmn., 2008—09. Served USAF. *

ROSS, RANDAL G., psychiatrist, educator; b. North Hollywood, Calif., Aug. 9, 1961; BS, U. Calif., Santa Barbara, 1983; MD, Yale U., 1987. Prof. U. Colo., Denver, 1993—. Office: PO Box F546 13001 E 17th Pl Aurora CO 80045 Business E-Mail: randy.ross@ucdenver.edu.

ROSS, RICHARD STARR, retired medical school dean, cardiologist, educator; b. Richmond, Ind., Jan. 18, 1924; s. Louis Francisco and Margaret (Starr) Ross; m. Elizabeth McCracken, July 1, 1950; children: Deborah Starr, Margaret Casad, Richard McCracken. Student, Harvard U., 1942—44, MD cum laude, 1947; ScD (hon.), Ind. U., 1981; LHD (hon.), Johns Hopkins U., 1994. Diplomate Nat. Bd. Med. Examiners, Am. Bd. Internal Medicine (subsplty. bd. cardiovasc. disease); cert. war cert. 1943. Successively intern, asst. resident, chief resident Osler Med. Service, Johns Hopkins Hosp., 1947—54; research fellow physiology Harvard Med. Sch., 1952—53; instr. medicine Johns Hopkins Med. Sch., 1954—56, asst. prof. medicine, 1956—59, assoc. prof., 1959—65, assoc. prof. radiology, 1960—71, prof. medicine, 1965—, Clayton prof. cardiovascular disease, 1969—75; dir. Wellcome Research Lab., Johns Hopkins; physician Johns Hopkins Hosp.; dir. cardiovascular div. dept. medicine, adult cardiac clinic Johns Hopkins Sch. Medicine and Hosp., dir. myocardial infarction research unit, 1967—75; dean med. faculty, v.p. medicine Johns Hopkins U., 1975—90, dean emeritus, 1990—. Sir Thomas Lewis lectr. Brit. Cardiac Soc., 1969; John Kent Lewis lectr. Stanford U., 1972; bd. dirs. emeritus Johns Hopkins Hosp., Francis Scott Key Med. Ctr.; mem. cardiovasc. study sect. Nat. Heart and Lung Inst., 1965—69, chmn. cardiovasc. study sect., 1966—69, mem. tng. grant com., 1971—73, chmn. heart panel, 1972—73, adv. coun., 1974—78; mem. Inst. Medicine, 1976—; chmn. vis. com. Harvard Med. and Dental Sch., 1979—86; bd. overseers Harvard U., 1980—86. Editor: Modern Concepts Cardiovascular Disease, 1961—65, The Principles and Practice of Medicine, 17th-22nd edits., 1968—88; mem. editl. bd.: Circulation, 1968—74, mem. editl. com.: Jour. Clin. Investigation, 1969—73; contbr. numerous articles to profl. jours. Capt. M.C. US Army, 1949—51. Recipient Flexner award, Assn. Am. Med. Coll., 1994, Pres.'s medal, Johns Hopkins U., 2005; named hon. fellow, UMDS, Guy's and St. Thomas's Hosps., London, 1996. Master: ACP; fellow: Am. Coll. Cardiology (Convocation medal 1990); mem.: Heart Assn. Md. (pres. 1967—68), Am. Heart Assn. (chmn. sci. sessions program com. 1965—67, chmn. publs. com. 1970—73, pres. 1973—74, dir. 1974—77, Gold Heart award 1976, Connor lectr. 1979, James B. Herrick award 1982), Assn. Univ. Cardiologists (councillor 1972—75), Am. Clin. and Climatol. Assn. (pres. 1978—79, councillor 1979—83, Metzger lecture 1986), Am. Soc. Clin. Investigation (councillor 1967—69), Sociedad Peruana de Cardiologie (corr.), Brit. Cardiac Soc. (corr.), Cardiac Soc. Australia and New Zealand (corr.), Assn. Am. Physicians, Am. Physiol. Soc., Am. Fedn. Clin. Rsch., Boylston Med. Soc., Elkridge Club, Interurban Club (pres. 1978), Peripatetic Club, Alpha Omega Alpha, Sigma Xi. Home: 830 W 40th St # 851 Baltimore MD 21211-2181 Office: Johns Hopkins U 1830 E Monument St Baltimore MD 21287 E-mail: rross@jhmi.edu.

ROSS, ROBERT D., cardiologist; b. Detroit, Nov. 6, 1955; BS, U. Mich., 1977, MD, 1981. Cardiologist Children's Hosp. Mich., 1987—, fellowship dir., 1991—2011, dir., pulmonary hypertension program, 2009—11. Pres. Soc. Pediatric Cardiology Tng. Program Dirs., 2011—. Mission leader, heart care and tchg., Santo Domingo, Dominican Republic; USTA capt. 4.0 Sr. Tennis Team. Recipient Tchg. award, Wayne State U. Sch. Medicine. Fellow: Am. Acad. Pediat., Am. Coll. Cardiology. Office: CHM Cardiology 3901 Beaubien Blvd Detroit MI 48201 Office Fax: 313-993-0894. Business E-Mail: rross@dmc.org.

ROSS, STEVEN ELLIOT, surgeon; b. Wilmington, Del., Sept. 12, 1951; s. Morris H. and Anita Selma (Luterman) R.; m. Carolyn Gross, June 13, 1981; children: Leah Jane, Asher Joshua, Tovah Jennifer. BA, U. Del., 1972; MD, Jefferson Med. Coll., Phila., Pa., 1976. Diplomate Am. Bd. Surgery, Am. Bd. Surg. Critical Care. Resident, general surgery York Hosp., York, Pa., 1976-81; fellow trauma and surgical critical care medicine Univ. Kansas Med. Ctr., Kansas City, 1981-82; attending surgeon Cooper Hosp., Camden, NJ, 1984—, head, divsn. trauma and emergency surgical services, vice chief, dept. surgery, fellowship dir. surg. critical care; prof. surgery Univ. Medicine Dentistry NJ/Robert Wood Johnson Med. Sch., Camden, NJ, 1984—. Contbr. several sci. articles to profl. jours. Chmn. NJ State Trauma Ctr. Coun., 1991-93, 97. Fellow Am. Coll. Surgeons (chmn. com. trauma NJ chpt. 1991-96, mem.), Am. Assn. Surgery Trauma, Soc. Critical Care Medicine, Western Trauma Assocs. (bd. dirs. 1993-95), Alpha Omega Alpha (faculty mem.), Am. Coll. Critical Care Medicine. Jewish. Office: Cooper Hosp Dept Surgery 3 Cooper Plz Rm 411 Camden NJ 08103 Address: 1 Cooper Plz Camden NJ 08103 Office Phone: 856-342-3041, 856-342-2657. Office Fax: 856-342-2817, 856-968-8306.

ROSSEAU, GAIL L., neurosurgeon, educator; b. Nov. 30, 1956; m. Rick Rosseau; children: Natalie, Brendan. BS, U. Iowa, 1978; MD, George Washington Med. Sch., Washington, DC, 1981. Cert. Neurosurgery. Intern, gen. surgery George Washington U., Washington, 1985—86, resident, neurol. surgery, 1986—91; cranial base surgery fellow H.I.A. du Val-de-Grace Hosp., Paris, 1990; cranial base surgery and microvascular surgery fellow U. Pitts. Presbyn.-U. Hosp., Pa., 1991—92; staff mem., neurol. surgery Gottlieb Meml. Hosp., 1992—99, Columbus Hosp., 1992—2001, Ingalls Hosp., 1998—2000, Elmhurst Meml. Hosp., 1999, Neurologic & Orthopedic Inst. Chgo., 2001—; mem. Chgo. Inst. Neurosurgery and Neuroresearch (CINN), Neurologic & Orthopedic Inst. Chgo., 1992—, dir., cranial base surgery, 1992—; staff mem., neurol. surgery Rush Med. Coll., Rush U. Med. Ctr., Ill., 1998, asst. prof., neurol. surgery Ill., 1998—. Lectr. in field. Contbr. articles to profl. jours., chapters to books. Recipient Harry B. Zehner, Jr. Meml Traveling Fellowship award, ACS, Chgo. Women of Yr. Mentor award; Health Policy fellowship, Am. Coll. Surgeons. Mem.: Congress Neurol., Am. Assn. Neurol. Surgeons. Achievements include pioneering the use of endoscopic techniques in treating pituitary tumors; leadership in international neurosurgicals organisation such as CNS, AANS, FIENS and more. Office: Chgo Inst Neurosurgery and Neuroreseach Neurologic & Orthopedic Inst Chgo 4501 N Winchester Ave 2nd Fl Chicago IL 60640 Address: Chgo Inst Neurosurgery and Neuroreseach Med Group 1200 S York Rd Elmhurst IL 60126 Office Phone: 773-250-0400, 773-250-0500.

ROSSETTO, ANNA, surgeon; b. Treviso, Italy, Jan. 17, 1977; Degree in Medicine, U. Udine, Italy, 2003, degree in Gen. Surgery, 2009. Vis. clinician Gen. Surgery and Transplant Unit U. Hosp. Udine, 2009—. Grant, AITF, U. Udine. Mem.: ESOT-ELITA. Avocations: cello, Judo, skiing. Home: Via Abbazia 24 Udine 33100 Italy Business E-Mail: rossettoannaar@libero.it.

ROSSI, A. CRISTINA, gynecologist, researcher, obstetrician, consultant; b. Bari, Italy, Sept. 6, 1974; d. Pasquale Rossi and Vannia Pascali. Degree in Medicine and Surgery, U. Bari, 1998. Resident ob-gyn. U. Bari, 2003, rsch. fellow, 2006—; cons. ob-gyn. Clinic Ob-Gyn., San Paolo Hosp., Bari, 2008—. Clin. rsch. fellow St. Joseph Hosp., Tampa, Fla., 2004. Contbr. articles to profl. jours. Recipient Jerome J. Hoffman Postgrad. 1st prize, 1999; Ob-Gyn. Rsch. grant, U. Foggia, Italy, 2006. Mem.: Internat. Soc. Ultrasound Ob-Gyn. London. Roman Catholic. Achievements include research in new sonographic criteria to diagnose twin transfusion syndrome in the first trimester; new staging system to assess severity of twin transfusion syndrome. Avocations: puzzles, chess, swimming. Office: IV Clinic Ob/Gyn Univ Bari Pzza Giulio Cesare Bari 70100 Italy Home: Via Marcello Celentano 42 70121 Bari BA Italy Home Fax: 011 080 5248039. Personal E-mail: acristinarossi@yahoo.it.

ROSSI, ALFREDO, medical educator; b. Avellino, Aug. 27, 1957; Laurea Medicina e Chirurgia, La Sapienza U., Rome, 1989, degree in Dermatology & Venereology, 1992. Assoc. prof. Dept. Dermatology, 1998—. Office: Viale del Policlinico 155 Rome 00185 Italy Business E-Mail: alfredo.rossi@uniroma1.it.

ROSSI, ENNIO C., internist, educator; b. Madison, Wis., Apr. 3, 1931; s. Joseph and Esther (D'Amelio) R.; m. Anna Maria Bianchi, June 22, 1957; children: Roberta, Marco. BA, U. Wis., 1951, MD, 1954. Diplomate Am. Bd. Internal Medicine. Intern Ohio State U. Hosps., 1954-55; resident medicine U. Wis. Hosps., 1958-61, fellow, 1961-63; instr. medicine Marquette U., Milw., 1963-64, asst. prof. medicine, 1964-66; assoc. prof. medicine Northwestern U., Chgo., 1966-72, prof. medicine, 1972-96, prof. emeritus, 1996—, chief hematology, 1967-84, chief transfusion medicine, 1984-96. V.p. med. affairs Life Source Blood Ctr., Glenview, Ill., 1988-93; vis. scientist Mario Negri Inst., Milan, 1977. Co-editor: Haemostasis and the Kidney, 1989; sr. editor: Principles of Transfusion Medicine, 1991, 2d edit., 1996, 3rd edit., 2002, 4th edit., 2009 Capt. U.S. Army, 1956-58. Fulbright scholar, U.S. Dept. State, U. Rome, 1955; Nat. Heart, Lung Blood Inst. Transfusion Medicine Acad. awardee, 1983; WHO travelling fellow, 1985. Fellow ACP; mem. Am. Soc. Hematology, Am. Soc. Pharmacology and Exptl. Therapeutics, Am. Assn. Blood Banks (chmn. acad. transfusion medicine com. 1988-93), Internat. Soc. Blood Transfusion. Home: 812 Oak St Apt 302 Winnetka IL 60093-2560

ROSSINI, MAURIZIO, medical researcher; b. Mantova, Italy, July 8, 1960; MD, U. Verona, PhD, 1985. Rschr. U. Verona, 2006. Office: Reumatologia Policlinico Borgo Roma Verona 37134 Italy E-mail: maurizio.rossini@libero.it.

ROSS-LEE, BARBARA, academic administrator; BS Biology and Chemistry, Wayne State U., M Tchr. Spl. Populations; grad., Mich. State U., 1973; DSc (hon.), N.Y. Coll. Osteo. Medicine; degree (hon.), Wilmington Coll., 2001. Legis. asst. Senator Bill Bradley; chmn. dept. family medicine, assoc. dean health policy Mich. State U. Coll. Medicine; dean Ohio U. Coll. Osteo. Medicine, 1993—2001; v.p. health sciences and med. affairs NY Inst. Tech., 2001—, dean sch. allied health and life sciences, 2001—02, dean NY Coll. Osteo. Medicine, 2002—06. Lectr. in field; dir. Osteo. Heritage Health Policy Fellowship Program; exec. dir. Inst. Nat. Health Policy and Rsch., NOMA (the osteo. affiliate NMA); mem. bd. dirs. Assn. Acad. Health Ctrs., Nat. Fund Med. Edn., Nat. Health Svs. Corps' Assn. Clinicians Underserved ; trustee Found. Appalachian Ohio; participant confs. Contbr. more than 30 scholarly articles med. and health-care issues. Recipient Magnificent 7 award, Bus. and Profl. Women/USA, 1993, Women's Health award, Blackboard African-Am. Nat. Bestsellers, Disting. Pub. Svc. award, Okla. State U. Coll. Osteo. Medicine, Walter F. Patenge medal pub. svc., Mich. State U. Coll. Osteo. Medicine, 2001; named to Ohio Women's Hall of Fame, 1998. Fellow: Am. Osteo. Bd. Family Physicians; mem.: NIH (adv. com. rsch. on women's health), Future Primary Care (Inst. Medicine's com.), U.S. Dept. Health and Human Svs. (nat. adv. com. rural health), Appalachian Health Policy (Appalachian regional commn.'s adv. coun.), AACOM Bd. Govs. (chair-elect exec. coun.), AOA Bur. Profl. Edn., Trilateral Internat. Med. Workforce Group. Achievements include first to be an osteopathic physician to participate in the prestigious Robert Wood Johnson Health Policy Fellowship. Office: NY Inst Tech Ctr Global Health Serota Bldg Rm 129 Old Westbury NY 11568 E-mail: brosslee@nyit.edu. *

ROSSMANN, JACK EUGENE, psychologist, educator; b. Walnut, Iowa, Dec. 4, 1936; s. Wilbert C. Rossmann and Claire L. (Mickel) Walter; m. Marilyn Martin, June 14, 1958; children: Ann, Charles, Sarah. BS, Iowa State U., 1958, MS, 1960; PhD, U. Minn., 1963; MA (hon.), Macalester Coll., St. Paul, 2007. Asst. prof. Macalester Coll., St. Paul, 1964-68, assoc. prof., 1968-73, prof., 1973—2007, prof. emeritus, 2007—, v.p. acad. affairs, 1978-86, chair dept. psychology, 1990-2000. Cons.-evaluator North Ctrl. Assn., 1975—2008; cons. Pers. Decisions Internat., Mpls., 1989—2000, Bush Found., 1993—2006; sr. advisor Spencer Found., 2004—09. Author: (with others) Open Admissions at CUNY, 1975; contbr. articles to profl. jours. Bd. dirs. Twin City Inst. for Talented Youth, St. Paul, 1978-91; trustee United Theol. Sem., New Brighton, Minn., 1984-96; pres. Minn. Intercollegiate Athletic Conf., 2003-06. 2d lt. US Army, 1959. Recipient Thomas Jefferson award, Macalester Coll., 1990, Outstanding Svc. award, Minn. Intercollegiate Athletic Conf., 2007; Adminstrv. fellow, Am. Coun. on Edn., 1977—78. Mem.: AAUP (pres. Minn. conf. 1993—95, chair nat. com. accrediation 2008—, Robert Sloan award, Minn. Conf. 2003), APA, Minn. Psychol. Assn. (treas. 2001, pres. 2003), Assn. Instl. Rsch., Assn. Psychol. Sci., Phi Kappa Phi, Phi Beta Kappa (hon.). Home: 99 Cambridge St Saint Paul MN 55105-1947 Office: Macalester Coll 1600 Grand Ave Saint Paul MN 55105-1801 Home Phone: 651-690-4370; Office Phone: 651-696-6110. Business E-Mail: rossmann@macalester.edu.

ROST, THOMAS LOWELL, retired botany educator; b. St. Paul, Dec. 28, 1941; m. Ann Marie Ruhland, Aug. 31, 1963. BS, St. John's U., Collegeville, Minn., 1963; MA, Minn. State U., 1965; PhD, Iowa State U., 1971. Postdoctoral fellow Brookhaven Nat. Lab., Upton, NY, 1970-72; asst. to full prof. dept. botany U. Calif., Davis, 1972-82, faculty asst. to chancellor, 1982-83, prof., chmn. plant biology sect., 1994-96, assoc. dean divsn. biol. sci., 1996—2003, exec. assoc. dean, 2003—05, prof. emeritus, 2006—. Cons. faculty of agronomy U. Uruguay, 1979, 89, 2005; vis. fellow Rsch. Soc. Biol. Sci., Canberra, Australia, 1979-80; vis. prof. U. Wroclaw, Poland, 1987, U. Exeter, Eng., 1993, Copenhagen U., 2003, Aristotle U., Thessalaniki, Greece, 2005; spl. asst. to vice provost Internat. Programs, 2007; interim dir. FSNEP, 2008; US AID cons. Kabul U., Afghanistan, 2008-10, curr. cons., Vietnam, 2010. Co-author: Botany: A Brief Introduction to Plant Biology, 1979, Botany: An Introduction on Plant Biology, 1982; co-editor: Mechanisms and Control of Cell Division, 1977, Plant Biology, 1998, 2d edit., 2005; contbr. articles to profl. jours. Internat. pres. Gamma Sigma Delta, 2004—06. Served to capt. US Army, 1965—67. Fellow Japan Soc. Promotion of Sci.; mem. Bot. Soc. Am. (Edwin E. Bessey award 2007, Merit award, 2008, Soc. Exptl. Biology, Am. Inst. Biol. Sci. Democrat. Roman Catholic. Avocation: community theatre. Office: U Calif Sect Plant Biology Davis CA 95616-8537 Office Phone: 530-752-0628.

ROSTAD, HANS, retired surgeon; s. Jens and Signe Rostad; m. Bjoerg Othilie Moxnes, Feb. 18, 1956; children: Grethe Liv, Britt Sigrun. MD (hon.), U. Oslo, 1955, PhD, 1974. Gen. and cardiovasc. surgeon U. Hosps., Oslo, 1960—2000, cons. surgeon. Rschr. Cancer Registry, Norway, 2000—. Contbr. scientific papers. Mem.: Norwegian and Nordic Surg. Socs. Office Phone: 47 22 45 1329. Business E-Mail: hans.rostad@kreftregisteret.no.

ROSTAIN, ANTHONY L., psychiatrist, educator; BA in Philosophy, Yale U., 1973, BA in Psychology, 1973; MS in Sci. Edn., So. Conn. State U., 1976; MD, NYU, 1980; attended Robert Wood Johnson Found. Clin. Scholars Program, U. Pa., 1983—85, MA in Sociology, 1985. Diplomate Am. Bd. Psychiatry adn Neurology-child and adolescent psychiatry, Am. Bd. Pediatrics. Resident in adult psychiatry Hosp. Univ. Pa, 1985—87; fellow in child psychiatry Phila. Child Guidance Ctr., 1987—88; prof. psychiatry U. Pa.; resident in pediatrics Children's Hosp. of Phila., 1980—83, prof. psychiatry, physician. Author: Assessing Parent's Willingness to Pursue Treatment for Children with Attention-Deficit Hyperactivity Disorder, 1993, Parent Acceptability and Feasibility of ADHD Interventions: Assessment, correlates, and predictive validity, 1996, Divorce: Pediatric Management, 1997, Sleep Disorders in Childhood, 1997, Relationship of Perceived Compentencies, Perceived Social Support, and Gender to Substance Use in Young Adolescents, 1997, Assessing and Managing Adolescents with School Problems, 1997, Family Function and Dysfunction, 1999, Medical expenditures among children diagnosed with psychiatric disorders in a Medicaid population, 2003, Growing Up with ADHD, 2003. Office: Children's Hospital of Philadelphia 34th St and Civic Center Blvd Philadelphia PA 19104-4399 Office Phone: 215-590-1000.

ROSTAS, LASZLO, cardiologist, hypertonologist; b. Görcsöny, Hungary, Sept. 8, 1947; s. Imre and Maria (Bodai) R.; m. Erzsebet Galambos; 1 child, Ildiko MD, Med. U. Pecs, 1972. Cert. in internal medicine and cardiology. Prof.'s asst. Inst. Patho physiology Med. U. Pecs, Hungary, 1969—72; asst. physician County Hosp., Szekszard, Hungary, 1972—83, asst. prof., 1983—90, head physician, 1990—91; head cardiology dept. Chest Hosp., Mosdos, Hungary, 1991—2006, Kaposi Mór Tchg. Hosp., Mosdos, 2007—; chief cardiology Somogy County, Hungary, 1992—. Co-author: Cardiac Arrhythmias, 1998, Clinical Cardiac Electrophysiology and Arrhythmology, 1999, 2009; contbr. numerous articles to profl. jours Chmn. Anti Smoking Assn., Somogy County, 1992— Recipient Diploma of Merit, Min. Health, Budapest, 1982, Batthyány-Strattmann Meml. award, Govt. of Hungarian Republic, Budapest, 2010. Mem. Hungarian Soc. Cardiology (bd. dirs., bd. dirs. arrhythmia and pacemaker working group) Avocations: nature, football, hiking. Office: Kaposi Mór Teaching Hosp Cardiac Dept Petofi Sr 4 7257 Mosdos Hungary Office Phone: 36-82-579 528. Business E-Mail: aritmros@hu.inter.net.

ROSTOFF, PAWEL ANDRZEJ, cardiologist, educator; b. Busko-Zdroj, Mar. 5, 1978; MD with honor, Jagiellonian U. Med. Coll., Cracow, Poland, 2002, PhD with Summa cum laude, 2011. Asst. Jagiellonian U. Med. Coll., Inst. Cardiology, Dept. Coronary Disease, John Paul II Hosp., Cracow, 2004—09, sr. asst., 2010—. Intern U. Hosp., Cracow, 2002—03; resident John Paul II Hosp., 2004—09; internal medicine specialist Polish Ministry Health, 2010—10. Contbr. articles to profl. jours. Fellowship, Polish Ministry Health, Warsaw, 2002, St. Estreicher fellowship, Jagiellonian U., 2002, Tng. fellowship, Polish Cardiac Soc., Warsaw, 2007. Mem.: Polish Cardiac Soc., European Soc. Cardiology, Polish Cardiac Soc. Avocations: travel, writing. Office: Pradnicka St 80 Cracow Malopolska 31-202 Poland Office Fax: 48 12 633 67 44. Business E-Mail: prostoff@vp.pl.

ROSTOKER, GUY PASCAL FRANCIS, nephrologist; b. Neuilly, France, June 11, 1956; s. Wolf Lucien Rostoker and Jeanne-Marie Balestrieri; m. Catherine Elisabeth Lerault; children: Pauline, Thomas. MD, St. Louis-Lariboisière, Paris, 1986; degree in biochemistry, U. Paris VII, 1986; PhD in Immunology, Paris VII Inst Jacques Monod, 1992; M in Immunology, U. Paris XII, Créteil, France, 1987. Intern, hosp. specialist Internat de Rouen (France), 1982-83; intern Internat. de Paris (Assistance Publique), 1983-87; chief resident Henri Mondor Hosp., Créteil, 1987-91, assoc. prof. nephrology, 1991-96; med. dir. divsn. nephrology Pvt. Hosp. Claude Galien, Quincy Sous Senart, France, 1997—. Mem. Am. Soc. Nephrology, French Soc. Nephrology, IgA Nephrophaty Club, Soc. for Mucosal Immunology, European Soc. for Clin. Investigation, Internat. Soc. Nephrology. Office: Svc de Nephrologie Hosp Prive Claude Galien 91480 Quincy Sous Senart France Office Phone: 0169399200. Office Fax: 0165399184. Business E-Mail: rostotom@orange.fr.

ROTA, EUGENIA, neurologist; d. Franco Eugenio Rota and Olga Anselmino. Medicine and Surgery, U. Turin, Italy, 1997. Diplomate Ordine Medici di Torino, 1997. Rsch. fellow Neuroimmunology Lab., Turin, Italy, 1997—98; specialization in neurology U. Turin, Italy, 1998—2003; rsch. fellow Headache and Facial Pain Unit, Pathophysiology Dept., Turin, 2003—05; asst. S. Croce Hosp., Neurology Dept., Mondovì, Italy, 2006—. Contract prof. U. Turin, 2004. Contbr. articles to profl. jours. Mem.: Italian Neurology Soc. Home: Strada Gariglio 14 CN Bra 12042 Italy Office: Alba Hosp Neurology Dept via Belli 26 Alba 12051 Italy Personal E-mail: eugenia.rota.mol@gmail.com.

ROTENBERG, VADIM SEMIONOVICH, psychiatrist, educator; b. Kirov, Russia, Aug. 5, 1941; arrived in Israel, 1990; s. Semion I. and Anna B. (Rogover) R.; m. Nataly (Samarovich) Rotenberg, Apr. 5, 1995; children: Simona, Anna. MD, 1st Moscow Med. Inst., 1964, PhD, 1970, DSc, 1979. Lic. physician. Unior doctor City Hosp., Moscow, 1964-66; unior scientist 1st Moscow Med. Inst., 1969-78, sr. scientist, 1978-88, head lab., 1988-90, Abarbanel Mental Health Ctr., Bat-Yam, Israel, 1992—2008. Sr. lectr. Tel-Aviv U., 1995—2008; vis. prof. Wuppertal U., 1989-90, Bar-Ilan U., 1993-94, U. Toronto, 1998, U. Osnabruck, 2004; head psychology project Zionistic Forum, 1996-2002; symposium chair World Assn. Dynamic Psychiatry, 1993, 97, 99, 2001, European Congress Sleep Rsch., 1990, European Congress Psychology, 1993, 95, World Congress Sleep, 1995, World Congress Psychosomatic Medicine, 1997. Author: The Adaptive Function of Sleep, 1982 (Best Ann. Sci. Publ. 1st Med. Inst., 1984); author: (with V.V. Arshavsky) Search Activity and Adaptation, 1984 (Best Ann. Sci. Publ. 1st Med. Inst., 1985); author: (with S.M. Bondarenko) Brain, Education, Health, 1989, Poems of 60th, 1996, Self Image and Behavior, 2000, Dreams, Hypnosis and Mental Activity, 2001; contbr. articles to profl. jours. Recipient Wolfson grant Tel-Aviv U., 1992. Mem. European Soc. Sleep Rsch., N.Y. Acad. Sci. Achievements include development of the search activity concept which integrates behavior, body resistance, REM sleep functions, brain monamines activity and brain laterality. Home: Levi Eshkol 22 B/6 Raanana 43703 Israel E-mail: vadir@post.tau.ac.il.

ROTH, ANDRÉ CH. D., ophthalmologist, consultant; m. Christiane Roth, July 11, 1959. MD, Med. Sch., Strasbourg, France, 1952—66. MD cert. Med. Sch. Strasbourg, 1966. Head ophthalmic depart. Country Hosp., Belfort, France, 1966—71; asst. prof. to prof. Med. Sch., Besançon, France, 1971—80, prof., head ophthalmic depart. Geneva, 1981—98, prof. emeritus, 1998—. Cons., strabismology ophthalmic depart. Hôpital de la Tour, Meyrin, Switzerland, 1999—. Author: (book) Eye Muscle Surgery. Pres. French Strabismological Assn., Paris, 2002—. Recipient Verriest Medal, Internat. Colour Vision Soc., 2003. Mem.: Med. Fedn. Switzerland (licentiate), German Ophthal. Soc. (licentiate), French Ophthal. Soc. (licentiate), Swiss Ophthal. Soc. (licentiate). Achievements include development of Color Vision Meter Interzeag 712. Office: Hôpital de la Tour Avenue Maillard 3 Geneva Meyrin 1217 Switzerland Home: Chemin de Grand Donzel 25 1234 Geneva Switzerland Office Fax: +41 22 719 67 01. Personal E-mail: andre_roth@bluewin.ch. E-mail: secretariat.ophtalmologie@latour.ch.

ROTH, BRADLEY JOHN, physicist; b. Clinton, Iowa, Aug. 15, 1960; s. Ronald Carl and Gayle Maxine (Granberg) R.; m. Shirley Sy Oyog, May 11, 1985; children: Stephanie Ann, Katherine Jane. BS in Physics, U. Kans., 1982; MS, Vanderbilt U., 1985, PhD, 1987. Rsch. asst. dept. physics Vanderbilt U., Nashville, 1982-87, rsch. assoc., 1987-88; staff fellow MES/BEIP/NCRR, NIH, Bethesda, Md., 1988-95; Robert T. Lagemann asst. prof. living state physics Vanderbilt U., 1995—98; assoc. prof. Oakland U., Dept. Physics, 1998—2008, prof., 2008—. NIH reviewer grant proposals. Contbr. numerous articles to profl. jours.; co-author Intermediate Physics for Medicine and Biology, 4th edit. NSF grad. fellow, 1982-85; Vanderbilt U. fellow, 1985-86; Am. Heart Assn.-Tenn. affiliate rsch. fellow, 1987-88; Summerfield scholar. Mem. Am. Phys. Soc. (fellow), Sigma Xi. Achievements include measurement of magnetic field of a single nerve axon; research in biomagnetism, magnetic stimulation, cardiac electrophysiology. Office Phone: 248-370-4871. Business E-Mail: roth@oakland.edu.

ROTH, JEFFREY DAVID, psychiatrist; MD, Yale U., New Haven, 1978. Diplomate Am. Bd. Psychiatry and Neurology-psychiatry, 1985, Am. Bd. Psychiatry and Neurology-addiction psychiatry, 1998. Intern The Univ. Chgo. Med. Ctr., 1979, resident psychiatry, 1979—82, hosp. affiliations includes. Fellow: Am. Soc. of Addictive Medicine. Office: The University of Chicago Medical Center 5841 S Maryland Ave Chicago IL 60637 Office Phone: 773-702-1000.

ROTH, JESSE, geriatrician; Grad., Columbia U., NYC; MD, Albert Einstein Coll. Medicine, 1959; D (hon.), U. Uppsala, Sweden, Yeshiva U., NYC, U. Rome. Intern, resident internal medicine Barnes Jewish Hosp./Washington U., St. Louis; fellowship Bronx VA Med. Ctr., NYC; various positions of increasing responsibility from clin. assoc., sr. investigator, chief diabetes sect., chief diabetes br. and sci. dir. Nat. Inst. Diabetes, Digestive & Kidney Diseases, NIH; asst. surgeon gen. USPHS, 1985—91; Raymond & Anna Lublin prof. medicine, dir. divsn. geriatric medicine & gerontology Johns Hopkins U. Sch. Medicine, Balt., dir. Johns Hopkins Ctr. Aging; pres., CEO Picower Inst. Med. Resh., Manhasset, NY; prof. medicine Albert Einstein Coll. Medicine; geriatrician-in-chief North Shore-LI Jewish Health Sys., rschr. Feinstein Inst. Med. Rsch. Sci. reviewer, mem. bd. governors Weizmann Inst. Sci., Rehovot, Israel. Contbr. articles to profl. jours. Recipient Lita Annenberg Hazen award, Nat. Inst. Diabetes, Digestive & Kidney Diseases, 1979, Disting. Svc. Medal, USPHS, A.C. Morrison award in natural scis., NY Acad. Scis., Nat. Med. Rsch. award, Nat. Health Coun., Gairdner Found. Ann. award for sci. excellence. Fellow: AAAS, ACP, Am. Acad. Arts & Scis.; mem.: Am. Diabetes Assn. (Banting Medal 1982, Albert Renold award 1993), Am. Soc. Clin. Investigation (past pres.), European Assn. Study of Diabetes (hon.), Endocrine Soc. (Koch award 1985, Robert H. Williams Disting. Leadership award 2001). Mailing: Feinstein Inst Med Rsch 350 Community Dr Manhasset NY 11030 Office: Albert Einstein Coll Medicine Yeshiva U 149 37 Powells Cove Blvd Whitestone NY 11357 Office Fax: 718-767-8952, 718-767-2215. E-mail: jesseroth md@hotmail.com, Jroth2@nshs.edu. *

ROTH, LOREN H., psychiatrist; b. May 9, 1939; m. Ellen A. Roth; children: Jonathan, Alexandra, Elizabeth. BA in Philosophy, Cornell U., 1961; MD cum laude, Harvard U., 1966, MPH, 1972; postgrad., Am. U., 1972-73. Diplomate Am. Bd. Psychiatry and Neurology; lic. physician, Conn., Md., Mass., Pa. Med. intern Univ. Hosps., Western Res. U., Cleve., 1966-67, resident psychiatry Yale U., New Haven, 1969-70, Mass. Gen. Hosp., Boston, 1970-72; staff psychiatrist Ctr. for Studies Crime and Delinquency, NIMH, Rockville, Md., 1972-74; co-dir., dir. law and psychiatry program Western Psychiat. Inst. and Clinic/U. Pitts., 1974—, chief adult clin. svcs., 1983-87, 88-89, chief clin. svcs., 1989-95, co-dir., dir. law and psychiatry program, 1974-94; vice-chmn. dept. psychiatry U. Pitts., 1988-97, asst. prof., 1974-78, assoc. prof., 1978-82, prof., 1982—; v.p. for managed care U. Pitts. Med. Ctr., 1993-97; assoc. vice chancellor for edn., health scis. U. Pitts Sch Medicine, 1995-97, assoc. sr. vice chancellor Health Scis., 1997—; sr. v.p., quality care U. Pitts. Med. Ctr. Health Sys., 2003—07, chief med. officer, 1997—2007, asst. special projects, office pres., 2007—; sr. advisor UPMC Health Plan Quality, Pitts., 2009—. Med. staff Presbyn.-Univ. Hosp., Pitts., 1983—; gen. med. officer Fed. Penitentiary, Lewisburg, Pa., 1967-69; William E. Schumacher disting. lectr. Maine Dept. Mental Health and Mental Retardation, Portland, 1982; mem. commn. on mentally disabled ABA, Washington, 1987; cons. law and psychiatry Dept. Welfare, Commonwealth Pa., 1974; cons. reviewer, site visitor crime and delinquency sect. NIMH, 1977; examiner Am. Bd. Psychiatry and Neurology, 1985; spl. asst. to pres. UPMC, 2007-. Author: (with others) Informed Consent: A Study of Decisionmaking in Psychiatry, 1984; editor: (with others) Psychiatry, Social, Epidemiologic and Legal Psychiatry, Vol. 5, 1986; contbr. articles to profl. jours., chpts. to books; editorial bd. Criminology, 1974-78, Law and Human Behavior, 1980-85, Internat. Jour. Law and Psychiatry, 1980-88, Behavioral Scis. and the Law, 1987-95; assoc. editor Am. Jour. Psychiatry, 1982-90; cons. editor Criminal Justice and Behavior, 1982-85. Lt. comrd. USPHS Res., 1967—. Recipient Steve Allen award United Mental Health, Inc., 1990, Sr. Vice Chancellor's Extraordinary Svc. award, U. Pitts. Med. Ctr.; grantee NIMH, 1979, 80-81, 89, Founds. Fund for Rsch. in Psychiatry, 1980-82. Fellow Am. Psychiat. Assn. (Isaac Ray award 1988), Am. Coll. Utilization Rev. Physicians, Am. Coll. Psychiatrists; mem. AMA, Am. Acad. Psychiatry and Law (pres. 1983-84), Group for Advancement Psychiatry (com. on psychiatry and law 1979-80, chmn. 1981-84), Am. Soc. Criminology, Am. Soc. Law and Medicine (bd. dirs. 1982-85), Internat. Acad. Law and Mental Health (bd. dirs.), Am. Psychopath. Assn., Phi Beta Kappa, Phi Kappa Phi. Office: U Pitts Med Ctr Forbes TWR 200 Lothrop St Ste 11016 Pittsburgh PA 15213-2546 Home: WPIC Ste 221 3811 OHara St Pittsburgh PA 15213 Office Phone: 412-647-4860. Business E-Mail: rothlh@upmc.edu.

ROTH, PAUL BARRY, dean, educator, emergency medicine physician; b. Glen Ridge, NJ, Oct. 7, 1947; s. Jerome M. and Selma (Leitner) R. BS, Fairleigh Dickinson U., 1969, MS, 1972; MD, George Washington U., 1976; postgrad., U. N.Mex., Albuquerque, 1976-79. Resident in family practice U. N.Mex. Sch. Medicine, Albuquerque, 1976—79; owner, pres. EMS of N.Mex., Albuquerque, 1978-82; owner, mem. of bd. Heights Urgent Care Ctr., Albuquerque, 1980-82; dir. divsn. emergency medicine dept. family, cmty. and emergency medicine U. N.Mex. Sch. Medicine, Albuquerque, 1982-91, prof. emerg. med., 1991—, chair dept. emergency medicine, 1991-93, interim chief med. officer, 1992—93, interim dean, 1994—95, dean, 1994—; interim dir. U. N.Mex. Med. Ctr., Albuquerque, 1994—95; med. dir. disaster medicine Nat. Disaster Med. Sys.; exec. v.p. U. N.Mex. Health Sci. Ctr., 2005—. Chair disaster com. U. N.Mex. Med. Ctr. Contbr. articles to Annals of EM, Current Practice of EM-Disaster Medicine, Jour. of AMA. Recipient Outstanding Individual Svc. award Nat. Disaster Med. Sys., 1986. Fellow Am. Coll. Emergency Physicians (chair sect. on disaster medicine, 1991-92), Am. Acad. Family Practice; mem. AMA, Soc. for Acad. Emergency Medicine, Am. Coll. Physician Execs., Am. Acad. Family Physicians. Office: U NMex Sch Medicine Health Scis Svcs Bldg, Suite 302 MSC09 5300 Albuquerque NM 87131-0001 Office Phone: 505-272-5849. Business E-Mail: PRoth@salud.unm.edu. *

ROTH, SANFORD IRWIN, pathologist, educator; b. McAlester, Okla., Oct. 14, 1932; s. Herman Moe and Blanche (Brown) R.; m. Kathryn Ann Corliss, Sept. 3, 1961; children: Jeffrey Franklin, Elisabeth Francine, Gregory James, Suzannah Joan. Student, Vanderbilt U., 1949-52; MD, Harvard U., 1956. Intern Mass. Gen. Hosp., Boston, 1956-57, resident in pathology, 1957-60, pathologist, 1962-75, Armed Forces Inst. Pathology, 1960-62; asst. prof. Med. Sch. Harvard U., 1962-69, assoc. prof. Med. Sch., 1969-75; faculty rsch. assoc. Am. Cancer Soc., 1967—72; pathologist, prof., chmn. dept. Coll. Medicine U. Ark., Little Rock, 1975-81; prof. Med. Sch. Northwestern U., Chgo., 1981—2000, asst. dean admissions, 1998-2000, prof. emeritus, 2000—; chief lab. svc. VA Lakeside Med. Ctr., Chgo., 1981—84. Attending pathologist Northwestern U. Hosp., 1981-2000; vis. prof. pathology Harvard Med. Sch., 2001-06, lectr., 2007—; cons. in pathology Mass. Gen. Hosp., 2001—. Emeritus mem. Soc. Investigative Dermatology. With M.C. US Army, 1960-62. Mem. AMA, AAAS, Coll. Am. Pathology, U.S.-Can. Acad. Pathology, Mass. Med. Soc. Home: 169 Tisquantum Rd Chatham MA 02633-2578 Office: Mass Gen Hosp Warren 225 Fruit St Boston MA 02114 Personal E-mail: siroth@northwestern.edu. Business E-Mail: sroth@partners.org.

ROTH, STEVEN E, dentist; Grad., Columbia U., U. Pa., NYU Rosenthal Inst. for Aesthetic Dentistry. Cert. Invisalign. Advanced dentistry residency program Beth Israel Med. Ctr.; faculty mentor Spear Advanced Dental Edn. Ctr.; established, inventor COSMALITE. Lectr. cosmetic dentistry, TMJ headaches and Bruxism Advanced Edn. Groups for Dental Professionals. Mem.: ADA, Am. Equilibration Soc., Am. Acad. of Cosmetic Dentistry. Office: SmilesNY Cosmetic & Implant Dentistry Lobby F 220 East 63rd St New York NY 10065 Office Phone: 888-757-7645. Office Fax: 212-421-0410. Business E-Mail: drroth@smilesny.com.

ROTH, SUSAN AMY, pediatrician; b. Chgo., Aug. 20, 1959; BA, Wash. U., St. Louis, 1981; degree, Rush Med. Coll., 1985. Pediatrician Northwestern Med. Faculty Found., 1988—96, Northshore U. HealthSys., 1997—. Asst. prof. pediat. Northwestern U. Med. Sch., 1988—2009, U. Chgo., 2009. Fellow: Am. Acad. Pediat. Avocations: jogging, swimming, golf. Office: 1000 Ctrl St Ste 765 Evanston IL 60201 Office Phone: 847-570-1507. Office Fax: 847-570-1577. Business E-Mail: sroth@northshore.org.

ROTH, WILLIAM STANLEY, hospital foundation executive; b. NYC, Jan. 12, 1929; s. Sam Irving and Louise Caroline (Martin) Roth; m. Hazel Adcock, May 6, 1963; children: R. Charles, W. Stanley Roth'. AA, Asheville-Biltmore Jr. Coll., NC, 1948; BS, U. NC, Chapel Hill, 1950. Dep. regional exec. Nat. coun. Boy Scouts Am., 1953-65; exec. v.p. Am. Humanics Found., 1965-67; dir. devel. Bethany Med. Ctr., Kansas City, Kans., 1967-74; exec. v.p. Geisinger Med. Ctr. Found., Danville, Pa., 1974-78; found. pres. Bapt. Med Ctrs., Birmingham, Ala., 1978-. Sec. Western Med. Systems, Cherokee County Homes, Cullman Sr. Housing, Dekalb Sr. Housing, Limestone Sr. Housing, Oxford Sr. Housing. Editor: Torch and Trefoil, 1960—61. Mem.-at-large Nat. coun. Boy Scouts Am., 1972-86; chmn. NAHD Ednl. Fund, 1980-82; ruling elder John Knox Kirk, Kansas City, Mo., Grove Presbyn. Ch., Danville, Pa. Recipient Silver award United Meth. Ch., 1970, Mid-West Health Congress, 1971; Seymour award for outstanding hosp. devel. officer, 1983, 70 Yr. Vet. award Boy Scouts Am., 2006. Fellow Assn. for Healthcare Philanthropy (life; nat. pres. 1975-76); mem. Nat. Soc. Fund Raising Execs. (pres. Ala. chpt. 1980-82, nat. dir. 1980-84, mem. ethics bd. 1993-98, advanced cert fund raising exec., Outstanding Fund Raising Exec., Ala. chpt. 1983), Mid-Am. Hosp. Devel. Assn. (pres. 1973-74), Mid-West Health Congress (devel. chmn. 1972-74), Am. Soc. for Healthcare Mktg. and Pub. Rels., Ala. Soc. for Sleep Disorders, Ala. Heart Inst., Ala. Assn. Healthcare Philanthropy (pres. 1991-93, chmn. bd. 1993-94), Ala. Planned Giving Coun. (bd. dirs. 1991-2000, pres. 1994-95), Alpha Phi Omega (nat. pres. 1958-62, dir. 1950—, Nat. Disting. Scv. award 1962), Delta Upsilon (pres. NC Alumni 1963-65), Rotary (pres. club 1976-77), Relay House, Summit Club, Green Valley Club (bd. govs.), Elks, Order of the Arrow (Nat. Disting. Svc. award 1958), Order of Holy Grail, Order of Golden Fleece. Home: 341 Laredo Dr Birmingham AL 35226-2325 Office: 3500 Blue Lake Dr Ste 101 Birmingham AL 35243-1908 Office Phone: 205-979-8285. Personal E-mail: billroth1@aol.com.

ROTHBAUM, BARBARA OLASOV, psychologist, educator; b. Charleston, SC, July 4, 1960; d. Sanford Patla and Faye (Rabinowitz) Olasov; m. John Edel Rothbaum, June 19, 1988; children: Alex Olasov, Jake Olasov. BA with highest honors, U. N.C., 1982; MS in Psychology, U. Ga., 1984, PhD in Clin. Psychology, 1986. Behavior therapist Middlesex Hosp. Med. Sch., London, 1984—85; instr. psychiatry Med. Coll. Pa., Phila., 1986—88, asst. prof. psychiatry, 1988—90; from asst. prof. to prof. Sch. Medicine Emory U., Atlanta, 1990—2005, prof. Sch. Medicine, 2005—, dir. Trauma and Anxiety Recovery Program Sch. Medicine. Project coord. Rape and Crime Victim Program, Phila, 1986-90; pvt. practice psychology, Phila., 1986-90; mem. sci. adv. bd. Anxiety Disorders Assocs., 2002—; mem. DSM-III-R work group on post-traumatic stress disorder. Contbr. articles to profl. jours., chpts. to books. Mem. APA, Ga. Psychol. Assn., Assn. for Advancement Behavior Therapy, Internat. Soc. for Traumatic Stress Studies (bd. dirs., pres. 2004). Democrat. Jewish. Avocations: art, outdoors, reading, bicycling. Office: Dept Psychiatry 1841 Clifton Rd Atlanta GA 30329 Office Phone: 404-712-8866. Business E-Mail: brothba@emory.edu.

ROTHBERG-BLACKMAN, JUNE SIMMONDS, retired nursing educator, psychotherapist; b. Phila., Sept. 4, 1923; d. David and Rose (Protzel) Simmonds; m. Jacob Rothberg, Sept. 7, 1952 (dec. Feb. 2001); children: Robert Rothberg, Alan Rothberg; m. Stanley F Blackman, May 27, 2002 (dec. July 2005). Diploma in nursing, Lenox Hill Hosp., 1944; BS, N.Y. U., 1950, MA, 1959, PhD (NIH fellow), 1965; Diploma in Psychotherapy and Psychoanalysis, Adelphi U., Inst. for Advanced Psychol. Studies, 1987. USPHS traineeship N.Y. U., 1957-59; sr. public health nurse Bklyn. Vis. Nurse Assn., 1951-53; prin. investigator in nursing, homestead study project Goldwater Hosp. and N.Y. U., 1959-61; instr. N.Y. U., 1964-65, asst. prof., 1965-68, assoc. prof., 1968-69, project dir. grad. program rehab. nursing, 1964-69, prof., 1969-87, prof. emeritus, 1987—; dean Adelphi U., Garden City, NY, 1969-85, v.p. acad. adminstrn., 1985-86; pvt. practice West Hempstead, NY, 1993-97. Pres. David Simmonds Co. Inc., Med. Supply Co., 1982-89; dir., chmn. compensation com. Quality Care, Inc.; cons. region 2 Bur. Health Resources Devel., HHS.; audit com. Ipco Corp. (formerly Sterling Optical Corp.), 1991; cons., spkr. in field. Contbr. articles to profl. jours. Mem. pres's coun. N.Y. U. Sch. Edn., 1973-75; treas. Nurses for Polit. Action, 1971-73; trustee Nurses Coalition for Action in Politics, 1974-76; bd. visitors Duke Med. Ctr., 1970-74; mem. governing bd. Nassau-Suffolk Health Systems Agy., 1976-79; leader People-to-People Internat. med. rehab. del. to People's Republic of China, 1981; mem. com. for the study pain disability and chronic illness behavior Inst. Medicine, 1985-86, com. on ethics in rehab. Hastings Ctr., 1985-87; trustee Paget's Disease Found., 1987-89. Recipient Disting. Alumna award NYU, 1974, recognition award Am. Assn. Colls. Nursing, 1976, Achievers award Ctr. for Bus. and Profl. Women, 1980 Fellow Am. Acad. Nursing (governing coun. 1980-82); mem. Nat. League Nursing (exec. com. coun. of baccalaureate and higher degree programs 1969-73), Am. Nurses Assn. (joint liaison com. 1970-72), Commn. Accreditation of Rehab. Facilities, Am. Congress Rehab. Medicine (pres. 1977-78, chmn. continuing edn. com. 1979-86, 34th Ann. John Stanley Coulter Meml. lectr. 1984, Gold Key award 1984, Edward W. Lowman award 1990), Am. Assn. Colls. Nursing (pres. 1974-76), L.I. Women's Network (pres. 1980-81), Kappa Delta Pi, Sigma Theta Tau, Pi Lambda Theta. Achievements include having June S. Rothberg collection in Nursing Archives, Mugar Meml. Library, Boston U. Home and Office: 401 E Linton Blvd Apt 252 Delray Beach FL 33483 Personal E-mail: stanleyb2@aol.com.

ROTHENBERG, ALBERT, psychiatrist, educator; b. NYC, June 2, 1930; s. Gabriel and Rose (Goldberg) R.; m. Julia C. Johnson, June 28, 1970; children: Michael, Mora, Rina. AB, Harvard U., 1952; MD, Tufts U., 1956. Diplomate Am. Bd. Psychiatry and Neurology. Intern Pa. Hosp., Phila., 1956-57; resident in psychiatry Yale U., West Haven (Conn.) VA Hosp., 1957-58, Grace-New Haven Hosp., 1958-59, Yale Psychiat. Inst., New Haven, 1959-60, chief resident, 1960-61; practice medicine specializing in psychiatry New Haven, 1960-61, 1963-75; chief neuropsychiatry Rodriguez U.S. Army Hosp., San Juan, P.R., 1961-63; practice medicine specializing in psychiatry Farmington, Conn., 1975-79, Stockbridge, Mass., 1979-94, Chatham, NY, 1994—2006, Canaan, NY, 2006—, Great Barrington, Mass., 1994-98; dir. rsch. Austen Riggs Center, Stockbridge, Mass., 1979-94. Asst. dir. Yale Psychiat. Inst., 1963-64, sr. staff mem., 1964-83; mem. staff Yale-New Haven Med. Ctr., West Haven VA Hosp., U. Conn. Health Ctr., Farmington; cons., mem. editorial bd. various jours. in psychiatry and psychology; instr. dept. psychiatry Yale U. Sch. Medicine, 1960-61, 63-64, asst. prof., 1964-68, assoc. prof., 1968-74, clin. prof., 1974-84; prof. psychiatry U. Conn. Sch. Medicine, Farmington, 1975-79, dir. residency tng., 1976-78, dir. clin. svcs., 1975-78; prin. investigator Studies in the Creative Process, 1964—; vis. prof. Pa. State U., 1971, adj. prof., 1971-78; vis. prof. dept. Am. studies Yale U., 1974-76, U. Capetown Med. Sch., South Africa, 1999, Salpêtrière Hosp., Paris, 1999; lectr. dept. psychiatry Harvard U. Med. Sch., 1982-86, clin. prof., 1986—; nominator, Nobel Prize in Medicine, 1990 . Author: (with B. Greenberg) Index of Scientific Writings on Creativity: Creative Men and Women, 1974, Index of Scientific Writings on Creativity: General 1566-1974, 1976; (with C.R. Hausman) The Creativity Question, 1976; The Emerging Goddess: The Creative Process in Art, Science and Other Fields, 1979; The Creative Process of Psychotherapy, 1988; Adolescence: Psychopathology, Normality, and Creativity, 1990; Creativity and Madness: New Findings and Old Stereotypes, 1990, Living Color, 2001; contbr. articles to profl. jours. Researcher on creativity in the arts, sci. and tech. Served with M.C. U.S. Army, 1961-63. Recipient Tufts Med. Alumni award 1956, Rsch. Scientist Career Devel. award NIMH 1964, 69, Golestan Found. award 1991, 92, Kovler award MESAB, 1999; Guggenheim Meml. fellow 1974-75, Ctr. Adv. Study in Behavioral Studies fellow 1986-87, Netherlands Inst. for Adv. Study in Humanities and Social Scis. fellow, 1992-93. Fellow Am. Psychiat. Assn.(disting. life), Am. Coll. Psychoanalysts; mem. AAAS, Mass. Psychiat. Soc., Am. Soc. Aesthetics, Rapaport-Klein Group, Sigma Xi. Democrat. Achievements include research in the creative process, schizophrenia, anorexia nervosa, and psychotherapy. Business E-Mail: albert_rothenberg@hms.harvard.edu.

ROTHER, JOHN, healthcare association administrator; b. Springfield, Mo., Apr. 18, 1947; s. Charles C. and Eleanor J. (Morrison) R. BA with honors, Oberlin Coll., 1969; JD with honors, U. Pa. Sch. Law, 1975. Bar: Pa. 1975, D.C. 1977. Appellate litigator NLRB, Washington, 1975-77; counsel Senator Jacob Javits US Senate Labor & Human Resources Com., Washington, 1977-81; staff dir., chief counsel US Senate Spl. Com. on Aging, Washington, 1981-84; exec. v.p. for policy, strategy, & internat. affairs AARP, Washington, 1984—2011; pres., CEO Nat. Coalition on Health Care (NCHC), Washington, 2011—. Chair Generations United; vice chair Nat. Quality Forum; founding mem. Nat. Acad. Social Ins., Corp. for Nat. Service. Named one of The 150 Who Make A Difference, The Nat. Law Jour., Washington, 1986. Mem. D.C. Bar, Gerontol. Soc. America Office: National Coalition on Health Care 1120 G St NW Ste 810 Washington DC 20005 Office Phone: 202-638-7151. Office Fax: 202-628-7166. *

ROTHERMUND, LARS, physician, researcher; b. Parchim, Meckelnburg-Vorpommern, Germany, Dec. 16, 1967; s. Alfred and Almut Rothermund; m. Eva Nassir; 1 child, Lea. Priv. Doz. Dr. med. habil., Charité U., Berlin, 2006. Rschr. dept. clin. pharmacology Charité U., 2000—06, oberarzt med. klinik iv nephrologie und endokrinologie, 2004—06, faculty mem., 2005—; leitender arzt KfH-Nierenzentrum, Ulm, Baden Wuertemberg, Germany, 2008—.

Contbr. rsch. articels to sci. jours. Office: KfH-Dialysezentrum Erlenstrasse 40 Ulm Baden-Wuerttemberg 89077 Germany Office Fax: 49 0731 175495 24. Business E-Mail: lars.rothermund@kfh-dialyse.de.

ROTHFIELD, NAOMI FOX, physician; b. Bklyn., Apr. 5, 1929; d. Morris and Violet (Bloomgarden) Fox; m. Lawrence Rothfield, Sept. 18, 1954; children: Susan, Lawrence, John, Jane. BA, Bard Coll., 1950; MD, NYU, 1955. Intern Lenox Hill Hosp., NYC, 1955-56; instr. NYU Sch. Medicine, 1956-62, asst. prof., 1962-68; assoc. prof. U. Conn. Sch. Medicine, Farmington, 1968-72, prof., 1972—, chief divsn. rheumatic diseases, 1972—99. Contbr. chpts. to books, articles to med. jours. Bd. dirs. Conn. Choral Artists, 1999-2008. Mem. Am. Soc. Clin. Investigation, Am. Rheumatism Assn., Assn. Am. Physics. Jewish. Home: 540 Deercliff Rd Avon CT 06001-2859 Office: U Conn Sch Medicine Divsn Rheumatic Diseases Farmington CT 06030-0001 Home Phone: 860-677-4781; Office Phone: 860-679-3604. E-mail: rothfield@nso.uchc.edu.

ROTHMAN, ABRAHAM, pediatrician; b. Bolivia, May 12, 1957; MD, UC San Diego, 1982. Physician Children's Heart Ctr., Nev., 2003—. Office: 3006 S Md Pky 690 Las Vegas NV 89109 Business E-Mail: arothman@childrensheartcenter.com.

ROTHMAN, JAMES EDWARD, cell biologist, educator; b. Haverhill, Mass., Nov. 3, 1950; BA summa cum laude, Yale U., 1971; PhD in Biochemistry, Harvard U., 1976; D h.c., U. Regensburg, 1995, U. Geneva, 1997. Fellow dept. biology MIT, Cambridge, 1976-78; asst. prof., dept. biochemistry Stanford U., Calif., 1978—81, assoc. prof., dept. biochemistry, 1981—84, prof., dept. biochemistry, 1984—88; E.R. Squibb prof. molecular biology Princeton U., NJ, 1988—91; chmn. cellular biochemistry and biophysics program Sloan-Kettering Inst., NYC, 1991—2003, vice chmn., 1994—2003; Paul A. Marks chair and chmn. cellular biochemistry and biophysics program Meml. Sloan-Kettering Cancer Ctr., NYC, 1991—2004; prof. dept. physiology and cellular biophysics Coll. Physicians and Surgeons, Columbia U., NYC, 2004—08, Clyde and Helen Wu prof. chem. biology, 2005—08; dir. Columbia Genome Ctr., 2005—08; chair dept. cell biology, head Ctr. High-Throughput Cell Biology Yale U., New Haven, 2008—, Fergus F. Wallace Prof. Biomedical Sciences, 2008—, prof. cell biology, 2008—, prof. chemistry, 2008—; exec. dir. Yale Ctr. for High Throughput Cell Biology. Editl. bd. Molecular and Cellulat Biology, 1982—84, Cell, 1984—94; chmn. Gordon Conf. on Molecular Membrane Biology, 1983; bd. editors Science, 1984—89; editl. com. Ann. Review Biochemistry, 1985—90, assoc. editor, 2003; study sect., Molecular Cytology NIH, 1990—94, coun., Nat. Inst. Digestive and Kidney Diseases, 1997—99; Devel. Therapeutics Review Group Nat. Cancer Inst., 1997—98; bd. sr. editors Jour. Clin. Investigation, 2002—07; assoc. editor Annual Review of Biochemistry, 2003—; sci. adv. bd. Ariz. Biodesign Inst., 2007—, U. Heidelberg, 2007—; invited lectr. in field. Contbr. several articles to profl. jours. Recipient Eli Lily award for Fundamental Rsch. in Biol. Chemistry, 1986, Passano Young Scientist award, 1986, Alexander Von Humboldt award, 1989, Heinrich Wieland prize, 1990, V.D. Mattia award, 1994, Fritz Lipmann award, 1995, Mayor's award for Excellence in Sci. and Tech., 1995, Harden medal, UK 1997, Jacobaeus prize, 1999, Heineken prize, 2000, Otto-Warburg medal, 2001, Beering award, 2005; co-recipient Rosenstiel award in Biomedical Sciences, 1994, Gairdner Found. Internat. award, 1996, King Faisal Internat. prize in Sci., 1996, Feodor Lynen award, 1997, Louisa Gross Horwitz prize of Columbia U., 2002, Albert Lasker award for Basic Medical Rsch., Lasker Found., 2002, Kavli award for Neuroscience Norwegian Acad. Sci. and Letters, Kavli Found. and Norway's Ministry of Edn. and Rsch., 2010; Fellow Andrew W. Mellon, 1979-1982; scholar Dreyfus Found. Teacher, 1981-86; commd. as a Kentucky Col., by Gov. State of Kentucky, 1997. Fellow: AAAS, Am. Acad. of Arts and Sciences, NAS (Richard Lounsbery award 1997); mem.: European Molecular Biology Orgn. (foreign assoc. 1995), Inst. Medicine, NAS, Japanese Biochemical Soc. (hon.). Office: Yale U Rothman Lab Sterling Hall Medicine PO Box 208002 C-207 New Haven CT 06520-8002 Address: Yale U Dept Cell Biology Sch Medicine Rothman Lab Sterling Hall of Medicine C-Wing 333 Cedar St SHM C-232 New Haven CT 06510 Office Phone: 203-737-5293. Office Fax: 203-737-3585. E-mail: james.rothman@yale.edu. *

ROTHMAN, PAUL B., dean, medical educator; MD, Yale U., 1984. Resident Columbia-Presbyn. Med. Ctr., NYC; Richard J. Stock prof. immunology and microbiology, chief pulmonary allergy and critical care medicine divsn. Columbia U. Coll. Physicians and Surgeons, NYC, 1997; head, prof. internal medicine Roy J. and Lucille A. Carver Coll. Medicine, U. Iowa, 2004—08, dean, 2008—. Mem. Immunologic Scis. Study Sect., NIH, Israel Cancer Rsch. Fund Internat. Sci. Adv. Bd., Am. Acad. Allergy, Asthma and Immunology Grant Review Com., Am. Thoracic Soc. Asthma Immunology and Inflammation Program Com. Contbr. articles to profl. jours. Recipient James S. McDonnell Found. Career Devel. Award, Pfizer Scholars Award, Pew Scholars Award, Leukemia Soc. of America Scholar Award, Pharmacia Allergy Rsch. Found. Internat. Award. Fellow: Am. Coll. Physicians; mem.: Assn. Am. Physicians, Collegium Internationale Allergologicum, Am. Soc. for Clin. Investigation, Coun. of Assn. of Am. Physicians, Assn. Profs. of Medicine. Office: U Iowa Carver Coll Medicine 212 CMAB Iowa City IA 52242-2600 Office Phone: 319-384-4547. E-mail: paul-rothman@uiowa.edu. *

ROTHMAN-BERNSTEIN-LEVIN, LISA J., occupational health nurse, medical abstract writer, nurse recruiter; b. Toledo, Dec. 29, 1949; 1 child, Daniel Karvinen. Diploma, Mercy Hosp. Sch. Nursing, Toledo, 1974; B Individualized Studies magna cum laude, Lourdes Coll., Sylvania, Ohio, 1989; AS in Bus., U. Toledo, 1970; cert. in Italian lang., history, art, U. Florence, Italy, 1972. Cert. hypnotherapist 2003. Buyer Lamson's of Toledo, Ga., 1971; owner, designer FUNKtional Art, Inc., 1984—; owner, baker Tres Bon Cheesecakes, Inc., Margate, Fla., 1984; cruise ship nurse Costa Cruise Line, Miami, Fla., 1979; sales Chandris Cruise Line, Greece, 1980, Bahama Cruise Line, Miami, Fla., 1980; home health nurse Upjohn, Ft. Lauderdale, Fla., 1983; patient svcs. coord. Fla. Med. Ctr., Lauderdale Lakes, Fla., 1983; sales and entertainment Norwegian Cruise Line, Miami, Fla., 1984—87; vol. nurse in ob-gyn. Yoseftal Hosp., Eilat, Israel, 1976—78; staff nurse in ob-gyn. Mt. Sinai Med. Ctr., Miami Beach, Fla., 1974—76; staff nurse on eye svc., oper. rm. St. Vincent Mercy Med. Ctr., Toledo, 1990, nursing and healthcare recruiter, 1991—, patient advocate, 1995—99; nurse recruiter Atlanta, 2007. Co-chair Lourdes Coll. Red Cross Blood Drive, 1988, 89; publicity chair St. Vincent Med. Ctr. 1993 Nurses' Week. Mem. Phi Theta Kappa, Kappa Gamma Pi.

ROTHSCHILD, MICHAEL ALAN, pediatric otolaryngologist, educator; b. Englewood, NJ, Mar. 26, 1962; s. Carl Eliot and Naomi Leah (Bloom) Rothschild; m. Jennifer Louise Hilmes, Aug. 1984; children: David Adrian, Dylan Frederick. BS cum laude, Yale U., New Haven, 1984; MD, Yale U. Sch. Medicine, 1988. Diplomate Am. Bd. Otolaryngology, Nat. Bd. Med. Examiners, lic. NY, NJ, Ohio. Resident gen. surgery Mt. Sinai Med. Ctr., NYC, 1988—90, resident otolaryngology, 1990-93; fellow pediat. otolaryngology Children's Hosp., Cin., 1993-94; attending physician Mt. Sinai Hosp., 1994—; asst. prof. otolaryngology and pediat. Mt. Sinai Sch. Medicine, 1994—98, assoc. prof. otolaryngology and pediat., 1998—2002, assoc. clin. prof. otolaryngology and pediat., 2003—. Instr. dept. otolaryngology U. Cin. Med. Ctr., 1993—94; cons. Englewood Hosp., NJ, 1995—, Mt. Sinai Cleft Palate & Craniofacial Team, 1995—. Editl. bd. (med. publs.) Archives of Otolaryngology-Head and Neck Surgery, Internat. Online Jour. of Otohrinolaryngology-Head and Neck Surgery, Virtual Reality in Medicine Jour.; contbr. articles to profl. jours. Mem. Bd. Health, Closter, NJ, 2003—. Recipient Faculty Tchg. award, Mt. Sinai Dept. Otolaryngology, 2000. Fellow: ACS, Am. Acad. Otolaryngology-Head and Neck Surgery (Honor award 1999), Am. Acad. Pediat.; mem.: Am. Med. Assn., NY Pediat Soc., Am. Med. Informatics Assn., Soc. Ear, Nose & Throat Advances in Children, Am. Broncho-Esophagological Assn., Am. Soc. Pediat. Otolaryngology (Charles F. Ferguson Clin. Rsch. award 2000). Office: Mt Sinai Med Ctr Dept Otolaryngology 1 Gustave L Levy Pl Box 1189 New York NY 10029 Office Phone: 212-241-5944. Office Fax: 212-996-2703.

ROTHSTEIN, FRED C., health facility administrator; b. Cleve. m. Jackie Rothstein; 2 children. BA, Miami U., Oxford, Ohio; MD, Chgo. Med. Sch. U. Health Scis., 1976. Bd. cert. pediatrics and pedatric gastroenterology. Pediat. intern Cleve. Metro Gen. Hosp., Ohio, 1976—77, Rainbow Babies & Children's Hosp., Ohio, 1976—77, pediat. resident Ohio, 1977—79, pediat. gastroenterology fellow Ohio, 1979—81, chief divsn. pediat. gastroenterology Ohio, practicing physician, pediat. gastroenterologist Ohio, pres., CEO; dir. dept. pediatrics, sr. v.p. med. affairs Mt. Sinai Med. Ctr., Cleve., 1989; sr. v.p. clin. integration U. Hosps. Health System, Cleve., 1990—96, acting pres., CEO, 2002—03; pres., CEO U. Hosps. Cleve., 2003—. Asst. prof. pediatrics Case Western Reserve U., Cleve., 1981—86; prof. pediatrics Case Western Res. U., Cleve., 2004—; bd. trustees Ctr. Health Affairs (CHA), 2004, Geauga Regional Hosp., Chardon, Ohio, 1997; bd. dirs. BioEnterprise. Contbr. more than 60 peer-reviewed abstracts, articles, and book chapters on issues concerning pediatric gastroenterology. Mem.: N.Am. Soc. Pediat. Gastroenterology and Nutrition, Am. Gastroenterological Assn., Am. Acad. Pediatrics, Am. Coll. Gastroenterology. Office: Univ Hosps Cleve 11100 Euclid Ave Cleveland OH 44106 Office Phone: 216-844-6217.

ROTHSTEIN-RUBIN, RENE R., oncologist; Grad., CUNY: Bklyn. Coll., 1977; MD, NYU, 1982. Diplomate Am. Bd. Internal Medicine, Am. Bd. Internal Medicine-med. oncology, Am. Bd. Internal Medicine-hematology, lic. Pa., 1984. Intern Cooper Univ. Hosp., 1983; resident Pa. Hosp., 1985, fellow, 1986; hosp. affiliations include Pa. Hosp.-Presbyterian Med. Ctr., Hahnemann Univ. Hosp.; physician Rittenhouse Hematology/Oncology. Office: Rittenhouse Hematology/Oncology 6th Fl 207 N Broad St Philadelphia PA 19107 Office Phone: 215-561-0809. Office Fax: 866-555-1112.

ROTMAN, MARVIN, radiation oncologist, radiologist, educator; b. Phila., Sept. 3, 1933; s. Herman Zelman and Edith (Solomon) R.; m. Marsha Vinson; children: David, Robert, Eve, Sydney. BS, Ursinus Coll., 1954; MD, Thomas Jefferson U., 1958. Asst. clin prof. radiology N.Y. Med. Coll., NYC, 1967-68, asst. prof. radiology, 1968-71, assoc. prof. clin. radiology, 1971-75, prof. radiology, 1975-79; prof., chmn. radiation oncology SUNY Health Sci. Ctr. at Bklyn., 1979—2003, Disting. Svc. prof., chair, 2003—; dir. radiation oncology Kings County Med. Ctr., NYC, 1979—, Long Island Coll. Hosp. Cons. Bklyn. VA Hosp., 1979—. Author textbook: (with others) Introduction to Radiotherapy, 1975, Genito-Urinary Malignancy, 1980; editor textbook: (with others) Clinical Applications of Continuous Infusion Chemotherapy and Comitant Radiation Therapy, 1986, others; contbr. more than 190 articles to profl. jours., textbooks. Bd. dirs. Young Concert Artists, N.Y.C., 1967—; nat. bd. dirs. Sante Fe Opera, 1987-93. Recipient Gold Medal award, Am. Soc. Therapeutic Radiology and Oncology, 2002, award of honor, Radiol. Soc. N.Am., 1991. Fellow Am. Coll. Radiology (counselor N.Y. State chpt. 1980—), Am. Coll. Radiation Oncology; mem. AMA (mem. radiology residency review com., Am. Bd. Radiology examiner on splty. bds.), Am. Radium Soc. (pres. 1994-96), Soc. Acad. Radiotherapy Programs (pres. 1984-86), N.Y. Cancer Soc. (pres. 1983-84), N.Y. Roentgen Soc. (chmn. radiotherapy sect. 1977-78), Med. Soc. Kings County (chmn. radiotherapy 1981—), Am. Soc. Therapeutic Radiology and Oncology (mem. exec. com., Gold medal), Kings Point Civic Assn. (pres. 2004—)Alpha Omega Alpha. Jewish. Avocations: tennis, piano, art.

ROTONDI, FRANCESCO, cardiologist; b. Naples, Oct. 26, 1962; MD, Naples U., 1988, degree in Cardiology, 1991. Asst. med. dir. Divsn. Cardiology San Giuseppe Moscati Hosp., Avellino, Italy, 2002—. Asst. med. dir. Cardiology Fatebenefratelli Hosp., Benevento, Italy, 1999—2002. Contbr. numerous articles to profl. jours. Pub. Luna di miele ad Auschwitz Riflessioni sul negazionismo della Shoah, 2005. Home: Via Benito Maffei 10 Avellino 83100 Italy Home Phone: 39082534987; Office Phone: 390825203239. Personal E-mail: francesco.rotondi@tin.it.

ROTT, MARILISE BRITTES, science educator; b. São Borja, Brazil, Apr. 3, 1964; Degree in Pharmacy, U. Fed. Santa Maria, 1986; D, U. Fed. Rio Grande do Sul, Porto Alegre, Brazil, 2000. Tchr. U. Fed. Rio Grande do Sul, 1989—. Office: Sarmento Leite Porto Alegre Rio Grande do Sul 90050170 Brazil Business E-Mail: marilise.rott@ufrgs.br.

ROTUNDA, ADAM MICHAEL, dermatologist; b. Mineola, NY, Aug. 2, 1974; s. Robert and Josephine Rotunda; m. Thuy Nguyen, July 20, 1997; 1 child, Tia Linh. BS in Nutritional Scis. summa cum laude with honors, Cornell U., Ithaca, NY, 1996; MD valedictorian, SUNY Downstate Med. Sch., Bklyn., 2001. Bd. Cert. Am. Bd. Dermatology, 2005. Intern St. Vincent's Hosp., NYC, 2001—02; resident, dermatology divsn. UCLA Sch. Medicine, 2002—05, asst. clin. prof. dermatology, 2006—; Mohs micrographic surgery and cutaneous oncology fellowship Bennett Surgery Ctr., Santa Monica, Calif., 2005—06; med. dir. dermatology R&D Allergan, Inc., 2006—08. Contbr. articles to profl. jours. Recipient Alumni Svc. award, SUNY Downstate Health Sci. Ctr., 2001, Lifetime Membership award, Downstate Student Ctr., 2001; named Review Article Incentive Program Competition winner, Dermatologic Surgery, 2006. Mem.: Am. Acad. Cosmetic Dermatology & Aesthetic Surgery (bd. dirs.), L.A. Met. Dermatologic Soc., Calif. Soc. Dermatology and Dermatologic Surgery, Pacific Dermatologic Assn., Am. Soc. Dermatologic Surgery, Am. Coll. Mohs Surgery, Am. Acad. Dermatology. Achievements include invention of Methods and related compositions for non-invasive reduction of fat and skin tightening. Office Phone: 949-760-0953.

ROUBIDEAUX, YVETTE, federal agency administrator; b. Pierre, SD, Jan. 29, 1963; MD, Harvard Med. Sch., 1989; MPH, Harvard Sch. Pub. Health, 1997. Cert. Am. Bd. Internal Medicine. Intern/resident primary care internal medicine program Brigham & Women's Hosp., Boston, 1989—92; med. officer, clin. dir. San Carlos Indian Reservation, Ariz., Gila River Indian Cmty., Sacaton, Ariz.; asst. prof. Dept. Family & Cmty. Medicine, U. Ariz. Coll. Medicine; dir. Indian Health Svc., US Dept. Health & Human Services, Washington, 2009—. Apptd. sec.'s adv. com. on minority health HHS, 2000—02; dir. training program U. Ariz. American Indian Rsch. Ctr. Health; dir. U. Ariz. Indians Into Medicine Program (INMED); co-founder Native Rsch. Network, Inc. Co-editor: Promises to Keep: Public Health Policy for American Indians and Alaska Natives in the 21st Century, 2001. Mem. Rosebud Sioux Tribe, SD. Recipient Outstanding American Indian Faculty award, U. Ariz., 2002, Addison B. Scoville award for outstanding vol. svc., American Diabetes Assn., 2008; grantee Minority Health Policy Fellowship, Commonwealth Fund/Harvard U., 1997. Mem.: Assn. American Indian Physicians (pres. 1999—2000, Indian Physician of Yr. 2004). Office: US Dept Health & Human Services 200 Independence Ave SW Washington DC 20201 Office Phone: 301-443-1083. E-mail: director@IHS.gov. *

ROUBIK, KAREL, biomedical engineer, educator; b. Nachod, Czech Republic, May 11, 1971; s. Karel Roubik and Jana (Klimesova) Roubikova. MSc in Engring., Czech Tech. U., 1994, PhD, 2001. Lectr. Charles U., Prague, 1995—; rschr. Czech Tech. U., Prague, 1997—2000, lectr., 2001—; assoc. prof. biomed. engring., 2006. Co-author (with J. Hozman): (educational videotape) Tomographical Imaging Systems in Medicine - CT, 2002 (Prize of Internat. Film Festival - Techfilm, 2002); co-author: (with J. Pachl) (monograph) Anaesthesiology and Resuscitation Fundamentals in Adults and Children, 2003; co-author: (with C. O'Neill and S. Smith) (textbook) English for Biomedical Professionals, 2005; co-author: (with E. Motyckova, P. Denny & E. Poncova) English for Biomedical And Electrical Engineering Scientists, 2009; author: Physical Chemistry for Biomedical Engineering, 2007; editor-in-chief: Clinician and Tech. Jour. Recipient Siemens prize, 2001, John H. Enmerson award, 2007, 2010; Devel. Biomedical Engring. grantee, Internat. Visegrad Fund, 2001—03. Mem.: Internat. Assn. Scis. & Tech. Devel., IMEKO Internat. Measurement Confedration (mem. tech. com. TC13), Am. Chem. Soc., Am. Assn. Respiratory Care, Czech Med. Assn. J. E. Purkynje, Czech Soc. Biomedical Engring. and Med. Informatics, Czech Speleological Soc. Achievements include patents for technical support of unconventional ventilatory regimens. Avocations: caving, speleology, extreme sports, Irish music. Home: Na Vlcovce 2040/2B CZ - 160 00 Prague Dejvice Czech Republic Office: Czech Tech U Faculty Biomed Engring nam Sitna 3105 CZ-272 01 Kladno Czech Republic Office Phone: 420-603479901. Office Fax: 420-312608204. E-mail: roubik@fbmi.cvut.cz.

ROUDEBUSH, JAMES GORDON, retired military officer; b. Scottsbluff, Neb., Feb. 23, 1948; B in Medicine, U. Nebr., 1971, MD, 1975; M in Pub. Health, U. Tex., San Antonio, 1983; attended, Aerospace Medicine Primary Course, Brooks AFB, Tex., 1980, Tri-Service Combat Casualty Care Course, Fort Sam Houston, 1981; attended by seminar, Air War Coll., 1988; attended, Inst. for Fed. Health Care Executives, George Washington U., Washington, DC, 1989, Nat. War Coll., Fort Lesley J. McNair, Washington, DC, 1991—92, Exec. Mgmt. Course, Def. Sys. Mgmt. Coll., Fort Belvoir, Va., 1993. Commd. 2d lt. USAF, 1972, advanced through grades to lt. gen., 2006; resident in family practice Wright-Patterson USAF Med. Ctr., Wright-Patterson AFB, Ohio, 1975-78; physician in family practice, flight surgeon USAF Hosp., Francis E. Warren AFB, Wyo., 1978-82; resident in aerospace medicine USAF Sch. Aerospace Medicine, Brooks AFB, Tex., 1982—84; chief of aerospace medicine 81st Tactical Fighter Wing, RAF Bentwaters, England, 1984-86, comdr., 1986-88, 36th Tactial Fighter Wing Hosp., Bitburg AB, Germany, 1988-91; vice comdr. Human Systems Ctr., Brooks AFB, Tex., 1992—94; command surgeon US Ctrl. Command (USCENTCOM), MacDill AFB, Fla., 1994-97, Pacific Air Forces, Hickam AFB, Hawaii, 1997-98; comdr. 89th Med. Group, Andrews AFB, 1998-2000; command surgeon US Transp. Command (USTRANSCOM) and Hdqs. Air Mobility Command, Scotts AFB, Ill., 2000—01; dep. surgeon gen. USAF, Bolling AFB, Washington, DC, 2001—06, surgeon gen., 2006—09. Decorated Legion of Merit with oak leaf cluster, Def. Superior Svc. Mmdal with oak leaf cluster, Meritorious Svc. medal with two oak leaf clusters, Air Force Commendation medal, Joint Meritorious Unit award, Air Force Outstanding Unit award with oak leaf cluster, Nat. Def. Svc. Medal with bronze star, Southwest Asia Svc. medal with bronze star, Air Force Overseas Long Tour Ribbon with oak leaf cluster, Air Force Longevity Svc. award Ribbon with silver oak leaf cluster, Small Arms Expert Markmanship Ribbon, Air Force Training Ribbon, Chief Physician Badge, Chief Flight Surgeon Badge. Mem. Soc. of USAF Flight Surgeons, Aerospace Med. Assn., Internat. Assn. of Mil. Flight Surgeons Pilots, Assn. of Mil. Surgeons of the U.S., Air Force Assn., Am. Coll. of Preventive Medicine, Am. Coll. of Physician Execs., AMA.

ROUMAN, JAMES CHRIST, anesthesiologist; b. Tomahawk, Wis., May 15, 1927; s. Christ John Rouman and Soteria Dendes. BS, Northwestern U., Evanston, Ill., 1949; MD, Northwestern U., Chgo., 1953. Diplomate An. Bd. Anesthesiology. Intern Meml. Hermann-Tex. Med. Ctr., Houston, 1953—54; resident Hartford Hosp./McGill U., Conn., 1956—59; attending staff Hartford Hosp., 1959—92; asst. prof. U. Conn., Sch. Medicine, Farmington, 1978—92. Author: (novels) Underwater Dreams, 2006, Uncertain Journey, 2011. With USN, 1945—47. Recipient Disting. Svc. award, Conn. State Soc. Anesthesiologists, 1995. Greek Orthodox.

ROUP, BRENDA JACOBS, nurse, retired military officer; b. Petersburg, Va., July 8, 1948; d. Eugene Thurman and Sarah Ann (Williams) Jacobs; m. Clarence James Roup, May 8, 1976. BSN, Med. Coll. Va., Richmond, 1970; MSN, Cath.U. Am., 1977; PhD, U. Md., 1995. Commd. 2d lt. U.S. Army, 1970; advanced through grades to lt. col. U.S. Army, 1986; infection control cons. 7th MEDCOM, Germany, 1982—83; chief infection control Brooke Army MEDCEN, San Antonio, 1983—86, Walter Reed MEDCEN, Washington, 1986—92; ret., 1992; Johnson & Johnson postdocgoral fellow Johns Hopkins U. Sch. Nursing, Balt., 1995—97; nursing cons. in infection control Md. Dept. Health and Mental Hygiene, 1999—. Nurse cons. in infection control to U.S. Army Surgeon Gen., 1986—92. Contbr. articles to profl. jours. Fellow: Soc. for Healthcare Epidemiology Am.; mem.: Assn. Profls. in Infection Control. Avocations: reading, gardening, cooking. Office: Md Dept Health & Mental Hygiene Baltimore MD 21201 E-mail: broup@dhmh.state.md.us.

ROUS, STEPHEN NORMAN, urologist, educator; b. NYC, Nov. 1, 1931; s. David H. and Luba (Margulies) R.; m. Margot Woolfolk, Nov. 12, 1966; children: Benjamin, David. AB, Amherst Coll., 1952; MD, N.Y. Med. Coll., 1956; MS, U. Minn., 1963. Diplomate: Am. Bd. Urology. Intern Phila. Gen. Hosp., 1956-57, resident, 1959-60, Flower-Fifth Ave. and Met. Hosp., NYC, 1957-59, Mayo Clinic, Rochester, Minn., 1960-63; practice medicine specializing in urology San Francisco, 1963-68; assoc. prof. urology N.Y. Med. Coll., NYC, 1968-72, assoc. dean, 1970-72; prof. surgery, chief div. urology Mich. State U., East Lansing, 1972-75; prof., chmn. dept. urology Med. U. S.C., Charleston, 1975-88; urologist-in-chief Med. U. S.C. and County hosps., Charleston, 1975-88; editorial dir. Norton Med. Books div. W.W. Norton and Co., 1988-94, editorial cons., 1994—; clin. prof. surgery Uniformed Svcs. U. of Health Scis., Bethesda, Md., 1992-2001; clin. prof. surgery,surgeon urology Brown U. Med. Sch., 2006—. Adj. prof. urology Med. U. S.C., 1988-99, prof. emeritus, 1999—; adj. prof. surgery Dartmouth Med. Sch., 1988-91, prof. surgery (urology), 1991-2001, prof. surgery emeritus, 2001—; staff urologist Dartmouth-Hitchcock Med. Ctr., 1991-99; cons. urologist Saginaw VA Hosp., 1971-75, Charleston VA Hosp., 1975-88; hon. cons. St. Peter's Hosp., London, 1981-82; sr. vis. fellow Inst. Urology, London, 1981-82; mil. cons. in urology USAF Surgeon Gen., 1982-85; chmn. alumni devel. com. Mayo Clinic, 1979-82; hon. staff The Exeter Hosp., N.H., 1988—; nat. bd. visitors N.Y. Med. Coll., 1988-97; chief urology VA Med. Ctr., White River Junction, Vt., 1991-2001; mem. reparative justice bd. Vt. Dept. Corrections, 2004; urologist VA Med. Ctr., Providence, 2005—. Author: Understanding Urology, 1973, Urology in Primary Care, 1976, Spanish edit., 1978, Russian edit., 1979, Urology: A Core Textbook, 1985, 2d edit., 1996, The Prostate Book, 1988, latest rev. edit., 2001, Portuguese edit., 2010, (with Judge Hiller B. Zobel) Doctors and the Law: Defendants and Expert Witnesses, 1993, (with Dr. Pamela Ellsworth) The Little Black Book of Urology, 2001; editor Urology Ann., 1987-97, Stone Disease: Diagnosis and Management, 1987, mem. editl. bd. Mil. Medicine, 1984-94; contbr. articles to med. jours. Mem. East Lansing (Mich.) Planning Commn., 1974-75; vestryman, jr. warden All Saints Episcopal Ch., East Lansing, 1973-75, lay reader, mem. diocesan com. on continuing edn., 1975-86; vestryman St. Michael's Episc. Ch., 1979-82, Charleston, S.C., chmn. every mem. canvas, 1979-80, chmn. lay readers, 1983-86; mem. fin. com., lay reader Christ Episc. Ch., Exeter, N.H., 1989-91; lector St. Thomas Episc. Ch., Hanover, N.H., 1991-96, vestryman, 1992-96, stewardship chmn., 1992-94; jr. warden 1994-96; chalicist, lector, del. to diocesan conv. Trinity Ch., Newport, RI 2006—, jr. warden, 2009-11, sr. warden, 2011-; mem. selectman's alt. Hampton Falls Planning Bd., 1989-91; alt. mem. Zoning Bd. Adjustment, Hanover, 1997-2000; bd. trustees, Nat. Hypertension Assn., N.Y.C., 2001-; bd. dirs. Med. Sci. Techs. Inc., Newport News, Va., 2001—; Dept. Morale Welfare Recreation adv. bd., US Naval Station Newport, 2008-. Col. USAFR, 1981-85, col. USAR, 1985-2000, col. AUS, ret., 2001—. Recipient "A" designator in urology, U.S. Army Surgeon Gen., 1986. Fellow ACS, Am. Acad. Pediatrics; mem. AMA, Soc. Univ. Urologists, Internat. Soc. Urology, Am. Urol. Assn., Nat. Urologic Forum, Soc. Pediatric Urology, Brit. Assn. Urol. Surgeons, German Urol. Assn. (hon.), English Speaking Union (v.p. Newport County br. 2006-08, pres. 2008-10), Newport Reading Room, Mayo Alumni Assn. (v.p. 1979-81, pres. 1983-85), Army and Navy Club (Washington), Lotos Club (N.Y.C.), Dartmouth Club of N.Y.C., Brown U. Faculty Club (bd. mgrs. 2006-10), Sigma Xi, Alpha Omega Alpha. Home: 421 Bellevue Ave #2A Newport RI 02840 Personal E-mail: stephen.n.rous@dartmouth.edu.

ROUSE, LEO E., dean, dental educator; DDS, Howard U. Coll. Dentistry, 1973; postgrad. studies in comprehensive dentistry, Watson Army Hosp., 1976—78. Assoc. dean clinical affairs Coll. Dentistry, Howard U., chmn. dept. clinical dentistry, interim dean, 2003—04, dean, 2004—. Examiner cons. and mem. exam. devel. com. N.E. Regional Bd. Dental Examiners. Col. (ret.) US Army, 1972—97, comdr. and COO dental command US Army, 1995—97. Recipient Alumni Achievement award, Howard U. Coll. Dentistry, 1997. Fellow: Am. Coll. Dentists; mem.: ADA, Am. Assn. Dental Examiners, Am. Dental Edn. Assn. (pres. 2011—), Nat. Dental Assn., Omicron Kappa Upsilon. Office: Howard Univ Coll Dentistry 600 W St NW Washington DC 20059 Office Phone: 202-806-0440. Business E-Mail: lrouse@howard.edu. *

ROUSSET CARON, MONIQUE MARIE, dentist, educator; b. Solesmes, North, France, Apr. 23, 1948; d. Alfred Caron and Augusta Ansart; children: Fabrice Rousset, Thomas Rousset, Stéphanie Rousset. PhD of Odontology, U. Lille II, 1994. Rsch. Mgmt. U. Lille 2, 2001. Asst. prof. U. Lille II, North, France, 1995—2002, prof., 2002—. Recipient prize, GIRSO, 1993. Mem.: IAPD. Achievements include research in Correction of radiographic errors. Office: Dept Paediatric Dentistry Place de Verdun F-59000 Lille North France E-mail: mrousset@univ-lille2.fr.

ROUTH, DONALD K(ENT), psychologist, historian, educator; b. Oklahoma City, Mar. 3, 1937; s. Ross Holland and Fay (Campbell) R.; m. Marion Starbird Wendler, Sept. 10, 1960(Dec. Sept. 10, 2008); children: Rebecca Ann (dec.), Laura Diane; m. Margaret Gonzalez, June 27, 2010. BA, U. Okla., 1962; PhD, U. Pitts., 1967; BA in History, Fla. Gulf Coast U., 2006. Diplomate Am. Bd. Profl. Psychology. Asst. prof. psychology and pediatrics U. Iowa, Iowa City, 1967-70, prof., 1977-85; assoc. prof. psychology Bowling Green State U., Ohio, 1970-71; assoc. prof. U. N.C., Chapel Hill, 1971-77; prof. psychology and pediat. U. Miami, Coral Gables, Fla., 1985—2002, prof. emeritus, 2002—. Chmn. behavioral medicine study sect. NIH, 1983-85 Editor Jour. Pediatric Psychology, 1976-82, Jour. Clin. Child Psychology, 1987-91, Jour. of Abnormal Child Psychology, 1992-98, Am. Jour. on Mental Retardation, 1998-2002, Internat. Clin. Psychologist, 2001—04; contbr. numerous articles to profl. jours., books Pres. Eno River Unitarian Universalist Fellowship, 1976-77; vol. faculty Fla. Gulf Coast U., 2002—05. Recipient award for disting. contbn. Soc. Pediatric Psychology, 1981, Presdl. award, 1988; Rsch. Psychologist of Yr. award Fla. Psychol. Assn., 1987, Reconocimiento, El Colegio Nacional de Psicologis de Mex., 1999, Disting. Alumni award Okla. Mil. Acad., 2004. Mem. APA (pres. div. child, youth and family svcs., 1984, pres. div. on mental retardation 1987, pres. divsn. clin. psychol. 1998, Wallace Russell lectr. divsn. history of psychology, 2011), Internat. Soc. Clin. Psychology (founder, pres. 1998-99), Disting. Profl. Contbns. to Clin. Psychology (sect. on clin. child psychology 1989, div. clin. psychology, 1992, Nicholas Hobbs award div. child youth and family svcs., 1996, Edgar A. Doll award divsn. mental retardation and devel. disabiities 2001), Assn. Southwest Fla. (founder, 2003),Phi Beta Kappa. Democrat. Home: 4528 Palm Tree Blvd Cape Coral FL 33904 Personal E-mail: donaldrouth@mac.com.

ROUX, FRANÇOIS XAVIER, neurosurgeon; b. Paris, Jan. 2, 1951; s. Jacques Daniel and Françoise Adrienne (Ruff) R.; m. Elisabeth Hue, Sept. 19, 1975 (div. 1984); children: Pierre, Caroline, Guillaume; m. Sophie Nguyen, Mar. 17, 1996 (div. 2004); children: Charles-Xavier, Mailys. MD, Paris U., 1979, PhD in Neuroanatomy, 1983; MBA, Ecole Superieure de Commerce, Paris, 1989. Cert. prof. medicine, France. Resident Hosp. Paris, 1977-81, chief resident, 1981-85, assoc. prof. neurosurgery, 1985-98, prof., 1998—, chief dept. neurosurgery, 2001—. Bd. dirs. Chain of Hope, Paris; mem. Nat. U. Coun., 1995—. Author: Laser Co2 Neurochirugical, 1985, Diode Lasers in Neurosurgery, 1999. Mem. Cabinet Paris Univs. Presidence, 1995—2000, Cabinet Health Ministry, Paris, 1992—93, 2001—02. Mem. Nat. Coun. Univs., Medecins du Monde, Assn. Humanitarian Action (bd. dirs.), French Soc. Neurosurgery (bd. dirs., pres. 1998-2000), European Laser Assn., French Soc. Laser Medicine (bd. dirs. 1985-98), Internat. Cooperation (South East Asia), French Speaking Neurol. Soc. (treas. 2000—, bd. dirs., pres. 2010-). Roman Catholic. Avocation: humanitarian medicine. Office: Hopital Sainte-Anne 1 Rue Cabanis 75014 Paris France Home: 27 Rue Leconte de Lisle 75016 Paris France Home Phone: +33 145254626. Business E-Mail: fx.roux@ch-sainte-anne.fr.

ROVEN, ALFRED NATHAN, surgeon; came to the U.S., 1949. BA in Psychology, Calif. State U., Northridge, 1969; MD, U. So. Calif., 1977. Diplomate Am. Bd. Plastic and Reconstructive Surgery, Am. Bd. Otolaryngology. Resident in otolaryngology U. So. Calif., 1977-82; clin. chief plastic surgery Cedars Sinai Med. Ctr., LA, 1989-91; resident in plastic and reconstructive surgery U. N.C., 1982-84; clin. chief burns Cedars Sinai Med. Ctr., LA, 1990-92, clin. chief hands, 1990-92. Qualified med. examiner State of Calif., 1985. Contbr. articles to jours. Avocation: reading. Office: 5757 Wishire Blvd 6 Los Angeles CA 90036

ROVEN, ROBERT BOCHNER, cardiologist, educator; b. NYC, Oct. 28, 1932; AB, Columbia U., NYC, 1953, MD, 1957. Diplomate Am. Bd. Internal Medicine, Am. Bd. Cardiovasc. Disease. Intern St. Luke's Hosp., NYC, 1957-58, resident, 1958-59, St. Bartholomew Hosp., London, 1959-60; NIH fellow in cardiology St. Luke's Hosp., NYC, 1962-64; staff Lenox Hill Hosp., NYC; sr. attending physician St. Luke's-Roosevelt Hosp. Ctr., NYC; active attending physician NYU Med. Ctr., NYC; pvt. practice, NYC, 1964—. Asst. clin. prof. medicine NYU Sch. Medicine Office: 654 Madison Ave New York NY 10065-8404 Office Phone: 212-371-8516. *

ROVINA, NIKOLETTA, medical educator; b. Athens, Greece, Oct. 12, 1967; d. Konstantinos Rovinas and Helen Rovina; m. Nick Antoniou, Dec. 27, 1999; children: Stelios Antoniou, Konstantinos Antoniou. MD, U. Crete, PhD, 1993. Lectr., dept. respiratory medicine U. Athens Med. Sch., Athens, Greece, 2007—. Translator med. books and jours. in greek; editor: (book) Asthma: Pathophysiology, Diagnosis, Therapy. Recipient Rsch. award, 1999, 2005, 2006. Mem.: Hellenic Thoracic Soc., ATS, ERS. Home: 8 Niki St Athens 17234 Greece Office: Sotiria Hosp Diseases of Chest 152 Mesogion Ave Athens GR-11527 Greece E-mail: nikrovina@med.uoa.gr.

ROVIT, RICHARD LEE, neurosurgeon; b. Boston, Apr. 3, 1924; s. Samuel and Frances (Ehrenberg) R.; m. Barbara Sayre Margolis, Mar. 29, 1953; children: Sandra Amy Golze, Adam John, Hugh Russel. Grad., U. Mich., 1944; MD, Jefferson Med. Coll., 1950; MSc, McGill U., 1961. Diplomate Am. Bd. Neurol. Surgery (dir. vice chmn. 1986-92). Intern in surgery Beth Israel Hosp., Boston, 1950-51; resident, then chief resident Mass. Gen. Hosp., Boston, 1951-58; USPH fellow in neurology The Nat. Hosp., London, 1956; sr. fellow in neurosurgery Lahey Clinic, Boston, 1957; fellow in neurophysiology and EEG Montreal (Can.) Neurol. Inst., 1958-59; prof. clin. neurosurgery NYU, 1967—; chmn. neurosurgery St. Vincent's Hosp. and Med. Ctr., NYC, 1967-92; prof. neurosurgery N.Y. Med. Coll., Valhalla, 1990—. Mem. claims com. med. Mut. Liability Ins. Co., 1985—. Editor, author: Trigeminal Neuralgia, 1991; contbr. articles to profl. jours. Trustee Sarah Neuman divsn. Jewish Home and Hosps., N.Y.C., 2004-. Lt. USN, 1952-54. Fellow ACS (v.p. 1994-95), Am. Assn. Neurol. Surgeons (v.p. 1980-81); mem. N.Y. Soc. Neurosurgeons (pres. 1974-76, 79-80), Soc. Neurol. Surgeons, Fairview Country Club (Greenwich, Conn.), Harvard Club of N.Y. Avocations: golf, running. Home: 4400 Theall Rd Rye NY 10580 Home Phone: 914-723-5936.

ROVNER, BARRY W., geriatric psychiatry, educator; Grad. in Natural Sciences cum laude, Muhlenberg Coll., 1976; MD, Thomas Jefferson U., 1980. Diplomate Am. Bd. Psychiatry and Neurology, 1985, Am. Bd. Psychiatry and Neurology-geriatric psychiatry, 1991, lic. admitted to practice Pa. Intern medicine Presby.-Univ. of Pa. Med. Ctr., 1980—81; resident psychiatry Johns Hopkins Univ. Sch. of Medicine, 1981—84, chief resident psychiatry, 1983—84, fellow neuropsychiatry dementia rsch., 1984—85; prof. psychiatry and human behavior Jefferson Med. Coll. Thomas Jefferson Univ., Phila., 1997, prof. neurology dept. Jefferson Med. Coll., 2004. Co-author: (publs.) The Prevalence and Management of Dementia and Other Psychiatric Disorders in Nursing Homes, 1986, Depression and Mortality in Nursing Homes, 1991, A Randomized Trial of Dementia Care in Nursing Homes, 1996, Practice Guideline for the Treatment of Patients with Alzheimer's Disease and Other Dementias, 2007, Preventing Depression in Age-Related Macular Degeneration, 2007, Activity Loss is Associated with Cognitive Decline in Age-Related Macular Degeneration, 2009, Variability in Depressive Symptoms Predicts Cognitive Decline in Age-Related Macular Degeneration, 2009. Office: Thomas Jefferson University 900 Walnut St 2nd Fl Philadelphia PA 19107 Office Phone: 215-503-1254. Office Fax: 215-503-1992. Business E-Mail: Barry.Rovner@jefferson.edu.

ROWE, DALE EDWARD, orthopedist, educator; b. Flint, Mich., Oct. 12, 1946; BS, Wayne State U., 1970, MD, 1971. Asst. program dir., orthop. resident Mich. State U., Kalamazoo Ctr. Med. Studies, 1993—2007, orthop. spine surgeon, 1993—, prof., surgery, Coll. Human Medicine, 2001—, prof., surgery, program dir., orthop. residency, 2007—. Fellow: Am. Acad. Orthop. Surgeons, Scoliosis Rsch. Soc.; mem.: Mich. Orthop. Soc., Clin. Orthop. Soc., Am. Orthop. Assn. Avocation: golf. Office: 1000 Oakland Dr Kalamazoo MI 49008 Office Fax: 269-337-6441. Business E-Mail: rowe@kcms.msu.edu.

ROWE, MICHAEL TERENCE, microbiologist; b. Belfast, Northern Ireland, Eng., July 14, 1953; s. Ann and Frank Rowe; children: Christopher George, Benjamin Michael. PhD, Queen's U. Belfast, 1982. Prin. sci. officer Agri-Food and Bioscis. Inst., Belfast, 1977—. Office: Agri-Food and Bioscis Inst Newforge Lane BT9 5PX Belfast England

ROWE, PETER STANLEY, nephrologist, educator; b. Crater, Oct. 1, 1954; BSc, Oxford Brookes U., Eng., 1977; PhD, U. Coll. London, 1981. MRC sr. rsch. fellow, hon. sr. lectr. U. Coll. London, 1981—2001; assoc. prof. U. Tex. Health Sci. Ctr. San Antonio, 2001—05; prof. with tenure U. Kans. Med. Ctr., 2005—. Rsch. grant, Children Cancer Rsch. Ctr., UTHSCSA, grant, NIH, NIDCR. Mem.: Bone Rsch. Soc., Endocrine Soc., Am. Physiol. Soc., Am. Soc. Nephrology, Am. Soc. Bone and Mineral Rsch. Office: University Kans Med Ctr Kansas City KS 66160 Office Fax: 913-588-9251. Business E-Mail: prowe@kumc.edu.

ROWE, VINCENT LOPEZ, physician, educator; b. LA, May 22, 1963; MD, U. Southern Calif., 1991. Assoc. prof. surgery Keck Sch. Medicine, U. Southern Calif., 1999—. Fellow: ACS. Office: 1520 San Pablo St Ste 4300 Los Angeles CA 90033 Office Fax: 323-442-5735. Business E-Mail: vincent.rowe@med.usc.edu.

ROWE, WILLIAM JOSEPH, internist; b. Cin., Oct. 31, 1927; s. Alvin Harold and Ida Claire (Omansky) R.; m. Mary Elaine Kenkel, Apr. 16, 1955. BS, U. Cin., 1950, MD, 1954. Diplomate Am. Bd. Internal Medicine. Asst. clin. prof. medicine Med. U. Ohio, Toledo, 1962—93; chmn. dept. medicine St. Vincent's Hosp., Toledo, 1979-83; chief adv. com. cardiac rehab. N.W. Ohio Heart Assn., Toledo, 1981-83. Del. citizen amb. program to China People to People, 1988. Contbr. articles to profl. jours., including Acta Astronautica, Lancet, Circulation. Capt. USAF, 1955-57. Fellow Brit. Interplanetary Soc.; mem. Nat. Space Soc. Republican. Achievements include research in describing only the second space syndrome, the Apollo 15 Space Syndrome; first to describe mechanisms for endothelial injuries of cardiovascular systems complicating extraordinary unremitting endurance exercise on earth or secondary to too little exercise and microgravity; show how inhalation of moon dust in the lunar module can cause severe hypertension; long space missions, gene therapy and the vital role of magnesium; research in how the international space station can be used to show used to show in experimental animals how the aging priocess may be offset by correcting magnesium deficits. Avocations: tennis, running, writing, travel. Home: 1485 Bremerton Ln Keswick VA 22947 Office Phone: 434-984-0079. Personal E-mail: rowerun@aol.com.

ROWEN, MARSHALL, radiologist; b. Chgo. s. Harry and Dorothy (Kasnow) R.; m. Helen Lee Friedman, Apr. 5, 1952; children: Eric, Scott, Mark. AB in Chemistry with highest honors, U. Ill., Urbana, 1951; MD with honors, U. Ill., Chgo., 1954, MS in Internal Medicine, 1954. Diplomate Am. Bd. Radiology. Intern Long Beach (Calif.) VA Hosp., 1955; resident in radiology Los Angeles VA Hosp., 1955-58; practice medicine specializing in radiology Orange, Calif., 1960—. Chmn. bd. dirs. Moran, Rowen and Dorsey, Inc., Radiologists, 1969—2002; asst. radiologist L.A. Children's Hosp., 1958; assoc. radiologist Valley Presbyn. Hosp., Van Nuys, Calif., 1960; dir. dept. radiology St. Joseph Hosp., Orange, 1961—2004, v.p. staff, 1972; dir. dept. radiology Children's Hosp. Orange County, 1964—2002, chief staff, 1977—78, v.p., 1978—83, v.p., trustee, 2008—10, 1993—98, 2000—06; asst. clin. prof. radiology U. Calif., Irvine, 1967—70, assoc. clin. prof., 1979—82, clin. prof. radiology and pediat., 1976—, pres. clin. faculty assn., 1980—81; trustee Choc. Padrinos; sec. Choco Health Svcs., 1987—89, v.p., 1990—93, trustee, 1995—, Found. Med. Care Orange County, 1972—76, Calif. Commn. Adminstrn. Svcs. Hosp., 1975—79, Profl. Practice Systems, 1990—92, Med. Splty. Mgrs., 1990—2004, St. Joseph Med. Corp., 1993—98; v.p. Found. Med. Care Children's Hosp., 1988—89; v.p., sr. v.p. St. Joseph Med. Corp. IPA, 1995—98; sr. v.p. Orange Coast Managed Care Svcs., 1995—98, Paragon Med. Imaging, 1993—2003, Calif. Managed Imaging, 1994—2009, Alliance Premier Hosps., 1995—96;

chmn. bd. dirs. Children's Healthcare Calif., 1995—2002, hon. chmn., bd. dirs., 2003—11, chair, investment com., 1995—2011; corp. bd. Blue Shield Calif., 1995—2006; mem. physician's rev. com. Blue Cross Calif., 1996—2011, mem. Blue Shield coun. advisors, 2001—07; trustee Children's Hosp. at Mission, 2004—09, sec. bd. dir., 2008—09, vice chair, 2009; cons. Imaging Adminstrn., 2005—; vice chair Childrens Healthcare Calif., 2003—, Choco Realty, bd. dir., 2008—11, chmn., 2010—11; Calif. dept. mgr. health care Patient Advocate Improvement Program, 2008—09; chmn. CRC Real Estate, 2008; bd. dir. CHOC/PSF Rsch. & Edn. Found., chmn., 2010—11; chair Fin. Comm., 2010—11; bd. dir. CHOC Found. Children, 2010—11. Mem. editl. bd. Western Jour. Medicine; contbr. articles to med. jours. Founder Orange County Performing Arts Ctr., mem. Laguna Art Mus., Laguna Festival of Arts, Opera Pacific, South Coast Reportory, Am. Ballet Theater, World Affairs Coun. Served to capt. M.C., U.S. Army, 1958-60. Recipient Rea sr. med. prize U. Ill, 1953; William Cook scholar U. Ill., 1951, Friend of Children award Children's Hosp. Guild, 1995, Charley award Children's Hosp., 1996, Outstanding Bd. Mem. Children's Hosp., 2010. Fellow Am. Coll. Radiology; mem. AMA, Am. Heart Assn., Soc. Nuclear Medicine (trustee 1961-62), Orange County Radiol. Soc. (pres. 1968-69), Calif. Radiol. Soc. (pres. 1978-79), Radiol. Soc. So. Calif. (pres. 1976), Pacific Coast Pediatric Radiologists Assn. (pres. 1971), Soc. Pediatric Radiology, Calif. Med. Assn. (chmn. sect. on radiology 1978-79), Orange County Med. Assn. (chmn. UCI liaison com. 1976-78), Cardioradiology Soc. So. Calif., Radiol. Soc. N.Am., Am. Roentgen Ray Soc., Am. Coll. Physician Execs., Center Club, Phi Beta Kappa, Phi Eta Sigma, Omega Beta Phi, Alpha Omega Alpha. Office: St Joseph Hosp 1100 W Stewart Dr Orange CA 92868 Home Phone: 714-349-8667. Personal E-mail: romarsh@aol.com.

ROWLAND, DIANE, foundation executive, health policy researcher; b. Bridgeport, Conn., Oct. 14, 1948; m. Brian L. Biles, Sept. 17, 1977. BA, Wellesley Coll., 1970; MPA, U. Calif., LA, 1973; SCD, Johns Hopkins U., 1987. Mem. staff U.S. House Rep., Washington, 1983—91; assoc. dir. Commonwealth Fund Commn. on Elderly People Living Alone, Balt., 1985—91; assoc. prof. Johns Hopkins U., Balt., 1987—93; exec. v.p. Kaiser Family Found., Washington, 1993—; fellow Acad. Health, 2002. Exec. dir. Kaiser Commn. on Future of Medicaid, Washington, 1991—98, Kaiser Commn. on Medicaid & the Uninsured, Washington, 1998—; pres. Assn. Health Svc. Rsch., Washington, 2000; mem. Sec. Task Force on Infant Mortality, Washington, 2000—. Contbr. articles to profl. jours. Fellow Brookdale Nat. fellow, Brookdale Found., 1987. Mem.: Inst. Medicine, 2004. Greek Orthodox. Avocations: travel, reading, sailing. Office: Henry J Kaiser Family Found 1330 G Street NW Washington DC 20005

ROWLAND, FRANK SHERWOOD, chemistry professor; b. Delaware, Ohio, June 28, 1927; m. Joan Lundberg, 1952; children: Ingrid Drake, Jeffrey Sherwood. AB, Ohio Wesleyan U., 1948; MS, U. Chgo., 1951, PhD, 1952, DSc (hon.), 1989, Duke U., 1989, Whittier Coll., 1989, Princeton U., 1990. Haverford Coll., 1992, Clark U. 1996, U. East Anglia, 1996, U. Urbino, Italy, 1998, Carleton Coll., 1998, Gustavus Adolphus Coll., 1997, Occidental Coll., 1998, Kanagawa U., Japan, 1999, LaTrobe U., Australia, 2000, U. Waterloo, Can., 2001, Ohio State U., 2002; LLD (hon.), Ohio Wesleyan U., 1989, Simon Fraser U., 1991, U. Calgary, 1997. Instr. chemistry Princeton U., NJ, 1952—56; asst. prof. chemistry U. Kans., 1956—58, assoc. prof., 1958—63, prof., 1963—64; prof. chemistry U. Calif., Irvine, 1964—, dept. chmn., 1964—70, Aldrich prof. chemistry, 1985—89, Bren rsch prof. chemistry, 1989—, Bren rsch prof. earth sys. sci. Vis. scientist Japan Soc. Promotion Sci., 1980; Humboldt sr. scientist Fed. Republic Germany, 1981; mem. acid rain peer rev. panel US Office Sci. Tech., The White House, 1982—84; mem. vis. com. Max Planck Inst., Heidelberg, Germany, 1982—96; ozone trends panel mem. NASA, 1986—88; chmn. Dahlem Conf. Changing Atmosphere, Germany, 1987; co-dir. western region Nat. Inst. Global Environ. Change, 1989—93; mem. Calif. Coun. Sci. Tech., 1989—95; del. Internat. Coun. Sci. Unions, 1993—98. Contbr. articles to profl. jours. Recipient John Wiley Jones award, Rochester Inst. Tech., 1975, Disting. Faculty Rsch. award, U. Calif., Irvine, 1976, Profl. Achievement award, U. Chgo., 1977, Alumni medal, 1997, Billard award, NY Acad. Sci., 1977, Tyler World Prize in Environ. Achievement, 1983, Dana award for Pioneering Achievements in Health, 1987, Wadsworth award, NY State Dept. Health, 1989, Japan prize in Environ. Sci., 1989, Dickson prize, Carnegie-Mellon U., 1991, Albert Einstein prize, World Cultural Coun., 1994, Nobel prize in chemistry, 1995, Nevada medal, 1997, Gold medal, Acad. Athens, 2003; named to, GTE Acad. All-Am. Hall of Fame, 2000; fellow Guggenheim Found., 1962, 1974. Fellow: AAAS (pres.-elect 1991, pres. 1992, chmn. bd. dirs. 1993), Am. Geophys. Union (Roger Revelle medal 1994), Am. Phys. Soc. (Leo Szilard award for physics in pub. interest 1979); mem.: NAS (mem. exec. com. 2000—02), Internat. Assn. Meteorology & Atmospheric Physics (hon. life), Royal Soc. London (fgn.), Inst. Medicine, Am. Philos. Soc., Am. Meteorol. Soc. (hon.), Korean Acad. Sci. Tech. (fgn. sec.), European Acad. Arts, Scis. & Humanities, Am. Chem. Soc. (chmn. divsn. nuclear sci. and tech. 1973—74, chmn. divsn. phys. chemistry 1974—75, Orange County award 1975, Tolman medal 1976, Zimmerman award 1980, Environ. Sci. & Tech. award 1983, Esselen award 1987, Peter Debye Phys. Chem. award 1993), Am. Acad. Arts & Scis., Sigma Xi, Phi Beta Kappa. Office: U Calif Irvine 571 Rowland Hall 2025 Irvine CA 92697-2025 Office Phone: 949-824-6016. Office Fax: 949-824-2905. E-mail: rowland@uci.edu.

ROWLAND, LEWIS PHILLIP, neurology professor, clinical investigator; b. Bklyn., Aug. 3, 1925; s. Henry Alexander and Cecile (Coles) Rowland; m. Esther Edelman Rowland, Aug. 31, 1952; children: Andrew Simon, Steven Samuel, Joy Rosenthal. BS, Yale U., New Haven, 1945; MD, Yale U. Sch. Medicine, 1948; PhD (hon.), U. Aix-Marseilles, France, 1986, U. Padua, Italy, 1996. Diplomate Am. Bd. Neurology. Intern neurology New Haven Hosp., 1949-50; asst. resident neurology NY Neurol. Inst./Columbia U. Med. Ctr., 1950-52, fellow, 1953; clin. assoc. neurology Nat. Inst. Neurol. Diseases & Blindness, NIH, Bethesda, Md., 1953-54; asst. to. prof. neurology Columbia U. Coll. Physicians & Surgeons, NYC, 1957—67, prof. dept. neurology, 1973—, chmn. dept. neurology, 1973-98; prof., chmn. dept. neurology U. Pa. Med. Sch., 1967-73. Assoc. physician neurology Montefiore Hosp., NYC, 1954—57; vis. fellow Nat. Inst.

Med. Rsch., London, 1956; asst. attending physician Columbia Presbyn. Med. Ctr., 1957—62, assoc. attending physician, 1962—67, dir. neurology svc., 1973—98; co-founder, co-dir. Neurol. Clin. Rsch. Ctr., Columbia Neurol. Inst., 1961—67, attending physician, 1973—, pres. med. bd., 1991—94; founder, co-dir. Eleanor & Lou Gehrig MDA/ALS Ctr., NYC, 1973—98; co-founder, co-dir. H. Houston Merritt Clin. Rsch. Ctr. Muscular Dystrophy & Related Diseases, Columbia U. Med. Ctr.; pres. Myasthenia Gravis Found., 1971—73, mem. med. adv. bd., Nat. Multiple Sclerosis Soc.; chmn. med. adv. bd. NYC Multiple Sclerosis Soc., 1977—92; pres. bd. dirs. Parkinson's Disease Found., 1979—; chmn. bd. sci. counselors Nat. Inst. Neurol. Disorders & Stroke, NIH, 1981—83, mem. nat. adv. coun., 1986—90. Author: NINDS at 50: Celebrating 50 Years of Brain Research, 2001, Legacy of Tracy J Putnam and H. Houston Merritt: Modern Neurology in the United States, 2008; editor: (med. textbooks) Merritt's Neurology, Amyotrophic Lateral Sclerosis (& Other Motor Neuron Diseases), Cerebral Hypoxia and Its Consequences; author: Current Neurologic Drugs; editor: Clinical Cases in Neurology; editor-in-chief Neurology, 1977—87, Neurology Today, 2001—, mem.editl. bd. Archives Neurology, 1968—76, Italian Jour. Neurol. Sci., 1979—99, Med. Letter, 1990—97, New Eng. Jour. Medicine, 1990—2000, Jour. Neuromuscular Disorders, 1991—97, Clin. Neurosci., 1995—98, Advances in Neurology, Handbook Clin. Neurology, Jour. Neurol. Sci. With USNR, 1942—44, with USPHS, 1953—54. Recipient Jerry Lewis award, Muscular Dystrophy Assn., 1993, Forbes Norris award, Internat. Alliance ALS/MND Associations, 2001, Lifetime Achievement award, Parkinson's Disease Found., 2008, NY State Neurol. Soc., 2011. Mem.: NAS, NYC Multiple Sclerosis Soc., Ea. Pa. Multiple Sclerosis Soc. (chmn. med. adv. bd. 1969—73), Assn. Univ. Professors Neurology (sec. 1971—74, pres. 1978), Assn. Rsch. Nervous Mental Disease (pres. 1969, v.p. 1980, chmn. bd. trustees 1992—98), Phila. Neurol. Soc. (pres. 1972), Am. Acad. Neurology (pres.-elect 1987—89, pres. 1989—91, past chmn. Edn. Rsch. Found., Sheil Essey rsch. award 1998), Am. Neurol. Assn. (hon.; pres. 1980, Geroge W. Jacoby award 1995). Office: Columbia U Med Ctr Neurological Inst 710 W 168th St New York NY 10032-2603 Office Phone: 212-305-8551. Business E-Mail: lpr1@columbia.edu.

ROWLAND, MICHAEL L., medical educator; b. Dayton, Ohio, Jan. 20, 1960; AB, Wittenberg U., 1978; PhD, Ohio State U., 1998. Asst. prof. Ohio State U. Coll. Dentistry, 2004—09, U. Louisville Sch. Medicine, 2009—. Home: Instructional Bldg B Rm 311W 50 Louisville KY 40202 Home Fax: 502-852-4038. Business E-Mail: michael.rowland@louisville.edu.

ROWLAND, NEIL E., psychology professor, department chairman; PhD. Prof., dept. psychology U. Fla., Gainesville, chmn., dept. psychology, 2007—. Contbr. articles to profl. jours. Office: Univ Fla Dept Psychology 330 Psychology Bldg PO Box 112250 Gainesville FL 32611-2250 Office Phone: 352-273-2178. Business E-Mail: nrowland@ufl.edu.

ROWLAND, THOMAS C., JR., retired obstetrician, retired gynecologist; b. Dawson, Ga., 1934; s. Thomas Clifford and Ethel (Cunningham) R.; m. Isabelle Hall, Aug. 3, 1957; children: Mary Hall Rowland Fagan, Thomas Clifford III. MA, U. S.C., 1955; MD, Med. U. S.C., 1959. Diplomate Am. Bd. Ob-Gyn. Intern Greenville Gen. Hosp., SC, 1959-60; resident in ob-gyn Nat. Naval Med. Ctr., Bethesda, Md., 1962-65; mem. staff Bapt. Med. Ctr., Columbia, SC, 1968—, chief ob-gyn svc., 1970, chief staff, 1979; clin. prof. ob-gyn U. SC Sch Medicine; clin. prof. ob.-gyn Med. U. SC, Charleston; pvt. practice ob.-gyn Palmetto Ob-Gyn, Columbia; ret., 2005. Mem. adv. bd. Nat. Bank S.C. Trustee Med. U. S.C., Charleston, 1981—, chmn. bd., 1990-94, 98-00. Fellow: ACOG (treas. 2000—03); mem.: AMA, S.C. Ob-Gyn. Soc. (pres.), So. Med. Assn. (pres.), South Atlantic Assn. Ob-Gyn. (pres.), Am. Fertility Soc., So. Gynecol. Soc. (chmn. bd. 1990—94, pres.).

ROWLANDS, DAVID THOMAS, pathology educator; b. Wilkes-Barre, Pa., Mar. 22, 1930; s. David Thomas and Anna Jule (Morgan) R.; m. Gwendolyn Marie York, Mar. 1, 1958; children: Julie Marie, Carolyn Jane. MD, U. Pa., 1955. Diplomate: Am. Bd. Pathology, Am. Bd. Allergy and Immunology. Intern Pa. Hosp., Phila., 1955-56; resident Cin. Gen. Hosp., 1956-60; asst. prof. U. Colo., 1962-64, Rockefeller U., 1964-66; assoc. prof. Duke U., Durham, NC, 1966-70; prof. pathology U. Pa., Phila., 1970-82, chmn. dept. pathology, 1973-78, prof. medicine, 1979-82; prof., chmn. dept. pathology U. So. Fla., Tampa, 1982-91, assoc. dean, 1983-84, prof. pediatrics, 1986-91; med. dir. Lifelink Tissue Bank, 1991-93. Mem. editorial bd.: Am. Jour. Pathology, 1971-81, Developmental and Comparative Immunology, 1977-79. Served with USNR, 1960-62. Recipient Lederle Med. Faculty award U. Colo., 1964, Jacob Ehrenzeller award Pa. Hosp., 1976 Mem. Am. Assn. Pathologists, Internat. Acad. Pathology, Am. Soc. Clin. Pathology, Am. Assn. Immunologists, Coll. Am. Pathologist, Arthur Purdy Stout Soc. Presbyterian. Home: 13804 Cypress Village Cir Tampa FL 33618-8406 Personal E-mail: drowland3@verizon.net.

ROWLETTE, HENRY ALLEN, JR., social worker, counseling psychologist; b. Phila., July 8, 1947; s. Henry Allen Sr. and Ophelia Alberta (Kilson) R.; m. Geraldine Lee Stevens, Mar. 1972 (div. Mar. 1986); children: Cessandra N., Deaeon D., Christiene A.; m. Carolyn Rowlette; 1 child, Janetta M.; m. Ann Laura Rowe, Mar. 19, 1989. BA, Cheyney State Coll., 1970; MEd, Boston U., 1981; MSW, Temple U., 1988; PhD, Suffield Coll. and U., 2003. Cert. sch. social worker, NJ; lic. clin. social worker; diplomate Am. Psychotherapy Assn., Nat. Bd. Cognitive Behavioral Therapists; ordained minister Bapt. Ch. Cardiac monitor technician Bapt. Med. Ctr., Little Rock, 1982-83; mental health technician The Horsham Clinic, Ambler, Pa., 1984; psychiat. technician The Lower Bucks Hosp., Bristol, Pa., 1984-90; mental health technician The Helene Fuld Med. Ctr., Trenton, NJ, 1988-90, psychiat. social worker, 1988-92; profl. sch. social worker The Willingboro Sch. Dist., NJ, 1990—96. Dist. crisis intervention team Willingboro Sch. Dist., 1994-96; therapist The NJ State Prison, Trenton, 1996-98, The Southwoods State Prison, Bridgeton, NJ; clinician Kennedy Meml. Health Ctr., Cherry Hill, NJ, 1998—, The Lumberton Schs./Sch. Social Worker, Lumberton, NJ, 1998; behavioral cons. Founds. Behavioral Health, Willow Grove, Pa., 1999; mental health technician The Children's Hosp. Phila., 1999-2000.

Clin. social worker Phila. Prison System, 2000; mem. NAACP, Trenton, 1990. With US Army, 1971-79. Mem. NASW, Am. Assn. Christian Counselors, Omega Psi Phi (Delta Upsilon chpt.), Phi Delta Kappa (Trenton chpt.), Am. Psychotherapy Assn., Nat. Bd. Cognitive Behavioral Therapists, Nat. Bd. Addiction Examiners, Nat. Assn. Forensic Counselors. Democrat. Baptist. Avocations: fishing, reading, computer technology/games. Home: 18 Foxchase Dr Burlington NJ 08016-3044 Office Phone: 609-953-5608. Personal E-mail: drhrowlettejr@comcast.net.

ROWLEY, BEVERLEY DAVIES, sociologist; b. Antioch, Calif., July 28, 1941; d. George M. and Eloise Davies; m. Richard B. Rowley, Apr. 1, 1966 (div. 1983). BS, Colo. State U., 1963; MA, U. Nev., 1975; PhD, Union Inst., 1983. Social worker Nev. Dept. Pub. Welfare, Reno, 1963—65, Santa Clara County Dept. Welfare, San Jose, Calif., 1965—66; field dir. Sierra Sage coun. Camp Fire Girls, Sparks, Nev., 1966—70; program coord. divsn. health scis. Sch. Medicine U. Nev., 1976—78, program coord., health analyst office rural health, 1978—84, acting dir. office rural health, 1982—84; exec. asst. to pres. Med. Coll. of Hampton Rds., Norfolk, Va., 1984—87; rsch. mgr. Office Med. Edn. Info. AMA, Chgo., 1987—88, dir. dept. data systems, 1988-91; dir. med. edn. Maricopa Med. Ctr., Phoenix, 1991—99; pres. Med. Edn. and Rsch. Assocs., Inc., Phoenix, Chgo., 1999—, Med. Edn. & Rsch. Assocs., Tempe, Ariz., 1999—; vis. prof. Ariz. State U. East, Mesa, 1999—2000, profl. and personal coach, 2004—; pres., exec. dir. Maricopa Med. Found., Phoenix, 2004—; adj. prof. sociology Scottsdale CC, Ariz., 2010—. Various positions as adj. prof. and lectr. in health scis. U. Nev. Sch. of Medicine, 1972-75; lectr. dept. family and cmty. medicine U. Nev., 1978-84; asst. dir., evaluator Health Careers for Am. Indians Programs, 1978-84; cons. Nev. Statewide Health Survey, 1979-84; interim dir. Health Max, 1985-86; asst. prof. dept. family and cmty. medicine Med. Coll. of Hampton Rds., Norfolk, Va., 1985-87. Editor of five books; contbr. numerous articles to profl. jours. Mem. Am. Sociol. Assn., Nat. Rural Health Assn. (bd. dirs. 1986-88), Assn. Behavioral Sci. and Med. Edn. (pres. 1986), Assn. Am. Med. Colls. (exec. coun. 1993-95), Coun. Acad. Scis. (adminstrv. bd. 1992-97), Assn. Hosp. Med. Edn. (bd. dirs. 1997—), Delta Delta Delta. Achievements include development of three computer systems including AMA-FREIDA; four internet-based educational programs for physicians. Avocations: hiking, skiing, gardening, sewing, ceramics. Office: MERA Inc 1903 E Sarah Ln Tempe AZ 85284-3430 E-mail: bdr@merainc.com.

ROWLEY, JANET DAVISON, physician; b. NYC, Apr. 5, 1925; d. Hurford Henry and Ethel Mary (Ballantyne) Davison; m. Donald A. Rowley, Dec. 18, 1948; children: Donald, David, Robert, Roger. PhB, U. Chgo., 1944, BS, 1946, MD, 1948; DSc (hon.), U. Ariz., 1989, U. Pa., 1989, Knox Coll., 1991, U. So. Calif., 1992, St. Louis U., 1997, St. Xavier U., 1999, Oxford U., Eng., 2000, Lund U., Sweden, 2003, Dartmouth U., 2004; degree (hon.), U. Calif. San Francisco, 2008; DSc, Lake Forest Coll. Harvard, 2008. Diplomate Am. Bd. Med. Genetics. Rsch. asst. U. Chgo., 1949—50; intern Marine Hosp., USPHS, Chgo., 1950—51; attending physician Infant Welfare and Prenatal Clinics Dept. Pub. Health, Montgomery County, Md., 1953—54; rsch. fellow Levinson Found., Cook County Hosp., Chgo., 1955—61; clin. instr. neurology U. Ill., Chgo., 1957—61; USPHS spl. trainee Radiobiology Lab. The Churchill Hosp., Oxford, England, 1961—62; rsch. assoc. dept. medicine and Argonne Cancer Rsch. Hosp. U. Chgo., 1962—69, assoc. prof. dept. medicine, 1969—77, prof. dept. medicine and Franklin McLean Meml. Rsch. Inst., 1977—84, Blum-Riese Disting. Svc. prof., dept. medicine and dept. molecular genetics and cell biology, 1984—, Blum-Riese Disting. Svc. prof. dept. human genetics, 1997—, interim dep. dean for sci. biol. scis. divsn., 2001—02; vis. prof. World Class U. Project, Republic of Korea. Bd. sci. counsellors Nat. Inst. Dental Rsch., NIH, 1972—76, chmn., 1974—76; mem. Nat. Cancer Adv. Bd., Nat. Cancer Inst., 1979—84, Nat. Adv. Coun. for Human Genome Rsch. Inst., 1999—2004; adv. com. Frederick Cancer Rsch. Facility, 1983—84; bd. sci. counsellors Nat. Human Genome Rsch. Inst., NIH, 1994—99, chmn., 1994—97; adv. bd. Howard Hughes Med. Inst., 1989—94, MD Anderson Cancer Ctr., 1998—2005; vis. com. dept. applied biol. scis. MIT Corp., 1983—86; bd. sci. cons. Meml. Sloan-Kettering Cancer Ctr., 1988—90; adv. com. Ency. Britannica U. Chgo., 1988—96; Presdl. Symposium Am. Soc. Pediatric Hematology/Oncology, 1995; chmn. sci. adv. com. Translational Genomics Rsch. Inst., Phoenix., 2004—; med. adv. bd. Calif. Inst. Regenerative Medicine, 2005—; mem. sci. adv. coun. Children's Hosp., Boston, 2005—. Co founder co editor: Genes, Chromosomes and Cancer, mem. editl. bd.: Oncology Rsch., Cancer Genetics and Cytogenetics Leukemia Rsch., Internat. Jour. Hematology, Genomics, Leukemia; past mem. editl. bd. Internat. Jour. Cancer, Blood, Cancer Rsch., Hematol. Oncology, Leukemia Rsch.; contbr. chapters to books, articles to profl. jours. Adv. com. for career awards in biomed. scis. Burroughs Wellcome Fund, 1994—98; selection panel for Clin. Sci. award Doris Duke Charitable Found., 2000—02, 2006; mem. Pres.'s Adv. Coun. on Bioethics, 2001—09; mem. med. rsch. material command leukemia program U.S. Army, 2002—04; mem. selection com. Rosalind Franklin young investigator award, 2004, 2007—, 2009; nat. adv. com. McDonnell Found. Program for Molecular Medicine in Cancer Rsch., 1988—98; adv. bd. Leukemia Soc. Am., 1979—84; selection com. scholar award in biomed. sci. Lucille P. Markey Charitable Trust, 1984—87; trustee Adler Planetarium, Chgo., 1978—; med. adv. bd. G&P Charitable Found., 1999—. Recipient Esther Langer award, Ann Langer Cancer Rsch. Found., 1983, First Kuwait Cancer prize, 1984, A. Cressy Morrison award in natural scis., NY Acad. Scis., 1985, Past State Pres. award, Tex. Fedn. Bus. & Profl. Women's Clubs, 1986, Karnofsky award and lecture, Am. Soc. Clin. Oncology, 1987, Antoine Lacassagne Lique prize, Nat. Francaise Contre le Cancer prize, 1987, Katherine Berkan Judd award, Meml. Sloan-Kettering Cancer Ctr., 1989, Steven C. Beering award, U. Ind. Med. Sch., 1992, Robert de Villiers award, Leukemia Lymphoma Soc., 1993, Return of the Child award., 2005, Kaplan Family prize for cancer rsch. excellence, Oncology Soc. Dayton, 1995, Cotlove award and lecture, Acad. Clin. Lab. Physicians and Scientists, 1995, Nilsson-Ehle lecture, Mendelian Soc. and Royal Physiographic Soc., 1995, Gairdner Found. Internat. award, 1996, Medal of Honor, Basic Sci. American Cancer Soc., 1996, Nat. Medal of Sci., The White House, 1998, Lasker-DeBakey Clin. Med. Rsch. award, Lasker Found., 1998, Woman Extraordinaire award, Internat. Women's Assocs., 1999, Golden Plate award, Am. Acad. Achievement, 1999, Women Achieving Excellence award, YWCA of Met. Chgo., 2000, Philip Levine award, Am. Soc. Clin. Pathology, 2001, Emile M Chamot award, State Microscopy Soc. Ill., 2001, Mendel medal, Villanova U., 2003, Benjamin Franklin medal, American Philos. Soc., 2003, Dist. Alumni Award, U. Chgo., 2003, Norman McLean Mentorship award, 2006, Medal, Lake Forest Coll., Harvard, 2008, Award for Excellence, Assn. Molecular Pathology, 2007, Disting. Scientist award, American Assn. Cancer Inst., 2009, Peter & Patricia Gruber Found. Genetics Prize, 2009, Presdl. Medal of Freedom, The White House, 2009; co-recipient King Faisal Internat. prize in medicine, 1988, Charles Mott prize, GM Cancer Rsch. Found., 1989, Pearl Meister Greengard prize, Rockefeller U., 2010; named Chicagoan of Yr., Chgo. mag., 1998. Fellow: AAAS (nominating com. 1998); mem.: NAS (chmn. sect. 41 1995—99, mem. com. 2004, Jessie Stevenson Kovalenko medal 2010), Chgo. Network (lectr. 2003—), Inst. Medicine (coun. 1988—90), Cancer Rsch. (G.H.A. Clowes Meml. award 1989, Charlotte Friend award 2003, Dorothy P. Landon award 2005), American Soc. Hematology (lectr. Millenium Symposium 1999, Presdl. Symposium 1982, Dameshek prize 1982, Ham-Wasserman award 1995, Henry M. Stratton medal 2003, Marion Spencer Fay Lifetime Achievement award 2006), Genetical Soc., American Soc. Human Genetics (pres.-elect 1992, pres. 1993, Allen award and lectr. 1991, Disting. Sci. lectr. 2003), American Philos. Soc., American Acad. Arts & Sciences (nominating com. 1998), Phi Beta Kappa (hon.), Sigma Xi (William Proctor prize for sci. achievement 1989), Alpha Omega Alpha (hon.). Episcopalian. Home: 5310 S University Ave Chicago IL 60615-5106 Office: U Chgo 5841 S Maryland Ave MC 2115 Chicago IL 60637-1463 Office Phone: 773-702-6117. Business E-Mail: jrowley@medicine.bsd.uchicago.edu.

ROWLINGSON, JOHN CLYDE, anesthesiologist, physician, educator; b. Syracuse, NY, Aug. 3, 1948; s. John Winthrop and Genevieve Estelle (Mahan) R.; m. Rosemary Colette Laney, Oct. 26, 1974 (div. 1992); children: Kristen, Andrew; m. Karen Wheeler, Aug. 4, 2001; stepchild, Isaac. BS, Allegheny Coll., 1970; MD, SUNY, Buffalo, 1974. Intern Millard Fillmore Hosp., Buffalo, 1974-75; resident in anesthesiology U. Va., Charlottesville, 1975-77; fellow in anesthesia pain mgmt. U. Va. Med. Ctr., 1977-78; asst. prof. anesthesiology U. Va. Sch. Medicine, Charlottesville, 1978-82, assoc. prof., 1982-86, prof., 1986—, Cosmo A. DiFazio prof. anesthesiology, 2005. Assoc. dir. Pain Mgmt. Ctr., U. Va. Health Sci. Ctr., 1978-79, dir., 1980-98, dir. acute pain svc., Acad. Disting. Educators, 1987-2007. Author: Regional Anesthesia, 1984; co-editor: Handbook of Critical Care Pain Management, 1993. Recipient Nils Lofgren award ASTRA, 1999; Nat. Inst. Handicapped Rsch. fellow, 1983-87, Pain fellow 1977-78. Fellow Am. Coll. Anesthesiology; mem. Am. Soc. Anesthesiologists, Am. Soc. Regional Anesthesia (rsch. grantee 1977, pres. 1996-97, recipient Disting. Svc. award 2007, Bonica Lectr., 2007), Am. Pain Soc., Internat. Assn. Study of Pain, Am. Acad. Pain Medicine (editl. bd. Anesthesia Analg 1996 , Reg. Anesthesia and Pain Medicine, 1997—), Va. Soc. Anesthesiology (sec, treas. 2005-07, pres. 2009-). Methodist. Avocations: running, tennis, skiing, biking. Home: 5006 Lake Tree Ln Crozet VA 22932 Office: U Va Hlth Sys Health Sci Ctr Anesthesiology PO Box 800710 Charlottesville VA 22908-0710 Home Phone: 434-823-9626; Office Phone: 434-924-2283. Business E-Mail: jcr3t@virginia.edu.

ROXO, PERSIO, JR., medical educator; b. Sao Paulo, Brazil, July 31, 1965; PhD, U. Sao Paulo, 1988. Prof. Faculty Medicine Ribeirao Preto-U. Sao Paulo, 2008—. Office: Ave Bandeirantes, 3900 Ribeirao Preto Sao Paulo 14049-900 Botswana Business E-Mail: persiorj@fmrp.usp.br.

ROY, HEMANT KUMAR, gastroenterologist, researcher; b. Calcutta, West Bengal, India, Dec. 30, 1964; s. Hirendra and Meena Roy; m. Urbi Ghosh, Dec. 30, 1993; children: Priya, Anjuli. BS, Vanderbilt U., Nashville, 1985; MD, Northwestern U., Chgo., 1989. Asst. prof. U. Nebr. Med. Ctr., Omaha, 1995—2002; assoc. prof. Northwestern U., Evanston, Ill., 2002—. Dep. editor: Archives Internal Medicine. Recipient Career Devel. award, Am. Soc. Clin. Oncology, 1996—99; grantee, Glaxo Inst. Digestive Health, 1997, NIH, 2004—. Mem.: Am. Coll. Gastroent. (rsch. com. 2000). Achievements include research in light scattering as a screening test for colon cancer. *

ROY, MANOJIT, research scientist; b. India, Sept. 4, 1967; PhD, Pune U., India. Rsch. scientist Howard Hughes Med. Inst., U. Mich., 2010—. Mem.: Soc. Conservation Biology, Ecol. Soc. America, Nature Conservancy. Avocation: reading. Office: 830 N University 2014 Kraus Bldg Ann Arbor MI 48109 Business E-Mail: roym@umich.edu.

ROY, PRANAB, biochemist; b. Calcutta, India, Sept. 12, 1950; s. Dhananjoy and Labanya (Adhya) Roy; m. Indrani Dey, May 8, 1977; 1 child, Kamala. BSc, Presidency Coll., Calcutta, 1970; MSc, IIT, New Delhi, India, 1973; PhD, Bose Inst., Calcutta, 1977. Postdoctoral assoc. Yale U., New Haven, Conn., 1978-80; postdoctoral fellow U. Conn., Farmington, 1980-82; lectr. Bose Inst., Calcutta, 1982-86; scientist Hind Lever Ltd., Bombay, 1986-95; biochemist Tea Rsch. Assn., Jorhat, India, 1995-96; dep. gen. mgr. Tata Tea Ltd., Calcutta, India, 1996—. Vis. scientist Unilever Rsch. Vlaardingen, 1990-91, Plant Breeding Internat., Cambridge, Eng., 1991; founder prof. dept. biotech. Burdwan U., West Bengal, India. Author: Subcellular Biochemistry, 1978; contbr. 40 articles to profl. jours. Mem. N.Y. Acad. scis., Indian Sci. Congress Assn., Soc. Biol. Chemists (life). Democrat. Hindu. Avocations: playing tabla, billiards, music, travel, reading. Home: 19A Linton St Kolkata WestBengal 700014 India Office: Burdwan University Dept Biotech Burdwan West Bengal 713104 India

ROY, ROB J., biomedical engineer, anesthesiologist, educator; b. Bklyn., Jan. 2, 1933; m. Carole Ann Apmann, Aug. 1, 1959 (div.); children: Robert Bruce, David John, Bruce Glenn; m. Judith Anne Webb, Oct. 6, 1996. BSEE, Cooper Union, NYC, 1954; MSEE, Columbia U., 1956; DEngSc, Rensselaer Poly. Inst., 1962; MD, Albany Med. Coll., NY, 1976. Profl. engr., N.Y.; diplomate Am. Bd. Anesthesiology. Prof. elec. engrin. dept. Rensselaer Poly. Inst., Troy, N.Y., 1962, prof. elec. engring. dept., 1980—, head biomed. engring. dept., 1985-94; prof. anesthesiology Albany (N.Y.) Med. Ctr., 1979—. Author: State Variables for Engineers, 1965, 2d edit., 1998; author over 200 papers in field. Mem.: IEEE (life), Am. Soc. Anesthesiologists, Sigma Xi. Office: Albany Med Ctr Dept Anesthesiology 47 New Scotland Ave Albany NY 12208-3412 E-mail: royr@rpi.edu, robjroy@att.net.

ROY, ROBERT RUSSELL, toxicologist; b. Mpls., Sept. 14, 1957; s. Rudolph Russell and Arlene Charlotte (Miller) R.; m. Barbara Jane Richie, Oct. 10, 1987; children: Andrew, Katherine. BA cum laude, Augsburg Coll., 1980; MS, U. Minn., 1986, PhD, 1989. Bd. cert. in toxicology. Toxicologist, project mgr. Pace Labs., Inc., Mpls., 1989-90; toxicologist Minn. Dept. Health, Mpls., 1990-93, Minn. Regional Poison Ctr., St. Paul, 1990-97; team leader, toxicology specialist 3M, St. Paul, 1997—, sr. toxicology specialist, 2000—. Lectr. U. Minn., Mpls., 1986-90, Midwest Ctr. Occupl. Health and Safety, St. Paul, 1990—, instr., 1989; adj. assoc. prof. U. Minn., 1993—; grad. faculty toxicology and pub. health U. Minn. Active Mt. Carmel Luth. Ch. Coun., Mpls., 1983-85. Mem. Soc. Toxicology, Am. Indsl. Hygiene Assn., Mt. Calvary Luth. Ch. (Excelsior, Minn.), Delta Omega. Home: 6301 Oxbow Bend Chanhassen MN 55317-9110 Office: Corp Toxicology 3 M Ctr Bldg 220-6E-03 Saint Paul MN 55144-1000 Business E-Mail: rroy@mmm.com.

ROYAL, HENRY DUVAL, nuclear medicine physician, educator, director; b. Norwich, Conn., May 14, 1948; BS, Providence Coll., 1970; MD, St. Louis U., 1974. Diplomate Am. Bd. Internal Medicine; Am. Bd. Nuclear Medicine. Intern R.I. Hosp., Providence, 1974, resident in internal medicine, 1975-76; resident in nuclear medicine Harvard Med. Sch., Boston, 1977-79; from assoc. to staff physician Barnes Hosp., St. Louis, 1987—; from assoc. to cons. staff physician Children's Hosp., St. Louis, 1987—; prof. nuclear medicine Washington U., St. Louis, 1993—; exec. dir. Am. Bd. Nuc. Medicine, St. Louis, 2004—. Co-team leader health effects sect. Internat. Atomic Energy Agy. Internat. Chernobyl Project, 1990; mem. com. on assessment of CDC radiation studies NRC/NAS, 1993-98; mem. sci. com. 1 and 4 Nat. Coun. on Radiation Protection and Measurements, 1993—; mem. coun. Nat. Coun. on Radiation Protection, 1996—, bd. dirs., 2000-05; adv. com. environ. hazards Vets., 1997—; bd. dirs. Am. Bd. Med. Specialties, 2005—. Contbr. articles to profl. jours. Mem.: Soc. Nuc. Medicine (v.p. 2002, pres. 2003), Alpha Omega Alpha. Office. W Pavilion B Rm 961 Box 8223 Washington Univ 660 S Euclid Ave Saint Louis MO 63110 Office Phone: 314-362-2809. Business E-Mail: royalh@mir.wustl.edu. *

ROY-BURMAN, ARUP, pediatrician; s. Pradip and Sumitra Roy-Burman; m. Sheila Dianne Jenkins; children: Sophia Anjali, Sage Milan, Sachin Keene. BA, U. Calif., Berkeley; MD, U. Calif., San Francisco. Diplomate in pediat. critical care medicine Am. Bd. Pediat. Assoc. clin. prof. pediat. U. Calif., San Francisco; pediat. intensivist Children's Hosp. & Rsch. Ctr., Oakland, Calif.; former pres. Children's Critical Care Med. Group, Inc., Oakland; chair Northern Calif. Pediat. Intensive Care Network, Oakland; med. dir. PED ICU UCSF, dir.transport access outreach. Co-founder and former dir. Roatan Vol. Pediat. Clinic, Coxen Hole, Honduras. Chair Global Healing, Berkeley, Calif. Named Best Doctors in America. Fellow: Am. Acad. Pediat., mem.: Soc. Critical Care Medicine, Phi Beta Kappa. Office: University Calif San Francisco 505 parnassus Ave M 680 San Francisco CA 94143 Office Phone: 415-476-5153.

ROY-BURMAN, PRADIP, molecular biology and virology educator; b. Comilla, Bengal, India, Nov. 12, 1938; came to U.S., 1963; s. Prafulla Nath and Mrinalini (Barman) Roy-Burman; m. Sumitra Ghosh, Nov. 26, 1963. BSc. with honors, Calcutta U., India, 1956, MSc., 1958, PhD, 1963. Rsch. assoc. dept. biochemistry Sch. of Medicine U. So. Calif., LA, 1963-66, Dernham sr. rsch. fellow in oncology Am. Cancer Soc., 1966-71, asst. prof. dept. biochemistry, 1967-72, assoc. prof. dept. pathology and biochemistry, 1972-78, prof. dept. pathology and biochemistry and molecular biology, 1978—, vice chmn. dept. pathology, 1987—2003. Interim chmn. dept. molecular microbiology and immunology, U. So. Calif., L.A., 1995-97, vis. prof. Med. U. Innsbruck, Austria, 2008; mem. pathology B study sect., NIH, 1990-94, 99-2003, reviewers res., 1994-98, 2005—, ad hoc mem. sci. tech. rev. bd. biomed. behavioral rsch. facilities NCRR, NIH, 1997—, prostate cancer rsch. program review panel, Dept. of Def., 2001—; chmn. NIH, ad hoc mem. TPM study seciton, 2006—, NCI Spl. Emphasis Rev. Panels, 1998—, European Comm. Program, 2006-05; symposium chmn. Internat. Congress Biochem. Molecular Biology, 1994; symposium co-chmn. Internat. Cancer Congess, 1994, chmn. workshop on pathogenesis of animal retrovirus, session immune interaction, 1996, 5th Internat. Symposium Hormonal Carcinegenesis, 2006; session chair Internat. Soc. Cell, Gene Therapy, 2007;sci. adv. bd. 6th Internat. Symp. Hormonal Oncogenesis, 2010; spkr. in field. Author (with others) books; contbr. articles to profl. jours.; book reviewer; inventor novel transcription regulatory elements for gene transfer vectors, mouse models for human prostate cancer, others; mem. editl. bd. Hematological Oncology, 1987—97, Cancer Biology and Therapy, 2001—, Jour. Cell Comm. Sign, 2007-, Hormonal Oncogenesis, 2007-. Rsch. grantee Am. Cancer Soc., NIH, Am. Diabetes Assn., Wright Found., Martell Found. Mem. Am. Soc. Microbiology, Am. Soc. Biol. Chemists and Molecular Biology, Am. Assn. Cancer Rsch., Am. Soc. Investigative Pathology, Internat. Assn. Comparative Rsch. on Leukemia and Related Diseases. Democrat. Hindu. Avocations: writing, hiking, golf. Office: Keck Sch Of Medicine HMR 210B 2011 Zonal Ave Los Angeles CA 90033 Office Phone: 323-442-1184. Business E-Mail: royburma@usc.edu.

ROYCE, MELANIE, oncologist, educator; b. Philippines, Aug. 21, 1961; MD, U. Cin. Sch. Medicine, 1994, PhD. Prof. medicine UNM Cancer Ctr., 2004—. Dir., breast multidisciplinary program & clinic UNM Cancer Ctr., 2004. Recipient Ann. Governors award, NM Commn. Status Women, Spirit Hope award, Nancy Floyd Haworth Found.; named Americas Top Physicians, Consumers Rsch. Coun. America, Americas Top Oncologists; named one of Best Doctors, Best Doctors, Inc. Mem.: AAAS, Am. Soc. Cell Biology, Am. Soc. Clin. Oncology, Am. Assn. Cancer Rsch. Office: 1201 Camino De Salud NE Albuquerque NM 87131 Business E-Mail: mroyce@salud.unm.edu.

ROYCE, PAUL CHADWICK, healthcare administrator; b. Mpls., July 2, 1928; BA, U. Minn., 1948, MD, 1952; PhD, We. Res. U., 1959. Diplomate Am. Bd. Internal Medicine. Intern U. Chgo. Clinics, 1952-53; fellow We. Res. U., Cleve., 1953—54, 1956—59; resident internal medicine Bronx Mcpl. Hosp., NYC, 1959-61; asst. prof. of medicine Albert Einstein Coll. of Med., NYC, 1961-69; sr. staff endocrinologist Guthrie Clinic, Sayre, Pa., 1970-81; assoc. prof. of medicine Hahnemann Med. Sch., Phila., 1973-81; emeritus prof. medicine Med. Coll. Pa./Hahnemann U., 1996—; dean and prof. clin. sci. and physiology Sch. Medicine U. Minn., Duluth, 1981-87; sr. v.p., clin. dir. Monmouth Med. Ctr., Long Branch, NJ, 1987-94; med. dir. The Segal Co. N.Y., 1995-98; prin. Royce Assocs., 1995—; tutor Writing Ctr., Monmouth U., NJ, 2001—03. Producer, host TV prgram Doctors on Call, 1983-87 (Nat. Friends of Pub. Broadcasting Hill award 1987), Author: Evoking Spirits, 2008 Lt. Med. USNR, 1954-56. Fellow, NSF, 1953—54, 1956—58, Upjohn Found., 1958—59. Mem. Am. Physiol. Soc., Physicians for Social Responsibility, Sigma Xi, Alpha Omega Alpha. Avocations: skiing, bicycling, canoeing. Personal E-mail: paul.royce1@verizon.net.

ROY-CHOWDHURY, JAYANTA, medical geneticist, educator; b. Kolkata, India, July 23, 1943; MBBS, Med. Coll., Kolkata, 1965. Prof. Albert Einstein Coll. Medicine, NYC, 1988—, sci. dir., gene therapy core facility, dir., cell culture and genetic engring. core, Marion Bessin Liver Ctr., 1988—. Photographer (exhibitions) Acad. Fine Arts, Kolkata; contbr. numerous articles to profl. jours., chapters to books. Recipient Alex Mowat award, Brit. Liver Trust, Spl. Svc. award, Am. Liver Found. Fellow: Am. Gastroent. Assn.; mem.: RCP (UK), Harvey Soc. (NY), NY Acad. Sci., Am. Assn. Study of Liver Diseases, Assn. Am. Physicians. Avocations: photography, painting. Office: 1300 Morris Park Ave Bronx NY 10461 Office Fax: 718-430-8975. Business E-Mail: jayanta.roy-chowdhury@einstein.yu.edu.

ROYE, DAVID P., JR., pediatric orthopaedic surgeon; b. Muskogee, Okla., Dec. 10, 1946; m. Carol Roye; 6 children. BA, U. Okla., Norman, 1971; MD, Columbia U. Coll. Physicians & Surgeons, 1975. Diplomate Am. Bd. Orthop. Surgery, AMA, Nat. Bd. Medicine, lic. NY, NJ, Conn., Ont., Can. Intern gen. surgery Roosevelt Hosp., NYC, 1975—76; resident orthop. surgery Columbia-Presbyn. Med. Ctr./NY Orthop. Hosp., 1976—78, jr. fellow orthop. surgery, 1978—79; fellowship pediat. orthop. surgery Hosp. for Sick Children, U. Toronto, 1979—80, St. Giles prof. pediat. orthop. surgery Columbia U. Coll. Physicians & Surgeons, 1980—; attending orthop. surgeon, dir. pediat. orthops. Children's Hosp. NY/Columbia-Prespyn. Med. Ctr., 1980—. Cons. med. staff, dept. orthop. surgery Helen Hayes Hosp., Greenwich Hosp., White Plains Hosp.; mem. alumni assn., awards com., devel. com. Columbia U. Coll. Physicians & Surgeons. Contbr. articles to profl. jours. Vol. cons. Healing the Children, Butler, NJ, Ea. Christian Children's Retreat, Wyckoff, NJ; vol. Children of China Pediat. Found., NY; vol. ops. com. Operation Smile, Norfolk, Va. Named one of America's Top Dr.'s, Castle Connolly Med. Ltd.; named to NY Mag.'s Best Dr.'s NY. Fellow: Orthop. Rsch. Soc., Scoliosis Rsch. Soc., Am. Acad. Cerebral Palsy and Devel. Medicine, Am. Acad. Pediat., NY Acad. Medicine, Am. Acad. Orthop. Surgeons (sec.); mem.: Am. Acad. Orthop. Surgeons Humanitarian of Leak, Pediat. Orthop. Soc. N. Am. (fin. com., Robert N. Hensiger Clin. Sci. award 2006), Am. Orthop. Soc., Am. Orthop. Assn., European Pediat. Orthop. Soc., Academic Orthop. Assn., Am. Bd. Orthop. Surgery (bd. examiners), Spine Club NYC, N. Am. Spine Soc., Pediat. Orthop. Club NY. Office: Childrens Hosp Columbia Presbyn Med Ctr 3959 Broadway Ste BHN 800 New York NY 10032 Office Phone: 212-305-5475. Office Fax: 212-305-8271.

ROYLE, JOHN PETERSON, vascular surgeon, educator; b. Glenhuntly, Victoria, Australia, July 12, 1934; s. John Eldred R. and Selena Lavinia Petersen; m. Pamela Ann More, Feb. 6, 1960; children: David, Susan, Jennifer, Julia MB, BS, U. Melbourne, Australia, 1957; AM (hon.), Acad. Medicine Malaysia, Kuala Lumpur, 1995. Lectr. prof. surg. unit St. Bartholomew's Hosp., London, 1964—65; acting prof. surgery U. Melbourne, 1971, assoc. prof. surgery, 1999—; surgeon Queen Elizabeth II, 1988; sr. vascular surgeon Austin & Repatriation Med. Ctr., Melbourne, 1977—81, dir. vascular surgery unit, 1981—2000, dir. gastroenterology, gen. surgery, vascular surgery unit, 1996—2002. Mem. fed. govt. task force on adverse events in hosps. Commonwealth Australia, Canberra, 1995-96; mem. medicare svcs. adv. com. endoluminal grafting, Canberra, 1999; prof. vascular surgery Shanghai Med. U., 1989; spl. advisor vascular surgery Govt. Tasmania, 2003; mem. surg. cons. coun. Govt. Victoria, 2001—, rural surgery task force, 2006-09. Co-author: (with W. Burnett) Multiple Choice Questions in the Basic Medical Sciences, 1978, (with V.C. Marshall) Multiple Choice Questions in Basic Surgical Sciences, 1985; prodr. (ednl. film on HIV/AIDS) Old Dogs and New Tricks, 1995 (cert. ednl. merit Brit. Med. Assn. Festival for Ednl. Videos 1995), Profunda Femoris Stenosis, 1971 (Bronze award Brit. Med. Assn. Film Competition 1971) Rep. ministerial task force on day surgery Victorian Govt., Melbourne, Australia, 1987; bd. dirs. Brockhoff Found., Melbourne, 1998— Recipient Rsch. award European Soc. Vascular Surgery, 1997, medal, Leader Australia Mc Queens Buttday Hon. List. Fellow Royal Australasian Coll. Surgeons (hon. treas. 1991-93, v.p. 1993-95, pres. 1995-96), ACS, Royal Coll. Surgeons Eng. (Hunterian professorship 1984), Royal Coll. Surgeons Edinburgh; mem. Internat. Soc. Cardiovasc. Surgery (pres. Australian & New Zealand chpt. 1982-83, 91-93, internat. v.p. 1993-95), Athenaeum Club, Melbourne Cricket Club, Lonsdale Golf Club, Scotchman's Creek Golf Club. Avocations: travel, golf, history. Home: 1 Myambert Ave Balwyn VIC 3103 Australia Home Phone: 61398362074. Home Fax: 61398301524. Personal E-mail: jroyle6@bigpond.com.

ROZANTINE, GAYLE STUBBS, psychologist; b. Atlanta, Dec. 1, 1944; d. William L. and Louise (Cash) Stubbs; children: Kathryn Patricia, Webb Black III, Gregory William, Benjamin Stubbs, John Paul; m. Barry Rozantine. BA in Psychology, Agnes Scott Coll., 1965; MA in Tchg., Emory U., 1966; MA in Clin. Psychology, Western Carolina U., 1990; PhD, U. Tenn., 1995. Lic. psychologist, Ga.; diplomate Am. Acad. Experts in Traumatic Stress; bd. cert. stress mgmt., 2008. Tchr. Fulton Co. Bd. Edn., Ga., 1967-68; psychology resident Med. Coll. of Ga., Augusta, 1994-95, clin. fellow, 1995-96; rsch. psychologist Pain Evaluation and Intervention Program Dept. of

VA Med. Ctr., Augusta, 1995-98; staff psychologist Compass Health Systems, Miami Beach, Fla., 1998, Charter Savannah Behavioral Health System, Ga., 1999-2000; CEO Ctr. Health and Well-Being, 2000—11, Optima Vita, 2010—11. Mem. critical incident stress debriefing team Med. Coll. Ga.; disaster mental health response team ARC; presenter in field. Author: The Clinician's Guide to At Ease Soldier, 2011, At Ease Soldier, The Wisdom of Wellness Program, 2010. Mem. APA, Coastal Area Psychologists, Ga. Psychol. Assn., Ga. Breast Cancer Coalition and Fund, Nat. Register Health Svc. Providers in Psychology. Office: The Ctr for Health and Well-Being PC 400 Commercial Ct Savannah GA 31406 Office Phone: 912-352-9500 ext. 105. Personal E-mail: gaylerozantine@yahoo.com. Business E-Mail: gaylerozantine@quietawakening.com. E-mail: gaylerozantine@comcast.net.

ROZATI, ROYA, gynecologist, consultant; b. Isfahan, Iran, Nov. 2, 1958; d. Taghi and Fouroogh Rozati; m. Dharma Rakshak, May 21, 1989; children: Gautham Mehdi, Vikram Aiman. MBBS, Gulbarga U., 1985; MD, All India Inst. Med. Scis., 1990. Jr. resident Nizams Inst. Med. Scis., Hyderabad, India, 1986—87; registrar Royal Samaritan Hosp., London, 1991—94, Ayrshire Ctrl. and Glasgow Royal Infirmary; prof. Owaisi Hosp. and Rsch. Centre, Hyderabad, Andhrapradesh, 1994—2001, med. supt., 1999—2000, prof., 2001—; cons., head Dept. Reproductive Medicine Mahavir Hosp. and Rsch. Centre, Hyderabad, 1994—. Author: (jour.) Asian Jour. Andrology, Indian Jour. Human Genetics, Fertility and Sterility, Toxiclolgy, Reproductive Toxicology, Mutagenesis, Food and Chem. Toxicology, Asian Jour. Obs-Gyn. Practice; contbr. articles to profl. jours. Master: Royal Coll. Gyn. Avocations: writing, reading. Home: 8-2-120/86/I/A Road # 3 Banjara Hills Andhrapradesh Hyderabad 500003 India Office: MHRI- Centre for Fertility Management 8-2-120/86/I/A Road # 3 Banjara Hills Andhrapradesh Hyderabad 500003 India E-mail: drrozati@rediffmail.com.

ROZBRUCH, S. ROBERT, orthopedist, researcher; b. Bklyn., Sept. 2, 1965; s. Max and Frieda Rozbuch; m. Yonina Jacobs, July 2, 1989; children: Jason, Elizabeth. BA magna cum laude, U. Pa., 1985; MD in Rsch. with honors, Cornell U. Weill Med. Coll., 1990. Resident orthop. Hosp. Spl. Surgery, NYC, 1990—95; fellow Internat. Ctr. Limb Lengthening, Balt., 1998—99; pres. S. Robert Rozbruch MD, PC, NYC, 1999—; now chief limb lengthening svc. Hosp. Spl. Surgery, NYC, dir. Inst. Limb Lengthening and Reconstruction, 2002—; assoc. prof. orthop. surgery Weill Med. Sch. Cornell U., 2002—. Treas. Limb Lengthening and Reconstruction Soc., 2002—, bd. dir., 2002; founder Limb Lengthening and Reconstruction Program Hosp. Spl. Surgery, NYC. Author: Fractures of the Knee in Clin. Orthop., 2000, Orthop. Knowledge Update-Trauma 3, 2003; contbr. articles to profl. jours. Bd. trustees Temple Israel Ctr., White Plains, NY, 2002—. Recipient Neer award, Am. Shoulder and Elbow Surgeons, 1991. Fellow: Am. Acad. Orthop. Surgeons; mem.: Orthop. Trauma Assn. Avocations: gardening, exercise. Office: Hosp Spl Surgery 535 E 70th St New York NY 10021 Office Phone: 212-606-1415. Business E-Mail: rozbruchsr@hss.edu.

ROZENBERG, LANA, cosmetic dentist; b. 1968; DDS, U. Pacific Sch. Dentistry, 1994. Founder, dir. Rozenberg Dental Day Spa, NYC. Named one of NY Top Cosmetic Dentists, NY Mag., 2002, 2004. Avocations: boating, golf, skiing, tennis, financial investments. Office: Rozenberg Dental Day Spa 8A E 63rd St New York NY 10065-7210 Office Phone: 212-265-7724. Business E-Mail: office@rozenbergdds.com.

ROZENTALE, BAIBA, medical association administrator; b. Cesis, Latvia, Aug. 13, 1955; MBA, Riga Internat. U. Economics and Bus. Adminstrn., 2007. Head clin. dept. Infectology Ctr. Latvia, 1993—94, dep. dir. in medicine field, 1994—99, dir., 1999—2009, 2010—, Min. of Health, State Chancellery, 2009—10. Prof., dept. infectology and dermatology Riga Stradins U., 2006, head infectology study program, postgrad. edn. faculty, 1999. Mem.: Mem. Operational Commn. Health, Min. of Health, Coun. Health Care Strategy, Min. of Health, Prin. Physican-infectologist Min. of Health, Rep. Infectology Ctr. Latvia, HIV/AIDS Think Tank Group European Com. Avocations: travel, theater, literature. Office: 3 Linezera St Riga LV-1006 Latvia Office Fax: 371 67014568. Business E-Mail: baiba.rozentale@rsu.lv.

ROZOV, TATIANA, retired pediatrician; b. Sremska Mitroviça, Yugoslavia, July 18, 1940; Grad, U. São Paulo, 1969, PhD, 1988. Chief pneumology unit Inst. Criança Hosp. da Clínicas-Faculdade Medicina U. São Paulo-FMUSP, 1971—96; postgrad. orientation prof. pediat. pulmonary rehab. Fed. U. São Paulo, 2000—. Cons., rschr. Roche of Brazil, 2004—08. Hon. pres. Brazilian Soc. Pediat. Pulmonology, 2009. Recipient Fifty Yrs. Commemoratory medal, Faculdade Medicina U. São Paulo. Avocations: painting, gardening, reading. Home: Estrada Vereador José Alves Barreto 3350 Ubatuba São Paulo 11680-000 Brazil Business E-Mail: rozov@uol.com.br.

ROZSÍVAL, PAVEL, ophthalmologist, educator, surgeon; b. Cheb, Czech Republic, Sept. 27, 1950; s. Vladimír and Věra (Matyašová) R.; m. Iva Fišerová, July 31, 1971; children: Kateřina, Pavel. MD, Charles U., Prague, Czech Republic, 1974, PhD, 1979. Sci. worker Charles U., Hradec Králové, Czech Republic, 1979-84; head dept. ophthalmology Dist. Hosp., Teplice, Czech Republic, 1984-86, Regional Hosp., Ústí n.Labem, Czech Republic, 1986-93, Charles U., 1993—, prof. ophthalmology, 1996—; head accreditation com. Czech Ministry of Health, 2005—. Cons. Nat. Med. Libr., Prague, 1978-92; mem. Czech Com. Ophthalmology, Prague, 1991—; mem. sci. adv. bd. Czech Chamber Physicians, 1993-98, Czech Ministry Health, 1999—2004; lectr. in field. Author: Ophthalmology for Family Physicians, 1994, Modern Cataract Surgery, 1995, Trends in Ophthalmology, 2005-11, Textbook Ophthalmology for Students of Medicine, 2006; contbr. over 350 articles to profl. jours. Mem. Am. Acad. Ophthalmology, Am. Soc. Cataract Refractive Surgery, Internat. Intraocular Implant Club, Czech Soc. Ophthalmology (pres. 1997—2005, v.p. 2005-09). Avocation: sport activities. Office: Charles Univ Tchg Hosp 500 05 Hradec Králové Czech Republic Home Phone: 420 4955 33586; Office Phone: 420-49-583 2325.

ROZTOCIL, KAREL, cardiologist; b. Prague, Czech Republic, Mar. 27, 1941; s. Karel and Libuse Roztocil; m. Jana Josefovic, June 16, 1965; children: Jan, Kristina. MD, Charles U., Prague, 1965; PhD in Internal Medicine, Czech Acad. Scis., 1975. Lic. internal medicine Postgrad. Med. Inst., Prague, 1971, angiology specialist Postgrad. Med. Inst., Prague, 2004. Physician dept. internal medicine Regional Hosp., Frydek-Mistek, Czech Republic, 1965—67; med. asst. dept. angiology Rsch. Inst. Exptl. Therapy, Prague, 1968—73; physician dept. cardiology Inst. Clin. and Exptl. Medicine (formerly Rsch. Inst. Exptl. Therapy), Prague, 1973, dep. head dept. cardiology, 1983—91, head dept. angiology, 1991—2004; study visit Charité Hosp., Berlin, 1974. Presenter in field. Mem. editl. bd. various jours.; contbr. over 200 publs. to profl. jours, chapters to books. Mem.: European Soc. Cardiology (mem. working group of peripheral circul., sci. sec.), Czech Med. Chamber Sci. Com., Angiology, Health Ministery Czech Rep. (chmn. 2005), Internat. Union Angiology (nat. del. Czech. Republic 1998—2002, assoc. treas., former com. mem. 2002—04, sec. gen. 2004—06), Ctrl. European Vascular Forum (sci. sec. 1998), Czech Soc. Angiology (sci. sec. 1994—99, pres. 2000). Achievements include clinical research in vascular diseases and cardiology. Office: Inst Clin and Exptl Medicine Videnska 1958 140 21 Prague Czech Republic Office Fax: 420261362732. Business E-Mail: karel.roztocil@medicon.cz.

RUAN, CHUN, radiologist, educator; b. China, Jan. 16, 1978; PhD, U. Tex. HSC, 2005. Asst. prof. U. Okla. Health Scis. Ctr., 2006—. Bd. dirs. Intersocietal Commn. Accreditation Magnetic Resonance Labs., 2009—; vice chair Okla. State Radiol. Soc., Med. Physics Sect., 2010—. Recipient Superior Tchg. award, U. Okla. HSC; Ednl. fellowship, Internat. Soc. Magnetic Resonance Medicine. Mem.: Am. Coll. Med. Physics, Am. Assn. Physicists Medicine. Avocations: music, movies, travel. Office: 940 NE 13th St Garrison Tower 4G4250 Oklahoma City OK 73104 Business E-Mail: chun-ruan@ouhsc.edu.

RUAN, FEI, physician; b. China, Dec. 18, 1975; M, Wuhan U., 2002. Physician Womens Hosp. Sch. Medicine Zhejiang U., 2002—. Office: XueShi Rd 2 HangZhou ZheJiang 310006 China E-mail: rf100@163.com.

RUAN, XIANGYAN, gynecologist; b. Zhu Madian, Henan, China, July 1, 1965; m. Junchao Gu, Oct. 1, 1989. MD, West China Med. U., Chengdu, 1997. Dir. endocrinology for gynecology Beijing Ob-Gyn. Hosp., Capital Med. U., Beijing, 1999—; assoc. prof. Beijing Ednl. Com., 2001; chief med. doctor Beijing Health Bur., 2004. Office: Beijing OB GYN Hosp 251 Yao Jia Yuan Rd Beijing 100026 China Business E-Mail: ruanxiangyan@163.com.

RUAT, MARTIAL, research scientist, director; b. Vergonzac, July 8, 1960; PhD, U. Paris VI, 1988; degree in engring., Insa Lyon, 1984. Dir. rsch. Inserm, 1990—. Mem.: Am. Soc. Neurosci., Soc. French Neurosci. Office: 1 Ave De La Terrasse Gif Sur Yvette 91198 France Office Fax: 0169823639. Business E-Mail: ruat@inaf.cnrs-gif.fr.

RUBAJ, ANDRZEJ, physician; b. Lublin, Poland, Nov. 1, 1970; PhD, Med. U. Lublin, 1995. Physician dept cardiology U. Hosp. Lublin, 1991—. Home: Paganiniego 12/147 Lublin 20-850 Poland Personal E-mail: arubaj@yahoo.com.

RUBEN, GEORGE COLLINS, biology professor; b. Berkeley, Apr. 29, 1941; BS in Chemistry, UC Davis, Calif., 1963; PhD in Phys. Chemistry, UC Berkeley, 1972. Head, electron Dartmouth Med. Sch., 1977—84, rsch. asst. prof., dept. pathology, 1982—84, dir., electron microscopy facility, 1977, Dartmouth Coll., NH, rsch. assoc. prof., biol. scis., 1984—94, rsch. prof., biol. scis., 1994—. Cons. Lawrence Livermore Nat. Lab., 1990—94; bd. dirs. Sun Farm Corp., 1995; editl. bd. mem. Synapse, J. Wiley Neurosci. Jour., 1995, editor-in-chief, microscopy rsch. and technique, 96. Recipient Citation award, UC Davis Chemistry Dept., 1963, Merit award, Chem. Engring. News, 1963, First prize, Tribology Conf.; grant, NSF, Phi Kappa Phi. Mem.: AAAS, Royal Microscopical Soc., Am. Chem. Soc., Cellulose, Paper & Textile Divsn., Soc. Neurosci., Microscopy Soc. America. Avocations: photography, sailing. Home: 10 Shaw St Lebanon NH 03766

RUBEN, ROBERT JOEL, pediatric otorhinolaryngologist, educator; b. NYC, Aug. 2, 1933; s. Julian Carl and Sadie (Weiss) R.; children: Ann, Emily, Karin, Arthur. AB, Princeton U., 1955; MD, Johns Hopkins U., 1959. Intern Johns Hopkins Hosp., Balt., 1959-60, resident, 1960-64, dir. neurophysiology lab., div. otolaryngology, 1958-64; practice specializing in pediatric otorhinolaryngology NYC, 1964—; asst. prof. otorhinolaryngology N.Y. U. Sch. Medicine, 1966-68; mem. staff hosps. Montefiore Med. Ctr., Bronx Med. Hosp. Ctr., N. Cen. Bronx Hosp., Montefiore Med., Jacobi Hosp., Bronx, NY, Children's Hosp. at Montefiore; prof., chmn. Montefiore Med. Ctr., Bronx Mcpl. Hosp. Ctr., N. Cen. Bronx, Bronx, 1979-99, prof., 1999—; prof. pediatrics Albert Einstein Coll. Medicine, Bronx, 1983—, assoc. prof. otorhinolaryngology NYC, 1968-70, prof., chmn. dept. otolaryngology, 1970-98, prof. dept. otolaryngology, 1970—, chmn. emeritus dept. otolaryngology, 1998—, disting. univ. prof., 1998—; prof. pediatrics Albert Einstein Coll. Medicine and Montefiore Med. Ctr., 1983—. Chmn. Nat. Com. for Rsch. and Neurol. and Communicative Disorders, pres., 1982-84; bd. dirs. Am. Bd. Otolaryngology-Head and Neck Surgery, 1989—; chmn. ENT devices com. FDA, 1993-96. Editor-in-chief: Internat. Jour. Pediatric Otorhinolaryngology, 1979—. Bd. dirs. N.Y. League Hard of Hearing, 1969-75, 76-85, Ctr. for Book Arts, 2006—, Ctr. for Book Arts, 2006—; bd. dirs. Friends of Princeton U. Libr., chair, 2001-05, v.p., 2007-; chairperson Friends of Princeton U. Libr., 2002-06; chairperson. sect. history of medicine & pub. health NY Acad. Medicine, 2010-. Served to surgeon USPHS, 1964-66. Recipient Rsch. award Am. Acad. Ophthalmology and Otolaryngology, 1962, Edmund Prince Fowler award Am. Rhinological-Laryngological-Otological Assn., 1973, Gold medal Best Didactic Film, IX World Congress Otorhinolaryngology, 1977, Pres.'s award Am. Acad. Otolaryngology-Head and Neck Surgery, 1992, Johns Hopkins U. Soc. of Scholars, 1993, George E. Schambaugh Otology prize, 1996, Merit award Am. Otological, 2004, Sylvian Tchg. award, Senta, 2005, Presdl. citation Trio, 2005. Fellow ACS, N.Y. Acad. Medicine; mem. AMA, Am. Assn. Anatomists, Audiology Study Group N.Y. (pres. 1964-66), Acoustical Soc. Am., Am. Acad. Ophthalmology and Otolaryngology, Soc. Univ. Otolaryngologists, Am. Otol. Soc. (sec.-treas. rsch. fund 1979—, award of merit 2004), Soc. for Ear, Nose and Throat Advances in Children (pres. 1973), Assn. for Rsch. in Otolaryngology (pres. 1985-86), Am. Acad. Pediat. (chmn. otol. bronchoesphology 1983-85), Am. Soc. Pediat. Otolaryngology (historian 1986-95), Am. Soc. Pediat. Otolaryngologists (historian 1986-93, pres.-elect 1993-94, pres. 1994-95), Internat. Fedn. Otolaryngic Socs. (chmn. com. on pediat. otolaryngology 2004-09), Nat. Inst. Deafness and Other Comm. Disorders (adv. coun. 1989-93), Am. Laryngol. Soc., Grolier Club (mem. coun. 2002-). Home: 1025 5th Ave Apt 12C S New York NY 10028-0134 Home Phone: 212-734-5368; Office Phone: 718-920-2487. E-mail: robert.ruben@einstein.yu.edu.

RUBENSTEIN, ANDREW, obstetrician, gynecologist, educator; Attended, MCP Hahnemann U., 1980. Diplomate Am. Bd. Ob-Gyn. Resident ob-gyn. Mt. Sinai Med. Ctr., 1990—94; with Hackensack Univ. Med. Ctr.; asst. clin. prof. ob-gyn. NJ Med. Sch. Office: Hackensack University Medical Center 82 E Allendale Rd 1 Saddle River NJ 07458 Office Phone: 201-934-5050.

RUBENSTEIN, ARTHUR HAROLD, retired dean, board member; b. Johannesburg, Dec. 28, 1937; arrived in U.S., 1967; s. Montague and Isabel (Nathanson) R.; m. Denise Hack, Aug. 19, 1962; children: Jeffrey Lawrence, Errol Charles. MB BCh, U. Witwatersrand, 1960, DSc (hon.) in Medicine, 2002. Diplomate Am. Bd. Internal Medicine. Intern, then resident Johannesburg Gen. Hosp., 1961, 63-65, 66-67; fellow in endocrinology Postgrad. Med. Sch., London, 1965-66; fellow in medicine University of Chicago, 1967-68, from asst. prof. to assoc. prof., 1968-74, prof., 1974—97, Lowell T. Coggeshall prof. med. sci., 1981—97, assoc. chmn., Medicine Dept., 1975—81, chmn., 1991—97; attending physician Mitchell Hosp., U. Chgo., 1968-97; dean, Gustave L. Levy disting. prof. Mount Sinai School Medicine, NYC, 1997—2001; exec. v.p. University of Pennsylvania Health Systems, Phila., 2001—11; dean University of Pennsylvania School Medicine, Phila., 2001—11. Bd. dirs. Lab. Corp. of America Holdings, 2004-, Glycadia; mem. study sect. NIH, 1973-77, Hadassah Med. Adv. Bd., 1986-95, adv. coun. Nat. Inst. Arthritis, Metabolism and Digestive Diseases, 1978-80; chmn. Nat. Diabetes Adv. Bd., 1982, mem., 1981-83. Mem. editl. bd. Diabetes, 1973-77, Endocrinology, 1973-77, Jour. Clin. Investigation, 1976-81, Am. Jour. Medicine, 1978-81, Diabetologia, 1982-86, Diabetes Medicine, 1987-91, Annals of Internal Medicine, 1991-96, Medicine, 1992—; contbr. articles to profl. jours. Mem. Am. Acad. of Arts & Sciences, Am. Assn. for the Advancement of Sci.; bd. dirs. Assn. of Academic Health Ctrs.; mem. Gov.'s Sci. Adv. Coun. State of Ill., 1989—96. Recipient David Rumbough Meml. award Juvenile Diabetes Found., 1978. Master: ACP (John Phillips Meml. award 1995); fellow: NY Acad. Medicine, Royal Coll. Physicians (London), South African Coll. Physicians; mem.: AAAS, Assn. Acad. Health Ctrs. (bd. dirs. 2005—), Assn. Am. Med. Colls. (mem. coun. of deans adminstrv. bd., Abraham Flexer award 2009), Assn. Profs. Medicine (councillor 1991—94, v.p. 1994—95, pres. 1995—96, Robert Williams award 1997), Inst. Medicine (coun. 1991—96), Residency Rev. Com., Am. Bd. Internal Medicine (bd. govs. 1985—93, exec. com. 1990—93, chmn. 1992—93), Assn. Am. Physicians (treas. 1984—89, councillor 1989—94, v.p. 1994—95, pres. 1995—96), Ctrl. Soc. Clin. Rsch. (v.p. 1988, pres. 1989), Am. Fedn. Clin. Rsch., Endocrine Soc., Brit. Diabetes Assn. (Banting lectr. 1987), Am. Diabetes Assn. (Solomon Berson Meml. lectr. 1985, Eli Lilly award 1973, Banting medal 1983), Am. Soc. for Clin. Investigation. Office: Laboratory Corp of America Holdings Bd Directors 531 S Spring St Burlington NC 27215 Office Phone: 336-436-5274. Office Fax: 336-436-1569. E-mail: Rubensteina@labcorp.com. *

RUBENSTEIN, DAVID AARON, military officer, healthcare administrator; b. Rockville Centre, NY, Nov. 23, 1954; s. Robert R. and Mona Sydney (Feder) R.; m. Patricia Barrier, Mar. 18, 1978; children: Sarah Elizabeth, William Robert. BS in Health Edn., Tex. A & M U., 1977; MHA, Baylor U., 1989; M of Mil. Arts and Sci., Command and Gen. Staff Coll., 1990. Commd. 2d lt. U.S. Army, 1977, advanced through grades to maj. gen., 2008, med. platoon leader 3d inf. div. Germany, 1977—79, ops. officer 3d med. battalion, 1979—80, pers. officer 307th med. battalion Ft. Bragg, NC, 1981—82, co. comdr., 1982—83, mil. instr. Acad. of Health Scis. Ft. Sam Houston, Tex., 1984—87, grad. student, 1987—88, adminstrv. resident William Beaumont Army Med. Ctr. Ft. Bliss, Tex., 1988—89, grad. student Command and Gen. Staff Coll. Ft. Leavenworth, Kans., 1989—90; adminstrv. asst. Office of the Army Surgeon Gen. Army Med. Svc. Corps, Washington, 1990—92; chief coordinated care Army Hosp., Ft. Belvoir, Va., 1992—93; hosp. comdr. 18th Mobile Army Surg. Hosp., Ft. Lewis, Wash., 1994—96; grad. student Army War Coll., Carlisle Barracks, Pa., 1996—97; dep. comdr. Eisenhower Army Med. Ctr., Ft. Gordon, Ga., 1997—99; hosp. comdr. 21st Combat Support Hosp., Ft. Hood, Tex., 1999—2001, Bosnia-Herzegovina, 1999—2000; cmdr. Landstuhl Regional Med. Ctr., Germany, 2001—03; chief of staff Europe Regional Med. Commd., 2003—04; cmdr. 30th Med. Brigade, 2004; asst. surgeon gen., 2005—06; commanding gen. Europe Med. Commd., 2006—08; major general, army deputy surgeon general US Army, 2008—10; comdr. Med. Ctr. & Sch., 2010—. Pres. Health Orgn. Network, El Paso, Tex., 1989, asst. surgeon gen. force sustainment, 2005; pres. Healthcare Execs. Ctrl. Savannah River Area, 1998-99; participant U.S. Army seminar Baylor U., Ft. Sam Houston, 1989. Author leadership seminar; reviewer books Lehigh U. Press, 1990, Mil. Rev. Jour., Mil. Medicine; contbr. articles to profl. jours. Religious lay leader Office of the Jewish Chapel, Ft. Bragg, 1982-83, Ft. Bliss, 1988-89, Ft. Leavenworth, 1989-90, Bosnia-Herzegovina, 1999-2000; fund drive coord. United Fund, Ft. Leavenworth, 1989; vol. Muscular Dystrophy Assn., Washington, 1990-91. Decorated Legion of Merit; recipient Fed. Healthcare Leadership award, 2003, Ray E. Brown award, Assn. Military Surgeons, US, 2006, Mentor of the Year award, U.S. Army Med. Svc. Corps., Federal Excellence in Healthcare Leadership award, Regent's healthcare Executive award, Am. Coll. Healthcare Executives. Fellow: Am. Coll. Healthcare Execs. (Regent's award 1993, regent 2000—02, gov. 2002—, chmn. 2008, Fed. Excellence in Healthcare Leadership award, Regent's Healthcare Exec. award); mem.: VFW, Assn. of U.S. Army, Am. Hosp. Assn., Assn. Mil. Surgeons of U.S. (Ray E. Brown 2006). Republican. Jewish. Avocations: flying, running, history, reading. Home and Office: 1839 Staff Post Fort Sam Houston TX 78234 Office Phone: 210-221-6325. Business E-Mail: david.rubenstein@us.army.mil.

RUBENSTEIN, EDWARD, physician, educator; b. Cin., Dec. 5, 1924; s. Louis and Nettie Rubenstein; m. Nancy Ellen Millman, June 20, 1954; children: John, William, James. MD, U. Cin., 1947. House staff Cin. Gen. Hosp., 1947—50; fellow May Inst., Cin., 1950; sr. asst. resident Ward Med. Svc., Barnes Hosp., St. Louis, 1953—54; chief of medicine San Mateo County Hosp., Calif., 1960—70; assoc. dean postgrad. med. edn., prof. medicine Stanford (Calif.) U., 1971—, emeritus, active. Faculty Stanford Photon Rsch. Lab.; affiliated faculty Stanford Synchortron Radiation Lab., 1971—; maj. materials facilities com. NRC, 1984—85, Nat. Steering Com. 6 GeV Electron Storage Ring, 1986—. Author (textbook): Intensive Medical Care; editor: Synchotron Radiation Handbook, 1988, vol. 4, 1991, Synchotron Radiation in the Biosciences, Molecular Medicine; mem. editorial bd.: Sci. Am., Inc., 1991—94; editor (textbook): Sci. Am. Medicine, 1978—94; editor: (series) Molecular Cardiovascular Disease, 1995, Molecular Oncology, 1996, Molecular Neuroscience, 1998. With USAF, 1950—52. Recipient Kaiser award for outstanding and innovative contbns. to med. edn., 1989, Albion Walter Hewlett award, 1993; named Disting. Scientist, SvrroMed, Inc., 2003. Master: ACP (Laureate 2002); fellow: AAAS, Royal Soc. Medicine; mem.: Am. Clin. and Climatol. Assn., Soc. Photo-Optical Engrs., Western Assn. Physicians, Calif. Acad. Medicine, Inst. Medicine, APS, Alpha Omega Alpha. Achievements include research in mechanisms of autoimmunity, dysfunction of the choroid plexus and cerebrospinal fluid circulatory system, synchrotron radiation, nonprotein amino acids, autoimmunity, molecular chirality; multiple sclerosis pathogenesis. Office: Stanford Med Ctr Dept Medicine Stanford CA 94305

RUBENSTEIN, HOWARD S., physician, writer; b. Chgo., June 14, 1931; s. Sidney Howard and Selma (Moldofsky) Rubenstein; m. Judith Ann Selig, May 26, 1968; children: Emily Rubenstein Engel, Adam Selig, Jennifer Rubenstein Zigun, John Stephen. BA, Carleton Coll., Northfield, Minn., 1953; MD, Harvard U., Boston, 1957. Intern and resident Los Angeles County Gen. Hosp., LA, 1957—60; rsch. fellow Harvard Med. Sch., Boston, 1960—64, rsch. assoc., 1964—68; physician, chief of allergy Harvard U. Health Svcs., Cambridge, Mass., 1968—89; med. cons. State of Calif., Dept. Social Svcs., Disability Program, San Diego, 1989—2000. Physician Albert Schweitzer Hosp., Deschapelles, Haiti, 1964; guest lectr. Chinese Med. Assn., China, 1984. Author: (epic in free verse) Maccabee, 2004, (plays) Brothers All, 2006, The Golem, Man of Earth, 2007, Tony and Cleo, 2008, (book and lyrics) Romance of the Western Chamber A Musical, 2010 (Asian Heritage award nominee, 2011); translator: Agamemnon: A Play by Aeschylus with Reconstructed Stage Directions, 1998, 2003, The Trojan Women: A Play by Euripides, 2002 (Billie awards, 2000, 2001), Britannicus: A Play by Jean Racine, 2009; contbr. articles to profl. jours. Fellow, US Pub. Health Svc., 1960—62; Harold C. Ernst fellow, Harvard Med. Sch., 1962—64 Mem.: Harvard Med. Sch., Carleton Coll., Ezekiel Hersey Coun. (life), Joseph Heywood Soc. (life), Sigma Xi, Phi Beta Kappa (life). Jewish. Home: 8677 Villa La Jolla Dr # 1114 La Jolla CA 92037 Personal E-mail: harubenstein@yahoo.com.

RUBENSTEIN, LISA V., medical association administrator, educator; MSPH, U. Calif.; MD, Albert Einstein Sch. Medicine. Dir. RAND Ctr. for the Study of Healthcare Provider Behavior VA Greater Los Angeles Med. Ctr., prof. medicine. Mem.: Soc. Gen. Internal Medicine (pres.). Office: 2501 M St NW Ste 575 Washington DC 20037 Office Phone: 310-393-0411 ext. 6303. E-mail: lisa_Rubenstien@Rand.org.

RUBIN, ALAN A., pharmaceutical and biotechnology consultant; b. NYC, July 10, 1926; s. Harry and Gertrude R.; m. Helen M. Feinstein; children: Jeffrey, Ronald, Howard. BS, NYU, 1950, MS, 1953, PhD, 1959. Pharmacologist Schering Corp., Bloomfield, N.J., 1954-64; dir. pharmacology Endo Labs., Garden City, N.Y., 1964-70, v.p. rsch., 1970-74; dir. rsch. DuPont Pharms., Wilmington, Del., 1974-82, dir. sci. info. and tech., 1982-87; dir. licensing tech. DuPont Merck Pharms., Wilmington, Del., 1987-91; pres. ARA Assoc., Rockland, Del., 1991—. Editor: Search for New Drugs, 1972, New Drugs: Discovery and Development, 1978; contbr. articles to profl. jours. With U.S. Army, 1944-46. Mem. AAAS, Am. Soc. Pharmacology and Exptl. Therapeutics, Soc. Exptl. and Biol. Medicine, N.Y. Acad. Sci. Home: 207 Hitching Post Dr Wilmington DE 19803-1914 Office: ARA Assoc PO Box 244 Rockland DE 19732-0244 Personal E-mail: alannaro@comcast.net.

RUBIN, AMIR DAN, hospital administrator; married; 2 children. B in Economics, U. Calif., Berkeley; M in Health Services Adminstrn, U. Mich., Ann Arbor, MBA. Assoc. cons., mgmt. cons. APM/CSC Healthcare Consulting, Calif., 1996—98; asst. v.p. ops. Meml. Hermann-Tex. Med. Ctr., Houston, 1998—2002; COO Stony Brook U. Hosp., NY, 2002—05, UCLA Health Sys., 2005—10; pres., CEO Stanford Hosp. & Clinics, Calif., 2011—. Office: Stanford Hosp & Clinics 300 Pasteur Dr Rm H3200 Stanford CA 94305 Office Phone: 650-723-4000. *

RUBIN, ARKADY, biostatistics and data management researcher, executive; b. St. Petersburg, Russia, Jan. 29, 1955; s. Mikhail Rubin and Mikhalina Rubina. BS in econ., Inst. of Nat. Economy, 1972—76, PhD, 1983—86. Prin. biostatistician Johnson & Johnson, Raritan, NJ, 1991—98; assoc. dir., biostatistics Pfizer, NYC, 1998—2003; exec. dir., biostatistics and data mgmt. NovaDel Pharma, Flemington, NJ, 2003—. Contbr. articles to profl. jours. Recipient Corp. award for the design of the low dose contraceptive clin. program, Johnson & Johnson, 1997. Mem.: Am. Statis. Assn. Achievements include design of clinical program for the contraceptive patch currently marketed as Evra; clinical program Norvasc/Lipitor combination pill (trade name Caduet); clinical program for the low-dose oral contraceptive currently marketed as Ortho Tri-Cyclen Lo; patents for Ortho Tri-Cyclen Lo. Office: NovaDel Pharma 25 Minneakoning Rd Flemington NJ 08822 Home: 28 Colts Ln Flemington NJ 08822-3401 E-mail: arubin@novadel.com.

RUBIN, BRUCE KALMAN, medical professor, researcher; b. Miami Beach, Fla., May 8, 1954; s. Arnold and Dorothy Bella (Firtel) Rubin; m. Tomomi Tainaka, July 29, 1990; children: Noah David, Max Aaron, Sam Tainaka. BSc, Tulane U., New Orleans, 1975, MEngr in Biomed. Engring., 1977, MD, 1979; MBA, Wake Forest U. Babcock Sch. Mgmt., Winston-Salem, NC, 2004. Diplomate Am. Bd. Pediat., cert. in Pediatric Pulmonology. Rhodes scholar Oxford U., 1978—80, intern pediat. England, 1979; resident Tulane U., 1980-81; respirology fellow Hosp. for Sick Children, Toronto, Ont., Canada, 1981-83; asst. prof., dir. pediat. ICU Queen's U., Kingston, Ont., 1983-87; asst. prof. pediat. U. Alberta, Edmonton, Canada, 1987-91; prof. pediat., dir. pulmonary medicine St. Louis U., Cardinal Glennon Hosp., 1991-97; prof., vice chair rsch., dept. pediat. Wake Forest U. Sch. Medicine, 1997—2009, chief pediat. pulmonology, 1999—2005; also prof. physiology and pharmacology, biomed. engring. Va. Tech.-Wake Forest U. Sch. Biomed. Engring., 1997—2009; faculty Internat. Course Pediat. Pulmology, 2002—; Jessie Ball duPont prof. & chmn. dept. pediat. Va. Commonwealth U., 2009—, prof., biomed. engring., prof. physiology & biophysics, 2009—; physician-in-chief Children's Hosp. Richmond, Va., 2010—. Pres. Internat. Congress Pediatric Pulmonology, 2004—06; bd. mem., treas. Internat. Soc. Aerosols Medicine, 2004—; trustee Am. Respiratory Care Found., 2005—; mem. editl. bd. 12 med. jours. Author: Therapy for Mucus Clearance Disorders (Lung Biology in Health and Disease), 2004, Antibiotics as Antiflammatory and Immunomodulatory Agents (Progress in Inflammation Research), 2005; contbr. over 200 articles to profl. jours., over 30 chapters to books. Recipient Achievement award for Excellence in Pulmonary Disease State Mgmt., Am Assn. Respiratory Care, 2007, Donald Egan Meml. Lectr. award, 2009, 27th Philip Kittredge Meml. Lectr. award, 2011, Forrest M. Bird Lifetime Sci. Achievement award, Am. Respiratory Care Found. & Am. Assn. Respiratory Care, 2008, Prix Extraordinaire, CRPP. Fellow: Am. Coll. Chest Physicians (Young Investigator award 1989, Critical Care Rsch. award 1990, Alfred Soffer award 2004), Am. Pediat. Assn., Royal Coll. Physicians Can.; mem.: Soc. Am. Magicians, Internat. Brotherhood Magicians, Assn. Med. Sch. Pediat. (dept. chair), Am. Pediatric Soc., Soc. Pediat. Rsch. Avocation: magic. Business E-Mail: brubin@vcu.edu.

RUBIN, DAVID T., medical educator; Assoc. prof. medicine U. Chgo. Med. Ctr., 1996—; co-dir. Inflammatory Bowel Disease Ctr.

RUBIN, DONALD BRUCE, statistician, educator, research and development company executive; b. Washinton, Dec. 22, 1943; s. Allan A. and Harriet Rubin. AB magna cum laude, Princeton U., 1965; MS, Harvard U., 1966, PhD, 1970. Rsch. statistician Ednl. Testing Svc., Princeton, NJ, 1971-75, chmn. stats., 1975-79, sr. statis. advisor, 1979-81, pres. Datamatrics Rsch. Inc., 1981—2008; prof. U. Chgo., 1982-84, Harvard U., Cambridge, Mass., 1984—, chmn. stats., 1985—94, 2000—02, John L. Loeb Prof. Stats., 2002—. Author: Handling Nonresponse in Sample Surveys by Multiple Imputation, 1980, Multiple Imputation for Nonresponse in Surveys, 1987, classic edit., 2004; author: (with others) Incomplete Data in Sample Surveys (Vol. 2): Theory and Bibliography, 1983; co-author: (with R.J.A. Little) Statistical Analysis With Missing Data, 1987, 2d edit., 2002, (with A. Gelman, J. Carlin. H. Stern) Bayasian Data Analysis, 1995, 2d edit., 2003, (with R. Rosenthal and R. Rosnow) Contrasts and Effect Sites in Behavioral Research: A Correlational Approach, 2000, Matched Sampling for Causal Effects, 2006; co-editor: (with P.W. Holland) Test Equating, 1982, contbr. over 350 articles to profl. jours. Recipient Parzen prize for statis. innovation, 1996; Woodrow Wilson Grad. fellow, 1965; NSF Grad. fellow, 1965, 68, John Simon Guggenheim fellow, 1977-78. Fellow AAAS (chmn. stats. 1992), Am. Statis. Assn. (editor jour. 1980-82, dir. 1980-82, statistician of yr. Boston chpt. 1995, Chgo. chpt. 2000, S.S. Wilks medal 1995, Mitchell prize 2001, 09), Inst. Math. Stats. (coun. mem. 1990-92, 99-2001, Fisher lectr. 2004), Von Humbolt Found., Brit. Acad.; mem. NAS (com. on nat. stats. 1989-92, mem. panel on confidentiality data 1989-92, panel on bilingual edn. 1990-92, working group on statis. analysis of com. on basic rsch. in behavioral and social scis. 1985-86, panel statis. in 21st century 1995, other coms.), Am. Acad. Arts and Sci., Biometric Soc., Internat. Assn. Survey Statisticians, Internat. Statis. Inst., Psychometric Soc., Royal Statis. Soc., European Assn. Methodology (hon.). Office: Harvard U Dept Statistics Cambridge MA 02138 Business E-Mail: rubin@stat.harvard.edu.

RUBIN, EMANUEL, pathologist, educator, department chairman; b. NYC, Dec. 5, 1928; s. Jacob and Sophie R.; m. Barbara Kurn, Mar. 27, 1955 (div. 1985); children: Raphael, Jonathan, Daniel, Rebecca; m. Linda A. Haegele, Oct. 13, 1985; children: Ariel, Ethan. BS, Villanova U., 1950; MD, Harvard U., 1954; Hon. Degree, U. Barcelona, 1994, U. Naples, 2003. Intern Boston City Hosp., 1954-55; resident Children's Hosp. of Phila., 1957-58; rsch. fellow in pathology Mt. Sinai Hosp., NYC, 1958-62, asst. attending pathologist, 1962-64, assoc. attending pathologist, 1964-68, attending pathologist, dir. hosp. pathology services, 1968-72, pathologist-in-chief, 1972-76; dir. labs. Hahnemann Hosp., Phila., 1977-86; physician-in-chief pathology Thomas Jefferson U. Hosp., Phila., 1986—2003. Prof. pathology Mr. Sinai Sch. Medicine, CUNY, 1966-72, Irene Heinz and John LaPorte Givien prof. pathology, chmn. dept., 1972-76; prof., chmn. dept. pathology and lab. medicine Hahnemann U. (now Drexel U.) Sch. Medicine, Phila., 1977-86; Gonzalo Aponte prof. pathology, chmn. dept. pathology and cell biology Thomas Jefferson U. Coll. Medicine, Phila., 1986-94, chmn. dept. pathology, anatomy and cell biology, 1994-2003, Gonzalo Aponte Disting. prof. pathology, chmn. emeritus dept. pathology, anatomy and cell biology, 2003-; adj. prof. biochemistry and biophysics U. Pa. Sch. Medicine, Phila., 1977-88. Author: (with J.L. Farber) Pathology, 1988, 94, 98; (with K.W. Miller and S.H. Roth) Cellular and Molecular Mechanisms of Alcohol and Anesthetics, 1991, Rubin's Pathology, 2004, 1st to 6th edit., 1988-2011; editor-in-chief Lab. Investigation, 1982-96; pathology editor: Fedn. Proc., 1982-86, Jour. Studies in Alcoholism, 1982-94, Alcoholism: Clin. Exptl. Rsch., 1999—, chmn. editl. bd., 2001—. Served with USN, 1955-57. Recipient K.F. Mostofi Disting. Svc. award, US-Canadian Acad. Pathology, 1996, Tom Kent Excellence in Pathology award, Group Rsch. Pathology Edn., 2001, Lifetime Sci. Achievement award, Sbarro Health Rsch. Orgn., 2004, Disting. Svc. award, Assn. Pathology Chairs, 2006, Gold medal, Internat. Acad. Pathology, 2006, Gold Headed Cane award, Am. Soc. Investigative Pathology, 2008. Mem. ACP, Am. Soc. Investigative Pathology, Internat. Acad. Pathology, U.S.-Can. Acad. Pathology, Am. Soc. Biol. Chemists and Molecular Biology, Am. Assn. Study of Liver Diseases, Am. Gastroent. Assn., Internat. Assn. Study of the Liver, Am. Coll. Toxicology. Home: 1505 Monk Rd Gladwyne PA 19035-1316 Office: 1020 Locust St Philadelphia PA 19107-6731 Business E-Mail: emanuel.rubin@jefferson.edu.

RUBIN, GERALD MAYER, biochemistry researcher, educator; b. Boston, Mar. 31, 1950; s. Benjamin H. and Edith (Weisberg) R.; m. Lynn S. Mastalir, May 7, 1978; 1 child, Alan F. BS, MIT, 1971; PhD in Molecular Biology, Cambridge U., Eng., 1974, ScD, 2002. Helen Hay Whitney Found. fellow Stanford U. Sch. Medicine, Calif., 1974-76; asst. prof. biol. chemistry Sidney Farber Cancer Inst.-Harvard U. Med. Sch., Boston, 1977-80; instructor, embryology Marine Biol. Lab., Woods Hole, Mass.; staff mem., dept. embryology Carnegie Instn. of Washington, Balt., 1980-83; John D. MacArthur prof. genetics, dept. molecular & cell biology U. Calif., Berkeley, 1983—2000, head, divsn. genetics, dept. molecular and cellular biology, 1987—95, HHMI investigator, 1987—2000, dir. Drosophila Genome Ctr., 1992—2006, prof. genetic dept. molecular & cell biology, 2000—09; v.p. biomedical rsch. Howard Hughes Med. Inst., Chevy Chase, Md., 2000—01, v.p., dir. planning Janelia Farm Rsch. Campus, Ashburn, Va., 2002—03, v.p., dir., 2003—. Adj. prof. dept. biochemistry and biophysics U. Calif. Sch. Medicine, San Francisco, 1987-; assoc. faculty mem., cell and molecular biology divsn. Lawrence Berkeley Nat. Lab., Calif.; mem. sci. adv. bd. Athena Neurosci., Inc., Tularik, Inc.; co-founder, chair sci. adv. bd. Exelixis Pharm., Inc. Predoctoral fellow, NSF, Helen Hay Whitney Found. Fellow; Recipient Young Scientist award Passano Found., 1983, Eli Lilly award in biol. chemistry, Am. Chem. Soc., 1985; co-recipient Newcomb Cleveland prize, AAAS, 2000, George W. Beadle Medal, Genetics Soc. Am., 2003; named Scientist of Yr., R&D Mag., 2006. Mem. AAAS, NAS (US Steel Found. award in molecular biology, 1985), Inst. Medicine, Genetics Soc. Am. Med., Phi Beta Kappa, Phi Lambda Epsilon, Royal Soc. UK (fgn.); Fellow Am. Acad. Arts & Sciences, Am. Acad. Microbiology. Office: Janelia Farm Rsch Campus Howard Hughes Med Inst 19700 Helix Dr Ashburn VA 20147-2408 Business E-Mail: rubing@janelia.hhmi.org.

RUBIN, KRISTA M., nurse; b. Boston, July 19, 1970; BS, U. Maine, 1992; MS, U. Mass., 2002. Nurse coord., cutaneous oncology program Beth Israel Deaconess Med. Ctr., 1997—2002; nurse practitioner, melanoma disease ctr. Mass. Gen. Hosp., 2002—. Editl. bd. mem. Jour. Dermatology Nurses Assn., 2009; bd. dirs. Children's Melanoma Prevention Found., 2009; med. adv. bd. New Eng. Melanoma Found., 2009. Recipient Academic Achievement award, Beth Israel Deaconess Med. Ctr., Dept. Nursing, 2001, Book award, U. Mass., 2002. Mem.: Am. Acad. Nurse Practitioners, Oncology Nursing Soc. (Excellence award 2010), Dermatology Nurses Assn. (chair, skin cancer com. 2009). Avocation: reading. Office: 32 Fruit St Yawkey Bldg Ste 9E Boston MA 02114 Office Fax: 617-724-6898. Business E-Mail: kmrubin@partners.org.

RUBIN, LEONARD SIDNEY, physiologist, educator, researcher; b. New York, Ny, Aug. 27, 1922; s. Hyman Hersh and Toba Rubin; m. Blanche Rubin, Mar. 30, 1950; children: Beth S., Joshua T., Matthew M. BS Chemistry, CUNY, New York, NY, 1943; PhD Neuroscience, NY Univ., New York, NY, 1950. Instr. NY Univ., New York, NY, 1943—44, rsch. assoc., 1950—53; chief psychophysiology br. Med. Labs, Army Chem. Corps., Edgewood, 1953—57; assoc. prof. Univ. Pa, Sch. of Medicine, Philadelphia, 1960—81; rsch. cons. Childrens Hosp. of Phila., Philadelphia, 1960—65, prof. Temple Univ. Med. Coll., Philadelphia, 1970—75; rsch. cons. St. Christopher's Hosp. for Children, 1964—67; cons., behavioral toxicology FDA, 1976—81; prof. Phila. Coll. of Med., Philadelphia, 1982—92; cons., biostatistics Cellcor Corp., Boston, 1988—92; prof., physiology/pharmacology Phila. Coll. of Osteo. Med., Philadelphia, 1981—. Armed forces nrc com. on vision, Washington, 1956—57; armed forces nrc com. on bioacoustics, Washington, 1956—57. Editl. cons. Jour. Studies on Alcohol, Jour. Nervous and Mental Disease, Psychophysiology, Psychopharmacologia, Am. Jour. Psychiatry. With US Army, 1944—46. Recipient Social Sci. Rsch. Award, Inst. of Math., Stanford U., 1955, A.E. Bennet Award, Soc. of Biol. Psychiatry, 1961; scholar Fgn. Exch. Scholar, NAS, Yugoslavia, 1974. Fellow: Am. Psychol. Soc., Soc. of Biol. Psychiatry, Am. Psychol. Assn.; mem.: Soc. for Psychophysiological Rsch., Acad. of Psychosomatic Medicine, Sigma Xi. Jewish. Achievements include Author, In Numerous Research Journals, 1952-1996. Avocation: studying philosophy, art, and music. Home: 706 Powder Mill Lane Wynnewood PA 19096-4035

RUBIN, LEWIS JOSEPH, physician, researcher; b. NYC, Aug. 5, 1950; s. Theodore and Erna Rubin; 1 child. BA, diploma in Hebraic studies, Yeshiva U., NYC, 1972; MD, Albert Einstein Coll. of Medicine, 1972—75. Am. Bd. Internal Medicine ABIM/ Wash., DC, 1978, diplomate Nat. Bd. Med. Examiners. Internship and residency Duke U. Med. Ctr., 1975—78, Am. Bd. Internal Med Medicine, 1980; assoc. in medicine Duke U., Durham, NC, 1978—79; assoc. prof. medicine U. Tex. Health Sci. Ctr., Dallas, 1980—84, 1984—85, U. Md., Balt., 1985—89, prof. medicine, 1989—98, dir. divsn. pulmonary medicine, 1985—98; prof. medicine U. Calif. San Diego, 1999—. Cons. in field. Contbr. more than 230 articles to sci. publs.;, editor 5 textbooks. Fellow: ACP, Am. Coll. Chest Physicians (bd. govs. 1997), Am. Heart Assn., Royal Coll. Physicians UK; mem.: Am. Soc. Clin. Investigation. Achievements include basic and clinical research in cardiopulmonary diseases, leading to drug developments and new treatments. Avocations: classical music, opera, travel. Home: 5550 Caminito Genio La Jolla CA 92037 Business E-Mail: ljrubin@ucsd.edu.

RUBIN, MARK GORDON, medical association administrator; b. NJ, Oct. 4, 1955; MD, Jefferson Med. Coll., 1981. Pres. APC, 1985—. Office: 153 South Lasky Dr Ste 1 Beverly Hills CA 90212 Office Fax: 310-556-0111. Personal E-mail: vjv429@aol.com.

RUBIN, MELVIN LYNNE, ophthalmologist, educator; b. San Francisco, May 10, 1932; s. Morris and May (Gelman) R.; m. Lorna Isen, June 21, 1953; children: Gabrielle, Daniel, Michael. AA, U. Calif., Berkeley, 1951, BS, 1953; MD, U. Calif., San Francisco, 1957; MS, State U. Iowa, 1961. Diplomate Am. Bd. Ophthalmology, 1963. Intern U. Calif. Hosp., San Francisco, 1957-58; resident in ophthalmology State U. Iowa, 1958-61; attending surgeon Georgetown U., Washington, 1961-63; asst. prof. surgery U. Fla. Med. Sch., Gainesville, 1963-66, assoc. prof. ophthalmology, 1966-67, prof. ophthalmology, 1967—97, prof. emeritus, 1997—, chmn. dept. ophthalmology, 1978-95, eminent scholar, 1989-97, eminent scholar emeritus, 1997. Author: Studies in Physiological Optics, 1965, Fundamentals of Visual Science, 1969, Optics for Clinicians, 1971, 2d edit., 1974, 25th ann. edit., 1995, The Fine Art of Prescribing Glasses, 1978, 3d edit., 2004; editor: Dictionary of Eye Terminology, 1984, Eye Care Notes, 1989, revised edit., 2001, Taking Care of Your Eyes, 2003; cons. editl. bd. Survey Ophthalmology; contbr. more than 100 articles to profl. jours. Co-founder Citizens for Pub. Schs., Inc., 1965, ProArteMusica Gainesville, Inc., 1969, pres., 1971-73; mem. Thomas Ctr. Adv. Bd. for the Arts, 1978-84, nat. sci. adv. bd. Helen Keller Eye Rsch. Found., 1989-96; bd. dirs. Hippodrome State Theater, 1981-87, Friends of Photography Ansel Adams Ctr., 1991-97, Friends of Classic 89 public radio, 2002-08, U. Fla. Found., 2005-, Friends of Music; trustee U. Fla. Performing Arts Ctr., 1995—2008; chmn. nat. art coun. U. Fla. Harn Mus. Art, 2005—; With USPHS, 1961-63. Recipient Best Med. Book for 1978 award Am. Med. Writers Assn., 1979, Shaler Richardson award for svc. to medicine Fla. Soc. Ophthalmology, 1995; M.L. Rubin Ann. Lectureship established in his honor by Fla. Soc. of Ophthalmology, 1993. Fellow ACS, Am. Acad. Ophthalmology (sec., dir. 1978-92, pres. 1988, Sr. Honor award 1987. Guest of Honor 1992; Spl. Recognition award 2010), Found. Am. Acad. Ophthalmology (bd. trustees, 1988-95, chmn., 1992-94), Joint Commn. on Allied Health Pers. in Ophthalmology (Statesman of Yr. award 1987); mem. Assn. Rsch. in Vision and Ophthalmology (trustee 1973-78, pres. 1979), Retina Soc., Macula Soc., Club Jules Gonin, NY Acad. Sci., Fla. Soc. Ophthalmology, Am. Ophthal. Soc. (coun. 1998-2002, chmn. 2002), Pan Am. Soc. Ophthalmology, Ophthalmic Photographers Soc., Alachua County Med. Soc., Fla. Med. Assn., AMA (editorial bd. Archives of Ophthalmology 1975-85), Sigma Xi, Alpha Omega Alpha., Phi Kappa Phi. Office: U Fla Med Ctr PO Box 100284 Gainesville FL 32610-0284 Office Phone: 352-273-8790. Business E-Mail: melrubin@eye.ufl.edu.

RUBIN, PHYLLIS GETZ, health association executive; b. NYC, Aug. 6, 1937; d. Joseph and Sylvia (Rosenberg) Getz; m. James Milton Rubin, Oct. 28, 1961; children: Felicia Sue, Andrea Faith. BA, Syracuse U., 1959; MA, Columbia U., 1961, Adelphi U., 1975. Physical edn. tchr. Hicksville (N.Y.) Pub. Schs., 1959-93; bd. dirs., pres. Assoc. Am. Acad. Allergy, Asthma and Immunology; owner JP Med Fit, 1997—, Phyllis Rubin, Ltd., A Med. Exercise Tng. Co., 1998—. Producer: (video) Aerobic Dancercise for Children, 1987. Bd. dir. COPAY, Great Neck, N.Y., 1986-91; v.p., sec. Pierpont Condominium Bd., 1986-90. Recipient Founder's Day award PTA, 1986. Mem.: N.Y. State Alliance for Health, Phys. Edn., REcreation and Dance (program spkr. 1984, 85, 93, v.p. Nassau zone 1987—2000, Zone Svc. award 1993). Avocations: tennis, reading, meditation, golf. Office Phone: 516-972-2342. E-mail: jpmedfit@aol.com.

RUBIN, RAPHAEL, medical educator, researcher; b. Seattle, Mar. 3, 1956; MD, Boston U., 1979. Prof., rschr. Thomas Jefferson Med. Sch., 1985—. Named Liver Specialist of Yr., NIH. Fellow: Am. Coll. Pathology. Avocations: violin, running. Home: 434 N Hoghland Ave Merion Station PA 19066 Home Fax: 610-668-1390. Personal E-mail: renerubin@hotmail.com.

RUBIN, ROBERT JOSEPH, internist, nephrologist, consultant; b. Bklyn., Feb. 7, 1946; s. B. Norman and Suzanne (Fried) R.; m. Fran Auerbach, June 14, 1970; children: Elyse Beth, David Jon. AB, Williams Coll., 1966; MD, Cornell U., 1970. Diplomate Am. Bd. Internal Medicine, Nephrology. Intern New England Med. Ctr. Hosps., Boston, 1970-71, resident, 1971-72, 74-76; epidemic intelligence officer, respiratory disease and spl. pathogens, divsn. viral diseases Ctr. for Disease Control, 1972-74; asst. dean govt. affairs Tufts U., 1979-84, assoc. prof. medicine, 1981-84. Chief renal divsn. Lemuel Shattuck Hosp., Boston, 1979-81; asst. sec. planning and evaluation U.S. HHS, Washington, 1981-84; clin. assoc. prof. Georgetown U., Washington, 1984-95, clin. prof., 1995—; exec. v.p. ICF, Inc., 1984-88; pres. Health and Scis. Internat., 1988-92, Lewin ICF Inc., 1992, Lewin-VHI, Inc., 1992-96, Lewin Group, 1996-99, CEO, 1999-2001. Contbr. articles to profl. jours. With USPHS, 1972-74, asst. surgeon gen., 1981-84. Robert Wood Johnson Health Policy fellow, 1977 Mem. ACP, AMA, Am. Soc. Nephrology, Internat. Soc. Nephrology, Mass. Med. Soc., Kenwood Club, Potomac Club, Phi Beta Kappa. Republican. Jewish. Office Phone: 202-444-9183.

RUBIN, ROBERT TERRY, psychiatrist, researcher, educator; b. LA, Aug. 26, 1936; s. Joseph Salem and Lorraine Grace (Baum) R.; m. Lynne Esther Mathews, Mar. 10, 1962 (div. Dec. 1980); children: Deborah, Sharon, Rachel; m. Ada Joan Mickas, Jan. 18, 1985. AB in premedical studies, UCLA, 1957; MD, U. Calif., San Francisco, 1961; PhD in physiology, U. So. Calif., 1977. Diplomate Am. Bd. Psychiatry and Neurology. Intern Phila. Gen. Hosp., 1961-62; resident in psychiatry Sch. Medicine UCLA, 1962-65, asst. prof. psychiatry, 1965-71, prof. psychiatry, 1972; prof. Pa. State U., Hershey, 1972-93; prof. neuroscis. Coll. Medicine Drexel U., Pitts., 1992—2006, prof. psychiatry, dir. Ctr. Neurosci. Rsch. Allegheny Campus, 1992—2005; prof. psychiatry UCLA Sch. Medicine, 2005—; chief dept. psychiatry VA Greater LA Healthcare System, 2005—. Cons. Naval Health Rsch. Ctr., San Diego, 1969-70; mem. Brain Rsch. Inst. UCLA, 1969—89; assoc. dir. Pitts. Tissue Engring. Initiative, 1994-2004; trustee Kinsey Inst. Sex Rsch., Ind. U., 1986-90. Contbr. articles to profl. jours. With USNR, 1967—69. Recipient Rsch. Sci. Devel. awards NIMH, 1972-77, Rsch. Scientist award, 1982, 87, 93. Fellow: AAAS, Am. Coll. Psychiatrists, Am. Psychiat. Assn.; mem.: Internat. Soc. Psychoneuroendocrinology (pres. 1984—87). Avocations: swimming, bagpipes. Office: VA Greater LA Healthcare System Dept of Psychiatry 116A 11301 Wilshire Blvd Los Angeles CA 90073 Home Phone: 310-231-0380; Office Phone: 310-268-3319. Business E-Mail: robert.rubin@va.gov.

RUBIN, SAMUEL HAROLD, internist, consultant; b. NYC, July 24, 1916; s. Joseph and Esther (Goldfarb) R.; m. Audrey Arndt, Nov. 20, 1943; children: James E., David A. AB, Brown U., 1938; MD, St. Louis U., 1943; MS, U. Chgo., 1957; DSc (hon.), N.Y. Med. Coll., 1997. Diplomate: Am. Bd. Internal Medicine. Intern Jewish Hosp., St. Louis, 1943-44; resident St. Louis U. Group Hosp., 1944-45, St. Mary's Hosp., Kansas City, Mo., 1945-46; practice medicine Asbury Park, NJ, 1948-61; vol. faculty mem. N.Y. Med. Coll., 1948-61, assoc. prof. dept. medicine, 1962-65, prof., 1965—, dir. Inst. Human Values in Med. Ethics, 1984-86; chief med. service N.Y. Med. Coll.-Met. Hosp. Center, 1966-71, assoc. dean, 1971-72, exec. dean, 1972-74, dean, v.p. acad. affairs, 1975, provost, dean, 1977-83, provost, dean emeritus, 1983—, cons., 1983—. Mem. bd. trustees St. Clares' Hosp., N.Y.C., 1985-2000, N.Y. Med. Coll., 1988-94. Contbr. articles to med. jours. With M.C. AUS, 1946-48. NIH program dir. grantee, 1966-71 Fellow A.C.P.; mem. N.Y. Acad. Sci. Home: 425E Heritage Hills Dr Somers NY 10589-1912

RUBIN, SETH ISAIAH, psychologist; b. Alexandria, La., Mar. 6, 1945; BA, Northwestern U., 1966, MA, 1968, PhD in Psychology, 1971. Diplomate in psychoanalysis and analytical psychology; cert. profl. qualification in psychology; lic. psychologist, Pa., Calif., Ariz., Mass., Aoo Oregon. Outpatient psychology fellow Hosp. U. Pa., 1978-80; tng. candidate, diploma candidate C.G. Jung Inst., Zurich, 1982-87; instr. dept. psychology Northwestern U., 1969-70; asst. prof. dept. psychology U. Ill. at Chgo. Circle, 1970-72; asst. rsch. prof. dept. psychiatry Med. Coll. Pa., 1974-75; asst. prof. dept. cmty. medicine U. Pa., 1975-76, asst. prof. dept. rsch. medicine, 1976-77, asst. prof. dept. ob-gyn., 1976-83, clin. assoc. dpet. psychiatry, 1987-88, clin. asst. prof./clin. assoc prof. psychology in psychiatry, 1987-92; allied health profl. Phila. Psychiat. Ctr., 1988-92; allied health affiliate, clin. psychologist Calif. Pacific Med. Ctr., 1994—2004. Adj. prof. Union Grad. Sch., 1989-96, Calif. Sch. Profl. Psychology, Berkeley/Alameda, 1992—; vis. prof. psychology Saybrook Inst., 1994-95; lectr. in field; dir. James Goodrich Whitney Clinic, C.G. Jung Inst. San Francisco, 2004. Contbr. articles to profl. jours. Fellow Am. Coll. Advanced Practice Psychologists, Internat. Coll. Prescribing Psychologists; mem. APA, Internat. Assn. for Analytical Psychology, Am. Soc. Clin. Psychopharmacology, Assn. Grad. Analytical Psychologists of the C.G. Jung Inst., San Francisco Jung Inst. (dir., James Goodrich Whitney Clin.), Soc. for Psychotherapy Rsch., othrs. Office: 2019 A Webster St San Francisco CA 94115-2329 Office Phone: 415-771-5115. E-mail: sirseth@well.com.

RUBIN, STEPHEN CURTIS, gynecologic oncologist, educator; b. Phila., May 24, 1951; s. Alan and Helen (Metz) R.; m. Anne Loughran, May 30, 1985; children: Michael, Elisabeth. BS, Franklin & Marshall U., 1972; MD, U. Pa., 1976. Diplomate Am. Bd. Ob-gyn. Intern in ob-gyn. U. Pa. Hosp., Phila., 1976—77, residency in ob-gyn., 1977—80, fellow in gynecologic oncology, 1980—92; asst. prof. ob-gyn. Med. Coll. Pa., Phila., 1982-85, dir. surg. gynecology, 1982-85, chief gynecol. oncology, 1984-85; asst. mem. gynecol. staff Meml. Sloan-Kettering Hosp., NYC, 1985—90, assoc. mem., 1990—93; asst. prof. ob-gyn Cornell U. Med. Coll., 1985—90, assoc. prof., 1990—93; prof. ob-gyn., chief gynecologic oncology U. Pa., Phila., 1993—, Franklin Payne prof., gyn. oncology, 2003—. Mem. divsn. gynecol. oncology, 1997-2003, dir. divsn. gynecol. oncology 2005-, mem. bd. dirs., 2005-, mem. exec. com., 2008-, chair Subspecialties Com., 2008-, Am. Bd. Ob.-Gyn. Editor: Ovarian Cancer, Cervical Cancer, Chemotherapy of Gynecologic Cancer, Uterine Cancer; contbr. over 250 articles to profl. publs. Recipient Career Devel. award Am. Cancer Soc., 1987, Boyer award Meml. Sloan-Kettering; grantee Nat. Cancer Inst., 1991, 96, 98, 99, 2005, 07, 10 Mem. ACS, ACOG, Am. Soc. Clin. Oncology, Soc. Gynecol. Oncologists (Pres.'s award 1993), Am. Gynecol. and Obstet. Soc., Soc. Gynecologic Investigation, Soc. Pelvic Surgeons, Gynecol. Cancer Found. (Karin Smith award 1996) Office: Univ Pa Med Ctr 3400 Civic Ctr Blvd Philadelphia PA 19104-4206 Office Phone: 215-662-3318.

RUBIN, THEODORE ISAAC, psychiatrist, writer; b. Bklyn., Apr. 11, 1923; s. Nathan and Esther (Marcus) R.; m. Eleanor Katz, June 16, 1946; children: Jeffrey, Trudy, Eugene. BA, Bklyn. Coll., 1946; MD, U. Lausanne, Switzerland, 1951; grad., Am. Inst. Psychoanalysis, 1964. Resident psychiatrist Los Angeles VA Hosp., 1953, Rockland State Hosp., NY, 1954, Bklyn. State Hosp., 1955, Kings County Hosp., NY, 1956; chief psychiatrist Women's House of Detention, NYC, 1957; mem. faculty Downstate Med. Sch., NY State U., 1957-59; pvt. practice NYC, 1956—. Tng. and supervising psychoanalyst Am. Inst. for Psychoanalysis of Karen Horney Clinic and Ctr.; mem. faculty Am. Inst. Psychoanalysis, 1962—; pres. emeritus bd. trustees Am. Inst. Psychoanalysis. Author: Jordi, 1960, Lisa and David, 1961, Sweet Daddy, 1963, In The Life, 1964, Platzo and the Mexican Pony Rider, 1965, The Thin Book by a Formerly Fat Psychiatrist, 1966, The 29th Summer, 1966, Cat, 1966, Coming Out, 1967, The Winner's Note Book, 1967, The Angry Book, 1969, Forever Thin, 1970, Emergency Room Diary, 1972, Doctor Rubin Please Make Me Happy, 1974, Shrink, 1974, Compassion and Self-Hate, An Alternative to Despair, 1975, Love Me, Love My Fool, 1976, Reflections in a Goldfish Tank, 1977, Alive and Fat and Thinning in America, 1978, Reconciliations, 1980, Through My Own Eyes, 1982, One to One, Understanding Personal Relationships, 1983, Not to Worry, The American Family Book of Mental Health, 1984, Overcoming Indecisiveness, 1985, Lisa and David, The Story Continues, 1986, Miracle at Bellevue, 1986, Real Love, 1990, Child Potential, 1990, Anti-Semitism: A Disease of the Mind, 1990, Little Ralphie and The Creature, 1998, Anti-Semitism: A Disease of the Mind, 2011; mem. editl. bd. Am. Jour. Psychoanalysis; also articles, columns.; co-writer (TV movie) Lisa and David, 1998. Served as officer USNR, World War II. Recipient Adolf Meyer award, Assn. Improvement Mental Health, 1963. Fellow Am. Acad. Psychoanalysis; mem. NY County Med. Soc., Am. Psychiat. Assn., Assn. Advancement Psychoanalysis, Authors Guild, Contemporary Authors, Writers Guild East. Office: 141 E 55th St Ste 9B New York NY 10022 Office Phone: 917-301-4889.

RUBINO, FRANCESCO, surgeon, educator; b. Cosenza, Italy, July 17, 1969; s. Ottavio Rubino and Anna Maria Manna. MD, Cath. U. Rome, 1994. Cert. Gen. Surgeon (Italy) 2000, ECFMG 1998, lic. Med. Practice Italy 1995. Resident gen. surgery Cath. U., Rome, Italy, 1996—2000; rsch. fellow laparoscopic surgery Cleve. Clinic Found., Cleve., 1996—97, Mt. Sinai Med. Ctr., New York, NY, 1999—2000; clin. fellow advanced laparoscopic surgery Rsch. Inst. Cancer of Digestive Sys.-European Inst. of Telesurgery, Strasbourg, France, 2001—07, instr. minimally invasive surgery, 2001, attending surgeon, 2003; assoc. prof. surgery Cath. U., Rome; chief gastrointestinal metabolic surgery, asst. prof. surgery Weill Cornell Med. Coll., NYC, 2007—; asst. attending surgeon NY-Presbyn.-Weill Cornell Med. Ctr., NYC, 2007—, head Diabetes Surgery Ctr., 2007—. Named one of 40 Under 40, Crain's NY Bus., 2009. Mem.: Internat. Club of Young Laparoscopic Surgeons, Brazilian Soc. for Bariatric and Metabolic Surgery, Am. Soc. for Metabolic and Bariatric Surgery, Italian Assn. Endoscopic Surgeons. Roman Catholic. Office: Weill Cornell Med Coll 525 East 68th St, P714 New York NY 10065 Office Phone: 212-746-5925. Office Fax: 212-746-8574. Business E-Mail: f.rubino@lycos.com. *

RUBINO, JOELLE L., physical therapist, athletic trainer; b. Latrobe, Pa., Feb. 23, 1978; d. Dennis L. and Nancy D. Rubino. BA in Psychology, W.Va. Wesleyan Coll., Buckhannon, BS in Sports Medicine, 2000; D in Phys. Therapy, Creighton U., Omaha, 2003. Athletic trainer cert. NATABOC. Lab./tchg. asst. W.Va. Wesleyan Coll., 1997—2000; tchg. asst. Creighton U., Omaha, 2002; clinician Brown and Assocs. PT, Dover, Del., 2003—; instr. Poly. Sch. District, Adult Edn., 2009—; instr. phys. therapy aide course Polytech Adult Edn., 2009—10. Presenter Sideline Sports Medicine. Vol. Sr. Olympics, Dover, 2004—06; life mem., vol. Girl Scouts US, Dover, 1996—2010; com. mem. Wyoming United Meth. Ch., Del., 2006; vol. Habitat for Humanity, 2000—06; vol. med. coverage DFRC, Newark, 2004—11. Recipient Most Creative Nat. Award, Nat. Athletic Tng. Month. Mem.: Del. Athletic Trainers Assn. (presenter, traumatic brain injuries 2008, chair PR com., Del. Athletic Trainer of the Yr. 2005), Nat. Athletic Trainers Assn., Am. Phys. Therapy Assn., Kappi Phi (life; pres. 1999—2000). Republican. Office: Brown & Assocs Phys Therapy APRO Phys Therapy Co 1288 S Governors Ave Dover DE 19904 Personal E-mail: rubinoj_2000@yahoo.com.

RUBINOFF, IRA, biologist, researcher, conservationist; b. NYC, Dec. 21, 1938; s. Jacob and Bessie (Rose) R.; m. Roberta Wolff, Mar. 19, 1961; 1 son, Jason; m. Anabella Guardia, Feb. 10, 1978; children: Andres, Ana. BS, Queens Coll., 1959; A.M., Harvard U., Cambridge, Mass., 1960, PhD, 1963. Biologist, asst. dir. marine biology Smithsonian Tropical Rsch. Inst., Balboa, 1964—70, asst. dir. sci., 1970—73, dir., 1973—2008, dir. emeritus and sr. staff scientist, 2008—. Assoc. in ichthyology Harvard U., 1965—; courtesy prof. Fla. State U., Tallahassee, 1976—; mem. sci. adv. bd. Gorgas Meml. Inst., 1964-88; trustee Rare Animal Relief Effort, 1976-85; bd. dirs. Charles Darwin Found. for Galapagos Islands, 1977—; chmn. bd. fellowships and grants Smithsonian Inst., 1978-79, acting under sec. sci., 2007-08; vis. fellow Wolfson Coll., Oxford U., Eng., 1980-81; vis. scientist Mus. Comparative Biology-Harvard U., 1987-88; dep. dir. US Nat. Mus. Natural History, 2001-02. Author Strategy for Preservation of Moist Tropical Forests; contbr. articles to profl. jours. Vice chmn. bd. dirs. Panama Canal Coll., 1989-93; bd. dirs. Internat. Sch. Panama, 1983-85, 90-93, Fundacion Natura, sec., bd. dirs., 1991—; bd. dirs. Ancon Panama, 1985-97, Earthwatch, 1995-97, City of Knowledge, 1996—, Charles Darwin Found. Inc., 2003-, Mpala Wildlife Found., 2003-; hon. dir. Instituto Latino Americano de Estudios Avanzados; dir. Biomusceo Panama. Awarded Order of Vasco Nunez de Balboa of Republic of Panama, Secs. Gold medal, 2008, Joseph Henry medal Smithsonion Inst., 2010. Bd. Regents, 2009. Fellow Linnean Soc. (London), AAAS, Am. Acad. Arts & Scis.; mem. Am. Soc. Naturalists, Soc. Study of Evolution, NY Acad. Scis. Clubs: Cosmos (Washington).

RUBINOW, DAVID R., psychiatrist, department chairman; b. Conn., Sept. 20, 1949; MD, U. Conn., 1975. Chief, psychiatry consultation svc. NIMH, 1982—92, chief, behavioral endocrinology br., 1996—2005, clin. dir., 1987—2005, dir., residency tng., 1990—96; clin. prof., psychiatry Georgetown U. Med. Sch., 1991—2005; chair, dept. psychiatry U. NC Sch. Medicine, Chapel Hill, 2005—. Fellow: Am. Coll. Neuropsychopharmacology; mem.: ACP (William C. Menninger Meml. award), NIMH (named Mentor of the year), Acad. Psychosomatic Medicine, Soc. Biol. Psychiatry (Rsch. award, Gold medal award, A.E. Bennett Neuropsychiatric rsch. found. award), Am. Coll. Psychiatrists (Mood Disorders Rsch. award). Office: 101 Manning Dr CB 7160 10514 Neuro Chapel Hill NC 27599 Office Fax: 919-966-7659. Business E-Mail: drubinow@med.unc.edu.

RUBINSON, HOWARD ALAN, physician; b. Bklyn., Aug. 24, 1949; s. Samuel and Hilda (Cohen) R.; m. Carol Berman, May 16, 1976; children: Roger, Abby. AB, Cornell U., Ithaca, NY, 1971; MD, Hahnemann Med. Coll., Phila., 1975. Diplomate Am. Bd. Radiology. Radiology instr. Sch. Medicine U. Miami, Fla., 1979-81, asst. prof. radiology Fla., 1981-84; mem. attending staff North Beach Hosp., Ft. Lauderdale, Fla., 1984-89, North Ridge Med. Ctr., Ft. Lauderdale, Fla., 1989—2006, Hollywood Med. Ctr., Fla., 1998—2006, Parkway Regional Med. Ctr., 2001—05; attending staff Holy Cross Hosp., Ft. Lauderdale, Fla., 2004—, Mercy Hosp., Miami, Fla., 2005—. Contbr. articles to profl. jours. Mem. Am. Coll. Radiology, Am. Soc. Emergency Radiology, Soc. Breast Imaging, Radiol. Soc. N.Am., Am. Roentgen Ray Soc., Soc. Thoracic Radiology, South Fla. Radiol. Soc. (pres. 1996-97), Fla. Radiol. Soc., Fla. Med. Assn., Broward County Med. Assn. Office: 2929 E Commercial Blvd Ste 600 Fort Lauderdale FL 33308 Personal E-mail: hrubinson@comcast.net.

RUBINSTEIN, ADAM JASON, plastic surgeon; b. NYC, Mar. 27, 1970; MD in Rsch. and Cmty. Svc. with distinctions, St. Louis U., 1996. Plastic surgeon Adam J. Rubinstein, MD PA, 2003—. Asst. prof. surgery FIU Sch. Medicine, NOVA Southeastern U. Sch. Medicine. Fellow: ACS; mem.: Am. Soc. Bariatric Plastic Surgeons, Internat. Soc. Aesthetic Plastic Surgery, Am. Soc. Aesthetic Plastic Surgery, Am. Soc. Plastic Surgeons. Avocations: sports, travel. Office: 19495 Biscayne Blvd Ste 200/201 Miami FL 33180 Business E-Mail: drr@dr-rubinstein.com.

RUBINSTEIN, ARYE, pediatrician, microbiologist, immunologist, educator; b. Tel Aviv, Oct. 02; came to U.S., 1971; s. Reuven and Kathe (Samson) R.; m. Orna Eisenstein, Dec. 7, 1965 (div. 1982); children: Ran, Yair, Avner, Noam; m. Charline Nezri, Dec. 27, 1983; children: Reuven, Rena, Rachel. MD, U. Berne, Switzerland, 1962. Diplomate Am. Bd. Pediatrics; bd. cert. in pediatrics, Israel, Switzerland; Am. Bd. Allergy and Immunology cert. in allergy and immunology. Intern, pediatrics resident, fellow U. Tel Aviv, 1962-67; rsch. assoc. divsn. immunology Med. Sch. Harvard Coll., 1971-73; dir.

divsn. immunology and bone marrow transplantation U. Berne, 1969-71; asst. prof. cell biology Albert Einstein Coll. Medicine, Bronx, 1973-80, asst. prof. pediatrics, 1973-77, assoc. prof., 1977-82, assoc. prof. microbiology and immunology, 1981-85, prof. pediatrics, 1982—, prof. microbiology and immunology, 1985—. Dir. divsn. clin. allergy and immunology Albert Einstein Coll. Medicine, dir. tng. program for allergy and immunology; dir. divsn. clin. allergy and immunology Albert Einstein Coll. Medicine, Montefiore Med. Ctr.; chief Ctr. Adult and Radioactive Chem. Immunology, Albert Einstein Coll. Medicine, Hosp. Albert Einstein Coll. Medicine; mem. study sect. on AIDS rsch. NIH; dir Focis affiliated Clin. Immunology Ctr. Albert Einstein Coll. Medicine Montegiare Med. Ctr. Mem. editl. bd. Annals of Allergy; reviewer New England Jour. Medicine, Jour. for Clin. Investigation, Jour. Pediatrics, Jour. Clin. Allergy and Immunology; contbr. over 175 articles to profl. publs. Lt. armed svcs., Israel, 1955-57. Recipient Lifetime award in Immunology, Humanitarian award DIFFA, Birch Svcs. for Children, Annual award U.S. Asst. Sec. of Health for excellence in AIDS rsch. and treatment, 1990, Bela Shick award for Pediatric Rsch., 1993, Ackerman award for Sci. and Humanity, 1995, Heroes in Medicine Internat. award, 2000; AIDS Rsch. Program grantee NIH, Bronx. Fellow Am. Acad. Allergy and Immunology, Am. Coll. Allergy & Immunology; mem. N.Y. Acad. Scis., Soc. Pediatric Rsch., The Harvey Soc., Am. Coll. Allergy, Clin. Immunology Soc., Clin. Immunology Soc. Office: Albert Einstein Coll Medicine 1625 Blondell Ave Bronx NY 10461-1926 Business E-Mail: arye.rublinslein@einskin.yu.edu. *

RUBINSTEIN, ROSALINDA, allergist, medical association administrator; b. Buenos Aires, Jan. 3, 1942; arrived in US, 1967; MD, U. Buenos Aires, 1965. Residence Beth Israel Hosp., 1968-70; fellow in allergy-asthma Harvard Med. Sch., Boston, 1970-71; allergy-asthma asst. pediatrician Columbia Presbyn., NYC, 1971—, Mt. Sinai Med. Ctr., NYC, 1973—78. Bd. dirs. NY Women's Agenda, Argentina Am. Med. Soc.; past pres. Nat. Coun. Women's Health, 1998—2000, pres., 2000—02. Recipient Recognition award, NY Women's Agenda, 1997, Cmty. award, Am. Med. Women's Assn., 1998. Mem.: AMA, Mt. Sinai Med. Ctr., Women's Med. Assn. (pres. 1995—97, Recognition award 1997), NY County Med. Soc., Am. Acad. Allergy-Asthma, Am. Coll. Allergy-Asthma, Harvard Club, Columbia Presbyn. Club. Home and Office: 1016 5th Ave New York NY 10028-0132 Office Phone: 212-737-2996. Personal E-mail: r.rubinsteinmdi@verizon.net.

RUBIO, FERNANDO GONGORA, medical educator; b. Bogotá, Colombia, Mar. 4, 1958; MD, U. Libre, 1985; PhD, Escola Paulista de Medicina UNIFESP, 2000. Adj. prof. Faculdade de Medicina de São José do Rio Preto, 1993—. Physician Hosp. de Base FUNFARME, 1993—2011. Mem.: Soc. Brasileira De Infectologia. Avocation: horseback riding. Home: Sebastiao Bernardino De Souza 100 São José do Rio Preto São Paulo 15062 001 Brazil Home Fax: 55-17-32015000 ext 1582. Personal E-mail: gongora@famerp.br.

RUBNITZ, MYRON ETHAN, pathologist, educator; b. Omaha, Mar. 2, 1924; s. Abraham Srol and Esther Molly (Jonich) R.; m. Susan Belle Block, Feb. 9, 1952; children: Mary Lu Rubnitz Roffe, Peter, Thomas (dec.), Robert. BSc, U. Nebr., 1945; MD, U. Nebr., Omaha, 1947. Diplomate Am. Bd. Pathology. Intern Mt. Sinai Hosp., Cleve., 1947-48, fellow in hematology NYC, 1948-49; resident in pathology Michael Reese Hosp., Chgo., 1949-51; pathologist VA Hosp., Hines, Ill., 1953-56, chief labs., 1956-93, cons., 1993—; assoc. prof. pathology Loyola U. Med. Sch., Maywood, Ill., 1963-70, prof., 1970-99, prof. emeritus, 1999—. Adj. prof. Ill. State U., Normal, 1979-96, 2003—, U. St. Francis, Joliet, Ill., 1989—, Ea. Ill. U. Charleston, 1991—, Western Ill. U., Macomb, 1991—; clin. instr. Augustana Coll., Rock Island, Ill., 1991—, med. dir. Myron Rubntz Sch. Med. Tech., 1974-. Chmn. candidates com. Village Caucus, Winnteka, Ill., 1969-70; bd. dirs. Chgo. Commons Assn., 1968—2000, North Shore Sr. Ctr., 1998-2009; mem. New Trier High Sch. Caucus, Winnetka, 1972-74. With AUS, 1943-46, PTO; lst lt. M.C., U.S. Army, 1951-53. Fellow Am. Soc. Clin. Pathologists, Coll. Am. Pathologists; mem. Internat. Acad. Pathology, Assn. VA Pathologists (pres. 1982-84), Chgo. Pathology Soc., Lake Shore Country Club (Glencoe, Ill.), Mich. Shores Club (Wilmette, Ill.). Avocation: travel. Home: 979 Sheridan Rd Winnetka IL 60093 Office: 456 Frontage Rd Winnetka IL 60093 Personal E-mail: susiebelle@sbcglobal.net.

RUCKDESCHEL, JOHN CHARLES, health facility administrator; b. Newport, RI, Jan. 5, 1946; s. John Adam and Rita Frances (Riley) R.; m. Angela Stone, June 15, 2002; children: Daniel, Emily, Darby, Haley. BSc, Rensselaer Poly. Inst., Troy, NY, 1967; MD, Albany Med. Coll., NY, 1971; Found. for Advanced Edn. in the Scis., NIH, 1973, Found. for Advanced Edn. in the Scis., NIH, 1983—84. Lic. NY, Fla., Mich., cert. Am. Bd. Internal Medicine, Med. Oncology. Straight med. intern Johns Hopkins Hosp., Balt., 1971-72; staff assoc. Nat. Cancer Inst., Balt. Cancer Rsch. Ctr., Balt., 1972-75; sr. asst. resident, medicine Beth Israel Hosp., Boston, 1975-76; asst. prof. medicine Albany Med. Coll., NY, 1976-79, assoc. prof. medicine NY, 1979-85, prof. medicine, 1985-91, head div. med. oncology NY, 1987-91, dir. joint ctr. for cancer and blood disorders NY, 1999—2001; dir., CEO H. Lee Moffitt Cancer Ctr., Tampa, 1991—2002; pres. H. Lee Moffitt Cancer Hosp., 1991—2002, Moffitt Cancer Found., 1994—2002, Lifetime Cancer Screening, Inc., 1994—2002; prof. oncology and medicine U. South Fla. Coll. Medicine, 1991—2002; pres., CEO Barbara Ann Karmanos Cancer Inst., Detroit, 2002—; prof. medicine & oncology Wayne State U. Sch. Medicine, Detroit, 2002—, assoc. dean, cancer affairs, 2002—, interim chair, radiation oncology, 2002—03; sr. v.p., cancer Detroit Med. Ctr., 2002—05; pres. The Cancer Hosp., 2002—05. Vis. scientist Nat. Cancer Inst.-Navy Med. Oncology Branch, Bethesda, Md., 1983—84; vis. prof. Found. for Promotion of Cancer Rsch., Nat. Cancer Ctr., Tokyo, 1990; lung cancer steering com. Eastern Cooperative Oncology Group, 1977—2002, lung cancer steering com. chmn., 1982—84, chmn., toxicity com., 1987—89, prin. investigator, Albany Med. Coll., 1989—91, prin. investigator, H. Lee Moffitt Cancer Ctr. & Rsch. Inst., 1991—94, chmn., cancer prevention com., 2002—02; mem. Lung Cancer Study Group, 1982—90, exec. officer, 1986—90; co-chair Nat. Cancer Inst., Lung Cancer Progress Review Group, 2001; bd. dir. Mich. Cancer Consortium, 2002—, Nat. Comprehensive Cancer Network, 1998—2002, exec. com., 2000—02; Ctr. and Inst. adv. com. Wayne State U. Divsn. Rsch., 2004—; mem. adv. bd. Cancer Control Rsch. Adv. Coun. State of Fla., 1992—2002, chmn., 1994—96; site visitor, ad hoc reviewer Nat. Cancer Inst., 1978—2003; external advisor, reviewer for several organizations and programs, 1986—; bd. dir., physicians group U. Southern Fla., 1992—2002, mem. Dean's exec. coun., 1992—2002, bd. dir., rsch. found., 1992, 2002, mem. presdl. search com., 1993, 99, bd. dir., Health Scis. Ctr. Self-Insurance Programs Coun., leadership coun., 1994—2002, mem. Inst. on Aging, 1996—2002, mem. adv. bd., PhD program in applied physicis, 1999—2002, mem. steering com., Ctr. for Entrepreneurship and Global Mgmt. Tech., 2000—02. Co-editor: (textbook) Thoracic Oncology, 1989, 95; Lung and Mediastinum. sect. editor Current Opinion in Oncology, 1996-99; lead author (lung cancer chpt.) Clinical Oncology, 3rd edit., 2004; editor-in-chief Evidence-Based Oncology 1999-2002; mem. editl. bd. Current Treatment Options in Oncology, Oncology Spectrums, Medical Oncology, Social Marketing Quarterly, Journal Cancer Education, Cancer Control: Journal Moffitt Cancer Ctr.; reviewer Annals Internal Medicine, Annals Oncology, Cancer Chemotherapy and Pharmacology, Cancer Research, Chest, Journal Clinical Oncology, Journal Nat. Cancer Inst., Journal Neuro-Oncology, Investigational New Drugs, Preventative Medicine, Proceedings for NAS; contbr. articles to med. jours. Gen. chair capital campaign Sacred Heart Ch., 1998; staff physician People's Free Med. Clinic, Balt., 1972—75; pres., bd. dir. United Urban Ministry Troy, NY, 1976—80; mem. Sand Lake Ambulance, NY, 1984—91, bd. dir. NY, 1984—85, line officer NY, 1985—87, bd. pres. NY, 1989—91; pres. West Sand Lake Vol. Fire Dept., NY, 1981—83, line officer NY, 1982—83, NY, 1985—86; bd. trustee, Suncoast Chpt. Leukemia Soc. Am., 1995—98; bd. dir. Jesuit HS Found., 1998—2000; chair, health/bio-med. com. Tampa C. of C., 1999, mem. steering com., Com. of 100, 2001—02; bd. trustee Jesuit HS, 2000—02; bd. dir., trust com. bd. Sun Trust Bank, 2000—02; mem. cmty. adv. bd. Jr. League Tampa, 2002. US Pub. Health Srv., 1972—75. Recipient Physicians Recognition award, AMA, 1974—, Excel award for Excellence in Comm. Leadership, 1994, Rensselaer Alumni Assn. Fellows award-Biology, 1996, Bellwether award for Lifetime Achievement, 1997, Town and Gown Cmty. Svc. award, 1999, 11th Ann. Fla. Med. Bus. Healthcare Physician Bus. Leadership award, 2000, Exemplary Alumni award, Albany Med. Coll., NY, 2000, Disting. Southern Oncologist award, 2001; named Brooks Brothers Man of Yr., 1994; named one of Best Doctors in Am., Americas Top Doctors, 1993—, The Med. Bus. Top 25: The Most Influential Physicians in Tampa Bay, 1998, Tampa Bay Mag. Doctors Chosen by Doctors, 2001. Fellow ACP, Am. Coll. Chest Physicians; mem. AMA, Am. Assn. Cancer Insts. (bd. dir. 1997-99, legis. com. 2001-), U. Liggett Sch. Grosse Pointe Woods, NJ, 2007-, Greater Detroit Area Health Coun., 2006-, Am. Cancer Soc. (jr. faculty clin. fellow, 1977-80, nat. adv. com. on psychosocial and behavioral rsch. 1986-89, chair, 1989, bd. dir. Greater Tampa, 1992-97, chair, rsch. com. fla. divsn., 1999-2000, bd. dir. Fla. divsn. 1997-2002, exec. com. Fla. divsn. 1998-2002, med. v.p., Fla. divsn. 1999-2000, pres. Fla. divsn., 2001-2002), Am. Assn. for Cancer Rsch. (mem. fin. com. 2001-), Am. Assn. for Cancer Edn., Am. Soc. Clin. Oncology (AJCC rep. 2000-), Am. Coll. Physician Execs., Am. Fedn. for Clin. Rsch. (coun., eastern sect. 1981-86), Internat. Assn. for the Study of Lung Cancer, Am. Assn. Med. Colls.(Coun. Tchg. Hosps. 1997-), Nat. Coalition for Cancer Rsch. (bd. dir. 1998-2002), US Nat. Com. for the Internat. Union Against Cancer Am. Joint Com. on Cancer, 2000-, Alpha Omega Alpha, Sigma Xi; hon. mem. U. South Fla. Golden Key Internat. Honour Soc. Office: Barbara Ann Karmanos Cancer Inst 4100 John R Detroit MI 48201 Office Phone: 313-576-8670, 313-993-7770. Business E-Mail: ruckdeschel@karmanos.org.

RUCKER, JOSEPH W., plastic surgeon, educator; MD, Mich. State U., East Lansing. Diplomate Am. Bd. Plastic Surgery. Gen. surgery tng.; resident in plastic surgery; fellow in breast reconstruction; clin. asst. prof. family practice dept. med. sch. Univ. Wis.; instr. Nat. Med. Assn.; pvt. practice Rucker MD Plastic Surgery Clinic, Wis., 1984—. Fellow: Internat. Soc. of Cosmetic Laser Surgery, Am. Soc. for Laser Medicine and Surgery, ACS; mem.: Internat. Soc. of Clin. Plastic Surgeons, Nat. Med. Assn., Wis. Soc. of Plastic Surgeons, Wis. State Med. Soc., Midwestern Assn. of Plastic Surgeons, Am. Assn. of Hand Surgeons. Office: Rucker MD Plastic Surgery Clinic 3221 Stein Blvd Eau Claire WI 54701 Office Phone: 800-456-8222.

RUCKER, STEVE, internist; MD, U. Pittsburgh, 1983. Diplomate Am. Bd. Internal Medicine, cert. nephrology. Intern Long Island Jewish Med. Ctr., resident; fellow Mt. Sinai Med. Ctr.; hospital affiliation includes St. Francis Hosp. Office: Saint Francis Hospital 100 Port Washington Blvd Roslyn NY 11576 Home: Ste 216 1999 Marcus Ave Lake Success New Hyde Park NY 11042 Office Phone: 516-562-6000.

RUCKMAN, ROGER NORRIS, pediatric cardiologist; b. Washington, Dec. 15, 1944; s. Norris Elliott and Eugenia (Campbell) R.; children: Robert, Karen, Stephen, Jonathan. BA in Chemistry, Williams Coll., Williamstown, Mass., 1966; MD, U. Va., 1970. Cert. in Pediat. 1976, in Pediatric Cardiology 1979. Intern Peter Bent Brigham Hosp., 1970-71; resident Med. Ctr. Hosp. of Vermont, 1973-75; fellow in cardiology Children's Hosp., Boston, 1975-77; asst. prof. pediatrics U. Nebr., Omaha, 1977-79, George Washington U., Washington, 1980-82, assoc. prof. pediatrics, 1982-90, prof. pediatrics, 1990—; pediatric cardiologist Children's Hosp. Nat. Med. Ctr., Washington, 1980—, chmn. cardiology, 1986-89. Contbr. articles to profl. jours. Served to capt. U.S. Army, 1971-73. Recipient Disting. Service award, Am.-Korea Found., 1972; NIH grantee, 1982—. Fellow Am. Acad. Pediatrics, Am. Coll. Cardiology; mem. Am. Heart Assn., Soc. Pediatric Research, Columbia Country Club (Chevy Chase, Md.). Republican. Presbyterian. Avocations: tennis, golf. Office: CNMC Dept Cardiology 111 Michigan Ave NW Washington DC 20010-2916 Office Phone: 202-476-2020. Business E-Mail: rruckman@cnmc.org.

RUDACILLE, SHARON VICTORIA, medical technician; b. Ranson, W.Va., Sept. 11, 1950; d. Albert William and Roberta Mae (Anderson) Rudacille. BS cum laude, Shepherd Coll., 1972. Med. technologist VA Ctr., Martinsburg, W.Va., 1972—. Instr. Sch. Med. Tech., 1972—76, assoc. coord. edn., 1976—77, edn. coord., 1977—78, quality assurance officer clin. chemistry, 1978—80, lab. svc. quality assurance and edn. officer, 1980—84, clin. chemistry sect. leader, 1984—86, staff med. technologist, 1986—94, supervisory med. technologist, 1994—95, sr. med. technologist, 1995—; adj. faculty mem. Shippensburg (Pa.) State Coll., 1977—78, Shepherd Coll., 1977—78. Mem.: Shepherd Coll. Alumni Assn., W.Va. Soc. Med. Technologists, Am. Soc. Clin. Pathologists, Am. Soc. Med. Tech., Sigma Pi Epsilon. Bapt.

RUDAS, MARCIN, neurosurgeon; b. Bydgoszcz, Jan. 12, 1974; MD, Mil. Med. Acad., PhD, 1999. Asst. Dept. Neurosurgery Mil. Clin. Hosp. Bydgoszcz, Poland, 2001—. Mem.: Polish Soc. Stereotactic and Functional Neurosurgery, Polish Soc. Neurosurgeons, European Soc. Stereotactic and Functional Neurosurgery. Avocations: tennis, bicycling, motorcycling. Office: Powstancow Warszawy 5 Bydgoszcz Kujawsko-Pomorskie 85-915 Poland Office Fax: 48523787094. Business E-Mail: marad@poczta.onet.pl.

RUDD, BETTY KYPRIANOU, psychologist; b. Nicosia, Cyprus, Jan. 13, 1949; arrived in Eng., 1954; d. Praxiteles Perdios Kyprianou and Loulla Maritsa Lorje; m. Ronald Keith Chalmers (div. 1979); children: Jason, Ben; m. Steven Ashley Rudd, Aug. 4, 1984; children: Maria, Sophia. Grad., Guildhall Sch. Music and Drama, London, 1969; licentiate, Royal Acad. Music, London, 1976; BA with honors, Open U., Eng., 1992; MSc, U. East London, 1995, MS in counseling psychology, 1997; PhD, City U., London, 2001. Cert. couples and family counselor, bereavement and loss therapist. Actress BBC, ITV, Children's Shakespeare Co., London, 1969-76; tutor speech and drama Poole (Eng.) Arts Ctr., 1977-87; counsellor Ashdown Natural Health Ctr., Uckfield, Eng., 1988-91; psychol. counsellor Mental Health Hosp., Uckfield, 1992-93, supr., 1994-96, course creator, convenor, 1997—. Vis. lectr. U. Surrey Roehampton, London, 2000—, U. E. London; cons. Nat. Assn. Substance Abuse, Gravesend, Eng., 1998-2000; dir., sec. Hygeia Health Ltd., 2002—; sr. lectr., placement coord. U. East London, 2005-07, dir Index Ind. Excellence Workshops, 2009 Author: The Counsellor's Basics, 1997, Talking is for Kids, 1999, Talking is for Us, 2001, EQ Book & EQ Game, 2002, EQ Pack, 2nd edit. 2009, Talking Is for All, 2008; co-author: Great Ways to De-Stress, 2002, Body Mind Update, 2003, Talking Is for Teens, 2003; editor Body Mind Pub., 2000—, Help Ypur Child Develop Emotional Literacy, 2009; rev. Crown Pub., Set of 10 EI" Games, 2005, Emotional Intelligence, 2005, Rainbow Game, 2011; cons. Incentive Plus Ltd Bd. dirs. Ashdown Natural Health Ctr., 1986—, Jolly Muffins Theatre Troupe, Uckfield, 1990—; co-founder Children's Theatre-in-Edn. Team, London, 1971, Forest Row Youth Club, East Grinstead, Eng., 1987; founder Two's Co. Theatre of Mime, London, 1977, Counsellor's Guild, Uckfield, 1996, cons., 1996—. Recipient Maj. award London Edn. Authority, 1967; named Best Mime of Yr., D. Jones Mimes, London, 1979. Mem. Brit. Psychol. Soc. (inaugural; divsn. transpersonal psychology 1995—, past press officer divsn. counselling psychology 1999-2003, chair 2002-04, divsn. psychology bd. examiners, examiner assessor and coord. tng., registered clin. & rsch. supr., 2011-), Brit. Assn. Counselling, Brit. Psychol. Soc. (divsn. counsel, psychol. rep. to Min. of Health in Parliament). Avocations: dinner parties, travel to mediterranean, theater, reading, swimming. Business E-Mail: info@emotionalliteracy.eu.

RUDDY, MICHAEL CONNOR, nephrologist; b. Albany, NY, Oct. 5, 1948; BS, Providence Coll., 1970; MD, UMDNJ-NJ Med. Sch., 1974. Assoc. prof. medicine UMDNJ-Robert Wood Johnson Med. Sch., 1980—2000, clin. assoc. prof. medicine and pharmacology, 2001—11; chief sect. nephrology U. Med. Ctr. Princeton, 2001—. Recipient Outstanding Faculty award, Alpha Omega Alpha. Fellow: ACP, Am. Soc. Hypertension; mem.: Am. Soc. Nephrology. Office: 88 Princeton-Hightstown Rd Princeton Junction NJ 08550 Office Fax: 609-750-7336. Business E-Mail: ruddy_m@msn.com.

RUDER, JOHN REGAN, physician; b. Colorado Springs, Colo., Oct. 23, 1947; s. Ralph Emerson and Rosemary Pierron (Regan) R.; m. Sheri Dee Rigby, July 6, 1985; children: Elizabeth, Lindsey, John. BA, Dartmouth Coll., 1969, MD, 1977. Intern in surgery U. N.Mex. & Affiliated Hosps., 1977-78; med. dir. Navajo Reservation, 1977-78; resident in surgery Dartmouth-Hitchcock Med. Ctr., 1978-81; resident in plastic and reconstructive surgery U. Utah, 1981-83, asst. clin. prof. plastic & reconstructive surgery Salt Lake City, 1986-90; chief plastic & reconstructive surgery VA Hosp., Salt Lake City, 1986-90; clin. instr. hand & upper extremity surgery Loma Linda (Calif.) U., 1990-91; v.p. Hand Surgery Assocs., Arlington Heights, Ill., 1991—. Co-author: (chpts.) Injuries and Rehabilitation of the Upper Extremity, 1998, Upper Extremity Compressive Neuropathies, 1998. Mem. ACS, Am. Soc. for Surgery of the Hand, Am. Soc. of Plastic and Reconstructive Surgery, Am. Assn. Hand Surgery, Alpha Omega Alpha. Office: Hand Surgery Assocs 515 W Algonquin Rd Ste 120 Arlington Heights IL 60005-4440

RUDERMAN, BRIAN SANDERS, pharmacist, phamacotherapist; s. Herman and Gloria Ruderman. BS in Pharmacy, L.I. U., Bklyn., 1981; MS in Immunology, U. Tex., Dallas, 1985; PharmD, U. Fla., 2001. Bd. cert. pharmacotherapy specialist Bd. Pharm. Specialties, 2001, lic. pharmacist Fla., 1988, N.Y., 1982, N.J., 1981. Pharmacist Parkland Meml. Hosp., Dallas, 1985—89, North Broward Med. Ctr., Pompano Beach, Fla., 1989—93, Delray Med. Ctr., Delray Beach, Fla., 1993—96; pharmacotherapist Westside Regional Med. Ctr., Plantation, Fla., 1996—, Fla. Med. Ctr., Ft. Lauderdale, 2002—. Cmty. spkr. HCA Healthcare Corp., Ft. Lauderdale, 1997—, Area Coun. on Aging of Broward County, Ft. Lauderdale, 2002—; presenter in field. Nursing continuing edn. provider Fla. Bd. Nursing, Plantation, 2000; clin. affiliate asst. prof. Nova Southeastern U., Ft. Lauderdale, 1999—2001. Recipient Proficiency in Pharmacokinetics, Lillian C. Zupko Found., 1980; named to, Nat. Soc. of Collegiate Scholars, 1999; J.S. Lindemann Scholarship for Excellence, J.S. Lindemann Found., 1981, N.Y. Alumni Chpt. scholar, Bernard Horvitz/AZO, 1981, Cancer Immunology Tng. grant, NIH, 1982. Mem.: Am. Soc. Health-System Pharmacists, Am. Coll. Clin. Pharmacy, U. Fla. Alumni Assn. Achievements include research that established the positive impact of a program to automatically adjust medication dosages based on renal function. Office: Westside Regional Med Ctr 8201 West Broward Blvd Plantation FL 33324-2798 Personal E-mail: rxcare@aol.com.

RUDLEY, LLOYD DAVE, psychiatrist; b. Phila., Aug. 7, 1955; s. John Frank and Ida (Rothman) R. BA summa cum laude, U. Pa., 1977; MD, Hahnemann U., 1981. Diplomate Am. Bd. Psychiatry and Neurology. Resident in psychiatry Med. Coll. Pa., Phila., 1981-85; pvt. practice Phila., 1985—, Elmer, NJ, 1986—; staff psychiatrist N.E. Cmty. Mental Health Ctr., Phila., 1985-87, Counseling Program N.J., Marlton, 1987-88; attending psychiatrist Hosp. U. Pa., Phila., 1985—. Attending psychiatrist Inst. of Pa. Hosp., Phila. Psychiat. Ctr.; cons. psychiatrist Horizon Ho, Phila, 1989—; mem. med. adv. bd. Juvenile Diabetes Found., Phila., 1986—. Mem. jr. com. Scheie Eye Inst., Phila., 1985—. Mem. AMA, Am. Psychiat. Assn., Pa. Psychiat. Soc., Pa. Med. Soc., Philadelphia County Med. Soc. (mental health subcom. 1988—, Janssen clin. scholar 1994), Phi Beta Kappa. Republican. Avocation: collecting maps.

RUDLOFF, UDO, surgical oncologist; b. Schweinfurt, Bavaria, Germany, Apr. 16, 1969; arrived in US, 2002; s. Herbert and Helga (Gall) Rudloff. PhD, German Cancer Rsch. Ctr., Heidelberg, 1994; MD, Ruprecht Karls U., Heidelberg, Germany, 1997. Rsch. fellow German Cancer Rsch. Ctr., Heidelberg, 1991—94, European Molecular Biology Labs., Heidelberg, 1993; ho. officer dept. surgery and orthop. Zomba Ctrl. Hosp., Malawi, 1997—98; ho. officer U. Hosp. Aintree, Liverpool, England, 1999, Leicester Gen. Hosp., England, 1999—2000, Hinchingbrooke Hosp., Huntington, England, 2000, Dewsbury Dist. Hosp., England, 2000—01; registrar Guy's and St. Thomas' Hosp., London, 2001—02; house officer North Shore - LI Jewish Health Sys., Manhasset, NY, 2002—05, NYU Sch. Medicine, NYC, 2005—07; fellow surg. oncology Meml. Sloan Kettering Cancer Ctr., NY, 2007—09; tenure track investigator Surgery Br. NCI, Bethesda, Md., 2009—. Recipient Young Talent award, Soc. Advancements Rsch. in Molecular Biology, Heidelberg, Germany, 1995, Young Investigator award, Am. Soc. Clin. Oncology, 2008; scholar, German Acad. Scholarship Found., 1994—97, Scholarship Found. Roman Cath. Ch., 1994. Mem.: Am. Bd. Surgery, Royal Coll. Obstetricians and Gynecologists. Office: Surgery Br NCI Hatfield Bldg CCR 4W 1 4-5940 10 Ctr Dr Bethesda MD 20892 Home Phone: 301-547-9226; Office Phone: 301-496-3098. Personal E-mail: udo_rudloff@hotmail.com. Business E-Mail: rudloffu@mail.nih.gov.

RUDNICK, ABRAHAM, psychiatrist, philosopher; b. Haifa, Israel, Jan. 13, 1964; s. Samuel and Ruth (Laufer) R.; children: Or, Niv, Lee. MD, Hebrew U., 1990; M in Psychiatry, Tel-Aviv U., 1999, PhD in Philosophy, 1999. Med. officer Israel Def. Forces, 1990—94; resident psychiatry Tel-Aviv Cmty. Mental Health Ctr., 1994—99; fellow psychiatry U. Toronto, 1999—2001; rehab. psychiatrist Abarbanel Mental Health Ctr., 2002, Beer Sheva Mental Health Ctr., Israel, 2003—04; head Can. Unit, Internat. Network UNESCO Chair in Bioethics, Haifa; assoc. prof. psychiatry and philosophy U. We. Ont., Canada, 2004—, chair, divsn. social rural psychiatry, 2008—; physician-leader psychosis prog. Regional Mental Health Care, London, Canada, 2004—. Lectr. in behavioral scis. and med. humanities Tel-Aviv U., 1998—2004. Contbr. books and articles to profl. jour. including Jour. Medicine and Philosophy, Internat. Jour. Law and Psychiatry, Biol. Psychiatry, Psychosomatics, Psychiatry Rehab. Jour. Avocation: music. Office: Regional Mental Healthcare 850 Highbury Ave PO Box 5532 Stn B London ON N6A4H1 Canada Home Phone: 519-6795375. Personal E-mail: harudnick@hotmail.com.

RUDNICK, ELLEN AVA, health facility administrator; b. New Haven; d. Harold and C. Vivian (Soybel) R.; children from previous marriage: Sarah, Noah; m. Paul W. Earle. BA, Vassar Coll., 1972; MBA, U. Chgo., 1973. Sr. fin. analyst Quaker Oats, Chgo., 1973-75; from with to pres. Baxter International, Inc., Deerfield, Ill., 1975—83; pres. Baxter Mgmt. Svcs., 1983-1990, HCIA, Balt., 1990-92, CEO Advisors, Northbrook, Ill., 1992—; prin., chmn. Pacific Biometrics, Lake Forest, Calif., 1993-99; exec. dir., clin. prof. Polsky Ctr. for Entrepreneurship University of Chicago, 1999—. Bd. dirs. Liberty Mut. Ins., Pattrson Dental Co., First Midwest Bank. Chief crusader Met. Chgo. United Way, 1982—85; mem. cir. friends Chgo. YMCA, 1985—89; bd. dirs. Evanston Northwestern-Highland Park Hosp., 1990—99, 2003—, Health Mgmt. Sys., 1997—, Evanston-Northwestern Hosp., 2000—02; pres. coun. Nat. Coll. Edn., Evanston, Ill., 1983—93. Office: Univ Chgo Booth Sch Bus 5807 S Woodlawn Chicago IL 60637

RUDOLPH, ABRAHAM MORRIS, pediatrician, educator; b. Johannesburg, Republic of South Africa, Feb. 3, 1924; s. Chone and Sarah (Feinstein) Rudolph; m. Rhona Sax, Nov. 2, 1949; children: Linda, Colin, Jeffrey. MBBCh summa cum laude, U. Witwatersrand, Johannesburg, 1946, MD, 1951; MD (hon.), U. Witwatersrand, Johannesburg, S. Africa, 2006; D (hon.), Rene Descartes U., Paris, 1996. Instr. Harvard Med. Sch., 1955—57, assoc. pediat., 1957—60; assoc. cardiologist in charge cardiopulmonary lab. Children's Hosp., Boston, 1955—60; dir. pediatric cardiology Albert Einstein Coll. Medicine, 1960—66, prof. pediat., assoc. prof. physiology NYC, 1962—66; vis. pediatrician Bronx Mcpl. Hosp. Ctr., NYC, 1960—66; prof. pediat. U. Calif., San Francisco, 1966—94, prof. physiology, 1974—88, Neider prof. pediatric cardiology, prof. ob-gyn and reproductive scis., 1974—94, chmn. dept. pediat., 1987—91, prof. pediatr. emeritus, 1994—; practice medicine, specializing in pediatric cardiology San Francisco. Mem. cardiovasc. study sect. NIH, 1961—65; mem. nat. adv. heart coun., 1968—72; established investigator Am. Heart Assn., 1958—62; career scientist Health Rsch. Coun., NYC, 1962—66; Harvey lectr. Oxford (Eng.) U., 1984; inaugural lectr. 1st Nat. Congress Italian Soc. Perinatal Medicine, 1985. Editl. bd. Pediat., 1964—70, Circulation, 1966—74, 1983—88, assoc. editor Circulation Rsch., 1970, Pediatric Rsch., 1970—77; editor: Rudolph's Pediatrics, Congenital Diseases of the Heart: Clinical-Physiological Considerations, 2001, 2009, Rudolph's Fundamentals of Pediatrics; contbr. articles to profl. jours. Recipient Merit award, Nat. Heart, Lung and Blood Inst., 1986, Arvo Yllpo medal, Helsinki (Finland) U., 1987, Jonxis medal, Children's Hosp. Groningen, 1993, Nils Rosen von Rosenstein award, Swedish Pediat. Soc., 1999, Pollin prize for pediat. rsch., N.Y. Presbyn. Hosp., Columbia U. Coll. Physicians and Surgeons, 2005, award, FRCP(Edin.), 1965, FRCP(Lond.), 1985, E. Mead Johnson award, 1964, Borden Award, Am. Acad. Pediat., 1979, Howland award, Am. Ped. Soc., 1999, Arvo Yilpo award, U. Helsinki, 1987, JMP Jonxis Medal, U. Groningen, 1992, Rosen Von Rosentein award, U. Uppsala; named Disting. Scientist, Am. Heart Assoc., 2003. Fellow: AAAS, Am. Assn. Adv. Sci., Royal Coll. Physicians (London), Royal Coll. Physicians (Edinburgh); mem.: Am. Heart Assn. (Rsch. Achievement award 1991, Founding Disting. Scientist award 2003), Am. Pediatric Soc. (coun. 1985—92, v.p. 1992—93, pres. 1993—94, Howland award 1999), Soc. for Pediatric Rsch. (coun. 1961—64), Soc. for Clin. Investigation, Am. Phys. Soc., Am. Acad. Pediat. (past chmn. sect. on cardiology, E. Mead Johnson award for rsch. in pediat. 1964, Borden award 1979, Lifetime Med. Edn. award 1992, Joseph St. Geme leadership award Pediat. 1993, Founder award, cardiology sect. 2001, Pollin Pediatric Rsch. prize 2005), NAS Inst. Medicine. Office: U Calif Cardiovascular Rsch Inst Calif Rm HSE 1424 Box 0544 San Francisco CA 94143-0544 Home Phone: 415-665-6841. Business E-Mail: abraham.rudolph@ucsf.edu.

RUDOLPH, ANDREW HENRY, retired dermatologist, educator; b. Detroit, Jan. 30, 1943; s. John J. and Mary M. Rudolph; children: Kristen Ann, Kevin Andrew. MD cum laude, U. Mich., 1966. Diplomate Am. Bd. Dermatology. Intern Univ. Hosp., U. Mich. Med. Ctr., Ann Arbor, 1966-67, resident dept. dermatology, 1967-70; pvt. practice medicine specializing in dermatology, 1972—2007; ret., 2007. Asst. prof. dermatology Baylor Coll. Medicine, Houston, 1972-75, assoc. prof., 1975-83, clin. prof., 1983—; chief dermatology svc. VA Hosp., Houston, 1977-82; mem. staff Meth. Hosp. Mem. editl. bd. Jour. Sexually Transmitted Diseases, 1977-85; contbr. to med. publs. Served as surgeon USPHS, 1970-72. Regent's scholar U. Mich., 1966. Fellow Am. Acad. Dermatology; mem. AMA, Am. Dermatol. Assn., Tex. Med. Assn., Harris County Med. Soc., Houston Dermatol. Soc. (past pres.), Tex. Dermatol. Soc., Skin Cancer Found., Am. Venereal Disease Assn. (past pres.), Mich. Alumni Assn. (life), Alpha Omega Alpha, Phi Kappa Phi, Phi Rho Sigma, Theta Xi.

RUDOLPH, SCOTT, pharmaceutical executive; b. 1958; s. Arthur Rudolph. Undergraduate, Dowling Coll. Chmn., CEO NBTY, Inc., Bohemia, NY, 1986—2010, chmn., 2010—. Past chmn. of bd. dirs. Dowling Coll., Long Island, NY, 1997—2000, vice chmn., 2004—10, pres., 2010—. Office: NBTY Inc 2100 Smithtown Ave Ronkonkoma NY 11779 Office Phone: 631-567-9500. Business E-Mail: srudolph@nbty.com. *

RUDRA, SONALI, medicinal chemist; d. Nimai Krishna and Manjula Rudra. B.Pharm with honors, Birla Inst. Tech. Sciences, Pilani, India, 1987—91; MS, NE La. U., Monroe, 1991—94, SUNY, Buffalo, 1994—98; PhD, Jamia Millia Islamia Ranbaxy, New Delhi, 2002—05. Rsch. scientist Ranbaxy Labs. Ltd., Gurgaon, Haryana, India, 1999—2002, sr. rsch. scientist, 2002—05, group leader, 2005—08, project leader, 2005—08, team leader, 2005—08; group leader Chembioteck, 2008—. Contbr. articles to profl. jours. Recipient Gold medal, Maharana Mewar Found., 1991; named G. P. Nair award, Indian Drug Mfrs. Assn., 1991. Mem.: Am. Chem. Soc. Achievements include patents for infectious diseases. Business E-Mail: sonalir@chembiotek.com.

RUDY, YORAM, biomedical engineer, biophysicist, educator; b. Tel Aviv, Feb. 12, 1946; arrived in U.S., 1973; s. Nahum and Yaffa (Krinkin) R. BSc, Technion/Israel Inst. Tech., Haifa, 1971, MSc in Physics, 1973; PhD in Biomed. Engring., Case Western Res. U., 1978. Asst. prof. dept. biomed. engring. Case Western Res. U., Cleve., 1981-86, assoc. prof., 1986-89, prof., 1989—2004, prof. dept. of physiology and biophysics, 1991—2004, prof. dept. medicine, 1992—2004, dir. cardiac bioelectricity rsch./tng. ctr., 1994—2004; Fred Saigh disting. prof. engring., prof. biomed. engring., cell biology and physiology, medicine, radiology and pediat. Washington U., St. Louis, 2004—, dir. Cardiac Bioelectricity and Arrhythmia Ctr., 2004—. Vis. prof. Technion/Israel Inst. Tech., 1982-83, U. Parma, Italy, 1986-87, U. Utah, Salt Lake City, 1990, Tel Aviv U., 1991, Russian Acad. of Scis., St. Petersburg, 1997, U. Berne, Switzerland, 1998, Johns Hopkins U., 2005, Columbia U., 2005, Nagoya U., Japan, 2005, Stamford U., 2007, U. Calif., San Francisco, 2008, The Cleve. Clinic, 2010; cardiovasc. and pulmonary study sect. NIH, 1984-88; lectr., spkr. in field. Hein Wellens Disting. prof. U. Maastricht, The Netherlands, 2008-09; mem. editl. bd. Jour. Electrocardiology, Jour. Cardiovasc. Electrophysiology, Cardiovasc. Rsch., Cardiac Electrophysiology Rev.; Heart Rhythmn Jour. contbr. articles to profl. jours. Grantee NIH, 1985—, Am. Heart Assn., 1990-95, NSF, 1987-94; recipient Gordon K. Moe Prof. award, 1997, NIH-Nat. Heart, Lung and Blood Inst. Merit award, 1998, Tawara Disting. Lectr. award Internat. Union Physiol. Scis., Kyoto, Japan, 2009. Fellow IEEE, Am. Physiol. Soc., Am. Inst. Med. and Biol. Engring., Am. Heart Assn., Heart Rhythm Soc. (named Disting. Scientist award 2010), Biomed. Engring. Soc. (Disting. Lectr. award 2001); mem. NAE, Biophys. Soc., Cardiac Electrophysiology Soc. (pres. 2006-08). Achievements include development of a novel imaging modality for non-invasive imaging of cardiac electrical events from electrical potentials measured on the body surface (electrocardiographic imaging, ECGI), of theoretical models of cardiac excitation at the cellular, sub-cellular and tissue levels; elucidation of the cellular mechanisms of cardiac arrhythmias and the role of tissue architecture in arrhythmogenesis. Office: Washington U St Louis Cardiac Bioelectricity Ctr 290 Whitaker Hall Campus Box 1097 Saint Louis MO 63130-4899

RUEGSEGGER, DONALD RAY, JR., radiological physicist, educator; b. Detroit, May 29, 1942; s. Donald Ray and Margaret Arlene (Elliot) R.; m. Judith Ann Merrill, Aug. 20, 1965 (div.); children: Steven, Susan, Mark, Ann; m. Patricia Ann Mitchell, Oct. 16, 1999. BS, Wheaton Coll., 1964; MS, Ariz. State U., 1966, PhD (NDEA fellow), 1969. Diplomate Am. Bd. Radiology. Radiol. physicist Miami Valley Hosp., Dayton, Ohio, 1969—, chief med. physics sect., 1983—. Physics cons. X-ray dept. VA Hosp., Dayton, 1970-73; adj. asst. prof. physics Wright State U., Fairborn, Ohio, 1973-74, clin. asst. prof. radiology, 1976-81, clin. assoc. prof. radiology, 1981—, group leader in med. physics, dept. radiol. scis. Med. Sch., 1978-85. Mem. AAAS, Am. Assn. Physicists in Medicine (pres. Ohio River Valley chpt. 1982-83, co-chmn. local summer sch. arrangements com. 1986), Am. Coll. Radiology, Am. Phys. Soc., Ohio Radiol. Soc. Home: 6252 Donnybrook Dr Centerville OH 45459-1837 Office: Radiation Therapy Miami Valley Hosp 1 Wyoming St Dayton OH 45409-2722 Home Phone: 937-433-6668; Office Phone: 937-208-4058. E-mail: drruegsegger@mvh.org.

RUEL, JENNIFER, family practice nurse practitioner; b. Mich., Jan. 14, 1976; FNP, U. Detroit Mercy, 2004; DNP, Oakland U., 2008. Nurse practitioner Henry Ford Hosp., 2008—. Interim FNP program coord., asst. prof. U. Detroit Mercy, 2008—11. Home: 18969 Alsie Dr Macomb MI 48044 Personal E-mail: jenfnp@sbcglobal.net.

RUENGSAKULRACH, PERMYOS, cardiologist, thoracic surgeon; b. Bangkok, Oct. 4, 1966; s. Joukaew Hau and Sujitra Mahattanapanich; m. Kanokrat Limnitda, July 29, 2003. MD (hon.), Prince Songkla U., Thailand, 1990; PhD in Cardiac Surgery, U. Melbourne, Australia, 2001; PhD in Math., U. Mahid, Thailand, 2007. Cert. surgeon Royal Coll. Surgeons, Thailand, 1994, cert. thoracic surgeon Royal Coll. Surgeons, Thailand, 1996. Govt. ofcl. grade 6, lectr., dept. of surgery, faculty medicine Prince Songkla U., Thailand, 1990—96; fellow in cardiac surgery Townsville Gen. Hosp., Queensland, Australia, 1997; fellow cardiac surgery U. Melbourne, Austin & Repatriation Med. Ctr., Melbourne, 1996—2001; cardiac surgeon Heart Inst., St. Louis Hosp. and Found., Bangkok, 2001—03; fellow in cardiovasc. surgery Schulich Heart Ctr., Sunnybrook & Women's Coll. Health Sci. Ctr., U. Toronto, Canada, 2003—04; cardiovasc. thoracic surgeon Bangkok Heart Hosp., Bangkok, 2004—. Vice chmn. rsch. ethics com. St. Louis Hosp. and Found., Bangkok, 2002—03, chief of med. record com., 2002—03, facilitator, 2002—03; dir. Cardiac Mercy Project. Cardiovascular Surgery Fellow, U. Toronto, 2004. Fellow: Am. Coll. Chest Physicians, Thailand Royal Coll. Surgeons; mem.: AHA, Internat. Soc. Cellular Therapy, Internat. Sci. Stem Cell Rsch., Soc. Thoracic Surgeons(US), European Assn. For Cardiothoracic Surgery, Thailand Heart Assn., Thailand Soc. Thoracic Surgeons, Asian Cardiovasc. & Thoracic Annal, Thailand Med. Assn. Achievements include research in TAG Young achievers award of 1998, 13th Inter Annual Scientific Congress, Cardio-Thoracic Section, Royal Australasian College of Surgeons; Finalist, 1998 RALPH READER Prize Presentation, 46th Annual Scientific Meeting of Cardiac Society of Australia and New Zealand; Finalist, 1998 VIVEN THOMAS Young Investigator Award, 71st Scientific Session, American Heart Association; Investigators Award in Clinical Research, Austin & Repatriation Medical Centre; Travel Award, 2000, The 8th Annual Meeting of the Asian Society for Cardiovascular Surgery; Finalist, TAG Young achievers award of 2000, 15th Inter Annual Scientific Congress, Cardio-Thoracic Section, Royal Australasian College of Surgeons. Home: 41-724 I House Condemenium RCA Rama 9 Rd Bangkapi Bangkok 10310 Thailand Office: Bangkok Heart Hosp Soi Soonvijai 7 New Petchburi Rd 2 10320 Bangkok Bangkok Thailand Office Phone: 662-3103323. Office Fax: 662-3103000; Home Fax: 662-2031523. Personal E-mail: lpermyos@hotmail.com. Business E-Mail: permyos@bangkokheart.com.

RUESINK, ALBERT WILLIAM, biologist, plant sciences educator; b. Adrian, Mich., Apr. 16, 1940; s. Lloyd William and Alberta May (Foltz) R.; m. Kathleen Joy Cramer, June 8, 1963; children: Jennifer Li, Adriana Eleanor. BA, U. Mich., 1962; MA, Harvard U., 1965, PhD, 1966. Postdoctoral fellow Swiss Fed. Inst. Tech., Zurich, 1966-67; prof. biology Ind. U., Bloomington, 1967—, spl. asst. to Pres. for Faculty Rels., 1999—2005. Recipient Amoco Teaching award Ind. U., 1980 Mem. AAUP (pres. chpt. 1978-79, 90-91), Am. Soc. Plant Biologists, Bot. Soc. Am. Democrat. United Church Of Christ. Home: 2605 E 5th St Bloomington IN 47408-4286 Office: Ind U Dept Biology 1001 E 3d St Bloomington IN 47405 Home Phone: 812-336-8366; Office Phone: 812-855-5555. Business E-Mail: ruesink@indiana.edu.

RUFF, ROBERT LOUIS, neurologist, physiologist, researcher; b. Bklyn., Dec. 16, 1950; s. John Joseph and Rhoda (Alpert) R.; m. Suzanne Ruff, June 7, 2003. BS summa cum laude, Cooper Union, 1971; MD summa cum laude, U. Wash., 1976, PhD in Physiology, 1976. Diplomate Am. Bd. Neurology and Psychiatry, Am. Bd. Phys. Medicine Rehab. Spinal Cord Medicine. Asst. neurologist N.Y. Hosp., Cornell Med. Sch., NYC, 1977—80; asst. prof. physiology and medicine U. Wash., Seattle, 1980—84; assoc. prof. neurology Case We. Res. Med. Sch., Cleve., 1984—92, prof. neurology and neuroscis., 1993—, residency dir., neurology dept., 1994—2003, vice chair neurology dept., 1995—2004; chief dept. neurology Cleve. VA Med. Ctr., 1984—2003, chief phys. medicine and rehab. svc., 1998—2000, 2006—, mgr. rehab. and spinal cord injury and disorder product line, 1999—2003; med. dir. Functional Elec. Stimulation Ctr., Cleve., 2000—; chief Spinal Cord Injury and Dysfunction Svc., Cleveland VA Med. Ctr., 2003—05; dir. neurology and acting rehab. rsch. svc. Office R & D Dept. VA Ctrl. Office, Washington, 2004—07; nat. dir. neurology Dept. Vet. Affairs, Washington, 2006—. Mem. adv. bd. for Neurology Dept. Vets. Affairs, 1989—, mem. study sect. for rehab. rsch. career devel. awards, 1998-, mem. merit rev. bd., rehab. rsch. devel. svc., 1999-2004; mem. NIH adv. couns. NINDS, 2006-, NICHD, 2006-08. Assoc. editor: Neurology, 1994—96, mem. editl. bd.:, 1996—97, Jour. Rehab. and Devel., 1999—, assoc. editor: Jour. Rehab. Rsch. and Devel., 2000—, ad hoc reviewer: various profl. and sci. jours., mem. editl. bd.: Muscle & Nerve, 2006—; contbr. articles to profl. jours., chapters to books. Advisor Child Devel. and Mental Retardation Ctr., Seattle, 1980-84, Burien Devel. Disability Ctr., Wash., 1982-84; med. adv. bd. Muscular Dystrophy Assn., Seattle, 1984, N.E. OH chpt. Multiple Sclerosis Soc.; chmn. med. adv. bd. N.E. OH chpt. Myasthenia Gravis Found., 1987—, mem. state bd. dirs., 1993-, nat. med. adv. bd., 1988-, nat. grant and fellowship com., 1990-2002, mem. nat. bd. dirs., 1990-2002, 2006-. Recipient Tchr. Investigator award NIH, Dr.'s award Periodic Paralysis Assn., 2005; NSF fellow, 1971; NIH grantee, Muscular Dystrophy Assn. grantee, Dept. Vets. Affairs, Rsch. Enhancement Advanced Ctr. awards, 1999—, Dr. award Myasthenia Gravis Found. Am., 2002; NY State Regents med. scholar, 1971. Fellow Am. Heart Assn. (stroke coun.), Am. Acad. Neurology (scientific issues com., legis. action com.); mem. AMA, IEEE, Am. Paraplegia Soc., Am. Soc. Neuro-Rehab., Am. Physics Soc., Neurosci. Soc., Biophys. Soc., Am. Neurol. Assn., N.Y. Acad. Sci., Am. Geriatrics Soc., Am. Physiol. Soc., Sigma Pi Sigma (v.p. 1970-71), Alpha Omega Alpha (v.p. 1975-76). Home: 935 Richmond Rd Lyndhurst OH 44124 Office: VA Med Ctr 10701 East Blvd Ste 128W Cleveland OH 44106-1702 Home Phone: 216-291-1643. Business E-Mail: robert.ruff1@va.gov.

RUFF, TILMAN ALFRED, physician; b. Adelaide, Australia, Mar. 23, 1955; s. Dietrich Paul and Irene (Wagner) R.; m. Charlotte Laemmle, Dec. 23, 1982; children: Ingrid Lara Laemmle-Ruff, Kristan Thomas Laemmle-Ruff. MB, BS with 1st class honors, Monash U., Melbourne, 1980. Intern, jr./sr. registrar, clin. supr. Prince Henry's Hosp., Melbourne, 1981-85; med. registrar Fairfield Infectious Diseases Hosp., Melbourne, 1986-87; sr. lectr. Monash Med. Sch., Melbourne, 1988-97; dir. travel health Fairfield Infectious Diseases Hosp., Melbourne, 1990-96; physician Macfarlane Burnet Centre for Med. Rsch., Melbourne, 1989-99; med. advisor Overseas Svc. Bur., Melbourne, 1988-96; head travel medicine svc. Royal Melbourne Hosp., 1996-98; assoc. med. dir. vaccines SmithKline Beecham Biologicals, Dandenong, Australia, 1998-2000; dir. clin. med. affairs GlaxoSmithKline Biologicals, 2001—04. Med. advisor internat. dept. Australian Red Cross, 1996—; assoc. prof. Nossal Inst. Global Health, U Melbourne, 2006—; project dir. Lombok Hepatitis B Model Immunization Project, 1989-91, Healthy Start for Child Survival in Indonesia Project, 1995-97, Healthy Mothers Healthy Babies Project, Indonesia, 1997-98; tech. advisor The Control of Hepatitis B Infection in Pacific Island Countries Project, 1996-2000, Expanded Programme Immunisation Pacific Island Countries Project, 2000-05; cons. tech. advisor immunization programs in Pacific Island Countries, Australian Agy. Internat. Devel., UNICEF, 2005—; dir. Poola Found., 1998-2000. Editor Pulse Jour., 1987-89; co-author: Manual of Travel Medicine, Victorian Infectious Diseases Service, Royal Melbourne Hosp., 1999, 2004; contbr. to books: Radioactive Heaven and Earth, 1991, A Textbook of Preventive Medicine, 1990; contbr. articles to profl. jours. Victorian com. mem. Amnesty Internat., Melbourne, 1972-73; co-organizer Save Life on Earth Internat. Art Exhbn., Melbourne, 1986; mem. Victorian Internat. Yr. of Peace Com., 1986; dir. Moonee Creek Coop. Ltd. Fellow: Royal Australasian Coll. Physicians; mem.: Internat. Commn. Nuclear Non-Proliferation and Disamament (adv. to co-chairs 2008—10), Internat. Campaign to Abolish Nuclear Weapons (chair 2006—), Med. Assn. for Prevention War (Australia) Inc. (v.p. 1989—97, 2000—02, pres. 2005—07, internat. coun. 2011—), Internat. Physicians for Prevention of Nuc. War (v.p. Asia Pacific 1989—93, cons. on policy and programs 1997—98, bd. mem. 2006—, v.p. South East Asia Pacific 2010—), Internat. Soc. Travel Medicine, Amnesty Internat., Pub. Health Assn. Australia, Australasian Soc. Infectious Diseases. Avocations: camping, skiing, music, writing, horseback riding. Personal E-mail: tilman.a.ruff@bigpond.com. Business E-Mail: tar@unimelb.edu.au.

RUFFIN, JOHN, federal agency administrator, researcher; b. New Orleans, June 29, 1943; s. Wesley and Olivia Ruffin; m. Angela Beverly Ruffin, Aug. 24, 1968; children: John Wesley, Meeka Dionne, Beverly Alaina. BS, Dillard U., New Orleans, 1965; MS, Atlanta U., 1967; PhD in Systematic and Devel. Biology, Kans. State U., 1971; DSc (hon.), Spelman Coll., Atlanta, Tuskegee U., Ala., U. Mass., Boston. Instr. biology So. U., Baton Rouge, 1967-68; asst. prof. biology Atlanta U., 1971-74; assoc. prof. Ala. A&M U., Huntsville, 1974-75; prof., chmn. dept. biology NC Ctrl. U., Durham, 1978—90, dean Coll. Arts & Scis., 1986—90; assoc. dir. rsch. on minority health NIH, Bethesda, Md., 1990—2001, dir. Nat. Ctr. Minority Health & Health Disparities, 2001—. Recipient Samuel L. Kountz award, NIH Dir.'s award, Nat. Hispanic Leadership award, Beta Beta Beta Biol. Honor Soc. award, Presdl. Meritorious Rank award. Mem.: AAAS, Assn. Environ. & Exptl. Botany, Assn. Southeastern Biologists, NC Acad. Scis., Botanical Soc. of America. Office: NCMHD 6707 Democracy Blvd Ste 800 Bethesda MD 20892-5465 Office Phone: 301-402-1366. Office Fax: 301-402-7040. E-mail: john.ruffin@nih.gov. *

RUFFIN, RICHARD A., orthopedic surgeon; b. Sept. 29, 1959; BS, U. Norte Dame, South Bend, Ind., 1981; MD, U. Okla., 1985. Cert. Am. Bd. Orthop. Surgery, Am. Bd. Orthop. Hand Surgery. Resident, orthop. U. iowa, Iowa City, 1985—90; fellow, upper extremity and microsurgery Kleinert Inst., Louisville, 1990—91; with Orthop. Assocs., Inc., Okla., 1991—. Named one of Golf Digest 2006 Top Golf Doctors in Am. Mem.: Arthoscopy Assn. N.Am., Am. Soc. for Surgery of the Hand, Am. Acad. Orthop. Surgeons. Office: Orthop Assocs Inc 3301NW 50th St Oklahoma City OK 73112 Office Phone: 405-947-0911. Office Fax: 405-942-5043.

RUGGIERI, MARTINO, child neurologist, educator; b. Catania, Italy, Apr. 21, 1962; s. Giuseppe and Giovanna (Rosolia) R.; m. Agata Polizzi, Sept. 9, 1996; 1 child, Giulio. MD, U. Catania, Italy, 1991, PhD, 2000; postgrad., U. Oxford, Eng., 1995—99. Resident in pediatrics U. Catania, 1991-95, postdoctoral fellow, 1999-2000, head Univ. neurocutaneous syndromes clinic, 1998—, sr. lect. Child Neurology/Neurogenetics, Nat. Rsch. Coun., 2000—, assoc. prof. pediat., 2006—; clin. asst. John Radcliffe Hosp., Oxford, Eng., 1995-98; fellow dept. child neurology Harvard U., Boston, 1996. Mem. cons. bd. Italian Assn. Neurofibromatosis, Parma, 1999—; cons. U. Neurocutaneous Syndromes, 2001—; Italian del. com. nat. advisors European Pediatric Neurology Soc.; cons. child neurology U. La Sapionza, Rome, 2002. Co-author: Internal Medicine, 1991, Neurologia Pediatrica, 1999, Pediatric Dermatology, 2000, Neurology of Autism, 2004; co-editor: Neurologia Pediatrica, 2001, 2006, Neurocutaneous disorders, 2007; dep. editor: JBPPNI, assoc. editor: Child Neur Syst; contbr. over 100 articles to profl. jours.; referee: 25 profl. jours. Grantee Nat. Rsch. Coun., Rome, 1996, Oxfordshire Rsch. Com., 1996-98, Ministry of Health, 2003. Mem.: European Pediatric Neurology Soc., Soc. Study Behavior Phenotype, Italian Soc. Pediatrics, Internat. Child Neurology Soc. Roman Catholic. Avocations: reading, playing classical guitar, motor boating, swimming. Home: Viale XX Settembre 21 95128 Catania Italy Office: Inst Neurol Sci CNR Viale Regina Margherita 6 95125 Catania CT Italy Office Phone: 39-095-3782487. Business E-Mail: m.ruggieri@isn.cnr.it. E-mail: rupo@ctonline.it.

RUIZ, JOSEPH RAYMOND, medical educator; b. Bitburg, Germany, Oct. 26, 1960; BSChemE, U. Tex. Austin, 1982; MD with honors, Cornell U. Med. Coll., 1986. Assoc. prof., anesthesiology U. Tex. MD Anderson Cancer Ctr., 2003—. Mem.: Am. Bd. Med. Quality, Am. Bd. Anesthesiology, Am. Soc. Anesthesiology. Home: 614 Timber Cir Houston TX 77079 Business E-Mail: jrruiz@mdanderson.org.

RUIZ, MARCO ANDRES, physician, educator; b. Lima, Peru, July 19, 1968; MD, U. Nacional Mayor San Marcos, 1994; MPH, U. Leeds, 1998. Asst. prof. clin. medicine La. State U., 2007—. Asst. prof. clin. medicine, infectious diseases La. State U., 2007, geriat. medicine fellowship assoc. dir., 09, cons. Stanley Scott cancer ctr., 10; editl. bd. mem. Infection and Virology Jour., 2011, Jour. AIDS and HIV rsch., 2011. Named one of Top Physicians of America, Rsch. Coun. America, 2009, Best Physicians of America, 2010. Mem.: ACP, Assn. Dir. Geriat. Medicine Fellowship Programs. Avocations: tennis, soccer, languages, travel, music. Office: 2235 Poydras Ave Office 227 New Orleans LA 70119 Business E-Mail: mruiz@lsuhsc.edu.

RUIZ-ARAGON, JESUS, microbiologist; b. Cadiz, Spain, Jan. 7, 1974; PhD, U. Seville, 1998; degree in Microbiology, U. Hosp. Cadiz, 2005. Pvt. practice, Cadiz, 1999—2001; microbiologist Hosp. Cadiz, 2001—05; microbiologist and biochemical analyser Hosp. Cruz Roja Seville, 2005—06; rsch. scientist Andalusian Agy. Health Tech. Assessment, 2006—. Adj. prof. U. Pablo Olavide, Seville, 2009—11. Recipient Jose Mira award. Mem.: Andalusian Agy. Health Tech. Assessment. Avocation: sports. Home: Chaparro 4 Bl 2 Esc 3 4 C Seville 41019 Spain Business E-Mail: jesusm.ruiz.ext@juntadeandalucia.es.

RUIZ BRAVO, NORKA, federal agency administrator; BS in Biology, Goucher Coll., Towson, Md., 1975; MS in Biology, Yale U., New Haven, PhD in Biology, 1983. Postdoc. fellow physiol. chemistry Johns Hopkins U., Balt.; postdoc. fellow biochemistry & molecular biology U. Tex. MD Anderson Cancer Ctr., faculty, 1983—89, Baylor Coll. Medicine, Houston, 1983—89; joined NIH, 1990, various positions including sci. rev. adminstr., Nat. Inst. Gen. Med. Scis. (NIGMS), prog. dir. Divsn. Genetics & Biology, 1992, acting dep. dir. NIGMS Divsn. Minority Opportunities in Rsch., spl. asst. NIGMS Office Extramural Activities, sci. rev. adminstr., Nat. Ctr. Human Genome Rsch., then dep. dir. cancer biology divsn., Nat. Cancer Inst., 1997—98, acting dir. cancer biology divsn., 1998—99, dep. assoc. dir. extramural activities, NIGMS, 1999—2000, assoc. dir. extramural activities, 2000—03, dep. dir. extramural rsch., dir. Office Extramural Rsch., 2003—08, spl. adv. to dir., 2008—. Mem.: AAAS, Soc. Devel. Biology, Am. Soc. Cell Biology. Office: NIH 9000 Rockville Pike Bethesda MD 20892 Office Phone: 301-496-1096. Office Fax: 301-402-3469. E-mail: nb9b@nih.gov.

RUIZ-COSANO, CARLOS, pediatrician, educator; b. Puente Genil, Córdoba, Spain, Sept. 30, 1960; MD, Medicine U. Granada, Spain, PhD in Medicine, 1984, degree in Medicine, 1990. Prof. pediat. Sch. Medicine, U. Granada, 1989. Office: Martínez Campos 2 Ave Madrid Granada 18002 Spain Office Fax: 34 958240740. Business E-Mail: cruiz@ugr.es.

RUMBOLDT, ZVONKO, internist, medical educator, dean; b. Zagreb, Croatia, Oct. 24, 1938; s. Zvonimir and Zorka (Habulin) R.; m. Mirjana Taraš, July 13, 1963; children: Zoran, Zvonimir. MD, U. Zagreb, 1963, PhD, 1979. Gen. practitioner Split (Croatia), 1963-69, staff mem. dept. medicine Clin. Hosp., Split, 1972—, head, 1990—2004, head dept. med. U. Hosp. Mostar, 2004—06. Rsch. fellow in clin. pharmacology U. Florence, Italy, 1975; rsch. fellow in hypertension Georgetown U., Washington, 1976; rsch. assoc. in clin. pharmacology Vanderbilt U., Nashville, 1976-77; assoc. prof. medicine U. Zagreb Sch. Medicine, 1981-86, prof. medicine, U. Split Sch. Med., 1986—2011, prof. emeritus, 2011-, dean, 1993-2001. Author, co-author 15 books including: Cardiovascular Clinical Pharmacology, 1988, 2d edit. 1991, Internal Medicine Practicum, 1985, 2nd edit. 2009, Handbook of Internal Medicine, 1991, 2d edit. 1997, Pharmacology in Medical Practice, 1984, 2d edit. 1992; editor translator, Harrison's Principles of Internal Medicine 13th edit., 1997, 16th Edit. 2011. Recipient Silver State Decoration for Sci. award State Govt., 1984, Roder Boskovic Decoration award, 1998. Mem. AAAS, AHA, Am. Coll. Clin. Pharmacology, Am. Soc. Clin. Pharmacology and Therapeutics, Croatian Soc. Hypertension (pres. 1997-2005). Roman Catholic. Avocations: swimming, spear fishing, tennis. Home: Lovretska 1 21000 Split Croatia Office: Split Univ Sch Med 11000 Split Croatia Office Phone: 0038521557928.

RÜMENAPF, GERHARD, vascular surgeon, educator; b. Dahn, Pfalz, Germany, June 4, 1957; s. Hans and Sitta (Kölln) R.; m. Nikola Burgemeister, Apr. 26, 1962; 1 child, Max. MD, U. Erlangen-Nuremberg, 1983, PhD, 1994. Resident exptl. surgery U. Erlangen-Nuremberg, Germany, 1984—87, resident surgery, 1987—95; chief resident vascular surgery Rhoen-Klinikum, Bad Neustadt, Germany, 1996—99; head surgeon dept. vascular and endocrine surgery Diakoniezentrum Speyer Krankenhaus, Germany, 1999—, prof. surgery, 2003; head Ctr. Vascular Medicine, Oberrhein Mannheim-Speyer-Landau, Germany, 2004. Contbr. articles to profl. jours. Capt. German Med. Corps, 1983-84. Mem. Deutsche Gesellsch Chirurgie, Deutsche Gesellsch Gefaesschirurgie, European Soc. Vascular Surgery. Office: Diakoniezentrum Speyer Hilgardstr 26 67346 Speyer Germany E-mail: gerhard.ruemenapf@diakonissen.de.

RUMLEY, JEFFREY P., lawyer, insurance company executive; BA, U. Detroit Mercy; JD, Mich. State U. Lic.: Mich. 1985. Joined Blue Cross Blue Shield of Mich., Detroit, 1992, dep. gen. counsel, v.p., gen. counsel various subs. corps., prin. counsel auto and nat. bus. unit. Office: Blue Cross Blue Shield of Michigan 600 E Lafayette Blvd Detroit MI 48226-2998 Office Phone: 313-225-9000. Office Fax: 313-225-6239. *

RUMMELT, ANDREAS, pharmaceutical executive; b. Erlangen, Germany, 1956; PhD in Pharmaceutical Sci., U. Erlangen-Nürnberg, Germany; training in gen. mgmt., IMD, INSEAD, Harvard Bus. Sch., Boston. Various positions including lab. head, then group head and dept. head, drug delivery systems Sandoz Internat. GmbH, 1985—94; head worldwide tech. rsch. & develop. Novartis Pharma AG, 1994—99, head, tech. ops., 1999—2004; CEO Sandoz Internat. GmbH, 2004—08, group head quality assurance and tech. ops., 2008—. Mem.: Soc. of Swiss Industrial Pharmacists, Soc. of Swiss Chemical Industry, Internat. Assn. for Pharmaceutical Tech. Office: Sandoz Internat GmbH Industriestrasse 25 83607 Holzkirchen Germany

RUMYANTSEVA, TATIANA, physician; b. Russia, Mar. 18, 1978; Degree, MGMSU, 1996. Physician Moscow City Clin. Hosp. 81, 2008. Home: Novgorodskaya St 30-237 Moscow 127572 Russia Personal E-mail: r197803@mail.ru.

RUND, DOUGLAS ANDREW, emergency physician; b. Columbus, Ohio, July 20, 1945; s. Carl Andrew and Caroline Amelia (Row) Rund; m. Sue E. Padavana, 1980; children: Carie, Emily, Ashley. BA, Yale U., 1967; MD, Stanford U., 1971. Lic. physician Ohio, diplomate Nat. Bd. Med. Examiners, Am. Bd. Family Practice, Am. Bd. Emergency Medicine. Intern U. Calif. San Francisco-Moffett Hosp., 1971—72; resident in gen. surgery Stanford U., 1972—74, Robert Wood Johnson Found. clin. scholar in medicine, 1974—76; med. dir. Mid-Peninsula Health Svc., Palo Alto, Calif., 1975—76; clin. instr. dept. medicine and preventive medicine Stanford U. Med. Sch., 1975—76; assoc. prof., dir. divsn. emergency medicine Ohio State Coll. Medicine, 1982—87, dir. emergency medicine residency program, assoc. prof. dept, 1976—87, prof., chmn. dept. preventive medicine, 1988—90, prof., chmn. dept. emergency medicine, 1990—, prof., interim chmn. dept. family medicine, 1994—95, assoc. dean, 2001—; pres. Ohio State Univ. Physicians, 2002—. Attending staff Ohio State U. Hosps., 1976—; med. dir. CSCC, Emergency Med. Svcs. Dept.; pres. Internat. Rsch. Inst. Emergency Medicine; sr. rsch. fellow NATO: Health and Med. Aspects of Disaster Preparedness, 1985—87; vis. epidemiology and injury control U. Edinburgh, Scotland, 1987; working group, emergency and critical care in space NASA, 2001—; bd. dirs. Am. Bd. Emergency Medicine, 1988—97, sr. editor in tng. exam., 1989—, pres., 1995—; pres., chmn. bd. dirs. Physicians of the Ohio State U. (POSU), 2002—; med. dir. Worthington Fire Dept. Author: Triage, 1981, Essentials of Emergency Medicine, 1982, 2d edit., 1986, Emergency Radiology, 1982, Emergency Psychiatry, 1983, Environmental Emergencies, 1985; editor: Emergency Medicine Ann., 1983—84, Emergency Medicine Survey, Annals of Emergency Medicine, Annals of Emergency Medicine Symposium, 1986; editor: (in chief) Ohio State Series on Emergency Medicine, Emergency Medicine Observer, 1986—87; mem. editl. bd.: Physician, Sports Medicine, Emergency Med. Svcs., Jour. Urgent Care Medicine; co-author: Family Medicine Pricples and Practice, 1978, 2d edit., 1983; contbr. articles to profl. jours. Recipient Faculty Tchg. award, Ohio State U., 1999, Douglas A. Rund Disting. Faculty award, Dept. Emergency Medicine, 2003. Fellow: Am. Coll. Emergency Physicians (task force on substance abuse and injury control, Outstanding Contbn. to Edn. award 1992); mem.: IAAA, Columbus Med. Review, Internat. Soc. for Emergency Med. Svcs. (med. dir.), Columbus Med. Forum (pres. 1993—), Soc. Acad. Emergency Medicine (chmn. internat. com. 1991—), Assn. Acad. Chairs Emergency Medicine (pres. 1992—93), Nat. Inst. on Alcohol Abuse and Alcoholism, Alpha Omega Alpha. Office: Ohio State U 146 Means Hall 1654 Upham Dr Columbus OH 43210-1240

RUNDMO, TORBJORN, psychology professor; b. Tromso, Norway, Feb. 7, 1955; s. Oddmar Strom and Tordis Rundmo. BA in Social Scis., U. Bergen, 1982, MA in Psychology, 1984; DPhil, Norwegian U. Sci. and Tech., 1993; DPhil (hon.), Stockholm Sch. Econs., 2005. Rsch. scientist SINTEF, Trondheim, Norway, 1986—91, Inst. Transport Econs., Oslo, 1991—92; assoc. prof. Norwegian U. Sci. and Tech., Trondheim, 1992—98, prof. organizational psychology, 1998—99, prof. cmty. psychology, 1999—. Office: Norwegian U Sci and Tech Dept Psychology 7491 Trondhein Norway Office Phone: 0047 73591656. E-mail: torbjorn.rundmo@svt.ntnu.no.

RUNER, EVELYN ROSARIO, endocrinologist; b. SI, NY, June 5, 1969; d. George and Evelyn (Yañez) R. BS, Temple U., 1991; MD, Mt. Sinai Sch. Medicine, 1995. Diplomate Am. Bd. Internal Medicine, Am. Bd. Endocrinology and Metabolism, 2005. Resident in gen. surgery Robert Packer Hosp., Sayre, Pa., 1995—96, Waterbury (Conn.) Hosp., 1996—97; resident in internal medicine Lehigh Valley Hosp., Allentown, Pa., 1997—2000; fellow in endocrinology U. S.C., Columbia, 2000—02. Mem.: ACP, AMA, Women in Endocrinology, Am. Assn. Clin. Endocrinologists, Endocrine Soc., Am. Soc. Internal Medicine. Democrat. Roman Catholic. Avocations: martial arts, medical history, military history, science fiction, guitar. Office: 1205 Langhorne Newtown Rd Ste 211 Langhorne PA 19047 Office Phone: 215-741-4016.

RUNER, PER THOMAS, otorhinolaryngologist, researcher; b. Stockholm, Oct. 4, 1956; m. Lena Maria Persson, Oct. 29, 1993; children: Felix, Hanna, Cecilia. MD, Lund U., Sweden, 1984, PhD, 1996. Med. diplomate, 1987. Intern Ystad (Sweden) Hosp., 1985-87; resident Dept. Otorhinolaryngology, Head and Neck Surgery, Lund, 1987-94, specialist in otorhinolaryngology, 1994-96; cons. otorhinolaryngology Ljungby (Sweden) Hosp., 1996-99, Blekinge Hosp., Karlskrona, Sweden, 1999—, vice dept. head dept. otorhinolaryngology, 2000—. Achievements include research on nitric oxide stimulate blood flow and mucociliary activity in the human nose; developed a method for in vivo studies of mucociliary activity in the human nose; research on endothelins 1, 2, and 3 stimulates mucociliary function and decreases blood flow in the upper respiratory tract. Office: Blekinge Hosp Dept Otorhinolaryngology 371 85 Karlskrona Sweden Home Phone: 0455-22814; Office Phone: 0455-735195. Office Fax: 0455-735212. Business E-Mail: thomas.runer@ltblekinge.se.

RUNNER, JACK CHARLES, health facility executive; b. Sandusky, Ohio, Mar. 31, 1955; s. Kenneth Earl and Mary Margaret Runner; m. Kathleen Marie Kahle, July 15, 1978; children: Kristen Marie, Kelly Marie. BS in Microbiology, Bowling Green State U., 1977; MBA, Ashland U., 1984. Staff technologist Sandusky Meml. Hosp., 1978-84; supr. microbiology dept. Firelands Cmty. Hosp., Sandusky, 1984-86; adminstrv. dir. North Coast Clin. Lab. Inc., Sandusky, 1985—. Mem. Am. Soc. for Microbiology, Drug. Info. Assn., Assn. Clin. Rsch. Profls., Am. Assn. Clin. Chemistry, Clin. Lab. Mgrs. Assn., U.S. Power Squadron (dist. comdr. 1999—), Kiwanis Internat., Sandusky Yacht Club, Boat U.S. Office: North Coast Clin Lab Inc 2215 Cleveland Rd Sandusky OH 44870-4485 Office Phone: 419-626-6012. Business E-Mail: jack@northcoastlab.com.

RUNOWICZ, CAROLYN DILWORTH, gynecologist, oncologist, researcher; b. Willimantic, Conn., May 1, 1951; d. S. Robert and Aline (Bergeron) Dilworth; m. Sheldon H. Cherry. BA, U. Conn., 1973;

MD, Thomas Jefferson Med. Coll., Phila., 1977. Diplomate Am. Bd. Ob-Gyn., Am. Bd. Gynecologic Oncology. Resident ob-gyn. Mt. Sinai Sch. Medicine & Med. Ctr., NYC, 1977-81, fellow gynecol. oncology, 1981-83; instr., dir. divsn. ob-gyn. Albert Einstein Coll. Medicine, NYC, 1983-88, asst. prof. dept. ob-gyn., 1988-93, assoc. prof., 1993—98; dir. gynecologic & oncology Our Lady of Mercy, Bronx, NY, 1988; prof., dir. gynecol. oncology Montefiore Med. Ctr., NYC, 1998—2001; prof. clin. obstetrics & gynecology Columbia U. Coll. Physicians & Surgeons, 2001—03; vice chmn. ob-gyn. St. Luke's Roosevelt Hosp., NYC, 2001—03; dir. Carole & Ray Neag Comprehensive Cancer Ctr., prof. ob-gyn. U. Conn. Health Ctr., Famington, NY, 2003—, NE utilities chair on exptl. oncology, 2003—. Presdl. appointee Nat. Cancer Adv. Bd., 2004—10, chair, 2006—10; lectr. in field. Author: To Be Alive: A Women's Guide to a Full Life After Cancer, 1995; co-author (with husband): Menopause Book: A Guide to Women's Health After 40, 1994, Answer to Cancer, 2004; co-author: (with Jeanne Petrek) Woman and Cancer: A Through and Compassionate Resource for Patients and Their Families, 1999; contbr. articles to profl. jours., chapters to books. Fellow: Am. Coll. Ob-Gyn.; mem.: AMA, Am. Soc. Clinical Oncology, Am. Gynecol. Club, Am. Cancer Soc. (pres. 2005—06), NY Obstet. Soc., Am. Gynecol. Obstetrics Soc., Soc. Gynecologic Oncologists (pres. 2000), Am. Med. Women's Assn. (Local Legend award), Alpha Omega Alpha, Phi Beta Kappa. Office: Carole & Ray Neag Comprehensive Cancer Ctr U Conn Health Ctr 263 Farmington Ave Farmington CT 06030-2875 Office Phone: 860-679-2809, 860-679-2100, 800-579-7822. Office Fax: 860-679-4815. Business E-Mail: crunowicz@uchc.edu. *

RUOSLAHTI, ERKKI, cell biologist, cancer researcher; b. Puumala, Finland, Feb. 16, 1940; B. in Medicine, U. Helsinki, Finland, 1961, MD, 1965, PhD in Immunology, 1967; MD (hon.), U. Lund, Sweden, 1991. Rsch./teaching asst. dept. serology and bacteriology U. Helsinki, 1964-66; head blood group dept. State Serum Inst., Helsinki, 1966-68; NIH rsch. fellow Calif. Inst. Tech., 1968-70; asst. prof., acting assoc. prof. dept. serology and bacteriology U. Helsinki, Finland, 1970-75; prof. bacteriology and serology U. Turku, Finland, 1975-76; sr. rsch. scientist dept. immunology City of Hope, Nat. Med. Ctr., Duarte, Calif., 1976, dir. immunobiology divsn. immunology, 1976—79; assoc. sci. dir. Cancer Rsch. Found. (now Sanford Bunham Med. Rsch. Inst.), La Jolla, Calif., 1979-80; scientific dir. Cancer Rsch. Found. (now The Burnham Inst.), La Jolla, Calif., 1980—95, v.p., COO, 1982-89, pres., CEO and dir. NCI Cancer Ctr., 1989—2001; disting. prof. Sanford Bunham Med. Rsch. Inst., La Jolla, Calif., 2002—. Adj. prof. dept. pathology U. Calif., San Diego, 1980-2004, dept. bioengring., 2003-; mem. pathobiochemistry study sect. Nat. Cancer Inst., 1981-85; Robert and Estelle Stadtler lectr. U. Tex., Sys. Cancer Ctr., 1984, Burton L. Baker Meml. lectr. U. Mich., Ann Arbor, 1987, Harvey Soc. lectr., 1988, Jeanette Piperno Meml. lectr. Temple U., Phila., 1989, G.H.A. Clowes award and lectr. Am. Assn. Cancer Rsch., 1990, Karl H. Beyer lectr. U. Wis., 1990, Walter Hubert lectr. 33d Ann. Meeting, Brit. Assn. for Cancer Rsch., 1992. Contbr. over 400 articles to profl. jours.; editl. bd. mem. Matrix, 1991—, Internat. Jour. Cancer, 1979—, Ann. Rev. of Cell Biology, 1987-90, Jour. Cell Biology, 1987-89, Jour. Biol. Chemistry, 1985-88, Cancer Rsch., 1979-82; reviewing editor Science, 1989—; editor-in-chief Cell Regulation, 1989-91. Recipient Barbara Robert Meml. medal French Soc. of Connective Tissue, 1988, Outstanding Investigator award Nat. Cancer Inst., 1986-93, G.H.A. Clowes award, 1990, Robert J. and Claire Pasarow Found. award, 1991, Leila Gruber Cancer Rsch. award Am. Acad. Dermatology, 1993, Abbott award Internat. Soc. for Oncodevelopmental Biology and Medicine, 1995, Gairdner Found. Internat. award, 1997, Jacobaeus Internat. prize, 1998, Jubilee award, British Biomedical Soc., 2003; co-recipient Japan prize: Cell Biology, 2005; knight Order of the White Rose of Finland, Academician grant, Finland, 2009, Order of Lion, Finland, 2010. Fellow Am. Acad. Arts and Scis.; mem. Finnish Acad. Scis., NAS, European Molecular Biology Orgn., Inst. of Medicine of the U.S. Nat. Academies; nobel fellow, Karolinska Inst., Stockholm. Office: Vascular Mapping Lab Ctr Nanomed Sanford Burnham Med Rsch Inst University Calif Santa Barbara CA 93106-9610 *

RUPP, PETER KARL, medical association administrator; b. Munich, Germany, Nov. 15, 1958; s. Werner Hans and Irmgard Annemarie Rupp; m. Anna Margarethe Bornhof; children: Sandra Carina, Veronika Maria, Felix Peter. Dr. med., Ludwig Maximilians U., Munich, 1978—84. MD State of Bavaria, 1984. Cons. intensive care and emergency medicine Krankenhaus München Schwabing, Munich, 1984—2002; chief emergency physician Town of Munich, Munich, 1991—2002; head of surg. dept., emergency dept. U. Berne Inselspital, Switzerland, 2002—04; head dept. Hirslanden Kliniken Bern, Switzerland, 2004—10. Author: Lehrbuch präklinische Notfallmedizin, Consilium Cedip Notfallmedizin; editor: Lehrbuch präklinische Notfallmedizin, Rettunsdienst. Capt., 1984, German Navy. Recipient Lebensrettungsmedaille, State of Bavaria, 1992. Mem.: Am. Coll. Emergency Physicians, German Soc. Internal Medicine, Bavarian Soc. Emergency Physicians, Swiss Emergency Physicians, German Soc. Intensive Care. Avocations: diving, skiing. Office: Linclenhofspital Schänzlistr 39 Bern 3000 Switzerland Office Fax: +41 (31) 337 8890; Home Fax: +49 (89) 1488 219527. Personal E-mail: dr-peter-rupp@gmx.de. Business E-Mail: peter.rupp@hirslanden.ch.

RUPPERT, RÜDIGER, orthopadic surgeon; b. Straubing, Germany, Mar. 1, 1971; s. Hans and Sieglinde Ruppert. MD, U. Regensburg, 1993; MD magna cum laude, Friedrich-Alexander-U., Erlangen, 1996. Scientific asst. Dr. Eichhorn/Strobel Straubing, Germany, 1997—99; sci. asst. Dep. Orthopedics and Traumatology U. Freiburg, Germany, 2001—03; orthop. surgeon Pro-spine Ctr. Dr. Bertagnoli, Bavaria, Germany, 2005; knee and spine dept. Orthopedic Surgery Ctr., 2006—. Contbr. scientific papers pub. to profl. jour. Mem.: Gesellschaft Orthop. Traumatologische Sportmedizin (assoc.).

RURIK, IMRE, physician, educator; b. Budapest, Hungary, June 30, 1953; s. Rurik Imre and Éva Szvetnik; children: Zsigmond children: Sarolta, Dénes. MD, Semmelweis Med. U., Budapest, 1979; MSc, Health Mgmt. Tng. Ctr., Budapest, 2002; PhD, Semmelweis U., 2003. Urologist Jahn Ferenc Hosp., Budapest, 1979—89; gen. practitioner Primary Health Ctr., Budapest, 1989—; sr. lectr. Semmelweis U., 1997—; magister Municipality of Pesterzsébet, Budapest; chair Dept. Family, Med. U. Debrecen. Mng. dir. Occupl. Med. Group, Budapest, 1995—2003; exec. mem. Primary Care Diabetes Europe. Mem.: Hungarian Bd. Gen. Practice. Roman Catholic. Avocations: tennis, skiing, jogging. Office: Primary Health Ctr XX Vörösmarty u5 1201 Budapest Hungary Office Fax: 361 285 8585. Personal E-mail: rurik.dr@t-online.hu. E-mail: rurik@med.unideb.hu.

RUSCH, VALERIE WILLIAMS, thoracic surgeon; b. NYC, Oct. 16, 1951; AB in Biochemistry, Vassar Coll., 1971; MD, Columbia U., 1975. Diplomate Nat. Bd. Med. Examiners, Am. Bd. Surgery, Am. Bd. Thoracic Surgery. Intern in gen. surgery U. Wash., Seattle, 1975-76, resident in gen. surgery, 1975-80, resident in cardiothoracic surgery, 1980-82; faculty assoc. dept. of thoracic surgery M.D. Anderson Cancer Ctr., Houston, 1982-83; thoracic surgeon Harborview Med. Ctr., Seattle, 1983-86, assoc. staff mem., 1986-89; thoracic surgeon Group Health Coop. of Puget Sound, Seattle, 1983-84; chief cardiothoracic surgery VA Hosp., Seattle, 1986-87; thoracic surgeon Univ. Hosp., Seattle, 1983-89; mem. courtesy med. staff Pacific Med. Ctr., Seattle, 1987-89; assoc. attending surgeon thoracic svc. Meml. Sloan-Kettering Cancer Ctr., NYC, 1989-94, attending surgeon, 1994—, chief thoracic surgery, 2000—. Asst. prof. div. cardiothoracic surgery U. Wash., 1983-88, assoc. prof., 1988-89; asst. mem. divsn. clin. rsch. Fred Hutchinson Cancer Rsch. Ctr., Seattle, 1985-89; assoc. mem. Meml. Hosp., Meml. Sloan-Kettering Cancer Ctr., N.Y.C., 1989-94, mem., 1994—; assoc. prof. surgery Cornell U. Med. Coll., N.Y.C., 1989-95, prof. surgery Cornell U. Med. Coll., 1995—; mem. cancer clin. investigations rev. com. Nat. Cancer Inst., 1991-98. Mem. editl. bd. Jour. Thoracic and Cardiovasc. Surgery, 1992-2007, Jour. Clin. Oncology, 2004-, Annals of Surgery, 2007; contbr. articles to profl. publs.; author abstracts in field. Grantee NIH, 1985-89, Deknatel Corp., 1986-87, Bard Electro Med. Systems, 1989, NeoRx Corp., 1989-90, Pfizer Corp., 1995-98. Fellow ACS (mem. bd. govs. 2002-, pres. bd. govs. 2007-), Am. Coll. Chest Physicians; mem. Am. Assn. Thoracic Surgery (mem. coun. 2006-), Soc. Thoracic Surgeons, Assn. Acad. Surgery, Soc. Surg. Oncology (mem. com. tng. 1993-95, mem. edn. com. 1993-95), Am. Soc. Clin. Oncology, (mem. program com. 1993, 96, bd. dirs. 2002-05), Am. Thoracic Soc., NY Cancer Soc., Internat. Assn. Study of Lung Cancer, Am. Med. Women's Assn., Am. Bd. Thoracic Surgery (mem. bd. dirs. 2003-), Henry Harkins' Surg. Soc., M.D. Anderson Assocs., Gen. Thoracic Surg. Club, Alpha Omega Alpha. Office: Meml Sloan-Kettering Cancer Thoracic Surgery Svc 1275 York Ave New York NY 10021-6094 Office Phone: 212-639-8695. Business E-Mail: ruschv@mskcc.org.

RUSH, DOMENICA MARIE, health facilities administrator; b. Gallup, N.Mex., Apr. 10, 1937; d. Bernardo G. and Guadalupe (Milan) Iorio; m. W. E. Rush, Jan. 5, 1967. Diploma, Regina Sch. Nursing, Albuquerque, 1958. RN N.Mex.; lic. nursing home adminstr.; cert. legal nurse cons., 2004. Charge nurse, house supr. St. Joseph Hosp., Albuquerque, 1958-63; dir. nursing Cibola Hosp., Grants, 1960-64; supr. operating room, dir. med. seminars Carrie Tingley Crippled Children's Hosp., Truth or Consequences, N.Mex., 1964-73; adminstr. Sierra Vista Hosp., Truth or Consequences, 1974-88, pres., 1989—90, adminstr., 1995—2003, CEO, 2008—, cons.; clin. nursing mgr. U. N.Mex. Hosp., 1990—94; adminstr. Nor-Lea Hosp., Lovington, N.Mex., 1990-94; with regional ops. divsn. Presbyn. Healthcare Svcs., Albuquerque, 1994—, regional ops., 1994—2003, regional adminstr., 2003—04, intern adminstrn. and spl. projects, 2004—06; founder Rush Consulting Svc., 2004—; CEO Trans Health, Inc., Balt., 2006—08; with Rush Consulting, LLC, 2009. Bd. dirs. N.Mex. Blue Cross/Blue Shield, 1977-88, chmn. hosp. relations com., 1983-85, exec. com. 1983—; bd. dirs. Region II Emergency Med. Svcs., CEO Truth Consequences Dissolved Rush Consultancy, LLC,interim CEO, Sierra Vista Hosp., 2008, permanent CEO, 2009. Originating bd. SW Mental Health Ctr., Sierra County, N.Mex., 1975; chmn. Sierra County Personnel Bd., 1983—. Recipient Frank Gabriel award N.Mex. Hosp. Health Sys. Assn., 2003, Govenor's award Emergency Med. Svcs., 2003, Govs.award for Outstanding Woman, N. Mex., 2004; Named Lea County Outstanding Woman, N.Mex. Commn. on Status of Women, Woman of Yr. for Lea County, N.Mex.; 1993. Mem. Am. Coll. Health Care Adminstrs., Sierra County C. of C. (bd. dirs. 1972, 75-76, svc. award 1973, Businesswoman of the Yr. 1973-74), N.Mex. Hosp. Assn. (bd. dirs., sec.-treas., pres.-elect, com. chmn., 1977-88, pres. 1980-81, exec. com., 1980-83, 84-85, recipient meritorius svc. award 1988), N.Mex. So. Hosp. Coun. (sec. 1980-81, pres. 1981-82), Am. Hosp. Assn. (N.Mex. del. 1984-88, regional adv. bd. 1984-88). Republican. Roman Catholic. Avocations: raising thoroughbred horses, cooking. Home: 1100 N Riverside Dr Truth Or Consequences NM 87901-9789 Office Phone: 575-740-2334, 575-894-2111. Personal E-mail: domrush@gmail.com.

RUSHDI, AHMED IBRAHIM, geologist, educator, marine chemist; arrived in U.S., 1997; s. Ibrahim Mohamed Rushdi and Fatima Hamoud Al-Attab; m. Faiza Ahmed Al-Saaidi, Sept. 30, 1980; children: Eman, Maryam. BSc, Sana'a U., Yemen, 1979; PhD, Oreg. State U., 1989. From demonstrator to assoc. prof. Sana'a (Yemen) U., 1980—94, assoc. prof., 1994—95; grad. rschr. Oreg. State U., Corvallis, Oreg., 1983—89, assoc. prof., 1998—; rsch. fellow U. Mich., Ann Arbor, Mich., 1995; vis. prof. U. Calif., San Diego, 1995—96. Dir. program Inst. Oceanography, Sana'a, 1991—94; expert marine sector Ministry Planning and Devel., Sana'a, 1992—95; mem. steering com. Global Environ. Facility, UN Devel. Environ. Program, Sana'a, 1993—95. Fellow, U. S. Am. Internat. Devel., Fulbright Found., 1995—96; scholar, UN Devel. Program. Mem.: Yemen Environ. Soc., Yemen Geol. Soc. Avocation: soccer. Home: 2951 SE Midvale Dr Corvallis OR 97333 Office: Coll Oceanic and Atmosphereic Scis Univ Oreg 104 Ocean Admin Bldg Corvallis OR 97331 Office Phone: 541-737-5707. Business E-Mail: rushdia@onid.orst.edu.

RUSHING, DEBRA FARROW, pharmacist; b. Indpls. d. Glenn Vernon and Betty Jean Farrow; m. David Earnest Rushing, Oct. 3, 1992 (dec. June 2002); children: Amber Marie, Dustin David, Zachary Glenn. BS in Pharmacy, Butler U., 1978. Resident pharmacy Ind. U. Med. Ctr., Indpls., 1981—82; staff pharmacist Ind. U. Hosp., Indpls., 1978—81, supr. pharmacy, 1982—83, staff pharmacist, 1983—2005, Health North Hosp., Carmel, Ind., 2005—. Mem.: Ind. Pharmacists Alliance, Am. Soc. Clin. Pharmacy, Am. Soc. Health Sys. Pharmacists. Republican. Methodist. Avocations: reading, bicycling, decorating, scrapbooking. Home: 14505 Dublin Dr Carmel IN 46033 Office: Indiana University Health North Hosp 11700 N Meridian St Carmel IN 46032 Office Phone: 317-688-2774. Business E-Mail: drushing@iuhealth.org.

RUSHING, PHILIP DALE, retired social worker; b. Carbondale, Ill., Mar. 15, 1932; S. Paul and Beulah Myrl (Benton) R.; m. Linda North, July 5, 1958 (div. July 1964); 1 child, Lisa Anne Rushing Burrow; m. Rosalie Anne Sturm, Aug. 20, 1966. BA, So. Ill. U., 1958; MSW, Washington U., St. Louis, 1960. Diplomate Am. Bd. Clinical Social Workers, Nat. Assn. Social Workers; LCSW Ill. Child welfare worker Ill. Dept. Pub. Welfare, Salem, East St. Louis, 1958-60, child welfare supr. East St. Louis, 1960-63; field rep. Nat. Assn. for Retarded Children, Dallas, Denver, 1963-65; dir. social svcs. A.L. Bowen Children's Ctr., Harrisburg, Ill., 1965-68; asst. zone dir. for mentally retarded Ill. Dept. of Mental Health, Harrisburg, 1968-74; regional coord. for devel. disabilities Ill. Dept. of Mental Health & Devel. Disabilities, Marion, 1974-83; social work adminstr. Choate Mental Health & Devel. Ctr., Anna, Ill., 1983-95; ret., 1995. Adj. asst. prof. So. Ill. U. Rehab. Inst., Carbondale, Ill., 1968-78; bd. dirs. Southeastern Ill. Pastoral Counseling Ctrs., chmn. pers. com., 1996-98. Bd. deacons First Presbyn. Ch., Harrisburg, 1974-77, bd. trustees, 1978-80, bd. elders, 1980-83, 96-98, 2003-06. With USN, 1951-55, Korea Fellow Am. Assn. Intellectual and Devel. Disabilities (life, chmn. social work divsn. Ill. chpt. 1973-74); mem. NASW (chmn. East St. Louis br. 1962). Home: 6542 Hwy 13 W Harrisburg IL 62946-4142 Personal E-mail: pr.rushing@juno.com.

RUSHTON, ALAN R., physician, medical researcher, historian; b. Oak Park, Ill., Mar. 10, 1949; s. Raymond H. and D. Loree (Swan) R.; m. Nancy Spencer, May 5, 1973; children: Andrew, Daniel. AB in Chemistry, Earlham Coll., Richmond, Ind., 1971; PhD in Genetics, U. Chgo., 1975, MD, 1977. Diplomate Am. Bd. Pediatrics, Am. Bd. Med. Genetics. Resident, intern Yale U.-New Haven Hosp., Conn., 1977-80; physician Hunterdon Med. Ctr., Flemington, NJ, 1980—; assoc. clin. prof. pediatrics Robert Wood Johnson Med. Sch., New Brunswick, NJ, 1980—. Lectr. genetics Princeton U., NJ, 1980-84; adj. prof. Med. U. Ams., Nevis, West Indies. Author: Genetics and Medicine in the United States 1800-1922, 1994, Royal Maladies: Inherited Diseases In The Ruling Houses Of Europe, 2008, Genetics and Medicine in Great Britain 1600 to 1938, 2009. Fellow Am. Acad. Pediatrics, Am. Coll. Med. Genetics, NY Acad. Medicine, Royal Soc. Medicine; mem. Am. Assn. History Medicine, History Sci. Soc. Office: Hunterdon Pediatric Assocs 6 Sand Hill Rd Ste 202 Flemington NJ 08822-4600 Personal E-mail: arrdoc@aol.com.

RUSK, MATTHEW H., internist, educator; BA, Harvard Coll., 1987; MD, U. Pa., 1992. Diplomate Nat. Bd. Med. Examiners, 1993, Am. Bd. Internal Medicine, 1996, recertification 2006. Intern medicine dept. Univ. of Pa. Hosp., 1992—93, resident medincine dept., 1993—95, chief resident medicine dept., 1995—96; staff internist gen. internal med. divsn. Univ. of Pa.; assoc. prof. clinical medicine dept. Author: (publs.) Review of Current Cardiac Studies, 1999, Ways to Stop Bleeding: Management of Common Injuries at home, 2000, Young Woman With Marked Lower Extremity Obesity, 2001, Coma and Altered Mental Status, 2002, and numerous others. Named one of the TOp Doctor, Phila. Mag., 2011. Office: PENN Presbyterian Medical Center Medical Arts Blgd Ste 102 39th & Market St Philadelphia PA 19104 Office Phone: 215-662-9990. Office Fax: 215-243-4600. E-mail: rusk@mail.med.upenn.edu.

RUSKIN, JEREMY N., cardiologist, director; b. South Africa, Oct. 19, 1945; MD, Harvard Med. Sch., 1971. Dir., cardiac arrhythmia svc. Mass. Gen. Hosp., 1978—. Recipient Michel Mirowski award, Mirowski Award Com. Fellow: Am. Coll. Cardiology; mem.: Heart Rhythm Soc. (Pioneer award in Pacing and Electrophysiology), Am. Heart Assn. Office: Mass Gen Hosp 55 Fruit St Boston MA 02114 Business E-Mail: jruskin@partners.org.

RUSSELL, ALAN JAMES, chemical engineering and biotechnology educator; b. Salford, Lancashire, Eng., Aug. 8, 1962; s. Francis Anthony and Yvonne (Heilbrunn) Russell; children: Hannah Justine Serena, Vincent Anthony Alexander, Christian Sebastian, Trevor Alan James, Emily Christine Samantha. BSc in Biochemistry and Applied Molecular Biology, with honors, U. Manchester Inst. Sci. & Tech., Eng., 1984; PhD in Biol. Chemistry, Imperial Coll., London, 1987. NATO rsch. fellow MIT, Cambridge, 1987-89; asst. prof. chem. engring. U. Pitts., 1989—95, assoc. dir. Ctr. Biotech., 1991-2001, Nickolas DeCecco prof., chmn. dept. chem. & petroleum engring., 1995—2001, dir. program in advanced biomaterials, prof. surgery, founding dir. McGowan Inst. Regenerative Medicine, 2001—, also Disting. Univ. prof. surgery. Co-founder Agentase LLC, Pitts., 1999; exec. dir. Pitts. Tissue Engring. Initiative; dir. Nat. Tissue Engring. Ctr., Pitts. Mem. editl. bd. Jour. Molecular Catalysis, Encyclopedia of Catalysis, Biocatalysis & Biotransformations; contbr. articles to profl. jours. Recipient Presdl. Young Investigator award, NSF, 1990, Chancellor's Disting. Rsch. award, U. Pitts., 1993, R&D 100 award, R&D Mag., 2000, Carnegie award for Excellence in Sci. & Tech., 2000, 2006, Am. Cyanamid Rsch. award; named one of The 100 Agents of Change, Rolling Stone mag., 2009. Fellow: Am. Inst. Med. & Biol. Engring.; mem.: Tissue Engring. Soc. N.Am., Am. Inst. Chem. Engineers, Biochemistry Soc., Am. Chem. Soc. Lutheran. Achievements include research on the symbiotic interface between enzymes and materials, the study of proteins in extreme environments and the development of rational approaches to biomaterial syntheses for tissue engineering; discovery of the decontamination and biotechnological destruction of chemical weapons using enzymes; patents in field. Office: McGowan Inst 450 Technology Dr Ste 300 Pittsburgh PA 15219 Office Phone: 412-624-5205. Business E-Mail: arussell@pitt.edu.

RUSSELL, ANDREW, child and adolescent psychiatrist, educator; MD, U. Colo., 1970. Diplomate Am. Bd. Psychiatry and Neurology, 1980, Am. Bd. Psychiatry and Neurology-child and adolescent psychiatry, 1988, Am. Bd. Psychiatry and Neurology-child and adolescent psychiatry, 2004. Intern medicine Orange County Med. Ctr., 1970—71; resident psychiatry UCLA Sch. Medicine, 1971—73, fellow child psychiatry, 1973—74, UCLA Neuropsychiatric Hosp., 1976—77; clin prof. psychiatry UCLA; hosp. affiliations include

Ronald Reagan UCLA Med. Ctr., Stewart and Lynda Resnick Neuropsychiatric Hosp. UCLA. Office: University of California Los Angeles NPI Semel Institute 760 Westwood Plz Los Angeles CA 90024 Office Phone: 310-825-0389.

RUSSELL, CADENE AMOY, lawyer; b. Orlando, Fla., Mar. 6, 1988; BA in Biol. Anthropology & Anatomy, Duke U., 2010. Asst. tchr., rschr., inst. genome sciences and policy, dept. African & African-Am. studies & genomics Duke U., 2009—10; writer Online Health Network, 2010—11; congl. intern US Congress, 2010—11; chamber intern DC Superior Ct., 2011; securities, litig. asst. Wilmer-Hale LLP, 2011—. Centennial conf. spkr. and organizer Nat. Urban League, 2010—11. Recipient Silver Knight award, Miami Herald, Miami Dade and Broward County, Fla. Mem.: Delta Sigma Theta Sorority, Inc. Home: 201 Massachusetts Ave NE Apt 201 Washington DC 20002 Personal E-mail: cadene.russell@gmail.com.

RUSSELL, ELBERT WINSLOW, neuropsychologist; b. Las Vegas, N.Mex., June 4, 1929; s. Josiah Cox and Ruth Winslow Russell; children from previous marriage: Gwendolyn Marie Harvey, Franklin Winslow, Kirsten Nash, Jonathan Nash; m. Sally Lynn Kolitz, Apr. 2, 1989. BA, Earlham Coll., Richmond, Ind., 1951; MA, U. Ill., 1953; MS, Pa. State U., 1958; PhD, U. Kans., 1968. Lic. psychologist Florida, 1973. Clin. psychologist Warnersville (Pa.) State Hosp., 1959-61; clin. neuropsychologist VA Med. Ctr., Cin., 1968-71, dir. neuropsychology lab. Miami, Fla., 1971-89, rsch. psychologist, 1989—. Adj. prof. Nova U., Ft. Lauderdale, 1980-87, U. Miami Med. Sch., 1980-94, U. Miami, 1979—. Author: (with C. Neuringer and G. Goldstein) Assessment of Brain Damage, 1970; (with R.I. Starkey) Halstead Russell Neuropsychology Evaluation System (manual and computer program), 1993, rev. 2001; contbr. articles to profl. jours. Recipient Life Time Achievement award, Am. Bd. Psychol. Assessment, 1999, Halstead award, Reitan Soc., 2000. Fellow APA., Am. Psychol. Soc., Nat. Acad. Neuropsychology; mem. Sigma Xi. Democrat. Mem. Soc. Of Friends. Home: 6091 SW 79th St Miami FL 33156-2944 Office: 9350 S Dixie Hwy Ste 1260 Miami FL 33156-2944 Home Phone: 305-667-3821; Office Phone: 305-670-2284. Personal E-mail: ewr@bellsouth.net.

RUSSELL, FINDLAY EWING, physician; b. San Francisco, Sept. 1, 1919; s. William and Mary Jane (Findlay) R.; m. Janet Louise Thiel. Feb. 14, 1950; children: Christa Ann, Sharon Jane, Robin Emily, Constance Susan, Mark Findlay. BA, Walla Walla Coll., Wash., 1941; MD, Loma Linda U., Calif., 1950; postgrad. (fellow), Calif. Inst. Tech., 1951 53; postgrad., U. Cambridge, Eng., 1962 63; PhD, U. Santa Barbara, Calif., 1974, LLD (hon.), 1989. Intern White Meml. Hosp., Los Angeles, 1950-51; practice medicine specializing in toxinology and toxicology Los Angeles, 1953—; mem. staff Los Angeles County-U. So. Calif. Med. Center, Loma Linda U. Med. Center, U. Ariz. Med. Ctr.; physiologist Huntington Inst. Med. Research, 1953-55; dir. lab. neurol. research Los Angeles County-U. So. Calif. Med. Center, 1955-80; mem. faculty Loma Linda U. Med. Sch., 1955—2007; prof. neurology, physiology and biology U. So. Calif. Med. Sch., 1966-81; prof. pharmacology and toxicology U. Ariz. Health Scis. Coll. Pharmacy, 1981—. Cons. USPHS, NSF, Office Naval Rsch., WHO, U.S. Army, Walter Reed, USAF, Brooks AFB. Author: Marine Toxins and Venomous and Poisonous Marine Animals, 1965, Poisonous Marine Animals, 1971, Snake Venom Poisoning, 1980; co-author: Bibliography of Snake Venoms and Venomous Snakes, 1964, Animal Toxins, 1967, Poisonous Snakes of The World, 1968, Snake Venom Poisoning, 1983, Bibliography of Venomous and Poisonous Marine Animals and Their Toxins, 1984, Venomous and Poisonous Marine Invertebrates of the Indian Ocean, 1996; editor: Toxicon, 1962-70. Served with AUS, 1942-46. Decorated Purple Heart, Bronze Star; recipient award Los Angeles County Bd. Suprs., 1960; award Acad. Medicine Buenos Aires, 1966; Skylab Achievement award, 1974; Jozef Stefan medal Yugoslavia, 1978, U.S. State Dept. medallion, 2006, Disting. Citizen award, 1992. Fellow A.C.P., Am. Coll. Cardiology, Royal Soc. Tropical Medicine, N.Y. Acad. Scis.; mem. Internat. Soc. Toxinology (pres. 1962-66, Francisco Redi medal 1967), Royal Soc. Medicine, Am. Soc. Physiology, Western Soc. Pharmacology (pres. 1973) Office: U Ariz Health Scis Coll Pharmacy Pharm/Tox Tucson AZ 85721 Office Phone: 520-626-4047.

RUSSELL, JOHN J., physician, educator; MD, Pa. State U. Coll. Medicine, Hershey; attended, Temple U. Sch. Medicine, Phila. Diplomate Am. Bd. Family Medicine. Resident Abington Meml. Hosp., Pa., assoc. dir. family practice residency program; asst. clin. prof. dept. family medicine Temple Univ. Sch. Medicine, Phila. Author: (articles) Tropical Therapy for Acne. Office: Abington Memorial Hospital 1200 Old York Rd Abington PA 19001 Office Phone: 215-481-2000.

RUSSELL, LIANE BRAUCH, retired geneticist; b. Vienna, Aug. 27, 1923; came to U.S., 1941; d. Arthur and Clara (Starer) Brauch; m. William Lawson Russell (dec.), Sept. 23, 1947; children: David Lawson, Evelyn Ruth. AB, Hunter Coll., 1945; PhD, U. Chgo., 1949; ScD (hon.), Hunter Coll., NYC, 1999; LHD (hon.), Berea Coll., 2005. Fellow U. Chgo., 1945-46, teaching asst., 1946-47; rsch. asst. Jackson Lab., Bar Harbor, Maine, 1945, 46; rsch. staff mem. Oak Ridge (Tenn.) Nat. Lab., 1947-75, sect. head., 1975-95, sr. rsch. fellow, 1988—2001; ret., 2002. Sci. advisor U.S. Del. at 1st Atoms for Peace Conf., Geneva, Switzerland, 1955; mem. numerous sci. bds. including Nat. Research Council com. on energy and environment, 1975-77, com. on biol. effects of ionizing radiation, 1977-80, bd. on environ. studies and toxicology, 1981-90, Nat. Council on Radiation Protection and Measurement Task Group, Washington, 1975-77, Genetox Program EPA, Washington, 1979—, Internat. Com. for Protection Against Environ. Mutagens and Carcinogens, Lausanne, Switzerland, 1977-83, Internat. com. on standardized genetic nomenclature for mice, 1977-91, office of tech. assessment, scientific adv. panel, 1985-86; mem. task group Internat. Agy. for Research on Cancer, Hanover, Fed. Republic of Germany, 1979, EPA review panel on mutagenicity guidelines, 1985-86; adj. faculty U. Tenn., 1980-. Assoc. editor Mutation Rsch., 1976-96, Environ. Mutagenesis, 1980-83; editor TCWP Newsletter, 1966—; editor: (book) Genetic Mosaics and Chimeras, 1979; contbr. more than 165 articles to profl. jours. Founder Tenn. Citizens for Wilderness Planning, Oak Ridge, 1966, pres. 1967-70, 86-87; active numerous environ. groups. Corp. fellow Union Carbide, 1983; corp. fellow Martin Marietta, 1985, sr. corp. fellow, 1988; recipient Merit award Mademoiselle, 1955, Roentgen medal City of Remscheid-Lennep, 1973, Disting. Assoc. award U.S. Dept. Energy, 1987; named to Hunter Coll. Hall of Fame, 1979, Sol Feinstone Environ. Achievement award SUNY, 1987, Lifetime Achievement award Tenn. Environ. Coun., 1990, Vocational Svc. award Oak Ridge Rotary, 1992, Marjorie Stoneman Douglas award Nat. Parks Conservation Assn., 1993, Enrico Fermi award U.S. Dept. Energy, 1993, Lifetime Conservation Achievement award So. Appalachian Forest Coalition, 1999, Lifetime Environ. Conservation award Tenn. Dept. Environment and Conservation, 2000; Tenn. Clean Water Network River Hero, 2008, River Network River Achievement award, 2009, YWCA Lifetime Achievement award, 2009. Fellow AAAS, Environ. Health Inst.; mem. Nat. Acad. Scis., Environ. Mutagen Soc. (pres. 1984-85, EMS award 1993), Tenn. Environ. Honor Soc. Avocation: environmental activism. Personal E-mail: lianerussell@comcast.net. Business E-Mail: russelllb@ornl.gov.

RUSSELL, LOUISE BENNETT, economist, educator; b. Exeter, NH, May 12, 1942; d. Frederick Dewey and Esther (Smith) B.; m. Robert Hardy Cosgriff, May 3, 1987; 1 child, Benjamin Smith Cosgriff. BA, U. Mich., 1964; PhD, Harvard U., 1971. Economist Social Security Adminstrn., Washington, 1968-71, Nat. Commn. on State Workmen's Compensation Laws, Washington, 1971-72, Dept. Labor, Washington, 1972-73; sr. economist Nat. Planning Assn., Washington, 1973-75; sr. fellow Brookings Instn., Washington, 1975-87; rsch. prof. Inst. for Health, Health Care Policy and Aging Rsch. Rutgers U., New Brunswick, N.J., 1987—, prof. econs., 1987—. Chmn. health care policy divsn. Rutgers U., 1988—. Author: Technology in Hospitals, 1979, The Baby Boom Generation and the Economy, 1982, Is Prevention Better Than Cure, 1986, Evaluating Preventive Care: Report on a Workshop, 1987, Medicare's New Hospital Payment System: Is It Working, 1989, Educated Guesses: Making Policy About Medical Screening Tests, 1994, (with MR Gold, JE Siegel and MC Weinstein) Cost-Effectiveness in Health and Medicine, 1996, (with M. Pignone, J. Wagner) Economic Models of Colorectal Cancer Screening in Average Risk Adults, 2005; contbr. over 100 articles to profl. jours.; assoc. editor Med. Decision Making, 2004—. Mem. U.S. Preventive Svcs. Task Force, 1984-88; co-chair Panel on Cost Effectiveness in Health and Medicine DHHS, USPHS, 1993-96. Mem. Inst. Medicine of NAS (elected 1983, com. to study future pub. health 1986-87, bd. on health scis. policy 1989-91, com. on clin. practice guidelines 1990-91, com. on setting priorities for practice guidelines 1994, nat. cancer policy bd. 2001-05). Office: Rutgers U Inst for Health Care Policy 30 College Ave New Brunswick NJ 08901-1293 Business E-Mail: lrussell@rci.rutgers.edu.

RUSSELL, MASON WEBSTER, economist, consultant; b. Beverly, Mass., July 28, 1956; s. Gordon Arthur and Elizabeth Mason (Webster) R.; m. Susanne Rachel Nadeau, Oct. 22, 1982. BA in Econs., Salem State U., 1978; MA in Polit. Economy, Boston U., 1981, postgrad., 1981-87. Lectr. econs. Boston U., 1979-82; asst. prof. econs. Bentley U., Waltham, Mass., 1982-85; sr. economist Policy Analysis Inc., Brookline, Mass., 1985-88, 94; exec. dir. White Mountain Health Svcs., Gorham, N.H., 1988-91; dir. corp. devel. North Care Corp., Berlin, N.H., 1991-92; dir., COO Mountain Health Svcs., Berlin, 1991-92; sr. economist Piedmont Group, Richmond, Va., 1992-94; sr. health economist Med. Rsch. Internat., Burlington, Mass., also London, 1994-98; dir. health econs. ICSL Healthcare Rsch., Burlington, Mass., also London, 1998-2000, v.p. outcomes rsch., gen. mgr. Waltham, Mass., 2000—02; dir. global health econ., pricing, reimbursement strategy Biogen, Inc., Cambridge, Mass., 2002—04; v.p. rsch. Boston Health Economics, Inc., Waltham, 2004—06; v.p. exec. dir. registries, pricing reimbursement Abt Bio Pharma Solutions, Lexington, Mass., 2006—10; head health economics RTI Internat. Health Solutions, Waltham, 2010—11; exec. dir., health econ. outcomes rsch. PharmNet 13, Princeton, NJ, 2011—. Faculty assoc. Sch. for Lifelong Learning, Univ. System N.H., Berlin, 1990-92; sec., dir. Gorham Devel. Corp., 1990-92; sr. adj. instr. Salem (Mass.) State U., 1995-2003; online faculty mem. U. Phoenix, 2005—. Contbr. articles to profl. jours. Pres., dir. United Way No. N.H., Berlin, 1990-92, Overlook VNA & Hosp. Inc., 2011-, dir., 2007-; vice chmn. gt. no. dist. Daniel Webster coun. Boy Scouts Am., 1990-92, dir. Masonic Health Sys., 2010-, The Groves Linclon Inc., 2010-, Grand Lodge Mass. AF & AM, 2009 Mem. Am. Coll. Healthcare Execs., Internat. Soc. Pharmacoecons. and Outcomes Rsch., Am. Coll. Clin. Pharmacy, Drug Info. Assn., Masons, Phi Kappa Phi. Democrat. Roman Catholic. Home Phone: 978-689-4792; Office Phone: 617-649-6152. Personal E-mail: masonwr@comcast.net. Business E-Mail: mrussell@pharmanet.com.

RUSSELL, PAUL SNOWDEN, surgeon, educator; b. Chgo., Jan. 22, 1925; s. Paul Snowden and Carroll (Mason) R.; m. Allene Lummis, Sept. 24, 1952; children: Katherine Swift, Paul Snowden, Allene, Laura Rice. PhB, U. Chgo., 1944, BS, 1945, MD, 1947; MA (hon.), Harvard U., 1962. Diplomate Am. Bd. Surgery, Am. Bd. Thoracic Surgery. From surg. intern, to resident Mass. Gen. Hosp., 1948-56, asst. surgery, 1957-60, chief gen. surg. svcs., 1962-69, chmn. com. on rsch., 1973-76; postdoctoral fellow USPHS, 1954-55; from tchg. fellow to clin. assoc. surgery Harvard Med. Sch., 1956-60, John Homans prof. surgery, 1962-98, John Homans Disting. prof. surgery, 1998—; assoc. prof. surgery Columbia Coll. Phys. and Surg., 1960-62; assoc. attending surgeon Presbyn. Hosp., NYC, 1960-62; assoc. vis. surgeon Francis Delafield Hosp., NYC, 1960-62, 74-94. Mem. com. tissue transplantation NRC-Nat. Acad. Scis., 1963-71, com. trauma, 1963-68; ad hoc com. to study clin. investigation and edn. in USN, 1971-73; allergy and immunology study sect. USPHS, 1963-65, chmn. allergy and immunology study sect. B, 1965-67; mem. transplantation and immunology com. Nat. Inst. Allergy and Infectious Diseases, 1967-69, chmn., 1970; mem. com. on cancer immunotherapy Nat. Cancer Inst., 1974-79. Contbr. papers in field.; Editorial bd.: Archives Surgery, 1963-72, Surgery, 1963-71, Transplantation, 1965-79, Annals of Surgery, 1966—, Transplantation Procs, 1966—, Jour. Immunology, 1977-80. Trustee Pine Manor Coll., Chestnut Hill, Mass., 1963-76, Groton Sch., 1964-79, The Conservation Law Found., 1997—; bd. dirs. Boston Fulbright Com., 1968, pres., 1980—; vice chmn. bd. govs., trustee corp. Jackson Lab. With USAF, 1951-53. Recipient Roche Pioneer award, Am. Soc. Transplant Surgeons, 2005. Fellow AAAS, ACS, Royal Soc. Medicine, Am. Acad. Arts and Scis., Assn. Immunologists, NY Acad. Scis., Mass. Med. Soc., New Eng. Surg. Soc., Boston Surg. Soc. (pres. 1994), Soc. Univ. Surgeons, Soc. Exptl. Biology and Medicine, Halsted Soc., Whipple Soc., Internat. Soc. Surgery, Am. Surg. Assn., Transplantation Soc. (pres. 1970, Medawar Prize 2005), Polish Acad. Sci. (fgn.), Sigma Xi. Home: 10 Longwood Dr Apt 148 Westwood MA 02090 Office: Dept Surgery Mass Gen Hosp Boston MA 02114 Office Phone: 617-726-2801.

RUSSELL, RICHARD OLNEY, JR., retired cardiologist; b. Birmingham, Ala., July 9, 1932; s. Richard Olney and Louise (Taylor) R.; m. Phyllis Hutchinson, June 15, 1963; children: Scott Richard, Katherine Hutchinson, Meredith Cooper, Stephen Wilbon. AB cum laude, Vanderbilt U., Nashville, 1953, MD, 1956. Diplomate Am. Bd. Internal Medicine, 1964, Am. Bd. Cardiovascular Disease, 1967. Intern Peter Bent Brigham Hosp., Boston, 1956-57, resident, 1959-60, 63-64; fellow in cardiology Med. Coll. Ala., Birmingham, 1960-62, instr., 1962-63; instr. medicine U. Ala., Birmingham, 1964-65, asst. prof., 1965-70, assoc. prof., 1970-73, prof., 1973-81, clin. prof., 1981—2006; pvt. practice medicine specializing in cardiology Birmingham, 1981—2006; ret., 2006. Mem. Jefferson County Bd. Health, 1977—81, chmn., 1979. Author: (with Charles Edward Rackley) Hemodynamic Monitoring in a Coronary Intensive Care Unit, 1974, 2d rev. and enlarged edit., 1981, Coronary Artery Disease: Recognition and Management, 1979, (with others) Radiographic Anatomy of the Coronary Arteries: An Atlas, 1976, Acute Ischemic Syndromes in American College of Cardiology Self Assessment Program, 1993; mem. editl. bd. Circulation, 1976-80, Am. Jour. Cardiology, 1977-82, Heart and Lung, 1978-83, Chest, 1978-83, Ala. Jour. Med. Scis, 1977-80, Jour. Am. Coll. Cardiology, 1987-90; sect. editor for Case Studies for Cardiosource for Am. Coll. Cardiology, 2001-06, assoc. editor, 2006-10; contbr. articles to profl. jours. Distbn. com. Greater Birmingham Found., 1984-90; exec. bd. Birmingham area coun. Boy Scouts Am., 1987-1998, v.p., 1990-96, coun. commr., 1996-98; vice chmn. Vulcan dist., 1988-89, chmn., 1989-91, bd. dirs. S.E. region, 1990-92, bd. dirs. southern region, 1992—; bd. dirs. Ctrl. Ala. United Way, 1988-92; mem. Newcomen Soc., 1988—; chmn. exec. com. Birmingham Bapt. Med. Ctr., Montclair, 1995, pres.-elect med. staff, 1998-99, pres. 1999-2000; chmn. Nat. Eagle Scout Assn. Scholarship Com. So. Region, 2001-03, chmn. area nine, 2009-11; asst. coun. cmmr. Greater Ala. coun. Boy Scouts Am., 1998-2000, coun. commr., 2001-04, v.p. bd., 2006, pres., 2007; mem. Am. Bd. Cardiovasc. Disease, 1991-96. Capt. U.S. Army. Decorated Commendation medal; recipient Dist. Award of Merit, Boy Scouts Am., 1991, Silver Beaver award, 1990, Disting. Eagle Scout, 1999, Silver Antelope award 2001, Vigil Honor, 2007; NIH rsch. fellow, 1966-67. Fellow: ACP, Am. Coll. Cardiology (bd. govs. 1979—81, trustee 1984—85, 1989—94, ann. sci. session program chmn. 1994, disting. fellowship 2001, Ala. chpt. named lectureship in honor); mem.: Med. Assn. State Ala. (spkr. house counselors dels. 1989—94, Laureate award 1999), Birmingham Soc. Internists (pres. 2001 03), Birmingham Cardiovascular Soc. (pres. 1981), Jefferson County Med. Soc. (v.p. 1982, pres. 1984), So. Soc. Clin. Investigation, Am. Fedn. Clin. Rsch., Am. Coll. Chest Physicians (bd. regents 1985—91), Am. Heart Assn. (pres. Ala. affiliate 1975—76, v.p. so. region 1986—87, task force on practice guidelines 1998—2000), Royal Soc. Medicine, NY Acad. Scis., Kiwanis (Brimingham sec. 1984—85, disting. pres. 1994 95), Leadership Birmingham, Omicron Delta Kappa, Alpha Omega Alpha, Phi Beta Kappa. Home: 4408 Kennesaw Dr Birmingham AL 35213-1826 Personal E-mail: rorussell@charter.net.

RUSSELL, ROBERT MITCHELL, gastroenterology educator; b. Boston, Apr. 9, 1941; s. Stanley Gordon and Martha Lillian (Johnson) R.; m. Sharon Stanton, Aug. 28, 1965; children: Kimberley, Brooke. BA cum laude, Harvard U., 1963; MD, Columbia U., 1967. Intern U. Chgo., 1967-69, resident, 1971-73, NIH fellow gastroenterology, 1973-75; from asst. to assoc. prof. medicine U. Md. Sch. Medicine, Balt., 1974-81; assoc. prof. medicine Tufts U., Boston, 1981-88, prof. medicine and nutrition, 1988—2008, emeritus prof. medicine and nutrition, 2008—, dir. human studies USDA Human Nutrition Rsch. Ctr. on Aging, 1981—99, assoc. dir. USDA Human Nutrition Rsch. Ctr. on Aging, 1983—2000, dir., 2000—08, sr. scientist, 1987—; emeritus staff physician dept. medicine sect. gastroenterology and clinical nutrition New England Med. Ctr. Hosps., Boston, 1981—. Chmn. sci. adv. bd. Nat. Dairy Coun., Chgo., 1987-91; mem. pretest com. Am. Bd. Internal Medicine, Phila., 1990-94; vice chair food and nutrition bd. NAS, 2001-04, chmn. 2004—06; chmn. U.S. nat. com. Internat. Union Nutrition Scientists; bd. dirs. Internat. Life Sci. Inst., trustee, 2004—06, spl. expert NIH, 2008- Author: Nutritional Status of Boston Elderly, 1991, Chronic Gastritis and Hypochlorhydria in the Elderly, 1992, Blomarkers for antioxitant defence and oxidative damage, 2010; editor: Present Knowledge in Nutrition, 2000, 06; editor-in-chief Nutrition Reviews, 2001-09; contbr. articles to profl. jours. Mem. Hyde Park Community Ctr., Chgo., 1972-74, Famine Policy Ctr. Com., Boston, 1985-88; mem. So. Iraq cons. team UNICEF, N.Y.C., 1991. Major U.S. Army, 1969-71, Vietnam; mem. bd. Nestle Found., 2008-; mem. bd. trustee US Pharmacopeia, 2010-, mem., Fetzer Inst. Adv. Coun. Health, 2011-. Recipient Global Medicine award Assn. U.S. Army, 1971, rsch. award Chgo. Soc. Gastroenterology, 1974, Rsch. Devel. award VA Career Devel. Program, 1975-78. Fellow ACP; mem. Am. Gastroent. Soc., Am. Soc. Nutrition Scientists (grad. nutrition edn. com. 1989-90), Am. Coll. Nutrition (Grace Goldsmith award 1994), Am. Soc. Clin. Nutrition (pres. 2002, Robert Herman award 1999), Soc. for Internat. Nutrition Rsch., Internat. Union Nutrition Scientists (chmn. U.S. nat. com. 2004—06, DSM award 2005), Am. Soc. Nutrition (v.p. 2009-, pres., 2010-, DSM Human Nutrition award 2005, Kritchevsky award 2008, Atwater award 2010). Democrat. Christian. Avocations: photography, sailing. Office: NIH ODS 6100 Executive Blvd Bethesda MD 20892-7517 Home Phone: 781-643-0069. Business E-Mail: rob.russell@tufts.edu, russellrz@od.nih.gov.

RUSSELL, STUART DEAN, cardiologist, educator; BS in Cellular and Molecular Biology, U. Wash., Seattle, 1986, MD, 1991. Bd. cert. in cardiology and internal medicine. Resident Johns Hopkins Hosp., Balt., 1991—94, assoc. prof. medicine, 2004—, chief of heart failure and transplantation; fellow Duke U. Med. Ctr., 1994—97; transplant fellow UCLA Med. Ctr., 1997—98. Contbr. several articles to profl.

jours. Office: Johns Hopkins Hosp Carnegie 568 600 N Wolfe St Baltimore MD 21287 Office Phone: 410-955-5708. Office Fax: 410-955-3478. E-mail: srusse14@jhmi.edu.

RUSSELL, SUE ANN, clinical psychologist; b. Connersville, Ind., Apr. 14, 1949; d. Hugh B. Russell and Martha Jane Meyer. BS, U. Colo., 1971; MDiv, Abilene Christian U., 1981; MS in Clin. Psychology, U. North Tex., 1984; PhD in Clin. Psychology, U. N.D., 1992. Intern Psychol. Svcs. Ctr. U. N.D., Grand Forks, 1986-92; intern Stone Ctr. Wellesley Coll., Wellesley, Mass., 1991-92; rsch. psychologist women's drinking project U. ND, Grand Forks, 1986-92; pvt. practice Grand Forks, 1993—. Founding fellow Jean Baker Miller Tng. Inst. of Wellesley Coll., 1996. Contbr. articles to profl. jours. Missionary to Tonga Tribe, Zambia, 1972—74. Fellowship Nat. Inst. on Alcohol Abuse and Alcoholism Nat. Inst. of Mental Health, 1991-92, Nat. Rsch. Svc. award 1988-91; pre-doctoral rsch. fellow Stone Ctr. of Wellesley Coll., 1991-92. Mem. Am. Psychol. Assn., N.D. Psychol. Assn., Assn. of Prevention and Cruelty to Animals Office: 628 7th Ave S Ste B Grand Forks ND 58201-4854 Office Phone: 701-746-8737.

RUSSO, JOSE, pathologist; b. Mendoza, Argentina, Mar. 24, 1942; came to US, 1971; s. Felipe and Teresa (Pagano) R.; m. Irma Haydee, Feb. 8, 1969; 1 child, Patricia Alexandra. BS, Agustin Alvarez Nat. Coll., 1959; MD, U. Nat. Cuyo, 1967. Instr. Inst. Gen. and Exptl. Pathology Med. Sch., Mendoza, 1961-66; asst. prof. Inst. Histology and Embryology, 1967-71; Rockefeller Found. postdoc. fellow Inst. Molecular and Cellular Evolution U. Miami, 1971—73; chief exptl. pathology lab. Mich. Cancer Found., Detroit, 1973-81; assoc. clin. prof. pathology Wayne State U., Detroit, 1979-91, chmn. dept. pathology, 1981-91; chmn. dept. pathology, sr. mem. Fox Chase Cancer Ctr., Phila., 1991-94, sr. mem., dir. Breast Cancer Rsch. and Environ. Ctr., 1994—, dir. med. outreach and minority affairs; sci. dir. League of Women Against Cancer. Mem. Mich. Cancer Found., 1982-91; adj. prof. pathology Jefferson Sch. Medicine, U. Pa. Sch. Medicine, Phila.; adj. prof. biochemistry Temple Med. Sch. Author: Tumor Diagnosis by Electron Microscopy, vol. 1, 1986, vol. 2, 1988, vol. 3, 1990, Immunocytochemistry in Tumor Diagnosis, 1985, Molecular Basis of Breast Cancer, 2004; editor-in-chief Jour. of Women's Cancer; contbr. over 380 articles to profl. jours USPHS grantee, 1978, 80, 84, 88, 90, 93-95, 98, 2000, 02, grantee Am. Cancer Soc., 1982, Dept. of Def., 1999-2003; NRC Argentina fellow, 1967-71 Mem. Am. Assn. Cancer Rsch., Am. Soc. Cell Biology, Soc. Exptl. Biology and Medicine, Tissue Culture Assn., Am. Soc. Clin. Pathology, Internat. Acad. Pathology, Am. Coll. Pathology, Sigma Xi Roman Catholic. Office Phone: 215-728-4782. Business E-Mail: jose.russo@fccc.edu, j.russo@fccc.edu.

RUSSO, PAUL, urologist; MD, Columbia U. Coll. of Physicians and Surgeons, 1979. Diplomate Am. Bd. Urology. Resident urology Barnes Hosp. Wash. Univ., St. Louis, 1980—84; fellow urologic oncology Meml. Sloan Kettering Cancer Ctr., 1984—88, urologist. Office: 1275 York Ave New York NY 10065 Office Phone: 800-525-2225.

RUSSO, VINCENT JOSEPH, surgeon; b. Phila., Apr. 15, 1939; s. Joseph Vincent Russo and Yolanda Italia D'Ambrosio; m. Sheila Kay Roos, June 8, 1963; children: Teresa, Joseph, Katrina, Anita. AB, Columbia U., 1960; MD, Boston U., 1964, MPH, 1983. Diplomate Am. Bd. Surgery. Staff surgeon Anna Jaques Hosp., Newburyport, Mass., 1971-88; clin. instr. surgery Harvard Med. Sch., Boston, 1984-98; med. dir. Blue Cross/Blue Shield, Methuen, Mass., 1990-98; sr. staff surgeon Lawrence (Mass.) Gen. Hosp., 1990-2000; med. dir. Ea. Mass. Health Ctrs., 1999—2000; clin. instr. Sch. Medicine Boston U., 2001—04; seaterm ship's physician Mass. Maritime Acad., 2001—06. Cons. surgeon Manchester (N.H.) VA Med. Ctr., 1985-98; pres. Essex North Med. Soc., Newburyport, 1988-89, 2002-04; dist. 3 med. examiner Essex County, 1986-2007; ship's doctor Mass. Maritime Acad., 2001-06. Bd. trustees, corporator, chmn. auditing com. Newburyport Savings Bank, 1987—; mem. UNICO, Andover, Mass., 1994-97. Lt. cmdr. USN, ships surgeon USS Forrestal Aircraft Carrier, 1969-71; selectmen, chmn. bd. Town of Newbury, Mass, 2004—09; selectman Town Newbury, 2004-2010; field rep., surveyor Joint Commn. on Accreditation of Health Orgns., 2004—; commr. mosquito control Commonwealth of Mass., 2005—; chmn. auditing comm. Newburyport Five Cents Savings Bank, 2006-; corporator Anna Jaques Hosp., Newburyport, Mass., 1985—. Lt. col. U.S. Army, 1990-91, Desert Storm. Named Physician of Yr., Mass. Med. Soc. Essex North Dist., 2009. Fellow ACS (councilor Mass. chpt. 1995-98); mem. AMA, Soc. Am. Gastrointestinal Endoscopic Surgeons, Mass. Med. Soc. (legis. com. 1990—, del. 2000—), Boston Surg. Soc., Essex North Dist. Med. Soc. (exec. com. 1986—, pres. 2002-04), Rotary (sr. active), Mass. Med. Soc. (reference com. 2002-04, trustee 2004—), U.S. Naval Inst. Roman Catholic. Avocations: theater, swimming, skiing, music. Office Phone: 978-852-8310. E-mail: vjrusso@massmed.org.

RUSSU, WADE A., pharmacist, educator; b. Santa Maria, Calif., May 4, 1969; BS, Calif. Poly. State U., 1992; PhD, U. Calif., Santa Barbara, 2000. Postdoc. scholar U. Calif., Irvine, 2000—05; assoc. prof. medicinal chemistry Thomas J. Long Sch. Pharmacy and Health Scis., U. Pacific, 2005—. New Investigator grant, Burroughs Wellcome Fund-AFPE-AACP. Mem.: Am. Assn. Cancer Rsch., Am. Chem. Soc., Rho Chi Soc., Phi Lambda Upsilon. Avocations: beer brewing, exercise. Office: 3601 Pacific Ave Stockton CA 95211 Office Fax: 209-946-2160. Business E-Mail: wrussu@pacific.edu.

RUST, EDWARD BARRY, JR., insurance company executive, lawyer; b. Chgo., Aug. 3, 1950; s. Edward Barry Sr. and Harriett B. (Fuller) R.; m. Sally Buckler, Feb. 28, 1976; 1 child, Edward Barry III. Student, Lawrence U., 1968-69; BS, Ill. Wesleyan U., 1972; JD, MBA, So. Meth. U., 1975. Bar: Tex. 1975, Ill. 1976. Mgmt. trainee State Farm Insurance Companies, Dallas, 1975-76, atty. Bloomington, Ill., 1976, sr. atty., 1976-78, asst. v.p., 1978-81, v.p., 1981-83, exec. v.p., 1983-85, pres., CEO, 1985—87, chmn., pres., CEO, 1987—. Bd. dirs. Helmerich & Payne, Inc., 1997-, The McGraw-Hill Companies, Inc., 2001-, Caterpillar Inc., 2003- Trustee Ill. Wesleyan U., 1985—; mem. adv. coun. Grad. Sch. Bus. Stanford U., 1987-94; mem. bus. adv. coun. Coll. Commerce and Bus. Adminstrn. U. Ill. mem., pres. George W. Bush's Transition Adv. Team Com. on Edn. Mem. Am. Enterprise Inst., Bus. Roundtable (chmn. edn. task force), Tex. State Bar Assn., Ill. Bar Assn., Am. Inst. Property and Liability Underwriters (trustee 1986-96), Ins. Inst. Am. (trustee 1986-96), Ins. Inst. for Highway Safety (vice chmn.), Nat. Alliance of Bus. (chmn. 1998—), Ill. Bus. Roundtable (chmn. 1998—), Bus. Advisory Coun. Univ. Ill. Coll. Commerce and Bus. Admin. Office: State Farm Ins Cos 1 State Farm Plz E-12 Bloomington IL 61710-0001 Office Fax: 309-766-2311, 309-766-3621. Business E-Mail: rust.edward@statefarm.com. *

RUST, ROBERT STANLEY, pediatrician, educator; b. Van Nuys, Calif., Aug. 11, 1948; s. Robert Bonham and Emily Frances Rust; m. Elizabeth Howe Merrill, June 26, 1976; children: James Robert Bonham, Merrill Alexander Campbell, David Armistead Lee, Thomas Ludwell Akers. BA, Kent State U., Ohio, 1970; MA, U. Va., Charlottesville, 1972, MD, 1981. Diplomate Am. Bd. Pediat., 1988, in neurology and child neurology Am. Bd. Psychiatry and Neurology, 1988, cert. in physician and surgeon Mo. State Bd. Medicine, 1984, in medicine and surgery Wis. State Bd. Medicine, 1990, Va. State Bd. Medicine, 1999. Assoc. dir. Internat. Coll., Salzburg, Austria, 1972—76; rsch. assoc. dept. plastic surgery U. Va., 1974—77, Worrell prof. neurology and pediat., 1999—, dir. child neurology, 1999—; resident dept. pediat. Yale U., New Haven, 1981—83; resident dept. neurology Wash. U., St. Louis, 1983—84, fellow dept. neurology and pediat., 1984—87, instr. and rsch. fellow, dept. pediat., neurology, 1987—90; asst. prof. pediat. and neurology U. Wis., Madison, 1990—97, dir. cerebral palsy clinic, 1990—97, dir. child neurology, 1991—97; assoc. prof. neurology and pediat. Harvard Sch. Medicine, Boston, 1997—99. Chair archives com. Child Neurology Soc., St. Paul, 1990—; clinic and tng. dir. child neurology Boston Children's Hosp., Harvard Med. Sch., 1997—99; chair child neurology sect. Am. Acad. Neurology, St. Paul, 2008—. Contbr. articles to profl. jours. Recipient Raven award, U. Va., 1981, Irwin P. Levy award, Wash. U., 1986, Outstanding Clin. Tchr. award, St. Louis Children's Hosp., 1989—90, Med. Alumni Assn. Disting. Tchg. award, U. Wis., 1997, Outstanding Physician award, Wis. Epilepsy Assn., 1998—99, Spl. award, mentorship and child neurology, Harvard Med. Sch., 1999, Hower award, lifetime achievement, Child Neurology Soc., 2008; Woodrow Wilson fellowship, 1970—72, 1974—76, Gov. Va. fellow, Commonwealth Va., 1974—76, Rsch. fellowship, NIH, 1991—96. Mem.: Internat. Child Neurology Assn. (presdl. adv. com. 2007—), Child Neurology Soc. (chair archives com. 1990—2008), Am. Headache Soc., Am. Acad. Neurology (chair sect. child neurology 2008—). Liberal. Presbyterian. Achievements include development of brain chemistry, neonatal brain injury, inflammatory neurologic diseases, headache, epilepsy. Avocations: carpentry, tennis, fishing, golf, horseback riding. Office: Univ Virginia Box 800394 Charlottesville VA 22908-0394

RUSTIA, ALESSANDRO, neurosurgeon, educator; b. Rome, Apr. 26, 1967; s. Ivo Rustia and Santina Rampini; life ptnr. Giovanna Schiavo; children: Elias Armando, Gabriel Alessandro, Jacopo Alessandro. MS in Neurosurgery, U. Firenze, 1993; PhD in Neurosurgery, 1998. Capt. med. army, Rome, 1993—2000; asst. med. dir. Azienza Ospedaliera, L'Aquila, Italy, 2000—02. Neurosurgeon asst. med. dir. Azienda San Giovanni, Roma, 2002—; prof. U. La Sapienza Laurea Physioterapy, Rome, 2003—. Capt. Army, 1987—2000, Firenze, Palmanova, Bosnia. Decorated Bronze medal Nato Army Cav. Roman Catholic. Achievements include research in oncology. Avocations: travel, running, photography, reading. Home Phone: 39 06 772 09295. Business E-Mail: r.alexx@tiscali.it.

RUSY, DEBORAH ANN, anesthesiologist, educator; b. Phila., May 16, 1959; MD, U. Wis. Med. Sch., 1992. Prof. U. Wis. Med. Found., 1996—. Mem.: AMA, ASA. Avocations: bicycling, skiing. Office: UW Madison Dept Anesthesiology Madison WI 53792 Business E-Mail: darusy@wisc.edu.

RUTHERFORD, GEORGE WILLIAMS, III, public health association administrator, educator; b. San Diego, Apr. 6, 1952; s. George Williams II and Anna Gwyn (Dearing) Rutherford; m. Lisa Anderson, Aug. 24, 1974 (div. 1984); children: Alicia Gwyn, George Williams IV; m. Mary Workman, Feb. 23, 1985; children: Alexandra Catherine, Anne Elizabeth Martha, Hugh Thomas Gwyn, Amanda Frances Julia. AB in Classics, Stanford U., Calif., 1974, BS in Chemistry, 1975, AM in Hist., 1975; MD, Duke U., Durham, NC, 1978. Diplomate Am. Bd. Pediat., Am. Bd. Preventive Medicine, Nat. Bd. Med. Examiners. Intern pediat. U. Calif. Med. Ctr., San Diego, 1978-79; resident pediat. U. Calif. Med. Ctr./Hosp. for Children, San Diego, 1979-80; resident Hosp. Sick Children, Toronto, 1980-81; chief resident Children's Hosp. & Health Ctr., San Diego, 1981-82; EIS officer divsn. viral diseases, divsn. field svcs Epidemiology Office Ctrs. Disease Control, Atlanta, 1982-84; dir. divsn. immunization, acting dir. divsn. tropical disease NYC Dept. Health, 1983-85; med. epidemologist AIDS program Ctrs. Disease Control, San Francisco Dept. Pub. Health, 1985-87; from med. dir. to dir. AIDS office San Francisco Dept. Pub. Health, 1986-90; chief, infectious disease br., state epidemologist Calif. Dept Health, Berkeley, 1990-92; state epidemologist Calif. Dept. Health, Berkeley, 1990—95; dep. dir. prevention svcs. Calif. Dept Health, Berkeley, 1992-95, state health officer, 1993-95; assoc. dean adminstrn., prof. epidemiology/health adminstrn. U. Calif. Sch. Pub. Health, Berkeley, 1995-97; prof. epidemiology & preventive medicine U. Calif., San Francisco, 1997—, Salvatore Pablo Lucia prof. preventive medicine, head divsn. preventative medicine & pub. health, dir. Prevention & Pub. Health Group (formerly Inst. Global Health), 2004—. Transport physician Children's Hosp. & Health Ctr., San Diego, 1981; asst. clin. prof. pediat. Emory U., Atlanta, 1982—83, Cornell U., NYC, 1984—85, U. Calif., San Francisco, 1986—92, asst. clin. prof. epidemiology & biostats., 1987—92, assoc. adj. prof. epidemiology, biostats. & pediat., 1992—95, adj. prof., 1996—; assoc. clin. prof. cmty. health U. Calif., Davis, 1991—95; cons. Pan-Am. Health Orgn. S.Am., 1986—89, WHO, 1988—90, Ctrs. Disease Control, Atlanta. Editor: Calif. Morbidity, 1990—92; mem. editl. bd. Calif. AIDS Update, 1988—, Current Issues in Pub. Health, 1993—97; translator: cardiology teaching manual; contbr. numerous articles to profl. jours., chapters to books. Fellow: Am. Acad. Pediat.; mem.: APHA, Assn. State & Territorial Health Ofcls., Soc. Epidemiol. Rsch., Internat. AIDS Soc., No. Calif. Pub. Health Assn., Infectious Diseases Soc. of America, Calif. Med. Assn., Am. Soc. Tropical Medicine & Hygiene, Am. Assn. Hist. of Medicine, Bay Area Communicable Disease Exch. Republican. Episcopalian. Avocation: tennis. Office: UCSF Prevention & Pub Health Group Global Health Scis 50 Beale St Ste 1200 San Francisco CA 94105 Office Phone: 415-597-8200. Office Fax: 415-597-8299. Business E-Mail: grutherford@psg.ucsf.edu. *

RUTHERFORD, ROBERT BARRY, vascular surgeon; b. Edmonton, Alta., Can., July 29, 1931; s. Robert Lyon and Kathleen Emily (Gunn) R.; m. Beulah Kay Folk, Aug. 20, 1955; children: Robert Scott, Lori Jayne, Holly Anne, Trudy Kay, Jay Wilson. BA in Biology, Johns Hopkins U., 1952, MD, 1956. Emeritus prof. surgery U. Colo., Denver, 1996—. Editor: (texts) Management of Trauma, 1968, 4 edits., Vascular Surgery, 1978, 6th edition, 2005, An Atlas of Vascular Surgery, Vol. 1, 1993, Vol. 2, 1998, Decision Making in Vascular Surgery, 2001; editor quar. rev. Seminars in Vascular Surgery. Fellow ACS, Royal Coll. Surgeons Glasgow, Soc. for Vascular Surgery (disting. fellow); mem. Phi Beta Kappa, Alpha Omega Alpha. Republican. Unitarian Universalist. Avocations: skiing, biking, wind surfing, sailing. Home: 14337 Dorsal St Corpus Christi TX 78418 Home (Summer): 345 Small Shore Trl Oakland ME 04963-4317

RUTHERFORD, THOMAS, gynecologic oncologist, educator; PhD, Med. Coll. Ohio, 1986, MD, 1989. Diplomate Am. Bd. Ob-Gyn., 1997, Am. Bd. Ob-Gyn.-gynecologic oncology, 2000. Resident ob-gyn. Cooper Hosp., 1990—93, fellow ob-gyn.; assoc. prof. ob-gyn. Yale Univ. Sch. Medicine; assoc. prof. reproductive sciences Yale Med. Group, sect. chief gynecology oncology; fellow Yale-New Haven Hosp., Conn., 1993—95. Co-author: (publs.) Overexpression of epithelial cell adhesion molecule in primary, metastatic, and recurrent/chemotherapy-resistant epithelial ovarian cancer: implications for epithelial cell adhesion molecule-specific immunotherapy, 2009, Brain metastases in epithelial ovarian and primary peritoneal carcinoma, 2009. Surgical care patients St. Joseph Hosp., 2005—09; volunteer surgical svcs. Shaanxi Univ. Chinese Medicine Univ. Beijing, 2009. Office: Yale-New Haven Hospital 20 York St New Haven CT 06510 Office Phone: 203-688-4242.

RUTKOW, IRA MICHAEL, surgeon, writer; b. Newark, Oct. 13, 1948; s. Al and Bea (Goldberg) R.; m. Beth Denise Greenwald, June 11, 1972; children: Lainie Wendy, Eric Ian. BS, Union Coll., 1970; MD, St. Louis U., 1975; MPH, Johns Hopkins U., 1978, DPH, 1981. Diplomate Am. Bd. Surgery. Intern then resident Boston City Hosp., Boston U., 1975—77; resident Johns Hopkins Hosp., 1977-80, U. Hosp. N.J. Med. Sch., 1980-82. Clin. prof. surgery N.J. Med. Sch., Newark, 1983—, surg. dir. Hernia Ctr., Freehold, NJ, 1984-2004, editor, Archives Surgery, 1992-2002. Author: Surgery: An Illustrated History, 1993 (N.Y. Times Notable Book of Yr. 1994), The History of Surgery in the United States, vol. 1, 1988, vol. 2, 1992, American Surgery: An Illustrated History, 1998, Bleeding Blue and Gray, 2005, James A. Garfield, 2006; Seeking the Cure, 2010, Socioeconomics of Surgery, 1989. Trustee Boys and Girls Club Newark, N.J., 1987—94; commr. Govs. Commn. on Health Care Costs, 1991. Recipient Med. Book award, Am. Med. Writers Assn., 1998, Fletcher Pratt Lit. award, Civil War Round Table NY, 2005, Founders Day medal, Union Coll., 2007; scholars, Johns Hopkins U., 2003. Fellow Am. Coll. Surgeons. Jewish. Home: 146 W 57th St Apt 55B New York NY 10019-3301 Office Phone: 212-541-8199. Personal E-mail: irarutkow@gmail.com.

RUTLEDGE, CHARLES OZWIN, pharmacologist, educator; b. Topeka, Oct. 1, 1937; s. Charles Ozwin and Alta (Seaman) R.; m. Jane Ellen Crow, Aug. 13, 1961; children: David Ozwin, Susan Harriett, Elizabeth Jane, Karen Ann. BS in Pharmacy, U. Kans., 1959, MS in Pharmacology, 1961; PhD in Pharmacology, Harvard U., 1966. NATO postdoctoral fellow Gothenburg (Sweden) U., 1966-67; asst. prof. U. Colo. Med. Ctr., Denver, 1967-74, assoc. prof., 1974-75; prof., chmn. dept. pharmacology U. Kans., Lawrence, 1975-87; dean, prof. pharmacology Purdue U., West Lafayette, Ind., 1987—2002, exec. dir. Discovery Park, 2001—05, interim vice provost rsch., 2002—05, v.p. rsch., 2005—07. Contbr. articles on neuropharmacology to profl. jours. Grantee NIH, 1970-87. Mem. AAAS, Am. Soc. Pharmacology and Exptl. Therapeutics (councillor 1982 84, sec.-treas. 1990-93, pres. 1996-97), Am. Assn. Coll. Pharmacy (chmn. biol. scis. sect. 1983-84, chmn. coun. faculties 1986-87, chmn. coun. deans 1993-94, com. implement change pharm. edn. 1989-92, pres. 1996-97). Avocations: gardening, skiing, travel. Home: 40 Brynteg Est West Lafayette IN 47906-5643 Office: Purdue U Hovde Hall 610 Purdue Mall West Lafayette IN 47907-2040 Office Phone: 765-494-6209. Business E-Mail: chipr@purdue.edu.

RUTMAN, MATTHEW P., urologist, educator; b. Bklyn., Oct. 11, 1972; BA, Emory U., 1994; MD, FUHS, Chgo. Med. Sch., 1998. Asst. prof. urology Columbia U., 2005—. Attending asst. NY Presbyn. Hosp., 2005. Mem.: Internat. Continence Soc., Soc. Urodynamics & Female Urology, Am. Urol. Assn., Alpha Omega Alpha. Avocations: running, travel, sports. Home: 5 Charlotte Ct Briarcliff Manor NY 10510 Home Fax: 914-941-3828. Business E-Mail: mr2423@columbia.edu.

RUTSTEIN, DAVID C., United States public health service administrator; Student, Morehouse Coll. Sch. Medicine; MD, Brown Univ., 1983; MD (hon.), Morehouse Sch. Medicine. Internal med. physician Salem Hosp., Mass., 1983—84; family med. residency Natividad Medical Center, Salinas, Calif., 1984—87; family physician Nat. Health Svc. Corps, Pohnpei and Yap, Federated States of Micronesia, 1987—2000, chief clin. officer to chief med. officer Washington, 2000—03; dep. assoc. adminstr. for Health Professions Health Resources and Svcs. Adminstrn., Washington, 2003—05; dir. Off.of Internat. Health Affairs, sr. adv., HRSA Administr., Washington, 2005; chief. med. officer US Public Health Service, Washington, 2005—; and dep. dir., Off. Disease Prevention and Health Promotion Off. Sec. Health and Human Svcs., Washington, 2005—; also family physician East of the River Comty. Health Ctr., Washington; capt. US Pub. Health Svc.; acting dir. Office of Force Readiness and Deployment, US Pub. Health Svc., 2007—; chief profl. officer Physicians Profl. Adv. Com. Recipient Disting. Alumnus award, Morehouse Sch. Medicine, Medal of Valor for leadership in pub. health after 2005 Indonesian Island of Nias earthquake, AMA, 2006. Mem.: Pacific Basin Med. Assn., Res. Officers Assn., Commissioned Officers Assn.,

Am. Pub. Health Assn., Am. Acad. Family Physicians. Office: US Dept Health and Human Svcs Off Disease Prevention and Health 1101 Wootton Pkwy Ste LL 100 Rockville MD 20852 Office Fax: 240-453-8282. Business E-Mail: david.rutstein@hhs.gov.

RUTTER, MICHAEL LLEWELLYN, child psychology educator; b. Brummanna, Lebanon, Aug. 15, 1933; arrived in Eng., 1936; s. Llewellyn Charles and Winifred Olive (Barber) Rutter; m. Marjorie Heys, Dec. 27, 1958; children: Sheila Carol, Stephen Michael, Christine Anne. MB, BChir, U. Birmingham, Eng., 1955, MD with honors, 1963; diploma in psychol. medicine, U. London, 1961; degree (hon.), U. Leiden, 1985, Cath. U., 1990, U. Birmingham, 1990, U. Edinburgh, 1990, U. Chgo., 1993, U. Minn., 1993, U. Ghent, 1994; degree, U. Warwick, 1999, U. East Anglia, 2000, U. North London, 2000, U. York, 2005, U. Oxford, 2005; EdD (hon.), U. Dublin, 2007. Various tchg. positions in pediat., neurology, internal, 1955-58; registrar then sr. registrar Maudsley Hosp., London, 1958-62; mem. sci. staff MRC Social Psychiatry Rsch. Unit, London, 1962-65; sr. lectr. then reader U. London Inst. Psychiatry, 1966-73, prof. child psychiatry, 1973-98, hon. dir. MRC Child Psychiatry unit, 1984-98, with Social Genetic and Devel. Psychiatry Rsch. Ctr., 1994—98; prof. devel. psychopathology Inst. Psychiatry, 1998—. Nuffield med. traveling fellow Albert Einstein Coll. Medicine, N.Y.C., 1961-62; fellow Ctr. for Advanced Study in Behavioral Scis., Stanford, Calif., 1979-80; hon. prof. U. Amsterdam, 2001. Author: Helping Troubled Children, 1975, Maternal Deprivation Reassessed, 2nd edit., 1981, (with H. Giller) Juvenile Delinquency: Trends & Perspectives, 1983, (with M. Rutter) Developing Minds: Challenge and Continuity Accross the Lifespan, 1993, (with H. Giller, A. Hagell) Antisocial Behavior by Young People, 1998, (with T. Moffitt, A. Caspi and P. Silva) Sex Differences in Antisocial Behavior: Conduct Disorder, Delinquency and Violence in the Dunedin Longitudinal Study, 2001, (with M. Tienda) Ethnicity and Casual Mechanisms, 2005, Genes & Behavior: Nature-Nurture Interplay Explained, 2006; co-editor: Autism: A Reappraisal of Concepts and Treatment, 1978, Stress, Risk and Resilience In Children and Adolescents: Processes, Mechanisms and Interventions, 1994, Development Through Life: A Handbook For Clinicians, 1994, Psychosocial Disorders in Young People: Time Trends & Their Causes, 1995, Antisocial Behavior by Young People, 1998, Child and Adolescent Psychiatry, 4th edit., 2002, Ethnicity and Casual Mechanisms, 2005; editor: Scientific Foundations of Developmental Psychiatry, 1980, Developmental Neuropsychiatry, 1983. Recipient Goulstonian lectr. award, Royal Coll. Physicians, 1973, rsch. award, Am. Assn. Mental Deficiency, 1975, Salmon lectr. award, N.Y. Acad. Medicine, 1979, C. Anderson Aldrich award, Am. Acad. Pediat., 1981, Adolf Meyer ward lectr. award, APA, 1985, Disting. Sci. Contbn. award, 1995, Castilla del Pino prize for achievement in psychiatry, Spain, 1995, Lifetime Achievement award, IMFAR, 2002, G. Stanley Hall award, APA, 2003, Marmor award, 2003, Arnold Lucius Gesell prize, 2004, Bronfenbrenner award, 2005, Camille Cosby World of Children award, 2005; fellow, Royal Soc., 1987; Belding travelling scholar, 1963, Rock Carling fellow, 1979. Fellow Royal Soc. Medicine (London, hon.), Royal Coll. Pediat. and Child Health (hon. founding fellow 1996), Royal Coll. Psychiatrists (London, hon.), Kings Coll. London, Brit. Acad., mem. AAAS (fgn. hon.), Internat. Soc. Rsch. in Child and Adolescent Psychiatry (pres. 1997-99), U.S. Nat. Acad. Edn. (fgn. assoc.), Brit. Pediat. Assn. (hon.), Assn. Child Psychology and Psychiatry (chmn. 1973-74), Brit. Psychol. Soc. (hon. fellow), Am. Acad. Child Psychiatry (hon. membership), NAS (fgn. assoc. Inst. Medicine, Sarnat Internat. prize in mental health 2001), Soc. Rsch. in Adolescence (John P. Hill award for excellence in theory devel. and rsch. 1992), Soc. Rsch. Child Devel. (pres. 1999-2001), Inst. Child Health (London, hon. fellow 1996), Internat. Acad. Rsch. in Learning Disabilities, Academia Europaea (founding mem.), Acad. Med. Scis. (founder, clin. v.p.). Home: 190 Court Ln London SE21 7ED England Office: SGDP Rsch Centre P080 Inst Psychiatry 16 de Crespigny Park SE5 8AF London England Office Phone: 44 2078480882. Business E-Mail: m.rutter@iop.kcl.ac.uk.

RUUSALEPP, ARNO, cardiac surgeon, researcher; b. Tartu, Estonia, Aug. 12, 1973; MD, Tartu U., 1998; PhD, Karolinska Inst., Stockholm, 2006. Cert. cardiovasc. surgeon Estonian Ministry Social Affairs, 2004. Cardiac surgeon Tartu U. Hosp., 2004—. Mem.: Soc. Thoracic Surgeons, European Assn. Cardio-Thoracic Surgery. Office: Tartu Univ Hosp L. Puusepa 8 51014 Tartu Estonia Office Fax: 3727318299. Business E-Mail: arno.ruusalepp@kliinikum.ee.

RUVKUN, GARY B., molecular geneticist; b. Berkeley, Calif., Mar. 26, 1952; s. Sam and Dora R.; m. Natasha Staller. AB in Biophysics, U. Calif., Berkeley, 1973; PhD in Biophysics, Harvard U., 1982. Postdoctoral fellow MIT and Harvard U., Cambridge, Mass., 1982-85; jr. fellow Soc. Fellows Harvard U., Cambridge, 1982-85; asst. prof. to prof. genetics Harvard U., Cambridge, 1985—. Mem. scientific adv. bd. Damon Runyon Walter Winchell Cancer Fund, 2001—05, Mass. Gen. Hosp. Cancer Ctr., 2003—07, Friedrich Meischer Rsch. Inst., Basel, Switzerland, 2005—06; mem. Harvard Microbial Sci. Initiative Organizing Com., 2003—, Harvard Origins of Life Initiative Organizing Com., 2004—; assoc. mem. Broad Inst. MIT/Harvard, 2003—; mem. NIH Nat. Adv. Coun. on Aging, 2004—07; mem. vis. com. Inst. Zoology, U. Zurich, 2005; invited presenter in the field. Contbr. several articles to jours.; editor: Developmental Biology, 1995—, Development, 1999—2005; bd. reviewing editors Science Mag., 2005—07. Recipient Faculty Rsch. award Am. Cancer Soc., 1989-, NIH Merit award, 2002-; co-recipient Lewis S. Rosenstiel award, Brandeis U., 2005, Warren Triennial prize, Mass. Gen. Hosp., 2007, Benjamin Franklin medal in Life Sci., Franklin Inst., 2008, Gairdner Found. Internat. award, 2008, Albert Lasker award for Basic Med. Rsch., Lasker Found., 2008, Louisa Gross Horwitz prize, 2009. Mem.: Am. Acad. Arts & Sciences, Soc. Fellows, Harvard U. Achievements include findings regarding molecular basis of temporal pattern formation, molecular basis of cell lineage asymmetry, scores of homeobox genes in C. elegans; patents in the field; patents pending in the field. Office: Ctr for Computational and Integrative Biology Mass Gen Hosp Richard B Simches Rsch Ctr 185 Cambridge St 7th Fl Boston MA 02114 also: Mass Gen Hosp Wellman 8 50 Blossom St Boston MA 02114 Office Phone: 617-726-5959. Office Fax: 617-726-6893. Business E-Mail: ruvkun@molbio.mgh.harvard.edu. *

RUZAL-SHAPIRO, CARRIE B., pediatric radiologist, educator; b. 1957; m. Peter Shapiro; children: Daniel, Billy. BS in Biochemistry, Princeton U., NJ; MD, Columbia U. Coll. Physicians & Surgeons, NY. Diplomate Am. Bd. Radiology; CAQ-Pediat. Radiology. Intern Babies & Children's Hosp.-Columbia Presbyn. Med. Ctr.; resident radiology Columbia Presbyn. Med. Ctr., 1984—88, clin. fellowship pediat. radiology, 1988—89; prof. clin. radiology, chief divsn. pediat. radiology Columbia U. Coll. Physicians & Surgeons, 1990—; attending dept. radiology NY Presbyn. Hosp.-Columbia U. Med. Ctr., 1990—. Dir., Office of Faculty Divsn., dept. radiology Columbia U. Coll. Physicians & Surgeons. Contbr. articles to profl. jours. Recipient Am. Coll. Med. Physics award, 2006. Office: NY Presbyn Hosp Dept Radiology 622 W 168th St New York NY 10032 Office Phone: 212-305-9335. Office Fax: 212-305-5777.

RUZIC, LANA, exercise physiologist; b. Zagreb, Croatia, May 13, 1970; MD, PhD, Med. Sch., Zagreb, 1993; MS, U. Zagreb, Zagreb, 2000. Cert. MD Ministry of Health, 1995. Gen. practitioner Ministry of Internal affairs, Zagreb, 1994—95; physician Reebok Health Clubs, Zagreb, 1995—98; lectr., rschr. kinesiology U. Zagreb, Dept. Sports and Exercise Medicine, 1998—. Past sec. Croatian Olympic Com. Med. Commn. Contbr. articles to profl. jours. Mem.: Croatian Med. Chamber, Am. Coll. Sports Medicine, Croatian Skiing Tchrs. Assn., Croatian Sports Medicine Assn., European Coll. Sports Sci. Roman Catholic. Avocations: skiing, travel, exercise. Office: Univ Zagreb Faculty Kinesiology Horvacanski Zavoj 15 10-000 Zagreb Croatia Office Fax: 00385 1 36 34 146. E-mail: lana.ruzic@kif.hr.

RUZYLLO, EDWARD EMIL, medical educator; b. Kosciaszyn, Oct. 13, 1909; s. Michael and Julie (Wyspianska) R.; m. Alina Zawadzka, Sept. 26, 1936; children: Witold, Jerzy. MD, Warsaw U., 1935; PhD, Warsaw Med. Acad., 1949, DSc, 1954; MD (hon.), Albert Schweitzer Acad. Med., 2000, Poznan Acad. Medicine, 2003. Intern in medicine Warsaw Ujazdowski Hosp., 1935-37; instr., reader in medicine 1st dept. medicine Med. Acad. Warsaw, 1947-54, head dept. gastroenterology and metabolism, 1958-70, assoc. prof. medicine, 1970-80; prof. medicine 2d dept. medicine Postgrad. Med. Sch., Warsaw, 1958-69. Chmn. sci. council Min. Health and Social Welfare, 1974-79, dir., dean Postgrad. Med. Ctr., 1961-74. Author 5 books in field; editor-in-chief Materia Medica Polona, 1968-70; contbr. articles to profl. jours. Served with Polish Army, 1937-46. Recipient 1st degree award, Min. of Health, 1965, 1973, award, Albert Jurzykowski Found., 1980. Mem.: Polish Med. Alliance (Chgo.), Internat. Soc. for Progress in Internal Medicine, Polish Soc. Endocrinology, Polish Soc. Rheumatology, Polish Soc. Medicine, Polish Soc. Internal Medicine (pres. 1970—76, hon. pres. 2001—), Roman Acad. Med. Scis. (hon.), Bulgarian Soc. Gastroenterology (hon.), Czechoslovak Soc. Internat. Medicine (hon.), Argentinean Soc. Medicine (hon.), German Soc. Internal Medicine (hon.), Swedish Soc. Medicine (hon.), Internat. Soc. Internal Medicine (hon.). Home: UL Rudawska 3 m8 PL 02 069 Warsaw Poland Office: 1 Goszcynskiego PL-02-616 Warsaw Poland

RYABCHUN, VADIM VALERYEVICH, research scientist; b. Krasnodar, Krasnodarskiy Kray, Russia, Dec. 20, 1977; s. Valery Yuryevich and Taisia Grigoryevna Ryabchun. Jr. rsch. scientist Russian Ctr. Functional Surg. Gastroenterology, Krasnodar, 1999—; head lab. functional diagnostics multiprofile med. diagnostic assn.Specialized Course Out-patient Treatment Polyclinic, Krasnodar, 2008—. Achievements include patents for functional diagnostics; pH-metry, manometry; invention of functional diagnostics. Office: Refsg 1st May street 167 Krasnodar Krasnodarskiy Kray 350086 Russia Personal E-mail: vvryabchun@hotmail.com. Business E-Mail: v.v.ryabchun@mail.ru.

RYAN, ARTHUR FREDERICK, retired diversified financial services company executive; b. Bklyn., Sept. 14, 1942; s. Arthur Vincent and Gertrude (Wingert) R.; m. Patricia Elizabeth Kelly; children: Arthur, Kelly Ann, Kevin, Kathleen. BA in Math., Providence Coll., 1963, D (hon.) of bus. adminstrn., 1994; student, Am. Coll., 1963—65; LHD (hon.), Dowling Coll.; DSc, NJ Inst. Tech., 2005. Area mgr. Control Data Corp., Washington, 1965-72; project mgr. data processing divsn. Chase Manhattan Corp., NYC, 1972-73, 2d v.p., 1973-74, v.p., 1974—77, sr. v.p., 1977—82, ops. exec., 1978-82, exec. v.p. corp. ops. and systems, 1982—84, exec. v.p. individual banking, 1984, head worldwide retail bank, 1984—90, vice chmn., 1985—90, pres., COO, 1990—94; chmn., pres., CEO Prudential Ins. Co. Am., Newark, 1994—99; (Prudential Ins. Co. Am. incorporated to become Prudential Fin., Inc., 1999); chmn., pres., CEO Prudential Fin., Inc., Newark, 2000—07, chmn., 2007—08. Bd. dirs. Prudential Fin., Inc., 1999—, Regeneron Pharmaceuticals, 2003—. Bd. trustees Providence Coll., 1992—, NY Presbyn. Hosp.; nat. bd. Local Initiatives Support Coalition; bd. dirs. New Am. Schools; co-chair Achieve, Inc., NJ United for Higher Sch. Standards, NJ Performing Arts Ctr. Lt. US Army, 1963—65. Recipient Nat. Alumni Personal Achievement Award, Providence Coll., 75th Anniversary Alumni Services Award, Diamond Anniversary Award, Keeper of the Dream award, Nat. Action Network, 2000, Patterson award, United Negro Coll. Fund/The Coll. Fund, 2000, Pub. Svc. award, NJ State CofC, 2001, Medal of Life award, PIUS XII Found., 2001, Cir. of Life Award, Million Dollar Round Table Found., 2002; co-recipient (with wife) Pelican award for Corp. and Cmty. Leadership, St. Vincent's Acad., 2001, (with wife) Inaugural Cmty. Leadership award, NJ Performing Arts Ctr. Women's Bd. Assn., 2002. Mem.: Am. Bankers Assn.

RYAN, GAIL FRANCES, radiation oncologist; d. Francis Ronald Ryan and Lorraine Frances McMahon; m. Ronald Allan Senior, July 10, 1981; children: Jaqueline Susan Speight, Katherine Francesca Senior, Stephanie Anne Senior, Natalie Lucy Senior. MBBS with honors, U. Queensland, Brisbane, 1976; MMedSci, Newcastle U., Australia, 1997. Intern Royal Melbourne Hosp., Victoria, Australia, 1977, jr. resident med. officer, 1978; sr. resident med. officer Royal Prince Alfred Hosp., Sydney, 1979; radiation oncology registrar Peter MacCallum Cancer Ctr., Melbourne, 1980—83, cons. radiation oncologist, 1984—; assoc. dir. Tattersall's Cancer Ctr. Epworth Hosp., Melbourne, 2007—. Mem., neurooncology study com. Victorian Coop. Oncology Group, Melbourne, 1994—; vis. radiation oncologist Royal Melbourne Hosp., 1999—, St. Vincent's Hosp., 2001—08; sr. lectr. dept. pathology U. Melbourne, 2000—; mem. glioma guidelines working com. Australian Cancer Network, Sydney, 2006—; mem., Hubert-Sterzl Award selection panel Med. Oncology Group Australia, Sydney, 2006—; mem. sci. adv. com. Coop. Trials Group for Neuro-Oncology, Sydney, 2008—. Contbr. scientific papers. Rsch. grants, Schering Plough Australia Pty Ltd., 2002, Clin. Oncological Soc. Australia, 2006, Nat. Health and Med. Rsch. Coun. Australia, 2007. Mem.: Royal Australian and New Zealand Coll. Radiologists (pathology examiner 1996—2002, clin. examiner 2002—), Australasian Leukaemia and Lymphoma Group, Internat. Extra Nodal lymphoma Study Group, European Assn. Neuro-oncology, European Soc. Therapeutic Radiology and Oncology. Avocations: travel, dance, singing. Office: Peter MacCallum Cancer Ctr Saint Andrews Pl Melbourne Victoria 3002 Australia

RYAN, JACK, physician, retired hospital corporation executive; b. Benton Harbor, Mich., Aug. 26, 1925; s. Leonard Joseph and Beulah (Southworth) R.; m. Lois Patricia Patterson; children: Michele, Kevin, Timothy, Daniel. AB, Western Mich. U., 1948; postgrad., U. Mich. Law Sch., 1949-50, Emory U., 1950-51; MD, Wayne State U., 1955. Intern St. Luke's Hosp., Saginaw, Mich., 1955-56; pres. Meml. Med. Ctr., Warren, Mich., 1956-77; v.p. med. affairs Detroit-Macomb Hosps. Corp., 1976-77, pres. and chief exec. officer, 1977-96; ret., 1996. Assoc. prof. medicine Wayne State U., Detroit, 1974—; bd. chmn. Mich. Hosp. Ins. Co., 1990—. Recipient Disting. Alumnus award Wayne State U. Med. Sch., 1974, Wayne State U., 1979, Western Mich. U., 1989, Disting. Key award Mich. Hosp. Assn., 1986, Tree of Life award Jewish Nat. Fund, 1996. Fellow Am. Coll. Family Physicians, Am. Coll. Physician Execs., Detroit Acad. Medicine; mem. Internat. Health Econs. and Mgmt. Inst. (charter), Econ. Club Detroit, Detroit Athletic Club, Renaissance Club, Red Run Club. Avocations: civil war, history, golf, tennis. Home: 175 Hendrie Blvd Royal Oak MI 48067-2412

RYAN, JAMES WALTER, physician, researcher; s. Lee W. and Emma E. (Haddox) R.; children: James P.A., Alexandra L.E., Amy J.S. AB in Polit. Sci., Dartmouth Coll., 1957; MD, Cornell U., 1961; D.Phil., Oxford U., Eng., 1967. Diplomate Nat. Bd. Med. Examiners. Intern, Montreal (Que.) Gen. Hosp., McGill U., Can., 1961-62, asst. resident in medicine, 1962-63; USPHS research asso. NIMH, NIH, 1963-65; guest investigator Rockefeller U., NYC, 1967-68, asst. prof. biochemistry, 1968; investigator Howard Hughes Med. Inst., 1968—71; assoc. prof. medicine U. Miami (Fla.) Sch. Medicine, 1968-79, prof. medicine, 1979-95, mem. vasc. biology ctr., 1995-00; prof. anesthesiology, pharmacology and toxicology Med. Coll. Ga., Augusta, 1995-00; sr. cons. ntGen, 2000—; chief scientist Ryogen, LLC, 2005—. Sr. scientist Papanicolaou Cancer Rsch. Inst., Miami, 1972-77; hon. med. officer to Regius prof. medicine Oxford U., 1965-67; vis. prof. Clin. Rsch. Inst. Montreal, 1974; mem. vis. faculty thoracic disease divsn., dept. internal medicine Mayo Clinic, 1974; vis. prof. Montreal Gen. Hosp./McGill U., 1985. Contbr. numerous articles on biochem. rsch. and pathology to sci. jours.; patentee in field. Rockefeller Found. travel awardee, 1962; William Waldorf Astor traveling fellow, 1966; USPHS spl. fellow, 1967-68; Pfizer travelling fellow, 1972; recipient USPHS Rsch. Career Devel. award NIH, 1968, Louis and Artur Luciano award for research of circulatory diseases McGill U., 1984-85. Fellow Am. Heart Assn. (mem. coun. cardiopulmonary diseases 1972—, coun. for high blood pressure rsch. 1976—); mem. AAAS, Am. Physiol. Soc., Am. Chem. Soc., Biochem. Soc., Am. Soc. Biochemist and Molecular Biology, Oxford and Cambridge Club (London), Sigma Xi. Baptist. Home: 3047 Lake Forest Dr Augusta GA 30909-3027 Office: ntGen Ryogen LLC 3047 Lake Forest Dr Augusta GA 30909

RYAN, JOHN JOSEPH, physician; b. Columbus, Ga., Sept. 5, 1957; s. Joseph Vincent and Annie Elizabeth R.; m. Sonia Francisca Ryan, Nov. 17, 1984; children: Annie, Joseph, Catherine. BS in Med. Tech., Columbus U., Ga., 1978; MD, Nuevo Leon U., Mex., 1990. Diplomate Am. Bd. Family Practice. Intern Anderson Family Practice, Anderson, SC, 1991—92, resident, 1991—94; physician Lowry's Family Medicine, Chester, SC, 1994—98; pvt. practice Chester, 1998—2003; physician Thomas Moore Health Clinic, Fort Hood, Tex., 2005—06, McAllen Primary Care Clinic, 2005—06, Mediplex Health Clinic, 2006—. Bass Brownsville Diocese Choir, Holy Spirit Parish Choir. Fellow: Am. Acad. Family Practice; mem.: AMA, Tex. Acad. Family Practice, Rotary, KC (Grand Knight). Roman Catholic. Avocations: fishing, golf, gardening.

RYAN, JUDITH W., geriatrics nurse, educator; b. Waterbury, Conn., Dec. 8, 1943; d. James Patrick Ryan and Edna (Swanson) Billings. BS, U. Conn., 1965; MS, Boston U., 1967; PhD, U. Md., 1984. RN, Md., Conn.; cert. adult nurse practitioner ANCC. Instr. U. Conn., Storrs, 1967-69; asst. prof. Ind. U., Purdue U., Indpls., 1969-73, U. Md., Balt., 1973-82, dir. primary care adult nurse pracitioner cert. program, dept. medicine, supportive care project, 1985-87, asst. prof. sch. nursing, 1987-95, asst. prof., 1976-82; clin. dir. EverCare, Balt., 1995-99; pres. Nurse Practitioners and Cons., P.C., 2000—10; ptnr. Prime Health Group, LLC, 2007—. Arbitrator Health Claims Arbitration Program, Md., 1976—; bd. mem. Md. Bd. Nursing, Balt., 1991-98, pres., 1993-96; trustee Md. Nurses Assn. Polit. Action Com., Balt., treas., 1989-91. Contbr. articles to profl. jours. Named Distinguished Practitioner Nursing, Nat. Acad. Practice, 1984-99. Mem. Am. Coll. Nurse Practitioners, Md. Nurses Assn. (2d v.p. 1986-88), Nurse Practitioner Assn. Md., Sigma Theta Tau, Phi Kappa Phi. Home: 1514 Woodside Ave Baltimore MD 21227 Office: 10989 Red Run Blvd Ste 208 Owings Mills MD 21117-3248 Office Phone: 410-654-8602 Ext. 103. Personal E-mail: jwryan128@comcast.net.

RYAN, KEVIN WILLIAM, virologist, clinical research administrator; s. Joseph Michael Ryan and Etoile Evelyn Werth; m. Mary Ellen Lyman, June 1, 1974; children: Matthew Lyman, Mark Joseph. BS, U. Iowa, 1978; PhD, U. Mich., 1984. Staff fellow Nat. Inst. Allergy and Infectious Diseases, NIH, Bethesda, Md., 1984-86; rsch. asst. dept. virology and molecular biology St. Jude Children's Rsch. Hosp., Memphis, 1986-89, asst. mem., 1989-98; asst. prof. pathology U. Tenn. Coll. Medicine, Memphis, 1994-98; sci. rev. adminstr. Nat. Inst. Allergy and Infectious Diseases, NIH, Rockville, Md., 1998-2000; program officer virology vaccine and prevention rsch. prog. divsn. AIDS, Nat. Inst. Allergy and Infectious Diseases, NIH, Bethesda, Md., 2000—05; deputy chief Prevention Scis. Br., 2001—02, chief, 2002—05, lead program officer grant-supported internat. clin. rsch. in

HIV/AIDS prevention, 2001—05; mem. working group NIAID, Comprehensive Internat. Program for Rsch. in AIDS (CIPRA), 2001—05; dep. dir. pediatrics, adolescent and maternal AIDS, Ctr. for Rsch. for Mothers and Children, Nat. Inst. Child Health and Human Devel., NIH, Rockville, Md., 2005—10; dep. dir. Vassiac Rsch. Program Divsn. AIDS NIAID, 2010—. Prin. investigator Nat. Inst. Allergy and Infectious Diseases, 1992—98; lead program officer HIV prevention trials network HPTN, 2002—05; govt. project officer HIV Network Prevention Trials (HIVNET) Internat. Master Contract for AIDS Rsch. NIAID, 2002—04; NIAID program officer Clin. Trials of Male Circumcision for HIV Prevention, 2002—04, Topical Microbicides Clin. Trials, 2002—05; NIAID Rep. HPTN Prevention Leadership Group, 2002—05; dep. chief Pediat., Adolescent and Maternal AIDS br. Ctr. for Rsch. Mothers and Children, Nat. Inst. of Child Health and Human Devel., NIH, 2005—10; lead NICHD program officer Adolescent Medicine Trials Network, 2005—10, Women and Infants HIV Transmission Study, 2005—10; program officer Pediatric HIV-AIDS Cohort Study, 2005—10; NICHD program officer Microbicide Trials Network, 2006—10, Clin. Trials Optimize Pediat. HN Therapy, Naiadi, Kenya, 2006—10, Clin. Trails HIV & Malaria, Tororo, Uganda, 2008—10; NICHD rep. on Internat. Working Group on Microbicides, 2007—10. Contbr. articles to profl. jours., chpts. to tech. manuals. Recipient Dir. award, NIH, 2002, Merit award, 2000, 2007; fellow postdoctoral Mich. Cancer Rsch. Inst., U. Mich., 1982. Mem.: Am. Soc. for Microbiology. Roman Catholic. Avocations: woodworking, golf. Office: Vaccine Rsch Program Divsn AIDS Nat Inst Allergy & Infections Disesse NIH 6700 B rocklodge Dr Bethesda MD 20892 Business E-Mail: kr90p@nih.gov.

RYAN, LISA KATHLEEN, environmental and medical science educator; b. Morgantown, W.Va., July 9, 1958; d. Richard Stoetzer and Ellen Stewart Wagner; m. Gill Diamond, Aug. 31, 1997; m. Niall Patrick Ryan, Oct. 3, 1981 (dec. Oct. 1, 1993); children: Allison Kathleen, Michael Richard Diamond, Sara Elana Diamond. BS in microbiology, Penn State U. Coll. of Sci., University Pk., 1980; MS in med. microbiology, W.Va. U. Med. Sch., Morgantown, 1983; PhD in toxicology, U. Pitts. Grad. Sch. Pub. Health, 1992. Rsch. biologist, immunotoxicology br. US EPA, Rsch. Triangle Pk., NC, 1995—2000; asst. prof., dept. of pathology UMDNJ-NJ Med. Sch., Newark, 2000—03; asst. prof. dept. oral biology UMDNJ-NJ Dental Sch., Newark, 2003—08; asst. prof. pulmonary divsn. Dept. Medicine, UMDNJ Med. Sch., 2008—; mem. Pub. Health Rsch. Inst. NJ Med. Sch. Devel. Enzyme-Linked ImmunoSorbent Assay endotoxin detection Hyclone Diagnostics/Travenol Labs., 1981—82; rsch. fellow in medicine Mass. Gen. Hosp./Harvard Med. Sch., Boston, 1992—95; ORD regional sci. advisor EPA region 2 US EPA Office Sci. Policy, Washington, 1998—2000. Contbr. articles to profl. jours. Recipient Individual Nat. Rsch. Svc. award, NIH Nat. Heart, Lung and Blood Inst., 1994—97; grantee grant, NIH Nat. Inst. Allergies and Infectious Diseases, 2000—03;, Allegheny-Erie Regional chpt. Soc. Toxicology, 1991, NIH Nat. Inst. Allergies and Infectious Diseases, 2007—, NIH Nat. Heart, Lung and Blood Inst., 2003—07, NIH Inst. Environ. Health Scis., 2009—, NIH Nat. Inst. Dental and Craniofacial Rsch., 2010—, UMDNJ Foundation, Antibody Sys., Inc. Mem.: AAAS, Sigma Xi, Am. Conf. of Govtl. Indsl. Hygenists, Am. Thoracic Soc., Am. Soc. for Microbiology, Soc. for Leukocyte Biology, Am. Assn. Immunologists, Soc. Toxicology. Achievements include patents for polymyxin agarose-lipopolysaccharide antigen and associated method. Avocations: swimming, ice skating, piano, clarinet, skiing. Office: Pub Health Rsch Inst UMDNJ NJ Med Sch Medicine Internat Ctr Pub Health 225 Warren St Newark NJ 07103 Office Phone: 973-854-3323. Office Fax: 973-854-3101. Personal E-mail: lkryan@aol.com. Business E-Mail: ryanlk@umdnj.edu.

RYAN, LOUISE, statistician, educator; b. Australia; BA in stats. and math., Macquarie U., Sydney, Australia, 1978; PhD in stats., Harvard U., 1983. From asst. prof. to Henry Pickering Walcott prof. biostatistics Harvard Sch. Pub. Health, Boston, 1985—2009, chair dept. biostatistics, 2006—09, adj. prof. biostatistics, 2009—; chief of math. and info. sciences Commonwealth Sci. and Rsch. Orgn., Australia, 2009—. Recipient Spiegelman award, Am. Pub. Health Assn., Mentors award, Harvard Sch. Pub. Health, Role Models award, Minority, Inc. Fellow: Internat. Stats. Inst., Am. Statis. Assn. (Disting. Achievement award, Environmetrics Sect., Elizabeth Scott award); mem.: Inst. Medicine. Office: CSIRO Math and Info Sciences Locked Bag 17 Bldg E6B Macquarie U Campus North Ryde NSW 1670 Australia Office Phone: 61 2 9325 3100. E-mail: louise.ryan@csiro.au.

RYAN, MELBAGENE T., retired food service and nutrition director; b. Arkadelphia, Ark., Jan. 6, 1927; d. Horace Samuel and Eunice Bridges (Moorman) Tull; m. Wayne Stuart Ryan, Dec. 26, 1954. BS in Edn., Henderson U., 1948; M in Edn., Tex. Women's U., 1951. Tchr. Eudora Pub. Schs., Ark., 1948-52; dir. food services Tex. Christian U., Ft. Worth, 1952-53, Tex. Women's U., 1953-58; dir. food and nutriton service Irving Ind. Sch. Dist., Tex., 1958-85. Project dir. to develop stds. excellence with a self study and evaluation Tex. Sch. Food Svc. Assn., 1985-88; cons. in field. Co-author and project dir.: (with others) Youth Advisory Council Resource Manual, 1978-79, Effective Food Service Management Using Computers, 1982. With child nutrition Tex. Sch. Food Svc. Assn., Washington, 1974-79; with legis. Am. Sch. Food Svc. Assn., Irving, 1980-85; mem. Denton Co. Hist. Commn., 1997—, Denton Co. Courthouse-on-the Square Mus., chmn. 1998—; mem. adv. bd. Lake Forest Good Samaritan Village, 1998—, Tex. Woman's U. Centennial Celebration, 2001, planning com., 1998-99, Denton Good Samaritan Village, 2003; chmn. Bayless Selby House Mus., 2002—. Recipient Food Facilities Design award Instns. Volume Feeding Awards Program, New Orleans, 1977, Trend Setter award, North Tex. Brokers Assn., Dallas, 1978; Melbagene Ryan Scholarship named in her honor by Dallas Profl. Friends, 1985. Mem. Denton Dietetic Assn. (pres. 1977-78), Tex. Dietetic Assn., Am. Dietetic Assn. (chmn. joint com. 1979-82), Tex. Sch. Food Svc. Assn. (pres. 1975-76, nutrition edn. 1975), Am. Sch. Food Svc. Assn. (conf. com. 1977-78, 1982-83), Tex. Women's U. Alumni Assn. Methodist.

RYAN, PATRICK GEORGE, diversified financial services company executive; b. Milw., May 15, 1937; m. Shirley Welsh, Apr. 16, 1966; children: Patrick Jr., Robert J., Corbett M. BS, Northwestern U., 1959. Sales agt. Penn Mut., 1959-64, Pat Ryan & Assocs. Chgo., 1964-71; chmn., pres. Ryan Ins. Group Inc., Chgo., 1971-82; pres., CEO Combined Internat. Corp, 1982—87, Aon Corp. (formerly Combined Internat. Corp.), Chgo., 1987—2005, exec. chmn., 1990—2008; founder, exec. chmn., CEO Ryan Specialty Group, LLC, Chgo., 2010—. Bd. dirs. Aon Corp. (formerly Combined Internat. Corp.), 1982-2008 Life trustee, past chmn., Rush U. Med. Ctr., Chgo.; chmn. bd., trustees Northwestern U.; chmn., CEO, Chgo. 2016, 2006-; past trustee Field Mus. Natural History, Chgo. Recipient Lifetime Achievement award, The Review-Worldwide Reinsurance, 2005, Internat. Exec. of the Yr., Brigham Young U., 2002, Golden Plate award, Acad. of Achievement, 2002; named to Chgo. Bus. Hall of Fame; named one of Forbes 400: Richest Americans, 2009. Fellow Am. Acad. Arts & Scis.; mem., past pres., Econ. Club Chgo. Office: Ryan Specialty Group 200 E Randolph 20th Fl Chicago IL 60601 Office Phone: 312-784-6001. Office Fax: 312-784-6002. *

RYAN, STEPHEN JOSEPH, JR., ophthalmologist, educator, health science association administrator; b. Honolulu, Hawaii, Mar. 20, 1940; s. S.J. and Mildred Elizabeth (Farrer) Ryan; m. Anne Christine Mullady, Sept. 25, 1965; 1 child, Patricia Anne. AB, Providence Coll., 1961; MD, Johns Hopkins U., 1965. Intern Bellevue Hosp., NYC, 1965—66; resident Wilmer Inst. Ophthalmology, Johns Hopkins Hosp., Balt., 1966—69, chief resident, 1969—70; fellow Armed Forces Inst. Pathology, Washington, 1970—71; instr. ophthalmology Johns Hopkins U., Balt., 1970—71, asst. prof., 1971—72, assoc. prof., 1972—74; Grace and Emery Beardsley prof. ophthalmology Keck Sch. Medicine, U. So. Calif., LA, 1974—, chmn. dept. ophthalmology, 1974—95, dean, 1991—2004, sr. v.p. for med. care, 1993—2004, Grace and Emery Beardsley Chair in Ophthalmology, med. dir. Doheny Eye Inst. (formerly Estelle Doheny Eye Found.), 1977—86, pres. Doheny Eye Inst., 1987—, chief of staff Doheny Eye Hosp., 1985—88; acting head ophthalmology divsn. dept. surgery Children's Hosp., 1975—77. Mem. adv. panel Calif. Med. Assn., 1975—. Editor (with M.D. Andrews): A Survey of Ophthalmology--Manual for Medical Students, 1970; editor: (with R.E. Smith) Selected Topics on the Eye in Systemic Disease, 1974; editor: (with Dawson and Little) Retinal Diseases, 1985; editor: (with others) Retina, 1989; editor:, 2000, 4t edit., 2005; assoc. editor: Ophthalmol. Surgery, 1974—85, mem. editl. bd.: Am. Jour. Ophthalmology, 1981—, Internat. Ophthalmology, 1982—, Retina, 1983—, Graefes Archives, 1984—; contbr. articles to med. jours. Recipient cert. of merit, AMA, 1971, Louis B. Mayer Scholar award, Rsch. to Prevent Blindness, 1973, Rear Adm. William Campbell Chambliss USN award, 1982, Mildred Weisenfeld Award for Lifetime Achievement in Vision Rsch., Fight for Sight, 2000. Mem.: AMA, Inst. Medicine NAS (home sec. 2006—), Jules Gonin Club, Rsch. Study Club, Nat. Eye Care Project, Retina Soc., Macula Soc., Pan-Am. Assn. Microsurgery, L.A. Acad. Medicine, Pacific Coast Oto-Ophthal. Soc., Los Angeles County Med. Assn., Calif. Med. Assn., L.A. Soc. Ophthalmology, Assn. Univ. Profs. of Ophthalmology, Pan-Am. Assn. Ophthalmology, Am. Ophthal. Soc., Am. Acad. Ophthalmology and Otolaryngology (award of Merit 1975), Wilmer Ophthal. Inst. Residents Assn., Soc. Scholars of Johns Hopkins U. (life). Office: 1450 San Pablo St Los Angeles CA 90033 also: Institute of Medicine 500 Fifth St NW NAS 316 Washington DC 20001 Office Phone: 323-442-6444. Business E-Mail: sryan@usc.org.

RYAN, TERENCE JOHN, dermatologist, educator; b. Hove, Sussex, Eng., July 24, 1932; s. Gerald John and Kathleen May (Knight) R.; m. Anne Trudie Merry; children: Josephine, James. MB BCh, Oxford U., Eng., 1957, MA, 1957, DM, 1977; PhD (hon.), Martin Luther U. Halle, 2007. House physician Sir George Pickering Gen. Medicine, Oxford, 1957-58; house surgeon Ear, Nose and Throat Surgery, Oxford, 1958-59; registrar in geriatrics Stoke Mandeville, Oxford, 1960-61, registrar in dermatology, 1962-65, sr. registrar, 1965-67; lectr., sr. lectr. Inst. Dermatology, London, 1968-71; physician Royal Postgrad. Med. Sch., London, 1968-71; chmn. faculty of medicine Oxford U., 1977-82, vice warden Green Coll.; hon. prof. dermatol. Nanjing, 2003—; adj. prof. Jefferson Med. Coll., Phila., 1988, U. Limerick, 2007, Mo. U., 2010; emeritus prof. Oxford U., 2008—, Oxford Brookes U., 2008—. Cons. dermatologist Churchill Hosp., oxford, 1971—; clin. prof. dermatology, oxford U., 1992—. Contbr. more than 600 articles to profl. jours. With Fuel Initiative Resources, Strategies and Tech., Brit. Skin Found.; bd. dirs. Oxford Internat. Biomed. Ctr.; dir. Global Initiatives for Traditional Systems (Gifts) of Health. Paul Harris fellow Internat. Rotary; recipient Knight of the Order of St. John, Nishimaru award Japanese Microcirculation Soc., 1991, John Boswick Meml. award, 2004, Ratschow medal Curatorium Angiologia Internat. Fellow Royal Coll. Physicians, World Conf. Microcirculation (pres. 1984), European Tissue Repair Soc. (pres. 1993, gold medal 1995), Brit. Assn. Dermatology (pres.); mem. Internat. Com. Dermatology, Internat. Soc. Dermatology (pres. 1994-99, hon. pres., chmn. task force), Internat. Found. Dermatology (sec.-treas. 1987-96, chmn. 1999—), Brasilian Acad. of Medicine (gold medal,2002), Internat. Soc. Dermatology Task Force Skincare for All Cmty. Dermatology (chmn.) Avocations: piano, painting. Office: Brook House Brook St Great Bedwyn Marlborough Wilts SN3 3LZ England Home Phone: 016722870375. Personal E-mail: userry282@aol.com.

RYBAKOWSKI, JANUSZ KAZIMIERZ, psychiatrist, educator, researcher; b. Krotoszyn, Poland, Jan. 8, 1946; s. Kazimierz Sylwester and Ludmila Maria (Ludwiczak) R.; m. Teresa Maria Tuszewska, July 29, 1972; 1 child, Filip. Grad., Med. Acad., Poznan, Poland, 1969, MD, 1973, postdoctoral degree, 1980. Diplomate Edn. Coun. Fgn. Med. Grads. Rsch. asst. Med. Acad., Poznan, 1970-76, assoc. prof., 1978-84; NIH Fogarty rsch. fellow psychiatry U. Pa., Phila., 1976-77; chmn. Med. Acad., Bydgoszcz, Poland, 1985-95, prof. psychiatry, 1990—; head dept. adult psychiatry U. Med. Scis., Poznan, 1994—. Vis. scientist U. Aarhus, U. Copenhagen, 1984-85, U. Pa., Phila., 1986, 88, 91. Author: Psychotropic Drugs in The Prophylaxis of Affective Illness and Schizophrenia, 1994, Faces of Manic-Depression, 2008, translator: Biological Bases of Psychiatric Disorders, 1982, Lithium Treatment of Manic-Depressive Illness, 1994; mem. editl. bd. jour. Lithium, 1990-94, Neuropsychobiology, 1996—, Bipolar Disorders, 2000—, Pharmacopsychiatry, 2000—, Acta Neuropsychiatrica, 2001-06, Internat. Jour. Psychiatry in Clin. Practice, 2005—, Cardiovasc. Psychiatry and Neurology, 2008-, field editor, World Jours. Biol. Psychiatry, 2009-, World Jour. Priblogial Psychiatry, 2009-, Cardiovascular Psychiatry & Neurology, 2008-; contbr. over 400 articles to profl. jours. Recipient award Polish Ministry of Health, 1992, 2002, award Newsweek Poland for Best Psychiat. Dept. in Country. Mem.: Internat. Soc. Psychiatric Genetics, Internat. Soc. Bipolar Disorders (bd. councillors 2003—06), Soc. Biol. Psychiatry, Assn. European Psychiatrists (bd. dirs. 1998—2004), N.Y. Acad. Scis., European Coll. Neuropsychopharmacology, Polish Psychiat. Assn. (v.p. 1992—98, pres. 1998—2001, chief psychopharmacology sect. 2004—), Internat. Neuropsychiatric Assn. (mem. internat. com. 1999—). Avocation: pop and jazz music. Office: U Med Scis Dept Adult Psychiatry Ul Szpitalna 27/33 60 572 Poznan Poland Home: Ul. Boleslawa Limanowskiego 15A/2 60-744 Poznan Poland Office Phone: 48-61-8475087. Business E-Mail: rybakows@wlkp.top.pl.

RYDELL, CATHERINE M., medical association administrator, former state legislator; b. Grand Forks, ND, May 8, 1950; d. Hilary Harold and Catherine F. (Ireland) Wilson; m. Charles D. Rydell, 1971; children: Kimberly, Jennifer, Michael. BS, U. N.D., 1971. Mem. ND House of Reps., 1984—96, mem. supreme ct. judicial planning, govt., vet. affairs com., past Republican caucus leader; exec. dir. ND Med. Assn., 1997—99, Am. Acad. Neurology, St. Paul, 1999—, Am. Acad. Neurology Found., Am. Acad. Neurology Enterprises, Inc. Coord. cmty. svc. Bismarck Jr. Coll.; bus. mgr. surg. svc. St. Alexius Med. Ctr. Bd. dirs. Mission Valley Family, YMCA, N.D. Early Childhood Tng. Ctr., Ronald McDonald Found., CHAND; mem. state adv. bd. Casey Family Program, Juvenile Justice; mem. lay adv. bd. St. Alexius; mem. regional adv. bd. Luth. Social Svcs.; mem. N.D. State Centennial Com., N.D. State Mus. Art. Recipient Outstanding Svc. award Tobacco Free N.D., Legislator of Yr. award Children's Caucus, Guardian of Bus. award Nat. Fedn. Ind. Bus. Mem. Philanthropic and Edn. Orgn. Sisterhood, N.D. Med. Assn. (v.p.), Gamma Phi Beta. Office: Am Acad Neurology 1080 Montreal Ave Saint Paul MN 55116-2386 *

RYDÉN, GÖRAN P.D., psychiatrist; b. Stockholm, Apr. 18, 1965; s. Per and Maud Rydén; m. Eleonore Poulsen, July 28, 1962; children: Johannes, Simon. MD, Sahlgrenska Acad., Gothenburg, Sweden, 1990. Intern Eksjö (Sweden)-Nässjö Hosp., 1990—92; psychiatry trainee Psychiat. Dept., Huddinge, Sweden, 1992—97, cons. psychiatrist, 2001—; sr. psychiatrist Psychiat. Policlinic, Tumba, Sweden, 1998—2001. Consulting psychiatrist TryggHansa Ins. Co., Stockholm, 2003—; head psychotherapy unit for borderline patients, Huddrige. Contbr. articles to profl. jours. Mem.: Bd. Section of Med. Psychology, Bd. Swedish Psychiat. Assn. (sec.), Swedish Med. Assn., Swedish Psychiat. Assn. (cert. completion of specialist tng. 1998), Swedish Psychoanalytic Soc. (assoc.). Home: Bergsgatan 2 S-112 23 Stockholm Sweden Office: Psychiatric Dept M56 Huddinge Univ Hosp S-141 86 Stockholm Sweden Personal E-mail: goran@ryden.nu. E-mail: goran.ryden@slpo.sll.se.

RYDSTEDT, LEIF WERNER, research scientist; b. Stockholm, June 30, 1952; s. A. Werner and Inger Anna (Kajsa) Nilsson; m. Alla Rydstedt, Feb. 3, 1990; 1 child, Filippa. BSc, Stockholm U., 1984, PhD, 1996. Rsch. asst. Stockholm U., 1986—95; lectr., project leader Karlstad U., 1997—98; rsch. fellow U. Surrey, 2001—, U. Coll. London, 2004—05; sr. lectr. HV, 1998—. Contbr. articles to profl. jours. Pvt. Swedish Air Force, 1973—74. Avocations: literature, writing.

RYLOVA, ANNA, anesthesiologist; b. Moscow, June 28, 1980; MD, Moscow Med. Acad., 2004; PhD, Burdenko Neurosurgery Inst., 2009. Anesthesiologist Burdenko Neurosurgery Inst., 2009—. Cons. Air Liquide Med. Sys., 2008. Mem.: Russian Soc. Anesthesiology, European Soc. Anesthesiology. Achievements include first to use xenon anesthesia in neurosurgery and in patients with severe cardiac dysfunction. Avocations: bicycling, cooking. Home: Novorogozhskaya 30-2 Moscow 109544 Russia Home Fax: 7 495 678 1195. Business E-Mail: asokhor@yandex.ru.

RYLTSEV, ROMAN YEVGENIEVICH, metallurgist; b. Nizhny Tagil, Russia, June 18, 1980; MS, Nizhny Tagil State Social-Pedagogical Acad., 2002; PhD, Ural State Pedagogical U., 2005. Sr. staff scientist Inst. Metallurgy Ural Divsn., Russian Acad. Scis., 2010—. Office: Amudsena St 101 Yekaterinburg Sverdlovsk 620016 Russia Business E-Mail: roman_ryltsev@uspu.ru.

RYOO, BAEK-YEOL, physician, educator; b. Seoul, Republic of Korea, Feb. 23, 1963; MD, Seoul Nat. U., 1988; PhD, Inje U., Republic of Korea, 2002. Prof. Asan Med. Ctr., 2009—. Office: 88 Olympic-ro 43-gil Songpa-gu Seoul 138-736 Republic of Korea Office Fax: 02-3010-6961. Business E-Mail: ryooby@amc.seoul.kr.

RYO-YANG, MIWA-MIHWA, physician; b. Osaka, Japan, Nov. 4, 1959; MD, Osaka U., 1996, PhD in Med. Sci., 2005. Physician Sumitomo Mitsui Banking Corp., Osaka Med. Clinic, 2006—. Recipient Circulation Jour. award, 1st prize, Japanese Circulation Soc. Home: 2-1-36-1205 Matsuzakicho Abenoku Osaka 5450053 Japan Home Fax: 81666292956. Personal E-mail: ryomw@gaia.eonet.ne.jp.

RYTLEWSKI, KRZYSZTOF, gynecologist, consultant, professor; s. Jerzy Rytlewski and Barbara Rytlewska; m. Aleksandra Billewicz, Mar. 1, 1984; children: Tomasz, Ewa Rytlewska. MD, Med. Acad., Kraków, Poland, 1975. Asst. Ob-Gyn. Dept. Med. Coll., Kraków, 1976—85, lectr., 1986—2000, cons., 2000—09, asst. prof., 2009—. Contbr. scientific papers. Achievements include research in L-arginine as a supporting treatment in preeclampsia.

RYU, BUOM-YONG, reproductive physiologist, educator; b. Seoul, Republic of Korea, July 24, 1964; PhD, Chung-Ang U., 2000. Rsch. Rschr. Genetic Engring. Ctr., Chung-Ang U., Republic of Korea, 1992—93, Inst. Reproductive Medicine and Population, Seoul Nat. U., Republic of Korea, 1993—2000; rsch. assoc. U. Pa., 2000—04, rsch. asst. prof., 2004—05; prof. Chung-Ang U., 2005—. Scholar Scholarship, Korea scholarship found. for the future leaders. Fellow: Korean Soc. Devel. Biology, Korean Soc. Animal Reproduction, Korean Soc. Animal Sci. Avocations: mountain climbing, golf, painting. Office: Dept Animal Science and Tech Chung Ang University 72-1 Nae-Ri Daedeok-Myeon Anseong-Si Gyeonggi-Do 456-756 Republic of Korea Office Fax: 82-31-676-0062. Business E-Mail: byryu@cau.ac.kr.

RYU, HYO SUB, dermatologist; b. Dae-gu, Republic of Korea, Mar. 24, 1974; s. Su Yeol Ryu and Hee Ja Lee; m. Ji Hyang Choi, Apr. 25, 2004; 1 child, Young Seo. BS in Gen. Med. Sci., Kyung-pook Nat. U.; MS in Dermatology, Kyungpook Nat. U., Dae-gu, Republic of Korea, 2002. Cert. physician Ministry Health & Welfare, Republic of Korea, 1998, Dermatologist Ministry Health & Welfare, Republic of Korea, 2003. Pres. Korean Intern & Resident Assn., Seoul, Republic of Korea, 2000—01; clin. & rsch. fellow, dept. dermatology Seoul Nat. U., Bundang Hosp., Sung-nam City, Kyung-gi do, Republic of Korea, 2006—07, asst. prof. dept. dermatology, 2007—09; CEO Bon Skin & Hair Clinic. Pub. health care Dr. Korean Hansen Welfare Assn., Jeju, 2003—05. Fellow: Am. Acad. Dermatology; mem.: Internat. Soc. Hair Restoration Surgery, Am. Soc. Laser Medicine and Surgery, Korean Dermatol. Assn. (Presdl. Citation award 2002). Office: Tuldream Hair Clinic 5th Fl Eunsung Bldg 205-6 Seohyundong Bundang-Gu Sungnam-Si Kyunggi-do 463-824 Republic of Korea Home: 101-401 Byuksan Apt Keumho-dong Sungdong-gu Seoul 133-778 Republic of Korea Personal E-mail: dermaryu@hotmail.com. Business E-Mail: bonin@hanmail.net.

RYU, JAE-JUN, dentist, educator; b. Daejeon, Choongnam, Republic Of Korea, Dec. 10, 1962; s. Kooangyeol Ryu and Kooangok Lee; m. Hee Cho, Oct. 27, 1994; 1 child, Joo Yeon. PhD, Korea U., Seoul, 1999. Cert. dentist 1988. Dir. Korean Acad. Oral & Maxillofacial Implantology, Seoul, 2000—, Korean Acad. Esthetic Dentistry, Seoul, 2002; chmn. Grad. Sch. Clin. Dentistry, Seoul, 2005—, Korea U. Ansan Hosp. Dept. Dentistry, Republic of Korea, 2007—. Contbr. articles to profl. jour. Office: Korea Univ Ansan Hosp Kojandong 425-070 Ansan Keongkido Republic of Korea Office Fax: 82-31-485-5373. Business E-Mail: kopros@hanmail.net.

RYU, JEE-YOUL, research scientist; b. Republic of Korea, Mar. 5, 1970; s. Nam-Jin Ryu and Jum-Soon Woo; m. Mi-Hwa Chang. PhD, Ariz. State U., 2004. Sr. rschr. Samsung Mobile Display Co. Ltd., Ulsan, Republic of Korea, 2005—. Achievements include patents for LVDS. Office: Samsung Mobile Display Co Ltd Kachun-Ri Samnam-Myun Ulju-Gun 818 689-701 Ulsan Ulsan Republic of Korea Personal E mail: ryujy88@hanmail.net.

RYU, JI KON, medical educator; b. Seoul, Republic of Korea, Feb. 27, 1965; s. Byung Kyu Ryu and Jun Sun Kim; m. Jung Eun Ha, Oct. 12, 1991; children: HyeCho, Sang Ho. MD, Seoul Nat. U., 1989, PhD, 2000. Asst. prof. Seoul Nat. U. Coll. Medicine, Republic of Korea, 2003—. Recipient Oral Presentation award, Asia Pacific Digestive Disease Week, 2005. Mem.: Korean Soc. Gastrointestinal Endoscopy. Office: Seoul National Univ Hosp 28 Yeongeon dong Jongno gu Seoul 110 744 Republic of Korea Office Fax: 82-2-762-9662. Business E Mail: jkr1965@medimail.co.kr.

RYU, KUM HEI, gastroenterologist; b. Republic of Korea, Dec. 18, 1974; MD, Ehwa Womans U., 2000, PhD, 2010. Intern Ewha Womans U. Med. Ctr., 2000—01, resident, internal medicine, 2001—05, fellow, gastroenterology, 2005—07; gastroenterology and gastroenteroscopy specialist Nat. Cancer Ctr., 2007—. Mem.: Korean Assn. Internal Medicine, Korean Soc. Gastrointestinal Endoscopy, Korean Soc. Gastroenterology, Am. Gastroent. Assn. Office: Nat Cancer Ctr Madu1-dong Ils Goyang Gyeonggi 410-769 Republic of Korea Office Fax: 82-31-920-0451. Business E-Mail: kumheiryu@hanmail.net.

RYU, KYEONG-SIK, orthopedist, educator; b. Seoul, Republic of Korea, Mar. 10, 1966; Degree, Cath. U., Seoul, 2009. Assoc. prof. Coll. Medicine, Cath. U., 2010—. Office: 505 Bapo-dong Seocho-gu Seoul 137-701 Republic of Korea Business E-Mail: nsdoc35@catholic.ac.kr.

RYU, KYUNG HA, physician, educator; b. Seoul, Republic of Korea, Jan. 18, 1960; d. Shi Keun and Dong Ju (Lee) Ryu; m. Ho Seong Han, Jan. 5, 1985; children: Yoon Suk Han, Jung Suk Han, Eun Sun Han. MD, Ewha Woman's U. Med. Sch. Coll. Medicine, Seoul, 1984, PhD, 1991. Cert. pediatrician Pediat. Bd., Republic of Korea, 1988. Resident dept. pediat. Ewha Woman's U. Hosp. Coll. Medicine, 1985—88, assoc. prof. dept. pediat., 1996—, assoc. prof., 2000—; clin. fellow dept. pediat. divsn. hematology and oncology Seoul Nat. U. Children's Hosp., 1995—96. Vis. dr. UCLA Umbilical Cord Blood Bank, 1998. Editor: (book) Diagnosis and Treatment of Clinical Medicine, Hematology, 2006, (editor) Textbook of Pediatrics, 2006; contbr. articles to profl. jours. Recipient Korean Sci. award, Assn. Immunobiologists, 2003. Mem.: Korean Soc. Hepatopoietic Stem Cell Transplantation (corr.), Korean Soc. Hospice and Palliative Care (corr.), Korean Soc. Pediatric Hematology and Oncology (corr.), Internat. Soc. Exptl. Hematology (assoc.), Internat. Soc. Hematology (assoc.), Korean Soc. Hematology (assoc.), Korean Soc. Pediat. (assoc.). Avocations: skiing, travel, golf. Office: Ewha Woman's U Coll Medicine Mokdong Hosp 911-9 MokDong Yangchun-ku Seoul 158-710 Republic of Korea Office Fax: 82 2 2653 3718. Business E-Mail: ykh@ewha.ac.kr.

RYU, MUNHO, biomedical engineer, educator; b. Seoul, Republic of Korea, Apr. 27, 1967; m. Jinsun Chang, Apr. 21, 1996; 1 child, Keunwoo. BS, Seoul Nat. U., 1990; PhD, Seoul Nationl U., 2004. Mgr. Daewoo Heavy Industries Co. Ltd., Changwon, Republic of Korea, 1990—2000; supervisory engr. Biomedlab Co. Ltd., Seoul, Republic of Korea, 2000—05; prof. Chonbuk Nat. U., Jeonju, Republic of Korea, 2005—. Office: Chonbuk Nat Univ Duckjin-Dong 1-Ga 664-14 Jeonju Jeonbuk 561-756 Republic of Korea Office Fax: 82-63-270-2247. Business E-Mail: mhryu@chonbuk.ac.kr.

RYU, SEONG YEOB, surgeon, educator; b. Gwangju, Republic of Korea, Feb. 6, 1967; MB, Chonnam Nat. U. Med. Sch., 1993; MD, Chonnam Nat. U. Grad. Sch., 2002. Assoc. prof., Med. Sch. Chonnam Nat. U., 2001—, cons., edn., rsch., Hwasun Hosp., 2004. Mem.: Korean Soc. Coloproctology, Korean Soc. Endoscopic & Laparoscopic Surgeons (Best Presentation award), Korean Gastric Cancer Assn. (7th Sanofi-Aventis Best Presentation award, 11th Sanofi-Aventis Best Presentation award), Korean Surg. Soc., Korean Med. Assn. Avocations: violin, mountain climbing, golf. Office: #160 Ilsim-ri Hwasun-eup Hwasun Jeollanam 519-809 Republic of Korea Office Fax: 82-61-379-7661. Business E-Mail: drrsy@chonnam.ac.kr.

RYU, SO YEON, medical educator; b. Gwangju, Republic of Korea, Jan. 31, 1968; PhD, Chosun U., 1999. Lectr. Dept. Preventive Medicine, Chosun U. Med. Sch., 2001—04, asst. prof., 2004—07, assoc. prof., 2007—. Mem.: Korean Soc. Medicine, Korean Soc. Preventive Medicine. Avocation: music. Office: #375 Seosuk-dong Dong-gu Gwangju 501-759 Republic of Korea Office Fax: 82-62-225-8293. Business E-Mail: canrsy@chosun.ac.kr.

RYU, YON JU, medical educator; b. Republic of Korea, Sept. 14, 1973; MD, Ewha Womans U. Sch. Medicine, PhD, 1998. Asst. prof., pulmonary and critical care medicine dept. medicine Ewha Med. Ctr. and Med. Rsch. Inst. Ewha Womans U. Sch. Medicine Mokdong Hosp., 2006—. Steering com. mem., Tb control program Korea Ctrs. Disease Control & Prevention, 2009—; steering com. mem. Korean Consortium E-Learning in Med. Edn., 2010—; steering com. mem., info. tech. & svc. Korean Assn. Lung Cancer Study, 2011—. Mem.: Korean Assn. Lung Cancer Study, Soc. Critical Care Medicine, Asian Pacific Soc. Respirology, European Respiratory Soc., Korean Acad. Tb and Respiratory Diseases. Office: Mokdong Hosp Mok 5-dong Yangcheon-gu Seoul 158-710 Republic of Korea Office Fax: 82-2-2650-2559.

RYZHAK, GALINA ANATOLIEVNA, pathologist, researcher; b. St. Petersburg, Russia, Jan. 15, 1955; d. Anatoliy Ivanovich Kuznetsov and Galina Pavlovna Kuznetsova; m. Peter Mikhailovich Ryzhak; 1 child, Anastasia Petrovna. MD, Med. Hygiene and San. Inst., St. Petersburg, PhD, 1978. Cert. prof. Highest Attestation Commn. Russian Fedn., 2005. Lt. Res. med. officer, 1978—2008; rschr. Vaccines & Serums Rsch. Inst., St. Petersburg, 1978—86; head biol. control dept. Mfg. Firm Bacteria & Virus Preparations Vaccine & Serums Rsch. Inst., St. Petersburg, 1986—96; dep. dir. rsch. work & new techs. St. Petersburg Inst. Bioregulation & Gerontolog, 1996—, head lab. ade-related clin. pathology, 1996—. Recipient Disting. Labour Achievements medal, 2003. Achievements include development of new medications and medical technologies for prevention and therapy of age-related pathologies. Avocations: literature, music, theater, travel. Office: Inst Bioregulation & Gerontology Dinamo pr 3 Saint Petersburg 197110 Russia Office Fax: 78122351832. Business E-Mail: galina@gerontology.ru.

SA, YINGLONG, urologist; b. Shanghai, Mar. 31, 1965; PhD, Shanghai Jiaotong U., 2010. Physician dept. urology Shanghai Sixth People's Hosp., 2001—. Office: 600 Yi-San Rd Shanghai 200233 China Business E Mail: sayinglong331@sina.com.

SAAD, ALI G., pathologist; b. Lebanon, Oct. 25, 1968; MD, Lebanese U., 1998. Postdoc. fellow, neuropathology Harvard Med. Sch., 2005—07, postdoc. fellow, pediat. pathology, 2007—08; head, anatomic pathology, dir., surg. pathology Ark. Children's Hosp., 2008—. Fellow: US and Can. Acad. Pathology. Avocations: tennis, hiking, bicycling. Office: 1 Childrens Way Lot #820 Little Rock AR 72202 Business E-Mail: agsaad@uams.edu.

SAAD, MARCELO, physician; b. Sao Paulo, Brazil, Feb. 26, 1968; MD, UNIFESP EPM, 1992, PhD, 2003. Physician Hosp. Israelita Albert Einstein, 2005. Home: R Montesquieu 371 Sao Paulo 04116-190 Brazil Business E-Mail: msaad@einstein.br.

SAAD, MOHAMED, surgeon; b. Desouk, Kafer Alshiekh, Egypt, Sept. 12, 1965; s. Saad Mohamed Abohalawa and Ensaf Amine Sharaf; m. Amal Said Alhesawi, Feb. 1, 1993; children: Yasmine Mohamed, Mae Mohamed, Salma Mohamed, Lobna Mohamed. MBChB, Alexandria U., Egypt, 1989, CM, 1993. Cons. surgeon Alzahraa Hosp., Jeddah, Saudi Arabia, 2004—, chief endoscopiest, 2004—. Contbr. articles. Fellow: Royal Coll. Surgeons. Achievements include patents pending for percutaneous endoscopic intragastric surgery cannula; introducing a new surgical technique called Fisherman's technique. Office: Alzahraa Hosp Prince Sultan Jeddah 15751 Saudi Arabia E-mail: mohsaad71@hotmail.com.

SAADA (REISCH), ANN, medical educator, researcher; b. Västerås, Sweden, Mar. 9, 1959; d. Frigyes and Susanna Reisch; m. Joel Saada, Aug. 11, 1981; children: Michael Saada, Gabriel Saada, Nathanel Saada, Jacob Saada. MSc, Hebrew U., Jerusalem, Isreal, 1980, MSc in Tchg., 1982, PhD, 1990. Lab. chief Shaare Zedek Med. Ctr., Jerusalem, 1994—2005, Hadassah Med. Ctr., Jerusalem, 2005—. Lectr. Michala and Lifshitz Colls., Jerusalem, 1994—; sr. lectr. Ben Gurion U. Negev, Beer Sheba, Israel, 2005—08. Contbr. articles to profl. jour. Rsch. grant, Israeli Acad. Sci., 2003—08, Iraeli Ministry Health, 1997, 2004—06, US-Isreali Binational Sci. Found., 2006—08, United Mitochondrial Disease Found., 2007—. Office: Hadassah Med Ctr Ein Kerem Jerusalem 91120 Israel

SAADEH, SHERIF NABIL, gastroenterologist, hepatologist, researcher; b. Amman, Jordan, Nov. 29, 1969; s. Nabil Ibrahim Saadeh and Helen Aziz Ibrahim; m. Claudia-Aghareed Jamal Haddad; children: Omar, Kareem, Celina. MBBS, U. Jordan Faculty Medicine, MD, 1993. Cert. internal medicine Am. Bd. Internal Medicine, 1999, gastroenterology Am. Bd. Internal Medicine, 2003, hon. diplomate Am. Bd. Hosp. Physicians, Am. Coll. Ethical Physicians. Staff gastroenterologist/hepatologist Baylor U. Med. Ctr., Dallas, 2003—. Contbr. Recipient Rsch. award, North Am. Conf. Gastroenterology Fellows, 2002, fellowship, Am. Bd. Hosp. Physicians, 2002, America's Top Physician award, Consumer's Rsch. Coun. Am., 2003; grantee medical rsch. grant-subinvestigator, Nat. Insts. Health, 2001, medical rsch. grant, Cleve. Clinic Hepatology Inst., 2001. Fellow: Am. Coll. Hosp. Physicians; mem.: ACP, Jordan Med. Assn., European Assn. for Study of Liver, Tex. Soc. Gastroenterology and Endoscopy, Am. Coll. Gastroenterology, Crohn's & Colitis Found. Am., Am. Liver Found., AMA (Physician's recognition award 2004—07), Am. Soc. Gastrointestinal Endoscopy, Am. Gastroenterol. Assn., Am. Ass. Study Liver Diseases. Roman Catholic. Office: Al-Khalidi Medical Plz P.O. Box 5321 11183 Amman Jordan Personal E-mail: saadeh@lycos.com.

SAALFELD, FRED ERICH, science educator, researcher; s. Eric Arthur and Milla (Kessler) S.; m. Elizabeth Renner, Nov. 22, 1958; 1 child, Fred E. Jr. (dec.). BS cum laude, So. East Mo. State U., 1957; MS in Phys. Chemistry, Iowa State U., 1959, PhD in Phys. Chemistry, 1961. Instr. Iowa State U., Ames, 1961—62; chemist Naval Rsch. Lab, Washington, 1962—63, head mass spectrometry sect., 1963—74, head phys. chem. br., 1974—76, supt. chem. divsn., 1976—82; chief scientist Office Naval Rsch., London, 1979—80, dir. rsch. Arlington, Va., 1982—87, dir., 1987—93, dep. chief naval rsch., tech. dir., 1993—98, exec. dir., tech. dir., 1998—2002; disting. rsch. prof. Ctr. for Tech. and Nat. Security Policy Nat. Def. U., 2003—04; sr. fellow Potomac Inst. for Policy Studies, 2002—, bd. regents, 2007—. Author more than 500 publications, reports, presentations on applications of mass spectrometry to fields of combustion, laser, environ. analysis. Recipient Disting. Rank awards U.S. Pres., Washington, 1989, 96, Meritorious Rank award U.S. Pres., Washington, 1986, Robert Conrad award Sec. USN, Washington, 1988, Disting. Civilian Svc. award Sec. of Def./Dept. Def., 1999; named Fed. Exec. of Yr., Fed. Exec. Inst., Washington, 1991, named Fred E. Saalfed award for lifetime achievement in sci., Chief Naval Rsch., 2001. Fellow AAAS, Potomac Inst. Policy Studies (sr.); mem. Am. Chem. Soc. (councilor 1973-89), Am. Soc. Mass Spectrometry (sec. 1970-74), Combustion Inst., Chem. Soc. Washington (pres. 1972). Achievements include provision for science base for life support systems used in enclosed environments; development of educational programs used by USN for scientist training. Office Phone: 703-887-2197. Personal E-mail: fsaalfeld@verizon.net.

SABAH, MUNA, pathologist, educator; b. Damascus, Syria, June 27, 1970; d. Anas Sabah and Falak Jallad; m. Hasan Mahayni, Aug. 20, 1993; children: Akram Mahayni, Sarah Mahayni. MD with first class honors, Damascus U., 1994; M in Med. Sci. with first class honors, U. Coll. Dublin, 1995. Cert. satisfactory completion specialist tng. Irish Com. on Higher Med. Tng., 2005, MD Royal Coll. Surgeons Ireland, 2005. Ho. officer in medicine Damascus U. Hosp., 1995, ho. officer in surgery, 1996; sr. ho. officer in histopathology dept. pathology Cork U. Hosp., Ireland, 1996—97, registrar in histopathology dept. pathology, 1998—99; sr. ho. officer in histopathology dept. pathology Waterford Regional Hosp., Ireland, 1997—98; lectr., specialist registrar in histopathology Royal Coll. Surgeons in Ireland and Beaumont Hosp., Dublin, 1999—2004, sr. lectr., cons. histopathologist, 2004—07; cons. histopathologist Connolly Hosp. Ireland, Dublin, 2007—. Contbr. articles to profl. jours. Fellow: Royal Coll. Physicians, Royal Coll. Pathologists; mem.: Royal Coll. Surgeons Ireland (undergrad. and postgrad. examiner 1999—, pathology curriculum planning 2005—). Achievements include research in Alterations of 9p21 may contribute to the progression and/or malignant transformation of GISTs. Loss of p16/LOH of 9p21 may be important in the pathogenesis of synovial sarcoma; pathogenesis of soft tissue sarcomas and gastrointestinal stromal tumors. Office: Connolly Hosp Blanchardstown Dublin D15 Ireland Home: 3 Park Manor Castleknock Dublin 15 Ireland Office Phone: 00353 876693643. Office Fax: 353-1-8207747. Personal E-mail: munasabah@gmail.com.

SABAT, SHYAMSUNDER B., radiologist, educator; b. Mumbai, Jan. 12, 1976; MBBS, Grant Med. Coll., 1999; MD, Jawaharlal Nehru Med. Coll., AMU, Aligarh, 2002. Lectr. radiology Grant Med. Coll. & Sir JJ Group Hosps., 2003—07; fellow vascular, interventional radiology U. Ala., Birmingham, 2007—08, fellow neuroradiology, 2008—09; asst. prof. neuro radiology Penn State Milton S Hershey Med. Ctr., 2009—. Com. mem., quality, safety com., dept. radiology Pa. State Milton S Hershey Med. Ctr., 2009; mem. editl. bd. Internet Jour. Radiology, 2010; com. mem., edni. com. Assn. U. Radiologists, 2011. Recipient Best Lectr. award, Grant Med. Coll. Mem.: Pa. Med. Soc., Assn. U. Radiologists, Am. Coll. Radiology, Radiologic Soc. N.America, Am. Soc. Neuroradiology. Avocations: writing, photography. Office: Dept Radiology MC H066 500 University Dr Hershey PA 17033 Office Fax: 717-531-0006. Business E-Mail: ssabat@hmc.psu.edu.

SABATH, LEON DAVID, internist, educator; b. Savannah, Ga., July 24, 1930; s. Sholom and Sarah (Cherkas) S.; children: Natasha, Joanna, Rachel. AB magna cum laude, Harvard U., 1952, MD, 1956. Diplomat Am. Bd. Internal Medicine, Am. Bd. Infectious Disease. Intern Peter Bent Brigham Hosp., Boston, 1956-57, sr. resident in medicine, 1962-63; jr. resident in medicine Bellevue Hosp., NYC, 1959-60; fellow in infectious disease Harvard U. and Thorndike Meml. Lab., Boston City Hosp., 1960-62; fellow in antibiotic resistance Sir William Dunn Sch. Pathology, Oxford U., Eng., 1963-65; mem. faculty dept. medicine Harvard U., also; staff physician Boston City Hosp., 1965-74; asst. Harvard Med. Sch., 1965-67, asst. prof., 1967-70, asso. prof., 1970-74; head sect. infectious diseases U. Minn., Mpls., 1974-83, prof. medicine, 1974—. Chmn. coms. U. Minn. Hosps.; adj. faculty Rockefeller U., 1990-91. Editor: Pseudomonas aeruginosa, 1980, Antibiotic Action in Patients, 1982; editl. bd. Clin. Pharmacology and Therapeutics, 1978-80; contbr. articles on antibiotics and their use, bacterial resistance to antibiotics, chlamydia and death associated wiht exercise to profl. jours. Trustee E.P.A. Cephalosporin Fund, Oxford U., 1970—. Capt. M.C. AUS, 1957—59. NIH spl. fellow, 1963-65; recipient Career Devel. award NIH, 1968-72 Fellow ACP, Infectious Disease Soc. Am.; mem. Am. Soc. Clin. Investigation, Am. Soc. Microbiology (vice chmn. div. antimicrobial chemotherapy 1976-77, chmn. 1977-78). Achievements include research in vancomycin resistance of staphylococcal aureus, and on sudden cardiac death associated with exertion. Avocation: cello. Home: 2504 Washburn Ave S Minneapolis MN 55416-4351 Office: U Minn Hosps Mayo Meml Blvd D416 Minneapolis MN 55455 Home Phone: 612-377-3770; Office Phone: 612-624-6661. Personal E-mail: leonsabath@yahoo.com.

SABATINI, LUCA CESARE, obstetrician, gynecologist; b. Spoleto, Italy, June 27, 1965; s. Domenico Sabatini and Alberta Corteggi; m. Donatella Proietti Picotti, July 2, 2000. MD with hons., U. La Sapienza, 1990; degree with hons. in Clin. Pathology, Umberto I U., 1997. Cert. in clin. pathology Italian Bd. Medicine, 1997, in ob.-gyn. Italian Bd. Medicine, 2003. Intern in clin. andrology and infertility Umberto I U. Hosp., Rome, 1988—91, resident in clin. pathology, 1992—97; lt. med. officer Italian Military Air Force, Florence, Italy, 1991—92; fellow in reproductive biology Med. Sch. St. Bartholomew's U., London, 1997—98; resident. in ob.-gyn London Deanery, 1999—2004; fellowship in reproductive medicine and surgery The Royal London and St. Bartholomew's Hosps., 2004—. Adminstrv. sr. registrar The Royal London (England) Hosp., 2003—05. Contbr. articles to profl. jours. Lt. med. officer Italian Air Force, 1992—93.

Scholar, Umberto I U. Hosp., Rome, Italy, 1995—97. Mem.: Royal Coll. Ob.-gyn., Brit. Fertility Soc., Italian Soc. Med. Andrology, Italian Med. Assn., Gen. Med. Coun., Italian Assn. Clin. Pathologists. Achievements include development of semiautomatic computer software for sperm analysis (SIAS). Office: St Bartholomew's Hosp Little Britain London EC1A 7BE England Office Fax: 0044 (0) 207 6017181. Business E-Mail: luca.sabatini@bartsandthelondon.nhs.uk.

SABATINI, SANDRA, physician; b. NYC, Dec. 1, 1940; BS in Chemistry, Millsaps Coll., 1962; MS in Pharmacology, Marquette U., 1966; PhD in Pharmacology, U. Miss., 1968; MD in Internal Medicine, Tex. Med. Sch., 1974. Lic. physician, Ill., Tex. Intern in medicine U. Ill. Hosp., Chgo., 1974-75; asst. prof. U. Tex. Med. Sch., San Antonio, 1968-70; assoc. dir. U. Ill. Hosp., Chgo., 1977-78; asst. prof. U. Ill. Coll. of Medicine, Chgo., 1977-83, assoc. prof. medicine and physiology, 1983-84; attending physician in nephrology VA, Chgo., 1977-84; med. dir. Dialysis Unit U. Ill., Chgo., 1978-84; prof. internal medicine and physiology Tex. Tech. U. Health Sci. Ctr., Lubbock, 1985—, chmn. dept. physiology, 1993-96; attending physician in nephrology U. Med. Ctr., Lubbock, 1985—. Lab. instr. Millsaps Coll., Jackson, Miss., 1961-62; instr. pharmacology Bapt. Hosp. Sch. Nursing, Jackson, 1966-68; merit rev. mem. NSF, 1987, 91, 92; rev. mem. several orgns. including Chgo. Heart Assn., 1984, NIH, 1983, 86, 89-93, 96, Nat. Kidney Found., 1987, 89—, Am. Heart Assn., 1981-84, others; cons. U.S. Med. Licensing Exam/Nat. Bd. Med. Examiners, Step 1 Physiology Test Com., 1996-99. Editl. referee Am. Jour. Kidney Disease, Am. Jour. Physiology, Am. Jour. Nephrology, Annals of Internal Medicine, others; mem. editl. bd. Am. Jour. Nephrology, 1989-93, Seminars in Nephrology, 1984—; co-editor Am. Jour. Kidney Diseases, 1997—; author numerous publs. and abstracts in field; contbr. articles to profl. jours. Bd. dirs. YWCA of Lubbock, 1994-99; mem. Leadership Tex., 1994. Predoctoral fellowship grantee Marquette U., 1963-66; pub. health predoctoral fellow U. Miss. Med. Sch., 1967-69, gen. medicine sci. rsch. grantee U. Tex. Med. Sch., 1968-70, post-grad. fellow Karolinska Inst., Swedish Med. Coun., 1971, 73, NIH grantee, 1979-82, 84-99, Chgo. Heart Assn. grantee-in-aid, 1979-85, 99; grantee Nat. Eye Inst., 1979-80; recipient Banes Charitable trust award U. Ill., 1984-85, U.S. Olympic com. Rsch. Foudn., 1986-87; recipient Outstanding Alumnus award Tex. Med. Sch., 1994, numerous other awards in field. Fellow: ACP; mem.: AAUP, AAAS, ADA (hon.), Lubbock Arts Alliance, Leadership Tex. Alumnae Assn., Nat. Kidney Found. West Tex. (bd. dirs. 1993—99, Outstanding Vol. 1995, 2001, Disting. Svc. award 1996), Nat. Kidney Found. (numerous offices including chmn. several coms.), Italian-Am. Nephrologists, Inc., Internat. Soc. Nephrology, Ill. Kidney Found., Ctrl. Soc. Clin. Rsch., So. Soc. Clin. Rsch. (councillor 1997—99, pres.-elect 1999, pres. 2000), Assn. Chairs Dept. Physiology (councillor 1995—97), Am. Soc. Renal Biochemistry and Metabolism (pres.-elect 1994), Am. Soc. Pharmacology and Exptl. Therapeutics, Am. Soc. Nephrology, Am. Physiol. Soc., Am. Heart Assn., Am. Fedn. Med. Rsch., Lubbock Women's Club, Rotary Internat. Office: Tex Tech U Health Sci Ctr 3601 4th St Lubbock TX 79430-0001

SABEL, BERNHARD AUGUST MARIA, psychologist, neuroscientist, educator; b. Trier, Federal Republic of Germany, Nov. 7, 1957; s. Hans and Ursula (Berekoven) S.; m. Kornelia Sabel; children: Torsten, Daniela. BA, U. Trier, 1978; MA, U. Düsseldorf, 1982; PhD, Clark U., 1984; Dr. med. habil., priv.-dozent, U. Munich, 1988. Postdoctoral assoc. and fellow MIT, Cambridge, 1984-86; rsch. scientist Inst. Med. Psychology U. Munich, 1986-92; prof., chmn. med. psychology U. Magdeburg (Germany) Med. Sch., 1992—; v.p. rsch. U. Magdeburg, 2008—10. Vis. neuroscientist Mass. Gen. Hosp./Harvard Med. Sch., 1991, 94-99; chmn. sci. adv. bd., bd. dirs. Ctr. Neurosci., Innovation and Tech., Magdeburg, vis. fellow, Princeton, U., 1999, v.p. U. Magdeburg, 2008-; founder, pres., CEO NovaVision AG, 2000-03, Nanopharm AG, Magdeburg, Germany, 2000—2006; founder NovaVision, Inc., Boca Raton, Fla., 2003, chief sci. officer; founder, CSO EBS Techs. GmbH, Kleinmachnow, Germany, 2007, v.p. rsch., 2008-10. Co-author: Brain Plasticity, 1997, Medical Psychology-Medical Sociology, 1993; co-editor: Pharmacological Approaches to the Treatment of Brain and Spinal Cord Injury, 1988, Medical and Biological Psychology, 1994, Communication and Aging, 2001; editor-in-chief Restorative Neurology and Neuroscience, 1997—; mem. editl. bd. Zeitschrift für Medizinische Psychologie, 1991—; contbr. articles on neurology and neurosci. to profl. jours.; patentee on controlled drug delivery system for treatment neural disorders, drug delivery system for small water soluble molecules, and nanoparticles to transport drugs across the blood brain barrier and computer-based vision tng. Mem. Cen. Mass. Symphony Orch., Worcester, 1978-86, Revere String Quartet, Boston, 1984-86. Fulbright scholar 1978, German Acad. Exch. Svc. grantee, 1982; Recipient Cinquegrani award Innovation Relay Ctrs., Florence, Italy, 2000, Leonardo da Vinci award, World Orgn. Achievement Human Potential, 2005. Mem. Soc. for Neurosci., Internat. Brain Rsch. Orgn., Internat. Neurochem. Soc., European Neurosci. Assn., Neurosci. Assn. (Germany), Controlled Release Soc., German Soc. Med. Psychology, European Brain and Behavior Soc., Internat. Bus. Club (bd. dirs. 1988-89), Internat. Brain Injury Assoc. (bd. gov. 2010-), Internat. Soc. Law Vision (exec. bd. mem. 2011-).

SABER, ASHRAF SOBHY, veterinarian, educator; b. Cairo, Cairo, Aug. 1, 1949; s. Sobhy Mohammad Saber and Nafesa Abdel-Maqsoud Abdel-Rahman; m. Brigitte Schenk, Dec. 19, 1983; 1 child, Dina Ashraf. B in Vet. Sci. with honors, Assiut U., M in Vet. Sci., Anatomy, 1976, PhD in Anatomy, 1979, M in Vet Sci., Surgery, 1992, PhD in Surgery 1st part, 1994; degree, Kassel U., 1983. Demonstrator to prof. anatomy faculty vet. medicine Assiut U., 1972—89, prof., 1989—98, head dept. anatomy, 1998—; vice dean Minoufiya U., Sadat City, Egypt, 1998—2004; editor Jour. Vet. Anatomy. Vis. prof. Free U., Berlin, 1993—94. Co-author: Selected Topics on Camileds, 2000; mem. editl. bd.: Jour. Camel Practice Rsch., contbg. author: 15 books in vet. field; contbr. more than 110 articles in vet. anatomy and history to profl. publs. Recipient Disting. Rsch. prize, Menoufiya U., 2000, Disting. Camel Scientist award, Rajasthan Agrl. U., 2007; scholar, German Academic Exch. Svc., 1988;, 1991, 1994, 1997, 2001, 2005. Mem.: Am. Assn. Vet. Anatomists, World Assn. History Vet. Medicine, African Assn. Vet. Anatomists (founder, pres.), Internat. Com. Vet. Gross Anatomical Nomenclature, Egyptian Soc. Arabian Horses, Egyptian Soc. Wildlife, Egyptian Assn. History Vet. Medicine Asst. (asst. mem. 1980, founder, gen. sec.), Egyptian Assn. Cattle Diseases, European Assn. Vet. Anatomists, Arab Vet. Medicine Assn., Egyptian Anatomical Soc., Egyptian Vet. Soc., Egyption Assn. History Vet. Medicine (Sadat city founder, pres. 2007), World Assn. Vet. Anatomists. Achievements include founding of the department and museums of veterinary anatomy and history of camels in the faculty of veterinary medicine at Minoufiya University. Avocations: painting, tennis, reading, stamp collecting/philately, shell collecting. Office: Faculty Vet Medicine Sadat City Egypt Office Phone: 048 260 3214. Personal E-mail: saberashraf_2@yahoo.com.

SABIA, PETER JAMES, cardiologist; MD, U. Md., 1984. Diplomate Am. Bd. Internal Medicine, Am. Bd. Internal Medicine-cardiovasc. disease, Am. Bd. Internal Medicine-interventional cardiology. Resident Univ. of Va. Med. Ctr., 1987, fellow, 1990; hosp. affiliations include Holy Cross Hosp., Suburban Hosp., Washington Adventist Hosp., Laurel Regional Hosp., Sibley Meml. Hosp. Named one of Top Doctors, Washingtonian Mag., 2011. Office: Associates in Cardiology Ste 200 1400 Forest Glen Rd Silver Spring MD 20910 Office Phone: 301-681-5700. Office Fax: 301-681-5599.

SABIR HUSIN ATHAR, PRIMUHARSA PUTRA, otolaryngologist, educator; b. Tanjung Enim, South Sumatra, Indonesia, May 12, 1964; s. Sabir Husin Athar and Aisyah Sutan Umar; m. Nor Mahani Harun, Nov. 18, 1993; children: Mohd Irfan Primuharsa Putra, Nurul Raihan Primuharsa Putra, Muhammad Hilmi Primuharsa Putra, Nurul Irdina Primuharsa Putra. MD, U. Kebangsaan Malaysia, Kuala Lumpur, 1991, MSurg in ORL-HNS, 2000. Internship Ministry Health Malaysia, Kota Bharu, 1991—92, med. officer Kuala Terengganu, 1992—96; residency programme Dept. Otorhinolaryngology-Head & Neck Surgery, U. Kebangsaan Malaysia, 1996—2000, sr. lectr. & cons. ent-head & neck surgeon, 2001—05, internal examiner, part i masters surgery — viva, 2001—04; resident cons. ent-head & neck surgeon KPJ Seremban Specialist Hosp., Malaysia, 2005—, chmn., risk mgmt. com., 2007, chmn., kpj patient safety goals com., 2008—; com. mem. KPJ Clin. Risk Mgmt., 2010, Malaysian Soc. Otorhinolaryngologist Head & Neck Surgeon, 2010—; adj. lectr. Liverpool John Moores U. Programs UPJ Internat. Coll. Nursing & Health Scis.; pres. elect. head & neck surgeon Malaysian Soc. ORL, 2011—. Exec. com. Malaysian Med. Assn., 1994—95, hon. sec., 1995—96, Malaysian Soc. Otorhinolaryngologists-Head Surgeon, 2001—02, exec. com., 2007—08, 2010—11; jour. reviewer Med. Jour. Malaysia, 2006; vis. cons. Dept. Oral & Maxillofacial Surgery, U. Kebangsaan Malaysia Med. Ctr., 2009—; vis. lectr. Cyberjaya U. Coll. Med. Scis.; jour. reviewer Malaysian Jour. Med. Scis., 2010, Dental Traumatology, 2010, Med. Case Studies Jour., 2010, Jour. Dentistry and Oral Hygiene, 2010—11, Philipine Jour. Otolaryngology Head & Neck Surgery, 2010; editl. bd. mem. Jour. Islamic Med. Assn. Malaysia, 2010. Contbr. articles to profl. jours.; co-editor: Commemorative book of Malaysian Soc. Otorhinolaryngologists Head And Neck Surgeon, 2011; reviewer Clin. Oncology & cancer Research, 2011. Recipient Excellent Svc. award, Ministry Health Malaysia, 1996, Best Participant award, U. Sci. Malaysia, 1996, Dato Harnam Third Prize, Malaysian Soc. Otorhinolaryngologists-Head & Neck Surgeon, 2000, UCB Pharma Third Prize, 2004. Fellow: Internat. Acad. Oral Oncology; mem.: Malaysian Soc. Quality Health, Asian Soc. Head & Neck Oncology, Islamic Med. Assn. Malaysia, Malaysian Med. Assn., Acad. Medicine Malaysia, Malaysian Soc. Otorhinolaryngologist - Head and Neck Surgeon, Asian Assn. Oral & Maxillofacial Surgeons, Asian Sleep Surg. Soc., Inter Am. Assn. Pediatric Otorhinolaryngology, Am. Acad. Otolaryngology-Head & Neck, Nat. Specialist Register, Malaysian Med. Coun., UKM Alumni Assn., Assn. Specialists Pvt. Med. Practice. Achievements include research in comparison between CO2 laser vaporization with swiftlase and submucosal diathermy in the treatment of patients with hypertrophy of inferior turbinate; cyclin d1 expression in nasopharyngeal carcinoma and association with grade, stage and response to radiotherapy; molecular characterization of Malaysian oral squamous cell carcinoma; oral cancer and precancer in Malaysia — risk factors, prognostic markers, genetic expression and impact on quality of life. Office: KPJ Seremban Specialist Hosp Jalan Toman 1 Kemayan Square Seremban Negeri Sembilan 70200 Malaysia Office Phone: 606-767-7800.

SABLE, ROBERT ALLEN, gastroenterologist; b. Bklyn., June 21, 1948; s. Benjamin and Sara S.; m. Valerie P. Kubie Kopelman, July 1, 1969 (div. Mar. 1982); 1 child, Jesse; m. Ellen Sue Finer, May 29, 1982; children: Scott, Eric. BS, MIT, 1969; MD, Albert Einstein U., 1973. Bd. cert. in internal medicine, gastroenterology and geriatrics Am. Bd. Internal Medicine. Staff physician N.Y. Telephone Co. Mid Manhattan Med. Dept., NYC, 1978-81; physician Riverdale Gastroenterology Cons., Bronx, 1981—; med. dir. Advanced Endoscopy Ctr., Bronx, 2007—09. Chief gastroenterology St. Barnabas Hosp., Bronx, 1982-2003, pres. med. bd., 1985-90; pres. divsn. coun. Montefiore Med. Ctr., 2001-03, pres. med. staff, 2005-08. Contbr. articles, reports, revs. to profl. jours. Fellow ACP, Am. Coll. Gastroenterology, Am. Gastroenterol. Assn.; mem. AMA, Am. Soc. for Gastrointestinal Endoscopy. Avocations: stamp collecting/philately, coin collecting/numismatics. Office: 3765 Riverdale Ave Ste 7 Bronx NY 10463 Home Phone: 914-591-6147; Office Phone: 718-549-4267. Personal E-mail: ra.sable@verizon.net.

SABOEIRO, ALESIA P., plastic surgeon; BS in Nutrition, U. Fla., Gainesville, 1984, MS in Nutrition, 1986; MD, U. Miami Sch. Medicine, 1992. Diplomate Am. Bd. Plastic Surgery, lic. Ga., 1998, NY, 2004. Resident gen. surgery St. Louis U. Hosp., 1992—95, resident plastic surgery, 1995—97; aesthetic surgery fellowship Paces Plastic Surgery & Recovery Ctr., Atlanta, 1998; asst. prof. surgery St. Louis U., 1998—2004; surgeon TriBeCa Plastic Surgery, NYC, 2004—. Contbr. articles to profl. jours. Fellow: ACS; mem.: Am. Soc. Plastic Surgeons, Am. Soc. Aesthetic Plastic Surgery. Office: TriBeCa Plastic Surgery 44 Hudson St New York NY 10013 Office Phone: 212-571-5200. Office Fax: 212-571-5255. *

SABOKBAR, AFSIE, cell biologist, researcher; b. Tehran, Iran, Sept. 6, 1961; d. Rokneddin Sabokbar and Forough Vahab-Zadeh; m. Richard Paul John Swannell, July 20, 1991; children: Sasha Omid Edward Swannell, Anushka Roya Amelia Swannell. BS (hon.), U. London, 1985; Doctorate (hon.), U. Essex, Eng., 1988. Postdoctoral rsch. officer U. Durham, County Durham, 1989—91, U. Cambridge, Cambridgeshire, 1991—94; sr. lectr., postdoctoral rsch. officer U. Oxford, Oxfordshire, 1994—, fellow Wolfson Coll., 1999—, dir. postgrad. studies, 2003—. Contbr. sci. papers to profl. jours. Achievements include research in cellular bone biology; patents pending for novel orthopaedic cement. Office: U Oxford Botnar Ctr Windmill Rd Oxfordshire Oxford OX3 7LD England E-mail: afsie.sabokbar@ndos.ox.ac.uk.

SABOL, JENNIFER L., breast surgeon; MD, Jefferson Med. Coll. Resident Baystate Med. Ctr., Springfield; fellow Baylor Univ. Med. Ctr.; hosp. affiliations include Bryn Mawr Hosp., 2006, Lankenau Med. Ctr., 2006, dir. breast care program; hosp. affiliations include Paoli Hosp., 2006; asst. prof. surgery Jefferson Med. Coll.; physician Main Line HealthCare. Co-author: (jours.) Concurrent Administration of Vinorelbine with Recombinant Human Granulocyte Colony-Stimulating Factor, 1999, Estrogern Replacement Therapy After Breast Cancer: A Twelve Year Follow-Up, 2001, Diagnosis, Treatment and Management of Breast Cancer inj Previously Augmented Women. Named one of the Top Doctor, Phila. Mag., 2011. Office: Main Line Health Medical Science Bldg Ste 275 100 Lancaster Ave Wynnewood PA 19096 Office Phone: 610-642-1908. Office Fax: 610-642-6808.

SABRI, SAHER S., radiologist, educator; b. Amman, Jordan, Apr. 3, 1976; MD, U. Jordan, 2000. Asst. prof., radiology U. Va., 2008—. Office: 1215 Lee St Charlottesville VA 22908 E-mail: saherss@hotmail.com.

SABRY, EHSAN YAHIA YOUSSEF, medical educator; b. Giza, Egypt, June 8, 1965; MBBch, Cairo U., Egypt, 1987, MD in Chest Diseases, 1997. Prof. Kasr Al-Aini Faculty Medicine Cairo U., Egypt, 1994—, Taif U., Saudi Arabia, 2006—09. Cons. Saudi German Hosp., Riyadh, 2009—11; reviewer Internat. Chest & Allergic Diseases Jours. Named one of Best Staff Mem., Taif U. Fellow: Am. Coll. Chest Physicians; mem.: French Soc. Allergy and Clin. Immunology, European Acad. Allergy and Clin. Immunology, European Respiratory Soc., Am. Thoracic Soc. Achievements include research in chest diseases. Avocations: reading, languages. Home: 17 Al-Falah St Shehabe St Giza Al-Mohandesseine 12411 Egypt Personal E-mail: ehsan_fr@yahoo.fr.

SACCHINI, VIRGILIO, surgeon, educator; b. Italy, Mar. 31, 1956; MD, U. Milan, 1981. Surgeon Meml. Sloan Kettering Cancer Ctr., 2000—. Prof. surgery Cornell U., 2000—. Mem.: MSKCC. Office: 300 East 66 St New York NY 10021 Office Fax: 16468884921. Business E-Mail: sacchinv@mskcc.org.

SACERDOTE, ALAN SCOTT, endocrinologist; b. Mount Vernon, NY, Mar. 11, 1948; s. Paul Emil and Pearl Rita (Quittell) Sacerdote; m. Nancy R. Sacerdote, Feb. 7, 1971; children: Derek, Allison. BA, NYU, 1970; MD, N.Y. Med. Coll., 1974. Dir. diabetes/endocrine ctr. The Bklyn. Hosp. Ctr., 1979-83; chief adult endocrinology sect. Woodhull Med. and Mental Health Ctr., Bklyn., 1983—; asst. prof. medicine SUNY Health Scis. Ctr., Bklyn., 1979-92, clin. assoc. prof. medicine, 1992—2007, clin. prof. medicine, 2007—, NYU Sch. Medicine, 2009—; prof. medicine St. George's U. Sch. Medicine. Adj. prof. endocrinology PA Program L.I. U., Bklyn., 1980—; endocrine cons. Bklyn. VA Med. Ctr., 1979—; adv. bd. mem. Juvenile Diabetes Found., Bklyn., 1979—. Co-author: Hope and Destiny, A Patient's and Parent's Guide to Sickle Cell Disease, 2002, 2d edit., 2005; mem. editl. adv. bd.: Endocrine Today; mem. editl. adv. bd. Endocrine Practices, 2007; reviewer: Diabetes Care. Mem., spkrs. panel Physicians Com. for Responsible Medicine, Washington, 1990—. Grantee travel, Westwood-Squibb Pharms., 1996, Merck Pharms., 1994, Hoechst-Celanese Pharms. (now Aventis Pharms.), 1994, multi-ctr. clin. rsch., 1993. Fellow: ACP; mem.: Am. Diabetes Assn. (clin. soc., govt. rels. com.), The Endocrine Soc., Rosicrucian Order. Democrat. Jewish. Avocations: antiques, underwater photography. E-mail: WalrusA@netscape.net.

SACHA, ROBERT FRANK, osteopath, educator; b. East Chicago, Ind., Dec. 29, 1946; s. S. Frank John and Ann Theresa S.; m. Linda T. LePage, 1988; children: Joshua Jude, Josiah Gerard, Anastasia Levon, Jonah Bradley. BS, Purdue U., 1969; DO, Chgo. Coll. Osteo. Medicine, 1975; PharmD, Creighton U., 2004. Diplomate Am. Bd. Pediatrics, Am. Bd. Allery and Immunology. Pharmacist, asst. mgr. Walgreens Drug Store, East Chicago, Ind., 1969-75; intern David Grant Med. Ctr., San Francisco, 1975-76, resident in pediatrics, 1976-78; fellow in allergy and immunology Wilford Hall Med. Ctr., 1978-80; staff pediatrician, allergist Scott AFB (Ill.), 1980-83; practice medicine specializing in allergy and immunology Cape Girardeau, Mo., 1983—. Assoc. clin. instr. St. Louis U., 1980—; clin. instr. Purdue U., 1971-72, Pepperdine U., 1975-76, U. Tex.-San Antonio, 1978-80, assoc. clin. instr. So. Ill. U. Pres., Parent Tchrs. League; bd. gov. Chgo. Coll. Osteopathic Medicine. Maj. M.C. USAF, 1975-83, comdr. USNR. Named one of Top Pediatricians 2002-2003, Pediatric Allergy, Immunology. Fellow Am. Coll. Allergy, Am. Coll. Chest Physicians, Am. Acad. Pediatrics, Am. Acad. Allergy-Immunology, Am. Assn. Cert. Allergists; mem. ACP, AMA, Am. Acad. Allergy, Assn. Mil. Allergists, Am. Coll. Emergency Physicians, Mil. Surgeons and Physicians. Republican. Lutheran. Home and Office: 351 Kelley Ct Cape Girardeau MO 63701 Office Phone: 573-651-4155. E-mail: bsacha@charter.net.

SACHAR, DAVID BERNARD, gastroenterologist, educator; b. Urbana, Ill., Mar. 2, 1940; s. Abram Leon and Thelma (Horwitz) Sachar; m. Joanna Maud Belford Silver, Aug. 29, 1961; children: Mark Benson, Kenneth Hulbert Belford(dec.). BA magna cum laude, Harvard Univ., 1959, MD cum laude, 1963. Cert. Am. Bd. Internal Medicine, diplomate Am. Bd. Gastroenterology. Intern Beth Israel Hosp., Boston, 1963-65, resident in internal medicine, 1967-68; asst. chief clin. rsch. Pakistan SEATO Cholera Rsch. Lab., Dhaka, Bangladesh, 1965-67; resident in gastroenterology Mt. Sinai Hosp., NYC, 1968-70, dir. divsn. gastroenterology, 1983-99, vice chmn. dept. medicine, 1992-99, dir. emeritus, 1999—, Arnold P. Gold Found. prof. medicine, 2005—08; instr. to prof. medicine Mt. Sinai Sch. Medicine, NYC, 1970-92, first Burrill B. Crohn prof. medicine, 1992-99; Dr. Hyman J. Zimmerman Meml. lectr. Georgetown U. Med. Sch., 2009; master educator Inst. Med. Edn., 2010—; John N. Edson vis. prof. LI Coll. Hosp., 2011. Co-chmn. work group on inflammatory bowel disease NIH, 1973—75; expert adv. panel gastroenterology and nutrition U.S. Pharmacopeial Conv., 1980—85; co-founder, sec., treas. Burrill B. Crohn Rsch. Found., NYC, 1984—; chmn. rsch. devel. com. Nat. Found. Ileitis and Colitis, 1984—89; K. H. Koster meml. lectr. Danish Soc. Gastroenterology, 1992; mem. Gastroenterology Leadership Coun. Task Force Fellowship Curriculum, 1994; guest lectr. Swedish Soc. Gastroenterology, 1995; internat. state art lectr. Falk Symposia, Germany, 1996; twentieth ann. Norman Tanner meml. lectr. St. George's Hosp. Med. Sch., London, 1997; internat. state art lectr., Belgium, 98, Brit. Soc. Gastroenterology, 1998, World Congresses Gastroenterology, Austria, 1998, Turkish Soc. Gastroenterology, 1998, World Congresses Gastroenterology, Italy, 1999, Hungarian Soc. Gastroenterology, 1999, Hellenic Soc. Gastroenterology, 1999; chmn. GI adv. bd. Solvay Pharm., Inc., 2000—02; internat. state art lectr. Falk Symposia, Germany, 2000—02; 25th ann. Nana Svartz meml. lectr., Örebro, Sweden, 2000; co chmn. 40th ann. post grad. course Portuguese Soc. Gastroenterology, 2000, internat. state art lectr., Italy, Belgium, Israel, 05; internat. state art lectr., Italy, 01, Spanish Soc. Gastroenterology, 2007, State Sci. Ctr. Coloproctology, Moscow, 2007, England, 05, internat. state art lectr., Germany, Portugal, 03, Shanghai, 11; 50th anniversary lectr. Romanian Soc. Gastroenterology & Hepatology, 2008, Indian Soc. Gastroenterology, 2009; mem. GI adv. com. FDA, 2004—08, chmn., 2005—08; Dr. Albert M. Yunich Memorial Lectr. Albany Med Coll., 2007; Keynote lectr. 3rd Internat. Symp. Molecular Tech. Shahid Beheshti U. Med. Sci., Tehran, 2009; 1st Burrill B. Crohn mem. lectr., Cuenca, Ecuador, 09. Editor: seven books and monographs on gastroenterology; contbr. 250 chapters to books, articles to profl. jours. Trustee Bangladesh Coun. Asia Soc., NYC, 1972—75, Englewood Cliffs Bd. Edn., 1973—75; campaign com. Shulman for Congress, NJ, 2007—08. Capt. USPHS. Recipient Jacobi Medallion for Disting. Achievement, Mt. Sinai Alumni Assn., 1994, Alexander Richman Commemorative award for Humanism in Medicine, 1996, Norman Tanner medal, St. George's Hosp. Med. Sch., 1997, Gold Headed Cane award, 1997. Master: Am. Coll. Gastroenterology (program dir. com. 1991, Henry Baker Presdl. Lectr. 1989, Berk/Fise clin. achievement award 2005); fellow: ACP, Am. Gastroent. Assn. (first chmn. clin. tchg. project 1984—90, nominating com. 1993—94, chmn. immuno inflammatory disorders sectional nominating com. 1995, Disting. Educator award 1996, Found. Mentors Rsch. Scholar award honoree 2007); mem.: Gold Humanism Honor Soc., Internat. Orgn. Study of Inflammatory Bowel Disease (first Am. elected chmn. 1989—92, chmn. task force clin. phenomics 1992—2007), Crohn's and Colitis Found. Am. (grant rev. com. and coun. 1990—94, Disting. Svc. award 1991, NY Gov. medal 1992, 2007), Brazilian Soc. Gastroenterology (patron 2003), Internat. Guild Miniature Artisans (trustee 2004—07), Alpha Omega Alpha, Phi Beta Kappa. Achievements include co developer of oral rehydration therapy for diarrhea; development of resources and standards for clin. tchg. in gastroenterology; established Joanna and David B. Sachar International Award and Visiting Professorship in Inflammatory Bowel Disease. Avocations: piano. Office: Mt Sinai Med Ctr One Gustave L Levy Pl New York NY 10029 Business E-Mail: david.sachar@mountsinai.org.

SACHDEVA, GEETANJALI, research scientist; b. New Delhi, Aug. 12, 1967; PhD, Jawaharlal Nehru U., 1996. Scientist D Nat. Inst. Rsch. Reproductive Health ICMR, 1997. Recipient 10th Royan Internat. Rsch. award, Royan Inst., Young Scientist award, Indian Soc. Human Genetics; Young Scientist fellowship, Cellular and Molecular Biology, Hyderabad, Long Term Biotech. Overseas fellowship, Dept. Biotech. Govt. of India. Mem.: Proteomics Soc. India, Indian Soc. for Study Reproduction and Fertility. Avocations: reading, music. Office: Jehangir Merwanji St Parel Mumbai Maharashtra 400012 India Business E-Mail: sachdevag@nirrh.res.in.

SACHDEVA, SILONIE, dermatologist, consultant; b. Jalandhar, Punjab, India, Jan. 21, 1976; d. Anoop Singh and Harinder Kaur Sachdeva; m. Pawan Prasher, Aug. 6, 2005. MBBS, Punjabi U., Patiala, Punjab, 1999; MD, Govt. Med. Coll., Patiala, 2003. Sr. resident, dermatology M. M. Inst. Med. Scis. & Rsch., Mullana-Ambala, Haryana, India, 2003—05, Dayanand Med. Coll. and Hosp., Ludhiana, Punjab, 2006; observer, dermatology UT Southwestern Med. Sch., Dallas, 2006; rsch. fellow Arlington Ctr. Dermatology, 2007; cons. dermatologist and dermatosurgeon VASAL Hosp. and Apollo Clinics, Jalandhar, Punjab, 2008—09; cons. dermatologist Carolena Skin Laser & Rsch. Ctr., Jalandhar, Punjab, 2010—11. Contbr. scientific papers. Fellow: Internat. Soc. Dermatology (fellowship 2008); mem.: Asian Soc. Pigment Cell Rsch., Internat. League of Deramtological Soc., Contact and Occupl. Dermatoses forum, India, Assn. Cutaneous Surgeons, India, Indian Soc. Dermatologists, Venereologists and Leprologists. Personal E-mail: siloniederm@yahoo.com.

SACHS, BENJAMIN PAUL, medical educator, dean; b. London, May 26, 1951; MBBS, Imperial Coll., London, 1975; DPH, U. Toronto, Can., 1977; completed bus. mgmt. program, Harvard U. Bus. Sch., 1987. Residency in ob-gyn. and fellowship in maternal-fetal medicine Brigham & Women's Hosp.; vis. scientist Centers for Disease Control and Prevention; faculty mem. Harvard U.; dept. chmn. ob-gyn. Beth Israel Deaconess Med. Ctr.; Harold Rosenfield prof. ob-gyn. and reproductive biology Harvard U. Med. Ctr.; prof. Harvard U. Sch. Pub. Health; sr. v.p., dean, sch. medicine Tulane U., 2007—. Recipient The Joint Commn. Eisenberg Nat. award, Nat. Quality Forum, 2007, Healthcare Excellence award, Blue Cross Blue Shield, 2007, Spencer Foreman award, Assn. Academic Med. Ctr., 2010. Office: Tulane University Sch Medicine Office of Dean 1430 Tulane Ave New Orleans LA 70112 Business E-Mail: bsachs@tulane.edu. *

SACHS, DAVID HOWARD, surgeon, immunologist, educator; b. NYC, Jan. 10, 1942; s. Elliot and Elsie (Hurvitz) S.; m. Kristina Olsson, Mar. 15, 1969; children: Michelle, Jessica, Karin, Teviah. AB, Harvard U., 1963; DES, U. Paris, 1964; MD, Harvard U., Boston, 1968. Intern in surgery Mass. Gen. Hosp., Boston, 1968-69, resident in surgery, 1969-70, dir. transplantation biology rsch. ctr. surgery dept., 1991—; chief immunology br. Nat. Cancer Inst., Bethesda, Md., 1982-90; prof. surgery and immunology Harvard U. Med. Sch., 1991—. Capt. PHS, 1970-91. Recipient Roche Ernest Hodge Meml. award, Am. Soc. Transplantation, 2005. Avocations: gardening, fishing, windsurfing, skiing. Office: Mass Gen Hosp East Bldg 149-9019 13th St Boston MA 02129

SACHS, GEORGE, biology professor, physician; b. Austria; BSc, U. Edinburgh, 1957, MB, ChB, 1960, DSc, 1980; MD, U. Gothenburg, 1987. Instr. Albert Einstein Coll., 1961—62; rsch. assoc. Columbia U., 1962—63; asst. prof. medicine and physiology U. Ala., Birmingham, 1963—65, assoc. prof., 1965—70, prof., 1970—82, dir. membrane biology, 1974—82; prof. medicine and physiology, Wilshire chair in medicine UCLA, 1982—, co-dir. ctr. ulcer rsch. and edn., 1987—2002, dir. membrane biology lab., 1987—; sr. med. investigator VAGLAHS, LA, 1984—99, staff physician, 1999—. Contbr. articles to profl. jours. Recipient Beaumont Prize in Gatroenterology, Am. Gastroenterological Assn., 1985, Hoffman LaRoche award, 1982, Gairdner Found. Internat. award, 2004, Ismar Boas Vorlesung Medal, German Gastroenterological Assn., 1992, others; named Dr. Norman Frankel Scholar, U. Chgo., 2005, Evans Scholor, Boston U., 2005. Office: UCLA 405 Hilgard Ave Los Angeles CA 90095 Office Phone: 310-268-3923. E-mail: gsachs@ucla.edu. *

SACHS, JEFFREY DAVID, economist, educator; b. Detroit, Nov. 5, 1954; s. Theodore and Joan Sachs; m. Sonia Ehrlich Sachs; children: Lisa, Adam, Hannah. BA summa cum laude, Harvard U., 1976, MA in Econs., 1978, PhD in Econs., 1980; degree (hon.), St. Gallen U., Switzerland, 1990, Lingnan Coll. Hong Kong, 1998, Varba Econs. U., Bulgaria, 2000, Iona Coll. N.Y., 2000. Prof. internat. trade Harvard U., Cambridge, Mass., 1984—2002; prof. sustainable devel. Columbia U., NYC, 2002—, dir. Earth Inst., 2002—. Dir. Harvard Inst. Internat. Devel. Harvard U., 1995—99, dir. Ctr. for Internat. Devel., 1998—2002; chmn. commn. on macroecons. and health WHO, 2000—01; spl. advisor on the millennium devel. goals UN, NYC, 2002—; pres., co-founder Millennium Promise Alliance, 2005—; cons. in field. Co-author: Macroeconomics in the Global Economy, 1992; author: Poland's Jump to the Market Economy, 1993, Development Economics, 1997, Macroeconomics in the Global Economy, 2003, The End of Poverty: Economic Possibilities of Our Times, 2005, Common Wealth: Economics from a Crowded Planet, 2008. Named one of The World's Most Influential People, TIME mag., 2005, New York's Influentials, New York mag., 2006, America's Best Leaders, US News & World Report, 2008. Mem.: Inst. Medicine. Office: The Earth Inst at Columbia Univ 314 Low Libr MC 4327 535 West 116th St New York NY 10027 Office Phone: 212-854-8704.

SACHS, LEO, geneticist, educator; b. Leipzig, Germany, Oct. 14, 1924; s. Elijah and Louise (Lichtblau) Sachs; m. Pnina Salkind; 4 children. BSc, U. Wales, Bangor, 1948; PhD, Trinity Coll., Cambridge U., 1951; DHC (hon.), Bordeaux U., 1985; MD (hon.), Lund U., 1997. Rsch. scientist John Innes Inst., 1951 52; mem. sci. staff Weizmann Inst. Sci., Rehovot, Israel, 1952—, prof., chmn. genetics dept., 1962—, Otto Meyerhof prof. molecular biology, 1968—. Contbr. articles to profl. jours. Recipient Israel prize for natural sci., 1972, Rothschild prize in biol. scis., 1977, Wolf Found. prize in medicine, Israel, 1980, Sloan prize, GM Cancer Rsch. Found., 1980, Warren Alpert prize, Harvard Med. Sch., 1997, Emet prize in life scis., 2002. Fellow: Royal Soc., mem.: NAS (fgn. assoc.), Israeli Acad. Sci. & Humanities, Internat. Cytokine Soc. (hon. life). Office: Weizmann Inst Sci Dept Molecular Genetics Rm 226 Arthur & Rochelle Belfer Bldg Biomed Rsch Rehovot 76100 Israel Office Phone: 972 8 934 4068. Business E-Mail: leo.sachs@weizmann.ac.il. *

SACK, GEORGE HENRY, JR., molecular geneticist, internist; b. Balt., Apr. 17, 1943; s. George Henry and Sophia Ann (Philippi) S. BA, Johns Hopkins U., 1965, MD, 1968, PhD, 1974. Diplomate Bd. Med. Genetics, Bd. Med. Examiners. Intern Johns Hopkins Hosp., Balt., 1968-69, asst. resident, 1969-70, fellow genetics, 1975-76; rsch. fellow Johns Hopkins Sch. Medicine, Balt., 1970-73; asst. prof. dept. medicine Johns Hopkins U., Balt., 1976-84, assoc. prof. dept. medicine and biol. chemistry, 1984—; molecular biologist Kennedy Inst., Balt., 1982-93, dir. exec. health program, 1996—2006; med dir. Hopkins USA, 2007—. Contbr. articles to profl. jours. Maj. USAR, 1973-75. Andrew W. Mellon scholar Johns Hopkins U., 1976, Kennedy Found. scholar, 1982-85. Fellow Am. Coll. Med. Genetics; mem. AMA, AAAS, Am. Soc. Human Genetics, Phi Beta Kappa. Office: Johns Hopkins Sch Medicine Dept Biol Chemistry P-615 Baltimore MD 21205 Office Phone: 410-955-4621, 410-735-6605. Business E-Mail: gsack@jhmi.edu.

SACKETT, KAY MARIE, nursing consultant; b. Aug. 24, 1952; BSN, Temple U., 1974, EdD, 1985. Clin. prof. nursing U. Buffalo Sch. Nursing SUNY, 1998—2008; dir. nursing edn., nursing Wake Forest U. Bapt. Med. Ctr., 2008—10; pvt. practice, 2010—. Cons. Spyglass Consulting, 2000—10. Named Co-Vol. of Yr., Shepherd's Ctr. Winston-Salem, NC, 2010; grant, NC Bapt. Hosp. Found., Jack Miller Family Found. Fellow: Marine Biology Lab., Nat. Libr. Medicine Med. Informatics (Med. Informatics fellow); mem.: Healing Touch Internat., Phi Delta Kappa, Sigma Theta Tau. Avocations: travel, reading. Home: 3213 Grant St Richmond VA 23221 Personal E-mail: kay.sackett@gmail.com.

SACKIN, CLAIRE, retired social work educator; b. NYC, Oct. 1, 1925; d. Harry and Diana (Mednick) Gershfeld; m. Milton Sackin, Feb. 4, 1955; children: William, Daniel, David, m. Hon Sackin, Feb. 4, 1955 (dec.). BA, Hunter Coll., 1946; MEd, U. Pitts., 1968, MSW, 1972, PhD, 1976. Tenured tchr. jr. high sch., Bronx, N.Y., 1947-57; rsch. asst. U. Pitts., 1973, instr. dept. urban mgmt., 1974; rsch. assoc. U. Pitts. Sch. of Social Work, 1975-76, Health & Welfare Planning Assn., 1974; prof. social work, dir. social work program St. Francis U., Loretto, Pa., 1976-97, prof. emerita, 1997—. Registered trainer alcoholism specialists cert. program; mem. adv. bd. Cedar Manor Treatment Ctr., Cresson, Pa., 1994-95; mem. Pa. Gov.'s Coun. Alcoholism, 1980, Nat. Assn. People with AIDS; presenter in field. Contbr. articles to jours. Mem. NASW (social action com. Pa. chpt. 1983-85, mem. Del. Assembly 1984, eastern regional coalition liaison 1984), Coun. on Social Work Edn., Amyotrophic Lateral Sclerosis Assn., Alpha Delta Mu (nat. bd. dirs.). Avocations: reading, crossword puzzles, opera, gardening, travel. Home: 531 Sandrae Dr Pittsburgh PA 15243-1727 Office: St Francis U Loretto PA 15940 Personal E-mail: sackin.dsl@verizon.net, claire.sackin@verizon.com.

SACKS, ANITA M., psychotherapist, educator; b. NYC, May 18, 1943; d. David and Sylvia Sacks; m. Henry Adam Majewski, Apr. 22, 1979 (dec.); 1 stepchild, Jennifer Majewski. BA, CCNY, NYC, 1965; MSW, Hunter Coll. Sch. Social Work, NYC, 1967; grad., Inst. Psychoanalytic Tng. and Rsch., 1987. Cert. social worker N.Y., LCSW Conn.; cert. psychoanalyst N.Y. Therapist Karan Horney Clinic, NYC, 1967—68, Jewish Bd. of Guardians, 1968—77; pvt. practice, 1977—; therapist and supr. Ctr. Marital and Family Therapy, NYC, 1977—83; tchr. and supr. family therapy unit, clin. instr. psychiatry Med. Ctr NYU, Bellevue, 1984—. Clin. supr. Jewish Family Svc., Stamford, Conn., 1997—2001; supr. family therapy St. Lukes-Roosevelt Hosp., NYC, 2004; tchr., supr. Barrier Free Living, NYC, 1993—95. Contbr. articles to profl. jours. Mem. co-op bd. dir., 1992—94. Mem.: Inst. Psychoanalytic Tng. and Rsch., N.Y. U. Bellevue Psychiatric Soc., Nat. Assn. Social Work, Am. Family Therapy Assn., Phi Beta Kappa. Avocations: pet training and therapy, walking, listening to music. Office: #5B 41 W 96th St New York NY 10025 Home Phone: 212-663-5962; Office Phone: 212-865-6959.

SACKS, CHARLES BERNARD, psychiatrist, educator; b. Cleve., May 14, 1939; s. Jerry and Frances (Shifrin) S.; m. Lora Jane Glickman, May 2, 1993; children: Eliza, Aaron. BA, Ohio State U., 1961, MD, 1965. Staff psychiatrist Washington Vets. Hosp., 1971-77; asst. clin. prof. Georgetown U., Washington, 1971—; staff psychiatrist Reston Clinic, Fairfax City, Md., 1976-77, Drug Treatment Adminstrn., Washington, 1971-72, Washington Free Clinic, 1971-73, Arlington & Fairfax City Hosp., 1977-88, Group Health Assocs., Washington, 1984-86; psychiatrist pvt. practice, McLean, Va., 1977—, Greenbelt, Md., 1977—; dir. Chevy Chase Psychiat. Clinic, Washington, 1987-89, Mt. Vernon Mental Health Ctr., 1994—2008. Maj. U.S. Army, 1969-71. Decorated Bronze medal with Oak Leaf Cluster. Avocations: sailing, photography, music, reading, sports. also: 1313 Vincent Pl Mc Lean VA 22101-3615 Office Phone: 703-821-1017.

SACKS, HERBERT SIMEON, psychiatrist, educator, consultant; b. NYC, Nov. 29, 1926; s. Maxwell Lawrence and Anne (Edelstein) S.; m. Helen Margery Levin, Dec. 26, 1948; children: Eric Livingston, Katharine Bird, Douglas Lowell, Russell Avery AB magna cum laude, Dickinson Coll., 1948; MD, Cornell U., 1952. Diplomate Am. Bd. Psychiatry and Neurology and subspecialty Child and Adolescent Psychiatry. Clin. assoc. Western New Eng. Psychoanalytic Inst., New Haven, 1955-63; intern in pediatrics Yale New Haven Med. Ctr., 1952-53; jr. asst. resident in psychiatry Yale Psychiat. Inst., 1953-54; sr. asst. resident in psychiatry, USPHS fellow Yale-New Haven Med. Ctr., psychiat. out patient dept., 1954-55; USPHS fellow in child psychiatry Yale U. Child Study Ctr., 1955-57; clin. dir. Mid-Fairfield Child Guidance Ctr., Norwalk, Conn., 1957-59; cons. Expt. in Internat. Living, Putney, Vt., 1962-69; sr. cons. U.S. Peace Corps, Washington, 1962-69; cons. AID, U.S. Dept. State, Office of Sahel, West Africa, 1974-84, Neurosci. Consultation Group, Grosse Point Farms, Mich., 1984-94; clin. prof. child and adolescent psychiatry Child Study Ctr., Yale U. Sch. Medicine, New Haven. Co-investigator, co-dir. Senegal River pilot health research program, New Haven and West Africa, 1976-78, co-investigator, co-dir. health sector, design team Senegal River integrated devel. project, 1981-83; vis. lectr. Yale Coll., 1969-71; mem. com. reviewers Dept. Commerce Nat. Bur. Standards, Inst. for Computer Scis. and Tech., Washington, 1975-77; mem. exec. com. Nat. Commn. on Confidentiality of Health Records, 1975-80 Author: Hurdles: The Admissions Dilemma in American Higher Education, 1978; contbg. author chpts. in books, articles on confidentiality, juvenile justice, higher edn., issues of youth in transition, other topics; author monographs Mem. Conn. Juvenile Justice Commn., Hartford, 1975-80; bd. advisors Dickinson Coll., Carlisle, Pa., 1980-85. Served to lt. (j.g.) U.S. Navy, 1944-46; PTO Fellow AMA, ACPO, Am. Psychiat. Assn. (trustee 1988-94, v.p. 1994-96, pres. 1997-98), Am. Acad. Child and Adolescent Psychiatry, Am. Orthopsychiat. Assn., Am. Coll. Psychiatrists; mem. Conn. Psychiat. Soc. (pres. 1976-77), Conn. Coun. Child and Adolescent Psychiatrists (pres. 1972-73), World Fedn. for Mental Health, Phi Beta Kappa. Avocations: farming, photography, fishing, lawn bowling. Home: 110 Laurel Rd New Haven CT 06515-2426 Office: 260 Riverside Ave Westport CT 06880-4804 also: Yale U Child Study Ctr PO Box 207900 New Haven CT 06520-7900 Office Phone: 203-227-0996.

SACKS, JOEL GERALD, ophthalmologist, educator; b. Chgo., Sept. 14, 1939; s. Louis and Rose S.; m. Cynthia Ann Dana, June 10, 1967; children: Charles, David, Martha. BA, Northwestern U., 1960, MS, 1962, MD, 1963; MBA, U. Cin., 1986. Diplomate, Am. Bd. Ophthalmology. NIH spl. fellow Md. Med. Legal Found., Balt., 1967-68; rsch. fellow Johns Hopkins Sch. Medicine, Balt., 1968-69; asst. prof. to assoc. prof. Northwestern U., Chgo., 1969-77; prof., dir. dept. ophthalmology U. Cin., 1977-94, prof. emeritus ophthalmology, 2005—; pres. Ophthalmic Cons., Inc., Cin., 1977-94; clin. prof. surgery Mich. State U., 1994-97; v.p. med. affairs, dir. med. edn. Butterworth Hosp., Grand Rapids, Mich., 1994-97; v.p., chief med. officer Touro Infirmary, New Orleans, 1998-99; clin. prof. ophthalmology Tulane U., New Orleans, 2000—06, prof. emeritus, 2006—. Pres. Med. Ctr. Fund Cin., 1985-88, Univ. Health Plan, Inc., Cin., 1987-89. Co-author: Neuropathology of Vision: an Atlas, 1973; contbr. articles to sci. jours. Founding mem. Beth Adam: The Cin. Congregation Humanistic Judaism, 1980. Capt. U.S. Army, 1967-74. Fellow Am. Acad. Ophthalmology (Honor award 1982); mem. Phi Beta Kappa, Alpha Omega Alpha. Home: 47 Fairway Oaks Dr New Orleans LA 70131-3339 *

SACKS, OLIVER WOLF, neurologist, writer; b. London, July 9, 1933; Came to U.S., 1960; s. Samuel and Muriel Elsie (Landau) S. BA, U. Oxford, 1954; MA, BM, BCh, Middlesex Hosp., London, 1958; DHL (hon.), Georgetown U., 1990, Coll. Staten Island, CUNY, 1991; DS (hon.), Tufts U., 1991, N.Y. Med. Coll., 1991; DS (hon.), Med. Coll. Pa., 1992, Bard Coll., 1992, U. Turin, 2003. Intern in medicine, surgery and neurology Middlesex Hosp., 1958-60; rotating intern Mt. Zion Hosp., San Francisco, 1961-62; resident in neurology UCLA, 1962-65; I.D. fellow in neuropathology and neurochemistry Albert Einstein Coll. Medicine, NYC, 1965-66, instr. neurology, 1966-75, asst. prof., 1975-78, assoc. prof., 1978-85, clin. prof. neurology, 1985—2007; prof. clin. neurology and clin. psychiatry Columbia U. Med. Ctr., NYC, 2007—; Columbia Artist Columbia U., NYC, 2007—. Adj. prof. psychiatry NYU, 1992-; sci. advisor Inst. Music and Neurologic Function, Beth Abraham Hosp., 1995-; cons. neurologist Comprehensive Epilepsy Ctr., Mt. Sinai Med. Ctr., 1999-;

cons., speaker, lectr. in field; hon. lectureships in field. Author: Migraine, 1970, Awakenings, 1973, (Hawthornden prize 1975), A Leg To Stand On, 1984, The Man Who Mistook His Wife for a Hat, 1985, Seeing Voices: A Journey into the World of the Deaf, 1989 (Mainichi Pub. Culture award 1996), An Anthropologist on Mars, 1995 (George S. Polk award for mag. reporting 1994, Nat. Assn. Sci. Writers award 1994, Esquire Apple Waterstone's Book of Yr. 1995), The Island of the Color Blind, 1996, Uncle Tungsten: Memories of a Chemical Boyhood, 2001, Oaxaca Journal, 2002, Musicophilia: Tales of Music and the Brain, 2007, The Mind's Eye, 2010 Bd. mem. N.Y. Bot. Garden. Recipient Oskar Pfister award APA, 1988, Harold D. Vursell Meml. award Am. Acad. and Inst. Arts and Letters, 1989, Communicator of Yr. Royal Nat. Inst. Deaf, 1991, Lewis Thomas prize Rockefeller U., 2002, Sloan Found. award, 2002, Pub. Comm. award NSF, 2004; Guggenheim fellow, 1989, others. Fellow Am. Acad. Arts and Scis., Am. Acad. Arts and Letters, NY Acad. Scis. (hon.); mem. Am. Acad. Neurology (presdl. citation 1991), Am. Fern Soc., Am. Neurological Assn. (hon.), Assn. Brit. Neurologists (hon.), Brit. Pteridological Soc., NY Mineralogical Club, NY Stereoscopic Soc., Soc. Neurosci., NY Inst. Humanities, Alpha Omega Alpha. Office: 2 Horatio St Apt 3G New York NY 10014-1638 also: Columbua U Med Ctr Neurological Inst of NY 710 W 168th St New York NY 10032 Office Phone: 212-633-8373. E-mail: mail@oliversacks.com, os2177@columbia.edu.

SADAH, ALAN Y., urologist; b. Mar. 10, 1961; m. Belmina Michael; children: Jacob, Alana. BS in Biology, U. Ill., Chgo., 1984; MD, Finch U., 1988. Diplomate Am. Bd. Urology. Resident gen. surgery U. Ill., Chgo., 1988—90; resident urology SUNY Stony Brook U. Hosp., Northpoint VA Med. Ctr., 1991—95; mem. staff Chgo. Prosthetic Ctr., Westmont, Ill., 1995—99, Unite Shock Wave Svcs., Des Plaines, Ill., 1995—99, Parkside Urol. Ctr., West Park Ridge and LaGrange, Ill., 1995—99, Oak Park (Ill.) Hosp., 1995—99, West Lake Hosp., 1995—99, Swedish Covenant Hosp., 1995—99, West Suburban Hosp., 1995—99, Lafayette (La.) Gen. Hosp., 1999—2000, Our Lady of Lourdes Hosp., Lafayette, 1999—2000, Acadiana Med. Group, Crowley, 1999—2000; clin. instr. surgery and family practice La. State U. Med. Ctr., Lafayette, 1997—2000; clin. urologist Am. Legion Hosp., Crowley, 1999—2000; clin. instr. West Suburban Hosp., 2001—, Advanced Urology Ctr., Forest Park, Ill., 2001—. Lectr. in field. Contbr. articles to profl. jours. Mem.: ACS, Acadia Parish Med. Soc., La. State Med. Soc., La. Urologic Soc., Am. Assn. Clin. Urologists, Am. Urol. Assn., U. Ill. Alumni Assn., Chgo. Med. Sch. Alumni Assn., Golden Key Nat. Honor Soc., Phi Kappa Phi, Phi Theta Kappa. Avocations: art, music, sports. Office: Advanced Urology Ctr PO Box 99 Forest Park IL 60130-0099

SADANA, AJIT, chemical engineer, educator; b. Rawalpindi, India, Feb. 14, 1947; arrived in US, 1980; s. Jai Chand and Jinder Sadana; m. Lopa Mudra Sadana, Jan. 16, 1953; children: Neeti, Richa. B, Indian Inst. Tech., 1969; M of Chem. Engring., U. Del., 1972, PhD, 1975. Project engr. Environengineering, Inc., Somerville, NJ, 1974—75; sr. scientific officer Nat. chem. Lab., Pune, India, 1975—80; assoc. prof. chem. engring. U. Miss., University, 1981—90, prof., 1990—. Vis. assoc. prof. Auburn U., Ala., 1980—81; engr. duPont, Inc., Newark, 1989; sr. fellow Naval Rsch. Lab., Washington, 1990, disting. fellow, 91; cons. in field. Author: Biocatalysis: Fundamentals of Enzyme Deactivation Kinetics, 1991, Bioseparations, 1997, Biosensors, 2002, 6th edit., 2010. Avocations: gardening, tennis. Home: 229 St Andrews Cir Oxford MS 38655 Office: U Miss Chem Engring Dept University MS 38677-1848 Home Phone: 662-513-6266; Office Phone: 662-915-5349. Business E-Mail: cmsadana@olemiss.edu.

SADATI, SAM S., dentist; m. Olivia Sadati; children: Sarah, Nadia. Grad. with honors, Creighton U., Omaha, 1992; postgrad in Esthetic Dentistry, U. Fla.; studied in Periodontal Esthetics, Atlantic Coast Dental Rsch. Clinic, studied in Dental Implantology, studied in Prosthetic Restoration and Dental Implantology; studied in Orthodontic Tng., US Dental Inst. Diplomate Am. Bd. of Cosmetic Dentistry. Fellow Acad. of Gen. Dentistry. Recipient gold medal, Am. Acad. of Cosmetic Dentistry's, 2003—07. Fellow: Internat. Acad. for Dental Facial Esthetics, Am. Acad. of Cosmetic Dentistry; mem.: Palm Beach County Dental Assn., Fla. Dental Assn., Am. Acad. of Implant Dentistry, ADA. Office: The Sadati Center for Aesthetic Dentistry 10140 Forest Hill Blvd 140 West Palm Beach FL 33414 Office Phone: 888-873-3558. Office Fax: 561-753-8585.

SADEGHI-NEJAD, ABDOLLAH, pediatrician, educator; b. Meshed, Iran, Apr. 29, 1938; s. Abdolhossein and Azizeh (Jabbari) S.-N.; m. Marion M. Marquardt, Jan. 26, 1974; children: Nathan R., Adrienne R. BA, Beloit Coll., 1960; MS in Pathology, U. Chgo., 1964, MD, 1964. Diplomate Am. Bd. Pediatrics. Intern then resident U. Chgo., 1964-67; fellow pediatric endocrinology U. Calif., San Francisco, 1969-70, Tufts Med. Ctr., 1967—69; from asst. prof. to prof. pediatrics Tufts U., Boston, 1970—; chief pediat. endocrinology and metabolism divsn. Tufts Med. Ctr., 1989—. Author and co-author books and articles. Mem. town meeting Town of Brookline, Mass., 1987-2001, 2005—, mem. adv. com., 1993-99; founding mem. Friends of Lost Pond. Fellow Am. Acad. Pediats.; mem. Am. Pediat. Soc., Am. Diabetes Assn., Endocrine Soc., European Soc. Pediatric Rsch., Pediat. Endocrine Soc., Soc. Pediat. Rsch. Office: Tufts Med Ctr 800 Washington St Boston MA 02111-1526 Office Phone: 617-636-5335.

SADICK, NEIL SCOTT, dermatologist; b. Bronx, NY, June 1, 1951; s. Harry and Shirley (Tompkins) Sadick; 1 child, Sydney. BA, SUNY, Binghamton, 1973; MD, SUNY, Syracuse, 1977. Diplomate Am. Bd. Internal Medicine, 1980, Am. Bd. Dermatology, 1983, Am. Acad. Cosmetic Surgery, 2000, Am. Bd. Hair Restoration Surgery, 2001. Pvt. practice, NYC, 1983—; mem. adv. bd. Dermatologic Soc. Greater NY, 1994—; clin. prof. dermatology Cornell U, Monroe Coll. Surg. advisor Archives Dermatology; global med. advisor Christian Dior Beauty; guest lectr. at med. seminar classes and workshops worldwide. Author: (book) Your Hair, Helping to Keep It, 1994; asst. editor (jour.) Jour. Am. Acad. Dermatology, 1994—; author: (book) Sclerotherapy of Varicose Veins, 1996; asst. editor (jour.) Jour. Aesthetic and Cosmetic Surgery, —; contbr. several articles in peer-reviewed scientific jours., chapters to books. Mem.: Internat. Soc. Hair Restoration Surgery (bd. examiner), Cosmetic Surgery Found. (pres.), Am. Soc. Dermatological Surgery (bd. dirs.), Am. Cancer Soc. (summer fellow 1977), Manhattan Met. Dermatology Soc. (pres. 1995—96), NY Acad. Medicine, Dermatology Found. (vice chmn. 1993—), Am. Soc. Cosmetic Surgery (bd. dirs.,), Am. Acad. Dermatology (adv. bd. 1995—), Dermatologic Soc. Greater NY (adv. bd. 1994, pres. 1995—96), Am. Coll. Phlebology. (pres. 2002—04, bd. dir., Jobst award 1990), LI Dermatology Soc. Avocations: tennis, travel. Office: Sadick Dermatology 911 Park Ave Ste 1A New York NY 10075 Home Phone: 212-288-8502; Office Phone: 212-772-7242. Business E-Mail: nssderm@sadickdermatology.com.

SADOCK, BENJAMIN JAMES, psychiatrist, educator; b. NYC, Dec. 22, 1933; s. Samuel William and Gertrude S.; m. Virginia Alcott, Oct. 20, 1963; children: James William, Victoria Anne. AB, Union Coll., 1955; MD, N.Y. Med. Coll., 1959. Rotating intern Albany (N.Y.) Hosp., 1959-60; resident Bellevue Psychiat. Hosp., NYC, 1960-63; instr. psychiatry Southwestern Med. Sch., Dallas, 1964-65, N.Y. Med. Coll., NYC, 1965-67, asst. prof., 1967-71, assoc. prof., 1972-74, prof., 1975-80, dir. student health psychiatry, 1980—; prof. psychiatry NYU Sch Medicine, 1981-99, Menas S. prof. psychiatry, 2000—, vice chmn. dept. psychiatry, 1984—2008, faculty scholar, 2000—. Hon. physician Lenox Hill Hosp.; attending psychiatrist Tisch Univ. Hosp. of NYU Med. Ctr., Bellevue Hosp.; cons. psychiatrist Franklin Delano Roosevelt VA Hosp., 1970-78, U.S. Dept. State, 1980-81, P.R. Inst. Psychiatry, 1976-80; examiner Am. Bd. Psychiatry and Neurology, 1970-80; mem. conf. on recert. Am. Bd. Med. Spltys.-Am. Psychiat. Assn., 1974; mem. Commn. on Continuing Edn. in Psychiatry, NIMH-Am. Psychiat. Assn., 1974-75. Co-author: Comprehensive Group Psychotherapy, 1971, 3d edit., 1993, 4th edit., 2010, 5th edit., 2011, The Sexual Experience, 1976, Pocket Handbook of Clinical Psychiatry, 1st edit., 1991, 2nd edit., 2003, 3rd edit., 2008, 5th edit., 2010, Comprehensive Glossary of Psychiatry and Psychology, 1991, Pocket Handbook of Drug Treatment in Psychiatry, 1992;: 4th edit., 2005, Pocket Handbook of Psychiatric Emergency Medicine, 1993, Pocket Handbook of Primary Care Psychiatry, 1996, Comprehensive Textbook of Psychiatry, 8th edit., 2005, 9th edit., 2009, Synopsis of Psychiatry, 10th edit., 2007; contbr. articles to profl. jours., chapters to books. Fellow Am. Psychiat. Assn. (treas. N.Y. County dist. br. 1973-76, mem. conf. on psychiatry and med. edn. 1967), N.Y. Acad. Medicine, A.C.P.; mem. AMA, Med. Soc. County and State N.Y., Am. Group Psychotherapy Assn., World Psychiat. Assn., Psychiat. Soc. N.Y. Med. Coll. (founder, pres. 1975-79), N.Y. Med. Coll. Alumni Assn. (gov. 1965-90), NYU-Bellevue Psychiat. Soc. (pres. 1981—2009), Alpha Omega Alpha. Achievements include research in psychiatric education, individual psychotherapy, anxiety disorders, depressive disorders, sexual disorders. Office: 4 E 89th St New York NY 10128-0636 also: NYU Med Ctr 550 1st Ave New York NY 10016-6402 E-mail: bjs6@nyu.edu.

SADOFF, ROBERT LESLIE, psychiatrist, educator; b. Mpls., Feb. 8, 1936; s. Max and Rose C. (Karroll) S.; m. Joan A Handleman, June 21, 1959; children: Debra, David, Julie, Sherry. BA, U. Minn., 1956, BS, 1957, MD, 1959; MS, UCLA, 1963. Intern L.A. VA Hosp., 1959—60; resident in psychiatry UCLA, 1960—63; asst. prof. psychiatry Temple U., Phila., 1966—72; clin. prof. U. Pa., Phila., 1972—; pvt. practice Jenkintown, Pa., 1965—. Lectr. law Villanova U., 1972-85. Author: (with Marvin Lewis) Psychic Injuries, 1975, Forensic Psychiatry, 1975, 2d edit., 1988, Legal Issues in the Care of Psychiatric Patients, 1982, Violence and Responsibility, 1988, (with Robert I. Simon) Psychiatric Malpractice, 1992; editor: Psychiatric Clinics of North America, 1984, Mental Health Experts, 2006, 2nd edit. 2007, Crime and Mental Illness, 2008, Issues in Pharmacy, Law of Ethics, 2008, Ethical Issues in Forensic Psychiatry, 2010. Bd. dirs. Joseph T. Peters Inst., Phila., 1980-92. Capt. M.C., U.S. Army, 1963-65. Recipient Earl Bond award U. Pa., 1979, VII ann. Nathaniel Winkelman award Phila. Psychiat. Ctr., 1988, Manfred Guttmacher award, 2993, Isaac Ray award Am. Psychiatric Assn., 2006, Disting. Alumni award, U. Minn Med. Sch., 2010, Deans Spl. award, U. Pa., 2008, Presdl. award, Pa. Psychiatry Soc., 2010. Fellow: Am. Coll. Legal Medicine, Am. Psychiat. Assn. (Manfred Guttmacher award 1993); mem.: Internat. Acad. Law and Mental Health (Philippe Pinel award 1995), Internat. Soc. for Philos. Enquiry (mentor 1987—), Am. Acad. Psychiatry and Law (pres. 1971—73), Am. Coll. Psychiatrists, Am. Red Magen David for Israel (nat. pres. 1986—2001). Avocation: collecting antique books. Office: The Pavilion Ste 326 261 Old York Rd Jenkintown PA 19046 Office Phone: 215-887-6144. Personal E-mail: sadoffbobsadoff@aol.com.

SADOSKY, ALESIA BETH, research scientist, director; b. Hartford, Conn., Oct. 21, 1962; BS, U. Vt., 1984; PhD, Pa. State Coll. Medicine, 1990; MPH, Columbia U., 1998; MBA, U. Conn., 2006. With Columbia U. Coll. Physicians & Surgeons, 1990—94; postdoc fellow Columbia U., 1995; rsch. scientist NYC Dept. Health, 1995—2000; dir. Pfizer Inc., 2000—; rsch. scientist, dir. Pa. State Coll. Medicine. Mem.: Am. Pain Soc. Achievements include research in health economics. Avocation: running. Office: Global Health Economics & Outcomes Research Pfizer Inc 235 East 42nd St New York NY 10017 E-mail: alesia.sadosky1@pfizer.com.

SADOUGHI, BABAK, physician, researcher; b. Beirut, Aug. 27, 1975; s. Hossein Abolghassem Sadoughi and Tahereh Sarkeshikian; m. Mahsa Mehrazin Sadoughi. MD summa cum laude, U. Pierre Marie Curie, Paris, 2000. House staff Assistance Publique - Hopitaux de Paris, Paris, 2000—04; rsch. assoc., program coord. Montefiore Med. Ctr. Albert Einstein Coll. Medicine, Bronx, NY, 2004—, house officer, dept. otorhinolaryngology, 2007—. Contbr. articles to profl. jours. Cons. Support for People with Oral and Head and Neck Cancer, Locust Valley, NY, 2005—05. Scholar, Mission Interuniversitaire Coordination Exchs. Franco-Ams. & U. Pa., 2000. Mem.: ARO, ACS, AMA, MSSNY, Triological Soc., AAOHNS, Mensa. Achievements include research in surgical training to reduce errors using virtual reality. Office: Montefiore Med Ctr 3400 Bainbridge Ave 3rd Floor Bronx NY 10467 Home: 1755 York Ave Apt 2N New York NY 10128 Office Fax: 718-405-9014.

SADOVE, ALAN MICHAEL, plastic surgeon; b. Chgo., Oct. 8, 1948; s. Max Samuel and Ethel (Segall) S.; m. Armin Altshuler, June 1, 1974; children: Scott Lawrence, Julia Claire. AB, Washington U., 1970; MD, Loyola U., Maywood, Ill., 1974; MS, U. Ill., Chgo., 1977. Intern Presbyn.-St. Luke's Hosp., Chgo., 1974—75, resident in gen. surgery, 1975—79; resident in plastic surgery U. Va., Charlottesville, 1979—81; fellow in plastic surgery NYU-Inst. Reconstructive Plastic Surgery, NYC, 1981—82; assoc. prof. surgery Ind. U. Sch. Medicine, 1982—; chief plastic surgery service, James Whitcomb Riley Hosp. for Children Ind. U. Med. Ctr., 1982—, med. dir. Burn Ctr., 1982—, dir. Oral-Facial Clinic, 1983—, med. dir. Craniofacial Anomalies team, 1982—; cons. VA Med. Ctr., Indpls.; mem. attending staff Wishard Meml. Hosp., Indpls. Mem. American Bd. Plastic Surgery (bd. dirs. 2003-10, chair), Chgo. Med. Soc., Ill. Med. Soc., AMA, ACS, Am. Soc. Plastic and Reconstructive Surgeons, Am. Cleft Palate Assn., Am. Burn Assn., Assn. Acad. Surgery, Am. Soc. Maxillofacial Surgeons, Marion County Med. Soc., Ind. State Med. Soc., Ohio Valley Soc. Plastic and Reconstructive Surgery, Sigma Xi. Office: Riley Towers Rm 1172 702 Barnhill Dr Indianapolis IN 46202-5128 also: Meridian Plastic Surgery Ctr 170 W 106th St Indianapolis IN 46290

SADOVSKY, RICHARD, medical educator; b. Yonkers, NY, Nov. 3, 1948; MD, SUNY, 1974; MS, NYU, 1988. Assoc. prof. SUNY-Downstate Med. Ctr., 1977—. Fellow: Am. Acad. Family Physicians. Avocations: tennis, music. Office: 450 Clarkson Ave Brooklyn NY 11203 Office Fax: 718-270-2125. Business E-Mail: richard.sadovsky@downstate.edu.

SADUN, ALFREDO ARRIGO, neuro-ophthalmologist, scientist, educator; b. New Orleans, Oct. 23, 1950; s. Elvio H. and Lina (Ottoleghi) S.; m. Debra Leigh Rice, Mar. 18, 1978; children: Rebecca Eli, Elvio Aaron, Benjamin Maxwell. BS, MIT, 1972; PhD, Albert Einstein Med. Sch., Bronx, NY, 1976, MD, 1978. Intern Huntington Meml. Hosp. U. So. Calif., Pasadena, 1978—79; resident Harvard U. Med. Sch., Boston, 1979—82, HEED Found. fellow in neuro-ophthalmology Mass. Eye and Ear Inst., 1982—83, instr. ophthalmology, 1983, asst. prof. ophthalmology, 1984; dir. residential tng. U. So. Calif. Dept. Ophthalmology, LA, 1984—85, 1990—2008; asst. prof. ophthalmology and neurosurgery U. So. Calif., LA, 1984—87, assoc. prof., 1987—90, full prof., 1990—, mem. internal review bd., F. Thornton endowed chair, prof. vision rsch., 2000—. Prin. investigator Howe Lab. Harvard U., Boston, 1981-84, E. Doheny Eye Inst., L.A., 1984—; examiner Am. Bd. Ophthalmology; mem. Nat. Residency Rev. Com. for Accreditations, 1993—, chmn., 1998—; mem. internal rev. bd. U. So. Calif.; mem. sci. exec. bd. K. Rasmussen Found.; mem. sci. adv. bd. Internat. Found. for Optic Nerve Diseases. Author: Optics for Ophthalmologists, 1988, New Methods of Sensory Visual Testing, 1989, 4 books; editor: Ophthalmology, 2000, Neuroprotection: Implications for Eye Disease, 2001; contbr. 250 articles to profl. jours., 70 chpts. to books. Recipient Pecan D. award, 1988—92, Rsch. to Prevent Blindness Sr. Investigator award, 1996—97, 1996, Lighthouse Internat. Pizart award, 1999, James Adams scholar, 1990—91, Sr. Investigator award, 1999—2000, Decade medal, Cuban Nat. Acad. Scis., Bradley Straatsma award, Am. Acad. Ophthalmology, 2003, Silver Fellow award, Assn. Rsch. Vision & Ophthalmogy, 2009. Fellow Am. Acad. Ophthalmology Neuro-Ophthalmologists, Assn. Rsch. in Vision and Ophthalmology; mem. NIH (Med. Scientists Tng. award 1972-78), Am. Assn. Anatomists, Assn. Univ. Prof. Ophthalmology (assoc.), Am. Bd. Ophthalmology (rep. to residency rev. com. 1994-2001), Soc. to Prevent Blindness, Nat. Eye Inst. (New Investigator Rsch. award 1983-86, rsch. grants 1988-91, 93-2002), Soc. Neuroscis., N.Am. Neuro-Ophthal. Soc. (chmn. membership com. 1990—, v.p. 1994—). Avocation: writing. Home: 2478 Adair St San Marino CA 91108-2610

SAEBO, ARVE, retired gastroenterological surgeon; b. Molde, Norway, Mar. 19, 1939; s. Asbjoern and Borghild (Oterholm) S.; m. Brit Olene Friestad, July 31, 1965; children: Asbjoern, Oystein, Sindre. Grad., Molde Gymnasium, 1958; MD, U. Oslo, 1966; DMS, U. Bergen, 1995. Diplomate in Gen. Surgery, Gastroenterol. Surgery. Resident Kristiansund County Hosp., Norway, 1968-70, Voss County Hosp., Norway, 1970-72, Akershus Ctr. Hosp., Nordbyhagen, Norway, 1972-76; cons. Lillestrom (Norway) Hosp., 1976-77; sr. resident Bergen (Norway) Univ. Hosp., 1977-81; cons. Bergen Casualty Dept., 1981-84, Volda County Hosp., Norway, 1984-85, Laksevag Hosp., Bergen, 1985-88, Molde Hosp., 1988—2004. Cpl. Norwegian Royal Guard, 1959. Mem. Norwegian Surg. Soc., Nordic Surg. Soc. Lutheran. Avocations: photography, painting.

SAE BYEOL, CHOI, surgeon, educator; b. Geochang, July 16, 1977; MD, Korea U., 2002, D, 2008. Surgeon, clin. instr. Yonsei U. Coll. Medicine, Severance Hosp., 2007—08, Korea U. Guro Hosp., 2009—. Mem.: Korean Assn. Hepato-Biliary-Pancreas Surgery, Korean Surg. Soc., Korean Med. Assn. Avocations: music, skiing. Office: 80 Gurogu Gurodong Seoul 152-703 Republic of Korea

SAEKI, TAKAKO, physician, director; b. Nagaoka, Japan, Dec. 1, 1960; MD, Niigata U., PhD, 1985. Chief Dept. Internal Medicine, Nagaoka Red Cross Hosp., 1995. Office: 2-297-1 Senshu Nagaoka Niigata 9402085 Japan Business E-Mail: saekit@nagaoka.jrc.or.jp.

SAEKI, TOHRU, science educator; b. Nagasaki, Japan, Oct. 10, 1965; married. PhD, Kyoto U., Japan, 1993. Asst. prof. Kyoto Prefectural U., Kyoto, 1995—2008. Office: Kyoto Prefectural Univ Nakaragi Shimogamo Sakyo-ku Kyoto 606-8522 Japan Office Phone: 81-75-703-5663. Business E-Mail: tsaeki@kpu.ac.jp.

SAEZ-DE-OCARIZ, MARIMAR, dermatologist; b. Mex. City, Nov. 25, 1971; MD, Mexican Sch. Medicine, La Salle U., 1995. Cert. dermatologist Hosp. Gen. Dr. Manuel Gea González, UNAM, 2000. Attending physician dermatology dept. Hosp. Gen. Dr. Manuel Gea González, 2001—02, cons. pediat. dermatology, 2002—; attending physician dermatology dept., adj. prof. pediat. dermatology, immunogenetics pediat. dermatologists Nat. Inst. Pediat., 2002—, adj. prof. dermatology, pediat. dermatology, 2006—. Recipient Brother Miguel medal, La Salle U., Academic Excellence prize, Upjohn Pharmaceutics, Gea-PUIS Rsch. prize, Hosp. Gen. Dr. Manuel Gea Gonzalez and PUIS. Mem.: Med. Soc. Hosp. Angeles del Pedregal, Ibero L.Am. Coun. Dermatology, Med. Assn. Nat. Inst. Pediat., Latinoamerican Soc. Pediat. Dermatology, Mexican Coll. Pediat. Dermatology. Avocations: reading, singing, running. Office: Insurgentes Sur 3700 C Insurgentes Cuicuilco Coyoacan Mexico City 04530 Mexico Office Fax: 5255 1045528. Business E-Mail: mariadelmar71@prodigy.net.mx.

SAFA, GILLES LOUIS, dermatologist; b. Nov. 11, 1966; s. Georges and Antoinette Safa; m. Sophie Ricordel, Aug. 14, 2002; children: Louis, Valentin. MD, U. Rouen, France, 1996. Cert. dermatologist U. Hosp. Rouen, 1996. Chief of svc, dept. dermotology Hosp. Ctr. St. Brieuc, St. Brieuc, France, 1998—. Fellow: Am. Acad. Dermatology (life). Office: Hosp Ctr St Brieuc 10 rue Marcel Proust 22000 St Brieuc France Office Fax: 33296017012. E-mail: gilles.safa@ch-stbrieuc.fr.

SAFAI, BIJAN, physician, investigator; b. Ardestan, Iran, Mar. 26, 1940; came to U.S., 1968; s. Abdol-Khalegh Safai and Kanom-Sadat Sadjaddi; m. Vera Plaskon, Sept. 16, 1978; 1 child: Matthew. MD, Tehran U., Iran, 1965; DSc, U. Gutenburg, Sweden, 1981. Diplomate Am. Bd. Dermatology, Am. Bd. Internal Medicine. Intern Nassau County Med. Ctr., East Meadow, NY, 1968-69; resident N.Y.U. Med. Coll. VA Hosp., NYC, 1969-70; resident in dermatology N.Y.U. Med. Coll., NYC, 1971-73; fellow in immunology Sloan-Kettering Inst. for Cancer & Allied Diseases, NYC, 1973-74; from asst. attending physician to chief dermatology svc. Meml. Hosp., NYC, 1974-93; from assoc. to attending physician in dermatology N.Y. Hosp., NYC, 1980-93; dir. dermatology Westchester County Med. Ctr., Valhalla, NY, 1993—; from asst. prof. to prof. in medicine/dermatology Cornell U. Med. Coll., NYC, 1974-93; prof., chmn. dept. dermatology N.Y. Med. Coll., NYC, 1993—, prof. dept. microbiology and immunology, 1994—. Teaching clin. asst. in dermatology NYU Med. Coll, N.Y.C., 1973-74; adj. mem. Rockefeller U., N.Y.C., 1982-84; rsch. assoc. Sloan-Kettering Inst. for Cancer and Allied Diseases, N.Y.C., 1977-79, asst. mem., 1979-83, assoc. mem., 1983-88; assoc. mem. Memorial Sloan-Kettering Cancer Ctr., N.Y.C., 1983-88, mem. 1988-93; mem. grad. sch. med. scis. N.Y. Med. Coll., Valhalla, 1994—; mem. adv. bd. Skin Cancer Found., 1982—; sec. dermatology sect. N.Y. Acad Medicine, 1988-89, chmn. 1989-90; mem. med. adv. bd. Cancer Rsch Instn., 1997—. Mem. editl. bd. Cancer Investigation, 1984-88, AIDS Rsch. and Human Retroviruses, 1986-90, Jour. of Acquired Immune Deficiency Syndromes, 1988—; contbr. numerous articles on immunodermatology to profl. jours. Mem. AIDS adv. task force, NCI/NIH, 1982-85; mem. AIDS Etiology task force, NCI, 1982-85; mem. ad hoc study sect. for AIDS, NIH, 1982-88; mem. spl. dermatology rev. group, GM2 study sect., NIH, 1990-96; mem. spl. rev. team NCI Intramural Rev., Lab. of Tumor cell Biology, 1987, 92, Medicine br., NCI, 1996; mem. study sect. on HIV, NCI, 1996; mem. spl. rev. group FDA Intramural Rev., 1995. Mem. AMA, Internat. Soc. Tropical Dermatology, Am. Fedn. for Clin. Rsch., Am. Acad. Dermatology (mem. AIDS com. 1989-91, task force on cutaneous oncology 1988-9, mem. adv. coun. 1988-91), Am. Dermatol. Soc. for Allery and Immunology, Soc. for Investigative Dermatology, Med. Soc. of State of N.Y., Med. Soc. of County of N.Y., N.Y. State Soc. Dermatology, Dermatol. Soc. of Greater N.Y., N.Y. County Health Svc. Rev. Orgn., N.Y. Acad. Scis., N.Y. Dermatol. Soc. (pres 1990-91, sec., treas. 1989-90), Dermatology Found., Z & E Fisher Med. Found. (pres. 1993—). Home: 340 E 64th St New York NY 10021-7503 Office: NY Med Coll Dept Dermatology Valhalla NY 10595 also: 625 Park Ave New York NY 10021-6545 Office Phone: 212 988 8918. Personal E-mail: safai@aol.com.

SAFFIOTTI, UMBERTO, pathologist; b. Milan, Jan. 22, 1928; came to U.S., 1960, naturalized, 1966; s. Francesco Umberto and Maddalena (Valenzano) S.; m. Paola Amman, June 21, 1958; children: Luisa M., Maria Francesca. MD cum laude, U. Milan, 1951, sply. diploma occupational medicine cum laude, 1957. Intern Inst. Pathol. Anatomy U. Milan, 1951-52, asst. to chmn. occupational medicine, chief lab. pathology, Inst. Occupational Medicine, 1956-60, fellow Inst. Gen. Pathology, 1957-60; rsch. asst. oncology, rsch. assoc. Chgo. Med. Sch., 1952-55, from asst. prof. to prof. oncology, 1960-68; mem. staff Nat. Cancer Inst., NIH, Bethesda, Md., 1968—, assoc. dir. carcinogenesis, 1968-76, chief lab. exptl. pathology, 1974-98, acting head Registry of Exptl. Cancers, 1988-98; scientist emeritus, 1998—; adj. prof., Environ. & Occ. Hlth. The George Washington U., Washington, 2000—07. Mem. pathology B study sect., NIH, 1964-68; former mem. various adv. coms. govt. agys.; mem. cancer prevention com. Internat. Union Against Cancer, 1959-66, panel on carcinogenicity, 1963-66; chmn. ad hoc com. evaluation low levels environ. carcinogens HEW, 1969-70. Co-editor books; contbr. articles to profl. jours. Bd. dirs. Rachel Carson Trust, 1976-79. Recipient Career Devel. award NIH, 1965-68, Superior Svc. Honor award HEW, 1971, Pub. Interest Sci. award Environ. Def. Fund, 1977, Spl. Recognition award USPHS, 1980 Fellow NYAS; mem. AAAS, Am. Assn. Cancer Rsch. (pres. Chgo. chpt. 1966-67), Am. Soc. Investigative Pathology, Soc. Toxicology, Sigma Xi. Democrat. Home: 5114 Wissioming Rd Bethesda MD 20816-2259 Office: NIH Nat Cancer Inst 6116 Executive Blvd Rm 7212 Bethesda MD 20892-2259 Business E-Mail: saffiotti@nih.gov.

SAFRONOV, DENIS LEONIDOVICH, pediatrician; b. Moldova, June 23, 1981; Magister, Ivanovo State Med. Acad., 2005. Dept. pediatrician neurology Russian Med. Acad. Postgrad. Edn., 2006—. Home: Kurkovaya St 11/49 Tula 300044 Russia Personal E-mail: d.l.s@rambler.ru.

SAFYER, STEVEN MICHAEL, hospital administrator; b. NYC, Feb. 16, 1949; m. Pamela Marcus; 2 children. MD, Albert Einstein Coll. of Med., 1982. Cert. internal medicine. Intern Montefiore Med. Ctr., Bronx, NY, 1978—82, resident, 1983—85, v.p. med. affairs, 1997, sr. v.p., chief med. officer, 1998—2008, pres., CEO, 2008—; assoc. prof., dept. medicine Albert Einstein Coll. Medicine, 1987—, assoc. prof., dept. epidemiology & population health, 1987—. Office: Montefiore Med Ctr MMC Centennial Bldg 111 E 210 St 4th Fl Bronx NY 10467 *

SAGALOWSKY, ARTHUR I., urologist, educator; b. Indpls., Aug. 19, 1948; s. Meyer and Goldie Sagalowsky; m. Hanne Albaek, June 11, 1972; children: Julie, Jordan. BA, Ind. U., 1970; MD, Ind. U. Med. Ctr., 1973; M, U. Tex. Southwestern Med. Sch., 2010—. Intern, resident Ind. U. Med. Ctr., Indpls., 1973—75, resident, 1975—78; clin. asst. prof. surgery and urology U. Tex. Southwestern Med. Ctr., Dallas, 1978—80, asst. prof. urology, 1980—84, assoc. prof. urology and surgery, 1984—89, prof. urology and surgery, 1989—. Fellow Clin. Pharmacology, U. Tex. Southwestern, 1978—80; surg. dir. renal transplantation U. Tex. Southwestern Med. Ctr., 1983—95, chief urologic oncology, dept. urology, 1995—2011, co-investigator NIH O'Brien Ctr. Urologic Rsch., 1993—2000, prin. investigator urology, 2000—, prin. investigator urology NIH Cancer Inst. Urologic Cancer Outreach Program, 1989—98. Avocations: piano, golf, fly fishing. Home: 4450 Cedarbrush Dallas TX 75346 Office: U Tex Southwestern Med Ctr Dept Urology 5323 Harry Hines Blvd Dallas TX 75390-9110 Office Phone: 214-648-3976. Business E-Mail: arthur.sagalowsky@utsouthwestern.edu.

SAGAN, ELIZABETH R., urologist; MD, U. of Pitts. Sch. of Medicine, 1979. Diplomate Am. Bd. Urology, lic. to practice Pa., 1982. Resident Univ. of Pitts. Med. Ctr. (UPMC); hosp. affiliations include Magee-Womens Hospital of UPMC, UPMC Mercy, UPMC Presbyn., St. Clair Hosp. Office: Magee-Womens Hospital University of Pittsburgh Medical Center 300 Halket St Pittsburgh PA 15213 Office Phone: 412-641-1000.

SAGARA, NAOHIKO, biology educator; b. Yamakuni-machi, Oita, Japan, Mar. 10, 1938; s. Nobuhiko Omori and Hisako Sagara; m. Masako Goto, May 30, 1968; children: Fuyuki, Miki, Maki. B in Agr., Kyoto U., 1960, M in Agr., 1962, D in Agr., 1975. Rsch. assoc. Kyoto U., 1966-75, assoc. prof. biology, 1975-89, prof. biology, 1989-92, prof. biol. coexistence, 1992-2001; prof. emeritus, 2001—. Vis. prof. U. Sheffield, 1986. Author: Mushrooms and Animals, 1989; contbg. author: The Fungal Community, 2d edit., 1992, Recent Advances in Biology of Japanese Insectivora, 1999, Soil Analysis in Forensic Taphonomy, 2008; contbr. articles to profl. jours. Mem. Mycol. Soc. Japan (mng. editor 1977-78), Brit. Mycol. Soc., Mammalogical Soc. Japan. Avocations: travel, fishing. Home: 230-128 Nagatani-cho Iwakura Kyoto 606-0026 Japan

SAGE, JACOB I., neurologist, educator; b. Sept. 26, 1946; s. Joseph and Fern (Ginsburg) S.; m. Cynthia Fox; children: Naomi, Rebecca, Abigail. AB, U. Chgo., 1968; MD, U. Pitts., 1972. Intern Yale-New Haven Hosp., 1972-73; resident in neurology U. Pitts., 1976-78; fellow in neurochemistry Cornell Med. Coll., NYC, 1978-80; asst. prof. neurology U. Medicine and Dentistry of N.J., New Brunswick, 1980-86, assoc. prof., 1986-90, prof. neurology, 1990—, dir. movement disorders divsn., 1995—. Mem. sci. adv. bd. Am. Parkinsons Disease Assn., N.Y.C., 1995—. Author: Parkinson's Disease: A Guide for Patients, 1996; editor: Practical Neurology of the Elderly, 1996; contbr. articles to profl. jours. Fellow Am. Neurol. Assn.; mem. Acad. of Neurology. Avocations: skiing, gardening. Office: UMDNJ Robert Wood Johnson Med Sch Dept Neurology New Brunswick NJ 08903 Home Phone: 609 921 1702; Office Phone: 732-235-7731. Business E-Mail: sage@umdnj.edu.

SAGE, WEBSTER LEGENE, JR., ophthalmologist; b. St. Louis, Oct. 22, 1925; s. Webster LeGene and Alice Virginia (Gollehon) S.; m. Claudine New, May 20, 1952 (dec. June 1986); children: Bryan LeGene, Evan Webster; m. Shirley Barr, Jan. 2, 1988. BS, U. Ariz., 1949; MD, Baylor U., 1953. Diplomate Am. Bd. Ophthalmology. Intern Good Samaritan Hosp., Phoenix; resident Loma Linda (Calif.) U.; pvt. practice Phoenix, 1956—. Chmn. dept. ophthalmology Good Samaritan Hosp., Phoenix, 1960-62, St. Joseph's Hosp., Phoenix, 1971-72; cons. Ariz. Bd. Med. Examiners, Phoenix; owner Surg. Eye Ctr. Ariz., Phoenix, 1985—. Chmn. bd. of elders and deacons Camelback Christian Ch., Scottsdale, Ariz. Maj. U.S. Army, 1962-64. Fellow ACS (life), Am. Acad. Ophthalmology, Internat. Coll. Surgeons; mem. Ariz. Ophthalmological Soc. (pres. 1963-64), Phoenix Ophthalmological Soc. (pres. 1967-68), Kiwanis Club, Paradise Valley Country Club, Phoenix Country Club. Avocations: travel, photography. Home: 8210 N Charles Dr Paradise Valley AZ 85253-2405 Office: 5133 N Central Ave Ste 100 Phoenix AZ 85012-1438

SAGESAKA, TOSHIAKI, obstetrician, gynecologist; b. Fujieda, Shizuoka, Japan, Aug. 20, 1951; s. Shouji and Tsuya Sagesaka; m. Fumiko Suzuki, Nov. 16, 1979; children: Akiko, Kazuaki, Takaaki. Grad., Juntendo U., Tokyo, 1977, PhD, 1983. Lectr. Juntendo U., Tokyo, 1984—88; vis. scientist Boston Biomedical Rsch. Inst., Boston, 1988—90; vis. lectr. Harvard Med. Sch., Boston, 1988—91; lectr. Teikyo U., Ichihara, Chiba, Japan, 1990—97; chief dept. ob-gyn. Self-Defense Forces Ctrl. Hosp., Setagaya-ku, Tokyo, Japan, 1997—2004; prof. Mita Hosp., Internat. U. Health and Welfare, Minato-ku, Tokyo, Japan, 2005—; with Atami Hosp., Internat. U. Health and Welfare, Atami-shi, Shizuoka, Japan, 2006—. Achievements include research in influence of red blood cell concentration on the initiation time of blood coagulation; anemia as a risk factor of hemorrhagic tendency during surgery; deoxyribonucleic acid replication in fetal cells. Office: Atami Hosp Internat U Health and Welfare 13-1 Higashikaigam-cho Atami 413-0012 Japan Office Fax: 81-3-3454-0067. Personal E-mail: qyt07667@nifty.ne.jp.

SAGGIORO, FABIANO PINTO, pathologist, researcher; b. Juiz de Fora, Minas Gerais, Brazil, Mar. 5, 1971; s. Roberto Gerken Saggioro and Carmem Maria Pereira Pinto; m. Maritcha Kirchmeyer David, June 22, 1996; children: Laura, Ana Clara. MD, Fed. U. Juiz de Fora, Brazil, 1994; MSc, U. São Paulo, Brazil, 2004, PhD, 2010. Med. resident pathology U. São Paulo State, Botucatu, São Paulo, 1995—98; forensic pathologist U. of São Paulo, Death Verification Svc. Cemel, Ribeirão Preto, São Paulo, 2002—; asst. pathologist U. São Paulo, Hospital Sch., Ribeirão Preto, São Paulo, 2004—. Cons. hematopathology U. São Paulo, Hosp. Sch., Ribeirão Preto, São Paulo, 2002—; trainee, surg. & forensic pathology Mayo Clinic, Rochester, Minn., 2009. Contbr. articles to profl. jours. Mem.: Internat. Acad. Pathology (assoc.), Brazilian Soc. Pathology (assoc.). Achievements include research in infectious disease (Hantavirus Cardiopulmonary Syndrome), neuropathology and hematopathology; colaborator pathologist in molecular research projects. Office: Univ Sƒo Paulo Hosp Sch Avenida Bandeirantes 3900 14048-900 Ribeirão Preto SP Brazil Business E-Mail: fsaggioro@terra.com.br.

SAGISAKA, SHONOSUKE, biologist; b. Hokkaido, Japan, Dec. 13, 1930; s. Katsuhei and Kiku (Kumeta) S.; m. Michiko Ito, Dec., 1964. BS, Tohoku U., Sendai, Japan, 1955, MS, 1957, PhD, 1960. Instr. Iwate Med. Coll., Morioka, Japan, 1960-63; asst. prof. Tohoku U., Sendai, 1963-67; assoc. prof. Hokkaido U., Sapporo, 1967-78, prof. biology, 1978-94, prof. emeritus, 1994—, dir., 1991. Contbr. articles to profl. jours. Avocations: travel, photography.

SAGRAVES, ROSALIE, pharmacy practice educator, former dean; b. Portsmouth, Ohio, Nov. 5, 1945; d. Estil and Bernice Ione (Newman) Sagraves; m. Arthur Kameshka, Mar. 30, 1985. Student, Miami U., Oxford, Ohio; BS in Pharmacy, Ohio State U., 1969; PharmD, Phila. Coll. Pharmacy & Sci., 1978. Clin. pharmacist Ohio State U. Hosp., Columbus, 1969-72, clin. pharmacy coord., 1973-75, clin. pharmacist, 1975-76; clin. instr. Ohio State U. Coll. Pharmacy, Columbus, 1972-76; asst. prof. U. Tex. Coll. Pharmacy, Austin, 1978-84, assoc. prof., 1984-85, U. Okla. Coll. Pharmacy, Oklahoma City, 1985-92, prof., 1992-95, U. Ill. Chgo. Coll. Pharmacy, 1995—, dean, 1995—2006, co-dir. Ctr. Excellence in Women's Health, 1998—2006. Clin. pharmacy specialist Brackenridge Hosp., Austin, 1978—85; adj. assoc. prof. U. Okla. Coll. Medicine, 1985—95; clin. specialist Children's Hosp. Okla., 1985—95; bd. dirs. Advanced Life Scis. Holdings, Inc., Woodridge, Ill., 2001. Co-author: Clinical Pharmacology and Therapeutics in Nursing, 1985, Handbook of Applied Therapeutics, 1989, Pediatric Pharmacotherapy, 1990, Applied Therapeutics: The Clinical Use of Drugs, 2005; assoc. editor Pharmacy Today, 1994—98, reviewer Am. Jour. Pharm. Edn., sect. editor Jour. Pediatric Health Care; contbr. articles to profl. jours. Recipient Outstanding Tchg. award, U. Okla. Coll. Pharmacy, 1990, KE/Merck Vanguard award, 1994, Outstanding Alumnus award, Ohio State U. Coll. Pharmacy, 1995, Career Achievement award, Profl. Fraternaties Assn., 1996. Fellow: Am. Coll. Clin. Pharmacy; mem.: Ill. Pharmacy Found., Am. Soc. Parenteral & Enteral Nutrition, Am. Soc. Health-Sys. Pharmacists, Am. Assn. Colleges of Pharmacy, Am. Pharm. Assn., Phi Kappa Phi, Rho Chi, Kappa Epsilon (treas. 1987—91, pres. 1991—93, nat. adv. 1993—95, Alpha Iota Tchg. award 1987, 1993, 1994). Avocations: travel, reading, writing. Office: Coll of Pharmacy U Ill 833 S Wood St M/C 874 Chicago IL 60612-7229 E-mail: sartros@aol.com.

SAGUA, HERNAN FRANCO, parasitology professor; b. Chuquicamata, Chile, Oct. 26, 1942; Degree in Med. Tech., U. Chile, 1967, MSc in Biology, Parasitology, 1987. Prof. Antofagasta U., 1967—. Dean Sci. Health Faculty, 2003—06; dir. Med. Tech. Dept., 2009—11. Mem.: Chilean Microbiology Soc., Chilean Bioethic Soc., Chilean Parasitolgy Soc. Office: Angamos Ave 608 Antofagasta 1240000 Chile Office Fax: 56-55-637802. Business E-Mail: hsagua@uantof.cl.

SAGY, SHIFRA, psychologist, researcher, educator; b. Tel Aviv, July 24, 1945; d. Israel and Jaffa Neeman; m. Alexander Sagy, Oct. 20, 1969; children: Eyal, Tehila. BA, Haifa U., Israel, 1972; MA, Ben-Gurion U., Beer-Sheva, Israel, 1985, PhD, 1990. Ednl. psychologist, counselor Ministry Welfare, Haifa, Israel, 1971—75; psychologist Boarding Sch., Israel, 1976—78; psychologist, therapist Kibbutz Clinic Child and Family Therapy, Israel, 1978—96; counselor Family Violence Ctr. Prevention and Treatment, Israel, 1990—92; prof. Ben-Gurion U., Beer-Sheva, 1993—, head cdn. dept., 2000—05, prof. ednl. psychology, 1993—, head conflicts mgmt. ctr., 2007—, head conflicts mgmt. and resolution programs, 2007—; head Ctr. Ednl. Enhancement, 2002—. Cons. Anti-Drug Authority, Israel, 1999—, Schneider Children Med. Ctr. Israel, 1999—, Israel Nat. Coun. Child, 2002—; chair steering com. Rsch. and Devel. Ctr. Bedouin Soc., 2005—07. Contbr. articles to profl. jours. Chair Mental Health Workers Advancement Peace, Israel, 1995; v.p. Friendship Across Borders, 2004—07, co-chair; chair Israeli Assn. Civil Rights, Beer-Sheva, 1992—93; co-chair Non-governmental orgns. Israeli, Palestinian, and German Cooperation, 2004—07; mem. Forum Coexistence in Negev; mem. cmty. adv. Bedouin Population in Negev. With Israeli Def. Force, 1965. Rsch. grantee, UNESCO and Rabin Ctr., 1992—93, People to People, 1999—2001, Abraham Fund, 2001—02, Isreali Sci. Found., 2005—09, German Academic Found., 2010—. Mem.: Israeli Sci. Found. (acad. adv. com. 2003—), Forum Coexistence in Negev, Friendship Across Borders (co-chmn. 2004—07, v.p. 2004—07), Peace Rsch. in Mid. East (exec. com. 1997—, co-dir. 2009—10). Meretz. Home: 7 Adad St 84965 Omer Israel Office: Ben Gurion U PO Box 653 84105 Beer Sheva Israel Home Phone: 97286469148; Office Phone: 972-50-867986, 97286461391. Business E-Mail: shifra@bgu.ac.il.

SAHA, RUMPA, microbiologist, educator; b. Kolkata, June 11, 1969; MBBS, Calcutta Nat. Med. Coll., 1993; MD in Microbiology, Postgrad. Inst. Med. Edn. and Rsch., 2002. Sr. resident U. Coll. Med. Scis. and Guru Teg Bahadur Hosp., 2002—05, sr. rsch. assoc., 2005—07, asst. prof., microbiology, 2007—. Co-editor: UCMS Newsletter; contbr. articles to sci. profl. publs. Recipient prize, Reunion Calcutta Nat. Med. Coll., 1991. Mem.: Hosp. Infection Soc. India (life), Indian Med. Assn., East Delhi Br. (life), Soc. Indian Animal and Human Mycologists (life First prize), Indian Assn. Med. Microbiologist (life). Avocation: sports. Office: Dilshad Garden Delhi 110095 India Office Fax: 0091-11-22590495. E-mail: rumpachatterjee@yahoo.co.in.

SAHAI, HARDEO, medical statistics educator; b. Bahraich, India, Jan. 10, 1942; m. Lillian Sahai, Dec. 28, 1973; 3 children. BS in Math., Stats. and Physics, Lucknow U., India, 1962; MS in Math., Banaras U., Varanasi, India, 1964; MS in Math. Stats., U. Chgo., 1968; PhD in Stats., U. Ky., Lexington, 1971. Lectr. math. and stats. Banaras U., Varanasi, India, 1964—65; asst. stats. officer Durgapur Steel Plant, West Bengal, India, 1965; statistician Rsch. and Planning divsn. Blue Cross Assn., Chgo., 1966; statis. programmer Cleft Palate Ctr. U. Ill., 1967; statis. programmer Chgo. Health Rsch. Found., 1968; mgmt. scientist Mgmt. Sys. Devel. Dept. Burroughs Corp., Detroit, 1971—72; from asst. prof. to prof. dept. math. U. PR, Mayaguez, 1972—82; vis. rsch. prof. Dept. Stats. and Applied Math. U. Ceara, Brazil, 1978—79; sr. rsch. statistician Travenol Labs., Inc., Round Lake, Ill., 1982—83; chief statistician US Army Hqrs., Ft. Sheridan, Ill., 1983—84; sr. math. statistician U.S. Bur. Census Dept. Commerce, Washington, 1984—85; sr. ops. rsch. analyst Def. Logistics Agy. Dept. Def., Chgo., 1985—86; prof. Dept. Biostats. and Epidemiology U. PR Med. Scis., San Juan, 1986—. Cons. PR Univ Cons., PR Driving Safety Evaluation Project, Water Resources Rsch. Inst., Travenol Labs., Campo Rico, PR, US Bur. Census, Washington,

Lawrence Livermore Nat. Lab., Calif., others; vis. prof. U. Granada, Spain, U. Veracruzana, Mex., patrimonial prof. stats., 1997—; vis. prof. U. Nacional de Colombia, U. Nacional de Trujillo, Peru, 1993-94, hon. prof. stats., 1994—; adj. prof. dept. math. U. P.R. Natural Scis. Faculty, 1995—; Patrimonial prof. stafs U. Veracruzana, 1997—. Author: Statistics and Probability: Learning Module, 1984; author: (with Jose Berrios) A Dictionary of Statistical Scientific and Technical Terms: English-Spanish and Spanish-English, 1981, (with Wilfredo Martinez) Statistical Tables and Formulas for the Biological Social and Physical Sciences, 1996, (with Anwer Khurshid) Statistics in Epidemiology: Methods, Techniques and Applications, 1996, (with Satish C. Misra and Amwer Khurshid) Quotations on Probability and Statistics with Illustrations, 2004, (with Anwer Khurshid) A Pocket Dictionary of Statistics, 2000, (with Mohammad I. Ageel) The Analysis of Variance: Fixed, Random and Mixed Models, 2000, (with Mario M. Ojeda) A Glossary of Statistical, Sciebtfic and Technical Terms: English-Spanish, 2004, (with Lucas López Segovia and Hector W. Colón-Rosa) A Glossary of Medical Epidemiologic and Demographic Statistics: English-Spanish, 2003, (with Mario M. Ojeda) Un Manual de Distribuciones t, x2y F Centrales Y No Centrales, 2000, (with Mario M. Ojeda) A Glossary of Computer and Management Terms: English/Spanish, 2004, (with Mario M. Ojeda) Comparisons of Approximations to the Percentiles of Noncentral t, x2 and F Distributions, 2001, (with A. Khurshid) Pocket Dictionary of Statistics, 2001, (with Mario M. Ojeda) Analysis of Variance for Random Models, Vol. 1: Balanced Data and Vol. 2: Unbalanced Data, 2004; mem. editl. bd. Sociedad Colombiana de Matematicas, P.R. Health Scis. Jour.; contbr. editor Current Index to Stats.; reviewer Collegiate Microcomputer, Comm. in Statistics, Indian Jour. Stats., Jour. Royal Statis. Soc. (series D, The Statistician), New Zealand Statistician, Biometrics, Can. Jour. Stats., Technometrics, Problems, Resources and Issues in Math. Undergrad. Studies; contbr. more than 150 articles and papers to profl. and sci. jours., numerous articles to tech. mags. Active Dept. Consumer Affairs Svcs. Commonwealth of PR, San Juan, Dept. Anti-Addiction Svcs., Commonwealth of P.R., San Juan., Inst. of AIDS, Municipality of San Juan, VA Med. Ctr. of San Juan, Caribbean Primate Rsch. Ctr., Ctr. Addiction Studies Caribbean Ctrl. U. Recipient Dept. Army Cert. Achievement award, 1984, U. Ky. Outstanding Alumnus award, 1993, medal of honor U. Granada, 1994, plaque of honor U. Nacional de Trujillo, 1994; fellow Coun. Sci. and Indsl. Rsch., 1964-65, U. Chgo., 1965-68, Harvard U., 1979, Fulbright Found., 1982; U.P. Bd. Merit scholar, 1957-59, Govt. India Merit scholar, 1959-64; grantee NSF, 1974-77, NIMH, 1987-90, 91—, NIDA, 1991—. Fellow AAAS, Am. Coll. Epidemiology, Inst. Statisticians (charter statistician), Inst. Math. and Its Applications (charter mathematician), N.Y. Acad. Scis., Royal Statis. Soc.; mem. Internat. Statis. Inst., Internat. Assn. Tchg. Stats., Soc. Epidemiol. Rsch., Inst. Math. Stats., Bernouilli Soc. for Math. Stats. and Probability, Internat. Biometric Soc., Am. Soc. for Quality Control, Am. Stats. Assn., Japan Statis. Soc., Can. Statis. Soc., Inter-Am. Statis. Inst., Internat. Assn. Statis. Computing, Sch. Sci. and Math. Assn., Sigma Xi. Avocations: religious studies, philosophy, reading, gardening. Home: Urb Mayaguez Ter 7083 Calle B Gaudier Texidor Mayaguez PR 00682-6617 Personal E-mail: hardeosahai@yahoo.com.

SAHEL, JOSÉ-ALAIN, ophthalmologist, researcher; b. Tlemcen, July 12, 1955; Med., Paris U. Med. Sch., 1980; degree in ophthalmology, 1984—. Chmn. dept. ophthalmology Quinze-Vingts Nat. Ophthalmology Hosp., Paris, 2001—, head clin. investigation ctr., 2005—, dir. nat. reference centre for inherited retinal dystrophies, 2005—; chmn. dept. ophthalmology and vitreo-retinal diseases Ophthalmology Found. A. de Rothschild, 2001; dir. Vision Inst., 2008. Hon. prof. Inst. Ophthalmology, U. Coll. London, 2001—, Cumberlege chair, prof. biomedical scis., 2001. Recipient, Alcon Rsch. Inst. Award, Trustee award, Found. Fighting Blindness, Innovation award, Altran Found. Mem.: European Vision Inst (mem. steering com.), French Acad. Sciences, Deutsche Opthalmologische Gesellschaft, Sci. Adv. Bd. - Faculty of Medicine of the Pierre & Marie Curie U., Sci. Adv. Bd. ERAB Allergan. Avocation: reading. Office: Institut de la Vision 17 rue Moreau Ile de France Paris 75012 France Office Phone: +33 1 53 46 25 04. Office Fax: +33 1 53 46 25 05. E-mail: j.sahel@gmail.com.

SAHN, STEVEN ALAN, internist, educator, pulmonologist; b. Bklyn., Jan. 25, 1943; s. Irwin H. and Mildred P. Sahn; m. Margaret Hoefer Sahn, June 8, 2002; children: Karen, Stacey, James, Michael, Rachel. BA, Duke U., 1964; MD, U. Louisville, 1968. Diplomate Am. Bd. Internal Medicine, Am. Bd. Pulmonary Medicine, Am. Bd. Critical Care Medicine. Intern in internal medicine U. Iowa Hosp., Iowa City, 1968-69, resident in internal medicine, 1969-71; fellow in pulmonary disease U. Colo. Health Sci. Ctr., Denver, 1971-73, instr. medicine, 1973-74, asst. prof. medicine, 1974-78, assoc. prof. medicine, 1978-83; prof. medicine, dir. divsn. pulmonary and critical care, allergy and sleep medicine Med. Univ. S.C., Charleston, 1983—. Vis. prof. U. Calif., San Francisco, 1980, Kans. U. Med. Ctr., Kansas City, 1981, U. Louisville Sch. Medicine, 1982, Wright State U. Med. Sch., Wright-Patterson AFB Hosp., Dayton, Ohio, 1982, Oreg. Health Scis. U., 1982, Vanderbilt U., Nashville, 1984, U. S.C. Sch. Medicine, 1985, U. Ariz. Health Sci. Ctr., Tucson, 1985, 92, 93, Yale U., New Haven, Conn., 1986, Hershey (Pa.) Med. Ctr., 1986, SUNY, Stonybrook, 1987, Dartmouth-Hitchcock Med. Ctr., Hanover, N.H., 1988, Maine Med. Ctr. U. Vt., Portland, Maine, 1988, Fitzsimmons Army Med. Ctr., Denver, 1989, Seton Hall U. Grad. Med. Edn., 1989, Newark, 1989, Loyola U. Med. Ctr., Chgo., 1989, Andrews AFB, Washington, 1990, Keesler AFB, Biloxi, Miss., 1990, U. Rochester, N.Y., U. Ala., Birmingham, 1990, N.Y. Med. Coll., 1990, Temple U. Sch. Medicine, Phila., 1990, U. Milan, Italy, 1990, Georgetown U. Med. Ctr., Washington, 1991, Albert Einstein Sch. Medicine, 1991, Johns Hopkins U. Sch. Medicine, Balt., 1991, Ind. U. Med. Ctr., 1994, Ohio State U. Sch. Medicine, 1994, 33 others; cons. Fitzsimons Army Med. Ctr., 1980-83, 88-90, DHEC of S.C., 1982—, USAF, 1989—93, FDA Office of Orphan Product Devel., 1993—95; presenter numerous seminars; vis. prof., keynote spkr. at numerous state thoracic meetings. Author: (with J.E. Heffner) Pulmonary Pearls, 1988, vol. II, 1994, Critical Care Pearls, 1989; editor: (with L.B. Reller and R.W. Schrier) Clinical Internal Medicine, 1979, Pulmonary Emergencies, 1982, Diseases of the Pleura: Seminars in Respiratory Medicine, 1987, Infections of the Pleural Space: Seminars in Respiratory Infections, Vol. III, 1988, (with J.E. Heffner) Internal Medicine Pearls, 1993, (with J.E. Heffner) Cardiology Pearls, 1993, Tuberculosis Pearls, 1996, Critical Care Pearls, II, 1997, Respieratory Care Pearls, 1997; mem. editorial bd. Chest, 1987—, Pulmonary and Critical Care Update, 1988—, editor 2007-; dept. editor Pulmonary and Critical Care Pearls Chest, 1992—, Pulmonary Pearls Jour. Respiratory Disease, 1990—, Critical Care Pearls Jour. Critical Illness, 1990—; cons. to 53 editorial bd. Am. Jour. Diseases of Children, Am. Jour. Medicine, Am. Jour. Respiratory Critical Care Medicine, Cancer, Cancer Rsch., Annals of Internal Medicine, Chest, Critical Care Medicine, Jour. Am. Acad. Dermatoloty, Jour. Am. Med. Assn., European Respiratory Jour., Jour. Applied Physiology, Jour. Intensive Care Medicine, Jour. Laboratory and Clin. Medicine, Jour. Respiratory Diseases, Lung, Mayo Clinic Proceedings, Med. Toxicology, N.Y. State Jour. Medicine, Tubercle and Lung Diseases, Western Jour. Medicine; contbr. to numerous articles, peer reviewed jours., revs. to profl. jours. & publs., chpts. to books. Recipient Young Investigator Pulmonary Rsch. award NHLBI, 1975-77, grantee 1975-77; named one of Outstanding Med. Specialists in the U.S. Town and Country Mag., 1990, one of Best Med. Specialists in N.Am., 1995, one of 400 Best Doctors in Am., Good Housekeeping Mag., 1991, one of Best Drs. in Am., Am. Health Mag., 1995; grantee Milheim, 1977-78, Beecham, 1977-78, 82-83, Warner-Chilcott, 1978-79, Squibb, 1978, 79-80, Lilly, 1979-80, 81-82, Boehringer-Ingelheim, 1980, 89-90, Med. Coll. S.C., 1985-86, ALASC, 1985-86, 86-87, 87-88, 88-89, Lederle, 1988-92, Hoescht-Roussel, 1988-90, Support Systems Internat., 1990-92, 92-93, Cutter Biological, Miles, Inc., Glaxo, 1991-92, Schering-Plough, 1992-93, Tap Pharmaceuticals, 1993. Fellow Am. Coll. Chest Physicians (annual meeting com. 1986, gov. S.C. 1988-91, 91-94, organizing com. nat. pulmonary bd. review course 1990, 92, 94, membership com. 1992-93, annual internat. sci. program com. 1993-95, reviewer MKSAP 1994), Am. Coll. Physicians, Am. Coll. Critical Care Medicine; mem. Am. Fedn. Clin. Rsch. (so. sect.), Am. Thoracic Soc. (respiratory care com. 1978-80, rsch. coord. com. 1985-87, annual meeting com. 1985-89, chmn. sci. assembly on clin. problems 1986-87, coun. chpt. reps. 1987-90), Am. Lung Assn. (adv. bd. S.C. coastal br. 1985-87, 89-91, 92-94, med. review com. 1985-89), We. Soc. Clin. Investigation, S.C. Thoracic Soc. (sci. planning com. 1985-86), Charleston County Med. Soc. Office: Med University SC Divsn Pulmonary Critical Care Allergy & Sleep Medicine 171 Ashley Ave Charleston SC 29425-0001 Office Phone: 803-792-3167. Business E-Mail: sahnsa@musc.edu.

SAHNI, RAKESH, pediatrician, educator; b. Nov. 2, 1960; MBBS, Maulana Azad Med. Coll., 1983. Prof., clin. pediat. Columbia U., 1988—. Mem.: Soc. Pediat. Rsch. Office: 3959 Broadway Rm MSCHN-1201 New York NY 10032 Office Fax: 212-305-8796. Business E-Mail: rs62@columbia.edu.

SAHOTA, AMRIK, medical researcher, educator, lab administrator; s. Sadhu Milkhy and Rao Kaur; m. Nirmala Thapar; children: Aneil, Jessica. BS in Biochemistry, Bath U., 1974; MS in Medicinal Chemistry, Loughborough U., 1976; PhD in Med. Genetics, Guy's Hosp. Med. Sch., London U., 1980. Diplomate in clin. molecular genetics Am. Bd. Med. Genetics, cert. Am. Bd. Med. Genetics, 1993, in molecular diagnostics Am. Bd. Clin. Chemistry, 2008; chartered biologist U.K. Postdoctoral fellow dept. molecular scis. Aston U., Birmingham, England, 1980—83; biochemist dept. hematology Gen. Hosp., Birmingham, England, 1983—85; rsch. assoc. dept. biology Ind. U., Bloomington, Ind., 1985—87; lab. dir. dept. med. and molecular genetics Ind. U. Med. Sch., Indpls., 1988—98; prof. genetics Rutgers U., Piscataway, NJ, 1998—; lab. dir. dept. pathology Robert Wood Johnson U. Hosp., New Brunswick, NJ, 2001—. Cons. Indpls.-Marion County Forensic Sci. Lab., 1991—98; adj. prof. dept. pathology Robert Wood Johnson Med. Sch., U. Medicine and Dentistry, NJ, 2001—05, clin. prof., 2005—, clin. prof. dept. surgery, 2009—. Contbr. articles to sci. jours.; editor conf. procs. Fellow: Acad Clin. Biochemistry, Royal Coll. Pathologists UK, Inst. Biology UK, Am. Coll. Med. Genetics; mem.: AAAS, Internat. Soc. for Nephrology, Assn. Molecular Pathology, Soc. for Study of Inborn Errors of Metabolism, Brit. Soc. Human Genetics, Am. Soc. Human Genetics, Am. Assn. Clin. Chemistry. Achievements include research in Genetic basis of kidney stone disease. Avocations: travel, reading, health and fitness. Office: Rutgers U Dept Genetics Life Scis Bldg 145 Bevier Rd Piscataway NJ 08854-8082 Business E-Mail: sahota@biology.rutgers.edu.

SAHU, GEETA RAM, medical researcher; b. Berhampur, Ganjam, India, June 23, 1973; PhD, Utkal U., India, 2004; postdoc., Nat. Inst. Health, 2007. Vis. fellow NIH, Bethesda, Md., 2005—07; orise fellow FDA, Bethesda, 2007—09; postdoc. fellow Lombardi Cancer Ctr., Georgetown U., Washington, 2009—10, U. Tenn. Health Sci. Ctr., Memphis, 2010—. Scientist IMGENEX India, Bhubaneswar, 2002—05. Mem.: Indian Assn. Cancer Rsch., Am. Physiol. Soc. Avocations: reading, cricket. Home: 37n Arcadian Cir Apt 103 Memphis TN 38103 Personal E-mail: sahugr@yahoo.com.

SAI, YAN, medical educator; b. Shandong, Mar. 6, 1976; D, Third Med. U., 2006. Assoc. prof. Third Med. U., 2008—. Office: Gaotanyan Rd #30 Shapingba Dist Chongqing 400038 China E-mail: sai2000cn@yahoo.com.cn.

SAIAG, PHILIPPE, dermatologist, educator; b. Neuilly, France, July 20, 1955; s. Andre and Jacqueline (Gambillard) S.; m. Marie-Claude Nedey, Mar. 9, 1983; children: Hadrien, Anne-Laure. MD, Paris-Ouest, 1985; PhD, Paris VII, 1984. Asst. prof. Hosp. Monton, Creteil, France, 1985-88, Hosp. Tenon, Paris, 1987-91, cons., 1991-93; prof. dermatology Hosp. A Paré, Boulogne, France, 1993—; chief dept. dermatology Hosp. a Paré, Boulogne, France, 1993—. Office: U Versailles 9 Ave Charles de Gaulle 92104 Boulogne-Billancourt France

SAID, OMAR, medical researcher; b. Nazareth, Israel, Feb. 18, 1960; PhD in Medicine, 1995. Sr. rschr. Galile Societ R & D Ctr., 1995—2004; CEO Antaki Ctr. Herbal Medicine, 2003—. Dir. Al-Maissam-Medicinal Plant Ctr. Rsch. & Edn., 2002—07; regional couns. mem. Nature Preservation. Achievements include research in diabetes, obesity, fertility, psoriasis, acne, hyperlipidemia and liver diseases. Home: Naqqara Kfar Canna Galilee 16930 Israel Home Fax: 0097246412713. Personal E-mail: omar@al-antaki.com.

SAID, QAYYIM, pharmacologist, educator; b. Lahore, Pakistan, Sept. 2, 1962; MA, U. Essex, 1994; PhD, U. Utah, 2002. Rsch. asst. prof., Pharmacotherapy Outcomes Rsch. Ctr. U. Utah, 2004—07, adj. faculty, Coll. Pharmacy, 2008—; asst. prof. Divsn. Pharm. Evaluation and Policy, U. Ark. Med. Scis., 2007—. Rsch. grant, Ark. Ctr. Health Disparities, NIH. Mem.: Internat. Soc. Pharmacoeconomics and Outcomes Rsch., Rho Chi Honor Soc. Avocations: movies, hiking. Home: University Ark Med Scis 4301 W Markham St # 522 Little Rock AR 72223 Home Fax: 501-686-5156. E-mail: qsaid@uams.edu.

SAIDO, KATSUHIKO, pharmacist, educator; b. Itako, Ibaraki, Japan, Sept. 30, 1947; s. Takehiko Saido and Sumie Suzuki; m. Hikari Sato, July 24, 1965; children: Masahiko, Tomohito. PhD, Nihon Univ., Funabashishi, Chiba, Japan, 1975. Cert. ACS, 2005. Prof. Coll. Pharmacy, Nihon Univ., 1998—. Rschr., IL, Japan. Recipient Appreciation award, ACS, 2005. Home: 3151 Tateishi Katsushika Tokyo 1240012 Japan Office: Coll Pharmacy Nihon Univ 771 Narashinodai Funabashi Chiba 2748555 Japan Home Fax: 81336915579. Personal E-mail: saido@s5.dion.ne.jp. Business E-Mail: saido.katsuhiko@nihon-u.ac.jp.

SAIFER, MARK GARY PIERCE, pharmaceutical executive; b. Phila., Sept. 16, 1938; s. Albert and Sylvia (Jolles) S.; m. Phyllis Lynne Trommer, Jan. 28, 1961 (dec.); children: Scott David, Alandria Gail; m. Merry R. Sherman, June 26, 1994. AB, U. Pa., 1960; PhD, U. Calif., Berkeley, 1966. Acting asst. prof. zoology U. Calif., Berkeley, 1966, fellow, 1967-68; sr. cancer rsch. scientist Roswell Park Meml. Inst., Buffalo, 1968-70; lab. dir. Diagnostic Data Inc., Palo Alto, Calif., 1970-78; v.p. DDI Pharms., Inc., Mountain View, Calif., 1978-94, Oxis Internat., Inc., 1994-95; v.p., sci. dir. Mountain View Pharms., Inc., Menlo Park, Calif., 1996—, also bd. dirs. Lectr., expert witness in field. Author, patentee in field:, mem. editl. bd.: Current Pharm. Biotechnology Jour. Mem. AAAS (life), Am. Assn. Pharm. Scientists, Parenteral Drug Assn. Office: Mountain View Pharms Inc 3475 Edison Way Ste S Menlo Park CA 94025-1821 E-mail: saifer@mvpharm.com.

SAIGO, MASAHIKO, cardiologist; b. Kobayashi, Miyazaki, Japan, July 10, 1961; m. Toshiko Kitada, 1990; children: Yuki, Keisuke, Ayano. MD, Kagoshima U., 1986, PhD, 1997. Resident in anesthesiology Kagoshima Univ. Hosp., Japan, 1986—87, clin. fellow in anesthesiology, 1987—89, clin. fellow in cardiology, first dept. internal medicine, 1989—95, staff physician, first dept. internal medicine, 1996—99; dir. internal medicine Ebino City Hosp., Miyazaki, Japan, 1999—2001, Ichihino Meml. Hosp., Kagoshima, Japan, 2005—09, Kibougaoka Hosp., 2009—; instr., first dept. internal medicine, faculty medicine Kagoshima U., 2002—03, asst. prof., dept. cardiovasc., respiratory, metabolic medicine, Grad. Sch., 2003—05. Vis. postdoctoral rsch. fellow, divsn. cardiology San Francisco Gen. Hosp., 2002—04; vis. postdoctoral rsch. fellow, dept. medicine U. Calif., San Francisco, 2002—04. Fellow: ACP, Japanese Circulation Soc., Japanese Coll. Cardiology, Am. Heart Assn., Coun. Clin. Cardiology, Japanese Soc. Internal Medicine; mem.: ACP, Am. Heart Assn., Japanese Coll. Cardiology, Japanese Circulation Soc., Japanese Soc. Internal Medicine. Office: Kibougaoka Hosp Dept Internal Medicine 5069 Hiramatsu Aira-shi Kagoshima 899 5652 Japan

SAIJUNTHA, WEERACHAI, biology professor; b. Thailand, Jan. 11, 1980; PhD in Med. Biochemistry, Khon Kaen U., 2007. Asst. prof. Walai Rukhavej Bot. Rsch. Inst., 2010—. Japan Soc. Promotion Sci. scholar, 2011. Office: Khamraing Kantharawichai Maha Sarakham 44150 Thailand Personal E-mail: wsaijuntha@yahoo.com.

SAIKI, HIROSHI, biotechnologist, educator; b. Kawasaki, Kanagawa, Japan, Feb. 24, 1950; BSc, Waseda U., 1973; PhD, Tohoku U., 1978. Prof., sch. biosci. and biotech. Tokyo U. Tech., 2004—. Mem.: Japan Chem. Soc., Am. Chem. Soc. Avocation: mountain climbing. Office: 1404-1 Katakura Hachioji Tokyo 192-0982 Japan Business E-Mail: saiki@bs.teu.ac.jp.

SAILER, SIGURD, physician, researcher; b. Rottenmann, Styria, Austria, Dec. 24, 1931; s. Franz and Hildegard (Schwarz) S.; m. Elisabeth Rosenberg, Mar. 20, 1939; children: Christine, Barbara. MD, U. Graz, Austria, 1955. Resident U. Vienna, 1955; sr. resident U. Innsbruck, 1964—82; chmn. med. dept. Landeskrankenanstalten, Salzburg, Austria, 1983-97. Contbr. more than 200 articles to profl. jours. Home and Office: Schwarzstrasse 23 A-5020 Salzburg Austria Office Phone: 43-662-876624. Business E-Mail: sailer@salzburg.co.at.

SAIMAN, LISA, epidemiologist; BA, Cornell U., 1977; MD, Albert Einstein Coll. of Medicine, 1983; MPH, Columbia U., 1999. Diplomate Am. Bd. Pediatrics, cert. pediatric infectious disease. Intership Babies & Children's Hosp., resident pediatrician, fellowship; prof. clin. pediat. Medicine Coll. of Physicians and Surgeons, Columbia Univ.; mem. sci. adv. bd. Transave Inc.; clin. cons. Aridis Pharmaceuticals LLC, mem. clin. adv. bd.; dir. CF Referral Ctr. for Susceptibility and Synergy Studies; divsn. chair Am. Soc. of Microbiology. Author numerous publs. on infectious disease and cystic fibrosis; editl. bd. (journals) Infection Control and Hospital Epidemiology and the Archives of Pediatric & Adolescent Medicine. Mem. CF Found. Clin. Rsch. Com. Office: Columbia University Medical Center 650 West 168th St PH 4W-470 New York NY 10032 Mailing: Aridis Pharmaceuticals LLC San Jose CA 95138 Office Phone: 212-305-9446. Office Fax: 212-342-5218. Business E-Mail: ls5@columbia.edu.

ST. CLAIR, DARET K., medical educator; b. Thailand, June 5, 1950; PhD, U. Iowa, 1984. Prof. U. Ky., 1996—. Recipient Kirwan prize, U. Ky. Mem.: Soc. Free Radical in Biology and Medicine. Office: 458 HSRB 1059 VA Dr Lexington KY 40536 Office Fax: 859-323-1059. Business E-Mail: dstcl00@uky.edu.

SAINT-CYR, MICHEL, plastic surgeon; b. Ottawa, Ontario, Canada, Aug. 9, 1968; s. Michelyne Rachel and Ian Hamilton; m. Rachel Lynne Merkord, May 25, 2007. BS, U. Ottawa, Can., 1997. MD U. Montreal, 1997, Fellow Royal Coll. Surgeons, 2002, cert. plastic surgery Royal Coll. Can., 2002. Assoc. prof. plastic surgery U. Tex. Southwestern Med. Ctr., Dallas, 2005—. Dir. hand surgery clinic

Parkland Meml. Hosp., Dallas, 2005—. Recipient Best Basic Sci. Study Presentation, Can. Soc. Plastic Surgeons, 2002, F.M. Woolhouse prize, Can. Soc. of Plastic Surgeons, 2002. Achievements include research in in vascular supply of the skin and flaps. Avocation: marathon running. Office: UT Southwestern Med Ctr 1801 Inwood Rd Dallas TX 75390-9132 Home: 3816 N Versailles Ave Dallas TX 75209 Business E-Mail: michel.saint-cyr@utsouthwestern.edu.

ST. GEME, JOSEPH W., III, pediatric and infectious diseases physician, educator; b. Mpls., Nov. 24, 1957; BS, Stanford U., Calif., 1979; MD, Harvard Med. Sch., 1984. Diplomate American Bd. Pediat., cert. in pediatric infectious diseases. Intern, resident pediat. Children's Hosp. Phila., 1984—87, chief resident pediat., 1987—88; postdoc. fellow dept. microbiology and immunology Stanford U., 1988—92, postdoc. fellow dept. pediat., divsn. infectious diseases, 1991—92; faculty, prof. pediat. and molecular microbiology Washington U. Sch. Medicine, St. Louis, 1992—2005; chair dept. pediat. Duke U. Sch. Medicine, Durham, NC, 2005—, James B. Duke prof. dept. pediat. & dept. molecular genetics and microbiology, 2007—. Contbr. articles to profl. jours. Recipient Calif. Rsch. Fellowship award, American Lung Assn., 1990, Young Investigator award in bacterial vaccine devel., Infectious Diseases Soc. America/Lederle-Praxis Biologics, 1993, Basil O'Connor award, March of Dimes Found., 1994, Established Investigator award, American Heart Assn., 1997, Squibb award, Infectious Diseases Soc. America, 1998; named Clin. Tchr. of Yr., Washington U. Sch. Medicine, 2001—03. Mem.: Assn. American Physicians, Inst. Medicine, Pediatric Infectious Diseases Soc. (Young Investigator award 1996), American Acad. Microbiology, American Soc. Clin. Investigation, Alpha Omega Alpha, Phi Beta Kappa. Achievements include research in pediatric infectious diseases, antibiotic resistance, respiratory tract infections, central nervous system infections, tick-borne infections, vaccine development and microbial pathogenesis. Office: Duke Univ Med Ctr Box 3352 Durham NC 27710 Business E-Mail: j.stgeme@duke.edu.

ST. GEORGE-HYSLOP, PETER HENRY, neurologist, educator; MD, U. Ottawa, 1976. Instr. neurology and genetics Harvard U.; asst. physician neurology and genetics Mass. Gen. Hosp.; asst. prof. medicine U. Toronto, 1991—96, dir. Ctr. for Rsch. in Neurodegenerative Disease, 1995—, prof., 1996—2003, university prof. medicine and neurology, 2003—; prof. exptl. neuroscience U. Cambridge, England. Internat. rsch. scholar Howard Hughes Med. Inst., 1997—. Recipient Met. Life award for Med. Rsch., 1987, Sci. award, Med. Rsch. Coun., 1996, Potamkin award, Am. Acad. Neurology, 1996, Disting. Sci. award, Can. Soc. Clin. Investigation, 1999, Giacchino da Fiore prize, 2000, Disting. Sci. award, Can. Inst. Health Rsch., 2001, Oon prize in Medicine, U. Cambridge, 2004. Fellow: Royal Coll. Physicians Can. (Gold medal in medicine 1993), Royal Soc. Can.; mem.: Inst. Medicine (fgn. assoc.), Am. Soc. Clin. Investigation. Office: CRND Tanz Neuroscience Bldg U Toronto 6 Queen's Park Cres W Toronto ON M5S 3H2 Canada

ST. JOHN, DONALD JAMES (BOURNE), clinical gastroenterologist, researcher; b. Melbourne, Australia, June 12, 1936; s. Reginald Arotio and Lilian Edith (Bourne) St. J.; m. Margaret Anne Watson, Mar. 10, 1962; children: David, Claire, James. Rebecca. MB BS, U. Melbourne, 1959, MD, 2001. Registered med. practitioner, Australia. Rsch. registrar West Middlesex Hosp., London, 1966—67; asst. physician, clin. rsch. unit Alfred Hosp., Melbourne, 1967—69; lectr. in medicine Monash U., Melbourne, 1969—71, sr. lectr. medicine, 1971—77; sr. assoc. in medicine U. Melbourne, 1977—99, assoc. prof., 1999—; dir. dept. gastroenterology Royal Melbourne Hosp., 1977—2001, hon. gastroenterologist, 2001—; sr. clin. cons. Nat. Cancer Control Initiative, 2001—06. Mem. Australian Screening Adv. Com., 2004—07; hon. sr. assoc. Cancer Coun. Victoria, 2006—. Contbr. numerous articles to Annals of Internal Medicine, Gastroenterology, Gut, Brit. Med. Jour., Clin. Chemistry, Australian and New Zealand Jour. Medicine, Archives of Pathology and Lab. Med., Bull. of WHO, others. Mem. governing coun. Orgn. Mondiale d'Endoscopie Digestive, 1986—94; mem. sci. adv. bd. WHO Ctr. for Prevention of Colorectal Cancer, 1988—98; mem. governing coun. Asian-Pacific Assn. of Gastroenterology, 1988—96. Named fellow, Asian-Pacific Soc. Digestive Endoscopy, 1991; named to, Order of Australia, 1998. Fellow: Am. Gastroenterol. Assn., Royal Coll. Physicians (London), Royal Australasian Coll. Physicians; mem.: Italian Soc. Gastroenterology (internat. mem.), Order of Australia, Australian Med. Assn., Australian Gastroenterol. Inst. (chmn. 1993—95), Gastroenterol. Soc. Australia (pres. 1987—89). Anglican. Avocations: gardening, history, music. Office: Cancer Coun Victoria 1 Rathdowne St Carlton VIC 3053 Australia Office Phone: 61 3 9635 5227. Business E-Mail: james.stjohn@cancervic.org.au.

ST. PIERRE, RONALD LESLIE, public health and medical educator, academic administrator; b. Dayton, Ohio, Feb. 2, 1938; s. Leslie Frank and Ruth Eleanor (Rhoten) St.P.; m. Joyce A. Guilford, Apr. 1, 1961; children: Michele Christine, David Bryan. BS, Ohio U., 1961; M.Sc., Ohio State U., 1962, PhD, 1965. Instr. anatomy Ohio State U., Columbus, 1965-67, asst. prof., 1967-69, assoc. prof., 1969-72, prof., 1972—2002, chmn. dept. anatomy, 1972-81, assoc. v.p. health scis., 1981-83, sr. assoc. v.p. health scis. and acad. affairs, 1983—2002, assoc. dean Coll. Medicine and Pub. Health, 1987-96, vice dean Coll. of Medicine and Pub. Health, 1996-2000, exec. vice dean, 2000—02, interim dean pub. health, 1999—2002, assoc. v.p., prof. emeritus, 2002—06, spl. asst. to sr. v.p. health scis., 2002—06; assoc. dir. Cancer Rsch. Ctr., 1974-78, interim provost, v.p. for acad. affairs Capital U., Columbus, 2006—09, mem. bd. trustees, 2011—. Vis. research asso. Duke U., 1966-67; cons. Battelle Meml. Inst., Columbus. Contbr. articles to profl. jours. Chmn. Ohio Gov.'s Com. on Employment of Handicapped, 1970-78; mem. state exec. com. Presdl. Commn. Employment of Handicapped, 1970-78, chmn., 1971-72; mem. planning and adv. council White House Conf. on Handicapped Individuals, 1975-78; mem. Columbus Mayor's Com. on Internat. Yr. of Disabled. Recipient Lederle Med. Faculty award, 1968-71, prize for basic research South Atlantic Assn. Obstetricians and Gynecologists, 1968, Outstanding Individual award Ohio Rehab. Assn., 1969, Gov.'s award for community service, 1973, Coll. Medicine Alumni Faculty Tchg. award, Ohio State U. Coll. Medicine, 2002, Univ. Disting. Svc. award, 2005. Mem. Am. Assn. Anatomists, Am. Assn. Immunologists, Soc. Exptl. Biology and Medicine, Sigma Xi (pres. Ohio State chpt. 1979-80) Republican. Presbyterian. Home: 8586 Button Bush Ln Westerville OH 43082-8675 Home Phone: 614-895-8123. Personal E-mail: rstpierre@insight.rr.com.

SAINZ, IGNACIO, cardiologist; b. Seville, Spain, Jan. 10, 1959; PhD, U. Seville, 1983; degree in Cardiologist, U. Cardiology Virgen del Rocio., 1988. Cardiology cons. Andalusian Med. Svc., 1983—. Mem.: Spanish Soc. Cardiology. Office: Doctor Jose Maria Bedoya 4 Seville 41004 Spain Office Fax: 00-34-954531750. Business E-Mail: ignacio.sainz.sspa@juntadeandalucia.es.

SAINZ DE BARANDA, PILAR, physical education educator; b. Albacete, Spain, Nov. 7, 1976; PhD, U. Murcia, 2002. Lic. U. Leon, 1999, cert. in health and phys. activity, spine, and flexibility. Prof. Cath. U. San Antonio Murcia, 2001—09, U. Castilla La Mancha, 2009—; dir. RAQUIS: Spine and Sport Rsch. Group. Sci. and tech. cons. Grupo Tratamiento Integral del Aparato Locomotor S.L., 1999—. Recipient Sport Rsch. award, Andalusian Sports Inst, Sport Sci. Rsch. award, Seneca Found. Region Murcia, Best Communication award, Faculty Phys. Activity and Sport Scis., Cath. U. San Antonio. Mem.: Promotion Physical Activity and Health Rsch. Group, Spanish Assn. Sport Scis., Spanish Soccer Strength and Conditioning Assn., Coll. Phys. Edn. Andalucia (licentiate Rsch. award 2008). Avocations: soccer, exercise. Home: C/ San Antonio 14 Guadalupe Murcia 30107 Spain Personal E-mail: psainzdebaranda@gmail.com.

SAINZ-FUERTES, RICARDO, psychiatrist; s. Ricardo Sainz-Estrada and Ana Fuertes-Ybañez; children: Guillermo Sainz-Arroyo, Jaime Sainz-Arroyo. LMS, Med. Sch., Barcelona, 1997; MSc, King's Coll., London, 2003; MRCPsych, Royal Coll. Psychiatrists, UK, 2005. Clin. rsch. tng. fellow Inst. Psychiatry, London, 2007—; specialist registrar psychiatry South London and Maudsley Trust, 2005—. Asst. combat scuba diver Spanish Navy, 1996—97. Decorated Cruz Mérito Naval Armada Española; Clin. Rsch. Tng. Fellowship, Med. Rsch. Coun., 2007—10. Mem.: Brit. Assn. Psychopharmacology, Gen. Med. Coun., Royal Coll. Psychiatrists. Achievements include research in protein expression in peripheral blood in psychosis. Avocations: sailing, diving, reading. Office Fax: 44 (0)20 7848 0632. Business E-Mail: drsainz@gmail.com.

SAITO, JUN, endocrinologist; b. Tokyo, June 27, 1960; MD, Ehime U., 1987; PhD, Chiba U., 1995. Chief, divsn. endocrinology and metabolism, dept. medicine Yokohama Rosai Hosp., 2004—. Mem.: Japan Endocrine Soc. Office: 3211 Kozukue-cho Kohoku-ku Yokohama Kanagawa 222-0036 Japan Office Fax: 81-045-474-8866. Business E-Mail: saitoj@yokohamah.rofuku.go.jp.

SAITO, MINORU, medical educator; b. Tokyo, June 25, 1959; D, Waseda U., 1992. Prof. Nihon U., 1999—. Office: 3-25-40 Sakurajosui Setagaya-ku Tokyo 156-8550 Japan Office Fax: 81-3-5317-9432. Business E-Mail: msaito@chs.nihon-u.ac.jp.

SAITO, MOTOAKI, urologist, researcher; b. Ueno, Mie, Japan, July 7, 1965; s. Hisanobu and Shigeyo (Inagaki) S.; m. Naomi Matsushita, Feb. 14, 1992; 1 child. MD, Tottori U., Yonago, Japan, 1991, PhD, 2000. Resident Tottori Univ. Hosp., Yonago, 1991-93; postdoctoral assoc. Yale U. Sch. Medicine, New Haven, Conn., 1993-96; lectr. Tottori U. Sch. Medicine, Yonago, 1995—. Contbr. articles to med. jours. Grantee Ministry Edn., Sci. and Culture of Japan, 1998. Mem. Internat. Continence Soc., Japanese Urol. Assn., Am. Urol. Assn., N.Y. Acad. Sci. Office: Tottori U Faculty Med Dept Urology 86 Nishmachi 683-0826 Yonago Tottori Japan

SAITO, SEIICHI, urologist, educator; b. Rubeshibe, Hokkaido, Japan, Apr. 6, 1956; s. Jiro and Eiko Saito; m. Ryuko Sakuraba, Aug. 22, 1981; children: Tetsuichi, Kaeko, Mitsuko. MD, Sapporo Med. Coll., Japan, 1982, PhD, 1986. Instr. Sapporo Med. Coll., 1986—87; rsch. fellow Mayo Clinic, Rochester, Minn., 1987—89; instr. Sapporo Med. Coll., 1989—91; sr. rsch. fellow Mayo Clinic, Rochester, Minn., 1989; dir. Art Pk. Urology Hosp., Sapporo, 1991—. Contbr. articles to profl. jour.; reviewer: jour. in field. Sex-check chief Asian Olympic Games, Sapporo, 1990, Universiade, Sapporo, 1991. Mem.: Hokkaido Hemodialysis Assn. (sec. 1998—), Sapporo Med. Assn. (acad. instr. 1998—), Endourology, Soc. Internat. Urology, Am. Urol. Assn. Avocations: skiing, badminton, music. Office: Art Park Urology Hosp Ishiyama Higashi 3-1-31 Sapporo 005-0850 Japan Fax: 81-11-591-7969.

SAITO, SHIRO, urologist, educator; b. Tokyo, July 16, 1956; s. Ken and Takako Saito; m. Mami Matsumoto, June 7, 1985; children: Yuki, Rina. MD, Keio U., 1982. Cert. med. doctor Japanese Ministry Health, Labor and Welfare, 1982. Rsch. fellow Meml. Sloan-Kettering Cancer Ctr., NYC, 1992—94; chief urology Keio U. Sch. Medicine, Shinjuku-ku, Japan, 1994—97, asst. prof., 1997—; chief dept. urology Nat. Tokyo Med. Ctr., Meguro-ku, 1997—; asst. prof. U. Ryukyus Sch. Medicine, Okinawa, 2000—. Mem.: Am. Assn. Cancer Rsch., Am. Urol. Assn. (corr.). Achievements include research in use of cancer seed implantation brachytherapy prostate. Office: Nat Tokyo Med Ctr 2-5-1 Higashigaoka Tokyo Meguro-ku 152-8902 Japan Office Phone: 81-3-3411-0111. Office Fax: +81-3-3412-9811. Business E-Mail: saitoshr@netjoy.ne.jp.

SAITO, TAKAO, medical association administrator; b. Ibaraki, Japan, Feb. 9, 1960; MS, Meiji Coll. Pharmacy, 1985; PhD, Osaka U., 1996. V.p. Takasago Internat. Corp., 2006—. Recipient award, Molecular Chirality Com. Japan, 2001. Home: 3-8-15 Yaguchi Ohta-ku Tokyo 146-0093 Japan

SAITO, YOSHIRO, medical educator; b. Furukawa, Miyagi, Japan, Feb. 3, 1973; s. Shigeo Saito; m. Maki Saito, June 18, 2001; children: Yoshihiro, Akari. PhD, Hokkaido U., Japan, 2001. Cert. pharmacist. Rsch. worker JSPS, Sapporo, Hokkaido, 2000—02; rsch. scientist AIST, Ikeda, Osaka, Japan, 2002—08; instr. Doshisha U., Kyotanabe, Kyoto, 2008—. Recipient Young Investigator award, SFRR Asia, 2005, SFRR Japan, 2007; fellowship, A NY Acad. Scis., 2004. Office: Doshisha Univ 1-3 Miyakodani Tatara Kyotanabe Kyoto 610-0394 Japan Business E-Mail: ysaito@mail.doshisha.ac.jp.

SAITO, YUTAKA, gastroenterologist; b. Japan, May 28, 1966; MD, Gunma U., 1992, PhD, 1996. Chief, gastrointestinal endoscopy divsn. Nat. Cancer Ctr. Hosp., 2003—. Office: 5-1-1 Tsukiji Chuo-ku Tokyo Kanto 104-0045 Japan Business E-Mail: ytsaito@ncc.go.jp.

SAK, ALI, radiobiologist, researcher; b. AksaraY, Turkey, Mar. 15, 1965; s. Mehmet and Neziha Sak; m. Dilek Peker, July 15, 1969; children: Sezer, Deniz. PhD, U. Essen, Germany, 1992. Diplomate Ruhr U. Bochum, U. Essen, 1992. Rsch. scientist U. Hosp. Essen, 1992—97, Humboldt U., Berlin, 1998—2001, U. Hosp. Essen, 2001—. Recipient Bristol-Myers-Squib rsch. award, Deutsche Gesellschaft for Radioonkologie, 1996, award, Hans-Langendorf Found., 2000. Mem.: DNA Repair Network (assoc.), European Soc. Therapeutic Radiology and Oncology (assoc.). Office: Dept Radiotherapy Hufelandstr. 55 45147 Essen Germany Office Fax: 492017235960. Business E-Mail: ali.sak@uni-due.de.

SAKAI, FUMIKAZU, radiologist, educator; b. Tokyo, Mar. 8, 1952; MD, Shisnhu U., 1978, PhD, 1990. Prof., diagnostic radiology Tokyo Women's Med. U. Med. Ctr., 2000—03; chief attending radiologist Tokyo Met. Komagome Hosp., 2003—07; vice chmn., prof., diagnostic imaging Saitama Med. U., Saitama Internat. Med. Ctr., 2007—. Mem.: Japanese Soc. Radiology. Office: 1397-1 Yamane Hidaka Saitama 3501298 Japan Office Fax: 81429844520. Business E-Mail: fmksakai@saitama-med.ac.jp.

SAKAI, KOJI, psychologist, educator; b. Suzuka City, Mie Prefecture, Japan, Aug. 25, 1972; s. Takeshi and Teruko (Hayashi) Sakai; m. Chiemi Sakai, Nov. 5, 2006; children: Ayane, Reona. BA, Tohoku U., Japan, 1995; MA, Kyoto U., Japan, 1997, PhD, 2000. Lectr. Kyoto Koka Women's U., 2000—05, assoc. prof., 2005—. Contbr. articles to profl. jours. Office: Kyoto Koka Women's Univ 38 Kadono-cho Nishikyogoku Ukyo-ku Kyoto 615-0882 Japan Office Phone: 81-75-325-5336. Office Fax: 81-75-325-5339. Business E-Mail: rb064@mail.koka.ac.jp.

SAKAI, KOYU, cardiologist, deputy director; b. Seattle, Dec. 18, 1969; s. Koken and Kiyoko Sakai; m. Tomoko Yasuda, Apr. 25, 2000; children: Yuka, Yuna, Michika. MD, Tokushima U., Japan, 1994; PhD, Kyoto U., 2003. Lic. in practice medicine Japan, 1994. Staff physician Kokura Meml. Hosp., Kitakyushu, Japan, 1998—2003, cardiologist-in-chief, 2003—06, dep. dir., 2006—. Contbr. articles to profl. jours. Fellow: ACP, Am. Heart Assn., Soc. Cardiovasc. Angiography Interventions, Am. Coll. Cardiology. Achievements include research in primary percutaneous coronary angioplasty is a feasible and effective procedure in high-risk patients with acute myocardial infarction. Avocation: reading. Office: Kokura Meml Hosp 3-2-1 Asano Kokurakita-Ku Kitakyushu 8020001 Japan

SAKAI, NAOTAKA, surgeon, educator; b. Japan, Dec. 22, 1953; MD, Yamagata U., 1979; PhD, U. Tokyo, 2010. Vis. clinician Mayo Clinic, 1992—93; instr. Yokohama City U., 1994—95, asst. prof., 1995—99; dir. Yokohama Citizen's Mcpl. Hosp., 1999—2001; prof. Utsunomiya U., 2001—. Fellow: Japan Coll. Rheumatology, Japanese Soc. Surgery Hand (award); mem.: Japanese Assn. Orrthop., Internat. Fedn. Soc. Surgery Hand, Performing Arts Medicine Assn. Avocation: classical music. Office: 7-1-2 Yoto Utsunomiya 321-8585 Japan Business E-Mail: naosakai@cc.utsunomiya-u.ac.jp.

SAKAI, TAKEHIRO, surgeon; b. Hirosaki, Aomori, Japan, Feb. 3, 1972; s. Yu and Noriko Sakai; m. Chiyo Sakai. MD, Hirosaki U. Sch. Medicine, Japan, 1997, PhD, 2001. Lic. Ministry of Health, Labour, and Welfare, Japan, 1997, bd. cert. surgeon Japan Surg. Soc., 2003, bd. cert. surgeon in gastroenterology Japan Soc. Gastroenterology Surgery, 2005. Surgeon, head surgeon Aomori Rosai Hosp., Hachinohe, Japan, 2001—03, head surgeon, 2007—08, 2011—, Kuroishi City Hosp., Aomori, Japan, 2003—05; surgeon Hirosaki City Hosp., 2005—07; asst prof., dept. thoracic and cardiovasc. surgery Hirosaki U. Sch. Medicine, 2008—11. Contbr. articles to profl. jours. Mem.: Japan Soc. Coloprotology, Japan Lung Cancer Soc., Japanese Assn. Acute Medicine, Japan Surg. Assn., Japanese Breast Cancer Soc., Japanese Soc. Gastroenterology (cert.), Japanese Gastric Cancer Assn., Japanese Assn. Thoracic Surgery, Japanese Soc. Abdominal Emergency Medicine, Japanese Soc. Gastroent. Surgery (cert.), Japan Surg. Soc. (cert.). Office: Aomori Rosai Hosp Dept Surgery 1 Minamigaoka Shirogane-machi Hachinohe 031-8551 Japan

SAKAI, YU, pathologist; b. Osaka, Japan, July 10, 1966; s. Kunisuke and Kazuko Sakai; m. Asako Kondo, June 10, 2000. MD, Nat. Def. Med. Coll., Tokorozawa, Japan, 1991; PhD, Juntendo U., Bunkyo-ku, Japan, 2002. Jr. resident Nat. Def. Med. Coll., Tokorozawa, 1991—93, sr. resident, 1995—97; physician Japan Self Def. Force Fukuoka Hosp., Kasuga, Fukuoka, Japan, 1993—94; pathologist Japan Self Def. Forces Ctrl. Hosp., Setagaya-ku, Tokyo, 1994—95, 1997—2005, Japan Self Def. Forces Sapporo Gen. Hosp., Japan, 2005—07; chief, test and evaluation sect. Mil. Medicine Rsch. Unit, Tokyo, 2007—09; chief, dept. pathology Kainan Hosp. Aichi Prefectural Welfare Fedn. Agrl. Coops., 2009—10, Anjo Kosei Hosp. Fellow: Japanese Soc. Pathology; mem.: Japanese Soc. Lab. Medicine, Japanese Soc. Clin. Cytology. Avocation: fishing. Office: Anjo Kosei Hosp Dept Pathology 28 Higashihirokute Anjo-cho Anjo Aichi 446 8602 Japan Personal E-mail: zwq04043@nifty.ne.jp.

SAKAI, YUZO, physician, educator; b. Chiba, Japan, Jan. 28, 1965; MD, Kochi Med. Sch., 1990; PhD, Chiba U., 1999. Staff physician dept. medicine Cancer Inst. Hosp., Tokyo, head Endoscopy Ctr., Social Ins. Funabashi Ctrl. Hosp., Japan, 2001—06; asst. prof. dept. medicine and clin. oncology Chiba U., 2006—10; dir. Chiba Ctrl. Clinic, 2009—. Mem. editl. bd. World Jour. Gastrointestinal Endoscopy, 2010—11. Grant, Pancreas Rsch. Found. Japan, Japanese Found. Rsch. and Promotion Endoscopy, 2009. Mem.: Japanese Soc. Internal Medicine, Japan Gastroent. Endoscopy Soc., Japanese Soc. Gastroenterology. Avocation: yachting. Office: 1-1-3F Honchiba-cho Chuo-ku Chiba 260-0014 Japan Office Fax: (81) 43 445 8262. E-mail: uzosakai@yahoo.co.jp.

SAKAKI, TOSHISUKE, hospital administrator; Dir. Nara Med. Univ. Hosp., Japan. Office: Nara Prefectural University Hospital 840 Shijo-cho Kashihara Nara 6348522 Japan Office Phone: 81744223051. *

SAKALIHASAN, NATZI, thoracic surgeon, educator, researcher; b. Komotini, Rodopi, Greece, 1957; s. Memet Sakalihasan and Macide Gur; m. Lise Anne Snytsers, Mar. 14, 1992; children: Sarah, Elif. MD, Cerrahpasa Med. Sch. U. Istanbul, Turkey, 1982; PhD, U. Liege, Belgium, 1994, agregation thesis, 2005. Cert. diploma equivalency U. Liege Faculty Medicine, Belgium, 1986, diplomate in surgery U. Liege, 1990, Agregation Thesis U. Liege, 2005. Residency gen. surgery U. Hosp., Sart Tilman, Liege, Belgium, 1986—90, fellow in cardiovascular surgery, 1990—94, sr. cardiovascular surgeon, 1994—. Grantee, Nat. Heart, Lung and Blood Inst. U.S., 2000. Mem.: European Soc. Vascular Surgery, French Soc. Vascular Surgery, Belgian Assn. Cardio-thoracic Surgery, Royal Belgian Soc. Surgery (reviewer 2000—05), Internat. Soc. Cardiovasc. Surgery, N.Y. Acad-.Scis. Achievements include development of use of positron emission tomography (PET) in evaluation of abdominal aortic aneurysm. Home: Rue des muguets 53 Liege Beaufays 4052 Belgium Office: Univ Hosp Liege Dept Cardiovasc Surgery Liege Sart Tilman 4000 Belgium Office Fax: 3243667114. Business E-Mail: nsaka@chu.ulg.ac.be.

SAKAMOTO, KAZUYOSHI, retired engineering educator; b. Tokyo, May 1, 1940; MS in Engring., Tokyo Kyoiku U., 1970, DSc, 1970. Prof. U. Electro-Comm., Tokyo, 1988—2006, prof., mem., Ctr. Promotion Alliances with Region, Industry and Govt., 2006—11. Avocation: travel. Office: Chofugaoka 1-5-1 Chofu Tokyo 182-8585 Japan Business E-Mail: sakamoto@crc.uec.ac.jp.

SAKARIASSEN, KJELL STEINAR, physiologist, educator, researcher; b. Tromsø, Norway, June 27, 1951; s. Steinar and Hjørdis Jensine (Eidissen) S.; m. Lucy Rigg, June 21, 1987 (div. Aug. 1991); m. Inger Johanne Lie, June 26, 1993. MSc in Cell Biology cum laude, U. Tromsø, 1979; PhD in Med. Biology cum laude, U. Utrecht, Netherlands, 1984. Postdoctoral fellow U. Wash., Seattle, 1985-87, F. Hoffmann-La Roche, Ltd., Basel, Switzerland, 1984-85, rsch. scientist, 1987—90; group leader U. Oslo, Norway, 1990-92; dir. rsch. Nycomed Imaging AS, Oslo, 1992-98; prof. physiology U. Oslo, 1993-98; dir. pharmacology Pharmacia & Upjohn, Pharmacia Corp., Biovitrum, Uppsala and Stockholm, Sweden, 1998—2001, Serono Internat. S.A., Ivrea, Italy, 2001—04, worldwide head of pharmacology and early safety evaluation Geneva, 2001—04, Boston, 2001—04; founder, head KellSa s.a.s., Biella, Italy, 2004—; mem. sci. adv. bd. Evolva SA, Basel, Switzerland, 2007—. Cons. Media Resource Svc., Ciba Found., London, 1991—; editl. asst. The Biochemical Jour., London, 1992-2006, Thrombosis Haemostasis, Stuttgart, 1999-2003, Jour. Thrombosis Haemostasis, Blackwell, 2003—; Owren lectr. U. Oslo, 1990; mem. sci. adv. bd. Evolva SA, Basel, Switzerland, 2007-. Contbr. chapters to books, articles to profl. jours. Am. Heart Assn. fellow, 2001; recipient Theodor Naegli prize, Basel, 1985, 5th Amalthée prize Animal Rights Orgn., Paris, 1993. Mem. Am. Soc. Hematology, Internat. Soc. Thrombosis and Haemostasis (chmn. subcom. rheology 1992-96, sci. and standardization subcom. pub. bd. 2000-04, sr. adv. coun. 2004—), Am. Heart Assn., NY Acad. Scis., Oslo Vascular Biology Soc. (founder 1990, chmn. 1990-97), Am. Diabetes Assn. Achievements include patents in field. Avocations: history, literature, music, skiing, speed-skating. Personal E-mail: kjell.sakariassen@gmail.com. Business E-Mail: kjell.sakariassen@kellsa.com.

SAKATA, SUSUMU, cardiologist, hematologist, researcher; b. Yonago, Tottori, Japan, Mar. 5, 1956; s. Sueyoshi and Masako (Tsubaki) S.; m. Atsuko Yamauchi, July 27, 1980; children: Naoya, Yuri, Ryusuke. BS, Osaka U., Japan, 1978, MS, 1980; D of Med. Sci., Nara Med. U., Japan, 1985. Assoc. prof. dept. physiology Nara Med. U., 1980—2008; prof. faculty health sci. Kio U., 2008—. Contbr. articles to profl. jours. Recipient rsch. grant Kurozumi Med. Found., 1993, Ministry of Edn., Sci. and Culture of Japan, 2008-, Ono Sports Sci. Found., 1997. Mem. Am. Physiology Soc., Physiol. Soc. Japan, Am. Heart Assn., Am. Soc. Gene Therapy. Avocations: sports watching, fishing, judging. Office: Kio Univ Faculty Health Sci 4-2-2 Umaminaka Koryo-cho Kitakatsuragi-gun Nara 635 0832 Japan Home Phone: +81-72-949-2024; Office Phone: 81-745-54-1601. Business E-Mail: s.sakata@kio.ac.jp.

SAKELLARIOU, GRIGORIOS T., rheumatologist; b. Serres, May 2, 1973; MD, 1998. Cons. rheumatologist 424 Gen. Mil. Hosp., 2008—. Office: Chalkeon 27 Thessaloniki Macedonia 546 31 Greece E-mail: sakelgr@gmail.com.

SAKELLARIS, GEORGIOS, physician, consultant; b. Arkalohori, May 29, 1958; MD, Heraklion, 1976. Cons. Pepagni, 1998. Home: Mel Piga 31 Heraklion Crete 71306 Greece Personal E-mail: gsakell@mycosmos.gr.

SAKHUJA, ANKIT, physician; b. Kanpur, India, Mar. 24, 1984; MD, All India Inst. Med. Scis., 2007. Resident Med. Coll. Wis., 2008—. House-staff rep. to grad. med. edn. coun. Med. Coll. Wis. Affiliated Hosps., 2010—11. Recipient Excellence award, Am. Soc. Nephrology, Ann. Sci. Award, Soc. Critical Care Medicine, 2011; nominee Rsch. award, Med. Coll. Wis. Affiliated Hosp.; Travel grant, Nat. Kidney Found., 2010. Mem.: AMA, ACP. Avocation: jogging. Home: 9112 W Dixon St Apt 204 Milwaukee WI 53214 Personal E-mail: dr.a.sakhuja@gmail.com.

SAKKA, SAMIR AKRAM, consultant orthopedic & spinal surgeon; b. Amman, Jordan, June 8, 1959; MB, BChir, St. Georges Hosp. Med. Sch., London, 1985; MS, London U., 1994. Register to sr. registar North Thames Region, London, 1991—; fellow Royal Nat. Orthop. Hosp., 1994-96, sr. fellow in spinal surgery, 1996; cons. orthop. and spinal surgeon U. Hosp. Levisham; hon. sr. lectr. London U. KGT. Hon. sr. lectr. United Med. and Dental Sch. Contbr. articles to profl. jours. Fellow Royal Soc. of Medicine; mem. Brit. Orthop. Trainers Assn. (BOTA prize 1995), Brit. Scoliosis Soc., Internat. Soc. Spinal Deformity Rsch., Brit. Orthop. Assn., Royal Coll. Surgeons of Edinburgh. Home: 11 Nelson Rd London SW191HS England Business E-Mail: ssakka@btinternet.in.

SAKMANN, BERT, physician, cell physiologist; b. Stuttgart, Germany, June 12, 1942; Grad, U. Tübingen, 1967; PhD, U. Göttingen, Munich, 1974; degree (hon.), U. Alicante, Spain, U. Liverpool, U. Bordeaux, France, U. Munich, Germany, U. Colorado, Denver, U. Coll. London, Weizmann Inst., Rehovot, Israel. Research asst. dept. of neurophysiology Max Planck Inst. for Psychiatry, Munich, 1969—70; council fellow dept. of biophysics University Coll., London, 1971—73; research asst. dept. of neurobiology Max Planck Inst. for Biophysical Chem., Göttingen, Germany, 1974—79, research assoc. membrane biology group, 1979—82, dir. membrane biology group, 1983—85, dir. dept. of cell physiology, 1985—89, Max Planck Inst. for Med. Research, Heidelberg, Germany, 1989—2008; sci. dir., rsch. group leader digital neuroanatomy Max Planck Fla. Inst., Jupiter, Fla., 2008—. Fgn. mem. NAS, Royal Society, London. Recipient Nernst prize, German Bunsen Soc. for Physical Chem., 1977, Feldberg prize, Feldberg Found., 1979, Magnes award, Magnes Found., 1981, Spencer prize, Columbia U., 1983, Adolf Fick prize, U. Würzburg, 1984, Zottermann prize, Swedish Physiological Soc., 1984, Gross-Horwitz prize, Columbia U., 1986, Leibniz prize, German Research Found., 1986, Louis Jeantet prize, Louis Jeantet Found., 1988, Gairdner prize, Gairdner Found., 1989, Ernst Hellmut Vits prize, U. Münster, 1990, Harvey prize, Technion, 1991, Gerard prize, Soc. for Neuroscience, 1991, Research prize, Min. of Sci., Research & Art, Baden-Württemberg, 1991, Nobel prize in physiology or medicine, Nobel Found., 1991. Mem.: Orden Pour le Mérite, Heidelberger Acad. of Sciences, Goettinger Acad. of Sciences, Bavarian Acad. of Sciences and Humanities, German Acad. of Natural Scientists Leopoldina (Carus medal 1991). Office: Max Planck Fla Inst 5353 Parkside Dr MC19-RE Jupiter FL 33458-2906 Office Phone: 561-972-9400. *

SAKOVETS, TATIANA GENNADIEVNA, medical researcher; b. Kazan, Dec. 17, 1974; Degree in Pediat., Kazan State Med. U., 1998, PhD, 2006. Asst. of chair neurology, rehab. Kazan State Med. U., 2006—. Mem.: Soc. Physiotherapists, Soc. Physicians Rehab. Medicine Physicians, Soc. Neurologists City of Kazan. Avocations: swimming, travel. Office: Butlerova 49 Kazan Tatarstan 420012 Russia Office Fax: 7(843)2618435. Business E-Mail: tsakovets@yandex.ru.

SAKS, KAI, education educator; b. Tartu, Estonia, July 30, 1955; d. Karl and Laine Viileberg; m. Jaan Saks, Jan. 31, 1976; children: Kalju, Silja Mikli. MD, U. of Tartu, 1979; PhD, Leningrad I Med. Acad., 1987. Rschr. U. of Tartu, Lab. of Cardiology, Tartu, Estonia, 1980—87; asst. prof. U. of Tartu, Dept. of Internal Medicine Propedeutics, 1987—91, U. of Tartu, Dept. of Cardiology, 1991—93, assoc. prof., 1993—99, U. of Tartu, Dept. of Internal Medicine, 2000—. Vice dean U. of Tartu, Faculty of Medicine, 1994—97. Anchorperson (series of tv broadcasts). Master: Internat. Assn. of Gerontology (coun. mem. 2004—), Estonian Assn. of Gerontology and Geriat. (pres. 2002—); fellow: InterRAI; mem.: Estonian Soc. of Cardiology. Avocations: gardening, bicycling. Office: Univ of Tartu Dept Int Med L. Puusepa 6-261 51014 Tartu Estonia Office Fax: +372 7318607. Personal E-mail: kai.saks@ut.ee. Business E-Mail: kai.saks@kliinikum.ee.

SAKSENA, MANSI, physician; b. India, Mar. 10, 1975; MD, Topiwala Nat. Med. Coll., 1999. Physician Mass. Gen. Hosp., 2007—, resident, radiology, 2011. Recipient Merit award, Radiol. Soc. N.Am. Home: 10 Chestnut Way Stratham NH 03885 Personal E-mail: mansisaksena@gmial.com.

SAKUDO, AKIKAZU, science educator; b. Ehime, Ehime Prefecuture, Japan, Mar. 28, 1977; PhD, U. Tokyo, 2004. Asst. prof. Osaka U., 2005—; assoc. prof. U. Ryukyus, 2009—. Contbr. scientific papers. Recipient Young Scientist award, Japanese Soc. Host Def. Rsch. Mem.: U. Industry Coop. Rsch. Coms. (Japan Soc. for Promotion of Sci. 2008—). Office: Uehara 207 Nishihara Okinawa 903-0215 Japan Office Phone: 81-98-895-3331. Business E-Mail: sakudo@med.u-ryukyu.ac.jp.

SAKURAI, HIROYUKI, surgeon; b. Urawa, Japan, Oct. 4, 1969; s. Yoshikane and Misako Sakurai; m. Masayo Tomioka Sakurai, June 28, 2003; 1 child, Yoshiki. MD, U. Yamanashi, 1994, PhD (hon.), 2005. Intern U. Yamanashi, Japan, 1994—95, med. staff, 1995—98, asst., 2003—04; resident Nat. Cancer Ctr. Hosp., Tokyo, 1998—2000, chief resident, 2001—02; chief Yamanashi Prefectrual Ctrl. Hosp., 2004—07; chief dept. thoracic surgery Saiseikai Ctrl. Hosp., 2007—. Office: Yamanashi Prefectural Ctrl Hosp Dept Surgery 1 1 Fujimi 1 chome Kofu Yamanashi 4000027 Japan Home: Saiseikai Ctrl Hosp Dept Thoracic Surgery 1-4-17 Mita Minato-Ku Tokyo 108-0073 Japan Office Phone: 81-55-253-7111. Business E-Mail: sakuraihm@ybb.ne.jp, h-sakurai2a@ych.pref.yamanashi.jp.

SALAHUDDIN, MD., research scientist; b. Bidar, July 20, 1976; BPharm, KLE, PhD, 2000. Sr. rsch. fellow KLE, 2008—. Fellowship, U. Grants Commn. New Delhi. Mem.: Pharmacy Coun. Avocations: sports, travel, music. Home: Outside Shah Ganj Afzal Pura Bidar Karnataka 585401 India Business E-Mail: salahuddin_md08@rediffmail.com.

SALAHUDDIN, PARVEEN, information scientist, researcher; d. Talat Salahuddin; m. Ziaul Islam. BS, Aligarh Muslim U., India, 1981, MS, 1984, MPhil, 1986, PhD, 1989. Sr. bioinformatics officer Aligarh (India) Muslim U., 1991—. Presenter in field. Contbr. articles to profl. jours. Mem.: AAAS, Protein Soc. Avocations: reading, gardening, travel, music, cooking. Personal E-mail: parveen_salahuddin@yahoo.com.

SALAJEGHEH, MOHAMMAD KIAN, neurologist, educator; b. Tehran, Iran, July 20, 1968; MD, Tehran U. Med. Scis., 1995. Instr., neurology Brigham and Women's Hosp. Harvard Med. Sch., 2007, asst. prof., neurology, 2010—. Recipient Med. Knowledge Competency award, Dept. Neurology U. Mass. Med. Sch., Recognition award, Am. Acad. Neuromuscular and Electrodiagnostic Medicine. Mem.: Am. Assn. Neuromuscular and Electrodiagnostic Medicine, Mass. Med. Soc., Am. Acad. Neurology. Office: 75 Francis St Tower 5D Boston MA 02115 Business E-Mail: msalajegheh@partners.org.

SALAMA, MAURICE A., dentist; married; 2 children. BA, SUNY, Binghamton, 1985—85; DMD, U. Pa., Phila., 1985—89. Cert. periodontics, orthodontics, implant surg. tng. Tchg. asst. dept. of biology SUNY, Binghamton, 1984—85; dental asst. to Dr. Mitchell Silverman Margate, 1987—89; extern Beth Israel Hosp., 1988, Hadassah Hosp., 1988; resident Maimonides Med. Ctr., Bkly., 1989—90; clin. asst. prof. periodontics and orthodontics shc. of dental medicine Univ. Pa., 1993—96, clin. asst. prof. of periodontics sch. of medicine, 1996—; clin. prof. of periodontics Med. Coll. of Ga., 1996—; vis. prof. of periodontics Nova Univ. Fla., 1996—; vis. prof. dept. of periodontics La. State Univ., 2000—; dentist Goldstein, Garber & Salama LLC. Scholar George Coslet award, Univ. Pa., Richard Chase award. Mem.: ADA, Ga. Dental Assn., Thomas P. Hinman Dental Soc, Alpha Omega Internat. Dental Frat., Acad. of Osseointegration, Am. Acad. of Periodontics, Am. Acad. of Orthodontics. Office: Goldstein, Garber & Salama LLC 300 Galleria Pkwy Atlanta GA 30339 Office Phone: 404-261-4941. Office Fax: 404-261-4946.

SALAMANCA-GOMEZ, FABIO, medical geneticist; b. Bogotá, Colombia, Nov. 3, 1940; s. Augusto Salamanca-Hurtado and Aminta (Gómez Uribe) Salamanca; m. Leonora Buentello, Feb. 24, 1971; 1 child, Fabio. MD, Nat. U. Colombia, 1964, Specialist in Med. Genetics, 1971, Master of Med. Scis., 1984. Acad. sec. faculty medicine Nat. U. Colombia, Bogotá, 1966-68; head dept. genetics Nat. Inst. Spl. Programs in Health, Bogotá, 1971-72; head sect. cytogenetics, div. investigation human genetics Mexicano del Seguro Social, 1974-78; head div. investigation human genetics Nat. Med. Ctr. Pediatric Hosp., IMSS, Mexico, 1978-80; head unit investigation human genetics Nat. Med. Ctr. Jefatura de Investigacion, IMSS, Mexico, 1980—; mem. divisional coun. Jefatura de Investigacion del Seguro Social, Inst. Mex., 1978—. Prof. faculty of medicine, U. Nat. Autonoma de Mex., 1973—; prof. U. Anahuac, Mex., 1975-86, Nat. Inst. Anthropology and History, Mex., 1975—, U. Nat. Autonoma de Mex., 1982—; mem. govt. bd. Inst. Biotech. Nat. U. Mex., mem. directive commn. faculty medicine, mem. directive commn. faculty odontology; mem. directive commn. Inst. Anthropology Rsch. Author: Gregor Mendel: The Garden's Forgotten Friar, 1988 (Nat. Med. Publs. award 1990), Human Cytogenetics: Principles and Clinical Practice, 1990 (Nat. Luis Soto-Allande award 1991); contbr. several chpts. books; co-editor Archives of Med. Rsch., 1991—; co-editor: Gac. Med. Mex., 1991-; contbr. articles to profl. jours. Recipient Nat. Med. Publs. award Nat. Acad. Medicine, 1987, Aaron Saenz award, Nat. Sec. of Health, 1995; grantee Nat. Coun. Scis. and Tech., 1983, 85, 87, 89, 91. Mem. AAAS, Mex. Assn. Human Genetics (pres. 1980-82), Mex. Assn. Biol. Anthropology (pres. 1985-87), Am. Soc. Human Genetics, Am. Coll. Human Genetics, Environ. Mutagen Soc., Internat. Fedn. Fertility Soc., Internat. Soc. Twin Studies, Latin Am. Soc. Human Genetics, Internat. Com. on Registry of Chromosome Abnormalities, Nat. Rsch. System (founder), Nat. Com. of Heath Scis. (pres. 1996), Nat. Commn of Health and Med. Scis. (pres. 1999), Nat. Coun. Human Genetics (founder), Nat. Acad. Medicine (Everardo Landa award 1983), Mex. Acad. Surgery (Gonzalez Castaneda award 1982), Mex. Acad. Pediatrics, Nat. Acad. Sci. Rsch., Assn. Investigation on Pediatrics, Mex. Assn. Clin. Pathology, Mex. Assn. for Study of Human Fertility & Reprodn. (basic rsch. award), Mex. Assn. Mutagenesis & Carcinogenesis, Mex. Assn. Ob-Gyn., Colombian Soc. Biol. Scis., Colombian Soc. Pathology, Colombian Soc. Human Genetics, Mex. Soc. Genomic Medicine. Office: Unit Investigation Human Genetics Nat Med Ctr Apartado Postal 12-951 3020 Mexico City Mexico E-mail: fasalam@prodigy.net.mx.

SALAMONSON, YENNA, nursing educator; b. Malaysia, Oct. 20, 1957; BSc, Macquarie U., 1984; PhD, U. Western Sydney, 2002. RN Campbelltown Hosp., 1985—87, clin. nurse specialist, 1997—2009; lectr. U. Western Sydney, 1987—2006, sr. lectr., 2007—09, assoc. prof., 2010—. Recipient Citation award, Australian Learning and Tchg. Coun., Coll. Health & Sci., Vice-Chancellor's Excellence award, U. Western Sydney. Mem.: Sigma Theta Tau Internat. (Xi Omicron chpt.). Office: Locked Bag 1797 Penrith NSW 2751 Australia Office Fax: 61 2 46203161. Business E-Mail: y.salamonson@uws.edu.au.

SALAND, LINDA CAROL, anatomist, neuroscientist, educator; b. NYC, Oct. 24, 1942; d. Charles and Esther (Weingarten) Gewirtz; m. Joel S. Saland, Aug. 16, 1964; children: Kenneth, Jeffrey. BS, CCNY, 1963, PhD in Biology, 1968; MA in Zoology, Columbia U., 1965. Rsch. assoc. dept. anatomy Columbia U. Coll. Physicians and Surgeons, NYC, 1968-69; sr. rsch. assoc. dept. anatomy Sch. Medicine U. N.Mex., Albuquerque, 1971-78, asst. prof. anatomy, 1978-83, assoc. prof., 1983-89, prof., 1989-97, prof. dept. neuroscis., 1997—. Ad hoc reviewer study sect. NIH, 1994, 1995, 1997, 2000, 2005, 2006-08, mem. site visit team. Mem. editl. bd. Anat. Record, 1980-98; contbr. articles to profl. jours. Recipient Khatali Tchg. Excellence award, U. N.Mex. Med. Class of 2001; fellow NDEA, 1966—68. Mem. Soc. for Neurosci., Women in Neurosci. (chmn. steering com. 1991-93). Office: U New Mex Sch Medicine Dept Neuroscis MSC 084740 Albuquerque NM 87131-0001 Business E-Mail: lsaland@salud.unm.edu.

SALANS, LESTER BARRY, physician, research scientist, educator; b. Chgo. Heights, Ill., Jan. 25, 1936; s. Leon K. and Jean R.; m. Lois Audrey Kapp, Dec. 21, 1958; children: Laurence Eliot, Andrea Eileen. BA, U. Mich., 1957; MD with honors, U. Ill., 1961. Internal medicine intern Stanford U. Med. Ctr., 1961, resident, 1962-64; USPHS postdoctoral and spl. fellow Rockefeller University, 1964-67, asst. prof., 1967-68; asst. prof. medicine Dartmouth Coll., 1968-70, assoc. prof., 1970-77; assoc. dir. diabetes, endocrinology, metabolism, also chief lab. cellular metabolism and obesity Nat. Inst. Arthritis, Metabolism and Digestive Diseases, NIH, Bethesda, Md., 1976-81; dir. Nat. Inst. Arthritis, Diabetes, Digestive and Kidney Diseases, NIH, Bethesda, Md., 1980—84; adj. prof. Dartmouth Coll., 1978-79, Rockefeller University, 1984—; v.p., head preclin. rsch. Sandoz Rsch. Inst., 1985-92; dean, v.p. Mt. Sinai Med. Sch., NY, 1987; prof. internal medicine Mount Sinai School Medicine, 1984-85, clin. prof. medicine, 1987—; v.p. scientific and acad. affairs Sandoz Rsch. Inst., 1985—97; pres. LBS Advisors, Inc., 1997—; prin. BioPharmAnalysis LLC, 2001—; adj. prof., dept. medicine Columbia U. Med. Ctr., 2005—10. Adj. prof. Rockefeller U., 1985—2001; vis. prof. U. Geneva, Switzerland, 1974—75; dir. Forest Labs., 1998—; mem. adv. bd. Naomi Berrie Diabetes Ctr. Columbia-Presbyn. Hosp., NYC, 1999—; mem. bd. dirs. PharmaIN, 2009—; adj. prof. medicine, dept. medicine physicians and surgeons Columbia U. Med. Ctr., 2005—10. Contbr. articles on insulin, diabetes mellitus, obesity to profl. jours., textbooks. Recipient NIH Rsch. Career Devel. award, 1972-76, NIH Dir. award, 1980, Juvenile Diabetes Fedn Pub. Svc. award, 1979 Fellow ACP; mem. AAAS, Am. Soc. Clin. Investigation, Am. Fed.

Clin. Rsch., Am. Diabetes Soc., Am. Diabetes Assn. (Charles H. Best award 1985), Endocrine Soc., Assn. Am. Physicians, Am. Soc. Clin. Nutrition. Office: Salans LLC Rockefeller Ctr 620 5th Ave 4th Fl New York NY 10020

SALA-PARCERISAS, ROBERT, tropical medicine physician; b. Torà, Spain, Sept. 8, 1949; s. Isidre Sala-Junyent and Maria Parcerisas-Vilaseca. Physician, U. Barcelona, Spain, 1976, M in Tropical Medicine, 1992, MD, 1995. Adj. physician residència sanitària Hosp. Arnau de Vilanova, Lleida, 1976; clin. physician Jospice (U.K.), Morazan, Honduras, 1978, Residencia Sanitaria Hosp. Arnav De Vilanova Lieida, 1976, Jospice Morazan Honduras, 1978, Ministério da Saúde, Tete and Quelimane, Mozambique, 1982—84, Médicos sin Fronteras Spain, N'Giva, Angola, 1992, Medicus Mundi Asturias Spain, Ntita, Burundi, 1994, FERS (Spain), Mbini, Equatorial Guinea, 1997. Asst. physician Hosp. Clinic i Provincial Eritropatologia, Barcelona, 2003—. Mem.: IBC (Ddir. Gen.'s Roll of Honor 2010—), ABI (rsch. bd. advisors 2006—). Roman Catholic. Achievements include research in theory of production of ultraviolet radiation by neutrophilic leukocyte during phagocytosis. Home: Plaça del Pati 5 2n 4a Lleida Torà 25750 Spain Business E-Mail: r.sala@antics.ub.edu.

SALAS, MAX, pediatrician, educator; MD, Nat. U. Mex., Mexico City, 1964. Diplomate Am. Bd. Pediats., 1969, Am. Bd. Pediatric Endocrinology, 1986. Rotating intern St. Luke's Hosp., St. Paul, 1963—64; resident in pediat. Children's Hosp., Boston, 1965—67, Sheffield, England, 1967—68; fellow in pediatric endocrinology Pitts. Children's Hosp., 1977—79, North Shore Univ. Hosp., Manhasset, NY, 1979—80; assoc. prof. pediat. Drexel U. Sch. Medicine, 2007. Office: St Peters Univ Hosp 254 Easton Ave New Brunswick NJ 08901-1977 Home Phone: 732-297-8562; Office Phone: 732-745-8574. *

SALAY, CINDY ROLSTON, software engineer; b. Roanoke, Va., July 18, 1955; d. Gilbert Wilson and Elinor Patterson (Sandridge) Rolston; m. John Matthew, July 7, 1988; 1 child, David. AAS, Va. Western Community Coll., 1976; AS, J. Sargeant Reynolds Community Coll., 1982; BS, Va. Commonwealth U., 1984. RN. Operating room RN Henrico Doctors Hosp., Richmond, Va., 1979-80; nursing supr. Johnston Willis Hosp., Richmond, 1980-87; systems analyst, coord. Health Corp Va., Richmond, 1983-87, sr. project leader, 1987-88; sr. systems analyst Hosp. Corp. Am., Nashville, 1987; sr. systems cons. IBAX Healthcare Systems, Reston, Va., 1988-94; sys. analyst MCV Hosps. Info. Sys., Richmond, Va., 1994-95; sr. sys. engr. McKesson, Atlanta, 1995—. Methodist. Avocations: reading, exercise. Home: 13800 Sunrise Bluff Rd Midlothian VA 23112-2512 Office: McKesson 5995 Windward Pkwy Alpharetta GA 30005-4184 Office Phone: 804-639-1070. E-mail: cindy.salay@mckesson.com.

SALCEDO, JOSE RODOLFO, pediatric nephrologist; b. Guadalajara, Jal, Mex., 1945; came to U.S., 1971; s. Rodolfo and Sara; m. Uma T. Salcedo, 1974; children: Nicholas A., Jonathan E. BA, U. Guadalajara, 1964, MD, 1970. Diplomate Am. Bd. Pediatrics, Pediatric Nephrology. Resident Martland Hosp., U. Medicine & Dentistry NJ, Newark, 1971-74; fellow in nephrology Children's Hosp., Washington, 1974-76, acting dir. pediatric nephrology, dir. dialysis unit, 1976-87, vice chmn., 1978—87; dir. pediatric nephrology divsn. N.J. Med. Sch., Newark, 1987-96; chief pediat. nephrology St. Joseph's Children's Hosp., Paterson, NJ, 1996—; assoc. prof. clin. pediats. and medicine U. Medicine and Dentistry NJ. Contbr. chpts. in books and articles to profl. jours. Fellow: Am. Soc. Nephrology, Am. Acad. Pediat. Office: Carolina Diabetes and Kidney Ctr 635 W Wesmark Blvd Sumter SC 29150 Home: 2162 Graytone Dr Sumter SC 29150 Office Phone: 803 469 7500. E mail: salcedojmd@yahoo.com.

SALDANHA, LEOPOLDO FREDERICO, nephrologist, physician, educator; b. Paranagua, Parana, Brazil, Feb. 11, 1942; s. Carlos and Silvia (Neves) S.; m. Elisabeth de Medeiros, Jan. 6, 1968 (div. Sept. 1986); children: Claudine, Gabriela; m. Morgana Bittencourt, Dec. 15, 2001 BS, Santa Catarina State Coll., 1959; MD, Fed. U. Sch. Medicine, 1966. Diplomate Bd. Nephrology, Bd. Internal Medicine. Resident internal medicine Hosp. Pub. Employees State, Rio de Janeiro, 1967—68; fellow nephrology U. Calif. Sch. Medicine, LA, 1970—73; rsch. fellow nephrology med. sch. Harvard U., Boston, 1973—75; chief dept. medicine State Hosp., Florianopolis, Brazil, 1979—81; chief nephrology divsn. Charity Hosp., Florianopolis, 1981—90; assoc. prof. medicine Fed. U., Florianopolis, 1987—2006. Cons. physician State Hosp., Florianopolis, 1969-89, Charity Hosp., Florianopolis, 1969—, Telecomm. Santa Catarina, Florianopolis, 1976-99; vis. assoc. prof. UCLA, 1991-92; rsch. scientist Cedars Sinai Med. Ctr., L.A., 1990-94; assoc. prof. medicine So. U., Tubarao, 2000—, Florianopolis, 2009-. Co-author: Principles of Nephrology, 1988, Handbook of Clinical Medicine, 2006; contbr. articles to profl. jours. including Brit. Med. Jour., Am. Jour. Medicine, Jour. Clin. Investigation, Trans. ASAIO, Am. Jour. Dis. Child, Am. Jour. Kidney Disease, Kidney Internat., Jour. Am. Soc. Nephrology, Nephron Rsch. grantee Brazilian Coun., 1993, Brazilian Ministry Edn. grantee, 1990; recipient Physician's Recognition award ACP, 1972 Mem. Am. Soc. Nephrology, Brazilian Med. Assn Avocations: classical music, films, books, napoleonic studies, tennis. Home: Apt 1001 Rua Bocaiuva 2268 Florianopolis 88015-530 Brazil Office Phone: 55-48-3622-1442. E-mail: lfsaldanha@hotmail.com.

SALDEEN, TOM GUSTAF PER, physician, educator; b. Stockholm, July 21, 1936; s. Bo G.E. and Eira O.S. Saldeen; m. Hill M. Wiesner, Nov. 14, 1959; children: Pia M.S., Nicoline E.M. Angergård, Katarina E.S. Saldeen-Nilèhn, Ann-Sofie E., Bo T.G. MD, U. Lund, 1961; PhD, U. Lund, Sweden, 1963. Vis. prof. Harvard Med. Sch., Boston, 1985—86; prof. and chmn. Dept. Forensic Medicine, U. Uppsala, Sweden, 1968—2001. Adj. prof. Brown U., Providence, 1985—87, U. Fla., Gainesville, 1988—, U. Ark., Little Rock, 1998—. Contbr. 800 sci. papers to numerous profl. jours. Fellowship, Am. Coll. Cardiology, 1989. Fellow: Am. Heart Assn. Achievements include patents in field. Avocations: cross country skiing, golf. Office: Univ of Uppsala Sweden Box 256 Uppsala 751 05 Sweden Home: Sodra Rudbecksgatan 4 SE 752 36 Uppsala Sweden Office Fax: 46 18 550510; Home Fax: 46 18 550510. Business E-Mail: tom.saldeen@surgsci.uu.se.

SALE, ALESSANDRO, biologist; b. Nuoro, Italy, July 19, 1977; Degree in Biol. Scis., U. Pisa, 2001; PhD in Neurobiology, Scuola Normale Superiore, Pisa, 2005. Medicine and biology fellow Italian Acad. Sci., 2003—05; postdoc. Lab. Neurobiology, Scuola Normale Superiore, Pisa, 2005—07, Ctr. Biology Memory, Norwegian U. Sci. and Tech., Trondheim, Norway, 2007; rsch. scientist, physiology Lab. Neurobiology, Scuola Normale Superiore, Pisa, 2007—09; rsch. scientist NRC (CNR), Inst. Neuroscience, Pisa, 2009—. Recipient Internat. award, Mario Benazzi e Giuseppina Benazzi Lentati, Italian Acad. Scis., Nat. prize, Venetian Acad. Scis. Mem.: Italian Soc. Study Animal Behavior, European Brain and Behavior Soc. Avocation: photography. Office: Inst Neurosci CNR via Moruzzi 1 Pisa Tuscany 56123 Italy Business E-Mail: sale@in.cnr.it.

SALEEM, FAHAD, pharmacist, researcher; b. Pakistan, July 4, 1977; MPhil, U. Balochistan, 2007; MBA, Iqra U. Quetta, 2008. Rsch. fellow U. Sains Malaysia, 2010—. Mem.: Internat. Network Rational Use of Drugs, ReAct, Internat. Soc. Pharmacoeconomics and Outcomes Rsch. Avocations: horseback riding, camping, hiking. Office: Universiti Sains Malaysia Discipline Social and Administrative Pharmacy Sch Pharmaceutical Scis Penang 11800 Malaysia Personal E-mail: drfahadsaleem@gmail.com.

SALEEM, SAHAR N., radiology professor, researcher; d. Atyat Mohammad Khalil and Nasr Abdu Saleem; m. Ahmed-Hesham Mohammad Saad Abdel Salam, Jan. 9, 1994; 1 child, Maha Said. MBBCh, Cairo U., 1987, MSc in Radiology, 1992, MD in Radiology, 1998. Resident Cairo U. Faculty Medicine, Radiology dept., 1989—92, asst. lectr., 1992—98, lectr., 1999—2004, asst. prof., 2004—08, prof., 2009—; fellow radiology U. Western Ont., London, 2004—05, postdoc. fellow in radiology and MRI Edn. Canada, 2004, postdoc. fellow neuroradiology rsch., 2005. MRI cons. Mahmod Mosque, Cairo, 1992—, n Egypt, Saudi Arabia. Contbr. chapters to books, articles to profl. jours. Profl. radiology trainer New Kasr Al Aini Tchg. Hosp., Cairo, Cairo, 1999. Recipient cert. of sci. achievement dept. radiology, Cairo U., 2003, cert. orgn. achievement dept. radiology, 2004, Summa Cum Laude award, Am. Soc. NeuroRadiology, 2005, Cert. of Appreciation, Radiol. Soc. Saudi Arabia, 2007, Cert. of Excellence in Publs., Cairo U., 2008—09, Med. Scis. Incentive award, 2009. Mem.: Can. Soc. Anthropology, Internat. Soc. Behcet's Disease, Internat. Soc. Magnetic Resonance in Medicine, Radiol. Soc. N.Am. (cert. of merit award 2005, Cum Laude award 2007), Egyptian Soc. Radiology. Muslim. Achievements include research in endovaginal and fetal MRI; neuro-imaging of brain malformation and genetic brain disorders, Neuro-Behcet's disease; diffusion tensor MR imaging of brain; Paleoradiology and CT of Royal Egyptian Mummies. Avocations: music, keyboards, painting, travel, poetry. Home: 4 St 49 Mokattam Cairo 11575 Egypt Office: Kasr Al Ainy Hosp Radiology Dept Manial Cairo 11111 Egypt Business E-Mail: saharsaleem1@gmail.com.

SALEHI, MOHAMMAD, health facility administrator, educator; b. Shahre Rey, Iran, Jan. 22, 1940; s. Mohammad Hasan Salehi and Zahra Mortazavi; m. Farideh Moili, Aug. 9, 1973; children: Ali Reza, Nahal. MD, Med. U. Tehran, Iran, 1967, specialization in pediat., 1972. Intern in pediat., internal medicine, gen., plastic surgery Med. U. Tehran affiliated hosps., 1966-67; resident in pediat. Dr. Ahari Hosp. (now Med. Ctr. for Children), Tehran, 1969-72; head chest pediat. ward, rschr. Rsch. Inst. Tuberculosis Lung Disease, 1977—; cons. VistaLink Travel Medicine affiliated U. Tex. Houston Med. Sch., 1999—; tech. supr. Tehran, Iran, 2006—. Editor articles in profl. jours. HVO (Health Vol. Overseas), 1998—. Fellow: ACCP (regent 2000—), Am. Acad Chest Physician Surgeons, Internat. Coll. Pediat. Child Care (hon.), Am. Acad. Pediat. (sr.); mem.: Am. Thoracic Soc. Muslim. Avocations: hunting, computers, electronics. Home: Apt 310 3rd Fl Ostad Motahhari Ave Yousefian St #36 Tehran 15667/86873 Iran Office: Nat Rsch Inst TB Lung Disease Niavaran Darabad 19556 Tehran Iran Office Phone: (+98-21) 33300191, (+98-21) 88874882. Personal E-mail: salehi8621@yahoo.com.

SALEHI OMRAN, AHMAD, cardiologist, consultant; b. Babol, Iran, Mar. 6, 1951; arrived in Saudi Arabia, 2001; s. Hasan Salehi Omran and Mahbibi Molla Mommadi; m. Rokhsareh Kazeminava, Mar. 20, 1986; children: Sina, Setareh. MD, U. Teheran, Iran, 1976. Cert. Am. Bd. Echocardiography. Head Emdad Hosp., Amol, Iran, 1978—79; resident in cardiology Teheran U., 1979—85; asst, prof. Babal (Iran) Med. U., 1985—92; clin. fellow Toronto (Can.) Gen. Hosp., 1992—96, clin. assoc. divsn. cardiology, 1996—2000; cons. cardiologist King Abdulaziz Med. City, Riyadh, Saudi Arabia, 2000—. Dep. chancellor, dean faculty of medicine Babal Med. U., 1985—92; dir. non-invasive lab. Dept. Cardiac Scis., Riyadh, 2001—. Fellow: Am. Soc. Echocardiography; mem.: Am. Coll. Cardiology, Iranian Med. Assn. Avocation: sports.

SALEM, HOSNI KHAIRY, urologist, educator; b. Egypt, Apr. 14, 1966; MD, Kasr Al Ainy Sch. Medicine, 1990. Asst. prof. Egyptian Urol. Assns., 2005—. Cons. French Tchg. Hosp., 2005—. Mem.: Internat. Endourol. Soc., Egyptian Soc. Urosurgery, Arab Soc. Urosurgery, Egyptian Soc. Andrology, European Assn. Urology, Internat. Soc. Sexual Medicine, Am. Urol. Assn., Soc. Internat. Urologie. Avocations: reading, travel. Home: PO Box 247 Giza 12515 Egypt Cairo El Haram 12515 Egypt Home Fax: 20235325873. Personal E-mail: dr_hosni@yahoo.com.

SALEM, SAMI (SAMI AHMAD), surgeon; Grad., Med. Sch., Hamburg, Germany, 1982—88. Gen. surg. tng., Hamburg, Germany, 1988—94; surg. tng. Gastrointestinal Surgery, England, 1995—2005; specialist Gen. and Gastrointestinal Surgery, England; cons. surgeon gastrointestinal and obesity surgery Jordan Hosp., Amman; cons. surgeon ctr. for morbid obesity and gastroesophageal reflux surgery Gastric Ctr., Stuttgart, Germany, 2005. Fellow: Royal Coll. of Surgeons; mem.: Internal Fedn. for the Surgery of Obesity, German Soc. for Morbid Obesity Surgery, German Soc. for Surgery. Achievements include leading the largest obesity surgery practice in the country; first to introduce the laparoscopic bariatric approach in Jordan. Office: Doctor Sami Salem Center Jabal Amman Medical Center Jordan Office Phone: 96265609039. Office Fax: 962795693683. *

SALENTINE, THOMAS JAMES, pharmaceutical executive; b. Milw., Aug. 8, 1939; s. James Edward and Loretta Marie S.; m. Susan Anne Sisk, Apr. 16, 1966; children: Anne Elizabeth, Thomas James Jr. BS in Acctg., Marquette U., Milw., 1961. CPA, Ind., Wis. Sr. audit mgr. Price Waterhouse, Milw., 1961-74; dir. corp. acctg. Ward Foods Inc., Wilmette, Ill., 1974-78; corp. contr. Johnson Controls Inc., Milw., 1984-85; v.p., contr. Stokely Van Camp Inc., Indpls., 1978-87; exec. v.p., CFO Bindley Western Industries Inc., Indpls., 1987—2001, also bd. dirs.; ptnr. Bindley Capital Ptnrs., LLC, 2001—. Bd. dirs. Priority Healthcare Corp., Nat. Refrigeration Svcs. Inc. Chmn. com. United Way, Indpls., 1989-90. Lt. USN, 1962-65. Mem. AICPA, Fin. Execs. Inst. Republican. Roman Catholic. Home: 3991 Gulf Shore Blvd Naples FL 34103 Office Phone: 317-704-4154.

SALERNO, JUDITH ALYCE, health science association administrator; b. Mar. 2, 1952; MSc in Health Policy, Harvard Sch. Pub. Health, 1976; MD, Harvard Med. Sch., 1985. Cert. Internal Medicine, Geriatric Medicine. Clin. and fellowship tng., internal medicine Georgetown U., George Washington U., NIH; assoc. chief staff Vet. Affairs Med. Ctr., Washington; chief cons., geriatrics and extended care Dept. Vet. Affairs, Washington; assoc. clin. prof., healthcare sciences and medicine George Washington U.; sr. clin. investigator, Nat. Inst. Aging NIH, US Dept. HHS, Bethesda, Md., 1989—92, guest researcher, Nat. Inst. Aging, 1992—95, dep. dir., Nat. Inst. Aging, 2001—08; exec. officer Inst. Medicine, 2008—. Co-founder Geriatric Edn. Ctr. Consortium, Washington; commr. Nat. Comm. for Quality Long-Term Care, Washington. Contbr. several articles to prof. jours. Recipient NIH Director's award for outstanding leadership and svc., Secretary's Meritorious Svc. award. Office: Institute of Medicine 500 Fifth St NW Keck 848 Washington DC 20001 Office Phone: 301-496-0216, 202-334-2177. Office Fax: 301-496-2525. Business E-Mail: salernoj@nia.nih.gov, jsalerno@nas.edu.

SALERNO, SISTER MARIA, advanced practice nurse, educator; b. Syracuse, NY; d. Joseph and Josephine (Ostrowski) S. Diploma in nursing, St. Joseph's Hosp., Syracuse, 1962; BSN summa cum laude, Cath. U. Am., Washington, 1974, MS in Nursing, 1976, PhD in Nursing, 1981; cert. nurse practitioner, U. Rochester, 1984. RN, N.Y., Md., Washington; cert. adult, geriatric nurse practitioner ANCC; joined Sisters of Third Franciscan Order, Roman Cath. Ch., 1963. Staff nurse St. Joseph Hosp. Health Ctr., Syracuse, 1962-63; sr. charge nurse ICU, gen. med. and surg. units St. Elizabeth Hosp., Utica, NY, 1965-66, head nurse pediat. unit, 1966-69; head nurse ECF Loretto Geriatric Ctr., Syracuse, 1969-72; lectr. Cath. U. Am., Washington, 1977—78, 1980—81, asst. prof. nursing, 1978-79, 81-92, assoc. prof., 1992—2009, dir. primary care adult/geriatric nurse practitioner programs, 1984—2009, co-dir. FNP program, 1994-97; dir. Adult CNS Nurse Educator Program, 2004—09; gen. councilor Sister St. Francis, 2008—. Contbr. chpts. to books; contbr. articles to profl. jours. Vol. nurse practitioner Cmty. of Hope, Washington, 1984-2009, instl. animal care and use com. George Washington U., 1996-2009, Cath. U. Am. 2000-09, Veteran's Adminstrn. Med. Ctr., 2004-09; scholarship com. Franciscan Found. for the Holy Land, 1996-. Grantee NIH, 1984-89, Cath. U. Am., 1989-90. Mem.: AAUP, ANA, D.C. League for Nursing (bd. dirs. 1995—97, 1999—2009), D.C. Nurse Practitioners Assn. (nom. com. 2006—07), Am. Coll. Nurse Practitioners, Am. Acad. Nurse Practitioners, Cath. U. Am. Nursing Alumni Assn. (pres. 1986—87, chpt. exec. bd. 1992—2003, treas. 1998—2003), Nat. Italian Am. Found. (assoc.), Sigma Theta Tau (grad. counselor Kappa chpt. 1985—87, awards com. 1987—89, grad. counselor Kappa chpt. 1991—97, eligibility com. 1991—97, 2002—03, grad. counselor Kappa chpt. 2006—09). Roman Catholic. Office: Sisters of St Francis Corp Office 2500 Grant Blvd Ste 3 Syracuse NY 13208 Business E-Mail: msalerno@sosf.org.

SALERNO, WILLIAM DOUGLAS, cardiologist; b. Passaic, NJ, 1956; MD, U. Autonoma de Guadalajara, 1982. Intern U. Medicine Dentistry N.J./Englewood Hosp., 1982-83, 83-84; resident Hackensack (N.J.) U. Med. Ctr., 1984-86, fellow in critical care medicine, 1987-89, 89-90, Norwalk Hosp./Yale U., New Haven, 1986-87; fellow in cardiovascular disease, 1987-89; fellow in interventional cardiology Hackensack U. Med. Ctr., 1989-90; dir. cardiac ICU, dir. coronary care unit Hackensack Med. Ctr.; clin. asst. prof. medicine to clin. assoc. prof. U. Medicine & Dentistry of NJ, sect. chief, coronary care unit. Clin. asst. prof. medicine U. Medicine and Dentistry N.J.-N.J. Med. Sch. Named NJ Health Sci. Libr. Assn. Clinician of Yr., 2003, Honored Citizen Mem., Honor Legion Police Depts. NJ; named one of Top Doctors in NY, NY mag., 2006, 2007. Mem. AMA, Am. Coll. Cardiology, ACP, Am. Coll. Chest Physicians, ATS, Soc. Critical Care Medicine, Internat. Soc. Endovascular Specialists, Am. Soc. Laser Medicine & Surgery, Am. Soc. Echocardiography, Soc. for Vascular Ultrasound. Office: 38 Mayhill St Saddle Brook NJ 07663-5307 also: Hackensack Univ Med Ctr 30 Prospect Ave Hackensack NJ 07601 Office Phone: 201-489-1766. Office Fax: 201-843-5910. Business E-Mail: wds@heart-care.org.

SALES, CLIFFORD M., surgeon; b. NYC, Jan. 29, 1961; MD, Mt. Sinai Sch. Medicine, NYC, 1986; MBA, Rutgers U., 2002. Diplomate Am. Bd. Surgery with added qualifications in vascular surgery. Intern Montefiore Med. Ctr., Bronx, NY, 1986-87, res. gen. surgery, 1987-91, fellow vascular surgery, 1991-93; chief divsn. vascular surgery Overlook Hosp. Recipient Honoree award, Rutgers Bus. Sch., 2007. Mem.: Am. Assn. Vascular Surgery, Soc. Clin. Vascular Surgery, Per. Vascular Surgery Soc., NJ Vascular Soc., Internat. Soc. Endosurgery, Internat. Soc. Cardiovasc. Surgery, East Vascular Surgery, Am. Venous Forum, Am. Coll. Surgeons. Office: 433 Ctrl Ave Westfield NJ 07090

SALFORD, LEIF G., neurosurgeon, educator; b. Malmö, Skåne, Sweden, Dec. 7, 1941; m. Eva K. Nordqvist, Apr. 15, 1967; children: Charlotte Sophia, Emelie Anne, Gustaf Nils. MD, Lund U., Skåne, PhD, 1974. Registered physician Sweden, 1969, cert. specialist in neurosurgery Sweden, 1975. Tchr., dept. anatomy Lund U., 1961—66, hosp. neurosurgeon, 1967—, prof. neurosurgery, 1996—, dir., Inst. Clin. Neuroscis., 1996—98, dir., head divsn. hosp., 1999—2004, hosp. mem., 1999—2006, dir., Inst. Clin. Scis., 2004—06; rsch. fellow Cornell Med. Ctr., NY Hosp., NYC, 1971—73; prof., dept. neurosurgery Kuwait U., Kuwait City, 1981—83; prof. neurosurgery, chief med. officer Gothenburg U. and Sahlgrenska Hosp., Sweden,

1994—97. Expert, info. soc. forum European Union, Brussels, 1995—2000; hon. prof. Med. Faculty Shantou U., China, 2001. Contbr. scientific papers to numerous rsch. publs. (Waerum prize, 2000). Co-founder, pres. European Assn. Neuro-Oncology, 1994—98; internat. mem. World Fedn. Neurosurg. Socs., 1986—2000. Fellow: Acad. Euroasiana Neurochirurgica (academician), Students' Med. Assn. (Lund) (hon.; master of tchg. 1991); mem.: Swedish Neuropsychol. Soc., Scandiavian Neuro-Oncology Soc. (hon.; founder, pres. 1990—97, pres. 1997), Am. Assn. Neurol. Surgeons (Harvey Cushing Soc.). Office: Lund Univ Hosp Dept Neurosurgery Ea-block 4th Fl Lund Skåne 22185 Sweden Business E-Mail: leif.salford@med.lu.se.

SALGADO, CASSANDRA, epidemiologist, educator; b. Calif., Jan. 31, 1968; BA, W.Va. U., 1990, MD, 1995; MS, U. Va. Hosp. epidemiologist Med. U. SC, 2004, asst. prof., 2004—08, assoc. prof., medicine, 2008—. Recipient Leadership award, CLSI, 2010—, MRSA Innovation award, SHEA, IDSA. Mem.: SC Med. Assn., Infectious Diseases Soc. America, Soc. Healthcare Epidemiology. Office: 135 Rutledge Ave Charleston SC 29425 Business E-Mail: salgado@musc.edu.

SALGADO, CLAUDIO GUEDES, dermatologist, educator; b. Belém do Pará, Brazil, Oct. 8, 1969; s. Ubirajara Imbiriba and Maria Helena (Guedes) Salgado; m. Ana Cristina Soeiro, Feb. 20, 1993; children: Renan Soeiro, Flávia Soeiro. MB, Pará State U., 1992; PhD, U. Tokyo, 1998. Cert. Japanese Soc. Investigative Dermatology, 1998, leprosy specialist Brazilian Soc. Leprosy, 2005. Tech. dir. Dr. Marcello Candia Reference Unit San. Dermatology Pará State, Marituba, 1999—2000; coord. Dermato-Immunology Lab., Marituba, 2001—. Vice-coord. Postgrad. Program Neuroscis. and Cellular Biology, Belém, 2004—; vis. prof. Pará Fed. U., Belém, Brazil, 2000—02, assoc. prof., 2002—. Contbr. articles to profl. jours. and mags. Recipient Best Poster Presentation award, Brazilian Fedn. Exptl. Biology Socs., 2005; grantee, Brazilian Nat. Rsch. Counseling, 2002—04, Pará State Fund Sci. and Tech., 2004—05, Brazilian Fed. Govt. Financing Agy., 2005—; scholar, Japanese Ministry of Edn., 1993—98. Mem.: Pará State Assn. Former Scholarship Students Japanese Ministry Edn., Pará State Soc. Medicine and Surgery (assoc.), Brazilian Soc. Leprosy (assoc.), Brazilian Soc. Immunology (assoc.). Home: Av Magalhães Barata 84 Apt 1603 Belém 66040 170 Brazil Office: Parß Fed Univ Avenida Joao Paulo 2 113 67200-000 Marituba PA Brazil Office Fax: 55-91-3256-9097; Home Fax: 55-91-3224-3907. Personal E-mail: csalgado@ufpa.br.

SALGADO, ROBERTO CARLOS, biomedical researcher; b. Mex., Dec. 10, 1977; D, U. Nat. Autónoma Méx., 2009. Rsch. scientist U. Nat. Autónoma Méx., 2005—, adj. prof. Office: Inst Investigaciones Biomedicas Mexico City 04510 Mexico Personal E-mail: otreborcarlos@hotmail.com.

SALGIN, SEMA, engineering educator, researcher; b. Ankara, Turkey, Nov. 6, 1970; PhD, Ankara U., 2004. Assoc. prof., rschr. Cumhuriyet U., 2008—, dir., bio-engring., 2010. Postdoc. Bursary grant, Sci. & Tech. Rsch. Coun. Turkey. Office: Cumhuriyet University Engineering Faculty Sivas 58140 Turkey Business E-Mail: ssalgin@cumhuriyet.edu.tr.

SALIH, MUHANNAD, pharmacist; b. Baghdad, Iraq, Aug. 26, 1978; PharmM in Clin. Pharmacy, U. Sains Malaysia, 2008. Pharmacist Clin. Pharmacy Discipline, Sch. Pharm. Scis., U. Sains Malaysia, 2008—; with Good Clin. Practice, Clin. Rsch. Ctr., Ministry of Health, Malaysia, 2009. Mem.: Syndicate Iraqi Pharmacists (registered mem. 2001—), Internat. Soc. Pharmacoeconomics and Outcomes Rsch. Avocations: swimming, badminton. Office: Sch Pharmacy University Sains Malaysia Minden Pulau Pinang 11800 Malaysia E-mail: muhanad_rmk@yahoo.com.

SALIH, MUSTAFA ABDALLA MOHAMED, pediatric neurologist, educator; b. Kosti, White Nile, Sudan, Jan. 5, 1950; arrived in Saudi Arabia, 1992; s. Abdalla Mohamed Salih and Noora Elhaj Saeed. MBBS in Medicine & Surgery, Khartoum U., Sudan, 1974, M in Pediatrics and Child Health, 1980, MD, 1982; DMS, Uppsala U., Sweden, 1990. Clin. rsch. fellow Regional Neurol. Ctr., Newcastle Upon Tyne, Eng., 1980-82; cons. pediatrician, neurologist U. Khartoum, 1982-92; fellow dept. neurophysiology Regional Neurol. Ctr., Newcastle Upon Tyne, 1986; fellow dept. pediatrics microbiology and immunology Uppsala U., 1985-90; prof. pediatrics U. Khartoum, 1990-92; prof. pediatrics, cons. neuropediatrician King Saud U., Riyadh, 1993—. Head dept. pediatrics U. Khartoum, 1990-92; pres. sci. com. Nat. Expanded Program on Immunization, Sudan, 1990-92; mem. coll. of medicine rsch. ctr. bd. King Saud U., Riyadh, 1992-98, 05—. Editor: Sudanese Jour. Paediatrics, 1985—92; guest editor Saudi Med. Jour. Supplement, 2006, internat. editor Sudan Med. Jour., 2009—, Sudanese Jour. Paediatrics, 2010—, mem. editl. bd. Jour. Pediatric Neurology, Open Pediatric Medicine Jour., Open Neurology Jour.; contbr. articles to profl. jour., chapters to books. U. Khartoum grantee, 1982-92, Postdoctoral fellow Med. Rsch. Coun., Gt. Britain, 1986, Swedish Commn. for Tech. Corp. and Med. Rsch. Coun., 1984, Riyadh Neuroscience award, 96, Medal of Excellence, Pres. Sudan. 2007, King Saud Univ. gold medal, 2010 Fellow Royal Coll. Pediatrics and Child Health; mem. AAAS, Internat. Child Neurology Assn., Sudan Assn. Paediatricians, World Fedn. of Neurology, Saudi Pediatric Assn., Saudi Neoroscience Soc. (award Pioneers & Promoters Neuroscience, 2008), World Muscle Soc., Am. Acad. Neurology, Am. Epilepsy Soc. Avocations: poetry, history. Personal E-mail: mustafa_salih05@yahoo.com. Business E-Mail: mustafa@ksu.edu.sa.

SALIK, JAMES M., gastroenterologist, educator; MD, NYU, 1980. Diplomate Am. Bd. Internal Medicine, 1983, Am. Bd. Internal Medicine-gastroenterology, 1985. Resident internal medicine NYU Med. Ctr., 1980—83, fellow gastroenterology, 1983—85, assoc. prof. medicine; attending physician NYU Langone Med. Ctr. Office: New York University Langone Medical Center 232 E 30th St New York NY 10016 Office Phone: 212-889-5544.

SALIM, DANA V., echocardiographer, educator; b. Lawton, Okla., May 3, 1960; d. Wilma June (Daniel) Collins; m. Muhammad Salim, July 17, 1998; children: Trey, Daniel, Saif, Safia. BS in Ultrasound, Okla U., 1993. Registered diagnostic cardiac sonographer Am. Registry Diagnostic Med. Sonography. Echocardiogher Norman (Okla.) Regional Hosp., 1993—97, Norman Clinic Inc., 1997—2001; educator cardiac ultrasound Okla. U. Health Scis. Ctr., Oklahoma City, 1996—. Mem. editl. bd.: Jour. Diagnostic Med. Sonography, 2000—. Mem. Cleve.-McClain County Med. Alliance, Norman, 1998—, Assistance League Norman, 2000—. Mem.: Am. Inst. Ultrasound in Medicine, Am. Heart Assn., Soc. Diagnostic Med. Sonography, Alpha Eta. Republican. Avocation: reading. Home: 4609 Flint Ridge Dr Norman OK 73072-4469 E-mail: dsalim1@cox.net.

SALISBURY, FRANKLIN C., JR., foundation administrator; s. Franklin and Tamara Salisbury. BA in Econs., Yale U., New Haven, 1978; MA, U. Chgo.; MDiv, Yale Divinity Sch.; JD, U. Ga., 1992. Chmn. Consumer Utilities Bd., Washington; joined Nat. Found. Cancer Rsch., Bethesda, Md., 1993, pres., CEO, 1997—. Chmn. bd. dirs. Asian Fund Cancer Rsch., Hong Kong. Office: Nat Found Cancer Rsch 4600 E West Hwy Ste 525 Bethesda MD 20814 *

SALITERMAN, STEVEN S., internist, educator; b. Mpls., June 6, 1951; s. Leonard S. and Dorothy Saliterman; m. Peg E. Maloney, Aug. 24, 1986; children: David Edward, Paul Wesley. BA in Physiology summa cum laude, U. Minn., 1972; MD, Mayo Med. Sch., Rochester, Minn., 1977; grad., Mayo Grad. Sch. Medicine, 1980. Diplomate Am. Bd. Internal Medicine 1983. Pvt. practice, St. Louis Park, Minn., 1981—; sr. aviation med. examiner FAA, Washington, 1981—. Rsch. com. Pk. Nicollet's Meth. Hosp., St. Louis Park, Minn., 1996—2003, chmn. dept. medicine, 2001—05; dept. biomed. engring. U. Minn., Mpls., 2002—, adj. assoc. prof., 2008—, faculty nano & microsystems applications ctr., 2006—; exec. com. Meth. Hosp., St. Louis Park, 2004—05, quality assurance com., 2004—05. Author: (textbook) Fundamentals of BioMEMS and Medical Microdevices, 2006; contbr. articles to profl. jours. Recipient Achievement award, US Army, 1969, Acheivement award, Profl. Engrs. Soc. Minn., 1969, Physician's Recognition award, AMA, 2006—10; fellow, NASA Johnson Space Ctr., 1973—74, NASA Ames Rsch. Ctr., 1976; Nat. Youth Sci. Camp scholar, Minn. State Sci. Fair, 1969. Fellow: ACP; mem.: Mayo Alumni Assn., Internat. Soc. for Optical Engring., Mayo Plummer Soc., Phi Beta Kappa. Achievements include patents for computerized simulator for critical care training & catheterization; design of 7027 computer system; laser activated amphibian monitor system. Avocations: swimming, hiking, photography, amateur radio. Office: 6490 Excelsior Blvd Ste W-110 Saint Louis Park MN 55426 Office Phone: 952-920-8771. Personal E-mail: stevensaliterman@comcast.net.

SALKOFF, LAWRENCE BENJAMIN, medical educator; b. NY, Mar. 3, 1954; BA in Economics, UCLA, 1967; PhD, U. Calif., Berkeley, 1979. Postdoc. fellow Yale U., 1979—83; prof. neurobiology and genetics Wash. U. Sch. Medicine, 1984—. Vol. US Peace Corps., 1967—70. Recipient award, Muscular Dystrophy Assn., John Belling prize, U. Calif.; grants, NIH, NSF, fellowship, Klingenstein Found. Rsch. Epilepsy. Mem.: Genetics Soc. America, Biophys. Soc., Soc. Neurosci. Avocations: sailing, tennis, jazz, classical music. Office: Washington University Dept Anat & Neurobiology Saint Louis MO 63110 Business E-Mail: salkoffl@pcg.wustl.edu.

SALKY, BARRY A., surgeon; b. Memphis, Nov. 10, 1944; s. Jake and Mary Salky; m. Alma Halski; children: Jonathan, Adam. MD, U. Tenn., Memphis, 1970. Diplomate Am. Bd. Surgery. Intern Mt. Sinai Hosp., NYC, 1971—73, resident in internal medicine, 1975—78, clin. prof. surgery, 1996—2004, prof. surgery, 2004—, chief divsn. laparoscopic surgery, 1992—96, 2004—. Author: Laparscopy for Surgeons, 1990, Advanced Laparoscopy for Surgeons, 1994. Maj. US Army, 1973—75. Recipient Ambassador's award, Am. Friends of Rambom Med. Ctr., 1995. Fellow: ACS, Am. Coll. of Gastroenterology; mem.: Soc. Surgery Alimentary Tract, Soc. Am. Gastrointestinal Endoscopic Surgeons (v.p. 1997—98). Jewish. Avocations: golf, travel. Office: Mt Sinai Hosp 5 E 98th St 14th Fl New York NY 10029 Office Phone: 212-241-6156. Business E-Mail: barry.salky@mountsinai.org. *

SALLAM, ISMAIL, government agency administrator, educator, cardiovascular surgeon; b. Monoufeya, Egypt, July 21, 1941; Diploma in surgery, Ain Shams U.; PhD, Glasgow U., 1955. Prof., head dept. heart surgery Ain Shams U., 1992—; head health & population com. Shura Consultative Assembly, 1990—; majority leader Upper House, 1992—96; min. health & population Ministry of Health & Population, Egypt, 1996—2002; chmn. Arab Health 6r. Min. Bd., 1997—2002; pres. Ptnrs. Population & Devel., 1998—2002; chmn. Gen. Orgn. Teaching Hosps. & Insts. (GOTHI). Chmn. founder Ismail Sallam Peace & Devel. Charitable Soc., 2010. Active WHO. Recipient United Arab Emirates Health Found. prize for health devel., 1999, UN Population award, 2000. Achievements include established Healthy Egyptians 2010 initiative, 1998, issued historical decree that abolished FMG in 1996, Nat. Health Ins., preschool children Egypt, 2002, lead, Health Peace Initiative Channel Health care Globally in areas of conflict. Home: 307 Dithrige St Apt 503 Pittsburgh PA 15213

SALLES, FREDERICO ASSIS DE, oral surgeon; b. Santo Amaro, Bahia, Brazil, June 1, 1932; s. Francisco Gonçalves de and Beatriz Assis de Salles; life ptnr. Ana Maria Cavalini Melo, Dec. 9, 2001; m. Maria Solange Freitas, Oct. 18, 1962 (dec. Dec. 15, 1980); children: Beatriz de Freitas, Emilia de Freitas, Paula de Freitas. Degree in Dentistry, Nat. Sch. Dentistry, Rio de Janeiro, 1961. Resident oral cancerology Hélio Angotti Hosp., Minas Gerais, Brazil, 1963; head maxillofacial surgery dept. Hosp. Found. Fed. Dist., Brasilia, Brazil, 1967—85. Vis. prof. Sch. Medicine Brasilia U., 1969—72; cons. dentistry and maxillofacial surgery Motor Disorders Hosp., Brasilia, 1974—2001. Dir.: (devel.) Technology in Navigator Surgery; contbr. articles to profl. jour. Dir. sci. dept. Brazilian Dental Assn., Brasilia, 1968—70. Recipient Ordem do Rio Branco, Brazilian Pres., 1989, Commendation, Fed. Dist. Gov., 2001, Hon. Recognition, Fed. Gov. Dist., 2007. Mem.: IAOMS. Roman Catholic. Avocations: sculpting, poetry, crafts. Home: SQN 105 Bloco B Apt 505 Brasília 70734-020 Brazil Office: Artis Tecnology Smdb Conjunto 12 71680-120 Brasília DF Brazil Home Phone: 55 61 32747817; Office Phone: 55 61 33665096. Office Fax: 55 61 33665096. Personal E-mail: salles.frederico@gmail.com. Business E-Mail: artis@artis.com.br.

SALLOUT, BAHAUDDIN IBRAHEEM, obstetrician; b. Riyadh, Saudi Arabia, Dec. 1, 1968; s. Ibraheem Ali Sallout and Jamilah Ahmed Zakout; m. Maha Ibrahim Zakout, Oct. 20, 1994; children: Luai, Rula, Mohammad, Jamilah. B.Medicine and Surgery, King Saud U., 1993. Clin. fellow maternal-fetal medicine Ottawa U., Ottawa, Ont., Canada, 2001—04; cons. ob-gyn. King Faisal Specialist Hosp., Riyadh, Saudi Arabia, 2004—05; cons. ob-gyn., head fetal medicine King Fahad Med. City, Riyadh, 2005—, instr., 2005—. Contbr. articles to profl. jours. Recipient Award of Excellence, Ottawa Hosp., 2004; grantee, Physician Svcs. Inc. Found., Can., 2002. Mem.: Saudi Ob-Gyn. Soc., Soc. of Ob-Gyn. Can., ACOG. Office: King Fahad Medical City Al Dhabab St Box 59046 Riyadh 11525 Saudi Arabia

SALMASSI, SADEGH, physician; b. Baghdad, Iraq, Aug. 14, 1946; s. Jafar and Kobra (Alavi) S.; m. Tahereh Ali Nazari, Jan. 17, 1970; children: Ali (dec.), Nahal. BS, Pahlavi U., 1966, MD, 1973. Diplomate Am. Bd. Pathology, Am. Bd. Gen. Practice in Medicine and Surgery. Instr. pathology U. Ill. Sch. Medicine, Chgo., 1975-80; asst. prof. pathology, assoc. chmn. dept., dir. blood bank U. Mo., Kansas City, 1980-84; chmn. family practice Delano (Calif.) Regional Med. Ctr., 1984-86, 2007—08; pres. Delano Regional Med. Group, 1989-96. Chief of staff Delano Regional Med. Ctr., 1989. Fellow Am. Coll. Internat. Physicians, Coll. Am. Pathologists, Am. Acad. Family Physicians, Am. Acad. Cosmetic Surgery, Am. Acad. Cosmetic Surgeons; mem. AMA, Am. Acad. Gen. Physicians, Calif. Med. Assn. Office: Sadegh Salmassi MD & Assocs Urgent Care Ctr 719 Main St Delano CA 93215-2935 also: Salmassi Cosmetic and Med Inst 719 Main St Delano CA 93215-2935 Office Phone: 661-725-5877, 661-725-7060. Personal E-mail: mdfcap@aol.com. Business E-Mail: salmassi@salmassimd.com.

SALMELA, LYNN MARIE, clinical nurse specialist; b. Albert Lea, Minn., Mar. 29, 1960; d. Melvin Raymond and Patricia Lou (Bushey) Salmela. BSN, Winona State U., Minn., 1982; MA, Coll. St. Scholastica, Duluth, Minn., 2000; compliant documentation mgmt. course, J.A. Thomas & Assocs., 2000; cert. emergency dept. electronic med. record tng., Epic Sys. Corp., 2004. RN Minn., Wis., cert. pub. health nurse, Minn., intravenous therapy nurse, 1997, in ambulatory electronic med. record application, Epic Sys. Corp., 2004. Staff nurse Milw. Children's Hosp. (now Children's Hosp. of Wis.), 1982—83, Mpls. Children's Hosp., 1983—86, St. Mary's Duluth (Minn.) Clinic, 1986—2001; adj. faculty mem. Coll. of St. Scholastica, Duluth, 1998—99; utilization mgmt./compliant documentation coord. St. Luke's Hosp., Duluth, 2000—03; clin. informatics analyst St. Mary's Duluth Clinic Health Sys., 2003—05, nurse clinician, nurse-on-line, 2005, EpicCare edn. specialist, 2005—07, tech. learning specialist, 2007—10; clin. proj. specialist Dept. Clin. Edn., 2010—; leader Process Excellence Process Tng., 2011. Author: (newsletter) Volunteer Link, St. Mary's Grief Support Ctr., 1993, 1995—96; contbr. articles to profl. publs. and newspapers. Vol. presch. screening programs, Winona, Minn., 1981—82; vol. blood screening clinic, Milw., 1982; vol. med. staff Grandma's Marathon, Duluth, 1989; vol. St. Mary's Grief Support Ctr., Duluth, 1993—97, Children's Asthma Camp, 1988. Recipient 1st Pl. award, Amateur Still Life Category, photography contest, 2001, 1st Pl. award portrait category, Photography Contest, 2002; scholar Presdl. scholar, Winona State U., 1978. Mem.: Nat. Assn. Clin. Nurse Specialists, Sigma Theta Tau. Republican. Avocations: camping, music, photography, writing, cooking. Home: 110 S 58th Ave E Duluth MN 55804 Office: Essentia Health 502 E 2nd St Duluth MN 55805 Office Phone: 218-786-1360. Business E-Mail: lynn.salmela@essentialhealth.org.

SALMI, TEEA T., dermatologist; b. Uusikaupunki, Finland, June 24, 1975; MD, U. Tampere, 2006. Lic. in medicine U. Tampere, 2002. Specialist physician dept. dermatology Tampere U. Hosp., Finland, 2005—. Mem.: Finnish Dermatol. Soc., Finnish Med. Soc. Avocations: travel, sports. Home: Hirvenhaukuntie 3 Lempäälä 37560 Finland Personal E-mail: teea.salmi@uta.fi.

SALMOIRAGHI, GIAN CARLO, physiologist, educator; b. Gorla Minore, Italy, Sept. 19, 1924; came to U.S., 1952, naturalized, 1958; s. Giuseppe Carlo and Dina (Rinetti) S.; m. Eva Tchoukourlieva, Dec. 5, 1970; 1 child, George Charles MD, U. Rome, 1948; PhD, McGill U., 1959; DSc (hon.), Hahnemann U., 1995. Sr. med. officer Internat. Refugee Orgn., Naples, Italy, 1949-52; research fellow Cleve. Clinic Found., 1952-55; lectr. dept. physiology McGill U., Montreal, Que., Canada, 1956-58; from neurophysiologist to dir., div. spl. mental health research NIMH, Washington, 1959-73; assoc. commr. research N.Y. State Dept. Mental Hygiene, Albany, 1973-77; assoc. dir. for research Nat. Inst. Alcohol Abuse, HHS, Bethesda, Md., 1977-84; prof. neurology and physiology Hahnemann U., Phila., 1984—94, vice provost for research affairs, 1984-85, chmn. dept. physiology, assoc. v.p sci. affairs, 1986-94; clin. prof. psychiatry George Washington U., 1966-73. Contbr. articles to profl. jours. Recipient Superior Service award HEW, 1970 Fellow Am. Coll. Neuropsychopharmacology; mem. AAAS, Am. Physiol. Soc., Am. Soc. Pharmacology and Exptl. Therapeutics, Internat. Brain Research Orgn., Internat. Soc. Psychoneuroendocrinology, Am. Psychiat. Assn., Soc. Neurosci., Royal Soc. Medicine, Soc. Biol. Psychiat., Assn. Research Neurol. and Mental Disease, Research Soc. Alcoholism, Assn. Chmn. Dept. Physiology, Sci. Research Soc., Sigma Xi. Clubs: Cosmos (Washington). Home: 8216 Hamilton Spring Ct Bethesda MD 20817-2714 Personal E-mail: gsalmoiraghi@pol.net.

SALMON, MARLA E., dean, nursing educator; b. Vermillion, SD, May 2, 1949; d. Everett Lloyd and Marceline Louise (Adamson) Salmon; m. Jerry Steven Anderson, Aug. 1, 1984; children: Jessica Louise White, Matthew Lawrence White. BA cum laude, U. Portland, 1971, BSN cum laude, 1972; MSN, 1999; ScD, Johns Hopkins U., 1977; DSc (hon.), UNMC, 2003. Dir. patient advocacy program Johns Hopkins U., Balt., 1974-75, instr., 1975-78; asst. prof. U. Minn., Mpls., 1978-82, asst. dir. PRONA, 1978-79, acting dir. PRONA, 1978-80, dir. pub. health nursing programs, 1980-85, assoc. prof., 1982-86; prof. pub. health nursing, chmn. dept. U. N.C., Chapel Hill, 1986-92; dir. nursing div., Bureau Health Professions HHS, Rockville, 1991-97; prof., dean Grad. Sch. Nursing U. Pa., Phila., 1997-99, dir. grad. studies; dean, prof. Nell Hodgson Woodruff Sch. Nursing Emory U., Atlanta, 1999—2008, founding dir., Lillian Carter Ctr. Internat. Nursing; Robert G. and Jean A. Reid endowed dean in nursing U. Wash., Seattle, 2008—, prof. psychosocial and cmty. health, prof. global health, 2008—. Bd. dirs. Nat. Adv. Coun. Nursing Rsch., NIH Inst. the Internat. Edn. Students, Joint Commn. on Accreditation

Healthcare Orgn. Nursing Adv. Coun.; cons. in field. Co-editor: News Outlook, 1989—91; author: Nurse: A World of Care, 2008 (Am. Jour. Nursing Book of Yr. award, 2008); contbr. articles to profl. jours. Trustee Robert Wood Johnson Found., 2002—; mem. Presdl. Task Force Health Care Reform, Washington, 1993; US del. WHO, Geneva, 1995. Recipient Recognition award, Assn. State Territorial Dirs. Nursing, 1993, Achievement award, Nat. Black Nurses Found., 1994, Presdl. award for Meritorious Exec., The White House, 1995; Fulbright scholar, 1972—73, W. K. Kellogg fellow, 1984—87, Reflective Leadership fellow, 1985—86, Rsch. grantee, 1975—78. Fellow: Am. Acad. Nursing; mem.: APHA, ANA (v.p. coun. cmty. health nursing 1988—, mem. task froce credentialing 1989), Women's Health Leadership Trust, Assn. Cmty. Health Nurses Educators, N.C. Nurses Assn., N.C. Pub. Health Assn., N.C. League Nursing, Nat. League Nursing, Am. Tae Kwon Do Assn., Sigma Xi, Delta Omega, Sigma Theta Tau. Avocations: athletics, gardening. Office: Univ Wash Sch Nursing Box 357260 Seattle WA 98195 Business E-Mail: msalmon@u.washington.edu.

SALOMON, DAVID SCOTT, oncology researcher; b. NYC, Sept. 30, 1947; s. Leicester and Elizabeth (Scott) S.; m. Jane Foran, May 7, 1984 (div.); 1 chld, Matthew; m. Kathy Chestnutt, July 3, 1994; children: Robin, Christopher. BS, Clark U., 1969; PhD, SUNY, Albany, 1973. Postdoctoral fellow Roche Inst. Molecular Biology, Nutley, NJ, 1973-75; staff fellow Lab. Devel. Biology NIDR/NIH, 1975-79; rschr. Lab. Pathophysiology Nat. Cancer Inst./NIH, Bethesda, Md., 1979-83, chief tumor growth factor sect. Lab. Tumor Immunology, 1983—, acting chief Mammary Biology and Tumorigenesis Lab., 2010—. Assoc. editor Breast Cancer Rsch. and Treatment, 1993—, Internat. Jour. Oncology, 1994—, Topics in Mammary Gland Biology and Neoplasia, 1995—, Cancer Reports Bull., 1995—; contbr. chpts. to books, some 150 articles to profl. jours.; patentee-cloned human cripto gene and applications thereof, human cripto-related gene. Mem. Am. Assn. Cancer Rsch., Am. Soc. for Biochemistry and Molecular Biology. Avocations: cycling swimming, backpacking. Office: Nat Cancer Inst Bldg 37 Rm 1114 37 Covenant Dr 20892 Office Phone: 301-496-9536. Office Fax: 301-402-8656. Business E-Mail: salomond@mail.nih.gov. *

SALOMON, RONALD M., medical educator; b. Boston, Apr. 7, 1954; MD, U. Liege, Belgium, 1987. Assoc. prof. psychiatry Vanderbilt U. Sch. Medicine, 1995—. Office: 1601 23rd Ave S 3rd Fl Nashville TN 37212 Business E-Mail: ron.salomon@vanderbilt.edu.

SALOMONE, JEFFREY PAUL, surgeon, educator; b. Reno, Nev., Dec. 6, 1961; s. Joseph Anthony and Peggy Ruth (Crompton) S. BS, U. Nev., 1983, MD, 1990. Diplomate Am. Bd. Surgery; cert. surg. critical care. Resident Tulane U. Med. Ctr., New Orleans, 1990-95, fellow in critical care, 1995-96; asst. prof. Emory U., Atlanta, 1996—2001, assoc. prof., 2001—. Cons. Nat. Registry of EMTs, Columbus, Ohio, 1996—. Fellow ACS; mem. AMA, Nat. Assn. Emergency Med. Svcs. Physicians, Am. Assn. for the History of Medicine, Soc. for Critical Care Medicine, Eastern Assn. Surgery of Trauma (pres. elect), Phi Kappa Phi. Avocations: gourmet cooking, photography, theater. Office: Emory U Dept Surgery TK Glenn Bldg Rm 312A 69 jesse Hill Jr Dr SE Atlanta GA 30303-3033 Home Phone: 404-658-9600; Office Phone: 404-616-7320. Business E-Mail: jsalomo@emory.edu.

SALOMONE, JOSEPH ANTHONY, III, emergency medicine physician; b. Reno, June 5, 1958; s. Joseph Anthony and Peggy Ruth (Crompton) S.; m. Cynthia Amelia Douglas, Aug. 10, 1980; children: Joseph Kenneth, Christopher Anthony. BS, U. Nev., 1979, MD, 1983. Diplomate Am. Bd. Emergency Medicine. Intern in gen. surgery Truman Med. Ctr., Kansas City, 1983-84, resident in emergency medicine, 1984-86, fellow in emergency medicine, 1986-87, rsch. dir. emergency medicine, 1987-88, assoc. residency dir., 1990-97, residency dir., 1997—, assoc. prof. emergency medicine, 1994—; med. dir. Met. Ambulance Svcs., Kansas City, 1988-89; staff physician St. Joseph's Med. Ctr., Asheville, N.C., 1989-90. Chmn. Emergency Physicians Adv. Bd., Kansas City, 1992-94; mem. edn. com. SAEM, 1997—. Author: Toxicology Guide for Emergency Medicine, 1988, Emergency Medicine, 1995; editor: Critical Decision in Emergency Medicine, 1995. Cubmaster Pack 397 Boy Scouts Am., Kearney, Mo., 1994-96, webelos leader, 1993-95, den leader, asst. adminstr., 1991-93. Fellow Am. Coll. Emergency Medicine, Am. Acad. Emergency Medicine; mem. Am. Coll. Emergency Physicians (mem. emergency med. svcs. com. Mo. chpt. 1990-94), Soc. for Acad. Emergency Medicine, Coun. Residency Dirs., Nat. Assn. Emergency Med. Svc. Physicians (state liaison 1988-90). Baptist. Avocations: computers, sailing. Office: Truman Med Ctr Dept Emergency Medicine 2301 Holmes St Kansas City MO 64108-2640 *

SALOMONSEN, RASMUS LYSHOLDT, physician; b. Copenhagen, Mar. 31, 1975; MD, U. Copenhagen, 2005. Physician Rigshospitalet, Clinic Otolaryngology Head and Neck Surgery, 2009—. Home: Ribegade 4 lth Copenhagen 2100 Denmark Personal E-mail: salomonsen@dadlnet.dk.

SALONEN, PAULA HANNELE, research scientist; d. Paavo and Eila Anelma Leskinen; m. Kimmo Tapani Salonen, July 24, 1976. Degree, Inst. Comml. Tng., Ikaalinen, 1976; MSc in Pub. Health, U. Tampere, 1998; cert. in funding in European Union, Tampere Poly., 1999; cert. in health care entrepreneurship and mng., U. Tampere, 2002. Rschr. Tampere Sch. Pub. Health, U. Tampere, 1994—95, Tampere Sch. Pub. Health, U. Tampere, 1997—98, 1999—2002, Nat. R&D Centre for Welfare and Health, Helsinki, Finland, 2003; rschr., cons. EviHealth Rsch. and Consulting, Pirkkala, Finland, 2005—. Mem. e-Business Rsch. Ctr., Tampere, 2001—05. Grantee, Alzheimer Found., 1998, Finnish Work Environment Fund, 2001, 2003—04, Nat. Tech. Agy., 2000; scholar employees - 11-years follow up study, Retirement Pension Ins. Inst. Varma-Sampo Ltd., 2000. Achievements include development of computer-based method lifestyle health control indicator; psyche indicator. Avocations: interior decorating, hiking, travel. Home: Spårentie 3 as 7 Pirkkala 33960 Finland Personal E-mail: pahasa@saunalahti.fi.

SALONIA, ANDREA, urologist, researcher; b. Como, Italy, May 6, 1971; s. Nello Salonia and Maria Enrica Mena. MD, U. Milan, 1996; Specialist in Urology, U. Trieste, Italy, 2001. Full staff urologist dept. urology H. San Raffaele, Milan, 2000—05. Mem.: Italian Soc. Andrology (assoc.). Office: Dept Urology - H San Raffaele Via Olgettina 60 20132 Milan Italy Office Fax: 00390226437298; Home Fax: 00390226437298. Business E-Mail: salonia.andrea@hsr.it.

SALOOJA, NINA, hematologist, consultant, medical educator; b. Cheshire, Eng., Jan. 9, 1962; d. Kailash Chander and Florence Ellen Salooja; m. Robin Russell-Jones, Sept. 18, 1993; children: Eleanor Russell-Jones, Lily Russell-Jones. MA, Oxford U., Eng., 1983; MB, BChir, St. Thomas's Hosp., London, 1986; DM, Oxford U., Eng., 2001; MSc, U. Coll. London, 2008. Diplomate med.edn. U. London, 2007. Cons. hematologist Charing Cross Hosp., London, 2000—; sr. lectr. faculty medicine Imperial Coll., London, 2000—. Fellow: Higher Edn. Acad., Royal Coll. Pathologists, Royal Coll. Physicians (U.K.); mem.: Inst. Learners and Tchrs. in Higher Edn. Avocations: violin, piano, contemporary dance, martial arts. Office: Hammersmith Hosp DuCane Rd London W12 0NN England also: Charing Cross Hosp Fulham Palace Road W6 8RF London England Office Fax: (0208) 8467111.

SALOVICH, DANIELLE, medical association administrator; BS in Biology and Soc., Ariz. State U., Tempe, 2005; MD, Robert Wood Johnson Med. Sch., NJ, 2011. Lectr. pre-matriculation program, rsch. asst. emergency dept., student doctor Promise Clinic Robert Wood Johnson Med. Sch., NJ, 2006—11. Mem.: American Med. Student Assn. (nat. pres. 2011—, sec., v.p. internal affairs, chair Constn. creation com., region II co-dir.), Alpha Kappa Alpha. Office: American Med Student Assn 1902 Association Dr Reston VA 20191 Office Phone: 703-620-6600 ext. 202. Business E-Mail: pres@amsa.org. *

SALSALI, MORTEZA, surgeon; b. Teheran, Iran, Dec. 25, 1920; s. Mahdi Salsali and Azizeh Sadri; m. Barbara Hobbord (div.). MD, Teheran Med. Sch., Iran, 1956; degree in Medicine and Surgery, SUNY, 1967. Diplomate Am. Bd. Surgery, 1965, Am. Bd. Thoracic Surgery, 1969. Intern St. Agnes Hosp., White Plains, NY, 1957; resident gen. surgery North Shore Hosp., Great Neck, NY, 1957—60; resident in pathology LI Coll. Hosp., Bklyn., 1960; fellow cardiac surgery United Hosp., Newark, 1961; fellow oncol. surgery Meml. Hosp., NYC, 1961—65; resident cardiovascular surgery U. Hosp., Balt., 1965—66; resident thoracic surgery VA Hosp., Bklyn., 1966—67; surgeon Pack Med. Group, Columbus Hosp., NYC, 1968—79; sr. rschr. Milan Cancer Inst., 1981—83; instr. cardiovascular surgery Rejai Hosp., Teheran, 1984—86; instr. gen. surgery Shahid Beheshti Med. Sch., Teleghanin Hosp., 1990—93; sr. rschr Iran Nat. Rsch. Ctr. in med. Sci., Teheran, 1993—2004. Contbr. articles to profl. jours. Named Profl. Yr., Internat. Health, 2007. Mem.: ACS, Am. Coll. Angiology, Uffiliale delle Nationi Unite, Inst. Promosioni, NY Cancer Soc. Achievements include invention of a technique for end-to-end anastomosis of superior vena cava and pulmonary artery without clamp occlusion of the superior vena cava, a safe technique for resection of the nonobstructed superior vena cava in lung cancer and bilateral mediastinal node dissection for tumor of anterior mediastingum; new technique for the treatment of Hirschsprungs disease; research and discovery of the reason why transfusion blood during surgery for solid tumor (cancer) is harmful. Avocations: music, singing, opera, painting. Home: Via Barce no 3 20146 Milan MI Italy Personal E-mail: salsali33@hotmail.com.

SALTER, EDWIN CARROLL, retired pediatrician; b. Oklahoma City, Jan. 19, 1927; s. Leslie Ernest and Maud (Carroll) S.; m. Ellen Gertrude Malone, June 30, 1962; children: Mary Susanna, David Patrick BA, DePauw U., 1947, MD, Northwestern U., 1951. Intern Cook County Hosp., Chgo., 1951-53; resident in pediatrics Children's Meml. Hosp., Chgo., 1956-58, Cook County Hosp., Chgo., 1956-58; practice medicine specializing in pediatrics Lake Forest, Ill., 1958-97; attending physician Lake Forest Hosp., 1958—97, pres. med. staff, 1981-82. Attending physician Children's Meml. Hosp., Chgo.; clin. faculty mem. dept. pediatrics Northwestern U. Med. Sch. Served to capt. M.C., U.S. Army, 1954-56 Mem. AMA, Ill. State Med. Soc., Lake County Med. Soc. (pres. 1984), Phi Beta Kappa Republican. Methodist. Home: 19 N Maywood Rd Lake Forest IL 60045-3233

SALTMAN, ROBERT JON, physician, medical educator; b. Holyoke, Mass., Jan. 15, 1954; s. Zailike and Adelaide Saltman; m. Linda Carolynn Eichler; children: Julie, Jane, Zachary. BA, Yale U., 1976; MD, Washington U., 1980. Diplomate internal medicine Am. Bd. Internal Medicine, endocrinology and metabolism Am. Bd. Internal Medicine. Chief resident, instr. medicine Barnes Hosp./Washington U., St. Louis, 1985—86; physician Barnes Jewish Christian Med. Group, St. Louis, 1986—2001; co-ptnr. West County Med. Specialists, St. Louis, 2001—; assoc. prof. clin. medicine Washington U. Sch. Medicine, St. Louis, 2001—. Co-editor: Washington University School of Medicine Manual of Medical Therapeutics, 1986. Mem.: ACP, Internat. Soc. Clin. Densitometry, Endocrine Soc., Am. Diabetes Assn. Avocations: tennis, skiing, wine collecting. Office: West County Med Specialists Ste 145 969 Mason Rd Saint Louis MO 63141 Home Phone: 314-432-6844; Office Phone: 314-878-6008. Personal E-mail: rlsalt@aol.com. *

SALTONSTALL, PETER L., medical association administrator; Sr. exec. Harvard U. Brigham and Women's Hosp., Tufts-New Eng. Med. Ctr., St. Elizabeth's Med. Ctr., Boston, Harvard U. Risk Mgmt. Found., U. Pitts. Med. Ctr. Strategic Bus. Initiatives; co-founder, CEO SafeCare Systems, LLC; pres., CEO Nat. Orgn. Rare Disorders, 2008—. Office: Nat Orgn Rare Disorders 55 Kenosia Ave PO Box 1968 Danbury CT 06813-1968 Office Phone: 203-744-0100. Office Fax: 203-798-2291. *

SALTZ, LEONARD BRUCE, oncologist; b. NYC, Apr. 25, 1957; s. Jack and Anita (Belfer) S.; m. Gail Michele Riess, June 17, 1989; children: Emily Nicole, Kimberly Julia, Victoria Paige. BSc, Stanford U., 1979; MD, Yale U., 1983. Diplomate Am. Bd. Internal Medicine, 1986, Diplomate Subspeciality of Hematology, Am. Bd. Internal Medicine, 1988, Diplomate Subspeciality of Med. Oncology, Am. Bd. Internal Medicine, 1989. Intern internal medicine The NY Hosp., NYC, 1983-84, resident internal medicine, 1984-86; postdoctoral assoc. Lab. of Immunology, Rockefeller U., NYC, 1986-87; fellow hematology-oncology The NY Hosp., Cornell U. Med. Ctr., NYC, 1986-89, asst. attending physician, 1988-89; clin. asst. attending physician Meml. Sloan-Kettering Cancer Ctr., NYC, 1989-93, asst. attending physician, asst. mem., 1993—98, assoc. attending physician, 1998—2005, attending physician, mem., 2005—, head, colorectal oncology sect., 2008—; chmn. pharmacy and therapeutics com. Weill Med. Coll., Cornell U., NYC, 1998—, prof. medicine, 2005—. Pres. NY Hosp. Housestaff Assn., NYC, 1985-86; instr. in medicine Cornell U. Sch. Medicine, NYC, 1992-93, asst. prof. medicine, 1993-98, assoc. prof. medicine, 1998—, prof. medicine, 2005-. Recipient Career Devel. award Am. Cancer Soc., 1993. Mem. ACP, Am. Soc. Clin. Oncology, Am. Assn. for Cancer Rsch.

SALTZ, RENATO, plastic surgeon; b. Uruguaiana, Brazil, Aug. 29, 1956; came to US, 1982; s. Jayme and Berta Saltz; m. Marcia Bartczak, Mar. 6, 1982; children: Bianca, Felipe. MD, U. Fed. Rio, Grande do Sul, Porto Alegre, 1980; postgrad., U. Ala., 1987-89, Med. Coll. Ga., 1990-92. Diplomate Am. Bd. Surgery, Am. Bd. Plastic Surgery. Mem. med. staff U. Fed. Rio, 1975-80; intern in gen. surgery Jackson Meml. Hosp., Miami, Fla., 1982-83, resident in gen. surgery, 1983-86, chief resident in gen. surgery, 1986-87; resident in plastic surgery U. Ala., Birmingham, Ala., 1987-88, chief resident in plastic surgery, 1989, fellow in hand, aesthetic and microsurgery, 1989-90; plastic surgeon Med. Coll. Ga., Augusta, 1990-94, asst. prof. sect. plastic surgery dept. surgery, 1990—94, dir. microsurgery and rsch. lab. sect. plastic surgery, 1990—94; assoc. prof. plastic reconstruct surgery U. Utah, 1994—2002, dir. Summit Plastic Surgery Ctr., 1994—2002; plastic surgeon Saltz Plastic Surgery & Spa Vitória, Salt Lake City, 2002—, Saltz Plastic Surgery & Skin Care Ctr., Park City, 2002—. Lectr., presenter in field; vis. prof. divsn. plastic surgery W.Va. U., Morgantown, 1989, vis. prof. divsn. plastic surgery, U. Ala., Birmingham, 1991; vis. prof. divsn. plastic surgery Fundaçã0o Faculdade Fed. Ciêcias Médicas de Porto Alegre, Brazil, 1993; founder Image Reborn Found. Utah Contbr. articles to profl. publs., chpts. to books; author videotapes. Recipient 3rd prize in resident competition Southeastern Soc. Plastic and Reconstructive Surgeons, 1988, 2nd prize in resident competition Southeastern Soc. Plastic and Reconstructive Surgeons, 1989. Fellow ACS, Internat. Coll. Surgeons; mem. AMA, Am. Burn Assn., Am. Soc. Reconstructive Microsurgery, Plastic Surgery Rsch. Coun., Am. Soc. Plastic and Reconstructive Surgery, Inc., Jackson Med. Soc., Brazilian Plastic Surgery Soc., Southeastern Surg. Congress, Richmond County Med. Soc., Rocky Mountain Assn. Plastic and Reconstructive Surgeons (past pres.), Am. Soc. Aesthetic Plastic Surgery (v.p.), Am. Soc. Plastic Surgery (v.p.), Salt Lake Surgical Soc., Salt Lake Plastic Surgery Soc., Internat. Soc. Aesthetic Surgery (chmn. edn. coun.). Utah plastic Surgery Soc. Office: Saltz Plastic Surgery and Spa Vitoria 5445 S Highland Dr Salt Lake City UT 84117 also: Saltz Plastic Surgery 5445 Highland Dr Salt Lake City UT 84117-7629 Office Phone: 801-274-9501, 435-655-6612. Business E-Mail: info@saltzplasticsurgery.com.

SALTZMAN, BRIAN, physician, surgeon, educator; b. July 24, 1953; BA, Tufts U., Medford, Mass., 1974, MD, Cornell U., Ithaca, NY, 1979. Fellow in endourology N.Y. Hosp., Cornell Med. Ctr., NYC, 1985-86; asst. prof. urology Mt. Sinai Med. Ctr., NYC, 1986-89; asst. prof. surgery Harvard Med. Sch., Boston, 1989-99, assoc. prof. surgery, 1999—. Office Phone: 617-332-0116. Business E-Mail: bsaltzma@caregroup.harvard.edu.

SALTZMAN, CHARLES L., surgeon, educator; b. Pa., Aug. 9, 1954; BA, Brown U., 1978; MD, U. NC, 1985. Prof., dir. resident rsch. U. Iowa Coll. Medicine, 1991—2005; prof., chmn. U. Utah, 2005—. Named Louis S. Peery, MD Presdl. Endowed Prof., U. Utah Dept. Orthop. Mem.: AAOS, AOFAS (past pres. 2010). Avocation: hiking. Office: 590 Wakara Way Salt Lake City UT 84108 Office Fax: 801-587-5411. Business E-Mail: charles.saltzman@hsc.utah.edu.

SALTZMAN, DANIEL, obstetrician-gynecologist, educator; BS, Stony Brook U.; MD, U. of Buffalo. Cert. maternal fetal medicine 2009, nuchal translucency assessment Fetal Medicine Found., fetal nasal bone assessment Fetal Medicine Found., diplomate Am. Bd. Ob-Gyn, 2009. Resident ob-gyn. George Washington Med. Ctr., 1980—83; fellow maternal and fetal medicine Brigham and Women's Hosp., Boston, 1983—85; fellow Harvard Med. Sch.; intern Univ. of Wis., 1979—80; clin. prof. Mt. Sinai Sch. of Medicine, NY, clin. assoc. prof. Co-author: (publs.) Anti-factor Xa plasma levels in pregnant women receiving low molecular weight heparin thromboprophylaxis, 2008, Outcomes of multiple gestations with advanced maternal age, 2009, Active second-stage management in twin pregnancies undergoing planned vaginal delivery in a U.S. population, 2010, Does glyburide negatively influence pregnancy outcomes in obese or non-obese gravidas with gestational diabetes?, 2011, and numerous others. Office: Mount Sinai Medical Center One Gustave L Levy Pl New York NY 10029 Office Phone: 212-241-6500.

SALUSKY, ISIDRO B., pediatric nephrologist, educator; b. Buenos Aires, Sept. 3, 1948; MD, U. Buenos Aires, 1971. Diplomate Am. Bd. Pediat., cert. in Pediat. Nephrology. Intern pediat. Pedro de Elizalde Hosp., Buenos Aires, 1972—73, resident pediat., 1973—75; fellowship pediat. nephrology Hosp. Enfants Malades, Paris, 1976—79; advanced rsch. fellow nutritional metabolism V.A. Wadsworth Med. Ctr., LA, 1979—81; fellowship pediat. nephrology UCLA Med. Ctr., 1981—82, prof. pediat. nephrology, 1982—; attending physician Mattel Children's Hosp./UCLA Med. Ctr. Dir. pediat. dialysis prog. UCLA Med. Ctr., 1984—, assoc. dir. dialysis prog., 1989—, prog. dir. gen. clin. rsch. ctr., 1991—. Contbr. articles to profl. jours. Dir. summer urban health rsch. prog. UCLA/Drew U. Ctr. of Excellence for Minorities, 1995—98; chair edn. com. USA Olympic Transplant Games, LA, 1992. Mem.: Nat. Kidney Found. (pres. elect medical adv. bd. 1991—92, pres. medical adv. bd. 1992—94), Am. Soc. Pediat. Nephrology, Internat. Pediat. Nephrology Assn., Internat. Soc. Peritoneal Dialysis, Soc. Bone and Mineral Rsch. Office: UCLA Med Ctr Dept Pediat Nephrology 10833 Le Conte Ave Los Angeles CA 90095 Office Phone: 310-206-6987. Business E-Mail: isalusky@pediatrics.medsch.ucla.edu.

SALVA, MIQUEL, biochemist, researcher; b. Palma de Mallorca, Balears, Spain, Dec. 9, 1962; s. Joan Salva and Magdalena Coll; m. Christelle Marie Ferra; children: Aina Maria, Christelle Maria. BSc, Universitat Autonoma de Barcelona, Spain, 1985, MSc, 1989, PhD, 1992. Rsch. scientist Laboratorios Almirall SA, Barcelona, 1991—95; sr. rsch. scientist Grupo Farmaceutico Almirall SA, Barcelona,

1995—99; head pharmacokinetics & drug metabolism Almirall Prodesfarma SA, Barcelona, 1999—2002, dep. dir. biol. devel., 2002—04, dir. prin. devel., 2005—. Fellow, European Molecular Biology Orgn., 1990. Mem.: ISSX, Can. Soc. Pharm. Scis., Groupe de Metabolisme et Pharmacocinetique, Am. Assn. Pharm. Scientists. Achievements include development of metabolism pathways of the antimigraine Almotriptan. Office: Almirall Prodesfarma SA Laurea Miro 408-410 E-08980 Barcelona Spain Office Fax: +34932912997. Business E-Mail: msalva@almirallprodesfarma.com.

SALVADORI, DAISY MARIA FAVERO, research scientist; b. Itu, São Paulo, Brazil, Feb. 14, 1959; MS, U. São Paulo, 1986, DSc, 1991. Adj. prof. Fed. U. Bahia, 1987—94; rschr. São Paulo State U., 1995—, advisor to v.p. grad. studies, 2005—. Master: Brazilian Mutagenesis Soc.; mem.: Brazilian Genetics Soc. Office: São Paulo State University Faculdade de Medicina de Botucatu Botucatu Sao Paulo 18618-000 Brazil Office Fax: 55-14-38117210. Business E-Mail: dfavero@fmb.unesp.br.

SALVADOR IZQUIERDO, RAFAEL, physician, consultant; b. Barcelona, July 19, 1979; MD, U. Barcelona, 2003. Cons. Hosp. Clínic Barcelona, 2008—. Office: Villarroel 170 Barcelona 08036 Spain Business E-Mail: rsalvado@clinic.ub.es.

SALVATI, EDUARDO A., orthopedist, surgeon, educator; MD, La Plata Medical Sch., 1963. Diplomate Am. Bd. Orthopedic Surgery, 1972, lic. NY. Resident orthopaedic surgery Clinica Ortopedica della Universita, Florence, Italy, 1964—65, Hosp. de Quilmes, Buenos Aires; fellow hip and knee surgery Hosp. for Spl. Surgery, NY, 1969—72, attending orthopaedic surgeon NY; clin. prof. orthopaedics surgery Weill Cornell Med. Coll. Co-author: (publs.) Total Hip Replacement Surgery (Arthroplasty) and Clot Formation, 2003. Recipient Eastern Orthopedic Assn. award, 1999, John Charnley award, Hip Soc., 2005, Nicholas Andry award, Am. Assn. of Bone and Joint Surgeons, Lifetime Achievement award, Arthritis Found., 2006, Hosp. for Spl. Surgery, 2007; named one of Best Doctors, NY Mag., 2009—11. Mem.: NY Acad. of Medicine, NY Med. Soc., Internat. Hip Soc. (former sec.), Am. Assn. of Hip and Knee Surgeons, Am. Hip Soc. (former pres.), Am. Acad. of Orthopedic Surgeons. Achievements include research in Prospective Evaluation of the Clinical and Economic Outcomes of Total Joint Replacement: The HSS Hip Arthroplasty Cohort; Prospective Evaluation of the Clinical and Economic Outcomes of Total Joint Replacement: The HSS Knee Arthroplasty Cohort; The Genetic Factor: Identifying Patients at High Risk for Developing Pulmonary Embolism (PE) After Orthopedic Surgery (Upper Extremity, Spine, THR, TKR) Using A Molecular Screening Test. Office: Hospital for Special Surgery Belaire Bldg 525 E 71st St New York NY 10021 Office Phone: 212-606-1472. Office Fax: 211-249-8617.

SALVATIERRA, OSCAR, JR., transplant surgeon, urologist, educator; b. Phoenix, Apr. 15, 1935; s. Oscar and Josefine S.; m. Pamela Moss; children: Mark, Lisa Marie. BS, Georgetown U., 1957; MD, U. So. Calif., 1961. Intern, resident in surgery and urology U. So. Calif.-Los Angeles County Med. Ctr., 1961-66; practice medicine Pomona, Calif., 1968-72; chief staff Casa Colina Hosp., 1972; post doctoral fellow in transplantation U. Calif.-San Francisco, 1972-73, asst. prof. surgery and urology, 1973-75, assoc. prof., 1975-81, prof., 1981-91, chmn. transplant service, 1974-91; attending surgeon and urologist Moffitt Hosp., 1973—; exec. dir. Pacific Transplant Inst., 1991-94; prof. surgery/pediatrics, dir. pediat. renal transplantation Stanford U. Med. Ctr., 1994—2006, attending surgeon, urologist and pediat.; advising dean Sch. Medicine Stanford U., 2005—; prof. surgery & pediat. Standford U., Emeritus Sch. Medicine, 2006—. Chair faculty senate Stanford U. Sch. Medicine, 2002—04; study sect. NIH, 1981-85, nat. adv. bd., 1986-92, chmn. nat. adv. bd. 1990-92, chmn. spl. study sect., 1997, 99 Mem. editl. bd. Transplantation and Immunology, 1984—, Transplantation, 1987—, Transplantation Procs., 1990—, Pediat. Transplantation, 1998—; assoc. editor Am. Jour. Kidney Diseases, 1987-89; contbr. over 290 articles and chpts. to med. lit. Nat. bd. advisors Agent Orange Class Assistance Program, 1988-96. With M.C., U.S. Army, Vietnam, 1966-68. Decorated Army Commendation medal, Grande Ufficiale of Italian Rep. Knighthood with title His Excellency; recipient Chancellor's award for pub. svc., U. Calif., 1986, Commendation resolution, Calif. State Legislature, 1990, Presdl. medal and Diploma of Honor, Argentina, 1999, Rambar-Mark award, Stanford U., 1999, Franklin Ebaugh award, 2003, Albion Walter Hewlett award, 2007, Stanford, 2007; named Oscar Salvatierra Symposium in his honor, 2001; grantee, NIH, 1974—76, 1980—83, 1988—90, 2003—, USPHS, 1986—89; Oscar Salvatierra Ann. Lectureship in Transplantation, in his honor, Stanford U., 2005—. Fellow ACS (bd. govs. 1986-92); mem. Am. Surg. Assn., Am. Soc. Transplant Surgeons (bd. dirs. 1977-85, pres. 1983-84, chmn. adv. com. on issues 1984-87), Soc. Univ. Surgeons, Soc. Univ. Urologists, N.Y. Acad. Scis., Am. Soc. Nephrology, Internat. Transplantation Soc. (bd. dirs. 1984—, pres.-elect 1996-98, pres., 1998-2000, Contbns. to Soc. medallion 2006), Soc. Pediatric Urology, Am. Urol. Assn., Nat. Kidney Found. (Pioneer award 2004, Nat. Kidney Found. Lifetime Champion of Hope award, 2009), Renal Physicians Assn. (bd. dirs. 1984-87), Pacific Coast Surg. Assn., San Francisco Surg. Soc., United Network Organ Sharing (bd. dirs. 1984-88, pres. 1985-86), Internat. Soc. for Organ Sharing (bd. dirs. 1991—, pres. 1993-95), Am. Soc. for Multicultural Health and Transplant Profls. (pres. 1992-94, Lifetime Achievement award, 2005), Nafziger Surg. Soc. Achievements include being the principle lay figure in passage and enactment of National Organ Transplant Act, 1984; introduction of Pope John Paul II to the 18th International Transplantation Congress for Encyclical on Organ Transplantation, 2000; Dr. Oscar Salvatierra award is named after him from Center of Excellence, Stanford University, 2009-. Office: Stanford University Sch Medicine CCSR 4245C Stanford CA 94305

SALVI, RICHARD, psychologist, otolaryngologist, educator; BS in Psychology, ND State U., 1968; PhD in Experimental Psychology, Syracuse U., 1975. Asst. prof. U. Tex., 1980—84, assoc prof., 1984—87; prof. dept. communicative disorders & sciences SUNY U. Buffalo; dir. Ctr. for Hearing & Deafness, 2003—. Editorial bd. Hearing Rsch., 1993—, Audiology & Neuro-Otology, 1995—, Internat. Tinnitus Jour., 1997—, Noise & Health, 1998—, Am. Acad. Audiology, 1999—, Jour. Audiological Medicine & Sciences Related to Communicative Disorders, 2005—; med. adv. bd. Martha Entenmann Tinnitus Rsch. Ctr.; internat. adv. bd. U. Coll. London Ctr. for Auditory Rsch. Mem.: Am. Tinnitus Assn. (Scientific Adv. com. 2001—). Office: Center for Hearing & Deafness 137Q Cary Hall Buffalo NY 14214 Office Phone: 716-829-5310. Office Fax: 716-829-2980. E-mail: salvi@buffalo.edu.

SALVO, JOHN P., JR., orthopaedic surgeon; MD, Thomas Jefferson U., Phila., Pa., 1961. Lic. NJ, 1964, Pa., 1973, diplomate Am. Bd. Orthopaedic Surgery. Intern William Beaumont Army Med. Ctr., 1962; hosp. affiliation include Bronson Methodist Hosp.; resident Thomas Jefferson Univ. Hosp., 1982, physician. Named one of the Top Doctors, Phila. Mag., 2011. Office: Thomas Jefferson University Hospital 2410 S Broad St Ste 200 Philadelphia PA 19148 Office Phone: 215-334-3350.

SALYER, KENNETH E., surgeon; b. Kansas City, Kans., Aug. 18, 1936; s. Everett A. and Laurene S.; m. Luci Lara-Salyer; children: Kenneth E. Jr., Leigh Green-Salyer. BS, U. Mo., 1958; MD, U. Kans., 1962. Intern Parkland Meml. Hosp., Dallas, 1962-63, resident in gen. surgery, 1963-67; fellow in surgery U. Tex. SW Sch. Med., Dallas, 1965-67, founder, dir. residency tng. program, 1969-78; prof. surgery, chair plastic surgery, 1969-78; resident in plastic surgery U. Kans. Sch. Med., Kansas City, 1967-69; founder, dir. Internat. Craniofacial Inst., Dallas, 1986—. Editl. bd. mem. Annals of Plastic Surgery, 1977-79, Jour. of Speech and Hearing Disorders (editl. cons.) 1982, Tex. Medicine (editl. cons.) 1981-85, Jour. of Craniofacial Surgery, 1990—, Italian Jour. Craniomaxillofacial Surgery, 1990—, Argentinian Jour. Plastic Surgery (internat. consultative coun. 1995—). Author: Techniques in Aesthetic Craniofacial Surgery, 1989, Cleft Lip and Palate Treatment Center: A Booklet for Parents, 1994, (with J. Bardach) Surgical Techniques in Cleft Lip and Palate, 1987, 2d edit. 1991, (with others) The Atlas of Craniomaxillofacial Surgery, 1982; editor: Symposium on Plastic Surgery in the Orbital Region, 1976; author various book chpts. Recipient Nat. Inst. Health award public health svc., sr. clin. traineeship Cancer Control Program 1967-69, Plastic Surgery Resident Program Participation award 2nd place 1967-69, scholar. competition (hon. mention) Edn. Found. Am. Soc. Plastic and Reconstructive Surgeons, 1972, Rsch. Grant award Ednl. Found. Am. Soc. Plastic and Reconstructive Surgeons 1975-76, Hektoen Gold medal for original investigation "Spectrum of Rsch. and Clin. Mgmt. of Craniofacial Anomalies" exhibit at AMA, San Francisco 1977, selected hon. mem. Japanese Soc. Craniofacial Surgery 1993, selected chmn. med. adv. bd. Children's Craniofacial Assn. 1993; grantee Internat. NIH Microvascular Surg. Rsch. 1969, Vets. Admin. Hosp. Maxillofacial Rsch. 1972-78, Sid Richardson Found. med. rsch. 1975-76, Gen. Electric Found. for Craniofacial Deformities 1985-87; recipient various awards for videos. Mem. AMA (mem. various coms.), Am. Acad. Pediat. (exec. com. section on plastic surgery, founding mem., sec.-treas. 1987-90, chmn. 1991—), Am. Assn. of Pediat. Plastic Surgery (founding mem., chmn. 1991—), Am. Assn. Plastic Surgery (mem. various coms.), Am. Burn Assn., Am. Cleft Palate Assn. (mem. various coms.), Am. Coll. Surgeons, Am. Soc. for Aesthetic Plastic Surgery, Am. Soc. Maxiofacial Surgery (pres. 2003-04), Am. Soc. Plastic and Reconstructive Surgery (mem. various coms.), Am. Soc. for Reconstructive Microsurgery, Argentine Soc. of Plastic Surgery, Children's Craniofacial Assn. (chmn. med. adv. bd.), Chirugio Soc., Craniofacial Biology Group, Dallas County Med. Soc., Dallas Soc. Plastic Surgery, Euro. Assn. for Craniomaxillofacial Surgery, Internat. Coll. Surgeons, Internat. Confederation for Plastic Reconstructive Surgery (founding mem.), Internat. Craniofacial Club, Internat. Craniofacial Travel Club, Internat. Soc. Clin. Plastic Surgery, Internat. Soc. Cranofacial Surgery (pres. 2001-03), Lipoplasty Soc. of N.A., Inc., Plastic Surgery Rsch. Coun. (chmn. 1978), Soc. for Biomaterials, Soc. Craniofacial Genetics, Soc. Head and Neck Surgery, So. Med. Assn., Southwestern Med. Found., Tex. Soc. Plastic Surgery (mem. various coms., pres.-elect 1982-83, pres. 1983-84), Tex. State Med. Assn., Wound Healing Soc, Craniofacial Surgery Fellowship (founder and dir. 1979-2006), Japanese Soc. Craniofacial Surgery, World craniofacial Found. (founder and chmn. 1990-), Am. Soc. Craniofacial Surgery (pres. 1996-99). Avocations: skiing, running, travel. Office Phone: 972-566-6669.

SALZ, JAMES JOSEPH, medical association administrator; m. Judith Salz; children: James, Mark, Heather, Elizabeth. MD, Duke U., SC, 1965. Diplomate Am. Bd. Ophthalmology, Calif., 1972. Pres. Laser Vision Med. Assocs., Beverly Hills, Calif., 1972—. Recipient Lifetime Achievement award, Am. Acad. Ophthalmology, 2008. Office: Laser Vision Med Assocs 11620 Wilshire Blvd #711 Los Angeles CA 90025 Personal E-mail: drjjsalz@gmail.com. Business E-Mail: drsalz@drsalz.com.

SALZBERG, C. ANDREW, plastic surgeon; b. Paterson, NJ, Mar. 14, 1951; MD, U. Fla., 1981. Ptnr. NY Group Plastic Surgery, 1987—. Mem.: Am. Soc. Plastic Surgery. Office: 155 White Plains Rd Ste 109 Tarrytown NY 10591 Personal E-mail: asalzbergmd@yahoo.com.

SALZER, HELMUT J. F., medical researcher; b. Austria, Sept. 12, 1981; MD, Med. U. Graz, Austria, 2008, MPH, 2011. Rsch. physician Med. U. Graz, Austria, 2008—. Mem.: Austrian Soc. Infectious Diseases, Am. Soc. Microbiology (grant 2010). Office: Auenbruggerplatz 15 Graz Styria A-8036 Austria Personal E-mail: salzer.helmut@gmail.com.

SAMAHA, A MICHAEL, JR., urologist, educator; Grad., St. Michael's Coll.; MD, Boston U. Diplomate Am. Bd Urology, 1984, lic. Pa. Resident gen. surgery and urology Temple Univ. Hosp., Phila., asst. clin. prof.; hosp. affiliation includes Fox Chase Cancer Ctr.; urologist Urology Health Specialists Ltd. Liability Co., Abington Meml. Hosp. Named one of the Top Doctors, Phila. Mag., 2011. Fellow: ACS; mem.: AMA, Montgomery County Med. Soc., Phila. Urol. Soc., Am. Assn. Clin. Urologists, Am. Urol. Assn. Office: Abington Memorial Hospital 1200 Old York Rd Abington PA 19001 Office Phone: 215-481-2000.

SAMANI, NILESH JAYANTILAL, medical educator, consultant; b. Nanyuki, Kenya, July 19, 1956; s. Jayantilal and Kantaben Samani; m. Varsha Raja, Aug. 11, 1984; children: Niraj, Rajiv. BSc, MB ChB, U. Leicester, Eng., 1981, MD, 1994, F Med. Sci., 2002. Cons. cardiologist Glenfield Hosp., Leicester, 1993—; prof. cardiology U. Leicester, 1997—. Fellow: Am. Heart Assn., Am. Coll. Cardiology, Royal Coll. Physicians. Office: Glenfield Hosp Groby Rd Leicestershire Leicester LE3 9QP England Home: 29 Berridge Ln Leicester LE4 7QB England Office Phone: 44 116 2563021. Office Fax: 44 116 2875792.

SAMANTA, AMALESH, medical educator; b. Midnapore, West Bengal, India, July 19, 1961; PhD, 1988. Lectr., pharm. tech. Jadavpur U., Kolkata, India, 1990—, tchr., rschr., divsn. microbiology dept. pharm. tech., 2007—11. Office: Raja S C Mallick Rd Kolkata West Bengal 700032 India Personal E-mail: asamanta61@yahoo.co.in.

SAMARANAYAKE, LAKSHMAN PERERA, dentistry educator; b. Colombo, Sri Lanka, Dec. 16, 1947; arrived in Scotland, 1977; s. Daniel Perera Samaranayake and Patikirige Dayawathi; m. Yuthika Hemamala Abeyagoonasekera, June 22, 1981; chidren: Dilani S., Asanka S. BDS, U. Ceylon, Peradeniya, Sri Lanka, 1971; DDS, U. Glasgow, UK, 1982; DSc (hon.), U. Peradeniya, 2005. Lectr. U. Peradeniya, 1975-77; registrar Glasgow (U.K.) Health Bd., 1977-85, hon. cons., 1985-90; assoc. prof. U. Alberta, Edmonton, Can., 1990-91; reader U. Hong Kong, 1991-97, chair, prof., 1997—. Chmn. sci. commn. Internat. Dental Fedn., 2003-06; assoc. dean Faculty of Dentistry, U. Hong Kong, 1998-2003, dean, 2004—; dir. Prince Philip Dental Hosp., 2004-. Author: (with others) Clinical Oral Microbiology, 1989, Infection Control for the Dental Team, 1991, Clnical Virology in Oral Medicine and Dentistry, 1992, Oral Candidosis, 1990, Essential Microbiology for Dentistry, 1999, 4th edit. 2011; contbr. articles to profl. 400 jours. Recipient Outstanding Rschr. award, U. Hong Kong, 2001, Outstanding Rsch. Student Supr. award, 2001, Disting. Scientist award, Internat. Assn. Dental Rsch. Wash., 2010. Fellow Royal Coll. Pathologists (U.K.), Dental Surgery Coll. Surgeons Edinburgh(hon.). Buddhist. Avocations: tennis, oenophile. Home: 7 Fl Block 30 Baguio Villas 555 Victoria Rd Hong Kong Hong Kong Office: Fac Dentistry U Hong Kong 34 Hospital Rd Hong Kong Hong Kong Office Phone: 2859-0342.

SAMARASINGHE, COLVIN ANANDA, neurosurgeon; b. Colombo, Sri Lanka, Dec. 11, 1946; s. Don Berty and Gladys Eleanor (Wijesingha) S.; m. Elizabeth Charlotte Siyambalapitiya, May 7, 1978; 1 child, Charmaine Minoli. Diploma, St. Thomas Coll., Mt. Lavinia, Sri Lanka, 1962, St. Thomas Coll., Sri Lanka, 1964; MBBS, Med. Coll., Colombo, 1970. Intern, sr. house officer/registrar Gen. Hosp., Colombo, 1971—76; registrar neurosurgery Nat. Hosp. Queen Square, London, 1977—79; cons., neurol. surgeon Nat. Hosp., Colombo, 1979—2006; sr. cons. neurosurgeon Nat. Hosp. Sri Lanka, Colombo, 1991—2006; ret. from Ministry of Health, Govt. Sri Lanka, 2006; pvt. neurosurgery practice Nawaloka Pvt. Hosps., Colombo, 2006—. Hon. cons., neurol. surgeon, Sri Lanka Air Force, Colombo, 1985—; sr. house officer gen. surgery Charing Cross Hosp., London, 1976-77. Contbr. articles to profl. jours Traveling fellow, U. Minn, Mayo Clinic Rochester, U. Rochester, U. Chgo., U. Ont., U. We. Ont., U. Columbia, 1989, Fujita Health U., 1998; recipient Brit. Coun. scholarship, Scotland, 1988 Fellow Royal Coll. Surgeons Eng., Edinburgh, ACS (internat. guest scholar), Coll. Surgeons Sri Lanka (hon. sec. 1991-92); mem. Am. Assn. Neurosurgeons (internat. assoc.), Congress Neurosurgeons, Asian Congress Neurosurgeons (exec. com.) Anglican. Avocations: photography, electronics, music. Office: Nawaloka Private Hospital Limited Department of Neurosurgery Sri Saugathodaya Mawatha Colombo 2 Sri Lanka Office Phone: 00-9411-5777816. Business E-Mail: drnivloc@sltnet.lk.

SAMBASIVAN, MAHADEVA IYER, neurosurgeon, consultant; b. Trivandrum, Kerala, India, May 1, 1936; s. Iyer Mahadeva and Ammal Avudai; m. Gomathy Sambasivan, May 8, 1963; children: Mahesh, Kumar, Srividya. MBBS, Trivandrum Med. Coll., India, 1955; MS in Neurosurgery, Vellore Christian Med. Coll., Trivandrum, 1960; MS in Gen. Surgery, Trivandrum Med. Coll., India, 1966. From asst. prof. to assoc. prof. Med. Coll., Trivandrum, 1966-75, prof., 1975-82, dir., 1982-91, vice prin., 1989-91; cons. neurosurgeon Cosmopolitan Hosp., Trivandrum, 1991—; pres. Kerala Brahmana Sabha, 2003. Sci. program dir. World Fedn. N.S. Socs., 1985-89, v.p. 1997—; dep. chmn. Neurotrauma Com. WFIVS, 1990—. Contbr. articles to med. jours. Chmn. Sankara Free Med. Ctr., Trivandrum, 1993—; v.p. Swati Tirunal Sangeetha Sabha, Trivandrum, 1994—; patron Ctr. for Human Rights Legal Aid Rsch., Trivandrum, 1994. Recipient Lifetime Achievement Gold medal, Hyderabad, 2009; named Silver Jubilee Orator, Med. Coll. Trivandrum, 1981. Fellow Royal Coll. Surgeons, Acad. Med. Scis.; mem. Neurol. Soc. (sec. 1981-89, pres. 1995—), World Fedn. Neurosurg. Socs. (v.p. 1997—, hon. pres. 2003). Avocations: sanskrit studies, vedie literature, nature. Home: Sivapriya Tagore Gardens 695011 Trivandrum India Office: Cosmopolitan Hosp Pattom 695004 Trivandrum Kerala India Home Phone: 04712442054; Office Phone: 04712448182. Personal E-mail: sambshiv@md4.vsml.net.in.

SAMBO, LUIS GOMES, international organization administrator, regional direrctor; b. Luanda, Angola, Jan. 1, 1952; s. José Ambrosio Sambo and Flavienne Ogandaga; 6 children. MD, U. Angola, 1977, U. Nova de Lisbon, Portugal; PhD in Mgmt. Scis., Sch. Bus. and Mgmt., U. Hull, Eng., 2004; D (hon.), U. Kinshasa, Democratic Republic Congo, 2009; diploma in Pub. Health, Med. Assn.; PhD (hon.), U. Kinshasa De Congo. Pub. health specialist Med. Postgrad. Coll., Luanda, 1988, cert. Portuguese Med. Assn., Lisbon, in epidemiology & bio stats. John Hopkins U., 1995, in epidemiol. methods planning & evaluating John Hopkins U., 1997, in relief ops. U. Geneva, 1992; in rsch. methods U. Hull, 2004; commendation decree Govt. of Angola, 1977, commendation diploma Govt. of Guinea Bissau, 1994, cert. Angolan Inst. State Adminstrn., 1985, in biostats. & epidemiology, in epidemiol. methodso planning evaluating, in relief ops. Angolan Inst. State Adminstrn. Physician Health Ctr., Ministry of Health, Cacuaco, Angola, 1977, Ministry of Health, Cabinda, Angola, 1978—81, dir. dept. human resources Luanda, 1981—83; vice min. health Govt. of Angola, Luanda, 1983—88; mem. exec. bd. WHO Exec. Bd., Geneva, 1978—80; chief strategic support team WHO, Harare, Zimbabwe, 1989—90, dir. programme mgmt., 1998—2005; rep. WHO Country, Bissau, Guinea-Bissau, 1990—94; health strategy coord. WHO, Brazzaville, Republic of the Congo, 1994—96, dir. health svcs. devel., 1996—98, regional dir. Africa, 2005—. Mem. consultative bd. U. Nova Lisbon, 2006—; mem. bd. editors Global

Libr. Women's Medicine, London, 2007—; mem. Portuguese Med. Assn. Contbr. more than 20 sci. articles pub. in internat. pub. health jours. Decorated Medal Commandeur de l'Ordre de Madagascar Republic of Madagascar; recipient Pub. Health medal, Republic of Niger, 2006, Silver Plate award, Angstan Med. Assn., Officer De L'Order Nat. award, Govt. Burkainfaso; Paul Harris fellow, Rotary Internat. Mem.: Portuguese Med. Assn., Angolan Med. Assn. (Silver Plate award 2008), Internat. Soc. Sys. Sci. Roman Catholic. Avocations: sports, music, fishing. Office: WHO Regional Office Africa Cite OMS Djoue Brazzaville Republic of the Congo Office Phone: 4724139351. Office Fax: 4724139506. Business E-Mail: sambol@afro.who.int. *

SAMDANI, AMER, medical association administrator; b. Lahore, Pakistan, Mar. 11, 1970; BA, Columbia U., 1991; MD, Johns Hopkins U., 1997. Dir. pediatric spine surgery Shriners Hosps. Children, 2005. Office: 3551 N Broad St Philadelphia PA 19140 Business E-Mail: asamdani@shrinenet.org.

SAMEC, JAMES RICHARD, psychotherapist; b. Chgo., May 6, 1941; arrived in Sweden, 1968; s. James and Sabine Samec; m. Lotta Flink, Jan. 23, 1965; children: Jennifer Iquique Maj, Joseph Malcolm. BS, Loyola U., Chgo., 1963, MA in History, 1969; psychotherapy magister, Carolingian Inst. and Stockholm U., 1997. Psychotherapy level 2 Carolingian Inst., 1989, psychotherapy supr. Ericastiftelsen, Stockholm, 1994, Eye movement desensitization and reprocessing supr. 2003. Tchr. St. Joseph's H.S., Westchester, Ill., 1965, Forrestville Upper Grade Ctr., Chgo., 1966—68, Kursverksamheten, Stockholm, 1969—73; day-care parent, "at home" therapist, recreation leader Sundbyberg (Sweden) Twp., 1971—79; mgr., supr., treatment asst., tchr. Liljeholmen's Therapy Sch., Stockholm, 1975—90; pvt. practice psychotherapist Stockholm, 1982—89; lic. psychotherapist pvt. practice Stockholm, Norrtälje, 1989—; mgr., supr. Upplands-Bro's Samskolan (Sweden) Twp., 1987—93; lic. psychotherapist, psychotherapy supr., head refugee project Child and Adolescent Psychiatry, Norrtälje, Sweden, 1994—2006. Contbr. articles to profl. jours. Chmn. PTA Sundbyberg's Sch., Sweden, 1973—79. Recipient scholarship and travel grant, Sven Jerring's Fund, Sweden, 1990, 2001, 2005, Stockholm County Bd. Health and Welfare, 1994, 1999. Mem.: Eye Movement Desensitization and Reprocessing-Sweden Assn. (vice auditor 2003), Swedish Family Therapy Assn., European Assn. for Psychotherapy (coord. working group for psychodynamic/psychoanalytic psychotherapy 1995—2000), Swedish Nat. Psychotherapy Assn. (bd. dirs. 1991—2001, chmn. internat. com. working group 2001—03, electoral bd. mem.). Avocations: literature, medieval and classical music. Home: Karlbergsvägen 49 2 tr 11335 Stockholm Sweden Office: Gambrinusgatan 2 112 27 Stockholm Sweden Office Phone: 46 8 31 33 08. Business E-Mail: james.samec@telia.com.

SAMELIS, GEORGIOS FOTIOS, oncologist, consultant; b. Athens, Attiki, Greece, Oct. 22, 1955; s. Fotios Samelis and Maria Samelis; 1 child, Eleni Samelis. MD, U. Athens, Greece, 1980, PhD, 1996. Cert. internal medicine Mcpl. Athens, 1986, med. oncology 1999. Cons. Hippokrateion Gen. Hosp., Athens, 1990—, dir. oncology dept., 2005; rsch. fellow Free U. Hosp., Amsterdam, 1992—94; med. oncologist Gustave Roussy Anticancer Hosp., Paris, 1994—95. Flight lt. Airforce, 1980—82, Athens. Recipient Greek Acad. award; Rsch. grant, Hippokrateio Gen. Hosp. Mem.: Greek Soc. Mastology (bd. dir., treas. 2009—), Hellenic Assn. Supportive Care Oral Cavity Cancer (bd. dir. 2006—11), Hellenic Assn. Preventive Medicine, Hellenic Assn. Med. Oncologists (bd. dir. 2006), Hellenic Coop. Oncology Group, Multidisciplinary Assn. Supportive Care Cancer, New Drug Devel., European Orgn. Rsch. Treatment Cancer, Am. Soc. Clin. Oncology, European Soc. Med. Oncologists, Med. Assn. Athens. Home: 46 Lykeiou St Athens Attiki 15341 Greece Office: Hippokrateion Gen Hosp Vasilissis Sofias 108 115 27 Athens Greece Office Phone: 00302107789736. Office Fax: 00302132088521; Home Fax: 00302299076704. Personal E-mail: gsamelis@otenet.gr. Business E-Mail: oncologydept.samelis@hippocratio.gr.

SAMELSON, LAWRENCE ELLIOT, medical researcher; b. Chgo., Apr. 18, 1951; s. Charles F. and Natalie (Rudeis) S.; m. Elizabeth Trosman, June 8, 1980; children: Seth Aaron, Rebecca Ellen. BA, U. Rochester, 1972; MD, Yale U., 1977. Resident in internal medicine U. Chgo. Hospitals, 1977-80; rsch. assoc. Lab. Immunology Nat. Inst. Allergy and Infectious Diseases, NIH, Bethesda, Md., 1980-85; sr. staff fellow Cell Biology and Metabolism Br., Nat. Inst. Child Health and Human Devel., NIH, Bethesda, 1985-87, named sr. investigator, 1988, chief Sect. Lymphocyte Signaling, 1995, dep. br. chief, 1995; chief Lab. Cellular and Molecular Biology Ctr. Cancer Rsch., Nat. Cancer Inst., NIH, Bethesda, 1999—, dep. dir., 2006—. Contbr. articles to profl. publs. Achievements include research in T cell antigen receptor structure and function, T cell activation, and biochemistry of signal transduction. Office: Ctr Cancer Rsch Lab Cellular and Molecular Biology 37 Convent Dr Bldg 37 Rm 2066 Bethesda MD 20892-4256 Office Phone: 301-496-9683. Office Fax: 301-496-8479. E-mail: samelson@helix.nih.gov.

SAMET, JONATHAN MICHAEL, epidemiologist, educator; b. Va., Mar. 26, 1946; BA in Chemistry and Physics, Harvard Coll., 1966; MD, U. Rochester, 1970; MS in Epidemiology, Harvard Sch. Pub Health, 1977. Diplomate Am. Bd. Internal Medicine, Nat. Bd. Med. Examiners. Intern in medicine U. Ky. Med. Ctr., Lexington, 1970-71; asst. resident in medicine U. N.Mex. Affiliated Hosps., Albuquerque, 1973-74, sr. resident, 1974-75; rsch. fellow in clin. epidemiology Channing lab. Harvard Med. Sch., Boston, 1975-78, rsch. assoc. in medicine, 1978-83; epidemiologist Cancer Rsch. and Treatment Ctr. U. N.Mex., Albuquerque, 1980-87, asst. prof. medicine, 1978-82, assoc. prof. medicine, 1982-88, assoc. prof. family, cmty., and emergency medicine, 1985-88, prof. family, cmty., and emergency medicine, 1986-94, prof. medicine, 1988-94, clin. prof. medicine, 1994—; prof., chmn. dept. epidemiology The Johns Hopkins U., Balt., 1994—, co-dir. risk scis. and pub. policy inst., 1995—; dept. preventive medicine, dir. U. Southern Calif., Inst. Global Health. Chief pulmonary divsn. U. N.Mex Hosp., Albuquerque, 1985—94, chief pulmonary and critical care divsn. dept. medicine, 1985—94; mem. indoor air quality and total human exposure com., sci. adv. bd. US EPA, 1987—95, 2007—, clean air sci. adv. com. chmn., 2008—; chmn. biol. effects ionizing radiation VI com. NRC, 1994—98, mem. bd. environ. studies and toxicology, 2002, chmn., 2003—09, chmn. com. rsch. priorities airborne particulate matter, 1998—2004; chmn. Inst. Medicine, 1997, chmn. com. asbestos, 2004—06, chmn. com. evaluation presumptive disability decision making process for vets., 2006—; co-dir. Inst. Global Tobacco Control, 1998—; chmn. epidemiology and disease control study sect. 2 NIH, 2002. Editor pro tem Am. Jour. of Epidemiology, 1991—92; editor: Am. Jour. of Epidemiology, 1992—98; assoc. editor Tobacco Control: An Internat. Jour., 1991—; editor: Epidemiologic Revs., 1994—2002, Epidemiology, 2002—07; co-editor-in-chief: Air Quality, Atmosphere and Health, 2007—. With US Army, 1971—73. Recipient Clinton P. Anderson award, Am. Lung Assn., N.Mex, 1988, Excellence in Environ. Health Rsch. award, Rochester Sch. Medicine and Dentistry, 2006, Distinguished Alumni award, U. Rochester, 2006, Tobacco Day award, WHO, 2007. Fellow: AAAS, Am. Coll. Epidemiology (pres. 2000—01, Surgeon Gen.'s medallion 2006); mem.: Am. Cancer Soc. (co-chair com. cancer and environment 2008—), US EPA (clean air sci. adv. com., sci. adv. bd. 2007—), Md. Thoracic Soc., Internat. Soc. Indoor Air Quality and Climate, Internat. Epidemiol. Assn., N.Mex. Thoracic Soc. (sec.-treas. 1982—83, v.p. 1983—84, pres. 1984—85), Am. Thoracic Soc. (long range planning com. environ. and occupational health assembly 1992—, program com. behavioral scis. sect. 1994—95, Pub. Svc. award 2006), Soc. for Epidemiol. Rsch. (pres.-elect 1988—89, exec. com. 1988—91, pres. 1989—90), Delta Omega Alpha, Alpha Omega Alpha. Office: Keck Sch Medicine Univ Southern Calif 1441 Eastate Ave NIT 4436 Los Angeles CA 90008-9175 Office Phone: 323-865-0803. Personal E-mail: jsamet@aol.com. Business E-Mail: jsamet@usc.edu.

SAMET, KENNETH ALAN, hospital administrator; b. Bklyn., Mar. 17, 1958; married. BA, Old Dominion U., 1990; MA, U. Mich., 1982. Pres., CEO MedStar Health, Inc.; adminstrv. intern Mt. Vernon Hosp., Fairfax, Va., 1981; asst. to pres. Washington Health Care Corp., 1983-85, dir., system devel., 1985-86; pres. Medlantic Enterprises, Washington, 1988-91; adminstrv. resident Washington Hosp. Ctr., 1982-83, pres., 1991; v.p., system devel. Medlantic Health Care Group, Washington, 1986-88, exec. v.p., sys. & bus. devel., 1988-91, exec. v.p., COO, 1991. Bd. dirs. Catalyst Health Solutions, Inc. Mem. D.C. Hosp. Assn., Md. Hosp. Assn., Va. Hosp. Assn. (bd. dirs.). Home: 8820 Burdette Rd Bethesda MD 20817-2807 Office: MedStar Health 5565 Sterrett Pl Columbia MD 21044 also: Catalyst Health Solutions Inc Bd Directors 800 King Farm Blvd Rockville MD 20850 Office Phone: 410-772-6500, 301-548-2900. Office Fax: 410-715-3905, 301-548-2991. Business E-Mail: ksamet@catalystrx.com. *

SAMMONS, MARY FRANCES, retail executive; b. Portland, Oreg., Oct. 12, 1946; d. Lee W. and Ann (Cherry) Jackson; m. Nickolas F. Sammons, Sept. 12, 1967; 1 child, Peter. BA, Marylhurst Coll., Oreg., 1970. Buyer Fred Meyer Inc., Portland, 1975-80, v.p., merchandiser, 1980-85, sr. v.p. apparel & home electronics group, 1996, exec. v.p., apparel, home & home electronics group, 1997—98; pres. Fred Meyer Stores, Inc., Portland, 1998—99, pres., CEO, 1999; pres., COO Rite Aid Corp., Camp Hill, Pa., 1999—2003, pres., CEO, 2003—07, chmn., pres., CEO, 2007—08, chmn., CEO, 2008—10, chmn., 2010—. Pres. The Rite Aid Found.; bd. dirs. Rite Aid Corp., 1999—, First Horizon Nat. Corp., 2003—08, StanCorp Financial Group, Inc., 2008—, Magellan Health Services, Inc., 2011—. Recipient Woman of Achievement award, YWCA, Portland, 1987; named one of The 100 Most Powerful Women, Forbes mag., 2005—09, 50 Most Powerful Women in Bus., Fortune mag., 2006, 2007, 50 Women to Watch, Wall St. Jour., 2006. Mem. American Mgmt. Assn. Office: Rite Aid Corp 30 Hunter Ln Camp Hill PA 17011 Office Phone: 717-761-2633. Business E-Mail: msammons@riteaid.com. *

SAMOJLIK, EUGENIUSZ, medical educator, health facility administrator; b. Kuchmy-Bialystok, Poland, Aug. 20, 1933; s. Michael and Anastazia S.; m. Anna Morozewicz, Apr. 10, 1965; children: Dorothy, Michael. BS in Biomedicine, U. Warsaw, 1958, PhD in Reproductive Endocrinology, 1964. Rsch. asst. Maternity Inst. Dept. Pharmacology, Warsaw, 1958-62, sr. asst., 1962-66; asst. prof., chief reproductive pharmacology & toxicology Inst. Pharmacy Dept. Pharmacology, Warsaw, 1966-70; assoc. prof., chief hormone rsch. lab. Med. Acad. Dept. Clin. Endocrinology, Warsaw, 1970-73; staff rschr. II Syntex, Inc. Rsch. Divsn., Palo Alto, Calif., 1974-75; asst. prof. physiology, dir. radioimmunoassay lab. Milton S. Hershey (Pa.) Med. Ctr., Divsn. Endocrinology, 1975-80; staff endocrinologist VA Med. Ctr. Dept. Medicine, Sect. Endocrinology, East Orange, NJ, 1980-82; dir. endocrine lab. Newark Beth Israel Med. Ctr., Dept. Medicine, 1982-92; assoc. prof. medicine divsn. endocrinology U. Medicine & Dentistry-N.J. Med. Sch., Newark, 1982—; chief endocrine lab. dept. Labs. NBIMC, 1994-96. Vis. researcher UCLA Sch. Medicine, Torrance, Calif., 1973; vis. scientist Nat. Inst. Child Health Human Devel., Reproductive Br., Bethesda, Md., 1973-74; lectr. in field. Mem. internat. adv. bd. Jour. Assisted Reproductive Tech. and Andrology, mem. editorial bd., 1996; contbr. articles to profl. jours. Grantee WHO, 1973-74, Ciba-Geigy, 1982-83, Nat. Cancer Inst., 1983-86, 85-88; tng. program fellow Worcester Found. Experimental Biology, Shrewsbury, Mass., 1967-69. Mem. AAAS, Am. Soc. Andrology, Am. Assn. Clin. Chemistry, Nat. Acad. Clin. Biochemistry, Acad. Medicine NJ, Endocrine Soc. Home: 73 Sykes Ave Livingston NJ 07039-1318 Fax: 973-972-5185. E-mail: samojleu@yahoo.com.

SAMOLINSKI, BOLELSLAW, physician, educator; b. Warsaw, Jan. 13, 1956; MD, Med. U. Warsaw, PhD, 1981. U. prof., 2005—. Office: Banacha 1a Warsaw PL-00-898 Poland Office Fax: 48225992041. Business E-Mail: boleslaw.samolinski@wum.edu.pl.

SAMPAYO, ESTHER MARIA, physician; b. NY, Mar. 2, 1973; MD, Albert Einstein Coll. Medicine, 1999; MPH, U. Pa., 2009. Chief resident Children's Hosp., Montefiore, 2002—03; attending physician Childrens Hosp. Phila., 2006—. Asst. prof. U. Of Pa. Sch. Medicine, 2006. Office: 3401 Civic Center Blvd Philadelphia PA 19104 Business E-Mail: sampayo@email.chop.edu.

SAMPINO, ANTHONY F., physician, obstetrician and gynecologist; b. Bklyn., Jan. 13, 1965; s. Frank Paul-Joseph and Lillian Katherine (Cucinotta) S. D Osteopathic Medicine, N.Y. Coll. Osteopathic Medicine, 1991. Diplomate Am. Bd. Ob-Gyn, Am. Coll. Osteo. Bd. Ob-Gyn. Rotating intern St. Barnabas Hosp., Bronx, N.Y., 1991-92; resident ob-gyn. St. Vincents Med. Ctr. of Richmond, Staten Island, N.Y., 1992-96; with dept. ob-gyn. Good Samaritan Hosp., West Islip, N.Y., 1996—; pvt. practice Comprehensive Ob-Gyn of L.I., West Islip, N.Y., 2000—; dir. osteo. internship program Good Samaritan Hosp., 1998—2002, dir. ob-gyn. residency, 2002—. Clin. asst. prof. N.Y. Coll. Osteo. Medicine, 1996—. Fellow: ACOG (jr., sect. chmn. 1992—94, bd. cert.); mem.: AMA, Suffolk County Med. Soc., N.Y. State Osteo. Med. Soc., Med. Soc. State of N.Y., Am. Assn. Gynecologic Laparoscopists (Outstanding Resident in Gyn. Endoscopy 1996), Am. Soc. Colposcopy and Cervical Pathology, Am. Osteo. Dirs. Med. Edn., Am. Coll. Osteo. Ob-gyn., Am. Osteo. Assn. Home: 55 West Ln Bay Shore NY 11706-8616

SAMPSON, HUGH ALBERT, JR., medical educator; b. Winnipeg, Man., Nov. 1, 1948; naturalized; BA, Hamilton Coll., 1971; MD, SUNY, Buffalo, 1975. Diplomate Am. Bd. Pediats., Am. Bd. Allergy and Immunology. Resident Children's Meml. Hosp.-Northwestern U., Chgo., 1975—78; fellow in allergy and immunology-pulmonary medicine Duke U. Med. Ctr., Durham, NC, 1978—80, mem. staff, 1980—86; prof. pediat. Johns Hopkins U., Balt., 1986—97; prof., pediat. Mt. Sinai Sch. of Medicine, NYC, 1997—. Co-author: Intestinal immunology and Food Allergy, 1995, Food Allergy: Adverse Reactions to Foods and Food Additives, 2003, Pediatric Allergy: Principles and Practice, 2008. Fellow Am. Acad. Allergy and Immunology; mem. Am. Pediat. Soc., Am. Acad. Pediats. (Brett Ratner award 2004), Am. Assn. Immunologists, Soc. Pediat. Rsch., Inst. Medicine, Henry Kunkel Soc., Sigma Xi, Alpha Omega Alpha. Mem. Soc. Of Friends. Avocations: jogging, sailing, skiing. Office: Mt Sinai Sch Medicine One Gustave L Levy Pl Box 1198 New York NY 10029 Office Phone: 212-241-5548. Business E-Mail: hugh.sampson@mssm.edu.

SAMPSON, UCHECHUKWU KACHI AMAKWENTA, medical educator; b. Nigeria, Oct. 31, 1970; MBBS, U. Ibadan, Nigeria, 1994; MPH, U. Medicine and Dentistry NJ, Sch. Pub. Health; MSc, Oxford U.; MBA, Rutgers U., 1998. Asst. prof. medicine, pathology, radiology and radiol. scis. Vanderbilt U., 2008—. Adj. prof. medicine Meharry Med. Coll., 2010; affiliate mem. Vanderbilt Inst. Global Health, 2011. Harold Amos Med. Faculty Devel. grant, Robert Wood Johnson Found., Career Devel. grant, Am. Coll. Cardiology Found., Gen. Electric Healthcare, Cardiovasc. Med. Rsch. grant, Merck-Schering Plough, Bowen Brooks Postdoc. fellowship, NY Acad. Medicine. Mem.: Assn. Black Cardiologists, Am. Coll. Cardiology, Am. Heart Assn. Avocations: piano, golf, philosophy, jazz. Office: 315 Preston Research Bldg 2220 Pierce Ave Nashville TN 37232 Business E-Mail: u.sampson@vanderbilt.edu.

SAMRANSAMRUAJKIT, RUJIPAT, pediatrician, educator; b. Prachinburi, Thailand, Apr. 3, 1967; s. Samran and Sutin Samransamruajkit; m. Jantarawan Sawetawong, Aug. 20, 1994; children: Pataramon, Sirapat. MD, Chulalongkorn U., Bangkok, 1992. Diplomate Am. Bd. Pediat., Seton Hall U., NJ, 1995, Am. Bd. Pediat. Pulmonary, U. Calif., Irvine, 1998, cert. in pediat. critcal care Loma Linda U., Ca., 1999. Clin. instr. pediat. Chulalongkorn U., Bangkok, 1999—2002, cons. pediat. pulmonary & critical care, 2000—, asst. prof. pediat., 2002—05, assoc. prof. pediat., 2005—. Contbr. articles to numerous internat. med. publs. Grantee, Local, Nat. & Internat. Med. Fundings, 2000—08. Mem.: Pediat. Pulmonary & Critical Care Assn. (Bangkok), Royal Pediat Assn. Thailand. Office: Chulalongkorn Univ Praram 4 Bangkok 10330 Thailand Home: 151 Lad Phrao 102 10310 Bangkok Bangkok Thailand Office Fax: 662 256-4911; Home Fax: 662 935-2655. Personal E-mail: rujsam@hotmail.com.

SAMS, MARY SUSAN, psychologist; b. Highland Park, Ill., June 25, 1964; d. Stephen Gary and Gail Perkins Rudisill; m. Patrick Edward Sams, Sept. 20, 2003. D in Psychology, Chgo. Sch. Profl. Psychology, 1997. Cert. clin. psychologist Ill., 1998. Pvt. practice, Evanston, Ill., 2000—; pediatric psychologist Children's Rsch. Triangle, Chgo., 2000—03. Bd. dirs. Ill. Profl. Soc. on the Abuse of Children, Chgo. Co-author: (treatment manual) Neurocognitive Habilitation for Children with FAS & ARND. Mem.: Ill. Psychol. Assn. Home: 742 Dexter St Santa Rosa CA 95404-2441 Personal E-mail: mssams@comcast.net.

SAMSON, LINDA FORREST, nursing educator, dean; b. Miami, Dec. 7, 1949; d. Alvin S. and Grace (Kanner) Forrest; m. Mark I. Samson, Jan. 29, 1972; children: Amy, Josh. BSN, Emory U., 1972, MN, 1973; PhD, U. Pa., 1989. RN, Fla., Ga., N.J., Pa., Ill. Nursing instr. Ga. State U., Atlanta, 1974-78; neonatal intensive care nurse Northside Hosp., Atlanta, 1976-78; perinatal clin. specialist Our Lady of Lourdes Med. Ctr., Camden, N.J., 1978-82, per diem staff nurse, ICU nursery, labor and delivery, 1982-88; asst. prof., nursing Kennesaw Coll., Marietta, Ga., 1988-89; asst. prof. Clayton Coll. and State U., Morrow, Ga., 1989-92, assoc. prof., 1992-98, prof., 1998—, head baccalaureate nursing dept. Morrow, Ga., 1991-94, acting dean Sch. Health Scis., 1992-94, dean Sch. Health Scis., 1994—2002; dean Coll. Health & Human Svcs. Govs. State U., University Park, Ill., 2002—, vice provost, rsch. & grad. studies, 2008—11. Adj. faculty Gloucester County Coll., 1981-83; adj. clin. preceptor U. Pa. Sch. Nursing, 1981-83, lectr. in perinatal nursing, 1983-88; nursing dir. So. N.J. Perinatal Coop., 1982-84; researcher and lectr. in field. Mem. editorial rev. bds.; contbr. chpts. to textbooks, articles to profl. jours. Bd. dirs., chmn. profl. adv. com. South Jersey chpt. March of Dimes, 1980-85. Named Nurse of Yr. N.J. State Nurses Assn., 1985; recipient Network Edn. grant N.J. State Dept. Health, 1982-84, numerous grants for rsch., 1983-89, Outstanding Svc. award March of Dimes, 1983, Disting. Leadership award March of Dimes, 1984; grantee Fuld Inst. Post Secondary Edn., 1997—, Nursing Workforce Diversity Grant, 2000-03, NCMHD, 2003—, Samhsa CSAP, 2002—08, DOL, 2010-. Mem. ANA (cert. advanced nursing adminstrn., RN, BC NEA), high risk perinatal nursing), AACN (program com. 1987-88, rsch. com. 1988-89, project devel. task force 1989, strategic planning com. 1989, bd. dirs. 1987-90, bd. dirs. certification corp. 1987-90, chair neonatal and pediatric appeal panels 1992), Am. Orgn. Nurse Execs. (planning com. 1994-95), Nat. Assn. Neonatal Nurses (pub. policy and legis. com. 1994-96), Assn. Women's Health, Obstetrics and Neonatal Nurses, Nat. Perinatal Assn. (program planning com. 1983-85, resolutions com. 1984-88, stds. devel. com. spl. interest group task force

1985-88, bd. dirs. 1985-89, chmn. resolutions com. 1988, fin. com. 1989, pub. health policy com.), Ill. Nurses Assn., Ga. Perinatal Assn. N.J. (pres. 1982-86), Sigma Theta Tau (bylaws com.), Am. Cancer Soc. (regional leader bd, sec. vice chair, v.p., pres.) Home: 20676 Francisca Way Frankfort IL 60423 Office: Govs State U Coll Health & Human Svcs Professions 1 University Pkwy University Park IL 60484-0975 Office Phone: 708-534-4389.

SAMUEL, CHRISHAN S., biomedical researcher; b. Colombo, Sri Lanka, Mar. 3, 1972; s. A. Joseph and Hilda A. Samuel; m. Justina N. Gunaseelan, Dec. 4, 1999. BS in Biochemistry with honors, Monash U., Australia, 1993; PhD, U. Melbourne, 1998. Postdoctoral fellow Dept. of Dermatology, Stanford U. Sch. of Medicine and Molecular Medicine Rsch. Inst., Palo Alto, Calif., 1999—2001; rsch. officer iii Howard Florey Inst., Parkville, Victoria, Australia, 2001, sr. rsch. officer, 2002—, rsch. fellow, 2006—, sr. rsch. fellow, 2009—, head Relaxin-Fibrosis Lab., 2002—, neurosci. faculty, 2010—. Mgr., molecular biology lab. Howard Florey Inst., Parkville, Victoria, Australia, 2003—05. Recipient Howard Florey Inst. Student Prize, Howard Florey Inst. Bd., 1995, Howard Florey Inst. Prize, 2007, rsch. award, Howard Florey Inst. Bd., Young Investigator Travel award, Faulding Australia Pty Ltd., 2000, Postdoctoral award, Applied Biosystems, 2002, Biomedical Rsch. award, Ramaciotti Biomedical Rsch. Found., 2003; fellow, Nat. Heart Found., Australian Health Med. Rsch. Coun., 2007—; Industry Postdoctoral fellow, Australian Rsch. Coun., 2002—04. Mem.: Endocrine Soc., Internat. Soc. for Heart Rsch., Endocrine Soc. of Australia, Matrix Biology Soc. of Australia and New Zealand, Australian Soc. for Med. Rsch. Office: The University of Melbourne Howard Florey Inst Gate 11 3010 Parkville VIC Australia Office Fax: + 61 3 9348 1707. E-mail: chrishan.samuel@florey.edu.au.

SAMUEL, ROBERT THOMPSON, optometrist; b. Kansas City, Mo., June 27, 1944; s. Manlius Thompson and Helen Evelyn (Syverson) S. BA, William Jewell Coll., 1966; postgrad., U. Mo., Kansas City, 1967; MS, U. Mo., 1968; DOptometry, U. Tenn., Memphis, 1971; postgrad., U. Mo., St. Louis, 1995, Northeastern State U., 1998. Cert. optometrist Mo. Buyer Recco, Inc., Kansas City, Mo., 1963-67; histology lab. instr. William Jewell Coll., Liberty, Mo., 1965-66; pvt. practice optometry Gladstone, Mo., 1972—; staff doctor O.H. Gerry Optical Clinics, 1996—. Panel doctor Ford Motor Co., Claycomo, Mo., 1985—, Union Pacific R.R., Kansas City, 1985—, TWA Airlines, 1990, Union Carbide, 1990. Publicity coord. Rep. Party, Kansas City, Mo., 1975-76; chmn. Save Your Vision Week, Kansas City, 1977; mem. Theatre League of Kansas City, 1976—, Kansas City Mus., 1986—, Friends of Art, 1985, Friends of Mo. Town 1955, 1980—. Recipient Outstanding Young Men of Am. award Jaycees, 1978, Good Citizens award DAR, 1962. Mem. Am. Optometric Assn., Mo. Optometric Assn., Optometric Soc. Greater Kansas City, Heart of Am. Contact Lens Congress, Am. Acad. Sports Vision, Vol. Optometric Svcs. for Humanity, Smithsonian Assocs., Lions (exec. bd. dir. Lions Eye Clinic 1974-84, bd. dirs. 1982—, Outstanding Svc. award 1973, 74, editor Lions Optometric Ctr. Quar. 1974-84), Kappa Alpha Order (treas. 1966). Republican. Lutheran. Avocations: photography, music, piano, swimming, travel. Home: 6325 N Monroe Ave Kansas City MO 64119-1923 Office: 1170 W 152 Hwy Liberty MO 64068-2035 also: 5601 NE Antioch Rd Kansas City MO 64119-2302 Office Phone: 816-453-7290.

SAMUELS, BRYAN HAYES, federal agency administrator; b. 1966; BA in Economics, U. Notre Dame, 1989; MA, U. Chgo., 1992. Prof. Sch. Social Svc. Adminstrn. U. Chgo.; dir. Ill. Dept. Children and Family Svcs., 2003—07; chief of staff Chgo. Pub. Schs., 2007—10; commr. Adminstrn. Children, Youth & Families, US Dept. Health & Human Services, Washington, 2010—. Office: US Department Health & Human Services 200 Independence Ave SW Washington DC 20201 *

SAMUELS, MARC, healthcare consultant; b. Bethesda, Md., Feb. 8, 1968; s. Monica (Leiter) Samuels; 1 child, Jeb. BA cum laude, U. Mich., 1989; MPH in Policy and Adminstrn., Yale U., 1992; JD, U. Tex., 1996. Staff asst. McManis Assocs., Health Care Consultants, Washington, Law Offices of Deborah L. Steelman, Washington, Office of Policy Devel., The White House, Washington, V.P.'s Domestic Policy Office, Washington; health care cons., legis. asst., health law sect. Jenkens & Gilchrist PC, Austin, Tex.; asst. to Gov. for Health Policy, Office of Gov. George W. Bush, Austin, Tex.; personal asst. to commr. Tex. Health and Human Svcs. Commn., Austin, Tex.; prin. Samuels Health Strategies, Austin, Tex. Mem. adv. bd. U. Houston Health Law and Policy Inst.; advisor Tex. Lifescience Found., Austin. Co-author: The Managed Care Answer Book, 1996, 4th edit., 1999, Risk Contracting and Capitation Answer Book, 1998, 2d edit., 1999; contbr. articles to profl. jours. Dep. rsch. dir. Kay Bailey Hutchison for U.S. Senate, 1993; health care policy advisor George W. Bush for Gov., 1994, Jeb Bush for Gov., 1998, Bush for Pres. Campaign Exploratory Com., 1999; chmn. A Policy Forum for Young Am., 1996. Spencer Scholar Risk & Ins. Mgmt. Soc., 1996; recipient Baker and Botts prize, 1996. Business E-Mail: msamuels@hillcopartners.com.

SAMUELS, RUMAME L., human resources specialist, director; b. Augusta, Ga., Aug. 22, 1975; BA in Psychology, Clemson U., 1995, MS in Applied Psycholgy, 1997. Dir., compensation and performance mgmt. MCG Health, Inc., 2009—. Mem.: WorldatWork, Soc. Human Resources Mgmt. Office: 1120 Fifteenth St FG-1185 Augusta GA 30912 Business E-Mail: rsamuels@georgiahealth.edu.

SAMUELSSON, BENGT INGEMAR, medical chemist; b. Halmstad, Sweden, May 21, 1934; s. Anders and Stina (Nilsson) Samuelsson; m. Inga Karin Bergstein, Aug. 19, 1958; children: Elisabet, Astrid. Degree in Med. Chemistry, Karolinska Inst., Stockholm, 1960, MD, 1961; DSc (hon.), U. Chgo., 1978, U. Ill., 1983. Asst. prof. Karolinska Inst., 1961—66, prof. med. and physiol. chemistry, chmn. dept. chemistry, 1972—95, dean Med. Faculty, 1978—83, pres., 1983—95, prof. emeritus, 1995—; prof. med. chemistry Royal Vet. Coll., Stockholm, 1967—72. Rsch. fellow Harvard U., 1961—62; mem. Nobel Com. Physiology & Medicine, 1984—89, chmn., 1987—89; mem. rsch. adv. bd. Swedish Govt., 1985—88; mem. Nat. Commn. Health Policy, 1987—90; chmn. Nobel Found., 1993—2005; mem. European Sci. & Tech. Assembly, 1994—97; spl. adv. to commr. for rsch. & edn. European Commn., 1995—97. Contbr. articles to profl. jours. Recipient A. Jahres award, Oslo U., 1970, Louisa Gross Horwitz award, Columbia U., 1975, Albert Lasker Basic Med. Rsch. award, 1977, Ciba-Geigy Drew award in biomed. rsch., 1980, Lewis S. Rosenstiel award in basic med. rsch., Brandeis U., 1981, Gairdner Found. Internat. award, 1981, Heinrich Wieland prize, 1981, Nobel prize in physiology/medicine, 1982, Waterford Bio-Med. Sci. award, 1982, Internat. Assn. Allergology & Clin. Immunology award, 1982, Abraham White Sci. Achievement award, 1984, Gregory Pincus Meml. award, 1984, Charles E. Culpepper award, 1985, Supelco award, Am. Oil Chemists Soc., 1985, Abraham White Disting. Sci. award, 1991, City of Medicine award, 1992, Maria Theresa medal, 1996, Medicus Magnus medal, 1997. Mem.: NAS (fgn. assoc.), AAAS (hon.), Spanish Soc. Allergology & Clin. Immunology, Royal Soc. London (fgn.), Internat. Soc. Hematology, Italian Pharm. Soc., Am. Soc. Biol. Chemists, Swedish Med. Assn., Assn. Am. Physicians, French Acad. Scis., Acad. Europaea (founding mem.), Mediterranean Acad. Sci., Royal Swedish Acad. Scis., Internat. Acad. Sci. (hon.), Royal Nat. Acad. Medicine Spain (hon.), Inst. Medicine (fgn.) (assoc.). Achievements include identification of endoperoxides, thromboxanes and the leukotrienes, studying the chemistry, biochemistry and biology of these compounds and their function in biological control system. Office: The Nobel Foundation Box 5232 SE-102 45 Stockholm Sweden

SAMUELSSON, ROLF G., physiologist, cardiologist, educator; b. Ludvika, Sweden, Aug. 7, 1942; MD, Uppsala Med. Sch., PhD, 1973. Cert. assoc. prof. in physiology and cardiology U. Uppsala, 1973. Assoc. prof. physiology and cardiology Danderyd Hosp., Stockholm, 1993—. John E. Fogarty Internat. Rsch. fellowship, NIH, 1979. Mem.: Swedish Assn. Cardiology and Physiology. Avocations: music, boating, travel. Office: Danderyds sjukhus Stockholm S-18288 Sweden Personal E-mail: samuelssonrg@yahoo.se.

SAMUKAWA, MINA, physical therapist, educator; b. Japan, Aug. 30, 1969; PhD, Grad. Sch. Health Scis., Sapporo Med. U., 2003. Asst. prof. Grad. Sch. Health Scis., Hokkaido U., 2003—. Office: Nishi 5 Chome Kita 12 jo Kitaku Sapporo Hokkaido 060-0812 Japan Business E-Mail: mina@cme.hokdudai.ac.jp.

SANAD, MAGDA MOSTAFA, biology professor; b. Egypt, Nov. 10, 1953; MBBCh, Zagazig U., Egypt, 1977, PhD in Basic Med. Scis., 1988. Demonstrator, prof. parasitology Zagazig U., 1979—2010; prof. parasitology Princess Noura U., Saudi Arabia, 1998—2007, King Saud U., Saudi Arabia, 2007—. Home: Olaya St Oruba St P.O. Box 22452 11495 Riyadh Saudi Arabia Personal E-mail: sand_mm2000@yahoo.com.

SANADA, SHOJI, cardiologist, educator; b. Japan, July 19, 1969; MD, Osaka U. Med. Sch., 1994; PhD, Osaka U. Grad. Sch. Medicine, 2002. Rsch. fellow, divsn. cardiology Brigham and Women's Hosp., Harvard Med. Sch., 2005—07; chief cardiology Osaka Prefectural Gen. Hosp., 2007—09; rsch. fellow Nat. Cerebral and Cardiovasc. Ctr., 2009—10; asst. prof. Osaka U. Grad. Sch. Medicine, 2010—. Rsch. grant, Japan Vascular Disease Rsch. Found., Japan Heart Found. Fellow: Japanese Coll. Cardiology (Young Investigator's award), European Soc. Cardiology, Am. Coll. Cardiology; mem.: Japanese Circulation Soc. (Young Investigator's award), Am. Heart Assn. (BCVS Travel grant). Office: 2-2 Yamadaoka Suita Osaka 5650871 Japan Personal E-mail: sanada4122@yahoo.co.jp.

SANADA, YUKIHIRO, surgeon; b. Japan, Apr. 20, 1978; MD, Yamagata U., 2003. With dept. transplant surgery Jichi Med. U., Shimotsuke, Tochigi, Japan, 2005. Office: Jichi Med. University dept Transplant Surgery 3311-1 Yakushiji Shimotsuke Tochigi 329-0498 Japan Office Fax: 81-285-58-7069. Business E-Mail: yuki371@jichi.ac.jp.

SAN AGUSTIN, MUTYA, pediatrician; b. Manila, Nov. 25, 1934; d. Dionisio and Trinidad (Tolentino) San A.; m. Barry Shaw, July 27, 1969; children: Noel, Ariel, Angela, Joanna. MD, U. Philippines, 1957. Diplomate Am. Bd. Pediats. Intern, resident Sinai Hosp., Balt., 1960, chief resident in pediats., 1961; chief phys. devel. rsch. divsn. Nat. Coordinating Rsch. Ctr., Philippines, 1962-64; dir. Montefiore-Morrisania Comprehensive Health Care Ctr., Bronx, NY, 1968-76; dir. ambulatory care medicine North Ctrl. Bronx Hosp.- Montefiore Med. Ctr., Bronx, 1976-97; dir. dept. primary care medicine Montefiore Med. Ctr., Bronx, 1997—. Cons. internat. ednl. br. HEW, 1969-74; cons. health com. US China People's Friendship Assn., 1975-81; cons. to pres. NYC Health and Hosps. Corp., 1979-89; dir. primary care residency in pediats. and internal medicine Albert Einstein Coll. Medicine, 1979-92, prof. pediat.-clin. epidemiology and social medicine, 1993; vis. prof. UCLA, 1985, Ben-Gurion U., Beer-Sheva, Israel; mem. NY State Coun. Grad. Med. Edn., 1988-90, NY State Hosp. Rev. and Planning Coun., 1990-95, NY State Gov.'s Health Adv. Bd., 1991-95; mem. residency tng. rev. com. divsn. medicine Bur. Health Profls., HHS, 1990-94; project dir. internat. pediat. fellowship program Montefiore Med. Ctr., Albert Einstein Coll. Medicine, 1989—; adj. prof. NYU A/P/A studies program and inst.; lectr. cultural diversity and cmty. health; vis. faculty dept. pediats. U. Philippines Coll. Medicine, pres. bd. dirs. Bronx Cmty. Health Network, 2008-; lectr. in field. Recipient Hon. Fellow award Philippine Pediat. Soc., Inc., 1996, Builder in Medicine Centennial award U. Philippines Coll. Medicine, 2006; pediats. fellow John Hopkins U., 1960-61; grantee NIH, 1967, NIMH, 1990-92; Atram Found. scholar, 1980; named one of 100 Most Influential Filipina Women in US, 2007. Mem. APHA, Am. Acad. Pediat., Am. Pediat. Soc., Royal Soc. Medicine, Soc. Gen. Internal Medicine, Ambulatory Pediat. Assn., NY Acad. Medicine, Philippine Ambulatory Pediat. Assn. (founding pres. 1995). E-mail: mutyasa@earthlink.net.

SAN ANDRÉS REBOLLO, FRANCISCO JAVIER, physician; b. Guadalajara, Spain, Dec. 21, 1962; s. Gaspar-Fructuoso San Andrés and Emiliana-Leonor Rebollo; m. Inmaculada De Pedro Andrés, June 13, 1998; children: David San Andrés, Carmen San Andrés, Javier San Andrés. BS, U. de Alcalá de Henares, 1986; MD, U. Complutense de Madrid, 2001. Family and cmty. med. resident Hosp. 12 de Octubre, NIH, Madrid, 1989—92; staff physician Health Ctr. Potes, NIH, Madrid, 1992—2002, Health Ctr. Embajadores, Madrid Inst. Health, 2002—. Med. dir. Health Ctr. Potes, NIH, Madrid, 1992—96, family and cmty. medicine tutor, 1994—97. Avocations: travel, swimming. Personal E-mail: maxjavibi2@saludalia.com.

SANANMAN, MICHAEL LAWRENCE, neurologist; b. Bklyn., Oct. 11, 1939; s. Jack and Sarey (Bykofsky) S.; m. Elisa Joan Freeman, Apr. 12, 1964; children: Amy, Peter. AB, Swarthmore Coll., 1960; MD, Columbia U., 1964. Diplomate Am. Bd. Psychiatry and Neurology. Intern U. Hosp., San Francisco, 1964-65; resident in neurology N.Y. Neurol. Inst., NYC, 1966-69; practice medicine specializing in neurology Elizabeth, N.J., 1972—. Cons. neurologist Rahway (N.J.) Hosp., Trinitas Hosp., N.J., Union Hosp., N.J.; instr. neurology Columbia U., N.Y.C., 1971-75; assoc. clin. prof. neurology U. Medicine and Dentistry N.J., Newark, 1975—. Lt. comdr. M.C., USNR, 1969-71. Mem. AMA, Am. Acad. Neurology, Am. Epilepsy Soc., N.J. Acad. Medicine, Am. Eastern EEG Socs., Am. Assn. EMG and Electrodiagnosis. Office: 700 N Broad St Elizabeth NJ 07208-2310 Office Phone: 908-354-3994. Personal E-mail: Mikesan48@aol.com.

SANBERG, PAUL RONALD, medical educator; b. Coral Gables, Fla., Jan. 4, 1955; s. Bernard and Molly (Spector) Sanberg BS with honors, York U., 1976; MS, U. B.C., 1979; PhD, Australian Nat. U., 1981, DSc, 1998; grad. diploma sci. edn., West Australia Inst. Tech., 1986; MD, St. James Sch., 2008. Postdoctoral fellow Johns Hopkins Med. Sch., Balt., 1981—83; asst. prof. Ohio U., Athens, 1983—86; assoc. prof. U. Cin., 1986—89; prof. Brown U., Providence, 1990—92, U. South Fla., Tampa, 1992—2003, assoc. v.p., 2003—10, disting. prof., 2003—, assoc. dean, 2003—06, sr. assoc. v.p., 2010—, spl. asst. to the pres., 2011—, chair neurosci., 1997—2005, exec. dir. Ctr. of Excellence for Aging and Brain Repair, 2000—. Co-founder Saneron CCEL Therapeutics, Inc., 2000—. Recipient award Am. Coll. Neuropsychopharmacology, Tourette Syndrome Assn., Sir. J.G. Crawford medal, Ove Ferno prize Coll. Internat. Neuropsychopharmacology; grantee NIH, Am. Heart Assn., Childrens Med. Rsch. Found., Hereditary Disease Found., Huntington's Disease Found., Outstanding Rschr. award Sigma Xi; named Healthcare Hero, Tampa Bay Bus. Jour., 2006, Everfront award, Taiwan, 2011. Mem. APA, Soc. for Neurosci., Internat. Brain Rsch. Orgn., Internat. Behavioral Neurosci. Soc. (pres. 1994, Outstanding Rschr. award 2004), Am. Soc. for Neural Transplant (pres. 1995), Cell Transplant Soc. (pres. 1996, editor), Nat. Acad. Inventors.(pres., 2010-). Home: 11751 Pilot Country Dr Spring Hill FL 34610-7912 Office: U South Fla Coll Medicine Dept NeuroSurgery & Brain Repair MDC 78 12901 Bruce B Downs Blvd Tampa FL 33612-4742 Business E-Mail: psanberg@health.usf.edu.

SANCHEZ, EDUARDO J., academic administrator, former state agency administrator, physician; m. Katherine Sanchez; 4 children. BS in Biomed. Engring. & Chemistry, Boston Univ.; MS in Biomed. Engring., Duke Univ., Durham, NC; MPH, Univ. Tex.; MD, Univ. Tex. Southwestern Med. Sch., 1988. Cert. family practice. Private family practice, Austin, Tex., 1992—2001; chief med. officer Austin-Travis County Dept. Health & Human Svc., 1994—98; commr. Tex. Dept. Health, Austin, 2001—04, Tex. Dept. State Health Svcs., Austin, 2004—06; dir., Inst. Health and Policy U. Tex. Recipient Louis B. Russell award, Am. Heart Assn., 2004, Public Health award, Am. Acad. Family Physicians, 2005. Office: Inst Health and Policy Univ Tex LBJ Sch Pub Affairs Rm SRH 3 312 Austin TX 78712-1536 Office Phone: 512-471-8970. Business E-Mail: Eduardo.J.Sanchez@uth.tmc.edu.

SANCHEZ, MIGUEL, pathologist, educator; Attended, U. Madrid, Spain, 1969. Diplomate Am. Bd. Pathology-anatomic pathology, Am. Bd. Pathology-clin. pathology, Am. Bd. Pathology-cytopathology. Resident in pathology Temple Univ., Phila., NY, 1972—73; fellow in pathology Meml. Sloan-Kettering Cancer Ctr., NY, 1973—74; fellow in clin. pathology St. Vincents Hosp., NY, 1974—75; assoc. prof. pathology Mt. Sinai Sch. Medicine; resident in pathology Englewood Hosp. and Med. Ctr., NJ, 1971—72, pathologist. Office: Englewood Hospital and Medical Center 350 Engle St Englewood NJ 07631 Office Phone: 201-894-3423. Office Fax: 201-871-2269.

SANCHEZ, VICTORIA WAGNER, science educator; b. Milw., Apr. 11, 1934; d. Arthur William and Lorraine Marguerite (Kocovsky) Wagner; m. Rozier Edmond Sanchez, June 23, 1956; children: Mary Elizabeth, Carol Anne, Robert Edmond, Catherine Marie, Linda Therese. BS cum laude, Mt. Mary Coll., 1955; MS, Marquette U., 1957; postgrad., U. N.Mex., 1979-86, U. Del., 1990. Cert. secondary tchr., N.Mex. Chemist Nat. Bur. Standards, Washington, 1958-60; tchr., chmn. sci. dept. Albuquerque Pub. Schs., 1979-94. Chmn. pub. info. area conv. Nat. Sci. Tchrs. Assn., 1984, mem. sci. rev. com. Albuquerque Pub. Schs., 1985-86, 92-93, dedication of N.W. Regional Sci. Fair, 1994, Gov.'s Summit on Edn., 1991, 92, Gov.'s Steering Com. Systemic Change in Math. and Sci. Edn.; panel mem. NSF, 1991-93. Bd. dirs. Encino House, Albuquerque, 1976-92, treas., 1977-79; leader Albuquerque troop Girl Scouts U.S., 1966-77; cmty. interpreter Environ. Open Space Divsn. City Albuquerque, N.Mex., 2000—. Named Outstanding Sci. Tchr., NW Regional Sci. Fair, Albuquerque, 1983, 88, 90, N.Mex. Parents of Yr., 2001; recipient St. George's award N.Mex. Cath. Scouting Com., 1978, Focus on Excellence award ASCD, Albuquerque, 1985, 89, Presdl. awards for excellence in sci. and math., 1989; Rozier and Victoria Sanchez Family, Outstanding Family in Philanthropy, 2007. Mem. AAUW (officer Albuquerque br. 1976-77, N.Mex. divsn. 1977-78), NSTA, N.Mex. Sci. Tchrs. Assn. (treas. 1988-90), Albuquerque Sci. Tchrs. Assn. (treas. 1984-85, v.p., pres.-elect 1986-87, pres. 1987-88, Svc. to Sci. award 1994), N.Mex. Acad. Sci., Am. Coun. on Edn. (math. and sci. edn. nat. com. 1990-92), DuPont Honors Workshop for Tchrs., Albuquerque Rose Soc. (sec. 1962-63). Democrat. Roman Catholic. Avocations: reading, fishing, hiking, needlecraft, camping. Home: 7612 Palo Duro Ave NE Albuquerque NM 87110-2315

SANCHEZ ALVARADO, ALEJANDRO, embryologist, molecular biologist, educator; b. Caracas, Venezuela, Feb. 24, 1964; came to U.S., 1982; s. Delfin Orestes and Vera Antonieta (Alvarado) S. BS, Vanderbilt U., 1986; PhD, U. Cin., 1992. Rsch. asst. U. Cin. Coll. Medicine, 1987-88, grad. student, 1988-92, rsch. assoc., 1992-93; postdoctoral fellow Carnegie Inst., Balt., 1994-96, staff assoc., 1996—2001; assoc. prof. U. Utah Sch. Medicine, 2002—04, prof.,

2005—11; investigator Howard Hughes Med. Inst., 2005—, Stowers Inst. Med. Rsch., Kans. City, Mo., 2011—. Sci. corr. El Nacional, Caracas, 1996; UNESCO lectr., Venezuela, 1997, 99; Kavli fellow NAS, 2008. Editor: Devel. Dynamics, 2002—, Cell Stem Cell, 2007—, Devel. Biology, 2007—; contbr. to conf. proceedings, articles to profl. jours.; editor: Regenerative Medicine, 2000—02. Recipient Marine Biol. Labs. Embryology rsch. award, 1995, Marcus Singer rsch. regeneration award, 1999. Mem. AAAS, Am. Soc. Cell Biology (E.E. Just Lectr. 2007), Soc. Devel. Biology, Singer Soc. for Regeneration, N.Y. Acad. Scis. Achievements include research in characterizing in vitro model for vertebrate cardiogenesis; development of an invertebrate model for the molecular study of regeneration. Office: U Utah Sch Medicine Dept Neurobiology and Anatomy 20N 1900 E Salt Lake City UT 84132

SANCHEZ ARELLANO, ELPIDIO, surgeon; b. Mazatlan, Sinalda, Mex., Mar. 4, 1934; s. Zatarain Francisco Sanchez and Loaiza Epifania Arellano; m. Lydia Aurora Mora Cerda, May 6, 1967; children: Daniel Sanchez Mora, Adrian Sanchez Mora, Abraham Sanchez Mora. MD, U. Nat. Autonomy Mex., 1960. Cert. neurologist Mex. Prof. neuroanatomy, neurology U. Nat. Autonomy Mex., 1960—71; gen. practitioner Hosp. Generalissa Mex., 1963—64, neurosurgery tng., 1964—68; neurologist, cardiologist Nat. Inst. Mex., 1969—78, neurosurgeon, 1970—86; pvt. practice Mexico, 1970—; neurologist Atizapan's (Mex.) Gen. Hosp., 1986—91; neurosurgeon Xoco's (Mex.) Gen. Hosp., 1988—91; neurologist ISSEMYN, Satálitz-Naucalpan, Mexico, 1989—90; neurosurgeon Newspaper Union, Mexico, 1993—96. Vol. Mex. State Police, 1995—. Fellow: N.Y. Acad. Scis., Am. Chem. Soc., Internat. Coll. Surgeons; mem.: Masons. Revolution Dem. Party. Home: Colina de Hernán 34 53140 Boulevares Mexico Office: Saint Tobasco 294-3o 06700 Boulevares Mexico

SANCHEZ PALACIOS, MANUEL, emergency physician, consultant; b. Santa Cristina, Zamora, Spain, Sept. 27, 1950; s. Manuel Sanchez Hernandez and Carmen Palacios Huertas; m. Francisca Sanchez Leon, July 7, 2000; 1 child, Maria Sanchez Sanchez. BS, Inst. Nacional, Laspalmas, Spain, 1967; PhD, U. Palmas, 1999. Lic. U. Laguna, 1976, cert. cardiologist Ministerio De Educacion Y Ciencias, 1979, intensivist 1982, intensive care med. resident Ministerio De Sanidad, 1979. Sect. JEFE, critical care unit Cabildo Insular, Las Palamas, 1986—2004; dir. critical care unit Svc. Canario Salud, Las Palmas, 2004—. Med. subdir. Hosp. Insular, Las Palmas, 1987—88. Vocal commn. etica Colegio Ofcl. Medicos, Las Palmas, 2005—07. Mem.: SEMICYUC. Avocation: singing. Office: Hosp Insular Drpasteur 35014 Las Palmas Spain Office Phone: 34928441392. Business E-Mail: msanpal@gobiernodecanarias.org.

SANCHEZ REGAÑA, MANUEL SANCHEZ, dermatologist, researcher; b. Villanueva Del Fresno, Badajoz, Spain, May 16, 1966; s. Francisco Sanchez and Clotilde Regaña; m. Teresa Serra, Mar. 30, 1966; 1 child, Jaume Sanchez. Bachelor, La Salle Gracia, Barcelona, Spain, 1984. Coord. psoriasis and phototherapy ctr. Hosp. Univ. Sagrat Corazon, Barcelona, 1995—, clin. head, 2005. Residents' s tutor Hosp. Univ. Sagrado Corazon, Barcelona, 2000—. Author: Psoriasis: Mitos Y Realidades, Psoriasis: Actualizacion Terapéutica. Recipient Premio Extraordinario De Licenciatura, Univ. De Barcelona, 1991. Mem.: Academia Española De Dermatologia (corr.). Achievements include research in Psoriasis And Pytiriasis Rubra Pilaris. Avocations: travel, music. Office: Hosp Univ Sagrat Cor Paris 83-85 Barcelona 08029 Spain Office Fax: 934941913. E-mail: ez.reg@terra.es.

SAND, MICHAEL STEVEN, clinical sexologist; s. Richard James Sand and Julia Ann Andrews; m. Arlene Sand, Sept. 3, 1982; children: Bryan Richard, Emily Carol, Stephen James. PhD, Maimonnides U., North Miami, Fla., 2006; MPH, Internat. Acad. Sex Rsch., San Francisco, 2004. Diplomate Am. Acad. Clin. Sexology, 2006. Assoc. dir., global sci. affairs Bayer Schering Pharma, Dusseldorf, Germany, 2004—06; dir., clin. rsch. Boehringer-Ingelheim, Ridgefield, Conn., 2006—. Bd. mem. Sex Info. and Edn. Coun. Can., Toronto, 1998—2008. Sgt. Spl. Forces US Army, 1973—76, Ft. Bragg, NC. Personal E-mail: mmichaelsand@yahoo.com.

SAND, TROND HALFDAN, neurologist, educator; s. Rolf and Ragna Lise Sand; m. Guri Elisabeth Gjerstad; children: Kjersti Irene, Ingeborg Maria. Cand Mag, U. Oslo, 1974, MD, 1977; PhD, U. Trondheim, Norway, 1991. Cert. clin. neurophysiologist Norwegian Med. Assn., 1987, neurologist Norwegian Med. Assn., 1989. Dept. head neurology St. Olavs U. Hosp., Trondheim, Norway, 2001—07, dept. head clin. neurophysiology, 1992—; clin. neurophysiology prof. Norwegian U. Sci. and Tech., Trondheim, 1994—. Leader Norwegian Soc. Clin. Neurophysiology, Oslo, 2007—. Contbr. articles to profl. med. jours. Lt. Army, 1979—80, Norway. Recipient Rsch. award, Trøndelag Med. Soc., 1991, Monrad Krohn Rsch. award, Norwegian Neurol. Soc., 1999; Rsch. grant, Norsk Medisinaldepot, 1983. Mem.: SASP, IHS, ESRS, IASP, AAEM, AASM. Office: St Olavs Univ Hosp Olav Kyrres gate 17 Trondheim 7006 Norway

SANDAHL, BONNIE BEARDSLEY, nursing administrator; b. Washington, Jan. 17, 1939; d. Erwin Leonard and Carol Myrtle (Collis) Beardsley; m. Glen Emil Sandahl, Aug. 17, 1963; children: Cara Lynne, Cory Glen. BSN, U. Wash., 1962, MN, 1974; cert. pediat. nurse practitioner, 1972. Dir. Wash. State Joint Practice Commn., Seattle, 1974-76; instr. pediatric nurse practitioner program U. Wash., Seattle, 1976, course coord. quality assurance, 1977-78; pediatric nurse practitioner/health coord. Snohomish County Head Start, Everett, Wash., 1975-77; clin. nurse educator (specialist), nurse mgr. Harborview Med. Ctr., Seattle, 1978-97, dir. child abuse prevention project, 1986-97; mgr. Children's Ctr., Providence Health Sys. Northwest, 1997-2000; v.p. clin. svcs. and ops., COO Seattle Children's Home, 2000—03, exec. dir., 2003—05; sch. nurse Seattle Pub. Schs., 2006—. Spkr. legis. focus on children, 1987; clin. assoc. dept. pediatrics U. Wash. Sch. Medicine, 1987—; clin. faculty U. Wash. Sch. Nursing, 1987—97; mgr. Providence Gen. Children's Ctr., Everett, 1997—2000; gov. appointee State Interagency Coord. Coun., 1998—2011, gov. appointee chair, 2003—11. Interim chair nat. coun. health planning and devel. HHS, 1980—87; mem. task force pharmacotherapeutic courses Puget Sound Health Sys. Agy., 1975—88, pres., 1980—82; mem. task force pharmacotherapeutic courses Wash. State Bd. Nursing, 1985—86; mem. child devel. project adv. bd. Mukiteo Sch. Dist., 1984—85; mem. parenting adv. com. Edmonds Sch. Dist.; chmn. hospice-hom health task force Snohomis County Hospice Program, Everett, 1984—85, bd. dirs. hospice, 1985—87, mem. adv. com., 1986—88; mem. Wash. State Health Coordinating Coun., 1977—82, chmn. nursing home bed projection methodology task force, 1986—87; mem. adv. com. uncompensated care Wash. State Legislature, 1983—84; mem. joint select com. Tech. Adv. Com. Managed Health Care Sys., 1984—85; pres. Alderwood Manor Cmty. Coun., 1983—85; treas. Wash. St. Women's Polit. Caucus, 1983—84; mem. com. examine changes in Wash. State Criminal Sex Law, 1987; appointee county needs assessment com. Snohomish County Govt. United Way, 1989, 1994; chair human svcs. adv. coun. Snohomish County Human Svcs. Dept., chmn. adv. com., 1998—; gubernatorial appointee state interagency coordinating coun. Health Svcs. Adv. Com. Wash. State, 1995—97. Recipient Golden Acorn award, Seattle-King County PTA, 1973, Katherine Rickey Vol. Participation award, 1987. Mem.: ANA (chair com. examiners maternal-child nursing practice 1988—90), King County Nurses Assn. (1st v.p. 1992—96, pres. 1996—97, Nurse of the Yr. 1985), Wash. State Nurses Assn. (chair healthcare reform task force 1992—96, elected mem. profl. nursing and healthcare coun., Hon. Leadership award 1981), Sigma Theta Tau. Home: 1814 201st Pl SW Lynnwood WA 98036-7060

SANDBERG, HANS-OLOF, chemist, director; b. Stockholm, June 30, 1943; s. Gunhild and Axel Olof Sandberg; m. Helena Sandberg, Aug. 14, 1971; 1 child, Eric Andres. MS in Chemistry, U. Uppsala, Sweden, 1970. Mktg. mgr. Scanditronix AB, Uppsala, Sweden, 1982—86; mng. dir. Med. Scandinavia AB, Bromma, Sweden, 1989—. Office: Medicall-Nordic AB Gustavslundsvägen 141B Bromma S-167 51 Sweden Office Fax: +46856484539. Personal E-mail: h-o.sandberg@medicall.se. E-mail: office@medicall.se.

SANDEN, BOUDEWIJN VAN DER, neuroscientist, director; b. Tilburg, Feb. 23, 1965; PhD, Academic Hosp. Nijmegen, 1999. Rschr. INSERM U836 Inst. Neurosci. Grenoble, 2002—, dir. intravital microscopy plateforme, 2007. Achievements include research in neuroscience epilepsy, Parkinson disease, Neuro-oncology, Small animal imaging like MRI, two-photon microscopy and endoscopy. Office: Inst Neurosci Grenoble Grenoble Isere 38000 France Business E-Mail: boudewijn.vandersanden@ujf-grenoble.fr.

SANDERS, ABRAHAM, pulmonologist, educator; BS, SUNY, Stony Brook, 1972; MD, SUNY Health Sci. Ctr., Bklyn., 1976. Diplomate Am. Bd. Internal Medicine-pulmonary disease, Am. Bd. Internal Medicine-critical care medicine, Am. Bd. Internal Medicine. Intern in internal medicine SUNY Downstate Med. Ctr., resident in internal medicine, 1976—80; intern in internal medicine Kings County Hosp., resident in internal medicine, 1976—80; intern in internal medicine Bklyn. Veterans Adminstrn. Med. Ctr., Bklyn., resident in internal medicine, 1976—80; chief resident pulmonary divsn. Kings County-Downstate Med. Ctr., 1979—80, hon. registrar Hammersmith Hosp. Royal Postgrad. Med. Ctr., London, 1980—81; assoc. prof. clin. medicine Weill Cornell Med. Coll.; assoc. attending physician NY Presbyn. Hosp. Co-author: (publs.) Coexistence of Sarcoidosis and Carcinoma in a Solitary Pulmonary Nodule, State Jour. or Medicine, 1986, Corticosteroids in Lung Diseases, Principles of Corticosteroid Therapy, 2002, Pulmonary Nodules in an Infliximab-Treated Rheumatoid Arthritis Patient, 2007, numerous other publs. Recipient J.J. Smith Meml. award, 1993, 2004, Excellence in Tchg., Weill Med. Coll. Cornell Univ., 1998, 2000—01, 2003, 2005, 2007, Leonard P. Tow Humanism award, Arnold P. Gold Found., Weill Cornell Med. Coll., 2006. Office: New York Presbyterian Hospital 1305 York Ave 4th Fl New York NY 10021 Office Phone: 646-962-2333. Office Fax: 646-962-0110.

SANDERS, AMY ELAINE, medical educator; b. Lancaster, Pa., Sept. 8, 1963; BA, Loyola U., Chgo., 1988; MD, SUNY Downstate Coll. Medicine, 2002. Asst. prof., neurology Albert Einstein Coll. Medicine, 2008—. Fellow, Nat. Inst. Aging NIMH, grant, Einstein CTSA Nat. Ctr. Rsch. Resources, Nat. Insts. Health, Nat. Inst. Aging. Mem.: Internat. Soc. Advance Alzheimer Rsch. and Treatment, Gerontol. Assn. America, Am. Acad. Neurology. Office: 1515 Blondell Ave Ste 220 Bronx NY 10461 Business E-Mail: amy.sanders@einstein.yu.edu.

SANDERS, GEORGIANA M., allergist, immunologist, educator; MD, U. Cin., 1975. Diplomate Am. Bd. Pediatrics, 1982, Am. Bd. Allergy and Immunology, 1985, lic. Mich., 1976. Resident pediat. Children's Hosp. of Mich., 1975—78; chief resident pediat. Boston City Hosp., 1978—79; fellow allergy & immunology Univ. of Mich. Hosp., 1981—84; clin. asst. prof. internal medicine dept. Univ. of Mich. Health System, clin. asst. prof. pediat. and communicable disease; hosp. affiliations include St. Joseph Mercy Hosp., Univ. of Mich. Hosps. and Health Ctr. Office: University of Michigan Hospitals and Health Centers 1500 E Medical Center Dr Ann Arbor MI 48109 Office Phone: 734-936-4000.

SANDERS, JACQUELYN SEEVAK, psychologist, educator; b. Boston, Apr. 26, 1931; d. Edward Ezral and Dora (Zoken) Seevak; 1 child, Seth. BA, Radcliffe Coll., 1952; MA, U. Chgo., 1964; PhD, UCLA, 1972. Counselor, asst. prin. Orthogenic Sch., Chgo., 1952—65; rsch. assoc. UCLA, 1965—68; asst. prof. Ctr. for Early Edn., LA, 1969—72; assoc. dir. Sonia Shankman Orthogenic Sch., U. Chgo., 1972—73, dir., 1973—93, dir. emeritus, 1993—; curriculum cons. day care ctrs. LA Dept. Social Welfare, 1970—72; instr. Calif. State Coll., LA, 1972; lectr. dept. edn. U. Chgo., 1972—80, sr. lectr., 1980—93, clin. assoc. prof. dept. psychiatry, 1990—93, emeritus, 1993—; instr. edn. program Inst. Psychoanalysis, Chgo., 1979—82. Cons. Osawatomie State Hosp., Kans., 1965—68; reading cons. Foreman HS, Chgo.; treas. Chgo. Inst. Psychoanalysis, 2003—. Author: Greenhouse for the Mind, 1989; editor (with Barry L. Childress): Psychoanalytic Approaches to the Very Troubled Child: Therapeutic Practice Innovations in Residential & Educational Settings, 1989; editor: Severely Disturbed Children and the Parental Alliance, 1992; editor: (with Jerome M. Goldsmith) Milieu Therapy: Significant Issues and Innovative Applications, 1993; editor: The Seevak Family, The Zoken Family; contbr. articles to profl. jours. Mem. vis. com. univ. sch. rels. U. Chgo.; bd. dirs. KAM Isaiah Israel Congregation, 1997—2001; bd. dirs., treas. Chgo. Inst. for Psychoanalysis. Recipient Alumna award, Girls' Latin Sch., Boston, Bettelheim award, Am. Assn. Children's Residential Ctrs., Disting. Svc. award, Radcliffe Assn., 2002; scholar Radcliffe Coll. scholar, 1948—52; Univ. fellow, UCLA, 1966—68. Mem.: Chgo. Inst. for Psychoanalysis, Assn. Children's Residential Ctrs. (past pres.), Harvard Club (bd. dirs. 1986—2001, Chgo.), Radcliffe Club (sec.-treas. 1986—87, pres. 1987—89, Chgo.). Home: 5842 S Stony Island Ave Apt 2G Chicago IL 60637-2033

SANDERS, JOAN E., biomedical engineer, educator; b. LA, May 11, 1961; BSME, Stanford U., 1983; degree in Bioengring., U. Wash., 1991. Wrangler Beartooth Ranch, 1979; rsch. engr. Baxter Travenol Labs., 1984; engr. Tyler Builders, 1985; dir., bioengring. rsch. Prosthetics Rsch. Study, 1990—93; prof. U. Wash., 1992—, adj. prof., rehab. medicine, 1993—, adj. prof., mech. engring., 1994—. Recipient Early Career Achievement award, IEEE Engring. Medicine and Biology Soc., George W. Thorn award, Whitaker Found., Lecture award, Orthotic and Prosthetic Edn. and Rsch. Found. Mem.: Am. Acad. Orthotists and Prosthetists (Thranhardt Lecture award, Rsch. award). Avocations: baseball, squash. Office: 3720 15th Ave NE Foege N430J Seattle WA 98195 Office Fax: 206-685-3300. Business E-Mail: jsanders@u.washington.edu.

SANDERS, JOE MAXWELL, JR., pediatrician; b. Hartsville, SC, July 5, 1940; m. Dorothy Garvin, June 6, 1963; children Joe M. III, Eric T. BS, The Citadel, 1962; MD, Med. U. S.C., 1967. Diplomate Am. Bd. Pediatrics. Rotating intern, resident in pediatrics Letterman Army Med. Ctr., San Francisco, 1967-70; fellow in adolescent medicine San Francisco Children's Hosp., 1970-71; chief adolescent medicine svc. Fitzsimmons Army Med. Ctr., 1971-86; dir. adolescent medicine svc. Med. Coll. Ga., 1986-88; assoc. exec. dir. Am. Acad. Pediatrics, Elk Grove Village, Ill., 1988-93, exec. dir., 1993—2004; ret., 2004. Asst. clin. prof. pediatrics U. Colo. Health Scis. Ctr., 1971-76, assoc. clin. prof., 1976-83, clin. prof. 1983-86; assoc. prof. pediatrics Med. Coll. Ga., 1986-88; clin. prof. pediatrics, U. Chgo., 1991—; cons. for adolescent medicine Surgeon Gen. Army, 1976-86; mem. med. com. Rocky Mt. Planned Parenthood, 1981-86; vis. prof. dept. pediatrics U. Kansas (Wichita), 1984, 87, dept. pediatrics and family practice, E. Tenn. State U., Johnson City, 1985, U. Fla., Gainesville, 1987, Fitzsimmons Army Med. Ctr., Denver, 1989, U. Chgo., 1991, Baylor Coll., Houston, 1994, others. Contbr. numerous articles and abstracts to profl. jours., chpts. to books; mem. editl. bd. Jour. Current Adolescent Medicine, 1979-81, Substance Abuse: A Guide for Profls., 1985-88; reviewer Pediatrics, 1984—, Jour. Pediatrics, 1986—, Jour. Adolescent Health, 1986—, Am. Jour. Diseases of Children, 1987—, Jour. Am. Med. Assn., 1987—, guest lectr., speaker at many sci. confs. and med. soc. meetings. Mem. teenage coord. coun. Richmond County Health Dept., 1986-88, head start health adv. com. CSRA Econ. Opportunity Authority, Inc., 1986-88; med. cons. Alexian Bros. Med. Rels. Com. Decorated Legion of Merit, U.S. Army, 1987; recipient Adele Hoffman award, Sect. on Adolescent Health, 1988. Fellow Am. Acad. Pediatrics (com. on adolescence 1980-87, chmn. 1983-87, chmn. uniformed svcs chpt. 1981, 84, mem. exec. com. mil. pediatrics sect. 1976-79, sec.-treas. 1976-77, chmn. 1977-79, mem. steering com. to establish non-geographic mil. dist. chpt., mem sect. on adolescent health 1979—, program com. 1981-83, task force on substance abuse, chmn. 1984-85, cons. 85-87, task force on sch. based clinics, 1987—), Soc. Adolescent Medicine (edn. com., ambulatory care com., 1975-80, chmn. nominating com. 1978, exec. com. 1980-83, chmn. awards com. 1990-93, pres. 1987-88, past pres's. coun. 1988—, Outstanding Achievement award 1994); mem. AMA (mem. planning com. nat. coalition on adolescent health, rep. Am. Acad. Pediatrics, Soc. Adolescent Medicine to Coalition 1987—, chmn. working group on rsch. agenda 1987-88, adv. com. on unintentional injuries 1987), Ambulatory Pediatric Assn., So. Soc. for Pediatric Rsch., Soc. Med. Cons. to Armed Forces, Order Mil. Med. Merit, Sigma Xi. *

SANDERS, W(ILLIAM) EUGENE, JR., retired internist; b. Frederick, Md., June 25, 1934; s. W(illiam) Eugene and E. Gertrude (Wilburn) Sanders; m. Christine Culp, Feb. 22, 1974. AB, Cornell U., 1956, MD, 1960. Diplomate Am. Bd. Internal Medicine. Intern Johns Hopkins Hosp., Balt., 1960-61, resident, 1961-62; instr. medicine Emory U. Sch. Medicine, Atlanta, 1962-64; chief med. resident, instr. U. Fla. Coll. Medicine, Gainesville, 1964-65, asst. prof. medicine and microbiology, 1965-69, assoc. prof., 1969-72; prof., chmn. dept. med. microbiology, prof. medicine Creighton U. Sch. Medicine, Omaha, 1972-95, prof. emeritus, 1995—. Cons-in-rsch. Fla. Dept. Health and Rehab. Svcs., 1966—. Editor: Am. Jour. Epidemiology, 1974—95; contbr. scientific papers to profl. jours. Med. officer USPHS, 1962—64. Recipient Rsch. Career Devel. award, NIH, 1968—72; John and Mary R. Markle scholar in acad. medicine, 1968—73. Mem.: N.Y. Acad. Scis., Thoracic Soc., Am. Lung Assn., Soc. Epidemiol. Rsch., Infectious Diseases Soc. Am., Am. Soc. Microbiology, Sigma Xi, Phi Beta Kappa, Phi Kappa Phi. Achievements include patents for enocin antibiotic and RBE limonene and perrilyl alcohol. Home: 1901 Pennsylvania Ave Englewood FL 34224-5530 E-mail: ecsanders@mac.com.

SANDERSON, DAVID R., physician; b. South Bend, Ind., Dec. 26, 1933; s. Robert Burns and Alpha (Rodenberger) S.; divorced, 1978; children: David, Kathryn, Robert, Lisa; m. Evelyn Louise Klunder, Sept. 20, 1980. BA, Northwestern U., 1955, MD, 1958. Cons. in medicine Mayo Clinic, Rochester, Minn., 1965—87, chmn. dept. thoracic disease, 1977—87, cons. in medicine Scottsdale, Ariz., 1987—2000, chmn. dept. internal medicine, 1988—96, vice chmn. bd. govs., 1987—94. Assoc. dir. Mayo Lung Project, Nat. Cancer Inst., Rochester., pres. Northwestern U., Med. Sch. Alumni Assn., 1995-97 Contbr. articles to profl. jours. Recipient Noble award Mayo Found., Rochester, Chevalier Jackson award Am. Bronchoesophagologic Assn., 1990. Fellow ACP, Am. Coll. Chest Physicians (gov. for Minn. 1981-87); mem. Am. Bronchoesophagologic Assn. (pres. 1986-87), World Assn. for Bronchology, Internat. Bronchoesophagologic Soc., Internat. Assn. Study of Lung Cancer, AMA, Sigma Xi, Sigma Chi (Significant Sig award 1989). Presbyterian. Home: 10676

E Bella Vista Dr Scottsdale AZ 85258-6086 Office: Mayo Clinic Arizona 13400 E Shea Blvd Scottsdale AZ 85259-5499 Home Phone: 480-860-6782; Office Phone: 480-301-8000. Personal E-mail: dsanderson958@cox.net.

SANDERSON, MARY LOUISE, medical association administrator; b. Fairmont, W.Va., Oct. 29, 1942; d. Lawrence Oliver and Frances Evelyn (Shuttleworth) Shingleton; m. William W. Olmstead III, Dec. 1966 (div. June 1974); children: William W. IV, Happy; m. Lester F. Davis, III, Oct. 1979 (div. Dec. 1986); m. David S. Sanderson, Sept. 1992. Student, Vassar Coll., 1960-62, Carnegie Mellon, 1962-63. Real estate broker, N.C. Exec. sec. Creative Dining, Raleigh, NC, 1980-83, Sea Pines Plantation Co., Hilton Head, SC, 1973-79; from adminstr. to exec. dir. Am. Bd. Neurol. Surgery, Houston, 1983—. Vol. Interact, Raleigh, 1984-86, M.D. Anderson Cancer Ctr./Camp Star Trails, 1994-96; docent Mordecai House Hist. Preservation, Raleigh, 1981-83; mem./vol. Reach to Recovery, 1995-2001, Houston Symphony, 2002-, Mus. of Fine Arts, Houston, 1999-. Recipient Vol. award N.C. State Gov., 1986. Mem. Am. Soc. Assn. Execs. Democrat. Episcopalian. Office: Am Bd Neurol Surgery 6550 Fannin St Ste 2139 Houston TX 77030-2718 *

SANDLER, ERIC STUART, oncologist; b. NY, Oct. 6, 1959; MD, U. Vt., 1985. Chief, divsn. hematology, oncology Nemours Children's Clinic, 1998—. Mem.: Am. Soc. Pediatric Hematology, Oncology, Am. Soc. Hematology, Am. Soc. Clin. Oncology. Office: Nemours Children's Clinic 807 Childrens Way Jacksonville FL 32207 Office Fax: 904-697-3792. Business E-Mail: esandler@nemours.org.

SANDLER, HOWARD M., medical educator; b. NYC, Dec. 2, 1956; MD, U. Conn. Sch. Medicine, 1985. Cert. Am. Bd. Radiology. Intern, radiological oncology St. Francis Hosp., Hartford, 1985—86; resident Hosp. U. Pa., Phila., 1989—89; asst. to prof., dept. radiation oncology and dept. urology U. Mich., Ann Arbor, 1989—. Office: University of Michigan Rm B2C490 1500 E Medical Center Dr Ann Arbor MI 48109-0010 Office Fax: 734-763-7371. E-mail: hsandler@umich.edu.

SANDLER, RICHARD H., pediatric gastroenterologist; MD, Mich. State U. Coll. Human Medicine. Resident, pediatrics Mich. State U., Lansing; fellow, pediatric gastroenterology, hepatology, and nutrition Harvard Med. Sch., Boston Children's Hosp.; fellow, human metabolism and nutrition Mass. Gen. Hosp., Boston; asst. in medicine, instr., divsn. of gastroenterology and nutrition The Children's Hosp., Harvard Med. Sch., Boston, 1989—90; dir. Biomed. Acoustics Rsch. Group, Evanston, Ill., 1990—, pres., CEO, 1997—; assoc. prof., pediatrics Rush Med. Coll., Chgo., 1990—; adj. assoc. prof., biomed. engring. U. Ill., Chgo., 2002—. Office: Rush Univ Med Ctr 1725 W Harrison St Chicago IL 60612 Address: 1725 W Harrison St Ste 946 Chicago IL 60612 Office Phone: 312-942-2889.

SANDLOW, LESLIE JORDAN, gastroenterologist, educator; b. Chgo., Jan. 7, 1934; s. Harry H. and Rose (Ehrlich) S.; m. Joanne J. Fleischer, June 16, 1957; children: Jay, Bruce, Lisa. BS, U. Ill., 1956; MD, Chgo. Med. Sch., 1960. Intern Michael Reese Hosp. and Med. Ctr., Chgo., 1961, med. resident, rsch. fellow gastrointestinal rsch., 1961-64, physician-in-charge clin. gastroenterology lab., 1963-74, asst. attending physician, 1964-67, assoc. attending physician, 1967-72, vice chmn. divsn. gastroenterology, dir. ambulatory medicine, 1968, dir. ambulatory care, 1969-76, attending physician, 1972—, assoc. med. dir., 1972-73; clin. asst. Chgo. Med. Sch., 1963-68, clin. instr., 1966; asst. prof. dept. medicine Pritzker Sch. Medicine, U. Chgo., 1973-76, assoc. prof., 1976-85, prof., 1985-90; prof. clin. medicine and med. edn. U. Ill. Coll. Medicine, Chgo., 1990-91, prof. medicine and med. edn., 1992—, sr. assoc. dean for grad. and continuing med. edn., 1993—, head dept. med. edn., 1993—, sr. assoc. dean for med. edn. affairs, 1994—. Dep. v.p. profl. affairs Michael Reese Hosp. and Med. Ctr., 1973-78, dir. Office Ednl. Affairs, 1976-81, assoc. v.p. acad. affairs, 1978-82, dir. quality assurance program, 1981-91, v.p. planning, 1982-83, v.p. profl. affairs and planning, 1983-88, dir. divsn. internal medicine, 1986-93, v.p. profl. and acad. affairs, 1988-91, med. dirs. acad. and med. affairs, 1992-94; med. dir. Michael Reese Health Plan, Inc., 1972-74, interim exec. dir., 1976-77; cons. gastroenterologist Ill. Ctrl. Hosp., 1978-80; vis. prof. Pontifica U. Catolica Rio Grande do Sul, Brazil, 1978, U. Fed. Espirito Santo, Brazil, 1978, Nordic Fedn. for Med. Understanding, Akureyri, Iceland, 1978, Seoul Nat. U. Sch. Medicine, 1981, Coll. Physicians and Surgsons, Kharachi, Pakistan, 1994, U. Tex., Ft. Worth, 1977, U. Ariz., Tucson, 1977, Loyola U. Med. Sch., Maywood, Ill., 1979; cons. in field; coord. Health Scis. Librs. in Ill.; mem. Midwest Med. Libr. Network; mem. subcom. on delivery of ambulatory med. care Inst. Medicine Chgo.; mem. cmty. resources task force Interinstnl. Cardiovascular Ctr.; chmn. steering group Ill. Regional Med. Program; past co-chmn. curriculum com. U. Chgo. Reviewer Rsch. in Med. Edn./Assn. Am. Med. Colls., 1985—, Acad. Medicine/Assn. Am. Med. Colls., 1989; contbr. numerous articles to profl. publs. Mem. Skokie (Ill.) Bd. Health, 1973-85, chmn., 1976-85; bd. dirs. Group Health Assn. Am., 1976-78, Portes Ctr., 1980—; bd. dirs. Good Health Program Skokie Valley Hosp., 1978-80; bd. dirs., exec. com. Rsch. and Edn. Found. of Michael Reese Hosp. Med. Staff, 1992—; pres.-elect Inst. Medicine Chgo., 2003-04, pres., 2004-06. Recipient numerous grants, including NIH 1988, Michael Reese Hosp. Found. 1994-95, Chgo. Cmty. Trust 1994-95, AOA faculty award 2007. Fellow Am. Coll. Gastroenterology; mem. N.Y. Acad. Scis., Inst. Medicine, Assn. Am. Med. Colls., Am. Coll. Physician Execs. (co-chair resource mgmt. com. of quality assurance forum), Soc. Dirs. Med. Coll. Continuing Med. Edn., Soc. Dir. Rsch. in Med. Edn. Home: 2314 N Lincoln Park W Chicago IL 60614-3455 Office: University Ill Coll Medicine Dept Med Edn MC 591 808 S Wood St 986 CME Chicago IL 60612-7309 Office Fax: 312-413-2048. Business E-Mail: ijs@uic.edu.

SANDORFI, NORA, rheumatologist, physician; MD, Semmelweis Med. U., 1983. Diplomate Am. Bd. Internal Medicine-rheumatology, lic. to practice Pa., 1998. Resident Allegheny Hosp. Grad. Sch., 1998, intern, 1996; fellow Thomas Jefferson Univ. Hosp. Office: Thomas Jefferson University Division of Rheumatology 1015 Walnut St Ste 613 Philadelphia PA 19107 Office Phone: 215-955-1410. Office Fax: 215-923-7885.

SANDOVAL, HORACIO, microbiologist, researcher; b. Mexico City, Oct. 1, 1946; s. Eduardo Sandoval and Yolanda Trujillo. BS in Bacteriology, Nat. Sch. Biolog. Scis., 1969; PhD, U. Lyon, 1974. Lectr. U. Met. Xochimilco, Mexico City, 1974—. Tchr. asst. Nat. Sch. Biolog. Scis, Mexico City, 1968—72. Office: U Autonoma Met Calzada Hueso 1100 04960 Mexico City Mexico

SANDRIAN, REZA, plastic surgeon; D Dental Surgery, U. Wash., Seattle; MD, Eastern Va. Med. Sch. Diplomate Am. Bd. Plastic Surgery, cert. oral and maxillofacial surgery. Resident oral and maxillofacial surgery Johns Hopkins Hosp., Univ. Md.; resident plastic surgery Tex. Med. Ctr., Houston; resident gen. surgery Univ. Washington, Seattle; med. staff Scripps Meml. Hosp. La Jolla; plastic surgeon Sadrian Cosmetic Surgery Ctr., San Diego Plastic Surgery Ctr. Author various sci. articles and lectures. Recipient multitude of prestigious awards. Office: San Diego Plastic Surgery Center Ste 300 and 380 9850 Genesee Ave La Jolla CA 92037 Office Phone: 858-587-9850. Office Fax: 858-622-2066. *

SANDS, ARTHUR T., biopharmaceutical executive, medical geneticist; BA in Econ. & Polit. Sci., Yale U.; MA, Baylor Coll. of Medicine, PhD, 1992. Former Am. Cancer Soc. postdoctoral fellow, dept. of human and molecular genetics Baylor Coll. of Medicine, 1992—95; co-founder (with Allan Bradley), pres., CEO Lexicon Pharmaceuticals (formerly Lexicon Genetics), The Woodlands, Tex., 1995—. Bd. mem. Tex. Inst. for Genomic Medicine. Recipient BioHouston Life Sci. award, 2004. Achievements include developing large-scale gene knockout technology for use in drug discovery. Office: Lexicon Pharms 8800 Technology Forest Pl The Woodlands TX 77381-1160 Office Phone: 281-863-3000. Office Fax: 281-863-8088. *

SANDS, STEPHEN ALAN, medical educator; b. NYC, July 11, 1964; PhD, NYU, 1997. Asst. prof. Columbia U. Med. Ctr., 2002—. Mem.: Childrens Oncology Group. Office: Columbia University Med Ctr New York NY 10032 Office Fax: 212-305-5848. Business E-Mail: ss2341@columbia.edu.

SANDSTEAD, HAROLD HILTON, physician, researcher, educator, director; b. Omaha, May 25, 1932; s. Harold Russel and Lula Florence (Hilton) S.; m. Kathryn Gordon Brownlee, June 6, 1959 (dec. May 13, 1989); m. Victoria Regan Liddle, Feb. 14, 1990 (div. Oct. 1993); m. Wilma Helen Carter Streaker, Sept. 25, 2004 (div. July 2008); children: Eleanor McDonald, James Brownlee, William Harold. BA in Pre-Medicine, Ohio Wesleyan U., 1954; MD, Vanderbilt U., 1958. Cert. Am. Bd. Internal Medicine, 1967, Am. Bd. Nutrition, 1967, Am. Bd. Physician Nutrition Specialists, 2001. Intern, internal medicine Barnes Hosp. Washington U., St. Louis, 1958—59, asst. resident, internal medicine, 1959—60; asst. resident, pathology Vanderbilt U. Hosp., Nashville, 1960-61; asst. surgeon USPHS U.S. NAMRU 3, Cairo, 1961-63; rsch. resident, internal medicine Thayer VA Hosp., Vanderbilt U., Nashville, 1963-64; chief med. resident, internal medicine Vanderbilt U. Hosp., Nashville, 1964-65; instr. internal medicine, asst. prof. biochemistry Med. Sch. Vanderbilt U., Nashville, 1965-70, asst. prof. internal medicine, assoc. prof. biochemistry in nutrition, 1970-71; dir. USDA-ARS Human Nutrition Rsch. Ctr., Grand Forks, ND, 1971-84; adj. prof. biochemistry and internal medicine Sch. Medicine U. ND, Grand Forks, 1971-84; dir. USDA-ARS Human Nutrition Rsch. Ctr. on Aging at Tufts U., Boston, 1984-85; prof. nutrition Tufts U., Medford, Mass., 1984-85; prof. preventive medicine and community health U. Tex. Med. Br., Galveston, 1985—2006; chmn. preventive medicine and community health Med. Br. U. Tex., Galveston, 1985-90, prof. internal medicine, biochem. and molecular biology, 1986—2006, prof. emeritus preventative medicine and cmty. health and internal medicine, 2006—. Cons. IAEA, FAO, WHO, Internat. Programme on Chem. Safety, UN Environment Programme, Agency Internat. Devel., Nat. Cancer Inst., Nat. Inst. Child Health and Human Devel., Nat. Eye Inst., Nat. Heart, Lung, and Blood Inst., Officer Internat. Rsch., NIH, FDA, EPA, USDA, Food Nutrition Bd., NRC, Inst. Medicine, NAS, Life Sciences Rsch. Office, Fedn. Am. Societies Exptl. Biology, US Pharmacopeia, Am.Acad.Pediat., ACS, Am. Soc. Parenteral and Enteral Nutrition, Am. Health Found., Mead Johnson Co., Internat. Lead Zinc Rsch. Org., Nat. Cattlemen's Beef Assn., NeuroBioTex; clinician, Nutrition Survey Panama, Interdepartmental Com. Nutrition & Nat. Devel., NIH, 1967; field team dir., Texas Nutrition Survey, 10 State Nutrition Survey, US Nutrition Program, NIH, 1968; clinician, Kentucky Nutrition Survey, 10 State Nutrition Survey, US Nutrition Program, NIH, 1969; panel mem., White House Conf. on Food, Nutrition & Health, 1969, Am. Bd. Nutrition, 1975-81, USDA, ARS, human studies rev. com. (chmn., 83-85), 1976-85; rsch. adv. com., NSLS X-Ray Microprobe, Brookhaven Nat. Lab., 1984-90; advisor, Am. Coun. on Sci. & Health, 1988-; FASEB Wellcome vis. prof. in Basic Med. Sci., Pa. State U., 1988; zinc information nutrition ctr. adv. bd. Am. Zinc Assn., 1999-, Permanent Commn. on Occupl. Health, 2004-07. Mem. editl. bd. Jour. Nutrition, 1972-76, 81-85, 2011-, Am. Jour. Clin. Nutrition, 1975-78, Annual Rev. Nutritional Rsch., 1975-1991, Jour. Lab. Clin. Medicine, 1978-1983, Biol. Trace Element Rsch., 1979—, Nutrition Rsch., 1981-85, Nutritional Reports Internat., 1981-88, Trace Elements Medicine Biology, 1983-98, Jour. Trace Elements Exptl. Medicine, 1982-2004, Jour. Am. Coll. Nutrition, 1987-88, Nutrition Rsch. Newsletter, 1989-98, Cancer Prevention, 1990-1994, assoc. editor history & biography; contbr. over 300 articles to profl. jours., chapters to books. 4 ISI Citation Classics. Recipient Future Leader award, Nutrition Found., 1968—71, Hull Gold medal, with HC Meng, AMA, 1970, Special Recognition award, Vanderbilt U. Sch. Medicine, 1971, Mead Johnson award, Am. Inst. Nutrition, 1971, WO Atwater award medal and lecture, US Dept. Agr., 1984, Ellen Swallow Richard Meml. Lecture, U. NC Inst. Nutrition, 1985, Sam & Mary Roberts Nutrition medal and Lecture, U. Kans. Sch. Medicine, 1985, Raymond Ewell Meml. lecture, U. Buffalo, SUNY Sch. Medicine, 1985, Special Recognition award, USDA Agrl. Rsch. Svc., 2004. Fellow ACP, Am. Soc. Nutrition (Mead Johson award 1972, fellow 1998); mem. Am. Soc. Clin. Nutrition (pres. 1982-83), Internat. Soc. for Trace Element Rsch. in Humans (pres. 2002-04, Raulin award 2007), Cosmos Club, Sigma Xi, Alpha Omega Alpha. Achievements include description of adverse effects of lead poisoning on renin-aldoserone function, pituitary-adrenal function, and pituitary-thyroid function; description of zinc deficiency in Egyptian adolescents, endocrine functions, and effects of zinc treatment; confirmation in rat of essentiality of zinc for nucleic acid and protein synthesis; confirmation in rats of the essentiality of zinc for wound healing; demonstration of some effects of zinc deficiency on development and function of rat on brain and on function later in life; demonstration of essentiality of zinc for neuropsychological functions of children and premenopausal women; demonstration of inhibition of zinc absorption by folic acid, demonstration by zinc kinetics of associations between iron status by serum ferritin and zinc status by zinc kinetics and plasma zinc concentration in premenopausal women; demonstration of zinc deficiency among low-income pregnant black US teenagers, Mexican-American children and premenopausal US women. Office: U Tex Med Br Ewing Bldg Galveston TX 77555-1109 Home: 77005 Seawall Blvd 407 Galveston TX 77551 Office Phone: 409-772-4661. Personal E-mail: hsandste@mac.com. Business E-Mail: hsandste@utmb.edu.

SANDY, LEWIS GORDON, physician, healthcare executive; b. Detroit, July 18, 1958; s. William Haskell and Marjorie Mindel (Mazor) S.; m. Kathleen Anne Morgan, June 17, 1984; children: Matthew, Natalie, Jonah. BS, U. Mich., 1979, MD, 1982; MBA, Stanford U., 1988. Diplomate Am. Bd. Internal Medicine, Nat. Bd. Med. Examiners. Intern Beth Israel Hosp., Boston, 1982-83, resident, 1983-85; Robert Wood Johnson clin. scholar U. Calif., San Francisco, 1985-86, clin. fellow in medicine, 1986-88; instr. Harvard Med. Sch., 1988-91; assoc. chief internal medicine Harvard Community Health Plan, Boston, 1988-89, dir. Health Ctr., 1989-91; v.p. Robert Wood Johnson Found., Princeton, NJ, 1991—96, exec. v.p., 1997—2003, UnitedHealthcare, Edina, Minn., 2003—07; sr. v.p. UnitedHealth Group, Minnetonka, Minn., 2007—; sr. fellow U. Minn. Sch. Pub. Health, 2004—; bd. dirs. America Health Ins. Plans, 2007—09; prin. United Health Ctr. Health Reform and Modernization, 2009—. Cons. Kaiser Found. Health Plan, Oakland, Calif., 1987-88. Fellow ACP; mem. AMA, Soc. Gen. Internal Medicine, Acad. Health, Alpha Omega Alpha. Home: 4800 Sunnyslope Rd E Edina MN 55424 Office: 9900 Bren Rd E Minnetonka MN 55343

SANETO, RUSSELL PATRICK, pediatric neurologist, epileptologist, neurobiologist; b. Burbank, Calif., Oct. 10, 1950; s. Arthur and Mitzi (Seddon) S.; m. Kathleen D. Saneto. BS with honors, San Diego State U., 1972, MS, 1975; PhD, U. Tex. Med. Br., 1981; DO, U. Osteo. Medicine and Surgery, 1994. Tchg. asst. San Diego State U., 1969-75; substitute tchr. Salt Lake City Sch. Dist., 1975; tchg. and rsch. asst. U. Tex. Med. Br., 1976-77, NIH predoctoral fellow, 1977-81, postdoctoral fellow, 1981; Jeanne B. Kempner postdoctoral fellow UCLA, 1981-82, NIH postdoctoral fellow, 1982-87; asst. prof. divsn. neurosci. Oreg. Regional Primate Rsch. Ctr., Beaverton, 1987-89; asst. prof. dept. cell biology and anatomy Oreg. Health Scis. U., Portland, 1988-90, U. Osteo. Medicine and Surgery, 1991-94, Cleve. Clinic, 1994-2001; assoc. prof. neurology and pediat. U. Wash. Seattle Children's Hosp., 2001—. Lectr. rsch. methods Grad. Sch., 1982; vis. scholar in ethics So. Bapt. Theol. Sem., Louisville, 1981; sci. advisor United Mitochondrial Disease Found. Mem. editl. bd. Epilepsy.com, Pediat. Neurology; contbr. articles to profl. jours. Mem. scientific adv. bd. United Mitochondrial Disease Found., Northwest Epilepsy Found., Hemispherectomy Found.; sec., treas. Mitochondrial Medicine Soc., 2007—08, pres., 2010—. Recipient Merit award Nat. March of Dimes, 1978; named one of Outstanding Young Men in Am., 1979, 81, one of Men of Significance, 1985, Best Drs. America, 2009-, Top Pediatricians in America, 2008-10. Mem. AAAS, Am. Acad. Pediats., Am. Acad. Neurology, Am. Epilepsy Soc., Bread for World, Winter Confs. Brain Rsch., Neuroscis. Study Program, NY Acad. Scis., Am. Soc. Neurochemistry, Soc. Neurosci., Sigma Sigma Phi. Democrat. Mem. Evangelical Free Ch. Office: Univ Wash Seattle Children's Neurology B-5552 4800 Sand Point Way NE Seattle WA 98105

SANFILIPPO, FRED PAUL, academic administrator, medical educator, pathologist; b. Racine, Wis., Aug. 30, 1949; s. Paul Joseph and Therese (Rhode) Sanfilippo; m. Janet Lee Thompson, 1973; children: Lisa, Joseph. Student, Max Planck Inst. Exptl. Medicine, Gottingen, Germany, 1966—68; BA in Physics, MS in Physics, U. Pa., 1970; PhD in immunology, Duke U., 1975, MD, 1976. Diplomate Am. Bd. Pathology, lic. physician NC, Md. Intern in anatomic pathology Duke U. Hosp., 1976—77, resident in anatomic and clin. pathology, 1977—79, postdoctoral rschr. divsn. tumor virology dept. surgery, 1976—79; asst. prof. pathology and exptl. surgery, lectr. immunology Duke U., 1979—84, from assoc. prof. to prof. pathology, 1984—93, from assoc. prof. to prof. exptl. surgery, 1985—93, prof. immunology, 1990—93; attending pathologist Duke U. and Durham VA Hosps., 1979—93; staff mem. Duke Surg. Pvt. Diagnostic Clinic, 1979—93; dir. Transplantation Lab Durham VA Hosp., 1979—93; dir. immunopathology Duke U. Med. Ctr., 1982—93, exec. com. dept. pathology, 1989—91; Baxley Prof. and chair pathology dept. John's Hopkins U., Balt., 1993—2000; pathologist-in-chief Johns Hopkins Hosp., Balt., 1993—2000; sr. v.p. health scis. Ohio State U., Columbus, 2000—07, exec. dean health scis., 2004—07, dean. coll. medicine, 2000—06; CEO Ohio State U. Med. Ctr., 2000—07; exec. v.p. health affairs, CEO Woodruff Health Scis. Ctr., chmn. Emory Healthcare Emory U., 2007—10. Mem. Duke Comprehensive Cancer Ctr., 1979—93; dir. rsch. Johns Hopkins Comprehensive Transplant Ctr.; mem. Third Frontier Commn. Adv. Bd., Ohio, 2004—; cons. Battelle Human Affairs Rsch. Ctrs., Seattle, 1985—93, NSF of Switzerland, 1992—93, numerous US govt. adv. coms.; mem. editl. bd. Transplantation, 1985—2001, Pathobiology, 1989—2001, Transplantation Now, Japan, 1989—2001, Pathology, Rsch. and Practice, 1990—2001, Human Immunology, 1992—2001, Lab. Investigation, 1993—2005, Xeno, 1994—2002, Virchows Archiv, 1998—2002, Transplant Immunology, 1998—2002; reviewer Am. Jour. Kidney Diseases, Am. Jour. Ophthalmology, Am. Jour. Pathology, New Eng. Jour. Medicine, Jour. of AMA, Jour. Am. Soc. Nephrology, Jour. Clin. Investigation, Jour. Leukocyte Biology, Kidney Internat., others; contbr. numerous articles to prof. jours.; speaker and presenter in field. Bd. trustees Omeris, Columbus, Ohio, 2004—. Recipient Kermit G. Osserman Award, Myasthenia Gravis Found., 1976, Wiley D. Forbus Award, NC Soc. Pathologists, 1979, Reach for Sight Physician Investigator Award, 1990; grantee numerous, NIH. Fellow: Am. Soc. Clin. Pathologists (coun. on edn. and rsch. 1994—96); mem.: Southeastern Organ Procurement Found. (exec. com 1992—97, sec. 1992—93, treas. 1993—94, v.p. 1994—95, pres. 1995—96), Assn. for Rsch. in Vision and Ophthalmology, Am. Soc. Nephrology, Am. Soc. Transplant Physicians (pres. 1985—86), Am. Soc. Histocompatibility and Immunogenetics, Transplantation Soc., US-Can. Acad. Pathology, Am. Assn. Med. Colls., Am. Assn. Immunologists, AMA, Am. Soc. Investigative Pathology (pres. 2002—03), Intersociety Pathology Coun., Assn. Pathology Chairs (sr. fellow), Am. Soc. Transplantation (past pres.), Alpha Omega Alpha. Office: Emory U Woodruff Health Scis Ctr 1440 Clifton Rd Atlanta GA 30322 Office Phone: 404-778-0234. Office Fax: 404-778-3100. E-mail: fred.sanfilippo@emory.edu.

SANFORD-HUGUS, BARBARA, geneticist, consultant; b. Brockton, Mass., Oct. 17, 1927; d. Arthur A. and Grace Brennan Hendrick; m. George R. Sanford, Nov. 25, 1950 (div. Jan. 15, 1971); children: Arthur, Jane, Brian, Paul; m. J. Edward Hugus, Apr. 14, 1992. BS, BA, Boston U., 1949; MA, Brown U., 1960, PhD, 1963; DSc (hon.), Bates Coll., 1986. Assoc. biologist Mass. Gen. Hosp., Boston, 1963—73; br. chief biology br. Nat. Cancer Inst., Bethesda, Md., 1973—78; assoc. prof. pathology Harvard Med. Sch., Boston, 1978—81; rsch. dir. Dana Farber Cancer Ctr., Boston, 1978—81; dir. Jackson Lab., Bar Harbor, Maine, 1981—88. Trustee U. Maine, Bangor, 1983—88, Jackson Lab., Bar Harbor, 1988—, Dana Farber Cancer Inst., Boston, 1981—. Contbr. numerous articles to sci. jours. Grantee, NIH, 1963—88. Mem.: Am. Assn. for Cancer Rsch. Home: 849 Coast Blvd Unit LC 202 La Jolla CA 92037 Personal E-mail: barbarahugus@hotmail.com.

SANGAMESWARAN, BALAKRISHNAN SANGAMESWARAN, principal; b. Tamilnadu, June 3, 1970; M in Pharmacy, 1996; PhD, Vinayaka U., 2009. Prof. Vinayaka Missions U., 1993—2009; prin. Adesh Inst. Pharmacy & Biomed. Scis., 2011—, rsch. & academic mem., 2011. Editl. bd. mem. numerous internat. jours. Contbr. articles to profl. jours. Mem.: AICTE. Office: Adesh Inst Pharmacy & Biomed Bathinda Punjab 151109 India Office Fax: 911642742901. Business E-Mail: sangar1970@yahoo.co.in.

SANGER, FREDERICK, biochemist; b. Rendcomb, Gloucestershire, Eng., Aug. 13, 1918; s. Frederick and Cicely Sanger; m. Margaret Joan Howe, 1940; children: Robin, Peter Frederick, Sally Joan. BA, St. John's Coll., U. Cambridge, 1940, PhD, 1943; DSc (hon.), Leicester U., 1968, Oxford U., 1970, Strasbourg U., 1970. Beit meml. med. rsch. fellow U. Cambridge, 1944-51, rsch. scientist, dept. biochemistry, 1944-61, rsch. scientist, divsn. head Med. Rsch. Coun. Lab. Molecular Biology, 1962-83. Contbr. articles to profl. jours. Decorated Comdr., Order of Brit. Empire, Order Companions of Honour; recipient Corday-Morgan medal and prize, Chem. Soc., 1951, Nobel prize for chemistry, 1958, 1980, William Bate Hardy prize, Cambridge Philos. Soc., 1976, Louisa Gross Horwitz prize, Columbia U., 1979. Fellow: Royal Soc., Royal Coll. Pathologists (hon.); mem.: Acad. Sci. Brazil, Acad. Sci. Argentina, Japanese Biochemical Soc. (hon.), Am. Soc. Biol. Chemists (hon.), Argentine Chem. Soc. (corr.), Am. Acad. Arts & Scis. (fgn. hon.). Achievements include discovery of the complete amino acid sequence of the two polypeptide chains of insulin; development of several methods to sequence the nucleic acids DNA and RNA including methods reading DNA using special bases called chain terminators, the use of very thin gel systems and the adaptation of efficient cloning methods to produce both DNA strands and the whole-genome shotgun.

SANGER, HEIDI, physician, director; b. Peekskill, NY, May 3, 1965; MD, ISU, 1994. Med. dir. Montefiore Med. Group, 2010—. Mem.: AMA. Avocations: swimming, tennis, gardening. Office: 440 White Plains Rd Eastchester NY 10709 Business E-Mail: heidisanger@pol.net.

SANGER, JAMES ROBERT, plastic surgeon, educator; b. Madison, Wis., Apr. 16, 1948; m. Mary Newton; children: Elizabeth, Susan, Peter, John. BS, U. Mich., Ann Arbor, 1970; MD, U. Wis., Madison, 1974. Plastic surgery sect. chief Zablocki VA Med. Ctr., Milw., 1981—; prof. surgery Med. Coll. Wis., Milw., 1992—, fellowship, 1981—82; resident gen. surgery Harbor gen. Hosp., UCLA, 1974—79; resident plastic surgery Med. Coll. Wis. Hosps., 1979—81. Contbr. chapters to books, articles to profl. jours. Recipient Robert H. Ivy Soc. award, Am. Soc. Plastic and Reconstructive Surgeons, 1992. Mem.: ACS, Plastic Surgery Rsch. Coun., Am. Soc. Surgery Hand, Am. Soc. Reconstructive Microsurgery, Midwest Assn. Plastic Surgeons (1st prize 1990—91), Wis. Soc. Plastic Surgeons, State Med. Soc. Wis., Med. Soc. Milw. County, Am. Soc. Plastic Surgeons, Milw. Acad. Medicine, Am. Soc. Peripheral Nerve, Am. Assn. Plastic Surgeons, Wound Healing Soc., Internat. Soc. Reconstructive Microsurgery, Am. Assn. Hand Surgery. Office: Med Coll Wis 8700 Watertown Plank Rd Milwaukee WI 53226-3595 Office Phone: 414-805-5451. Office Fax: 414-259-0901. *

SANGER, JOSEPH JAY, radiologist, nuclear medicine physician, educator; MD, NYU, 1977. Diplomate Am. Bd. Nuc. Medicine, Am. Bd. Medical Specialties, lic. NY, 1980. Resident NYU Med. Ctr., 1977—80, fellow, 1980—81; assoc. prof. NYU Radiology Assocs., dir. radiology informatics dept. of radiology. Named one of Best Doctors in NY, NY Mag., 2010. Achievements include research in Database Applications in Medicine. Office: NYU Langone Medical Center and School of Medicine 550 1st Ave New York NY 10016 Office Phone: 212-263-7300.

SANG-HA, OH, plastic surgeon, educator; b. Seoul, Republic of Korea, July 1, 1970; MD, Chungnam Nat. U., 1997. Chief Dept. Plastic and Reconstructive Surgery, 2010—. Asst. prof. Chungnam Nat. U., Coll. Medicine, 2007—. Mem.: Korean Soc. Aesthetic Plastic Surgery, Korean Cleft Palate-Craniofacial Assn., Korean Soc. Plastic and Reconstructive Surgeons. Office: Chungnam Nat University Hosp Daejeon 301-721 Republic of Korea Office Fax: 82-42-280-7384. Business E-Mail: djplastic@cnu.ac.kr.

SANGHI, VINAY, cardiologist, researcher; MD, Osmania Med. Sch., Hyd, 1994. Cert. in neurorescue interventions, in vascular medicine Am. Bd. Internist Chgo. Med. Sch., 1996—99; fellow Luth. Gen. Hosp., Park Ridge, Ill., 1999—2002; fellow Lahey Clinic Tufts U., Boston, 2002—03; interventional cardiologist Health First / HOlmes Regional Med. Ctr., Melbourne, Fla., 2003—07; asst. prof. Southern Ill. U., Carbondlae, 2008—10; dir. cath lab. Heartland Regional Med. Ctr., 2008—10; sr. cons. Fortis Escorts Heart Inst., New Delhi, 2010—. Named one of Top Cardiologists USA, Consumer Rsch. Coun. America, 2009—10. Fellow: Soc. Coronary Angiogroaphy and Intervention, Am. Coll. Cardiology, ACP.

SANG-HOON, KANG, oral surgeon, educator; b. Republic of Korea, May 11, 1973; DDS, Coll. Dentistry, Yonsei U., 1999. Clin. asst. prof. Coll. Dentistry, Yonsei U., 2008—. Office: 1232 Baeksok-dong Ilsandong-gu Goyang Gyounggi 410-719 Republic of Korea

SANG HYUN, PAIK, medical educator, director; b. Seoul, Republic of Korea, Nov. 17, 1969; MD, Soon Chun Hyang Med. U., PhD, 1995. Rsch. fellowship Duke U. Med. Ctr. Vivo Microscopy, 2006—07; rsch. fellowship, instr., asst. prof., divsn. radiology Soon Chun Hyang U. Bucheon Hosp., 2003—10, assoc. prof., divsn. radiology, 2010—. Head, dept. plan & mgmt. Korean Inst. Accreditation Med. Image, 2008—; med. and ins. dir. Korean Soc. Thoracic Radiology, 2008—; mem. Com. Quality Evaluation Korea Nat. Cancer Screening, 2008—, Com. Med. Devices Health and Ins. Rev. and Assessment Svc., 2011. Recipient award, 37th Ann. Meeting Korean Soc. Ultrasound in Medicine, 2005, Rakcheon Med. award, 2006; Rsch. grant, Nat. Rsch. and Found., 2008. Mem.: Korean Assn. Study of Lung Cancer, Korean Soc. Thoracic Radiology, Korean Med. Assn., Korean Soc. Ultrasound in Medicine, Korean Radiol. Soc. Office: 1174 Jung-Dong Wonmi-Gu Bucehon-Si Gyeonggi-Do 420-767 Republic of Korea Business E-Mail: radpsh@schmc.ac.kr.

SANG-KEUN, WOO, medical researcher; b. Republic of Korea, Nov. 20, 1972; PhD, Konkuk U., 2003. Sr. rschr. Korea Inst. Radiol. and Med. Scis., 2008—. Grant, IEEE NSS, MIC Com. Mem.: IEEE, Soc. Nuc. Medicine. Avocations: golf, baseball. Office: 75 Nowon-gil Gongneung-dong Seoul Nowon-Gu 139-706 Republic of Korea Office Fax: 82-2-970-1341.

SANG-WON, UM, pulmonologist, educator; b. Seoul, Republic of Korea, Apr. 5, 1972; MD, Seoul Nat. U., 1998, PhD, 2010. Clin. fellow Samsung Med. Ctr., Sungkyunkwan U. Sch. Medicine, Seoul, Republic of Korea, 2007—08, clin. asst. prof., 2008—09, asst. prof., 2009—. Intern Seoul Nat. U. Hosp., 1998—99, resident, 1999—2003, clin. fellow, 2006—07. Recipient Young Investigator's award, World Congress Bronchology. Mem.: Korean Med. Assn., Korean Assn. Study Lung Cancer, Korean Acad. Tb and Respiratory Diseases, Asian Pacific Soc. Respirology, Internal Assn. Study Lung Cancer. Avocations: skiing, jogging. Office: Sungkyunkwan University Sch Medicine Samsung Med Ctr 50 Irwon-Dong Seoul 135-710 Republic of Korea Office Fax: 82-2-3410-3849. Business E-Mail: sangwonum@skku.edu.

SAN JOSE AZA, BEGOÑA, health services researcher; b. Bilbao, Spain, Dec. 30, 1972; married; 2 children. Diploma in Psychology, Deusto U., 1995; MSc, Erasmus U., 1996, PhD, 2000. Rsch. assoc. dept. hygiene and epidemiology Athens Med. Sch., Greece, 2000—06; rsch. and mktg. positions Interamerican Ins. Co., Athens, 2006—. Mem.: Spanish Greek Assn. E-mail: bego@panafonet.gr, bego@vodafone.net.gr.

SANKAR, RAMAN, pediatric neurologist; b. India, Mar. 04; PhD, U. Wash., Seattle, 1971, MD, Tulane U. Sch. Medicine, New Orleans, 1986. Diplomate Am. Bd. Psychiatry & Neurology, special qualifications in child neurology. Postdoc. rsch. assoc. U. Wash., 1974—75; asst. then assoc. prof. medicinal chemistry Xavier U., New Orleans, 1975—82; intern pediat. Children's Hosp. LA, 1986—87, resident pediat., 1987—88; resident neurology UCLA Sch. Medicine, 1988—89, fellowship pediat. neurology, 1989—91; prof. pediat. neurology Mattel Children's Hosp. at UCLA, 1991—; staff UCLA Med. Ctr. Mem. profl. adv. bd. Epilepsy Found., 2000—. Contbr. articles to profl. jours. Fellow: Am. Acad. Neurology; mem.: Child Neurology Soc. (mem. rsch. com. 2000—), Soc. Neurosci., Am. Epilepsy Soc. Office: UCLA Med Ctr Dept Pediat Neurology 10833 Le Conte Ave 22 474MDCC Los Angeles CA 90095-1752 Office Phone: 310-825-9169. Business E-Mail: RSankar@ucla.edu.

SAN-LANG, WANG, chemistry professor; b. Taiwan, Nov. 20, 1957; PhD, Osaka Prefecture U., 1990. Prof. Tamkang U., 2003—. Office: 151 Yinchuan Rd Tamsui New Taipei 251 Taiwan Business E-Mail: sabulo@mail.tku.edu.tw.

SANNITA, WALTER GEROLAMO, neurologist, neuroscientist, educator; b. Stazzano, Italy, May 29, 1945; s. Giuseppe C. Sannita and Elodia A. Marchiori; m. Piera Antonietta Uglioni, 1982; children: Simona, Francesca. MD, U. Med. Sch., Genova, Italy, 1970; MD, cert., Ednl. Commn. Fgn. Med. Grads., NYC, 1976; Bd. Neurology, U. Med. Sch., Parma, Italy, 1978; Bd. Clin. Neurophysiology, U. Med. Sch., Genova, Italy, 1981. Cert. neurologist, clin. neurophysiologist. Rschr. Nat. Coun. Rsch., Genova, 1970-76; rsch. fellow in neurosurgery U. J.W. Goethe, Frankfurt, Germany, 1971-72; fellow Internat. Assn. Psychiat. Rsch., NYC, 1975—76; asst. prof. psychiatry SUNY, Stony Brook, NY, 1975-77, assoc. prof. psychiatry, 1986—; prof. neuro-ophthalmology U. Med. Sch., Genova, 1994—2006; dir. ctr. neuroactive drug U. Genova, 1984—2004; prof. clin. neurophysiology U. Med. Sch., Genova, 1985—; head Ctr. Clin. Neuro-ophthalmology U. Genova, 1995—2004; dir. Inst. of Neurophysiopathology, 1998—2004; dir., postgrad. tng. clin. neurophysiology U. Med. Sch., 2002—04, dir., undergrad. tng. clin. neurophysiology, 2003—04; sci. dir. Si Life Consortium Advanced Rsch. Disabled Genova, Italy; prin. investigator Rsch. Advanced Neurorehab. Crotone, Italy. Prin. investigator neurophysiology Italian Space Agy. ALTEA Project, 1998—; nat. del. EU Cost Action, 2004—09. Assoc. editor Neuropsychobiology Jour., 1995-2005, Jour. Psychophysiology, 2000-; editorial bd. Italian Jour. Clin. Neurophysiology, 1977-93; editorial bd. Rsch. Comm. Psychol. Psychiat. Behavior, 1979-2000; contbr. over 200 articles to sci. jours., handbooks and books. Fellow Nat. Inst. Nuc. Physics; mem. N.Y. Acad. Sci., Internat. Pharmaco-EEG Soc. (sec. 1988-94, v.p. 1994-96, pres. 1996-2000), Italian Soc. Psychophysiology (mem. exec. bd. 1995-2000, pres. elect 2001-03, pres. 2003—08), Delegate Mgmt. Com., Italian Nat. Inst. Nuc. Physics. Avocations: archeology, modern art. Office: Dept Neurosci Ophthalmology Genetics U. Genova Largo P Daneo Genova Italy Office Phone: 0039-010-3537464. Office Fax: 39010-3533848. E-mail: wgs@dism.unige.it.

SANO, AKIHIKO, research scientist; m. Kazumi Takeuchi, Mar. 18, 1984. MS, Osaka U., Japan, 1981. Mgr. pharm. rsch. group Dainippon Sumitomo Pharma Co., Ltd., Ibaraki-Shi, Japan, 1981—. Recipient Nikkei BP Tech. awards, 2000. Office: Dainippon Sumitomo Pharma Co Ltd 3-45 Kurakakiuchi 1-chome Ibaraki 567-0878 Japan Office Fax: 81-72-627-8140; Home Fax: 81-6-6856-3016.

SANO, HAJIME, medical educator; b. Yokohama, Japan, Nov. 4, 1960; MD, Yamanashi Med. Coll., 1986. Assoc. prof. Kitasato U., Sch. Medicine, 2006—. Office: 1-15-1 Kitasato Minamiku Sagamihara Kanagawa 2520374 Japan Business E-Mail: sanohj@med.kitasato-u.ac.jp.

SANPAKIT, SANYAPONG, orthopedist, educator; b. Bangkok, Oct. 23, 1969; MD, Mahidol U., 1992. Diplomate Thai Bd. Orthop. Surgery, Khon Kaen U., 1996. Fellow spine surgery Mass. Gen. Hosp., Harvard U, 1997—98; asst. prof. dept. orthop. surgery Siriraj Hosp., 2002—. Cons. Bumrungrad Hosp., 2001. Recipient Best Resident Orthop. Surgery award, Khon Kaen U.; Pediat. Orthop. Surgery fellowship, U. Tenn., Campbell Clinic, Memphis, 1998—2000. Mem.: Thai Orthop. Assn., Royal Coll. Orthop. Surgeons Thailand (Best Resident Rsch. award 1996). Avocations: tennis, piano. Office: Dept Orthop Surgery Siriraj Hosp 2 Prannok Rd Bangkok Bangkoknoi 10700 Thailand Office Fax: 662-4128172. Business E-Mail: sisap@mahidol.ac.th.

SANSONE, GUY, restructuring company executive; BA, SUNY, Albany. CPA. Accounting and auditing mgr. Deloitte & Touche, LLP; CFO Telegroup, Inc.; pres., co-CEO, bd. dirs. Rotech Healthcare, Inc.; sr. v.p. Integrated Health Svcs., Inc.; interim CFO, mem. leadership team HealthSouth Corp.; mng. dir., head Healthcare Industry Group Alvarez & Marsal LLC, NYC; pres., CEO, chief restructuring officer Saint Vincent Cath. Med. Ctr., NYC, 2005—09. Office: Alvarez & Marsal LLC 600 Lexington Ave New York NY 10022 Office Phone: 212-759-4433. Office Fax: 212-759-5532.

SANTACROCE, LUIGI, medical educator, researcher; b. Bari, Italy, Sept. 16, 1965; MD, 1990. Asst. prof., med. rschr. U. Bari, 2004—, chmn., Sch. Dental Hygiene Taranto, 2008—10, chmn., Sch. Nursing, 2010—. Recipient prize, Chini Found.; fellow, Prof. Giuseppe Marinaccio Found. Avocations: football, reading. Office: Pzza G Cesare 11 Bari 70124 Italy Business E-Mail: l.santacroce@doc.uniba.it.

SANTAMARÍA, LUIS, histopathologist, researcher, professor; b. Madrid, Aug. 25, 1952; s. Gaudencio Santamaría and Teresa Solís. Degree in medicine, Autonomous U. Madrid, 1975, degree in histopathology, 1978, D, 1980. Diplomate Ministry of Health, Spain, 1975. Resident in histopathology Hosp. La Paz, Madrid, 1975—78; asst. prof. histology Sch. Medicine, Autonomous U. Madrid, 1978—82, assoc. prof. histology, 1982—84, titular prof. histology, 1984—. Sec. grad. com. Sch. Medicine, Autonomous U. Madrid, 1983—87, sec. doctorate com., 1995—, vice-dir. dept. morphology, 2000—. Contbr. articles to profl. jours. Grantee, Ministry of Health, Spain, 1993—94, Autonomous Cmty. Madrid, 1999—2000, fellow, Ministry of Edn. and Sci., Spain, 1990—91. Mem.: NY Acad. Scis., Soc. Study Reproduction, Internat. Soc. Stereology, Nat. Royal Acad. Medicine (Spain) (corr.). Roman Catholic. Avocations: jogging, mountain hicking. Office: UAM/Sch Medicine Dept Anatomy Histology and Neuroscience Calle Arzobispo Morcillo 2 28029 Madrid Spain Business E-Mail: luis.santamaria@uam.es.

SANTANGELO, MARIO VINCENT, retired dentist; b. Youngstown, Ohio, Oct. 5, 1931; s. Anthony and Maria (Zarlenga) S. Student, U. Pitts., 1949-51; DDS, Loyola U., Chgo., 1955, MS, 1960. Instr. Loyola U., 1957—60, asst. prof., 1960-66, assoc. prof., 1966-70, chmn. dept. radiology, 1962-70, dir. dental aux. utilization program, 1963-70, chmn. dept. oral diagnosis, 1967-70, asst. dean, 1969-70; pvt. practice Chgo., 1960-70; ret., 1970. Cons. Cert. Bd. Am. Dental Assts. Assn., 1967-75, VA Rsch. Hosp., 1969-75; counselor Chgo. Dental Assts. Assn., 1966-69; mem. dental student tng. adv. com. divsn. dental health USPHS, HEW, 1969-71; cons. dental edn. rev. com. NIH, 1971-72; cons. region IV, USPHS, HEW, Atlanta, 1973-76, region V, Chgo., 1973-77; mem. Commn. on Dental Edn. and Practice, Fedn. Dentaire Internat., 1984-92; mem. bd. visitors Washington U. Sch. Dental Medicine, St. Louis, 1974-76; mem. project staff Dental Edn. in the US, 1976. Contbr. articles to dental jours. 1st Lt. USAF, 1955—56, Capt. USAF, 1956—57. Recipient Dr. Harry Strusser Meml. award NYU Coll. Dentistry, 1985. Fellow Am. Coll. Dentists (life); mem. ADA (life, asst. sec. coun. dental edn. 1971-81, acting sec. 1981-82, sec. 1982-90, dir. 1990-92, asst. sec. commn. on dental accreditation 1975-81, acting sec. 1981-82, sec. 1982-90, dir. 1990-92, acting sec. commn. continuing dental edn. 1981-82, sec. 1982-90, dir. 1990-92), Ill. State Dental Assn. (life), Chgo. Dental Assn. (life), AMA (edn. work group 1982-86), Assembly Specialized Accrediting Bodies (coun. on postsecondary accreditation 1981-92, award of merit 1992), Am. Assn. Dental Schs., Odontographic Soc. Chgo. (life), Am. Acad. Oral Pathology, Am. Acad. Dental Radiology, Can. Dental Assn. (commn. on dental accrediation award of merit 1992), Am. Acad. Oral Medicine, Am. Assn. Dental Examiners (hon.), Blue Key Honor Soc., Omicron Kappa Upsilon, Xi Psi Phi. Home: 1440 N Lake Shore Dr Chicago IL 60610-1626

SANTHOSH, JAYASHREE, engineering educator, researcher; b. Kochi, Kerala, India, Jan. 27, 1962; PhD, Indian Inst. Tech., Delhi, 2006. Tchr., rschr. Indian Inst. Tech. Delhi, 1988—. Recipient Silver award, Technol. Conf., Pragathy Maidan, India. Fellow: IETE (India) (Gowri Meml. award). Avocations: reading, music. Office: Indian Inst Tech Delhi Computer Ctr Hauz Khas N New Delhi 110016 India Office Fax: 9126581058. Business E-Mail: jayashree@cc.iitd.ac.in.

SANTHRANI, THAKUR, pharmacist, educator; b. Hanamkonda, Dec. 28, 1961; BPharm, Kakatiya U., Warangal, Andhra Pradesh, 1983; MPharm, PhD, Andhra U., Waltair, 1995. Asst. prof. Rural Coll. Pharmacy, Devanhalli, Karnataka, 1992—95, St Peter's Inst. Pharm. Tech., Warangal, 1995—96; prof. Inst. Pharm. Tech., Sri Padmavati Mahila U., 1996—, head dept., 2007—10. Chmn. bd. studies faculty pharmacy Sri Padmavati Mahila U., 2008—11. Recipient Pres.'s Cert., Bharat Scouts And Guides; Jr. Rsch. fellowship, Indian Coun. Med. Rsch., Sr. Rsch. fellowship, Coun. Sci. and Indsl. Rsch., grant, U. Grants Commn., India. Mem.: All Pharmacy Tchrs. India, Indian

Pharmacol. Soc. Avocations: travel, reading, writing. Office: Sri Padmavati Mahila University Chittoor Dist Tirupati Andhra Pradesh 517 502 India Office Fax: 918772248416. E-mail: drsanthrani@gmail.com.

SANTIAGO-BORRERO, PEDRO J., dean, pediatrician, educator; MD, U. PR, San Juan, 1960. Cert. American Bd. Pediat. Residency in pediat. U. PR Med. Sciences Campus, fellowship in pediatric hematology-oncology, dean sch. medicine, 1978—85, prof. pediat., 1983—, dir. hematology-oncology sect. and pediatric hematology svc., chancellor, acting dean sch. medicine. Coord. human molecular genetics unit, prin. investigator U. PR Med. Sciences Campus Rsch. Centers in Minority Institutions. Mem.: American Acad. Pediat., Internat. Soc. Hematology, American Soc. Hematology, American Fedn. Clin. Rsch. Office: University PR A-878 Main Bldg Med Scis Campus PO Box 365067 San Juan PR 00936-5067 Office Phone: 787-765-2363. Office Fax: 787-756-8475. Business E-Mail: pedro.santiago@upr.edu. *

SANTINA, DALIA, nutritionist, writer, skin care specialist; b. Amman, Jordan, Sept. 24, 1954; d. Mahmoud Dauod Abbasi, Widad Abbasi; m. Mohammed Shafiq Santina. BA in English Lit., U. Riyadh, Saudi Arabia, 1977; diploma in computer programming, Western Bus. Coll., 1980; diploma in Skin Aesthetics, Career Acad. Beauty, 1989; PhD in Holistic Nutrition, Clayton Coll. Natural Health, 1994. Cert. paramedical acne 1990, glycolic acid services 1991, mgmt. aging and sun-damaged skin 1992, natural pharmacology 1992, aesthetic peeling 1992, oxygenation of the skin 1993, lymphatic drainage massage techniques 1994, homeopathic esthetiocology 1994, iridology diploma 1995, cert. chem. peels 1996, hydrotherapy 1997, glycolic treatments 1998, diploma in iridology 2003, cert. in herbology 2003. Exec. asst. to v.p. Am. Health Ctr., Newport Beach, Calif., 1988—89; skin care co. Skinclub, Huntington Beach, Calif., 1991—96; lectr. holistic nutrition/skin health issues, 1999—. Translator computer sys. tng. manuals, Dallas, 1983—84; tech. translator England and No. Ireland, 1984. Author: Holistic Skin Is...In, 2001, Super Supplements for Skin, Body & Mind, 2004; contbr. articles to profl. jours. Recipient Gold medal in Table Tennis, Sports Bd., Kuwait, 1972. Avocations: horseback riding, reading, antiques. Home Phone: 949-786-0672. Personal E-mail: dalia4skin@msn.com.

SANTINI, ARIO, dental educator, researcher; b. Glasgow, Scotland, June 19, 1942; s. Ario and Maria (McLaughlin) Santini; m. Sheelah Mary Murphy, Sept. 14, 1968; children: Alasdair John, Christopher Paul, Marie-Louise, Annabelle Rose. BDS, U. Edinburgh, Scotland, 1966, DDS, 1982; PhD, U. Nijmegen, Holland, 2000. House officer Edinburgh Dental Hosp., 1966; gen. dentist Lothian Health Bd., 1967—. Vis. dental surgeon H.M.P. Shotts & Edinburgh, 1982—99; clinical lectr. Edinburgh U., 1983—91, sr. lectr., 1992—94, dir. biomaterials rsch., 2002; rsch. collaborator U. Nijmegen, 1997—2000; founder, chmn. rsch. com. Faculty Gen. Dental Practitioners, London; with Nat. Dental Adv. Bd., 1996—2000. Contbr. articles to profl. jours. Active West Lothian Primary Care Trust, 1999—2002; chmn. subcom. Lothian Area Dental Com., 2003—. Fellow Rsch. fellow, Edinburgh U., 1981—84. Fellow: Soc. Antiquaries Scotland; mem.: Fedn. Dentair Internat., British Dental Assn. Avocations: Egyptology, history, sports. Office: Univ Edinburgh Dental Dept EH14 2EP Edinburgh Scotland

SANTISTEBAN-PONCE, JAVIER, pediatrician, researcher; b. Arequipa, Peru, June 3, 1964; s. Rene Santisteban-Grillo and Teresita Ponce-Pardo. MD, Univ. Peruana Cayetano Heredia, Lima, 1991; diploma in med. informatics, Univ. Nacional Autonoma de Mex., 2001. Cert. med. practitioner Colegio Medico del Peru, 1992. Rsch. fellow Univ. Peruana Cayetano Heredia, Lima, 1992—95, resident in pediat., 1995—98, cons., 1998—2000; attending physician Hosp. Nacional Edgado Rebagliati, Lima, 2000—. Author: Manual de Atencion a las Enfermedades Prevalentes de la Infancia; contbr. articles to profl. jours. Fellow: Am. Acad. Pediat. (corr.; internat.), Sociedad Peruana de Pediatria (corr.); mem.: Am. Med. Informatics Assn. (corr.). Roman Catholic. Office: Edgardo Rebagliati Nat Hosp Av Salaverry s/n Jesus Maria Lima 11 Peru Home: Donatello 357 San Borja Lima Peru Personal E-mail: flogisto@usa.net.

SANTORA, DOREEN, hospital administrator; Chief oper. officer Blue Horizon Internat.; former sr. v.p. ops. Hackensack Univ. Med. Ctr., former v.p. ops. Recipient Individual Spirit of Caring Nat. award, The Planetree Alliance Orgn.; named one of The 44 Top Cardiac Care Centers for Women, Good Houekeeping Mag., 2004. Office: Hackensack University Medical Center 30 Prospect Ave Hackensack NJ 07601 Office Phone: 201-996-2000.

SANTORO, GIULIO ANIELLO, colon and rectal surgeon, educator; b. Salerno, Italy, Dec. 8, 1966; s. Giuseppe Santoro and Antonietta Mazzarella; m. Anna Milito, May 2, 1998; children: Giuseppe, Paolo, Marco. Cert. U. Medicine, Italy, 1991. Cons. colorectal surgeon Regional Hosp., Treviso, Italy, 1997—, head pelvic fl. unit, 2007; hon. prof. Med. U., Shandong, China, 2006—. Head Sect. Anal Physiology & Ultrasound. Author: (books) Benign Anorectal Diseases, Atlas Of Endoanal And Endorectal Ultrasonography. Mem.: Pelvic Fl. Disorders, Italia Soc. Colorectal Surgery (bd. mem 2007). Achievements include invention of proctoscope for endorectal ultrasonography; first to ultrasonography of pelvic floor. Office: Depf Surgery Regional Hosp Piazzale Ospedale 1 Treviso 31100 Italy Office Phone: 39 0422 322354. Business E-Mail: gasantoro@ulss.tv.it.

SANTORO, GIUSEPPE, human anatomy professor; b. Messina, Italy, Apr. 4, 1965; MD, U. Messina Med. Sch., 1989. Navy med. officer Armed Forces, 1990—91; rschr., human anatomy U. Messina Med. Sch., 1991—98, assoc. prof., human anatomy, 1998—2010, U. Messina Sch. Pharmacy, 2010—; resident, sport's medicine U. Messina Med. Sch., 1997. Mem.: Italian Soc. Histochemistry, Italian Soc. Anatomy and Histology. Office: Dept Biomorphology AOU Viale Gazzi Messina 98125 Italy Office Fax: 39090692449. Business E-Mail: giuseppe.santoro@unime.it.

SANTORO, JEROME, infectious disease physician; MD, Temple U. Diplomate Am. Bd. Internal Medicine, 1975, Am. Bd. Internal Medicine-infectious disease, 1978. Intern Temple Univ. Hosp., resident; fellow Med. Coll. Hosp. of Pa.; with Lankenau Med. Ctr., 1979, Paoli Hosp., 1997, Bryn Mawr Hosp., 1997; clin. prof. medicine Thomas Jefferson Univ.; chmn. medicine dept. Main Line Health Hosp., mem. med. exec. com., Lankenau Hosp. Sr. clin. investigator Lankenau Inst. for Med. Rsch., mem. lankenau med. rsch. bd. Mem. Lankenau Hosp. Found., Sharpe Found., Nat. Found. for Infectious Diseases. Mem.: ACP, AMA, Am. Venereal Disease Assn., Coll. of Physicians of Phila., Infectious Disease Soc. of America, Am. Soc. of Internal Medicine, Pa. Soc. for Infectious Diseases, Am. Soc. of Microbiology. Office: Lankenau Medical Center MOB E Ste 164 100 Lancaster Ave Wynnewood PA 19096 Office Phone: 610-896-0210. Office Fax: 610-896-5101.

SANTOS, EDIL LUIS, biomedical researcher, educator; b. Curitiba, Parana, Brazil, Aug. 8, 1974; BSc, U. Fed. Rio de Janeiro, 1996, PhD, 2004. Adj. prof. Fed. U. Rio de Janeiro, 2008—. Mem.: Brazilian Soc. Biomed. Engring. Avocations: drawing, volleyball. Office: Federal University Rio de Janeiro PO Box 68 510 Rio de Janeiro 21945-970 Brazil Office Fax: 55 21 2562 8591. Business E-Mail: edil.luis@peb.ufrj.br.

SANTOS, ELMER BULURAN, nuclear medicine physician, nuclear scientist; b. Manila, Philippines, July 17, 1970; arrived in U.S., 1994; s. Vedasto Buluran Santos and Rosario Santiago Buluran-Santos. BS in Biology, U. Santo Tomas, Manila, 1987, MD, 1991; PhD in Cellular Molecular Pathology, U. Cambridge, Eng., 2000. Lic. Philippine Regulation Commn., 1992, Ednl. Commn. Fgn. Med. Grads., 1993, Fedn. State Med. Bds., 1993. Rotating intern Dept. Health-Jose Reyes Med. Ctr., Manila, 1991—92; med. intern Hosp. St. Raphael-Yale U. Sch. Medicine, New Haven, 1994—95; resident nuc. medicine Meml. Sloan-Kettering Cancer Ctr., N.Y. Hosp. Cornell Med. Ctr., NYC, 1995—97; chief resident Meml. Sloan-Kettering Cancer Ctr., NYC, 1996—97, fellow, 2001—03, rsch. assoc., 2003—. Coll. fellow Christ's Coll., U. Cambridge, 1999—2001, coll. lectr., 1999—2001, dir. studies in pathology, 1999—2000, admissions com. mem.; rsch. cons. Merck Pharmaceuticals, West Point, Pa., 1999—2000, Glaxo-Wellcome, Stevenage, England, 2000—01. Grantee, Glaxo-Wellcome, 1997—2000; fellow Nuc. Medicine, Meml. Sloan-Kettering Cancer Ctr., 1997, In-vivo Cellular and Molecular Imaging Ctr., 2001, Molecular Imaging Tng. in Oncology, 2003; Coll. Sci. Devel. Found. scholar, U. Santo Tomas, 1984—87, Cambridge Overseas Trust scholar, U. Cambridge, 1997—2000, Christ's Coll. scholar, 1997—2000. Achievements include research in HPV DNA Vaccine; Adoptive Immunotherapy; Radioimmunotherapy; Molecular Imaging. Avocations: piano, swimming, archery. Office: Meml Sloan-Kettering Cancer Ctr 1275 York Ave New York NY 10021

SANTOS, PAULO ROBERTO, physician, educator; b. Rio de Janeiro, Mar. 26, 1963; MD, Fluminense Fed. U., 1989; PhD in Med. Scis., Fed. U. Ceará, 2009. Assoc. prof. Sobral Sch. Medicine, Fed. U. Ceará, 2006—. Bd. dirs. Renal Unit Santa Casa Sobral Hosp., 1992. Recipient Patron award, Fed. U. Ceará. Mem.: Brazilian Soc. Nephrology. Home: Rua Tenente Amauri Pio 380 Apt 900 Fortaleza Ceará 60160090 Brazil Home Fax: 55-85-34611727.

SANTOS, RAUL D., physician; b. Sao Paulo, Brazil, Sept. 26, 1963; MD, Paulista Med. Sch., 1986; PhD, U. Sao Paulo, 1999. Dir. lipid clinic Heart Inst. Incor U. Sao Paulo, 2004—. Pres. Internat. Task Force Coronary Heart Disease Prevention-L.Am., 2005—06; mem. at large bd. dirs. Internat. Atherosclerosis Soc., 2010—; assoc. editor jour. clin. lipidology Nat. Lipid Assn., 2010. Recipient award, Astra Zeneca, BIMBO award, Bimbo Bakeries, Ignacio Chavez award, Interam. Soc. Cardiology. Mem.: European Atherosclerosis Soc. (assoc. editor atherosclerosis 2008), Sao Paulo Soc. Cardiology, Brazilian Soc. Cardiology (pres. dept. atherosclerosis 2010—11). Avocation: music. Office: Av Dr Eneas C Aguiar 44 Sao Paulo 05403900 Brazil Business E-Mail: raul.santos@incor.usp.br.

SANTOS, ROSEANE MAIA, pharmacist, educator; b. Rio de Janeiro, Nov. 17, 1954; d. Humberto Annibal and Maria Carlinda Maia Santos; 1 child, Cristiano Maia Lima. BS in Biochem. Pharmacy, Fed. U. Rio de Janeiro, 1979, M in Hosp. Pharmacy, 1990; PhD in Pharmaceutics, U. Buffalo, 2004—. Technician Bioanalysis Clin. Lab., Rio de Janeiro, 1977—79; tech. asst. Don Baxter Chem. Industry, Rio de Janeiro, 1981—82; sanitarist Ministry Health, Nat. Divsn. Drugs, Brazilia, 1982—83; hosp. pharmacist Fed. U. Rio de Janeiro, 1983—94, rsch. asst., 1984—91; head rschr. Inst. Clin. Pharmacology, Rio de Janeiro, 1986—91; asst. prof. U. Rio de Janeiro, 1994—. Contbr. articles to profl. jours. Mem.: Am. Assn. Pharm. Scientists. Office: Nova Southeastern Univ 3200 S Univ Dr Terry Bldg Office Room 1334 Fort Lauderdale FL 33328 Personal E-mail: roseane_santos@yahoo.com.

SANTOS, SILVIA REGINA CAVANI JORGE, pharmacist, educator; b. Sao Paulo, Feb. 18, 1948; Degree in Pharmacy and Biochemistry, U. Sao Paulo, 1972, PhD, 1982. Dir. rsch. lab. clin. pharmacokinetics Inst. Coracao Med. Sch. U. Sao Paulo, 1983—2001, prof. chair, pharmacokinetics pharmacotherapy pharmacy dept. Sch. Pharm. Sci., 1988—. Contbr. scientific papers. Recipient Best Sci. Presentation award, 2007. Fellow: Clin. Pharmacology Therapeutics Brazilian Soc. Avocations: music, travel, movies. Home: Perucaia 63 Sao Paulo 05578-070 Brazil Home Fax: +55 11 3091-2189. Personal E-mail: pharther@usp.br.

SANTOS, VITORINO MODESTO, physician; b. Uberaba, Minas Gerais, Brazil, Dec. 24, 1942; MD, Fed. U. Triângulo Mineiro, 1966, PhD, 2002. Preceptor, intern, med. residence program Health Sec. Brasília, 1969—94; adj. prof., internal medicine Fed. U. Triângulo Mineiro, 1994—2004; coord., internal medicine Cath. U. Brasília, 2004—. Adj. prof., internal medicine, preceptor, med. residence program Armed Forces Hosp., 2004. Office: Estrada do Contorno do Bosque Cruze Brasilia 70630-900 Brazil Office Fax: 55-61 32341367. E-mail: vitorinomodesto@gmail.com.

SANTOS-GUZMÁN, JESUS, research scientist, educator; b. Monterrey, Oct. 22, 1961; MD, Intituto Tecnológico y de Estudios Superiores Monterrey, 1989; PhD, UCLA, 2011. Prof., rschr. Intituto Tecnológico y de Estudios Superiores de Monterrey, 2004—. Office: Ave Morones Prieto #3000 Pte Col lo Monterrey Nuevo Leon 64710 Mexico Business E-Mail: jsg@itesm.mx.

SANTOSH, KOLANGARA VEETIL, medical educator; b. Kerala, India, Mar. 10, 1971; MBBS, Vijayanagar Inst. Med. Scis., Bellary, 1995, MD, 2000. Casualty med. officer Devamatha Hosp., Koothattukulam, Kerala, 1995—97; lectr. Sree Siddhartha Med. Coll., Tumkur, 2000—02; lectr., asst. prof. Vydehi Inst. Med. Scis. and Rsch. Ctr., Bangalore, 2002—06, assoc. prof., 2006—10, prof., 2010—. Cons. pathologist RV Metropolis Diagnostic Lab., Bangalore, 2002—11. Recipient Merit award, Edn. Dept. Govt. of Karnataka, 1987; Nat. scholarship, Ministry of Human Resource Devel., Govt. of India, 1987—88. Mem.: Indian Assn. Cytologists, Indian Assn. Pathologists and Microbiologists. Avocations: crossword puzzles, reading, computers. Home: 12 3rd Main Venkatamma Ramaiah Layout Bangalore Karnataka 560054 India Personal E-mail: santoshpath@yahoo.com.

SANTRA, AMBURANJAN, nuclear medicine physician; b. Jalbenti, West Bengal, India, Mar. 18, 1973; MBBS, R G Kar Med. Coll., Kolkata, 1996; MD in Nuclear Medicine, All India Inst. Med. Scis., New Delhi, 2009. Resident, dept. nuc. medicine and PET-CT All India Inst. Med. Scis., 2006—09; asst. prof., head, dept. nuc. medicine Med. Coll. & Hosp., Kolkata, 2009—. Recipient Young Scientist award, Asian Regional Coop. Coun. Nuc. Medicine; Nat. Merit scholarship, Govt. of India, Travel grant, 2010, CSIR, ICMR, 2010. Mem.: Soc. Nuc. Medicine. Avocations: sports, exercise, movies, music. Home: 3/3B Ballygunge Pl Ground Fl Kolkata West Bengal 700019 India Personal E-mail: a_ranjan_santra@yahoo.co.in.

SANTRA, GOURANGA, medical educator; b. Medinipur, West Bengal, India, Nov. 26, 1974; MBBS, NRS Med. Coll., Kolkata, 1997; MD, IPGME&R, 2003. Asst. prof. Med. Coll., Kolkata, 2005—. Recipient Bharat Jyoti award, IIFS, Glory of India Gold medal; Nat. scholarship, WB Secondary & Higher Secondary Bd. Mem.: IMA, IACM, RSSDI, API. Avocations: travel, music, reading. Home: P-306 Binayak Enclave 59 K C Ghosh Rd Kolkata West Bengal 700050 India Personal E-mail: g.santra@yahoo.com.

SANTUCCI, KAREN, pediatrician, director; b. NY, Sept. 25, 1962; BS, CMSV, 1984; MD, SUNY Downstate, 1989. Med. dir., sect. chief PEM, Yale Children's, 2007—. Office: 100 York St 1F New Haven CT 06511 Office Fax: 203-737-7447. Business E-Mail: karen.santucci@yale.edu.

SANZANA, EDGARDO SANTIAGO, orthopedic surgeon, educator; b. Concepcion, Chile, Sept. 11, 1957; s. Santiago Sanzana and Raquel Salamanca. MD, U. Concepcion, 1981; MSC in Orthopaedic Surgery, Austral U. of Chile, Valdivia, 1989; PhD Outstanding Cum Laude, U. Barcelona, Spain, 2004. Cert. orthopedic surgeon Chile. Orthopedic surgeon; gen. practitioner Gen. Hosp., Concepcion, 1982—86; resident orthopedic surgery Univ. Hosp., Valdivia, 1987—89; orthopedic surgeon Hosp. del Trabajador, Concepcion, 1990—2000; fellow arthroscopy surgery Hosp. Clinic, Barcelona, Catalonia, 2001—04; asst. prof. orthopedic surgery U. of Concepcion, 1995; sr. orthopedic surgeon Hosp. del Trabajador, Concepcion, 2005. Mem.: So. Chilean Soc. Orthopedic Surgery, Med. Soc. of Santiago (corr.), Latin Am. Soc. of Arthroscopy (corr.), Spanish Soc. of Orthopedic Surgery (corr.; gen. sec. 1997—98, pres. 2000), Chilean Soc. of Surgeons (corr.), Chilean Soc. of Orthopedic Surgery (corr.). Business E-Mail: esanzana@udec.cl.

SANZ-DE-BRUGOA, VERONICA, physician; b. Madrid, May 13, 1965; MD, 1991. With med. dept. Sigma-Tau, 1992—93; med. advisor Pfizer Spain, 1995—. Recipient Rsch. San Lucas award, Med. Assn. Seville; grantee, Puerta De Hierro Hosp., Madrid, Newton-Wellesley Hosp., Newton, Mass. Avocations: reading, opera. Home: Costa Brava 18 8J Madrid 28034 Spain Personal E-mail: lorenzo.jose@telefonica.net.

SANZ-DE-BURGOA, VERONICA, physician; b. Madrid, May 13, 1965; MD, Sch. Medicine Seville, 1990. Mem. med. dept. SIGMA-TAU, 1992—93; CRA PFIZER, 1995—96, med. advisor, 1996—. Grant, Med. Assn. Seville, 1991, Puarta De Hierro Hosp., Madrid, Newton-Wellesley Hosp., Mass. Avocations: opera, reading. Home: Costa Brava 18 8°J Madrid 28034 Spain Personal E-mail: veronica.sanz.de.burgoa@pfizer.com.

SAPEGA, ALEXANDER A., sports medicine physician, orthopedic surgeon; BS with distinction, Cornell U., 1975; MD, Temple U., Havertown, Pa., 1980. Diplomate Am. Bd. Orthopaedic Surgery; lic. physician, Kanstown, Pa., Mt. Laural, N.J. Intern, residency, fellowship U. Pa. Sch. of Medicine, Phila., 1982-85; fellow in sports medicine Temple U., Phila., 1985-86; asst. instr. orthopaedic surgery U. Pa. Sch. Medicine, Phila., 1982-85; clin. instr. orthopaedic surgery Temple U. Sch. Medicine, Phila., 1985-86; asst. prof. U. Pa. Sch. Medicine, Phila., 1986-92; asst. prof., clin. educator Hosp. U. Pa., Phila., 1992-95, assoc. prof., clin. educator, 1995—97; dir. post-grad. fellowship Knee Surgery Program Hosp. U. Pa., Phila., 1995—97; chief sports medicine svc. Hosp. U. Pa., Phila., 1995—97. Faculty lectr. for symposia and ednl. groups; invited lectr. to med. and sci. meetings. 1983—; clin. rsch. assoc. Inst. of Sports Medicine and Athletic Trauma, 1975-76; attending surg. staff Dept. Orthopaedic Surgery, Temple U., Phila., 1985-86; attending staff dept. orthopaedic surgery Hosp. Univ. Pa., Phila, 1986-97, dept. orthopaedic surgery The Grad. Hosp., Phila, 1986-92; chief of sports medicine svc., Phila. VA Hosp., 1986-92; attending staff dept. orthopaedic surgery, Mt. Sinai Hosp., Phila., 1989-92, dir. U. Pa. Sports Medicine Ctr., Phila., 1995-97, pvt. practice, 1997. Contbr. over 40 articles to profl. jours. including Am. Jour. Bone and Joint Surgery, Am. Jour Sports Medicine, Jour. Orthopaedic Rsch.; also revs., monographs and chpts. in books; mem. edtl. bd. Am. Jour. Knee Surgery, 1988-95. Post Grad. Advances in Sports Medicine, 1988-91; cons. reviewer Medicine and Sci. in Sports and Exercise, 1983-86, The Am. Jour. of Bone and Joint Surgery, 1988-95, Jour. of Orthopaedic Rsch., 1988-91; mem. editl. bd. for rsch., Am. Jour. Bone and Joint Surgery, 1990-99; inventor: Apparatus for Reconstructive Knee Ligament Surgery, 1988, Method for Reconstructive Knee Ligament Surgery, 1990. Mem. Orthop. Rsch. Soc., 1991—2008. Recipient N. Am. Traveling fellowship Am. Orthopaedic Assn.; grantee: NIH, 1982-85, VA, 1985-86, 88-90. Advanced Tech. Ctr. S.E. Pa., 1986. Fellow Am. Acad. Orthpaedic

Surgeons (Elizabeth Winston Lanier Kappa Delta award 1986); mem. Arthroscopy Assn. N.Am. Office: NJ Knee and Shoulder Ctr 1288 Rte 73 S Ste 100 Mount Laurel NJ 08054 Office Phone: 856-273-8900.

SAPER, JOEL R., neurologist, educator; b. Joliet, Ill., Feb. 6, 1943; s. Leonard and Jeanette (Kristal) S.; children: Lisa, Justin, Lauren. BS in History, U. Wis., 1965; MD, U. Ill., Chgo., 1969. Diplomate Am. Bd. Psychiatry and Neurology, Am. Bd. Pain Medicine, diplomate headache bd. United Coun. Neucological Subspecialists, 2006. Intern Michael Reese Hosp., Chgo., 1969-70; resident U. Mich. Med. Ctr., Ann Arbor, 1970-73; instr. U. Mich. Med. Sch., Ann Arbor, 1973-75, asst. prof., 1975-78; founder, dir. Mich. Head Pain and Neurol. Inst., Ann Arbor, 1978—; dir. Head Pain Treatment Program, Chelsea, Mich., 1978—; clin. prof. neurology Mich. State U., Lansing, 1989—. Author: Freedom from Headaches, 1978, Soft Back Edition, 1981, Consumer Report Edition, 1981, Clinical and Basic Neurology for Health Professionals, 1981;: Help for Headaches, 1983, Headache Disorders, 1983, Controversies and Clinical Variants of Migraine, 1987, Handbook of Headache Management, 1992, 2nd edition, Handbook of Headache Management, 1999; Topics in Pain Mgmt., 1985—2001; contbr. chapter to book. Chair physicians' subcom. State of Mich. House Health Care Task Force, 1993-94; chair Mich. Coun. on Pain, 1995-96; nat. chmn. Pain Care Coalition, 1995-. Recipient John Graham Sr. Clinician award, Am. Headache Soc., 1995, Phillip M. Lippe MD award, 1996. Fellow: ACP; mem.: Am. Coun. on Headache Edn. (chmn. 1994—95), Am. Pain Soc. (cons. to bd. 1992—), Am. Headache Soc. (pres. 1992—94, bd. mem.), Am. Acad. Neurology (cdn. com. 1992—), Am. Acad. Pain Medicine (bd. mem. 1992, 1998—). Office: Mich Head Pain and Neurol Inst 3120 Professional Dr Ann Arbor MI 48104-5131

SAPHIR, RICHARD LOUIS, pediatrician; b. NYC, May 1, 1933; s. Samuel and Grace (Greenberg) Saphir; m. Judith Schwartz, Dec. 6, 1958; 1 child, Steven. BA, NYU, 1954; MD, SUNY, NYC, 1958. Diplomate Nat. Bd. Med. Examiners, Am. Bd. Pediat. Asst. attending pediatrician Mt. Sinai Hosp., NYC, 1965—71, asst dir., pediat. acute care clinic, 1970—78, 1971—82, assoc. clin. prof. pediat., 1982—88, attending pediatrician, 1982—; chief, pediatric svcs. U.S. Naval Hosp., Newport, RI, 1967—69; clin. prof. pediat. Mt. Sinai Sch. Medicine, NYC, 1988—. Bd. dirs. Mt. Sinai Children's Ctr. Found., NYC, 1987—. Contbr. articles to profl. jours. Chmn. cmty. and adv. com. N.Y.C. Info. and Counseling Program for Sudden Infant Death Syndrome, 1979—81; med. bd. YMHA, NYC, 1982—86. Comdr. USNR, 1967—69. Fellow: NY County Med. Soc. (vice chmn. com. child welfare 1974—85), NY Pediat. Soc. (pres. 1978—79), Am. Acad. Pediats. (com. sci. meetings 1985—97, chmn. prep course 1991—96, editl. adv. bd. Continuing Med. Edn. audiotapes 1991—2001, ednl. program rep. ambulatory care quality improvement program 1992—2002, ednl. advisor proficiency testing program 1996—99, editl. bd. Pediat. in Rev. 1997—2003, ednl. adv. Uniformed Svcs. pediat. seminar 1997—2010, mem. super cont. med. edn. planning com. 2000—08, chmn super cont. med. edn. planning com. 2002—06, com. on continuing med. edn. 2002—06, editl. bd. Pediat. 2009—), NY Acad. Medicine (treas. 1987—89) Office: BSM Pediatrics PC 55 E 87th St New York NY 10128-1043 Office Phone: 212-722-4950.

SAPORITO, FRANCESCO, cardiologist, researcher; b. Messina, Italy, May 9, 1959, s. Santo Saporito and Antonina Marino, m. Rosa Maria Puglisi, Apr. 9, 1988; children: Fabrizio, Isabella. Medicine, U. Messina, Italy, 1983. Rschr. dr., cardiologist Azienda Ospedaliera U., Messina, 1987—. Contbr. scientific papers (Best Commn. Poster, 1999). Local councillor Commune of Messina, 1998—2003. Roman Catholic. Avocations: travel, gym, movies, English study. Office: Azienda Ospedaliera Univ Via Consolare Valeria 98124 Messina ME Italy E-mail: francosaporito@tiscali.it.

SAPORTA, JACK, retired psychologist, educator; b. NYC, Oct. 21, 1927; s. David and Victoria (Fils) S.; m. Judith Hammond, May 28, 1967 (div. 1979); children: David J., Victoria G. Johnson. AB cum laude, Adelphi U., 1951; PhD, U. Chgo., 1962. Diplomate Am. Bd. Profl. Psychology; lic. clin. psychologist. Pvt. practice, 1962-99; supt. Tinley Park (Ill.) Mental Health Ctr., 1975-78; chief manpower tng. and devel. Ill. Dept. Mental Health, Chgo., 1978-82; dean, prof. Forest Inst. Profl. Psychology, Des Plaines, Ill., 1982-85; mem. faculty Fielding Grad. U., Santa Barbara, Calif., 1984—2005, Ill. Sch. Profl. Psychology, Chgo., 1985-97; doctoral psychologist, emeritus Luth. Gen. Hosp. Mem. adj. faculty psychology Lake Forest Grad. Sch. Mgmt., 1987-97; mem. Ill. State Clin. Psychology Lic. and Disciplinary Com., Springfield, 1984-93; profl. staff Forest Hosp., Des Plaines, 1977-96; mem. attending doctoral profl. staff Luth. Gen. Hosp., Park Ridge, Ill., 1986-2000, emeritus, 2000—; founding dean Forest Inst. Profl. Psychology; founding pres. Psy Chi Hon., Adelphi U. Served with US Army, 1946—47, Germany. Named Educator of Yr., Forest Inst., 1982, Outstanding Faculty Mem. Lake Forest Grad. Sch. Mgmt. Fellow Acad. Clin. Psychology, NTL-Inst. (faculty); mem. APA (accreditation site vis. team 1990-2000), Ill. Psychol. Assn., Chgo. Psychol. Assn. (mem. exec. bd., Cert. of Recognition 1999). Avocations: tennis, computers, do-it-yourself home projects. Home: 13077 Stone Creek Court Huntley IL 60142

SAR, VEDAT, psychiatrist, educator, researcher; b. Istanbul, Turkey, June 23, 1955; s. Mehmet Cavit and Muazzez (Barut) S.; m. Ilknur Özütemiz, Oct. 24, 1983; 1 child, Meric. MD, Istanbul U., 1981; postgrad., Hacettepe U., Ankara, Turkey, 1986. Resident in psychiatry Hacettepe Univ. Medical Faculty Hosp., Ankara, 1981-86; attending psychiatrist Gümüssuyu Mil. Hosp., Istanbul, 1987-88, Sagmalcilar Correctional Ctr. Hosp., Istanbul, 1988-89; fellow Cerrahpasa Medical Faculty Istanbul U., Istanbul, 1989-90, assoc. prof. psychiatry, 1990-92, Istanbul Med. Faculty U., Istanbul, 1992-96; prof. psychiatry Istanbul U., Istanbul, 1996—. Dir. Clinical Psychotherapy Unit, 1993— Istanbul Med. Faculty Hosp., Dissociative Disorders Program, 1994—. Contbr. articles to profl. jours. Recipient David Caul Meml. award, Internat. Soc. Study of Dissociation, 1995, 99, Morton Prince award, 2001, 10, Cornelia Wilbur award, 2004. Mem. Am. Psychiat. Assn. (internat. mem. and adv. DSM-V task force, 2009), Internat. Soc. Study Trauma and Dissociation (pres. 2007-08), European Soc. Traumatic Stress Studies. Office: Istanbul Tip Fakultesi Psikiyatri Klinigi Capa 34390 Istanbul Turkey Business E-Mail: vsar@istanbul.edu.tr.

SARABU, RAMAKANTH, biochemist; b. India, June 20, 1955; PhD, Indian Inst. Tech., Chennai, 1984. Project leader in metabolic, inflammation and virology areas Roche, sr. rsch. leader, 1989—. Mem.: Am. Chem. Soc. Office: 340 Kingsland St Nutley NJ 07110 Business E-Mail: ramakanth.sarabu@roche.com.

SARACEVIC, TEFKO, information science educator; married; 2 children. MS in Libr. Sci., Case Western Reserve U., 1962, PhD in Info. Sci., 1970. Prof. comm., info. and libr. studies Rutgers U., New Brunswick, NJ. Editor-in-chief: Info. Processing and Mgmt., 1985—. Avocations: reading, skiing. Office: Rutgers U Sch Comm Info & Libr Studies 4 Huntington St New Brunswick NJ 08901-1071 Office Phone: 732-932-7500 Ext. 8222. E-mail: tefko@scils.rutgers.edu.

SARAFIDIS, PANTELIS, nephrologist, clinical hypertension specialist, clinical researcher; s. Anastasios Sarafidis and Maria Sarafidou. MD, Sch. Medicine, Aristotle U. Thessaloniki, 2000, PhD, 2005; MSc in Health Units' Adminstrn., Hellenic Open U., Patrae, Greece, 2006. Cert. med. dr. Prefecture Halkidiki, Hellenic Republic, 2000. Physician, rschr. and jr. lectr. sect. nephrology & hypertension, dept. medicine AHEPA Hosp., Aristotle U. Thessaloniki, 2006—10; rsch. fellow Rush U. Med. Ctr., Chicago, 2005—06. Cons. physician Pharm. Co., Thessaloniki, 2006—08. Contbr. articles to profl. jours. Recipient Several awards, European Soc. Hypertension, Jiri Widmisky Sr. award, ESH and ISH, 2008; grants, Am. Soc. Hypertension, Rsch. fellow, Hellenic Soc. Hypertension. Mem.: Several Nat. and Internat. Med. Socs. Office: AHEPA Hosp Aristotle Univ St Kiriakidi 1 Thessaloniki 546 36 Greece Business E-Mail: psarafidis11@yahoo.gr.

SARAO, LOVELEEN KAUR, research scientist; b. New Delhi, Sept. 19, 1984; PhD, Punjab Agrl. U., Ludhiana, India. Rsch. scholar Punjab Agrl. U., 2008—. Lectr. APS Coll. Nursing, 2007—08; mem. numerous Internat. Conf. Contbr. articles to profl. publs. Mem.: Indian Soc. Agr. Engrs. Avocations: reading, languages. Home: 36-C BRS Nagar Ludhiana Punjab 141002 India Personal E-mail: loveleen_sarao84@yahoo.com.

SARAVANAN, R., lab administrator; b. Dharmapuri, Andhra Pradesh, India, June 5, 1977; PhD, 1998. Screening bioactive compounds nature Micro Lab., Bangalore, 2011—. Office: Annamalai University CAS Faculty Marine Biology Parangipettai Tamil Nadu 608502 India Personal E-mail: saran_prp@yahoo.com.

SARAVO, ANNE COBBLE, clinical psychologist, mental health consultant; b. Atlanta, Feb. 23, 1938; d. William Edwin and Iris Benny (Norman) Cobble; m. James Vincent Saravo, Sept. 27, 1958 (dec.); children: Stacy Anne Nathan, Lisa Ames Furmanek. BA, Tex. Tech. U., 1959, MS, U. Mass., 1964, PhD, 1965, postgrad., Regional Health Authority, London, 1978-79, U. So. Calif., 1980-81. Lic. psychologist, Calif., Ga., SC. Assoc. prof. psychology Antioch Coll., Yellow Springs, Ohio, 1966-69; cons. Winchester (Eng.) Day Treatment Nursery Sch., 1971-73; sch. psychologist Muroc Unified Sch. Dist., Edwards AFB, Calif., 1974-75; clinical psychologist Antelope Valley Hosp., Lancaster, Calif., 1975-76, Farnborough Hosp., Kent, Eng., 1978-80, Orange County Mental Health Svc., Calif., 1981—97, chief adult out-patient svc., 1984-87, chief adult inpatient svcs., 1987-95; pvt. practice clin. psychology Seal Beach, Calif., 1981, Atlanta, 2004—, Beaufort, SC, 2007—; program mgr. Medi-Cal Inpatient Managed Care, 1995-97; med. advisor Medicare, Calif. Nat. Heritage Ins. Corp., 1995—2010. Bd. dirs. High Hopes Neurol. Recover Group, Costa Mesa, Calif., chair profl. adv. bd., 1988-2001; oral examination commr. Calif. Bd. Psychology, 1989-1999; geriatric coord. Orange County Mental Health Svcs., 1985-87; profl. adv. bd. Orange County Caregiver Resource Ctr., 1989-1999; mem. Alzheimers Disease rev. panel Calif. Dept. Mental Health, 1990-91; expert reviewer Calif. Bd. Psychology, Med. Bd. Calif., 2000—2010; invited spkr. in field. Contbr. articles to profl. jours. Chairperson Conf. Geriatric Mental Health, Asilomar, Calif., 1986, So. Calif. Geriatric Mental Health Coordinators, 1985-87; vol. disaster mental health team Red Cross, 2001-; bd. dirs., Citizens Opposed Domestic Abuse, 2010, Living with Covenants Com. Dataw Island, 2009-11, pianist Beaufort Orch., 2004-05; performer TCU, Van Cliburn Inst., 2004-05; piano recital Beaufort Orch. League Benefit, 2009. U.S. Pub. Health fellow Fels Research Inst., 1966-67. Mem. APA, Calif. Psychol. Assn. (chair medicare/pub. sector subcom. 1990-96, co-chair reimbursement and managed care com. 1996-97, bd. dirs. divsn. pvt. practice 1998), Ga. Psychol. Assn. (mem. legislative com. 2003-09), SC Psychol. Assn., Nat. Acad. Neuropsychology (grad.), Brit. Psychol. Soc., Gerontol. Soc. Am. Avocation: piano. Home Phone: 865-657-9667; Office Phone: 770-597-3261. Personal E-mail: chateaucobble@yahoo.com.

SARAVOLATZ, LOUIS DONALD, epidemiologist, medical educator; b. Detroit, Feb. 15, 1950; s. Samuel and Saya Betty (Chonich) S.; m. Yvette Susanne Braymer, Oct. 6, 1990; children: Samuel Francis, Louis Donald II, Stephanie Nicole. BS, U. Mich., Ann Arbor, 1972, MD, 1974. Fellow Am. Coll. Epidemiology. Intern Henry Ford Hosp., Detroit, 1974-75, 1975-77, fellow, 1977-79, dir. hosp. epidemiology, 1979-82, divsn. head infectious diseases, 1982-96, dir. infectious diseases rsch. lab., 1982-96; prof. medicine Case-Western Res. U., 1993-96, Wayne State U. Sch. Medicine, Detroit, 1996—. Clin. prof. medicine U. Mich. Med. Sch., Ann Arbor, 1986-96; mem. AIDS clin. drug devel. com. NIH, 1990-95; chmn. dept. internal medicine St. John Hosp. and Med. Ctr., 1996—. Contbr. over 170 articles to profl. publs. Active Blue Ribbon Com. on AIDS State of Mich., Detroit, 1990; chmn. physician com. on AIDS Greater Detroit Health Coun., 1989. Master: ACP, Am. Coll. Physicians; fellow: Royal Soc. Medicine (London), Infectious Diseases Soc. Am. (chmn. antimicrobial use and clin. trials com. 2000—03). Office Phone: 313-343-3362. Business E-Mail: louis.saravolatz@stjohn.org.

SARELA, ABEEZAR I., surgeon, consultant; b. Bombay, Dec. 22, 1965; s. Ismail and Khadija Sarela; m. Ibtisam Tapia, Aug. 16, 1997; 1 child, Shazia. MBBS, U. Bombay, 1989, MS in Gen. Surgery, 1993; MSc in Surg. Sci., U. London, 1996. Cert. Ednl. Commn. for Foriegn Med. Grads. US, 1990, specialist tng. gen. tng. Royal Coll. Surgeons, 2002, Fellow Royal Coll. Sugreons (FRCS) Intercollegiate Bd. Gen. Surgery. Resident, lectr. in surgery King Edward VII Meml. Hosp., Bombay, 1990—95; registrar Hammersmith Hosp., London, 1995—96; registrar in surgery Ashford Hosp., London, 1996—97; lectr., sr. registrar in surgery St. James's U. Hosp., Leeds, England, 1997—2001; internat. fellow in surg. oncology Meml. Sloan Kettering Cancer Ctr., NYC, 2001—03; cons. surgeon, sr. lectr. in surgery Leeds Tchg. Hosps. U. Leeds, 2003—. Mem. Royal Coll. Surgeons, 1995—; clin. rschr. Leeds Gen. Infirmary, 2003—, U. Leeds, 2003—. Contbr. articles to profl. jours. Recipient Best Paper award, Soc. Surg. Oncology, 2000; grantee Rsch. grant, Yorkshire Cancer Rsch., 1999. Fellow: Royal Coll. Surgeons, Soc. Surg. Oncology (corr.). Achievements include research in metastatic gastrointestinal cancer; Barrett's esophagus; lymphadenectomy for gastric and duodenal cancer; laparoscopic adrenalectomy; high grade dysplasia; staging laparoscopy and apoptosis in cancer; advanced and revisional laparoscopic surgery for cancer and obesity. Avocations: reading, travel. Office: Gen Infirmary at Leeds Great George Street LS1 3EX Leeds England Office Fax: 44113 3922788. Business E-Mail: abeezar.sarela@leedsth.nhs.uk.

SAREMBOCK, IAN JOSEPH, internist, cardiologist; b. Cape Town, South Africa, June 9, 1951; arrived in US, 1986, naturalized, 1994; m. Ghita Marueen Sarembock; children: Craig Murray, Kerri Lauren. MD, U. Cape Town, 1975, PhD, 1988. Diplomate Am. Bd. Internal Medicine, Am. Bd. Cardiovasc. Medicine, Am. Bd. Interventional Cardiology. Sr. house officer dept. internal medicine U. Cape Town and Groote Schuur Hosp., Cape Town, 1979-80, resident in internal medicine, 1980-83, sr. registrar Cardiac Clinic, 1985-86; Velva Schrire meml. rsch. fellow Cardiac Clinic Groote Schur Hosp., 1983-85; postdoctoral rsch. assoc. divsn. cardiology Yale U., New Haven, 1986-88; attending cardiologist divsn. cardiology VA Ctr., West Haven, Conn., 1987-88; asst. prof. internal medicine cardiovasc. divsn. U. Va. Health Scis. Ctr., Charlottesville, 1988-93, assoc. prof. internal medicine cardiovasc. divsn., 1993-99, dir. coronary care unit, 1988—2007, prof. internal medicine cardiovasc. divsn., 1999—2007; interventional cardiologist, 1988—2007; cardiology cons. Salem VA Med. Ctr., Va., 1988—2000; dir. Ctr. Interventional Cardiology, U. Va. Health System, 2005—07, Ohio Heart & Vascular Ctr., Cin., 2007—. Lectr., presenter in field; invited prof. Heart-Lung Inst., Utrecht, Netherlands, 1992; mem. faculty restenosis summits, Cleve. Clinic, 1992, 93, 97. Contbr. articles to profl. publs. Mem. policy working com., house staff supervision Commonwealth of Va., 1990-2007. With South African Def. Force, Med. Corps, 1977—78. Grantee U. Va. Sch. Medicine, 1989, Beecham Labs., 1989-90, Am. Heart Assn., 1989-91, 91-92, 95-98, NIH, 1991-94, 2000-05; named Harrison Disting. Tchg. Prof. Internal Medicine, 2006-07. Fellow ACP, Coll. Physicians South Africa, Am. Coll. Cardiology (allied health profls. com. 1993—), Coun. Thrombosis Atherosclerosis and Vascular Biology, Soc. Catheterization & Intervention; mem. AAAS, Am. Heart Assn. (bd. dirs. Charlottesville/Albermarle divsn. 1991—, mem. Va. affiliate rsch. peer rev. subcom. 1992—, thrombosis coun. 1987, fellow coun. on clin. cardiology 1989), South African Med. and Dental Coun. Jewish. Office: Ohio Heart Vascular Ctr 4750 E Galbraith Rd Ste 103 Cincinnati OH 45236 Office Phone: 513-985-0022. E-mail: sarembock@ohioheart.org.

SARESELLA, MARINA, research scientist; b. Milan, June 24, 1961; PhD, U. Milano, 1987. Fondazione don c gnocchi onlus Rsch. Inst., 1988—. Office: Via Capecelatro 66 Milan 20148 Italy Business E-Mail: msaresella@dongnocchi.it.

SARGENT, ARLENE ANNE, nursing educator; b. Little Falls, Minn, Jan. 11, 1944; d. Anton Clarence and Eleanor Anne (Buerman) Hondl; m. Ken William Sargent, June 16, 1972; children: Lisa, Michelle. BSN, Coll. St. Catherine, 1969; MSN, U. Minn., 1972; EdD, No. Ill. U., 1980. Staff nurse U. Wash., Seattle, 1969-70, U. Minn. Hosp., Mpls., 1970-72; instr. Loyola U., Chgo., 1972-75; asst. prof. U. Dubuque, Iowa, 1975-76, assoc. prof., chairperson, 1976-79; assoc. prof. No. Ill. U., DeKalb, 1979-83; prof., chairperson Holy Names Coll., Oakland, Calif., 1983-98; assoc. dean St. Mary's-Samuel Merritt Intercollegiate Nursing Program, Oakland, Calif., 1999—2004, dean nursing program, 2000—04; mng. dir. for edn. and workforce Kaiser Permanente, Oakland, Calif., 2004—07; assoc. dean academic affairs Samuel Merritt U., Oakland, Calif., 2007. Bd. mem. Calif. Strategic Planning Commn., 1993—, John Muir Physicians Network. Mem. Sigma Theta Tau (mem. heritage com. 1994—), Pi Lambda Theta, Kappa Delta Pi. Presbyterian. Avocations: playing piano, hiking. Office: Samuel Merritt University 3100 Summit St Oakland CA 94609 Personal E-mail: sargentak@gmail.com. Business E-Mail: asargent@samuelmerritt.edu.

SARGENT, JOHN, psychiatrist; b. Mar. 27, 1947; MD, U. Rochester, 1973. Diplomate in psychiatry, child and adolescent psychiatry Am. Bd. Psychiatry and Neurology; diplomate Am. Bd. Pediats.; approved clin. supr. Am. Assn. Marriage and Family Therapy. Intern and resident pediat. U. Wis., Madison, 1973—77; resident child and adolescent psychiatry Phila. Child Guidance Ctr., 1978—80; resident gen. psychiatry Hosp. U. Pa., Phila., 1984—87; dir. child and adolescent psychiatry U. Pa. Med. Sch., 1989—97, dir. adult residency program, 1989—97; mem. staff Children's Hosp. Phila., Phila. Child Guidance Ctr., 1980—97; dir. edn. and rsch., dean Karl Menninger Sch. Psychiatry & Mental Health Svcs., Topeka, 1997—2001; prof. psychiatry Baylor Coll. Medicine, Houston, 2001—08; dir., divsn. child and adolescent psychiatry Ben Taub Hosp., Houston, 2001—08, Tufts Med. Ctr., 2008—; prof. psychiatry and pediats. Tufts U. Sch. Medicine, 2009—. Assoc. prof. psychiatry and pediat. U. Pa. Med. Sch., 1987-97; Pfeiffer/Adams prof. psychiatry Karl Menninger Sch. Psychiatry. Mem. editl. bd. Jour. Am. Acad. Child and Adolescent Psychiatry, Family Process, Bull. of Menninger Clinic; co-author: Madness, Chaos and Violence: Therapy with Families at the Brink; co-editor: Primary Care Pediatrics; contbr. over 60 articles to profl. jours. Dep. dir. Ea. European Child Abuse and Child Mental Health Program, Soros Found. and Children's Mental

Health Alliance, 1997-2003. Office: Tufts Medical Center Dept of Psychiatry 800 Washington St Box 1007 Boston MA 02111 Home Phone: 781-259-0667; Office Phone: 617-636-8768. Business E-Mail: jsargent@tuftsmedicalcenter.org.

SARI, YAVUZ SELIM, surgeon; b. Osmaniye, Turkey, June 1, 1961; s. Hamza and Fatma Sari; m. Demet Bayram, Jan. 28, 1989; children: Yuksel Asli, Orhan Selcuk. MD, Cukurova U., Adana, 1986. Cert. gen. surgeon SB Istanbul Tng. Hosp., 1993. Gen. practice Saglik Bakanligi, Sinop, Turkey, 1986—88, asst. gen. surgeon. Contbr. articles to profl. publ. Achievements include research in surgical technique. Office: SB Istanbul Egitim Hastanesi Fahrettin Koraltan Istanbul 34310 Turkey Office Fax: 90 212 3251742. Personal E-mail: yssari@hotmail.com.

SARIC, MARKO, physician, consultant; b. June 22, 1924; s. Dragutin and Pina (Kurilic) S.; m. Sonja Bartulica, Mar. 12, 1957 (dec. 1981); m. Biserka Bujas, 1983; 1 child, Lana. MD, U. Zagreb, Croatia, 1951, PhD, 1959. Physician Univ. Hosp., Zagreb, 1952-57; rschr. Inst. for Med. Rsch. and Occupl. Health, U. Zagreb, 1957-64, dir. of Inst., 1964-91, prof. occupl. health, 1964—. Cons. WHO, Geneva; mem. Parliament Assembly of Yugoslavia, Belgrade, 1965-67; chmn. Council Health and Social Welfare, Parliament, Republic of Croatia, Zagreb, 1967-74. Author: Occupational Health, 1962; co-author: Pathology of Work—Occupational Diseases in Mining, Industry and Agriculture, 1964, Occupational Medicine, 1978, 84, Working Ability, 1984; editor: Assessment of Temporary Disability, 1982, Occupational and Environmental Health, 2002; contbr. articles to sci. jours. Recipient award City of Zagreb, City Coun. Zagreb, 1967, 1978, Ruder Boskovic award Republic Com. Sci., Tech. and Informatics of Republic of Croatia, 1977, US EPA medal, 1980, award Antifascist Coun. Nat. Liberation of Yugoslavia, Fed. Assembly of Yugoslavia, 1983, Croation Nat. Life Achievement Biomedical Scis. award, 2000, Disting. award Commn. Internat. Occupl. Health, 2006. Mem. Acad. Med. Scis. Croatia (laureate 2002), Croatian Acad. Scis. and Arts, Permanent Commn. and Internat. Assn. Occupl. Health (bd. dirs. 1978-84), Yugoslav Assn. Occupl. Health (pres. 1969-74, bd. dirs. 1978-83), Med. Assn. Croatia (pres. sect. occupl. health 1974-91), NY Acad. Sci., Am. Occupl. Med. Assn. Office: Inst Med Rsch/Occupl Health Ksaverska Cesta 2 10000 Zagreb Croatia Home: Radicevo Setaliste 27 10-000 Zagreb Croatia Office Phone: 385 01 4673188. Business E-Mail: marko@imi.hr.

SARICI, SERDAR UMIT, neonatologist; b. Agri, Turkey, May 2, 1966; s. Niyazi and Fatma Sarici. MD, Gulhane Med. Faculty, Ankara, Turkey, 1990. Practitioner Turkish Army, Ankara, 1991—93; pediatrician Gulhane Mil. Med. Acad., Ankara, 1993—2000, neonatologist, 2000—, asst. prof. pediat., 2002—04, assoc. prof. pediat., 2004—10, chief divsn. neonatology, 2005—, prof. pediat., 2010—. Adv. bd. Turkish Jour., Ankara, 2004—; adv. bd., reviewer Pediat., 2004—. Editor: Gulhane Med. Jour., 2005—; contbr. articles to profl. jours. Recipient Sci. award, Bayindir Hosp., 2005, TUBITAK, 2006. Mem.: Sci. & Technol. Rsch. Council Turkey, Turkish Neonatology Soc. Avocation: jogging. Office: Gulhane Mil Med Acad Dept Pediat Etlik Ankara 06018 Turkey Home: Soyer Sokak 8/3 Incirli Kecioren 06290 Ankara Ankara Turkey Office Phone: 90 312 304 4397, 90 312 430 4350, 90 530 885 2015. Business E-Mail: s.umitsarici@tr.net, umit@umitsarici.com.

SARIOGLU, TAYYAR, cardiovascular surgeon; b. Gaziantep, Turkey, Apr. 19, 1951; s. Ali and Necmiye Sarioglu; m. Ayse Isin, Sept. 17, 1978; children: Hande, Omer. MD, Ankara U., Turkey, 1974. Cardiovasc. surgery trainee Hacettepe U., Ankara, 1974—79, assoc. prof., 1984; cardiovasc. fellow Klokkenberg, Netherlands, 1984; spl. cardiovasc. fellow U. Ala., Birmingham, 1985—86; prof. Istanbul (Turkey) U., 1987—2000; dir. cardiovasc. surgery dept. Inst. Cardiology Istanbul U., 1995—2000; founder, gen. dir. Istanbul Meml. Hosp., project and mgmt. leader, 1996—2003; chief cardiovasc. dept. Acibadem Hosp. Bakirkoy, Istanbul, 2003—; prof., chief, dept. cardiovasc. surgery Acibadem U., Istanbul. Editor: (textbook) Cardiovascular Surgery, Jour. Turkish Thoracic and Cardiovascular Surgery, 1992—97; contbr. more than 120 study pubs. Active Turkish Heart Found., Istanbul, 1990; pres., founder Istanbul Cardiac Surgery Found., 1995. Fullbright scholar, 1984. Mem.: AAAS, Turkish Soc. Pediat. Cardiology, Turkish Soc. Cardiology, European Soc. Cardiology, Turkish Cardiovasc. Soc., European Cardio-Thoracic Surgery Soc., NY Acad. Sci. Achievements include development of newborn and complex cardiac surgery program in Turkey, 1986-90. Office: Acibadem Hosp Bakirkoy Halit Ziya Usakligil Cad 1 34140 Bakirkoy Turkey Home: Atakoy Konaklari A 7 Bakirkoy Istanbul Turkey Office Phone: 90 212 4144408. Personal E-mail: atsarioglu@hotmail.com. E-mail: tsarioglu@asg.com.tr.

SARKAR, JAYANTA, medical researcher; b. Kolkata, India, July 2, 1978; B in Vet. Sci., West Bengal U. Animal and Fishery Scis., AH, 2000; PhD, Indian Vet. Rsch. Inst., 2006. Scientist Ctrl. Drug Rsch. Inst., Lucknow, India, 2006—. Young Scientists fellow, Dept. Sci. and Tech., Govt. of India, 2010. Mem.: Am. Assn. Cancer Rsch. Office: DTDD Divsn Ctrl Drug Rsch Inst Lucknow Uttar Pradesh 226001 India Business E-Mail: j_sarkar@cdri.res.in.

SARKAR, RASHMI, dermatologist, educator; b. Lucknow, Uttar Pradesh, India, Sept. 20, 1967; d. Asim Kumar and Chhobi Sarkar; m. Srikanta Basu, Feb. 21, 1996; 1 child, Abhik Sarkar Basu. BSc, M.C.M. Dav Coll. for Women, Chandigarh, 1986; MBBS, Dayanand Med. Coll., Ludhiana, India, 1990; MD, Postgrad. Inst. Med. Edn. and Rsch., Chandigarh, 1995. Sr. resident in dermatology Lady Hardinge Med. Coll., Delhi, India, 1997—99, Govt. Med. Coll., Chandigarh, 1999—2000, sr. lectr., 2000—01; asst. prof. Vardhman Mahavir Med. Coll./Safdarjung Hosp., New Delhi, 2001—. Editor: Asian Pigment Bull.; mem. editl. bd.: Indian Jour. Pediat. Dermatology, reviewer: Indian Pediat. Jour., 2002—06, Med. Sci. Monitor Jour., 2002—03, Clin. Exptl. Dermatology, 2004—05, BMC Dermatology, 2004—05, Indian Jour. Med. Scis.; contbr. chapters to books, articles to profl. jours. Mem.: Indian Med. Assn., European Soc. Pigment Cell Rsch., Indian Soc. Pediat. Dermatology (life), Indian Assn. Dermatologists, Venereologists and Leprologists (life). Avocations: singing, creative writing, reading, travel. Office: Vardhman Mahavir Med Coll Safdarjung Hosp Dept Dermatology New Delhi 110029 India Home: PLOT NO 104 110 092 New Delhi India Office Phone: 0091-11-26190698. Personal E-mail: rashmisarkar@yahoo.com.

SARKER, SHAH-JALAL, medical educator; s. Abdul Wadud Sarker and Nurjahan Begum; m. Farzana Parveen Huq, Apr. 30, 2003; children: Abdullah, Abdurrahman, Ibrahim. BSc in Stats. with hons., U. Dhaka, Bangladesh, 1990, MSc in Stats., 1991; MSc in Epidemiology, Erasmus U., Netherlands, 1998; PhD, U. Surrey, Eng., 2001. Statis. analyst Bangladesh Rural Advancement Com., Dhaka, 1995—96; lectr. stats. Shahjalal U. Sci. & Tech., Sylhet, Bangladesh, 1996—98, asst. prof. stats., 1999—2003; rsch. fellow Med. & Pharm. Stats. Rsch. Unit, U. Reading, England, 2002—05, Stroke Rsch. Group, King's Coll. London, 2005—08. Statis. cons. Divsn. Health and Social Care Rsch., King's Coll. London, 2005—08; statis. cons. actuarial firm Watson Wyatt LLP, London, 2005—06; rsch. mem. Guy's & St Thomas' Nat. Health Svc. Trust, London, 2005—08; lectr. cancer biostatic Queen Mary U., London, 2009—. Contbr. articles to profl. jours. Treas., exec. com. mem. ASLU, 2009—; bd. mem. Human Devel. Found., Dhaka. Netherlands Fellowship Program grant, 1997—98. Fellow: Royal Statis. Soc.; mem.: SCT, Bangladesh Statis. Assn., Statisticians in Pharm. Industries. Avocations: reading, bicycling. Office: Barts Cancer Inst Ctr Exptl Cancer Medicine Queen Mary University London Old Anatomy Bldg Charterhouse Sq London EC1M 6BQ England Office Phone: 44 (0) 207 882 8495. Personal E-mail: s.sarker@qmul.ac.uk.

SARKIS, ELIAS HENRY, psychiatrist; s. Henry Elias and Yvonne Sarkis; m. Stephanie Anne Moulton, Oct. 17, 1998; 1 child, Daniel Agop. BS in Biology and French, CCNY, NYC, 1971—75; MD, U. Lille, France, 1979—85. Cert. Child and Adolescent Psychiatrist Am. Psychiat. Assn, Fla., 1992. Med. dir. Sarkis Family Psychiatry, Gainesville, Fla., 1991—, Daytop Therapeutic Cmty., Citra, Fla., 1993—98. Clin. assoc. prof. U. Fla., Gainesville, 1996—. Pres., founder Fla. Psychiat. Edn., Gainesville, 1999—2003. Recipient Leadership Award, AMA, 1990. Fellow: Am. Psychiat. Assn.; mem.: Alachua County Mental Health Assn. (assoc.; pres. 1990—91), Fla. Psychiat. Soc. (assoc.; pres. 2002—03). Office: Sarkis Family Psychiatry 529 NW 60th St Gainesville FL 32607 Personal E-mail: ok@ehsfamily.com. Business E-Mail: drsarkis@afpmed.com.

SARKISIAN, EDWARD GREGORY, dentist; m. Anna Svirid; children: Sara, Aram. BS, cert. in med. tech., U. Mich., 1974; DDS, U. Detroit, 1978. Lic. Bd. Dentistry, Mich. Gen. practice dentistry, Dearborn, Mich., 1978—. Mem. staff Harper Grace Hosp., Detroit, 1978-88; clin. instr. Dept. Otolaryngology Sch. Medicine Wayne State U., Detroit, 1982-90. Trustee St. Nerses Sem., 2005—07. Fellow Am. Coll. Dentists, Pierre Fauchard Acad. (treas. Mich. sect., 1996-2009); mem. ADA, Mich. Dental Assn. (ho. of dels. 1999-2001), Detroit Dist. Dental Soc. (strategic planning com., del. 1999-2001, ethics com. 2005—, Det. Dist. Dental Soc. Ethics Peer Reeview chmn., 2009-), Detroit Dental Clinic Club (pres. 2008-10), Armenian Gen. Benevolent Union Am., Francis Vedder Soc. Crown and Bridge Prosthodontics, Nat. Eagle Scout Assn., U. Mich. Alumni Assn., U. Mich. Club of Greater Northville (bd. govs., pres., 2004-2005), North East Regional Bd Dentistry(cons. examiner, 2009-), Armenian Orthodox. Clubs: U. Mich. Pres.'s, U. Mich. Victors. Lodge: Knights of Vartan (Nareg chpt. comdr. 1984-85, midwest rep. 1986-87). Office: 22190 Garrison Suite 201 Dearborn MI 48124

SARKISIAN, STEVEN R., ophthalmologist, educator; b. Phila., May 2, 1972; MD, Jefferson Med. Coll., 1999. Glaucoma fellow dir., clin. assoc. prof. Dean McGee Eye Inst., U. Okla., 2006—. Named one of Best Doctors in Am., Woodward and White, Best Doctors in Okla., Okla. Mag., America's Top Ophthalmologists, Consumers Rsch. Coun. Am. Office: Dean McGee Eye Inst 608 Stanton Yo Oklahoma City OK 73104 Office Fax: 405-271-6088. Business E-Mail: steven-sarkisian@dmei.org.

SARKISSIAN, ASHOT, nephrologist; b. Yerevan, Armenia, July 30, 1961; Prof. Yerevan State Med. U., 1984; head, divsn. nephrology Arabkir Joint Med. Ctr., 2003—. Bd. dir. Mem.: Swiss Soc. Nephrology, Internat. Pediatric Nephrology Assn., European Soc. Pediatric Nephrology. Office: Mamikonyants 30 Yerevan 0014 Armenia Office Fax: 374-10-284170. Business E-Mail: ashsark@arminco.com.

SARKS, SHIRLEY HEATHER, ophthalmologist; b. Harrogate, Yorkshire, UK, May 19, 1934; d. Frederic Knowles and Irene Knowles (nee Bye); m. John Peter Sarks, Dec. 9, 1964. MBBS, Royal Free Hosp. Sch. Medicine, 1958; MD, U. NSW, 1978. Cert. Royal Australian and New Zealand Coll. Ophthalmologists, 1977. Hon. cons. ophthalmologist Prince of Wales Hosp., Randwick, NSW, 1986. Pvt. med. retina practice, Sydney. Founding ptnr. Ptnr. Sight Program. Co-recipient Paul Kayser Internat. award, Retina Rsch. Found., Houston, 1991. Mem.: Royal Coll. Surgeons, Commonwealth Australia. Anglican. Achievements include clarification of natural history and manifestations of age-related macular degeneration; research in correlation of clinical and pathological findings in retinal disease. Office: JP and SH Sarks 15 Parnell St Strathfield NSW 2135 Australia Business E-Mail: jssarks@bigpond.net.au.

SARLE, CHARLES RICHARD, health facility executive; b. Saratoga Springs, NY, Sept. 21, 1944; s. John Robert and Marjorie Elizabeth (Swick) S.; m. Marion D. Wallace, June 21, 1968; children: Richard Charles, Robert Edmond. BBA cum laude, Northea. U., 1968; MBA, Babson Coll., 1973. CPA, Mass., Vt. Staff acct. Price Waterhouse & Co., Boston, 1968-70, George Kanavich, CPA, Wellesley, Mass., 1970-72; controller Human Resource Inst., Boston, 1972-73, adminstr., 1973-77; controller Brattleboro (Vt.) Retreat, 1977-78, dir. adminstrn., 1978-85, v.p., 1985-88, chief exec. officer, 1988-97; pres., CEO Carrier Clinic, Belle Mead, NJ, 1997—. Speaker in field. Mem. commn. Vt. Health Bldg. Fin. Agy., 1978—90; trustee Austine Sch. for Deaf and Hard of Hearing, 1990—97, pres., 1994—97; trustee Winston Prouty Ctr. for Child Devel., 1982—97, treas., 1983—90, sec., 1991—97; trustee Health Rsch. and Edn. Trust NJ, 1998—99, NJ Hosp. Assn., 2000—06, policy devel. com., 1998—2001, fin. com., 2000—, investment com. mem., 2001—10, audit compliance commn. mem., 2006—; bd. govs. NCCJ, 1998—2003, exec. com., 1999—2003. Recipient recognition award Brattleboro C. of C., 1985. Fellow AICPA, Mass. Soc. CPA, Am. Coll. Healthcare Execs. (regent Va. br. 1991-95); mem. Am. Hosp. Assn. (del.-at-large 1988-92, del.-at-large to regional policy bd.), Nat. Assn. Pvt. Psychiat. Hosps. (bd. dirs. polit. action com. 1983-93, trustee 1998-2000, 2007-10), Nat. Psychiat. Alliance (trustee 1989-96, pres. 1994-96), Vt. Soc. CPA (Cmty. Svc. award 1984), Hosp. Fin. Mgmt. Assn. (hosp. cost com. 1985-96), Rescue, Inc. (trustee 1982-83), New Eng. Healthcare Assembly (trustee 1995-97). Avocations: skiing, fishing, tennis, photography. Home: PO Box 840 Belle Mead NJ 08502-0840 Office: Carrier Clinic Rt 601 Belle Mead NJ 08502 E-mail: rsarle@carrierclinic.com.

SARMA, APURBA KUMAR, cardiologist, surgeon, consultant; b. Nalbari, India, Mar. 1, 1967; s. Bhabendra Nath Devsarma and Sabitri Devi; m. Hiramoni Sarma, Oct. 3, 1996; children: Bipasha(Daughter), Hrishikesh(Son). MBBS, MS, 1982. Lic. surgeon Sctimst, Kerala State, India., 1999. Registrar Dept. Cardiovascular Thoracic Surgery Indraprastha-Apollo Hosps., New Delhi, 1995—96; sr. resident Dept. Cardiovascular Thoracic Surgery Sree Chitra Tirunal Inst. Med. Scis. and Tech., Trivandrum, India, 1997—99, asst. prof. Dept. Cardiovascular Thoracic Surgery, 2000—04; chief cardiac surgeon Zh Sikder Women's Med. Coll. and Hosp., Dhaka, Bangladesh, 2004—. Cons. in field. Contbr. articles to profl. jours. Scholar, Govt. India, 1982—84. Mem.: Indian Assn. Cardiovascular-Thoracic Surgeons (life). Achievements include discovery of there is no difference in free flow of blood from pediclled left internal thoracic artery in varying degree of twists up to 360 degrees of twists. Avocations: travel, sports. Office: Zhs Women'S Medical Coll & Hospital Monica Estate West Dhanmondi Dhaka 1209 Bangladesh Business E-Mail: drapurbaks@yahoo.co.uk.

SARMA, NANDAKUMARA D., senior scientist; naturalized; s. Nalini Dandapantula and Venkateshwara Dandapantula Sarma; m. Polasani Vandana; 1 child, Prahlad. PhD in Pharm. Scis., Banaras Hindu U., Varanasi, India, 1994. Registered pharmacist. CRTA fellow Nat. Cancer Inst., Bethesda, Md., 2004—05; pharmacist, 2004—; sr. scientist US Pharmacopeia, Rockville, Md., 2006—; adj. prof. Thomas J. Long Sch. Pharmacy U. Pacific, Stockton, Calif. Spkr. Adverse Event Assessment and Reporting of Dietary Supplements: A US Perspective. Drug Info. Assn. Annual Meeting, San Diego, 2009; contbr. scientific papers to profl. jours. Mem.: Inst. Food Technologists, Drug Information Assn., Indian Pharm. Assn. (life). Avocations: walking, reading. Office: 12601 Twinbrook Pky Rockville MD 20852 Office Phone: 301-816-8354. Business E-Mail: dns@usp.org.

SARMA, PODILA S., retired health facility administrator; b. Parlakimidi, Orissa, India, May 4, 1950; s. Podila Surya Prakasa Rao and Podila Ramalakshmi Devi; m. Janaki Radhakrishnan, Aug. 28, 1978; 1 child, Podila Krishna Prakash. MBBS, Andhra U., 1971, MD, 1980. Diplomate Indian Bd. Internal Medicine, Nat. Bd. Examiners; cert. tchr. Intern Andhra U., 1971—73; jr. med. officer Jawaharlal Nehru Hosp. Rsch. Ctr., Bhilainagar, India, 1973—78, sr. med. officer, 1978—82, sr. specialist, 1982—86, speciaist in charge, 1986—90, sr. specialist in charge, 1990—94, sr. dep. dir., 1994—99, jt. dir., 1999—2004, dir., 2005—; resident Guntur Med. Coll., 1977—80; dir., 2005—06; dir.-in-charge, 2006—10; cons. physician Dr. Sharma's Clinic, Bhilai, 2010—. Grad. instr. Andhra Med. Coll., Visakhapatnam, India, 1980—97; lectr. Bhilai (India) Steel Plant, 1982—93, Jawaharlal Nehru Hosp., Bhilainagar, 1990—; reviewer Jour. Med. Sci. Monitor, 2001—; clin. observer Kieo U., Juntendo U., Japan, 1990; presenter in field. Editor: Jour. Soc. Ecol. Environ. Devel., 1998—; author: Advances in Internal Medicine, 1993; contbr. (chpt. to book) Recent Advances in Internal Medicine for the Asian Pacific Physicians, 1993, Modern Trends in the Prophylaxis and Treatment of Malaria, 1993; contbr. articles to profl. journals including Jour. Assn. Physicians India. Fellow, Guntur Med. Coll., 1972—73, Guntur Govt. Hosp., 1977—80, Andhra U., 1980. Fellow: ACP, Soc. Internal Medicine, Indian Coll. Physicians, Royal Coll. Tropical Medicine Hygiene; mem.: Phoenix Network Expert Clinicians, Indian Rheumatism Assn. (life), Indian Soc. Clin. Pharmacology Therpeutics (life), Assn. Physicians India (life; Madhya Pradesh chpt.), Indian Soc. Hosp. Infection Control (life), Internat. Soc. Infectious Diseases, Assn. Physicians (v.p. 1997—99, pres. 2002—, Durg chpt.). Avocations: reading, writing, music. Home: MIG II 437 Hudco Amdinagar 490 009 Bhilainagar India Office: Dr. Sarma's Clinic 187 Zonal Market A Sector 10 Bhilainagar 490009 India Office Phone: +919479123938. Personal E-mail: podilassarma@rediffmail.com, psasarma@gmail.com.

SARMA, SMITA, physician, consultant; b. Guwahati, Assam, Feb. 19, 1974; MBBS, GMC, 1998; MD in Microbiology, AMC, 2004. Assoc. cons. microbiology Medanta the Medicity, 2009—. Mem.: Indian Assn. Med. Microbiology. Office: Sector 38 Gurgaon Haryana 122001 India E-mail: sarma.smita@rediffmail.com.

SARMAY, GABRIELLA, immunologist; b. Budapest, July 20, 1948; d. Gyula Szentpeteri and Izabella Petrakovics; m. Ivan Sarmay, July 20, 1970; children: Monika, Balazs. Biologist, Lorand Eotvos Univ., Budapest, 1972, PhD, 1983, DSc, 1993. Rsch. scientist Nat. Inst. Haematology, Budapest, 1972-74; asst. prof. Lorand Eotvos U., Budapest, 1974-82, lectr., 1982-94, prof., 1994—. Sr. rschr. Sandoz Forschunsinstitute, Vienna, 1992-95. Contbr. articles to profl. jours. Recipient Acad. award Hungarian Acad. of Sci., 1990, Novicardin award 2008. Mem. Hungarian Soc. Immunology, Hungarian Biochem. Soc., EFIS & IUIS. Avocations: reading, skiing, sailing, swimming, travel. Office: Lorand Eotvos U Dept Immunology Pazmany Peter S 1/c Budapest Hungary Office Phone: 3613722500 ext. 8662. Business E-Mail: sarmayg@elte.hu.

SARN, JAMES, physician, health association administrator; b. Orange, NJ, July 17, 1941; s. Chester Walter and Grace Marie (Lang) S.; m. Leslie Barton Warren, June 28, 1971; children: Fiona Rachel, Audrey Pearmain, Nicola Warren, Philip Hamilton. BS, U.S. Military Acad., 1963; MPH, U. N.C., 1972; MD, Duke U., 1973. Diplomate Bd. Med. Examiners. Dir. health, nutrition, population USAID, Managua, Nicaragua, 1974-78; dir. disease control Ariz. Dept. Health Svcs., Phoenix, 1978-80, health dir., 1980-83; agency dir. health and population U.S. Agency Internat. Devel., Washington, 1983-85, dir. health, nutrition, population Khartoum, Sudan, 1985-87, dir. health and nutrition Cairo, Egypt, 1987-91; dep. asst. sec. internat. and refugee health Dept. Health and Human Svcs., Washington, 1991-93; dir. health, nutrition and population Save The Children, Westport, Conn., 1993—. Contbr. articles to profl. jours. U.S. delegate Internat. Conf. Nutrition, Rome, Italy, 1992, Pan Am. Health Orgn. Governing Coun., Washington, 1991-93, World Health Assembly, Geneva, 1991-93; mem. bd. Nat. Coun. Internat. Health, Washington, 1984, 85, 91-93. Capt. U.S. Army 1963-68, Vietnam. Recipient Bronze Star U.S. Army, 1965, 68, Medal Honor 1st Class Govt. Vietnam,1968, Peacemaker medal Govt. Brazil, 1965, Surgeon General's Exemplary Svc. award Pub. Health Svc. Dept. Health and Human Svcs., 1993. Mem. AMA, APHA, Am. Coll. Preventative Medicine, Am. Soc. Tropical Medicine, Nat. Coun. Internat. Health (bd. dirs. 1991—). Home: 426 Judd Rd Easton CT 06612-1024 Office: Save the Children 54 Wilton Rd Westport CT 06880-3131 *

SARNA, SUSHIL, biology professor; b. India, Mar. 2, 1942; BE, Delhi Coll. Engring., 1963; PhD, U. Alta., 1971. Prof. internal medicine, cell biology and neurosci. U. Tex. Med. Br., 2002—. Recipient Outstanding Achievement award, AGA. Home: 3406 Acorn Wood Way Houston TX 77059 Business E-Mail: sksarna@utmb.edu.

SARNAT, BERNARD GEORGE, plastic surgeon, educator, researcher; b. Chgo., Sept. 1, 1912; s. Isadore M. and Fanny (Silverman) S.; m. Rhoda Elaine Gerard, Dec. 25, 1941; children: Gerard, Joan. SB, U. Chgo., 1933, MD, 1937; MS, DDS, U. Ill., 1940. Diplomate Am. Bd. Plastic Surgery, 1947. Intern Los Angeles County Gen. Hosp., 1936-37; resident oral and plastic surgery Cook County Hosp., Chgo., 1940-41; asst. to Dr. Marshall Davison (gen. surgery) Univ. Hosp., Chgo., 1942-43; asst. to Drs. Vilray P. Blair and Louis T. Byars (plastic and reconstructive surgery), St. Louis, 1943-46; practice medicine specializing in plastic surgery Chgo., 1946-56, Beverly Hills, Calif., 1956-91; asst. histology U. Ill. Coll. Dentistry, 1937-40, prof., head dept. oral and maxillofacial surgery, 1946-56; asst. dept. surgery, divsn. plastic surgery Washington U. Sch. Medicine, St. Louis, 1944-46; prof., dir. dept. oral and plastic surgery St. Louis U. Coll. Dentistry, 1945-46; clin. asst. prof. surgery (plastic surgery) U. Ill. Coll. Medicine, 1949-56; adj. prof. oral biology Sch Dentistry UCLA, 1969—2010, mem. Dental Rsch. Inst., 1974-95, adj. prof. plastic surgery Sch. Medicine, 1974—2010, emeritus prof., 2010; attending staff Cedars-Sinai Med. Ctr., LA, 1956-91, emeritus, 1991—, mem. staff, sr. rsch. scientist, chief plastic surgery, 1961-81. Cons. in gen., plastic and maxillofacial surgery VA Regional Office, Chgo., 1956; lectr. in field. Sr. author: (with Isaac Schour) Oral and Facial Cancer, 2d edit., 1957, (with Daniel Laskin) Surgery of the Temporomandibular Joint, 1964; editor: (with Daniel Laskin) The Temporomandibular Joint A Biological Basis for Clinical Practice, 4th edit., 1991, (with Andrew D. Dixon) Factors and Mechanisms Affecting Growth of Bone, 1982, Normal and Abnormal Bone Growth: Basic and Clinical Research, 1985, Fundamentals of Bone Growth: Methodology and Applications, 1991, (with James Bradley) Craniofacial Biology and Craniofacial Surgery, 2010; contbr. chpts. to books, articles to profl. jours. Co-winner Joseph A. Capps prize for med. rsch. Inst. Medicine, Chgo., 1940, Frederick B. Noyes prize, 1940; recipient Kerbs award for rsch. plastic and reconstructive surgery, 1950, 1st prize, sr. award Found. Am. Soc. Plastic and Reconstructive surgeons, 1957, Beverly Hills Acad. of Medicine award, 1959, Nat. Achievement award medicine Phi Epsilon Pi, 1964, 1st prize Am. Rhinologic Soc., 1980, medal Hebrew U., Jerusalem, 1985, medal Tel Aviv U., 1985, Disting. Svc. Alumni award U. Chgo. Pritzker Sch. Medicine, 1987, hon. award Am. Soc. Maxillofacial Surgeons, 1990, Dallas B. Phemister Profl. Achievement award Dept. Surgery U. Chgo., 1993, Disting. Alumnus award U. Ill. Coll. Dentistry, 1994, Craniofacial Biology Rsch. award Internat. Assn. for Dental Rsch., 1995, Disting. Scientist award, Pioneer in Medicine award Cedars-Sinai Med. Ctr., L.A., 1999, Profl. Achievement citation U. Chgo. Alumni Assn., 2003, citatioon of excellence in rsch. Plastic Surgery Ednl. Found., 2003, Profl. Achievement award U. Ill. Alumni Assn., 2004. Fellow ACS, AAAS, Am. Assn. Plastic Surgeons (hon. award 1993); mem. Calif. Med. Soc., L.A. Med. Soc., Am. Soc. Plastic and Reconstructive Surgeons, Plastic Surgery Rsch. Coun. (founding mem., chmn. 1957), Am. Soc. Maxillofacial Surgeons (hon.), Calif. Soc. Plastic Surgeons, Beverly Hills Acad. Medicine (pres. 1962-63), Internat. Assn. Craniofacial Biology, Am. Assn. Pediat. Plastic Surgeons (hon.), Am. Assn. Phys. Anthropologists, Internat. Assn. Study Dento-Facial Abnormalities (hon.), Sigma Xi, Omicron Kappa Upsilon, Zeta Beta Tau, Phi Delta Epsilon, Alpha Omega (Internat. Achievement medal 1988). Home: 1875 Kelton Ave Apt 301 Los Angeles CA 90025-8505

SARNOFF, DEBORAH SUSAN, dermatologist, educator; b. Bklyn., Jan. 8, 1954; d. Norman and Ruth Sarnoff; m. Robert H. Gotkin, May 28, 1983. BA summa cum laude, Cornell U., 1975; MD, George Wash. U., 1980. Diplomate Am. Bd. Dermatology, 1984. Internship Wash. Hosp. Ctr., 1980-81; resident in dermatology NYU Med. Ctr., NYC, 1981-83, chief resident, 1983-84, fellow in Mohs skin cancer surgery, 1985-86; dermatologic surgeon Cosmetique Dermatology, Laser & Plastic Surgery, LLP, Greenvale, NY, 1985—; clin. asst. prof. NYU Med. Ctr., 1989—2001, clin. assoc. prof., 2001—08, clin. prof., 2009—; pvt. practice Cosmetique Dermatology Laser & Plastic Surgery LLP NYC, 1988—; active med. staff North Shore LIJ, Glen Cove. Clin. rsch. dermatology br. NIH, Bethesda, Md., 1987-88; sr. v.p. Skin Cancer Found. NYC 2007-. Author: (books) Beauty and the Beam, 1998, Instant Beauty, 2002. Fellow: Am. Soc. Laser Medicine & Surgery, Nat. Council Medical Soc., Am. Acad. Dermatology, Am. Coll. Physicians. Office: 625 Park Ave New York NY 10065 also: Cosmetique Dermatology, Laser & Plastic Surgery LLP 31 Northern Blvd Greenvale NY 11548 Office Phone: 212-794-4000, 516-484-9000. Office Fax: 212-794-0231, 516-484-7549. Business E-Mail: sarnoffandgotkin@aol.com.

SARODE, RAVINDRA (RAVI SARODE), physician; b. Indore, India, Dec. 9, 1957; MBBS, MGM Med. Coll. Indore, 1982; MD, Postgrad. Inst. Med. Edn. & Rsch., 1985. Dir. transfusion medicine and reference hemostasis lab. UT Southwestern Med. Ctr., 2000—. Mem.: Am. Soc. Apheresis (pres. elect 2011—), AABB, Am. Soc. Hematology. Avocation: tennis. Office: 5323 Harry Hines Blvd Dallas TX 75390-9073 Business E-Mail: ravi.sarode@utsouthwestern.edu.

SARPONG, SAMPSON, allergist; b. Ghana, July 10, 1956; MD, Howard U., 1990. Postdoc. fellow John Hopkins U., 1995; dir. Ctr. Allergic Diseases LLC, 2007—. Prof. Howard U., 2000. Rsch. grant, NIH. Mem.: AAAAI. Avocation: tennis. Home: 14819 Kimberwick Dr Bowie MD 20715 E-mail: ssarpong@howard.edu.

SARRAMON, JEAN-PIERRE FERNAND LOUIS, urologist, educator; b. Toulouse, France, Jan. 18, 1938; s. Henri and Jacqueline (Pellegrin) S.; m. Marie-France Lhez, Mar. 19, 1964; children: Christine, Benedicte. Baccalaureate in Lit. and Philosophy, St. Joseph Coll., Toulouse, 1956; MD, Med. Faculty Toulouse, 1970. Intern in medicine U. Hosp., Toulouse, 1964; prosector in anatomy Med. Sch., Toulouse, 1970, chief of clinic in surgery, 1970-71, asst. prof. urology, 1972-77, assoc. prof., 1978-90, prof., 1990—2006, prof. emeritus, 2006—; chief of svc., chmn. urology, renal transplantation/ANDrdo U. Hosp., 1982—; dir. exptl. surgery dept. C.H.U. Purpan, Toulouse, 1985—. Mem. U. Nat. Counsel, 1987; mem. faculty, lectr. European Sch. Urology; pres. 96th French Congress Urology, 2002; expert Supreme Ct. Appel, 2003. Mem. editl. bd. Le Progres en Urologie, 1990, Internat. Jour. Impotence Rsch., 1990, Les Annales d'Urologie, Archivio Italiano di Urologia, Nephrologia Andrologia, 2001; contbr. chpts. to books. Hon. officer French Armed Forces, 1975—. Decorated chevalier Legion of Honor (France); recipient clin. rsch. prize Languedoc Acad., 2005; named Prof. Exceptional Class Univ., 2000, Prof. Emeritus U., 2007. Mem. French Transplantation Soc., French Soc. Urology (pres. 2002-03), French Coll. Urologists (mem. adminstrv. coun.), European Urol. Assn., Am. Urol. Assn. (corr.), Soc. Internat. d'Urologie, Belgium Urol. Assn., European Orgn. for Rsch. and Treatment of Cancer, European Soc. Male Genital Surgery (v.p.), Adminstrv. French Urol. Counsel, Internat. Microsurgery Soc., European Soc. Organ Transplantation, Internat. Soc. Impotence Rsch., Conseil Nat. des Univs., Nat. French Surgery Acad. (titular mem. 2009), Expert Supreme Nat. Court Appeal, Languedoc Acad. Roman Catholic. Avocations: horseback riding, mountain climbing, sailing, golf, skiing, racing cycles. Home: 9 Rue Espinasse 31000 Toulouse France Office: Urological Dept CHU Rangueil-Chemin Du Vallon 31000 Toulouse France Office Phone: 0561323201, 0561323201. Business E-Mail: sarramon.jp@chu-toulouse.fr.

SARTORELLI, ALAN CLAYTON, pharmacologist, educator; b. Chelsea, Mass., Dec. 18, 1931; m. Alice C. Anderson, July 7, 1969. BS, New Eng. Coll. Pharmacy Northeastern U., 1953; MS, Middlebury Coll., Vt., 1955; PhD, U. Wis., 1958; MA (hon.), Yale U., 1967. Rsch. chemist Samuel Roberts Noble Found., Ardmore, Okla., 1958—60, sr. rsch. chemist, 1960—61; mem. faculty dept. pharmacology Yale Sch. Medicine, New Haven, 1961—, prof., 1967—, head devel. therapeutics program Comprehensive Cancer Ctr., 1974—90, chmn. dept. pharmacology, 1977—84, 1998—2000, dir. Comprehensive Cancer Ctr., 1984—93, Alfred Gilman prof. pharmacology, 1987—, prof. epidemiology, 1991—97. Head devel. therapeutics program Comprehensive Cancer Ctr., 1974—90, chmn. dept. pharmacology, 1977—84, 1998—2000, dep. dir., 1982—84, dir., 1984—93, Alfred Gilman prof. pharmacology, 1987—; Charles B. Smith vis. rsch. prof. Meml. Sloan-Kettering Ctr., 1979; William N. Creasy vis. prof. clin. pharmacology Wayne State U., 1983; Mayo Found. vis. prof. oncology Mayo Clinic, 1983; Walter Hubert lectr. Brit. Assn. Cancer Rsch., 1985; Pfizer lectr. in clin. pharmacology U. Conn. Health Ctr., 1985; William N. Creasy vis. prof. clin. pharmacology Bowman Gray Sch. Medicine, 1987; Wellcome vis. prof. basic sci. U. Pitts. Sch. Medicine, 1990; sci. adv. bd. ImmunoGen, Inc., 1981—90, U. Ind. Cancer Ctr., 1992, Cancer Inst. NJ, 1993—2000, Cell Pathways, Inc., 1993—2003; chmn. cancer sci. adv. bd. ViraChem., Inc., 1986—93, The Liposome Co., 1986—2001, Vion Pharms., 1993—, bd. dirs., chmn. sci. adv. bd.; chmn. vis. sci. adv. com. Columbia U. Comprehensive Cancer Ctr., 1986—99; chmn. pres.'s cancer adv. bd. Fox Chase Cancer Ctr., 1992—2007; clin. investigation rev. com. Nat. Cancer Inst., 1968—72, mgmt. cons. to dir. divsn. cancer treatment, 1975—77, bd. sci. counselors, divsn. cancer treatment, 1978—81, chmn. com. to establish nat. coop. drug discovery groups, 1982—83, chmn. spl. rev. com. Outstanding Investigator grant applications, 1992, chmn. ad hoc contracts tech. rev. group, 93; instnl. rsch. grants com. Am. Cancer Soc., 1971—76, coun. analysis and projection, 1978—79; cons. in biochemistry U. Tex. M.D. Anderson Hosp. and Tumor Clinic, Houston, 1970—76; cons. Sandoz Forschungs-Institut, Vienna, 1977—80; mem. exptl. therapeutics study sect. NIH, 1973—77, working cadre nat. large bowel cancer project, 1973—76; adv. com. Cancer Rsch. Ctr., Washington U. Sch. Medicine, 1971—75, SLSB Ptnrs., L.P., 1992—96; sci. adv. com. U. Iowa Cancer Ctr., 1979—83; external adv. com. Wis. Clin. Cancer Ctr., 1978—79, Duke Comprehensive Cancer Ctr., 1983—94; external adv. bd. U. Ariz. Cancer Ctr., 1982—92, U. So. Calif. Cancer Ctr., 1983—93, Clin. Cancer Rsch. Ctr., Brown U., 1980—86; nat. program com. 13th Internat. Cancer Congress, 1979—81; cons. Bristol-Myers Co., 1982—93, selection com. prize in cancer rsch., 1977—85, chmn., 1979—81, chmn. selection com. award for disting. achievement in cancer rsch., 1989—92; bd. advisors Drug and Vaccine Devel. Corp. (Ctr. for Pub. Resources), 1980—81, Specialized Cancer Ctr., Mt. Sinai Med. Ctr., 1981—90, Grace Cancer Drug Ctr., Roswell Park Meml. Inst., 1986—89; med. and sci. adv. com. grants rev. subcom. Leukemia Soc. Am., 1983—88; program planning com. Mary Lasker-Am. Cancer Soc. Conf., 1986; external sci. rev. com. Massey Cancer Ctr., 1989—94; bd. visitors Moffit Cancer Ctr. U. South Fla., 1989—92; dep. dir. Cancer Prevention Rsch. Unit for Conn., 1989—93, acting dir., 1991—93; nat. bd. Look Good...Feel Better program Cosmetic Toiletry and Fragrance Assn., 1989—91; organizing com. Conf. on Bioreductive Drug Activation, 1993—94; chmn. bd. spl. cons. Inst. for Cancer Therapeutics, 1993; sci. adv. bd. U. Ill. Cancer Ctr., 2001; chmn. sci. adv. bd. Celator Pharms. Inc., 2002—. Regional editor Am. Continent Biochem. Pharmacology, 1968—2003, exec. editor, 1993—2003, editor-in-chief Cancer Comm., 1969—93, Oncology Rsch., 1993—; editor: Handbuch der experimentellen Pharmakologie vols. on antineoplastic and immunosuppressive agts., series on cancer chemotherapy Am. Chem. Soc. Symposium, 1976; founder, exec. editor Pharmacology and Therapeutics, 1975—2003, editl. bd. Internat. Ency. Pharmacology and Therapeutics, 1972—94, Seminars in Oncology, 1973—83, Chemico-Biol. Interactions, 1975—78, Jour. Medicinal Chemistry, 1977—82, Cancer Drug Delivery, 1982—85, Jour. Enzyme Inhibition, 1984—2002, Jour. Liposome Rsch., 1986—92, In Vivo, 1990—2002, Cancer Biotherapy, 1992—97, Cancer Rsch., Therapy and Control, 1993—97, Oncology Reports, 1995—, Molecular and Cellular Differentiation, 1996—, mem. adv. bd. Advances in Chemistry Series, ACS Symposium Series, 1977—80, editl. adv. bd. Cancer Rsch., 1970—71, assoc. editor, 1971—78, Current Awareness in Biol. Scis., Current Advances in Pharmacology and Toxicology, 1983—88, Cancer Cells, 1989—91, Jour. Exptl. Therapeutics and Oncology, 1995—, exec. adv. bd. Ency. of Human Biology, 1987—90, Dictionary of Sci. and Tech., 1989—91, editl. cons. Biol. Abstracts, 1984—88; contbr. articles to profl. jours. Bd. dirs. Schubert Performing Arts Ctr., 1992—2001, Schubert Opera Bd., 1991—2000, chmn., 1993—. Recipient Outstanding Alumni award, Northeastern U., 1987, Mike Hogg award, M.D. Anderson Cancer Ctr., U. Tex., 1989, Alumni Achievement award, Middlebury Coll., 1990, AACR-Bruce F. Cain Meml. award, 2001, Drug Discovery and Devel. award, Glaxo SmithKline, 2002. Fellow: AAAS, N.Y. Acad. Scis.; mem.: Coun. Biology Editors, Conn. Acad. Sci. and Engring., Inst. Medicine NAS (com. on govt. industry collaboration in biomed. rsch. and edn. 1989, mem. Forum on Drug Devel. and Regulation 1989—93), Assn. Am. Cancer Insts. (v.p. 1986, liaison rep. to Nat. Cancer Inst. 1986, bd. dirs. 1986—89, pres. 1987—88, chmn. bd. dirs. 1989), Am. Soc. Pharmacology and Exptl. Therapeutics (award com. 1988, chmn. 1992, award in exptl. therapeutics 1986, Otto Krayer award 2002), Am. Soc. Cell Biology, Am. Soc. Biochemistry and Molecular Biology, Am. Soc. Microbiology, Am. Chem. Soc., Am. Assn. Cancer Rsch. (dir. 1975—78, chmn. publs. com. 1981—88, dir. 1984—87, v.p. 1985—86, fin. com. 1985—88, exec. com. 1985—89, pres. 1986—87, chmn. exec. com. 1987, chmn. awards com. 1987, chmn. nominating com. 1993—95, mem. devel. com. 1995—97). Home: 4 Perkins Rd Woodbridge CT 06525-1616 Office: Yale U Dept Pharmacology 333 Cedar St New Haven CT 06520-8066 Office Phone: 203-785-4533. Business E-Mail: alan.sartorelli@yale.edu.

SARTORI, STEFANO, dentist; b. Levico Terme, Italy, July 11, 1972; s. Carlo Sartori and Rafaella Heidegger; m. Rosanna Bovenzi, June 1, 2002; 1 child, Alessandro. DDS Biomedical Stats., U. Pavia, Italy, 2000. Pvt. practice Studio Sartori-Bovenzi, Piacenza, Italy, 1997—. Home: via Scalabrini nr 31 29100 Piacenza Italy Office: Studio Dentistico Sartori - Bovenzi Via Giovanni Battista Scalabrini nr 31 29121 Piacenza PC Italy Office Phone: 39-0523-314248. Office Fax: +39-0523-314248; Home Fax: +39-0523-314248. Personal E-mail: stefanodoc@fastwebnet.it.

SARUK, MICHAEL, dermatologist, educator; b. Chgo., Nov. 1, 1951; s. Marvin Saruk and Geraldine Ruth Freeman; m. Louise Link, 1991; m. Anne Faulkner, 1977; children: Benjamin Dov, Jonathan Simon, Evan Samuel. BS, U. Ill., 1973; MD, Rush U., 1977. Diplomate Am. Bd. Dermatology, 1983, Am. Bd. Pathology, 1981, Am. Bds. Pathology and Dermatology, 1981. Asst. prof. pathology and dermatology U. Pitts. Sch. Medicine, 1982—83; instr. dermatology U. Pa. Sch. Medicine, Phila., 1984—86; clin. instr. dermatology Mt. Sinai Sch. Medicine, NYC, 1987—92; clin. asst. prof. dermatology U. Pa. Sch. Medicine, 1993—99, clin. assoc. prof., dermatology, 1999—. Cons., advisor Novartis Pharms., 2002—; cons., clin. investigator Aventis Pharms., 2002—04, Astellas Pharms., 2004—, Allergan Pharms., 2002—05, Galderma Pharms., 2004—05, Centocor - subs. of Johnson and Johnson, 2005—; asst. med. examiner Office of Med. Examiner, New Haven County, Conn., 1978—82, Celgene, 2008—. Co-author: (medical text) Soft Tissue Tumors; contbr. articles to profl. jours. Founding sponsor Magnolia Speech Sch. Demonstration Program, Berwyn, Pa., 2002. Fellow: Am. Soc. Dermatologic Surgery, Am. Soc. Mohs Surgery, US & Can. Acad. Pathology, Am. Acad. Dermatology, Am. Soc. Dermatopathology; mem.: Dermatology Found. (vice-chair Ea. Pa. 1997—2000), Del. Acad. Dermatology (pres. 1997—98), Pa. Acad. Dermatology, Soc. Investigative Dermatology, Phi Beta Kappa. Achievements include Start of the pigmented lesion clinic for the diagnosis and treatment of pigmented disorders of the skin, including moles and melanoma, in the department of dermatology, University of Pittsburgh, 1982; Start of What Is Now One Of The Largest Private Group Dermatology And Plastic Surgery Practices In The Delaware Valley, Employing A Multidisciplinary Approach To The Treatment Of Cutaneous Diseases. Office: Delaware Valley Dermatology Group LLC 3411 Silverside Rd Ste 107 Wilmington DE 19810 Office Fax: 610-296-3963.

SARUTA, MASAYUKI, medical researcher, gastroenterologist; b. Shinjuku Ku, Tokyo, Mar. 3, 1972; MD, Jikei U. Sch. Medicine, Minato-Ku, Tokyo, 1997, PhD, 2005. Resident Jikei U. Sch. Medicine, 1997—2002; postdoc. rschr. Cedars-Sinai Med. Ctr., LA, 2005—07. Office: Jikei Univ Sch Medicine 3-25-8 Nishi Shinbashi Minato Ku Tokyo 105-8461 Japan Business E-Mail: m.saruta@jikei.ac.jp.

SARWAL, VIRENDAR, cardiac surgeon, researcher; b. Chandigarh, India, Sept. 22, 1960; s. Kanahiya Lal and Daya Rani (Puri) S.; m. Rashmi Singhal, Jan. 22, 1984; children: Ridhima, Varun. MBBS, Panjabi U., Patiala, India, 1981, MS in Gen. Surgery, 1988; MCh, PGIMER, 1991. Attending cardiac surgeon Escorts Heart Inst., New Delhi, 1992-94; cons. cardiac surgeon Batra Cardiac Care Ctr., New Delhi, 1994-95; asst. prof. Pgimer, Chandigarh, India, 1995-96; assoc. cons. Apollo Heart Hosp., New Delhi, 1997-98; med. dir., sr. cons. cardiac surgeon City Hosp. and Heart Care Ctr., Chandigarh, 1998-99; sr. cons. cardia surgeon Malhatra Heart Inst. & Med. Rsch. Ctr., New Delhi, 2000—01; sr. cons. cardiac surgeon Fortis Hosp., Mohali, India, 2001—. Contbr. articles to profl. jours. Mem. Indian Assn. Cardiovascular & Thoracic Surgeons, N.Y. Acad. Scis. Avocations: playing badminton, music, writing. Home: House #1184 Sector 8-C Chandigarh 160018 India Office: Fortis Hosp Heart Sector 62 Phase VIII Mohali 160062 India

SARWAR, TAHIRA PARVEEN, dietician; b. Doncaster, England, Nov. 6, 1972; d. Mohammed and Zebeadah Sarwar. BS in Applied Human Nutrition, Dietetics with honors, U. Wales, Cardiff, 1996; diploma in Advanced Dietetic Practice, Brit. Dietetic Assn., 2002; post grad. cert. in Diabetes, U. Surrey, Eng., 2002. Registered dietician Health Professionals Coun., 1996, dietitian Brit. Dietetics Assn., 1996, in dietetics, lic. DAFNE educator Dose Adjustment For Normal Eating, 2002. Dietitian Fosse Health NHS Trust Glenfield Hosp., Leicester, England, 1996—98; sr. primary care dietitian

Parkside Health NHS Trust, London, 1999—2001; sr. project dietitian Brent NHS Authority, 2001—04; sr. diabetes dietitian Ctrl. Derby Primary Care Trust & Derby Hosps. NHS Trust, 2002—08; cmty. specialist dietitian Diabetes and Obesity Nottingham City Primary Care Trust, 2008—. Mem. nutrition subcommittee Diabetes UK, London, 2001—03, sr. dietitian Primary Care, 1999—; sr. dietitian Multicultural Nutrition Group Of The Brit. Dietetics Assn., Birmingham, 1996—. Author: (tng. pack) Global Nutrition- Developing Multicultural Dietary Competancies, 2004; contbr., star: (films) Apnee Sehati, 2006; contbr. articles to profl. jours. Recipient poster presentation prize, So. Derbyshire Acute Hosps. NHS Trust, 2003, Health and Social Care Team award, Dept. Health Eng., 2005. Mem.: Dose Adjustment For Normal Eating (mem. collaborative group 2003, exec. group mem. 2003), Nat. Obesity Forum, Health Professions Coun., Brit. Dietetics Assn. (sr. dietician Diabetes Mgmt. Edn. Group 2002—). Muslim. Home: 8 Middleton Blvd Nottingham NG8 1BH England Personal E-mail: tsarwar_srd@yahoo.co.uk.

SARWARK, JOHN FRANCIS, orthopaedic surgeon, educator; b. Aurora, Ill., Jan. 24, 1954; m. Maria Panico Sarwark; children: John, Robert, Annie. BS, U. Ill., Champaign, 1975; MD, Northwestern U., 1979. Resident in orthop. surgery Northwestern U., 1979—84; attending pediat. orthop. surgeon Childrens Mercy Hosp., Kansas City, Mo., 1985—88, Childrens Meml. Hosps., Chgo, 1988, divsn. head pediat. orthop. surgery Chgo., 2003—; asst. prof. orthop. surgery Northwestern U. Med. Sch., Chgo, 1988—94, assoc. prof. orthop. surgery, 1994—2001; med. dir. ctr. childhood safety Childrens Meml. Hosp., Chgo., 1997—; prof. orthop. surgery Northwestern U. Med. Sch., Chgo., 2001—. Faculty Med. Ethics and Humanities Program, Northwestern U. Med. Sch., Chgol, 1996-99. Contbr. articles to profl. jours. Mem. Pathways Awareness Found., Glenview, 1993—. Recipient Berkheiser award, Inst. Medicine, Chgo., 1990. Fellow: Pediat. Orthop. Soc. N.Am. (mem.-at-large 1992—93, 2002—04, bd. dirs.), Scoliosis Rsch. Soc. (edn. com. 1996—2000, fellow com. 2000—), Am. Acad. Pediat. (exec. com. orthopedic sect. 1997—, chair 2002—04), Am. Acad. Orthop. Surgeons (faculty chmn. com. on pub. edn. 1998—2001, assoc. editor Orthopedic Knowledge Online 2003—), Am. Orthop. Assn., Alpha Omega Alpha. Avocations: fines arts, travel. Office: Divsn Pediat Orthopaedic Surgery Childrens Meml Hosp 2300 N Childrens Plz Box 69 Chicago IL 60614-3363 Office Phone: 773-327-1270. Business E-Mail: jsarwark@childrensmemorial.org.

SASAGURI, SHIRO, medical educator; b. Izuhara, Nagasaki, Japan, Dec. 1, 1951; s. Hiromichi and Kuniko Sasaguri; m. Atsuko Sasaguri, Apr. 23, 1978; children: Daigo, Seigo, Shiho. MD, PhD, Tokyo med. & Dental U., 1978. Prof. surgery Kochi U., Nankoku, Japan, 1999—. Achievements include patents pending for effect of deep sea water on the progression of atherosclerosis. Office: Kochi Univ Dept Surgery Kohasu Okoh Nankoku Kochi Prefecture 783-0085 Japan Office Phone: 81-88-880-2375. Office Fax: 81-88-880-2376. Business E-Mail: sasaguri@kochi-u.ac.jp.

SASAHARA, ARTHUR ASAO, cardiologist, educator, researcher; b. Del Rey, Calif., May 11, 1927; s. Harold Hango and Blanche (Takayama) S.; m. Alice Ann Guenther, Apr. 2, 1955; children: Ann Mariko, Claire Michiko, Ellen Reiko, Karen Hideko, Mark Tadao. AB, Oberlin Coll., 1951; MD, Case Western Res. U., 1955; AM (hon.), Harvard U., 1987. Diplomate Am. Bd. Internal Medicine. Intern Boston City Hosp., 1955-56; jr. asst. med. resident Mass. Gen. Hosp., Boston, 1956-57; fellow in cardiology West Roxbury VA Med. Ctr., Mass., 1957-58, Children's Hosp. Med. Ctr., Boston, 1958-59; sr. resident in medicine Yale-New Haven Med. Ctr., 1959-60; asst. chief med. svc., dir. cardiopulmonary lab., dep. chmn. rsch. and edn. com. VA Hosp. West Roxbury, 1960-70, chief cardiopulmonary sect., 1971-74, assoc. chief staff for rsch. and edn., 1970-76, chief med. svc., 1974-82, West Roxbury-Brockton VA Hosp., 1982-87; prof. medicine Harvard Med. Sch., Boston, 1974-93, prof. emeritus, 1993—; cons. cardiovascular-pulmonary diseases Boston, 1965-87; cons. pediatric cardiology Children's Hosp. Med. Ctr., Boston, 1976-86; physician Brigham and Women's Hosp., Boston, 1979-82, sr. physician, 1982—. Dir. thrombolytics rsch. pharm. products divsn. Abbott Labs., Abbott Park, Ill., 1987—95, sr. med. dir., 1995—97; sr. physician cardiovascular divsn. Brigham and Women's Hosp., 1998—; sr. physician Venous Thromboembolism Rsch. Group Brigham and Womens Hosp., Boston, 2000—; co-founder & co-dir. North Am. Thrombosis Forum, 2006—. Author-editor: Pulmonary Embolic Disease, 1965, Pulmonary Emboli, 1975, New Therapeutic Agents in Thrombosis and Thrombolysis, 1997, 2d edit., 2002; contbr. articles to profl. jours.; designer constant infusion med. pump, Harvard Apparatus Co., 1973; mem. editl. bd. New Eng. Jour. Medicine, 1971-73, Jour. Nuclear Medicine, 1981-83, Am. Jour. Medicine, 1971-72, Circulation, 1973-78, VASA, 1978-85, Jour. Cardiovasc. Medicine, 1980-86, Primary Cardiology, 1986-89. With U.S. Army, 1945-47. NIH grantee, 1963-82; VA grantee, 1961-87. Fellow ACP, Am. Coll. Chest Physicians, Am. Coll. Cardiology; mem. AAAS, Internat. Soc. Fibrinolysis and Thrombolysis, Am. Fedn. Clin. Rsch., Internat. Soc. Thrombosis and Hemostasis, Am. Heart Assn., N.Am. Thrombosis Forum (founding dir. 2006-), Alpha Omega Alpha. Democrat. Episcopalian. Home: 1115 Beacon St # 12 Newton MA 02461-1154 Personal E-mail: aasasahara@comcast.net.

SASAKI, AKIHIKO, cardiologist; s. Kozo and Yukiko Sasaki; m. Yoko Sano, Sept. 12, 1992; children: Hiroki, Miki. MD, Tokyo Med. U., 1988, PhD, 1996. Diplomate Japan, 1988. Instr. Tokyo Med. U., Shinjuku-ku, 1995—2000; dir. Sasaki Med. Clinic, Nakano-ku, Tokyo, 2000—. Vis. lectr. Tokyo Med. U., Shinjuku-ku, 2001—. Contbr. articles to profl. jours. Recipient Jos Willems Young Investigators award, Internat. Soc. for Computerized Electrocardiology, 1997, award, Japanese Soc. of Electrocardiology, 1997, Jos Willems Young Investigators award, Internat. Soc. for Computerized Electrocardiology, 1998, 1999, Sasa Meml. award, Tokyo Med. U., 2000; grantee Rsch. grant, 1995. Fellow: Japanese Soc. Internal Medicine; mem.: Japanese Soc. Electrocardiology, The Japanese Coll. Cardiology, Internat. Soc. Electrocardiology, The Japanese Circulation Soc. (bd. cert. 1997—), The Japan Med. Assn. Achievements include research in symmetrical T waves using a first derivative electrocardiogram. Home and Office: Sasaki Med Clinic 3-36-12 Yayoi-cho Nakano-ku Tokyo 164-0013 Japan Personal E-mail: a-sasaki@fa2.so-net.ne.jp. Business E-Mail: a-sasaki@sasaki-medical-clinic.jp.

SASAKI, CLARENCE TAKASHI, surgeon, educator; b. Honolulu, Jan. 24, 1941; s. Tsutomu and Carla Harumi (Mirikitani) S.; m. Carolyn Elizabeth Lindahl, June 26, 1967; children: Peter Gordon, John Eric. BA, Pomona Coll., 1962; MD, Yale U., 1966. Diplomate: Am. Bd. Otolaryngology. Intern San Francisco Hosp., U. Calif., 1966-67; resident in surgery Dartmouth Med. Sch., 1967-68; resident in otolaryngology Yale U. Med. Sch. Hosps., New Haven, 1970-73, faculty mem., 1973—, assoc. prof., 1977-82, prof. surgery, 1982—, chief sect. otolaryngology, 1981—, Charles Ohse prof. surgery, 1988—, vice chmn. dept. surgery, 1996. Author: Surgery of the Skull Base, Head and Neck Surgery, Vol. 1 Atlas Otolarynogology, Vocal Fold Physiology, Laryngeal Function in Phonation and Respiration, Neurological Diseases of the Larynx, Laryngeal Physiology for the Surgeon, 2008; mem. editl. bd. profl. jours. Served to maj. M.C. U.S. Army, 1968-70. Recipient award Fowler Triological Soc., 1979. Mem. Am. Acad. Otolaryngology (1st prize clin. rsch.), Am. Soc. Head and Neck Surgery (coun.), Assn. Rsch. Otolaryngology, Am. Laryngol. Rhinol. and Otol. Soc. (coun., sec. ea. sect. 1990, v.p. 1998), New Eng. Otolaryngology Soc. (pres. 1987, coun.), Assn. Acad. Depts. Otolaryngology (coun.), Am. Laryngol. Assn. (coun. 2008, Casselberry award 1999, ALA award, 2010), Pan Pacific Surg. Assn., Soc. for Neurosci., Soc. Neurovascular Surgery, Soc. for Head and Neck Surgeons, Am. Neurotolog. Soc., Pan Am. Assn. Oto-rhinolaryngology and Bronchoesophagology, Conn. Med. Soc., N.Y. Acad. Scis., Soc. Univ. Otolaryngologists, Collegium ORLAS, Cartesian Soc. (co-dir.), Am. Bronchoesophagological Assn. (mem. coun., treas. 2003, pres. 2007, Broyles-Maloney award 2004, Chevalier Jackson award 2010), N.Am. Skull Base Soc., Laryngeal. Cancer Assn. (Padua), Am. Otol. Soc., Dysphagia Rsch. Soc. (treas., pres.), Lawn Club, Mory's Assoc., Yale Club, Phi Beta Kappa, Sigma Xi. Office: Yale U Med Sch Dept Surgery PO Box 208041 333 Cedar St New Haven CT 06520-8041 Office Phone: 203-785-2592.

SASAKI, KEN-ICHIRO, cardiologist, educator; b. Japan, Apr. 28, 1969; D, Kurume U., 2002, MD. Physician. asst. dept. internal medicine III Kurume U. Sch. Medicine, 1994—2002; physician. asst. Divsn. Cardiovasc. Medicine, Dept. Internal Medicine III, Kurume U. Sch. Medicine, 2002—11, physician, asst. prof., 2011—. Office: 67 Asahi-machi Kurume Fukuoka 830-0011 Japan Office Phone: 81-942-31-7562. Office Fax: 81-942-33-6509. Business E-Mail: sasaken@med.kurume-u.ac.jp.

SASAKI, KENROH, pharmaceutical science educator, researcher; b. Onoda Miyagi, Japan, 1964; s. Ken-ichi and Sachiko Sasaki; m. Naomi Furusawa; children: Kentaro, Koutaro, Atsuro. PhD, Tohoku Pharm. U., Sendai, 1992. Cert. pharmacist Ministry of Welfare, Japan. Asst. prof. Tohoku Pharm. U., 1992—2002, univ. lectr., 2003—; rsch. assoc. U. Miss. Med. Ctr., Jackson, 2000—01. Acad. councilor Japanese Pharmacol. Soc., Tokyo, 2000—. Contbr. articles to profl. jours. Mem.: Oriental Med. Soc. Japan, Pharmacognosy Soc. Japan, Neurophyschopharmacological Soc. Japan, Pharm. Soc. Japan. Achievements include patents in field. Office: Tohoku Pharm U Komatsushima 4-4-1 Aoba-ku Sendai 981-8558 Japan Office Fax: 81 22 727 0220. E-mail: kenrs@tohoku-pharm.ac.jp.

SASAKI, NOBUHISA, orthopaedic surgeon; b. Miyako, Japan, Oct. 22, 1972; s. Osamu and Reiko Sasaki; m. Yoko Hatayama, July 20, 2000; 1 child, Keigo. MD, Fukushima Med. U., Japan, 1998, PhD, 2004. Postdoctoral fellow dept. orthopaedic surgery Fukushima Med. U., Sch. Medicine, 2004—. Guest rschr. dept. orthopaedics Inst. Clin. Scis., Sahlgrenska Acad., Göteborg U., Gothenburg, Sweden, 2005—07; clin. dr. Yurin Hosp., Kitakata, Japan, 2007—08, Minami Souna City Gen. Hosp., Japan, 2008—10, Takasu Orthops. & Internal Medicine, Urayasu, Japan, 2010—; vis. assoc. prof. Ryotokuji U., Urayasu, 2010—. Recipient Incentive award, Japanese br. office Internat. Soc. for the Study of the Lumbar Spine, 2006. Shinto. Achievements include research in anti TNF-alpha antibody reduces pain-behavioral changes induced by epidural application of nucleus pulposus in a rat model depending on the timing of administration; anti nociceptive effect of bovine milk derived lactoferrin in a rat lamber disc herniation model. Avocation: travel. Office Phone: 81-47-380-5050. Business E-Mail: non@fmu.ac.jp.

SASAKI, SATOSHI, engineering educator; b. Japan, July 16, 1966; MS, U. Tokyo, 1992, DEng, 1998. Prof. Tokyo U. Tech., 2010—. Lectr. J. F. Oberlin U., 2010. Avocations: photography, guitar. Office: 1404-1 Katakura Hachioji Tokyo 192-0982 Japan Business E-Mail: sasaki@bs.teu.ac.jp.

SASENICK, JOSEPH ANTHONY, health care company executive; b. Chgo., May 18, 1940; s. Anthony E. and Caroline E. (Smicklas) S.; m. Betty Cheung, Dec. 22, 2007; children: Richard Allen, Susan Marie, Michael Joseph. BA, DePaul U., 1962; MA, U. Okla., 1966. With Miles Labs., Inc., Elkhart, Ind., 1963-70; product mgr. Alka-Seltzer, 1966-68, dir. mktg. grocery products divsn., 1968-70; with Gillette Corp., Boston, 1970-79, dir. new products/new ventures, personal care divsn., 1977; v.p. diversified cos. and pres. Jafra Cosmetics Worldwide, 1977-79; mktg. dir. Braun AG, Kronberg, W. Ger., 1970-73; chmn. mng. dir. Braun U.K. Ltd., 1973-77; with Abbott Labs., North Chicago, 1979-84, corp. v.p., pres. consumer products divsn., 1979-84; pres., CEO, Moxie Industries, 1984-87; pres., CEO Personal Monitoring Technologies, Rochester, NY, 1987; pres. Bioline Labs., Ft. Lauderdale, Fla., 1988; mng. dir., ptnr. Vista Resource Group, Newport Beach, Calif., 1988-90; pres., CEO, Alcide Corp., Redmond, Wash., 1991-92, chmn., CEO, 1992—2004; founder Board Romm Ltd., 2004; life sci. commercialization cons. Washington Biotech. & Biomed. Assn., Seattle. Mem. Columbia Tower Club, Wash. Athletic Club. Home and Office: Board Room Ltd 1301 Spring St # 24J Seattle WA 98104 Office Phone: 206-732-6703. Personal E-mail: jasasenick@msn.com.

SASHIN, DONALD, physicist, educator; b. NYC, Dec. 11, 1937; s. David and Pearl (Taub) S.; m. Kathleen Flaherty, July 24, 1967; children: Deirdre Moira, Courtenay Aileen. BS in Physics, MIT, 1960; MS in Physics, Carnegie Inst. Tech., 1962; PhD in Physics, Carnegie Mellon U., 1968. Instr. radiology and radiation health U. Pitts., 1967-70, asst. prof. radiology, 1970-74, asst. prof. indsl and environ. health, 1970-77; asst. prof. radiation health, 1977-87; assoc. prof. radiology U. Pitts., 1974—, assoc. prof. radiation health, 1987-89, assoc. prof. environ. and occupl. health, 1989-2000. Contbr. articles to profl. jours., patentee in field. Recipient Cum Laude award sci. exhibit Radiol. Soc. N.Am., 1977, cert. of merit sci. exhibit, 1979. Mem. IEEE, AAAS, Am. Phys. Soc., Am. Assn. Physicists in Medicine, Soc. Nuclear Medicine, Health Physics Soc., Rotary Internat. (Pitts.) (pres., Oakland chpt. 2011-), Sigma Xi. Democrat. Roman Catholic. Avocations: golf, fishing, swimming, sailing. Home: 4360 Centre Ave Pittsburgh PA 15213-1403 Office: PET Facility B938 PUH/UPMC 200 Lothrop St Pittsburgh PA 15213-2546 Home Phone: 412-683-1468; Office Phone: 412-647-0713.

SASHIYAMA, HIROSHI, surgeon; b. Japan, Mar. 5, 1963; MD, Chiba U., 1994, PhD, 2001. Dir. endoscopy unit Tsujinaka Hosp. Kashiwanoha, 2009—. Mem.: Japanese Bd. Cancer Therapy (gen. clin. oncologist), Japan Gastroent. Endoscopy Soc. (bd. cert. endscopist in gastroenterology), Japanese Soc. Gastroenterology (bd. cert. gastroenterologist), Japanese Soc. Gastroent. Surgery (bd. cert. surgeon in gastroenterology), Japan Surg. Soc. (bd. cert. surgeon). Office: 178-2 Wakashiba Kashiwa Chiba 277-0871 Japan Office Fax: 81-4-7137-3738. E-mail: sasiyama@hotmail.com.

SASLOW, DEBBIE L., cancer control specialist, director; d. H. Arnold and Ann E. Weinstat; children: Kayla M., Rianna N. BS, Brown U., 1983—87; PhD, Yale U., 1987—92. Coord., president's nat. action plan on breast cancer PHS Office on Women's Health, Washington, 1995—97; dir., breast and gynecologic cancers Am. Cancer Soc., Atlanta, 1997—. Spkr. in field. Office: 250 Williams St 6th Floor Atlanta GA 30303

SASMAL, PRAKASH KUMAR SASMAL, surgeon, educator; b. India, June 3, 1974; MBBS, SCB Med. Coll., Odisha, MS in Gen. Surgery, 1999; degree in Minimal Access Surgery, ILS Hosp., Kolkata, 2010. Asst. prof. IMS & SUM Hosp., Bhubaneswar, 2010—. Cons., advanced laparoscopic and bariatric surgeon Swarna Hosp., 2011. Contbr. articles to sci. profl. jours. Recipient Gold medal, Dr. Kasinath Mishra U., Utkal U. Fellow: Nat. Bd.; mem.: Assn. Minimal Access Surgeons India, Assn. Surgeons India. Avocations: travel, gardening, painting. Home: Plot- 5F/746/2 Sector - 9 CDA Cuttack Odisha 753014 India Personal E-mail: drpksasma@gmail.com.

SASS, CYNTHIA, dietician, health expert; BS, MS in Nutrition Sci., Syracuse U., NY; MPH, U. South Fla. Cert. specialist in sports dietetics American Dietetic Assn., registered dietitian. Adj. faculty Sch. Phys. Edn. & Exercise Sci., U. South Fla., 2000—07; pres. Sass Consulting Svcs, Inc., 2004; nutrition dir., columnist Prevention Mag., 2007—08; nutrition cons. Phila. Phillies, 2007—09; sports nutritionist NY Rangers, Tampa Bay Rays. Author: Your Diet is Driving Me Crazy: When Food Conflicts Get in the Way of Your Love Life, 2004, Cinch! Conquer Cravings, Drop Pounds and Lose Inches, 2011 (NY Times Bestseller); co-author: Flat Belly Diet!, 2008 (NY Times Bestseller), Flat Belly Diet! Cookbook, 2009 (NY Times Bestseller), The Ultimate Diet Log, 2009; contbg. editor, columnist, nutritionist Athletes Quarterly, contbg. editor, blogger Shape mag., Food Coach columnist Remedy mag., sports nutrition columnist Tennis mag., mem. editl adv. bd. Martha Stewart Whole Living, Taste of Home, Healthy Cooking, numerous TV appearances include Today Show, Good Morning America, The Early Show, Rachel Ray Show, The Biggest Loser, Dr. Oz Show, Martha Stewart Show, Nightline, ABC World News Tonight, CNN, Extra, The Insider, MSNBC, Fox News Live, others. Mem.: American Coll. Sports Medicine, Tampa Dietetic Assn. (pres., webmaster, media rep 2006—07, Disting. Dietitian 2006), American Dietetic Assn. (nat. media spokesperson 2001—07, one of Recognized Young Dietitians of Yr. 2005), Eta Sigma Gamma (pres. Delta Kappa chpt. 2002—03). Office: c/o HarperCollins Publishers Inc 10 E 53rd St New York NY 10022 Office Phone: 212-207-7000. Office Fax: 212-207-7145.

SASS, NEIL LESLIE, toxicologist; b. Balt., Oct. 24, 1944; s. Samuel and Blanche (Radoon) S.; m. Anita Paige Hoswell, June 29, 1984. BS, Wake Forest Coll., 1966; MS, W.Va. U., 1969, PhD, 1971; MS, Johns Hopkins U., 1984. Commd. officer USPHS, 1966, advanced through grades to capt., 1988, comdr. Preventive Medicine unit, 1989; served as rsch. toxicologist med. labs. U.S. Army, Edgewood Arsenal, Md., 1971-74; chief clin. investigations William Beaumont Army Med. Ctr., El Paso, Tex., 1974-77; toxicologist Bur. of Foods FDA, Washington, 1977-82; spl. asst. to dir. Ctr. for Food Safety and Applied Nutrition, FDA, Washington, 1982-99; dir. divsn. toxicological rsch. Ctr. for Food Safety and Applied Nutrition, Washington, 1996-99; chief toxicologist, state counterterrorism coord., chem. lab. dir. Ala. Dept. Pub. Health, Montgomery, 1999—2010. Jewish. Office: Ala Dept Pub Health The RSA Tower 201 Monroe St Ste 1450 Montgomery AL 36104-3735 Home: 904 Longfellow Pl Dauphin Island AL 36528-4432 Home Phone: 334-832-2322; Office Phone: 334-206-5973. Business E-Mail: nsass@adph.state.al.us.

SASSO, ENRICO, medical educator; b. Naples, Italy, Feb. 5, 1956; Laureate, U. Naples, 1981, PhD, 1988. Head epileptic care unit U. Parma, 1999, prof., dept. neuroscience, 2001—. Mem.: Italian League Against Epilepsies. Avocations: painting, music. Office: Via Gramsci 14 Parma 43126 Italy Office Fax: 390521704115. Business E-Mail: enrico.sasso@unipr.it.

SASSO, LOREDANA, nursing educator; b. Sanremo, Nov. 28, 1957; MSN, U. Genoa, Rome, 2006. Ednl. coord., tutor Cath. U. Sacro Cuore U. Genoa, 1986—2001, assoc. prof. dept. health scis., 2005—, dir. PhD course nursing rsch., 2006—. Pediat. nurse Inst. G. Gaslini Hosp. Genoa, 1976—80; expert healthcare and ednl. processes Provincial Ctr. Infancy, Imperia, 1980—86; dir. Healthcare Edn. & Tng. Ctr. San Martino Hosp., U. Genoa, 1993—2005. Master: Fedn. Nat. dei Coll. IPASVI (Rome) (Italian regulatory bd. nursing nat. sec., exec. bd. mem.), European Coun. Nursing Regulators (Brussels) (v.p. past pres., founding mem.). Avocations: jogging, reading, travel. Office: via A Pastore 1 Genoa Liguria 16132 Italy Office Fax: 39 353 8552. Business E-Mail: l.sasso@unige.it.

SASSON, J. PIERRE, radiologist, director; b. NYC, Aug. 6, 1962; MD, Tufts U. Sch. Medicine, 1989. Vice chair, radiology residency program dir. Mt. Auburn Hosp., 1998—. Recipient Excellence Tchg. award, Radiology Residents. Mem.: Assn. Program Dirs. Radiology, Radiologic Soc. N.America, Am. Soc. Neuroradiology (sr.). Office: Mt Auburn Hosp 330 Mt Auburn St Cambridge MA 02138 Office Fax: 617-499-5546. Business E-Mail: psasson@gmail.com.

SASTROWARDOYO, TERESITA MANEJAR, nurse; b. Iloilo, Philippines; came to U.S., 1960; d. Timoteo and Monica (Casianan) Manejar; m. Sumarsongko H. Sastrowardoyo, June 8, 1962; children: Timoteo, Daniel (dec.), Benjamin. BSN, Ctrl. Philippine U., Iloilo, 1957; cert. operating rm. and surgical nursing, St. Luke's Hosp Ctr., NYC, 1960-61. Head nurse med. unit Emmanuel Hosp., Roxas City, Philippines, 1957-58; supr. oper. rm. Brent Hosp., Zamboanga City, Philippines, 1958-60; staff nurse oper. rm. Jewish Meml. Hosp., NYC, 1961-62; evening staff nurse oper. rm. Flower and Fifth Ave Hosp., NYC, 1963-65; staff nurse oper. rm., charge nurse night shift St. Lukes Hosp. Ctr., NYC, 1966-76; staff nurse oper. rm. South Side Hosp., Bayshore, NY, 1976—, asst. head nurse operating room, 2003—. Mem.: N.Y. State Nurses Assn., Ctrl. Philippine U. Alumni Assn. N.Y., N.J. and Conn. (bd. dirs. 1994—95, 1995—97). Baptist. Avocations: gardening, reading.

SATAKE, KATSUSUKE, surgeon, educator; b. Osaka, Japan, Apr. 6, 1935; s. Jutaro and Toshi (Izuma) S.; m. Michiko Kitamoto, May 28, 1967; children: Makoto, Akira, Shinobu. MD, Osaka U., Japan, 1961, D in Med. Sci., 1973. Intern Tachikawa USAF Hosp., Tokyo, 1961-62; resident surgery Osaka (Japan) City Univ. Hosp., 1962-69, instr. surgery, 1969-74; surg. fellow Hahnemman Med. Coll., Phila., 1970-72; asst. prof. Osaka (Japan) City U., 1974-89, assoc. prof., 1989-2001. Chmn. surgery Osaka (Japan) Socio-Med. Ctr., 1992-2001; vis. prof. Kyto Univ. Sch. Medicine, 2000—; pres. (hon.) Minami Ashiyahama Hosp., 2001—. Assoc. editor: Pancreas, 1986; co-editor: Jour. Hepato-Biliary Pancreatic Surgery, 1992—, 2001; editor-in-chief: Jour. of the Japan Pancreas Soc., 1999—2001; editor: Pancreatology, 1999—. Grantee for pancreatic cancer Japanese Ministry Health and Welfare, Tokyo, 1986—, grantee for acute pancreatitis Pancreatic Rsch. Found. Tokyo Japan, 1993. Fellow ACS, Japanese Assn. Gastroenterology, Japan Pancreas Soc. (mem. coun. 1987); mem. Soc. for Surgery of the Alimentary Tract, Internat. Assn. Pancreatology (coun. 1998), Pancreatic Rsch. Found. of Japan (coun. 1997—, exec. dir. 2001—), Asia Oceanica Pancreatic Assn. (councilor 2004—). Home: 4-3-9 Shinimazato Ikuno-ku Osaka 544-0001 Japan Office: Higashi Nagahara Hosp 4-3-13 Nagata Nishi Osaka 577-0018 Japan Home Phone: 81 6 6758 4321; Office Phone: 81 6 6766 0111. Fax: 81-797-23-6117. E-mail: satakek@f8.dion.ne.jp.

SATALOFF, DAHLIA, surgeon, educator; MD, U. Mich. Intern in gen surgery St. Joseph Mercy Hosp.; resident in gen. surgery Pa. Hosp., dir. integrated breast cancer, vice chair dept. of surgery; clin. prof. surgery Univ. of Pa. Sch. of Medicine. Profl. adv. bd. mem. Breast Cancer.org. Named Top Doc, Phila. Mag., 2002, 2011, Best Doctors in America, 2007—08, 2009—10; named one of Top Physicians, Suburban Life Mag., 2010. Mem.: Ea. Coop. Oncology Group, Am. Soc. of Breast Surgeons, Soc. of Surg. Oncology, Am. Soc. of Clin. Oncology. Office: Hospital of the University of Pennsylvania 3400 Spruce St Philadelphia PA 19104 Office Phone: 215-662-4000.

SATCHER, DAVID, public health service officer, former Surgeon General of the United States; b. Anniston, Ala., Mar. 2, 1941; s. Wilmer and Anna Satcher; m. Nola Satcher; children: Gretchen, David, Daraka, Daryl. BS, Morehouse Coll., 1963; MD, PhD, Case Western Reserve U., 1970; recipient of many honorary degrees and numerous disting. honors. Resident and fellow Strong Mem. Hosp., U. Rochester, UCLA, and King Drew; former faculty UCLA Sch. Medicine and Pub. Health; faculty, chair dept. family medicine King-Drew Med. Ctr., LA, interim dean, 1977—79; dir. King-Drew Sickle Cell Rsch. Ctr.; prof., chmn. dept. cmty. and family medicine Morehouse Sch. Medicine, Atlanta, 1979—82; pres. Meharry Med. Coll., Nashville, 1982—93; dir. Ctrs. for Disease Control and Prevention, Atlanta, 1993—98; adminstr. Agy. for Toxic Substances and Disease Registry, 1993—98; surgeon gen. US Dept. Health & Human Services, Washington, 1998—2002, asst. sec. health, 1998—2001; sr. vis. fellow Kaiser Family Found., Washington, 2002—; dir. Nat. Ctr. for Primary Care Morehouse Sch. Medicine, Atlanta, 2002—, interim pres., 2005—06, founder, dir. Satcher Health Leadership Inst., 2006—. Apptd. mem. Coun. of Grad. Med. Edn., 1986, chmn.; former Robert Wood Johnson Clin. Scholar; former Macy Faculty Fellow; bd. dir. Jonhson & Jonhson, 2002—, MetLife Inc., 2007—. Recipient Watts Grassroots award for cmty. leadership, 1979, Nat. Conf. Christians and Jews awards, 1985, Black Achievment award, Ebony Mag., 1994, Brewslow award in pub. health, 1995, Dr. Nathan B. Davis award, AMA, 1996, Lifetime Achievement award, NY Acad. Medicine, 1997, Bennie Mays Trailblazer award, Nat. Found. for Infectious Diseases, Jimmy and Roslyn Carter award, Discovery Health Channel Med. Honors, 2004; named Nashvillian of Yr., 1992. Fellow: Am. Acad. of Family Physicians; mem.: Inst. Medicine NAS, Alpha Omega Alpha, Phi Beta Kappa. Focuses on promoting healthly lifestyles and ending disparities in health; as director of the CDC, he raised childhood immunization rates to 78% in 1996 from 55% in 1992. Office: Nat Ctr for Primary Care at Morehouse Sch Medicine 720 Westview Dr SW Atlanta GA 30310 Office Fax: 404-756-5767. *

SATHYANARAYANA, SHEELA, pediatrician, educator; BA, Duke U., 1997; MD, U. Southern Calif. Sch. Medicine, 2002; MPH, U. Wash. Sch. Pub. Health, 2007. Resident U. Wash. CHRMC, 2002—05; asst. prof. divsn. gen. pediatrics U. Wash. Office: University of Washington Dept of Pediatrics 1100 Olive Way Ste 500 M/S 8-1 Box 35930 Seattle WA 98101 Office Phone: 206-884-1037. E-mail: sheela.sathyanarayana@seattlechildrens.org.

SATHYAVAGISWARAN, LAKSHMANAN, pathologist, county official; b. Madras, India, Mar. 17, 1949; MD, Stanley Med. Coll., Madras U., 1971. Intern,anatomical clin. pathology Jewish Hosp. Med. Ctr., Bklyn., 1972—73; resident, forensic pathology Columbia U., St. Luke's Hosp., NY, 1973—77; resident, internal medicine County of LA, 1977—78, dep. med. examiner, 1978—92, chief med. examiner-coroner, 1992—; resident, infectious diseases Bklyn. Cumberland Med. Ctr., NY, 1980—81; fellow, infectious disease Columbia U. Harlem Hosp., NY, 1981—82; fellow UCLA King Drew Med. Ctr., 1982—83; staff mem. LA County, U. Southern Calif. Med. Ctr. Clin. prof., pathology U. Southern Calif. Keck Sch. Medicine, UCLA Geffen Sch. Medicine. Achievements include being the medical examiner during the O.J. Simpson murder trial and testified during the criminal and civil trials; testified in the trials of Dean Carter and Phil Spector; performed the autopsy of the body of Micheal Jackson on June 26, 2009. Office: 623 W Duarte Rd Ste 2 Arcadia CA 91007 Office Phone: 626-574-7587.

SATO, CHIFUMI, physician, educator; b. Agatsuma, Japan, July 16, 1949; s. Chiharu and Keiko (Ito) Sato; m. Mayumi Nakanishi, Nov. 2, 1975; 1 child. MD, Tokyo Med. and Dental U., 1975, PhD, 1983. Resident Tokyo Med. and Dental U., 1975-77, Bronx VA Med. Ctr., NYC, 1977-81; sr. resident Tokyo Med. and Dental U., 1981-82, from asst. prof. to assoc. prof., 1982—94, prof., 1994—. Sr. specialist sci. affairs Ministry of Edn., Sci. and Culture, Japan, 1987—89. Mem.: Japanese Gastroent. Assn., Japanese Assn. Study of Liver. Avocation: running. Office: Tokyo Med & Dental U Dept Analytical Health Sci/1-5-45 Yushima Bunkyo-ku Tokyo 113-8519 Japan Office Phone: 81-3-5803-5335. E-mail: c.sato.ns@tmd.ac.jp.

SATO, ETSURO, pulmonologist; b. Saku, Japan, May 4, 1964; s. Tsugunobu and Hisako Sato; m. Kazue Ito, June 18, 1994. MD, Shinshu U., 1984—89, PhD, 1989—98. Staff dr. Koseiren Shinmachi Hosp., Nagano, Japan, 2000—; resident Shinshu U. Hosp., Nagano, Japan, 1989—90, staff dr., 2000—00; vis. investigator Ariz. State U., 1999—2000, La. State U. Med. Ctr., Shreveport, 1998; staff dr. Shinshu U. Hosp., Nagano, Japan, 1997—98, Nat. Chusin Matsumoto Hosp., Nagano, Japan, 1996—97, Shinshu U. Hosp., Nagano, Japan, 1992—96, Asama Gen. Hosp., Nagano, Japan, 1991—92; resident Nagano Red Cross Hosp., Japan, 1990—91. Contbr. articles to profl. jours. Mem.: Japanese Soc. Allergology, Japanese Respiratory Soc., Japanese Soc. Internal Medicine. Avocations: golf, travel, skiing. Home: Tanbajima 1-611-1 Nagano 381-2246 Japan Office: Shinmachi Hosp Kamijo 137 Shinshushinmachi Nagano 381-2404 Japan Office Phone: 026-262-3111. Office Fax: 026-262-3411. Personal E-mail: angiorensin2@yahoo.co.jp.

SATO, FÁBIO RICARDO LOUREIRO, oral and maxillofacial surgeon, researcher, professor; BA, Fundação Getúlio Vargas, São Paulo, Brazil, 2003, MBA, 2006; DDS, U. São Paulo, 2009; MS, OMFS, Piracicaba Dental Sch., State U. Campinas-Unicamp, 2008, PhD, 2010. Mgr. Hosp. Sírio-Libanês, São Paulo, 2005—06, Hosp. Des Defileoda Fore OMFS, 2010. Home: Rua Santa Catarina 03086-025 Sao Paulo SP Brazil

SATO, HIROKAZU, pediatrician; b. Youkaichiba, Chiba, Japan, Mar. 13, 1956; s. Tadayoshi and Nobuko Sato; m. Chizuru Hatori, Nov. 14, 1982; children: Asuka, Hayato. Degree, Gunma U., Japan, 1981. Resident dept. pediat. Chiba U., 1981—89; chief physician pediat. dept. Funabashi Ctrl. Hosp., 1989—93; chief physician divsn. endocrinology Chiba Children's Hosp., 1993—2002; asst. prof. Saitama Med. U., Moroyama, Japan, 2002—04; visc-dir. Sunrise Children's Clinic, Funabashi, 2004—. Contbr. scientific papers (Pharmacia Corp. Internat. award, 2000). Office: Sunrise Children's Clinic 4-22-10 Motonakayama Funabashi 273 0035 Japan Office Phone: 81 47 333 8222. Office Fax: 81 47 333 2733. Personal E-mail: hschiba@aol.com.

SATO, KEN, physician, researcher; s. Seiichi and Kinuko Sato; m. Tomomi Sekiguchi, Apr. 23, 1995; children: Yuuki, Naoki. MD, Jichi Med. Sch., Japan, 1990; PhD, Gunma U., Japan, 1998. Physician Gunma U., 1990—91, physician in affiliated hosps., 1991—98, sr. resident, 1998—2000, 2003—04, assoc., 2004—06, asst. prof., 2007—. Rschr. U. Calif., Irvine, 2000—03. Author: Trends in Bone Cancer Research, 2006, Focus on Vitamin E Research, 2006. Grantee, Japan Soc. for Promotion Sci., 2005—06, 2008—; grant, Japanese Found. Rsch. and Promotion Endoscopy, 2009. Fellow: Japan Gastroenterological Endoscopy Soc. (diplomate), Japan Soc. Hepatology (diplomate), Japanese Soc. Gastroenterology (diplomate), Japanese Soc. Internal Medicine (diplomate). Achievements include application of combinatorial molecular engineering using phage display; validation of effective therapy for chronic hepatitis B and C; research in actual situation of liver tumors with non-alcoholic steatohepatitis; identification of werner syndrome as a possible cause of non-alcoholic steatohepatitis; elucidation of the role and mechanism of transforming growth factor-alpha in hepatic fibrosis; validation of partial splenic embolization for antiviral therapy in chronic hepatitis C with thrombocytopenia; elucidation of the antifibrotic and antixidant effects of azelnidipine on models of experimental liver fibrosis.

SATO, MASAYUKI, retired medical educator; b. Hokkaido, Japan, June 30, 1943; BS, Thohoku U., 1966, PhD, 1972. Asst. prof., Sch. Pharm. Scis. Tohoku U., 1974—98; prof. U. Shizuoka, 1998—2009, councilor, 2001—03. Mem.: Chem. Soc. Japan, Am. Chem. Soc., Pharm. Soc. Japan (editor, chem. and pharm. bull. 1995—97, Promotion award). Avocations: golf, fishing.

SATO, MASUKO, pediatrician, clinical psychologist; b. Osaka, Japan, Nov. 4, 1938; d. Yoshida Kikuzo and Yoshida (Nishimura) Yone; m. Sato Yoshinobu, May 28, 1963; children: Mayumi, Naomi. Grad., Kyoto Prefectural Med., MD, 1963; PhD Pathological Studies Brain Damage, 1967. Pediatrician Japan Bapt. Hosp., Kyoto, 1967, vis. pediat. investigator NYU Med. Ctr., 1967; assoc. prof. preventive medicine pediat., dept. child health Kyoto Women's U., 1972-82, prof., 1982—2004; hon. prof. Bukkyo U., 2004—08; prof. clin. psychology dept. edn.; pediatracian Developmental Disorder Clinic, Uji Takeda Hosp., 2005—. Author: Recent Child Health, 1983, rev. edit., 1994; author, editor: Practice Guide in Child Health, 2003, Practice in Child Health, 2006, rev., 2009 Child Health-Theory and Practice 3rd rev., 2009; contbr., editor Ency. of Infant Devel., 1985. Dir., Yukawa Social Gathering of World Federalists, Kyoto, 1989-2008. Recipient Awards of fostering for nursery, Japanese assn. of social welfare. Mem. Japan Soc. Child Health (councilor 1985-2003). Home: 8 Shimogamo-Maehagicho Sakyo-ku Kyoto 606-0833 Japan Office: Dept Pediatrics Uji Takeda Hosp 24-1 Azamonji Uji 611-0021 Japan

SATO, MINORU, chemist, educator; b. Kesennuma, Miyagi, Japan, Oct. 1, 1948; s. Denzho and Hashime Sato; m. Tokuko Onodera, Apr. 11, 1976; children: Motohiro, Kana, Tomonori. BS, Tohoku U., Sendai, 1971, PhD, 1981. Rschr. Nissin Food Products, Co. Ltd., Takatsuki, Osaka, Japan, 1971—73; rsch. asst. Kitasato U., Sanriku, Iwate, Japan, 1973—81, lectr., 1981—83, assoc. prof., 1983—90, Tohoku U., Sendai, Miyagi, Japan, 1990—99, prof., 1999—, dir. dept. applied biosci., 2005—. Editor, author: Micronutrients and Health of Cultured Fish, 2003. Recipient Collaborative Rsch. award, Iron and Steel Inst. Japan, 2004. Fellow: Japanese Soc. Fisheries Sci. (Achievement award for Young Scientist 1989). Achievements include patents for freshness checker and histamine checker of simple and quick freshness and histamine analyzer. Avocations: travel, bowling. Office: Tohoku Univ Tsutsumidori Amamiyamachi 1-1 Miyagi Sendai 981-8555 Japan Office Fax: 81-22-717-8739. E-mail: msato@bios.tohoku.ac.jp.

SATO, TAKAMI, pediatrician, medical oncologist; b. Oita-shi, Japan, July 27, 1955; s. Takao and Miyoko (Tashima) S.; m. Chiyo Motoyoshi, Dec. 4, 1983; children: Takahiro, Shingo, Rino, Youki. MD, Jichi Med. U., 1980. Med. dr. Kiyokawa-mura Clin., Onogun, Japan, 1985—88; assoc. dir. div. pediatrics and internal medicine Oita Prefectural Hosp., Onogun, 1988—90; instr. Jichi Med. Sch., Kawachi-gun, Japan, 1990—92; asst. prof. dept. medicine Thomas Jefferson U., Phila., 1993—98, assoc. prof. dept. medicine, 1998—2007, prof. dept. med. oncology, 2007—. Contbr. articles to profl. jours. Mem.: AACR, Japanese Pediatric Soc., Am. Soc. Clin. Oncology. Office: Thomas Jefferson U 925 Chestnut St Philadelphia PA 19107-5005 Office Phone: 215-955-8875.

SATO, YOSHINOBU, clinical pathologist, otolaryngologist; b. Kyoto, Dec. 16, 1934; s. Juhei and Aya Nakamura S.; m. Masuko Yoshida Sato; children: Mayumi Sato Morimoto, Naomi Sato Matsumoto. Grad., Kyoto Prefectural U. Med., 1961, MD, 1962, PhD Biochem. Studies, 1967. Asst. prof. Kyoto Prefectural U. Med., 1970-75; prof. clin. pathology, dep. med. tech. Kobe Tokiwa U., 1979—2000. Cons. Biomed. and Environ. Cons., Inc., Richland, Wash., 1989—; invited guest investigator, tchg. asst. NYU Med. Ctr., 1967-68; exec. bd. Internat. Soc. Aerosols Medicine, 1977-95, pres. Symposium 1990 of 3rd Internat. Aerosol Conf., 1990-91, pres. Symposium of 5th Internat. Aerosols Conf., Tokyo, Kobe, 1984; v.p. Japan Assn. Aerosol Sci. and Tech. (JAAST), 1990-91, hon. mem., 2008-; hon. pres. Japan Soc. Aerosols Medicine, 1995—, founder, pres., chmn., bd. dirs. Kanto Total Health Care and Promotion Plan Clinic, 1994—2011, Kinki Preventive Med. Labs., Inc., 1995—. Editor Jour. Aerosol Medicine, N.Y., 1988-93. Recipient Iinoya prize Japan Assn. Aerosol Sci. and Tech., 1994, Career Achievement award Internat. Soc. Aerosols Medicine, 1997. Home: 8 Shimogamo Maehagicho Sakyoku Kyoto 606-0833 Japan Office: Kinki Preventive Med Labs Inc 19-9 Kojogaoka Otsu 520-0821 Japan Office Phone: 81-77-522-7699. Business E-Mail: labthp@ezweb.ne.jp. E-mail: labthp@softbank.ne.jp.

SATO, YUKIHITO, internist; b. Hyogo, Japan, Aug. 31, 1962; MD, Kyoto U., 1987, PhD, 1995. Trainee Kyoto U. Hosp., 1987—88, Hamamatsu Rosni Hosp., 1988—90; chief internal medicine Hyogo Prefectural Amagasaki Hosp., Japan, 1995—2001, 2004—; asst. cardiology Kyoto U., 2001—04, clin. asst. prof. cardiology, 2004—. Office: Hyogo Prefectural Amagasaki Hosp Higashidaimotsucho 1-1-1 Hyogo Amagasaki 660-0828 Japan Office Fax: 06-6482-7430. Business E-Mail: cardioys@kuhp.kyoto-u.ac.jp.

SATOH, KOICHI, oral surgeon; s. Ken-Ichi and Michiko Satoh; m. Tomoko Mukae, Apr. 22, 1989; children: Nobuaki, Hirofumi, Toshiharu, Masako. DDS, Kyushu Dental Coll., Kitakyushu, Japan, 1988; PhD, Osaka U., Japan, 1995. Cert. Japanese Bd. Oral and Maxillofacial Surgery, 1998. Asst. prof. Kyushu Dental Coll., Miyazaki, 1995—97, Miyazaki Med. Coll., 1997—99, assoc. prof., 1999—2001, Kyushu Dental Coll., Kitakyushu, Fukuoka, Japan, 2001—. Oral and maxillofacial surgeon Japanese Cleft Palate Found., Dahka, Bangladesh, 2000, La Marsa, Tunisia, 02, Sfax, Tunisia, 05, Clinica de Labio y Paladar Hendido, Monterrey, Mexico, 2002; presenter and spkr. in field. Editor: Cleft Palate Speech (Japanese edition); contbr. articles to profl. jours. Grantee, Ministry Edn., Sci., Sports and Culture in Japan, 1995—96, 2004—05. Mem.: Japanese Assn. Oral and Maxillofacial Surgeons, Japanese Cleft Palate Assn., Internat. Assn. Oral and Maxillofacial Surgeons, Am. Cleft Platate-Craniofacial Assn. Office: Kyushu Dental Coll 2-6-1 Manazuru Kokurakita-ku Kitakyushu Fukuoka 803-8580 Japan Office Fax: +81-93-582-1286. Business E-Mail: satoh@kyu-dent.ac.jp.

SATOH, TOMOHIDE, pathologist; b. Tokyo, Jan. 3, 1960; s. Shoichi and Tsuyako Satoh. DDS, Tokyo Dental Coll., Chiba, Japan, 1984, PhD, 1988. Invited scientist U. Milan (Italy), 1988-89; rsch. assoc. Tokyo Dental Coll., Chiba, 1990-92, Tokyo Med. and Dental U., Tokyo, 1992-93, oral pathologist, 1994-95; freelance scientist Tokyo, 1995—2002; dir. Tomo Dental Office, Hamamatsu-cho, Tokyo, 2002—. Mem. AAAS, Japanese Soc. Pathology, Japanese Soc. Electron Microscopy. Avocations: windsurfing, skiing, swimming, jogging, opera.

SATOH, TOYOMI, oncologist, educator; b. Sendai, Miyagi, Japan, Sept. 21, 1963; s. Satoh Isamu and Satoh Kyoko; m. Yuki Miyazaki, Mar. 8, 1968; children: Satsuki, Aoi, Maika, Ibuki. MD, U. Tsukuba, Medicine, 1989, PhD, 2001. Diplomate Japan, 1989. Dir. ob-gyn dept. Ibaraki Seinan Ctrl. Hosp., Sakai, Japan, 1996—2002; asst. prof. U. Tsukuba, Ibaraki, 2002—. Councilor Japan Soc. Gynecol. Oncology, Tokyo, 2004—. Gynecol. oncologist U. Tsukuba, Ibaraki, 2002—08. Office: Univ of Tsukuba Tennoudai 1-1-1 Ibaraki Tsukuba 305-8575 Japan Office Phone: +81-29-853-3073. Office Fax: +81-29-853-3072. Business E-Mail: toyomi-s@md.tsukuba.ac.jp.

SATOH, YOSHIHIDE, physiologist; b. Niigata, Japan, Oct. 12, 1967; DDS, Nippon Dental U., Japan, 1992, PhD, 1996. Postdoc. fellow U. Leicester, England, 1997—98; rsch. assoc. Nipon Dental U., Niigata, 1996—2003, asst. prof., 2004—08, assoc. prof., 2009—. Recipient Encouragement award, Nippon Dental U., 1999; grant,

Ministry Edn., Culture, Sports, Sci., Tech. Japan, 2006—07. Avocation: sports. Office: Nippon Dental Univ Dept Physiology 1-8 Hamaura-cho Niigata 951-8580 Japan Business E-Mail: ysatoh@ngt.ndu.ac.jp.

SATORU, OGAWA, anesthesiologist; b. Osaka, Japan, Mar. 7, 1978; MD, Hyogo Coll. Medicine, Nishinomiya, Japan, 2004. Rsch. fellow Emory U. Sch. Medicine, 2010—. Recipient Morimura award, Hyogo Coll. Medicine, 2004. Office: Dept Anesthesiology 1364 Clift Atlanta GA 30322 E-mail: satoru.ogawa78@gmail.com.

SATRIANO, GIUSEPPE SALVATORE, surgeon; b. Baragiano, Italy, June 20, 1946; s. Pietro and Maria (Alberico) S. Degree in medicine and surgery, U. Naples, Italy, 1973; degree in heart and vascular surgery, U. Naples, 1984; degree in anesthesia and intensive care, U. Catania, 1991. Med. diplomate. 1st aid surgeon S. Giovanni di Dio e Ruggi d'Aragona Hosp., Salerno, Italy, 1976, 1st aid and emergency surgeon, 1978-82, gen. surgeon, 1987-91, asst. surgeon, 1991—; fellow Italian Hosp., Buenos Aires, 1976-78; cardiovascular surgeon San Carlo Hosp., Potenza, Italy; prof. emergency and nursing care Medicine and Surgery Faculty, U. Naples, Italy, 2002—. Local authority dr., Amalfi, Italy, 1974, Salerno, 1975; chief dir. emergency med. svc., Salerno, 1992-95, Salerno Emergency Med. System, 1999; cons. 1st Aid Hosp., Salerno, 1995-96; basic life support instr. Italian Resuscitation Coun.; designer devel. project Euroambulance-Third Millenium Industrias Metalomecanicas Tecnologia Avançada, Portugal; sci. dir. tng. program paramedic staff, ambulances and helicopter crews S. Giovanni Dio e Ruggi d'Aragona Hosp. Emergency Dept. Salerno; chief dir. Salerno Emergency Med. Sys., 1999; health chief dir. Soc. Di Saluamento, Genova, 2004. Author: (book) Protezione Civile: Che Cosa Fare e Come, 1984, (booklet) La Mia Salute, 1984, L'Elisoccorso, Linee guida, Protocolli, Procedure, 2000, Nozioni di Primo Intervento, 2001. Founder vol. rescue team Soccorso Amico, 1974; dir. Emersalerno Emergency Med. Svc., 1992; mem. adv. coun. Dr. for Disaster Preparedness, Starke, Fla., 1988. Decorated knight comdr. Fedn. Autonomous Priories of Sovereigh Order St. John of Jerusalem Knights of Malta; recipient S. Valentino d'Oro award, 1983, Gold medal Marcello Candia, Naples, 1988, Sicurezza Europea award, 1992, Pericle d'Oro award, 1996; Paul Harris fellow Rotary Internat., 1992. Mem. Italian Resuscitation Coun., Am. Civil Def. Assn. (Recognition of Excellence award 1992). Avocations: travel, collecting old medical books, scuba diving, photography, parachuting, helicopter piloting. Office: S Giovanni Hosp Emerg Dept Di Dio e Ruggi d'Acagona 84100 Salerno Italy Home: Via Giovanni Lanzalone 26 84126 Salerno SA Italy Office Phone: 39-089-339999. E-mail: s.amico@starnet.it.

SATTA, JARI, thoracic surgeon; b. Kolari, Finland, Oct. 5, 1957; MD, Oulu U., 1982, PhD. Cardiac surgeon Oulu U. Hosp., 1987—2011. Mem.: European Cardiothoracic Soc. Home: Veijolankuja 6 Oulu 90150 Finland

SATTUR, ATUL PRALHAD, dental educator; b. Belgaum, Apr. 15, 1972; BDS, St. Paul's HS, MDS, 1986. Prof. SDM Coll. Dental Scis., 1989—. Mem.: IDA, IAOMR. Avocation: gymnastics. Office: SDM Coll Dental Scis Sattur Dharwar Karnataka 580 009 India Personal E-mail: atulsattur@yahoo.com.

SAUDEK, CHRISTOPHER D., endocrinologist, educator; b. Bronxville, NY, Oct. 8, 1941; s. Robert and Elizabeth (Koch) Saudek; m. Susan Saudek; children: Mark S., Deborah M., Christina A., Anthony C. AB, Harvard U., Cambridge, Mass., 1963; MD, Cornell U. Med. Coll., Ithaca, NY, 1967. Diplomate Am. Bd. Internal Medicine. Intern, resident Presbyn. St. Luke's Hosp., Chgo., 1967-69; resident internal medicine Boston City Hosp., 1969-70; fellow in metabolism Thorndike Meml. Lab, Harvard Med. Sch., 1970-72; asst prof. Cornell U., 1973-80; assoc. prof. Johns Hopkins U. Sch. Medicine, Balt., 1981—91, prof., 1991—, Hugh P. McCormick prof. endocrinology & metabolism, dir. Johns Hopkins Diabetes Ctr. & Gen. Clin. Rsch. Ctr. Cons. ABCNews.com OnCall+ Diabetes Ctr. Co-author: The Johns Hopkins Guide to Diabetes: For Today and Tomorrow, 1997, The Complete Diabetes Prevention Plan: A Guide to Understanding the Emerging Epidemic of Prediabetes and Halting Its Progression to Diabetes, 2004; contbr. articles to profl. jours. Mem.: Am. Diabetes Assn. (pres. 2001—02, Outstanding Clinician in Diabetes award 1991). Office: Johns Hopkins U Sch Medicine Osler 576 600 N Wolfe St Baltimore MD 21287-0005 Office Phone: 410-955-0309. Office Fax: 410-614-9586. E-mail: csaudek@jhu.edu. *

SAUER, WILLIAM HENRY, cardiologist; MD in Cardiac Electrophysiology, U. Pa., 1999. Cardiac electrophysiology program dir. U. Colo. Hosp., faculty staff physician, 2006—. Recipient Outstanding Cardiology Faculty award, UCD, 2010; named one of Best Doctors, 2009—11. Office: 12401 E 17th Ave Mailstop B136 Leprino Bldg 5th Fl Aurora CO 80045

SAUERBRUCH, TILMAN, internist, educator; b. Lauingen, Germany, July 9, 1946; s. Peter and Annemarie (v. Rosenberg) Sauerbruch; m. Almuth v. Plettenberg, 1973 (dec. 1987); children: Sophie, Florens, Friederike; m. Astrid v. Reitzenstein, 1994. MD, U. Heidelberg, 1971. Intern, resident internal medicine U. Heidelberg, Mcpl. Hosps. Pforzheim, U. Munich, 1973—79; specialist for internal medicine and gastroenterology Munich, 1979—92; assoc. prof. internal medicine U. Munich, 1984—92; prof. internal medicine, chmn. med. dept. U. Bonn, 1992—. Vice dean med. faculty U. Bonn, 2000—02, dean, 2002—03. Contbr. articles to profl. jours. Bd. mem. Boehringer Ingelheim Fonds, 2004—10; supervisory bd. mem. U. Hosp. Munich. Recipient Foerderpreis fur die Europaischen Wissenschaften, Koerber Found. Hamburg, 1986, Clin. Rsch. prize, SKD Munich, 1989. Fellow: Am. Gastroenterology Assn.; mem.: German Assn. Study Liver (pres. 2010), Deutsche Gesellschaft Verdauungs und Stoffwechselkrankheiten (pres. 2002), Am. Assn. Study Liver. Office: Medizinische Univ Klinik Sigmund-Freud-Str 25 D-53105 Bonn Germany Office Phone: 004922828715216. Business E-Mail: sauerbruch@uni-bonn.de.

SAULACIC, NIKOLA, dentist, researcher; b. Herceg Novi, Montenegro, Yugoslavia, Dec. 27, 1968; s. Andrija and Ksenija Saulacic; m. Sandra Perunski, June 16, 2005; 1 child, Lea. DDS, Faculty od Stomatology, U. Belgrade, Serbia, 1995, MSc, 2000, Degree in Oral surgery, 2000; PhD, U. Santiago de Compostela, Spain, 2005. ITI scholar Dept. Oral Surgery, U. Bonn, Germany, 2003—04; rsch. and tchg. assoc. dept. Oral Surgery and Stomatology Sch. Dental Medicine, U. Geneva, 2005—06; pot-doc fellow ITI Rsch. Inst. Dental and Skeletal Biology, U. Berne, Switzerland, 2006—07; rsch. asst. dept. Cranio-Maxillofacial Surgery U. Hosp., U. Berne, 2007—. Contbr. to resch. papers (Premio Extraordinario, 2006). Fellow: Internat. Team Implantology. Achievements include patents pending for device and method for distraction osteogenesis. Office: Univ Hos Univ of Berne Freiburgstrasse 10 Berne 3010 Switzerland Business E-Mail: nikola.saulacic@insel.ch.

SAULSBURY, FRANK T., pediatric immunologist and rheumatologist; b. Lexington, Nebr., Aug. 27, 1947; MD, U. Nebr. Coll. Medicine, 1972. Diplomate Am. Bd. Pediat. Intern pediat. Johns Hopkins U. Hosp., Balt., 1972—73, resident pediat., 1973—75, fellowship pediat. immunology, 1977—79; med. alumni. prof. pediat. U. Va. Sch. Medicine, 2002—; head divsn. pediat. immunology and rheumatology U. Va. Health Sys. Contbr. articles to profl. jours. Mem.: Am. Pediat. Soc. Office: U Va Sch Medicine Dept Pediat PO Box 800386 Charlottesville VA 22908 Office Phone: 434-924-1906. Office Fax: 434-982-4246. Business E-Mail: fts@virginia.edu.

SAUNDERS, BRENT L., medical products executive, lawyer; BA in Econ. & East Asian Studies, U. Pitts., 1992; MBA, Temple U., JD, 1996. Chief compliance officer Thomas Jefferson U. Health Sys.; sr. v.p. compliance, legal & regulatory Home Care Corp. of America; chief risk officer Coventry Health Care; ptnr., head Compliance Bus. Advisory PricewaterhouseCoopers LLP, 1999—2003; sr. v.p. Global Compliance & Bus. Practices Schering-Plough Corp., 2003—07, pres. Global Consumer Health Care, 2007—09; CEO, bd. dirs. Bausch + Lomb Inc., 2010—. Instr. health law, adj. faculty mem. Widener Sch. of Law; bd. dirs. ElectroCore LLC; spl. advisor Gen. Atlantic, 2010. Mem. NJ Gov. Elect Chris Christie; bd. dirs. Overlook Hosp. Found. Named Compliance Officer of the Yr., Health Care Compliance Assn., 1997. Mem.: Health Care Compliance Assn. (co-founder, former pres.), American Heart Assn. (bd. dirs.). Office: Bausch + Lomb Inc One Bausch & Lomb Pl Rochester NY 14604-2701 Office Phone: 585-338-6000. Office Fax: 585-338-6007. Business E-Mail: brent.saunders@bausch.com. *

SAUNDERS, CRAIG RAYMOND, neurosurgeon; MD, U. Iowa, 1970. Lic. Calif., 1980, NJ, 1998, diplomate Am. Bd. Thoracic Surgery. Intern Wilford Hall Med. Ctr., 1971; resident Univ. Iowa Hosp., 1978, Cleve. Clinic, 1980, former head affiliate programs cardiothoracic surgery dept.; chmn. cardiothoracic surgery St. Barnabas Health Care System; physician Newark Beth Israel Med. Ctr. With editl. and adv. bds. Nat. Peer Rev. Jour. Fellow: ACS; mem.: Thoracic Surgery Dirs. Assn., Am. Coll. Chest Physicians, AMA, Soc. Thoracic Surgeons, Western Thoracic Surg. Assn. Office: Beth Israel Medical Center 201 Lyons Ave Ste G5 Newark NJ 07112 Office Phone: 973-926-6938.

SAUNDERS, JAMES C., neuroscientist, educator; b. Elizabeth, NJ, May 8, 1941; s. Charles Oliver and Elizabeth Veronica (Drake) S.; m. Elaine Priscilla Edwards, Oct. 14, 1967; children: Breton Morris, Drew Charles. BA, Ohio Wesleyan U., 1963; MA, Conn. Coll., 1965, U. Pa., 1979; PhD, Princeton U., 1968. Lectr. dept. psychology Monash U., Victoria, Australia, 1969-72; rsch. assoc. Cen. Inst. for Deaf, St. Louis, 1972-73; asst. prof., then prof. dept. otorhinolaryngology U. Pa., Phila., 1973-89, acting dir. Inst. Neurol. Scis., 1980-83. Guest scientist Karolinska Inst., Stockholm, 1984-85; exec. com. CHABA, Nat. Rsch. Coun., Washington, 1986-89; chmn. disorders rev. com. NIDCD, Bethesda, Md., 1987-89; mem. exec. coun., long range planning com., Assn. Rsch. Otolaryngology, Chgo., 1988-91; mem. com. on hearing and bioacoustics Nat. Inst. on Deafness and Other Comms. Disorders; chair Med. Sch. Fac. Senate, U. Pa., 1998-99; chair faculty 2000 project U. Pa., 1999—; guest scientist Victor Segelan U. Bordeaux, 2003—, dir. neurobiology Otorhinolaryngology Tng. Program, 2003. Contbr. chpts., rev. papers to books on biology of hearing; contbr. articles on auditory neurobiology to profl. jours; author abstracts of meeting presentations on hearing. Recipient Basic Sci. Rsch. award Am. Acad. Otolaryngology, 1978, 87, Pa. Acad. Otolaryngology, 1982, Basic Sci. Excellence award (Claude Pepper award) NIDCD, 1988, award for extraordinary leadership Sch. Medicine, U. Pa., 2002. Mem. AAAS, Acoustical Soc. Am., Soc. Neurosci., NY Acad. Sci., Sigma Xi (legal cons. effects of noise on hearing). Democrat. Office: Univ Pa 5 Ravdin ORL 3400 Spruce St Philadelphia PA 19104-4206 Home: 417 Bryn Mawr Ave Bala Cynwyd PA 19004-2619 Business E-Mail: saundrej@mail.med.upenn.edu.

SAUNDERS, SCOTT, pediatrician, educator; b. Internat. Falls, Minn., Aug. 25, 1961; BS, U. Minn., 1983; MD, Stanford Med. Sch., PhD, 1990. Pediat. resident Boston Children's Hosp., 1990—93; postdoc. fellow, newborn medicine Harvard Med. Sch., 1993—97; asst. prof. Wash. U. Sch. Medicine, 1997—2005, assoc. prof., 2005—. Mem.: Soc. Pediat. Rsch. Avocation: politics. Office: Wash University Sch Medicine Saint Louis MO 63141 Business E-Mail: saunders_s@kids.wustl.edu.

SAUR, PETRA, anesthesiologist; b. Kassel, Germany, Apr. 13, 1962; d. Karl-Heinz and Helga (Knierim) Saur. MD, U. Goettingen, Germany, 1988, PhD, 1998; diploma in health econs., Germany, 2001. Cert. specialist sports medicine, in emergency medicine, in manual therapy, in pain therapy, in psychotherapy, in intensive care medicine, in health cons., in palliative care medicine; in quality mgmt. Med. asst. U. Goettingen, 1988-98, sr. physician, 1998—, sr. physician emergency, 1997—. Physician Civic Sports Orgn., Goettingen, 1992—. Recipient 1st award pain therapy, 1994, 2d award, 1999. Mem.: German Assn. Sports Medicine, German Assn. Manual Medicine, German Assn. Anesthesia Intensive Care Medicine. Avocation: dance. Office: Sana Luebeck and Ostholstein GmbH Kronsforder Allee 71-73 Luebeck 23560 Germany Home: Sonnenweg 46 23611 Bad Schwartau Germany E-mail: psaur@psaur.de.

SAUSVILLE, EDWARD ANTHONY, oncologist; b. Albany, NY, Apr. 3, 1952; s. Edward Adolphus and Pauline (Zamenick) S.; m. Carol Ann Cassidy, Feb. 1, 1975(dec., 2009); children: Justin, Brendan, Elizabeth, Rebecca, Paul. BS, Manhattan Coll., 1973; MD, PhD, Albert Einstein Coll. Medicine, 1979. Med. house staff Brigham & Women's Hosp., Boston, 1979-82; med. staff fellow Nat. Cancer Inst., Bethesda, Md., 1982-85, sr. investigator, 1985—88, 1990—2004, assoc. dir. Devel. Therapeutics Program, 1994—2004; assoc. prof. medicine Georgetown U. Sch. Medicine, Washington, 1988-90; assoc. dir. clin. rsch. Marlene and Stewart Greenebaum Cancer Ctr. U. Md., 2004—, prof. Sch. Medicine, 2004—. Mem. editl. bd. Cancer Rsch., Jour. Nat. Cancer Inst., Molecular Cancer Therapeutics, Cancer Letters, others; contbr. chapters to books, articles to profl. jours. Mem. Am. Assn. Cancer Rsch., Am. Soc. Clin. Oncology, Am. Soc. Biochem. Molecular Biology, Phi Beta Kappa, Alpha Omega Alpha. Achievements include research on mechanisms of bleomycin action; bombesin-related peptide gene expression and response in lung cancer; optimal treatment and staging of cutaneous T-cell lymphoma; preclinical, Phase I and Phase II trials of novel antineoplastic agents. Home: 709 Bonifant Rd Silver Spring MD 20905-5950 Office: U Md Marlene and Stewart Greenebaum Cancer Ctr 22 S Greene St Baltimore MD 21201-1595 Office Phone: 410-328-7394. Business E-Mail: esausville@umm.edu.

SAUTE, ROBERT EMILE, drug and cosmetic consultant; b. West Warwick, RI, Aug. 18, 1929; s. Camille T. and Lea E. (Goffinet) S.; m. Arda T. Darnell, May 18, 1957; children: Richard R., Steven N., Allen K. BS, RI Coll. Pharmacy, 1950; MS, Purdue U., 1952, PhD, 1953. Registered pharmacist. Tech. asst. to pres. Lafayette (Ind.) Pharmacal, 1955-56; sr. rsch. and devel. chemist H.K. Wampole Denver Chem. Co., Phila., 1956-57; supt. Murray Hill (NJ) plant Strong Cobb Arner Inc., 1957-60; adminstrv. dir. rsch. and devel. Avon Products Inc., Suffern, NY, 1960-68; dir. rsch. and devel. toiletries divsn. Gillette Co., Boston, 1968-71; group v.p. Dart Industries, LA, 1972-75; pres. Saute Cons., Inc., LA, 1975—. Bd. dirs. Joico Labs., Inc., Cosmetics Enterprises, Ltd.; chmn., bd. dirs. Zerran Internat. Corp. Contbr. to books; patentee in field. With U.S. Army, 1953-55. Recipient Alumnus award, U. RI; named Old Master, Disting. Alumnus, Purdue U. Fellow Soc. Cosmetic Chemists (bd. dirs. 1987-89, 94-96, chmn. Calif. chpt. 1986, Robert A. Kramer Lifetime Svc. award 2010); mem. AAAS, N.Y. Acad. Scis., Soc. Investigative Dermatology, Am. Assn. Pharm. Scientists, Purdue U. Alumni Assn. (old master, disting. alumnus), Sigma Xi, Rho Chi. Avocations: travel, art, music, cooking, wine. Office Phone: 818-896-1444.

SAVAGE, JOSEPH GEORGE, academic administrator; b. Bklyn. s. Joseph George Jr. and Eileen (Schnell) S.; m. Lynn Ann Campbell; children: Kimberly, Patricia, Joseph IV. BA, Oswego Coll., 1977; postgrad., Seton Hall U., 1985. With Nat. Multiple Sclerosis Soc., NYC, 1977—80; dir. devel., mktg. Clara Mass Meml. Med. Ctr., Belleville, N.J., 1980-81; exec. dir. Found. of St. Joseph's Hosp. Med. Ctr., Paterson, N.J., 1981-89; sr. v.p. St. Francis Hosp. Heart Ctr., Roslyn, N.Y., 1989-92; v.p. St. Vincents Hosp. and Med. Ctr., NYC, 1992-98; exec. v.p. Cathedral Health Care Sys., Newark, 1998—2001; v.p. exec. adminstrn. Caldwell Coll., NJ, 2001—. Commr. health City of Clifton, 1990-94; bd. dirs. N.Y. Heart Coun., 1989-93, Cath. Family and Cmty. Svcs., 1992-2006, Osweo Coll. Alumni, 1992—, St. Mary's Hosp., Passiac, N.J., 1993-99, 2000—; bd. trustees Caldwell Coll. Fellow Nat. Assn. Hosp. Devel. (communication chair 1982-85, edn. chair 1985-86, bd. dirs., regional dir. 1988-89), Friendly Sons of St. Patrick NY, Ancient Order of Hibernians, Rotary (past pres. Clifton Club, Paul Harris fellow, Walter Head fellow), Caldwell Club(chmn. project Iraci Freedom). Roman Catholic. Avocations: swimming, golf. Office: Caldwell Coll 9 Ryerson Ave Caldwell NJ 07006-1558 Home Phone: 973-885-6715. E-mail: jsavage@caldwell.edu.

SAVANI, RASHMIN CHANDULAL, pediatrician, educator; s. Chandulal Bhagwanji and Hemlata Chandulal Savani; m. Nimisha Kotak, Dec. 28, 1991; m. Dora Veronica Duarte Miranda, July 14, 1983 (div. Feb. 2, 1988); children: Milan Rashmin, Anand Miranda, Meera Anisha. MBChB, U. Sheffield, Eng., 1982. Diplomate Am. Bd. Pediat., 1988, Am. Bd. Neonatal Perinatal Medicine, 1989. Jr. ho. officer internal medicine Hallamshire Hosp., Sheffield, South Yorkshire, England, 1982—83; jr. ho. officer gen. surgery No. Gen. Hosp., Sheffield, South Yorkshire, England, 1983; sr. ho. officer Peterborough (Eng.) Gen. Hosp., 1983—84; intern then resident Duke U. Med. Ctr., Durham, NC, 1984—87; asst. prof. pediat. Children's Hosp. U. Man., Winnipeg, Canada, 1991—96, U. Pa., Phila., 1996—2002, assoc. prof. pediat., 2002—06; prof. pediat., William Buchanan chair U. Tex. Southwestern Med. Ctr., 2006—. Contbr. articles. Recipient Young Investigator award, Am. Acad. Pediat., 1998; grantee, NIH, 1999—; Neonatology and Pulmonary Biology fellow, Children's Hosp. Med. Ctr., 1987—91. Mem.: Perinatal Rsch. Soc., Am. Thoracic Soc., Soc. Pediat. Rsch., Ea. Soc. Pediat. Rsch. (Young Investigator award 1997). Office: Univ Tex Southwestern Med Ctr 5323 Harry Hines Blvd K4 222 Dallas TX 75390-9063 Business E-Mail: rashmin.savani@utsouthwestern.edu.

SAVITS, BARRY SORREL, surgeon; b. Phila., Feb. 14, 1934; s. Frank and Sophia (Cohen) S.; children: George, Frank, Alexander. BA, Princeton U., 1955; MD, U. Pa., 1959; cert. surg. residency, Mt. Sinai Hosp., NYC, 1965. Prof. surgery Project Hope, Ecuador, 1965-66; instr. surgery Albert Einstein Med. Coll., Bronx, NY, 1966-67; surgeon LaGuardia Med. Group, Queens, NY, 1970-72; dir. surgery St. Mary's Hosp., Bklyn., 1973-91, Kingsbrook Jewish Med. Ctr., Bklyn., 1991-2000; attending N.Y. Meth. Hosp., 2000—, SUNY-Univ. Hosp. of Bklyn., 1995—; clin. asst. prof. surgery SUNY Health Scis. Ctr., Bklyn., 1975—. Vis. surgeon Hope-Ecuador, 1965-66, Care-Medico, Afghanistan, 1976. Comdr. USN, 1967-69. Fellow ACS (gov. 1991-97); mem. Soc. Am. Gastrointestinal Endoscopic Surgeons, Assn. Acad. Surgery, Assn. Surg. Program Dirs., Bklyn. Surg. Soc. (pres. 1992-93). Jewish. Avocation: reading. Office: 263 7th Ave Ste 4E Brooklyn NY 11215 Home Phone: 212-675-2327; Office Phone: 718-832-4992. Office Fax: 718-832-4692. Personal E-mail: bsavits@aol.com.

SAVITSKY, MAUREEN ELIZABETH, pharmacist; b. Plainfield, NJ, Aug. 12, 1959; d. Jerome Joseph and Mary Elizabeth (Leonard) S. BS in Pharmacy, Mercer U., Atlanta, 1982, PharmD, 1983. Clin. pharmacy resident U. Nebr. Med. Ctr., Omaha, 1984-85; drug info. resident U. Mich. Med. Ctr., Ann Arbor, 1985-86; dir. drug info. svc. U. Chgo. Hosps., 1986-88; coord. clin. and drug info. svcs. Geisinger Med. Ctr., Danville, Pa., 1988-97; dir. formulary svcs. Pa. State

Geisinger Health Sys., 1997-2000, Geisinger Health Sys., 2000—, program dir. pharmacy practice residency, 2000—; clin. asst. prof., group facilitator for working profl. Doctor of Pharmacy program, U. Fla. Coll. Pharmacy, 2000—. Contbr. articles to profl. jours.; reviewer jour. manuscripts for sci. publs.; mem. editl. bd. Jour. Pharmacy Practice, 1993-96, Formulary, 2002—. Fellow Am. Soc. Health Sys. Pharmacists, mem. Pa. Soc. Hosp. Pharmacists (pres. No. Ctrl. chpt. 1991-92, bd. dirs. 2000-2002), Drug Info. Assn., Kappa Epsilon, Phi Kappa Phi, Phi Lambda Sigma, Rho Chi. Office: Geisinger Med Ctr 100 N Academy Ave Danville PA 17822-4201 Office Phone: 570-271-8013. E-mail: msavitsky@geisinger.edu.

SAVITZ, DAVID A., epidemiologist; BA, Brandeis U.; MS, Ohio State U., 1978; PhD, U. Pitts., 1982. Rschr. Battelle-Columbus Labs., Columbus, Ohio, 1977—79; pub. health svc. trainee in epidemiology U. Pitts., 1979—81; asst. prof. preventive medicine and biometrics U. Colo. Sch. Medicine, Denver, 1981—85; asst. prof. epidemiology U. NC Sch. Pub. Health, Chapel Hill, 1985—89, assoc. prof. epidemiology, 1989—92, prof. epidemiology, 1993—2005, chair epidemiology, 1996—2005, Cary C. Boshamer disting. prof., 2003—05; Charles W. Bludhorn prof. cmty. and preventive medicine Mt. Sinai Sch. Medicine, NYC, 2005—, prof. obstetrics, gynecology and reproductive sci., 2005—, dir. Ctr. Excellence in Epidemiology, Biostatistics and Disease Prevention, 2005—. Author: Interpreting Epidemiologic Evidence. Fellow: Am. Coll. Epidemiology; mem.: Inst. Medicine, Am. Epidemiological Soc., Soc. Pediatric and Perinatal Epidemiologic Rsch., Internat. Soc. Environ. Epidemiology, Internat. Epidemiological Assn., Soc. Epidemiologic Rsch. (sec.-treas. 1987—91, exec. com. 1994—97, pres. 2000—01), Am. Pub. Health Assn., Delta Omega (Theta chapt.). Office: 17 E 102 St New York NY 10029 Office Phone: 212-241-7025. Office Fax: 212-996-0407. E-mail: david.savitz@mssm.edu.

SAVOLA, SUVI, medical researcher; b. Espoo, Finland, Feb. 15, 1979; MSc, U. Helsinki, 2005, PhD, 2009. Rsch. scientist dept. pathology U. Helsinki, 2005—09; sr. scientist MRC-Holland, 2009—11, head tumour diagnostics, 2011—. Home: Reguliersgracht 114 -2 Amsterdam Noord Holland 1017 LX Netherlands

SAVONEN, KAI PETTERI, physiologist; b. Hartola, Finland, Apr. 13, 1969; s. Tuula Marita and Arto Kalervo Savonen; children: Olli Mikael, Vili Aleksi. MS in Sport Coaching, U. Jyväskylä, Finland, 2003; DMed Sc, MA, U. Kuopio, Finland, 2008. Lic. physician U. Kuopio, 2006. Exercise physiologist Vuokatti Sports Inst., Sotkamo, Finland, 1995—2000; specialising physician Kuopio Rsch. Inst. Exercise Medicine, 2006—08, 2009—10; family physician Kuopio Health Ctr., 2008—09; specializing physician Kuopio U. Hosp., 2011—. Chmn. Northern Savo Med. Soc., 2011—. Cpl. Inf., 1988—89, St. Micheal, Finland. Recipient Heikki Wendelin award, Finnish Soc. Clin. Physiology, 2007, Martti Hämäläinen award, Northern Savo Med. Soc., 2008, Young Investigator's award, Finnish Physiol. Soc., 2009. Mem.: Am. Coll. Sports Medicine. Office: Kuopio Rsch Inst Exercise Medicine Haapaniemenkatu 16 Kuopio 70100 Finland Office Phone: 358-44-7744040. Personal E-mail: savonen@student.uef.fi.

SAVOY, SUZANNE MARIE, nursing educator; b. NYC, Oct. 18, 1946; d. William Joseph and Mary Patricia (Moclair) Savoy. BS, Columbia U., 1970; M in Nursing, UCLA, 1978; PhD in Nursing, Loyola U., 2010. RN, cert. clin. nurse specialist, clin. nurse leader. Staff nurse MICU, transplant Jackson Meml. Hosp., Miami, 1970 72; staff nurse MICU Boston U. Hosp., 1972-74, VA Hosp., Long Beach, Calif., 1974-75; staff nurse MIRU Cedars-Sinai Med. Ctr., LA, 1975-77; critical care clin. nurse specialist Anaheim (Calif.) Meml. Hosp., 1978-81; practitioner, instr. Rush-Presbyn.-St. Luke's Med. Ctr. Coll. Nursing, Chgo., 1982-88; rsch. assoc. dept. neurosurgery Rush U., 1984-88; clin. rsch. assoc. Medtronic, Inc. Drug Adminstrn. Sys., Mpls., 1988-91; staff nurse critical care Harper Hosp., Detroit, 1992-93; clin. nurse specialist, surg./trauma crit. care Detroit Receiving Hosp., 1993-95; clin. instr. Wayne State U. Coll. of Nursing, Detroit, 1991-96; adult crit. care clin. nurse specialist Saginaw (Mich.) Gen. Hosp., 1996—98; cardiac clin. nurse specialist Covenant Healthcare Sys., Saginaw, 1998—2005; asst. prof. Saginaw Valley State U. Coll. Nursing, 2005—10, assoc. prof., 2010—. Adj. faculty Wayne State U. Coll. Nursing, 1996—98, program coord. Crit. Care ACNP-CC MSN, 1993—96; neurosci. clinician acute stroke unit Harper Hosp., Detroit, 1989; edn. cons. Critical Care Svcs., Inc., Orange, Calif., 1979—81; mem. staff Convenant Healthcare, 2005—08. Contbr. articles to profl. jours. Mem.: RN Aim East Ctr. Region (treas. 2008—), Am. Assn. Spinal Cord Injury Nursing (mem. rsch. com. 1993—95), Mich. Assn. Health Care Quality (treas. 2002—04), Am. Assn. Crit. Care Nurses (bd. dirs. Long Beach chpt. 1981—82, treas. NEMC chpt. 1999—2001), Am. Assn. Neurosci. Nurses (treas. Ill. chpt. 1983—85, pres. 1986—87, SE Mich. chpt. 1992—96, bd. dirs., treas., program chair), Theta Chi (nominating com. chair 2008—11), Sigma Theta Tau, Lambda Gamma Phi (bd. dirs. 1994—96). Roman Catholic. Office Phone: 989-964-7026. Personal E-mail: cardioapn@aol.com. Business E-Mail: smsavoy@svsu.edu.

SAWAGUCHI, TOSHIKO, forensic pathologist, educator; b. Shibuya, Tokyo, May 31, 1959; d. Shigenori and Akiko Sawaguchi. MD, DMS, Keio U., Shinjuku, Tokyo, 1988. Assoc. prof. Tokyo Women's Med. U., awdnjuku, 1998—. Invited prof. Free U. Brussels, 1998-99; cons. Japanese SIDS Soc., Shinjuku, 1998—. Author: books and rsch. papers in field of forensic medicine from clinical view. Supporter SIDS rsch. Japanese SIDS Family Assn., Shinjuku, 1995-2001. Recipient award for med. rsch. Assn. Med. Drs. in Tokyo. Achievements include research in SIDS, apoptosis. Home: Sendagaya 2-37-2 Shibuya Tokyo 151-0051 Japan Office: Tokyo Women's Med U Kawada-cho 8-1 Shinjuku Tokyo 162-8666 Japan Office Fax: 81 3 5269 7300; Home Fax: 81 3 3404 7937. E-mail: tsawagy@research.twmu.ac.jp.

SAWAYA, GEORGE F., obstetrician, gynecologist, educator; BS in Organic Chemistry, Hendrix Coll., 1985; MD, Vanderbilt U. Sch. Medicine, 1990. Resident UCSF, 1990—94, fellow, 1994—96, asst. adj. prof. dept. obstetrics, gynecology & reproductive sciences, 1996—97, asst. prof. dept. obstetrics, gynecology & reproductive sciences, 1997—2003, assoc. prof. dept. obstetrics, gynecology & reproductive sciences, 2003—. Recipient Rhoda Goldman Rsch. award, Mt. Zion Health Sys., 1997, Tchg. award, UCSF Med. Sch., 1998, Edn. Contributions award, 2003. Mem.: APGO (Tchg. award 2000), Alpha Omega Alpha. Office: UCSF Box 0856 San Francisco CA 94143-0856 Office Phone: 415-502-4090. Office Fax: 415-502-4065. E-mail: sawayag@obgyn.ucsf.edu.

SAWAYA, RAYMOND, neurosurgeon; b. Latakia, Syria, May 5, 1949; s. Emile and Josephine (Boulos) S.; m. Kristin Tveit; children: Marc-Emile, Corinne Marguerite. MD, St. Joseph U., Beirut, 1974. Diplomate Am. Bd. Neurol. Surgery. Intern Beeckman-Downtown Hosp., NYC, 1974-75; resident in surgery SUNY, Syracuse, 1975-76; resident in neurosurgery U. Cin., 1976-80, Johns Hopkins Hosp., Balt., 1981; vis. scientist NIH, Bethesda, Md., 1981-82; assoc. prof. U. Cin., 1983-90, dir. div. neuro-oncology, 1983-90; neurosurgeon Mayfield Neurol. Inst., Cin., 1983-90; prof., chmn. dept. neurosurgery U. Tex. M.D. Anderson Cancer Ctr., Houston, 1990—; prof., chmn. Baylor Coll. Medicine, 2005—. Contbr. numerous articles on neurosurgery to profl. jours. Research Adv. Group grantee VA Med. Ctr., 1984. Mem. Am. Radium Soc., Tex. Med. Assn., Am. Assn. Neurol. Surgeons, Congress of Neurosurgeons, Soc. Surg. Oncology, Houston Neurol. Soc. (pres.), Johns Hopkins Alumni Assn. Roman Catholic. Avocations: music, bridge, swimming. Office: 1515 Holcombe Blvd # 442 Houston TX 77030-4009 E-mail: rsawaya@mdanderson.org.

SAWCZUK, IHOR S., urologist; b. NYC, Oct. 5, 1952; s. Stefan and Stefania (Mruczkewycz) S. BA, NYU, 1974; MD, Med. Coll. of Pa., 1979. Diplomate Am. Bd. Urology. Chief Allen Pavilion Urology Columbia-Presbyn. Med. Ctr., NYC, 1988—99; prof. urology Columbia U., NYC, 1993—, vice chmn. Dept. of Urology, 1994—2001; chmn. urology Hackensack (NJ) U. Med. Ctr., 2001—, chief urologic oncology Cancer Ctr.; prof. surgery U. Medicine and Dentistry NJ, Newark, 2003—07, v.p., chief academic officer, 2010. Adv. bd. Kidney Cancer Assn., 1994—, Kidney and Urology Found., 2002—; dep. dir. Internat. Coop. Urological Edn. Project, 1994-96. Co-editor: (book) Urologic Clinics of North America, 1993. Bd. dirs. Children of Chernobyl, Short Hills, N.J., 1992-98. Recipient Young Investigator award Nat. Kidney Found., 1987, Alpha Omega Alpha Vol. Clin. Faculty award N.J. Med. Sch., 2003. Mem. ACS, Am. Urol. Assn. (scholar 1986), N.Y. Acad. Scis., Soc. Urologic Oncology, Minimally Invasive Robotics Assn. Office Phone: 201-336-8090.

SAWH, LALL RAMNATH, urologist; b. Couva, Trinidad and Tobago, June 1, 1951; s. Ramnath Rooplal and Ramkumaria (Sinanan) S.; m. Sylvia Sheila Ragobar, Dec. 22, 1973; children: Sean Lall, Shane Stefan. MBBS, U. W.I., Mona, Jamaica, 1975. Intern Gen. Hosp. San Fernando, Trinidad, 1975-76, sr. housr officer, 1976-77, sr. registrar in urology, 1980-86, acting cons. urologist, 1987—; clin. asst. Royal Infirmary Edinburgh, Scotland, 1978-79; clin. attachment Inst. Urology, London, 1979. Examiner Nursing Coun., Trinidad, 1984-86, examiner surgery U. of the West Indies, 1991—, assoc. lectr. surgery, 1990—; cons. urologist Gen. Hosp., Port of Spain, Trinidad, 1988, Eric Williams Med. Scis. Complex, Mt. Hope, Trinidad; head local kidney transplant team, 1990; chmn. sci. com. Trinidad and Tobago Kidney Found., 1989-93; lectr. in urology to various Caribbean countries; surgeon Gen. Hosp., San Fernando, Port of Spain; cons. Eric Williams Med. Sci. Complex, 1994—, Mt. Hope, Trinidad; cons. urologist Port-of-Spain Gen. HOsp., 1988—. Author: Renal Hypothermic Surgery, 1982, Button-Hole Kidney Surgery, 1986; contbr. articles to profl. jours. Recipient award for Outstanding and Meritorious Svc. to Trinidad and Tobago, Caroni County Coun., 1989, Chaconia Gold medal Trinidad and Tobago, 1993; honored by city coun. for contbn. to medicine in San Fernando, 1989, Chamber of Commerce award Point Lisas/Couva, 1995; Rotary Club awards, Chaguanas, Tobago. Fellow Royal Coll. Surgeons; mem. Am. Urol. Assn. (corr. mem.), Med. Assn. Trinidad and Tobago (chmn. 1984-85), Endo-urol. Soc. U.S., Med. Bd. Trinidad and Tobago (specialist, med. officer), Caribbean Assn. of Nephrologists & Urologists, Caribbean Prostatic Health Coun. (Trinidad rep.), Surg. Edn. Com. (founder), Soc. Surgeons (treas. 1986-93). Clubs: Lawn Tennis (Point a Pierre, Trinidad). Achievements include performing first successful kidney transplant in Trinidad and Tobago, 1988, performed the first renal hypothermic surgery in Trinidad in 1981, performed the first button hole renal lithotripsy in the West Indies in 1986, operation of the only Dornier Lithotriptor in West Indies. Office: Goodhealth Med Centre 7 Firzblackmer Dr Port-of-Spain Trinidad and Tobago Office Phone: 868-657-7294.

SAWTELLE, CARL S., psychiatric social worker; b. Boston, July 14, 1927; s. Carl Salvador and Martha (Bellamacina) Sawtelle; m. Thelma Florence Ramsay Sawtelle, Aug. 20, 1950; children: Tracy Lynn, Lisa June. BA, Suffolk U., Boston, 1951; MSW, Simmons Sch. Social Work, 1953. Lic. 1st social worker Mass., 1980. Social worker Tewksburry State Hosp., Mass., 1952; psychiat. social worker, head psychiat. social worker, dir. clin. social work Taunton State Hosp., Mass., 1953—74, 1st dir. clin. social work Plymouth, Mass., 1964—70; co-founder, v.p. 1st legally established War On Poverty Program Triumph, Inc., Taunton; co-founder 1st Greater Taunton Coun. Alcoholism, 1972. Mentor to young social workers. With USCG, 1944—46. Mem.: Mass. Mental Health Social Workers Assn. (co-founder, pres. 1972—74, other offices), Am. Legion, Acad. Cert. Social Workers (chmn. 1962—72), Nat. Assn. Social Workers (co-founder Southeast Mass. chpt. 1957, pres. 1957, Spl. Mass. Chpt. award 1978). Achievements include invention of innovated programs, resources, opportunities, services to state mental hosp. patients and their families; contributer advancement of knowledge, practice quality & standards of psychiat. social work, father of licensing & registration of social workers in Mass. Home: 9 Tracywood Rd Canton MA 02021-3501

SAWYER, DONALD E., urologist; b. Cambridge, Mass., Sept. 11, 1944; m. Anne Ross, June 30, 1968. BA, U. Vt., 1966; MD, N.Y. Med. Coll., 1970. Diplomate Am. Bd. Urology. Intern N.Y. Med. Coll., 1970-71, resident, 1971-72, Lahey Clinic, 1972-75; urologist in pvt. practice, Long Beach, Calif., 1979-99, Los Alamitos, Calif., 1979-99, Ocean Springs, Pascagoula, Miss., 1999—2001, VA Med. Ctr., Jackson, 2001—. Asst. prof. urology U. Miss. Med. Ctr., 2001—. Contbr. articles to profl. jours. Lt. comdr. MC USN, 1975—79. Recipient Commanding Officer's Letter of Commendation, USN. Fellow: ACS; mem.: Soc. U. Urologists, Soc. Govt. Svc. Urologists, Am. Assn. Clin. Urologists, Am. Urol. Assn. Avocations: travel, walking, physical fitness. Office: VA Med Ctr 1500 E Woodrow Wilson Dr Jackson MS 39216 Office Phone: 601-364-1358. Business E-Mail: Donald.Sawyer@va.gov.

SAWYER, MARY CATHERINE, retired hospital administrator; b. Borger, Tex., Dec. 8, 1931; d. Andrew Rodgers and Mary Elizabeth (Slater) Hill; m. Edmond Eugene Sawyer, Aug. 26, 1963; children: Slater Shane, Anthony Barrett, Maronda Rae. BBA, Tex. Tech U., 1956; cert. in med. records, U. Tex. Med. Br., Galveston, 1957. Registered med. adminstr.; cert. coding specialist. Med. record adminstr. Taylor Hosp., Inc., Lubbock, Tex., 1957-63; pvt. practice cons. Paris, Tex., 1963-79; med. record adminstr., coding specialist St. Joseph's Hosp., Paris, 1979-98; ret., 1998. Mem. DAR (corr. sec. 1989-91, treas. 1991-93, 1st vice regent 1994-96, def. chmn. 1990-96), Gordon Country Club, Phi Gamma Nu. Methodist. Avocation: genealogy. Home: 216 Glover Deport TX 75435-2305

SAWYER, PHILIP NICHOLAS, surgeon, educator, health science facility administrator; b. Bangor, Maine, Oct. 25, 1925; s. Frank S. and Linda (Makanna) S.; m. Grace Makla, June 13, 1953; children: Margaret Ann, Elizabeth Lynn, Susan Jean, Philip Michael. BS, Harvard U., 1947; MD, U. Pa., 1949. Diplomate Am. Bd. Surgery, Am. Bd. Thoracic Surgery. Intern Hosp. of U. Pa., Phila., 1949-50, resident in surgery, fellow, 1953-56; chief resident in surgery, fellow in pathology St. Luke's Hosp., NYC, 1956-57; instr., asst. prof. surgery SUNY Downstate Med. Ctr., Bklyn., 1957-62, assoc. prof., 1962-66, prof., head vascular surgery svc., 1966-84, prof. emeritus, 1985—; pres. Interface Biomed. Labs. Corp.; prof. surgery N.Y. Med. Coll., 1991-96; vis. surgeon, head vascular surg. svcs. Kings County Hosp., Bklyn., 1972-85. Hon. cons. Meth. Hosp., Bklyn.; hon. assoc. attending, head vascular surg. svcs. St. John's Episcopal Hosp., Far Rockaway, N.Y.; hon. attending surgery VA Hosp., Bklyn.; hon. cons. cardiovascular and thoracic surgeon Norwalk (Conn.) Hosp.; hon. cons. vascular surgeon Caledonian Hosp., Bklyn.; prin. investigator Office Naval Rsch., NIH, Am. Heart Assn., 1953-84, NIH, 1957-86; disting. lectr. worldwide. Founding editor Jour. Investigative Surgery; assoc. editor: Am. Jour. Med. Electronics, Jour. Biomed. Rsch. Engring.; editor: Biophysical Mechanisms in Vascular Homeostasis & Intravascular Thrombosis, 1965, Vascular Grafts, 1976, Modern Vascular Grafts, 1987; co-editor: Surgical Resident's Manual, 1980, Vascular Diseases, Current Controversies, 1981; contbr. over 300 articles to med. jours., numerous patents on heart valves, vascular grafts, hemostatic agts., vascular wall protective agts. Recipient Clemson award for basic biomaterials rsch. Soc. for Biomaterials, 1985; Markle scholar, 1959-64. Mem. Acad. Surg. Rsch. (Jacob Markowitz award 1986), AAAS, Am. Assn. for Thoracic Surgery, Am. Chem. Soc., Am. Coll. Cardiology, ACS, Am. Coll. Chest Physicians, AMA, Am. Heart Assn., Am. Nuclear Soc., Am. Soc. for Artificial Internal Organs, IEEE, Internat. Cardiovascular Soc., Soc. for Thoracic Surgeons, Soc. Univ. Surgeons, Soc. for Vascular Surgery, European Soc. for Microcirculation, Fedn. Am. Socs. for Exptl. Biology, Cardiovascular Soc. (pres.), Harvard Club (N.Y.C.), Sigma Xi, others. Avocation: collecting historical weapons. Office: 7324 Ridge Blvd Brooklyn NY 11209

SAWYER, WILLIAM DALE, internist, educator, dean, foundation administrator; b. Roodhouse, Ill., Dec. 28, 1929; s. Cloyd Howard and Eva Collier (Dale) S.; m. Jane Ann Stewart, Aug. 25, 1951; children: Dale Stewart, Carole Ann. Student, U. Ill., 1947-50; MD cum laude, Washington U., St. Louis, 1954; ScD (hon.), Mahidol U., Bangkok, 1988; DPH (hon.), Chiang Mai U., Thailand, 1993, Chulalongkorn U., 1998. Intern Washington U.-Barnes Hosp., 1954-55, resident, 1957-58, fellow, 1958-60; asst. prof. microbiology Johns Hopkins U., Balt., 1964-67; prof., chmn. dept. microbiology Rockefeller Found.-Mahidol U., Bangkok, 1967-73, Ind. U. Sch. Medicine, Indpls., 1973-80; prof. depts. medicine, microbiology and immunology Wright State U., Dayton, Ohio, 1981-87, dean Sch. Medicine, 1981-87; pres. China Med. Bd. N.Y., Inc., 1987-97. Adj. prof. biology Ball State U., Muncie, Ind., 1978-80; hon. prof. microbiology Sun Yat Sen U. Med. Sci., 1987; hon. prof. Peking Union Med. Coll., 1989; hon. advisor Beijing Med. U.; cons. U.S. Army Med. R & D Command, WHO Immunology Ctr., Singapore, 1969-73; mem. bd. sci. advisers Armed Forces Inst. Pathology, 1975-80, chmn., 1979-80; adj. prof. medicine and microbiology and immunology N.Y. Med. Coll., Valhalla, 1990-96; hon. prof. China Med. U., 1995, West China U. Med. Sci., 1995, Zhejiang Med. U., 1995, Jiujang Med. Coll., 1995, Hunan Med. U., 1996, Xian Med. U., 1996, Shanghai Med. U., 1996. Contbr. numerous articles to profl. jours. Mem. Lobund adv. bd. U. Notre Dame; dir. Georgetown Area Cmty. Found., 1998-2002, pres. 1999; mem. exec. com. Georgetown Cmty. Resource Ctr., 2000-03. Served to maj. M.C., USA, 1955-64. Recipient Gold medal of merit Airlangga U., Indonesia, 1992, Pub. Health Recognition award Asia-Pacific Acad. Consortium Pub. Health, 1993, China Health medal, 1996, White Magnolia award, 1996. Fellow ACP; mem. AAAS, Am. Soc. Microbiology (br. pres. 1976), Sci. Rsch. Soc. Am., Am. Fedn. Clin. Rsch., Ctrl. Soc. Clin. Rsch., Infectious Diseases Soc. Am., Soc. Exptl. Biology and Medicine, Am. Acad. Microbiology, Am. Assn. Pathologists, Assn. Am. Med. Colls. (coun. deans 1980-87), Phi Beta Kappa, Sigma Xi, Alpha Omega Alpha. Home: Temple Meridian # 14 4312 S 31st St Temple TX 76502 Personal E-mail: wllmsawyer@aol.com.

SAWYER-MORSE, MARY KAYE, nutritionist, educator; b. Ft. Stockton, Tex. BA in Psychology, S.W. Tex. State U., 1978; MS in Nutrition, Incarnate Word Coll., 1987; PhD, U. Tex., 1997. Lic. dietitian. Nutrition svcs. con. Christian Sr. Svcs., 1985-87, exec. dir., 1987-90; nutrition svcs. cons. Alternative Adult Day Care Ctr., 1989-90; pvt. cons. dietitian, 1990—; cmty. dietitian Health Enhancement Ctr. Humana Hosp. Met., 1990-91; assoc. prof., dietetic program dir. U. Incarnate Word, San Antonio, 1991—2004; dir. Heath Mgmt., UMR, 2004—. Presenter Innovative Nutrition Svc. Model S.W. Tex. Gerontol. Soc. Ann. Meeting, 1988, Diabetic Homebound Svcs. Nat. Conf. Meals-On-Wheels Am., 1989; spkr. in field. Contbr. articles to profl. jours. Recipient Disting. Rsch. award, 1977, 1978, Acad. Excellence award, 1978, Women's Leadership award, YWCA, 1988, Creative Tchg./Rsch. award, 1994; named Tex. Dietetic Educator,

2003; grantee, U.S. Dept. Edn., 1997—2000; Carnation Corp. scholar, 1995. Mem.: Nat. Spkrs. Assn. (devel. dir. 2000—01, Tex. Dietetic Educator of the Yr. 2003), San Antonio Dist. Dietetic Assn., Tex. Dietetic Assn., Am. Dietetic Assn. (sec. 1990—92, mem. nominating com. 1993—94, dietetic educators practice group). Office Phone: 830-997-1552. Personal E-mail: morsemk@msn.com.

SAWYERS, CHARLES L., oncologist, hematologist, educator; b. Nashville, Jan. 26, 1959; s. John L. and Julia Edwards Sawyers; m. Susan Gail Schneck, Oct. 21, 1990. BA in history of sci., Princeton U.; MD, Johns Hopkins U., 1985. Cert. Internal Medicine, 1988, Hematology, 1992, Medical Oncology, 1991. Intern in medicine U. Calif., San Francisco, 1985—86, resident in hematologic oncology, 1986—88; Howard Hughes fellow in hematologic oncology UCLA, 1988—91, prof. medicine, molecular pharmacology and urology; investigator Howard Hughes Med. Inst., 2003—06, 2008—; chmn. human oncology and pathogenesis program Meml. Sloan-Kettering Cancer Ctr., NYC, 2006—. Sci. adv. bd. Agios Pharmaceuticals, Cambridge, Mass.; bd. sci. councilors Nat. Cancer Inst. Recipient Richard and Hinda Rosenthal Found. award, Am. Assn. Cancer Rsch., 2005, Dorothy P. Landon prize for Translational Cancer Rsch., 2009, David A. Karnofsky award, Am. Soc. Clin. Oncology, 2005; co-recipient Lasker-DeBakey Clin. Med. Rsch. award, Lasker Found., 2009. Mem.: NAS, Inst. Medicine. Achievements include development of imatinib (Gleevec), 2001; dasatinib (Sprycel), 2006. Office: Meml Sloan-Kettering Cancer Ctr 1275 York Ave New York NY 10065 Office Phone: 646-888-2594, 646-888-2163. Office Fax: 646-888-2595. E-mail: martinb@mskcc.org. *

SAX, MARY RANDOLPH, speech and language pathologist; b. July 13, 1925; d. Bernard Angus and Ada Lucile (Thurman) TePoorten; m. William Martin Sax, Feb. 7, 1948. BA magna cum laude, Mich. State U., 1947; MA, U. Mich., 1949. Supr. speech correction dept. Waterford Twp. Schs., Pontiac, 1949—69; lectr. Marygrove Coll., Detroit, 1971-72; pvt. practice in speech and lang. pathology Wayne and Oakland Counties, Mich., 1973—. Co-investigator Support Pers. Profl. Practice of Speech-Lang. Pathology; counselor to divsn. stroke liaisons Am. Heart Assn. Mich.; liaison between Am. Heart Assn. of Mich. and Am. Heart Assn., Dallas, 1996—98; adj. speech pathologist, Southfield, Mich.; lectr. on stroke Mich. Spkrs. Bur., Am. Heart Assn., 1990—; pub. spkg. coach, 1989—; mem. adj. faculty SS Cyril and Methodius Sem., Orchard Lake, Mich., 1989—90; adj. St. Mary's Prep. Sch., Orchard Lake, 1990—; mem. Met. Detroit Operation Stroke com. Am. Stroke Assn., 1999—2004, mem. med. subcom. to move area hosps. to become primary stroke ctrs. with active stroke teams; founder, mem. Stroke Project Task Force for Detroit, 1993—98; com. mem. Charette, study Arch. and Design for phys. restructuring Franklin, Mich., 1993; invited speech pathology del. Internat. Health Programs People to People Citizen Amb. Program, 1996; mem. sci. coun. on stroke Am. Heart Assn., Dallas, 1980—2002; mem. quality improvement and med. edn. subcom. Am. Heart Assn. New Heart and Stroke Network Metro Detroit; mem. stroke adv. com./stroke advocacy com. States of Midwest affiliate Am. Heart Assn., 1995—2005; invited USA rep., speech & lang. pathology Med. People to People Amb. Program Neurol. Ctrs., Czech Republic, Hungary, Austria, 2001; mem. stroke advocacy and stroke advisory coms., Am. Heart Assn. Greater Midwest Affiliate, Mich., Ind., Ill., Wis., ND, SD, Minn.; pvt. instr. Oral Reading Before Large Groups, 2010; invited del. Am. Speech, Lang. & Hearing Assn., Brazil, 2011—; join fellow experts People to People Amb. Program., Brazil, 2011. Contbr. articles to profl. jours. including Lang. and Lang. Behavior Abstracts, Lang. Speech and Hearing Svcs., Speech Lang. Hearing Jour. Active Franklinites for Responsible Govt.; mem. stroke com. Mich. Heart Assn., 1978—2005; trustee Southfield Twp, 2007; founder, pres. Lakeview Assn. Sylvan Lake, Mich., 2006—. Recipient Svc. Recognition award Coll. Edn. Mich. State U.; grantee Inst. Articulation and Learning, 1969, others; Christian svc. commn. St. Owen, Birmingham co-chmn. blood dr. Red Cross, Franklin, Mich., 1991—. Mem.: Founders Soc. of Detroit Inst. Arts, Franklin Found. (mem. natural resources adv. coun. 1991—99, bd. dirs. 1994—98), Pvt. Practitioners Speech-Lang. Pathology (co-founder), Internat. Assn. Logopedics and Phoniatrics (Switzerland), Am. Heart Assn. Mich. (mem. stroke awareness seminars, continuing edn. for physicians and other profls., planning and operation edn.), Mich. Speech-Lang.-Hearing Assn. (cmty. & hosp. com., pvt. practitioner liason, developer structural parameters, State Clin. Svcs. award, Selection Com. State award), Am. Speech-Lang.-Hearing Assn., Mich. Humane Soc., Gamma Phi Beta, Kappa Delta Pi, Phi Kappa Phi, Theta Alpha Phi. Achievements include research in language and speech acquisition in children in reference to the development of and prediction of biological speech change; research interests in developmental phonatory voice disorders, and in adult acquisition of language and speech relative to central and autonomic nervous systems. Office: 31320 Woodside Dr Franklin MI 48025-2027

SAXENA, AMULYA KUMAR, surgeon, director; s. Gopal Krishna and Kesar Bala Saxena. MD, Med. U. Pecs, Hungary, 1992; PhD, Med. U. Graz, Austria. Surg. rsch. fellow Boston's Children Hosp., Harvard Med. Sch., 1996—97; cons. pediatric surgeon Dept. Pediatric Surgery, Westfälische Wilhelms U., Münster, Germany, 2002—03; chief cons. pediatric surgeon Westfälische Wilhelms U., Münster, 2003—04, interim chief of pediatric surgery, 2004—04; dep. dir. Dept. Pediatric and Adolescent Surgery, Med. U. Graz, Austria, 2005. Guest physician Divsn. Infectious Diseases, Dept. Pediatric, Boston's Children Hosp., Harvard Med. Sch., 1996—97, Dept. Pediatric Surgery, Children's Mercy Hosp., U. Mo., Kans. City Sch. Medicine, Kansas City, Mo., 1999—99, Dept. Pediatric Surgery, Hosp. 12 de Octubre, U. Complutense, Madrid, 2001—01; guest prof. Dept. Pediatric Surgery, Children's Hosp. Med. Ctr., U. Cin., Ohio, 2007—07. Editor: (pediatric surgery book) Essentials of Pediatric Endoscopic Surgery, Springer Verlag; contbr. articles to profl. jours. Chmn. STEPS (Strategies & Trends in European Pediatric Surgery), Graz, Europe, 2004—08; dir. ChildcAIR, Münster, Germany, ED-BEC, Münster, Germany; sci. advisor Med. U. of Monastir, Monastir, Tunisia, 2004. Recipient Medal Honor, Mayor Monastir, Tunisia, 1997, Outstanding Clin. Applied Rsch. award, European Rsch. Inst., 2007, Dr. Farooq Abdullah Best Rsch. Paper award, 2009, Vis. Scientist award, Bank Austria Creditanstalt; grantee Pediatric Surgery fellowship, Westfälische Wilhelms U., Münster, Germany, 2002; European Rsch. Grant, European Union, Brussels, 2007—. Mem.: Tunisian Assn. Pediat. Surgery (life), Tissue Engring. and Regenerative Medicine Internat. Soc. (life), Austrian Soc. Pediatric and Adolescent Surgery (life), European Pediatric Surgeons Assn. (life; vice-secretary 2004—08), Internat. Pediatric Endosurgery Group (life), German Soc. Surgery (life), European Tissue Engring. Soc. (life; founding mem. 1999). Achievements include research in cell scaffold interactions for tissue engineering; development of instruments for Endoscopic Surgery; first to skeletal muscle tissue engineering. Office: Med Univ Graz Auenbruggerplatz 34 Graz Steiermark A-8036 Austria Business E-Mail: amulya.saxena@meduni-graz.at.

SAXENA, ANUJ, pharmaceutical business executive; b. Delhi, India, July 31, 1967; s. Jagdish and Sneh (Talwar) Saxena. MBBS, Grant Med. Coll., Bombay, India, 1990. Mng. dir. Elder Group of Cos., Bombay, 1991—; founder Maverick Prodn. House, 2005—; restaurateur Blue Waters, Mumbai, India. Lead actor (television series) Aasman Ke Agay, 1993, (cinema) Sar Ankhon Par, 1999, (television serial) Karm, 1995, Kkusum. Avocations: cinema, painting, travel, reading, music. Office: Elder Pharms Ltd C9 Dalia Industrial Estate off New Link Rd Andheri - W Mumbai 400 053 India Office Phone: 00912226730058—65. Office Fax: 009122 667564 68.

SAXENA, BRIJ B., endocrinologist, biochemist, educator; PhD, India; DSc, U. Muenster, W.Ger.; PhD, U. Wis., 1961; DSc (hon.), Bundelkhand U., India, 2002. Asst. prof. biochemistry and endocrinology N.J. Coll. Medicine., 1966-74; assoc. prof. biochemistry Cornell U. Med. Coll., NYC, 1974—, prof. biochemistry, 1974—, prof. endocrinology, 1981—, dir. div. reproductive endocrinology, Harold and Percy Uris endowed prof. reproductive biology, 2000—. Contbr. articles to profl. jours. Recipient Career Scientist award N.Y.C. Health Research Council; Upjohn research award; Campoz da Paz award. Fellow Royal Soc. Medicine (London); mem. Am. Soc. Biol. Chemists, AAAS, Endocrine Soc., Harvey Soc., Am. Physiol. Soc., Am. Chem. Soc. Office: Cornell U Med Coll 515 E 71st St Ste 412 New York NY 10021-4805 Office Phone: 212-746-3067. Business E-Mail: brs2003@med.cornell.edu.

SAXENA, PIKEE, obstetrician, gynecologist; d. Suresh Kumar and Manju Gupta; life ptnr. Rohit Saxena, Jan. 26, 1996; 1 child, Abhyuday. MBBS, Delhi U., MD, 1998; postgrad. diploma in Clin. Rsch., Catalyst India, Delhi, 2007. Cert. postgrad. in hosp. mgmt. Nat. Inst. Health & Family Welfare, New Delhi, 2006. Lectr. Nat. Inst. Health and Family Welfare, 2002—08; asst. prof. Lady Hardinge Med. Coll., New Delhi, 2008—, cons. Contbr. scientific papers to profl. rsch. publs. (eleven awards). Mem.: Nat. Assn. Reproductive & Child Health India, Fedn. Ob-Gyn. Soc. India. Achievements include research in reproductive endocrinology. Home: J-36 New Delhi 110017 India Office: Lady Hardinge Med Coll Cannaught Pl New Delhi 110001 India Personal E-mail: pikeesaxena@hotmail.com.

SAXENA, ROMIL, pathologist, educator; d. Rajendra Mohan and Rani Saxena; m. Sunil Badve. MBBS, MD, Grant Med. Coll., Mumbai, India. Diplomate Am. Bd. Pathology, 1998. Resident pathologist Sir JJ Group of Hosps., Bombay, 1985—87; sr. registrar, histopathology Tata Meml. Hosp. for Cancer, Bombay, 1987—88, sr. registrar, hematopathology, 1988—90; registrar, dept. pathology, S.E. Thames Regional rotation King's Coll. Hosp., Farnborough Hosp., 1990—91; lectr., dept. pathology King's Coll. Hosp., London, 1991—95; resident, dept. pathology Albert Einstein Sch. Medicine, Bronx, NY, 1995—96; fellow, gene therapy and liver pathology Mt. Sinai Med. Ctr., NYC, 1996—98; fellow, gastrointestinal pathology Yale U. Sch. Med., New Haven, 1998—2002; asst. prof., dept. pathology Mt. Sinai Sch. Medicine, NYC, 2002; asst. prof. depts. pathology and lab. med. Ind. U. Sch. Medicine, Indpls., 2002—08, assoc. prof. depts. pathology and lab. med., dept. medicine, 2008—. Dir., anatomic pathology Richard L. Roudebush VA Med. Ctr., Indpls., 2002—04; lectr. in field in liver & transplantation pathology. Editor: Practical Hepatic Pathology, 2011; contbr. articles to profl. jours., chapters to books. Fellow: Royal Coll. Pathologists (assoc.); mem.: Am. Assn. Study Liver Diseases, Internat. Acad. Pathology (assoc.), Laennec Hepatopathology Soc. (assoc.), Hans Popper Hepatopathology Soc. (assoc.), US and Can. Acad.Pathology (assoc.). Achievements include expertise in liver hepatopathology and transplantation pathology. Avocation: writing. Office: Ind Univ Clarian Health 350 W 11th St Indianapolis IN 46202

SAXENA, TARUN, internist, researcher; b. Sirohi, Rajasthan, India, Dec. 4, 1971; s. Vinod Kumar and Anjana Rani Saxena; m. Manjari Saxena, June 15, 2002; 1 child, Bhasat. Higher Secondary, St.Paul's, Ajmer, India, 1987; MD Internal Medicine, Rajasthan Med. Coun., India, 1999. Med. officer physician State Govt., Ajmer, 2000—. Cons. physician State Govt., Ajmer, 2000—. Author: Serum Insulin Assay an Important Therapeutic Tool in Mgmt. of Freshly Diagnosed Type 2 Diabetes, 2000. Recipient Best Physician award, Tehsil Bhinai Ajmer, 2000, 2001. Mem.: Vivekan and Yoga Centre Ajmer (Best Assoc. Mem. 2002). Achievements include first to Non pharmacological methods in possible cure of fresh cases of type 2 diabetes mellitus. Avocations: reading, writing. Home: E-196 Shastri Nagar Rajasthan Ajmer 305001 India Office: Gheexiboi Meml Mittal Hosp Rsch Ctr Pushkar Rd Rajasthan Ajmer 305001 India Personal E-mail: yogadiab@rediffmail.com. E-mail: t_saxena71@yahoo.com.in.

SAXINGER, WILLIAM CARL, microbiologist; b. Chgo., Oct. 4, 1941; s. Otto and Mary Saxinger; m. Judith Ann Conroy, Aug. 17, 1967; children: Justin, Daniel, Anne. BS in Chemistry, U. Ill., Champaign, 1963, PhD in Microbiology, 1969. NAS, NRC, postdoc. rsch. assoc. NASA, AMES Rsch. Ctr., Exobiology Divsn., Moffett Field, Calif., 1969—71; rsch. assoc. lab. chem. evolution, dept. chemistry U. Md., Coll. Pk., 1971—72, asst. rsch. prof., lab. chem. evolution, 1972—76; sr. staff fellow, lab. tumor cell biology NIH, Nat. Cancer Inst., Bethesda, Md., 1972—75, sr. investigator, microbiologist, 1975—85, sr. investigator, supervisory microbiologist, office dir. Ctr. cancer rsch. Frederick, Md., 1996—, sr. investigator, supervisory microbiologist, lab. tumor cell biology, 1985—96. Cons. devel. of blood bank screening Ortho Diagnostics, Raritan, NJ, 1987; del. US Dept. State, Washington. Contbr. scientific papers. Computer support for spl. needs classes Ivymount Sch., Rockville, Md., 1998—2005. Recipient Tech. Transfer award, Dirs. Nat. Cancer Inst. and Divsn. Cancer Etiology, 1992. Independent. Lutheran. Achievements include patents for polypeptides comprising IL-6 ligand binding receptor domains; polypeptides that bind HIV gp120 and related nucleic acids, antibodies; discovery of markers for possible infection by human leukemia virus HTLV-I in US blood donors; HIV bind to cell receptors in a preliminary promiscuous fashion rendering the design of a multivalent vaccine more feasible; patents for competitive ELISA for the detection of antibodies; identified possible risk to recipients of blood from US donors carrying serum markers of human retovirus; identified risk of human retrouirus contamination in US blood bank supply; development of technologies stuctural definition of cell surface receptor-ligand binding sites proving pathways to development of biological system level response modification and vacclne. Avocations: computers, photography, music, Aikido. Home: 6814 Renita Ln Bethesda MD 20817 Office: Nat Cancer Inst NIH Bldg 37 1041A Bethesda MD 20892 Business E-Mail: carl.saxinger@gmail.com.

SAY, BURHAN, retired physician; b. Istanbul, Turkey, Feb. 26, 1923; came to U.S. 1951; s. Ethem Serif and Ayse Say; m. Elizabeth E. Jackson, Nov. 5, 1955; children: Tony, Daniel Demir. MD, U. Istanbul, 1946. Diplomate Am. Bd. Pediatrics, Am. Bd. Med. Genetics. Asst. prof. pediatrics Hacettepe U., Ankara, Turkey, 1960-64, prof. pediatrics, 1964-73; clin. prof. of pediatrics U. of Okla./Tulsa Med. Coll., 1975—; ret. Dir. H.A. Chapman Inst., Tulsa, 1982—; v.p. Children's Med. Ctr., Tulsa, 1988—. Contbr. articles to profl. jours. Pres. Am. Cancer Soc., Tulsa, 1980-90, Great Plains Genetics Soc., Tulsa, 1993. Lt. Turkish Army, 1946-48, Turkey., Fulbright scholar, Boston, 1966—68. Avocation: sports. Home: 6216 E 99th St Tulsa OK 74137-5503 Home Phone: 918-299-5891. Personal E-mail: mbsay@cox.net.

SAYANA, SHILPA, medical association administrator; b. Zambia, Feb. 28, 1977; BA, Leigh U., 2004; MD, U. Vt.; MPH, Yale U., 2004. HIV fellow AIDS Healthcare Found., 2007—08, global HIV clinician, 2008—10, dir., global quality mgmt., 2010—. Clin. instr., dept. medicine UCLA, 2010—11. Recipient Most Humanistic Resident award, UCLA-SFVP Residency Program, 2005, 2006, 2007, Most Humanistic Intern award, 2004, 2005; named Women of World, UN Assn. Pasadena & 50/50 Leadership; fellow, Albert Schweitzer Found., 2001. Mem.: AAHIVM. Avocations: meditation, yoga, hiking. Home: 4162 Farmdale Ave Studio City CA 91604 Business E-Mail: shilpa.sayana@aidshealth.org.

SAYED, M. GARY, healthcare administrator, educator, scientist; BS in Nuclear Med. Sci., U. of Incarnate Word, San Antonio, 1985; MS in Radiochem., U. Iowa, 1989; PhD in Radiol. Scis., Med. Coll. Ohio, 1993. Med. health physicist U. Iowa, Iowa City, 1989-91; asst. prof. nuclear medicine U. Findlay, Ohio, 1992-97, asst. dir. Nuclear Medicine Inst., 1992-96, acting dir. Nuclear Med. Inst., 1997; assoc. prof. Thomas Jefferson U., Phila., 1998—2003, chmn. dept. diagnostic imaging, 1998—2003, clin. prof., 2002—; prof. Coll. Sci. and Health Charles Drew U. Medicine and Sci., 2003—, dean Coll. Sci. and Health, 2003—. Vis. prof. radiology Dokuz Eylul U., Izmir, Turkey, 1996; vis. prof. nuc. medicine Kuwait U., Kuwait, 2001—02; pres. Am. Bd. of Sci. in Nuc. Medicine. Editor: Nuclear Medicine Science Syllabus, 3d edit., 1999; guest editor: Radiologic Sci. and Edn. Jour. Recipient Leadership award Assn. Schs. of Health Professions, 1998; sr. Fulbright scholar, 1996. Fellow Am. Coll. Nuclear Medicine. Office: Charles Drew U Medicine and Science 1731 E 120th St Los Angeles CA 90059 Home Phone: 856-625-1166; Office Phone: 323-357-3440. Office Fax: 323-357-3433. Business E-Mail: gasayed@cdrewu.edu.

SAYED, SUHAIL I., surgeon, researcher; b. Shrirampur, Maharashtra, India, June 29, 1982; s. Iftekhar Yousuf and Shakila I. Sayed. MBBS in Medicine and Surgery, Govt. Med. Coll., Miraj, Maharashtra, 2006; MS in Otolaryngology and Head & Neck Surgery, Maharashtra U. Health Scis., Nashik, 2009. Cert. diploma in otolaryngology and head & neck surgery. Coll. Physicians and Surgeons, Mumbai, 2009. Surg. registrar Grant Med. Coll. and Sir JJ Group Hosp., Mumbai, 2006—09; sr. rsch. fellow Tata Meml. Hosp., Mumbai, 2009—. Contbr. articles to profl. med. jours. Clin. fellow Cancer Aid and Rsch. Found., Mumbai, 2006. Office: Grant Medical College & Sir JJ hospital Byculla Maharashtra Mumbai 400008 India Home: 6B Pcmc Colony Ajmera Complex Pimpri 411 018 Pune India Office Phone: 912223739034. Personal E-mail: drsuhailsayed@yahoo.com.

SAYERS, MARTIN PETER, pediatric neurosurgeon; b. Big Stone Gap, Va., Jan. 2, 1922; s. Delbert Bancroft and Loula (Thompson) S.; m. Marjorie W. Garvin, May 8, 1943; children: Daniel Garvin Sayers, Stephen Putnam Sayers, Julia Hathaway Sayers Bolton, Elaine King Sayers Buck. BA, Ohio State U., 1943, MD, 1945; postgrad., U. Pa., 1948-51. Intern Phila. Gen. Hosp., 1945-46; resident in neurosurgery U. Pa. Hosps., Phila., 1948-51; practice medicine specializing in neurosurgery Columbus, Ohio, 1951—; mem. faculty Ohio State U., Columbus, 1951-87, clin. prof. neurosurgery, 1968-87, emeritus, chief dept. pediatric neurosurgery, 1960-87. Cons. Bur. Crippled Children Services Ohio.; Neurosurgeon Project Hope, Ecuador, 1964, Ceylon, 1968, Cracow, Poland, 1979. Served as lt. jr. grade M.C. USN, 1946—48. Mem. Am. Assn. Neurol. Surgeons (chmn. pediatric sect.), Congress Neurol. Surgeons (pres.), Neurosurg. Soc. Am. (pres.), Am. Soc. Pediatric Neurosurgery, Soc. Neurol. Surgeons. Office: 931 Chatham Ln Columbus OH 43221-2417

SAZEL, MILOS, physician, physiologist, consultant; b. Plzen, Czech Republic, Apr. 1953; s. Frantisek Sazel and Magdalena Sazelova; m. Petra Novotna, Aug. 29, 1981; children: Vojtech, Anezka, Marie. MD, Charles U., 1978, diploma in internal medicine, 1983, PhD in Physiology, 1992, diploma in aviation medicine, 1993, diploma in hyperbaric med. oxygenotherapy, 2006. Ho. officer Ctrl. Mil. Hosp., Prague, 1978—79; head med. svc. Anti-Aircraft Rgt., Marianské Lazne; commd. sr. officer, med. dept. Staff of Corps, Pribram, 1980—82; head med. svc. Radio Reconnaissance Bn., Kladno, 1982—83; sr. rsch. worker Inst. Aviation Medicine, Prague, 1983—92, head dept. flight safety, 1993—; cons. Hyperban Aviation Med., 2009; dir. CMAS P Nitrox Advanced. Lectr. Czech Tech. U., Prague, 1997—2009. Lt. col. Czech Mil., 1972—2004. Mem.: Czech Med. Soc. J. E. Purkyne (life), Czech Med. Chamber (life). Achievements include research in aviation and diving physiology; Hyperbaric Oxygen Therapy. Home Phone: 420222951310; Office Phone: 420973208139. Personal E-mail: milos.sazel@seznam.cz, sazel@ulz.cz.

SBUTTONI, MICHAEL JAMES, orthodontist, contractor; b. Albany, NY, Aug. 6, 1953; s. Michael Francis and Mary Susan (Walsh) Sbuttoni; m. Karen Sbuttoni, Aug. 9, 1975; children: Michael Louis, Ashley Ryan. BS, SUNY, Albany, 1975; DDS, SUNY, Buffalo, 1979; cert. in orthodontics, Eastman Dental Ctr., Rochester, NY, 1981. Real estate salesman Tri City Realty-Albany Bd. Realtors, 1971—; bldg. contractor M. Sbuttoni Constrn., Albany, 1972-86; practice dentistry specializing in orthodontics Dr. Serling and Decker DDS. P.C., Albany, 1981—. Staff orthodontist St. Peter's Hosp., Albany, 1984—; bldg. contractor Craftsmens Guild, Albany, 1987—; pres. Eastern Broadcasting Group, 2002. Mem.: ADA, Angle Soc. Orthodontists, Coun. Govt. Rels. (chmn.), Northeastern Soc. Orthodontists, 3d Dist. Dental Soc. (bd. dirs. 1985—89, v.p. 1987—88, pres. 1988—90, ADA rep. 1990—96), Dental Soc. State N.Y. (pub. rels. 1985—88, coun. edn. 1992—93), Am. Assn. Lingual Orthodontists (charter), Internat. Coll. Dentists, Am. Assn. Orthodontists (coun. govt. rels.), Am. Coll. Dentists, Elks, Kiwanis (fund raising dir. 1985—87). Republican. Roman Catholic. Avocations: marathon running, golf, skiing, sailing, gardening. Home: 92 Middlesex Ct Slingerlands NY 12159-9636 Office: Drs Serling & Decker DDS PC 1004 Western Ave Albany NY 12203-2743 Office Phone: 518-439-8891. Business E-Mail: quickmick9@aol.com.

SCACCIA, FRANK JOHN, facial surgeon, otolaryngologist; b. Teaneck, NJ, June 21, 1959; s. Ralph John and Angelina Josephine Scaccia. BS magna cum laude, Duke U., Durham, NC, 1981; MD, Wake Forest U., Winston-Salem, NC, 1985. Diplomate Am. Bd. Facial Plastic and Reconstructive Surgery, Am. Bd. Otolaryngology and Head and Neck Surgery. Resident in gen. surgery Monmouth Med. Ctr., Long Branch, NJ, 1985—88; resident in otolaryngology Case Western Res. U., Cleve., 1988—92; surgeon Otolaryngology Assocs., Red Bank, NJ, 1992—98; surgeon, CEO Riverside Plastic Surgery and Sinus Ctr., Red Bank, 1998—. Mem. staff Riverview Med. Ctr., Red Bank, Bayshore Cmty. Hosp., Holmdel, NJ. Contbr. articles to med. jours. Vol. surgeon Face to Face, 1992—; vol. Parker Clinic, Red Bank. Recipient Jack Anderson prize for scholastic excellence, Am. Bd. Facial Plastic and Reconstructive Surgery, 1995; named Top Beauty Dr., NJ Savvy Living, 2005—09, Top NY Metro Dr., Castle Connolly, 2006, 2007, Am. Top Dr., 2006, 2007. Fellow: ACS, Internat. Coll. Surgeons, Am. Acad. Facial Plastic and Reconstructive Surgery, Am. Acad. Otolaryngology; mem.: NJ Med. Soc., Monmouth County Med. Soc., Phi Beta Kappa. Avocations: running, bicycling, guitar. Home: Grand Pointe Condo 700 Ocean Ave Unit # 1 Sea Bright NJ 07760 Office: 70 E Front St Ste 3 Red Bank NJ 07701 Home Phone: 732-747-0845; Office Phone: 732-747-5300. Personal E-mail: acce000007@yahoo.com.

SCADDEN, DAVID THOMAS, hematologist, oncologist, research scientist; b. 1953; BA in English Lit., Bucknell U., 1975; MD, Case Western Res. U., 1980. Diplomate Am. Bd. Internal Medicine. Intern Brigham-Women's Hosp., Boston, 1980-81, resident in internal medicine, 1981-83, fellow in hematology/oncology, 1983-86; with Dana Farber Inst. Brigham & Women's Hosp., Boston; Gerald & Darlene Jordan prof. medicine Harvard U.; co-dir. Harvard Stem Cell Inst., 2004—; dir. Center for Regenerative Medicine, Mass. Gen. Hosp.; chief of hematologic malignancies Mass. Gen. Hosp. Co-chmn. Dept. of Stem Cell and Regenerative Biology, Harvard U.; mem. bd. of scientific counselors Nat. Cancer Inst.; bd. of external experts Nat. Heart, Lung and Blood Inst.; assoc. mem. Broad Inst. Recipient Clin. Scientist award in Translational Rsch., 2002, award, Burroughs Wellcome Fund, Doris Dute Found. Mem.: Inst. of Medicine, Nat. Acad. Scis. Achievements include research in defining hematopoietic stem cell niche translating stem cell research to medical therapy; adult hematopoietic stem cells with emphasis on their interaction with the microenvironment and cell cycle control. Office: AIDS Rsch Ctr Mass Gen Hosp Fruit St Boston MA 02114 also: Ctr for Regenerative Medicine and Tech Mass Gen Hosp 13th St Bldg 149 Rm 5212D Boston MA 02129 Office Phone: 617-726-5615. Office Fax: 617-724-2662. Business E-Mail: scadden.david@mgh.harvard.edu.

SCALA, JAMES, health facility administrator, consultant, writer; b. Ramsey, NJ, Sept. 16, 1934; s. Edvigi and Lorene (Hendricksen) Scala; m. Nancy Peters, June 15, 1957; children: James, Gregory, Nancy, Kimberly. BA, Columbia U., 1960; PhD, Cornell U., 1964; postgrad., Harvard U., 1968; LHD (hon.), Hofstra U., 1998. Cert. nutrition specialist. Staff scientist Miami Valley Labs., Procter and Gamble Co., 1964-66; head life scis., dir. fundamental rsch. Owens Ill. Corp., 1966-71; dir. nutrition T.J. Lipton Inc., 1971-75; dir. health scis. Gen. Foods Corp., 1975-78; v.p. sci. and tech. Shaklee Corp., San Francisco, 1978-85, sr. v.p. sci. affairs, 1986-87. Lectr. Georgetown U. Med. Sch.; instr. U. Calif., Berkeley; nutritionist U.S. Olympic Ski Team, 1981—87. Author: Making the Vitamin Connection, 1985, The Arthritis Relief Diet, 1987, 2d edit., 1989, Eating Right for a Bad Gut, 1990, 2d edit., 1992, Eating Right for a Bad Gut, new edit., 1999, The High Blood Pressure Relief Diet, 1988, 2d edit., 1990, Look 10 Years Younger, Feel 10 Years Better, 1991, 2d edit., 1993, Prescription for Longevity, 1992, 2d edit., 1994, If You Can't/Won't Stop Smoking, 1993, The New Arthritis Relief Diet, 1998, 25 Natural Ways to Manage Stress and Avoid Burnout, 2000, 25 Natural Ways to Relieve Irritable Bowel Syndrome, 2000, 20 Natural Ways to Reduce the Risk of Prostate Cancer, 2001, 25 Natural Ways to Lower Blood Pressure, 2002; editor: Nutritional Determinants in Athletic Performance, 1981, New Protective Roles for Selected Nutrients, 1989; columnist: Dance mag.; contbr. articles to profl. jours. With USAF, 1953—56. Disting. scholar, U. Miami, Fla., 1977, Atlantic U., 1977. Fellow: Am. Coll. Nutrition; mem.: AAAS, Am. Diabetic Assn., Mt. Diablo Astron. Soc., Eastbay Astron. Soc., Astron. Soc. Pacific (bd. dirs., chmn. devel. coun.), Inst. Food Technologists, Am. Soc. Cell Biology, Sports Medicine Coun., Brit. Nutrition Soc., Am. Inst. Nutrition, Oakland Yacht Club, Olympic Club (San Francisco), Sigma Xi. Libertarian. Avocations: astronomy, photography. Personal E-mail: jscala2@comcast.net.

SCALES, JAMES LEONARD, JR., orthopedic surgeon; b. Sacramento, May 15, 1952; s. James Leonard and Ruth Marie S.; m. Donna Marie Coppola, Oct. 11, 1983; children: James C., Steven, Kevin. AB in Psychology cum laude, Harvard U., Cambridge, Mass., 1974; MD, UMDNJ, Rutgers Med. Sch., Piscataway, 1979; MS in Physiology, Rutgers U., New Brunswick, NJ, 1978, PhD prog. in Physiology, 1980—82. Diplomate Am. Bd. Orthopedic Surgery, 2008. Resident in gen. surgery U. Medicine and Dentistry N.J., Rutgers Med. Sch., Piscataway, 1979—80; resident in orthop. surgery U. Medicine and Dentistry N.J., N.J. Med. Sch., Newark, 1982—86; staff physician med. unit Meadowlands Sports Complex, NJ Sports & Exposition Authority, East Rutherford, NJ, 1980—88; gen. practitioner Catholine Gibbs Meml. Health Ctr., 1982—86; orthop. surgeon D'Ascoli Orthop. Surgery, Sparta, NJ, 1986—88; pres. Andover Orthop. Surgery & Sports Medicine Group, PA, Newton, 1988—; ind. med. examiner CFO Med. Svcs., Roseland, NJ, 2006—08. Cons. orthop. N.J. Cardinals, Profl. Baseball Team, Augusta, 1997—2005; chief surgery Newton Meml. Hosp., 1994—96; med. dir. N. Jersey Surgery Ctr., Newton, 2002—05; vol. physician US Olympic Com., US Olympic Tng. Ctr., Lake Placid, NY, 1997; chmn. Quality Performance Com.; exec. bd. dirs. Garden State Orthop. Network, IPA, 1996—2000, Med. Mgmt. Com., Wes-Com Health Care Inc., PHO, 1996—98; med. staff rep. Newton Meml. Hosp. Found., 1996—98; vice chief med. staff Newton Meml. Hosp., Newton, NJ, 1998; football sideline physician at 4 HS, 91. Interviewer Harvard Club N.J., 1975—. Recipient Track Champion, NJ State HS, 1969, Jr. Olympic Track Champion, NJ AAU, 1969. Fellow: Am. Acad. Orthop. Surgeons; mem.: AMA, US Olympic Sports Medicine Soc., Sussex County Med. Soc., Am. Med. Soc., N.J. Med. Soc., Pa. Orthop. Soc., N.J. Orthop. Soc. Avocations: music, exercise. Office: Andover Orthop Surgery 280 Newton-Sparta Rd Newton NJ 07860 Office Phone: 973-579-7443. Office Fax: 973-579-5628.

SCALF, RENE DENISE, veterinary medical technician; d. Robert Joseph and Judith Ann Austin. BS magna cum laude, U. Colo., 1987; AAS, Bel Rea Inst. Animal Tech., 1990. Cert. vet. technician Colo. Assn. Cert. Vet. Technicians, 1990, vet. technician specialist in emergency and critical care Acad. Vet. Emergency and Critical Care Technicians, 1998. Student tutor Bel Rea Inst. Animal Tech., Aurora, Colo., 1989—90; night technician team leader Allpets Clinic, Boulder, Colo., 1990—95; intensive care technician Vet. Ctrs. Am. Vet. Referral Assocs., Gaithersburg, Md., 1995—97; vet. technologist III Colo. State U. Vet. Tchg. Hosp., Ft. Collins, 1997—. Coord. Boulder Bloodworx Canine and Feline Bloodbank, 1993—95, guest lectr. in field. Contbr. chapters to books. Recipient Animal Dietary Mgmt. award, Hill's Pet Products, 1989; Regent's scholar, U. Colo., Boulder, 1983, Women's Ctr. scholar, 1986, Dean's scholar, 1986, Kenneth M. Good Bus. scholar, U. Colo., 1987. Mem.: Acad. Internal Medicine for Vet. Technicians (organizing com. 2006, dir.-at-large small animal internal medicine 2006, mem.-a-large 2003—06), Nat. Assn. Vet. Technicians Am., Vet. Emergency and Critical Care Soc., Acad. Vet. Emergency and Critical Care Technicians (assoc., bd. regents, mem. at large 2003—, chair credential appeals com., chair exam com.), Colo. Assn. Cert. Vet. Technicians (assoc.), Golden Key Nat. Honor Soc., Beta Gamma Sigma. Avocations: piano, guitar, tennis, national park enthusiast.

SCALING, SAM T., obstetrician, gynecologist; b. Fort Monmouth, NJ, Aug. 16, 1945; s. Sam T. and Helen Louise Scaling; m. Lisa Janine Peck, Aug. 6, 1988; 1 child, Micah;children from previous marriage: Traci, Craig, Chad, Chris, Cory, Tiffany. BS, U. N.Mex., Albuquerque, 1967; MD, U. Tenn., Memphis, 1971. Diplomate Am. Bd. Ob/Gyn. Intern Confederate Meml. Med. Ctr., Shreveport, La., 1971—72; resident in ob gyn. Baylor Coll. Medicine, Houston, 1975—78, chief resident ob/gyn., 1977—78; pvt. practice Obstetrics, Gynecology and Infertility Casper, Wyo., 1978—; founder, pres. Women's Health Assocs. Wyo., Casper, 2001—; med. staff Wyo. Med. Ctr., 1978—; chmn. dept. ob/gyn. Wyo. Med. Ctr., Meml. Hosp. Natrona County, 1981—83, 1986—88, 2001, 2002—05, sec. med. staff, 1989—91, vice chief of staff, 1991—93, chief of staff, 1993—95. Clin. asst. prof., instr. ob/gyn. Wyo. Family Practice Program, Casper, 1978—; v.p. Wyo. State Bd. Med. Examiners, 1984—92, 1989—90, pres., 1990—92; presenter in field; med. dir. Casper Family-Centered League Lamaze Prepared Childbirth, 1980—84, Christ-Centered Childbirth, 1984—87, Caring Ctr., Casper, 1986—90, Wyo. Med. Ctr. PMS Clinic, 1987—90. Author childrens books. Mem. Little Dilly Golf Tournament com. Casper Country Club, 1994—96; mem. adv. bd. Caring Ctr., 2001—; mem. Healing Pl. Counseling Ctr. adv. bd. Highland Park Cmty. Ch., 1994—95; v.p. bd. dirs. Casper Children's Chorale, 1981—82; bd. dirs. Wyo. Cmty. Health Care Alliance, 1997—, Christian Solidarity Worldwide-USA, 1997—2000. Maj. USAF, 1972—75. Named to Am.'s Top Obstetricians and Gynecologists, Consumers Rsch. Coun. Am., 2002—03, 2007; NSF summer scholar, N.Mex. Highlands U., 1962. Fellow: ACS, ACOG, Am. Fertility Soc.; mem.: Am. Soc. Reproductive Medicine (mem. nat. adv. coun. 1997), Natrona County Med. Soc., Am. Assn. Pro Life Obstetricians and Gynecologists, Am. Coll. Physician Execs., Soc. Reproductive Surgeons, Am. Assn. Gynecologic Laparoscopists, Wyo. State Med. Soc., Ctrl. Assn. Obstetricians and Gynecologists, Found. N.Am. Wild Sheep (life), Alaska Profl. Hunters Assn., Bass Anglers Sportsman Soc. (life), N.Am. Hunting Club (life), Boone and Crockett Club (life), Safari Club Internat. (life), Rocky Mountain Elk Found., Alpha Omega Alpha. Republican. Mem. Ch. Of God. Avocations: hunting, fishing, hiking, gun collecting, coin collecting/numismatics. Office: Women's Health Assocs Wyo 1125 E 2d Casper WY 82601 Office Phone: 307-577-4226.

SCAMMAN, W. WIKE, retired pathologist; b. Hamburg, Iowa, Feb. 3, 1932; s. Willard Sedgwick and Agnes Louise Scamman; m. Donna Ruth Garceau, Feb. 27, 1960; children: George, Sara, Amy, Will, Glenn. BA, Westminster Coll., 1953; MD, Vanderbilt U., 1957. Intern U. Ill. Hosps., Chgo., 1957—58, pathology resident, 1958—62; assoc. pathologist Kennestone Hosp., Marietta, Ga., 1962—63, Lattimore-Fink Lab., Topeka, 1963—70; pathologist, dir. Damon Labs., Topeka, 1970—82, Scamman Pathology Svcs., Topeka, 1982—2009. Pres. Kans. Assn. Blood Banks, Topeka, 1967—68, Topeka Blood Bank, Inc., 1974—75, Kans. Soc. Pathologists, 1969—70. Co-founder S.W. Youth Athletic Assn., Topeka, 1968; charter mem. Washburn Rural Optimist Club, Topeka, 1970. Mem.: Am. Soc. Clin. Pathologists, U.S. Can. Acad. Pathologists, Coll. Am. Pathologists, Kans. Med. Soc. Home: 4635 SW Urish Rd Topeka KS 66610

SCANDALIS, THOMAS A., dean, educator, osteopath, researcher; b. Northport, NY; BA in Biol. Sciences, Adelphi U., Garden Center, NY; DO, NY Inst. Tech. NY Coll. Osteo. Medicine, Old Westbury, 1987. Cert. in family practice, in sports medicine. Post doctoral tng. Massapequa Gen. Hosp., Seaford, NY; prof. NY Inst. Tech. NY Coll. Osteo. Medicine, chmn. dept. family medicine, 1996—2005, assoc. dean academic affairs, 2005—07, dean, 2007—. Team physician NY Inst. Tech. Athletics, 1988—, US Nat. Boxing Team, 1994—98. Peer reviewer, editor: Clin. Jour. Sports Medicine, peer reviewer: Jour. of American Osteo. Assn. (George Northrup Writing award, 1998), Physician and Sports Medicine. Clin. specialist, combat medic US Army, 1976—80. Osteo. Heritage Health Policy fellow. Fellow: American Osteo. Acad. Sports Medicine (bd. mem., pres. 2004); mem.: NY State Bd. Profl. Med. Conduct, American Osteo Assn., American Coll. Osteo. Family Physicians, NY State Osteo. Med. Soc., American Med. Soc. Sports Medicine. Office: NY Inst Tech NY Coll Osteo Medicine Office of Dean Rockefeller Rm 107 Northern Blvd PO Box 8000 Old Westbury NY 11568-8000 Office Phone: 516-686-3722. Business E-Mail: tscandal@nyit.edu. *

SCANGOS, GEORGE A., biotechnology company executive; b. 1948; BA in Biology, Cornell U., 1970; PhD in Microbiology, U. Mass. Postdoctoral fellow Yale U., New Haven; with Bayer Corp., 1987—93, pres., biotechnology, 1993—96; chmn. Anadys Pharmaceuticals, Inc., 2005—; CEO, pres. & bd. dirs. Biogen Idec, Inc., Cambridge, Mass., 2010—. Bd. mem. Global Alliance for TB Drug Devel.; nat. bd. visitors U. Calif. Davis Sch. Medicine; bd. dirs. TaconicArtemis GmbH (formerly Artemis Pharmaceuticals GmbH)); adj. prof., biology Johns Hopkins U., prof., biology, 1981—87; pres., CEO Exelixis, Inc., 1996—2010, bd. dirs., 1996—, Entelos, Inc., 1997, Onyx Pharmaceuticals Inc., 2000—05. Chmn. Calif. Healthcare Inst. (CHI); bd. dirs. Global Alliance for TB Drug Devel., Fond. Sante, BayBio; bd. overseers U. of Calif. Davis Sch. of Medicine; bd. visitors U. Calif. San Francisco Sch. of Pharmacy, San Francisco Sch. Pharmacy. Office: Biogen Idec Inc 133 Boston Post Rd Weston MA 02493 Office Phone: 781-464-2000. Business E-Mail: george.scangos@biogenidec.com. *

SCANIFFE, JOSEPH ALBERT, anesthesiologist, consultant; s. Angelo and Agnes Mary Scaniffe; m. Lidia Brigette Munteanu, Apr. 8, 2006, children: Richard Anthony, Christopher Michael, Brigette Annette Mocan. BS in Engring., US Mil. Acad., West Point, NY; MBA, U. So. Calif., LA; MD, Uniformed Svcs. U. Health Scis., Bethesda, Md., 1985. Diplomate Am. Bd. Anesthesiology, 1990. Commd. 2d lt. US Army, airborne ranger, pathfinder Air Assault, Aviation, advanced through grades to lt. col., nuc. weapons assembly team chief 9th Inf. Divsn., Ft Lewis, Wash.; exec. officer D/1/84th FA, Ft Lewis, Wash.; attack helicopter platoon comdr. 101st Airborne Divsn., Ft Campbell, Ky.; task force logistics officer 101st Airborne Divsn. Task Force, Germany; comdr. A/3/319th FA 101st Airborne Divsn., Ft Campbell; instr. advanced ground/air tactics Armor Ctr., Ft Knox, Ky.; staff anesthesiologist Madigan Army Med. Ctr., Tacoma, 1989—90, chief clin. svcs./vascular anesthesia Ft Lewis, Wash., 1991—97; asst. chief anesthesia 82d Airborn Divsn. 5th Mobile Army Surg. Hosp., Iraq, Saudi Arabia, Kuwait, Persian Gulf War; ptnr. Swedish Med. Ctr., Seattle, 1998—2003; ptnr. Milford Anesthesia Assocs. Bristol Hosp., Conn., 2003—, chief dept. anesthesia, 2009—. Asst. prof. Uniformed Svcs. U. Sch. Medicine, Bethesda, 1991—97; faculty Acad. Health Scis., San Antonio, 1991—97; clin. instr. U. Wash., Seattle, 2000—03. Humanitarian Med. Aid Mission, Dominican Republic, 2007, Bolivia, 2009. Decorated Meritorious Svc. medal US Army, Army Commendation medal, Army Achievement medal, Nat. Def. Svc. medal, SW Asia Svc. medal, Armed Forces medal, Kuwait Liberation medal Kingdom of Saudi Arabia and Kingdom of Kuwait; recipient Expert Field Medicine award, Profiles in Medicine award, Bristol Hosp. Conn., 2010; named one of Am.'s Top Anesthesiologists, Consumers' Rsch. Coun. America, 2006—10. Master: Am. Bd. Anesthesiology; mem.: Milford Anesthesia Assn. (bd. dir.), Assn. Mil. Surgeons (life, Outstanding Leadership and Acad. award 1985), Conn. State Soc. Anesthesiology, Soc. Cardiovasc. Anesthesiologists, Internat. Anesthesia Rsch. Soc., Am. Soc. Regional Anesthesia, Am. Soc. Anesthesiologists. Independent. Roman Catholic. Achievements include development of operational/combat anesthesia machine. Avocations: hiking, bicycling, racquetball, fishing, woodworking. Home: 11 Glenmore Dr Farmington CT 06032

SCANTLEBURY, VELMA PATRICIA, surgeon; b. Barbados, Oct. 6, 1955; came to U.S., 1970; d. Delacey Whitstanley and Kathleen (Jordan) S.; 2 children. BS, LI U., 1977; MD, Columbia U., 1981; DS (hon.), LI U., 1998, Seton Hall Coll. PA. Intern in surgery Harlem Hosp. Ctr., NYC, 1981-82, resident in surgery, 1982-86; fellow in transplantation U. Pitts., 1988, assoc. prof. surgery, 1998—2002; prof. surgery, dir. transplantation U. South Ala. Med. Ctr., Mobile, 2002—. Mem. med. advisory bd. Nat. Kidney Found. Vol. King County Hosp., Bklyn., 1972. Recipient Martin Luther King Sch. award, 1973-74, Am. Fedn. Tchrs. Sch. award, 1973-75, Nat. Med. Found. award 1977-78, Joseph Collins Found. Sch. award 1978, Gift of Life award Nat. Kidney Found., OMNI Life Models award, Women of Spirit award Carlow Coll.; named Outstanding Young Women of Am. 1988. Fellow, ACS; mem. AMA (listed by AMA as nation's first African-Am. female transplant surgeon), P&S Alumni Assn., Black and Latin Students Orgn. (treas. N.Y.C. 1979-80), Slpha Epsilon Delta, Phi Sigma Soc. (sec. Bklyn. chpt. 1976-77), Am. Soc. Transplantation, Am. Soc. Transplant Surgeons, Soc. Black Academic Surgeons, Am. Soc. Minority Health and Transplant Professionals (bd. dirs.), Internat. Women's Forum We. Pa., Nat. Assn. Negro Bus. and Profl. Women. Democrat. Office: Univ S Ala Med Ctr 2451 Fillingim St Mobile AL 36617-2293

SCAPINELLI, RAFFAELE, orthopaedic surgeon, educator; b. Reggio Emilia, Italy, Feb. 15, 1932; s. Pietro Scapinelli and Beatrice Franzini; m. Emilia Bucciante, Sept. 24, 1958; children: Anna Carola, Luisa, Filippo, Francesca. Degree in medicine, U. Padua, Italy, MD, 1956, splty. degree in orthop. and traumatology, 1959, splty. degree in radiology, 1961; splty. degree in physiotherapy, U. Florence, Italy,

1970; postgrad., Nuffield Orthop. Ctr., Oxford, Eng., 1961—62. Asst. orthop. clinic U. Padua, 1962—73, prof., dir. orthop. clinic, 1986—2004, hon. prof. orthop., 2006; prof., dir. orthop. clinic U. Chieti, Italy, 1973—86. Dir. sch. specialization in orthop. and traumatology U. Chieti and U. Padua. Author: Handbook of Traumatology of the Locomotor Apparatus, 3d edit., 2000; contbr. over 230 articles to profl. jours. Mem.: Soc. Orthopaedics and Traumatology Ctrl. Italy (pres. 1982—84), Posterior Cruciate Ligament Study Group, Internat. Patello-Femoral Study Group, Italian Soc. Orthop. and Traumatology, Internat. Soc. Orthop. and Traumatology Surgery. Achievements include first to describe sesamoid bones in the ligamentum nuchae of man; describe blood supply of the human knee joint; development of two operative methods for shoulder disorders, one for recurrent posterior instability and one for cuff tear arthropathy; investigation on the fields of knee, the spine, paediatric orthopaedics & paleopathology, the latter including studies on the bones of St. Luke the Evangelist (1st centuryAD) and Poet Francesco Petrarca 1304-1374. Avocation: painting. Business E-Mail: raffaelescapinelli@libero.it.

SCARABIN, PIERRE-YVES, physician, researcher; b. Le Mans, France, Aug. 25, 1948; s. Pierre Scarabin and Emilienne Ténette; m. Maryvonne Le Poulichet, June 28, 1975; children: Catherine, Laure, Valérie. MD, Med. U., Rennes, 1975. Lic. Rennes U., France, 1980. Dir. rsch. Nat. Inst. of Health and Med. Rsch. (INSERM), Paris, 1992—; rschr. INSERM, Paris, 1984—92. Prof. Paris XI U., 1985—. Contbr. scientific papers. Mem.: French Soc. for Haemostasis and Thrombosis. Liberal. Achievements include research in estrogen replacement therapy associated with an increased risk of venous thromboembolism in postmenopausal women; the effect of estrogen on blood coagulation; hormone replacement therapy and the reduction of vascular inflammation. Home: 34 Rue Aristide Briand Orsay 91400 France Office: INSERM Unit 258 16 Avenue Paul Vaillant-Couturier Villejuif 94807 France Office Fax: +33147269454. Personal E-mail: pyscarabin@wanadoo.fr. E-mail: scarabin@vjf.inserm.fr.

SCARAVILLI, MARIA SERENA, dentist; b. Italy, July 23, 1983; Degree in Dentistry, U. Naples Federico II, 2006, degree in Oral Surgery, 2010. Dentist, oral surgeon Dental Offices, 2007—. Referee Jour. Pediats., 2008—. Fellow: SENAME Mediterranean Soc. Implantology (Best Lectr. award), Italian Oral Surgery Soc.; mem.: Internat. Congress Oral Implantologist (Best Lectr. award). Avocations: reading, music, jogging. Office: Via Petrarca 57 Caserta I-81100 Italy E-mail: serena.scaravilli@gmail.com.

SCARBOROUGH, MARION NICHOLS, nutritionist, recreational facility executive; b. Enosburg Falls, Vt., July 26, 1915; d. George Leonard and Clara May (Woodward) Nichols; m. Mat. Scarborough, Aug. 30, 1950 (dec. Mar., 1960); 1 child Mary Anne Scarborough O'Donnell Adams. ASS, Green Mountain Coll., Poultney, Vt., 1935; BS, Kans. State U., 1937; MPH, Harvard U., 1947. Chief dietitian Newton (Mass.) Wellesley Hosp., 1938-43, 182d Gen. Hosp., U.S. Army, 1943-45; nutritionist, author food exch. list U.S. Pub. Health Diabetes Sect., Boston, 1947-50; nutritionist Fla. Bd. Health, Jacksonville, 1950-52; owner Happy Acres Ranch, Inc., Jacksonville, 1953—. Sec. Fla. Assn. Children Under Six ECA, 1965, pres., 1966, 67. Commd. officer USPHS, 1948-50. Mem. APHA, Am. Dietetic Assn., Am. Camping Assn., Nat. Assn. Edn. of Young Children. Episcopalian. Home and Office: Happy Acres Ranch Inc 7117 Crane Ave Jacksonville FL 32216-9012

SCARDINO, PETER T., urologic oncologic surgeon; b. Portsmouth, Va., Sept. 28, 1945; m. Alice Barrow Myrick, 1965 (div.); children: Allison Kelly, Peter Daniel Robinson, Elizabeth Barrow; m. Judith Kelman, 2007. BA in Religious studies, Yale U., New Haven, 1967; MD, Duke U. Sch. Medicine, Durham. NC, 1971. Diplomate Am. Bd. Urology. Resident surgery Mass. Gen. Hosp., Boston, 1971-73; clin. assoc. surgery br. Nat. Cancer Inst., NIH, 1973-76; resident urology UCLA Sch. Medicine, 1976-79, instr., 1978-79; asst. to assoc. prof. Baylor U. Coll. Medicine, Houston, 1979-86, prof. urology, 1986-98, Russell & Mary Hugh Scott prof., chmn. dept. urology, 1989-98; chief urology svc., Murray F Brennan chair surgery Meml. Sloan-Kettering Cancer Ctr., NYC, 1998—99, head prostate cancer program, 1998—, chmn. dept. urology, 1999—2006, Alfred P Sloan chair, 1999—2000, Florence & Theodore Baumritter/Enid Ancell chair urologic oncology, 2000—08, chmn. dept. surgery, 2006—, David H. Koch chair, 2008—. Prof. dept. urology Cornell U. Weill Med. Coll., 1998—, SUNY Downstate Med. Ctr., 2000—. Co-author (with Judith Kelman): Dr. Peter Scardino's Prostate Book, 2005; editor: Comprehensive Textbook of Genitourinary Oncology; editor-in-chief Nature Clinical Practice Urology; contbr. numerous articles to profl. jours., chapters to books. Recipient Presdl. Citation, Am. Found. Urologic Disease, 1996, Alumnus award, Duke U. Med. Ctr., 1999; named one of Best Doctors in NYC, NY mag., 2000—09. Fellow: ACS (past v.p., Disting. Svc. award 2000), Am. Surg. Assn. (past pres.); mem.: Inst. Medicine, NY Acad. Sci., Am. Assn. Cancer Rsch., Am. Soc. Clin. Oncology, Am. Assn. Genitourinary Surgeons, Clin. Soc. Genitourinary Surgeons., Am. Urol. Assn. (Gold Cytoscope award 1989, Eugene Fuller Triennial Prostate award). Office: Meml Sloan Kettering Cancer Ctr Dept Urology 1275 York Ave New York NY 10021-6094 Office Phone: 646-422-4329. *

SCARLATA, PAUL ANTHONY, oral surgeon; b. McKeesport, Pa., Apr. 3, 1935; s. Joseph Mario and Josephine Gloria (Battaglia) S.; m. Mary Jane Parks, June 15, 1963 (dec. 1982); children: Stephanie, Anthony, Christopher, Matthew, Sarah; m. Darla K. Hosler, May 27, 1988 (div. 1994); m. Helen Walterick Meyers, Jan. 3, 2006. BS, U. Pitts., 1957, DDS, DMD, U. Pitts., 1961. Resident in oral surgery Western Pa. Hosp., Pitts., 1962-63, St. Luke's Hosp., NYC, 1963-64; practice gen. dentistry and oral surgery Chambersburg, Pa., 1967—; chief dental svc. Chambersburg Hosp., 1974-76, 82-84. Treas. Franklin County (Pa.) Heritage, 1971—, pres., 1977-78; fgn. student exch. host Youth for Understanding, appointed regional field dir. Capt., oral surgeon AUS, 1964—67, Mannheim, Germany. Recipient Buhl Planetarium Sci. award 1st prize Astronomy 6″ Newtonian Reflector, 1952. Mem. ADA (life), Pa. Dental Assn., We. Pa. Assn. Oral Surgeons, Gt. Lakes Soc. Oral Surgeons, N.Y. Soc. Clin. Oral Pathologists, Am. Dental Soc. of Anesthetists, Cumberland Valley Dental Soc. (pres. 1982-83), Am. Legion (life), Chambersburg Club, Antique Studebakers Club, Antique Auto Assn. (life), K.C., Pitts. Athletic Club. Home: 6703 Congressional Terr Fayetteville PA 17222-9403 also: 6703 Congressional Ter Fayetteville PA 17222-9403 Personal E-mail: poppars@comcast.net.

SCARNATI, RICHARD ALFRED, forensic psychiatrist; b. Pitts., Dec. 18, 1940; Diploma in Phys. Therapy, D.T. Watson Sch. Physiatrics, Leetsdale, Pa., 1966; BS in Phys. Therapy, U. Pitts., 1966; MA in Health and Safety, Calif. State U., LA, 1969; DO, Chgo. Coll. Osteo. Medicine, 1976. Diplomate Am. Bd. Psychiatry and Neurology, 1981, Subspecialty Certification, Forensic Psychiatry, 1999, cert. physician Va. State Bd. Medicine, DEA, Ohio State Med. Bd., Fla. Bd. Med. Examiners, osteopathic physician, Ind. Med. Lic. Bd., physician & surgeon Md., Tex. Med. Bd., physician Pa., osteo physician & surgeon, registered physical therapist, Calif. Bd. Med. Quality Assurance. Residency in psychiatry Ill. State Psychiat. Inst., 1976-77, Med. Coll. of Va., 1977-79; psychiatrist Monroe Ctr. for Mental Health, Richmond, Va., 1979; prison & forensic psychiatrist Ohio Dept. Mental Health, Columbus, 1979—81, Cin., 1985—91; psychiatrist VA Hosp., Hampton, Va., 1981-82, VA Outpatient Clinic, Harrisburg, Pa., 1982-83, Harrisburg (Pa.) Hosp., 1984; president Ohio Dept. Mental Health Med. Dir. Assn., 1987—88; psychiatrist North Ctrl. Mental Health Svcs., Columbus, 1992—. Clin. asst. prof. psychiatry U. Cinn., 1985-92, Tex. Coll. Osteo. Medicine, Ft. Worth, 1990-94, Ohio State U., Columbus, 1981-82, 1992—, 2004, Ohio U. Coll. Osteo. Medicine, Athens, vol. faculty, 1987—93, clin. asst. prof. psychiatry, 1993—96, clin. assoc. prof. psychiatry, 1996-2000, clin. prof. forensic psychiatry, 2000-09; clin. prof. psychiatry & forensic psychiatry, 2009-. Author (book) Soul Explosion; contbr. articles to profl. jours. With U.S. Army, 1960-63, Korea. Recipient Hon. Mention for Disting. Svcs., Spl. Olympics, 1979, Psychiatric Svc. awards, Outstanding Svc. award, North Ctrl. Mental Health Svcs. Staff, 1993, 95, 98, 99, 2000, 01, Appreciation award, A. T. Still U., Health Source Ohio, Ohio U., 2010-11. Fellow. Am. Psychiatrist Assn.(life); mem. Am. Acad. Psychiatry and the Law, Am. Osteo. Assn., Am. Coll. Neuro Psychiatrists (assoc.), World Psychiat. Assn. (America's Top Psychiatists award, 2010, Man of Yr. award, The Leading Physicians of the World) Physicians for Human Rights, Physicians for Social Responsibility, Ohio Psychiat. Physicians Assn. (counselor), Psychiat. Soc. Ctrl. Ohio (pres. 2007-08), Christian Med. Dental Soc., Amnesty Internat., Common Cause, Sierra Club (life), Pub. Citizen, Chgo. Coll. Osteopathic Medicine Alumni Assn., Amnesty Internat. USA, MENSA, Sierra Club(life), Catholic Alumni Club, Am. Legion, Nat. Writers Union. Roman Catholic. Avocations: weightlifting, hiking, dance, travel, computers. Home: PO Box 20203 Columbus OH 43220-0203 Office: North Ctrl Mental Health Svcs 1301 N High St Columbus OH 43201-2460

SCARPA, ANTONIO, federal agency administrator, physiologist, medical educator; b. Padua, Italy, July 3, 1942; s. Angelo and Elena (DeRossi) Scarpa. MD cum laude, U. Padua, 1966, PhD in Pathology, 1970; student, Weizmann Inst. Sci., Israel, U. Utrecht, Netherlands, U. Bristol, Eng.; MA (hon.), U. Pa., 1978. Asst. prof. biochemistry/biophysics U. Pa., Phila., 1973-76, assoc. prof., 1976-80, prof., 1980-86, dir. biomed. instrumentation group, 1983-86; prof. medicine Case Western Res. U., Cleve., 1986—98, David & Inez Myers prof., 1998—2005, chmn. dept. physiology & biophysics, 1986—2005; dir. Ctr. Sci. Rev., NIH, Bethesda, Md., 2005—. Permanent mem. peer review com.'s NIH, 1983—2003. Mem. editl. bd. Circulation Rsch., 1978—81, Biophys. Jour., 1979—82, Jour. Muscle Rsch., 1979—85, Physiol. Rev., 1982—90, Magnesium, 1982—95, FASEB Jour., 1987—92, Molecular Cellular Biochemistry, 1988—2005;, editor (numerous med. text. and journs.); contbr. articles to profl. jours. Grantee Nat. Heart, Lung & Blood Inst., Nat. Inst. Alcohol Abuse & Alcoholism, Nat. Inst. Diabetes & Digestive & Kidney Diseases, Am. Heart Assn. Mem.: Fedn. Am. Societies Exptl. Biology, Assn. Am. Med. Colleges, Biophys. Soc. (exec. coun. 1980—83, 1985—89, 1994—97, treas. 1998—2003), Am. Soc. Biol. Chemistry, Am. Soc. Physiologists. Avocations: farming, sailing, painting. Office: NIH CSR Two Rockledge Ctr 3030 6701 Rockledge Dr MSC 7776 Bethesda MD 20892-7776 Office Phone: 301-435-1114. Office Fax: 301-480-3965. Business E-Mail: toni.scarpa@nih.gov. *

SCARPIGNATO, CARMELO, pharmacologist, educator; b. Catania, Sicily, Italy, Oct. 8, 1948; s. Giuseppe Scarpignato and Grazia Martino; life ptnr. Iva Pelosini. MD, U. Modena, Italy; DSc in Biochemistry, U. Messina; PharmD (hon.), Constantinian U. Cert. in gastroenterology & hepatology U. Messina, 2000. Prof. pharmacology & therapeutics U. Parma Med. Sch., Italy, 1985—; assoc. prof. gastroenterology U. Nantes, France, 1994—96. Cons. clin. pharmacologist U. Hosp., Parma, 1992—. Fellow: Am. Coll. Gastroenterology, Am. Coll. Clin. Pharmacology, Royal Coll. Physicians; mem.: NY Acad. of Sciences, Brit. Pharmacological Soc., Am. Gastroenterology Assn. Achievements include research in rational drug use in gastroenterology. Office: U Parma Med Sch Via Volturno 39 Emilia Romagna Parma 43100 Italy Office Fax: +1-603-843-5621; Home Fax: +1-603-843-5621. Personal E-mail: scarpi@tin.it.

SCARR, SANDRA WOOD, retired psychology educator, researcher; b. Washington, Aug. 8, 1936; d. John Ruxton and Jane (Powell) Wood; m. Harry Alan Scarr, Dec. 26, 1961 (div. 1970); children: Phillip, Karen, Rebbecca, Stephanie; m. James Callan Walker, Aug. 9, 1982 (div. 1994). AB, Vassar Coll., 1958; AM, Harvard U., 1963, PhD, 1965. Asst. prof. psychology U. Md., College Park, 1964-67; assoc. prof. U. Pa., Phila., 1967-71; prof. U. Minn., Mpls., 1971-77, Yale U., New Haven, 1977-83; Commonwealth prof. U. Va., Charlottesville, 1983-95, chmn. dept. psychology, 1984-90; CEO, chmn. bd. dirs. KinderCare Learning Ctr., Inc., 1995-97; ret., 1997. Mem. nat. adv. bd. Robert Wood Johnson Found., Princeton, N.J., 1985-91; coord. coun. psychology SUNY Bd. Regents, N.Y.C., 1984-92; prof. Kerstin Hesselgren, Sweden, 1993-94. Author: Race, Social Class and Individual Differences in IQ, 1981, Mother Care/Other Care, 1984 (Nat. Book award APA 1985), Caring for Children, 1989; editor Jour. Devel. Psychology, 1980-86, Current Directions in Psychol. Sci., 1991-95. Fellow Ctr. for Advanced Studies, Stanford U., Calif., 1976-77; grantee NIH, NSF, others, 1967-95. Fellow AAAS, APA (chmn. com. on human rsch. 1980-83, coun. of reps. 1984-89, bd. dirs. 1988-90, Award for Disting. Contbn. to Rsch. on Pub. Policy 1988), Am. Psychol. Soc. (bd. dirs. 1992—, pres. 1996-97, James McKeen Cattell award 1993); mem. Am. Acad. Arts and Scis. (coun. mem. 1995-2000), Behavior Genetics Assn. (pres. 1985-86, exec. coun. 1976-79, 84-87, Dobzhansky award 2004), Soc. for Rsch. in Child Devel. (governing coun. 1974-76, 87-93, chmn. fin. com. 1987-89, pres. 1989-91), Internat. Soc. for Study of Behavioral Devel. (exec. bd. 1987-94). Avocations: gardening, growing Kona coffee, breeding dogs. Home: 78-6915 Palekana Rd Holualoa HI 96725-8708 Office Phone: 808-322-9445. Personal E-mail: sandrascar@aol.com.

SCARSE, OLIVIA MARIE, cardiologist, consultant; b. Chgo., Nov. 10, 1950; d. Oliver Marcus and Marjorie Ardis (Olsen) S. BS, North Park Coll., 1970; MD, Loyola U., Maywood, Ill., 1973. Diplomate Am. Bd. Internal Medicine, Am. Bd. Cardiovascular Diseases. Surg. intern Resurrection Hosp., Chgo., 1974; resident in internal medicine Northwestern U., Chgo., 1974-77; cardiovascular disease fellow U. Ill., Chgo., 1977-80; dir. cardiac catherization lab. Cook County Hosp., Chgo., 1981; dir. heart sta. MacNeal Hosp., Berwyn, Ill., 1983; dir. electrophysiology Hines VA Hosp., Maywood, Ill., 1984-85; dir. progressive care Columbus Hosp., Chgo., 1985-88, pvt. practice, 1984—, Ill. Masonic Hosp., Chgo., 1989-96. Founder Physician Cons. for Evaluation of Clin. Pathways, Practice Parameters and Patient Care Outcomes, 1991—. Dir. continuous quality improvement Improvement Columbus, 1990-95; mem. presdl. ad hoc com. on prevention and treatment of domestic violence Chgo. Med. Soc., 1997—. Pillsbury fellow Pillsbury Fund, 1980. Fellow Am. Coll. Cardiology; mem. AMA, ACP, Chgo. Med. Assn., Ill. State Med. Assn., Am. Heart Assn. (coun. on clin. cardiology), Crescent Countries Found. for Med. Care, Physicians Health Network, Cen. Ill. Med. Rev. Orgn. Avocations: dance, acting, modeling, singing. Home and Office: 2650 N Lakeview Ave Apt 4109 Chicago IL 60614-1833 *

SCARTOZZI, RICHARD, ophthalmologist; BS in Biochemistry, SUNY, Stony Brook, 1998; MD, Johns Hopkins U., 2002. Vitreoretinal surgeon New Eng. Retina Assocs., 2008—. Med. intern LI Jewish Hosp., 2002—03; ophthalmology resident Wills Eye Hosp., 2003—06; retina fellow Doheny Eye Inst. U. Southern Calif., 2006—08. Recipient Valedictorian award, State U. NY at Stony Brook; named one of America's Top Ophthalmologists award, Consumers' Rsch. Coun. America; Nat. Eye Inst. Travel grant, Barry M. Goldwater Rsch. scholarship, Howard Hughes Med. Inst. Rsch. fellowship, Nat. Sci. Found. RAIRE fellowship. Fellow: Am. Coll. Surgeons, Am. Acad. Ophthalmology; mem.: Rsch. Prevent Blindness, Assn. Rsch. Vision and Ophthalmology, Am. Soc. Retina Specialists, Phi Beta Kappa. Avocation: poetry.

SCARVELL, JENNIFER MARY, physiotherapist, educator and researcher; b. Adelaide, South Australia, Australia, Apr. 9, 1963; d. Ian Robert and Mary Elizabeth Falconer; m. Christopher Richard Scarvell, Jan. 27, 1996; children: Jasmin, Jessica Roberts, Juliette Roberts, Callum. BSc, U. Sydney, Australia, 1985, PhD, 2004. Registered physiotherapist Australia. Staff physiotherapist Prince of Wales and Prince Henry Hosps., Sydney, NSW, 1985—86, Western Suburbs Hosp., Sydney, NSW, 1986—89, Foothills Hosp., Calgary, Alta., Canada, 1989; sr. physiotherapist Canberra Hosp., ACT, 1990—99, rschr. trauma and orthpaedic rsch. unit, 2000—; adj. sr. lectr. Australian Nat. U.; lectr. U. Canberra, ACT, 2004—, adj. sr. lectr., assoc. prof., head & physiotherapy, 2011—. Contbr. articles to health jours. Recipient Dora Lush Biomed. scholarship, Nat. Health and Med. Rsch. Coun. of Australia, 2002—04. Mem.: Australian Physiotherapy Assn. (ACT Br. Svc. Award for Quality and Rsch. 2005). Office: Trauma and Orthopaedic Rsch Unit Canberra Hosp Woden 2601 Australia

SCARZELLO, GIOVANNI, physician; b. Puteaux, France, Nov. 10, 1957; MD, Sch. Medicine Padova, 1983, postgrad. in Radiation Oncology, 1988; postgrad. in Med. Oncology, U. Padova. Physician U. Hosp. Padova, 1989—2005; physician, cons. Oncologic Inst. Veneto, 2006—. Adj. prof. Med. Sch. U. Padova, 1995—. Grant, Oncologic Inst. Veneto. Mem.: Italian Sarcoma Group, Italian Soc. Pediat. Hematlogy Oncology, Italian Soc. Radiation Oncology, Internat. Soc. Pediat. Radiation Oncology, Internat. Soc. Pediat. Oncology. Avocations: sports, reading. Office: via Gattamelata 164 Padua 35128 Italy Office Fax: 390498212958. Business E-Mail: g.scarzello@unipd.it.

SCEMES, ELIANA, medical educator; b. Cairo, Jan. 19, 1956; B, Biosci. Inst., U. Sao Paulo, 1979; PhD, U. Sao Paulo, 1986. Prof. neurosci. Albert Einstein Coll. Medicine, 2010—. Rsch. grant, NIH. Mem.: Am. Soc. Neurochemistry, Am. Soc. Cell Biology, Soc. Neurosci. Avocations: flute, saxophone. Office: 1410 Pelham Pky Bronx NY 10461 Business E-Mail: eliana.scemes@einstein.yu.edu.

SCEUSA, NICHOLAS A., retired pharmacologist; b. Bklyn., July 22, 1948; s. Nicolo Sceusa and Maria Rita Anastasi; m. Donna Lynn Klein, Feb. 23, 1973; children: Amanda, Nicholas. BS in Biology, Syracuse U., 1971; BS in Pharmacy, L.I. U., 1977; PharmD, U. Ill., Chgo., 1996. Registered pharmacist, N.Y. Sr. staff pharmacist King Khalid Univ. Hosp., Riyadh, Saudi Arabia, 1984-86, Tawam Hosp., Al Ain, United Arab Emirates, 1986-87; staff pharmacist II St. Luke's - Roosevelt Hosp., NYC, 1987—90; staff pharmacist St. Clare's Hosp., 1990—95; pres., CEO Gelsus Rsch. and Consulting, Inc., 1997—2010. Author (with others): The Secret History of Italian-American Evacuation and Internment during World War II; contbr. articles to profl. jours. Advisor to Sch. Bd. Dist. 3, N.Y.C., 1996-98. Mem.: Am. Assn. Pharm. Scientists, Masons (treas.). Episcopalian. Achievements include patents for biofiltration and (Teorell-Meyer) dosage forms; invention of RAPID drug delivery system; rechargeable cardiac stent; new forms of surgical bandages and novel nutraceutical products. Avocations: hunting, fishing, outdoors, science, invention. Home and Office: 145 W 96th St Ste 1A New York NY 10025-6449 Personal E-mail: gelsus@verizon.net.

SCHAAL, BARBARA ANNA, evolutionary biologist, educator; b. Berlin, 1947; naturalized, 1956; BS in Biology with honors, U. Ill., Chgo., 1969; MPhil, Yale U., New Haven, 1971, PhD, 1974. Postdoc. rsch. fellow U. Ga., 1973—74; asst. prof. biology U. Houston, 1974—76; asst. prof. botany, asst. prof. genetics Ohio State U., 1976—80; assoc. prof. biology Washington U., St. Louis, 1980-86, prof., 1986—, prof. genetics, Sch. Medicine, 1986—, chair dept. biology, 1993-97, Spencer T. Olin prof. arts & sci. in biology,

2001—09, Mary-Dell Chilton disting. prof. arts & scis., 2009—. Rsch. assoc. Mo. Bot. Garden, 1980—; mem. Pres.'s Coun. Advisors on Sci. & Tech. (PCAST), 2009—. Assoc. editor Molecular Biology & Evolution, 1993—99, Am. Jour. Botany, mem. editl. bd. Functional Ecology, Molecular Ecology, Conservation Genetics. Bd. trustees Mo. chpt. Nature Conservancy. Recipient Sigma-Xi Rsch. award, Ohio State U., 1980, Young Investigator award in molecular evolution, Alfred P. Sloan Found., 1995—98, Leadership award, St. Louis YWCA, 1996, Disting. Faculty award, Washington U., 1998, Arthur Holly Compton Faculty Achievement award, Wilbur Cross medal, Yale U., Key award, Am. Genetics Assn.; fellow John Simon Guggenheim Meml. Foind., 1997—98. Fellow: AAAS, St. Louis Acad. Sci. (bd. trustees), Am. Acad. Arts & Scis.; mem.: NAS (v.p. 2005—), Soc. Study of Evolution (coun. mem. 1982—85, exec. v.p. 1988—91), Bot. Soc. America (pres. 1995—96, Merit award 1999). Achievements include research in the use of molecular genetic data to understand evolutionary processes such as gene flow, geographical differentiation and the domestication of crop species. Office: Washington U Dept Biology Campus Box 1137 304 McDonnell Hall 1 Brookings Dr Saint Louis MO 63130-4899 Office Phone: 314-935-6822. Business E-Mail: schaal@biology.wustl.edu.

SCHAAL, SHLOMIT, ophthalmologist, vitreoretinal specialist, educator, scientist; BSc, Technion Inst. Tech., Haifa, Israel, 1992, MD, 1996, PhD, 2006. Vitreo-retina fellow U. Louisville, 2006—08, asst. prof., 2008—, dir., PCC Retina Laser Clinic, 2008; dir. Diabetic Retinopathy Svc., U. Lousville, 2011—. Lt. IDF Naval Force, 1996—2000, Haifa, Israel. Office: University Louisville 301 East Muhammad Ali Blvd Louisville KY 40202 Office Phone: 502-852-5466.

SCHACHTEL-GREEN, BARBARA HARRIET LEVIN, retired epidemiologist; b. May 27, 1921; d. Lester and Ethel (Neiman) Levin; m. Hyman Judah Schachtel, Oct. 15, 1941 (dec. Jan. 1990); m. Louis H. Green, Feb. 26, 1995; children: Bernard, Ann Molly. Student, Wellesley Coll., 1939—41; BS, U. Houston, 1951, MA in Psychology, 1967; PhD, U. Tex., Houston, 1979. Psychol. examiner Meyer Ctr. for Devel. Pediat., Tex. Children's Hosp., Houston, 1967-81; instr. dept. pediat. Baylor Coll. Medicine, Houston, 1967-81, asst. prof. dept. medicine, 1982—2005; ret., 2005. Asst. dir. biometry and epidemiology Sid W. Richardson Inst. for Preventive Medicine, Meth. Hosp., Houston, 1981-88, dir. quality assurance, 1988-93; instl. rev. bd. for human rsch. Baylor Coll. Medicine, Houston, 1981-87, 97—; devel. bd. U. Tex. Health Sci. Ctr., Houston, 1987-97; dean's adv. bd. Sch. Arch., U. Houston, 1987-89. Contbr. articles to profl. jours. V.p., bd. dirs. Houston-Harris County Mental Health Assn., 1966—67; vice-chmn. bd. mgrs. Harris County Hosp. Dist., Houston, 1974—90, chmn., 1990—92, bd. dirs., 1970—93; trustee Inst. Religion in Tex. Med. Ctr., 1990—, vice chmn., 2000—; sec. Bo Harris County Hosp. Dist. Found. Bd., 1993—; bd. dirs. Congregation Beth Israel, 1993—95, Planned Parenthood of Houston, Inc., 1994—2000, Houston Ind. Sch. Dist. Found., 1993—2001, Crisis Intervention, 1994—96. Named Great Texan of Yr., Nat. Found. for Iletis and Colitis, Houston, 1982, Outstanding Citizen, Houston-Harris County Mental Health Assn., 1985, Robert Eckles County Judge, 2006; recipient Good Heart award B'nai Brith Women, 1984, Women of Prominence award Am. Jewish Com., 1991, Mayor's award for outstanding vol. svc., 1994. Mem. APA, APHA, Wellesley Club of Houston (pres. 1968-70). Avocations: golf, tennis, reading. Home: 2527 Glen Haven Blvd Houston TX 77030-3511 Home Phone: 713-668-3600. Personal E-mail: barabara.louis@gmail.com.

SCHACHTER, AARON KALMAN, sports medicine physician; b. Cin., Apr. 22, 1976; BS, Wake Forest U., 1998; MD, U. Louisville, 2002. Physician, sports medicine, arthroscopy and shoulder surgery Orthop. Health, 2008—. Fellow: Am. Bd. Orthop. Surgery; mem.: AOSSM, Arthroscopy Assn. N.Am., Am. Acad. Orthop. Surgery. Office: Orthopedic Health 849 Boston Post Rd S Milford CT 06460 Personal E-mail: schac19@yahoo.com.

SCHACHTER, EDWIN NEIL, pulmonologist, educator; b. NYC, May 10, 1943; s. Franz and Feiga (Zeltzman) S.; m. Deborah Chase, Nov. 15, 1969; children: Karen, Lauren. BA, Columbia U.; MD, NYU, 1968. Cert. internal medicine, pulmonary medicine, critical care medicine. Intern, medicine Bellevue Hosp. Ctr., NY, 1968—69, resident NY, 1969—70, NY, 1972—73; fellow Yale U. Sch. Medicine, Lung Rsch. Ctr., 1973—74; asst. prof. to assoc. prof. medicine Yale U., 1975—84; chief pulmonary divsn. St. Albans Naval Hosp.; med. dir. respiratory care dept. Yale New Haven Hosp.; prof. cmty. medicine Mt. Sinai Med. Ctr., dir. Respiratory Care Dept.; chmn. pulmonary medicine Mt. Sinai Med. Sch. Author: Life and Breath, 2003, The Good Doctor's Guide to Colds & Flu, 2005; contbr. articles to profl. jours., chpts. to books. Chmn. Sci. Adv. Com. Am. Lang. Assn., 2008—; bd. dirs. Lung Assn. N.Y., NYC, 1994, pres., 1998, Nat. Assn. Med. Dirs. of Respiratory Care, Washington, 1990—92, Conn. Respiratory Assn., 1983; del. nat. coun. Am. Lung Assn., 2001. Lt. comdr. USN. Grantee Nat. Inst. Occpl. Safety and Health, 1987—; Am. Lung Assn. honoree City N.Y. Annual Gala, 2005. Fellow ACP, ACCP; mem. Am. Thoracic Soc., Am. Assn. Respiratory Care, Am. Physiol. Soc. Office: Pulmonary Associates 5 E 98th St 8th Fl New York NY 10029 Office Phone: 212-241-5656. E-mail: Neil@thegooddoctor1.com.

SCHACHTER, LINDA MICHELE, pulmonologist; b. Melbourne, Australia, Mar. 2, 1965; MBBS, U. Melbourne, 1989; PhD, U. Sydney, 2006. Respiratory and sleep physician Austin and Repatriation Med. Ctr., 1999—2006; respiratory and sleep physician, med. dir. Sleep Svcs. Australia, 2005—. Fellow: Royal Australasian Coll. Physicians; mem.: Thoracic Soc. Australia and New Zealand, Australasian Sleep Assn., Am. Assn. Sleep Medicine, Am. Thoracic Soc. Office: Unit 2/787 Dandenong Rd East Malvern Victoria 3122 Australia Office Fax: 61398322295. Business E-Mail: lindams@bigpond.com.

SCHAEFER, FRANK WILLIAM, III, microbiologist; b. Dayton, Ohio, Sept. 1, 1942; s. Frank William Jr. and Irene Josephine (Krouse) S. BA, Miami U., 1964; PhD, U. Cin., 1973. Sr. microbiologist Nat. Homeland Security Rsch. Ctr., 1978—. Adj. asst. prof. U. Cin. Med. Sch., 1984—2011. Recipient Gold medal, US EPA, 1994, 1999, Bronze medal, 2004. Mem. ASTM, AAAS, Am. Soc. Parasitology, Am. Soc. Microbiology, Am. Water Works Assn., Soc. Protozoologists, Sigma Xi. Office: US Environmental Protection Agency 26 Cincinnati OH 45268 Office Fax: 513-487-2555. Business E-Mail: schaefer.frank@epa.gov.

SCHAEFER, HEIDI MAREE, nephrologist, educator; b. Wauseon, Ohio, Jan. 5, 1972; MD, U. Cin., 1998. Asst. prof. medicine Vanderbilt U. Med. Ctr., 2004—. Kidney-pancreas transplant adv. bd. Am. Soc. Transplantation, 2006—09, membership com., 2010—; program com. Nat. Kidney Found., 2007—. Recipient 5 Star Customer Svc. award, Profl. Rsch. Consultants, Inc, 2007—11. Mem.: Am. Soc. Nephrology, Am. Soc. Transplantation, Nat. Kidney Found. Avocation: reading. Office: Vanderbilt University 912 Oxford House Nashville TN 37232 Business E-Mail: heidi.schaefer@vanderbilt.edu.

SCHAEFER, JOANN, public health service officer; MD, Creighton Univ., 1995. Cert. family medicine. Private practice, Omaha, 1995—2002; instr. Creighton Univ. Sch. Med., Omaha, 1997—2003, assoc prof., 2003; dep. chief med. officer Nebr. Dept. Health & Human Svc., Lincoln, 2002—05, chief med. officer, dir. regulation & licensure, 2005—. Named a Local Legend, Am. Med. Women's Assn. Mem.: Am. Acad. Family Physicians, AMA, Nebr. Acad. Family Physicians, Metro Omaha Med. Soc., Nebr. Med. Assn. (Physician of the Yr. 2004). Office: Nebr Dept Health & Human Svc 301 Centennial Mall S Lincoln NE 68509 Mailing: Nebr State Health Dept PO Box 95026 Lincoln NE 68509-5026

SCHAEFER, MARY ANN, health facility administrator, consultant; b. Chgo., May 18, 1942; d. Joseph and Mary A. (Kozyra) Strosnik; m. Robert Earl Schaefer, May 18, 1963 (dec.); children: Debra Ann, Robert Joseph, James Edward (dec.). Diploma in nursing, St. Francis Hosp. Sch. Nursing, Evanston, Ill., 1962; BA, Nat. Coll. Edn., Evanston, 1980; MBA in Health Svc. Mgmt., Webster U., 1990; MJ in Health Law, Loyola U., Chgo., 1993. Med. and surg. nurse Resurrection Med. Ctr., Chgo., 1962-79, charge nurse labor and delivery, 1978-79; coord. maternal child care Humana, Hoffman Estates, Ill., 1979-81; nurse mgr. labor and delivery Resurrection Med. Ctr., Chgo., 1981-91; mgr. Family Birthplace Resurrection Med. Ctr., Chgo., 1991-98; cons., prin. M/B Assocs.-Consultants Perinatal Healthcare and Edn., Barrington, 1994-98; mgr. Maternal-Child Health Sherman Hosp., Elgin, Ill., 1998-00, dir. women's svcs., 2000—06; dir. bd. Elgin Well Child Ctr., 2002—06; cons. Good Shepherd Hosp., Barrington, Ill., 2006—10; nurse Valley Plastic Surgery, West Dundee, 2006—; adj. faculty health careers divsn. Harper Coll., Paletine, Ill. Seminar leader on childbirth edn., legal issues in nursing; adj. faculty law & ethics Harper Coll. Palatine, Ill. Contbr. to Motor Facilitation Handbook; editorial bd. Essentials publ., Resurrection Med. Ctr. Mem. Assn. Women's Health, Obstetric and Neonatal Nurses (cert. in inpatient obstetric nursing, instr. principles and practice electronic fetal monitoring), Assn. Healthcare Accrediation Profls., Chgo. Health Care Risk Mgmt. Soc. Home: 5806 Prairie Ridge Rd Crystal Lake IL 60014-4601 Personal E-mail: maryannschaefer@aol.com.

SCHAEFER, ROBERT ANTHONY, internist, gastroenterologist, educator; b. NYC, Mar. 1, 1939; s. George John Schaefer, Regina Marie Farrell; m. Mary Jeanne Kreek, Jan. 24, 1970; children: Robert A. Jr., Esperance A.K. AB, Yale U., 1959; MD, Columbia U., 1963. Diplomate Am. Bd. Internal Medicine with subspecialty in gastroenterology. Intern, resident Vanderbilt U. Hosp., Nashville, 1963—65, resident in internal medicine U. Vt., 1967—68, chief resident, 1968—69; fellow gastroenterology N.Y. Hosp.-Cornell Med. Ctr., NYC, 1969—71; asst. prof. medicine Cornell U. Med. Coll., NYC, 1971—77, clin. assoc. prof. medicine, 1977—99, assoc. prof. clin. medicine, 1999—. Lt. comdr. USNR, 1965—67. Fellow: ACP, Am. Coll. Gastroenterology; mem.: Am. Soc. Gastroenterological Endoscopy, Am. Assn. for Study of Liver Disease, Am. Gastroenterology Assn. Office: 1305 York Ave New York NY 10021 Office Phone: 646-962-4000.

SCHAEFFER, EVELYNE, molecular biologist, researcher; b. Strasbourg, France, Oct. 1, 1952; d. Andre and Jeanne (Lieber) S. MS, U. Louis-Pasteur, Strasbourg, 1974, DS, 1976, PhD, 1979. Rschr. Ctr. Nat. Rsch. Sci., Strasbourg, 1977-79, Pasteur Inst. Ctr. Nat. Rsch. Sci., Paris, 1982-93, INSERM U338/U575 Ctr. Nat. Rsch. Sci., Strasbourg, 1993—2006; postdoctoral rschr. U. Calif., Berkeley, 1979-82; with Inst. de Biologie Moleculaire et Cellulaire, 2007—. Investigator Gladstone Inst. Virology and Immunology, San Francisco, 1999—2001. Contbr. rsch. articles to profl. jours. Office: IBMC UPR 9021 15 Rue René Descartes 67084 Strasbourg France Business E-Mail: e.schaeffer@ibmc.u-strasbg.fr.

SCHAEFFER, LEONARD DAVID, management consultant, educator, former health insurance company executive; b. Chgo., July 28, 1945; s. David and Sarah (Levin) Schaeffer; m. Pamela Lee Sidford, Aug. 11, 1968; children: David, Jacqueline. BA, Princeton U., 1969. Mgmt. cons. Arthur Andersen & Co., 1969—73; dep. dir. mgmt. Ill. Mental Health/Devel. Disability, Springfield, 1973—75; dir. Ill. Bur. of Budget, Springfield, 1975—76; v.p. Citibank, N.A., NYC, 1976—78; asst. sec. mgmt. and budget HHS, Washington, 1978, adminstr. HCFA, 1978—80; exec. v.p., COO Student Loan Mktg. Assn., Washington, 1980—82; pres., CEO Group Health, Inc., Mpls., 1983—86; chmn., CEO Blue Cross of Calif., Woodland Hills, 1986—96, WellPoint Health Networks Inc., Thousand Oaks, Calif., 1992—2004; chmn. WellPoint Inc., 2004—05; prin. North Bristol Partners, Santa Monica, Calif., 2005—; sr. advisor TPG Group, 2006—; chmn. Surg. Care Affiliates, Birmingham, 2007—; Judge Robert Maclay Widney chair and prof. University Southern Calif., LA, 2008—. Bd. dirs. Allergan, Inc., Irvine, Calif., 1993—, AMGEN Inc., Thousand Oaks, 2004—, Quintiles Transnational Corp., 2008—; bd. councilors U. So. Calif. Sch. Policy, Planning & Devel., 1988—; bd. dirs., exec. com. Blue Cross-Blue Shield Assn., Chgo., 1986—2004; mem. Congl. Prospective Payment Assessment Commn., 1987—93, Pew Health Professions Com., Phila., 1990—93; chmn. bd. trustees Nat. Health Found., LA, 1992—2001; chmn. bd. dirs. Nat. Inst. Health Care Mgmt., 1993—2006; co-chair adv. coun. dept. health care policy Harvard Med. Sch., 1998—2003, bd. fellows, 2003—; founding chmn. Coalition for Affordable and Quality Healthcare, 2000; regents lectr. U. Calif., Berkeley, Calif., 2005—06. Bd. govs. Town Hall, LA, 1989—2006; trustee The Brookings Inst., Nat. Health Mus., 2000—; adv. coun. Dept. Econs. Princeton U., NJ; adv. group Coun. on Health Care Econs. and Policy. Recipient Citation for Outstanding Svc., Am. Acad. Pediat., 1981, Disting. Pub. Svc. award, HEW, Washington, 1980; fellow, Kellogg Found., 1981—89; Internat. fellow, King's Fund Coll., London, 1990—. Mem.: Am. Assn. Health Plans (bd. dirs. 2001—04), Health Ins. Assn. Am. (chmn. 1999), Inst. Medicine NAS, Regency Club, Princeton Club, Cosmos Club. Office: North Bristol Partners LLC 1733 Ocean Ave Ste 325 Santa Monica CA 90404 also: Sch Policy Planning and Devel University Southern Calif Lewis Hall 312 Los Angeles CA 90089-0626 Business E-Mail: ldschpe@usc.edu. *

SCHAFER, ANDREW I., hematologist, department chairman; b. Budapest, Hungary; married; 3 children. MD, U. Pa., Phila. Cert. in hematology, internal medicine, oncology. Resident U. Chgo.; fellow in hematology Brigham and Women's Hosp.; asst. prof. medicine Harvard U. Med. Sch., 1981—87, assoc. prof. medicine, 1987—89; chief hematology and oncology West Roxbury VA Hosp., Brockton VA Hosp., Mass., 1984—89; prof. medicine, assoc. dean Baylor U. Sch. Medicine, Houston, 1989—98; chmn. dept. medicine, chief internal medicine svc. The Meth. Hosp., Houston, 1998—2002; chmn. dept. medicine U. Pa. Sch. Medicine, 2002—07, Weill Cornell Med. Coll., NYC, 2007—, E. Hugh Luckey Disting. prof. medicine, 2007—; physician-in-chief NY-Presbyn. Hosp. Weill Cornell Med. Ctr., 2007—. Adj. prof. biomed. engring. Rice U., Tex.; prin. investigator NIH; bd. extramural advisors Nat. Heart, Lung and Blood Inst.; bd. dirs. Assn. Professors of Medicine; pres. Am. Soc. Hematology, 2007; pres. elect Assoc. Profs. Medicine, 2009—. Founding editor-in-chief: The Hematologist, mem. editl. bd.: Platelets, Circulation, Jour. Cardiovascular Risk, Am. Jour. the Med. Scis., Am. Jour. Medicine, Annual Rev. Medicine, Current Medicinal Chemistry; contbr. articles to profl. jours., chapters to books. Recipient Milton Fund award, Harvard U. Med. Sch., 1984; named Established Investigator, Am. Heart Assn. Fellow: Am. Heart Assn. Coun. on Arteriosclerosis, Thrombosis and Vascular Biology; mem.: Assn. Am. Physicians, Am. Soc. Clin. Investigation. Office: Office of the Chmn NY Presbyn Hosp Weill Cornell Med Coll 530 E 70th St M 522 New York NY 10021 Office Phone: 212-746-4720. Office Fax: 212-746-8793.

SCHAFER, JOSHUA, pharmaceutical executive; b. 1971; m. Jennifer Schafer; 3 children. BS, U. Notre Dame; MS, Northwestern U.; MBA, Northwestern U. Kellogg Sch. Mgmt. With Anderson Consulting; with global medical mktg. Searle; sr. product mgr. new product planning Takeda Pharmaceuticals North America Inc.; v.p. global oncology strategy Astellas Pharma Inc., Deerfield, Ill., 2009—. Named one of The 40 Under 40, Crain's Chgo. Bus., 2010. Office: Astellas Pharma US Inc Three Parkway North Deerfield IL 60015-2548 Office Phone: 800-695-4321. *

SCHAFER, SHARON MARIE, anesthesiologist; b. Detroit, Mar. 23, 1948; d. Charles Anthony and Dorothy Emma (Schweitzer) Pokrieffka; m. Timothy John Schafer, Nov. 12, 1977; children: Patrick Christopher, Steven Michael. BS in Biology, Wayne State U., 1971, MD, 1975; MBA in Practice Mgmt., Madonna U., 2000. Diplomate Am. Bd. Anesthesiology. Intern, resident Sinai Hosp. Detroit, 1975-78; pvt. practice anesthesiology Troy, Mich., 1988—. Mem. AMA, Am. Soc. Anesthesiologists. Roman Catholic. Home and Office: 5741 Folkstone Dr Troy MI 48085-3154 Office Phone: 248-879-6246. E-mail: sharschafer@att.net.

SCHAFERMEYER, ROBERT WILLIAM, emergency physician, educator, health policy consultant; b. St. Louis, Jan. 9, 1948; s. William Jacob and Virginia Rose S.; m. An-ping Yuan, May 12, 1973; children: Christina, David, Matthew, Joseph. Student, St. Louis U., 1966-69; MD, U. Mo., 1973. Diplomate Am. Bd. Emergency Medicine, Am. Bd. Pediats., sub-bd. pediat. emergency medicine. With. dept. emergency medicine East Tenn. Children's Hosp., Knoxville, 1979—81; mem. dept. emergency medicine Carolinas Med. Ctr., Charlotte, NC, 1981—; clin. assoc. prof. pediats. U. N.C. Sch. Medicine, Chapel Hill, 1981-85, clin. prof. emergency medicine and pediats., 1994—; assoc. chair dept. emergency medicine Carolinas Med. Ctr., Charlotte, 1982—, chief dept., 2007—. Dir. E.D. Cons. and Lectrs., Charlotte, 90—. Assoc. editor: Pediatric Emergency Medicine Concepts and Clinical Practice, 1992; editor: Pediatric Emergency Medicine: A Comprehensive Study Guide, 1995, 2002, 3rd edit., 2009; contbr. articles and revs. to profl. jours. including Annals Emergency Medicine Jour.; reviewer Pediat. Emergency Medicine, Acad. Emergency Medicine; past mem. editl. bd. Pediat. Emergency Med. Jour. Com. mem. MEMAC Adv., Mecklenberg County, 1991-93; mem. task force Drug Abuse for County Commrs., Mecklenberg, 1989-90. Lt. commdr. USPHS, 1974—76. EMS-C grantee Maternal and Child Health, 1992-94. Fellow Am. Coll. Emergency Physicians (bd. dirs. 1994-2002, pres.-elect 1999-2000, pres. 2000-01, past pres. 2001-02, Weigenstein Outstanding Leadership award 2004); mem. Am. Acad. Pediats., NC chpt. Am. Coll. Emergency Physicians (councillor 1984-94, bd. dirs. 1983-89, pres. 1986-88, Leadership/Svc. award 1988, George Podgorny Emergency Medicine Svc. award 1996), Soc. Acad. Emergency Medicine (bd. dirs. 2004-07), Mecklenburg County Med. Soc. (bd. dirs. 2009-, pres. elect 2010). Roman Catholic. Avocations: tae kwan do, photography, skiing. Office: Carolinas Med Ctr 1000 Blythe Blvd Charlotte NC 28203-5812 Office Phone: 704-355-3181.

SCHAFF, HARTZELL VERNON, surgeon; b. Holdenville, Okla., Feb. 24, 1948; s. Hartzell Vernon and Ruth N. (Stuckey) Schaff; m. Voni Faith Schafer, Mar. 3, 1973. Diplomate Am. Bd. Surgery, Am. Bd. Thoracic Surgery. Intern dept. surgery Johns Hopkins Hosp., Balt., 1973—74; asst. resident, 1974—75; fellow cardiovasc. surg. rsch. lab., 1975—76; sr. asst. resident, 1976—78; resident cardiac & thoracic surgery, 1978—80; cons. thoracic & cardiovasc. surgery Mayo Med. Sch., Rochester, Minn., 1980—; asst. prof. surgery, 1980—85; assoc. prof., 1985—92; co-dir. cardiovasc. surg. rsch. lab., 1985—; prof. surgery, 1992—94; Stuart W. Harrington prof. surgery, 1994—; chair divsn. cardiovasc. surgery. Mem. editl. bd. Jour. Thoracic & Cardiovasc. Surgery. Contbr. articles to profl. jours., chapters to books. Recipient L.G. Moorman award, 1973, George D. Zuidema Resident Rsch. award, 1980; Fulbright Vis. Prof. Cardiac

Surgery, 1986—87. Fellow: ACS; mem.: AMA, Johns Hopkins Med. & Surg. Assn., Priestley Soc., Internat. Assn. Cardia Biol. Implants, Am. Assn. Clin. Anatomists, Soc. Thoracic Surg. Edn., Soc. U. Surgeons, Am. Heart Assn., Assn. for Acad. Surgery, Am. Coll. Cardiology, Alpha Omega Alpha, Phi Eta Sigma, Sigma Xi. Republican. Episc. Home: 433 9th Ave SW Rochester MN 55902-2923 Office: Mayo Clinic 200 1st St SW Rochester MN 55905-0002 Office Phone: 507-284-2511. Office Fax: 507-284-0161.

SCHAFFER, JULIE V., pediatric dermatologist, researcher; MD, Yale U. Sch. Medicine, New Haven, 2000. Diplomate Am. Bd. Pediat., Am. Bd. Dermatology. Resident dermatology Yale U. Sch. Medicine, 2001—04; clin. fellowship pediat. dermatology NYU Med. Ctr., 2004—05, asst. prof. dermatology and pediat.; dir. pediat dermatology NYU Dermatol. Assoc. Contbr. articles to profl. jours. Mem.: Women's Dermatol. Soc., Am. Acad. Dermatology (Young Investigator award 2007), Dermatology Found. (Med. Career Devel. award 2007, 2008). Achievements include research in clinical and molecular investigation of genetic and congenital skin diseases. Office: NYU Dept Dermatology Faculty Practice Tower 530 1st Ave New York NY 10016 Office Phone: 212-263-5889.

SCHAFFER, STEPHEN WARD, medical educator; b. San Diego, Oct. 15, 1944; BS, Buena Vista Coll., 1966; PhD, U. Minn., 1971. Postdoc. fellow U. Pa., 1971—74; asst. prof. Lehigh U., 1974—81; prof. U. South Ala., 1981—. Cons. NIH, Am. Heart Assn., 1980—2011. Recipient Vincenzo Panagia Disting. Scientist award, Internat. Acad. Cardiovasc. Scis., Norman Alpert Established Investigator award. Mem.: Am. Soc. Biochemistry and Molecular Biology, Am. Soc. Pharmacology and Exptl. Therapeutics, Internat. Soc. Heart Rsch., Internat. Acad. Cardiovasc. Scis., Am. Heart Assn. Avocations: gardening, reading. Office: University South Ala Coll Medicine Mobile AL 36688 Business E-Mail: sschaffe@jaguar1.usouthal.edu.

SCHAFFNER, ADAM DAVID, plastic surgeon, educator; b. Chgo., Sept. 26, 1971; s. Robert Schaffner and Dorann Gerstman, Marjorie Schaffner (Stepmother), George Gerstman (Stepfather); m. Marcie Suzanne Rubin, June 10, 2007; children: Brett Spencer, Miles Scott. BS in Biology summa cum laude, Emory U., Atlanta, 1993; MD, Rush U., Chgo., 1998. Diplomate Am. Bd. Otolaryngology, 2004, Am. Bd. Facial Plastic and Reconstructive Surgery, 2007, lic. NY, 2000, Calif., 2003, Conn., 2004, Mich., 2007, DC, 2009, Va., 2009. Clin. asst. inst. SUNY, Stony Brook, 1998—2003, intern surgery, 1998—99, resident otolaryngology-head and neck surgery, 1999—2003; AAFPRS fellowship, facial plastic & reconstructive surgery Mittelman Facial Plastic Surgery Ctr., 2003—04; mem. med. staff Stanford Hosp., 2003—04, Sound Shore Med. Ctr. Westchester, New Rochelle, NY, 2004—07, Greenwich Hosp., Conn., 2004—07, Georgetown U. Hosp., 2009—10; clin. asst. prof. Weill Cornell Med. Coll., 2005—08; resident plastic & reconstructive surgery Detroit Med. Ctr. Wayne State U, 2007—09; asst. prof. clin. plastic and reconstructive surgery Georgetown U. Sch. Medicine, 2009—10; ASAPS fellowship plastic surgery Georgetown U. Hosp., 2009—10; clin. asst. prof. Weill Cornell Med. Coll., 2010—; mem. med. staff Lenox Hill Hospital, 2010—, Manhattan Eye, Ear & Throat Inst., 2010—, NY Eye & Ear Infirmary, 2010—, Ctr. Specialty Care, Inc., 2010—; dir. Plastic Surgery Inst. NY, 2006—; dir., plastic surgery JUVA Plastic Surgery, 2010—. Rsch. assoc. CDC, Atlanta, 1992—93; summer rsch. fellow NCI, Bethesda, Md., 1994; vol. cons. in field ABC News, 2004—; trainer, cons., mem. spkrs. bur. Sanofi-Aventis, 2005—06; cons. Pfizer Upper Respiratory New Products N.Am. Market Coun., 2005, BioForm Med., 2005, Scientiae, 2011—, Gerson Lehrman Healthcare Coun., Kythera Pharm., 2007—08; mem. med. com. US Open Championship Golf Tournament, 2006; reviewer Aesthetic Plastic Surgery, 2011—, Aethetic Surgery Jours., 2011—. Contbr. articles to profl. jours., chapters to books. Participant FACE to FACE Domestic, 2004—, FACE to FACE Internat., 2006—; mem. exec. com. Rush Cmty. Svc. Initiatives Program, Chgo., 1996—98; steering com. co-chmn. St. Basil's Free People's Clinic, Chgo., 1996—98; vol. Children's Healthcare of Atlanta at Egleston, Atlanta, 1991—93; mem. Med. Adv. Bd., Little Baby Face Found., 2011—; hon. mem. FACES, 2010—, Oroject CARE, 2010—; mem., bd. dirs. Elec. Pear Prodns., 2006—. Recipient Jack Boozer, PhD award for Social and Religious Ethics, Emory U., CibaGeneva award; named America's Cosmetic Drs., Castle Connolly Med.; named one of America's Top Surgeons, Consumers' Rsch. Coun. America, 2009—11; Messing Meml. Merit scholar, Zeta Beta Tau Found. Fellow: ACS, Am. Acad. Otolaryngology-Head and Neck Surgery (Humanitarian Efforts Travel grantee 2002), Am. Acad. Facial Plastic and Reconstructive Surgery (mem. Found. Continuing Med. Edn. com. 2004—10, mem. Emerging Trends and Technologies com. 2004—10, mem. Ad Hoc com. on Patient Advocacy 2008—09, mem. FACE to FACE com. 2008—); mem.: AMA, NY State Soc. Otolaryngology-HNS, NY County Medical Soc., Medical Soc. State NY, NY Facial Plastic Surgery Soc. Avocations: piano, swimming, theater, travel, skiing. Office: 60 East 56th St 2nd Fl New York NY 10022-3350 Office Phone: 212-688-6600. Office Fax: 212-688-6602; Home Fax: 914-819-0488. Personal E-mail: aschaffner@gmail.com.

SCHAFFNER, WILLIAM, medical educator; b. Jersey City, Aug. 12, 1937; BA, Yale U., New Haven, 1957; MD, Cornell U. Med. Coll., Ithaca, NY, 1962. Diplomate Am. Bd. Internal Medicine, Am. Bd. Preventive Medicine, cert. in pediatric infectious diseases. Intern, resident then fellow infectious diseases Vanderbilt U. Med. Ctr., Nashville, 1962—66; epidemic intelligence svc. officer Ctrs. Disease Control, USPHS, 1966—68; faculty Vanderbilt U. Sch. Medicine, 1969—, chief divsn. infectious diseases, 1982—89, now prof. preventive medicine, medicine and infectious diseases and chmn. dept. preventive medicine. Bd. dirs. Nat. Found. Infectious Diseases, v.p. bd. dirs., 2007—; mem. steering com. Nat. Network Immunization Info.; pub. health policy & communicable disease control cons. Tenn. Dept. Health; bd. dirs. Internat. Fedn. Infection Control. Mem. editl. bd. Clin. Rsch., 1974—84, Infection, 1985—, Am. Jour. Epidemiology, 1987—97, European Jour. Clin. Microbiology & Infectious Diseases, 1993—; sr. assoc. editor Infection Control & Hosp. Epidemiology, 1981—, assoc. editor Jour. Infectious Diseases, 2003—; contbr. articles to profl. jours., chapters to books. Recipient Philip S. Brachman award, Ctrs. Disease Control, 1985, William J. Darby award, Vanderbilt U. Sch. Medicine, 2005; Ford Found. Scholar, Yale

U., 1953—57, Fulbright Scholar, Albert Ludwigs U., Freiburg, Germany, 1957—58. Fellow: Infectious Diseases Soc. America (bd. dirs. 2000—03); mem.: ACP (master mem.), Am. Soc. Microbiology (chair divsn. nosocomial infections 1983—84), Soc. Healthcare Epidemiology America (pres. 1983, Lecturer award 1996). Office: Vanderbilt U Med Ctr Office A 1124 MCN 1211 Med Ctr Dr Nashville TN 37232 Business E-Mail: william.schaffner@vanderbilt.edu. *

SCHAIE, K(LAUS) WARNER, human development and psychology educator; b. Stettin, Germany (now Poland), Feb. 1, 1928; came to U.S., 1947, naturalized, 1953; s. Sally and Lottie Luise (Gabriel) S.; m. Coloma J. Harrison, Aug. 9, 1953 (div. 1973); 1 child, Stephan; m. Sherry L. Willis, Nov. 20, 1981. AA, City Coll., San Francisco, 1951; BA, U. Calif., Berkeley, 1952; MS, U. Wash., 1953, PhD, 1956; DPhil (hon.), Friedrich-Schiller U., Jena, Germany, 1997; ScD (hon.), W.Va. U., 2002. Lic. psychologist, Calif., Pa. Fellow Washington U., St. Louis, 1956-57; asst. prof. psychology U. Nebr., Lincoln, Nebr., 1957-64, assoc. prof., 1964—67; prof. chmn. dept. psychology W.Va. U., Morgantown, W.Va., 1968—73; prof. psychology, dir. Gerontology Rsch. Inst., U. So. Calif., 1973-81; Evan Pugh prof. human devel. and psychology Pa. State U., University Park, 1981—2008, Evan Pugh prof. emeritus, 2008—, dir. Gerontology Ctr., 1985—2003; affiliate prof. psychiatry and behavioral scis. U. Wash., 1991—. Devel. behavior study sect. NIH, Bethesda, Md., 1970-72, chmn., 1972-74, chmn. human devel. and aging study sect., 1979-84, expert panel in comml. airline pilot retirement, 1981, data and safety bd. shep project, 1984-91. Author: Developmental Psychology; A Life Span Approach, 1981, Adult Development and Aging, 1982, 5th rev. edit., 2002, Japanese, Chinese, Serbo-Croat and Spanish edits., 2003, Intellectual Development in Adulthood: The Seattle Longitudinal Study, 1996, Developmental Influences on Adult Intelligence, 2005; editor: Handbook of Psychology of Aging, 1977, 7th rev. edit., 2011, Longitudinal Studies of Adult Development, 1983, Cognitive Functioning and Social Structure over the Life Course, 1987, Methodological Issues in Research on Aging, 1988, Social Structure and Aging: Psychological Processes, 1989, Age Structuring in Comparative Perspective, 1989, The Course of Later Life, 1989, Self-Directedness: Cause and Effects Throughout the Life Course, 1990, Aging, Health Behaviors and Health Outcomes, 1992, Caregiving Systems: Formal and Informal Helpers, 1993, Societal Impact on Aging: Historical Perspectives, 1993, Adult Intergenerational Relations: Effects of Societal Change, 1995, Older Adults Decision Making and the Law, 1996, Impact of Social Structures on Decision Making in the Elderly, 1997, Impact of the Workplace on Older Persons, 1998, Handbook of Theories of Aging, 1999, Mobility and Aging, 2000, Evolution of the Aging Self, 2000, Effective Health Behavior in the Elderly, 2002, Mastery and Control in the Elderly, 2003, Influence of Technology on Successful Aging, 2003; Independent Aging: Living Arrangements and Mobility, 2003, Religious Influences on Health and Wellbeing in the Elderly, 2004, Historical Influences on Lives and Aging, 2005, Social Structures, Self-Regulation and Aging, 2006, Demographic Influences on Health and Wellbeing in the Elderly, 2007, Social Structures and Aging Individuals, 2008; editor Ann. Rev. Gerontology and Geriat., vol. 7, 1987, vol. 11, 1991, vol. 17, 1997, series editor, 1996—2009; contbr. articles to profl. jours. Fellow APA (coun. reps. 1976-79, 83-86, 2011-, Disting. Contbn. award, 1992), Am. Psychol. Soc., Gerontol. Soc. (Kleemeier award, 1987, Disting. Mentorship award, 1996, Lifetime Achievement award, 2008); mem. Psychometric Soc., Internat. Soc. Study Behavioral Devel., Mensa (Lifetime Achievement award, 2000). Unitarian Universalist. Avocations: hiking, stamps. Home: 2500 6th Ave North Apt 1 Seattle WA 98109 Office Phone: 206-281-4050. Business E-Mail: schaie@u.washington.edu.

SCHALÉN, WILHELM ARVID, neurosurgeon; b. Uppsala, Oct. 4, 1951; MD, Lund U., 1977, PhD, 1992. Cons. Skåne U. Hosp., 2003—. Dir. neurosurg. studies faculty medicine Lund U., 1999. Mem.: Scandinavian Neurosurg. Soc., Swedish Neurosurg. Soc., Swedish Med. Assn. Office: Getingevägen 4 Skåne University Hosp Lund Skåne SE-221 85 Sweden Business E-Mail: wilhelm.schalen@med.lu.se.

SCHALICK, WALTON O., III, medical educator; b. Pittsfield, Mass., Oct. 18, 1964; MD, Johns Hopkins U., PhD, 1995. Asst. prof. U. Wis., 2007—. Office: 1300 University Ave #1440 Madison WI 53706 Business E-Mail: schalick@wisc.edu.

SCHALLER, JANE GREEN, pediatrician; b. Cleve., June 26, 1934; d. George and May Alice (Wing) Green; children: Robert Thomas, George Charles, Margaret May. AB, Hiram Coll., Ohio, 1956; MD cum laude, Harvard U., 1960. Diplomate Am. Bd. Pediat., Am. Bd. Med. Examiners. Resident in pediat. Children's Hosp.-U. Wash., Seattle, 1960-63; fellow immunology Children's Hosp. U. Wash., 1963-65; faculty U. Wash. Med. Sch., 1965-83, prof. pediat., 1975-83; head divsn. rheumatic diseases Children's Hosp., Seattle, 1968-83; prof., chmn. dept. pediat., pediatrician-in-chief Tufts U. Sch. Medicine/New Eng. Med. Ctr., 1983-98; Karp prof. pediat. Tufts U. Sch. Medicine, Boston, 1983—, disting. prof., 1995—. Vis. physician Med. Rsch. Coun., Taplow, Eng., 1971-72; adj. prof. diplomacy The Fletcher Sch. Law and Diplomacy, Tufts U., 1998-2000. Contbr. articles to profl. jours. Bd. dirs: Seattle Chamber Music Festival, 1982-85; trustee Boston Chamber Music Soc., 1985—; mem. Boston adv. coun. UNICEF, tech. advisor UN Study on the Impact of Armed Conflict on Children, 1995-97; chmn., adv. com. children's rights divsn. Human Rights Watch, 1995—; mem. adv. com. Middle East divsn., 1998—; exec. com. Women's Commn. for Refugee Women and Children Internat. Rescue com., 1989-94, adv. coun. 1994—. Mem.: AAAS, Royal Coll. Pediats. U.K., Internat. Women's Forum, Mass. Women's Forum, Harvard U. Med. Sch. Alumni Coun. (v.p. 1977—80, pres. 1982—83), Physicians for Human Rights (founding pres. 1986—89, exec. com. 1986—), Com. Health in So. Africa (exec. com. 1986—92), Assn. Med. Sch. Pediat. Chmn. (exec. com. 1986—89, rep. to coun. on govt. affairs and coun. acad. socs.), New Eng. Pediat. Soc. (pres. 1991—93), Am. Coll. Rheumatology, Internat. Pediat. Assn. (pres.-elect 1998—2001, pres. 2001—04, exec. dir. 2004—), Am. Acad. Pediat. (exec. com. sect. on internat. child health, head children's rights program, rep. to UNICEF), Am. Pediat. Soc., Soc. Pediat. Rsch., Inst. Medicine of NAS, Saturday Club, Tavern Club, Aesculapian Club (pres 1988—89). Office: 737 Olive Wat #2505 Seattle WA 98101

SCHALLHORN, STEVEN, ophthalmologist; Former dir. cornea & refractive surgery Naval Med. Ctr.; former mgr. refractive surgery program US Navy; ophthalmologist Clearview Eye & Laser Med. Ctr. Visiting prof. Harvard, USC, Baylor Coll. Medicine; cons. NASA, NATO, FAA. Ret. capt. USN. Decorated Legion of Merit USN; recipient Joint Chiefs of Staff award, Lans Refractive Surgery award. Fellow: Am. Acad. Ophthalmology; mem.: ASCRS, AMA, Am. Bd. Ophthalmology. Office: Clearview Eye & Laser Medical Care 6255 Lusk Blvd Ste 100 San Diego CA 92121

SCHALLY, ANDREW VICTOR, endocrine oncologist, researcher; b. Wilno, Poland, Nov. 30, 1926; arrived in USA, 1957, naturalized, 1962; s. Casimir Peter and Maria (Lacka) Schally; m. Ana Maria Comaru, Aug. 1976 (dec. Sept. 2004). BSc, McGill U., Montreal, Can., 1955, PhD in Biochemistry, 1957; MD (hon.), Tulane Med. Sch., New Orleans, 1978. Rsch. asst. dept. biochemistry Nat. Inst. Med. Research, London, 1949—52; rsch. asst. endocrine unit Allan Meml. Inst. Psychiatry, McGill U., 1952—57; rsch. assoc. dept. physiology Baylor Coll. Medicine/Tex. Med. Ctr., Houston, 1957—60, asst. prof. biochemistry, 1960—62; assoc. prof. Tulane U. Sch. Medicine, 1962—67, prof., 1967—2006; Disting. Leonard Miller prof. pathology Miller Sch. Medicine, U. Miami, 2006—, prof. divsn. hematology/oncology, 2007—. Chief Endocrine, Polypeptide & Cancer Inst., VA Med. Ctr., New Orleans, 1962—2005, VA Med. Ctr., Miami, Fla., 2005—; sr. med. investigator US Dept. Vets Affairs, 1973—99, disting. med. rsch. scientist, 1999—. Author: The Hypothalamus and Pituitary in Health and Disease, 1972; contbr. articles to profl. jours. Recipient Van Meter prize, Am. Thyroid Assn., 1969, Ayerst-Squibb award, Endocrine Soc., 1970, Charles Mickle award, U. Toronto, 1974, Gairdner Found. Internat. award, 1974, Borden award, Assn. Am. Med. Colleges/Borden Co. Found., 1975, Albert Lasker award for basic med. rsch., 1975, Nobel prize for medicine, 1977. Fellow: AAAS; mem.: NAS, Internat. Brain Rsch. Found., Am. Soc. Reproductive Medicine, Am. Chem. Soc., Am. Assn. Cancer Rsch., Royal Acad. Medicine Spain, Acad. Sci. Russia, Nat. Acad. Medicine Venezuela, Nat. Acad. Medicine Brazil, Nat. Acad. Medicine Mex., Internat. Soc. Rsch. Biology & Reproduction, Soc. Exptl. Biology & Medicine, Soc. Biol. Chemists, Am. Physiol. Soc., Endocrine Soc., Mex. Acad. Sci. (corr.), Chilean Endocrine Soc. (hon.), Spanish Soc. Fertility (hon.), Can. Soc. Endocrinology & Metabolism (hon.), Polish Acad. Medicine (hon.), Hungarian Acad. Scis. (hon.), Sigma Xi, numerous other internat. organizations. Achievements include research in TRH, the releasing factor of the thyroid stimulating hormone; hypothalamic luteinizing hormone releasing factor, LH-RH, the brain's master key to the body's control reproductive function; the application of hypothalamic hormones for cancer therapy. Avocations: swimming, soccer. Office: VA Hosp Research 151 1201 NW 16 St Miami FL 33125 Office Phone: 305-575-3477. Office Fax: 305-575-3126. Business E-Mail: andrew.schally@va.gov.

SCHALM, EVERETT W., physician; Studied, U. of Medicine and Dentistry of NJ, New Brunswick, 1986. Diplomate Am. Bd. Family Medicine, cert. sports medicine, adolescent medicine. Intern Mountainside Hosp., resident family medicine, 1987—89, physician; with Merit Mountainside LLC, St. Josephs Wayne Hosp. Office: Mountainside Hospital Ste 201 799 Bloomfield Ave Verona NJ 07044 Office Phone: 973-746-7050. Office Fax: 973-857-2831.

SCHANDLER, JON B., hospital administrator; b. Paterson, NJ, Apr. 19, 1950; s. Jack Morris and Deborah Londner Schandler; m. Amy Miller, Mar. 23, 1975; children: Matthew, Karen. BS, Villanova U., 1972; MBA, Fordham U., 1979. CPA NY. Sr. acct. Price Waterhouse & Co., NYC, 1973—76; contr. White Plains Hosp. Ctr. (WPHC), White Plains, NY, 1976—80, COO, 1980—81, pres., CEO, 1981—. Mem.: No. Met. Hosp. Assn., NY Soc. C.P.A.'s, Am. Inst. C.P.A.'s, Gamma Phi. Office: White Plains Hosp Med Center 41 E Post Rd White Plains NY 10601

SCHARGORODSKI, LEO, medical association administrator; Mem. ctrl. staff, exec. dir. March of Dimes Birth Defects Found., Buffalo, Miami, Fla., Washington; exec. dir. Am. Diabetes Assn. Rsch. Found., Am. Nurses Fedn.; chief devel. officer Am. Nurses Assn., 1998—2006; exec. dir., CEO Nat. Osteoporosis Found., Washington, 2006—09; v.p. Events Mgmt. Group, 2009—11; exec. dir. Dr. Cyrus and Myrtle Katzen Cancer Rsch. Ctr., Washington, 2011—. Recipient C Flag award, Pres. Ronald Reagan, Emmy award. Office: Dr Cyrus & Myrtle Katzen Cancer Rsch Ctr 2150 Pennsylvania Ave NW Ste 1-200 Washington DC 20037 Office Phone: 202-741-2250. Office Fax: 202-741-2487. *

SCHARHAG, JÜRGEN WALTER, cardiologist, researcher; s. Theo and Karin Scharhag; 1 child. Asst. dept. cardiology U. Mainz, Germany, 1997—; asst. inst. sports preventive medicine U. Saarland, Saarbrücken, Germany, 1999. Achievements include research in Sportscardiology. Office: Inst Sports Preventive Medicine U Saarland Saarbrücken 66123 Germany Office Fax: 0049-681-302-4296. E-mail: j.scharhag@mx.uni-saarland.de.

SCHAROLD, MARY LOUISE, psychoanalyst, psychiatrist, educator; b. Wichita Falls, Tex., Mar. 3, 1943; d. Walter John and Louise Helen (Hartmann) Baumgartner; m. William Ballew McCollum, Aug. 23, 1964 (div. 1981); m. Harry Karl Scharold, June 19, 1982; children: Margaret Louise, Walter Ballew. BA with highest distinction, U. Kans., 1964; attended, U. Kans. Sch. Medicine, 1964—66; MD, Baylor Coll. Medicine, 1968; attended, Houston-Galveston Psychoanalytic Inst., 1974—76; postgrad., Topeka Inst. Psychoanalysis, 1981. Diplomate Am. Bd. Psychiatry and Neurology, 1975, cert. adult psychoanalysis Am. Psychoanalytic Assn., 1982. Intern Meml. Bapt. Hosp., Houston, 1968-69; resident in psychiatry Baylor Coll. Medicine, Houston, 1969—72, chief resident, 1971-72; psychiatrist Houston, 1972—; psychoanalyst, 1981—. Asst. prof. Baylor Coll. Medicine, Houston, 1973-76, asst. clin. prof., 1981-84, assoc. clin. prof. 1984—; dir. Baylor Psychiat. Clinic, Houston, 1973-76; co-dir. Rice U. Psychiat. Svc., Houston, 1981-82; asst. clin. prof. U. Kans. Sch. Medicine, Kansas City, 1977-81; tchg. assoc. Topeka Psychoanalytic Inst., 1984-86; tchg. analyst, Houston-Galveston Psychoanalytic Inst., 1986-90, tng. and supervising analyst, 1990—2008, emeritus, 2008-, v.p., 1994-96, pres., 1996-01, bd. dirs., 2001-04; acting pres. bd. trustees Child Devel. Ctr., 2005-06, sec. bd. trustees, 2005-08. Contbr.

articles to profl. pubs. Adv. bd. Leavenworth (Kans.) Mental Health Assn., 1977-81 Watkins scholar U. Kans., 1961-64; Grad. Fellowship award, Pi Beta Phi, 1965; recipient Hilltopper, Ten Outstanding Sr. Women, U. Kans., 1963, Greater U. Fund award, 1964, U. Kans., Eugen Kahn award, Outstanding Baylor Psychiatry Resident, 1972, 1st Disting. Svc. award, Houston-Galveston Psychoanalytic Soc., 2004; named Outstanding Woman Med. Student, AMWA, Houston Branch, 1968; named to Best Doctors in America, 1996- Mem. Am. Psychiat. Assn. (disting. life fellow, mem. com. quality assurance 1986-87, chair Tex. peer rev. 1984-88), Am. Coll. Psychoanalysts, Am. Psychoanalytic Assn. (cert. 1982, peer rev. com. 1985-90, prof. ins. commn. 1986-93, bd. profl. stds. 1994-2001, CME com. 1994-96, exec. coun. 1994-96, cert. com. 1995-98, preparedness and progress com. 1998-2006, chair preparedness and progress com. 2000-06, coordinating com. bd. profl. stds. 2000-06, bylaws com. 2001—09, fin. com. 2003—09, councilor-at-large 2005-09, chair councillors-at-large, 2007—09, hon. membership com, 2005-09, election oversight com., 2005-09, compliance task force, 2006-07, com. on coun., 2006—2008, annual meeting task force 2008, audit com. 2008—09, co-chair, 2000-10), Am. Group Psychotherapy Assn., Ctr. Advanced Psychoanalytic Studies, Houston Psychiat. Soc. (v.p. 1984-85, pres.-elect 1985-86, pres. 1986-87), Houston-Galveston Psychoanalytic Soc. (sec.-treas. 1984-86, pres.-elect 1986-88, pres. 1988-90, alt. councillor 1994-96), Houston Group Psychotherapy Soc. (adv. bd. 1984-85), Mortar Bd., Phi Beta Kappa, Delta Phi Alpha, Alpha Omega Alpha, Pi Beta Phi Alumni Assn. Republican. Lutheran. Office: 1406 E Main St Ste 200 Fredericksburg TX 78624 Home Phone: 713-590-2301; Office Phone: 713-590-2302. Personal E-mail: mlscharold@mindspring.com.

SCHARSCHMIDT, BRUCE FREDERICK, physician; b. Cleve., Mar. 6, 1946; s. Lewis Wilson and Roselyn Elizabeth (Klein) Scharschmidt; m. Peggy Sue Crawford Scharschmidt, June 4, 1977; children: Tiffany, Brent. BS, Northwestern U., 1966, MD, 1970. Diplomate Am. Bd. Internal Medicine. Intern U. Calif., San Francisco, 1970—71, resident medicine, 1971—72, fellow, 1975—77, asst. prof. medicine, 1977—81, assoc. prof. medicine, 1981—85, prof., 1985—96; assoc dir. Liver Ctr., 1983—96; cons. liver transplantation US, Calif. govts., 1983—; v.p. Chiron Corp., 1996—2006, Novartis, 2006—08; sr. v.p. Hyperion Therapeutics Inc., 2008—. Editl. bd. Hepatology Jour., 1981—86; assoc. editor Gastroenterology, 1981—86; editor Jour. Clin. Ivestigation, 1987—92. Contbr. articles to profl. jours. Lt. comdr. USPHS, 1972—75. Recipient Rsch Career Devel. award, 1977—82; grantee, NIH, 1980—2000. Mem.: Northwestern Med. Sch. CTSA, Assn. Am. Physicians, Western Assn. Physicians, Western Soc. Clin. Investigation, Soc. Exptl. Biology & Medicine, Am. Liver Found. (bd. dir.), Internat. Assn. Study Liver, Am. Gastroenterol. Assn., Am. Assn. Study Liver Disease, Am. Soc. Clin. Investigation (pres. 1992—93), Am. Fedn. Clin. Rsch., Nathan Smith Davis Club (alumni bd. & pres.), Western Gut Club, Phi Eta Sigma, Alpha Omega Alpha. Republican. Office Phone: 650-745-7851 Personal E-mail: bruce.scharschmidt@gmail.com.

SCHARWÄCHTER, LEENDERT PETER, clinical psychologist; b. Renkum, Gelderland, Netherlands, Mar. 27, 1961; s. Leendert Peter Scharwächter and Adriana Hendrika Penseel; m. Brigitte Maureen Bernarde Liklikuwata; children: Sabine Christine Adriana, Veronique Mara Linde. MS in Clin Psychology & Philosophy, Radhoud U., Nijmegen, 1989. Clin. psychologist Rynstate, Arnhem, Gelderland, Netherlands, 2011—. Home and Office: Parksingel 135 Bemmel Gelderland 6681 ND Netherlands Office Phone: 31481450434. Office Fax: 31 481 451 591. Business E-mail: scharwachter@freeler.nl.

SCHATTEN, GERALD PHILLIP, stem cell biologist, reproductive biologist, educator; b. NYC, Nov. 1, 1949; s. Frank and Sylvia Schatten; m. Irene Fonseca; children, Daniel, Madeline, Samantha, Marta, Andre. BS, U. Calif., Berkeley, 1971, PhD, 1975. Instr. U. Calif., Berkeley, 1975; postdoctoral fellow Rockefeller Found., 1976-77; from asst. prof. to prof. Fla. State U., Tallahassee, 1979-86; prof. molecular biology, zoology and obstetrics gynecology U. Wis., Madison, 1986-97, rsch. dir. women's health rsch., 1997—, dir. integrated microscopy resource for biomed. rsch., 1986-92, dir. gamete and embryo biol. tng. program, 1989-97; program dir. Mellon Ctr. of Excellence in Reproductive Biology, 1996-97, 99—; prof. ob-gyn. and cell-devel. biology, sr. scientist Oreg. Regional Primate Rsch. Ctr. Oreg. Health Scis. U., Portland, 1997-2001; dir. Pitts. Devel. Ctr., dep. dir. Magee-Women's Rsch. Inst., Pitts., 2001—, vice chair, prof. dept. ob/gyn./reproductive scis., prof. cell biology and physiology, 2001—. Dir. gamete and embryo biol. tng. program U. Wis., Madison, 1989-97; exec. bd. UNESCO's Internat. Cell Rsch. Orgn., 1995—, pres., 2011—; co-dir. frontiers in reprodn. course Marine Biol. Lab., Woods Hole, Mass., 1998-2001, NIH Course Frontiers Stem Cells & Regeneration, 2003-. Editor Current Topics in Devel. Biology, 1996-2007 Recipient Rsch. Career Devel. award NIH, 1981-86, Merit award, 1997-2008, Sadler award, 1998; Purkinje medal of sci. Czech Acad. Scis., 2000, Patrick Steptoe medal, brit. Fertility Socs., 2005, Stem Cell Sci. and Policy award, Genetics Policy Inst., 2005, Pioneer Human Embryonic Stem Cell award, Stanford U., 2005. Mem.: UNESCO, Internat. Cell. Rsch. Orgn. (pres. 2011—), Nat. Inst. Aging Coun. Office: Univ Pitts Pitts Devel Ctr 204 Craft Ave Pittsburgh PA 15213

SCHATZ, GOTTFRIED, biochemistry educator; b. Strem, Austria, Aug. 18, 1936; arrived in Switzerland, 1974; s. Andreas and Anna (Lantos) S.; m. Merete Petersen, Aug. 11, 1962, children: Isabella, Peer, Kamilla. PhD in Chemistry and Biochemistry (summa cum laude), U. Graz, Austria, 1961; Doctorate (hon.), Comenius U., Bratislava, 1996, U. Stockholm, 2000. Asst. prof., dept. biochemistry U. Vienna, Austria, 1961-68; postdoctoral fellow Pub. Health Rsch. Inst., NYC, 1964-66; assoc. prof. biochemistry and molecular biology Cornell U., Ithaca, NY, 1968-73, prof. biochemistry and molecular biology, 1973-74; prof. biochemistry Biozentrum, U. Basel, Switzerland, 1974—2000, chmn., 1983-85, prof. emeritus, 2000 —. Adv. panel, biochemistry and biophysics, US Sci. Found., 1973-74; mem. fellowship com., European Molecular Biology Orgn., 1978-82; mem. scientific adv. com., European Molecular Biology Lab., Heidelberg, 1986-89; adv. bd. Max-Planck Inst. Biochemistry, Martinsried/Munich, 1984-86; mem. Swiss adv. bd., Basel Inst. Immunology, 1985-88; mem. adv. bd. Maurice E. Müller Inst. für hochauflosende Elektronenmikroskopie am Biozentrum, Basel, 1983-85; sec.-gen. European Molecular Biology Orgn., Heidelberg, Fed. Republic Germany, 1984-89; mem. adv. bd., Max-Planck Inst. Cell Biology, Ladenburg/Heidelberg, 1983-; chmn. adv. bd., Inst. for Molecular Pathology, Vienna, 1987-99; scientific adv. bd., biology dept., Princeton U., NJ, 1988-91; mem. adv. bd. Swiss Cancer Rsch. Inst., Lausanne, 1990-92; mem. Swiss Nat. Rsch. Coun., Berne, 1990-2000; chmn. adv. bd., Ctr. for Molecular Biology, Heidelberg, 1990-92; adv. bd., Inst. for Molecular Biology and Biotechnology, Iraklion, Crete, 1990-92; chmn. evaluation com., Max Delbrück Centrum, Berlin, 1996, Nat. Coun. Scientific Rsch. (CNRS), divsn. Inst. Curie, Paris, 1998-; strategic adv. com., Inst. Pasteur, Paris, 2000-. Contbr. numerous papers to sci. jours. Recipient Innitzer prize, 1967, Emil Christian Hansen Gold medal Carlsberg Found., Copenhagen, 1983, Sir Hans Krebs medal Fedn. European Biochem. Socs., Berlin, 1986, Otto Warburg medal German Biochem. Soc., 1988, Schleiden medal Germany Acad. Scis., 1993, Marcel Benoist prize Benoist Found., Berne, 1993, Gairdner Found. Internat. award, 1998, Order of Merit, Republic of Austria, 2000, Wilson medal, Am. Soc. Cell Biology, 2000, Antonio Feltrinelli Internat. prize, 2004; co-recepient Louis Jeantet prize for medicine Jeantet Found., Geneva, 1990, Order for Arts and Scis. Republic of Austria, 1992, Lynen medal, U. Miami (U.S.A.), 1997. Mem. AAAS (fgn.), NAS (U.S.-fgn. mem.), German Acad. Leopoldina, Japanese Biochem. Soc.(hon. mem.), Austrian Acad. Scis., Royal Swedish Acad.(fgn. mem.), Protein Soc. (coun. 1993-99), Austrian Acad. Sciences (mem. adv. bd., Molecular Biology Inst., Salburg, 1994-96), Royal Netherlands Acad. Scis., Rheinland-Westphalian Acad. Scis., Swiss Sci. and Tech. Coun. (pres. 2000-03). E-mail: gottfried.schatz@unibas.ch. *

SCHATZ, IRWIN JACOB, cardiologist, educator; b. St. Boniface, Man., Can., Oct. 16, 1931; came to US, 1956, naturalized, 1966; s. Jacob and Reva S.; m. Barbara Jane Binder, Nov. 12, 1967; children: Jacob, Edward, Stephen and Brian (twins). Student, U. Man., Winnipeg, 1951, MD with honors, 1956. Diplomate: Am. Bd. Internal Medicine. Intern Vancouver (B.C.) Gen. Hosp., 1955-56; resident Hammersmith Hosp., U. London, 1957, Mayo Clinic, Rochester, Minn., 1958-61; head sec. peripheral vascular disease Henry Ford Hosp., Detroit, 1961-68; asso. prof. medicine Wayne State U., 1968-71, chief sect. cardiovascular disease, 1969-71; assoc. prof., asso. dir. sect. cardiology U. Mich., 1972-73, prof. internal medicine, 1973-75; prof. medicine John A. Burns Sch. Medicine, U. Hawaii, 1975—, chmn. dept. medicine, 1975-90, interim chmn. dept. medicine, 2003—05. Author: Orthostatic Hypotension, 1986; contbr. numerous articles to med. jour. Mem. jud. coun. State of Hawaii Supreme Ct., 2000—; mem. disciplinary coun. Hawaii Supreme Court, 2010—. Rockefeller Found. scholar, 1991. Master ACP (bd. gov. 1984-89, Laureate award Hawaii chpt. 1992, Mayo Clinic Disting Alumni award, 2009); fellow Am. Coll. Cardiology (bd. gov. 1980-84); mem. Am. Heart Assn. (fellow coun. cardiology), Am. Fedn. Clin. Rsch., Asian-Pacific Soc. Cardiology (v.p. 1987-91), Accreditation Coun. for Grad. Med. Edn. (chmn. residence rev. com. internal medicine 1989-95), Hawaii Heart Assn. (pres.), Western Assn. Physicians, Am. Autonomic Soc. (chmn. bd. gov., pres. 1996-98), Pacific Interurban Club. Jewish. Office: 1356 Lusitana St Honolulu HI 96813-2421 *

SCHATZBERG, ALAN FREDERIC, psychiatrist, researcher; b. NYC, Oct. 17, 1944; s. Emanuel and Cila (Diamand) S.; m. Nancy R. Silverman, Aug. 27, 1972; children: Melissa Ann, Lindsey Diamand. BS, NYU, 1965, MD, 1968; MA (hon.), Harvard U., 1989. Diplomate Nat. Bd. Med. Examiners, Am. Bd. Psychiatry and Neurology. Intern Lenox Hill Hosp., NYC, 1968-69; resident in psychiatry Mass. Mental Health Ctr., Boston, 1969-72; clin. fellow in psychiatry Harvard Med. Sch., Boston, 1969-72, asst. prof. psychiatry, 1977-82, assoc. prof., 1982-88, prof., 1988-91; interim psychiatrist-in-chief McLean Hosp., Belmont, Mass., 1984-86, dir. depression rsch. facility, 1985—, svc. chief, 1982-84, 86-88; psychiatrist adv. panel Eli Lilly & Co., Indpls., 1986-93; clin. dir. Mass. Mental Health Ctr., Boston, 1988-91; Kenneth T. Norris, Jr. prof. psychiatry and behavioral scis. Stanford (Calif.) U., 1991—, chmn. dept. psychiatry and behavioral scis. Sch. Medicine, 1991— Cons. AMA Videoclinics, Chgo., 1979-83; mem. AMA/FAA panel on health regulations, Chgo., 1984-86; mem. NIH Biol. Psychopathology and Clin. Neuroscis. Intitial Rev. Group, 1991-95, chmn., 1993-94, ITMA Rev. Group, 2007-09. Co-author: Manual of Clinical Psychopharmacology, 1986, 7th edit., 2010; co-editor: Depression: Biology, Psychodynamics and Treatment, 1978, Hypothalamic-Pituitary-Adrenal Axis, 1988, Textbook of Psychopharmacology, 1996, 4th edit., 2009; mem. editl. bd. McLean Hosp. Jour., 1975—88, Jour. Psychiat. Rsch., 1988—, co-editor-in-chief, 2000—, mem. editl. bd. Harvard Rev. Psychiatry, 1992— Anxiety, 1993, Jour. Clin. Psychopharmacology, 1993—, Archives of Gen. Psychiatry, 1995—, Psychoneuroendocrinology, 1995—, Am. Jour. Psychiatry, 2002—05, assoc. editor-in-chief Depression and Anxiety, 1992—2007, translational field editor Neuropsychopharmacology, 2002—07; contbr. more than 500 articles to profl. publs., chapters to books. Maj. USAF, 1972-74. Rsch. grantee NIMH, 1984-87, 94—, Poitras Charitable Found., 1985-93, Pritzker Found., 1997—; recipient Mood Disorders Rsch. award Am. Coll. Psychiatrists, 2002, Klerman Lifetime Rsch. award Nat. Depressive and Manic Depressive Assn., 1998, Strecker award U. Pa., 2002, Falcone award Nat. Alliance Rsch. in Schizophrenia and Affective Diseases, 2005. Fellow: APA (pres. 2009—10, Rsch. award 2002), Soc. Biol. Psychiatry (pres. 2005—06), Am. Coll. Psychiatrists (Disting. Svc. award 2005, Mood Disorders Rsch. award 2002), Am. Psychopathol. Assn., Am. Coll. Neuropsychopharmacology (coun. 1994—97, pres. 2000—01); mem.: NAS, Inst. Medicine. Avocations: travel, swimming, fine arts, theater. Office: Stanford U Sch Medicine 401 Quarry Rd Rm 3313 Stanford CA 94305-5797 Office Phone: 650-723-6811. Business E-mail: afschatz@stanford.edu.

SCHAUER, MATTHIAS CHRISTIAN, physician; b. Munich, Oct. 7, 1973; s. Alfred and Sieglinde Schauer. Dr. med., Albert-Ludwig-U., Freiburg im Breisgau, Germany, 1998; MD, U. Freiburg, 1998; degree in Gen. Surgery and Emergency Medicine, Technische U. Muenchen, 2006; PhD, U. Duesseldorf, 2011. Cert. surgery specialist Tech. U. Munich, 2006, in emergency medicine Tech. U. Munich, 2007, in surgical endoscopy and natural orifice transluminal endoscopic surgery U. Tuebingen and Hamburg, 2009. Resident surgery Klinikum Augsburg Germany, Tech. U. Munich, 1999—2008; staff mem. Dept. Gen., Visceral & Pediat. Surgery Heinrich Heine U. Düsseldorf, 2008—. Emergency physician acute and polytraumatized patients, 2007—; chief surg. endoscopy, asst. resident, 2008; adv. dept. intensive care medicine; surg. cons. Internal Medicine, 2008—; surg. adv. surg. oncology, 2008—; sr. physician gen., visceral and pediat. surgery, 2011—. Co-author: Sentinel Node Concept, 2005, Update Oncology, 2011; contbr. articles to profl. jours. Mem.: German Soc. Surgery. Achievements include research in natural orifice transluminal endoscopic surgery with development of wound closures for the transluminal access; development of multimodal programs concerning chemotherapy and following surgical resection in the treatment of Barrett's carcinoma; evaluation of chemotherapy response and its prediction for further individualized therapy concepts with the goal to avoid ineffective chemotherapy cycle; evaluation and prediction of chemotherapeutical side effects on the basis of the patient's individual immune status; significance of tyrosine kinase receptors and cadherin for metastases and treatment options; research in surgical strategies in the treatment of advanced renal cell carcinoma. Avocation: bicycling. Office: Heinrich Heine University Duesseldorf Gen Visceral & Childrens Surgery Duesseldorf 40225 Germany Office Phone: 49-211-81-17350. Office Fax: 49-211-81-17359. Business E-mail: matthias.schauer@med.uni-duesseldorf.de.

SCHAUER, PHILIP R., surgeon; b. Jan. 31, 1961; BS, Tex. A&M U., Coll. Station; MD, Baylor Coll. Medicine, Houston, 1986. Intern, surgery U. Tex. Health Sci. Ctr., San Antonio, resident, surgery, 1993, chief resident, gen. surgery; fellow, laparoscopic surgery Duke U. Med. Ctr., Durham, NC, 1995; dir., endoscopic surgery, dir. bariatric surgery, dir. Mark Ravitch/Leon Hirsh Ctr. for Minimally Invasive Surgery U. Pitts. Med. Ctr.; dir., Bariatric and Metabolic Inst. Cleve. Clinic, Ohio, 2004—, chief, minimally invasive gen. surgery, 2004—; prof. surgery Cleve. Clinic Lerner Coll. Medicine of Case Western Reserve U. Mem. adv. coun. Am. Bd. Surgery; bd. gov. Fellowship Coun.; fiduciary role MISS Surgery Symposium, Physician Reviews of Surgery, LLC, RemedyMD, Inc., Surgical Excellence; invited spkr. in field; cons. in field. Assoc. editor Surgery for Obesity and Related Diseases, mem. several editl. bds. Named one of Best Doctors in America. Fellow: ACS; mem.: Obesity Soc., Soc. Clin. Surgery, Cul. Surgical Soc., Soc. Surgery Alimentary Tract, Soc. U. Surgeons, Am. Surgical Assn., N.Am. Soc. for the Study of Obesity, Internat. Fedn. Surgery for Obesity, Am. Soc. for Bariatric Surgery (past. chmn. rsch., tng. and credentialing com.), Soc. Am. Gastrointestinal and Endoscopic Surgeons (bd. govs.), Am. Soc. for Metabolic and Bariatric Surgery (immediate past pres.). Achievements include being the innovator in the development of numerous minimally invasive gastrointestinal procedures and also bariatric surgical techniques and devices for weight loss and diabetes control. Office: Cleve Clinic Main Campus Mail Code M61 9500 Euclid Ave Cleveland OH 44195 Office Phone: 216-444-4794.

SCHAUF, VICTORIA, pediatrician, educator; b. NYC, Feb. 17, 1943; d. Maurice J. and Ruth H. (Baker) Bisson; m. Michael Delaney; 2 children. BS in Microbiology with honors, U. Chgo., 1965, MD with honors, 1969. Intern in pediat. U. Chgo. Hosp., 1969—70; resident in pediat. Sinai Hosp. of Balt., 1970—71; chief resident pediat. Children's Hosp. Nat. Med. Ctr., Washington, 1971—72; rsch. trainee NIH, Bethesda, Md., 1972; adj. asst. prof. microbiology Rush Med. Coll., Chgo., 1972—74; prof. pediat., head pediatric infectious diseases U. Ill., Chgo., 1974—84; med. officer FDA, Rockville, Md., 1984—86; chmn. dept. pediat. Nassau County Med. Ctr., East Meadow, NY, 1986—90; prof. pediat. SUNY, Stony Brook, 1987—94; pvt. practice, 1995—; chief pediatric svcs. Ridgecrest Regional Hosp., 2005—, chief staff, 2009—. Vis. prof. Rockefeller U, 1990; mem. vis. faculty Chiang Mai (Thailand) U., 1978; mem. ad hoc com. study sects. NIH, Bethesda, 1981-82; bd. dirs. Pearl Stetler Rsch. Found., Chgo., 1982-84; cons. FDA, 1987-88, 93-95, Can. Bur. Human Prescription Drugs, Ottawa, 1990-2004, Biotech. Investors, 1993-95, Calif. Children's Svcs., 2005—09; course dir. pediat. infectious diseases rev. course Cornell U. Med. Coll., N.Y.C., 1994, faculty, 1995. Co-author: Pediatric Infectious Diseases: A Comprehensive Guide to the Subspecialty, 1997; prodr. radio and TV programs in field; contbr. articles to profl. jours., chpts. to books. Vol. physician Cook County Hosp., Chgo., 1974-84; mem. adv. com. Nat. Hansen's Disease Ctr., La., 1986, Nassau County Day Care Coun., N.Y., 1988-90; mem. adv. bd. Surg. Aid to Children of World, N.Y., 1986-90; commr., sec. Kern County Children and Families Commn., 1999-2002; bd. dirs. Indian Wells Valley Cmty. Found., 2001-. Am. Lung Assn. grantee U. Ill., 1977; recipient contract NIH, U. Ill., 1978-81, grantee, 1979-84. Fellow Infectious Diseases Soc. Am.; mem. Pediatric Infectious Diseases Soc. (exec. bd.), Soc. Pediatric Rsch., Am. Pediatric Soc., AAAS, Am. Soc. Microbiology, Am. Acad. Pediat., Phi Beta Kappa, Alpha Omega Alpha. Avocation: walking. Home Phone: 760-384-2399; Office Phone: 760-371-2128. Business E-Mail: vschauf@pol.net.

SCHAUMBURG, HERBERT HOWARD, neurology educator; b. Houston, Nov. 6, 1932; m. Joanna Jane Austin; children: Barnabas Paul, Kristin Elizabeth. AB cum laude, Harvard Coll., 1956; MD, Washington U., 1960. Instr. in neurology Albert Einstein Coll. of Medicine, NYC, 1964-67, asst. prof. neurology, 1967-69, assoc. prof. neurology, 1972-76, prof., 1976—, vice chmn., 1977-84, acting chmn., 1984-86, chmn., 1986—; instr. pathology Harvard Med. Sch., Boston, 1969-71. Mem. Am. Acad. Neurology, Am. Assn. Neuropathologists, Am. Neurol. Assn., Soc. Toxicology, Soc. Neurosci. Home: 616 King Ave City Island Bronx NY 10464 Office: Albert Einstein Coll Medicine 1300 Morris Park Ave Bronx NY 10461-1926 Office Phone: 718-430-2002. Personal E-mail: Schaumbu@optimum.net. Business E-Mail: herbert.schaumb@einstein.yu.edu.

SCHECHTER, ALAN NEIL, medical researcher; b. NYC, June 28, 1939; s. Sidney S. and Mildred (Levy) S.; m. Geraldine Poppa, Feb. 6, 1965; children: Daniele, Andrew. AB, Cornell U., 1959; MD, Columbia U., 1963. Lic. MD, N.Y., Calif. Intern, resident Albert Einstein Coll. Medicine, NYC, 1963-65; from rsch. assoc. to med. officer Nat. Inst. Arthritis and Metabolic Diseases, NIH, Bethesda, Md., 1965-72; sect. chief Chem. Biology Lab Nat. Inst. Diabetes and Digestive and Kidney Diseases, NIH, Bethesda, 1972-81, lab. chief

Chem. Biology Lab., 1981—. Bd. dirs. Found. for Advanced Edn. in Sci., Bethesda, Stetten Mus. Med. History, Bethesda. Patentee in field; editor 5 books; contbr. numerous articles to profl. jours. Capt. USPHS, 1983—2001. Home: 5405 Beech Ave Bethesda MD 20814-1733 Office: NIH Chem Biology Lab Nat Inst Diab Digest Kidney Dis 9000 Rockville Pike Bethesda MD 20892-0003

SCHECHTER, CLYDE B., preventive medicine physician, medical association administrator; MD, Columbia U. Fellowship Mt. Sinai Medical Ctr., resident, adj. assoc. prof. community and preventive medicine; chief resident St. Luke's- Roosevelt Hosp. Ctr.; assoc. prof., dept. family and social medicine Albert Einstein Coll. Medicine, assoc. prof., dept. epidemiology and population health. Mem.: American Bd. Preventive Medicine (chair 2009). Office: Albert Einstein Coll Medicine Mazer Bldg Room 110 1300 Morris Park Ave Bronx NY 10461

SCHECHTER, MICHAEL D., obstetrician, gynecologist; MD, NYU, 1988. Diplomate Am. Bd. Ob-Gyn. Resident St. Luke's-Roosevelt Hosp., 1989—92; with Greenwich Hosp., Putnam Gynecology & Obstetrics. Office: Putnam Gynecology & Obstetrics 500 W Putnam Ave Greenwich CT 06830 Office Phone: 203-622-0303.

SCHECHTER, NEIL LAWRENCE, pediatrician, educator; b. NYC, Sept. 12, 1947; s. Stanley and Sylvia Schechter; m. Carlota Patricia Geyer, Aug. 27, 1977; children: Benjamin Birch, Anna Carlota. BA, Northwestern U., Evanston, Ill., 1969; DO, Mich. State U., East Lansing, 1973; MD, U. Conn. Sch. Medicine, Farmintgon, 1982. Diplomate Am. Bd. Pediat., 1979. Dir. devel. pediat. St. Francis Hosp. Med. Ctr., Hartford, 1979—; prof. pediat. U. Conn. Sch. Medicine, Farmington, 1992—; dir. pain relief program Conn. Children's Med. Ctr., Hartford, 2000—. Editor: Pain in Infants, Children and Adolescents, 2000; contbr. articles to profl. jours. Recipient medal, Copernicus Med. Inst., Poland, 1989, Jeffrey Lawson award, Am. Pain Soc., 2000; scholar Bellagio Study Ctr., Rockefeller Found., 2004; Dozor Vis. Prof., Ben Gurion U., 2005. Fellow: Am. Acad. Pediat.; mem.: Soc. Devel. Behavioral Pediat., Academic Pediatric Assn., Internat. Assn. Study of Pain. Achievements include one of the first to report on the disparity in pain management between adults and children. Office: Conn Children's Med Ctr 282 Washington St Hartford CT 06106 Office Fax: 860-545-8661. Business E-Mail: nschech@ccmckids.org.

SCHECTER, ARNOLD JOEL, public health physician, researcher; b. Chgo., Dec. 1, 1934; s. Benjamin and Leonore Natalie (Lyon) S.; m. Martha-Jean Berenson, Feb. 14, 1964; children: Benjamin, David, Anna. BA in Liberal Arts, U. Chgo., 1954, BS in Physiology-Neurophysiology, 1957; MD, Howard U., 1962; MPH, Columbia U., 1975. Diplomate Am. Coll. Preventive Medicine; med. lic., Ky., N.Y., N.J., N.C. Postdoc. dept. anatomy Harvard Med. Sch., Boston, 1962—64; instr. dept. medicine Mass. Gen. Hosp., Harvard Med. Sch., Boston, 1964-65; intern Beth Israel Hosp., Boston, 1966, US Army Med. Corp., 1967—69; gen. practitioner, sr. aviation med. examiner West Point, Ky., 1969-70; med. dir. inpatient rehab. ctr., drug and alcohol rehab. program Region Eight Mental Health and Mental Retardation Bd., Inc., Louisville, 1971-72; asst. prof. dept. psychiatry, divisional drug and alcohol abuse SUNY Downstate Med. Ctr., Bklyn., 1973-75; clin. assoc. prof. dept. preventive medicine N.J. Med. Sch., Newark, 1975-79; prof. dept. preventive medicine SUNY Upstate Med. Ctr., Binghamton, 1979—98; prof. environ. & occpl. health scis. U. Tex. Sch. Pub. Health, Dallas, 1999—; pres. Zumwalt Inst. for Environ. Health Inc., 1996—; cons. Health Canada, Environment Canada, 2010. Spl. expert Nat. Inst. Environ. Health Scis. NIH, 1997—98; cons. U.S. EPA, Washington, 1985—86, Washington, 1999—2000, WHO, 1986—90; sci. peer reviewer dioxin U.S. EPA, 1995, 2000, 2010—11; peer reviewer A.T.S.D.R. of C.D.C., 1995—2005; dir. clin. rsch. in drug abuse, coord., faculty mem. Career Tchr. Tng. Ctr., SUNY Downstate, 1972—75; assoc. dir. office primary health care edn., office of the dean NJ Med. Sch., 1976—79; advisor Environ. Def. Fund, 1991—92, Nat. Vets. Legal Svcs. Project, 1991—92; co-founder assoc. editor Am. Jour. Drug and Alcohol Abuse, NYC, 1973—78, editl. bd., 1978—86; editl. adv. bd. Substance and Alcohol Actions/Misuse, Elmsford, NY, 1979—85; adj. prof. epidemiology U. N.C. Sch. Pub. Health, 1998—2004; adj. prof. occupl. medicine Duke Med. Ctr., 1998—99; editl. adv. bd. mem. Environ. Health Perspectives, 2008—; mem. USEPA Dioxin Reassessment Panel, 2010—11. Editor: Rehabilitation Aspects of Drug Dependence, 1977, Treatment Aspects of Drug Dependence, 1978, Biomedical Issues in Drug Abuse, 1981, Sociological Issues in Drug Abuse, 1981, Dioxins and Health, 1994; sr. editor: 2d edit., 2003; environmental sect.editor Maxcy Rosenau Last Public Health and Preventive Medicine, 14th edit., 1998; editor: 15th edit., 2007; co-editor: Drug Abuse: Modern Trends, Issues and Perspectives, 1978; co-editor: (with H. Alksne, E. Kaufman) Critical Concerns in the Field of Drug Abuse, 1978; contbr. over 200 articles to profl. jours., books. Capt to maj., physician MC US Army, 1967-69. Recipient Pacesetter award Commonwealth Mass., 1990. Fellow: ACP, Am. Coll. Occupl. and Environ. Medicine, Am. Coll. Preventive Medicine; mem.: AAAS, APHA (chair Vietnam caucus), Internat. Soc. Environ. Epidemiology, Internat. Soc. Exposure Scis., Soc. Epidemiology Rsch., Tex. Pub. Health Assn., Soc. Epidemiologic Rsch., Am. Occupl. and Environ. Medicine Assn., Am. Coll. Epidemiology. Achievements include discovery of dioxin and furan levels in US population, US food contaminated with dioxins, dibenz furans; Polybrominated diphenyl ethers (PBBEs), which are found mainly in meat, fish & diary products; PBDE brominated flame retardant contamination in breast milk of all US mothers tested, and that these levels as well as blood are highest in the world; PBDES can be measured in all total tissues studied; PCB transformer fires can lead to contamination of buildings by dioxins; Agent Orange elevated dioxin body burden exists decades after exposure in Vietnamese and in American Vietnam Veterans; dioxin contamination exists in body tissues of the general population of the US; dioxin hot spots in Vietnam with current contamination of some Vietnamese by contaminated food; development of congener specific tissue dioxin analysis as biomarker for dioxin exposure; developed naltrexone, a narcotic antagonist in rehabilitation of oplate addicts now used in other drug rehabilitation programs; US food is contaminated with PBDE brominated flame retardants and some contaminated with hexabromocyclododecane, and perfluorinated compounds and Bisphenol A., PFC and BPA. Home: 16606 Loch Maree Ln Dallas TX 75248-1711 Office: U Tex Sch Pub Health 6011 Harry Hines Blvd Dallas TX 75248 Office Phone: 214-336-8519. Personal E-mail: ajschecter@aol.com. Business E-Mail: arnold.schecter@utsouthwestern.edu.

SCHEFFLER, LINDA WEINGARTEN, psychologist, educator; b. NYC, Feb. 15, 1936; d. Robert Lee and Helen (Sonnenstrahl) Weingarten; m. Philip B. Scheffler, July 1, 1966. BA, U. Mich., 1957, MA, 1958, PhD, 1963. Asst. prof. to assoc. prof. counseling Hunter Coll., CUNY, NYC, 1969—91. Pvt. practice psychology, N.Y.C., 1972—. Author: Help Thy Neighbor-How Counseling Works and When It Doesn't, 1984. Pres. Met. Coll. Mental Health Assn., N.Y.C., 1983-84. Avocations: gardening, studio art, water colour. Home Phone: 212-744-3014; Office Phone: 212-744-3321. Business E-Mail: lws3@mac.com.

SCHEIB, GARRY L., hospital administrator; m. Susan Scheib; 3 children. BS with honors, Lehigh U., MBA. V.p., network ops., mgr., rels. U. Pa. health sys., affiliated hosps.; with Am. Medicorp, Humana; pres., bus. group Mediq, Inc.; pres., grad. health sys. Rancocoas Hosp., 1990—93; exec. dir., health sys. office network devel., v.p. network ops. NJ divsn. Rancocas Hosp., Zurbrugg Hosp., 1997—98; exec. dir. Hosp. U. Pa., 1999—; sr. v.p., hosp. ops. University of Pennsylvania Health Systems, 2002—04, COO, 2004—. Pres. Burlington C. of C.; mem. bd. dirs. various cmty. orgns. Office: Hospital University of Pennsylvania 3400 Spruce St Philadelphia PA 19104-4283 Office Phone: 215-662-4000.

SCHEIBE, KARL EDWARD, psychology professor; b. Belleville, Ill., Mar. 5, 1937; s. John Henry and Esther Julia (Friesen) S.; m. Elizabeth Wentworth Mixter, Sept. 10, 1961; children: David Sawyer, Robert Daniel. BS, Trinity Coll., 1959; PhD, U. Calif.-Berkeley, 1963; MA (hon.), Wesleyan U., 1973. Faculty mem. Wesleyan U., Middletown, Conn., 1963—73, prof. psychology, 1973—2005, prof. emeritus, 2005—. Vis. prof. U. So. Calif., 1974; dir. rev. panels NSF Sci. Profl. Devel. Program, 1975-81; cons. Am. Council Edn., 1975-81; exec. dir. Saybrook Counseling Ctr., 1990-2008; dir. Wasch Ctr. Ret. Faculty, 2004-. Author: Beliefs and Values, 1970, Mirror, Masks, Lies and Secrets, 1979, Studies in Social Identity, 1983, Self Studies: The Psychology of Self and Identity, 1995, The Drama of Everyday Life, 2000. Trustee Trinity Coll., Hartford, Conn., 1977-83; moderator congregation First Ch. of Christ, Middletown, 1981-82. Woodrow Wilson fellow, 1959; NSF fellow, 1961; NIMH research grantee, 1964-68; Fulbright fellow Cath. U. Sao Paulo, Brazil, 1972-73, 84. Mem. Am. Psychol. Assn., Eastern Psychol. Assn., Conn. Acad. Arts and Scis., Phi Beta Kappa Congregationalist. Home: 11 Long Ln Middletown CT 06457-4046 Office: Wesleyan U Wasch Ctr for Ret Faculty Middletown CT 06459-0001 Office Phone: 860-685-2273. Business E-Mail: kscheibe@wesleyan.edu.

SCHEIBEL, ARNOLD BERNARD, psychiatrist, educator, research director; b. NYC, Jan. 18, 1923; s. William and Ethel (Greenberg) Scheibel; m. Madge Mila Ragland, Mar. 3, 1950 (dec. Jan. 1977); m. Marian Diamond, Sept. 1982. BA, Columbia U., NYC, 1944, MD, 1946; MS, U. Ill., 1952. Intern Mt. Sinai Hosp., NYC, 1946-47; resident in psychiatry Barnes and McMillan Hosp., St. Louis, 1947-48, Ill. Neuropsychiat. Inst., Chgo., 1950-52; asst. prof. psychiatry and anatomy U. Tenn. Med. Sch., 1952-53, assoc. prof., 1953-55, UCLA Med. Ctr., 1955-67, prof., 1967—, mem. Brain Rsch. Inst., 1960—, acting dir. Brain Rsch. Inst., 1987-90, dir., 1990-95. Cons. in field. Contbr. numerous articles to tech. jours, chpts. to books.; mem. editl. bd. Brain Rsch., 1967-77, Developmental Psychobiology, 1968—, Internat. Jour. Neurosci., 1969—, Jour. Biol. Psychiatry, 1968—, Jour. Theoretical Biology, 1980—; assoc. editor News Report, 1989—. Mem. Pres.'s Commn. on Aging, Nat. Inst. Aging, 1980—. Served with AUS, 1943-46; from lt. to capt. M.C. AUS, 1948-50. Guggenheim fellow (with wife), 1953-54, 59; recipient Disting. Svc. award Calif. Soc. Biomed. Rsch., 1998. Fellow Am. Acad. Arts and Scis., Norwegian Acad. Scis., Am. Psychiat. Assn. (life, Harriet and Charles Luckman Disting. Tchg. award 1997) AAAS; mem. Am. Neurol. Assn., Soc. Neurosci., Pyschiat. Rsch. Assn., Soc. Biol. Psychiatry, So. Calif. Psychiat. Assn. Home: 16231 Morrison St Encino CA 91436-1331 Office: UCLA Dept Neurobiology Los Angeles CA 90024 Business E-Mail: scheibel@mednet.ucla.edu.

SCHEIBER, STEPHEN CARL, psychiatrist; b. NYC, May 2, 1938; s. Irving Martin and Frieda Olga (Schor) S.; m. Mary Ann McDonnell, Sept. 14, 1965; children: Lisa Susan, Martin Irving, Laura Ann. BA, Columbia Coll., 1960; MD, SUNY, Buffalo, 1964. Diplomate Am. Bd. Psychiatry and Neurology. Intern Mary Fletcher Hosp., Burlington, Vt., 1964-65; resident in psychiatry Strong Meml. Hosp., Rochester, NY, 1967-70; asst. prof. U. Ariz., Tucson, 1970-76, assoc. prof., 1976-81, prof., 1981-86; exec. sec. Am. Bd. Psychiatry and Neurology, Inc., Deerfield, Ill., 1986-89, exec. v.p., 1989—2006; pres., CEO Isaac Ray Ctr., Inc., Chgo., 2008—10. Adj. prof. psychiatry Northwestern U., Chgo., 1986—, Med. Coll. Wis., Milw., 1986-2006, clin. prof. psychiatry, 2006—. Co-editor: The Impaired Physician, 1983, Certification, Recertification and Lifetime Learning in Psychiatry, 1994, Core Competencies for Psychiatric Practice, 2003, Core Competencies for Neurologists, 2003; contbr. articles to profl. jours. Mem. med. adv. com. Casas de los Ninos, Tucson, 1974-86; mem. mental health adv. com. Tucson Health Planning Coun., 1974-75; med. student interviewer Office of Med. Edn., 1975; mem. Glenbrook (Ill.) North H.S. Boosters Club, 1988-91; treas. Robert E. Jones Found., 1988-96. Surgeon USPHS, 1965-67. Recipient Outstanding Tchr. award, U. Ariz., 1986, Disting. Life and Career Achievement award, SUNY, Buffalo Med. Alumni Assn., 1998; grantee Group Therapy Outcome Studies on Inpatient Svc., 1980, Dialysis and Schizophrenia Pilot Project, NIH, 1978. Fellow: Am. Assn. Dirs. Psychiat. Residency Tng. (pres. 1981—82), Am. Coll. Psychiatrists (bd. regents 1992—2001, treas. 1995—2001, Disting. Svc. award 2007), Group for Advancement of Psychiatry (life; invited mem., chmn. mem. edn. com. 1987—91, bd. dirs., sec. 1993—97, pres.-elect 1997—99, pres. 1999—2001), Am. Psychiat. Assn. (life; chmn. impaired physician com. 1985—88, cons. 1988—92, 2008—09, life sec. 2006—08, v.p. 2008—10, pres. 2010—, Disting. Life Fellow 2002, Vestermark award 2007), Assn. Acad. Psychiatry (life; parliamentary sec. 1979—84, treas. 1984—88, pres.-elect 1988—89, pres. 1989—90, Lifetime Educator award 2002, Disting. Life Fellow 2006); mem.: Am. Bd. Med. Specialties (Disting. Svc. award 2007), Benjamin Rush Soc. (sec. treas. 2004—06, v.p. 2006—08, pres. 2008—10), Oracle Heights Club (pres. 1983—84). Democrat. Jewish. Office: Isaac Ray Ctr Inc 1725 W Harrison St #110 Chicago IL 60612

SCHEINER, DAVID LAWRENCE, internist; b. Buffalo, Sept. 3, 1938; MD, Columbia U. Coll. Physicians and Surgeons, 1963. Cert. Am. Bd. Internal Medicine, 1970, lic. Ill.; cert. advocate, attending physician, advocate Ill. Mo. Hosp. Med. intern U. Chgo. Hosp., 1963—64, resident, 1964—67, gen. internist; advocate Hyde Pk. Med. Group. Primary care physician Barak Obama, 1987—2009. Office: Advocate Med Group Hyde Pk 1301 E 47th St Chicago IL 60653 Office Phone: 773-493-8212. Office Fax: 773-955-2166.

SCHEINMAN, STEVEN JAY, dean, medical educator; b. Monticello, NY, Oct. 22, 1951; 2 children. AB summa cum laude, Amherst Coll., 1973; MD cum laude, Yale U., 1977. Diplomate Am. Bd. Internal Medicine in Nephrology, lic. physician N.Y., Conn. Resident internal medicine Yale-New Haven Hosp., 1977-80; chief resident internal medicine Upstate Med. Ctr., Syracuse, NY, 1980-81, fellow nephrology, 1981-83, Yale-New Haven Hosp., 1983-84; asst. prof. medicine SUNY Upstate Med. U., Syracuse, 1984-90, asst. prof. pharmacology, 1988-90, assoc. prof. medicine and pharmacology, 1990-94, prof. medicine and pharmacology, 1994—, chief nephrology divsn. dept. medicine, 1994—2004, exec. v.p., dean Coll. Medicine, 2004—, officer-in-charge, 2006. Vis. scientist MRC Molecular Medicine Group, Royal Postgrad. Med. Sch. Hammersmith Hosp., London, 1992, London, 95; vis. scholar dept. biochemistry U. Oxford, 1985; attending physician U. Hosp., Syracuse, Crouse-Irving Meml. Hosp., Syracuse, VA Med. Ctr., Syracuse; dir. Nephrology Fellowship Program, 1993—; mem. NY State Coun. on Grad. Med. Edn.; spkr. seminars, confs., orgns. Assoc. editor Neph SAP, 2002—04; mem. editl. bd. Yale Jour. Biology and Medicine, 1975—77, Jour. Am. Soc. Nephrology, 2000—02, mem. NIDDK Spl. Rev. Group, 1998—; contbr. articles to profl. jours. Recipient Lange award, Yale U. Sch. Medicine, 1976, Resident Merit award, ACP (Conn. chpt.), 1980, Nat. Rsch. Svc. award, NIH, 1981—83, Clin. Investigator award, 1985—90, Charles R. Ross Rsch. award, SUNY-Health Sci. Ctr., 1992, Pres.'s award for Excellence and Leadership in Rsch., SUNY Upstate Med. U., 2001, Chancellor's Rsch. Recognition award, SUNY, 2002; grantee, Nat. Inst. Arthritis Diabetes Digestive and Kidney Diseases, 1981—83, 1985—90, 1995—2002, 2000—04, 2003—, Am. Heart Assn., 1985, 1988—90, 1990—91, 1992—95, 1995—97, NATO, 1995—98. Mem.: Rsch. Found. SUNY (bd. mem. 2007—), Assn. Am. Med. Colls. Coun. Deans, Assn. Subspecialty Profs., Nat. Kidney Found., Am. Heart Assn. Coun. on Kidney, Am. Soc. Bone and Mineral Rsch., Am. Physiol. Soc., Internat. Soc. Nephrology, Am. Soc. Nephrology (mem. editl. bd. Jour. 2000—02), Am. Fedn. Med. Rsch., Am. Soc. Clin. Investigation, Alpha Omega Alpha, Phi Beta Kappa. Office: Office of Dean SUNY Upstate Med Univ 1257 Weiskotten Hall Syracuse NY 13210 Office Phone: 315-464-9720. Business E-Mail: scheinms@upstate.edu. *

SCHEKMAN, RANDY W., molecular biology administrator, biochemist; b. St. Paul, Dec. 30, 1948; married, 1973; 1 child. BA, UCLA, 1970; PhD in Biochemistry, Stanford U., 1975; PhD (hon.), U. Geneva, 1997. Fellow U. Calif., San Diego, 1974-76, from asst. to assoc. prof. Berkeley, 1976-83, prof., 1983—, head divsn. biochemistry and molecular biology, 1990-97, co-chair dept. molecular and cellular biology, 1997—. Fellow Woodrow Wilson Found., 1970, Cystic Fibrosis Found., 1974, John S. Guggenheim Found., 1982-83; recipient Research award in microbiology & immunology, Eli Lilly, 1987, Lewis S. Rosenstiel award in basic biomedical sci., 1994, Gairdner Found. Internat. award, 1996, Albert Lasker award for basic med. rsch., Albert and Mary Lasker Found., 2002, Louisa Gross Horwtiz prize, Columbia U., 2002; named Amgen award lecturer, Protein Soc., 1999, Berkeley Faculty Rsch. lecturer, U. Calif., 1999. Mem. Am. Soc. Microbiology, Am. Soc. Biochemists & Molecular Biologists, Am. Acad. of Arts & Sciences (elected 2000), NAS (elected 1992); hon. mem. Japanese Biochemical Soc.; foreign assoc. EMBO. Achievements include research on molecular mechanism of secretion and membrane assembly in eucaryotic cells. Office: U Calif Dept Molecular Cell Bio 401 Barker Hall Spc 3202 Berkeley CA 94720-3202 Office Phone: 510-642-5686. E-mail: schekman@uclink4.berkeley.edu. *

SCHELBERT, HEINRICH RUEDIGER, nuclear medicine physician; b. Wuerzburg, Germany, Nov. 5, 1939; MD, U. Würzburg, Germany, 1964. Diplomate Am. Bd. Nuclear Medicine. Intern Mercy Med. Ctr., Phila., 1966-67, resident, 1967-68, 70-71; resident in cardiology U. Dusseldorf, Germany, 1971-72; fellow in cardiology, resident in nuclear medicine U. Calif., San Diego, 1968-69, asst. rsch. cardiologist, 1972-75, assoc. rsch. radiologist, 1975-76; hosp. assoc. UCLA Med. Ctr., 1977—; prof. radiol. scis. UCLA Sch. Medicine, 1980-90, prof. pharmacol. and radiol. scis., 1993—. Editor-in-chief: Jour. Nuc. Medicine, 2004. Recipient Georg von Hevesy prize 2d Internat. Congress World Fedn. Nuclear Medicine and Radiation Biology, 1978, 3d Internat. Congress World Fedn. Nuclear Medicine and Radiation Biology, 1982, Disting. Sci. award, Acad. Molecular Imaging, 2006. Fellow Am. Coll. Cardiology; mem. Am. Heart Assn. (disting. scientific achievement award 1989), Soc. Nuclear Medicine (Herrman L. Blumgart pioneer lectr. award 1989, George De Hevesy Nuclear Medicine Pioneer award 1998), German Soc. Nuc. Med. (hon.), Swiss Soc. Nuc. Medicine (hon.; editor-in-chief, nuc. medicine). Office: David Geffen Sch Medicine UCLA Dept Molecular Med B2 085J Box 956948 Los Angeles CA 90095-6948 Office Phone: 310-825-3076. Business E-Mail: hschelbert@mednet.ucla.edu.

SCHELL, CATHERINE LOUISE, physician; b. Niskayuna, NY, Jan. 27, 1948; m. Richard J. Rathe, Jan. 7, 1986. BA, Ind. U., 1970, MA, 1974; MLS, Simmons Coll., 1975; MD, Am. U. Caribbean, Montserrat, 1983. Diplomate Am. Bd. Family Practice; cert. CAQ Geriatrics. Libr. Calder Med. Libr., U. Miami, Fla., 1975-78; libr., dir. Mercy Hosp., Miami, 1978-79; libr. Miami-Dade C.C., 1978-80; intern Med. Coll. Ga., Rome, 1983; resident U. Wyo., Cheyenne, 1985-87; staff physician Vets. Hosp., Cheyenne, 1986-88, Dept. of Army, U.S. Dept. Def., Ft. Devens, Mass., 1988-90, Vets. Hosp., Lake

City, Fla., 1990-93, staff physician, fellow Gainesville, Fla., 1993-95; fellow in geriatrics U. Fla., 1993-95, fellow in geriatrics internal medicine, 1995, fellow geriatrics internal medicine, 1995; physician Dept. of Navy, 1995-96; pres. Med. Decisions Software, Inc., 1999—; physician Vets. Outpatient Clinic, 2004—, Va. Hosp., 2007—, Bay Pines Va, 2008—. Tchr. ESL YMCA Internat., Taipei, Taiwan, 1970-71. Title IIB fellow Simmons Coll., 1974-75; Ford Found. grantee, Ind. U., 1969-70. Fellow Am. Acad. Family PRactice; mem. Acad. Health Sci., Med. Libr. Assn.

SCHELL, NORMAN BARNETT, preventive medicine physician, consultant; b. NYC, May 25, 1925; s. Jack and Ada Sylvia (Rosen) S.; m. Lila Barbara Mendelsohn, Aug. 27, 1950; children: Martin, Judith, Steven. AB cum laude, NYU, 1946, MD, 1950; MPH, Harvard U., 1971. Diplomate Am. Bd. Pediats., Am. Bd. Preventive Medicine, Nat. Bd. Med. Examiners; lic. physician, N.Y. Rotating intern Beth Israel Hosp., NYC, 1950-51; asst. resident in pediats. Mt. Sinai Hosp., NYC, 1951—52; clin. fellow in pediats. N.Y.-Cornell Med. Ctr., NYC, 1952-53; pvt. practice Jericho and Hicksville, NY, 1956-69; pub. health physician Nassau County Health Dept., Mineola, NY, 1969-76, dep. commr., 1976-90. Asst. prof. preventive medicine SUNY, Stony Brook, 1974-90; pediat. cons. N.Y. State Health Dept., 1956-69, HEW Project Head Start, N.Y.C., 1968-75; emeritus pediat. staff Nassau County Med. Ctr. Author: Keys to Childhood Illnesses, 1992; contbr. articles to profl. jours. Lt. M.C., USN, 1953-55, capt. M.C., USNR, 1981-85. Recipient Physician Recognition award AMA, 1970, Grade 1A Health Officer N.Y. State Health Dept., 1973. Fellow Am. Acad. Pediats. (com. on sch. health 1971-77, citation com. on med. edn. 1977), Am. Coll. Preventive Medicine, N.Y. Acad. Medicine; mem. Am. Coll. Legal Medicine (assoc.), Nassau County Med. Soc. (chmn. sch. health com.), Harvard Club N.Y.C., West Point Club, Phi Beta Kappa. Avocations: photography, classical music, computer technology. Home and Office: 999 Hwd Rd NE Apt 130 Marietta GA 30068

SCHELLER, REINHOLD, psychologist; b. Wuerzburg, Germany, Oct. 16, 1941; s. Philipp Scheller and Rosa Hummel; m. Mall Maesak, Aug. 17, 1968; children: Christin, Bjoern. Diploma in Psychology, U. Erlangen-Nuernberg, Germany, 1967, PhD, 1970. Cert. client-ctr. therapist U. Trier, Germany, 1979, lic. psychol. psychotherapist 2000. Wissenschaftlicher mitarbeiter U. Erlangen-Nuernberg, 1967—71; asst. prof. U. Trier, 1972, wissenschaftlicher rat und prof., 1973—74, abteilungsvorsteher und prof., 1975—86, prof., 1987—. Author: (book) Psychologie der Berufswahl und der beruflichen Entwicklung, 1976; editor: Brennpunkte der Klinischen Psychologie (6 Vols.), 1981—83, Sucht und Rueckfall, 1995. Mem.: Deutsche Gesellschaft fuer Psychologie. Avocations: hiking, swimming. Home: Am Knieberg 15 Trier 54293 Germany Office: Univ Trier Fachbereich I Psychologie Trier 54286 Germany Home Phone: 4906512019980116; Office Phone: 4906512012057. Office Fax: 4906512012059. Business E-Mail: scheller@uni-trier.de.

SCHELLER, RICHARD H., physiologist, science educator; b. Milw., Oct. 30, 1953; BA in Biochemistry with honors, U. Wis., Madison, 1975; PhD in Chemistry, Calif. Inst. Tech., 1980. Postdoctoral fellow divsn. biology Calif. Inst. Tech., 1980—81; postdoctoral fellow in molecular neurobiology Columbia U. Coll. Physicians and Surgeons, 1981—82; asst. prof. dept. biol. sciences Stanford U., Calif., 1982—87, assoc. prof. dept. biol. sciences Calif., 1987—90, assoc. prof. dept. molecular and cellular physiology and dept. biol. sciences Calif., 1990—93, assoc. prof. dept. biol. sciences by courtesy Calif., 1990—93, prof. dept. molecular and cellular physiology and dept. biol. sciences Calif., 1993—2001, prof. dept. biol. sciences Calif., 1993; assoc. investigator Howard Hughes Med. Inst., Stanford U. Med. Ctr., 1990—94, investigator, 1994—2001; sr. v.p., research Genentech, Inc., 2001—03, exec. v.p., research, 2003—08, chief scientific officer, 2008—09, exec. v.p., research and early develop., 2009—. Mem. molecular, cellular and devel. neurobiology rev. com. NIMH, 1993—96; mem. sci. adv. bd. Hereditary Disease Found., 1995—96; mem. neurobiology adv. bd. Cold Spring Harbor Lab., 1995; mem. sr. rev. com. McKnight Endowment Fund, 1995; mem. adv. bd. Nat. Adv. Mental Health Coun., NIH, 1996; adj. prof. biochemistry and biophysics, Sch. Medicine U. Calif., San Francisco, 2004—. Mem. editl. bd. Jour. Neurosci., 1984—90, DNA, 1984—, Ann. Rev. Neurosci., 1985—90, Molecular Brain Rsch., 1985, Cellular and Molecular Neurobiology, 1986, Synapse, 1989—91, Neuron, 1990, Current Opinion in Neurobiology, 1990, sect. editor Jour. Neurosci., 1991—95, monitoring editor Jour. Cell Biology, 1991, assoc. editor Genes to Cells, 1995; contbr. articles to profl. jours. Recipient Basil O'Connor award, March of Dimes Found., 1983, Presdl. Young Investigator award, 1985, Alan T. Waterman award, NSF, 1989, Merit award, NIMH, 1992, W. Alden Spencer award, Columbia U., 1993, Life Sciences Disting. Alumni award, U. Wis.-Madison Coll. Agricultural and Life Sciences, 2009; co-recipient Kavli prize for Neuroscience, Norwegian Acad. Sci. and Letters, Kavli Found. and Norway's Ministry of Edn. and Rsch., 2010; fellow, NIH, 1976—80, 1981—82, Alfred P. Sloan Found., 1984, Klingstein fellow in Neurosci., 1985; scholar, McKnight Found., 1983, Pew scholar in biomed. scis., 1986, Camile and Henry Dreyfus Tchr. scholar, 1986. Fellow: Acad. of Arts and Sciences; mem.: NAS (award in Molecular Biology 1997), Soc. for Neurosci. (young investigator award selection com. 1996). Office: Genentech Inc 1 DNA Way South San Francisco CA 94080-4990 Office Phone: 650-225-1000.

SCHELLING, THOMAS CROMBIE, economist; b. Oakland, Calif., Apr. 14, 1921; s. John and Zelda (Ayres) Schelling; m. Corinne T. Saposs, Sept. 13, 1947 (div. 1991); children: Andrew, Thomas, Daniel, Robert; m. Alice M. Coleman, Nov. 8, 1991. AB in Economics, U. Calif., Berkeley, 1944; PhD in Economics, Harvard U., 1951; D (hon.), Yale U., 2009. Economist US Bur. of Budget, Washington, 1945—46, The Marshall Plan, Paris, Copenhagen, 1948—50, Exec. Office of Pres., The White House, Washington, 1951—53; assoc. prof., then prof. economics Yale U., New Haven, 1953-58; prof. economics Harvard U., Cambridge, Mass., 1958-90, Lucius N. Littauer prof. polit. economy, 1969—90; prof. economics and pub. affairs U. Md., College Park, 1990—2003, disting. prof. economics emeritus, 2003—. Sr. staff mem. RAND Corp., Santa Monica, Calif., 1958—59; chmn. rsch. adv. bd. Com. Econ. Devel., Washington, 1978—81, 1984—85; mem. mil. econ. adv. panel CIA, 1980—85; dir. Inst. Study of Smoking Behavior & Policy, Harvard U., 1984—90; co-faculty mem. New Eng. Complex Systems Inst. Author: Nat. Income Behavior, 1951, Internat. Economics, 1958, The Strategy of Conflict, 1960, Arms and Influence, 1966, Micromotives and Macrobehavior, 1978, Thinking Through the Energy Problem, 1979, Choice and Consequence, 1984, Strategies of Commitment, 2006; co-author (with Morton H. Halperin): Strategy and Arms Control, 1961. Recipient Frank E. Seidman Disting. award in polit. economy, 1977; Nobel Prize in Econ. Sci., 2005. Fellow AAAS, Assn. for Pub. Policy Analysis and Mgmt., Am. Econ. Assn. (pres. 1991, Disting. Fellow award); mem. NAS (Award Behavioral Rsch. Relevant to the Prevention of Nuclear War, 1993), Inst. Medicine, Ea. Econ. Assn. (pres. 1996). Office: U Md Dept Economics 3105 Tydings Hall College Park MD 20742-0001 Mailing: 4506 Wetherill Rd Bethesda MD 20816 Business E-Mail: tschelli@umd.edu.

SCHENCK, JOHN FREDERIC, physician; b. Decatur, Ind., June 7, 1939; s. John C. Schenck and Mildred Blosser; m. Jane Stark, Oct. 12, 1962 (div. 1982); children: Brooke, Kimberly, David; m. Susan J. Kalia, Oct. 8, 1994; 1 stepchild, Tania. BS in Physics, Rensselaer Poly. Inst., 1961, PhD in Physics, 1965; MD, Albany Med. Coll., NY, 1977. Staff scientist electronics lab. GE, Syracuse, NY, 1965-73; assoc. prof. elec. engring. Syracuse (NY) U., 1970-73; intern Albany Med. Ctr. Hosp., 1977-78; staff mem., sr. scientist GE Global Rsch., Schenectady, NY, 1973—; mem. med. staff Ellis Hosp., Schenectady, 1981—98. Adj. asst. prof. dept. radiology U. Pa., 1983-2000; adj. prof. neurology Albany Med. Coll., 2003-; chmn. Workshop on Advances in Magnetic Resonance Imaging Safety and Compatibility, McLean, Va., 1996; dir. Magnetic Resonance Imaging rsch. Neuroscis. Rsch. Ctr., Albany Med. Ctr., 2001-11. Contbr. articles pub. to profl. jours. Recipient S.S. Greenfield award Am. Assn. Physicists in Medicine, 1993; Nat. Merit scholar, 1957-61; NSF fellow, 1962-63, Coolidge fellow GE, 2003. Fellow: Am. Phys. Soc., Internat. Soc. Magnetic Resonance Medicine (Gold medal, 2009); mem. IEEE, AAAS, NY Acad. Scis., Sigma Xi. Achievements include 20 patents for magnetic resonance imaging. Home: 22 E Claremont Dr Voorheesville NY 12186-9104 Office: GE Global Rsch Bldg K1 NMR Schenectady NY 12309 Office Phone: 518-387-6543. Business E-Mail: schenck@research.ge.com.

SCHENCK, ROBERT ROY, hand surgeon; s. Isaac Barrett Schenck and Pearl Irene Murnan; m. Ruth Helm (div.); children: Rebecca VanNydeggen, Karen Schmidt, Heidi McCluskey, Robert Paul; m. Marcia Anne Whitney, June 13, 1982. B cum laude, Taylor U., 1952; MD, U. Ill., Chgo., 1955. Diplomate Am. Bd. Plastic Surgery. Asst. attending plastic and orthop. surgery Rush U., Chgo., 1972—80, dir. sect. hand surgery, 1972—2008, assoc. attending plastic and orthop. surgery, 1980—85, sr. attending plastic and orthop. surgery, 1985—, prof. emeritus plastic surgery, 2008—. Cons. orthop. and gen. surgery West Suburban Hosp., Oak Park, Ill., 1973—2008; pres. Hand Therapy Ltd., Chgo., 1985—95. Bd. dirs. Bishop Anderson House, Chgo., 2004—08; founding pres. The Hand Surgery Endowment, 1996—2001. Sr. surgeon USPHS, 1957—59. Mem.: Am. Assn. Hand Surgery. Episcopalian. Achievements include invention of dynamic traction for finger fracture. Avocations: photography, art, sculpting. Home: 1100 N Lake Shore Dr Apt 33-A Chicago IL 60611 Office: Hand Surgery Ltd Box 220580 Chicago IL 60622-9998 Office Phone: 312-738-3426. Personal E-mail: rschenckmd@aol.com. Business E-Mail: handsurgeryltd@aol.com.

SCHENDEL, STEPHEN ALFRED, surgeon, educator; b. Mpls., Oct. 10, 1947; s. Alfred Reck and Jeanne Shirley (Hagquist) S.; children: Elliott, Mélisande. BA, St. Olaf Coll., Northfield, Minn., 1969; BS with high distinction, U. Minn., 1971, DDS, 1973; diplome asst. etranger with high honors, U. Nantes, France, 1980; MD, U. Hawaii, 1983. Diplomate Am. Bd. Plastic Surgery, Nat. Bd. Med. Examiners, Nat. Bd. Dental Examiners, Am. Bd. Oral and Maxillofacial Surgery (adv. com., bd. examiner 1991-95). Intern, then resident in oral and maxillofacial surgery Parkland Meml. Hosp., Dallas, 1975-79; resident in gen. surgery Baylor U. Med. Ctr., Dallas, 1983-84, Stanford (Calif.) U. Med. Ctr., 1984-86, resident in plastic surgery, 1986-89, acting assoc. prof. surgery, 1989-91, assoc. prof., 1991-95, head divsn. plastic and reconstructive surgery, 1992—2002, dir. residency tng., 1992-98, chmn. dept. functional restoration, 1994—2001, prof. surgery, 1995—2002, prof. emeritus surgery, 2007; head plastic surgery, dir. Craniofacial Ctr. Lucile Salter Packard Children's Hosp., Stanford, 1991—2007, chief pediat. surgery, 1997—2002. Asst. to Dr. Paul Tessier, Paris, 1987-88; asst. dept. stomatology and maxillofacial surgery Centre Hospitalier Regional Nantes, 1979-80; med. bd. Lucile Salter Packard Children's Hosp. at Stanford, 1991—. Assoc. editor Selected Readings in Oral and Maxillofacial Surgery, 1989—; mem. editl. bd. Jour. Cranio-Maxillofacial Surgery; contbr. articles to profl. jours., chpts. to books. Recipient Disting. Alumnus award St. Olaf Coll., 1993; Fulbright fellow, Nantes, 1979-80, Chateaubriand fellow Govt. of France, 1987-88. Fellow ACS, Am. Acad. Pediat.; mem. Internat. Soc. Craniofacial Surgeons, European Assn. Cranio-Maxillofacial Surgeons, Am. Soc. Pediat. Plastic Surgeons, Am. Assn. Plastic Surgery, Soc. Baylor Surgeons (founding), Am. Cleft Palate-Craniofacial Assn., Am. Soc. Plastic Surgeons (sec. 1996—), Am. Soc. Maxillofacial Surgeons (sec., pres. 2000-01), Assn. Acad. Chairmen Plastic Surgery, Zedplast (bd. dirs. 1993—), Omicron Kappa Upsilon. Avocations: fly fishing, painting and sculpture. Office: Stanford U Med Ctr Divsn Plastic Reconstr Surg 770 Welch Rd Ste 400 Palo Alto CA 94304 Home Phone: 650-261-1031; Office Phone: 650-723-5824, 650-328-0511. Business E-Mail: sschendel@stanford.edu.

SCHENK, DALE BERNARD, pharmaceutical executive, neuroscientist; m. Elizabeth O. Sarah (dec.); children: Anais, Sara, Max, Sam; m. Maria Torres. BA cum laude, U. Calif., San Diego, 1979, PhD, 1984. Scientsit Scios/Nova, Mountain View, Calif., 1984-87; sr. scientist and project leader Athena Neuroscis., South San Francisco, 1987-90, sr. scientist, dir. immunochemsitry, 1990-93, project leader, mgr., 1993-94, dir. neurobiology, 1994—98; v.p. neurobiology Elan Corp., plc, South San Francisco, 1998—99, sr. v.p. discovery rsch., 1999—2003, sr. v.p., chief sci. officer, 2003—, exec. v.p., chief sci. officer, 2007—. Presenter in field. Ad Hoc reviewer jours.; contbr. numerous articles to profl. jours.; patentee in field. Grantee Am. Liver Found., 1983, NIH, 1986, 89, 90. Mem. AAAS, Am. Soc. Hypertension (founder), US Chess Fedn. Office: Elan Corp plc 800 Gateway Blvd South San Francisco CA 94080 Office Phone: 650-877-0900.

SCHENK, QUENTIN FREDERICK, retired social work educator, psychologist, mayor; b. Fort Madison, Iowa, Aug. 25, 1922; s. Fred Edward John and Ida (Sabrowsky) S.; m. Patricia J. Kelley, Aug. 6, 1946 (div. Apr. 1970); children: Fred W. (dec. 1972), Patricia, Karl, Martha; m. Emmy Lou Willson, May 23, 1970 (dec. Dec. 7, 2007). BA, Willamette U., 1948; MS, U. Wis., 1950, MS in Social Work, 1953, PhD, 1953. Lic. ind. clin. social worker, Wis.; cert. longterm care, Ariz. Asst. prof. social work U. Wis.-Madison, 1953-55, prof., chmn. extension social work, 1961-63; prof., former dean Sch. Social Welfare, Milw., 1962-68, prof. emeritus, 1990—; assoc. prof. U. Mo., 1955-61; project specialist Ford Found., 1968-71. Spl. cons. on urban mission in Africa United Presbyn. Ch., 1971-, World Council Chs., 1971-; advisor to Haile Sellassie I U., Addis Ababa, Ethiopia, 1968-71; Alderman City of Cedarburg (Wis.), 1974-82, mayor, 1982-86. Author: (with Emmy Lou Schenk) Pulling Up Roots, 1978, Welfare Society and the Helping Professions, 1981; author sect. on Ethiopia, Welfare in Africa, 1987; contbr. articles, bulls., reports to profl. lit. Mem. Nat. Trust for Hist. Preservation, Wis. Hist. Preservation Negotiating Bd., 1975-76; chmn. bd. Guest House, Milw., 1987-89; mem. Sierra Club, Planned Parenthood, Unitarian Ch. S.E. Ariz. (v.p. 1999), ACLU, Dem. Party of Ariz. With USNR, 1942—46, carrier pilot WWII, ret. lt. Decorated Air medal with four gold stars, Disting. Flying Cross; recipient Presdl. citation Pres. Harry Truman, 1948; scholar Fulbright Found., 1959-60. Mem. DAV (life), Am. Assn. Ret. Persons, Aircraft Owners and Pilots Assn., Nat. Audubon Soc., Nature Conservancy. Democrat. Unitarian Universalist. Avocations: hiking, boating, travel. Home: 4400 Avenida Cochise Sierra Vista AZ 85635-5712 Personal E-mail: qschenk@mac.com.

SCHENKER, JOSEPH GEORGE, physician, obstetrics and gynecology educator; b. Cracow, Poland, Nov. 20, 1933; s. Ignancy and Anna (Greshler) S.; m. Ekaterina Idels, 1959; children: Inon, Eran. MD, Hebrew U., Jerusalem, 1959. Intern Tel Hashomer Hosp., 1958-59; resident in ob-gyn. Hadassah Med. Ctr., Jerusalem, 1962-68, temp. chief physician ob-gyn., 1965-72, permanent chief physician ob-gyn., 1973-78, chmn. dept. ob-gyn., 1978—; rsch. fellow divsn. of reprodn. U. Pa., Phila., 1972-73; dep. dir. Hadassah Med. Ctr., 1977-80; ob-gyn. lectr. Sch. Medicine Hebrew U., Jerusalem, 1968-71, sr. lectr., 1971-76, assoc. prof. ob-gyn., 1976-79, prof. ob-gyn., 1979—, chmn. com. postgrad. tng. in ob-gyn., 1973-78, exec. chief tchg., 1977-80, 82-85, mem. com. for med. edn. Med. Sch., 1981-85. Chmn. directory bd. exam. in ob-gyn. State of Israel, 1979-83; chmn. adv. com. ob-gyn. Ministry of Health, State of Israel, 1979-86, chmn. com. residency tng., 1985-90, dep. chmn. sci. coun., 1985-90, chmn. com. for lic. and internship exam., 1988—, mem. pub. coun. demography, 1994—, chmn. bd. examination for med. lic. and internship, 1988—; mem. coun. for syllabus residency tng. Israel Sci. Coun., 1980-85; chmn. European Residency Exch. Program, Extended European Bd. Gyn. and Obstetrics, 1992—; mem. Internat. Sci. Adv. Bd. Jewish Physicians, 1985—; judge Ministry of Justice of Israel, Dist. Ct. of Appeals, 1986—; mem. com. on control of experiments in animals Israel Acad. Scis., 1987—; mem. adv. com. Physician Licensing, State of Israel, 1988—; mem. adv. bd. ob. interventions WHO, 1989, com. on recent advances in medically assisted reprodn., 1990, com. on assisted reprodn., 1991; chmn. Fedn. Internat. Gynecology and Obstets. Com. Study of Ethical Aspects of Human Reproduction, 1994. Editor: Recent Advances in Pathophysiol. Conditions in Pregnancy, 1984, The Intrauterine Life: Management and Treatment, 1986, Advances in Assisted Reproductive Technologies, 1990; mem. editl. bd. Human Reprodn., Internat. Jour. Gynecology and Obstets., Gynecol. Endocrinology, Asia-Oceania Jour. Ob-Gyn., Fertility and Sterility, Jour. Assisted Reprodn. and Genetics, Fetal Diagnosis and Therapy, Internat. Jour. Feto-Maternal Medicine, Global Bioethics, European Jour. Ob., Gyn., and Reproductive Biology, Early Pregnancy: Biology and Medicine, Jour. of the Russian Assn. of Human Reproduction; contbr. more than 430 articles to profl. jours. With Israel Med. Corps, 1959-62. Fellow Am. Coll. Ob. Gyn. (hon.); mem. German Soc. Ob-Gyn. (hon.), Polish Soc. Ob-Gyn. (hon.), Fertility and Sterility Soc. Peru (hon.), Rumanian Soc. Ob-Gyn. (hon.), Implantation Soc. Japan (hon.), Hungarian Soc. Ob-Gyn. (hon.), Macedonian Assn. Gynecologists and Obstetricians (hon.), Israel Med. Assn. (sci. coun. 1980-85, pres. coun. 1980-84, 84-88), Israel Soc. Ob-Gyn. (pres. Jerusalem chpt. 1976—, pres. 1984-89, 89-92, dep. pres. 1993—), Hadassah Chief Physician Orgn. (chmn. 1977-79), Hadassah Orgn. Heads of Dept. (active chmn. 1983-84), Women Coun. Israel, Fallopian Internat. Corr. Soc. (bd. dirs. 1984—), European Soc. Human Reprodn. (founder), Internat. Acad. Reproductive Medicine, Internat. Soc. for the Study of Pathophysiology of Pregnancy (founder), Internat. Soc. of the Fetus as a Patient (founder), European Soc. Reproductive and Embryology (mem. adv. com.), European Assn. Ob-Gyn. (mem. adv. com.), Asia-Oceania Soc. Ob-Gyn. (mem. adv. com.), Internat. Soc. Gynecol. Endocrinology (founder), Israel Soc. Endoscopic Surgery (founder), Am. Fertility Soc., Am. Assn. Planned Parenthood Physicians, Internat. Coll. Surgeons, Internat. Menopausal Soc., Internat. Soc. Study of Twins, Am. Assn. Laparoscopy, Soc. for Advancement of Contraception, Israel Soc. Family Planning, Israel Soc. Gerontology, Israel Soc. Endocrinology, Internat. Acad. Human Reproduction (pres. 1996), Royal Coll. Ob-Gyn. (hon.), among others. Jewish. Office: Hadassah U Dept Ob-Gyn 91120 Jerusalem Israel Office Phone: 972-50-784779. Business E-Mail: schenker@cc.huji.ac.il.

SCHENKER, MARC BENET, preventive medicine physician, medical educator, department chairman; b. LA, Aug. 25, 1947; s. Steve and Dosella Schenker; children: Yael, Phoebe, Hilary. BA, U. Calif., Berkeley, 1969; MD, U. Calif., San Francisco, 1973; MPH, Harvard U., Boston, 1980. Instr. medicine Harvard U., Boston, 1980-82; asst. prof. medicine U. Calif., Davis, 1982-86, assoc. prof., 1986-92, prof., 1992—, chmn. dept. pub. health scis., 1995—. Fellow ACP; mem. Am. Thoracic Soc., Am. Pub. Health Assn., Soc. Epidemiologic Rsch., Am. Coll. Epidemiology, Soc. Occupl. Environ. Health, Internat. Commn. Occupl. Health, Assn. Tchrs. Preventive Medicine, Phi Beta Kappa, Alpha Omega Alpha. Office Phone: 530-752-5676.

SCHENKER, STEVEN, internist, educator; b. Poland, Oct. 5, 1929; came to US, 1943, naturalized, 1946; s. Alfred and Ernestyna S.; m. Sally Ann Wood, May 11, 1956; children: Julie C. Schenker Burn, Steven A., David S., Andrew G., Jennifer E. Schenker Campeggi; m. Jo Ann Neumann, Nov. 24, 1985. BA, Cornell U., Ithaca, NY, 1951, MD, 1955. Intern Harvard Service-Boston City Hosp., 1955-56, resident in medicine, 1956-58; asst. prof. medicine U. Cin. Sch. Medicine, 1961-63; asst. prof. U. Tex., Southwestern Sch. Medicine, 1963-67, assoc. prof. medicine, 1967-70; prof. medicine, biochemistry, dir. div. gastroenterology Vanderbilt U. Sch. Medicine, Nashville VA Hosp., 1970-82; prof. medicine and pharmacology U. Tex. Sch. Medicine, San Antonio, 1982—2009, dir. divsn. gastroenterology, 1982—2001, prof. emeritus, 2010—. Chmn. study sect. Nat. Inst. on Alcohol Abuse and Addiction, 1980-83; chmn. study sects. VA, 1985-88. Editor: Hepatology, 1985-90; contbr. numerous articles in field to profl. jours. Recipient Markle award, 1963; Career Devel. award NIH, 1968; Jurzykowski Found. for Research in Medicine award, 1979, Alcoholism Research Soc. award 1987. Mem. Am. Assn. for Study of Liver Diseases (pres. 1980, Disting. Svc. award 1997), Am. Soc. Clin. Investigation, Assn. Am. Physicians, Am. Gastroent. Soc., Am. Soc. Pharm. and Exptl. Therapeutics, Am. Soc. Clin. Nutrition, Internat. Soc. for Study of Liver Diseases, Alpha Omega Alpha. Home: 26025 Mesa Oak Dr San Antonio TX 78255-3533 Office: U Tex Med Sch San Antonio TX 78284 Office Phone: 210-567-4878.

SCHEPERJANS, FILIP, physician; b. Castrop-Rauxel, Germany, Jan. 23, 1981; MD, Heinrich Heine U., Düsseldorf, Germany, 2006; doctoral student summa cum laude, C. & O. Vogt Inst. fur Hirnforschung, Düsseldorf, 2001—06; student, Nat. Hosp. Neurology and Neurosurgery, London, 2005, Mt. Sinai Sch. Medicine, NYC, 2005, U. Ctrl. Hosp., Helsinki, Finland, 2005—06. Rschr. Forschungszentrum Jülich, Germany, 2006—07; physician Health Ctr., Tuusula, Finland, 2007—08, HUS, Finland, 2008—; with U. Dusseldorf, 2008. Tutor Inst. Anatomy, Düsseldorf, 2002—03; lectr. Sch. Child Nursing, Düsseldorf, 2003—04. Contbr. scientific papers to profl. publs. Pilot, gen. aviation, 1999. Scholar, German Nat. Merit Found., 2002—06, German Academic Exch. Svc., 2005. Mem.: Duodecim, Finnish Med. Assn. Achievements include research in anatomical and neurochemical characterization and probabilistic mapping of the human brain.

SCHEPP, WOLFGANG, internist; b. Aachen, Germany, Sept. 23, 1955; s. Otto and Hildgegard (Buch) S.; m. Susanne Schwonzen, Apr. 1, 1958; children: Lukas, Johanna, Nicola. MD, Bonn U. Med. Sch., 1981; DSc, Munich U. Tech., 1988. Intern Bonn U. Med. Sch., Germany, 1983-84; resident Munich Tech. U., 1985-88; rsch. assoc. UCLA, 1989; cons. gastroenterologist Tech. U. Munich, 1990-97; head dept. gastroenterology Bogenhausen Acad. Tchg. Hosp., Munich, 1997—, med. dir., 2003—06. Fellow Am. Gastroenterol. Assn. (internat. mem.); mem. German Gastroenterol. Assn., German Soc. Internal Medicine, German Cancer Assn. Avocations: classical music, sailing, mountain hiking. Office Phone: +49-8992702061. E-mail: schepp.wolfgang@t-online.de.

SCHER, JORDAN MAYER, pharmacologist, psychiatrist, alcohol and drug abuse services professional; b. Balt. s. Robert Samuel and Marye Kremen Scher; m. Jeanne Nonken, July 20, 1954 (div. June 1960); children: Jan. Jo, Jill; Linda Anderson, 1960; 1 child: Gabhriel. BS, Wesleyan U., Middleton, Conn., 1945; MD, U. Md., Balt., 1949; PhD in Neuropsychopharmacology, Northwestern U., Evanston, Ill., 1957. Diplomate Am. Bd. Psychiatry and Neurology, Am. Bd. Med. Hypnosis, cert. addiction specialist Am. Acad. Health Care Providers in Addiction Disorders. Resident and fellow in psychiatry U. Md. Psychiat. Inst., Balt., 1953—55; fellow in psychiatry NIMH, Bethesda, Md., 1955—57; fellow in medicine, hypertension studies Cleve. Clinic Found., 1950—51; project dir., rsch. psychiatrist NIMH, 1955-57; dir. narcotics project Cook County (Ill.) Jail and Criminal Ct., 1957—59; coor. undergrad. psychiatry Northwestern U. Med. Sch., 1957—60; pvt. practice psychiatry Chgo., 1957—79; cons. Sheriff's Office and Cook County Jail, 1958—63; from asst. to assoc. prof. dept. neurology and psychiatry Northwestern U. Med. Sch., Chgo., 1960—63; dir. Chgo. Psychiat. Found. and Ontoanalytic Inst., Chgo., 1960—70; prof. dept. neurology and psychiatry Northwestern U., 1963—65; dir. psychiat. svcs. Bd. of Health, 1963—65; exec. dir. Nat. Coun. Drug Abuse, Chgo., 1971—79; dir. sct. on psychiatry and religion Yeshiva Torat Israel, Jerusalem, 1972—74; exec. dir. Methadone Maintenance Inst., Chgo., 1972—79; advisor acupuncture Nat. Inst. Acupuncture and Herbal Medicine, Taiwan, 1974—; psychiatrist cons. Diaspora Yeshiva, Jerusalem, 1980—; pvt. practice psychiatry Jerusalem, 1982—; dir. psychiatric unit Cook County Jail, 1958—63, dir., death row, 1958—63. Vis. prof. psychiatry and drug abuse Hebrew U., 1982-89; cons. psychiatry, Israel and numerous orgns.; rschr. in field; dir. Jerusalem Inst. Drug Abuse, 1980-85, Jerusalem House, Israel, 1989—; dir. drug abuse unit Ezrat Nashim, Detox, NYC, 1997-; advisor on drugs and alcohol Min. of Health, Israel; commn. on addiction, chmn. Adult Subcom. on Drug Abuse, City of Jerusalem. Author: Narcotic Detoxification as Acute Induced Panic Disorder: Neuropsychopharmacological Causes, 1996, Treatment, and Implications, A Monograph, 1992, (with L. Appleby, J. Cumming) Chronic Schizophrenia, 1959, Theories of the Mind, 1963, Drug Abuse in Industry: Growing Corporate Dilemma, 1973; co-editor: (with M. Segal): Drugs and the Law, vol. 1, Perspectives in Drug Abuse, 1989; founder, editor The Jour. Existential Psychiatry, 1959-70, Nat. Coun. Drug Abuse Drug/Health Alert, 1972-79; cons. Am. Psychiat. Assn. Jour., 1963-70, Jour. AMA, 1964-71; mem. editl. bd. Psychosomatics Jour., 1965-67, Human Context Jour., 1970-72, Medica Judaica Jour., 1971-72; co-editor: Perspectives in Drug Abuse, 1989; contbr. numerous articles to profl. jours.; patentee in field. Co-chair bus. adv. coun. Nat. Rep. Congl. Com., 2002-03; mem. Democratic Nat. Congregational Com., 2002-07. Lt. USNR, 1949-57. Recipient Key to City of St. Louis, 1969, Wisdom award of honor, Wisdom Soc., 1972, Pawlowski Peace prize, 1974, Physician's Recognition award, AMA, 1975—2004, DeQuincey prize in addiction rsch., 1993, Cert. of Honor 50 Yrs. of Dedicated Svc. to Med. Profession, AMA, 2002. Fellow AAAS, Royal Soc. Medicine, Am. Acad. Psychosomatic Medicine (program com.), World Med. Assn. (hon.; US com.), Comprehensive Medicine Assn., Am. Assn. Clin. and Exptl. Hypnosis, Nat. Acad. Religion and Mental Health, Am. Geriatric Soc., NY Acad. Scis.; mem. AMA, Am. Coll. Forensic Psychiatry, Am. Acad. Psychiatry and Law, Am. Acad. Psychiatry in Alcohol and Drug Abuse, Am. Soc. Neuroimaging, Am. Soc. Addiction Medicine, Am. Soc. Addiction Psychiatry, Am. Ontoanalytic Assn. for Existential Psychiatry (founder), Am. Soc. Psychoanalytic Physicians, Inc., Am. Med. Soc. Alcoholism, Am. Acad. Orthomolecular Psychiatry, Am. Med. Record Assn., Am. Soc. Group Psychotherapy and Psychodrama, Chgo. Soc. Assn. Execs., Ill. Rehab. Assn., Nat. Rehab. Assn., Nat. Coun. Crime and Delinquency, Chgo. Assn. Commerce and Industry, Assn. Advancement of Psychotherapy, Am. Soc. Group Psychotherapy and Psychodrama, Am. Assn. Psychoanalytic Physicians, Internat. Soc. Med. Hypnosis, Internat. Assn. Group Psychotherapy, Am. Psychiat. Assn., Internat. Ontoanalytic Assn., Vienna Med. Psychol. Soc. (hon.), Assn. Am. Med. Colls., Am. Acad. Neurology, Washington Psychiat. Soc., Am. Humanistic Psychology Assn., Am. Acad. Psychotherapists, Am. Soc. Psychoanalytic Medicine, Am. Group Psychotherapy Assn., Psychosynthesis Rsch. Found., Soc. Advancement of Gen. Systems Theory, Soc. Sci. Study of Sex, Human Ecology Found., Soc. Biol. Psychiatry, Am. Soc. Photobiology, Ill. Med. Soc., Sigma Xi, Phi Delta Epsilon. Jewish. Avocations: Biblical/Jewish-Christian studies, archaeology, cosmology, paleoanthropological studies on the origin and evolution of human mind and communication. Home Phone: 646-861-0047; Office Phone: 212-245-9585. Personal E-mail: jmsmdphd@gmail.com, jordanscher@yahoo.com.

SCHERER, MARCIA JOSLYN, psychologist, researcher, educator; b. Buffalo, June 9, 1948; d. Alfred John and Marjorie (Greene) J.; m. John Vincent Scherer Jr., Jan. 2, 1976. BS, Syracuse U., NY, 1970; MS, SUNY, Buffalo, 1977; MPH, PhD, U. Rochester, NY, 1986. Cert. rehab. counselor. Editor Mental Health Assn., Buffalo, 1973-80; psychotherapist Erie County Dept. Mental Health, Buffalo, 1980-82; asst. prof. Nat. Tech. Inst. for Deaf, Rochester, NY, 1986-95, assoc. prof., 1995-96; pres., dir. Inst. Matching Person and Tech., Inc., 1997—; dir. consumer evaluations, sr. rsch. assoc. Ctr. Assistive Tech., Occupl. Therapy U. at Buffalo, 1996-98; assoc. prof. phys. medicine and rehab. U. Rochester Med. Ctr., 1997—2008, prof. phys. medicine and rehab., 2008—. Asst. prof. psychology Eastman Sch. Music, Rochester, 1989-95; sr. rsch. assoc. Internat. Ctr. Hearing and Speech Rsch., Rochester, 1989—2007; prof. Rocky Mountain U. Health Professions, 2008-, project dir., Burton Blatt Inst. Syracuse U., 2009-. Author: Communication in the Human Services: A Guide to Therapeutic Journalism, 1980, Living in the State of Stuck, 1993, 4th edit., 2005, Connecting to Learn: Educational and Assistive Technology for People with Disabilities, 2004, (assessment instruments) Assistive Technology Device Predisposition Assessment, 1989, (assessment instrument) Educational Technology Predisposition Assessment, 1990, (assessment instruments) Workplace Technology Predisposition Assessment, 1991, Health Care Technology Predisposition Assessment, 1992, Matching Assistive Technology and Child, 1997, Matching Assistive Technology and Child School Version, 2008, Hearing Tech. Predisposition Assessment, 2004, Cognitive Support Technology Predisposition Assessment, 2007, (CD) Improving The Match Of Person and Technology, 2005; co-author: Assistive Technology in the Workplace, 2006; editor: (book) Assistive Technology: Matching Device and Consumer for Successful Rehabilitation, 2002, (jour.) Disability and Rehabilitation: Assistive Technology, 2005—; co-editor: Psychological Assessment in Medical Rehabilitation, 1995, Evaluating, Selecting and Using Appropriate Assistive Technology, 1996; mem. editl. bd.: Tech. and Disability, 1990—98, Disability and Rehab., 1998—, Assistive Tech., 1996—2003, Spinal Cord Injury Psychosocial Process, 2004—10, Rehabilitation Psychology, 2005—07; contbr. articles to profl. jours. Mem. adv. bd. Nat. Ctr. Med. Rehab. Rsch., NIH, 2006—10. NIH grantee, 2000, 02, 06, Ctr. Disease Control, 2007; recipient Literary award Rho Chi Sigma, 1984, James Hanson Humanitarian award Grad Sch. Edn. U. Buffalo, 2005, Sam McFarland Meml. Mentor award, Rehab. Engring. Assistive Tech. Soc. N. Am., 2011, Roger G. Berkar award, Am. Psychol. Assn. Divsn. Rehab. Psychology, 2010. Fellow: APA (treas. Divsn. 22 2001—04), Rehab. Engring. and Assistive Tech. Soc. N.Am. (bd. dirs. 1997—99, fellow 2008), Am. Congress Rehab. Medicine (fellow 2002, sec. 2002—07, Disting. Svc. award 2007); mem.: AAUW (life grantee 1983), Authors League Am. Inc., Authors Guild Inc., NY Acad. Scis., Assn. for Advancement of Assistive Tech. in Europe, Australian Rehab. and Assistive Tech. Assn., Am. Bd. Med. Psychotherapy and Psychodiagnosticians, Chi Sigma Iota (life). Methodist. Avocations: creative writing, fossils and minerals. Home and Office: 486 Lake Rd Webster NY 14580-1055 Personal E-mail: impt97@aol.com.

SCHERER, RONALD CALLAWAY, voice scientist, educator; b. Akron, Ohio, Sept. 11, 1945; s. Belden Davis and Lois Ramona (Callaway) S.; children: Christopher, Maria. BS, Kent State U., 1968; MA, Ind. U., 1972; PhD, U. Iowa, 1981. Research asst. U. Iowa, Iowa City, 1979-81, asst. research scientist, 1981-83, adj. asst. prof., 1983-88, adj. assoc. prof., 1988—; adj. asst. prof. U. Denver, 1984-86; asst. adj. prof. U. Colo., Boulder, 1984-93, adj. assoc. prof., 1993-96; rsch. scientist Denver Ctr. Performing Arts, 1983—88, sr. scientist, 1988—96; lectr. voice and speech sci. Nat. Theatre Conservatory, Denver, 1990-94; asst. clin. prof. Sch. Medicine U. Colo., Denver, 1988—96; assoc. prof. Bowling Green State U., Ohio, 1996—2001, prof., 2001—05, 2006—. Adj. assoc. prof. U. Okla., 1992-96; affiliate clin. prof. U. No. Colo., 1993-96; Oberlin Coll. affiliate scholar, 1996—; mem. exec. and legis. bd. Nat. Ctr. Voice and Speech, 1990-96; adj. prof. Drexel U., Phila., 2006-; G. Paul Moore lectr., The Voice Found., 2002; rsch. prof. U. Cin., 2005-06. Author: (with Dr. I. Titze) Vocal Fold Physiology: Biomechanics, Acoustics and Phonatory Control, 1983; contbr. articles to profl. jours. Nat. Inst. Dental Research fellow, 1972-76. Fellow: Internat. Soc. Phonetic Scis. (auditor 1988—91); mem.: Am. Assn. Phonetic Scis. (nominating com. 1985—87, counselor 2000—03, councelor 2000—03), Internat. Assn. Logopedics and Phoniatrics, Acoustical Soc. Am., Am. Speech-Lang.-Hearing Assn., Internat. Arts Medicine Assn., Collegium Medicorum Theatri, Sigma Xi, Pi Mu Epsilon (G. Paul Moore lectr.). Office Phone: 419-372-2515.

SCHERER, SIEGFRIED, biologist; b. Oberndorf, Germany, Apr. 7, 1955; s. Hans-Georg and Sofia (Sturm) S.; m. Sigrid Hartwig, Dec. 23, 1980. Diploma in biology, U. Konstanz, 1979, dr. rer. nat., 1983, habil., 1991. Univ. lectr. U. Konstanz, Germany, 1983-88, rsch. fellow, 1990, Va. Poly. and State U., Blacksburg, 1989; prof., dir. inst. of microbiology Tech. U. München, Germany, 1991-99; mng. dir. Rsch. Ctr. Milk and Food, Weihen-Stephan, Germany, 1999—2003; chair microbial ecology Tech. U. Munich, 2003—, vice dean faculty biosci., 2008—. Mem. extended bd. dirs. Tech. U. Munich, 2001—04. Author: (books) Photosynthese, 1983, 2nd edit., 1996; co-author: Entstehung und Geschichte der Lebewesen, 1986, Russian edit., 1996, Evolution-ein Kritisches Lehrbuch, 1998, Finnish edit., 2000, Brasilian edit., 2002, Serbian edit., 2003, 3rd edit., 2006; editor: Typen des Lebens, 1993; contbr. more than 180 articles in field. Recipient Byk award Byk-Gulden, 1984, Otto von Guencke Rsch. award, 2005, Good Tchg. award, 2007. Mem. Am. Soc. for Microbiology. Office: Inst Microbiologie ZIEL Weihenstephauer Berg 3 D-85354 Freising Germany

SCHERGER, JOSEPH EDWARD, family physician, educator; b. Delphos, Ohio, Aug. 29, 1950; m. Carol M. Scherger, Aug. 7, 1973; children: Adrian, Gabriel. BS summa cum laude, U. Dayton, 1971; MD, UCLA, 1975. Family practice residency U. Wash., Seattle, 1975-78; clin. instr. U. Calif. Sch. Medicine, Davis, 1978-80, asst. clin. prof., 1980-84, assoc. clin. prof., 1984-90, clin. prof., 1990—, dir. predoctoral program, 1991-92; med. dir. family practice and community medicine Sharp Healthcare, San Diego, 1992-96; assoc. dean primary care, chair dept. family medicine U. Calif., Irvine, 1996—2001, prof. dept. family medicine, 1996—2001, prof. family and preventive medicine San Diego, 2003—; dean Fla. State U., Coll. Medicine, Tallahassee, 2001—03; v.p. primary care Eisenhower Med. Ctr. Med. dir. AmeriChoice, 2006—09; consulting med. dir. Lumetra, 2007—. Editor (in chief): (med. jour.) Hippocrates. Recipeient Hippocratic Oath award UCLA, Calif. Physician of Yr. award Am. Acad. Family Physicians. Mem. NAS (mem. Inst. Medicine), Am. Acad. Family Physicians, Soc. Tchrs. Family Medicine. Office Fax: 760-610-7301. Business E-Mail: jscherger@emc.org.

SCHERL, SHARON, dermatologist; BSN, Columbia U., 1981; attended, NY Med. Coll., 1984—88. Diplomate Am. Bd. Dermatology. Chief dermatology dept. Englewood Hosp.; with Am. Acad. of Dermatology; mem. AAD com. Recertification Edn. Task Force; hosp. affiliations include Columbia-Presbyterian Med. Ctr.; resident gen. medicine dept. Mt. Sinai Hosp. Med. Ctr.; student rep. NY Med. Coll., tng. Named to Am.'s Top Doctors, Castle Connolly, 2000. Mem.: Am. Acad. of Dermatology, Alpha Omega Honor Soc. Office: Englewood Hospital and Medical Center 350 Engle St Englewood NJ 07631 Office Phone: 201-894-3000.

SCHERR, DOUGLAS, urologist; BA, Cornell U., 1989; MD, The George Washington U. Med. Sch., 1994. Diplomate Am. Bd. Urology. Intern gen. surgery The George Washington Univ. Hosp., 1994—95, jr. asst. resident gen. surgery, 1995—96; resident urology The James Buchanan Brady dept. of urology The New York Hosp.-Cornell Med. Ctr., 1996—99, chief resident urology The James Buchanan Brady dept. of urology, 1999—2000; fellow urologic oncology Meml. Sloan Kettering Cancer Ctr., 2000—02; clin. dir. dept. of urology Weill Med. Coll. of Cornell Univ., 2002—; visiting assoc. physician Rockefeller Univ. Hosp., 2003—. Urology instr. Weill Med. Coll. of Cornell Univ., 2002, asst. prof. urology, 2002—. Lectr. Am. Austrian Found. Mem.: AMA, Cancer and Leukemia Group B GU Core, Soc. of Univ. Urologists, NY Sect. of Am. Urol. Assn., Am.Urol. Assn., Soc. for Basic Urol. Rsch., Soc. of Urologic Oncology. Office: New York Cornell Medical Center 525 E 68th Starr 900 New York NY 10021 Office Phone: 212-746-5788.

SCHERR, LAWRENCE, internist, healthcare educator, historian; b. NYC, Nov. 6, 1928; s. Harry and Sophia (Schwartz) S.; m. Peggy L. Binenkorb, June 13, 1954; children: Cynthia E., Robert W. AB, Cornell U., 1950, MD, 1957; DSc (hon.), Long Island U., 1990, North Shore-LIJ Health Sys. Grad Sch., 2004. Diplomate Am. Bd. Internal Medicine (bd. dirs., sec.-treas. 1979-86). Intern Cornell Med. divsn. Bellevue Hosp. and Meml. Ctr., NY, 1957-58, asst. resident, 1958-59, rsch. fellow cardiorenal lab., 1959-60, chief resident, 1960-61, co-dir. cardiorenal lab., 1961-62, asst. vis. physician, 1961-63, assoc. vis. physician, 1963-65, dir. cardiology and renal unit, 1963-67, assoc. dir., 1964-67, vis. physician, 1966-68; physician to out-patients NY Hosp., 1961-63, asst. attending physician, 1963-66, assoc. attending physician, 1966-71, attending physician, 1971-2000; asst. attending physician, cons. Sloan-Kettering Cancer Ctr., 1962—2000. Chmn. dept. medicine North Shore Univ. Hosp., 1967-01, chmn. emeritus, 2001-, dir. acad. affairs, 1969-93, sr. v.p. med. affairs, 1993-00; exec v.p. med. and acad. affairs North Shore-LI Jewish Health Sys., 1998-00, trustee, 2000—, chief acad. officer, sr. v.p. acad. affairs, 2000-05, Betsey Cushing Whitney acad. dean emeritus, historian, 2005—; asst. in medicine Med. Coll. Cornell U., 1958-59; rsch. fellow NY Heart Assn., 1959-60; instr. medicine Cornell U. Med. Coll., 1960-63, asst. prof., 1963-66, assoc. prof., 1966-71, David J. Greene disting. prof. medicine Weill Cornell Coll. Medicine, 1971-96, assoc. dean, 1969-96, Betsey Cushing Whitney prof. emeritus medicine, 2006-; prof. medicine NYU Sch. Medicine, 1996-05; career scientist Health Rsch. Coun., NYC, 1962-66; tchg. scholar Am. Heart Assn., 1966-67; pres. NY State Bd. Medicine, 1974-75; chmn. Accreditation Coun. for Grad. Med. Edn., 1988, NY State Coun. on Grad. Edn., 1990-92, with Korean Warfare Amphibious Force US Navy, 1950-53. Contbr. articles to profl. jours. Mem. US White House Rev. Coun., Nat. Health Policy devel., 1993. Combat officer USN, 1950—53, Republic of Korea. Decorated NY State Conspicuous Svc. medal, Korean Pres. Unit Citation for Meritorious Svc. Fellow NY Acad. Medicine, Am. Heart Assn. (coun. on clin. cardiology); master ACP (chmn. and gov. Downstate NY region II 1975-80, regent 1980-86, chmn. bd. regents 1985-86, chmn. bd. regents emeritus, nat. pres. 1987-88, pres. emeritus, Alfred Stengel Meml. medal); mem. AMA, Am. Fedn. Clin. Rsch., Harvey Soc., NY Med. Soc., Nassau County Med. Soc., Assn. Am. Med. Colls., Am. Clin. and Climatologic Assn., Fed. Law Enforcement Found. (Cmty. Svc. award, 2008), Am. Coun. Grad. Med. Edn.(chmn. 1987), Am. Bd. Internat. Medicine(Sec. Treasured bd. 1984-86). Office: N Shore LIJ Health Sys 125 Community Dr Great Neck NY 11021-5502 Office Phone: 516-465-2536.

SCHERZER, ALFRED L., developmental pediatrician; s. Morris Scherzer and Elizabeth Levitch; children: Elizabeth S. Herbster, Andrea L., Martha E. MSPH, Columbia U. Sch. Pub. Health, 1950; EdD, Tchrs. Coll., Columbia U., 1954; MD, Columbia U. Coll. Physicians and Surgeons, 1963; MA in Med. Sociology, Yale U., New Haven, 1957. Diplomate Am. Bd. Pediat., 1969. Emeritus clin. prof. pediat. Weill-Cornell U. Med. Coll., NYC, 1963—94; prof. clin. pediat. & preventive medicine SUNY, Sch. Medicine, Stony Brook, 2005—. Med. dir. NYC Bd. Edn., Divsn. Spl. Edn., 1970—95; pres. Am. Acad. for Cerebral Palsy and Devel. Medicine, 1985—86. Contbr. articles to profl. jour. Achievements include research in early diagnosis of development and childhood disability in the developing world. Office: Stony Brook Children's Svc 15 W 2nd St Riverhead NY 11901 Business E-Mail: alfred.scherzer@stonybrook.edu. *

SCHEXNIDER, VIRGINIA REEVES, school psychologist; d. Curtis Reeves Sr. and Virginia Cundiff Reeves; m. Alvin James Schexnider, July 1, 1978; children: Alvin James, Elena Cundiff. BA, Fisk U., Nashville, 1975; MA, U. Va., Charlottesville, 1978. Dir. student assessment ctr. Va. State U., Petersburg, 1980—81; sch. psychologist Richmond City Pub. Schs., Richmond, 1993—96; lic. sch. psychologist Winston-Salem/Forsyth County Pub. Schs., NC, 1996—2002; cert. sch. psychologist Va. Beach City Pub. Schs., 2002—. Directorship The Richmond Symphony, 1989—94, Reynolda Ho. Mus. of Am. Art, Winston-Salem, NC, 1997—2003. Mem.: NASP (assoc.), Va. Acad. Sch. Psychologists (assoc.), Fisk U. Alumni Assn. (life), U. Va. Alumni Assn. (life), Phi Beta Kappa.

SCHIAVON, MAURIZIO, sports medicine physician, educator; b. Padova, Veneto Region, Italy, Sept. 28, 1951; s. Mario Schiavon and Bruna Giacchetto; m. Angiola Paganotto, July 2, 1977; children: Mattia Paolo, Nicolò. Diploma in Grammer, Tito Livio Grammar Sch. Padova, Italy, 1970; MD, U. Padova, Italy, 1976; degree in Pulmonary Diseases, U. Padoua, Italy, 1979; degree in Occuptl. Medicine, U. Trieste, Italy, 1983; degree in Sports Medicine, U. Padoua, Italy, 1987. Lic. in sports medicine Ministry Health, Italy, 1978. Gen. medicine asst. ULSS 12 Hosp., Pieve di Soligo, Treviso, Veneto Region, Italy, 1979—81; specialist sports medicine Ctr. Sports Medicine, NHS, ULSS 16, Padova, 1982—90, coord., 1991—2002; ann. contract prof. postgrad. sch. sports medicine U. Padova, 1998—; med. exec. Ctr. Sports Medicine, NHS, ULSS 16, 2002—04; person in charge Sports Medicine & Phys. Activities Unit, Nat. Health Svc. (NHS) ULSS 16, 2005—. Mem. Tech. Com. Sports Medicine, Venice, Veneto Region, Italy, 2005—, ptnr. Ministry Health Target Project "Sudden Death in Young Athletes", Roma, 2002—05; cons. Naval Underwater Med. Inst., Egyptian Naval Forces, Alexandria, Egypt, 2001—01; regional diving med. cons. Med. Ctr. www.scuba-doc.com, Ono Island, Ala., 1999—; diving med. cons. Divers Alert Network Europe, Roseto Abruzzi, Italy, 1992—; prof. medicine Sant'anna sch. advanced studies and Inst. clin. physiology Nat. Rsch. Coun., Pisa, Italy, 2006—. Co-editor: (book) Respiratory Apparatus and Underwater Activity, 2000, The Diver's Travels. Practical Advice for Safe Diving, 2002, Pulmonary Diseases and Underwater Activity, 2008; contbr. chapters to books. Mem. Panathlon Internat., Padova, 1983. Master: Italian Fedn. Sports Medicine; mem.: Undersea and Hyperbaric Med. Soc., European Underwater Baromedical Soc., Italian Soc. Underwater and Hyperbaric Medicine, Italian Soc. Sports Cardiology, Italian Fedn. Sports Medicine. Office: UO Medicina dello Sport/Attività Motorie Azienda ULSS 16 via dei Colli 4 Padova 35143 Italy Office Phone: 39 049 8216001. Business E-Mail: maurizio.schiavon@sanita.padova.it.

SCHICK, VOLKER, urologist; b. Neun Kirchen, Germany, July 30, 1949; s. Jakob and Irma (Theis) S.; m. Hedda Wulff, Jan. 23, 1972; children: Kerstin, Martina, Oliver, Michael. MD, U. Saarland, Saarbrucken, 1982. Internship resident, dept. urology, surg. dept. St. Joseph Hosp., Minden, Germany, 1981—85; asst. dept. urology Minden, Germany, 1981-85; head physician, 1985-89; chief urologist Robert Koch Hosp., Gehrden, Germany, 1989—. Contbr. articles on surg. treatment of urol. tumors, stone treatment erectile dysfunction to profl. jours. Fellow European Bd. Urology; mem. Soc. for Minimal Invasive Therapy. Office: Robert Koch Dist Hosp Von Reden Str 1 30989 Gehrden Germany Home Phone: 491716393318; Office Phone: 49-5108-692700. Business E-Mail: volker.schick@krh.eu.

SCHICKLER, PAUL E., chemicals executive; BSBA, Drake U., Des Moines, MA in Bus. Adminstrn. Acct. and various adminstrv. positions E.I. Du Pont de Nemours & Co., 1974—84, contr., 1984—95, v.p. human resources learning and devel., comm. and real estate mgmt., 1995—99, v.p., dir. L.Am., Mex. & African ops., Pioneer, 1999—2003, v.p. internat. ops., 2003—07, pres. Pioneer Hi-Bred, 2007—. Bd. dirs. Grand View Coll., Juvenile Diabetes Rsch. Found. Internat. Office: E I du Pont de Nemours and Co 1007 Market St Wilmington DE 19898 Office Phone: 302-774-1000. Office Fax: 302-999-4399. Business E-Mail: paul.e.schickler@usa.dupont.com. *

SCHIEBLER, GEROLD LUDWIG, pediatrician, educator; b. Hamburg, Pa., June 20, 1928; s. Alwin Robert and Charlotte Elizabeth (Schmoele) Schiebler; m. Audrey Jean Lincourt, Jan. 8, 1954; children: Mark, Marcella, Kristen, Bettina, Wanda, Michele. BS, Franklin and Marshall Coll., 1950; MD, Harvard U., 1954. Intern pediat. and internal medicine Mass. Gen. Hosp., Boston, 1954—55, resident, 1955—56; resident pediat. U. Minn. Hosp., Mpls., 1956—57, fellow pediatric cardiology, 1957—58, rsch. fellow, 1958—59; rsch. fellow sect. physiology Mayo Clinic and Mayo Found., 1959—60; from asst. prof. pediatric cardiology to prof. emeritus U. Fla., 1960—2001, prof. emeritus, 2001—. Dir. divsn. Children's Med. Svcs. State of Fla., 1973—74, area med. dir., 1974—2000, cons., 2001—. Author (with L.P. Elliott): The X-ray Diagnosis of Congenital Cardiac Disease in Infants, Children and Adults, 1968, 1979; author: (with L.J. Krovetz and I.H. Gessner) Pediatric Cardiology, 1979. Recipient Lifetime Achievement award, Coll. Medicine, 2004; named Children's Med. Svcs. Pediatrician of Decade, Gov. Jeb Bush, 1999. Mem.: AMA (Benjamin Rush award 1993), AAAS, Fedn. State Med. Bds. (Svc. award 2008), Fla. Med. Assn. (past v.p., bd. govs., pres. 1991—92, Cert. Of Merit 2008), Fla. Heart Assn. (past pres.), Fla. Pediat. Soc. (exec. com.), Soc. Pediatric Rsch. (emeritus), Am. Coll. Cardiology, Am. Acad. Pediat. (Abraham Jacobi award 1993), Inst. Medicine NAS, Alpha Omega Alpha, Phi Beta Kappa. Home: 408 Beachside Villas Amelia Island Plantation Amelia Island FL 32034-6551 Home Fax: 904-277-7211. Business E-Mail: gls@health.ufl.edu.

SCHIESSER, HEATH G., former health products executive; Grad. cum laude, Trinity U.; MBA, Harvard U., Mass. Worked in devel. of new ventures; co-founder online pharmacy Express Scripts; mgmt. cons. McKinsey & Co.; sr. v.p. mktg. and sales WellCare Health Plans, Tampa, Fla., 2002—05, pres. prescription ins., 2005—06, sr. advisor, Medicare products, 2006—08, pres., CEO, 2008—09. Bd. dirs. WellCare Health Plans, 2004—.

SCHIEVINK, WOUTER, neurosurgeon, director; b. Amsterdam, Nov. 4, 1963; MD, U. Amsterdam, 1989. Dir. vascular neurosurgery Cedars-Sinai Med. Ctr., 1998. Office: 8631 W 3rd St 800E Los Angeles CA 90046 Business E-Mail: schievinkw@cshs.org.

SCHIFF, DONALD WILFRED, pediatrician, educator; b. Detroit, Sept. 11, 1925; s. Henry and Kate (Boesky) S.; m. Rosalie Pergament; children: Stephen, Jeffrey, Susan, Douglas. Student, Wayne State U., 1943-44, Oberlin Coll., 1944-45; MD, Wayne State U., 1949. Diplomate Am. Bd. Pediatrics. Intern Detroit Receiving Hosp., 1949-50; resident in pediatrics U. Colo., 1954-55, chief resident in pediatrics, 1955-56; instr. U. Colo. Health Scis. Ctr., Denver, 1956-59, asst. clin. prof., 1959-69, assoc. clin. prof., 1969-78, clin. prof., 1978-87, prof., 1987—; pvt. practice Littleton (Colo.) Clinic, 1956-86, chmn. bd., 1973-79; med. dir. HMO Colo., Denver, 1980-86; med. dir. Child Health Clinic The Children's Hosp., Denver. Contbr. articles to profl. jours. Bd. dirs. Sch. Dist. VI, Colo., 1962; pres. Arapahoe Mental Health Clinic, Denver, 1968-70, bd. dirs., 1964-70; adv. coun. State of Colo. Medicaid, Denver, 1981—. With USN, 1944-46, USPHS, 1952-54, Turtle Mountain Indian Reservation, N.D. Recipient 25 Yrs. Teaching award U. Colo. Sch. Medicine, 1981. Mem. Am. Acad. Pediatrics (chmn. Colo. chpt. 1973-79, alternate dist. chmn. 1977-81, chmn. dist. 8 1981-86, nat. pres. 1988-89), Rocky Mountain Pediatric Soc., Colo. Med. Soc. Home: 600 Front Range Rd Littleton CO 80120-4052 Office: The Childrens Hospital 13123 E 16th Ave Aurora CO 80045-7106

SCHIFF, GILBERT MARTIN, virologist, microbiologist, educator; b. Cin., Oct. 21, 1931; married, 1955; 2 children. BS, U. Cin., 1953, MD, 1957. Intern U. Hosp., Iowa City, 1957-58, resident internal medicine, 1958-59; med. officer lab br. Communicable Diseases Ctr., Ga., 1959-61; head tissue culture investigation unit, perinatal rsch. br. Nat. Inst. Neurol. Diseases and Blindness, 1961-64; dir. clin. virology lab. U. Cin., 1964-78, asst. prof. medicine and microbiology, 1964-67, asst. prof. microbiology, 1967-71, prof. medicine Coll. Medicine, 1971—, pres. James N. Gamble Inst. Medical Rsch., 1981—. Attending physician dept. medicine Emory U., Atlanta, 1959-61; cons. com. maternal health Ohio State Med. Assn., 1964-70, Hamilton County Neuromuscular Diagnostic Clinic, 1966, 75, Contract Immunization Status in U.S., 1975-77; mem. com. viral hepatitis among dental pers. VA; mem. immunization practice adv. com. Surgeon Gen., 1971-75; dir. Christ Hosp Inst. Med. Rsch., Cin., 1974-83, chairperson libr. com., 1974—, mem. com. cancer programs, 1979—, mem. com. human rsch., 1980—, chairperson search com., dir. radiotherapy, 1980-82; mem. com. infection control, 1981—, mem. com. univ. liaisons, 1982—; mem. subcom. antimicrobial agents U.S. Pharmacopeia, 1977-80; mem. study sect., adv. com., review com. NIH, mem. com. Rubella immunization Ohio Dept. Health; com. Rubella control Cin. Dept. Health. Trustee Children's Hosp. Med. Ctr., rsch. com., 1985—; community adv. com. Hoxworth Blood Ctr., 1991—. Recipient career rsch. devel. award Nat. Inst. Child Health and Human Devel., 1970-74; grantee USPHS, 1964-67, Nat. found., 1965-67. Fellow ACP; mem. AAAS, Am. Soc. Microbiology, Am. Fedn. Clin. Rsch. (sec.-treas. 1967-70), Am. Pub. Health Assn., Sci. Rsch. Soc. Am., Ctrl. Soc. Clin. Rsch. (sec.-treas. 1977-81, v.p. 1983, pres. 1984), Infectious Disease Soc. Am. Am. Soc. Clin. Investigation, Sigma Xi. Office: Dept Pediatrics U Cincinnati Coll Med 3333 Burnet Ave Cincinnati OH 45229-3026 E-mail: gilbert.schiff@cchmc.org.

SCHIFF, HOWARD IRWIN, urologist; b. Bklyn., May 15, 1948; s. Frank and Mildred Schiff; m. Debbie Mathews Schiff, Aug. 29, 1970; children: Jonathan, Richard, Robin, Meredith, Amanda. BA, Hofstra U., 1970; MS, W.Va. U., 1973, MD, 1975. Diplomate Am. Bd. Urology, lic. physician N.Y. Intern dept. surgery Montefiore Hosp., Bronx, 1975—77; intern dept. urology Mt. Sinai Med. Ctr. N.Y., 1977—80; asst. attending physician Mt. Sinai Med. Ctr., NYC, 1980—; consulting urologist City Hosp. Ctr., Elmhurst, NY, 1980—2004; attending urologist Beth Israel Med. Ctr., NYC, 1983—2003; asst. attending physician Weill-Cornell Med. Ctr., NYC, 2001—; asst. attending urologist North Shore U. Hosp., Manhasset, NY, 2005—; cons. urologist Hosp. Special Surgery, NYC, 2008—. Asst. clin. prof. urology Mt Sinai Sch. Medicine, NYC, 1982—; adj. asst. clin. prof. urology Weill-Cornell Sch. Medicine, NYC, 2001—. Contbr. articles to profl. jours. Recipient Ferdinand Valentine Residents Essay award, N.Y. Acad. Mag., 1979, Physicians Recognition award, AMA, 1980—, award, Castle Connelly Guide, 1997—2011; named one of Best Drs. in N.Y., N.Y. Mag., 1998, 2000, 2001, Best Drs. in NY Metro Region, Castle Connelly Guide, 1997—2011, NY Times Super Drs., 2009—11. Fellow: ACS; mem.: Am. Urol. Assn. Office: 1120 Park Ave New York NY 10128 Office Phone: 212-996-6660. Personal E-mail: hschiff@prodigy.net, hschiffmd@gmail.com.

SCHIFF, LAWRENCE ALAN, dentist; b. NYC, June 11, 1954; s. Leonard Julius and Mildred Ruth Schiff; m. Susan Lynn Zemmel, Aug. 17, 1986; children: Chelsea Ann, JonDavid. BA, Colgate U., Hamilton, NY, 1976; DMD, Fairleigh Dickinson U., Hackensack, NJ, 1980. Residency in gen. practice U. Pa., Phila., 1981; clin. assoc. instr., sch. dental medicine U Pa., 1981—86; pvt. practice Erdenheim, Pa., 1986—. Coach SE Pa. Youth Lacrosse Assn. Named one of America's Top Dentists, Top Dentist in Cosmetic Dentistry, Phila. Mag., 2011. Fellow: Acad. Gen. Dentistry; mem.: ADA, Phila. County Dental Assn., Montgomery Bucks Dental Assn., Am. Acad. Cosmetic Dentistry, Beta Beta Beta. Achievements include research in effects of estrogen on collagen crosslinking. Avocations: golf, skiing. Office: DMD 813 Bethlehem Pike Erdenheim PA 19038 Office Phone: 215-233-1163. Business E-Mail: smilsvr@comcast.net, lschiff@theschiffdentalgroup.com.

SCHIFF, NICHOLAS D., neurologist; b. June 30, 1965; BA with honors, Stanford U., Calif., 1987; MD with honors, Cornell U. Med. Coll., NY, 1992. Diplomate Am. Bd. Psychiatry & Neurology. Resident neurology NY Hosp.; prof. neurology & neurosci. Weill Cornell Med. Coll., also dir. Lab. Clin. Neurophysiology. Assoc. attending neurologist NY-Presbyn. Hosp.; cons., advisor IntElect Med. Inc. Co-author: (med. text) Diagnosis of Stupor and Coma, 2007; contbr. articles to profl. jours., chapters to books. Recipient Rsch. award for Innovation, Soc. Neurosci., 2007; named one of The 100 Most Influential People in the World, TIME mag., 2008, The 100 Agents of Change, Rolling Stone mag., 2009. Mem.: American Neurol. Assn. Achievements include research in pathophysiology of impaired consciousness, the neurophysiological mechanisms of arousal regulation, and the effects of deep brain electrical stimulation techniques on forebrain integration. Office: Weill Cornell Med Coll 520 E 70th St K 615 New York NY 10021 Office Phone: 212-746-2372. Office Fax: 212-746-8532.

SCHIFF, PETER B., radiation oncologist, educator; MD, Albert Eistein Coll. of Medicine, 1980—84. Diplomate Am. Bd Radiology-radiation oncology, 1990. Resident in radiation oncology meml. Sloan-Kettering Cancer Ctr., NY, 1985—88; prof. of radiation oncology sch. of medicine NYU Lnagone Med. Ctr.; assoc. chair for translational rsch. dept.of radiation oncology NYU Langone Med. Ctr. Author: (journ.) Lung Tumor Motion and Deformation during the Respiratory Cycle: Potential Implications for Radiation Therapy, Radical hysterectomy versus radiation for early-stage cervical cancer: How big is too big?, Stage IIIA endometrial carcinoma: Outcome and predictors of survival, A feasibility study or novel ultrasonic tissue characterization for prostrate-cancer diagnosis: 2D spectrum analysis of in vivo, Optimizing the management of stage II endometrial cancer: the role of radical hysterectomy and radiation, Patterns of care and access to fertility-conserving surgery for patients with ovarian sex cord stromal and germ cell tumors, Racial disparities for uterine corpus tumors: changes in clinical characteristics and treatment over time, Safety of ovarian preservation in premenopausal women with endometrial cancer, Implementation and validation of an ultrasonic tissue characterization technique for quantitative assessment of normal-tissue toxicity in radiation therapy, Early metastatic spread after a complete response in locally advanced vulvar cancer treated with neoadjuvant chemoradiation: a case report, Uterine carcinosarcomas and grade 3 endometrioid cancers: evidence for distinct tumor behavior, various journs. in publs. Office: NYU Langone Medical Center 550 1st Ave New York NY 10016 Office Phone: 212-263-7300.

SCHIFF, ROBERT, healthcare consulting company executive; b. NYC, Jan. 7, 1942; s. Henry and Jeanette (Levine) S.; m. Adrianne Bendich, Aug. 16, 1964 (div. July 1979); children: Jorden, Debra; m. Joann McTaggart, Aug. 24, 1986. BS, CCNY, 1964; MS, Iowa State U., 1966; PhD, U. Calif., Davis, 1968. Cert. Regulatory Affairs Profl. Soc. Asst. prof. anatomy Tufts U. Sch. Medicine, Boston, 1969-72; mgr. serology rsch. Hyland divsn. Baxter Labs., Costa Mesa, Calif., 1972-74; dir. R & D J.T. Baker Diagnostics, Bethlehem, Pa., 1974-77; dir. diagnostic R & D Hoffmann-LaRoche, Nutley, N.J., 1977-80, group v.p. Warner Lambert Co., Morris Plains, N.J., 1980-82; pres., CEO Schiff & Co., Inc., West Caldwell, N.J., 1982—. Del. Nat. Commn. for Clin. Lab. Stds., 1979-80; vice chmn. R & D Coun. N.J., 1980-82; bd. dirs. E.P.I. subs. E-Z-EM, Westbury, N.Y., 1991-98. Contbr. numerous articles to profl. jours., patentee in field. Bd. dirs. Pharm. Tng. Inst., 2002. Post Doctoral fellow U. Calif., Davis, 1969; Aid to Cancer Rsch. grantee, Mass., 1970. Fellow Regulatory Affairs Profl. Soc.; mem. NY Acad. Sci., Regulatory Affairs Profl. Soc. (bd. editors Focus 2006), Am. Soc. Quality Control (cert. quality auditor), Am. Assn. Clin. Chemistry, Brit. Inst. Regulatory Affairs, Parenteral Drug Assn., Sigma Xi. Avocation: flying. Office: Schiff & Co 1129 Bloomfield Ave West Caldwell NJ 07006-7123 Office Phone: 973-227-1830. Personal E-mail: rschiff13@aol.com.

SCHIFF, SAMI, medical technician; b. Peschiera del Garda, Verona, Italy, Nov. 20, 1972; Degree in Psychology, U. Padova, 2000; PhD in Psychologica and Psychiat. Sci., 2004. Tech. asst., dept. clin. and exptl. medicine U. Padova, 2007—. Mem.: CIRMAMNEC. Avocation: running. Home: Via Giustiniani 2 Padova 35128 Italy Business E-Mail: sami.schiff@unipd.it.

SCHIFFER, CHARLES ALAN, oncologist, educator; b. Bklyn., Apr. 11, 1944; s. Mortimer and Esther (Ginsberg) S.; m. Judy T. Schiffer, June 14, 1970 (dec. Aug. 1992), Pamela Schiffer; 1 child, Joshua T. MD, Brandeis U., 1968, NYU, 1968. Diplomate Am. Bd. Internal Medicine, Am. Bd. Med. Oncology. Intern, resident, chief resident NYU Sch. Medicine, 1968-72; staff fellow, sr. investigator Nat. Cancer Inst., Balt., 1972-81; chief divsn. malignancies, hematology U. Md. Cancer Ctr., Balt., 1981—97; prof. medicine and oncology Barbara Ann Karmanos Cancer Inst., Wayne State U. Sch. Medicine, Detroit, 1997—; prin. investigator, clinical trials of Gleevec Wayne State U. Sch. Medicine, Detroit, 1999—. Prof. oncology and medicine U. Md. Sch. Medicine, Balt., 1983-1997; chair oncology drug adv. com. FDA, Rockville, Md., 1992-95; chair leukemia com. Cancer and Leukemia Group B, Chgo.; cons. various pharm. cos.; vis. prof. numerous univs. Editor: Neoplastic Diseases of Blood, Leukemia sect., Current Opinion in Oncology; mem. editl. bds. Blood, Jour. Clin. Oncology, Internat. Jour. Hematology, Transfusion Medicine Reviews and Transfusions; contbr. chpts. in books and articles to profl. jours. Lt. comdr. USPHS, 1972-81. Recipient Humanitarian award Arlene Wyman Guild, 1992, Dr. John J. Kenney award, Leukemia/Lymphoma Soc. Am., 2006, Celegene award for Career Acheivement in Hematology, 2006; named Best Doctor, Am. Health Mag., Best Cancer Specialist in the US, Good Housekeeping Mem. Am. Soc. Hematology (coms.), Am. Soc. Clin. Oncology (coms.). Avocations: skiing, biking, music, reading. Office: Hudson-Webber Cancer Rsch Ctr 4100 John R Detroit MI 48201 Address: Weisberg Cancer Treatment Ctr 31995 Northwestern Hwy Farmington MI 48334 Office Phone: 313-576-8737. Business E-Mail: schiffer@karmanos.org, schiffer@wayne.edu.

SCHIFFRIN, MILTON JULIUS, physiologist; b. Rochester, NY, Mar. 23, 1914; s. William and Lillian (Harris) S.; m. Dorothy Euphemia Wharry, Oct. 10, 1942; children: David Wharry, Hilary Ann. AB, U. Rochester, 1937, MS, 1939; PhD cum laude, McGill U., 1941. Instr. physiology Northwestern U. Med. Sch., Chgo., 1941—45; lectr. pharmacology U. Ill. Med. Sch., 1947—57, clin. asst. prof. anesthesiology, 1957—61; with Hoffmann-La Roche, Inc., Nutley, NJ, 1946—79, dir. drug regulatory affairs, 1964—71, asst. v.p., 1971—79; pres. Wharry Rsch. Assn., Seattle, 1979—. Chmn. Everglades Health Edn. Ctr., 1986—87. Author: (with E.G. Gross) Clinical Analgesics, 1955; editor: Management of Pain in Cancer, 1957. Bd. dirs. Univ. Adult Day Ctr., 1993—; mem. adv. bd. Regional Ombudsman Program, 1998—, Residents Coun. Washington, 1998—. Capt. USAAF, 1942-46. Mem. Am. Med. Writers Assn. (bd. dirs. 1967-70, pres. N.Y. chpt. 1967-68, nat. pres. 1972-73), Am. Physiol. Soc., Internat. Coll. Surgeons, Am. Therapeutic Soc., Coll. Clin. Pharmacology and Therapeutics, Am. Chem. Soc. Home and Office: Unit 308 4400 Stone Way N Seattle WA 98103-7486 Home Phone: 206-284-8809. Personal E-mail: grampared@comcast.net.

SCHILDER, RUSSELL J., oncologist, educator; M, U. Miami. Intern internal medicine Temple Univ. Hosp., resident internal medicine; assoc. prof. medicine Temple Univ.; fellow hematology and oncology Fox Chase Cancer Ctr., mem., dept. med. oncology, 1986—. Co-author: (publs.) Relevant molecular markers and targets, 2006, Increased expression of the pro-protein convertase furin predicts decreased survival in ovarian cancer, 2007, Platinum resistance: the role of DNA repair pathways, 2008, A phase II evaluation of bortezomib in the treatment of recurrent platinum-sensitive ovarian or primary peritoneal cancer: A Gynecologic Oncology Group study, 2009, Sorafenib in combination with gemcitabine in recurrent epithelial ovarian cancer. A study of the Princess Margaret Hospital Phase II Consortium, 2010, and numerous other publs. Mem.: ACP, Eastern Coop. Oncology Group, Soc. for Biologic Therapy, Am. Soc. for Blood and Marrow Transplantation, Am. Soc. of Hematology, Am. Soc. of Clin. Oncology. Office: Fox Chase Cancer Center 333 Cottman Ave Philadelphia PA 19111 Office Phone: 215-728-6900.

SCHILDGEN, OLIVER, virologist, researcher; b. Nuremberg, Germany, July 23, 1974; adopted s. Klaus and s. Andrea Schildgen, s. Albert Schlaf; m. Verena Maiworm, Apr. 4, 2003. Diploma in biology, U. Cologne, Germany, 1998; D, U. Essen, 2001. Rsch. scientist U. Cologne, Max-Planck-Inst. Neurol. Rsch., Germany, 1998—99, U. Essen, 1999—2001, U. Bonn, 2002—. Mem.: German Soc. Virology, Reiterkorps Jan von Werth (assoc.). Evangelist. Achievements include research in human metapneumovirus (HMPV); hepatitis B viruses (WHV, HBV); herpes simplex virus (HSV-1); patents pending for HBV drug resistance and uses thereof. Avocations: Judo, Ninjutsu, cooking, dance, sightseeing. Office Fax: 4902282874433. Personal E-mail: oliver.schildgen@freenet.de.

SCHILLER, JOAN HOFF, oncologist, educator; b. Chgo., Nov. 10, 1954; MD, U. Ill. Coll. Medicine, Chgo., 1980. Diplomate Am. Bd. Internal Medicine, Am. Bd. Internal Medicine, Med. Oncology, cert. Nat. Bd. Med. Examiners. Intern, internal medicine Northwestern Meml. Hosp., Chgo., 1980—81, resident, oncology, 1981—83; fellow, human oncology U. Wis. Clin. Cancer Ctr., Madison, Wis., 1984—86, rsch. assoc.; asst. prof. U. Wis., Madison, Melanie Heald prof., dept. medicine, sect. med. oncology; dep. dir., Harold C. Simmons Comprehensive Cancer Ctr. U. Tex. Southwestern Med. Ctr., Dallas, chair, hematology/oncology, prof., dept. hematology/oncology. Mem. internat. scientific com. 10th World Conf. on Lung Cancer; head, lung cancer disease-orientated working group U. Wis. Hosp. and Cancer Ctr.; spkr. in field. Contbr. articles to profl. jours., chapters to books. Mem. med. com. Joan's Legacy Lung Found.; founder, pres. Women Against Lung Cancer. Mem.: Am. Soc. Clin. Oncology, Eastern Co-operative Oncology Group (chairperson, thoracic oncology com.). Office: U Tex Southwestern Med Ctr at Dallas 5323 Harry Hines Blvd Dallas TX 75390-8852 Office Phone: 214-648-4180. Office Fax: 214-648-1955.

SCHILLER, WILLIAM RICHARD, surgeon; b. Bennett, Colo., Jan. 14, 1937; s. Francis T. and Frances M. (Finks) S.; m. Beverlee Schiller; children from previous marriage: Julie, Lisa. BS, Drury Coll., Springfield, Mo., 1958; MD, Northwestern U., 1962; MA in Liberal Arts, St. John's Coll., 2005. Diplomate Am. Bd. Surgery; cert. of added qualifications in surg. critical care, 1987, recertified in surg. critical care, 1994. Intern Passavant Meml. Hosp., Chgo., 1962-63; resident Northwestern U. Clin. Tng. Program, Chgo., 1963-68; assoc. prof. surgery Med. Coll Ohio, Toledo, 1970-78; prof. surgery U. N.Mex, Albuquerque, 1978-83; dir. Trauma Ctr. St. Joseph's Hosp., Phoenix, 1983-89; dir. burn and trauma ctr. Maricopa Med. Ctr., Phoenix, 1989-98; prof. surgery So. Ill. U., Springfield, 1998—2002; ret., 2002. Clin. prof. surgery U. Ariz. Health Sci. Ctr.; prof. surgery Mayo Grad. Sch. Medicine, Rochester, Minn. Contbr. chpts. to books, articles to profl. jours. Served as maj. M.C. U.S. Army, 1968-70, Vietnam. Recipient Disting. Alumnus award for career achievement, Drury Coll., 2004. Fellow ACS; mem. Am. Assn. Surgery of Trauma, Cen. Surg. Assn., Western Surg. Assn., Soc. Surgery of Alimentary Tract, Am. Burn Assn., Internat. Soc. of Surgery. Republican. Home: 784 Aspen Compound Santa Fe NM 87501 Personal E-mail: wrschiller@hughes.net.

SCHILLINGER, ERIKA, medical educator; b. NYC, Sept. 19, 1964; BA, Harvard U., 1986; MD, Stanford U., 1994. Clin. assoc. prof. Stanford U. Med. Sch., 1997—. Recipient Bloomfield award, Stanford U. Avocations: singing, hiking, crafts. Office: 900 Blake Wilbur Dr W3045 Palo Alto CA 94304 Business E-Mail: erikas@stanford.edu.

SCHILSKY, RICHARD LEWIS, oncologist, researcher; b. NYC, June 6, 1950; s. Murray and Shirley (Cohen) S.; m. Cynthia Schum, Sept. 24, 1977; children: Allison, Meredith. BA cum laude, U. Pa., Phila., 1971; MD with honors, U. Chgo., 1975. Diplomate Nat. Bd. Med. Examiners, Am. Bd. Internal Medicine (subspecialty med. oncology); lic. physician, Mo., Ill. Intern, resident medicine Parkland Meml. Hosp., Southwestern Med. Sch., Dallas, 1975-77; clin. assoc. medicine br. and clin. pharmacology br. Divsn. Cancer Treatment, Nat. Cancer Inst., Bethesda, Md., 1977-80, cancer expert clin. pharmacology br., 1980-81; asst. prof. dept. internal medicine U. Mo. Sch. Medicine, Columbia, 1981-84; asst. prof. dept. medicine U. Chgo. Pritzker Sch. Medicine and Michael Reese Med. Ctrs., 1984-86, assoc. prof. dept. medicine, 1986-89; assoc. dir. joint sect. hematology and med. oncology U. Chgo. and Michael Reese Med. Ctrs., 1986-89; assoc. prof. dept. medicine, assoc. dir. sect. U. Chgo. Pritzker Sch. Medicine, 1989-91, prof. dept. medicine sect. hematology-oncology, 1991—; dir. U. Chgo. Cancer Rsch. Ctr., 1991-99; chmn. Cancer and Leukemia Group B, Chgo., 1995—2010; assoc. dean clin. rsch. biol. scis. divsn. U. Chgo., 1999—2007. Vivian Saykaly vis. prof. oncology McGill U., 1992; sci. com. Internat. Congress on Anti-Cancer Chemotherapy, 2002; adv. panel on hematologic and neoplastic disease U.S. Pharmacopeial Conv., 1991-95; cancer ctr. support grant rev. com. Nat. Cancer Inst., NIH, 1992-95; expert panel on advances in cancer treatment, 1992-93; mem. Cancer Ctrs. Working Group, 1996-97; oncologic drugs adv. com. FDA, 1996-2000, chmn., 1999-2000; mem. clin. trials implementation com. Nat. Cancer Inst., 1997-98, mem. bd. sci. advisors, 1999—, chmn., 2009-, mem. clin. trials working group, 2004-05, mem. translational rsch. working group, 2005-07, mem. clin. trials adv. com., 2007-. Mem. editl. bd. Investigational New Drugs, 1988-95, Jour. Clin. Oncology, 1990-93, Contemporary Oncology, 1991-95, Jour. Cancer Rsch. and Clin. Oncology, 1991—, Seminars in Oncology, 1997—; assoc. editor Clin. Cancer Rsch., 1994—, Cancer Therapeutics, 1997-99, Cancer, 2000—07; contbr. articles to profl. jours., chpts. to books. With USPHS, 1977-80. Recipient Spl. Advancement for Performance award VA, 1983, Fletcher Scholar award Cancer Rsch. Found., 1989; grantee VA, 1981-87, Am. Cancer Soc., 1983-86, 92-95, Ill. Cancer Coun., 1985-86, Michael Reese Inst. Coun., 1985-86, Nat. Cancer Inst., 1987, 88-90, Burroughs-Wellcome Co., 1987-88, NIH/Nat. Cancer Inst., 1988— Fellow ACP; mem. AAAS, Am. Soc. Clin. Oncology (bd. dirs. 2002-05, pres.-elect 2007, pres. 2008-2009, immediate past pres., 2009-10), Am. Assn. Cancer Rsch., Am. Fedn. Clin. Rsch. (senator Midwest sect. 1983-84, councilor 1983-86, chmn. 1988-89), Am. Cancer Soc. (bd. dirs. Ill. divsn. 1997-2002), Am. Assn. Cancer Edn., Am. Soc. Clin. Pharmacology and Therapeutics, Ctrl. Soc. Clin. Rsch., N.Y. Acad. Scis., Assn. Am. Cancer Insts. (bd. dirs. 1995-99), Chgo. Soc. Internal Medicine, Am. Fedn. for Med. Rsch., Am. Soc. Clin. Oncology, Assn. Patient Orientated Rsch., Sigma Xi, Alpha Epsilon Delta, Alpha Omega Alpha. Office: University Chgo Biol Scis Divsn 5841 S Maryland Ave MC 2115 Chicago IL 60637-1463 Office Phone: 773-834-3914. Office Fax: 773-834-3915. Business E-Mail: rschilsk@medicine.bsd.uchicago.edu.

SCHIM, STEPHANIE MYERS, nursing educator; b. Mt. Vernon, Ohio, Mar. 15, 1951; d. Herbert Gardner and Bertha Aileen (Milligan) Myers; m. Carl Christopher Schim, June 5, 1976 (div. Feb. 1998); 1 child, Michael Myers Schim. BA, U. Mich., 1973; BSN, Cornell N.Y. Hosp., 1977; MSN, Wayne State U., Detroit, 1981, PhD, 1997. Cert. pub. health clin. nurse specialist. Pub. health nurse Visiting Nurses, Detroit, 1977-79; staff nurse, charge nurse Rehab. Inst., Detroit, 1979-81; adjunct faculty Madonna U., Livonia, Mich., 1981-82; dist. supr. Visiting Nurses, Detroit, 1982-85; pub. health supr. Oakland County Health Dept., Pontiac, Mich., 1985-87, chief of field nursing, 1987-94, chief of clinics, 1994-97; nurse scholar Henry Ford Health Sys./Oakland U. Ctr. Acad. Nursing, Detroit, 1997—2002; asst. prof. Wayne St. U., Detroit, 2000—06, assoc. prof., 2006—. Contbr. articles to profl. jours. Mem. Midwest Nursing Rsch. Soc., Transcultural Nursing Soc., Assn. Cmty. Health Nurse Educators, Sigma Theta Tau. Episcopalian. Avocations: sewing, reading. Home: 1203 Etowah Ave Royal Oak MI 48067-3473 Office: 240 Cohn Detroit MI 48202 Business E-Mail: s.schim@wayne.edu.

SCHINDERLE, ROBERT FRANK, retired hospital administrator; b. Mayville, Wis., Aug. 3, 1923; m. Elizabeth, June 23, 1949; children: David, Gary, Mary. BS, Marquette U., Milw., 1949; MS, Northwestern U., Evanston, Ill., 1959. Asst. office mgr. Western Leather Co., Milw., 1949-51; mgr. bus. office St. Francis Hosp., Peoria, Ill., 1951-55; credit mgr. Mercy Hosp., Chgo., 1955-59, asst. to adminstr., 1957-58, controller, 1958-59, asst. adminstr., 1959-65, St. Joseph Hosp., Joliet, Ill., 1965-70, assoc. adminstr., 1970-71, adminstr., 1971-76, exec. dir., 1976—86; adminitr., chief exec. officer St. Joseph Med. Ctr., 1976—86; ret. dir. corp. legis. affairs and devel. Franciscan Sisters Health Care Corp., Mokena, Ill., 1989; dir. Current Affairs & Devel., 1986—89, chmn. bd. dirs., 1994—97. Chmn. Areawide Hosp. Emergency Svcs. Coun. Bd. dirs. Region IX Health Systems Agy., Our Lady of Angels Retirement Home, Joliet, Joliet YMCA, St. Joseph Coll. Nursing, Joliet. Recipient Sister Borameo award. Fellow Am. Coll. Health Care Execs. (life); mem. Am. Hosp. Assn., Ill. Hosp. Assn. (chmn. 1975-78), Ill. Hosp. Licensing Bd. (chmn. 1982-97, vice chmn. 1997-), Catholic Hosp. Assn. (bd. dir., 1975-78), Ill. Cath. Hosp. Assn. (chmn. 1972-73), Lodges: Rotary, Elks, KC, Delta Sigma Pi Bus. Frat., Beta Gamma Sigma. Roman Catholic. Home: 24017 W Newkirk Dr Plainfield IL 60544-1838

SCHINDLER, SEPP ROLF, psychologist; b. Vienna, Dec. 14, 1922; s. Josef Schindler and Josefine Augesky; m. Elfriede Onder, Aug. 28, 1964; 3 children. PhD, U. Vienna, 1949; Univ. Doz., U. Salzburg, Austria, 1969. Cert. clin. psychologist, public officer. Tchr. prison adminstr., Vienna, 1949—56; psychologist Vienna, 1957—60; dir. probation svc., 1960—73; prof. U. Salzburg, 1973—87, head of psychology dept., 1985—87. Recipient Gold medal, Fed. Republic of Austria, 1983. Home: Nonntaler Hauptstrasse 37D A-5020 Salzburg Austria

SCHINFELD, JAY S., obstetrician, gynecologist, educator; MD, Thomas Jefferson Med. Coll. Diplomate Am. Bd. Ob-Gyn, Am. Bd. Ob-Gyn-reproductive endocrinology. Resident ob-gyn. Albert Einstein Coll. Medicine; fellow gynecologic endocrinology and fertility Brigham and Women's Hosp.; hosp. affiliations include Doylestown Hosp., Holy Redeemer, Lower Bucks Hosp., Albert Einstein Hosps., Grand View Hosp.; clin. prof. Jefferson Med. Coll.; dir. divsn. reproductive endocrinology & infertility Abington Meml. Hosp., Pa. Mem.: PA. Med. Soc., Phila. Obstet. Soc., Phila. Area Reproductive Endocrine Soc., Am. Soc. Reproductive Medicine, Am. Coll. Obstetricians and Gynecologists. Office: Abington Memorial Hospital Towamencin Corporate Ctr 1690 Sumneytown Pk Ste 190 Lansdale PA 19446 Office Phone: 215-855-7511. Office Fax: 215-855-7611.

SCHINGALE, FRANZ JOSEF, physician; b. Helmstedt, Germany, Dec. 21, 1946; s. Kurt and Annerose Schingale; m. Bernadette Anna Katherina Schwegel, June 12, 1982; children: Philine Valeria, Vanessa Verena, Sebastian Kurt Heinrich. MD, Philipps U., 1977. Asst. St. Johannis Hosp., Landstuhl, Germany, 1975—77; asst. surgeon City Hosp., Bamberg, 1977—80; surgeon pvt. practice, Vorra, 1980—2004. Med. dir. Lympho-Opt clinic, Pommelsbrunn, Germany, 1982—; ptnr. H&S funds, Vorra; med. instr. lymphtherapists Lymphologic, Augsburg, 2001—. Author: (book) lymphoedema, lipoedema, Diagnosis and Therapy; co-author: Practical Ambulant Lymphology. Lieutnant German Mil., 1966—68. Master: Soc. German Speaking Lymphologists, Fed. Assn. Lymphologists (pres.), Lympho-Opt Network (pres.); mem.: Assn. Phlebology, Assn. Lymphology Czech Republic (hon.), Assn. Lymphology (assoc.). Home: Zelchstrasse 12 Vorra D-91247 Germany Office: Lympho-Opt Clinic Happurgerstrasse 15 Pommelsbrunn D-91224 Germany Office Fax: +49 9154 911 202. Personal E-mail: schingale@lympho-opt.de.

SCHIOLDANN, JOHAN ANDREAS, psychiatrist, educator; b. Aalborg, Denmark, Oct. 16, 1941; arrived in Australia, 1984; s. Karl Rasmus Rudolf Nielsen and Ela Larsen; m. Marianne Moritz, May 18, 1968 (div. Jan. 2, 1972); m. Ann-Marie Marr, Oct. 7, 1978; children: Hannah, Sophie, Eliza, Heloise, Lise-Lotte. MD, U. Copenhagen, 1969; DMSc, Odense U., Denmark, 1983. Lic. diploma of psychiatry Denmark. Sr. cons. psychiatrist Glenside Hosp., Eastwood, Adelaide, Australia, 1985—87; dir. psychiatry Townsville Gen. Hosp., Queensland, Australia, 1987—88; sr. cons. psychiatrist Graylands Hosp., Claremont, Perth, Western Australia, 1988—95; forensic psychiatrist Justice Dept., Copenhagen, 1990—91; from clin. assoc. prof. to clin. prof. U. Western Australia, 1992—96; dir. Psychiat. Emergency Svcs. South Australia, 1995—97; clin. prof. U. Adelaide, 1996—2008, emeritus prof., 2008; sr. cons. psychiatrist Glenside Hosp. and Royal Adelaide Hosp., Adelaide, 1997—2006; private practice Adelaide, 2007—11. Vis. neuropsychiatrist Julia Farr Svc., Adelaide, 1997—2001. Author: D.G. Monrad. A Pathography, 1983, Famous and Very Important Persons, 1960-1984, 1986, The Life of D. G. Monrad (1811-1887), 1988, In Commemoration of the Centenary of the Death of Carl Lange. The Lange Theory of Periodical Depressions. A Landmark in the History of Lithium Therapy, 2001, History of the Introduction of Lithium into Medicine and Psychiatry: Birth of Modern Psychopharmacology 1949, 2009; author: (with others) Pre-Durkheim Suicidology: The 1892 Reviews of Tuke and Savage, 2002; editor: King Christian VII's Insanity, 1906, 1978, Memory of Woe of the Sixth Department, 1897, 1978, Extracts of Professor Herholdt's Diaries Regarding the Illness of Rachel Hertz, 1807-1826, 1987, On Possession States, 1924, On Diseases in the Bible. A Medical Miscellany, 1672, 1994; author: Erik Stromgren (1909-1993), 1996; author: Famous and Very Important Persons, Vol. 2: 1985-1999, 2005; editor: Erik Stromgren Talks About His Life in Psychiatry, 2002; trans., editor: Psychogenic Psychoses (1916), 2003; editor: Bibliotheca Danorum Medica or Full Conspectus of Medical and Related Treatises in Denmark, Norway, 2004, Schleswig and Holstein Down to the Year 1832, 2004, Handbook of the Literature of the Natural Sciences in Denmark, Norway and Holstein From the Year 1829, 2006, Introduction to the Bibliography of Practical Medicine 1806, 2006; contbr. articles to profl. med. jours. Fellow: Royal Australian and New Zealand Coll. Psychiatrists; mem.: World Psychiat. Assn. (sect. clin. psychopathology, sect. history pyschiat.), Australian Soc. Authors. Avocations: history, biography. Office: U Adelaide Discipline of Psychiatry Royal Adelaide Hosp Adelaide 5006 Australia Home: 26 Blackburn St Adelaide 5000 Australia Fax: 61 83646961. Business E-Mail: schioldann@senet.com.au, johan.schioldann@three.com.au.

SCHIRBER, ANNAMARIE RIDDERING, retired speech and language pathologist, educator; b. Somerset County, NJ, Dec. 18, 1941; d. Pieter C. and Marie Louise (Kerk) Riddering; m. Eric R. Schirber, Aug. 25, 1960; children: Stefan Rene, Ashley Brooke. BA in Speech and Hearing Therapy, Rutgers U., 1964; MA in Edn. of Deaf and Hard of Hearing, Smith Coll., 1968; postgrad., Rutgers U., 1987-93. Speech therapist Manatee County Bd. Edn., Bradenton, Fla., 1968-69; speech-lang. specialist Lawrence Twp. Pub. Schs., Lawrenceville, NJ, 1969—2002, Montgomery Twp. Bd. Edn., Skillman, NJ, 2003, Rock Brook Sch., Skillman, 2003—07. Adj. instr. comm. dept. Trenton (N.J.) State Coll., 1983-87; vis. lectr. Rutgers U., New Brunswick, 1993. Author: Teaching Auditory Processing Skills to Children, 1994; co-author: (with Erica Winebrenner) Speech Activities for Children, 1994, Language Activities to Teach Children at Home, 1994. Mem. exec. com. Women's Coll. Symposium, Princeton, N.J., 1982-84; mem. nat. alumnae admissions com. Smith Coll., Northampton, Mass., 1984-86. Grantee Lawrence Twp. Bd. Edn., 1973, 89, 90, Lawrence Twp. Edn. Found., 1999, 2001. Mem. AAUW (Venice, Fla. br. sec. 2009-11), Princeton Area Smith Coll. Club (exec. com. 1996-2007, pres. 1998-2000), Smith Coll. Club Sarasota, Fla. (exec. com. mem. 2008-10), Southbay Women's Club (pres. 2010). Home: 1505 Danforth Ln Osprey FL 34229

SCHIZA, SOPHIA E., medical educator; b. Greece, Mar. 17, 1967; MD, Med. Sch. U. Crete, 1991, PhD, 1998. Lectr. to asst. prof., thoracic medicine U. Crete, 2002—, head sleep disorders unit, dept. thoracic medicine, med. sch., 2002. V.p., accreditation sleep labs. Hellenic Thoracic Soc., 2008, coord., sleep breathing disorders group, 08. Mem.: Am. Coll. Chest Physicians, Am. Thoracic Soc., Am. Acad. Sleep Medicine, European Sleep Rsch. Soc., European Respiratory Soc. Avocations: music, tennis. Office: University Hosp Dept Thoracic Me Heraklion Crete 71110 Greece Office Fax: 30 2810 542650. Business E-Mail: schiza@med.uoc.gr.

SCHIZAS, CONSTANTIN, spinal surgeon, researcher; b. Athens, Greece, Oct. 27, 1961; m. Anne-Sophie Rieben, Aug. 10, 1992. MD, U. Louvain, Brussels, 1986; MS in Orthop., U. Coll. London, 1994; PhD, U. Lausanne, Switzerland, 1995; postgrad. diploma in Bioengring., U. Strathclyde, Glasgow, Eng., 1995. Intern, resident Royal Nat. Orthopaedic Hosp., London; oberarzt Schulthess Clinic, Zurich, Switzerland, 1995—96; cons. orthop. and spinal surgeon Queen Mary's Hosp., London, 1996—2000; hon. cons. St Luke's Hosp. for Clergy, London, 2000—; cons. orthop. and spinal surgeon Whittington Hosp., London, 2000—03; hon. cons. orthop. surgeon Royal Nat. Orthop. Hosp., Stanmore, Middlesex, England, 2002—. Hon. sr. lectr.

U. London, London, 2000—03; spinal surgeon U. Lausanne, Switzerland, 2003—. Contbr. chpt. to book. Fellow: Royal Coll. Surgeons Eng., Swiss Orthop. Assn., Brit. Orthop. Assn.; mem.: Swiss Spine Soc. (sec.), Assn. Study Internal Fixation (faculty 2002—), Cervical Spine Rsch. Soc., Eurospine Spinal Soc. Europe. Achievements include research in minimally invasive techniques in spinal surgery; gait analysis in scoliosis surgery; back pain treatment; hip replacement surgery; disc bioengineering. Avocations: skiing, mountain climbing. Office: Hosp Orthopedique Da La Suisse Romande Lausanne 1011 Switzerland Office Phone: 413149609.

SCHLEGEL, PETER NILES, urologist, educator; b. Malden, Mass., Feb. 17, 1958; s. Niles Matthew and Mary Patricia (McIntyre) S.; children: Andrew Peter, Lucy Filice, Nicholas Halloran. AB, Hamilton Coll., 1979; MD, U. Mass., 1983. Diplomate Am. Bd. Urology, Nat. Bd. Med. Examiners; lic. physician, N.Y. Intern in gen. surgery and resident Johns Hopkins Hosp., Balt., 1983-85, resident, chief resident in urology, 1985-89, instr. urology, 1989; fellow-in-residence The Population Coun., NYC, 1989-91, staff scientist, 1991—; asst. attending surgeon New York Hosp., NYC, 1991-96; assoc. attending surgeon N.Y. Hosp., NYC, 1996—; assoc. vis. physician Rockefeller U., NYC, 1991—; asst. prof. urology Cornell Med. Coll., NYC, 1991-96, assoc. prof. urology, 1996—2004, prof., 2004—, vice chmn. urology, 1999-2001, acting chmn., 2001—03, chmn., 2003—. Vis. prof. Austria, Israel, Indonesia, Japan, Saudi Arabia, Brazil, others; vis. fellow Royal Coll. Surgeons, 1993; co-dir. Ctr. for Male Reproduction and Microsurgery, Cornell Inst. for Reproductive Medicine, 2000—03; lectr. in field. Former co-editor Jour. Audiology; mem. numerous editl. bds.; contbr. numerous articles, abstracts to profl. jours., chpts. to books. Trustee Am. bd. Urology. Recipient Edwin Beer Program award N.Y. Acad. Medicine, 1996-98, New Investigator award Am. Found. for Urol. Disease, 1993-95, fellow, 1989-91; fellow Am. Cancer Soc., 1986-87, NIH, 1989-91; established Clinician award ESHRE, 1996; named one of Medical Marvels, New York Mag., 2006 Mem.: Am. Bd. Urology (trustee 2009—), Soc. for Male Reprodn. /Urology (pres.), Soc. for Study of Male Reprodn. (pres.), Am. Urol. Assn., Soc. for Basic Urol. Rsch., Soc. for Study of Reprodn., Am. Soc. Andrology, Am. Soc. Reproductive Medicine (bd. dirs.), Alpha Omega Alpha. Roman catholic. Avocation: sailing. Office: New York Hosp Dept Urology 525 E 68th St New York NY 10021-4885 Office Phone: 212-746-5491. E-mail: pnschleg@med.cornell.edu. *

SCHLEGEL, TOBIAS JOHANNES, orthopedist, surgeon; b. Cologne, Germany, Sept. 3, 1963; s. Karl Friedrich and Sigrun Karin Betty Schlegel; m. Nicola Kremser, Sept. 23, 1993; children: Carla Marie, Ella Alberta. MD, U. Essen, 1992. Lic. in orthopaedy Aerztekammer Nordrhein, 1998. Resident Huyssens-Stiftung, Essen, Germany, 1992—93, Lutherhaus, Essen, 1993—94, St. Vinzenz-Krankenhaus, Duesseldorf, Germany, 1994—95, St. Marien-Hosp. Kaiserswerth, Duesseldorf, Germany, 1995—96, head physician, 1997—99; med. supt. Orthopaedic Clinic, Muelheim an der Ruhr, Germany, 1999—. Author: Schmerz-Manual, 2002; contbr. articles to profl. jours. Mem.: Sueddeutsche Orthopaeden Assn., German Press Assn., German Pain Assn., Internat. Soc. Thermology, German Soc. Orthopaedics. Achievements include research in thermology, pharmacology and others. Home: Hans-Luther-Allee 15 Nordrhein-Westfalen Essen 45131 Germany Office: Praxisklinik Friedrichstrasse Friedrichstrasse 12 Nordrhein-Westfalen Muelheim an der Ruhr 45468 Germany Office Fax: +49(208)382386; Home Fax: +49(201)8776864. Personal E-mail: schlegel.ortho@t-online.de.

SCHLEIFER, STEVEN J., psychiatrist, educator; b. NYC, Mar. 10, 1950; s. Jack and Caroline (Rapps) S.; m. Sarah L. Rosenberg, Dec. 1971; children: Jonathan, Jason, Justin, Tara. MD, Mt. Sinai Sch. of Medicine, 1975; BA, Columbia Coll., 1971. Diplomate Nat. Bd. Med. Examiners, Am. Bd. Psychiatry and Neurology. Asst. prof. of psychiatry Mt. Sinai Sch. of Medicine, New York, NY, 1982—87; assoc. prof. of psychiatry UMDNJ-New Jersey Med. Sch., Newark, 1987—92, prof. of psychiatry NJ, 1992—, chair, dept. of psychiatry NJ, 1992—2001. Cons. NIH, Bethesda, Md., 1984—, Hackensack U. Med. Ctr., NJ, 1988—2010, Veterans Adminstrn. Med. Ctr., East Orange, NJ, 1988—2002; chief of svc., dept of psychiatry UMDNJ-Univ. Hosp., Newark; chief of svc. UMDNJ-Univ. Behavioral Healthcare, Newark, 1992—2002. Contbr. articles to profl. jours. Grantee NIMH, 1982, Chernow Found., N.Y.C., 1983, Upjohn Co., Kalamazoo, 1989, NIAAA, 1990. Fellow Am. Psychiat. Assn. (disting.); mem. NJ Psychiat. Assn., Soc. Biol. Psychiatry, Am. Psychosomatic Soc., Psychoneuroimmunology Rsch. Soc., Acad. Psychosomatic Medicine, Brain, Behavior and Immunity (editl. bd. mem). Avocations: opera, skiing. Office: UMDNJ-New Jersey Med Sch 183 South Orange Ave Newark NJ 07103 E-mail: schleife@umdnj.edu.

SCHLESINGER, IRWIN D., neurologist; b. Brooklyn, Sept. 13, 1935; s. Edward Schlesinger and Eva Parkoff; m. Marcia Rubinstein; 1 child, Lisa. BS, Bklyn. Coll., 1956; MD, SUNY, Med. U., Syracuse, 1961. Diplomate Am. Bd. Psychiatry and Neurology, Am. Bd. Clin. Neurophysiology. Intern then resident medicine Cornell med. divsn. Bellevue Hosp., NYC, 1961—63; resident neurology Albert Einstein Coll. Medicine Bronx Mcpl. Hosp., 1965—68; neurologist Neurol. Specialities L.I., Manhasset, NY, 1968—. Attending neurologist N. Shore Univ. Hosp., Manhasset, 1968—; staff neurologist L.I. Jewish Med. Ctr., Glen Oaks, NY, 1969—; cons. neurologist St. Francis Hosp., Roslyn, NY, 1975—; clin. assoc. prof. neurology Cornell U. Med. Coll., NYC, 1971—95, NYU Med. Sch., NYC, 1995—. Capt. USAF, 1963—65. Fellow: ACP, Am. Acad. Neurology; mem.: AMA, Am. Acad. Sleep Medicine, Am. Clin. Neurophysiology Soc., Am. Assn. Electrodiagnostic Medicine, Alpha Omega Alpha. Office: 3 Delaware Dr Lake Success NY 11042

SCHLESINGER, SARAH JANE, medical educator, researcher; b. Chgo., Feb. 28, 1960; d. Edward S. and Renee C. Schlesinger; m. Terrace Room, June 20, 1982. Grad., Wellesley Coll., Mass.; MD, Rush Med Coll., Chgo., 1985. Cert. Anatomic Pathology. Intern otolaryngology Albert Einstein Coll. Medicine, Bronx, NY, 1985—86, resident anatomical pathology, 1986—87, NY Hosp., NYC, 1987—89, resident, 1989—90; asst. prof. pathology Cornell U., 1990, SUNY, Buffalo, 1991—94; asst. prof. Georgetown U. Med. Coll., Washington, 1994—2001; adj. faculty Rockefeller U., NYC, 2001—03, assoc. prof. clin. investigation, 2003—, rschr. Aaron Diamond AIDS Rsch. Ctr. Lab head Walter Reed Army Med. Ctr., Washington, 1990—2002; attending physician Buffalo Gen. Hosp., 1991—94; rschr. pathology Roswell Pk. Cancer Inst., NY, 1991—94; staff Armed Forces Inst. Pathology, Md., 1994; staff divsn. retrovirology Walter Reed Army Inst. Rsch., Rockville, Md., 1995. Contbr. articles to profl. jours.

SCHLESSINGER, JOSEPH, pharmacologist, biochemist, medical educator; b. Topusko, Croatia, Mar. 26, 1945; BSc in Chemistry/Physics magna cum laude, Hebrew U., Jerusalem, 1968, MSC in Chemistry magna cum laude, 1969; PhD, The Weizmann Inst. Sci., Rehovot, Israel, 1974. Postdoctoral assoc. Dept. Chemistry Sch. Applied Physics, Cornell U., 1974—76; vis. scientist Immunology Br. Nat. Cancer Inst., NIH, Bethesda, Md., 1977—78; sr. scientist Dept. Chem. Immunoloy The Weizmann Inst. Sci., Rehovot, 1978—80, assoc. prof., 1980—84, prof. Dept. Chem. Immunology, Ruth & Leonard Simon prof., 1984—91; dir. div. molecular biology Biotech. Rsch. Ctr. Meloy Labs., Inc., Rockville, Md., 1985—86, dir. Biotech. Rsch. Ctr., 1986—88; rsch. dir. Rorer Biotech., Inc., King of Prussia, Pa., 1988—90; Milton and Helen Kimmelman prof., chmn. Dept. Pharmacology NYU Med. Sch., NYC, 1990—2001; dir. Skirball Inst. Biomolecular Medicine NYU Med. Ctr., NYC, 1998—2001; William H. Prusoff prof., chmn. Dept. Pharmacology Yale U. Sch. of Medicine, New Haven, 2001—; founding dir. Cancer Biology Inst. Yale Cancer Ctr., New Haven, 2010—. Founder Plexxikon, 2001; co-founder, dir. and chmn. Sci. Adv. Bd. Kolltan. Mem. editl. bd. European Molecular Biology Orgn. Jour., Jour. Cell Biology, Cell Regulation, Cancer Rsch., Receptors, Growth Factors, Cell Crowth & Differentiation, Protein Engring., Oncogenes and Growth Factor Abstracts; contbr. articles to profl. jours. Recipient Sara Leedy prize, Weizmann Inst. Sci., 1980, Hestrin prize, Biochem. Soc. Israel, 1983, Levinson prize, 1984, Antoine Lacassagne prize, 1995, Disting. Svc. award, Miami Nature Biotechnology, 1999, AACR Internat. Award for Cancer Rsch., Pezcoller Found., 2010; co-recipient Drew-Ciba Prize, 1995, Taylor prize, 2000. Mem.: NAS, Inst. Medicine, Am. Acad. Arts and Scis., European Molecular Biology Orgn., Japanese Biochemical Soc. (hon.). Office: Yale University School of Medicine Department of Pharmacology PO Box 208066 New Haven CT 06520-8066 Office Phone: 203-785-7395. Office Fax: 203-785-3879. E-mail: joseph.schlessinger@yale.edu. *

SCHLEY, WILLIAM SHAIN, otolaryngologist; b. Columbus, Ga., Sept. 21, 1940; s. Frances Brooking Schley and Susie (Smith) Mathews. BA, Emory U., 1962, MD, 1966. Intern mixed surg. The Roosevelt Hosp., NYC, 1966-67, resident in surgery, 1967-68; resident in otorhinolaryngology N.Y. Hosp.-Cornell Med. Ctr., NYC, 1970-73; clin. instr. otorhinolaryngology Cornell U. Med. Coll., 1972-75, clin. asst. prof., 1975-81, assoc. prof., 1982—, acting chmn. dept. otorhinolaryngology, 1988-94, chmn. dept. otorhinolarygology, 1994—2005. Otorhinolaryngologist to outpatients with pvt. patient privileges N.Y. Hosp., 1973-75, asst. attending otorhinolaryngologist with pvt. patient privileges, 1975-81, assoc. attending, 1992—, acting otorhinolaryngologist-in-chief, 1988-94, otorhinolaryngologist-in-chief, 1994-2005; assoc. asst. surgeon otolaryngology Manhattan Eye, Ear, Nose and Throat Hosp., 1988-99; v.p. and sec. med. bd. N.Y. Hosp., 1994-97, pres., 1998-99, pres., v.p. med. bd. The N.Y. and Presbyn. Hosp., 1998, pres., 1998-99, mem. ex officio bd. trustees, 1998-99; mem. co-chmn. vis. day com. The N.Y. Hosp.-Cornell Med. Ctr., 1995-98; pres. N.Y. Hosp.-Cornell Med. Coll. Alumni Coun., 1996-98; course dir. Salzburg Cornell Med. Seminars, 1996—2007, steering com., 1999—, Homes fellow, 1998 Author: (with others) Pulmonary Diseases of the Fetus Newborn and Child, 1978; contbr. numerous articles to profl. publs. Vestry St. James Ch., N.Y.C., 1994-97, chmn. The Third Age Coun. St. James Ch., 2007-09; mem. ad hoc bd. visitors Emory U., 1994-95; bd. dirs. Health Advs. for Older People, 1997—, v.p., 2000—; mem. adv. bd. Sch. Medicine Emory U., 2000—, chmn. adv. bd., 2002—. Lt. comdr. USNR. Recipient The Emery medal, 2001, Austrian Cross of Merit, 2010; named NY Treasure, Health Advocates For Older People, 2010. Fellow ACS (Manhattan dist. #2 com. on applicants 1991-97, Manhattan Credentials Com. 1991-99); mem. Am. Acad. Otolaryngology-Head and Neck Surgery, Med. Soc. State of N.Y., N.Y. State Soc. Otolaryngology-Head and Neck Surgery (exec. coun. 1974-80, dist. dir. 1980), County Med. Soc. N.Y., N.Y. Laryngol. Soc. (sec.-treas. 1981-84, v.p. 1984-85, pres. 1985-86), N.Y. Bronchoscopic Soc. (v.p. 1986-94, pres. 1994-97), N.Y. Clin. Soc. (v.p. 1998-99, pres. 1999-2000, sec.-treas, 2005-07), Assn. Emory Alumni (bd. govs. 1990-97, pres.-elect 1993-94, pres. 1994-95), Omicron Delta Kappa. Episcopalian. Avocations: astronomy, ornithology. Home: 430 E 63d St Apt 5E New York NY 10065-7927 Office: DS10 449 E 68th St New York NY 10065-6310 Office Phone: 212-746-2223. E-mail: schley@med.cornell.edu.

SCHLICHTING, NANCY MARGARET, hospital administrator; b. NYC, Nov. 21, 1954; BA in Pub. Policy Studies magna cum laude, Duke U., 1976; MBA in Hosp. Adminstrn. and Acctg., Cornell U., 1979. Adminstrv. resident Meml. Sloan-Kettering Cancer Ctr., NYC, 1978; adminstrv. fellow American Hosp. Assn./Blue Cross-Blue Shield Assn., Chgo., 1979-80; fellow healthier cmtys. Health Care Forum; asst. dirs. ops. Akron (Ohio) City Hosp., 1980-81, assoc. dir. planning, 1981-83, exec. v.p., 1983-88, Riverside Meth. Hosps., Columbus, Ohio, 1988-92, pres., COO, 1992-93, pres., CEO, 1993-96; pres. Eastern region Cath. Health Initiatives, Aston, Pa., 1996-97; exec. v.p., COO Summa Health Sys., Akron, Ohio, 1997—98; sr. v.p., chief adminstrv. officer Henry Ford Healthcare Sys., Detroit, 1998—99, exec. v.p., COO, 1999—2003, pres., CEO, 2003—, Henry Ford Hosp., 2001—03. Bd. dirs. Fifth Third Bank Corp., First Nat. Bank of Ohio, Mich. Health and Hosp. Assn., Greater Detroit Area Health Coun., Walgreen Co., 2006—, Fifth Third Bank of Eastern Mich., Mayor's Time, Gilda's Club; bd. mem. Franklin Univ., Akron Regional Devel. Bd., AmeriTrust Columbus Adv. Br.; bd. mem. Coll. Bus. Adminstrn. Advancement Coun. Univ. Akron; past pres. Sloan Alumni Assn. Cornell Univ.; served as preceptor and lectr. in various schs. Bd. mem. Arthritis Found., Leadership Akron, ARC, Inter-Health, United Way of Franklin County, United Way of Summit County, YMCA Capital Campaign, Young Women's Christian Assn. (YWCA); trustee Kresge Found. Named an Up and Comer, Modern Healthcare, 1991; named one of Top 100 Most Influential Women in Detroit, Crain's Bus., 2002, Top 25 Women in Healthcare, Modern Healthcare mag., 2011; named to Macomb Hall of Fame. Office: Henry Ford Health Sytems 1 Ford Pl Ste 1C Detroit MI 48202 Office Phone: 313-874-6677. *

SCHLOERB, PAUL RICHARD, surgeon, educator; b. Buffalo, Oct. 22, 1919; s. Herman George and Vera (Gross) S.; m. Louise M. Grimmer, Feb. 25, 1950; children: Ronald G., Patricia S. Johnson, Marilyn A. Hock, Dorothy S. Hoban, P. Richard. AB, Harvard U., 1941; MD, U. Rochester, 1944. Intern U. Rochester Med. Sch., 1944—45, asst. resident, 1947—48, instr. surgery, 1952; rsch. fellow, resident Peter Bent Brigham Hosp., Boston, 1948—52; faculty U. Kans. Med. Ctr., Kansas City, 1952—79, prof. surgery, 1964—79, 1988—2006, prof. surgery emeritus, 2006—, dean for rsch., 1972—79, dir. nutritional support svc., 1993—2002; prof. surgery U. Rochester (NY) Med Ctr., 1979—88, adj. prof. surgery, 1988—90; surgeon Strong Meml. Hosp., 1979—88, dir. Surg. ICU, 1979—85, dir. surg. nutritional support service. Contbr. over 100 articles to profl. jours. Lt. (j.g.), M.C. USNR, 1944-55; to lt. 1953-55. Mem. AMA, ACS, AAAS, Am. Surg. Assn., Soc. U. Surgeons, Am. Physiol. Soc., Internat. Soc. Surgery, Ctrl. Surg. Assn., Am. Assn. for Surgery of Trauma, Am. Assn. Cancer Rsch., Biomed. Engring. Soc., Am. Inst. Nutrition, Am. Soc. Clin. Nutrition, Surgery Biology Club 2, Sigma Xi. Achievements include first to measure total body water in humans J. Clin. Invest. Office: Dept Surgery U Kansas Med Ctr Kansas City KS 66160-0001 Business E-Mail: pschloer@kumc.edu.

SCHLOM, JEFFREY BERT, research scientist; b. NYC, June 22, 1942; s. David and Anna Schlom; m. Kathleen; children: Amy Melissa, Steven Michael. BS (Pres.'s scholar), Ohio State U., 1964; MS, Adelphi U., 1966; PhD, Rutgers U., 1969. Instr. Columbia Coll. Phys. and Surg., 1969-71, asst. prof., 1971-73; chmn. breast cancer virus segment Nat Cancer Inst., NIH, Bethesda, Md., 1973-76, chief Lab. Tumor Immunology and Biology, 1983—, head Exptl. Oncology Sect., 1976-83, head Immunotherapeutics Group; prof. George Washington U., Washington, 1975—. Disting. lectr. Can. Cancer Soc., 1985 Contbr. articles to profl. jours. Recipient Dir.'s award NIH, 1977, 89, Tech. Transfer award NIH, 1994, 95, 96, Disting. Scientist award Turin U., 1996, others. Mem. Am. Assn. Cancer Rsch. (Rosenthal award 1985), Am. Soc. Cytology (Basic Rsch. award 1987). Office: Nat Cancer Inst / Ctr Cancer Rsch Bldg 10 Rm 8B09 10 Center Dr MSC 1750 Bethesda MD 20892 Office Phone: 301-496-4343. Office Fax: 301-496-2756. Business E-Mail: js141c@nih.gov. *

SCHLOSE, WILLIAM TIMOTHY, human services administrator; b. West Lafayette, Ind., May 16, 1948; s. William Fredrick and Dora Irene (Chitwood) Schlose; m. Linda Lee Fletcher, June 29, 1968 (div. 1978); children: Vanessa Janine Schlose Hubert, Stephanie Lynn; m. Kelly Marie Martin, June 6, 1987; 1 child, Taylor Jean Martin-Schlose. Student, Bowling Green State U., 1966-68, Long Beach City Coll., 1972-75. Cert. tchr. Calif. Staff respiratory therapist St. Vincent's Med. Ctr., LA, 1972-75; cardio-pulmonary chief Temple Cmty. Hosp., LA, 1975-76; adminstrv. dir. spl. svcs. Santa Fe Meml. Hosp., LA, 1976-79, mktg. and pub. rels. staff Nat. Med. Homecare Corp., Orange, Calif., 1979-81, Medtech of Calif., Inc., Burbank, Calif., 1981-84; regional mgr. Mediq Health Care Group Svcs., Inc., Chatsworth, Calif., 1984-88; pres. Baby Watch Homecare, Whittier, Calif., 1988-90, Tim Schlose and Assocs., Brea, Calif., 1990—. Staff instr. Montebello (Calif.) Adult Schs.; v.p. Naptime Diagnostics, Brea, 1990—. Author: Fundamental Respiratory Therapy Equipment, 1977; mem. editl. bd. RT, Jour. Respiratory Care Practitioners, 1997—. With USN, 1968—72. Mem.: Calif. Perinatal Assn., LA Pediat. Soc., Am. Assn. Physicians Assts., Nat. Assn. Apnea Profls., Nat. Bd. Respiratory Care, Calif. Soc. Respiratory Care (past officer), Am. Assn. Respiratory Care, So. Calif. Fiat Club (co-founder), Spl. Vehicle Team Owners Assn. (founder So. Calif. chpt.), SVTOA (charter dir. Calif. chpt.), Saleen Mustang Owners Group (founder), Mustang Club Am., SVT Cobra Owner's Club So. Calif., Saleen Owners Enthusiasts Club. Republican. Methodist. Avocations: boating, auto racing, auto restoration, fly fishing. Office: Tim Schlose Assocs 4195 Chino Hius Pky Ste 365 Chino Hills CA 91709 Office Phone: 800-822-1115. E-mail: naptimedx@verizon.com, timschlose@aol.com.

SCHLOSSER, BETHANEE, dermatologist, educator; b. Erie, Pa., Sept. 23, 1974; MD, Pa. State U., PhD, 2003. Asst. prof. Northwestern U. Feinberg Sch. Medicine, 2007—. Fellow: Am. Acad. Dermatology; mem.: Internat. Soc. Study Vulvovaginal Disease, Women's Dermatologic Soc. Office: Dept Dermatology 676 N St Clair Chicago IL 60611 Business E-Mail: bschloss@nmff.org.

SCHLOTTERBECK, DAVID L., health products executive; BSEE, GM Inst.; MSEE, Purdue U.; grad., Stanford U. Exec. Inst., 1984. Exec. v.p., COO Nellcor, Inc., 1991—94; pres., CEO Vitalcom, Inc., 1995—97; pres., COO Pacific Sci. Co., 1997—98, ALARIS Med. Systems, 1999—2004; CEO clinical technologies & services Cardinal Health, Inc., 2004—06, CEO clinical & medical products, 2006—09; chmn., CEO CareFusion Corp., San Diego, 2009—. Bd. dirs. Virtual Radiologic Corp., 2008—; vice chmn. Cardinal Health Inc., 2008—09. Office: CareFusion Corp 3750 Torrey View Ct San Diego CA 92130 Office Phone: 858-480-6000. Business E-Mail: david.schlotterbeck@carefusion.com.

SCHLUSSEL, RICHARD, urologist; MD, Albert Einstein Coll. of Medicine, 1986. Diplomate Am. Bd. Urology. Resident urology Mt. Sinai Med. Ctr., 1988—92; fellow urology Harvard Univ. Childrens Hosp., Boston, 1992—94. Asst. prof. urology Columbia Univ. Coll. of Physicians and Surgeons. Office: 65 E 96th St New York NY 10128 Office Phone: 212-305-1114.

SCHMETZER, ALAN DAVID, psychiatrist; b. Louisville, Sept. 3, 1946; s. Clarence Frederick and Catherine Louise (Wootan) Schmetzer; m. Janet Lynn Royce, Aug. 25, 1968; children: Angela Beth, Jennifer Lorraine. BA, Ind. U., 1968, MD, 1972. Diplomate Am. Bd. Psychiatry and Neurology, subsplty. cert. in addiction psychiatry; diplomate Am. Psychotherapy Assn., Am. Bd. Forensic Med. Examiners, Assn. Convulsive Therapy. Intern Ind. U. Hosps., Indpls., 1972-73, resident, 1972-75; dir. clinics PCI, Inc., Anderson, Beech Grove, Kokomo, Ind., 1975-79; psychiat. cons. Cmty. Addiction Svcs. Agy., Indpls., 1975-80; instr. psychiatry in primary care Family Practice Residency Programs St. Francis Hosp., St. Vincent's Hosp.

and Ind. U. Hosps., Indpls., 1975-91; med. dir. Child Guidance Clinic of Marion County, Indpls., 1980-81; chmn. psychiatry dept. St. Francis Hosp., Beech Grove, 1980-82; med. dir. Crisis Intervention Unit Midtown Mental Health Ctr., 1980-90, dir., 1990-96, med. dir., 1996-98; coord. emergency psychiat. svcs. Ind. U. Med. Ctr., Indpls., 1980-90, asst. prof. psychiatry, 1975-94, assoc. prof. psychiatry, 1994—2002, prof. psychiatry, 2002—, coord. psychiat. edn. of med. students, 1989-95, asst. chmn. dept. psychiatry, 1993-96, dir. psychiat. edn., 1995-97, vice chmn. edn. dept. psychiatry, 1997—, dir. psychiatry residency tng., 1998—, dir. addiction psychiatry residency tng. Indpls., 1999—; chief psychiatry Wishard Meml. Hosp., 1990-98; chief rsch. unit, pres. med. staff Larue D. Carter Meml. Hosp., 2007—. Primary psychiat. cons. Ind. Dept. Mental Health and Addiciton, 1988-89; med. dir. Ind. Divsn. Mental Health, 2001-03; supt. Larue D. Carter Meml. Hosp., 2003-05; examiner Am. Bd. Psychiatry and Neurology; addiction psychiatrist Midtown Mental Health Ctr., 2006-07; med. dir. Ind. U. Psychiat. Mgmt., Inc., 2007—. Contbr. articles to profl. jours. Maj. Ind. N.G., 1972-79. Decorated Army Commendation medal, 1978; recipient Residents award for outstanding teaching, 1985, 90, 97, 2003, Roeske Excellence in Teaching award, 1992, Med. Student Psychiatry Clin. Tchg. award, 2000, Irma Bland Residency Tchg. award, 2005, Alumnus of the Yr., Silver Creek H.S., 2005, Eugene E. Levitt svc. award in psychology, 2003, Exemplary Psychiatrist award NAMI, 2004, named one of Best Doctor's in Am., 2003-04, 06-07, Am. Top Psychiatrists, 2006. Fellow Am. Psychiat. Assn., Am. Ortho-psychiat. Assn.; mem. AMA (Physicians Recognition award 1978-), Ind. Med. Assn., Indpls. Med. Soc., Ind. Psychiat. Soc. (pres. 1989-90, 97-98), Am. Acad. Clin. Psychiatry, Univ. Faculty Club Indpls. (v.p. 1999-2000, pres. 2000-01), Athenaeum Turnverein Club, Alpha Phi Omega, Phi Beta Pi, Psi Chi, Alpha Epsilon Delta. Presbyterian. Office: Dept Psychiatry 1111 W 10th St PB-A212 Indianapolis IN 46202-4800 Office Phone: 317-274-1224. Business E-Mail: aschmetz@iupui.edu.

SCHMICKLER, STEFANIE, surgeon; b. Ahaus, Germany, Feb. 15, 1964; d. Dieter and Rosemarie Pietsch; m. Franz-Peter Schmickler, Apr. 16, 1988. MD, U. Muenster, Germany, 1989. Asst. Augenaerzte Gemeinschaftspraxis, Ahaus, 1989—91, St. Johannes Hosp., Dortmund, Germany, 1991—93. Pres. VSDAR, Munich, 1999—2000. Contbr. articles (Best paper, 2006). Recipient Video and Poster prize, DOC, 1996—2008. Mem.: ESCRS (Video prize 2002), AAO, ASCRS (Video and Poster prize 1996—2010), BAO, DOG, DGII, Ocunet. Conservative. Roman Catholic. Achievements include research in different surgical videos. Office: Augenaerzte Gemeinschaftspraxis Domhof 15 Ahaus North Rhine Westphalia D-48683 Germany also: Augen Zentrum Anaus Wuellenerstr 97a Ahaus North Rhine Westphalia D 48683 Germany Office Phone: 49256193000. Office Fax: 4925619300138. Business E-Mail: schmickler@augenpraxis.de.

SCHMID, LYNETTE SUE, child and adolescent psychiatrist; b. Tecumseh, Nebr., May 28, 1958; d. Mel Vern John and Janice Wilda (Bohling) S.; m. Vijendra Sundar, June 13, 1987; children: Jesse Christopher Mikaéle, Eric Lynn Kalani, Christina Elizabeth Ululani. BS, U. Nebr., 1979; MD, U. Nebr., Omaha, 1984; postgrad., U. Mo., 1984—89. Diplomate Am. Bd. Med. Examiners, Am. Bd. Psychiatry and Neurology. Child and adolescent psychiatrist Fulton (Mo.) State Hosp., 1990-91, Mid-Mo. Mental Health Ctr., Columbia, Mo., 1991-96; owner Fairview Motel, Kemmerer, Wyo., 1996—. Clin. asst. prof. psychiatry U. Mo., Columbia, 1990-96. Contbr. articles to profl. jours. Mem. Am. Psychiat. Assn., Am. Acad. Child and Adolescent Psychiatry, Ctrl. Mo. Psychiat. Assn. (sec.-treas. 1992-93, pres.- elect 1993-94, pres. 1994-95), U. Nebr. Alumni Assn., Phi Beta Kappa, Alpha Omega Alpha. Republican. Avocations: walking, reading, studying scripture.

SCHMID, OSKAR ALFRED EDUARD, orthopedist, surgeon, researcher; s. Oskar A. J. and Maria T. Schmid; m. Kirsten Trotnow, Aug. 13, 1996; children: Constantin Johannes Oskar Trotnow, Carlotta Marie Elisabeth Trotnow. MD, U. Regensburg, Germany, 1986. Dir. R&D Albatros Entwicklungs and Vertriebs Gmbh, Nittenau, Germany, 1988—; dir. motion lab. U. Erlangen (Germany)-Nuremberg, 1995—, team leader children and youth traumatology, 2002—, team leader children and youth orthopedics trauma dept, 2002—, team leader foot surgery, 2002—05; dir. orthopedic and trauma surgery Dist. Hosp. SA, 2005—. Team capt. Tennisclub Nittenau, Germany, 1986—89. Mem.: European Soc. of Movement Analysis in Adults and Children, German Orthopedist Assn., Internat. Soc. Biomechanics (pres. 3-D human movement group 2000—02, runner up Young Investigator award). Home: Fichtenweg 7 D-93149 Nittenau Germany Office: U Erlangen-Nuernberg Krankenhausstrasse 12 D-91054 Erlangen Germany Personal E-mail: schmid.oskar@t-online.de. E-mail: oskar.schmid@chir.imed.uni-erlangen.de.

SCHMID-SCHOENBEIN, GEERT WILFRIED, biomedical engineer, educator; b. Albstadt, Baden-Wurttemberg, Germany, Jan. 1, 1948; came to U.S., 1971; s. Ernst and Ursula Schmid; m. Renate Schmid-Schoenbein, July 3, 1976; children: Philip, Mark, Peter. Vordiplom, Liebig U., Giessen, Germany, 1971; PhD in Bioengring., U. Calif., San Diego, 1976. Staff assoc. dept. physiology Columbia U., NYC, 1976-77, sr. assoc., 1977-79; asst. prof. dept. applied mechs. & engring. scis. U. Calif., San Diego, 1979-84, assoc. prof., 1984-89, prof., 1989-94, prof. dept. bioengring., 1994—. Editor: Frontiers in Biomechanics, 1986, Physiology and Pathophysiology of Leukocyte Adhesion, 1994, Molecular Basis of Microcirculatory Disorders, 2002; author more than 330 rsch. reports. Chair World Coun. & Biomechanics, 2010. Recipient Melville medal ASME, 1990, Ratschow medal European Soc. Phlebology, 1999. Fellow Am. Inst. for Med. and Biol. Engring., Am. Heart Assn.; mem. NAE, Biomed. Engring. Soc. (pres. 1991-92), Am. Microcirculatory Soc. (pres. 2003-04), N.Am. Soc. Biorheology (pres. 1989-99, Landies award 2008), European Microciculatory Soc., Am. Physiol. Soc., Am. Mech. Engring. Soc. Achievements include bioengineering research on cardiovascular disease, microcirulation, bioengineering, and lymphology. Office: U Calif San Diego Dept Bioengineering Gilman Dr 9500 0412 La Jolla CA 92093-0412

SCHMIDT, AXEL, physician, philosopher, researcher; b. Krefeld, Germany, May 29, 1962; s. Eckhard C.F. and Juliane (Blehs) S.; m. Doris Bade, July 19, 1969; children: Julia Maria, Sabrina Cornelia. Abitur, Gymnasium Fabritianum, Krefeld, 1981; Candidate Philosophy, U. Düsseldorf, 1987, MD, 1988. Cert. MD, clin. microbiologist. Clin. microbiologist U. Hosp., Düsseldorf, Germany, 1986—93; assoc. prof. Inst. für Mikrobiologie und Virologie U. Witten/Herdecke, Germany, 1997—. Pres. North-Rhine Westfalia Union of German Clin. Microbiologists, Germany, 1995—; mem. bd. curators Manfred Plempel Stipendium for Med. Mycology, 1997—, Dorothy Hegarty award, 1997—; bd. dirs. German Diagnostic Group. Editor: (book series) Contributions to Microbiology, 1996—, Birkhauser's Advances in Infectious Diseases, 2003—; mem. editl. bd. Chemotherapy, 1996—, Drug Rsch., 1996—, Haut, 1996—, Alternatives to Lab. Animals, 1997—, Mikrobiologe, 1998—, Luft, 1998—; mem. sci. bd. (jour.) Progress in Medicine, 1996—, Skin, 1997—, Mycoses, 1998—; reviewer New Eng. Jour. Medicine, 1997—; contbr. numerous sci. papers; patentee in field. Mem. Cold Spring Harbor Lab. Assn., German Soc. Mycology, Paul Ehrlich Assn., Internat. Soc. Human/Animal Mycoses, Robert Koch Found., German Soc. Philosophy. Christian Democrat. Roman Catholic. Avocation: hunting. Home: Ludgerweg 36 D-42329 Wuppertal Germany Office: U Witten/Herdecke Inst Microbiol, Stockumer Str 10 D-58448 Witten Germany Personal E-mail: axel780961@t-online.de.

SCHMIDT, JOSEPH DAVID, urologist; b. Chgo., July 29, 1937; s. Louis and Marian (Fleigel) S.; m. Andrea Maxine Herman, Oct. 28, 1962. BS in Medicine, U. Ill., 1959, MD, 1961. Diplomate Am. Bd. Urology, 1971. Rotating intern Presbyn. St. Luke's Hosp., Chgo., 1961-62, resident in surgery, 1962-63; resident in urology The Johns Hopkins Hosp., Balt., 1963-67; faculty U. Iowa Coll. Medicine, Iowa City, 1969-76, U. Calif., San Diego, 1976—, prof., head divsn. urology, 1976—2006; prof., emeritus, 2006—; vice-chmn. dept. surgery U. Calif., San Diego, 1985-97. Cons. U.S. Dept. Navy, San Diego, 1976—; attending urologist Vets. Affairs Dept., San Diego, 1976—; assoc. dir. for clin. rsch. U. Calif. San Diego Cancer Ctr., 1997-98. Author, editor: Gynecological and Obstetric Urology, 1978, 82, 93. Capt. USAF, 1967-69. Recipient Francis Senear award U. Ill., 1961. Fellow ACS, Am. Urol. Assn. Inc., Alpha Omega Alpha. Avocations: collecting antique medical books, manuscripts. Office: U Calif Med Ctr Divsn Urology 200 W Arbor Dr San Diego CA 92103-8897 Office Phone: 619-543-2628. Office Fax: 619-543-6573. Business E-Mail: jdschmidt@ucsd.edu.

SCHMIDT, LISBETH SAMSOE, pediatrician, researcher; b. Copenhagen, Feb. 26, 1970; MD, U. Copenhagen, 1999, PhD, 2010. Dist. physician Aasiat Hosp. Greenland, 2003; physician, dept. anesthesiology Bispebjerg Hosp., 2003—04; pediat. trainee U. Hosp. Hillerød, 2004—06, U. Hosp. Herlev and Rigshospitalet, 2010—; rsch. asst. Danish Cancer Soc., 2006—10. Mem.: Young Pediatricians in Denmark (v.p., bd. mem. 2006—11), Nordic Soc. Pediat. Hematology and Oncology (mem., brain tumor bd. 2007—11, Young NOPHO prize 2009). Avocations: running, tennis, kayaking. Home: Hans Rostgardsvej 2 Humlebæk 3050 Denmark Business E-Mail: samsoe@cancer.dk.

SCHMIDT, LYNDA WHEELWRIGHT, psychotherapist; b. Beijing, July 29, 1931; came to the U.S., 1931; d. Joseph Balch and Jane Byers (Hollister) Wheelwright; m. Klaus Dieter, May 8, 1930; children: Karen Calley, Claudia Lewis. BA, U. Calif., Berkeley, 1965, MSW, 1968. Cert. Jungian analyst; bd. cert. diplomate Am. Bd. Examiners Clin. Social Work. Staff psychiat. social worker Pacific Med. Ctr., San Francisco, 1968-71; pvt. practice psychotherapy and Jungian analysis San Francisco, 1971-87, Brooklin, Maine, 1985—. Tng. analyst CG Jung Inst., San Francisco, 1978—; mem. certifying com. CG Jung Inst., San Francisco, 1980-84; cons. and lectr. in field. Author: Time Out of Mind: Trekking the Hindu Kush, 1978, The Long Shore, A Psychological Experience of the Wilderness, 1991; contbr. articles to profl. jours. Fellow Calif. Soc. Clin. Social Workers; mem. NASW, Acad. Cert. Social Workers, Inc., CG Jung Inst. (chair certifying com. 1980-84), Alpha Phi Sorority. Democrat. Avocations: reading, horseback riding, travel, music. Home and Office: PO Box 269 Brooklin ME 04616-0269

SCHMIDT, MARKUS H., medical association administrator, educator; b. Ohio, 1966; MD, Med. Coll. Ohio, PhD, 1997. Med. dir. Ohio Sleep Medicine Inst., 2001—. Adj. asst. prof. Ohio State U., 2001—11. Recipient Pres. award, Med. Coll. Ohio, 1990, Young Investigator award, Sleep Rsch. Soc., Am. Sleep Disorders Assn., 1999, Neuroscience Investigator award, Cleve. Clinic Found., 1999, 2000, 2001; named one of Best Drs., 2008, 2009, 2010. Mem.: AMA, World Assn. Sleep Medicine, European Sleep Rsch. Soc., Sleep Rsch. Soc., Am. Acad. Sleep Medicine. Office: 4975 Bradenton Ave Dublin OH 43017 Office Fax: 614-766-2599. Business E-Mail: mschmidt@sleepmedicine.com.

SCHMIDT, NANCY ANNE, psychotherapist; b. Jersey City, July 18, 1958; d. William John Lawrence and Ruth Martha (Morant) S. BA summa cum laude, Fordham U., 1986; MA summa cum laude, N.J. City State U., 1990; cert. pastoral counselor, World Christianship Ministries, 1994. Cert. social worker, criminal justice specialist, hypnotherapist, addiction counselor, eating disorders specialist; cert. domestic violence counselor, cert. crisis counselor. Adj. prof. N.J. City State U. (formerly Jersey City State Coll.), 1988-91, adj. prof. psychology, 1990-94; pvt. practice West New York, 1990—; counselor Substance Abuse Treatment Ctr., Union City, NJ, 1994-96; substance abuse program dir. Sr. Treatment and Edn. Program, Union City, 1994-96; staff psychotherapist North Hudson Cmty. Action Corp. Mental Health Ctr., West New York, 1996-98, dir. mental health, addictive svcs., social work, psychiatry, 1998—. Bd. dirs. Hudson Health Care Partnership, Jersey City; bd. dirs. Hudson County Healthy Families 2000, mem. Hudson County Task Force on Women & Addiction, co-dir. Union City Police Dept./North Hudson Cmty. Action Corp. Domestic Violence Outreach Program, Union City Police Dept. stress reduction cons.; presenter in field. Mem. APA, Am. Counseling Assn., Am. Assn. Family Counselors (cert.), Nat. Assn. Alcohol and Drug Abuse Counselors, Am. Assn. Christian Counselors, Am. Psychotherapy Assn., Alpha Sigma Lambda, Phi Kappa Phi, Psi Chi. Avocations: swimming, walking, reading, writing, poetry. Office: North Hudson Cmty Action Corp Mental Health Addictive Svc 5301 Broadway West New York NJ 07093-2622

SCHMIDT, RENÉ STEFFEN, orthopedic surgeon; b. Stuttgart, Germany, Apr. 27, 1971; s. Erich and Renate Schmidt; m. Sandra Schmidt-König. MD, U. Tübingen, 1999; PhD, U. Ulm, Germany, 2007. Physician U. Ulm, 1999—2001, 2003—07, Katharinen Hosp., Stuttgart, 2001—02, Clinic Göppingen, Germany, 2008—09, U. Clinic Mannheim, Germany, 2007—08, 2009—; prof. U. Mannheim, 2010. Office: Univ Clinic Mannheim Theodor Kutzer Ufer 1-3 Mannheim 68167 Germany Office Phone: 004917161640. Personal E-mail: rene.schmidt@gmx.de.

SCHMIDT, RICHARD GEORGE, orthopaedic surgeon; MD, Pa. State U., 1980. Lic. Pa., 1982, NJ, 1989, diplomate Am. Bd. Orthopaedic Surgery, 1988. Intern gen. surgery Pa. Univ. Hosp., fellow orthop. oncology, resident orthop. surgery, 1985; fellow orthop. oncology Shands Hosp., 1986; active staff surgeon St. Christopher's hosp. for Children, St. francis Med. Ctr., Fox Chase Cancer Ctr., Graduate Hosp.; chief orthop. oncology surgery Lankenau Hosp. Contbr. chapters to books Palliative Orthopaedic Surgery, Principles and Practice of Supportive Oncology, 1998, articles Metabolic Characterization of Human Soft Tissue Sarcomas In Vivo and In Vitro Using Proton decoupled Phosphorus Magnetic Resonance Spectroscopy, 1996, An Unusual Complications of an Ankle Arthroscopy and its Management, 1998, Knee Pain Following Fracture Repair, 1998. Named one of the Top Doctors, Phila. Mag., 2010—11. Mem.: Pa. Orthop. Soc. (bd. dirs.), Eastern Orthop. Assn., NJ Orthop. Soc., Phila. Orthop. Soc. Office: Lankenau Hospital Medical Science Bldg St 275 100 Lancaster Rd Wynnewood PA 19096 Office Phone: 610-667-2663.

SCHMIDT, ROBERT MILTON, preventive medicine physician, educator, medical association administrator; b. Milw., May 7, 1944; s. Milton W. and Edith J. (Martinek) S.; children Eric Whitney, Edward Huntington. AB, Northwestern U., 1966; MD, Columbia U., 1970; MPH, Harvard U., 1975; PhD in Law, Medicine and Pub. Policy, Emory U., 1982; MA, San Francisco State U., 1999. Diplomate Am. Bd. Preventive Medicine, Am. Bd. Internal Medicine, Am. Bd. Hematology. Resident in internal medicine Univ. Hosp. U. Calif.-San Diego, 1970-71; resident in preventive medicine Ctr. Disease Control, Atlanta, 1971-74; commd. med. officer USPHS, 1971; advanced through grades to comdr., 1973; dir. hematology div. Nat. Ctr. for Disease Control, Atlanta, 1971-78, spl. asst. to dir., 1978-79, inactive res., 1979—; clin. asst. prof. pediatrics Tufts U. Med. Sch., 1974-86; clin. asst. prof. medicine Emory U. Med. Sch., 1971-81, clin. assoc. prof. community health, 1976-86; clin. assoc. prof. humanities in medicine Morehouse Med. Sch., 1977-79; attending physician dept. medicine Wilcox Meml. Hosp., Lihue, Hawaii, 1979-82, Calif. Pacific Med. Ctr., San Francisco, 1983—; dir. Ctr. Preventive Medicine and Health Rsch., 1983—, dir. Health Watch, 1983—; sr. scientist Inst. Epidemiol. and Behavioral Medicine, Inst. Cancer Rsch., Calif. Pacific Med. Ctr., San Francisco, 1983-88; prof. hematology and gerontology, dir. Ctr. Preventive Medicine and Health Rsch., chair health professions program San Francisco State U., 1983-99, prof. medicine, 1983—, prof. emeritus, Calif. State U. Sys., 1999—; founding dir. Health Watch Internat., 1994—, CEO, pres. Cons. WHO, FDA, Washington, NIH, Bethesda, Md., Govt. of China, Mayo Clinic, Rochester, Minn., Northwestern U., Evanston, Ill., Chgo., U. R.I., Kingston, Pan Am. Health Orgn., Inst. Pub. Health, Italy, Nat. Inst. Aging Rsch. Ctr., Balt., U. Calif., San Diego, U. Ill., Chgo., Columbia U., NYC, Harvard U., Johns Hopkins U., U. Chgo., UCLA, U. Calif. Berkeley, Brown U., Providence, U. Calif., San Francisco, Stanford U., Boston, Emory U., Atlanta, Duke U., NC, U. Tex., Houston, Ariz. State U., U. Hawaii, Honolulu, U. Paris, U. Geneva, U. Munich, Heidelberg U., U. Frankfurt, U. Berlin, Cambridge U., England, U. Singapore, others; vis. rsch. prof. gerontology Ariz. State U., 1989—90; mem. numerous sci. and profl. adv. bd., panels, com. Mem. editorial bd. Am. Jour. Clin. Pathology, 1976-82, The Advisor, 1988—, Generations, 1989—, Contemporary Gerontology, 1994—, Alternative Therapies in Health and Medicine, 1995—, Aging Today, 1997—; book and film reviewer Sci. Books and Films, 1988—, many other jours.; author: 17 books and manuals including Hematology Laboratory Series, 4 vols., 1979-86, CRC Handbook Series in Clinical Laboratory Science, 1976—; assoc. editor: Contemporary Gerontology, 1993—; contbr. more than 400 articles to sci. jours. Alumni regent Columbia U. Coll. Physicians and Surgeons, 1980—. Northwestern U. scholar, 1964-66; NSF fellow, 1964-66; Health Professions scholar, 1966-70; USPHS fellow, 1967-70; Microbiology, Urology, Upjohn Achievement, Borden Rsch. and Virginia Kneeland Frantz scholar awards Columbia U., 1970; recipient Am. Soc. Pharmacol. and Exptl. Therapy award in pharmacology, 1970, Commendation medal USPHS, 1973, Meritorious Performance and Profl. Promise award, 1989, Student Disting. Teaching and Svc. award Pre-Health Professions Student Alliance, 1992, Leadership Recognition awards San Francisco State U., 1984-89, 91-96, Meritorious Svc. award, 1992. Fellow: ACPM, AAAS (med. scis. sect.), ACP (commentator ACP Jour. Club/Annals of Internal Medicine 1993—), Internat. Soc. Hematology, Am. Soc. Clin. Pathology, Am. Coll. Preventive Medicine (sci. com.), Am. Geriat. Soc., Royal Soc. Medicine (London), Gerontol. Soc. Am.; mem.: APHA, AMA, Emory Sch. Pub. Health, Calif. Coun. Gerontology and Geriat., Nat. Assoc. Adv. for Health Professions, Internat. Health Eval. Assn. (v.p. for Ams. 1992—94, bd. dirs. 1992—, pres. 1994—96), Calif. Med. Assn., San Francisco Med. Soc., NY Acad. Sci., Am. Soc. Aging (editl. bd. 1990—, Dychtwald Pub. Speaking award 1991), Am. Soc. Microbiology, Assn. Tchr. Preventive Medicine (edn. com., rsch. com.), Am. Coll. Occupl. and Environ. Medicine, Calif. Coun. Gerontology and Geriat., Am. Assn. Med. Info., Nat. Assn. Advisors for Health Professions (bd. dirs.), Am. Assoc. Blood Banks, Acad. Clin. Lab. Physicians and Scientists, Internat. Soc. Thrombosis and Hemostasis, Am. Soc. Hematology (hon.; emeritus), Internat. Commn. Standardization in Hematology, Am. Assn. Med. Info. (chair prevention and health evaln. informatics WG), Nat. Gallery of Art (Washington), Columbia U. Club No. Calif., Circle Club (Washington), Army and Navy Club, Golden Key (hon. faculty mem.), Harvard Club (NY and San Francisco), Northwestern U. Club. No. Calif., Cosmos Club (mem. art com. 1997—), Knights of Malta, Sigma Xi, Phi Beta Kappa. Home: Whaleship Plaza 25 Hinckley Walk San Francisco CA 94111-2303 Office: Health Watch Med Ctr Calif Pacific Med Ctr San Francisco CA 94120-7999 Home Phone: 415-956-5670; Office Phone: 415-956-5670. Personal E-mail: rmschmidtmd@aol.com.

SCHMIDT, THOMAS CHARLES, biomedical engineer, researcher; b. Jersey City, Feb. 21, 1947; s. Ernest J. and Shirley J. Schmidt; m. Marilyn I. Karcheski, Aug. 3, 1968; 1 child, Thomas M. B in Engring., Stevens Inst. Tech., 1968, M in Engring., 1973. Registered profl. engr., Fla., Calif. Vis. lectr. physiol. psychology Stevens Inst. of Tech., Hoboken, NJ, 1974—76; engr. Perry Techs., Riviera Beach, Fla., 1976—80; sr. rsch. engr., rsch. specialist, staff engr., sr. staff engr. Lockheed-Martin, San Diego, 1980—, Riviera Beach, Fla. Participant NASA Med-Ops. Task Group (Clin. Care Capability Project), Houston, 2000; chair ASME PVHO design sub-com., 2003—. Contbr. The Underwater Handbook: A Guide to Physiology and Performance for the Engineer, 1976, articles to profl. jours.; patentee in field. Dir., pub. safety chair Clairemont Town Coun., San Diego, 1997—2008; chair Balboa Ave. Citizens Adv. Com., San Diego, 1999—2003, Healty Cmtys. & Lifestyles Initiative, County Health & Human Svcs., 2005—08; mem. Cmty. Engagement Action Forum County Health and Human Svcs., San Diego, 1999—2008, participant strategic planning process, 1999—2003; mem. Clairemont-Mesa Planning Com., San Diego, 2000—08. Recipient cert. of appreciation, State of Calif. (78th Assembly Dist.), 1999, cert. of recognition, 2000, 2001, State of Calif. (76th Assembly Dist.), 2003, 2004, spl. commendation, City of San Diego (6th Dist. Councilmember), 1998, 1999, cert. of appreciation, County of San Diego (3rd Dist. Supr.), 1999, County of San Diego (Asst Dir. Health and Human Svcs.), 2000, spl. commendation, City of San Diego (6th Dist. Councilmember), 2000, 2001, 2002, 2004, Cmty. Svc. award, City of San Diego (Dir. of Planning), 2001, 2002, commendation, Gov. of Calif., 2003, spl. commendation, City of San Diego (6th Dist. Councilmember), 2004, cert. of recognition, U. S. Congress (Calif. 50th Dist.), 2004, cert. of appreciation, ASME (Codes and Standards), 2004, cert. of aclamation, 2008. Mem.: ASME (ASME safety code com. - pressure vessels for human occupancy 1987—, chair PVHO design sub-com. 2003—), Calif. Environ. Health Assn. (exec. bd. S.W. chpt. 2000—), Undersea and Hyperbaric Med. Soc. (safety com. 1981—, submarine medicine com. 1984—). Home: 5953 Castleton Dr San Diego CA 92117 Office: Lockheed Martin MS2 100 E 17th St Riviera Beach FL 33404 Office Phone: 561-494-2064. E-mail: thomas.c.schmidt@lmco.com.

SCHMIDT-NIELSEN, BODIL MIMI (MRS. ROGER G. CHAGNON), retired physiologist, educator; b. Copenhagen, Nov. 3, 1918; came to U.S., 1946, naturalized, 1952; d. August and Marie Jorgensen Krogh; m. Knut Schmidt-Nielsen, Sept. 20, 1939 (div. Feb. 1966); children: Astrid, Bent, Bodil; m. Roger G. Chagnon, Oct. 1968 (dec. 2003). DDS, U. Copenhagen, 1941, DOdont, 1946, DPhil, 1955; DS (hon.), Bates Coll., 1983; MD (hon.), U. Aarhus, Denmark, 1997. Mem. faculty Duke U., Durham, NC, 1952-64; prof. biology Case Western Res. U., Cleve., 1964-71, chmn. dept., 1970-71, adj. prof., 1971-74; trustee Mt. Desert Island Biol. Lab., Maine, rsch. scientist Maine, 1971-86, exec. com. Maine, 1978-85, v.p. Maine, 1979-81, pres. Maine, 1981-85; prof. dept. physiology U. Fla., Gainesville, 1985—. Adj. prof. Brown U., Providence, 1971-75, dept. physiol. U. Fla., Gainesville, 1986—; mem. tng. grant com. NIGMS, 1965-71. Author: August and Marie Krogh, Lives in Science, 1995, Danish edit., 1997; editor: Urea and the Kidney, 1970; assoc. editor Am. Jour. Physiology: Regulatory, Integrative and Comparative Physiology, 1978-81. Trustee Coll. of Atlantic, Bar Harbor, Maine, 1972-92. Recipient Career award NIH, 1962-64, John Simon Guggenheim Meml. fellow, 1952-53; Bowditch lectr., 1958, Jacobaeus lectr., 1974. Fellow AAAS (del. coun. 1977-79), NY Acad. Scis., Am. Acad. Arts and Scis.; mem. Am. Physiol. Soc. (coun. 1971-77, pres. 1975-76, Ray G. Daggs award 1989, Orr Reynolds award 1994, August Knogh lectr. 1994, Berliner award 1998), Soc. Exptl. Biology and Medicine (coun. 1967-71). Achievements include research, publications on biochemistry of saliva, water metabolism of desert animals, urea excretion, peristalsis of renal pelvis and concentrating mechanism, comparative kidney physiology, comparative physiology of excretory organs. Office: U Fla Dept Physiology 2015 SW 16th Ave Gainesville FL 32605 also: 2680 SW 53 Ln #1528 Gainesville FL 32608 Business E-Mail: bodil@gator.net.

SCHMIEDEL, OLE, endocrinologist, consultant; b. Berlin, Sept. 17, 1965; s. Bernd and Edeltraut Schmiedel; m. Carolyn Schmiedel; 1 child, Jann. Degree, Humboldt U. Berlin, 1996. Trainee physician NHS Scotland, Edinburgh, England, 1997—2002, Freeman Hosp., Newcastle upon Tyne, England, 2002—03; tutor endocrinology U. Wales Coll. Medicine, Wrexham, England, 2003—04, med. rschr., 2003—08; specialist registrar, diabetes & endocrinology All Wales Tng. Rotation, Cardiff, England, 2003—06, U. Hosp. Wales, Cardiff, 2006—08. Contbr. scientific papers. Mem.: RCP, Soc. Endocrinology. Achievements include microvascular research in diabetes mellitus. Office: Univ Hosp Wales Heath Pk Cardiff Wales CF14 4XW England Business E-Mail: schmiedelo@cardiff.ac.uk. E-mail: oleschmiedel@doctors.net.uk.

SCHMIEGEL, KLAUS KURT, retired organic chemist, researcher; b. Chemnitz, Saxony, Fed. Rep. Germany, June 28, 1939; came to U.S., 1951; s. Walter Eugen and Martha Marie (Wendisch) S.; m. Joel Marie Larkin, Apr. 16, 1966; children: Karen, Susan, Kurt, Eric. BS in Chemistry, U. Mich., Ann Arbor, 1961; AM, Dartmouth Coll., 1963; PhD, Stanford U., 1968. Sr. chemist Eli Lilly & Co., Indpls., 1968—78, rsch. scientist, 1979—93. Author: (book chpt.) Microtubules and Microtubules Inhibitors, 1985; contbr. articles to profl. jours. Mem. Am. Chem. Soc., AAAS. Co-inventor, with Bryan Molloy, of Prozac, 1988, other achievements include 14 patents related to central nervous system, cancer, cardiovascular, obesity and animal health and diabetes.

SCHMITT, BARTON DOUGLAS, pediatrician, educator; b. Chgo. Heights, Ill., 1937; married; 4 children. MD, Cornell U., Ithica, NY, 1963. Cert. in pediat. Am. Bd. Med. Specialties, 1968. Intern Minn. Hosps., 1963—64, resident, 1964—66; fellow Colo. Gen. Hosp., Denver, 1968—69; med. dir. after-hours call ctr. The Children's Hosp., Denver, 1988—; pediatrician, prof. pediat. U. Colo. Sch. Medicine, Denver. Author: The Child Protection Team Handbook, 1977, Guidelines for the Hospital and Clinic: Management of Child Abuse and Neglect, 1979, Your Child's Health, 1987, Your Child's Health: The Parents' Guide to Symptoms, Emergencies, Common Illnesses, Behavior, and School Problems, 1991, Instructions for Pediatric Patients, 1992, 1998, Pediatric Telephone Advice, 2004, Your Child's Health: The Parents' One-Stop Reference Guide, 2005, Pediatric Telephone Protocols, 2006, (computer software program) The Pediatric Advisor. Recipient Child Devel. award, Am. Acad. Pediat., 1994, Edn. award, 2004. Achievements include first to write computerized protocols for pediatric triage, 1994. Office: The Childrens Hospital 13123 E 16th Ave Aurora CO 80045-7106 Office Phone: 720-777-6179. Business E-Mail: Barton.Schmitt@uchsc.edu.

SCHMITZ, NICOLE M.R., biomedical researcher; b. Luxembourg City, Luxembourg, Oct. 6, 1962; d. Fernand M.J-P. Schmitz and Renate Marie Schmitz-Kröhl. Cert., U. Luxembourg, 1984; student, U. Karlsruhe, Germany, 1985; diploma in Biology, U. Zurich, 1990; PhD, Swiss Inst. Exptl. Cancer Rsch., 1994. Postdoctoral fellow U. Bern, Switzerland, 1994—96, rsch. asst., 1997—2004, co-project leader, 2000—04; vis. scientist ETH, Zurich, 2004—05; rsch. fellow Inst. Cancer Studies U. Birmingham, England, 2006. Lectr. Lycée Des Garçons, Luxembourg, 1985; cons. Nat. Mus. Natural History, Luxembourg, 1984; mem. Found. for Bone Marrow Transplantation, U. Children's Hosp., Bern, Switzerland, 2000. Contbr. articles to profl. jours. Recipient Honor Fell Travel award, Brit. Soc. Cell Biology, 1993, 1994, Pub. award, Santa Cruz Biotech. Inc., 1999, 2001, 2007; grantee Rsch. grant, Found. for Clin. and Exptl. Cancer Rsch., 1997, 2000, Swiss Nat. Rsch. Found., 2000—02, Found. for Bone Marrow Transplantation, 2000, Found. for Clin. and Exptl. Cancer Rsch., 2001, Am. Order Excellence, 2006; fellowship, Ministry Cultural Affairs, Luxembourg, 1991—94. Mem.: Swiss Soc. Oncology, Brit. Soc. for Cell Biology, European Assn. Cancer Rsch., Internat. Soc. Computational Biology, NY Acad. Scis., Union Swiss Socs. for Exptl. Biology (Congress Travel grant 1993), European Life Sci. Org., Am. Assn. Cancer Rsch. Achievements include post-translational modifications in the retinoblastoma protein family in acute lymphoblastic leukemia; SER 612 phosphorlycation by CDK4 in acute lymphoblastic leukemia; research in acute lymphoblastic leukemia; detection of the MCM4/NFI/RB complex in NALM-6 leukemia cells. Personal E-mail: nmrschmitz@hotmail.com, nschmitz@freesurf.ch.

SCHMOLL, HANS JOACHIM, hematology and oncology educator; b. Hannover, Germany, June 21, 1946; s. Johannes and Edeltraut (Schneider) S. MD, Med. U. Hannover, 1970, PhD, 1982. Rsch. assoc. Med. U., Hannover, 1971—84, prof. medicine and hematology-oncology, 1984—95; prof. medicine and hematology, chair hematology/oncology Martin Luther U., Halle-Wittenberg, Germany, 1996—. Mem. exec. bd. ESMO, 2006—. Author, editor: Kompendium Intern Onkologie, 1986, 4th edit., 2005; assoc. editor Cancer Rsch., 2002—2010; editor-in-chief Onkologie, 2001—, Ongotargets and Therapic Done Press; mem. editl. bd. European Jour. Cancer Future Oncology. Recipient German Cancer award, 2001, Sci. award, German Assn. Med. Oncologists, 1998. Mem.: German Assn. Med. Oncology (pres., chmn. 2001—09). Home: Ludwig Barnay Strasse 9 D-30175 Hannover Germany Office: Martin Luther Univ Dept Oncol Hematol Int Med IV D-06120 Halle Germany Home Phone: 0049-0171 3111667; Office Phone: 01149 345 557 2921. Personal E-mail: hjschmoll@yahoo.de. Business E-Mail: haematologie@medizin.uni-halle.de.

SCHMÖLZER, GEORG MARCUS, physician, researcher, author; b. Graz, Austria, July 9, 1974; s. Felix and Brigitte Schmölzer. MD, Med. U. Graz, 2002; PhD, Monash U., Melbourne, Australia, 2011, Med. U Graz, 2011. Vis. fellow Gt. Ormond St. Hosp., London, 2002; paediatric clin. and rsch. fellow Med. U. Graz, 2003—07; rsch. clin. fellow Royal Women's Hosp., Melbourne, Victoria, Australia, 2007—; rsch. fellow Med. U. USAR, 2011. Head orgn. com. Styrian Soc. Emergency Medicine, Graz, 2003—04; med. dir. project European Union, Graz, 2003; exec. com. mem. Austrian Resuscitation Coun., Vienna, 2003—07, orgn. com. mem., 2004—; med. advisor Children's Mus., Graz, 2006—07; chairmen spl. interest group resuscitation Austrian Soc. Paediatrics, Graz, 2009—; mem. spl. interest group resuscitation Perinatal Soc. Australia and New Zealand, Brisbane, Australia, 2010—. Contbr. articles to profl. jours. Recipient Pub. Svc. Award, The UN, 2006, Jo White Bequest, Royal Women's Hosp., Melbourne, Australia, 2009, Rsch. award, Australia, Innovation Rsch. award; grantee, Royal Women's Hosp., Melbourne, Australia, 2008; Travel grant, German Soc. Neonatology and Paediatric Intensive Care Medicine, 2003, Sci. and Rsch., Provincial Govt. Styria, Austria, 2007, Postgrad. Rsch. scholarship, Monash U., Melbourne, 2009—. Mem.: Am. Thorax Soc., Austrian Resuscitation Coun., European Resuscitation Coun., Academic Pediatric Assn., Australian Soc. Med. Rsch. Avocations: acting, travel, reading, running, snowboarding, swimming, hiking, art. Office: Royal Melbourne Hosp PO Box 2120 3050 Parkville Victoria Australia Office Fax: 61 3 8345 3789. Business E-Mail: georg.schmoelzer@me.com.

SCHNAGL, ROGER DIETER, retired microbiology educator, virologist, researcher; b. Reitendorf, Austria, Oct. 10, 1944; s. Heinz Günther and Elfriede Gerhild (Prandstetter); m. Heather York Syme, Feb. 25, 1978. BSc, U. Melbourne, 1968, BSc (honors), 1969, PhD, 1975. Postdoctoral rsch. fellow microbiology dept. U. Melbourne, 1975—78; lectr. dept. microbiology LaTrobe U., Melbourne, 1979—86, sr. lectr. dept. microbiology, 1987—2004, head dept. microbiology, 1993—95, 2000—04, dep. head, 1996—2000; ret., 2004. Demonstrator, tutor U. Melbourne, 1968—77; tutor Ormond Coll., 1970—77, St. Hilda's Coll., 1978—80; mem. human ethics com. LaTrobe U., 1987—94, dep. chair, 1991—94, dir. advanced electron microscope facility, 2001—02. Contbr. articles to profl. jours. Numerous rsch. grants and awards, 1979—. Mem. NY Acad. Scis., Rich River Golf Club, Royal Automobile Club of Victoria. Avocations: squash, tennis, scuba diving, stamp collecting/philately. Business E-Mail: rschnagl@netspace.net.au.

SCHNALL, EDITH LEA, microbiologist, educator; b. NYC, Apr. 11, 1922; d. Irving and Sadie (Raab) Spitzer; m. Herbert Schnall, Aug. 21, 1949 (dec. Feb. 17, 2005); children: Neil David, Carolyn Beth. AB, Hunter Coll., 1942; AM, Columbia U., 1947, PhD, 1967. Clin. pathologist Roosevelt Hosp., NYC, 1942-44; instr. Adelphi Coll., Garden City, N.Y., 1944-46; tchg. asst. Columbia U., 1946; asst. med. mycologist Columbia Coll. Physicians and Surgeons, NYC, 1946-47, 49-50; instr. Bklyn. Coll., 1947; mem. faculty Sarah Lawrence Coll., Bronxville, N.Y., 1947-48; lectr. Hunter Coll., NYC, 1947-67; adj. assoc. prof. Lehman Coll., CUNY, 1968; hon. curator N.Y. Bot. Garden, 1968; asst. prof. Queensborough C.C., CUNY, 1967, assoc. prof. microbiology, 1968-75, prof., 1975—2002, adminstr. Med. Lab. Tech. program, 1985—2003, prof. emerita, 2003—10. Vis. prof. Coll. Physicians and Surgeons, Columbia U., N.Y., 1974; advanced biology examiner U. London, 1970—. Editor: Newsletter of Med. Mycology Soc. N.Y., 1969-85; founder, editor Female Perspective newsletter of Queensborough Community Coll. Women's Club, 1971-73. Mem. Alley Restoration Com., N.Y.C., 1971—; mem. legis. adv. com. Assembly of the State of N.Y., 1972; mem. Cmty. Bd. 11, Queens, N.Y., 1974-98, 3d vice-chmn., 1987-92, 2d vice chmn., 1992-97; pub. dir. of bd. dirs. Inst. Continuing Dental Edn. Queens County, Dental Soc. N.Y. State and ADA, 1973-97. Rsch. fellow NIH, 1948-49; faculty rsch. fellow, grantee-in-aid Rsch. Found. of SUNY, 1968-70; faculty rsch. grant Rsch. Found. CUNY, 1971-74. Mem. AAAS, Internat. Soc. Human Animal Mycology, Am. Soc. Microbiology (coun., N.Y.C. br. 1981—, co-chairperson ann. meeting com. 1981-82, chair program com. 1982-83, v.p. 1984-86, pres. 1986-88), Med. Mycology Soc. N.Y. (sec.-treas. 1967-68, v.p. 1968-69, 78-79, archivist 1974—, fin. advisor 1983-97, pres. 1969-70, 79-80, 81-82, Lifetime Achievement award, 2002), Bot. Soc. Am., Med. Mycology Soc. Americas, Mycology Soc. Am., N.Y. Acad. Scis., Torrey Bot. Club (N.Y. State), Queensborough Community Coll. Women's Club (pres. 1971-73, N.Y.C.), Sigma Xi, Phi Sigma. Home: 21406 29th Ave Flushing NY 11360-2622

SCHNALL, ROBERT I., urologist; Grad., Tufts U., Bedford; MA, MD, Temple U. Lic. Pa., 1982, diplomate Am. Bd. Urology, 1990. Resident gen. surgery and urology Temple Univ. Hosp.; clin. asst. prof. Temple Univ.; hospital affiliations include Bryn Mawr Hosp., 1997—, Paoli Hosp., 1998—, Urology Health Specialists Ltd. Liability Co.; system chief Main Line Health; intern Lankenau Hosp., resident gen. surgery and urology, urologist, 1998—, divsn. chief. Contbr. Grade III Vesico-ureteral Reflux-To Re-implant or Not?. Named Top Dr., Phila. Mag., 2010. Mem.: Pa. Urol. Soc., Am. Urol. Assn. Office: Lankenau Hospital Medical Office Bldg E Ste 361 100 Lancaster Ave Wynnewood PA 19096 Office Phone: 610-649-6420. Office Fax: 610-649-4689.

SCHNECK, STUART AUSTIN, retired neurologist, educator; b. NYC, Apr. 1, 1929; s. Maurice and Sara Ruth (Knapp) S.; m. Ida I. Nakashima, Mar. 2, 1956; children: Lisa, Christopher. BS magna cum laude, Franklin and Marshall Coll., 1949; MD, U. Pa., 1953. Diplomate Am. Bd. Psychiatry and Neurology (bd. dirs., sec. 1990-91, v.p. 1991-92, pres. 1992-93). Intern Hosp. U. Pa., Phila., 1953-54; resident in medicine U. Colo. Med. Center, Denver, 1954-55, 57-58, resident in neurology, 1958-61; instr. neurology U. Colo. Sch. Medicine, 1959-61; instr. neuropathology Columbia U., NYC, 1961-63; vis. fellow in neuropathology Columbia-Presbyn. Med. Ctr., NYC, 1961-63; asst. prof. neurology and pathology U. Colo., 1963-67, assoc. prof., 1967-70, prof., 1970-95, assoc. dean clin. affairs Sch. Medicine, 1984-89, emeritus prof., 1996—. Cons. Fitzsimons Army Hosp., VA, Nat. Jewish Hosp.; pres. med. bd. Univ. Hosp., Denver, 1983-89, bd. dirs., 1989-90; mem. benefits adv. bd. U. Colo., 1999—, v.p. retired faculty assn. health sci. ctr., 1998-99, pres., 1999-2001. Author (with Ida I. Nakashima) The Geezers' Guide to Colo. Hikes, 2002; contbr. articles to profl. jours. Served with USAF, 1955-57. USPHS fellow, 1961-63. Mem. Am. Acad. Neurology, Am. Assn. Neuropathologists, Am. Neurol. Assn., Univ. Srs. Assn. (chmn. bd. dirs. 1997-2002), Rocky Mountain Stroke Assn. (bd. dirs. 1998—2006), Ctr. for Personalized Edn. Physicians (bd. dirs. 1999—2008), Alpha Omega Alpha (bd. dirs. 1979-89, treas., pres. 1990-93, editl. bd. 1994—2006).

SCHNEEWEISS, SEBASTIAN, medical educator, pharmacoepidemiologist; MD, Munich U. Med. Sch., 1992; SM, Harvard Sch. Public Health, 1994, ScD, 2000. Assoc. prof. medicine, dept. epidemiology Harvard Medical Sch., Boston, 2000—; vice chief Divsn. Pharmacoepidemiology and Pharmacoeconomics Brigham and Women's Hosp.; principal investigator Developing Evidence to Inform Decisions about Effectiveness Rsch. Ctr. Brigham & Women's Hospital. Office: Brigham and Women's Hosp 1620 Tremont St Ste 2020 Boston MA 02120

SCHNEIDER, ALAN IRA, cardiologist; MD, U. Md., 1989. Diplomate Am. Bd. Internal Medicine, Am. Bd. Internal Medicine-cardiovasc. disease, Am. Bd. Internal Medicine-clin. cardiac electrophysiology. Intern Mercy Med. Ctr., resident, 1992; resident internal medicine Univ. of Md. Hosp., chief resident internal medicine, fellow cardiology, 1995, fellow cardiac electrophysiology, 1996; chief cardiology Holy Cross Hosp. Named one of Top Doctors, Washingtonian Mag., 2011. Office: Holy Cross Hospital 1500 Forest Glen Rd Silver Spring MD 20910 Office Phone: 301-754-7000.

SCHNEIDER, ALLAN STANFORD, biophysics, neuroscience and pharmacology educator, biomedical research scientist; b. NYC, Sept. 26, 1940; s. Harry and Edith (Gonsky) S.; m. Mary-Jane Beekman Tunis, Dec. 14, 1968; children: Henry Seth, Joseph Benjamin B.Chem. Engring., Rensselaer Poly. Inst., 1961; MS, Pa. State U., 1963; PhD, U. Calif.-Berkeley, 1968. Chem. engr. E.I. du Pont de Nemours & Co. Exptl. Sta., Wilmington, Del., 1963-64; postdoctoral fellow Weizmann Inst. Sci., Rehovot, Israel, 1969-71; staff fellow NIH, Bethesda, Md., 1971-73; assoc. Sloan-Kettering Inst. Cancer Rsch., NYC, 1974-80, assoc. mem., 1980-85; asst. prof. Cornell U. Grad. Sch. Med. Scis., NYC, 1974-80, assoc. prof. biochemistry, 1981-83, assoc. prof. cell biology and genetic, 1983-85, chmn. biochemistry unit Sloan-Kettering div., 1982-83; assoc. prof. pharmacology and toxicology Albany Med. Coll., NY, 1985-86, prof. pharmacology and toxicology, 1986-94, prof. pharmacology and neurosci., 1995—, dir. grad. studies, 1987-91. Adjunct prof. Biomedical Sci., Sch. of Public Health, St. U. N.Y., Albany, 1987—; vis. prof. Weizmann Inst. Sci., Rehovot, Israel, 1987; vis. rsch. scholar U. Bergen, Norway, 1989, 95; vis. rsch. scholar, U. of Melbourne, Australia, 1998. Contbr. chpts to books, sci. articles to profl. jours. Rsch. grantee Am. Cancer Soc., 1980-83, Am. Heart Assn., 1977-82, 90-93, NIH, 1982-93, 2001—05, NSF, 1977-79, 1997-2002, Cystic Fibrosis Found., 1980-82; established investigator Am. Heart Assn., 1977-82. Mem. Biophys. Soc., Soc. Neurosci., Soc. of Gen. Physiologist, Am. Heart Assn. (coun. on basic sci. 1977-95), Phi Lambda

Upsilon, Tau Beta Pi (internat. com. for chromaffin cell biology 1987-93). Achievements include first isolation and characterization of chromaffin cells of the adrenal gland now widely used as a model neuronal cell culture system; determination of the relation between cytosolic calcium signals and neurohormone (adrenaline) secretion, relevant to cellular mechanism of hormone and neurotransmitter release; determination of hydration of biomembranes; spectroscopic characterization of protein structure in situ in biomembranes and cells; theoretical and experimental analysis of optical activity spectra of turbid biological suspensions; research on neurochemistry of adrenal chromaffin cells, regulation of cell calcium and hormone and neurotransmitter release; mechanisms of nicotine dependence and fetal nicotine syndrome and effects of maternal smoking on fetal brain development. Office: Ctr for Neuropharmacology & Neurosci Albany Med Coll MC 136 Albany NY 12208 Office Phone: 518-262-5837. Business E-Mail: schneia@mail.amc.edu.

SCHNEIDER, ARTHUR SANFORD, medical educator; b. LA, Mar. 24, 1929; s. Max and Fannie (Ragin) S.; m. Edith Kadison, Aug. 20, 1950; children: Jo Ann Schneider Farris, William Scott, Lynnellen. BS, UCLA, 1951; MD, Chgo. Med. Sch., 1955. Diplomate Am. Bd. Internal Medicine, Am. Bd. Pathology. Intern, Wadsworth VA Hosp., Los Angeles, 1955-56, resident, 1956-59, chief clin. pathology sect., 1962-68; mem. faculty UCLA, 1961-75, clin. assoc. prof., 1971-75; chair dept. clin. pathology City of Hope Med. Ctr., Duarte, Calif., 1968-75; prof., chair dept. clin. pathology Whittier Coll., 1974-75; prof., chair dept. pathology Chgo. Med. Sch. Rosalind Franklin Medicine & Sci., 1975—; chief lab. service VA Med. Ctr., North Chicago, Ill., 1975-86, chief lab. hematology, 1986-94. Sr. author: BRS Pathology, 1993; sr. author 4th edit., 2009; contbr. chapters to books, articles to profl. jours. Served to capt. M.C., USAF, 1959-61. Fellow: ACP, Am. Soc. Clin. Pathologists, Coll. Am. Pathologists; mem.: AMA, AAUP, Group Rsch. in Pathology Edn., Lake County Med. Soc., Ill. Med. Soc., Am. Soc. Clin. Rsch., Am. Assn. Blood Banks, Am. Soc. Hematology, Acad. Clin. Lab. Physicians and Scientists, Assn. Pathology Chairs, Am. Assn. Investigative Pathology, Internat. Acad. Pathology, Alpha Omega Alpha, Sigma Xi, Phi Delta Epsilon. Office: Chgo Med Sch Rosalind Franklin U Medicine and Sci 3333 Green Bay Rd North Chicago IL 60064-3037 Home Phone: 847-234-5693; Office Phone: 847-578-3260. E-mail: arthur.schneider@rosalindfranklin.edu.

SCHNEIDER, BENJAMIN, psychology professor, consultant; b. NYC, Aug. 11, 1938; s. Leo and Rose (Cohen) S.; m. H. Brenda Jacobson, Jan. 29, 1961; children: Lee Andrew, Rhody Yve. BA, Alfred U., 1960; MBA, CUNY, 1962; PhD, U. Md., 1967. Lic. psychologist, Md. Asst. prof. adminstrv. scis. and psychology Yale U., New Haven, 1967-71; prof. psychology-mgmt. U. Md., College Park, 1971-79, prof. psychology and mgmt., 1982—2004, prof. emeritus, 2004—; sr. rsch. fellow Valtera Corp., 2003—; John A. Hannah prof. orgnl. psychology Mich. State U., East Lansing, 1979-82. Vis. prof. Inst. Adminstrn. and Enterprise, U. Aix-Marseille, 1993, 99, 2001, Peking U., 1988, Tuck Sch. Bus. Adminstrn., Dartmouth Coll., 1999. Author: (with D.T. Hall) Organizational Climates and Careers, 1973, Staffing Organizations, 1976, (with N. Schmitt) 2d edit., 1986, (with F.D. Schoorman) Facilitating Work Effectiveness, 1988, Organizational Climate and Culture, 1990, (with D.E. Bowen) Winning the Service Game, 1995, (with S.S. White) Service Quality: Research Perspectives, 2004, (with D.B. Smith) Personality and Organizations, 2004, (with R.E. Ployhart and N. Schmitt) Staffing Organizations, 3rd edit., 2006, (with W. Macey, K. Barbera & S. Young) Employee Engagement: Tools for Analysis, Practice and Competitive Advantage, 2009; mem. editl. rev. bd. Jour. Applied Psychology, 1988-98, 2002-, Jour. Svc. Mgmt., 1989—, Jour. Svc. Rsch., 1998—, Orgnl. Behavior and Human Decision Processes, 2002-, Cornell Quar., 2002-. Fulbright grantee, 1973—74. Fellow APA, Am. Psychol. Soc., Soc. for Indsl. and Orgnl. Psychology (pres. 1984-85, Disting. Sci. Contbns. award 2000, Scholarly Contbn. award 2004), Acad. Mgmt. (pres. orgnl. behavior divsn. 1982-83, Haneman Career Contbns. award, Human Resource Divsn. 2009), Am. Mktg. Assn. (svcs. mktg. spl. interest group, Career Contbns. award 2006), San Diego Indsl. and Orgnl. Profls. (pres. 2005-06), Soc. Human Resources Mgmt. (Michael Losey Human Resource Rsch. award 2009). Office: 1363 Caminito Floreo Ste G La Jolla CA 92037 Office Phone: 858-488-7594. Business E-Mail: bschneider@valtera.com.

SCHNEIDER, BENJAMIN EDWARD, medical educator; b. Ill., May 21, 1970; MD, U. Colo., 1997. Instr. Harvard Med. Sch., 2003—. Office: 330 Brookline Ave Boston MA 02215 Personal E-mail: boston1776@comcast.net.

SCHNEIDER, CALVIN, physician; b. NYC, Oct. 23, 1924; s. Harry and Bertha (Green) S.; m. Elizabeth Gayle Thomas, Dec. 27, 1967. AB, U. So. Calif., 1951, MD, 1955; JD, LaVerne Coll., 1973. Intern LA County Gen. Hosp., 1955—56, staff physician, 1956—57; pvt. practice medicine West Covina, Calif., 1957—. Staff Inter-Community Med. Ctr., Covina, Calif. With USNR, 1943-47. Republican. Lutheran.

SCHNEIDER, DARREN BRENT, surgeon; BS, Stanford U., 1988; MD, U. Calif., San Diego, 1992. Diplomate in gen. surgery American Bd. Surgery, 2000, in vascular surgery 2002. Postdoctoral fellowship Gladstone Inst. Cardiovascular Surgery, San Francisco, 1995—98; gen. surgery residency training U. Calif., San Francisco, 2000, fellowship interventional radiology, 2000—01, vascular surgery fellowship, 2001—02, assoc. prof. surgery, radiology, 2002—10; chief vascular & endovascular surgery, dir. Ctr. for Vascular & Endovascular Surgery NY Presbyterian Hosp./Weill Cornell Medical Ctr., NYC, 2010—; assoc. prof. surgery Weill Cornell Medical Coll., NYC, 2010—. Recipient Lange Medical Publication award, 1991, Student Rsch. award, American. Assn. Acad. Surgery, 1992. Fellow: American Coll. Surgeons; mem.: Peripheral Vascular Surgery Soc. Office: Weill Cornell Medical College 525 East 68th St Starr 8 New York NY 10065 Office Phone: 212-746-5192. Office Fax: 212-746-5812. *

SCHNEIDER, GEORGE T., obstetrician, gynecologist; b. New Orleans; s. George Edmond Schneider and Erna Marie Kraft; 1 child, Lynne Schneider Cantrell. Diploma, U. Heidelberg, Fed. Republic Germany, 1938; BS, Tulane U., 1941, MD, 1944. Intern Touro Infirmary, New Orleans, 1944-45, resident ob-gyn, 1945-47, U.S. Naval Hosp., Creat Lakes, Ill., 1947-48; vice chmn. Ochsner Med. Instns., New Orleans, 1960-86, cons., 1986—. Prof. ob-gyn Sch. Medicine, La. State U., New Orleans, 1965—. Contbr. articles to profl. jours. Bd. dirs. Assn. Internat. Edn., Houston, 1984—, YMCA New Orleans, 1985—, Am. Cancer Soc. La. Lt. USNR, 1945. Recipient Cert. of Merit Cancer Soc. El Salvador, 1980; named hon. counsul Honduras, 1988. Fellow ACS, Am. Coll. Ob-Gyn; mem. Ob-Gyn Soc. New Orleans (past pres.), Internat. Soc. Reproductive Medicine (past pres.), Hospitaliers Order St. Lazarus, Southern Ob-gyn. Seminar (Asheville, NC) (past pres.). Presbyterian. Office Phone: 504-866-1082. Fax: 504-842-4141. E-mail: gtschneidermd@bellsouth.net.

SCHNEIDER, GERALD L., plastic surgeon; b. Mechanicsburg, Pa., Oct. 25, 1945; s. Gordon Henry and Pauline Emma (Rife) S.; 1 child, Ross Roberts. BS, No. Ariz. U., 1968; MD, U. Ariz., 1973. Intern Naval Regional Med. Ctr., San Diego, 1973-74; resident in gen. surgery U.S. Naval Hosp., San Diego, 1974-78, resident in plastic surgery Portsmouth, Va., 1978-80, staff surgeon divsn. plastic surgery San Diego, 1981-83, chief divsn. plastic surgery, 1983-84; pvt. practice Flagstaff, Ariz., 1984-90; staff surgeon La Jolla (Calif.) Cosmetic Surgery Ctr., 1990-91; surgeon Scripps Clinic & Rsch. Found., La Jolla, 1991—. Capt. USNR Fellow ACS; mem. Am. Soc. Plastic Surgeons. Avocation: golf. Office: Scripps Clinic & Rsch Found 10666 N Torrey Pines Rd La Jolla CA 92037-1092 Office Phone: 858-554-9606. Business E-Mail: schneider.gerald@scrippshealth.org. *

SCHNEIDER, HOLM, pediatrician, educator; b. Leipzig, Germany, Jan. 1, 1969; m. Anne-Therés Schneider, 1989; 5 children. MD, U. Leipzig, Germany, 1995; PhD, U. Erlangen-Nuernberg, Germany, 2001. Resident U. Hosp., Leipzig, Germany, 1995—97, Imperial Coll. Sch. Medicine, London, 1997—99, U. Hosp., Erlangen, Germany, 1999—2006; rsch. group leader U. Erlangen-Nuernberg, 1999—2006, prof., 2008—, Med. U. Innsbruck, Austria, 2006—08. Recipient Zeise prize, U. Leipzig, 1996, Rolf Emmrich prize, Med. Soc. Saxony, Germany, 1996, Young Investigator Award, Soc. Thrombosis and Hemostasis Rsch., Germany, 2002, Arthur Vick prize, Assn. Orthop. Rheumatology, Germany, 2004, Gottron Just sci. prize, U. Ulm and City Ulm, Germany, 2006, prize, Union European Neonatal and Perinatal Soc., 2008. Mem.: European Soc. Cell and Gene Therapy. Office: Children's Hosp Univ Erlangen-Nuernberg Loschgestr 15 Erlangen 91054 Nuremberg Germany Office Fax: 4991318533013. Business E-Mail: holm.schneider@uk-erlangen.de.

SCHNEIDER, JAN, retired obstetrics and gynecology educator; b. Prague, Czechoslovakia, Dec. 10, 1933; came to US, 1963, naturalized, 1967; s. Evzen and Erika S.; m. Sandra Wilson, May 20, 1961 (dec. 2009); children: Hana, Donald, Kathryn, Jonathan; m. Nancy Berezin, 2010. M.B., U. London, 1957; M.P.H., U. Mich., 1967. Prof. ob-gyn, chief obstetric service dept. ob-gyn U. Mich. Med. Sch., Ann Arbor, 1963-77; prof., chmn. ob-gyn. Med. Coll. Pa. and Hahnemann U. (now Drexel U. Coll. Medicine), Phila., 1978-97, assoc. dean, 1997-99, prof. and chmn. emeritus of ob-gyn., 1999—. Editor: (with R. J. Bolognese and R. H. Schwarz) Perinatal Medicine, 2d edit, 1981. Fellow Am. Coll. Obstetricians and Gynecologists, Soc. Perinatal Obstetricians, Am. Gynecol. and Obstet. Soc., Phila. Obstet. Soc. Presbyterian.

SCHNEIDER, JOEL P., biochemist, researcher; b. 1968; BS in Chemistry, U. Akron, Ohio, 1991; PhD in Chemistry, Tex. A&M U., College Station, 1995. George W. Raiziss fellow dept. biochemistry and biophysics U. Pa. Sch. Medicine, Phila., 1996—99; asst. then assoc. prof. dept. chemistry and biochemistry U. Del., Newark, 1999—2009, prof. dept. chemistry and biochemistry, prof. material sci. and engring., 2009—10; chief Chem. Biology Lab., head peptide design and materials sect. Nat. Cancer Inst. at Frederick, Ctr. Cancer Rsch., Md., 2010—. Editor-in-chief: Biopolymers-Peptide Sci. of American Peptide Soc.; contbr. articles to profl. jours. Office: Nat Cancer Inst at Frederick Bldg 376 Rm 104 1050 Boyles St Frederick MD 21702 Office Phone: 201-846-5954. Business E-Mail: joel.schneider@nih.gov. *

SCHNEIDER, KIRK J., psychologist, writer; b. Cleve., July 27, 1956; s. Murray Harold Schneider and Laura Siegal; m. Jurate Elena Raulinaitis, Sept. 17, 1989. BA in Psychology, Ohio State U., 1978; MA in Psychology, West Ga. Coll., 1979; PhD in Psychology, Saybrook Inst., 1984. Lic. psychologist Mass., Calif. Suicide prevention staff Columbus Mental Health Ctr., 1977—78; family therapy trainee Ohio State U., 1978—79; counseling intern West Ga. Coll., 1978—79, grad. tchg. asst., 1978; adv. psychology trainee N.E. Cmty. Mental Health Ctr./Fairhill Psychiat. Hosp., East Cleveland, Ohio, 1979—80; intern, supervisee InterLogue-James F.T. Bugental, PhD, Santa Rosa, Calif., 1980—83; post-doctoral trainee Massillon (Ohio) State Hosp., 1984—85; staff psychologist Human Resources Inst., Norton, Fall River, Mass., 1985—87; pvt. practice, founder Ctr. for Existential Therapy, San Francisco, 1987—. Staff psychologist Ctr. for Nutritional Rsch., Quincy, Mass., 1987—88; mem. crisis counseling team Merrill-Lynch & Co., Boston, 1988; staff psychologist South Shore Coun. on Alcohol, Quincy, 1988—89; co-founder v.p. Existential-Humanistic Inst., San Francisco, 1997—; adj. faculty Lesley Coll., Cambridge, 1986—90, Bentley Coll., Waltham, Mass., 1989, Union Inst., Cin., 1989—90, Calif. Sch. Profl. Psychology, Berkeley, Alameda, 1990—96, The Profl. Sch. Psychology, San Francisco, 1992, Saybrook Grad. Sch., San Francisco, 1995—, Calif. Inst. Integral Studies, San Francisco, 1996—, clin. supr., 1990—; adj. faculty Ctr. for Humanistic Studies, Detroit, 2001—; spkr. in field. Author, editor: The Paradoxical Self: Toward an Understanding of Our Contradictory Nature, 1990, Horror and the Holy: Wisdom-teachings of the Monster Tale, 1993, The Psychology of Existence: An Integrative, Clinical Perspective, 1995, The Handbook of Humanistic Psychology: Leading Edges in Theory, Research, and Practice, 2001, Rediscovery of Awe: Splendor, Mystery and the Fluid Center of Life, 2004, Existential-Integrative Psychotherapy, 2008; author: Awakening to Awe, 2009; author: (editor) Existential-Humanistic Therapy, 2010; contbr. articles to profl. jours., chapters to books. Vice pres. Existential-Humanistic Inst., San Francisco, 1999—. Fellow: APA (Rollo May award 2004, Cultural Innovator award 2009); mem.: AAAS, Assn. for Humanistic Psychology.

SCHNEIDER, MANFRED, chemical and pharmaceutical company executive; b. Bremerhaven, Germany, Dec. 21, 1938; Student in bus. mgmt., U. Freiburg, U. Hamburg, U. Cologne; doctorate, Tech. U. Aachen, Germany. With orgn., auditing and cost acctg. dept. Bayer AG, Leverkusen, Germany, 1966-71, head dept. regional coord., corp. auditing and controlling corp. staff divsn., 1984-87, chmn. mgmt. bd. com. logistics and svcs., mem. bd. coms. R&D, investment and tech., spokesman Western-European activities, chmn. mktg. com., 1987-92, chmn. bd. mgmt., 1992—2002, chmn. supr. bd., 2002—; head divsn. fin. and acctg. dept., then chmn. bd. mgmt. Duisburger Kupferhütte (subs. Bayer AG), 1971-81, chmn. supr. bd., 2002—; asst. to prof. bus. mgmt. Aachen Tech. U. Mem. supr. bds. Daimler AG, Stuttgart, TUI AG, Hannover, RWE AG, Essen; head supr. bd. Linde AG, Wiesbaden. Mem.: German Chem. Industry Assn. (pres. 1999—2001). Office: Bayer AG D-51368 Leverkusen Germany *

SCHNEIDER, MARCIE, pediatrician; Grad., Brown U., Albert Einstein Coll. Diplomate Am. Bd. Pediatrics. Pediat. resident Montefiore Med. Ctr., 1984—86; fellowship adolescent medicine North Shore Univ. Hosp., NY, 1986—88, assoc. chief divsn. of adolescent medicine NY, medical dir. NY; founder Greenwich Adolescent Medicine LLC, 2005, practiced adolescent medicine, 2005—. Author various publs. Fellow: Soc. for Adolescent Medicine, Am. Acad. of Pediat.; mem.: Acad. of Eating Disorders. Office: Greenwich Adolescent Medicine 239 Glenville Rd Greenwich CT 06831 Office Phone: 203-532-1919. Office Fax: 203-532-1518.

SCHNEIDER, PHILLIP HARRY LEONARD (PHIL SCHNEIDER), healthcare organization executive; b. Saginaw, Mich., Jan. 29, 1947; s. Leonard Franklin and Marjory Avalon (Reed) S.; m. Patricia. BA in Journalism, Ctrl. Mich. U., 1969, BS in Polit. Sci., 1969, MA in Polit. Sci., 1970. Editor-in-chief Midland Daily News, Mich., 1970—75; mgr. fin and pub. rels. Dow Chem. Co., Midland, Mich., 1975-78, mgr. media relations, 1978-82, dir. pub. rels., 1982-86; v.p. corp. comm. Medlantic Healthcare Corp., Washington, 1986—91; v.p. external rels., program devel. Nat. Assn. Chain Drug Stores, Alexandria, Va., 1991—2009; pres. Nat. Assn. Chain Drug Stores Found., 1998—2009; founder, pres. Tier One Assocs., 2009. Comm. chmn. Am. Indsl. Health Coun., 1984-86; pub. rels. chmn. Mich. Chem. Coun., Lansing, 1984-86; dir. Am. Found. Pharm. Edn., Pub. Affairs Coun., Washington; chmn. Nat. Coun. on Patient Info. and Edn., Washington; founder, bd. dirs. Sun Safety Alliance. Contbr. articles to profl. jours. Councilman, Midland City Council, 1982-86; bd. dirs. Big Brothers, Jr. Achievement, United Way. Named Outstanding Citizen City of Midland, 1983. Mem.: Assn. Fundraising Profls., Am. Mktg. Assn., Am. Med. Writers Assn., Pub. Rels. Soc. America, Nat. Press Club, Sigma Delta Chi. Roman Catholic. Achievements include playing a key role in establishing and directing the Small Business Coalition on Health Care Reform. Avocations: golf, racquetball, biking, reading. Office Phone: 703-549-3001, 703-395-9411. *

SCHNEIDER, ROBERT JAY, oncologist; b. Miami, Fla., May 31, 1949; s. Irving and Ethel (Pack) S.; m. Barbara Cunningham, June 1, 1974; children: Matthew, Kirsten. Student, Washington U., 1967-69; BA cum laude, Boston U., 1971; MD, Albert Einstein Coll. Medicine, NYC, 1975. Diplomate Am. Bd. Internal Medicine, Am. Bd. Oncology; lic. physician, N.Y. Intern, jr. and sr. resident internal medicine Bronx Mcpl. Hosp., NYC, 1975-78; fellow med. oncology Meml. Sloan-Kettering Cancer Ctr., NYC, 1978-80, adj. attending physician/cons. dept. medicine, 1981—; asst. prof. medicine N.Y. Med. Coll., Valhalla, 1980-81. Clin. instr. medicine Cornell U. Med. Coll., 1978-80; jr. clin. faculty fellow Am. Cancer Soc., 1980-81; mem. N.Y. Met. Breast Cancer Group, 1990—; cons. cancer program No. Westchester Hosp. Ctr., Mt. Kisco, N.Y., 1981-82; mem. staff Westchester County Med. Ctr., Valhalla, N.Y., No. Westchester Hosp. Ctr., Mt. Kisco, Meml. Sloan-Kettering Cancer Ctr., N.Y.C. Contbr. articles to profl. jours. Mem. adv. bd. Cancer Care, Inc. Conn., 1997-99. Recipient Clin. Fellowship award Am. Cancer Soc., 1978-79. Mem. Am. Soc. Clin. Oncology, Westchester County Med. Soc., Soc. Integrative Oncology, Am. Soc. Breast Disease, N.Y. State Med. Soc., Woodway Country Club. Republican. Presbyterian. Achievements include research in detection and treatment of early breast cancer, the human spirit in the fight against cancer, salvage chemotherapy with etoposide, ifosfamide and cisplatin in refractory germ cell tumors. Office: 101 S Bedford Rd Ste 202A Mount Kisco NY 10549-3456

SCHNEIDER, STEPHEN HARLEY, medical educator; b. Neptune, NJ, Apr. 1, 1948; s. Joseph and Edith (Himmelman) S.; m. Carole Robin Lowenstein, Aug. 31, 1981; children: Ari, Rachel. BA, MD, Boston U., 1972. Cert. in internal medicine and endocrinology, N.J. Rsch. assoc. Boston City Hosp., 1975-76, fellow divsn. diabetes and metabolism, 1976-77, asst. dir. diabetes clinic, 1976-77, dir. diabetes clinic, 1977-78, dir. diabetes and metabolism svcs., 1978-79; instr. medicine Boston Univ. Sch. Medicine, 1978-79; asst. prof. medicine U. Medicine and Dentistry N.J.-Robert Wood Johnson Med. Sch., New Brunswick, NJ, 1979-85, assoc. prof. clin. medicine, 1985-88, assoc. prof. medicine, 1988-95, prof. medicine, 1995—. Mem. editl. bd. Diabetes Forcast Mag.; contbr. numerous articles to profl. jours. including Jour. Clin. Endocrinology and Nutrition, New Eng. Jour. Medicine, Diabetes Care, Atherosclerosis, Japanese Heart Jour., Diabetologia, Metabolism. Bd. dirs. Juvenile Diabetes Assn., East Brunswick Jewish Ctr. Youth Com.; founding mem. affiliate Internat. Diabetic Athlete's Assn. Recipient McKeen Cattell award Am. Coll. Clin. Pharmacology, 1986; rsch. fellow Am. Heart Assn., 1976. Fellow ACP; mem. Am. Soc. Internal Medicine, Am. Coll. Sports Medicine, Am. Fedn. Clin. Rsch., Begg Soc., Phi Beta Kappa, Alpha Omega Alpha. Jewish. Avocations: football, soccer, history, theology, bicycling. Office: UMDNJ-Robert W Johnson Med Divsn Endocrinology PO Box 19 New Brunswick NJ 08903-0019 Office Phone: 732-235-7751, 732-234-7219, 732-235-7748. Business E-Mail: schneide@umdnj.edu. *

SCHNEIDER, STEVEN JACK, neurosurgeon; b. Bklyn., June 22, 1958; children: Samantha, Daniel, Russell, Sierra, Aspen. BA in Biology cum laude, NYU, 1979; MD magna cum laude, Baylor Coll. Medicine, 1982. Diplomate Am. Bd. Neurological Surgeons, 1992, Am. Bd. Pediatric Neurosurgery, 1997. Intern, pediatric neurological surgery Baylor Coll. Medicine and Affiliated Hosps., Houston, 1982-83, resident, pediatrics, 1983-88; fellow in pediatric neurological surgery NYU Med. Ctr., NYC, 1988-89; asst. attending physician, pediatric neurological surgery Winthrop U. Hosp., Mineola, NY, 1989—; assoc. attending physician, pediatric neurological surgery LI Jewish Med. Ctr., NY, 1989—, dir., neurosurgery residency NY, chief, pediatric neurological surgery NY, 2002—, dir., surgical services, Comprehensive Epilepsy Ctr. NY; chief attending physician neurosurgery Nassau County Med. Ctr., East Meadow, NY, 1989—; asst. attending physician North Shore U. Hosp., Manhasset, N.Y., 1992-93, head sect. pediatric neurological surgery, asst. attending physician, 1989—, chief, pediatric neurological surgery, 2002—, Schneider Children's Hosp., New Hyde Park, NY, 2002—, dir., surgical services, Comprehensive Pediatric Movement Disorder Ctr.; clin. instr., Leo M. Davidoff Dept. Neurological Surgery Albert Einstein Coll. Medicine, Yeshiva U., Bronx, NY, 1989—; clin. instr. Cornell U. Med. Ctr., NY, 1993—; clin. asst. prof. neurosurgery NYU Sch. Medicine; pediatric neurosurgeon, sr. ptnr. LI Neurosurgical Associates, PC, New Hyde Park, NY, 1989—. Contbr. articles to profl. jours.; serves as ad hoc editor for multiple scientific jours., including Pediatric Neurosurgery. Mem. adv. coun. Children's Brain Tumor Found., Epilepsy Found., Think First Found. Fellow Am. Coll. Surgeons, Am. Acad. Pediatrics; mem. Am. Epilepsy Soc., Am. Acad. Pain Medicine, Harris County Med. Soc., Tex. Med. Assn., Congress Neurol. Surgeons, Am. Assn. Neurol. Surgeons (mem. sect. on pain, mem. joint sect. on disorders spine & peripheral nerves), AMA, Am. Modulation Soc., Complex Regional Pain Syndrome Assn., Hydrocephalus Assn., Guardians of Hydrocephalus, Nat. Neurofibromatosis Found., Am. Syringomyelia Alliance Project, Congress Neurological Surgeons, Nassau County Med. Soc., NY State Neurosurgical Soc., NY Soc. Neurosurgery, Alpha Omega Alpha, Beta Lambda Sigma. Office: 410 Lakeville Rd Ste 204 New Hyde Park NY 11042 Office Phone: 516-354-3401. Office Fax: 516-354-8597. Business E-Mail: sschneid@lij.edu.

SCHNEIDER, THIERRY, physician; b. Paris, June 21, 1962; BS, Louis Le Grand, 1989; MD, U. Lille, 1993. Regional dir. EFS, 2004. Med. cons. French Fed. Blood Donors. Office: 34 Blvd Monnet Nantes 44011 France Business E-Mail: thierry.schneider@efs.sante.fr.

SCHNEIDER, THOMAS AQUINAS, retired surgeon, educator; b. St. Charles, Mo., Dec. 22, 1934; s. Vincent Augustine and Anna Maria (Marheineke) Schneider; m. Joyce Elaine Diehr, June 7, 1958; children: Lisa, Thomas, Dawn, Tracy. BS, Loras Coll., 1954; MD, St. Louis U., 1958. Diplomate Am. Bd. Surgery. Resident surgery St. Louis City Hosp., 1958—63; pvt. practice St. Charles, 1963—2001; ret., 2001. Clin. instr. St. Louis U., 1966—91, asst. clin. prof., 1991—; med. dir. vascular lab. St. Joseph Health Ct., St. Charles, 1991—, dir. trauma svc., 1981—91. Fellow ACS; mem. St. Louis Vascular Soc. (pres. 1993—95), St. Louis Surg. Soc. (councilor 1988—91, v.p. 1996—97), Mo. Com. on Trauma, Hodgen Club (pres. 1988), Alpha Omega Alpha. Roman Catholic. Avocations: golf, music, history. Personal E-mail: opas@sbcglobal.net.

SCHNEIDER, VIVIAN I., psychologist, researcher; b. Wichita Falls, Tex., Sept. 6, 1949; d. Robert and Vivian H. Davis; m. Robert Jordan Schneider, June 8, 1972 (dec. Mar. 13, 2002); children: Kayt, Amy J. Kim, Jay Robert. BA in Psychology, Met. State Coll. Denver, 1972; MA in Psychology, U. Colo., Boulder, 1988, PhD in Psychology, 1991. Sr. rsch. assoc. U. Colo., Boulder, 1991—. Co-author: (chpts.) Learning and Memory of Knowledge and Skills: Durability and Specificity, Foreign Language Learning: Psycholinguistic Studies on Training and Retention, The Psychology of Learning and Motivation: Advances in Research and Theory; contbr. articles to profl. jours. Ham radio operator Boulder County Amateur Radio Emergency Svcs., 1995—; vol. Lamb's Lunch, Boulder, 2004—; Sunday sch. tchr. Boulder Chinese Bapt. Ch., 2003—; children's leader Bible Study Fellowship, Boulder, 1975—85, 2006—08, 2010—; Sunday sch. tchr. Bethany Ch., Boulder, 1976—2008. Mem.: Psychonomic Soc. Avocations: reading, quilting. Office: U Colo Ucb 345 Boulder CO 80309 Home: 3010 Birch Ave Boulder CO 80305-3457 Office Fax: 303-492-8895. Business E-Mail: vivian.schneider@colorado.edu.

SCHNEIDEWIND, JANA-MARIA, medical association administrator, nephrologist, rheumatologist; b. Leipzig, Germany, July 17, 1965; d. Ulrich Franz Oskar and Eva-Maria Gertrud (Herzberg) Schneidewind. MD, U. Rostock, Germany, 1991; postgrad. mgmt. in healthcare sys., Cologne, Germany; postgrad., Malmö U. Hosp., 1999, Harvard Med. Sch., 2000; diploma econ. and mgmt. in healthcare, Cologne, 2001. Physician U. Rostock, Germany, 1991-93, Southern Clinic, Rostock, Germany, 1994-96; splst. Inst. Blood Purification, Homburg, Germany, 1996, Dialysis Cmty. North, Rostock, Germany, 1996 97, Charité Campus Virchow Humboldt U., Berlin, Germany, 1997-98; nephrologist CreaTief & Care LLC, Rostock, Germany, 1998-99; head physician CreaTief & Care GmbH, 1999-2001, Galenos GbR, Homburg, Germany, 2001—03; CEO German Ctr. Extracorporeal Detoxification, 2003—08, ind. cons., sci. advisor, 2008—. Contbr. articles to profl. jours. Mem. Internat. Soc. for Apheresis, European Renal Assn.-European Dialysis and Transplant Assn., Soc. German Internists. Avocations: running, swimming, music. Business E-Mail: j.schneidewind@deed.com. E-mail: j.schneidewind@laotze.de.

SCHNEIDMAN, BARBARA SUE, psychiatrist; b. Mpls., Jan. 18, 1944; d. Barbara Sue and Mildred (Roberts) Schneidman; m. William McAllister. BA, U. Minn., Mpls., 1966, MD, 1970; MPH, U. Wash., 1974. Diplomate Am. Bd. Psychiatry and Neurology. Resident ob-gyn. U. Wash., Seattle, 1972-74, dir. gynecology, 1974-78, resident in psychiatry, 1978-81, cons. primary care, 1981-88; pvt. practice Seattle, 1981-93; cons. Sexual Assault Ctr., Seattle, 1981-93, Ctrl. Area Mental Health, Seattle, 1990-92; pres. Fedn. State Med. Bds., Dallas, 1991—92, interim pres., CEO, 2009, pres. OCEG, 2009; assoc. v.p. Am. Bd. Med. Specialties, Evanston, Ill., 1993-98; dir. divsn. med. edn. liaison and outreach AMA, 1998—2002, v.p. med. edn., 2002—08. Mem., chair Wash. State Bd. Med. Examiners, 1982—93. Mem.: Am. Bd. Psychiatry & Neurology (psychiatry dir. 2007—), Wash. Psychiat. Soc., Am. Psychiat. Assn. Avocation: bicycling. Office: c/o American Bd Psychiatry and Neurology Inc 2150 E Lake Cook Rd Ste 900 Buffalo Grove IL 60089 *

SCHNELLER, EUGENE STEWART, supply chain management and health administration and policy educator; b. Cornwall, NY, Apr. 9, 1943; s. Michael Nicholas and Anne Ruth (Gruner) Schneller; m. Ellen Stauber, Mar. 24, 1968; children: Andrew Jon, Lee Stauber. AA, SUNY, Buffalo, 1965; BA, LI U., 1967; PhD, NYU, 1973; grad. physician assoc. (hon.), Duke U., 2004. Rsch. asst. dept. sociology NYU, NYC, 1968-70; project dir. Montefiore Hosp. and Med. Ctr., Bronx, NY, 1970-72; asst. prof. Med. Ctr. and sociology Duke U., Durham, NC, 1973-75; assoc. prof., chmn. dept. sociology Union Coll., Schenectady, 1975-79, assoc. prof., dir. Health Studies Ctr., 1979-85; prof., dir. Sch. Health Mgmt. and Policy, Ariz. State U., Tempe, 1985—91, assoc. dean rsch. and adminstrn. Coll. Bus., 1992-94; dir. L. William Seidman Rsch. Ctr., Tempe, 1992-94, counselor to pres. for health profl. edn., 1994-96; clin. prof. cmty. and family medicine U. Ariz., 1995-96, clin. prof. prevention, rsch., 1997—2002; prof., dir. Sch. Health Mgmt. and Policy W.P. Carey Sch. Bus. Ariz. State U., 1996—2002, prof. Sch. Health Mgmt. and Policy, 2002—10; dir. Health Sector Supply Chain Initiatives, 2002—; prin. Health Care Sector Advances, 2004—, Dean's Coun. of 100 Disting. Rsch. Scholars, 2007—, prof. dept. chain supply mgmt., 2010—, prof. dept. supply chain mgmt., 2010—. Mem. health rsch. coun. N.Y. State Dept. Health, 1977—85; vis. rsch. scholar Columbia U., NYC, 1983—84; fellow Accrediting Commn. Edn. Health Svcs. Adminstrn., 1983—84; chmn. Western Network Edn. Health Adminstrn., Berkeley, Calif., 1987—92; commr. Calif. Commn. Future Med. Edn., 1996—97; mem. Ariz. Medicaid Adv. Bd., 1990—92, Ariz. Data Adv. Bd., 1989—91, Ariz. Health Care Group Adv. Bd., 1989; Dean's Coun. 100 Disting. Rsch. scholar Ariz. State U., 2007—. Author: The Physician's Assistant, 1980, Strategic Management of the Health Care Supply Chain, 2006; mem. editl. bd. Work and Occupations, 1975—93, Hosps. and Health Svcs. Adminstrn., 1989—92, Health Adminstrn. Press, 1991—94, Health Mgmt. Rev., 1996, Electronic Hallway, 1999; contbr. articles to profl. jours., chapters to books; mem. editl. mem. with Mitrix Wallacy and Michael Fretil Managing Chaese Pub. Svcs., 2007. Trustee Barrow Neurol. Inst., Phoenix, 1989—95; chair nat. adv. com. Investigator Awards Health Svcs. Rsch. Robert Wood Johnson Found., 1993—96. Mem.: APHA, Pharm. and Therapeutics Soc. (trustee 1999—2005, sec. 1999—2005), Assn. Univ. Health Programs Health Adminstrn. (bd. dirs. 1990—96, chmn. bd. dirs. 1994—95), Am. Sociol. Assn. (bd. dirs. vomaris 2011—). Home: 11843 N 114th Way Scottsdale AZ 85259-2609 Office: Ariz State U Dept Supply Chain Mgmt WP Carey Sch Bus Tempe AZ 85287 Office Phone: 602-320-1512, 480-965-6334. Business E-Mail: gene.schneller@asu.edu.

SCHNITZER, BERTRAM, hematopathologist; b. Frankfurt, Germany, June 21, 1929; arrived in Can., 1940; s. Robert Julius and Eva (Rosen) S.; m. Anna-Ercoli, June 2, 1959; children: Bret, Robert, Stefan. BS, NYU, 1952; MD, U. Basle, Switzerland, 1958. Lic. physician, Conn., Va., Mich.; diplomate in anatomic pathology and clin. pathology Am. Bd. Pathology. Intern Balt. City Hosps., 1958-59; resident pathology Georgetown U. Hosp., Washington, 1959-63; pathologist, hematopathologist Armed Forces Inst. Pathology, Washington, 1963-66; instr. pathology U. Mich., Ann Arbor, 1966-67, asst. prof., 1967-69, assoc. prof., 1969-73, prof. pathology, dir. hematopathology, 1973—. Cons. VA Hosp., Ann Arbor, 1966—; mem. hematology test com. Am. bd. Pathology, 1980 85; chair hematology com. Checkpath Am. Soc. Clin. Pathology, 2002—. Co-author: Monocytes, Monocytosis and Monocytic Leukemia, 1973, Refractory Anemia, 1975; contbr. articles to profl. jours., chpts. to books; cover photograph Sci., 1972. Recipient First DiGuglielmo Prize in Hematology Italian Nat. Soc., Rome, 1976, S.W. Oncology Group grantee U.S. Govt., Washington. Mem. Soc. Hematopathology (pres. 1988-90), Am. Soc. Clin. Pathologists (expert panel hematology com. 1986—, com. on continuing edn. spl. topics 1989—), Am. Soc. Hematology, Internat. Inflammation Club. Achievements include research on tumors of the head and neck, surgical pathology of lymph nodes and neoplastic hematology. Home and Office: Univ Mich Dept Pathology 1301 Catherine St Ann Arbor MI 48109-0602 Business E-Mail: raven@med.umich.edu.

SCHNUR, RHONDA E., medical geneticist, pediatrician, educator; Attended, Baylor Coll. Medicine. Diplomate Am. Bd. Pediatrics, Am. Bd. Medical Genetics-med./clin. cytogenetics, Am. Bd. Medical Genetics-med./clin. biochemical genetics. Intern Mt. Sinai Med. Ctr., resident; fellow Children's Hosp., Phila., Univ. Pa. Sch. Medicine; prof. pediat. Cooper Univ. Hosp., head genetics divsn. With Cooper Univ. Physician; reviewer Am. Jour. Human Genetics, Archieves of Dermatology, Jour. Am. Acad. Dermatology, Am. Jour. med. Genetics, Pediatric Dermatology, Human Genetics, Human Molecular Genetics, Genes, Chromosomes and Cancer. Recipient Top Dr. Clin. Genetics, SJ Mag., NJ Monthly Mag., Best Doctor, Best Doctors in America, Top Dr. Clin. Genetics, Phila. Mag.; named one of the Top Doctors, 2011; grantee Metabolic Diseases and Newborn Screening Grant. Mem.: Phila Genetics Group, Human Genetics Assn. NJ, Nat. Incontinentia Pigmenti Found., Sci. Adv. Coun., Soc. for Craniofacial Genetics, Soc. for Inherited Metabolic Disorders, Am. Cleft Palate Assn., Am. Coll. Med. Genetics, Soc. Pediatric Dermatology, Am. Soc. Human Genetics, AMA. Office: Cooper University Hospital Three Cooper Plz Ste 200 Camden NJ 08103 Office Phone: 856-968-7255. Office Fax: 856-541-6213.

SCHOBER, WOLFGANG KLAUS, toxicologist, researcher; b. Rosenheim, Germany, Dec. 26, 1970; s. Klaus Manfred Hans and Ursula Roswitha Schober; m. Nicole Elisabeth Dagmar Aumüller, Sept. 7, 2001; 1 child, Dominik Pascal. Degree in Food Chemistry with high distinction, Ludwig-Maximilians-U., Munich, Germany, 1997; DSc summa cum laude, Technische U. München, Germany, 2000, Habilitation in Exptl. Allergology, 2010. Registered toxicologist Fedn. European Toxicologists & European Socs. Toxicology, 2005, German Soc. Exptl. and Clin. Pharmacology and Toxicology, 2005. Postdoctoral rsch. fellow GSF nat. rsch. ctr. environ. and health/Technische U. München, 2000—02; postdoctoral lectr. Ctr. Allergy and Environ. Technische U. München, 2003—05, asst. prof. Ctr. Allergy and Environ., 2006—. Sci. sec. organizing com. internat. congresses divsn. environ. dermatology and allergy Helmholtz Zentrum München/Technische U. München. Editor: Metabolic activation of polycyclic aromatic hydrocarbons with bay and fjord regions by cytochromes P450 of mouse, rat and man; contbr. articles to profl. jours. Recipient Nat. prize, Bavarian State Ministry Scis., Rsch. and the Arts, 2002, Best Paper award, 2004, 2006, 2008, Best Lectr. award, Technische U. München, 2010. Mem.: German Soc. Allergology and Clin. Immunology, German Soc. Exptl. and Clin. Pharmacology and Toxicology (Toxicology award 2007), World Allergy Orgn., Fedn. European Toxicologists & European Socs. Toxicology, European Acad. Allergology and Clin. Immunology (Best Poster awards 2004, 2006, 2008). Achievements include research in metabolic activation of polycyclic aromatic hydrocarbons with bay and fjord regions by cytochromes P450 of mouse, rat and man; adjuvant effects of anthropogenic air pollutants on development and maintenance of IgE-mediated allergic diseases. Avocation: sports. Office: ZAUM Ctr Allergy and Environ Biedersteiner Str 29 Bavaria Munich 80802 Germany Office Fax: +49 (0)89 41 40 34 53. Business E-Mail: schober@lrz.tum.de.

SCHOCHET, BARRY P., health care executive; b. NYC, Mar. 13, 1951; s. George and Freda Schochet. BA in Zoology, U. Maine, 1973; MA in Health Care Adminstrn., George Washington U., 1975. Asst. adminstr. Doctors Hosp., Hollywood, Fla., 1975-76, Cypress Community Hosp., Pompano Beach, Fla., 1976-77, adminstr., 1977-78, exec. dir., 1978-79; asst. regional v.p. Nat. Med. Enterprises, St. Petersburg, Fla., 1979-80, asst. v.p. Los Angeles, 1980-81, v.p. ops. Tampa, Fla., 1981-83, sr. regional v.p., 1984-87, sr. divisional v.p., 1987-89, exec. v.p., 1989-91, sr. exec. v.p. and COO Santa Monica, Calif., 1991-93, pres., COO hosp. group, 1993-95; exec. v.p. operations Tenet Healthcare (formerly Nat. Med. Enterprises), Dallas, 1995—99; vice chmn. Tenet Healthcare, 1999—. Mem. Am. Hosp. Assn., Fedn. Am. Health Care Systems (bd. govs. 1985—, bd. dirs. 1989—, chmn. 2000), Am. Coll. Health Care Execs., Fla. League Hosps. (bd. dirs. 1981—, chmn. 1988-89), bd. dir. Healthcare leadership coun., 1999—. Office: Tenet Healthcare 13737 Noel Rd Ste 100 Dallas TX 75240-2017

SCHOEN, NORBERT, cardiologist; b. Muehldorf, Germany, Dec. 14, 1962; s. Gerhard and Gisela Schoen; m. Brigitte Skora; children: Christian, Katrin. MD, Ludwig Maximilians U., Munich, 1989. Jr. physician German Heart Ctr., Radiology, Munich, 1989—90; guest physician U. Essen, Germany, 1991—93; jr. physician Dist. Hosp., Muehldorf, Germany, 1991—96; sr. physician Mueller Clinic Catheter Lab., Munich, 1996—97, guest physician, 1997—2000; pvt. practice Muehldorf, Germany, 1997—. Fellow: Am. Heart Assn., Am. Coll. Cardiology, Internat. Coll. Angiology, European Soc. Cardiology; mem.: Soc. Cardiovascular Angiography Interventions, Am. Soc. Nuc. Cardiology.

SCHOEN, ROY MILES, physician; b. Staten Island, NY, Sept. 24, 1940; s. Herbert Edyane and Mary Ann (Levenstein) S. AB, Dartmouth Coll., 1962; DDS, NYU, 1966; MD, Hadassan Med. Sch., Jerusalem, 1971. Diplomate Am. Bd. Psychiatry and Neurology, Am. Bd. Ob-Gyn. Intern Booth Meml. Med. Ctr., Flushing, N.Y., 1969-71; resident in psychiatry Payne Whitney clinic N.Y. Hosp., NYC, 1971-73; resident in child psychiatry N.Y. Psychiatric Inst., NYC, 1973-75; dir. child, adolescent psychiatry North Shore Hosp., Manhasset, N.Y., 1975-79; resident in ob-gyn. Lenox Hill Hosp., NYC, 1979-82; obstetrician/gynecologist Orlando & Schoen, MD, PC, NYC, 1982—2004; sr. attending dept. ob-gyn. Lenox Hill Hosp., NYC, hon. attending. Maj. Army Res. N.G., 1971-81. Fellow Am. Coll. Ob-Gyn., N.Y. Gynecologic Soc.

SCHOEN, WILLIAM JACK, finance company executive; b. LA, Aug. 2, 1935; s. Jack Conrad and Kathryn Mabel (Stegmayer) S.; m. Sharon Ann Barto, Oct. 1, 1966; children: Kathryn Lynn, Karen Anne, Kristine Lea, William Jack. BS in Fin. magna cum laude, U. So. Calif., 1960, MBA, 1963. Mktg. mgr. Anchor Hocking Glass Co., 1964-68; v.p. sales and mktg. Obear-Nester Glass Co., 1968-71; pres. Pierce Glass Co., Port Allegheny, Pa., 1971-73; pres., chief exec. officer, dir. F.&M. Schaefer Brewing Co., NYC, 1973-81; now chmn., pres. Wilshar Management Co. Inc., Naples, Fla., 1981—; chmn. Health Management Associates, Inc., Naples, 1983—, also bd. dirs. Contbr. to indsl. publns. Founder Marine Corp. Heritage Found.; mem. Bus. Coun. of 100 of Fla.; bd. dir. Internat. Coll. Found.; chmn. Schoen Found.; mem. bd. advisors U. So. Calif. Bus. Sch.; trustee U. So. Calif., 2006-. Served with USMC, 1953-56, Korea. Mem. Hole in the Wall, Naples Yacht Club, Port Royal Club, Teton Springs Club, Phi Kappa Phi. Republican. Lutheran. Office: Health Mgmt Assocs 5811 Pelican Bay Blvd Ste 500 Naples FL 34108-2711 Office Phone: 239-598-3175.

SCHOENBERGER, STEVEN HARRIS, physician, research consultant; b. Cleve., Nov. 26, 1950; s. Stanford L. and Irene (Gold) S. BA, Tulane U., 1972; MD, U. Autonoma Guadalajara, Mex., 1976. Diplomate Am. Bd. of Urology. Asst. prof. Tulane U. Sch. Medicine, New Orleans, 1983—. Rsch. assoc. Delta Regional Primate Rsch. Ctr., Covington, La., 1983-85, chief section of urology Lawrence and Meml. Hosp., New London, Conn.; chmn. laser com., Lawrence and Meml. Hosp., New London, Conn., 1989—, chief sect. urology, 2003—; rsch. cons. Pfizer Med. Group, Groton, Conn., 1989—. Fellow ACS, Am. Soc. Laser Medicine and Surgery; mem. Soc. Univ. Urologists, N.Y. Acad. Scis., New Eng. Escadrille. Office: 3 Shaws Cv Ste 206 New London CT 06320-4968 Office Phone: 860-443-0622.

SCHOENBRUN, LOIS, medical association administrator; Grad., U. Md., College Park. Membership dir. Nat. Abortion Fedn., 1983—88; dep. dir. Am. Med. Women's Assn., Alexandria, Va., 1988—95; exec. dir., found. dir. Am. Acad. Optometry, Rockville, Md., 1996—; owner ILYEO Martial Arts, LLC, Takoma Pk., Md., 2006—. Fellow: Am. Acad. Optometry. Avocation: Tae Kwon Do. Office: Am Acad Optometry #506 6110 Executive Blvd Rockville MD 20852 Office Phone: 301-984-1441 ext. 3006. Office Fax: 301-984-4737. Business E-Mail: LoisS@aaoptom.org. *

SCHOENEBERGER, MARLIES LUISE, alcohol and drug abuse services professional, gerontologist, sociologist; b. Wemmetsweiler,

Saarland, Germany, Dec. 27, 1947; d. Nikolaus Andreas and Katharina Regina Schoeneberger. BA summa cum laude, Spalding U., 1991; MA, U. Ky., 1994, PhD magna cum laude, 2000. Cert. gerontology, postgrad. cert. in med. behavioral sci.; women's studies. Health educator Ctr. Drug and Alcohol Rsch., U. Ky., Lexington, 1996—99, rsch. analyst, 1999—2000, rsch. coord., 2000—02; asst. project dir. NDRI-CIRP, Denver, 2002—03, project dir., 2003—. Contbr. articles to profl. jours. and procs. Mem.: Am. Correctional Assn., Sigma Xi. Home: 2868 Central Park Blvd Denver CO 80238 Office: 3600 Havana St DWCF Admin Bldg 2d Fl A 213 Denver CO 80239 Office Phone: 303-371-8155. Business E-Mail: maria.schoeneberger@doc.state.co.us.

SCHOENER, EUGENE PAUL, medical educator; b. NYC, Oct. 22, 1943; BS, CCNY, 1964; PhD, Rutgers U., 1970. Rsch. assoc. Columbia U. Coll. Physicians & Surgeons, 1972—74; prof. pharmacology and psychiatry Wayne State U. Sch. Medicine, 1974—. Mem.: APHA, Assn. Med. Edn. and Rsch. in Substance Abuse, Rsch. Soc. on Alcoholism, Soc. Neurosci. Avocations: photography, travel. Office: 2761 E Jefferson Ave Detroit MI 48207 Office Fax: 313-577-5062. Business E-Mail: eschoen@med.wayne.edu.

SCHOENFELD, ELINOR RANDI, epidemiologist; b. NYC, Apr. 9, 1956; d. Samuel and Helen (Goldstein) S.; m. Eric Gottesman, 1998. BS, SUNY, Stony Brook, 1977; MS, SUNY, Buffalo, 1980, PhD, 1988. Clin. assoc. Columbia U. Sch. Pub. Health, NYC, 1980-82; data mgr. cmty. oncology program Hackensack (NJ) Med. Ctr., 1982-83; rsch. affiliate Roswell Park Cancer Inst., Buffalo, 1984-85, cancer rsch. scientist, 1985-88; epidemiology cons. Joel Bernstein, MD Otolaryngology, Buffalo, 1984-89; rsch. scientist SUNY Sch. Medicine, Stony Brook, 1988-93, rsch. instr., 1989-90, asst. prof., 1990-98, rsch. assoc. prof. preventive medicine, 1998—, dir. ops., 1992—, sr. rsch. scientist, 1993—, rsch. assoc. prof. opthalmology, 1998—. Epidemiology cons. Univ. Hosp., Stony Brook, 1990-92; dir. Suffolk County Diabetes Study, 1992-99; mem. admissions com. SUNY, Buffalo, 1985-87; founder Elke Images, NYC; presenter, invited spkr. in field. Author: Applications of Diffusion Theory to Cancer Care in the United States: 1972-81, 1990, (with others) On Diabetes, Breast and Skin Cancers, Cataracts, Diabetic Retinopathy, Otitis Media, Myopia, Clinical Trials, Biomedical Informatics, Osteoporosis, Minority Health, Prostate Cancer, 1988-2008; developer (with others) Tailored Web-Edn. Sys. known as TWEEDS; contbr. articles to profl. jours. Bd. dirs. Essential Needs for Srs. Efforts, Inc., N.Y.C., 1995-97, BJ Spoke Gallery, NYC, 2006—; mem. health svcs. rsch. working group Nat. Eye Inst., 1997; mem. nat. health adv. com. Hadassah USA, 1998-2001; mem. Suffolk County Cancer Task Force, 2004—; mem. exec. com. Witness Project L.I., 2002-06. Predoctoral fellow Stony Brook U., 1977-78, Epidemiology Program fellow U. Minn., 1980, fellow in cancer epidemiology Columbia U., 1980-82; Nat. Cancer Inst. grantee NIH, 1987-88, 95—; Nat. Eye Inst. grantee, NIH, 1992-06, Nat. Inst. Dental & Craniofacial Rsch., 2008-; Carol Baldwin Fund grantee, 2001-05; N.Y. State grantee, 2003—, disting. alumni award for univ. svc., StonyBrook U., 2004, u. award for cmty. svc., 2008. Mem. APHA, Soc. Clin. Trials, Soc. Behavioral Medicine, Soc. Epidemiologic Rsch. Jewish. Achievements include minority health, community based participatory research. Office: SUNY Stony Brook Sch Med Dept Prev Med Stony Brook NY 11794-0001 Office Phone: 631-444-2142. E-mail: eschoenfeld@notes.cc.sunysb.edu.

SCHOENFELD, MARK H., cardiac electrophysiologist; Grad., Harvard U. Diplomate Am. Bd. of Internal Medicine-cardiovasc. disease, Am. Bd. of Internal Medicine-clin. cardiac electrophysiology. Fellow Mass Gen. Hosp., resident. Mem.: Cmty. Med. Group (CMG). Office: Hospital of Saint Raphael 1450 Chapel St New Haven CT 06511 Office Phone: 203-867-5400.

SCHOENHARD, WILLIAM CHARLES, JR., health system executive; b. Kansas City, Mo., Sept. 26, 1949; s. William Charles S. and Joyce Evans (Thornsberry) Bell; m. Kathleen Ann Klosterman, June 3, 1972; children: Sarah Elizabeth, Thomas William. BS in Pub. Adminstrn., U. Mo., 1971; M of Health Adminstrn. with honors, Washington U., St. Louis, 1975. V.p., dir. gen. svcs. Deaconess Hosp., St. Louis, 1975-78; assoc. exec. dir. St. Mary's Health Ctr., St. Louis, 1978-81; exec. dir. Arcadia Valley Hosp., Pilot Knob, Mo., 1981-82, St. Joseph Health Ctr., St. Charles, Mo., St. Joseph Hosp. West, Lake St. Louis, 1982—86; exec. v.p., COO SSM Health Care, St. Louis, 1986—2009, dep. under sec. health ops. & mgmt., dept. veterans affairs Washington, 2009—. Adv. bd. dirs. Firstar Bank, 1998-01, Midwest Bank Ctr., 2004, Coll. Bus. Mgmt. U. Mo., Columbia, Mo., 2005-09. Contbr. articles to profl. jours. Mem. Mo. Commn. on Patient Safety, 2003—04, Organ Donation and Transplantation Alliance, 2006—08; mem. adv. bd. St. Louis chpt. Lifeseekers, St. Louis, 1985—94; mem. bd. mgrs. Kirkwood-Webster (Mo.) YMCA, 1990—96, sec., 1996; mem. healthcare adv. bd. Sanford Brown Colls., 1992—94; bd. dirs. St. Andrews Mgmt. Svcs., Inc., 1994—2002, Mid Am. Transplant Svcs., 1995—2009, sec., 2005—09, vice chmn., 2009—; exec. com. mem. Lindenwood U., 2004—09, bd. dirs., 1997—2009, Civic Entrepreneurs Orgn., 1997—2000, Greater St. Louis Boy Scouts Am., 1997—2009, Benedictine Health Sys., 2002. With USN, 1971—72, Vietnam. Fellow Am. Coll. Health Care Execs. (regent Mo.-Gateway area 1997-01, bd. govs. 2002—, chmn. 2006-07); mem. VFW, Am. Hosp. Assn. (del. regional policy bd. 1999-2005, bd. trustees, 2007—09, exec. com., 2008-09, ops. com. 2007—09), Mo. Hosp. Assn. (bd. trustees 1999-2005, chmn. 2000), Am. Heart Assn. (mem. bd. Greater St. Louis chpt. 2001-03), Cath. Health Assn. U.S. (mem. fin. com. 1999-01), Am. Legion, US Navy League, Westborough Country Club, Phi Eta Sigma, Pi Omicron Sigma, Delta Upsilon, Delta Sigma Pi. Roman Catholic. Avocations: reading, walking. Home: 420 Fairwood Ln Saint Louis MO 63122-4429 Office: Dept Veterans Affairs 810 Vermont Ave NW Washington DC 20420

SCHOENHOEFER, PETER SEBASTIAN, retired editor, pharmacologist; b. Wuppertal, Germany, Sept. 16, 1935; s. Friedrich and Erna Schoenhoefer; m. Erika Pretz, 1965; 1 child, Danja. Diploma in chemistry, U., Bonn, 1960; MD, U., Cologne, 1963. Diplomate bd. cert. in medicine U. Cologne, 1963. Asst. pharmacology, Bonn, Germany, 1964—67; internat. postdoctoral fellow NHLI NIH, Bethesda, Md., 1967—69; asst. prof. U. Bonn, 1970—72; prof. pharmacology Med. Acad., Hannover, Germany, 1972—79; chief dept. Fed. Health Office, Berlin, 1979—84; dir. inst. clin. pharmacology Ctrl. Hospitals Bremen, Germany, 1984—86; senatsdirector State Health Adminstrn., Bremen, 1986—88; dir. inst. clin. pharmacology Ctrl. Hospitals Bremen, 1989—2000; co-editor Arznei-Telegramm, Berlin, 2000—10. Recipient Integrity Award 2002, Transparency Internat., 2002. Home: Ruetenhoefe 7B D-28355 Bremen Germany

SCHOENRICH, EDYTH HULL, internist, preventive medicine physician; b. Cleve., Sept. 9, 1919; d. Edwin John and Maud Mabel (Kelly) Hull; m. Carlos Schoenrich, Aug. 9, 1942; children: Lola, Olaf. AB, Duke U., Durham, NC, 1941; MD, U. Chgo., 1947; MPH, John Hopkins U., Balt., 1971. Diplomate Am. Bd. Internal Medicine, Am. Bd. Preventive Medicine. Intern John Hopkins Hosp., Balt., 1948-49, asst. resident medicine, 1949-50, fellow medicine, 1950-51, chief resident, pvt. wards, 1951-52; asst. chief, acting chief dept. chronic and cmty. medicine Balt. City Hosp., Balt., 1963-66; dir. svc. to chronically ill and aging Md. State Dept. Health, Balt., 1966-74; dir. divsn. pub. health adminstrn. Sch. Pub. Health, John Hopkins U., Balt., 1974-77, assoc. dean acad. affairs, 1977-86, dir. part time profl. programs and dep. dir. MPH program, 1986—, prof. dept. health policy and mgmt., 1974—, joint appointment medicine, 1978—. Contbr. articles to profl. jours. Trustee Friends Life Care Cmty., 1984—, Kennedy-Krieger Inst., Balt., 1985—, Vis. Nurses Assn., 1990-95, Md. Home and Cmty. Care Found., 1995—. Recipient Stebbins medal John Hopkins U., 1989, Disting. Med. Alumna award, 1997, Golden Apple award, 2007; named to Md. Women's Hall of Fame, 2005 Fellow ACP, Am. Coll. Preventive Medicine; mem. APHA, Assn. Tchrs. Preventive Medicine, Med. and Chirurg. Soc. Md., Balt. City Med. Soc., Phi Beta Kappa, Alpha Omega Alpha, Delta Omega. Avocations: gardening, music, theater, swimming. Home: 1402 Boyce Ave Baltimore MD 21204-6512 Office: Johns Hopkins Bloomberg Sch Sch Pub Health 7420 N Honeysuckle Ct Brimfield IL 61517-8901 Office Phone: 410-955-1291. Business E-Mail: eschoenr@jhsph.edu.

SCHOEPF, DIETER, psychiatrist, psychotherapist; s. Ernst and Heidi Schoepf; m. Andrea Brummermann; 1 child, Isabelle. MD, Dept. Neurology, Hamburg, 1994. LCSW in FA Psychiatrie und Psychotherapie Ärztekammer NRW, 2002. Oberarzt U. clinic, Bonn, Germany, 2002; supr. CBASP Nat. Tng. Programme, Inc., Richmoond, 2007, provider, 2007—, therapist, 2007—. Contbr. articles to profl. publs. V.p. CBASP-Netzwerk e.V., Freiburg, Germany, 2008. Office: Univ Clinic Bonn Dept Psychiatry & Psychotherapy Sigmund-Freud St 25 Bonn 53105 Germany Office Phone: 0049-228-287-15794.

SCHOETZ, DAVID JOHN, JR., colon and rectal surgeon, educator; b. Milw., Oct. 29, 1948; s. David John and Beverly (Rogers) S.; m. Ruthanne Brennan, Mar. 25, 1972; children: Elizabeth Anne, David John III. BA, Coll. of Holy Cross, Worcester, Mass., 1970; MD, Med. Coll. Wis., Milw., 1974. Diplomate Am. Bd. Surgery, Am. Bd. Colon and Rectal Surgery. Resident in surgery Boston U. Med. Ctr., 1974-81; resident in colon/rectal surgery Lahey Clinic Med. Ctr., Burlington, Mass., 1981-82, staff colon-rectal surgeon, 1982—, chmn. dept. colon-rectal surgery, 1987—2002, acad. dean, 2006—; prof. surgery Med. Sch. Tufts U., Boston, 1999—, chmn. dept. med. edn., 2000—. Fellow ACS (commn. on cancer 1998-2003, gov., 2004—10), Am. Bd. Colon and Rectal Surgery (sr. examiner 1996—, assoc. exec. 2005-06, exec. dir. 2006—), ABMS (bd. dirs. 2009—), Am. Soc. Colon and Rectal Surgeons (sec. 1999-2002, pres.-elect 2002-03, pres. 2003-04). Office: Lahey Clinic Med Ctr 41 Mall Rd Burlington MA 01803-4521 Office Phone: 781-744-8889. *

SCHOIFET, SCOTT DAVID, orthopaedic surgeon; MD, Columbia U., NY, 1983. Lic. NJ, 1989, diplomate Am. Bd. Orthopaedic Surgery. Intern gen. surgery St. Vincent's Cath. Med. Ctr., 1984, resident gen. surgery, 1985; resident orthop. surgery Strong Meml. Hosp., 1988; fellow orthop. surgery Mayo Clinic Minn., 1989, fellow gen. surgery, 1990; hosp. affiliations include Virtua Ambulatory Surgery Ctr., Virtua Meml. Hosp., Virtua WJ Hosp., Marlton, Virtua West Jersey Hosp., Berlin, Virtua Hosp., Voorhees, Marlton. Named one of the Top Doctors, Phila. Mag., 2010—11. Fellow: Am. Acad. Orthop. Surgeons; mem.: ACS. Office: Virtua Hospital Elmwood Business Pk 773 Rt 70 E Ste E100 Marlton NJ 08053 Office Phone: 856-673-3960.

SCHOLEFIELD, PETER GORDON, health facility administrator; b. Newport, Wales, June 26, 1925; emigrated to Can., 1947, naturalized, 1952; s. Tom and Margaret (Bithell) S.; m. Erna Mary Cooper, Sept. 29, 1951; children: David, John, Paul. B.Sc., U. Wales, 1944, M.Sc., 1946, D.Sc., 1960; PhD, McGill U., Montreal, Que., Can., 1949. Rsch. fellow to prof. biochemistry McGill U., 1949—69, dir. cancer research unit, 1965-69; asst. exec. dir. Nat. Cancer Inst. Can., Toronto, 1969-80, exec. dir., 1980-91, spl. adviser to chief exec. officer, 1991-92; dir. grants and awards Alta. Heritage Found. for Med. Rsch., Edmonton, 1992-94; coord. acad. affairs Samuel Lunenfeld Rsch. Inst. Mt. Sinai Hosp., Toronto, 1994-99. Chair rsch. policy com., bd. dirs. Alzheimer Soc. of Can., 1994-2000; mem. health adv. com. Alta. Heritage Found. Med. Rsch, 1994-99; bd. dirs. Ont. Neurotrauma Found., 1999-2004, sec., 2003-04, chmn. rsch. com., 2003-04; mem. adv. bd. Inst. Neuroscis. Mental Health and Addiction, Can. Insts. Health Rsch., 2001-04, mem. standing com. on grants and awards competitions, 2005-07, mem. sub-com. on programs and peer rev., 2007-09; chair Can. Tobacco Control Rsch. Initiative, 2007-09. Home: 1503-2010 Islington Ave Etobicoke ON Canada M9P 3S8 Personal E-mail: peter.scholefield@rogers.com.

SCHOLZ, HASSO, pharmacologist, educator; b. Stettin, Germany, Aug. 24, 1937; s. Hans Friedrich and Ruth (von Langendorff) S.; m. Elke Ries, 1962; children: Kristin, Inken. MD, U. Mainz, Germany, 1966. Prof. pharmacology U. Mainz, 1972-75; prof., head dept. biochem. pharmacology Med. Sch., U. Hannover, Germany, 1976-81; prof. pharmacology U. Hamburg, Germany, 1982—; head div. pharmacology Univ. Hosp. of Eppendorf, U. Hamburg, Germany, 1982—2002. Contbr. numerous articles to profl. publs. Mem. German Soc. Pharmacology and Toxicology (pres. 1987-90), German Cardiac Soc. (pres. 1991-92), Leopoldina German Soc. Sci., Academia Europaea, Acad. Sci. Hamburg. Home: Fuhlsbuetteler Weg 28 D-22453 Hamburg Germany Office: Univ Hosp Dept Pharmacology Martinistrasse 52 D-20246 Hamburg Germany E-mail: h.scholz@uke.uni-hamburg.de.

SCHOLZ, PETER M., surgeon, director; MD, U. Basel, Switzerland, 1970. Diplomate Am. Bd. Surgery, 1983, Am. Bd. Thoracic Surgery, 1985. Intern in Surgery Duke U. Med. Ctr., Durham, NC, 1974—75, resident gen. and thoracic surgery, 1975—83; physician divsn. thoracic surgery Robert Wood Johnson U. Med. Group, New Brunswick, NJ, 1983—, chief divsn. cardiovasc. surgery, 2005—10; assoc. dean clin. & transtional rsch., 2010—. Office: Clin Acad Bldg Ste 4100 125 Paterson St New Brunswick NJ 08901-0019 Office Phone: 732-235-7642.

SCHOLZ, WOLF-ULRICH, psychologist, consultant; b. Frankfurt am Main, Germany, Sept. 6, 1950; Diploma in psychology, Goethe Univ., Frankfurt am Main, 1978, diploma in ednl. scis., 1991. Cert. clin. psychologist, 1984, supr., 1994, psychol. psychotherapist, 1999, trainer in suggestopedia, 1994, clin. hypnosis, 1987. Counseling psychologist pvt. practice, Frankfurt am Main, 1980—; acad. tutor Goethe U., 1985-91; trainer, instr. FIRST, Frankfurt am Main, 1990—. Lectr. clin. psychology cognitive behavior therapy and hypnosis, health promotion Deutsche Psychologen Akademie, Bonn, 1989-99; trainer Didactic Ctr., Goethe U., 1990-97; pers. cons. Goethe U., 1999—; trainer, instr. hypnosis multimodal stress competence autogenic tng., 2003—. Author: Hypnosis and Hypnotherapy, 1994, The Ruse of Reason, 1999, Continuing Developments in Cognitive Behavioral Therapies, 2001, Recent Currents and Approaches in Cognitive-Behavioral Therapies, 2002; co-author: FIRST Papers in REBT, 1995, 2002. Mem. Berufsverband Deutscher Psychologen (substitute del. 1996-98, del. 1999—2009), European Coaching Assn. Achievements include development of metalogue approach of rational-emotive behavior therapy and counseling, training for multimodal stress competence, symbolization theory for the context of the fostering of development. Office: FIRST Sandweg 53 D-60316 Frankfurt Germany

SCHONFELD, GUSTAV, medical educator, researcher, administrator; b. Mukacevo, Ukraine, May 8, 1934; arrived in US, 1946, naturalized, 1951; s. Alexander Schonfeld and Helena Gottesmann; m. Miriam Steinberg, May 28, 1961; children: Joshua Lawrence, Julia Elizabeth, Jeremy David. BA, Washington U., St. Louis, 1956, MD, 1960. Diplomate Am. Bd. Internal Medicine. Intern. Bellevue Med. Ctr. NYU, 1960—61, resident in internal medicine, 1961—63; chief resident in internal medicine Jewish Hosp., St. Louis, 1963—64; from NIH trainee in endocrinology & metabolism to Kountz prof. medicine Washington U., St. Louis, 1964—96, Busch prof., chair medicine, 1996—99, Samuel E. Schechter prof. medicine, 2002—; rsch. assoc. Cochran VA Hosp., St. Louis, 1965—66, clin. investigator, 1968—70, cons. in internal medicine, 1972—; rsch. flight med. officer USAF Sch. Aerospace Medicine, Brooks AFB, Tex., 1966—68; from asst. physician to physician Barnes Hosp., St. Louis, 1972—96; physician-in-chief Barnes Jewish Hosp., St. Louis, 1996—99; clin. instr. medicine Harvard U. Med. Sch., Boston, 1970—72; assoc. prof. metabolism and human nutrition, asst. dir. Clin. Rsch. Ctr. MIT, Cambridge, 1970—72. Mem. rsch. com. Mo. Heart Assn., 1978-80; expert witness working group on atherosclerosis Nat. Heart, Lung and Blood Inst., 1979, Nat. Diabetes Adv. Bd., 1979; mem. endocrinologic and metabolic drugs adv. com. USPHS, FDA, 1982-86; mem. nutrition study sect. NIH, 1984-88, spl. reviewer metabolism study sect.; mem. adult treatment guidelines panel Nat. Cholesterol Edn. Program, 1986; mem. Consensus Devel. Conf. on Triglyceride, High Density Lipoprotein and Coronary Heart Disease, 1992; cons. Am. Egg Bd., Am. Dairy Bd., Inst. Shortening and Edible Oils, Ciba-Geigy, Sandoz, Fournier, Parke-Davis, Bristol-Meyers Squibb, Monsanto/Searle; adj. prof. medicine Columbia U. Coll. Physicians & Surgeons, 2006. Past editor: Atherosclerosis, past mem. editl. bd.: Jour. Clin. Endocrinology and Metabolism, Jour. Clin. Investigation, Jour. Lipid Rsch., past assoc. editor: Circulation. Recipient Berg Prize in Microbiology, 1957, 58, Faculty/Alumni award Washington U., 1995; named Physician honoree Am. Heart Assn. Mo. Affiliate, 1995; grantee MERIT status NIH, Vascular Biology Spl. Merit award, Am. Heart Assn. Fellow ACP, AAAS; mem. Assn. Am. Physicians, Am. Soc. for Clin. Investigation, Am. Physiol. Soc., Am. Soc. Biol. Chemists, Am. Inst. Nutrition, Am. Diabetes Assn., Am. Heart Assn. (program com. coun. on atherosclerosis 1977-80, 86-88, nutrition com. 1980-84, pathology rsch. com. 1980-83, budget com. 1991, awards com. 1992, exec. com. 2001—, Spl. Vascular Biology award 2005, G.L. Duff lecture award, 2006), Endocrine Soc., Alpha Omega Alpha. Democrat. Jewish. Office: Washington U Sch Medicine Box 8046 660 S Euclid Ave Saint Louis MO 63110-1010 Office Phone: 314-362-8060. Business E-Mail: gschonfe@wustl.edu.

SCHÖNICKE, GERRIT, nephrologist; b. Oberhausen, Germany, May 12, 1971; s. Walter Schönicke and Monika Lehmkuhl. MD, U. Düsseldorf, Germany, 1997. Nephrologist U. Düsseldorf, 1997—. Contbr. articles to profl. jours. Office: U Düsseldorf Moorenstr 5 D-40225 Düsseldorf Germany Home: kirchsoren 9 24226 Heihendorf Germany Office Fax: +49 211 811 7722; Home Fax: +49 211 7008821. E-mail: schoenic@uni-duesseldorf.de.

SCHOOLAR, JOSEPH CLAYTON, psychiatrist, pharmacologist, educator; b. Marks, Miss., Feb. 28, 1928; s. Adrian Taylor and Leah (Covington) S.; m. Betty Jane Peck, Nov. 2, 1960; children: Jonathan Covington, Cynthia Jane, Geoffrey Michael, Catherine Elizabeth, Adrian Carson AB, U. Tenn., Knoxville, 1950, MS, 1952; PhD, U. Chgo., 1957, MD, 1960. Diplomate Am. Bd. Psychiatry and Neurology. Chief drug abuse research TRIMS, Houston, 1966-72; assoc. prof. U. Tex. Grad. Sch. Biomed. Scis., Houston, 1968—; prof. psychiatry Baylor Coll. Medicine, Houston, 1975—, prof. pharmacology, 1974—2002, prof. emeritus pharmacology and psychiatry, 2003—, chief div. psychopharmacology, 1973-82; dir. Tex. Research Inst. Mental Scis., Houston, 1972-85. Mem. Nat. Bd. Med. Examiners' Task Force on Drug Abuse and Alcoholism, 1982-; mem. Drug Abuse Adv. Com., FDA, Washington, 1983-85, chmn., 1984; chmn. profl. needs planning task force Nat. Inst. Drug Abuse, Washington, 1977- Editor: Current Issues in Adolescent Psychiatry, 1973, Research and the Psychiatric Patient, 1975, The Kinetics of Psychiatric Drugs,

1979, Serotonin in Biological Psychiatry - Advances in Biochemical Psychopharmacology, 1982. Cons. Parents' League Houston, 1972-74; mem. coordinating com. Citizens Mental Health Service, Houston, 1976; mem. acad. com. for study of violence Houston Police Dept., 1979; bd. dirs. Can-Do-It, Houston, 1982-. Served with U.S. Army, 1945-47, to 1st lt. USAR, 1950-62. Recipient Eugen Kahn award Baylor Coll. Medicine, Houston, 1964, Alumni award for Disting. Svc., U. Chgo., 1995, Psychiat. Excellence award Tex. Soc. Psychiat. Physicians, 1995. Fellow Am. Psychiat. Assn. (disting. life), Am. Coll. Psychiatrists, Am. Coll. Neuropsychopharmacology, Collegium Internationale NeuroPsychopharmacologicum, Am. Soc. Pharmacology and Exptl. Therapeutics. Episcopalian. Home: 1111 Hermann Dr Unit 17E Houston TX 77004-6930 Office: Baylor Coll Medicine PO Box 66575 Houston TX 77266-6575 Home Phone: 713-523-6979; Office Phone: 713-524-9700. E-mail: jschoolar@pol.net.

SCHOOLEY, ROBERT T., medical educator; b. Washington, Nov. 10, 1949; s. Robert Enoch and Lelia Francis (Barnhill) S.; m. Constance Benson; children: Kimberly Dana, Elizabeth Kendall. BS, Washington and Lee U., 1970; MD, Johns Hopkins U., 1974. Diplomate Am. Bd. Internal Medicine. Intern Johns Hopkins Hosp., Balt., 1974—75, resident, 1975—76; clin. assoc. lab. clin. investigation Nat. Inst. Allergy & Infectious Disease, NIH, Bethesda, Md., 1976—77, chief clin. assoc. lab. clin. investigation, 1977—78, med. officer lab. clin. investigation, 1978—79; from instr. to assoc. prof. medicine Harvard Med. Sch., Boston, 1979—90; prof. medicine U. Colo., Denver, 1990—2005, U. Calif., San Diego, 2005—, head Divsn. Infectious Diseases, 1990—2004. Dir. Colo. Ctr. for AIDS Rsch., 2003—05; head divsn. infectious diseases U. Calif., San Diego, 2005—, vice chair dept. medicine, 2007—. Mem. editl. bd.: Antimicrobial Agts. and Chemotherapy, 1987—2000, Biotherapy, 1987—95, Jour. Acquired Immune Deficiency Syndromes, 1988—, Clin. and Diagnostic Lab. Immunology, 1992, assoc. editor: Clin. Infectious Diseases, 2002—; contbr. articles to profl. jours. Clin. and rsch. fellow Infectious Disease Unit, Mass. Gen. Hosp., Boston, 1979-81; rsch. fellow Medicine Harvard Med. Sch., 1979-81; recipient Bonfils-Stanton award for sci. and medicine. Fellow Infectious Disease Soc. Am., mem. AAAS, Am. Assn. Immunologists, Am. Soc. Clin. Investigation, Assn. Am. Physicians, Omicron Delta Kappa. Office: U Calif San Diego Mail Stop 0711 9500 Gilman Ave La Jolla CA 92093 Home Phone: 858-350-9610; Office Phone: 858-822-0216. Business E-Mail: rschooley@ucsd.edu.

SCHOON, DORIS VIVIEN, ophthalmologist; b. Luverne, Minn., Dec. 31, 1928; d. Jacob and Esther Viola S. BA, U. Minn., 1950, MD, 1954; MSEE, Calif. State U., 1991. Diplomate Am. Bd. Ophthalmology. Intern Kings County Hosp., Bklyn., 1954-55; physician Embudo Presbyn. Hosp., N.Mex., 1955-57; resident in clin. pathology U. Colo. Med. Ctr., Denver, 1957-58; gen. practice medicine Anaheim, Calif., 1958-61; resident in ophthalmology L.A. Eye and Ear Hosp. at Hollywood Presbyn. Hosp., 1961-64; ophthalmologist Anaheim, 1965-75; pvt. practice electrophysiology related to vision, 1997—2003, prof. clin. ophthalmology U. Calif., Irvine, 2004—. Physician Long Beach Vets. Hosp., 1998—. Fellow Am. Acad. Ophthalmology; mem. IEEE, Am. Women's Med. Assn., Internat. Soc. Clin. Electrophysiology in Vision, Soc. of Women Engrs., Order Eastern Star. Republican. Presbyterian. Achievements include research in field of using fast random stimuli to obtain electroretinograms and visually evoked potentials.

SCHORR, LISBETH BAMBERGER, policy analyst; b. Munich, Jan. 20, 1931; d. Fred S. and Lotte (Krafft) Bamberger; m. Daniel L. Schorr, Jan. 8, 1967; children: Jonathan, Lisa. BA with highest honors, U. Calif., Berkeley, 1952; LHD (hon.), Wilkes U., 1991, U. Md., 1994, Bank St. Coll. Edn., 1999, Wheelock Coll., 2000, Lewis & Clark Coll., 2001, Whittier Coll., 2003. Med. care cons. U.A.W. and Community Health Assn., Detroit, 1956—58; asst. dir. Dept. Social Security AFL-CIO, Washington, 1958—65; acting chief CAP Health Svcs., OEO, 1965—66; chief program planning Office for Health Affairs, OEO, Washington, 1967. Cons. Children's Def. Fund, Washington, 1973—79; scholar-in-residence Inst. of Medicine NAS, 1979—80; chmn. Select Panel on Promotion Child Health, 1979—80; adj. prof. maternal and child health U. N.C., Chapel Hill, 1981—85; lectr. social medicine Harvard U. Med. Sch., 1984—; dir. project on effective interventions, 1988—2007; founder www.PathwaysToOutcomes.org; sr. fellow Ctr. for Study Soc. Policy, 2008; nat. coun. Alan Gutmacher Inst., 1974—79, 1982—85; pub. mem. Am. Bd. Pediat., 1978—84; vice chmn. Found. for Child Devel., 1978—84, bd. dirs., 1976—84, 1986—94; mem. coun. Nat. Ctr. for Children in Poverty, 1987—96; mem. children's program adv. com. Edna McConnell Clark Found., 1987—97; bd. dirs. Pub. Edn. Fund Network, 1991—93; co-chair Roundtable on Cmty. Change Aspen Inst., 1992—2006, mem. exec. com. Roundtable on Cmty. Change, 2006—; mem. bd. on children and families NAS, 1993—95; mem. Nat. Commn. State and Local Pub. Svcs., 1992—94; mem. task force on young children Carnegie Corp., 1992—94; mem. sec.'s adv. com. Head Start quality and expansion, 1993—94; mem. nat. selection com. Ford Found./Kennedy Sch. Awards for Innovations in Am. Govt., 1998—2006; dir. Pathways Mapping Initiative, Project on Effective Interventions, 2000—. Author: Within Our Reach: Breaking the Cycle of Disadvantage, 1988, Common Purpose: Strengthening Families and Neighborhoods to Rebuild America, 1997. Co-chmn. Boundaries task force Harvard Children's Initiative, 1998—2000; mem. Brookings Children's Roundtable, 1999—2002; bd. dirs. Nat. Student Partnerships, 2001—03, Eureka Cmtys., 1995—2005, Civic Ventures, 1997—99. Recipient Dale Richmond Meml. award, Am. Acad. Pediat., 1977, 9th ann. Robert F. Kennedy Book award, 1989, Nelson Cruikshank award, Nat. Coun. Sr. Citizens, 1990, Porter prize, 1993, PASS award, Nat. Coun. on Crime and Delinquency, 1997, Marian F. Langer award, Am. Orthopsychiat. Assn., 1999, Empatheia award, Vols. of Am., 1999. Mem.: Nat. Acad. on Social Ins., Inst. Medicine NAS, Phi Beta Kappa. Home and Office: 3113 Woodley Rd NW Washington DC 20008-3449 Home Phone: 202-483-7150; Office Phone: 202-462-3071. Business E-Mail: lisbeth_schorr@hms.harvard.edu.

SCHORR-RIBERA, HILDA KEREN, psychologist; b. NYC, May 2, 1942; d. Leon and Rosa Schorr-Ribera; m. Ira Eli Wessler, Aug. 6, 1971; children: Mike, Daniel. BA, Hunter Coll., 1963; MEd, U. No. Fla., 1982; PhD, U. Pitts., 1988. Lic. psychologist, Pa.; diplomate Am. Bd. Forensic Examiners; diplomate, fellow Am. Bd. Med. Psychotherapists and Psychodiagnosticians; diplomate Am. Bd. Forensic Medicine, Am. Acad. Experts in Traumatic Stress; cert. in clin. hypnosis. Psychotherapist South Hills Interfaith Ministries, Bethel Park, Pa., 1989-92, Profl. Psychol. Assn. of Greater Pitts., 1992; pvt. practice psychologist Pitts., 1993—. Child therapist Forbes Hospice, 1993—; group facilitator of adult wellness group and children's support groups Burger King Cancer Caring Ctr., Pitts., 1989—, Allegheny Hospice, Pitts., 1994—96; psychol. evaluator Washington (Pa.) County Ct., 1993—2005, Allegheny County Ct., Pitts., 1995—98; cons. psychologist to sch. dists. Allegheny and Washington Counties. Author (with others): Educating the Child With Cancer, 1993. Keynote spkr. on illness and bereavement to profl. assns., hosps., schs. and agys., Pitts., 1989—. Mem. APA, Am. Soc. Clin. Hypnosis, Am. Bd. Med. Psychotherapists and Psychodiagnostics, Pa. Psychol. Assn., Greater Pitts. Psychol. Assn. Avocations: music, reading, walking, travel. Office: 117 Ridgeway Ct Pittsburgh PA 15228-1729 Office Phone: 412-344-0222. Personal E-mail: schorrribera@yahoo.com.

SCHOTLAND, DONALD LEWIS, retired medical educator, neurologist; b. Orange, NJ, Sept. 21, 1930; s. Joseph Henry and Elsie (Block) S.; m. Marilyn Goldfeder, July 6, 1955 (dec. 1974); m. Estherina Shems, Jan. 11, 1976; children: John, Thomas, Peter. AB, Harvard U., 1952, MD, 1957; spl. student, MIT, 1955-56; MA (hon.), U. Pa., 1973. Diplomate Am. Bd. Psychiatry and Neurology 1964. Intern U. Ill. Research and Edn. Hosp., 1957-58; asst. resident in neurology Columbia Presbyn. Med. Center, NYC, 1958-61, asst. neurologist, 1961-65, asst. attending neurologist, 1965-66; asst. in neurology Coll. Physicians and Surgeons, Columbia U., NYC, 1960-61, vis. fellow in neurology, 1961-64, assoc. in neurology, 1964-66, asst. prof. neurology, 1966-67; assoc. prof. Sch. Medicine, U. Pa., Phila., 1967-72, prof., 1972-98, prof. emeritus, 1998—. Speaker profl. confs., U.S., Can., Italy, Japan, China, France, Israel, Finland; dir. Henry M. Watts, Jr. Neuromuscular Disease Rsch. Ctr., 1974-90. Editor: Diseases of the Motor Unit, 1982; contbr. articles, papers to profl. publs. Served to 1st lt. USAR, 1958-65. NIH postdoctoral fellow, 1961-64; recipient Research Career Devel. award, 1966-67, various grants NIH and Muscular Dystrophy Assn. Fellow Coll. of Physicians of Phila.; mem. Am. Acad. Neurology, Am. Neurol. Assn., Phila. Neurol. Soc., Muscular Dystrophy Assn. (sci. adv. com. 1974-86, chmn. fellowship com. 1974-86, chmn. 6th Internat. Conf. 1980). Home: 1310 Wyngate Rd Wynnewood PA 19096-2455 Office: Hosp of Univ Pa 3400 Spruce St Philadelphia PA 19104-4283 Personal E-mail: dlschotl@mail.med.upenn.edu.

SCHOTT, KATHARINE SUE, nursing educator; d. Francis Earl and Gertrude Betty (Brown) S. BSN, Mt. Mercy Coll., Cedar Rapids, 1975; MA, U. Iowa, 1987, PhD, 1991. Charge nurse ICU, critical care unit, recovery rm., nurse tng. officer Nursing Corp., US Army, various locations, 1975; advanced through grades to major U.S. Army, 1987; ret. lt. comdr., officer in charge fleet hosp. unit USN, 1993; adj. asst. prof. & instr., pathophysiology and neurological and behavioral pathology U. Iowa, 1987—2010; staff nurse Vis. Nurses Assn. Johnson County, Iowa City, 1993-97. Rsch. in computer-based instrn. Co-founder K-9 Potty Patrol, Milw., 1998—2003, Just Like Home Doggie Motel, Watertown, Wis., 2003—. Decorated numerous mil. awards. Home: W8264 County Road J Watertown WI 53098-3631 Personal E-mail: drschott@aol.com.

SCHOTTE, CHRIS KAMIEL WILLY, psychologist, researcher; b. Ukkel, Belgium, Dec. 12, 1956; s. Henri Schotte and Marie-Louise Meyers; m. Fabienne Schroeders, Apr. 9, 1983; children: Sophie, Anouk. M in Psychol. Sci., Vrije U. Brussel, 1981, PhD in Psychol. Sci., 1996. Cert. cognitive behavioral therapist VVGT, Vlaamse Vereniging Gedrags Therapie, 1993. Clin. psychologist Dept. Psychiatry U. Hosp. Anwterp, Edegem, Belgium, 1983—2007; asst. prof. Faculty Psychology and Ednl. Scis. Vrije U. Brussels, 1995—; head dept. clin. psychology U. Hosp. Brussels, 2008—. Mem.: European Assn. Behavioral and Cognitive Therapies, Flemish Soc. Clin. Psychologists, Internat. Soc. Study of Personality Disorders, Collaborative Antwerp Rsch. Inst. Home: Tonnetgaarde 29 Brussels b-1090 Belgium Office: UZ Brussels Clin Psychology Laarbeeklaan 101 1090 Brussels Belgium Office Phone: 3224763461. Business E-Mail: christiaan.schotte@uzbrussel.be.

SCHOTTENFELD, DAVID, retired epidemiologist, educator; b. NYC, Mar. 25, 1931; m. Rosalie C. Schaeffer; children: Jacqueline, Stephen. AB, Hamilton Coll., 1952; MD, Cornell U., 1956; MS in Pub. Health, Harvard U., 1963. Diplomate Am. Bd. Internal Medicine, Am. Bd. Preventive Medicine. Intern in internal medicine Duke U., Durham, NC, 1956-57; resident in internal medicine Meml. Sloan-Kettering Cancer Ctr., Cornell U. Med. Coll., NYC, 1957-59; Craver fellow med. oncology Meml. Sloan-Kettering Cancer Ctr., 1961-62; clin. instr. dept. pub. health Cornell U., NYC, 1963—65, asst. prof. dept. pub. health, 1965-70, assoc. prof. dept. pub. health, 1970-73, prof. dept. pub. health, 1973-86; John G. Searle prof., chmn. epidemiology sch. pub. health U. Mich., Ann Arbor, 1986—2004, prof. internal medicine, 1986—2004, prof. emeritus internal medicine and epidemiology Sch. Pub. Health, 2004—; adj. prof. dept. family medicine and cmty. health U. Mass. Med. Sch., Worcester, 2006—. Vis. prof. epidemiology U. Minn., Mpls., 1968, 71, 74, 82, 86; W.G. Cosbie lectr. Can. Oncology Soc., 1987. Editor: Cancer Epidemiology and Prevention, 1982, 2d. edit., 1996, 3d edit., 2006; author 10 books; contbr. more than 250 articles to profl. jours. Served with USPHS, 1959-61. Recipient Acad. Career award in Preventive Oncology, Nat. Cancer Inst., 1980-85, Disting. Achievement award Am. Soc. Preventive Oncology, 1992, Alumni award Harvard U. Sch. Pub. Health, 2010; vis. scholar Nat. Cancer Inst., 2007. Fellow AAAS, ACP, APHA (John Snow award 2007), Am. Coll. Preventive Medicine, Am. Coll. Epidemiology (Abraham Lilienfeld award 2002), Armed Forces Epidemiology Bd.; mem. Soc. Epidemiologic Rsch. (pres. 1998-99), Phi Beta Kappa. Office: U Mich Sch Pub Health Dept Epidemiology 109 Observatory St Ann Arbor MI 48109-2029 Home: 25 River Birch Ln Dalton MA 01226-2104 Business E-Mail: daschott@umich.edu.

SCHOTTENFELD, RICHARD STEVEN, psychiatrist; b. East Orange, NJ, Apr. 27, 1949; s. Alvin Carl and Pearl Natalie (Feller) S.; m. Tanina Rostain. BA, Yale U., 1971, MD, 1976. Diplomate Am. Bd. Psychiatry and Neurology. Intern Mt. Sinai Hosp., NYC, 1976-77; resident Yale U. Sch. Medicine, New Haven, 1979-82, Robert Wood Johnson clin. VA fellow, 1982-84; asst. prof. psychiatry Yale U., New Haven, 1984-90, assoc. prof. psychiatry, 1990—; dir. alcohol treatment Conn. Mental Health Ctr., New Haven, 1984-87, dir. evaluation unit, 1984-87, assoc. dir. substance abuse treatment unit, 1987-89, co-dir. substance abuse treatment unit, 1989-91, dir. substance abuse treatment unit, 1991—2001; med. dir. APT Found., New Haven, 1987—, acting chief exec. officer, 1989-91, chief exec. officer, 1991—99. Mem. Conn. Psychiat. Soc. (co-chair AIDS subcom. 1988-89). Avocations: cross country skiing, backpacking, bicycle riding. Office: Conn Mental Health Ctr 34 Park St Rm S-103 New Haven CT 06519-1187 Office Phone: 203-974-7349. Business E-Mail: richard.schottenfeld@yale.edu.

SCHOVER, LESLIE RUTH, psychologist; b. Chgo., Sept. 17, 1952; d. Donald Sanford and Janet June (Moss) Schover; m. Menachem Shoham, Oct. 21, 1990 (div. 2000). BA magna cum laude, Brown U., 1974; MA in Psychology, UCLA, 1975, PhD in Psychology, 1979. Lic. psychologist, Tex. Postdoctoral fellow SUNY, Stony Brook, 1979-81; instr., dept. psychiatry Baylor Coll. Medicine, Houston, 1981; asst. prof. urology (psychology), asst. clin. psychologist M.D. Anderson Hosp. and Tumor Inst., Houston, 1981-86; staff psychologist, dept. urology with joint appointments in the Cancer Ctr. and dept. psychiatry and psychology Cleve. Clinic Found., 1986—99; assoc. prof., behavioral sci. U. Tex. M.D. Anderson Cancer Ctr., 1999—2003, prof., behavioral sci., 2004—. Author: Prime Time: Sexual Health for Men Over 50, 1984, Sexuality and Chronic Illness, 1988; contbr. many articles to profl. jours. Active nat. task force for breast cancer control Am. Cancer Soc., Atlanta, 1988-91. Woodrow Wilson grantee, 1979. Mem. APA, Internat. Acad. Sex Rsch., Am. Soc. Reproductive Med., Phi Beta Kappa. Democrat. Jewish. Office: U Tex MD Anderson Cancer Ctr MDA CPB3 3241 Unit 1330 PO Box 301439 Houston TX 77230-1439 Business E-Mail: lschover@mdanderson.org.

SCHOWALTER, JOHN ERWIN, child and adolescent psychiatry educator; b. Milw., Mar. 15, 1936; s. Raymond Phillip and Martha (Kowalke) S.; m. Ellen Virginia Lefferts, June 11, 1960; children: Jay, Bethany. BS, U. Wis., 1957, MD, 1960. Diplomate Am. Bd. Psychiatry and Neurology (com. on cert. in child psychiatry 1983-85, chmn. 1986-87, bd. dirs. 1993-2000, chmn. com. added qualifications forensic psychiatry 1993-97); cert. in adult and child psychiatry also psychoanalysis. Intern in pediat. Yale-New Haven Hosp., 1960-61; asst. resident in psychiatry Cin. Gen. Hosp., 1961-63; fellow in child psychiatry Yale U. Child Study Ctr., New Haven, 1963-65; psychiatrist Mental Hygiene Clinic U.S. Army, Ft. Ord, Calif., 1965-67; asst. prof. Yale U. Child Study Ctr., 1967-70, assoc. prof. Sch. Medicine, 1970-73, dir. tng., 1971-96, prof. pediat. and psychiatry, 1975-09, chief child psychiatry, 1982-90, dir. child psychiatry clin. svcs., 1990—2003, Albert J. Solnit prof. child psychiatry and pediat., 1989—2003, interim chmn., 2001—02, prof. emeritus, sr. rsch. scientist, 2003—, mem. adv. com., 2009—. Mem. publ. com. Yale U. Press., 1992-97; mem. sci. adv. bd. Sophia Found. Med. Rsch., Rotterdam, The Netherlands, 1984-89; dir. mental health and substance abuse Yale Preferred Health Plan, 1995-99. Co-author: The Family Handbook of Adolescence, 1979, contbr. numerous articles, book revs.; mem. editl. bd. Pediatrics, 1976-81, Children's Health Care, 1977-2003, Jour. Am. Psychoanalytic Assn., 1978, Pediatrics in Rev., 1978-85; asst. editor: Jour. Am. Acad. Child and Adolescent Psychiatry, 1988-97; co-editor: Yearbook Psychiatry and Applied Mental Health, 1988-97. Capt. U.S. Army, 1965-67. Fellow Am. Acad. Child and Adolescent Psychiatry (sec. 1985-87, pres. 1989-91, Simon Wile award 1996, mem. fin. planning com. 2000-04, chair governance com. 2001-04, chmn. presdl. scholars com. 2005—, chmn. policy statements com. 2005—, chmn. task force policies and procedures, 2007—09, mem. fin. planning com. 2007-, mem. devel. com. 2009-, chair, Life Fellowship Group 2010-), Am. Coll. Psychiatrists (chair Laughlin fellowship com. 2000-01, chair membership com. 2002-07), Am. Acad. Pediat.; mem. AMA (residency rev. com. psychiatry 1983-87, 89-94), Am. Pediatric Soc., Am. Psychoanalytic Assn. (cert. adult and child), Group Advancement Psychiatry (life fellow, com. on child psychiatry 1981, bd. dir. 1989-91, pres. 1993-95, mem. fin. com. 2008-), Assn. Care Children's Health (pres. 1984-86), Am. Psychiat. Assn. (chmn. McGavin award selection com., 2007—, McGavin award, 2006), Soc. Profs. Child Psychiatry (pres. 1984-86), Western New Eng. Inst. Psychoanalysis (mem. faculty in child psychoanalysis 1984-2011, pres. 1986-88), Conn. Med. Soc., New Haven Med. Soc., Conn. Coun. Child Psychiatrists (pres. 1979-81), Benjamin Rush Soc. (sec., treas. 1998-99, v.p. 1999-2000, pres. 2000-02), Sigma Xi. Lutheran. Home: 256 Ives St Hamden CT 06518-2200 Office: Yale U Child Study Ctr PO Box 207900 230 S Frontage Rd New Haven CT 06520-7900 Office Phone: 203-785-2516.

SCHRADER, WOLFGANG FRIEDRICH, surgeon; b. Berlin-Charlottenburg, Germany, Aug. 17, 1958; s. Bernhard Kurt and Christa Margareta Schrader; m. Betina Sigrid Gruner, June 15, 1985; children: Julian Joachim, Johannes Sebastian, Nikolas Benedikt, Viola Lavinia. MD, U. Tuebingen, 1984. Cons. vitreoretinal dept. U., Dept. Ophthalmology, Freiburg, Germany, 1988—95, head vitreoretinal dept. Wuerzburg, 1995—2008, Nuerenberg, 2008; prof HS U. Iasi, Romania; prof U. Würzburg. Contbr. articles to profl. jours. Achievements include patents for Device for the in vivo determination of an optical property of the aquous humor of the eye. Office: Dept Opthalmology Erlenstegenstr 30 Nurenberg D90491 Germany Office Phone: 499119199450. Office Fax: 499119199459. E-mail: mail@profschrader.de.

SCHRAFF, SCOTT, otolaryngologist; b. NY, Feb. 21, 1964; MD, Eastern Va. Med. Sch., 2000. Fellow pediat. otolaryngology Cin. Children's Hosp. Med. Ctr., 2005—07; pediat. otolaryngologist Ariz. Otolaryngology Cons., 2007—. Adj. asst. prof. otolaryngology Mayo Sch. Medicine. Recipient Resident Rsch. award, Am. Acad. Otolaryngology. Fellow: Am. Acad. Pediat.; mem.: Am. Acad. Otolaryngology,

Soc. Ear, Nose and Throat Advancements Children, Am. Soc. Pediat. Otolaryngology. Avocations: running, bicycling, skiing. Office: 2222 E Highland Ave Ste 204 Phoenix AZ 85016 E-mail: schraffs@hotmail.com.

SCHREIBER, ADAM L., physiatrist, educator; b. NJ, Aug. 10, 1976; MA, Coll. William and Mary, 1999; DO, Kirksville Coll. Osteo. Medicine, 2003. Asst. prof., rehab. medicine Jefferson Med. Coll., 2008—. Fellow: Am. Acad. Phys. Medicine & Rehab.; mem.: Am. Assn. Neuromuscular & Electrodiagnostic Medicine, Assn. Academic Physiatrists, Am. Osteo. Assn., Am. Osteo. Coll. Phys. Medicine and Rehab. Office: 25 S 9th St Philadelphia PA 19107 E-mail: schreiberdo@yahoo.com.

SCHREIBER, MARK TRAUDT, psychiatrist; b. Denver, Oct. 6, 1947; s. Charles William and Sophie Emily Schreiber; m. Constance Anne Rabe, Nov. 27, 1976; children: Vanessa, Laura, Charles, Anne, John. BS, U. Nebr., Lincoln, 1970; MD, Washington U., St. Louis, Mo., 1975. Diplomate Am. Bd. Psychiatry and Neurology, 1980, Am. Bd. Addictionology, 1986. Resident Barnes Hosp. Washington U., St. Louis, 1975—78; psychiatrist Hearst, Fischer & Schreiber, Virginia Beach, Va., 1978—84, Crossroads Clin., Virginia Beach, 1984—89, Atlantic Psychiatric, Virginia Beach, 1989—. Med. dir. Serenity Lodge, Chesapeake, Va., 1984—91; assoc. med. dir. Va. Beach Psychiat. Ctr., 1991—. Contbr. articles to profl. jours. Dist. coun. bd. mem. & v.p. Boys Scout America, 2008; elder Bayside Presbyn. Ch., Va. Beach, 1980—, chmn. com., 2008—; chmn. internat. partnership com. Presbytery Ea. Va., Portsmouth, 1982—. Named Am.'s Top Psychiatrists, Consumers' Rsch. Coun. Am. Fellow: Am. Soc. Addiction Medicine (regional chmn. 2000—04), Am. Psychiat. Assn. (Disting. fellow 2005). Avocations: ballroom dancing, skiing, reading, camping, travel. Office: Atlantic Psychiatric 780 Lipshua Pkwy Ste 450 Virginia Beach VA 23452 Office Phone: 757-468-0550.

SCHREIBER, MICHELLE, insurance company executive; m. Ted Schreiber; 2 children. Grad., Case Western Reserve U. Sch. Med., Ohio. Intern and resident New York Hosp., Cornell Med. Ctr.; staff mem. at several New York City based med. centers; sr. staff physician Henry Ford Health Sys., assoc. program dir. internal medicine residency program, divsn. head gen. internal medicine; assoc. med. dir. Henry Ford Hosp.; sr. v.p., chief quality and safety officer Detroit Med. Ctr. Sys.; sr. v.p., chief med. officer Trinity Health. Faculty Wayne State U. Sch. of Medicine. Mem.: ACP, Michigan Hosp. Assn. (mem. quality and safety com.), Michigan State Med. Soc. Office: Trinity Health 27870 Cabot Dr Novi MI 48377-2920 *

SCHREIER, ANN M., nursing educator; b. Springfield, Mass., May 22, 1950; BSN, Boston U., 1972; PhD, Stanford U., Calif., 1981. Assoc. prof. East Carolina U. Coll. Nursing, 1992—. Pres. Am. Soc. Pain Mgmt. Nursing, 2010—11. Office: Health Scis Bldg East Carolina Greenville NC 27858 Business E-Mail: schreieran@ecu.edu.

SCHREINER, ALBERT WILLIAM, internist, educator; b. Cin., Feb. 15, 1926; s. Albert William and Ruth Mary (Neuer) S.; m. Jean Tellstrom, Dec. 12, 1953; 1 child, David William. BS, U. Cin., 1947, MD, 1949. Diplomate Am. Bd. Internal Medicine, 1958. Clin. investigator VA Hosp., Cin., 1957-59, chief med. svc., 1959-68, dir. dept. internal medicine, 1968-93; dir. resident program internal medicine Christ Hosp., Cin., 1978-87; mem. faculty U. Cin. Coll. Medicine, 1955—, assoc. prof. medicine, 1962-67, prof. internal medicine, 1967-98, emeritus prof. internal medicine, 1998—; attending physician Cin. Gen. Hosp., 1957—95. Cons. to med. dir. Gen. Electric, 1987-96; med. dirs. United Home Care Hospice, 1993-99, United Home Care Agy.; chair, instl. rev. bd. IRB Christ Hosp., 1988-2008, investigator Sterling Rsch. Group, 2003-, rschr., 2008. Contbr. articles to profl. jours. Bd. dirs., chmn. health com. Cmty. Action Commn., 1968-71; trustee Drake Meml. Hosp., 1975-78, Leukemia Found. Southwest Ohio, Cancer Control, Am. Cancer Soc., bd. dirs. Hamilton County unit, 1990; bd. dirs., chair profl. affairs com. United Home Care Agy., 1998; bd. dirs. Gamble Inst. Med. Rsch., Cin., 1991-96; chmn. IRB Hilltop Rsch., 2007-09. Fellow: ACP; mem.: Am. Soc. Clin. Rsch. Program Dirs. Internal Medicine, Assn. Program Dirs. Internal Medicine, Clin. Soc. Internal Medicine (pres. 1979—80), Ohio Soc. Internal Medicine (trustee 1978, sec.-treas. 1981—85, v.p. 1982—83, pres. 1984—85), Ohio Med. Assn., Am. Fedn. Clin. Rsch., N.Y. Acad. Scis., Am. Cancer Soc. (bd. dirs. Hamilton County unit 1990—92), Phi Beta Kappa, Sigma Xi. Roman Catholic. Home: Deupree House II 3939 ERIE Ave Apt 3060 Cincinnati OH 45208-1487 Office: Sterling Rsch Group Ltd 375 Glensprings Dr Springdale OH 45246 Office Fax: 513-671-8090. Business E-Mail: aschreiner@sterling.research.org.

SCHRIEFER, ALBERT, science educator; b. Salvador, Bahia, Brazil, June 4, 1966; s. Nicolaus Dieter and Eliane Maria Borges Schriefer; m. Ana Lúzia Dourado Fernandes, July 6, 2002. MD, U. Fed. Bahia, Brazil, 1990; MS, U. Fed. Bahia, 1995; PhD, U. São Paulo, Brazil, 2001. Fellow Cornell U. Med. Coll., Divsn. Internat. Medicine and Infectious Dieases, NYC, 1992—95; rschr. Hosp. Universitário Prof. Edgard Santos, Serviço de Imunologia, Salvador, Bahia, Brazil, 2001—; prof. parasitology Universidade Fed. da Bahia, Salvador, Bahia, Brazil, 2004—. Coord. parasitology discipline Universidade Fed. da Bahia, Instituto de Ciências da Saúde, Salvador, Bahia, Brazil, 2005—. Contbr. articles various sci. publs. Recipient 1st pl., Nat. Young Physician Nat. award, Unibanco Saúde de Medicina, 1997, Nat. Rsch. award, Roche, 1998; Fogarty Tng. scholarship, NIH, 1992 - 1995, fellow in Med. Rsch., Divsn. Internat. Medicine and Infectious Diseases, Cornell U. Med. Coll., 1992 - 1995. Achievements include development of a live oral vaccine candidate for the prophylaxis of Enteropathogenic E. coli caused childhood diarrhoea; discovery of multiclonal structure among Leishmania braziliensis parasites with implication on form of human disease. Home: Dr Hosannah de Oliveira 115 apto 1304 Salvador 41 815-215 Brazil Office: Hosp Univ Prof Edgard Santos João das Botas s/n 5o andar Salvador 40 110-160 Brazil Office Fax: 5571-32457110; Home Fax: 5571-32457110. Personal E-mail: aschriefer@globo.com. E-mail: aschriefer@hupes.ufba.br.

SCHRIER, ROBERT WILLIAM, physician, educator; b. Indpls., Feb. 19, 1936; s. Arthur E. and Helen M. Schrier; m. Barbara Lindley, June 14, 1959; children: David, Debbie, Douglas, Derek, Denise. BA, Depauw U., Greencastle, Ind., 1957; DSc (hon.), DePauw U., Greencastle, Ind., 2004; MD, Ind. U., 1962; DSc (hon.), U. Colo., 1996, Silesian Acad. Medicine, Katowice, Poland, 1997. Intern Marion County Hosp., Ind., 1962; resident U. Wash., Seattle, 1963-65; asst. prof. U. Calif. Med. Ctr., San Francisco, 1969—72, assoc. dir. renal divsn., 1971-72, assoc. prof., 1972; prof., head renal disease U. Colo. Sch. Med., Denver, 1972-92, prof., chmn. dept. medicine, 1976—2002; prof. renal disease, 2002—. Editor 45 textbooks in internal medicine, geriat., drug usage, and kidney disease; contbr. over 1000 sci. articles to profl. jours. Pres. Western Soc. Clin. Investigation, 1981, Nat. Kidney Found., 1984-86. With US Army, 1966—69. Recipient David Hume award Nat. Kidney Found., 1987, Louis Pasteur medal U. Strasburg, 1987, Mayo Soley award Western Soc. Clin. Investigation, 1989, Robert H. Williams award Assn. Profs. Medicine, 1996, Torchbearer award 1997, Edward N. Gibbs Meml. award NY Acad. Medicine, 2000, Alexander von Humboldt Rsch award 2004, Grand Hamdan Internat. Med. Scis. award 2004. Mem. ACP (master, John Phillips award 1992), Am. Soc. Nephrology (treas. 1979-81, pres. 1983, John Peters award 1997), Internat. Soc. Nephrology (treas. 1981-90, v.p. 1990-95, pres. 1995-97, Jean Hamburger award 2003), Am. Clin. and Climatol. Assn. (v.p. 1986), Assn. Am. Physicians (pres. 1994-95, Francis Blake award 1995), Western Assn. Physicians (pres. 1982), Inst. of Medicine of NAS, Alpha Omega Alpha. Achievements include research contributions centered on the pathogenesis of acute renal failure, genetic renal disorders, mechanisms of cell injury, diabetic nephropathy and renal and hormonal control of body fluid volume; advancement of a unifying hypothesis of sodium and water regulation in health and disease which has stimulated world-wide interest in the medical science community. Business E-Mail: robert.schrier@ucdenver.edu.

SCHRIER, STANLEY LEONARD, hematologist, educator; b. NYC, Jan. 2, 1929; s. Harry and Nettie (Schwartz) S.; m. Peggy Helen Pepper, June 6, 1953; children: Rachel, Leslie, David. AB, U. Colo., 1949; MD, Johns Hopkins U., 1954. Diplomate Am. Bd. Internal Medicine (chmn. subsplty. bd. hematology). Intern Osler Med. Service, Johns Hopkins Hosp., 1954-55; resident U. Mich., Ann Arbor, 1955-56, U. Chgo. Hosp., 1958-59; sr. asst. surgeon USPHS, 1956-58; instr. medicine Stanford Sch. Medicine, Calif., 1959-60, asst. prof. medicine, 1960-63, assoc. prof., 1963-72, prof. medicine, 1972-95, chief divsn. hematology, 1968-94, prof. medicine emeritus, hematology, 1996—. Vis. scientist Weizmann Inst., Rehovot, Israel, 1967-68; vis. prof. Oxford U., Eng., 1975-76, Hebrew U., Jerusalem, 1982-83 John and Mary Markle scholar, 1961; recipient Kaiser award Stanford U., 1972, Kaiser award, 1974, 75, David Rytand award, 1982, Eleanor Roosevelt Union Internationale Contre le Cancer award, 1975-76, Albion Walter Hewlett award, 1996, Walter J. Gores award, 2002. Fellow ACP; mem. Am. Soc. Hematology (pres. 2004), Am. Physiol. Soc., Soc. Exptl. Biology and Medicine, Am. Soc. Clin. Investigation, Western Assn. Physicians, Assn. Am. Physicians. Democrat. Jewish. Office: Stanford U Sch Medicine Rm 1155 MC 5156 269 Campus Dr Palo Alto CA 94305-5156 E-mail: sschrier@stanford.edu.

SCHROEDER, DAVID J. DEAN, retired psychologist; b. Hutchinson, Kans., Mar. 21, 1942; s. D.J.W. and Louise (Wedel) S.; m. Nevonna Joyce Thomas, May 24, 1964; children: Taryn Dee Schroeder Dye, Anita Joy Fitch. BA, Tabor Coll., 1964; MS, Kans. State Tchrs. Coll., 1967; PhD, U. Okla., 1971. Lic. psychologist, Kans. Rsch. psychologist Civil Aerospace Med. Inst., Oklahoma City, 1970-72, clin. rsch. psychologist, 1980-89, supr., 1989-90, mgr. human factors rsch. lab., 1990-91, mgr. aerospace human factors rsch. divsn., 1991—2008; intern Norfolk (Nebr.) Regional Ctr., 1972-73; clin. psychologist VA Hosp., Murfreesboro, Tenn., 1973-75, Topeka, 1975-80. Co-author: FAA Employee Survey: National Report, 1984, 86, FAA Employee Survey: Regional/Center Reports, 1984, 86, FAA Job Satisfaction Survey National Report, 1988, FAA Job Satisfaction Survey: Regional/Center/Work Group Reports, 1988; mem. adv. editl. bd. Aviation Space and Environ. Medicine, 1993-95, 99-2001, 2006-09. Mem. senate adv. com. Tabor Coll., Hillsboro, Kans., 1987-89; Christian edn. com. chmn. So. Dist. Conf. Mennonite Brethren Ch., Hillsboro, 1989; Sunday Sch. tchr. Western Oaks Christian Ch., Oklahoma City, 1990—; co-chair cmty. investment subcom. United Way Ctrl. Okla., 2006-09, Okla. City Friends Libr. Bd., 2008-09, treas., 2009-11; vice chair Com. Investment United Way Ctrl. Okla., 2009-11, chair, 2011-; bd. dirs. United Way Ctrl. Okla., 2011-. Fellow APA, Aerospace Med. Assn. (chmn. sci. program com. 1990-91, mem. coun. 1992-95, v.p. 1996-97, v.p. edn. and rsch. 1999-2002, pres.-elect, 2002-03, pres. 2003-04, program com. chair APA divsn. applied exptl. and engring. psychology 1996-97, sec.-treas. 1998-2001, pres. 2002-03, rep. APA Coun. 2008-10, chmn. aerospace human factors com. 1999-2002, Raymond F. Longacre award for outstanding accomplishmnts in psychol. and psychiat. aspects of aerospace medicine 1997), Aerospace Human Factors Assn. (pres. 1994-95, sec. 2008-, Henry L. Taylor Founders award 2001); mem. Okla. Psychol. Assn. (bd. dirs. 1988-89, pres.-elect 1991, pres. 1992), Internat. Acad. Aviation and Space Medicine, IAASM Sci. Com. 2007-, Nat. Rsch. Coun. Nat. Acads.(mem. Com. Pilot Fatigue 2010-11). Democrat. Achievements include research in assessing the interactive effects of alcohol, age and drugs on dynamic tracking and cognitive performance, personality characteristics and training success of air traffic control students, biofeedback, anxiety and burnout in government employees, human factors of air traffic control operational errors, fatigue and shiftwork. Home: 6109 Walnut Ln Oklahoma City OK 73132 Home Phone: 405-470-1184. Personal E-mail: davids20@cox.net.

SCHROEDER, DONALD J., orthopedic surgeon; b. Omaha, Nebr., Nov. 5, 1938; s. Francis A. and Maire L. (Schlueter) S.; m. Patricia A. Speer, Feb. 11, 1962 (div. June 1980); children: Cynthia, Douglas; m. Carol E. Schaan, Aug. 20, 1983. BS, Creighton U., 1960, MD, 1964. Diplomate Am. Bd. Orthopedic Surgery. Intern Detroit Receiving Hosp., 1964-65; resident in orthopedic surgery Wayne State U., Detroit, 1964-71; resident with affiliate hosp. Shriners Hosp., St. Louis, 1969-70; attending surgeon Sacred Heart Gen. Hosp., Eugene, Oreg., 1971—2001. Pres. Marist Found., Eugene, 1993. Smith Kline fellow, 1964. Fellow Am. Acad. Orthopedic Surgeons; mem. AMA (alt. del. 1993-98, del. 1998—2010), Oreg. Med. Assn. (pres. 1993-94), Lane County Med. Soc. (pres. 1987-88), Western Orthopedic Assn., Am. Bd. Forensic Medicine (vice chair, chair 2000-02), Alpha Omega Alpha. Republican. Roman Catholic. Avocation: ranching. Office: 3203 Willamette St Eugene OR 97405 Home Phone: 541-688-2023. Personal E-mail: dschro1475@aol.com.

SCHROEDER, STEFAN, anesthesiologist, consultant, research scientist; b. Hamburg, Germany, Feb. 22, 1965; MD, U. Hamburg, 1993; PhD, U. Bonn, 2002. Diplomate Pub. Health Auth., Hamburg, 1994. Intern Marienkrankenhaus, Hamburg, 1993—94; resident anesthesiologist U. Kiel, Schleswig-Holstein, Germany, 1994—96, U. Bonn, Nordrhein Westfalen, Germany, 1996—2000, sr. physician, 2000—04; head sr. physician Westkuestenklinikum Heide, Germany, 2004—. Cons. anesthesiologist U. Bonn, 2000—04, lectr. anesthesiology and intensive care medicine, 2002—; cons. anesthesiologist Westkuestenklinikum Heide, 2004—, cons. intensive care medicine, 2004—. Contbr. over 50 sci. articles to med. jours. Diving physician German Red Cross, Bonn, 2000—. Achievements include research in inflammatory response syndrome, oxygen radicals, apoptosis. Office: Westkuestenklinikum Heide Esmarchstr 50 Schleswig-Holstein Heide 25746 Germany Business E-Mail: sschroeder@wkk-hei.de.

SCHROEDER, STEVEN ALFRED, medical educator; b. NYC, July 26, 1939; s. Arthur Edward and Norma (Scheinberg) Schroeder; m. Sally B. Ross, Oct. 21, 1967; children: David Arthur, Alan Ross. BA, Stanford U., 1960; MD, Harvard U., 1964; LHD (hon.), Rush U., 1994; DSc (hon.), Boston U., 1996, U. Mass. Med. Ctr., 1997, Georgetown U., 2000; DSc, Med. Coll. Wis., 2002; DHL (hon.), U. Medicine Dentistry NJ, 2003. Diplomate Am. Bd. Internal Medicine. Intern and resident in internal medicine Harvard Med. Svc., Boston City Hosp., 1964—66, 1968—70; asst. prof., then assoc. prof. George Washington Med. Ctr., Washington, 1971—76; vis. prof. St. Thomas' Hosp. Med. Sch., London, 1982—83; prof. medicine, chief div. gen. internal medicine, mem. Inst. Health Policy Studies U. Calif., San Francisco, 1976—90; pres., CEO Robert Wood Johnson Found., Princeton, NJ, 1990—2002; clin. prof. medicine U. of Medicine and Dentistry N.J., 1990—2002; disting. prof. health and health care U. Calif., San Francisco, 2003—, dir. smoking cessation leadership ctr., 2003—. Conv. various govtl. and philanthropic health orgns.; chair internat. adv. com. faculty medicine Ben Gurion U., Israel. Sr. editor: Current Med. Diagnosis and Treatment, 1987—93, mem. editl. bd.: New Eng. Jour. Medicine Mag.; contbr. numerous articles to profl. jours. Mem. U.S. Prospective Payment Assessment Commn., 1983—88; bd. overseers Harvard Coll., 2000—06; bd. dirs. Am. Legacy Found., 2000—05, vice chair, 2001—03, chair, 2003—05; dir. James Irvine Found., Charles R. Drew U. Medicine and Sci., 2005—. Named a Nat. Pub. Health Hero, U. Calif. Berkeley, 2004. Master: ACP (James Bruce award 2007); fellow: Am. Acad. Arts & Scis.; mem.: AAAS, APHA, Assn. Am. Med. Coll. (David Rogers award 2008), Albany Med. Ctr. (Medicine prize 2000—), Soc. Gen. Internal Medicine (past pres.), Inst. Medicine, Assn. Am. Physicians, Physicians for Social Responsibility, Harvard Med. Alumni Assn. (past pres.), Alpha Omega Alpha, Phi Beta Kappa. Office: U Calif San Francisco 3333 California St Ste 430 San Francisco CA 94143-1211 Home Phone: 415-435-3872; Office Phone: 415-502-1881. Business E-Mail: schroeder@medicine.ucsf.edu.

SCHROEDER, TOBIAS, radiologist; b. Ulm, Germany, Feb. 28, 1968; s. Karl-Eugen and Sigrid Maria (Eppenauer) Schroeder; m. Eva Wembacher; children: Theodor Tobias, Carla Pauline. MD, Rheinische Friedrich-Wilhelms-U., Bonn, Germany, 1992, Ludwig-Maximilians-U., Munich, 1995. Bd. cert. radiologist Govt. Nordrhine-Westfalia, Duesseldorf, Germany. Resident dept. surgery U. Hosp. Zurich, Switzerland, 1996—99; resident dept. diagnostic and interventional radiology and neuroradiology Univ. Hosp. Essen, Germany, 1999—2003, attending physician, mem. staff, 2003—06, assoc. prof. radiology, sr. staff radiologist, 2006—. Home: Dodelle 55 45239 Essen Germany Office: Inst Fur Diagnostische und Interventionelle Radiologle und Neuroradiologie Universitatsklinikum Essen Germany

SCHROEPFER, TRACY A., social sciences educator; b. Little Rock, Ark., June 26, 1954; MSW, U. Mich., 1996, PhD, 2003. Instr., rsch. and stats. cons. U. Ark., Little Rock, 1989—94; assoc. prof. U. Wis., Madison, 2003—. Bd. mem. Wis. Cancer Coun., 2006—; editl. bd. mem. Jour. Social Work End-of-Life and Palliative Care, 2007—; mem., editl. bd. exec. com. Jour. Gerontol. Social Work, 2009—; pres. Assn. Gerontology Edn. Social Work, 2010. Contbr. chapters to books, articles to profl. jours. Treas. Social Work Hospice & Palliative Care Orgn., 2007—. Recipient Faculty Achievement award, Assn. Gerontology Edn. Social Work, Chancellor's Disting. Tchg. award, U. Wis., Faculty Excellence award; fellowship, John A. Hartford Found. Mem.: Internat. Soc. Advance Care Planning & End Life Care, Gerontol. Soc. America, Am. Acad. Hospice and Palliative Medicine. Avocations: reading, bicycling. Office: 1350 University Ave Madison WI 53706 Office Fax: 608-263-3836. Business E-Mail: tschroepfer@wisc.edu.

SCHROTH, JOYCE ABLE, social worker; b. Bloomington, Ill., Apr. 4, 1948; d. Raymond Daniel Able and Lois Martha Vielhak; m. Thomas H. Schroth, July 22, 1972; children: Bradley, Michael. BA, Ill. Wesleyan U., 1971. Dir. City of Westlake, Ohio, 1998—. Mem. cmty. adv. bd. Lakewood Hosp., Ohio, 1998—, St. John West Shore Hosp., Westlake, 1998—, mem. mission & values com., 1998—; pres. adv. coun. Retired Sr. Vol. Program, Brookpark, 1999—; mem. adv. bd. Westlake Healthcare Ctr., 2002—04; pres. Cuyahoga County Mcpl. Offices on Aging Assn.; mem. cmty. adv. bd. Fairview Hosp., 2003—; mem. Cuyahoga County Adv. Coun. Dept. Sr. and Adult Cmty. Svc. Chmn. citizen's adv. com. Westlake City Schs., 1985—88, chair levy com., 1988; mem. Westlake Bd. Edn., 1987—90, Cuyahoga County Adv. Coun. on Sr. and Adult Svcs., 2003; bd. dirs. Univ. Settlement, 2005—08. Recipient Cmty. Leadership award, St. John West Shore Hosp., 2002, Cleve. State U., 2005, Luth.'s Maldonado award, 2005. Mem.: Westlake Lions Club, Sigma Kappa. Republican. Mem. Lds Ch. Avocations: travel, reading, genealogy. Office: City Westlake 29694 Ctr Ridge Rd Westlake OH 44145-5114 Office Phone: 440-899-3544. Business E-Mail: jschroth@cityofwestlake.org.

SCHROYER, MICHAEL KEVIN, healthcare consultant, hospital executive; b. Kewanee, Ill., Sept. 14, 1959; s. Jesse Wayne and Shirley Ann (Brown) S.; m. Joy Anne, June 20, 1987; children: Tiffany Marie, Rebecca Ann, Adam Michael. Diploma, Moline Pub. Hosp. Sch. Nursing, 1980; BSN, Loyola U., 1984; MBA, Auburn U., 2006. Cert. healthcare exec. (CHE). Nurse mgr., CCU, ICU, PICU, CCFP Jersey Shore Med. Ctr., Neptune, NJ; assoc. dir., critical care nursing Hyde Park Hosp., Chgo.; adminstrv. dir., transplant svcs. Rush-Presbyn./St. Lukes Med. Ctr., Chgo.; adminstrv. coord., v.p. cardiovasc. and med. svcs. United Med. Ctr., Moline, Ill.; adminstrv. leader, v.p. Regional CardioLife Ctr., Tenet Brookwood Med. Ctr., Birmingham, Ala., 1993-96; v.p. clin. svcs. MedCath McAllen (Tex.) Heart Hosp., 1996-98, MedCath Dayton (Ohio) Heart Hosp., 1998-2000, interim CEO, 2000, v.p. ops./COO, 2000—01; pres. / CEO Okla. Heart Hosp., Oklahoma City, 2001—03; prin., cons. TRG Cardiovascular, Denver, 2001—07; exec. dir. cardiac and vascular svcs. Meml. Heart & Vascular Inst., Meml. Health Sys., Springfield, Ill., 2004—07; COO St. Vincent Heart Ctr. of Ind., Indpls., 2007—; v.p. Ind. Ops., Care Group Cardiovasc., Navion Healthcare Solutions, 2008—. Author: Emergency Nursing, 1989, Nursing Spectrum, 1989, Comprehensive Nursing Care Plans, 1995. Former bd. dirs. Rock Island County chpt. Am. Heart Assn. Fellow: Am. Col. Healthcare Executives, Am. Coll. Healthcare Execs. (cert. healthcare exec.); mem.: Am. Heart Assn. (bd. dirs. Oklahoma City chpt., bd. dirs. Springfield chpt., Greater Indpls. chpt.), Am. Coll. Cardiology (assoc.; cardiac care assoc. liason Ind., cochair, Advocacy Task Group, mem., Nat. Advocacy Steering Com., mem., Nat. Ptnrs. in Quality Com.), Sigma Theta Tau. Home: 9065 Pebblepointe Cir Zionsville IN 46077 Office: St Vincent Heart Ctr of Ind 10580 N Meridian St Indianapolis IN 46290 Personal E-mail: mschroyerl@indy.rr.com.

SCHTEINGART, DAVID EDUARDO, internist; b. Buenos Aires, Oct. 17, 1930; came to U.S., 1957; s. Mario and Flora (Garfunkel) S.; m. Monica Naomi Starkman, July 3, 1960; children: Miriam, Judith, M. Daniel. MD, U. Buenos Aires, 1955. Diplomate Am. Bd. Internal Medicine. Fellow Mt. Sinai Hosp., NYC, 1957-58, Maimonides Hosp., Bklyn., 1958-59, U. Mich., Ann Arbor, 1959-62, instr., 1962-63, asst. prof., 1963-68, assoc. prof., 1968-72, prof., 1972—. Contbr. articles to profl. jours., books. Pres. Beth Israel Congregation, Ann Arbor, 1974-79, Hebrew Day Sch., Ann Arbor, 1984-86, Jewish Fedn. Washtenaw County, Ann Arbor. Recipient rsch. grants NIH, Bethesda, Md., 1985—. Fellow Am. Coll. Physicians; mem. Endocrine Soc., N.Y. Acad. Scis., Am. Soc. Clin. Nutrition, Cen. Soc. Clin. Rsch., Am. Fedn. Clin. Rsch. Jewish. Avocations: tennis, running, community activities. Office: U Mich Med Sch 1150 W Medical Center Dr Ann Arbor MI 48109-0726

SCHUBEL, JERRY ROBERT, marine scientist educator, dean; b. Bad Axe, Mich., Jan. 26, 1936; s. Theodore Howard and Laura Alberta (Gobel) S.; m. Margaret Ann Hostetler, June 14, 1958; children: Susan Elizabeth, Kathryn Ann. BS, Alma Coll., 1957; MA in Tchg., Harvard U., 1959; PhD, Johns Hopkins U., 1968; DSc (hon.), Mass. Maritime Acad., 1997. Rsch. assoc. Chesapeake Bay Inst., Johns Hopkins U., Balt., 1968-69, rsch. scientist, 1969-74, adj. rsch. prof., assoc. dir., 1973-74; dir. Marine Sci. Rsch. Ctr. SUNY, Stony Brook, 1974-83, dean, leading prof., 1983-94, acting dir. Waste Mgmt. Inst., 1985-87, provost, 1986-89, dir. COAST Inst., 1989, disting. svc. prof., 1994-95, prof. emeritus, 1995—; pres. emeritus, CEO New Eng. Aquarium, Boston, 1994—2001; vis. prof. Wash. Coll., Chestertown, Md., 2002—03, dir. Alternative Futures Forum, 2002—03; pres., CEO Aquarium of Pacific, Long Beach, Calif., 2002—. Hon. prof. East China Normal U., Shanghai, 1985—; sec. exec. com. Commn. on Food, Environ. and Renewable Resources, 1993, chair steering com., 1994; mem. governing bd. Regional Marine Rsch. Program, Greater N.Y. Bight, 1993-94; v.p., founding dir. Gulf of Maine Ocean Observing Sys., 1998-02; adv. panel Nat. Whale Conservation Fund Found., 2001-05; mem. NOAA Sci. Adv. Bd., 2008-, Nat. Sea Grant Adv. Panel, 2002-07, chair, 2004-05; bd. dirs. Internat. Resources Group, 2002—09, rev. panel Census of Marine Life, U.S. Nat. Com., 2003-07, mem. NSF Edn. and Human Resources Adv. Com., 2003-05, South Bay Salt Pond Restoration, Nat. Sci. Panel, 2003-06; nat. assoc. Nat. Acads. Sci. and Engring.; mem. marine bd. NRC, 1989-94, 2002—08; bd. dirs. Inst. for Learning Innovation, 2004—; mem. adv. panel Ocean Rsch. and Resources, 2006—09, vice chair, 2007—, chmn., 2007-09; mem. Calif. Ocean Protection Coun., Sci. Adv. Team, 2009-, NOAA Sci. Adv. Bd., 2009-. Author: The Living Chesapeake, 1981, The Life and Death of the Chesapeake Bay, 1 986; (with H.A. Neal) Solid Waste Management and the Environment, 1987, Garbage and Trash: Can We Convert Mountains Into Molehills?, 1992; editor: (with B.C. Marcy Jr.) Power Plant Entrainment, 1978; (with others) The Great South Bay, 1991; sr. editor Coastal Ocean Pollution Assement News, 1981-86; co-editor in chief Estuaries, 1986-88; mem. editl. bd. CRC Revs. in Aquatic Scis.; contbr. articles to profl. jours. Mem. adv. bd. Environ. Sci. Com. Outer Continental Shelf, Minerals Mgmt. Scs., 1984-86, chmn., 1986; bd. dirs. N.E. Area Remote Sensing Sys., 1983-85, L.I. Incubator Corp.; v.p. L.I. Forum for Tech., 1989-92; chair Mass. Outfall Monitoring Task Force, 1995-98; mem. sci. adv. bd. EPA, 1996-98; commr. Nat. Rsch. Coun.'s Commn. on Engring. Tech. Sys., 1996-200; mem. vis. com. dept. ocean engring MIT, 1995-2002; trustee Natural Heritage Insts., 1995-2001; mem. Boston Artery Bus. Bd. Dirs., 1994-2001; mem. Boston Mcpl. Rsch. Bur. Bd. Dirs., 1994-2001; mem. Annenberg Challenge Adv. Com., 1995-2002; hon. trustee Sci. Mus. L.I., 2000-02. Recipient L.I. Sound Am. Environ. Edn. award, 1987, Stony Brook U. medal, 1989, Matthew Fontaine Maury award, 1990, Ocean Champion award Monmouth U. Uchan Coast Instn., 2007, Ben Gurion U. medal, 1993, sci. achievement award Sci. Mus. L.I., 2000; Alfred P. Sloan fellow, 1959; Wheaton Coll. Disting. fellow, 2000. Mem. NAS (com. on Coastal Ocean 1989-93), Nat. Assn. State Univ. and Land Grant Colls. (bd. dirs. marine divsn., chmn. 1986-88), L.I. Environ. Coun., L.I. Marine Resources Adv. Coun. (chair 1990-94), L.I. Rsch. Inst. (bd. dirs. 1992-94), L.I. Environ.-Econ. Roundtable (co-chair 1991-92), Suffolk County Recycling Commn., (chmn. 1987-88), Estuarine Rsch. Fedn. (v.p. 1982-83, pres. 1985-87), N.Y. Sea Grant Inst. (chmn. governing bd. 1988-90, mem. gov.'s task force on coastal resources 1990-91), Census Marine Life (mem. U.S. nat. com. 2003—08), The Nature Conservancy (trustee L.I. chpt. 1991-94), Franklin Electronic Pubs. (bd. dirs. 1991—), Taproot (bd. dirs. 1988-93, vice chair 1990-93), Internat. Resources Group (bd. dirs., 2002—08), Sigma Xi, Phi Sigma Pi. Avocation: photography. Office: Aquarium of the Pacific 100 Aquarium Way Long Beach CA 90802 Home Phone: 564-437-5722; Office Phone: 562-951-1608. Business E-Mail: jschubel@lbaop.org.

SCHUBERT, GUENTHER ERICH, pathologist; b. Mosul, Iraq, Aug. 17, 1930; s. Erich Waldemar and Martha Camilla (Zschitzschmann) Schubert; children: Frank, Marion, Dirk. MD, U. Heidelberg, Germany, 1957; pvt. docent in pathology, U. Tuebingen, Germany, 1966. Asst. med. dir. U. Tuebingen, Germany, 1966—76; prof. pathology, 1972; head Inst. Pathology, Wuppertal, Germany, 1976—96; chair of pathology U. Witten-Herdecke, Germany, 1985—96. Co-author: Coloratlas of Cytodiagnosis of the Prostate, 1975, Pathologie, 1984, 1997, Endoscopy of the Urinary Bladder, 1979, Textbook of Pathology, 1981, 1987. Mem. Wissenschaftlicher Beirat, Bundesarztekammer, Bonn, Germany, 1976—85; pres. Medizinisch Naturwissenschaftliche Gesellschaft, Wuppertal, 1984—85, Onkologischer Schwerpunkt, Wuppertal, 1985—93, OSP Bergisch-Land, 1992—95, Bergische Arbeitsgemeinschaft fur Gastroenterologie, Wuppertal, 1987—88, 1990—91, 1994—95. Mem.: NY Acad. Scis., Internat. Acad. Pathology, Deutsche Gesellschaft fur Urologie, Deutsche Gesellschaft fur Nephrologie, Deutsche Gesellschaft fur Pathologie, Lions. Avocations: music, diving, photography. Office: Inst Pathology Am Anschlag 71 42113 Wuppertal Germany

SCHUBERT, HERMANN D., ophthalmologist, educator; MD, Heinrich Heine U., Duesseldorf, Germany. Intern, Duesseldorf, NY; resident pathology Columbia Presbyn. Hosp., NY, resident ophthalmology; rsch. fellow Columbia Univ.; hon. fellow Spaeth Internat.; fellow Am. Acad. of Ophthalmology, NY Acad. of Medicine; prof. clin. ophthalmology and pathology Columbia Univ.; fellowship Wills Eye Hosp., Phila.; dir. retina clinic Presbyn. Hosp., NY, dir. ophthalmic pathology. Recipient Honor award, Am. Acad. Ophthalmology Tchg. awards, Wills Eye Hosp. and Columbia Univ. Mem.: Club Jules Gonin, Am. Ophthal. Soc. (AOS), NY Ophthal. Soc., Assn. for Rsch. in Vision (ARVO), Am. Retina Soc., German Ophthal. Soc. Office: NewYork-Presbyterian Columbia University Medical Center 622 West 168th St New York NY 10032 Office Phone: 212-305-2500.

SCHUBERT, MARK S., allergist, immunologist, educator; MD, U. Ariz., 1983. Diplomate Am. Bd. Internal Medicine, 1987, Am. Bd. Allergy and Immunology, 2009, Nat. Bd. of Med. Examiners, lic. Ariz., 1984, Calif., 1987. Resident neurological surgery Barrow Neurological Inst., 1984—85; resident internal medicine Good Samaritan Med. Ctr., 1985—87; fellow allergy immunology & rheumatology Stanford Univ. Med. Ctr., 1987—89; assoc. clin. prof. medicine Univ. of Ariz. Coll. of Medicine; hosp. affiliations include Banner Desert Med. Ctr., Banner Good Samaritan Med. Ctr., Banner Thunderbird Med. Ctr., John C. Lincoln North Mountain Hosp., St. Joseph's Hosp. and Med. Ctr. Author: (publs.) Allergic fungal sinusitis, 2007, Allergic fungal sinusitis: Pathophysiology, diagnosis and management, 2009, Expert Commentary in: Salazar KC, Nelson MR, Stone KD. A 42-year-old woman with chronic rhinosinusitis and allergic mucin, 2009, Distinctions between allergic fungal rhinosinusitis and chronic rhinosinusitis, 2010. Named one of Top Doctors, Phoenix Mag., 2002, 2004—11, Best Doctors in America, 2003, 2007, 2010—11. Fellow: ACP, Am. Coll. of Chest Physicians, Am. Acad. of Allergy, Asthma, and Immunology, Am. Coll. of Allergy, Asthma & Immunology; mem.: Am. Coll. of Rheumatology, Western Soc. of Allergy, Asthma and Immunology, Phoenix Rheumatology Assn., Maricopa County Med. Soc., Ariz. Infectious Diseases Soc., AMA, Am. Acad. for the Advancement of Sci., Arizona Allergy and Asthma Soc. (former pres.), Greater Phoenix Allergy and Asthma Soc. (former pres.). Office: Banner Good Samaritan Medical Center 1111 E McDowell Rd Phoenix AZ 85006-2666 Office Phone: 602-239-2000.

SCHUBERT, THOMAS, orthopedist, consultant; b. Neugersdorf, Germany, Mar. 9, 1952; s. Christian and Ingeborg Schubert; m. Christina Gnauck, Nov. 7, 1982; children: Friedrich, Agnes, Josephine, David, Sara; m. Ulrike Tietze, May 10, 1978 (div. Aug. 7, 1980). Degree in Medicine, Med. Acad., Dresden, 1978, DSc, 1982. Lic. physician Med. Acad., 1988. Registrar Dept. Orthopaedics Med. Acad., Dresden, Germany, 1978—82, cons. Dept. Orthopaedics, 1982—88, sr. cons. Dept. Orthopaedics, 1988—92; specialist cons. orthopaedics Pvt. Orthopaedic Clinic, Dresden, 1992—. Contbr. articles to profl. jours. Lt. inf. German Army, 1968—70. Recipient Ganse award, 1977, Virchow award, 1980. Mem.: Am. Assn. Orthopaedic Surgeons, Assn. Osteologists, Assn. Orthopaedic Sugeons, Assn. Acupuncture, Assn. Foot Surgeons, Assn. Foot Surgery. Achievements include development of bioceramics as bone substitutes. Office: Orthopaedische Gemeinschaftspraxis Tharandter Strasse 43 Saxony Dresden D-01159 Germany Personal E-mail: t.schubert@praxisklinik-ortho.de. Business E-Mail: thomas_schubert@jsk-medianet.de.

SCHUCHAT, ANNE, federal agency administrator; BA in Philosophy, with minor in Biology, Swarthmore Coll., 1980, DS (hon.); MD, Dartmouth U., 1984. Resident in internal medicine Manhattan VA Hosp.; epidemic intelligence svc. officer Centers for Disease Control, Atlanta, 1988, chief respiratory diseases br., acting dir. Nat. Ctr. Infectious Diseases, dir. Nat. Immunization Program, 2005—06, dir. Nat. Ctr. Immunization and Respiratory Diseases, 2006—, interim dep. dir. Sci. and Pub. Health Prog., 2009; clin. asst. prof. medicine Emory U.; rear adm., asst. surgeon gen. USPHS, 2006—. Contbr. chapters to books, articles to profl. jours. Recipient Maternal and Child Health Young Investigator award, Am. Pub. Health Assn., Meritorious Svc. medal, USPHS; named Physician Rsch. Officer of Yr. Mem.: Inst. Medicine. Office: Nat Immunization Program CDC Mailstop C23 1600 Clifton Rd Atlanta GA 30333 E-mail: aschuchat@cdc.gov. *

SCHUCHTER, LYNN M., oncologist, educator; MD, U. Chgo. Diplomate Am. Bd. Internal Medicine, 1986, Am. Bd. Internal Medicine-hematology/oncology, 1989. Intern Michael Reese Hosp., 1982, resident internal medicine, 1983—85; fellow med. oncology Johns Hopkins Hosp., 1987—89; prof. medicine Univ. Pa.; chief hematology oncology, dept. medicine Hosp. of Univ. Pa.-UPHS. Named one of Best Doctors in America, 2003—04, 2005—06, 2007—08, 2009—10, Top Docs, Phila. Mag., 2004—11, America's Top Doctors, 2007, 2008, 2010. Office: Hospital of the University of Pennsylvania - UPHS W Pavilion, 4th Fl 3400 Civic Ctr Blvd Philadelphia PA 19104 Office Phone: 800-789-7366.

SCHÜCK, OTTO, nephrologist, researcher; b. Prague, Czech Republic, Aug. 26, 1926; s. Pavel and Marie (Sedlačková) S.; m. Ladislava Čizková, Aug. 16, 1950. MD, Charles U., Prague, 1950, PhD, 1956, DSc, 1966. Rsch. fellow First Med. Clinic, Prague, 1950-61; asst. dir. Inst. for Exptl. Therapy, Prague, 1962-65; rsch. fellow Med. Clinic, Manchester, Eng., 1966-67; dir. Clinic of Nephrology, Prague, 1967-85; rschr. Inst. Clin. Exptl. Medicine, Prague, 1985—2007; cons. internal clinic, second med. faculty Charles U., Prague, 2008—. Head dept. nephrology Postgrad. Med. Sch. Prague, 1976-92; cons. Nat. Med. Care, Prague, 1994-97. Author: Examination of Kidney Function, 1984 (medal Czech Soc. Internal Medicine 1985), Clinical Nephrology, 1995 (Cilag Found. award 1996); contbr. articles to profl. jours. Recipient Bruno Watschinger award Danube Symposia for Nephrology, 1987, Purkynje award Czech Soc. Medicine, 1996. Mem. Czech Soc. Nephrology (hon. pres. 1996, medals 1962, 72), NY Acad. Scis., Soc. for Nephrologie. Avocations: music, swimming. Home: Kratochvilova 4 162 00 Prague Czech Republic Office: Dept Internal Medicine 2nd Faculty Medicine V Úvalu 84 Prague 150 06 Czech Republic Business E-Mail: otto.schuck@lfmotol.cuni.cz.

SCHUENING, FRIEDRICH, medical educator; b. Trier, Germany, Nov. 20, 1942; MD, U. Hamburg, Germany, 1975. Prof. Vanderbilt U., 1999—2011; rof. St. Louis U., 2011—. Mem.: CIBMTR, ASCO, ASH. Office: 3655 Vista Ave West Pavilion Cancer Ctr Saint Louis MO 63110 Office Fax: 314-773-1167. Business E-Mail: fschueni@slu.edu.

SCHUGER, CLAUDIO D., cardiac electrophysiologist, educator; MD, Univesidad De Buenos Aires, 1977. Diplomate Am. Bd. Internal Medicine, Am. Bd. Internal Medicine-cardiovasc. disease, 2007, Am. Bd. Internal Medicine-clin. cardiac electrophysiology, 2008. Resident internal medicine Hacarmel Hosp., Israel, 1980—82; fellow cardiovasc. disease Bikur Cholim Hosp., 1983—85; fellow cardiac electrophysiology Harper Hosp., 1987—90; prof. medicine Wayne State Univ. Co-author: (publs.) Misdiagnosis of atrial fibrillation and its clinical consequences., 2004, Focal atrial tachycardia originating from the right hepatic vein., 2009, Percutaneous intravascular defibrillator: preliminary data and many questions., 2011, numerous publs. Office: Henry Ford Hospital Main Campus 2799 W Grand Blvd Detroit MI 48202 Office Phone: 313-916-2417.

SCHUKER, ELEANOR SHEILA, psychiatrist, educator; b. NYC, Jan. 3, 1941; d. Louis Aaron and Millicent (Milchman) S.; m. Alan Melowsky, Dec. 26, 1974; 1 child, Julie. BA, Swarthmore Coll., 1961; MD, Columbia U., 1965; cert. in psychoanalytic medicine, Columbia U. Ctr. for Psychoanalytic Training and Rsch., 1975. Diplomate Am. Bd. Psychiatry and Neurology. Intern Mt. Sinai Hosp., NYC, 1965-66; resident in psychiatry NY State Psychiat. Inst., Columbia U., NYC, 1966-69; attending psychiatrist Columbia U. Health Svc., NYC, 1969-90; co-dir. psychiat. emergency svcs. St. Luke's Hosp., NYC, 1970-72, founder, dir. rape intervention program, 1977-80, assoc. attending psychiatrist, 1978-99; collaborating psychoanalyst Columbia U. Psychoanalytic Ctr., NYC, 1975-85, training and supervising analyst, 1985—, mem. exec. com., 1996—99, sr. assoc. dir., 2007—; asst. clin. prof. psychiatry Columbia U., 1980—90, assoc. clin. prof. psychiatry, 1990—. Cons. Women's Counseling Project, N.Y.C., 1974-89. Editor: (with Nadine Levinson) Female Psychology: An Annotated Psychoanalytic Bibliography, 1991; contbr. articles to profl. jours. Recipient Founders award, Crime Victims Treatment Ctr., 2002. Fellow Am. Psychiat. Assn.; mem. Am. Psychoanalytic Assn. (cert., alt. del. to exec. coun. 1986-93), Assn. for Psychoanalytic Medicine (pres. 1995-97, George E. Daniels Merit award 1999), Alumni Assn. Columbia Psychoanalytic Ctr. (pres. 1978-80). Office: 150 W End Ave Apt 26A New York NY 10023-5743 Office Phone: 212-799-4922.

SCHULER, CHRISTINE R., medical researcher; b. Pitts., June 30, 1959; PhD, U. NC, Chapel Hill, 1999; MA, Temple U., 1992. Rsch. epidemiologist Nat. Inst. Occupl. Safety and Health, 1999—. Office: Nat Inst Occupational Safety and Health 1095 Willowdale Rd Morgantown WV 26505 Office Fax: 304-285-5820. Business E-Mail: cschuler@cdc.gov.

SCHULERI, ERWIN WILHELM, physician, consultant; b. Deva, Romania, Feb. 4, 1933; arrived in Germany, 1979; s. Wilhelm Friedrich Schuleri and Ida (Breckner) Baltres; m. Liane Gilda Schuster, June 10, 1959; children: Ingo, Jessie. Diploma dr. med., Med.-Pharm. Inst., Cluj, Romania, 1958; Diploma in Philosophy, Babes-Bolyay U., Cluj, 1974. Paediatrician Govt. Med. Sta., Baita, Deva, Romania, 1958-63; asst. physician pathology County Hosp., Deva, 1963-67, med. specialist, head dept., 1967-79; asst. physician pathology Town Hosp., Pforzheim, Germany, 1979-81, head physician, 1981-83, Schweinfurt, Germany, 1983-87, head dept. pathology, 1987-98. Contbr. articles to profl. jours. Capt. Romanian Res. Army, 1975-. Mem. NY Acad. Scis. Avocations: fishing, travel, literature on history, philosophy and art. Home: Altstadtstr. 26 97422 Schweinfurt Germany Personal E-mail: erwin.schuleri@gmx.de.

SCHULLER, DIANE ETHEL, allergist, immunologist, educator; b. Bklyn., Nov. 27, 1943; d. Charles William and Dorothy Schuller. AB cum laude with honors in Biology, Bryn Mawr Coll., 1965; MD, SUNY, Bklyn., 1970. Diplomate Am. Bd. Allergy & Immunology, Am. Bd. Pediatrics, Nat. Bd. Med. Examiners. Intern, resident in pediats. Roosevelt Hosp., Bklyn., 1970-72; resident in allergy Cooke Inst. Allergy, 1972-74; assoc. in pediatrics Geisinger Med. Ctr., Danville, Pa., 1974-78, dir, dept. pediat. allergy, immunology & pediat. diseases, 1978-95; asst. clin. prof. pediats. Hershey Med. Coll. Pa. State U., 1974-79, assoc. clin. prof., 1979-88; clin. prof. Jefferson Med. Coll., Phila., 1989-95; dir. pediat. allergy, immunology, pulmonology Pa. State U./Hershey Med. Coll., 1995—2007, emeritus dir., 2007—, prof. pediats., 1995—. Bd. dirs. Ctrl. Pa. Lung and Health Assn.; bd. dirs., exec. com. Am. Lung Assn. Pa., sec., 1992—; chmn. Susquehanna Vly. Lung Assn., 1983—; scholarship com. Bryn Mawr Club, N.Y., 1970-75; Columbia-Montour Home Health Svcs. Adv. Group Profl. Personnel, 1975-95. Editl. bd. Annals of Allergy,

Asthma and Immunology. Recipient physician's recognition award AMA, 1973-76, 74-76, 75-78, 79-82, 83-86, 87-90, 91-94, 95-98, 1999-2005. Fellow Am. Acad. Pediats. (exec. com. 1998-2004), Am. Coll. Allergy Asthma and Immunology (2d v.p. 1988, bd. regents 1989-92, exec. com. 1990-93, v.p. 1992-93, pres.-elect 1993-94, pres. 1994-95), Am. Acad. Allergy and Immunology, Am. Assn. Clin. Immunology and Allergy (regional dir., exec. com.), Joint Coun. Allergy and Immunology (bd. dirs. 1986-95, treas. joint coun. 1991-93); mem. Am. Assn. Cert. Allergists (v.p. 2002, pres.-elect 2002-03, pres. 2003-04), Pa. Allergy and Asthma Assn. (bd. dirs. 2007-, sec.-treas. 2010-11, pres.-elect 2011-), NY State Allergy Soc., NY State Med. Soc., NY County Med. Soc., Network Mothers Asthmatics (chmn., bd. dir. 2007-), Allergy & Asthma Network Mothers Asthmatics (chair 2007-09), Joint Task Force on Practice Parameters. Office: Milton S Hershey Med Coll Pa State U Hershey PA 17033 Office Phone: 717-531-1846. Business E-Mail: dschuller@psu.edu.

SCHULMAN, AMY WEINFELD, pharmaceutical company executive, lawyer; b. NYC, Oct. 16, 1960; d. Alvin Harold and Ann Schulman; m. David Eli Nachman; children: Ezra, Gideon, Rafael. BA, Wesleyan U., 1982; JD, Yale U., 1989. Bar: NY 1990, US Dist. Ct. (so. & ea. dist. NY), US Supreme Ct. Law clk. to Hon. Harold Ackerman US Dist. Ct. (Dist. NJ), Newark, 1989; assoc. Cleary Gottlieb, NYC, 1990—97; of counsel Piper & Marbury, NYC, 1997; ptnr. Piper Rudnick, NYC, 1998—2004; ptnr. litigation practice, mem. exec. com., policy com. DLA Piper Rudnick Gray Cary, NYC, 2005—08; sr. v.p., gen. counsel Pfizer, Inc., NYC, 2008—10, exec. v.p., gen. counsel, bus. lead nutrition, 2010—. Mem. steering com. DI-Drug and Med. Device, 1999—; mem. commn. on jury N.Y. State, 1999—; mem. exec. com. Yale Univ. & Yale Law Sch., 1999—; bd. dirs. N.Y. Lawyers Pub. Interest, NYC; nat. coord. counsel, trial counsel. Contbr. articles to profl. jours. Bd. dir. Bklyn. (N.Y.) Acad. Music, 2002—. Recipient Arthur Liman Public Interest award, Legal Action Ctr., 2010; named a Top Comml. Litigator, The American Lawyer mag., 2006; named one of The 500 Leading Lawyers in America, Lawdragon, 2006, 2007, The 21 Rising Female Litigators, Minority Corporate Counsel Assn., 2007, The 100 Most Powerful Women, Forbes mag., 2009, The 20 Most Influential General Counsels, The Nat. Law Jour., 2009; named to The 45 Under 45, The American Lawyer mag, 2003. Mem.: ABA (vice chmn. Products Liability com.), Internat. Assn. Def. Counsel, Def. Rsch. Inst. (vice chmn. Alternative Dispute Resolution sect.), Fed. Bar Council. Achievements include design of and implements alternative resolution programs for Fortune 500 companies and has handled nearly 750 mediations. Office: Pfizer Inc 235 E 42nd St New York NY 10017 Office Phone: 212-835-6108. Office Fax: 212-835-6001. *

SCHULMAN, HAROLD, obstetrician, gynecologist; b. Newark, Oct. 26, 1930; m. Rosemarie Vincenti; children: Stanley H., Sandra C., Gina M. BS, U. Fla., 1951; MD, Emory U., 1955. Diplomate Am. Bd. Ob-Gyn., Am. Bd. Maternal and Fetal Medicine; registered diagnostic med. sonographer. Intern Jackson Meml. Hosp., Miami, Fla., 1955-56, resident, 1958-61; instr. dept. ob-gyn. U. Miami (Fla.) Sch. Medicine, 1961; instr., asst. prof. dept. ob-gyn. Temple U. Sch. Medicine, Phila., 1961-65; asst. prof. dept. ob-gyn. Albert Einstein Coll. Medicine, Bronx, 1965-67, assoc. prof., 1968-71, prof., 1971—, acting dept. chmn., 1972—80, chmn., 1973-80; assoc. dir. dept. ob-gyn Bronx Mcpl. Hosp. Ctr., 1967-70, dep. dir., 1970-72; chmn. dept. ob-gyn. Winthrop U. Hosp., Mineola, NY, 1984-93; prof. ob-gyn SUNY, Stony Brook, 1984-93; chmn. dept. ob-gyn. Lawnwood Regional Med. Ctr., Ft. Pierce, Fla., 1995-2000; cons. ob-gyn. Wyckoff Hosp. Med. Ctr., Bklyn., 2002—. Author: Techniques of Abortion, 1972, Tipping the Scales, 2005, Women's Secrets, Mens Muscles Unveiled, 2009; contbr. articles to profl. publs. Served to capt. U.S. Army, 1956-58. Am. Cancer Soc. fellow, 1959-60; USPHS trainee, 1965-66 Fellow ACOG (vice chmn. Dist. II 1972-75); mem. Bronx County Obstet. Soc. (pres. 1974), AAAS, Obstet. Soc. (sec. 1978-80, pres. 1982-83), N.Y. Obstetrical Soc., Soc. Maternal Fetal Medicine, Am. Gynecologic and Obstetric Soc., Am. Gynecol. Obstetrics, N.Y. Obstetics Soc. (pres. 1982), Phi Beta Kappa, Alpha Omega Alpha; hon. mem. Miami Ob-Gyn. Soc., South Atlantic Obstetricians and Gynecologists Soc., Buffalo Gynecologic and Obstetric Soc. (E.G. Winkler meml. lectr.), Croatian Ultrasound Soc. (hon.). Democrat. Jewish. Office Phone: 914-747-4168. Personal E-mail: hschulman29@optonline.net.

SCHULMAN, JOSEPH DANIEL, physician, health facility administrator, medical geneticist, educator; b. Bklyn., Dec. 20, 1941; s. Max and Miriam (Grossman) S.; m. Dixie A. King; children: Erica N., Julie K. BA, Bklyn. Coll., 1961; MD, Harvard U., 1966. Diplomate Am. Bd. Pediat., Am. Bd. Ob-Gyn., Am. Bd. Med. Genetics. Intern, then resident in pediat. Mass. Gen. Hosp., Boston, 1966-68; clin. assoc. Nat. Inst. Arthritis and Metabolic Diseases, 1968-70; resident in obstetrics and gynecology and fellow in pediatrics N.Y. Hosp.-Cornell Med. Ctr., 1970-73; Gilbert and Nat. Found. fellow Cambridge (Eng.) U., 1973-74; head sect. human biochem. genetics Nat. Inst. Child Health and Human Devel., NIH, Bethesda, Md., 1974-83; dir. med. genetics program NIH, Bethesda, 1979-1983; prof. ob-gyn., pediat., genetics George Washington U., 1983-84; CEO Genetics & IVF Inst., Fairfax, Va., 1984-98, chmn., 1984—2001, 2004—; prof. human genetics, pediat., ob-gyn. Med. Coll., Va. Commonwealth U., 1984—; with dept. ob-gyn. Fairfax Hosp., 1984—. Affiliate prof. ob-gyn. U. Cal., San Diego, 2003—; advisor to numerous govt. and pvt. orgns. Author 4 books; contbr. numerous articles to med. jours.; editorial bd. Molecular Human Reproduction, 1995—, numerous other sci. jours. With USPHS, 1968-70, 74-83. Fellow ACOG; mem. Soc. Pediat. Rsch., Soc. Gynecologic Investigation, Am. Soc. Clin. Investigation, Am. Soc. Human Genetics, Am. Fertility Soc., Harvard Club, Cosmos Club, Calif. Club, Phi Beta Kappa, Sigma Xi. Office: 3015 Williams Dr Fairfax VA 22031

SCHULMAN, SIDNEY, neurologist, educator; b. Chgo., Mar. 1, 1923; s. Samuel E. and Ethel (Miller) S.; m. Mary Jean Diamond, June 17, 1945; children— Samuel E., Patricia, Daniel. BS, U. Chgo., 1944, MD, 1946. Asst. prof. neurology U. Chgo., 1952-57, assoc. prof., 1957-65, prof., 1965-75, Ellen C. Manning prof., divsn. biol. scis., 1975-93, Ellen C. Manning prof. emeritus, 1993—. Served with M.C. AUS, 1947-49. Mem. Am. Neurol. Assn., U. Chgo. Med. Alumni Assn. (pres. 1968-69, Norman Maclean award 1997), Chgo. Neurol. Soc. (pres. 1964-65)

SCHULTE, KLAUS-MARTIN HEINRICH, general, visceral, and endocrine surgeon, consultant, researcher; b. Bochum, Germany, July 26, 1964; s. Armin and Margrit S. Gen. student, Coll. de France, Paris, 1986-88; med. student, Faculté Broussais, Paris, 1986-88; student, Harvard U., 1990; MD, U. Clinics, Essen, Germany, 1990. Med. diplomate. Intern in nephrology Hôpital Henri Mondor U. Paris XII, Creteil, 1990-91; resident in surgery Alfried-Krupp-Krankenhaus, Essen, 1991-95; fellow of surgery, mem. faculty med. Heinrich-Heine U., Düsseldorf, Germany, 1995-98; ind. researcher, 1998-2000; head rsch. lab. dept. surgery, 2000—04; cons. endocrine and gen. surgery King's Coll. Hosp., London, 2004—05, hon. sr. lectr. surgery, 2005—, lead clinician emergency, gen. and trauma surgery, 2006—. Cons. in field. Ind. reviewer med. jours., 1997-; contbr. articles to profl. jours. Grantee German Nat. Scholarship Orgn., 1985-90, Alfried-Krupp-von-Bohlen-und-Halbach Found., 1990-91, German Nat. Rsch. Found. (DFG), 1998-2000; recipient Oberdisse award Soc. Endocrinology, 1997, Dr. G. Wille Award, 2001, von-Langenbeck Award German Soc. Surgery, 2002. Mem. Am. Soc. Endocrinology. Roman Catholic. Avocations: singing, rowing, writing. Office: Kings Coll Hosp Denmark Hill London SE 59RS England Home: Kahrstr. 82 41372 Nieder Krüchten-Brempt Germany Office Phone: 0044-20-3299 1925. Business E-Mail: klaus-martin.schulte@kch.nhs.uk.

SCHULTZ, DANIEL G., former federal agency administrator; b. NYC, Sept. 28, 1949; BA in Polit. Sci., CCNY, 1971; MD, U. Pitts., 1974. Cert. in Gen. Surgery and Family Practice. Intern in pediatrics and medicine U. N.Mex; gen. med. officer, clin. dir. Tuba City Indian Hosp., Navajo Reservation, Ariz., 1975—78; resident gen. surgery Pub. Health Svc. Hosp., San Francisco; fellowship in pediatric surgery Denver, 1981; med. officer Gen. Surgery Br. Ctr. Devices and Radiological Health, FDA, 1994, chief med. officer, Divsn. Reproductive, Abdominal and Radiological Devices, divsn. dir., dep. dir., dir. Office Device Evaluation, acting dir., 2004, dir., 2004—09. Fellow: Am. Coll. Surgeons.

SCHULTZ, ERIC H., health insurance company executive; m. Kim Schultz; 2 children. BS in Biology, U. Conn., BA in Economics; MBA in Health care, Yale U.; D in Economics (hon.), Mass. Coll. of Pharmacy and Health Sciences, 2009. Med. group adminstr. Nashville Healthcare Group; held exec. positions with CIGNA Healthcare; pres., CEO Fallon Cmty. Health Plan (FCHP), 2010, Harvard Pilgrim Health Care Inc., 2010—. Past pres. Mohegan Coun., Boy Scouts of America; bd. dirs. Kenneth Schwartz Ctr., America's Health Ins. Plans, Mass. Assn. of Health Plans, New England Coun., Worcester Regional Rsch. Bureau. Office: Harvard Pilgrim Health Care Inc 93 Worcester St Wellesley MA 02481 Office Phone: 617-509-1000.

SCHULTZ, RICHARD CARLTON, plastic surgeon; b. Grosse Pointe, Mich., Nov. 19, 1927; s. Herbert H. and Carmen (Huebner) S.; m. Pauline Zimmermann, Oct. 8, 1955; children: Richard, Lisa, Alexandra, Jennifer. MD, Wayne State U., 1953. Diplomate Am. Bd. Plastic Surgery. Intern Harper Hosp., Detroit, 1953-54, resident in gen. surgery, 1954-55, U.S. Army Hosp., Ft. Carson, Colo., 1955-57; resident in plastic surgery St. Luke's Hosp., Chgo., 1957-58, U. Ill. Hosp., Chgo., 1958-59, VA Hosp., Hines, Ill., 1959-60; practice medicine specializing in plastic surgery Park Ridge, Ill., 1961-96; ret., 1996; clin. asst. prof. surgery U. Ill. Coll. Medicine, 1966-70, assoc. prof. surgery, 1970-76, prof., 1976-96; prof. emeritus, 1997—; head divsn. plastic surgery U. Ill. Coll. Medicine, 1970-87; pres. med. staff Luth. Gen. Hosp., Park Ridge, 1977-79; prof. emeritus surgery U. Ill., 1997. Vis. prof. U. Pitts., 1972, U. Miss., 1973, U. Pisa, Italy, 1974, Jikei U. Coll. Medicine, Tokyo, 1976, Ind. U., 1977, U. Helsinki, 1977, U. N.Mex., 1978, U. Milan, 1981, So. Ill. Sch. Medicine, 1982, Tulane U. Med. Sch., 1983, Shanghai 2d Med. Coll., 1984, U. Guadalajara (Mex.), 1986, Gazi U., Turkey, 1988, U. Coll. Medicine Tsuksba, Japan, 1996, Taegu (Korea) U., 1996; sr. Fulbright lectr. U. Uppsala, Sweden, 2003; participant, guest surgeon Physicians for Peace, Turkey and Greece, 1988, Israel and Occupied Ters., 1990, Egypt, 1991, Lithuania, Estonia, 1993 (team leader); leader citizen amb. People to People Internat. Del. Plastic Surgeons to Albania & Russia, 1994, del. leader, Tibet and China, 1998. Author: Facial Injuries, 1970, 3d edit., 1988, Maxillo-Facial Injuries from Vehicle Accidents, 1975, Outpatient Surgery, 1979. Mem. sch. bd., Lake Zurich, Ill., 1966-72, pres., 1968-72; pres. Chgo. Found. for Plastic Surgery, 1966-. Served to capt. M.C., AUS, 1955-57. Fulbright Found. scholar, Sweden, 1960-61; recipient Auto Safety award Med. Tribune, 1967, Robert H. Ivy award 1969, Disting. Sci. Achievement award Wayne U. Coll. Medicine Alumni, 1975, Sanvenero-Rosselli award, 1981; McGregor scholar, U. Mich., 1946-49; grantee Ednl. Found. Am. Soc. Plastic and Reconstructive Surgery, 1964-65. Fellow ACS (pres. local commn. on trauma 1985-87); mem. Am. Assn. Plastic Surgeons (trustee 1990-91), Am. Soc. Plastic and Reconstructive Surgeons, Midwestern Assn. Plastic Surgeons (pres. 1978-79), Chgo. Soc. Plastic Surgeons (pres. 1970-72), Midwestern Assn. Plastic Surgeons (pres. 1978-79), Am. Soc. Maxillofacial Surgeons (pres. 1988-89, award of honor 1986), Am. Assn. Automotive Medicine (pres. 1970-71, A. Merkin award 1982), Am. Cleft Palate Assn., Am. Soc. Aesthetic Plastic Surgery, Tord Skoog Soc. Plastic Surgeons (pres. 1971-75), Can. Soc. Plastic Surgery, Chilean Soc. Plastic Surgery (corr.), Japanese Soc. Plastic Surgery (corr.), Cuban Soc. Maxillofacial Surgery (corr.), Korean Soc. Plastic Surgery (corr.). Home (Summer): PRS Enterprises PO Box 357 Northport MI 49670-0357 Business E-Mail: schultz5@coslink.net.

SCHULTZ, RICHARD H., state agency administrator; MS, Ctrl. Wash. Univ. Adminstr., divsn. health Idaho Dept. Health & Welfare, Boise, 1986—, dep. dir. health services. Office: Idaho Dept Health and Welfare 450 W State St PO Box 83720 Boise ID 83720-0036 Office Phone: 208-334-5945. Office Fax: 208-334-6581.

SCHULTZ, RICHARD M., biology professor; b. Malden, Mass., Mar. 20, 1949; s. Samuel and Marylyn (Schaffer) S.; m. Nicola Thomsen Neff, Oct. 20, 1979. BA, Brandeis U., Waltham, Mass., 1971; PhD, Harvard U., 1975. Postdoctoral fellow Harvard Med. Sch., Boston, 1975-78; asst. prof. biology U. Pa., Phila., 1978-84, assoc. prof., 1984-90, Patricia Williams prof. biology, former chmn. dept. biology, Charles and William L. Day disting. prof. biology, assoc. dean natural sciences. Contbr. over 140 articles to profl. jours. Recipient Jan Purkinje medal Czech Acad. Sci., 1994. Fellow AAAS. Office: 204B Carolyn Lynch Lab Dept Biology University Pa Philadelphia PA 19104 Office Phone: 215-898-7869. Business E-Mail: rschultz@sas.upenn.edu.

SCHULTZ, RICHARD MICHAEL, biochemistry educator, researcher; b. Phila., Oct. 28, 1942; s. William and Beatrice (Levine) S.; m. Rima M. Lunin, Mar. 7, 1965; children: Carl M., Eli J. BA, SUNY, Binghamton, 1964; PhD, Brandeis U., 1969. Rsch. fellow Harvard U. Med. Sch., Boston, 1969-71; asst. prof. Loyola U. Stritch Sch. of Medicine, Maywood, Ill., 1971-78, assoc. prof., 1978-84, prof., 1984—, chmn. dept. molecular and cellular biochemistry, 1984-2000. Mem. adv. med. bd. Leukemia Rsch. Found., Chgo., 1987-91. Co-author: Textbook of Biochemistry; contbr. articles to profl. jours., chapters to books. Recipient Rsch. grants NIH. Achievements include in vivo evidence for the role of protease enzymes and their inhibitors in regulating tumor cell metastasis, ras oncogene pathways in cancer, role of JNK and c-Jun in cancer cell protease expression, obtaining evidence on the nature of the transition-state in serine protease enzyme catalysis, regulation of gene expression by histone modification. Office: Divsn Molecular & Cellular Biochemistry Loyola U Sch Medicine Maywood IL 60153 Home Phone: 708-383-7026; Office Phone: 708-216-9378. E-mail: rschult@lumc.edu.

SCHULTZ, RICHARD OTTO, ophthalmologist, educator; b. Racine, Wis., Mar. 19, 1930; s. Henry Arthur and Josephine (Wagoner) S.; m. Diane Haldane, Sept. 29, 1990; children: Henry Reid, Richard Paul, Karen Jo. BA, U. Wis., 1950, MS, 1954; MD, Albany Med. Coll., 1956; MSc, U. Iowa, 1960. Diplomate Am. Bd. Ophthalmology. Intern, Univ. Hosps., Iowa City, 1956-57, resident in opthalmology, 1957-60; chief ophthalmology sect. div. Indian health USPHS, Phoenix, 1960-63; practice medicine specializing in ophthalmology Phoenix, 1963; NIH spl. fellow in ophthalmic microbiology U. Calif., San Francisco, 1963-64, clin. assoc., 1963-64, research assoc., 1963-64; assoc. prof., chmn. dept. ophthalmology Marquette U. Sch. Medicine (now Med. Coll. Wis.), Milw., 1964-68, prof., chmn., 1968-97, prof. ophthalmology, 1997—2000, prof. emeritus, 2000—. Mem. nat. adv. eye coun. NIH, 1984-88; cons. Froedert Hosp., Milw. Contbr. articles to profl. jours. Served with USPHS, 1960-63. Fellow: ACS (life), Am. Ophthalmol. Soc. (emeritus), Am. Acad. Ophthalmology (life); mem.: Oxford Ophthalmol. Congress (Eng.), N.Y. Acad. Scis. (emeritus), Assn. Rsch. Vision and Ophthalmology (emeritus), Pan Am. Assn. Ophthalmology (life), Milw. Ophthal. Soc., Assn. Univ. Profs. Ophthalmology (past pres., trustee). Home: 4487 Granny Smith Ct Egg Harbor WI 54209 Home Phone: 920-868-5021. Personal E-mail: eyeotto@aol.com.

SCHULTZ, STANLEY GEORGE, physiologist, educator, retired dean; b. Bayonne, NJ, Oct. 26, 1931; s. Aaron and Sylvia (Kaplan) S.; m. Harriet Taran, Dec. 25, 1960; children: Jeffrey, Kenneth. AB summa cum laude, Columbia U., NYC, 1952; MD, NYU, 1956. Intern Bellevue Hosp., NYC, 1956-57, resident, 1957-59; research assoc. in biophysics Harvard U., 1959-62, instr. biophysics, 1964-67; assoc. prof. physiology U. Pitts., 1967-70, prof. physiology, 1970-79; prof., chmn. dept. physiology U. Tex. Med. Sch., Houston, 1979-96, prof. dept. internal medicine, 1979—, prof. dept. integrative biol. pharm. physiology, 1997—2010, vice chmn., 1999—2003, Fondren chair in cell signalling, 1999—2009, dean Sch. Medicine, 2003—06, H. Wayne Hightower Dist. prof. biomed. sci., 2005—07, assoc. dean sch. medicine, 2007—10, emeritus prof., 2010—. Cons. USPHS, NIH, 1970—; mem. physiology test com. Nat. Bd. Med. Examiners, 1974-79, chmn., 1976-79 Editor Am. Jour. Physiology, Jour. Applied Physiology, 1971-75, Physiol. Revs., 1979-85, Handbook of Physiology: The Gastrointestinal Tract, 1989-91—; mem. editl. bd. Jour. Gen. Physiology, 1969-88, Ann. Revs. Physiology, 1974-81, Current Topics in Membranes and Transport, 1975-81, Jour. Membrane Biology, 1977—, Biochim. Biophys. Acta, 1987-89; assoc. editor Ann. Revs. Physiology, 1977-81; assoc. editor News in Physiol. Scis., 1989-94, editor, 1994-2003; contbr. articles to profl. jours. Served to capt. M.C. USAF, 1962-64. Recipient Rsch. Career award NIH, 1969-74, Solomon Berson award NYU, 2003; overseas fellow Churchill Coll., Cambridge U., 1975-76, Prince Mahidol award, Thailand, 2007. Mem. Am. Heart Assn. (estab. investigator 1964-68), Am. Physiol. Soc. (councillor 1989-91, pres.-elect 1991-92, pres. 1992-93, past pres. 1993-94, Guyton award 1997, Orr Reynolds award 1999, Daggs award 2003), European Acad. Sci., Fed. Am. Soc. Exptl. Biology (exec. bd. 1992-95), Internat. Cell Rsch. Orgn., Internat. Union Physiol. Scis. (chmn. internat. com. gastrointestinal physiology 1977-80, chmn. U.S. nat. com. 1992-98), Assn. Am. Physicians, Am. Assn. Ob-Gyn. (hon. fellow), Assn. Chmn. Depts. Physiology (pres. 1985-86), Houston Philos. Soc., Phi Beta Kappa, Sigma Xi. Office Phone: 713-500-5012, 713-500-6204. Business E-Mail: stanley.g.schultz@uth.tmc.edu. *

SCHULTZ, VICTOR M., physician; b. Pitts., Aug. 14, 1932; s. Irvin and Rose (Reiss) S. BS, Kent State U., Ohio, 1955; MD, Ohio State U., Columbus, 1958. Diplomate Am. Bd. Dermatology. Pvt. practice, Santa Monica, Calif., 1965—. Fellow Am. Acad. Dermatology, Pacific Dermatologic Assn.; mem. AMA, Am. Coll. Physicians, Calif. Med. Assn., L.A. County Med. Assn. Avocations: skiing, tennis, golf, music, swimming. Office: 2461 Santa Monica Blvd Santa Monica CA 90404-2049 Home Phone: 310-826-6832; Office Phone: 310-828-7492.

SCHULTZE-MOSGAU, STEFAN, oral and maxillofacial surgeon, plastic surgeon; b. Mainz, Germany, Feb. 20, 1965; s. Helmut and Maritta Schultze-Mosgau; married; 2 children. Habil, PhD, 2000. Cert. prof. Germany, in medicine Germany, 1995, TQM-EFQM assessor Germany, 2002, lic. in dentistry 1989, in medicine 1996, cert. oral surgeon 1999, oral and maxillofacial surgeon 2000. Resident dept. oral and maxillofacial surgery Med. HS Hannover, Germany, 1990—95, Friedrich-Alexander-U. Erlangen-Nuremberg, Germany, 1995—2000, sr. hosp. cons., attending, 2000—05, prof., 2005; prof., head & chmn. Dept. Oral & Maxillofacial Surgery-Plastic Schiller-U., Jena, Germany, 2005—. Contbr. scientific papers to numerous profl.

jours. Recipient Dt. Millerpreis Award, Dt. Ges. f. Zahn, Mund, Kieferheilkunde, 2002, First Pl. Gold Camera Award, US Int. Film and Video Festival, 2000, First Pl. Couronne d'or, XVe Festival Int. du Film Dentaire, Paris, 2000, Intermedia-Globe Gold Award, World Media Festival Hamburg, 2000. Fellow: European Bd. Oral and Maxillofacial Surgery; mem.: German Assn. Oral Health and Dentistry, German Assn. Oral Implantology, Internat. Assn. Oral and Maxillofacial Surgeons, German Assn. Oral- and Maxillofacial Surgery, European Found. Quality Mgmt. (qkb 2002). Office: Dept Oral & Maxillofacial Surgery Erlanger Allee 101 Jena 07747 Germany Office Phone: 4936419323601. Business E-Mail: stefan.schultze-mosgau@med.uni-jena.de.

SCHULZ, RAYMOND ALEXANDER, medical marketing professional, consultant; b. Paris, June 2, 1946; s. Helmut W. and Colette (Prieur) S.; m. Dixie Lee Suzanne Specht, Apr. 9, 1977 (div. Dec. 1990); children: Christopher, William; m. Casey Elizabeth Watson, Apr. 10, 1999; 1 child, Francis John. BA in Physics, W.Va. U., Morgantown, 1970; MS in Computer Sci., Columbia U., NYC, 1975. Sr. programmer Meml. Sloan Kettering Cancer Ctr., NYC, 1972-74; program coord. Neurol. Inst. Columbia Presbyn. Hosp., NYC, 1974-76; engring. mgr. EMI Med. Systems, Northbrook, Ill., 1976-78; product mgr. Johnson & Johnson (Technicare), Solon, Ohio, 1978-80; group product mgr. Siemens Corp., Iselin, NJ, 1980-82; mktg. mgr. Toshiba Am. Med. Systems (formerly Diasonics MRI), South San Francisco, Calif., 1983-92; dir. mktg. Voxel, Laguna Hills, Calif., 1992—98; v.p. mktg. and customer support Voxel, Inc., Provo, Utah, 1999—2001; prin. RAenterprises, San Mateo, Calif., 2001—; v.p. mktg. and sales Scanis, Inc., Foster City, Calif., 2002—03; tech. dir. Accuray, Sunnyvale, Calif., 2004—07; mktg. mgr. Varian Med. Sys., Palo Alto, Calif., 2007—. Former bd. dirs. Dynecology, Harrison, NY, 2004—07; presenter in field. Mng. editor, pub. Robtoic Radiosurgery vol 1, 2005, Treating Tumors that Move with Respiration, 2007, Shaped Beam Radiosurgery, 2011; contbr. articles to profl. jours., chapters to books. Mem. vestry St. Matthews Episcopal Ch., San Mateo, Calif., 2006—09. Recipient first prize Roentgen Centenary Congress, 1995, Best Paper prize Am. Assn. Neurol. Surgeons, San Francisco, 2000, 06, RX Club award, 2009. Mem. Am. Assn. Physicists in Medicine, Internat. Stereotactic Radiosurgery Soc., Internat. Assn Study Lung Cancer, Med. Mktg. Assn., Larchmont Yacht Club, Commonwealth Club Calif., Eta Kappa Nu. Avocations: skiing, running, hiking, swimming, mountainbiking. Office: Varian Med Sys & Surg Svcs Varian Surgical Scis 3100 Hansen Way Palo Alto CA 94304 Business E-Mail: ras257@columbia.edu, raymond.schulz@varian.com.

SCHULZE, ARTHUR EDWARD, biomedical engineer, researcher; b. Richmond, Tex., Nov. 22, 1938; s. Arthur Dorwin and Ida (Bockhorn) S.; m. Sharon Kay Havemann, Sept. 2, 1962; children: Keith E., Mark A. BSEE, U. Tex., 1962, MSEE, 1963; MS Biomed. Sci., U. Tex., Houston, 1968. Registered profl. engr., Tex. Sr. aerosystems engr. Gen. Dynamics, Ft. Worth, 1963-67; rsch. assoc. U. Tex. Grad. Sch. Biomed. Scis., Houston, 1967-68, mgr., biomed. engr. SCI Systems, Inc., Houston, 1968-74; v.p. Telecare, Inc., Houston, 1974-79, gen. mgr. Tex. Sci. Corp., Houston, 1979-81; dir. R & D Narco Bio-Systems, Houston, 1981-84, pres., 1984-86; v.p. Lovelace Sci. Resources, Inc., Houston, 1986-92; pres. Healthcare Tech. Group, 1993—; chmn., founder 20th Century Tech. Mus., 2005—. Contbr. articles to sci. publs. Mem. IEEE, Aerospace Med. Assn., Assn. Advancement Med. Instrumentation, AAAS, Biomed. Technology Club. Avocations: photography, beekeeping. Home: 114 Bluebonnet Ln Wharton TX 77488-3076 Office: Healthcare Tech Group 625 N Fulton St Wharton TX 77488-3941 Office Phone: 979-282-8808. Personal E-mail: schulze@neosoft.com.

SCHULZE, KEITH E., dermatologist, surgeon; b. Ft. Worth, Nov. 6, 1963; s. Arthur E. and Sharon E. Schulze; m. Betsy S. Nance, Apr. 29, 1989; children: Sarah E., Kristen E. BA in Chemistry summa cum laude, Tex. Luth. U., 1985; MD, U. Tex., 1989. Diplomate Am. Bd. Dermatology, 1993. Physician, ptnr. South Tex. Med. Clinics, P.A., Wharton, 1993—96, sec., treas., 1996—2000; clin. asst. prof. dept. dermatology U. Tex. Med. Sch., Houston, 2000—01; v.p., co-dir. Dermatologic Surgery Ctr., 2001—06; pres. Ft. Bend Skin Cancer Ctr., Sugar Land, Tex., 2006—. Trustee St. Thomas Episcopal Sch., Wharton, Tex., 1999—2001; dir. Wharton C. of C. and Agr., 1996—99. Recipient Eugene D.Jacobson award Highest Achievement Mammalian Physiology, U. Tex. Med. Sch., Houston, 1986, award Highest Achievement Microbiology, 1986. Fellow: Am. Soc. Dermatologic Surgery, Am. Coll. Mohs Micrographic Surgery and Cutaneous Oncology, Am. Acad. Dermatology, Am. Soc. Mohs Surgery; mem.: Houston Dermatologic Soc., Harris County Med. Soc., Tex. Dermatologic Soc., Tex. Med. Assn., Alpha Omega Alpha. Achievements include research in numerous clinical pharmacologic trials. Avocations: fishing, hunting. Office: Ft Bend Skin Cancer Ctr 15400 SW Fwy Ste 150 Sugar Land TX 77478 Office Phone: 281-980-6647.

SCHULZE, PAUL C., cardiologist, educator; Attended, U. Leipzig, Germany, 1998. Diplomate Am. Bd. Internal Medicine, Am. Bd. Cardiology-cardiovascular disease, Am. Bd. Cardiology-echocardiography, Am. Bd. Cardiology-nuc. cardiology. Resident in internal medicine Boston Univ. Med. Ctr., 2005—07; fellow in cardiovascular disease NY Presbyn. - Columbia Med. Ctr., 2007—09; cardiologist NY Presbyn. Hosp. Office: New York Presbyterian Hospital 662 W 168th St 12th Fl Rm 1273 New York NY 10032 Office Phone: 212-305-4680.

SCHUMACHER, H(ARRY) RALPH, internist, rheumatologist, medical educator, researcher; b. Montreal, Canada, Feb. 14, 1933; s. H. Ralph and Dorothy (Shreiner) S.; m. Elizabeth Jean Swisher, July 13, 1963; children: Heidi Ruth, Kaethe Beth. BS, Ursinus Coll., 1955; MD, U. Pa., 1959. Intern Denver Gen. Hosp., 1959-60; resident in medicine Wadsworth VA Hosp., LA, 1960-62, fellow in rheumatology, 1962-63, Robert B. Brigham Hosp. and Harvard U. Med. Sch., Boston, 1965-67; chief arthritis-immunology ctr. VA Med. Ctr., Phila., 1967—2006; faculty mem. U. Pa. Sch. Medicine, Phila., 1967—, prof. medicine, 1979—, acting arthritis divsn. chief, 1978-80, 91-95, prof. orthopaedics, 1998—2002. Vis. scholar NIH, 1994-99; lectr. in field. Author: (books) Gout and Pseudogout, 1978, Essentials of a Differential Diagnosis of Rhematoid Arthritis, 1981, Rheumatoid Arthritis, 1988, Case Studies in Rheumatology for the House Officer, 1989, Atlas of Synovial Fluid and Crystal Identification, 1991, A Practical Guide to Synovial Fluid Analysis, 1991, The Spondylarthropathies, 1998, Classic Papers in Rheumatology, 2001, Crystal-induced Arthropathies, 2006; editor: Primer on Rheumatic Disease, 1981—97, Jour. Clin. Rheumatology, 1994—, OMERACT, —, Crystal Diseases Section, 2005—; mem. editl. bd. Jour. Rheumatology, 1973—, Arthritis and Rheumatism, 1981—88, Revue du Rhumatisme (now Joint, Bone, Spine), 1992—2007, Internat. Jour. Clin. Practice, 1992—, New European Rheumatology, 1993—, Asian Pacific League Against Rheumatism Internat. Jour. Rheumatology, 1997—, Current Rheumatology Reports, 1999—, Indian Jour. Rheumatology, 2000—, Portuguese Jour. Rheumatology, 2000—; mem. editl. bd. Resident and Staff Physician, 2001—08; mem. editl. bd.: Vojnosanitetski, 2005—, Chinese Jour. Integrative Medicine, 2007—, Brazilian Journal of Rheumatology, 2008—; contbr. articles to profl. jours. Pres. Ea. Pa. chpt. Arthritis Found., 1980-82; chmn., founder Phila. Garden Tours, 1987—95; bd. dirs. Hemochromatosis Rsch. Found., 1984—, Am. Bd. Med. Advancement China, 1983-99. With M.C. USAF, 1963-65. Recipient VanBreeman award Netherland Rheumatism Soc., 1988, Philip Hench award Assn. Mil. Surgeons, 1986, Hollander award Arthritis Found., 1996; named Alumnus of Yr. Ursinus Coll, 1995; named to Sports Hall of Fame Ursinus Coll., 1997; Deposition VA grantee, 1967-95, NIH grantee, 1981, 94—2010. Master PANLAR; fellow ACP; mem. AAAS, Am. Coll. Rheumatology (master; pres. Southeastern region 1981-82, Klemperer lectr. 2002), Phila. Rheumatism Soc. (pres. 1980), Phila. Electron Microscopy Soc. (chmn. 1975-76), Rheumatism Soc. Mex., Rheumatism Soc. Australia, Rheumatism Soc. Colombia, Rheumatism Soc. Chile, Rheumatism Soc. China, Rheumatism Soc. Argentina, Med. Soc. Argentina, Slovak Soc. Rheumatology. Office: VA Med Ctr 151 K University and Woodland Aves Philadelphia PA 19104 Business E-Mail: schumacr@mail.med.upenn.edu.

SCHUNK, WERNER WALTHER, neurologist, toxicologist; b. Sundhausen, Germany, Jan. 12, 1938; s. Walther and Marie Schunk; m. Christine Margarethe Seyfert, 1960; children: Suhr, Claudia Dr. medicina, Med. Akademie, Erfurt, Germany, 1963; Dr.habilitatus, Martin Luther U., Halle, Germany, 1974. Dir. Inst. Arb.medicine MAE, Erfurt, 1968—72; prorektor Medizin Acad., Erfurt, 1972—92, prof., 1976; leiter Inst. Arbeitsmed., Gotha, 1992—. Author (editor): Pollutants in the Rubber Industry, 1995, Occupational Toxicology, 1997, 5th edit., 2001, Registrar of Pollutants of Baking Occupations, 2003—06, 3d edit., 2005; author: numerous poems. Mem. Soc. Arbeitsmedizin, Soc. Med. Rehab. (pres. 1978-85). Achievements include patents for biomaterialen, de-toxikationen and new polymers. Home: Gallettistrasse 2 99867 Gotha Germany Office: Arbeitmedizinisches Inst Gallettistr 2 D99867 Gotha Germany Office Phone: 03621 893903. Office Fax: 03621-893904.

SCHUPP, WILFRIED JOHANNES, physiatrist, neurorehabilitation specialist; b. Saulgau, Germany, Nov. 27, 1955; s. Albert and Klara Johanna (Bautz) S.; m. Centa Maria Hoesle, Mar. 28, 1984 MD, U. Ulm, 1981. Diplomate Neurology and Psychiatry, Bavarian Chamber of Physicians, 1987, Social medicine, 1989, Physiatrist, 1993. Asst. mem. Psychiatric Clinic Reichenau, Konstanz, Germany, 1981-82; mem. Max Planck Inst. Psychiatry, Munich, Germany, 1982-84, Dept Neurology, Fachklinik Enzensberg, Füssen, Germany, 1984-86; med. vice head dept. neurology Fachklinik Enzenberg, Füssen, 1987-90, med. head dept. neurology, 1990-96; mem. Neurological Univ. Clinic, Munich, 1986-87; med. head dept. neurology Fachklinik Herzogenaurach, Germany, 1996—. Assoc. mem. Ctr. for Neuromuscular Diseases, Erlangen; lectr. rehab. and sports medicine U. Erlangen, 1998—; mem. adv. com. for rehab. Fedn. German Pension Ins. Insts., Frankfurt, 1988-91, leader adv. bd. on neurorehab., 1991-2006; vice leader adv. bd. on neurorehab. Fedn. Bavarian Social Health Insurances, Munich, 1994—; adviser Bavarian Chamber of Physicians, Munich, 1994—; advisor Fed. German Assn. for Rehab. of Disabled, Frankfurt, 1998—, adv., German Assn. Pub. Work Accident Ins., Berlin, 2001-; mem. adv. bd. neuro-rehab. Social German Pension Insurances, Berlin, 2007-. Co-author: Posture and Gait, 1990, Rehabilitation of the Disabled, 1992, EMG-Biofeedback in Neuromuscular Diseases, 1994, Rehabilitation and Care for Neurologically Disabled Patients in Germany, 1995, Rehabilitation Medicine--Rehabilitation of Neurological Diseases, 1995, 2d edit., 1998, Stroke (and its Rehabilitation), 1996, Structure and Process of Rehabilitation in Germany, 2002, Neuromuscular Diseases and Sports, 2003, Neurological Rehabilitation, 2004, Job Oriented Medical Rehabilitation, 2006, 09, Vocational and Travelling Aspects in Neurological Diseases, Rehabilitation Nursing; contr. to jour. articles. Mem. German Soc. for Neurology (working group neurology and sports), German Soc. for Neurorehab., German Soc. for Neurotraumatology and Clin. Neuropsychology, German Soc. for Phys. and Rehabilitative Medicine (Award of Yr. 3d prize 1996), German Soc. for Muscular Ills, Internat. Assn. for Study of Pain (German sect., Award of Yr. 3d prize 1999), Internat. Soc. Phys. and Rehab. Medicine, German Stroke Soc., European Neurological Soc., Soc. Rsch. and Treatment in Aphasia, World Muscle Soc., Rotary Club. Roman Catholic. Avocations: travel, art, cooking. Office: Fachklinik Herzogenaurach In der Reuth 1 D-91074 Herzogenaurach Bavaria Germany Office Phone: 49-9132-831035. Personal E-mail: wschupp@gmx.net.

SCHUR, WALTER ROBERT, physician; b. Webster, Mass., June 17, 1914; s. Robert O. and Alma L. (Gatzke) S.; m. Delta Jean Newman, June 17, 1944; children: Paul, David, Jonathan, Ruth, Timothy, Peter, Stephen, Mary, Joel, Daniel, Rhoda. Student, Valparaiso U., 1931-34; MD, Middlesex U.Sch. of Med., 1940. Resident Milford (Del.) Meml. Hosp., 1940-41, Grace Hosp., Cleve., 1942-43; intern Luth. Hosp., Cleve., 1941-42; pvt. practice Oxford, Mass., 1944—. Bd. dirs., pres. Doctors Hosp., Worcester, Mass., chmn. bd., 1978-87; bd. dirs. AdCare Hosp., 1987—, chmn. bd dirs., 1987-91, Atlantic dist. Luth. Ch.-Mo. Synod, 1978-87, mem., sec. edn. com., missions com., 1960-77, mem. stewardship com., youth com., edn. com., 1951-57, chmn. edn. com. Atlantic dist., 1954-57, mem. commn. on mission and ministry in ch., named Dist. Layman of Yr., 1966, chmn. com. on ministry Atlantic dist., 1970; bd. dirs. Luth. Assn. Works of Mercy, assn. Evang. Luth. Chs.; bd. dirs. Valparaiso U., 1969-99, sec., 1984-99; pres., scholarship chmn. N.E. dist. Luth. Laymen's League, 1957; vice chmn. Luth. Hour Oper. Com., 1958, chmn., 1959-61; New Eng. bd. dirs. Assn. Evang. Luth. Chs., 1977-87, trustee East Coast Synod, 1977-87, mem. nat. bd. dirs., 1979-88; mem. coun. New Eng. Synod Evang. Luth. Ch. Am., 1988-94; bd. dirs., vice chmn. French River Edn. Ctr., 1985—; mem. Oxford Sch. Com., 1961-86, Mass. Commn. on Christian Unity; assoc. charter mem. Park Ridge Ctr., 1986. Recipient award of merit Internat. Luth. Laymen's League, 1963, Soli Deo Gloria award New Eng. Synod, Evang. Luth. Ch. Am., 1994. Fellow Am. Acad. Gen. Practice, Am. Acad. Family Physicians (charter); mem. AMA, Mass. Med. Soc., Worcester Dist. Med. Soc., Am. Geriatrics Assn., New Eng. Ob-gyn. Soc., Valparaiso U. Alumni Assn. (past pres.), Luth. Acad. for Scholarship (bd. dirs. 1977-86), Concordia Hist. Inst., New Eng. Luth. Hist. Soc. (charter), Internat. Platform Assn., New Eng. Huguenot Soc., Rotary (past pres.). Home: 168 Charlton St Oxford MA 01540-2008 Office: 367 Main St Oxford MA 01540-1746

SCHUREK, HANS JOACHIM FRANZ, nephrologist; b. Stuttgart-Bad Cannstatt, Germany, Jan. 28, 1941; s. Adalbert Heinrich Eugen and Frieda Anna Emma Hedwig (Freitag) S.; m. Marianne Ursula Elisabeth Bialetzki, Aug. 25, 1967; children: Jens-Uwe, Eva-Maria. MD, U. Tuebingen, Germany, 1968; Habilitation, U. Hannover Med. Sch., Germany, 1982. Rschr. and clinician Freie U./U. Klinikum Benjamin Franklin, Berlin, 1969—75, U. Hannover Sch. Medicine, 1975—79, cons. and rschr., 1979—86, head physician and rschr., 1986—88; chief nephrology St. Bonifatius Hosp., Lingen, 1988—, emeritus, 2006—. Cons. U. Hannover Sch. Medicine, 1979-86; guest rschr. physiology U. Zurich, Switzerland, 1988; guest rschr. U. Muenster, Germany, 2006-. Contbr. articles to profl. jours.; patentee in field. Grantee Deutsche Forschungsgemeinschaft, 1974-89. Mem. Internat. Soc. Nephrology, Am. Soc. Nephrology, European Renal Assn. Roman Catholic. Avocations: music, painting, pedersen-cyclist, journeys.

SCHURMAN, DAVID JAY, orthopedic surgeon, educator; b. Chgo., Apr. 25, 1940; s. Shepherd P. and Dorothy (Laskey) S.; m. Martha Ellen Rocker, Mar. 8, 1967; children: Hilary Sue, Theodore Shepherd. BA, Yale U., 1961; MD, Columbia U., 1965. Intern Baylor U., Houston, 1965-67; resident in gen. surgery Mt. Sinai Hosp., NYC, 1966-67; resident in orthop. surgery UCLA, 1969-72; asst. rsch. surgeon UCLA Med. Sch., 1972-73; asst. prof. orthopedic surgery Stanford Med. Sch., 1973-79, assoc. prof., 1979-87, prof., 1987—. Acting chief divsn. orthop. surgery Stanford U. Med. Ctr., 1990-93, fellowship dir. total joint replacement, 1983—, fellowship dir. sports medicine, 1992-95, dir. orthop. rsch. lab., 1973—. Capt. USAF, 1967-69. Fellow NIH, 1972-73; grantee NIH, 1976-96; recipient Top Dr. award, San Francisco Mag., 02, 03, 05. Mem. Am. Orthopaedic Assn. (bd. dirs. 1994-95), Clin. Orthopaedics and Related Rsch. (bd. dirs. 1994-00), Assn. Bone and Joint Surgeons (v.p. 1996-97, pres. 1997-98). Office: Stanford U Sch Medicine R145 Divsn Orthop Surgery 300 Pasteur Dr Palo Alto CA 94304-2203 Office Phone: 650-723-7608. Business E-Mail: djsortho@standford.edu.

SCHUSS, STEVEN, pediatrician, educator; Grad., Albert Einstein Coll. Medicine, 1979. Diplomate Am. Bd. Pediatrics, lic. NJ. Resident in pediat. Montefiore Hosp. Med. Ctr., Bronx, NY, 1980—83; asst. clin. prof. pediat. Albert Einstein Coll. Medicine; with Hackensack Univ. Med. Ctr.; pediatrician Englewood Hosp. & Med. Ctr. Office: Englewood Hospital and Medical Center Metropolitan Pediatric Group 704 Palisade Ave Teaneck NJ 07666 Office Phone: 201-836-4301. Office Fax: 201-836-5110.

SCHUSSLER, OLIVIER, cardiac surgeon, researcher; b. Grenoble, Isere, France, Apr. 7, 1966; s. François and Simone Schussler; m. Magali Boissin; children: Julie, Timothée, Loïc. MD, U. Paris, 1999, PhD, U. Paris XI, 1999. Cert. in cardiothoracic surgery Paris U. Sch. Medicine, 1999. Postdoc. clin. fellow, thoracic surgery APHP CHU Ht Dieu Hosp., Paris, 2000—02; thoracic surgeon APHP CHU Hôtel Dieu Hosp., 2004—08; postdoc. rsch. fellow Scripps Rsch. Inst., La Jolla, Calif., 1999—2001; scientist Biosurg. Rsch. Lab. Georges Pompidou European Hosp., Paris, 2001—08; postdoc. clin. fellow cardiac surgery APHP CHU Georges Pompidou Hosp., Paris V U., 2002—04; postdoc. clin. and rsch. fellow Ottawa Heart Inst., Ont., Canada, 2008—11. Co-founder ACM Biomatrix Biotech Startup, 2010. Recipient Postdoc. Rsch. award, Heart & Stroke, Can., 2010; fellow European Bourse Lavoisier, 1999. Achievements include research in tissue engineering, cardiac regeneration; patents for tissue engineering. Office: Department Cardiothoracic Vascular Hospital University de Geneve HUG 24 Rue Micheli du Crest 1211 Geneve France

SCHUSTER, CARLOTTA LIEF, psychiatrist; b. NYC, Sept. 16, 1936; d. Victor Filler and Nina Lincoln (Rayevsky) Lief; m. David Israel Schuster, Sept. 2, 1962; 1 child, Amanda. BA, Barnard Coll., 1957; MD, NYU, 1964. Cert. Am. Bd. Psychiatry and Neurology; cert. addiction psychiatry. Intern Lenox Hill Hosp., NYC, 1964-65; resident St. Luke's Hosp., NYC, 1965-68; fellow Inst. Sex Edn. U. Pa., Phila., 1968-69; instr. N.Y. Med. Coll., NYC, 1969-72; asst. attending Met. Hosp., NYC, 1969-72; assoc. attending St. Luke's-Roosevelt Hosp. Ctr., NYC, 1972-95; staff psychiatrist Silver Hill Hosp., New Canaan, Conn., 1972-95; clin. assoc. instr. Columbia U., NYC, 1990-95. Chief substance abuse svc. Silver Hill Hosp., New Canaan, 1976-95; dir. Recovery Clinic Bellevue Hosp., N.Y.C., 1995-2003; mem. faculty Dept. Psychiatry Sch. Medicine NYU, 1995—. Author: Alcohol and Sexuality, 1988; co-author: Chapter in Advances in Alcohol and Substance Abuse, 1987; contbr. chpts. to books. Mem. Am. Psychiat. Assn., Am. Med. Soc. on Addictions, Am. Acad. Addiction Psychiatry. Democrat. Jewish. Avocations: cooking, attending concerts, opera, films. Home: 130 E 30th St New York NY 10016-8230 Home Phone: 212-725-0978; Office Phone: 212-213-2513. Personal E-mail: carlotta_schuster@msn.com.

SCHUSTER, MICHAEL, hematologist, educator, internist; MD, Dartmouth Coll., Hanover, NH, 1980. Diplomate Am. Bd. Internal Medicine, Am. Bd. Internal Medicine-hematology. Intern New England Deaconess Hosp., Boston, resident internal medicine, 1981—83; fellow hematology and oncology Beth Israel Med. Ctr., Boston, 1983—87; assoc. prof. medicine NY-Presbyn./Weill Cornell

Univ., NYC; with Stony Brook Univ. Med. Ctr., NY. Office: Stony Brook University Medical Center East Loop Rd Stony Brook NY 11794 Office Phone: 631-444-4000.

SCHUSTER, VICTOR LEONARD, nephrologist, educator; b. Beatrice, Nebr., Mar. 3, 1952; Degree, U. Nebr., 1973; MD, Wash. U., St. Louis, 1977. Baumritter prof. & chair, dept. medicine Albert Einstein Coll. Medicine, 2001—. Treas. Internat. Soc. Nephrology, 2008. Fellow: ACP, Am. Heart Assn., Am. Soc. Nephrology; mem.: AAUP, Am. Soc. Clin. Investigation. Office: 1300 Morris Pk Ave Belfer 1008 Bronx NY 10025 Office Fax: 718-430-8659. Business E-Mail: victor.schuster@einstein.yu.edu.

SCHÜTZER, KAJS-MARIE, physician; b. Stockholm, Nov. 29, 1956; MD, Sahlgrenska U. Medicine, 1982, PhD. Specialist, lung medicine Sahlgrenska U. Hosp., 1982—95; sr. rsch. physician AZ Pharma, 1995. Mem.: Göteborgs Läkarsällskap, Svenska Läkarsällskapet. Avocations: golf, travel. Office: AstraZeneca R & D Möndal S-431 83 Sweden Business E-Mail: kajs-marie.schutzer@astrazeneca.com.

SCHUVAL, SUAN JILL, physician; b. NYC, Oct. 17, 1960; MD, SUNY, Buffalo, 1986. Attending physician North Shore-Long Island Jewish Health Sys., 1991—. Home: 11 Elaine Pl Plainview NY 11803 Home Fax: 516-622-5060. Business E-Mail: sschuval@nshs.edu.

SCHWAB, ERNEST ROE, III, physiology educator, researcher, academic administrator; b. Denver, July 19, 1950; s. Ernest Roe and Mary Ellen (Murray) S.; m. Patty Ann Millspaugh, May 16, 1974. BA, Union Coll., Lincoln, Nebr., 1975; MS, Andrews U., Berrien Springs, Mich., 1978; PhD, Loma Linda U., Calif., 1989. Assoc. prof. allied health studies, assoc. dean academic affairs Sch. of Allied Health Professions, Loma Linda U., Loma Linda, Calif., 1996—; assoc. prof. biology La Sierra U., Riverside, Calif., 1991—96; asst. prof. biology Loma Linda U., 1983—91. Contbr. articles to profl. jours. Planner, grant writer So. Calif. Young Artists Symphony, Redlands, Calif., 1998—2001; judge Calif. State Sci. Fair, L.A., Calif., 1998—2011. Recipient Godfrey T. Anderson award for Excellence in Tchg., Loma Linda U., 1990, Cert. of Merit, Nat. Acad. Advising Assn., 1994, Disting. Svc. award, Loma LInda U. Sch. Allied Health Professions, 2004; grantee Rsch. Opportunity award, NSF, 1989. Mem. Union Concerned Scientists, Scientists Action Network, N.Y. Acad. Scis., Sigma Xi (Grad. Student Research grantee 1979), Nat. Acad. Adv. Assn. (Cert. of Merit 1994), Soc. for Neurosci., Internat. Soc. for Neuroethology, Soc. Integrative and Comparative Biology, Soc. Coll. & U. Planners. Democrat. Seventh-Day Adventist. Avocations: photography, travel, backpacking, piano. Home: 423 Marilyn Lane Redlands CA 92373 Office: Loma Linda University 11234 Anderson St Loma Linda CA 92350-0001 Personal E-mail: acheta1@earthlink.net. Business E-Mail: eschwab@llu.edu.

SCHWAB, FRANK J., orthopedist, educator; b. Calif., May 17, 1964; MD, Columbia U., 1990; BA in Chemistry, Princeton U., 1986. Lic. physician State of NY, diplomate Am. Bd. Orthop. Surgery, Nat. Bd. Med. Examiners. Assoc. attending physician, dept. orthop. surgery Maimonides Med. Ctr., Bklyn., 1996—; attending physician Hosp. Joint Diseases Orthop. Inst., NYC, 1996—; dir., Spine Clinic Maimonides Med. Ctr., 1997—, dir. residency edn., 1998—2000, dir., dept. orthop. rsch., 1998—2006; orthop. spinal surgeon NYU Sch. Medicine, 1999—, clin. asst. prof., 1999—2006, clin. assoc. prof., 2006—, chief spinal deformity svc., divsn. spinal surgery, Hosp. Joint Diseases, 2007—. Editl. bds. mem. Bull. Hosp. Joint Diseases, 2008—; assoc. editl. bd. SPINE, 2009—. Recipient Andrew Puperre award, 1990, 3rd Pl., NY Acad. Medicine, Pediat. Orthop. Soc. NY, 1995, SRS Russell A. Gibbs Clin. award, Scoliosis Rsch. Soc. Ann. Meeting, 2009; Postdoc. Rsch. fellowship, NATO-NSF, 1990—. Mem.: AMA, Internat. Spine Study Group, Spinal Deformity Study Group, Spinal Deformity Edn. Group (bd. dirs. 2002—), Am. Acad. Orthop. Surgeons, Scoliosis Rrch. Soc. (aging spine com. mem. 2005—, patient based outcomes com. mem. 2006—, adult deformity com. mem. 2006—), N.Am. Spine Soc. Achievements include research in pain predictors and prognostic parameters; force plate analysis in the setting of spinal deformity; interbody fusion techniques; porcine animal model for scoliosis and non-fusion corrective techniques. Mailing: 306 E 15th St Ste 1F New York NY 10003 Office: 305 2nd Ave Ste 19 New York NY 10003 Address: 255 Hudson St PHE New York NY 10013 Office Fax: 646-602-6926. Business E-Mail: fschwab@worldnet.att.net, frank.schwab@nyumc.org.

SCHWAB, JOEL GERSON, pediatrician, educator; Grad., U. Mich., 1967; MD, NY Med. Coll., 1971. Cert. in pediat. Am. Bd. Med. Specialties. Resident in pediat. Northwestern U. Children's Meml. Hosp.; asst. prof. pediat. Northwestern U.; pvt. practice Child Life Ctr., 1974—86; assoc. prof. pediat. U. Chgo. Med. Ctr., dir. med. student edn., dept. pediat.; faculty dir. health professions advising office U. Chgo. Collegiate Divsn., 2003—. Mem. admissions com. Pritzker Sch. Medicine, Chgo., mem. com. on promotions. Recipient Faculty Tchg. award, Faculty Dean Med. Edn., 1998, Outstanding Clinical Tchg. award, Pritzker Sch. Medicine, Leonard Tow Humanism in Medicine award, 2006; named Tchr. of Yr., Pediatric Residents, 1998. Mem.: Am. Assn. Pediat. Office: U Chgo Med Ctr MC3055 5841 S Maryland Ave Chicago IL 60637 Office Phone: 773-702-6169. Office Fax: 773-702-4786. Business E-Mail: jschwab@peds.bsd.uchicago.edu.

SCHWAB, RICHARD J., pulmonologist, educator; Diplomate Am. Bd. Internal Medicine, 1986, Am. Bd. Internal Medicine-sleep medicine, Am. Bd. Internal Medicine-pulmonary disease, 1990, cert. critical care 1991. Intern Univ. of Pa. Med. Ctr.; resident Thomas Jefferson Univ. Hosp., fellow; assoc. prof. medicine Univ. of Pa.; co-med. dir. Penn Sleep Ctr. Named one of the Top Docs, Phila Mag., 2004, 2005, 2007, 2008, 2011, Best Doctors in America, 2003—04, 2005—06, 2007—08, 2009—10, America's Top Doctors, 2007, 2008, 2010. Mem.: ACP, Am. Sleep Disorders Assn., Am. Thoracic Soc., Am. Coll. of Chest Physicians. Office: Penn Sleep Center Ste 201 3624 Market St Philadelphia PA 19104 Office Phone: 800-789-7366.

SCHWAB, STEVEN J., academic administrator, nephrologist; b. Cape Girardeau, Mo., Jan. 20, 1953; s. Norman J. and Virginia Louise (Schaefer) Schwab; m. Carol A. Schermann, May 31, 1975. BS, Southeast Mo. State U., 1975; MD with honors, U. Mo., 1979. Diplomate Am. Bd. Internal Medicine, Am. Bd. Nephrology. Intern U. Kans. Med. Ctr., Kansas City, resident in internal medicine, 1979—82; fellow in nephrology, renal divsn. Wash. U. Barnes Hosp., St. Louis, 1982—84; asst. prof., dir dialysis dept. Duke U. Med. Ctr., Durham, NC, 1985—2003, vice chmn. dept. medicine; prof. and chmn, dept. medicine Med. Coll. Ga., Augusta, 2003—06, interim dean medicine, 2005—06; exec. dean. Sch. Medicine U. Tenn. Health Sci. Ctr., 2006—10, interim chancellor, 2009—10, chancellor, 2010—. Med. adv. bd. Vasca, Inc., Mass. Contbr. articles to profl. jours. Named one of best doctors in Augusta in nephrology, Augusta mag., 2004. Fellow: Nat. Kidney Found. (mem. profl. coun.); mem.: Am. Heart Assn. (mem. sci. coun.), Internat. Soc. Nephrology, Am. Fedn. Clin. Rsch., Am. Soc. Nephrology, ACP, Alpha Omega Alpha. Office: University Tennesee Health Sci Ctr Office of Chancellor 62 S Dunlop Ste 220 Memphis TN 38163 Office Phone: 901-448-4796. Business E-Mail: sschwab@uthsc.edu. *

SCHWABE, ROBERT, medical educator; b. Hannover, Germany, Nov. 6, 1969; MD, Ludwig-Maximilians-U. Munich, Germany, 1996. Asst. prof. Columbia U., 2003—. Office: 1150 St Nicholas Ave New York NY 10032 Business E-Mail: rfs2102@columbia.edu.

SCHWAN, SEVERIN ANTON, pharmaceutical executive; b. Hall, Austria, Nov. 17, 1967; s. Konrad and Ingeborg (Frank) S.; m. Ingeborg Stix, June 10, 1995. M of Law, Innsbruck U., 1991, M of Econ., 1991, D of Law, 1993. Corp. fin. positions Roche Basel, Switzerland, 1993—95; head fin. & adminstrn. Roche Brussels, Belgium, 1995—98; head fin. & informatics, mem. exec. bd. Roche Deutschland Holding GmbH, Germany, 1998—2000; head global fin. & services Roche Diagnostics, Basel, Switzerland, 2000—04, head Asia Pacific region Singapore, 2004—06, div. CEO Basel, Switzerland, 2006—08; CEO Roche Group, Basel, Switzerland, 2008—. Avocations: violin, trick filming, skiing. Office: Roche Group Grenzacherstrasse 124 4058 Basel Switzerland *

SCHWARTZ, ALAN LEIGH, pediatrician, educator; b. NYC, Apr. 25, 1948; s. Robert and Joyce (Goldner) S.; m. Judith Child, June 22, 1974; 1 child, Timothy Child. BA, Case Western Res. U., 1974, PhD in Pharmacology, 1974, MD, 1976. Diplomate Am. Bd. Pediatrics. Intern Children's Hosp., Boston, 1976-77, resident, 1976-78, fellow Dana Farber Cancer Inst., 1978-80; instr. Harvard Med. Sch., Boston, 1980-81, asst. prof., 1981-83, assoc. prof., 1983-86; prof. pediatrics, molecular biology and pharmacology Washington U. Sch. Medicine, St. Louis, 1986—, chmn. dept. pediatrics, 1995—; chmn. faculty practice plan Washington U., 1999—2001. Vis. scientist MIT, Boston, 1979-82; mem. sci. adv. bd. Nat. Inst. Child Health and Human Devel., NIH, Bethesda, Md., 1988-94; investigator Am. Heart Assn. Alumni Endowed Prof. Pediats. Wash. U. Sch. Medicine, 1987-97, Harriet B. Spoehrer Prof. Pediats., 1997—. Mem. Inst. Medicine of NAS. Office: Washington U Sch Medicine Dept Pediatrics Box 8116 One Children's Pl Saint Louis MO 63110-1093 E-mail: schwartz@kids.wustl.edu.

SCHWARTZ, ALLAN, cardiologist, medical educator; b. NYC, Mass., Jan. 22, 1947; BS magna cum laude, CCNY, 1967; MA in Physics, Harvard U., 1968; MD, Columbia U. Coll. Physicians & Surgeons, 1974. Diplomate Am. Bd. Internal Med., cert. in cardiovasc. disease. Intern NY Presbyn. Hosp./Columbia U. Med. Ctr., 1974—75, cardiology resident, 1975—76; clin. cardiology fellowship Mass. Gen. Hosp./Harvard Med. Sch., Boston, 1976—78; asst. prof. clin. med. Columbia U. Coll. Physicians & Surgeons, 1978—87, assoc. prof. clin. med., 1987—90, clin. prof. med., 1990—93, dir. cardiac catheterization lab., 1990—99, Margaret Milliken Hatch clin. prof. med., 1993—99, Harold Ames Hatch prof. clin. med., 1999—. Vis. fellow Columbia U. Coll. Physicians & Surgeons, 1974—76; asst. attending physician NY Presbyn. Hosp./Columbia U. Med. Ctr., 1978—87, assoc. attending physician, 1987—90, attending physician, 1990—94, assoc. dir. divsn. cardiology, 1994—99, chief divsn. cardiology, 1999—. Contbr. articles to profl. jours. Recipient Janeway prize, Columbia U. Coll. Physicians & Surgeons, 1974, Robert F. Loeb award, 1974; named one of America's Top Doctors, Castle Connolly Med. Ltd., NY's Best Doctors, NY Mag.; fellow Woodrow Wilson Nat. Fellowship Found., 1967—68. Fellow: ACP, Am. Coll. Cardiology, Am. Heart Assoc. (Coun. Clin. Cardiology, Coun. Circulation); mem.: NY State Soc. Med., Paul Dudley White Soc., Phi Beta Kappa, Alpha Omega Alpha. Office: Columbia U Med Ctr 161 Ft Washington Ave Ste 551 New York NY 10032 also: NY Presbyn 622 W 168th St New York NY 10032 Office Phone: 212-305-1606, 212-305-5367, 212-305-2500. Business E-Mail: as20@columbia.edu. *

SCHWARTZ, ANDREW B., neuroscientist, educator; PhD in Physiology, U. Minn., 1984. Fellow Johns Hopkins Sch. Medicine; researcher Barrow Neurological Inst., 1988—95, Neurosciences Inst., San Diego, 1995—2002; prof. neurobiology & researcher U. Pitts., 2002—. Achievements include development of three-dimensional trajectory representation in the motor cortex.

SCHWARTZ, ANNA L., oncological nurse, educator, nursing researcher; b. Inverness, Calif., Sept. 29, 1963; PhD, U. Utah, 1997. Affiliate rsch. prof. U. Wash.; oncology nurse practitioner St. John's Med. Ctr., 1997—. Various Rsch. grants, NIH, Rsch. grant, Dept. Defs. Fellow: Am. Acad. Nursing. Avocations: bicycling, horseback riding. Office: PO Box 1468 Wilson WY 83014 Business E-Mail: annaschwartz@peoplepc.com.

SCHWARTZ, BENNETT K., dermatologist; MD, U. Vt., Burlington, 1983. Intern Thomas Jefferson U. Hosp., Phila., 1983—84; resident in dermatology Dartmouth-Hitchcock Med. Ctr., Hanover, NH, 1984—87; pvt. practice Voorhees, NJ, 1987—. Contbr. articles to profl. jours. Fellow: Am. Acad. Dermatology. Office: 2301 Evesham Rd Ste 403 Voorhees NJ 08043

SCHWARTZ, BRADFORD S., biochemist, educator, former dean; BA, U. Ill., Urbana-Champaign, 1974; MD, Rush U., 1977. Postdoctoral rschr. Scripps Rsch. Inst., 1979—81; prof. biochemistry U. Ill. College Medicine, Urbana-Champaign, former regional dean. Mem.: Am. Soc. Hematology (chmn. com. on publications). Office: University Ill Coll Medicine 190 Med Sciences Bldg 506 S Mathews Ave Urbana IL 61801 Office Phone: 217-333-5465. Office Fax: 217-244-7078. E-mail: schwart2@illinois.edu. *

SCHWARTZ, BRIAN S., medical educator, academic administrator; MD, Northwestern U. Med. Sch., 1984; MS in Clin. Epidemiology, U. Pa. Sch. Medicine, 1989. Assoc. prof. to prof. Johns Hopkins U., Balt., dir. occupl. and environ. health. Office: Johns Hopkins U Dept Occupl & Environ Hlth 615 N Wolfe St W7041 Baltimore MD 21205 Office Phone: 410-955-4158. Office Fax: 410-955-1811. Business E-Mail: bschwart@jhsph.edu.

SCHWARTZ, CHARLES E., medical geneticist, medical association administrator; BA in Chemistry, Colgate U.; MS in Biochemistry, Okla. State U., 1972; PhD, Vanderbilt U., 1978. NCI Postdoctoral Fellow, Dept. Biochemistry U. Vt., 1978—80; rsch. scientist La Jolla Cancer Rsch. Found., 1980—81; rsch. assoc., dept. human genetics U. Utah Sch. Medicine, 1983—85; dir. molecular genetics lab. Greenwood Genetics Ctr., 1985—95, dir., center for molecular studies, JC Self Rsch. Inst., 1996—, dir. rsch., head JC Self Rsch. Inst., 2004—. Adj. prof., dept. genetics and biochemistry Clemson U., Clemson, SC, 1987—; asst. prof. pediatrics U. South Carolina, Columbia, 1987—, adj. asst. prof. biology, 1988—. Recipient Robert Guthrie award for Advances in Biochemical and Molecular Genetics, American Assn. Mental Retardation, 2003; named Professional of the Year, SC Chap. American Assn. Mental Retardation, 2002. Mem.: American Bd. Medical Genetics (diplomate 1993—, dir. clinical molecular genetics 2006—, treas. 2007, v.p. 2008, pres. 2009). Office: Ctr Molecular Studies JC Self Research Inst 113 Gregor Mendel Circle Greenwood SC 29646-2307

SCHWARTZ, DAGAN, medical educator, researcher; b. Israel, Oct. 16, 1960; MD, Hebrew U., 1991. Head, paramedic edn., asst. med. dir. M.D.A., 2000—08; attending physician Rabin Med. Ctr., 2005—11; dir., emergency dept. Rambam Med. Ctr., 2008—09; lectr., rschr. Ben-Gurion U., 2004—. Fellow: ACEP. Home: 68 Stern Rd Kiryat Ono 55602 Israel Business E-Mail: sdagan@bgu.ac.il.

SCHWARTZ, DAVID A., genetics, environmental sciences and pulmonology medicine physician, former federal agency administrator; m. Louise Sparks; 3 children. BA in Biology, U. Rochester, NY, 1975; MD, U. Calif., San Diego, 1979; MPH in Occupl. Medicine, Harvard U., 1985. Diplomate Nat. Bd. Med. Examiners, Am. Bd. Internal Medicine, Am. Bd. Occupl. Medicine, Am. Bd. Pulmonary Medicine, lic. NC, Iowa, DC, Tex., SC. Training in tropical medicine Walter Reed Army Inst. Rsch., 1979; pub. svc. sci. resident NSF, 1979—80; intern/resident Boston City Hosp., 1980—83, chief resident, 1983—84; rsch. fellow Robert Wood Johnson Clin. Scholars Prog., U. Wash., Seattle, 1985—87, pulmonary/critical care fellow, 1985—88; asst. prof. pulmonary disease divsn. Dept. Internal Medicine, U. Iowa, Iowa City, 1988—92, assoc. prof. pulmonary disease, critical care & occupl. medicine, 1992—96, prof., 1996—2000, dir. occupl. medicine, 1988—2000, assoc. chair prog. devel., Dept. Internal Medicine, 1996—2000; prof. medicine & genetics, chief divsn. pulmonary & critical care medicine Duke U. Med. Ctr., Durham, NC, 2000—05, dir. Ctr. Environ. Genomics, Inst. Genome Sci. & Policy, 2000—05, Walter Kempner prof. medicine, 2001—05, vice chair. rsch., Dept. Medicine, 2003—05; prof. environ. scis. & policy Duke U. Nicholas Sch. Environment & Health Scis., 2001—05, adj. prof., 2005—; dir. Nat. Inst. Environ. Health Scis., NIH, Rsch. Triangle Pk., NC, 2005—08, dir. Nat. Toxicology Prog., 2005—08; provost, dir. ctr. Genes environ. health Nat. Jewish Health, Denver, 2008—10; chair dept. medicine U. Colo. Sch. Med., 2011—. Contbr. over 200 articles to profl. jours. in environ. genetics. Named one of America's Top Dr.'s, Castle Connolly Ltd., 2000—. Mem.: Am. Thoracic Soc. (Lifetime Sci. Achievement award), Assn. Am. Physicians, Am. Soc. Clin. Investigation, Am. Fedn. Clin. Rsch., Phi Beta Kappa. Office: University Colo 12631 E 17th Ave B178 Aurora CO 80045 Office Phone: 303-398-1903. Business E-Mail: schwartzd@njhealth.org.

SCHWARTZ, DONALD F., city health department administrator; BA, Brown Univ., 1977; MD, MPH, Johns Hopkins Univ., 1982; MBA, Wharton Sch. Bus. Univ. Pa., 1987. Resident in pediatrics Yale-New Haven Hosp., 1982—85; Robert Wood Johnson Found. clin. scholar Univ. Pa. Sch. Med., 1985—87; physician, fellow through dep. physician-in-chief & chief adolescent med. Children's Hosp., Phila., 1987—2008; Mary D. Ames assoc. prof. of child advocacy Univ. Pa. Med. Sch., vice-chair dept. pediatrics; health commr. & dep. mayor health & opportunity Phila. Dept. Health, 2008—. Sr. fellow Leonard Davis Inst. for Health Econ.; sr. scholar Ctr. for Clin. Epidemiology & Biostatistics; mem. gov. coun. Am. Pub. Health Assn.; adv. Mayor's Cabinet for Children, Youth Violence Task Force. Past pres. bd. dir. Phila. Citizens for Children & Youth; mem. adv. bd. Phila. Children's Network; mem. adv. com. Phila. Sch. District; mem. Pulse adv. bd. Univ. Pa. Sch. Law; bd. dir. Healthier Babies, Healthier Mothers; mem. Phila. Child Welfare Adv. bd. Office: Commr of Health Rm 600 1401 JFK Blvd Philadelphia PA 19102 Office Phone: 215-686-9009. Office Fax: 215-686-5212.

SCHWARTZ, GARY E., psychologist, educator; PhD, Harvard U. Prof. psychology & psychiatry Yale U., dir. Psychophysiology Ctr., co-dir. Behavioral Medicine Clinic; dir. VERITAS rsch. program U. Ariz., prof. psychology, medicine, neurology, psychiatry & surgery, dir. Lab. for Advances in Consciousness & Health, dir. Ctr. for Frontier Medicine in Biofield Sci. Author: The Afterlife Experiments, The G.O.D. Experiments, The Truth About Medium; co-author: The Living Energy Universe. Office: Univ of Arizona Psychology Bldg Rm 312 1503 E University Blvd PO Box 210068 Tucson AZ 85721 Office Phone: 520-318-0286. E-mail: gschwart@email.arizona.edu.

SCHWARTZ, HEDWIGA (HEDWIGA PLESS), physician; b. Beius, Bihor, Romania, Oct. 15, 1932; arrived in Israel, 1975; s. Adalbert and Piri (Neumann) P.; m. Carol Schwartz, Apr. 23, 1958; 1 child, Richard. MD, U. Medicine, Cluj, Romania, 1959. Med. diplomate. Pvt. practice in internal medicine, Oradea, Romania, 1959-75; pvt. practice in gen. and internal medicine Petach-Tikva, Israel, 1975—. Home: Salant 66 Petah Tiqwa Israel Office: PO Box 2064 Herzl 24 Petah Tiqwa 49120 Israel E-mail: drchwa@zahav.net.il.

SCHWARTZ, HENRY P., psychiatrist, educator; MD, SUNY Health Sci. Ctr., Bklyn. Cert. American Bd. Psychiatry and Neurology. Internship in gen. surgery Yale U.-New Haven Hosp., residency in psychiatry; fellowship in child and adolescent psychiatry NY Hosp., Westchester Divsn.; pvt. practice psychiatrist NYC; tng. dir. child and adolescent psychiatry Mt. Sinai Med. Ctr., NYC, adj. asst. clin. prof. psychiatry & pediat.; lectr. in child psychiatry NYU, NYC; lectr. in psychiatry Columbia U., NYC. Contbr. articles to profl. jours. Mem.: Assn. Psychoanalytic Medicine (pres. 2011—). Office: 41 Union Sq W Rm 402 New York NY 10003 Office Phone: 212-462-2389. Business E-Mail: hps@verizon.net. *

SCHWARTZ, HOWARD ALAN, periodontist; b. Paterson, NJ, Dec. 27, 1944; s. Samuel and Ruth (Dimond) S.; m. Rita Blumenthal, Dec. 29, 1968 (dec. Sept. 2000); children: Andrew David Schwartz, Steven Austin Schwartz. BS, Fairleigh Dickinson U., 1967, DDS, 1970; cert. in periodontology, Georgetown U., 1972. Lic. dentist, N.J., N.Y., Mass., Pa., Md., Washington. Clin. instr. in periodontics Georgetown U., 1970-72; chief resident periodontal sect. dept. dentistry VA Hosp., Washington, 1972; asst. prof. periodontics and oral medicine Fairleigh Dickinson U. Sch. Dentistry, Hackensack, NJ, 1972-73, part time clin. asst. prof. periodontics and oral medicine, 1973-79, part time clin. assoc. prof. periodontics and oral medicine, 1979-87, part time clin. prof. periodontics and oral medicine, 1987-89; pvt. practice periodontics and oral medicine, 1972—. Author: (with W.A. Gibson) Immunofluorescent Demonstration of IgG, IgM, and IgA in Human Dental Plaque, (with others) Histochemical Localization of Selected Dehydrogenases in Frozen Sections of Human Dental Plaque, (with others) Salvary Composition as related to Dental Calculus Formation in Humans. Mem. dentists divsn. com., Hon. Cabinet, United Jewish Cmty. of Bergen County, 1984-85. Fellow Am. Coll. Dentists, Internat. Coll. Dentists. Fellow Acad. Dentistry Internat.; mem. ADA, Am. Acad. Periodontology, N.J. Dental Assn. (trustee, treas. 1994-96, v.p. 1996-97, pres.-elect 1997-98, pres. 1998-99), Internat. Assn. Dental Rsch., Northeastern Soc. Periodontists, Am. Acad. Oral Medicine, N.J. Soc. Periodontists (pres. 1978-79), Bergen County Dental Soc. (pres. 1989-90), Am. Coll. Dentists, Internat. Coll. Dentists, Acad. Dentistry Internat., Delta Dental NJ (bd. trustees 2006-). Jewish. Avocations: running, photography, computers. Home: 10 Wood Hollow Trail Saddle River NJ 07458-1346 Office: 97 N Dean St Englewood NJ 07631-2806 Office Phone: 201-567-7766. E-mail: howard@howardschwartz.org.

SCHWARTZ, J. SANFORD, internist, educator; b. Detroit, Mar. 8, 1949; AB, U. Rochester, 1970; MD, U. Pa., 1974. Cert. Nat. Bd. Med. Examiners, 1975, Internal Medicine, 1977. Fellow USPHS, 1972; intern in medicine Hosp. U. Pa., Phila., 1974—75, resident, 1975—77; chief ambulatory health care Phila. VA Med. Ctr., 1977—78; Robert Wood Johnson clin. scholar U. Pa., Phila., 1976—79, prof. medicine, health care mgmt. and economics, 1989—, Robert D. Eilers prof. health care mgmt. and economics, 1989—98, exec. dir. Leonard Davis Inst. Health Economics, 1989—98, Leon Hess prof. internal medicine, 2007; dir. clin. efficiency assessment ACP, 1981—83. Mem.: Inst. Medicine. Office: Blockley Hall Ste 1120 423 Guardian Dr Philadelphia PA 19104-6021 Office Phone: 215-898-3563. E-mail: schwartz@wharton.upenn.edu.

SCHWARTZ, JARED NAPHTALI, Aperio chief medical officer; s. Victor and Ruth Regina Schwartz; m. Diane Gail Herman, Aug. 31, 1969; children: Rachael Leah, Sarah Rebecca Wainberg. BS, Ohio State U., Columbus, 1968, MSc, 1969; MD, Duke U., Durham, 1973, PhD, 1975. Cert. NC Med. Bd., 1974, diplomate Am. Bd. Pathology, 1977, Am. Bd. Pathology, 1984, in cytopathology Am. Bd. Pathology, 1995. Pres. Coll. Am. Pathologists, 2007—09; dir. pathology & lab medicine Presebyterian Healthcare, 1981—2009; cons. prof., dept. pathology Stanford Med. Ctr. Pres. Mecklenburg County Med. Soc., 1987—88; mem. CLIAC, Atlanta, 2003—09. Pres. Leadership Charlotte, Metrolina Lung Assn., Charlotte, NC. Recipient award, Coll. Am. Pathologists. Home: 3429 Wynington Dr Charlotte NC 28226 Office: Presbyterian Pathology Group PLLC 200 Hathorne Ln Charlotte NC 28207 Office Phone: 760-539-1152. Office Fax: 704-384-5770. Personal E-mail: jnsduke@gmail.com. Business E-Mail: Jschwartz@aperio.com, jnschwartz@stanford.edu.

SCHWARTZ, JUDY ELLEN, thoracic surgeon; b. Mason City, Iowa, Oct. 5, 1946; d. Walter Carl and Alice Nevada (Moore) Schwartz. BS, U. Iowa, Iowa City, 1968, MD, 1971; MPH, Johns Hopkins U., Balt., 1996. Diplomate Am. Bd. Surgery, Am. Bd. Thoracic Surgery, Am. Bd. Med. Mgmt., cert. physician exec. Cert. Commn. Med. Mgt. Intern Nat. Naval Med. Ctr., Bethesda, Md., 1971-72, gen. surgery resident, 1972-76, thoracic surgery resident, 1976-78, staff cardiothoracic surgeon, 1979-82, chief cardiothoracic surgeon, 1982-83; chmn. cardiothoracic surg. dept. Naval Hosp., San Diego, 1983-85, quality assurance program dir., 1985-88. Exec. office Rapidly Deployable Med. Facility Four, 1986—88; asst. prof. surgery Uniformed Svcs. U. Health Sci., Bethesda, 1983—99; sr. policy analyst quality assurance Profl. Affairs and Quality Assurance, 1988—90, dep. dir. quality assurance, 1990; dir. clin. policy Health Svcs. Ops., Washington, 1990—94; head performance evaluation and improvement Nat. Naval Med. Ctr., 1994—99; cardiothoracic splty. cons. to naval med. command USN, Washington, 1983—84; Dept. Def. rep. to task force info. mgmt. Joint Commn. Accreditation Health Care Orgn., 1990—93, chmn., 1991—93, mem. task force IMS Tech., 1993—94; chmn. info. mgmt. workshop Fed. Health Care Study Commn.'s Coord. Fed. Health Care, 1993; corp. med. dir. Medcenter One Health Sys., 1999—2002, trustee, 1999—2003; corp. med. dir. ND Dept. Corrections & Rehab., 1990—2002; v.p. med. affairs Medcenter One, 2002; v.p. Surg. Svc. and Electronic Med. Records Informatics, 2003—05, Surg. Svc., 2005—06; bd. dirs. SCCI; mem. adv. com. Blue Cross Blue Shield Care Mgmt., 1999—2002, v.p. med. affairs, 2002; chmn. rsch. and bioethics com. Instnl. Rev. Bd., 2000—06; mem. exec. adv. bd. Surg. Info. Sys., 2005—08; examiner Nat. Baldridge award, 2006—09; v.p. med. affairs Knox Cmty. Hosp., 2007—. Contbr. articles to various publs. Mem. nat. physician's leadership coun. VHA, 2000—02; trustee St. Vincent's Nursing Home, 2001—05. Capt. USN, 1969—99, ret. USN, 1999. Decorated Legion of Merit, Commendation Medal Navy and Marine Corps, Meritorious Unit Commendation. Fellow: ACS (mem. com. allied health pers. 1985—91, mem. exec. com. 1987—91, mem. accreditation rev. com. edn. physician asst. 1988—94, treas. accreditation rev. com. 1991—93, sr. mem. com. allied health pers. 1991—94), Am. Coll. Cardiology; mem.: AMA, Am. Coll. Physician Execs., Am. Mgmt. Assn., Am. Med. Women's Assn., Am. Thoracic Soc.

SCHWARTZ, LINDEN MATTHEW, physiatrist; MD, NJ Med. Sch. Lic. Pa., 1988, diplomate Am. Bd. Physical Medicine and Rehab.-pain medicine, Am. Bd. Physical Medicine and Rehab., Am. Bd. Medical Specialties. Intern Overlook hosp. Columbia Univ., 1988; resident Pa. Hosp., 1989, Thomas Jefferson Univ. Hosp., 1991; physician Chestnut Hill Hosp. Office: Chestnut Hill Hospital Hill 8601 Stenton Ave Glenside PA 19038 Office Phone: 215-233-6226. Office Fax: 215-233-6380.

SCHWARTZ, LOUIS WINN, ophthalmologist; b. Pa., Apr. 19, 1942; s. Edward and Sylvia Beatrice (Winn) Schwartz; m. Linda Weinberg, June 14, 1964; children: Joanne Karen, Geoffrey Paul. AB, Bowdoin Coll., 1963; MD, Jefferson Med. Coll., 1967. Diplomate Am. Bd. Ophthalmology. Intern Phila. Gen. Hosp.-U. Pa., 1967-68; resident in ophthalmology Wills Eye Hosp., Phila., 1970-73; ophthalmologist Ophthalmic Assocs., Lansdale, Pa., 1973—; clin. prof. ophthalmology Jefferson Med. Coll., Phila., 2008—; attending surgeon Glaucoma Svc. Wills Eye Hosp., Phila., 1994—, sec.-treas., 1998-2000, v.p., 2000—02, pres., 2002—04. Chief ophthalmology North Penn Hosp., 1995—2000. Co-author: Laser Therapy of Anterior Segment, 1988, 9 other books; assoc. editor: Contact Lens Assn. Ophthalmology Jour., 1988; contbr. articles to profl. jours. Recipient Honor award, Am. Acad. Ophthalmology, 1988. Mem.: InterCounty Ophthalmol. Soc. (pres. 1985—86), Pa. Acad. Ophthalmology, Am. Glaucoma Soc., Ophthalmic Club Phila. (life; pres. 1985—86, honored life mem. 2006). Office: Ophthalmic Assocs 1000 N Broad St Lansdale PA 19446-1138 Office Phone: 215-368-1646. Personal E-mail: oalandsdale@aol.com.

SCHWARTZ, MARSHALL ZANE, pediatric surgeon; b. Mpls., Sept. 1, 1945; s. Sidney Shay and Peggy Belle (Lieberman) S.; m. Michele Carroll Walker, Oct. 16, 1971; children: Lisa, Jeffrey. BS, U. Minn., 1968, MD, 1970. Diplomate Am. Bd. Surgery, Am. Bd. Pediatric Surgery. Intern NY Hosp., NYC, 1970—71; resident gen. surgery U. Minn., Mpls., 1971—73, 1975—76, rsch. fellow, 1974—75; jr. resident in pediat. surgery Children's Hosp. Med. Ctr., Harvard Med. Sch., 1973—74, sr. resident in pediat. surgery, 1976—77, chief resident in pediat. surgery, 1977—78; instr. Med. Sch. Harvard U., Boston, 1978—79; asst. surgery Children's Hosp. Med. Ctr., Boston, 1978—79; asst. prof. Med. Br. U. Tex., Galveston, 1979—81, assoc. prof., 1981—83, chief. pediat. surgery, 1980—83; assoc. prof. U. Calif., Davis, 1983—86, prof., 1986—92, chief pediat. surgery, 1983—92, vice chmn. faculty Sch. Medicine, 1990—91, chmn. faculty Sch. Medicine, 1991—92; prof. surgery and pediat. George Washington Sch. Medicine, 1992—96; surgeon-in-chief, chmn. dept. surgery Children's Nat. Med. Ctr., Washington, 1992—96; assoc. med. dir. Dupont Hosp. for Children, Wilmington, Del., 1996—2001, vice chmn. dept. surgery, 1996—2003; prof. surgery and pediat. Thomas Jefferson U., 1996—, vice chmn. dept. surgery, 1996—2003; sr. scholar Sch. Health Policy Thomas Jefferson U., 2005—; mem. staff St. Christopher Hosp. for Children, Phila., 2004—06, surgeon-in-chief, chief divsn. pediat. surgery, 2006—; prof. surgery and pediat. Drexel U. Sch. Medicine, Phila., 2004—; bd. dirs. Phila. Acad. Surgery, 2005—08; prof. surgery Temple U., 2008—; mem. surgery residency review com. ACGME, 2009—; mem. bd. regent ACS. Bd. dirs. Am. Bd. Surgery, 2003—09, chmn. pediat. surgery bd., 2006—09; bd. dirs. Am. Coll. Surgeon Health Policy Inst., 2008—. Mem. editl. bd. Jour. Pediat. Surgery, 1988—, Jour. ACS, 1999—. Vice chmn. Bd. of Childrens Faculty Assocs., Childrens Nat. Med. Ctr.; bd. dir. Am. Pediat. Surg. Assn., 2001—04; pres. bd. dir. Sacramento Children's Hosp. Found., 1990—92; chmn. bd. dir. Delaware Valley Transplant Program, 2000—02; bd. dirs. Gift of Life, 2005—, chmn. Med. Adv. Bd., 2009—11; bd. dirs. St. Christophers Hosp. Children, 2007—, St. Christophers Found. Children, 2007—. Recipient Basil O'Connor Rsch. award March of Dimes Found., 1981, Young Investigator award NIH, 1982, Found. for Children Rsch. award, 1982, James W. McLaughlin award U. Tex., 1983, ASPEN-Rhodes Rsch. award, 1999, Rsch. award Am. Colon and Rectal Surg. Assn., 2000. Fellow: ACS (chmn. adv. coun. pediat. surgery 2004—08, chmn. adv. coun. chairs 2005—08, mem., bd. regents 2009—); mem.: Internat. Soc. Surgery (exec. com. 2004—07), Pacific Assn. Pediat. Surgeons (pres. 1997—98), Soc. Surgery Alimentary Tract, Am. Pediat. Surg. Assn. (bd. govs. 2001—04, pres. elect 2009—, pres. 2010—11, immediate past pres. 2011—), Soc. Univ. Surgeons, Am. Surg. Assn. (prog. com. 2007—09, chmn. 2008—09). Jewish. Avocations: photography, fishing, woodworking. Office: St Christopher Hosp for Children Erie Ave at Front St Philadelphia PA 19134 Office Phone: 215-427-5446. Personal E-mail: mzschwartz@msn.com. Business E-Mail: marshall.schwartz@tenethealth.com.

SCHWARTZ, MICHAEL L., plastic surgeon; Attended, Columbia U.; MD, Baylor Coll. of Medicine, Houston, Tex. Diplomate Am. Bd. of Facial Plastic & Reconstructive Surgery, Am. Bd. of Otolaryngology. Internship in gen. surgery Beth Israel Med. Ctr.; resident in otolaryngology, facial plastic surgery Columbia Presbyn. Med. Ctr.; fellow Am. Coll. of Surgeons; hosp. affiliations include Good Samaritan Hosp., St. Mary's Hosp. Office: Michael L. Schwartz MD Ste 7600 1411 North Flager Dr. West Palm Beach FL 33401 Office Phone: 561-829-5212.

SCHWARTZ, MICHAEL ROBINSON, management consultant; b. St. Louis, Mar. 18, 1940; s. Henry G. and Edith C. (Robinson) Schwartz; m. Kathleen Nowicki, Dec. 9, 1989; children from previous marriage: Christine, Richard. AB, Dartmouth Coll., 1962; MHA, U. Minn., 1964. Asst. in adminstrn. Shands Tchg. Hosp., Gainesville, Fla., 1966-67, asst. dir., 1967-68, assoc. dir., 1968-73; assoc. adminstr. St. Joseph Mercy Hosp., Pontiac, Mich., 1973-76, pres., 1976-85; exec. v.p. Mercy Health Svcs., Farmington Hills, Mich., 1985-96, COO, 1988-96; exec. v.p. Ea. Mich. region Sisters of Mercy Health Corp., 1991-92; pvt. practice Birmingham, Mich., 1996—2004, 2007—; dir. provider rels. Blue Cross Blue Shield of Mich., 2003—04, v.p. contracting, 2004—05, sr. v.p. network rels. contracting, pharmacy Mich., 2005—07. Non-resident lectr. U. Mich., 1982—93; cons. prof. Oakland U., 1980—88; asst. prof. hosp. adminstrn. U. Fla., 1967—73; pres. Eastern Mich. Regional Bd. Sisters of Mercy Health Corp., 1976—79; v.p. Lourdes Nursing Home, 1981—84, United Way-Pontiac/North Oakland, 1982—84; treas. Oakland Health Edn. Program, 1978—79; bd. dirs. Blue Cross/Blue Shield of Mich., 1982—86, coms., 1978—86, chair hosp. contingent to participating hosp. agreement adv. com., 1989—96; bd. dirs. Vis. Nurse Assn., Inc., 1997—2005, treas., 1998—2004, vice chair, 1999—2000, chair, 2000—02; chmn. bd. dirs., pres. Accord Ins. Co. Ltd., 1983—88; chmn. bd. dirs. Mercy Health Plans, 1986—96, Venzke Svc. Co., 1983—88, pres., 1983—84; chmn. bd. dirs., pres. Venzke Ins. Co. Ltd., 1988—96; mem. audit and fin. com. Am. Healthcare Sys., 1988—92; mem. S.E. Mich. Hosp. Coun., chmn. pub. rels. com., 1983—85; mem. Commonfund Healthcare Coun., 1999—2005, U. Detroit Mercy Health Professions Adv. Bd., 2002—07; trustee Sisters of Mercy Health Corp., 1991—93, sec. bd. trustees, 1993; bd. dirs. Hosp. Fund, 1986—96, Visiting Nurse Svc. Corp., 2007—, DenteMax, 2007—09, vice chair, 2009. Mem. charitable trust Sisters of Mercy, Regional Cmty. Detroit, 1999—2004; bd. mem. Am. Red Cross Southeastern Mich. Blood Region, 2008—; adv. bd. mem. Global Health Svcs. Network, 2008—. With US Army, 1964—66. Fellow: Am. Coll. Healthcare Execs. (life; mem. exec. com. higher edn. 1990—93, Mich. Regent's award 1992); mem.: Comprehensive Health Planning Coun. (com. mem. 1976—81), Am. Healthcare Sys. Risk Retention Group (bd. dirs. 1990—91), Mich. Hosp. Assn. (at-large rep. corp. bd. 1990—96, exec. com. 1992—96), Pontiac Urban League (pers. com. 1979). Office Phone: 313-378-8400. Business E-Mail: mschwartzbham@aol.com.

SCHWARTZ, MILES JOSEPH, retired cardiologist; b. Richmond, Va., Aug. 7, 1925; s. Hugo and Ella ((Kramer)) Schwartz; m. Margery Baer Schwartz, June 7, 1956 (div. 1972); children: Elizabeth, James, Margaret; m. Katherine Rush, May 26, 1980. BS, Queens Coll., NYC, 1947; MD, N.Y. Univ., 1951. Diplomate Am. Bd. Internal Medicine, Am. Bd. Cardiovasc. Disease. Interne Mt. Sinai Hosp., NYC, 1951-52; resident Bronx VA Hosp., NY, 1952-53, Mt. Sinai Hosp., NYC, 1953-54; fellow Bronx VA Hosp., NY, 1954—55, asst. med. sect. chief, 1956-58; resident, to chief resident St. Luke's Hosp. Ctr., NYC, 1955-56, asst. attending physician to assoc. cardiologist, 1959-69, chief hypertension clinic, 1959-81, dir. clin. cardiology tng. program, 1966—97, attending physician, 1970-98, clin. dir. pvt. med. svc., 1974-78, assoc. dir. medicine, 1978-84, assoc. dir. cardiology divsn., 1987—97; acting dir. cardiology divsn. St. Luke's Roosevelt Hosp., NYC, 1995—96; pres. Williamsburg Healthcare Consortium, 2001—03; ret., 2003. Cons. Sharon (Conn.) Hosp., 1976—91; prof. emeritus clin. med. Columbia U., Physicians and Surgeons, NYC, 1998; mem. animal, human instl. rev. bds. Coll. of William and Mary, Williamsburg, Va., 2003—07. Served in USNR, 1944—46. Fellow: ACP, Am. Heart Assn., Am. Coll. Cardiology; mem.: Phi Beta Kappa, Alpha Omega Alpha. Jewish. Avocations: travel, history. Home: 26 Stratford Ridge Mashpee MA 02649 Personal E-mail: mjs64berry@gmail.com. *

SCHWARTZ, NEENA BETTY, endocrinologist, educator; b. Balt., Dec. 10, 1926; d. Paul Howard and Pauline (Shulman) S. AB, Goucher Coll., 1948, DSc (hon.), 1982; MS, Northwestern U., 1950, PhD, 1953. From instr. to prof. U. Ill. Coll. Medicine, Chgo., 1953—72, asst. dean for faculty, 1968—70; prof. physiology Northwestern U. Med. Sch., Chgo., 1973—74; Deering prof. Northwestern U., Evanston, Ill., 1974—99, chmn. dept. biol. scis., 1974-78, acting dean, Coll. Arts and Scis., 1996-97, prof. emeritus, 2000—. Contbr. articles to profl. jours., chapters to books. NIH rsch. grantee, 1955—. Fellow: AAAS (exec. bd. 1998—2002, Lifetime Mentor award 2003); mem.: Soc. for Neurosci., Am. Physiol. Soc., Soc. for Study of Reproduction (dir. 1975—77, exec. v.p. 1976—77, pres. 1977—78, Carl Hartman award 1992), Endocrine Soc. (v.p. 1970—71, mem. coun. 1979—83, pres. 1982—83, Williams award 1985, Disting. Educator award 1998), Am. Acad. Arts and Scis. Home: 1511 Lincoln St Evanston IL 60201-2338 Office Phone: 847-491-5529. Business E-Mail: n-schwartz@northwestern.edu.

SCHWARTZ, PETER EDWARD, physician, medical educator; b. NYC, Mar. 28, 1941; s. Bernard and Marcia (Firkser) S.; m. Arlene Harriet Eigen, Aug. 13, 1966; children: Bruce, Andrew, Kenneth. BS, Union Coll., Schenectady, NY, 1962; MD, Yeshiva U., NYC, 1966; MA (hon.), Yale U., 1985. Diplomate Am. Bd. Ob-Gyn., Am. Bd. Gynecol. Oncology. Surg. intern U. Ky. Med. Ctr., Lexington, 1966-67; resident in ob-gyn. Yale-New Haven Hosp., 1967-71; fellow in gynecol. oncology U. Tex. M.D. Anderson Hosp., Houston, 1973-75; asst. prof. Yale U. Sch. Medicine, New Haven, 1975-80, assoc. prof., 1980-85, prof., 1985—, now vice chmn. dept. ob-gyn., 1992—. Maj. USAF, 1971-73. John Slade Ely Prof. of obstetrics and gynecology at Yale U. (hon. chair). Home Phone: 203-795-6813; Office Phone: 203-785-4014. Business E-Mail: peter.schwartz@yale.edu.

SCHWARTZ, RICHARD HARVEY, pediatrician; b. Bklyn., July 6, 1938; s. Hy and Ruth (Marshak) S.; m. Rose Lynne Hass, May 29, 1960; children: Lisa, Keith, Keira. BA, George Washington U., 1960; MD, Georgetown U., 1965. Diplomate Am. Bd. Pediat., Am. Soc. Addiction Medicine. Intern U.S. Army, 1965-66, resident in pediat., 1969-71; pvt. practice, Vienna, Va., 1972—. Contbr. more than 300 articles to med. jours. Maj. U.S. Army, 1965-69. Mem. AMA (Outstanding Contbn. in Adolescent Medicine award 1990), Am. Acad. Pediatrics (rsch. award 1989). Jewish. Avocations: walking, travel. Office: Advanced Pediatrics 100 East St SE Ste 301 Vienna VA 22180 Office Phone: 703-938-5555.

SCHWARTZ, ROBERT HENRY, pediatrician, allergist; b. Bklyn., Apr. 20, 1936; s. Emanuel and Rose (Mantel) S.; m. Carol Susan Lauretz, May 18, 1938; children: Rhonda Lynn Schwartz Slovic, Lisa Meredith Schwartz Weiss. AB, Dartmouth Coll., 1957; MD with honors, U. Rochester, NYC, 1962. Diplomate Am. Bd. Pediatrics in pediatric allergy, Am. Bd. Allergy and Immunology. Intern medicine Strong Meml. Hosp., Rochester, 1962-63, resident pediatrics, 1963-64; clin. assoc. NIH, Bethesda, Md., 1964-66; sr. resident Babies Hosp., Columbia-Presbyn. Med. Ctr., NYC, 1966-67; fellow allergy U. Rochester, 1967-69, asst. prof. pediatrics, 1969-73, assoc. prof., 1973-78, prof., 1978—. Dir. Cystic Fibrosis Ctr., Strong Meml. Hosp.,

Rochester, 1967-85, dir. allergy tng. program, 1970-85, dir. pediatric allergy clinic, 1970-85, dir. pediatric clin. allergy, 1991—; dir. Allergy Asthma Immunology of Rochester, 1985—; dir. Am. Bd. Allergy and Immunology, 1978-83, pres., 1983. Sr. editor Pediatric Asthma Allergy and Immunology, 1992—. Pres. Allergy and Asthma Rochester Resource Ctr., 1995—. Lt. comdr. USPHS, 1964-66. Recipient McCurdy-Stornont award Monroe County Med. Soc. Fellow Am. Acad. Allergy Asthma and Immunology, Am. Assn. Cert. Allergists; mem. Soc. Pediatric Rsch., Am. Pediatric Soc., Phi Beta Kappa. Republican. Jewish. Avocation: photography. Home: PO Box 1429 Cannon Beach OR 97110-1429 *

SCHWARTZ, ROBERT PAUL, pediatric endocrinologist; b. Lakeland, Fla., Sept. 29, 1941; s. Sydney and Edythe (Racz) Schwartz; m. Rebecca Chambers, Apr. 29, 1965; children: Sharon, Michael. BS, U. Fla., 1964, MD, 1968. Diplomate Am. Bd. Pediat. Intern, resident Charlotte Meml. Hosp., NC, 1968-70; fellowship pediat. endocrinology Duke U. Med. Ctr., Durham, NC, 1970-71, 73-74; asst. chmn. dept. pediat. Carolinas Med. Ctr., Charlotte, 1974-92; prof., chief pediat. endocrinology Wake Forest U. Sch. Medicine, Winston-Salem, NC, 1992—. Mem. editl. bd.: Jour. Pediatrics, 1996—2003; contbr. articles to profl. jours. Mem.: Pediat. Academic Soc., Lawson Wilkins Pediat. Endocrine Soc., Am. Diabetes Assn., NC Pediat. Soc. (pres. 1987—89), Am. Bd. Pediat., Am. Acad. Pediat. (chair endocrine sect. 1996—99). Office: Wake Forest U Sch Medicine Med Ctr Blvd Winston Salem NC 27157-0001 Office Phone: 336-716-3199. Office Fax: 336-716-9229. Business E-Mail: rschwrtz@wfubmc.edu.

SCHWARTZ, ROBERT S., geriatrician, educator; MD, Ohio State U., 1974. Diplomate Am. Bd. Internal Medicine, 1977, Am. Bd. Internal Medicine-endocrinology, 1981, Am. Bd. Internal Medicine-geriatric medicine, 2000. Resident internal medicine Univ. Washington Med. Ctr., 1975—77, fellow endocrinology, diabetes, metabolism nutrition & gerontology, 1977—80; hosp. affiliations include: Univ. Colo. Hosp., Veterans Affairs Eastern Colo.Health Care System; Goodstein prof. medicine Univ. Colo., head divsn. geriatric medicine. Office: University of Colorado Hospital PO Box 6511 12401 E 17th Ave Aurora CO 80045 Office Phone: 720-848-0000. E-mail: robert.schwartz@ucdenver.edu.

SCHWARTZ, STANLEY S., endocrinologist, educator; BA, U. Pa., 1969; MD, U. Chgo., 1973. Cert. Nat. Bd. Med. Examiners, 1974, diplomate Am. Bd. Internal Medicine, 1976, Am. Bd. Internal Medicine-endocrine and metabolism, 1979. Intern Univ. of Pa., 1973—74; resident Hosp. of the Univ. of Pa., 1974—76; fellow Univ. of Chgo., 1976—78; assoc. prof. Univ. of Pa. Co-author: (publs.) Diabetic Glycemic Control and Retinal Blood Flow, 1990, Erectile Dysfunction in Diabetes, 1991; author: Synergy in diabetes treatment, 2008, Nutrition and Diabetes, 1999, numerous publs. Office: Philadelphia Heart Institute Penn- Presbyterian Hospital Suite 28 Philadelphia PA 19104

SCHWARTZ, STEPHEN GREGORY, ophthalmologist; b. Queens, NY, Nov. 28, 1969; s. Charles F. and Patricia Schwartz; m. Melanie Rebak, June 15, 1996; children: Jessica Hope, Reid Alexander, Oliver Mason. BS with honors, Cornell U., Ithaca, NY, 1991; MD, NYU, NYC, 1995; MBA, J.L. Kellogg Sch. Mgmt., Evanston, Ill., 2008. Diplomate Am. Bd. Ophthalmology. Intern Lenox Hill Hosp., NYC, 1995—96; resident NYU Sch. Medicine, NYC, 1996—99; fellow Baylor Coll. Medicine, Houston, 1999—2001; asst. prof. ophthalmology Va. Commonwealth U. Sch. Medicine, Richmond, 2001—04, program dir. ophthalmology, 2002—04; asst. prof. clin. ophthalmology U. Miami (Fla.) Miller Sch. Medicine, 2004—09, assoc. prof. clin. ophthalmology, 2009—; med. dir. Bascom Palmer Eye Inst. Naples, Fla., 2004—. Bd. govs. Prevent Blindness Fla., Tampa, 2006—; bd. dirs. Va. Voice for Print Handicapped, Inc., Richmond, 2002—04. Grantee Investigator award, Prevent Blindness Am., 2005; Nat. Glaucoma Rsch. grantee, Am. Health Assistance Found., 2003. Fellow: Am. Acad. Ophthalmology (Achievement award 2006); mem.: AMA, Collier County Med. Soc., Fla. Soc. Ophthalmology (bd. dirs. 2006—, pres. 2010—, Outstanding Young Ophthalmologist Leadership award 2006), Fla. Med. Assn., Assn. Rsch. in Vision and Ophthalmology (members in tng. com. 2003—06), Am. Soc. Retina Specialists. Office: Bascom Palmer Eye Inst 311 9th St N # 100 Naples FL 34102 Office Phone: 239-659-3937. Office Fax: 239-659-3982. Business E-Mail: sschwartz2@med.miami.edu.

SCHWARTZ, STEVE WENDELIN, physician; b. Bethesda, Md., May 16, 1955; s. Wallace John and Gwynne June (Lingenfelter) S. AB in Chemistry summa cum laude, Duke U., 1977, MD, 1981. Diplomate Am. Bd. Family Practice. Rotating intern Med. U. S.C., Charleston, 1981-82, resident in family practice, 1982-84; emergency rm. physician Coastal Emergency Svc., 1985-86; family physician Carolina Health Care, Myrtle Beach, SC, 1984—; CEO Cactus Internat., Inc. Data processing dir. HMI, 1984—; pres. Flu Trends Internat., 2006-10, Unitrends Software Corp., 1989-2003, chief tech officer, 2004-05; rschr. Symbol Theory; programmer langs. Columnist SCO World Mag.; contbr. articles to profl. jours. Del. ann. meeting N.C. Med. Soc., 1980; participant Intramural Soccer, 1977-80; mem. Intramural Track, 1980, Blacknall Meml. Presbyn. Ch., 1977-80; coord. Boy Scouts Phys. Exam. Program, 1983; vol. cmty. health care project for poor East End Cmty. Health Ctr.; tchr. seminars on alcoholism for drug edn. project Holistic Medicine Group, 1980; Bible study coord. Valley of Achor. With USAF. 1973-75. First Place Durham Open Chess Tournament, 1974; recipient Grand Strand Leadership, 1986. Fellow Am. Acad. Family Physicians; mem. AMA (Physicians Recognition award 1986), So. Med. Assn., Horry County Med. Soc., Phi Beta Kappa, Upsilon Pi Epsilon. Achievements include patents for flu nose and throat spray to treat all. Avocations: chess, soccer. Office: Carolina Health Care 4605 Hwy 17 Byp S Myrtle Beach SC 29577-6681 Personal E-mail: steves@sc.rr.com.

SCHWARTZ, THEODORE H., neurosurgeon, medical educator; BS, Havard U., 1987, MD magna cum laude, 1993. Resident, chief resident neurosurgery Neurological Inst. of NY Columbia-Presbyn. Med. Ctr.; fellowship Yale-New Haven Med. Ctr.; dir. brain tumor surgery, attending neurological surgeon NY-Presbyn. Hosp., NYC, 2001—; prof. neurological surgery Weill Cornell Med. Coll., prof. neurological surgery in otorhinolaryngology. Dir. inst. minimally invasive skull base and pituitary surgery NY Presbyn. Hosp. Office: New York Presbyterian Hospital 525 East 68th St Box #99 New York NY 10021 Office Fax: 212-746-2004. Personal E-mail: schwarh@med.cornell.edu.

SCHWARTZ, WILLIAM J., cardiologist, educator; MD, Albert Einstein Coll. Medicine, 1975. Diplomate Am. Bd. Cardiology-cardiovascular disease, Am. Bd. Internal Medicine. Resident in internal medicine Bronx Mcpl. Hosp., NY, 1976—79, fellow in cardiovascular disease, 1978—79; fellow in cardiac catheterization NYU Med. Ctr.; with Lenox Hill Hosp.; asst. prof. medicine, cardiology Mt. Sinai Sch. Medicine, cardiologist. Office: Mount Sinai School Medicine 31-41 45th St Astoria NY 11103 Office Phone: 718-721-1500. Office Fax: 718-777-1623.

SCHWARTZBERG, ALLAN ZELIG, psychiatrist, educator; b. Cleve., Dec. 5, 1930; s. Joseph and Jeanette (Eisenman) S.; m. Katherine Weiss, June 19, 1955; children: Shana, Robert. BS cum laude, Case Western Res. U., 1951; MD, Ohio State U., 1955. Diplomate Am. Bd. Psychiatry and Neurology, Am. Bd. Forensic Medicine. Intern, resident in psychiatry Johns Hopkins Hosp., Balt., 1955—59; pvt. practice Gaithersburg, Md.; assoc. clin. prof. psychiatry Georgetown U. Sch. Medicine, Washington, 1979—89, clin. prof., 1989—. Vis. prof. faculty seminar in cmty. psychiatry Harvard U. Med. Sch., Boston, 1965-67; cons. Dept. Energy, 2002-. Editor-in-chief Internat. Annals Adolescent Psychiatry, 1988—2000; co-editor Adolescent Psychiatry, Vols. 8-19; contbr. articles to med. jours. Recipient Vicennial medal Georgetown U., 1984. Fellow AMA, Am. Psychiat. Assn. (disting. life), Am. Soc. for Adolescent Psychiatry, Am. Soc. Psychoanalytic Physicians (pres. 1986-87, 2000-01), Am. Coll. Psychiatrists; mem. Am. Group Psychotherapy Assn., B'nai B'rith, Phi Beta Kappa. Republican. Jewish. Home: 6616 Kenhill Rd Bethesda MD 20817-6014 Office: Comprehensive Behavioral Svcs 9021 Shady Grove Ct Gaithersburg MD 20877-1308 Office Phone: 301-590-9000. Personal E-mail: azsmd@aol.com.

SCHWARTZBERG, JOANNE GILBERT, physician; b. Boston, Nov. 30, 1933; d. Richard Vincent and Emma (Cohen) Gilbert; m. Hugh Joel Schwartzberg, July 7, 1956; children: Steven Jonathan, Susan Jennifer. BA magna cum laude, Radcliffe Coll., 1955; MD, Northwestern U., 1960. Diplomate Am. Bd. Quality Assurance and Utilization Rev. Physicians. Founder, med. dir. Chgo. Home Health Svc., 1972—95; founder, v.p., med. dir. Suburban Home Health Svc., Chgo. area, 1975—87; clin. asst. prof. preventive medicine and cmty. health U. Ill. Coll. Medicine, 1985—. Dir. Aging and Cmty. Health AMA, 1990—; pres. Inst. Medicine of Chgo., 1994—95, bd. dirs., 1990—2000, 2005—; co-chair Ill. Health and Social Svc. Caucus to the White House Conf. on Aging, 1995; presdl. appointee to adv. com. White Ho. Conf. on Aging, 2005. Contbr. articles to profl. jours. Pres. Near North Montessori Sch., Chgo., 1972—75, bd. dirs., 1970—83. Recipient Mayor's citation, City of Chgo., 1963, Physician of Year award, Nat. Assn. Home Care, 1988, Henry P. Russe Exemplary Compassion in Medicine citation, Inst. Medicine Chgo. & The Rush Presbyn. St. Luke's Med. Ctr., 2001. Mem.: Alexander Graham Bell Assn. for Deaf (bd. dirs. 1984—90, gen. chmn. internat. conv. 1986, chmn. internat. parents orgn. 1988—90), Am. Geriat. Soc, Chgo. Med. Soc., Ill. Med. Soc., Ill. Geriat. Soc. (pres. 1990—92), Am. Coll. Med. Quality, Am. Acad. of Home Care Physicians (founding bd. dirs. 1987—, pres. 1992—94, Physician of Yr. 1994). Jewish. Home: 853 W Fullerton Ave Chicago IL 60614-2412 Office: 515 N State St Chicago IL 60610-4325 *

SCHWARTZ-GIBLIN, SUSAN TOBY, neuroscientist, educator, dean emeritus; b. NYC, Dec. 27, 1938; d. David Jack and Anne Lila (Garfinkle) S.; m. Denis Richard Giblin, Sept. 9, 1966 (dec.); children: Vanessa Elizabeth Giblin Bibby, Timothy Norris Giblin. BA in Zoology, Columbia U., 1959; PhD in Physiology, Albert Einstein Coll. Medicine, 1965. NATO postdoctoral fellow McGill U., Montreal, Can., 1965-66; instr. exptl. psychiatry NYU Med. Ctr., NYC, 1966-75, head neurophysiology lab., 1966-72; adj. asst. prof. CUNY, 1975-78; guest investigator Rockefeller U., NYC, 1978-81, asst. prof. neurobiology and behavior, 1981-87, assoc. prof. neurobiology and behavior, 1987-93; prof. physiology, dean grad. sch. Med. Coll. Pa., Hahnemann U. (now Drexel U. Med. Sch.), Phila., 1993—97; dean, sch. grad. studies, prof. neurology SUNY Downstate Med. Ctr., 1997—2008; developer joint PhD biomedical engring. program SUNY Downstate Med. Ctr., Polytechnic U., 2004—. Lectr. in field. Reviewer jours.; contbr. numerous articles to peer-reviewed profl. jours. Recipient: Citation Classic Current Contents Jour., 1981; Mark S. Cohen fellow, 1982-85, Philip Femano fellow, 1982-86, Sandra Cottingham fellow, 1983-86, Ann Robbins Sakai fellow, 1986-90, Margaret M. McCarthy fellow, 1989-92, David Holtzman fellow, 1990-92; grantee USPHS, 1968-71, 81-87, 91-95, Whitehall Found., 1990-92. Mem. AAAS, Internat. Brain Rsch. Orgn., Soc. Neurosci., Sigma Xi. Office: SUNY Downstate Medical Ctr Sch Graduate Studies 450 Clarkson Ave Box 41 Brooklyn NY 11203 Office Phone: 212-861-5478, 718-270-2740. Office Fax: 718-270-3378. Business E-Mail: susan.schwartz-giblin@downstate.edu.

SCHWARTZMAN, SERGIO, rheumatologist, educator; MD, Mt. Sinai Sch. Med., 1982. Lic. NY, diplomate Am. Bd. Internal Medicine, 1985, Am. Bd. Internal Medicine-rheumatology. Resident internal medicine LI Jewish Med. Ctr., 1983—85; fellow rheumatology Hosp. Spl. Surgery, 1985—87, assoc. attending physician; assoc. prof. medicine Weill Cornell Med. Coll. Contbr. articles Uveitis and Other Eye Conditions in Rheumatology Patients, Eye Problems in Lupus, Rheumatoid Arthritis and Eye Concerns. Named one of Best Doctors in NY, NY Mag., 2011. Office: Hospital for Special Surgery 7th Fl 535 E 70th St New York NY 10021-4892 Office Phone: 212-606-1557. Office Fax: 212-794-2527.

SCHWARZ, BERTHOLD ERIC, psychiatrist; b. Jersey City, Oct. 20, 1924; s. Berthold Theodore Dominick and I. Thyra W. (Ericson) Schwarz; m. Ardis Marilyn Peterson, Jan. 22, 1955; children: Lisa Thyra, Eric Rolf. AB, Dartmouth Coll., 1945; MD, NYU, 1950; MS, Mayo Grad. Sch. Medicine, 1957. Intern Mary Hitchcock Meml. Hosp., Hanover, NH, 1950-51; psychiatrist, researcher pvt. practice, Montclair, NJ, 1955-82; Mayo Found., Rochester, Minn., 1951-55; psychiatrist, researcher pvt. practice, Vero Beach, Fla., 1982—2002. Cons. Essex County Hosp. Ctr., Cedar Grove, N.J., 1965-82, Med. Correctional Assn., Ossining, N.Y., 1960-72; exec. dir. Internat. Psychosomatics Inst., Mountain Lakes, N.J., 1995—. Contbr. articles to med. jours. With USNR, 1943-45. Fellow AAAS, Am. Psychiat. Assn., Am. Soc. Psychical Rsch., Am. Geriatric Soc. Republican. Avocations: ufos, parapsychiatry, swimming, walking. Office: 642 Azalea Ln Vero Beach FL 32963-1832 Home: PO Box 644030 Vero Beach FL 32964-4030 Office Phone: 772-231-5220. Personal E-mail: ardisps@aol.com.

SCHWARZ, ERNST RUEDIGER, cardiologist, researcher; s. Ernest Johann Ferdinand and Friedel Elise Schwarz; m. Juana Rocio Angel, Nov. 19, 1999; children: Aubriana d'Iwana Angel, Lujain Vanessa. MD, Philipps U. Marburg, Germany, 1987, U. Vienna, Austria, 1989; PhD, RWTH U. of Tech., Aachen, Germany, 2000. Diplomate in internal medicine German Physicians Chamber, in cardiology German Physicians Chamber, in intensive care medicine German Physicians Chamber. Assoc. prof. RWTH U. Hosp., Aachen, 1998—2000; chmn. cardiology Dr. S. Fakeeh Hosp.-Harvard Med. Internat., Jeddah, Saudi Arabia, 2000—03; prof. medicine U. Tex. Med. Br., Galveston, 2003—06, dir. cardiology clinics, 2005—06; prof. medicine UCLA, 2006—. Co-dir. cardiac transplant Cedars Sinai Med. Ctr., LA, 2006; dir. heart failure and transplantation U. Tex. Med. Br., Galveston, 2003—06, dir. heart failure fellowship program, 2004—06, dir. multidisciplinary clinic for sexual health, 2005—06; spkr. in field. Contbr. articles to profl. jours., chapters to books. Recipient Young Investigator award, Internat. Soc. Nuc. Cardiology, 1995. Fellow: Soc. Coronary Angiography and Interventions, European Soc. Cardiology, Am. Coll. Cardiology; mem.: Saudi Heart Assn., German Cardiac Soc., Heart Failure Soc. Am. Achievements include first to transesophageal echocardiography with IVUS catheters in rodent model; research in intenisve invasive hemodynamic work in myocardial bridges; clinical and morphologic work in hibernating myocardium; evaluation, assessment and treatment of sexual dysfunction in patients with severe cardio-vascular diseases. Office: Cedars Sinai Med Ctr 8700 Beverly Blvd 6215 Los Angeles CA 90048 Office Fax: 310-423-1498.

SCHWARZ, HERMANN KARL, orthopaedic surgeon; b. Wuerselen-Bardenberg, Germany, Sept. 5, 1957; s. Rudi and Hiltrud Schwarz; m. Irmgard Maria Wilhelms, Apr. 16, 1983; children: Irene Maria, Michael Christoph, Sebastian Rudolf, Matthias Walter. Grad., U. Rheinisch-Westfaelische Hochschule, Aachen, Germany, 1978, Rheinische Friedrich-Wilhelms-Univ., Bonn, Germany, 1982; MD, U. Bonn, 1984. Cert. rehab. and phys. therapy specialist Germany, algesiology specialist Germany, pub. health specialist Germany, orthop. lab. medicine specialist Germany, chiropractic specialist Germany, sports medicine specialist Germany. Resident neurol. dept. Knappschafts-Hosp. Bardenberg, Wuerselen, Germany, 1982—83, resident dept. surgery, 1984—86; army dr. Bundeswehr, Euskirchen, Germany, 1983—84; resident, sr. resident dept. orthop. surgery Bethlehem Hosp., Stolberg, Germany, 1987—91; head orthop. dept. Clinic Bad Rippoldsau, Germany, 1991—97; external cons. physician Orthopaedische Praxis, Freudenstadt, Germany, 1997—. Spkr., expert in field, 1984—; cons. clin. quality mgmt. Bundesversicherungsanstalt fuer Angestellte, Berlin, 1993—96; cons., mem. adv. boards several pharm. cos., Germany, 1996—. Co-editor: (med. jour.) Hans-Huber-Verlag. Surgeon maj. Heimatschutzbrigade, 1993—94, Euskirchen. Decorated Ehrenmedaille der Bundeswehr German Fed. Armed Forces; grantee, German Cath. Ch., Cusanuswerk, Bonn, 1978—82. Mem.: VSO, Verband sueddeutscher orthopaeden, IGOST, Internationale gesellschaft fuer orthopaedische schmerztherapie, DGSS, Deutsche gesellschaft zum studium des schmerzes, Berufsverband der Fachaerzt für Orthopaedie, IOF, internat. osteoporosis found. (del. for the orthopaedische gesellschaft fuer osteologie 2004—06), DGO, Deutsche Gesellschaft für Osteologie (bd. mem. 2005—06), DGOOC, Deutsche Gesellschaft für Orthopaedie und orthopaedische Chirurgie (vicechairman of the rsch. group for osteology 2004—06), DVO, Dachverband Osteologie e.V. der deutschsprachigen wissenschaftlichen Gesellschaften (chmn. of the working group for edn. and tng. in osteology 2002—06), DGPMR, Deutsche gesellschaft fuer physikalische medizin und rehab., OGO, Orthopädische Gesellschaft für Osteologie (chmn. 2002—06). Roman Catholic. Avocations: violin, skiing, Nordic walking. Home: Konrad-Schott-Strasse 24 Freudenstadt 72250 Germany Office: Orthopaedische Praxis Lauterbadstrasse 4 Freudenstadt 72250 Germany Office Fax: +49744185212. E-mail: schwarz-freudenstadt@t-online.de.

SCHWARZ, MARKUS J., psychoneuroimmunologist, neurochemist; b. Ingolstadt, Germany, Apr. 16, 1966; s. Georg and Maria (Riemer) Schwarz; divorced; 1 child, Marie Sophie. Diploma in medicine, U. Munich, 1996; MD in Exptl. Psychiatry, Ludwig-Maximilian U., Munich, 1998. Physician Ludwig-Maximilian U., Munich, 1996-97; rsch. asst. dept. neurochemistry Psychiat. Hosp., Munich, 1998—2004, head lab. sect. psychoneuroimmunology and therapeutic drug monitoring, 2004—; habilitation in exptl. psychiatry, 2005. External project ptnr. Expo 2000 Psychoneuroimmunology, Hannover, Germany, 1997—; mem. adv. bd. European Psychiatry, 1999—; mem. expert group therapeutic drug monitoring AGNP; vice chair Found. "Immunity and Soul". With Mountain Inf. German Army, 1986—87. Fellow, Arbeitsgem Neuropsychopharmacology, 1999, World Psychiat. Assn., 1999, 2001, German Soc. Biol. Psychiatry, 2001, 2002. Mem.: World Psychiat. Assn. (sec. sect. immunology and psychiatry, NY, Washington 1999—2009, mem. Ednl. Liaisons Network, fellow 1999, 2001), German Soc. Immunology, European Coll. Neuropsychopharmacology (Poster award, fellow 1999), Am. Psychiat. Assn. Roman Catholic. Achievements include patents in field. Avocations: mountain biking, travel, opera, walking, skiing. Office: U Munich Psychiat Hosp Nussbaumstr 7 D-80336 Munich Germany

SCHWARZ, RICHARD HOWARD, obstetrician, gynecologist, educator; b. Easton, Pa., Jan. 10, 1931; s. Howard Eugene and Blanche Elizabeth (Smith) S.; m. Patricia Marie Lewis, Mar. 11, 1978; children by previous marriage: Martha L., Nancy Schwarz Tedesco, Paul H., Mary Katherine Schwarz Murray. MD, Jefferson Med. Coll., 1955; MA (hon.), U. Pa., 1971. Diplomate Am. Bd. Ob-Gyn. (examiner 1977-95), Divsn. Maternal Fetal Medicine 1974. Intern, then resident Phila. Gen. Hosp., 1955-59; prof. U. Pa., Phila., 1963-78; prof., chmn. Downstate Med. Ctr., Bklyn., 1978-90, dean, v.p. acad. affairs, 1983-89, provost, v.p. clin. affairs, 1988-93, interim pres., 1993-94, prof. ob.-gyn., 1990-96, disting. Svc. prof. ob.-gyn. emeritus, 1996; chmn. ob.-gyn. NY Meth. Hosp., Bklyn., 1996—2002; prof. ob.-gyn. Cornell U. Med. Coll., NYC, 1996—2002; vice chair for clin. svc. dept. Ob/GYN Maimonides Med. Ctr., 2002—; prof. ob-gyn. and reproductive sci. Mt. Sinai Sch. Medicine, NY, 2005—08. Obstetrical cons. March of Dimes Birth Defects Found., 1995-2008. Author: Septic Abortion, 1968. Editor: Handbook of Obstetric Emergencies, 1984, mem. editorial bd. jour. Ob-Gyn., Milw., 1983-87; contbr. over 200 articles to profl. jours. Bd. dirs. March of Dimes, NYC, 1985-95. Capt. USAF, 1959-63. Recipient Career Achievement award, Infectious Disease Soc. Ob-Gyn., 1999, Founder's award, 2004, Wyeth Ayerest Career Achievement award, 2000. Fellow Royal Coll ObGyn (ad eundem), 1999; mem. ACOG (chmn. dist. 2 1984-87, v.p. 1989-90, pres. elect 1990-91, pres. 1991-92, Lifetime Achievement award dist. II 2005). Republican. Presbyterian. Office: Maimonides Med Ctr 967 48th St Brooklyn NY 11219-3645 Business E-Mail: rhsch@optonline.net.

SCHWARZ, RODERICH EGBERT, surgeon, oncologist; b. Braunschweig, Germany, Aug. 18, 1960; came to U.S., 1987; s. Peter and Ilse Schwarz; m. Margaret A. Schwarz, Feb. 26, 1994; children: Anna Magdalena, Johann Richard, Carla, Liesa, Edward. PhD, Med. Sch. Hannover, Germany, 1985, MD, 1984. Diplomate Am. Bd. Surgery. Resident in gen. surgery U. Pitts., 1989-94; rsch. fellow Pitts. Cancer Ctr., 1987-89; fellow in surg. oncology Meml. Sloan-Kettering Cancer Ctr., NYC, 1994-96; attending surgeon City of Hope Nat. Med. Ctr., Duarte, Calif., 1996—2001; prof., surgical oncology U. Tex. Southwestern Med. Ctr., Dallas, 2007—, pancreatic and gastrointestinal cancer specialist; assoc. prof. surg. oncology UMDN Robert Wood Johnson Med. Sch., NB, NJ, 2001—07. Author chpts. to books; contbr. several articles to profl. jours. Recipient Deutsche Forschungsgemeinschaft Internat. Rsch. Tng. award, 1989. Fellow ACS; mem. Am. Assn. for Cancer Rsch., Am. Soc. Clin. Oncology, Soc. Surg. Oncology(award, 1995), Soc. Surgery of the Alimentary Tract, German Surg. Soc., Soc. U. Surgeons. Avocation: music. Office: U Tex Southwestern Medical Ctr at Dallas 5323 Harry Hines Blvd Dallas TX 75390-8548 also: Simmons Comprehensive Cancer Ctr Seay Bldg 2201 Inwood Rd 3rd Fl Dallas TX 75390 Office Phone: 214-648-5865. Office Fax: 214-648-1118. *

SCHWARZBERG, MOSHE NAFTALY, physician, medical educator, b. Tel-Aviv, Israel, Mar. 29, 1954; s. Yehoshua and Sali (Weiss) Schwarzberg. MD, Bologna U., Italy, 1983; diploma in Family Medicine, Tel-Aviv U., 1995. Intern Ichilov Hosp., Tel-Aviv, 1983—84, physician emergency rm., 1984—89; responsible physician in shifts Rabin Med. Ctr., Petach Tikva, Israel, 1990—91, resident, 1992—96; sr. physician Clalit Health Orgn., Tel-Aviv, 1996—. Clin. instr. Tel-Aviv U., 1997—; lectr. Med. Force Israeli Army, 2002—03. Author: Headache, Medical Hypotheses; contbr. articles to profl. jours.; author: The Rights of the Hebrew Israeli Nation in The Land of Israel-Evidence Based Argumentations. Instr. Home Front Commd and Clalit Health Orgn., Tel-Aviv. Recipient Excellent Clinic award, Clalit Health Orgn., Tel-Aviv Dist. Dir., 1998, Quality Clinic award, Clalit Health Orgn. Gen. Dir., 2005. Mem.: Israel Family Practitioners Assn., Israel Med. Assn. Jewish. Avocation: reading. Home: 52100 Ramat Gan Israel Personal E-mail: mswny@netvision.net.il. Business E-Mail: mosheshw@clalit.org.il.

SCHWEBEL, MILTON, psychologist, educator; b. Troy, NY, May 11, 1914; s. Frank and Sarah (Oxenhandler) S.; m. Bernice Lois Davison, Sept. 3, 1939; children: Andrew I., Robert S. AB, Union Coll., 1934; MA, SUNY, Albany, 1936; PhD, Columbia U., NYC, 1949; Cert. in Psychotherapy, Postgrad. Ctr. Mental Health, NYC, 1958; LHD, LHD, Saybrook U., 2010. Lic. psychologist, NY, NJ; diplomate Am. Bd. Examiners Profl. Psychology. Asst. prof. psychology Mohawk Champlain Coll., 1946-49; asst. to prof. edn., dept. chmn., assoc. dean NYU, 1949-67; dean, prof. Grad. Sch. Edn., Rutgers U., New Brunswick, NJ, 1967-77; dean emeritus Grad. Sch. Applied and Profl. Psychology, 1977—, prof., 1977-85, prof. emeritus, 1985—. Vis. prof. U. So. Calif., U. Hawaii; postdoctoral fellow Postgrad. Ctr. Mental Health, NYC, 1954-58, lectr. psychology, 1958-90; cons. NIMH, US, state and city depts. edn., UNESCO, ednl. ministries in Europe, Asia, univs. and pub. schs., UNESCO; pvt. cons. psychologist and psychotherapist, 1953—; disting. cons. & faculty Saybrook Grad. Sch. & Rsch. Ctr., 1999—, adj. rsch. faculty Inst. Transactional Psychology, 2005-. Author: A Guide to a Happier Family, 1989, Personal Adjustment and Growth, 1990, Student Teachers Handbook, 3d edit., 1996, Interests of Pharmacists, 1951, Health Counseling, 1953, Who Can Be Educated?, 1968, Remaking America's Three School System: Now Separate and Unequal, 2003; editor: Mental Health Implications of Life in the Nuclear Age, 1986, Facilitating Cognitive Development, 1986, Promoting Cognitive Growth Over the Life Span, 1990, Behavioral Science and Human Survival, 1965, The Impact of Ideology on the I.Q. Controversy, 1975; editor Peace & Conflict: Jour. Peace Psychology, 1993-2000 (vol. 9, no. 4. named Pioneer in Peace Psychology: Milton Schwebel); co-editor Bull. Peace Psychology, 1991-94; mem. editl. bd. Am. Jour. Orthopsychiatry, Readings in Mental Health, Jour. Contemporary Psychotherapy, Jour. Counseling Psychology, Jour. Social Issues, others. Mem. sci. adv. bd. Internat. Ctr. for Enhancement of Learning Potential, 1988—; trustee Edn. Law Ctr., 1973-81, Nat. Com. Employment Youth, Nat. Child Labor Com., 1967-75, Union Exptl. Colls. and Univs., 1976-78; pres. Nat. Orgn. for Migrant Children, 1980-85; pres. Inst. of Arts and Humanities, 1984-95. Served with AUS, 1943-46, ETO. Recipient Disting. Leader in Edn. award, Grad. Sch. Edn. Rutgers U., 2006; Met. Applied Rsch. Coun. fellow, 1970—71. Fellow APA, Am. Psychol. Soc., Am. Orthopsychiatry Assn., Soc. Psychol. Study Social Issues, Jean Piaget Soc. (trustee), Am. Ednl. Rsch. Assn., NY Acad. Scis., Psychologists for Social Responsibility (pres.), Sigma Xi. Home and Office: 431 S Brighton Ln Tucson AZ 85711 Office Phone: 520-745-1725. Business E-Mail: mschwebe@rci.rutgers.edu. *

SCHWEBIG, ANNICK, pharmaceutical executive; b. Dakar, Sénégal, Aug. 30, 1950; MD, Faculty Medicine, Paris, 1974. V.p. r & d in Europe Bristol-Myers Squibb, 1993—2000; gen. mgr. Actelion Pharm. France, 2000—. Pres. working group rare diseases-orphan drug LEEM-French Pharm. Cos. Assn., v.p. biotech com., sec. alliance rsch. and innovation in health industries. Recipient Chevalier dans l'Ordre Nat. Légion d'Honneur, Health Ministry. Mem.: Paris C. of C. Avocations: opera, golf. Office: 21 Blvd de la Madeleine Paris 75001 France Office Fax: 00 33 1 58 62 32 31. Business E-Mail: paulette.maina@actelion.com.

SCHWEIKERT, EDGAR OSKAR, dentist; b. Heidelberg, Germany, Aug. 30, 1938; arrived in US, 1972; s. Oskar and Priska (Zehr) Schweikert; m. Mary Lou Como Schweikert, Apr. 7, 1969; 1 child, Marisa. Degree, Hamburg Dental Sch., 1966; Dr. Med. in Dentistry, U. Munich, 1969. Lic. dentist Calif. NY dentist US Army, Frankfurt, Germany, 1969—72; gen. practice dentistry LA, 1972—73, Bklyn., 1973—; lectr. in field. Author: Multiple Cantilevers in Fixed Prosthesis, 1988, Spanish edit., 1990; contbr. articles to profl. jours. Served as capt. German Air Force, 1967—69. Mem.: ADA, Guild Dental Craftsmen, Bay Ridge Dental Soc., Second Dist. Dental Assn., German Dental Assn. Home and Office: 429 77th St Brooklyn NY 11209-3205 Office Phone: 718-680-4717.

SCHWEINS, MICHAEL JOSEF, surgeon; b. Kaiserslautern, Germany, July 29, 1958; s. Bernd M. and Josefine (Wallrafen) S.; m. Birgit Maria Dolle, June 19, 1961; children: Julian Benedikt, Moritz Michael, Felix Simon. MD, U. Cologne, Germany, 1984; PhD, U. Cologne. Diplomate in surgery and trauma surgery. Fellow in intensive care U. Cologne, 1984-85, fellow in surgery, 1985-90, surgeon cons., 1990-93; chief, owner Outpatient Clinic for Surgery, Orth. Surgery and Sports Med., Cologne, 1993—, Hernia Ctr. Cologne, 2004—. Author: Sonografie in Surgery, 1988, Hygiene Procedures in German Hospitals, 1993; editor: Hygiene Procedures in Surgery, 1993; contbr. articles to profl. jours. Cpl. Air Def., German Army, 1977-78. Mem. German Soc. Surgery, German Soc. Orthopedic Surgery, Orgn. Ambulatory Surgery (bd. mem.). Roman Catholic. Avocations: skiing, golf, hunting, collecting modern art. Office: Hernia Ctr Cologne Zeppelin St 1 50667 Cologne Germany Office Phone: 0049-221-8026330, 00492212776433. Personal E-mail: michaelschweins@web.de.

SCHWEITZER, PAUL, cardiologist; b. Slovak, Poland, July 3, 1929; MD, Med. Sch. Slovak U., 1953. Jr. assoc. cardiology Peter Bent Brigham Hosp., 1971—72; attending physician medicine Flower and Fifth Ave. Hosp., 1972—73; chief, cardiovasc. lab. Jersey City Med. Ctr., 1973—76; chief, divsn. cardiology VA Med. Ctr., 1976—92; assoc. chief, divsn. cardiology Beth Israel Med. Ctr., 1992—. Prof. Albert Einstein Coll. Medicine, 1994—2011. Recipient Tchg. Excellence award, Med. Svc. Bronx VA Med. Ctr., Simon Dack award, Mt. Sinai Hosp., Solomon Berson Award. Office: Beth Israel Med Ctr First Ave 16th St New York NY 10003 Office Fax: 212-420-4222. Business E-Mail: pschweit@chpnet.org.

SCHWEITZER, VANESSA GAYL, otorhinolaryngologist; b. Pomona, Calif., Jan. 26, 1952; d. Elford J. Nelson and Patricia Wilma (Sherman) Schweitzer. BS in Zoology, U. Mich., 1973; md, 1977. Diplomate Am. Bd. Otolaryngology. Intern in gen. surgery U. Mich., 1977—79, resident in otorhinolaryngology, 1979—83; emergency physician Chelsea Cmty. Hosp., Mich., 1979—83, Saline Cmty. Hosp., Mich., 1979—80, Beyer Meml. Hosp., Ypsilanti, Mich., 1980—83; sr. staff physician dept. otolaryngology, head and neck surgery Henry Ford Hosp., Detroit, 1983—; clin. prof. dept. otolaryngology, head and neck surgery U. Mich., Ann Arbor, 1984—; rschr. Kresge Hearing Inst., Otology Rsch. Lab. Henry Ford Hosp. & U. Mich. Lectr. in field; emergency physician Emergency Physicians' Med. Group, Inc., Ann Arbor, 1979—83; med. examiner Washtenaw County, Ann Arbor, 1980—84. Contbr. articles to med. jours. Recipient Branstrom Freshman award, 1970, Triological Soc Fowler Rsch award; scholar, Angell, 1969—75. Fellow: ACS; mem.: ASCO, AMA, Alpha Lambda Delta, Phi Beta Kappa, Internat. Photodynamic Therapy Assn., Walter P. Work Soc. (Resident Paper Competitive award 1982), Am. Acad. Facial Plastic and Reconstructive Surgery, Am. Acad. Otolaryngology, Am. Coll. Emergency Physicians. Republican. Office: Henry Ford Health Sys 2799 W Grand Blvd Detroit MI 48202-2608 Office Phone: 313-916-3279. Business E-Mail: uschwei1@hfhs.org.

SCHWENK, THOMAS L., dean, physician, educator; b. Kalamazoo, Mich., Oct. 26, 1949; s. Lee G. and Katherine J. Schwenk; m. Jane K. Kindig, Dec. 22, 1970; children: Sarah J., Andrew T. BChE, U. Mich., 1971, MD, 1975. Cert. Am. Bd. Family Medicine, Am. Bd. Sports Medicine. Residency family medicine U. Utah, 1975—78, fellow family medicine, 1980—82; joined as asst. prof. dept. family medicine U. Mich., Ann Arbor, 1984, chmn. dept. family medicine, 1986—2007, prof. dept. med. edn., assoc. dir. depression ctr., 1993—2011, prof., George A. Dean chair dept. family medicine, 2007—11, prof. emeritus; v.p. health sciences, dean U. Nev. Sch. Medicine, Reno, 2011—. Contbr. chapters to books, several articles to publications; writer Journal Watch, 1994—. Fellow: Am. Coll. Sports Medicine; mem.: Inst. of Medicine, Am. Bd. Family Practice (former v.p. bd. dirs.). Office: Office of Dean MS 0332 University Nev Sch Medicine Reno NV 89557 Office Phone: 775-784-6001. Office Fax: 775-784-6979. Business E-Mail: tschwenk@medicine.nevada.edu. *

SCHWENN, LEE WILLIAM, retired health facility administrator; b. Morrisonville, Wis., Dec. 23, 1925; s. LeRoy William and Vivian Mae (Kramer) S.; m. Glenna Edith Mehne, Jan. 16, 1947; 1 son, William Lee. BS, U. Wis., 1948; M.P.H., U. N.C., 1956. Tchr. pub. schs., Appleton, Wis., 1948-52; teaching cons. Wis. Health Dept., 1952-53; adminstrv. asst. Madison (Wis.) Health Dept., 1953-57; adminstrv. cons. U.S. Children's Bur., Atlanta Regional Office, 1957-58; adminstr. USPHS, Washington, 1958-66; assoc. dir. D.C. Dept. Health, 1966-70, D.C. Dept. Human Resources, 1970-71; exec. v.p. Maimonides Med. Center, Bklyn., 1971-88, pres., 1988-89, spl. cons. Bd. Trustees, 1989-96. Recipient Distinguished Pub. Service award D.C. Govt., 1970 Mem. Delta Omega. Home: 200 Tabernacle Rd B15 Black Mountain NC 28711

SCHWENZER, MICHAEL, psychologist, researcher; b. Ludwigsburg, Germany, May 12, 1966; s. Herbert and Else Schwenzer; 1 child. Abitur, Ellental Gymnasium, Bietigheim-Bissingen, 1978—86; Dr. sc. hum., U. Tübingen, Germany, 2004; Diploma in Psychology, U. Tübingen, 1994. Cert. in theology, psychology U. Tübingen; specialization in perception, basic cognitive processes, hypochondriasis, depression. Doctorate Dept. Sports Medicine, Tübingen, 1995—2003; post-doc rschr. Ctr. for Neurology, Tübingen, 2004—05, Dept. Psychiatry and Psychotherapy, Aachen, Germany, 2006—. Psychotherapist tchr. DGVT, Bonn, Germany. Contbr. articles various profl. jours. Intern social welfare Diakonische Bezirksstelle, Heilbronn, Germany, 1986—87. Grantee Free Accommodation, Evangelische Kirche Württemberg, 1988; fellow Fortüne, Dept. Medicine, Tübingen, 1994—95, 2000; fellowship, Deutsche Forschungsgemeinschaft, 2005—, START fellowship, Dept. Psychiatry and Psychotherapy, Aachen, 2006—11, fellowship, Interdisciplinary Ctr. Clin. Rsch., 2009—10. Mem.: German Soc. Behavior Therapy. Avocations: walking, chess, history. Office: Dept Psychiatry Psychotherapy and Psychosomatics Pauwelsstr 30 Aachen 52074 Germany Office Phone: 49 241/8089730. Business E-Mail: mschwenzer@ukaachen.de.

SCHWILK, BERNHARD, physician, researcher; b. Kaisersbach, Baden-Württemberg, Germany, Feb. 3, 1952; s. Walter and Maria Eva (Rothweiler) S.; m. Christina Säps Ernst, Aug. 23, 1985; children: Max, Nora. Examin as Phys., U. Ulm, Germany, 1982; MBA, U. Applied Scis., Neu Ulm, 2002. Resident Karl-Olga-Krankenhaus, Stuttgart, Germany, 1982-85; resident anaesthesiology U. Ulm, 1986-91, sr. physician anaesthesiology, 1991-98, sr. physician, asst. prof. anaesthesiology, 1998—2002; mgr. Univ. Hosp. Charite, Berlin, 2003—06, hosp. bus. mgr.; med. dir. Hosp. Luedenscheid, 2006—. Advisor biomedical industry. With German Army, 1971-72. Mem. Physicians Prevention Nuc. War, European Soc. Intensive Care Medicine, NY Acad. Sci., European Soc. Computing Tech. Anaesthesiology Intensive Care (gen. sec. 1996-2001, founding mem. 1989), Bd. German Anaesthesiologists (commn. quality assurance 1993—), Bd. Physicians (chairperson coun. quality assurance anaesthesiology Baden-Württemberg 1998-2001, clin. advisor cos. med. tech. IT). Avocations: anthropology, economics, ethical discussions.

SCIALES, CHRISTOPHER W., dermatologist; Grad., Fordham U.; MD, Yeshiva U., 1988. Lic. NJ, 1989, diplomate Am. Bd. Dermatology. Resident internal medicine Montefiore Med. Ctr., Bronx; resident dermatology NJ Med. Sch., Newark; owner Livingston Dermatology Assocs., 1993—, dermatologist; owner Warren Dermatology Assocs., 1996—; clin. instructor St. Barnabas Med. Ctr., East Orange Veterans Adminstrn. Med. Ctr. Mem.: Am. Acad. of Dermatology, Am. Soc. for Dermatologic Surgery, Dermatol. Soc. of NJ (past pres.). Office: Livingston Dermatology Associates 201 S Livingston Ave Livingston NJ 07039 Office Phone: 973-994-1170.

SCIARRA, JOHN J., obstetrician, gynecologist, educator; b. West Haven, Conn., Mar. 4, 1932; s. John and Mary Grace (Sanzone) S.; m. Barbara Crafts Patton, Jan. 9, 1960; chidren: Vanessa Patton, John Crafts, Leonard Chapman. BS, Yale U., 1953; MD, Columbia U., NYC, 1957, PhD, 1963. Asst. prof. Columbia U., NYC, 1964-68; prof., dept. head U. Minn. Med. Sch., Mpls., 1968-74; prof. Northwestern U. Med. Sch., Chgo., 1974—; chmn. ob-gyn Northwestern Meml. Hosp. and Northwestern U. Med. Sch., Chgo., 1974—2003. Guest prof. Peking U., China, 2005. Editor Gyn-Ob Reference Series, 1973-2005, Internat. Jour. Gyn-Ob, 1985-2006, Global Library of Women's Medicine, 2008-. V.p. med. affairs Chgo. Maternity Ctr., Chgo., 1974—2003; treas. Soc. Family Planning, 2005-. Fellow ACS, Am. Coll. Ob-Gyn. (chmn. internal affairs com. 1985-89), Royal Coll. Ob Gyn. (ad eundem); Internat. Fedn. Gyn-Ob. (pres. 1991-94, pres. Supporters Assn. 1994-2000); mem. Assn. Profs. Gyn-Ob. (sec. 1976-79, pres. 1980-81, Achievement award 1998, Tchg. award 2003), Am. Assn. Maternal and Neonatal Health (pres. 1980-89), Coun. Resident Edn. in Ob-Gyn., Am. Fertility Soc. (Hartman award 1965, bd. dirs. 1971-73), Assn. Profs. Gyn-Ob. Med. Edn. Found. (sec.-treas. 1987-91, pres. 1991-93), Ctrl. Assn. Ob-Gyn. (trustees 1986-90, pres. 1990-91), Chgo. Gynecol. Soc. (pres. 1990-91), Internat. Soc. Gynecol. Endoscopy (hon. 2005, v.p. 1997-99, pres. 1999-01), Am. Gynecol. Club (pres. 2007-08), Soc. Family Planning (treas., 2006-10), Internat. Acad. Human Reprodn. (v.p., 2011-), Yale Club N.Y.C., Carleton Club (Chgo.). Avocations: photography, travel. Office: Northwestern U Med Sch Dept Ob-Gyn 680 N Lake Shore Dr Ste 1015 Chicago IL 60611-8702 Office Phone: 312-695-5107. Business E-Mail: jsciarra@northwestern.edu.

SCIARRA, LUIGI, cardiologist; b. Italy, July 11, 1970; MD, U. Rome Tor Vergata, 1995, degree in Cardiology, 1998. Cardiologist interventional arrhythmology Ospedale di Portogruaro, 2000—02, Ospedale di Conegliano Veneto, 2003—06; cons. cardiology ablation Ospedale Civile di Teramo, 2006—09, Ospedale Grassi di Ostia, 2007—; cardiologist interventional arrhythmology Policlinico Casilino, 2007—. Prof. in fields, 2001—; reviewer in fields, 2004—; bd. dirs. Assomedico, 2010—. Mem.: Italian Assn. In-Hosp. Cardiologists, Italian Fedn. Cardiology, European Heart Rhythm Assn., Italian Assn. Arrhythmology & Cardiostimulation, European Soc. Cardiology. Avocations: running, skiing, sailing. Home: via Montaione 20 Rome 00139 Italy Personal E-mail: lui.sciarra@libero.it.

SCIBETTA, MARIA T., internist; MD, U. Medicine and Dentistry og NJ, Newark. Diplomate Am. Bd. Internal Medicine. Resident internal medicine Mt. Sinai Hosp., NY, 1991—93; med. staff The Valley Hosp., NJ. Recipient Patient's Choice award; named one of Top Doctors, Castle Conolly. Office: The Valley Hospital 223 N Van Dien Ave Ridgewood NJ 07450 Office Phone: 201-447-8000.

SCIOLARO, CHARLES MICHAEL, surgeon; b. Kans. City, Kans., July 5, 1958; s. Gerald Michael and Charleen Gwen Sciolaro; m. Vicki Lynn Mizell, Sept. 29, children: Rachel, Lynsey, Ryan, Jonathan. BA in Biology, Chemistry with magna cum laude, Mid Am. Nazarene U., Olathe, Kans., 1980; MD, Kans. U. Med. Ctr., Kans. City, 1984. Diplomate Am. Bd. Gen. Surgery, Thoracic and Cardiac; lic. La., Fla., Kans., Mo., Penn., SC; cert. ACLS, PALS, ATLS, Calif. x-ray supr. and operator, transesophageal echocardiography. Intern gen. surgery Tucson hosps. surg. program U. Ariz., 1984—85, resident gen. surgery, 1985—89, chief resident gen. surgery, 1989—90; instr. surgery Loma Linda U. Med. Ctr., Tucson, 1991—93; physician divsn. cardiac, thoracic and vascular surgery MacArthur Surg. Clinic, Alexandria, 1993—96; staff physician Bethany Med. Ctr., 1996—2001, Overland Pk. Med. Ctr., 2001—, Rsch. Med. Ctr., 2006—09, Docs Who Care, 2007—. Emergency rm. physician, cons. Nat. Emergency Corp., Tucson, 1986-87; emergency care attendent Vets. Med. Ctr., Tucson, 1985-89, Cigna Urgent Care, 1985-89; staff physician Kanza Multispecialty Clinic, Kansas City, 1996-2003, Rapides Regional Med. Ctr., Alexandria, 1993-96, Providence Med. Ctr., Kans. City, 1996-2007, Bapt.-Luth. Med. Ctr., 2003-06; pres. Kans. Heart and Lung Surgery, Chartered, 2003—; rschr., lectr., presenter in field. Contbr. articles to profl. jours. Active mem. Pres. Bus. Com., 2005—08, Christ Cmty. Ch., Leawood, Kans. Recipient Congl. Order of Merit, 2005; named one of America's Top Surgeons, 2005; Biochemistry Rsch. fellowship, U. Kans., 1978—79. Mem. ACS, Soc. Thoracic Surgery, Soc. Internat. Coll. Surgeons. Republican. Mathodist. Avocations: photography, softball, woodworking. Office: 8101 Parallel Pky Ste 500 Kansas City KS 66112 Office Phone: 913-660-0438. Office Fax: 913-676-6059.

SCIOT, RAF MARIA EMIEL, pathologist, educator; b. Hasselt, Belgium, Jan. 3, 1960; s. Paul Sciot and Gaby Francen; m. Hilde Sijmons, Aug. 24, 1985; children: Eline, Bram, Hanne. MD, PhD, Cath. U. Leuven, Belgium, 1985. Prof. pathology U. Leuven, 2001—; sr. staff mem. dept. pathology U. Hosp., Leuven. Contbr. articles to profl. jours. Mem. acad. coun. Cath. U. Leuven, 2004—. Grantee, Flemish Rsch. Funding Orgn., 1999, 2005. Achievements include research in cancer diagnosis and pathogenesis. Office: Univ Hosp Dept Pathology Herestraat 49 3000 Leuven Belgium Office Fax: 003216336548. Personal E-mail: raf.sciot@med.kuleuven.be. Business E-Mail: raf.sciot@uz.kuleuven.ac.be.

SCITOVSKY, ANNE AICKELIN, economist, researcher; b. Ludwigshafen, Germany, Apr. 17, 1915; arrived in U.S., 1931, naturalized, 1938; d. Hans W. and Gertrude Margarete Aickelin; 1 child, Catherine Margaret. Student, Smith Coll., 1933—35; BA, Barnard Coll., 1937; postgrad., London Sch. Econs., 1937—39; MA in Econs., Columbia U., 1941. Mem. staff legis. reference svc. Libr. of Congress, 1941—44; mem. staff Social Security Bd., 1944—46; with Palo Alto (Calif.) Med. Found./Rsch. Inst., 1963—, chief health econs. div., 1973—94, sr. staff scientist, 1994—. Lectr. Inst. Health Policy Studies, U. Calif., San Francisco, 1975—94; mem. Inst. Medicine of NAS, Nat. Acad. Social Ins., Pres.'s Commn. for Study of Ethical Problems in Medicine and Biomed. and Behavioral Rsch., 1979—82, U.S. Nat. Com. on Vital and Health Stats., 1975—78, Health Resources and Svcs. Adminstrn., AIDS adv. com., 1990—94; cons. HHS, Inst. Medicine Coun. on Health Care Tech. Assessment, 1986—90. Home: 161 Erica Way Portola Valley CA 94028-7439 Office: Palo Alto Med Found Rsch Inst Ames Bldg 795 El Camino Real Palo Alto CA 94301-2302 Personal E-mail: ascitovsky@aol.com.

SCIUPOKAS, ARUNAS, medical educator, neurologist, pain physician; b. Kaunas, Lithuania, Mar. 10, 1953; s. Petras Sciupokas and Sofija Sciupokiene; m. Elona Sakalauskaite, Feb. 18, 1977; children: Giedre, Arune, Algirdas. MD, Univ. Medicine, Kaunas, 1977, specialization in neurology, 1985, PhD, 1994. Physician Emergency Sta., Siauliai, Lithuania, 1978—82, Regional Hosp., Siauliai, 1983—88; asst. prof. Clin. Neurology Univ. Medicine, 1988—98, assoc. prof., 1998—, vice dean med. faculty, 1999—. Dir. pvt. clin., Siauliai, 1995—; pain physician, Pain Clinic Kaunas U. Hosp., 2002—. Author: Chronic Noncancer Pain and Its Treatment by Opioid Analgesics, 2006; co-author: Clinical Neurology, 2003; editor: Diseases of Peripheral Nervous System, 1997, Pain Medicine, 1998; editor-in-chief: newspaper Pain News, 1999—, jour. Pain Medicine, 2002—; editor: Neurological Damage in General Practice, 2002. Grantee, Open Soc. Inst. N.Y.C., 2000, EFIC, 2006. Mem.: Internat. Assn. Study of Pain, Lithuanian Pain Soc. (pres. 1998—), Lithuanian Neurologists Assn. (v.p. 1997—2002). Avocations: sports, chess, travel. Office: Univ Medicine Mickeviciaus 9 3000 Kaunas Lithuania Home: C. Sasnausko G. 22 44149 Kaunas Lithuania Home Phone: +370-37 797416. Office Fax: 370.37.333514. Business E-Mail: neurpain@kmu.lt. E-mail: asciupokas@hotmail.com.

SCLAFANI, ANTHONY PAUL, plastic surgeon, educator, biomedical researcher; b. Bklyn., Oct. 3, 1963; BA, Columbia U., 1985; MD, U. Pa., 1989. Diplomate Am. Bd. Otolaryngology, Am. Bd. Facial Plastic and Reconstructive Surgery. Intern in gen. surgery Beth Israel Med. Ctr., NYC, 1989-91; from resident in otolaryngology, head and neck surgery to prof. N.Y. Eye and Ear Infirmary, NYC, 1991—2004, prof., 2004—, dir. facial plastic surgery, 1996—, surgeon dir., 2005—; fellow in facial plastic and reconstructive surgery St. Louis U. Sch. Medicine, 1995-96; pvt. practice NYC, 1996—, Chappaqua, NY, 1998—. Editor-in-chief Facial Plastic Surgery; assoc. editor Facial Plastics Clinics N.Am.; contbr. articles to profl. jours. Fellow ACS, Am. Acad. Facial Plastic and Reconstructive Surgery (Sir Harold Delf Gillies award 1996, Ira Tresley Rsch. award 2002, 04), Am. Acad. Otolaryngology and Head and Neck Surgery; mem. Am. Soc. Laser Medicine and Surgery, Triological Soc. Office: NY EE Infirm/Facial Pl Surg Dept Otolaryng/Head Neck 310 E 14th St 6th Fl New York NY 10003-4201 also: 59 S Greeley Ave Chappaqua NY 10514-3321 also: 200 W 57 th St New York NY 10019 Office Phone: 914-238-5500. Personal E-mail: docs@nyface.com.

SCOCCIANTI, MARCO, vascular surgeon; b. Jesi, Ancona, Italy, Sept. 29, 1952; s. Renato Scoccianti and Luisa Piscini; m. Rosella Santini, June 21, 1981; children: Matteo, Margherita. Medicine and Surgery laude, Università La Sapienza, 1978; diploma Specialist Gen. Surgery, U. Pisa, 1984; diploma in Thoracic Surgery, U. Ancona, 1990. Cert. Specialist in Vascular Surgery European Bd. Surgery, 1996. Registrar in cardiothoracic surgery U. Witswatersrand, Johannesburg, 1983—86, Humberside Cardiothoracic Centre, Cottingham, England, 1987—87; staff vascular surgeon S. Filippo Neri Hosp., Rome, 1988—92; vascular fellow Harbor-UCLA Med. Ctr., Torrance, 1993—94; staff vascular surgeon I.D.I., Rome, 1996—99, S.Giovanni - Addolorata Hosp. Complex, Rome, 1999—2001; head endovascular surgery unit S.Giovanni - Addolorata Hospial Complex, Rome, 2002—04; chief vascular and endovascular surgery Pescara City Hosp., Italy, 2005—. Project leader European Biomed. II Program, Rome, 1995—98; investigator European GROWTH Program, Rome, 1999—. Mem.: Italian Soc. of Vascular and Endovascular Surgery (licentiate; full mem. 1998—2003). Achievements include patents for A new method of cell seeding of sinthetic vascular grafts; design of New Endovascular Devices To Facilitate Endovascular Procedures Such As An Aortic Multifunctional Aortic Calibrator And A Polydirectional Guiding Catheter; European Expert evaluateur for researc projects of the European Commission, Directorate L; research in investigator European BIOMED II Program Grant to control intimal hyperplasia after vascular injury (surgery or angioplasty) by adenovirus mediated gene transfer; Project Leader European BIOMED II Program Grant to prevent small diameter graft failure by ex-vivo gene therapy with genetically modified fibroblasts; investigator European GROWTH Program Grant to develop a new small diameter prosthetic vascular graft with a new silicone/polyurethane based material; Evaluation Of Endoluminal Grafts Compliance After Exclusion Of Abdominal Aortic Aneurysms With Stent-Grafts; development of An Innovative Method Of Cell Seeding To Increase The Patency Rates Of Small Diameter Vascular Grafts; patents for European Patent related to a new method of cell seeding on vascular grafts; development of Development And Improvement In The Deployment And Evaluation Of Endoluminal Grafts During Exclusion Of Abdominal And Thoracic Aortic Aneurysms With Stent-Grafts; New Technique To Decrease Limb Ischemia During Complex Peripheral Endovascular Procedures; expert in the treatment of abdominal aortic dissection with endoluminal grafts. Office: Ospedale Civile Spirito Santo via R Paolini 45 65124 Pescara Italy Home: Via Santa Maria di Galeria 351 123 Rome Italy Office Phone: (39) 335-5221701. Personal E-mail: mscoccianti@tiscali.it.

SCOGNAMIGLIO, GIANCARLO, cardiologist; b. Naples, Nov. 11, 1973; Degree in Medicine & Surgery, Second U. Naples, 1997, specialist in Cardiology, 2001. Cardiologist Clinica 'Villa dei Fiori', Acerra, 2002—05, Pellegrini Hosp., Naples, 2006—08, Monaldi Hosp., 2nd U. Naples, 2008—. Mem.: European Soc. Cardiology, Italian Soc. Cardiology. Avocations: football, travel, movies. Home: Via Montedoro 25 Torre del Greco Naples 80059 Italy Home Fax: 390818819648. Personal E-mail: gianca.scog@tiscali.it.

SCOLLARD, PATRICK J., hospital executive; b. Chgo., Apr. 20, 1937; s. Patrick J. and Kathleen (Cooney) S.; m. Gloria Ann Carroll, July 1, 1961; children: Kevin, Maureen, Daniel, Thomas, Brian. BS in Econs., Marquette U., 1959; grad. sr. exec. program, MIT, 1976. With Equitable Life Assurance Soc. U.S., NYC, 1962-79, asst. v.p., 1969-71, v.p., personnel dir., 1971-75, v.p. corp. adminstrv. svcs., 1975-79; sr. v.p. Chem. Bank, NYC, 1979-80, exec. v.p., 1980-87, chief adminstrv. officer, 1987-92; pres., CEO St. Francis Hosp., Roslyn, NY, 1992-99; pres. Scollard Assocs. LLC, Garden City, NY, 1999—; pres., CEO Cath. Health Svcs. of L.I., Melville, NY, 2003—04, also bd. dirs. Bd. dirs. Cath. Health Svcs. L.I.; chmn. LI Healthcare Network, 2010—, Scollard Family Found. Inc., 1999—, bd. dirs.

SCOMMEGNA, ANTONIO, obstetrician, gynecologist, educator; b. Barletta, Italy, 1931; came to U.S., 1954, naturalized, 1960; s. Francesco Paola and Antonietta S.; m. Lillian F. Sinkiewicz, May 3, 1958; children: Paola, Frank, Roger. BA, State Lyceum A. Casardi, Barletta, 1947; MD, U. Bari, Italy, 1953. Diplomate: Am. Bd. Obstetrics and Gynecology, also sub-bd. endocrinology and reprodn. Rotating intern New Eng. Hosp., Boston, 1954-55; resident obstetrics and gynecology Michael Reese Hosp. and Med. Center, Chgo., 1956-59, fellow dept. research human reprodn., 1960-61, research asso., 1961; fellow steroid tng. program Worcester Found. Exptl. Biology, also Clark U., Shrewsbury, Mass., 1964-65; asso. prof. obstetrics and gynecology Chgo. Med. Sch., 1965-69; mem. staff Michael Reese Hosp. and Med. Center, 1961—89, attending physician obstetrics and gynecology, 1961—89, dir. sect. gynecologic endocrinology, 1965-81; dir. ambulatory care obstetrics and gynecology Mandel Clinic, 1968-69, chmn. dept., 1969-89; attending, chief svc. U. Ill. Chgo. Hosp. and Med. Ctr., 1989-98; trustee Michael Reege Med. Ctr., 1977—80; prof. dept. ob-gyn. Pritzker Sch. Medicine, U. Chgo., 1969-89; prof., head dept. ob-gyn. Coll. Medicine, U. Ill. Chgo., 1989-98, prof. emeritus, 1999—. Contbr. articles to profl. jours. Fulbright fellow, 1954-55 Fellow Am. Coll. Obstetricians and Gynecologists, Endocrine Soc., Chgo. Inst. Medicine, Am. Gynecol. and Obstet. Soc.; mem. AMA, Ill., Chgo. med. socs., Am. Fertility Soc., Chgo. Gynecol. Soc. (sec. 1976-79, pres. 1981-82), Soc. Study Reprodn., AAAS, Soc. for Gynecologic Investigation. Home: 2645 N Dayton Chicago IL 60614 Office Phone: 312-996-0222. Business E-Mail: anmis@uic.edu.

SCORCIA, VINCENZO, ophthalmologist, educator; b. Bari, Italy, Mar. 4, 1977; MD, Liceo G. De Sanctis Roma, 1995. Aggregate prof. U. Magna Graecia, 2008—. Mem.: Am. Acad. Ophthalmology. Home: Via Bevagna 46 Rome 00191 Italy Personal E-mail: vscorcia@libero.it.

SCOTT, DAVID MICHAEL, pharmacist, educator; b. St. Paul, July 5, 1949; s. David Marvin and Cecelia (Ventura) S.; m. Patti L. Anderson, May 1, 1976; children: Michael, Justin, Nathan. BS, U. Minn., Mpls., 1972, MPH, 1982, PhD, 1987. Lic. pharmacist Minn. Pharmacy intern United Hosps., St. Paul, 1972-73, staff pharmacist, 1973-75; pharmacy dir. Cmty.-Univ. Health Care Ctr., Mpls., 1975-84; clin. instr. pharmacy U. Minn., Mpls., 1975-86; assoc. dir. orthop. rsch. St. Paul Ramsey Med. Ctr., 1984-86; asst. prof. U. Nebr. Med. Ctr., Omaha, 1986-95, assoc. prof., 1996—2009, prof., 2009—; assoc. prof. N.D. State U., Fargo, 2003—. Epidemiologist Toward a Drug-Free Nebr., Nebr. Dept. Edn., Lincoln, 1989-94; mem. Springville Elem. Sch. Drug Abuse, Omaha, 1988-97; faculty advisor Acad. Student Pharmacists, APhA, Omaha, 1994-2003; assessment specialist N.D. Telepharmacy Project, 2003-. Contbr. articles to sci. jours. Coach Keystone Little League, Omaha, 1991-94; bd. dirs. Butler-Gast YMCA, Omaha, 1992-96; vice chmn. bd. dirs., 1994-95; chmn. Nebr. Pulling Am. Cmtys. Together Sch. Truancy Task Force, Lincoln, 1994-97. Grantee, Am. Assn. Colls. Pharmacy, Alexandria, Va., 1995—97, U.S. Dept. Edn., Washington, 1996—97, U.S. Dept. Health and Human Svcs. Health Resources and Svcs. Adminstrn., 2000—03, 2003—. Mem.: APHA (mem. program com. 1991—93), Internat. Soc. Pharmacoeconomics and Outcomes Rsch., Nat. Cmty. Pharmacists Assn. (faculty liasion 1987—2003), Internat. Soc. Pharmacoepidemiology (mem. program com. 1992—97), Am. Assn. Colls. of Pharmacy (mem. program com. 1990—92, grant 1995—97). Avocations: jogging, golf, reading, basketball, nature. Office: ND State U Coll Pharmacy 118K Sudro Hall Fargo ND 58108-6045 Office Phone: 701-231-5867. Business E-Mail: david.scott@ndsu.edu.

SCOTT, GREGORY W., healthcare company executive; B in Math. Econ., Colgate U.; MS, U. Mich. cert. CLU. Sr. v.p. Prudential Capital Corp.; gen. ptnr. RRY Ptnrs.; v.p. corp. fin. Salomon Brothers, Inc.; exec. v.p., CFO Prudential Securities; pres. no. ctrl. group, healthcare & employee benefits ops. Prudential Ins. Co., v.p., treas., sr. v.p., CFO health care group; COO, CFO Medsite, 1999-01; exec. v.p., CFO PacifiCare Health Sys. Inc., Cypress, Calif., 2001—. Mem. Fin. Exec. Inst. Office: PacifiCare Health Sys 5995 Plaza Dr Cypress CA 90630

SCOTT, JAMES ARTHUR, radiologist, educator; b. Cleve., Aug. 23, 1950; s. Robert James and Margaret Emma (Hinz) S.; m. Phyllis Virginia Gauthier, Oct. 3, 1981. SB, MIT, 1972; MD, Boston U., 1976. Diplomate Am. Bd. Radiology, Am. Bd. Nuc. Medicine. Resident Harvard U. Med. Sch.-Mass. Gen. Hosp., Boston, 1976-80, fellow, 1980-81, instr., 1982-83, asst. prof., 1984-93, assoc. prof., 1994—. Mem. editl. adv. bd. Jour. Nuc. Medicine, Am. Jour. Roentgen. Recipient New Investigator Rsch. award NIH, 1984-87. Mem. Soc. Sci. Exploration, Sigma Xi, Am. Coll. Radiology, AAAS, Phi Lambda Upsilon, Theta Xi. Lutheran. Avocations: writing, golf, history. Office: Div Nuclear Medicine Mass Gen Hosp Boston MA 02114 Personal E-mail: jas.scott@verizon.net. Business E-Mail: scott@helix.mgh.harvard.edu.

SCOTT, JAMES L., emergency physician, educator; MD, U. Ariz., 1983. Diplomate Am. Bd. Emergency Physicians, Nat. Bd. Med. Examiners. Internal medicine intern U. Ariz.; resident Georgetown U.; emergency medicine resident George Washington U.; with George Washington U. Sch. Medicine and Health Sciences, Washington, 1986—, residency dir., asst. dean grad. med. edn., asst. dean student affairs, prof. dept. emergency medicine, 1998—, assoc. dean, 2000—03, interim dean, 2003—04, dean, 2004—10. Recipient Nat. Tchg. award, Am. Coll. Emergency Physicians, 1998. Mem.: Soc. Acad. Emergency Medicine, Am. Coll. Emergency Physicians. Office: GWU Sch Med and Health Science Dept Emergency Medicine 2300 K St NW Ste 327 Washington DC 20037 Office Phone: 202-994-7936. E-mail: jscott@gwu.edu, msdijls@gwumc.edu. *

SCOTT, JANE VICROY, microbiologist; b. Selma, Ala. d. C.E. and Eileen (Yeager) Vicroy; m. Jeffrey Glassberg, Jan. 9, 1977; 1 child, Matthew Scott. Attended, Judson Coll., 1962-64; BA, Tex. Christian U., 1966, MS, 1968; PhD in Microbiology and Immunology, Baylor Coll. Medicine, 1976. Postdoctoral fellow U. Calif., San Francisco, 1976-79; rsch. assoc. Rockefeller U., NYC, 1979-82; rsch. microbiologist Lederle Labs., Pearl River, N.Y., 1982-84, group leader, 1985, dept. head vaccines R & D, 1986-89, sect. head, 1989-90, dir. bus. devel., 1991-95; dir. indsl. liaison NYU Med. Ctr., NYC, 1996-2000; dir. bus. devel. PLIVA, Inc., Livingston, NJ, 2000—05; prin. HVA, Inc., Livingston, 2005—. Adj. faculty Rockefeller U., N.Y.C., 1982-84. Campaign mgr. for Town Supr., 1990; dist. leader Dem. Com., New Castle, N.Y., 1988-94. Mem. Am. Soc. for Microbiology, Assn. U. Tech. Mgrs., N.Am. Butterfly Assn. (sec.-treas. 1997—), Licensing Execs. Soc., Sigma Xi. Achievements include identification of lymphocytes as carrier of virus; antigenic variation in visna; development of acellular pertussis vaccine for U.S.; patent for purification of acellular pertussis vaccine; research in various drugs and delivery technology, licensing transactions. Office: HVA Inc 205 Park Ave Morristown NJ 07960 Office Phone: 973-214-3732.

SCOTT, JOHN ATWOOD, JR., hypnoanalyst, psychologist, marriage and family therapist; b. Darby, Pa., July 14, 1949; s. John Atwood and Mary Joyce (Forrester) S.; m. Edna Vera Newhouse, June 12, 1971; children: Abigail Rae, John Benjamin. BS, Empire State Coll., 1976; MA in Religion, Harding Grad. Sch. Religion, 1979; postgrad., Memphis State U., 1979; EdD, U. Memphis, 1991. Ordained to ministry Ch. of Christ, 1969. Min., youth worker Shiloh, Inc., NYC, 1969-71; youth worker, adminstr. Ctrl. Coleman Youth Devel. Project, Rochester, NY, 1971-75; counselor, hypnoanalyst John. A. Scott, PhD and Assocs., P.C., Memphis, 1975—2003; clin. psychology intern Jersey Shore Med. Ctr., Neptune, NJ, 1986-87; dir. social svcs. office Linden-Camilla Towers, Memphis, 2001—03; clin. dir. Brief Psychotherapy Inst. of the Rockies, Broomfield, Colo., 2003—; mil. family life cons. MHN Govt. Svcs., 2009—. Author: The Little Book of Wisdom: Ten Steps for Healing and Personal Growth; assoc. editor: Med. Hypnoanalysis, 1980-86; contbr. articles and book revs. to profl. publs. Bd. dirs. Drug and Alcohol Coun., Rochester, 1973-75; mem. 16th Ward Coalition for Neighborhood Devel., Rochester, 1973-75, chmn., 1974; mem. adv. bd. Genessee Valley Mental Health Ctr., 1974-75, chmn., 1975; neighborhood rep. to bd. dirs. Action for Better Cmty., 1974-75; founder, dir. Rochester City-Wide Basketball League, 1974-75; minister outreach to city program White Station Ch. of Christ, Memphis, 1976-91. Mem. Am. Acad. Med. Hypnoanalysts (bd. dirs. 1981—, pres. 1990-92, chmn. 1994-96, pres. 1998-2000, chmn. 2000-02), Soc. Med. Hypnoanalysts, Am. Inst. Hypnosis, Hypnosis Rsch. Found., Am. Assn. Sex Educators, Counselors and Therapists, Nat. Alliance for Family Life. Office: 1022 Depot Hill Rd Broomfield CO 80020 Office Phone: 303-465-2323. E-mail: drjascott2003@yahoo.com.

SCOTT, KAMELA KOON, psychologist, educator; b. Carson City, Nev., July 28, 1964; d. Ray Harold and Bert Gardner Koon; m. David Keitt Scott, Feb. 13, 1993; children: Nicolas Keitt, Isaac David. BA, Baylor U., Waco, Tex., 1986; PhD, U. No. Tex., Denton, 1992. Lic. Clin. Psychologist Divsn. Med. Quality Assurance, Fla., 1994. Psychology intern U. Tex. Med. Br. and Shriner's Burns Inst., Galveston, Tex., 1991—92; instr. dept. psychiatry Emory U. Sch. Medicine, Atlanta, 1992—93; asst. prof. dept. of Pediat. U. Fla. Coll. Medicine, Jacksonville, Fla., 1993—96, asst. prof., 1996—2002, assoc. prof. dept. surgery, 2002—. Program dir., psychol. svcs. U. Fla., Dept. Pediat., Dist. Hematology/Sickle Cell Program, Jacksonville, 1993—96, U. Fla. Regional Trauma Sys., Jacksonville, 2001—; chmn. Sexual Harassment Com. U. Fla., Jacksonville, 1997—; mem. Jacksonville Pediat. Injury Control Sys., 1996—; bd. mem. Shands Jacksonville Ethics Com., 1996—, Shands Jacksonville Emergency Preparedness Com., 1998—; adv. bd. mem. Shands Jacksonville Clin. Pastoral Edn. Adv. Bd., 1998—2004; supervising psychologist Shands Jacksonville Trauma Psychology Post-Doctoral Fellowship, 1998—; site reviewer Fla. Brain and Spinal Cord Injury Program, Tallahassee, 1998—; lectr. U. Fla. Risk Mgmt. Ednl. Series, Gainesville, 2002—. Author: (book chapter) Surg. Clinics of North Am., (book chapters (2)

Behavioral Aspects of Pediatric Burn Injuries, (jour. article) Current Surgery, Jour. of Trauma, Jacksonville Medicine. Adv. bd. mem. Partnerships for Preventing Violence, Jacksonville, 1998—2003, Serving Child Victims of Traumatic Abuse, Jacksonville, 2002—03; active mem. Compassionate Families, Inc., Jacksonville, 1998—2003. Named Outstanding Alumnae of Yr., U. North Tex., 2005; grantee, City of Jacksonville, Fla., 2001—05, State of Fla. Byrne Grant, 2001-2002, The Blue Found. for a Healthy Fla., 2001—05, The Jacksonville Jaguars Found., 1999-2001, U. of Fla. Dean's Fund, 1997-1998; scholar, Pres. U.S., Washington, D.C., 1982. Mem.: APA. Republican. Baptist. Avocations: scuba diving, skiing, deep sea fishing, camping. Office: U Fla Surgery 655 West 8th St Jacksonville FL 32209 Business E-Mail: kamela.scott@jax.ufl.edu.

SCOTT, KATHLEEN A., speech educator; b. Chgo., Jan. 7, 1960; PhD, Temple U., 2007. Asst. prof. Hofstra U., 2007—. Grant, Shoolman Found. Mem.: Am. Speech Lang. Hearing Assn. Avocations: reading, yoga, golf. Home: PO Box 132131 Spring TX 77393 Business E-Mail: kathleen.scott@hofstra.edu.

SCOTT, MATTHEW PETER, biology educator; b. Boston, Jan. 30, 1953; s. Peter Robert and Duscha (Schmid) S.; m. Margaret Tatnall Fuller, May 13, 1990; children: Lincoln Fuller, Julia Fuller. BS, MIT, 1975, PhD, 1980. Postdoctoral tng. Ind. U., Bloomington, 1980-83; from asst. prof. to assoc. prof. U. Colo., Boulder, 1983-90; prof. Stanford (Calif.) U., 1990—, chmn. dept. devel. biology, 1997-98, assoc. chmn. dept. devel. biology, 1999—; assoc. investigator Howard Hughes Med. Inst., 1989-90, investigator, 1993—. Vis. prof. genetics Harvard Med. Sch., 1994-95. Recipient Passano Young Investigator award Passano Found., 1990. Mem. NAS, Inst. Medicine, Am. Acad. Arts and Scis. Achievements include research in developmental genetics, in particular, homeotic genes, signaling systems, and cancer biology. Office: Stanford U Sch Med Dept Devel Biology 279 Campus Dr Beckman B300 Stanford CA 94305-5329

SCOTT, MIMI KOBLENZ, psychotherapist, actress, journalist, playwright; b. Albany, NY, Dec. 15, 1940; d. Edmund Akiba and Tillie (Paul) Koblenz; m. Barry Stuart Scott, Aug. 13, 1961 (dec. Nov. 1991); children: Karen Scott Zantay, Jeffrey B. BA in Speech and English Edn., Russell Sage Coll., 1962; MA in Speech Edn., SUNY, Albany, 1968; M in Social Welfare, SUNY, 1985; PhD in Psychology, Pacific Western U., Encino, Calif., 1985. Cert. tchr., social worker. Tchr. English, speech Albany Pub. Schs., 1961-63; hostess, producer talkshow Sta. WAST-TV 13, Albany, 1973-75; freelance actress NYC, 1975-77; producer, actress Four Seasons Dinner Theater, Albany, 1978-82; instr. of theatre Albany Jr. Coll., 1981-83; pvt. practice psychotherapy Albany, NY, 1985-92, NYC, 1992—; exec. prodr. City of Albany Park Playhouse, 1989-92; actor self-employed NYC, 1992—2007; actor Off Broadway show Grandma Sylvia's Funeral, 1996-98, Split Ends, 2004, Grease, Albany, 2007. Guest psychotherapist Sally Jessy Raphael Show, 1992, 93, Jane Whitney Show, 1994, A Current Affair, 1995, News Talk TV, 1995; founder, producing artistic dir. Manhattan Playwrights Inc., 2001—07, actress So Jewtastic VH1, 2006; group therapist Women's Health and Resource Ctr. South Fla., Hollywood, 2008. Scriptwriter, dir., actor (TV films) To Liberty and Justice for All, 1985, featured writer Backstage, 1995—96, featured in ind. film Mr. Vincent, Sundance, 1997, book and lyricist (musical) Dressing Room, Soho Playhouse, N.Y.C., 2000; author: Mind Tricks, 2003; dir.: Mind Tricks, 2003; featured on NBC Dateline, 2005; author, dir., prodr.: SPLIT! Tales from Children of Divorce in Upstate New York, 2008; author (performer): Broadway to Hollywood: My Life in Song, 2009, Doin What Came Natur'lly, The Merry, Madcap and Moxie Memoirs of Mimi Scott, 2011. Event organizer AmFar, 1985; co-chmn. March of Dimes Telethon, 1985-86; fundraiser Leukemia Found., 1987, AIDS Benefit Albany, NY, 1986, North Miami Beach, Fla., 1988; elected to SUNY Albany U. Found., 1990. Recipient FDR Nat. Achievement award March of Dimes, 1985, Recognition Cert. Capital Dist. Psychiat. Ctr., 1983-85; named Woman of Yr. YWCA, 1986, Commr. Albany Tricentennial Celebration, 1986; named Mimi Scott Day in her honor Mayor of Albany, 1989. Mem.: NASW, AFTRA, AEA, SAG, Hollywood Fla. C. of C., Drama League of N.Y., N.Y. League Profl. Theatre Women. Jewish. Avocations: writing, painting. Home and Office: 1965 Broadway #11D New York NY 10023 Office Phone: 917-846-2449. Personal E-mail: mscott13@aol.com.

SCOTT, NANCY L., information technology manager, health facility administrator, consultant; b. Berwyn, Ill., Sept. 11, 1962; d. Kenneth N. and Lolita L. Unger; m. Paul A. Scott, Dec. 29, 1990 (div. Sept. 1995). BS, Univ. of Ill., 1983; MBA with hons., U. of Chgo., 1991. Cert. CHE Am. Coll. of Healthcare Execs., Chgo., 2000. Various positions including implementation specialist to fin. product mgr. Enterprise Systems, Inc., Wheeling, Ill., 1993—96; cytogenetics technologist Univ. of Chgo., 1986—88; supr. Reproductive Genetics Inst., Chgo., 1988—90; dist. agt. The Prudential, Des Plaines, Ill., 1992; mgr., sr. cons. Cap Gemini Ernst & Young U.S., Chgo., 1996—2003; acct. exec. AHA Fin. Solutions, Inc., Chgo., 2003—04; payroll project mgr. Hewitt Assocs. LLC, Chgo., 2005—. Home: 3238 Elm Ave Brookfield IL 60513 Office: Hewitt Assocs LLC 120 S Riverside Plz Chicago IL 60606 Office Phone: 312-279-6643. Personal E-mail: NLScott@aol.com.

SCOTT, PAMELA MOYERS, physician assistant; b. Clarksburg, W.Va., Jan. 5, 1961; d. James Edward and Norma Lee (Holbert) Moyers; m. Troy Allen Scott, July 19, 1986. BS summa cum laude, Alderson-Broaddus Coll., 1983; M Physician Asst. Studies, U. Nebr., 1999. Cert. physician asst. Physician asst. Weston (W.Va.) State Hosp., 1983-84, Rainelle (W.Va.) Med. Ctr., 1984-2000, Brierwood Med. Ctr., 2000—01; pvt. practice Williamsburg, W.Va., 2001—. Adj. faculty Mountain State U., Beckley, W.Va., 2003, Alderson Broaddus Coll., 2009-10, physician asst. adv. coun., 2010-; support faculty physician asst. program Coll. W.Va., 1994-99, mem. physician asst. adv. coun. 1993-94, physician asst. program admission selection com., 1994-99; keynote spkr. Alderson-Broaddus Coll. Ann. Physician Assn. Banquet, 1992, 2001, 1st Physician Asst. Convocation Ceremony, 1998, guest spkr., 2010; spkr., presenter in field; guest Lifetime TV med. program Physician Jour. Update, 1993; adv. coun. W.Va. Rural Health Networking, 1994-95, W.Va. Rural Networking Managed Care Policy Group, 1996, W.Va. Coalition for Managed Care Options, 1997; mem. coalition W.Va. Comprehensive Cancer Ctr., 2004-06; people to people physician asst. del. China, 1992, 04, Brazil, 2003, del. leader 2003, 2004, mem., Advance NPST PAs, 2010-. Author: (textbook) Cases In Council Medicine, 2011; mem. editl. bd. Jour. Am. Acad. Physician Assts., 1995-98, 04-05, manuscript reviewer, 1995-2007; dept. editor Procedures in Family Practice Dept., 1996-04, When the Patient Asks, 2005-07; author, illustrator Mikie Meets the Physician Assistant, 2005; mem. editl. bd. Advance for Physician Assts., 2007—10, Cases to Clinical medicine; contbr. articles to profl. jours., chpts. to textbook. Mem. W.Va. State Task Force on Adolescent Pregnancy and Parenting, 1992-2000, sec., 1996-98; mem. W.Va. Rural Networking Managed Care Study Group, 1995, W.Va. Rural Networking Managed Care Policy Group, 1996; mem. adv. com. W.Va. State Bur. Pub. Health Family Planning, 1997-2000; mem. Greenbrier County P.A.T.C.H. Spkr.'s Bur., 1996-2003; mem. Meadow Bridge Cmty. Adv. Group, 1997-2000, Meadow Bridge Domestic Violence Prevention Task Force, 1998-2000; mem. heart profl. edn. adv. panel Nat. Heart, Lung & Blood Inst., 2003-2005; mem. N.H.L.B.I. profl. edn. dissemination adv. panel, 2005; bd. trustees Physician Asst. Found., 2002-03; mem. physician asst. alumni subcom. for renewing the promise campaign Alderson-Broadus Coll., 2004-2005; mem. Am. Heart Assn. Childhood Obesity Healthcare Expert Panel, 2005-07, liaison Am. Acad. Pa., Heart Truth Profl. Edn. Dissemination Campaign Adv. Panel, Nat. Heart, Lungs & Blood Inst., 2005-06, Heart Truth Profl. Edn. Devel. Panel, 2004-05; bd. dirs. W.Va. Med. Profls. Health Program, 2007—, mem. Case Mgmt. Com., 2009-. Named Young Career Woman of Yr. Rainelle chpt. and Dist. V of W. Va., Citation of Honor at State Level of Competition, Bus. and Profl. Women's Club, 1986, W.Va. Women's Commn. Celebrate Women award, Mountaineer Spirit, 2005; recipient W.Va. Gov.'s award for Outstanding Rural Health Practitioner, 1997, Alderson Broaddus Coll.'s Alumni Achievement award, 1995, Harry Bennington Meml. award, 2001, Hu C. Avanelle Myers award, 2004. Fellow: Assn. Family Practice Physician Assts. (newsletter editor 2001—02, med. matters installment writer, editor 2002—, Appreciation award 2002, 2004), W.Va. Assn. Physician Assts. (chmn. membership com. 1989—91, nominations and elections com. 1990—91, pres. 1991—94, chair ann. med. Jeopardy tournament 1997—2001, student activities com. 1999—2000, chmn. mentoring program 1999—2000, ann.scholarhsip named in honor 2005, Outstanding Physician Asst. of Yr. 2003), Am. Acad. Physician Assts. (mem. rural health caucus 1991—98, W.Va. chief del. Ho. of Dels. Nat. Conv. 1992, W.Va. del. 1992—98, mem. pub. edn. com. 1992—98, W.Va. chief del. Ho. of Dels. Nat. Conv. 1994—98, W.Va. chief del. house of dels. nat. conv. 1994—98, chair pub. edn. com. 1996—98, bd. advisor elections com. 1998—99, dir.-at-large 1998—2002, bd. on fin. 1998—2005, alt. del. 1999—2000, chmn. bd. commn. on external affairs 1999—2001, bd. advisor pub. rels. com. 2000—01, chair bd. commn. internal affairs 2001—02, bd. advisor clin. affairs coun. 2001—02, chmn. bd. on appts. 2002—03, chmn. bd. commn. on external affairs 2002—03, mem. coord com. 2002—03, pres.-elect 2002—03, bd. advisor to constituent rels. com. 2002—03, co-chair ad hoc work group on governance 2002—03, bd. on budget 2002—05, mem. exec. com. 2002—05, clin. and sci. affairs coun. 2002—05, edn. coun. 2002—05, mem. found. bd. trustees 2002—05, profession practice coun. 2002—05, bd. advisor leadership adv. commn. 2002—05, pres. 2003—04, chair exec. com. 2003—04, alt. del. 2003—07, bd. rep. nominating com. 2005—06, Outstanding Physician Asst. of Yr. 1991); mem.: Case Mgmt. Com., Soc. Physician Assts. in Rheumatology (news column editor & writer 2006—), Optum Health Educator's Ednl. Rsch. Panel, Amgen's Osteoporosis Allied Health Care Practitioner (adv. bd. mem. 2008—10), W.Va. Med. Profls. Health Program, Soc. Preservation Pa. History (chair publicity com., newsletter editor 2004—06, founding mem., bd. dirs. 2004—08, pres. elect 2005—06, pres. 2006—07, immediate past pres. 2007—08). Republican. Baptist. Avocations: reading, handicrafts, shopping. Home and Office: PO Box 43 Williamsburg WV 24991-0043 E-mail: pamscottpa@citlink.net.

SCOTT, PHILIP JOHN, medical educator, general physician; b. Auckland, New Zealand, June 26, 1931; s. Horace MacDonald and Doris Annie (Ruddock) S.; m. Elizabeth Jane MacMillan, Oct. 3, 1956 (dec. Mar. 03, 2002), Margaret Fernie Wann (dec. Nov. 11, 2007); children: Janet Elizabeth, Michael John, Jennifer Margaret, Philippa Anne; m. Alison Rhona Roberton. B of Med. Sci., U. Otago, 1952, MB, BChir, 1955; MD, U. Birmingham, England, 1962. Internship Auckland, Green Lane and Middlemore Hosps., Auckland, New Zealand, 1956-57; postgrad. Royal Postgrad. Med. Sch. London, 1959-60; residency Auckland Hosp., 1958; jr. med. officer Auckland Hosp. Bd., 1956-58; house physician Royal Postgrad. Med. Sch., London, 1959; med. registrar, jr. rsch. fellow Nat. Health Svc. and Med. Rsch. Coun. Gt. Britain, Birmingham, England, 1960-62, Queen Elizabeth Hosp., Birmingham, England, 1960-62, U. Birmingham; from assoc. prof. to prof of medicine, head dept. medicine U. Auckland, 1973-87; head acad. unit Middlemore Hosp., Auckland, 1988-97; prof. emeritus U. Auckland, 1997—. Chmn. allocation and orgn. com. New Zealand Bd. Health, Wellington, 1985-87; bd. dirs. Counties Manakau Health Ltd. Contbr. articles to profl. jours. Com. mem. Hosp. and Related Svcs. Task Force, Wellington, 1987-88. Decorated knight comdr. Her Majesty the Queen, 1987. Fellow Royal Australasian Coll. Physicians, Royal Coll. Physicians London, Royal Soc. London, Royal Soc. New Zealand (lead in environment report 1986, pres. 1997-2000). Avocations: pottery, gardening, literature, medical history. Home and Office: 64 Temple St Meadowbank 1072 Auckland New Zealand Office Phone: 0064-9-5215384. Business E-Mail: maesket@clear.net.nz.

SCOTT, RALPH MASON, retired radiologist, educator; b. Leemont, Va., Nov. 23, 1921; s. Benjamin Thomas and Marion Hazel (Mason) S.; m. Alice Latine Francisco, Dec. 21, 1946; children: Susan Taylor, Ralph Mason, John Thomas. BA, U. Va., 1947; MD, Med. Coll. Va., 1950. Diplomate Am. Bd. Radiology (trustee 1965-76, treas. 1969-70, v.p. 1970-72, pres. 1972-74). Intern Robert Packer Hosp., Sayre, Pa., 1953-54, resident, 1954-57, dir. radiation therapy and nuclear medicine sect., 1957-59; fellow Christie Hosp. and Holt Radium Inst., Manchester, England, 1956-57; asst. prof. radiology U. Chgo. Med. Sch., 1959-60; assoc. prof. radiology, dir. radiation therapy and radioisotopes U. Louisville Med. Sch., 1960-64, prof., dir. radiation therapy, 1964-77; prof. and chmn. dept. rad. oncology U Lousiville, 1974-77; prof. radiation therapy U. Louisville Med. Sch., 1981-82; prof. emeritus U. Louisville, 1995; dir. J. Graham Brown Regional Cancer Ctr., Health Scis. Ctr. U. Louisville Med. Sch., 1981-82; dir. dept. radiation medicine Christ Hosp., Cin., 1982-93; ret. Clin. prof. radiology U. Cin. Coll. Medicine, 1982-93; prof., chmn. dept. therapeutic radiology U. Md. Sch. Med., 1977-80; dir. radiation therapy program div. cancer rsch. resources and ctrs., Nat. Cancer Inst. (on leave from U. Louisville), 1976-77. Pres. Ky. divsn. Am. Cancer Soc., 1972-73; bd. dirs. Living Arrangements for the Developmentally Disabled, 1993-95, No. Ky. Assn. for the Retarded, 1993-95, Day Spring Inc., 1993-95, United Health Care, 1994-95, Seven Counties Svcs., Inc., 1997-2003, J. Graham Brown Regional Cancer Ctr. Corp., 1997—. Lt. (j.g.) USNR, 1943-46, PTO. Mem. Am. Roentgen-Ray Soc. (exec. coun. 1968—, chmn. exec. coun. 1972-73), AMA, Am. Coll. Radiology (vice chmn. commn. on cancer 1968-69), Am. Radium Soc., Am. Soc. Therapeutic Radiologists, Assn. U. Radiologists, Radiol. Soc. N.Am., Pi Kappa Alpha, Phi Chi. Home: Treyton Oak Towers 211 W Oak St Apt 922 Louisville KY 40203 Personal E-mail: ramsco1@earthlink.net.

SCOTT, RICHARD MALACHI, psychologist; b. Bklyn., Dec. 15, 1968; s. David Malachi and Olive Scott. AA in Gen. Studies, Mira Costa Coll., 1990, AS in Psychology, 1990, AA in Visual Arts, 1990; BA in Psychology, U. Calif., San Diego, 1991; MA in Clin. Psychology, We. Am. U., 1993; PhD in Clin. Psychology, Saybrook Inst., 2000; postgrad., Coll. Medicine & Health Scis., St. Lucia; D Clin. Hypnosis, Nat. Bd. Ethical Stds., 2008. Lic. clin. psychologist. Social worker, case worker Salvation Army, Family Svcs. Divsn., San Diego, 1993—2000; social worker Dept. Pub. Social Svcs., Riverside, Calif., 1996—98; psychol. asst. various orgns., Calif., 1997—2009; clin. psychologist Calfi. Dept. Corrections, Chino, Calif., 2000—08; pvt. practice San Diego, 2004—. Project and clin. dir. So. Calif. Alcohol and Drug Program, Inc., Downey, Calif., 2004; clin. psychologist Geriatric Cons., Inc., San Diego, 2003—08, Dept. of Corrections, San Diego. Mem.: Nat. Acad. Sports Medicine, San Diego Psychol. Assn., APA. Avocations: dance, drawing, painting, sculpting, singing. Home: 3474 Del Sol Blvd Condo C San Diego CA 92154-3508 Personal E-mail: research2005@hotmail.com.

SCOTT, RICHARD THOMAS, JR., reproductive endocrinologist; b. Selma, Ala., Nov. 28, 1958; s. Richard Thomas and Cynthia Marvin (Coleman) S.; m. Blair MacKerer, June 16, 1979; children: Whitney Blair, Katherine Leigh, Richard Thomas III. BS in Chemistry, Randolph Macon Coll., 1979; MD, U. Va., Charlottesville, 1983. Diplomate Nat. Bd. Med. Examiners, Am. Bd. Ob-Gyn., reproductive endocrinology divsn; bd. cert. high complexity lab dir. embryology, andrology, endocrinology, Am. Bd. Bioanalysts. Commd. 2nd lt. USAF, 1979, advanced through grades to lt. col., 1993; intern Wilford Hall USAF Med. Ctr., San Antonio, 1983-84, resident, 1984-87, chief reproductive endocrinology Lackland AFB, Tex., 1989-93, fellow Jones Inst. for Reproductive Medicine, Ea. Va. Med. Sch., Norfolk, 1987-89; chief reproductive endocrinology Uniformed Svcs. U. Health Scis., Bethesda, Md., 1993—, asst. prof., 1990—, assoc. prof., 1993—. Adj. scientist S.W. Found. Biomed. Rsch., 1990—, dir. Assisted Reproductive Technology, Reproductive Medicine Assocs. of N.J., Morristown, N.J. Ad hoc reviewer Fertility and Sterility, Jour. Clin. Endocrinology and Metabolism, Ob-Gyn., Am. Jour. Ob-Gyn., Contraception, Maturitas, Jour. Pediatric and Adolescent Gynecology, Internat. Jour. Infertility, Jour. In Vitro Fertilization and Embryo Transfer; contbr. articles to profl. jours. and abstracts. Lt Col USAF, 1993—95, Uniformed Services University of the Health Sciences. Grantee Surgeon Gen., Wyeth Rsch., Solvay Pharm. Rsch., Hitachi of Am., Tap Pharms. Fellow Am. Coll. Obstetricians and Gynecologists (chmns. award Armed Forces dist. meeting 1988, Searle award 1989, Prof. of Yr. 1991); mem. Am. Fertility Soc. (Best Poster award 1988), N.Am. Menopausal Soc., Soc. Air Force Clin. Surgeons, Endocrine Soc., Soc. Reproductive Endocrinologists, Phi Beta Kappa, Chi Beta Phi, Omicron Delta Kappa. Achievements include receiving several awards for research. Office: RMA of NJ 111 Madison Ave Ste 100 Morristown NJ 07960-6083 Home: 170 Post Kennel Rd Far Hills NJ 07931-2408

SCOTT, RICK (RICHARD LYNN SCOTT), Governor of Florida, investment company executive; b. Bloomington, Ill., Dec. 1, 1952; s. Orba and Esther Scott; m. Annette Holland, 1971; children: Allison, Jordan. BSBA, U. Mo., 1975; JD, Southern Meth. U., 1978. Bar: Tex. Chmn., CEO Columbia/HCA Healthcare Corp., Nashville, 1987-97; pres., CEO Richard L. Scott Investments, LLC, Naples, Fla., 1997—2001; co-founder, chmn. Solantic Corp., Jacksonville, Fla., 2001—11; founder Conservatives For Patients' Rights (CPR), 2009—19; gov. State of Fla., 2011—. Bd. dirs. CyberGuard, 2001—03, Solantic Corp., 2001—11, Secure Computing Corp., 2006—08. Mem. nat. bd. The United Way, 1997—2003. Served in USN, 1971—74. Recipient Second Century award for Excellence in Health Care, Columbia U. Sch. Nursing, 1995, Entrepreneurship award, George Washington U., 2007; named CEO of the Yr., Financial World mag., 1995; named one of The Top 25 Performers, US News & World Report, 1995, America's 25 Most Influential People, TIME mag., 1996. Mem.: Bus. Coun., Bus. Roundtable, Healthcare Leadership Coun. Republican. Christian. Office: Office of Governor The Capitol 400 S Monroe St Tallahassee FL 32399-0001 also: Richard L Scott Investments LLC 1400 Gulfshore Blvd N Ste 148 Naples FL 34102 Office Phone: 239-263-9030, 212-398-2020, 850-488-2272. Office Fax: 239-263-9031, 212-398-2033. *

SCOTT, WALTER JOSEPH, thoracic surgeon; MD, U. Chgo., 1981. Diplomate Am. Bd. Thoracic Surgery, lic. Pa., 2001. Resident gen. surgery The Univ. Chgo. Med. Ctr., 1987, fellow cardiovascular physiology and cardiothoracic surgery, 1988; chief thoracic surgery Fox Chase Cancer Ctr. Named one of Top Doctors, Phila. Mag., 2008, 2011. Fellow: ACS; mem.: Am. Soc. of Clin. Oncology, Soc. of Thoracic Surgeons. Office: Fox Chase Cancer Center 333 Cottman Ave Philadelphia PA 19111-2497 Office Phone: 215-728-6900.

SCOTTI, DENNIS JOSEPH, educator, researcher, consultant; b. NYC, Apr. 20, 1952; s. Joseph and Theresa (Giancola) S. BS, Stony Brook U., 1974; MBA, Adelphi U., 1977; MS, Temple U., 1980, PhD, 1982. Bd. cert. in healthcare mgmt.; cert. managed care and healthcare fin. profl. Dep. chief administr. Dept. Mental Health Devel. Ctr., Suffolk, N.Y., 1975-77; asst. prof. Rutgers U., N.J., 1980-83; assoc.

prof. Fairleigh Dickinson U., N.J., 1983-88, prof., 1989—, sr. prof. Ctr. Healthcare Mgmt. Studies, 2001—06, Alfred E. Driscoll endowed prof., 2006—. Exec. v.p. Presscott Assocs., Ltd., Avon, Conn., 1989—. Co author: Strategic Management in the Health Care Sector, 1988; contbr. articles to profl. jours. Mem. Regents Adv. Coun. N.J.; bd. trustees, quality of paitent com. CentraState Healthcare Sys., N.J. Recipient Tchg. Excellence award Exec. MBA, 1997, HFMA medal, 2011. Fellow Am. Coll. Healthcare Execs., Healthcare Fin. Mgmt. Assn. (William G. Fulmer Bronze award 1997, Robert H. Reeves Silver award 2001, Frederick T. Muncie award 2004, co-recipient Helen M. Yerger Spl. Recognition award 2002, ACHE Svc. award 2009, ACHE Regents Leadership award 2010); mem. Med. Group Mgmt. Assn., Health Planning and Mktg. Soc., Acad. Mgmt. (co-recipient Best Theory to Practice award 2003), Health Decisions Assembly, Phi Theta Kappa, Delta Mu Delta, Beta Gamma Sigma. Office: Fairleigh Dickinson U 1000 River Rd Teaneck NJ 07666-1996

SCOVEL, MARY ALICE, retired music therapy educator; b. Grand Rapids, Mich., Jan. 28, 1936; d. Carl Edward and Alice Bertha (Bieri) Sennema; m. Ward Norman Scovel, July 7, 1956; children: Marcia, Katherine, Steven (dec.), Carl (dec.). MusB, Western Mich. U., 1969; MusM, Mich. State U., 1975. Registered music therapist; bd. cert. Asst. prof. music Grand Valley State U., Allendale, Mich., 1969-75; instr. U. Dayton (Ohio), 1975-78, Muskegon (Mich.) Community Coll., 1978-80; intern dir. Battle Creek (Mich.) Adventist Hosp., 1980-84; prof. music therapy Western Mich. U., Kalamazoo, 1984-95; ret., 1995; owner, pvt. practice Health Harmonics, Honolulu, 1997-98; ret., 1998; dir. Sun Tones Women's Barbershep Chorus, 2010—. Cons. Pre-sch. Physically Handicapped, Wyo., Mich., 1974, Doris Klausen Devel. Ctr., Battle Creek, 1985-86; music therapist, sound practitioner and trainer, Tahlequah, Okla., 1995-97; pvt. practice health harmonics, 1997—; chmn. Multi-clinic, Kalamazoo, 1988-89. Author: Music Therapy in Treatment of Adults, 1990, Surviving Suicide: My Journey to the Light Within, 2003; co-editor Music Therapy Perspectives; cited in The Mozart Effect by Don Campbell, 1997; contbr. articles to profl. jours. Lay del. United Meth. Ch., Albion, Mich., 1991; vol. coord. United Hospice Beaufort, SC, 2005-06, dir. choir chimes PEP/Programs for Exceptional People, 2005—; music therapist Hospice Care Low Country, Bluffton, SC, 2006—. Mem. Am. Music Therapy Assn. (del., Life Achievement award), Nat. Assn. Mental Illness, Great Lakes Region Music Therapy (past pres.), Mich. Music Therapists, AAUW, Pi Delta Alpha, Pi Kappa Lambda. Avocations: reading, cross country skiing, singing, swimming, quilting. Home: 112 Doncaster Ln Bluffton SC 29909 Home Phone: 843-705-3633. Personal E-mail: mwscovel@sc.rr.com.

SCRANTON, RICHARD, medical association administrator; b. New Hartford, NY, Oct. 14, 1966; MD, Quillen Coll. Medicine, 1994; MPH, Harvard Sch. Pub. Health, 2002. Dir. spl. projects Vet. Affairs, 2002—06; assoc. physician Brigham and Women's Divsn. Aging, 2002—09; co-dir. gen. medicine fellowship va campus Harvard Med. Sch., 2004—06; chief med. officer VeroScience, 2006—. Asst. prof. Harvard Med. Sch., 2006—10. Decorated Navy and Marine CORPS Commendation medal US Navy. Mem.: Am. Diabetes Assn. Office: 1334 Main Rd Tiverton RI 02878 Office Fax: 401-816-0524. Business E-Mail: richard_scranton@veroscience.com.

SCRIMSHAW, NEVIN STEWART, physician, nutritionist, educator; b. Jan. 20, 1918; m. Mary Ware Goodrich, 1941; 5 children. BA with honors, Ohio Wesleyan U., 1938; MA in Biology, Harvard U., 1939, PhD in Physiology, 1941, MPH, 1959; MD with honors, U. Rochester, 1945. Intern Gorgas Hosp., 1945-46; Rockefeller postdoctoral fellow U. Rochester, NY, 1946—47, Merck NRC fellow NY, 1947—49; asst. resident in ob-gyn. Strong Meml. Hosp., Genesee Hosp., NY, 1948—49; dir. Inst. Nutrition C.Am. and Panama, Guatemala, 1949—61, cons. dir., 1961—65, cons., 1965—. Cons. nutrition Pan-Am. San Bur. WHO, 1948—49, regional advisor on nutrition, 1949—53; dir. Clin. Rsch. Ctr. MIT, 1962—66, 1979—83, dir. internat. food and nutrition program, 1976—88, prof. human nutrition, 1961—76, head dept. nutrition and food sci., 1961—79, inst. prof., 1976—87, emeritus, 1988—; vis. prof. Columbia U., NYC, 1976—88, vis. lectr., 1961—66, Harvard U., 1968—85; adj. prof. Tufts U.; mem. govt. adv. com. NIH; chmn. internat. com. NRC; dir. devel. studies divsn. UN U., 1985—86, food nutrition program, 1975—97, sr. advisor, 1998—; mem. adv. com. WHO, Nutrition Found., others. Editor (with others): Amino Acid Fortification of Protein Foods, 1971, Nutrition, National Development and Planning, 1973, The Economics, Marketing and Technology of Fish Protein Concentrate, 1974, Development: Significance and Potential for the Tropics, 1976, Single-Cell Protein: Safety for Animal and Human Feeding, 1979, Nutrition Policy Implementation: Issues and Experience, 1983, Diarrhea and Malnutrition: Interactions, Mechanisms and Interventions, 1983, Chronic Energy Deficiency, 1987, Acceptability of Milk and Milk Products in Populations with Lactose Intolerance, 1988, Nutrition in the Elderly, 1989, Activity, Energy Expenditure and Energy Requirements of Infants and Children, 1990, RAP: Rapid Assessment Procedures: Qualitative Methodologies for Planning and Evaluation of Health Related Programs, 1992, Protein-energy Interactions, 1992, Community-based Longitudinal Nutrition and Health Studies: Classical Examples from Guatemala, Haiti, and Mexico, 1995, The Effects of Improved Nutrition in Early Childhood: The Institute of Nutrition of Central American and Panama Follow-up Study, 1995, The Nutrition and Health Transition of Democratic Costa Rica, 1995, Energy and Protein Requirements, 1996, Causes and Consequences of Intrauterine Growth Retardation, 2000; contbr. articles to profl. jours. Trustee Rockefeller Found., 1971—83, Pan-Am. Health and Edn. Found., 1986—92; pres. Internat. Nutrition Found. for Developing Countries, 1982—. Recipient Osborne and Mendal award, 1960, Internat. award, Inst. Food Technologists, 1969, medal of honor, Fundacion F. Cuenca Villoro, Spain, 1978, Bristol-Myers prize, 1988, Alan Shawn Feinstein award, 1991, World Food prize, 1991, Kellogg award in internat. nutrition, 2002, Lifetime Achievement award, UN, 2004. Fellow: APHA (v.p. 1978, award of excellence in promoting and protecting health of people 1974), AAAS, Am. Soc. Clin. Nutrition, Royal Soc. Health, Am. Soc. Nutritional Scis.; mem.: NAS (chair applied biol. sect. 1973—76, 1988—91), Nat. Inst. Medicine, others, Internat. Epidemiol. Assn., Internat. Union Nutritional Scis. (pres. 1978—81), Am. Epidemiol. Soc., Am. Physiol. Soc., Mass. Med. Soc., New Eng. Pub. Health Assn., Mass. Pub. Health Assn., Am. Bd. Nutrition, Am. Coll. Preventive Medicine, Am. Coll. Nutrition, Am. Acad. Arts and Scis., Inst. Medicine NAS. Home and Office: Sandwich Mountain Farm 115 Sandwich Notch Rd PO Box 330 Campton NH 03223-0330 Office Phone: 603-726-4200. Office Fax: 603-726-4614. Business E-Mail: nscrimshaw@inffoundation.org.

SCRIMSHAW, SUSAN CROSBY, academic administrator; b. Nov. 12, 1945; m. Allan Stern; 1 child from previous marriage, Mary Corey March. AB, Barnard Coll., 1967; MA, Columbia U., 1969, PhD in Anthropology, 1974. Rsch. assoc. Internat. Inst. for Study of Human Reporduction, 1969—75; asst. prof. health adminstrn. Columbia U., 1975; asst. prof. pub. health Div. Population, Family and Internat. Health, Sch. Pub. Health UCLA, 1975—80, assoc. prof. Div. Population and Family Health, 1980—85, assoc. dir. Latin Am. Ctr., 1984—88, prof. pub. health and anthropology, 1985—96, acting chair Dept. Pub. Health, 1988—89, assoc. dean Academic Programs, 1988—94, acting dean, 1991—92, 1992—93; dean, prof. cmty. heath scis. and anthropology U. Ill. Sch. Pub. Health, Chgo., 1995—2006; pres. Simmons Coll., Boston, 2006—09; interim pres. Sage Colleges, 2009—. Co-editor: The Handbook of Social Studies in Health & Med. Recipient Margaret Mead award, 1985. Fellow: AAAS; mem.: Nat. Soc. Med. Anthropology (pres. 1985), Soc. Applied Anthropology, Am. Anthropology Assn., Inst. Medicine (coun. mem. 2006—). Office: Simmons Coll Office of Pres 300 The Fenway Boston MA 02115

SCRIVER, CHARLES ROBERT, medical researcher, human geneticist, retired medical educator; b. Montreal, Que., Can., Nov. 7, 1930; s. Walter deM. and Jessie (Boyd) S.; m. E.K. Peirce, Sept. 8, 1956; children: Dorothy, Peter, Julie, Paul. BA cum laude, McGill U., Montreal, 1951, MDCM cum laude, 1955; DSc (hon.), U. Man., 1992, U. Glasgow, 1993, U. Montreal, 1993, Utrecht U., 1999, U. B.C., 2002, U. We. Ont., 2007, McGill U., 2007. Intern Royal Victoria Hosp., Montreal, 1955-56; resident Royal Victoria and Montreal Children's Hosps., 1956-57, Children's Med. Ctr., Boston, 1957-58; McLaughlin travelling fellow Univ. Coll., London, 1958-60; chief resident pediat. Montreal Children's Hosp., 1960-61; asst. prof. pediat. McGill U., 1961, prof. biology Faculty of Sci., prof. pediat. Faculty of Medicine, 1969—, Alva prof. human genetics, 1994—2002, prof. emeritus, 2002—. Mem. med. adv. bd. Howard Hughes Med. Inst., 1981-88; dir. Med. Rsch. Coun. Group in Genetics, 1972-94; assoc. dir. Can. Genetic Diseases Network, 1989-98. Co-author: Amino Acid Metabolism and Its Disorders, 1973, Garrod's Inborn Factors in Disease, 1989; sr. online editor Metabolic and Molecular Bases Inherited Disease, 1986—2008; sr. editor emeritus, 2008-, contbr. more than 600 rsch. publs. in field. Decorated Order of Can., Que., Mont.; recipient Wood Gold medal, McGill U., 1955, Gairdner Internat. award, Gairdner Found., 1979, Prix Michel-Sarrazin, Club de Rech Clin du Que., 1988, Ross award, Can. Pediatric Soc., 1990, Award of Excellence, Genet Soc. Can., 1992, Prix d'Excellence, Inst. Rsch. Clin. de Montreal, 1993, Prix du Quebec, Wilder Penfield, 1995, Lifetime Achievement award, Montreal Children's Hosp., 1995, Medal of Merit, Can. Med. Assn., 1996, Lifetime Achievement award, March of Dimes Birth Defects Found., 1997, Querci Found. prize, Italy, 2001, Founders award, Can. Coll. Med. Geneticist, 2003, Folling medal, European PKU Rsch. Group, 2010, Pollin Pediat. Rsch. prize, Columbia U. NY Presbyn. Hosp., 2010, Medicine Alumni Global Lifetime Achievement award, Mc Gill U., 2009; named Royal Coll. lectr., 1992, Disting. Scientist, Med. Rsch. Coun., 1995—; named to Can. Med. Hall of Fame, 2001, Can. Sci. Engring. Hall of Fame, 2001; Markle scholar, 1962—67. Fellow: AAAS, Royal Soc. London (Can. Rutherford lectr. 1983), Royal Soc. Can. (McLaughlin medal 1981), Royal Coll. Physicians of Ireland (hon.), Am. Coll. Med. Genetics (hon.); mem.: Am. Acad. Pediat. (Mead Johnson award for rsch. in pediat. 1968), Soc. Francaise de Pediat., Brit. Pediat. Assn. (50th Anniversary lectr. 1978), Assn. Am. Physicians, Am. Soc. Clin. Investigation, Am. Pediat. Soc. (pres. 1994—95, Howland award 2010), Am. Soc. Human Genetics (dir. 1971—74, pres. 1986—87, William Allan award 1978, Award of Excellence in Human Genetics Edn. 2001), Soc. Pediat. Rsch. (pres. 1975—76), Can. Soc. Clin. Investigation (pres. 1974—75, G. Malcolm Brown Meml. award 1979, Henry Friesen award 2001). Office: McGill Univ-Montreal Childrens Hosp Rsch Inst 2300 Tupper St Montreal PQ Canada H3H 1P3 Business E-Mail: charles.scriver@mcgill.ca.

SCULATI, MICHELE, nutritionist, consultant; b. Bergamo, Italy, July 23, 1974; s. Delfina Ghilardi-Sculati and Oliviero Sculati; m. Laura Zanolin, Dec. 14, 2007. MD, U. Pavia, Italy, 1999, cert. in Clin. Nutrition cum laude, 2003—, PhD, 2009. Exec. com. mem. Centri Mara Selvini, Milan, 2005—. Self employed Med. Ambultory, Bergamo, Italy, 2002—; cons. Galbusera, Sondrio, Italy, 2007—, Edelman, Milan, 2008—, Nutrition Found. Italy, 2011. Performer: (radio program) Gastronauta on Radio 24. Recipient award, Italian Dietetic Assn. Congress, 2004, European Assn. for the Study of Obesity, Congress, 2008. Mem.: Italian Ice Cream Inst. Sci. Com., Italian Obesity Soc., Italian Dietetic Assn. Office: Dr Michele Sculati Piazza Oberdan 7 Bergamo 24127 Italy Office Phone: 035258723. Office Fax: 035258723; Home Fax: 0350797841. Business E-Mail: info@sculati.it.

SCULCO, THOMAS PETER, surgeon; b. NYC, Feb. 20, 1944; s. Alfred Francis and Mary Jacqueline Sculco; m. Cynthia Davis, June 4, 1966; children: Sarah Jane, Peter. BA in Classics, Brown U., 1965; MD, Coll. of Physicians and Surgeons Columbia U., 1969. Intern in gen. surgery Roosevelt Hosp., NYC, 1969-70, resident in orthopedic surgery, 1970-71; orthop. fellowship London Hosp., 1974—75; asst. attending orthopedic surgery Meml. Hosp., NYC, 1977-83; resident in orthopedic surgery Hosp. for Spl. Surgery, 1971-74, asst. attending orthopedic surgery, 1977-83, assoc. attending orthopedic surgery, 1983-91, attending surgeon in orthopedics, 1991—, Korein-Wilson prof. orthopedic surgery, surgeon-in-chief, med. dir.; asst. attending orthopedic surgery NY Hosp., 1977-83, attending surgeon in orthopedics, 1991—; cons. orthopedic surgeon Mary Manning Walsh Nursing Home, 1978—, Meml. Hosp., 1983—, Bronx Vets. Adminstrn. Hosp., 1987—; from asst. to assoc. prof. clin. surgery Cornell U., 1977-91; dept. chmn., prof. clin. surgery in orthopedics Weill Med. Coll., Cornell U., 1991—. Chief surg. arthritis svc. Hosp. for Spl. Surgery, 1993-2003, dir. orthopedic surgery, 1993-2003, surgeon-in-chief, 2003—; sr. scientist Hosp. for Spl. Surgery, 1996—. Mem. editl. bd. Surg. Blood Mgmt. Forum, 1997. Trustee NY chpt. Arthritis Found., 1997—; mem. Carnegie Hill Assn., St. Bernard's Sch.; bd. dirs. Westerley (RI) Cmty. Chorus, 190-96; sponsor Westerley Pub. Libr., 1996; patron Met. Opera, Carnegie Hall. MC maj. USAF, 1975—77. Recipient Clint Compere award Twentieth Century Orthopedic Assn., 1997, Lifetime Achievement award Arthritis Found., 1999,; recipient numerous grants; named Best Doctors in NY, NY Mag., 2003 Mem. AMA, NY County Med. Soc., Am. Acad. Orthopedic Surgeons (com. on data svcs. chmn. 1981-85, coun. musculoskeletal specialty socs. 1986-90, coord. com. on health policy 1986-89, task force on data chmn. 1987, com. on clin. policies 1991—, patent edn. com. 1999—, liaison to bd. trustees Arthritis Found. 1999—, bd. dirs. 1999-2001), NY Acad. Medicine, NY State Orthopedic Soc., Eastern Orthopedic Soc., Am. Orthopedic Soc., Austrian Orthop. Soc. (hon.), Interurban Orthopedic Assn., Am. Rheumatism Assn., Orthopedic Rsch. and Edn. Found., Knee Soc. (founding mem. 1983, exec. com. 1983-84, program chmn. 1986, membership com. 1986-93, chmn. 1992-93, edn. com. 1990-94, chmn. 1993-94), Assn. VA Orthopedic Surgeons (founder 1986, sec.-treas. 1986-88), Assn. for Arthritis Hip and Knee Surgery, Acad. Orthopedic Soc., Physicians Sci. Soc., Med. Strollers, Internat. Soc. Tech. in Arthroplasty, Am. Austrian Found. (bd. dirs. 2000—), Hip Soc. (membership com. 2000—, Otto Aufranc Rsch. award 1991, Charnley Rsch. award 1995), Austrian Orthop. Assn. (hon.). Office: The Hosp for Spl Surgery 535 E 70th St New York NY 10021 Address: Belaire Bldg 525 East 71st St 2nd Fl between York Ave and East River New York NY 10021 Office Phone: 212-606-1475. Office Fax: 212-734-9572. Business E-Mail: sculcot@hss.edu.

SCULLY, JAMES HENRY, JR., psychiatrist, educator; b. New Britain, Conn., Jan. 14, 1944; s. James Henry and Marietta (Maguire) S.; m. Mary Elizabeth Hailey, Sept. 6, 1969; children: Jennifer, Sarah. A.B., Georgetown U., 1965 MD, Tulane U., 1969. Diplomate Am. Bd. Psychiatry and Neurology. Resident in psychiatry U. Colo., Denver, 1975—76, instr. psychiatry, 1976—78, dir. med. student edn. in psychiatry, 1978—86, asst. prof. psychiatry, 1978—82, assoc. prof. psychiatry, 1983—92, dir. residency training, 1985—92; former prof., chair neuropsychiatry U. SC; CEO, med. dir. American Psychiatric Assn., Arlington, Va. Chief cons. Denver VA, 1978-92; dir. profl. edn. Colo. State Hosp., 1979-87, vice chmn. dept. psychiatry, 1987-92; sr. examiner Am. Bd. Psychiatry and Neurology, bd. dirs., 2000—; mem. fin. com. Am. Bd. Med. Spltys., 2000—. Editor: Psychiatry, 3rd edit., 1996, 4th edit., 2001; editor-in-chief PRITE, 1995-98; contbr. chpts. to books. Trustee Ctr. for Creative Arts Therapy; pres. univ. trust U. S.C. Sch. Medicine, 2000. Served to lt. comdr. USN, 1969—73. Recipient Kaiser Permanente teaching award Colo. U., 1982, AACAP award, 2000; co-recipient VA Award for Valor, 1984. Fellow Am. Psychiat. Assn. (dep. med. dir. 1992-96, chair coun. on med. edn. 1997); mem. AMA (chair sect. coun. on psychiatry 2000—), Am. Coll. Psychiatrists (bd. regents 2000—, chair sci. program com.), Colo. Psychiat. Soc. (trustee), Assn. of Dirs. of Med. Student Edn. in Psychiatry, Assn. Dirs. Psychiatry Residency Tng., Assn. Acad. Psychiatry, Denver Barbarians Rugby Football Club, Cosmos (Wash.) Club. Democrat. Office: Am Psychiatric Assn Ste 1825 1000 Wilson Blvd Arlington VA 22209 E-mail: jscully@psych.org. *

SCULLY, MARTHA SEEBACH, speech and language pathologist; b. S.I., Nov. 1, 1951; d. Henry F. and Rose Anne (Callahan) Seebach; m. Roger Tehan Scully, Dec. 29, 1979; 1 child, Roger Tehan. BA, Trinity Coll., 1972; MS, George Washington U., 1974; postgrad., Syracuse U., NY, 1976-79. Lic. speech-lang. pathologist, Md. Clin. supr. Syracuse U., 1976-79; speech-lang. pathologist Fairfax (Va.) County Pub. Schs., 1979—. Bd. dirs. Trinity Coll., Washington, Nat. Children's Choir, 1987-91; trustee Davis Meml. Goodwill Industries, 1994-96, bd. dirs. Goodwill Guild, 1990—, chair ball; docent Folger Shakespearean Libr.; chmn. Nat. Challenge Com. of Disabled, 1985; mem. Ear Ball, 1988, 89; mem. Internat. Children's Festival, 1990, 91; co-chmn. Jr. League of Washington Capital Collection, 1990; chmn. Salvation Army Garden Party, 1992, Washington Embassy Tour, 1993; mem. bd. edn. Holy Cross Sch., Garrett Park, Md., 2001-. Recipient First Order Affiliation Order of Franciscans mirror, 1985; named Outstanding Woman in Am., 1987, 88. Mem. Am. Biog. Inst., Am. Speech-Lang.-Hearing Assn., Coun. for Exceptional Children, Montgomery County Assn. for Hearing Impaired Children, Benevolent and Protective Order Elks (mem. Washinton-Rockville lodge, lecturing knight 1999, esteemed loyal knight 2000, 2008-; chaplain, 2006-07), Christ Child Soc., John Caroll Soc., Chevy Chase Women's Republican Club, Junior League Wash. Home: 14621 Edelmar Dr Silver Spring MD 20906-1762

SCULLY, THOMAS A. (TOM SCULLY), lawyer, former federal agency administrator; b. 1957; BA, U. Va., 1979; JD, Catholic U. America, 1986. Staff asst. Fed. Election Commn., 1979—81; staff asst. to Senator Slade Gorton US Senate, 1981—85; atty. Akin, Gump, Strauss, Hauer & Feld, LLP, 1986—88; comm. staff Bush-Quayle Campaign, 1988, dep. dir. congressional affairs; assoc. dir. for human resources, veterans & labor Office Mgmt. & Budget (OMB), Exec. Office of the Pres., Washington, 1989—92, counselor to the dir., 1992—93; dep. asst. to Pres. The White House, Washington, 1992—93; ptnr. Patton Boggs, LLP, Washington, 1993—95; pres., CEO Fedn. American Hospitals, 1995—2001; adminstr. Centers. for Medicare and Medicaid Services (CMS) US Dept. Health & Human Services (HHS), Washington, 2001—03; sr. counsel Alston & Bird LLP, Washington, 2003—. Republican. Office: Alston & Bird LLP 10th Fl N Bldg 950 F St NW Ste 1 Washington DC 20004-1439 Office Phone: 202-239-3459. Office Fax: 202-654-4969. E-mail: thomas.scully@alston.com. *

SEABORG, DAVID MICHAEL, evolutionary biologist; b. Berkeley, Calif., Apr. 22, 1949; s. Glenn Theodore and Helen Lucille (Griggs) S.; m. Adele Fong Yee, June 17, 1990. BS, U. Calif., Davis, 1972; MA, U. Calif., Berkeley, 1974. Biology tchr. U. Calif., Berkeley, 1972-73; biol. rschr., photographer Trans Time Labs, Berkeley, 1978; pvt. practice, 1974—; hypnosis and self-hypnosis tchr. Open Edn. Exchange, Oakland, Calif., 1978—81; biol. tchr. Oakland Mus., Calif., 1983-87; rsch. biologist, dept. ecology and evolutionary biology U. Calif., Irvine, 1987; pres. dir. Rsch. Found.

for Biol. Conservation and Rsch., Walnut Creek, Calif., 1983—; radio talk show host Sta. KPFA, Berkeley, 1996; biology and life sci tchr. Phillip and Sala Burton Acad. H.S., San Francisco, 1996-97; lab. Chem. Biodynamics U. Calif., Berkeley, 1975; amateur comedian, 1969—. Vol. asst. to curator Smithosonian Instn. 1966-67; lectr. sci, philos., environ. issues, 1974—; Inventor game, Sum-It, 1981; originator, theory of evolution based on organisms as integrated systems; originator, idea that genetic code is on an adaptive peak & how populations cross from one adaptive peak to another in evolution, 2010; chmn. Com. for Arts and Lectures, U. Calif., Berkeley, 1974-75; chmn. Bastille Day, Lafayette (Calif.)-Langeac Soc., 1982, master of ceremonies, 1982-86, 98-2000. Contbr. articles to profl. sci. jours.; author: (poetry book) Honor Thy Sowbug, 2008. Environ. organizer; founder, pres. U Turn Soc., Glenn Seaborg Open Space Fund, World Rainforest Fund, Found. for Biol. Conservation and Rsch.; creator, organizer press conf. on global environ. and social issues 100th Nobel Prize Festivities, Stockholm, 2001, alternate del. Dem. Party Nat. Convention, Denver, 2008. Recipient Meritorius Svc. award Smithsonian Inst., 1967, Animal Photograph award Soc. Photographic Scientists and Engrs., 1967, Best of Show Photo Contest award Klamath Basin Audubon Soc., 1991; award Nat. Libr. Poetry, 1995, 99, 2006, 07, award Big Yr. Environ. Competition, 2008. Mem.: UN Assn. of USA (East Bay chpt. bd. dirs. 2006—09), Nat. Resources Def. Coun., Earth Island Inst., World Wildlife Fund, Desert Tortoise Preserve Com., Population Connection, Save the Bay Assn., Greenpeace, Rainforest Action Network, Nature Conservancy, Calif. Alumni Assn., Calif. Aggie Alumni Assn., Sierra Club, Club of Rome USA (bd. dirs. 1995—2008, v.p. 1998—2001). Democrat. Address: 1888 Pomar Way Walnut Creek CA 94598-1424 E-mail: davidseaborg@juno.com.

SEAGER, DAUNA GAYLE OLSON-STOKES, speech therapist; b. Logan, Utah, Sept. 22, 1925; d. Helmar Alexander and La Rena Barnes (Jones) Olson; m. Arch Jr. Stokes, Aug. 5, 1943 (dec. Apr.il 1970); children: Jeffrey David, John Phillip, Jeannette; m. Floyd W. Seager, July 7, 1973 (dec. Oct. 1996). AS, Weber State U., Ogden, Utah, 1964; BS, Utah State U., Logan, 1969, MS in Audiology Speech Pathology, 1969. X-ray ech., physician asst. Robins X-Ray, Ogden, Utah, 1946-52; asst. to supt. Lyman Pub. Schs., Wyo., 1952-60; clinic supr. Utah State U., Logan, 1965-69; speech, language, hearing therapist Weber/Davis Sch. District, Ogden, Farmington, Utah, 1969-73, various, Utah, 1970-90; co-founder, coord. Clinic at O.R.M., Ogden, Utah, 1988—, chair coord. Bd. dirs. Weber County DUP Mus., Ogden. Author: Pioneer Settlers, 1990; contbr. articles to profl. jours. Co-founder Seager Indigent Clinic, Ogden Mission, Utah, 1988—; organized Stroke Club for Families of CVA Support Group, Ogden, 1972-74, Stroke Unit St. Benedict's Hosp., Ogden, 1972-74, Parent Child Tchr. Group, Ogden, 1970-73; mem. Ogden Sesquicentennial Com., OgSesqui, 2000—, Weber County Sesquicentennial, 2000; co-chair Ogden Mayor's Cemetery Enhancement Commn; mem. cmty rels com McKay Dee Hosp, 2000—. Fellow Utah State U., Logan, 1967-68, 68-69; recipient Point of Light award #101 Gov. Utah, 2003. Mem.: DAR, Mus. Action Team, Fedn. Ogden Bus. Profl. Women Internat., Weber County Women's Legis. Coun. and Rep. Women, Weber Far South Ctr. Co., Utah Mus. Assn. (bd. dirs.), Ogden Mayors Project (cemetery com., sesquicentennial com.), Altrusa Internat., Daus. of Utah Pioneers, Child Culture Club, Aglaia Club. Mem. Lds Ch. Avocations: historian/lecturer, writing, golf, bridge, swimming, ballroom dancing. Home and Office: 4046 South 895 East Ogden UT 84403-2416 Personal E-mail: dgoseager@goggle.com.

SEAGLE, EDGAR FRANKLIN, environmental engineer, consultant; b. Lincolnton, NC, June 27, 1924, s. Franklin Craig and Lillie Mae (James) S.; m. Doris Elaine Long, Mar. 23, 1958; children: Rebecca Jane, Mary Elaine, James Craig, William Franklin. AB in Chemistry, U. N.C., 1949, MS in Pub. Health, 1954; BCE, U. Fla., 1961; DPH, U. Tex., 1974. Registered profl. engr., Ala. Sr. sanitarian Health Dept., City of Charlotte, NC, 1950-52, chief indsl. hygiene sect. NC, 1956-59; sanitation cons. N.C. State Bd. Health, Raleigh, 1954-56; engr. dir. USPHS, Rockville, Md., 1961-78; asst. dir. Fellowship Office Nat. Acad. Scis., Washington, 1978-83; pub. health engr. Dept. of Environ., State of Md., Balt., 1985-88; ind. engring. cons. Rockville, 1984-85, 88—. Contbr. articles to profl. publs. With USN, 1943-46, PTO. Mem. ASCE, APHA, Am. Acad. Environ. Engrs. (diplomate). Methodist. Home and Office: 14108 Heathfield Ct Rockville MD 20853-2760 Personal E-mail: edgarseagle@comcast.net.

SEAH, STEVE, surgeon; MB and Surgery, 1984, M of Medicine in Ophthalmology, 1989. Fellow Royal Coll. physicians and Surgeons, Glasgow, 1989, Royal Coll. Ophthalmologist, England, 1989, Royal Coll. Surgeons, Edinburgh, 1989, Acad. Medicine, 1994; internat. sci. advisor Tianjin Eye centre; head and sr. cons. glaucoma svc. Singapore Nat. Eye Centre (SNEC), 1993—2005; head glaucoma rsch. unit Singapore Eye rsch. inst. (SERI), 1993—2005; tng. with dr. Alain Telandro, 2004; cons. Xiamen Eye Centre; sr. cons. ophthalmic surgeon eye clinic Gleneagles Hosp., Singapore; dir. Optimax Lasik Centre Pte Ltd., Singapore, Steve Seah Hosp. Svcs. Pte Ltd., Steve Seah Hosp. Pte Ltd. Founding exec. mem. Asian Oceanic Glaucoma Soc. (AOGS), organizing chmn. inaugural sci. meeting, Singapore, 1997; clin. sr. lectr. Nat. Univ., Singapore, 1999—2006; conf. organizing chmn. Asia Pacific Acad. of Ophthalmology, Singapore, 2006. Co-author numerous book chpts., sci. papers, articles and abstracts in various sci. jours. Lt. col. Combat Support Hosp. Recipient Local Merit Scholarship, Pub. Svc. Commn., 1979—84, 1st Prize on Biology Essay Competition, Ministry of Edn., 1978, Merit award for free Paper presentation, Singapore Nat. Eye Centre, 1993, Spl. Achievement award, 1997, Disting. Svc. award, Asia Pacific Acad. of Ophthalmology, 2001, 2006. Fellow: Acad. of Medicine Singapore (fellow 1993); mem.: Ministry of Healt (drug evaluation panel), Singapore Med. Coun., Asia-Pacific Acad. of Ophthalmology, Assn. for Rsch. in Vision and Ophthalmology (ARVO), Singapore Soc. of Ophthalmology (pres. 2002—07). Achievements include design of a divide and scoop technique which make phacoemulsification surgery for cataract faster and safer. Office: Steve Seah Eye Centre Camden Medical Centre One Orchard Blvd Number 16-01/02 248649 Singapore Office Phone: 6565656888. Office Fax: 6565659988. *

SEALY, LINDA, physiologist, educator; b. Kans. City, Mo., May 22, 1955; BA, Ill. Wesleyan U., 1976; PhD, U. Iowa, 1980. Assoc. prof., molecular physiology, biophysics, cell and devel. biology, cancer biology Vanderbilt U. Med. Sch., 1986—. Office: Dept Molecular Physiology Nashville TN 37232 Business E-Mail: linda.sealy@vanderbilt.edu.

SEAMAN, JILL, infectious diseases physician; b. Moscow, Idaho, May 26, 1952; BA, Middlebury Coll., Vt., 1974; MD, U. Wash. Sch. Medicine, Seattle, 1979; diploma, London Sch. Hygiene & Tropical Medicine, 1989. Diplomate Am. Bd. Family Medicine. Residence in family practice Natividad Med. Ctr., Salinas, Calif.; physican Doctors Without Borders, Old Fangak, Sudan, 1989—, also Yukon-Kuskokwim Health Corp., Bethel, Alaska. Contbr. articles to profl. jours. Named a MacArthur Fellow, John T. & Catherine MacArthur Found., 2009; named one of 10 Heroes of Medicine, TIME mag., 1997. Office: Yukon Kuskokwim Health Corp PO Box 528 Bethel AK 99559 Business E-Mail: jill_seaman@ykhc.org. *

SEAR, JOHN WILLIAM, retired medical educator; b. Enfield, Middlesex, Eng., Sept. 3, 1947; BSc, MBBS, U. London, 1972; PhD, U. Bristol, 1981. MRC tng. fellow, lectr. U. Bristol, 1977—81; anaesthetics reader U. Oxford, 1982—2002, anaesthetics prof., 2002—. Cons. anaesthetist Oxford Radcliffe Hosp. NHS Trust, 1982—2010. Recipient Henry Featherstone award, Assn. Anaesthetists Gt. Britain and Ireland. Fellow: Coll. Anaesthetists, Coll. Medicine South Africa, Australian and New Zealand Coll. Anaesthetists, Royal Coll. Anaesthetists (London). Avocations: music, sports. Home: 6 Whites Forge Appleton Abingdon Oxon OX13 5LG England Business E-Mail: john.sear@nda.ox.ac.uk.

SEARLES, LYNN MARIE, registered nurse; b. Cherryvale, Kans., Oct. 29, 1949; d. Darrell Eugene and Beva Caroline (Waller) Stringer; m. Martin Dale Searles, Aug. 23, 1970; children: Jeremy Dale, Michelle Le Anne. Degree in Fine Arts, Labette Cmty. Jr. Coll., Parsons, Kans., 1969, ADN, 1970. RN Kans. Evening med.-surg. charge nurse Coffeyville (Kans.) Meml. Hosp., 1970-72, med.-surg. head nurse, 1972-73, relief evening house supr. and emergency rm. nurse, 1974, head nurse recovery rm., 1974-81, head nurse recovery rm., ambulatory care unit Coffeyville Meml. Med. Ctr., 1981-83, head nurse recovery rm., ambulatory care unit and surgery, 1983-84; dir. family planning, rural home health aide and multi phasic screening clinics, AIDS edn. and counseling Jefferson County Health Dept., Oskaloosa, Kansas, 1984-87; health facility surveyor Kans. Dept. Health and Environ., Topeka, 1988—2004, edn. coord., risk mgmt. specialist, 2004—. Mem.: Am. Soc. Post Anesthesia Nurses (charter), Kans. Pub. Health Assn., Nazarene Healthcare Fellowship. Republican. Nazarene Ch. Avocations: needlecrafts, gardening, interior decorating.

SEARS, DAVID O'KEEFE, psychology professor; b. Urbana, Ill., June 24, 1935; s. Robert R. and Pauline (Snedden) S.; children: Juliet, Olivia, Meredith. BA in History, Stanford U., 1957; PhD in Psychology, Yale U., 1962. Asst. prof. to disting. prof. psychology and polit. sci. UCLA, 1961—, dean social scis., 1983-92. Dir. Inst. for Social Sci. Rsch., 1993-2008. Author: Public Opinion, 1964, Politics of Violence, 1973, Tax Revolt, 1985, Political Cognition, 1986, Social Psychology, 12th edit., 2005, Racialized Politics, 2000, Oxford Handbook of Political Psychology, 2003, The Diversity Challenge, 2008, Obama's Race, 2010. Recipient Edward L. Bernays award, Soc. for Psychol. Study of Social Issues, 1979, Warren E. Miller Career award, Am. Polit. Sci. Assn., 2003; fellow, Guggenheim, 1988—89. Fellow Am. Acad. Arts and Scis.; mem. Soc. for Advancement Socio-Econs. (pres. 1991-92), Internat. Soc. Polit. Psychology (pres. 1994-95, Harold D. Lasswell award 1994). Office: UCLA Psychology Dept Los Angeles CA 90095-0001 Office Phone: 310-825-2160. Business E-Mail: sears@psych.ucla.edu.

SEARS, JIM (JAMES M. SEARS), pediatrician; m. Diane Sears; children: Lea, Jonathan. MD, St. Louis U., 1996. Pediatric resident Northeastern Ohio U. Coll. Medicine and Tod Children's Hosp., Youngstown, 1996—99; pvt. practice Capistrano Beach, Calif.; med. expert The Doctors, 2008—. Lectr. in field. Co-author: The Baby Book, 2003, The Premature Baby Book, 2004, The Healthiest Kid in the Neighborhood, 2006, Father's First Steps-Twenty-Five Things Every New Father Should Know, 2006, The Baby Sleep Book, 2006; contbr. Parenting mag., Baby Talk mag. Avocations: bicycling, skiing, hiking. Office: Sears Family Pediatrics 26933 Camino De Estrella Capistrano Beach CA 92624 *

SEARS, NICHOLAS J., cardiovascular surgeon; MD. Cert. cardiovascular surgeon. Sr. v.p., clin. svcs. Aspen Healthcare Metrics, 2004; chief med. officer MedAssets, Inc., 2006—. Asst. prof., surgery U. South Florida Coll. of Medicine. Vice chief, cardiothoracic surgery, vice chief, surgery Tampa Gen. Hosp. Office: MedAssets Inc Ste 200 100 N Point Ctr E Alpharetta GA 30022 Office Phone: 678-323-2500. Office Fax: 678-323-2501. Business E-Mail: n.sears@medassets.com. *

SEARS, WILLIAM, pediatrician; Resident Harvard Med. Sch. Children's Hosp.; assoc. ward chief Hosp. for Sick Children, Toronto, assoc. prof. pediatrics; assoc. clinical prof. pediatrics U. Calif. Sch. Medicine, Irvine. Med. & parenting cons. BabyTalk mag., Parenting mag.; pediatric cons. Parenting.com. Fellow: Royal Coll. Pediatricians, Am. Acad. Pediatrics. Office: 26933 Camino De Estrella Ste A Capistrano Beach CA 92624 Office Phone: 949-493-5437. Office Fax: 949-493-0535.

SEASHORE, MARGRETTA REED, physician, educator; b. Red Bank, NJ, June 20, 1939; d. Robert Clark and Lillie Ann (Heaviland) Reed; m. John Seashore, Dec. 26, 1964; children: Robert H., Carl J., Carolyn L. BA, Swarthmore Coll., 1961; MD, Yale U., 1965. Diplomate Am. Bd. Pediatrics, Am. Bd. Med. Genetics, Nat. Bd. Med. Examiners. Intern in pediat. Yale U. Sch. Medicine, New Haven, 1965-66, asst. resident in pediat., 1966-68, postdoctoral fellow in genetics and metabolism, depts. pediat. and medicine, 1968-70, asst. clin. prof. human genetics and pediat., 1974-78, from asst. prof. to assoc. prof., 1978-90, prof. genetics and pediatrics, 1990—; clin. asst. prof. pediat. U. Fla. Coll. Medicine, Gainesville, 1970-71, asst. prof., 1971-73; attending physician Duvall Med. Ctr., U. Hosp. Jacksonville, 1970-73, asst. prof., 1970-71; attending physician Hope Haven Children's Hosp., Jacksonville, Fla., 1970-73, Shands Tchg. Hosp., Gainesville, 1971-73, Danbury (Conn.) Hosp., 1977—, Yale-New Haven Hosp., 1974—, dir. Genetic Consultation Svc., 1977-86, 1989—; cons. physician Bridgeport (Conn.) Hosp., 1974—, Lawrence and Meml. Hosp., New London, Conn., 1979—, Norwalk (Conn.) Hosp., 1981—. Contbr. chapters to books. Fellow: Am. Coll. Med. Genetics (founding fellow), Am. Acad. Pediat. (mem. screening com. Conn. chpt. 1977—, mem. genetics com. 1989—94, chair com. genetics 1990—94); mem.: AAAS, AMA, New Eng. Genetics Group (chmn. outreach com. 1979—89, mem. steering com. 1979—98, chmn. screening com. 1989—93, co-dir. 1992—95), Soc. Study Inborn Errors of Metabolism, Am. Bd. Med. Genetics (bd. dirs. 2004—), Soc. Inherited Metabolic Disorders (bd. dirs. 1989—, sec. 1991—96, pres. 1997), Am. Soc. Human Genetics (mem. genetic svcs. com. 1986—91). Avocations: music, gardening, sewing, computers. Office: Yale U Sch Med Dept Genetics 333 Cedar St New Haven CT 06510-3289 Home Phone: 203-565-6267; Office Phone: 203-785-4938. Business E-Mail: margretta.seashore@yale.edu.

SEAVER, LAURIE H., clinical geneticist, educator; MD, U. Ariz., Tucson, 1987. Diplomate Am. Bd. Pediatrics, 2005, cert. Am. Bd. Clin. Genetics, 2006. Resident pediat. Univ. Ariz., 1988—90, fellow clin. genetics, 1990—93; assoc. prof. pediat. JA Burns Sch. Medicine U. Hawaii; hosp. affiliation includes Queen's Med. Ctr., Kapiolani Med. Ctr. for Women. Office: Kapoilani Medical Center for Women Hawaii Community Genetics 1441 Kapiolani Blvd Ste 1800 Honolulu HI 96814 Office Phone: 808-973-3403.

SEAVEY, CHRISTOPHER GORDON, psychotherapist, alcohol and drug abuse services professional; b. Syracuse, NY, Dec. 4, 1942; s. Gordon Crowell and Shirley Edith Seavey; m. Eudene Sawyer, Aug. 8, 1965 (div. Mar. 1983); children: Sandra, Sherry, Gordon; m. Nancy Bowen, 1983. BA in Human Svcs., U. Mass., 1986; MA in Rehab. Counseling, U. South Fla., 1991; PhD in Psychotherapy, Internat. U. Grad. Studies, 2001. Sr. counselor Project Turnabout, Hingham, Mass., 1982—86; counselor Coastal Cmty. Counseling, Braintree, Mass., 1986—87, South Shore Coun. on Alcoholism, Quincy, Mass., 1987; chem. dependency counselor II David Lawrence Ctr., Naples, Fla., 1989—90; cons. vocat. rehab. Intracorp, Naples, 1990—96; acting dir. Addiction Recovery Ctr., Ft. Myers, Fla., 1993—98; clin. dir. Assisted Addiction Recovery, Naples, 1995—2004; dir. Christopher Seavey LMHG PA, 2004—. Mem. adv. bd. Naples Rehab. Inc., 1994-97. Chmn. Collier County Depression Coalition, Naples, 1997. Recipient Book award U. Mass., Boston, 1986; U. Calif. San Francisco fellow, 1986; Tobacco Coalition grantee, 1998. Mem. NADAAC, ACA, Internat. Assn. Rehab. Profls., Internat. Coun. on Alcohol and Addictions, Fla. Rehab. Assn. (pres. S.W. Fla. chpt. 1994-95, Svc. award 1999), Fla. Mental Health Counselors, Gulf Coast Mental Health Counselors Assn. (past pres.), Internat. Soc. Study Women's Sexual Health, Am. Assn. Sexuality Educators, Counselors and Therapists, Phi Kappa Phi. Office: 9853 N Tamiami Trail Ste 213 Naples FL 34108 Office Phone: 239-595-7775. Business E-Mail: chriseavey@earthlink.net.

SEBASTIAN, VINOD, surgeon, educator; b. India, Sept. 9, 1977; MBBS, Med. Coll. Kottayam, 2001; degree in Pediatric Cardiothoracic Surgery, Stanford U., 2011. Fellow UT Southwestern Med. Ctr., Dallas, 2007—10; oak found. rsch. fellow, fetal cardiac intervention Stanford U., 2010—, clin. instr., 2011—. Guest editor Annals Transplantation, Cardiology Young. Recipient Ellen Cosgrove Rsch. Ho. Staff Competition award, Monmouth Med. Ctr., Charles L Zukaukus Chief Resident award. Office: 300 Pasteur Dr Stanford CA 94305 Business E-Mail: v1977@stanford.edu.

SEBASTIANELLI, MARIO JOSEPH, internist, nephrologist, health facility administrator; b. Jessup, Pa., Sept. 14, 1935; s. Carlo and Antonia (Antonelli) S.; m. Alena Marie Drazdauskas, June 26, 1993 (div. July 2004); children: Mario, Alexa, Marco. BS in Biology, U. Scranton, 1958; MD, Jefferson Med. Coll., 1962. Diplomate Am. Bd. Internal Medicine. From sr. instr. to assoc. prof. medicine Hahnemann U., Phila., 1969—87; pvt. practice Scranton, Pa., 1971—; chief nephrology, founding dir. hemodialysis Moses Taylor Hosp., Scranton, 1972—76; founding med. dir. Pa. Regional Tissue Bank, Scranton, 1983—91; founding dir. inpatient hemodialysis svcs. Comty. Med. Ctr., Scranton, 1996—2006; founding med. dir. Fresenius Med. Care Dialysis Svcs. Dunmore, Scranton, 2001—. Mem. senateconfirmed gov. apptd. Govs. Renal Disease Adv. Com., Harrisburg, Pa., 1973-76; creator, owner Comprehensive Health Svcs. Ctr., Dunmore, Pa., 1979—; founding med. dir. Diagnostic Lab., Dunmore, 1981-95. Contbr. articles to profl. jours. Bd. dirs. Scranton Lackawanna Human Devel. Agy., Scranton, 1977-82. Lt. USNR, 1963-65. Fellow: ACP; mem.: KC (4th degree), AMA, Renal Physicians Assn., Internat. Soc. Nephrology, Am. Soc. Nephrology, Alpha Omega Alpha. Republican. Roman Catholic. Avocations: fishing, swimming, travel, sports cars, reading. Office: Comprehensive Health Svcs Ctr 1416 Monroe Ave Ste 206 Dunmore PA 18509-2477 Home Phone: 570-876-2086; Office Phone: 570-347-5212. E-mail: drmjseb@hcrn.com.

SEBAT, JONATHAN, geneticist, educator; Grad., U. Calif., Santa Barbara, 1995; PhD, U. Idaho, 2002. Adj. prof. biology Stony Brook U.; assoc. prof. genetics Cold Spring Harbor Lab.; founding mem. Stanley Ctr. for Psychiatric Genomics. Office: One Bungtown Rd Cold Spring Harbor NY 11724 Office Phone: 516-422-4196. E-mail: sebat@cshl.edu.

SEBATI, KONJI, health management planner; 2 children. BSc, U. North, South Africa, 1974; MB ChB, U. Nairobi, Kenya, 1981; diploma in Child Health, Coll. Medicine South Africa, 1985; diploma in Mgmt., U. Witwatersrand, South Africa, 1993. Med. advisor Roche Pharms., Johannesburg, 1993—94; med. dir. Pfizer Labs., Johannesburg, 1993—2000, corp. affairs dir., 1998—2000, human resource dir., 1999—2000; med. dir. Pfizer Inc, NYC, 2000—05; South Africa amb. to Switzerland and the Holy See Bern, 2005—08; South Africa amb. to France, 2009—. Team leader Diflucan program Pfizer Inc., NYC, 2000—. Office: South African Embassy 59 quai D'orsay F 75343 7 Paris France Personal E-mail: konji24@yahoo.com. Business E-Mail: sebatik@foreign.gov.38.

SEBELIUS, KATHLEEN, United States Secretary of Health and Human Services, former Governor of Kansas; b. Cin., May 15, 1948; d. John J. and Mary K. (Dixon) Gilligan; m. Keith Gary Sebelius, 1974; children: Edward Keith, John McCall. BA in Polit. Sci., Trinity Coll., Washington, 1970; MPA, U. Kans., 1977. Dir. planning Ctr. Cmty. Justice, Washington, 1971—74; spl. asst. Kans. Dept. Corrections, Topeka, 1975—78; exec. dir. Kans. Trial Lawyers Assn., Topeka, 1978—86; mem. Dist. 56 Kans. House of Reps., Topeka, 1987—95; ins. commr. State of Kans., Topeka, 1995—2002, gov., 2003—09; sec. US Dept. Health & Human Services, Washington, 2009—. Mayor City of Potwin, Kans., 1985—87; mem. Presdl. Adv. Com. Consumer Protection & Quality in Health Care, 1997; chair Democratic Govs. Assn., 2007. Mem. nat. gov. bd. Common Cause, 1975—81; bd. dirs Kans. Kids Count. Recipient Breaking the Glass Ceiling award, Women in Govt., 1997, Svc. award, Kansas City YMCA; named Pub. Ofcl. of Yr., Governing Mag., 2001; named an Outstanding Elected Officer, Nat. Fedn. Democratic Women, 1996; named one of America's Top Five Governors, TIME mag., 2005, The 100 Most Powerful Women, Forbes mag., 2009, 2010, 2011, The 100 Most Powerful Women in DC, Washingtonian mag., 2009, The 10 Most Powerful Women in Washington, Fortune mag., 2010, The Top 25 Women in Healthcare, Modern Health mag., 2011. Mem.: Kans. Women's Political Caucus (founder), Nat. Assn. Ins. Commrs. (chair). Democrat. Roman Catholic. Office: US Department Health & Human Services 200 Independence Ave SW Rm 615 F Washington DC 20201 Office Phone: 877-696-6775. E-mail: Kathleen.Sebelius@hhs.gov. *

SECHI, GIANPIETRO, neurologist, educator; b. Bultei, Sassari, Italy, Mar. 4, 1950; MD, 1975. Assoc. prof. U. Sassari, 2001, neurologist, prof., 2001—. Avocation: swimming. Office: Viale S Pietro 10 Sassari Sardegna 07100 Italy Business E-Mail: gpsechi@uniss.it.

SECRETI, LALAINIA, emergency physician; b. NY, Sept. 16, 1969; BS, LeMoyne Coll., 1991; MD, St. George's U., 1996. Attending physician emergency medicine Upstate Med. U., 2001—. Fellow: ACEP. Office: Upstate Med University 750 E Adams Syracuse NY 13210 Office Fax: 315-464-4854. Business E-Mail: secretil@upstate.edu.

SEDAGHATIAN, MOHAMAD REZA, retired pediatrician; b. Shiraz, Fars, Iran, Feb. 11, 1938; s. Habib and Roghayeh (Hodjati) Sedaghatian; m. Nezhat Khalili, Sept. 4, 1970. MD, Shiraz Med. Sch., Iran, 1964. Diplomate Am. Bd. Pediatrics, Am. Bd. Neonatal Perinatal Medicine. Pediatric resident Tulane U., 1969-71; neonatal fellow U. Ariz., Phoenix, 1972; asst. prof. pediatrics Shiraz Med. Sch., 1973-79, assoc. prof. pediatrics, 1979-84, prof. pediatrics, 1984; sr. cons. Ministry of Health, Abu Dhabi, United Arab Emirates, 1985—2011; prof. pediatrics Gulf Med. Coll., 2004—09, chmn. dept. pediatrics, 2005. Dir. neonatal units Shiraz U., 1973—85, dir. pediatric residency, 1981—85, head, dept. neonatal medicine and surgery, 1985—2004; dep. med. dir. Mafraq Hosp., 2003—, acting med. dir., 2003—05. Contbr. articles to profl. jours. 1st lt. Health Corp., 1966—68. Fellow: Emirates Neonatal Soc. (pres. 2005—08), Emirate Perinatal Soc. (pres. 2000—04), Am. Perinatal Assn., United Arab Emirates Med. Assn., Am. Acad. Pediatrics, Tulane Pediat. Alumni Assn.; mem.: Bayler Pediat. Alumni Assn. Achievements include discovery of of the Sedaghatian congenital lethal metaphyical chontrodysplasian syndrome. Avocations: tennis, movies, music, ping pong/table tennis, volleyball. Office Phone: 514-677-7151.

SEDDON, JOHANNA MARGARET, ophthalmologist, epidemiologist; b. Pitts. BS, U. Pitts., 1970, MD, 1974; MS in Epidemiology, Harvard U., 1976. Intern Framingham (Mass.) Union Hosp., 1974-75; resident Tufts New Eng. Med. Ctr., Boston, 1976-80; fellow ophthalmic pathology Mass. Eye and Ear Infirmary, Boston, 1980-81, clin. fellow vitreoretinal Retina Svc., 1981-82; instr. clin. ophthalmology Harvard Med. Sch., Boston, 1982-84, asst. prof., asst. surgeon ophthalmolgy, 1984, assoc. prof., 1989—; assoc. surgeon, dir. ultrasound svc. Mass. Eye and Ear Infirmary, Boston, 1989—, founder, dir. epidemiology rsch. unit, 1984—85, dir. epidemiology unit, 1985—2007, surgeon in ophthalmology, 1992—2007; assoc. prof. faculty dept. epidemiology Harvard Sch. Pub. Health, Boston, 1992—2007; founding dir. ophthalmic epidemiology and genetics svc. New Eng. Eye Ctr., Tufts Med. Ctr., 2007—; prof. ophthalmology Tufts U. Sch. Medicine, 2007—. Mem. com. vision Commn. Behavioral and Social Scis. and Edn., NRC, NAS, Washington, 1984; mem. divsn. rsch. grants NIH, 1987-89, 94—; mem. sci. adv. bd. Found Fighting Blindness, 1994—, Macular Degeneration Internat., 1994—, adv. panel, Age-Related Macular Degeneration Alliance Internat.; internat. spkr. in field; lectr. in field. Author books and articles in field, especially in field of ocular tumors and macular degeneration nutrition & genetic epidemiology; mem. editl. staff ophthalmic jours. Recipient NIH Nat. Svc. Rsch. awards, 1975, 80-81, Lewis R. Wasserman Merit award Rsch. to Prevent Blindness for seminal findings in ophthalmic rsch., 1996, 1st Maurice Rabb, Jr. award Prevent Blindness Am. Orgn., 2005; Inaugural Gold fellow, Assn. rsch. Vision & Ophthalmology, grantee, Prin. Investigator Nat. Eye Inst., 1984—, Nat. Cancer Inst., 1986; med. sch. scholar, 1970-74, Henry H. Clark Med. Edn. Found. scholar, 1973, voted one of Am.'s top ophthalmologists, Consumer Rsch. Coun. Am., 2004-10. Mem. AMA (Sr. Honor award 2003), APHA, Am. Acad. Ophthalmology (Honor award 1990, Sr. Honor award 2003), Am. Med. Women's Assn., Assn. Rschr. Vision & Ophthalmology (elected, chair epidemiology sect. 1990, trustee clin. vision epidemiology sect. 1992-97. v.p. 1996-97, Spl. Recognition award 1997, Gold fellow 2009), Soc. Epidemiologic Rsch., New Eng. Ophthal. Soc., Am. Coll. Epidemiology, Retina Soc., Macula Soc. (mem. com. 2006—), Mass. Soc. Eye Physicians and Surgeons (v.p. 2000-02, mem. com. 2006—), Am. Epidemiol. Soc., Am. Soc. Ret. Surgeons (Hon. award 2005). Achievements include discovery of association between nutrition, dietary antioxidants, and systemic inflammatory biomarkers and age-related macular degeneration; genetic markers associated with onset and progression of macular degeneration; novel genetic variants associated with age related macular degeneration; environmental lifestyle modifiers of genetic susceptibility for macular degenrations; development of first prediction models for macular degeneration. Office Phone: 617-636-9000. Personal E-mail: jseddon@earthlink.net.

SEDEI RODDEN, PAMELA JEAN, psychologist, director; b. Johnstown, Pa., Jan. 31, 1956; d. Joseph and Betty Ruth (Watkins) Sedei; m. William Eugene Rodden, Dec. 4, 1982; 1 child, Gretchen Jean Rodden. BA, Southwestern Coll., Winfield, Kans., 1977; MS, Pitts. State U., Kans., 1979; PhD, Western Colo. U., 1983. Lic. profl. counselor Colo., diplomate in psychotherapy, cert. cognitive behavior therapist, nat. cert. counselor, domestic violence counselor, criminal justice specialist. Staff psychologist Autumn Manors Inc., Florence, Kans., 1982-83; clin. psychologist Richmond (Tex.) State Hosp., 1984-86; unit psychologist Wheat Ridge (Colo.) Regional Ctr., 1986-89, acting unit dir., 1989; dir. behavioral svcs. Colo. State Divsn. Devel. Disabilities, Denver, 1989-97; dir. Forensic Mental Health Svcs., Boulder, Colo., 1997—2001, Pamela JS Rodden & Assocs., Fort Collins, Colo., 2001—. Dir. Rodden Consultants, Longmont, Colo., 1986—90, Rodden Assocs., 2001—. Co-author: A Model For Interdisciplinary On Site Evaluation of People Who Have Dual Diagnosis, 1991. Fellow: Am. Coll. Forensic Examiners; mem.: ACA. Republican. Roman Catholic. Address: 1420 Blue Spruce Dr Ste G Fort Collins CO 80524 Office Phone: 970-482-8553. E-mail: Pjsrodden@juno.com.

SEDMAK, DANIEL D., academic administrator; b. Columbus, Ohio, Apr. 18, 1952; m. Peggy Sedmak; 5 children. BS in biology, U. Cin.; MD, Ohio State U., 1980. Resident in pathology Cleve. Clinic Found., 1980—84, fellow in immunopathology, 1984—85; joined faculty Ohio State U., 1985; dir. nephropathology and transplant pathology programs Ohio State U. Hosp.; prof. and chair pathology Coll. Medicine and Pub. Health, Ohio State U., 1997, interim dean, sr. assoc. v.p. health sci. and exec. vice dean; exec. dean Georgetown U. Sch. Medicine, 2003—04, exec. v.p. health sci., 2003—04; exec. vice dean, assoc. v.p. health sciences Ohio State Med. Ctr., Columbus, 2003—. Office: Ohio State Univ Med Ctr 200 Meiling Hall 370 West 9th St Columbus OH 43210 Office Phone: 202-687-4600. Business E-Mail: sedmak@georgetown.edu.

SEDO, MANUEL ARTURO, psychologist, researcher; b. Barcelona, 1932; arrived in US, 1972; s. Manuel Sedo and Manuela Garcia-Tunon; m. Asuncion Sastre, July 10, 1965; children: Silvia Johnson, Natalia C., Arturo. PhD, Boston Coll., Chestnut Hill, 1978; diploma, Inst. Psychology, Sorbonne, 1960. Lic. psychologist Commonwealth of Mass. Staff psychologist Children's Hosp. Med. Ctr., Boston, 1975—78; sch. psychologist Boston Pub. Schs., 1980—2000. Author, rschr.: psychol. tests with low lang.-load and high-cognitive processing load Five Digit Test, 2007 (Edith Kaplan award, 2004). Recipient Fulbright Fellowships, 1990, 1991; fellow, Harvard Coll., 1972. Mem.: APA, Mass. Neuropsychol. Soc. (mem. bd.). Achievements include design of Neuropsych tests of prefrontal maturity 3 to 11 comparing knowledge and fluid effort. Office: Testing 9 Ingleside Rd Natick MA 01760 Office Phone: 508-655-6970. Business E-Mail: manuel@sedo.net.

SEEBACH, LYDIA MARIE, physician; b. Red Wing, Minn., Nov. 9, 1920; d. John Henry and Marie (Gleusen) S.; m. Keith Edward Wentz, Oct. 16, 1959; children: Brooke Marie, Scott. BS, U. Minn., 1942, MB, 1943, MD, 1944, MS in Medicine, 1951. Diplomate Am. Bd. Internal Medicine. Intern Kings County Hosp., Bklyn., 1944; fellow Mayo Found., Rochester, Minn., 1945-51; pvt. practice Oakland, Calif., 1952-60, San Francisco, 1961—. Asst. clin. prof. U. Calif., San Francisco, 1981—; mem., vice chmn. Arthritis Clinic, Presbyn. Hosp., San Francisco, 1961-88, pharmacy com., 1963-78; chief St. Mary's Hosp. Arthritis Clinic, San Francisco, 1968-72; exec. bd. Pacific Med. Ctr., San Francisco, 1974-76. Contbr. articles to med. jours. Fellow ACP; mem. AMA, Am. Med. Womens Assn. (pres. Calif. chpt. 1968-70), Am. Rheumatism Assn., Am. Soc. Internal Medicine, Pan Am. Med. Womens Assn. (treas.), Calif. Acad. Medicine, Calif. Soc. Internal Medicine, Calif. Med. Assn., San Francisco Med. Soc., San Francisco Med. Assn., San Francisco Soc. Internal Medicine, No. Calif. Rheumatism Assn., Internat. Med. Women's Assn., Mayo Alumni (bd. dirs. 1983-89), Iota Sigma Pi. Republican. Lutheran. Avocations: music, cooking, gardening, needlepoint. Office: 490 Post St Ste 1536 San Francisco CA 94102-1414 Office Phone: 415-362-6398. Personal E-mail: lseebach@sbcglobal.net.

SEEBACHER, CLAUS, retired physician; b. Mannheim, Germany, Oct. 10, 1935; s. Franz and Emmy Seebacher; m. Beate Gebert; 1 child, Anne Ullmann. Med. dr., Med. Acad., Dresden, 1960. Cert. prof. Acad. Med. Edn., Berlin, 1985. Med. asst. Med. Acad., Germany, 1960—72, cons., 1972—76; head physician Muncipal Hosp. Dresden-Friedrichstadt, 1976—2001. Co-author (with Gustav Fischer Verlag Jena): (text book) Mykosen - Epidemiologie-Diagnostik-Therapie; author: Dermatomykosen, Grundlagen und Therapie, Springer-Verlag. Mng. chair Found. Deutschsprachigen Mykologischen Gesellschft, Münster, Germany, 2005—. Mem.: Internat. Soc. Human and Animal Mycology, Deutschsprachige Mykologische Gesellschaft. Home: Merseburger St 5 Dresden 01309 Germany

SEELER, RUTH ANDREA, pediatrician, educator; b. NYC, June 13, 1936; d. Thomas and Olivia Seeler. BA cum laude, U. Vt., 1959, MD, 1962. Diplomate Am. Bd. Pediat., Am. Bd. Pediatric Hematology/Oncology. Intern Bronx (N.Y.) Mcpl. Hosp., 1962—65; pediats. hematology/oncology fellow U. Ill., 1965—67; dir. pediatric hematology/oncology Cook County Hosp., 1967—84; prof. pediatrics and pediatric edn. Coll. Medicine U. Ill., Chgo., 1984—; assoc. chief pediatrics Michael Reese Hosp., Chgo., 1990—97, acting chief pediatrics, 1997—99; pediatrician St. Anthony's Hosp./U. Ill. Coll. Medicine, 1999—2001. Course coord. pediats. Nat. Coll. Advanced Med. Edn., Chgo., 1987-96; mem. subboard Pediatric Hematology/Oncology, Chapel Hill, 1990-95; chief, prof. Midwest Am. Bd. Pediat., 1990-2011. Mem. editl. bd. Am. Jour. Pediat. Hematology/Oncology, 1985-95. Founder med. dir. camp for hemophiliacs Ill. Hemophilia Found., 1973—2000, pres. Ill., 1981—85; jr. and sr. warden, treas. Ch. Our Saviour, Chgo., 1970—92. Mem.: U. Vt. Med. Sch. Alumna Assn. (pres. 2008—10, exec. com. mem.), Phi Beta Kappa, Gamma Phi Beta Found. (trustee 1994—2011, 2002—08, grants chair). Avocations: triathalons, biking, swimming. Office: U Ill Coll Medicine Pediats M/C 856 840 S Wood St Chicago IL 60612-7317 Office Phone: 312-355-1021. Business E-Mail: seeler@uic.edu.

SEELEY, WILLIAM WARD (BILL SEELEY), neurologist, educator; s. John Arthur and Ruthann Bickel Seeley. AB in Psychology, Brown U., 1993; MD, U. Calif., San Francisco, 1999. Diplomate American Bd. Psychiatry & Neurology, lic. Calif. Resident in neurology Harvard Med. Sch., Boston, 2000—03; clin. fellow in behavioral neurology U. Calif., San Francisco, 2003—05, faculty mem., 2005—, assoc. prof. neurology Memory & Aging Ctr., dir. Neurodegenerative Disease Brain Bank. Contbr. articles to profl. jours. including PNAS, Neuron and Jour. of Neuroscience. Named a MacArthur Fellow, John D. & Catherine T. MacArthur Found., 2011. Mem.: American Acad. Neurology. Office: UCSF Memory and Aging Ctr 350 Parnassus Ave Ste 706 San Francisco CA 94143-1207 Office Phone: 415-476-6880. Business E-Mail: wseeley@memory.ucsf.edu. *

SEELY, ELLEN WELLS, endocrinologist; b. NYC, Sept. 25, 1955; m. Jonathan David Strongin, June 11, 1983; children: Jessica, Mathew. BA magna cum laude, Brown U., 1977; MD, Columbia U., 1981. Diplomate Am. Bd. Internal Medicine, Endocrinology and Metabolism. Residency internal medicine Brigham & Women Hosp., Boston, 1981-84, fellow in endocrinology, 1984-87; rsch. fellow medicine Harvard U., Boston, 1984-87; dir. clin. rsch. endocrine hypertension divsn. Brigham & Women's Hosp., Boston, 1987—, assoc. physician, 1987-95; prof. medicine Harvard Medical Sch., Boston, 2010; physician Brigham & Women's Hosp., 1996—. Mem. admissions com. Harvard Med. Sch., 2009—; vice chair Dept. Medicine, DVLPT Bringham Womans Hosp. Contbr. articles to profl. jours. Capps scholar in diabetes Harvard Med. Sch., 1994-96, Harvard Med. Sch. scholar in medicine, 1998-99. Fellow: Coun. for High Blood Pressure Rsch.; mem.: ADA, Internat. Soc. Study of Hypertension in Pregnancy, Endocrine Soc., Sigma Xi. Office: Brigham & Women's Hosp 221 Longwood Ave Boston MA 02115-5804

SEELY, ROBERT DANIEL, cardiologist, medical association administrator; b. Woodmere, NY, Nov. 4, 1923; s. Harry and Ethel (Weil) S.; m. Marcia Ann Wells, June 19, 1953; children: Ellen Wells, Anne Wells. BS, NYU, 1943; MD, Columbia U., 1946. Intern Mt. Sinai Hosp., NYC, 1946-47, asst. resident in medicine, 1950-51, resident in pathology, 1951-52, chief resident in medicine, 1952-53; Sara Welt fellow in cardiovascular research Presbyn. Hosp., NYC, 1953-54; instr. dept. physiology, cardiovascular research Western Res. U., Cleve., 1947-48; chief rheumatic heart disease clinic Mt. Sinai Hosp., NYC, 1961-70, attending physician medicine and cardiology, 1978—, chief of service dept. medicine, 1979—, clin. prof. medicine, cardiology Sch. Medicine, 1970—; practice medicine specializing in cardiovascular disease NYC, 1953—. Contbr. articles to profl. jours. Served to capt. M.C. AUS, 1948-50. Recipient Solomon Berson Meml. award Mt. Sinai Hosp., 1977 Fellow Am. Coll. Cardiology, ACP; mem. N.Y. Heart Assn., AMA, N.Y. County Med. Soc., Soc. Cert. Internists N.Y., Phi Beta Kappa, Alpha Omega Alpha, Beta Lambda Sigma Office: 49 E 96th St # 11D New York NY 10128-0782 Personal E-mail: billybobseedy@gmail.com.

SEET, BENJAMIN HY, ophthalmologist, administrator; b. Manchester, Eng., Jan. 27, 1965; s. Chay-Tuan and Noi-Cher Seet; m. Boon-Shya Tan; children: Darren, Alicia. MBBS, Nat. U. Singapore, 1989, M of Medicine in Ophthalmology, 1994; MPH, Johns Hopkins U., 2000. Ophthalmic resident Singapore Nat. Eye Ctr., 1991—94; med. officer Singapore Armed Forces, 1994—2004, chief army med. officer, 2006—09, chief med. corps., 2009—11; Med. Staff Officer UN Dept. Peacekeeping Ops., NYC, 1998—99, chief med. support sect., 2004—06; dep. exec. dir. Agy. Sci. and Tech. Rsch., 2011—; brig. gen., 2007—09. Adj. rsch. fellow Def. Med. Rsch. Inst., Singapore, 1996—2002; dir. Agri-food Vet. Authority Singapore, 2007—09; cons. Ministry Health, Singapore, 2008—; dir. Health Promotion Bd., 2009—; chmn. Nat. Trauma Com., 2009—10. Contbr. (manual) Medical Support Manual for United Nations Peacekeeping Operations, 2nd Ed., 1999; contbr. articles to profl. jours. Col. Singapore Mil., 2009—, Singapore. Recipient Master of Medicine Gold Medal in Ophthalmology, Nat. U. Singapore, 1994, UN medal, 1999, 2006, Garland W. Clay award, Am. Acad. Optometry, 2006, Pub. Adminstrn. medal, 2009. Fellow: Royal Coll. Surgeons (Edinburgh); mem.: Delta Omega (Alpha chpt.). Avocation: collecting military ephemera. Personal E-mail: benseet@starnet.gov.sg. *

SEFF, RONALD A., ophthalmologist; MD. Ophthalmologist, 1977—. Bd. dirs. Universal Security Instruments, Inc., 2002—. Office: Universal Security Instruments Inc Bd Directors 11407 Cronhill Dr Ste A Owings Mills MD 21117 Office Phone: 410-363-3000. Office Fax: 410-363-2218. *

SEFFRIN, JOHN REESE, health science association administrator, educator; b. Hagerstown, Ind., May 19, 1944; s. Theodore H. and Mary Ellen (Reese) Seffrin; m. Carole Sue Washburn, Apr. 16, 1966; 1 child, Mary. BS in Edn., Ball State U., Muncie, Ind., 1966, DSc (hon.), 1994; MS, U. Ill., Champaign-Urbana, 1967; PhD in Health Edn., Purdue U., West Lafayette, Ind., 1970, D (hon.) in Social Sci., 2003; DSc (hon.), Thomas Jefferson U., Med. Coll. Phila., 2008, Ind. U., Bloomington, 2008. Asst. prof. health edn. Purdue U., 1970—76, assoc. prof., chair health & safety edn., 1976—79; prof., chmn. dept. applied health sci. Ind. U., Bloomington, 1979—92; exec. v.p., chief staff officer Am. Cancer Soc., Atlanta, 1992—95, CEO, 1995—. Trustee Am. Cancer Soc. Found., 1992—; commr.-at-large Nat. Commn. Health Edn. Credentialing, 1995—2000; charter mem., mem. steering com. C-Change (formerly Nat. Dialog on Cancer), 1999; mem. subcom. on cessation HHS, Washington, 2002—03; bd. dirs. Healthcare Inc. Nat. bd. dirs. Am. Lung Assn., 1980—90; treas. Partnership for Prevention of Premature Death, Disease and Disability, 1991—; mem. Pres.'s Commn. on Improving Econ. Opportunity in Cmtys. Dependent on Tobacco Prodn. While Protecting Pub. Health, 2000—01; trustee Ctr. Advancement Health, 2003—05; pres. State Welfare Bd. Ind. Dept. Pub. Welfare, 1979—80, 1982—84; treas. Midwest Nuc. Bd., 1973—75; chmn. cmty. edn. com. Am. Lung Assn., 1981—83, v.p., 1980, pres., 1982; bd. dirs. Nat. Ctr. Tobacco-Free Kids, 1996—; chmn. bd. dirs. Nat. Health Coun., 1998—2000; past pres. Internat. Union against Cancer; bd. dirs. Wabash Ctr. for the Mentally Retarded, 1970—73. Recipient Outstanding Alumnus award, Ball State U., 1982, Surgeon Gen.'s Cert. appreciation, USPHS, 1992, Presdl. citation, Soc. Pub. Health Edn., 2007; named Sagamore of Wabash, State of Ind., 1980, 1988. Fellow: Am. Sch.

Health Assn. (mem. governing coun. 1979—81, 1982—89, pres. 1987—88, Howe award 1991); mem.: NAS (Nat. Cancer Policy Bd. 1997—2002), AMA, Am. Acad. Family Physicians (pub. adv. bd. 1999—), Rsch. Am. (bd. dirs. 1996—), Independent Sector (bd. dirs. 1997—2006), Nat. Interagy. Coun. on Smoking and Health (bd. dirs. 1979—), Internat. Union Against Cancer (ex-officio mem. US nat. com. 2000—, pres. 2002—06), Ind. Assn. for Health, Phys. Edn. and Recreation (pres. 1976, Cert. of Appreciation 1977, Honor award 1982), Am. Cancer Soc. (dir. Ind. Divsn. 1977—90, chmn. Ind. Divsn. 1982—85, dir.-at-large to nat. bd. dirs., chmn. nat. pub. edn. com. 1984—87, nat. v.p. 1986—87, chmn. nat. bd. dirs. 1989—91), Ind. Thoracic Soc. (mem. governing coun. 1977—84), Ind. Family Health Coun. (dir. 1979—81, v.p. 1980—81, pres. 1981), Ind. Assn. Health Educators (pres. 1975—76, chair 1997—2000), Assn. for Advancement Health Edn. (bd. dirs. 1989—92), Nat. Assn. State Bds. of Edn. (commn. on sch. cmty. role in improving adolescent health 1989—90), Eta Sigma Gamma, Phi Delta Kappa. Roman Catholic. Office: Am Cancer Soc Inc 250 Williams St NW Atlanta GA 30303 Business E-Mail: john.seffrin@cancer.org. *

SEFTOR, ELISABETH ANN, research scientist; b. LA, July 17, 1952; d. Paul and Bernice Annette (Kerman) Rabinek; m. Richard Edward Barnet Seftor, Aug. 30, 1972; 1 child, Rebecca Merle. BS, Calif. State U., Northridge, 1975. Staff rsch. assoc. U. Calif., Berkeley, 1975—77, UCLA, 1977—83; sr. rsch. specialist U. Ariz., Tucson, 1983—93; sr. rsch. assoc. St. Louis U., 1993—96; sr. rsch. asst. U. Iowa, Iowa City, 1996—2004; sr. rsch. scientist Children's Meml. Rsch. Ctr., Chgo., 2004—. Coord. George Engelmann Rsch. Scholar Program, St. Louis, 1994—96. Reviewer: BioTechniques Mag., 1992—2000, Brit. Jour. Cancer, 1999; contbr. articles to profl. jours. Grantee, NIH, 1996—, 1997—, 1998—. Mem.: Am. Assn. Cancer Rsch. Achievements include research in genetic profiling of melanoma cells; identification of aggressive tumor cell plasticity and tumor stem cell potential; design of invitro invasion assay systems; development of characterized unique cell lines. Avocations: reading, cooking, swimming. Office: CMRC 2300 Childrens Plaza 222 Chicago IL 60614 Home: 6329 N Le Mai Ave Chicago IL 60646-4827 Home Phone: 773-631-9445; Office Phone: 773-755-6366. Business E-Mail: eseftor@childrensmemorial.org.

SEGAL, BERNARD LOUIS, cardiologist, educator; b. Montreal, Feb. 13, 1929; came to U.S., 1961, naturalized, 1966; s. Irving and Fay (Schecter) S.; m. Idajane Fischman, Feb. 17, 1963; 1 dau., Jody Segal Reinbold. BSc cum laude, McGill U., 1950, postgrad., 1930-31, MD, C.M. high standing, 1955. Diplomate Am. Bd. Internal Medicine. Intern Jewish Gen Hosp., Montreal, 1955-56; resident Balt. City Hosp., 1956-57, Beth Israel Hosp., Boston, 1957-58, Georgetown Med. Ctr., Washington, 1958-59, St. George's Hosp., London, 1959-61; pvt. practice internal medicine and cardiology Phila., 1961—; prof. medicine Med. Coll. Pa., Hahnemann U., 1996 ; prof. medicine, sr. attending physician Jefferson Med. Coll./Thomas Jefferson U., 1998—2008. Dir. emeritus cardiology Thomas Jefferson U., 1998 Author: Auscultation of the Heart, 1965; Editor: Theory and Practice of Auscultation, 1964, Engineering in the Practice of Medicine, 1966, Your Heart, 1972, Arteriosclerosis and Coronary Heart Disease, 1972; mem. editl. bd. Am. Jour. Cardiology, 1970—, Clin. Echocardiography, 1978; contbr. articles to profl. jour. Fellow ACP, Am. Coll. Cardiology (chmn. scholar-trainee com., trustee 1969-71), Am. Coll. Chest Physicians; mem. NY Acad. Sci., Alpha Omega Alpha. Home: 1156 Red Rose Ln Villanova PA 19085-2121 Office: Jefferson Heart Inst 925 Chestnut St Mezzanine Philadelphia PA 19107-4824 also: 401 E City Line Ave Ste 525 Bala Cynwyd PA 19004-1125 Office Phone: 215-955-8145.

SEGAL, BRAHM, epidemiologist; b. Can., Apr. 9, 1965; MD, Albert Einstein Coll. Medicine, 1992. Head infectious diseases Roswell Pk. Cancer Inst., 2002—. Fellow: IDSA. Office: Roswell Pk Cancer Inst Carlton St Buffalo NY 14263 Office Fax: 716-845-5777. Business E-Mail: brahm.segal@roswellpark.org.

SEGAL, HERMAN B., cardiologist, educator; Attended, Bowdoin Coll.; MD, Tufts U. Diplomate Am. Bd. Internal Medicine, Am. Bd. Internal Medicine-cardiovasc. disease. Tng. internal medicine Kings County Hosp./Downstate Med. Ctr., Bklyn., Boston Veterans Affair Hosp.; fellow The West Roxbury Veterans Affair Hosp., Brigham and Women's Hosp.; asst. chief medicine Washington DC Veterans Affair Med. Ctr., chief medicine, staff cardiologist; faculty Georgetown Univ. Med. Sch.; pvt. practice Silver Spring, Md., 1981. Office: Number 308 10313 Georgina Ave Silver Spring MD 20902 Office Phone: 301-681-9095. Office Fax: 301-681-8156.

SEGAL, RODICA, science educator; b. Satu-Nou, Ismail, Romania, June 6, 1938; d. Mihai and Vasilica (Anghel) Gheorghiu; m. Brad Segal, Oct. 18, 1962; 1 child, Mugur. Degree in engring., Inst. Poly., Galati, Romania, 1961; MSc, PhD, U. Dunarea de Jos, Galati, 1971. Asst. prof. Inst. Poly., Galati, 1961-68, lectr., 1968-90; prof. U. Dunarea de Jos, Galati, 1990—. Author (with B. Segal, V. Teodoru, V. Gheorghe) Nutritional Value of Food Products, 1983, (with I. Mincu, B. Segal) News Orientation in Nutrition, 1997, (with G. Popa, B. Segal, S. Dumitrache) Toxicology of Food Products, 1987 (award Romanian Acad. 1989); editor (with G.M. Costin) Functional Foods, 1999, Food for Particular Nutritional Uses, 2001, Nutrition Principles, 2002, Biochemistry of Food, 2006, (with D.M. Cheta) How to Live Longer and Better, 2008, (with G.M. Costin) Ecological Food, 2008. Mem. Acad. Agrl. Sci. (corr.), Romanian Soc. Biochemistry and Molecular Biology. Avocations: travels, recreational activities. Home: Eroilor 32A 6200 Galati Romania Office: U Dunarea de Jos Domneasca 47 6200 Galati Romania Business E-Mail: rodica.segal@ugal.ro.

SEGALL, LIVIU, physician, educator; b. Iasi, Romania, Feb. 18, 1967; MD, Gr. T. Popa U. Medicine and Pharmacy Iasi, 1991. Asst. prof. Gr. T. Popa U. Medicine and Pharmacy Iasi, 1999—. Home: Canta nr 36 bl 532 sc A ap 17 Iasi 700529 Romania Personal E-mail: l_segall@yahoo.com.

SEGALL, MALCOLM MAURICE, retired pediatrician, health system analyst; b. London, Dec. 19, 1935; s. Mark and Sophie Segall; m. Ivana Segall; 1 child, Veronika. MBChB, U. Sheffield, Eng., 1959. Cert. MRCP London, 1963. Tng. posts Sheffield tchg. hosps., 1959—63; house physician, cardiology Hammersmith Hosp., London, 1961—62; rsch. fellow & paediatric registrar Nuffield Inst. Med. Rsch., U. Oxford & Radcliffe Infirmary, Oxford, 1963—65; rsch. fellow & sr. registrar Inst. Child Health & Gt. Ormond St. Hosp. Sick Children, London, 1966—69; sr. paediatric registrar St Thomas's Hosp., London, 1969—70; prof. paediatrics & child health U. Dar es Salaam, Tanzania, 1970—72; fellow Inst. of Devel. Studies, U. Sussex, Brighton, England, 1973—99, head, health unit, 1989—98; health planner Ministry Health, Maputo, Mozambique, 1977—79; European Commn.-financed spl. advisor dir. gen. Nat. Dept. Health, Pretoria, South Africa, 1995—97, 2001—04. Cons. govts. & internat. agys., 1973—2005; cons. min. health Ministry Health, Harare, Zimbabwe, 1980—81; vis. prof. Pub. Health Shanghai Med. U., China, 1993—96. Author academic publs. Vol. Med. Aid Com. Vietnam, 1969—70; founder mem. Guiné, Angola, Mozambique Med. Action, 1973—76. Fellow: Royal Soc. Medicine; mem.: Keep Our NHS Pub., Internat. Soc. Equity Health, Editl. Bd., Internat. Jour. Health Planning & Mgmt., Brit. Med. Assn. Avocations: writing, tennis. Home: 27 Wilbury Ave Hove BN3 6HS England Business E-Mail: ivanamalc@msegall.freeserve.co.uk.

SEGELMARK, MARTEN, medical educator; b. Lund, Sweden, Nov. 11, 1957; MD, Lund U., 1984, PhD, 1995. Jr. cons. Lund U. Hosp., 1998—2001, sr. cons., 2001—10; prof. Linköping U., 2010—. Sr. cons. Östergötland U. Hosp., 2010; adj. prof. Lund U., 2008—10, dep. head dept. nephrology, 2001—10, assoc. prof., 2000—. Recipient Anna-Lisa Crafoord award, Lund Med. Assn. Master: European Vasculitis Assn.; mem.: Am. Soc. Nephrology, European Dialysis and Transplantion Assn., Swedish Soc. Nephrology. Avocations: sailing, skiing, kayaking. Office: Avdelningen läkemedelsforskning Häl Linköping Östergötland 58185 Sweden Business E-Mail: marten.segelmark@liu.se.

SEGNI, MARIA, endocrinologist, researcher; b. Rome, Dec. 11, 1957; d. Celestino Segni and Paola Satta Branca. MD, Cath. U., 1982. Cert. in pediatrics Italy, in endocrinology Italy. Asst. prof. U. La Sapienza, Rome, 1990—. Tchg. in pediat. and pediatric endocrinology La Sapienza U.; vis. physician Mayo Clinic, Rochester, Minn., 1999—2001, Children's Meml. Hosp., Chgo., 2002. Contbr. scientific papers. Recipient Roche award, Internat. Conf. Thessaloniki, 2001. Mem.: Am. Diabetes Assn., European Soc. Pediat. Endocrinology, European Thyroid Assn., Endocrine Soc. Home: Via Giuseppe Vaccari 3 Rome 00194 Italy Office: La Sapienza Univ Dept Pediat Via Regina Elena 324 00161 Rome Italy Office Fax: 00390649978520. Business E-Mail: m.segni@mclink.it.

SEIBOLD, JAMES RICHARD, physician, educator; b. Washington, Apr. 5, 1950; s. Herman Rudolph and Clara Bond (Taylor) S.; m. Tracey Elizabeth Thompson, Jan. 9, 2009; children: Jon Drew, Zachary Bennett, Gabriel Louis Eyde, Olivia Katherine Eyde. BS, La. State U., 1972; MD, SUNY, Stony Brook, 1975. Diplomate Am. Bd. Internal Medicine, Am. Bd. Rheumatology. Intern in medicine L.I. Jewish Hosp., New Hyde Park, NY, 1975-76, resident in medicine, 1976-78; fellow in rheumatology U. Pitts., 1978-80; asst. prof. medicine Robert Wood Johnson Med. Sch. U. Medicine and Dentistry N.J., New Brunswick, 1980-86, assoc. prof., 1986-92, prof., 1992—, chief rheumatology, 1986-91, dir. clin. rsch. ctr., 1989-95; prof., dir. scleroderma program U. Mich., Ann Arbor, 2004—10, prof. chief divsn. rheumatology U. Conn. Health Ctr., Farmington, 2010. Mem. adv. bd. Ctr. for Advanced Biotech. and Medicine, Piscataway, N.J., 1989-95, dir. Scleroderma program 1995—2004, W.H. Conzen chair clin. pharmacology Schering-Plough Found., 1989; prof. internal medicine Scleroderma Program U. Mich., 2006, Marvin and Betty Danto rsch. prof., 2006—10, prof., chief rheumatology U. Conn. Health Ctr. Farmington, dir., founder Scleroderma Rsch. Cons. LLC Author: (chpt.) Rheumatology, 1988, 91, 94, 95, 99, 2001, 03, 05; contbr. over 400 articles to profl. jours. Bd. dirs. Arthritis Found. Fellow ACP, Am. Coll. Rheumatology (regional coun. 1985), Scleroderma Clin. Trials Consortium (founder 1994, pres. 2004—08). Mem. Soc. Of Friends. Home and Office: Scleroderma Rsch Cons LLC 97 Deer Run Avon CT 06001 Office Fax: 860-404-2983. Personal E-mail: jamesrseibold@gmail.com.

SEIÇA, RAQUEL, medical educator, researcher; b. Leiria, Portugal, Jan. 31, 1957; d. Virgilio Seiça and Rosária Fino; m. Rui Carvalho, Nov. 28, 1981; children: Ana Carvalho, Mariana Carvalho. D, U. Coimbra, 1981, PhD, 1999. Physician Hosp. Figueira da Foz and Hosp. Guarda, Portugal, 1982—85, Health Ctr. Coimbra, 1985—87; investigator Ctr. Neurosci. and Cell Biology, U. Coimbra, 1992—2007; head Inst. Physiology Faculty of Medicine, U. of Coimbra, asst. estagiaria, 1987—91, asst., 1991—99, asst. prof., 1999—2004, prof. metabolism and physiology, 2005—, head, Inst. Physiology, 2006—, prof. and coord., 2007—, investigator, IBILI, 2007—, investigator, CIMAGO, 2007—, tchr. acupuncture postgrad. course, tchr. & coord. advanced course doctoral program health scis. & biomed. rschs., 2009—. Mem. adminstrn. coun. Faculty Medicine, U. Coimbra, 1993—97; mem. U. senate U. Coimbra, 1994—96; mem. representation senate Faculty Medicine, U. Coimbra, 1997—99, mem. commn. evaluation, 2001—01; pres. com rsch. projects Faculty of Medicine, U. of Coimbra, 2005—09; mem. comm. implementation bologne process Faculty Medicine, U. Coimbra, 2006—09, mem. schoolar com., 2007—, coord., 2008—. Office: Inst Physiology Faculty Medicine Pólo III Azinhaga de Santa Comba Celas Coimbra 3000-354 Portugal

SEIDEL, ANDREW J., medical association administrator; b. Washington, Aug. 22, 1952; MBA, U. Balt., 1985. Asst. v.p. St. Luke's Hosp. & Health Network, 1998—. Bd. dirs. Adventist Whole Health Network, 2008—. Mem.: Am. Soc. Healthcare Human Resource Admin., Soc. Human Resource Mgmt. (SPHR Cert.). Avocations: motorcycling, golf. Office: 360 W Ruddle St Tamaqua PA 18218 Business E-Mail: seidela@slhn.org.

SEIDEL, GEORGE ELIAS, JR., zoology educator; b. Reading, Pa., July 13, 1943; s. George E. Sr. and Grace Esther (Heinly) S.; m. Sarah Beth Moore, May 28, 1970; 1 child, Andrew. BS, Pa. State U., 1965; MS, Cornell U., 1968, PhD, 1970; postgrad., Harvard U. Med. Sch., Boston, 1970-71. Asst. prof. physiology Colo. State U., Ft. Collins, 1971-75, assoc. prof., 1975-83, prof., 1983-93, univ. disting. prof., 1993—. Vis. scientist Yale U., 1978-79, MIT, 1986-87; mem. bd. on agr. NRC. Co-editor: New Technologies in Animal Breeding, 1981; contbr. articles to profl. jours. Recipient Alexander Von Humboldt award, N.Y.C., 1983, Animal Breeding Research award Nat. Assn. Animal Breeders, Columbia, Mo., 1983, Clark award Colo. State U., 1982, Upjohn Physiology award, 1986; Gov's. award for Sci. and Tech., Colo., 1986. Mem. AAAS, NAS, Am. Dairy Sci. Assn., Am. Soc. Animal Sci. (Young Animal Scientist award 1983, Physiology, Endocrinology award, 2008), Soc. for Study of Reprodn., Internat. Embryo Transfer Soc. (pres. 1979, disting. svc. award 2001, Pioneer award 2008). Home: 3248 Arrowhead Rd Laporte CO 80535-3022 Office: Colo State U Animal Repro Biotech Lab Fort Collins CO 80523-1683 Office Phone: 970-491-5287. Business E-Mail: gseidel@colostate.edu.

SEIDEN, MICHAEL VAN, hospital administrator, physician; b. NYC, Oct. 9, 1958; s. Stanley and Patricia (Guzewicz) Seiden; m. Jean A. Lambert, Oct. 6, 1981; children: Stanley, Stephanie. BA, Oberlin Coll., 1980; MA, MD, Washington U., 1986, PhD in Humoral Immunology, 1986. Diplomate Am. Bd. Internal Medicine. Intern, resident Mass. Gen. Hosp., Boston, 1986-89, chief med. resident, 1991, asst. in medicine, 1992, chief clin. rsch. unit Divsn. Cancer Medicine; oncology fellow Dana Farber Cancer Inst., Boston, 1990; post-doctoral fellow Brigham and Women's Hosp., Boston, 1992; chmn. clin. rsch. com. Gynecologic Cancer Program Dana-Farber/Harvard Cancer Ctr., Boston, coord. cancer stem-cell project; pres., CEO, prof. Fox Chase Cancer Ctr., Phila., 2007—. Assoc. prof Harvard U. Med. Sch., 1991; asst. to the dir. Mass. Gen. Hosp. Cancer Ctr., 1993. Mem. editl. bd. Clin. Cancer Rsch., Jour. Clin. Oncology, The Oncologist; contbr. articles to profl. jours. Recipient Mass. Breast Cancer Scholar, 2001; named, 1995, 2000. Office: Fox Chase Cancer Ctr 333 Cottman Ave Philadelphia PA 19111-2497 *

SEIDLER, RACHAEL D., psychology professor; b. Houston, Dec. 19, 1969; MS, Ariz. State U., 1995, PhD, 1999. Assoc. prof. U. Mich., 2003—. Grant, NIH. Mem.: Soc. Neural Control Movement, Soc. Neurosci. Office: 401 Washtenaw Ave Ann Arbor MI 48109-2214 Office Fax: 734-936-1925. Business E-Mail: rseidler@umich.edu.

SEIDMAN, JONATHAN G., geneticist, educator; m. Christine Edry, 1973; 3 children. BA in Biochemistry, Harvard U., 1971; PhD, U. Wis. Postdoctoral studies Nat. Inst. Child Health and Human Develop.; Henrietta B. and Frederick H. Bugher Prof. Cardiovascular genetics Harvard Med. Sch., Boston; investigator Howard Hughes Med. Inst. Contbr. articles to profl. jours. Recipient (with wife) Bristol-Myers Squibb award for Disting. Achievement in Cardiovascular Rsch., 2002. Mem.: Inst. Medicine, NAS. Avocations: sailing, gardening. Office: Havard Med Sch, Seidman Lab Dept Genetics 77 Avenue Louis Pasteur Boston MA 02115 Business E-Mail: seidman@genetics.med.harvard.edu.

SEIFER, DAVID BRIAN, reproductive endocrinologist, educator; Studied, U. Ill., 1981. Diplomate Am. Bd. Ob Gyn, cert. reproductive endocrinology-infertility. Resident Stanford Univ. Hosp.; fellow Yale Univ., Cleveland Clin. Hosp.; clin. prof. NYU Sch. of Medicine; prof. ob-gyn. Mt. Siani Sbc. Med.; co-dir. genesis fertility and reproductive medicine Maimonides Med. Ctr. Mem. editl. bd. Fertility and Sterility and the Jour. of Pelvic Medicine and Surgery; cons. FDA. Co-editor: (textbook) Clinical Reproductive Medicine, The Physiologic Basis of Gynecology, and Obstetrics, and Office Infertility. Mem.: NIH. Office: Maimonides Medical Center 1355 84th St Brooklyn NY 11228 Office Phone: 718-283-8600. Office Fax: 718-283-6580.

SEIFERT, DANIEL, physicist; b. Praha, Jan. 10, 1979; Dergree in Engrng., CTU Prague, 2005, PhD. Nuc. physics Inst. ASCR, v.v.vi. Acad. Scis. Czech Republic, 2002—. Mgr. computer radiography PAPCO s.r.o., 2010. Fellow: IAEA, Inst. Advanced Study Pavia, IUSS (Pavia). Avocations: tennis, football, swimming, piano, computers. Home: Kurkova 1209 Praha 18200 Czech Republic Personal E-mail: danielseifert@seznam.cz.

SEIFERT, JULIA JOHANNA, orthopaedic surgeon; b. Siegburg, Germany, July 13, 1967; d. Hans-Juergen and Ute Karin Seifert. Study of Human Medicine, Free Univ. Berlin, 1987—94, Dr., 1995, specialist surgery, 1999, specialist orthopedic surgery and emergency medicine, 2001. Resident DRK Hosp. Berlin, 1990—92; intern Unfallkrankenhaus Berlin, Berlin, 1992—2000, sr. physician, 2003; intern U. Greifswald, 2000—03. Adviser Workers Compensation, Berlin, 2003. Contbr. articles to profl. jours. Recipient scholarship for postdoctoral lectr. qualification, Ministry of Health, 2001—03. Mem.: German Assn. Orthopaedic Surgeons, Am. Fracture Assn. (Henry Meyerding award 2002). Avocations: climbing, marathon. Office: Unfallkrankenhaus Berlin Warener Str 7 Berlin 12683 Germany

SEIFERT, MATHIAS SIEGFRIED, chemist, researcher; b. Wanne-Eickel, Germany, Nov. 8, 1965; s. Max Siegfried and Ria Elisabeth Seifert; m. Annette Maria Schneider, Sept. 5, 1992; children: Christine, Lea-Michelle. Diploma in chemistry, U. Dortmund, Germany, 1993; diploma in environ. sci., Friedrich Schiller U., Jena, Germany, 1995, PhD, 1998. Scientific asst. Heinrich Heine U., Duesseldorf, Germany, 1998—2000; scientific cons. BG Inst. Work and Health, Dresden, Germany, 2000—04; lab. mgr. Fed. Rsch. Ctr. for Nutrition and Food, Detmold, Germany, 2004—07; plant mgr. smelting works, aluminum recycling Bruch Group, Dortmund, 2007—08; mem. environ. protect dept. Aurubis AG, Luenen, 2008—. Presenter in field. Mem. editl. bd.: Jour. Trace and Microprobe Techniques, 1999—2003, Elements and Their Compounds in the Environ., 2002—03, Jour. Elementology, 2004—10, Trace Elem. Electrolytes, 2007—; contbr. articles to profl. jours. Local mgr. Christlich Demokratische Union, 1998—. Mem.: Martin Heidegger Soc., German Physikalische Soc., Soc. German Chemists. Democrat. Home: Bergelchen-Ort 3 Dortmund 44339 Germany Office Phone: 492306108490. Personal E-mail: mathias.seifert@gmx.de.

SEIFF, STEPHEN S., ophthalmologist; b. LA, Sept. 30, 1925; s. Max and Minnie F. (Feldman) S.; m. Gloria Louise Holtzman, Apr. 16, 1950; children: Stuart R., Sherri Seiff Sloane, Karen Seiff Sacks. AA, UCLA, 1945; AB, U. Calif., Berkeley, 1946; MD, U. Calif., San Francisco, 1949. Diplomate Am. Bd. Ophthalmology. Intern County Gen. Hosp., LA, 1949-50; fellow in anesthesiology Lahey Clinic,

Boston, 1950-51; resident in ophthalmology U. Calif., San Francisco, 1952-55; clin. prof. dept. ophthalmology UCLA, 1956—2002, sr. status clin. prof., 2002—11; pvt. practice Beverly Hills, Calif., 1995—2011; clin. chief divsn. ophthalmology Cedars/Sinai Med. Ctr., LA, 1957—2011; attending ophthalmologist Children's Hosp., LA, 1956-94. Lectr. in field; assoc. examiner Am. Bd. Ophthalmology; past pres., former mem. LA Soc. Ophthalmology. Collaborating author: Clinical Anticoagulant Therapy, 1965; contbr. articles to profl. jours. Hon. bd. dirs. That Man May See Inc., San Francisco; former exec. com. mem. UCLA Hosp. Lt. M.C. USNR, 1950-52. Recipient Sr. Honor award UCLA Dept. Ophthalmology, 1994. Fellow ACS, Am. Acad. Ophthalmology; mem. Frederick Cordes Eye Soc. (past nat. pres.), Am. Soc. Cataract and Refractive Surgery (founding mem.). Avocation: sailing. Personal E-mail: sseiff@aol.com.

SEIFTER, JULIAN L., physician, educator; m. Betsy Seifter. MD, Einstein, Bronx, NyY, 1975. Diplomate in internal medicine Am. Bd. Internal Medicine, 1980, in nephrology Am. Bd. Internal Medicine, 1982. Assoc. prof. medicine Harvard Med. Sch., Boston, 1982—; physician Brigham And Women's Hosp., Boston, 1982—. Author (writer): After the Diagnosis: Transcending Chronic Illness, 2010. Office: Brigham and Women's Hosp 75 Francis St Boston MA 02108 *

SEIGLER, RUTH QUEEN, college nursing administrator, educator, consultant; b. Conway, SC, July 31, 1942; d. Charles Isaac and Berneta Mae (Weaks) Queen; m. Rallie Marshall Seigler, Sept. 1, 1963; children: Rallie Marshall Jr., Scot Monroe. ADN, Lander Coll., 1962; BSN, U. S.C., 1964, M of Nursing, 1980. Pub. health nurse Richland County Health Dept., Columbia, SC, 1964—66; dir. nurses Columbia Area Mental Health Ctr., 1966—69; program nurse specialist Midlands Health Dist., 1969—72; discharge planner Richland Meml. Hosp., 1972—73, clin. dir., 1973—75; exec. dir. S.C. State Bd. Nursing, 1976—83; v.p. nursing dept. Self Meml. Hosp., Greenwood, SC, 1983—86; exec. dir. S.C. Commn. on Aging, Columbia, 1986—95; asst. dean Coll. Nursing U. S.C., Columbia, 1995—96, assoc. clin. prof., 1996—. Cons. intergenerational family studies, 1999—; dir. Cockcroft Leadership Program for Nurse Execs., 2002—, Ctr. for Nursing Leadership, 2004-05, sr. cons., 2005—; bd. dirs. Queen Gas Co., Barnwell, SC; nurse cons. Creative Nursing Mgmt., Mpls., 1984—. Advisor: The Role of Cmty. Mental Health Nurse, 1971. Elder Spring Valley Presbyn. Ch., 2001—04, 2010—; moderator Trinity Presbytery, 2003—. Recipient Disting. Alumni award Lander Coll., 1978, Career Woman Recognition award Columbia YWCA, 1980, William S. Hall award SC Assn. Residential Care Homes, 1988, U. SC Coll. Nursing Disting. Alumni award, 1993, award for excellence SC League for Nursing, 1995, Svc. Recognition award SC AARP, 1995; named one of Ten Women of Achievement, SC March of Dimes, 1987, hon. fellow AVC Leadership, 2002, Excellence in Leadership award, 2004, Ordie P. Taylor Humanitarian award, 2005, Palmetto Gold award Top 100 Nurses in SC, 2006, Spirit of Giving award U. SC Coll Nursing Partnership Bd., 2011. Mem. ANA, APHA, SC Nurses Assn. (sec. 1965-68, bd. dirs. 1986-88, Excellence award 1984, Recognition award 1984), SC Hosp. Assn., SC Gerontol. Soc., SC Nurses Found., SC Healthy People 2000 (vice chair), Partnership for Older South Carolinians (founder, chair bd. dirs.), Columbia Luncheon Club (pres. 1997-98), SC Fedn. Older Ams., Evening Mission Action Group, Bd. Nursing Home Examiners, Pilot Club, Inc. (pres. 1988-89, 97-98), Vols. of Am.-Carolinas (bd. dirs., chair, 1998-00, elder, 1999-01, 2010-), Rotary Internat., Sigma Theta Tau, Beta Sigma Phi (pres. chpt. 1997-98, 2011-12). Presbyterian. Avocations: gardening, travel. Home: 6 Beaver Dam Ct Columbia SC 29223-3100 Office: University SC Coll Nursing Office of Dean Columbia SC 29208-0001

SEIGNEURIC, RENAUD GUILLAUME, medical researcher; b. Dijon, France, July 22, 1972; PhD in Medicine, Biology, U. Grenoble, France, 2000; PhD in Biomedical Engring., U. Montreal, 2001. Math tchr. Rectorat de Toulouse, 2001—04; postdoc. fellow MAASTRO Clinic, Maastricht, Netherlands, 2004—07; rschr. U. Bourgogne, INSERM, 2007—. Cons. La main à la pâte, 2007—11; cons. physics baseball EEPHY, 2008; rschr. Or - Nano, 2009; coord. INSERM, 2010—. Avocation: baseball. Office: Faculty Medicine and Pharmacy 7 Bld Jeanne d'Arc Dijon 21000 France

SEIJIRO, SHIMADA, medical educator; b. Osaka, Japan, Apr. 19, 1963; MD, Kinki U., 1990, PhD, 1996. Instr., faculty medicine Sakai Hosp., Kinki U., 2009—. Office: 2-7-1 Harayamadai Minamiku Sakai Osaka 590-0132 Japan Office Fax: 072-298-6691.

SEIKEN, GAIL L., nephrologist, educator; MD, Uniformed Svcs. U. Health Sciences, 1986. Diplomate Am. Bd. Internal Medicine, Am. Bd. Internal Medicine-nephrology. Resident Walter Reed Army Mc, Washington, 1992; asst. prof. Uniformed Svcs. Univ. of the Health Sciences. Decorated Army Svc. Medal, Army Achievement Medal; recipient Hon. Mention, Nat. Kidney Found. Fellows Competition, 1991. Mem.: Am. Soc. of Nephrology, Nat. Kidney Found. (sec. South Tex. chpt.), Alpha Omega Alpha Med. Honor Soc. Office: Washington Nephrology Associates 4915 Auburn Ave Ste 104 Bethesda MD 20814 Office Phone: 301-593-6844, 301-907-4646. Office Fax: 301-907-7796.

SEIL, FREDRICK JOHN, retired neuroscientist; b. Nove Sove, Yugoslavia, Nov. 9, 1933; s. Joseph and Theresa (Krieger) S.; m. Daryle Faith Wolfers, July 2, 1955; children: Jonathan Fredrick, Joel Philip Timothy. BA, Oberlin Coll., 1956; MD, Stanford U., 1960. Intern Kaiser Found. Hosp., San Francisco, 1960-61; resident in neurology Stanford U., Calif., 1961-64, fellow in neurology, 1964-66; staff neurologist VA Med. Ctr., Palo Alto, Calif., 1969-76, clin. investigator Portland, Oreg., 1976-79, staff neurologist, 1979-81, dir. VA office regeneration research programs, 1981—2001, ret., 2001. Asst. prof. neurology Stanford U., 1969-75, assoc. prof. neurology Oreg. Health and Sci. U., Portland, 1976-78, prof. neurology, 1978-2001, prof. cell and devel. biology, 1990-2001, prof. emeritus neurology, 2001—. Editor: Nerve, Organ and Tissue Regeneration: Research Perspectives, 1983, Neural Regeneration, 1987, 94, Current Issues in Neural Regeneration Rsch., 1988, Neural Regeneration and Transplantation, 1989, Advances in Neural Regeneration Research, 1990, Neural Injury and Regeneration, 1993, Multiple Sclerosis: Current Status of Research and Treatment, 1994, Neural Regeneration, Reorganization, and Repair, 1997, Neural Plasticity and Regeneration, 2000; contbr. articles to profl. jours. Capt. US Army Med. Corps, 1966—68. Grantee VA, 1970-2001, NIH, 1986-95. Mem. Internat. Brain Rsch. Orgn., Internat. Soc. Develop. Neurosci., Am. Neurol. Assn., Am. Assn. Neuropathologists, Soc. Neurosci., Soc. Exptl. Neuropathology. Democrat. Achievements include founding of biennial International Symposium on Neural Regeneration; co-founding of biennial Asia Pacific Symposium on Neural Regeneration. Home: 1 Twain Ave Berkeley CA 94708 Personal E-mail: seilf@comcast.net.

SEINFELD, DAVID, cardiologist, educator; MD, Albert Einstein Coll. Medicine, 1973. Diplomate Am. Bd. Cardiology-cardiovascular disease, Am. Bd. Internal Medicine. Resident Beth Israel Med. Ctr.; resident in internal medicine Montefiore Med. Ctr., Bronx, NY, 1974—76, fellow in cardiovascular disease, 1976—78, with; assoc. clin. prof. medicine Albert Einstein Coll. Medicine; cardiologist Lenox Hill Hosp. Office: Lenox Hill Hospital 100 E 77th St New York NY 10075 also: Montfiore Medical Center 20 E 68th St Ste 214 New York NY 10065 Office Phone: 212-288-1538. Office Fax: 212-439-1665.

SEITZ, WILLIAM HENRY, JR., surgeon; b. NYC, Jan. 12, 1950; s. William Henry and Catherine (Kehoe) Seitz; m. Susan Andrea Versenyi, June 4, 1972; children: David William, Eric Alexander, William Henry III, Elizabeth Andrea. BS, Fairfield U., 1971; grad. cert. phys. therapy, Columbia U., 1972, MD, 1979. Diplomate Am. Bd. Medical Examiners. Resident in gen. surgery St. Vincent's Med. Ctr., NYC, 1979-81; resident in orthopaedic surgery Columbia Presbyn. Med. Ctr., NYC, 1981-83, chief resident, 1983-84, Annie C. Kane fellow in hand surgery, 1984-85; clin. instr. Case Western Res. U. Sch. Medicine, Cleve., 1985-87, asst. clin. prof., 1987-94, assoc. clin. prof., 1995—; clin. prof. orthop. surgery dept. Cleve. Clinic Lerner Coll. Medicine, 2005—; chief prof. Surgery Svc. Cleave. Lerner Coll. Medicine, Cleve., 2009—. Chmn. dept. orthop. surgery Orthop. Inst., Cleve., 1997—99, Mt. Sinai Med. Ctr., Cleve., 1997—99; dir. Cleve. Orthop. & Spine Hosp./Luth. Med. Ctr., Cleve., 1999—, Cleve. Clin. Health Sys., 1999—; head of hand and upper extremity surgery, orthop. rehab. Mt. Sinai Med. Ctr., Clevel., 1985—99; cons. Nisonger Ctr. for Child Devel., Columbus, Ohio, 1985—, Cuyahoga County Md. Mental Retardation, Cleve., 1986—; spkr., presenter in field; dept. staff Orthop. Surgery Cleve. Clin. Found., 2000—. Editor: Current Opinion on Orthops.-Hand and Wrist, 1994—99; mem. editl. bd. Jour. Hand Surgery, 1994—99; reviewer: JBJS, 1993—; contbr. articles to profl. jours. Fellow: Am. Acad. Orthop. Surgeons (chmn. exhibit com. mem. 2009—); mem.: Acad. Medicine Edn. Found. (trustee 2005—), No. Ohio Med. Assn., Acad. Medicine Cleve. (bd. dirs. 1999—, exec. com. 2001—, pres. 2004—, 2004—, Outstanding Svc. award 2004), Cleve. Orthop. Soc. (pres. 2001—02), Orthop. Trauma Assn., Orthop. Rsch. Soc., Am. Shoulder and Elbow Surgeons, Am. Orthop. Assn. (mem. com. 2008—), Am. Soc. Surgery Hand (chmn. indsl. rels. com. 1999—, Summer L. Koch award 1990, Sterling Bunnel fellow 1992, internat. travelling fellow 1992—93). Roman Catholic. Home: 3398 Kenmore Rd Shaker Heights OH 44122-3462 Office: Cleve Orthop & Spine Hosp 1730 West 25th St Cleveland OH 44113 Office Phone: 216-363-2331. Business E-Mail: seitzw@ccf.org. *

SEIWALD, ROBERT J., retired inventor; b. Ft. Morgan, Colo., Mar. 26, 1925; BS in Chemistry, U. San Francisco; PhD in Organic Chemistry, St. Louis U., 1954. Prof. organic chemistry U. San Francisco, 1957-89; ret., 1989. Served in WWII. Inducted Nat. Inventors Hall of Fame, 1995. Achievements include invention of first patented antibody labeling agent. Office: Nat Inventors Hall of Fame 3701 Highland Park NW North Canton OH 44720-4535

SEIZER, FERN VICTOR, retired health services administrator; b. NYC, Oct. 29, 1934; d. David L. and Florence Maisel Victor; m. Robert J. Seizer, Aug. 28, 1955; children: Steven P., Susan A. BA, UCLA, 1956. Dir. pub. affairs and edn. Nat. Coun. Jewish Women, LA, 1968—80; exec. dir. Fair Housing Coun. San Fernando Valley, LA, 1980—82, Venice Family Clinic, LA, 1982—94, Valey, La., 1980—82, exec. advisor, 1994; dir. cmty. rels. Didi Hirsch Cmty. Mental Health Ctr., Culver City, Calif., 1994—2000; ret., 2000; exec. dir. Venice Family Clinic, LA, 1982—94. Mng. editor, city editor UCLA Daily Bruin, 1953—54; mem. corp. coun. execs. United Way of Greater L.A., 1991—93; mem. Adminstrs. Forum and Cmty. Outreach Task Force UCLA Sch. Medicine, 1990—93. Adv. com. on primary care Calif. State Dept. Health Svcs., Sacramento, 1990—93; mem. managed care planning coun. L.A. County, 1989—90; mem. social svcs. commn. City of Santa Monica, 1998—99; bd. dirs. Nat. Multiple Sclerosis Soc., LA, 1995—, St. John's Hosp. and Health Ctr., Santa Monica, Calif., 1994—2000, Venice Family Clinic, 1996—. Recipient Alumni Award for excellence in Profl. Achievement, UCLA, 1995, Unsung Hero award, Calif. Cmty. Found., 2000, Most Valuable Trustee award, Nat. Multiple Sclerosis Soc., 1999, Outstanding Contbn. to the Cmty. award, L.A. City and County, 2000. Mem.: Phi Beta Kappa. Avocations: movies, theater, travel, bridge. Home: 257 S Rodeo Dr Beverly Hills CA 90212

SEIZI, SUZUKI, research scientist; b. Japan, Oct. 11, 1970; D, Hokkaido U., 2001. Postdoc Grad. Sch. Agr., Hokkaido U., 2010—. Home: Fukuyama 1051-103 Nagaoka Niigata 940-2122 Japan Personal E-mail: seizis@res.agr.hokudai.ac.jp.

SEJNOWSKI, TERRENCE JOSEPH, science educator; b. Cleve., Aug. 13, 1947; s. Joseph Francis and Theresa (Cudnik) Sejnowski; m. Beatrice Alexandra Golomb, Mar. 24, 1990. BS, Case Western Res. U., 1968; PhD, Princeton U., 1978. Rsch. fellow Harvard Med. Sch., Boston, 1979-82; prof. biophysics Johns Hopkins U., Balt., 1982-90; prof. Salk Inst. U. Calif. San Diego, La Jolla, 1988—, dir. computational neurobiology tng. program, 2001—; Francis Crick prof. Salk Inst., 2005—. Investigator Howard Hughes Med. Inst., 1991—; bd. dirs. San Diego McDonnell-Pew Ctr. for Cognitive Neurosci., 1990-98, Inst. for Neural Computation, U. Calif. San Diego., 1990—. Editor-in-chief Neural Computation, 1989—; co-inventor: (with others) the Boltzmann machine and NET talk; mem. editl. bd. Sci. Mag., 1990—2010. Pres. Neural Info. Processing System Found. Recipient Presdl. Young Investigator award NSF, 1984, Wright prize Harvey Mudd Coll., 1996; Sherman Fairchild Disting. scholar Calif. Inst. Tech., 1993. Fellow: AAAS, IEEE (Neural Network Pioneer award 2002), Johns Hopkins U. Soc. Scholars, Soc. Neuroscience; mem.: NAE, NAS, Soc. Math. Biology, Internat. Soc. Neuroethology, Soc. Neuroscience, Fedn. Am. Soc. Exptl. Biophysics, NY Acad. Scis., Am. Psychol. Assn., Optical Soc. Am., Am. Psychol. Soc. (sr.), Biophys. Soc., Am. Assn. Artificial Intelligence, Assn. Rsch. in Vision and Ophthalmology, Am. Math. Soc., Internat. Neural Network Soc. (gov. bd. 1988—92, Hebb prize 1999), Am. Phys. Soc., Inst. Medicine. Achievements include the Boltzmann machine, NETtalk, a neural network for text-to-speech and infomax Independent Component Analysis (ICA). Office: Salk Inst PO Box 85800 San Diego CA 92186-5800 Business E-Mail: sejnowski@salk.edu. *

SEKI, EKIHIRO, gastroenterologist, educator; b. Kobe, Japan, May 23, 1969; MD, Hyogo Coll. Medicine Grad. Sch., 1994, PhD, 2002. Asst. prof. U. Calif., San Diego, 2010—. Editl. bd. mem. Jour. Hepatology, 2010, World Jour. Gastroenterology, 2010. Rsch. fellowship, Yamanouchi Found., 2004, Uehara Meml. Found., 2005, Postdoc. fellowship, ALF, 2006. Fellow: Am. Assn. Study of Liver Diseases (Rsch. prize 2006); mem.: Am. Gastroent. Assn. Office: Leichtag Biomed Rsch Bldg Rm #332 MM 9500 Gilman Dr MC0702 La Jolla CA 92093-0702 Office Fax: 858-822-5370. Business E-Mail: ekseki@ucsd.edu.

SEKI, HUMITAKE HUGH, scientist, educator; b. Okayama, Japan, Dec. 14, 1937; s. Masaji and Sakae (Sentou) S.; m. Atsuko Yamamoto, May 31, 1970; children: Junko, Tsunetake. B in Agr., U. Tokyo, 1961, M in Agr., 1963, PhD in Agr., 1966. Rsch. assoc. U. Tokyo, 1966-76, vis. fellow, 2006—07; postdoctoral fellow NRC Can., 1967—69; lectr. Waseda U., Tokyo, 1973-75; assoc. prof. microbiology U. Tsukuba, Japan, 1976-89, prof., 1989-2001, dean master's program in biosys. studies, 1998-2001, prof. emeritus, 2001; lectr. Miyazaki U., Japan, 2004—05, Ocean U. China, 2005, Yamagata U., 2008; expert com. mem. FAO, 1971—93, UNESCO, 1972—90, UNEP, 1981—91. 19th headmaster Kashima-shinryû, Japan Traditional Martial Art, heir to the headmaster Kashima-shinryû, Japan Patent Office, 2007; councilor U. Tokyo, 1992-96, 98-2002; mem. com. cons. Ministry of Edn., Tokyo, 1994-96; sec. gen. ann. meeting Oceanographic Soc., 1997. Author: Microbiological Studies on the Decomposition of Chitin in Marine Environment, 1965, The Role of Microorganisms in the Marine Food Chain with Reference to Organic Aggregate, 1972, Kashima-Shinryû Originator of Samurai Martial Arts, 1976, Organic Materials in Aquatic Ecosystems, 1982, A Historical Perspective of Biological Studies in the Ocean, 1995, Microbial Function in the Geochemical Cycles of Marine Ecosystem, 1996, Techniques, Physical Strength and Trance (in Japanese), 1998, Original Achievements Leading Inductively Towards Quantitative Evaluation of Detritus Food Chains in the Marine Food Web, 2000, Kashima-Shinryû and the Education Principles of the Samurai Class (in Japanese), 2001, Divine Martial Art of Kashima (in Japanese), 2009, The Historical Milieu of Kashima-Shinryû Martial Art in Traditional Japanese Culture, 2010; mem. editl. bd. Water, Air, and Soil Pollution, 1980-2001, Aquatic Living Resources, 1991-2001; editor-in-chief Oceanography in Japan, 2003-07. Recipient Okada prize Oceanog. Soc., 1966, Disting. Svc. awards Pacific region Dept. of Def. Dependent Schs., U.S., 1983, ann. Waka column prize Mainichi newspaper, 1984, Oceanog. Soc. prize, 1996. Mem.: Shintou, Japanese Acad. Budô Am. Soc. Microbiology (emeritus mem.), Oceanographic Soc. Japan (emeritus mem.), Soc. Franco-Japonaise d'Océanographie 2000 Prix, Japan Sci. Coun. (com. 1991—2000). Shintou. Achievements include research in microbiological studies on the decomposition of chitin in marine environment; role microorganisms in the marine food chain with reference to organic aggregate. Avocations: haiku, waka. Home: Narita-Higashi 4-32-9 Suginami-ku Tokyo 1660015 Japan

SEKI, MINORU, engineering educator; b. Tokyo, Sept. 26, 1957; PhD, U. Tokyo, 1994. Assoc. prof. U. Tokyo, 1996—2003; prof. Osaka Prefectural U., 2003—06, Chiba U., 2007—. Office: 1-33 Yayoi-cho Inage-ku Chiba 263-8522 Japan Business E-Mail: mseki@faculty.chiba-u.jp.

SEKI, TAKAYUKI, pharmaceutical executive; b. Japan, Jan. 27, 1969; M, U. Tokyo, 1996, PhD, 2005. Mgr. Tisho Pharm. Co. Ltd., 2011—. Office: 403 Yoshino-Cho 1-Chome Kita Ku Saitama-shi Saitama 331-9530 Japan Business E-Mail: takayuki.seki@po.rd.taisho.co.jp.

SEKIGUCHI, JUNICHI, molecular microbiologist and educator; s. Shinichi and Harue (Saiga) S.; m. Masae Amoh; 3 children. BSc, Osaka U., 1968, PhD, 1973. Fellow U. Calgary, Alta., Can., 1973-76; assoc. prof. Kumamoto (Japan) Inst. Tech., 1976-85; prof. microbiology Shinshu U., Ueda, Japan, 1985—2011, emeritus and spl. appoinment prof., 2011—, prof. emeritus, 2011—. Mem. Soc. for Biosci. and Bioengring. Japan (Saito award 1977), Japan Soc. for Biosci. Biotech. and Agrochemistry, Molecular Biology Soc. Japan, Am. Soc. Microbiology. Avocations: tennis, skiing. Office: Shinshu University Faculty Textile Sci and Tech 3-15-1 Tokida Ueda 386-8567 Japan Office Phone: 81-268-21-5344. Business E-Mail: jsekigu@shinshu-u.ac.jp.

SEKINE, IKUO, oncologist; b. Yokkaichi, Mie, Japan, Apr. 12, 1963; s. Juichi and Hiroko Sekine; m. Yuki Sekine; children: Yuta, Ayano. PhD, Chiba U., 2000, MD, 1989. Diplomate National Board of Medical Doctor Japan, 1989. Intern Chiba U. Sch. of Medicine, Japan, 1989—90; internist Shioya Gen. Hosp., Yaita, Tochigi, Japan, 1990—92; resident Nat. Cancer Ctr. Hosp. East, Kashiwa, Chiba, Japan, 1992—97; mem. med. staff Nat. Cancer Ctr. Hosp., Tsukiji, Chuo-ku, Tokyo, Japan, 1997—2003, head, 2004—; post doctoral fellow Southwestern Med. Ctr. U. Tex., Dallas, 2002—03. Contbr. articles to profl. jours. Rsch. Fellowship for collaborative works in fgn. inst., Found. for Promotion of Cancer Rsch., 2002, 31st Grants-in-Aid for Cancer Rsch., 1998. Mem.: Internat. Assn. for Study Lung Cancer, Am. Soc. Clin. Oncology. Office: National Cancer Center Hospital 5-1-1 Tsukiji Chuo-ku Tokyo 104-0045 Japan Office Fax: 81-3-3542-3815. Business E-Mail: isekine@ncc.go.jp.

SEKINE, JOJI GEORGE, professor, maxillofacial surgeon, consultant, cytopathologist; b. Nagasaki, Japan, Feb. 18, 1961; s. Takeshi and Kyoko (Sugamura) Sekine; m. Yoshimi Sekime. DDS, Fukuoka Dental Coll., Japan, 1989; PhD, Nagasaki U., 1996. sr. cons. accredited oral and maxillofacial surgeon. Sr. cons. Maxillofacial Implant Surgery; postgrad. second dept. oral anatomy Fukuoka Dental Coll., Japan, 1989-90; resident second dept. oral and maxillofacial surgery Nagasaki U. Sch. Dentistry, 1990-91, resident dept. anesthesiology, 1991-92, asst. prof. second dept. oral and maxillofacial surgery, 1991-99, lectr. second dept. oral and maxillofacial surgery, 1999—2007; resident ICU Nagasaki U. Med. Hosp., 1992; prof. dept. oral and maxillofacial surgery Shimane U. Faculty Medicine, Izumo, Japan, 2007—. Vis. prof. dept. oral and maxillofacial surgery Umeå U., 2006—07. Contbr. articles to profl. publs. Named regents of Japanese Acad. Maxillofacial Implant. Fellow Internat. Coll. Surgeons; mem. Japanese Soc. Oral and Maxillofacial Surgeons, Internat. Assn. Oral and Maxillofacial Surgeons, Japanese Soc. Clin. Cytology (cert. cytopathologist), Am. Assn. Oral and Maxillofacial Surgeons, Asian Assn. Oral and Maxillofacial Surgeons. Avocations: yacht racing, jazz. Office: Dept Oral and Maxillofacial Surgery Shimane Univ Faculty Medicine 89-1 Enya-cho Izumo 693-8501 Japan Home Phone: 81 853 21 7515; Office Phone: 81 853 20 2301. Business E-Mail: georges@med.shimane-u.ac.jp.

SEKINE, YOSHIMOTO, psychiatrist, researcher; b. Shizuoka, Japan, Nov. 19, 1968; s. Hideji and Akie Sekine; m. Yuko Kato, Feb. 5, 2000; 1 child, Kippei. MD, U. Ryukyus, Japan, 1995; PhD in Medicine, Hamamatsu U., 2000. Lic. psychiatrist Japan, 1996. Trainee psychiatrist Hamamatsu U. Hosp., Shizuoka, Japan, 1995—96, rsch. psychiatrist Sch. Medicine, 1996—2000, asst. prof. Sch. Medicine, 2000—08; assoc. prof. Ctr. Forensic Mental Health, Chiba U., 2008—09, prof., 2009—. Vis. rschr. Ctrl. Rsch. Lab. Hamamatsu (Japan) Photonics, KK, 2002—04; vis. rschr. NIDA NIH, 2006—08. Contbr. articles to profl. jours. Resarch, treatment for patients, and edn. Psychiatry, Hamamatsu U Sch of Med, Hamamatsu, Shizuoka, Japan. Recipient Dr. Kenjiro Takayanagi Rsch. award, 2001, Dr. Paul Janssen Rsch. award, 2002, Rsch. award, Pub. Health Rsch. Found. Japan, 2003, Japan Brain Rsch. Soc., 2004; grantee, The Japan Ministry, 2001—04, The Stantley Med. Rsch. Inst., 2002. Mem.: AAAS, The Japanese Soc. Biol. Psychiatry (Travel award 2001, Rsch. award 2002). Achievements include patents for new treatment for patients with schizophrenia. Office: Divsn Med Treatment & Rehab Ctr Forensic Mental Health Chiba Univ 1-8-1 Inohana Chou-ku Chiba 260-8690 Japan Business E-Mail: sekiney@faculty.chiba-u.jp.

SEKOWSKI, CYNTHIA JEAN, health products executive, medical consultant, eyecare practitioner; b. Chgo., Feb. 14, 1953; d. John L. and Celia L. (Matusiak) S. PhD in Health Svcs. Adminstrn., Columbia Pacific U., 1984, PhD in Health Scis., 1984; grad., Realtor Inst., 1998. Chief contact lens dept. Lieberman & Kraff, Chgo., 1974—87; pres., CEO Seko Eye Care, Inc., Chgo., 1988—; realtor Country Club Realty Group, Naples, Fla., 1995—2002, John R. Wood, Inc. Realtors, 2002—09, Luxury Relocation Svcs., Inc., 2010—. Rschr., technologist U. Ill., Chgo., 1976-78. Active Chgo. Zool. Soc., 1984—, Little City Inner Cir., 1991—, Aurora Lakeland Med. Ctr. Found.; sponsor Save the Children Orgn., 1983—; asst. to campaign mgr. Rep. state senatorial candidate, Chgo., 1972; mem. Am. Mensa, Intertel Internat. Soc.; pres. Compass Point Condo Assn., Naples, 1996-99; budget com. Windstar Country Club Master Homeowner's Assn., Naples, 1996-99; mem. ptnrs. coun. Habitat for Humanity, mem. Dem. Nat. Com. Fellow: Contact Lens Soc. Am.; mem.: Intertel Soc., Winners Cir. Spl. Olympics, Women's Coun. Realtors, Naples Area Bd. Realtors, Nat. Assn. Realtors, Fla. Assn. Realtors, Nat. Contact Lens Examiners, Better Vision Inst., Opticians Assn. Am., Ill. Soc. Opticianry, Am. Fedn. Police and Concerned Citizens (sustaining mem.), Geneva Lakes Conservancy, The Phoenix Soc. (med. profl.), Columbia Pacific U. Alumnae Assn., US Golf Assn., Nat. Geog. Soc., SW Fla. Conservancy, Nat. Wildlife Fedn. (charter mem. Guardians of the Wild), Soc. of the Little Flower, Wis. Hist. Soc., Bear's Paw Country Club (mktg. com. 2002—), Vanderbilt Country Club (residents adv. bd. 1999—2001, vice-chmn. adminstrn. com. 2001—03). Roman Catholic. Avocations: gardening, reading, photography, golf, writing poetry. E-mail: csekowski@wi.rr.com.

SELA, MICHAEL, immunologist, chemist; b. Tomaszow, Poland, Mar. 6, 1924; arrived in Israel, 1941; s. Jakob and Roza (Aleskowski) Salomonowicz; m. Margalit Liebmann, June 20, 1948 (dec. Jan. 1975); children: Irit, Orlee; m. Sara Kika, Jan. 25, 1976; 1 child, Tamar. Grad., Ecole de Chimie, U. Geneva, 1947; MS, Hebrew U., Jerusalem, 1946, PhD in Biochemistry, 1954, D (hon.), 1995, U. Bordeaux II, 1985, Nat. Autonomous U. Mex., 1985, Tufts U., Mass., 1989, Colby Coll., Maine, 1989, U. Tel Aviv, 1999, Ben-Gurion U., Israel, 2001. Faculty Weizmann Inst. Sci., Rehovot, Israel, 1950—, chmn. dept. immunology, 1963-75, W. Garfield Weston prof. immunology, 1966—, v.p., 1970-71, dean faculty biology, 1970-73, bd. govs., 1970—, pres., 1975-85, dep. chmn. bd. govs., 1985—2005. Vis. scientist NIH, Bethesda, Md., 1956—57, 1960—61; vis. prof. molecular biology U. Calif., Berkeley, 1967—68; chmn. Coun. European Molecular Biology Orgn., 1975—79; pres. Internat. Union Immunol. Socs., 1977—80; chmn. sci. adv. com. European Molecular Biology Lab., 1978—81; spl. program rsch. & tng. tropical diseases WHO, 1979—81; staff dept. biology MIT, Cambridge, Mass., 1986—87; sci. adv. group experts Programme Vaccine Devel., 1987—92; adv. bd. Tables Rondes Roussel UCLAF, France, 1980—; mem. coun. Paul Ehrlich Found., Frankfurt, 1980—97; mem. intern guidance panel Israel Inst. Gifted Children, 1987; founding mem., bd. dirs. Internat. Found. Survival & Devel. Humanity, Moscow, Washington, 1988—92. Mem. editl. bd. numerous sci. pubs.; contbr. articles to profl. jours., chapters to books. Decorated Comdr.'s Cross Order of Merit Germany, 1986, officer l'Ordre de la Legion d'Honeur France, 1987; recipient Israel prize in natural scis., 1959, Rothschild prize in chemistry, 1968, Emil von Behring prize, Germany, 1973, Otto Warburg medal, German Soc. Biol. Chem., 1968, Gairdner Found. Internat. award, 1980, prix de l'Institut de la Vie, France, 1984, Albert Einstein Golden medal, UNESCO, 1995, Cabellero Order de San Carlos, 1997, Interbrew-Baillet Latour Health prize, Belgium, 1997, Wolf Found. prize in medicine, Israel, 1998; Fogarty Internat. scholar, 1973—74. Fellow: AAAS (hon. fgn.); mem.: NAS (assoc.; fgn.), Italian Acad. Sci. (fgn. assoc.), French Acad. Scis. (fgn.), Am. Philos. Soc. (fgn.), Internat. Coun. Scientific Unions, Pontifical Acad. Scis., Israel Acad. Scis. & Humanities, Max Planck Soc. (fgn., Harnack medal 1996), Acad. Medicine Mex. (hon.), Am. Acad. Arts & Scis. (hon.; fgn.), Romanian Acad. (hon.), Chilean Soc. Immunology (hon.), French Soc. Immunology (hon.), Am. Assn. Immunologists (hon.), Scandinavian Soc. Immunology (hon.), Am. Soc. Biol. Chemists (hon.). Office: Weizmann Inst Sci Wolfson Bldg 708 Box 26 Rehovot 76100 Israel Office Phone: 972 8 934 4022. E-mail: michael.sela@weizmann.ac.il. *

SELARU, FLORIN M., gastroenterologist, educator; b. Romania, Mar. 15, 1975; MD, Carol Davila U. Medicine, 1999; degree in Gastroenterology, Johns Hopkins U., 2009—09. Asst. prof. Johns Hopkins U., 2009—. Fellowship to Faculty Transition Award, American Gastroenterology Assn. Mem.: Am. Gastroent. Assn. Office: 720 Rutland Ave Ste 950 Baltimore MD 21205 Business E-Mail: fselaru1@jhmi.edu.

SELBEKK, TORMOD, research scientist; b. Orkdal, Sor-Trondelag, Norway, May 27, 1969; MSc, Norwegian U. Sci. and Tech., 1994. Sr. rsch. scientist SINTEF, 2001—. Mem.: Norsk Forening Ultralyd-Diagnostikk. Avocations: motorcycling, mountain climbing, boating. Office: PO Box 4760 Sluppen Olav Kyrres Gate Trondheim Sor-Trondelag 7465 Norway Office Fax: 47 930 70 800. Business E-Mail: tormod.selbekk@sintef.no.

SELBY, JOHN BAYNE, SR., retired radiologist, medical educator; b. Cheyenne, Wyo., Feb. 17, 1924; s. John Edwin Selby and Caroline Lansdale Duckett; m. Jane Claire Dentry, June 11, 1950 (dec. Mar. 3, 2011); children: John Bayne Jr., Henry Gordon, Rebecca Jane. BS, U. Tenn., 1948, MD, 1946; MS in Medicine, U. Minn., 1957. Diplomate Am. Bd. Internal Medicine, Am. Bd. Nuc. Medicine. Asst. in pathology Johns Hopkins U., Balt., 1950—51; intern Evanston (Ill.) Hosp., 1947—48; resident Garfield Hosp., Washington, 1948—50; fellow in pathology Johns Hopkins U., Balt., 1950—51, Mayo Clinic, Rochester, Minn., fellow in medicine, 1954—57, asst. staff mem., 1957; assoc. prof. medicine U. Ky., Lexington, 1958—75; chief nuc. medicine VA Hosp., Lexington, 1966—75, Charleston, SC, 1975—89; prof. radiology Med. U. SC, Charleston, 1995—2000, emeritus prof. radiology, 2001—. Mem. editl. bd. Clin. Nuc. Medicine, Phila., 1985—2005, Jour. SC Med. Assn., Columbia, 2000—06. Author: Self Assessment Nuclear Medicine, 1977, 1981, Mission in Space, 1994. Mem. Med. Discipline Commn., SC, 1985—88; pres. Ky. Diabetes Assn., Lexington, 1968—69; bd. dirs. Sch. Applied Radiol. Sci., Med. U. SC, Charleston, 1984—86. Capt. US Army, 1952—54, Korea, col. USAR, 1956—74. Fellow: ACP; mem.: Soc. Nuc. Medicine, Endocrine Soc., Alpha Omega Alpha. Avocation: tennis. Home: 2602 Atlantic Ave Sullivans Island SC 29482 Personal E-mail: selbysr2@aol.com.

SELECKY, MARY C., state agency administrator; BA, Univ. Pa. Adminstr. NE Tri-County Health District, Colville, Wash., 1979—99; sec. Wash. Dept. Health, Olympia, 1999—. Mem.: Assn. State & Territorial Health Officials (past pres., McCormack award 2004), Nat. Assn. City & County Health Officials (bd. dir.), Wash. State Assn. Local Public Health Officials (past pres.). Office: Dept Health 101 Israel Rd SE Olympia WA 98501

SELETZ, JULES M., surgeon; b. Chgo., 1930; BA in Biology, Va. Mil. Inst., 1953; MD, U. Health Scis., Chgo., 1958. Diplomate Am. Bd. Surgery, FACS. Intern, then resident in gen. surgery Boston City Hosp., 1958-63, mem. staff, 1963-74; mem. faculty Sch. Medicine Tufts U., 1963-82; mem. staff Newton Weslesley Hosp., 1963-82; mil. surgeon U.S. Army, 1982-94; mem. staff Keller Army Cmty. Hosp., West Point, N.Y., 1990-94; physician surveyor Joint Com. Accreditation Healthcare Orgn., 1994-01. Author mystery/med. thriller novels and hist. fiction. Home: PO Box 1087 Lincoln NH 03251-1087 Office Phone: 781-631-4317. E-mail: jseletz@earthlink.net. *

SELF, WILLIAM THOMAS, microbiologist, educator; b. Birmingham, Ala., Mar. 17, 1971; s. Lawrence Thomas Self and Paula June Adams; m. Marianne Stearns, June 24, 1995; children: Zachary Thomas, Ryan Thomas, Matthew Thomas, Michael Thomas. BS in Microbiology, U. Fla., Gainesville, 1993; PhD in Microbial Physiology, U. Fla., 1998. Staff fellow NIH, Bethesda, Md., 1999—2003; asst. prof. U. Ctrl. Fla. Coll. Medicine, Orlando, 2003—08, assoc. prof., 2009—. With rev. panels NSF, NIH. Contbr. articles to profl. jours. Recipient Outstanding Tchr. award, 2009, Outstanding Rsch. award, 2010; grants, NIH, NSF, NASA, 2004—. Mem.: Am. Soc. Microbiology (pres. Fla. br. 2008—10). Home: 3600 Foxcroft Cir Oviedo FL 32765 Office: Univ Ctrl Fla 4000 Central Florida Blvd Bldg 20 Rm 124 Orlando FL 32816-2364 Business E-Mail: wself@mail.ucf.edu.

SELFRIDGE, GEORGE DEVER, retired dentist, retired military officer; b. Pitman, NJ, Sept. 24, 1924; s. William John and Edith (Gorman) S.; m. Ruth Motisher, 1948; children: Pamela Ruth, Kimberly Dawn, Cheryl Beth. Student, Gettysburg Coll., 1942-43, Muhlenburg Coll., 1943-45; DDS, U. Buffalo, 1947; MA, George Washington U., 1974. Commd. lt. (j.g.) USN, 1948, advanced through grades to rear adm., 1973; intern Naval Dental Sch., Bethesda, Md., 1948-49, Naval Hosp., St. Albans, NY, 1949-50; asst. dental officer U.S.S. Midway, 1949-51; with USN, 1951-64; sr. dental officer U.S.S. Randolph, 1958-60, U.S.S. Cadmus, 1964-65, U.S.S. Vulcan, 1965-66, Svc. Force, 1964-66, Submarine Force, Atlantic Fleet, 1967-69; from asst. dir. grad. edn. to comdg. officer Navy Grad. Dental Sch., Bethesda, 1969-76; exec. officer Norfolk (Va.) Navy Dental Clinic, 1972-73; ret. USN, 1976; dean Dental Sch., Washington U., St. Louis, 1976-86; dir. dental services Barnes Hosp., St. Louis, 1976—87, Children's Hosp., St. Louis, 1976-87; exec. dir. Am. Bd. Orthodontics, 1986-97; ret., 1998. Adv. bd. VA Hosp., St. Louis, 1977-79; mem. exec. coun. Cen. Region Testing Svc., 1976-86; adv. com. St. Louis Jr. Coll. Dist., 1976-86. Contbr. articles to med. jours. Decorated Legion of Merit; recipient commendation medals, Greater St. Louis Gold Medallion award, 1995, Spl. Recognition award Am. Bd. Orthopedics, 1996. Mem. ADA, Am. Coll. Dentists (past pres.), Internat. Coll. Dentists (dep. registrar, sec. U.S. sect., Spl. Recognition award), Assn. Mil. Surgeons U.S., Omicron Kappa Upsilon. Republican. Home: 14545 Foxham Ct Chesterfield MO 63017-5620

SELIGSON, FREDERIC LEE, physician, cardiothoracic surgeon; b. Erie, Pa., July 12, 1956; BA, Dartmouth Coll., 1978; MD, U. Pitts., 1982. Diplomate Am. Bd. Thoracic Surgery, Am. Bd. Surgery. Intern, resident in surgery Beth Israel Hosp., Boston, 1982-87; resident in cardiothoracic surgery U. Ill., Chgo., 1987-89; cardiothoracic surgeon Thoracic and Vascular Surgeons, P.C., Prairie Village, Kans., 1989—. Office Phone: 816-523-7088.

SELIKTAR, DROR, engineering educator; b. Glasgow, Scotland, Oct. 3, 1972; BSc in Mech. Engring., Drexel U., 1994; PhD in Bioengring., Ga. Inst. Tech., 2000. Assoc. prof. Technion - Israel Inst. Tech., 2002—. Office: Faculty Biomed Engineering Tech Technion Haifa 32000 Israel E-mail: dror@bm.technion.ac.il.

SELIN, LISA K., physician; b. Helsinki, Finland, Apr. 8, 1952; d. Lauri Oscar and Hilma K Selin. BSc, Dalhousie Univ, 1970—74; MD, Dalhousie U., 1974—79, FRCP, 1980—84; PhD, Univ. Man., 1986—93. Med. intern Dalhousie U., Halifax, Canada, 1979—80, resident in internal medicine, 1980—84; fellow in infectious diseases Univ. of Man., Winnipeg, Canada, 1984—86; doctoral student Univ of Man., 1986—91; postdoctoral fellow Univ. Mass. Med. Sch., 1992—95, instr., 1995—96; asst. prof. Univ. Mass. Med Sch., 1996—2001; assoc. prof. Univ. Mass. Med. Sch., 2001—08, prof., 2008—. Contbr. articles to profl. jours. Med. Coun. of Can. Student fellowship, Med. Coun. of Can., 1986—91, Dalhousie Entrance schoarship, Dalhousie Univ, 1970, Izaak Walton Killam scholarship, Izaak Walton Killam Found., 1984—86, Clin. Investigator award, Nat. Inst. of Health, 1996—99, Rsch. grant, NIH- NIAID, 2000—, NIH-NIAID, 2001—, 1999—2003. Mem.: Can. Infectious Disease Soc., Am. Assn. of Immunologists. Achievements include research in T cell-mediated heterologous immunity in viral infections. Avocations: painting, cross country skiing, swimming, gardening, travel. Office: Univ Mass Med Sch 55 Lake Ave North Worcester MA 01655 E-mail: liisa.selin@umassmed.edu.

SELKOE, DENNIS JESSE, neurologist, researcher, educator; b. NYC, Sept. 25, 1943; s. Herbert E. and Mary P. (Lille) S.; m. Polly Ann Strasser, June 24, 1967; children: Gregory, Kimberly. BA, Columbia U., 1965; MD, U. Va., 1969. Diplomate Am. Bd. Psychiatry and Neurology, Nat. Bd. Med. Examiners. Intern in medicine Hosp. U. Pa., Phila., 1969-70; rsch. assoc. NIH, Bethesda, Md., 1970-72; resident in neurology Peter Bent Brigham/Children's Hosp., Boston, 1972-74, chief resident in neurology, 1974-75; rsch. assoc. Harvard Med. Sch., Boston, 1975-78, asst. prof. neurology, 1978-82, assoc. prof., 1982-85, assoc. prof. neurology and neurosci., 1985-90, faculty mem. divsn. on aging, 1980—, prof. neurology and neurosci., 1990—, Vincent and Stella Coates prof. neurol. diseases, 2001—; co-dir. Ctr. Neurologic Diseases Brigham and Women's Hosp., Boston, 1985—. Mem. sci. adv. bd. Alzheimer's Disease Assn., Chgo., 1983-89; mem. Gov.'s Commn. on Alzheimer's Disease, Mass., 1985-87; neurosci. adv. com. Howard Hughes Med. Inst., 1996—. Author over 200 articles, book chpts. on biochemistry and molecular biology of Alzheimer's Disease. Recipient Wood-Kalb Found. prize Alzheimers Disease Assn., 1984, Med. Rsch. award Met. Life Found., 1986, LEAD award Nat. Inst. on Aging, 1988, NIH Merit award, 1991—, Arthur Cherkin award UCLA, 1995, Mathilde Solowey award in neurosci. Found. for Advanced Edn. in Scis., NIH, 1998, Rita Hayworth award Alzheimer's Assn., 1995, Boerhaave medal U. Leiden, 1998, Pioneer award Alzheimer's Assn., 1999, Lifetime Achievement award, Alz Assn., 2008; grantee Bristol-Myers Squibb Neurosci., 1990. Fellow AAAS, Am. Acad. Neurology (Potamkin prize 1989, Dr. A.H. Heineken prize for Medicine 2002, Lifetime Achievement award, Alzheimers Assn., 2008); mem. Am. Neurol. Assn., Soc. for Neurosci., Am. Assn. Neuropathologists, World Fedn. Neurologists, Inst. Medicine NAS, Assoc. Am. Physicians. Office: Harvard Med Sch Brigham & Womens Hosp 77 Avenue Louis Pasteur Boston MA 02115-5727

SELLER, ROBERT HERMAN, cardiologist, physician; b. Phila., Mar. 21, 1931; s. David and Elsie (Straussman) S.; m. Maxine Schwartz, June 3, 1956; children: Michael, Douglas, Stuart. AB, U. Pa., 1952, MD, 1956. Intern. Grad. Hosp. of U. Pa., Phila., 1956-57; research asst. dept. pharmacology U. Pa., 1953-55; resident in cardiology, research fellow Am. Heart Assn., Phila. Gen. Hosp., 1957-58; resident in internal medicine Albert Einstein Med. Ctr., Phila., 1958-59, chief resident, 1959-60; instr. medicine Hahnemann Med. Coll. and Hosp., Phila., 1960-64, asst. prof., 1964-69, assoc. prof., 1969-72, dir. Service F, 1962-67, asst. coordinator mil. edn. for nat. def., 1961-64, dir. div. family medicine, 1967-72, acting chmn. dept. family medicine and community health, 1972-74, prof. medicine, family medicine and community health, 1973-74; practice medicine, specializing in cardiology Buffalo, 1974—; prof., chmn. dept. family medicine, prof. medicine SUNY-Buffalo, Deaconess Hosp., 1974-82, chmn. dept. family practice and dir. family practice residency program, 1974-82; prof. medicine and family medicine SUNY-Buffalo, 1974-2000; emeritus prof. medicine and family medicine, 2000—. Author: Differential Diagnosis of Common Complaints, 1986, 5th edit., 2007, Diagnosis of Common Complaints, 2004; contbr. articles to profl. jours. NIH grantee, 1972-75; Deaconess Hosp. family practice resident tng. grantee, 1975-; health professions spl. projects grantee, 1975- Fellow ACP, Am. Coll. Cardiology, Am. Acad. Family Physicians, Phila. Coll. Physicians; mem. AMA, N.Y. Med. Soc., Erie County Med. Soc., Am. Fedn. Clin. Research, Am. Heart Assn., Soc. of Tchrs. of Family Medicine, N.Y. Acad. Sci., N.Y. Acad. Family Physicians.

SELLEVOLD, OLAV FREDRIK MÜNTER, anesthesiologist; b. Oslo, July 31, 1947; s. Ragnar and Astrid (Münter) S.; m. Anne Brit Misund; children: Fredrik Ragnar, Kristin Liv, Jorgen Tormod. MD, U. Bergen, Norway, 1974; specialist in anesthesiology, U. Trondheim, Norway, 1981, PhD, 1988. Gen. practice medicine, 1976; trainee in pediatrics Haukeland Hosp., Bergen, 1976; trainee in anesthesiology U. Hosp., Trondheim, 1976-81, trainee in cardiology, 1979-80; prof., chmn. dept. anaesthesia and intensive care Haukeland U. Hosp., Bergen, Norway, 1997-99; prof. dept. anaesthesia and intensive care Univ. Hosp., Trondheim, 1999—. Cons. Univ. Hosp., Trondheim, 1986—, dir. cardiac anesthesia/intensive care, 1993—; prof. anaesthesiology U. Trondheim, 1996—97; academician European Acad. Anaesthesiology, 2001—. Author: Glucocorticoids in Myocardial Protection; mem. editl. bd. Jour. Cardiothoracic and Vascular Anaesthesia, others; guest editor Acta Anaesth Scand, European Jour. Anaesthesiology. Bd. dirs. several nat. and internat. orgns. Mem.:

Royal Norw. Acad. Scis., Nat. Anaesthesia Soc. (com. chmn.), European Soc. Anesthesiology (ptnr. amalgamation com. 2004—05), Union European de Medicins Specialists (rep. 1994—2002), Norwegian Soc. Anesthesiology (chmn. 1991—93, Excellent Rsch. prize 1999), Confedn. European Nat. Socs. Anesthesiology (hon.; treas. 1998, pres.-elect 2004), European Assn. Cardiothoracic Anesthesiology (hon.; dep. chmn. 1993—95, pres. 1995—98, editor EACTA News 1995—2004). Home: Heimstadvn 16 N 7040 Trondheim Norway Office: Dept Cardiothoracic Anaesthesiology and Intensive Care St Olavs University Hosp Prinsesse Kristines Gt 3 No 7330 Trondheim Norway Fax: 47 7386 7029. Business E-Mail: olav.sellevold@ntnu.no.

SELLICK, KATHLEEN A., hospital administrator; b. Phoenix; m. Phil Sellick; 1 child, Grace. BS, Ariz. State U.; MBA, U. Chgo. Grad. Sch. Bus., 1984. With Am. Med. Internat., Beverly Hills, Calif., Westgate Med. Ctr., Denton, Tex.; adminstrv. resident Mayo Clinic, Rochester, Minn.; v.p. adminstrn. and dir. outreach devel. Hoag Meml. Hosp. Presbyn., Newport Beach, Calif.; exec. v.p. and COO St. Joseph Hosp., Orange, Calif., 1995—99; assoc. exec. dir. and COO U. Wash. Med. Ctr., Seattle, 1999—2001, acting exec. dir., 2000—01, exec. dir., 2001—06; pres., CEO Rady Children's Hosp., San Diego, 2006—. Clin. asst. prof., dept. health services U. Wash. Sch. of Public Health and Community Medicine. Recipient Leadership in Action award, Mental Health America San Diego County, 2010. Office: Rady Children's Hospital 3020 Children's Way San Diego CA 92123 Office Fax: 206-598-6292. *

SELLKE, FRANK WILLIAM, cardiothoracic surgeon, researcher; b. Ft. Wayne, Ind., Feb. 5, 1956; s. Erwin A. and Anna Luise (Schumacher) S.; m. Amy Marie Brill, Jan. 31, 1987; children: Michelle, Eric, Nicholas, Amanda. AB summa cum laude, Wabash Coll., 1978; MD, Ind. U., Indpls., 1981. Diplomate Am. Bd. Thoracic Surgery, Am. Bd. Surgery. Intern Ind. U. Hosp., Indpls., 1981-82; emergency physician Culver Union Hosp., Crawfordsville, Ind., 1982-83; resident in surgery Akron (Ohio) City Hosp., 1983-87; postdoctoral fellow cardiac surgery U. Iowa, Iowa City, 1987-90; from instr. to asst. prof. surgery Harvard Med. Sch., Boston, 1990-95, assoc. prof. surgery, 1995—2000, prof. surgery, 2000—; cardiothoracic surgeon Beth Israel Hosp., Boston, 1990—; chief cardiothoracic surgery Beth Israel Deaconess Med. Ctr., Boston, 1999—2006, chief cardiothoracic surgery rsch., 2006—08; chief cardiothoracic surgery & prof. Brown Med. Sch., 2009—. Chmn. dept. cardiovascular surgery and medicine Landmark Med. Ctr., 2005—08. Mem. editl. bd. Jour. Thoracic and Cardiovascular Surgery, Jour. Cardiac Surgery, Shock; contbr. rsch. articles to profl. jours. Fellow Am. Coll. Cardiology, Am. Coll. Surgeons; mem. AMA, Am. Surg. Assn., Am. Heart Assn., Am. Physiol. Soc., Am. Coll. Chest Physicians, Soc. Univ. Surgeons, Assn. Acad. Surgeons, Am. Assn. for Thoracic Surgery, Soc. Thoracic Surgeons, Phi Beta Kappa. Lutheran. Home: 121 Monadnock Rd Chestnut Hill MA 02467-1136 Office: Beth Israel Deaconess Med Ctr 110 Francis St Boston MA 02215 Office Phone: 617-632-8385, 401-444-2732. Business E-Mail: fsellke@bidmc.harvard.edu, fsellke@lifespan.org.

SELLS, BRUCE HOWARD, biomedical sciences educator; b. Ottawa, Ont., Can., Aug. 15, 1930; s. Charles Henry and Nell (Worth) S.; m. Bernice May Romain, Sept. 19, 1953; children: Jennifer, Monica, David, Lisa. BS, Carleton U., 1952; MA, Queen's U., 1954; PhD, McGill U., 1957. Demonstrator McGill U., Montreal, Ont., Can., 1954-57; rsch. assoc. Columbia U., NYC, 1961-62; asst. prof. St. Jude Children's Hosp.-U. Tenn., Memphis, 1962-68; assoc. prof. St. Jude Children's Hosp., Memphis, 1964-72, mem., 1968-72; prof., dir. molecular biology Meml. U. Nfld., St. John's, Can., 1972-83, assoc. dean, 1979-83; prof. molecular biology U. Guelph, Ont., Can., 1983-96, dean biol. sci. Ont., 1983-95, univ. prof. emeritus, 1997—; exec. dir. Can. Fed. Biol. Socs., 1999—2007, exec. dir. emeritus, 2007—08; interim dir. Nat. Inst. Nutrition, 2003—04. Adv. com. Ont. Health Rsch. Coun., 1992; bd. mem. Med Biogene, 2004-08, Alzheimer Soc., Lanark County, 2009-, bd. mem., Ont., 2011-, dir., ASO Eastern Regional, 2011-. Contbr. articles to profl. jours. Rsch. fellow Damon Runyon Meml. Fund, Brussels, 1957-59, Copenhagen, 1959-60; Killam Sr. Rsch. fellow U. Paris, 1978-79; grantee NIH, 1963-72, NSF, 1965-69, Med. Rsch. Coun. Can., 1972-93, Damon Runyon Meml. Fund for Cancer Rsch., 1962-76, Nat. Found.-March of Dimes, 1974-78, Muscular Dystrophy Assn. Can., 1974-78, Nat. Cancer Inst. Can., 1979-83, Nat. Scis. and Engring. Rsch. Coun., 1990-2001, Vis. Prof. award Institut Pasteur, Paris, 1989; Exch. fellow Natural Scis. and Engring. Rsch. Coun. of Can., 1994. Fellow Royal Soc. Can. (rapporteur microbiology and biochemistry divsn. 1985-87, convenor 1987-89); mem. Acad. Sci. of Royal Soc. Can. (life scis. divsn. fellowship rev. com. 1990-92), Can. Biochemistry Soc. (pres. 1981-82, Ayerst award selection com. 1990), Med. Rsch. Coun. (Centennial fellowships com., chmn. com. on biotech. devel. grants 1983-85, standing com. for Can. Genetic Disease Network 1991-92, chmn., 1992-97, mem. coun. 1979-83), Nat. Rsch. Coun. Can. (biol. phenomena subcom. 1983-86, chmn. steering group, sci. criteria for environ. quality com. 1986, E.W.R. Steacie Prize com. 1986-88), Assn. Can. Deans of Sci. (co-founder 1989). Home: 277 Coutts Bay Rd RR 5 Perth ON Canada K7H 3C7 E-mail: Bruce.Sells@sympatico.ca.

SELMAN, JAY E., neurologist; b. 1945; AB in Polit. Sci., Washington U., St. Louis, 1967, MS in Speech and Hearing, 1969; MD, U. Tex. Southwestern Med. Sch., Dallas, 1973. Diplomate Am. Bd. Pediat., Am. Bd. Psychiatry & Neurology with added qualification in clin. neurophysiology, special competence in child neurology. Intern pediat. Albert Einstein Coll. Medicine/Bronx Mcpl. Hosp., NY, 1973—77, resident pediat. and neurology NY, 1974—78, fellowship pediat. neurology NY, 1976—77; assoc. clin. prof. neurology Columbia U. Coll. Physicians and Surgeons, NYC, 1992—; attending neurologist No. Westchester Hosp., Mount Kisco, NY. Head Stroke Liaison Com. No. Westchester Hosp.; mem. profl. adv. bd. Epilepsy Found.; mem. learning network Jewish Bd. Family and Child Svcs. NY; vis. clin. asst. prof. neurology Albert Einstein Coll. Med.; neurological cons. Blythedale Children's Hosp., Valhalla, NY, 2002—, chief pediat. neurology, 2008—. Contbr. articles to profl. jours. Named one of NY's Top Dr.'s, Castle Connolly Med. LTD. Mem.: Epilepsy Soc. So. NY, Child Neurology Soc., Am. Acad. Neurology and Movement Disorders, Am. Epilepsy Soc. Home: 95 Bradhurst Ave Valhalla NY 10595-1637 Office Fax: 914-666-7371. Personal E-mail: jay_selman@yahoo.com.

SELTMAN, MARTIN I., geriatrician, educator; MD, Med. Coll. of Pa. Diplomate Am. Bd. Family Practice, Am. Bd. Family Practice-geriatric medicine. Intern Shadyside Hosp., Pa., resident Pa.; faculty family medicine Drexel Univ. Coll.; dir. Forbes Family Practice Residency Program; hosp. affiliations include Forbes Regional Hosp., West Penn Hosp. Office: Metro Family Practice 901-B West St Pittsburgh PA 15221 Office Phone: 412-247-2310.

SELTSER, RAYMOND, epidemiologist, educator, preventive medicine physician; b. Boston, Dec. 17, 1923; s. Israel and Hannah (Littman) S.; m. Charlotte Frances Gale, Nov. 16, 1946; children: Barry Jay, Andrew David. MD, Boston U., 1947; MPH, Johns Hopkins U., 1957. Diplomate Am. Bd. Preventive Medicine (trustee, sec.-treas. 1974-77), Am. Bd. Med. Specialties (mem. exec. com. 1976-77). Asst. chief med. info. and intelligence br. U.S. Dept. Army, 1953-56; epidemiologist divsn. internal health USPHS, 1956-57; from asst. prof. to prof. epidemiology Johns Hopkins U. Sch. Hygiene and Pub. Health, Balt., 1957-81, assoc. dean, 1967-77, dep. dir. Oncology Ctr., 1977-81; dean U. Pitts. Grad. Sch. Pub. Health, 1981-87, prof. epidemiology, 1981-88, emeritus dean, emeritus prof. epidemiology, 1988—; assoc. dir. USPHS Ctrs. for Disease Control, Rockville, Md., 1988-90; assoc. dir. Ctr. for Gen. Health Svcs. Extramural Rsch. Agy. for Health Care Policy and Rsch., Rockville, 1990-95, sr. advisor spl. population rsch. Ctr. Primary Care Rsch., 1995-98; med. and healthcare advisor Dept. Va Office Inspector Gen. Office Health Care Inspections, Chevy Chase, Md., 1997—2000. Cons. NIMH, 1958-70, also various govtl. health agys., 1958-79; expert cons. Pres.'s Commn. on Three Mile Island, 1979-80; mem. Three Mile Island Adv. Panel Health, Nat. Cancer Inst. Cancer Control Grant Rev. Com., Pa. Dept. Health Preventive Health Service Block Grant Adv. Task Force, Gov.'s VietNam Herbicide Info. Commn. Pa.; chmn. Toxic/Health Effects Adv. Com., 1985-87. Trustee, exec. com., chmn. profl. adv. com. Harmarville Rehab. Ctr., Pitts., 1982-87; bd. dirs. Health Edn. Ctr., Media Info. Svc.; chmn. USPHS Task Force on Improving Med. Criteria for SSA Disability Determination, 1988-92. Capt. AUS, 1951-53, Korea Decorated Bronze Star; recipient Centennial Alumni citation Boston U. Sch. Medicine, 1973; elected to Johns Hopkins Soc. of Scholars, 1986. Fellow AAAS, APHA (mem. governing coun. 1975-77, chmn. EPI sect. coun. 1979-80), Pa. Pub. Health Assn. (bd. dirs. 1985-88, pres.-elect 1986-88), Am. Coll. Preventive Medicine, Am. Heart Assn.; mem. Am. Epidemiol. Assn., Internat. Epidemiol. Assn., Am. Soc. Preventive Oncology, Am. Cancer Soc. (bd. dirs. Pa. divsn. 1985-87, exec. com. 1986-87), Assn. Schs. Pub. Health (sec. 1969-71, exec. com., chmn. edn. com. 1983-87), Soc. Med. Cons. Armed Forces, Soc. Epidemiologic Rsch., Nat. Coun. Radiation Protection and Measurements (consociate), Johns Hopkins Alumni Coun. (exec. com. 1994-97), Sigma Xi, Delta Omega. E-mail: rseltser@verizon.net.

SELTZER, VICKI LYNN, obstetrician, gynecologist; b. June 2, 1949; d. Herbert Melvin and Marian Elaine (Willinger) Seltzer; m. Richard Stephen Brach, Sept. 2, 1973; children: Jessica Lillian Brach, Eric Robert Brach. BS, Rensselaer Poly. Inst., 1969; MD, NYU, 1973. Diplomate Am. Bd. Ob-Gyn. (examiner 1988-2001). Intern Bellevue Hosp., NYC, 1973—74, resident ob-gyn., 1974—77; fellow gynecol. cancer Am. Cancer Soc., NYC, 1977—78, Meml. Sloan Kettering Cancer Ctr., NYC, 1978—79; assoc. dir. gynecol. cancer Albert Einstein Coll. Medicine, NYC, 1979—83, prof. ob-gyn., 1989—. Assoc. prof. ob-gyn SUNY, Stony Brook, 1983—89; Edie & Marvin H. Shur prof. ob-gyn & women's health Albert Einstein Coll. Medicine, NYC, 2003—08; dir. ob-gyn. Queens Hosp. Ctr., Jamaica, NY, 1983—93, pres. med. bd., 1986—89; chair ob-gyn LI Jewish Med. Ctr., 1993—2008, emeritus chair ob-gyn, 2008—; chair ob-gyn North Shore U. Hosp., 1999—2008, emeritus chair ob-gyn, 2008—; v.p. women's health svcs. North Shore-LI Jewish Health Sys., 1999—2008; chair med. bd. North Shore U. Hosp., 2001—; mem. steering com. N.Y. State Coun. Grad. Med. Edn., 2005—, chair subcom. primary care; mem. U.S. Coun. Grad. Med. Edn., 2006—10. Author: Every Woman's Guide to Breast Cancer, 1987; editor: Women's Primary Health Care, 1995, 2000; editor-in-chief: Primary Care Update for the Ob-Gyn, 1993—; mem. editl. bd. Women's Life mag., 1980—82, Jour. Jacobs Inst. Women's Health, 1990—95, Ob-Gyn. Survey, 2005—, Jour. Reproductive Medicine, 2005—, mem. internat. editl. bd. Jour. Soc. Obstreticians and Gynecologists Can., 2000—; contbr. articles to profl. jours.; host (TV series) Weekly Ob-Gyn. program, Lifetime Med. TV; author: Prolog Taskforce for Gynciolog Oncology and Critical Care, 2011. Mem. Mayor Beame's Task Force on Rape, NYC, 1974—76; chair health com. Nat. Coun. Women, NYC, 1979—84; bd. govs. Nat. Coun. Women's Health, 1985—94; chair Coun. Resident Edn. Ob-Gyn., 1987—93. Recipient citation, Nat. Safety Coun., 1978, Achiever award, L.I. Ctr. Bus. and Profl. Women, 1987; Galloway Fund fellow, 1975. Fellow: ACOG (gynecol. practice com. 1981, v.p. 1993—94, pres.-elect 1996—97, pres. 1997—98), N.Y. Obstet. Soc. (pres. 1999—2000, com. internat. affairs 2010—, com. contuning med. edn. 2010—, mentor of yr. award 2010); mem.: Am. Hosp. Assn. (governing coun. maternal and child health 2004—, chair-elect 2007, chair 2008), N.Y. Cancer Soc., Am. Med. Women's Assn. (com. chair 1975—79, editl. bd. jour. 1986—2002, citation 1973), Internat. Fedn. Gynecology and Obstetrics (internat. steering com. to reduce maternal mortality 2000—02), Women's Med. Assn. (v.p. N.Y. 1974—79, resident rev. com. ob-gyn 1993—98, Lila Wallis Lifetime Achievement award 2002), NYU Sch. Med. Alumni Assn. (bd. govs. 1979—, v.p. 1987—91, pres. 1992—93), Alpha Omega Alpha.

SELVAGGI, FRANCESCO, surgeon, educator; b. Naples, Italy, Mar. 24, 1957; MD, U. Naples, 1981. Cert. specialist in gen. surgery Naples, 1991. Assoc. prof. gen. surgery Second U. Naples, 1999—. Chief neapolitan unit colo-proctology Italian Soc. Colorectal Surgery SICCR, 2004—11. Mem.: Italian Soc. Gastroenterology, European Soc. Coloproctology, European Crohn's Colitis Orgn., Italian Soc. Surgery. Home: Via Francesco Giordani 42 Naples Campania 80122 Italy

SELVAM, LATHA, medical educator; b. Salem, June 15, 1972; MSc, Dr. ALM PG IBMS, Taramani, 1995; PhD, CMC, Vellore, 2008. Assoc. prof. SVMCH & RC, 2008—. Home: 201 Faculty Quarters Ariyur Puducherry 605 102 India Home Phone: 9486419659; Office Phone: 04132644482. Personal E-mail: lathaphysio@yahoo.co.in.

SELVAMANI, PALANISAMY, medical educator; b. Tiruchirappalli, Jan. 23, 1978; MPharm, Jadavpur U., 2001, PhD, 2010. Prof. Anna U. Tech. Tiruchirappalli, 2003. Mem.: Tamilnadu Pharamcy Coun., Indian Pharmacol. Soc., Indian Pharmacists Assn., Assn. Pharm. Tchrs. India, Indian Pharm. Assn. Avocation: painting. Office: Dept Pharm Tech Tiruchirappalli Tamil Nadu 620024 India Office Fax: 91 431 2407333. E-mail: pselvamani@rediffmail.com.

SELVIN, JOSEPH, biology professor; b. Marthandam, Tamilnadu, India, Feb. 3, 1972; s. Joseph R. and Ponnesam P.; m. Seghal G. Kiran; 1 child, Sanfrey Joseph. BSc in Chemistry, Christian Coll., Marthandam, 1993; MSc in Environ. Biotech., Manonmaniam Sundaranar U., Tirunelveli, 1996; PhD in Marine Biotech., Ctrl. Marine Fiheries Rsch. Inst., Thiruvananthapuram, 2002. Head, dept. biotech., Mariagin, 2001—04; rsch. officer ICFRE, Bangalore, Karnataka, India, 2005; sr. lectr. Bharathidasan U., Tiruchirappalli, Tamilnadu, 2005—11, Prof., 2011—. Fellow guide Indian Acad. Sci., Bangalore, 2008—. Contbr. articles to profl. jours. Recipient Jawarharlal Nehru award, ICAR, New Delhi, 2003, Young Scientist award, DST, New Delhi, 2004, Nature Pub. Group award, 2006, Young Scientist medal, INSA, 2006, Prof. L.S.S. Kumar Endowment award, 2006, Young Investigator Project award, DBT, New Delhi, 2008; Rsch. grant, 2006, Internat. Found. Sci., Sweden, 2004, CSIR, New Delhi, 2006, UNESCO, 2006, MoES, New Delhi, 2008. Office: Bharathidasan Univ Dept Bioinformatics Tiruchirappalli Tamilnadu 620024 India Office Fax: 91-431-2407045. E-mail: selvinj@rediffmail.com.

SELWYN, PETER ALAN, family practice, educator; MD, Harvard U. Diplomate Am. Bd. Family Practice. Resident Montefiore Med. Ctr., dir. cmty. health and wellness, med. dir. substance abuse program, 1984; hospital affiliation includes Yale Univ., 1992; prof. Yeshiva Univ., 1992, chair dept. family and social medicine, 1999. Co-author: Palliative Care in the Management of Advanced HIV/AIDS, Developing a Multidisciplinary Model of Comparative Effectiveness Research Within a Clinical and Translational Science Award, An Epidemic in Evolution: The Need for New Models of HIV Care in the Chronic Disease Era, Complications of HIV infection: a systems-based approach, Comorbidity-Related Treatment Outcomes among HIV-Infected Adults in the Bronx, NY, various publs. Office: Yeshiva University Jack and Pearl Resnick Campus 1300 Morris Park Ave Bronx NY 10461 Office Phone: 718-430-2000.

SEMENZA, GREGG L., medical geneticist, educator; AB in Biology, magna cum laude, Harvard Coll., Cambridge, Mass., 1974; MD, PhD in Genetics, U. Pa., Phila., 1978. Diplomate Nat. Bd. Med. Examiners, Am. Bd. Pediat., Am. Bd. Med. Genetics. Intern, resident petiat. Duke U. Med. Ctr., Durham, NC, 1984—86; postdoc. fellow med. genetics Johns Hopkins U. Sch. Medicine, Balt., 1986—90, asst. prof. dept. pediat., 1990—94, assoc. prof., 1994—99, prof., 1999—, also prof. dept. medicine, oncology & radiation oncology, McKusick-Nathans Inst. Genetic Medicine, founding dir. vascular program, Johns Hopkins Inst. Cell Engring., 2003—. Vis. prof. dept. physiology Med. Coll. Wis., 1998; Iyengar meml. lectr. U. Pa. Sch. Vet. Medicine, 2001; Abelson meml. vis. prof. Washington U. Sch. Medicine, St. Louis, 2001; Woznicki lectr. cardiovasc. pathology & genetics Baylor Coll. Medicine, Houston, 2001; Fisher disting. lectr. Tulane U. Sch. Medicine, New Orleans, 2003. Author: (med. textbook) Transcription Factors and Human Disease, 1998; editor-in-chief Jour. Molecular Medicine, 2007—, mem. editl. bd. Jour. Clin. Investigation, 2000—, Antioxidants & Redox Signaling, 2003—, Cancer Rsch., 2003—, Molecular & Cellular Biology, 2008—; contbr. articles to profl. jours. Recipient Lucille P. Markey Scholar award in biomed. sci., 1989, Established Investigator award, American Heart Assn., 1994, Jean & Nicholas Leone award, Children's Brain Tumor Found., 1999, Chancellor's award in neurosci., La. State U. Health Scis. Ctr., 2002, Gairdner Found. Internat. award, Can., 2010. Fellow: Am. Coll. Med. Genetics (founding fellow 1992); mem.: NAS, Am. Soc. Clin. Investigation, Soc. Pediatric Rsch. (E. Mead Johnson award 2000), Assn. Am. Physicians, Alpha Omega Alpha. Office: Johns Hopkins U Sch Medicine Inst Genetic Medicine 733 N Broadway Rsch Bldg Ste 671 Baltimore MD 21205 Office Phone: 443-287-5618. E-mail: gsemenza@jhmi.edu. *

SEMER, NADINE BETH, plastic surgeon; b. Balt., Dec. 3, 1960; MD, U. Md., 1986; MPH, Harvard U. Sch. Pub. Health, 2008. Plastic surgeon, ptnr. Southern Calif. Permanente Med. Group, 1999—. Fellow: ACS. Avocations: travel, reading. Home: 2409 Cloy Ave Venice CA 90291 Personal E-mail: nadinesemer@gmail.com.

SEMIGLAZOV, VLADIMIR FEDOROVICH, oncologist, surgeon; b. Urgum, Russia, Sept. 16, 1941; s. Fedor Prokópjevich and Nina Mihailovna (Smorkalova) S.; m. Svetlana Ivanovna Shabalina, June 16, 1970; children: Vladislav, Feodor. MD, Leningrad Med. Inst., 1965; PhD in Oncology, N.N. Petrov Rsch. Inst., 1971, MD, 1981. Clin. coord. N.N. Petrov Rsch. Inst. Oncology, 1965-67, attending physician, 1970-74, head dept. surgery and breast cancer clinic, 1980—, dir., 2005; sr. rsch. Surg. Dept. Rsch. Inst. Oncology, 1974-80; dir. WHO Collaborative Ctr. and Breast Cancer Clinic, St. Petersburg, 1985—. Author: Early Detection of Breast Cancer, 1989, Minimal Breast Cancer, 1992, Treatment of Advanced BREAST Cancer, 1997, Noninvasive and Invasive Breast Cancer, 2005. Grantee Russian Acad. of Scis., 1995; recipient N.N. Petrov Oncol. awards Russian Acad. of Med. Sci., I. Pavlov golden medal Russian Acad. Nat. Scis., 2000. Mem. Am. Soc. Clinical Oncology, Soc. of Oncology of Russia, European Soc. Mastology, European Orgn. Rsch. and Treatment Cancer, St. Petersburg Scientific Soc. Oncologists (chmn. 1999—), European Soc. Surg. Oncology, Russian Acad. Med. Scis., 2000 (corres. mem.). Office: NN Petrov Rsch Inst Oncology Leningradskaya Str 68 Pesochny 2 Saint Petersburg 197758 Russia Home: Dept 117 Engyel'Sa Pr-Kt 28 194156 Saint Petersburg Sankt-Pyetyerburg Russia Office Phone: +7(812)596-89-18. E-mail: fsemig@mail.ru, ssemiglazov@mail.ru.

SEMINARA, DONNA, geriatrician, educator; Grad., Universidad Autonoma de Guadalajara Facultad de Medicina, 1986. Diplomate Am. Bd. of Internal Medicine, Am. Bd. of Internal Medicine-geriatric medicine. Fellow Am. Coll. of Physicians; resident Staten Island Univ. Hosp., 1987—90, dir. geriat. Office: Staten Island University Hospital 475 Seaview Ave Staten Island NY 10305 Office Phone: 718-226-8851.

SEMPLE, JANE FRANCES, health facility director; b. Lakewood, Ohio, Feb. 14, 1951; d. Frank Joseph and Margaret Eleanor (Carpenter) Semple; m. Nick N. Morana, June 24, 1977 (div. Sept. 1981). AAB, Cuyahoga CC, Cleve., 1977; BA, Baldwin-Wallace Coll., 1980; MBA, Case Western Res. U., 1984; ND, Trinity Coll. Natural Health, 1999. Diplomate Am. Bd. Naturopaths. Adminstrv. asst. DeVilbiss Co., Cleve., 1969—77; project dir. Nat. Survey Rsch. Ctr., Cleve., 1977—80; market rsch. mgr. Sherwin-Williams Co., Cleve., 1980—85; instr. Cuyahoga CC, Cleve., 1986—92, Baldwin-Wallace Coll., Berea, Ohio, 1992—93; dir. Alternative Healing Inst., 1987—. Author: Naturopathic Health Series Family Promise. Mem. S. B. Anthony Soc. Womenspace, Cleve., 1980—88; vet. vol. Family Homeless Shelter. Mem.: Sunshine Health Freedom Coalition, Am. Botanic Coun., Am. Assn. Nutritional Cons., Am. Naturopathic Med. Assn. Democrat. Home: 26969 Greenbrooke Dr Olmsted Falls OH 44138 Office: Alternative Healing Inst 4965 Doven Ctr Rd North Olmsted OH 44070 Office Phone: 440-777-2665. Personal E-mail: dr.jane@bright.net.

SEMPRINI, GLORIA, plastic surgeon; b. Rimini, Italy, Jan. 18, 1980; Liceo scientifico, 1998, laurea in Medicina E Chirurgia, 2005. Resident plastic surgery Palstic and Reconstructive Dept., 2007—. Office: Piazza Rodolone 3 Gemona Del Friuli Udine 33013 Italy Business E-Mail: semprini-gloria@libero.it.

SEN, CHANDRANATH, neurosurgeon, educator; MS, U. Med-.Coll., India, 1976. Diplomate Am. Bd. Neurol. Surgery. Resident Univ. of Wis. Hosp., 1979—80; fellow Univ. of Pitts., 1985—86; vis. fellow Nat. Hosp. for Nervous Disorders, London, 1989; chmn. of neurosurgery St. Luke's-Roosevelt Hosp. Ctr.; adj. prof. Mt. Sinai Sch. of Medicine. Mem. bd. of certifications Am. Board of Neurol. Surgery, 1989; trustee Continuum Health Ptnrs. Inc.; mem. of med. bd. Beth Israel Med. Ctr. Named one of Best Doctors, NY Mag., 2008, Top Doctors in NY, Castle Connolly's, 2009. Office: Mount Sinai Hospital Ste 4E 425 W 59th St New York NY 10019 Office Phone: 212-523-6720.

SEN, ELIF, pulmonologist; b. Ankara, Turkey, Dec. 2, 1974; d. Hasan Oral Sen and Hatice Betul Saglik. BA with hons., Tevfik Fikret Lisesi, Ankara, 1992; MD (hon.), Ankara U., 1998. Intern Ankara U. Med. Sch., resident; rsch. asst. chest medicine Ankara U., 1998—2003, specialist in chest diseases dept., faculty medicine, 2003—. Mem.: Thorax Soc., European Respiratory Soc. Office: Ankara U Mamak Cad Ankara 06100 Turkey Personal E-mail: elifsen2001@yahoo.com.

SEN, PIYAL, psychiatrist; b. Kolkata, West Bengal, India, Dec. 23, 1965; s. Paramesh Chandra and Utsa Sen; m. Ishita Ghosh, Nov. 23, 1993. MBBS, Nil Ratan Sircar Med. Coll., Kolkata, 1989, DPM, Inst. Postgrad. Med. Edn. and Rsch., Kolkata, 1992; diploma in Forensic, Inst. Psychiatry, London, 1998; PGCAP, Queen Mary and Westfield Coll., London, 2000. Cons. forensic psychiatrist East London Forensic Svc., Hackney, London, 2000—01, Priory Healthcare Svc., Milton Keynes, Buckinghamshire, England, 2001—03, lead cons., 2003—05, cons. forensic psychiatrist, 2005—07, Surrey, England, 2007—08; cons., assoc. med. dir. St. Andrews Healthcare Bd. Basildon, Essen & Northampton, 2009—. Contbr. scientific papers. Jour. editor Brit. Indian Psychiat. Assn., London, 2008; brochure editor London Durga Puja Dusserah Assn., Mont., 2007—08. Recipient India Internat. Friendship award, 1999. Fellow: RCP (cpd coord., oxford region 2007—, cpd exec. 2007—). Office: Saint Andrews Healthcare Clara House Pound Ln N Benflect Essen 55129 JP Germany Home: Athenaeum Rd N20 9AH Whetstone England Office Phone: 02168723847. Office Fax: 01268723801. Personal E-mail: piyal@freeuk.com. Business E-Mail: psen@standrew.co.uk.

SEN, SRIJAN, medical educator; b. Nov. 25, 1975; MD, Mich. U., 2005, PhD. Asst. prof. U. Mich., 2009. Office: 5047 BSRB 109 Zina Pitcher Pl Ann Arbor MI 48109 Business E-Mail: srijan@umich.edu.

SENCZUK, ANNA MARIA, cell biologist, researcher; b. Czestochowa, Poland, Nov. 3, 1965; arrived in US, 2000, permanent resident, 2006; d. Janusz and Halina Senczuk; m. Miroslaw Josef Studzinski, Dec. 29, 1990; children: Tom Studzinski, Lukas Studzinski. Attended, Academia Medyczna, Wroclaw, Poland, 1990; BS in Cell, Molecular and Microbiology, U. Calgary, Alta., Can., 1996, MS in CMMB, 1999. Assoc. U. Calgary, 1999—2000; scientist Amgen, Seattle, 2000—; dir. Polish-Am. Chamber of Commerce, 2010—. Presenter in field; contribr. Radiowisla.com, 2010—. Contbr. articles to profl. jours. Mentor Bio Expo., Seattle, 2002—. Mem.: Sigma Xi. Achievements include patents for HIC dual salt. Office: Amgen 1201 Amgen Ct West AW2D2152 Seattle WA 98119 Office Phone: 206-265-8338. Personal E-mail: senczukowa@hotmail.com. Business E-Mail: senczuka@amgen.com.

SENDAX, VICTOR IRVEN, retired dentist, educator, dental implant researcher; b. NYC, Sept. 14, 1930; s. Maurice and Molly R. S.; m. Deborah deLand Cobb, Dec. 17, 1969 (div. June 1976); 1 child, Jennifer Reiland; m. Marcia Ayer Pearson, Dec. 13, 1986; children: Anneliese Chase, Cordelia Ayer. Grad., Tanglewood Music Ctr., 1953; BA, NYU, 1951, DDS, 1955; postgrad., Harvard U. Sch. Dental Medicine, Cambridge, Mass., 1969-72. Diplomate Am. Bd. Oral Implantology/Implant Dentistry (pres. 1996, dir.). Commr. NY State Dental Svc. Corp., 1969-73; pres., dir. BioDental Rsch. Found., Inc., NYC, 1975—2010; pres. Victor I. Sendax, D.D.S., P.C., NYC, 1972—2010, Sendax Mini Dental Implant Ctrs. Mgmt., Inc., 1985—2010; sr. emeritus attending oral implantologist mini-dental implant program, dept. demtistry & oral surgery, divsn. otolaryngology St. Lukes-Roosevelt Hosp., NYC, 1979—; ret., 2010. Adj. assoc. prof. implant prosthodontics Columbia U. Sch. Dental and Oral Surgery, NYC, 1974-92; vis. lectr. dept. implant dentistry Harvard U. Sch. Dental Medicine, NYU Coll. Dentistry; faculty NY County Dental Soc. Sch. for Continuing Dental Edn.; mem. dental implant rsch. programs adv. com. Nat. Inst. Dental Rsch., HHS; cons. Julliard Sch. Voice and Drama, NYC, 1972—90, Vocal Dynamics Lab. Dept. Otolaryngology, Lenox Hill Hosp., NYC, 1970-90; founder Sendax Implant Seminars; 1st dir. implant prosthodontics resident program Columbia U. Sch. Dental and Oral Surgery and Columbia Presbyn. Hosp. Editor: Dental Clinics of North America: HA-Coated Dental Implants, 1992; mem. editl. bd. Oral Implantology, 1979-98; patentee in mini-implants, oral implant magnetics, implant abutments and sinus graft implant stabilizers; co-developer: MDI/SENDAX mini-dental implant system, author: (profl. text book) Mini Dental Implant Innovations, 2011, Luciano Pavarotti Redux, 2011 Mem. bd. dirs. City Ctr. Music and Drama, Inc. divsn. Lincoln Ctr. Performing Arts, NYC, 1966-75; mem. adv. bd. Amagansett (N.Y.) Hist. Assn., 1969-89; trustee Leukemia Soc. Am., NYC, 1967; bd. dirs. Schola Cantorum, 1980-90, Soc. Asian Music, 1965-76. Capt. Dental Corps USAF, 1955-57. Recipient Cert. of Honor, Brit. Dental Implant Assn., 1988., Aaron Gershkoff Meml. award for Outstanding Contbns. and Dedication to Oral Implantology Am. Acad. of Implant Dentistry, 1996. Fellow: Royal Soc. Medicine Gt. Britain, Am. Acad. Implant Dentistry (nat. pres. 1981), Internat. Coll. Dentists, Am. Coll. Dentists; mem.: ADA (ho. of dels. 1969), Japan Soc., N.Y. Acad. Scis., Internat. Assn. Dental Rsch., Am. Assn. Dental Rsch. (implant group), Fedn. Dentaire Internat., Am. Analgesia Soc., Acad. of Osseointegration, Am. Dental Edn. Assn. (former chmn. spl. interest group on dental implant edn.), Century Assn. Home: 70 E 77th St Apt 6A New York NY 10075-1811 E-mail: vis@sendax-minidentimpl.com.

SENEL, ENGIN, dermatologist; b. Ankara, Ankara, Turkey, Apr. 24, 1980; s. Ramazan and Armagan Senel. MD, Hacettepe U., Ankara, 2004; PhD in Dermatology, Baskent U., Ankara, 2008. Diplomate Hacettepe U., 2004; Computer MEB, Turkey, 1998. Med. dr. Baskent U., 2004—. Author poem novels. Mem.: Turkish Soc. Dermatology, EAVD, Soc. Dermatology (assoc.), TEMA (assoc.). Home: Sehitlik Uslu Sokak Saray Apt 41/9 6620 Ankara Ankara, Ankara Turkey Personal E-mail: enginsenel@enginsenel.com.

SENER, STEPHEN FRANCIS, oncologist, surgeon; b. Chgo., Jan. 30, 1950; s. Charles J. and Helen Sener; m. Sherri Abbott, June 21, 1971; children: Matthew Charles, Michael Stephen. BA in Chemistry, Northwestern U., Evanston, Illinois, 1972; MD, Northwestern U., Chgo., 1977. Lic. surgeon Am. Bd. Surgery, 1983, surg. oncologist Soc. of Surg. Oncology, 1988. Asst. prof. surgery Northwestern U., Chgo., 1987—92, assoc. prof. surgery, 1992—98; prof. of surgery Northwestern U. Dept. of Surgery, 1998—; head, divsn. gen. surgery Evanston Northwestern Healthcare, 1996—2001, attending surgeon, 1984—, vice-chairman, dept. surgery, 1999—. Contbr. articles to profl. jours. Recipient Departmental Honors award, Northwestern U. Dept. Chemistry, 1972, Faculty Tchr. Yr., Northwestern U. Dept. Surgery, 1998. Fellow: Soc. Surg. Oncology; mem.: Am. Surg. Assn., Midwest Surg. Assn. (mem. exec. com. 2000—), Am. Cancer Soc. (Ill. pres. 1992—94, nat. bd. dirs. 1992—2006, nat. pres. 2004—05, pres. 2004—05, immediate past pres. 2005—06, St. George medal 1998), Chgo. Surg. Soc. (sec. 1999—2003), Am. Soc. Clin. Oncology, Ctrl. Surg. Assn. Achievements include first to organize and lead six surgical teams from Evanston Northwestern Healthcare on humanitarian surgical missions to Moscow State University, Latvia Cancer Inst., and Peking University. Office: Evanston Northwestern Healthcare 2650 Ridge Walgreen Bldg Rm 2507 Evanston IL 60201

SENG, JULIA S., nurse midwife, educator; b. Ohio, Dec. 17, 1960; MS, U. Mich., 1995, PhD, 1999. Rsch. assoc. prof. U. Mich., 2008—. Recipient Best Book of Yr. award, Am. Coll. Nurse Midwives. Fellow: Am. Acad. Nursing; mem.: Internat. Soc. Studies of Trauma and Dissociation, Am. Coll. Nurse Midwives. Office: 204 S State St Rm G120 Lane Hall Ann Arbor MI 48109-1290 Business E-Mail: jseng@umich.edu.

SENGER, HARRY L., psychiatrist; b. Cin., Apr. 15, 1931; AB, Harvard U., 1953; MD, Harvard Med. Sch., 1957. Cert. Diplomate Am. Bd. Psychiatry and Neurology. Pvt. practice clin. psychiatry, Cambridge, Mass., 1963—2002, Boston, 2002—. Contbr. articles to profl. jours. Fellow: Mass. Psychiat. Soc. (chmn. edn. com. 1990—, Disting.), Am. Psychiat. Soc. (life; disting. mem.). Office: 77 Warren St Brighton MA 02135 Office Phone: 617-782-5550.

SENGOTTUVELU, G., cardiologist, educator; b. Salem, Aug. 13, 1969; married. MD, DM, MMC, DNB, 1991. Diplomate Nat. Bd., 2000. Prof., rschr. Apollo Hosps., 2009—, sr. cons., 2009. Sr. cons. Apollo Hospitals, 2009. Editor: Focus Issue on TransRadial (Kongu Achiever award, 2008); editor: (reviewer) Indian Heart Jour.; contbr. articles to profl. jours. Organiser, camps & heart disease prevention activities Dr. G.S. Heart Found., Chennai, 2006—08. Recipient Young Interventionalist Award, Asian Interventional Cardiovasc. Therapeutics; Internat. Cardiology fellowship, ICPS, 2003. Fellow: SCAI. Avocation: writing. Office: Apollo Hosp Greams Ln Off Greams Rd Chennai Tamil Nadu 600006 India Personal E-mail: gsengottuvel@yahoo.co.in.

SEN GUPTA, ROBIN, pathologist; b. Hamburg, Germany, Mar. 25, 1966; s. Achintya Kumar and Irmgard Sen Gupta; m. Cornelia Kuchel, Sept. 11, 1992; children: Mina Sophie, Paula Marie, Hanna Lotte, Louisa Lynn. Dr. in Med., U. Hamburg, 1997. Diplomate in med. U. Hamburg, 1994. Head Dept. Pathology, Bocholt, Germany, 2007—. Office: St-Agnes-Hosp Bocholt Barloer Weg 125 Bocholt 46397 Germany

SENIOR, JUAN, cardiologist; b. Barranquilla, Nov. 4, 1964; MB, U. PB, 1988; degree in Internal Medicine, U. Antioquia, 1993. Chief, heart transplantation program, heart failure clinic U. Antioquia, 2001—07, chief, cardiology clinic posgrad. program, 2008—10, cardiologist, interventional cardiology, 2008—. Fellow: ACP; mem.: Heart Failure Assn. European Soc. Cardiology, Soc. Colombiana Cardiologia y Cirugia Cardiovasc., Assn. Colombiana Medicina Interna (Premio Docente-Investigador award). Avocations: literature, sports. Office: Calle 64 No 51 D - 154 Medellin Antioquia 57 Colombia Business E-Mail: mmbt@une.net.co.

SENNERBY, LARS GERHARD, medical educator; b. Linköping, July 29, 1960; DDS, U. Gothenburg, 1986, PhD, 1991. Cons., asst. prof. Brånemark Clinic, Gothenburg Pub. Health Svc., Sweden, 1989—2002; prof. U. Gothenburg, 2000—. Editor-in-chief Clin. Implant Dentistry & Related Rsch., Wiley Publ., 1999. Avocations: travel, cooking, gardening. Office: Medicinaregatan 12C PO Box 450 Gothenburg Västra Götaland SE 405 30 Sweden Business E-Mail: lars.sennerby@telia.com.

SENOL, VESILE, medical educator; b. Isparta, Turkey, Sept. 11, 1960; PhD, Sch. Medicine, Pub. Health, 2004. Asst. prof. Faculty Health Edn., 1996, eRCIYES U., 2004—, Erciyes U., 2004—. Bd. dirs. 1st & Emergency Aid, 1996—. Recipient Success Encouragement award, eRCIYES U. Mem.: HASAK. Avocations: swimming, reading. Office: Halil Bayraktar Health Svcs Vocatio Kayseri 38039 Turkey Office Fax: 903524375936. Personal E-mail: drvesilesenol@gmail.com.

SENOL DURAK, EMRE, clinical psychologist, educator, researcher, psychotherapist; b. Ankara, May 5, 1977; Degree in Clin. Psychology, Mid. East Tech. U. Clin. Psychology, 2003, PhD, 2007. Psychologist UNICEF and Turkish Psychology Assn., 1999—2000, Ministry Justice Prison Detention Houses Ankara Number 1 F Type Prison, 2000—03; clin. psychologist Ministry Justice Prison Detention Houses, 2003—04; lectr. Dept. Psychology, Abant Izzet Baysal U., Bolu, Turkey, 2004—08, asst. prof., 2008—. Cons. Ministry Justice Prison Detention Houses Edn. Program, 2003—04. Grant, Jacop Found. Mem.: Internat. Family Therapy Assn., Turkish Psychology Assn. Avocations: photography, theater, jazz, classical music. Office: Abant Izzet Baysal University Dept Psychology Bolu 14280 Turkey Personal E-mail: emresenoldurak@yahoo.com.

SENSENIG, DAVID MARTIN, retired surgeon; b. May 4, 1921; s. Wayne and Elizabeth Long (Crawford) S.; m. Constance Campbell, June 6, 1947; children: Philip Campbell, David Martin, Andrew Wilson, Thomas O'Brien; m. Bernice Evans, Dec. 20, 1975. BS, Haverford Coll., 1942; postgrad., U. Pa., 1942-43; MD, Harvard U., 1945; JD, Temple U., 1998. Diplomate Am. Bd. Surgery, Am. Bd. Thoracic Surgery. Rotating intern Allentown (Pa.) Hosp., 1945-46; surg. ho. officer, jr. asst. resident Peter Bent Brigham Hosp., Boston, 1948-50, sr. asst. resident, resident surgeon New Eng. Ctr. Hosp., Boston, 1950-52; surg. resident Westfield (Mass.) State Sanatorium, 1952-53; asst. chief surg. svc., dir. surg. rsch. lab. VA Med. Tchg. Group Hosp., Memphis, 1953-55; asst. chief surg. svc. VA Hosp., Albany, N.Y., 1955-57; resident in thoracic and cardiac surgery Univ. Hosp. State U. Iowa, Iowa City, 1957-59, instr. in surgery, 1957-58, assoc. in surgery, 1958-59, from asst. prof. to assoc. prof., 1960-62; chief thoracic surgery sect. VA Hosp., Phila., 1959-60, asst. chief surg. svc., 1963-66; cardiothoracic surgeon Pa. Hosp., Phila., 1962-63; asst. prof. surgery U. Pa., Phila., 1962-66, supr. Animal Rsch. Lab., 1963-66; pvt. practice medicine specializing in surgery Bangor, Maine, 1966-88; attending surgeon Ea. Maine Med. Ctr., Bangor, 1966-88, St. Joseph Hosp., Bangor, 1966-88, chief surg. svc., 1974-79, VA Hosp., Togus, Maine, 1988-95, ret., 1995. Contbr. articles to profl. jours. Capt. US Army, 1943—48. Mem. ACS (gov. at large 1985-91), Am. Thoracic Soc., Internat. Cardiovasc. Soc., Am. Geriatric Soc., Am. Coll. Chest Physicians, New Eng. Surg. Soc., New Eng. Soc. Vascular Surgery v.p. 1991), Maine Vascular Soc. (pres. 1978), Iowa Acad. Surgery, Pa. Assn. Thoracic Surgery, N. Am. Soc. Pacing and Electrophysiology, Penobscot County Med. Soc. (pres. 1974), Phila. Acad. Surgery, Bangor Med. Club (pres. 1970). Republican. Lutheran. Home: 101 Sunset Dr Lansdale PA 19446-1706 Home Phone: 215-393-3409.

SENTER, HOWARD J., neurosurgeon, educator; Attended, Tufts U., Boston. Diplomate Am. Bd. Neurol. Surgery. Intern Tufts New Eng. Med. Ctr., Boston; resident Yale Univ. Sch. of Medicine, New Haven, NY Univ.-Bellevue Hosp., NYC; interim chmn. neurosurgery dept. The Western Pa. Hosp., The Western Pa. Hosp. Forbes Regional Campus; clin. asst. prof. neurosurgery Temple Univ. Office: West Penn Allegheny Health System Mellon Pavilion 4815 Liberty Ave Ste 448 Pittsburgh PA 15224 Mailing: West Penn Allegheny Health System 320 E N Ave Pittsburgh PA 15212 Office Phone: 412-682-6800, 412-359-3131. Office Fax: 412-682-2036.

SENTURK, EKREM, retired thoracic surgeon; b. Turkey, May 8, 1966; MD, Sch. Medicine, 1983. Physician Adnan Menderes U., 2006—11, cons., 2006—11; asst. prof. Sch. Medicine, 2006—11.

SENZEL, ALAN JOSEPH, chemist, consultant, music critic; b. LA, May 26, 1945; s. Bernard and Esther Mildred (Shykin) s.; m. Phyllis Sharon Abt, June 22, 1969; children: Richard Steven, Lisa Beth. BS in Chemistry, Calif. State U., Long Beach, 1967; MS, UCLA, 1969, PhD, 1970. Assoc. editor Am. Chem. Soc., Washington, 1970-74; methods editor Assn. Ofcl. Analytical Chemists, Washington, 1974-78; info. dir. Chemistry Industry Inst. Toxicology, Research Triangle Park, NC, 1978-79; pvt. cons. Raleigh, NC, 1978—. Sr. tech. writer Cardinal Health, Morrisville, N.C., 2002-2004; music critic Raleigh News and Observer, 1982-90, Spectator Mag., 1990-94; dep. mgr. Environ. Sys. Group, Environ. Resources Mgmt. Inc., Exton, Pa., 1988; project scientist Agrl. divsn. Residu Chem. dept. CIBA-GEIGY Corp., Greensboro, N.C., 1989-93; analytical contract lab. mgr. Entropy, Inc., 1995-96. Editor: Instrumentation in Analytical Chemistry, 1973, Newburger's Manual of Cosmetic Analysis, 1977 (FDA award 1978), Safety in the Laboratory, 1984 (STC award 1985); assoc. editor: Official Methods of Analysis, 1975; editor Inclusions Quar., 1993-94; publs. mgr. Internat. Union Pure and Applied Chemistry, 1999-2002. Pres. Congregation Sha'arei Israel, 1981-83, Raleigh Chamber Music Guild, 1997-99. Mem. Soc. Tech. Comm. (treas. 1983-85, v.p. 1985-87, achievement award 1985, excellence award 2002), Am. Chem. Soc., Assn. Ofcl. Analytical Chemists, Bridge Club (Raleigh), Capitol Club, Vanderbilt Club, B'nai B'rith. Republican. Jewish. Avocations: music, tennis, basketball, bridge. Home and Office: 7704 Audubon Dr Raleigh NC 27615-3403 Office Phone: 919-559-4814, 919-483-7882. E-mail: asenzel@yahoo.com.

SEO, DAISUKE, chemistry professor; s. Kouichi and Noriko Seo. DSc, Waseda U., Shinjuku, Tokyo, 2002. Rsch. assoc. Waseda U., 2001—03; asst. prof. Kanazawa U., Ishikawa, Japan, 2003—. Office: Kanazawa University Kakuma Kanazawa Ishikawa 920-1192 Japan Office Phone: 81-76-264-5683. Business E-Mail: dseo@se.kanazawa-u.ac.jp.

SEO, DONG WAN, internist; b. Daejeon, Choongnam, Korea, Jan. 12, 1963; s. Ho-Jin and Hyang-Sup (Kim) S.; m. Hye-Kyung Lee; children: Jung-Hee, Jae-Duk. BS, Seoul Nat. U. Med. Coll., 1987; MS, U. Ulsan, Seoul, 1995, MD, 1997. Korean med. diplomate with qualification for gastroenterology bd., gastrointestinal endoscopy. Dir. Boeun Sanitary Ctr., Seoul, 1988-90; resident Asan Med. Ctr., Seoul, 1991-94, fellow in gastroenterology, 1995-96; instr. Asan Med. Ctr./U. Ulsan, Seoul, 1997-98, prof. medicine, 1999—. Vis. prof. divsn. gastroenterology U. Wash. Med. Coll., Seattle, 2001—03. Author: Cholangioscopy, 2001-02, Hepatobiliary Surgery, 2004, Endoscopic Retrograde Cholangiopancratography, 2008, Diseases of the Gallbladder and Bile Duct, 2008, Cholangiocarcinoma 2009; contbr. articles to profl. jours. Recipient Young Investigator's award Asian Pacific Congress of Gastroenterology, 1996, Internat. Jour. Pancreatology, 1998, Korean Min. Health, 1998-99, Audio-Visual award, Am. Soc. Gastrointestinal Endoscopy, 1999. Mem. Am. Gastroenterol. Assn., Am. Soc. Gastrointestinal Endoscopy (Audio-Visual award 1999), Internat. Assn. Pancreatology. Achievements include research in MR spectroscopy, cholangioscopy/gastrointestinal endoscopy. Home: Apt Pungnapdong Songpagu 102-1101 Hyundai Seoul 138-040 Republic of Korea Office: Asan Med Ctr Div Gastroent 388-1 Pungnapdong Songpagu Seoul 138-736 Republic of Korea Business E-Mail: dwseoamc@amc.seoul.kr.

SEO, HEE-SOO, orthopedist; b. Seoul, Dec. 24, 1977; MD, Hallym U., 2003. Chief dir. Cartilage Repair Ctr. affiliated with Himchan Hosp., 2009—. Home: Ichon 1-dong Hangaram Apt 203-1503 Seoul KSXX0022 Republic of Korea Home Phone: 82-10-4423-5364. Personal E-mail: mdseohs@naver.com.

SEO, ILLYOUNG, urologist, educator; s. Myoungkon Seo and Youngsook Jo; m. Suna Kim, Dec. 27, 1992; children: Jaewon, Jiwoo. B in Gen. Medicine, Wonkwang U. Sch. Medicine, Iksan, Republic of Korea, 1992; M Medicine, Wonkwang U., Iksan, Republic of Korea, 1995. Resident Wonkwang U. Hosp., Iksan, Jeonbuk, Republic of Korea, 1993—97, clin. fellow, 2000—01, Nagoya U. Hosp., Nagoya, Aichiken, Japan, 2002—03; assoc. prof. Wonkwang U., Iksan, 2001—; chmn. dept. urology Wonkwang U. Hosp., Iksan, 2005—; dir. Internat. Health Care Ctr., Wonkwnag U. Hosp., Iksam, 2010—. Author: (book) Laparoscopic Surgery for Urologic Oncology, Recent Advance in Endourology vol. 9. Consulting dir. Korea Labor Welfare Corp., 2006—; tutor of med. svc. Med. Student's Assn. Won-Buddism, Iksan, 2003—04; urologist examiner Korean Acad. Med. Sci., 2003—. Capt. Korean Army, 1997—2000, Republic of Korea. Recipient Travel award, Internat. Soc. Andrology, 2005. Mem.: Korean Endourological Soc. (sec. gen. 2003—, Olympus grant 2002, Pambio-Rowa award 2005), Korean Soc. Urological Oncology (exec. bd. mem. 2006—), Korean Urological Assn. (bd. mem. sci. com. 2006—, Acad. award 1995, 2009), Korean Soc. Andrology (exec. bd. mem. 2004—), Internat. Soc. for Sexual Medicine (corr.), Endourology (corr.). Achievements include research in vitamin D gene study for stone. Home: Posco The Sharp Apt101-1104 Hyoja-dong Jeonbuk Jeonju 560-894 Republic of Korea Office: Wonkwang Univ Dept Urology 344-2 Sinyong-Dong 570-711 Iksan Jeollabuk-do Republic of Korea Office Fax: 82-63-842-1455. Business E-Mail: seraph@wonkwang.ac.kr.

SEO, JEONG KEE, pediatrician, educator; b. Seoul, Jan. 19, 1949; s. Byung Seoul Seo and Hyung Kee Park; m. Kyo Sun Kim, June 15, 1978; children: Sang Hyun, Seung Hyun, Ju Hyun. MD, Seoul Nat. U., 1973, PhD, 1981. Lic. physician Korea, diplomate Korean Bd. Pediats. Rsch. fellow divsn. pediat. gastroenterology and nutrition Children's Hosp. and Mass. Gen. Hosp., Boston, 1984—86; instr., asst. prof., assoc. prof. divsn. gastroenterology and nutrition, dept. pediats Coll. of Medicine, Seoul Nat. U., Seoul, 1981—94, prof. pediats., 1994—, chmn. dept. pediats., 2004—05. Congress pres. 11th Seoul Congress Asian panPacific Soc. Pediat. Gastroentenology Hepatology & Nutrition, 2009. Author: 24 textbooks on Pediatric Gatroenterology, Hepatology and Nutrition; contbr. more than 265 articles to profl. jours., Govt. and Seoul Nat. U. Hosp. grantee, 1991—. Mem.: Asian Panpacific Soc. Pediat. Gastroenterology, Hepatology and Nutrition (pres. 2009—), Nat. Acad. Medicine, Korean Soc. Pediat. Gastroenterology, Hepatology and Nutrition (pres. 1994—, 2001—03), Korean Soc. Gastrointestinal Motility, Korean Soc. Gastroenterology, Korean Soc. Gastrointestinal Endoscopy (pres. 2008), Korean Soc. Pediat., Korean Med. Assn. Achievements include founding of the first training center in Korea for pediatric endoscopy and gastroenterology at the Seoul Nat. U. Children's Hospital. Office: Seoul Nat U Children's Hosp 28 Yongon-dong Chongno-gu Seoul 110-744 Republic of Korea Office Fax: 82-2-743-3455. Business E-Mail: jkseo@snu.ac.kr.

SEO, JOON BEOM, radiologist, educator; b. Yeosu, Republic of Korea, Mar. 5, 1969; s. Seong Hoon Seo and Ok Sun Lee; m. Hoyun Lee, June 9, 1996; children: Geo, Jinew. MD, Seoul Nat. U., Republic of Korea, 1993, MS, 1998, PhD, 2001. Nat. med. lic. Korea, 1993, cert. Bd. Radiology Korea, 1998. Instr. radiology Gachon Med. Sch., Inchon, Republic of Korea, 2000—01; attending radiologost Asan Med. Ctr., Seoul, 2002—; instr. radiology U. Ulsan Coll. Medicine, 2002—03, asst. prof. radiology, 2004—07, assoc. prof. radiology, 2008—. Presenter in field. Contbr. articles to profl. jours. Recipient Best Sci. Paper of Sci. and Tech. award, Korean Fedn. of Sci. and Tech. Socs., 2000; grantee, Asan Inst. Life Sci., 2003, 2005, 2007, Korea Rsch. Found., 2005, 2007, Korea Sci. and Engring. Found., 2006—. Mem.: Soc. Thoracic Radiology, Korean Computer Aided Diagnosis Soc. (assoc.), Korean Soc. Cardiac Imaging (assoc.), Korean Soc. Thoracic Radiology (assoc. Best Sci. Paper award 2001, 2003, 2006), Korean Radiol. Soc. (life), Korean Med. Assn. (life). Office Fax: 82-2-476-4719. Business E-Mail: joonbeom.seo@gmail.com.

SEO, MIN-HYO, chemist, researcher; b. Gosung, Kyang Sang Nam-Do, Republic of Korea, Dec. 26, 1962; s. Tae-Gyo Seo and Nam-Jo Bae; life ptnr. Yi-Kyoung Choi, Mar. 12, 1999; children: Won-Jun, Ho-Jeong. B, Seoul Nat. U., Republic of Korea, 1985, M, 1988, PhD, 1992. Rschr. Samyang Corp., Seoul, 1991—92; sr. rschr. Samyang Pharm. R&D Ctr., Daejeon, Republic of Korea, 1993—95, program coord., 2003—; prin. rschr. Samyang Ctr. R&D Ctr., Daejeon, 1998—2002; rsch. assoc. dept. pharms. and pharm. chemistry U. Utah, Salt Lake City, 1996—97. Contbr. articles to profl. jours. Mem.: Am. Chem. Soc., Am. Assn. Pharm. Scientists. Achievements include development of paclitaxel loaded Polymeric Micelle(Genexol-PM) was launched; invention of ionically fixed Polymeric nanoparticle; patents for negatively charged amphiphilic block copolymer; composition for sustained delivery of hydrophobic drugs; biodegradable poly (alkylene oxide)-poly(p-dioxanone) block copolymer. Avocations: mountain climbing, fishing, reading, golf, soccer. Office: Samyang Pharms R&D Ctr 63-2 Hwaam-Dong Yusung-Gu 305-717 Daejeon Daejeon Republic of Korea Office Fax: 82-42-865-8299. Business E-Mail: seo@samyang.com.

SEO, WAN SEOK, psychiatrist, educator; b. Andong, Republic Of Korea, July 6, 1968; s. Jae Yoon Seo and Chun Ja Yoon; m. Kwang Ok Jeong; children: Hye Rin, Jee Eun. MD, Yeungnam U., Daegu, Republic of Korea, 1993; PhD, Chungnam U., Daejeon, Republic of Korea, 2006. Cert. physician Korean Ministry Health and Welfare, 1993, Bd. Psychiatry 1998. Spkr. Seoul U. Hosp., Republic of Korea, 2001, Yeungnam U. Hosp., Daegu, 2001—03; prof. Yeungnam U., Coll. Medicine, Daegu, Republic of Korea, 2003—; exch. prof. Johns Hopkins, Sch. Medicine, Balt., 2006—07. Sec. pub. Korean Soc. Biol. Therapies in Psychiatry, Deagu, 2007—. Contbr. articles to profl. jours. Cons. North Daegu Com. Domestic Violence, 2005—08. Capt. US Army, 1998—2001, Pochon. Mem.: Korean Psychiatry Assn. Office: Yeungnam Univ Hosp Daemyung Dong Namgu 705-717 Daegu Daegu Republic of Korea Home Phone: 82-53-583-5742. Office Fax: 82536290256; Home Fax: 82536290256. Business E-Mail: sws3901@ynu.ac.kr.

SEO, YEON SEOK, gastroenterologist, educator; b. Incheon, Republic of Korea, Nov. 11, 1970; s. Jeong Hwa Seo and Chung Ja Jung; m. Hyun Kyung Kweon; children: Jang Won, Ji Ye. BS in Med. Sci., Korea U. Coll. Medicine, Seoul, MD in Med. Sci., 1996; MS in Med. Sci., Grad. Sch. Korea U., Seoul, 1999, PhD in Med. Sci., 2006. Lic. physician Korean Ministry Health, Welfare & Family Affairs, 1996, cert. in internal medicine Korean Ministry Health, Welfare & Family Affairs, 2001, in gastroenterology Korean Assn. Internal Medicine, 2006. Clin. asst. prof. Korea U. Guro Hosp., Seoul, 2005—06, Korea U. Anam Hosp., Seoul, 2006—07, asst. prof., 2007—. Mem. editl. com. Korean Assn. Study Liver, Seoul, 2008—; mem. acturial com. Korean Soc. Gastroenterology, Seoul, 2008—. Contbr. articles to profl. jours. Capt. med. officer, 2001—04, Kyungki-Do, Republic of Korea. Recipient Best Presentation award, Korean Assn. Study Liver, 2005, Best Poster award, Asian Pacific Assn. Study Liver, 2008. Mem.: Korean Liver Cancer Study Group, Korean Soc. Gastrointestinal Endoscopy, Korean Assn. Internal Medicine, Korean Med. Assn., Korean Soc. Gastroenterology, Korean Assn. Study Liver. Avocations: swimming, running, golf, cooking. Office: Korea Univ Anam Hosp 126-1 5-Ga Anam-Dong Seongbuk-Gu Seoul 136-705 Republic of Korea Business E-Mail: drseo@korea.ac.kr.

SEO, YOO-JIN, occupational health educator; b. Pusan, Republic of Korea, May 1, 1952; s. Seo Soo-hak and Shin Yeon-rae; m. Kim Yang-sook; children: Seo Yong-hoon, Seo Soo-yeon. PhD, Toua U., Shimoseki, Japan, 1997. Vis. prof. dept. ergonomics U. Eivnron. Health, Kitakyushu, Japan, 1989—93; dir. gen., Office Pub. Rels. Kyungnam U., Masan, Republic of Korea, 1999—2002, dean acad. affairs, 2006—. Home: Doosan Apt 207-1201 Gyungsangnamdo Masan 631-763 Republic of Korea Office: Dept Exercise/Sci Sport Studies Weolyoung-Dong 449 631-701 Gyungsangnamdo Masan Gyeongsangnam-do Republic of Korea Office Phone: +82-11-586-7787. Business E-Mail: yoojin@kyungnam.ac.kr.

SEOKRAN, YEOM, physician, educator; b. Republic of Korea, May 2, 1971; MD, Chonnam Nat. U., 1997, PhD, 2008. Asst. prof. Pusan Nat. U. Hosp., 2005—, chief, Trauma Ctr., 2010—. Mem.: Korean Assn. CPR, Korean Soc. Traumatology, Korean Soc. Clin. Toxicology, Korean Soc. Disaster Medicine, Korean Soc. Emergency Medicine. Avocations: art, movies, travel. Office: 1-10 Ami-dong Seo-gu Busan 603-739 Republic of Korea Office Fax: 82-51-253-6472. Personal E-mail: seokrany@yahoo.com.

SEOL, GEUN HEE, nursing educator; d. Byoung Tae Seol and Ok Sung Lee; m. Sun Seek Min, Nov. 14, 1999; children: Ji Hong Min, Ji Hwang Min. PhD, Ewha Womans U., Seoul, 2004. Postdoc. fellow Johns Hopkins U., Balt., 2004—06; prof. Korea U., Seoul, 2006—. Psychiat. nurse Korea U. Med. Ctr., Anam Hosp., Seoul, 1996—98; part-time instr. Dankook U., Chunan, 2002—03; postdoc. fellow & part-time instr. Eulji U., Daejeon, 2006. Contbr. articles to profl. jours. Grant, Korea Sci. and Engring. Found., 2004, Nat. Rsch. Found. Korea, 2007, 2009. Mem.: Korean Soc. Brain and Neural Sci., Korean Soc. Biol. Nursing Sci., Korean Soc. Nursing Sci., Korean Physiology Soc., Soc. Neurosci. Office Phone: 82-2-3290-4922. Business E-Mail: ghseol@korea.ac.kr.

SEONG, CHU-MYONG, oncologist, researcher; b. Seoul, Republic of Korea, Sept. 9, 1955; m. Ahna Seong; children: Paul, Ashley. BS, Yonsei U., Seoul, 1976, MD, 1980. Lic. medical Oncologist Am. Bd. Internal Medicine, 1991. Resident in internal medicine U. Ill., 1982—85; fellow in med. oncology M.D. Anderson Cancer Ctr., 1985—87; fellow in hematology U. Tex., 1987—88; prof. Ewha Women's U., Seoul, 1997—; dir. cancer ctr. Ewha BMT Ctr., Seoul, 1997—. Author: Dr. Seong's BMT Clinic, 2004, Leukemia Clinic, 2005. Recipient Best Dr. award, Ewah Med. Ctr., 2004. Mem.: Am. Soc. Hematology (licentiate). Home: 13-702 Si-Bum Apt Yeidodong Yeindenpogu Seoul 150 761 Republic of Korea Office: Ewha U Mok-dong Hosp 911-1 Mok-dong Yangcheongu Seoul 158 710 Republic of Korea Office Fax: 82 2 2650 5062; Home Fax: 82 2 761 7631. Business E-Mail: cmseong@ewha.ac.kr.

SEONG, SANG-CHEOL, hospital administrator, orthopedist; b. Kyeongnam, Geochang, Republic of Korea, Nov. 10, 1948; BS, Seoul Nat. U. Coll. Medicine, 1973; D in Orthopedics, Seoul Nat. U., 1996, MS in Orthopedics, 1976. Intern Seoul Nat. U. Hosp., Republic of Korea, 1973—74, residence, 1974—78; Dr. of Med. Affairs 15th Infantry, 1978—79; dir., orthopedic surgery Seoul Dist. Military Hosp., 1979—81; v.p., in charge of student Seoul Nat. U. Coll. Medicine, 1992—94; dir., planning dept. Seoul Nat. U. Hosp., 1995—98, vice-dir., chmn., info. propulsion com., 1999—2001, bd. dirs., 2004—, Bundang Seoul Nat. U. Hosp.; chief dir. Korean Human Body Basic Tech. Rsch. Found., 1995—98. Lectr., asst. prof. assoc. prof. Seoul Nat. U., Republic of Korea, 1981—94; orthopedic surgery rschr. Harvard U.; rchr. Karolinska Hosp., Sweden, 1990; bd. dirs. Korea Orthopedic Assn., 1992—96; vp. Korean Elderly Disease Assn., 1995—97; vice chmn., orgnl. com. Internat. Assn. Gerontology, 1997—99; chmn. Korean Knee Soc., 1997—2001, v.p., 2001—02; pres. Korean Joint Knee Soc., 2002—03, Korean Arthroscopy Soc., 2003—04, Korean Soc. Gerontology. Served to major in Army. Mem.: Korean Soc. Sports Medicine (pres. 2001—). Office: Seoul National Univ Hospital 28 Yeongeon-dong Jongno-gu Seoul 110 744 Republic of Korea Office Phone: 01182220722890. Office Fax: 01182220720785. *

SEOW-CHOEN, FRANCIS, colorectal surgeon; b. Singapore, May 6, 1957; s. Hong-Teng and Lay-Keng (Kong) Seow; m. Ching-Peng Siow, May 28, 1983; children: Isaac Seow En, Samuel Seow An, Olivia Seow Wen. M.B.BS, Nat. U. Singapore, 1981. House surgeon Ministry of Health, Singapore, 1981-82, orthopaedic resident, 1984-87; med. officer Ministry of Def., Singapore, 1982-84; registrar in surgery Singapore Gen. Hosp., 1987-89, registrar in colorectal surgery, 1989, sr. registrar coloproctology, 1989-92, cons. surgeon, 1992-95, head, sr. cons., 1996—; rsch. fellow St. Mark's Hosp., London, 1989-90; head and sr. cons. surgeon Singapore Gen. Hosp., 1995—, clin. assoc. prof., 1998—; dir. surg. oncology Nat. Cancer Ctr. Instr. advanced trauma life support ACS, 1992-94; officer in charge operating theatre Singapore Navy, 1990-94; dir. Endoscopy Ctr., Singapore, 1994—; officer-in-charge med. flight Rep. of Singapore Air Force, 1982-83; chmn. 1st Clin. Nutrition Meeting, 1994; treas. 25th Combined Surg. Meeting, 1992, vice chmn. 26th, 1992, chmn. 28th, 1994; sci. chmn. 28th Malaysia-Singapore Congress, 1994. Mem. editl. bd. Techniques in Coloproctology, Brit. Jour. Surgery, Colorectal Diseases, Diseases of the Colon and Rectum, 1990—, Indian Jour. Coloproctology; contbr. articles to med. jours. Vol. aftercare officer Singapore Anti-Narcotics Assn., 1977-79; organizing com. Steering Com. on Trauma Mgmt., Singapore, 1992, Practice Guidelines of Endoscopists, Singapore, 1992. Capt. Singapore Navy, 1982-94. Beecham scholar Nat. U. Singapore, 1980-81; Manpower Devel. Plan fellow Ministry of Health, Singapore, 1989-90, Overseas Fund fellow Royal Coll. surgeons, Edinburgh, 1989, Internat. Travel fellow Am. Soc. Colon and Rectal Surgeons, 1993. Fellow Acad. Medicine Singapore (sec. 1992-94). Ch. of Eng. Avocation: writing. Home: 22 Saraca Road Singapore 807368 Singapore Office: Seow Choen Colorectal Ctr Pte Ltd 3 Mount Elizabeth 240 Orchard Rd #06-06 Paragon Singapore 238859 Singapore Home Phone: 65-64813898; Office Phone: 61 6738 6887. Business E-Mail: seowchoen@colorectalcentre.com.

SEPE, DANA, physician; b. Bklyn., July 22, 1978; BS in Biology, Lehigh U., 2000; MD, Robert Wood Johnson U., 2004. Pediat. resident Children's Hosp. Phila., 2004—07, pediat. hematology, oncology fellow, 2007—10, attending physician, 2010—. Recipient Young Investigator award, Alex's Lemonade Stand Found. & Ctr. Childhood Cancer Rsch., Children's Hosp. Phila. Mem.: Am. Soc. Clin. Oncology, Children's Oncology Group, Am. Soc. Pediat. Hematology & Oncology. Avocation: running. Office: Children's Hosp Phila Philadelphia PA 19104 Business E-Mail: sepe@email.chop.edu.

SEPLOWITZ, ALAN, endocrinologist; Attended, Columbia U. Diplomate Am. Bd. of Internal Medicine-endocrinology, Am. Bd. of Internal Medicine. Intern NY Presbyn. Hosp., resident, fellow, with. Office: New York Presbyterian / Columbia University Medical Center 622 West 168th St. New York NY 10032 Office Phone: 212-305-2500.

SEQUEIRA, PATRICK, dentist, researcher; b. London, July 3, 1965; s. Jerome and Margrit Sequeira; m. Donna R. Byron, Jan. 1, 2000. BDS, Guy's Hosp. Dental Sch., London, 1988; DMD, Zürich U., Switzerland, 1992; MSc, Green Coll., Oxford, England, 2001. Cert. bd. endodontist SSE, SFZ, SSO Switzerland, 2004. Resident prosthetic dentistry Guy's Dental Hosp., London, 1988—89; pvt. practice Cham, Zug, Switzerland, 1992—. Mem. editl. bd. Evidence Based Dentistry. Contbr. articles to profl. jours. Chmn. sci. com. Swiss Soc. Endodontology, 2006. Lt. Swiss Army M.C. Mem.: Royal Soc. Medicine, London, Internat. Assn. Dental Rsch., Swiss Dental Assn., Cochrane Collaboration. Office: Dental Practice Alte Steinhauserstrasse 3 Cham Zug CH-6330 Switzerland

SEQUEIRA, RAFAEL FRANCIS, cardiologist, educator; b. Nairobi, Kenya, Apr. 10, 1939; came to U.S., 1979; m. Kathleen Patricia Sequeira, Apr. 20, 1975; children: Raphael, Anthony, John. MD, U. Coll. Dublin, 1964. Diplomate Am. Bd. Cardiology. Intern Mater Hosp. Univ. Coll. Dublin (Ireland), 1969-70; resident Stobhill Hosp. Univ. Glasgow (Scotland), 1970-73; fellow in cardiology Univ. Bristol (Eng.) Royal Infirmary, 1974-77; prof. medicine U. Miami, Fla.; prin. investigator divsn. cardiology U. Miami Sch. Medicine. Contbr. articles to profl. jours. Fellow Am. Coll. Cardiology, Royal Coll. Physcians U.K. Office: U Miami Divsn Cardiology PO Box 16960 Miami FL 33101-6960 Home Phone: 305-361-6009; Office Phone: 305-585-5530. Business E-Mail: rsequeir@med.miami.edu. *

SEQUEIRA, SHIEFA NECIA, lab administrator, researcher; b. India, May 21, 1976; PhD in Biochemistry, Manipal Acad. Higher Edn., 2007. Asst. prof. Fr. Muller Med. Coll., 2000—07; asst. prof. biochemistry Ueims Sch. Medicine, 2007—10; lab mgr. Fetal Medicine Found., 2010—. Recipient Pres. Guide award, India. Avocation: reading. Office: Fetal Medicine Found Dist 8 Dubai 505010 United Arab Emirates Office Fax: 0097143624946.

SERAFIN, DONALD, plastic surgeon, educator; b. NYC, Jan. 18, 1938; s. Stephen Michael and Julia (Sopko) S.; m. Patricia Serafin; children: Allison Elizabeth, Christina Julia, Donald Stephen, Lara Leigh. AB, Duke U., 1960, MD, 1964. Diplomate Am. Bd. Surgery, Am. Bd. Plastic Surgery. Surg. intern Grady Meml. Hosp., Atlanta, 1964-65; resident in surgery Emory U. Hosp., Atlanta, 1965-69; asst. resident in plastic and reconstructive surgery Duke U. Med. Ctr., Durham, NC, 1971-73, chief resident, 1973-74; Christine Kleinert fellow in hand surgery U. Louisville Hosp., 1972-73; practice medicine specializing in plastic surgery, Durham; plastic reconstructional surgery cons. Womack Semy Medicine Ctr., Fort Bragg, NC. Mem. staff N.C. Splty. Hosp., Durham Regional Hosp., Maria Parham Hosp.; asst. prof. plastic, reconstructive and maxillofacial surgery

Duke U., 1974-77, assoc. prof., 1977-81, prof., 1981-2000, prof. emeritus, 2000—, chief divsn. plastic reconstructive and maxillofacial and oral surgery, 1985-95, chmn. Plastic Surgery Rsch. Coun., 1983. Assoc. editor Jour. Reconstructive Microsurgery; contbr. articles to profl. jours. Ret. col. USAR, 2004. Decorated Air Force Commendation medal, Army Commendation medal, Army Achievement medal, Army Meritorious Svc. medal. Fellow ACS; mem. AMA, Internat. Soc. Reconstructive Microsurgery, Am. Soc. Plastic Surgeons, Am. Assn. Plastic Surgeons, Am. Soc. Aesthetic Plastic Surgery, Am. Soc. Surgery Hand, Am. Assn. Hand Surgery, Am. Burn Assn., Plastic Surgery Rshc. Coun., N.C. Soc. Plastic, Maxillofacial and Reconstructive Surgeons, Southeastern Soc. Plastic and Reconstructive Surgeons. Office: 511 Ruin Creek Rd Ste 104B Henderson NC 28350 Office Phone: 252-438-8252, 919-220-7711. Personal E-mail: seradonald@aol.com.

SERANE, V. TIROUMOUROUGANE, pediatrician; b. Pondicherry, India, Sept. 4, 1973; arrived in England, 2003; s. Vidjayarangane and Canagammalle Serane; m. Bhuvaneswari Kothendaraman. MBBS, Jawaharlal Inst. Postgraduate Med. Edn. and Rsch., Pondicherry, 1996, MD, 2000. Diplomate Nat. Bd., New Delhi. Sr. resident Jawaharlal Inst. Postgraduate Med. Edn. and Rsch., Pondicherry, India, 2000—03; pediatrician Lister Hosp., Stevenage, England, 2003—. Mem.: Nat. Acad. Med. Scis. Achievements include research in Tuberculin test 24 hour prediction and Qualitative interpretation. Home: 34 III Cross St 605 001 Pondicherry India Personal E-mail: drtmserane@yahoo.com.

SERBAN, TOVARU, dentist, educator; b. Sinaia, Prahova, Romania, Apr. 5, 1948; s. Tovaru Aurelian and Tovaru Ani-Eliza; m. Tovaru Tudose, Nov. 13, 1993; 1 child, Tovaru Alexandra. Cert. Faculty Stomatology, Romania, 1972. Stomatologist CFR Hosp., Policlinic Unit, Bucarest, Romania, 1974—98; prof. oral medicine Faculty Dental Medicine Carol Davila U. Medicine, Bucarest, Romania, 1998—, assoc. dean, 2008—. Contbr. articles to profl. sci. jours. Physician Mountain Rescue Team-Salvamont, Sinaia, Romania, 1976—89. Mem.: Eaom, Aaom. Office: Faculty Dental Medicine Calea Plevnei nr 19 Bucarest 010221 Romania Home: Strada Eminescu Mihai NR 29 10513 Bucarest Romania Office Fax: 0040213126765. Personal E-mail: serban.tovaru@gmail.com.

SEREJINE, IGOR NIKOLAEVICH, ophthalmologist; b. Termes, Uzbekistan, May 28, 1958; PhD, Moscow Inst. Eye Deseases Helmholz, 1990; MD, Ufa Eye Rsch. Inst. Physician, surgeon, ophthalmologist Ufa Eye Rsch. Inst., 1981—2008, Ophthalmology Dept. Clin. Ctr. JST Tatneft, 2008—. Recipient Honor award, Rep. Bashkortostan. Mem.: Ophthalmology Soc. Russian Fedn., European Vitreoretinal Soc. Office: Radisheva 67 Almetievck Tatarstan 423450 Russia Office Fax: 78553311120. Personal E-mail: serejine@mail.ru.

SERES, DAVID S., physician, director; b. Phila., Apr. 1, 1958; MD, Jefferson Med. Coll., Thomas Jefferson U., 1985; MS in Healthcare Mgmt., Harvard U. Sch. Pub. Health, 2010. Dir. med. nutrition Columbia U. Coll. Physicians and Surgeons, and Inst. Human Nutrition, 2008—. Fellow. Am. Coll. Physician Execs.; mem.: Am. Soc. Parenteral and Enteral Nutrition (chair med. practice sect. 2010—), Am. Soc. Nutrition, FASEB. Office: Columbia University Medical Ctr 630 New York NY 10032 Business E-Mail: dseres@columbia.edu.

SERFLING, G. AUBREY, hospital administrator; married, V.p. corporate services Pacific Medical Ctr., San Francisco; COO Pacific Presbyterian, exec. v.p.; CEO Calif. Pacific Medical Ctr., 1991—95; sr. v.p. system devel. Sutter CHS, San Francisco, 1995—97; sr. v.p., CFO Crozer-Keystone Health Systems, 1997—98; CFO, CIO Columbia-Cornell Care, LLC, 1998—2000; exec. v.p., CFO Eisenhower Med. Ctr. (includes Annenberg Ctr., Betty Ford Ctr., and Barbara Sinatra Children's Ctr.), 2000—01, pres., CEO Rancho Mirage, Calif., 2001—. Office: Eisenhower Med Ctr 39000 Bob Hope Dr Rancho Mirage CA 92270

SERGIO, D'ADDATO, medical researcher, educator; b. Bologna, Italy, Jan. 28, 1961; Degree in Medicine, U. Bologna, 1986; PhD, U. Siena, 1995. Cert. specialist in geriat. and gerotology U. Bologna. Rschr. U. Bologna, 2001—, aggregate prof., 2004. Office: via Albertoni 11 Bologna 40138 Italy Office Fax: 39051391320. Business E-Mail: sergio.daddato@unibo.it.

SERGIO, GAINI MARIA, neurosurgeon; b. Milan, July 10, 1942; MD, U. Milan, 1968. Prof. head neurosurg. dept. U. Milan, 1982—. Office: Via Francesco Sforza 35 Milan Lombardia 20129 Italy Business E-Mail: sergiomaria.gaini@nimi.it.

SERGOTT, ROBERT C., ophthalmologist; BA, Johns Hopkins U., 1967—71, MD, 1971—75. Diplomate Am. Bd. Ophthalmology. Intern Mary Imogene Bassett Hosp, Coopertown, 1975—76; resident Wills Eye Hosp., Phila., 1976—79; fellow neuro-ophthalmology Bascom Palmer Eye Inst., 1979—80; fellow U. Pa., 1980—81; attending neuro-ophthalmologist Lankenau Hosp., 1980—; co-dir. neuro-ophthalmology svc. Wills Eye Hosp., 1994—; asst. prof. ophthalmology Thomas Jefferson Med. Coll., 1981—, clin. asst. prof. neurology, 2000—. Recipient James Shipman award, 1978, National Research Service award, National Eye Inst., 1979—80, Golden Apple award for Best Clinical Teacher, 1989; named one of The Best Doctors in America, 1994—95, Best Ophthalmologist in America, Ophthalmology Times, 1996, 100 Best Ophthalmologists in America; Heed Ophthalmic Foundation fellowship, 1980—81. Mem.: Am. Ophthalmological Soc. Office: Wills Eye Institute 9th Fl 840 Walnut St Philadelphia PA 19107 Office Phone: 215-928-3130. Office Fax: 215-592-1923.

SERLING, JOEL MARTIN, educational psychologist; b. Seneca Falls, NY, Feb. 8, 1936; s. Philip and Cecil Serling; children: Meredith Anne, Rebecca Lynne, Heather Lee. AA, U. Buffalo, 1957; BS in Edn., Ohio Northern U., 1959; MA, Columbia U., 1960. Cert. sch. psychologist NY, NC. Instr. psychology West Liberty State Coll., W.Va., 1961—63; vocat. psychologist Divsn. Child Welfare, Cleve., 1963—64; sch. psychologist Steuben County Bd. Coop. Ednl. Svcs., Bath, NY, 1964—65, Chenango County Bd. Coop. Ednl. Svcs., Norwich, NY, 1965—67, Delaware County Bd. Coop. Ednl. Svcs., Walton, NY, 1967—68, Vestal Ctrl. Sch., NY, 1968—70, Whitesboro Ctrl. Sch., NY, 1970—92. Bd. edn., bd. dirs Hillel Day Sch., Utica-Rome, 1971—75; instr. psychology Am. Inst. Banking, 1971—; bd. profl. advisors Mohawk Valley Learning Disabilities Assn., 1972—76; cons., mentor Empire Coll., SUNY, 1975—; adj. prof. psychology Utica Coll., Syracuse U., 1971—75, 1986—, Mohawk Valley CC, 1971—91, SUNY Coll. Tech., Utica-Rome, NY, 1975—, CC Southern Nev., 1995—; presenter in field. Co-author, co-developer: Early Identification Screening Index, 1971; contbr. articles to profl. publs. Recipient Cert. recognition, Mohawk Valley Learning Disabilities Assn., 1973. Mem.: APA, Phi Delta Kappa, Whitesboro Tchrs. Assn., NY State United Tchrs. Assn., United U. Professions, Ctrl. NY Psychol. Assn., Sch. Psychologists Upper NY, NY Assn. Sch. Psychologists (cert. of recognition 1977), Nat. Assn. Sch. Psychologists (charter), Odd Fellows Club, Zeta Beta Tau. Jewish. Home: 2133 Idaho Fall Dr Henderson NV 89044 E-mail: jssp@cox.net.

SERNA THOME, MARÍA GUADALUPE, nutritionist, consultant; b. San Luis Potosi, Mexico, Dec. 18, 1968; d. Ramón Serna Vargas and Olga María Thome Del Castillo. BS in Nutrition and Food Sci., Iberoamericana U., 1993. Nutritionst with kidney patients Nat. Inst. of Nutrition and Med. Sci. Salvador Zubirán, Mexico City, 1992—95; nutritionist with oncology patients Nat. Cancer Inst., México City, 1994—. Mem.: Mex. Coun. Clin. Nutrition (cert. Nutritionist 1998), Mex. Soc. Parenteral and Enteral Nutrition. Office: Nat Cancer Inst Av San Fernando No 22 Tlalpan 14000 Mexico City DF Mexico Office Fax: 00115255 55-60-29-01. E-mail: gpeserna@hotmail.com.

SERNYAK, AUDREY H., cardiologist; b. 1986; BA in Religious Studies, U. Va., 1987—91; MD, Va. Commonwealth U., 1991—95. Diplomate Am. Bd. Internal Medicine, Am. Bd. Internal Medicine-cardiovasc. diseases, Am. Bd. Internal Medicine-interventional cardiology. Intern internal medicine Parkland Meml. Hosp. Southwestern Med. Sch., 1995—96, resident internal medicine Parkland Meml. Hosp., 1996—98, fellow cardiovasc. disease Parkland Mem. Hosp., 1998—2002, fellow interventional Parkland Meml. Hosp., 2001—02; hosp. affiliations include Virtua-West Jersey Health System, Camden, NJ, Our Lady of Lourdes Med. Ctr., Camden, NJ. Co-author: (publs.) Early management of acute MI, 1999, Prevalence of coronary artery disease in patients with aortic stenosis with and without angina pectoris, 2001, Clinical consequences of anomalous coronary arteries, 2001, Hemodynamic characteristics and procedural outcomes of patients with mitral stenosis and depressed cardiac output, 2001, Relationship of pulmonary artery diastolic and mean arterial wedge pressure in patients with and without pulmonary hypertension, 2001, (book chpt.) Cocaine and Other Causes of Acute Coronary Syndromes, 2003. Office: Lourdes Medical Associates Ste 101 63 Kresson Rd Cherry Hill NJ 08034 Office Phone: 856-428-4100. Office Fax: 856-428-4058.

SEROTA, RONALD D., psychiatrist, educator; MD, Jefferson Coll., 1968. Diplomate Am. Bd. of Psychiatry and Neurology, Am. Bd. of Psychiatry and Neurology-addiction psychiatry, Am. Bd. of Internal Medicine. Resident in internal medicine Mt. Zion Hosp. and Med. Ctr., San Francisco, 1970, Univ. of Oreg., Portland, Oreg., 1973; resident in psychiatry Thomas Jefferson Univ. Hosp., 1981; asst. prof. psychiatry & human behavior Thomas Jefferson Univ. Author: (publs.) Correlates of employment: A cohort study, Learned helplessness and cocaine dependence. An investigation, A therapeutic use of the methadone fluvoxamine drug interaction, and numerous others. Named one of Top Docs, Phila. Mags., 2010. Office: Thomas Jefferson University Hospital - Center City Campus 111 S 11th St Philadelphia PA 19107 Office Phone: 215-955-6000.

SEROTA, SCOTT, medical association administrator; BA, Purdue U.; MA in Health Admin. and Planning, Wash. U. Sch. of Med., St. Louis. Creator, leader Physicians Preferred Health Inc., Mo.; v.p. health care mgmt. PruCare, St. Louis, 1980; v.p. group ops., v.p. health care mgmt. Prudential Ins. Co., Chgo.; pres., CEO Rush Prudential Health Plans, Chgo., 1993—96; exec. v.p. system devel. Blue Cross and Blue Shield Assn., COO, 1994—96, exec. v.p. sys. devel., 1996—2000, pres., CEO, 2000—. Founding mem. Inst. on Healthcare Costs and Solutions Wash. Bus. Group on Health; bd. mem. Council for Affordable Quality Healthcare, Nat. Ctr. for Healthcare Leadership, Partnership for Prevention, Nat. Alliance for Health Info. Tech., Accrediting Commn. on Edn. for Health Services Admin.; mem. Am. Coll. of Healthcare Executives. Office: Blue Cross Blue Shield Assn 225 N Michigan Ave Chicago IL 60601 *

SERRA, ALESSANDRO, physician; b. Sassari, Italy, Aug. 4, 1972; MD, U. Sassari, 1997, PhD, 2007. Rsch. asst. Daroff-Dell'Osso Ocular Motility Lab. VA Med. Ctr. Case Western Res. U., 2006—08; resident physician, PGY4 U. Hosps. and Case Med. Ctr., 2008—. Mem.: Am. Acad. Neurology. Home: 2921 Corydon Rd Cleveland Heights OH 44118 Business E-Mail: alessandro.serra@uhhospitals.org.

SERRA, JOSE A., medical association administrator; b. Madrid, June 15, 1960; Degree in Medicine, U. Complutense, Madrid, 1984, PhD, 1993. Med. dir. Hosp. Gen. U. Gregorio Marañón, 2002—04, chair, geriatric dept., 2000—. Grant, Fondo De Investigación Sanitaria. Mem.: European Geriatric Soc., Spanish Geriatric Soc. Office: Doctor Esquerdo 46 Madrid 28007 Spain Office Fax: 91.586.67.04. Business E-Mail: jserra.hgugm@salud.madrid.org.

SERRI, RICCARDA, dermatologist, consultant; b. Milan, Apr. 29, 1955; d. Ferdinando Serri and Marisa Rusconi; 1 child, Luca Forcignanó Serri. MD, U. Milan, 1982. Rschr. Istituto Clinica Dermatologica, Milan, 1982—86; prof. Scuola Medicina Estetica, Rome, 1988—95. Editor: (newsletter) Dermocosmonews; author: (book) Skin Care. Fellow: Am. Acad. Dermatology (assoc.). Achievements include first to biotech natural cosmetics. Office: Studio Dermatologico 22 via Solferino Milan 20121 Italy Home: 7 Via della Moscova 46 20121 Milan MI Italy Office Fax: 39-02-6597143; Home Fax: +39-02-6597143. Personal E-mail: riky riky@enter.it. E-mail: riky@enter.it.

SERT, HUSEYIN, medical educator; b. Turkey, Dec. 25, 1975; Asst. prof. Fatih U. Sch. Medicine, 1999—. Office: Alparslan Turkes St Ankara Yenimahalle 06520 Turkey Personal E-mail: drhuseyinsert@yahoo.com.

SERVELLO, DOMENICO, neurosurgeon; b. Trieste, Italy, Oct. 18, 1955; s. Antonio Servello and Giovanna Sponza; life ptnr. Stella Rinaldi; 1 child, Silvia. PhD in Medicine and Surgery, U. Statale Trieste, 1979. Cert. Parma State U., Neurological Bd., 1983, Milan State U., Neurosurg. Bd., 1988. Neurosurgeon Inst. Neurologico Besta IRCCS, Milan, 1980—2000; head functional neurosurgery unit Galeazzi IRCCS, Milan, 2000—. Grantee, Henry Jur Found., 1980—89, Am. Tourette Syndrome Assn., 2006. Mem.: Lega Italiana Malattia Parkinson Disordini Extrapiramidali, European Soc. Stereotactic & Functional Neurosurgery, Movement Disorder. Roman Catholic. Avocations: music, reading, travel. Office: Galeazzi IRCCS Galeazzi St Milan 20161 Italy Home: Via Comune Antico 51 20125 Milan MI Italy Office Fax: 00390266214916. Business E-Mail: servello@libero.it.

SESAY, MUSA BAHAZID, anesthesiologist, researcher; s. Alhaji Alimamy and Haja Bomwarah Sesay; m. Valerie Elfrida Davies; children: Sulaiman Musa, Ishmael Mamud. MD, Victor Segalen U., Bordeaux, France, 1992. Cert. Coll. Francaise d'Anesthésie-Réanimation, 1996. Dir. xenon rsch. project Pellegrin U. Hosp., Bordeaux, 1999—, chief anesthesiologist, interventional radiology unit, 2003—. Contbr. articles to profl. jour. Founder non-govtl. orgn. ADARI, Bordeaux, 2006—08. Mem.: Soc. Francaise d'Anesthésie-Réanimation (grant 1998). Achievements include research in detection of autonomic hyperreflexia by heart rate variability. Home: 20 Rue Jean Bart Merignac 33700 France Office: Pellegrin Univ Hosp Pl Amelie Raba Leon Bordeaux 33076 France Home Phone: 33614301782; Office Phone: 33556795403. Office Fax: 33556796155. Personal E-mail: musa.sesay@wanadoo.fr.

SESSA, ANTONINO, physician; b. Fisciano, Salerno, Italy, May 20, 1957; MD, U. Federico Ii Napoli, 1986, degree in Nephrology, 1993. Med. dir. hosp., 1993. Avocations: reading, acting. Home: Via Della Veterinaria 59 Naples Campania 80137 Italy Home Fax: 0039 081210452. Personal E-mail: dhtr.pellegrini@libero.it.

SESSIONS, ROY BRUMBY, otolaryngologist, educator; b. Houston, July 28, 1937; s. Roy Brumby and Elizabeth (Compton) S.; m. Mary Cousart, Aug. 28, 1976; children: Kate, Elizabeth, Abigail, Matthew. BS, La. State U., Baton Rouge, 1958; MD, La. State U., New Orleans, 1962. Resident gen. surgery and otolaryngology Washington U. Sch. Medicine, St. Louis, 1965-69; asst. prof. Baylor Coll. Medicine, Houston, 1969-73, assoc. prof., 1973-83; prof. head and neck surgery Meml. Sloan Kettering Cancer Ctr., NYC, 1983-89; prof., chmn. dept. otolaryngology, head and neck surgery Med. Sch. Georgetown U., Washington, 1989-97; chmn. dept. otolaryngology, head and neck surgery Beth Israel Med. Ctr., NYC, 1998—, assoc. dir. Cancer Ctr., co-dir. Inst. Head and Neck Surgery, 1998—. Contbr. articles to profl. jours., chpts. to books; author one textbook. Lt. comdr. USN, 1962-65. Roman Catholic.

SETHI, JASWINDER K., biomedical research scientist; b. Oct. 4, 1970; d. Inderjit Singh and Joginder Kaur Sethi. BSc with first class honors, Birkbeck Coll. U. London, 1993; DPhil, Brasenose Coll. Oxford U., Oxford, 1997. Rsch. technician U. Coll. London, 1989—93; Fulbright rsch. scholar Harvard U. Sch. Pub. Health, Boston, 1996—97, Wellcome Trust Internat. prize travelling fellow, 1997—99; R.D. Lawrence fellow Cambridge U. Dept. Clin. Biochemistry, England, 2001—02, David Phillips rsch. fellow, 2002—; sr. scholar elect Trinity Hall Cambridge U., 2004—. Mentoring program dir. Brit. Fulbright Scholars Assn., London, 2002—. Author: Regulation of Cyclic ADP-Ribose Mediated Calcium Signalling, 1997; contbr. over 37 articles to profl. jours., chapters to books. Scholar, Med. Rsch. Coun., 1993—96; Internat. prize Travelling Postdoctoral fellow, Wellcome Trust, 1997—2001, R.D. Lawrence fellow, Diabetes UK, 2001—02, David Phillips Rsch. fellow, Biotechnology and Biol. Sciences Rsch. Coun., 2002—. Office: Cambridge Univ Dept Clin Biochemistry Inst Metabolic Sc Addenbrookes Hosp Hills Rd Cambridge CB2 2QQ England Office Phone: 44 (0) 1223 762 633. Business E-Mail: jks30@cam.ac.uk.

SETHI, JYOTI, physiologist, educator; b. New Delhi, Jan. 23, 1971; MBBS, Pt. J.L.N. Med. Coll., Raipur, India, 1994; MD in Physiology, Pt. B.D. Sharma Postgrad. Inst. Med. Scis., Rohtak, 2002. Asst. prof. Pt. B.D. Sharma Postgrad. Inst. Med. Scis., Rohtak, 2004—08, assoc. prof., 2008—, cons. physiologist, 1999—2008. Mem.: Assn. Physiology & Pharmacology India. Home: 44/9-J Medical Campus Rohtak Haryana 124001 India Personal E-mail: jsethi23@rediffmail.com.

SETHI, YASH PAL, radiologist, consultant; MBBS, U. Delhi, India, 1987, MD, 1992. Diplomate Am. Bd. Radiology, 2001. Resident physician internal medicine SUNY Health Sci. Ctr., Bklyn., 1995—96; resident radiology Wayne State U. Med. Ctr., Detroit, 1996—98; radiology resident and chief resident St. Vincents Cath. Med. Ctr., NY, 1998—2000; clin. instr. imaging fellow U. Mo., Columbia, 2000—01, asst. prof., 2001—09; staff radiologist Harry S Truman VA Med. Ctr., Columbia, 2001—04; svc. chief radiology Kans. City Va. Med. Ctr., 2010—. Dir., residency program U. Mo., Columbia, Mo., 2006—09, dir. med. students radiology curriculum, 2002—06, dir., MRI fellowship Hosp. and clin. radiology dept., 2005—09. Contbr. scientific papers in field. Recipient Physician Recognition, 2001, Order of Socrates award, 2005, Svc. Quality Hero, U. Mo., 2002, 2004; named Tchr. of Year, 2002, 2003, 2004. Mem.: AMA, Mo. State Radiol. Soc. (bd. dirs. 2005—09), Mo. State Med. Assn. (Marconi Phillips Aur award Faculty Devel. 2004), Clin. Magnetic Resonance Soc., N.am., Am. Roentgen Ray Soc., Am. Coll. Radiology, Soc. Gastrointestinal Endoscopists (life). Office: Univ Missouri Hosp One Hospital Dr Columbia MO 65212 Home: 405 E Minor Dr Kansas City MO 64131

SETHURAMAN, USHA, medical educator; b. India, Mar. 11, 1968; MBBS, Chengalpet Med., 1991; MD in Pediat. Emergency Medicine, Children's Hosp. Mich., Wayne State U., 2001. Clin. asst. prof. Children's Hosp. Mich., Wayne State U., 2001—07, asst. prof., 2007—. Expert witness Detroit County Courts, 2001—11; course dir.

Pediatric Advanced Life Support, Am. Heart Assn., 2002—11; mem. Children's Hosp. Childhood Obesity and Wellness Task Force, 2007—11. Investigator Initiated Program grant, Blue Cross Blue Shield Mich. Found., Physican Investigator Rsch. grant, Cardinal Health E3 grant, Cardinal Health. Mem.: Am. Acad. of Pediat. Avocations: reading, tennis. Office: 3901 Beaubien Blvd Detroit MI 48201 Office Fax: 313-993-7166. Business E-Mail: usethu@dmc.org.

SETHY, DAMAYANTI, occupational therapist, educator; b. Dhenkanal, Orissa, India, May 15, 1980; MS in Occupl. Therapy, Swami Vivekananda Nat. Inst. Rehab. Tng. & Rsch., 2002, MOT, 2004. Lectr. occupl. therapy Nat. Inst. Orthopaedically Handicapped, India, 2006—. Mem.: Hand Therapy Assn., All India Occupl. Therapists Assn. Avocation: dance. Office: Bt Rd Bonhoogly Kolkata West Bengal 700090 India E-mail: damayanti.sethy@gmail.com.

SETIA, MONIKA, medical researcher; b. India, Oct. 14, 1978; PhD, Pa. State U., 2010. Process developer GE Capital Internat. Svcs., 2002—05; grad. asst. Pa. State U., 2005—10; rsch. fellow Duke-NUS Grad. Med. Sch., 2010—. Recipient 2nd Pl., 22nd Ann. Grad. Exhbn., Pa. State U., 1st Pl., Genworth Ctr. Excellence, GE Capital Internat. Svcs.; Rsch. grant, Children, Youth, and Families Consortium, Pa. State U. Mem.: Population Assn. America, Gerontol. Soc. America, AcademyHealth. Office: Duke-NUS Graduate Med Sch 8 College Rd Singapore 169857 Singapore Business E-Mail: monika.setia@psu.edu.

SETO, CRAIG KAILANI, physician; b. Mar. 30, 1962; Degree in Biology, U. SC, 1984; MD, Eastern Va. Med. Sch., 1988. Family physician Irwin Army Cmty. Hosp. US Army, 1991—94, family and sports medicine tchg. physician Martin Army Cmty. Hosp., 1995—2000; primary care sports medicine fellow Hughston Sports Medicine Ctr., 1994—95; asst. residency dir. family medicine residency program U. Va., 2000—10, team physician athletic dept., 2009, dir., Sch. Medicine-Health Sys., 2010—. Vol. physician US Olympics-Women's Softball, Atlanta, 1996; team physician Covenant HS, 2001, Western Albemarle HS, 2001. Recipient Tchg. award, U. Va. Sch. Medicine, Resident Tchg. award, U. Va. Fellow: Am. Acad. Family Medicine; mem.: Christian Med. Assn., Am. Coll. Sports Medicine, Soc. Tchrs. Family Medicine, Am. Med. Soc. Sports Medicine. Avocations: running, swimming, bicycling, exercise. Office: Dept Family Medicine University Va Charlottesville VA 22911 Office Fax: 434-243-2916. Business E-Mail: cks2n@virginia.edu.

SETTY, ARATHI, rheumatologist; b. India, Mar. 7, 1976; MD, SUNY Upstate Med. U., 2001; MPH, Harvard, 2007. Chief rheumatology Mt. Auburn Hosp., Harvard Med. Sch., 2007—. Office: 625 Mount Auburn St Ste 106 Cambridge MA 02138 Personal E-mail: asetty21@gmail.com.

SETZER, MATTHIAS, neurosurgeon; b. Erbach/Odenwald, Aug. 23, 1968; Abitur, Gymnasium Michelstadt, 1987; MD, J.W. Goethe U., Frankfurt, 1994. Neurosurgeon J.W. Goethe U., 1994—. Mem.: GMDS, Soc. Neurosci., Deutsche Wirbelsäulen Gesellschaft, CNS, Deutsche Gesellschaft für Neurochirurgie. Office: Schleusenweg 2-16 Frankfurt am Main Hessen 60528 Germany Business E-Mail: matthias.setzer@kgu.de.

SEUNG-HEON, SHIN, medical educator; b. Daegu, Republic Of Korea, Sept. 13, 1963; s. Kim Ok-Hee; m. Kim Hyun-Ji, Mar. 1, 1990; children: Shin Hyun-Wook, Shin Jeong-Wook. PhD, Kyungpook Nat. U., Daegu, 2001. Diplomate Bd. Korean Otolaryngology, 1992. Prof. Daegu Cath. U. Med. Ctr., 1995—; mem. fgn. relationship Korean Rhinologic Soc., Seoul, Republic of Korea, 2004—06, editor, 2006—08. Lt. Navy, 1992—95, Pohang. Grantee, Korean Health Assn., 2004. Achievements include research in role of fungi in pathogenesis of chronic rhinosinusitis. Office: Daegu Catholic Univ Med Ctrr 3056-6 Daemyung 4dong Namgu Daegu 705-718 Republic of Korea Home Phone: 82536504526; Office Phone: 82-53-650-4530. Office Fax: 82-53-650-4533. Business E-Mail: hsseung@cu.ac.kr.

SEUNG-HUN, CHO, psychiatrist; b. Seoul, Republic of Korea, Sept. 9, 1974; s. Cho Dongchan and Chae Sogun; m. Lee Eunpa. MD, Kyung Hee U., Seoul, 2007. Cert. physician Seoul, 2000. Prof. Kyung Hee U., Seoul, 2007—09, med. clin. prof., 2007—09. Contbr. articles to profl. jours. Med. svc. pub. health physician Korean Ministry of Health & Welfare, 2004—07. Recipient Med. awards, KyungHee U. Med. Ctr., 2009. Fellow: Korean Soc. Health Info. and Health Stats. (Seoul) (staff 2009). Achievements include invention of herbal medication for treating alcohol dependence. Home and Office: Hosp Korean Medicine Kyung Hee University #1 Hoegi-Dong Dongdaemun-Gu Seoul 130-701 Republic of Korea Office Phone: 82-2-958-9186. Personal E-mail: choshkh@gmail.com.

SEUNG-HYUN, KIM, ophthalmologist; b. Seoul, Seoul, Apr. 22, 1968; MD., Korea U. Coll. Medicine, 1993, PhD, 2002. Prof. Korea U. Coll. Medicine, 2003—. Office: 516 Gojan-dong Ansan Gyunggi 425-707 Republic of Korea Business E-Mail: ansaneye@hanmail.net.

SEVCIK, PAVEL, anesthesiologist; b. Cesky Tesin, Moravia, Czech Republic, Aug. 14, 1953; s. Vladimir Sevcik and Marta Sevcikova; m. Alena Slavikova, July 7, 1978; children: Lenka, Eva. MD, J. E. Purkynje U., Brno, Czech Republic, 1978. Cert. anesthesiologist 1st degree, anesthesiologist 2d degree. Resident St. Anne Hosp., Brno, 1978—83, head physician ICU, 1983—88, head dept. anesthesiology and intensive care medicine, 1996—; head dept. anesthesiology Mcpl. Hosp., Brno, 1989—91; head ICU U. Hosp., Brno, 1992—95. Assoc. prof., mem. sci. bd. U. Brno, 1997—2001; prof. Masaryk U., Brno, 2001—. Author: (books in Czech) Sepsis in Intensive Care, 1993, The Control of Pain, 1994, Intensive Care Medicine, 2000, 2d edit., 2003, Preumonias in Intensive Care Medicine, 2004; mem. editl. bd. Jour. Anesthesiology and Emergency Medicine, 1991—. Sci. bd. Ministry of Health, Czech Republic, 2000—04. Avocations: hiking, photography. Office: Hosp Dept Anesthesiology and Intensive Care M 62500 Brno Czech Republic Office Phone: 420 532233850. Office Fax: 4205 32233801. Business E-Mail: psevcik@fnbrno.cz.

SEVENING, DIANE KAY, alcohol/drug abuse studies educator, researcher; b. Platte, SD, July 27, 1951; d. James Clayton (Stepfather) and Florence June Rommen; m. Douglas Lee Sevening, Aug. 15, 1981; children: Rodney Justin, Ryan Lee. D of edn., U. SD, 1998—99. Instr. U. SD Arts & Sciences Alcohol & Drug Abuse Studies Dept., Vermillion, 1984—89, 1989—99, asst. prof. Internat. pres. Internat. Coalition for Addiction Studies Edn. (INCASE), Vermillion, SD, 2000—02. Contbr. articles to profl. jours.; co-author: A Comparison of Traditional Teaching Methods and Problem-Based Learning in Addictions Studies Class, 2002. Sec. U. SD Student Affairs Com., 2001—03; mem. U. SD Academic Integrity Task Force, 2002—03; presenter Internat. Coalition for Addiction Studies Edn. (INCASE) Conf., Portland, Oreg., 2003, Nat. Drug and Alcohol Recovery Month, Sioux Falls, SD, 2003, Vol. Am., Sioux Falls, SD, 2003—03. Mem.: Internat. Coalition for Addiction Studies Educators (assoc.; immediate past pres. 2002—03), Gamma Sigma Delta (assoc.), Phi Delta Kappa (assoc.). Home: 602 W Dartmouth St Vermillion SD 57069 Office: Univ SD 414 E Clark St Vermillion SD 57069 Business E-Mail: dsevenin@usd.edu.

SEVER, JOHN LOUIS, medical researcher, educator; b. Chgo., Apr. 11, 1932; s. John Louis and Harriet (Link) Sever; m. Gerane Werle, Mar. 3, 1956; children: Kimberly, Beverly, Valerie. BA, U. Chgo., 1952; BS, MD, MS, PhD, Northwestern U., 1957. Head sect. infectious diseases NINDS, NIH, Bethesda, Md., 1960—71, chief infectious diseases, 1971—88; chmn. pediat. Children's Nat. Med. Ctr., Washington, 1988—90, prof. pediat., ob-gyn., immunology, microbiology and tropical medicine, 1988—. Cons. Rotary Internat., Evanston, Ill., 1964—, NIH, Bethesda, 1988—, WHO, Geneva, 1991—. Editor: 11 med. books; contbr. more than 600 articles to profl. jours. Capt. USPHS, 1960—88. Recipient Kimbel award, Am. Soc. for Microbiology, 1979, Wellcome Diagnostics award, Pan Am. Med. Virology, 1989, Meritorious Alumni award, Northwestern U., 1989, Pasteur award, Microbiology Soc., 1987, Abbott award, 1996, Soc. for Biomolecular Screening award, 2001. Mem.: Pan Am. Soc. Rapid Viral Diagnosis (pres. 1995—96), Assn. Med. Lab. Immunologists (pres. 1994—95, Erwin Niter award 1997), Teratology Soc. (pres. 1976—77), Assn. Med. Clin. and Lab. Immunologists (pres. 1992—94), Infectious Disease Soc. of Ob-gyn. (pres. 1994—96, Ortho-McNeill award 1998), Country Glen Club, Potomac Rotary Club. Avocation: gardening.

SEVER, PETER SEDGWICK, pharmacologist, educator; b. Manchester, Eng., July 23, 1944; s. Harry Sedgwick and Lillian Maria Sever; m. Judith Alexandra Mackay, Dec. 28, 1982; m. Victoria Cattell, Mar. 15, 1969 (div. Mar. 1981); children: Richard, Charlotte; children: Alexander, Emily, Harry, Hugo. M.B.,B.Chir., MA, U. Cambridge, 1968; PhD, U. London, 1974. Sr. house officer Brompton Hosp., London, 1969—70; med. rsch. coun. fellow London U., 1971—74; lectr. in medicine St. Mary's Hosp. Med. Ctr., London, 1974—76, sr. lectr. medicine, 1976—80, prof. clin. pharmacology, 1980—87, Imperial Coll., London, 1988—. Dir. Internat. Ctr. for Circulatory Health, 2003—. Author: Clinical Atlas of Hypertension, 1991; editor-in-chief Jour. of Renin-Angiotension Aldosterone System, 1999—; editor: Cardiovascular Disease Prevention, 1993—, Current Advances in Ace Inhibition, vols. 1-3, —. Trustee Hypertension Trust U.K., 1998—, Brit. Heart Found., 2001—06; gov. Imperial Coll. London, 1989—93. Scholar Lord Moran scholar, St. Mary's Hosp. Med. Sch., 1965—68. Fellow: European Soc. Cardiology, Trinity Hall (Cambridge) (hon.); mem.: Nat. Inst. Health Rsch. (sr. investigator 2009—), European Coun. for Blood Pressure and Cardiovascular Rsch. (pres. 1998—99), Brit. Hypertension Soc. (pres. 1989—91). Avocations: travel, sports. Home: Hedgerley House Andrew Hill Ln Hedgerley SL2 3UL England Office: Imperial Coll London Internat Ctr for Circulatory Health 59 North Wharf Rd W2 1NY London England Business E-Mail: p.sever@imperial.ac.uk.

SEVERS, WALTER BRUCE, pharmacology educator, researcher; b. Pitts., June 10, 1938; s. Walter Bruce and Pauline Marie (Sever) S.; m. Anne Elizabeth Daniels, Apr. 25, 1970; children: Mary, Jane, Steven, William, Katherine. BS, U. Pitts., 1960, MS, 1963, PhD, 1965. Postdoctoral fellow NIH, Bethesda, Md., 1966-68; asst. prof. pharmacology Coll. Medicine, Pa. State U., Hershey, 1968-71, assoc. prof., 1971-77, prof., 1977-99, prof. emeritus, 1999—. Cons. pharmacology/toxicology, 1999—; v.p. for sci. affairs Ednl. Horizons, Inc., Lemoyne, Pa., 1998—; ad hoc grant cons. NIH, U.S. Army, NSF; vis. prof. physiology U. Belgrade Med. Sch., 1994—. Mem. editl. Bd. Am. Jour. Physiology, 1978-98; assoc. editor Pharmacology, 1998-2000; contbr. numerous articles, chpts., revs. to profl. publs. Recipient Disting. Alumnus award U. Pitts., 1978, I.M. Setchenov medal Acad. Med. Sci. USSR, 1983, Blue medal for sci. Acad. Med. Sci., Bulgaria, medal for sci. U. Belgrade; NASA grantee, 1976-98. Fellow Am. Coll. Clin. Pharmacology; mem. Am. Physiol. Soc., Am. Soc. Pharmacology and Exptl. Therapeutics, Soc. for Neurosci., Soc. for Exptl. Biology and Medicine, Sigma Xi (pres. Pa. State U. chpt. 1981-82), Kiwanis (pres. Hershey area 1980, bd. dirs.). Republican. Roman Catholic. Avocations: reading, camping, hiking. Home: 1011 Grubb Rd Palmyra PA 17078-3510 Office: Pa State U Coll Medicine Dept Pharm Mail Code H78 500 University Dr Hershey PA 17033-2360 Office Phone: 717-531-8291. Business E-Mail: wbs2@psu.edu.

SEWARD, JAMES PICKETT, internist, educator; b. NYC, Oct. 14, 1949; s. George C. and Carroll Frances (McKay) S. AB, Harvard U., 1971; M of Pub. Policy, U. Calif. Berkeley, 1977; MD, U. Calif. San Francisco, 1977; M of Med. Mgmt., Tulane U., 2003. Diplomate Am. Bd. Internal Medicine, Am. Bd. Occupational Medicine, Am. Bd. Med. Mgmt. Resident U. Calif. Hosps., San Francisco, 1977—80; med. dir. health svcs. Lawrence Livermore Nat. Lab., Calif., 1994—; Robert Woods Johnson postdoctoral fellow U. Calif., San Francisco, 1980—82, clin. prof., 1983—, dir. preventive medicine residency Berkeley, 1991—95, dir. occupl. health program, 1982—94, clin. prof. Sch. Pub. Health, 1986—. Fulbright scholar, 1972-73. Fellow Am. Coll. Preventive Medicine (occupl. med. regent 2005-07), Am. Coll. Occupl. an Environ. Medicine (bd. mem. 2010-), Am. Coll. Physicians Execs., Calif. Acad. Preventive Medicine (past pres.), We. Occupl. and Environ. Med. Assn. (past pres.), Calif. Med. Assn. Office: HSD L723 LLNL PO Box 808 Livermore CA 94551-0808

SEWARD, TROILEN GAINEY, retired psychologist; b. Petersburg, Va., Nov. 26, 1941; d. Troy L. and Mary (Nester) Gainey; m. William E. Seward III, June 29, 1963; children: Susan Blair, William E. IV. BA, Coll. William and Mary, 1963, MEd, EdS, Coll. William and Mary, 1980; MEd, Va. Commonwealth U., 1977. Tchr. elem., Petersburg, 1963—67; tchr. secondary Surry Acad., Va., 1967—76, guidance counselor, 1976—77; headmistress Tidewater Acad., Wakefield, Va., 1977—79; psychologist Peninsula Child Devel. Clinic, Newport News, Va., 1980—82; sch. psychologist Dinwiddie Pub. Sch., Va., 1982—89, dir. pupil pers. svcs., spl. edn., 1990—93, dir. student svcs., 1993—95, supt., 1996—2001; ret., 2002; edn. lobbyist, 2002—. Human rights com. Southside Tng. Ctr., Petersburg, 1986—; cons. in field. Trustee Ritchie Meml. Ch., Claremont, Va., 1971—; mem. Town Coun., Claremont, 1984-90, fin. com., 1984-90, mayor, 2006—. Mem. Nat. Assn. Sch. Psychologists (del. 1992-94), Va. Assn. Sch. Psychologists (chair cert. and licensure com. 1985-87, legis. chair 1987—, pres. 1989-91), Va. Literacy Found. (bd. mem. 2008-), Va. Edn. (adult edn. adv. bd. mem. 2009-) Delta Kappa Gamma, Phi Kappa Phi. Episcopalian. Home: PO Box 266 Claremont VA 23899-0266

SEWELL, JILLIAN RUTH, paediatrician, consultant; b. Melbourne, Australia, Jan. 19, 1949; d. John and Nell Shaw; m. Richard B. Sewell (div. 1996); children: Robert, Catherine. MBBS, Univ. Melbourne, 1971; FRACP, RACP, Sydney, Australia, 1984. Fellow Royal Children's Hosp., Melbourne, 1984—85, pediatrician, 1986—, RACP chair bd. pediat. censors, 1993—97, chair divsn. pediat., 1998—2002, pres., 2004—06; chair Nat. Inst. Clin. Studies, 2002—04, Order Australia, 2005, Alfred Health Bd., 2006—. Avocations: bushwalking, reading, theater. Office: Royal Childrens Hosp Flemington Rd Parkville 3052 Australia Office Phone: 6139345950. Business E-Mail: jill.sewell@rch.org.an.

SEXTON, JOHN JOSEPH, oral and maxillofacial surgeon, educator; b. Boston, Dec. 4, 1947; s. Bernard Thomas and Margaret Theresa (Carrigg) S.; m. Judith Whelden, Aug. 21, 1971; 1 child, Benjamin. BS, Boston Coll., 1970; DMD, Tufts U., 1975; MScD, Boston U., 1978, CAGS, 1979. Diplomate Am. Bd. Oral and Maxillofacial Surgery. Orthognathic fellow Boston U. Inst. for Correction of Facial Deformities, 1976-77; intern, jr. resident, chief resident Boston U./Tufts U., 1975-79; asst. prof. Goldman Sch. Dental Medicine, Boston U., 1979-81; chief oral and maxillofacial surgery Beth Israel Hosp., Boston, 1981—2001, dir. maxillofacial trauma svc., 1990—2001, dir. mucosal disorders unit, 1990—2001; chief oral and maxillofacial surgery Lahey Clinic Med. Ctr., Burlington, Mass., 2001—04. Cons. dermatology Beth Israel Hosp.; asst. prof. oral and maxillofacial surgery Harvard Med. Sch., Boston, 1999-2006. Contbr. numerous articles to profl. jours. Avocations: philosophy, physics, history, travel. Office: 372 Washington St Ste 2500 Wellesley MA 02481-6202 Business E-Mail: jsexton@bidmc.harvard.edu.

SEYA, TSUKASA, immunologist, research director; b. Koriyamashi, Fukushima, Japan, Oct. 18, 1950; s. Noboru Seya and Midori (Konnai) S.; m. Michiyo Matsumoto; 2 children. PhD, Hokkaido U., Sapporo, Japan, 1984, MD, 1987. Resident Hokkaido U. Sch. Medicine, 1976-79, rsch. fellow, 1979-84; rsch. assoc. Washington U., St. Louis, 1984-87; assoc. dir. Osaka Med. Ctr. Cancer and Cardiovascular Diseases, Japan, 1987—95, dir., 1996—2001, chmn., 2001—04; prof. Grad. Sch. Medicine, Hokkaido U., Japan, 2004—. PRESTO, Tokyo, 1994-97, OPSR, Tokyo, 1997-2002, CREST, Tokyo, 2002-07, Kosezaho grant, 2008-. Mem. Am. Assn. Immunologists, N.Y. Acad. Scis. Office: Hokkaido Univ Kita-15 Nishi-7 Kita 060-8638 Japan Sapporo Office Phone: 81-11-706-5073. Business E-Mail: seyatu@pop.med.hokudai.ac.jp.

SEYFERT, HOWARD BENTLEY, JR., podiatrist; b. Clifton Heights, Pa., July 10, 1918; s. Howard Bentley and Mabel (Ashenbach) S.; m. Anna Mary van Roden, June 26, 1942; 1 child, Joanna Mary Irwin. D of Podiatric Medicine, Temple U., 1940. Cert. Nat. Bd. Podiatric Med. Examiners (past pres.), Ariz. State Bd. Podiatry Examiners (past pres.). Pvt. practice podiatric medicine and surgery, Phoenix, 1950-82, Sedona, Ariz., 1982-93. Mem. med. staff Marcus J. Lawrence Meml. Hosp., Cottonwood, Ariz., Drs. Hosp., Phoenix; computer programs instr.; peer rev. cons. to Medicare for Ariz., 1975-93; mem. health svcs. adv. group, Ariz., 1980-85. Capt. USAF, 1942—46, ETO, Lt. Col. USAF (ret.) USAF, 1978. Decorated Bronze Star. Fellow Acad. Ambulatory Foot Surgery, Am. Coll. Foot and Ankle Surgeons; mem. Air Force Assn. (life), Res. Officers Assn. Am. (life), Mil. Officers Assn. Am., Assn. Mil. Surgeons of U.S., Ariz. Podiatric Med. Assn. (past pres.), Am. Podiatric Med. Assn., Gen. Old Golf Club, Oak Creek Country Club (Sedona), Continental Country Club (Flagstaff). Republican. Presbyterian. Avocations: golf, gardening, landscaping. Home: 17040 Amold Dr Riverside CA 92518-2813

SEYMOUR, RICHARD BURT, health educator; b. San Francisco, Aug. 1, 1937; s. Arnold Burt-Oakley and Florence Marguerite (Burt) S.; m. Michelle Driscoll, Sept. 15, 1963 (div. 1972); children: Brian Geoffrey, Kyra Daleth; m. Sharon Harkless, Jan. 5, 1973. BA, Sonoma State U., 1969, MA, 1970. Freelance writer, Sausalito, Calif., 1960—; coord., adminstr. Coll. of Mendocino, Boonville, Calif., 1971-73; bus. mgr. Haight Ashbury Free Clinics, San Francisco, 1973-77; exec. adminstr., dir. tng. and edn. projects Height Ashbury Free Clinics, San Francisco, 1977-87; instr. John F. Kennedy U., Orinda, Calif., 1986—; asst. prof. Sonoma State U., Rohnert Park, Calif., 1985—; pres., chief exec. officer Westwind Assocs., Sausalito, Calif., 1988—. Cons. Haight Ashbury Free Clinics, San Francisco, 1987—, treas., bd. dirs.; chmn. World Drug Abuse Treatment Network, San Francisco, 1988—; coord. Calif. Collaborative Ctr. for Substance Abuse Policy Rsch., 1997—; bd. dirs. Slide Ranch. Author: Physician's Guide to Psychoactive Drugs, 1987, Drug Free, 1987, The New Drugs, 1989, The Psychedelic Resurgence, 1993, Compost College, 1997, Clinicians' Guide to Substance Abuse, 2001; editor-in-chief Internat. Addictions Infoline, 1995; editor-in-chief Jour. of Psychoactive Drugs, 1996; exec. editor: Alcohol MD.com, 1999—; contbr. articles to profl. jours. Mem. Calif. Health Profls. for New Health Policy, Washington, 1976-80; chmn. Marin Drug Abuse Adv. Bd., San Rafael, Calif., 1979-81, CalDrug Abuse Svcs. Assn., Sacramento, 1975-79; mem. Alcohol and Drug Counselors Edn. Project, 1985—, San Francisco Delinquency Prevention Commn., 1981—, Calif. Primary Prevention Network, 1980—. Grantee NIMH, 1974—, Nat. Inst. on Drug Abuse, 1974—. Mem. Internat. Platform Assn., Commonwealth Club of Calif., Internat. Soc. Addiction Jour. Editors (bd. dirs., treas. 2000—).

Democrat. Episcopalian. Avocations: travel, writing, landscape painting, camping. Office: Westwind Assocs 90 Harrison Ave Apt C Sausalito CA 94965-2240 Office Phone: 415-565-1904. Business E-Mail: journal@comcast.net.

SEYREK, NESLIHAN, nephrologist, educator; b. Adana, Turkey, May 22, 1963; d. Enver and Tumay Arca; m. Ertugrul Vasfi Seyrek, Nov. 3, 1990; children: Neslisah, Hanzade. MD, U. Istanbul Cerrahpasa Med. Sch., Turkey, 1986; MD in internal medicine, Cukurova U. Sch. Medicine, Turkey, 1992; MD in nephrology, Cukurova U. Sch. Medicine, 1997. Internal medicine specialist Cukurova U. Sch. Medicine, Adana, Turkey, 1987—92, nephrology specialist, 1992—97, assoc. prof., 1997—2004, prof. nephrology, 2004—, chmn. nephrology, 2006—; nephroloy rsch. fellow U. So. Calif., LA, 1996—97. Nephrology cons. U. Hosp., Adana, 2004—; lectr. Eczacibasi Pharmaceuticals Inc., Istanbul, Turkey, 2004—. Author: Hypertension and Treatment in IIIrd Millenium, Hemodialysis Handbook; contbr. articles various profl. jours. Lectr. Local GNO's, Adana, 2000—05. Recipient Jr. Sci. award, Sci. and Tech. Rsch. Coun. of Turkey, 1977, Oral Presentation award, Hypertension and Renal Diseases Assn. of Turkey, 2003, Presentation award, European Renal Assn., 2004; Training scholarship, Giessen U., Germany. Mem.: Internat. Soc. Nephrology (assoc.), European Renal Assn. European Dialysis and Transplant Assn. (assoc.), Turkish Soc. Nephrology (assoc.), Turkish Med. Assn. (assoc.). Avocations: tennis, swimming, travel. Office: Cukurova U Med Faculty Balcali Hastanesi Adana 01330 Turkey Home: Kurtulus Mah 19 Sok Eyup Unal Apt 32/4 1120 Adana Adana Turkey Home Fax: +903224574292. E-mail: nseyrek@cu.edu.tr.

SFAKIANAKI, OURANIA, research scientist; b. Heraklion, June 8, 1976; PhD in Medicine, U. Crete, Greece, 2010. Biologist U. Parma, Italy, 2004. Rsch. scientist Liver Rsch. Lab., U. Crete, 2006—09. Recipient Better Oral Announcement award, Greek Soc. Study Liver, 2009. Avocations: reading, travel, music. Home: Stef Saxliki 44 Heraklion Crete 71304 Greece Personal E-mail: rsfaki@yahoo.gr.

SGAMBATI, KATHLEEN, former state legislator; m. Frank Sgambati; children: Eric, Michael. With NH Dept. HHS, 1977—2004; dep. commr. to Gov. Steve Merrill State of NH, dep. commr. to Gov. Jeanne Shaheen; cons. Sgambati & Assocs., 2004—06; mem. Dist. 4 NH State Senate, 2006—11, chair Health and Human Svcs. Com., mem. Fin. Com. & Pub. and Mcpl. Affairs Com., dep. majority leader. Mem., energy, environment and economic develop. com. NH State Senate, mem., fin. com., vice-chair, health and human svcs. com., mem., pub. and mcpl. affairs; mgr. Childrens' Health Initiative. Recipient Nathan Davis award for Outstanding Govt. Svc., AMA, 2008; Caroline Gross Fellowship, Harvard U., 1997. Democrat. Home Phone: 603-286-8931; Office Phone: 603-271-3074, 603-271-2111. Office Fax: 603-271-2105. Business E-Mail: kathleen.sgambati@leg.state.nh.us. *

SGARRO, DOUGLAS A., retail executive, lawyer; b. NY, 1959; m. Breda Sgarro; 3 children. Grad, Hamilton Coll., 1981; law degree, Univ. of Va. Sch. of Law, 1984. Assoc. Brown & Wood LLP, New York, NY, 1984—93, ptnr., 1993—97; sr. v.p. and chief legal officer CVS Pharmacy, Woonsocket, RI, 1997—2004; pres. CVS Realty Co., Woonsocket, RI, 1999—2009; sr. v.p. and chief legal officer CVS Corp., Woonsocket, RI, 2000—04; exec. v.p. strategy, chief legal officer CVS Corp., CVS Pharmacy, Woonsocket, RI, 2004—07; exec. v.p., chief legal officer CVS Caremark Corp., Woonsocket, RI, 2007—. Dir. Providence Children's Mus., United Way, Rye, NY. Mem.: Am. Bar Assoc. Bus. Law Sect., Internat. Assoc. of Atty. Exec. in Corp. Real Estate. Avocations: reading, exercise. Office: CVS Caremark Corp One CVS Dr Woonsocket RI 02895 *

SHABAYEK, MOHAMED HELMY, ophthalmologist; b. Aug. 1, 1973; MD, Cairo U., 2002; PhD, U. Miguel Hernandez, 2007. Ophthalmology specialist Internat. Eye Hosp., Egypt, 2003; clin. and rsch. fellow U. Miguel Hernandez, Spain, 2003—06; clin. and rsch. fellow, cornea and refractive surgery dept. VISSUM Inst. Oftalmologico de Alicante, Spain, 2003—06, ophthalmology cons., 2006—07; pvt. practice Egypt, Spain, 2007—. Contbr. articles to profl. publs. Recipient Hon. Collaborator award, U. Miguel Hernandez, Acknowledgement award, European Soc. Cataract and Refractive Surgery, Gov. North Sinai. Home: 12 El Koroum St 3 El Dokki Giza 12311 Egypt Personal E-mail: shabayek@coma.es.

SHABOT, MYRON MICHAEL, hospital system administrator; b. Houston, Aug. 5, 1945; s. Sam and Mona Doris (Stalarow) S.; 1 child, Samuel Laib. Student, Tulane U., 1963-64; BA, U. Tex., Austin, 1966; MD, U. Tex., Dallas, 1970. Intern Parkland Meml. Hosp., Dallas, 1970—71; resident Harbor Gen. Hosp., Torrance, Calif., 1973—78; lectr. surgery UCLA Sch. Medicine, 1977-78, asst. prof., 1978-82, clin. assoc. prof. surgery and anesthesiology, 1983-97, prof. surgery, 1997—; dir. surg. ICU, LA County Harbor Med. Ctr.-UCLA Sch. Medicine, 1980-82; med. dir. Enterprise Info. Svcs. Cedars-Sinai Med. Ctr., LA, dir. surg. ICU, 1982—, vice chief of staff, 2000—01, chief of staff, 2002—03, also bd. dirs. Sec. Cedars-Sinai Med. Ctr. Attending Staff, 1999-2000; bd. dirs. eHealth Initiative and Found., 2006—; adj. prof. U. Tex. Health Scis. Ctr., Houston; supr. sys. chief quality officer Meml. Hermann Healthcare Sys., Houston, 2007, sr. v.p., sys. chief medcial officer, 2007-. Contbr. articles to profl. jours. Served to lt. comdr. USPHS, 1971-73. Fellow ACS (So. Calif. chpt. bd. dirs. 1988—, pres. 1992-93, gov., 1992—), Am. Coll. Critical Care Medicine, Am. Coll. Med. Informatics; mem. Western Surg. Assn., Pacific Coast Surg. Assn., Soc. Critical Care Medicine, Am. Assn. Surgery of Trauma, Soc. Computers in Critical Care and Pulmonary Medicine (bd. dirs. 1988—, treas. 1989—, pres., 1993-94), Soc. Clin. Data Mgmt. Systems (pres. 1985-86), L.A. Surg. Soc. (pres. 1997-98), Phi Eta Sigma. Jewish. Office: 929 Gessner Rd Ste 2700 Houston TX 77024 Home Phone: 713-647-9894. Business E-Mail: michael.shabot@memorialhermann.org.

SHABSIGH, RIDWAN, urologist; MD, Damascus U. Med. Sch., Syria. Diplomate Am. Bd. Urology. Resident urology Baylor Coll. of Medicine, Houston, fellow sexual medicine, urinary incontinence, urologic prostheses; urologist urology dept. Columbia Univ.; dir. urology divsn. Maimonides Med. Ctr., Bklyn. Faculty mem. dept. of urology Columbia Univ.; prof. clin. urology Columbia Univ. Coll. of Physicians and Surgeons; mem. editorial bd. World Journal of Urology, Journal of Sexual Medicine, The Aging Male, Andrologia, The Internat. Journal of Men's Health and Gender. Author: (books) Sensational sex in 7 Easy Steps; contbr. The New England Journal of Medicine, Lancet, British Medical Journal and other several journals. Recipient The John K. Lattimer award for Excellence in Clin. Instrn., Am. Found. of Urologic Disease Young Investigator award, Internat. Soc. of Sexual Medicine female sexual dysfunction prize. Fellow: ACS; mem.: Sexual Health Coun. of the Am. Urol. Assn. Found., Internat. Soc. for the Study of Women Sexual Health, Sexual Medicine Soc. of America, Internat. Soc. of Sexual Medicine, Am. Urol. Assn. Office: 3121 Ocean Ave Brooklyn NY 11235 Office Phone: 718-283-7746.

SHACK, ROBERT BRUCE (BRUCE SHACK), plastic surgeon, department chairman; b. Vernon, Tex., Oct. 7, 1947; s. Nathan Lee and Patsy Lee (Holliday) S.; m. Sharon Summers Frazier, Aug. 16, 1969 (div. 1982); children: Robert David, Nathan Andrew; m. Wanda Kaye, Nov. 11, 1984; children: Jerion Elizabeth, Austin Ryan. BS, Midwestern U., Wichita Falls, Tex., 1969; MD, U. Tex., Galveston, 1973. Diplomate Am. Bd. Surgery, Am. Bd. Plastic Surgery with added qualifications in surgery of the hand. Extern St. Paul's Hosp., Dallas, 1971, St. Bartholomew's Hosp., London, 1971; intern surgery Vanderbilt U. Med. Ctr., Nashville, 1973—74, asst. resident surgery, 1974—77, chief resident surgery, 1977—78, resident plastic surgery, 1978—79, chief resident plastic surgery, 1979—80, asst. prof. plastic surgery, 1982—87, assoc. prof. plastic surgery, 1987—96, interim chmn., assoc. prof. dept. plastic surgery, 1996, chmn. and prof. dept. plastic surgery, 1997—; asst. prof. plastic surgery Johns Hopkins Hosp., Balt., 1980—82, U. Med. Sch. Medicine, Balt., 1981—82. Attending surgeon Children's Hosp. and Ctr. for Reconstructive Surgery, Balt., 1980—82; attending surgeon plastic surgery Md. Inst. for Emergency Medicine, 1980—82, Children's Hosp., Balt., 1980—82, Vanderbilt U. Med. Ctr., Nashville, 1982; attending head and neck surgeon John Hopkins Hosp., Nashville, 1980—82; staff privileges Baptist Hosp., 1982, Centennial Med. Ctr., Nashville, 1982; courtesy privileges in surgery Nashville Gen. Hosp., 1982—93; prof., chmn. dept. plastic surgery Vanderbilt Ctr. for Cosmetic Plastic Surgery; cons. head and neck surgery VA Hosp., 1982—; mem. instrnl. course com. Plastic Surgery Ednl. Found., 1985—86, 1986—87, 1987—88, mem. in svc. exam com., 1985—86, 1987—88, chmn. breast/aesthetic subcom. in-svc. exam. com. plastic surgery, 1988—94, chmn. in-svc. exam com., 1994—97, assoc. vis. prof., 1996; mem. adv. bd. Tenn. chpt. Neurofibromatosis Found., 1990—; sr. guest examiner Am. Bd. Plastic Surgery, 1999—2002, CAQSH exam cons., 1999—2002; mem. carrier adv. com. Tenn. Medicare Part B, 2004—; vis. prof. plastic surgery Scott-White Clinic, Tex. A&M, Temple, 1996; vis. prof. dept. plastic surgery U. Miss., Jackson, 1997; XV Marzoni lectr. and vis. prof. U. Ala., Birmingham, 2000; IX Ann. Coleman lectr. and vis. prof. U. Va., 2001; vis. prof. plastic surgery So. Ill. Sch. Medicine, 2003, Baylor Coll. Medicine, 2003; presenter and lectr. in field. Contbr. chapters to books, articles to profl. jours. Recipient Disting. Alumnus award, Midwestern State U. Divsn. Scis., 1998; named one of Outstanding Young Men in Am., 1969; grantee, LPG, Inc., 1998—99, Aesthetic Surgery Edn. and Rsch. Found., 1998, 1999, Southeastern Soc. for Plastic Surgeons, 2002—03. Fellow: ACS (mem. Tenn. dist. 2 com. on applicants 1990—2000); mem.: AMA, Southern Med. Law (pres. 2009—10), Am. Soc. Plastic and Reconstructive Surgeons (treas. practice rels. commn. 1983—84, mem. fin. com. 1983—84, treas. practice rels. commn. 1984—85, mem. fin. com. 1984—85, 1985—86, socioeconomic com. 1985—86, mem. fin. com. 1986—87, socioeconomic com. 1986—87, 1987—88, v.p. associated mgmt. svcs. 1988—90, chmn. fin. com. 1988—90, mem.-at-large bd. dirs. 1991—93, chmn. profl. liability ins. com. 1991—94, pres. associated mgmt. svcs. 1991—98, chmn. mktg. com. 1995—97, asst. sect. 1997), Tenn. Soc. Plastic and Reconstructive Surgery (pres. 2002—), Tenn. Med. Assn., So. Surg. Assn., So. Med. Assn. (asst. sec. plastic surgery sect. 1984—85, sec. plastic surgery sect. 1986—88, assoc. councilor State of Tenn. 1986—, chmn. elect plastic surgery sect. 1989, chmn. plastic surgery sect. 1990, councilor 2004—, pres. elect 2008—09, pres. 2008—), Southeastern Soc. Plastic and Reconstructive Surgeons (resident and rsch. com. 1984—85, chmn. So. Med. Assn. liaison com. 1986—90, chmn. resident and rsch. com. 1993—95, trustee bd. dirs. 1995—, chmn. spl. edn. com. 1998, 2001—02, pres. 2007, grantee 1998—99), Nashville Surg. Soc. (sec.-treas. 1993—96, pres.-elect 1996, pres. 1996—97), Nashville Acad. Medicine, John Staige Davis Soc. Plastic Surgeons Md., John B. Lynch Soc. (v.p. 1984—85, pres. 1985—), H. William Scott, Jr. Soc. (sec. 1993—97, pres.-elect 1999, pres. 2000—01), Am. Soc. for Aesthetic Plastic Surgery (grantee 1997—98), Am. Soc. for Reconstructive Microsurgery, Am. Soc. Plastic Surgeons (sec. 1998—2001, alt. del. AMA 2000—02, practice commr. 2000—, chmn. by-laws com. 2001—, v.p. 2002), Am. Soc. Maxillofacial Surgeons (mem. fin. com. 1993—98), Am. Cancer Soc., Am. Burn Assn., Am. Assn. Plastic Surgeons, Sigma Xi, Mu Delta, Beta Beta Beta. Republican. Methodist. Avocations: golf, shooting. Office: Vanderbilt U Med Ctr Dept Plastic Surgery 1161 21st Ave S D-4207 MCN Nashville TN 37232-2345 Office Phone: 615-936-0169. Business E-Mail: bruce.shack@vanderbilt.edu.

SHADE, GEORGE HENRY, JR., obstetrician, gynecologist, educator; b. Detroit, Jan. 4, 1949; s. George Henry Shade, Sr. and Julia M. Bullard-Shade; m. Carlotta Ann Johnson, July 24, 1976; children: Carla Nicole, Ryan McNeal. BS in Psychology, Wayne State U., Detroit, 1971, MD, 1974. Diplomate Am. Bd. Ob-gyn., 1980. Resident physician dept ob-gyn. Wayne State U., 1974—78; ptnr. Vincent, Combs, Massé & Shade, MD, PC, Detroit, 1978—2000; chmn. physicians adv. coun. St. John Health, 2000—02; chief dept. ob-gyn. Sinai-Grace Hosp. Detroit Med. Ctr., 2002—07, v.p. med. affairs Sinai-Grace Hosp., 2005—. Clin. instr. Wayne State U., 1978—82, asst. prof., 1982—2002, assoc. prof., 2002—; asst. prof. Mich. State U., 1982—2002, assoc. prof., 2002—; nat. spkrs. bureau Wyeth Pharm. Corp., 2000—; vice chmn. bd. medicine State Mich., Lansing, 2006—. Contbr. articles to profl. jours. Bd. dirs. Omnicare Health Plans, Detroit, 2001—03. Recipient Psi Chi Nat. honor Soc., Dept. of Psychology-Wayne State U., 1971. Mem.: Sigma Pi Phi, Kappa Alpha Psi (life). Democrat. Baptist. Achievements include research in pelvic endometriosis in the Africian Amercian female. Avocations: horseback riding, music, photography, art, sports cars and auto racing. Office: Sinai Grace Hosp Wayne State U 6071 W Outer Dr Ste M541 Detroit MI 48235 Office Fax: 313-966-4296. Business E-Mail: gshade@dmc.org.

SHADER, RICHARD IRWIN, psychiatrist, pharmacologist, educator; b. Mt. Vernon, NY, May 27, 1935; s. Myer and Beatrice (Epstein) Shader; m. Aline Brown, Sept. 21, 1958 (dec. Aug. 10, 2002); children: Laurel Beth, Jennifer Robin, Robert Andrew; m. Cynthia H. Livingston, Dec. 6, 2003. Student, Harvard U., Cambridge, Mass., 1952-56; MD, NYU, 1960; grad., Boston Psychoanalytic Inst., 1970. Diplomate Am. Bd. Psychiatry and Neurology (dir. 1977-84, treas. 1982-83, pres. 1984). Intern Greenwich Hosp., Conn., 1960-61; resident in psychiatry Mass. Mental Health Ctr., Boston, 1961-62, 64-65, NIMH, Bethesda, Md., 1962-64; assoc. prof. psychiatry Harvard Med. Sch., 1970-79; psychiatrist in chief New Eng. Med. Ctr. Hosp., Boston, 1979-91; prof. dept. psychiatry Tufts U. Med. Sch., Boston, 1979—2007, prof. emeritus, 2007—10, chmn. dept., 1979-91, prof. pharmacology, 1989—2007, prof. emeritus, 2007—11, chmn. dept. pharmacology and exptl. therapeutics, 1991-93, dir. grad. program dept. pharmacology and exptl. therapeutics, 1999—2010, sr. rsch. fellow, med. cons. Ctr. for the Study of Drug Devel., 2007—, prof. emeritus, dept. molecular physiology and pharmacology, 2011—; lectr. psychiatry Harvard Med. Sch., 1979—. Author (with A. DiMascio): Psychotropic Drug Sides Effects, 1970; author: (with D. J. Greenblatt) Benzodiazepines in Clinical Practice, 1974; author: Manual of Psychiatric Therapeutics, 1975, 1998, 2003; editor: Psychiatric Complications of Medical Drugs, 1972; editor: (with A. DiMascio) Clinical Handbook of Psychopharmacology, 1970, Butyrophenones in Psychiatry, 1972; editor: (with D. J. Greenblatt) Pharmacokinetics in Clinical Practice, 1985, MAOI Therapy, 1988; editor: (with J. P. Tupin and D. S. Harnett) Handbook of Clinical Psychopharmacology, 1988; editor: (with D.A. Ciraulo) Pharmacotherapy of Depression, 2004; editor: 2d edit., 2007, 3d edit., 2010; editor: (with others) Drug Interactions in Psychiatry, 1989, 3d edit., 2005; editor: Clinical Manual of Chemical Dependence, 1991; editor-in-chief Jour. Clin. Psychopharmacology, 1980—. Past mem. Am. Soc. Pharmacology and Exptl. Therapeutics; bd. dirs. Med. Found., Inc., 1980—87. With USPHS, 1962—64. Recipient Seymor Vestermark award, Am. Psychiat. Assn., 1988, 1990; fellow, Ctr. Advanced Study Behavioral Scis., Stanford, Calif., 1990—91; Joseph J. Michaels Merit scholar, 1968—69. Fellow: Am. Coll. Neuropsychopharmacology (v.p. 1984, pres. 1990, emeritus 2005); mem.: AMA (emeritus), Am. Soc. Clin. Pharmacology and Therapeutics (emeritus), Mass. Med. Soc. (emeritus,). Democrat. Jewish.

SHADOW, RUBY L. WESLEY, nursing educator, administrator, researcher; b. Detroit, Nov. 25, 1949; d. David Williams and Leatrice (Gragg) Williams; m. Thomas Shadow, 2007; 1 child, Nathaniel Rogers Wesley III. Diploma, Providence Hosp. Sch. Nursing, Southfield, Mich., 1971; BS in Nursing, Wayne State U., Detroit, 1974, MEd, 1977; PhD, U. Md., Balt., 1987. Clin. instr. U. Tenn. Sch. Nursing, 1978-79; community health nursing instr. U. Md., Balt., 1984-85; assoc. prof. Bowie State U., 1985-89; asst. dean Coppin State Coll., Balt., 1989-90; asst. prof. Wayne State U., 1991—; nurse researcher Rehab. Inst. Mich., 1992, dir. nursing practice Detroit, 1992-93, dir. nursing, 1993-96; asst. v.p. med./surg. rehab. nursing Sinai Hosp., Detroit, 1996—98; chief oper. officer Detroit Inst. for Children, 1998—99; pres., CEO Big Bros./Big Sisters of Metro Detroit, 2000—02; v.p. programs Detroit Urban League, 2002—03; exec. dir. Wayne County Patient Care Mgmt. Sys., 2003—06; assoc. chief nursing edn. and rsch. VA Med. Ctr., Washington, 2006—. Henry C. Welcome fellow, 1986 87; Nat. Inst. Disability and Rehab. rsch. fellow, 1991-92. Office: Washington VA Med Ctr 50 Irving St NW Washington DC 20422-0002 Office Phone: 202-745-8486. Personal E-mail: drrlwesley@hotmail.com.

SHAEFFER, CHARLIE WILLARD, JR., cardiologist; b. Phila., Feb. 8, 1938; s. Charlie Willard and Lucy Virginia (Chambliss) S.; m. Claire Brightwell, Feb. 24, 1959; children: Charlie Willard III, James Robert. BS, Fla. State U., 1960; MD, Washington U., St. Louis, 1964. Diplomate Am. Bd. Internal Medicine, Am. Bd. Cardiovascular Disease, Am. Bd. Clin. Lipidology. Rotating intern Naval Hosp., Bethesda, Md., 1964-65, resident in internal medicine Oakland, Calif., 1965-68, fellow cardiology Bethesda, 1968-70, staff cardiology Portsmouth, Va., 1970-71, chief, cardiology, 1971-74; cardiologist, corp. sec. Desert Cardiology Cons., Inc., Rancho Mirage, Calif., 1974—. Cons. Naval Hosp., San Diego, 1974-75; head cardiology Eisenhower Med. Ctr., Rancho Mirage, Calif., 1976-78, pres., med. staff, 1982-83, bd. dirs., 2002—; instr. Advanced Cadiopulmonary Life Support, Am. Heart Assn., Dallas, 1983—; Am. Bd. Lipidology, 2007. Contbr. articles to profl. jours. Pres. Riverside County Heart Assn., Calif., 1978—79; Calif. affiliate Am. Heart Assn., Burlingame, Calif., 1984—85, Desert divsn. Palm Desert, Calif., 1989—90, chmn. S.W. Region, 1989—90, 1992—93, vol. advocate, 2006, chmn. pub. policy subcom., 1996—99, chair tobacco issues subcom., 1998—; bd. dirs. Eisenhower Med. Ctr., Rancho Mirage, 1990—93, 2002—09, Eisenhower Meml. Hosp., Rancho Mirage, 1990—93. Recipient Bronze Svc. award Calif. affiliate Am. Heart Assn., 1982, Silver Svc. award 1983, 85, 87, Gold Svc. award 1988, Sol Azteca award La Prensa Hispansa, 2000, Cmty. Svc. award Riverside County Med. Assn., 2002; named Physician Vol. of Yr., 1996; honoree Eisenhower Med. Ctr. Aux., 1999, Am. Heart Assn. Desert Divsn., 2004., Gold Heart award, Am. Heart Assn., 2010. Fellow ACP, Clin. Cardiology Am. Heart Assn. (Jefferson award, 2005, named Advocacy Vol. Yr. 2006), Am. Coll. Cardiology, Am. Coll. Chest Physicians. Avocations: jogging, music, reading, travel. Office: Desert Cardiology Cons 39000 Bob Hope Dr Rancho Mirage CA 92270-3221 E-mail: cshaeffer@desertcard.com.

SHAFER, FRANK E., pediatric hematologist, oncologist; Grad., Creighton U., Omaha, 1983. Diplomate Am. Bd. Pediatrics, Am. Bd. Pediatrics-pediatric oncology & pediatric hematology. Intern Univ. Colo., Denver, 1984, resident, 1986; fellow Children's Nat. Med. Ctr., Washington, 1990; with St. Christophers Hosp. for Children, Phila. Office: St Christophers Hospital for Children 3601 A St Philadelphia PA 19134 Office Phone: 215-427-5096.

SHAFFER, ANITA MOHRLAND, counselor, educator; b. Racine, Wis., Apr. 5, 1939; d. Milton Arthur and Gudrun Amanda Stoffel. BS magna cum laude, U. Wis., 1961; MEd, U. Wash., 1966; postgrad., Ariz. State U., 1971-76. Cert. in elem. edn., social sci. secondary edn., spl. edn., Tex.; lic. profl. counselor, Tex. Tchr. Racine Unified Dist. 1, 1961-63, Edmonds Sch. Dist. 15, Lynnwood, Wash., 1963-70, Ariz. Dept. Corrections, Phoenix, 1971-77; tchr. spl. edn. Pasadena (Tex.) Ind. Sch. Dist., 1977-78, spl. edn. counselor, 1978-90, elem. counselor, 1990-98; supr. U. Houston, 1998—2008. Ednl. cons., 1998—. Violin, Houston Sinfonietta, 2002—. Mem. Tex. Counseling Assn., Houston Counseling Assn., Mus. Fine Arts Houston (patron), Houston Lic. Profl. Counselors Assn., Pi Lambda Theta, World Affairs Coun. Home: 5905 Woodway Place Ct Houston TX 77057-2005 *

SHAFFER, KITT, radiologist, educator; b. Kans. City, Mo., Apr. 9, 1954; d. William Elias and Anna Mae Johnston Shaffer; m. Timothy Paul Titcomb, Feb. 14, 1980. MD, Tufts Sch. Medicine, Boston, 1983; PhD, U. Kans., 1983—83. Diplomate Am. Bd. Radiology, 1987. Co-dir., thoracic imaging Brigham & Women's Hosp., Boston, 1991—92, dir., med. student edn. radiology, 1996—2005, radiology ednl. cons., 2008—; asst. chief radiology Dana-Farber Cancer Inst., Boston, 2001—04; dir., human body course anatomy Harvard Med. Sch., Boston, 2003—07, lectr. radiology, 2008—; vice-chair Dept. Radiology, Boston Med. Ctr., 2008—; prof. radiology Boston U. Med. Sch. Radiology ednl. cons. Brigham and Women's Hosp., Boston, 2008—; vis. prof. radiology Dartmouth Med. Ctr., Hanover, NH, 2003—07, U. Wash., Seattle, 2007; vis. prof. radiology St. Luke's Healthcare Sys., Kans. City, Mo., 2008, U. Ind., Indpls., 2009—, U. Western Ont., London, 2009—, U. Md., Balt., Emory U., Atlanta; anatomy question writer Nat. Bd. Med. Examiners, Phila., 2006—08; thoracic bd. examiner Am. Bd. Radiology, Louisville, 2000—; chair, edn. com. Alliance Med. Student Educators Radiology, 2006—. Panelist Dana-Farber Cancer Inst., Boston, 2002—04. Recipient Warren Widrich Edn. award, Boston Va. Med. Ctr. Dept Radiology, 1988, Faculty prize, Harvard Med. Sch., 2005, Profl. Leadership award, Am. Assn. Women Radiologists, 2004, Outstanding Tutor award, Acad. Harvard Med. Sch., 2007; named one of Best First Yr. Tutor, Harvard Med. Sch., 2003, Tutor of Yr., 2004; fellowship, Harvard Macy Insst., 1999, Bok Ctr. Edn., Harvard U., 2000, fellow, Shapiro Ctr. Beth Israel, Boston, 2001, Provost IT Innovation grant, Harvard U., 2000, Provost Equipment grant, 2005. Mem.: Soc. Breast Imaging, Soc. Thoracic Radiologists, Am. Coll. Radiology, Am. Roentgen Ray Soc. (mem. edn. com.), Alliance Med. Student Educators Radiology (pres., founding mem. 2005—06), Assn. U. Radiologists, Am. Assn. Women Radiologists, New Eng. Roentgen Ray Soc., Radiologic Soc. North America (named Outstanding Educator 2010), Alpha Omega Alpha. Achievements include first to development of web-based teaching modules of radiologic anatomy. Avocations: painting, ceramics. Office Fax: 617-638-6602. Business E-Mail: kitt.shaffer@bmc.org.

SHAFFER, WILLIAM ORLON, surgeon; b. Wichita Falls, Tex., Nov. 9, 1951; BS, U. Mich., 1974, MD, 1976. Diplomate Am. Bd. Orthop. Surgeons, 1984. Chmn. orthopaedic surgery Nat. Naval Med. Ctr., Bethesda, Md., 1987—89; spine surgeon Ventura Orthopedic and Sports Surgeons, 1989—94; prof., orthoapedic surgery & neurol. surgery St. Louis U., 1994—2001; prof., vice chmn. & residency program dir. U. Ky. Orthopaedic Surgery, 2001—10; physician ptnr. Northwwest Iowa Bone, Joint & Sports Surgeons, 2010—. Reviewer Spine, 1986, Spine Jour., 1994; mem. guideline oversite com. Am. Acad. Orthopaedic Surgery, 2007—11; co-chmn. evidence based guideline devel. com. North Am. Spine Soc., 2009—. Decorated Commendation medal US Navy Dept., Meritorious Unit Commendation (Desert Storm), Overseas Svc. medal; recipient Acromed award, North Am. Spine Soc., Volvo award, Internat. Soc. Study Lumbar Spine. Fellow: Am. Orthop. Assn., North Am. Assn. Spine Surgeons, Am. Acad. Orthop. Surgeons; mem.: Internat. Soc. Study Lumbar Spine, Iowa Orthop. Soc. Avocations: photography, gardening, movies. Office: 1200 1st Ave E Ste C Northwest Spencer IA 51301 Office Fax: 712-262-5638.

SHAFRITZ, DAVID ANDREW, physician, research scientist; b. Phila., Oct. 5, 1940; s. Saul and Ethel (Kohn) S.; m. Sharon C. Klemow, Aug. 16, 1964; children: Gregory S., Adam B., Keith M. AB in Chemistry with honors, U. Pa., 1962, MD, 1966. Diplomate Nat. Bd. Med. Examiners, Am. Bd. Internal Medicine. Intern, then asst. resident U. Md. Hosp., Balt., 1966-68; rsch. assoc. NIH, Bethesda, Md., 1968-71; clin. and rsch. fellow Mass. Gen. Hosp., Boston, 1971-73; instr. Harvard Med. Sch., Boston, 1971-73, asst. prof. medicine, 1973; asst. prof. medicine and cell biology Albert Einstein Coll. Medicine, Yeshiva U., Bronx, NY, 1973-76, assoc. prof., 1976-81, prof. medicine and cell biology, 1981—, dir. Marion Bessin Liver Rsch. Ctr., 1985—, Herman Lapota prof. liver disease rsch. (endowed chair), 1992—. Cons. integrated Genetics, Inc., Framingham, Mass., 1981-86, Immuno, Vienna, Austria, 1986-91, Innovir, Inc., N.Y.C., 1991-98, Eugenetech Internat., Inc., Ramsey, N.J., 1991-93, Ctrs. for Med. Innovation, 1997-2001; temp. advisor WHO, Geneva, 1983; mem. Nat. Com. for Clin. Lab. Stds., Villanova Pa., 1983—, Renaissance Techs., 1996—, Affymetrix, Inc., 1997—; sci. adv. bd. com. liver cancer program Inst. for Cancer Rsch., Fox Chase and Phila., 1987—, mem. rev. panel C. study sect. Nat. Inst. Diabetes and Digestive and Kidney Diseases, 1988-92, chmn., 1991-92; mem. cen. coord. com. Liver Tissue Procurement and Distbn. Sys., 1986-95, Nat. Inst. Health Metabolic Pathology Study sect., 1995-99; mem. Nat. Bd. Med. Examiners and U.S. Med. Exam. Com., 1996-98. Co-author: The Liver: Biology and Pathobiology, 1982, 5th edit., 2009, Hepatobiliary Diseases, 1991; assoc. editor Hepatology, 1981-86; mem. editl. bd. Jour. Med. Virology, 1982-93, Hepatology, 1990-96, Jour. Virology, 1992-98; contbr. more than 200 rsch. articles and revs. to profl. publs.; contbr. chpts. to books; patentee in field. Trustee Westchester Jewish Ctr., Mamaroneck, N.Y., 1980-86. Lt. comdr. USPHS, 1968-71. Recipient Merck award U. Pa., 1962, Morton McCutcheon Meml. Rsch. prize Sch. Medicine, 1966, Career Scientist award Irma T. Hirschl Trust, N.Y.C., 1974-79, NIH Merit award, 1994, Disting. Rsch. Achievement award Am. Liver Found., 2000, AGA Rsch. Mentor award, 2007; European Molecular Biology Orgn. fellow, 1978; recipient Rsch. Career Devel. award NIH, 1975-80, spl. rsch. fellow, 1971-73, rsch. grantee, 1974—. Mem. Am. Assn. for Study of Liver Diseases, Internat. Assn. for Study of Liver, Am. Gastroenterol. Assn. (Mentors award 2007), Am. Soc. Biochemistry and Molecular Biology, Am. Soc. Investigative Pathology, Am. Soc. Clin. Investigation, Assn. Am. Physicians, N.Y. Acad. Scis., Harvey Soc., Interurban Clin. Club (sec./treas. 1996-99, pres. 1999-2000). Democrat. Jewish. Avocations: jogging, tennis. Home: 4 Pheasant Run Larchmont NY 10538-3423 Office: Yeshiva U Albert Einstein Coll Med Marion Bessin Liver Rsch Ctr 1300 Morris Park Ave Bronx NY 10461-1926 Office Phone: 718-430-2098. Business E-Mail: david-shafrtz@einstein.yu.edu.

SHAGAN, BERNARD PELLMAN, endocrinologist, educator; b. Bklyn., Sept. 29, 1935; s. Samuel David and Pearl (Pellman) S.; m. Maureen Helen Oshever Amster, June 24, 1957 (div. 1970); children: Ellen Ruth Basch, Brian Ross; m. Phoebe Orange, Aug. 24, 1972; 1 child, Adam Irwin. AB, Harvard U., 1956; MD, NYU, 1960. Diplomate Am. Bd. Internal Medicine; bd. cert. endocrinology and metabolism. Chief sect. endocrinology Coney Island Hosp., Bklyn., 1968-79; chief sect. endocrinology, assoc. prof. medicine East Tenn. State U. Quillen Dishner Coll. Medicine, Johnson City, 1979-84; assoc. chmn., then acting chmn. dept. medicine Nassau County Med. Ctr., East Meadow, NY, 1984-87; assoc. prof. clin. medicine SUNY, Stony Brook, 1985-87; chmn., program dir. dept. medicine Monmouth Med. Ctr., Long Branch, NJ, 1987-96, dir. Diabetes Edn. Ctr., 2002—06; pvt. practice in endocrinology and metabolism Shrewsbury, NY, 1997-98, West Long Branch, NJ, 1998—2002; pvt. practice of endocrinology Long Branch, NJ, 2002—04; clin. prof. medicine Drexel U. Med. Ctr.; chief med. dir. Health Pia Am., Newark, 2004—06; cons. endocrinology Chemed, Lakewood, NJ, 2010—. Clin. prof. medicine Med. Coll. Pa. Hahnemann U., Phila., 1988—2002; clin. prof. medicine Coll. Medicine Drexel U., Phila., 2004—. Contbr. articles to med. jours. Capt. M.C., U.S. Army, 1966-68. Master ACP (gov. N.J. 1996-2000, fellowship); fellow Am. Coll. Endocrinologists; mem. Am. Assn. Clin. Endocrinologists, Am. Diabetes Assn., Endocrine Soc. Jewish. Avocations: music, singing, piano. Office Fax: 732-415-8773. Business E-Mail: bshagan@optonline.net. *

SHAGIDULLIN, ROAL'D RIFGATOVICH, research scientist; b. Tersy Village, Russia, Aug. 5, 1928; s. Rifgat Samatovich Shagidullin and Amina Bagautdinovna (Khusnutdinova) Shagidullina; m. Bacirova Aida Zaudjatovna, July 1, 1960; children: Rifgat Roal'dovich, Guzel' Roal'dovna Fatcullina. B Physico-math. Scis., U. Kazan, Russia, 1967; D Chem. Scis., U. Kazan, 1996; diploma, Arbuzov Inst. Kazan, 1997. Seasonal agrl. worker Kolkhoz, Menzelinsk, Tatarstan, Russia, 1942—45; sec. Dist. Regional Komsomol Coms., Kazan, 1950—53; lab. asst., aspirant Physico-tech Inst. Kazan Br. Russian Acad. Scis., 1953—56, jr. scientist, sci. sec., chief lab., chief scientist Arbuzov Inst. Kazan, 1956—2007. Invited lectr. Phys. Faculty of Univ., Kazan, 1969—71; sci. chief Spectroanalitical Ctr. Acad. Scis. Tatarstan and Inst., Kazan, 1990—, prof. physico-chem scis., 1997. Co-author (with A.V. Chernova et.al.): Atlas of IR Spectra, 1974, 1984, 1990; editor: A.E. Arbuzov Inst.: Facts, People, Photo-Memory, 2001, author (and co-author) over 450 articles. Mem. Komsomol Coms., Kazan, 1948—58; dep. Dist. Soviet of Peoples Deps., Kazan, 1950—55. Recipient Badge Honor, Russia, 1970, Disting. Pub. Svc. and Merits medals, 1945, 1970, 1987, 1995, 2000, 2005, 2005, 2006, 2010, Meritorious Sci. Worker award, Republic of Tatarstan, 1999. Mem.: Rosochotribolov Soc. (Hon. Hunter 1992). Achievements include research in molecular structure and properties determination of hundreds new physiological active elementoorganical compounds, drugs; IR-Spectra and diagnosis of cancer. Office: AE Arbuzov Inst Organic and Phys Chemistry Arbuzov St 8 420088 Kazan Russia Office Phone: 7 843 2 73 18 92. Business E-Mail: arbuzov@iopc.knc.ru.

SHAH, AMY S., medical educator; b. Sarnia, Ont., Can., Sept. 3, 1979; MD, St. George's U. Med. Sch., 2004; MS, U. Cin., 2011. Asst. prof. Cin. Children's Hosp. Med. Ctr., 2011—. Mem.: Pediatric Endocrine Soc., Am. Heart Assn. Office: 3333 Burnet Ave ML 7012 Cincinnati OH 45226 Business E-Mail: amy.shah@cchmc.org.

SHAH, IRA BALWANT, pediatrician, researcher; MBBS, Grant Med. Coll., 1997; MD, Seth Gordhandas Sunderdas Med. Coll., 2000. Lic. pediatrician Maharashtra Med. Coun., 2000, diplomate Nat. Bd. Examinations, 2000. Lectr. B.J.Wadia Hosp. Children, Mumbai, India, 2001—, incharge Pediatric HIV Clinic, 2002—, incharge Pediatric Hepatobiliary Clinic, 2005—; incharge pediatric TB Clinic, 2007—. Asian editor Journal Pediat. Infectious Diseases, 2008—10; editl. bd. mem. Annals of Tropical Pediats., 2010; writers group mem. Pediat. HIV Guidelines for Nat. AIDS Control Orgn., India, 2006, 10; cons. pediat. infections diseases & pediat. hepatology Nanavati Hosp., Mumbai; editl. cons. Annals Tropical Pediat., 2011—. Editor: (medical journal and child health website) Pediatric Oncall (Golden Web award, 2001); author: Management of Pediatric HIV, 2005, Dengue, Leptospirosis, Malaria, 2007, IAP Textbook of Pediatric HIV, 2007—, Tuberculosis, 2009, Macronutrients, 2011, Micronutrients, 2011, Diet and Nutrition, 2011, Typhoid Fever, 2011; editor: Pediatric Oncall, 2000—; contbr. articles to profl. jours. Trustee Bhikubhai Chandula L Jalandwala Gen. Hosp., Mumbai, 2004. Recipient Distinction in Biochemistry award, U. Mumbai, 1993, Distinction in Physiology award, 1993. Fellow: Coll. Physicians and Surgeons (Gold medal 1997—99); mem.: Gen. Practioners Assn. (assoc.), Indian Med. Assn. (life), Indian Acad. Pediat. (life; convenor task force pediat. HIV 2006). Office: Pediatric Oncall Levioza 1/B Saguna 271/B St Francis Rd 400 056 Maharashtra Vile Parle W Mumbai India

SHAH, JATIN PREMANAND, head and neck surgeon, educator; b. Visnagar, Gujarat, India, Dec. 31, 1940; came to U.S., 1967; s. Premanand C. and Sarla P. (Mehta) S.; m. Bharti N. Gandhi, May 11, 1967; 1 child, Mili MD, Baroda Med. Coll., India, 1964, MS in Surgery, 1967; PhD (hon.), U. Athens, Catholic U. Louvain, Belgium. Diplomate Am. Bd. Surgery. Attending surgeon Meml. Sloan Kettering Cancer Ctr., NYC, 1974—, chief head and neck svc., 1992—, E.W. Strong chair in head and neck oncology; prof. surgery Cornell U. Med. Coll., NYC, 1987—. Vis. prof. Royal Soc. Medicine, London, 1997. Author: Head and Neck Surgery, 1996 (prize Royal Soc. Medicine 1996), rev. edit., 1997 (1st prize Brit. Med. Assn. 1997), 3d edit., 2003 (George D. Howells prize U. London 2003). Blokhin Gold medal Russian Acad. Scis., Ellis Island Medal of Honor, 2009 Fellow ACS, Royal Coll. Surgeons Edinburgh (hon.), Royal Australian Coll. Surgeons (hon.), Dental Surgery Royal Coll. Surgeons (London) (hon.); mem. Soc. Head and Neck Surgeons (pres. 1991), Internat. Fedn. Head and Neck Oncological Socs. (founder, CEO 1987), NY Cancer Soc. (pres. 1984), NY Head and Neck Soc. (pres. 1985), North Am. Skull Base Soc. (pres. 2003), Internat. Acad. Oraloncology (pres. 2005), AAPI(Disting. Physician award, 2011). Office: Meml Sloan Kettering Cancer Ctr 1275 York Ave New York NY 10021-6094 Office Phone: 212-639-7604. *

SHAH, KIRTIKANT CHIMANLAL, retired dermatologist; b. Baroda, Gujarat, India, Nov. 3, 1936; s. Chimanlal Bhailal and Kantaben Chimanlal Shah; m. Kirtiben Kirtikant Shah, May 13, 1963; children: Rima, Rupa, Radha, Joy. MB, BChir, Govt. Med. Coll., Baroda, 1961, MD, 1964, postgrad. diploma, 1966. Cert. Med. Coun. India. Lectr. Govt. Med. Coll., Baroda, 1964—66; med. exec. Alembic Ltd., Baroda, 1966—68; prof., head dept. dermatology Govt. Med. Coll. and New Civil Hosp., Surat, 1968—96; postgrad. tchr., prof. in charge postgrad. ctr., dermatology and sexually transmitted diseases South Gujarat U., Surat, 1968—96; ret., 1996. Chmn. bd. clin. studies South Gujarat U., Surat, 1976—96; chief dir., dermato-surgeon Kirti Skin Laser Surgery Inst., Surat, 1996—; cons. in field. Contbr. articles to profl. jours. Recipient Ambady Oration award, Indian Assn. Dermatologists, 1987, Bishnupniya Debi award, 1990; grantee, Health Dept. Govt. Gujarat, 1980. Mem.: Indian Med. Assn. (life), Indian Leprosy Assn. (life), Indian Assn. Sexually Transmitted Diseases (life), Indian Assn. Dermatologists, Venereologists, Leprologists (life). Achievements include research in animal models in vitiligo, cherry anglomas, cutaneous angiopathy, others. Avocations: sports, writing, travel, reading, driving. Home: 12 Sangna Society Rander Rd Surat 395009 India Office: Kirti Laser Inst 1 Premjinagar Soc Adajan Rd Surat 395009 India Office Phone: 02613056789. Business E-Mail: drkcshah@kirtilaser.com, beautyncurves@kirtilaser.com, drmegha@kirtihealthcare.com.

SHAH, MODASER, psychiatrist; b. Mardan, Pakistan, June 1, 1942; arrived in U.S., 1972; s. Syed Ahmad and Sultana Shah; m. Keiko Sakina Anzai, June 1, 1969; children: Omar Ali Kenji, Samina, Rehana. MD, Tokyo Med. and Dental U., 1968, PhD, 1972. Diplomate Am. Bd. Psychiatry and Neurology. Intern, Phila., 1972—73; resident in internal medicine NY, 1973—74, Warren, Pa., 1974—76, St. Louis, 1976—77; staff psychiatrist St. Louis State Hosp., 1977—82; med. dir. Great Rivers Mental Health Ctr., St. Louis, 1982—86; chief of med. staff St. Louis State Hosp., St. Louis, 1986—87; sr. psychiatrist Malcolm Bliss Mental Health Ctr., St. Louis, 1987—92; psychiatrist, cons. Internat. Clinic, Tokyo, 1992—98; v.p., psychiatrist Hachinohe City, Japan, 1998—2001; staff psychiatrist Ozark Ctr., Joplin, Mo., 2001—. V.p., med. dir. Matsudaira Hosp., Hachinohe City, Japan. Contbr. articles to profl. jours. Active in promotion of med./psychol. needs of minorities in Japan, Tokyo, 1992—98. Mem.: Mo. State Med. Assn., Am. Psychiatric Assn. Sufi Muslim. Achievements include research in psychology and psychopathology of Muslim migrant workers in Japan, at risk for radicalization; integration of aspects of Sufism and Zen. Avocation: classical Western, Indian and Japanese music. Office: Ozark Ctr 530 E 34th St # 203 Joplin MO 64803

SHAH, MONA, corporate financial executive; b. Lahore, Pakistan, July 25, 1972; B, Rutgers U., 1995. Account asst. Edelman Pub. Rels., 1995—97; office mgr. Mercer Surg. Group, 2006—. Avocation: travel. Office: 2063 Klockner Rd Hamilton NJ 08690 Personal E-mail: monazui@yahoo.com.

SHAH, NIKHIL L., urologist, surgeon; BA, MPH, U. Mich.; MD, Kirksville Coll. Osteopathic Medicine. Fellow Henry Ford Hosp. Vattikuti Urology Inst., chief resident; dir. minimally invasive & robotic urology St. Joseph's Ctr. for Robotic Surgery. Mem.: AMA, AUA. Office: Saint Joseph's Hospital 5665 Peachtree Dunwoody Rd NE Atlanta GA 30342

SHAH, NIRAV RAMESH, state official; b. Buffalo, May 7, 1972; s. Ramesh and Rekha Shah; m. Nidhi Shah; 2 children. Grad. with honors, Harvard Coll.; MD, MPH, Yale U., New Haven, 1998. Diplomate American Bd. Internal Medicine. Intern Yale-New Haven Hosp., 1998—99, resident, 1999—2001; Robert Wood Johnson Clin. scholar UCLA, 2001—03; Nat. Rsch. Svc. fellow NYU; asst. prof. medicine, sect. value and comparative effectiveness NYU Langone Med. Ctr.; attending physician Bellevue Hosp. Ctr., NYC; commr. NY State Dept. Health, 2011—. Assoc. investigator Geisinger Ctr. Health Rsch., Danville, Pa., 2004—10. Contbr. articles to profl. jours. Fellow: ACP, NY Acad. Medicine. Achievements include recognition as an expert in the use of systems-based methods to improve patient outcomes and as a leading researcher in use the of large scale clinical laboratories and electronic health records to improve the effectiveness and efficiency of care. Office: New York State Dept Health Corning Tower Empire State Plz Albany NY 12237 *

SHAH, PREDIMAN K., cardiologist, educator; MBBS, Govt. Med Coll. Srinagar, India, 1969. Diplomate Am. Bd. Internal Medicine. Intern, cardiology Mt. Sinai Hosp., Milw., 1971-72; resident All India Inst. Med. Scis., New Delhi, 1970-71, Montefiore Hosp., NYC, 1973-74, fellow cardiology, 1974-76; hosp. apptd. Cedar Sinai Med. Ctr., LA, dir., divsn. cardiology, dir., Atherosclerosis Rsch. Ctr., Shapell and Webb Family Endowed Chair, Cardiology; prof. medicine UCLA Sch. Medicine; dir. Cardiology & Atherosclerosis Rsch. Ctr., Cedars Sinai Heart Inst. Mem. scientific adv. bd. Larry King Cardiac Found.; nat. chmn. Entertainment Industry Found. Nat. Cardiovascular Rsch. Initiative, 2001—; vis. prof. Cleveland Clinic, Mayo Clinic, Tex. Heart Inst., U. Utah, U. Va., U. Calif., San Diego, U. Calif., San Francisco, U. Tex. Galveston Med. Branch, U. San Antonio & Mass. Gen. Hosp. Harvard Med. Sch.; Fullbright vis. prof. to Japan, Argentina, Chile and Taiwan; spkr. in field. Contbr. scientific papers; mem. editl. bd. Circulation, Am. Jour. Cardiology, Internat. Jour. Heart Failure, Indian Heart Jour., Jour. Preventative Cardiology, Reviews in Cardiovascular Medicine, Current Cardiology Reports, Jour., Jour. Am. Coll. Cardiology, Arteriosclerosis, Thrombosis and Vascular Biology, Cardiovascular Pharmacology &Therapeutics. Recipient Medicine award, Ceders-Sinai, 2007, Herrick award, Am. Heart Assn., 2008, Leadership, 2008; named one of Top Cardiovascular Specialist, Am. Health Mag. Fellow Am. Coll. Cardiology (mem. of several committees including Ann. Scientific Program Com., chairperson Clin. Cardiology Spotlight Program (ClinCard), ACP, Coll. Chest Physicians; mem. Am. Heart Assn. (vol., chmn. ednl. task force, LA bd., mem. Western Regional Bd., pres. LA chpt. 2001-2002 (Lifetime Achievement award, 2002, mem. rsch. com., chmn. fall symposium, mem. Young Investigators Award Group, mem. Western Regional Peer-Review Group), European Acad. Scis. Office: Cedars-Sinai Med Ctr 8700 Beverly Blvd Rm 5531 Los Angeles CA 90048-1865 Office Phone: 310-423-3884. Office Fax: 310-423-0144. Business E-Mail: shahp@cshs.org.

SHAH, RAHUL K., surgeon, researcher; b. Jackson, Mich., Feb. 14, 1975; s. Kanaiyalal R. and Dakshaben K. Shah; m. Banu Abbas Karimi, June 3, 2000; children: Nishrin R., Amir R. BA, Boston U., MD, 2000. Diplomate Am. Bd. Otolaryngology, 2006. Surg. intern St. Elizabeth Med. Ctr., Boston, 2000—01; otolaryngology resident Tufts-NEMC, Boston, 2001—05, adminstrv. chief resident, 2004—05; fellow in pediatric otolaryngology Children's Hosp., Boston, 2005—06; asst. prof. otolaryngology/pediat. Children's Nat. Med. Ctr., George Washington U. Sch. Medicine, Washington, 2006—, assoc. prof., 2011—, med. dir., peri-operative svcs. Mem. peri-operative task force and co-chair standardization com. Children's Nat. Med. Ctr., Washington, 2007—, pres. elect, med. staff; others; cons. in field. Contbr. articles to profl. jours. Fellow: ACS, Triologic Soc., Am. Acad. Otolaryngology; mem.: Phi Beta Kappa, Alpha Omega Alpha. Office: Childrens Nat Med Ctr Divsn Otolaryngology 111 Michigan Ave NW Washington DC 20010 Office Phone: 202-476-3852.

SHAH, RAJAL B., pathologist; arrived in U.S., 1995; s. Bipin S. and Sharmishtha Shah; m. Ami R. Patel, June 15, 1995; children: Ansh R., Alay R. MD, Gujarat U., Ahmedabad, Gujarat, India, 1989. Bd. cert. in anatomic and clin. pathology Am. Bd. Pathology, 2000. Resident physician dept. pathology Gujarat Cancer and Rsch. Inst., India, 1989—93, lectr. Ahmedabad, 1993—95; resident anatomic and clin. pathology St. John Hosp. and Med. Ctr., Detroit, 1995—99; fellow genitourinary/surg. pathology dept. pathology U. Mich., Ann Arbor, 1999—2001, asst. prof. pathology and urology, 2001—07, assoc. prof. pathology and urology, 2007—09; dirs., urologic pathology Caris Life Scis., Dallas, 2010—. Prin. investigator and dir. Specialized Program of Rsch. Excellence in Prostate Cancer, Tissue Core Program U. Mich., Ann Arbor, 2004—. Contbr. articles to profl. jours. Grantee Specialized Program Rsch. Excellence in Prostate Cancer, Nat. Cancer Inst., 2003—09. Fellow: Am. Coll. Pathologist; mem.: Am. Urology Assn., U.S. and Can. Acad. Pathology. Home: 1812 Kings Isle Dr Plano TX 75093-2422 Office Fax: 214-596-2274. Business E-Mail: rshah@carisls.com.

SHAH, RAJESH PRAVINCHAND, cardiologist, consultant, medical researcher; b. Georgetown, Penang, Malaysia, Dec. 7, 1964; s. Pravinchand Punamchand and Jeet Pravinchand Shah; m. Jagruti Bhaskerrai Upadhyaya, Aug. 30, 1994; children: Prathik Rajesh, Sonya Rajesh. MBBS, Nat. U. Singapore, 1989, M of Medicine in Internal Medicine, 1994; academician, Acad. Medicine Malaysia, 1997. Med. officer Ministry of Health, Singapore, 1989—93; registrar in cardiology Nat. Heart Ctr., Singapore, 1993—96; specialist in cardiology Penang Gen. Hosp., Malaysia, 1996—99; lectr. in cardiology Penang Med. Coll., 1999—; cons. cardiologist Gleneagles Med. Ctr., Penang, 1999—. Prin. investigator Ontarget/Transcend Multicentre Trial, Penang, 2002—; mem. Joint Penang Ind. Ethics Com., Malaysia, 2003. Dir.: (plays) The Teahouse of the August Moon, 1987. Active Nat. Heart Assn., Kuala Lumpur, Malaysia, 1998—; med. cons. Temple Fine Arts Charity Med. Clinic, Penang, 2005—. Fellow: Nat. Heart Assn. Malaysia, Am. Coll. Cardiology, Acad. Medicine Singapore, European Soc. Cardiology, Royal Coll. Physicians Edinburgh; mem.: Penang Med. Practitioners' Soc. (mem. exec. com. 2000—), Malaysian Med. Assn. (life), Alumni Assn. KE VII Coll. Medicine (pres. 2005—06), Old Frees' Assn. (life), Masons (master mason 2003). Avocations: music, travel, computers, swimming. Office: Gleneagles Med Ctr Jalan Pangkor 1 10050 Penang Malaysia Personal E-mail: dr_rajesh_shah@hotmail.com.

SHAH, SAPNA RATAN, engineering educator; b. Kanpur, India, July 1, 1980; PhD, Harcourt Butler Technol. Inst., 2000. Asst. prof. Harcourt Butler Technol. Inst., 2004—. Office: Harcourt Butler Technological Inst Nabawganj Kanpur Uttar Pradesh 208002 India Office Fax: 0512-2533812. Personal E-mail: sapnasingh1980jan@rediffmail.com.

SHAH, SHIRISH ANANTLAL, pharmacist; b. Bombay, Apr. 26, 1938; s. Anantlal T. and Lilavati A. (Choksi) Shah; m. Portia Rose Dahling, Apr. 30, 1966; children: Sanjay, Kishan, Kinnari. BS in Pharmacy, U. Bombay, 1961; MS, U. Conn., Storrs, 1964; PhD, U. Iowa, Iowa City, 1975. Scientist product devel. Armour Pharm. Co., Kankakee, Ill., 1963-69; head pharm. product devel. sect. Pennwalt Corp., Rochester, NY, 1969-72; sr. pharm. scientist USV Pharm. Corp., Tuckahoe, NY, 1975-76; asst. mgr. pharm. rsch. Johnson & Johnson Baby Products Co., Piscataway, NJ, 1976-79; dir. rsch. and tech. svcs. Zenith Labs., Inc., Northvale, NJ, 1979-85; v.p. devel. and tech. affairs Lemmon Co., Sellersville, Pa., 1985-87; dir. product devel. Ciba Consumer Pharm., Edison, NJ, 1988-89; mgr. R & D DuPont Pharm., Garden City, NY, 1990-91; mgr. new product devel. Perrigo Co., Allegan, Mich., 1992—2001; v.p. sci. affairs Paddock Labs, Inc., Mpls., 2002; dir. R & D Allergan, Inc., Irvine, Calif., 2002—03; exec. dir. R & D Watson Pharm., Corona, Calif., 2003—05; dir. formulation sci. ICON Devel. Solutions, Redwood City, Calif., 2006—. Mem.: Am. Assn. Pharm. Scientists, Am. Pharm. Assn., Drug Info. Assn., Am. Chem. Soc., Masons, Rho Chi, Phi Lamda Upsilon. Hindu. Office: 555 Twin Dolphin Dr Redwood City CA 94065 Home: 2814 W Wildwood Dr Phoenix AZ 85045 Home Phone: 480-659-8964; Office Phone: 480-659-8963. Personal E-mail: shirishashah@msn.com. Business E-Mail: shirish.shah@iconplc.com.

SHAH, SHIRISH KALYANBHAI, computer science, chemistry and environmental science educator; b. Ahmedabad, India, May 24, 1942; came to U.S., 1962, naturalized, 1974; s. Kayyanbhai T. and Sushilaben K. S.; m. Kathleen Long, June 28, 1973 (dec. July 31, 2007); 1 son, Lawrence. BS in Chemistry and Physics, St. Xavier's Coll. Gujarat U., 1962; PhD in Phys. Chemistry, U. Del., 1968; cert. in bus. mgmt., U. Va., 1986; PhD in Cultural Edn. (hon.), World U. West, 1986. Asst. prof. Washington Coll., Chestertown, Md., 1967-68; dir. quality control Vita Foods, Chestertown, Md., 1968-72; asst. prof., assoc. prof. sci., adminstr. food, marine sci. and vocat. programs Chesapeake Coll., Wye Mills, Md., 1968-76; rsch. grant Food Tech. Program, 1973—75; assoc. prof., prof. sci., chmn. dept. tech. studies CC Balt., 1976—91; assoc. prof. chemistry Coll. Notre Dame Md., 1991—2002. Cons. joint apprentice com. Balt. City Govt., 1980-91; chmn. computer sys. and engring. techs. CC Balt., 1979-89, project facilitator telecom. curriculum and lab., 1985-89, coord. tech. studies, 1989-91; mem. Balt. City Adult Edn. Adv. Com., 1982-89, Distance Learning Task Force, 1996-97, chmn. Coll. wide computer user com., 1985-91; higher edn. eval. team Mid. Atlantic States Assn., 1987-2008; adj. prof. Phys. Sci. Coppin State Coll., 1996-98; coun. mem. Faculty R&D, 1994-97; reviewer AAAS, 1996-2005, NIH Edn. grant, 2000-02; adj. prof. chemistry Villa Julie Coll., 2002-05; lectr., prof. chemistry Towson U., 1998—, FYE advisor, 1999-, Morgan State U., 1999—. Contbr. numerous sci. projects, articles to profl. jours. Permanent mem. Rep. Senatorial Com.; charter mem. Rep. Presdl. Task Force; mem. Congl. Adv. Com., 1983—; tchr., developer prison programs Patuxent Inst., Jessup, Md., 1982-91; developer joint program for computer aided design between Coll. and HS, 1989-91; adviser Young Reps., 1992-2002; vol. Gilchrist Hospice Ctr., 2008-. Recipient award, Am. Chem. Soc., 2007, Nat. award, 2009, Pub. Rels. award, 2009, Gold medal, St Johns Coll., Cambridge, Eng., 2010, Silver medal, WISDOM, Cambridge, Eng., Lifetime Achievement award, Calif. Conf.; Comm. grant, Mayor's Manpower Office for release of prisoners, 1980—81, Md. Dept. Transp. grant, 1981—82. Fellow Am. Inst. Chemists (co-chair internat. com. 2002); mem. IEEE, APHA, NSTA, Am. Lung Assn. (chair environ. affairs com., 1976-80), Am. Lung Assn. Md. (bd. dir. 1971-80), Am. Chem. Soc. (chmn.-elect Md. sect. 1995-96, chmn. 1996-98, chair kids and chemistry program Md. sect. 1996-99, sec. Mid-Atlantic regional conf., 2002-04, chmn. com. govt. rels. Md. sect. 1998-, chair pub. rels. com. 2000-, pres.-elect Chesapeake sect. 2002-03, 2010, co-coord. chemagination program 2005, pub. rels. mem. 2009, Phoenix award 1996-97, Pub. Rels. award, 1996, Sci. Policy award, 2000, Salute to Excellence award, 2004, Outstanding Coord. Chemagination, 2005), Indsl. Hygiene Assn. (pres. Chesapeake sect. 2003-04, 10-), Nat. Environ. Tng. Assn., Nat. Assn. Indsl. Tech. (dir. local region, bd. dir. 1989 95), Md. Pub. Health Assn. (bd. dir., chair pub. health nursing edn. 2005), Am. Vocat. Assn., Am. Tech. Edn. Assn., Am. Fedn. Tchrs., Md. State Tchrs. Assn., Md. Assn. Cmty. and Jr. Colls. (v.p. 1977-78, pres. 1978-97), Moose Lodge, Pub. Relations Nat. Am. Chem. Soc., Sigma Xi, Epsilon Pi Tau, Iota Lambda Sigma Nu. Roman Catholic. Avocations: racquetball, tennis, bowling. Home: 5605 Purlington Way Baltimore MD 21212-2950 Office: Chemistry Dept Towson University Towson MD 21252- Office Phone: 410-704-2720. Personal E-mail: dr.shah@juno.com. Business E-Mail: sshah@towson.edu.

SHAH, SIDDHARTH ASHVIN, preventive medicine physician; b. Houston, July 12, 1972; s. Ashvin and Hema Shah; m. Nisha Gautam. BA in Religious Studies, cum laude, Rice U., Houston, 1994; MD, Baylor Coll. Medicine, Houston, 2000; MPH, Mt. Sinai Sch. Medicine, NYC, 2003. Diplomate American Bd. Preventive Medicine, lic. NY, DC. Intern psychiatry Menninger Sch. Psychiatry, Topeka, 2000—01; resident preventive & behavioral medicine Mt. Sinai Sch. Medicine, 2001—03, clin. instr., 2003—, founder, exec. dir. Psychosocial Assistance Without Borders, 2001—07; founder, med. dir. Greenleaf Integrative Strategies LLC, Washington, 2002—. Psychosocial cons., mind/body medicine practitioner Olive Leaf Wholeness Ctr., NYC, 2004—05; program dir. preventive medicine, attending physician family medicine Wyckoff Heights Med. Ctr., Bklyn., 2004—06; med. staff, group leader Ctr. Integrative Medicine, Washington, 2006—08. Narrator numerous guided meditation/yoga albums dealing with sleep aid and stress management; contbr. articles to profl. jours. Mem.: Mid-Atlantic Group Psychotherapy Soc., American Group Psychotherapy Assn. Achievements include provided specialized psychosocial trauma services to multiple ethnic communities affected by hate crimes and bigotry perpetrated by people looking for revenge against innocents after the 9/11 terrorist attacks; traveled to Gujarat, India to provide psychosocial training and vicarious trauma prevention to workers in different humanitarian organizations; in 2004, traveled to tsunami-affected Nagapattinam district in South India where he gave educational programs on vicarious trauma prevention to workers who were working with human remains, family reunion and survivor rehabilitation; after Hurricanes Katrina and Rita, traveled to the Gulf Coast to consult to fire fighters and rescue personnel on operational stress and vicarious trauma; traveled to South Asia in 2006 to give tsunami relief workers a program in self-care. E-mail: drshah@greenleaf-is.com. *

SHAH, SUNIL, surgeon, educator; b. Nairobi, Kenya, Feb. 23, 1963; s. Jitendra and Rama Shah; m. Anne Cole; children: Ruan Jon, Tia Alissa, Camrun Jay Shah. MBBS, Haberdashers' Aske's, Elstree, Hertfordshire, Eng., 1981, FRCophth. Cons. ophthalmic surgeon Birmingham & Midland Eye Ctr., England, 2000—, Midland Eye Inst., Solihull, England, 2004—; prof. Aston U., Birmingham, 2007—, U. Ulster, Belfast, England, 2007—. Dir. & coun. mem. Brit. Contact Lens Assn., London, 2004—; dir. Midland Eye Inst., Solihull, 2004—10, Laser & Lens Network, Birmingham, 2008—. Fellow: RCS (Edinburgh), Royal Coll. Ophthalmologists (refractive surgery working party 2003—09); mem.: Ophthalmology Times (editl. bd. 2007—09), Contact Lens and Anterior Eye (editl. bd. 2007—09), Clin. & Exptl. Ophthalmology (sect. editor 2005—09), Brit. Jour. Ophthalmology (sect. editor 2007—), Brit. Med. Assn. Achievements include research in accuracy of refractive surgery; patents pending for treatment of infections; highly respected corneal and refractive surgeon internationally. Office: Laser & Lens Network 6 Bow St Birmingham West Midlands B1 1DW England Business E-Mail: info@laserandlens.com.

SHAH, UDAYAN KANAIYALAL, surgeon; b. Lexington, Va., Mar. 6, 1968; s. Kanaiyalal Ramanlal and Daksha Kanaiyalal Shah; m. Barbara Ziv; children: Henry S.U., Silas L.U. MD, Boston U. Sch. Medicine, 1992. Cert. Am. Bd. Otolaryngology-Head & Neck Surgery, 1998. Attending surgeon Children's Hosp. Phila. & U. Pa. Sch. Medicine, 1998—2007; attending surgeon, dir., of fellow resident edn. Nemous Alfred I duPont Hosp. for Children & Thomas Jefferson U. Sch. Medicine, Wilmington, Del., 2007—, assoc. prof., 2007—; chair Medical Devices Drugs Com., Am. Acad. Otolaryngology. Author: sci. papers in field; editor: Tonsil and Adenoid Techniques. Treas. Soc. Ear, Nose and Throat Advances in Children, 2004—11, pres.-elect, 2011. Fellow: ACS, Am. Soc. Pediatric Otolaryngology; mem.: Am. Soc. Pediat. (chair fin. com.), Am. Acad. Pediatrics. Office: Alfred I duPont Hosp for Children Divsn Otolaryngology 1600 Rockland Rd Wilmington DE 19803 Office Phone: 302-651-5895. Business E-Mail: ushah@nemours.org.

SHAH, VIRAL N., endocrinologist; b. India, July 11, 1980; MD, Postgrad. Inst. Med. Edn. and Rsch., 2007. Physician, clin. fellow Postgrad. Inst. Med. Edn. and Rsch., 2009—. Avocation: reading. Office: Postgrad Inst Med Education and Research Dept Endocrinology Sector 12 Chandigarh 160012 India Business E-Mail: viralshah_rational@yahoo.co.in.

SHAHABI, SHOHREH, gynecologist, researcher; b. Kerman, Iran, May 31, 1961; d. Fakhrolmolouk Adhami and Ali Mohammad Shahabi; m. Taghi Makani, Aug. 26, 1979; 1 child, Anais Rameau. MD magna cum laude, U. Brussels, Belgium, 1992; Univ. Diploma in Maternal Fetal Medicine, U. of Paris V, René Descartes., 1993; Univ. Diploma in Ultrasound, U. of Paris V, René Descartes, 1995, Univ. Diploma in Breast Disease, 1996. Diplomate Am. Bd. Ob-Gyn., ob-gyn. bd. cert. Belgium, 1997, France, 1998. Assoc. rsch. scientist, specialist in ob-gyn. Yale Sch. of Medicine, New Haven, 1999—2003; instr. in ob-gyn. Albert Einstein Sch. of Medicine, Bronx, NY, 2003—, fellow in gynecologic oncology., 2003—. Postdoctoral rsch. fellow Yale Sch. of Medicine, New Haven, 1998—99. Contbr. articles to profl. jours. (Akzo-Nobel Rsch. Award for outstanding rsch., 2003, award Am. Assn. for Clin. Chemistry, 1999). Mem.: AMA (assoc.), French Soc. Sonography (assoc.), AIUM (assoc.), Belgian Gynecol. Soc. (assoc.), French Soc. Colposcopy (assoc.), Am. Assn. Ob-Gyn. (assoc.; associated mem. 1999—2003). Achievements include research in forefront of laboratory science and clinical practice involved in the explanation of false positive hCG; establishing the importance of hyperglycosylated hCG as a very specific marker in choriocarcinoma; immunology of ovarian cancer; microtubule stabilizing agents; use of doppler imaging in different gynecological oncologic complications; phenoxodiol a novel drug which induces FLIP/XIAP function in chemoresistant ovarian cancer through fas- mediated apoptosis. Office: Albert Einstein Sch Medicine Dept Ob/Gyn 300 Morris Park Ave Bronx NY 10461 Home: 350 W 42nd St Apt 51c New York NY 10036-6962 Personal E-mail: shohreh_shahabi@yahoo.com.

SHAHAPUR, PRAVEEN RAJASHEKHAR, medical educator; b. Bijapur, July 15, 1971; MBBS, Blde Med. Coll., 1995; MD, Manipal Acad. Higher Edn., 2003. Asst. prof. Blde Shri B. M. Patil Med. Coll. Bijapur, 2003—08, assoc. prof., cons., 2008—. Bd. fellowship, Hiv Medicine. Mem.: Blde Assn. Bijapur, Indian Redcross Soc., Hosp. Infection Soc. India, Indian Assn. Med. Microbiology. Avocations: movies, reading, travel. Home: Beside Naveen Diamontiles Opp ITI Coll Bijapur Karnataka 586103 India Personal E-mail: drprshahapur@gmail.com.

SHAHEEN, NICHOLAS J., epidemiologist, educator; Grad., Harvard U.; MD, U. Chgo. Pritzker Sch. Medicine; MPH, U. NC Sch. Pub. Health. Fellow in epidemiology Nat. Inst. Health; assoc. prof. medicine & epidemiology U. NC Sch. Medicine, dir. Ctr. for Esophageal Diseases & Swallowing. Fellow: Am. Coll. Physicians, Am. Coll. Gastroenterology, Am. Gastroenterological Assn.; mem.: NC Med. Soc., Am. Med. Soc., Am. Soc. Gastrointestinal Endoscopy. Office: University of North Carolina Center for Functional GI Bioinformatics Bldg CB #7080 Chapel Hill NC 27599-7080

SHAHI, KEDAR SINGH, surgeon; b. Uttarakhand, India, Mar. 25, 1971; MBBS, BRD Med. Coll. Gorakhpur, 1995; MS, King George Med. Coll. Lucknow, 2000. Chief resident paediat. surgery King George Med. Coll., 2000—02; sr. resident MCKR Hosp., Delhi, 2002—03; sr. resident plastic surgery MAMC and Lok Nayak Hosp., 2003—04; assoc. prof. Govt. Med. Coll. Haldwani, 2004—. Recipient Chikitsa Ratan, India Internat. Soc. Fellow: Assn. Indian Surgeons, Internat. Coll. Surgeons; mem.: Indian Assn. Gastrointestinal Endoscopic Surgeons, Assn. Surgeons India, Indian Med. Assn. Avocations: painting, writing, photography. Home: Rampur Rd N Manpur Haldwani Uttarakhand 263139 India Home Fax: 91234423. Personal E-mail: kedar_shahi@rediffmail.com.

SHAHIDULLAH, MOHAMMAD, medical researcher, educator; b. Village Ruhuli, Bangladesh, Nov. 1, 1959; s. Akkel Ali Mondal and Saleha Khatun; m. Sadequn Nahar, Aug. 19, 1988; children: Asif, Archie. PhD, U. Glasgow, 1994; DVM, Bangladesh Agrl. U., 1982. Lectr. pharmacology Bangladesh Agrl. U., Mymensingh, 1983—87, asst. prof., 1987—94; postdoctoral rsch. fellow U. Glasgow, 1994—2001; rsch. fellow, lectr. Hong Kong Poly. U., Kowloon, 2001—05; asst. prof. U. Louisville, 2005—06, U. Ariz., 2006—. Contbr. articles to profl. jours. Recipient U. Prize, Bangladesh Agrl. U., 1985, Rsch. Louisville award, 2005; Merit scholar, Dhaka Edn. Bd., Bangladesh, 1975, Bangladesh Agrl. U., 1977—83, Commonwealth scholar, Assn. Commonwealth Univs. UK, 1990. Mem.: Am. Physiol. Soc., Internat. Soc. Eye Rsch., Fedn. U. Tchrs. Bangladesh, Assn. U. Tchrs. UK, Assn. Rsch. Vision and Ophthalmology. Achievements include development of isolated eye preparation as an experiemtal model for diverse ocular research; in vitro eye model to study retinal physiology using multifocal electroretinogram; discovery of link between intracellular calcium movement and aqueous humor formation; first to show in the isolated whole eye preparation that chloride ion is involved in the secretion of eye's aqueous humor; development of novel method of isolating and culturing ocular nonpigmented ciliary epithelial cells. Office: U Ariz Dept Physiology Tucson AZ 85724 Office Phone: 520-626-7351. Office Fax: 620-626-2382. Business E-Mail: shahidua@email.arizona.edu.

SHAHIN, EMAN SALEH, nursing educator; b. Egypt, Mar. 9, 1973; B in Nursing, 1996; PhD, Ctr. Humanities and Health Scis., 2008. Lectr. Faculty Nursing Port Said U., 2008—. Fellowship, Ministry of Egypt Edn. Avocations: reading, cooking. Office: Oraby and Elethad St Port Said 0020 Egypt Business E-Mail: eman.shahin@nur.psu.edu.eg.

SHAHSUVARYAN, MARIANNE LEVON, ophthalmologist, surgeon, researcher, educator; d. Levon Vaghinak Shahsuvaryan and Svetlana Alexander Bakhshinova. Diploma in medicine with honors, Yerevan State Med. U., 1989; PhD, 1996, DSc, 2003. Cert. in specialization in ophthalmology Ctrl. Physicians Advancing Tng. Inst., Russia, 1991. Gen. ophthalmologist Ophthalmologic Ctr., Yerevan, 1991—, dir. med. edn. tng., 2004—; prof. ophthalmology Yerevan State Med. U., 2005—. Author: Comprehensive Eye Examination, Eye Diseases, Essentials of Ophthalmology, Red Eye: Telling the Truth about a Danger, Handbook of Practical Ophthalmology, Emergency in Ophthalmology, The Red Eye: Telling the Truth About A Danger; contbr. articles to profl. jours. Recipient award Cert. for the paper presented at the Young Medic's Second Internat. Conf., Armenian Med. Assn., 2003; fellow, Moorfield's Eye Hosp., London, 2000, Dept. Ophthalmology, Leuven U., Belgium, 2000. Fellow: Armenian Med. Assn., Armenian Ophthalmologic Assn. Avocations: knitting, billiards. Personal E-mail: mar_shah@hotmail.com.

SHAHWAN-AKL, LINA JOSEPH, nursing educator; b. Beirut, July 31, 1954; d. Joseph Hanna and May Amin (Doumit) Shahwan; m. Fouad Antoine Akl; 1 child, Christian Antoine. BS, Am. Univ., Beirut, 1977; MS, Boston U., 1983; PhD, Victoria U., Australia, 2002. RN. Staff nurse Am. U. Med. Ctr., Beirut, 1977-79; instr. Am. U. Beirut, 1979-81, asst. prof., 1983-87; sr. lectr. Phillip Inst. Technology, Melbourne, Australia, 1987-89, prin. lectr., 1989-91; assoc. prof. Royal Melbourne Inst. Tecch., 1991—. Cons. Maternal Child Health Svcs., Melbourne, 1989-93, Maternal Child Telephone Svcs., 1991-92. Author/presenter health program series on SBS radio in Arabic lang., 1988-89. Named Nurse of Yr. for vol. work with vaccination of children in Palestinian camps in Lebanon, Internat. Coun. of Nurses, 1982. Christian Maronite. Avocations: reading, walking, swimming, music, cooking. Home: 1 North Ave Victoria Bulleen 3105 Australia Office: Royal Melbourne Inst Tech Plenty Rd Bundoora Vic 3083 Australia Business E-Mail: lina.shahwan-akl@rmit.edu.au.

SHAI, SEN-EI (SHENG-YI HSIEH), thoracic surgeon, researcher; b. Taipei, Taiwan, Dec. 26, 1961; s. Chih-San Hsieh and Shou-Fun Chen; m. Ching-Jung Yang; children: Chi-Chen Hsieh, Chi-Wei Hsieh. MD, Nat. Def. Med. Ctr., Taipei, 1988. Cert. Bd. Thoracic and Cardiovasc. Surgery, Bd. Chinese Surg. Assn., Bd. Chinese Chest and Critical Care Medicine Assn., Bd. Surg. Soc. Gastroenterology, Bd. Endoscopic Surgery Assn. Resident in surgery Taipei Vet. Gen. Hosp., 1988—93, attending surgeon thoracic surgery, 1993—94; chief gen. surgery Chia-I Vet. Gen. Hosp., Taiwan, 1994—96; attending surgeon thoracic divsn. Taichung Vet. Gen. Hosp., Taiwan, 1996—; rsch. fellow thoracic divsn. Mass. Gen. Hosp., Boston, 1998—99. Avocation: Swimming,reading. Home: Shi-Tun Rd Sec 3 No 303-3 2F-1 Taichung 407 Taiwan Office: Taichung Vet Gen Hosp 160 Sec 3 Taichung Kang Rd Taichung 407 Taiwan Home Phone: 886-4-24620593; Office Phone: 886-4-23592525 ext 5050. Office Fax: 886-4-23599715; Home Fax: 886-4-24619383. Personal E-mail: sse50@yahoo.com.

SHAIB, YASSER HANI, gastroenterologist, educator; b. Beirut, Feb. 20, 1971; MD, Am. U. Beirut, 1995; MPH, U. N.Mex., 2002. Chief endoscopy, Michael E. DeBakey Va. Med. Ctr. Baylor Coll. Medicine, 2010—, assoc. prof. medicine, 2010—. Recipient Spl. Contbn. award, Michael E. DeBakey Va. Med. Ctr. Fellow: Am. Soc. Gastrointestinal Endoscopy. Avocations: bicycling, soccer. Home: 2131 Mcclendon St Houston TX 77030 Business E-Mail: yshaib@bcm.edu.

SHAIBANI, AZIZ, neurologist, director; b. Baquba, Iraq, Jan. 14, 1959; MD, Mosul Med. Coll., 1993. Dir. Nerve and Muscle Ctr. Tex., 1998—. Office: 6624 Fannin St # 1670 Houston TX 77030 Personal E-mail: ataher@aol.com.

SHAIKH, BAHU SULTAN, physician, educator; b. Karachi, Sind, Pakistan, 1945; came to US, 1969; s. Noor Mohammad and Shahkhatoon Shaikh.; m. Yasmeen Khamisani, 1972 (div. Nov. 1995); children: Maheen, Sasha Ghulam Mohammad; m. Mona Sayed, July 1996; 1 child: Aneesa. Student, St. Patrick's Coll., Karachi, Pakistan, 1963; MBBS, Dow Med. Coll., Karachi, 1968. Intern Ellis Hosp., Schenectady, NY, 1969; resident in internal medicine Thomas Jefferson U., Phila., 1970-72, rsch. fellow, 1972-74; asst. prof. coll. medicine Penn State U., Hershey, Pa., 1974-80; assoc. prof. Med. Coll. Ohio, Toledo, 1980-87, clin. assoc. prof., 1987—99, clin. prof., 1999—. Cons. Toledo Clinic, Ohio, 1987—. Contbr. several chpts. in books related to cancer and AIDS, 1983-87, numerous articles to prof. jours. Recipient Key to the Golden Door award, Internat. Inst. Greater Toledo, 1999. Fellow. ACP, Pakistan Acad. Med. Scis.; mem. Am. Soc. Clin. Oncology, Am. Soc. Hematology, Assn. Internat. Physicians of NW Ohio,, Assn. Pakistani Physicians N.Am. Office: Toledo Clinic 4235 Secor Rd Toledo OH 43623-4299

SHAIN-ALVARO, JUDITH CAROL, physician assistant; b. Bronx, NY, Aug. 13, 1953; d. Frank and Pearl (Crausman) Shain; m. Virgilio S. Alvaro, May 13, 1990; 1 child, Jessica Blaire. BS in Biology, Fairleigh Dickinson U., 1975; BS, Physician Asst. Cert., Baylor Coll. Medicine, Houston, 1978. Lic. physician asst., N.Y., N.J.; BLS, ACLS, Am. Heart Assn. Postgrad. surg. residency program for physician assts. Montefiore Med. Ctr. and Albert Einstein Coll. Medicine, Bronx, NY, 1979—81; physician asst. dept. cardiothoracic surgery North Shore U. Hosp., Manhasset, N.Y., 1981-84; lic. med. officer Passenger Cruise Ships, Miami, Fla., 1984-88; med. cons. The Floating Hosp., Bankers Trust Co., NYC, 1988-89; sr. physician asst. pers. health svcs. St. Vincent's Hosp. and Med. Ctr., NYC, 1990—93; sr. physician asst. N.J. Med. Sch. Nat. Tuberculosis Ctr., 1993—2001, Pa. Orthop. Surgery, St. Michael's Med. Ctr., Newark, 2011—. Faculty NJ Aids Edn. Tng. Ctr., physician asst. rep. to NJ AIDS Edn. Tng. Ctr., 1995-01; mem. Nat. Physician Asst. Working Group to Nat. AIDS Edn. Tng. Ctr., 1995-01; physician asst. Interventional Radiology, U. Radiology Group, East Brunswick, NJ, 2007-08, St. Vincent's Cath. Med. Ctr., 2009-10; clin. advanced physician asst. orthop. oncology surgery Mt. Sinai Med. Ctr., NYC, 2010-; lectr. in field. Trustee Sisterhood Congregation B'nai Israel, Congregation B'nai Israel; mayoral appointee Fair Lawn Boro Coun. Planning Bd. Adv. Com. Broadway Redevel., 1999-01; vol. Capital Fundraising, Devel. Dept. Solomon Schechter Day Sch., New Milford, NJ, 2000-08; trustee Sisterhood Fair Lawn Jewish Ctr., 2007-08; capital fundraiser Frisch Sch., 2008-, bd. trustees, Frisch Parent Asson., 2010-. Fellow Am. Acad. Physician Assts., N.J. State Soc. Physician Assts.; mem. Filipino Am. Assn. Fair Lawn. Avocations: travel, theater, reading.

SHAKED, ABRAHAM, surgeon, educator; MD, Hebrew U. Jerusalem, 1982; PhD, City U. of NY, 1989. Diplomate Am. Bd. Surgery-gen. surgery, 1989, cert. transplantation surgery 1991. Resident Mt. Sinai Hosp.; fellow Univ. Calif.; chief divsn. of transplant surgery Hosp. of the Univ. of Pa., dir. penn transplant inst.; prof. surgery Univ. Pa. Sch. of Medicine. Named Top Docs, Phila. Mag., 2002, 2010, 2011; named one of Best Doctors in America, 2005—06, 2007—08, 2009—10. Mem.: ACS, Am. Assn. for the Study of Liver Diseases, Soc. of Univ. Surgeons, Am. Soc. of Transplant Surgeons (pres.). Office: Hospital of the University of Pennsylvania 3400 Spruce St 2 Dulles Philadelphia PA 19104 Office Phone: 215-662-6723. Office Fax: 215-662-2244.

SHAKED, YUVAL, medical educator; b. Israel, Mar. 12, 1973; PhD, Hebrew U., 2004. Asst. prof. to sr. lectr. Israel Inst. Tech.-Technion., 2008—. Grant, Israel Ministry Health, Israel Cancer Rsch. Found., Israel Cancer Assn. Office: Efron 1 Haifa 31096 Israel Business E-Mail: yshaked@tx.technion.ac.il.

SHAKESPEARE, THOMAS PHILIP, oncologist; b. Middlesex, Surrey, Eng., Aug. 5, 1967; arrived in Australia, 1969; s. Thomas Francis and Claudette Shakespeare (Stepmother), Senya Shakespeare; m. Lisa Belinda Coates; children: Thomas Jay, Zachary James. MB, BChir, U. Sydney, Australia, 1990, grad. diploma in medicine, 2000; MPH, U. NSW, Sydney, 2003. Sr. cons. radiation oncologist The Cancer Inst., Singapore, 2000—05; assoc. prof. Nat. U. Singapore, 2003—05; dir. cancer svcs. Tan Tock Seng Hosp., Singapore, 2003—05; dir. area cancer svcs. North Coast Area Health Svc., Coffs Harbour, NSW, Australia, 2005—, sr. cons. radiation oncologist, 2005—; conjoint assoc. prof. U. NSW, Sydney, 2005—. Dir. PRIMER Collaboration, Sydney, 2004—; auditor radiation oncology Victorian Dept. Health, Victoria, Australia, 2005—; auditor in radiation oncology Internat. AEC, Vienna, 2005—; mem. clin. svcs. adv. com. NSW Cancer Inst., Sydney, 2005—. Reviewer: Internat. Jour. Radiation Oncology, Biology, Physics; contbr. articles to profl. jours. Recipient Fellowship award, Human Manpower Devel. Project, Singapore, 2003. Fellow: Acad. Medicine Singapore, Royal Australian and New Zealand Coll. Radiologists (examiner, Novartis prize for rsch. 2001, 2002, Faculty Prize for rsch. 2004, C.E. Eddy prize 1996); mem.: Am. Soc. Therapeutic Radiology and Oncology (mem. health svcs. rsch. com. 2004—05). Office: North Coast Cancer Institute Coffs Harbour Health Campus Locked Bag Coffs Harbour NSW 2450 Australia Business E-Mail: tshakespeare@mncahs.health.nsw.gov.au.

SHAKIROV, ZAIR SAATOVICH, biologist, researcher; b. Tashkent, Uzbekistan, Nov. 1, 1955; s. Saat Shakirov and Muborak Bakhadirova; m. Akida Zakirovna Nazarova, Aug. 20, 1983; children: Sodiq Zairovich, Rustam Zairovich, Suhrob Zairovich. MSc in Biology, Tashkent State U., 1981; PhD, Uzbekistan Acad. Scis., Tashkent, 1989. Jr. rsch. scientist Inst. Microbiology Uzbekistan Acad. Scis., Tashkent, 1986—91, sr. rsch. scientist, 1991—2003, head lab., 2003—. Supr. PhD student Inst. Microbiology Uzbekistan Acad. Scis., Tashkent, 1993—96, Tashkent, 2001—06. Grantee, European Commn., 1998—2002, Cooperative Devel. Rsch., Ctrl. Asian Republics, US Agy. Internat. Devel., 1998—2002, 2003—07, Sci. Tech. Ctr. Ukraine Found., USDA, 2005—, 2006—. Fellow: Uzbekistan Soc. Biochemistry (assoc.), Uzbekistan Soc. Microbiology (assoc.); mem.: Internat. Union Microbiol. Socs. (assoc.). Pacific. Muslim. Achievements include research in structure and physical- chemical properties of glutamine synthetase of Ankistrodemus braunii; comparative analysis of nitrogen-fixators of Uzbekistan arid Yemen soils; bacteria of Azospirillum genus from salt-affected soils of Uzbekistan; biotechnology for the improved adaptation of leguminous trees to stress conditions; use of symbiotic biodiversity to enhance plant tolerance to environmental stresses; adaptation of Onobrychis, a salt and drought tolerant perennial legume grass species of Central Asia deserts, for crop production and to combat desertification. Avocations: singing, science, high technology, travel, computers. Office: Uzbekistan Acad Scis Inst Microbiology A Kadyri Build 7 B 100128 Tashkent Uzbekistan Home: Jangoh C-15 H-12a Flats 56-57 100128 Tashkent Uzbekistan Office Phone: 998 71 1427120. Office Fax: 998 71 1427129. Personal E-mail: zair@dostlink.net. Business E-Mail: info@microbio.uz.

SHAKNO, ROBERT JULIAN, hospital and social services administrator; b. Amsterdam, Holland, Aug. 15, 1937; came to U.S., 1939, naturalized, 1944; s. Rudy C. and Gertrude S.; m. Linda, June 10, 1962; children: Steven Lee, Deborah Sue. BBA (scholar 1955), So. Methodist U., 1959; M.H.A., Washington U., St. Louis, 1961. Adminstrv. asst. Mt. Sinai Hosp., Chgo., 1961—63; asso. adminstr. Tex. Inst. Rehab. and Research, Houston, 1963—65; asst. adminstr. Michael Reese Hosp., Chgo., 1965—70, v.p., hosp. dir., 1970—73; asso. exec. dir. Cook County Hosp., Chgo., 1973—75; pres. Hackensack Med. Center, NJ, 1975—85, Mt. Sinai Med. Ctr., Cleve., 1985—96; dir. nat. strategy practice KPMG Peat Marwick, 1996-98; v.p. med. affairs, vice dean sch. of medicine Case Western Res. U., 1998—2002; pres., CEO Jewish Family Svc., Cleve., 2002—05; ptnr. Tatum Ptnrs., LLC, Deerfield, Ill., 2005—; adv. bd. Med. Svcs. Co., Cleveland, Ohio, 2005; ptnr. exec. svc. corp., Chgo., 2007—. Bd. dirs. Ohio Hosp. Inc. Co. Mem. editorial bd. Mgmt. Series, Am. Coll. Healthcare Execs. Mem. Leadership Cleve.; bd. dirs. Premier Hosp. Alliance, chmn., 1994-96; bd. dirs. The New Cleve. Inc., Univ. Circle Inc., Cleve., Cleve. Sight Ctr.; trustee Hope Lodge, Cleve. chpt. Am. Cancer Soc.; chmn. elect, bd. dirs. Jewish Family Svcs.; chmn. social svcs. divsn. United Jewish Appeal, Cleve., 1987-88, chmn. health cabinet, 1990, gen. co-chmn., 1990—; chmn. Hosp. Pacesetter campaign United Way, chmn. health svcs. portfolio, 1988-89, oversight commn., 1992-93; bd. trustees Mount Sinai Health Sys., Chgo., 2006-. Served to 1st lt. USAR, 1960-66. Named Young Adminstr. of Yr., Washington U., 1968 Fellow Am. Coll. Hosp. Adminstrs.; mem. Am. Hosp. Assn. (coun. urban hosps., del. coun. on met. hosps., rep. regional policy bd.), Washington U. Alumni Assn. (past pres.), Greater Cleve. Hosp. Assn. (bd. dirs.), Ohio Hosp. Assn. (bd. dirs.), Cleve. Sight Ctr. (trustee, bd. dirs.), Sigma Alpha Mu (past pres.). Home: 908 Island Ct Deerfield IL 60015 Office Phone: 312-909-2022. Personal E-mail: lbs1shak@sbcglobal.net.

SHALAEV, SERGEY V., cardiologist, researcher; b. Omsk, Russia, Apr. 23, 1959; s. Vasilii E. Shalaev and Venera S. Shalaeva; m. Irina V. Medvedeva; 1 child, Vasilii S. MD, Tyumen Med. Inst., Russia, 1987; PhD, Tyumen Med. Inst., 1993. Rschr. All-Union Cardiology Ctr., Moscow, 1989—93; chief dept. urgent cardiology Tyumen Cardiology Ctr., 1993—2005; chief cardiology care dept. Regional Clin. Hosp., Tyumen, 2005—. Editor: Therapy, 1999; author: Acute Coronary Syndrome, 2005. Mem.: Russian Sci. Soc. Cardiology. Home: 84-45 Sovetskaya 625000 Tyumen Russia Office: Regional Clin Hospital ul Kotovskogo 55 625023 Tyumen Tyumyenskaya obl Russia E-mail: shalaev@tokb.ru.

SHALALA, DONNA EDNA, academic administrator, former United States Secretary of Health and Human Services; b. Cleve., Feb. 14, 1941; d. James Abraham and Edna (Smith) S. AB, Western Coll., 1962; MSSC, Syracuse U., 1968, PhD, 1970; 44 hon. degrees, 1976—2008. Vol. US Peace Corps, Iran, 1962-64; asst. prof. polit. sci. Bernard M. Baruch CUNY, 1970-72; assoc. prof., chair, program in politics & edn. Tchrs. Coll. Columbia U., 1972-79; asst. sec. for policy devel. & rsch. US Dept. Housing & Urban Devel. (HUD), Washington, 1977-80; prof. polit. sci., pres. Hunter Coll., CUNY, 1980-87; prof. polit. sci. & ednl. policy studies, chancellor U. Wis., Madison, 1987-93; sec. US Dept. Health & Human Services (HHS), Washington, 1993-2001; pres. U. Miami, 2001—, prof. polit. sci., 2001—, secondary faculty Dept. Epidemiology, 2002—. Dir., treas. Mcpl. Assistance Corp. NYC, 1975—77; vis. prof. Yale Law Sch., 1976; co-chair Pres. Commn. on Care for Am. Returning Wounded Warriors, 2007—; bd. dirs. Lennar Corp., 2001—, Gannett Co., Inc, 2001—, MEDNAX, Inc., 2010—. Author: Neighborhood Governance, 1971, The City and the Constitution, 1972, The Property Tax and the Voters, 1973, The Decentralization Approach, 1974. Mem. Trilateral Commn., 1988—92, Knight Commn. on Intercollegiate Sports, 1989—91, Homes for Working Families, 2004—08; bd. govs. American Stock Exch., 1981—87; trustee TIAA, 1985—89, Com. Econ. Devel., 1982—92, Brookings Inst., 1989—92, John F. Kennedy Ctr. for the Performing Arts, Washington, 1993—2001, Henry J. Kaiser Family Found., 2001—11; bd. dirs. Children's Def. Fund, 1980—93, American Ditchley Found., 1981—93, Spencer Found., 1988—92, M&I Bank of Madison, 1991—92, NCAA Found., 1991, Inst. Internat. Econs., 1981—, Gannett Co., Inc., McLean, Va., 2001—, Michael J. Fox Found. for Parkinson's Rsch., 2001—08, United Health Group, Inc., Mpls., 2001—07, Lennar Corp., Miami, 2001—, US Soccer Fedn., 2008—; co-chair (with Ann Veneman) Mother's Day Every Day, 2009—. Recipient Donald C. Stone award, American Soc. for Pub. Adminstrn., 1981, Elizabeth Morrow Cutter award, YWCA of Greater NY, 1982, Disting. Svc. medal, Columbia U. Tchrs. Coll., 1989, Ryan White Youth Svc. award for Outstanding Contributions to the Fight Against Teen HIV/AIDS, 1997, Margaret E. Mahoney award for Outstanding Contributions to Health Policy, NY Acad. Medicine, 1997, League of Women Voters-Disting. Leader award for a Lifetime of Pub. Svc., 2000, U. Calif. San Francisco medal, 2002, American Assn. of Colleges of Nursing John P. McGovern award, 2003, Nat. Conf. for Cmty. & Justice, Silver Medallion award for Svc. to Humanity, 2005, Images in Excellence award, Black Coaches Assn., 2007, Urban Leadership award, U. Pa. Inst. for Urban Rsch., 2008, Statue of Liberty-Ellis Island Found., Ellis Island Family Heritage award in Edn., 2008, Radcliffe medal, Radcliffe Inst. for Advanced Study, Harvard U., 2008, Presdl. Medal of Freedom, The White House, 2008; named Women of the Yr., Glamour mag., 1994; named one of America's 200 Most Influential Women: Legends, Leaders and Trail Blazers, 1998, 100 of America's Most Important Women, 1999, America's Best Leaders, US News & World Report and the Ctr. for Pub. Leadership at Harvard U. Kennedy Sch. Govt., 2005, The 25 Great Pub. Servants, Coun. for Excellence, 2008; Ohio Newspaper Women's scholar, 1958, Western Coll. Trustee scholar, 1958—62, Carnegie fellow, 1966—68, Spencer Fellow, Nat. Acad. Edn., 1972—73, Guggenheim fellow, 1975—76. Fellow American Acad. Polit. & Social Sci., Inst. Medicine (coun. mem.), Nat. Acad. Pub. Adminstrn.; mem. ASPA (Nat. Pub. Svc. award, 1992), American Polit. Sci. Assn.(v.p. 1984-85, Annual Career Achievement award for Disting. Scholarships in Urban Politics, 1992, Hubert Humphrey award, 1994), Nat. Acad. Social Insurance, American Acad. Arts & Sciences, Coun. Fgn. Rels., American Philosophical Soc., Soc. for Women's Health Rsch., Japan Soc.(Leadership Fellow, 1987), Nat. Acad. Edn. Office: U Miami Office Pres 230 Ashe Administration Bldg 1252 Memorial Dr Coral Gables FL 33146 E-mail: dshalala@miami.edu. *

SHALEV, BARUCH ABA, geneticist; b. Jerusalem, Feb. 20, 1936; s. Zwi and Hana (Cherstien) Shwieg; m. Rina Cohen, Sept. 13, 1965; children: Ofra, Zwi, Itay. BS, Hebrew U., Jerusalem, 1961; MS, U. Calif., Davis, 1962; PhD, U. Reading, England, 1977. Sr. supr. Goldman's Egg City, Moorpark, 1962-63; geneticist Ministry of Agr., Israel, 1963-99, statistician in charge experiments, 1965-99, rschr., 1965-99, in charge computer unit, 1977-99, sr. geneticist, 1977-99, ret., 1999; pvt. cons., 2000—. Lectr. Hebrew U., Israel, 1970-74; cons. FAO, UN, Rome, 1990-92, China, 2002; cons. in field. Author: Poultry Genetics, 1980, Poultry Production, 1995, Field Experiments in Poultry, 1996, 100 Years of Nobel Prizes And More, 2002, 2005, 2009; contbr. over 200 articles to profl. jours. Brit. Coun. fellow, 1974-77. Mem. European Poultry Genetics Working Group (prize of excellence 1989). Achievements include development of 2 genetic lines of geese. Avocations: swimming, music, aerobics. Home: 23, Hameginim St 46686 Herzliya Israel Office Phone: 972-52-3368518. Personal E-mail: baruchshalev@hotmail.com.

SHALIMAR, gastroenterologist; b. New Delhi, May 22, 1977; MBBS, AIIMS, 2000, DM in Gastroenterology, 2009. Physician AIIMS, 2009—. Office: All India Inst Med Scis New Delhi 110029 India Personal E-mail: drshalimar@yahoo.com.

SHALINSKY, JOSEPH GEORGE, pharmacist, pharmaceutical executive; b. Kansas City, Kans., July 6, 1916; s. Herman and Freda (Iskowitz) S.; m. Charlotte Louise Zolotor, Jan. 18, 1953; children: Robert Alan, Lee Bryan, Jonathan Neil. BS in Pharmacy, U. Mo., Kansas City, 1939. Registered pharmacist, Kans., Mo. Dir., chmn. Druggist Mut. and Pharmacists Mut. Ins. Cos., 1976—89; pres. Shalinsky Drug Co. Inc., Kansas City and Overland Park, Kans., 1953—; staff pharmacist Waggoner Pharmacy, Bonner Springs, Kans., Brewer's Price Chopper Pharmacy, Bonner Springs. Mem. adv. coun. U. Kans. Sch. of Pharmacy, 1967—; mem. Kans. Drug Abuse Adv. Coun., 1974, Gov.'s Conf. on Eradication of Marijuana, 1969; procurement chmn. Wyandotte County "Sabin on Sunday" Cmty. Polio Immunization Program; chmn. Johnson County Pharmacy Theft Prevention Program, 1978; bd. dirs. Salvation Army, 1953—; mem. exec. com. Crosslines Retirement Ctr., 1953—. Recipient Alumni Achievement award U. Mo. Kansas City, 1974, Disting. Svc. award U. Kansas City Alumni Assn., 1961, 50-Yr. Pharmacist award Kans. Bd. Pharmacy, Mo. Bd. Pharmacy. Fellow Am. Coll. Apothecaries; mem. VFW, Am. Pharm. Assn. (pres. Greater Kansas City chpt. 1947), Nat. Assn. Bds. of Pharmacy (chmn. com. on continuing edn. 1967, blue ribbon com. on exams. 1967, exec. bd. 1975-76, treas. 1977, 2d v.p. 1977, pres. 1980, chmn. bd. dirs. 1981), Nat. Assn. Retail Druggists, Am. Assn. Colls. of Pharmacy, Kans. Pharmacists Assn. (exec. com. 1967-84, dist. dir. Wyandotte/Johnson County 1947, Bowl of Hygeia award 1989, Pharmacist of Yr. award 1981), Mo. Pharm. Assn., Kans. Pharmacy Tripartite Com., Greater Kansas City Pharmacists Assn., U. Mo. Kansas City Pharmacy Alumni Assn. (pres. 1960-61), U. Mo. Kansas City Pharmacy Found. (pres. 1963-64, bd. dirs. 1964-75, chmn. bd. dirs. 1975—, Joseph G. Shalinsky Scholarship Fund established in his honor 1996), Am. Legion, Fleet Res. Assn., Ret. Officers Assn., Optimist, Kansas City C. of C., Argentine Activities Assn. (pres. 1972-74, Cmty. Svc. award 1988), B'nai B'rith. Home: 9201 Fontana St Shawnee Mission KS 66207-2632 E-mail: shaljos@att.net.

SHALITA, ALAN REMI, dermatologist; b. Bklyn., Mar. 22, 1936; s. Harry and Celia; m. Simone Lea Baum, Sept. 4, 1960; children: Deborah (dec.) and Judith (twins). AB, Brown U., 1957; BS, U. Brussels, 1960; MD, Bowman Gray Sch. Medicine, 1964; DSc (hon.), L.I. U., 1990. Intern Beth Israel Hosp., NYC, 1964-65; resident dept. dermatology NYU Med. Ctr., 1967-68, NIH tng. grant fellow dept. dermatology, 1968-70, instr. dermatology, 1970-71; asst. prof. NYU, 1971-73, Columbia U., 1973-75; assoc. prof. medicine, head divsn. dermatology SUNY Downstate Med. Ctr., Bklyn., 1975-79, prof., 1979—, head divsn. dermatology, 1979-80, chmn. dept. dermatology, 1980—, asst. dean, 1977-83, acting dean Queens campus, 1983-84; assoc. dean clin. affairs SUNY Health Sci. Ctr., Bklyn., 1989-92, assoc. provost for clin. affairs, 1992-93, assoc. v.p. clin. affairs, 1992-2005, assoc. dean grad. med. edn., 1999—2006. Disting. tchg. prof. SUNY Health Sci. Ctr., Bklyn., 1996—; asst. attending in dermatology U. Hosp., NYC, 1970-73, Bellevue Hosp. Ctr., 1970-73, Manhattan VA Hosp., 1971-73, Presbyn. Hosp., 1973-75; bd. dirs. Kings County Hosp. Ctr.; cons. dermatology Bklyn. VA Hosp., 1975—; chief dermatology U. Hosp. Bklyn., 1975—, Brookdale Med. Ctr., 1977-90, Kings County Hosp. Ctr., Bklyn., 1975—, acting med. dir., 1989-92; med. dir. U. Hosp. Bklyn., 1992-96. Pres. Temple Shaaray Tefila, N.Y.C., 1982-86, chmn. bd. trustees, 1987-95. Lt. M.C. USNR, 1965-67. Recipient Torch of Liberty award Anti-Defamation League, 1987, Surg. and Pediat. awards Beth Israel Hosp., NYC, 1965, Leah Dickstein Man of Good Conscience award Women's Med. Assn. NY, 1999, Leadership in Urban Med. Edn. award Arthur Ashe Inst. for Urban Health, 1999; Spl. fellow NIH, 1970-73. Mem.: AMA, Venezuelan Dermatology Soc., Argentina Dermatology Soc., Brit. Assn. Dermatologists, N.Y. Dermatol. Soc. (pres. 1989—90), Dermatol. Soc. Greater N.Y. (pres. 1980—81), N.Y. State Dermatol. Soc., N.Y. Acad. Medicine, N.Y. State Med. Soc., N.Y. Acad. Scis., Internat. Soc. Dermatology, Assn. Profs. Dermatology (sec.-treas. 1988—94, pres. 1996—98), Am. Soc. Dermatol. Surgery (past bd. dirs.), Dermatology Found. (past trustee), Soc. Investigative Dermatology, Polish Dermatology Soc. (hon.), Soc. Francaise de Dermatology (hon.), Am. Dermatol. Assn. (hon.; sec.-treas. 1996—2001, pres. 2001—02), Am. Acad. Dermatology (hon.; bd. dirs. 1983—87, v.p. 1995—96), Alpha Omega Alpha. Republican. Home: 70 E 77th St Apt 9B New York NY 10021-1811 Office: 450 Clarkson Ave Brooklyn NY 11203-2056 Office Phone: 718-270-1229. Business E-Mail: ashalita@downstate.edu.

SHAMALY, HUSSEIN IBRAHIM, pediatrician, consultant; b. Arraba, Israel, Oct. 10, 1950; s. Ibrahim Abed and Fatma Hassan Shamaly; m. Zahra Mohammad Assaf, July 13, 1984; children: Shamaly, Ayman, Lama, Amir. MD, Bucharest Med. Faculty, Romania, 1982. Resident in pediat. Afula (Israel) Hosp., 1989-93; resident in pediat. gastroenterology Rambam Hosp., Haifa, Israel, 1996-99; sr., pediat. dept. French Hosp., Nazareth, Israel, 1993—, cons. pediat. gastroenterology, 1999—. Mem. Tel-Aviv Gastroenterology Assn. Muslim. Avocation: travel. Home: POB 191 Arraba 24945 Israel Office: French Hosp Nazareth Galilee Israel Fax: +97246574747; +97246740603. E-mail: shamaly5@bezeqint.net.

SHAMBAUGH, GEORGE ELMER, III, internist, educator; b. Boston, Dec. 21, 1931; s. George Elmer, Jr. and Marietta Susan (Moss) S.; m. Katharine Margaret Matthews, Dec. 29, 1956 (dec.); children: George, Benjamin, Daniel, James, Elizabeth; m. Martha Repp Davis, Jan. 3, 1987 (dec.); m. Roberta Smith Ravan, Sept. 19, 1998. BA, Oberlin Coll., 1954; MD, Cornell U., 1958. Diplomate Am. Bd. Internal Medicine. Gen. med. intern Denver Gen. Hosp., 1958-59; rsch. fellow physiologic chem. U. Wis., Madison, 1967—69; asst. prof. medicine Northwestern U. Med. Sch., Chgo., 1969-74, assoc. prof., 1974-81, prof., 1981—99; prof. emeritus Northwestern U, Chgo., 1999; prof. Emory U. Med. Sch., 1999—. Mem. Divsn. Endocrinology, Metabolism and Molecular Medicine, 1969-1999; chief endocrinology and metabolism VA Lakeside Med. Ctr., Chgo., 1974-1999, dir. geriatric evaluation unit, 1997-1999; attending physician Northwestern Meml. Hosp., Chgo., 1969-1999; prof. medicine Emory U. Sch. Med., Atlanta, 1999-, attending physician Grady Meml. Hosp. divsn. endocrinology, dept. med. Contbr. articles to text books and profl. jour. Served with M.C., US Army, 1959-67 NIH spl. postdoctoral fellow, 1967-69; Schweppe Found. fellow, 1972-75, Nanette Wenger Svc. award 2008, Dept. Medicine Emory U., Atlanta; named one of Class Pres. of Yr., Oberlin Coll. Alumni Assn. 2008, Henry G. Heedy award Asheville Sch., 2009. Fellow ACP, Am. Coll. Endocrinology, Am. Assn. Clin. Endocrinology; mem. Am. Fedn. Med. Rsch., Sci. Rsch. Soc., Am. Endocrine Soc., Am. Thyroid Assn., Am. Inst. Nutrition, Am. Soc. Clin. Nutrition, Am. Physiol. Soc., Ctrl. Soc. Clin. Rsch., Inst. Medicine Chgo., Taipei Internat. Med. Soc. (pres. 1960), N.Y. Acad. Sci., Euro Diabetes Assn., Am. Men and Women of Sci., Sigma Xi, Nu Sigma Nu. Home: 7655 Blandford Pl Atlanta GA 30350-5603 Office: Emory Univ Dept Medicine 49 Jesse Hill Jr Dr SE Atlanta GA 30303 Business E-Mail: gshamba@emory.edu. *

SHAMBUREK, ROLAND HOWARD, physician; b. Adell, Wis., June 7, 1928; s. William and Catherine (Illig) Shamburek; m. Gladys Irene Gibbons, June 21, 1952 (dec. Feb. 5, 2010); children: Steven J., Robert D., Daniel J. Grad., Monroe HS, Wis., 1946; BS, U. Wis., 1950, MD, 1953; MPH, Harvard U., 1960; grad., U.S. Army War Coll., Carlisle Barracks, Pa., 1972. Diplomate Am. Bd. Preventive Medicine. Commd. 1st lt. M.C., U.S. Army, 1953, advanced through grades to col., 1968; intern St. Joseph's Hosp., Marshfield, Wis., 1953-54; grad. U.S. Naval Sch. of Aviation Medicine, Pensacola, Fla., 1957; resident in preventive (aerospace) medicine USAF Sch. Aerospace Medicine, Brooks AFB, 1960-63; service in 216th Field Artillery (Atomic) Battalion, 1954—56, 1966, Office of Army Surgeon Gen., Washington, 1966—70, 1972—75; comdr. 67th EVAC Hosp., Vietnam, 1970-71, U.S. Army Med. Pers. Support Agy., 1975-77; ret. U.S. Army, 1977; exec. v.p. Aerospace Med. Assn., 1977-79; clin. practice Pentagon Health Clinic, Washington, 1981-85; med. researcher Office of Army Surgeon Gen., 1985-87. Med. monitor Canary Island Tracking Sta. for Gemini missions NASA, 1965—66. Contbr. scientific papers in field. Decorated Legion of Merit with oak leaf cluster, Army Commendation medal, Meritorious Svc. medal; recipient Gold Palm Eagle Scout award, Boy Scouts Am., 1945. Mem.: AMA (del. 1978), Internat. Acad. Aviation and Space Medicine, Soc. NASA Flight Surgeons, U.S. Army Flight Surgeons, Soc. Med. Cons. Armed Forces, Aerospace Med. Assn. (v.p. 1968—69), Am. Coll. Preventive Medicine (v.p. 1968—69), Assn. Mil. Surgeons (John Shaw Billings award 1968). Address: 3700 Moss Dr Annandale VA 22003-1915

SHAMIR, JUDITH, health science association administrator; BA in Early Childhood Edn., CUNY, Bklyn. Coll., 1977. Previous positions with Am. Nurses Credentialing Ctr., Nat. Assn. Alcoholism; sr. staff specialist Am. Nurses Assn., 1994—96, dir., leadership services, 1996—2004; dir., office of coun. and membership services Inst. of Medicine, 2004—. Mem.: Greater Washington Soc. Assn. Executives, Am. Soc. Assn. Executives, BoardSource (Nat. Ctr. for Non-Profit Boards). Office: Institute of Medicine 500 Fifth St NW NAS 319 Washington DC 20001 Office Phone: 202-334-2175.

SHAMMA, ASAD R., surgeon; BS in Biology, Am. U. of Beirut, Lebanon, 1977, MD, 1981; resident, chief resident gen. surgery, SUNY, Syracuse, 1981—96; fellow, U. Iowa, Iowa City, 1986—87. Diplomate #32353, Am. Bd. of Surgery, 1987, cert. in Vascular Surgery #100019 1988, ECFMG #3211422, 1980, Recertified Am. Bd. of Surgery, 1994, Recertified in Vascular Surgery 1997, lic. Lebanon, 1981, NY #149625, 1981, Iowa #26345, 1986, Md. #D39511, 1990, Md. #D39511, 1991, UAE-Dubai #201013003090749, 2009, Qatar #1599, 2010. Assoc. surgery Univ. of Iowa, 1987—89, asst. prof., 1989—90; staff surgeon Veterans' Adminstrn. Med. Ctr., 1987—88, chief, vascular surgery, 1988—90; staff surgeon Holmes Regional Med. Ctr., 1990—2003, chief, vascular surgery, 1992—2000, sec., med. staff, 2000—02; v.p. Med. Staff Holmes Regional Med. Ctr., 2002—03; chmn. Credentials Com. Holmes Regional Med. Ctr., 2002—03; attending physician Najjar Hosp., Beirut, 2004; workshopsmed. dir. Internat. Varicose Vein Conf., 2003; chief, vascular surgery Hammoud Univ. Ctr., 2003—; staff surgeon Clemenceau Med. Ctr., 2006—; med. dir. HM Med. Diagnostics BV, Landgraaf, Netherlands, 2006—. Recipient Fredrick Hyde Resident Tchg. award, Health Sci. Ctr., 1986. Fellow: Am. Coll. of Surgeons; mem.: Am. Venous Forum, Laser Inst. of America, Am. Coll. of Phlebology, Soc. for Vascular Surgery, Fla. Vascular Soc., Soc. for Clin. Vascular Surgery, Peripheral Vascular Surgery Soc., Alpha Omega Alpha (hon.). Office: Sodeco Center Block B 8th fl Beirut Lebanon Office Phone: 9611611212. *

SHAMOVA, OLGA, medical researcher; b. St. Petersburg, Aug. 15, 1964; PhD, St. Petersburg State U., 1987. Sr. rschr. Inst. Exptl. Medicine, 2002—. Office: 12 Academic Pavlov Str Saint Petersburg 197376 Russia Office Fax: 7-812-234-9493. Business E-Mail: oshamova@yandex.ru.

SHAMS, SHAHZAD, neurosurgeon; BSc, Punjab U., Lahore Pakistan, 1984; MBBS, King Edward Med. U. KEMU, Lahore Pakistan, 1981—87. Sr. house surgeon north surg. unit Mayo Hosp., Lahore, Pakistan, 1987, sr. house physician east med. unit, 1988, med. officer accident emergency dept., 1990, med. officer north surg. unit, 1990, registrar north surg. unit., 1991; demonstrator anatomy dept. King Edward Med. Coll. (KEMC), Lahore, Pakistan, 1989; registrar neurosurgery dept. Lahore Gen. Hosp. (LGH), Pakistan, 1992, sr. registrar neurosurgery dept., 1994—96; clin. attachment Falkirk and Dist. Royal Infirmary NHS Trust, England, 1993; clin. fellow neurol. surgery dept. George Wash. Univ., DC, 1997—98; attending neurosurgeon neurosurgery dept. Allied Hosp., Faisalabad, 1998—2001, Civil Hosp., Faisalabad, 1998—2001; cons. neurosurgeon Saahil Hosp., Faisalabad, 1998—2002; head neurosurgeon dept. & neurosurgeons attending Svcs. Hosp., Lahore, Pakistan, 2003—04, attending neurosurgeon, 2003—10; attending neurosurgeon neurosurgery dept. Svcs. Inst. Med. Sciences (SIMS), Lahore, Pakistan, 2003—10; cons. neurosurgeon Omar Hosp., Lahore, Pakistan, 2003—; head neurosurgery dept. Sir Ganga Ram Hosp. (SGRH), Lahore, Pakistan, 2010—. Asst. prof. neurosurgery dept Punjab Med. Coll., Faisalabad, 1998—2002; assoc. prof. & PGMI head neurosurgery dept. Post Grad. med. Inst. (PGMI), Lahore, Pakistan, 2003; head neurosurgery dept. and assoc. prof. Svcs. Inst. Med. Sciences (SIMS), Lahore, Pakistan, 2004—10; prof. Fatima Jinnah Med. Coll. (FJMC), 2010—. Fellow: George Wash. Univ. (fellow 1998), Coll. of Physicians and Surgeons, Karachi Pakistan (fellow 1996), Royal Coll. of Physicians and Surgeons, Glasgow UK (fellow 1994). Avocations: reading poetry, golf. Office: Omar Hospital jail Rd Lahore Pakistan also: Services Institute for Medical Sciences & Services Hospital Department of Neurosurgery Jail Rd Lahore Pakistan Office Phone: 924237576400, 9242111127127. Personal E-mail: drshahzadshams@hotmail.com. *

SHAMSHAM, FADI MICHEL, cardiologist; b. Beirut, Nov. 28, 1968; arrived in U.S., 1994; s. Michel Salim Shamsham and Marie Assi Gemayel. BS, Am. U. of Beirut, 1989, MD, 1993. Diplomate Am. Bd. Internal Medicine, Am. Bd. Internal Medicine with subspecialities in cardiovascular diseases and interventional cardiology, cert. in vascular & endovascular medicine Am. Bd. Vascular medicine, in nuc. cardiology, cardiac device specialist Internat. Bd. Heart Rhythm Soc. Resident in internal medicine S.I. U. Hosp., SI, NY, 1994—97; fellow in cardiovascular diseases SUNY, Bklyn., 1997—2000; fellow in interventional cardiology Kaiser Permanente Found. Hosp., LA, 2000—01; fellow in vascular medicine Charleston Area Med. Ctr., W.Va., 2001—02; cardiologist Med. Group of North Fla., Tallahassee, 2002—06, Heart and Vascular Ctr., Venice, Fla., 2006—08, Chester County Heart & Vascular Ctr., 2009, Southern Ill. Heart & Vascular Ctr., 2009—; med. staff Tallahassee Meml. Hosp., Fla., 2002—06, Capital Regional Med. Ctr., 2002—06, Venice Regional Med. Ctr., 2006—08, Sarasota Meml. Hosp., 2007—08, Brandywine Hosp., 2009, Jennersville Regional Hosp., 2009, St. Mary's Good Samaritan Hosp., 2009—, Crossroads Cmty. Hosp., 2010—. Clin. inst. SUNY, Bklyn., 1997—2000. Contbr. articles to profl. jours. Fellow: Soc. Cardiac Angiography and Interventions, Am. Coll. Cardiology. Home: 4113 Victoria Ave Mount Vernon IL 62864 Office Phone: 618-204-5462. Office Fax: 618-204-5472. Personal E-mail: fshamsham@aol.com.

SHAMSUDDIN, MOHAMED HUSSAIN QADER, health facility administrator, consultant pediatrician; b Aden, Yemen, Apr. 16, 1951; came to U.S., 1996; s. Kader Ali and Ruqaiya (Adam Ali) S.; m. Salwa A.A. Ramzo, Nov. 20, 1979; children: Samar, Samir. MBBS, U. Delhi, India, 1976; MD, Inst. Med. Edn. & Rsch., Chandigarh, India, 1984. Registrar, sr. registrar pediatrics Mansoora Children Hosp., Aden, 1978-82; resident, tchg. fellow PGIMER, Chandigarh, 1982-84; cons. pediatrician Aden Refinery Co. Hosp., 1985—, acting dir., 1987—, asst. dir., 1992—, dir., 1995—. Hon. registrar St. Mary's Hosp., Manchester, Eng., 1988-89; mem. Med. Coun. of Yemen for So. & Eastern Provinces Ministry of Health, 1991—; mem. bd. mgmt. Aden Refinery Co., 1995—; mem. rsch. bd. advisers Am. Biog. Inst., 2004. Cultural and ednl. sec. Nat. Gen. Union for Yemeni Students (India br.), 1972-77. Recipient Thomas Jefferson fellowship for MPH program at U. Ariz. (USAID), 1996-98, British Coun. scholarship, 1988-89, fellowship for postgrad. studies in Paediatrics, 1997—; nominee Internat. Health Profl. of Yr. award Internat. Biog. Inst., 2006. Mem. APHA, Pi Lambda Theta. Muslim. Avocations: swimming, reading. Office: Aden Refinery Hosp PO Box 0003 Aden Yemen

SHANAHAN, SHEILA ANN, pediatrician, educator; m. Justin Laurence Cashman Jr., Sept. 14, 1968; children: Justin III, Gillis. BA, Trinity Coll., 1963; MD cum laude, Med. Coll. Pa., 1969. Diplomate Nat. Bd. Med. Examiners, Am. Bd. Pediats. Intern Presbyn. Hosp., NYC, 1969-70, resident in pediats., 1970-72, asst. in clin. pediats., 1972-75, assoc. clin. pediats., 1975-78; pvt. practice specializing in pediats. Greenwich, Conn., 1972-78; asst. attending Greenwich Hosp., 1972-73, assoc. attending, 1973-78; from instr. to assoc. Columbia Coll. Physicians and Surgeons, NYC, 1972-78; asst. prof. pediats. George Washington U. Sch. Medicine, Washington, 1980—, Georgetown U. Sch. Medicine, Washington, 1984—; pvt. practice specializing in pediats. Washington, 1984—. Attending dept. ambulatory medicine Children's Hosp. Nat. Med. Ctr., Washington, 1980—84; courtesy staff Georgetown U. Hosp., Washington, 1984—, Sibley Meml. Hosp., Washington, 1984—, Children's Hosp. Nat. Med. Ctr., 1984—. Fellow Am. Acad. Pediats. Office: 4900 Massachusetts Ave NW Washington DC 20016-4358 Office Phone: 202-966-5000. *

SHANE, JOHN MARDER, endocrinologist; b. Kans. City, Mo., Oct. 5, 1942; s. Henry Kamsler and Ruth (Marder) S.; m. Eileen Goodart, June 18, 1967; children: Robert M., Edward G. BS, U. Okla., 1964, MD, 1967. Diplomate Am. Bd. Ob-Gyn., Am. Bd. Reproductive Endocrinology; cert. master gardener. Resident Harvard Med. Sch., Boston, 1970-73, fellowship, 1973-75, instr., 1970-75, asst. prof., 1975-78; pvt. practice Tulsa, 1978-99. Lectr., cons. Tutorial Svcs. Internat., England, 1984—; bd. dirs. St. Francies G.I.F.T. Lab., Tulsa; cons. to preimplantation genetics project Chapman Genetics Inst., Children's Med. Ctr., Tulsa. Author: CIBA Symposium Infertility: Diagnosis and Treatment; contbr. articles to profl. jours. and publs.; exhibitions include Okla. Woodturners, The Philbrook Mus. Active Tulsa Garden Ctr., 1988—; bd. dirs. Temple Israel, Tulsa, 1985-86, Up With Trees Found., 2000—, Tulsa, master gardener. Capt. USAF, 1967-69. Recipient Annual award Boston Obstet. Soc., 1977; named one of Best Doctor's in Am., Tulsa's Best Doctors, Tulsa People Mag. Mem. ACS, Tulsa Gynecol. Soc. (past pres. 1986-87), Soc. Reproductive Endocrinologists, Tulsa bonsai Soc. (bd. dirs. 1988—), Am. Coll. Ob-Gyn. (v.p. 1971-92, pres. New England Jr. divsn. 1972-73), Am. Bonsai Soc. (nat. bd. dirs.), Chanie des Rotisseurs (l'Ordre Mondial, Tulsa v.p., advisor to bd., Bronze Star 2001), Southside Rotary of Tulsa (bd. dirs., pres. 1997-98, Nat. Arboretum Bonsai Pavillion (nat. bd. dirs.), Rotary Club Tulsa (past pres. Southside club). Independent. Jewish. Avocations: gardening, cooking, bonsai, collector Oriental arts, woodturning.

SHANES, JEFFREY GLENN, cardiologist; b. Elkhart, Ind., Nov. 14, 1949; s. Harry and Doris Shanes; m. Mara Davis, Sept. 5, 1999; children: Ira Gary, Morris Mordecai, Fran Merzel, Yehuda Poupko, Chaim Poupko, Eli Sheva Schreiber, Chaya Segal. BS, Roosevelt U., Chgo., 1972; MD, Finch U. Health Scis./Chgo. Med. Sch., 1976. Diplomate Am. Bd. Internal Medicine, 1979, in cardiovasc. disease 1981. Chmn. cardiology dept. Gottlieb Hosp., Melrose Park, 1991—2001; instr. medicine Wash. U., St. Louis, 1979—81, U. Ill., Chgo., 1982—83, asst. prof. medicine, 1983—88, dir. cardiac catheterization lab, 1982—88, assoc. prof. medicine, 1988—2004, Rosalind Franklin U. Medicine and Sci., Chgo., 2004—; pres. Cons. in Cardiovasc. Medicine, Melrose Park, Ill., 1990—. Contbr. articles to profl. jours. Recipient Lange Med. Publs. award, 1976; Studies Left Ventricular Dysfunction grant, NIH, 1986. Mem.: ACP, Am. Heart

Assn., Am. Coll. Cardiology. Avocations: photography, travel, scuba diving. Office: Consultants in Cardiovascular Medicine 675 W North Ave Melrose Park IL 60160 Office Fax: 708-344-0508.

SHANFIELD, STEPHEN B., psychiatrist, educator; b. Toronto, Ont., Can., Aug. 14, 1939; s. Joseph P. and Mildred Lenore (Neiman) S.; m. Carmen Lynn Kight, Aug. 15, 1971 (div. Mar. 1990); 1 child, Jason Gabriel; m. Alicia Debra Leff, Sept. 1, 2000. BA, UCLA, 1961; MD, U. So. Calif., 1965. Intern Montefiore Hosp. and Med. Ctr., NYC, 1965-66; resident in psychiatry Sch. of Medicine Yale U., New Haven, 1966-69; maj. USAF, 1969-79; staff physician Wilford Hall USAF Med. Ctr., San Antonio, 1969-71; from asst. prof. to prof. Coll. Medicine U. Ariz., Tucson, 1973-85; prof. Health Sci. Ctr. U. Tex., San Antonio, 1985—2006, prof. emeritus, 2006—. Contbr. articles to prof. jours. Fellow Am. Psychiat. Assn., Am. Coll. Psychiatrists; mem. Group Advancement Psychiatry. Home: 122 Chester St # 2 San Antonio TX 78209-5679 Personal E-mail: stephen.shanfield@gmail.com.

SHANG, HONGCAI, medical educator; b. China, July 4, 1972; PhD, Tianjin U. TCM, 2005. Prof. Tianjin U. TCM, 2010. Office: #88 Yuquan Rd Nankai Dist Tianjin 300193 China Business E-Mail: shanghongcai@foxmail.com.

SHANG, YINGBIN, dermatologist; b. Shenyang, China, Jan. 30, 1971; MD, China Med. U., 2006; PhD, Shanghai Jiaotong U., 2009. Vice chief physician Suzhou Mylike Cosmetic Hosp., 2010. Office: 889 W Ganjiang Rd Suzhou Jiangsu 215000 China Office Phone: 86-0512-88169999. Business E-Mail: shangyingbin@126.com.

SHANGLONG, YAO, anesthesiologist; b. Anhui, Mar. 12, 1956; MD, Huazhong U. Sci. and Tech., PhD, 1990. Dir., dept. anesthesiology Union Hosp., Tongji Med. Coll., Huazhong U. Sci. and Tech., 1997—, v.p., 2004—. Recipient First prize, Hubei Provincial Govt. of China. Master: Chinese Assn. World Soc. Pain Clinician, Assn. Anesthesiology Chinese Med. Assn., Chinese Assn. Anesthesiologists. Avocation: travel. Office: Jiefang Rd Wuhan Hubei 430022 China E-mail: yao_shanglong@yaoo.com.cn.

SHANGRAW, ROBERT EDWARD, medical educator, researcher; b. Troy, NY, Mar. 16, 1954; s. Robert Dixon and M. Janice (Bonacker) S.; m. Patricia Mary Ford, May 25, 1985; children: Kirsten Celanire, Sarah Elizabeth, Kathleen Ford. BS, Rensselaer Poly. Inst., 1976; PhD, Albany Med. Coll., NY, 1981, MD, 1985. Resident in surgery U. Wash., Seattle, 1985-86; rsch. assoc. U. Tex. Med. Br., Galveston, 1986-87; resident in anesthesia Hosp. U. Pa., Phila., 1987-90; asst. prof. anesthesiology Oreg. Health and Sci. U., Portland, 1990—96, assoc. prof., 1996—2001, prof., 2001—. Cons. NIH Study Sects., 1998—. Contbr. articles on biomedicine to profl. jours. Fellow NIH, 1977-80, 82, 83. Mem. AMA, Am. Physiol. Soc., Am. Soc. Anesthesiologists, Internat. Anesthesia Rsch. Soc., Biochem. Soc., Assn. Univ. Anesthesiologists, Sigma Xi, Alpha Omega Alpha. Roman Catholic. Avocations: skiing, sailing, hiking, kayaking, swimming. Home: 5776 SW Calusa Loop Tualatin OR 97062-9757 Office: Oreg Health and Sci U Dept Anesthesiology and Periop Medicine 3181 SW Sam Jackson Park Rd Portland OR 97239-3098 Office Phone: 503-494-7641. Business E-Mail: shangraw@ohsu.edu.

SHANI, JACOB, interventional cardiologist, educator; MD, Technion-Israel Inst. of Tech., 1977. Diplomate Am. Bd. Internal Medicine, 1981, Am. Bd. Internal Medicine-cardiovasc. disease, 1983, Am. Bd. Internal Medicine-interventional cardiology, 2009, lic. NY, 1979, Mass., 1981. Resident in internal medicine Maimonides Med. Ctr., Bklyn., 1978—81, program dir. interventional cardiology, chmn. cardiac inst., dir. divsn. cardiology, program dir. adult cardiovascular disease; fellow in cardiovascular disease Beth Israel Hosp., Boston, 1981—83; prof. clin. med. SUNY; prof. interventional cardiology Univ. Rome La Sapienza. Recipient Jack Aron medal award for Disting. Svc., 2001, Physician of the Year award, Guardians of the Sick Orgn., 2001, Ohel Found. Physician of the Year award as Director of Cardiology, Maimonides Med. Ctr., 2002; named one of Best Doctors of NY, NY mag., 25 Best Doctors in the Met. Area, NY Post, 2001. Office: Maimonides Medical Center 2nd Fl 4802 10th Ave Brooklyn NY 11220 Office Phone: 718-871-4600. Office Fax: 718-283-7480.

SHANKAR, HARIHARAN, anesthesiologist, educator; MBBS, Stanley Med. Coll., 1982. Assoc. prof. Med. Coll. Wis., 2005—, dir., pain medicine fellowship program, 2010—. Named Tchr. of Yr., Dept. Anesthesiology, Med. Coll. Wis. Office: 5000 W Nat Ave Milwaukee WI 53295 Business E-Mail: hshankar@mcw.edu.

SHANKAR, JAI JAI SHIVA, medical educator; b. Kharia, Bihar, India, Sept. 5, 1975; DM in Neuroradiology, NIMH & NeuroScis., 2007. Asst. prof., cons. QE II Hosp., Halifax, 2010—. Recipient Best Paper award, Indian Soc. Neuroradiology, Bursary award, Internat. Epilepsy Congress, Honour Your Hero Star, Toronto Western Hosp. Found., 2010; Diagnostic & Interventional Neuroradiology fellowship, U. Ottawa & U. Toronto, 2010. Mem.: Am. Soc. Neuroradiology. Avocations: swimming, running, painting. Home: 5770 Spring Garden Rd Halifax NS Canada B3H4J8 Personal E-mail: shivajai1@rediffmail.com.

SHANKEL, DELBERT MERRILL, microbiologist, biologist, educator; b. Plainview, Nebr., Aug. 4, 1927; s. Cecil Wilfred and Gladys Dalton (Dodd) Shankel; m. Carol Jo Mulford, Sept. 10, 1962; children: Merrill, Jill, Kelley. BA, Walla Walla Coll., 1950; PhD, U. Tex., 1959. Tchr. Walla Walla Coll. Acad., College Place, Wash., 1950-51; instr. San Antonio Coll., 1954-55; asst. prof., assoc. prof. microbiology and biology U. Kans., Lawrence, 1959-68, prof., 1968—, asst. dean, assoc. dean arts and sci., 1966-72, acting dean, 1973, exec. vice chancellor, 1974-80, 86, 90-92, acting chancellor, 1980-81, chancellor, 1994-95, chancellor emeritus, 1996. Commr. N. Ctrl. Assn. Colls. and Schs., Chgo., 1991—95, cons., evaluator, 1969—96, NW Comm. Coll., 1997—. Editor: Artimutagenesis and Anticarcinogenesis: Mechanisms vols. I-III, 1986, 1988, 1993; assoc. editor: Mutation Rsch., 1992—95. Active numerous civic orgns. With US Army, 1952—54. Recipient Outstanding Educator award, Mortar Bd., U. Kans., 1982, 1985, 1990; named Disting. Alumnus of the Yr., Walla Walla Coll., 1989; numerous rsch. grantee. Fellow: Am. Acad. Microbiology; mem.: Radiation Rsch. Soc., Soc. Gen. Microbiology (Eng.), Genetics Soc. Am., Environ. Mutagen Soc. (chmn. pub. policy com. 1991—93, mem. nat. coun. 1994—97), Am. Soc. Microbiology (past chmn. edn. com., chmn. numerous coms.), U. Kans. Alumni Assn. (interim pres., CEO 2004), Sigma Xi (pres. U. Kans. chpt. 1967). Republican. Unitarian Universalist. Avocations: sports, music, theater, reading. Office: U Kans 1002 Haworth Hl Lawrence KS 66045-0001 Office Phone: 785-864-3150. Business E-Mail: shankel@ku.edu.

SHANKLIN, CAROL W., dietician, educator; BS in Home Econs. Edn., U. Tenn., Martin, 1973; MS in Food Sys. Adminstrn., U. Tenn., Knoxville, 1974, PhD in Food Sys. Adminstrn., 1976. Asst. prof. foods and nutrition Tex. Tech. U., 1977—78; asst. food svc. dir. Highland Hosp., Lubbock, Tex., 1978; asst. prof. food sys. mgmt. Tex. Women's U., 1978—82, assoc. prof. food sys. mgmt., 1982—88, assoc. prof., chair dept. nutrition and food scis., 1985—87, prof., chair dept. nutrition and food scis., 1987—90; tech. advisor, cons. Miss. Inst. Higher Learning, 1988—89; grad. program dir., prof. dept. hotel, restaurant, instn. mgmt. and dietetics Kans. State U., Manhattan, 1990—2001, asst. dean. Grad. Sch., prof. dept. hotel, restaurant, instn. mgmt. and dietetics, 2001—04, assoc. dean. Grad. Sch., prof. dept. hotel, restaurant, instn. mgmt. and dietetics, 2004—07, prof. Grad. Sch., prof. dept. hotel, restaurant, instn. mgmt. and dietetics, 2007—09, interim dean, Grad. Sch., prof. dept. hotel, restaurant, instn. mgmt. and dietetics, 2008—09, dean grad. sch., prof. dept. hospitality mgmt. & dietetics, 2009—. Contbr. articles to profl. jours. Recipient Michael Olsen Rsch. Achievement award, U. Del. Mem.: Am. Dietetic Assn. (Medallion award 2001). Achievements include research on environmental issues in the food service and hospitality industry; dietetics and hospitality education; quality service in food service operations; research in food service management, food safety and security in food service operations. Office: Kansas State U Graduate Sch 103 Fairchild Manhattan KS 66502-1404 Office Phone: 785-532-7927. Business E-Mail: shanklin@k-state.edu. *

SHANKLIN, DOUGLAS RADFORD, physician; b. Camden, NJ, Nov. 25, 1930; s. John Ferguson and Muriel (Morgan) S.; m. Virginia McClure, Apr. 7, 1956; children: Elizabeth, Leigh, Lois Virginia, John Carter, Eleanor. Student, Wilson Tchrs. Coll., 1949; AB in Chemistry, Syracuse U., 1952; MD, SUNY, Syracuse, 1955. Intern in pathology Duke U., 1955-56, resident, 1958; resident in pathology SUNY, Syracuse, 1958-60; practice medicine specializing in pathology Gainesville, Fla., 1960-67, 78-83; mem. faculty U. Fla., 1960-67; prof. pathology, ob-gyn. U. Chgo., 1967-78; prof. dept. pathology U. Tenn., Memphis, 1983—2008, prof. obstetrics, 1986—2008, vice chmn. dept. pathology, 1983-90, prof. emeritus, 2008—. Vis. prof. U. Okla., 1967, Duke U., Mich. State U., 1969, Leeds U., Dundee U., Karolinska, 1974, Leeds U., 1978, 85, Emory U., 1980, London U., Edinburgh U., 1981, 85, U. Brit. Coll., 1987; jr. investigator Marine Biol. Lab., Woods Hole, Mass., 1951-54, sr. investigator, 1966—, mem. corp., 1970—; parliamentarian, 1990-94; mem. Marine Resources Adv. Com., 1988-90, mem. election com., 1994-96; chmn. nat. adv. com. W-I-C evaluation U.S. Dept. Agr., 1979-86; lectr. Coll. Law U. Fla., 1963-67, 77-83; cons. Pan Am. Health Orgn., 1973-89; sr. cons. Santa Fe Found., 1976-79, exec. dir., 1979-83; course dir. Ctr. Continuing Edn., U. Chgo., 1980-82. Author: Syllabus for Study of Gynecologic-Obstetric-Pediatric Disease, 1961, Diseases of Woman, Pregnancy, Child, 1964, Maternal Nutrition and Child Health, 1979, 2nd edit., 2000, Tumors of Placenta and Umbilical Cord, 1990; editor Interscience Devel. Disorders, 1971-80; assoc. editor Jour. Reproductive Medicine, 1968-70, 79-85, editor in chief, 1970-75; mem. editl. bd. Exptl. Molecular Pathology, 1999—; contbr. articles to profl. jours. Trustee Coll. Light Opera Co., Falmouth, Mass., 1970—, Hippodrome Theatre, Gainesville, 1975-83, Opera Memphis, 1989-92. With M.C., USNR, 1956-58. Recipient Best Basic Sci. Tchg. award U. Fla., 1967, Excellence in Tchg. award, Grad. Coll. Med. Scis., U. Tenn., 2002, Enid Gilbert-Barness prize, 2010; named freeman citizen of Glasgow, 1981. Fellow: Royal Soc. Medicine (london); mem.: AAAS, Coll. Physicians and Surgeons Costa Rica, Internat. Physicians for Prevention Nuc. War, Physicians Social Responsibility, Am. Coll. Ob-gyn., N.Y. Acad. Scis., So. Med. Assn., So. Soc. Pediat. Rsch., Math. Assn. Am., Internat. Acad. Pathologists, Soc. Pediat. Rsch., Am. Coll. Rheumatology (spl. study com. 1995—96), Hosp. Assn., Am. Chem. Soc., Am. Soc. Molecular Marine Biology and Biotech., Am. Soc. Exptl. Pathology, Cosmos Club, Pediat. Pathology Club (sec.-treas. 1970—75, pres. 1981—82), Navy League, Sigma xi, Phi Beta Kappa. Home: PO Box 1267 Gainesville FL 32602-1267 also: PO Box 511 Woods Hole MA 02543-0511 Home Fax: 352-372-5487, 508-457-9635. Personal E-mail: radfordcrawford@juno.com.

SHANKLIN, KENNETH DALE, plastic surgeon; b. Toluca, Ill., Dec. 21, 1931; s. Walter Arthur and Elsie Ida Josephine (Holz) S.; m. Doris Gay Minton, July 24, 1955 (div. Jan. 21, 1971); 1 child, Steven Dale; m. Colleen Jean Wheeler, July 30, 1978. BS, U. Ill., 1954; MD, U. Utah, 1967. Diplomate Am. Bd. Med. Specialists in gen. surgery, plastic surgery; lic. Calif. Commd. 2d lt. USAF, 1954, advanced through grades to lt. col., ret., 1977; intern Wilford Hall USAF Med. Ctr., San Antonio, 1967-68, resident in plastic surgery, 1972-74, resident in gen. surgery Travis AFB, Calif., 1968-72; assoc. clin. prof. plastic surgery U. Tex., San Antonio, 1974-77; asst. clin prof. plastic surgery U. Calif., Davis, 1977-84, assoc. clin. prof. plastic surgery San Francisco, 1984—2004; pvt. practice plastic surgery Fresno, Calif., 1977-93; acting chief med. officer Mil. Entrance Processing Sta., Sacramento, 1994—2001. Bd. dirs., pres. Valley Children's Hosp. Med. Staff, Fresno; bd. dirs. Liga Flying Physicians, Fresno, 1995-98. Prodr., dir. films sci. meetings (Outstanding award 1976). Mem. Am. Soc. Plastic Surgeons, Internat. Congress Plastic and Reconstructive Surgeons (bd. dirs. 1983-91), Am. Med. Soc. Vienna, Mil. Order of the World Wars (dept. N. Calif. comdr. 1996-97, region 14 comdr. 1998-99, nat. surgeon gen. 2004-10, Disting. Chpt. Comdr. 1997, Silver Patrick Henry Patriotism award, 1997), Am. Legion (dist. vice comdr. 1998-99, dist. comdr. 1999-2000, vice comdr. Calif. 2001-02), Rotarian, Comml. Pilot Single Multi Engine Airplane Rotorcraft Helicopter, Instrument Airplane (Lic.) Avocations: teaching, flying. Home and Office: Mil Order World Wars 5100 John D Ryan Blvd 2211 San Antonio TX 78245-3513

SHANKS, KATHRYN MARY, health facility administrator; b. Glens Falls, NY, Aug. 4, 1950; d. John Anthony and Lenita (Combs) S. BS summa cum laude, Spring Hill Coll., 1972; MPA, Auburn U., 1976. Program evaluator Mobile (Ala.) Mental Health, 1972-73; dir. spl. projects Ala. Dept. Mental Health, Montgomery, 1973-76; dir. adminstrn. S.W. Ala. Mental Health/Mental Retardation, Andalusia, 1976-78; adminstr. Mobile County Health Dept., 1978-82; exec. dir. Coastal Family Health Ctr., Biloxi, Miss., 1982-95; cons. med. group practice, 1995—; ptnr. Shanks & Allen, Mobile, 1979—; healthcare consulting pvt. practice, 1995—; practice dir. USA Health Svcs. Found., 1999—2001; practice mgr. Humana Mil. Healthcare Svcs., 2002—06; interim dir. Lynn Meadows Discovery Ctr., 2006—08; practice mgr Humana Military Healthcare Svcs., 2008—; bus. mgr. dept. pediat. U. South Ala., 1997—99, instr., mgr. dept. pediats., 1997—99. Cons. S.W. Health Agy., Tylertown, Miss., 1984-86; preceptor Sch. Nursing, U. So. Miss., Hattiesburg, 1983, 84; advisor Headstart Program, Gulfport, Miss., 1984-95; LPN Program, Gulf Coast C.C., 1984-95; lectr. Auburn U., Montgomery, 1977-78. Bd. dirs. Mobile Cmty. Action Agy., 1979-81, Moore Cmty. House; mem. S.W. Ala. Regional Goals Forum, Mobile, 1971-72, Cardiac Rehab. Study Com., Biloxi, Miss., 1983-84, Mothers and Babies Coalition, Jackson, Miss., 1983-95, Gulf Coast Coalition Human Svcs., Biloxi, 1983-95; exec. dir. Year for Miss., 1993-94. Pres.'s scholar, Spring Hill Coll., 1972. Mem. ACLU, Miss. Primary Health Care Assn. (pres.), Med. Group Mgmt. Assn., Soc. for Advancement of Ambulatory Care, Spring Hills Alumni Assn., HOSA Group(treas.), Wings Youth Theatre Troup (adv. bd. mem.), Mary C. Okeefe Cultural Ctr.(Ocean Springs)(bd. dirs.) Avocations: home restoration, golf, community sservice.

SHANMUGARATNAM, KANAGARATNAM, medical educator, consultant; b. Singapore, Apr. 2, 1921; s. Kanagaratnam Shanmugam and Achimuthu Kanther; m. Sarvambikai Viswalingam, Aug. 17, 1950; children: Vani, Santhan, Tharman. LMS, Coll. Medicine, Singapore, 1947; MD, U. Malaya, Singapore, 1954; PhD, U. London, 1957. Pathologist Govt. Med. Svc., Singapore, 1948—60; prof. pathology U. Singapore, 1960—86, Dean faculty medicine, 1962—65, emeritus prof., 1986—; emeritus cons. Nat. U. Hosp., Singapore, 1986—. Dir. Singapore Cancer Registry, 1967—2002; chmn. epidemiology programme Internat. Union Against Cancer, Geneva, 1974—78; head ctr. upper respiratory tract tumors WHO, Geneva, 1972—95, mem. com. internat. classification diseases oncology, 1998—2000. Mem. Singapore Med. Coun., 1962—68; master Acad. Medicine, Singapore, 1966—68; pres. Internat. Assn. Cancer Registries, Geneva, 1984—88. Recipient Pub. Adminstrn. Gold medal, Singapore Govt., 1976, Disting. Academician award, Singapore Acad. Medicine, 2005; Queen's fellowship, Singapore Govt., 1954. Mem.: Royal Coll. Pathologists, Royal Coll. Pathologists Australasia (Disting. Fellow award 2006). Office: Pathology Nat Univ Hosp 5 Lower Kent Ridge Rd Singapore 119074 Singapore Office Fax: 65-6773-6021. Business E-Mail: k_shanmugaratnam@nuhs.edu.sg.

SHANMUGAVELU, SABESAN, research and development company executive; b. Kumbakonam, Jan. 10, 1952; PhD, Secondary Sch. Bd., 1973. Sr. dep. dir. Vector Control Rsch. Centre, 2003—. Chief, human resources devel. Vector Control Rsch. Centre, 2003—; adj. assoc. prof. Georgetown U., Washington. Mem.: Sci. Societies (life). Office: Med Complex Indira Nagar Pondicherry 605006 India Office Fax: 91 413 2272041. Personal E-mail: sabesan1@yahoo.com.

SHANNON, MARY LOU, adult health nursing educator; b. Memphis, Apr. 4, 1938; d. Sidney Richmond Shannon and Lucille (Gwaltney) Shannon Cloud. BSN, U. Tenn., 1959; MA, Columbia U., 1963, MEd, 1964, EdD, 1972. Staff nurse City of Memphis Hosps., 1959—60, instr. Sch. Nursing, 1960—62; asst. prof. U. Tenn., Memphis, 1964—70, assoc. prof., 1970—73, prof., 1973—89; prof., chair adult health dept. Sch. Nursing U. Tex., Galveston, 1989—98, prof., 1989—2000, prof. emeritus, 2000—. Bd. dirs. Nat. Pressure Ulcer Adv. Panel, Buffalo, 1987-96; vis. prof. U. Alta., Edmonton, Can., 1982, Union U., Memphis, 2001, Bapt. Coll. Health Scis., 2003, U. Tex., Galveston, 2004; mem. project adv. bd. RAND, Santa Monica, Calif., 1994. Contbr. chpts. to books in field and to periodicals; mem. editl. bd. Advances in Wound Care, 1987-2000. Trustee Nurses Edn. Funds, N.Y.C., 1972-86. Mem. AAAS, ANA, Nat. League Nursing (bd. of rev. 1983-86), Orthopedic Nurses Assn., So. Nursing Rsch. Soc., Am. Assn. for History of Nursing, Sigma Xi, Sigma Theta Tau, Phi Kappa Phi. Avocations: travel, reading.

SHAO, WAN-JIN, colon and rectal surgeon, educator; b. Nanjing, China, Nov. 20, 1963; BS, Nanjing U. Chinese Medicine, 1986. Clin. prof., chief cons. colorectal surgeon Nanjing U. Chinese Medicine Hosp., 2005—. Fellow: Am. Soc. Colon & Rectal Surgeons. Avocations: swimming, bicycling, travel. Office: 155 Hanzhong Rd Nanjing Jiangsu 210029 China Business E-Mail: njdoctorswj@163.com.

SHAO, ZONGHONG, medical association administrator; b. Hebei, China, Dec. 10, 1958; B, Shanghai Med. Sch., 1982. Dir. hematological dept. Gen. Hosp. Tianjin Med. U., 2004—. Master: Hematological Group Chinese Med. Assn.; mem.: Am. Soc. Hematology. Avocation: literature. Office: Anshan St 154# Heping Dist Tianjin 300052 China Business E-Mail: shaozonghong@sina.com.

SHAO-LIANG, HAN, medical educator; b. Liaoning, China, Mar. 29, 1963; PhD, China Med. U., 1987. Prof. First Affiliated Hosp. Wenzhou Med. Coll., 2004—. Office: 2 Fuxue Ln Lucheng Dist Wenzhou Zhejiang 325000 China Office Fax: 86-0577-88069307. E-mail: slhan88@126.com.

SHAPEERO, LORRAINE G., physician, researcher, educator; d. Ezra and Goldine Shapeero. BA, U. Calif., Berkeley, 1964; MD, U. Calif., San Francisco, 1968. Diplomate Am. Bd. of Radiology, 1974. Resident to faculty U. Pa., Phila., 1970—74; fellowship Inst. of Orthop. Royal Nat. Orthop. Hosp., London, 1975—76; faculty U. Calif., San Francisco, 1977—82, 1984—95, Columbia U., NY, 1982—84, Institut Gustave Roussy, France, 1990—; chief Musculoskeletal Radiology sect. Uniformed Svcs. U., Bethesda, Md., 1995—; attending radiologist Walter Reed Army Med. Ctr., Wash., 1995—; dir. Bone and Soft Tissue Sarcoma Program US Mil. Cancer Inst., Wash., 2000—. Contbr. articles various profl. jours. and rsch. publs. Mem.:

Musculoskeletal Radiology (mem. editl. bd. 1999—2002), Investigative Radiology (mem. editl. bd. 1990—94), Internat. Skeletal Soc., Radiology (mem. editl. bd., cons. to editor 1995—2001), Acad. Radiology (mem. editl. bd. 1994—), Assn. U. Radiologists (bd. dirs.), Alliance Med. Student Educators in Radiology (exec. com.), Am. Roentgen Ray Soc., Am. Coll. Radiology, Radiol. Soc. North Am., Internat. Soc. Magnetic Resonance in Medicine, Connective Tissue Oncology Soc., Radiology Rsch. Alliance (pres. 2005—06), Phi Beta Kappa. Office: Uniformed Svcs U 4301 Jones Bridge Rd Bethesda MD 20814

SHAPIRO, BURTON LEONARD, dentist, maxillofacial pathologist, geneticist, educator; b. NYC, Mar. 29, 1934; s. Nat Lazarus and Fay Rebecca (Gartenhouse) S.; m. Eileen Roman, Aug. 11, 1958; children: Norah Leah, Anne Rachael, Carla Faye. Student, Tufts U., Medford, Mass., 1951-54; DDS, NYU, 1958; MS, U. Minn., 1962, PhD, 1966. Faculty U. Minn. Sch. Dentistry, Mpls., 1962—, assoc. prof. div. oral pathology, 1966-70, prof., chmn. div. oral biology, 1970-79, prof., chmn. dept. oral biology, 1979-88, prof. dept. oral pathology and genetics, 1979-88, dir. grad. studies, mem. grad. faculty genetics, 1966—, prof. dept. oral sci., 1988—2006, mem. grad. faculty pathobiology, 1979; prof. dept. lab. medicine and pathology U. Minn. Sch. Medicine, 1985—; prof. emeritus U. Minn., 2006; mem. Human Genetics Inst. U. Minn. Sch. Medicine, 1988—, univ. senator, 1968-72, 88-93; also mem. med. staff U. Minn. Health Scis. Center; exec. com. Grad. Sch. U. Minn., chmn. health scis. policy rev. council, chmn. univ. faculty consultative com., 1988-92; chmn. univ. fin. and planning com. Grad. Sch. U. Minn., 1988. Hon. research fellow Galton Lab. dept. human genetics Univ. Coll., London, 1974; spl. vis. prof. Japanese Ministry Edn., Sci. and Culture, 1983 Mem. adv. editorial bd.: Jour. Dental Research, 1971—; Contbr. articles to profl. jours. Served to lt. USNR, 1958-60. Am. Cancer Soc. postdoctoral fellow, 1960-62; advanced fellow, 1965-68; named Century Club Prof. of Yr., 1988. Fellow Am. Acad. Oral Pathology, AAAS; mem. Internat. Assn. Dental Research (councilor 1969), Am. Soc. Human Genetics, Craniofacial Biology Soc. (pres. 1972), Sigma Xi, Omicron Kappa Upsilon. Office: U Minn Sch Dentistry Dept Oral Sci Minneapolis MN 55455 Business E-Mail: burt@umn.edu.

SHAPIRO, DAVID BENJAMIN, researcher; b. Chgo., Apr. 7, 1954; s. Leopold Julius and Virginia Lucille Shapiro. BA, Reed Coll., 1982; MA, Northwestern U., Evanston, Ill., 1986, U. Chgo., 1988; PhD, U. Ill., 1993. Computer operator Joslyn Mfg., Chgo., 1974—75; rschr. Survey Ctr., Chgo., 1982—83; rsch. analyst AMA, Chgo., 1988—89, United Way, Chgo., 1990—92; rschr. Inst. on Disability and Human Devel., U. Ill., Chgo., 1993—95. Mem.: Am. Polit. Sci. Assn. Avocations: reading, parrots.

SHAPIRO, EDWARD ROBERT, psychiatrist, educator, health facility administrator, psychotherapist; b. Boston, Sept. 13, 1941; s. Jacob and Ruth (Yankelovich) S.; m. Donna Elmendorf; 1 child, Joshua Jackson; 1 child from previous marriage, Jacob Matthew; 1 stepchild, Zachary Andrew Robbins. BA magna cum laude, Yale U., 1962; MA in Anthropology, Stanford U., 1966; MD, Harvard U., 1968. Diplomate Am. Bd. Psychiatry and Neurology. Intern in medicine Beth Israel Hosp., Boston, 1968-69, resident in psychiatry Mass. Mental Health Ctr., Boston, 1969-72, chief resident in psychiatry, 1971-72; clin. assoc. NIMH, Bethesda, Md., 1972-74; dir. Adolescent and Family Treatment and Study Ctr. McLean Hosp., Belmont, Mass., 1974-89, dir. Psychosocial Tng. and Consultation, 1989-91; bd. dirs. Ctr. for Study of Groups and Social Systems, Boston, 1983-90, A.K. Rice Inst., Washington, 1983-90, dir. Nat. Group Rels. Conf., 1989-91; faculty mem. Boston Psychoanalytic Inst., 1978—; assoc. clin. prof. psychiatry Harvard Med. Sch., Boston, 1982—; med. dir., CEO The Austen Riggs Ctr., Stockbridge, Mass., 1991—2011; tng. and supr. analyst Psychoanalytical Inst. of the Berkshires, 2003—; clin. prof. psychiatry Yale U. Sch. Medicine, 2009—. Dir. The Erik H. Erikson Inst. for Edn. and Rsch., 1994-2000. Co-author: (with A.W. Carr) Lost in Familiar Places: Creating New Connections Between the Individual and Society, 1991; editor: The Inner World in the Outer World: Psychoanalytic Perspectives, 1997; mem. editorial bd. Jour. Adolescence, 1977-82, Psychiatry, 1988—; assoc. editor Jour. Adolescence, 1982-84; contbr. articles to profl. jours. Mem. Yale Russian Chorus. With USPHS, 1972-74. Recipient Isenberg Teaching award McLean Hosp., 1980, Rsch. prize Soc. for Family Therapy and Rsch., 1984, Felix and Helen Deutsch Sci. prize Boston Psychoanalytic Inst., 1980, Outstanding Psychiatrist for Advancement of the Profession award Mass. Psychiat. Assn., 2007, Top Doctors award, 2011. Fellow Am. Psychiat. Assn. (disting. life), Am. Coll. Psychoanalysis, A.K. Rice Inst.; mem. Am. Psychoanalytic Assn. Achievements include helping develop the Erik H. Erikson Inst. for Edn. and Rsch. as a vehicle for applying the clinical insights developed at Riggs to larger social issues. Avocation: music. Office: The Austen Riggs Ctr PO Box 962 25 Main St Stockbridge MA 01262-0962

SHAPIRO, EUGENE DAVID, pediatrician, epidemiologist, educator; s. Jonah R. and Rita R. Shapiro; m. Susan K. Bowers; children: Lauren R., Amy E., Daniel J. BA, Yale Coll., New Haven, Conn., 1970; MD, U. Calif., San Francisco, 1976. Resident Children's Hosp. Pitts., 1976—79; asst. prof. pediat. Yale Sch. Medicine, New Haven, 1983—89, assoc. prof. pediat., 1989—93, prof. pediat., 1993—. Grantee, NIH, 1983—; fellow, Children's Hosp. Pitts., 1979—81; Robert Wood Johnson scholar, Yale Sch. Medicine, 1981—83. Fellow: Am. Acad. Pediat.; mem.: Am. Epidemiologic Assn., Pediatric Infectious Disease Soc., Infectious Disease Soc. Am., Soc. Pediatric Rsch., Am. Pediatric Soc., Am. Bd. Pediatrics-Infectious Diseases. Achievements include research in assessment of clinical effectiveness of vaccines. Office: Yale U Dept Pediatrics 333 Cedar St PO Box 208064 New Haven CT 06520-8064

SHAPIRO, HAROLD TAFLER, economics professor, former academic administrator; b. Montreal, Que., Can., June 8, 1935; s. Maxwell and Mary (Tafler) Shapiro; m. Vivian Bernice Rapoport, May 19, 1957; children: Anne, Marilyn, Janet, Karen. BComm, McGill U., Montreal, 1956; PhD in Econs. (Harold Helm fellow, Harold Dodds sr. fellow), Princeton U., NJ, 1964. From asst. prof. to assoc. prof. econ. University of Michigan, Ann Arbor, 1964—70, prof., 1970—76, prof. econ. and pub. affairs, 1977, chmn. dept. econ., 1974—77, v.p. acad. affairs, 1977—79, pres., 1980—87; rsch. adv. Bank Can., 1965-72; pres. Princeton University, 1988—2001, pres. emeritus, prof. economics & pub. affairs Woodrow Wilson Sch., 2001—. Mem. exec. com. Assn. of Am. Universities, 1985—89; trustee NJ Commn. Sci. and Tech., 1988—91; mem. Pres.'s Coun. Advisors Sci. and Tech., 1990—92, Stem Cell Inst. of NJ Joint Bd. Mgrs., 2005—; chmn. com. employer-based health benefits Inst. Medicine, 1991, Nat. Acad. Sci. Com. Americas Energy Future, 2007—; bd. overseers Robert Wood Johnson Med. Sch., 2000—; bd. dir. The Hastings Ctr., Reading is Fundamental, Knight Found. Comm. on Intercollegiate Athletics, Merck Vaccine Adv. Bd., Princeton Healthcare Sys.; bd. trustees U. Medicine & Dentistry NJ, 2006—; trustee tech. Israel Inst. Tech., 2002—; chmn. Orgn. NIH Nat. Sci., 2000—03, mem. adv. com. Human Embryonic Stem Cell Rsch., 2006—; chmn. bd. DeVry Inst., 2008—. Author: A Larger Sense of Purpose: Higher Education and Society, 2005; editor (with William G. Bowen): Universities and Their Leadership, 1998; editor: (with James F. Childress & Eric M. Meslin) Belmont Revisited: Ethical Principles for Research With Human Subjects, 2005. Chair Nat. Bioethics Adv. Commn., 1996—2001; chmn. spl. Presdl. com. Rsch. Librs. Group, 1980—89; mem. Gov.'s High Tech. Task Force, Mich., 1980—87, Gov.'s Commn. Jobs and Econ. Devel., Mich., 1983—87, Carnegie Commn. Coll. Retirement, 1984—86; dir. Am. Coun. Edn., 1989—91; mem. Pres. Bush Coun. Advisors Sci. and Tech., 1990—93; trustee Alfred P. Sloan Found., 1980—, Interlochen Ctr. Arts, 1988—95, U. Pa. Med. Ctr., 1992—, Univ. Corp. Advanced Internet Devel., 2000, Am. Jewish Com., 2002—, Ednl. Testing Svc., 1994—2000. Recipient Lt. Gov.'s medal in commerce, McGill U., 1956, William D. Carey Lectureship award Leadership in Sci. Policy, 2006. Fellow: AAAS, Mich. Soc. Fellows (sr.); mem.: Am. Philos. Soc., Inst. Medicine of NAS/NRC, Univs. Rsch. Assn. (trustee 1988—2001). Office: Princeton Univ Woodrow Wilson Sch 359 Wallace Hall Princeton NJ 08544 Office Phone: 609-258-6184. Business E-Mail: hts@princeton.edu.

SHAPIRO, JOAN ISABELLE, lab administrator, medical/surgical nurse; b. Aug. 26, 1943; d. Macy James and Frieda Lockhart; m. Ivan Lee Shapiro, Dec. 28, 1968; children: Audrey, Michael. Diploma, Peoria Meth. Sch. Nursing, 1964. RN. Nurse Nurse Grant Hosp., Columbus, Ohio, 1975—76, Cardiac Thoracic and Vascular Surgeons Ltd., Geneva, Ill., 1977—97, mgr. non-ivasive lab., 1979—97. Owner operator Shapiro's Mastiff's 1976-82; sec.-treas. Sounds Svcs., 1976—, Mainstream Sounds Inc., 1980-84; co-founder Cardio-Phone Inc., 1982-99, Edgewater Vascular Inst., 1987-89, Associated Profls., 1989-92; v.p. Computer Specialists Inc., 1986-89; founder, pres. Vein Ctr., Edema Ctr. Ltd., mem., Esther Aynes Chpt. NSDAR, 2009-. Mem. DAR (sec. Katahdin Valley-Lydia Putman chpt. 2004—08), Soc. Non-invasive Technologists, Soc. Peripheral Vascular Nursing (cmty. awareness com. 1984-2004), Kane County Med. Soc. Aux. (pres. 1983-84, adviser, 1984-85), Katahdin Valley Putnam Cpt. of DAR (sec. 2004-08). Lutheran. Home: Cardiac Thoracic/Vas Surg PO Box 325 Fort Fairfield ME 04742-0325 Business E-Mail: joan@ivanshapiro.com. *

SHAPIRO, LARRY J., dean, educator, pediatrician; b. July 6, 1946; s. Philip and Phyllis Shapiro; m. Carol-Ann Uetuke; children: Jennifer, Jessica, Brian. AB, Washington U., St. Louis, 1968, MD, 1971. Diplomate Am. Bd. Pediat., Am. Bd. Med. Examiners, Am. Bd. Med. Genetics. Intern St. Louis Children's Hosp., 1971—72, resident, 1971—73, rsch. assoc. NIH, Bethesda, Md., 1973—75; asst. prof. Sch. Medicine UCLA, 1975—79, assoc. prof., 1979—83, prof. pediat. and biol. chemistry, 1983—91; investigator Howard Hughes Med. Inst., 1987—91, investigator, W.H. and Marie Wattis Disting. prof.; prof., chmn. dept. pediat. U. Calif.-San Francisco Sch. Medicine, 1991—2003; chief pediat. svcs. U. Calif.-San Francisco Med. Ctr., 1991—2003; Spencer T. and Ann W. Olin Disting. prof., exec. vice chancellor for med. affairs, dean Washington U. Sch. Medicine, St. Louis, 2003—. Contbr. numerous articles to profl. publs. Served to lt. comdr. USPHS, 1973—75. Fellow: AAAS, Am. Acad. Pediat. (E. Mead Johnson award in rsch. 1982); mem.: Am. Acad. Arts and Scis., Am. Pediatric Soc. (coun. mem. 1999—2001, pres. 2003—04), Am. Soc. Clin. Investigation, Am. Soc. Human Genetics (coun. 1985—88, pres.-elect 1995, pres. 1997), Assn. Am. Physicians, Soc. for Inherited Metabolic Disease (coun. 1983—88, pres. 1986—87), Western Soc. for Pediatric Rsch. (coun. 1983—87, pres. 1989—90, Ross award in rsch. 1981), Soc. Pediatric Rsch. (coun. 1984—87, pres. 1991—92), Inst. Medicine (coun. mem.). Office: Wash U 660 S Euclid campus box 8106 Saint Louis MO 63110 *

SHAPIRO, LAWRENCE R., clinical geneticist, educator; BS, Tufts U., Medford, Mass., 1958; MD, NYU, 1962. Lic. NY, 1964, diplomate Am. Bd. Pediatrics, 1967, cert. Am. Bd. Clin. Genetics-Med. Genetics, 1982, Am. Bd. Clin. Cytogenetics-Med. Genetics, 1982. Intern Children's Hosp., Los Angeles, 1963, resident pediat., 1963—64, Bellevue Hosp., 1964—65; fellow clin. genetics Mt. Sinai Med. Ctr., 1967—68; prof. pediat. NY Med. Coll.; hosp. affiliation includes Good Samaritan Hosp., Nyack Hosp., Vassar Brothers Med. Ctr., Westchester Med. Ctr. Office: Westchester Medical Center 19 Bradhurst Ave Number 1600 Hawthorne NY 10532 Office Phone: 914-593-8900. Office Fax: 914-593-8938.

SHAPIRO, LIZA J., anthropologist, educator; BA in Anthrop. & Psychology summa cum laude, SUNY, Albany, 1983; PhD in Anthrop., SUNY, Stony Brook, 1991. Asst. prof. dept anthrop. U. Tex., Austin, 1990—97, assoc. prof. dept. anthrop., 1997—2008, prof. dept. anthrop, 2008—. Assoc. editor Jour. Human Evolution, 2004—07, Am. Jour. Physical Anthrop., 2005. Contbr. several srticles to profl. jours. Mem.: Soc. Integrative & Comparative Biology, Am. Assn. Physical Anthropologists, Phi Beta Kappa. Office: University of Texas Dept Anthropology 1 University Sta C3200 Austin TX 78712-1086 Office Phone: 512-471-7533. Office Fax: 512-471-6535. E-mail: liza.shapiro@mail.utexas.edu.

SHAPIRO, LOUIS A., hospital administrator; BA, U. Pitts., M in Health Adminstrn. Diplomate Am. Coll. Healthcare Execs. Exec. v.p., chief adminstrv. officer Grad. and Mt. Sinai Hosps., Phila.; v.p. Allegheny Hosp., Pitts.; sr. practice cons. McKinsey and Co.; chief adminstrv. officer Geisinger Clinic, Danville, Pa., 2002—04; exec. v.p., clin. enterprise COO Geisinger Health Sys., Danville, Pa., 2004—06; pres., CEO Hosp. for Spl. Surgery, NYC, 2006—. Office: Hosp for Spl Surgery 535 E 70th St New York NY 10021 *

SHAPIRO, LUCY, molecular biology educator; b. NYC, July 16, 1940; d. Philip and Yetta (Stein) Cohen; m. Roy Shapiro, Jan. 23, 1960 (div. 1977); 1 child, Peter; m. Harley H. McAdams, July 28, 1978; stepchildren: Paul, Heather. BA, Bklyn. Coll., 1962; PhD, Albert Einstein Coll. Medicine, 1966. Asst. prof. Albert Einstein Coll. Medicine, NYC, 1967-72, assoc. prof., 1972-77, Kramer prof., chmn. dept. molecular biology, 1977-86, dir. biol. scis. divsn., 1981-86; Eugene Higgins prof., chmn. dept. microbiology, Coll. Physicians and Surgeons Columbia U., NYC, 1986-89; Joseph D. Grant prof. devel. biology Stanford (Calif.) U. Sch. Medicine, 1989-97, chmn. dept. devel. biology, 1989-97, Virginia and D.K. Ludwig prof. cancer rsch., dept. devel. biology, 1998—; dir. Beckman Ctr. Molecular and Genetic Medicine, Stanford U., 2001—. Mem. bd. sci. counselors NIH, Washington, 1980—84; mem. bd. sci. advisors G.D. Searle Co., Skokie, Ill., 1984—86; trustee Scientists Inst. for Pub. Info., 1990—94; mem. sci. adv. bd. SmithKline Beecham, 1993—2000, Anacor Pharms., Inc., 2001—, PathoGenesis, 1995—2000, Ludwig Inst. Cancer Res., 2000—, Glaxo Smith Kline, 2001—07, Hatteras Ventures, 2008—09, Pasteur Inst., Paris, 2009—; mem. adv. bd. Biodesign Inst., Ariz. State U., 2006—08, Singapore Inst. Molecular & Cell Biology, 2006—08, Lawrence Berkeley Nat. Labs., 2006—; bd. dirs. Anacor Pharms. Inc., 2001—, Gen-Probe Inc., 2008—. Editor: Microbiol. Devel., 1984; mem. editl. bd. Jour. Bacteriology, 1978-86, Trends in Genetics, 1987—, Genes and Development, 1987-91, Cell Regulation, 1990-92, Molecular Biology of the Cell, 1992-98, Molecular Microbiology, 1991-96, Current Opinion on Genetics and Devel., 1991—; contbr. articles to profl. jours. Mem. sci. bd. Helen Hay Witney Found., N.Y.C., 1986-94, Biozentrum, Basel, 1999-2001, Hutchinson Cancer Ctr., Seattle, 1999; mem. grants adv. bd. Beckman Found., 1999—; co-chmn. adv. bd. NSF Biology Directorate, 1988-89; vis. com., bd. overseers Harvard U., Cambridge, Mass., 1987-90; mem. sci. bd. Whitehead Inst., MIT, Boston, 1988-93; mem. sci. rev. bd. Howard Hughes Med. Inst., 1990-94, Cancer Ctr. of Mass. Gen. Hosp., Boston, 1994; mem. Presidio Coun. City of San Francisco, 1991-94; mem. pres. coun. U. Calif., 1991-97. Recipient Hirschl Career Scientist award, 1976, Spirit of Achievement award, 1978, Alumna award of honor Bklyn. Coll., 1983, Excellence in Sci. award Fedn. Am. Soc. Exptl. Biology, 1994, Gairdner Found. Internat. award, 2009, Swedish Royal Acad. Sci., 2008, John Scott award 2009, Abbott Lifetime Achievement award ASM, 2010, Disting. Alumna award Albert Einstein Coll. Medicine, 2010, named Hitchcock Prof. U. Calif., Berkeley, 2008; Jane Coffin Child fellow, 1966; resident scholar Rockefeller Found., Bellagio, Italy, 1996. Fellow AAAS, Am. Acad. Arts and Scis., Am. Acad. Microbiology, Calif. Coun. on Sci. and Tech.; mem. NAS (Selman A. Waksman award 2005), Inst. Medicine of NAS, Am. Philos. Soc., Am. Soc. Biochemistry and Molecular Biology (nominating com. 1982, 87, coun. 1990-93), Am. Heart Assn. (sci. adv. bd. 1984-87). Avocation: watercolor painting. Office: Stanford U Sch Medicine Beckman Ctr Dept Devel Biology Stanford CA 94305 Office Phone: 650-725-7678. *

SHAPIRO, MARCIA HASKEL, speech and language pathologist; b. NYC, Nov. 6, 1949; d. Ben and Edna Haskel; m. Louis Shapiro, Aug. 1, 1981 (dec. 2005); m. Thomas Nardone, 2006. BA, Hunter Coll., 1982; MA, NYU, 1983; MA in Speech Pathology, U. Ctrl. Fla., 1991; PhD, Barrington U., 2001. Cert. deaf educator, Fla. Tchr. deaf Pub. Sch. 47, NYC, 1983-84; speech pathologist St. Francis Sch. for the Deaf, Bklyn., 1984-86, Seminole County Schs., 1986-87, Lake County Schs., 1987-89, Orange County Schs., Orlando, Fla., 1989-91, West Volusia Meml. Hosp., Deland, Fla., 1991-93, Orlando Regional Med. Ctr., 1993, Sand Lake Hosp., 1993-98; staff head swallowing dept. Leesburg Regional Med. Ctr., 1994; dir. speech pathology Fla. Hosp., Waterman, 1995—, rsch. assoc. dysphasia study. Mem. adv. bd. Libr. Spl. Edn., 2002—04. Recipient Profl. Alumni award, U. Ctrl. Fla., 2006. Mem. AFTRA, EQUITY, Am. Speech and Hearing Assn. (v.p. continuing edn. Fla. 2002-2004), Annals of Deaf, Coun. Am. Instrs. of the Deaf, Alexander Graham Bell Assn. for Deaf. E-mail: marcy6116@aol.com.

SHAPIRO, MARIAN KAPLUN, psychologist; b. NY, July 13, 1939; d. David and Bertha (Pearlman) Kaplun; m. Irwin Ira Shapiro, Dec. 20, 1959; children: Steven, Nancy. BA, Queens Coll., 1959; MA in Tchg., Harvard U., 1961, EdD, 1978. Cert. psychologist. Tchr. North Quincy (Mass.) HS, 1962-64; instr. Carnegie Inst., Boston, 1968-74; staff psychologist South Shore Counselling Assn., Hanover, Mass., 1978-80; pvt. practice Lexington, Mass., 1980—. Adj. instr. Mass. Sch. Profl. Psychology, Dedham, 1985—. Author: (book) 2nd Childhood: Hypnoplay Therapy with Age--Regressed Adults, 1989; contbr. articles to profl. jours., poetry to lit. jours.; author: (poetry books) Players in the Dream Dreamers In THe Play, 2007, THe End of The World, Announced on Wednesday, 2007, Your Third Wish, 2007. Fellow: Am. Coll. Forensic Examiners Inst., Am. Orthopsychiatric Assn.; mem.: APA, Worldwide Leaders in Healthcare, New Eng. Soc. Clin. Hypnosis, Internat. Soc. Study Dissociation, New Eng. Soc. Treatment Trauma and Dissociation, Am. Soc. Clin. Hypnosis (cert. cons.), Am. Soc. Group Psychotherapy (clin.), N.E. Soc. Group Psychotherapy, Mass. Psychol. Assn., Pi Lambda Theta, Sigma Alpha. Avocations: music, singing, piano, violin, poetry. Home and Office: 17 Lantern Ln Lexington MA 02421-6029 Office Phone: 781-862-3728.

SHAPIRO, MARK LOUIS, surgeon, educator; b. Kans. City, Mo., Sept. 29, 1967; BA in Psychology, Mich. State U., 1989; MD, Ross U. Sch. Medicine, 1997. Surg. resident Jewish Hosp. Cin., 1997—2002; fellow, surg. critical care. instr. surgery U. Cin., 2002—03; asst. prof. surgery U. Mass., Worcester, 2003—06; assoc. prof. surgery, assoc. dir. trauma svcs., dir., total parenteral nutrition tpn svcs. Duke U. Med. Ctr., 2006—. Recipient Joel Essig Excellence award, Jewish Hosp. Cin. Ohio, 2001, Excellence award, U. Mass., Worcester, 2006, Strength, Hope & Caring award, Duke U. Med. Ctr., 2008; named Med. Student Govt., Ross U., 1995. Mem.: ACS, Am. Trauma Soc., Pres. NC Chpt., Western Trauma Assn., Ea. Assn. Surgery Trauma, Soc. Critical Care Medicine. Avocation: golf. Office: Duke University Med Ctr 2837 Durham NC 27710 Office Fax: 919-668-4369. Business E-Mail: ml.shapiro@duke.edu.

SHAPIRO, NELLA IRENE, surgeon, educator; b. NYC, Nov. 13, 1947; d. Eugene and Ethel (Pearl) Shapiro; m. Jack Schwartz, Oct. 16, 1977; children: Max Schwartz, Molly Schwartz. BA, Barnard Coll., 1968; MD, Albert Einstein Coll., 1972. Resident in gen. surgery Montefiore Hosp., NYC, 1972-76; mem. staff N. Ctrl. Hosp., Bronx, NY, 1976-77, Bronx Mcpl. Hosp., 1977-87, chief gen. surgery, 1983-87; mem. staff gen. surgery Albert Einstein Coll. Hosp., Bronx, 1977-93, chief gen. surgery, 1991-93; atty. Lear Surg. Assocs., 1993-94; pvt. practice Bronx, 1994—; dir. breast surgery Eastchester Ctr. Cancer Care, Bronx, 2004—. Asst. prof. surgery Albert Einstein Coll., Bronx, 1980—; assoc. dir. gen. surgery Weller Hosp., Bronx, 1991—93; co-founder Whaecom Breast Ctr., Bronx, 1991—. Fellow: ACS. Avocations: travel, opera. Office: Eastchester Ctr Cancer Care 2330 Eastchester Rd Bronx NY 10469 Home Phone: 914-238-3544; Office Phone: 718-405-0400, 718-732-4000.

SHAPIRO, PAULA, retired maternal and women's health nurse; b. Pitts., Nov. 16, 1927; d. Ben and Esther (Halpert) Cohn; m. Bernard Shapiro, July 17, 1982; children: Eugene Hershorin, Abby Hershorin, Marc Hershorin, Jay Hershorin, Ellen Fenerty, Kenneth, Fred, Stacy Pierce. RN, Montefiore Hosp. Sch. Nursing, 1948; BS, Phila. U., 1987. RN, Pa. Nursing care coord. Thomas Jefferson U. Hosp., Phila.; asst. supr. operating rm. Wakefield (R.I.) Gen. Hosp.; staff RN operating rm. Jefferson Hosp., Phila., ret., 1993. Contbr. articles to profl. jours. Vol. Thomas Jefferson U. Hosp.; vol. o.r. nurse Tel Aviv, Israel, 1977. Home: 1500 Locust St Apt 2216 Philadelphia PA 19102-4317 Personal E-mail: paulashapiro@hotmail.com.

SHAPIRO, RICHARD L., surgeon, educator; Grad. summa cum laude, U. Pa.; MD, NYU, 1988. Diplomate Am. Bd. Surgery. Dir. melanoma and breast cancer rsch. fund NYU Med. Ctr.; mem. melanoma clin. trials rev. com. NYU Langone Med. Ctr., intern in gen. surgery, chief resident in gen. surgery, 1989—93, exec. chief resident, fellow in surgical oncology, 1993—95, surgeon. Pub. (100 peer-reviewed articles, book chapters, and abstracts). Named one of Top Doctors, NY. Fellow: ACS; mem.: Assoc. for Acad. Surgery, Alpha Omega Alpha, Am. Assoc. for Cancer Rsch., Am. Soc. of Clin. Oncology, Soc. of Surgical Oncology. Office: New York University Langone Medical Center 160 E 34th St New York NY 10016 Office Phone: 212-731-5347. Office Fax: 212-731-5574.

SHAPIRO, THEODORE, psychiatrist, educator; b. NYC, Feb. 26, 1932; s. Herman Alexander and Nettie (Rosenblatt) S.; m. Joan May Itkin, June 26, 1955; children: Susan, Alexander Herman. BA, Wesleyan U., 1953; MD, Cornell U., 1957. Diplomate Am. Bd. Psychiatry and Neurology, Am. Bd. Child Psychiatry, Am. Psychoanalytic Assn. Intern Montefiore Hosp., NYC, 1957—58; resident in psychiatry NYU-Bellevue Hosp., 1958—61; instr. to prof. NYU Sch. Medicine, 1960—76; rsch. assoc. child psychiatry NYU-Bellevue Hosp., 1961—65; asst. lectr. N.Y. Psychoanalytic Inst., NYC, 1970—86; prof. psychiatry and pediatrics Cornell U. Med. Coll., NYC, 1976—2002; tng. and supervising analyst N.Y. Psychoanalytic Inst., NYC, 1986—; vice chair for child and adolescent psychiatry, 1995—2002; emeritus prof. Cornell U. Med. Coll., NYC, 2002—. Cons. alcohol, drug abuse and mental health adminstrn. WHO, Washington, Geneva and Copenhagen, 1980—82; chair com. on stewardship Task Force Future, 1980—82, acad. sec., 1981—83, chair work group on sci. issues, 1988—89, chair com. editorship and stewarship of jour., 1984—86, 1990—92; participant APA bilateral exch. in Ea. Europe, 1992; mem. reviewer child psychopathology and treatment rev. com. NIMH, 1994—98; lectr. Jefferson Med. Coll., 2007; lectr. in field; spkr. in field. Author: Clinical Psycholinguistics, 1979; co-editor: Infant Psychiatry, 1976; editor: Psychoanalysis and Contemporary Science, 1976, Structure in Psychoanalysis, 1991, Affect: Psychoanalytic Perspectives, 1992; co-author: Manual of Panic-Focused Psychodynamic Psychotherapy, 1996, Psychodynamic Treatment of Depression, 2004, Psychodynamic Approaches to the Adolscent with Panic Disorder, 2004; editor Jour. Am. Psychoanalytic Assn., 1984-93; book rev. editor Internat. Jour. Psychoanalysis, 1993-2002; co-editor Research in Psychoanalysis, 1995; contbr. articles to profl. jours. Keynote lectr. Am. Psychoanalytic Assn., Boston, 2003, H. Hartmann Meml. NY Psychoanalytic Inst., 2004. Recipient Wilfred C. Hulse award, N.Y. Coun. Child Psychiatry, 1982, Harry Bakwin Meml. award, NYU, 1982, Heinz Hartmann award, N.Y. Psychoanalytic Inst., 2004; grantee, NIMH, 1976—86; grant, 2009—. Fellow Am. Acad. Child Psychiatry (sec. 1981-83), Am. Psychiat. Assn.; mem. Internat. Acad. Child/Adolescent Psychiatry (chmn. com. 2006), Soc. Profs. Child Psychiatry (chmn. com. on edn. 1982-90), Group for Advancement of Psychiatry (chmn. com. on child psychiatry 1985-90, elected GAP bd., 2008-), Am. Bd. Psychiatry & Neurology (com. on child and adolescent psychiatry 1987-93, chmn. 1992-93), N.Y. Psychoanalytic Soc. Jewish. Office: Weill Med Coll Cornell U Payne Whitney Clinic PO Box 140 New York NY 10021-0012 Office Phone: 212-746-5713. E-mail: tshapiro@med.cornell.edu.

SHAPIRO, WILLIAM MAURICE, emergency medicine physician, administrator, researcher; b. Phila. m. Jane Catherine Fitzgerald, Sept. 26, 1992; 1 child, Erin Rose. BA, Temple U., 1972; MD, Hahnemann U., 1976. Diplomate Am. Bd. Internal Medicine, Am. Bd. Emergency Medicine. Dir. emergency dept. Herrick Meml. Hosp., Tecumseh, Mich., 1986-87, Villa View Comty. Hosp., San Diego, 1989-90; physician Scripps Clinic and Rsch. Found., La Jolla, Calif., 1991—; dir. San Diego divsn. Staticon Internat., 1990-99; prin. investigator n Touch Rsch. San Diego, 2000—04; med. dir. Accelovance Rsch. of San Diego, 2005—07; staff physician Kaiser Permanent Emergency Medicine, Orange, Calif. Dir. EMT course Raisin Twp. Fire Dept., Tecumseh, 1985-86; dir. ACLS courses Harborview Med. Ctr., San Diego, 1990-93; expert reviewer Med. Bd. Calif. Recipient commendation Tecumseh City Coun., 1985. Fellow ACP, Am. Coll. Emergency Physicians, Am. Acad. Emergency Medicine. Avocations: music, skiing, windsurfing. Office: Kaiser Permanente Orange County Emergency Medicine 441 N Lakeview Ave Anaheim CA 92807

SHAPSHAY, STANLEY M., otolaryngologist, educator; b. Bklyn., Dec. 22, 1942; s. Samuel and Mollie Shapshay; m. Ruth E. Shapshay, Oct. 1, 1967; children: Sandra Lynne, Mara Rachelle. BS, Bklyn. Coll., 1964; MD, Med. Coll. Va., Richmond, 1968. Diplomate Am. Bd. Othlaryngology. Intern surgery Boston City Hosp., 1968-69; resident otolaryngology Tufts-New Eng. Med. Ctr., Boston, 1969-71, 1972-75; fellow otolaryngical head & neck surgery Serafimer Hosp., Karolinska Med. Sch., Stockholm, 1971-72; asst. prof. otolaryngology Boston U. Sch. Medicine, 1977-86, clin. assoc. prof. otolaryngology, 1986—91, prof. otolaryngology, 1991—2005; prof., chair dept. otolaryngology Tufts U. Sch. Medicine, Boston, 1994—2001; prof. otolaryngology-head & neck surgery Mt. Sinai Sch. Medicine & Med. Ctr., NYC, 2005—06; prof. dept. otolaryngology Albany Med. Coll., NY, 2006—; staff Univ. Ear, Nose & Throat of Northeastern NY, LLP, 2006—. Clin. instr. U. Wash., Seattle, 1975—77; chief otolaryngology dept. VA Med. Ctr., Boston, 1977—80, attending otolaryngologist, 1980—82; asst. vis. surgeon otolaryngology Univ. Hosp., Boston, 1977—82; vis. surgeon Children's Hosp. Med. Ctr., Boston, 1977—87; chief ambulatory surgery/otolarygology Boston City Hosp., 1980—82; staff dept. otolaryngology/head & neck surgery Lahey Clinic Med. Ctr., Burlington, Mass., 1982—94, chmn. clin. laser com., 1984—93, bd. govs., 1993—94, New Eng. Med. Ctr. Hosps., 1995—97; vis. prof. Stanford U., Calif., 1995, Vanderbilt U. Med. Ctr., Nashville, 1995, U. Istanbul, Turkey, 1997; adj. prof. dept. surgery/otolaryngology Brown U. Sch. Medicine, Providence, 1997—; vis. scientist spectroscopy lab. MIT, 1996—. Mem. editl. bd. Lawers in Surgery and Medicine, Medical Laser Industry Report, Otolaryngoloty-Head & Neck Surgery; contbr. articles to profl. jours., chapters to books; spkr. in field. Maj. US Army, 1975—77. Fellow: ACS, Am. Rhinological Soc., Am. Coll. Chest Physicians, Am. Broncho-Esophagol. Assn. (coun. mem. 1985—, chmn. prevention fgn. body accidents and caustic ingestion com. 1988—89), Am. Soc. Head & Neck Surgery (mem. prevention com.), Am. Acad. Otolaryngology & Ophthalmology; mem.: AMA, Am. Laryngological Assn., Am. Coun. Otolaryngology (subcom allied health pers. 1975—76), Am. Acad. Otolaryngology (Young Otolaryngologist 1981—82), Triological Soc. (coun. mem. 1997—, pres 2005—06, Edmund Prince Fowler award), Biomed. Optics Soc., Am. Bd. Laser Surgery (founding mem.), New Eng. Otolaryngol. Soc. (sec.-treas. 1984—88, pres. 1990—91), Am. Soc. Laser Medicine & Surgery (chmn. postgrad. edn. com. 1986—87, membership/awards com. 1989—90, v.p. 1989—90). Avocations: reading, tennis, ballroom dancing. Office: Albany Med Coll Dept Otolaryngology 43 New Scotland Ave Albany NY 12208 also: Univ ENT Northeastern NY 35 Hackett Blvd Albany NY 12208 Office Phone: 518-262-3125, 518-262-5575. Office Fax: 518-262-3165, 518-262-6670.

SHARARA, FADY IHSAN, reproductive endocrinologist, infertility specialist; b. Beirut, Feb. 26, 1962; s. Ihsan A. Sharara and Samia R. Mouneimneh; m. Roula Mohsen Dalloul; children: Yasmeen, Noora. BS, Am. U. Beirut, 1982, MD, 1986. Asst. prof. U. Ill., Chgo., 1994—95; co-dir. divsn. reprodn. endocrinology and infertility Michael Reese Hosp. and Fertility Ctr., 1995—96; asst. prof., assoc. prof. U. Md. Sch. Medicine, Balt., 1996—2000; dir. assisted reproductive techs. Fertility and Reproductive Health Ctr., Annandale, Va., 2000—01; founder, med. dir. Va. Ctr. Reporductive Medicine, Reston, 2001—; clin. assoc. prof. George Washington U. Sch. Medicine, Washington, 2001—. Dir. asst. reproductive techs. U. Md. Sch. Medicine, 1997—2000. Recipient Serono Young Investigator award, Chgo. Area Reproductive Endocrinologists, 1995. Fellow: ACOG; mem.: ESHRE, ASRM, Am. Infertility Assn. (bd. dirs. 2001—03), Mid. East Fertility Soc., Endocrine Soc. Office: Va Ctr Reproductive Medicine 11150 Sunset Hills Rd Ste 100 Reston VA 20190 Home Phone: 301-320-9320; Office Phone: 703-437-7722. Business E-Mail: fsharara@vcrmed.com.

SHARAWY, MOHAMED M., science educator; b. Cairo, Mar. 13, 1941; DDS, Coll. Dental Medicine, 1962; PhD, U. Rochester, 1970. Prof. Ga. Health Scis. U., 1970—. Dir. oral biology, anatomy Coll. Dental Medicine, 1970. Scholarship, Fullbright. Mem.: Exptl. Biology & Medicine, Internat. Assn. Dental Rsch. Avocations: walking, tennis, travel. Office: Laney Walker Blvd Augusta GA 30912 Office Fax: 706-721-9415. Business E-Mail: msharawy@georgiahealth.edu.

SHARER, KEVIN W., medical products executive; b. Clinton, Iowa, Mar. 2, 1948; m. Faye M. Sharer (div.); children: Heather, Keith; m. Carol Sharer. BS in Aero. Engring., US Naval Acad., 1970; MS in Aero. Engring., US Naval Postgraduate Sch., 1971; MBA, U. Pitts., 1982. Commd. lt. to lt. comdr. USN, 1970—78; with AT&T Inc. (merger of SBC Communications & AT&T Corp.), 1978-82; cons. McKinsey & Co., 1982-84; pres., CEO General Electric Co., Princeton, NJ, 1984-89; exec. v.p., pres. bus. markets divsn. MCI Communications, Washington, 1989—92; pres., COO Amgen, Inc., Thousand Oaks, Calif., 1992-2000, pres., CEO, 2000—01, chmn., pres., CEO, 2001—10, chmn., CEO, 2010—. Bd. dirs. Amgen Inc., 1992—, 3M Corp., 2001—07, Northrup Grumman Corp., 2003—, Chevron Corp., 2007—. Chmn. bd. trustees LA County Mus. Natural Hist.; bd. trustees U. So. Calif. Office: Amgen Inc 1 Amgen Ctr Dr Thousand Oaks CA 91320-1799 Office Phone: 805-447-1000. Office Fax: 805-447-1010. *

SHARFSTEIN, JOSHUA MOSES, public health service officer, state official; b. Sept. 26, 1969; s. Steven and Margaret (Shiling) Sharfstein; m. Yngvild Olsen; 2 children. BS, Harvard Coll., 1991; MD, Harvard Med. Sch., 1996. Pediatrics resident Boston Med. Ctr., 1999, Boston Children's Hosp., 1999; gen. pediatrics fellow Boston U. Sch. Med., 2001; pediatrician Children's Nat. Med. Ctr., Mt. Wash. Pediatric Hosp.; sr. public health aide for Rep. Henry A. Waxman US House of Reps., Washington; commr. Balt. Health Dept., 2005—09; prin. dep. commr. FDA, 2009—11, acting commr., 2009; sec. Md. Dept. Health & Mental Hygeine, Baltimore, 2011—. Named Pub. Official of Yr., Governing Mag., 2008. Office: Maryland Dept Health & Mental Hygeine 201 West Preston St 5th Fl Baltimore MD 21201 Office Phone: 410-767-4639. E-mail: JSharfstein@dhmh.state.md.us. *

SHARIF, NAJ, pharmaceutical executive, researcher; b. Pakistan, Nov. 22, 1956; BS with joint honors, Southampton U., Eng., 1978, PhD, 1982. Staff scientist Warner-Lambert Pfizler, 1985—88; staff rschr. II Syntex Rsch., Roche, 1988—91; group leader Synaptic Pharm. Corp., 1991—92; dir. Alcon Rsch., Ltd., 1992—. Adj. prof. U. North Tex. CNS & Ophthal. Expertise, 2005—. Contbr. articles to profl. 180 jours. 19 patents. Travel fellowship, Weizman Inst., Rehovot, Israel. Mem.: Am. Soc. Pharmacology & Exptl. Therapeutics, Assn. Ocular Pharmacology & Therapeutics, Assn. Rsch. Vision & Ophthalmology. Avocations: tennis, ping pong/table tennis, music. Office: Alcon Research Ltd R6 19 6201 South Freeway Fort Worth TX 76134 Business E-Mail: naj.sharif@alconlabs.com.

SHARIF, SULEIMAN IBRAHIM, pharmacologist, researcher; b. Benghazi, Libya, Aug. 1, 1951; s. Ibrahim Saleh Sharif and Gamra Saleh Abar; m. Fatima Azzahra Mohamed Hyba; children: Ibrahim Suleiman, Rubian Suleiman. BPharm, Cairo, 1974; PhD, Nottingham, 1980. Chmn., dept. pharmacology Faculty of Medicine, Garyounis U., Benghazi, Libya, 1981—86; dean, med. grad. studies Al-Arab Med. U., Benghazi, 1992—99, dean, faculty of pharmacy, 1996—99; chmn., dept. of pharmacology and toxicology Faculty of Pharmacy and Health Sciences, AUST, Ajman, United Arab Emirates, 2000—05; prof. and chmn., dept. of pharmacology U. of Sharjah, United Arab Emirates, 2005—. Dir., med. supply orgn. Ministry of Health, Libya, 1995—96. Author: (text book) Pharmacology Synopsis with MCQ's, 1995, (book) Hashish, Medicinal Plants in Quran. Mem. Narcotics Prohibition Com., Benghazi, Libya, 1985—99. Grant, Garyounis U. Rsch. Ctr., 1985—90, 1985—89. Fellow: Innovative and Med. Environ. Commn.; mem.: Union of Arab Pharmacists, Newyork Acad. of Sci. (patron mem. 2003—), Libyan Pharm. Assn. (chmn., sci. com. 1980—96), Internat. Brain Rsch. Orgn.

SHARIFI, AZALEA A., orthodontist and general dentist; b. Hays, Kans., Mar. 2, 1967; d. Iraj Alagha Sharifi and Sara D. Salehian; m. Ramin Farmand; 1 child, Shayan-Daniel Farmand. DDS, Westfalian U., Muenster, Germany, 1995, MSc in Orthodontics and Dentofacial Orthopedics, 2001; PhD, U. Muenster, 1997; DMD, U. Pa., Phila., 2004. Cert. orthodontics. Orthodontics fellow Clinic for Orthodontics, Osnabrueck, Germany, 1996—98; pvt. practice Collegeville, 2004—. Interdisciplinary cons. dentofacial anomalies and clefts dept. maxillofacial surgery U. Muenster Dental Sch., 1998—2001, instr., 1998—2001; instr. restorative dentistry dept. U. Pa., 2004—. Translator dentistry articles in internat. jours. Mem.: ADA, Acad. Gen. Dentistry, Montgomery-Bucks (Pa.) Dental Assn., Pa. Dental Assn., German Dental Assn. Avocations: travel, arts, skiing. Office: Market Place at Collegeville 201 S 2nd Ave Collegeville PA 19426 Office Phone: 610-454-7991. Personal E-mail: azaleasharifi@yahoo.com.

SHARKEY, PETER F., orthopaedic surgeon, educator; MD, SUNY, 1984. Cert. orthopaedic surgery. Intern St. Joseph Health Ctr.; resident Thomas Jefferson Univ. Hosp., fellow, prof.; hosp. affiliations include Riddle Hosp., 2008—, Bryn Mawr Hosp., 2008—. Office: Thomas Jefferson University Hospital 925 Chestnut St 5th Fl Philadelphia PA 19107 Office Phone: 800-321-9999.

SHARLIP, IRA D., urologist, educator; MD, U. Pa., 1961. Urologist Pan Pacific Urology, San Francisco, 1980—. Clin. prof. urology U. Calif., San Francisco. Maj. US Army, 1967—69. Mem.: Internat. Soc. for Sexual Medicine (pres.). Office: Pan Pacific Urology 2100 Webster St Ste 222 San Francisco CA 94115 Office Phone: 415-202-0250.

SHARMA, DAYANANDA SHAMURAILATPAM, physicist; b. Imphal, Manipur, India, Jan. 1, 1969; MSc in Physics, Manipur U., 1992; diploma, Mumbai U., 1997. Lectr. Govt. Med. Coll., 1999—2000; med. physicist Tata Meml. Hosp., 2000—07, with sci. execution and implementation, 2000—11; chief med. physicist & RSO Kokilaben Dhireubhai Ambani Hosp. & Med. Rsch. Inst., 2007—, gen. mgr., cons., devel., execution & improvement, 2007—11. Mem.: ESTRO, AROI, AMPI. Office: Four Bungalows Andheri W Mumbai Maharashtra 400053 India Office Fax: 91 22 30972030. Business E-Mail: dayananda.sharma@relianceada.com.

SHARMA, MADAN KUMAR, broadcast executive; b. Nepal; Acting dep. gen. mgr. Nepal TV (NTV) Corp., Kathmandu, gen. mgr., 2002—. Mem.: Asia-Pacific Broadcasting Union. Office: Nepal TV Corp PO Box 3826 Singh Durbar Kathmandu Nepal Office Phone: 0119774228447. Office Fax: 0119774227452.

SHARMA, PANKAJ, neurologist, researcher; s. Kewal Krishan and Janak Sharma. MD, U. London; PhD, U. Cambridge; DHMSA, Soc. Apothecaries, London. Lic. MD London, 1988. Brit. heart found. clinician scientist U. Cambridge, 1994—2000; cons. neurologist & reader Hammersmith Hospitals & Imperial Coll., London, 2003—; sr. fellow Dept. Health, UK. Bd. trustees South Asian Health Found., London, 1997—; pres. Brit. Fulbright Scholars Assn., London, 2004—06; med. dir. Different Strokes, London, 2004—. Contbr. articles to profl. jours. Pres. Gonville Hall Debating Soc., Cambridge U., 1995-97. Fulbright scholar Harvard U./Mass. Gen. Hosp., 1998-99. Mem. Royal Coll. Physicians London; British Fulbright Scholars Assn. (pres.). Avocations: collecting anitquarian medical books, theater, tennis, fencing, debating. Office: Hammersmith Hospitals & Imperial College Fulham Palace Rd London W6 8RF England Office Fax: +2088467487. E-mail: psharma@cantab.net, secretary.sharma@londonmedicalpractice.com.

SHARMA, RAJEEV, anesthesiologist, consultant; b. New Delhi, Mar. 20, 1978; MD, Maulana Azad Med. Coll., New Delhi, 2000. Cons. anaesthesiologist ESI Hosp., New Delhi, 2009—. Mem.: Difficult Airway Soc., Indian Soc. Anaesthesiologists. Avocations: chess, board games. Office: ESI Hosp Rohini Sector-15 New Delhi 110085 India Personal E-mail: rajeevkrsharmaji@email.com.

SHARMA, SAMIN KUMAR, internist, interventional cardiologist, educator; b. Alwar, India, May 28, 1955; Undergraduate degree, Maharaja Coll., India, 1972; MD, SMS Med. Coll., Rajasthan U., Jaipur, 1978. Cert. Internal Medicine, Cardiovascular Disease, Interventional Cardiology. Intern, internal medicine SMS Hosp., Jaipur, India, 1978—79, resident, internal medicine, 1979—82, NYU Downtown Hosp., 1983—86; fellow, cardiology City Hosp. Ctr. at Elmhurst, 1986; prof., medicine, cardiology Mt. Sinai Med. Sch., NY; dir., interventional cardiology Mt. Sinai Med. Ctr., NY. Serves on Cardiac Adv. Bd. NY State; travels to India 4 to 6 times a yr. to teach the art of angioplasty to Indian cardiologists; founder, dir. Live Symposium of Complex Coronary Cases, 1998—. Contbr. several articles to profl. jours.; featured on or in Today Show, NY Times, Wall Street Journal, NY Mag., Barron's, Forbes, Newsweek, Washington Post, Crain's NY Bus., Newsday, NY Post, NY Sun, Earthtimes, India Abroad and India Today. V.p. Rajasthan Develop. Found., India. Recipient Best Med.

and Chief Resident, NY Infirmary-Beekman Downtown Hosp., Ctr. of Excellence award for Rotational Coronary Atherectomy, 1996—2000, Simon Dack award for Best Tchr., Cardiovascular Inst., Mt. Sinai Hosp., 2000, Prestigious Jaipur, Rajasthan Govt. India, 2002, Governor's award Excellence, NY State, 2006, Jacobi Medallion award, 2007, Mt. Sinai Physician Yr. award, 2007; named one of Best Doctors, US News and World Report, Top Physicians, Consumer Rsch. Coun. America, Castle Connelly. Office: 5 E 98th St 3rd Fl New York NY 10029 Office Phone: 212-427-1540. Business E-Mail: samin.sharma@mountsinai.org.

SHARMA, SANJAY, anesthesiologist; b. Eng., June 6, 1974; MBBS, UNSW, 1999. Vis. obstetric fellow Queen Charlottes Hosp. London, 2009—10; obstetric anaesthetist Westmead Hosp., 2010—. Cons. obstetric anaesthetist South West Area Health Svc., 2010. Fellow: ANZCA; mem.: Obstetric Anaesthetists Assn. Office: Dept Anaesthesia Westmead Hosp Westmead NSW 2145 Australia Personal E-mail: sanger007@hotmail.com.

SHARMA, SANJIV, cardiologist; s. Sohan Lal and Inder Mohini Sharma; m. Geetanjali Sharma, May 2, 1994; children: Rohan, Rhea. Degree in Premed., Multani Mal Modi Coll., Punjabi U., 1983; MBBS, All India Inst. Med. Scis., New Delhi, India, 1988, MD, 1993. Diplomate Am. Bd. Internal Medicine, 1996, Am. Bd. Cardiovasc. Disease, 1999, Am. Bd. Interventional Cardiology, 2000. Jr. resident All India Inst. Med. Scis., New Delhi, 1989—91, sr. resident, 1992—93; resident Mass. Gen. Hosp., Harvard Med. Sch., Boston, 1993—94, Boston U. Sch. Med., 1994—96; cardiology fellowship West LA VA Med. Ctr., 1996—99; interventional cardiology fellowship Cedars Sinai Med. Ctr., LA, 1999—2000; interventional cardiologist Bakersfield Heart Hosp., Calif., 2000—, chmn. dept. medicine Calif. Dir. rsch. and edn., chmn. health edn. and continuing med. edn. com. Bakersfield Heart Hosp., Calif., 2000—; instr. clinical medicine UCLA, 2005. Contbr. articles to rsch. papers. Fellow: Am. Coll. Cardiology, Soc. Cardiac Angiography and Intervention. Achievements include invention of guiding catheter for coronary intervention-patent pending; research in novel strategy for preventing the complication of slow-flow and no-reflow phenomena in saphenous vein graft interventions; first to use of drug eluting stent and filter-wire in vertebral artery percutaneous intervention; research in status paper advocating the use of intracoronary administration of abciximab in percutaneous coronary interventions; intragraft administration of abciximab and verapamil prevents slow-flow and no-reflow phenomena during saphenous vein graft percutaneous coronary interventions; invention of carotid fixation guilding catheter sheath. Office: Ctrl Cardiology Medical Clinic 2901 Sillect Ave Ste 100 Bakersfield CA 93308 Personal E-mail: sanjiv1122@yahoo.com.

SHARMA, SANTOSH DEVRAJ, obstetrician, gynecologist, educator; b. Kenya, Feb. 24, 1934; arrived in US, 1972; d. Devraj Chananram and Lakshmi (Devi) S. BS, MB, B.J. Medical Sch., Pune, India, 1960. House surgeon Sasson Hosp., Poona, India, 1960-61; resident in ob-gyn. various hosps., England, 1961-67; house officer Maelor Gen. Hosp., Wrexham, U.K., 1961-62; asst. prof. ob-gyn. Howard U. Med. Sch., Washington, 1972-74; assoc. prof. John A. Burns Sch. Med., Honolulu, 1974-78, prof., 1978—. Fellow Royal Coll. Ob-Gyn., Am. Coll. Ob-Gyn. Avocations: travel, photography. Office: 1319 Punahou St Rm 824 Honolulu HI 96826-1032 Business E-Mail: santosh@hawaii.edu.

SHARMA, VINAY, oncologist, educator; b. Jammu and Kashmir, India, Dec. 12, 1955; MD, Tata Meml. Ctr., 1987; PhD, Cancer Rsch. Inst., 2002. Prof. U. Witwatersrand, 2003—, cons., prof., dept. radiation oncology CMJAH, 2003—. Mem.: Internat. Soc. Diseases Esophagus (Rsch. fellow). Avocations: reading, travel. Office: Steve St Victory Pk Johannesburg Gauteng 2195 South Africa Office Fax: 27116429185. Business E-Mail: vinay.sharma@wits.ac.za.

SHARON, LYNN WALSH, research scientist; b. Darby, Pa., Nov. 21, 1961; BA, Shippensburg U., 1982; MS, Rutgers State U., NJ, PhD, 1990. Prof. Johns Hopkins U., 1990—2005; exec. dir. U. Ky., 2005—09, dir. ctr. drug and alcohol rsch., 2009—. Bd. dirs. Coll. Problem Drug Dependence, 2005—11, past pres., 2008—09; adv. panel mem. FDA, 2009—11; safety adv. panel, chair Meda Pharms., 2009—11. Recipient Betty Ford award, Assn. Med. Edn. and Rsch. Substance Abuse, Joseph Cochin Young Investigator award, Coll. Problems Drug Dependence, Presdl. Early Career award, US White House. Fellow: Coll. Problems Drug Dependence; mem.: APA. Office: 515 Oldham Ct Lexington KY 40503 Office Fax: 859-257-5232. Business E-Mail: sharon.walsh@uky.edu.

SHARP, CHRISTINA KRIEGER, retired nursing educator; b. Ft. Montgomery, NY, Aug. 4, 1928; d. Joseph Lewis and Mary Agnes Krieger; m. Andrew Asa Sharp, Jr., Feb. 3, 1957 (dec. Jan. 31, 1969); children: Shawn Patrick(dec.), Sharon Paula Zegers, Jill Ann(dec.). RN, cadet nurse, St. Lukes Hosp., Newburgh, NY, 1948; BS, Coll. William and Mary, 1955; MA, NYU, 1974. RN N.Y. Staff nurse Vets. Hosp., Richmond, Va., 1948—53, Army Hosp., West Point, NY, 1954—56, Anaheim Meml. Hosp., Calif., 1960, Petaluma Gen. Hosp., Calif., 1960—61, Arlington Gen. Hosp., 1963, Cornwall Hosp., NY, 1964; instr. nursing Orange County CC, Middletown, NY, 1956—57, Santa Rosa (Calif.) Jr. Coll., 1961—62; supr. nursing Vocat. Edn. and Extension Bd., New City, NY, 1957—60; coord. practical nursing program Newburgh Sch. Dist., 1963—83; resident Saigon Vietnam, 1962; nursing instr., dir. Govt. Manpower Program, Newburgh, NY, 1964—65. Cons. N.Y. State Edn. Dept. Nursing, Albany, 1973—84; mem. del. gen. assembly Newburgh NY Tchrs. Assn., 1983—91; ret. del., 1983—91; bd. dirs. Coun. NY State Practical Nursing Programs, 1969—75, pres., 1971—73, treas., 1974—75. Mem.: AARP, AAUW (sec. 1999—2001), Cassleberry Vets. Aux., Vets. Fgn. Wars Aux., Widowed Friends Fla., AFL-CIO, Nat. Edn. Assn., Am. Fedn. Tchrs. (Everyday Hero award 2011), Am. Fedn. Labor and Congress of Indsl. Orgn., Fla. Educators Assn., NY State United Tchrs. (Fla. retiree coun. mem. 1992—2011, Orlando unit pres. 1997—2002, 2005—, Cmty. Svc. award 1998), Fla. Alliance Ret. Ams. (pres. 2001—, bd. mem. 2002—, sec. ctrl. Fla. chpt. 2004—), Tchr. Retirees Fla., Fla. Soc. RNs Ret., Inc. (Orlando dist. pres. 1994—97, NY state retired tchr. Fla. state coun. 43 pres. 1995—2009, editor yearbooks 1997—, state pres. 1998—2002, Fla. state coun. 43 pres. 2001—10, RNR Chapt. Svc. award 2003), Widow and Widowers Soc. Ctrl. Fla. (pres. 1999—2002), Orange County Ret. Educators Assn., Golden Rod Civic Club (bd. dirs. 2001—, chair 2003—), Am. Legion Aux. Avocations: travel, opera, ballet, Broadway shows, ice shows. Home: 2735 Mystic Cove Dr Orlando FL 32812-5344 E-mail: tisharp@aol.com.

SHARP, PHILLIP ALLEN, geneticist, molecular biologist, educator; b. Ky., June 6, 1944; s. Joseph Walter and Katherin (Colvin) S.; m. Ann Christine Holcombe, Aug. 29, 1964; children: Christine Alynn, Sarah Katherin, Helena Holcombe. BA in Chemistry and Math., Union Coll., Barbourville, Ky., 1966; PhD Chemistry, U. Ill., Urbana, 1969; DSc (hon.), U. Ky., 1994, Bowdoin Coll., 1995, U. Tel Aviv, Israel, 1996, Albright Coll., 1996, U. Glasgow, 1998, Thomas Moore Coll., 1999, U. Buenos Aires, 1999; LHD (hon.), Union Coll., 1991; MD (hon.), Uppsala U., 1999; PhD (hon.), Northern Ky. U., 2001. Rsch. asst. U. Ill., 1966—69; postdoc. fellow Calif. Inst. Tech., 1969—71, Cold Spring Harbor Lab., NY, 1971—72, sr. rsch. investigator NY, 1972—74; assoc. prof. dept. biology & Ctr. Cancer Rsch. MIT, 1974—79, prof., 1979—99, assoc. dir. Ctr. Cancer Rsch., 1982—85, dir., 1985—91, head dept. biology, 1991—99, Salvador E. Luria prof. biology, 1991—99, Inst. prof., 1999—, dir. McGovern Inst. Brain Rsch., 2000—04. Bd. dirs. Biogen Idec Inc., 1978—2009; mem. adv. coun. dept. molecular biology Princeton U., NJ, 1987—2003; mem. Pres.'s Com. Advisors on Sci. & Tech., The White House, 1994—97; chmn. awards assembly GM Cancer Rsch. Found., 1994—2006; mem. adv. bd. Nat. Cancer Inst., 1996—2000, chmn., 2000—02; mem. sci. bd. Ludwig Inst. Cancer Rsch., 1998—2008; mem. bd. sci. governers Scripps Rsch. Inst., 1999—; chair com. rsch. & edn. Partners HealthCare Systems, Inc., 2003—. Mem. editl. bd.: Molecular and Cellular Biology, 1974—85, Jour. Virology, 1974—86, Cell, 1974—95, RNA, 1995—; contbr. articles to profl. jours. Chair sci. & med. adv. bd. Huntsman Cancer Found., 1995—2001; trustee Alfred P. Sloan Found., 1995—2004; mem. sci. adv. bd. Van Andel Inst., Grand Rapids, Mich., 1996—, Ontario Inst. Cancer Rsch., Canada, 2006—; bd. trustees Mass. Gen. Hosp., 2002—; bd. dirs. Whitehead Inst. Biomed. Rsch., Cambridge, Mass., 2005—, FDA Reagan-Udall Found., 2008—. Recipient Career Devel. award, Am. Cancer Soc., 1974—79, Eli Lilly award in biological chemistry, 1980, Howard Ricketts award, U.Chgo., 1985, Gairdner Found. Internat. award, 1986, NY Acad. Scis. award in biological and med. scis., 1986, Alfred P. Sloan Jr. prize, GM Cancer Rsch. Found., 1986, Louisa Gross Horwitz prize, Columbia U., 1988, Albert Lasker award for basic med. rsch., 1988, Dickson prize, U. Pitts., 1990, Nobel prize in physiology/medicine, 1993, Mendel Medal award, Villanova U., 1993, James R. Killian, Jr., Faculty Achievement award, MIT, 1993, Walker prize, Boston Mus. Sci., 2001, Biotech. Heritage award, Biotechnology Industry Orgn./Chem. Heritage Found., 2002, Alumni Achievement award, U. Ill., 2003, Novartis Drew award in biomed. rsch., 2003, Nat. Medal Sci., 2004, Winthrop-Sears award, Chemists' Club NY, 2007. Fellow: AAAS, Royal Soc. Edinburgh (hon.); mem.: NAS (councilor 1986, Double Helix medal 2006, US Steel Found. award in molecular biology 1980), Ky. Acad. Scis. (hon. life), Am. Assn. Cancer Rsch., Soc. Biol. Chemists, Inst. Medicine, European Molecular Biology Orgn. (assoc.), Am. Philos. Soc. (Benjamin Franklin medal 1999), Am. Soc. Biochemistry & Molecular Biology, Am. Acad. Arts & Scis., Am. Soc. Microbiology. Office: MIT David H Koch Inst Integrative Cancer Rm E17529B 40 Ames St Cambridge MA 02139-4307 Business E-Mail: sharppa@mit.edu. *

SHARRAR, WILLIAM G., pediatrician, educator; MD, U. Pa. Sch. Medicine; BA in Biology, Franklin and Marshall Coll. Diplomate Am. Bd. Pediatrics. Intern Phila. Gen. Hosp.; resident pediatric Children's Hosp. Phila., chief resident, 1972—73; developer Divsn. Gen. Pediat., Cooper, 1983; chief pediat. The Children's Regional Hosp., Cooper; chief pediat. dept. pediat. Cooper Univ. Hosp.; prof. pediat. Univ. Medicine and Dentistry NJ-Robert Wood Johnson Med. Sch. Trustee Cooper Health Sys. Recipient Physician Recognition, Horizon NJ Health, Born To Shine Gala honoree, The March of Dimes; named Top Doc, Inside Jersey Mag., South Jersey Mag., New Jersey Monthly Mag. Mem.: AMA, Phila. Pediatric Assn., Am. Cleft Palate Craniofacial Assn., Am. Acad. Pediat. NJ Chpt., Am. Acad. Pediat., Ambulatory Pediatric Assn. Office: Three Cooper Plaza Ste 200 Camden NJ 08103 Office Phone: 856-342-2001. Office Fax: 856-968-8297.

SHASHKIN, PAVEL NIKOLAYEVICH, biochemist; b. Ulyanovsk, Russia, Sept. 23, 1957; s. Nikolay I. Shashkin and Maria Ya Shashkina; m. Tamara S. Shashkin; children: Alexey, Alice Shashkina, Veronika. M in Physics, M.V. Lomonosov Moscow State U., 1980; PhD in Biology, Cancer Rsch. Ctr., Moscow, 1990. Rsch. scientist Cancer Rsch. Ctr., Moscow, 1991—97, sr. rsch. scientist, 1997—99; vis. instr. U. Md., Balt., 1998—2000; rsch. assoc. U. Winnipeg, Man., Canada, 2000—01, U. Va., Charlottesville, 2002—04, Cleve. Clinic, 2004—07; sr. scientist BPS Biosci. Inc., 2008—09, group leader, 2010—. Contbr. articles to profl. jours. Grantee, Karolinska Inst. Stockholm, Sweden, 1995, 1996. Mem.: Am. Heart Assn., Am. Diabetes Assn. Avocations: tennis, travel. Office: BPS Bioscience Inc 11526 Sorrento Valley Rd #A2 San Diego CA 92121 Home: 12984 Carmel Creek Rd Unit 155 San Diego CA 92130-2131 Office: BPS Biosci Inc 6044 Corherstone Ct W #E San Diego CA 92121 Office Phone: 858-202-1404 ext. 117. Business E-Mail: pshashkin@bpsbioscience.com.

SHASTRY, SHAMEE, medical educator; b. Mangalore, Jan. 11, 1980; MBBS, Kasturba Med. Coll., 2003; MD, Sanjay Gandhi Postgrad. Inst. Med. Scis., 2008. Med. officer Manipal U., 2009, asst. prof., 2009—. Contbr. articles to profl. jours. Mem.: Indian Soc. Blood Transfusion. Avocations: chess, embroidery. Office: Dept Transfusion Medicine Kast Manipal Karnataka 576104 India E-mail: shameegirish@gmail.com.

SHATILA, AHMAD HUSSAIN, surgeon, oncologist; arrived in U.S., 1970; s. Hussain Ahmad and Yisir Omar Shatila; m. Bonnye Lynn Oliver, June 24, 1972; children: Suzanne, Sarah, David. BS in Biology, Am. U. Beirut, 1965, MD, 1970. Diplomate Am. Bd. Surgery. Resident surgery U. Louisville, 1970—72, SUNY, Syracuse, 1972—75; fellow surg. oncology Luth. Med. Ctr., Cleve., 1975—76, Cleve. Met. Health Med. Ctr., Case We. Res. U., 1976—78; pvt. practice Cleve., 1976—2008. Mem. med. staff MetroHealth Med. Ctr., Case Western Res. U., Divsn. Surg. Oncology, 1976—2008, emeritus staff, 2008—; asst. clin. prof. surgery Case Western Res. U., Cleve., 1984—; chmn. dept. surgery S.W. Gen. Health Ctr., Middleburg Heights, Ohio, 1989—91, chief surg. oncology, 1990—2008, co-founder cancer program; pres. med. staff S.W. Med. Corp., 1986—94, 2000—08; founder Cleve. Breast Clinic, Middleburg Heights; presenter in field. Contbr. articles to profl. jours. Com. mem. S.W. Cmty. Health Found., Middleburg Heights, 1990—2010. Fellow: ACS, U.S. Soc. Surg. Oncology; mem.: Dean's Soc. CWRU Med. Sch., Ea. Coop. Oncology Group (investigator 1976—2005, mem. breast steering com. 1980—86, vice chair toxicity com. 1983—88, mem. surgery steering com. 1984—87), Ohio State Med. Assn., Am. Cancer Soc. (med. adv. com.), Am. Soc. Clin. Oncology. Conservative. Muslim. Achievements include being the surgical oncology co-chair of the first US Intergroup clinical trial: Efficacy of Adjuvant Chemotherapy in High Risk Node Negative Breast Cancer. Avocations: golf, photography, boating, gardening. Office: For Corresponder PO Box 30849 Middleburg Heights OH 44130 Personal E-mail: ahshatila@adelphia.net.

SHATKIN, AARON JEFFREY, biochemistry educator; b. Providence, July 18, 1934; s. Morris and Doris S.; m. Joan A. Lynch, Nov. 30, 1957; 1 son, Gregory Martin. AB, Bowdoin Coll., 1956, DSc (hon.), 1979; PhD, Rockefeller Inst., 1961. Sr. asst. scientist NIH, Bethesda, Md., 1961-63, rsch. chemist, 1963-68; vis. scientist Salk Inst., La Jolla, Calif., 1968-69; assoc. mem. dept. cell biology Roche Inst. Molecular Biology, Nutley, N.J., 1968-73, full mem., 1973-77, head molecular virology lab., 1977-86, head dept. cell biology, 1983-86; dir. N.J. Ctr. Advanced Biotech. Medicine, 1986—; prof. molecular genetics UMDNJ, 1986—; univ. prof. molecular biology Rutgers U., New Brunswick, N.J., 1986—. Adj. prof. cell biology Rockefeller U.; vis. prof. molecular biology Princeton U. Mem. editl. bd. Jour. Virology, 1969-82, Archives of Biochemistry and Biophysics, 1972-82, Virology, 1973-76, Comprehensive Virology, 1974-82, Jour. Biol. Chemistry, 1977-83, 94-99, RNA Jour., 1995-96, Procs. of NAS, 1997-2001; editor Advances in Virus Rsch., 1983—, Jour. Virology, 1973-77; founding editor-in-chief Molecular and Cellular Biology, 1980-90. Served with USPHS, 1961-63. Recipient U.S. Steel Found. NAS prize in molecular biology, 1977, N.J. Sci. and Tech. Pride award, 1989, Thomas Edison Sci. award State of N.J., 1991, award for Disting. Rsch. in the Biomed. Scis., Assn. Am. Med. Colls., 2003, Edward J. H Excellence Medicine Outstanding Scientist award, 2009, Rockefeller fellow, 1956-61 Fellow AAAS, Am. Acad. Arts and Scis., Am. Acad. Microbiology, N.Y. Acad. Scis.; mem. NAS, Am. Soc. Microbiology, Am. Soc. Biol. Chemists, Am. Soc. Virology, Am. Chem. Soc., Am. Soc. Cell Biology, Harvey Soc. Home: 1381 Rahway Rd Scotch Plains NJ 07076-3452 Office: Ctr Advanced Biotech and Medicine 679 Hoes Ln Piscataway NJ 08854-5627 E-mail: shatkin@cabm.rutgers.edu.

SHATZ, CARLA J., neurobiology professor; b. NYC; BA in Chemistry, Radcliffe Coll., 1969; MPhil, Univ. Coll., London, 1971; PhD, Harvard U., 1976, postdoc., 1976—78. Assoc. prof. neurobiology Sch. Medicine Stanford U., Palo Alto, Calif., 1985—89, prof. neurobiology, 1989—92, investigator Howard Hughes Med. Inst., 1994—2000, Class of 1943 prof. neurobiology U. Calif., Berkeley, 1992—2000; prof., chair dept. neurobiology Harvard Med. Sch., Boston, 2000—07, Nathan Marsh Pusey prof. neurobiology; head Bio-X program, prof. biology and neurobiology Stanford U., 2007—. Mem. commn. on life scis. NRC, 1990—96; nat. adv. NIH, 1996—99; mem. coun. NAS, 1998—2001. Fellow. Inst. Medicine, Am. Philos. Soc., NAS, AAAS. Office: Clark Ctr 318 Campus Dr W 1 1 Rm W157 Stanford CA 94305-5437 Office Phone: 650-723-0534. Business E-Mail: cshatz@stanford.edu.

SHAVER, JOAN LOUISE FOWLER, dean, women's health nurse; b. Can. 1 child. BS in Nursing, U. Alberta, Can., 1966; M in Nursing, U. Wash., 1968-70, PhD in Physiology and Biophysics, 1976. Nursing instr. chair med. surgical prog. Holy Cross Hosp. Sch. Nursing, Calgary, Canada, 1966-68; staff nurse Virginia Mason Hosp., Seattle, 1970-71; asst. prof. Sch. Nursing U. Ariz., Tucson, 1976-77; assoc. prof. U. Calgary, Canada, 1977-80; asst. prof. Dept. Physiological Nursing U. Wash., Seattle, 1980-85, rsch. affil. Regl. Primate Rsch. Ctr., 1983-86, assoc. prof., 1985-89, chair Dept. Physiological Nursing, 1988-95, prof., 1989-95, prof., chair Dept. Biobehavioral Nursing & Health Systems, 1995-96, co-dir. Ctr. Women's Health Rsch., 1989-96; prof. biobehavioral health sci., dean Coll. Nursing U. Ill., Chgo., 1996—, co-dir. Rsch. Core Nat. Ctr. Excellence in Women's Health, 1997—. Bd. dirs. Advocate HealthCare, Chgo.; ednl. adv. coun. Select Comfort Corp.; pres. Am. Acad. Nursing, 2003—05. Mem. editl. bd. Health Care for Women Internat., 1984—, Heart and Lung: The Jour. Critical Care, 1988-90, Jour. Applied Nursing Rsch., 1988-91, IMAGE: Jour. Nursing Scholarship, editl. adv. bd. Nursing Rsch., 1997—, Biol. Rsch. for Nursing, 1999—, Jour. Nursing Scholarship, 2000—; contbr. articles to profl. jours. Mem. nat adv. coun. NIH Nat. Inst. Nursing Rsch.; mem. governing coun. Advocate Ill. Masonic Med. Ctr.; mem. health adv. com. Alberta Heritage Found. Med. Rsch. Abe Miller Meml. scholar Alberta Assn. Registered Nurses, 1968-69; Kathryn McLaggen Meml. fellow Can. Nurses Found. Fellow: Am. Acad. Nursing Am. Nurses Assn.; mem.: Inst. Medicine Chgo., Sigma Theta Tau Internat. Office: U Ill Chgo Coll Nursing MC 802 845 S Damen Ave Chicago IL 60612-7350 Business E-Mail: jshaver@uic.edu.

SHAW, ANTHONY, pediatric surgeon, retired educator; b. Shanghai, Oct. 31, 1929; s. Bruno and Regina (Hyman) S.; m. Iris Violet Azian, Mar. 12, 1955 (dec. Oct. 09, 2009); children: Brian Anthony, Diana Shaw Clark, Daniel Aram. BA cum laude, Harvard Coll., 1950; MD, NYU, 1954. Diplomate Am. Bd. Surgery; cert. spl. competence pediat. surgery. Intern and resident in surgery Columbia-Presbyn. Med. Ctr., NYC, 1954-56, 58-62; resident in pediat. surgery Babies Hosp., NYC, 1962; asst. prof. surgery Columbia U. Coll. Physicians and Surgeons, NYC, 1965-70; chief pediat. surgery St. Vincent's Hosp., NYC, 1963-70, Harlem Hosp. Ctr., NYC, 1965-70; prof. surgery U. Va., Charlottesville, 1970-81, chief pediat. surgery Med. Ctr., 1970-81; prof. surgery UCLA, 1981-2001, emeritus prof. surgery, 2001—; chief pediat. surgery Olive View-UCLA Med. Ctr., Sylmar, 1986-2001, cons. surgeon, 2003—. Expert witness on child abuse L.A. Superior Ct., 1986—; chmn. gov.'s adv. com. child abuse and neglect Commonwealth of Va., 1975-80; vis. prof. pediat. surgery People's Republic of China, 1985. Contbr. more than 220 articles to profl. jours. Mem. Gov.'s Task Force on Child Abuse Va., 1973-74. Capt. U.S. Army, 1956-58. Recipient Commrs. award Va. Dept. Social Svcs., 1980, award Gov.'s Adv. Bd., Cert. of Recognition HEW, 1978. Fellow Am. Pediat. Surg. Assn. (sec. 1982-85), ACS (v.p. 1987-89); mem. AMA, Pacific Coast Surg. Assn. (v.p. 1989-90), Am. Soc. Law, Medicine, and Ethics, Am. Profl. Soc. on Abuse of Children, Alpha Omega Alpha. Avocation: writing humor. Home and Office: One S Orange Grove Blvd # 9 Pasadena CA 91105 Home Phone: 626-796-8588; Office Phone: 626-796-8588. Personal E-mail: shawpas@pacbell.net.

SHAW, DANIEL STEPHEN, psychology professor, department chairman; b. Washington, Feb. 8, 1958; s. Milton and Natalie Jane (Bisguyer) S.; m. Ann Caroline Plough, May 9, 1987; three children. BA, Oberlin Coll., 1980; MA, U. Va., 1985, PhD, 1988. Lic. clin. psychologist, Pa. Rsch. asst. Children's Hosp. Nat. Med. Ctr., Washington, 1980-82; clin. intern in psychology dept. psychology U. Va., Charlottesville, 1984-85, clin. intern in psychology dept. family practice, 1986-87; clin. intern Med. Coll. of Hampton Roads, Norfolk, Va., 1987-88; asst. to full prof. clin. and devel. psychology U. Pitts., 1989—, asst. to full prof. psychiatry, 1989—, dir. psychology clinic, 1990, 1992, 1997—98, dir. grad. admissions, 1990—92, 1995, 1997, dir. Pitt early steps project, 2000—, faculty assoc., Univ. Ctr. Social and Urban Rsch., 2000—, chmn. dept. psychology; behavioral scientist, child and family ctr. U. Oreg. Dept. Psychology, 2002—. Divorce mediator L.A. Conciliation Ct., 1983; rsch. asst. U. Va., 1983-86, teaching asst., 1986-87. Bd. dirs. SUPPORT, Inc., Pitts., 1989-91. Grantee U. Pa., 1988-91, Buhl Found., Jewish Health Found., NIMH, 1994—, recipient Mid-career Rsch. Svc. award, 1999-2009, SR. Rsch. Svc. award NIDA, 2009-. Mem. APA (div. devel. psychology, Boyd McCandless Young Investigator award 1995), Pa. Psychol. Assn., Greater Pitts. Psychol. Assn. (task force 1988-89), Soc. for Rsch. in Child Devel., Soc. for Rsch. on Child and Adolescent Psychopathology, Life History Rsch. Soc. (Young Scholar award 1990). Democrat. Jewish. Avocations: tennis, photography, computers. Office: U Pitts Dept Psychology Sennott Sq Bldg Rm 4101 210 S Bouquet St Pittsburgh PA 15260-0001 Office Phone: 412-624-1836. Office Fax: 412-624-8827. Business E-Mail: casey@pitt.edu.

SHAW, RICHARD EUGENE, cardiovascular researcher; b. Springfield, Ohio, Jan. 20, 1950; s. Eugene Russell and Marjorie Caroline Shaw; m. Nov. 26, 1976; 2 children. BA, Duquesne U., 1972; MA, U.S. Internat. U., San Diego, 1977; PhD, U. Calif., San Francisco, 1984. Cert. nuc. med. technologist. Nuclear Medicine Tech. Cert. Bd. Staff nuc. med. technologist Scripps Meml. Hosp., La Jolla, Calif., 1975-79; rsch. asst. U. Calif. San Francisco Sch. Medicine, 1980-85; mgr. rsch. programs San Francisco Heart Inst., Daly City, Calif., 1985-87, dir. rsch., 1988-90, dir. rsch. and ops., 1991—2003; dir. rsch., quality and edn. Sutter Pacific Heart Ctrs., 2003—08, Calif. Pacific Med. Ctr.'s Heart & Vascular Ctr., 2009—; rsch. dir. Cardiology Fellowship Program, 2010—. Sr. advisor steering com. for databases Daus. of Charity Nat. Health Sys., St. Louis, 1993-96. Editor-in-chief Jour. Invasive Cardiology, 1989—; contbr. articles to profl. jours; chpts. to books. Coach Am. Youth Soccer Orgn. and Youth Baseball Assn., bd. dirs., Burlingame, Calif., 1990-94; pres. Burlingame H.S. Athletic Boosters, 2000—. Recipient Founding Father award, Am. Coll. Cardiology Nat.l Cardiovascular Data Registry, 2008, Training Program Tchr. of Yr., Calif. Pacific Med. Ctr., 2009; named Impact Player of Yr. award, Mi-Co Corp., 2005. Fellow Am. Coll. Cardiology (nat. cardiac database com., outcomes assessment subcom. 1998—, NCDR task force 2001—, publs. subcom. 2001—), Am. Coll. Angiology; mem. Am. Heart Assn., Soc. for Clin. Trials, N.Y. Acad. Scis., Am. Statis. Assn., Am. Med. Informatics Assn., Soc. Behavioral Medicine. Avocation: music. Office: Sutter Pacific Heart Ctr CPMC 2200 Webster # 303 San Francisco CA 94115 Home Phone: 650-678-2375. Business E-Mail: shawr@sutterhealth.org.

SHAW, RONALD AHREND, physician, educator; b. Toledo, July 20, 1946; s. Harold Michael and Eve Helen (Ganch) S.; m. Carol Ann Rapp, June 13, 1970; children: Robert, Benjamin, Daniel. BS, U. Toledo, 1968; MD, Washington U., 1972. Diplomate Am. Bd. Emergency Medicine. Intern, then resident in surgery St. Luke's Hosp., St. Louis, 1972-73, resident in surgery, 1973; mem. staff Bapt. Med. Ctr.-Montclair, Birmingham, Ala., 1976-81, chief emergency svc., 1979-81; assoc. dir. lifesaver flight ops. Caraway Meth. Med. Ctr., Birmingham, 1981-85; dir. emergency svc. sch. medicine U. Ala., 1985-89; asst. dir. emergency svc. R.I. Hosp., Providence, 1989-95; attending physician emergency dept. Bapt. Med. Ctr., Montgomery, Ala., 1996—; med. dir. emergency dept. Jackson Hosp., 2000—01; sec.-treas., med. staff Bapt. Med. Ctr., 2001—03. Cons. U. Tex., Houston, 1986, Bell Helicopter, Ft. Worth, 1986, Mut. Assurance, Birmingham, 1986-89, NYU, 1988-89, R.I. State Med. Examiners Office, 1991-96, Fla. Dept. Health, EMS Office, 1991—, Joint Underwriters Assocs. of R.I., 1991-96; chmn. adv. bd. emergency svc. Ala. Dept. Pub. Health, 1986-89; med. dir. Emergency Med. Svcs. div. R.I. Dept. Health, 1990-95; med. dir. Health Care Rev., Inc., 1995-96. Bd. dirs. MADD, Ala., 1986, Univ. Emergency Medicine Found., 1995-96; mem. planning com. Youth Baseball, Vestavia Hills, ala., 1986, 87; mem. disaster com. City of Birmingham, 1984-89; mem. 911 Commn., State of R.I., 1991-96. Recipient Disting. Achievement award Birmingham Emergency Med. Svc., 1988. Fellow Am. Coll. Emergency Physicians (bd. dirs. Ala. chpt. 1984-89, steering com. EMS sect. 1991-94, sec.-treas. R.I. chpt. 1995-96); mem. AAAS, ACS (state com. on trauma R.I. chpt. 1990-96), N.Y. Acad. Sci., Med. Assn. Ala. (mem. coun. med. svc. 1985-86). Republican. Avocations: hunting, stamp collecting and computer programming. Office Phone: 334-272-1050. Personal E-mail: kd1hp@msn.com.

SHAW, STANLEY MINER, retired pharmacist, educator; b. Parkston, SD, July 4, 1935; s. George Henry and Jensina (Thompson) S.; m. Excellda J. Watke, Aug. 13, 1961; children: Kimberly Kay, Renee Denise, Elena Aimee. BS, S.D. State U., 1957, MS, 1959; PhD, Purdue U., 1962. Instr. S.D. State U., 1960-62; asst. prof. bionucleonics Purdue U., West Lafayette, Ind., 1962-66, assoc. prof., 1966-71, prof. nuclear pharmacy, 1971—2005, prof. emeritus nuclear pharmacy, 2005—, head. divsn. nuclear pharmacy, 1990—2004, acting head Sch. Health Scis., 1990-93. Bd. pharm. spltys. Splty. Council Nuclear Pharmacy, 1978-82. Contbr. articles to profl. jours. Recipient Lederle Pharmacy faculty award, 1962, 1965, Parenteral Drug Assn. Rsch. award, 1970, Henry Heine Outstanding Tchr. award, Sch. Pharmacy Purdue U., 1989, 1993, 1999, Disting. Alumnus award, S.D. State U., 1991, Coll. Pharmacy Disting. Alumnus award, 2006, Disting. Pharmacy Educator award, Am. Assn. Colls. Pharmacy, 1994. Fellow Acad. Pharmacy Practice (chmn. sect. nuclear pharmacy 1979-80, historian 1981-85, mem.-at-large 1993-95, chmn.-elect 1995-96, chmn. 1996-97, Disting. Achievement award 1998), Am. Soc. Hosp. Pharmacy, Am. Pharm. Assn. (ho. of dels. 1977, 79, 86, 92, Founder's award, Daniel B. Smith Practice Excellence award 2000), Internat. Pharm. Fedn.; mem. Health Physics Soc., Sigma Xi, Phi Lambda Upsilon, Phi Lambda Sigma, Rho Chi. Home: 7208 W Greenview Dr Battle Ground IN 47920-9732 Office: Purdue Univ Sch Pharmacy West Lafayette IN 47907-1336 Business E-Mail: shaws@purdue.edu.

SHAYAKUL, CHAIRAT, nephrologist; b. Bangkok, Oct. 16, 1961; MD, Siriraj Hosp., 1984, Dip Thai Bd Nephrology, 1992. Physician Siriraj Hosp., 1985—. Mem.: Thai Royal Med. Coll. Avocations: stamp collecting/philately, travel. Office: Dept Medicine 2 Prannok Rd Bangkok 10700 Thailand Office Fax: 662 4121360. Personal E-mail: cshayakul@hotmail.com.

SHE, JINHUA, electrical engineer, educator; b. Jinshi, Hunan, China, May 23, 1963; s. Yuan-guang She and Shao-ai Liu; m. Yoko Miyamoto, Nov. 26, 1988; 1 child, Koh Miyamoto. BS, Ctrl. South U., 1983; MS, Tokyo Inst. of Tech., 1990, PhD, 1993. Assoc. engr., Automation Rsch. Inst. of Ministry of Metallurgy Industry, Beijing, 1983. Assoc. engr. Automation Rsch. Inst. of Ministry of Metall. Industry, Beijing, 1983—86; lectr. Tokyo U. of Tech., Hachioji, Japan, 1993—2000, assoc. prof., 2001—. Contbr. articles to profl. jours. (Internat. Fedn. Automatic Control Best paper award, 1999). Mem.: IEEE, Japan Soc. Mech. Engrs., IEE of Japan, The Soc. Instrument & Control Engrs. Office: Tokyo Univ Technology 1404 1 Katakura Hachioji 192 0982 Japan Office Fax: 81-426-37-2487. E-mail: she@cs.teu.ac.jp.

SHEAFFER, SUZANNE FRANCES, geriatrics nurse; b. Harrisburg, Pa., Feb. 8, 1963; d. Walter Richard and Catherine Frances (Mourawski) Markham; children: William Chester, Sarah Suzanne, Katye Iona; m. Paul L. Sheaffer Jr. ADN, Harrisburg CC, Pa., 1984; BSN, York Coll., Pa., 1997; B in Criminal Justice Adminstrn., Ctrl. Pa. Coll., Summerdale, 2005; postgrad. in Criminal Justice, St. Leo U., Fla., 2005—06; postgrad., North Ctrl. U., 2007—; PhD student, 2009—. RN; lic. nursing home adminstr., Pa. Nurse ICU and critical care unit Meml. Hosp., York, Pa., 1987-88; staff nurse emergency dept. Polyclinic Med. Ctr., Harrisburg, 1988-91; assoc. prof. Nat. Edn. Ctr.-Jr. Coll., Harrisburg, 1991; dir. nursing Camp Hill Care Ctr., Pa., 1991-92; resident assessment supr. Susquehanna Ctr., Harrisburg, 1992-94; dir. nursing Susquehanna Luth. Village, Millersburg, Pa., 1994-95; asst. adminstr. Dauphin Manor, Harrisburg, 1995—; mgr. clin. svcs. ea. divsn. HCR Manor Care; med. analyst Medicaid Fraud Control Unit Pa. Atty. Gen. Office, 2003—. ACLS, CPR instr. Am. Heart Assn., Harrisburg, 1989—; BCLS, CPR instr. ARC, Harrisburg, 1992—; RN, paramedic Lebanon County First Aide and Safety Patrol, Pa., 1992-. Sec. Little People PTA, Harrisburg, 1991-92; pres. Student Human Resource Mgmt. Club, York Coll., Pa., 1992—; v.p. Prince of Peace PTO, 1997-98; cheerleading coach, Midget Footbal Assoc., 2002—; cheerleading coord. Susquehanna Twp. Midget Football Assn., 2003, HNJ, 2006-; acad. adviser Eta Sigma Alpha Chi Beta chpt., 2003-05; home room parent Holy Name Jesus Sch., 2002-, cheer coord., 2006-09. Recipient Nurse of Hope award Am. Cancer Soc., Dauphin County, Harrisburg, 1983-84. Mem. AACN, Pa. Nurses Assn., Pa. Dir. Nursing Assn. for Long Term Care, PANPHA (advocate), York Coll. Alumni Assn. (bd. dirs. Susquehanna Valley), Pa. Homesch. Assn., Ctrl. Pa. Alumni Assn. Roman Catholic. Avocations: ceramics, ballet, flute. Office Phone: 717-712-2033. Personal E-mail: sheafferfam@msn.com.

SHEARES, BRADLEY T. (BRAD SHEARES), retired pharmaceutical executive; b. Jan. 23, 1957; BA in Chemistry, Fisk U., Nashville, 1978; PhD in Biochemistry, Purdue U., Ind., 1982. Rsch. fellow dept. biochemical regulation Merck Inst. Therapeutic Rsch./Merck Rsch. Labs., Rahway, NJ, 1987—90; various positions Merck & Co., Inc. (formerly Schering-Plough Corp.), 1990—2007, dir. external bus. devel., US Human Health (USHH) divsn., 1992—93, sr. dir. hosp. bus. group, 1993—94, exec. dir. anti-infectives bus. group, 1995—96, v.p. anti-infectives bus. group, 1996—98, v.p. hosp. mktg. and sales, 1998—2000, pres. USHH divsn. Whitehouse Station, NJ, 2001—07; CEO Reliant Pharmaceuticals, Inc., Liberty Corner, NJ, 2007. Bd. dirs. Progressive Corp., 2003—, Honeywell Internat. Inc., 2004—, Covance Inc., 2009—, IMS Health Inc., 2009—, Henry Schein, Inc., 2010—. Bd. dirs. Spelman Coll., Atlanta, Pa. Bus. Roundtable; mem. sci. adv. coun. Montclair State U., NJ. Named one of Most Powerful Black Execs., Fortune mag.; NIH rsch. fellow, MIT Ctr. Cancer Rsch., 1983—85, Lucille P. Markey scholar, 1985—87. Mem.: AAAS, American Soc. Microbiology, American Soc. Biol. Chemists (assoc.). Office: Covance Inc Bd Directors 210 Carnegie Ctr Princeton NJ 08540 Office Phone: 609-452-4440, 609-452-9375. Business E-Mail: bradley.sheares@covance.com. *

SHEBEL, HEATHER A., editor; d. Jack Raymond and Martha Ann Heminger; m. Shebel John M., Oct. 10, 2001. BA in math., U. Chgo., 1996. Rsch. tech. U. Chgo. Hosp., 1996—2001; sr. manuscript editor Jour. AMA, Chgo., 2001—. Editor (copy editor): (cd-rom) Multimedia Textbook of Coronary Arteriography and Interventions, 1997; co-author: Journal of Hand Surgery, 2002 (Joseph H. Boyes award, 1998). Mem.: Coun. Sci. Editors (cert.). Office: Am Med Assn 515 N State St Chicago IL 60654

SHEDD, DONALD POMROY, surgeon; b. New Haven, Aug. 4, 1922; s. Gale and Marion (Young) S.; m. Charlotte Newsom, Mar. 17, 1946 (dec. Apr. 28, 2007); children: Carolyn, David, Ann, Laura BS, Yale U., New Haven, Conn., 1944, MD, 1946. Diplomate Am. Bd. Surgery. Intern Yale New Haven Hosp., 1946-47, asst. resident, resident, 1949-53; instr. surgery Yale U. Med Sch., New Haven, 1953-54, asst. prof., 1954-56, assoc. prof., 1956-67; chief dept. head and neck surgery Roswell Park Cancer Inst., Buffalo, 1967-96, prof. emeritus, 1996—; rsch. prof. emeritus SUNY at Buffalo, 1996—. Co-editor: Surgical and Prosthetic Speech Rehabilitation, 1980, Head and Neck Cancer, 1985, (with Prof. Abel Fink) The Early History of Hospice Buffalo, 2003; author: Historical Landmarks in Head and Neck Cancer Surgery, 2000; contbr. numerous articles to profl. jours. Founding bd. dirs. Hospice Buffalo, Inc., 1973—83. Capt. US Army, 1947—49. Mem. Am. Head and Neck Soc., Soc. Univ. Surgeons, Soc. Surg. Oncology, New Eng. Surg. Soc., Soc. Head and Neck Surgeons (pres. 1976-77). Avocations: sailing, windsurfing, tennis, history of medicine.

SHEDLARZ, DAVID L., retired pharmaceutical executive; b. NYC, 1948; m. Patricia Shedlarz; 1 child, Danielle. BS in Econs. and Math., Mich. State U., 1970; MBA in Fin. and Acctg., NYU, 1975. Various position including sr. fin. analyst, Pharmaceutical divsn., fin. mgr. & controller mktg./sales/prodn., Diagnostics divsn. Pfizer, Inc., NYC, 1976-79, prodn. contr. U.S. pharms. divsn., 1979-81, asst. group contr. U.S. Pharms. divsn., 1981-84, group contr., 1984-89, v.p. fin. U.S. pharms. group, 1989-92, corp. officer, v.p. fin. parent co., 1992-95, CFO, 1995—2005, sr. v.p., 1997—99, exec. v.p., 1999—2005, vice chmn., 2005—07. Bd. dirs. Pitney Bowes Inc., 2001—, Nat. Multiple Sclerosis Bd.; mem. NYU Stern Sch. Bd. Overseers, J.P. Morgan Chase & Co. Nat. Adv. Bd., Nat. Assn. Mfrs. Bd., Internat. Acctg. Standards Bd., Standing Adv. Group, Pub. Acctg. Oversight Bd.; bd. dirs. The Hershey Co., 2008—. Mem. Nat. Jr. Achievement Bd.; chmn. Nat. Jr. Achievement NY. Office: The Hershey Co 100 Crystal A Dr Hershey PA 17033 Office Phone: 717-534-4200. Office Fax: 717-534-7873. Business E-Mail: david.schedlarz@pb.com.

SHEDROFF, SHARON D., psychologist, anthropologist, researcher, consultant; b. Middletown, Conn. d. Leon and Sylvia Shedroff. BA summa cum laude, Syracuse U., NYC, 1974; MA, Calif. Sch. Profl. Psychology, San Diego, 1979. Lic. marriage, family and child counselor Calif., 1981. Psychology intern T.R.I. Cmty. Svcs., San Diego, 1978—81, marriage, family & child counselor, 1981—82; rsch. psychologist Grid Rsch., San Diego, 1983—85; founder, ptnr. Edwards Assocs., San Diego, 1985—, Strategic Vision Inc., San Diego, 1989—, Inst. for Value-Centered Life, San Diego, 1999—. Author: (novels) Dakota Dreams, 2003; contbr. articles to profl. jours. Mem.: Am. Morgan Horse Assn., U.S.A. Equestrian. Avocations: skiing, competitive horseback riding. Home: PO Box 420036 San Diego CA 92142 Office: The Edwards Assocs PO Box 420429 San Diego CA 92142 Office Phone: 858-576-7141.

SHEEAN, PATRICIA M., nutritionist, educator; BA in Nutrition & Dietetics, U. Ariz., 1992; MA in Nutrition, U. Ill., Chgo., 1999, PhD in Nutrition Epidemiology, 2005. Prof. dept. preventive medicine Feinberg Sch. Medicine Northwestern U., 2005—. Rsch. editor Jour. Am. Dietetic Assn. Mem.: Am. Soc. for Parenteral & Enteral Nutrition, Am. Dietetic Assn. Office: Northwestern University Dept of Preventive Medicine 680 N Lake Shore Dr Ste 1102 Chicago IL 60611 Office Phone: 312-503-3438. E-mail: p-sheean@northwestern.edu.

SHEEHAN, DAVID VINCENT, medical educator; b. Drogheda, Ireland, Mar. 23, 1947; MD, Nat. U. Ireland, MBA, 1970. Clin. fellow psychiatry Harvard Med. Sch., 1972—75, instr. psychiatry, 1975—80, asst. prof. psychiatry, 1980—85; prof. psychiatry U. South Fla. Coll. Medicine, 1985—2010, disting. health prof., 2008—10, disting. emeritus health prof., 2011—; prof. psychology U. South Fla. Coll. Arts and Scis., 2006—10. Recipient Lifetime Achievement award, Nat. Anxiety Found.; named one of Best Drs. in America, Woodward, White. Fellow: Am. Psychiat. Assn.; mem.: Am. Coll. Psychiatrists. Avocations: tennis, classical music, chess. Home: 611 Warren Rd Lutz FL 33548 Business E-Mail: dsheehan@health.usf.edu.

SHEEN, LEE-YAN, nutritionist, researcher; b. Kaohsiung, Taiwan, June 7, 1962; s. Ching-Kuwei Sheen and Hwei-May Sheen-Juang; m. Shuw-Yuan Lin, July 19, 1987; children: Chih-Hsin, Chih-Chao. BS, Nat. Chung-Hsing U., Taiwan, 1984, MS, 1986, PhD, 1990. Assoc. prof. China Med. Univ., Taichung, Taiwan, 1992—2001, chair, 1997—2000; assoc. prof. Grad. Inst. of Food Sci. and Tech., Nat. Taiwan U., Taipei, 2001—. V.p. Assn. for the Study of Health Foods in Taiwan, Taipei, 1994—97, pres., 1997—. Author: (book) Nutrition and Cosmetology; mng. editor Nutritional Scis. Jour., 2003—. Exec. bd. mem. Health Food Soc. of Taiwan, Taipei, 1998; bd. mem. Nutrition Soc. of Taiwan, Taipei, 2001. 2d lt. US Army. Decorated Outstanding Officer in Army Ministry of Def.; recipient Outstanding Dietitian, Assn. of Dietitian in Taiwan, 2000. Fellow: Inst. of Food Tech.; mem.: The Chinese Agrl. Chem. Soc., Taiwanese Inst. of Food Sci. and Tech., Nutrition Soc. of Taiwan (Prof. Joseph S.Chen Meml. award 2001), Health Food Soc. of Taiwan, Assn. for the Study of Health Foods in Taiwan. Achievements include development of Representative of the initiators for establishing the Health Food Soc. of Taiwan; Establish the guideline for the evaluation the liver protection effect of Health Foods in Taiwan; research in Evaluation and analysis of physiological functions and active principles of functional foods, especially on garlic. Office Fax: 886-2-23620849. E-mail: lysheen@ntu.edu.tw.

SHEEN, VOLNEY L., neurologist, educator; b. Lexington, Ky., Aug. 15, 1968; BS, Johns Hopkins, 1990; MD, Harvard, PhD, 1997. Cert. in neurology, in neurophysiology. Med. intern Mass. Gen. Hosp., 1997—98, neurology fellow, 1998—2001; instr., neurology, epilepsy attending Beth Israel Deaconess Med. Ctr., Harvard Med. Sch., 2001—04, asst. prof., neurology, 2004—09, assoc. prof., neurology, 2010—. Attending physician, epilepsy Beth Israel Deaconess, Boston, 2001, dir., epilepsy, Needham, 2009—; editl. bd. mem. Case Reports Neurol. Medicine, 2011. Recipient Young Investigator award, Beckman Coulter, award, Ellison Found., Nat. Rsch. award, Alzheimer's Assn., Clin. Investigators award, Doris Duke Found.; grant, NINDS. Mem.: Soc. Neurosci. Avocations: travel, interior decorating, gardening. Office: 330 Brookline Ave Dept Neurology Boston MA 02215 Business E-Mail: vsheen@bidmc.harvard.edu.

SHEEN-AARON, JULIA, public health service officer; MPH, Emory U., Atlanta; grad. pub. health cert. program, U. Wash. Sch. Pub. Health and Cmty. Medicine. Dir. chronic disease program VI Dept. Health, St. Thomas, 1993—2004, project mgr., cardiovascular health program, 1993—2004, project coord., behavioral risk factor surveillance systems, 1994—2004, project mgr., breast and cervical cancer program, 1995—98, project mgr., tobacco prevention and control program, 1995—2005, territorial asst. commr., St. Croix dist., 2007—, acting commr., 2009—11. Office: VI Dept Health 48 Sugar Estate St Thomas VI 00802 Office Phone: 340-774-0117. Office Fax: 340-773-6551. Business E-Mail: julia.sheen@usvi-doh.org. *

SHEERAN, PAUL W., anesthesiologist, pediatrician, educator; BA in Spanish and Lit. cum laude with honors, Whitman Coll., 1987; MD, U. Wash., 1991. Diplomate Am. Bd. Anesthesiology, Am. Bd. Pediatrics-pediatric critical care medicine, Am. Bd. Pediatrics. Intern Harbor UCLA Med. Ctr., 1992, resident pediat., 1994—97; resident anesthesia UT Southwestern Med. Ctr., 1998—2000; fellow Children's Med. Ctr. of Dallas; fellow, pediatric critical care medicine UT Southwestern Med. Ctr., 1995—97, chief fellow, pediatric critical care medicine, 1997—98, fellow pediatric anesthesia, 2000—01, asst. prof. Office: UT Southwestern Medical Center 5323 Harry Hines Blvd Dallas TX 75390-9003 Office Phone: 214-648-3111.

SHEFI, SHAI, urologist, consultant; b. Haifa, Israel, Jan. 30, 1964; MD, Hebrew U.-Hadassah Med. Sch., Jerusalem, 1993. Cert. urologist Israel Bd. Urology, 2002. Urology resident Urology Dept., Tel Hashomer, Israel, 1997—2002; andrology fellow U. Calif., San Francisco, 2004—06; attending urologist Male Infertility Unit, Sheba Med. Ctr., Tel Hashomer, 2006—08; founding andrologist Comprehensive Andrology Practice, Petach Tikva, Israel, 2006—; male infertility cons. Maccabi Health Care Program, Israel, 2008—. Contbr. articles to profl. jours. Lt. paratrooper divsn., 1982—86, Israel. Recipient Astellas Best Abstract award, Am. Urol. Assn., 2005, Rsch. award, Israel Cancer Assn., 2005, Cook Urology Travel award, Am. Soc. Andrology, 2006; Am. Physician fellowship, Israel, 2005, Andrology fellowship, U. Calif., San Francisco, 2006. Mem.: Israely Soc. Sexual Medicine, Israeli Urol. Assn. Achievements include research in human spermatogonial stem cells.

SHEHADI, SAMEER IBRAHIM, plastic surgeon; b. Zahle, Lebanon, Mar. 3, 1931; came to U.S., 1984; s. Ibrahim A. and Mounira D. (Dumit) S.; m. Leila A. Nassif, June 18, 1960; children: Ramzi Richard, Kamal Sameer, Imad Edward. BA, Am. U. Beirut, 1952, MD, 1956. Diplomate Am. Bd. Surgery, Am. Bd. Plastic Surgery. Intern. Am. U. Hosp., Beirut, resident gen. surgery, 1956-59, chief resident gen. surgery, 1959-60, resident plastic surgery St. Louis U. Hosps., 1960-62; fellow hand surgery Pitts. U. Hosps., 1962; resident head and neck surgery Roswell Park Meml. Inst., Buffalo, 1963; clin. asst. prof. Am. U. Beirut, 1963-79, clin. prof. surgery, 1979-84, chmn. dept. surgery, 1976-79, 81-84; prof., dir. div. plastic surgery St. Louis U., 1984-97, emeritus prof. surgery, 1997—. Contbr. articles to profl. jours. Recipient Chevaliers award Order of the Cedars, Govt. Lebanon, 1960. Fellow ACS (gov. at large Lebanon chpt. 1981-84); mem. AMA, St. Louis Met. Med. Soc., St. Louis Surg. Soc., Mo. Med. Assn., Lebanese Order of Physicians, Am. U. Beirut Med. Alumni Assn., Am. Soc. Plastic and Reconstructive Surgeons, Am. Soc. Maxillofacial Surgeons, Am. Assn. Chmn. Plastic Surgery, Am. Assn. Plastic Surgeons, Am. Assn. Hand Surgeons, Lebanese Soc. Plastic and Reconstructive Surgeons (pres. 1974-84), Internat. Soc. Burn Injuries (Lebanon rep. 1968-84). Home: Shobshob Bldg Cairo St Beirut Lebanon Office: Nassif Bldg Sourati Hamra Beirut Lebanon Office Phone: 961-1746345. E-mail: sshehadi@gmail.com.

SHEIKH, ALEEMUZZAMAN, medical educator, writer; Lectr. Nihon U. Sch. Medicine, Tokyo, 1989—. Vice chmn. Japan Bangladesh Soc. Organizer.

SHEIKH, AZEEM, cardiologist; b. Quetta, Balochistan, Pakistan, Dec. 11, 1968; s. Abdul Samad Sheikh and Surrayya Perveen. MBBS, Allama Iqbal Med. Coll., Lahore, Pakistan, 1995; BSc, Punjab U., 1997. Trainee registrar Shaikh Zayed Hosp./Fed. Postgrad. Med. Inst., Lahore, 1997—2000; med. officer Shaikh Zayed Hosp., 2000—03; clin. fellow cardiology Nottingham U. Hosps. NHS Trust, 2004—06; specialist registrar cardiology Addenbrooke's Hosp., Cambridge, England, 2009—10, Southend U. Hosp., England, 2010—11. Author: First Aid for the FCPS, 2000, Hand Book of Differential Diagnosis for Postgraduate Examinations, 2003, Pool Questions for FCPS-I, 20th edit., 2011; contbr. articles to profl. jours. Recipient Gold Medal Best Outgoing Grad. of Yr., 1988, Gold Medal All Pakistan Essay Competition, 1985—86, Gold Medal award, Pakistan and the New Millennium Photography Competition, 1999. Fellow: Coll. Physicians and Surgeons (Pakistan); mem.: Royal Coll. Physician (London), Brit. Soc. Echocardiography, European Soc. Cardiology, Brit. Jr. Cardiologists Assn., Brit. Cardiovasc. Soc. Personal E-mail: drazeemsheikh@yahoo.com.

SHEIKH, HASSAN, physician; b. Lahore, Pakistan, Apr. 17, 1979; MD, Aga Khan U., 2003. Fellow Pa. State Hershey Cancer Inst., Pa. State U., 2009—. Mem.: ACP, Am. Med. Dirs. Assn., Am. Geriat. Soc., Am. Soc. Hematology, Am. Soc. Clin. Oncology. Office: 500 University Dr Hershey PA 17033 E-mail: hasansheryar@yahoo.com.

SHEINFELD, JOEL, urologist; MD, U. of Florida Coll. of Medicine, 1981. Diplomate Am. Bd. Urology. Resident urology Strong Meml. Hosp., Rochester, NY, 1982—86; fellow urologic oncology Meml. Sloan Kettering Cancer Ctr., 1986—89. Assoc. prof. urology Cornell Univ.-Weill Med. Coll. Author Evaluation of lymph node counts in primary retroperitoneal lymph node dissection, Surgery for retroperitoneal relapse in the setting of a prior retroperitoneal lymph node dissection for germ cell tumor and other several articles. Named one of Best Doctors in NY, NY Mag., 2010. Office: Memorial Sloan Kettering Cancer Center 1275 York Ave New York NY 10021 Office Phone: 212-639-2000.

SHEINKOP, MITCHELL, orthopedist, surgeon, educator; BS, Univ. Ill., Champaign-Urbana, 1963; MD, Chgo. Med. Sch., 1967. Cert. Ill., Orthopedic Bd., 1974, Am. Bd. Orthopedic Surgery, 1983. Intern Cook County Hosp., Chgo., 1967—68; resident in orthopedic surgery Northwestern U. Sch. Medicine, Chgo., 1968—71, orthodontic and prosthesis rsch., 1973—78; asst. prof. surgery, orthopedics Univ. Chgo. Hosp. and Pritzker Sch. Medicine, Chgo., 1972—73; hosp. chief Univ. Chgo. Hosp. Childrens Orthopedic Clin., 1972—73; sr. attending surgeon Rush Presbyn. St. Lukes Med. Ctr., 1973—; orthopedic surgeon Chgo. Police Dept., 1985—87; attending surgeon Oak Park Hosp., 1994—; dir., adult reconstruction program Rush Affiliated Network Orthopedic Residency Program, 1995—; attending surgeon Ill. Masonic Hosp., 1996; faculty dir. The Nat. Ctr. Advanced Med. Edn., 1997—98; prof. orthopedics, prof. emeritus Rush Univ., 1999—; prof., dept. orthopedics Neurologic & Orthopedic Hosp. Chgo., dir. joint replacement program. Fellow in pediatric orthopedics and trauma Hadassah Med. Ctr., Jerusalem; fellow in hand surgery Passavant Meml. Hosp., Chgo.; orthopedic cons. Ill. State Pediatric Inst., 1973—74. Vol. attending surgeon Children's Meml. Hosp. First lt., capt. USAF, 1967—76. Mem.: AMA, Inst. Medicine Chgo., Ill. Orthopedic Soc., Chgo. Rheumatism Soc., Am. Acad. Orthopedic Surgeons, Am. Coll. Surgeons, Chgo. Com. Trauma, Chgo. Med. Soc. Office: Midwest Orthopedics Ste 1063 1725 W Harrison St Chicago IL 60612 also: Neurologic & Orthopedic Hosp Chgo 4501 N Winchester Ave Chicago IL 60640 Office Phone: 773-250-0000.

SHEKA, KEDAMBADY P., surgeon; b. Bellare, India, Sept. 8, 1942; s. Marayana and Rukmini N. Sheka; married; children: Karthik, Satya. B Medicine, B Surgery, Kasturba Med. Coll., Mangalore, India, 1965, MS, 1971. Diplomate Am. Bd. Thoracic Surgery. Chmn. surg. svcs. Coney Island Hosp., Bklyn., 1993—2009; pres. Univ. Group Med. Assocs., Bklyn., 2000—09. Pres. Bklyn. Surg. Soc., 2010—11. Fellow: ACS; mem.: Assn. Surgeons India, Soc. Thoracic Surgery. Avocation: tennis. Home: 366 Ramona Ave Staten Island NY 10312 Office Phone: 718-616-3445.

SHEKARI YAZDI, MOHAMMAD, dermatologist, researcher; s. Shekariyazdi and Heravi; 1 child, Shahabeddin Shekariyazdi. Rschr. Med. U. Vienna, 1999—2008. Rschr. Austrian Orient Acad., Vienna, 2004—06. Fellow: Am. Acad. Dermatology; mem.: European Acad. Dermatology and Venerology, Austrian Ethnomedicine Soc., Austrian Soc. Dermatology and Venerology (cert.), Soc. Social Dem. Academicians. Achievements include research in persian ethnomedicine. Personal E-mail: mdshekariyazdi@yahoo.com.

SHEKHAR, STEPHEN S., obstetrician, gynecologist; b. New Delh, Jan. 13, 1944; arrived in U.S., 1972; s. S.P. Jain and Shakuntala Mithal; m. Claudette Dorita, Jan. 6, 1978; children: Sasha, Stephen. MBBS, Punjabi U., Patiala, India, 1966. Surgeon Nat. Health Svc. U.K., 1966-72; intern Roosevelt Hosp.-Columbia Coll. Physicians and Surgeons, NYC, 1972-73; resident in ob-gyn. St. Clare's Hosp., N.Y. Med. Coll., NYC, 1973-76, Harlem Hosp.-Columbia U., NYC, 1976-77; pvt. practice Studio City, Calif., 1977—. Mem. staff L.A. County-U. So. Calif. Med. Sch.; clin. prof. ob-gyn. and family medicine U. So. Calif. Sch. Medicine, Oreg. Health Scis. U. Sch. Medicine. Fellow ACS, Am. Coll. Ob-Gyn., L.A. Soc. Ob-Gyn.; mem. AMA, Calif. Med. Assn., L.A. County Med. Assn., Oreg. Med. Assn., Jackson County Med. Assn. Home and Office: 377 Lantern Hill Dr Ashland OR 97520 Home Phone: 323-423-6566; Office Phone: 323-963-3032. E-mail: drssshekhar@gmail.com.

SHELBURNE, JOHN DANIEL, pathologist; b. Washington, Aug. 27, 1943; s. Clarence Daniel and Edith (McDanel) S.; m. Katherine Howard Parrish, June 17, 1966; children: Mark, Kerri. BA, U. N.C., 1966; PhD, Duke U., 1971, MD, 1972. Intern, then resident Duke U. Med. Ctr., Durham, NC, 1972-76; asst. prof. Duke U., Durham, 1973-78, assoc. prof., 1978-85, prof. pathology, 1985—; dir. electron microscopy lab. VA Med. Ctr., Durham, 1976-92, chief lab. svc., 1983-99, chief of staff, 1999—. Adv. WHO, Manila, 1990; panel mem. VA Program, Washington, 1987—; participant Nordrhein/Westfalen Exchange, Germany, 1988. Editor: Basic Methods in Biological X-Ray Microprobe, 1983; author, editor: Microprobe Analysis in Medicine, 1989, Biomedical Applications of Microprobe Analysis, 1999. Mem. Appalachian Trail Conf., Harpers Ferry, West, Va., 1970—; bd. dirs. Cen. Carolina Youth Soccer, Durham, 1987-90; founding mem. N.C. Soc. for Electron Microscopy and Microprobe, Research Triangle Park, N.C., 1980—. Recipient Morehead scholarship, 1961-66, AOA Med. Honorary Duke Med. Sch., 1970; named Med. Scientist Tng. Program participant NIH, 1966-72, Shelley Meml. lectr., 1985, Florey Meml. lectr., 1988. Fellow Coll. Am. Pathologists; mem. Am. Assn. Pathologists, Microscopy Soc. Am., Microbeam Analysis Soc. Democrat. Episcopalian. Home: 4302 Malvern Rd Durham NC 27707-5451 Office: Duke U Dept Pathology PO Box 3712 Durham NC 27710-3712

SHELBY, JAMES STANFORD, surgeon, researcher; b. Ringgold, La., June 15, 1934; s. Jesse Audrey and Mable (Martin) S.; m. Susan Rainey, July 15, 1967; children: Bryan Christian, Christopher Linden. BS in Liberal Arts, La. Tech. U., New Orleans, 1956; MD, La. State U., Houston, 1958. Diplomate Am. Bd. Surgery, Am. Bd. Thoracic Surgery. Intern Charity Hosp. La., New Orleans, 1958-59, resident in surgery and thoracic surgery, 1959-65; fellow in cardiovasc. surgery Baylor U. Coll. Medicine, Houston, 1965-66; practice medicine specializing in cardiovasc. surgery Shreveport, La., 1967—2004; ret., 2004. Mem. staff Schumpert Med. Ctr., Highland Hosp., Willis-Knighton Med. Ctr.; assoc. prof. surgery La. State U. Sch. Medicine, Shreveport, 1967—; pres. Shelby Oil and Gas. With M.C., AUS, 1961-62. Recipient Medallion award La. Tech. U., 1982. Mem. AMA, Am. Coll. Cardiology, Soc. Thoracic Surgeons, Am. Heart Assn., Southeastern Surg. Congress, So. Thoracic Surgery Assn. Home: 6003 E Ridge Dr Shreveport LA 71106-2425 Office: 2751 Albert Bicknell Dr Ste 5C Shreveport LA 71103-3970 Office Phone: 318-632-9438.

SHELDON, ELEANOR HARRIET BERNERT, sociologist, writer; b. Hartford, Conn., Mar. 19, 1920; d. M.G. and Fannie (Myers) Bernert; m. James Sheldon, Mar. 19, 1950 (div. 1960); children: James, John Anthony. AA, Colby Jr. Coll., 1940; AB, U. N.C., 1942; PhD, U. Chgo., 1949. Asst. demographer Office Population Rsch., Washington, 1942-43; social scientist USDA, Washington, 1943-45; assoc. dir. Chgo. Community Inventory, U. Chgo., 1947-50; social scientist Social Sci. Rsch. Coun., NYC, 1950-51, rsch. grantee, 1953-55, pres., 1972-79; rsch. assoc. Bur. Applied Social Rsch. Columbia U., 1950-51, lectr. sociology, 1951-52, vis. prof., 1969-71; social scientist UN, NYC, 1951-52; rsch. assoc., lectr. sociology UCLA, 1955-61; assoc. rsch. sociologist, lectr. Sch. Nursing U. Calif., 1957-61; sociologist, exec. assoc. Russell Sage Found., NYC, 1961—72; vis. prof. U. Calif., Santa Barbara, 1971. Author: (with L. Wirth) Chicago Community Fact Book, 1949, America's Children, 1958, (with R.A. Glazier) Pupils and Schools in N.Y.C, 1965; editor: (with W.E. Moore) Indicators of Social Change, Concepts and Measurements, 1968, Family Economic Behavior, 1973; contbr. articles to profl. jours. Bd. dirs. Colby-Sawyer Coll., 1979-85, UN Rsch. Inst. for Social Devel., 1973-79; trustee Rockefeller Found., 1978-85, Nat. Opinion Rsch. Ctr., 1980-87, Inst. East-West Security Studies, 1984-88, Am. assembly, 1976-95. William Rainey Harper fellow, U. Chgo., 1945—47. Fellow AAAS, Am. Acad. Arts and Scis., Am. Sociol. Assn., Am. Statis. Assn.; mem. U. Chgo. Alumni Assn. (Profl. Achievement award), Sociol. Rsch. Assn. (pres. 1971-72), Coun. on Fgn. Rels., Am. Assn. Pub. Opinion Rsch., Ea. Sociol. Soc., Internat. Sociol. Assn., Internat. Union Sci. Study of Population, Population Assn. Am. (2d v.p. 1970-71), Inst. of Medicine (chmn. program com. 1976-77), Cosmopolitan Club. Home and Office: 630 Park Ave New York NY 10065-6544 E-mail: ehbsheldon@aol.com.

SHELDON, GEORGE FRANK, medical educator; b. Dec. 20, 1934; s. Richard Robert and Helen Irene (Zerzan) S.; m. Ruth Guy, Aug. 28, 1959; children: Anne Anderson, Elizabeth, Julia. BA, U. Kans., Lawrence, 1957, MD, 1961; postgrad., Mayo Clinic Grad. Sch., 1965. Asst. instr. we. civilization U. Kans., 1955—57; intern Kans. U. Med. Ctr.; resident in surgery U. Calif., San Francisco, 1965-69; fellow in surg. biology Harvard Med. Sch. of Peter Bent Brigham Hosp., 1969-71; from asst. to prof. U. Calif., 1971-82; Dr. Zack D. Owens Disting. prof. surgery, dept. chmn. U. NC, Chapel Hill, 1984—2001. Chmn. residency rev. com. accreditation Coun. Grad. Med. Edn.; mem. Coun. Grad. Med. Edn. of Health and Human Svcs., 1986, chmn. 1998; mem. adminstrv. bd. Coun. Acad. Socs., chair, 1998-99; chmn. Merit Rev. Bd. Surgery Va., AAMC, 2000, 01; pres. vis. bd. UN Formed Svcs. U. Health Scis., 2002-03; mem. Coun. on Physician and Nurse Shortage Wharton Sch. Bus. U. Penn. Author: (with J.B. Runnell) Pictorial History of Kansas Medicine, 1961; (with Jill Ridky) Managing in Academics, 1993; editor: (with J.B. Davis) Clinical Surgery, 1995; editor-in-chief: E-Facs.org. With USPHS, 1962-64. Recipient Surgeon's Dist. award for Svc. to Safety, Nat. Safety Coun., 1993, Douglass Stubbs award Nat. Med. Assn., 1991, Disting. Faculty award Med. Alumni Assn. U. N.C., 2001; named Disting. Med. Alumnus, Kans. U., 2000. Fellow Royal Coll. Surgeons of Edinburgh (hon.), Royal Coll. Surgeons Eng., European Surg. Assn., Assn. of Surgeons of Gt. Britain and Ireland, Phila. Acad. Surgeons (Hunterian Orator 2001); mem. ACS (sec. bd. govs., regent 1984-93, pres. 1998, editor-in-chief e.facs.org web portal 2004—, dir. Inst. Health Policy Rsch., Surgeon of Yr. 2001, Fitts Orator, 1987, Scudder Orator Honored Surgeon, editor E facs.org web ponta 2004-), Am. Bd. Surgery (chmn. 1989-90), Nat. Bd. Med. Examiners (test com. 1981-84), Am. Assn. Surgery of Trauma (pres. 1984, Fitts medal), Am. Surg. Assn. (sec. 1989-94, pres. 1994-95), Assn. Am. Med. Colls. (exec. com., chair elect 1999, chair 2000-01, disting. svc. mem.), Soc. Surg. Chmn. (pres.), Coun. Acad. Socs. (chmn. 1998—, com. on gender equity and com. on health workforce), Inst. Medicine (sec. com. on employer based health ins. and tech. assessment edn. bds., Fluid Resuscitation com. on Nation's Physician Workforce 1996, Reviewer Poison Ctrs), Hunter Soc. (172nd Hunterian Orator). Achievements include being recognized as the leading authority on surgical workforce. Office: U NC at Chapel Hill Dept Surgery Campus Bx 7050 4006 Burnett-Womack Bldg Chapel Hill NC 27599-7050 Office Phone: 919-900-4053. Business E-Mail: gsheldon@med.unc.edu.

SHELDON, GEORGE H., federal agency administrator; b. Wildwood, NJ, June 3, 1947; BA, Fla. State U., 1969; JD, Fla. State U. Coll. Law. Legis. aide to Senator Reubin O.D. Askew Fla. Dept. State; asst. to dep. sec. Fla. Dept. Health & Rehabilitative Services; mem. Fla. House of Reps., 1975—82; atty. Levine, Freedman, Hirsch & Levinson, Tampa, Fla.; co-founder, lobbyist Sheldon, Cusick & Associates, Tallahassee, 1987—99; dep. atty. gen. State of Fla., 1999—2003; assoc. dean student & alumni services St. Thomas U., Miami, Fla., 2003—07; asst. sec. for ops. Fla. Dept. Children & Families (DCF), 2007—08, sec. DCF, 2008—11; acting asst. sec., adminstrn. for children & families US Dept. Health & Human Services, Washington, 2011—. Democrat. Office: US Department Health & Human Services 200 Independence Ave SW Washington DC 20201 *

SHELDON-MORRIS, TIFFINI ANNE, clinical psychologist, consultative examiner; b. Berkeley, Calif., Apr. 20, 1976; d. Terry E. and Jan L. Sheldon; m. John Christopher Morris, Aug. 6, 2000. BS in Psychology, Abilene Christian U., 1997; MS in Psychology, Fla. Inst. Tech., 2001, D of Psychology, 2001. Lic. psychologist NC, 2010; Licensed Clinical Psychologist Tex., 2004. Postdoctoral fellow Houston Veterans Affairs Med. Ctr., Houston, 2001—02; team leader and counselor Sr. Connections, Houston, 2003—04; clin. psychologist VeriCare, 2004—10, ind. contractor, quality mgmt., 2010—; cons. examiner Disability Determination Svcs., Raleighnn, NC, 2011—. Consultative examiner Dept. of Assistive and Rehabilitative Svcs., Austin, Tex., 2004—10; cons. examiner Disability Determination Svcs., Raleigh, NC, 2011—. Active mem. Monterey Ch. Christ, Lubbock, Tex., 2004—10, Pinedale Christian Ch., 2010—. Scholar Grad. Student Tchg. Assistantship, Fla. Inst. of Tech., 1998-2000. Mem.: APA, Alpha Kappa Delta Internat. Hon. Soc., Alpha Chi Nat. Honor Soc., Girls Aiming Toward Achievement. Avocations: travel, reading, swimming, music, theater. Office: VeriCare 4715 Viewridge Ave Ste 230 San Diego CA 92123 Home: 552 Old Cypress Dr Winston Salem NC 27127 Office Fax: 800-819-1655. Personal E-mail: drtiffini@yahoo.com.

SHELOV, STEVEN PATRICK, pediatrician, educator; b. Honolulu, Nov. 19, 1944; s. Sidney M. and Faith R. S.; m. Marsha Liberman, Aug. 30, 1968; children: Joshua, Danielle, Eric. BS, Yale, 1966; MD, Med. Coll. Wisc., 1971; MS in Med. Admin., U. Wisc., 1995. Diplomate Am. Bd. Pediatrics. Intern, then resident Montefiore Med. Ctr., Bronx, 1971-74, chief resident, 1974-75; asst. dir. ambl. pediat. Albert Einstein Coll. Med., Bronx, NY, 1977-79; dir. pediat. edn. Montefiore Med. Ctr., Bronx, 1980—, prof. and vice chmn. pediat., 1989-97; chmn. pediat. Infants and Children's Hosp. of Bklyn., Maimonides Med. Ctr., Bklyn., 1997—2010, prof. pediat. medicine; assoc. chief staff Cohen Childrens Hosp., 2010; prof. pediats. SUNY Downstate Sch. Medicine; prof. pediat Hofstra Sch. Medicine, 2010. Editor: Caring for Your Baby and Young Child: Birth to 5, 1991, 1996,

2004, 10, Pediatrics for Medical Students, 2003, 11, Guide to Your Child's Symptoms, 1997, The First Year of Life, 2004, 10, Interim Chair of Pediatrics Cohen Children's Medical Center-NJ/LIJ, 2010-. Bd. trustees NACHRI, 2008. Recipient Geo. Armstrong award Ambulatory Pediat. Assn., 1996, Lifetime Achievement in Edn. award, Am. Acad. Pediat., 2002; named Alumnus of Yr., Med. Coll. Wis., 2011. Mem.: Vis. Nurse Svc. (Lillian Wald award 2008), Nat. Assn. Children's Hosps. (bd. trustees 2008—), Am. Acad. Pediats. (Holroyd-Sherry award 2004, Clifford Grulee award 2009). Home Phone: 914-472-2714; Office Phone: 718-470-3248. Business E-Mail: sshelov@nsus.cav.

SHELTON, JAMES D. (DENNY SHELTON), hospital investment company executive; BA in Polit. Sci. and History, La. State U.; MS in Pub. Adminstrn., U. Mo. Hosp. adminstr. La., Iowa, NC, Ga., Ill., Mo.; exec. dir. Westbank Hosp. Ops. Nat. Med. Enterprises (now Tenet Healthcare Corp.), New Orleans, 1984—86, v.p. ops., 1986—90, sr. v.p. ops., 1990—93, exec. v.p. ctrl. divsn., 1993—94; pres. ctrl. group Columbia/HCA, 1994—98, pres. Pacific group, 1998—99; chmn., CEO Triad Hosps. Inc., 1999—2007; chmn. Legacy Hospital Partners, Inc., 2007—; sr. advisor CCMP Capital Advisors, LLC; interim CEO Omnicare Inc., Covington, Ky., 2010; non-exec. chmn. Omnicare, Inc., Covington, Ky., 2011—. Chmn. Fedn. Am. Hosps., 1999, mem. bd. govs., 1999—2002; bd. dirs. Am. Hosp. Assn., Ventas, Inc., Omnicare, Inc. Office: Legacy Hosp Partners Inc 2800 N Dallas Pky Ste 200 Plano TX 75093 *

SHELTON, RONALD M., dermasurgeon; b. NYC; BS summa cum laude, Union Coll., 1980; MD, SUNY, Syracuse, 1984. Bd. cert. Am. Bd. Dermatology. Gen. surgery resident L.I. Jewish Med. Ctr., New Hyde Park, NY, 1984—85; dermatology resident Brooke Army Med. Ctr., San Antonio, 1987—90; cosmetic dermatologic surgery and Mohs surgery fellow U. Calif., San Francisco, 1992—93; asst. prof. Mount Sinai Med. Ctr., NYC, 1993—98; co-dir. Dermatology, Laser & Plastic Surgery, LLP, NYC, 1998—2001; dir., founder The N.Y. Aesthetic Cons. LLP, NYC, 2001—. Author: Botox, 2003, Liposuction, 2004. Capt. USAF, 1985—92. Recipient Tchr. of Yr. award, Mt. Sinai Med. Ctr. Dept. Dermatology. Mem.: Am. Coll. Mohs Micrographic Surgery, Am. Soc. for Dermatologic Surgery (winner Young Investigator's Competition), Phi Beta Kappa. Office: NY Aesthetic Cons LLP 260 E 66th St New York NY 10065 Office Phone: 212-593-1818.

SHEMIN, RICHARD JAY, cardiothoracic surgeon, educator; b. Little Rock, Sept. 25, 1950; s. Saul and Beverly (Newfield) S.; m. Susan Helaine Packer, Aug. 25, 1971; children: Stephanie Leigh, Michael Andrew, Michelle Elizabeth. BA magna cum laude, Boston U., 1970, MD magna cum laude, 1974. Cert. Am. Bd. Thoracic Surgery. Intern, gen. surgery Peter Bent Brigham Hosp./Harvard Med. Sch., Boston, 1974—75, resident, cardiothoracic vascular surgery, 1975—76, 1978—80; asst. prof., cardiothoracic surgery Harvard Med. Sch., Boston, 1982—87; fellow in cardiothoracic surgery NYU Sch. Medicine, NYC, 1980-82; clin. assoc., cardiothoracic surgery NHLBI/NIH, The Clinical Ctr., Bethesda, Md., 1976-78; sr. resident in surgery Brigham and Women's Hosp./Harvard Med. Sch., Boston, 1978-80, assoc. surgery, cardiac surgeon, prof., 1982-87; med. dir., cardiac surgery, ICU Brigham and Women's Hosp., Boston, 1984—87; assoc. cardiothoracic surgery Children's Hosp. Med. Ctr., Boston, 1984; prof., chmn. Boston U. Sch. Medicine, 1987—2007, chief, cardiothoracic surgery, 1995—2007, vice chair dept. cardiothoracic surgery, 1997—2007; chair dept. cardiothoracic surgery Boston Med. Ctr., 1987—2007, co-dir., Cardiovascular Ctr., 2000—07; prof., surgery David Geffen UCLA Sch. Medicine, 2007—; vice-chmn., dept. surgery UCLA Med. Ctr., 2007—, chief cardiothoracic surgery, chmn. cardiothoracic surgery, 2007—, co-dir., Cardiovascular Ctr., 2007—. Cons. Dana Farber Canc Inst, Boston, MA, 1983, Baxter Healthcare, Orange County, Calif., 1990-; pres., Boston U. Cardiothoracic Surgery Found., Inc.; presenter in the field Contbr. several articles to profl. jours; assoc. editor Circulation, Jour. Cardiac Surgery; reviewer for several jours. including Annal of Thoracic Surgery, Jour. Thoracic and Cardiac Vascular Surgery. Lt. comdr. USPHS, 1996-98. Recipient Roche award Boston U. Med. Sch., 1974, Boston U. Sch. Medicine Alumni award, 1987, Outstanding Leadership, Thoracic Surgery Found. for Rsch. and Edn. Fellow ACS (coun. Mass. Chpt.), Am. Surg. Assn., Am. Coll. Cardiology (coun. Mass. Chpt.), Am. Heart Assn. (pres. greater Boston divsn.), Am. Coll. Chest Physicians; mem. Soc. Thoracic Surgeons (chair workforce com. 1998-), Am. Assn. Thoracic Surgery, Thoracic Surgery Tng. Dirs. Assn. (exec. com., editor Adult Cardiac Surgery), Algonquin Club Boston (exec. com., bd. dirs.), Northeast Cardiac Surgery Soc. (immediate past pres.), Phi Beta Kappa, Alpha Omega Alpha. Avocations: sailing, hunting, golf, reading history and biographies. Office: UCLA Divsn Cardiothoracic Surgery 10833 LeConte Los Angeles CA 90095 Office Phone: 310-206-8232. Office Fax: 310-825-7473.

SHEMMERI, THAFUR, pediatric dentist; m. Nida Kazzaz, July 17, 1977; children: Ealaf, Esel, Aws. BDS, Baghdad U., 1977; DMD, Boston U., 1991, MSc in Dentistry, 1990, DSc in Dentistry, 1991. Cert. in pediatric dentistry Boston U., 1988. Pvt. practice, Baghdad, Iraq, 1977—86; pvt. practice in pediatric dentistry Mass., 1992—. Mem.: Mass. Dental Soc., Am. Orthodontic Soc., Am. Acad. Pediatric Dentistry, ADA, Am. Acad. Pediat. (assoc.). Office: Wachusett Pediatric Dentistry 100 Whalon St Fitchburg MA 01420 Office Phone: 978-342-3004. Office Fax: 978-343-5979. Personal E-mail: dmd4kids@hotmail.com.

SHEMS, ESTHERINA, retired child psychiatrist; b. Tel Aviv, Apr. 15, 1932; came to US, 1950; d. Aaron and Rachel (Yehuda) S.; m. Donald L. Schotland, Jan. 11, 1976. BS cum laude, Lynchburg Coll., 1954, DSc (hon.), 2009; MD, Woman's Med. Coll. Pa., 1958. Rotating intern Lankenau Hosp., Phila., 1958-59; fellow in adult psychiatry U. Pa., Phila., 1960-63; child psychiatry affiliate Child Study Ctr. Phila., 1961-63; asst. instr., dept. psychiatry U. Pa. Sch. Medicine, Phila., 1962-63, Irving Schwartz Inst. for Children and Youth, 1964-66, various staff, adminstrv. positions Phila. Psychiat. Ctr. Phila., 1964-81; clin. assoc. in psychiatry U. Pa. Sch. Medicine, Phila., 1979-81; cons. early intervention programs Cmty. Coun. for Mental Health/Mental Retardation, Inc., Phila., 1981—2002; ret. Numerous cons. and tchg. positions in field including invited lectr., Inst. Pediatrics Chinese Acad. Med. Scis., Beijing, People's Republic of China. Exec. bd. Trust Fund of Alumnai Assn. Woman's Med. Coll., Med. Coll. Pa., 2001—; vice-chair. Woman's Med. Coll., Med. Coll. Pa., 2003—. Named one of Outstanding Young Women of America, 1967, one of Outstanding Young Women of Pa., 1967; recipient T. Gibson Hobbs Outstanding Alumni award Lynchburg Coll., 1969, Disting. Alumni award, 1990, Richard H. Thornton award for Excellence, 1995, Lifetime Achievement award, Va. Found. Ind. Colls., 2002. Fellow Am. Orthopsychiat. Assn., Coll. Physicians Phila.; mem. Med. Women's Internat. Assn. (US del. and session co-chmn. XIX Internat. Congress 1984, XX Internat. Congress 1987, XXII Congress 1995, mem. sci. rsch. com. 1990-98, nat. coord. for USA 1992-98, v.p. N.Am., exec. bd. 1998-2001), Am. Psychiat. Assn. (life mem.), Am. Med. Women's Assn. (life, mem. exec. com., bd. dirs. 1986-88, 92-98, councilor of orgn. 1986-88, mem. various coms. and task forces 1970—, Bertha Van Hoosen MD award 2002), Psychiat. Physicians Pa., Phila. Psychiat. Soc., Phi Kappa Phi, Chi Beta Phi (various offices), others. Avocations: travel, photography, music, reading. Home: 1310 Wyngate Rd Wynnewood PA 19096-2455

SHEN, ALFRED C., neurosurgeon; b. Ithaca, NY, Oct. 5, 1964; s. C. C. and Helen H. Shen; m. Kim Nguyen, Feb. 12, 2000; children: Eric Y., Erin Y. BSEE, Rice U., Houston, 1987; MD, U. Tex., Dallas, 1991. Diplomate Am. Bd. Neurol. Surgery, 2004. Spine fellow U. Tenn., 1999; neurosurgeon Desert Spine and Neurosurg. Inst., Rancho Mirage, Calif., 2002—; chief neurosurgery Eisenhower Med. Ctr., 2008—. Mem.: AMA, Congress Neurol. Surgeons, Am. Assn. Neurol. Surgeons.

SHEN, DANIEL HUENG-YUAN, medical researcher; b. Taipei, Taiwan, Dec. 30, 1964; s. Bao-Che and Li-Chu Shen; m. Julie Chin-Wen Che; children: Michael, Alice. MD, Nat. Def. Med. Coll., Taipei, 1990; MS, Ohio State U., 2001, PhD, 2003. Intern Tri-Service Gen. Hosp, Taipei, Taiwan, 1988—90; resident Tri-Service Gen. Hosp., Taipei, Taiwan, 1992—96; nuclear medicine physician Tri-Svc. Gen. Hosp., Taipei, 1992—; rschr. Ohio State U., Columbus, 1998—2003. Cons. PET Ctr., Nat. Def. Med. Ctr., 2003. Contbr. articles to profl. jours. Rep. Kuo-Ming Party, Taipei, 1985—88. Maj. Taiwan Mil., 1990—2003. Recipient, Beierwalts award, Detroit, 2000. Achievements include research in modified NIS proteins and genes for imaging and cancer therapy. Avocations: reading history, chess, swimming, classical music. Home: 2F 38-11 Ting-Chow Rd Sect 3 Taipei 100 Taiwan Office: Tri-Service Gen Hosp 325 Cheng-Kung Rd Sec 2 Taipei 114 Taiwan

SHEN, DAVID, orthodontist; married; 1 child. BS, SUNY, Stony Brook; DDS, U. Pa., Phila., 1981. Cert. in orthodontic specialty U. Pa., 1981, phase II Am. Bd. Orthodontics. Faculty mem. U. Calif., San Francisco; orthodontist OrthoWorks, San Francisco, 1983—. Spkr. in field. Fellow: Acad. Dentistry Internat.; mem.: Calif. Dental Assn., Am. Assn. Orthodontics, Am. Dental Assn., San Mateo County Dental Soc. (past chmn. mem. com.), No. Calif. Asian Dental Assn. (past pres.), Align Century Club. Avocations: photography, water sports, travel. Office: OrthoWorks Ste 2418 450 Sutter St San Francisco CA 94108

SHEN, DEMIN TEHMIN, hospital administrator, surgeon, educator; b. Jakarta, Indonesia; s. Woo Pow Shen and Pow Djin Tjhing; m. Geraldine Waligorski, July 4, 1969; children: Paul, Michelle. MD, U. Indonesia, Jakarta, 1960; PhD, U. Bogor, Indonesia, 1992. Resident in gen. surgery U. Pa., Phila., 1962-67; resident in thoracic and cardiovasc. surgery St. Vincent Hosp., Cleve., 1967-68, Cleve. Clinic, 1968-69; chief ICU, Govt. Hosp., Bandung, Indonesia, 1970-76; chief gen. surgery Cibabat Hosp., Cimahi, Indonesia, 1976-78; chief surgery Rajawali Hosp., Bandung, 1978-80, dir., 1980—; assoc. prof. Maranatha U., Bandung, 1972—; hon. prof. surgery PUMC, Beijing, 1995; hon. prof. Anzhen Hosp., Beijing Capital U., 2011. Chmn. Humanity Found., Bandung, 2010—. Fellow ACS, Royal Coll. Surgeons (Can.), Indonesian Surgeons Assn.; mem. Lions (Melvin Jones award 1982). Avocation: swimming. Home: 22 Bahureksa Bandung W Java Indonesia Office: Rajawali Hosp 38 Rajawali Bandung W Java Indonesia Business E-Mail: biotek@bdg.centrin.net.id.

SHEN, HSIU-YING YU, pharmacist, educator; b. Taipei, Taiwan, Republic of China, July 12, 1936; s. Zu-Tian and Chong (Jou) Yu; m. Yu-Zen Shen Oct. 1, 1961; children: Fa-Chih, Ying-Fen, Fa-Hui. BSc, Nat. Tiawan U., Tapei, Republic of China, 1959; PhD, U. Tokyo, Japan, 1988. Pharmacist Nat. Taiwan U. Hosp., Taipei, 1959-61, chief pharmacist pharm. sect., 1961-62, chief pharmacist sterile solution sect., 1962-63, chief pharmacist dispensing sect., 1964-65, chief pharmicist inventory control sect., 1965, chief pharmacist quality control sect., 1966-81; lectr. Nat. Taiwan U., Taipei, 1966-81, assoc. prof., 1981-85, prof., 1985—2001, emeritus prof., 2001—. Trustee The Chen's Pharm. Rsch. Found., Tapei, 1993— Editl. bd. Jour. of Pharmacy, Tapei, 1985—, The Chinese Pharmacopoeia, 3d edit., 1970, 7th edit., 2009, The Chinese Pharm. Jour., 1999—; reviewer Pharm. Rsch, Jour. Pharmaceutical Sci., Med. Sci. Monitor, Jour. Food and Drug Analysis. Trustee The Su-Quen-Po Medicinal rsch. Found., Sin-Chu, 2004—. Recipient Annual Excellent Rsch. Achievement award Nat. Sci. Coun., Tapei, Taiwan, 1984—. Mem. Pharm. Soc. Taiwan (comptroller 2004-), Japan Soc. Drug Delivery Sys., (organizing com. Taiwan local chpt. 1997—), Internat. Pharm. Fedn., Taipei Pharmacists Assn. (chair internat. affairs com. 2002-2008). Home: # 12 Ln 12 Pa-Teh Rd Sect 3 105 Taipei Taiwan Office: Nat Taiwan U Sch Pharmacy #1 Jen-ai Rd Sect 1 100 Taipei Taiwan

SHEN, JIN WEN, orthopedist, educator; b. Hangzhou, China, Jan. 20, 1962; BA, Zhejiang Med. U., 1982; MD, Zhejiang TCM U., 2004. Acting assoc. chief staff for orthop. dept. Hangzhou No. 4 Mcpl. Hosp., 2001—05; tutor, dept. orthop. Zhejiang TCM U., 2008; chief physician Zhejiang Province TCM Hosp. and Zhejiang TCM U. Hosp., 2009—. Office: 54 Youdian Rd Hangzhou Zhejiang 310006 China Office Fax: 86-571-87077785. Business E-Mail: shenjw100@163.com.

SHEN, TSUNG YING, medicinal chemistry educator; b. Beijing, Sept. 28, 1924; came to U.S., 1950; s. Tsu-Wei and Sien-Wha (Nieu) S.; m. Amy T.C. Lin, June 20, 1953; children: Bern, Hubert, Theodore, Leonard, Evelyn, Andrea. B.Sc., Nat. Ctrl. U., Chongqing, China, 1946; diploma, Imperial Coll. Sci. and Tech., London, 1948; PhD, U. Manchester, Eng., 1950, D.Sc., 1978. Research assoc. Ohio State U., Columbus, 1950-52, MIT, Cambridge, 1952-56; sr. research chemist Merck, Sharp & Dohme Research Labs., Rahway, NJ, 1956-65, dir. synthetic chem. research, 1966-76, v.p. membrane chem. research, 1976-77, v.p. membrane and arthritis research, 1977-86; A. Burger prof. medicinal chemistry U. Va., Charlottesville, 1986-96, emeritus and rsch. prof., 1996—2001. Vis. prof. U. Calif., Riverside, 1973, U. Calif., San Francisco, 1985; adj. prof. Stevens Inst. Tech., Hoboken, NJ, 1982-85; hon. prof. Beijing Med. U., Chinese Acad. Med. Sci., Inst. Material Medica, China Pharm. U.; mem. sci. bd. CytoMed, 1989-96, T Cell Sci, 1988-93, Gene Labs., 1989-94, Osteo Arthritis Sci, 1993-95, Argonex, 1994-98; advisor Academica Sinica Taiwan, 1992-97. Mem. editl. bd. Clinica Europa Jour., 1977, Prostaglandins and Medicine, 1978, Medicinal Rsch. Revs., 1979-94, Jour. Medicinal Chemistry, 1980-83, Medicinal Chem. Rsch., 1991-; patentee in field. Recipient Outstanding Patent award NJ Research and Devel. Council, 1975, Merck Dirs. sci. award, 1976, Galileo Meml. medal, U. Pisa, 1976, Rene Descartes medal U. Paris, 1977, medal of Merit Giornate Mediche Internazionali del Collegium Biologicum Europea, 1977, cert. of merit Spanish Soc. Therapeutic Chemistry, 1983, achievement award Chinese Inst. Engrs.-USA, 1984. Mem. AAAS, Am. Chem. Soc. (1st Alfred Burger award in medicinal chemistry 1980, inaugural mem., named to Hall of Fame, Divsn. Medicinal Chemistry, 2007), NY Acad. Scis., Acad. Pharm. Assn. (hon.), Chinese Am. Chem. Soc. (bd. dirs. 1995-97), Acad. Pharm. Scis. (hon.). Achievements include discovery of indomethacin, sulindac, diflunisal and other antiinflammatory agents; synthesis of bioactive natural product derivs and drug targeting ligands. Home: 238 Eliot St Chestnut Hill MA 02467-1447 Personal E-mail: tysal42@verizon.net.

SHEN, YI, engineering educator; b. Fuyu, PR, China, Feb. 8, 1965; M, Harbin Inst. Tech., 1988, PhD, 1995. Prof. Harbin Inst. Tech., 1997—. Editor Jour. Astronautics, 2008, Electric Machines & Control, 2008. Contbr. scientific papers. Recipient New Century Excellent Talents award, Ministry of Edn., PR China, U. Key Tchr. award, Ministry Edn., PR China. Office: No 92 West Da-Zhi St Harbin Heilongjiang 150001 China Business E-Mail: shen@hit.edu.cn.

SHENAQ, SALWA A., anesthesiologist; b. Jordan, Feb. 11, 1948; arrived in U.S., 1975; d. Ahmed M. and Hoson M. Saleh; m. Saleh M. Shenaq (dec. Mar. 17, 2007); children: Deana, Amir, Farris. MD, Cairo U., 1972; MBA, U. Houston, 1997. Diplomate Am. Bd. Anesthesia, Am. Bd. Quality Assurance and Utilization Rev. Chief cardiovasc. anesthesia Meth. Hosp., Houston, 1990—92, dir. cardiovasc. anesthesia rsch., 1992—98; chief anesthesiology VA Med. Ctr., Houston, 1998—. Fellow: Am. Heart Assn., Am. Coll. Cardiology; mem.: Am. Coll. Physician Exec., Internat. Anesthetic Rsch. Soc., Am. Soc. Echocardiography, Am. Coll. Managed Care Medicine (adv. bd. 1996—), Tex. Soc. Anesthesiologists (del. 2001), Soc. Cardiovasc. Anesthesiologists (bd. dirs. 1992—95), Assn. Univ. Assocs., Am. Soc. Critical Care Anesthesiologists, Am. Soc. Anesthesiologists. Home: PO Box 27882 Houston TX 77227-7882 Personal E-mail: salwashenaq@gmail.com.

SHENEFELT, PHILIP DAVID, dermatologist; b. Colfax, Wash., July 31, 1943; s. Roy David and Florence Vanita (Cagle) S.; m. Debrah A. Levenson; children: Elizabeth, Sara, Shaina. BS with honors, U. Wis. Madison, 1966, MD, 1970, MS in Adminstrv. Medicine, 1984. Diplomate Am. Bd. Dermatology, Am. Bd. Med. Hypnosis. Intern U.S. Naval Hosp., Bethesda, Md., 1970-71; gen. practice Oreg. (Wis.) Clinic, 1975; resident in dermatology U. Wis. Hosp., Madison, 1975-78, mem. staff, 1978-87; asst. prof. dermatology U. South Fla., Tampa, 1987—97, assoc. prof., 1997—2011, prof., 2011—. Chief dermatology sect. VA Hosp., Bay Pines, Fla., 1987—89, asst. chief, Tampa, 1988—2002, chief, 2002—07; dermatologist Univ. Health Svc. U. Wis., Madison, 1978—87, VA Hosp., Madison, 1982—85. Served to lt. comdr. USN, 1969-74; capt. USNR (ret.); med. corps officer Submarine and Diving. Kellogg fellow, 1980-82. Mem.: AMA, Fla. Med. Assn., Soc. Clin. Exptl. Hypnosis, Noah Worcester Dermatol. Soc., Fla. West Coast Dermatol. Soc., Fla. Dermatol. Soc., Am. Soc. Clin. Hypnosis, Am. Coll. Physician Execs., Am. Acad. Dermatology. Office: U South Fla Dermatol # 79 12901 Bruce Downs Blvd Tampa FL 33612-4742 Office Phone: 813-974-2188. Business E-Mail: pshenefe@health.usf.edu.

SHENG, ZHI (CHIH) YONG, surgeon, educator; b. Shanghai, July 1, 1920; m. Yun Xui Zhang, Oct. 9, 1943; children: Ai-lun, Jia-lun, Pei-lun MD, Shanghai Med. Coll., 1942. Resident dept. surgery Red Cross First Hosp., Shanghai, 1942—45, chief resident, dept. surgery, 1945—46; rsch. fellow Surgical Rsch. Lab., U. Tex. Med. Br., Galveston, 1947—48; vis. surgeon Yangtzepoo Hosp., Shanghai, 1949—50, Chong-san Hosp., Shanghai, 1950—52; assoc. rschr., deputy chief, dept. experimental surgery Acad. Mil. Med. Sci., PLA, China, 1952—61; chief, dept. gen. surgery Surgical Emergency Hosp., Shanghai, 1956—57; chief, faculty of topographical anatomy and operative surgery Second Mil. Med. Coll., Shanghai, 1956—57; chief, dept. trauma and burns Gen. Hosp. of PLA, Beijing, 1961—82; prof. of surgery Postgraduate Med. Coll. of PLA, Beijing, 1978—; dir. trauma ctr. Postgraduate Med. Coll. of PLA, 304th Hosp., Beijing, 1982—96; vice dir. 304th Hosp., Beijing, 1982—88, dir. Burns Inst., 1996—97; hon. dir. Burns Inst. First Affiliated Hosp. to Gen. Hosp. of PLA (formerly 304th Hosp.), Beijing, 1997—; academian Chinese Acad. Engring., 1996—2000, sr. academian, 2000—; hon. prof. Jinan U. Med. Coll., 2002—; prof. of surgery Qinghua U. Med. Coll., 2005; prof., burn and plastic surgery hosp. Gen. Hosp. PLA, 2006—. Editor-in-chief: Med. Jour. of PLA, hon. chief editor: Chinese Jour. Trauma, Chinese Jour. Burns, mem. editl. bd.: Chinese Jour. Critical Care Medicine, formerly mem. editl. bd.: Burns, Jour. of Internat. Soc. Burn Injuries, mem. editl. bd.: Chinese Jour. Clinical Nutrition, Academic Jour. of Second Mil. Med. U., mem. adv. bd.: Chinese Hour. Traumatology, Chinese Jour. Emergency Medicine, Modern Rehabilitation, author chpts. to books, monographs in field. Recipient First prize, State Prize of Advances in Sci. and Tech., 1985, 2002, Second prize, 1992, 1993, 2005, 2008, Third prize, 1995, 1998, First Prize, Army Prize of Advances in Sci. and Tech., 1996, 1998, 1999, 2001, 2004, Second Prize, 1988—2001, First Prize, Army Prize of Achievement in Clin. Medicine, 2001, Advances in Sci. and Tech.,

State Bureau of Seismology, 1978, Merit of Honor, Headquarters of Gen. Staff, Gen. Dept. Politics and Logistics, PLA, 1987, Gen. Dept. Logistics, PLA, 1987, Second-class merit, 1987, Third-class merit, 1989, First-class merit, Military Commn., People's Republic of China, 2000, Ho Leung Ho Lee prize, 1999, award for Important Achievements in Sci. and Tech. of Mil. Svc., 1996, Bo Le prize, Gen. Dept. Logistics, PLA, 2000, Master of Era, Gen. Logistic Dept., prize, Guanghua Engring. Sci. & Tech., Chinese Acad. Engring., 2010. Mem.: AAAS (internat. mem.), Burns Soc. of PLA (advisor), Trauma Soc. of PLA (advisor), Med. Assn. of PLA, Chinese Soc. for Trauma, Chinese Surgical Soc., Chinese Med. Assn. (hon. mem. bd. trustees), Chinese Burns Soc. (co-founder 1975, vice chmn. 1986—91, chmn. 1991—94, hon. chmn. 1994—2002), Israel Burn Assn. (hon.), Trauma Assn. Can. (hon.), Am. Assn. for Surgery of Trauma (hon.), Internat. Soc. for Burn Injuries (sr.). Avocation: classical music. Office: Burns Inst First Affiliated Hosp Gen Hosp of PLA formerly 304th Hosp 51 Fucheng Rd Beijing 100048 China Office Phone: 86-10-68989158. Personal E-mail: shengzhy@cae.cn. Business E-Mail: shengzy@public.bta.net.cn.

SHENGKAI, YAN, pathologist, educator; Postdoc., U. Sask., Can., 2007; PhD, Peking Union Med. Coll. & Chinese Acad. Med. Scis., 2002. MS Coll. Medicine, Wuhan U., China, 1993—96; rsch. asst. Dept. Lab. Medicine, Peking Union Med. Coll. Hosp., 1996—99, assoc. prof. to dir. asst., 2005; postdoc. fellow Dept. Pathology & Lab. Medicine, U. Sask., Saskatchewan, Canada, 2005—07; dept. head to assoc. prof. Dept. Lab. Medicine, China-Japan Friendship Hosp., Beijing, 2007—. Mem. rev. com. China Nat. Accreditation Svc. Conformity Assessment, Beijing, 2008—; mem. Nat. Expert Com. Prevention and Control Cardiovasc. Disease, Beijing. Recipient 2nd prize, Govt. Wuhan City, Hubei Province, China, 2000, 2004, Best Paper award, Chinese Soc. Lab. Medicine, 2004. Mem.: Am. Assn. Clin. Chemistry (younger fellow 2005—, Gallwas Membership grant), Chinese Soc. Biochemistry and Molecular Biology (mem. lipoprotein profession com. 2006—). Achievements include research in effects of hydrogen sulfide on homocysteine-induced oxidative stress in vascular smooth muscle cells. Office: China-Japan Friendship Hosp No2 East Yinghua Rd Beijing 100029 China Office Fax: 86-10-64288578. Personal E-mail: yanshengkai@yahoo.com.cn.

SHENK, THOMAS EUGENE, molecular biology educator, academic administrator; b. Bklyn., Jan. 1, 1947; s. Eugene Richard and Helen Marie (Deffenbaugh) S.; m. Susan Mary Hillman, July 4, 1979; children: Christopher Thomas, Gregory Thomas BS in Biology, U. Detroit, 1969; PhD in Microbiology, Rutgers U., 1973. Postdoctoral fellow, molecular biology Stanford Med. Ctr.; asst. prof. molecular biology U. Conn., Farmington, 1975-80; prof. molecular biology SUNY, Stony Brook, 1980-84, Elkins prof., dept. molecular biology Princeton U., 1984—, Am. Cancer Soc. prof., 1986—, chmn. dept. molecular biology, 1996—. Bd. dirs. Merck & Co., Inc., 2001—, CV Therapeutics, Inc., Palo Alto, Calif., 2001—, Cell Genesys, Inc., 2001—, mem. scientific adv. bd., 1997—, Novalon Pharm. Corp.; investigator Howard Hughes Inst.; mem. pres. adv. group Fox Chase Cancer Ctr.; chair Sloan General Motors prize Selection Com.; spkr. in field; chair NIH Virology Study Sect.; bd. trustee Cold Spring Harbor Lab. Co-editor: Enhancers and Eukaryotic Gene Expression, 1983; contbr. articles to profl. jours.editor, Journal of Virology, 1984-94. Recipient NIH Rowe award. Mem. Am. Soc. Microbiology (Eli Lilly award 1982, pres.), NAS, Inst. Medicine, Am. Soc. for Virology (past pres.); fellow Am. Acad. Arts and Sciences., Am. Acad. Microbiology. Achievements include patents in field. Office: Princeton U Dept Molecular Biology Lewis Thomas Lab 203 Princeton NJ 08544-0001

SHENOT, PATRICK J., urologist, educator; MD, SUNY, 1991. Diplomate Am. Bd. Urology. Intern Thomas Jefferson Univ. Hosp., resident, fellow gen. surgery, 1991—93, fellow urology, 1993—97, 1997—98, hospital affiliations include, Meth. Hosp.; physician Thomas Jefferson Univ., asst. prof. urology dept. Jefferson Med. Coll., residency program dir. Jefferson Med. Coll., vice chmn. academic affairs dept. Jefferson Med. Coll. Co-investigator clin. trials involving genitourinary disorders. Co-author: Lyme Cystitis And Neurogenic Bladder Dysfunction, 1992, Urinary Dysfunction in Lyme Disease, 1993, Latex Allergy Manifested in Urological Surgery And Care of Adult Spinal Cord Injured Patients, 1994, Radial Dilatation in the Insertion of the Multi-Component Inflatable Penile Prosthesis, 1995, Urological Symptomatology in Patients With Reflex Sympathetic Dystrophy, 1996, several book chpts. and publs. Named one of the Top Physicians, Guide to America, the Top Doctors, Phila. Mag., 2010. Mem.: ACS, Internat. Soc. of Pelvic Neuromodulation, Internat. Continence Soc., Am. Paraplegia Soc., Am. Spinal Cord Injury Assn. (recipient of awards of excellence in rsch.), Am. Urol. Assn. Office: Thomas Jefferson University Hospital 111 S 11th St Philadelphia PA 19107 Office Phone: 215-955-6961. Office Fax: 215-923-1884. Business E-Mail: Patrick.Shenot@jefferson.edu.

SHENOY, PREMNATH K.R., research pharmacist, medical educator; s. Ramakrishna Kudbail and Lalitha Shenoy; m. Poonam Nayak, May 31, 1986; children: Pooja, Shweta. B in Pharm., Govt. Coll. of Pharmacy, Bangalore, 1972—77, M in Pharm., 1979—81; diploma in Mgmt. studies, Bombay U., 1988—90; PhD, Regional Rsch. Lab., Bangalore, 2000—02. R & d officer FDC Ltd., Bombay, 1981—84; asst. mgr. Cyanamid India Ltd., Atul, 1984—86; tech. mgr. Sigma Labs., Bombay, 1986—91, Wallace Pharm., Ponda, 1991—94; head, qa & tech. svcs. Astrazeneca Pharma India Ltd., Bangalore, 1991—. Author: (rsch. article) Indian Drugs. Mem. RMS residents Assn., Bangalore, 2001—02. Recipient State Award, Youth Services Dept, Govt. of Karnatak, 1978, IDMA gold Medal, Indian Drug Manufacturers Assn., Bombay, 1978, IPA gold medal, Indian Pharm. Assn., 1978; UGC Scholarship, U. Grants Commn., 1978—80. Mem.: Assn. Pharm. Tchrs. India (life), Quality Cir. Forum of India, Bangalore chpt. (life; exec. mem., editor 1999—2001), Indian Pharm. Assn. (life), PSG Coll. Pharmacy (hon.; mem., governing coun. 2001—03). Hindu. Avocations: reading, travel, coin collection. Home: Opp Rms Watertank 560 094 RMV II stage, Sanjay Nagar, Bangalore 560 094 India Office Fax: 91 80 846 2208. Personal E-mail: krpshenoy@yahoo.com.

SHENOY, VIJENDRA, otolaryngologist, educator; b. Mangalore, Dec. 6, 1977; MBBS, Manipal U., 2000, MS, 2005. Assoc. prof. Manipal U., 2005—. Recipient Best Outgoing award, Manipal U., 2005. Mem.: Assn. Otolaryngologist India. Office: Dept ENT Kastur Mangalore Karnataka 575001 India E-mail: drvijendras@gmail.com.

SHEPARD, BEATRICE L., retired microbiologist, historian; b. Hillsdale, Mich., May 15, 1919; d. James Wesley Shepard and Ona Ola Kinney. AB in Zoolog., U. Calif., Berkeley, 1940. Regional lab. dir. L.A. County Health Dept., LA, 1945-46; sr. biologist, sr. chemist S.E. Regional Lab., Juneau, Alaska, 1946-67; acting chief of labs. Alaska Dept. Health & Social Svcs., Juneau, 1967-70; microbiologist in charge S.E. Regional Lab., Alaska Dept. Health and Social Svcs., 1967—77; ret., 1977. Chemist L.A. County Health Dept., 1944-45, L.A. County Gen. Hosp., 1943-44; dir. pub. health lab. Health Dept. Riverside (Calif.) County, 1942-43. Author: Praise the Lord and Pass the Penicillin, 1979; co-author: Have Gospel Tent, Will Travel, History of 100 Years of Alaskan Methodism, 1986; editor: (newsletter) Western Cir. Rider, 1998—2005, Eagle River United Meth. Camp, 1998—; contbr. articles to profl. jours., chapters to books. Docent Alaska State Mus., 1992—2004; mem. Juneau Borough Commn. on Aging, 1997—2009; curator Alaska State Mus., 2003; mem. gen. commn. archives and history United Meth. Ch. Archives Ctr., Madison, NJ, 1988—96; historian Alaska Meth. Ch., Alaska Missionary Conf., Anchorage, 1980—2008; bd. dirs., advocacy chair Mus. Alaska, 1992—2005; sec. bd. dirs. Eagle River Meth. Camp, 1955—2005; bd. dirs. Western Jurisdictional Commn. on Archives and History, 1984—2005; chair Alaska Missionary Conf. Commn. on Archives and History, 1980—2004. Named Outstanding Lay Person of Yr. award Alaska Missionary Conf. of United Meth. Ch., 1986; recipient Meritorious Health Svc. award Alaska Pub. Health Assn., 1990, Lifetime Achievement award Juneau C. of C., 1997-. Mem.: Friends of Alaska State Mus. (hon.; life), Museums Alaska (hon.; life). Avocation: photography. Home: 12585 Glacier Hwy Juneau AK 99801 E-mail: BShep98308@aol.com.

SHEPARD, RICHARD BLOUNT, surgeon, educator; b. Birmingham, Ala., May 9, 1926; m. Winyss Renee Acton, Mar. 26, 1955; children: Winyss Elizabeth, Kathryn Bouchelle, Richard Kesniel, Karen Acton. BS in Physics, Pa. State U., 1949; MD, U. Pa., 1953. Intern, resident in surgery U. Pa. Hosp., Phila., 1953-59; instr., rsch. assoc. in physiology U. Pa., Phila., 1954-56; chief resident Fitkin Hosp. Hahnemann Med. Coll., Neptune, NJ, 1959-60; from instr. to prof. surgery U. Ala., Birmingham, 1960-98, prof. surgery, emeritus, 1998—. Engr. Victoreen Instrument Co., Cleve., 1946; engr. Haller, Raymond & Brown, State College, Pa., 1948; cons. for device implant mfrs. and electronics mfr., 1960-2004; chmn. USRA-NASA biomed. com. for studies selection, shuttle orbital flight tests, 1981-83. Contbr. articles to profl. jours. and chpts. to books. With US Army, 1943—46, spl. engr. detatchment Manhattan Project US Army, 1945—46. Grantee Heart Assn. S.E. Pa., NIH. Fellow ACS, Am. Coll. Cardiology, Soc. for Vascular Surgery (disting.); mem. IEEE (life), Heart Rhythm Soc., Soc. Thoracic Surgeons. Achievements include research in blood flow and energy characteristics, especially as related to cardiopulmonary bypass operations and underlying physiology; one of the first to implant cardiac pacemakers and investigational defibrillators; application of physics and tissue biology to clinical and laboratory implantable device development, teaching and problem solutions. Office Phone: 205-934-4672. Business E-Mail: RShepard@uab.edu.

SHEPARD, S. JEFF, physicist; b. Guntersville, Ala., Apr. 1, 1953; BS, Oakland U., 1977; MS, UTHSC Dallas, 1981. Med. physicist Wheaton Regional Cancer Ctr., Millville Hosp., 1982—86, Baylor U. Med. Ctr., 1986—2004; sr. med. physicist U. Tex. M. D. Anderson Cancer Ctr., 1994—. Resident Henry Ford Hosp., 1978—80. Fellow: Am. Assn. Physicists Medicine (chair 1990—99, 2004—08, chair, Rad, Fluoro Subcom. 2006—08, chair, Imaging Physics Com. 2008—, fellowship); mem.: Soc. Imaging Informatics Medicine. Office: 1400 Pressler St Unit 1472 Houston TX 77030-3721 Office Fax: 413-745-0581. Business E-Mail: jshepard@mdanderson.org.

SHEPARD, THOMAS HILL, physician, educator; b. Milw., May 22, 1923; s. Francis Parker and Elizabeth Rhodes (Buchner) S.; m. Alice B. Kelly, June 24, 1946; children: Donna, Elizabeth, Ann. AB, Amherst Coll., 1945; MD, U. Rochester, 1948. Intern Strong Meml. Hosp., Rochester, NY, 1948-49, resident, 1950-52, Albany (N.Y.) Med. Ctr., 1949-50; pediatric endocrine fellow Johns Hopkins Hosp., 1954-55; pediatrician U. Wash., Seattle, 1955-61, teratologist, 1961—, prof. pediat., head ctrl. lab. for human embryology, 1961-93, prof. emeritus, 1993—; embryologist dept. anatomy U. Fla., 1961-62; rsch. assoc. dept. embryology Carnegie Inst., 1962, U. Copenhagen, 1963. Cons. NIH, FDA, EPA, 1971-; vis. prof. pediat. U. Geneva, 1972, 73-74. Author: A Catalog of Teratogenic Agents, 2006, 13th edit., 2011; contbr. articles to profl. jours. With US Army, 1946—48, with USAF, 1952—54. Mem.: Am. Pediatric Soc., Western Soc. Pediatric Rsch. (pres. 1970), Orgn. for Teratogen Answering Svcs. (hon. Thomas Shepard Ann. lectr.), Japanese Teratology Soc. (hon.), Teratology Soc. (hon.; pres. 1968). Home: 3015 98th Ave NE Bellevue WA 98004-1818 Office: U Wash Sch Medicine Dept Pediatrics Seattle WA 98195-0001 Home Phone: 425-454-2146. Business E-Mail: shepard@u.washington.edu.

SHEPHARD, BRUCE DENNIS, obstetrician, educator, medical writer; b. San Francisco, Apr. 21, 1944; s. Richard G. and Madelyn (Rogers) S.; children: Christopher, Carleton, Elizabeth. BA in History, U. Calif., Berkeley, 1966; MD, U. Calif., San Francisco, 1970. Diplomate Am. Bd. Ob-Gyn. Intern Jackson Meml. Hosp.-U. Miami (Fla.), 1970-71, resident in ob-gyn., 1971-74; pvt. practice Tampa, 1976—; clin. assoc. prof. obstetrics U. So. Fla. Sch. Medicine, Tampa, 1976—. Bd. dirs. Ctr. of Excellence, Humana Women's Hosp., Tampa, Fla., 1983-90, Gulf Coast Health Systems Agy., 1980-83; mem. midwifery adv. com. Fla. Dept. Health and Human Resources, Tallahassee, 1982-86; cons. physician KePRO, 2010-. Prin. author: The Complete Guide to Women's Health, 1982, 3d rev. edit., 1997; prin., writer, spokesperson (series of TV commls.) The Healthy Woman (Gold Link award 1987); mem. med. adv. bd. Baby Talk mag., 1992-2004; bd. dirs. PBS affiliate WEDU, 1998-2005; contbr. articles to profl. jours. and women's mags. Lectr. Continuing Edn., Inc., 2002—; mem. Agy. Health Care Adminstrn., Dept. Health and Rehab. Svcs., Fla., cert. med. expert Fla., 2001—; mem. Healthier Fla. Provider Adv. Bd., 2007—; med. adv. bd. Welcare HMO, 1996—; pres. coun. AVMED HMO, 1999—2002; bd. dirs. Mus. Sci. and Industry, Tampa, 2007—09. Served as maj. USAF, 1974—76. Mem. AMA, Am. Coll. Ob-Gyn. (patient edn. com. 1984-86, John McCain fellow 1981), Hillsborough County Med. Assn. (v.p. 2003-05, pres. elect. 2005-06, pres. 2006-07, named one of Best Drs. in America 2011-), Phi Beta Kappa. Democrat. Lutheran. Avocations: tennis, photography, golf, antique glass collecting, running. Home: 14516 Nettle Creek Rd Tampa FL 33624 Office: 4302 N Habana Ave Ste 300 Tampa FL 33607 Personal E-mail: shephardmd@verizon.net.

SHEPHERD, ALISON ANNE, nursing educator; b. Desborough, Northamptonshire, Eng., June 15, 1965; d. Brian and Dorothy Laywood; life ptnr. John Burton. BSc in Biomed. Scis. with honors, Kingston U., 1993; MSc in Nutritional Medicine, U. Surrey, 2004. RN Kettering Gen. Hosp. Sch. Nursing Kettering Northamptonshire; registered nutritionist Nutrition Soc. London, postgrad. cert. in academic practice King's Coll. London, cert. nursing tchr. Nursing lectr. De Montfort U., Leicester, England, 2002—04; nurse tutor Florence Nightingale Sch. Nursing Kings Coll. U. London, 2009—. Guest lectr. Mt. Carmel Coll. Nursing, Columbus, Ohio, Health Sci. Ctr. U. Tex., San Antonio, Robert Morris Coll. Nursing, Chgo. Spkr. Excellence Nursing Conf. Singapore, 2004, Nursing Practice Event Birmingham, London, 2009, Internat. Nutrition and Health Conf. Olympia, 2009; contbr. articles. Recipient Queens Nurse award, 2010. Mem.: Health Care Profl. Adv. Bd. Innocent Smoothie Co., Sci. Com. Internat. Nutrition and Health Conf. (London), Editl. Bd. Complete Nutrition. Anglican. Avocations: theater, reading, cooking, singing. Office: James Clerk Maxwell Bldg 57 Waterlo SE1 8WA London England Office Phone: 2078483613. Personal E-mail: alison.shepherd@kcl.ac.uk.

SHEPHERD, DOUGLAS, hospital administrator; b. Aug. 1, 1944; married; three children. BA in Zoology, Miami U., 1966, postgrad., 1966-68; MHA, U. Mich., 1970. Grad. rsch. asst. in zoology Miami U., Oxford, Ohio, 1967-68; resident Ohio State U. Hosp., Columbus, 1969; asst. to adminstrv. officer Nat. Naval Med. Ctr., Bethesda, Md., 1970-73, hosp. project officer, 1973-79; assoc. adminstr. for clin. affairs Washington Hosp. Ctr., Washington, 1979-84; COO, sr. v.p. Nat. Rehab. Hosp., Washington, 1984—2004; with Laurel Regional Hosp., 2005—. Bd. trustees Commn. on Accreditation of Rehab. Facilities; faculty George Washington U., Washington, Ithaca Coll., N.Y. Cons. editor: Hospital Topics mag.; editl. adv. bd. Aspen Publishers, Inc., Jour. of Rehab. Adminstrn. Lt. comdr USN, 1970. Fellow Am. Coll. of Healthcare Execs. (bd. govs., regent-at large dist. 2, 1993-2002); mem. Am. Hosp. Assn. (governing coun. sect. of rehab. hosps. and programs 1986, chmn. 1991, former house of dels.), D.C. Hosp. Assn. (past chmn.), Md. Hosp. Assn. (past pres.), Va. Hosp. Assn. (past pres.), Am. Congress Rehab. Medicine, Assn. Health Care Adminstrs. of Nat. Capital Area (pres. 1978-79), others. Home Phone: 301-407-0201; Office Phone: 301-497-7978. E-mail: douglas.shepherd@dimensionshealth.org. *

SHEPHERD, GILLIAN MARY, physician; b. Mar. 12, 1948; d. John Thompson and Helen (Johnston) S.; m. Eduardo Goar Mestre, Aug. 4, 1973; children: Laura Elena, Cristina Alicia, Eduardo Goar. BA, Wheaton Coll., Norton, Mass., 1970; postgrad., Tufts U., 1970-73; MD, N.Y. Med. Coll., 1976. Diplomate Am. Bd. Internal Medicine, Am. Bd. Allergy and Immunology. Intern, resident Lenox Hill Hosp., NYC, 1976-79; fellow in allergy and immunology N.Y. Hosp./Cornell Med. Sch., NYC, 1979-81; assoc. prof. medicine Cornell U. Med. Coll., NYC, 1988—, clin. assoc. prof. medicine, 1995—. Assoc. attending physician N.Y. Hosp., N.Y.C.; cons. allergy and immunology dept. medicine Meml. Sloan-Kettering Cancer Ctr., N.Y.C., 1982—. Contbr. articles in field to profl. jours. Fellow ACP, Am. Acad. Asthma, Allergy and Immunology (chair Edn. and Rsch. Trust 1999-2001, bd. dirs. 2000-2003); mem. AAAS, Am. Fedn. for Clin. Rsch., Joint Coun. Allergy and Immunology, N.Y. Allergy Soc. (exec. com. 1982-94, pres. 1991-92), N.Y. County Med. Soc. Office: 235 E 67th St Rm 203 New York NY 10021-6040 Office Phone: 212-288-9300.

SHEPHERD, JOHN H., gynecologist; b. London, July 11, 1948; s. Henry Robert and Mimika Shepherd; m. Alison Sheila Brandram-Adams, May 27, 1972; children: David, Katy, Emily. MBBS, St. Bartholomews Hosp, 1971. Cons. ob-gyn. St. Bartholomews Hosp., London, 1981—83, cons. gynecologist, 1983—2008; cons. surgeon Royal Marsden Hosp., 1983—; prof. surg. gynecology London U., 1999—2008. Head surgery Royal Marsden Hosp., 2003—05, head gynaecological oncology, 2009—. Fellow, U. South Fla., Tampa, 1979—81. Fellow: Royal Coll. Gynecologists (coun. mem. 2003—10, Gold medal), Royal Soc. Medicine (pres. sect. ob-gyn. 2006—07), Royal Coll. Surgeons; mem.: Soc. Pelvic Surgeons (pres. 2007—08), Royal Ocean Racing Club (rear commodore 2011—), Marylebone Cricket Club. Achievements include development of techniques in pelvic reconstruction & fertility sparing surgery. Office: London Clinic Consulting Room 5 Devonshire Place W1G 6HL London England Home: Market Hill Cowers Isle of Wight PO31 7TR England Office Phone: 0044 0 207 935 4444. Business E-Mail: dr.jhs@thelondonclinic.co.uk.

SHEPHERD, JOHN THOMPSON, physiologist; b. No. Ireland, May 21, 1919; s. William Frederick and Matilda (Thompson) S.; m. Helen Mary Johnston, July 28, 1945; children: Gillian Mary, Roger Frederick John; m. Marion G. Etzwiler, Apr. 22, 1989. Student, Campbell Coll., Belfast, No. Ireland, 1932-37; MB, BCh, Queen's U., Belfast, 1945, MChir, 1948, MD, 1951, DSc, 1956, DSc (hon.), 1979; MD (hon.), U. Bologna, 1984, U. Gent, 1985. Lectr. physiology Queen's U., 1948-53, reader physiology, 1954-57; assoc. prof. physiology Mayo Found., 1957-62, prof. physiology, 1962—, chmn. dept. physiology and biophysics, 1966-74; bd. govs. Mayo Clinic, 1966-80; trustee Mayo Found., 1969-81, dir. rsch., 1969-77, dir. for edn., 1977-83, chmn. bd. devel., 1983-88; dean Mayo Med. Sch., 1977-83; assoc. dir. Gen. Rsch. Ctr. Mayo Clinic, Rochester, 1992-94. Chmn. U.S. Nat. Com. for the Internat. Union of Physiol. Scis., 1991-95; vis. prof. U. Auckland, New Zealand, 1997; vis. prof. cardiovasc. divsn. U. Minn., 1995; Soma Weiss meml. lectr. Third Internat. Congress

WHMA, Pecs, Hungary, 1996. Author, editor: Physiology of the Circulation in Human Limbs in Health and Disease, 1963, Cardiac Function in Health and Disease, 1968, Veins and Their Control, 1975, Human Cardiovascular System, 1979, Handbook of Physiology, The Cardiovascular System Peripheral Circulation and Organ Blood Flow, 1983, Vascular Diseases in the Limbs, 1993, Nervous Control of the Heart, 1996; co-editor: Exercise: Regulation and Integration of Multiple Systems. Handbook of Physiology, 1996; mem. editl. bd. Hypertension, 1973—, Am. Jour. Physiology, Am. Heart Jour., Microvascular Rsch.; cons. editor Circulation Rsch., 1981—; editor-in-chief News in Physiol. Sci., 1988-94; mem. editl. adv. bd. Clin. Autonomic Rsch., 1990—, Jour. Autonomic Nervous Sys., 1994—, Exptl. Physiology, 1994—, Vascular Medicine, 1995—, Internat. Angiology Adv. Com., 1994—, Cardiovasc. Rsch., 1997—; contbr. more than 590 sci. articles to profl. jours. Recipient NASA Skylab Achievement award, 1974, A. Ross McIntyre medal for achievement, 1991; Brit. Med. Assn. scholar, 1949-50, Fulbright scholar, 1953-54; Anglo-French Med. exch. bursar, 1957; Internat. Francqui chair, 1978; Einthoven lectr. 1981, Volhard lectr., 1990. Fellow Am. Coll. Cardiology (hon.), Royal Coll. Physicians (London, hon.), Royal Coll. Physicians Ireland (hon.), Royal Acad. Medicine (Belgium); mem. NAS (space sci. bd. 1973-74, chmn. com. space biology and medicine 1973), Am. Physiol. Soc. (Disting. Svc. award 1990, Ray G. Daggs award 1997), Louis Rapkine Assn., Am. Heart Assn. (dir. 1968—, pres. 1975-76, chmn. vascular medicine and biology task force 1990, hon. fellow coun. clin. cardiology), Physiol. Soc. Gt. Brit., Med. Rsch. Soc. London, Assn. Am. Physicians, Internat. Union of Angiology (hon.), Worldwide Hungarian Med. Acad. (hon.), Rappaport Inst. Israel (sci. adv. bd.), Sigma Xi. Office: Mayo Clinic Plummer Bldg N-10 Rochester MN 55905 Home Phone: 612-333-2036; Office Phone: 507-284-2691.

SHEPHERD, SUSAN J, nutritionist; b. Australia, Victoria, Oct. 23, 1974; BS in Applied Sci. (Health Promotion), Deakin U., Melbourne, Australia, 1995, MS in Nutrition and Dietetics, 1997; PhD, Monash U., Melbourne, 2008. Advanced accredited practising dietitian Dietitians Assn. Australia, 2008. Dietitian Dept. Gastroenterology, Box Hill, Victoria, 2002—, Box Hill Hosp., Victoria, 2002—. Dir. Shepherd Works Pty Ltd, Melbourne, Victoria, 1999—. Author: (cookbooks) A Wealth of Health, (cookbook) Irresistible for the Irritable, Two Irresistible for the Irritable, Gluten Free Cooking (Gourmand Cookbook award Best Health and Nutrition Cookbook (Australia), 2007), Gluten Frei Kotchen, 2009; researcher (dietetic research) Dietary Guidelines for Fructose Malabsorption (Gastroent. Soc. of Australia Young Investigator award, 2006), (dietetic) Dietetic Professional Development (Dietitian's Assn. of Australia Award of Achievement, 2003), Dietitians Association of Australia Coeliac Disease presentation (Rsch. in Practice award, 2007), Dietary Management For Irritable Bowel Syndrome; contbr. articles to profl. jours.; researcher Food Intolerance Management Plan, 2011. Dora Lush Biomedical Rsch. scholarship, Nat. Health and Med. Rsch. Coun., 2004—07. Mem.: Dietitians Assn. of Australia. Office: Dept Gastroenterology Box Hill Hosp Level 2 5 Arnold St Box Hill Victoria 3128 Australia Home: 402 150 Kerr St Fitroy Victoria 3065 Australia Office Phone: 61 3 9890 49411. Office Fax: + 613 9890 4944. Business E-Mail: info@shephardworldcom.au. E-mail: info@coeliac.com.au.

SHEPP, BRYAN EUGENE, psychologist, educator; b. Cumberland, Md, Sept. 13, 1932; s. Bryan Evert and Dorothy Lorene (Stell) S.; m. June Lee Langeluttig, Jan. 31, 1953; children: Karen Suzanne, David Bryan. BS, U. Md., 1954, MS, 1956, PhD, 1960; MS with honors, Brown U., 1966. Rsch. prof. U. Conn., 1961-63; asst. prof. psychology George Peabody Coll., Nashville, 1963-64, Brown U., Providence, 1964-66, assoc. prof., 1966-69, prof., 1969-98, prof. emeritus, 1998—, chmn. dept. Providence, 1983-88, assoc. dean faculty, 1988-91, dean faculty, 1991-96. Cons. in field; vis. scientist Oxford (Eng.) U., 1970 Contbr. numerous articles to profl. publ.; ad hoc editor for several psychol. jour. Served with USN, 1955-59. Decorated letter of commendation Sec. of Navy; USPHS postdoctoral fellow, 1959-61; Nat. Inst. Child Health and Human Devel. grantee, 1965—82. Fellow APA, Am. Psychol. Soc. (founding fellow); mem. AAAS, AAUP, Psychonomic Soc., Univ. Club. Home Phone: 207-633-4703. Personal E-mail: beshepp@yahoo.com.

SHEPPARD, MICHAEL T., medical association administrator; MBA, Loyola Coll. Sellinger Sch., Balt. Several high level positions including dir. fin., dir. fin. and info systems, COO, dep. exec. dir. Am. Urol. Assn., Md., exec. dir. Ret. USNR. Recipient Inst. Internal Auditors award, Acctg. Academic Excellence award, Towson U. Mem.: Am. Soc. Assn. Executives., Am. Inst. Cert. Pub. Accountants, Greater Wash. Soc. Assn. Execs., Inst. Mgmt. Accountants Assn., Md. Assn. Cert. Pub. Accountants, Alpha Sigma Lambda. Office: Am Urol Assn 1000 Corporate Blvd Linthicum Heights MD 21090 Office Phone: 410-689-3700. Office Fax: 410-689-3800. *

SHEPPE, JOSEPH ANDREW, surgeon; b. Huntington, W.Va., Sept. 24, 1953; m. Kathy Chapman; children: Sheree Nicole, Natalee Marie, Brittany Lee. BS summa cum laude in Chemistry and Zoology, Marshall U., 1975; MD, W.Va. U., 1979. Diplomate Am. Bd. Surgery, Am. Bd. Colon and Rectal Surgery. Intern in gen. surgery Charleston (W.Va.) Area Med. Ctr., 1979-84; fellow in colon and rectal surgery William Beaumont Army Med. Ctr., Royal Oak, Mich., 1984-85; pvt. practice Columbia, SC, 1985—. Physician Bapt. Med. Ctr., Columbia, Providence Hosp., Columbia, Richland Meml. Hosp., Columbia, Lexington Med. Ctr., West Columbia, S.C.; clin. instr. in gen./colorectal surgery U. S.C. Med. Sch. Fellow ACS, Am. Soc. Colon and Rectal Surgery; mem. S.C. Med. Soc., Columbia Med. Soc. Home: 204 Leaning Tree Rd Columbia SC 29223-3009 Office: 1333 Taylor St Ste 4-a Columbia SC 29201-2949 Office Phone: 803-779-5600.

SHERERTZ, ROBERT J., epidemiologist, educator; b. Greensboro, NC, July 16, 1950; MD, U. Va., 1976. Hosp. epidemiologist Wake Forest U. Sch. Medicine, 1982—2011, prof., medicine, 1988—2011. Fellow: Infectious Diseases Soc. America. Office: Wake Forest University Sch Medicine Winston Salem NC 27157-1042 Business E-Mail: sherertz@wfubmc.edu.

SHERICK, DANIEL G., plastic surgeon, educator; b. Ann Arbor; married; 2 children. MD, Mich. State U., 1991. Diplomate Am. Bd. Plastic Surgery. Resident in gen. surgery Univ. of Mich. Med. Ctr., rsch. fellow in plastic surgery; resident in plastic surgery Dartmouth-Hitchcock Med. Ctr., NH; tchg. staff Univ. of Mich. Med. Ctr.; vol. Interplast; staff Chelsea Cmty. Hosp., St. Joseph Mercy Ann Arbor Hosp., St. Joseph Mercy Livingston Hosp., St. Joseph Mercy Saline Hosp.; plastic surgeon St. Joseph Mercy Health System, Ctr. for Plastic and Reconstructive Surgery, Mich. Mem.: Am. Soc. of Aesthetic Plastic Surgeons. Office: Center for Plastic and Reconstructive Surgery PO Box 994 5333 McAuley Dr Suites 5001 and 5008 Ann Arbor MI 48106 Office Phone: 734-712-2323. Office Fax: 734-712-2312.

SHERIDAN, BRETT C., thoracic surgeon, educator; b. Aug. 18, 1965; BS, Stanford U., 1988; MD, Baylor Coll. Medicine, 1992. Assoc. prof. UNC, 2002—. Fellow: ACS; mem.: Soc. Thoracic Surgeons. Office: UNC CB 7065 3037 Burnett Womack Bldg Chapel Hill NC 27599 Office Fax: 919-966-3475. Business E-Mail: sheridan@med.unc.edu.

SHERIF, CAMILLO, neurosurgeon, researcher; b. Vienna, Apr. 9, 1977; s. Kamel Sherif. MD, Med. U. Vienna, 2003. Resident neurosurgery Med. U. Vienna, 2003—07, sr. rsch. fellow, dept. neurosurgery, 2005—10, head, cerebrovascular rsch. group, Dept. Biomed. Rsch., 2011—; sr. rsch. fellow U. Berne, Cerebrovascular Rsch. Group, Switzerland, 2007—10; sr. resident neurosurgery Cantonal Hosp. Aarau, Switzerland, 2007—, fellow, 2009—10, Neurosurgery Hosp. Rudolfstiftung, Vienna, 2010—. Contbr. articles to profl. jours. Recipient Sci. award, Med. U. Vienna, 2005, Austria Soc. Neurosurgery, 2006. Fellow: Swiss Soc. Neurosurgery, Austrian Soc. Neurosurgery. Achievements include research in introduction of a new method for the evaluation of embolized cerebral aneurysms. Office: Rudolfstiftung Juchgasse Vienna A1030 Austria Business E-Mail: camillo.sherif@meduniwien.ac.at.

SHERIF, KATHERINE, internist, educator; MD, Pa. Med. Coll. Diplomate Am. Bd. Internal Medicine. Intern internal medicine Med. Coll. of. Pa., 1992, resident internal medicine, 1993—94, chief resident internal medicine, 1995; co-dir. Ctr. for Polycystic Ovary Syndrome Univ. of Chgo., 2000; hosp. affiliation includes Hahnemann Univ. Hosp.; chief and clin. dir. Medicine Ctr. for Women's Health Drexel. Univ.; assoc. prof. internal medicine dept. Coll. Medicine Drexel Univ. Author: (publs.) Screening Mammography for Women 40-49 Years of Age: A Clinical Guideline, 2007, Guidelines for Cardiovascular Disease Prevention in Women, 2007, 2008, and several others. Recipient Agent of Change award, Women's Way 25th Anniversary Year; named one of the Top Doctor, Phila. Mag., 2011. Office: Hahnemann University Hospital Broad and Vine Philadelphia PA 19102 Office Phone: 215-762-7000. Office Fax: 215-762-8109.

SHERMAK, MICHELE, plastic surgeon; b. Philippines, June 25, 1966; MD, Johns Hopkins U., 1992. Plastic surgeon Plastic Surgery Ctr. Md., Johns Hopkins Sch. Medicine, 2010. Office: 1304 Bellona Ave Lutherville MD 21093 Personal E-mail: shermakmd@gmail.com.

SHERMAN, IRWIN WILLIAM, biological sciences educator, academic administrator; b. NYC, Feb. 12, 1933; s. Morris and Anna (Ezaak) S.; m. Vilia Gay Turner, Aug. 25, 1966; children: Jonathan Turner, Alexa Joy. BS, CCNY, 1954; MS, Northwestern U., Evanston, Ill., 1959, PhD, 1960. Asst. prof. U. Calif., Riverside, 1962-67, assoc. prof., 1967-70, prof. biology, 1970—2005, chmn. biology dept., 1974-79, dean Coll. Natural and Agrl. Scis., dir. agrl. expt. sta., 1981-88, exec. vice chancellor, 1993-94, emeritus prof., 2006—; vis. scientist Scripps Rsch. Inst., 2006—. Instr. marine biol. lab., Woods Hole, Mass., 1963-68; mem. study sect. tropical medicine NIH, 1970-73; cons. Agy. Internat. Devel., 1978-90; mem. ad hoc study group U.S. Army, 1975-78. Author: The Invertebrates: Function and Form, 1976, Biology: A Human Approach, 1989, Malaria: Parasite Biology, Pathogenesis, Protection, 1998, Molecular Approaches to Malaria, 2005, The Power of Plagues, 2006, Twelve Diseases That Changed Our World, 2007, Reflections on a Century of Malaria Biochemistry, 2008, The Elusive Malaria Vaccine, 2009, Magic Bullets to Conquer Malaria: From Quinine to Qinghaosu, 2011. Steering com. World Health Orgn., 1978-87. With U.S. Army, 1954-56. USPHS fellow Rockefeller Inst., 1960-62, Guggenheim fellow, 1967, NIH/Nat. Inst. Med. Rsch. fellow 1973-74, Walter and Eliza Hall Inst. for Med. Rsch. fellow, 1986; Wellcome Trust lectr. Brit. Soc. Parasitology, 1987, Scripps Rsch. Inst. fellow 1991, 2003-. Fellow AAAS, Am. Acad. Microbiology; mem. Am. Soc. Tropical Medicine and Hygiene. Democrat. Jewish. Avocations: painting, reading. Office: Scripps Rsch Inst Dept Genetics SP-273 10550 N Torrey Pines La Jolla CA 92037 Business E-Mail: isherman@scripps.edu.

SHERMAN, JEFFREY SCOTT, hospital administrator, lawyer; b. Bklyn., Oct. 26, 1955; s. Martin and Beatrice (Matrick) S.; m. Susan Ellen Ganz, Aug. 13, 1981; children: Elisabeth Faye, Andrew Harris. BA cum laude, SUNY, Albany, 1976; JD magna cum laude, Bklyn. Law Sch., 1980. Bar: NY 1980. Assoc. Proskauer, Rose et al, NYC, 1980-83, Shereff, Friedman, Hoffman & Goodman, NYC, 1983-87, ptnr., 1988—90; v.p., treas. Tenet Healthcare, 1990; joined Wyeth, 1990, v.p., assoc. gen. counsel, 2001—03; v.p., gen. counsel Becton, Dickinson & Co., Franklin Lakes, NJ, 2004—06, sr. v.p., gen. counsel, 2006—; joined LifePoint Hosps., 2009, exec. v.p., CFO. Mem. ABA, Assn. of the Bar of the City of NY (young lawyers com. 1983-86). Office: LifePoint Hospitals Inc 103 Powell Ct Ste 200 Brentwood TN 37027 Office Phone: 614-372-8500. E-mail: jeffrey.sherman@lpnt.net. *

SHERMAN, JOHN ERIC, plastic surgeon; b. NYC, 1951; m. Emily Sherman; 2 children. MD, NY Med. Coll., 1975. Internship & residency Montefiore Hospital Med. Ctr., NYC, 1975—78; chief resident plastic surgery Cornell Med. Ctr., 1978—80; fellowship reconstructive plastic surgery Memorial Sloan Kettering Cancer Ctr., 1979—80; plastic surgeon priv. practice, NYC, 1980—; attending plastic surgeon NY Hospital, Lenox Hill Hospital; clinical assist. prof. surgery Cornell U. Med. Coll. Author: Surgery of Facial Bone Fractures, 1987. Fellow: Am. Coll. of Surgeons (pres. Manhattan Chapter 2007—09, treas. NY State 2009—11); mem.: Am. Soc. of Maxillofacial Surgeons, Am. Soc. of Aesthetic Plastic Surgeons, Am. Soc. of Plastic & Reconstructive Surgeons. Avocation: golf. Office: 1016 5th Ave New York NY 10028

SHERMAN, JOHN FOORD, biomedical consultant; b. Oneonta, NY, Sept. 4, 1919; s. Henry C. and Ruth (Foord) Sherman; m. Betsy Deane Murray, Feb. 8, 1944 (dec.); children: Betsy Deane, Mary Ann. BS, Union U., 1949, DSc, 1970; PhD, Yale U., 1953. With NIH, 1953—74; assoc. dir. extramural programs Nat. Inst. Neurol. Diseases and Blindness, 1961—62, Nat. Inst. Arthritis and Metabolic Disease, 1962—63; assoc. dir. for extramural programs Office Dir. NIH, 1964—68, dep. dir., 1968—74; v.p. Assn. Am. Med. Colls., Washington, 1974—91, exec. v.p., 1987—91, spl. cons., 1991—94. Bd. advisors Am. Bd. Internal Medicine, 1991—98; sr. advisor Rsch!Am., 1994—. Asst. surgeon gen. USPHS, 1964—68; spl. rsch. chemotherapy and neuropharmacology; panel on data and studies NRC, 1976—87; biomed. libr. rev. com. NIH, 1981—98; bd. dirs. Spinal Cord Injury Edn. and Tng. Found., 1986—92, Musculoskeletal Transplant Found., 1987—2003. With US Army, 1941—46. Decorated Bronze Star; recipient Meritorious Svc. award, USPHS, 1965, Disting. Svc. award, HEW, 1971, Sec.'s Spl. Citation award, 1973, Nat. Civil Svc. League award, 1973, Disting. Alumnus award, Union U.-Pharmacy Coll. Coun., 1974, Lifetime Achievement award, Nat. Assn. for Biomed. Rsch., 1990, Spl. Recognition award, Assn. Am. Med. Colls., 1996. Fellow: AAAS; mem.: Inst. Medicine NAS, Cosmos Club, Sigma Xi. Congregationalist. Personal E-mail: johnfsherman@msn.com.

SHERMAN, MICHAEL SCOTT, anesthesiologist, insurance company executive; b. Bklyn., June 20, 1961; m. Heather Sherman, Dec. 28, 1996. BA in Anthropology and Natural Sciences, U. Pa., 1982, MS in Biomedical Anthropology; MD, Yale U., 1986; MBA, Harvard U., 1997. Diplomate Am. Bd. Anesthelogist, Am. Bd. Cardiac Anesthesiology, Am. Bd. Med. Mgmt. Intern St. Luke's/Roosevelt Hosp. Ctr., NYC, 1986-87, resident in gen. surgery, 1987-88; resident in anesthesiology SUNY Health Sci. Ctr., Bklyn., 1990-93; emergency medicine attending physician Comty. Hosp. Bklyn., 1988-90; anesthesiologist Good Samaritan Regional Med. Ctr., Phoenix, 1993-95; dir. corp. devel., managed care and integrated programs Total Renal Care, 1997-99; mng. dir. physician network devel. Total Nephrology Care Network, 1997-99; v.p. provider bus. devel. and product mgmt. HealthAllies.com., Glendale, Calif., 1999—2001; v.p. med. and clin. affairs Immusol, Inc., San Diego, 2001—05; dir. bus. develop. Total Renal Care (now known as Da Vita); v.p., gen. mgr. Thomson Medstat (now Thomson Reuters); various roles UnitedHealth Group, v.p. network and consumer solutions, Ingenix, chief bus. develop. officer, Medicare Part D bus.; corp. med. dir., physician strategies Humana, Minn.; sr. v.p., chief med. officer Harvard Pilgrim Health Care, 2011—. Spkr. in field; guest lectr. Harvard Bus. Sch. Mem. editl. bd. Biotechnology Healthcare. Bd. dirs. Hennepin County History Mus. Fellow Am. Coll. Physician Execs.; mem. AMA, Am. Soc. Anesthesiologists, Am. Coll. Healthcare Execs., Am. Coll. Legal Medicine, Calif. Soc. Anesthesiologists, Calif. Med. Assn. Office: Harvard Pilgrim Health Care 93 Worcester St Wellesley Hills MA 02481 E-mail: msherman@immusol.com. *

SHERMAN, RICHARD ARTHUR, nephrologist, educator; b. NYC, Jan. 3, 1950; s. Stanley L. and Gloria L. (Wisotsky) S.; children: Eric, Gregory, Stefano. BS, CCNY, 1971; MD, Yeshiva U., 1975. Intern, then resident Met. Hosp. Ctr., 1975-77; fellow in nephrology Bronx Mcpl. Hosp. Ctr., 1977-79; asst. prof. medicine Robert Wood Johnson Med. Sch., New Bruswick, 1979-85, assoc. prof., 1985—93, prof., 1993—. Med. adv. bd. Kidney and Urology Found. Am., 2002—; creator, organizer confs. hemodialysis therapy, N.Y., San Diego, 1984, 85. Editor-in-chief jour. Seminars in Dialysis, 1987—. Mem. coun. on dialysis Nat. Kidney Found., 1996—. Mem. Internat. Soc. Nephrology, Am. Soc. Nephrology, Nephrology Soc. N.J. (pres. 1984-85). Office: Robert Wood Johnson Med Sch Dept Medicine POB 19 1 Robert Wood Johnson Pl New Brunswick NJ 08903-0019 Business E-Mail: sherman@umdnj.edu.

SHERMAN, SPENCER E., ophthalmologist; AB cum laude, Princeton U., Sigma XI, 1958; MD, Columbia Coll. Physicians & Surgeons, 1962. Diplomate Am. Bd. Ophthalmology. Intern Mt. Sinai Hosp., NYC, 1962-63, attending ophthalmologist, 1968—, resident in ophthalmology, 1965-68; asst. clin. prof. ophthalmology NYU Sch. Medicine, NYC; staff Mt. Sinai Hosp., 1998—. Attending ophthalmologist Manhattan Eye & Ear Hosp., NYC, 1968—, Lenox Hill Hosp., NYC, 1968—, NY Eye and Ear Infirmary, Mt. Sinai Hosp., 1970—. Capt. USAMC, 1963-65. Named one of Best Drs. in NY, Castle Connolly Group, 1980—, Top Drs. in US, Ctr. for Study of Svc. Fellow ACS, Internat. Coll. of Surgeons, Am. Acad. of Ophthalmology (Honor and Svc. award); mem. AMA, Nat. Soc. Prevention Blindness, Found. Children with Learning Disabilities, Am. Soc. Refractive Surgeons, NY Acad. Medicine, NY Ophthalmologic Soc., Internat. Soc. Refractive Surgery, Am. Soc. Cataract & Refractive Surgery, Harmonie Club, Sunningdale Country Club, Maidstone Gun Club, Peconic Sportsman Club, East Hampton Tennis Club. Office: 166 E 63rd St New York NY 10021-7636 Office Phone: 212-753-8300. Fax: (212) 752-4285. E-mail: sesmdpc@aol.com.

SHERMAN, VADIM, surgeon, director; b. Bobruisk, Belarus, Jan. 29, 1976; s. Jack and Rita Sherman; m. Erica Hundorfean Sherman. MD, U. Western Ont., Can., 2000; MS, McGill U., Montreal, Quebec, Can., 2007. Cert. Am. Bd. Surgery, 2006, in Healthcare Mgmt. Rice U., 2008. Dir., comprehensive bariatric surgery ctr. Baylor Coll. Medicine, Houston, 2006—10, program dir., minimally invasive surgery fellowship, 2006—10, dir. meth. bariatric and metabolic surgery, assoc. program dir. meth. gen. surgery resident, 2011—. Contbr. chapters to books. Fellow: RCS (Can.); mem.: ACS, Soc. Am. Gastrointestinal and Endoscopic Surgeons, Can. Assn. Gen. Surgeons, Am. Soc. Metabolic and Bariatric Surgery (rsch. com. 2006). Office: Methodist Hosp SM 1661 6550 Fannin St Houston TX 77030 Office Phone: 713-441-5155. Office Fax: 713-790-6470. Business E-Mail: vsherman@tmhs.org.

SHERN, DAVID L., mental health services professional, former dean; b. Pueblo, Colo., Feb. 23, 1951; BA in Psychology, U. Colo., 1973, MA in Social Psychology, 1977, PhD in Social Psychology,

1980; cert. in advanced epidemiologic methods, NIMH Staff Coll., 1980. Asst. dir. research and evaluation sect. Denver Dept. Health and Hosps. Mental Health Programs, 1981-82; research assoc. evaluation services sect. Colo. div. Mental Health, Denver, 1982-84, mgr. sponsored research program, 1984-88; project dir., investigator estimating residential services for chronically mentally ill Colo. divsn. Mental Health, Denver, 1983-87; investigator validation models for estimating mental health need U. Denver, 1983-88; dir. bur. evaluation and svcs. rsch. NY Office of Mental Health, Albany, 1988-95; dean, prof. Louis de la Parte Fla. Mental Health Inst., U. South Fla., Tampa, 1995—2006; pres., CEO Mental Health America, Alexandria, Va., 2006—. Cons. several health facilities, Denver, 1976—88; chmn. Fla. Commn. Mental Health and Substance Abuse, 1999—2000; prin. investigator Treatment Outcome Study, 1988; prin. investigator rsch. grants NIMH Substance Abuse and Mental Health Svcs. Adminstrn., 1988—2000; dir. NIMH Ctr. for Sudy Issues in Pub. Mental Health, 1993—95; mem. Govs. Suicide Prevention Task Force, 2003—06. Contbr. articles to profl. jours. Bd. dirs. Travelers Aid of Denver, 1981-83, Karis Cmty., 1986-88, pres. 1988; founding mem. Albany County Land Conservancy, 1992-95, pres., 1992-95; treas. USF Charter Sch., 1998-2006;active Crisis Ctr. of Tampa Bay, 2004-06. Mem. APA, APHA (chair mental health sect. 1992-93, governing coun. 1995-97), Orgn. for Program Evaluation in Colo. (pres. 1982-83, assoc. editor bull.), Am. Evaluation Assn. Independent. Avocations: hiking, gardening, travel. Office: Mental Health America 2000 N Beauregard St 6th Fl Alexandria VA 22311 Office Phone: 703-838-7500. *

SHERR, VIRGINIA TRUITT, psychiatrist; b. Washington, Mar. 19, 1931; d. Reginald Van Trump and Mary Harrington Truitt; m. Paul C. Sherr, Apr. 28, 1957; children: Donald, Paul B., Suzanne, Gregory. BS, U. Md., 1952; MD, U. Md., Sch. Medicine, Balt., 1956. Diplomate Am. Bd. Psychiatry and Neurology. Intern Allentown Gen. Hosp.; adminstrv. officer Norristown (Pa.) State Hosp.; pvt. practice, 1976—. Mem. Montgomery County Task Force Aged; med. writer; spkr. in field. Contbr. articles to profl. jours. Mem. med. bd. George Sch.; bd. dirs. Sr. Adult Activity Ctr. Montgomery County. Recipient Ann. Clin. Rsch. award Montgomery County Med. Soc., 1975. Fellow: APA (Disting. life); mem.: Am. Chronic Pain Assn., Am. Pain Soc., Internat. Lyme and Associated Diseases Soc. (founding mem., 1st membership chair), Cultural Environ. Movement (founding bd. dirs.), Internat. Physicians Prevention Nuclear War, Physicians Social Responsibility (bd. dirs.). Office: 47 Crescent Dr Holland PA 18966-2105 Office Phone: 215-322-6567. Personal E-mail: vts1234@verizon.net.

SHERROD, LLOYD BRUCE, retired nutritionist; b. Goodland, Kans., Mar. 5, 1931; s. Charles and Helen S.; m. Judith Harms Sherrod, Dec. 21, 1963; children: Donna L, Barbara E. BS, S.D. State U., Brookings, 1958; MS, U. Ark., Fayetteville, 1960; PhD, Okla. State U., Stillwater, 1964. Rsch. assoc. Okla. State U., Stillwater, 1963, asst. prof. U. Hawaii, Hilo, 1964-67; from assoc. prof to prof. Tex. Tech. U. Ctr., Pantex, 1967-79; nutrition-chemistry instr. Frank Phillips Coll., Borger, Tex., 1979-88; part-time nutrition instr. Amarillo (Tex.) Coll., 1989-95; ret., 1995. Rschr. in field. Contbr. articles to sci. jours. Served with U.S. Army, 1951-53. Mem. AAAS, Am. Soc. Animal Science, Am. Dairy Science Assn., Am. Soc. Agronomy, Am. Inst. Biol. Scis., Tex. Jr. Coll. Tchrs. Assn., Am. Men and Women of Sci., Plains Nutrition Coun., Sigma Xi., Phi Kappa Phi, Gamma Sigma Delta. Home and Office: PO Box 1017 Panhandle TX 79068-1017

SHERRY, BETTYLOU, epidemiologist; b. St. Johnsbury, Vt., June 13, 1941; BS, U. Vt., 1963; PhD, U. Wash., 1986. Asst. prof. U. Wash., 1986—93; epidemiologist Ctr. Disease Control and Prevention, 1993—2007, lead epidemiologist, 2008—. Recipient Performance awards, Ctrs. Disease Control and Prevention. Fellow: Obesity Soc.; mem.: Am. Dietetic Assn. Avocations: guitar, gardening, hiking. Office: 4770 Buford Hwy NE MS K-26 Atlanta GA 30341 Business E-Mail: bsherry@cdc.gov.

SHERRY, MICHAEL MCCLAIN, internist; MD, U. Pitts., 1980. Diplomate Am. Bd. Internal Medicine, Am. Bd. Internal Medicine-med. oncology, Am. Bd. Internal Medicine-hematology, lic. Pa., 1981. Intern Mercy Hosp., 1981, resident, 1983, Vanderbilt Univ. Med. Ctr., 1985; fellow Univ. Physicians Med. Ctr. Montefiore Hosp., 1986; hosp. affiliation includes Heritage Valley Sewickley, Pa. Office: Heritage Valley Sewickley 720 Blackburn Rd Sewickley PA 15143 Office Phone: 412-329-2500.

SHERWOOD, ARTHUR MONTGOMERY, research scientist; b. Johnson City, Tenn., Dec. 28, 1942; BEE, Ga. Inst. Tech., 1966; PhD, Duke U., 1970. Sci. & tech. advisor Nat. Inst. Disability & Rehab. Rsch., 2002—. Exec. dir. Internat. Soc. Restorative Neurology, 2009. Mem.: IEEE. Office: 550 12th St SW PCP 5157 Washington DC 20202

SHESHEER KUMAR, MUNPALLY, biotechnologist, director; b. Nizamabad, Andhra Pradesh, India, June 11, 1974; PhD, Osmania U., 2006. Software designer Premier Biosoft India Pvt. Ltd., 1998—99; rsch. scientist Shantha Biotechnics Ltd., 1999—2001; scientist Sudershan Biotech Ltd., 2001—03; dir. Anoop Labs. Pvt. Ltd., 2006—08; mng. dir. RAS Lifescis. Pvt. Ltd., 2008—. Recipient DST Lockheed Martin Innovation Growth award, Dept. Sci. and Tech., Govt. India. Office: RAS Lifescis Pvt Ltd 13 4-7-18/13/2. Raghavendra Nagar Nachar Hyderabad Andhra Pradesh 500076 India Personal E-mail: shesheer@gmail.com.

SHETE, ABHIJEET RAJENDRA, dentist, educator; b. India, Mar. 29, 1982; B in Dental Surgery, Vasantdada Patil Dental Coll., Sangli, 2004; M in Dental Surgery, Govt. Dental Coll., Calicut, 2009. Lectr. Tatyasaheb Kore Dental Coll. And Rsch. Ctr., New Pargaon, 2010—. Mem.: Indian Soc. Periodontology. Avocations: travel, sports. Home: 203 Govinda Complex 6th Ln Rajaram Kolhapur Maharashtra 416008 India Personal E-mail: drabhijeetshete@rediffmail.com.

SHETH, JAYESH JAYANTILAL, biochemist, researcher; b. Modasa, Gujarat, India, Feb. 26, 1957; s. Jayantilal Nathalal and Rmilaben Chunilal S.; m. Frenny Jayesh Sheth, Feb. 3, 1959; children: Riddhi, Harsh. BS, J&J Sci. Coll., Nadiad, India, 1976; MS, Sir Hurkisondas Nurrotumdas Ho, Bombay, 1979, PhD, 1983. Jr. rsch. assoc. M.P. Shah Cancer Hosp., Ahmedabad, India, 1983-85; in charge, Hosp. Sheth V.S. Hosp., Ahmedabad, 1989—; assoc. prof. endocrinology N.H.L. Mcpl. Med. Coll., Ahmedabad, 1989; ptnr. Shah Pathoology Lab and Endocrine Unit, Ahmedabad, 1985—; dir. Inst. Human Genetics & Found. Rsch. Genetics & Endocrinology, Ahmedabad, 1994—; fellow Indian Coll. of Mother and Child Health, 2002. Vis. scientist Jiwaji U., Gwalior, 1995—; trustee Sheth Rasiklal Shah Sarvjanik Hosp., Modasa, 1996—, Diagnostic Sys. Lab. Inc., Houston, 1997—; sci. mem. Jivraj Mehta & Bakesi Med. Rsch. Hosp., Ahmedabad, 1998—; mem. adv., sec. Hosp. Growth Colloquia Pharmacia Upjohn, Bombay, 1999—. Contbr. articles to profl. jours.; inventor on thyroid & lysosomal storage disorders. Exec. mem. Maharaja Agrasen Kendriy Vidyalaya, Ahmedabad, 1997—; mng. trustee Sheth Charitable Trust, Ahmedabad, 1991—; founder, Inst. Human Genetics, Ahmedabad. Jr. rsch. fellow Indian Coun. Med. Rsch., 1990—, summer fellow med. rsch. Erasmus U., 1991, fellow, WHO 11 th PG course in Reproductive Medicine and Reproductive Biology, Geneva, 2002, travel fellowship Internat. Soc. New Born Screening, 2007. Fellow UICC, mem. Endocrine Soc. India, Endocrine Soc. (we. zone), Endocrine Soc. (U.S.A.), Indian Soc. Fetal Medicine (founder). Avocations: spiritual discourses, reading, gardening, badminton, yoga. Office: FRIGE House Inst Human Genetics 15 Kapidhwaj Jodhpur Vill Rd Satellite Ahmedabad 380015 India Home: 42 Ashwraj Bunglows Prahladnagar Gardens Satellite Amedabad 380051 India Office Phone: 91-79-26921414. Personal E-mail: jshethad1@sancharnet.in.

SHETH, RAJ D., neurologist; b. India, Sept. 16, 1958; MD, U. Malta, 1982. Prof. neurology U. Wis., 1997—2008, Mayo Clinic Coll. Medicine, 2008; chief neurology Nemours Children's Clinic, Jacksonville, Fla., 2008; prof. pediat. U. Fla., 2011. Mem. editl. bd. Epilepsia, 2011; dir. Pediat. Epilepsy Ctr. at Wolfson Children's Hosp., Jacksonville. Fellow: Am. Acad. Pediat., Am. Acad. Neurology. Office: 807 Children's Way Jacksonville FL 32207 Business E-Mail: rsheth@nemours.org.

SHETTER, ANDREW GEORGE, neurosurgeon; b. Florence, SC, July 3, 1944; s. George A. and Dorothy L. Shetter; children: Sarah, Drew; m. Mary Sheltor. BA, Pomona Coll., 1966; MD, U. Calif., San Francisco, 1970. Diplomate Am. Bd. Neurol. Surgery. Surg. intern Med. Coll. Va., Richmond, 1970—71; resident neurosurgery Barrow Neurol. Inst., Phoenix, 1971—76, neurosurgeon. Office: Barrow Neurosurgical Associates 2910 N 3rd Ave Phoenix AZ 85013-4434 Office Phone: 607-406-3469. *

SHETTY, ASODE ANANTHRAM, orthopedic surgeon, consultant; s. Barkur Vittal and Kamala Shetty; m. Saritha Ananthram Alva, May 20, 1983; 1 child, Neha Ananthram. MBBS, Karnatak Med. Coll., India, 1978; MCh in Orthops., U. Liverpool, Eng., 1996; diploma in orthops., Kings' Coll., London, 2003; MSc in Orthops., U. Brighton, Eng., 2005. Specialist registrar Guys' Kings' & St Thomas ' Sch. Medicine, London, 2000—04; sr. fellow Kings' Coll Hosp., London, 2004—05; cons. orthops. and trauma Medway Maritime Hosp., Gillingham, England, 2005—. Cons. surgeon King's Coll. Hosp., London; sr. lectr. King's Coll., London. Author: Who was Who in Orthopaedics, Self Assessment in Orthopaedics & Trauma; contbr. articles to profl. jours. Fellow: Brit. Orthop. Assn., Royal Coll. Surgeons. Achievements include development of Patello femoral joint; research in autologous chondrocyte implantation, HAC coated implants. Home: 6 Barncroft Dr Hempstead Gillingham ME7 3TJ England Office: Medway Maritime Hosp Windmill Rd Gillingham ME7 5NY England E-mail: mraashetty@yahoo.co.uk.

SHETTY, DEVI PRASAD, surgeon; b. May 8, 1953; MBBS, CM, Kasturba Med. Coll. Gov. Med. Coun. of India; founder Narayana Hrudayalaya, Bangalore, India, chmn. Prof. Rajiv Gandhi Univ. of Med. Sciences, Bangalore, India. Recipient Padma Shree Award, Govt. of India, Social Entrepreneurship Award, World Econ. Forum, Ernst & Young Entrepreneur of the Yr. Award. Fellow: Royal Coll. of Surgeons. Achievements include being the first in India to perform heart surgery on newborns; pioneer in elevating the technology landscape of cardiovascular surgery in India; first to use a microchip camera to close holes in the heart. Office: Narayana Hrudayalaya Pvt Ltd No 258/A Bangalore 560 099 India Office Phone: 918027835000. Office Fax: 918027832648. *

SHETTY, KAUP RAJMOHAN, endocrinologist, educator; came to U.S., 1966; s. Muddanna and Girija M. Shetty; m. Vasanthi R. Shetty; children: Sandeep, Suparna. MB BChir, Mysore Med. Coll., Karnataka, 1965. Diplomate Am. Bd. Internal Medicine, cert. in internal medicine, endocrinology and metabolism, geriatric medicine. Resident in internal medicine VA Med. Ctr., Chgo. and Milw., 1967-70; fellow in endocrinology and metabolism Med. Coll. Wis. and Affiliated Hosps., Milw., 1970-72, attending physician in endocrinology and metabolism, 1972—; attending physician in geriatrics and gerontology VA Med. Coll., Milw., 1991—; assoc. prof. medicine Med. Coll. Wis., Milw., 1991-95, prof. medicine, 1995-2000, prof. medicine emeritus, 2000—. Contbr. articles to profl. jours., chapters to books. Fellow ACP, Royal Coll. Physicians Can., Am. Coll. Endocrinology; mem. Endocrine Soc., N.Y. Acad. Scis. Achievements include research in hormones and aging, post-polio syndrome, metabolic accompaniments of inactivity. Avocation: tennis. Office: VA Med Ctr 5000 W National Ave Milwaukee WI 53295-0001

SHETTY, MULKI RADHAKRISHNA, retired oncologist; b. Hiriadka, Karnataka, India, July 10, 1940; arrived in U.S., 1974; s. Sunderram and Kusumavati Shetty. MBBS, Stanley Med. Coll., Madras, 1964; DTM, U. Liverpool, Eng., 1968; LMCC, Med. Coun., Can., 1975. House surgeon and physician Bombay Hosp., 1965-66; sr. house officer Manor Pk. Hosp., Bristol, Eng., 1966-67, Torbay Hosp., 1967-68, St. Lukes Hosp., Huddersfield, 1969-70; sr. resident Gen. Hosp. Meml. U., New Foundland, 1971-72; intern Ottawa Gen. Hosp., 1972-73; fellow in chemotherapy Ont. Cancer Found., Ottawa, Can., 1973-74; fellow in clin. oncology U. Fla., Gainesville, 1974-75; attending oncologist N.W. Community Hosp., Arlington Heights, Ill., 1975-2000; ret., 2000. Cons. N.W. Cmty. Hosp., Arlington Heights, Ill., 1975—2000. Author: (book) Lung Cancer, 1980, Recent Advances in Chemotherapy, 1985, Wildlife Adventures, 1997, Chicago, 1997, Quotes and Notes, 2003, The Itinerant Indian, 2005, Encyclopaedia of Quotable Couplets, 2005, English Couplets Vol. II, 2007, Vol. III, 2007, Quotable English Couplets, 2007; Rhymning English Couplets, 2009; coined new word calcifectomy; contbr. chapters to books, articles to profl. jours. Recipient Cert. for Oustanding Svc., Am. Cancer Soc., 1982. Hindu. Achievements include Reached the North Pole by icebreaker YAMAL, Aug. 5, 2001; discovery of biological equation memory=Emotion x Rhyme x Rythm.

SHETTY, SHISHIR RAM, dental educator; b. Calicut, Kerala, Jan. 22, 1981; BDS, SDM Coll. Dental Scis., 2004; MDS, Yenepoya Dental Coll., 2008; PhD student in Oral Precancer and Micronutrients, 2011—. Asst. prof. AB Shetty Meml. Inst. Dental Scis., 2008—. Contbr. articles to profl. jours. publs. Recipient Prof Nagesh Gold medal, Rajiv Gandhi U. Health Scis. Mem.: Indian Red Cross Soc., Indian Dental Assn., Indian Assn. Oral Medicine & Radiology. Avocation: stamp collecting/philately. Office: Nitte University Deralakatte Mangalore Karnataka 575018 India E-mail: divyahegde31@yahoo.co.in.

SHETTY, TEENA, neurologist, educator; b. Bangalore, India, 1974; 3 children. Attended, Oxford U., England, 1993—94; M in Philosophy, U. Cambridge, England, 1999; MD with honors, Brown U., 2000. Diplomate American Bd. Psychiatry & Neurology, 2005, American Bd. Electrodiagnostic Medicine, 2007, neuromuscular medicine American Bd. Psychiatry & Neurology, 2008, cert. NY. Vis. rsch. fellow Inst. of Neurology, London, 1996; resident Cornell-NY Presbyn. Hosp., 2001—04; fellow neuromuscular diseases, neurophysiology and electromyography Harvard-Brigham and Women's Hosp., 2004—05; fellow electromyography and intraoperative monitoring neurophysiology Hosp. for Spl. Surgery, 2005—06, editl. bd. mem. jour., asst. attending neurologist; asst prof. neurology Weill Cornell Med. Coll. Cons. minor traumatic brain injury and neurologist NY Giants Football Team; columnist Providence Jour.-Bull., 1994—99. Recipient Leah J. Dickstein award, 2000; named one of The 40 Under 40, Crain's NY Bus., 2011; scholar Sigma Xi Honor Soc. Fulbright Scholarship, 1998—99, Fulbright Scholar, 1998—99. Fellow: American Assn. Neuromuscular & Electrodiagnostic Medicine; mem.: American Acad. of Neurology. Achievements include research in Peripheral nerve injuries following total hip and knee replacement surgeries; Peripheral neurological complications from anesthesia; Serial diffusion tensor imaging in football players after concussions; Post-op neuropathies; Spine disorders. Office: Hospital for Special Surgery Belaire 5th Fl 525 E 71st St New York NY 10021 Office Phone: 212-774-2138. Office Fax: 212-249-9185. *

SHEU, SHENG HSIUNG, physician, educator; b. Tainan, Taiwan, July 3, 1945; m. Su Hsin Chung. MD, Kaohsiung Med. U., Taiwan, 1970. Physician Kaohsiung Med. U. Hosp., Taiwan, 1970—; prof. Kaohsiung Med. U., Taiwan, 1991—; supt. Kaohsiung Med. U. Hosp., Taiwan, 2003—. Prof. Kaohsiung Med. U., 1991—. Office: Kaohsiung Med Univ Shih-Chuan 1st Rd Kaohsiung 80708 Taiwan Business E-Mail: sheush@kmu.edu.tw.

SHEWRY, SANDRA, telehealth company executive; BS, Univ. Calif., Santa Cruz; MS, MPH, Univ. Calif., Berkeley. Asst. sec. Calif. Health & Welfare Agency; exec. dir. Calif. Managed Risk Med. Ins. Bd.; dir. health Ctr. for Best Practices, Nat. Governors Assn.; dir. Calif. Dept. Health Svcs., Sacramento, 2004—07, Calif. Dept. Health Care Services, 2007—08; pres., CEO Calif. Ctr. Connected Health, 2008—. Mem. Commn. on High Performance Health Sys., Commonwealth Fund; bd. mem. Insure the Uninsured Project. Office: Calif Ctr Connected Health 1331 Garden Hwy Sacramento CA 95833-9755 Office Phone: 916-488-8607. Office Fax: 916-484-7643.

SHI, GUO-PING, medical educator; b. Zhejiang, China, Sept. 2, 1961; MSc, Beijing Agr. U., 1987; DSc, Harvard U., 1995. Assoc. prof. Harvard Med. Sch., 2009—. Office: NRB-7 77 Ave Louis Pasteur Boston MA 02115 Office Fax: 617-525-4380. Business E-Mail: gshi@rics.bwh.harvard.edu.

SHI, HONG-JIAN, physician; b. Nantong, Jiangsu, China, Aug. 22, 1970; MD, SE U., PhD, 2009. Physician Affiliated Wujin Hosp., Jiangsu U., 2010—. Mem.: RSNA. Office: 2 North Yongning Rd Changzhou Jiangsu 213002 China Business E-Mail: shihongjian@sina.com.

SHI, LEIYU, medical educator, educator; b. Shanghai, July 7, 1961; s. Yongchun Shi and Zhengku Guan; m. Lirong Shi, Jan. 29, 1991; children: Sylvia M., Jennifer T. BA, Shanghai Fgn. Lang. U., 1982; MPA, Seton Hall U., South Orange, NJ, 1986; MBA, U. Calif., Berkeley, 1990, D of Pub. Health, 1990. Health adminstr. Shanghai Pub. Health Dept., 1982-84; rsch. assoc. U. Calif., Berkeley, 1986-90; asst. prof. U. SC, Columbia, 1991-94, assoc. prof. dept. health adminstn., 1995-97, chair dept. health adminstrn., 1995-97; assoc. dir. Primary Care Policy Ctr., Balt., 1997—2006; assoc. prof. Johns Hopkins U., Balt., 2006—, prof., 2007—. Cons. US Dept Health and Human Svcs., Washington, 1991—, Grad. Coun. of Med. Edn., Washington, 1994, various health orgns., 1986—; adv. bd. Ryan White Title II Care Act Svcs., SC, 1994-98. Author: Delivering Health Care in America, 1998, Health Services Research Methods, 1997, Physician Recruitment and Retention, 1993; contbr. numerous articles to profl. jours. Grantee Managed Care and Cmty. Health Ctr., 1998—, Robert Wood Johnson Found., 1999—, Bur. of Primary Health Care, HRSA, 1996—, Ctrs. for Disease Control, 1995-99. Mem.: APHA, Assn. for Health Svcs. Rsch. Office: Johns Hopkins U 624 N Broadway Rm 409 Baltimore MD 21205-1900 Home: 3121 Tilden Dr Baltimore MD 21211 Office Phone: 410-614-6507. Business E-Mail: lshi@jhsph.edu.

SHI, SONGTAO, dentist, educator; DDS, Peking U. Sch. Stomatology, Beijing, 1983, MS in Pediatric Dentistry, 1986; PhD in Craniofacial Biology, U. Southern Calif., 1994. Asst. prof. dept. pediatric dentistry Beijing Med. U., 1986—89; rsch. assoc. Doheny Eye Inst. U. Southern Calif., 1989—94; fellow in Skeletal Biology UCSF, 1994—97; pvt. practice S&S Best Dental Ctr., 1998—99; fellow in craniofacial & skeletal diseases NIDCR-NIH, 1999—2001, clinical fellow supr. craniofacial & skeletal diseases, 2002—03, section chief craniofacial & skeletal diseases, 2003—06; asst. prof. U. Southern Calif. Ctr. for Craniofacial Molecular Biology, 2006—08, assoc. prof.,

2008—. Recipient Travel award, NIDCR-NIH, 2000. Office: University of Southern California School of Dentistry CSA 148 HSC 9062 Los Angeles CA 90033 Office Phone: 323-442-3038. Office Fax: 323-442-2981. E-mail: songtaos@usc.edu.

SHI, WEI, nephrologist; b. Henan, China, June 22, 1956; PhD, Sun Yat-sen Med. U., 1996. Attending physician Third Hosp. XinXiang Med. U., 1991—93; resident, internal dept. Zhumadian Ctrl. Hosp., Henan, China, 1983—88; dir. renal divsn. Guangdong Gen. Hosp., 1998, med. dir., 1999, chief physician, divsn. nephrology, Guangdong Acad. Med. Scis. China, 2002—. Master instr. Nanfang Med. U., 2006, phd supr., 06. Mem.: Guangdong Soc. Nephrology (v.p.), Guangdong Province Hosp. Assn. (v.p.), Standing Com. Mem. Chinese Soc. Blood Purification Adminstrn., Nephrology Br. Chinese MD Assn. (standing com. mem.), Chinese Soc. Nephrology (standing com. mem.). Office: 106 Zhongshan Rd 2 Guangzhou Guangdong 510080 China Office Fax: 86-20-83850849. Personal E-mail: weishi_gz@126.com.

SHIA, JINRU, physician; b. Hunan, China, June 19, 1962; MD, Hunan Med. Coll., 1983. Assoc. mem. Meml. Sloan-Kettering Cancer Ctr., 1998—. Office: 1275 York Ave New York NY 10065 Business E-Mail: shiaj@mskcc.org.

SHIBAHARA, TOMOYUKI, veterinarian, researcher; b. Kawanabe, Kagoshima, Japan, Oct. 25, 1969; s. Kouichi and Yasuko Shibahara; m. Naoko Tsurubayashi, Nov. 4, 1970; children: Runa, Souga, Eina. PhD in Veterinary Medicine, Hokkaido U., Sapporo, Japan, 2004. Cert. vet. Ministry of Agr., Forestry and Fisheries Japan. Rschr. dept. epidemiology Nat. Inst. Animal Health, Ibaraki, 1994—. Mem.: Japanese Soc. Vet. Sci. Achievements include research in pathological study of several infectious diseases in domestic animals. Avocations: kendo, tennis. Office: Nat Inst Animal Health 3-1-5 Kannondai Tsukuba 305-0856 Japan Business E-Mail: tshiba@affrc.go.jp.

SHIBAMOTO, YUTA, radiation oncologist; b. Kakogawa, Hyogo, Japan, Dec. 13, 1955; s. Yoshio and Setsuko (Matsumoto) S.; m. Hiromi Yanagawa, May 3, 1980; children: Ai, Megumi, Jun. MD, Kyoto U., 1980, DMS, 1987. Resident Kyoto U. Hosp., 1980; asst. prof. Shimane Med. U., Izumo, 1980-83, Kyoto U., 1987-92, lectr., 1992, assoc. prof., 1992—2002; prof., chmn. Nagoya City U., Japan, 2002—. Guest rschr. U. Essen, Germany, 1989-90. Contbr. articles to profl. jours. including Cancer, Cancer Rsch., and Brit. Jour. Cancer; inventor fluorine-containing 2-nitroimidazole radiosensitizer drug. Recipient Hanns-Langendorff prize German Radioprotection Assn. and Hanns-Langendorff Found., Germany and Austria, 1992. Mem. Internat. Assn. for the Sensitization of Cancer Treatment (bd. dirs. 1994—), Japanese Soc. for Therapeutic Radiology and Oncology (councilor 1994—), Japan Radiol. Soc. (councilor 2002--), Japanese Cancer Assn., Japan Soc. for Cancer Therapy, Japan Radiation Rsch. Soc., Japan Lung Cancer Soc. Office: Nagoya City U Mizuho-ku Nagoya 467-8601 Japan Home: 3-29 Ota-cho Nagoya 467-0874 Japan Office Phone: 8152 853 8274.

SHIBANO, MAKIO, pharmaceutical educator, researcher; b. Kawachinagano, Osaka, Japan, Sept. 8, 1967; s. Hirofumi and Machiko Shibano; m. Yukiko Furuya; children: Masaki, Yuna. BS in Pharm. Scis., Osaka U. Pharm. Scis., Takatsuki, 1991, PhD in Pharm. Scis., 1999. Rsch. assoc. Osaka U. Pharm. Scis., 1991—2006, lectr., 2006—; vis. asst. prof. U. NC, Chapel Hill, 2006—07. Office: Osaka Univ Pharm Scis 4-20-1 Nasahara Takatsuki Osaka 569-1094 Japan Office Fax: 81-72-690-1005. Business E-Mail: shibano@gly.oups.ac.jp.

SHIBATA, AKIRA, internal medicine educator, academic administrator; b. Niigata City, Japan, Sept. 3, 1930; s. Tsuneichiro and Hideko (Iijima) S.; m. Yoriko Hashimoto, Oct. 8, 1960; 3 children. MD, Niigata U., 1955; PhD, Tohoku U., Sendai, Japan, 1960. Assoc. prof. internal medicine Akita (Japan) U. Sch. Medicine, 1970-75, prof., chmn. dept., 1975-77, Niigata U. Sch. Medicine, 1977-96, prof. emeritus, 1996—, dean, 1992-94. Dir. Univ. Hosp. Niigata U., 1990-92, Tachikawa Gen. Hosp., 1996-2000, Niigata Minami Hosp., 2001—; pres. Japan Russia Med. Collaboration Orgn., 1992-94; hon. head Harbin (China) Inst. Hematology, 1991—. Author: Textbook of Internal Medicine, 1979, Leukemia: Diagnosis and Treatment, 1981, Essential Hematology, 1983; editor: Diagnosis of Internal Medicine, 1994, History of Japanese Hematology, 2005. Fellow: ACP (hon.), Japanese Soc. Reticuloendothelial Sys. (hon.; trustee, pres.1995), Japanese Soc. Internal Medicine (hon.; trustee, pres. 1994), Japanese Soc. Hematology (hon.; trustee, pres. 1994), Acad. Medicine Malaysia (hon.). Home: 252-7 Hamaura-cho 1chome Niigata 951-8151 Japan Office: Niigataminami Hosp 1-7-1 Meikeshinmei Niigata 950-8601 Japan

SHIBATA, KOHEI, surgeon, oncologist; b. Kitsuki, Japan, Apr. 1966; s. Tsuneo and Noriko Shibata; m. Ayako Yoshimatsu; children: Shunsuke, Saki, Ryogo. Degree in medicine, Oita U., 2000. Rsch. assoc. Oita U. Faculty of Medicine, Hasama-machi, 2002—. Contbr. articles to profl. jours. Home: 2-2 Syonoharu Oita 870-0876 Japan Office: Oita Univ Faculty of Medicine 1-1 Idaigaoka Hasama-machi Yufu 879-5593 Japan Oira Office Fax: 81-97-549-6039. E-mail: shibata@med.oita-u.ac.jp.

SHIBATA, MASA-AKI, medical educator, researcher; b. Ichinomiya, Aichi, Japan, Dec. 18, 1956; s. Yoshitake Shibata; m. Eiko Shibata, Apr. 2, 1983; children: Rihito, Arisa. DMS, Nagoya City U. Med. Sch., Aichi, 1994. Cert. pathologist Japanese Soc. Toxicology Pathology, 1994. Rschr. Nagoya City U. Med. Sch., 1981—94, Nat. Cancer Inst., NIH, Bethesda, Md., 1994—99; assoc. prof. Osaka Med. Coll., Takatsuki, Japan, 1999—. Contbr. articles to profl. jours. Music player Tsugaru Shamisen Club, Osaka, 2002—. Recipient grant-in-aid, MEXT Japanese Govt., 1999—2008; Rsch. Excellence fellow, 1998. Achievements include research in the functional roles of bax in mammary cancer progression; haploid loss of bax leads to accelerated mammary cancer development. Avocation: tsugaru shamisen. Office: Osaka Medical Coll 2-7 Daigaku-Machi Takatsuki Osaka 569-8686 Japan Office Fax: 81-72-684-6511. Business E-Mail: shibatam@art.osaka-med.ac.jp.

SHIBATA, SEIICHI, chemist; b. Nagasaki, Japan, Mar. 20, 1949; s. Hidetoshi and Ritsuko Shibata; m. Setsuko Kageyama Shibata, May 4, 1978; children: Satoko, Tomohiro, Atsushi. B in Chemistry, Kyushu U., Fukuoka, Japan, 1971, M in Chemistry, 1973, PhD in Chemistry, 1976. Rsch. assoc. Inst. Nuc. Study U. Tokyo, Tanashi, Japan, 1976—96, assoc. prof., 1996; prof. Rsch. Reactor Inst. Kyoto U., Kumatori, Osaka, Japan, 1996—. Mem. internat. adv. com. 2d Tallin Symposium on Neutrino Physics, Lohusalu, Estonia, 1993; chmn. Ann. Symposium on Radiochemistry, Izumisano, Japan, 2003. Author, translator: Radiochemistry, 2005; contbr. articles to profl. jours. Mem.: Geochem. Soc. Japan, Atomic Energy Soc. Japan, Phys. Soc. Japan, Chem. Soc. Japan (rep. 1998—99, sec. 2001—), Japan Soc. Nuc. and Radiochem. Scis. (dir. 1999—2003, v.p. 2006—08, pres. 2008—). Avocations: reading, classical music. Home: Asashiro-nishi 2-1232 Osaka 590-0458 Japan Office: Kyoto U Rsch Reactor Inst Asashiro-nishi 2-1010 Osaka 590-0494 Japan E-mail: shibata@rri.kyoto-u.ac.up.

SHIBATA, SHIGEHIRO, medical educator; b. Morioka, Iwate, Japan, May 23, 1967; s. Shigeji and Shigeko Shibata; m. Miho Shibata; 1 child, Kaho. MD, Akita U. Sch. Medicine, Japan. Contbr. scientific papers to profl. jours. Achievements include discovery of predict the post-resuscitative outcome of patients with out-of-hospital cardiac arrests. Home: Yamagishi Morioka Iwate 020-0004 Japan Office Phone: 81-19-651-5111. Office Fax: 81-19-651-5151. Business E-Mail: shibatas@iwate-med.ac.jp.

SHIBATA, YO, dentist, researcher; b. Aichi, Japan, Jan. 25, 1972; s. Shibata Miho and Shibata Hikaru. Dentistry, Showa U., Sch. of Dentistry, 1990—96. Lic. Dentist Ministry of Welfare/Tokyo, 1996. Asst. prof. Oral Biomaterials and Tech., Showa U., Sch. of Dentistry, Tokyo, Japan, 2000—. Recipient L.D.Caulk Student Award for Operative Dentistry, DENTSPLY, 1996; grant, Acad. of Dental Materials, 2000, Grant, Ministry of Edn., Culture, Sports, Sci. and Tech., 2003—. Mem.: Japanese Soc. for Dental Materials and Devices (assoc.), Internat. Assn. For Dental Rsch. (assoc.). Office: Showa Univ Sch Dentistry 1-5-8 Hatanodai Shinagawa-ku Tokyo 142-8555 Japan Office Fax: +81-3-3784-8179. Business E-Mail: yookun@dent.showa-u.ac.jp.

SHIBAYAMA, HIDETARO, physiology and biomechanics educator; b. Tokyo, Dec. 22, 1934; s. Hidefumi and Koi (Tani) S.; m. Noriko Inoue, Sept. 7, 1963; children: Masaaki, Hideaki. EdB, U. Tokyo, 1961, MEd, 1963; PhD, Jikeikai Med. Sch., Tokyo, 1984. Rschr. Phys. Fitness Rsch. Inst., Tokyo, 1966—73, chief, 1973-80, vice dir., 1980-83; prof. physiology and biomechanics Nat. Inst. Fitness and Sports, Kagoshima, Japan, 1983—99, pres., 2000—. Co-author: Physiology of Middle and Elderly Persons, 1982, Health Promotion in Children, 1987, Exercise Physiology, 1989; co-translator: Physical and Physiological Conditioning, 1976. Avocation: traditional research members of japanese sumo wrestling. Office: Nat Inst Fitness and Sports 1 Branch Shiromizu-cho Kanoya 891-2393 Japan

SHICHIJO, KAZUKO, pharmacist, researcher; b. Nagasaki, Japan, Apr. 27, 1957; d. Akira and Reiko Matsuo; m. Toshiyuki Shichijo, Mar. 20, 1984; children: Shichijo Wataru, Shichijo Satoru. BS, Nagasaki U., 1980, PhD in Philosophy, 1992. Registered pharmacist Japan, 1980. Asst. prof. Grad. Sch. Ngasaki (Japan) U., 1980—. Rsch. assoc. Duke U., Durham, NC, 1996. Grantee, Japan Soc. Promotion of Sci., 1996. Home: Shiroyamadai 1-7-4 Nagasaki 852-8027 Japan Office: Nagasaki Univ Grad Sch Sakamoto 1-12-4 Nagasaki 852-8523 Japan Office Fax: 81-95-849-7108; Home Fax: 81-95-862-0980. Business E-Mail: shichijo@net.nagasaki-u.ac.jp.

SHICHIRI, MASAYOSHI, medical researcher; b. Osaka City, Japan, Jan. 5, 1956; s. Seisuke and Yasuko Shichiri; m. Yuko Tsukada, Dec. 4, 1988. MD, PhD, Tokyo Med. Dental U., 1984. Diplomate Ministry Welfare, Japan, 1980. Contbr. scientific papers. Fellow: Soc. Cardiovasc. Endocrinology Metabolism, Japanese Soc. Nephrology, Japan Endocrine Soc., Japanese Soc. Hypertension; mem.: Japan Diabetes Soc. Achievements include discovery of bioactive peptide hormones using bioinformatics; identification of salusin peptides; patents for retard the progression of cancer and other diseases; patents pending for use of peptide, antibodies to treat cancer and other diseases; research in diagnostic strategy for hematuria. Office: Kitasato University Dept Endocrinology Diabetes & Metabolism 1-15-1 Kitasato Minamiku Sagamihara Kanagawa 252-0374 Japan

SHIELDS, ADELE RIKE, transparent pharmacist, medical researcher, educator; b. Washington, Pa., Aug. 13, 1979; PharmD, U. Pitts., 2003. Rsch. assoc. prof., surgery U. Cin., 2004—, adj. prof., pharmacy, 2007—. Recipient Healthcare Heroes award, Cin. Bus. Courier, Young Investigator award, Am. Transplant Congress. Mem.: Am. Soc. Health Sys. Pharmacists, Am. Coll. Clin. Pharmacists, Am. Soc. Transplantation, Kappa Psi Pharm. Frat. Avocations: travel, music, reading. Office: 2123 Auburn Ave Ste A42 Cincinnati OH 45219 Office Fax: 513-558-3580. E-mail: rikea@ucmail.uc.edu.

SHIELDS, CAROL L., ophthalmologist; Grad., U. Notre Dame, 1979; MD, U. Pitts., 1983. Diplomate Am. Bd. Ophthalmology, 1989. Resident Wills Eye Hosp., 1987, fellow ocular pathology, 1987—88, fellow ocular oncology, 1988—89; fellow orbital & eyelid tumors & reconstruction Moorfields Eye Hosp., 1988; assoc. dir. ocular oncology svc. Wills Eye Inst.; prof. ophthalmology Thomas Jefferson Univ.; cons. Children's Hosp. of Phila. Office: Wills Eye Institute 14th Fl 840 Walnut St Philadelphia PA 19107 Office Phone: 215-928-3105. Office Fax: 215-928-1140.

SHIELDS, LAWRENCE THORNTON, orthopaedic surgeon, educator; b. Boston, Oct. 2, 1935; s. George Leo and Catherine Elizabeth (Thornton) S.; m. Karen S. Kraus, Sept. 21, 1968; children: Elizabeth Coulter, Laura Thornton, Sarah Daley, Michael Lawrence. AB, Harvard U., 1957; MD, Johns Hopkins U., 1961. Diplomate Am. Bd. Orthop. Surgery. Intern Barnes Hosp., Washington U., St. Louis, 1961—62, resident, 1962—63; resident orthop. surgeon Children's Hosp. Med. Ctr., Boston, 1966—67, Mass. Gen. Hosp., Boston, 1967—68, Peter Bent Brigham, Robert Breck Brigham Hosps., Boston, 1968—69, Harvard Med. Sch., Boston, 1965—69, instr., 1969—; orthop. surgeon Peter Bent Brigham & Women's Hosp., Children's hosps., 1969—, Waltham (Mass.)-Weston Hosp. and Med. Ctr., 1969—, also chief orthop. surgery, pres. med. staff; mem. Conf. Des Chev. Du Tastevin. Mem. Waltham-Weston Orthop. Assocs.; proprietor Boston Athenaeum; mem. staff Hahnemann Hosp., Boston, Newton-Wellesley (Mass.) Hosp.; cons. orthop. surgeon VA Hosp., Boston; mem. faculty Harvard Med. Sch.; vis. scholar Trinity Hall Cambridge U., 1987; hon. prof. New Eng. Coll., Henniker, NH, Sussex, England, 1995; bd. dirs. Wal-West Health Sys., 1986—; pres. Mass. Bay Investment Trust; dir. Waltham Investment Group. Contbr. articles to med. jours. Bd. dirs. Mass. Acad. Emergency Med. Technicians, Waltham Boys' Club; bd. of overseers Boston Lyric Opera, 1993—; trustee, exec. com. Waltham-Weston Hosp. and Med. Ctr. Lt. M.C. USNR, 1963-65. Fellow: ACS, Mass. Hist. Soc. Libr., Am. Acad. Orthop. Surgeons, Mass. Hist. Soc., Olser Club London (corr.); mem.: Irish Networking Boston, Eire Soc., Charitable Irish Soc., Cox & Co., Napoleonic Hist. Soc., Dictionary Soc. N. Am., World Future Soc., Am. Acad. Poets, Irish Georgian Soc., Thomas B. Quigley Sports Medicine Soc. (pres. 2001—, v.p.), R. Austen Freeman Soc. (v.p.), Mass. Med. Soc. (v.p. 1982—83, councillor), Mass. Orthop. Assn. (sec. 1986—, bd. dirs.), Royal Soc. Medicine, N.Y. Acad. Scis., Confrérie des Chevaliers du Tastevin, Boston Opera Assn. (bd. dirs.), Harvard Mus. Assn., Thoreau Soc., Emerson Soc., Trollope Soc. (founding mem., bd. dirs., London), Handel and Hayden Soc. (bd. overseers), Waltham Hist. Soc., Les Amis d'Escoffier Soc., Confrerie de La Chaine des Rotisseurs (elected 1996), Internat. Consular Corps (hon.), Charles River Dist. (pres. 1982—83, treas., exec. com.), Titanic Hist. Soc., Boston Lyric Opera (bd. overseers 1993), English Speaking Union (bd. dirs.), St. Crisplin's Soc. Boston (pres. 1991—, founding mem.), L'Ordre Mondial (elected 1999), Academie Brillat-Savarin, Theodore Roosevelt Assn. New Eng. (founding), USS Wasp CV-19 Assn., Osler Club London, New Eng. Orthop. Club, Boston Orthop. Club, St. Botolph Club (Boston), Harvard Club, Algonquin Club Boston (pres. 1990—, bd. dirs.), East India, Devonshire Sports and Pub. Schs. Club (London), Rotary, Bull Dog Terriers, Union Club Boston, Clover Club Boston (pres. 2011—), 33 Touchdown Club/Found. (founding), Pi Eta (Harvard). Home: 9 Beverly Rd Newton MA 02461-1112 Office: 721 Huntington Ave Boston MA 02115-6010 also: Lawrence T Shields Md 9 Beverly Rd Newton Highlands MA 02461-1112 Business E-Mail: ltshields@mcb.harvard.edu.

SHIELDS, PETER G., oncologist, educator; BA in Biochemistry & Am. Civilization, U. Pa., 1979; MD, Mt. Sinai Sch. Medicine, 1983. Diplomate Nat. Bd. Med. Examiners, Am. Bd. Internal Medicine, Am. Bd. Internal Medicine-Oncology, Am. Bd. Internal Medicine-Hematology. Intern, internal medicine George Washington U. Hosp., Washington, 1984; clin. fellow, hemotology and oncology Joint Program at George Washington Univ. Hosp. and Nat. Cancer Inst., 1987; med. dir. La Clinica del Pueblo, Inc., Washington, 1984—96, chairperson bd. dirs., 1997—2005, mem. hon. coun., 2007—; intensivist Capital Hill Hosp., 1985—87, emergency medicine physician Washington, 1986—87; sr. clin. assoc. Washington Occupational Health Assocs., Inc., DC, 1986—87; commissioned officer, capt. US Pub. Health Svc., 1990—99; sr. clin. investigator NIH, Nat. Cancer Inst., Divsn. Cancer Etiology, Lab. Human Carcinogenesis, Bethesda, Md., 1990—95; acting sect. chief NIH, Nat. Cancer Inst., Divsn. Cancer Etiology, Lab. Human Carcinogenesis, Molecular Epidemiology Sect., Bethesda, Md., 1995—97, sect. chief, 1997—99, tenured investigator, 1997—99; clin. instructor, dept. medicine Georgetown Univ. Med. Ctr., 1986—90, asst. prof. medicine, divsn. hemotology and oncology, 1990—97, assoc. prof., divsn. hematology and oncology, 1997—99, prof., medicine and oncology, 2000—, dir., divsn. cancer genetics and epidemiology program, dept. oncology, 2000—08, interim academic chair, dept. medicine, 2007—; program leader, cancer genetics and epidemiology program Lombardi Comprehensive Cancer Ctr., Georgetown Univ. Med. Ctr., 2000—08, assoc. dir. for cancer control and population sciences, 2000—08, dep. dir., 2008—; sr. med. dir. Capital Breast Care Ctr., Washington, 2006—08; vice-chair, dept. oncology Georgetown Univ., 2006—09; prof., dept. pediat. and child health Howard U., Washington, 2004—; prof., dept. biology U. DC, 2008—. Spl. vol. lab. human carcinogenesis, divsn basic sciences Nat. Cancer Inst., 2000—; bd. dirs. La Clinica del Pueblo, Inc., Washington, 2005—06, Metropolitan Capitol Coll. Occupational and Environ. Medicine, 1992—96; mem. scientific review panel Cancer Rsch. and Prevention Found., 2006—; rsch./clinician chair DC Tobacco Coalition, 2007—; scientific reviewer Ga. Cancer Coalition, 2006—; mem. DC Bd. Medicine, 2001—; med. dir. Avon Walk for Breast Cancer, Washington, 2004—; mem. exec. com. Lombardi Cancer Ctr., Georgetown U. Med. Ctr., Washington, 2000—08. Contbr. several articles to peer-reviewed jours.; reviewer for several scientific jours., mem. adv. editl. bd. Cancer Epidemiology, Biomarkers and Prevention, 1996—99, assoc. editor, 1999—2002, sr. editor, Null Results, 2002—, sr. editor, Biomarkers, Omics and Systems Biology, 2008—, mem. adv. editl. bd. Pharmacogenetics, 1998—2003, mem. editl. bd. Carcinogenesis, 1999—2002, 2008—, Journal of Cancer Epidemiology, 2008—, Oncology Reports, 1997—99, associate editor International Journal of Cancer Prevention, 2003—07, Molecular Carcinogenesis, 2005—. Mem. Am. Cancer Soc. DC Govtl. Relations Com., 2007—08, chair, 2008—; even co-host Cancer Action Network, Am. Cancer Soc., Washington, 2007, mem. organizing host com., 2008. Recipient Janice Jirau award for Cmty. Svc., Comprehensive AIDS Resources and Edn. Consortium, 1994, Physician Recognition award, AMA, 1994, Med. Achievement award, Avon Found., NY, 2007, Pro Bono Health Care award, John Carroll Soc., 2008; named to America's Top Doctors for Cancer, Castle Connolly, 2005, 2007, 2006, 2009. Mem.: Metropolitan Capital Coll. Occupational and Environ. Medicine, Med. Soc. DC, Am. Soc. Preventive Oncology, Am. Conf. Govt. Indsl. Hygienists, Am. Coll. Occupational and Environmental Medicine, Am. Assn. of Cancer Rsch. (Molecular Epidemiology Group) (mem. task force on behavioral sci. and cancer 2005—), Soc. for Rsch. on Nicotine and Tobacco, Alpha Omega Alpha. Office: Georgetown University Medical Ctr 3800 Reservoir Rd NW LL (s) Level Rm 150 Box 571465 Washington DC 20057-1465 Office Phone: 202-687-0003. Business E-Mail: pgs2@georgetown.edu.

SHIELDS, WILLIAM DONALD, physician, educator; b. Salt Lake City, Oct. 29, 1941; s. F. Alburn and Ruth (Clawson) Shields; m. Virginia Mary Howell, May 19, 1970; children: Stephen Christopher, Justin Michael, Christine Rebecca. BA in chemistry, U. Utah, 1967;

MD, U. Utah Sch. Medicine, Salt Lake City, 1967—71. Cert. in neurology with special competence in child neurology Am. Bd. Psychiatry and Neurology, 1977, diplomate Am. Bd. Pediat., 1978. Resident U. So. Calif., LA, 1971—73; fellow U. Utah, Salt Lake City, 1973—76; asst. prof. UCLA Sch. Medicine, 1976—83, assoc. prof., 1983—90, prof., 1990—2009, guest prof., 2009—, Rubin Brown prof., 1999—2005. Chief, divsn. pediatric neurology UCLA Sch. Medicine, 1980—2005. Contbr. chapters to books, articles to profl. jours. Pres., bd. mem. Epilepsy Found. L.A., 1981—88; mem. profl. adv. bd. Epilepsy Found. Am., Landover, Md. Recipient Maxwell J. Schleifer Disting. Svc. Award, Exceptional Parent Found., 2004; named a Top Dr., Am.'s Top Doctors, 2001—10; grantee, Milken Family Found., 1986—2004, NIH, 1992—98. Fellow: Am. Acad. Pediat.; mem.: Nat. Inst. Neurologic Disease and Stroke, L.A. County Epilepsy Soc. (chmn, profl. adv. bd. 1981—86, pres. 1986—89), Am. Acad. Neurology, Profs. Child Neurology, Am. Epilepsy Soc. (Svc. Award 1996), Child Neurology Soc. (counselor 1994—96). Office: David Geffen Sch Medicine UCLA 10833 LeConte Ave Los Angeles CA 90095-1752 Office Phone: 310-825-6196. Office Fax: 310-825-5834.

SHIFFMAN, KENNETH, orthopedist, surgeon; MD, Univ. So. Fla. Coll. Medicine, Tampa, Fla. Cert. Am. Bd. Orthopaedic Surgery, added qualification in hand surgery. Intern, resident Loyola Univ. Med. Ctr., assoc. prof., orthopaedic surgery; staff physician Hinsdale Hosp., Good Samaritan Hosp., Hinsdale Surg. Ctr., Salt Creek Surgery Ctr.; ptnr. Hinsdale Orthopaedic Associates, S.C., 1990—. Fellow, hand and upper extremity surgery Princess Margaret Rose Hosp., Edinburgh; fellow, orthopaedic trauma Sunnybrook Med. Ctr., Toronto, Canada. Mem.: Chgo. Soc. Surgery of the Hand, Am. Soc. Surgery of the Hand, Am. Acad. Orthopaedic Surgeons. Office: Hinsdale Orthopaedic Associates SC 550 W Ogden Ave Hinsdale IL 60521

SHIFRIN, DONALD LEE, pediatrician; b. Portland, Oreg., Jan. 10, 1949; m. Barbara Sue Chamberlin, Nov. 3, 2002; children: Max Burton, Alexis Chamberlin. MD, Georgetown U., Washington, 1970. Cert. Am. Bd. Pediatics, 1981. Physician Pediatric Assocs., Bellevue, Wash., 1978—. Clin. prof. pediat. U. Wash. Sch. Medicine, Seattle. Chair Maimonides Soc. Jewish Fedn. Greater Seattle, 2000—. Fellow: Am. Acad. Pediat. Office: Pedatric Associates 2700 Northup Way Bellevue WA 98004 Home: 4317 Forest Ave Mercer Island WA 98040 Office Phone: 425-827-4600. Office Fax: 425-828-2256; Home Fax: 206-275-3244. Business E-Mail: dshifrin@peds-associates.com.

SHIGEKI, YAMADA, pharmacist; b. Nagoya, Aichi, Japan, Jan. 15, 1967; m. Yamada Chiho; children: Yamada Sayumi, Yamada Kazutaka. PhD, Nagoya U. Grad. Sch. Medicine, 2004. Gen. mgr. Nagoya Kyoritsu Hosp., Aichi, 1997—. Office: Nagaya Kyoritsu Hosp 1-172 Hokke Nakagawaku Nagoya Aichi 454-0933 Japan Office Fax: 81-52-353-9112. Business E-Mail: syamada@kaikou.or.jp.

SHIGEMITSU, TOSHIRO, ophthalmologist, researcher; b. Kyoto, Feb. 7, 1953; s. Yoshito and Eiko (Yoshioka) S.; m. Kumiko Nakahori, Oct. 27, 1990. MD, Fujita Health U., Toyoake, Japan, 1982, DMS, 1987. Asst. prof. ophthalmology Fujita Health U., Toyoake, 1988-91, assoc. prof. ophthalmology, 1991—2001, vis. assoc. prof. ophthalmology, 2002—. Dir. ophthalmology Hojinkai Med. Found., Kawade Hosp., Toyota, 1984—99; dir., head Shigemitsu Eye Clinic & Rsch. Found., Inc., 2002—. Patentee in field; contbr. articles to profl. jours. Mem. judging com. Fund Med. Security Sys., Aichi, 1996—2002. Recipient Japan Soc. Clin. Ophthalmology poster prize, 1998, Silver medal, Japan Ophthalmol. Soc., 1990; grantee Eye Bank Assn. Aichi, 1993, 94, 95. Mem.: Am. Acad. Opthalmology, Toikai Med. Assn. (bd. dirs. 1999—2005), Japanese Soc. Pathology (sci. councillor 2001—), Toukai Soc. Glaucoma (bd. dirs. 1998—2002), Asia Pacific Intraocular Implant Assn. (faculty 1997—98), Japanese Ophthalmic Pathology Soc. (councillor 1997—), Am. Aging Assn., European Soc. Cataract and Refractive Surgeons, Am. Soc. Cataract and Refractive Surgery. Avocations: travel, movies, golf, art. Office: Shigemitsu Eye Clin & Rsch Fdn Inc 3-6-23 Kuzuha-Asahi Hirakata 573-1111 Japan Office Phone: 81 72 866 2238.

SHIGEMURA, KATSUMI, urologist; b. Nishinomiya, Hyogo, Japan, Oct. 9, 1972; s. Yutaka and Yuko Shigemura; m. Megumi Mochimatsu; children: Yuto, Shunta. MD, Kochi Med. Sch., Japan, 1999; BSc, Kobe U. Grad. Sch. Medicine, Japan, 2006; grad, Kobe U. Grad. Sch. Medicine, 2004; PhD in Med., Kobe U. Grad. Sch. Medicine, Japan, 2006. Cert. urological specialist Japanese Urol. Assn., 2008. Neurosurgery resident Kobe U. Hosp., Hyogo, 1999, urol. resident, 2000, urol. clin. fellow, 2007, urol. rsch. stuff, 2007—; neurosurgery resident Rokko Island Hosp., Kobe, 1999—2000; urol. resident Nishiwaki Mcpl. Hosp., Hyogo, 2000—02; postdoc. fellow U. Ark. Med. sci., Little Rock, 2004, Emory U. Sch. Medicine, Atlanta, 2004—07; sub-head urologist Akashi Municial Hosp., Hyogo, 2007—; grad. rschr. Kobe U. Sch., 2002—. Contbr. scientific papers. Recipient Sakaguchi award, 65th Japanese Urol. Assn., 2007, Kobe Urol. rsch. Forum award, 2008, 3rd Shinsui-kai award, 2008; grant, Japanese Antibiotic Rsch. Assn., 2004, Hyogo Prefecture Health Promotion Assn., 2008, Japan Soc. Promotion Sci., 2008. Mem.: Japanese Soc. Renal Cancer, Tokyo, Japanese Endourology, ESWL Assn., Tokyo, Japanese STD Assn., Tokyo, Japanese Infectious Assn., Tokyo, Japanese Chemotherapy Assn., Tokyo, Asian Assn. UTI, STD, Kitakyushu, Fukuoka, Japan, Japanese Urol. Assn. (Tokyo). Office: Akashi Mcpl Hosp 1-33 Takasho-cho Akashi 673-8501 Japan Office Fax: 81-78-914-8374.

SHIGESADA, NANAKO, mathematical biology educator, researcher; b. Kurashiki, Okayama, Japan, July 7, 1941; d. Yutaro and Toshiko Inoue; m. Katsuya Shigesada, May 15, 1966; 1 child, Yukihiko. BS, Kyoto U., Japan, 1964, MS, 1966, DSc (hon.), 1971. Instr. Kyoto U., 1971-92; vis. prof. SUNY, Stony Brook, 1979-80; vis. scientist Stanford (Calif.) U., 1980-81; prof. info. and computer sics. Nara (Japan) Women's U., 1992—2005, Doshisha U., 2005—. Author: Mathematical Perspective of Life Sciences, 1975, Mathematical Models of Biological Invasions, 1992, Biological Invasions: Theory and Practice, 1997; contbr. articles to profl. jours. Trustee, v.p. Nara Women's U., 2000—05. Mem. Japanese Assn. Math. Biology (sec. gen. 1990-92), Am. Acad. Arts & Scis. (hon. fgn.). Home: 13-49 Hirata Kawara Kyotanabe 610-0361 Japan Office: Dept Culture and Sci Doshisha Univ Kyo-Tanabe Kyoto 610 0321 Japan

SHIGEYOSHI, OBA, nephrologist, educator; b. Tokyo, June 27, 1965; PhD, U. Tokyo, MD, 1991. Asst. prof. U. Tokyo Sch. Medicine, 2003—. Contbr. scientific papers. Grants-in-Aid, Kato Meml. Biosci. Found., Ministry Edn., Culture, Sports, Sci. and Tech. Japan. Mem.: Japanese Soc. Internal Medicine, Japanese Soc. Nephrology, RNA Soc. Japan, Internat. Soc. Nephrology, Am. Soc. Nephrology. Avocation: music. Office: 7-3-1 Hongo Bunkyo-ku Tokyo 1138655 Japan Office Fax: 81338140021. Business E-Mail: oba-2im@h.u-tokyo.ac.jp.

SHIH, CHUN-CHING, medical educator; b. Chiayi City, Taiwan, Jan. 26, 1962; PhD, China Med. U., 2002. Asst. prof., dept. beauty sci. Meiho U., Pingtung, Taiwan, 2002—03; asst. prof., dept. nursing Ctrl. Taiwan U. Sci. and Tech., Taichung, Taiwan, 2003—08; asst. prof. Inst. Pharm. Sci. and Tech. Ctrl. Taiwan U. Sci. and Tech., 2008—09, assoc. prof., 2009—. Contbr. articles to profl. publs. Fellow: Taiwan Pharmacist Assn. Avocations: reading, music, ballet. Office: 666 Buzih Rd Beitun Dist Taichung City 40601 Taiwan Office Fax: 886-4-22394256. Business E-Mail: ccshih@ctust.edu.tw.

SHIH, HUNG-CHE, pharmacist; b. Kaoshiung, Taiwan, May 25, 1949; PhD, Tokyo Med. U., 1988. Cert. in pharmacy Govt., 1979. Physician Tokyo Med. U., 1982—88. Grantee, Tchr. Abuse Inhibitation, 1996. Office: Chung-Shan Med Univ 110 Sect 1 Chien-Kou N Rd Taichung 400 Taiwan Office Phone: 886424730022 ext. 11664. Business E-Mail: shj525@csmu.edu.tw.

SHIH, JUI-TIEN, surgeon, consultant; s. Luby Geou; m. Jessica Yi, June 15, 1990; children: Peggy, Jenny. MD, Nat. Def. Med. Ctr., 1989. Cons. Armed Forces Taoyuan Gen. Hosp., Taiwan, 1995—. Office: Armed Forces Taoyuan General Hospital 168 Joing-Shing R Long-Tan Taiwan Taoyuan 325 Taiwan Office Fax: 886-3-4898976. Personal E-mail: jui_tien_shih@hotmail.com.

SHIH, YANG-HSIN, environmental studies educator; b. Kaohsiung, Taiwan, Mar. 5, 1972; PhD, Nat. Taiwan U., 2002. Asst. prof., dept. soil and environ. scis. Nat. Chung Hsing U., 2004—08, adj. assoc. prof., ctr. nanosci. and nanotech., 2004—08, assoc. prof., dept. soil and environ. scis., 2008—10; assoc. prof., dept. agrl. chemistry Nat. Taiwan U., 2010—. Sec. Chinese Soc. Soil and Fertilizers Scis., 2006—07, bd. dirs., 2008—10. Chinese Soc. Land Resource and Protection, 2007—10; vis. asst. prof., dept. civil and environ. engring. MIT, Mass., 2007. Recipient Disting. Young Tchr. award, Nat. Chung Hsing U.; Vis. fellowship, Nat. Sci. Coun., Taiwan. Mem.: Am. Chem. Soc. Avocations: reading, bicycling, swimming. Office: Nat Taiwan University Dept Agricultural Chemistry Rm 225B 1 Sect 4 Roosevelt Rd Taipei 106 Taiwan Business E-Mail: yhs@ntu.edu.tw.

SHIHADA, RABIA, otolaryngologist; b. Israel, Feb. 17, 1975; BMSc, Hebrew U., Hadassah Med. Sch., Jerusalem, 1998, MD, 2002. Sr. otolaryngologist Dept. Otolaryngology-Head and Neck Surgery, Bnai-Zion Med. Ctr., Haifa, Israel, 2003—. Sr. otolaryngologist Maccabi Healthcare Svcs., Clalit Healthcare Svcs.; lectr., speech and hearing, spl. edn. Gordon Coll. Edn., Haifa; lectr., ear nose and throat diseases, continuing med. edn. Dr. Y. Zaida Nursing Sch., Haifa; lectr., ear nose and throat diseases Faculty of Social Welfare and Health Studies, Dept. Communication Disorders, U. Haifa. Named Outstanding Lectr., Faculty of Medicine, Technion, Haifa. Mem.: Israeli Head and Neck Surgery Soc., Israeli Neuro-Otological Soc., Israeli Otolaryn. Soc., Israeli Med. Assn. Avocations: piano, photography. Home: Hillel 58/56 Haifa 33728 Israel Home Phone: 97248539485. Personal E-mail: dr.shihada@gmail.com.

SHIH-CARDUCCI, JOAN CHIA-MO, food service executive, medical technologist, biochemist, writer, educator; b. Rukuan, Chunghua, Taiwan, Dec. 21, 1933; came to U.S., 1955; d. Luke Chiang-hsi and Lien-chin Shih; m. Kenneth M. Carducci, Sept. 30, 1960 (dec. July 1988); children: Suzanne R., Elizabeth M. BS in Chemistry, St. Mary Coll., Xavier, Kans., 1959; intern in med. tech., St. Mary's Hosp., Rochester, NY, 1960. Med. rschr. Strong Meml. Hosp. U. Rochester, 1960-61; pharm. chemist quality control Strasenburgh Labs., Rochester, 1961-62; cooking tchr. adult edn. Montgomery County Pub. Schs., Rockville, Md., 1973-79; tchr. The Chinese Cookery Inc., Rockville, 1975-86, Silver Spring, Md., 1986—, pres., bd. dirs., 1975—; chemist NIH, Bethesda, 1987-2000; analytical chemist NIH/WRAIR, Rockville, Md., 1994-96. Author: The Chinese Cookery, 1981, Hunan Cuisine, 1984, Vegetarian Cuisine, 2000, The Art of The Chinese Cookery, 2001 (The Cook Book Winner of Pinnacle Book award 2005). Mem. Am. Chem. Soc., Internat. Assn. Cooking Profls. (Woman of Yr. 1994-2004). Republican. Roman Catholic. Avocations: piano, music, dance, gardening. Office: The Chinese Cookery Inc PO Box 24 Highland MD 20777-0024 Office Phone: 301-236-5311. Personal E-mail: chinesecookery@aol.com.

SHIJUN, FU, medical researcher, director; b. Feixian, Shandong, China, July 29, 1980; PhD, Zhejiang U., 2008. Dir. Shandong Binzhou Animal Sci. and Vet. Medicine Acad., 2008—. Mem.: Chinese Assn. Animal and Vet. Scis. Avocation: basketball. Office: 169 Yellow River II Rd Binzhou Shandong 256600 China Personal E-mail: fsj729@yahoo.com.cn.

SHIKOWITZ, MARK JAY, otolaryngologist; b. NY, Oct. 3, 1954; MD, U. Dominica, 1981. Vice chmn., otolaryngology dept. North Shore LIJ Health Sys., 1997—. Grant, Nat. Inst. Deafness and Other Communicative Disorders. Mem.: LI Soc. Otolaryngology Head and Neck Surgery, Am. Acad. Otolaryngology. Office: 430 Lakeville Rd New Hyde Park NY 11042 Office Fax: 718-470-4514. Business E-Mail: mshikowi@lij.edu.

SHILLINGBURG, HERBERT THOMPSON, JR., dental educator; b. Mar. 21, 1938; s. Herbert Thompson and Stefi Marie (Schuster) Shillingburg; m. Constance Joanne Murphy, June 11, 1960; children: Lisa Grace, Leslie Susan, Lara Stephanie. Student, U. N.Mex., 1955-58, 65-66; DDS, U. So. Calif., 1962; Dr (hon.), U. Medicine and Pharmacy Targu Mures, Romania, 2006. Gen. practice dentistry, Albuquerque, 1964-67; asst. prof. fixed prosthodontics sect. UCLA Sch. Dentistry, 1967-70, chmn., 1970-72; chmn. dept. fixed prosthodontics U. Okla. Coll. Dentistry, Okla. City, 1972—2003, David Ross Boyd Disting. prof., 1983, prof. emeritus, 2003—. Cons. VA Hosp., Muskogee, Okla., 1975—84, Oklahoma City, 1977—93, U.S. Army Dental Activity, Ft. Knox, Ky., 1980—94. Author: (also in Japanese, German, Greek, Spanish, Italian, French, Portuguese, Polish, Korean, Chinese, Russian and Croation) Preparations for Cast Gold Restorations, 1974, Fundamentals of Fixed Prosthodontics, 1976, 3d edit., 1997, 4th edit., 2011, Guide to Occlusal Waxing, 1979, 3d edit., 2000, Restoration of the Endodontically Treated Tooth, 1984, Fundamentals of Tooth Preparations for Cast Metal and Porcelain Restorations, 1987; co-editor: Quintessence of Dental Technology, 1984—88; sect. editor: Quintessence Internat., 1988—2001, mem. editl. coun.: Jour. Prosthetic Dentistry, 1996—99. Capt. US Army, 1962—64. Recipient Award for tchg. excellence, UCLA Sch. Dentistry, 1969, 1972, 1973, Okla. Coll. Dentistry, 1976, 1978, 1982, 1987, 1993, 1994, 1997, 1st prize, Am. Med. Writers Assn., 1988, La Mèdaille de la Ville de Paris (èchelon Argent), 1990, Outstanding Profl. Achievement award, O U Coll. Dentristy, 2003, Prof. of Hon., U. Medicine and Pharmacy Targu-Mures, 2004; named Disting. Lectr., O U Assoc., 1989, Herbert T. Shillingburg Endowed Professorship Fixed Prosthodontics, Coll. Dentistry, 2006. Fellow: Am. Coll. Dentists; mem.: ADA, Okla. State Dental Assn., Internat. Assn. Dental Rsch., Am. Coll. Prosthodontists (hon.), Am. Acad. Restorative Dentistry, Am. Acad. Fixed Prosthodontics (George H. Moulton award 1998), Am. Acad. Operative Dentistry, Phi Kappa Phi, Omicron Kappa Upsilon (Stephen H. Leeper award for Tchg. Excellence Supreme Ch. 2000). Independent. Episcopalian. Avocations: travel, photography. Home: 1312 Brixton Rd Edmond OK 73034-3314 Office: U Okla Coll Dentistry PO Box 26901 Oklahoma City OK 73190-0001

SHIM, BONGSUK, medical educator; b. Busan, Republic of Korea, Dec. 17, 1957; m. Miran Han, May 30, 1984; children: Younjoo, Heejoo. BS, Younsei U., Seoul, Republic of Korea, 1981; MS, Hanyang U., Seoul, 1990, Dr., 1993. Cert. Ministry of Health, Welfare and Family Affairs, Republic of Korea, 1982, med. specialist 1986. Instr. Ewha Womans U., Seoul, 1989—90, asst. prof., 1990—97, assoc. prof., 1997—2002, chief mgmt. and planning office, Dongdaemun Hosp., 1998—, chief emergency ctr., Dongdaemun Hosp., 1999—2000, chmn. dept. urology, 2002—06, prof., 2002—, dir., Dongdaemun Hosp., 2007—. Vis. fellow U. Calif., San Francisco, 1997—98; exec. dir. planning com. Korean Prostate Soc., Seoul, 1997—2000, sec. gen., 2001—02; exec. dir., gen. Korean Soc. Nutritional Medicine, Seoul, 2006—. Author: (textbook) QA of Benign Prostatic Hyperplasia, Urinary Tract Infection, Textbook of Benign Prostatic Hyperplasia, Urinary Tract Infection, Textbook of Urology. Capt. Korean Army, 1986—89. Named one of Ewha Hosp. Best Dr., 2007. Master: Korean Assn. Urinary Tract Infection (Seoul) (exec. dir. academic com. 2003—07, v.p. 2007—); mem.: Soc. Internat. Urology (Montreal, Can.), Am. Urologic Assn. (Washington), Korean Urol. Assn. (Seoul) (exec. dir. med. info. com. 2001—04, exec. mem. 2004—), Korean Med. Assn. (Seoul). Roman Catholic. Avocations: travel, photography, computers. Office: Ewha Womans Univ Hosp 911-1 Mok-6-Dong Yangcheon Ku Seoul 158 710 Republic of Korea Office Phone: 82-2-2650-2863. Office Fax: 82-2-2654-3682. Business E-Mail: bonstone@ewha.ac.kr.

SHIM, CHAN SUP, physician; b. Seoul, Korea, Jan. 21, 1949; s. Shim Sang Sool and Chin Keum-I; m. Yoon Young Sook, Jan. 29, 1979; children: Shim Hyoung Joon, Shim Jae Youn. MD, Chonnam Nat. U., Kwangju, Korea, 1976; MMS, Choong-ang U., Seoul, Korea, 1982; PhD, Korea U. Sch. Medicine, Seoul, Korea, 1987. Instr. divsn. gastroen., dept. internal medicine Soon Chun U. Hosp., Seoul, Korea, 1981-86, asst. prof. divsn. gastroen., dept. internal medicine, 1986-89, assoc. prof. divsn. gastroen., dept. internal medicine, 1990-94, prof. divsn. gastroen., dept. internal medicine, 1995—, dir. Inst. Digestive Rsch., 1995—. Faculty mem. 10th Internat. Symposium Endoscopic Ultrasonography, Cleve., 1995, 11th Internat. Symposium Endoscopic Ultrasonography, Kyoto, Japan, 1998, Congreso Artentino Gastroen. Endoscopia Digestiva, Buenos Aires, 1998, 7th United European Gastroen Week, Rome, 1999, 12th Internat. Symposium Endoscopic Ultrasonography, Monaco, 2000, 11th Asian Pacific Congress Gastroen & 8th Asian Pacific Congress Digestive Endoscopy, Hong Kong, 2000; pres. 98' Internat. Workshop Endoscopic Ultrasonography and Advanced Therapeutic Endoscopy, Seoul, 1998, 15th Internat. Therapeutic Endoscopy, Hong Kong, 2000; spkr. in field. Author: Abdominal Realtime Ultrasound, 1988, Therapeutic Gastrointestinal Endoscopy, 1992, Gallstone and Dietary Therapy, 1996, Overview of Geriatrics, 1998, Gallstone, 1998, Textbook of Geriatrics, 2000, Textbook of Hepato-biliary-pancreas Surgery, 2000, Abdominal Ultrasound, 2d edit., 2000; translator Harrison's Principles of Internal Medicine, 1997, The CIBA Collection of Medical Illustrations, 2000; editor-in-chief Atlas of Endoscopic Retrograde Cholangiopancreatography, 1999. Recipient Min. Edn. award, 1994, 6th Acad. Encouragement award, Korean Fedn. Sci. & Tech. Socs., 1996, 8th, 1998, Korean Soc. Med. Ultrasound award, 1997, Korean Soc. Gastroen. Endoscopy award, 1998, Korean Soc. Gastroen. Investigator award, 1998, Nakchun Acad. Encouragement Fund award, 1999, Min. Cluture & Travel award, 2000, Japanese Soc. Gastroen. Endoscopy award, 2000; grantee Cancer Rsch. Fund, 1994, Korean Soc. Ultrasound in Medicine, 1994. 97, Korean Motility Soc., 1997, Paul Jassen Found., 1997., Chong Kun Dang Fund, 1999. Mem. Korean Soc. Gastroen. Endoscopy (exec. bd. 1983—, scientific bd. 1988-89, 91-92, editl. bd. 1989-91, editor-in-chief 1991-92, sec. gen. 1992-94), Japanese Soc. Gastroen. Endoscopy, Korean Assn. Internal Medicine (editl. bd. 1989—), Assn. Internat. Gastro-Surg. Club (corr.), Am. Soc. Gastroen. Endoscopy (corr.), Korean Soc. Gastroen. (scientific bd. 1994—, exec. bd. 1994—), Korean Acad. Med. Scis. (editl. bd. 1995—), Crohn's & Colitis Found. Am., Am. Gastroel. Assn., Am. Motility Soc. (corr.), Korean Soc. Pancreas and Biliary Tract, Korean Soc. Med. Ultrasound. Office: Inst Digestive Rsch 657 Hannam Dong Seoul 140-743 Republic of Korea

SHIM, CHANG KI, agriculturist; b. Jinju, July 1, 1970; PhD, Gyeongsang Nat. U., 2005. Rschr. Plant Molecular Biology and Biotechnology Rsch. Ctr., Republic of Korea, 1994—2001; postdoc. rschr. Nat. Inst. Agr. Sci., Rural Devel. Adminstrn., Republic of Korea, 2005—07; rsch. Nat. Agrobiodiversity Ctr., Rural Devel.

Adminstrn., Republic of Korea, 2007—10, Nat. Acad. Agrl. Sci., Rural Devel. Adminstrn., Republic of Korea, 2011—. Tchg. asst. Gyeongsang Nat. U., Republic of Korea, 2001—05. Mem.: Korean Soc. Organic Agr., Korean Soc. Hort. Sci., Korean Soc. Plant Pathology. Achievements include development of environmental friendly control management of disease and insect. Avocations: photography, hiking. Office: 249 Seodun-dong Gwonseon-gy Suwon Gyeonggi 441-707 Republic of Korea Office Fax: 82-31-290-0507. Business E-Mail: ckshim@korea.kr.

SHIM, JAE YONG, physician; b. Seoul, Republic Of Korea, May 5, 1962; s. Kwan Sup Shim and Kyou Soon Son; m. Shinwhi Lee, June 5, 1992; children: Keysun, Haesun. MPH, Yonsei U., Seoul, 1998; PhD, Korea U., Seoul, 2004. Cert. med. dr. Ministry for Health, Welfare and Family Affairs, 1987, family medicine specialist 1990. Hon. fellow, hon. registrar Flinders U., Repatriation Gen. Hosp., Adelaide, Australia, 2004—05; assoc. prof. Yonsei U. Med. Coll., 2006—; leader med. outreach team, mission awareness com. Gangnam Severance Hosp., Seoul, 2006—08, head dept. family medicine, 2008—, dir. Clin. Trials Ctr., 2008—. Dir. Korean Palliative Medicine Rsch. Group, Seoul, 2007—; editor-in-chief Korean Jour. Hospice and Palliative Care, Seoul, 2008—. Lt., med. officer Korean Army, 1990—93, Republic of Korea. Grant, Korea Nat. Enterprize Clin. Trials, 2008. Mem.: Korean Soc. Hospice and Palliative Medicine, Korean Acad. Family Physician. Office: Gangnam Severance Hosp 146-92 Dogok-Dong Gangnam-Gu Seoul 135-720 Republic of Korea Office Fax: 82-2-3463-3287. Business E-Mail: hope@yuhs.ac.

SHIM, SANG KOO, mental health services professional; b. Tokyo, Oct. 1, 1942; arrived in U.S., 1968; s. Sang Taek and Kum Ryon (Bae) Shim; m. Jae Hee Lee, July 12, 1972; children: Tammy, David. BS, Seoul Nat. U., Republic of Korea, 1967; MBA, No. Ill. U., 1970; MS, U. Wis., Madison, 1975. CPA Ill., cert. valuation analyst. Acct. Vaughn Mfg. Co., Chgo., 1970-72, Stewart-Warner Corp., Chgo., 1972-73; fin. cons. Cen. Acctg. Assn., New Baden, Ill., 1977-79; auditor Ill. Dept. Mental Health, Springfield, 1980-82, CFO, 1983-97; chief bur. gen. acctg. Ill. Dept. Human Svcs., Springfield, 1997—2002. Bd. dirs. Metro City Bank, Doraville, Ga. Treas. Korean Assn. Greater St. Louis, 1982. Mem.: Am. CPA Soc., Korean-Am. Assn. St. Louis (pres. 2008—10), Nat. Assn. Cert. Valuation Analysts, Assn. Govt. Accts. (cert. govt. fin. mgr.), Ill. CPA Soc., Mo. CPA Soc. Office: Shim & Co CPA 1600 Lebanon Ave Ste 102 Belleville IL 62221 Home: 1157 Stonewolf Trl Fairview Heights IL 62208-4187 Office Phone: 618-257-1788. Personal E-mail: skshim@aol.com, skshim42@gmail.com.

SHIM, SEUNG-CHEOL, medical educator; b. Seoul, Republic of Korea, Dec. 14, 1964; MD, Hanyang U., 1989, PhD, 2000. Asst. prof. Eulji U., 1998—2002, assoc. prof., 2004—10, prof., 2010—; vis. prof. U. Wash., 2002—04; chief, medicine UN PKO, 2006. Chief Divsn. Rheumatology, 1998—2011; chmn. Dept. Medicine, 2004—11; dir. Instnl. Rev. Bd., 2004—10, Internat. Health Svc. Ctr., 2004—11, Clin. Trial Ctr., 2010—11. Recipient Disting. Rsch. Prof. award, Eulji U., Disting. Clinician Prof. award, Disting. Investigator award, Korean Rheumatism Assn., 2001, 2004. Mem.: Med. R & D Forum, Korean Soc. Internal Medicine, Korean Coll. Rheumatology. Office: Seogu Dunsandong 1306 Daejeon 302-799 Republic of Korea Office Fax: 82-42-611-3853.

SHIM, WON JOON, ecotoxicologist, environmental chemist, researcher; b. Seoul, Republic of Korea, Mar. 4, 1968; s. Dong Ro Shim and Ok Hee Lee; m. Sun Wook Hong, Mar. 5, 1967; children: Jong Hoon, Jong Hyo. BS, Seoul Nat. U., 1990, MS, 1996, PhD, 2000. Rsch. scientist Korea Ocean Res. and Dev. Inst., Ansan, Republic of Korea, 1995—2000; sr. rschr. Korea Ocean Res And Dev. Inst., Ansan, Republic of Korea, 2003—; lab. dir. Envitech Inc., Daejeon, Republic of Korea, 2000—01; exec. officer NeoEnBiz Inc., Seoul, Republic of Korea, 2001—03. Mem. Endocrine Disrupting Chemicals Adv. Com., Seoul, 2003—; sci. adv. com. mem. People's Party For Reform, Seoul, 2002—03. Lt. j.g. Naval Operation Command, 1991—94, Jinhae. Fellow Fellowships for advanced study, Korea Sci. Found., 1999; scholar Full Scholarships for undergraduate study, Seoul Nat. Univ. Alumni Assn., 1986—90, Daewoo Grad. Scholarships, Daewoo Found., 1996. Mem.: Korean Soc. Environ. Analysis, Korean Soc. Oceanography, Korean Soc. Environ. Toxicology (Best Poster Presentation award 2001, 2002), Soc. Environ. Toxicology and Chemistry. Achievements include research in Effects of Organotins on Marine Organisms. Avocation: scuba diving. Office: Korea Ocean Res And Dev Inst Jangmok-Ri 391 656-834 Geoje Gyeongsangnam-do Republic of Korea Office Fax: +82-55-639-8689. Personal E-mail: wjshim@kordi.re.kr.

SHIM, YOUNGBO, neurosurgeon, director; b. Daegu, Feb. 7, 1962; s. JaeGwang Shim and JungHee Yoon; m. MinJin Kim, May 5, 1987; children: KyuSung, SunAh. MD, KyungPook Nat. U., Daegu, 1986; PhD, Hallym U., Seoul, 1997. Diplomate Ministry Health and Welfare, 1986, cert. neurol. surgeon Korean Neurosurg. Soc., 1991, in critical care medicine Korean Soc. Critical Care Medicine. Clin. neurosurgeon InCheon Christian Hosp., Republic of Korea, 1993—94; assoc. prof. Sch. Medicine Hallym U., Seoul, Republic of Korea, 1994—2001; dir. St.Peter's Hosp., Uijeongbu, Republic of Korea, 2001—. Editor Neurosurg. Text Compilation Com. Korean Neurosurg. Soc., Seoul, 1999—2001; internat. mem. Congress Neurol. Surgeon, Schaumburg, Ill., 2008—; dir. 4th detailed rsch. Korea Health Industry Devel. Inst., Seoul, 2009—. Contbr. articles to profl. jours. Capt. Korean Army, 1991—93. Mem.: Korean Neurosurg. Soc., Steering Com. KyungIn Neurosurgical Soc. Achievements include first to introduction of spinal cord stimulator in Korea; patents pending for neuropeptides for dementia. Avocations: golf, travel. Office: St Peter's Hosp 228-22 Uijeongbudong 480-844 Uijeongbu Gyeonggi-do Republic of Korea Office Phone: 82-31-840-1700 ext. 201. Office Fax: 82-31-843-3781. Business E-Mail: leherring40@naver.com.

SHIMA, KOHJI, neurologist, consultant; b. Sapporo, Hokkaido, Japan, Sept. 30, 1945; s. Yoshichika and Ura Shima; m. Fumiko Hayashi, June 10, 1973; children: Hiroaki, Kuniaki, Akiko. MD, Sapporo Med. U., 1970; PhD, Hokkaido U. Sch. Medicine, Sapporo, 1984. Cert. bd. neurologist Japanese Soc. Neurology, 1981. Vice dir. Sapporo Minami Nat. Hosp., 2000—07; advisor Sapporo Neurology Clinic, 2008—. Vis. clin. prof. Hokkaido U. Sch. Med, Sapporo, 2008—, vis. prof., 2005—06. Examiner judging com. specified intractable diseases, Hokkaido. Mem.: NY Acad. Sci., Am. Acad. Neurology. Achievements include first to establishment of Hokkaido medical care network for intractable disease. Home: 4-11 N43 E14 Higashi-ku Sapporo Hokkaido 007-0843 Japan Office: Sapporo Neurology Clinic 2-17 N21 E21 Higashi-ku Sapporo Hokkaido 065-0021 Japan Office Fax: 81-11-780-2255.

SHIMADA, ATSUYOSHI, neuropathologist, researcher; b. Awaji City, Hyogo, Japan, Feb. 12, 1963; s. Atsunobu and Mineko Shimada; 1 child, Tomo-oki. MD, Kyoto U., Japan, 1988, D in Med. Sci., 1992. Lic. physician Japan, cert. Edn. Commn. Fgn. Med. Graduates. Fellow Japan Soc. Promotion Sci., Kyoto, 1992—93; vis. fellow NIH, Balt., 1993—95; resident Columbia U. Med. Ctr., NYC, 1995—97; rsch. scientist Columbia U., NYC, 1997; rsch. assoc. Nagasaki U., Japan, 1998; lab. dir. Inst. Develop. Rsch., Aichi Human Svc. Ctr., Kasugai, Japan, 1998—. Contbr. articles to profl. jours. Mem.: Psychoneuroimmunology Rsch. Soc., Japanese Biochem. Soc., NY Acad. Scis., Japan Soc. for Biomed. Gerontology (treas. 2006—), Japanese Neurosci. Soc., Japanese Soc. Neuropathology (treas. 2004—), Am. Soc. Investigative Pathology, Soc. Neurosci., Japanese Soc. Pathology (treas. 2000—). Achievements include research in mechanism of brain aging and neural functions of lipid mediators. Office: Inst Develop Rsch Aichi Human Svc Ctr 713-8 Kamiya Aichi Kasugai 480-0392 Japan Business E-Mail: ats7@inst-hsc.jp.

SHIMADA, YASUYUKI, surgeon; b. Kyoto, May 12, 1960; s. Kojiro and Jun Shimada; m. Rika Shimada, Nov. 30, 1963; children: Syunji, Chiho, Wataru, Hideki. PhD, Kyoto Prefectural U., Japan, 1994. Physician's license Min. of Welfare/Japanese govt., 1985. Sr. lectr. Kyoto Prefectural U. Medicine, 1999—2003; cons. cardiac surgery Saiseikai Suita Hosp., Japan, 2003—. Dir.: (research works) Myocardial protection against ischemia/reperfusion injury (Commendation/ Gen. meeting in Japan Surg. Soc., 2000). Fellow: JATS; mem.: Japanese Med. Assn. Achievements include research in ischemia/reperfusion injury of myocardium; publication to medical journals. Home: 1-14 Kamiadachi Yoshida Sakyo Kyoto 606-8307 Japan Office Fax: +81-6-6382-2498. Personal E-mail: yasuyuki.shimada@ma8.seikyou.ne.jp. E-mail: shimada1087d@suita.saiseikai.or.jp.

SHIMAMOTO, TAKASHI, hospital administrator, hematologist; b. Katsushika-ku, Tokyo, Japan, Jan. 30, 1964; s. Hiroshi and Chiyoko Shimamoto. MD, Tokyo Med. U., 1988, DMS, 1994. Mem. med. staff Tokyo Med. U., 1988—95, instr., 1997—99, asst. prof., 1999—2003; post doctoral fellow NYU Med. Ctr., NYC, 1995—97; dir. Kamata Gen. Hosp., Tokyo, 2003—04, Sanofi-Aventis Group, Tokyo, 2004—. Contbr. articles to profl. jours. Recipient Cancer Rsch. award, Tokyo Med. U., 1998; grantee, Ministry of Edn., Sci. and Culture, 2000; fellow Leukemia Rsch. fellow, 1996. Fellow: Japanese Bd. Hematology, Japanese Soc. Internal Medicine; mem.: European Soc. Med. Oncology, Japanese Bd. Internal Medicine, Am. Assn. Cancer Rsch., Am. Soc. Hematology, Am. Soc. Clin. Oncology. Office: Sanofi-Aventis K K 3-20-2 Nishi Sinjuku Tokyo Shinjuku 163-1488 Japan Business E-Mail: takashi.shimamoto@sanofi-aventis.com.

SHIMAMURA, TADAKATSU, microbiology educator; b. Atsugi, Japan, Aug. 16, 1942; s. Umeo and Fuku (Hosoya) S.; m. Yoshiko Sakakibara, Jan. 23, 1969; children: Yuko, Tadao. MD summa cum laude, Showa U., 1968; D of Med. Sci., Keio U., 1973. Instr. Keio U. Sch. Medicine, Tokyo, 1972-74; rsch. assoc. Rutgers U., New Brunswick, N.J., 1972-73; asst. prof. Tokai U. Sch. Medicine, Isehara, Japan, 1974-83, assoc. prof, 1983-87; prof., chmn. Showa U. Sch. Medicine, Tokyo, 1987—2008; prof. emeritus Showa U., 2008—. Vis. prof. Rutgers U., 1977, vis. investigator, 1983; vis. asst. prof. Harvard Med. Sch., Mass., 1977. Author: Microbiology, 1989, Microbiology and Immunology for Medical Students, 1991, Immunology, 1993; inventor in field. Bd. dirs. Waksman Found. Japan Inc., 2001—. Postdoctoral fellow Yale U. Sch. Medicine, Conn., 1978; recipient Kamijo prize Showa U., 1968, Tea Meritorious award Japan Tea Ctrl. Assn., 1996. Mem. Japanese Soc. Bacteriology (councilor 1991—, chmn. bd. dirs. Kanto br. 1991-94, dir. 1997-99, 2006-08), Japanese Assn. Infectious Diseases (councilor 1994—), Japanese Assn. Germfree Life and Gnotobiology (dir. 1994-08), Japanese Soc. Catechinology (pres. 2004—). Avocations: tennis, golf, reading.

SHIMAZU, SEIICHIRO, pharmacologist, researcher; b. Asiya-shi, Hyogo-ken, Japan, Jan. 26, 1961; s. Kazuo and Toshiko Shimazu. BSc, Kagoshima U., Japan, 1983, MSc, 1985; PhD, Kyoto U., Japan, 2003. Rschr. Fujimoto Diagnostics Inc. Habikino Inst., Habikino-shi, Osaka, Japan, 1986—93; rschr., sect. mgr. Fujimoto Pharm. Corp. Rsch. Inst., Matsubara, Osaka, Japan, 1993—; rschr. Kagoshima U., 1985—86. Contbr. articles to profl. jours. Mem.: Movement Disorder Soc., Japan Bioindustry Assn., Societas Neurologica Japonica, Japanese Biochem. Soc., Japanese Pharmacol. Soc., Assn. Sci. Tech. and Managerial (licentiate; com. mem. 2003), Instn. Profl. Engrs. Japan (licentiate; assoc. profl. engr. 1993). Achievements include patents for anti-allergic substance and production; anti-allergic substance and the production; nevel ethylamine derivatives; patents pending for nevel optically active aminopropane derivatives; acetylcholinergic agent. Home: 4-11-18-208 Matsugaoka Osaka Matsubara 580-0042 Japan Office: Fujimoto Pharmaceutical Corporation 1-3-40 Nishiotsuka Osaka Matsubara 580-0011 Japan Office Fax: +81-72-332-8482. Personal E-mail: sshimazujp@yahoo.co.jp. Business E-Mail: soyaku@fujimoto-pharm.co.jp.

SHIMER, JULIE A., health products executive; m. Jary Shimer. BS in Physics, Rensselaer Polytechnic Inst., Troy, NY; MSEE, Lehigh U., Bethlehem, Pa., PhD in Elec. Engring. Exec. positions Bethlehem Steel Co., AT&T Bell Labs.; v.p. semiconductor products sector Motorola, v.p., gen. mgr. paging divsn.; gen. mgr., v.p. networking products 3Com Corp.; pres., CEO Vocera Comm., Cupertino, Calif., Welch Allyn, Inc., Skaneateles Falls, NY, 2007—. Bd. dirs. Netgear. Bd. dirs. Engring. Info. Found. Mem.: IEEE, Soc. Women Engrs., Sigma Xi. Office: Welch Allyn Inc Corp Hdqs 4341 State Street Rd Skaneateles Falls NY 13153-0220 *

SHIMIZU, ICHIRO, hematologist; b. Osaka, Japan, May 7, 1952; m. Harumi Miyamoto, Mar. 15, 1981; children: Shun, Kaori, Yu. MD, U. Ehime, 1980; PhD, U. Tokushima, 1987. Resident Hosp. Tokushima U., Japan, 1980-81; rsch. assoc. U. Tokushima, 1985-87; postdoctoral fellow U. Pa., Phila., 1989-91; from rsch. assoc. to assoc. prof. U. Tokushima, 1991—; mgr. Seirei Yokohama Hosp., 2009—; dir. Showa Clinic, 2011—. Mem. Am. Gastroenterol. Soc., Am. Assn. Study of Liver Disease, World Soc. Gastroenterology, Japan Soc. Gastroenterology. Office: Showa Clinic 1-11-11 Shin Yokohama,Kohoku-Ku Yokohama Kanagawa 222-0033 Japan Office Phone: 81 45715 3111. Business E-Mail: ichiro.shimizu@showaclinic.jp.

SHIMIZU, MAYUMI, radiologist, educator; b. Fukuoka, Japan, Apr. 22, 1962; DDS, Kyushu U., 1998, PhD, 1994. Asst. prof. Kyushu U., 1993. Vis. rsch. fellow Hamburg U., Germany, 1993—95. Mem.: Internat. Assn. Dento-Maxillo-Facial Radiology. Office: Dept Oral & Maxillofacial Radiology Maidashi 3-1-1 Higashi-ku Fukuoka-shi 812-8582 Japan Office Fax: 81-92-642-6410. Business E-Mail: shimizu@rad.dent.kyushu-u.ac.jp.

SHIMIZU, TATSUO, pediatrician, researcher; b. Osaka, Japan, Feb. 28, 1952; s. Jiro and Shizuko Shimizu; m. Noriko Moriwaki, Apr. 7, 1990; 1 child, Yuhei. MD, Osaka Med. Coll., 1976, PhD, 1983. Diplomate Japan Pediatric Soc., 1988, Japanese Circulation Soc., 1995. Resident Kanto Teishin Hosp., Tokyo, 1976—78, The Heart Inst. Japan, Tokyo Women's Med. Coll., 1978—80; rsch. fellow UCLA, 1980—82; tchg. fellow Osaka Med. Coll., Takatsuki, 1982—85; chief pediatrician Hirakata City Hosp., Hirakata, Japan, 1985—89; asst. prof. Osaka Med. Coll., Takatsuki, 1989—90; v.p. Shujinkai Hosp., Takatsuki, Japan, 1990—93; chief pediatrician Ikoma Gen. Hosp., Nara, Japan, 1993—2004, Hokusetsu Gen. Hosp., Takatsuki, Japan, 2004—. Councilor Japanese Soc. of Pediatric Cardiology and Cardiac Surgery, Tokyo, 2000—, Kinki Kawasaki Disease Soc., Osaka, 1998—. Contbr. articles to profl. jours. Fellow UCLA clin. fellow, Am. Heart Assn. Fellow: Japanese Soc. of Pediat. Cardiology and Cardiac Surgery; mem.: Japanese Circulation Soc., Japan Pediat. Soc. Avocation: music appreciation. Home: 5-8-11 Kosobe-cho Osaka Takatsuki 569-1115 Japan Office: Hokusetsu Gen Hosp 6-24 Kitayanagawa-cho Osaka Takatsuki 569-8585 Japan Office Phone: 81-72-696-2121. Office Fax: 81-72-694-2657. Business E-Mail: tatsuoshimizu-circ@umin.ac.jp.

SHIMIZU, TOSHIO, neurologist; b. Japan, Nov. 9, 1960; MD, Kanazawa U., 1985. Chief physician Tokyo Met. Neurol. Hosp., 1988—. Grant, ALS Rsch., 'Inochi-no-Aya', Japan Epilepsy Rsch. Found. Fellow: Tokyo Met. Neuromuscular Electrodiagnosis Study Group. Office: 2-6-1 Musashidai Fuchu Tokyo 183-0042 Japan Office Fax: 81-42-322-6219. Business E-Mail: toshio_shimizu@tmhp.jp.

SHIMMIN, MARGARET ANN, retired women's health nurse practioner; b. Forbes, ND, Oct. 26, 1941; d. George and Reba S. Diploma in Nursing, St. Luke's Hosp. Sch. Nursing, Fargo, ND, 1962; BSW, U. West Fla., Pensacola, 1978; cert. ob-gyn nurse practitioner, U. Ala., Birmingham, 1983, MPH, 1986. Lic. nurse, Fla., ND, Ala. Head nurse, emergency room St. Luke's Hosps., Fargo, 1962-67; charge nurse, labor and delivery, perinatal nurse educator Sacred Heart Hosp., Pensacola, Fla., 1970-82; ARNP Escambia County Pub. Health Unit, 1983-89; cmty. health nursing cons. Dist. 1 Health and Rehab. Svcs., 1989-96; sr. cmty. health nursing supr. Escambia County Health Dept., 1996—2002, nurse program specialist OSHA staff tng. and quality assurance, 2002—05, nurse program specialist diabetes intervention program, 2005—07; ret., 2007. Capt. nurse corps U.S. Army, 1967-70, Japan. Mem. NAACOG (cert. maternal-gynecol.-neonatal nursing, ob-gyn nurse practitioner), Fla. Nurses' Assn., ANA, N.W. Fla. ARNP (past sec./treas.), Fla. Perinatal Assn., Nat. Perinatal Assn., Healthy Mothers/Healthy Babies Coalition, Fla. Pub. Health Assn., U. West Fla. Alumni Assn., U. Ala. at Birmingham Sch. of Public Health Alumni Assn., Phi Alpha. Republican. Presbyterian. Avocations: cooking, music, travel, photography, reading.

SHIMODA, KATHLEEN JANE, infection control nurse; b. Des Moines, Jan. 16, 1947; d. Kikuo George and Tamae Shimoda; 1 child, Leslie Kikue. BSN, Calif. State U., LA, 1969. RN Calif. Infection control nurse VA Long Beach (Calif.) Healthcare Sys., 1973—78, infection control coord., 1979—. Clin. asst. prof. family medicine Coll. of Osteo. Medicine of the Pacific, Pomona, Calif., 1989—. Contbr. articles to profl. jours. Mem.: Assn. for Practitioners in Infection Control. Office: VA Long Beach Healthcare System 5901 East Seventh St Long Beach CA 90822 Personal E-mail: shimodacreations@cs.com. E-mail: kathleen.shimoda@med.va.gov.

SHIMOFUSA, RYOTA, radiologist; b. Tokyo, Apr. 29, 1975; MD, Akita U., 2000; PhD, Chiba U., 2005. Asst. prof. Chiba U. Hosp., 2000. Office: 1-8-1 Inohana Chuo-ku Chiba 260-8677 Japan Business E-Mail: mofu@indigo.plala.or.jp.

SHIMOKAWA, KEN-ICHI, pharmacist, educator; b. Japan, Apr. 4, 1964; PhD, Meiji Pharm. U., 1994. Assoc. prof. Meiji Pharm. U., 2010—. Office: 2-522-1 Nozawa Kiyose Tokyo 204-8588 Japan Office Fax: 81-42-495-8953. Business E-Mail: kshimoka@my-pharm.ac.jp.

SHIN, BYUNG SEOP, anesthesiologist, educator; b. Seoul, Republic of Korea, Mar. 1, 1964; MD, Sch. Medicine, Hanyang U., 1992; PhD, Chungbuk Nat. U., 2011. Clin. asst. prof. Dept. Anesthesiology and Pain Medicine, Samsung Med. Ctr., 2001—07, assoc. prof., 2011—; rsch. fellow U. Calif., San Francisco, 2006—07. Vis. scientist Stanford U., 2006—07. Mem.: Korean Soc. Molecular and Cellular Biology, Soc. Neurosci., Korean Soc. Critical Care Medicine, Korean Soc. Anesthesiology. Avocation: travel. Office: Samsung Med Ctr Dept Anesthesiology and Pain Medicine Seoul 135-710 Republic of Korea Office Phone: 82-2-3410-0358. Office Fax: 82-2-3410-6626. Business E-Mail: smcsbs@skku.edu.

SHIN, CHOL, physician, researcher; Dir. Inst. Human Genomic Study, Ansan-si, Gyeonggi-do, Republic of Korea, 2005—. Office Phone: 82-31-412-5603. Office Fax: 82-31-412-5604. Business E-Mail: shinchol@pol.net.

SHIN, CHOONGSOO S., engineering educator; b. Seoul, Republic of Korea, Aug. 11, 1972; PhD, Stanford U., 2006. Asst. prof. Sogang U., 2009—. Recipient New Investigator Recognition award, Orthopaedic Rsch. Soc., Patellofemoral Rsch. Excellence award, Internat. Soc. Arthroscopy, Knee Surgery and Orthopaedic Sports Medicine. Mem.: Korean Soc. Precision Engring., Korean Soc. Mech. Engr., Orthopaedic Rsch. Soc. Avocations: photography, astronomy. Office: 1 Shinsu-dong Sogang University Seoul 121-742 Republic of Korea Personal E-mail: scslove@gmail.com.

SHIN, DONGHYEOK, surgeon, educator; b. Seoul, Republic of Korea, Aug. 19, 1969; MD, Med. Sch. Konkuk U., 1995; PhD, Chungnam Nat. U., 2008. Fellowship Konkuk U. Med. Ctr., 2000—01, clin. instr., 2002—04, asst. prof., 2004—08, assoc. prof., 2008—. Mem. info. and communication com. Korean Soc. Plastic and Reconstructive Surgery, 2004—06, mem. legislation com., 2006—08, mem. internal affairs com., 2008—10, mem. ins. com., 2011. Mem.: Korean Soc. Microsurgery, Korean Soc. Surgery Hand, Korean Soc. Aesthetic Plastic Surgery, World Soc. Reconstructive Microsurgery. Avocation: skiing. Office: 4-12 Hwayang-dong Gwangjin-gu Seoul 143-729 Republic of Korea Office Fax: 82-2-2030-5249. Business E-Mail: sdhplastic@kuh.ac.kr.

SHIN, DONGWOO, medical educator; b. Seoul, Republic of Korea, May 2, 1973; PhD, Seoul Nat. U., 2002. Assoc. prof. Sungkyunkwan U. Sch. Medicine, 2007—. Office: 300 Chunchun-dong Suwon Gyeonggi-do 440-746 Republic of Korea Business E-Mail: shind@skku.edu.

SHIN, EAK KYUN, cardiologist, educator; b. Incheon, Republic of Korea, Apr. 3, 1949; m. Mee Lee Kim, Nov. 9, 1954; children: Hyun Jik, Hyun Jae. MD, Korea U., Seoul, 1974; PhD, Cath. U., Seoul, 1987. Korean Ministry Health, 1974. V.p. Gachon U. Medicine and Sci., Incheon, 2005—; pres. Gil Med. Ctr., Gachon Med. Sch., Incheon. Recipient Academic Achievement award, Korean Soc. Circulation, 2000. Sentinal Party. Home: # 603 Garden Ste Mok-5-Dong Yanchon-gu Seoul 158-729 Republic of Korea Office: Gil Medical Center Heart Center Kuwol-Dong Namdong-Gu # 1198 405-760 Incheon Incheon Republic of Korea Business E-Mail: ekshin@gilhospital.com.

SHIN, EUI-CHEOL, medical researcher; b. Seoul, Republic Of Korea, Aug. 29, 1971; s. Hyun-Po Shin and Young-Ja Park; m. Sue Haksoo Kim, June 7, 2003. MD, Yonsei U. Sch. Medicine, Seoul, Republic of Korea, 1996; PhD, Yonsei U., Seoul, Republic of Korea, 2001. Lic. doctor Korean Med. Assn., 1996. Chief med. scientist Armed Forces Rsch. Inst. Medicine, Daejon, Republic of Korea, 1999—2002; rsch. fellow Nat. Inst. Diabetes and Digestive and Kidney Diseases, NIH, Bethesda, Md., 2002—07; asst. prof. Grad. Sch. Med. Sci. and Engring., Korea Advanced Inst. Sci. and Tech., Daejon, Republic of Korea, 2007—. Home: 239 Winter Walk Dr Gaithersburg MD 20878 Office: GSMSE KAIST 373-1 Guseong-dong Yuseong-gu Daejeon 305-701 Republic of Korea Office Fax: 82 42 350 4240. Personal E-mail: ecshin@hotmail.com. Business E-Mail: ecshin@kaist.ac.kr.

SHIN, EUN-SEOK, cardiologist; b. Republic of Korea, Jan. 25, 1968; MD, Chung-Ang U., 1993; PhD, Andong U., 2005. Mgr. Local Cardiovasc. Com., 2011—. Avocations: snowboarding, reading, singing. Office: 290-3 Jeonha-dong Dong Ulsan 682-714 Republic of Korea Office Fax: 82-52-250-7058.

SHIN, HEE SUN, nursing educator; b. Seoul, Republic of Korea, Mar. 10, 1956; BS, Seoul Nat. U., 1979; PhD, U. Pitts., 1990. Asst. prof. Chosun U., 1991—94; prof. Dankook U., 1994—. Rsch. Environ. Health Ctr., Dankook Med. Ctr., 2008—11. Rsch. grant, Korea Rsch. Found. Mem.: Korean Nurses Assn., Korean Soc. Nursing Sci. Avocation: travel. Office: Dankook University Nursing Dept Cheonan Choongnam 330-714 Republic of Korea Office Fax: 82 41 559 7902. Business E-Mail: sw724@dankook.ac.kr.

SHIN, HEUNG MOOK, vascular pharmacologist, vascular physiologist; b. Sangju, Gyeongbuk, Republic Of Korea, Aug. 11, 1960; s. Won Jong Shin and Jong Soon Kim; m. Jeong Hee Seo, Oct. 1, 1989; children: Woo Chul, Woo Hong. PhD, Dongguk U., Seoul, 1992. Diplomate oriental medicine Ministry Health and Welfare, 1985. Dir. Dongguk U. Oriental Med. Rsch. Inst., Gyeongju, 2003—07; com. mem. Nat. Health Pers. Licensing Exam. Bd., Seoul, 2006; full prof. Dongguk U. Coll. Oriental Medicine, Gyeongju, Gyeongbuk, 1993—, dean, 2003—07. Adv. com. traditional oriental medicine industry Gyeongsangbuk-Do Province, Daegu, Republic of Korea, 2003—06. An adv. com. med. attendance Dongeuynandal, Seoul, 2001. Grants, Ministry Health and Welfare, Republic of Korea, 1998—2001, 2003—05, 2009—. Mem.: Korea Sci. & Engring. Found, Korean Soc. Oriental Physiology (dir., editor 2001—), Koreran Assn. Lab. Animal Sci. (licentiate), Korean Soc. Smooth Muscle Rsch. (licentiate), Korean Soc. Molecullar and Cell Biology (licentiate), Korean Soc. Physiology (licentiate). Achievements include patents for extracts of siegasbeckiae herba for treatment of anti-cancer, hypertension and oxidants; HMC05 as a herbal remedy to treat and prevent hypertension; HMCO5 as aherbal remedy to treat and prevent atherosclerosis. Office: Dongguk Univ Oriental Med Coll 707 Seokjangdong Gyeongbuk Gyeongju 780-714 Republic of Korea Home: 102-502 Daeduk Apt 1329-2 Bongdukdong 705-502 Namgu Daegu Republic of Korea Office Fax: 82-54-742-5441; Home Fax: 82-54-742-5441. Business E-Mail: heungmuk@dongguk.ac.kr.

SHIN, HO SIK, medical educator; b. Daegu City, Republic of Korea, Sept. 25, 1974; s. Myeong U. Shin and Tae Hwa Yang; m. Jeong Hyun Kim, Oct. 22, 2005; children: Seong Jin, Min Chan. MB, Kosin U., Busan City, Republic of Korea, 1999, MS in Medicine, 2006. Lic. physician Ministry of Health and Welfare, 1999, cert. Bd. Internal Medicine, 2004, Bd. Dialysis, Korean Soc. Nephrology, 2005, bd. cert. in nephrology Korean Soc. Internal Medicine, 2006. Physician, dept. internal medicine, Republic of Korea Army Armed Forces Yangju Hosp., Gyeonggi, 2007—09; assoc. prof. dept. internal medicine Coll. Medicine, Kosin U. Gospel Hosp., 2009—. Mem.: Korean Soc. Internal Medicine, Korean Soc. Nephrology. Office: Kosin University Gospel Hosp 34 Amnam-dong Seo-gu Busan City 602-702 Republic of Korea Office Fax: 82-51-248-5686. Personal E-mail: kidneymd@hanmail.net. Business E-Mail: danieljoseph@hanmail.net.

SHIN, HO-JOON, parasitologist, educator; b. Seoul, Republic of Korea, July 18, 1959; m. Jong-Ran Kim, Feb. 18, 1984; children: Ihn-Sohn, Sang-Min. BSc, Chung-Nam Nat. U., Republic of Korea, 1982; MSc, Yonsei U., 1985; PhD, Chung-Nam Nat. U., Republic of Korea, 1992. Rsch. asst. Sch. Medicine Hanyang U., Seoul, Republic of Korea, 1982—85; rsch. asst. Coll. Medicine Yonsei U., Seoul, 1987—90, rsch. fellow Coll. Medicine, 1990—94; post doctoral rschr. Tenn. U., Knoxville, Tenn., 1994—95; lectr. Sch. Medicine Ajou U., Suwon, Republic of Korea, 1995—97, asst. prof. Sch. Medicine, 1997—2001, assoc. prof. Sch. Medicine, 2001—. Mem.: Korean Soc. Parasitology (sec. social affairs 2003—, Academic award 2004), Am. Soc. Microbiology. Office: Dept Microbiology Ajou Univ School of Medicine Suwon 443-752 Republic of Korea Office Fax: 82 31 219 5079. Business E-Mail: hjshin@ajou.ac.kr.

SHIN, HYE SOOK, nursing educator; b. Seoul, Republic of Korea, Nov. 5, 1958; d. Jung Soo Shin and Am Nyo Kim; m. Kwon Sik Lee, Oct. 4, 1986; children: Ha Neui Lee, Woo Lam Lee. BSN, Kyung Hee U., Seoul, 1983, MSN, 1986, PhD, 1994. RN Ministry Health Welfare & Family Affairs, 1983, cert. sch. nurse, 1983; drill tchr. Ministry Edn., Sci. & Tech., 1983. Staff nurse Kyung Hee Med. Ctr., Seoul, 1983—84; tchg. asst. Dept. Nursing, Kyung Hee U., Seoul, 1987—90, lectr., 1997—99; vis. scholar U. Calif., LA, 1994—95; asst. prof. Coll. Nursing Sci., Kyung Hee U., 1999—2003, assoc. prof., 2003—08, assoc. dean, 2008—, prof., 2008—; vis. scholar Sch. Nursing, Johns Hopkins U., Baltimore, 2004—05; head East-West Nursing Rsch. Inst., Kyung Hee U., 2007—. Mgr. Korean Acad. Women's Health Nursing, Seoul, 1996—97, East-West Nursing Rsch. Inst., Kyung Hee U., Seoul, 1997—99, mgr., Tng. Course Oriental Nursing Specialists, 2000—01, reviewer, 1997—, Jour. Korean Acad. Women's Health Nursing, Seoul, 1997—, Nursing Policy Rsch. Inst. Yonsei U., Seoul, 2003, Korean Academic Soc. Nursing Edn., Seoul, 2007—, Award Nursing Scientist, Korean Soc. Nursing Sci., Seoul, 2007; commr. numerous orgns., Seoul, 2000—; dir. RN-BSN Dept. Nursing, Kyung Hee U., 2000—01; fin. dir. RN-BSN Soc., 2000—01; chmn. Kyung Hee U. Grad. Sch., Seoul, 2001—02, Grad. Sch. Edn. Kyung Hee U., 2006—07; evaluation bd. Support Project Jump Study Outstanding Women Scientist, Korea Sci. & Engring. Found., Seoul, 2002; dir. Coll. Nursing Sci., Kyung Hee U., Seoul, 2002—04; acad. chairperson Korean Acad. Women's Health Nursing, Seoul, 2006—07; acad. commr. Korean Acad. Nursing, Seoul, 2006—07; evaluation bd. mem. Selection Seoul City Face Project Investment Support, Seoul Devel. Inst., 2007—08; fin. dir. Korean Academic Soc. Nursing Edn., Seoul, 2007—. Author: (book) Guide for Problem Based Learning in Maternity; co-author: The Health Life of Modern Women, Introduction of Korean Traditional (Oriental) Nursing, Intervention for East-West Nursing, Women's Heath Nursing Care I.II, revised edit., Korean American Women Living in Two Cultures -Elderly Korean American Women Living in Two Culture; translator (co-author): Maternal & Women's Health Care I, II, (Korean version), revised edit., author, Practice and Intervention of Nursing Diagnosis(Maternity); contbr. articles to nursing jours. Recipient A Slogan award, Kyung Hee U., 1996; grantee, Office Rsch. and U.-Industry Cooperation, Kyung Hee U., 1997, Korea Rsch. Found., 1998, Office Rsch. and U.-Industry Cooperation, Kyung Hee U., 2003, 2004, 2007, 2008, Korea Rsch. Found., 2006; fellow, Grad. Sch., Kyung Hee U., 1992. Mem.: Korean Academic Soc. Nursing Edn., Korean Soc. Maternal and Child Health, Sigma Theta Tau Internat., Lambda Alpha Chpt. (fin. commr. 1999—2002), Korean Subjectivity Acad., Korean Acad. Women Health Nursing, Korean Nurses Assn., Korean Acad. Nursing, Social Meeting Women Prof. (mgr. 2003—04), Global Common Soc. EuiH wang Club (mgr. 2000—02). Presbyterian. Avocations: singing, golf, table-tennis, travel, movies. Home: 270 Hagye-dong Woosung Apt 109-806 Nowon-gu 139-940 Republic of Korea Office: Kyung Hee Univ 1 Hoegi-dong Dondaemun-gu Seoul 130-701 Republic of Korea Office Phone: 82-2-961-9143. Office Fax: 82-2-961-9398; Home Fax: 82-2-977-0001. Personal E-mail: 58suksh@hanmail.net. Business E-Mail: suksh@khu.ac.kr.

SHIN, JAE IL, pediatrician; b. Seoul, Republic of Korea, June 23, 1974; s. Soon Dug Song and Seong Seop Shin. MD, Yonsei U. Wonju Coll. Medicine, 1999. Diplomate Ministry Health and Welfare Affairs, Seoul, 1999. Intern Severance Hosp., Seoul, 1999—2000, resident, 2000—04; gen. pediatrician Yeoncheon County Hosp., Republic of Korea, 2004—07; fellow Severance Children Hosp., 2007—, pediatric nephrologist, 2007—. Contbr. numerous sci. articles to med. jours. Recipient Grad. Sch. awards, IPPP, 2007. Mem.: Korean Med. Assn. Office: Yonsei Univ Coll Medicine 250 Sungsan-Ro Seodaemun-Ku Seoul 120-752 Republic of Korea Office Fax: 8223939118. E-mail: pedshin2000@yahoo.co.kr.

SHIN, JAE-GOOK, pharmacologist, educator; b. Miryang, Republic of Korea, Nov. 25, 1962; s. Young Taek Shin; m. Pil Ock Lee; children: Seung Jin, Dong Jin. B with honors, Inje U., Busan, Republic of Korea, 1986, MD with honors, 1987; MS with honors, Seoul Nat. U., Republic of Korea, 1990, PhD with honors, 1992. Lic. Ministry of Health and Welfare, 1983. Internship Seoul Paik Hosp., Seoul, Republic of Korea, 1986—87; asst. Inje U., Busan, 1987—90, rsch. fellow. dept. of pharmacology, 1990—91, lectr., 1990—92, prof., 2005—, asst. prof. Busan Paik Hosp., 1996—97, dir. Clin. Pharmacology Ctr., 2001—04, dir. Pharmacogenomics Rsch. Ctr., 2003—, dep. dir. Busan Paik Hosp., 2004, vice dean rsch. affair, 2005—; mem., dir. instl. rev. bd. Busan Paik Hosp., 1996—2005; clin. pharmacology fellow, divsn. of clin. Georgetown U. Med. Ctr., Wash., 1997—99; guest prof. Ctrl. South U., Changsha, China, 2003—; dir. Bio-Marker Rsch. Ctr. Personalized Therapy, 2007—; dir. clin. trial ctr. Busan Paik Hosp., 2008—. Mem. pharmacy and therapeutics com. Busan Paik Hosp., 2001—06; guest prof. Ctrl. S. U., Changsha, China, 2003—; com. mem. local coun. Clin. Trial Ctr., Busan, 2005—; com. mem. Korea Ctrs. Disease Control and Prevention, Seoul, 2005—. Mem. editl. bd. Pharmacogenetics and Genomics Jour., 2007—, The Open Drug Metabolism, —, Korean Jour. Clin. Pharmacology Therapeutics, —, Personalzed Medicine, 2004—. Mem. bioequivalence study subcom. Ctrl. Pharm. Affair Coun. Korean Food and Drug Adminstrn., 2001—, mem. bridging study subcom., 2001—; mem. profl. e-mail club Korean Food and Drug Adminstrn., 2002—03; mem. Busna Bio Forum, 2002—03; mem. sci. adv. com. dept. pharm. rsch. Nat. Inst. Toxicological Rsch., 2003—05; mem. Supreme Prosecutor's Office, Busan, 2004—06, Busan Support Network, 2005—; columnist sci. issues Busan Daily News, 2006—07; mem. sci. adv. com. Daegu Hanny U., 2006—; mem. BioIndustry Assn. Busan, 2006—; mem. adv. com. Busan Techno Park, 2007—. Lt. Republic of Korea Navy, 1992—95. Recipient 12th Outstanding Rsch. award in Sci. and Tech., Korean Fedn. Sci. and Tech. Socs., 2002, 1st Disting Scholar award, Inje U., 2005; fellow, Georgetown U. Med. Ctr., 1997—99; Merck Foun. Internat. fellow, 1997. Mem.: Korean Pharms. & Society Forum, Korean Soc. Pharmacoepidemiology and Risk Mgmt., Korean Soc. Gender Specific Medicine (com. mem. 2005—), Korean Soc. Psychopharmacology, Korean Soc. Cellular and Molecular Biology, Korean Soc. Toxicology, Korean Soc. Med. Biochemistry and Molecular Biology, Pharmacogenomics Study Group, Korean Assn. Instl. Rev. Bds., Internat. Soc. Pharmacogenomics, Drug Info. Assn., Korean Med. Assn., Korean Soc. Pharmacology (dir. sci. com. 2007—), Korean Soc. Clin. Pharmacology and Therapeutics, Korean Soc. Med. Edn., Am. Soc. Clin. Pharmacology and Therapeutics, Internat. Soc. Study Xenobiotics, Korea Genome Orgn. Democrat. Roman Catholic. Achievements include patents for Genetic marker for decreased activity of cytochrome P450 2J2 protein; patents pending for Method for detection of genetic variants of thiopurine methyltransferase gene; Method for detection of genetic variants of human organic cation transporter gene; htSNP for determining a genotype of cytochrome P450 2D6 gene and uses thereof revice to genotyping chip using thereof; patents for Genetic marker for decreased activity of cytochrome P450 3A7 protein; Cocktail incubation liquid and high-throughput screening system for evaluation of major human cytochrome P450 enzyme activities and drug-drug interactions; patents pending for Single nucleotide polymorphic of UDP-glucuronosyltransferase 1A4 and use thereof; patents for Method for analysis of mutant genotype of human cytochrome P450 2B6 gene; Method of analysis of genetic variants of hyman cytochrome P450 2D6 gene; Method for detection of genetic variants of breast cancer resistance protein gene; Single nucleotide polymorphism of HNF-4a gene and use thereof; Inje cocktail kit for high-throughput evaluation of human cytochrome P450 enzyme. Office: Inje U Coll Medicine 633-165 Gaegum2 Dong Busanjingu 614-735 Busan Busan Republic of Korea Office Fax: 82-51-893-1232. Business E-Mail: phshinjg@inje.ac.kr.

SHIN, JUNG HO, emergency physician; b. Seoul, Republic of Korea, Nov. 29, 1969; s. Cheol Jae Shin and Mae Ja Jung; m. Kyeong Soon Kim, Nov. 20, 2005. B, Korea U., 1997, M, 2003. Lic. MD Korea Med. Assn., 1997, Emergency Physician Korea Assn. of Emergency Physician, 2002. Fellowship Seoul Nat. U. Hosp., 2002—03; instr. Seoul Nat. U. Bundang Hosp., 2003—05, asst. prof., 2005—. Contbr. book. Mem.: Am. Coll. of Emergency Physician (assoc.). Achievements include research in optimal depth of central venous catheter in Korean, using 3 demensional computed tomography. Office: Seoul Nat Univ Bundang Hosplt Gumi-Dong Bundang-Gu 300 462-707 Seongnam Gyeonggi-do Republic of Korea Office Fax: 82-31-787-4055. E-mail: shinjho@gmail.com.

SHIN, JUNG-HO, gynecologist, educator; s. Chong Hoon and Kwang Ja Shin; m. Nam Yon Jong, Oct. 21, 2000; children: Shin Ji-Won, Shin Hye-Won. MS, Korea U., Grad. Sch., Seoul, 2000, MD, 2006. Clin. lectr. Korea U. Med. Ctr., Guro-gu, Seoul, 2006—08, assoc. prof., 2008—. Sec. gen. East Asian Union Human Genetics Socs. Mem.: Korean Soc. Gynecologic Endocrinology. Office: Korea Univ Med Ctr Gurogongil 97 Guro-gu Seoul 152703 Republic of Korea Office Fax: 822 838 1560. Business E-Mail: shinjh@korea.ac.kr.

SHIN, JUNGPIL, computer scientist, educator; b. Busan, Republic of Korea, Sept. 3, 1967; s. Chulje Shin and Junghee Kack; m. Sunghee Hong; children: Juung, Borin. PhD, Kyushu U., 1994—99. Assoc. prof. U. of Aizu, Japan, 2004—, asst. prof., 1999—2003. Achievements include research in character recognition, pattern recognition, image processing, and computer vision; pen-based interacting system, real-time system, oriental character processing, mobile computing, computer education, human recognition, and Machine intelligence. Office: Univ of Aizu Tsuruga Ikki-machi Fukushima Aizu-Wakamatsu 965-8580 Japan Office Fax: +81-242-37-2731. Business E-Mail: jpshin@u-aizu.ac.jp.

SHIN, KENJI, pediatrician, educator; b. Kumamoto, Japan, Aug. 11, 1956; MD, Tsukuba U., 1983, PhD, 1990. Clin. rschr. Veiden Mcpl. Gen. Hosp., 1986; lectr. Hahnemann U., 1990—92; assoc. prof. Ibaraki Prefectural U., 2008—. Mem.: Japanese Soc. Child Neurology, Japan Pediat. Soc. Office: Ami 4733 Inashiki-gun Ami Ibaraki 300-0331 Japan Office Fax: 0298-88-9277. Business E-Mail: sin@ami.ipu.ac.jp.

SHIN, SANG YOUNG, endodontist; s. Chung Ho Shin and Soon Hun Chung; m. Jiyoun Chung, June 17, 1995; children: Brian, Alexander S. BS, U. Utah, Salt Lake City, 1995; DMD, Nova Southeastern U. Sch. Dental Medicine, Davie, Fla., 2001, degree in Advanced Edn. Gen. Dentistry, 2002. Cert. endodontics Temple U. Sch. Dental Medicine, 2004, Am. Bd. Endodontics, 2009. Endodontist Endodontic Assocs. Palm Beaches P.A., West Palm Beach, Fla., 2003—. Co-chmn. Atlantic Coast Dental Rsch. Clinic, Lake Worth, Fla., 2006—. Contbr. articles to jours. Deacon Korean Presbyn. Ch. Palm Beach, West palm Beach, 2008—10. Mem.: ADA, Coll. Diplomates Am. Bd. Endodontics, Atlantic Coast Dental Rsch. Clinic, Ctrl. Palm Beach County Dental Assn., Fla. Dental Assn., Am. Assn. Endodontists, Omicron Kappa Upsilon. Achievements include research in revascularization; bacteriocin production by strains of enterococcus faecalis.

SHIN, SANG-JIN, medical educator; b. Seoul, Republic of Korea, June 22, 1968; MD, Yonsei U., 1993, PhD, 2005. Assoc. prof. Ewha Womans U., 2003—. Home: Seocho-Ku Seocho-Dong Woosung Apt Seoul 137-070 Republic of Korea Personal E-mail: sjshin622@ewha.ac.kr.

SHIN, SUE, physician; b. Seoul, Aug. 24, 1970; MD, Seoul Nat. U. Coll. Medicine, 1994, PhD, 2004. Resident Dept Lab. Medicine, Seoul Nat. U. Boramae Hosp., 1996—99, clin. prof., 2000—02, dir., 2003—10; med. dir. Seoul Met. Govt. Pub. Cord Blood Bank, 2006; asst. prof. dept lab. medicine Seoul Nat. U. Coll. Medicine, 2007—, asst. dean academic affairs, 2009—10, assoc. prof. dept lab. medicine, 2011—. Bd. specialist Instl. Rev. Bd. Boramae Hosp., 2007—10. Recipient Academic Rsch. award, Korean Med. Women's Assn., Korean Soc. Blood Transfusion, Best Academic award, Korean Assn. Quality Assurance Clin. Lab.; Sci. fellowship, Takeda Sci. Found., Japan. Mem.: European Com. Clin. Microbiology and Infectious Disease, Korean Soc. Lab. Medicine (referee lab. qualification com. 2001), Internat. Soc. Stem Cell Rsch., Am. Assn. Blood Bank. Office: Lab Medicine Boramae Hosp Seoul 156-707 Republic of Korea E-mail: jeannie@snu.ac.kr, sshinmd@gmail.com.

SHIN, SUJIN, nursing educator; b. Seoul, Republic of Korea, Nov. 19, 1973; PhD, Ewha Womans U., 2006. Staff nurse Asan Med. Ctr., Seoul, 1996—2000; rschr. Ewha Womans U., 2000—03, part time lectr., 2003—06, postdoc. rsch. fellow, Coll. Nursing Sci., 2006—07; asst. prof. Soon Chun Hyang U., 2007—. Recipient Award of Pres., Korean Nurses Assn. Mem.: Korean Gerontol. Nurses Assn. (bd. mem., chair publ. com. 2011—), Sigma Theta Tau Internat. Honor Soc. Nursing, Korean Soc. Adult Nursing (bd. mem., chair edn. com. 2010—11), Korean Soc. Nursing Sci. Office: 31 Soonchunhyang 6th Rd Dongnam-gu Cheonan Chungnam 330-100 Republic of Korea Office Fax: 82-41-574-3860. Business E-Mail: ssj1119@sch.ac.kr.

SHIN, SUNG JAE, microbiologist, educator; b. Republic of Korea, May 5, 1975; PhD, Seoul Nat. U., 2004. Rsch. assoc. Dept. Population Medicine and Diagnostic Scis., Coll. Vet. Medicine, Cornell U., 2001—02; postdoc. fellow PathoBiol. Scis., U. Wis., Madison, 2004—07; asst. prof. Dept. Microbiology, Coll. Medicine, Chungnam Nat. U., 2007—. Mem., bd. evaluation and cons. Korea Ctrs. Disease Control and Prevention, 2007—, Nat. Vet. Rsch. & Quarantine Svc., 2007—, Korea Health Industry Devel. Inst., 2008—. Recipient Young Scientist award, 10th Korea-Japan Internat. Symposium Microbiology, Korea Inst. Medicine, 2011. Mem.: Korean Soc. Microbiology (mem., bd. academic and ethic cons. 2008—), Am. Soc. Microbiology. Avocations: soccer, Judo, Tae Kwon Do. Office: 6 Munwha-dong Jung-ku Daejeon Chungnam 301-747 Republic of Korea Office Phone: 82-42-580-8246. Office Fax: 82-42-585-3686. Business E-Mail: sjshin@cnu.ac.kr.

SHIN, SUNG-HEUI, medical educator; b. Gwangju, Republic of Korea, Apr. 16, 1966; s. Jong-Soo Shin and Tae-Ja Kim; m. Hae Jung Lee; children: Seung-Hyun, Ji-Hae. PhD, Choonam Nat. U., Republic of Korea, 1998. Contbr. articles to profl. med. jours. Mem.: Korean Soc. Microbiology, Am. Soc. Microbiology. Achievements include research in relationship between Iron and Vibrio vulnificus septicemia. Office: Chosun Univ Medical Sch Seosuk-Dong Dong-Gu 375 501-759 Gwangju Republic of Korea Office Fax: 82-62-233-6052; Home Fax: 82-62-513-7589. Business E-Mail: shsin@chosun.ac.kr.

SHIN, TAE YONG, pharmacist, educator, researcher; b. Milyang, Gyungnam, Republic of Korea, Mar. 3, 1955; s. Deuk Eui Shin, Sam Suk Kim; m. On Suk Kim, Nov. 25, 1984; children: Jae Sun, Jae Keun. PhD in Pharmacy, Wonkwang U., Iksan, Jeombuk, 1987. Lic. pharmacist. Prof. Coll. Pharmacy Woosuk U., 1989—, chief health ctr., 1991—96, chief natural sci. rsch., 1994—95, chief Inst. Drug Rsch., 1995—97, dean Coll. Pharmacy, 1998—2000, v.p. acad. info., 2002—. Mem. com. Ctrl. Pharm. Affairs Coun. Korea Food and Drug Adminstrn., Seoul, 1999—; dir. Jeombuk chpt. Korea Anti-Drug Campaign Ctr., Jeonju, 2000—. Editor: Oriental Pharmacy and Experimental Medicine, 2001—; contbr. numerous articles to profl. jours. Mem.: Jeonbuk Pharm. Assn. (vice-chmn. 1994—95). Office: Woosuk Univ Coll Pharm Hujeong Ri 490 565-701 Wonju Republic of Korea Home Phone: 063-226-0268. Office Fax: 82-63-290-1567. E-mail: tyshin@mail.woosuk.ac.kr.

SHIN, WON-HAN, medical educator; b. Hamyang, Gyeongsangnam-Do, Republic of Korea, Mar. 15, 1949; m. Myung-Hee Lee; children: Sun-Woo, Bong-Gon. MD, Pusan Nat. U., Republic of Korea, 1977; PhD, Soonchunhyang U., Seoul, 1991. Prof. Soonchunhyang U. Bucheon Hosp., Gyeonggi-Do, Republic of Korea, 1996—, dir., 2004—. Mem.: Assn. Am. Neurosurgeon (corr.), Internat. Lions Club. Citizens. Roman Catholic. Avocations: travel, golf. Office: Soonchunhyang U Hosp 1174 Jung-Dong Wonmi-Ku Bucheon 420767 Republic of Korea Office Fax: 82-32-621-5107. Personal E-mail: shinwh@schbc.ac.kr.

SHIN, YONG BEOM, research scientist; b. Seoul, Republic of Korea, Dec. 29, 1967; PhD, POSTECH, 1999. Prin. rsch. scientist Korea Rsch. Inst. Biosci. and Biotech., 2003. Office: Gwahak-ro 125 Yuseong-gu Daejeon 205-806 Republic of Korea Business E-Mail: ybshin@kribb.re.kr.

SHIN, YONG SAM, neurosurgeon, educator; b. Pusan, Republic of Korea, Apr. 15, 1964; s. Jeong Soon Um; m. Mina Kang, Jan. 4, 1965; children: In Hye, In Young. MD, Yonsei U., Seoul, Republic of Korea, 1988. Assoc. prof. Ajou U., Suwon, Kyung-Gi, Republic of Korea, 2001—. Neurosurgery cons. Am. Gen. Hosp., Seoul, 1993—2005. Capt. Republic of Korea Army, 1993—95. Decorated Army Commendation medal. Mem.: World Fedn. of Interventional Neuroradiology, Congress of Neurol. Surgery, Am. Assn. Neurol. Surgery. Office Fax: 82-31-219-5238. Business E-Mail: nsshin@ajou.ac.kr.

SHIN, YOUNG-HEE, education educator; b. Kyungsang Namdo, Republic of Korea, Aug. 21, 1955; PhD, Busan Nat. U., Republic of Korea, 1988. Prof. Kyungsung U., Busan, 1989—. Office: Coll Pharmacy Kyungsung Univ Daeyeon-Dong Nam-Gu 608-736 Busan Busan Republic of Korea Office Fax: 82-51-663-4804. Business E-Mail: yhshin@ks.ac.kr.

SHIN, YOUNGSOO, international organization official; b. Seoul, South Korea, Oct. 15, 1943; MD magna cum laude, Seoul Nat. U., 1969, MPH summa cum laude, 1971; DPH in Health Policy and Mgmt., Yale U., New Haven, 1977. Prof. dept. health policy & mgmt. Coll. Medicine, Seoul Nat. U., 1978—2009; mem. exec. bd. WHO, Geneva, 1995—98, dir. Western Pacific regional office, 2009—. Pres. Korea Inst. Health Svcs. Mgmt., Ministry Health & Welfare, 1992—99, chmn. Nat. Commn. Hosp. Svc. Evaluation Program, 1994—97; pres. Korea Nat. Health Ins. Rev. & Assessment Svc., 2002—03. Mem.: Korean Soc. Med. Informatics (v.p. 1994—98), Korean Soc. Health Policy & Adminstrn. (pres. 1996—98), Korean Soc. Preventive Medicine (pres. 2005—06), Korean Soc. Quality Assurance in Health Care (pres. 2006—08). Mailing: WHO Regional Office Western Pacific PO Box 2932 1000 Manila Philippines *

SHINDO, KATSUHISA, surgeon; b. Osaka, Japan, Nov. 2, 1939; s. Tomoo and Setsue (Danyasu) Shindo; m. Takako Inoue, June 15, 1968; children: Masahisa, Tokuhisa. MD, Tokyo Med. and Dental U., 1966; PhD, Osaka U., 1974. Intern U.S. Naval Hosp., Yokosuka, Japan, 1966-67; resident in surgery Osaka U. Hosp., 1967-69, Temple U. Hosp., Phila., 1969-71; rsch. fellow Osaka U. Sch. Medicine, 1971-75, asst. in surgery, 1976-84; asst. pathology Heidelberg U., Germany, 1975-76; vice adminstr. Kawachi Gen. Hosp., Higashi-Osaka, 1984-86; assoc. prof. Kinki U. Sch. Medicine, Osaka-Sayama, Japan, 1987-94, prof. surgery, 1994—2010, chief dept. surgery, 1999—2003, head Health Affairs Ctr., 2003—10, hon. prof., 2010—. Judge Exam. Bd. Social Ins. Med. Fee Payment Fund, Osaka, 1991—; chief judge Exam. Bd. Health Ins. Claims Review & Reimbursement Svc., 1999—; med. auditor Health Ins. Claims Rev. & Reimbursement Svc., Tokyo, 2010—; del. Japan ISO TC173/SC3, Stockholm, 1991—; convenor ISO TC173/SC3/WG4&5, Tokyo, 1996—; cons. indsl. hygiene, 1993—. Author: Stoma Rehabilitation, 1974, How to be Free from Piles, 1994, Informed Consent Manual, 1995, Terminology of Stoma-Rehabilitation Science, 1997, Clinical Skills and Practical Materials for Informed Consent, 1999, The Science of Stoma Rehabilitation, 2007, Extend a Passionate Hand to Stoma, 2010; editor-in-chief: STOMA, 1982—, Asian Ostomy, 2002—. Recipient 1st award, Internat. Acad. Proctology, 1972, Hon. award, 1975; grantee Osaka Anticancer Assn. Rsch. grantee, 1980. Mem.: Japan Cytometry Soc. (councillor 2001—05), Asian Soc. Stoma Rehab. (founder 1999, dir. gen. 2002—), Asian Fedn. Colo-proctology (founder 1975, spl. mem. 2008—), Japan Surg. Assn. (councillor 1998—), Japanese Soc. Surg. Pathology (councillor 1996—2005), Japanese Soc. Abdominal Emergency Surgery (councillor 1995—2005, spl. mem. 2005—), Japanese Soc. Hepato, Biliary and Pancreatic Surgery (councillor 1995—2006), Japan Soc. Clin. Oncology (councillor 1995—2005), Japanese Soc. Genetics Aspects Human Malignancy (gov. 1986—2004), Japanese Coll. Surgeons (councillor 1995—2006, spl. mem. 2006—), Japanese Soc. Gastroent. Surgery (councillor 1989—2005, spl. mem. 2005—), Japan Soc. Colo-Proctology (v.p. 1991—92, dir. 2001—08, spl. mem. 2008—), Internat. Soc. Univ. Colon and Rectal Surgeons (continental sec. 1978—98, continental v.p. 1998—2000, congress convenor 2000—02, v.p. 2004—06, sec. of treasury 2010—), Japanese Soc. Cancer Colon Rectum (hon.; sec. gen. 1992—2000), Japanese Soc. Stoma Rehab. (hon.; bd. dirs. 1984—2005, pres. 1998). Achievements include research in new histochemical examination of phosphoamidase and its application to the digestive epithelium; diagnostic pattern of DNA-content in the borderline neoplasm of the large intestine. Avocation: computers. Home: 13-4 Ohnodai 7-chome Osaka Sayama 589-0023 Japan Office: Health Insurance Claims Review & Reimbursement Services 2-12 Tsuruno-cho Osaka 530-8327 Japan

SHINE, JOHN, molecular geneticist, researcher, biochemist; b. Brisbane, Australia, July 3, 1946; arrived in US, 1984; s. Patrick and Molly Gertrude (Hoare) Shine; m. Kathleen Mary Morgan, Feb. 15, 1969; children: Rebecca Kathleen, Michael Patrick. BS with honors, Australian Nat. U., 1972, PhD, 1975; DSc (hon.), U. New South Wales, 2006. Rsch. fellow molecular biology unit Australian Nat. U., Canberra, 1978—80, fellow dept. genetics, 1980—83, sr. fellow, 1983—84, founder Ctr. Recombinant DNA Rsch., 1982; v.p. rsch. & devel. Calif. Biotech., Inc., Mountain View, 1984—86, pres., chief sci. officer, 1986—87; prof. molecular biology U. New South Wales, 1987—, prof. medicine; dep. dir. Garvan Inst. Med. Rsch., Australia, 1987—90, exec. dir., 1990—2011. Bd. dirs. Biotech. Rsch. Ptnrs., Mountain View, 1984—87, Calif. Biotech., Inc., 1986—90; adj. prof. medicine U. Calif., San Francisco, 1985—87; chmn. bd. dirs. Pacific Biotech. Ltd., 1987—90; chmn. Australian Nat. Health & Med. Rsch. Coun., 2003—06. Editor: Molecular Biology & Medicine, DNA; contbr. articles to profl. jour. Decorated Officer, Gen. Divsn. Order Australia, 1996; recipient Boehringer-Mannheim medal, Australian Biochem. Soc., 1980, Centenary medal, 2001. Fellow: Royal Coll. Pathologists Australasia, Australian Acad. Sci. (Gottschalk medal 1982). Achievements include first to clone a human hormone gene; demonstrate that hormone genes cloned in bacteria could be expressed in a biologically active form; patents in field. Office: University NSW Faculty Medicine Sydney 2052 Australia *

SHINE, KENNETH IRWIN, academic administrator, cardiologist, educator; b. Worcester, Mass., 1935; Grad., Harvard Coll., 1957; MD, Harvard U., 1961. Diplomate Am. Bd. Internal Medicine. Intern Mass. Gen. Hosp., Boston, 1961—62, resident, 1962—63, 1965—66, fellow in cardiology, 1966—67; surgeon USPHS, 1963—65; instr. Harvard Med. Sch., 1968—; asst. prof. medicine UCLA Sch. Medicine, 1971—73, assoc. prof., 1973—77, prof., 1977—92, prof. emeritus, 1993—, dir. CCU, 1971—75, chief div. cardiology, 1975—79, vice chmn. dept. medicine, 1979—81, exec. chmn., 1981—86, dean, 1986—92, provost for med. scis., 1991—92; clin. prof. medicine Georgetown U. Med. Ctr., Washington, 1993; pres. Inst. of Medicine, Washington, 1992—2002; dir. RAND Center for Domestic and International Health Security, 2003; exec. vice chancellor for health affairs U. Tex. Sys., 2003—, interim chancellor, 2008—09. Master: Am. Coll. Physicians; fellow: Am. Coll. Cardiology; mem.: Inst. Medicine, Assn. Am. Med. Colls. (adminstrv. bd. coun. deans 1989—92, exec. bd. 1990—92, chmn. coun. deans 1991—92), Am. Heart Assn. (pres. 1986—87). Office: U Texas Sys O Henry Hall Room 204 601 Colorado St Austin TX 78701 Office Phone: 512-499-4224. E-mail: kshine@utsystem.edu.

SHINER, ROBERT JOSEPH, physician, researcher; b. London, Feb. 10, 1950; s. Margot and Alex Shiner; m. Claudie Lagnado, Aug. 8, 1971; children: Lisa Sara, Tamar. Cert. specialist, pulmonary diseases Am. Bd. Internal Medicine, 1984, specialist, respiratory medicine Royal Coll. Physicians and Surgeons Can., 1984. Resident, dept. internal medicine Chaim Sheba Med. Ctr., Tel Hashomer Hosp., Tel Aviv U., 1977—79, 1984—85, staff specialist, dept. respiratory medicine, 1986—87, head, Inst. Clin. Respiratory Physiology, 1989—2001; resident, fellow, dept. respiratory diseases McGill U. Respiratory Diseases Tng. Program, Montreal, Canada, 1980—83; vis. cons., respiratory medicine Royal Brompton Hosp. - Asthma Rsch. Coun. UK, London, 1988—89; hon. sr. lectr., cons. Nat. Heart and Lung Inst., London, 1997—. Contbr. rsch. articles to med. jours. Fellow, Royal Coll. Physicians and Surgeons Can., 1982, Royal Coll. Physicians London, 2006, Am. Coll. Chest Physicians, 2008. Mem.: Brit. Thoracic Soc., European Respiratory Soc. (Israel nat. rep. 1991—95), Am. Thoracic Soc. Achievements include research in the role of methotrexate in steroid dependent asthma, severe asthma, physiology and pathophysiology of COPD. Office: Respiratory Med Hammersmith Hosp Du Cane Rd London W12 ONN England Office Fax: 44-208-383-3260. Business E-Mail: r.shiner@imperial.ac.uk.

SHINICHI, UENO, surgeon, educator; b. Kagoshima, Dec. 29, 1958; MD, Kagoshima U., 1982, PhD. Prof. Dept. Surg. Oncology, 1984—. Mem.: Japan Surg. Soc. Office: Sakuragaoka 8-35-1 Kagoshima 890-8520 Japan E-mail: ueno1@m.kufm.kagoshima-u.ac.jp.

SHINN, SUNG HO, cardiovascular surgeon; b. Seoul, Republic of Korea, Mar. 24, 1970; s. Kyung Sub Shinn and Soon Ja Chung; m. Hee Yong Ahn, Aug. 23, 1999; children: Yae Rim, Hong Gyun. PhD, Coll. Medicine, Hanyang U., Seoul, 2006. Diplomate Korean Med. Assn., 1996, cert. specialist Korean Soc. Thoracic and Cardiovasc. Surgery, 2001, Korean Soc. Critical Care Medicine, 2009. Clin. fellow Asan Med. Ctr., Seoul, 2004—06, Sejong Gen. Hosp., Bucheon, Gyeonggi-Do, Republic of Korea, 2006—07; clin. assoc. prof. Hanyang U. Guri Hosp., Gyeonggi-Do, 2007—. Mem.: Korean Soc. Critical Care Medicine, Korean Soc. Thoracic and Cardiovasc. Surgery. Avocations: sports, travel. Office: Hanyang University Guri Hosp Gyomun-Dong 249-1 471-710 Guri Gyeonggi-do Republic of Korea

SHINNAR, SHLOMO, pediatric neurologist, educator; b. Haifa, Israel, Nov. 11, 1950; s. Reuel and Miryam (Halpern) S.; m. Shoshana Ellen Cohen, Aug. 11, 1974; children: Ora Rivka, Aviva Batya, Avraham Ever. BA in Physics summa cum laude, Columbia Coll., 1971; PhD, Albert Einstein Coll. Medicine, 1977, MD, 1978. Diplomate Am. Bd. Pediat., Am. Bd. Psychiatry and Neurology, Am. Bd. Child Neurology and Clin. Neurophysiology. Intern, asst. resident in pediatrics, fellow Johns Hopkins Hosp., Balt., 1978-80, asst. resident, resident in neurology, fellow, 1980-83; from asst. prof. to prof. neurology and pediat. Albert Einstein Coll. Medicine, Bronx, 1983—; from asst. attending to attending neurology and pediat. Montefiore Med. Ctr., Bronx Mcpl. & North Ctrl. Bronx Hosps., 1983—; prof. neurology and pediat. Montefiore Med. Ctr., Bronx, Hyman Climenko prof. neurosci. rsch., 2002—. Co-dir. Epilepsy Mgmt. Ctr. Montefiore Med. Ctr. Albert Einstein Coll. Medicine, Bronx, 1983-86, dir., 1986—; mem. adv. bd. Epilepsy Inst., N.Y.C., 1984—, chair 1996—, instnl. rev. bd. protection of human subjects Montefiore Med. Ctr., Bronx, 1985—, vice-chmn., 1989—, prof. of neuroscience rsch., 2002—; adj. sch. scientist Gertrude Sergievsky Ctr. Columbia Coll. Physicians and Surgeons, N.Y.C., 1985—, Sergievsky Scholar, 1986—; cons. in field. Field editor Epilepsy Advances, 1987-93; editl. bd. The Neurologist, 1993—, Epilepsia, 1994-2000, Pediatric Neurology, 1996—; contbr. articles to profl. jours. NY State Regents scholar, 1967-71; Martin and Emily L. Fisher fellow, 1991— Fellow Am. Acad. Pediats., Am. Acad. Neurology; mem. Am. Epilepsy Soc. (chmn. childhood onset epilepsy com. 1993-95, councillor 1992-95, Rsch. Recognition award 1989), Epilepsy Found. America, Child Neurology Soc., Eastern EEG Soc., Internat. Child Neurology Soc., Nat. Assn. Epilepsy Ctrs., Soc. Pediat. Rsch., Am. Neurol. Assn., Epilepsy Inst. Office: Montefiore Med Ctr 111 E 210th St Bronx NY 10467 Business E-Mail: sshinnar@montefiore.org.

SHINNAR, SHOLOMO, neurologist, pediatrician, educator; Attended, Albert Einstein Coll. of Medicine, 1978. Diplomate Am. Bd. of Psychiatry and Neurology, Am. Bd. of Pediatrics. Resident pediat. Johns Hopkins Hosp., 1979—80, resident neurology, 1980—83; fellow Am. Acad. of Neurology, Am. Acad. of Pediat.; prof. neurology & pediat. Montefiore Med. Ctr., Albert Einstein Coll. of Medicine, Bronx, NY. Editor: (book) Childhood Seizures; co-editor: Febrile Seizures. Recipient Rsch. Recognition award, Am. Epilepsy Soc. Mem.: Epilepsy Inst., Epilepsy Found. of So. NY, Epilepsy Found. of America, Am. Epilepsy Soc., Soc. for Pediat. Rsch., Am. Neurol. Assn. Office: Montefiore Medical Center Henry & Lucy Moses Division 111 East 210th St Bronx NY 10467 Office Phone: 718-920-4321.

SHINOHARA, YUKITO, neurologist, director; b. Tokyo, May 17, 1938; MD, Keio U. Sch. Med., PhD, 1963. Prof. Tokai U. Sch. Medicine, 1976—2005; dir. Fedn. Nat. Pub. Svc. Pers. Mut. Aid Assns. Tachikawa Hosp., 2006—. Mem.: Am Neurol. Assn., Am Heart Assn., World Fedn. Neurology, Asia Pacific Stroke Orgn., World Stroke Orgn. Avocations: tennis, golf. Office: 4-2-22 Nishiki-cho Tachikawa Tokyo 190-8531 Japan Business E-Mail: yshinoha@tachikawa-hosp.gr.jp.

SHINOZAKI, TAMOTSU, retired physician, anesthesiologist; b. Dairen, Japan, Mar. 18, 1934; s. Yuichi and Shizue Shinozaki; m. Kazuko Sakanaka Shinozaki, Feb. 14, 1940; children: Aritomo, Yuji, Emiko. MD, Okayama U., 1958, D in Med. Scis., 1963. Diplomate Am. Bd. Anesthesiology; cert. spl. qualifications in critical care medicine. Intern St. Luke's Internat. Hosp., Tokyo, 1958—59; resident in anesthesiology Mary Fletcher Hosp., 1964—67; attending anesthesiologist Med. Ctr. Hosp. of Vt., Burlington, 1967—99; asst. prof. Med. Sch. U. Vt., Burlington, 1967—72, assoc. prof., 1972—90, clin. prof., 1990—99, med. co-dir. surg. ICU, 1985—99, prof. emeritus, 2000—; adminstrv. dir. surg. ICU Fletcher Allen Healthcare, Burlington, 1997—99, attending emeritus, 2000—. Cons. med. divsn. Hewlett Packard Co., Waltham, Mass., 1972-77, Intelligent Med. Sys., Carlsbad, Calif., 1987. Recipient Quality Cup award, Excellance in the Quality Movement, 1994. Fellow Am. Coll. Critical Care Medicine; mem. Sigma Xi. Home: 335 Dorset Hts South Burlington VT 05403 Business E-Mail: tshinoza@uvm.edu.

SHINTAKU, HARUO, medical educator, researcher; b. Osaka, Japan, Oct. 30, 1952; s. Keiji and Sumiko Shintaku; m. Tsuneko

Tsuga, July 10, 1956; children: Masayuki, Kanako. Med. diplomate, Osaka City U. Med. Sch., 1978; PhD, Osaka City U. Grad. Sch. Medicine, 1982. Diplomate Ministry of Health, Labour and Welfare, 1982, cert. pediat. specialist Japan Pediatric Soc., 2002, attending physician Japanese Soc. Human Genetics, 2002. Instr. Osaka City U. Grad. Sch. Medicine, 1988—94, asst. prof., 1994—99, lectr., 1999—2010, assoc. prof., 2010—. Dir. Osaka Pediat. Assn. Contbr. articles to profl. jours. Adviser Meeting of Parents of Children with PKU, Osaka, 2000—, Meeting of Parents of Children with MPS, Osaka, 2000—. Grantee, Ministry Health, Labor and Welfare, 2006—, Environ. Restoration Conservation Agy. Japan, 2007—, Ministry Edn., Culture, Sports, Sci. and Tech., Japan, 2008—. Achievements include patents for preventives or remedies for drug-induced renal disturbance. Home: 1-24-17 Kitabatake Abeno-ku Osaka 545-0035 Japan Office: Osaka City Univ Grad Sch 1-4-3 Asahimachi Abeno-ku Osaka 545-8585 Japan Office Fax: +81-6-6636-8737; Home Fax: +81-6-6626-2516. Personal E-mail: biopterin@mac.com. Business E-Mail: shintakuh@med.osaka-cu.ac.jp.

SHINTANI, YASUSHI, molecular and cellular biologist, researcher; b. Yokohama, Japan, May 18, 1958; s. Isao and Miyoko Shintani; m. Kiyoko Mizuno, Mar. 19, 1989; 2 children. BS, Kobe U., 1982; SM, Kyoto U., 1984, PhD, 1993. Rschr. Takeda Chem. Industries, Ltd., Osaka, Japan, 1984—89, 1992—98, assoc. rsch. head, 1994—96, rsch. head, 1997—2010, assoc. dir., 2010—; rsch. assoc. Harvard Med. Sch., Boston, 1990—91. Author: G-Protein-Coupled Receptor, Anti_Cancer Drugs, Cytokines, Cerebral Ischemia Metabolism; contbr. scientific papers to sci. jours. Mem.: Japanese Assn. Animal Cell Tech., Japanese Biochemical Soc., Am. Soc. Biochemistry, Molecular Biology. Achievements include patents in field; invention of serum-free cell culture, G-protein Coupled Receptor, Cytokines. Avocations: travel, mountain climbing. Home: 1-33-5-401 Midorigaoka Toyonaka 560 0002 Japan Office: Takeda Pharm Co Ltd Yodogawa ku 17-85 Jusohonmachi 2 Chome Osaka 532 8686 Japan Home Phone: 06-6853-1567; Office Phone: 06-6300-6142. Business E-Mail: Shintani_Yasushi@takeda.co.jp.

SHIOKAWA, KOICHIRO, biologist, educator, academic administrator; b. Fukuoka, Kurate-gun, Japan, Jan. 31, 1941; s. Mitsuo and Teruko Shiokawa; m. Chizuyo Ariyoshi, Apr. 29, 1965; children: Aya, Ken, Yoko, Kayo. BSc, Kyushu U., Fukuoka, 1963, MSc, 1965, DSc, 1967. Postdoctoral fellow Kyushu U., Fukuoka, 1968—69, asst. prof. faculty sci. dept. biology, 1974—81, assoc. prof. faculty sci. dept. biology, 1981—89; rschr. Takeda Pharm. Industries Ltd., Osaka, Japan, 1969—72; vis. scientist N.Y. Blood Ctr. Cell Biology Lab., NYC, 1972—74; full prof. faculty sci. U. Tokyo, 1989 2001, prof. emeritus, 2001—; lectr. Daiichi Pharm. U., Fukuoka, 2001—02, Daiichi Welfare U., Fukuoka, 2002—; prof. Teikyo U., 2003—, chair, dept. judo therapy, faculty med. tech., 2008—. Violinist Kyushu U. Philharmonic Orch., 2001; vis. prof. Ctrl. U. for Nationalities, Beijing, 2003—. Author: (book) Molecular Biology of an African Clawed Toad, 1985, (textbook) Molecular Embryology, 1990, University Fundamental Biology, 2002. Recipient prize, Japanese Zool. Soc., 1981. Mem.: Japanese Soc. Molecular Biologists, Japanese Soc. Cell Biologists, Japanese Soc. Develop. Biology, Japanes Zoological Soc. Achievements include discovery of activiation of RNA transcription during cleavage stage and execution in SAMDC-expressed protein synthesis-inhibited embryos in early embryonic development of an African clawed toad. Avocation: violin. Home: Fukumaru 213 Wakamiya-cho Fukuoka 822-0101 Japan Office: Cell Biology Dept Biosciences Sch Sci Engring Tiekyo Utsunomiya 320 8551 Japan Office Phone: 81-28-627-7145. Business E-Mail: shiokawa@nasa.bio.teikyo-u.ac.jp.

SHIOTA, KOHEI, anatomist, embryologist, educator; b. Ueno, Mie, Japan, Sept. 1, 1946; s. Kiyoshi and Fumiko Shiota; m. Mitsuko Maeda, May 19, 1974; children: Hirokatsu, Hirotaka. MD, Kyoto U., Japan, 1971, PhD, 1976. Lectr. anatomy Kyoto U. Faculty Medicine, 1979, assoc. prof. teratology, 1981—90, prof., chmn. dept. anatomy and devel. biology, 1990—2009, dir. Congenital Anomalies Rsch. Ctr., 1992—2008; v.p. Kyoto U., 2001—04; assoc. dean Kyoto U. Grad. Sch. Medicine, 2005—07, dean, 2007—08; assoc. mem. Sci. Coun. Japan, 2006—; exec. v.p. Kyoto U., 2008—. Vis. scientist U. Wash., Seattle, 1980-82; vis. prof. Free U., Berlin, 1988, 89; mem. Adv. Com. Japanese Ministry of Health & Welfare, Tokyo, 1985-2000; hon. vis. fellow U. Leicester, Eng., 1993. Co-author (with H. Nishimura and other): Atlas of Human Prenatal Histology, 1983; co-author: (with K.L. Moore and T.V. N. Persaud) Color Atlas of Clinical Embryology, 2000; editor: Jour. Congenital Anomalies, 1990—, Jour. Reproductive Toxicology, 1995—99, Jour. Birth Defects Rsch., 2003—, Jour. Anatomy, 2006—10. Fellow World Acad. Perinatal Medicine (assoc.); mem. Japanese Teratology Soc. (pres. 1996-97, chmn. bd. dirs. 2004—), Japanese Assn. Anatomists (bd. dirs. 1997-98, 2005-09), Internat. Fedn. Teratology Socs. (coun. 1995-2006), US Teratology Soc., Sci. Council Japan. Home: 45-1 Kamihonmachi Shichiku Kita-Ku Kyoto 603-8116 Japan Fax: 81-753-5546. Business E-Mail: shiota@hq.kyoto-u.ac.jp.

SHIOTANI, SEIJI, diagnostic radiologist; b. Kyoto, Dec. 22, 1965; s. Kiyoshi and Aichiyo Shiotani; m. Kuniko Oka, Sept. 8, 1991; 1 child, Nobuaki. MD, Shimane Med. U., Izumo, Japan, 1991. Intern Shimane Med. U., 1991—93; resident Kanagawa Cancer Ctr., Yokohama, Japan, 1993—96; fellow Shimane Med. U., 1996—99; chief Tsukuba Med. Ctr., Japan, 1999—2011. Contbr. articles to various profl. jours. Mem.: Japanese Assn. Acute Medicine, Japanese Coll. Radiology, Japan Soc. Legal Medicine, Japan Radiol. Soc. Achievements include research in Postmortem Computed Tomography (PMCT); Establishment of Radiol. Thanatology, contributions to establish PMCT findings in Cardiopulmonary arrest on arrival patients and to evaluate the usefulness at PMCT of detection of the cause of death. Office: Tsukuba Med Ctr Hosp 1-3-1 Amakubo Tsukuba 305-8558 Japan Business E-Mail: shiotani@tmch.or.jp.

SHI-PING, LUH, thoracic surgeon, educator, medical researcher, health facility administrator; b. Taipei, Taiwan, Jan. 14, 1964; s. Shu-Ka Luh; married. PhD, Nat. Taiwan U. Inst. Clin. Medicine, Taipei, 2000. Cert. prof. Nat. Chung-Cheng U., 2008. Surgeon, prof., Nat. Chung-Cheng U. Chia-Yi Christian Hosp., Taiwan, 2007—08, chief thoracic surgery, Clin. Rsch. and Faculty Devel. Ctr., 2007—, vice supr. & chief thoracic surgery. Edtl. bd. mem. J. Zhechiang U. Sci., 2006—. Fellow: Am. Congress Chest Physicians. Home and Office: Chia-Yi Christian Hosp 539 Chung-Shiao Rd Chia-Yi 600 Taiwan Personal E-mail: luh572001@yahoo.com.tw.

SHIPKO, JANET M., human resources specialist; b. Schenectady, NY, Nov. 3, 1953; d. Frederick J. and Elizabeth Shipko. MSc in Health Care Mgmt., U. Md., 1996. Asst. chief of staff, res. affairs Tripler Army Med. Ctr., Honolulu, 2003—06; chief res. policy Office of Surgeon Gen., Falls Church, Va., 2006—07; program dir. res. affairs Office of Sec. of Def., 2007—08; chief of staff 807th MDSC, Salt Lake City, 2008—. Col. USAR, 1982. Decorated Meritorious Svc. medal US Army, Army Commendation medal, Army Superior Unit award, Armed Forces Res. medal, Army Achievement medal, Nat. Def. Svc. medal, Global War on Terrorism medal, Def. Meritorious Svc. medal. Office Phone: 801-656-4073, 703-474-6646. Business E-Mail: janet.m.shipko@us.army.mil.

SHIRAISHI, HIROHIKO, pediatrician, educator; b. Kawasaki, Kanagawa, Japan, June 14, 1954; s. Mitsuo and Sumako Shiraishi; m. Yukie Shiraishi; children: Hiroko, Tomohiko, Yuri. MD, Japan, 1980; PhD, Jichi Med. U., Tochigi, 1986. Assoc. prof. Jichi Med. U., Shimotsuke, Japan, 2000—04, prof. subdir. pediat., 2004—. Achievements include first to developing occluder for patent ductus arteriosus made from nitnol. Office: Jichi Med Univ Yakushiji 3311-1 Shimotsuke Tochigi 329-0498 Japan Office Fax: 81-285-44-6123. Business E-Mail: shiraish@jichi.ac.jp.

SHIRAKASHI, SANSHIRO, psychologist; b. Tokyo, Sept. 21, 1936; s. Shigeo and Takako Shirakashi; m. Masu Baba, Jan. 3, 1938; children: Ayumi, Yutaka. BA, Kyushu U., 1960, MA, 1962, PhD, 1972. Asst. prof. Seinan Gakuin U., Fukuoka, Japan, 1966—68, assoc. prof., 1968—73, prof., 1973—85, Naruto U. Edn., Naruto, Japan, 1985—90, Osaka U., Japan, 1990—99, prof. emeritus, 1999—2009; prof. dept. humanities Koshien U., Takarazuka, Hyogo, Japan, 1999—2009; vis. prof., dept. human scis. Osaka U. Economics, 2009—. Author: Psychology of Leadership, 1985, Leadership and Human Relations, 1992; editor: Introduction to Social Psychology, 1997, Introduction to Industrial Organizational Psychology, 2009. Mem.: Japanese Assn. Orgnl. Sci. (standing dir. 1997—99), Japanese Assn. Indsl. Orgnl. Psychology (standing dir. 1994—2004). Personal E-mail: sanshiro@zag.zag.jp.

SHIRAKI, KEIZO, physiology researcher; b. Shiga, Japan, July 17, 1936; s. Kenji and Fuji Shiraki; m. Yasuko Shiraki, Nov. 21, 1936; 1 child, Midori. MD, Kyoto Prefectural U. of Medicine, Japan, 1961, PhD, 1967. Sr. instr. Kyoto Prefectural U. of Medicine, 1967-68; asst. prof. U. Alaska, Fairbanks, 1968-69; assoc. prof. U. Tokushima Sch. Medicine, Japan, 1970-78; prof. U. Occupational and Environ. Health, Kitakyushu, Japan, 1978—2002, prof. emeritus, 2002—, chmn. dept. physiology, dean postgrad. affairs, 1999—2002. Mem. Am. Physiol. Soc., Am. Coll. Sports Medicine, Undersea Biomed. Soc., N.Y. Acad. Sci. Avocation: fishing.

SHIRWAIKAR, ANNIE, medical educator; arrived in India, 1973; d. Kuruvilla Thomas and Annamma Kuruvilla; m. Arun Shirwaikar, Apr. 28, 1986; children: Anusha, Anil. B in pharm., Dept. of Pharm. Sciences, 1979—81; M in pharm., Ph.D, Coll. of Pharm. Sciences, 1990 95. Lectr. K.M. Coll. of Pharmacy, Madurai, Tamilnadu, India, 1982—83, Coll. of Pharm. Sciences, Manipal, India, 1983—85, asst. prof., 1985—87, reader, 1987—2000, assoc. prof., 2000—01, prof. and head of the dept. of pharmacognosy, 2001—. Examiner for ug, pg and ph.d Various Universities, India, 1983—; chmn. bd. studies Manipal Acad. Higher Edn., India, 2001—; cons. Various Ayurveda Colleges, India, 2001 ; fellow of acad. gen. edn. Manipal Acad. of Higher Edn., 1983—; mem. Bd. of Studies, Mangalore U., India, 1993—96; mem. editl. bd., Druglines Coll. of Pharmacy. SRIMPS, Coimbatore, India, 1998—. Mem. editl. bd.: Phcog mag.; contbr. articles to profl. jours. Warden MAHE Hostel, Manipal, India, 1996—2003; mem. Hostel Adv. com., Manipal Acad. of Higher Edn., India, 1996—2003. Recipient Outstanding Alumni award, Manipal Acad. Higher Edn., 2001; grantee, 2002, All India Coun. Tech. Edn., India, 2003, Manipal Acad. Higher Edn., 2002; fellow, Lee Found., Singapore, 1980, Manipal Found., 2002—, Nat. Soc. Ethropharm., Inc.; scholar, Govt. of India, 1975—79. Fellow: Nat. Soc. Ethnopharmacology (hon.); mem.: Indian Pharm. Assn. (hon.; pres. Manipal 2003), Assn. Pharm. Teachers of India (life). Syrian Christian. Achievements include patents for herbal composition for improving anticancer activity, anti-inflammatory activity and protecting body from oxidative damage and method of preparing the same. Avocations: singing, reading, bible study, cooking, music. Office: Coll Pharm Scis Mahe Campus 576 104 Manipal India Office Phone: 91-0820-2922430. Office Fax: 0820-2571998, 2578062. E-mail: annieshirwaikar@yahoo.com.

SHIRYAJEV, YURI N., surgeon, educator; b. Voronezh region, Russia, Aug. 11, 1971; s. Nikolay A. Shiryajev and Zinaida A. Shiryajeva. MD, State Med. U., St. Petersburg, Russia, 1996. Cert. surgeon Pediat. Med. Acad., 1998. Asst. lectr. State Pediat. Med. Acad., St. Petersburg, 1999—. Surgeon Mariinsky Hosp., St. Petersburg, 1997—. Contbr. scientific papers. Achievements include research in palliative esophageal resections. Office: State Pediatric Med Acad ul Litovskaya 2 194100 Saint Petersburg Russia Office Fax: 7(812)275-73-26. Personal E-mail: shiryajev@yandex.ru.

SHITTU, GAFFAR M., pediatrician, consultant; b. Kano, Nigeria, June 24, 1948; s. Shittu Colony Aliyu and Gama Fagge Yarliiman; m. Gabriella Hulicsko, May 6, 1972; children: Gaffar Jr., Kamilu, Ismail. MD, Med. U. Debrecen, Hungary, 1976; degree, Inst. Pediat., Miskolc, Hungary, 1982. Med. dir., cons. pediat. Classic Clinics Ltd., Kano, Nigeria, 1984—. Mem. Guild Med. Dirs. (nat. soc. sec. 1992-96, nat. treas., state chmn. 1996—02), Nigerian Med. Assn. (vice chmn. 1999-2000, state chmn. HIV/AIDS com. 2001-02), Hungarian Coll. Pediat., Rotary (dir. cmty. svc. 1996-2000, v.p. 1999-2000, pres.-elect 2000-01). Muslim. Avocations: football, tennis, swimming, ping pong/table tennis. Home: 1a Abbas Rd Arakan Ave PO Box 244 Kano Nigeria Office: Classic Clinics Ltd Abbas Rd/Arakan Ave PO Box 9098 Kano Nigeria Fax: 064-648282.

SHIVAM, KUMAR, engineering educator; b. Delhi, India, Mar. 16, 1983; MSc, DDU Gorakhpur U., 2004, PhD, 2009. Asst. prof. IMS Engring. Coll., Ghaziabad, 2009—. Mem.: Process Biochemistry Reviewers Com. Office: IMS Engineering Coll NH 24 Adhyatmi Ghaziabad Uttar Pradesh 201009 India Personal E-mail: k.shivam@rediffmail.com.

SHJIN, YIN, science educator; b. Hubei, China, Sept. 20, 1974; PhD, Wuhan U., 2009. Assoc. prof. Southern Ctrl. U. Nationalities, 2009—. Office: Hongshan Dist Mingyuan Rd 708# Wuhan Hubei 430074 China Business E-Mail: yinshijinyf@163.com.

SHKLAR, GERALD, pathologist, periodontist, educator; b. Montreal, Que., Can., Dec. 2, 1924; came to U.S., 1950, naturalized, 1955; s. Louis and Ann (Schleifstein) S.; m. Judith Nisse, June 16, 1948 (dec. Sept. 18, 1992); children: David, Michael, Ruth; m. Se-Kyung Oh, July 13, 1997. BS, McGill U., 1947, DDS, 1949; MS, Tufts U., 1952; MA (hon.), Harvard U., 1971; D (hon.), U. Athens. Diplomate Am. Bd. Oral Pathology, Am. Bd. Periodontology. Asst. prof. oral pathology Sch. Dental Medicine Tufts U., Boston, 1953—59, assoc. prof. Sch. Dental Medicine, 1960—61, prof. oral pathology, rsch. prof. peridontology Sch. Dental Medicine, 1961—71, lectr. oral pathology Sch. Dental Medicine, 1971—. Head dept. oral medicine and oral pathology Sch. Dental Medicine Harvard U., Boston, 1971-93, Charles A. Brackett prof. oral pathology, 1971-2000, Charles A. Brackett prof. oral pathology emeritus, 2000—; sr. clin. investigator Forsyth Inst., Boston, 1994—2000; cons. oral pathology Children's Hosp. Med. Ctr., Brigham and Women's Hosp., Mass. Gen. Hosp. Author: Oral Cancer, 1984; co-author (with Edmund Cataldo and Henry Goldman): Oral Pathology: An Atlas of Microscopic Pathology, 1975; co-author: (with Philip L. McCarthy) The Oral Manifestations of Systemic Disease, 1976, Diseases of the Oral Mucosa, 2d edit., 1982; co-author: (with David Chernin) Libellus De Dentibus, 1563, of Bartholomaei Eustachii, 1999, A Sourcebook of Dental Medicine, 2002; co-author: (with Fermin Carranza) History of Periodontology, 2003; contbr. over 350 articles to profl. jours., chapters to books. Fellow AAAS, Am. Acad. Dental Sci., Am. Acad. Oral Medicine, Am. Acad. Oral Pathology, Am. Coll. Dentists, Internat. Coll. Dentists; mem. ADA, Internat. Assn. Dental Rsch., Am. Acad. Periodontology, Am. Cancer Soc., Am. Assn. Cancer Rsch., Am. Assn. Cancer Edn., Am. Acad. History Dentistry, History of Sci. Soc., Sigma Xi, Omicron Kappa Upsilon. Avocations: harpsichord, flute. Home: 154 Evelyn Rd Waban MA 02468-1042 Home Phone: 617-332-6452.

SHKOLNIK, EVGENY, physician, educator; b. Moscow, June 5, 1979; MD, Moscow State U. Medicine & Dentistry, 2002, PhD, 2006. Asst. prof. functional methods internal medicine dept. Moscow State U. Medicine & Dentistry, 2007—. Mem.: ESC. Office: Delegatskaya 20/1 Moscow 107473 Russia Office Fax: 74992692498. Business E-Mail: eshkolnik@mail.ru.

SHLANKSY-GOLDBERG, RICHARD, intervention radiologist, educator; MD, U. Rochester. Diplomate Am. Bd. Radiology-radiology, Am. Bd. Radiology-interventional radiology. Resident Thomas Jefferson Univ. Hosp., fellow Hosp. of the Univ. of NJ, Pa.; hosp. affiliation include Hosp. of the Univ. of Pa., assoc. prof. Named one of the Best Doctors in America, 2005—10, the Top Doctors, Phila. Mag., 2004 05, 2008, 2011. Fellow: Soc. of Interventional Radiology. Office: Hospital of the University of Pennsylvania 1 Silverstein 3400 Spruce St Philadelphia PA 19104 Office Phone: 800-789-7366.

SHLOFMITZ, RICHARD ALAN, cardiologist; b. NYC, Jan. 22, 1955; MD, NYU Sch. Medicine, 1980. Cert. Internal Medicine, 1984, Cardiovascular Disease, 1987, Interventional Cardiology. Intern, medicine North Shore U. Hosp., Manhasset, NY, 1980—81, resident, cardiology, 1981—84; fellow Columbia Presbyn. Med. Ctr., NYC, 1984—87; with St. Francis Hosp., Roslyn, NY, 1987—, dir., cardiac catheterization lab and interventional cardiology, attending physician. Prin. investigator in numerous percutaneous interventional trials St. Francis Hosp., Roslyn, NY. Office: 100 Port Washington Blvd Roslyn NY 11576 Office Phone: 516-390-9640. Office Fax: 516-390-9650.

SHLYAKHTIN, OLEG ALEKSANDROVICH, materials scientist, researcher; b. Tula, Russia, Dec. 29, 1958; s. Alexander G. Shlyakhtin and Julia I. Shlyakhtina; m. Anna V. Voronkova, Sept. 17, 1983; children: Roman, Alexandra. MSc in Chemistry, Moscow State U., 1981, PhD in Chemistry, 1985. Rsch. scientist Dept. Chemistry Moscow State U., 1984—88, sr. rsch. scientist Dept. Chemistry, 1988—2002; sr. rsch. scientist Inst. Chem. Physics Russian Acad. Scis., Moscow, 2002—09; prin. res. scientist, dept. chemistry Moscow State U., 2009—. Vis. rsch. scientist Korea Inst. Sci. and Tech., Seoul, Republic of Korea, 2001—08. Contbr. articles to profl. jours. Fellow, Ministry Sci. and Tech., Republic of Korea, 1998, 1999, 2001, 2002, 2004; fellowship, Ministry Sci. & Tech., Russian Fedn., 2000. Avocations: travel, hiking. Office: Moscow State Univ Divsn Inorganic Chemistry Dept Chemistry/ Moscow 119991 Russia Personal E-mail: olegshl@mail.ru. Business E-Mail: oleg@kist.re.kr, oleg@inorg.chem.msu.ru.

SHLYAKHTO, EVGENY VLADIMIROVICH, medical association administrator; b. Russia, June 29, 1954; PhD, Pavlov Med. U., St. Petersburg, Russia, 1983, DMS, 1991. Dir. Fed. Almazov Heart Blood Endocrinology Ctr., St. Petersburg, 2001—. Mem. editl. bd. Jhypertension.com; vice editor-in-chief Pavlov State Med. U. Sci., editor-in-chief; head chair internal medicine Pavlov Med. State U. St. Petersburg, 1997. Contbr. articles to profl. med. jours. Mem.: Russian Soc. Cardiologists (v.p.), Russian Soc. Internal Medicine, Am. Heart Assn., Am. Coll. Cardiology, Internat. Soc. Hypertension. Achievements include research in arterial hypertension, metabolic cardiovascular syndrome, chronic heart failure, molecular cardiology, clinical pharmacology. Office: Federal Almazov Heart Blood Endocrinology Ctr Akkuratova Str 2 Saint Petersburg 197341 Russia Office Fax: 7 812 7023701. Business E-Mail: shlyakhto@inbox.ru.

SHOCHAT, STEPHEN JAY, pediatrician, surgeon; b. Balt., Dec. 17, 1938; s. Albert J. and Rose (Blechman) S.; m. Sheila Floam, July 1960 (div. July 1979); children: Francine Lynne, Alisa Joy; m. Carla Ann Centi, Jan. 26, 1980; children: David Robert, Sarah Elizabeth. BS, Randolph Mason Coll., 1959; MD, Med. Coll. Va., 1963. Surg.

resident Washington U. Med. Ctr., St. Louis, 1963-68; pediatric surg. resident Boston Children's Hosp., 1968-70; thoracic surg. resident Queen Elizabeth Hosp., Birmingham, Eng., 1970, George Washington Hosp., Washington, 1972; chief pediatric surgery Hershey (Pa.) Med. Ctr., 1973-77, Stanford (Calif.) Med. Ctr., 1977-94; sr. surgeon Children's Hosp. Phila., 1994-96; surgeon-in-chief, chmn. dept. surgery St. Jude Children Rsch. Hosp., Memphis, 1996—2009, mem. dept. surgery, 2009—; prof. pediats. and surgery U. Tenn., Memphis, 1996—. Lt. col. USAF, 1970-72. Office: St Jude Children Rsch Hosp Dept Surgery Memphis TN 38105 Office Phone: 901-595-2911. Business E-Mail: stephen.shochat@stjude.org.

SHOCKLEY, CAROL FRANCES, psychologist, psychotherapist; b. Atlanta, Nov. 24, 1948; d. Robert Thomas and Frances Lavada (Scrivner) Shockley. BA, Ga. State U., Atlanta, 1974, MEd, 1976; PhD, U. Ga., Athens, 1990. Cert. in gerontology, diplomate Am. Bd. Forensic Examiners. Counselor Rape Crisis Ctr., Atlanta, 1979-80; emergency mental health clinician Gwinnett Med. Ctr., Lawrenceville, Ga., 1980-86; psychotherapist Fla. Mental Health Inst., Tampa, 1987-89, Tampa Bay Acad., Riverview, Fla., 1990-91; sr. psychologist State of Fla. Dept. of Corrections, Bushnell, 1991-92; pvt. practice psychologist Brunswick, Ga., 1992—2000, Griffin, Ga., 2002—. Mem. adv. bd. Mental Health/Mental Retardation, 1992—94. Author (with others): (book) Relapse Prevention with Sex Offenders, 1989. Vol. Ga. Mental Health Inst., Atlanta, 1972; leader Alzheimer's Disease Support Group, Athens, Ga., 1984; vol. therapist Reminiscence Group Elderly, Athens, 1984—85. Recipient Meritorious Svc. award, Beta Gamma Sigma, 1975. Mem.: APA, Ga. Psychol. Assn., Psi Chi, Sigma Phi Omega. Avocations: astronomy, archaeology, music, travel. Office: 315 W Solomon St Ste 210 Griffin GA 30223

SHOEMAKER, RITCHIE C., medical association administrator; b. Charlotte, NC, June 13, 1951; BS, Duke U., 1973; MD, Duke Med. Sch., 1977. Med. dir. Ctr. Rsch. Biotoxin Associated Illnesses, 2001—. Pvt. practice, 1980—. Office: 500 Market St Suite 102 Pocomoke City MD 21851 Business E-Mail: ritchieshoemaker@msn.com.

SHOEMAKER, WILLIAM JOSEPH, neuroscientist; b. Boston, Sept. 20, 1941; s. William McCune and Clementine Shoemaker; life ptnr. Teena Gravel; children: Monica Yvette Anschel-Geraghty, Benjamin John. BA in Zoology, U. Mass., Amherst, 1964; PhD in Biochemistry and Metabolism, MIT, Cambridge, 1971. Assoc. sect. chief NIMH, Bethesda-Washington, 1972—76; sr. scientist The Salk Inst., La Jolla, Calif., 1976—84; prof. U. Conn. Health Ctr., Farmington, 1985—. Cons. rsch. programs at numerous instns. Contbr. articles to numerous profl. jours., chapters to books. Mem. leadership group Unitarian Soc. Hartford, Conn., 1987. Unitarian. Achievements include life master rating one-star by American Cribbage Congress. Avocations: bicycling, cribbage. Home: 175 Thistle Pond Dr Bloomfield CT 06002 Office: Univ Conn Health Ctr 263 Farmington Ave Farmington CT 06030-1410 Personal E-mail: wshoemaker17@comcast.net.

SHOENLEBEN, ROBBIE JOE, mental health services professional; b. Greenville, Ohio, May 31, 1964; s. Eldon and Shirley Shoenleben; m. DeeAnne Lackey, Nov. 23, 1990; 1 child, Ian Tristan. BS in Edn., Wright State U., Dayton, Ohio, 1985, M in Art Therapy, 1987. Lic. profl. counselor S.C., 2003. Art therapist Marshall I. Pickens Hosp., Greenville, SC, 1989—95, social worker I, 1995—97, lead clin. therapist, 1997—2000, clin. therapy coord., 2000—01, mgr., clin. assessment, 2001—. Adj. prof. Converse Coll., Spartanburg, SC, 1993—96. Mem.: Am. Mental Health Counselors Assn. Home: 109 Bracken Ct Liberty SC 29657 Office: Marshall I Pickens Hosp 701 Grove Rd Greenville SC 29605 Personal E-mail: shoenleben@earthlink.net. E-mail: rshoenleben@ghs.org.

SHOGO, ISHIUCHI, neurosurgeon, educator; b. Ashikaga, Tochigi, Japan, Jan. 9, 1959; married. MD, Gunma U. Sch. Medicine, Maebashi, Japan, PhD, 1985. Cert. specialist Japan Neurosurg. Soc., 1992. Assoc. prof. Gunma U. Hosp., 2002—, physician, med. treatment, 2008—09; prof., chmn. dept. neurosurgery faculty medicine U. Ryukyu, 2009—. Recipient Hoshino Brain Tumor prize, Japan Brain Tumor Soc., 2003. Mem.: Soc. Neurosci. Achievements include patents for remedy for brain cancer. Office: University Ryukyu 207 Uehara Nishihara-ch Okimawa 903-0215 Japan Office Phone: 81-98-895-1171. Office Fax: 81-98-895-1425. Business E-Mail: ishogo@showa.gunma-u.ac.jp.

SHOHAT, BATYA, cellular immunologist; b. Iasi, Romania, May 2, 1934; arrived in Israel, 1950; d. Leopold and Sofi (Ghingold) Bercovici; m. Isaac Shohat, Sept. 18, 1956; children: Ronit, Michael. MSc, Tel Aviv U., 1958; PhD, Hebrew U., Jerusalem, Israel, 1965. Head exptl. cancer pharmacol. unit Beilinson Med. Ctr., Petah Tiqva, Israel, 1967-70, mem. chemotherapy sect., 1970-87; head cellular immunology unit Clin. lab. Hematological Inst., Petah Tiqva, 1987-94. Internat. Union Against Cancer fellow Meml. Sloan-Kettering Cancer Inst., 1980; Israel Cancer Rsch. Fund grantee, 1986-88; WHO grantee, 1987-89. Mem. N.Y. Acad. Scis., Am. Soc. for the Immunoloy of Reprodn., Israel Hematol. Assn., Israel Immunol. Soc. Achievements include research in human T Lymphotropic virus. Home: 15A Nordau St Ramat Gan Israel Office: Beilinson Med Ctr Cellular Immunology Unit Petah Tiqwa 49100 Israel E-mail: bishohat@bezeqint.net.

SHOHEN, SAUNDRA ANNE, health facility administrator, public relations executive; b. Washington, Aug. 22, 1934; d. Aaron Kohn and Malvina (Kleiman) Kohn Blinder; children: Susan, Brian. BS, Columbia Pacific U., 1979, MS in Health Svcs. Adminstrn., 1981. Adminstr. social work dept. Roosevelt Hosp., NYC, 1978-79; adminstr. emergency dept. St. Luke's-Roosevelt Hosp. Ctr., NYC, 1979-83, assoc. dir. pub. rels., 1983-87; pres. Saundra Shohen Assocs., Ltd., NYC, 1987-92; v.p. Prism Internat., NYC, 1988-91; bd. dirs. Tureck Bach Inst., NYC, 1985—. Panelist ann. Emmy awards NATAS, N.Y.C., 1983, 84; tchr. healthcare mktg. Baruch Coll., N.Y.C., 1994. Author: Health Scripts for Radio, 1983, Voice of America, 1983 (Presdl. Recognition award, 1984); author: (with others) AIDS: A Health Care Management Response, 1987; author: EMERGENCY!, 1989. Mem. NATAS, Internat. Hosp. Fedn., Am. Soc. Hosp. Mktg. and Pub. Rels., Vols. in Tech. Assistance. Democrat. Jewish. Home: 240 Central Park S Apt #13N New York NY 10019-1413

SHOHET, MICHAEL ROBERT, plastic surgeon, educator; b. Cin., Nov. 24, 1967; BS, U. Cin., 1990, MD, 1994. Assoc. clin. prof. Mt. Sinai Sch. Medicine, 2001—. Pres. NY Facial Plastic Surgery Soc., 2008—. Fellow: ACS; mem.: Am. Acad. Otolaryngology, Head & Neck Surgery, North Am. Skull Base Soc., Am. Bd. Facial Plastic & Reconstructive Surgery. Office: 620 Columbus Ave 2nd Fl New York NY 10024 Office Fax: 917-441-6829. Business E-Mail: michael.shohet@mssm.edu.

SHOKAT, KEVAN, pharmacology professor; b. 1964; BA in Chemistry, Reed Coll., Portland Oreg., 1986; PhD in Chemistry, U. Calif., Berkeley, 1991. Asst. prof. chemistry and molecular biology Princeton U., NJ, 1994—98, assoc. prof., 1998—99; assoc. prof. cellular and molecular pharmacology U. Calif., San Francisco, 1999—2001, prof., 2001—, vice chair dept. cellular and molecular pharmacology, 2004—10, chair, 2010—; assoc. prof. chemistry U. Calif., Berkeley, 1999—2002, prof., 2002—. Investigator Howard Hughes Medical Inst., 2005—. Assoc. editor Molecular & Cellular Proteomics, 2001—, Chemistry & Biology, 2002—, mem.internat. editl. adv. bd. Organic & Biomolecular Chemistry, 2003—; contbr. articles to profl. pubs. Recipient NSF Early Career Devel. award, 1995—97, Young Investigator award, Protein Soc., 2001, Eli Lilly award, American Chem. Soc., 2002, Outstanding Mentor award, U. Calif. San Francisco, 2006; Regents fellow, U. Calif. Berkeley, 1986—87, Postdoc. fellow, Life Scis. Rsch. Found., 1992—94, Pew scholar in biomedical scis., 1996—2000, Glaxo-Wellcome scholar in organic chemistry, 1997—98, Searle scholar, 1997—2000, Cottrel scholar, 1997—2000. Mem.: NAS, Soc. Biomolecular Scis., Inst. Medicine, Phi Beta Kappa. Achievements include research in using the tools of synthetic organic chemistry, structural biology, genetics and mathematical modeling to gain insight into how signaling networks transmit information in normal and disease settings; development of chemical methods to decipher the role of individual kinases and their cellular signaling networks. Office: Univ California 600 16th St MC 2280 San Francisco CA 94143 E-mail: shokat@cmp.ucsf.edu. *

SHOMAKER, SAM (THOMAS SAMUEL SHOMAKER), dean, anesthesiologist, former lawyer; b. Vincennes, Ind. m. Suzanne Yandow; 3 children. Grad. summa cum laude, St. Louis U., 1976; JD, Georgetown U., Washington, 1979; MD, U. Hawai'i John A. Burns Sch. Medicine, 1986. Legis. intern to John. C. Danforth US Senate, legis. asst. to Daniel K. Inouye; intern in surgery U. Hawaii; residency in anestesiology U. Utah, U. Fla.; prof. anestesiology, residency program dir. anestesiology, assoc. dean curriculum & minority affairs, sr. assoc. dean academic affairs U. Utah Coll. Medicine, interim dean, 1998—99; vice dean acad. affairs, COO, v.p. faculty group practice Univ. Clin., Edn. and Rsch. Associates U. Hawaii John A. Burns Sch. Medicine, 2000—06, acting dean, 2005—06; prof. anestesiology U. Tex. Med. Br., 2006—10, dean Austin Programs, 2006—09; Jean and Thomas McMullin dean medicine, v.p. clin. affairs Tex. A&M U. Health Sci. Ctr., 2010—. Lt. USNR. Mem.: Assn. American Med. Colleges. Avocations: Karate, Kung Fu, Ju Jitsu, running, youth soccer coach. Office: Tex A&M Health Sci Ctr Office of Dean 3rd Fl Health Professions Edn Bldg 8447 Hwy 47 Bryan TX 77807 Office Phone: 979-436-0200. Business E-Mail: shomaker@medicine.tamhsc.edu. *

SHOME, GOUTAM, immunologist, educator; b. Bangladesh, Sept. 17, 1961; MD, Dhaka Med. Coll., 1984; PhD, U. Tsukuba, Japan, 1992. Attending allergist, immunologist Covenant Health Sys., 2007—. Adj. assoc. prof. Tex. Tech. U., 2007—. Fellow: Am. Coll. Physician, Am. Acad. Allergy, Asthma, & Immunology. Home: 9812 Slide Rd Lubbock TX 79424 Home Fax: 806-783-9059.

SHON, WON YONG, orthopedist, surgeon, educator; b. GyeongJoo, Gyeongsangbuk-Do, May 29, 1953; s. Yoon Soo Shon and Boo Ok Yoo; m. Kae Jeoung Kang, Aug. 31, 1988; children: Soo Min, Woo Jeoung. MB, Korea U., Seoul, 1978, M of Medicine, 1981, PhD of Medicine, 1987. Registered orthopedic surgeon Republic of Korea, physican Republic of Korea. Prof. Korea U., Med. Coll., Seoul, 1986—. Cons. Korean FDA, Seoul, 2004—07; cons., com. mem. Korea Health Ins. Rev. Agy., Seoul, 2004—07. Translator: (book) Revision of Total Hip Arthroplasty; contbr. articles to profl. jours. Lt. Korean Navy, 1983—86. Fellow, Endo-Klinik, Hamburg,Germany, 1989—90, Hosp. Spl. Surgery, NYC, 1999—2000. Fellow: Internat. Soc. Tech. Arthroplasty (first v.p. 2007, pres. 2008), Korea Orthop. Soc., Korean Hip Soc. (pres. 2004—05); mem.: Korean Musculoskeletal Transplantation Soc. (pres. 2003—04), European Orthop. Rsch. Soc. Buddhist. Avocation: mountain climbing. Office: Korea Univ Guro Hosp Orthopedic Dept 80 Guro Dong Guro Gu Seoul 152 703 Republic of Korea Home Phone: 82-2-6678-2213; Office Phone: 82-2-2626-3085. Office Fax: 82-2-2626-1164. Personal E-mail: shonwy@hotmail.com. Business E-Mail: wonyong@kumc.or.kr.

SHONKOFF, JACK P., dean; AB, Cornell U., 1968; MD, NYU Sch. Medicine, 1972. Intern, asst. resident, sr. resident in pediatrics Bronx Mcpl. Hosp. Ctr., Albert Einstein Coll. Medicine, 1972-75; clin. trainee divsn. child psychiatry Albert Einstein Coll. Medicine, Bronx, 1974-75, rsch. asst. child developmental psychology unit, 1974-75; fellow in medicine developmental eval. clinic Children's Hosp. Med. Ctr. and Harvard Med. Sch., Boston, 1975-76; coord. developmental consultation svc. Martha Eliot Health Ctr., Jamaica Plain, Mass., 1975-76; cons. cmty. eval. and rehab. ctr. Wrentham (Mass.) State Sch., 1975-76; asst. in medicine Children's Hosp. Med. Ctr., Boston, 1976-79; attending pediatrician U. Mass. Med. Ctr., Worcester, Mass., 1979-94; pediatric coord. masters program Wheelock Coll., Boston, 1981-90; coord. early intervention study group U. Mass., Brandeis U., Wellesley Coll, Mass. Dept. Public Health, 1982-84; prin. investigator, project dir. early intervention collaborative study U. Mass. Med. Sch., 1984-94, Florence Heller Grad Sch. Brandeis U., Waltham, Mass., 1994-98, dean, 1994—. Instr. pediatrics Harvard Med. Sch., 1976-79, lectr. 1997—. Simmons Coll., Boston, 1976-79, instr. dept. early childhood edn. Wheelock Coll., Boston, 1979-80, adj. asst. prof. grad. sch., 1980-85, adj. assoc. prof. grad. sch., 1985-90; asst. prof. pediatrics U. Mass. Med. Sch., Worcester, Mass., 1979-85, assoc. prof. 1985-89, prof. 1990-94; Samuel F. and Rose B. Gingold prof. human devel. Brandeis U., Waltham, Mass., 1994—; adj. prof. family medicine and cmty. health Tufts U. Sch. Medicine, Boston, 1997—; chair bd. on Children, Youth and Families Inst. Medicine and Nat. Rsch. Coun./Nat. Acad. Scis., com. on integrating the science of early childhood devel. bd.; bd. dirs. Zero to Three: Nat. Ctr. for Infants, Toddlers and Families; Robert Wood Johnson vis. rsch. prof. U. Rochester Sch. Medicine and Dentistry, Rochester, N.Y., 1986; Arthur L. Tuuri Interdisciplinary lectr. Mott Children's Health Ctr., Flint, MI, 1986; vis. prof. Sistema Nacional para el Desarrollo Integral de la Familia, Mexico City, Mexico, 1986, U. Puerto Rico Sch. Medicine, San Juan, Puerto Rico, 1988, A.I. Dupont Inst., Wilmington, Del., 1989, U. Vermont Sch. Medicine, Burlington, 1990, Koret vis. prof. pediatrics Pacific Presbyn. Med. Ctr., San Francisco, Calif., 1990, Harrie R. Chamberlin lectr. and vis. prof. U. N.C., Chapel Hill, 1991, vis. prof. in pediatrics Children's Hosp., Oakland, Calif., 1991, Children's Nat. Med. Ctr., Washington, 1991, Omer H. Foust lectr. and vis. prof. Riley Hosp. for Children, Ind. U. Med. Ctr., Indpls., 1991, Dr. Louis W. Sauer lectr., vis. prof. Evanston Hosp., Ill., 1991, Sydney Rosen Commemorative lectr. Hosp. for Sick Children, Toronto, Ontario, 1992, vis. prof. Tel Aviv U., Israel, 1992, Felton Bequests' vis. lectr. Royal Children's Hosp. and Monash Med. Ctr., Melbourne, Australia, 1993, John B. Welsh Meml. lectureship and vis. prof. U. Calif. San Diego Med. Ctr., Calif., 1994, Warren Weiswasser lectr., vis. prof. Yale U. Sch. Medicine, New Haven, CT, 1995, Dr. Howard R. Rappaport Meml. lectureship, Mt. Sinai Sch. Medicine, N.Y.C., 1997, Raymond Keefe/Joseph Bellizzi Meml. lectr. St. Francis Hosp. and Med. Ctr., Hartford, Ct., 1998. Editl. bd.: Jour. Child Neurology, 1985-90, Jour. Early Intervention, 1989-94, Topics in Early Childhood Special Education, 1987-94, Infant Mental Health Jour., 1983-86; consulting editor: Child Development, 1983-90, Infant Mental Health Jour., 1993-95, Zero to Three, 1985—; assoc. editor: Infant Mental Health Jour., 19987-92, Rudolph's Pediatrics, 20th edit., 1993-94, 21st edit., 1998—; ad hoc manuscript review Am. Jour. Diseases of Children, Am. Jour. Pub. Health, Child Development, Clinical Pediatrics, Infant Mental Health Jour., Jour. of Am. Med. Assn., Jour. Child Psychology and Psychiatry, Jour. Devel. and Behavioral Pediatrics, Jour. Early Intervention, Jour. Division of Early Childhood, Jour. Special Edn., Pediatrics. Fellow W.K. Kellogg Found., 1980-83, Nat. Ctr. for Clin. Infant Programs, 1981-82; recipient Senator Gerard D'Amico award Mass. Early Intervention Consortium, 1986, award for Excellence Boston Inst. for Devel. of Infants and Parents, 1992, Disting. Contribution to Child Advocacy award APA Divsn. Child, Youth and Family Svcs., 1995; grantee in field. Mem. Am. Pediatric Soc. (elected mem.), Inst. Medicine (elected mem.). Office: Brandeis U Florence Heller Grad Sch PO Box 9110-MS 035 Waltham MA 02454-9110 Fax: (781) 736-3852. E-mail: shonkoff@brandeis.edu.

SHONS, ALAN RANCE, plastic surgeon, surgical oncologist, educator; b. Freeport, Ill., Jan. 10, 1938; s. Ferral Caldwell and Margaret (Zimmerman) S.; children: Lesley, Susan. AB, Dartmouth Coll., 1960; MD, Case Western Res. U., 1965; PhD in Surgery, U. Minn., 1976. Diplomate Am. Bd. Surgery, Am. Bd. Plastic Surgery. Intern U. Hosp., Cleve., 1965-66, resident in surgery, 1966-67; rsch. fellow transplantation immunology U. Minn., Mpls., 1969-72, asst. prof. plastic surgery, 1976-79, assoc. prof., 1979-84, prof., 1984; resident in surgery U. Minn. Hosp., 1972-74; resident plastic surgery NYU, 1974-76; dir. divsn. plastic and reconstructive surgery U. Minn. Hosp., St. Paul Ramsey Hosp., Mpls. VA Hosp., 1976-84; cons. plastic surgery St. Louis Park Med. Ctr., 1980-84; prof. surgery Case Western Res. U., Cleve., 1984-93, dir. divsn. plastic and reconstructive surgery, 1984-92; prof. surgery, assoc. dir. comprehensive breast program, H. Lee Moffitt Cancer Ctr. and Rsch. Inst. U. South Fla., Tampa, 1992—2003; surgeon pvt. practice, Great Neck, NY, 2004—. Examiner Am. Bd. Plastic Surgery, 1987-2000; dir. divsn. plastic surgery Glen Cove Hosp., NY, 2006-. Author: (with G.L. Adams and D. McQuarrie) Head and Neck Cancer, 1986; (with R. Jensen) Plastic Surgery Review, 1993. Capt. USAF, 1967-69. Fellow ACS (chmn. Minn. com. on trauma 1978-84); mem. AMA, Am. Soc. Plastic and Reconstructive Surgeons, Am. Assn. Plastic Surgeons, Minn. Acad. Plastic Surgeons (pres. 1981-82), Soc. Head and Neck Surgeons, Transplantation Soc., Plastic Surgery Rsch. Coun., Am. Soc. Aesthetic Plastic Surgery, Am. Soc. Maxillofacial Surgeons, Am. Assn. Immunologists, Soc. Exptl. Pathology, Am. Cleft Palate Assn., Am. Soc. Craniofacial Surg. Assn., Fla. Soc. Plastic and Reconstructive Surgeons, Sigma Xi. Office: 935 Northern Blvd Great Neck NY 11021 Office Phone: 516-482-6893.

SHOOTER, ERIC MANVERS, retired neurobiology professor, consultant; b. Mansfield, Eng., Apr. 18, 1924; arrived in U.S., 1964; s. Fred and Pattie (Johnson) Shooter; m. Elaine Staley Arnold, May 28, 1949; 1 child, Annette Elizabeth. BA, Cambridge U., Eng., 1945, MA, 1949, PhD, 1950, ScD, 1986; DSc, U. London, 1964. Sr. scientist biochemistry Brewing Industry Rsch. Found., 1950—53; biochemistry lectr. Univ. Coll., London, 1953—63; assoc. prof. genetics Stanford U., 1963—68, prof. genetics and biochemistry, 1968—75, prof., chmn. neurobiology dept., 1975—87, prof. neurobiology, 1987—2004, prof. neurobiology emeritus, 2004—, chmn. Neurosci. PhD Program, 1972—82. Assoc. Neurosci. Rsch. Program, NYC, 1979—89; mem. tchg. staff Internat. Sch. Neurosci., Praglia, Italy, 1987—93; sr. cons. Markey Charitable Trust, Miami, Fla., 1985—97; bd. dirs. Regeneron Pharm., Inc., Tarrytown, NY. Assoc. editor (book series) Ann. Rev. Neuroscis., 1984—2001; contbr. articles to profl. jours. Recipient Wakeman award, Duke U., 1988, Award for Disting. Achievement in Neurosci. Rsch., Bristol-Myers-Squibb, 1997; scholar, Josiah Macy Jr. Found., N.Y.C., 1974—75. Fellow: AAAS, Am. Acad. Arts and Scis., Royal Soc. (London); mem.: NAS, Am. Philos. Soc., Internat. Brain Rsch. Orgn., Internat. Soc. Neurochemistry, Am. Soc. Neurochemistry, Am. Assn. Biol. Chemists, Soc. for Neurosci. (Ralph W. Gerard prize 1995), Inst. Medicine of NAS, Alpha Omega Alpha (hon.). Avocation: travel. Home: 370 Golden Oak Dr Portola Valley CA 94028-7757 Office: Stanford U Sch Medicine Dept Neurobiology 299 Campus Dr Stanford CA 94305-5125 Business E-Mail: eshooter@stanford.edu.

SHORE, ELEANOR GOSSARD, retired medical school dean; b. Ottawa, Ill., Aug. 11, 1930; d. Arthur Paul and Mary Catherine (Lineberger) Gossard; m. Miles Frederick Shore, July 4, 1953;

children: Miles Paul, Rebecca Shore Lewin, Susanna Shore LeBoutillier. BA magna cum laude, Radcliffe Coll., 1951; MD, Harvard U., 1955, MPH, 1970. Diplomate Am. Bd. Preventive Medicine. Med. intern New Eng. Med. Ctr. Hosp., Boston, 1955-56; resident in occup. medicine Harvard U. Health Svcs., Cambridge, Mass., 1966-68; Macy scholar Radcliffe Inst., Radcliffe Coll., Cambridge, 1966-68; resident in preventive medicine Harvard Sch. Pub. Health, Boston, 1970-71; asst. physician Radcliffe Coll., 1959-61, Harvard U. Health Svcs., 1961—96; rsch. assoc. dept. microbiology Harvard U. Sch. Pub. Health, 1971-76; asst. to pres. Harvard U., 1972-81; assoc. dean for faculty affairs Harvard Med. Sch., 1978-89, mem. faculty, 1978—2004, dean for faculty affairs, 1989—2004, sr. cons. to office acad. and clin. programs, 2005—. Mem. editl. bd. Harvard Med. Alumni Bull., 1976—. Bd. dirs. Mass.-Ukraine Citizens Bridge, Brockton, Mass., 1989-94, pres., 1991-92; bd. dirs. Needham (Mass.) Found. for Pub. Sch. Edn., 1990-94; bd. dirs. Mass. Health Rsch. Inst., Inc., 1990-99, sec., 1995-99; overseer to overseer emeritus Boston Mus. Sci., 1981—; trustee Schepens Eye Rsch. Inst., Boston, 1993—; mem. acad. coun. Real Colegio Complutense, Harvard U., 1995—; dep. dir. Harvard Med. Sch. Ctr. for Excellence in Women's Health, 1998-2004. Recipient Pres.'s Recognition award Am. Med. Women's Assn., 1996. Fellow Am. Acad. Preventive Medicine; mem. AAAS, APHA, Mass. Pub. Health Assn., Mass. Med. Soc., Aesculapian Club (treas. 1986-89, pres. 1990-91). Business E-Mail: eleanor_shore@hms.harvard.edu.

SHORE, JAMES H(ENRY), psychiatrist; b. Winston-Salem, NC, Apr. 6, 1940; s. James Henry and Ellen Elizabeth (Hayes) S.; m. Christine Lowenbach, Aug. 24, 1963; children— Ellen Ottilie, James Henry. MD, Duke U., 1965. Diplomate Am. Bd. Psychiatry and Neurology. Intern U. Utah Med. Ctr., 1965-66; resident in psychiatry U. Wash., 1966-69; chief mental health office Portland Area Indian Health Svc., Oreg., 1969-73; assoc. prof. psychiatry, dir. cmty. psychiatry tng. program U. Oreg. Health Sci. Ctr., 1973-75, prof., chmn. dept. psychiatry, 1975-85; from chmn. dept. psychiatry Health Sci. Ctr. to chancellor U. Colo., Aurora, 1985—2004, chancellor Health Scis. Ctr., 2004—05, chancellor emeritus Health Scis. Ctr., 2006—. Mem. exptl. and spl. edn. com. NIMH-Internal Rev. Group, 1976-80; dir. Colo. Psychiatry Hosp., 1985-99; interim dir. U. Colo. Hosp., Denver, 1987-88, interim exec. vice chancellor, 1995-97, chancellor, 1998-2005; cons. in field. Contbr. numerous articles to profl. publs. Mem. Various community bds. Served with USPHS, 1969-73. Decorated USPHS Commendation medal; various grants. Fellow Am. Psychiat. Assn., Am. Coll. Psychiatry (pres. 2003-04); mem. Am. Assn. Chmn. Depts. Psychiatry (pres. 1989), Am. Bd. Psychiatry and Neurology (dir. 1987—, pres. 1994), Residency Rev. Com. for Psychiatry (chmn. 1991-92). Office: U Colo Health Scis Ctr Mail Stop F800 PO Box 6508 Aurora CO 80045

SHORENSTEIN, ROSALIND GREENBERG, internist; b. NYC, Jan. 14, 1947; d. Albert Samuel and Natalie Miriam (Sherman) Greenberg; m. Michael Lewis Shorenstein, June 18, 1967; children: Anna Irene, Claire Beth. BA in Chemistry, Wellesley Coll., 1968; MA in Biochemistry and Molecular Biology, Harvard U., 1970, PhD in Biochemistry and Molecular Biology, 1973; MD, Stanford U., 1976. Diplomate Am. Bd. Internal Medicine. Resident in internal medicine UCLA Med. Ctr., 1976-79; pvt. practice internal medicine Santa Cruz, Calif., 1979—. Mem. dept. internal medicine Dominican Hosp., Santa Cruz, 1979—; co-dir. med. svcs. Health Enhancement & Lifestyle Planning Systems, Santa Cruz, 1983—. Contbr. articles to profl. journals. Dir. Santa Cruz Chamber Players, 1993-94, pres., bd. dirs., 1994—. Recipient Charlie Parkhurst award Santa Cruz Women's Commn., 1989; NSF fellow, 1968-72, Sarah Perry Wood Med. fellow Wellesley Coll., 1972-76. Mem. Am. Soc. Internal Medicine (del. 1994, 95), Calif. Soc. Internal Medicine (trustee 1994—, sec.-treas. 1996-2000), Am. Med. Women's Assn. (Outstanding Svc. award 1987, br. #59 pres. 1986—), Calif. Med. Assn. (com. on women 1987-93), Santa Cruz County Med. Soc. (mem. bd. govs. 1993—, sec. 1997-99, pres. 2000-01, sec. 2002-), Phi Beta Kappa, Sigma Xi. Jewish. Office: 700 Frederick St Ste 103 Santa Cruz CA 95062-2239 Office Phone: 831-458-1002.

SHORT, ELIZABETH M., internist, educator, retired federal agency administrator; b. Boston, June 2, 1942; d. James Edward and Arlene Elizabeth (Mitchell) Meehan; m. Michael Allen Friedman, June 21, 1976; children: Lia Gabrielle, Hannah Ariel, Eleanor Elana. BA in Philosophy magna cum laude, Mt. Holyoke Coll., 1963; MD cum laude, Yale U., 1968. Diplomate Am. Bd. Internal Medicine, Am. Bd. Med. Genetics. Resident in internal medicine Yale New Haven Hosp., 1968-70; postdoctoral fellow in human genetics Yale Med. Sch., 1970-72; resident U. Calif., San Francisco, 1972-73; sr. chief resident Stanford (Calif.) Med. Sch., 1973-75, asst. prof. medicine, 1975-83, assoc. dean student affairs, med. edn., 1978-83; dep. dir. acad. affairs, dir. biomed. rsch. Assn. Am. Med. Colls., Washington, 1983-88; dep. assoc. chief med. dir. for acad. affairs VA, Washington, 1988-92, assoc. chief med. dir. for acad. affairs, 1992-96; health policy cons. HHS, 1996—2001; emerita prof. clin. medicine Georgetown U. Sch. Medicine; ret., 2001. Vis. prof. human biology Stanford U., 1983-86; mem. Accreditation Coun. Grad. Med. Edn., 1988-97; mem. White House Task Force on Health Care Reform, 1993. Assoc. editor Clin. Rsch. Jour., 1976-79, editor 1980-84; contbr. articles to profl. jours. Mem. Nat. Child Health Adv. Coun., NIH, 1991-97; com. edn. and tng. Office Sci. and Tech. Policy, White House, Washington, 1991-96, Calif. Philharm., 2003-07; bd. dirs., 2003-07, treas.,06-07, Hillsides Home Children, 2003-, bd. dirs., 2003-, exec. com., 2004-11, mem. program assesment com., 2006-, chair, 2006-11, search com., 2009, mem. centennial com., 2011-, Pacific Asia Mus., 2008-; bd. trustees, 2008-, planning com., 2009-, chair acquisitions com., 2009-, Mus. Am. Western Coun., 2008-. Recipient Maclean Zoology award; Munger scholar, Markle scholar, Sara Williston scholar Mt. Holyoke Coll., 1959-63, Yale Men in Medicine scholar, 1964-68; Bardwell Meml. Med. fellow, 1963. Mem. AAAS, Am. Soc. Human Genetics (pub. policy com. 1984-95, chmn. 1986-94), Am. Fedn. Clin. Rsch. (bd. dirs. 1973-83, co-chmn. com. status women 1975-77, editor Clin. Rsch. Jour., 1978-83, nat. coun., exec. com., pub. policy com. 1977-87), Western Soc. Clin. Investigation, Calif. Acad. Medicine, Phi Beta Kappa, Alpha Omega Alpha. Home and Office: 3535 Ranch Top Rd Pasadena CA 91107 Personal E-mail: elizshort@aol.com.

SHORT, MARION PRISCILLA, neurogenetics educator; b. Milford, Del., June 12, 1951; d. Raymond Calistus and Barbara Anne (Ferguson) S.; m. Michael Peter Klein; 1 child, Asher Calistus Klein. BA, Bryn Mawr Coll., 1973; diploma, U. Edinburgh, Scotland, 1975; MD, Med. Coll. Pa., 1978. Diplomate Am. Bd. Psychiatry and Neurology, Am. Bd. Internal Medicine. Intern in internal medicine Hahnemann Med. Coll. Hosp., Phila., 1978-79; med. resident in internal medicine St. Lukes-Roosevelt Hosp., NYC, 1979-81; neurology resident U. Pitts. Health Ctr., 1981-84; fellow in med. genetics Mt. Sinai Med. Ctr., NYC, 1984-86; fellow in neurology Mass. Gen. Hosp., Boston, 1986-90, asst. neurologist, 1990-95; asst. prof. dept. neurology Harvard Med. Sch., Boston, 1990-95; asst. prof. dept. neurology, pediat. and pathology U. Chgo., 1995—2000, clin. assoc. pediat. neurosurgery, 2000—08, fellow McLean Ctr. for Clin. Med. Ethics, 2002—03, sr. fellow McLean Ctr. for Clin. Med. Ethics, 2003—04; program dir. genetics, transplantation and clin. rsch. AMA, Chgo., 1997—2002; dir. office sci. Am. Med. Assn., 1997—2002. Recipient Clin. Investigator Devel. award, NIH, 1988—93; fellow, Inst. Medicine, Chgo., 1999. Mem. AMA, Am. Acad. Neurology, Am. Soc. for Human Genetics, Am. Coll. Med. Genetics. Office: Pediat Neurosurgery U Chgo MC 4066 5481 S Maryland Ave Chicago IL 60637-4325 Office Phone: 773-702-2475. Business E-Mail: mpshort@surgery.bsd.uchicago.edu. *

SHORTEN, GEORGE DECLAN, anesthesiologist; b. Cork, Ireland, Mar. 30, 1961; s. Owen and Geraldine (Hickey) S. MB BCh, Univ. Coll. Cork, 1985, MD, 1994. Diplomate Am. Bd. Anesthesiology. From instr. to asst. prof. Harvard Med. Sch., Boston, 1990-96; prof. anesthesia and intensive care medicine Univ. Coll. Cork, 1997—. Cons. Cork U. Hosp., U.S. Dept. Health; hon. cons. South Infirmary, Victoria Hosp., Cork, Ireland; nat. dir. Masters Program in Anesthesia Coll. of Anesthaetists, Ireland; reviewer multiple med. jours. including: Anesthesiology, Anesthesia and Analgesia, European Jour. Anesthesia, Am. Jour. Kidney Diseases, granting agys. Euroean Soc. Anaesthesists, Health Rsch. Bd. Ireland. Editor: (Book) Eur. Soc. Anaesthetists Refresher Course Book, Bd. Internat. Anesthesiology Clinics. Named Hon. Pres., Irish Anesthetic and Recovery Nurses Assn. Fellow Royal Coll. Anesthesthetists, Royal Coll. Surgeons Ireland; mem. Am. Soc. Anesthesiologists, Soc. Airway Mgmt.European Soc. Anesthetists, AAAS, Coun. of Healthcare Advisors (Gerson Lehrman Group)

SHORTLIFFE, EDWARD HANCE, internist, medical educator, computer scientist; b. Edmonton, Alta., Can., Aug. 28, 1947; s. Ernest Carl and Elizabeth Joan Shortliffe. AB, Harvard U., 1970; PhD, Stanford U., 1975, MD, 1976. Diplomate Am. Bd. Internal Medicine. Trainee NIH, 1971—76; intern Mass. Gen. Hosp., Boston, 1976—77; resident Stanford Hosp., Palo Alto, Calif., 1977—79; asst. prof. medicine Stanford U. Sch. Medicine, Palo Alto, 1979—85, assoc. prof., 1985—90, chief divsn. gen. internal medicine, 1988—95, prof., 1990—2000; assoc. chair medicine Primary Care, 1993—95; assoc. dean info. resources and tech. Stanford U. Sch. Medicine, 1995—2000; prof., chair dept. biomed. informatics Columbia U. Coll. Physicians and Surgeons, NYC, 2000—07, Rolf H. Scholdager prof. biomed. informatics, 2005—07; deputy v.p. Info. Tech., Health Scis., Columbia U., NYC, 2002—07; founding dean U. Ariz. Coll. Medicine, Phoenix, 2007—08, prof. basic med. scis., prof. medicine, 2007—09; prof. biomed. informatics Ariz. State U., 2007—09, U. Tex. Houston, 2009—; pres., CEO Am. Med. Informatics Assn., Bethesda, Md., 2009—. Advisor Nat. Bd. Med. Examiners, Phila., 1987—93; pres. Symposium on Computer Applications in Med. Care, Washington, 1988—89; mem. Nat. Fed. Networking Adv. Coun., NSF, 1991—93; mem. computer sci. and telecomm. bd. NRC, 1991—96; bd. regents ACP, 1996—2002; mem. Pres.'s Info. Tech. Adv. Com., 1997—2002; chmn. com. on healthcare and next generation internet NRC, 1998—2000; mem. Nat. Com. on Vital Health Stats., 2000—03; trustee N.Y. Acad. Medicine, 2005—; bd. dirs. Medco Health Solutions, Inc., 2003—07. Editor: Rule-Based Expert Systems, 1984, Readings in Medical Artificial Intelligence, 1984, Medical Informatics: Computer Applications in Health Care, 1990, Medical Informatics: Computer Applications in Health Care and Biomedicine, 2d edit., 2000, Biomedical Informatics, 3d edit., 2006. Com. sci. engring. and pub. policy NAS, 2001—03, 2005—07. Recipient Grace M. Hopper award, Assn. Computing Machinery, 1976, Young Investigator award, Western Soc. Clin. Investigation, 1987, Rsch. Career award, Nat. Libr. of Medicine, 1979—84; scholar, Kaiser Family Found., 1983—88. Fellow: Am. Coll. Med. Informatics (pres. 1992—94), Am. Assn. Artificial Intelligence; mem.: Am. Clin. and Climatol. Assn., Assn. Am. Physicians, Am. Med. Informatics Assn., Am. Soc. for Clin. Investigation, Inst. Medicine (mem. coun. 2000—03, 2005—07), Soc. for Med. Decisionmaking (pres. 1989—90). Achievements include development of several medical computer programs including MYCIN and ONCOCIN. Avocations: skiing, jazz. Office: Am Med Informatics Assn 4915 St Elmo Ave Ste 401 Bethesda MD 20814-6052 Home: 2938 Brompton Sq Dr Houston TX 77025-1551 Office Phone: 301-657-1291. Business E-Mail: shortliffe@amia.org.

SHORTLIFFE, LINDA MARIE DAIRIKI, urology educator, researcher; b. Boston, Feb. 28, 1949; d. Setsuo and Norma Masako (Yoshida) Dairiki; children: Lindsay Ann, Lauren Leigh. AB in Hist. and Sci., Harvard U., 1971; MD, Stanford U. Sch. Medicine, Calif., 1975. Diplomate Am. Bd. Urology. Resident gen. surgery Tufts-New Eng. Med. Ctr., Boston, 1976-77; intern Stanford U. Med. Ctr., 1975-76, resident urology, 1977-81, chief pediat. urology, 1991—, chair dept. urology, 1995—; asst. prof. surgery urology Stanford U. Sch. Medicine, 1981-88, assoc. prof., 1988-93, prof., 1993—. Com. mem. spl. grants Nat. Inst. Diabetes, Digestive and Kidney Diseases, Bethesda, Md., 1990—94; pres. elect, trustee Am. Bd. Urology, 2001—07; pres. Soc. Univ. Urologists, 2004—05; bd. dirs. VIVUS, Inc., 1999—; dir. Am. Found. Urol. Disease, Balt., 2004—. Contbr. articles to profl. jours. Named one of Best Dr.'s in America, Woodward and White, Inc., America's Top Dr.'s, Castle Connolly Med. LTD; named to Nat. Libr. Med. Fellow: ACS, Am. Acad. Pediat. (chair-elect urology sect. 2007—08); mem.: Soc. Pediat. Urology, Am. Urol. Assn. Office: Stanford U Med Ctr Dept Urology 300 Pasteur Dr S287 Stanford CA 94305-5118 Office Phone: 650-498-5042. Business E-Mail: lindas@stanford.edu.

SHOSHANI, DAVID, medical researcher; s. Zion and Ora Shoshani; m. Shoshana Kaminski, Aug. 20, 1978; children: Ron, Gadi Dennis. MD, Tel Aviv U., 1978. Med. dir. Eli Lilly, Tel Aviv, 1989—97, HemoDynamics, Yoqneam, Israel, 1997—2000; v.p. med. affairs Mor Rsch. Applications, Petach-Tiquva, Israel, 2000, ColBar Life Sci., Herzliya, Israel, 2002—. Contbr. articles to profl. jours., scientific papers (Excellent Leadership award, 2006). Vol. Cancer Assn., Tel Aviv, 1995—2005. Maj. paratrooper, 1968—71, Israel. Achievements include patents for new catheter for minimal invasive procedures; research in successful clinical study for new dermal filler approval. Home: 16, Sold 43100 Raanana Israel Home Fax: 972-97480124. Personal E-mail: daviddsh@netvision.net.il.

SHOTTS, EMMETT BOOKER, JR., microbiology educator, researcher; b. Jasper, Ala., Sept. 23, 1931; s. Emmett Booker and Will Laceye (Brown) Shotts; m. Martha C. Monroe, Sept. 7, 1997; children: Elizabeth, Dan, Evelyn, Georgia Alice Maria. BS, U. Ala., 1952; MS, U. Ga., 1958, PhD, 1966. Epidemic intellegence svc. Ctr. for Disease Control, Atlanta, 1959-61; rsch. microbiologist Ctrs. for Disease Control, Atlanta, 1962-64; rsch. assoc. U. Ga., Athens, 1957-59, prof., 1966—97, prof. emeritus, 1997—; dir. Nat. Fish Health Rsch. Lab. US Dept. Interior, 1997—2001; cons., 2001—. Contbr. chapters to books, abstracts and articles to profl. jours. Vice chmn. Bd. Health, White County, Ga., 2009-; With US Army, 1954-56. Recipient Rsch. award Beecham Pharm., 1986, 87, Edwards award Am. Soc. for Microbiology southeastern br., 1990, Feeley award, 1992, Disting. Svc. award Wildlife Disease Assn., 1992, Sneiszko award Fish Health Am. Fisheries Soc., 1995. Fellow Am. Acad. Microbiology (specialist med. microbiology); mem. Am. Soc. Clin. Pathology (med. technologist), Am. Coll. Vet. Microbiology (hon. diplomate), Am. Vet. Epidemiology Soc. (hon. diplomate). Office: Dept Med Microbiology U Ga Athens GA 30602 Personal E-mail: emshotts@windstream.net.

SHOUL, MELVIN I., retired surgeon; b. Newburyport, Mass., 1922; MD, Tufts U., 1947. Diplomate Am. Bd. Surgery. Intern Boston City Hosp., 1947-49, resident in surgery, 1949-52; chief gen. surgery Murphy Army Hosp., 1954; pvt. practice surgery, 1954—94; clin. instr. surgery Harvard Med. Sch., 1954—94; ret., 1994. Contbr. articles to profl. jours. With US Army, 1953—54, Korea. Fellow ACS; mem. AMA, Boston Surg. Soc. Personal E-mail: melvinshoul2@live.com. *

SHOULSON, IRA, neurologist, pharmacologist, educator; b. Erie, Pa., Apr. 4, 1946; BA, U. Pa., 1967; MD, U. Rochester, 1971. Cert. Internal Medicine, 1974, Neurology, 1980. Intern in internal medicine Strong Meml. Hosp., Rochester, NY, 1971—72, resident in neurology, 1972—73, 1975—77; fellow NIH, Bethesda, Md., 1973—75; mem. faculty U. Rochester Med. Ctr., 1977—, prof. neurology, prof. pharmacology and physiology, Louis C. Lasagna prof. in exptl. therapeutics, 2004—; founder Parkinson Study Group, 1985, Huntington Study Group, 1994. Mem.: Inst. Medicine, Movement Disorder Soc. (hon.), Alpha Omega Alpha. Office: U Rochester Sch Medicine and Dentistry 601 Elmwood Ave Box 673 Rochester NY 14642

SHOYAMA, YUKIHIRO, pharmacist, educator; b. China, Apr. 21, 1943; PhD, Kyushu U., 1968. Dir., herbal garden Faculty Pharm. Sci., Kyushu U., 1991—2004, prof., 1991—2007, dean, 2004—06, prof. emeritus, 2007—, guest prof., 2007—10; prof. Faculty Pharm. Sci., Nagasaki Internat. U., 2007—. Contbr. articles to sci. profl. jours. Recipient award, Senji Miyata Found. Mem.: Pharm. Soc. Japan, Japanese Soc. Pharmacognosy (pres. 2007—09, award). Avocation: art. Office: 2825-7 Huis Ten Bosch Sasebo Nagasaki 859-3298 Japan Office Phone: 81-956-20-5653. Business E-Mail: shoyama@niv.ac.jp.

SHREEDHARA, CHANDRA SHEKARA SHASTRY, medical educator; b. Shimoga, Karnataka, India, Nov. 29, 1954; PharmM, Govt. Coll. Pharmacy, Bangalore, 1983; PhD, Jnana Sahyadri, 2003. Prof. RGUHS Nat. Coll. Pharmacy, Shimoga, 1986—2005, Manipal U. Manipal Coll. Pharm. Scis., 2005—. Avocations: music, cricket, reading. Office: Madhav Nagar Manipal Karnataka 576 104 India Office Fax: 91-820-2571998. Business E-Mail: css.shim@manipal.edu.

SHRESTHA, BADRI MAN, transplant surgeon, consultant; b. Gaurigunj, Jhapa, Nepal, Apr. 16, 1955; s. Durga Lal and Ganga Shrestha; m. Sita Kumari, Apr., 1981; children: Alice, Anne, Donna. MB BChir, Assam Med. Coll., India, 1979; MS in Surgery, U. Colombo, Sri Lanka, 1987; MPhil, U. Cardiff, Wales, 1996. Lic. transplant surgeon. Med. officer Health Dept. Nepal, 1980-83; registrar in surgery Colombo U., 1984-87, Bir Hosp., Kathmandu, Nepal, 1987-90, Nat. Health Svcs., U.K., 1991-92, sr. registrar, 1993-96; cons. surgeon Bir Hosp., Kathmandu, 1996—; dir. transplantation Sheffield Kidney Inst.; regional rep. UK Transplant; mem. Ct. Examiners RCS Eng., London; examiner U. Sheffield, England; peer reviewer editl. bd. mem. numerous jours. Postgrad. tutor Bir Hosp., 1996—; coll. tutor Royal Coll. Surgeons Edinburgh, 1997—. Contbr. articles to profl. jours. Recipient Svc. medal His Majesty King Birendra, 1983. Fellow Royal Coll. Surgeons Eng. (overseas dr.'s tng. scheme award 1996), Internat. Coll. Surgeons; mem. Brit. Transplantation Soc., Soc. Surgeons Nepal, N.Y. Acad. Scis. Avocations: composing Nepalese songs, flute, keyboards, singing. Office: SKI Divsn Transplantation Herries Rd Sheffield 557 England Home: 507 Fulwood Road S10 3QB Sheffield England E-mail: shresthabm@doctors.net.uk.

SHRESTHA, NABIN K., physician, researcher; married;; children: Priyanka, Nishan. B in Medicine and Surgery, Delhi U., Maulana Azad Med. Coll., 1994; MPH, Cleve. State U., 2006. Diplomate in internal medicine Am. Bd. Internal Medicine, 1999, in infectious diseases Am. Bd. Internal Medicine, 2001, in med. microbiology Am. Bd. Pathology, 2005. Asst. prof. B.P. Koirala Inst. Health Scis., Dharan, Nepal, 2002—04, assoc. prof., 2004; assoc. staff physician Cleve. Clinic, 2004—06, quality rev. officer, dept. infectious disease, 2005—, staff physician, 2006—, program dir., clin. microbiology fellowship program, 2006—; asst. prof. Case Western Res. U., Cleve., 2009—. Contbr. articles to profl. jours. Recipient Joseph Cash Meml. award, Cleve. Clinic, 2002, Innovator award, 2010. Fellow: ACP, Coll. Am. Pathologists, Infectious Diseases Soc. America; mem.:

AAAS, Am. Nepal Med. Found. (bd. dirs. 2008—, sec. 2009—), Soc. for Healthcare Epidemiology Am., Am. Soc. Microbiology, Beta Gamma Sigma (life). Office: Cleveland Clinic 9500 Euclid Ave / G-21 Cleveland OH 44195

SHREVE, SUE ANN GARDNER, retired health products company administrator; b. Bklyn., Jan. 26, 1932; d. Homer Frank and Grace Emily (Kohlhagen) Gardner; m. Eugene Sheldon Shreve II, Nov. 20, 1954; children: Pamela Ann, Cynthia Ann Shreve Richard. BBA, Hofstra U., 1955. Co. rep. N.Y. Tel. Co., Bay Shore, 1954-55; engr. Republic Aviation, Farmingdale, N.Y., 1955-58; substitute tchr. East Islip (N.Y.) Sch. Dist., 1966-71; mgr. Patchogue Surg. and Athletic Supplies, Sayville, N.Y., 1971-81, ret., 1981. Invited guest writer Nat. Geneal. Soc. newsletter, 1996, 99, 2004; lectr. in genealogy, 1997—; condr. genealogy workshops, 1996—. Author, editor, pub.: The Kohlhagen Family Genealogy, 1994, The Shreve Family Genealogy, an update from 1641, 1997, Hendrickson Genealogy England to Illinois before 1840, 1999, Piscitelli Genealogy Italy to NYC before 1912, 2000; compiler, editor newsletter Gardner/Gardiner Rschrs., 1993—, Amos F.F. Gardner His Maternal Ancestors—Kirkpatrick & Barkley & Descendants, 2001, The Coates Family Genealogy, 2002, The Ridgeway Family Genealogy, 2003, The Mendenhall Family Genealogy, 2003, The Stockton Family Genealogy, 2003, The Becker Family Genealogy Germany to St. Clair County Ill. and Madison County Ill. in 1846-2005,The Gardner Connection Pres. Ulysses S. Grant issue reviewer Geneal. Helper Mag., 1995., The Shreve Connection to Pres. George Washington, The Shreve Connection to Pres. Richard M. Nixon, The Gardner Connection to William Williams a Signer of the Declaration of Independence Life mem. N.Y. State Congress of Parents and Tchrs., 1963—, past pres.; mem. Penataquit Aux. Southside Hosp., 1985—; mem., fundraiser Hospice of South Shore, 1983—; mem. Bay Shore N.Y. Hist. Soc., 1997—, Bay Shore Beautification Soc., 2000—; rec. sec. Bradish Ln. Homeowners Assn., 1997—2008, treas., 2002—; mem. Sagtikos Manor Hist. Soc., 2003—; maj. sponsor Bay Shore Arts Festival, 2001—08; mem. Bay Shore C. of C. Recipient Ofcl. proclamation Village of Frankfort, Ill., 1996; named one of Outstanding Young Women of Am., 1967. Mem.: DAR/Nat. Soc. DAR (vice regent 2001—05, regent 2005—09, rec. sec. 2009—, Nat. DAR Conservation award 2009), AAUW (hon.; charter, past pres., past treas. Islip area br., life mem. 2010, rsch. and project grantee 1989), Colonial & Antebellum America (descs. of sheriffs, cons.), The Order of Descendants of the Ancient & Honorable Artillery Comp Inc., Nat. Soc. Daughters Founders & Patriots, Nat. Soc. Colonial Dames XVII Century, The Plymouth Hereditary Soc., 1st Families of Mass., 1st Families of RI and Providence Plantations, 1st Families of Conn., Hereditary Soc. Pres. and First Ladies America, Nat. Soc. Sons of the Am. Revolution (Medal of Appreciation 2005), Bay Shore C. of C., 1st Families of Ohio, Daus. Union Vets. of Civil War (rec. sec. 2004—), German Genealogy Group of L.I. (rec. sec. 2003—), Bay Shore Garden Club (past pres., treas., dir., 2d v.p. 2000—, Woman of Yr. 1997, 2003). Republican. Methodist. Avocations: tennis, gourmet cooking, gardening, needlecrafts, international travel. Home: 5 Anderson Ct Bay Shore NY 11706-7701 Personal E-mail: sue12632@aol.com.

SHRIER, DIANE KESLER, psychiatrist, educator; b. Mar. 23, 1941; d. Benjamin Arthur and Mollie (Wortman) Kesler; m. Adam Louis Shrier, June 10, 1961; children: Jonathan Laurence, Lydia Anne, Catherine Jane, David Leopold. BS in Chemistry/Biology magna cum laude, Queen's Coll., CUNY, 1961; postgrad., Washington U. Sch. Medicine, St. Louis, 1960-61; MD, Yale U., 1964. Diplomate Am. Bd. Psychiatry and Neurology. Pediat. intern Bellevue Hosp., NYC, 1964-65; psychiat. resident Albert Einstein Coll. Medicine-Bronx Mcpl. Hosp. Ctr., 1966-68, child psychiatry fellow, 1968-70; staff cons. Family Svc. and Child Guidance Ctr. of the Oranges, Maplewood, Milburn-Orange, N.J., 1970-73, cons., 1973-79; pvt. practice Montclair, N.J., 1970-92, Washington, 1994—. Cons. Cmty. Day Nursery, East Orange, NJ, 1970—79, Montclair State Coll., 1976—78; psychiat. cons. Bloomfield (N.J.) pub. schs., 1974—75; clin. instr. Albert Einstein Coll. Medicine, 1970—73; clin. asst. prof. psychiatry U. Medicine and Dentistry N.J., 1978—82, clin. assoc. prof., 1982—89, prof. clin. psychiatry, 1989—92; vice-chmn., dir. clin. psychiat. svcs. dept. psychiatry Children's Nat. Med. Ctr., 1992—94, attending staff, 1994—; prof. psychiatry and pediats. George Washington U. Med. Ctr., 1992—94, clin. prof. psychiatry, behavioral scis. and pediat., 1994—; cons. Walter Reed Med. Ctr., 1994—. Contbr. articles to med. jours. Trustee Montessori Learning Ctr., Montclair, 1973-75. Regents scholar Queen's Coll., 1961., Disting. LIPE fellowship Am. Psychiatric Assn. Fellow Am. Psychiat. Assn., Acad. Child Psychiatry; mem. Tri-County Psychiat. Assn. (exec. com., rec. sec. 1977-78, 2d v.p. 1978-79, 1st v.p. 1979-80, pres. 1977-81), N.J. Psychiat. Assn. (councillor 1981-84), Am. Acad. Child and Adolescent Psychiatry (councillor at large 1992-95), Phi Beta Kappa. Home: 4000 Cathedral Ave NW Apt 317B Washington DC 20016-5267 Office: Ste 104 1616 18th St NW Washington DC 20009-2521 Office Phone: 202-667-9005. Personal E-mail: dianeshrier@rcn.com. Business E-Mail: diane.shrier.med.64@aya.yale.edu.

SHROPSHIRE, DONALD GRAY, hospital executive; b. Winston-Salem, NC, Aug. 6, 1927; s. John Lee and Bess L. (Shouse) S.; m. Mary Ruth Bodenheimer, Aug. 19, 1950; children: Melanie Shropshire David, John Devin. BS, U. NC, 1950; postgrad Erickson fellow, U. Chgo., 1958-59; LLD (hon.), U. Ariz., 1992; EdD (hon.), Tucson U., 1994. Personnel asst. Nat. Biscuit Co., Atlanta, 1950-52, asst. personnel mgr. Chgo., 1952-54; adminstr. Eastern State Hosp., Lexington, Ky., 1954-62; assoc. dir. U. Md. Hosp., Balt., 1962-67; adminstr. Tucson Med. Ctr., 1967-82, pres., 1982-92, pres. emeritus, 1992—; pres. Tucson Hosps. Med. Edn. Program, 1970-71, sec., 1971-86; pres. So. Ariz. Hosp. Council, 1968-69; bd. dirs. Ariz. Blue Cross, 1967-76, chmn. provider standards com., 1972-76; chmn. bd. Healthways, Inc., 1985-92. Mem. bd. La Posada at Pk., Inc., Green Valley, Ariz., 1996-2000, chmn., bd. emeritus, 2000—. Bd. dirs. Health Planning Coun. Tucson, mem. exec. com., 1969-74; chmn. profl. divsn. United Way, Tucson, 1969-70, vice chmn. campaign, 1988, Ariz. Health Faciltities Authority, bd. dirs., 1992-2005; chmn. dietary svcs. com., vice chmn., 1988, Md. Hosp. Coun., 1966-67; bd. dirs. Ky. Hosp. Assn., 1961-62, chmn. coun. profl. practice, 1960-61; past pres. Blue Grass Hosp. Coun.; trustee Assn. Western Hosps., 1974-81, pres., 1979-80; mem. accreditation Coun. for Continuing Med. Edn., 1982-87, chair, 1986; bd. govs. Pima C.C., 1970-76, sec., 1973-74, chmn., 1975-76, bd. dirs. Found., 1978-82, Ariz. Bd. Regents, 1982-90, sec., 1983-86, pres., 1987-88; mem. Tucson Airport Authority, 1987—, bd. dirs., 1990-95, pres., 1995; v.p. Tucson Econ. Devel. Corp., 1977-82; founder, dir., bd. dirs. Vol. Hosps. Am., 1977-88, treas., 1979-82; mem. Ariz. Adv. Health Coun. Dirs., 1976-78; bd. dirs. Tucson Tomorrow, 1983-87, Tucson Downtown Devel. Corp., 1988-95, Rincon Inst., 1992-97, Sonoran Inst., 1992-97, Pima County Med. Res. Corps, 2006—; dir. Mus. No. Ariz., 1988-2002, dir. emeritus, 2002—; nat. bd. advisors Eller Coll. Mgmt. U. Ariz., 1990-2007, mem. Dean's Bd. Coll. Fine Arts, 1992—, chmn., 1992-96, pres. Ariz. Coun. Econ. Edn., 1993-95; vis. panel Sch. Health Adminstrn. and Policy Ariz. State U., 1990-92; bd. dirs. Cmty. Found. So. Ariz., 1996-2001; mem. adv. bd. Steele Meml. Rsch. Ctr., U. Ariz. Coll. Medicine, 1996-2004; mem. student health adv. com. U. Ariz., 1990-07. Named to Hon. Order Ky. Cols.; named Tucson Man of Yr. 1987, Tucson Father of Yr. 1997, Hon. Alumnus, Coll. Nursing, U. Ariz., 1998; recipient Disting. Svc. award Anti-Defamation League B'nai B'rith, 1989, Sticking-Your-Neck-Out award Pima Coun. on Aging, 1991, Il Magnifico award U. Ariz. Coll. Fine Arts, 1996, Humanitarian award Arthritis Found. S.Am., 2001, Crystal Apple Lifetime Achievement award Tucson Metro Edn. Commn., 2004, Pima Med. Found. award, 2005, Humanitarian Achievement award, Ednl. Enrichment Found., 2005; co-recipient Paloma Family Svcs. Commitment to Children award, 2005; Pima CC Dinner honoree, 1986, 92. Mem. Am. Hosp. Assn. (nominating com. 1983-86, trustee 1975-78, ho. dels. 1972-78, chmn. coun. profl. svc. 1973-74, regional adv. bd. 1969-78, chmn. joint com. with NASW 1963-64, Disting. Svc. award 1989), Ariz. Hosp. Assn. (Salisbury award 1982, bd. dirs. 1967-72, pres. 1970-71), Ariz. C. of C. (bd. dirs. 1988-93), Assn. Am. Med. Colls. (mem. assembly 1974-77), Health Care Execs. Study Soc., 1975-, Tucson C. of C. (bd. dirs. 1968-69, 1974), Nat. League for Nursing, Ariz. Town Hall (bd. dirs. 1982-92, chmn. 1990-92, treas. 1985, Circle of Disting. Svc. award 2002, Agnos Legacy Award, 2010), Pima County Acad. Decathlon Assn. (dir. 1983-85), Rotary Club (Tucson) (pres. 1993-94, McPherson award, 2008), U. Ariz. Alumni Assn. Coll. Nursing (hon. alumnus 1998), Pi Alpha Alpha (hon.). Baptist/Presbyterian (ch. moderator, chmn. finance com., deacon, ch. sch. supt., trustee, bd. dirs. ch. found.) Office: Tucson Med Ctr 5301 E Grant Rd Tucson AZ 85712-2805

SHRUM, KAYSE, dean, educator, pediatrician; AS, Connors State Coll., Warner, Okla., 1992; DO, Okla. State U., 1998. Resident in pediat. Tulsa Regional Med. Ctr., 1998—2001; pvt. practice Muskogee Children's Clinic, Okla., 2001—02; co-course coord. health promotion & disease prevention Okla. State U. Ctr. Health Sciences, 2002—04, asst. residency program dir., 2003—04, asst. prof. dept. pediat., 2002—07, acting chair dept. pediat., 2003, chmn. dept. pediat., 2004—11, St. Francis Health Systems endowed chair pediat., 2004—, assoc. prof. dept. pediat., 2007—09, prof. pediat., 2009—, interim v.p. acad. affairs, 2009—11, provost, dean Coll. Osteopathic Medicine and George Kaiser Family Found. chair in med. excellence and svc., 2011—. Mem. Okla. Med. Res. Corps, 2005—; bd. mem. Tulsa Coalition Children's Health, 2004—; mem. med. exec. com. St. Francis Children's Hosp., 2006—; bd. trustees Okla. State U. Med. Ctr., 2006—08; bd. dirs. Ronald McDonald House Charities, 2006—09. Mem.: Nat. Bd. Osteopathic Med. Examiners, American Osteopathic Bd. Pediat. (bd. trustees 2007—), American Osteopathic Assn. (mem. house dels. 2000, 2009), Okla. Osteopathic Assn. (mem. legis. com. 2002—03, post grad. edn. com. 2003—05, mem. Okla. State genetics bd. 2002—, bd. trustees 2008—, alt. mem. house dels. 2009—, mem. physician grievance com. 2009—10), Phi Theta Kappa, Ark. Alpha Epsilon Delta, Golden Key Honor Soc., Sigma Sigma Phi, Phi Kappa Phi. Office: Okla State University Ctr Health Sciences Office of Provost/Dean 1111 W 17th St Tulsa OK 74107 Office Phone: 918-582-1972. Business E-Mail: kayse.shrum@okstate.edu. *

SHU, HUNG-YU, biology professor; b. Taoyuan, Taiwan, Sept. 25, 1970; PhD, Nat. Yang-Ming U., 2002. Asst. prof. Chang Jung Christian U., 2007—. Mem.: Am. Soc. Microbiology. Office: 396 Sect 1 Changrong Rd Gueiren Tainan 71101 Taiwan

SHU, JENNIFER A., pediatrician, writer; b. May 21, 1967; MD, Med. Coll. Va., 1992. Cert. Pediat. Resident, pediat. U. Calif., San Francisco, 1992—96; mem. pediat. staff Dartmouth Hitchcock Med. Ctr., Lebanon, NH, 2004—. Cons. in field. Host (blogspot) parentingsense.blogspot.com; author: Heading Home with Your Newborn from Birth to Reality, 2005, Baby and Child Health, 2006, Food Fights, 2007; interviewed by NBC Nightly News, CNN Headline News, MSNBC, Discovery Health Channel, US News and World Report, USA Today, US Weekly and local and nat. TV, newspapers and radio shows and multiple parenting magazines and websites, regular host ReachMD on XM satellite radio.

SHUB, HARVEY ALLEN, surgeon; b. Bklyn., Oct. 28, 1942; s. Irving and Sara (Levin) S.; m. Susan Jayne Smith, Dec. 26, 1970; children: Carolyn, Todd. Student, NYU, 1960-61, 64-65; BS in Zoology, Physics, U. Miami, 1964; MD, U. Rome, Italy, 1971. Diplomate Am. Bd. Colon and Rectal Surgery. Intern Beth Israel Med. Ctr., NYC, 1971-72, resident in surgery, 1972-76; fellow in colon and rectal surgery Muhlenberg Hosp., Plainfield, NJ, 1976-77; practice medicine specializing in colon and rectal surgery Orlando, Fla., 1977—; chmn. dept. surgery Fla. Hosp., 1988-89, dept. colon and rectal surgery, 1999—2001. Pres. med. staff Fla. Hosp., 1992-93; asst. cons. prof. dept. surgery Duke U., 1995; mem. staff Winter Park Meml. Hosp., South Seminole Cmty. Hosp., Fla. Hosp. and Med. Ctr., Orlando Regional Healthcare Sys.; clin. asst. prof. dept. family medicine U. South Fla., Tampa, 1982—; med. dir. Brevard Profl. Network, 2002-2004. Consulting editor Jour. Fla. Med. Assn.; contbr. articles to profl. jours. Chmn. pub. edn. com. Am. Cancer Soc. Orange County, 1982—86. Capt. M.C., USAR, 1971-77. Recipient Physician's Recognition awards AMA. Fellow ACS, Am. Soc. Colon and Rectal Surgeons, Internat. Coll. Surgeons, Southeastern Surg. Congress, Internat. Soc. Univ. Colon and Rectal Surgeons; mem. AMA, So. Med. Assn., Fla. Med. Assn. (sect. splty. medicine), Orange County Med. Assn., Piedmont Soc. Colon and Rectal Surgeons (pres. elect 1997, pres. 1998-2000), Orange County Ostomy Assn. (med. adviser), Fla. Soc. Colon and Rectal Surgeons (sec.-treas. 1980-82, pres. 1983-84, sec.-treas. 1986-98, pres. 1998-2000, treas. 2005—), Am. Soc. Gastrointestinal Endoscopy, Am. Soc. Laser Medicine and Surgery, Soc. Am. Gastrointestinal Endoscopic Surgeons. Home: 5252 Vista Club Run Sanford FL 32771-7153 Personal E-mail: tushmd4@aol.com.

SHUEN-KUEI, LIAO, medical association administrator, educator; b. Morioka, Japan, June 28, 1940; BSc, Tunghai U., 1964; PhD, McMaster U., 1971. Sect. head, divsn. head, dir., academic affairs Biotherapeutic Inc. and Biol. Therapy Inst., 1986—90; adj. prof., dept. microbiology and immunology NY Med. Coll., Vahalla, 1986—92; vis. sr. scientist, oncology lab. Hoag Cancer Ctr., Newport Beach, Calif., 1990—92; prof. Grad. Inst. Clin. Med. Scis. Chang Gung U., 1992—2010; prof., dir. Cancer Immunotherapy Ctr. Taipei Med. U. Hosp., 2010—. Peer-review referee manuscripts Jour. Cancer Rsch. Inst., Cancer Rsch., Biochemistry and Cell Biology, Molecular Biotherapy, Tumor Biology, BMC Cancer, Jour. of Bion, 1978—2011; mem. grants panel, study section site visit rev. team Med. Rsch. Coun. Can., Nat. Cancer Inst., Nat. Cancer Inst., Nat. Inst. Health, 1979—86; institional rev. bd. mem. Min-Shen Hosp., Taoyuan, Taiwan, 2002—07; reviewer, faculty promotion com. and tenure com. Jefferson Thomas U., Phila., 2008—09. Mem.: Internat. Soc. Immuno and Biotherapy, Am. Assn. Cancer Rsch. Office: 250 Wu-Xing St Shing-Yi Dist Taipei 110 Taiwan Business E-Mail: liaosk@tmuh.org.tw.

SHUER, LAWRENCE MENDEL, neurosurgery educator, dean; b. Toledo, Apr. 12, 1954; s. Bernard Benjamin and Estelle Rose (Drukker) S.; m. Paula Ann Elliott, Sept. 4, 1976; children: Jenna, Tammy, Nichole. BA with high distinction, U. Mich., 1975, MD cum laude, 1978. Diplomate Am. Bd. Neurol. Surgery, Nat. Bd. Med. Examiners. Fellow in neurology Inst. Neurology, London, 1979; intern in surgery Stanford U. Sch. Medicine, Calif., 1978-79, resident in neuropathology, 1980, resident in neurosurgery, 1980-84, clin. asst. prof. surgery and neurosurgery, 1984-90, assoc. prof., 1990—2002, assoc. dean Grad. Med. Edn., 1996—, assoc. chair neurosurgery, 2004—; chief of staff Stanford U. Hosp. and Clinics, 1996—2008, prof., 2002—. Numerous presentations in field. Contbr. articles and abstracts to med. jours., chpts. to books. Recipient Kaiser tchr. award Stanford U., 1993; James B. Angell scholar. Mem. AMA, Am. Assn. Neurol. Surgeons, Congress Neurol. Surgeons, Western Neurosurg. Soc., Calif. Assn. Neurol. Surgeons (bd. dirs., treas. 1995—98, 2nd v.p. 1998-99, 1st v.p. 1999-2000, pres.-elect 2000-01, pres. 2002-03), Calif. Med. Assn., Am. Heart Assn. (fellow stroke coun.), Santa Clara County Med. Assn., San Francisco Neurol. Soc., Alpha Omega Alpha. Conservative. Jewish. Avocations: skiing, swimming, travel. Office: Stanford U Med Ctr 300 Pasteur Dr R229 Palo Alto CA 94304-5327 Home Phone: 650-222-5433; Office Phone: 650-723-6093. Business E-Mail: lshuer@stanford.edu.

SHUFANG, NIE, biomedical researcher, educator; b. Wuhan, Mar. 14, 1977; PhD, Shenyang Pharm. U., 2004. Postdoc. rschr. Shenyang Pharm. U., 2004—09, Sch. Chinese Medicine, Hong Kong Bapt. U., 2009—10; rsch. prof., dept. pharm. engring. Wuhan Bioengineering Inst., China, 2010—. Office: Han-Shi Rd 1 Wuhan Hubei 430415 China Business E-Mail: niesf77@163.com.

SHUGALEV, NICOLAY PETROVICH, neurologist; b. Moscow, July 20, 1942; PhD, Moscow Sch.; MD, Moscow Med. Sechenov Acad., 1965. Rsch. scientist, brain rsch. dept., Rsch. Ctr. Neurology Russian Acad. Med. Scis., 1965—. Head Lab. Exptl. Pathology Nervous Sys., 1996. Avocation: travel. Office: Obukha 5 Moscow 105064 Russia Office Fax: (495)9178007. Business E-Mail: nshugalyov@yandex.ru.

SHUKLA, DHANANJAY, ophthalmologist; b. Gwalior, India, July 30, 1967; s. Bhartendu and Sudha Shukla; m. Kamalpreet Likhari, May 6, 1995; children: Manu, Dev. MS, Gajara Raja Med. Coll., 1994. Prof. Aravind Eye Hosp. and Postgrad. Inst., Madurai, India, 2004, cons., 2004. Recipient Gold medal, Gajara Raja Med. Coll., 1988, 1989. Mem.: Am. Familial Exec. Vitreo-Retinopathy Consortium (indian mem.), Ocular Trauma Soc. of India (life), All India Ophthal. Soc. (life), Vitreo-Retinal Soc. of India (life). Office: Aravind Eye Hosp 1 625 020 Madurai 625020 India Office Fax: 91-452-253984. Personal E-mail: daksh66@gmail.com.

SHUKLA, SHRUTI, microbiologist; b. Uttar Pradesh, India, Mar. 22, 1984; M in Microbiology, Jiwaji U., Gwalior, Madhya Pradesh, 2005; PhD, Dr. Hari Singh Gour U., Sagar, Madhaya Pradesh, 2009. Microbiologist Alkem Lab. Pvt. Ltd., Mumbai, 2005—06; prof. Yeungnam U., Republic of Korea, 2009—. Editl. mem. Tang Jour., Republic of Korea. Rsch. Project grant, Nat. Medicinal Plant Bd., New Delhi. Mem.: Rsch. Jour. Biotechnology, India, Indiam Assn. Microbiologists. Avocations: writing, sports. Home: C/O Dr Anil Sharma 6 C Sagar Madhaya Pradesh 470003 India Personal E-mail: s.microb@yahoo.com.

SHUKOR, SHEIKH MUSZAPHAR, surgeon; b. July 26, 1972; B in Medicine and Surgery, Kasturba Med. Coll., Manipal India; CM in Orthopaedic Surgery, U. Kebangsaan, Malaysia. With Seremban Hosp., 1998, Gen. Hosp., Kuala Lumpur, 1999, Selayang Hosp., 2000—01; orthopedist Univ. Kebangsaan Malaysia Hosp. Joined Angkasawan Program; prime mem. of the 16 mem. crew Soyuz 11 Spacecraft. Finalist Angkasawan Program. Achievements include 1st Malaysian to go to space under the "Angkasawan Program" in collaboration with Russia; renowned medic in Medicine at the University Kebangsaan in Malaysia and a Popular Orthopedic Surgeon. Office: University Kebangsaan Malaysia Hospital Jalan Yaacob Latif Bandar Tun Razak Cheras Kuala Lumpur 56000 Malaysia Office Phone: 60391733333. *

SHUKOR, SHIEKH MUSZAPHAR, orthopedic surgeon; b. Malaysia, July 27, 1972; married. Grad. in Medicine and Surgery, Kasturba Med. Coll., Manipal, India; MS in Orthopedic Surgery, U. Kebangsaan, Malaysia. Orthopedist Univ. Kebangsaan Malaysia Hosp., Kuala Lumpur; spaceflight participant Soyuz TMA-11 / Soyuz TMA-10, 2007. Avocations: yoga, meditation, swimming, gymnastics. Office: c/o Universiti Kebangsaan Malaysia Medical Centre Jalan Yaacob Latif Bandar Tun Razak Kuala Lumpur Malaysia Office Phone: 60391455555. Office Fax: 60391724530. *

SHULDINER, ALAN RODNEY, endocrinologist, educator; b. Irumagawa, Japan, Feb. 5, 1957; parents Am. citizens; s. Julius and Janet (Gursky) S.; m. Jill Francie Bresman, June 27, 1984; children: Seth David, Scott Ross. AB in Chemistry magna cum laude, Lafayette coll., 1979; MD with honors, Harvard U., 1984. Diplomate Am. Bd. Internal Medicine, Am. Bd. Endocrinology and Metabolism. Intern in medicine Columbia-Presbyn. Hosp., NYC, 1984-85, resident in medicine, 1985-86; med. staff fellow Diabetes Br. Nat. Inst. Diabetes and Digestive and Kidney Diseases NIH, Bethesda, Md., 1986-88, sr. staff fellow, 1988-90; asst. prof. div. geriatric medicine and gerontology Sch. Medicine Johns Hopkins U., Balt., 1990-91, assoc. prof. div. geriatric medicine and gerontology, 1993—97; prof., head division of diabetes, obesity and nutrition U. Maryland Medical Sch., 1997—99, prof., head division of endocrinology, diabetes and nutrition, 1999—, John Whitehurst Professor of Medicine, 2005—, dir., Interdepartmental Program in Genetics and Genomic Medicine, 2005—; core investigator, geriatric rsch. and education clinical ctr. Balt. Veterans Administration Medical Ctr.; network dir., Joslin Diabetes Ctr. U. Maryland. Guest rschr. Nat. Inst. on Aging NIH, Balt., 1991—96; prof., head divsn. diabetes, obesity and nutrition U. Md. Sch. Medicine, 1997—99; dir. Joslin Diabetes Ctr, 1997—, head divsn. endocrinology, diabetes & nutrition, 1999—; lectr. Endocrine Soc. meetings, 1996, 99, Japan Diabetes Soc. meeting, 1996, Am. Heart Assn. meeting, 1996, FASEB meeting, 1997, Am. Diabetes Assn. meeting, 1997, 99, VII Internat. Symposium on Insulin Action, 1998, with, 2000, NAASD, 2001, FASEB, 2002. Co-author: Current Therapy in Endocrinology and Metabolism, 3d edit., 1988, 4th edit., 1991, Handbook of Endocrine Research Techniques, 1993, Diabetes Mellitus: A Fundamental and Clinical text, 1996, 3d edit., 2003; contbr. articles to profl. jours. including Archives Biochem. Biophysics, Jour. Biol. Chemistry, New Eng. Jour. Medicine, Diabetes, Analytical Biochemistry, Endocrinology, Gene, Nucleic Acids Rsch., Procs. NAS, Biotechniques, Jour. Clin. Endocrinology Metabolism, Diabetes. Recipient Paul Beeson Physician Faculty Scholar award Am. Fedn. Aging Rsch., 1996. Fellow: ACP (Betty Stevens award 2003); mem.: AMA, AAAS, Endocrine Soc., Am. Diabetes Assn. Office: Univ Maryland 660 W Redwood St Rm 494 Baltimore MD 21201-1009 E-mail: ashuldin@medicine.umaryland.edu.

SHULI, LIANG, surgeon; b. Hebei, China, July 7, 1976; PhD, Nanfang Med. U., 2000. Chief, prof. Epilepsy Ctr., 1st affiliated Hosp., Gen. Hosp. PLA, 2004—. Vice sec. gen. Beijing Assn. Against Epilepsy, 2008—, bd. dirs., 2009—. Mem.: China Med. Assn. Avocation: mountain climbing. Office: 51 Fucheng Rd Beijing 100048 China Business E-Mail: liangsl_304@sina.com.

SHULKIN, BARRY, physician; b. Amarillo, Tex., Apr. 2, 1952; s. Stanley and Harriet Shulkin; m. Patricia Ann Mandel, June 17, 1990; children: Zachary David, Jeffrey Daniel. BA, U. Tex., Austin, 1974; MD, U. Tex., Dallas, 1978; MBA, U. Mich., Ann Arbor, 2002. Prof. radiology U. Mich., Ann Arbor, 1999—2004; dir. nuc. medicine St. Jude Children's Rsch. Hosp., Memphis, 2004—. Chair fin. com. Am. Bd. Nuc. Medicine, St. Louis, 2004. Grantee, NIH, 1991—2001. Fellow: ACP. Avocation: running. Office: St Jude Children's Research Hospital 262 Danny Thomas Place Mail Stop 220 Memphis TN 38105 *

SHULMAN, ABRAHAM, otolaryngology educator, hospital administrator; b. NYC, Feb. 24, 1929; s. Ben and Libby (Sarnoff) S.; m. Arlene P., Sept. 8, 1957; children: Rachel, Melanie. BS, CCNY, 1950; MD, U. Berne, 1955; PhD student, Martha Entenmann Tinnitus Rsch. Ctr., Inc., 2010—. Bar:; diplomate Am. Bd. Otolaryngology., 1962. Rotating surg. intern Queens County Gen. Hosp., 1955—56; resident in otolaryngology Kings County Hosp., Bklyn., 1957—60; clin. instr. Downstate Med. Ctr. SUNY, 1962—64, assoc. prof. Downstate Med. Ctr., 1975—89; prof. clin. otolaryngology SUNY Health Sci. Ctr., Bklyn., 1989—92, prof. emeritus clin. otolaryngology, 1992—; clin. instr. Albert Einstein Coll. Medicine, 1966—68, asst. clin. prof. otolaryn. surgery, 1968—75. Asst. surgeon Bklyn. Eye & Ear Hosp., 1966-69; otology cons. College Point chief of otolaryngology Lincoln Hosp., 1967-70, Bklyn. VA Med. Ctr., 1977-85, chief otolaryngology, staff attending otolaryngologist, 1985—, acting chief of otolaryngology, 1990-91; lectr., asst. attending otolaryngologist Mt. Sinai Hosp., 1974; chief otolaryngology Lincoln Hosp., 1967-1970; asst. attending otolaryngology Bronx Mcpl. Hosp., 1967-75; chief Otolaryngologist, asst. attending otolaryngologist, Kings County Hosp., 1962-64, dir. otolaryngology, 1975-92, attending otolaryngologist, 1975—, Brookdale Med. Ctr., 1982-86; chief otolaryngology Cath. Med. Ctr., Bklyn. and Queens, 1969-94, attending otololaryngologist St. John's Queens Hosp., 1969-94; chmn. Internat. Tinnitus Forum, 1982—; Martha Entenmann Tinnitus Rsch. Ctr., Inc., dir. otology neurotology 1994—. Editor (co-chief): Internat. Tinnitus Jour., 1994—; editor: (text) Tinnitus Diagnosis and Treatment, 1991—; contbr. articles to jours. Cons. Children's Devel. Ctr., 1975; med. cons. Office Vocat. Rehab., 1974; dir. med. svc. Lexington Sch. of the Deaf, 1972-74. Lt. comdr. USNR, 1960-62. Recipient Cert. of Appreciation, Am. Speech and Hearing Assn., 1989—, Hocks award, Am. Tinnitus Assn., 1990, Honor award, Am. Acad. Otolaryngology, 1994, Myrtle Reed award, Hadassah Zionist Orgn. Am., 150 Yrs. Med. Edn. Achievement award, SUNY Downstate Med. Ctr., 2010. Fellow ACS, AMA, Am. Acad. Ophthalmology and Otolaryngology (Head & Neck Surgery mem., 2010-), Am. Neurotology Soc., Am. Acad. Otolaryngology-Head & Neck Surgery, Am. Audiology Soc., Am. Soc. Ophthalmologic and Otolaryngology Allergy, Am. Soc. Facial Plastic Surgery, Internat. Coll. Surgeons, Adam Politzer Soc.; mem. Am. Coun. Otolaryngology, Am. Soc. Contemporary Medicine and Surgery, Pan-Am. Assn. Otorhinolaryngology and Bronchoesophagology, NY Acad. Sci., Soc. for Cryosurgery, Queens County Med. Soc., Soc. Univ. Otolaryngologists, Bklyn. Oncology Soc., Assn. for Rsch. in Otolaryngology, Neuroequilibrimetric Soc. (Neurotological Rsch. award 2010), Harvey Soc., Centurion Club, Sigma Xi. Office Phone: 718-773-8888.

SHULMAN, GERALD I., physician, scientist, endocrinologist, educator; b. Detroit, Feb. 8, 1953; BS with high honors and distinction, U. Mich., 1974; MD, PhD, Wayne State U., 1979; MA, privatim (hon.), Yale Univ., 1997. Intern Duke U., Durham, NC, 1979-80, residency, 1980-81; fellowship in endocrinology and metabolism Mass. Gen. Hosp., Boston, 1981-84; asst. prof. medicine Harvard U., Boston, 1985-87; assoc. prof. Sch. Medicine Yale U., New Haven, 1989-96; assoc. dir. Yale MD-PhD Program Sch. Medicine Yale U., New Haven, 1993—, prof. internal medicine, cellular and molecular physiology, 1996—; mem. elected Nat. Academy Sci., 2007. Vis. prof. Vanderbilt U., 1994, Albert Einstein Coll. Medicine, 1999, Washington U. Sch. Medicine, 2001, Cambridge U., 2002, U. Md., 2004; assoc. dir. Yale Diabetes Endocrine Rsch. Ctr., 1996—; investigator Howard Hughes Med. Inst., 1997—; Sipersten lectr. U. Calif., San Francisco, 2006; program dir. Yale/New Haven Hosp. Gen. Clin. Rsch. Ctr.; Pfizer prof. U. Colo.; mem. NIH study sects.; Marble lectr. Joslin Diabetes Ctr., 2007; lectr. in field. Mem. editl. bd. Diabetes, Am. Jour. Physiology; assoc. editor: Diabetic Medicine, Jour. Clin. Investigation, Am. Jour. Medicine, Diabetologia, Internat. Jour. Molecular Medicine, Am. Jour. Physiology, Jour. Biol. Chemistry, Cell Metabolism, 2004—, PLoS Medicine, 2004—; contbr. articles to profl. jours. Recipient Outstanding Investigator award for Clinical Rsch., 1994, Am. Fed. Med. Rsch., 1997, Diabetes Care Rsch. award, Boehriger Mannheim/Juvenile Diabetes Found. Internat., 1997, Young Investigator award in diabetes, Novartis, 1999, Mary June Kugel award, Juvenile Diabetes Rsch. Found. Internat., 1999, E.H. Ahrens Jr. award, Assn. for Patient-Oriented Rsch., 2001, Josiah Brown award in Diabetes, UCLA, 2002, John Shaw Lectureship, Australia-SE Asia- New Zealand, 2006, Miami Berie award for outstanding Achievement in Diabetes Rsch., Columbia U., 2007, Calloway Leadership, U. Calif., Berkeley, 2008, Einstein Lectureship, Baystate Med. Ctr., Springfield, Mass., 2008, Naomi Berrie award. Fellow: ACP, Am. Coll. Endocrinologists, Internat. Soc. Magnetic Resonance in Medicine; mem.: NAS, European Assn. Study of Diabetes, Am. Physiol. Soc., Inst. Medicine of NAS, Endocrine Soc., Am. Soc. Clin. Investigation, Assn. Am. Physicians, Am. Diabetes Assn. (clin. rsch. grantee 1996, Outstanding Sci. Achievement Lilly Lectr. award 1997, Mentor award 1997, 1999, Disting. Clin. Scientist award 2004), Interurban Clin. Club. Office: Howard Hughes Med Inst Yale U Sch Medicine PO Box 9812 New Haven CT 06536-0812 Address: Yale Univ Sch Medicine New Haven CT 06536-8012 Fax: 203-737-4059. Business E-Mail: gerald.shulman@yale.edu.

SHULMAN, ROBERT JAY, pediatrician, nutritionist, gastroenterologist, educator; b. Newark; s. Irving Jack and Shirley Shulman; children: David Ian, Hannah Rachel. BA, Emory U., 1972; MD, Chgo. Med. Sch., 1976. Diplomate in pediatrics and pediatric gastroenterology Am. Bd. Pediatrics. Asst. prof. pediat. Baylor Coll. Medicine, Houston, 1982-89, assoc. prof., 1989—96, prof., 1996—2008; dir. nutritional support team Tex. Children's Hosp., Houston, 1982—2008. Chmn. sub-bd. in pediatric gastroenterology Am. Bd. Pediatrics, 2003—06; chmn., nutrition com. North Am. Soc. Pediat. Gastroenterology, Hepatology and Nutrition, 2007—08. Author: Young Chef's Nutrition Guide and Cookbook, 1990, Keys to Child Nutrition, 1991; author: (with others) Pediatric Gastroenterology and Nutrition in Clinical Practice, 2001, Principles and Practice of Pediatrics, 2006, Pediatric Nutrition Support, 2007; co-editor: Nutrition in Your Pocket, 2002; mem. editl. bd. Jour. Pediat. Gastroenterology and Nutrition, 1994—96. Fellow: Am. Acad. Pediat.; mem.: Soc. Pediat. Rsch., N.Am. Soc. Pediat. Gastoenterology and Nutrition (exec. coun. 1997—99), Am. Inst. Nutrition, Am. Soc. Patenteral and Enteral Nutrition (chmn. pediatric sect. 1997—99, pres. 1997—99), Am. Gastroent. Assn. Avocation: guitar. Office: Baylor Coll Medicine 1100 Bates Ave Houston TX 77030-2600

SHULSTAD, ANDREW ROBERT, pediatrician; s. Robert Norman and Carol Ann Shulstad; m. Jennifer Shulstad, children: Mary Claire, Christopher, Connor. BSA, U. Ga., Athens, 1992; MD, Med. Coll. Ga., Augusta, 1996. Intern, then resident Med. Coll. Ga., 1996—99; pediatrician Charlotte Pediat. Clinic, NC, 1999—; exec. bd. NC Pediat. Soc., 2006—09; owner & Med. Dir. Satin Med. Spa, 2010—. Camp physician YMCA Camp Thunderbird, Lake Wylie, SC, 2005—07; chief pediat. Levine Children's Hosp., Charlotte, 2006—09, Charlotle Jr. League, 2005—09. Chmn. bd. dirs. Reach Out and Read-Charlotte, 2003—05; mem. adv. panel Charlotte Jr. League, 2005—. Recipient Pres. award, Mecklenburg County Med. Soc., Charlotte, 2004, Best Pediat. award, Charlotte Mag., 2007—10, Opetims Bd. Charlotle Pediat. Clinic, 2003—. Fellow: Am. Acad. Pediat.; mem.: Carolina Physicians Network (exec. bd. 2007—), NC Pediat. Soc. (exec. bd. 2006—). Avocations: soccer, basketball, water sports, horseback riding, travel. Office: Charlotte Pedia Clinic 4501 Cameron Valley Dr Charlotte NC 28211

SHUM, CHEUK FAN, surgeon; b. Hong Kong, Jan. 23, 1979; m. Hoi Shan Cheung, Dec. 30, 2004; 1 child, Hei Yi. MBBS, Nat. U., Singapore, 2003, MMed in Surgery, 2008. House officer Singapore Health Svcs. Ltd., 2003—04, med. officer, 2004—08; registrar Alexandra Health Pte. Ltd., 2008—11. Contbr. articles to profl. jours. Mem.: Singapore Urol. Assn., Royal Coll. Surgeons Edinburgh, Singapore Med. Assn. Office: Alexadra Health Pte Ltd 90 Yishun Central Singapore 768828 Singapore

SHUMAN, CAROLYN RAE (THORBURN), psychologist, writer; d. Donald Spencer and Eileen Mary Thorburn; m. Gary H. Shuman, Nov. 22, 1975; m. Dennis Lee Atkin, June 15, 1963 (div. July 20, 1968); 1 child, Dennis Lee Atkin, Jr. PhD, Tex. A&M U., Commerce, 1985—96; MS, East Tex. State U., Commerce, 1985—90; BS, Bapt. Coll. of Charleston, SC, 1977—78; AA, Armstrong State Coll., Savannah, Ga., 1972—76. RN 1975. Owner Ctr. for Cognitive Therapy, Hamilton, Bermuda, 1999—2003, Carol Shuman PhD LLC, 2010—; dir. family svc. ctr. USNAS-Bermuda, St David's, 1992—95; psychotherapist/psychologist Ashton Associates, Hamilton, 1994—99; clin. supr. USNAS-Bermuda, St. David's, 1991—94; adj. prof. Webster U., U. of Md., City Colleges of Chgo., USNAS-Bermuda, 1991—97. Cons. King Edward Hosp. VII EAP, Hamilton, 2001—03, Family Learning Ctr., Hamilton, 1994—96. Author: (book) Jenny Is Scared: When Sad Things Happen in the World, 2003 (Psychology Grad. Faculty Scholarship, Tex. A&M-Commerce, 1987), Kill The Once... Kill Me Twice: Murder on The Queen's Playground, 2010. Mem., spkr. Bermuda Chamber of Commerce, Hamilton, 2000—03; mem. Fairhaven Christian Care/ Nat. Drug Strategy/, Hamilton, 1998—2001. Recipient Journalism Enterprise, Ga. AP, 1972; scholar Honors Scholarship, Armstrong State Coll., 1973-1975, Grad. Faculty Honors, Tex. A&M Psychology Dept., 1987. Mem.: Am. Soc. Criminology, Am. Psychol. Assn., Nat. Writer Assn., APA (life). Achievements include research in cross culture, health, cognitive behavior therapy, hardiness; death studies (Psychology Journal, 1992); presentations, Death & Dying, SWPA, 1993-1997. Avocations: writing, swimming, travel, music. E-mail: drcshuman@datkin.net.

SHUNSUKE, YAMADA, medical educator; b. Oita, Japan, Feb. 10, 1958; MD, Tokai U. Sch. Medicine, 1983, PhD, 1993. Prof. Tokai U. Sch. Medicine, 2011—. Fellow: Japan Soc. Endoscopic Surgery, Japanese Assn. Chest Surgery; mem.: Japan Lung Cancer Soc., Japan Surg. Soc., Japanese Assn. Thoracic Surgery. Avocations: skiing, diving. Office: Tokai University Hachioji Hosp 1838 Hachioji Tokyo 192-0032 Japan Office Fax: 81-426-39-1144. Business E-Mail: yamada.shunsuke@hachioji-hosp.tokai.ac.jp.

SHURE, MYRNA BETH, psychologist, educator; b. Chgo., Sept. 11, 1937; d. Sidney Natkin and Frances (Laufman) Shure. Student, U. Colo., 1955; BS, U. Ill., 1959; MS, Cornell U., Ithaca, NY, 1961, PhD, 1966. Asst. prof. U. RI; head tchr. Nursery Sch., Kingston, 1961-62; asst. prof. Temple U., Phila., 1966-67, assoc. prof., 1967-68; instr. Hahnemann Med. Coll., Phila., 1968-69, sr. instr. psychology, 1969-70, asst. prof., 1970—73, assoc. prof., 1973—80, prof., 1980—2002, Drexel U., Phila., 2002—. Spl. cons. PBS Children's TV Show The Puzzle Place; adv. bd. Parents Mag., 2004—07. Author (with George Spivack): Social Adjustment of Young Children, 1974; author: (with George Spivack and Jerome Platt) The Problem Solving Approach to Adjustment, 1976; author: (with George Spivack) Problem Solving Techniques in Childrearing, 1978; author: (child curricula manual) I Can Problem Solve, 1992; author: (trade book) Raising a Thinking Child, 1994; author: (audiotape, workbook, paperback) Raising a Thinking Preteen, 2000 (Parents' Choice award, 2001, Parent's Guide Classic award, 2001); author: Thinking Parent, Thinking Child, 2004; mem. editl. bd. Jour. Applied Devel. Psychology. Recipient Lela Rowland Prevention award, Nat. Mental Health Assn., 1982, Sarah award, Women in Comm. (Phila. chpt., 1998, Psychology in the Media award, Pa. Psychol. Assn., 1999, award, Ctr. for Substance Abuse Prevention, 2001; rsch. grantee, NIMH, 1971—75, 1977—79, 1982—85, 1987, 1988—93, Office Juvenile Justice and Delinquency Prevention grantee, 1966. Fellow: APA (divsn. clin. psychology, child sect. 1994, Disting. Contbn. award divsn. cmty. psychology 1984, Task Force on Prevention award 1987, Task Force on Model Programs award 1994, U. Utah and Juvenile Justice Dept. of Delinquency Prevention award 1996, US Dept. Edn. award 2001, Collaborator for Academic, Social and Emotional Learning award 2002); mem.: Phila. Soc. Clin. Psychologists, Soc. Rsch. in Child Devel., Nat. Assn. Edn. Young Children, Nat. Assn. Sch. Psychologists. Office: Drexel U Dept Psychology 245 N 15th St MS 626 Philadelphia PA 19102 Office Phone: 215-762-7205. Business E-Mail: mshure@drexel.edu.

SHURIN, SUSAN B., federal agency administrator, oncologist, researcher; BA in Biology, Harvard U., 1965; MD, Johns Hopkins U., 1971. Pediat. intern Johns Hopkins Hosp., 1971—72; pediat. resident Boston U., Boston City Hosp., 1972—74; hematology/oncology fellowship Children's Hosp. Med. Ctr., Boston, 1974—76, Mass. Gen. Hosp., 1976—77; prof. pediatrics and oncology Case Western Reserve U., Cleve., 1977—2004; dir. pediatric oncology Case Comprehensive Cancer Ctr.; dir. pediatric hematology-oncology Rainbow Babies and Children's Hosp.; v.p., sec. Corp. at Case Western Reserve U.; dep. dir. Nat. Heart, Lung, and Blood Inst. (NHLBI) NIH, Bethesda, Md., 2006—09, acting dir. Eunice Kennedy Shriver Nat. Inst. Child Health and Human Devel. (NICHD), 2009—10, acting dir. Nat. Heart, Lung, and Blood Inst. (NHLBI), 2009—. Office: NHLBI Office of Dir Bldg 31 Rm 5A52 31 Center Dr MSC 2486 Bethesda MD 20892-2486 Office Phone: 301-496-5166. Office Fax: 301-402-0818. Business E-Mail: susan.shurin@nih.gov. *

SHUSS, JOHN LOGAN, surgeon; b. Kansas City, Dec. 7, 1949; s. J. Logan and Marian Ruth (Brain) S.; m. Linda Lea Trower, Sept. 6, 1980; 1 child, Samantha Lea. BA, U. Kans., 1972; MD, U. Kans., Kansas City, 1975. Resident in gen. surgery La. State U., New Orleans, 1975—76, U. Kans. Coll. Health Scis., 1976—80; surgeon Garden City, Kans., 1980—85, Twin Falls (Idaho) Clinic and Hosp., 1985—2001, Magic Valley Regional Med. Ctr., 2002—. Fellow ACS (pres. Idaho chpt. 1995-96), Southwestern Surg. Congress.; mem. Soc. Am. Gastrointestinal Endoscopic Surgeons, Phi Beta Kappa. Avocations: skiing, white-water rafting, tennis, golf. Home: 3185 Boehm Estates Dr Twin Falls ID 83301-8122 Office: 630 Addison Ave W Ste 200 Twin Falls ID 83301 Home Phone: 208-733-9225.

SHUSTER, FREDERICK, retired internist, gastroenterologist; b. Newark, Sept. 12, 1933; s. Ralph and Anne (Weinstein) S.; m. Jane A. Block, June 11, 1958; children: Alan R., Robert G. BS, Rutgers U., 1955; MD, U. Chgo., 1959. Diplomate Am. Bd. Internal Medicine, Am. Bd. Gastroenterology. Intern U. Mich. Hosp., Ann Arbor, 1959-60, resident internal medicine, 1960-62; resident gastroenterology VA Hosp. U. Miami, Fla., 1962-63; pvt. practice N. Miami Beach, Fla., 1963-97; from clin. instr. to assoc. prof. medicine U. Miami, Fla., 1963—; pvt. practice Aventura, Fla., 1997-98, North Miami Beach; ret., 1998. Chmn. dept. medicine Parkway Regional Med. Ctr., N. Miami Beach, 1967, 70, chief of staff, 1974-75, chief divsn. gastroenterology, 1976-77, chmn. pharmacy and therapeutics com., 1978-98. Chmn. med. advisory com. Crohn's and Colitis Found., S. Fla. chpt., Miami, 1979-81. Major U.S. Army, 1967-69. Recipient Physician's Recognition award in Continung Edn., AMA, Chgo., 1970—. Fellow Am. Coll. Physicians, Am. Coll. Gastroenterology, Alpha Omega Alpha. Jewish. Avocations: bowling, ballroom dancing, stock market research and investing. E-mail: fred991@att.net.

SHUSTER, LYNNE THERESE, internist; b. Oct. 3, 1958; BA, St. Olaf Coll.; MD, Mayo Med. Sch., Rochester, Minn., 1987. Resident, internal medicine Mayo Grad. Sch. Medicine, Mayo Clinic, Rochester, Minn.; fellow, advanced gen.medicine Mayo Grad. Sch. Medicine; asst. prof. medicine Mayo Clinic, Rochester, dir., Women;s Health Clinic. Contbr. several articles to profl. jours. Office: Mayo Clinic 200 1st St SW Rochester MN 55905

SHUTO, TAKASHI, neurosurgeon; b. Yokohama, Kanagawa, Japan, Sept. 27, 1963; s. Akira and Keiko Shuto; m. Keiko Nakao. MD, Yokohama City U., Japan. Cert. Neurosurgeon Japan Neurol. Soc., 1995. Resident in internal medicine Yokohama City U. Hosp., Japan, 1989—91, asst. prof. neurosurgery, 1991—92, staff neurosurgery,

1996—97, asst. prof. neurosurgery, 1997—2001; staff neurosurgery Kanagawa Childrens Med. Ctr., Yokohama, Japan, 1992—93, Yokohama Rosai Hosp., 1993—95, asst. chief neurosurgery, 2001—; staff neurosurgery Odewara Mcpl. Hosp., Japan, 1995—96. Contbr. scientific papers. Grantee, Yokohama Found. for Advancement of Med. Sci., 1998. Office: Yokohama Rosai Hosp 3211 Kozukue Kohoku-ku Kanagawa Yokohama 2220036 Japan Office Fax: +81-45-474-8110. E-mail: shuto@yokohamah.rofuku.go.jp.

SHUTTLEWORTH, ANNE MARGARET, psychiatrist; b. Detroit, Jan. 17, 1931; d. Cornelius Joseph and Alice Catherine (Rice) S.; m. Joel R. Siegel, Apr. 19, 1959; children: Erika, Peter. AB, Cornell U., 1953, MD, 1956. Intern Lenox Hill Hosp., NYC, 1956-57; resident Payne Whitney Clinic-N.Y. Hosp., 1957-60; practice medicine specializing in psychiatry Maplewood, NJ, 1960—. Cons. Maplewood Sch. System, 1960-62; instr. psychiatry Cornell U. Med. Sch., 1960; mem. Com. to Organize New Sch. Psychology, 1970. Mem. AMA (Physicians Recognition award 1975, 78, 81, 84, 87, 90, 93, 96, 99, 02, 05, 08), Am. Psychiat. Assn., Am. Med. Women's Assn., NY Acad. Scis., Acad. Medicine NJ, Phi Beta Kappa, Phi Kappa Phi. Office: 2066 Millburn Ave Maplewood NJ 07040-3715

SIBITZ, INGRID, psychiatrist, researcher; b. Klagenfurt, Austria, 1966; MD, Med. Sch., Vienna, 1993. Physician dept. psychiatry Kaiser-Franz-Josef-Hosp. Vienna, 1994; psychiat. trainee Dr. G. Schönbeck and Ctr. Social Psychiatry Caritas, Vienna, 1995; gen. med. trainee SMZ-Ost Hosp., Vienna, 1996—97; psychiat. trainee dept. social psychiatry and evaluative rsch. Med. U. Vienna, 1997—2002, psychiatrist clin. dept. social psychiatry, 2003—, leading psychiatrist day clin. dept. social psychiatry, 2005—, wahringer Gurtel; guest rschr. Dublin City U., 2010. Contbr. articles to profl. psychiat. jours. Office: Med Univ Vienna Währinger Gürtel 18-20 Vienna 1090 Austria Office Phone: 43 140400 3546. Business E-Mail: ingrid.sibitz@meduniwien.ac.at.

SICARD, GREGORIO A., surgeon, educator; b. Ponce, PR, Oct. 8, 1944; permanent resident; BS, St. Louis U., 1965; MD cum laude, U. PR Sch. Medicine, San Juan, 1972. Lic. Flex Licensure Exam., 1974, diplomate Am. Bd. Surgery, 1978, cert. in gen. vascular surgery recertification 1983. Intern, surgery Barnes Hosp. Washington U. Sch. Medicine, St. Louis, 1972—73, asst. resident, surgery, 1973—76, chief resident, surgery, 1976—77; renal transplant fellow Washington U. Sch. Medicine, St. Louis, 1977—78, instr., surgery & vascular sect., 1977—78, asst. prof., surgery & vascular sect., 1978—83, assoc. prof., surgery & vascular sect., 1983—88, sect. chief, surgery & vascular surgery, 1983—, prof., surgery, vascular sect., 1988—, divsn. chief, gen. surgery, 1998—2007, prof., radiology interventional radiology, 1998—, exec. vice-chmn., dept. surgery, 2000—, prof., dept. surgery, 2006—. Attending surgeon Barnes Jewish Hosp., St. Louis, 1976—, St. Louis City Hosp., 1977—81, St. Louis Regional Med. Ctr., 1977—97, St. Louis Children's Hosp., 1978—, Jewish Hosp. St. Louis, 1990—; staff surgeon Vets. Adminstrn. Hosp., St. Louis, 1977—. Contbr. articles to profl. jours. Co-investigator NIH, 1996—99, 2004—08. Recipient Scholastic Achievement award, PR Med. Assn., 1972, WUSM Alumni Faculty award, 2003, Barnes-Jewish Hosp. Lifetime Achievement award, 2006; named to America's Top Drs. List, 2004, 2005, 2006, 2007; grant, Shering-Piough Rsch. Inst., 1998—99, Prograft Med. Inc., 1998—2000. Fellow: Am. Coll. Surgeons; mem.: Internat. Soc. Vascular Surgery, Brazilian Vascular Jour. Internat. Adv. Coun., Cirujanos Vasculares de Habla Hispana, Cirujanos Endovasculares de Latinoamerica, Fed. Drug Adminstrn. Endovascular Devices Adv. Panel, PR Soc. Vascular and Endovascular Surgery (hon.), Mexican Angiology and Vascular Surgery Soc. (hon.), Colombian Soc. Gen. Surgeons (hon.), Internat. Fedn. Surg. Coll. (assoc.), Assn. Program Dirs. Gen. Vascular Surgery (assoc.; program dir., issues com. 1993—), Ecuadorian Soc. Angiology and Vascular Surgery (hon.), Eastern Vascular Soc. (hon.), Eastern Vascular Soc. (hon.), Midwestern Vascular Surg. Soc., Midwest Surg. Assn., Mid-America Transplant Svcs. (bd. dirs., pres. elect 1997, pres. 1999), Vascular Surgery Biology Club. Office: Washington University Sch Medicine Surgery 660 S Euclid Campus Box 8109 Saint Louis MO 63110 Home: 10370 Whitebridge Ln Saint Louis MO 63143 Office Fax: 314-454-3923. Business E-Mail: sicardg@wustl.edu.

SICHERER, SCOTT H., pediatric allergist, researcher; MD, Johns Hopkins U. Sch. Medicine, NY. Diplomate Am. Bd. Pediat., Am. Bd. Allergy & Immunology. Resident pediat. Mt. Sinai Hosp.; fellowship allergy and immunology Johns Hopkins U. Hosp.; assoc. prof. pediat. Mt. Sinai Sch. Medicine; rschr. Jaffe Food Allergy Inst.-Mt. Sinai Hosp. Mem. med. adv. bd. Food & Allergy Anaphylaxis Alliance. Author: (children's book) Maya and Andrew Learn About Food Allergies, 2000, (book) Understanding and Managing Your Child's Food Allergies, 2006; co-author: The Complete Peanut Allergy Handbook, 2005; contbr. chapters to books, articles to profl. jours. Fellow: Am. Acad. Allergy, Asthma, and Immunology; mem.: Am. Acad. Pediat. Achievements include research in allergic diseases caused by specific foods such as peanuts, tree nuts, egg, seafood and milk; the natural history,epidemiology and genetics of food allergy; gastrointestinal manifestations of food allergies; psychosocial issues associated with food allergies. Office: Mt Sinai Sch Medicine Dept Pediat Box 1198 5 E 98th St 10th Fl New York NY 10029 Office Phone: 212-241-5548. Office Fax: 212-426-1902. Business E-Mail: scott.sicherer@mssm.edu.

SICHEWSKI, VERNON ROGER, physician; b. Winnipeg, Man., Can., Dec. 10, 1942; came to U.S., 1980; s. Nicholas and Helen (Sabanski) S. BS, U. Man., 1963; MD, Cairo U., 1979. Diplomate Am. Bd. Emergency Medicine. Resident Charity Hosp. La., New Orleans, 1980-83, Bellevue Hosp., NYC, 1980-83; pvt. practice Broward Gen. Med. Ctr., Ft. Lauderdale, Fla., 1983-86, Trauma Care Assocs., North Miami, Fla., 1986—. Flight physician Nat. Jets, Ft. Lauderdale, 1986—; mem. Aero Jet Internat. Air Ambulance Profls., 1998; attending physician trauma unit Jackson Meml. Hosp. U. Miami, 1989-97; attending physician Cleve. Clin. Found. Hosp., Ft. Lauderdale, 1999—. Flight lt. RCAF, 1963-74. Fellow Am. Coll. Emergency Physicians; mem. AMA, So. Med. Assn. Republican. Roman Catholic. Avocations: stamp collecting/philately, hunting, fishing, antiques. Home: 1108-2841 N Ocean Blvd Fort Lauderdale FL 33308

SICHLETIDIS, LAZAROS TH, medical educator, director; b. Thessaloniki, Greece, Aug. 10, 1943; Diploma in Medicine, Aristotle's U. Thessaloniki, 1969, diploma in Pulmonary Medicine, 1975. Asst., pulmonary clinic Aristotle's U. Thessaloniki, 1972—75, cons., 1975—84, asst. prof., medicine, 1984—85, assoc. prof., medicine, 1995—2006, prof., medicine, dir., pulmonary clinic, 2006—10. Post-grad. fellow Inst. Di Medicina Del Lavoro, Milan, 1986—87. Grant, European Union, Greek Ministry of Edn., Greek Ministry of Employment. Fellow: Am. Coll. Chest Physicians; mem.: Thoracic Assn. Northern Greece, Greek Soc. Environ. Medicine, Hellenic Thoracic Soc., European Respiratory Soc. Avocations: skiing, mountain climbing. Office: 3 Charles Deal Thessaloniki 54623 Greece Office Fax: 302310260858. Business E-Mail: sichlet@med.auth.gr.

SICHUK, GEORGE, entrepreneur, creator and builder mental analyst, writer, atomic scientist, biochemist, physiologist, transcendental academic theologian, physician; b. Butler Twp., Pa., May 10, 1933; s. Stephan Nicholas and Eva (Hawranick) Sichuk; m. Georgiana Nadya Stroyen, July 27, 1968. BA, Drew U., 1954; DS, Rutgers U., 1962. Rsch. assoc. Sloan-Kettering Inst. Cancer Rsch., NYC, 1961—71; asst. prof. biology Montclair State Coll., Upper Montclair, NJ, 1972—75, William Paterson Coll., Wayne, NJ, 1975; lectr. interdisciplinary studies Bloomfield (N.J.) Coll., 1976; sci. tchr. Eastside H.S., Paterson, NJ, 1988—93; entrepreneur author Lincoln Park, NJ, 1993—. Author: My Presidential Library, 1959, Gabriel's Voice, 1996, Uriel's Light, 1997, One Man's Testament, 1998, Constitutional Imperatives for Rational Government, 2003, Common Sense Plus, 2004, The Pentian Truth: Thomas Paine, the Mozart of Reason, 2004, Miracles of Evolution, Tragedies of Evolution Voodoo Religions, 2007, Invisible Essentials of the Biosphere, 2007, The Pythagorean Fact: Life is not a Theory, 2008, Miracles of Spring, Evolution Equals Food, Splitting the Photon, 1945, Walking on Air, 1960, The Star People, Life is a Rohrshach test, 2009, Living Phosphates: Photon Spin Resonance, Judge of Judges, Founding Mothers; contbr. articles to profl. med. jours. Good will amb. U.S. Govt., Cuba, 1960; coach Police Athletic League, Lincoln Park, 1977—79; CEO NJ Citizens Orgn., 1967—68; exec. and coach Orthodox Citizens' Club, NJ, 1980—90. Achievements include clarification of relationship of the endocrine and immune systems to cancer to direct attention to the nucleic acids (DNA and RNA); clarification of transplantation immunology; proof that "butter yellow" a dibenzanthracene used to give margarine a yellow color is a carcinogen; research in the role of sex hormones in thrombotic disease; dynamic relationship between dietary protein quality and function of adrenal cortex in mammals; nanotechnology and peaceful use of atomic energy; harmonic function of the human brain, denial of monotheism; and proof of origin of viruses, identifying vectors of disease; kidney transplantation; proof that DES can cause thromboembolic disease. Avocations: geo-politics, house maintenance engineering, golf, flying, music. Home: 18 Sewanois Ave Lincoln Park NJ 07035-1710

SICKINGER, STEPHAN, molecular biologist, biomedical researcher; b. Germany, Jan. 28, 1962; Diploma, U. Erlangen-Nuremberg, Germany, 1989, PhD, 1995; postdoc, Inst. Food Rsch. Novaich, 1995—98. Postdoc. scientist Leibniz Inst. Natural Products Rsch. and Infection Biology, Hans-Knoell-Inst., Jena, Germany, 2001—05; sub-project leader exp. Rheumatology Unit Med. U., Jena, Germany, 1998—2001; postdoc. scientist sub project leader Daniel-Swarovski-Rsch.-Lab. Innsbruck Med. U., 2007—09, sci. advisor Daniel-Swarovski-Rsch.-Lab., 2008, postdoc. asst. divsn. neurobiochemistry, biocenter, 2010—11, postdoc. rsch. scientist Cardiac Rsch. Lab., 2011—; postdoc. scientist, vis. scientist U. Leipzig, Dept. Biochemistry, 2005—07. Mem.: Austrian Soc. Transplantation, Transfusion, and Genetics, Austrian Assn. Molecular Life Scis. and Biotechnology, Soc. Gen. and Applied Microbiology (Germany). Avocations: music, guitar, bicycling, squash. Office: Carsiac Rsch Lab Innrain 66 Innsbruck Tirolia 6020 Austria Business E-Mail: stephan.sickinger@i-med.ac.at.

SICKLICK, MARC JOSEPH, pediatrician, allergist, immunologist, educator; MD, Yeshiva U. Diplomate Am. Bd. Pediatrics, Am. Bd. Allergy and Immunology, registered NY, 1975. Resident in pediat. Bronx Mcpl. Hosp. Ctr., NY, 1974—77; fellow in allergy and immunology Montefiore Med. Ctr., 1977—79; pediat. assoc. clin. prof. Albert Einstein coll. med. Yeshiva Univ.; hosp. affiliations include LI Jewish Med. Ctr., North Shore Univ. Hosp. Recipient Best Doctors, NY Mag., 2010. Fellow: Am. Coll. of Allergy, Asthma, and Immunology, Am. Acad. of Allergy, Asthma, and Immunology. Office: North Shore University Hospital 123 Grove Ave Ste 110 Cedarhurst NY 11516 Office Phone: 516-569-5550.

SICOLI, MARY LOUISE CORBIN, psychologist, educator; b. Delaware County, Pa., Nov. 15, 1944; d. C.M. Lewis and Lucille (Weber) Corbin; m. Thomas Sicoli, Aug. 27, 1967; children: Michael, Kathryn Francesca. BS, West Chester U., Pa., 1966, MS, 1974, U. Wis., Madison, 1967; PhD, Bryn Mawr Coll., Pa., 1977. Tchr. music, supr. Unionville-Chadds Ford (Pa.) Sch. Dist., 1967-70; supr. student tchrs. Rosemont (Pa.) Coll., 1976-78; prof. psychology, campus psychologist, coord. psychol. svcs. Cabrini Coll., Radnor, Pa., 1974—. Cons. Children's Svcs. Southea. Pa., 1974-80; supr. doctoral interns in psychology Bryn Mawr Coll., 1979-86; presenter in field. Contbr. articles to profl. jours., scientific papers at profl. Confs. Founding mem. bd. dirs. Maternal Support Sys. Chester County, 1981—; mem. Citizens Action for Better TV, 1981—; founder, chair Psychol. Aspects Popular Culture, Popular Culture Assn. Recipient Legion of Honor award Chapel of the Four Chaplains, 1980, Christian and Mary Lindback award for Disting. Coll. Tchg., 1984; named hon. alumnus Cabrini Coll., 2005. Fellow Pa. Psychol. Assn. (founder campus psychologist network); mem. AAUP, Am. Psychol. Assn. (reviewer rsch. papers 1980-), Ea. Psychol. Assn., Jean Piaget Soc., Assn. Moral Devel., Kappa Delta Pi, Psi Chi (founding adv., reviewer rsch. papers 1980-, Ea. Region Chptr. award 2005), Delta Epsilon Sigma. Home: 404 Darlington Dr West Chester PA 19382-2139 Office: Cabrini Coll Dept Psychology Radnor PA 19087 Home Phone: 610-696-8116. Personal E-mail: mlcorbin@verizon.net. Business E-Mail: mlsicoli@cabrini.edu.

SIDBURY, ROBERT, pediatrician; b. Durham, NC, Sept. 23, 1963; s. James Buren Jr. and Alice Rayle Sidbury; 1 child, Claire Winnie. BS in Psychology, Duke U., 1985, MD, 1993; MPH, Harvard Sch. Pub. Health, 2008. Diplomate Am. Bd. Dermatology, Am. Bd. Pediat. Dermatology. Intern U. Calif., San Francisco, 1993—94, rsch. fellow, 1994—95; resident in dermatology Oreg. Health & Sci. U., Portland, Oreg., 1995—98; fellow pediat. dermatology Childrens Meml. Hosp., Chgo., 1998—2000; asst. prof. pediat. Childrens Hosp., Seattle, 2000—; rsch. fellow Harvard Pediat. Health Svc., 2007—08; asst. prof., dept. dermatology Harvard Med. Sch., Boston Children's Hosp., 2006—09; chief, div. dermatology assoc. prof., dept. pediat. Seattle Children's Hosp., U. Wash. Sch. Medicine, 2009—. Faculty U. Wash. Sch. Medicine, 2004—05; instr. dermatology Bastyr U.; presenter, lectr. in field. Mem. editl. bd.: Derm Clips; contbr. articles to profl. jours., chapters to books. Recipient Dermatology Investigator award, Dermatology Found., 1998; named Tchr. of Yr., Providence Family Practice, 2003, Top Doctor, Seattle Mag., 2004, Boston Mag., 2007, Seattle Met. Mag., 2010. Fellow: Am. Acad. Pediatrics, Am. Acad. Dermatology (edn. slide series task force 2004); mem.: Soc. for Pediat. Dermatology. Democrat. Office: Childrens Hosp University Wash Sch Med A7916 4800 Sand Point Way NE Seattle WA 98105 Office Phone: 206-987-2158. Office Fax: 206-987-2217. Business E-Mail: robert.sidbury@seattlechildrens.org.

SIDDARAJU, NEELAIAH, cytologist, educator; s. Neelaiah and Shakunthalamma; m. Savita Sk, Aug. 8, 1993; 1 child, Chirag. MBBS, Kasturba Med. Coll., Mangalore, Karnataka; MD, Mysore Med. Coll., Karnataka, 1991, Diploma in Clin. Pathology. Sr. resident Lady Hardinge Med. Coll., New Delhi, 1991—94; asst. prof. gen. pathology Mahatma Gandhi Dental Coll., Pondicherry, India; assoc. prof. pathology Maulana Azad Med. Coll., New Delhi; asst. prof. pathology Jawaharlal Inst. Postgrad. Med. Edn. and Rsch. (JIPMER), Pondicherry, prof. pathology, 2002—. Spkr. World Cancer Congress, Singapore, 2010. Contbr. sci. articles to profl. journals; reviewer med. journals. Recipient Rashtriya Gaurav award, India Internat. Friendship Soc., 2010, Indira Gandhi Achievers award, 2010, Rajiv Gandhi Excellence award, 2010, Glory of India Gold medal, Best Citizens of India award, Internat. Pub. House, 2010. Personal E-mail: rajusiddaraju@yahoo.com. E-mail: rajusiddaraju@gmail.com.

SIDDIQUI, FOUZIA, neurologist; d. Ajaz Ahmed Siddiqui and Rakhshanda Ajaz. PECHS, Govt. Coll. Women, Karachi, 1988; MBBS, Dow Med. U., Karachi, 1996; FCPS in Medicine, Coll. Physician and Surgeons Pakistan, Karachi, 2001. Internship Cert. Civil Hosp. Karachi, 1997, residency cert. Liaquat Nat. Hosp., 2001. Internship psychiatry Civil Hosp. Karachi, 1996, internship surgery, 1997, internship medicine, 1997; emergency med. officer Liaquat Nat. Hosp., Karachi, 1998, resident medicine; asst. prof. Hamdard U., Karachi, 2002—03; cons. physician PECHS trauma and gen. Hosp., Karachi; externship neurology Regions Hosp., St. Paul, 2001; rsch. fellow NJ Neurosci. Inst. JFK Med. ctr., Edison, NJ, 2003—06, sleep medicine fellow; preliminary medicine U. Toledo Med. Ctr., 2006—07, resident neurology, 2007—10; cons. Rockingham Meml. Hosp., attending neurologist Harrisonburg, Va., 2010—, cons. neurologist & sleep specialist. Rsch. fellow NJ Neurosci. Inst. JFK Med. ctr., Edison, NJ, 2003—06. Contbr. articles to profl. med. jours. Vol. worker Patients Welfare Orgn., Karachi, 1991—96; asst. editor Amnesty Internat., Karachi, 1994—98. Recipient Travel award, Internat. Restless legs Group, 2004, Gold Found. award, U. Toledo Med. Ctr., 2010. Mem.: Internat. Restless Legs Study Group, Am. Acad. Neurology. Avocations: travel, reading. Office: Rockingham Memorial Hosp 2006 Health Campus Dr Harrisonburg VA 22801 Office Phone: 540-689-5755. Office Fax: 419-383-3093. Personal E-mail: drfsid@yahoo.com.

SIDDIQUI, KHUSHNOOD AHMED, biotechnologist; b. Indore, India, June 15, 1937; BSc, N.Mex. State U., 1956; PhD, U. Reading, Eng., 1964, DSc, 2001. Lectr. botany Agr. Coll., Tando Jam, Pakistan, 1956—61; sr. rsch. scientist Can. Dept. Agr., Lethbridge, Alta., Canada, 1964—66; sr. sci. officer Atomic Energy Agrl. Rsch. Ctr., 1967—70, prin. sci. officer, head plant genetics, 1973—86, chief sci. officer, head plant genetics, 1986—96, chief sci. officer, dir., 1992—96, chief scientist, dir., 1996—97; vis. sr. scientist Danish Atomic Energy Commn., Denmark, 1970—72; chief rsch. coord., rsch. prof. Internat. Assn. Promotion of New Genetical Approaches to Crop Improvement, Tando Jam, 1986—; HEC eminent prof. biotechnology, genetic engring. and environ. scis. U. Sindh, Jamshoro, Pakistan. Recipient Pakistan Atomic Energy Commn. award, Norman Borlaug award, 1986, Underwood award, AFRC, UK, 1993, Latif Gold medal, 1994, Al-Khwarizmi Internat. award, Govt. Iran, 1995, Internat. Award in Agr., Third World Network of Sci. Orgns., Italy, 1996, Internat. Man of Millennium award, UK, 1999, Am. Medal of Honor, U.S.A., 2003. Fellow: Royal Hort. Soc., Linnean Soc., Third World Acad. Scis., Pakistan Acad. Scis. (Open Gold medal 1988); mem.: Brit. Soc. for Philos. of Sci., Agrl. Inst. Can. Mailing: A 387 Talpur Colony 70050 Tando Jam Pakistan Office Phone: (92-221) 765759. Office Fax: (92-221) 765284. E-mail: khushnood@justice.com.

SIDDIQUI, RAZIA SULTANA, retired psychotherapist, educator; d. Gurcharan Singh and Bhupinder Kaur Sangha; m. Mohammed Sadiq Siddiqui, May 2, 1963; children: Niloufer Siddiqi Dennis, Adeeba Sultana Siddiqi, Khalid Mohammed Siddiqi. BA, Dayanand Mathradas Coll., Moga, India, 1956, BT, 1959; MA in Psychology, Lucknow U., India, 1958; diploma in Med. & Social Psychology, Mysore U., Bangalore, India, 1962; cert. in psychotherapy, Southwestern Med. Sch., Dallas, 1972; PhD in Neuropsychology, Postgrad. Inst. Med. Edn. and Rsch., Chandigarh, India, 1994. Asst. prof. ednl. psychology Saraswati Tng. Coll., Amritsar, India, 1959—60; clin. psychologist Niloufer Pediat. Hosp., Hyderabad, India, 1962—65; asst. prof. med. psychology Nangrahar Med. Sch., Jalalabad, Afghanistan, 1965—80, dir. publs., 1968—80; assoc. prof. psychology Kabul U., Afghanistan, 1980—88, assoc. prof. ednl. psychology Faculty Edn., 1980—88, dir. fgn. rels., 1982—88. Asst. editor Kabul Times, 1967—68. Election officer tech. Registrar of Voters, San Diego, 2006—. Home: 2162 Crystal Clear Dr Spring Valley CA 91978 Personal E-mail: razias@juno.com. E-mail: goodie65@hotmail.com.

SIDERIDOU, IRINI D., chemist, educator; b. Greece, Oct. 26, 1952; PhD, Aristotle U. Thessaloniki, 1984. Assoc. prof., chemistry dept. Aristotle U. Thessaloniki, 1998—. Home: Olympiados 7 Sykies Thessaloniki Macedonia 56626 Greece

SIDERIS, CHRISTOS, orthodontist, dental association administrator; b. Agios Petros, Greece, Feb. 16, 1951; s. Antonios and Maria Sideris; m. Maria Grigoriou, Nov. 6, 1983; children: Antonios, Konstantinos, Sofia. DDS, Nat. Kapodistrian U. Athens, 1975, D Odontology, 1991; MSD, Fairleigh Dickinson U., 1983. Cert. NY Higher Edn. Orgn., 1981. Pvt. practice, Neo Psichico, Greece, 1983—; rschr. in orthodontics Nat. and Kapodistrian U. Athens, Greece, 1986—92, vis. lectr., 1994—; pres. Dental Star Co., Anixi, Greece, 2002—. Pres. -elect 4th Panhellenic and Internat. Orthodontic Congress, Athens, 1996—96; clin. instr. Fairleigh Dickinson U., Hackensack, NJ, 1981—83. Editor: Greek Orthodontic News, 2001—03. Recipient William Ketcham award, 1983; fellow Rschr. Fellowship and Clin. Instr., Fairleigh Dickinson U., 1981. Mem.: European Orthodontic Orgn., Greek Assn. Orthodontic Study and Rsch. (founder 1985, trustee-elect 1986—94, mem. congress organizing coms. 1988—96, v.p.-elect 1994—2000, pres.-elect 2000—02, rep. 6th internat. orthodontic congress 2005), Dental Assn. Athens (rep. for Greek Assn. Orthodontic Study Rsch. 1998—2000), Civilization Club Dionysos, Athletic Club Dionysos, Cleft Palate Profl. Study Club Greece. Office: 9 Solomou St Neo Psichico 154 51 Greece Office Fax: 302106723544; Home Fax: 302108145776. Personal E-mail: siderisc@otenet.gr.

SIDHU, GURMEET SINGH, medical association administrator; b. India, Nov. 6, 1950; MD, Maulana Azad Med. Coll., 1972. Pres. Premier Radiology, 2005—. Mem.: Medchi, SVIR, ACR, RSNA. Office: Dept Radiology Prince Georges Cheverly MD 20785 Office Fax: 301-618-3964. Personal E-mail: gurmeet50@netscape.net.

SIDHU, PRITAM KAUR, toxicologist; b. Khanna, Punjab, India, Mar. 18, 1962; B in Vet. Sci., M in Vet. Sci., Punjab Agrl. U., Ludhiana, AH, 1989; PhD, U. London, 2001. Asst. prof. Punjab Agrl. U., 1991—96, asst. toxicologist, 1991—2001; toxicologist Guru Angad Dev Vet. & Animal Sci. U., Ludhiana, 2001—09, asst. prof., rsch. & tchg., 2001—09, sr. toxicologist, 2009—, prof., rsch., tchg. & adminstrn., 2009—11. Guest spkr. RVC, London; postdoc. fellow U. SC, 2003—04; rsch. assignment Royal Vet. Coll. U. London, 2008—09. Nat. Merit scholarship, Punjab Govt., Brit. Coun., grant, Bayer Pharms., 1999, RVC London, 2003, UK and INSA, 2006, New Delhi, 2009. Mem.: Indian Vet. Jour., Punjab Acad. Scis., Indian Assn. Advancement Vet. Rsch. (Izatnagar), Vet. Alumni Assn. (Punjab), Vet. Coun. India & Punjab, Soc. Toxicology (India). Avocations: reading, gardening. Office: Dept Epidemiology & PVM COVSC Ludhiana Punjab 141004 India Personal E-mail: psidhu25@rediffmail.com.

SIDI, AVNER, anesthesiologist, educator; b. Haifa, Israel, Dec. 5, 1949; MD, Hebrew U., Jerusalem, 1973. Asst. prof. anesthesiology Hebrew U., Jerusalem, 1979—87; assoc. prof. anesthesiology U. Fla., 1985—, Tel-Aviv U., Israel, 1997—2011. Vice-chmn., dir. PACU dept. anesthesiology Sheba Med. Ctr., Israel, 1997—2009. Recipient 1st pl., Soc. Simulation in Healthcare, 2011, Rsch. grant, European Soc. Anesthesiology, 2002. Mem.: Israel Soc. Anesthesiologists (chmn. quality control & rev. com. 2008—11), Israel Med. Assn. (mem. supreme com. bd. exams, sci. coun. 2010—, chmn. bd. exam. com. anesthesiology, sci. coun. 2001—08), Am. Soc. Anesthesiologists. Avocation: travel. Home: 16020 SW 75th St Archer FL 32618 Business E-Mail: asidi@anest.ufl.edu.

SIDKY, ISLAM H., perinatologist, consultant; b. Cairo, July 7, 1957; m. Rana J. Abbas, July 15, 1979; 1 child, Fatima I. MD, Cairo U., 1982. Diplomate American Board Of Obstetrics/Gynecology Am. Bd. Ob-Gyn. Resident ob.-gyn. Union Meml. Hosp., Balt., 1987—91; staff physician North Hills Med. Ctr., Greenville, SC, 1991—94; sr. staff physician Henry Ford Hosp., Detroit, 1994—97; sr. cons. physician Al-Corniche Hosp., Abu-Dhabi, United Arab Emirates, 1997—. Fellow: Am. Coll. Ob/Gyn. (assoc.); mem.: Emirates Perinatal Soc. Office: Al Corniche Hosp Po Box 3788 Abu Dhabi United Arab Emirates Business E-Mail: islamsidky@maktoob.com.

SIDOTI, PAUL A., ophthalmologist, educator; s. Eugene J. and RoseMarie Sidoti; m. Maria N. Enriquez, July 14, 2001; children: Matthew P., Michael A. MD, Albert Einstein Coll. Medicine, 1988. Diplomate Am. Bd. Ophthalmology. Prof. ophthalmology N.Y. Med. Coll., Valhalla, 2008—; dir. comprehensive ophthalmology svc. N.Y. Eye & Ear Infirmary, NYC, 1999—; ophthalmology residency program dir. NYC, 2007—. Fellow: Am. Acad. Ophthalmology; mem.: Assn. Rsch. in Vision in Ophthalmology, N.Y. Ophthal. Soc., Am. Glaucoma Soc. Office: NY Eye & Ear Infirmary 310 E 14th St New York NY 10003 Office Fax: 212-979-4512.

SIEBERT, BRIAN DAVID, retired biochemist; b. Adelaide, South Australia, Feb. 14, 1935; s. Reginald James and Florence Barbara Siebert; m. Ann Elizabeth Morgan, Apr. 4, 1959; children: David John, Richard Edward, Rachel Ann Rundle, Elizabeth Jane. BS, U. Adelaide, 1958, PhD, 1968. Biochemist Commonwealth Serum Labs., Melbourne, Australia, 1957—61; rsch. biochemist Animal Rsch. Lab., Alice Springs, Australia, 1961—64; rsch. scientist CSIRO, Australian Govt., Townsville, Qld., 1968—76, officer in charge Rockhampton, Qld., 1980—83, chief rsch. scientist, human nutrition Adelaide, 1983—94; traveling fellow Grassland Rsch. Inst., Hurley, England, 1972—73; sr. rsch. fellow U. Adelaide, 1977—80, 1994—2009; vis. fellow USDA Forage Rsch. Ctr., Madison, Wis., 1982. Pvt. practice, Adelaide, 1994—. Contbr. scientific papers. Presiding officer Strata Corp., Adelaide, 2002—08. Grant, Australian Meat Rsch. Com., 1985—86, Res. Bank Australia, 1986—88, South Australia Cattle Compensation Fund, 1988—90, 1994—96, Australian Meat & Livestock Rsch. Corp., 1990—92, Meadow Lea Foods Ltd., 1993—94, Australian Rsch. Grants Com., 1997—2000. Fellow: Royal Soc. South Australia; mem.: Am. Oil Chemists Soc. Office: Univ Adelaide Roseworthy Campus Roseworthy 5371 Australia Personal E-mail: banda.siebert@bigpond.com. Business E-Mail: brian.siebert@adelaide.edu.au.

SIEBERT, JOHN WESTON, plastic surgeon; b. Madison, Wis., Feb. 8, 1955; MD, U. Wis. Med. Sch., 1981. Cert. Surgery, Plastic Surgery. Resident in surgery Mass. Gen. Hosp., 1981—86; resident in plastic surgery NYU Med. Ctr., 1986—88, clin. fellow in microsurgery, 1988—89, assoc. prof., surgery, 1989, adj. prof. plastic surgery; attending surgeon Manhattan Ear, Eye and Throat Hosp., NYC, 1989—, Bellevue Hosp. Ctr., NYC, 1989—, NY Ear and Eye Infirmary, NYC, 1989—; prof. surgery U. Wis. Med. Sch. Recipient Golf Digest Top 100 Golf Doctors in Am., 2006. Achievements include pioneering microsurgery on facial deformities, aesthetic surgery. Office: Clin Sci Ctr 600 Highland Ave Madison WI 53792 also: 630 Park Ave New York NY 10065 Office Phone: 212-737-8300. Office Fax: 212-737-8340. Business E-Mail: johnwSiebert@minuspring.com.

SIEBZEHNRUEBL, ERNST ROBERT, gynecologist, consultant; b. Passau, Germany, Oct. 4, 1956; s. Franz Xaver and Rosa (Rudolf) S.; m. Christine Oeller, Aug. 4, 1978; 1 child, Florian. Abitur, Adalbert-Stifler Gymnasium, Passau, 1977, MD, 1984, PhD, 1995. Med. diplomate. Rsch. fellow U. Erlangen, Germany, 1983-84, registrar dept. ob-gyn., 1984-88, sr. registrar dept. ob-gyn., 1988-90, cons., dir. in-vitro fertilization and asst. reproduction, 1991-2000; prof., head divsn. gyn. endocrinology & reproductve med. U. Frankfurt, 2001—04; dir. fertility Ctr. Frankfurt, 2004—. Fellow Am. Fertility Soc., Soc. for Cryobiology, German Fertility Soc. Home: Stormstr 10a 63110 Rodgau Germany Office Phone: +49-69-4260-770. Business E-Mail: siebzehnruebl@ivf-ffm.de.

SIEGAL, GENE PHILIP, pathology educator; b. Bronx, NY, Nov. 16, 1948; s. Murray H. and Evelyne (Philips) S.; m. Sandra Helene Meyerowitz, Aug. 3, 1972; children: Gail Deborah, Rebecca Stacey. BA, Adelphi U., Garden City, NY, 1970; MD, U. Louisville, 1974; PhD, U. Minn., 1979; cert. in hosp. mgmt., U. N.C., 1988. Diplomate Nat. Bd. Med. Examiners, Am. Bd. Pathology. Intern, resident, rsch. fellow Mayo Clinic Found., Rochester, Minn., 1974-79; rsch. assoc. Lab. Pathophysiology, Nat. Cancer Inst., NIH, Bethesda, Md., 1979-81; fellow surg. pathology U. Minn., Mpls., 1981-82; asst. prof. pathology U. N.C., Chapel Hill, 1982-88, assoc. prof. pathology, 1988-90; mem. Lineberger Comprehensive Cancer Ctr., Chapel Hill, 1983-90; prof. pathology U. Ala., Birmingham, 1990—2008, prof. cell biology, prof. surgery, 1991—, sr. scientist, group leader breast, ovary, prostate program, Comprehensive Cancer Ctr., 1993—99, Robert W. Mowry Endowed prof. Pathology, 2008—; exe. vice chair, pathology U. Ala. Health Sys., 2008—. Mem. Children's Cancer Study Group, 1987-90, Pediatric Oncology Group, 1990-2000, Children's Oncology Group, 2001—, mem. osteosarcoma pathology com., sr. scientist Ctr. for Aging, Cell Adhesion and Matrix Rsch. Ctr., 1995—, Ctr. Metabolic Bone Disease, 1997—, Gene Therapy Ctr., 2000—.; editor-in-chief Lab. Investigation, 2008-. Co-editor: Molecular Antibodies in Diagnostic Immunohistochemistry, 1988, Updates in Diagnostic Pathology, 2003; sr. assoc. editor Am. Jour. Pathology, 2003-08; assoc. editor Archives of Pathology and Lab. Medicine, 1989-90; sect. editor, 2006-; mem. editl. bd. Yearbook of Pathology, 1983-91, Archives of Pathology and Lab. Medicine, 1990-91, Am. Jour. Clin. Pathology, 1990—, Modern Pathology, 1996—, Advances in Anat. Pathology, 1999-, Am. Jour. Surg. Pathology, 2000-, Annals Diagnostic Pathology, 2003—, Skeletal Radiology, 2003—, Lab. Investigation, 2004-08, Jour. Molecular Medicine, 2005-, CAP Today, 2005-, Human Pathology, 2005-, Am, jour. Translocational Res., 2009-, Open Breast Cancer Jour., 2009-, Musculoskeletal and Spinal Diseases, 2009-, Cancer Growth and Metastasis, 2009-, clin. Medicine: Pathology, 2009-. With USPHS, 1979-81. Clin. fellow Am. Cancer Soc., Chapel Hill, 1981-82, jr. faculty fellow, 1983-86, Jefferson-Pilot fellow in acad. medicine, U. N.C., Chapel Hill, 1985-86. Fellow Am. Soc. Clin. Pathologists (bd. dirs. 2005-06, chair fellows coun. 2005-06, mem. ann. meeting com. 2004-, membership com. 2005-), Coll. Am. Pathologists (insp. 1990—, mem. surg. pathol. and vice chair pub. coms. 2005-), Royal Soc. Medicine (London); mem. AMA, AAAS, Internat. Skeletal Soc. (exe. com. 2007-), Am. Soc. for Investigative Pathology (councilor 2002-05, mem. publs. com. 2005-08), U.S. and Can. Acad. Pathology (abstract rev. bd. 1989-91, 2003-05), A.P. Stout Surg. Pathologists (pres. 2005-07, chair exec. com. 2005-09), Metastasis Rsch. Soc., Am. Assn. Cancer Rsch., Assn. Dirs. Anatomic and Surg. Pathology (coun. 2000-05, mem. Castleman award com. 2005-08), Intersoc. Pathology Coun. (sec.-treas. exec. com. 2003-07, chair 2007-09), Sigma Xi (pres. chpt. 1989-90), Alpha Omega Alpha, Phi Beta Delta. Democrat. Jewish. Office: Univ Ala at Birmingham Dept Pathology 506 Kracke Birmingham AL 35233 Office Phone: 205-934-6608. Business E-Mail: gsiegal@uab.edu.

SIEGEL, BARRY ALAN, radiologist; b. Nashville, Dec. 30, 1944; s. Walter G. Siegel and Lillian B. Ivener; m. Pamela M. Mandel, Aug. 18, 1968 (div. Mar. 1981); children: Peter A., William A.; m. Marilyn J. Siegel, Jan. 29, 1983. AB, Washington U., St. Louis, 1966, MD, 1969. Diplomate Am. Bd. Nuc. Medicine, Am. Bd. Radiology. Intern Barnes Hosp., St. Louis, 1969-70; from resident in radiology to prof. Mallinckrodt Inst. Radiology Washington U., 1970—79, prof. radiology Mallinckrodt Inst. Radiology, 1979—, dir. divsn. nuc. medicine Mallinckrodt Inst. Radiology, 1973—, mem. Siteman Cancer Ctr., 1996—. Dir. Am. Bd. Nuc. Medicine, LA, 1985—90, sec., 1990; chmn. adv. com. on med. uses of isotopes NRC, Washington, 1990—96; chmn. radiopharm. drugs adv. com. FDA, Rockville, Md., 1982—85, radiol. devices panel, 1992—95; mem. U.S. Pharmacopeia Adv. Panel on Radiopharms., 1975—2000, Armed Forces Radiobiol. Rsch. Inst., Bethesda; coun. experts, chair radiopharm. expert com. U.S. Pharmacopoeial Conv., 2000—05; co-chair working group Nat. Oncologic PET Registry, 2005—; cons. in field. Author, editor 33 books; contbr. articles to profl. jours., chpts. in books. Maj. USAF, 1974—76. Recipient Commr.'s Spl. citation U.S. FDA, 1988, Honor citation U.S. Pharmacopeial Conv., 1995, 2000. Fellow: ACP, Am. Coll. Nuc. Physicians, Am. Coll. Radiology (vice chmn. commn. nuc. medicine 1981—93, editor-in-chief profl. self evaluation program 1988—2002, chmn. nuc. medicine com. imaging network 1998—2006, med. dir. PET core lab. imaging network 2006—, Gr. Deputy Co-Chair Imaging Network 2008—); mem.: ACS (chmn. diagnostic imaging com. oncology group 1998—2007, mem. exec. com. 2000—07), AMA, Acad. Molecular Imaging (chair inst. Clin. PET coun. 2001—02, bd. dirs. 2004—07, Disting. Clin. Scientist award 2008), Soc. Nuc. Medicine (trustee 1981—85, 1987—91, Georg Charles de Hevesy Nuclear Pioneer award 2003), Radiol. Soc. N.Am. Office: Washington U Mallinckrodt Inst Radiology 510 S Kingshighway Blvd Saint Louis MO 63110-1016 Home Phone: 314-367-3650; Office Phone: 314-362-2809. Business E-Mail: siegelb@mir.wustl.edu.

SIEGEL, BRUCE, hospital and health association executive; m. Maura Cooper; 2 children. AB, Princeton U.; MD, Cornell U.; MPH, John Hopkins U. Cert. Preventive Medicine. Commissioner of health State of NJ; dir., Ctr. for Health Care Quality, prof. health policy George Washington U. Sch. Pub. Health and Health Services; pres., CEO Tampa Gen. Healthcare, NYC Health and Hosp. Corp., Nat. Assn. of Public Hospitals and Health Systems, 2010—. Chair Nat. Adv. Coun. for Healthcare Rsch. and Quality; dir. Accreditation Coun. for Grad. Med. Edn.; bd. of stewardship trustees of Catholic Health Initiatives; sr. fellow New Sch. U.; advisor Inst. of Medicine, World Bank, hospitals, hospital associations, philanthropies, county and state governments and pharm. firms; written and spoken extensively on health care mgmt., policy and pub. health issues. Named one of 50 Most Influential Physician Executives, 100 Most Influential People in Healthcare, Modern Healthcare Mag., 2011. Office: National Assn of Public Hospitals and Health Systems 1301 Pennsylvania Ave NW Ste 950 Washington DC 20004 Office Phone: 202-585-0100. Business E-Mail: bsiegel@naph.org.

SIEGEL, DAVID, physician; b. Bronx, NY, June 19, 1948; BA with high honors, Wesleyan U., 1969; MD, Albert Einstein Coll. Medicine, 1973. Chief medicine VA Northern Calif. Health Care Sys., 1995—. Prof., vice chair dept. medicine U. Calif., Davis, 1995—2011; mem. bd. trustees Wesleyan U. Preventive Cardiology Academic fellow, Nat. Heart, Lung, Blood Inst. Fellow: ACP, Am. Heart Assn.; mem.: Assn. Profs. Medicine. Avocations: fishing, gardening, motorcycling. Office: Sacramento Mather VA Med Ctr 10535 Hospital Way T-3 Mather CA 95655 Business E-Mail: david.siegel@va.gov.

SIEGEL, EBERHARD GOTTFRIED, endocrinologist, gastroenterologist, educator; b. Grötzingen, Germany, Sept. 21, 1950; s. Guenther Joachim and Gisela Siegel; m. Gerlinde Wöhlert; children: Melanie, Christine, Markus. MD, U. Heidelberg, Germany, 1976; Habilitation, U. Göttingen, Germany, 1988. Asst. physician Dept. Medicine, Tübingen, 1977; rsch. fellow Inst. Clin. Biochemistry, Geneva, 1977-80; asst. physician Dept. Medicine, Göttingen, 1980-88, oberarzt, 1988-91, prof. medicine, 1992; head St. Vincentius Hosp., Karlsruhe, Germany, 1991—. Contbr. articles to profl. jours. Mem. City Coun., Wolfschlugen, 1971—77. Sci. grantee, Deutsche Forschungsgemeinschaft, 1982—91. Mem.: Am. Diabetes Assn., Acad. Ethics in Medicine, German Endocrine Soc., German Gastroenterol. Assn., European Diabetes Assn., German Diabetes Assn. (exec. bd. 2001—05, Bertram prize 1989, förderpreis 1977), Rotary. Avocations: music, mountain climbing, skiing. Office: St Vincent Hosp Südendstr 32 76137 Karlsruhe Germany

SIEGEL, MARC OLIVER, physician, educator; b. Munich, Dec. 30, 1970; BS, Georgetown U., 1992; MD, Georgetown Med. Sch., 1998. Asst. prof. medicine George Wash. U., 2009—. Office: 2150 Pennsylvania Ave NW Ste 5-41 Washington DC 20037 Office Fax: 202-741-2241. E-mail: marc.siegel@comcast.net.

SIEGEL, MICHAEL ELLIOT, nuclear medicine physician, educator; b. NYC, May 13, 1942; s. Benjamin and Rose (Gilbert) S.; m. Marsha Rose Snower, Mar. 20, 1966; children: Herrick Joye, Meridith Ann. AB, Cornell U., 1964; MD, Chgo. Med. Sch., 1968. Diplomate Nat. Bd. Med. Examiners. Intern Cedars-Sinai Med. Ctr., LA, 1968-69, resident in radiology, 1969-70; NIH fellow in radiology Temple U. Med. Ctr., Phila., 1970-71; NIH fellow in nuclear medicine Johns Hopkins U. Sch. Medicine, Balt., 1971-73, asst. prof. radiology, 1972-76; assoc. prof. radiology and medicine U. So. Calif., LA, 1976—, prof. radiology, 1989—, dir. divsn. nuclear medicine, 1982-99. Dir. Sch. Nuclear Medicine, Los Angeles County-U. So. Calif. Med. Ctr., 1976-99; dir. divsn. nuclear medicine Kenneth Norris Cancer Hosp. and Rsch. Ctr., L.A., 1983-99; dir. dept. nuclear medicine Orthopaedic Hosp., L.A., 1981-2006, Intercmty. Hosp., Covina, Calif., 1981-2006, U. So. Calif. Univ. Hosp., L.A., 1993—; clin. prof. radiology U. Calif., San Diego, 2000—. Author: Textbook of Nuclear Medicine, 1978, Vascular Surgery, 1983, 88, numerous other textbooks; editor: Nuclear Cardiology, 1981, Vascular Disease: Nuclear Medicine, 1983. Mem. Maple Ctr., Beverly Hills. Served as maj. USAF, 1974-76. Recipient Outstanding Alumnus award Chgo. Med. Sch., 1991. Fellow Am. Coll. Nuclear Medicine (sci. investigator 1974, 76, nominations com. 1980, program com. 1983, trustee 1993, disting. fellow, 1993, bd. reps. 1993—, bd. dirs. 1994—, treas. 1996—, chmn. ann. sci. program 1996—, pres.'s award 1997, v.p. 1997-98, pres. 1999—, CEO 2005—); mem. Soc. Nuclear Medicine (sic. exhbn. com. 1978-79, program com. 1979-80, Silver medal 1975), Calif. Med. Assn. (sci. adv. bd. 1987—), Radiol. Soc. N.Am., Soc. Nuclear Magnetic Resonance Imaging, Friars So. Calif., Alpha Omega Alpha. Achievements include research on development of nuclear medicine techniques to treat recurrent joint effusions, evaluate cardiovascular disease and diagnose and treat cancer; clinical utilization of video digital displays in nuclear medicine development; invention of pneumatic radiologic pressure system. Office: U So Calif Med Ctr Rm 5250 1200 N State St Los Angeles CA 90033-1029 Business E-Mail: mesiegel@usc.edu.

SIEGEL, ROBERT STEVEN, internist, oncologist, educator; b. Phila., Pa., Feb. 5, 1951; MD, George Washington U. Sch. Medicine, 1977. Cert. Internal Medicine, Hematology, Med. Oncology. Intern, internal medicine Duke U. Med. Ctr., Durham, NC, 1977—78, resident, hematology oncology, 1978—80, fellow, 1980—82; hosp. appointment George Washington U. Med. Ctr., Washington, prof. medicine, dir., divsn. hematology and oncology, mem., Med. Faculty Assocs. Named one of Top Doctors, Washingtonian.com, 2005, 2010. Office: George Washington U Med Ctr 2150 Pennsylvania Ave NW Ste 1-200 Washington DC 20037 Office Phone: 202-741-2478, 202-741-2210. Office Fax: 202-741-2487.

SIEGEL, SHELDON C., pediatrician, immunologist, allergist; b. Mpls., Jan. 30, 1922; s. Carl S.; m. Priscilla Rikess, Mar. 3, 1946; children— Linda, Nancy. AA, Va. Jr. Coll., 1940; BA, BS, U. Minn.,

1942, MD, 1945. Intern U. Minn. Hosp., 1946, resident in pediatrics, 1947-48; fellow in pediatric allergy Rochester, NY, 1949-50; practice medicine specializing in pediatric allergy and pediatrics St. Paul, 1950-52, San Antonio, 1952-54, Los Angeles, 1954—; clin. instr. pediatrics U. Rochester, 1949-50, U. Minn., 1950-51; asst. prof. pediatrics U. Tex., 1952-54; asst. clin. prof. U. Calif. at Los Angeles Med. Sch., 1955, clin. asso. prof., 1957-62, clin. prof., 1963—, co-chief pediatric allergy clinic, 1957—. Editorial bd.: Jour. Allergy, 1973-75; contbr. articles to med. jours. Fellow Am. Acad. Allergy (pres. 1974), Am. Coll. Allergists, Am. Acad. Pediatrics; mem. AMA, Allergy Found. Am. (pres. 1976), Calif. Med. Assn., LA County Med. Assn., LA Pediatric Soc., Calif. Soc. Allergy, LA Soc. Allergy, Western Pediatric Rsch. Soc., Am. Bd. Med. Specialists, Sigma Xi.

SIEGEL, STUART ELLIOTT, pediatric oncologist, educator; b. Plainfield, NJ, July 16, 1943; s. Hyman and Charlotte Pearl (Freinberg) S.; m. Linda Wertkin, Jan. 20, 1968 (dec. 2003); 1 child, Joshua; m. Barbara Frankel, May 29, 2005. BA, MD, Boston U., 1967. Diplomate Am. Bd. Pediatrics, Am. Bd. Pediatric Oncology. Intern U. Minn. Hosp., Mpls., 1967-68, resident, 1968-69; clin. assoc. NIH, Bethesda, Md., 1969-72; asst. prof. pediatrics U. So. Calif. Sch. Medicine, LA, 1972-76, assoc. prof., 1976-81, prof., 1981—, vice chmn. dept. pediat., 1994—2010; head div. hematology-oncology Childrens Hosp. LA, 1976—, dep. physician-in-chief, 1987-90; dir. Childrens Ctr. for Cancer and Blood Diseases, LA, 1996—. Mem. clin. cancer program project com. NIH, Nat. Cancer Inst., HEW, Bethesda, Md., 1978-82; pres. So. Calif. Children's Cancer Services, LA, 1977-95. Bd. dirs. Nat. Leukemia Broadcast Coun., 1987—2010, Ronald McDonald Children's Charities, 1988-95, Make-A-Wish Found., 1987-95, Children's Hosp. LA Found., 1994-2000, Ronald McDonald House Charities, 1995—, LA Regional Coun. Am. Cancer Soc., 1996—, Nat. Childhood Cancer Found., 1995-2003, 2005-, pres. 2011-; pres. Ronald McDonald House Charities So. Calif., 1996-2008; bd. trustees, Children's Hosp., LA, 2000—; treas. Padres Contra El Cancer, 2003-04; mem. steering com. Live Strong Young Adult Alliance, 2005—, v.p. Thinkcare Bd. Dirs., 2008-; sec., mem., bd. dirs. Children's Speciality Care Coalition, Calif., 2009-10, pres., bd. dirs., 2010-, Children's Cancer Rsch. Fund, chair, 1990-, grants com., Alex's Lemonade Stand Found., 2010-, St. Baldrick's Found., 2010, Hyundai Hope on Wheels Found., 2010-; Surgeon USPHS, 1969-72. Named to NAt. Caring Hall of Fame, 2001. Fellow Am. Acad. Pediatrics. Office: Childrens Hospital Of La PO Box 27980 Los Angeles CA 90027-0980 Office Phone: 323-361-2205. Business E-Mail: ssiegel@chla.usc.edu. *

SIEGELMAN, EVAN SPENCER, diagnostic radiologist; BA, Franklin and Marshall College, 1984; MD, John Hopkins U., 1988. Diplomate Am. Bd. of Radiology-diagnostic radiology, 1993. Resident diagnostic radiology Thomas Jefferson Univ. Hosp., 1989—93, fellow body MRI, 1993—94; chief MRI sect. Hosp. of the Univ. of Pa. Assoc. prof. radiology Hosp. of the Univ. of Pa. Author: (articles) Female Urethra and Vagina, 2002, Gadolinium susceptibility artifact causing false positive stenosis isolated to the proximal common carotid artery in 3D dynamic contrast medium enhanced MR angiography of the thorax--a brief review of causes and prevention, 2003, Magnetic resonance-defined periportal steatosis following intraportal islet transplantation: a functional footprint of islet graft survival?, 2003, MR Imaging of Hepatic Cysts and Hemangiomas, 2004, Imaging of the Malignant Liver Disease, 2004, MR Imaging of the Bladder, 2004, The young cervical spine, 2004, MR imaging of the bladder, 2004, Magnetic resonance imaging of focal splenic and hepatic lesions in the dog, 2004, (books) Body MRI, 2005. Office: University of Pennsylvania Medical Center !st Fl Founders Mrj 3400 Spruce St Philadelphia PA 19104 Office Phone: 215-662-3034. Office Fax: 215-662-3013.

SIEGELOVÁ, JARMILA MARCELA, internist, physiology educator; b. Brno, Czech Republic, Jan. 4, 1942; d. Jaromír and Alžběta (Milionová) S. MD, Masaryk U., Brno, 1965, PhD, 1977, DSc, 1990. Qualified in internal medicine Brno. Asst. prof. Masaryk U., 1965-77, sci. worker, 1977-86, sr. sci. worker, 1986-90, assoc. prof., 1990-97, prof., 1997—, dept. head, 1996—. Asst. prof. U. Tübingen, Germany, 1966-67; vis. scientist Med. Faculty, Paris, 1993, 95, U. Graz, Austria, 1994, U. Minn., Mpls., 1995-2002. Author: Breath By Breath Analysis of Breathing, 1993; editor: Scientific Meeting, 1993, Chronobiology in Health and Disease, 1994, 96, 98, 2000. Grantee U. Minn., 1989, Czech Republic Ministry of Health, 1990-95, 96-98, 98-2000, Med. Faculty Paris, 1992, U. Graz, 1993, Min. Wsn., 1998-2002, U. Minn., 1995, 2000. Mem. European Respiratory Soc., Internat. Soc. Hypertension, Assn. Physiologists France, N.Y. Acad. Scis. Office: Masaryk Univ Dept Physiotherapy Pekarská 53 656 91 Brno Czech Republic Office Phone: 00420543182977. Business E-Mail: jsiegel@med.muni.cz, jarmila.siegelova@fnusa.cz.

SIEGERT, BARBARA (MARIE), health care administrator; b. Boston, May 22, 1935; d. Salvatore Mario and Mary Kathleen (Wagner) Tartaglia; m. Herbert C. Siegert (dec. Apr. 1974); children: Carolyn Marie, Herbert Christian Jr. Diploma, Newton Wellesley Hosp., Mass., 1956; MEd, Antioch U., 1980. Diplomate Am. Bd. Med. Psychotherapists. Supr. nursing Hogan Regional Ctr., Hathorne, Mass., 1974-78; community mental health nursing advisor Cape Ann area office Dept. Mental Health, Beverly, Mass., 1978-79, dir. case mgmt., 1979-87, dir. case mgmt. north shore area office, 1988-91; dir. case mgmt. Dept. Mental Health-north shore area-Lynn (Mass.) site, Lynn, Mass., 1991-92. Mem. interdisciplinary faculty, profl. cons. com., lecture staff clin. pastoral counseling program Danvers State Hosp./Hogan/Berry Regional Ctrs., Hathorne, Mass., 1982-86; nursing edn. adv. com. North Shore Community Coll., Beverly, 1983-91; tng. staff Balter Inst., Ipswich, Mass., 1987-88. Mem. Internat. Cultural Diploma Honor, 1989—. Recipient Spl. Recognition award Lexington (Mass.) Pub. Schs., 1973, Peter Torci award Lexington Friends of Children in Spl. Edn., 1974. Home: 63 Willow Rd # B Boxford MA 01921-1218

SIEGFRIED, JAY W., physiatrist, educator; MD, U. Cin. Diplomate Am. Bd. Physical Medicine and Rehab. Intern Thomas Jefferson Univ. Hosp., resident; hops. affiliations include Paoli Hosp., 1997—, Bryn Mawr Rehab. Hosp., 1992—, rehab. medicine cons.; rehab. dir. Saunders House; clin. asst. prof. dept. of rehab. medicine Thomas Jefferson Univ. Hosp.; hops. affiliations include Lankenau Med. Ctr., 1981—, chief divsn. of rehab. medicine. With Lower Merion Rehab. Assocs. Co-author: (publ.) The Role of Epineurotomy in the Operative Treatment of Carpal Tunnel Syndrome, 1997. Named one of the Top Doctors, Main Line Health, 2002, Phila. Mag., 2002, 2011. Office: Lankenau Medical Center Ste B7 100 Lancaster Ave Wynnewood PA 19096 Office Phone: 484-476-3391. Office Fax: 484-476-8005.

SIEGFRIED, JILL MARIE, medical educator; b. Milw., June 12, 1954; BA, Wellesley Coll., 1976; PhD, Yale U., 1981. Prof. U. Pitts., 1988—. Co-dir., lung and thoracic malignancies program U. Pitts. Cancer Inst., 1998—. Recipient Alton Ochsner award, Am. Assn. Chest Physicians; Rsch. grant, Nat. Cancer Inst. Mem.: Nat. Lung Cancer Partnership, Am. Assn. Cancer Rsch. Avocations: singing, gardening, cooking. Office: Hillman Cancer Ctr 5117 Centre Ave Pittsburgh PA 15213 Office Fax: 412-623-7768. Business E-Mail: siegfriedjm@upmc.edu.

SIEGLER, RICHARD LOUIS, pediatric nephrologist, educator; b. Vallejo, Calif., May 5, 1939; s. Alfred Charles and Loyola Ann (Wolf) S.; m. Karen Koenig, June 25, 1963; children: Mark, Matthew, Amy. BA in Life Sci., Calif. State U., Sacramento, 1961; MD, Creighton U., 1965. Diplomate Am. Bd. Pediats., Am. Bd. Pediat. Nephrology. Intern in mixed medicine-pediatrics Creighton Meml. - St. Joseph's Hosp., Omaha, 1965-66, resident in pediatrics, 1966-67, U. Utah Med. Ctr., 1969-71; fellowship in nephrology Dept. Medicine, U. Utah Med. Ctr., 1971-72; asst. prof. U. Utah Sch. Medicine, Salt Lake City, 1972—78, chief pediat. nephrology dept. pediats., 1972—2001, assoc. prof., 1978—90, acting chmn. dept. pediats., 1982-83, vice chair clin. affairs, 1983-87, prof., 1990—2005, prof. emeritus, 2005—; prof. affilate, sch. medicine San Carlos U., Guatemala, 2008—. Mem. exec. com. Primary Children's Med. Ctr., Salt Lake City, 1982-83; dir. pediat. renal disease program U. Utah Health Scis. Ctr., Salt Lake City, 1982-86; bd. dirs. Sacramental Children's Home, 2008-. Contbr. articles to profl. jours., book chpts. Bd. trustees Utah Children, Salt Lake City, 1989-90. Capt. U.S. Army, 1967-68, Viet Nam. Decorated Bronze Star; recipient Rsch. awards Southern Ariz. Found., 1990-91, Svc. to Children award Am. Acad. Pediat., Utah Chpt., 2006; Thrasher Rsch. Fund grantee, 1978-79, 82-85, RO1 grantee NIH, 1996-2001, R21 co-grantee NIH, 2006-08. Fellow Am. Acad. Pediats. (mem. exec. com. Utah chpt. 1986-90, pres. Utah chpt. 1988-90, chair legis. com. 1990-92); mem. Am. Soc. Nephrology, Am. Soc. Pediat. Nephrology. Achievements include being credited with the initial description of a new inherited disorder known as the "Siegler-Brewer-Syndrome"; being honored by the president of Guatemala at the opening ceremony of the Richard L. Siegler Pediatric Hemodialysis Center (the first such facility in the country). Avocations: bicycling, violin, photography. Home: 2840 Prado Ln Davis CA 95618 Office Phone: 530-297-7007. Personal E-mail: rlsieglerconsulting@gmail.com.

SIEGMAN, MARION JOYCE, physiologist, educator; b. Bklyn., Sept. 7, 1933; d. C. Joseph and Helen Siegman. BA, Tulane U., 1954; PhD, SUNY, Bklyn., 1966. Instr. physiology Med. Coll. Thomas Jefferson U., Phila., 1967-68, asst. prof., 1968-71, assoc. prof., 1971-77, prof., 1977—, chair dept. physiology, 2001—. Mem. physiology study sect. NIH. Editor: Regulation and Contraction of Smooth Muscle, 1987. Recipient award for excellence in rsch. and teaching Burlington No. Found., 1986, award for excellence in teaching Lindback Found., 1987, Outstanding Alumna award, Newcomb Coll./Tulane U., 1990; grantee NIH, 1967—. Mem. Am. Physiol. Soc., Biophys. Soc. Avocation: photography. Office: Jefferson Med Coll 1020 Locust St Philadelphia PA 19107-6731 Office Phone: 215-503-7761, 215-503-7893. E-mail: marion.siegman@jefferson.edu.

SIEGMUND-SCHULTZE, ELISABETH, health facility administrator, director; b. Speyer, Germany, July 20, 1962; d. Gerhard and Gertha Siegmund-Schultze; children: Tillmann, David. MD, U. Kiel, Germany, 1991. Physician Hosp., Heilbronn, Germany, 1990—91; phsician Hosp. of the U. Bochum, Herne, Germany, 1991—99, referee to dir. adminstrn., 1999—2000; dir. product innovation Kaufmännische Krankenkasse, Hannover, Germany, 2000—08; head dept. managed care KKH-Allianz, Hannover, 2008—. Asst. chmn. Ärztekammer Westfalen-Lippe, Münster, Germany, 1993—2000. Scholar, Evangelisches Studienwerk Villigst, 1982—89. Mem.: Dt. Fisellsh F Ferundheits Okonomic Dt. Arztinmenbuund, Soc. for Quality Mgmt. in der Gesundheitsversorgung. Lutheran. Avocations: literature, art, films, sports. Office: KKH-Allianz Karl-Wiechert Allee 61 Hannover D-30625 Germany Business E-Mail: e.siegmund-schultze@kkh-allianz.de.

SIEMIONOW, MARIA, microsurgeon; b. Poznan, Poland, May 3, 1950; came to U.S., 1989; d. Bronislaw and Zofia (Jackowska) Kusza; m. Wlodzimierz Siemionow, Apr. 26, 1975; 1 child, Krzysztof. MD, Med. Acad. (Karol Marcinkowski Univ. Faculty of Medicine), Poznan, 1974; degree in Orthopedics, Med. Acad., Poznan, 1981, PhD in Microsurgery, 1985, DSc in Microcirculation, 1992. Fellow Univ. Hosp., Helsinki, Finland, Univ. Louisville Hosp., Ky.; intern Univ. Hosp., Pozan, Poland; resident Inst. for Orthopaedics and Rehabilitation Medicine, Pozan, Poland, Mcpl. Hosp., Piekary Slaskie, Finland; asst. clin. instr. Inst. Orthopedics/Rehab. Medicine, Poznan, 1978-81, sr. asst. lectr., 1982-86, adj. orthopedics, hand and microsurgery, 1990-95; rsch. assoc. prof., rsch. dir. U. Utah, Salt Lake City, 1995—; rsch. dir. Cleve. Clinic Found., 1995—, current sect. head plastic surgery rsch., dir. plastic surgery rsch., head, microsurgery tng., current mem., Transplantation Ctr., current mem., Orthopaedic Surgery, current mem., Immunology. Vis. prof. U. Guadalajara, Mex., 1986, U. Monastir, Tenesia, 1989, Mount Vernon Hosp., London, 1992, Chang Gung Meml. Hosp, Taipei, Taiwan, 1994. Editl. bd. Jour. Investigative Surgery, 1991-93, Jour. Reconstructive Microsurgery; author: Tissue Surgery, 2005, Transplanting a Face: Notes on a Life in Medicine, 2007; contbr. articles to sci. jours. Christine Kleinert Hand Surgery fellow, 1985; recipient: James Barrett Brown award, Am. Assn. Plastic Surgeons, 2007 Mem. Am. Soc. Reconstructive Microsurgery (pres. 1992), Internat. Soc. Reconstructive Microsurgery (pres. 1993), Plastic Surgery Rsch. Coun., Physicians for Peace (pres. 1993), Interplast-Turkey (pres. 1993). Achievements include being the first surgeon to perform a face transplant in the United States, 2008. Avocations: art, skiing, hiking, photography, languages. Office: Dept of Plastic Surgery (A60) Cleve Clinic Found 9500 Euclid Ave Cleveland OH 44195 Office Phone: 216-445-2405.

SIEMONS, GARY OTTO, colon and rectal surgeon; BS in Biology, Rutgers U., 1973; MD, U. Va., 1980. Diplomate Am. Bd. Surgery, Am. Bd. Colon and Rectal Surgery, lic. NJ, 1982. Intern Rutgers med. sch. Univ. Medicine and Dentistry NJ, NB, resident Rutgers med. sch., chief resident in surgery, fellow in colorectal surgery, Muhlenberg Hosp., Plainfield; hosp. affiliations include Our Lady of Lourdes Med. Ctr., Kennedy Health System, Centennial Surgery Ctr., Virtua West Jersey Hosp., Voorhees. Fellow: Am. Soc. of Colon and Rectal Surgeons, ACS; mem.: Pa. Soc. of Colon/Rectal Surgeons, NJ Soc. of Colon/Rectal Surgeons Camden County Med. Soc., Med. Soc. of NJ, AMA. Office: Virtua West Jersey Hospital 502 Centennial Blvd Ste 5 Voorhees NJ 08043 Office Phone: 856-429-8030. Office Fax: 856-428-2718.

SIERLES, FREDERICK STEPHEN, psychiatrist, educator; b. Bklyn., Nov. 9, 1942; s. Samuel and Elizabeth (Meiselman) S.; m. Laurene Harriet Cohn, Oct. 25, 1970 (div. Aug. 1990); children: Hannah Beth Alterson, Joshua Caleb; m. Terrie Lee Stengel June 28, 2008. AB, Columbia U., 1963; MD, Rosalind Franklin U., 1967. Diplomate Am. Bd. Psychiatry and Neurology. Intern Cook County Hosp., Chgo., 1967-68; resident in psychiatry Mt. Sinai Hosp., NYC, 1968-69, assoc. attending psychiatrist Chgo., 1973-74; resident in psychiatry Rosalind Franklin U., North Chgo., Ill., 1969-71, chief resident, 1970-71, instr. psychiatry, 1973—74, asst. prof., 1974-78, assoc. prof., 1978-88, dir. med. student edn., 1974—94, chair, 1994—2002, residency dir., 1999—2001; inaugural mem. Master Tchr.'s Guild, 2009—; staff psychiatrist U.S. Reynolds Army Hosp., Ft. Sill, Okla., 1971-73. Cons. psychiatry Cook County Hosp., 1974-79, St. Mary of Nazareth Hosp., 1979-82, Gt. Lakes Naval Hosp., 1987-90, Jackson Park Hosp., 1987-89, Mt. Sinai Hosp., 1988—, Elgin Mental Health Ctr., 1997—; chief mental health clinic, North Chicago VA Hosp., 1982-85, chief psychiatry svc., 1983-85mem, internat. editl. bd. Acad. Psychiatry, 2008-. Author: (wth others) General Hospital Psychiatry, 1985, Behavioral Science for the Boreds, 1987, rev. 2d edit., 1989, rev. 3d edit., 1993, USMLE Behavioral Science Made Ridiculously Simple, 1998; editor: Clinical Behavioral Science, 1982, Behavioural Science for Medical Students, 1993; mem. editl. bd. Acad. Psychiatry, 2000-07; contbr. articles to profl. jours. Coach Glenview (Ill.) Youth Baseball, 1987-89, mgr. 1990 (age 10-12 Glenview World Series winner 1990), Glenview Tennis Club, 1986-90 (3.5 Men's Doubles League winner 1989-90). Maj. M.C., U.S. Army, 1971-73. N.Y.State Regents scholar, 1959-63; NIMH grantee, 1974-83, Chgo. Med. Sch. grantee, 1974-83; recipient Seymour Vestermark award NIMH/Am. Psychiat. Assn., 2003. Fellow Am. Psychiat. Assn. (disting. life fellow, 2006-, coun. edn. and career devel. 1993-95); mem. Ill. Psychiat. Soc. (fellowship com. 1985-99), Columbia Coll. Alumni Secondary Schs. Com., Assn. Dirs. Med. Student Edn. in Psychiatry (exec. coun. 1985-99, chmn. program com. 1987-88, treas. 1989-91, pres-elect 1991-93, pres. 1993-95, immediate past pres. 1995-99), Alliance for Clin. Edn., Am. Assn. Dirs. Psychiat. Residency Tng. (exec. coun. 2000-03, chair workforce coalition 2000-03), Sigma Xi, Alpha Omega Alpha, Phi Epsilon Pi. Office: Rosalind Franklin Univ Chgo Med Sch 3333 Green Bay Rd North Chicago IL 60064-3037 Business E-Mail: frederick.sierles@rosalindfranklin.edu.

SIEROCKI, JOHN STANLEY, oncologist; b. New Haven, 1947; MD, Hahnemann U., 1973. Diplomate Am. Bd. Internal Medicine, Am. Bd. Med. Oncology. Intern Hahnemann U., Phila., 1973—74, resident in medicine, 1974—76; fellow in med. oncology Meml. Sloan-Kettering Cancer Ctr., NYC, 1976—78; attending physician in medicine, hematology and med. oncology Med. Ctr. at Princeton, NJ, 1983—. Assoc. clin. prof. medicine U. Medicine and Dentistry N.J.-R.W. Johnson, 1985—. Recipient Syear Recognition award; named one of Top Drs. in N.Y. Metro Area, Castle Connolly, Top Drs. 2003, N.J. Monthly Mag., Top Drs. in NY Metro Area Castle Connolly, 2006—, Best Drs. in America, 2009—10. Office: Princeton Med Group 419 N Harrison St Princeton NJ 08540-3521 Home Phone: 609-575-4809; Office Phone: 609-924-9300. Business E-Mail: jsierocki@princetonhcs.org.

SIERPINSKA, TERESA, dentist; b. Wlodawa, Poland, Oct. 15, 1966; MD, Med. U. Bialystok, 1999; PhD, Med. U. Lodz, 2010. Head, dept. dental technologies Med. U. Bialystok, 2010—, adj. prof., dept. prosthetic dentistry, 2000—11. Mem.: Polish Dental Assn., OSIS-EDI. Avocations: classical music, travel, reading. Office: Waszyngtona 13 Bialystok 15-276 Poland Business E-Mail: teresasierpinska@net.bialystok.pl.

SIEVING, PAUL A., federal agency administrator, ophthalmologist, educator; BS in Physics and Hist., with honors, Valparaiso U., Ind., 1970, DS (hon.), 2003; MS in Physics, Yale U., New Haven, 1973; MD, U. Ill. Med. Sch., 1978; PhD in Bioengring., U. Ill. Grad. Sch., 1980. Diplomate Nat. Bd. Med. Examiners, Am. Bd. Ophthalmology, lic. Ill., Calif., Mass., Mich. Resident ophthalmology U. Ill. Eye & Ear Infirmary, 1978—82; postdoc. fellow retinal physiology U. Calif., San Francisco, 1982—84; clin. fellow retinal degenerations Harvard Med. Sch., Mass. Eye & Ear Infirmary, 1984—85; asst. prof. ophthalmology U. Mich., Ann Arbor, 1985—89, assoc. prof., 1989—94, prof., 1994—2001, Paul R. Lichter prof. ophthalmic genetics, 1990—2001, founding dir. Ctr. Retinal & Macular Degeneration, Dept. Ophthalmology & Visual Scis., 1990—2001; dir. Nat. Eye Inst. (NEI), NIH, Bethesda, Md., 2001—. Vice-chair clin. rsch. Found. Fighting Blindness, 1996—2001; jury mem., award vision rsch. Champalimaud Found., Portugal. Contbr. articles to profl. jours., chapters to books. Recipient Disting. Alumnus award, Valparaiso U., 1991, Rsch. to Prevent Blindness Sr. Sci. Investigator award, 1998, Alcon award, Alcon Rsch. Inst., 2000, Pisart Vision award, NY Lighthouse Internat. for Blind, 2005, Health Care Leadership award, Am. Optimetric Assn., 2007; named one of Best Dr.'s in America, 1996—98, 2001, 2005. Mem.: Am. Acad. Opthal., NAS Inst. Medicine, Internat. Soc. Clinical Electrophysiology of Vision (tres. 1986—94), Am. Ophthal.

Soc., Retina Soc. (assoc.), Sigma Xi. Office: Nat Eye Inst Bldg 31 Claude D Pepper Bldg 6A03 31 Center Dr Bethesda MD 20892-2510 Office Phone: 301-496-2234. Business E-Mail: paul.sieving@nih.gov. *

SIFFEL, CSABA, medical epidemiologist; b. Mór, Hungary, May 29, 1968; s. József Siffel and Rozália Németh; m. Sarolta Tulipán; children: Gábor, Ádám. MD, Semmelweis U. Medicine, Budapest, Hungary, 1992; PhD, Eötvös U., Budapest, 2003. Cert. PMP, PMI. Project mgmt. profl. Project Mgmt. Inst., Newtown Sq., Pa.; programme dir. Hungarian congenital abnormality registry, dept. human genetics and teratology WHO Collaborating Ctr., "Bela Johan" Nat. Ctr. Epidermiology, Budapest, 1997—2000; med. epidemiologist Nat. Ctr. Birth Defects & Devel. Disabilities, Atlanta, 2003—. Sec., treas. Internat. Clearinghouse, Rome, 1998—2000; conf. chair Ctrl. & Ea. European Summit, Budapest, 2008. Contbr. articles to public health (Pro Hygiene award, 1999), to profl. jours. Recipient Career Devel. award, Assn. Tchrs. Preventive Medicine, USA, 2000—03; Rsch. grant, European Commn., 1998—2002. Mem.: Am. Med. Infomatics Assn., Internat. Clearinghouse Birth Defects Surveillance & Rsch., Nat. Birth Defects Prevention Network, U.S.A., The Teratology Soc. Office Phone: 404-498-3821. Business E-Mail: csiffel@cdc.gov.

SIFFERT, ROBERT SPENCER, orthopedic surgeon; b. NYC, June 16, 1918; s. Oscar and Sadye (Rusoff) Siffert; m. Miriam Sand, June 29, 1941; children: Joan, John. AB in Biology with honors, NYU, 1939, MD, 1943. Diplomate Am. Bd. Orthrop. Surgery, Nat. Bd. Med. Examiners. Intern Kings County Hosp., Bklyn., 1943; resident in orthop. surgery Mt. Sinai Hosp., NYC, 1946-49, fellow in pathology, 1949-52, mem. staff, 1949—, attending orthop. surgeon, 1986—, dir. orthop. surgery, orthop. surgeon in chief, 1960-86, Lasker/Siffert Disting. Svc. prof., 1986—, chmn. emeritus, 1990—; pvt. practice NYC, 1949—. Sr. orthop. cons. N.Y.C. Dept. Health, 1952—60; attending orthop. surgeon Blythedale Children's Hosp., Valhalla, 1960—86, cons., 1986—90; dir. dept. orthops. City Hosp., Elmhurst, 1965—86; prof., chmn. dept. orthrops. Mt. Sinai Sch. Medicine, 1966—86, Dr. Robert K. Lippman prof., 1983—86, acting chmn., 1993—94, emeritus prof. and chair, 1986—, disting. prof. orthop., 2011—. Author (with J. F. Katz): Management of Hip Disorders in Children, 1983; author: See How They Grow, 1985; contbr. articles to profl. jours. Bd. dirs., mem. profl. adv. com. Easter Seal Soc. Crippled Children and Adults, 1st v.p., 1977—79; mem. adv. bd. CARE-MEDICO, 1972—83, bd. dirs., chmn., 1981—83; bd. dirs. CARE, 1983—90; mem. adv. bd. Orthopaedics Overseas, 1981—93. Capt. USAAF, 1944—46, CBI. Decorated 4 Battle Stars; recipient Ann. award in medicine, N.Y. Pub. Health Assn., 1956, N.Y. Philanthropic League, 1959, Richman award for humanism in medicine, Mt. Sinai Sch. Medicine, 1989, Lifetime Achievement award, NY Arthritis Found., 2004, Disting. Svc. Prof. award, Mt. Sina Sch. Medicine, 1990. Fellow: APHA, ACS; mem.: N.Y. State Med. Soc. (chmn. orthrop. sect. 1967—68), N.Y. Acad. Medicine (fellow orthop. sect. 1952, sec. 1962—63, chmn. 1963—64), Orthop. Rsch. Soc., Internat. Skeletal Soc., Internat. Soc. Orthop. Surgery and Traumatology, Assn. Bone and Joint Surgeons, Am. Acad. Orthop. Surgery (chmn. com. care handicapped child), Am. Orthop. Assn., Century Assn. (N.Y.C.), Phi Beta Kappa, Alpha Omega Alpha. Personal E-mail: rssiffert@aol.com.

SIFRI, COSTI D., medical educator; b. Oreg., Sept. 15, 1966; BS, U. Oreg., 1989; MD, U. Rochester, 1995. Instr. medicine Harvard Med. Sch., 2002—04; asst. prof. medicine U. Va. Health Sys., 2004—10, hosp. epidemiologist, med. dir. transplant & compromised host infectious disease program, 2009, assoc. prof. medicine, 2010—. Recipient Maxwell Finland award, Mass. Infectious Disease Soc., Mass. Gen. Hosp., Physician-Scientist Early Career award, Howard Hughes Med. Inst., Clin. Excellence award, Dept. Medicine, U. Va. Health Sys. Fellow: ACP; mem.: Soc. Healthcare Epidemiology America, Infectious Disease Soc. America. Office: University Va Health Sys PO Box 800473 Charlottesville VA 22908 Office Fax: 434-924-1225. Business E-Mail: csifri@virginia.edu.

SIGAL, ELLIOTT C., pharmaceutical executive; b. 1952; BS in Indsl. Engring., MS in Indsl. Engring., Purdue U., 1973, PhD, 1977; MD, U. Chgo., 1981. V.p., co-founder Pritsker Assocs., 1973—75; clin. fellow, rsch. fellow pulmonary medicine University of California, San Francisco, 1984—88, instr. medicine, 1988—89, asst. prof. medicine, 1989—92, asst. dir. Cystic Fibrosis R & D prog., 1990—92; exec. dir. Ctr. Inflammation Rsch. Syntex, 1992—95; v.p. inflammation and immunology rsch. Roche Bioscience, 1995—96; pres., CEO Mercator Genetics, 1996—97; v.p. dept. applied genomics Bristol-Myers Squibb Co., 1997—99, sr. v.p. early discovery & applied tech., 1999—2001, sr. v.p. drug discovery and exploratory devel., 2001—02, sr. v.p. global clin. and pharm. devel., co-chair brand devel. oper. com., 2002—04, exec. v.p., chief sci. officer, pres. R & D, 2004—, mem. exec. com., 2009—. Asst. adj. prof. medicine U. Calif., San Francisco, 1992—94, assoc. adj. prof., 1994; bd. dir. Bristol-Myers Squibb Co., 2011—. Office: Bristol-Myers Squibb Co 345 Park Ave New York NY 10154-0037 *

SIGAL, ROBERT K., plastic surgeon; Attended magna cum laude, Harvard U., 1977—81; MD, Thomas Jefferson U., 1981—85; post grad., U. Pa., 1987—89. Diplomate Am. Bd. Plastic Surgery. Intern Univ. Calif. LA Med. Ctr., 1985—87, resident gen. surgery, 1989—92; resident plastic surgery Univ. of Pa., 1992—94; hosp. affiliations include Fairfax Hosp., Reston Hosp.; med. dir. Austin-Weston Ctr. for Cosmetic Surgery. Co-author: (publs.) The immunology of silicone in a murine model, 1993, Rejuvenating the Aged Face, 2000, Surgical Treatment of the Aged Mouth, 2003, Lip Recontouring, 2005, and numerous other publications. Recipient Sigma Xi medical student research award, 1984, Clin. Surgery prize, 1985, Basic Sci. award, 1993—94; fellow NIH Cancer and Nutrition Fellowship, 1987—89. Mem.: Nat. Capital Soc. of Plastic Surgeons (former pres.), Va. Soc. of Plastic Surgery, Am. Assn. for the Advancement of Sci., NY Acad. of Sciences, ACS (mem. candidates group), US Rowing Assn., Friends of Harvard Rowing, Univ. Barge Club. Office: Austin-Weston Center for Cosmetic Surgery 1825 Samuel Morse Dr Reston VA 20190 Office Phone: 703-893-6168.

SIGEL, ERIC J., pediatrician, educator; MD, Case Western Res. U., 1988. Diplomate Am. Bd. Pediatrics-adolescent medicine, 2005, Am. Bd. Pediatrics, 2007. Resident pediat. Rainbow Babies & Children's Hosp., 1990—92; fellow adolescent medicine Children's Hosp. Boston, 1992—93; assoc. prof. Univ. Colo.; physician Children's Hosp. Colo. Office: Children's Hospital Colorado B025 13123 E 16th Ave Aurora CO 80045 Office Phone: 720-777-6131. Office Fax: 720-777-7339.

SIGETY, CHARLES BIRGE, investment company executive; b. NYC, Sept. 30, 1952; s. Charles Edward and Katharine Kinne (Snell) S.; m. Elizabeth Ross Pennington, Nov. 27, 1976; children: Austin Douglas, Katharine Colyer, Alexander Birge. BA in English Lit., Bates Coll., 1975. Lic. nursing home adminstr. Adminstr. in tng. Florence Nightingale Nursing Home, NYC, 1972, asst. dir. facility ops., 1975, dir. facility ops., 1975-78, assoc. adminstr., 1978-81, exec. dir., 1981-82; pres., CEO Profl. Med. Products, Inc., Greenwood, SC, 1982-96; pres. Upper Savannah Internat. Trade Assn., Greenwood, 1993; CEO Bison Investments, Inc., Tampa, Fla., 1996—, Aerial Machine & Tool Corp., Vesta, Va., 1998—2006, Polyten Plastics, LLC, Washington, 1998-2006, Coeur Acquisition, LLC, Washington, NC, 1999, Polyten, LLC, Washington, NC, 2000—03; mng. ptnr. Bison Mgmt. Solutions LLC, 2008—. Mem. adv. bd. Liberty Mut. Ins. Cos. S.C., 1986—96, NationsBank (Bank of Am.), Greenwood, SC, 1984—96; vice chmn. Upper Savannah Bus. Group on Health Care, 1981—87, S.C. Bus. Roundtable for the Initiative for Work Force Excellence, Columbia, 1988—92; dir. exec. com. Osteo Am., Inc., 1993—96; bd. advisors Capital South Ptnrs., 2004—06; pres. Petersburg Landing Devel., Inc., 2005—, Boonsborough, LLC, 2006—; mem. bd. adv. MD Internat., 1992—2000, 2003—09. Bd. visitors Med. U. S.C., 1988; treas. YPO HealthCare Focus Forum, 1997; bd. dirs. Stewards Found., 2003-07; active Soc. Internat. Fellows 1999-2006, Defense Orientation Conf. Assn. 2004-. Mem. Health Industry Mfrs. Assn. (ofcl. rep. 1982-96, 99-2002), Upper Savannah Internat. Trade Assn. (pres. 1993), Young Pres.'s Orgn., Chief Execs. Orgn., World Pres.' Orgn., Def. Orientation Conf. Assn. Avocations: hunting, boating. Office: Bison Investments Inc 3225 S Macdill Ave # 129-236 Tampa FL 33629-8171 Office Phone: 813-832-6359. Business E-Mail: cbs@bisoninvestments.com.

SIGETY, CHARLES EDWARD, lawyer, financial planner; b. NYC, Oct. 10, 1922; s. Charles and Anna (Toth) S.; m. Katharine K. Snell, July 17, 1948; children: Charles, Katharine, Robert, Cornelius, Elizabeth. BS, Columbia U., 1944; MBA, Harvard U., 1947; LLB, Yale U., 1951; LHD (hon.), Cazenovia Coll., 1994. Bar: NY 1952, DC 1958. With Bankers Trust Co., 1939-42; instr. adminstrv. engring. Pratt Inst., 1948; instr. econs. Yale U., 1948-50; vis. lectr. acctg. Sch. Gen. Studies Columbia U., NYC, 1948-50, 52; rapporteur com. fed. taxation for U.S. coun. Internat. C. of C., 1952-53; asst. to com. fed. taxation Am. Inst. Accts., 1950-53; with Compton Advt. Agy., NYC, 1954; vis. lectr. law Yale U., 1952; pvt. practice law NYC, 1952—; pres., dir. Video Vittles, Inc., NYC, 1953—67; dep. commr. FHA, 1955-57; of counsel Javits and Javits, 1959-60; 1st asst. atty. gen. NY, 1958-59, dir., mem. exec. com. Gotham Bank, NYC, 1961—63; dir. NY State Housing Fin. Agy., 1962—63; chmn. Met. Ski Slopes, Inc., NYC, 1962—65; pres., exec. adminstr. Florence Nightingale Health Ctr., NYC, 1965—05, dir. Schaerer AG, Wabern, Switzerland, 1982-88; chmn. Kenbar Group, NYC, 1997—, Internat. Bioimmune Sys., Inc., Great Neck, NY, 1999—2010. Professorial lectr. Sch. Architecture, Pratt Inst., NYC, 1962-66; mem. Sigety Assocs., cons. in housing mortgage financing and urban renewal, 1957-67; ho. cons. Govt. of Peru, 1956; mem. missions to Hungary, Poland, Fed. Republic Germany, Malta, Czechoslovakia, Russia, Israel, Overseas Pvt. Investment Corp., 1990-92; owner, operator Peppermill Farms, Pipersville, Pa., 1956—. Bd. dirs., sec., v.p., treas. Nat. Coun. Health Ctrs., 1969-85; bd. dirs. Am.-Hungarian Found., 1974-76, Pritikin Rsch. Found., 1991—2010, Stratford Arms Condo Assn., 1992-93, 2002-08, Global Leadership Inst., 1993—2008, Hepatitus B Found., Doylestown, 2005-2010; founding mem., bd. dirs., Natl. Assn. for Continence, 1982, trustee Cazenovia Coll., NY, 1981-2002, Delaware Valley Coll. Sci. and Agr., Doylestown, Pa., 1998-2005; trustee, v.p. Woodmere Art Mus. Phila., 2000-05, Navy Supply Corps Found., Athens, Ga., 2000—; del. White House Conf. on Aging, 1971, White House Conf. on Mgmt. Tng. and Market Econs. Edn. in Ctrl. and Ea. Europe, 1991; bd. visitors Lander Coll., U. SC, Greenwood, 1982-84; mem. fin. com. World Games, Santa Clara, 1981, London, 1985, Karlsruhe, 1989, The Hague, 1993, Confrerie des Chevaliers du Tastevin, Confrerie de la Chaine des Rotisseurs, Wine and Food Soc., Wednesday 10; chmn. Alumni Assn. Townsend Haris HS, NYC, 2005-. Lt. (j.g.) Supply Corps, USNR, 1942-46. Recipient President's medal Cazenovia Coll., 1990, George Washington laureate Am. Hungarian Found., 1996; named Prin. for Day, Townsend Harris HS NYC Bd. Edn., 1997-2001, 2006, Disting. Alumnus US Navy Supply Corps Sch., Athens, Ga., 1998; Baker scholar Harvard U., 1947. Mem. DOCA (Defense Orientation Conf. Assn.). Presbyterian. Office Phone: 212-410-8787. Personal E-mail: sigety@msn.com.

SIGH, ROBERT VIRGIL, public health physician; b. Houston, Aug. 9, 1964; s. Odea D. and Rosie L. Sigh; m. Miriam Lynette Sigh, July 21, 1991; 1 child, Caleb Robert. BA, Oakwood Coll., Huntsville, Ala., 1985; MPH, Loma Linda U., Calif., 1992, MD, 1996. Residency in family practice Fla. Hosp., Orlando, 1996—99; residency in preventative medicine, pub. health Loma Linda Univ., Calif., 1999—2000; med. dir. Adventist Whole Health Network, Reading, Pa., 2001—03, Margaret J. Weston Cmty. Health Ctr., Clearwater, SC, 2003—06; clin. dir., ready responder HRSA/NHSC, Rockville, Md., 2003—06; with USPHS, 2003—; staff physician Oakhurst Med. Ctr., 2006—09; regional med. cons., pub. health analyst HRSA Office Performance Review, Atlanta Regional Office, 2009—. Decorated Field Med. Readiness Badge; recipient Crisis Response award, Health Resource Svc. Adminstrn., Rockville, 2005, 2008; named Outstanding Unit Citation; named one of America's Top Family Drs. Mem.: Commd. Officers Assn., Rres. Officer Assn., Delta Sigma Phi. Avocations: saxophone, woodworking, hiking, camping. Home: 140 Barcelona Dr Covington GA 30016-6526

SIGMON, J. LEWIS, JR., medical educator; b. Newton, NC, July 8, 1940; MD, U. N.C., 1966. Intern David Grant USAF Hosp., 1966-67; resident Charlotte (N.C.) Meml. Hosp., 1969-71; chmn. dept. family medicine Carolinas Med. Ctr., Charlotte, 1984-95, clin. coord. Charlotte Ofcl Reg. Primary Care Edn., 1995—2001, sr. ind. cons. in grad. med. edn., family medicine, 2001—, dir. family medicine residency program Monroe, 1997—2001; prof. family medicine U. NC, 1993—2004, prof. emeritus, 2004—. Cons. Residency Assistance Program Family Medicine, Kans. City, Mo., 1989—97; acad. coun. Nat. Inst. for Program Dir. Devel., Kansas City, Mo., 1999—2003; chair Am. Bd. Family Medicine Found., 2000—; residency rev. com. for family medicine ACGME, 1997—2003, specialist site visitor for residency rev. com., 2004—; step 3 test material devel. com. USMLE/NBME, 2005—09, step 3 test devel. com. scriptor, 2009—; mem. Am. Bd. Family Medicine, 1995—2000. Recipient Disting. Svc. award, U. NC Sch. Medicine, 2005. Mem. AMA, N.C. Acad. Family Physicians. Office Phone: 704-578-1416. Personal E-mail: sigmonjr@aol.com.

SIGNORELLO, LISA BETH, epidemiologist; b. June 29, 1968; BS, U. Pa., 1990; ScD, Harvard Sch. Pub. Health, 1998. Sr. epidemiologist Internat. Epidemiology Inst., 1999—. Rsch. assoc. prof. Vanderbilt U. Sch. Medicine, 2000—. Recipient David S. Fine Meml. award, U. Pa., Travel award, Am. Assn. Cancer Rsch., Tng. award, NIH, Nat. Cancer Inst. Fellow: Am. Coll. Epidemiology; mem.: APHA, Am. Assn. Cancer Rsch., Soc. Epidemiologic Rsch. Home: 211 Midsummer Cir Gaithersburg MD 20878 E-mail: lisa.signorello@vanderbilt.edu.

SIGNORILE, JOSEPH, medical educator; b. NYC, Mar. 26, 1947; PhD, Tex. A&M U., 1990. Prof. U. Miami, 1989—. Rsch. health sci. specialist Vets. Adminstrn., 1999—2011. Mem.: Nat. Strength and Conditioning Assn., Am. Geriat. Soc., Am. Coll. Sports Medicine. Office: PO Box 248065 Coral Gables FL 33124 Business E-Mail: jsignorile@miami.edu.

SIGNORILE, PIETRO GIULIO, medical association administrator; b. Martina Franca, Italy, Sept. 2, 1953; Degree in Medicine, U. La Sapienza Rome, 1978. Ob-Gyn. specialist U. La Sapienza Rome, 1982. Pres. Italian Endometriosis Found., 2007—. Avocations: golf, tennis, painting. Office: Via Emilio Longoni 69 Rome 00155 Italy Office Fax: 0039-06-2255261. Business E-Mail: signorilepg@endometriosi.it.

SIGURDSSON, KRISTJAN, gynecological oncologist, consultant; b. Reykjavík, Iceland, Dec. 14, 1943; s. Sigurdur Sigurdsson and Brynja Helga Kristjansdottir; m. Sigrun Osk Ingadottir, Apr. 23, 1966; 1 child, Vilborg Ragnheidur Kristjansdottir. Diploma, U. Iceland, Reykjavik, 1972; PhD, U. Lund, Sweden, 1982; DPH, Nordic Sch. Pub. Health, Gothenburg, Sweden, 1999. Med. diplomate Iceland, Sweden, cert. health care adminstrn. Iceland. Clin. amanuensis dept. gynecologic oncology Univ. Hosp., Lund, 1979—82, chief physician sect. gynecologic oncology Reykjavik, 1986—2001, med. dir. dept. gynaecology & obstetrics, 1995—99; chief physician Icelandic Cancer Detection Clinic Icelandic Cancer Soc., Reykjavik, 1982—, med. dir., 1987—; clin. prof. med. faculty U. Iceland, 2007—. Mem. steering com. Mercks Future II Internat. HPV vaccination trial, 2002—07. Contbr. articles to profl. jours.; mem. internat. adv. bd. CME Jour. Gynecologic Oncology, 1996, mem. editl. bd. Scandinavian Jour. Pub. Health, 2000—06. Mem.: Icelandic Med. Assn., Internat. Gynecologic Cancer Soc. (licentiate), Nordic Soc. Gynecologic Oncology (licentiate; bd. dirs. 1993—2000), Scandinavian Assn. Obstetrics and Gynecology (licentiate). Avocations: swimming, outdoor activities, travel. Office: Icelandic Cancer Soc Skogarhlid 8 125 Reykjavik Iceland Office Fax: +354-5401920. Business E-Mail: kristjan@krabb.is.

SIGWART, ULRICH, cardiologist, educator; b. Mar. 9, 1941; s. Christine Sartorius, Sept. 2, 1967; children: Anne, Philip, Jan, Catherine. MD, U. Münster, Germany, 1967; DSc magna cum laude in Medicine, U. Freiburg, Germany, 1967; DSc in Medicine, U. Düsseldorf, Germany, 1978; DSc (hon.), U. Lausanne, 1999. Intern Cmty. Hosp. Loerrach, 1967-68; resident Framingham Union Hosp., Boston VA Hosp., 1968-71; fellowship in cardiology Baylor Coll. Medicine, 1971-72; chief of cath lab. Gollwitzer Meier Inst., Bad Oeynhausen, 1973-79; chief invasive cardiology U. Hosp., Lausanne, 1979-89; dir. dept. invasive cardiology Royal Brompton Hosp., London, 1989—2001; chief cardiology U. Geneva, 2001—06, emeritus prof., 2006—. Hon. cons. Royal Brompton Hosp., London, 2007—; lectr. in field. Author: Automation in Cardiac Diagnosis, 1978; editor: Ventricular Wall Motion, 1984, Coronary Stents, 1992, Endoluminal Stenting, 1996, Handbook of Cardiovascular Interventions, 1996, Intraluminal Stents, 1996; editl. bd. Jour. Am. Coll. Cardiology, Clin. Cardiology, Cardiac Imagin, Interventional Cardiology, Frontiers in Cardiology, Stents, Latinamer Jour. Hemodyn., Angiogr. & Therap. Cath.; co-editor Handbook on Cardiovascular Interventions; contbr. over 500 articles to profl. jours. Past chmn. Swiss Cultural Fund, Gt. Britain. Recipient Gruentzig prize, 1996, 2006, Forssmann prize, 2001, Sven Effert prize, 2003, King Faisal Internat. prize for medicine, 2004, Polzer prize, 2007, ACC, 2007. Fellow Am. Coll. Cardiology, European Soc. Cardiology (founding fellow, past chmn. working group myocardial function), Am. Coll. Angiology, Royal Coll. Physicians; mem. Swiss Acad. Med. Sci., Swiss Soc. Cardiology (founding chmn. working group PTCA & Lysis)(hon.), Swiss Soc. Cardiol.(hon.), Russian Soc. Interventional Cardiology (hon.), Brit. Cardiac Soc., Soc. Vandoise de Mèdicine, German Soc. Cardiology, Am. Soc. Cardiac Interventionists, Internat. Andreas Grüntzig Soc., Internat. Soc. for Endovascular Surgery, Am. Coll. Angiology, Am. Heart Assn., Brit. Cardiac Interventionist Soc., Royal Soc. Medicine, Med. Pilots Assn., Polish Cardiac Soc. (hon.), Argentinian Soc. Cardiology (corr.). Business E-Mail: ulrich.sigwart@unige.ch.

SIHOE, ALAN DART LOON, cardiothoracic surgeon; b. Hong Kong, China, Jan. 19, 1971; s. Kok Keng Sihoe and Sun Ming Chan; m. Yuen Ling Tong, Jan. 29, 1999; 1 child, Ewan. B Medicine B Surgery, MA, U. Cambridge, England, 1994. Ho. officer medicine and surgery Glasgow Royal Infirmary, Scotland, 1995—96; sr. ho. officer cardiothoracic surgery Nottingham City Hosp., England, 1996; med. and health officer cardiothoracic surgery Chinese U. Hong Kong, Prince of Wales Hosp., Shatin, Hong Kong, 1997—2006; assoc. cons. in cardiothoracic surgery U. Hong Kong, Grantham Hosp., 2006—, U. Hong Kong, Queen Mary Hosp., 2006—. Hon. clin. tutor cardiothoracic surgery Chinese U. Hong Kong, 1998—2006; hon. clin. asst.

prof. surgery U. Hong Kong, 2006—. Recipient Runner-up, Best Young Investigator award, 14th Ann. Internat. Surg. Symposium, Hong Kong, 2003; fellow, Hong Kong Lung Found., 2007; scholar Ezra Abraham English and Math. scholar, English Schools Found., Hong Kong, 1983—87; Ezra Abraham Yr. scholar, 1983—89. Fellow: Coll. Surgeons Hong Kong, Hong Kong Acad. Medicine, Royal Coll. Surgeons Edinburgh, Am. Coll. Chest Physicians; mem.: Hong Kong Thoracic Soc., Internat. Chinese Soc. Thoracic Surgery. Achievements include research in impact and management of pain following thoracic surgery. Office: Univ Hong Kong Dept Cardothoracic Surgery Queen Mary Hosp Hong Kong Personal E-mail: adls1@excite.com. Business E-Mail: adls1@lycos.com.

SIJANOVIC, SINISA, obstetrician, gynecologist, researcher; b. Vukovar, Croatia, Sept. 4, 1967; s. Andrija and Marija Sijanovic; m. Ivanka Genda, Jan. 21, 1974. MD, U. Zagreb, Croatia, 1992, MSc in Biomedicine Scis., 1997, PhD, 2003; degree in gynecologic endoscopy and open Surgery, Friedrich Schiller U., 2000. Lic. Ob/Gyn physician Croatia, 1999. Asst. in anatomy Med. Sch. U. Zagreb, 1993—98; intern, resident Clin. Hosp. Osijek, dept. ob/gyn, 1994—99; ob.-gyn. Clin. Hosp. Osijek, Croatia, 1999—. Fellow, Internat. Fedn. Gynecology and Obstetrics, 2000, Darthmouth Hitchcock Med. Ctr. Mem.: WHO. Roman Catholic. Office: Clinical Hospital Osijek Josipa Huttlera 4 Osijek 31000 Croatia Home: Vijenac Ivana Cesmickog 12 31-000 Osijek Croatia Office Fax: +38531512234. E-mail: sinisa.sijanovic@os.hinet.hr.

SIJENS, PAUL EDUARD, clinical scientist, associate professor; b. Maarssen, Utrecht, The Netherlands, Apr. 1, 1959; s. A.P. Sijens and C.E. Slagt. Bsc, U. Utrecht, 1981, MSc, 1983, PhD, 1988. Rsch. scientist U. Utrecht, 1983-89; postdoctoral scientist Cleve. Clinic-NIH, 1989-91; rsch. assoc., mem. staff Dr. Daniel den Hoed Clinic, Rotterdam, Netherlands, 1991—2000; assoc. prof. radiology Univ. Med. Ctr., Groningen, Netherlands, 2000—. Reviewer Brit. Jour. Cancer, Cancer Rsch. European Jour. Radiology, NMR Biomed., Radiotherapy and Oncology, Investigational Radiology, Thromb Haemost, Hepatology, Clin. Sci., Jour. Hepotology. Editor European Radiology; contbr. articles to sci. jours., including EMBO Jour., Cancer Rsch., Radiology, Internat. Jour. Hyperthermia, NMR Biomedicine, European Jour. Cancer, Magnetic Resonance in Medicine, Magnetic Resonance Imaging, Investigative Radiology. Tournament leader Netherlands Bridge League, 1988—. Rsch. grantee Dutch Cancer Found., travel grantee European Soc. Med. Oncology, 1988, rsch. grantee Sandoz, 1991. Mem. Internat. Soc. for Magnetic Resonance in Medicine, Magnetic Resonance of Cancer Study Group. Achievements include first to publish magnetic resonance spectra of human breast and breast tumors. Home: Noorderhaven 54 9712 VL Groningen Netherlands Office: UMCG Groningen Hanzeplein 1 9713 GZ Groningen Netherlands

SIKICH, LINMARIE, psychiatrist; b. Rock Springs, Wyo., Dec. 6, 1958; BA, Wash. U., St. Louis, 1981, MA/MD, 1987. Diplomate in psychiatry Am. Bd. Psychiatry and Neurology, 1995, in child, adolescent pyschiat. 1996. Med. dir. Treatment and Edn. of Austic Handicapped Children and Related Comm. (TEACCH) Med. Consultation Clinic, 2002—04; prin. investigator NC Children & Adult's Clin. Rsch. Found., 2003—04; assoc. prof., divsn. tchg. and divsn. of child and adolescent psychiatry UNC, Chapel Hill, 2003—; attending physician Dorothea Dix Hosp., Raleigh, NC, 2007—10; dir. ASPIRE (Adolescent, School-age & Preschool Psychiat. Intervention Rsch. and Evaluation) Program, U. NC, Chapel Hill, 2005—. Chair, grant rev. panel NIMH Interventions for Children and Families Study Sections, 2010—11; editl. bd. Jour. Child and Adolescent Psychiatry, 2010; mem. NIMH Spl. Emphasis Panel Peer Rev., 2010; component mem. Autism and Devel. Disorders, 2010. Recipient Chair, NIMH Interventions for Children and Families Study Sect., Career Devel. award, NIMH, Young Investigator's award, NARSAD; named to, Best Doctor's in Am. Mem.: Nat. Alliance for the Mentally Ill, Autism Soc. of Am. /Autism Soc. of NC, NC Coun. for Child and Adolescent Psychiatry (exec. bd. 2002—07), NC Med. Soc., NC Psychiat. Assn. Achievements include research in child psychopharmacology. Office: University NC Dept of Psychiatry 101 Manning Chapel Hill NC 27599-7160 Office Phone: 919-966-8653. Office Fax: 919-966-8004. Business E-Mail: lsikich@med.unc.edu.

SIKORSKA, ANNA JOLANTA, physician, educator; d. Czeslaw Jan Sikorski and Zofia Maria (Kiewlak) Sikorska. Med. diploma, Med. Acad., Warsaw, Poland, 1989; I degree specialization in internal diseases, Med. Ctr. Postgrad. Edn., Warsaw, Poland, 1994, II degree specialization in internal diseases, 1997, II degree specialization in hematology, 2004; PhD, Inst. Hematology and Blood Transfusion, Warsaw, Poland, 2003. Jr. asst. Inst. Hematology and Blood Transfusion, Warsaw, 1989—94, asst. lectr., 1994—2003, prof. asst., 2003—. Contbr. articles to profl. jours. Mem.: Polish Soc. Hematology and Blood Transfusion. Avocations: classical music, mountain climbing, swimming. Office: Inst Hematology and Blood Transfusion Chocimska Str 5 00-957 Warsaw Poland

SILBER, DENISE ARLENE, health science association administrator; b. NYC, May 19, 1953; BA, Smith Coll., 1974; MBA, Harvard Bus. Sch., 1979. Pres. Basil Strategies, 2001—. Pres. PHARMBA Assn.; rsch. author Inst. Montaigne, 2004—09; founder Drs. 2.0 & You Conf., 2011. Recipient Chevalier in French Legion of Honor award, French Nat. Order Legion of Honor. Mem.: HBS Club France, Smith Coll. Alumnae Club France, HBS Alumni Health Initiative. Office: Basil Strategies 1 Rue Jacques Offenbac Paris IDF 75016 France Business E-Mail: denise.silber@basilstrategies.com.

SILBER, SHERMAN J., urologist, consultant; b. Chgo., Dec. 18, 1941; BA in English, U. Mich., 1966, MD, 1966. Lic. Alaska, Calif., Mich., Mo., NY, cert. Am. Bd. Urology, 1977, Am. Urologic Assn., 1978. Intern Stanford U., 1966—67; gynecology asst. US Pub. Health Svc., 1967—69; resident in nephrology U. Mich., 1969—70, resident in urology, 1970—73; urologist & reproductive microsurgeon St. Luke's Hosp., dir. Infertility Ctr. of St. Louis; assoc. dir. New Hope Infertility Ctr. Instr. U. Melbourne Med. Sch., 1973—74, U. Calif. Med. Sch., 1974—76; cons. Dutch-Speaking Free U., Tel Hashomer Hosp., Tel Aviv, Kato Ladies Clinic, Tokyo, MIT Whitehead Inst. Author: How to Get Pregnant, 2007. Office: 224 S Woods Mill Rd Ste 730 Chesterfield MO 63017 Office Phone: 314-576-1400. Office Fax: 314-576-1442.

SILBERBERG, DONALD H., neurologist; b. Washington, Mar. 2, 1934; s. William Aaron and Leslie Frances (Stone) S.; m. Marilyn Alice Damsky, June 7, 1959; children: Mark, Alan. MD, U. Mich., 1958; MA (hon.), U. Pa., 1971. Intern Mt. Sinai Hosp., NYC, 1958-59; clin. assoc. in neurology NIH, Bethesda, Md., 1959-61; Fulbright scholar Nat. Hosp., London, 1961-62; NINDB spl. fellow in neuro-ophthalmology Washington U., St. Louis, 1962-63; assoc. neurology U. Pa., 1963-65, asst. prof., 1965-67, assoc. prof., 1967-71, prof., 1971-73, acting chmn. dept., 1973-74, prof., vice chmn. neurology, 1974-82, chmn., 1982-94, sr. assoc. dean, dir. internat. programs, 1994—2004, emeritus prof. hon. staff, 2010. Hon. staff U. Pa. Med. Ctr., Phila.; pres., CEO Betasteron Found., Inc., 1994-2007 Contbr. articles to profl. jours., abstracts, chpts. in books. Recipient grants in study of multiple sclerosis. Mem.: Global Network for Rsch. on Mental and Neurol. Health (founding v.p.), World Fedn. Neurology, Phila. Neurol. Soc. (pres. 1978—79), Assn. Univ. Profs. Neurology (pres.-elect 1993), Nat. Multiple Sclerosis Soc. (trustee 1997—99, 2001—03), Coll. Physicians Phila., Am. Acad. Neurology, Am. Neurol. Assn. (hon.), Alpha Omega Alpha. Office: U Pa Med Ctr Dept Neurology 3400 Spruce St Philadelphia PA 19104-4206

SILBERBERG SINAKIN, INGA, dermatologist; b. Kassel, Germany, Sept. 16, 1934; arrived in U.S., 1938; d. Willi and Erna (Rosenbaum) S.; m. Herbert M. Sinakin, Feb. 16, 1969; 1 child, William Elias. BA, Hunter Coll., 1955; MD, SUNY, 1959; MS in Dermatology, NYU, 1965. Diplomate Am. Bd. Dermatologists, 1964. Instr., clin. dermatology NYU Med. Ctr., NYC, 1963-65, clin. asst. prof., 1965-66, asst. prof. dermatology, 1966-71, clin. assoc. prof. dermatology, 1971-76; cons., dermatology Newcomb Hosp., Vineland, N.J., 1975-98. Recipient Henry Silver award Dermatologic Soc. Greater N.Y., 1962, 65, Dermatology Found. Discovery award, 1993, Dr. Rose Hirschler award Women's Dermatologic Soc., 1999; Jonas Salk scholar, City of N.Y., 1955-59. Fellow Am. Acad. Dermatology; mem. AMA. E-mail: hmsina@aol.com. *

SILBERFARB, PETER MICHAEL, psychiatrist, educator; b. Jersey City, Oct. 28, 1938; m. Anne Wagner, 1962; children: Benjamin, Leah S. BS, Bucknell U., 1960; postgrad., NYU, 1960-61; MD, Hahnemann Coll., 1965; MA (hon.), Dartmouth Coll., 1986. Diplomate Nat. Bd. Med. Examiners, Am. Bd. Psychiatry and Neurology (pres. 1998). Intern Hahnemann Med. Coll. Hosp., Phila., 1965-66; resident in internal medicine Dartmouth Affiliated Hosps., Hanover, NH, 1966-68, resident in internal medicine and psychiatry, 1968-69, psychiatry resident, 1971-72, chief resident in psychiatry, 1972-73; instr. in psychiatry Med. Sch., Dartmouth Coll., Hanover, 1972-73, asst. prof. of psychiatry, 1973-77, dir. tng. and edn., 1976-86, assoc. prof. clin. psychiatry, assoc. prof. clin. medicine, 1977-80, dir. grad. edn. and residency tng., 1978-86, assoc. prof. psychiatry, assoc. prof. medicine, 1980-82, dir. tng. and edn., 1984—2002, prof. psychiatry, prof. medicine, 1986—2002, chmn. dept. psychiatry, 1986—2002, Raymond Sobel prof. psychiatry, 2003, prof. emeritus. Cons. psychiatrist Mary Hitchcock Meml. Hosp., Hanover, 1973—; dir. psychiat. in-patient svc. Dartmouth-Hitchcock Med. Ctr., 1973-75, dir. cancer psychiatry program Norris Cotton Cancer Ctr., 1975-2002, acting dir. psychiatry consultation svc., 1977-79, assoc. dir. cancer control Norris Ctr., 1981-86; sec. psychiatry com. Cancer and Leukemia Group B, 1976-79, vice chmn., 1979-2000; mem. grant rev. com. for cancer control Nat. Cancer Inst., 1979, 80, mem. spl. grant rev. com., 1981, 82, 85, cons. to bd. sci. counselors, 1982, mem. cancer control grant rev. com., 1986-90; vice chmn. adv. com. for psychosocial and behavioral rsch. Am. Cancer Soc., 1982-88, chmn., 1988-89; cons. collaborative ctr. for cancer pain relief WHO, Milan, 1985; mem. accreditation coun. for grad. med. edn. Appeals Bd. for Psychiatry, Chgo., 1983, specialist site visitor, 1985-90, mem. residency rev. com. for psychiatry, 1991-96; dir. Am. Bd. Family Practice, 1996-2000; mem. exec. com. Am. Bd. Med. Specialties, 1996-99. Author chpts. to books; mem. editl. bd. Jour. Psychosocial Oncology, 1983-91, Internat. Jour. Psychiatry in Medicine, 1986-90, Contemporary Psychiatry, 1987-91, Psychooncology, 1991-96; referee numerous manuscripts; contbr. articles to profl. jours. Surgeon USPHS, 1969-71. Fellow Am. Psychiat. Assn. (cons. to task force on treatment if psychiat. disorders 1989), Am. Coll. Psychiatrists; mem. AMA, Am. Soc. Psychiat. Oncology/AIDS, Am. Soc. Clin. Oncology, Am. Assn. Dirs. Psychiat. Residency Tng. (mem. curriculum com. 1979-88, mem. task force on med. students and residents, chmn. com. regional dirs. 1984-88, mem. exec. com. 1984-88), Am. Psychosomatic Soc., N.H. Psychiat. Soc. (chmn. membership com. 1974-76, chmn. continuing edn. com. 1977-79), N.H. Med. Soc., Assn. Rsch. in Nervous and Mental Disease, Assn. Acad. Psychiatry, Benjamin Rush Soc. Home: Bragg Hill Norwich VT 05055 Office: Dartmouth Coll Med Sch Dept Psychiatry Lebanon NH 03756-0001

SILBERSTEIN, EDWARD BERNARD, nuclear medicine educator, oncologist, hematologist, researcher; b. Cin., Sept. 3, 1936; s. Bernard Gumpert and Harriet Louise (Kahn) S.; m. Jacqueline Rose Mervis, Oct. 2, 1988; children: Scott, Lisa. BS magna cum laude, Yale U., 1958; MD, Harvard U., 1962; MA in History of Art, U. Cin., 2010. Bd. cert. in Internal Medicine, Hematology, Nuclear Medicine, Med. Oncology Am. Bd. Internal Medicine. Intern Cin. Gen. Hosp., 1962—63, resident in internal medicine, 1963—64; resident Univ. Hosps. Cleve., 1966—67; NIH fellow in hematology New Eng. Med. Ctr., Boston, 1967—68; asst. prof. radiol. medicine U. Cin. Med. Ctr., 1968—72, assoc. prof. radiol. medicine, 1972—76, prof. radiol. medicine, 1976—, Eugene L. and Sue R. Saenger prof. radiol. scis., 1998—2000, prof. emeritus of radiology and medicine, 2000—. Assoc. dir. E.L. Saenger Radioisotope Lab., 1980—; chmn. Environ. Safety Health Com. Dept. Energy Fernald Facility, 1986-91; mem. U.S. Pharmacopeia Com. of Revision, 1990—; mem. Nat. Coun. on Radiation Protection and Measurement, 1997—; cons. Nuc. Regulatory Commn., 1988—; dir. divsn. nuc. medicine Jewish Hosp., 1976-95; cancer pain panel Agy. for Health Care Planning and Rsch., 1992-93; mem. Am. Nuclear Soc. Com. on Isotope Assurance, 2003-05, Am. Coll. Radiology Appropriateres Panel, vis. prof. various lecturerships; reviewer in field. Author: Differential Diagnosis in Nuclear Medicine, 1984, Bone Scintigraphy, 1984, Diagnostic Patterns in Nuclear Medicine, 1998; contbr. articles to profl. jours., chpts. to books. Active Race Rels. Commn. Greater Cin., 1995—2000; trustee Cin. Opera Assn., 1993—, v.p., 2003—; active Jewish Cmty. Rels. Coun., 1992—2005; trustee Isaac M. Wise Temple, 1992—2000, treas., 1997—2000; bd. dirs. Talbert House, 1969—, Air Pollution Control League, Cin., 1980—95. Capt. US Army Med. Corps, 1964—66. Recipient Pearl S. Gantz award for Cmty. Svc., United Way of Cin., 2002, VIP Volunteerism award, Hamilton County Mental Health Bd., 2005; fellow, Am. Col. Nuc. Physicians. Mem.: Am. Bd. Nuclear Medicine (chmn. 1999), Soc. Nuc. Medicine (sec. 1989—92, 1989—92, bd. dirs. 1989—99, pres. S.E. chpt. 1990—91, chair sci. program 1992—94, spkr. Ho. of Dels. 2002—04, Speaker's award 2004, Marshall Brucer award 2002), Literary Club, Sigma Xi, Phi Beta Kappa. Jewish. Avocations: tennis, history of art, archaeology, travel. Office: U Cin Med Ctr Mont Reid Pavilion G026 234 Goodman St Cincinnati OH 45219-2364 Office Phone: 513-584-9032. Business E-Mail: silbereb@healthall.com.

SILBERSTEIN, STEPHEN DAVID, health facility administrator, neurologist; b. June 6, 1942; MD, U. Pa., 1967. Intern U. Pa., 1967-68; resident in neurology HUP, Phila., 1968-69; rsch. assoc. in pharmacology, toxicology Nat. Inst. Mental Health, Bethesda, MD, 1969-72; resident in neurology HUP, Phila., 1972-75; chief sect. neurology Germantown Hosp. & Med. Ctr., Phila., 1975-97; prof. neurology Thomas Jefferson U. Hosp., Phila., 1997-98; dir. Comprehensive Headache Ctr., Phila., 1982-97, Jefferson Headache Clinic, Phila., 1997—. Fellow: American Academy of Neurology, American Headache Soc., ACP. Office: Jefferson Headache Ctr Ste 8130 Gibbon 111 South 11th St Philadelphia PA 19107

SILBIGER, MARTIN L., radiologist, educator, dean; b. Ravenna, Ohio, Mar. 17, 1938; s. Alfred James and Evelyn Norma (Cheswick) Silbiger; m. Ruth Hope Steele, June 4, 1957; children: Martin, Eve, Jonathan, Holly, Wendy. BA, U. Pa., 1958; MD, Western Reserve U., 1962; MBA, U. South Fla., 1989. Diplomate Am. Bd. Radiology, Am. Bd. Nuc. Medicine. Intern Univ. Hosps. Cleve., 1962—63; resident Johns Hopkins Hosp., 1963—66; with NIH, 1966—68; radiologist Tampa (Fla.) Gen. Hosp., 1968—; prof. U. South Fla., Tampa, 1982—; chief of staff Tampa Gen. Hosp., 1978—80; chmn. dept. radiology U. South Fla. Coll. Medicine, 1982—95; dean coll. medicine U. South Fla., 1995—2000, v.p. health scis., 1995—2000. Founder Hillsborough County Med. Assn. Found., Tampa, 1992; treas. Cmty. Found. Tampa, 1993—95; bd. dirs. Moffitt Cancer Ctr., Tampa, 1985—2000, Moffitt Cancer Ctr. Found., 1994—2000. Avocations: reading, rollerblading, golf, tennis. Home: 1827 Bayshore Blvd Tampa FL 33606-3210 Office: 3301 Alumni Dr Tampa FL 33612-9413 also: 1209 Bruce B Downs Blvd PO Box 66 Tampa FL 33601-0066

SILLANPAA, PETRI J., orthopedist; b. Finland, Sept. 27, 1977; s. Esa and Irma Sillanpaa; m. Krista Kankaanranta, Aug. 2, 2003; children: Minttu, Maiju. MD, U. Tampere, 2003, PhD, 2008. Orthop. resident Kanta-Hame Ctrl. Hosp., Hameenlinna, Finland, 2004—07; rsch. fellow Rsch. Dept., Ctrl. Mil. Hosp., Helsinki, Finland, 2004—; orthop. surgeon Tampere U. Hosp., Finland, 2007—. Contbr. articles and scientific papers to profl. jours. Mem.: Finnish Orthop. Assn. Achievements include invention of a mini-invasive surgical technique for patellar instability. Office: Tampere Univ Hosp Tampere PL 2000 Finland Business E-Mail: petri.sillanpaa@uta.fi.

SILLEN, HENRIK LARS, research and development company executive; b. Sweden, Nov. 22, 1971; MS, U. Stockholm, 1995. Alliance mgr. AstraZeneca, 2011—. Avocation: sailing. Office: Pepparedsleden Molndal 43183 Sweden E-mail: henrik.sillen@astrazeneca.com.

SILLER, KEITH A., neurologist, psychiatrist; MD, NYU, 1989. Cert. Neurology. Intern in psychiatry NYU Med. Ctr., 1989—90, resident in neurology, 1990—93, clin. fellow in cerebrovascular disease, 1993—95, asst. prof. neurology and psychiatry; med. dir. NYU Comprehensive Stroke Care Ctr. Office: NYU Langone Med Ctr HCC 5 5A 530 1st Ave New York NY 10016 Office Phone: 212-263-1485. Office Fax: 212-263-7871. E-mail: keith.siller@nyumc.org.

SILLMAN, ARNOLD JOEL, physiologist, educator; b. NYC, Oct. 10, 1940; s. Philip and Anne L. (Pearlman) S.; m. Jean Fletcher Van Keuren, Sept. 26, 1969; children: Andrea Jose Callaway, Diana Van Keuren Taylor. AB, UCLA, 1963, MA, 1965, PhD, 1968. Asst. prof. UCLA, 1969-73, U. Calif., Davis, 1975-78, assoc. prof., 1978-85, prof., 1985—2007, prof. emeritus, 2007—; asst. prof. U. Pitts., 1973-75, interim dir. aquaculture and fisheries program, 1994—95, vice chair sect. neurobiology, physiology and behavior, 1998—2007, acting chair, 2001. Contbr. articles to profl. jours. USPHS trainee, UCLA, 1966-67; fellow NSF, 1967-68, Fight for Sight, Inc., 1968-69. Recipient Acad. Senate Disting. Tchg. award, 1996. Jewish. Avocations: backpacking, gardening, woodworking. Home: 1140 Los Robles St Davis CA 95618-4927 Office: U Calif Dept Neurobiology Physiology & Behavior Coll Biol Scis Davis CA 95616 Business E-Mail: ajsillman@ucdavis.edu.

SILLS, EDWARD M., pediatric rheumatologist; b. Bklyn., Jan. 8, 1938; MD, NYU Sch. Medicine, 1963. Diplomate Am. Bd. Pediat. Intern pediat. Bronx Mcpl. Hosp. Ctr., 1963—64, resident pediat. rheumatology, 1964—67; dir. pediat. rheumatology Johns Hopkins Children's Ctr., Balt., 1969—; assoc. prof. pediat. Johns Hopkins U. Sch. Medicine, Balt., 1969—. Med. dir. pediat Johns Hopkins Home Health Grp.; prog. dir. pediat continuing edn. Johns Hopkins U. Sch. Medicine. Contbr. articles to profl. jours. Named one of America's Top Dr.'s, Castle Connolly Med. LTD. Mem.: Am. Coll. Rheumatology.

SILVA, ANDREZA, medical researcher; b. Rio de Janeiro, Oct. 16, 1981; Grad. in Vet. Medicine, U. Fed. Rural do Rio de Janeiro, 2005; PhD in Vet. Medicine, Sch. Vet. and Animal Sci., 2011. Vet. rsch. scientist Sch. Vet. Medicine and Animal Sci., São Paulo State U., 2006—. Office: Ursula Camargo de Barros street 488 Botucatu São Paulo 18610-301 Brazil Personal E-mail: andrezamedvet@yahoo.com.br.

SILVA, ANTÓNIO MENEZES, surgeon, educator; b. Luanda, Portugal, Aug. 18, 1949; s. António and Maria Natália Silva; m. Maria Isabel Dias Da Silva; children: Miguel Menezes De Silva, Mónica Menezes Da Silva. MD, U. Luanda, 1973. Postgrad. fellow Hosp. Santa Maria, Lisbon, Portugal, 1976—79; resident surgery Hosps. Civis de Lisboa, 1979—85; gen. surgeon Hosp. De Cascais, Portugal, 1988—94; grad. asst. Hosp. Pulido Valente, Lisbon, 1994—99, head of dept., 1999—. Adj. prof. New Univ. Lisbon, 2001—. Editor-in-chief Archivos Internationales Hydatidology, 1997, dir. (jour.) Revista Portuguesa Hydatidology, 2003. Mem.: Internat. Assn. Hydatidology (pres. 2001, Cave Canem medal 1997). Office: Hosp Pulido Valente SA Al Linhas De Torres 117 1769-001 Lisbon Portugal Home: Estrada da Luz 59-8o D 1600-152 Lisbon Portugal Office Phone: +351 217587232. E-mail: mensilvapt@yahoo.com.

SILVA, ARTUR OLIVEIRA, pathologist, researcher; b. Oporto, Portugal, Dec. 2, 1974; s. Artur Gonçalves and Maria José Silva; m. Helena Guedes Pinto, July 21, 2001; children: André, Diogo. MD, Oporto U., 1998, MSc, 2004. Gen. practitioner Hosp. de Sao Joao, Oporto, 1998—2000, resident in surg. pathology, 2001—05, pathologist, 2006—. Rschr. in field. Contbr. articles to profl. jours. Tchr. Christian Sch., Oporto, 1991—2001. Recipient Honor award, Hosp. de Sao Joao, 2002. Mem.: Internat. Acad. Pathology. Avocations: writing, reading, singing, tennis, chess. Office Phone: 0351 22 5090591. Business E-Mail: artosilva@elix.pt.

SILVA, CELSO, medical educator; b. Sao Paulo, Brazil, Aug. 20, 1964; MD, Jundiai Med. Sch., Brazil, 1991; M in Translational Rsch., U. South Fla., 2011. Postdoc. rsch. fellow Brown U., 1996—99, resident physician, ob-gyn., 1999—2003; clin. fellow, reproductive endocrinology and infertility U. Pa., 2003—06; mem., instl. rev. bd. U. South Fla., asst. prof., 2007—. Recipient Presdl. award, Soc. Gynecol. Investigation. Fellow: Am. Congress Ob-Gyn.; mem.: Am. Soc. Reproductive Medicine (Tng. Rsch. award). Home: 1014 Bay Harbour Pl Tampa FL 33602 Business E-Mail: csilva@health.usf.edu.

SILVA, CLASSIUS FERREIRA, engineering educator; b. Tupi Paulista, Oct. 1, 1973; Degree in Chem. Engring., State U. Maringá, 1996; DSc in Chem. Engring., State U. Campinas, 2006. Prof. U. Fed. São Paulo, 2009—. Adj. prof. State U. West Paraná, 1999—2009. Mem.: European Stevia Assn. Avocations: music, theater, films. Office: Rua Artur Riedel 275 Diadema São Paulo 09927-270 Brazil Office Fax: 551123560023. E-mail: classiusferreira@yahoo.com.br.

SILVA, ELCIO DIAS, urologist, b. Goiania, Goias, Brazil, June 20, 1951; s. Nardine and Denir Silva; Postdoc., U. Estadual Campinas, São Paulo, Brazil, 2006. Diplomate Med. Sch. Minas, Gerais, Brazil, 1975. Titular mem. Brazilian Urologic Soc., São Paulo, 1981—; coord. urologic laparoscopic surgery Hosp. Santa Marcelina, São Paulo, 2004—; coord. urologic svc. Maternidade Campinas, 2004—; pres. laparoscopic dept. Campinas Med. and Surgery Soc., 2006—; coord. laparoscopic course Vet. Med. Sch., São João Boa Vista, São Paulo, 2006—. Contbr. articles to profl. jours. Master: Campinas Rotarian Assn. (pres. 2000—01), Rotary Club Campinas Oeste (pres. 1999—2000); mem.: Older House (pres. 1994—97). Office: Urologic Clinic Avenida Andrade Neves 784 13013-161 Campinas SP Brazil E-mail: doutorelcio@terra.com.br.

SILVA, FÁTIMA MARIA HELENA SIMÕES PEREIRA DA, statistician, educator; b. São Carlos, Brazil, Nov. 21, 1953; PhD, U. São Paulo, 2001. Prof. U. São Paulo, 1993—. Home: Rua Chile 1026/13 Ribeirão Preto São Paulo 14020 610 Brazil Business E-Mail: fsimoes@fcfrp.usp.br.

SILVA, FERNANDA CAMPOS, obstetrician; b. Brazil, July 15, 1978; D, U. Fed. Rio de Janeiro, 2002; PhD, U. Fed. Fluminense, 2011. Obstetrician Clínica Perinatal Barra, 2004—11, Hosp. Fed. de Bonsucesso, 2006—. Mem.: Federação Brasileira de Ginecologia e Obstetrícia. Office: Av Embaixador Abelardo Bueno 201 Rio De Janeiro 22775-040 Brazil Business E-Mail: fernandacampos@cpdt.com.br.

SILVA, GRACIELA E., medical educator; b. Mex., Aug. 8, 1962; PhD, U. Ariz., 2004. Asst. prof. Ariz. State U., 2006—. Recipient Young Investigator award, Am. Acad. Sleep Medicine. Mem.: AASM. Avocation: bicycling. Office: 500 North 3rd St Phoenix AZ 85004-0698 Office Fax: 602-496-0849. Business E-Mail: graciela.silva@asu.edu.

SILVA, ILCE FERREIRA, healthcare educator; b. Montanha, Feb. 7, 1978; MS in Epidemiology, Brazilian Nat. Sch. Pub. Health, 2003, PhD in Pub. Health, 2008. Pub. health program coord. Secretariat State of Health in Espirito Santo, 1998—2000; rsch. coord. Brazilian Nat. Cancer Inst., 2002—08; adj. prof. epidemiology U. Federal Fluminense, 2009—. Home: Rua Itacuruca 26/Apto 205 Tijiica Rio de Janeiro 20210150 Brazil Personal E-mail: ilceferreira@yahoo.com.br.

SILVA, JANE MARY ALVES DA, ophthalmologist; b. Arapiraca, Alagoas, Brazil, Nov. 5, 1973; Degree, U. Fed. Alagoas, 1997. Ophthalmologist U. Fed. Pemambuco, 1998—2001. Fellow U. Estadual Campinas, 2005. Mem.: Eye's Inst. Recife (award). Avocation: reading. Home: Caio Pereira St 175 1202 Rosarinho Recife Pernambuco 52014010 Brazil Home Fax: 81 2122 5000. Personal E-mail: janemary.alves@gmail.com.

SILVA, JOSE ROBERTO V., biology professor; b. Itatira, Ceara, Brazil, Mar. 8, 1973; Degree in Vet. Medicine, State U. Ceara, 1999; PhD, Utrecht U., Netherlands, 2005. Adj. prof. Fed. U. Ceara, 2005—. Rsch. scientist Cearense found., FUNCAP, Brazil, 2008—10, Nat. Coun. Sci. & Technol. Devel., CNPq, 2010—. Recipient Young Scientist award, State U. Ceara. Mem.: Brazilian Soc. Embryo Transfer. Avocation: bicycling. Office: Comand Mauricelio Rocha Ponte 100 Sobral Ceará 62042280 Brazil Office Fax: 55 88 3611 8000. Personal E-mail: roberto_viana@yahoo.com.

SILVA, MARCIO DE OLIVEIRA, epidemiologist; b. Salvador, Bahia, Brazil, Feb. 9, 1979; MD, Fed. U. Bahia, 2003. Cert. in infectious diseases 2007. Physician infectious diseases SESAB, 2011—. Home: Plinio Moscoso Salvaor Bahia 40155812 Brazil Personal E-mail: oliveiras_m@yahoo.com.br.

SILVA, MARTINHO BRAGA, research scientist; b. Brasília, Brasil, Mar. 17, 1976; Degree in Psychology, U. Brasília, 1999; D in Social Anthropology, U. Fed. Rio de Janeiro, 2011. Vis. rschr. FIOCRUZ Brasília, rsch. scientist, 2008—. Cons. Ministry Health, 2008—10. Mem.: Assn. Brasileira Antropologia. Avocations: astrology, volleyball. Home: Squadron 203 - D Apt 503 Brasília 70833-040 Brazil Personal E-mail: martinho02003@yahoo.com.br.

SILVA, OMEGA LOGAN, physician; b. Washington, Dec. 14, 1936; d. Louis Jasper and Ruth (Dickerson) Logan; m. C. Francis A. Silva, Oct. 25, 1958 (div. 1981); 1 child, Frances Cecile; m. Harold Bryant Webb, Nov. 28, 1982. BS cum laude with honors in chemistry, Howard U., Washington, 1958, MD, 1967. Bio-chemist NIH, Bethesda, Md., 1958-63; resident in medicine Vets. Affairs Med. Ctr., Washington, 1967—70, fellow in endocrinology, 1970—71, rsch. assoc., 1971—74, clin. investigator, 1974—77, asst. chief endocrinology, 1977-96, dir. diabetes clin., 1977—96; assoc. prof. medicine George Washington U., Washington, 1975-91; physician Mitchell-Trotman Med. Group, P.C., Washington, 1996-97; prof. George Washington U., Washington, 1991-98, prof. emeritus, 1999—; prof. Howard U., Washington, 1977-96. Mem. exec. com. Health Care Coun. Nat. Capital Area, 1995—, bd. dirs.; med. rev. officer Employee Health Programs, Bethesda, 1998-2004; bd. dirs. NRC Women and Families. Author: (with others) Endocrinology, 1990; featured Nat. Libr. Medicine's Changing the Face of Medicine, an Exhibition on America's Women Physicians, 2003; contbr. articles to profl. jours. Charter mem. Nat. Mus. of Women in the Arts, Washington, 1986; trustee Howard U., 1991-97, chair, hon. com. 140 Gala Anniversary Coll. Medicine, Howard U., 2008. Recipient Disting. Alumni award Howard U. Coll. Medicine, 1997 Master ACP (mem. com. 2003-06, Best Sci. Presentation award 1974); fellow African Am. Inst. 2006; mem. Am. Med. Women's Assn. (br. I v.p. 1986-87, pres. 1987-88, anti-smoking task force 1989-92, chair govtl. affairs, 1992-96, mem. nominations com. 1992, gov. region III 1996-97, v.p. program 1997-99, chmn. leadership com. 1996-97, pres. elect 1999-00, pres. 2000-02, chair policy & advocacy com. 2006-, founder Internat. Women in Medicine Hall of Fame, 2001, AMWA Bertha Van Hoosen award, 2008), Howard U. Med. Alumni (pres. 1983-88, bd. dirs. 1983-), Endocrine Soc. (life), Alpha Omega Alpha, ACS (emeritus mem., 2007), Am. Diabetes Assn. (DC) (cmty. leadership bd. 2009), Univ. Club (Foremother award Nat. Rsch. Ctr. Women and Families, Washington, 2010).

SILVA, RICARDO HENRIQUE ALVES DA, orthodontist, educator; b. Bauru, São Paulo, Brazil, July 11, 1980; PhD, U. Sao Paulo, 2007. Dentist, Bauru Dental Sch. U. Sao Paulo, 2002, prof., rschr., forensic dentistry, Sch. Dentistry Ribeirao Preto, 2008—; prof. Paulista U., 2004—07. Writer Editora Santos, 2010. Author: (book) Professional Guidance to Dentist: Ethics and Law. Mem.: Forensic Dentistry and Ethics Brazilian Soc. (bd. dirs., exec. sec. 2010—), SBPqO - Brazilian Divsn. - Internat. Assn. Dental Rsch. Avocations: running, films, soccer. Office: FORP/USP - Avenida do Café Ribeirão Preto Sao Paulo 14040-904 Brazil Business E-Mail: ricardohenrique@usp.br.

SILVA, RUI A., gastroenterologist; b. Matosinhos, Dec. 12, 1965; Grad in Medicine, Oporto Med. Sch., 1980. Gastrenterologist Inst. Português De Oncologia, 1992—, sr. gastroenterologist. Mem.: Portuguese Soc. Gastroenterology. Home: Av Republica 1921 6 Esquerdo Vila Nova Gaia 4430-206 Portugal Personal E-mail: rsgastro@sapo.pt.

SILVAGNI, ANTHONY JOSEPH, dean, osteopath; b. Atlantic City, Apr. 18, 1940; s. Anthony Serafino and Madeline (Valentino) S.; m. Marlene Scherr, Mar. 12, 1961 (div. July 1977); children: Paul, Michelle; m. Dianna Poole, Oct. 1, 1977. BS in Pharmacy, Phila. Coll. of Pharmacy and Sci., 1963, MS in Hosp. Pharmacy, 1966, PharmD, 1970; postgrad., Purdue U., 1963-64; DO, Phila. Coll. Osteo. Medicine, 1982. Resident in hosp. pharmacy Thomas Jefferson U. Hosp., Phila., 1965-66, assoc. dir. pharmacy services, 1969-73; chief pharmacist prescription div. cen. pharm. services Appalachian Regional Hosp., Williamson, W.Va., 1966-67, asst. dir. cen. pharm. services, 1967-68; dir. pharmacy services Presbyn. U. Pa. Hosp., Phila., 1968-69; dir. pharmacy programs Lake Area Health Edn. Ctr., Erie, Pa., 1973-74; assoc. dir. clin. pharmacy services Peter Bent Brigham Hosp., Boston, 1974-76; clin. pharmacist U. Ariz., Tucson, 1976-78; faculty Health Care Edn. Programs Am., Chestnut Hill, Mass., 1980-82; intern Tucson Gen. Hosp., 1982-83; physician Dakota Family Practice, Parkston, S.D., 1983—; dean Nova Southeastern Univ. Coll. of Osteopathic Med., 1998—. Instr. in clin. pharmacy Phila. Coll. Pharmacy and Sci., 1969-73; asst. profl clin. pharmacy U. Ariz., 1977-78; chmn. dept. clin. practice Mass. Coll. Pharmacy, Boston, 1974-76; cons. clin. pharmacy Tucson Gen. Hosp., 1977-78, dir. clin. pharmacy services, 1977-78, vis. cons. staff dept. medicine, 1978; vis. faculty hypertension, Smith, Kline & French, Phila., 1980-82; lectr. to nat., state, county and local health profl. orgns. Contbr. articles to profl. jours. Mem. curriculum com. Mass. Coll. Pharmacy, 1974-76, chmn. PharmD admissions com., 1975-76; mem. bldg. com. U. Ariz. Coll. Pharmacy, 1976-78, grad. thesis com., 1977-78, faculty voting rights com., 1978, chmn. grade grievance com, 1978. Served with U.S. Army, 1961-62. Pa. State U. grantee, VA grantee, Lakes Area Regional Med. Program grantee, Smith, Kline and French grantee; Merck Sharp and Dohme scholar, 1979, Nat. Student Osteo. Med. Assn. scholar, 1980. Fellow Am. Found. for Pharm Edn.; mem. AMA, Am. Acad. Gen. Practitioners, Am. Osteo. Assn. (grantee), Am. Pharm. Assn. (review panel for handbook 1975—, practitioner panel 1973—), Am. Soc. Hosp. Pharmacists (adv. panel on student membership 1975-76), Am. Pharm. Assn. Acad. of Pharmacy Practice (charter), S.D. Med. Assn., Dist. 6 Med. Soc., Kappa Psi, Phi Sigma Gamma, Rho Chi. Avocations: flying, skiing, motorcycling, camping. Office: Nova Southeastern Univ Coll Medicine Rm 1401 Terry Bldg 3200 S University Dr Fort Lauderdale FL 33328 *

SILVA GUNAWARDENE, YASANTHI ILLIKA NILMINI, medical educator; b. Sri Lanka, Feb. 24, 1968; BSc with honors, U. Colombo, Sri Lanka, 1994; PhD, U. Hong Kong, 2003. Demonstrator, biochemistry and molecular biology Faculty Sci. U. Colombo, Sri Lanka, 1994—95; demonstrator, parasiotology Faculty Medicine U. Kelaniya, Sri Lanka, 1997—99, sr. lectr., molecular medicine, 2003—, dept head, molecular medicine, 2010—; rsch. & tech. asst. U. Hong Kong, 1999—2003. Recipient Vice-Chancellor's award, U. Kelaniya, Sri Lanka, 2007, Zonta Woman of Achievement award, Zonta Internat. Club 1 Colombo, Sri Lanka, 2009, Presdl. Rsch. award, Dem. Socialist Republic of Sri Lanka, 2010; IAEA fellowship, 2007. Office: Faculty Medicine Thalagolla Rd RA Ragama GQ 11010 Sri Lanka Office Fax: 94-011-2958337. Business E-Mail: nilminis@graduate.hku.hk.

SILVA-LOVATO, CLÁUDIA HELENA, dental educator, researcher; b. Sertãozinho, São Paulo, Brasil, May 8, 1974; Degree, Faculty Odontology Ribeirão Preto, 1996; PhD, MMS, U. São Paulo, Ribeirão Preto, DDS student, 2002—. Assoc. prof., rschr. faculty odontology U. São Paulo, 2009. Office: Avenida do Café sn Ribeirão Preto São Paulo 14040-904 Brazil Business E-Mail: chl@forp.usp.br.

SILVEIRA, ERIKA APARECIDA, nutritionist; b. Bambuí, Minas Gerais, Brasil, Sept. 28, 1974; Nutrição, U. Fed. Goiás, 1999; Doutorado em Epidemiologia, U. Fed. Minas Gerais, 2006. Adj. prof., rsch. scientist U. Fed. Goiás, 2005—11, coord. ambulatório de nutrição e obesidade, hosp. das clínicas, 2007—11, coord. especialização em epidemiologia, 2008—10, coord. programa de pós-graduação nutrição e saúde, 2011—. Recipient Prêmio Helena Feijó, Conselho Fed. de Nutricionista, Menção Honrosa Trabalho, Comissão Científica V Encontro Brasileiro de Obesidade e Transtornos alimentares. Avocations: movies, travel. Office: Rua 227 Goiânia Goiás 74605-080 Brazil Office Fax: 55(62)3209-6273. Business E-Mail: erikasil@terra.com.br.

SILVEIRA, PAULO CESAR LOCK, research scientist; b. Criciúma, Santa Catarina, Apr. 29, 1982; Grad, U. do Extremo Sul Catarinense, 2005, M, 2008. Rsch. fellow, grad. program biochemistry & capes U. Fed. de Santa Catarina, 2009—. Avocations: soccer, cooking. Office: Campus Universitário - Bloco C - 2°andar Florianópolis Santa Catarina 88040-900 Brazil Personal E-mail: silveira_paulo2004@yahoo.com.br.

SILVEIRA, VERA MAGALHAES, epidemiologist, educator; b. Recife, Brazil, Aug. 19, 1960; Degree in Medicine, Fed. U. Pernambuco, 1984; PhD in Infectious Diseases, UNIFESP, 1992. Prof., infectious diseases Fed. U. Pernambuco, 2005, coord., discipline infectious diseases, 2005. Recipient Prof. Honored Dedication Tchg. award, Fed. U. Pernambuco. Avocation: tai chi. Office: Av Prof Moraes Rego 1235 Recife Pernambuco 50670-901 Brazil Office Fax: 11-81-21268528. Business E-Mail: vemagalhaes@uol.com.br.

SILVER, DEE EDWARD, physician, neurologist; b. Keystone, Iowa, Dec. 8, 1939; s. Grant Mason and Cora Ann (Larson) S.; m. Penelope Neena Diumenti (div. May 1988); 1 child, Helen Diumenti Silver; m. Marilyn Janet Lyddy, Mar. 8, 1998. BA, Iowa State Tchrs. Coll., Cedar Falls, 1961; MD, U. Iowa, Iowa City, 1967. Diplomate Am. Bd. Neurology. Head dept. electroencephalography and neurophysiology Balboa Naval Hosp., San Diego, 1971—73; physician, ptnr., head dept. neurology Coastal Neurol. Med. Group, La Jolla, Calif., 1973—. Med. dir. San Diego Parkinsons Disease Info. Ctr., 1986—; bd. dirs. Ellen Browning Scripps Soc., San Diego, 1986-94, 1996-2005; mem. exec. cabinet Scripps Inst. Medicine and Sci., San Diego, 1994-2004; head neurology dept. Balboa Naval Hosp., 1972-73 Author and editor publs. in field Lt. comdr. USN, 1971-73 Mem. AMA, Calif. Med. Assn. (del. 1981-84), Am. Acad. Neurology, Movement Disorder Soc., Rotary Internat. (Paul Harris fellow 1986), Purple Key Soc Republican. Avocations: tennis, fly fishing, hunting, golf, trumpet. Home: PO Box 224 Rancho Santa Fe CA 92067-0224 Office: 9850 Genesee Ave Ste 740 La Jolla CA 92037-1218

SILVER, DONALD, surgeon, educator; b. NYC, Oct. 19, 1929; s. Herman and Cecilia (Meyer) S.; m. Helen Elizabeth Harnden, Aug. 9, 1958; children: Elizabeth Tyler, Donald Meyer, Stephanie Davies, William Paige. AB, Duke U., 1950, BS in Medicine, MD, 1955. Diplomate Am. Bd. Surgery, Am. Bd. Gen. Vascular Surgery, Am. Bd. Thoracic Surgery. Intern Duke Med. Ctr., 1955-56, asst. resident, 1958-63, resident, 1963-64; mem. faculty Duke Med. Sch., 1964-75, prof. surgery, 1972-75; cons. Watts Hosp., Durham, 1965-75, VA Hosp., Durham, 1970-75, chief surgery, 1968-70; prof. surgery, chmn. dept. U. Mo. VA Med. Ctr., Columbia, 1975-98, chmn. univ. physicians, 2002—05. Cons. Harry S. Truman Hosp., Columbia, 1975—2000; mem. bd. sci. advisers Cancer Research Center, Columbia, 1975—; mem. surg. study sect. A NIH; dir surg. svcs. U. Mo. Health System, 2001-2003. Contbr. articles to med. jours., chpts. to books; editorial bds.; Jour. Vascular Surgery, Postgrad. Gen. Surgery, Vascular Surgery. Served with USAF, 1956-58. James IV Surg. traveler, 1977 Fellow ACS (gov. 1995-99), Deryl Hart Soc.; mem. AMA, AAAS, Mo. Med. Assn., Boone County Med. Soc., Internat. Cardiovascular Soc., Soc. Univ. Surgeons, Am. Heart Assn. (Mo. affiliate rsch. com.), Soc. Surgery Alimentary Tract, Assn. Acad. Surgery, So. Thoracic Surg. Assn., Internat. Soc. Surgery, Soc. Vascular Surgery, Am. Assn. Thoracic Surgery, Am. Surg. Assn., Ctrl. Surg. Assn. (pres.-elect 1990-91, pres. 1991-92), Western Surg. Assn., Midwestern Vascular Surg. Soc. (pres. 1984-85), Ctrl. Surg. Assn. Found. (treas. 1992-93, 2d v.p. 1993-94, 1st v.p. 1994-95, pres. 1995-96). Home: 3 Silver Maple Ct Durham NC 27705-5642 Personal E-mail: retdoc@frontier.com.

SILVER, HERBERT, physician; b. Bklyn., Feb. 18, 1932; s. Ben and Sylvia (Weinstock) S.; m. Judith Elaine Miller, Aug. 28, 1966; children: Rand Kenneth, David Jeffrey. BA, Adelphi U., 1953; MD, SUNY, Buffalo, 1957. Diplomate Am. Bd. Pathology. Intern Maimonides Med. Ctr., 1957-58; resident Nassau Univ. Med. Ctr., 1958-60, Hosp. of U. of Pa., 1960-62; assoc. pathologist, dir. blood bank/hematology Barnes-Jewish Hosp., St. Louis, 1964-70; dir. transfusion medicine Hartford (Conn.) Hosp., 1970—2001; assoc. prof. U. Conn. Med. Ctr., Farmington, 1970-90, U. Conn. Sch. of Allied Health, Storrs, 1977—2002. Cons. St. Francis Med. Ctr., Hartford, Conn., 1978-2002, Conn. Children's Med. Ctr., 1980-2002; med. dir. Hartford Med. Lab, 1985-99; adv. bd. Capital Cmty. Coll. Found., Hartford, Conn., 2002—. Author, editor: Probability of Inclusion in Paternity Testing, 1982, Problem Solving in Immunohematology, 1987; guest editor Transfusion Jour., 1992-96; contbr. articles to profl. jours. Bd. dirs. Emanuel Synagogue, West Hartford, Conn. Capt. U.S.

Army Med. Corps, 1962-64. Mem.: AMA, Coll. Am. Pathologists, Am. Soc. Clin. Pathology, Am. Assn. Blood Banks (bd. dirs. 1987—92, Disting. Svc. award 1993, John Elliott Meml. award 2000). Democrat. Jewish. Avocations: bicycling, clarinet. Home: 32 Beacon Hill Dr West Hartford CT 06117-1003

SILVER, MALCOLM DAVID, pathologist, educator; b. Adelaide, South Australia, Apr. 29, 1933; s. Eric Bertram and Stella Louisa (Riley) S.; m. Meredith May Galloway, Jan. 19, 1957; children: Stuart Faulkner, Claire Eleanor, Caryl Louise. MD, U. Adelaide; PhD, McGill U. Diplomate: Am. Bd. Pathology. Resident med. officer Royal Adelaide Hosp., 1957-58; resident in pathology Royal Victoria Hosp.-Pathol. Inst., McGill U., Montreal, Que., Canada, 1958-63; research fellow dept. exptl. pathology John Curtin Sch. Med. Research, Australian Nat. U., Canberra, 1963-65; asst. prof. pathology U. Toronto, 1965-68, assoc. prof., 1968-74, prof., 1974—79, chmn. dept. pathology, 1985-95, prof. dept. lab. medicine and pathobiology, 1996—98; staff pathologist Toronto Gen. Hosp., 1965-72, sr. staff pathologist, 1972-79; prof., chmn. dept. pathology U. Western Ont., London, Ont., Canada, 1979-85; chief pathology Univ. Hosp., London, 1979-85; pathologist in chief Toronto Gen. Hosp., 1985-89, The Toronto Hosp. (Toronto Gen. and Toronto Western Divs.), 1989-91, sr. staff pathologist, 1991-98; bd. mem. sec. Grey County Woodlot Assn.; bd. mem. Escarpment Biosphere Conservancy Ontario. Prof. emeritus U. Toronto, 1998—. Contbr. articles to profl. jours. Fellow Royal Coll. Patholologists Australasia, Royal Coll. Physicians and Surgeons Can.; mem. Can. Assn. Pathologists, Ont. Assn. Pathologists, Internat. Acad. Pathology, Can. Cardiovasc. Soc., Soc. for Cardiovasc. Pathology. E-mail: md.silver@utoronto.ca.

SILVERMAN, GARY A., pediatrician; PhD, U. Chgo., 1982, MD, 1984. Lic. Nat. Bd. of Med. Examiners, diplomate Am. Bd. Pediatrics, Am. Bd. Pediatrics-neonatal-perinatal medicine. Resident Children's Hosp., Boston, 1987; fellow newborn medicine dept. St. Louis Children's Hosp., St. Louis, 1989; postdoc. rsch. fellow Wash. Univ., 1991; chief UPMC newborn medicine program Magee-Womens Hosp., dir. neonatal-perinatal tng. program; prof. pediatrics cell biology physiology Univ. of Pitts. Co-author of numerous publications. Recipient National Research Service award, The Medical Alumni prize, Univ. of Chgo., Individual National Research Service award, FIRST award, Nat. Inst. of Child Health and Human Devel., William Randolph Hearst award, March of Dimes Birth Defects Foundation award, Elsa U. Pardee Foundation award, Biology Smokeless Tobacco Research Council award, Inaugural Class Hartwell Individual Biomedical Research award; named one of Best Doctors in Pittsburgh, Pitts. Mag.; Leukemia Society Special fellowship, Lucille P. Markey Trust Child Health fellowship, The Stewart Trust of Washington D.C. Alexander and Margaret Stewart Trust grant. Mem.: Assn. of Am. Physicians, Midwest Soc. for Pediatric Rsch., Am. Thoracic Soc., Am. Acad. of Pediatrics Sect. on Perinatal Pediatrics, Am. Acad. of Pediatrics, Am. Soc. for Biochemistry and Molecular Biology, Am. Soc. for Clin. Investigation, Am. Pediatric Soc., Perinatal Rsch. Soc., Soc. for Devel. Biology, Am. Assn. for Cancer Rsch., Am. Soc. for Cell Biology, Human Genome Orgn. (HUGO), Am. Soc. of Human Genetics, Soc. for Pediatric Rsch., Am. Fedn. for Clin. Rsch., Am. Assn. of Immunologists, Am. Assn. for the Advancement of Sci. Office: University of Pittsburgh Physicians Neonatal Medicine Magee-Womens Hospital 300 Halket St Pittsburgh PA 15213 Office Phone: 412-641-4111.

SILVERMAN, JAN F., cytopathology, anatomic and clinical pathologist; MD, Va. Commonwealth U., Richmond, 1970. Diplomate Am. Bd. Pathology-cytopathology, Am. Bd. Pathology-anatomic and clin. pathology, lic. Pa., 1997, Tex., 1978. Intern Mt. Sinai Hosp.; resident pathology Med. Coll. of Va. Hosp., fellow; prof. pathology and lab. medicine Temple Univ., Drexel Univ. Coll. of Medicine; chmn. dept. of medicine Allegheny Gen. Hosp. Forbes Regional Campus; chmn. dept. of pathology West Penn Hosp.; chmn. dept. of lab. medicine Allegheny General Hosp. Named one of the Top Doctors, Pitts. Mag., 2011. Office: Western Pennsylvania Hospital 320 E N Ave Pittsburgh PA 15212 Office Phone: 412-359-6886. Office Fax: 412-359-3598.

SILVERMAN, MERVYN F., health science association administrator, consultant; BS cum laude, Washington and Lee U., 1960; MD, Tulane U., 1964; MPH, Harvard U., 1969. Cert. Am. Bd. Preventive Medicine. Physician Peace Corps, Thailand, 1965-67, regional med. dir. East Asia and the Pacific Washington, 1967-68; spl. asst. to commr. FDA, Washington, 1969-70, dir. Office of Consumer Affairs, 1970-72; dir. health Wichita (Kans.)-Sedgwick County Dept. Cmty. Health, 1972-77; med. dir. Planned Parenthood Kans., Wichita, 1976-77; dir. health Dept. Health, San Francisco, 1977-85; health care cons. Mervyn F. Silverman & Assocs., Inc., 1985—; dir. AIDS health svcs. program Robert Wood Johnson Found., 1986-92; nat. spokesperson Am. Found. for AIDS Rsch., 1986-96, pres., also bd. dirs. Resident physician Sta. KPIX-TV, San Francisco, 1979-85; dir., prodr., host weekly health program Sta. KMPX Radio, 1980-82; sr. tech. advisor Acad. Ednl. Devel.-AIDSCOM, 1990-92; former med. advisor to bd. dirs. Golden Gate chpt. ARC, San Francisco; past vice chmn. Adv. Health Coun., State of Calif.; former assoc. clin. prof. Wichita State U.; former assoc. clin. prof. U. Hawaii; former adj. assoc. prof. Sch. Pub. Health and Tropical Medicine Tulane U.; former adj. prof. Inst. Health Policy Studies, Sch. Medicine, U. Calif., San Francisco; former mem. nat. adv. coun. Harvard AIDS Inst.; spkr., presenter in field. Author: (with others) Humanistic Perspectives in Medical Ethics, 1972, What to Do About AIDS, 1986, AIDS and Patient Management: Legal, Ethical and Social Issues, 1986, AIDS: Facts and Issues, 1986, AIDS in Children, Adolescents and Heterosexual Adults: An Interdisciplinary Approach to Prevention, 1988, others; contbg. and consulting editor Modern Medicine Publs., Mpls., 1970-75; contbg. editor Healthline, 1983-85; contbr. articles to profl. jours. Bd. dirs., vice-chmn. U.S.-China Ednl. Inst. Recipient Award for Courageous Leadership, San Francisco Found., Award of Excellence, KAIROS Support for Care Givers, Civic Achievement award Bay Area Non-Partisan Alliance, Heroes in Medicine award Internat. Assn. Physicians in AIDS Care, Pub. Health Hero award U. Calif., Berkeley, 2001; Wear Found. fellow Wichita State U., scholar Kans. Newman Coll., Courage award Am. Found. AIDS Rsch., 2008. Mem. APHA, AMA, Omicron Delta Kappa, Delta Omega. Address: 9 Crolona Heights Dr Crockett CA 94525

SILVERMAN, NORMAN HENRY, cardiologist, educator; b. Johannesburg, Sept. 29, 1942; came to U.S., 1972; s. Simon Cecil and Jean (Krawitz) S.; m. Heather Silverman. DSc in Medicine, U. Witwatersrand, Johannesburg, 1985, postgrad. Diplomate Am. Bd. Pediatrics. Prof. pediat. Stanford U. Med. Ctr., Palo Alto, Calif., 1974—75, prof. pediat. cardiology, 2002—; asst. prof. pediatrics U. Calif., San Francisco, 1975—79, assoc. prof. radiology, 1979—85, prof. pediat. in residence, 1985—2002, prof. radiology in residence, 1985—2002. Co-author: Two Dimensional Echocardiography, 1982, Congenital Heart Disease, 1990; author: Pediatric Echocardiography, 1993; co-editor: Fetal Cardiology, 2003. Lt. South African Def. Force, 1968-69. Grantee March Dimes, 1977-79, Am. Heart Assn., 1978-80, 90-92; Roma and Marvin Auerback scholar pediat. cardiology Lucile Packard Children's Hosp. and Stanford U. Med. Ctr. Fellow Am. Coll. Cardiology, Coll. Physicians South Africa, Soc. Pediatric Rsch., Am. Pediatric Soc., Am. Heart Assn., Am. Soc. Echocardiography. Achievements include research in echocardiography of congenital heart disease in infants and children; fetal echocardiography and treatment. Office: Stanford U Med Ctr 750 Welch Rd #305 Palo Alto CA 94304 Office Phone: 650-723-7913. E-mail: norm.silverman@stanford.edu. *

SILVERMAN, WENDY K., psychologist, educator; PhD, Case Western Reserve Univ. Prof., psychology Fla. Internat. Univ., Miami. Author: 4 books; editor: Journ. Clin. Child and Adolescent Psychology. Mem.: Soc. Clin. Child and Adolescent Psychology (pres. 2005—06), Am. Psychological Assn. Office: Dept Psychology Fla Internat Univ DM256 11200 SW 8th St Miami FL 33199 Business E-Mail: silverw@fiu.edu.

SILVERS, ANN, peri-operative nurse, educator; b. Omaha, Mar. 1, 1943; d. John Stephen and M. Georgina Marie Mary McNeil; m. Ralph L. Silvers, Oct. 30, 1993. Diploma, St. Joseph Hosp. Sch. Nursing, Phoenix, 1966; BS in Health Care Scis., Chapman Coll., Travis AFB, Calif., 1979. RN Ariz. Pvt. scrub nurse Drs. Nelson, Brown, Cornell, Phoenix, 1969; staff nurse operating room St. Joseph Hosp., Phoenix, 1966-69, 70, Tucson, 1970—71, Washoe Med. Ctr., Reno, 1976—77; staff nurse U. Ariz. Med. Ctr., Tucson, 1971—75, asst. oper. rm. supr., 1975—76; oper. rm. staff nurse David Grant Med. Ctr., Travis AFB, Calif., 1977—81; coord. oper. rm. edn. Seton Med. Ctr., Daly City, Calif., 1981—85; staff nurse operating room Yavapai Regional Med. Ctr., Prescott, Ariz., 1985—88, John C. Lincoln Hosp., Phoenix, 1988—2000. Instr. surg. technician program and perioperative nurse program Gateway C.C., Phoenix, 1989-91, also extern preceptor. Capt. USAF, 1977-81. Mem. Assn. Operating Room Nurses (cert.), Sigma Theta Tau.

SILVERS, WILLYS KENT, geneticist; b. NYC, Jan. 12, 1929; s. Lewis Julian and Miriam Elizabeth (Rosenzweig) Silvers; m. Abigail M. Adams, Sept. 29, 1956 (dec. June 18, 2005); children: Deborah Elizabeth, Willys Kent. BA, Johns Hopkins U., 1950; PhD, U. Chgo., 1954. Assoc. staff scientist Jackson Lab., Bar Harbor, Maine, 1956-57; assoc. mem. Wistar Inst., Phila., 1957-65; mem. faculty U. Pa. Med. Sch., 1965—, prof. genetics, 1967-98, prof. emeritus, 1998—. Mem. allergy and immunology study sect. NIH, 1962—66, adv. bd. primate rsch. ctrs., 1968—71; mem. com. cancer immunobiology Nat. Cancer Inst., 1974—78; bd. sci. overseers Jackson Lab., Bar Harbor, 1980—89. Author: The Immunobiology of Transplantation, 1971, The Coat Colors of Mice: A Model for Mammalian Gene Action and Interaction, 1979; mem. editl. bd. Transplantation, 1963—71, Jour. Exptl. Zoology, 1965—70, 1981—86, Jour. Immunology, 1973—77, Jour. Reticuloendothelial Soc., 1974—77; contbr. articles to profl. jours. Mem.: Am. Genetic Assn. (coun. 1980—83, pres. 1983). Home: 1500 Monk Rd Gladwyne PA 19035 Personal E-mail: wsilvers@aol.com.

SILVERSOO, SHAWNA, dentist; b. July 5, 1971; BS in Chemistry, Ohio State Univ., 1993, MD, 1997, DDS, 2000. Dentist Hawkins Dental Team, 2000—05, dental surgeon, 2003—05; adj. prof. Ohio State Univ., 2003—08; sr. dentist Meriks, Silversoo and Pertey Dentist Assoc., Cincinnati, 2006—. Intern Johnson Dental Practice, 1994—96; resident, dental surgery wing Grant-Lee Hosp., 1996—98. Author: (textbook) Your Dental Tools and You, 2003, (children's book) Getting To Know Your Buddy -- Cousin Toothbrush!, 2007. Republican. Avocations: guitar, aviation.

SILVERSTEIN, ARTHUR MATTHEW, ophthalmic immunologist, educator, historian; b. NYC, Aug. 6, 1928; s. Sol and Beatrice (Pearl) S.; m. Frances Swimmer, 1950; children— Alison, Mark, Judith AB, Ohio State U., 1948, M.Sc., 1951; PhD, Rensselaer Poly. Inst., 1954; D.Sc. (hon.), U. Granada, Spain, 1986. Research asst. Sloan Kettering Inst., NYC, 1948-49; biochemist N.Y. Health Research Lab., NYC, 1949-52, sr. biochemist Albany, 1952-54; chief immunobiology Armed Forces Inst. Pathology, Washington, 1956-64; assoc. prof. Johns Hopkins Sch. Medicine, Balt., 1964-67, prof., 1967-89, prof. emeritus, 1989—. Cons. NIH, 1963-77. Author: Pure Politics and Impure Science: The Swine Flu Affair, 1981, A History of Immunology, 1989, 2nd edit., 2009, Paul Ehrlich's Receptor Immunology, 2002; mem. editl. bd. various sci. jours.; contbr. articles to profl. jours. Served to 1st lt. U.S. Army, 1954-56. Recipient Doyne Meml. medal Oxford Ophthal. Congress, Eng., 1974, Endowed Professorship Ind. Order Odd Fellows, 1964-89; Congl. Sci. fellow Fedn. Am. Socs. Exptl. Biology, 1975-76. Mem. AAAS, Am. Assn. Immunologists, Brit. Soc. Immunology, Assn. Research in Vision and Ophthalmology (trustee 1984-87, pres. 1988), Phi Beta Kappa, Sigma Xi. E-mail: arts@jhmi.edu.

SILVERSTEIN, CHARLES, psychologist; b. NYC, Apr. 23, 1935; PhD, Rutgers U., 1975. Supervisior Inst. Human Identity, 1973. Founding editor Jour. Homosexuality, 1974—80; supr. NYU Sch. Medicine, 1985—2010. Contbr. chapters to books. Recipient Gold medal, Am. Psychol. Found., Honors award, Gay & Lesbian Psychiatrists NY. Fellow: APA (Disting. Profl. Contbn. award, divsn. 44, Presdl. citation); mem.: NY State Psychol. Assn. Avocations: travel, art. Office: 233 W 83 St New York NY 10024 Business E-Mail: csilverstein2@nyc.rr.com.

SILVERSTEIN, JANET HOPE, pediatrician, educator; b. Bronx, NY, June 21, 1944; d. Jesse and Beatrice (Zuckerman) Fisher; m. Burton Silverstein, Aug. 18, 1978; children: Craig Darryl, Todd Alan. BS, U. Rochester, 1966; MD, U. Pa., 1970. Diplomate Am. Bd. Pediat. Clin. assoc., pediat. Duke U. Med. Ctr., Durham, NC, 1977-78; instr. in pediat., cmty. health U. Fla., Gainesville, 1978-80, asst. prof. pediat., cmty. health, 1980-84, assoc. prof., 1984-90, prof. pediat., 1990—, chief divsn. pediat. endocrinology, 1994—, med. dir., Pediatric Clinic, 1998—2004. Med. dir. Fla. Diabetes Camp, Gainesville, 1988—, Diabetes Project Unit, Gainesville, 1979—2002; gov.'s diabetes adv. coun., Tallahassee, 1984—2000, 2004—; sci. adv. bd. Diabetes Action Rsch. and Edn. Found., Washington, 1990—; program dir. U. Fla. Diabetes Rsch., Edn. and Treatment Ctr., 1991—; com. Am. Bd. Pediat.; mem. editl. bd. Jour. Pediat. & Endocnne Today, 1994—2005. Contbr. articles to profl. jours. Co-creator Diabetes Resdl. Unit for Children Having Trouble Coping with Diabetes; creator Bring a Friend to Camp, After Hours Pediat. Clinic. Named Olympic Torch Bearer, 1996. Mem.: Soc. Pediatric Rsch. (elected), Ambulatory Pediat. Assn., Lawson Wilkins Pediat. Endocrinology Soc. (chair diabetes com. 2000—01, bd. dirs. 2003—07, past chmn. drug, therapeutics com., pres. elect 2010—), Endocrine Soc., Am. Diabetes Assn. (chair coun. on youth 2001—03), Am. Acad. Pediats. (chair exec. com. sect. on endocrinology 2000—04), Am. Pediat. Soc., Nat. Diabetes Edn. Program (chmn. children's work group 2004—). Avocations: jogging, bicycling, art, reading. Home: 1932 NW 24th St Gainesville FL 32605-3848 Office Phone: 352-334-1390.

SILVERSTEIN, JEFFREY HAROLD, anesthesiologist, educator; b. St John's, Newfoundland, Can., Aug. 13, 1956; BD, Mich. State U., 1978; MD, U, Extremadura, 1983. Prof., assoc. dean Mt. Sinai Sch. Medicine, 1991—. Office: Mount Sinai Med Ctr Dept Anesthesiology Box 1010 1 Gusta New York NY 10029-6574 Office Fax: 212-876-3906. Business E-Mail: jeff.silverstein@mssm.edu.

SILVERSTEIN, SAMUEL CHARLES, cellular biology and physiology professor, researcher; b. NYC, Feb. 11, 1937; s. Paul Robert and Jeanette (Kamen) S.; m. Jo Ann Kleinman, Apr. 2, 1967; children: David Paul, Jennifer Kate. AB, Dartmouth Coll., 1958; MD, Albert Einstein Coll. Medicine, 1963. Intern in medicine U. Colo. Med. Center, 1963-64; postdoctoral fellow dept. cell biology Rockefeller U., 1964-67; resident in medicine Mass. Gen. Hosp., 1967—68; asst. prof. cellular physiology and immunology Rockefeller U., 1968-71, assoc. prof., physician, 1972—; John Dalton prof. physiology, prof. medicine Columbia U. Coll. Physicians and Surgeons, NYC, 1983—, chmn. dept., 1983—2003. Founder, dir. Columbia U. Summer Rsch. Program for Secondary Sch. Sci. Tchrs., 1990—; prin. investigator, program dir. Pre and Post-doctoral Tng. Immunology, 1997—2005. Editor: Transport of Macromolecules in Cellular Systems, 1979; chmn. editl. bd. Jour. Cell Biology, 1979-82, editor, 1978-89. Bd. dirs. Arnold P. Gold Found., 1998—, Cancer Rsch. Fund, Damon Runyon Found., 1990—; bd. dirs. Rsch. Am., 1993-2005, mem. exec. com., 1996-2006. Recipient John Oliver LaGorce medal, Nat. Geog. Soc., 1967, Marie Bonazinga Rsch. award, Soc. Leukocyte Biology, 1984, Disting. Alumnus award, Albert Einstein Coll. Medicine, 1987, N.Y.C. Mayor's award Publ. Understanding of Sci. and Tech., 2003, Westy award Contbns. Sci. Edn. N.Y.C. Schs., 2004, Fountain Valley Sch. Trustees 75th Anniversary award, Colorado Springs, 2005, Silverstein Peak, Sentinel Range, Antarctica named in his honor by, US Geol. Survey, 2006; fellow Helen Hay Whitney, 1964—67, John Simon Guggenheim, 2005, Pres. Lasker/Funding First, 2001—04. Fellow: AAAS (chair sect. medicine 1998), N.Y. Acad. Sci. (edn. com.), Am. Soc. Microbiology; mem.: Am. Acad. Arts and Scis., Inst. Medicine Nat. Acad. Scis., Fedn. Am. Socs. for Exptl. Biology (bd. dirs. 1991—96, v.p. 1993—94, pres. 1994—95, chmn. pub. affairs adv. com. 1995—96), Practitioners Soc. N.Y., Assn. Am. Physicians, Am. Physiol. Soc., Am. Soc. Biol. Chemists, Infectious Diseases Soc. Am., Am. Assn. Immunologists, Am. Soc. Clin. Investigation, Am. Soc. Cell Biology (Bruce Alberts award for Excellence in Sci. Edn. 2005), Century Assn., Explorers Club, Am. Alpine Club (dir. 1963—64, 1969—74), Dartmouth Coll. Chpt. Phi Beta Kappa (elected 2008). Achievements include research and numerous publications in field of virology, cell biology, immunology, seconary science education, science policy, and mountaineering. Office: Columbia U Coll Physicians & Surgeons 630 W 168th St New York NY 10032-3795 Office Phone: 212-305-3546. Business E-Mail: scs3@columbia.edu.

SIM, FIONA M., public health service officer, editor; d. David and Doris Sim; m. Martin S. Swerdlow; children: D. Swerdlow, O. Swerdlow. BSC, MB, BS, U. Coll. London, 1978; MSc, London Sch. Hygiene and Tropical Medicine, 1982; LLM, U. Hertfordshire, Eng., 1998. Joint editor Pub. Health Royal Inst. Pub. Health, London, 2001—04; head pub. health devel. Dept. Health Eng., London, 2001—04. Fellow: Royal Coll. Physicians London, U.K. Faculty Pub. Health. Home: 4 Church Close WD7 8BJ Hertfordshire Radlett England E-mail: fiona.sim@doh.gsi.gov.uk.

SIM, KWEE-BO, engineering educator; b. Jinju, Gyeongnam, Republic of Korea, Sept. 20, 1956; B in Engring., Chung-Ang U., 1984; PhD, U. Tokyo, 1990. Prof. Chung-Ang U., 1991—, dir. tech. transfer ctr., 2004—08, dir. ctrl. libr., mus., 2009—10. Pres. Korean Inst. Intelligent Sys. Soc., 2006—07. Recipient Academic award, Chung-Ang U., 2001, 2007, Cert., Small & Medium Bus. Adminstrn., Republic of Korea, 2009. Fellow: Korean Inst. Intelligent Sys. Soc. (Academic award 2000, 2009), Inst. Control, Robotics & Systems, Republic of Korea (Fumio Harashima Mechatronics award 2004, Academic award 2005); mem.: IEEE, Inst. Electronics Engrs., Republic of Korea, Inst. Electronics, Info. & Communication Engrs., Japan. Avocations: surfing, reading, travel, mountain climbing. Office: 221 Heukseok-Dong Dongjak-Gu Seoul 156-756 Republic of Korea Home Phone: 82 2 823 1251; Office Phone: 82-2-820-5319. Office Fax: 82-2-817-0553. E-mail: kbsim@cau.ac.kr.

SIMARI, ROBERT DAVID, physician; b. Weymouth, Mass., June 6, 1960; BS, Notre Dame, 1982; MD, U. Kans., 1986. Dean clin. and translational rsch. Mayo Clinic, 1993—. Mem.: Am. Soc. Clin. Investigation. Home: 2001 1st St SW Rochester MN 55902 Business E-Mail: simari.robert@mayo.edu.

SIMBERKOFF, MICHAEL S., epidemiologist; b. Mt. Vernon, NY, Nov. 20, 1936; AB, Dartmouth Coll., 1936; MD, NYU Sch. Medicine, 1962. Staff physician, infectious diseases sect., med. svc. NY Va. Med. Ctr., 1970—86, chief, infectious diseases sect., med. svc., 1986—2001, assoc. chief staff, r & d, 1996—97, chief, 1997—99, Va. NY Harbor Healthcare Sys., 1999—. Asst. prof. NYU Sch. Medicine, 1969—77, assoc. prof., 1977—2005, asst. dean veterans affairs, 1997—2008, prof. medicine, 2005, assoc. dean veterans affairs, 08. Fellow: ACP; mem.: Infectious Diseases Soc. America, Alpha Omega Alpha. Avocations: swimming, running, kayaking. Office: 423 E 23rd St New York NY 10010 Business E-Mail: mike.simberkoffmd@va.gov.

SIMBERLOFF, DANIEL, biologist, educator; b. Easton, Pa., Apr. 7, 1942; s. Isaac and Ruth (Koplowitz) Simberloff. AB, Harvard U., 1964, PhD, 1969. Asst. prof. biology Fla. State U., Tallahassee, 1968—73, assoc. prof., 1973—78, prof., 1978—97, Robert O. Lawton Disting. prof., 1986; Nancy Gore Hunger prof. environ. studies dept. ecology and evolutionary biology U. Tenn., 1997—. Vis. prof. U. Mich., 1974, U. Minn., 1980, Hebrew U., Jerusalem, 1984; bd. dirs. Nat. Sci. Bd., 2000—06; mem. species survival commn. Internat. Union Conservation Nature and Natural Resources. Editor: Jour. Biogeography, 1974—, Biodiversity and Conservation; co-editor: Ecological Communities: Conceptual Issues and the Evidence, 1984; co-editor: (with D. Schmitz and T. Brown) Strangers in Paradise: Impact and Management of Nonindigenous Species in Florida, 1997; mem. editl. bd.: Jour. Biogeography, Northeast Gulf. Sci., Environ. and Ecol. Statistics, Raffles Bulletin of Zoology, Ecologia, Oecologia, BioSci., Biol. Invasions; contbr. articles to sci. jours. Recipient Developing Scholar award, Fla. State U., 1977, Rector's medal, U. Helsinki, Finland, 1983, Disting. Statistical Ecologist award, Internat. Assn. Ecology, 1994. Mem.: Soc. for Systematic Zoology, Brit. Ecol. Soc., Soc. for Study Evolution, Am. Soc. Naturalists, Ecol. Soc. Am., Nature Conservancy, Soc. Conservation Biology, Brit. Ecol. Soc., Am. Acad. Arts and Scis. Jewish. Home: 2145 Indian Hills Dr Knoxville TN 37919-8914 Office: Ecology and Evolutionary Biology Univ Tenn 480 Dabney Hall Knoxville TN 37996-1610 Office Phone: 865-974-0849. Office Fax: 865-974-3067. E-mail: dsimberloff@utk.edu.

SIMBIRI, KENNETH OMOLLO, medical researcher; b. Kenya, June 4, 1958; PhD, Temple U., 2006. Rsch. assoc. NYU, 1989—94; rsch. scientist U. Pa., 2007—. Bd. dir. Calcutta House, 2007—11. Mem.: Internat. Soc. Neurovirology, Royal Inst. Pub. Health, Am. Assn. Pub. Health. Avocations: jogging, soccer, tennis, squash. Office: 202A Johnson Pavilion Philadelphia PA 19104 Business E-Mail: simbiri@mail.med.upenn.edu.

SIMEONE, DIANE M., general surgeon, educator; b. Providence, Nov. 26, 1962; m. Welling Ted, June 20, 1999; children: Sam Welling, Amelia Welling. BS, Brown U., Providence, 1984; MD, Duke U. Sch. Medicine, Durham, NC, 1988. Diplomate American Bd. Surgery. Resident, gen. surgery U. Mich. Health Systems, Ann Arbor, 1988—95, asst., then assoc. prof., 1995—2007, prof. dept. surgery, 2007—, Lazar J. Greenfield prof. surgery, prof. molecular & integrative physiology, chief divsn. gastrointestinal surgery. Co-dir. gastrointestinal oncology program U. Mich. Comprehensive Cancer Ctr., 2005—, dir. Multidisciplinary Pancreatic Cancer Clinic. Contbr. articles to profl. jours. Mem. sci. adv. bd. Lustgarten Found., NYC, 2007—. Fellow. ACS, mem.: Inst. Medicine, American Pancreatic Assn. Achievements include research in pancreatic cancer stem cells and molecular profiling in pancreatic cancer, and in the surgical treatment of pancreatic adenocarcinoma. Office: University Mich 2922D Taubman Ctr SPC 5331 1500 E Med Center Dr Ann Arbor MI 48109 Business E-Mail: simeone@umich.edu. *

SIMINOVITCH, LOUIS, geneticist, educator, scientist; b. Montreal, Que., Can., May 1, 1920; s. Nathan and Goldie (Wachman) S., m. Elinore Esther Faierman, July 2, 1944 (dec. 1995); children: Harriet Jane, Katherine Anne, Margo Ruth. B.Sc., McGill U., 1941, PhD, 1944; D honoris causa, Meml. U., 1978, McMaster U., 1978, U. Montreal, 1990, McGill U., 1990, U. Western Ont., 1990, U. Toronto, 1995, U. Ottawa, Can., 1999; DSc, U. Guelph, 2001. Mem. staff Nat. Research Council Can., 1944-47; Canadian Royal Soc. fellow Pasteur Inst., Paris, 1947-49; mem. staff Centre Nationale de la Recherche Scientifique, 1949-53; Nat. Cancer Inst. Can. fellow U. Toronto, Ont., Can., 1953-56, asst. prof. dept. med. biophysics, 1956-58, assoc. prof. med. biophysics, 1958-60, prof. med. biophysics, 1960-85, prof. Inst. Med. Sci., 1968-85, prof., chmn. dept. med. cell. biology, 1969-70, prof. dept. med. genetics, 1970-85, chmn. dept. med. genetics, 1970-81, assoc. prof. pediatrics, 1972-78, univ. prof., 1976-85, univ. prof. emeritus, 1985—; dir. rsch. Samuel Lunenfeld Rsch. Inst. Mt. Sinai Hosp., Toronto, 1985-94, dir. emeritus Samuel Lunenfeld Rsch. Inst., 1994—; sr. fellow Massey Coll, U. Toronto, 2009. Scientist divsn. biol. rsch. Ont. Cancer Inst., Toronto, 1956-69, head microbiology sect. divsn. biol. rsch., 1957-63, head divsn. biol. rsch., 1963-69; geneticist-in-chief Hosp. Sick Children, Toronto, 1970-85; mem. virology and rickettsiology sect. NIH, 1966-68; mem. health research com. Ont. Coun. Health, 1966-82; mem. panel sect. Nat. Cancer Inst., Can., 1965-69, mem. rsch. adv. group, 1969-74, chmn., 1970-72, bd. dirs. 1975-85, pres. 1982-84; bd. dirs. Can. Weizmann Inst. Sci., 1972—; mem. adv. bd. Ont. Mental Health Found., 1974-78; chmn. Ont. Health R&D Com., 1974-82; task force on genetic services Ont. Ministry Health, 1974-76; mem. Ont. Task Force On Health Research Requirements, 1974-76; mem. grants com. for cancer, growth and differentiation Med. Rsch. Coun. Can., 1967-70, mem. grants com. for genetics, 1971-74, chmn. com. on guidelines for Recombinant DNA, 1975-77, mem. exec., 1977-83; bd. dirs. Mount Sinai Hosp., Toronto, 1975-82; mem. United Ch. Can. Gen. Coun. Commn. on Genetic Engring., 1974-78; mem Killam selection com. The Can. Coun., 1975-78; bd. advisors Clin. Rsch. Inst. Montreal Center Bioethics, 1976-80; mem. adv. com. on genetic services Ont. Ministry Health, 1976-82; mem. Sci. Coun. Can., 1976-80; mem. Ont. Coun. Health, 1976-82; mem. bd. sci. counsellors Nat. Cancer Inst., NIH, 1978-83; G. Malcolm Brown Meml. lectr. Royal Coll Physicians and Surgeons, 1978; bd. dirs. Cancer Care Ont. (formerly Ont. Cancer Treatment and Rsch. Found.), 1979-93, chmn. rsch. adv. panel, 1986-98, mem. exec. com., bd. dirs., 1991-93; mem. Alfred P. Sloan Jr. selection com. Gen. Motors Cancer Rsch. Found., 1980-81, 83-84; nat. bd. dirs. Canadian Cancer Soc, 1981-84; mem. sci. adv. bd. Huntingtons Soc. Can., 1984-89; adv. com. Coll. Biol. Scis., Guelph, Ont., 1986-90; mem. rsch. coun. Can. Inst. Advanced Rsch., Toronto, 1982-91, chmn. adv. com. evolutionary biology, 1986-93; mem. med. adv. bd. The Gairdner Found., 1983-93; mem. bd. govs. Baycrest Centre Geriatric Care, 1987—, bd. dirs.; chmn. adv. bd. Allelix, Inc., 1987-91; mem. sci. tech. svcs. sub-com. Sci. Coun. Can., 1988-89; chmn. steering com. for evaluation of MRC grants program MRC, Ottawa, 1989-91; chmn. sci. adv. com. Rotman Rsch Inst., Baycrest Centre, 1990—; mem. Can. Inst. Acad. Medicine, 1992—; mem. Montreal Neurol. Inst. adv. bd. Montreal, 1992—; spl. adv. rsch. to dean Sch. Medicine U. Toronto, 1994—, chmn. program adv. com., sci. adv. com. Tanenbaum Chairs, 1995-02; mem. sci. adv. bd. Med. Discoveries Fund, 1994-01; bd. dirs. Glycodesign, Toronto, 1995-96, chmn. sci. adv. com., 1996-01; mem. sci. and med. adv. bd. Hybrisens, Ltd., Toronto, 1995-96; mem. sci. adv. bd. Apoptogen, 1995-99, GeminX, 1997-2003, Genesense Techs., 1998-99, Ottawa Gen. Hosp. Rsch. Inst., 1998-2000; chmn. sci. adv. bd. Lorus Therapeutics, 1999—; mem. rev. panel rsch. resources program med. scholars Howard Hughes Med. Inst., 1995; chmn. external adv. com. Loeb Inst. Med. Rsch., 1987-00; bd. dirs. Ottawa Civic Hosp. Loeb Rsch. Inst., 1996-00; chmn. sci. adv. bd. Bioniche, 1996-98; bd. dirs. U. Med. Discoveries, Inc., 1996-05; mem. neuro adv. coun. Montreal Neurol. Inst. and Hosp., 1997-00; chmn. sci. adv. com. The KLARU, Baycrest Ctr. Geriatric Care, Toronto, 1997—, bd. dirs., 1998—; chmn. sci. adv. com. Phagetech, 1998-2004; bd. dirs. Premier's Rsch. Excellence Awards Program, 1998-05; chmn. sci. adv. bd. Cytochroma Inc., 1999-06; bd. dirs. Viventia Biotech, 1999-2006; mem. sci. adv. bd. Aurelium Bioplasma, 2002-04; mem. sci. adv. com. Genetic Diagnosis, Inc., 2003-05, chair sci. & rsch. com. Thunder Bay Regional Rsch. Inst., 2007-. Editor Virology, 1960-80, Bacteriological Revs., 1969-72, Jour. Molecular and Cellular Biology, 1980-90; founding mem., pres. editl. bd. Sci. Forum, 1966-79; mem. editl. bd. Cell, 1973-81, Somatic Cell Genetics, 1974-84, Jour. Cytogenetics and Cell Genetics, 1974-80, Mutation Rsch., 1976-82, Jour. de Microscopie et de Biologie Cellulaire, 1976-86, Cancer Genetics and Cytogenetics, 1979-84, Jour. Cancer Surveys, 1980-89; corr. editor Proc. Royal Soc. B, 1989-93; contbr. numerous articles to sci. jours. Recipient Lifetime Achievement award, Toronto Biotech. Initiative, 2005; named to Canadian Med. Hall of Fame, 1997, Canadian Sci. & Engring. Hall of Fame, 2008. Fellow Royal Soc. Can. (mem. AIDS study steering com. 1987-88, mem. adv. com. on evaluation rsch. 1989-92, Centennial medal 1967, Flavelle medal 1978), Royal Soc. London, Nat. Acad. Scis. US (fgn. assoc.). Home: 130 Carlton St # 805 Toronto ON Canada M5A 4K3 Office: Samuel Lunenfeld Rsch Inst Mt Sinai Hosp 600 University Ave Toronto ON Canada M5G 1X5 Home Phone: 416-975-5535; Office Phone: 416-586-4800 8223. Business E-Mail: lsimin@mshri.on.ca.

SIMJEE, AISHA, ophthalmologist, educator; b. Surat, India, Jan. 23, 1944, came to U.S., 1970; d. Yusuf Esmail Simjee and Amina Ahmed Badat; m. Sabbir A. Dadabhai, Apr. 28, 1978; children: Alia Dadabhai, Sufia Dadabhai. Intermediate Sci. degree, Rangoon U., Burma, 1963; MB, BS, Inst. Medicine, Rangoon, 1968. Diplomate Am. Bd. Ophthalmology. Intern Rangoon Gen. Hosp., 1968-69, South Balt. Gen. Hosp., 1970-71; rschr. in ophthalmology Johns Hopkins Hosp., Balt., 1971-72; resident in ophthalmology Eye Dept. Howard U. Hosp., D.C. Gen. Hosp., Armed Forces Inst. Pathology, Washington, 1972-75; fellow in cornea external diseases Wills Eye Hosp., Phila., 1975-76, fellow in ophthalmic pathology and med. retina Scheie Eye Inst., Phila., 1976-77; asst. prof. ophthalmology Howard U., Washington, 1977-78; clin. assoc. prof. ophthalmology U. Calif., Irvine, 1978—; pvt. practice Orange, Calif. Mem. med. adv. bd. Orange County Eye & Tissue Bank, 1990—; attending physician St. Joseph Hosp., Orange, 1978—, U. Calif. Irvine Med. Ctr., 1978—. Contbr. articles to profl. jours. Vol. ophthalmologist La Amistad de Jose Clinic, Sponsor Care Program of St. Joseph Hosp., 1988—, Testing 1-2-3 Screening Clinic St. Joseph Hosp., ann. eye screening for local sch. children, Project Orbis, S.E.E. Internat., Santa Barbara, Am. Eye Care Project, Hope World Wide, 2002—, Internat. Asst. Mission, 2002—. Named Woman of Achievement, Rancho Santiago Coll., Santa Ana, 1990; recipient certs. of recognition Calif. state senator John Seymour, Calif. congressman Christopher Cox, Calif., lt. gov. Leo McCarthy; recipient Pride in the Profession award AMA Found., 2005, Woman of Vision award We Give Thanks or Orange County, 2006, Values in Action award St. Joseph Hosp. Fellow ACS, Am. Acad. Ophthalmology (Nat. Eye Care Project 1986—); mem. AMA (Pride in Profession award 2005), Calif. Med. Assn., Orange County Med. Assn. (bd. dirs. 1995-02, Physician of Yr. 2010), Orange County Soc. Ophthalmology (exec. com. 1992-02). Office: 1310 W Stewart Dr Ste 501 Orange CA 92868-3856 Home Phone: 714-771-2033; Office Phone: 714-771-2020. Personal E-mail: drsimjee@sbcglobal.net.

SIMMEN, HANS-PETER, surgeon, educator; b. Chur, Switzerland, Oct. 1, 1951; s. Martin and Anna-Maria (Fravi) S.; m. Elisabeth Gugler, Jan. 3, 1983; children: Christian, Daniela. MD, U. Zurich, Switzerland, 1978. Prof. surgery U. Zurich, 1978—2001, prof., 2001—; resident dept. surgery Cantonal Hosp. St. Gallen, Switzerland, 1979-86; staff mem. dept. surgery U. Med. Sch. Zurich, Switzerland, 1987-96; head dept. surgery Spital Oberengadin, Samedan, 1987—2008; head trauma divsn. dept. surgery U. Hosp. Zurich, 2008—. Contbr. articles to profl. jours. Mem. Am. Soc. for Microbiology, Surg. Infection Soc. Europe, German Soc. for Surgery, Swiss Soc. for Surgery. Avocation: cross country skiing. Office: Trauma Divsn Univ Hosp Zürich CH-8091 Zurich Switzerland Personal E-mail: simmen.samedan@bluewin.ch. Business E-Mail: hanspeter.simmen@usz.ch.

SIMMER, THOMAS L., insurance company executive; Assoc. program dir., internal medicine program Henry Ford Hosp.; v.p. health and med. affairs, med. dir. Health Alliance Plan; joined Blue Cross Blue Shield of Michigan, 1999, sr. v.p. for health care programs and provider services, 1999—2006, chief med. officer, 1999—, sr. v.p., health care value & provider affiliation, 2006—. Bd. chair Ctr. for Healthcare Rsch. and Transformation; chair Michigan Health and Safety Coalition, 2004. Recipient of several disting. svc. awards; named Health Care Heroes, Crain's Detroit Bus., 2010. Fellow: ACP; mem.: Michigan State Med. Soc. Office: Blue Cross Blue Shield of Michigan 600 E Lafayette Blvd Detroit MI 48226

SIMMONS, ANTHONY, virology educator, physician, researcher; b. Leicestershire, U.K., Mar. 12, 1954; s. Alfred William and Sarah Sylvia Simmons; m. Mary-Jane Potter, June 8, 2002; children: Katie Anne, Matthew James. MD, PhD, Cambridge, UK, 1976—86. FRC-Path Royal Coll. Pathologists, 1986. Sr. med. specialist Inst. Med. and Vet. Sci., Adelaide, Australia, 1986—2001; prof. pediat. pathology: microbiology and immunology U. Tex., Galveston, 2001—. Mem. editl. bd. Jour. Virology, Herpes Jour.; contbr. articles to profl. jours. Mem.: Australian Herpes Mgmt. forum (founding mem.), Am. Social Health Assn. (sci. adv. com.), Am. Soc. Virology, Am. Assn. Immunologists. Achievements include patents for compositions and methods for herpes simplex prophylaxis and treatment. Avocations: sailing, rock climbing, snowboarding. Home: 1001 Postoffice St Galveston TX 77550 Office: U Tex Med Br 301 University Blvd Galveston TX 77555-0372 Business E-Mail: ansimmon@utmb.edu.

SIMMONS, DAVID, medical educator; b. Hampton Court, Middlesex, England, Aug. 22, 1959; s. Leslie and Stella Simmons; m. Denise Simmons, Nov. 11, 1988; children: Daniel, Benjamin. BA with honors, U. Cambridge, 1981, MA, 1984, MD, 1991; MBBS, U. London, 1984. MRCP Royal Coll. Auatralian Physicians New Zealand, 1987, FRACP Royal Coll. Physicians UK, 1992. Registrar diabetes rsch. Sheikh Rashid Diabetes Unit, Oxford, 1987—89; registrar Middlemore Hosp., 1989—90, fellow diabetes rsch., 1990—90; sr. lectr. medicine U. Auckland, 1992—92; prof. rural health U. Melbourne, 1999—2003; prof. medicine U. Auckland, 2003—07; cons. diabetes Cambridge U. Hosp. NHS Found. Trust., England, 2007—. Founder, med. dir. Diabetes Projects Trust, Auckland, 1991—98; vis. prof. Pfizer, 2002; lectr. Nat. Health Found., New Zealand, 2004. Author: over 190 jour. papers, 14 book chpts., over 60 other publs. (Glaxo Young Investigators Prize, 1990). Co-chair Nat. Gestational Diabetes Mellitus Working Party, New Zealand, 2006; chair Nat. Diabetes in Pregnancy Com., Australia, 2001—02. Recipient David Large prize, So. Auckland Health, 1996, Joeseph Moet award, 2009. Mem.: Internat. Assn. Diabetes in Pregnancy and Study Groups, ADIPS (coun. mem. 1988—2006). Avocations: travel, walking. Office: Inst Metabolic Sci Addenbrookes Hosp Cambridge CAMBS CB20QQ England

SIMMONS, DONNA MARIE, neuroscientist, histotechnologist, consultant, lecturer, scientific editor, research ethics instructor; b. Hartford, Conn., Oct. 13, 1943; d. John Henry and Ellen Louise (Meehl) Strayer; m. Corvin Gale Simmons, Sept. 17, 1964. Student, We. Wash. State U., U. Wash.; PhD, U. So. Calif., 2006. Histologic technician, instr. Tacoma Gen. Hosp. Sch. Med. Tech., Tacoma, 1963; lab. technician Med. Sch. U. Wash., 1964; histologic technician Northgate Med. Lab., Seattle, 1964—67; rsch. technologist in neuroanatomy Regional Primate Rsch. Ctr. U. Wash., 1967—82; rsch. asst. Devel. Neurobiology Lab. Salk Inst., La Jolla, Calif., 1982—85, sr. technician. lab. mgr. Neural Sys. Lab. Howard Hughes Med. Inst., 1985—90, vis. faculty neurosciences dept. Baylor U. Med. Sch., 1990; rsch. assoc. dept. biol. scis.-neurobiology U. So. Calif., LA, 1990—2002, Neurosci. Rsch. Inst., 2002—09; vis. scholar Brain Arch. Ctr. USC, 2009—; sci. editor freelance, 2008—; instr., rsch. ethics Beckman Rsch. Inst., City of Hope, 2010—. Cons., lectr. in field; judge Greater San Diego Sci. and Engring. Fair, 1987-89, Calif. Sci. Fair, 1992—; leader sci. del. to People's Rep. of China, 1986; chair China Scientist Exch. Fund, 1986-87; mem. Swiss Histology Meeting Exch., 1990. Author tech. articles, revs. in field; mem. editl. bd. Jour. Histotech, 1982-2002. Recipient Diamond Cover award Jour. Histotech., 1990; various svcs. awards; best non-clin. pub. in field, 1985; Hudson Hoagland USA-Australia Exch. Med. Rsch. fellow Prince Henry's Rsch. Inst. Monash U., 1996. Mem. AAAS, Am. Neuroendocrine Soc., Am. Soc. Clin. Pathologists (affiliate), Am. Physiol. Soc., Wash. State Histology Soc. (past pres., histology liason Am. Soc. Med. Tech.), Nat. Soc. Histotech. (charter, regional dir. 1980-82, jud. chair 1983-86), Calif. Soc. Histotech. (San Diego dir. protem 1985-86), Assn. Women in Sci. (San Diego charter, bd. dirs. 1985-90), Soc. for Neurosci., Women in Neurosci., NY Acad. Sci., J.B. Johnston Club, Cajal Club, Sierra Club, NOW, Am. Alpine Club, Sigma Xi. Business E-Mail: dsimmons@mizar.usc.edu.

SIMMONS, GEOFFREY STUART, physician, lecturer, writer; b. Camp Gordon, Ga., July 28, 1943; s. Ted R. and Jane A. (Lavander) Simmons; m. Sherry Simmons, Sept. 7, 1985; children: Bradley, Anais. BS, U. Ill., 1965, MD, 1969. Diplomate Am. Bd. Internal Medicine; cert. instr., ham operator, trainer Cmty. Emergency Response Team. Intern U. So. Calif., LA, 1969-70, resident, 1971-74; pvt. practice Astoria, Oreg., 1974-77, Eugene, Oreg., 1977—; chmn. internal medicine dept. Peace Health Med. Group, 1996-98, 2000—. Med. corres. KUGN Radio, 1993—95; chair Med. Res. Corps Coun., 2002—; trainer Cmty. Emergency Response Team; bd. govs. Am. Acad. Disaster Medicine, 2006—; bd. dirs. Physicians and Surgeons Sci. Integrity, 2006—; advisor Regional Adv. FEMA Region X. Author: (book) The Z Papers, 1977, The Adam Experiment, 1978, Pandemic, 1980, Murdock, 1982, The Glue Factory, 1995, To Glue or Not to Glue, 1997, What Darwin Didn't Know, 2004, Billions of Missing Links, 2007, Common Source and Disaster Preparedness, 2011; med. commentator KABC Radio, 1970. Fellow: Discovery Inst. (sr.); mem.: Eugene Citizen Corps., Lane County Med. Soc. (chmn. task force for disaster preparedness 2001—02, trainer cmty. emergency response team 2004—, vol. mgr. cert. program 2004—, lead cert. trainer cmty. emergency response teams). Avocations: writing, teaching disaster preparedness. Office Phone: 541-687-6041.

SIMMONS, LYNDA TEEL, nurse, healthcare executive; d. A. Stokes. ADN in Nursing, Columbus Coll., 1969, BA in Psychology, 1973; BSN, Troy State U., 1984, MSN magna cum laude, 1986; ADM in Nursing. RN State Med. Agy., Clin. Nurse Specialist. Head nurse emergency room Columbus Med. Ctr., Ga., 1972—75; hosp. supr. Drs. Hosp. Hosp. Corp. Am., 1975—80; dir. Columbus Med. Ctr., Surgical Nursing Divsn., 1980—82; critical care instr. BSN Program Auburn U., Auburn, Ala., 1985; RN State Med. Agy., Columbus, Ga., 1988—93; CEO Simmons Healthcare Enterprises, 1996—. Lectr. Sepsis, Legal Nursing, Neurology, Renal, 2004—08. Mem.: Am. Assn. Critical Care Nurses, Emergency Nurse Assn., Soc. Critical Care Medicine, Am. Assn. Legal Nurse Cons., Sigma Theta Tau.

Avocations: horseback riding, fencing, tennis, swimming. Office: Simmons Healthcare Enterprises 1303 Pagoda Dr Columbus GA 31907 Office Phone: 706-563-1891.

SIMMONS, MICHAEL ANTHONY, pediatrician; m. Margaret Clare Martindale (div.); children: Kristen Ann, Jeffrey Michael, Jennifer Clare Roe, Jason Davis. AB cum laude, Harvard Coll., 1963, MD, 1967. Diplomate Am. Bd. Pediatrics, Am. Bd. Neonatal-Perinatal Medicine. Intern Harriet Lane Svc., Johns Hopkins Hosp., Balt., 1967—68, asst. resident, 1968—69, sr. asst. resident, 1969; chief resident Dept. Pediatrics, U. Colo. Med. Ctr., Denver, 1971—72, rsch. fellow in perinatal medicine, 1972—74, clin. instr. in pediatrics, 1974—77, assoc. prof. pediatrics, 1977; assoc. prof. pediatrics and obstetrics Johns Hopkins U. Sch. Medicine, Balt., 1977—83; prof., chmn. dept. pediatrics U. Utah Sch. of Medicine, Salt Lake City, 1983—94; dean U. N.C. at Chapel Hill Sch. Medicine, 1994—97, prof. pediatrics, 1994—, interim chief, 1997. Adj. prof. dept. obstetrics and gynecology U. Utah Sch. of Medicine, Salt Lake City, 1984-94; co-dir. newborn svcs. U. Colo. Med. Ctr., Denver, 1974-77, Johns Hopkins Hosp., 1977-83; mem. staff Denver Gen. Hosp., 1976-77, Denver Children's Hosp., 1976-77; vice chmn. clin. affairs dept. pediatrics Johns Hopkins Hosp., 1981-83; chief of pediatrics U. Utah Med. Ctr., Salt Lake, City, 1983-94; med. dir. Primary Children's Med. Ctr., 1983-94; bd. dirs. Triangle Univs. Licensing Consortium, U. N.C. Hosps. Contbr. numerous articles to profl. jours. Fellow Am. Acad. of Pediatrics (excellence in pediatric rsch. com. 1991—, coun. on govt. affairs 1992—); mem. Perinatal Rsch. Soc. (coun. 1982-84, pres.-elect 1985-87, pres. 1989), Western Soc. for Pediatric Rsch. (coun. 1985-86, pres.-elect 1987, pres. 1988), Soc. for Pediatric Rsch., Am. Bd. Pediatrics (sub-bd. of neonatal-perinatal medicine 1983-89, chmn. 1984-88). Office: UNC Health Care 101 Manning Dr Chapel Hill NC 27514 Office Phone: 336-832-6160. Personal E-mail: michael.simmons@mosescone.com. *

SIMMONS, RACHE M., surgeon, educator; MD, Duke U., 1988. Diplomate Am. Bd. Surgery. Med. cons. Woman's World mag.; resident in surgery Univ. NC Hosp., 1989—93; dir. NY Hosp.; fellow in surgical oncology NY Hosp.- Cornell Hosp., 1993—94; assoc. prof. surgery Cornell Univ. - Weill Med. Coll.; bd. mem. Am. Soc. of Breast Surgeons, pres.; surgeon NY- Presbyn Hosp./ Weill Cornell Med. Ctr.; asst. dir. Strang-Cornell Breast Ctr. Author numerous sci. publs. and presentations. Mem.: Met. Breast Cancer Group, Assn. of Women Surgeons, ACS. Office: New York- Presbyterian Weill Cornell Medical Center 525 E 68th St New York NY 10065 Office Phone: 212-746-5454.

SIMOES, EDUARDO JARDIM, epidemiologist, educator; b. Recife, Brazil, Mar. 5, 1957; came to U.S., 1989; s. Mauro Simoes Jr. and Maria do Carmo de Almeida Jardim; m. Suyenne Mulatinho; children: Julia, Raisa. MD, U. Pernambuco, Recife, 1981; MSc, London U., 1987; MPH, Emory U., 1991. Primary care physician Secretariat of Health, Recife, 1982-89, med. officer, 1985-86, asst. health planner, 1986-89, cons. health planner, 1989; vis. assoc. Ctrs. Disease Control, Atlanta, 1991-93; asst. rschr. Emory U. Sch. Medicine, Atlanta, 1993-95; med. epidemiologist Mo. Dept. Health, Columbia, 1995—, chief of office epidemiology, state epidemiologist Jefferson City, 2000—. Asst. prof. epidemiology, St. Louis U. Sch. Pub. Health, 1995—, U. Mo. Sch. Medicine, Columbia, 1998—; cons. Coun. State and Territorial Epidemiologists, 1995—, Mo. Patient Care Rev. Found. Task Force, 1998—. Contbr. articles to profl. jours. Mem. APHA, Am. Coll. Epidemiology, Assn. State and Territorial Chronic Disease Program Dirs. Office: Mo Dept Health Office of Epidemiology 920 Wildwood Dr Jefferson City MO 65109-5796 Home: 1438 Wembley Ct NE Atlanta GA 30329-3968 Fax: 573-526-4102. E-mail: simoes@mail.health.state.mo.us.

SIMON, ALAIN CHRISTIAN, clinician, medical researcher; s. Bernard Emmanuel and Anne Hélène Simon; m. Hélène Françoise-Marie Ycard, July 27, 1977; 1 child, Olivier Alain. MD, Faculte de Medecine, 1976. Asst. chief clinic Hosp. Broussais & Faculté de Médecine, Paris, 1976—83; prof. therapeutics Faculty Medicine, Paris, 1986; head dept. preventive cardiovasc. medicine Hosp. Broussais & Faculty Medicine René Descartes, Paris, 1998—; practitioner Assistance Publique Hosp. de Paris, 1986. Coord. prevention and rehab. pole Hôpital Européen Georges Pompidou, Paris, 2002—05; co-dir. unit rsch. Centre Nat. de Recherche Scientifique, Paris, 2002—. Mem. editl. bd.: Jour. Hypertension; contbr. articles to numerous profl. jours. Mem.: Internat. Soc. Hypertension. Avocations: reading, running, mountaineering, antiques. Home: 112 ter Avenue de Suffren Paris 75015 France Office: Hosp European Georges Pompidou 20Rue Leblanc Paris 75908 France Office Fax: 33156095028. Business E-Mail: alain.simon@egp.aphp.fr.

SIMON, BARRY I., periodontist, educator; b. Jersey City, June 29, 1940; BA, Brandeis U., 1961; DDS, Fairleigh Dickinson U.; MSD, Boston U., 1966. Pvt. practice, 1972—2001; prof. NJ Dental Sch., 1972—. Mem.: NJ Dental Assn., Am. Acad. Periodontology (Educator award), Am. Dental Assn. Avocations: flying, bicycling, skiing. Home: 35 Cherry Tree Rd Loudonville NY 12211 Home Fax: 973-972-2594. Business E-Mail: simonbi@umdnj.edu.

SIMON, BERNECE KERN, retired social worker; b. Denver, Nov. 27, 1914; d. Maurice Meyer and Jennie (Bloch) Kern; m. Marvin L. Simon, Feb. 26, 1939 (dec.); 1 child, Anne Elizabeth. BA, U. Chgo., 1936, MA, 1942. Social worker Jewish Children's Bur. Chgo., 1938-40, U. Chgo. Hosps. and Clinics, 1940-44; mem. faculty U. Chgo., 1944-81, instr., 1944-48, asst. prof., 1948-60, prof. social casework, 1960—81, prof. emeritus, 1981—, Samuel Deutsch prof. Sch. Social Service Adminstrn., 1960—. Mem. bd. editors 17th Edit. Ency. Social Work, 1975—77, Social Svc. Rev., 1975—99, Social Work, 1978—82; book rev. editor: Social Work, 1982—87, cons. editor: Jour. Social Work Edn.; contbr. articles to profl. jours., chapters to books. Mem.: NASW, Nat. Acads. Practice Social Work, Acad. Cert. Social Workers, Coun. Social Work Edn. (mem. nat. bd. dirs., sec. 1972—74). Home Phone: 773-753-4603.

SIMON, ERIC JACOB, neuroscientist, educator; b. Wiesbaden, Germany, June 2, 1924; came to U.S., 1938, naturalized, 1945; s. Joseph and Paula (Meyer) S.; m. Irene M. Ronis, Aug. 9, 1947; children: Martin A., Faye Ruth, Lawrence D. BS, Case Inst. Tech., Cleve., 1944; MS, U. Chgo., 1947, PhD, 1951; doctorate (hon.), U. René Descartes Sorbonne, Paris, 1982. Postdoctoral trainee in biochemistry Columbia U. Coll. Physicians and Surgeons, 1951-53; lectr. in chemistry CCNY, 1952-59; research assoc. Cornell U. Med. Coll., 1953-59; asst. prof. medicine NYU Med. Center, 1959-64, assoc. prof. exptl. medicine, 1964-72, prof. exptl. medicine, 1972-80, prof. psychiatry and pharmacology, 1980—. Harry Williams Meml. lectr. Dept. Pharmacology Emory U., Atlanta, 1986; mem. initial rev. com. Nat. Inst. Drug Abuse, 1976-80, chmn. 1979-80, mem. Nat. Adv. Coun. on Drug Abuse, 1989-92; Sterling-Winthrop lectr. Albany Med. Coll., 1977; vis. prof. Coll. de France, Paris, 1990; vis. lectr. Shanghai and Beijing, 1985. Trustee Teaneck (N.J.) Bd. Edn., 1975-79. Served with U.S. Army, 1944-46. Recipient Rsch. Pace Setter award Nat. Inst. Drug Abuse, 1977, Louis and Bert Freedman Found. award N.Y. Acad. Scis., 1980, Nathan B. Eddy Meml. award Coll. on Problems of Drug Dependence, Lexington, Ky., 1983, Alumni Profl. Achievement award U. Chgo., 1986, Founder's Lectr. award Internat. NArcotics Rsch. Conf., 1999; Health Rsch. Coun. NYC career scientist, 1959-75. Fellow AAAS, N.Y. Acad. Scis. (trustee 1986-89); mem. Am. Soc. Biol. Chemists, Am. Soc. Neurochemistry, Am. Soc. Pharmacology, Internat. Soc. Neurochemistry, Am. Chem. Soc., Sigma Xi. Lodges: B'nai B'rith. Research, publs. on opiate receptors, endorphins, biochemistry of analgesic action, vitamin E metabolism, acyl-coenzyme A synthesis. Office: 550 1st Ave New York NY 10016-6402 Home: 245 Prospect Ave Apt 6A Hackensack NJ 07601-2571 Office Phone: 212-263-5637. Business E-Mail: eric.simon@nyu.edu.

SIMON, GARY LEONARD, internist, educator; b. Bklyn., Dec. 18, 1946; s. Bernard and Dorothy (Ligeti) Simon; m. Vicki Thiessen, Aug. 29, 1970; children: Jason, Jessica. BS, U. Md., 1968, MD, 1975; PhD, U. Wis., 1972. Diplomate Am. Bd. Internal Medicine, Am. Bd. Infectious Diseases. Resident in internal medicine U. Md. Hosp., Balt., 1975—78; fellow infectious diseases Tufts-New Eng. Med. Ctr., Boston, 1978—80; asst. prof. dept. medicine George Washington U., Washington, 1980-84, assoc. prof., 1984-89, assoc. chmn. medicine, 1984-97, prof., 1989—, dir. divsn. infectious diseases, 1993—, vice chmn. medicine, 1997—, Walter G. Ross Prof. Medicine, 2006. Cons. on AIDS Assn. Am. Med. Coll., Washington, 1990—. Contbr. articles to profl. jours. Recipient Outstanding Attending Physician award, George Washington U., 1981, Disting. Rschr. award, 2002, Oscar and Shoshana Trachtenburg award, 2005; named Walter G. Ross Prof. in Clinical Rsch., 2006; named one of Best Doctors in Am., 2004—. Master: ACP (Laureate award 2000); fellow: Infectious Disease Soc.; mem.: Internat. AIDS Soc., Assn. Subspecialty Profs., Am. Soc. Microbiology, Alpha Omega Alpha. Office: George Washington U 2150 Pennsylvania Ave NW Washington DC 20037-3201 Home Phone: 301-983-2873; Office Phone: 202-741-2234. Business E-Mail: gsimon@mfa.gwu.edu.

SIMON, GREGORY E., psychiatrist, researcher; MD, U. N.C., 1982; MPH, U. Wash., 1990. Diplomate Am. Bd. Internal Medicine 1985, Am. Bd. Adult Psychiatry 1990. Scientific investigator Ctr. for Health Studies, Group Health Coop., Seattle, 1990—2000, staff psychiatrist, 1990—, sr. scientific investigator Seattle, 2000—; rsch. prof. psychiatry and behavioral sciences U. Wash., Seattle, 2005—. Named one of Best Doctors, Seattle Met. mag., 2006, Puget Sound Consumers' Checkbook, 2007. Mem.: Am. Psychiatric Assn. (Eli Lilly "Welcome Back" award 2002, sr. scholar health services rsch. award 2002), Depression and Bipolar Support Alliance (sci. adv. bd., Gerald R. Klerman sr. investigator award 2005). Office: Group Health Coop 1730 MInor Ave #1600 Seattle WA 98112 Business E-Mail: simon.g@ghc.org.

SIMON, JIMMY LOUIS, pediatrician, educator; b. San Francisco, Dec. 27, 1930; s. Sylvain L. and Hilda H. (Netter) S.; m. Marilyn S. Wachter, June 21, 1953; children: Kent, Nancy. AB, U. Calif.-Berkeley, 1952; MD, U. Calif.-Berkeley, San Francisco, 1955. Diplomate Am. Bd. Pediats. Intern U. Calif., San Francisco, 1955-56; resident Grace-New Haven Hosp., 1956-57; sr. asst. resident Boston Children's Hosp., 1957-58; instr., asst. prof. pediats. U. Okla., Oklahoma City, 1960-64; asso. prof. U. Tex. Med. Br., Galveston, 1966-72, prof. pediatrics, 1972-74; prof., chmn. pediats. Bowman Gray Sch. Medicine, Wake Forest U., Winston-Salem, NC, 1974-96; prof., chmn. emeritus Wake Forest U. Sch. Medicine, Winston-Salem, NC, 1996—. With USAF, 1958-60. Mem. Am. Pediat. Soc., Am. Acad. Pediats., Am. Bd. Pediats., Ambulatory Pediat. Assn., Alpha Omega Alpha. Office: Wake Forest U Sch Medicine Dept Pediatrics Medical Center Blvd Winston Salem NC 27157-0001

SIMON, NORMA PLAVNICK, psychologist; d. Mark and Mary Plavnick; m. Robert G. Simon, Dec. 18, 1949; children: Mark Allan, Susan. BA, NYU, 1952, cert. in psychoanalysis, 1977; MA, Columbia U., 1953, EdD, 1968. Diplomate Am. Bd. Profl. Psychology, Am. Bd. Counseling Psychology, Am. Bd. Psychoanalysis. Psychologist Queens Coll. Counseling Ctr., Flushing, NY, 1968-70, asst. dir., 1970-76, dir., 1976; gen. practice psychology NYC, 1970—. Faculty, supr. New Hope Guild, Bklyn., 1976—, dir. child and adolescent tng. prog., 1988-98; adj. prof. clin. psychology Columbia U., N.Y.C., 1986-2002; supr. NYU Postdoctoral Prog. in Psychoanalysis, 1988—; mem. com. on profl. practice and ethics Nat. Register Health Svc. Providers, 1998-2003. Author: (with Robert G. Simon): Choosing a College Major: Social Science, 1981; co-author 3 book chpts. on licensure and ethics in psychology; mem. editl. bd. The Counseling Psychologist jour., 1986-89, Profl. Practice and Rsch. in Psychology, 1994-99, Jour. Infant, Child and Adolescent Psych Therapy, 1999—. Vice chair N.Y. State Bd. for Psychology State Edn. Dept., Albany, 1978-82, chair, 1982-88; bd. dirs. Pelham (N.Y.) Guidance Coun., 1980-83; pres.-elect Assn. State and Provincial Psychology Bds., 1990, pres., 1991. Recipient Morton Berger award, Assn. State and Provincial Psychology Bds., 1998, Outstanding Psychologist award, Acad. Counseling Psychology, 2003. Fellow: APA (mem. bd. profl. affairs 1987—89, chair bd. profl. affairs 1988—89, policy and planning bd. 1991—93, mem. ethics com. 1995—97, vice chair ethics com. 1996—97, chair ethics com. 1997, workgroup on telehealth 1998—2000, mem. accreditation com. 2004—, non-govtl. orgnl. UN assoc. team mem. 2006—, Karl Heiser award 1993, John Black award 1994, Disting. Psychologist of Yr., Divsn. Ind. Practice 2004), Am. Bd. Counseling Psychology (bd. dirs. 1992—2000, pres.-elect 1999, pres. 2001—03), Nat. Acads. Practice (elected disting. practitioner), Am. Bd. Profl. Psychology (trustee 1998—2001, pres.-elect 2001—, pres. 2004—05); mem.: UN NY (mem., Com. Aging, Mental Health and Family NGO), Internat. Coun. Psychologists (exec. com. mem., NGO UNTeam), NGO UN (commn. ageing recording sec. 2009—, mem. at large 2011—, com. mental health mem.-at-large), ABPP (Russell Bent award 2009), Internat. Assoc. Applied Psychology (non-govtl. orgnl. UN team mem.).

SIMON, SUZANA KATALENIC, cytologist; b. Zagreb, Croatia, June 2, 1971; MD, U. Medicine, Zagreb, 1997. Cert. specialist in clin. cytology U. Zagreb, Sch. Medicine, 2005. Clin. cytologist Clin. Hosp. Merkur, Zagreb, 1999—. Office: Zajceva Ulica 19 Zagreb 10 000 Croatia E-mail: katalenicsimon.suzana@gmail.com.

SIMONELLI, CHRISTINE, internist; b. Stockton, Calif., Sept. 12, 1948; BS, U. Colo., 1970; MD, U. N.Mex Sch. Medicine, 1977. Internist St. Paul Ramsey Med. Ctr., 1980—96; med. dir., osteoporosis care HealthEast Clin., 1996—. Mem.: Am. Soc. Bone and Mineral Rsch., Nat. Osteoporosis Found., Internat. Osteoporosis Found., Internat. Soc. Clin. Densitometry. Avocations: dance, golf. Office: 1875 Woodwinds Drive Site WL-30 Woodbury MN 55125 Office Fax: 651-232-0070. Personal E-mail: msciao@comcast.net.

SIMONIAN, SIMON JOHN, surgeon, scientist, educator, health science association administrator, philanthropist, writer, quaker peace activist; b. Antioch, French Ter., Apr. 20, 1932; arrived in U.S., 1965, naturalized, 1976; s. John Simon and Marie (Tomboulian) Simonian; m. Arpi Ani Yeghiayan, July 11, 1965; children: Leonard Armen, Charles Haig, Andrew Hovig. First MB, U. London, 1951, MD, 1957; BA in Animal Physiology, St. Edmund Hall, U. Oxford, Eng., 1964; MSc in Nutrition, Immunology and Genetics, Harvard U., 1967, ScD in Nutrition, Immunology and Genetics, 1969; MA in Animal Physiology, U. Oxford, 1969; DSc (hon.), Nat. Acad. Scis., Armenia, 1998. Diplomate Am. Bd. Surgery, 1977, lic. Mass., 1970, Ill., 1974, Pa., 1978, Mich., 1988, Va., 1990, cert. Ednl. Coun. Fgn. Med. Grads., 1970. Rsch. asst., team mem. smallpox vaccine lyophilization immunology unit Lister Inst. Preventive Medicine, U. London, Elstree, Essex, England, 1951—52; intern in medicine Univ. Coll. Hosp., London, 1957; intern in surgery Edinburgh Royal Infirmary, U. Edinburgh, Scotland, 1957—58; resident tutor in surgery Edinburgh Royal Infirmary, Scotland, 1961—62; clin. clk. Nat. Hosp. & Inst. of Neurology, U. London, 1958; resident Edinburgh Western Gen. Hosp., U. Edinburgh, 1958—59, City Hosp., U. Edinburgh, Birmingham Accident and Burns Hosp., U. Birmingham, England, 1959—60; demonstrator dept. anatomy Edinburgh U., 1960-61; rsch. fellow in surgery and biochemistry Am. U. Beirut Lebanon, 1964—65; rsch. fellow in pathology Lab. Chem. Pathology Harvard U., Harvard Med. Sch. & Peter Bent Brigham Hosp., Boston, 1965-68; trainee NIH US Army Devel. Command Immunology Rsch. Harvard Med. Sch., 1967; instr. immunology Harvard Med. Sch., Boston, 1966-70, instr. in surgery and immunology, 1968—69, surg. dir. course on transplantation, biology and medicine, 1968-70, faculty assoc. in surgery and immunology, 1969—70; vis. prof., invited spkr. Harvard Med. Sch., Mass. Gen. Hosp., Brigham and Womens Hosp., New Eng. Deaconess Hosp., 1982; dir. transplantation immunology unit & lab., asst. in surgery Brigham and Womens Hosp., Boston, 1968-70; resident and chief resident in surgery Boston City Hosp., 1970—74; attending surgeon in transplantation and gen. surgery svcs. U. Chgo. Med. Ctr., 1974—77; asst. prof. surgery, mem. com. immunology U. Chgo., 1974-77; dir., surgeon-in-chief divsn. renal transplantation Hahnemann U. Sch. Medicine and Hosp., Phila., 1978-87, prof. surgery, 1978-88, chmn. Transplantation Com., 1983-88, chmn. quality assurance of surgery com., 1986-88; dept. surgery coord. with joint commn. for accreditation of hosps. Hahnemann U. Sch. Medicine, 1986—88; chief and chmn. dept. surgery twelve divsns. and surg. residency program St. John Hosp. and Med. Ctr., Detroit, 1988-89, chmn. credentials com. of surgery and oper. rm. com., 1988-89, assoc. v.p. for med. affairs, 1989-90; pres., CEO Vein Inst. Met. Washington, Inc., 1990—2006; assoc. attending staff Fairfax Hosp., Falls Church, Va., 1990-92, active attending faculty, 1992—2006; guest lectr., 1994, 99; clin. assoc. prof. surgery Georgetown U. Sch. Medicine, Washington, 1992-95, guest lectr., 1994, clin. prof. surgery, 1995—2006; vis. prof. Ctr. Study Religion UCLA, 2009—, Profl. Hypnotherapy Certification Program, Hypnotherapy Motivation Inst., Calif.; bd. mem., primary dir., rep. Quaker Religion Interreligious Coun. Southern Calif. Vis. prof., invited spkr. Vanderbilt U., 1968, Cedars-Sinai Med. Ctr., UCLA, 1977, Addenbroke's Hosp., Cambridge U., England, 1977, Karolinska Inst., Stockholm, 1977, Huddinge Hosp., U. Stockholm, 1977, Med. Coll. Pa. and Hosp., Phila., 1980, 81, 85, Grad. Hosp., U. Pa., Phila., 1981, 85, U. Athens, 1981, U. Coll. Hosp., U. London, 1981, Western Gen. Hosp. Edinburg U., 1981, VA Hosp., Tufts U., Boston, 1982, John Radcliffe Hosp., U. Oxford, 1982, Nat. Acad. Scis., Yerevan, Armenia, 1995, St. Edmund Hall, U. Oxford, England, 1997, Christ Ch. Hosp., Chgo., 1974—77, South Chgo. Hosp., 1974—77, Del. Med. Ctr., Wilmington, 1977, Wilkes Barre (Pa.) Gen. Hosp., 1979, Robert Packer Hosp., Sayre, Pa., Guthrie Clinic, Sayre, 1980, Abington Meml. Hosp., Phila., 1982, Crozer Chester Med. Ctr., Pa., 1982, St. Agnes Hosp. Med. Ctr., Phila., 1982, Sacred Heart Hosp., 1982, Riverview Hosp., Red Bank, NJ, 1983, Easton (Pa.) Hosp., Allentown, 1983, Newcombe Med. Ctr., Vineland, NJ, 1983, Cath. Med. Ctr., Manchester, NH, 1984, Burlington County Med. Ctr., Mount Holly, NJ, 1984; cons. Michael Reese Hosp., Chgo., 1976—77; cons. gen. surgery City of Phila., 1986—88; cons. vascular surgery Coll. Podiatry, Phila., 1986—88; cons. venous vascular surgery Podiatry Residence Program, No. Va. Med. Coll., Richmond, 1994—2000; cons. surgery John F. Kennedy Meml. Hosp., Stratford, NJ, 1982—86, St. Agnes Hosp. Med. Ctr., Phila., 1982—86; chief & surgeon in chief, med. team support U.S. Pres. Ronald W. Reagan, 1988; chief & surgeon in chief, med. team support pres. George H. W. Bush, 1989; vis. surgeon Inst. Vein Disease, Mich., 1989—90; vis. scientist Argonne Nat. Lab., Ill., 1969, vis. scientist, collaborator, 1974—77; founding mem. sci. bd. ctr. regenerative biology and medicine Ind. U., 2001—; invited spkr., panelist 8th Internat. Congress of Nephrology, Athens, 1981, 1st Internat. Soc. for Edn. and Rsch. in Vascular Disease, San Diego, 1992, 4th Internat. Dialogue Transition to Global Soc., U. Md., College Park, 1995; invited spkr. 3d Armenian Med. World Congress, Montreal, 1986, 4th Armenian Med. World Congress, LA, 1989; invited spkr., chairperson of session 5th Armenian Med. World Congress, Paris, 1992; invited spkr. 6th

Armenian Med. World Congress, Boston, 1995, 7th Armenian Med. World Congress, Lyon, France, 1998, Internat. Forum Plebology, Frankfurt, Germany, 2000, 01, 02, 03, 04, 8th Armenian Med. World Congress, Toronto, 2001, 9th Armenian Med. World Congress, San Fransisco, 2005, 10th Armenian Med. World Congress, NY, 2009, Internat. Soc. Lymphology, 2001; eminent scholar external assessor for chair dept. surgery U. Zambia, Lusaka, 1994; mem. faculty, moderator internat. consensus panel The Investigation Chronic Venous Insufficiency, Paris, 1997; mem. faculty and moderator internat. consensus panel venous Thromboembolism, Rhodes, Greece, 1999; mem. faculty and moderato internat. consensus panel Thrombophilia, Limasol, Cyprus, 2003; mem. internat. consensus panel The Prevention, Investigation and Treatment of Venous Thromboembolism and Thrombophilia, Windsor, England, 2005; sci. advisor, invited spkr., panelist 8th Pan-Am. Congress Phlebology and Lymphology, Campo Grande, Brazil, 1998; lectr, invited spkr., panelist 9th Pan-Am. Congress Phlebology and Lymphology, Cordoba, Argentina, 2000; hon. mem. Internat. Forum Phlebology and Minisurgery of Varicose Veins, Frankfurt, Germany, 2000; Guthrie lectr. Robert Packer Hosp., Pa., 1980; Venus lectr., Rhodes, Greece, 99, Internat. Union Angiolo European Chpt. Congress, 2003; Diomed. lectr., 03; Kwang Dong lectr. Phlebological Soc. Korea Ann. Congress, Seoul, 2003; BSN Jobst lectr. Internat. Union Phlebology USA Congress, San Diego, 2003; keynote spkr. 18th Internat. Union Angiolo World Congress, Tokyo; Jonathan E. Rhoads ann. orator Phila. Acad. Surgery, 1984; invited spkr. LA Day Nonviolence, 2010, Unity & Diversity World Coun., 2010, Interfaith Cmtys. United Justice & Peace, 2011; invited spkr. in 300 insts. Co-author: (books) Manual of Vascular Access Procedures, 1987, Prevention of Venous Thromboembolism, 2002, Diagnosis and Treatment of Lymphedema, 2006, Prevention and Treatment of Venous Thromboembolism, 2006; cons. to editl. bd. Dateline: Issues in Transplantation, 1985—87, mem. editl. bd. Phila. Medicine, 1988, Transplantation Procs., 1987—96, Jour. Transplantation Abstracts, 1969—70, Internat. Angiology, 1998—2009, assoc. editor Am. Coll. Phlebology Vein Line, 2000—06, reviewer Jour. Oncology and Dermatologic Surgery, 1993, Jour. Dermatologic Surgery, 1997, Jour. Vascular Surgery, 2000, The Surgeon Journal Royal College of Surgeons Edinburgh and Ireland, Venous Digest, 2002; editor (translator in English): Short Saphenous Vein issue, Jour. de Phlebologie, 1999; contbr. articles to profl. jours. and books, over 300 rsch. papers; appeared in med. movie Giving. Leader, concert master Friends Sch. Orch., 1948-49, Med. Sch. and Hosp. Orch., 1956-57;co-founder Armenian Youth Soc., London, Eng., 1953, pres. 1953-54, Armenia House Cmty. Ctr., London, 1956; Armenian Studies Program U. Chgo., 1975; bd. govs. Friends Sch., London, 1964-65; Mass. del., Armenian Assembly of Am., Washington, 1972; fellow-trustee, 1978-2010, affiliate, 2011-, co-founder Entry into Manhood of Armenian Youth at Age 13, 1981; co-founder Armenian Am. Health Assn. of Greater Washington, 1992, mem. pharms. com. 1992, chmn. nominating com. 1993; sec., bd. dirs. Woodrock Inc., Potomac, Md., 1993-94; mem. Am. Friends of St. Edmund Hall, U. Oxford, 1992—, U.S. Campaign for St. Edmund Hall, 1995—, mem. bd. advisors, 1999-03, mem. campaign steering bd., 2000-05; benefactor St. Edmund Hall, Oxford U.; mem. St. Mary's Armenian Apostolic Ch., Washington, guest preacher, 1994, 95, 96; guest spkr. Armenian Ch. Youth Orgn. Am., Washington, 1998; bd. dirs. Am. Friends State U. Armenia, Yerevan, 1994-, Arlington (Va.) Symphony Orch., 1992-96, sci. com. Armenia-U.S.A., 1996—; mem. regional com. U.S. Campaign for Univ. Oxford, 1993; active amphitheatre endowment fund Boston City Hosp., 1994; fundraiser Eurasia Found., 1996; sci. advisor, chmn. session, invited spkr. Internat. Union Plebology, World Congress, 11th, Monreal, Can., 1992, 12th, London, Eng., 1995, 13th, Sydney, Australia, 1998, 14th, Rome, 2001; sci. advisor, chmn. session, invited spkr. Internat. Union Angiology World, Congress 17th, London, Eng., 1995, 18th, Tokyo, 1998, 19th, NYC, 2001, 20th, Rome, 2004, 05; invited spkr. Internat. Meeting Neurochemistry Immounogy, Nat. Acad. Scis., Armenia, 2007, Internat.Vascular Meeting, Armenia, 2007; bd. advisors Georgetown U. Ctr. for Advancement, 2007, Am. U. of Armenia Devel. Coun., 2007—; philanthropist, Hahnemann U., 1980-, St. Edmund Hall, Oxford U., 1987-, Georgetown U. Hosp. Med. Ctr., 1991-, State U. Armenia, 1995-, Harvard Sch. Pub. Health, 1998-, Va. U. Inova Campus, 2005-, Brigham and Women's Hosp., Boston Harvard U. Med. Sch., 2007—, Cornell U. Weill Med. Coll., 2007-, NY Presbyn. Hosp., 2007—, U. Mich. Med. Ctr., Ann Arbor, 2007—, Tufts U., Boston, 2007-, Am. U. Armenia, 2007-, Nat. Acad. Scis. Armenia, 2008-, Interfaith Worship Islamic Ctr. Southrn Calif., 2011, Islamic Ctr. Orange County, Irving, 2011, invited spkr., Santa Monica Friends Adult Edn. Com., mem. US Organising Com. internat. meetin European Acad. Scis. & Arts, 2010, Non-Violent Peaceful March: For Nuclear Test Ban Treaty, Aldermaston, Eng., 1957, For Abolition of Nuc. Bombs City Hall, LA, 2009, For World Peace march, Santa Monica & LA, 2009, Against Budget Cuts UCLA, 2009, Non Violent Peace Vigils, 2011-; pres. Greater Del. Valley Soc. Transplant Surgeons, 1982-85; mem. Friend Ctr. Armenian Langs. & Lit., UCLA, sponsor, Saalam Shalom Found., 2010, Inner City Law Ctr., LA, 2009, Abolotion Dealth Penalty Calif., 2010, Planned Parenthood, Doctors Without Borders, Nonviolent Peace Force Sudan, Amnesty Internat., Peace Sunday, mem. Interfaith Com. United Justice & Peace, Unity Diversity World Coun., Southern Calf. Com. Parliament World Religions, mem. steering com., LA Day Non Violence, Nonviolence Workshop Reverend James Lawson. H.J. Turtle scholar, 1943-46, R. Wright scholar, 1943-46, A. Koundakjian scholar, 1943-48, K. Clay scholar, 1946-48, Nairn scholar London U., 1949-52, Middlesex scholar London U., 1952-57; recipient N.K. Harris award, 1946, Leadership award, 1949, Valedictorian award Friends Sch., 1949, Suckling prize obstetric rsch. U. London, 1956, Brit. Med. Rsch. Coun. award Lab. Physiology Oxford U., 1962-64, NIH award transplantation and immunology rsch. Harvard Med. Sch. and Peter Bent Brigham Hosp., 1970, R. Alt prize surg. rsch. Boston City Hosp. and Beverly Hosp., 1973, Thompson award immunological rsch. U. Chgo., 1974-77, Johnson award immunological rsch. U. Chgo., 1975-77, Upjohn award, Hahneman U., 1982, Presdl. Rep. Ronald Reagan Medal of Merit, 1982, U.S. Pres. Ronald W. Reagan Seal and Medal, 1988, Richard Kabakjian award eradication of small pox Armenian Student Assn. Am., 1986, Disting. Alumni award Med. Soc. St. Edmund Hall, U. Oxford, 1997, Kaken award Tokyo, 1998, STD award Cordoba, Argentina, 2000, Contbns. to Health Rsch. award; named Outstanding New Citizen of Citizenship Coun. Met. Chgo. and Dept. Justice, Washington, 1976; Businessman of Yr. Leadership award Nat. Rep. Congl. Com., 2003, Physician of Yr. Leadership award, 2003, named Famous Grad. Saint Edmund Hall, Oxford U., co-endowed Stanley N. Gershoff PhD prize Friedman sch. nutrition, sci. and policy Tufts U., Boston, 2006; co-endowed Stanley Gershoff, Simon & Arpi Simonian prize Tufts U., Boston, 2008-; co-endowed The John and Marie J. Simonian award, St. Nerces Sem., 1981, sponsor, Endowmwnt John R. Pfeifer, MD Rsch. award, Providence Hosp., Southfield, Mich., 1992, Joseph E. Murray, MD prof. plastic surgery Harvard Brigham Women and Children's Hosps., Boston, 1999, Major donor, John R. Pfeifer MD prof. vascular surgery U. Mich., Ann Arbor, 2006, and David B. Skinner MD prof. thoracic surgery Weill Cornell Med. Coll. NY Presbyn. Hosp., 2006; endowed Marie J. Simonian Prize, Dept. Surgery, Georgetown U. Hosp. Med. Ctr., 1991 (prize com. 1991—), co-endowed The Thomas J. Gill III MD prize dept. pathology Brigham Women's Hosp., Boston, 2006, Simon J. and Arpi A. Simonian Prize for scholastic excellence for doctoral candidates, dept. nutrition sch. pub. health Harvard U., 2006, co-endowed Simon and Arpi Simonian prize in Excellence Leadership, St. Edmund Hall, Oxford U., 2007, endowed Joseph E. Murray & Simon J. Simonian prize, Dept. Surgery Brigham & Women's Hosp., Harvard Med. Sch, Boston, 2009; endowed Thomas J. Gill, III & Simon Simonian Rsch. Excellence prize Dept. Pathology, Brigham Women's Hosp., Harvard Med. Sch., 2008-, co-establised venous Vascular Phlebology Program, Divsn. Vascular Surgery, Georgetown U. Hosp., Reston, Va., 2006; Philanthropy Recognition award Hahnemann U., 1980—; named to Legacy Soc. Wall of Brigham, Women's Hosp. Harvard Med. Sch., Boston, Wall Inova's Claude Moore Health Edn. Ctr., Med. Coll. Va., Fairfax, Va., 2006, Guide to Am.'s Top Surgeons, Consumer's Rsch. Coun., 2006—, Founding Sponsor award. Martin L. King Jr. Meml., Washington, 2009, Stop Wars award, LA, 2011; grantee U.S. Govt., industry cos., founds.; fellowship Am. Profl. Soc. Fellow: ACS (Phila., Mich. and Washington chpts.), Am. Coll. Phlebology (invited spkr. La Quinta 2001, invited spkr. Ft. Lauderdale 2005), Phila. Acad. Surgery (Jonathan E. Rhoads ann. orator 1984, Samuel D. Gross prize com. 1988), Royal Coll. Surgeons Edinburgh; mem.: APHA, AAAS, AMA, AAUP, Clerk & Chair Peace & Social Action Com. (nominating com. mem.), Santa Monica Meeting, Southern Calif. Soc. for Clin. Hypnosis, Faculty Club UCLA, Pacific Coun. Internat. Policy, U. Coll. London Med. Soc. (treas. 1952—53), Presdl. Soc., U. Mich., Ptnrs. Soc., Cornell Weill Med. Coll., Friends Soc., Brigham and Womens Hosp., Armenian Orthodox Ch., Nat. Nutrition Round Table, Harvard U., Sch. Pub. Health, Alumni Giving Harvard Sch. Pub. Health (co-chair 2007—09), Leadership Coun., Harvard Sch. Pub. Health (founding mem. 2003—09), Phlebological Surgery Sect., Am. Coll. Phlebology (founding chair, bd. dirs. 2002—03, past chair 2003—04), Ambulatory Phlebectomy Sect., Am. Coll. Phlebology (chmn. program com. and sec. treas. 1999—2001, sect. chair elect 2000—01, chair, bd. dirs. 2001—02), European Acad. Scis. and Arts, Northern Va. Med. Soc., North Am. Soc. Phlebology, Chgo. Soc. Gastroenterology, Transplantation Soc. (membership com. 1980—82), Pa. Med. Soc., Phila. County Med. Soc. (rep. ctr. city br. 1981—83, pres. 1984, bd. dirs. 1985—87, chairperson long range planning com. 1986—98), Greater Del. Valley Soc. Transplant Surgeons (councilor 1978—80, pres. elect 1980—82, pres. 1982—85, councilor 1985—88, advocate govs. 1985), Phila. Acad. Scis. (invited spkr. 1982, co-chmn. membership com. 1982—88), Chgo. Soc. Gastroenterology, Assn. of Ill. Transplant Surgeons, Am. Venous Forum (co-chair session, ofcl. disscussant 10th ann. meeting 1999, invited spkr. Ft. Myers 2001, chair Internat. Rels. Com. 2001—02, invited spkr. La Jolla 2002), Am. Soc. Transplant Surgeons (co-founding charter mem. 1974, chair immunosuppression studies com. 1974—77, membership com. 1980—82), NY Acad. Scis., Samuel Hahnemann Surg. Soc., Am. Coll. Phlebology (curriculum devel. projects com. 1992—2006, co-chmn. symposiums and session 1992—2006, faculty 1993—2006, panelist 10th ann. congress 1996, membership com. 1998—2000, chmn. sci. program com. 13th ann. congress 1999, program chair 14th ann. congress, Atlanta 2000, invited spkr. Atlanta 2000, invited spkr. Ft. Lauderdale 2002), Internat. Cardiovasc. Soc. (chair session 22d world congress 1995, N.Am. chpt., Kyoto), European Soc. Organ Transplant, UCLA Libr. (assoc.), Korean Soc. Phlebology (hon.), Internat. Forum Phelbology(Germany) (hon.), Am. Soc. Artificial Internal Organs, Am. Technion Soc., Wayne County Med. Soc., Greater Washington Telecomm. Assn. (pres.' club 1994), Am. Soc. Lymphology (nat. adv. bd., chair sci. com. 1999—2001, pres.-elect 2000—01, invited spkr. La Quinta 2001, pres. 2001—03, invited spkr. Kansas City 2002, re-elected pres. 2003—06), Am. Fedn. Clin. Rsch., Transplantation Soc. Mich., Assn. Acad. Surgery, Armenian Med. and Dental Assn. Greater Phila. (co-founder 1983, pres. 1983—85, Outreach award 1986), Assn. for Study of Med. Edn., Physicians for Social Responsibility, Cancer Rsch. Assn. Boston, Am. Venous Found. (bd. dirs. 2002—06), Brit. Med. Assn., Am. Armenian Med. Assn. (co-founder & treas. 1972, 25th anniversary co-founder award 1997), Nat. Assn. Armenian Studies and Rsch. (rep. Midatlantic region 1994—2003, bd. dirs. 2004—06), Royal Coll. Physicians of London Licentiates, Med. Soc. Va., Fairfax County Med. Soc., Mich. State Med. Soc., Chgo. Assn. Immunologists, Detroit Surgical Assn., Detroit Acad. Surgery, Am. Coll. Physician Execs., Am. Assn. Vascular Surgery (invited spkr. 2000), Royal Coll. Surgeons of Eng., Nat. Acad. Scis. Armenia (fgn.), Mus. Musical Compositions Alan Hovhaness (bd. advisors 2007—), Organ Procurement Agy. Mich. (adv. bd. 1988—89), End Stage Renal Disease Network 24 (med. rev. bd. 1980—82, 1986—87), Armenian Gen. Benevolent Union (invited spkr. 1982, pres.' club 1990—2005), Soc. Brigham Surg. Alumni, Harvard Club (South Calif.), Immunology Club Boston, Med. Club (Phila.), Harvard Club (Washington), Oxford and Cambridge Soc., Oxford Soc., Sigma Xi. Mem. Soc. Of Friends. Achievements include bilateral lung reimplantation resulting in normal function without vagus nerves; reversal of renal allograft rejection using IgG concentrate of antilymphocyte serum (ALS) and of antihymocyte globulin (ATG); prevention and treatment of massive gastroduodenal hemorrhage from hemorrhagic gastritis using pioneering antacids to neutralize gastric acid pH7; first co-discovered essential amino acids phenylalanine and tryptophan that are essential for antibody formation; participated in the production of the first Freeze dried, heat stable, globally effective smallpox vaccine which was used by the WHO in 1966; to vaccinate everybody resulting in eradication of smallpox in 1977 which was the first and only major disease eradicated in the history of medicine and public health and saving two million lives; co-discoverer of immunogenetic control of antibody formation that will lead to design future drugs to treat patients as genetically unique to the prevention of hypertension and autimmune genetic and chronic diseases; research advantages and disadvantages and prevention of splenectomy in renal transplant recipients; stage-enmasse cardiopulmonary reimplantation that resulted in normal function without vagus nerves; zinc deficiency depresses the action of zinc dependent enzymes, priming the recipient with donor antigen improves kidney transplant survival; discovery of stable bonding protein carrier and cytotoxic agent for treatment of organ transplant rejection and cancer; combined surgery and sclerotherapy corrects abnormal structure, function and aesthetics of leg varicose veins; pioneering conversion of arteriovenous shunt to arteriovenous fistula for immediate long term hemodialysis; first to use needle phlebectomy in USA; first to use beaver microblade phlebectomy; first to use bupivacaine wound infiltration in venous surgery wounds to minimize post operative pain; abolition of concurrent deep and perforator vein incompetence by surgical correction of superficial vein incompetence; evolving concepts in management of accute superficial and deep thromboembolism, phlebolymphedema; first to develop the largest phlebology organization participating with insurance in the United States; first to use the name Vein Institute; first to establish successful venous vascular program in medical school hospital; discovery of immunogenetics; kidney transplantation as a medical specialty; establishment of lymphatic vascular disease lymphology; establishment of venous vascular disease phlebology as a medical specialty; advocate for the government to provide the cost of winter heating for all the Buildingsof the institutes of the national academy of sciences was signed into law by the prime minister of Armenia. Avocations: exercise, music, reading.

SIMONS, HELEN, retired school psychologist, psychotherapist, educator; d. Leo and Sarah (Shrayer) Pomper; m. Broudy Simons, May 20, 1956 (div. May 1972); children: Larry, Sheri. BA in Biol., Lake Forest Coll., 1951; MA in Clin. Psychology, Roosevelt U., 1972; D of Clin. Psychology, Ill. Sch. Profl. Psychology, 1980. Sch. psychologist Chgo. Bd. Edn., 1974—2010; with Chgo. Pub. Schs., 1974—2010; intern Cook County Hosp., Chgo., 1979-80; pvt. practice psychotherapist Chgo., 1980—2010. Faculty Internat. Soc. for Prevention of Child Abuse and Neglect; lectr., presenter at workshops. Contbr. articles to profl. jours. Mem.: APA, Internat. Sch. Psychologists Assn., Internat. Soc. for Prevention of Child Abuse and Neglect, Chgo. Sch. Psychol. Assn., Ill. Sch. Psychologists Assn., Nat. Sch. Psychologists Assn. Avocations: music, dance, reading. Home: 6145 N Sheridan Rd Apt 29D Chicago IL 60660-6855 Personal E-mail: hpompers@aol.com.

SIMONS, JOHN NELSON, surgeon, consultant; b. Lawrence, Kans., Sept. 19, 1932; s. Dolph Collins and Marie Nelson Simons; children: John Jr., Andrea, James, Suzanne, Melissa. BA, U. Kans., 1954; MD, U. Pa., 1958; M in Surgery, U. Minn., 1963. Cert. Am. Bd. Surgery, 1965, Am. Bd. Plastic Surgery, 1967. Cons. plastic surgery Mayo Clinic, Rochester, Minn., 1965—66, asst. prof. plastic surgery, 1965—72, head sect. plastic surgery, 1967—73, assoc. prof. plastic surgery, 1972—73. Founder, CEO Health Campus Internat. Consultants in Health Care Delivery, East Gulf Lake, Minn., 1995—. Republican. Home: 10999 Pine Beach Rd East Gull Lake MN 56401

SIMONS, KAI, cell biologist; b. Helsinki, Finland, May 24, 1938; s. Lennart Jacob and Rut Gunhild (Waselius) S.; m. Carola Marita Smeds, June 19, 1965; children: Mikael, Katja, Matias. MD, U. Helsinki, 1964; PhD (hon.), U. Louvain, Belgium, 2003, U. Oulu, Finland, 2003. Postdoctoral fellow Rockefeller U., NYC, 1965-67; researcher U. Helsinki, 1967-75, prof., 1976; group leader European Molecular Biology Lab, Heidelberg, Germany, 1975—2000, program coordinator, 1982-97; hon. prof. U. Heidelberg, 1995—2006; dir. Max Planck Inst. Molecular Cell Biology and Genetics, Dresden, 1998—, group leader, 2006—08; co-dir. Shanghai Inst. Advanced Studies Chinese Acad. Sci. Dunham lectr. Harvard U. Med. Sch., Boston, 1996; Li lectr. U. Calif., Berkeley, 1998. Contbr. over 250 articles to profl. jours.; former editor Jour. Cell Biology, Current Opinion of Cell Biology. Recipient prize Fedn. European Biochem. Socs., 1975, Jahre prize, 1991, Ayrāpāā prize, 2003, Prix Mondial Nessim Habif, U. Geneva, 2003, Virchow Lecture and medal, U. Wuerzburg, Germany, 2004, Laurens van Deenen medal, Utrecht, Netherlands, 2005. Mem. European Molecular Biology Orgn., Soc. Scientiarum Fennica, Heidelberg Acad. Scis., Acad. Europaea, Am. Acad. Arts and Scis., Nat. Acad. Scis. (U.S.), European Life Scientist Orgn. (pres.), Akademie Leopoldina. Office: Max Planck Inst Molec Cell Biology Pfotenhauer Str 108 D-01307 Dresden Germany Business E-Mail: simons@mpi-cbg.de.

SIMONSEN, ANNE, medical educator; b. Norway, May 29, 1967; PhD, U. Oslo, 1996. Sr. scientist Norwegian Radium Hosp., 2004—09; prof. U. Oslo, 2009—. Mem. Autophagy Editl. Bd. Recipient Ragnar Moerks Legacy prize, Norwegian Radiumhospital. Mem.: Norwegian Acad. Scis. Avocation: running. Office: Inst Basic Med Scis PB 1112 Blindern Oslo N-0317 Norway Business E-Mail: anne.simonsen@medisin.uio.no.

SIMONSON, STEWART GERARD, retired federal agency administrator; b. May 11, 1963; BA, U. Wis., 1986, JD, 1994. Bar: Wis., DC. Legal counsel to Gov. State of Wis., 1995—99; corp. sec., counsel Nat. Railroad Passenger Corp. (AMTRAK), 1999—2001; dep. gen. counsel US Dept. Health & Human Services, 2001—03, spl. counsel to sec., 2003—04, asst. sec. for pub. health emergency preparedness, 2004—06.

SIMONSON, SUSAN KAY, social worker; b. La Porte, Ind., Dec. 5, 1946; d. George Randolph and Myrtle Lucille (Opfel) Menkes; m. Richard Bruce Simonson, Aug. 25, 1973. BA with honors, Ind. U., 1969; MA, Washington U., St. Louis, 1972. Perinatal social worker Yakima Valley Meml. Hosp., Yakima, Wash., 1979-81, dir. patient support program, 1981—98, dir. social svc., 1982-98; instr. Spanish, ethnic studies, sociology Yakima Valley Coll., Yakima, Wash., 1981—93. Pres. Yakima Child Abuse Council, 1983-85; developer nat. patient support program, 1981. Contbr. articles to profl. jours. Mem. adv. council Robert Wood Johnson Found. Rural Infant Health Care Project, Yakima, 1980, Pregnancy Loss and Compassionate Friends Support Groups, Yakima, 1982—, Teen Outreach Program,

Yakima, 1984—. Recipient NSF award, 1967, discharge planning program of yr. regional award Nat. Glasrock Home Health Care Discharge Planning Program, 1987; research grantee Ind. U., 1968, Fulbright grantee U.S. Dept. State, 1969-70; Nat. Def. Edn. Act fellowship, 1970-73. Mem. AAUW, Am. Hosp. Assn. (regional award 1989), Phi Beta Kappa, Assn. Gravestone Studies.

SIMONSSON, STINA, research scientist; b. Göteborg, Sweden, Mar. 21, 1969; d. Anders Sören and Sylvia Gunilla Odén; m. Tomas Jan Simonsson, Sept. 17, 1994; children: Linn Amanda, Klara Sofie, Hannes William. MS in Chem. Engring., Chalmers U. Tech., Sweden, 1992; PhD, Göteborg U., Sweden, 2000. Postdoctoral fellow Cambridge (Eng.) U., 2000—04; asst. prof. Göteborg (Sweden) U., 2005—. Grantee, Biotech. and Biol. Scis. Rsch. Coun., Eng., 2000, 2004, Swedish Rsch. Coun., 2005—. Achievements include patents for nuclear reprogramming by amphibian oocytes. Home: Fotbollsgatan 27 431 69 Mölndal Sweden Office: Göteborg Univ Med Biomedicine PO Box440 40530 Göteborg Sweden

SIMONYAN, KRISTINA, medical educator; b. Yerevan, Armenia, Jan. 27, 1975; MD, Yerevan State Med. U., U. Goettingen, 2004; PhD, U. Hannover, 2003. Asst. prof. Mt. Sinai Sch. Medicine, 2009—. Recipient Rsch. Excellence award, NIH. Mem.: Orgn. Human Brain Mapping, Soc. Neurosci. Office: One Gustave L Levy Place Box 1137 New York NY 10029 Business E-Mail: kristina.simonyan@mssm.edu.

SIMOPOULOS, THOMAS T., physician; b. Marlborough, Mass., Jan. 3, 1969; MA, Brandeis U., 1991; MD, U. Mass., 1995. Dir. interventional pain mgmt. Beth Israel Deaconess Med. Ctr., 2003—. Named Tchr. of Yr. Mem.: ASIPP. Avocation: travel. Office: One Brookline Pl Brookline MA 02445 Office Fax: 617-278-8065. Business E-Mail: tsimopou@bidmc.harvard.edu.

SIMPSON, ANDREW J.G., molecular biologist, researcher; b. Newcastle Under-Lyme, Eng. s. Hubert G. and Barbara M.C. Simpson; m. Catarina B.C. Simpson, Aug. 26, 1993; children: Victoria, William, Leila. PhD, Nat. Inst. Med. Rsch., London, 1980. Postdoc. fellow NIH, Bethesda, Md.; faculty Nat. Inst. Med. Rsch., 1983—89; vis. scientist Centro de Pesquisas René Rachou, Belo Horizonte, Brazil, 1989—95; head lab. cancer genetics Ludwig Inst. Cancer Rsch., São Paulo, Brazil, 1995—2002, dir. James R. Kerr prog., spl. asst. to dir. NYC, 2002, sci. dir. Office: Ludwig Inst Cancer Rsch 605 Third Ave 33rd Fl New York NY 10158 Office Phone: 212-450-1500. Office Fax: 212-450-1555. *

SIMPSON, CHRISTOPHER, medical association administrator; b. Norwich, NY, Mar. 25, 1981; BS in Human Devel., Binghamton U., 2004. Practice mgr., neuroscis. Albany Med. Ctr., 2006—08; practice adminstr. Tenn. Phys. Medicine and Pain Mgmt., 2008—. Mem.: NMGMA, TNMGMA, MGMA. Home: 1738 Lincoya Bay Dr Nashville TN 37214 Personal E-mail: simpsc@gmail.com.

SIMPSON, DAVID ALLEN, osteopath; b. Highland Park, Mich., Mar. 29, 1955; s. Fred Raymond and Mary Theresa (Rossi) S.; m. Anne M. Pawlak, Oct. 20, 1984. BS in Biology with distinction, Wayne State U., Detroit, 1977, MS in Human Anatomy, 1979; DO, Kirksville Coll. Osteo. Medicine, 1983. Diplomate Am. Bd. Neurology and Psychiatry (examiner), Fellow Electrodiagnostic Medicine (examiner). Commd. 2d lt. U.S. Army, 1979, advanced through grades to lt. col., 1997; resident in neurology Botsford Gen. Hosp., Farmington Hills, 1988-91; staff neurologist Mich. Inst. for Neurologists, Farmington Hills, 1991—; from asst. to assoc. clin. prof. U. Mich., 1992—2002, Mich. State U., 2001—, prof. neurology, 2008. Dir. fellowship tng. in neuromuscular disease Mich. Inst. Neurol. Disorder, U. Mich., MDA Clinic, Mich. State U.; dir. Muscular Dystrophy Clinic of Southeastern Mich., Famington Hills, Mich., dir. MDA Clinic, Mich. State U., Lansing, Mich., 2001-, dir. MDA-ALS ctr., 2008-, Farmington Hills, 2009-, Mich. Inst. Neurol. Disorders, MDA Clinic, Farmington Hills, Mich., 2007-, MDA, ALS Ctr., 2008-; physician Wheel-Chair Hockey League, 1999—; lectr. in field. Patentee in field; contbr. articles to profl. jours.; chief editor: Jour. of Am. Coll. of Neurologists and Psychiatrists. 2nd lt. USAR, 1979—84, lt. col. US Army, 1997. Decorated Meritorious Svc. medal, Disting. Svc. medal, Army Commendation medal, Humanitarian Svc. medal, Army Achievement medal, Good Conduct medal, Army Res. medal. Mem. Am. Osteo. Assn., Mich. Assn. Osteo. Physicians and Surgeons, Am. Coll. Neuropsychiatrists, Psi Sigma Alpha, Sigma Sigma Alpha. Roman Catholic. Avocations: golf, skiing, boating. Home: 19550 Laurel Dr Livonia MI 48152-1141 Office: Mich Inst Neurologic Disord Dept Neurology Farmington Hills MI 48045 Office Phone: 734-525-4466, 248-553-0010. Personal E-mail: wchlphysician@msn.com, dr.simpson.mda.mi@gmail.com.

SIMPSON, ELIZABETH, medical research scientist; b. Carshalton, Eng., Apr. 29, 1939; d. Jack Henry Gordon and Olive Rosina Wood; 1 child, Emma Jane. BA, Cambridge U., Eng., 1960, B of Vet. Medicine, 1963. Pvt. practice veterinarian, Fredericton, Canada, 1963-66; virologist Dept. Health and Welfare, Ottawa, Canada, 1965—66; lectr. Cambridge U., Canada, 1966-69; rsch. scientist Nat. Inst. Med. Rsch., Harrow and Mill Hill, England, 1969—71, WHO cons. immunologist Delhi, India, 1970—71; rsch. scientist CRC, Harrow, 1971—84, summer vis. scientist, Jax Lab., 1976—; head transplant biology group Clin. Rsch Ctr. Imperial Coll., Harrow, 1984—2004, head transplant biology group Clin. Sciences Ctr., Hammersmith Hosp. London, 1994—2004, dep. dir. Clin. Sciences Ctr., 1999—2004, emeritus prof. transplantation biology, 2004—, sr. rsch. investigator dept. medicine. Vis. scientist NIH, Bethesda, Md., 1972—73; com. and bd. mem. MRC, 1983—2003, AFRC, UK, 1989—2002; mem. various panels Wellcome Trust Cancer Rsch., 1992—; dir. adv. bd. mem. Roslin Inst., 1994—2001; cons. Ridley Internat. (Cotswold), London, 1998—2001; mem. sci. adv. bd. Cobra Pharms., Keele, England, 1998—2000, Gensel, 1999—2001; mem. programmes com. Cancer Rsch. UK, 2002—06, projects com. chmn., 2003—06, sci. exec. bd. mem., 2004—06, mem. fellowship interview panel, 2002—07; sci. funding advisor Govt. of Republic of Korea, 2006—. Contbr. articles to internat. profl. jours. Fellow: Royal Soc. London, Acad. Med. Sciences London, Royal Vet. Coll. (hon.). Avocations: music, reading, sailing, skiing. Office: Imperial College London Dept Medicine S Kensington Campus SW7 2BU London England Office Phone: 44 020 8383 8282. Business E-Mail: elizabeth.simpson@imperial.ac.uk. *

SIMPSON, GREG B., psychology professor, department chairman; PhD, U. Kansas, Lawrence, 1979. Prof. cognitive psychology U. Kans., chmn. dept. psychology. Contbr. articles to profl. jours. Office: Univ Kans Dept Psychology 1415 Jayhawk Blvd Rm 426 Lawrence KS 66045-7556 Office Phone: 785-864-4131. Office Fax: 785-864-5696. Business E-Mail: gsimpson@ku.edu.

SIMPSON, JACK BENJAMIN, medical technologist, business executive; b. Tompkinsville, Ky., Oct. 30, 1937; s. Benjamin Harrison and Verda Mae (Woods) S.; m. Winona Clara Walden, Mar. 21, 1957; children: Janet Lazann, Richard Benjamin, Randall Walden, Angela Elizabeth. Student, Western Ky. U., 1954-57; grad., Norton Infirmary Sch. Med. Tech., 1958. Asst. chief med. technologist Jackson County Hosp., Seymour, Ind., 1958-61; chief med. technologist, bus. mgr. Mershon Med. Labs., Indpls., 1962-66; founder, dir., officer Am. Monitor Corp., Indpls., 1966-77; founder, pres., dir. Global Data, Inc., Ft. Lauderdale, Fla., 1986—. Mng. ptnr. Astroland Enterprises, Indpls., 1968—, 106th St. Assocs., Indpls., 1969-72, Keystones Ltd., Indpls., 1970-82, Delray Rd. Assoc. Ltd., Indpls., 1970-71, Allisonville Assocs. Ltd., Indpls., 1970-82, Grandview Assocs. Ltd., 1977—, Rucker Assocs. Ltd., Indpls., 1974—; mng. ptnr. Raintree Assocs. Ltd., Indpls., 1978—, Westgate Assocs. Ltd., Indpls., 1978—; pres., dir. Topps Constrn. Co., Inc., Bradenton, Fla., 1973-91, Acrovest Corp., Asheville, N.C., 1980—; dir. Indpls. Broadcasting, Inc.; founder, bd. dirs. Bank of Bradenton, 1986-92; founder, CFO Biomass Processing Tech., Inc., West Palm Beach, Fla., 1996—2008; also bd. dirs. Mem. Am. Soc. Med. Technologists (cert.), Indpls. Soc. Med. Technologists, Fla. Soc. Med. Technologists, Am. Soc. Clin. Pathologists, Am. Assn. Clin. Chemistry, Royal Soc. Health (London), Internat. Platform Assn., Am. Mus. Natural History, Columbia of Indpls. Club, Harbor Beach Surf Club, Fishing of Am. Club, Marina Bay Club (Ft. Lauderdale), Elks. Republican. E-mail: jack_simpson@msn.com.

SIMPSON, JOE LEIGH, obstetrics and gynecology educator; b. Birmingham, Ala., Apr. 9, 1943; s. Robert S. and Winnie (Leigh) S.; m. Sandra A. Carson, May 6, 1978; children: Scott, Reid MD, Duke U., Durham, NC, 1968. Diplomate Am. Bd. Ob-Gyn, Am. Bd. Med. Genetics. Fellow in genetics Cornell Med. Coll., NYC, 1968-73; clin. assoc. NY Blood Ctr., NYC, 1969-73; asst. clin. prof. ob-gyn U. Tex., San Antonio, 1973-75; assoc. prof. ob-gyn., head humsn genetics Northwestern U. Med. Sch., Chgo., 1975-79, prof. ob-gyn, 1979-86; Faculty prof. chmn. dept. ob-gyn U. Tenn., Memphis, 1986-94; prof., chmn. dept. ob-gyn Baylor Coll. Medicine, Houston, 1994—2006, prof. dept. molecular and human genetics, 1994—2006, Fla. Internat. U. Coll. Medicine, Miami, prof. ob-gyn., prof. human molecular genetics; exec. assoc. dean Academic Affairs. Mem. genetics grant rev. and adv. bd. HHS, 1979-82; mem. clin. rsch. panel March of Dimes, 1986-94, chmn. adv. panel reproductive hazards, 1988-92, mem. sci. adv. bd., 1994—; mem. accreditation coun. grad. med. edn. Residency Rev. Com. Med. Genetics, 1993-98; mem. adv. com. Nat. Inst. Child Health and Devel., 1994-97; mem. bd. sci. counselors Intramural Rsch. Nat. Inst. Child Health and Devel., 2005-08. Author: Disorders of Sexual Development, 1976; author: (with others) Genetics in Obstetrics and Gynecology, 1982, 3d edit., 2003, Obstetrics: Normal and Problem Pregnancies, 1986, 5th edit., 2007; co-editor: Genetic Diseases in Pregnancy, 1981, Material Serum Screening for Fetal Genetic Disorders, 1992, Essentials of Prenatal Diagnosis, 1993; contbr. articles to profl. jours. and chpts. to books. Maj. US Army, 1973—75. Recipient numerous awards Nat. Insts. Child Health and Devel., March of Dimes, Dept. Def., Wyeth-Ayerest pub. recognition award Assn. Profs. Ob-Gyn, Dept. Def., 1992. Fellow ACOG (chmn. genetics subcom. 1981-84), Am. Coll. Med. Genetics (treas. 1996-02, pres., 2007-09), Royal Coll. Obstetricians and Gynecologists (hon.); mem. NAS, Inst. Medicine, Am. Gynecol. and Obstet. Soc. (mem. coun. 1997-99), Am. Soc. Reproductive Medicine (bd. dirs. 1984-87, pres. 1993-94), Soc. Gynecologic Investigation (pres. 1998-99, Pres.'s Achievement award 1986, Pres. Disting. Scientist award 2002), Soc. Advancement Contraception (pres. 1995-98), Am. Soc. Human Genetics (mem. program com. 1988-91), Internat. Soc. Prenatal Diagnosis (pres. 1994-98), Internat. Fedn. Fertility Socs. (pres. elect 2010-), Preimplantation Genetic Diagnosis Internat. Soc. (pres. 2006-09). Republican. Presbyterian. Achievements include research in reproductive genetics and prenatal genetic diagnosis including elucidating disorders of sex differentiation and ovarian failure, safety with prenatal genetic diagnosis; recovery fetal cells from maternal blood. Avocations: opera, tennis, travel. Office: Fla Internat Univ Coll Medicine 11200 SW 8th St HLSII 693 Miami FL 33199 Office Phone: 305-348-0653. Business E-Mail: simpsonj@fiu.edu.

SIMPSON, JOHN NOEL, health facility administrator; b. Durham, NC, Feb. 27, 1936; m. Virginia Marshall, June 27, 1959; children: John Noel, William M. Asst. adminstr. Riverside Health Sys., Newport News, Va., 1962-65, assoc. adminstr., 1965-70, Richmond (Va.) Meml. Hosp., 1970-74, sr. v.p., adminstr., 1974-77, exec. v.p., 1977-80, pres., 1980-85, Health Corp. Va., 1985-96; chmn. bd. Bon Secours-Richmond Health System, 1996-97, regional v.p., CEO, 1997-2000, divisional cons., 2000—. Preceptor Sch. Health Adminstrn. Duke U. and Med. Coll. Va., Washington U., St. Louis; bd. dirs. Sun Health, Inc./Sun Alliance, 1979-92, vice-chmn., 1984, chmn., 1985-87; vice-chmn. Med./Bus. Coalition, 1981-83; participant Leadership Met. Richmond; bd. dirs. Ctrl. Va. Health Sys. Agy., 1980-84, Richmond chpt. ARC, 1980-83; mem. Va. Bd. Med. Assistance, 1980-84; mem. joint subcom. studying Va. med. malpractice laws divsn. legal svcs. Gen Assembly of Comm. of Va., 1984; chmn. Va. Health Network, 1989-91; chmn. Hanover Bus. Coun., 1994-95; mem. Gov. Regional Econ. Devel. Adv. Coun., 1994-95. Served with Med. Svc. Corps U.S. Army, 1959-62. Fellow Am. Coll. Healthcare Execs. (Coun. of Regents 1976-82, Edgar C. Hayhow award 1976, bd. govs. 1990-94, regents award sr. exec. level 1995). Fellow Am. Coll. Healthcare Execs. (coun. of regents 1976-82, Edgar C. Hayhow award 1976, bd. govs. 1990-94, regents award sr. exec. level 1995); mem. Am. Hosp. Assn. (chmn. RPBIII 1994-97, del. 1989-93, mem. bd. trustees 1994-97, Va. Hosp. Assn. (dir. 1974-97), del. 1989-93, mem. bd. trustees 1994-97, Va. Hosp. Assn. (dir. 1974-97, chmn.-elect, chmn. 1984-85, Disting. Svc. award 1998), Va. Ins. Reciprocal (chmn. 1977-79), Met. Richmond C. of C. (bd. dirs), Richmond Acad. Medicine (Disting. Svc. award 2000). Republican. Presbyterian. Home Phone: 804-740-0283; Office Phone: 804-379-2930. Personal E-mail: JSIMP22736@aol.com.

SIMPSON, STEVEN QUINTON, physician, researcher; b. Miami, Okla., Aug. 17, 1957; s. Dallas James and Carolyn Sue (Moberly) S.; m. Pamela Janette Nicklaus, May 20, 1989; children: Nathan Edward, Andrew Dallas. BS, Baker U., 1979; MD, U. Kans., 1983. Diplomate Am. Bd. Internal Medicine, Am. Bd. Pulmonary Disease, Am. Bd. Critical Care Medicine; cert. Nat. Inst. Occupational Safety and Health. Intern in internal medicine Kans. U. Med. Ctr., Kansas City, 1983-84, resident in internal medicine, 1984-86; fellow in pulmonary and critical care medicine Rush-Presbyn. St. Luke's Med. Ctr., Chgo., 1986-89, instr. medicine Divsn. Pulmonary and Critical Care Medicine, 1986-89, asst. prof. Divsn. Pulmonary and Critical Care Medicine, 1989-90, U. N.Mex., 1990—; attending physician Rush-Presbyn. St. Luke's Med. Ctr., Chgo., 1989-90, U. N.Mex. Hosp., Albuquerque, 1990—. Adj. scientist Inhalation Toxicology Rsch. Inst., Lovelace Biomed. and Environ. Rsch. Inst., Albuquerque, 1991—; consulting physician Miner's Colfax Med. Ctr., Raton, N.Mex., 1990—, dir. Cardiopulmonary Outreach Program and Black Lung Clinic, 1992-95; attending physician Albuquerque VA Med. Ctr., 1992—, dir. med. ICU, 1993—; presenter 19th Ann. Am. Thoracic Soc. Lung Disease Symposium, N.Mex., 1991, 94, 96, program chair, 1996, U. N.Mex., 1993, Soc. of Critical Care Medicine, 1994. Author: (with others) The Physiologic and Pathologic Effects of Cytokines, 1990, Pulmonary and Critical Care Medicine, 1996, Current Pulmonology and Critical Care Medicine, 1996; contbr. articles to profl. jours. Grantee Chgo. Lung Assn., 1989-91, Am. Lung Assn., 1991-93, Miner's Colfax Med. Ctr., 1992—, N.Mex. Dept. Health, 1993-94. Mem. AAAS, ACP (Cecile Lehman Mayer Rsch. award finalist 1988, 92, Alfred Soffer Rsch. award 1992, DuPont Young Investigator award 1993), Am. Coll. Chest Physicians, Am. Thoracic Soc. (sec.-treas. N.Mex. chpt. 1994-95, pres. 1995-96), Am. Fedn. for Clin. Rsch., N.Y. Acad. Scis., Soc. Critical Care Medicine, Blue Key Nat. Honor Soc., Alpha Delta Sigma. Avocations: writing prose, guitar, hiking. Office: U N Mex Dept Med Pulmonary Divsn 2211 Lomas Blvd NE # 5-acc Albuquerque NM 87106-2745 *

SIMS, ELIZABETH LANEAL, retired healthcare association executive; b. Manila, Ark., May 22, 1948; d. Aaron Neal and Mary Elizabeth (Butler) Shedd; m. Jared Preston Sims, Aug. 31, 1968; children: Jared Neal, David Paul, Christopher Wayne. BA in English, James Madison U., Harrisonburg, Va., 1974. Tchr. English Buffalo Gap HS, Augusta County, Va., 1977—79, Wilson Meml. HS, 1981—88, tchr., sponsor, high sch. yr. book The Hornet's Nest, 1981—88; vol. coord., case mgr. Family Children's Svc., Richmond, 1989—93, program adminstr. sr. svcs., 1993—98; exec. dir. Hanover Mental Health Assn., Inc., Ashland, 1998—2005; exec. dir. Va. affiliate Nat. Alliance on Mental Illness, 2005—06; ret., 2007. Pres. bd. dirs. Hanover Mental Health Assn., 1996-98; bd. dirs. Va. Coalition for Aging Mem. adminstrv. bd. Ctr. United Meth. Ch., 1981—83; mem. staff/parish com. Duncan Meml. United Meth. Ch., 2002—, sec. to adminstrv. bd., 2003—, mem. lay leadership com., 2006—09; sec. Mission Team; bd. dirs. United Way, Richmond, 1995—97, campaign cabinet, 1998—2000; v.p. bd. dirs. Urban League Greater Richmond, 1999—2004; bd. dirs. Urban League Found., 2002—04, Friends of Hanover, 2003—05. Recipient Cert. of Appreciation for Profl. Excellence in Edn., Aug. Co., 1987, Cert. of Appreciation, Urban League, 1998, United Way Svcs., 1997, 1998, 1999, 2000. Mem. Internat. Assn. Psychosocial Rehab. Svcs., Mental Health Assn. Va. (bd. dirs. 1998—), Beta Sigma Phi (Laureate Rho chpt. pres. 2003-07, treas. 2007-, sec. Richmond City Coun.). United Methodist.

SIMS, PAMELA JAN (CERUSSI), writer, minister; b. Little Rock, Sept. 10, 1933; 2 children. Attended, Mt. St. Mary's Acad., St. Scholastica's Coll., Sydney, Delgado Coll., Nola, Tulane U., 1951; DD (hon.). Lic. rev. in Christian ministry specialized svcs. Fla., 2006. Past pres. Ikebana Internat., Le Gals, Inc., 1979—89; pres. Titanic Bead Co.; journalist, notary pub. Fla., 1986—. Tchr. legal secretarial classes, Nola; support writer Pres. George W. Bush, 1999—2008. Author: Pensacola Today mag., Climate mag., introduction to Bonsai & Basic Ikebana; featured on local TV Guide mag. cover Anskebara Design; prin. works include Bonsai and Ikebana design articles; contbr. articles in mags. and newspapers. Vol. Pensacola Art Mus.; leader Girl Scout; team leader Bush/Cheney Inc., 2002—08; mem. Rep. Nat. Com., Rep. Nat. Woman's Club, Pensacola Christian Women's Club, United Intercessors Inc. Recipient Cert. of Recognition, Rep. Nat. Party, 2002, 2006, Congl. Award of Merit, 2004, 8 Blue ribbons and 3 Tri-Color ribbons, Fla. Fedn. Garden Clubs, 2004, Cert. of Appreciation, Rep. Nat. Com., 2005. Mem.: Coxes of FFGC Claneder, Facdar Club, Sweet Bay GC, Dogwood Club, Pensacola Camellia Club & WRL. Achievements include patents pending for AIDS cure other medical discourses. Office Fax: 850-457-1022.

SIMS, RICHARD LEE, retired hospital administrator; b. Columbus, Ohio, Jan. 6, 1929; s. Dorwin Delos and Christine Anna (Hanstein) Sims; m. Marilyn Lou Atkinson, June 2, 1951 (dec. July 2005); children: John Christopher, Steven Paul; m. Norma W. Shilliday, Nov. 17, 2006. BS, Ohio State U., Columbus, 1951. Pres. Doctors Hosp. Found., Columbus, 1977-95; preceptor faculty Ohio State U. Coll. Health Care Adminstrn.; past chmn. Hosp. Coun. Franklin County; ret., 1995. Past chmn. Hosp. Shared Svc. Inc. Past chmn. 1st Cmty. Village Bd.; past chmn. governing bd. 1st Cmty. Ch.; pres. Scioto Valley Health Systems Agy., 1999-2002; pres. Employment for Srs., 1999-2000, Probus, 2003; past chair Columbus area chpt. ARC, emeritus bd. dirs.; mem. 1st Cmty. Found., Drs. Hosp. Devel. Found. Recipient Disting. Svc. award Columbus Jr. C. of C., 1960-63. Fellow Am. Coll. Healthcare Execs. (life), Am. Coll. Osteo. Healthcare Execs. (life); mem. Am. Osteo. Healthcare Assn. (chmn. 1988), Ohio Soc. of Assn. Execs. (past pres.), Ohio Hosp. Assn. (past chmn. bd.), Ohio Osteo. Hosp. Assn. (past pres.), Am. Legion (past post comdr.), Rotary (pres. 1978-79), Columbus Club, Sigma Chi (named Significant Sig 2003). Home: 4848 Slate Run Ct Columbus OH 43220

ŠIMUNIC, SLAVKO, radiologist, educator, consultant; b. Brèko, Bosnia and Herzegovina, Dec. 6, 1931; s. Franjo and Marija Šimunic; 1 child, Romana Šimunic Cvrtila. MD, Faculty Medicine, U. Zagreb, Croatia, 1958; PhD, Faculty Medicine, 1980. Gen. practitioner Med. Ctr. Sisak, Croatia, 1959—64, radiologist, 1967—69; radiology fellow Clin. Hosp. Ctr., Zagreb, 1964—67, radiologist, 1969—97, radiologist,head division angioradiology, 1976—80, radiologist, head dept. diagnostic &intervention radiology, 1980—91, head inst. diagnostic &intervention radiology, 1991—97; head dept. radiology Clin Hosp Osijek, 1997—2002. Prof. radiology Faculty Medicine, U. Zagreb, Croatia, 1982—97, Faculty Medicine, U. Osijek, Osijek, 1997—2002, prof. emeritus, 2002—; asst. dir. Clin. Hosp. Ctr., Zagreb, 1994—2000. Co-editor: (book) Round Table of Interventional Radiology, 1981, Percutaneous Transluminal Angioplasty, 1985; editor-in-chief (book) Who is Who in Croatian Medicine, 1994; mem. editl. bd.: Revue Radiologia Iugoslavica, 1984—91, Radiology and Oncology, 1991—2001. Mem.: Croatian Soc. Radiology (pres. 1992—96), Cardiovasc. & Interventional Radiological Soc. Europe, European Assn. Radiology, Croatian Med. Assn. (Special Appreciation award 2000), Hungarian Soc. Radiology (hon.), Croatian Med. Assn. (hon.). Home: Šubiceva 21 Zagreb 10000 Croatia Home Phone: 385-1-46-40-014. E-mail: slavko.simunic@xnet.hr.

SIMURINA, TATJANA, anesthesiologist; b. Zadar, Croatia, May 28, 1961; d. Joso and Manda Simurina. MD, U. Zagreb, Sch. Medicine, 1988, PhD in Biomedicine and Health, 2011; MSc in Biomedicine & Health, 1996; postgrad, U. Split, Med. Sch., 2005. Cert. Specialist Anesthesia & Intensive medicine Ministry Health, Croatia, 1997. Physician, resident anesthesia Ministry Health, Zagreb, 1992—97; staff anesthesiologist & intensive care practitioner Gen. Hosp., Zadar, 2009—. Mem Croation Med. Assn., 1988, Croation Soc Anesthesiology & intensive Care Unit, 1993; pres. ethics com. Gen. Hosp., 2008—. Active mem., Croatia, 2002—08. Mem.: ESA, ASA, HDRAA, HDAIW, HLZ. Home: Put Simunova 7 Zadar 23000 Croatia Office: Gen Hosp Boze Pericica 5 Zadar 23000 Croatia Office Phone: 385315677. Office Fax: 38523311969; Home Fax: 38523231316. Personal E-mail: tatjana_simurina@yahoo.com.

SINAKIN, HERBERT MORRIS, dermatologist; b. Jersey City, Jan. 26, 1931; s. Richard and Florence Sinakin; m. Inga Silberberg Sinakin; 1 child, William Elias. BS, Rutgers U., New Brunswick, NJ, 1952; MD, SUNY, Bklyn., 1956. Dermatologist pvt. practice, Jersey City, 1960 75, Vineland, NJ, 1975 97; ret., 1997. Mem.: AMA, Am. Acad. Dermatology, NJ State Med. Soc. Avocations: bicycling, exercise, bowling. Home: 1083 E Landis Ave Vineland NJ 08360

SINCLAIR, DANIEL, law educator; b. London, June 30, 1950; LLB, London U., 1972; LLM, Monash U., 1978; PhD, Hebrew U., 1988. Prof. Striks Law Sch., 1997; fellow Jewish law, vis. prof. law Fordham U. Law Sch., 2005—. Home: Ben Tabbai 3 # 21 Jerusalem 93590 Israel Business E-Mail: dsinclair@law.fordham.edu.

SINCLAIR, DAVID A., science educator, researcher; BS with first class honors, U. New South Wales, Sydney; PhD in Molecular Genetics, 1995. Postdoctoral researcher MIT; prof., pathology Harvard Med. Sch., co dir., Paul F. Glenn Laboratories for the Molecular Biology of Aging; assoc. mem. Broad Inst. for Systems Biology; co-founder Sirtris Pharmaceuticals, Waltham, Mass. Mem. steering com. Harvard med. curriculum, Harvard Med. Sch. Bioinformatics Initiative. Contbr. articles to profl. jours. Recipient Helen Hay Whitney Postdoctoral award, Genzyme Outstanding Achievement in Biomedical Sci. award, 2004; Spl. Fellowship, Leukemia Soc., Ludwig Scholarship, Harvard-Armenise Fellowship, Am. Assn. for Aging Rsch. Fellowship, New Scholar, Ellison Med. Found. Achievements include research focused in finding genes and small molecules that slow the pace of aging and prevent the diseases of old age. Office: Dept Pathology Harvard Med Sch New Rsch Bldg Rm 931 77 Avenue Louis Pasteur Boston MA 02115 Office Phone: 617-432-3931. Office Fax: 617-432-6225. Business E-Mail: david_sinclair@hms.harvard.edu.

SINCLAIR, JAMES BURTON, retired plant pathology educator, consultant; b. Chgo., Dec. 21, 1927; s. James Lawrence Sinclair and Helen Marie (Thompson) Owens. BSc, Lawrence U., 1951; PhD, U. Wis., 1955. Grad. rsch. asst. U. Wis., Madison, 1951-55, grad. rsch. assoc., 1955-56; from asst. prof. to assoc. prof. La. State U., Baton Rouge, 1956-65, prof., 1965-68, adminstrv. asst. to chancellor, 1966-68; prof. U. Ill., Urbana, 1968-96, dir. nat. soybean rsch. lab., 1992-96; ret. Co-author: Basic Plant Pathology Methods, 1985, 1995, Principles of Seed Pathology, 1987, 1997, Anatomy and Physiology of Diseased Plants, 1991; contbr. articles to profl. jours. Pres. bd. dirs. W.R. and C.V. Spurlock Mus., Urbana, 1998-00; sec., editor Greater Cmty. AIDS Project, 1996-00; sec. Econ. Devel. Commn., Savoy, 2004-; fin. planning com. Carle Hospice, 2001-02; mem. (docent), dir bd. Spurloch Mus. World Culture, 1998-, mem. pub. com., 2005—; mem., chmn. catalogue collection com. Choir Krannert Art Mus. and Kincaid Pavilion, 1998-2009, docent; active Village Savoy Econ. Devel. Com., 2004-. Sgt. US Army, 1946-47. Recipient Soybean Rsch. Recognition award, Am. Soybean Assn., 1983, Prodn. Rsch. award, 1989, Paul A. Funk award, 1984, Sr. Faculty award for Excellence Rsch., Coll. Agrl. Consumer and Environ. Svc., 1988, Disting. Svc. award, USDA, 1988, Devel. Diagnostic Guide for Soybean Disease award, Am. Soybean Assn., 1899, Disting. Svc. award, Phytopathol. Soc. (north ctrl. divsn.), 1991, Rsch. award, Land of Lincoln Soybean Assn., 1992, Lucia R. Briggs Disting. Achievement award, Lawrence U., 2001. Fellow Am. Phytopathol. Soc., Nat. Acad. Scis. (India); mem. Ill. Crop Improvement Assn. (hon.), Am. Soc. Agronomy (hon.), Rotary (chmn. internat. com. Savoy chpt. 1990-91, v.p. 1991-93, pres. 1993-94, chmn. club svc. conf. 2003-04, chmn. bd. dirs. Inter Global Techs. 2010-). Home: 408 Arbours Dr Savoy IL 61874-9752 Personal E-mail: jsinclai@illinois.edu.

SINCLAIR, JOHN DAVID, psychologist; b. Bluefield, W.Va., Mar. 28, 1943; s. John Thornton and Carolyn June (Biddle) Sinclair; children: Stephanie, Joanna, Pamela, Annette. BA, U. Cin., 1965, MA, 1967; PhD, U. Oreg., 1972. Tchg. asst. U. Cin., 1963—67, rsch. asst., 1964—67; NDEA fellow U. Oreg., Eugene, 1967—70, NSF trainee, 1970—71; coord. psychol. rsch. Alko Group Ltd., Helsinki, 1972—96; sr. rschr. dept. mental health and alcohol rsch. Nat. Inst. Health & Welfare, Helsinki, 1996—; sci. dir. Lightlake Sinclair Ltd., Helsinki, 2003, Lightlake Therapeutics, Inc., 2009—. Docent U. Helsinki, 1994—, lectr., 1978; vis. scientist Ctr. for Advanced Study in Theoretical Psychology, Edmonton, 1979, U. N.C., Chapel Hill, 1980, Ind. U. Sch. Medicine, Indpls., 1988, 90; chmn. bd. ContrAl Clinics, Espoo, Finland, 1996-2000. Co-author: Analyzing Data, 1970, Effect of Centrally Active Drugs on Voluntary Alcohol Consumption, 1975, Animal Models in Alcohol Research, 1980; author: The Rest Principle, A Neurophysiological Theory of Behavior, 1981; permanent exhibit designer Finnish Sci. Ctr., Vantaa, 1984-92, Løten, Norway, 1994— Mem. Internat. Soc. for Biomed. Rsch. on Alcoholism, Internat. Soc. Addiction Medicine, Rsch. Soc. on Alcoholism Achievements include patents for extinction treatment with naloxone, naltrexone and nalmefene for alcoholism, drug addiction and eating disorders; sinclair method. Avocations: painting, writing. Home: Kylmalantie 172A FIN 02550 Evitskog Finland Office: THL Dept MH & Alco Rsch PO Box 33 FIN-00251 Helsinki Finland Office Phone: 358 20 610 8122. Personal E-mail: sinclair_finland@yahoo.com. Business E-Mail: david.sinclair@thl.fi.

SINCLAIR, SARA VORIS, health facility administrator, registered nurse; b. Kansas City, Mo., Apr. 13, 1942; d. Franklin Defenbaugh and Inez Estelle (Figenbaum) Voris; m. James W. Sinclair, June 13, 1964; children: Thomas James, Elizabeth Kathleen, Joan Sara. BSN, UCLA, 1965; grad., Great Basin Pub Health Leadership Inst., 2011. RN, Utah; lic. health care facility adminstr.; cert. health care adminstr. Staff nurse UCLA Med. Ctr. Hosp., 1964-65; charge nurse Boulder Meml. Hosp., 1966, Boulder Manor Nursing Home, 1974-75, Four Seasons Nursing Home, Joliet, Ill., 1975-76; dir. nursing Home Health Agy of Olympia Fields, Joliet, Ill., 1977-79, Sunshine Terr. Found., Inc., Logan, Utah, 1980, asst. adminstr., 1980-81, adminstr., 1981-93; dir. divsn. health systems improvement Utah Dept. Health, Salt Lake City, 1993-97; CEO Sunshine Terr. Found., 1997—2007; long term care cons., 2007; contracted RN monitoring surveyor Ctrs. for Medicare/Med. Svcs., 2007—08; cons. Long Term Care with Haffenreffer & Assocs., Inc., Portland, Oreg., 2008—09; med. surg. dir. Bear River Health Dept., 2010—. Long term care profl. and tech. adv. com. Joint Commn. on Accreditation Healthcare Orgns., Chgo., 1987—91, chmn., 1990—91; adj. lectr. Utah State U., 1991—93, search com. for dir. major gifts, 2001; adj. clin. faculty Weber State U., Ogden, Utah; moderator radio program Healthwise Sta. KUSU-FM, 1985—93; del. White House Conf. on Aging, 1995; chmn. Utah Dept. of Health's Ethics, Instl. Rev. Bd. Com., 1995—97, Utah Dept. Health Rist Mgmt. Com., 1993—97; exec. com. Utah Long Term Care Coalition, 1995, chmn., 1997—2001; oversight com. and long term care tech. adv. group Utah Health Policy Commn., 1996—2000, Health Insight Utah State Coun., 1996—2001; adj. vol. faculty U. Utah Gerontology Ctr., 1997—2008; moderator Living Well Longer Utah Pub. Radio weekly program, 1998—; bd. dirs. Logan Regional Hosp., chair quality assurance, 2001—07; mem. regional adv. bd. Zions Bank, 2001—08; chair quality subcom. Am. Health Care Assn., 2003—05, chair clin. practice com., 2006; chmn. adv. bd. No. Utah Area Health Edn. Ctr., 2001—07; spkr., presenter in field. Contbg. author: Associate Degree Nursing and The Nursing Home, 1988; contbr. articles to profl. jours. Deans adv. coun. Coll. Bus. Utah State U., Logan, 1989—91, mem. presdl. search com., 1991—92; chmn., co-founder Cache Cmty. Health Coun., 1985, chair, 2000; bd. dirs. Bridgerland Area Tech. Coll., 2001—08, Utah Assistive Tech. Found., 2001—04, vice chair; chmn. bd. Hospice of Cache Valley, Logan, 1986, apptd. chmn. Utah Health Facilities Com., 1989—91; chmn. health and human svcs. subcom. Cache 2010, 1992—93; mem. long term care tech. adv. group oversight com. Utah Health Policy Commn., 1997; dir. Health Insight, 1996; trustee Utah State U., 1997—2001; chmn. Utah State U. Trustee's Acad. Affairs Com., 1999—2001; co-chair Living Well Longer Coun., 1997—2004, Cache Cmty. Health Coun., 2000—07; apptd. Utah State Bd. Regents, 2001, re-apptd., 2007; apptd. mem. Utah State Bd. Edn., 2002—06, officer, 2006, chair Am. Coll. of Health Care Adminstrs., 2005; appointee med. care adv. coun. Utah Dept. Health, 2007; bd. dirs. Utah Higher Edn. Assistance Authority, 2002—03; govtl. appointee Utah Commn. on Aging, 2005, 2007, vice chmn., 2005—07; mem. bd. trustees Utah Coll. Applied Tech., 2006—08; mem. exec. com. Utah Partnership Edn., Inc., 2006, bd. trustees, 2006. Recipient Disting. Svc. award, Utah State U., 1989, Total Citizen award, Cache C. of C., 2002, Pioneer award, Utah Area Health Edn. Ctr., 2003, Utah AHEC Pioneer award, 2003, Mary Meredith Dist. Pub. Health Nurse award, Utah Pub. Health Assn., 2004, Disting. Svc. to Cmty. award, Utah State U. Cmty. Assocs., 2007; named Rotarian of Yr., Logan Rotary Club, 2002; named one of Those Who Dare to Care, U. Utah Coll. Nursing Alumni Assn., 2005. Fellow: Am. Coll. Health Care Adminstrs. (convocation and edn. coms. 1992—93, v.p. Utah chpt. 1992—94, bylaws com. 1996—2000, region IX vice gov. 1998—2000, chmn. bylaws com. 1999—2000, chair edn. com. 2000, nominating com. 2000, bd. dirs. 2002—07, chmn. bd. 2005—06, immediate past chair 2006—); mem.: Logan Bus. and Profl. Women's Club (pres. 1989, Woman of Achievement award 1982, Woman of Yr. 1982), Utah Gerontol. Soc. (bd. dirs. 1992—93, chmn. nominating com. 1993—94, bd. dirs. 1995—97, chmn. ann. conf. 1996, pres. 1997), Utah Health Care Assn. (pres. 1983—85, treas. 1991—93, pres. 2000—01, Disting. Svc. award 1991, Sv. award for long term care 1996), Am. Health Care Assn., Nat. Ctr. Assisted Living (non-proprietary v.p. 1986—87, region v.p. 1987—89, exec. com. 1993, cert. facilitator 2002, chmn. quality subcom. 2003—05, chmn. clin. practice com. 2007, Quality award, bd examiners 2009), Am. Assn. Retired People (co-chmn. 2007—), Cache C. of C. (pres. 1991, named Total Citizen of Yr. 2002), Rotary (Logan chpt. chair cmty. svc. com. 1989—90, pres. Logan club 1999—2000, Rotarian of Yr. 2002), Golden Key Nat. Honor Soc. (hon.). Avocations: walking, reading. Office Phone: 435-757-7266. Business E-Mail: saravsinclair@yahoo.com, ssinclair@brhd.org.

SING, ROBERT FONG, physician; b. Camden, NJ, May 29, 1953; s. William Fong and Elizabeth (Maxwell) S.; m. Lauren McNamee, May 11, 1991. BS in Biology, Ursinus Coll., 1975; DO, Coll. Osteo. Medicine and Surgery, 1978. Intern Met. Hosp., Phila., 1978-79, resident in family practice, 1979-80; dir. emergency dept. Springfield (Pa.) Hosp., 1984—2000; dir. sports medicine Sports Sci. Ctr., 1987—; med. dir. Emergency Ambulance Svcs., Inc., 1994-95, Universal Ambulance Svcs., 2005—; owner J. Enright Jewelers, Inc., Swarthmore, Pa., 1995-97; owner, pres. Springfield Sports Emergency Med. Corp., 1999—. Owner, pres. Finish Line Sports, Inc., Phila., 1988-94; sch. and team physician Springfield Sch. Dist., 1989—, Rose Tree-Media (Pa.) Sch. Dist., 1987—; chief med. officer Kent Profl. Bicycling Tour of China, 1995, U.S. Olympic Cycling Trials, 1996. Author: Dynamics of the Javelin Throw, 1984. Med. dir. Springfield Ambulance Corp., 1988—., med. dir. Springfield Fire Co., 2006-. Named to Ursinus Coll. Athletic Hall of Fame, 1985. Fellow Am. Coll. Sports Medicine, Am. Osteo. Acad. Sports Medicine; mem. Am. Coll. Osteo. Emergency Physicians, Am. Coll. Emergency Physicians., NFL Players Assn. (physician, 1995-), Internat Javelin Competition (Finland) (chief med. officer, 2008) Avocations: track and field, classical music, bicycling. Home: 1274 Gradyville Rd Glen Mills PA 19342-9614 Office: Sports Sci Ctr 166 Saxer Ave Springfield PA 19064-2335 Office Phone: 610-328-7262. Personal E-mail: sing3035@aol.com.

SINGAL, PANKAJ, medical educator; b. Haryana, India, Feb. 22, 1977; BDS, MDS, M.C.O.D.S., Mangalore, 1999. Assoc. prof. Dental Coll. & Hosp., 2004—. Recipient Gold medal, M.A.H.E. U. Mem.: ISP. Avocations: music, golf. Office: 173 Red Square Market Hisar Haryana 125001 India Office Phone: 09896150506. E-mail: pankajsingal@rediffmail.com.

SINGER, ALFRED, immunologist, researcher; MD, Columbia U. Clin. tng. Columbia-Presbyn. Med. Ctr., NY; fellow in immunology Rockefeller U., NY; chief Exptl. Immunology Br. Cancer Rsch., Nat. Cancer Inst., NIH, Bethesda, Md., head lymphatic devel. sect. Office: Exptl Immunology Br Ct Cancer Rsch 10 Center Dr Bldg 10 Rm 4B36 Bethesda MD 20892 Office Phone: 301-496-5461. Office Fax: 301-496-0887. E-mail: singera@nih.gov. *

SINGER, DINAH S., federal agency administrator, immunologist, researcher; Grad., MIT, 1969; MPhil, PhD, Columbia U. Post-doctoral fellow Lab. Biochemistry Nat. Cancer Inst., sr. investigator Immunology Branch; sr. sci. officer Howard Hughes Med. Inst., 1998—99; dir. divsn. cancer biology Nat. Cancer Inst., 1999—, chief molecular regulation sect., exptl. immunology br. Mem.: Am. Assn. Immunologists. Office: Nat Cancer Inst Bldg 10 Rm 4836 10 Center Dr Bethesda MD 20892 Office Phone: 301-496-9097. Office Fax: 301-480-8499. Business E-Mail: singerd@mail.nih.gov. *

SINGER, JEFFREY ALAN, surgeon; b. Bklyn., Feb. 2, 1952; s. Harold and Hilda (Ginsburg) S.; m. Margaret Sue Gordon, May 23, 1976; children: Deborah Suzanne, Pamela Michele. BA cum laude, Bklyn. Coll., 1973; MD, N.Y. Med. Coll., 1976. Diplomate Am. Bd. Surgery. Intern Maricopa County Gen. Hosp., Phoenix, 1976-77, resident, 1977-81, mem. teaching faculty, 1981-96; trauma cons. John C. Lincoln Hosp., Phoenix, 1981-83; pvt. practice Phoenix, 1981-87; group pvt. practice Valley Surg. Clinics, Ltd., Phoenix, 1987—, S.W. Surg. Clinics, P.C., Phoenix, 1996-97. Sec.-treas. med. staff Humana Desert Valley Hosp., Phoenix, 1987-89, chief surgery, 1985-87, 91-93, exec. com., 1993-95; adj. asst. prof. divsn. clin. edn. Ariz. Coll. Osteo. Med., Midwestern U., 1998—; mem. adj. clin. faculty Kirksville (Mo.) Coll. Osteo. Medicine. Assoc. editor Ariz. Medicine, 1994-2000, contbg. writer, 2001—. Rep. precinct committeeman, Phoenix, 1986-2000; exec. com. bd. dirs. Goldwater Inst. Pub. Policy Rsch., 2002—; bd. dirs. Ariz. Fedn. Taxpayers, 2007-09; treas., Arizonans Healthcare Freedom, 2009-2010, US Health Freedom Coalition, 2009-. Named Top Doc, Phoenix Mag., 1999. Fellow: ACS, Am. Soc. Abdominal Surgeons, Southwestern Surg. Congress, Internat. Coll. Surgeons; mem.: Med. Choice Ariz. (treas. 2007—09), Maricopa County Med. Soc. (v.p. 1998, bd. dirs. 1998—2002), Ariz. Med. Assn. (bd. dirs. polit. com. 1985—, legis com. 1986—, chmn. bd. dirs. polit. com. 1991—93, Walk the Talk award 2001), Ariz. Sch. Choice Trust (bd. dirs. 1998—2004, adv. bd. 2004—), Alpha Omega Alpha. Avocations: philosophy, politics, history, travel, underwater sports, writing. Office Phone: 602-996-4747. Personal E-mail: dr4liberty@aol.com. Business E-mail: jsinger@valleysurgicalclinics.com.

SINGER, MAXINE FRANK, retired biochemist, science association director; b. NYC, Feb. 15, 1931; d. Hyman S. and Henrietta (Perlowitz) Frank; m. Daniel Morris Singer, June 15, 1952; children: Amy Elizabeth, Ellen Ruth, David Byrd, Stephanie Frank. AB, Swarthmore Coll., 1952, DSc (hon.), 1978; PhD, Yale U., 1957, DSc (hon.), 1994, Wesleyan U., 1977, U. Md.-Baltimore County, 1985, Cedar Crest Coll., 1986, CUNY, 1988, Brandeis U., 1988, Radcliffe Coll., 2000, Williams Coll., 1990, Franklin and Marshall Coll., 1991, George Washington U., 1991, NYU, 1992, Lehigh U., 1992, Dartmouth Coll., 1993, Harvard U., 1994, Yale U., 1994, U. Nebr., 2004; PhD honoris causa (hon.), Weizmann Inst. Sci., 1995. USPHS postdoctoral fellow NIH, Bethesda, Md., 1956—58, rsch. chemist biochemistry, 1958—74; head sect. on nucleic acid enzymology Nat. Cancer Inst., 1974—79; chief Lab. of Biochemistry, Nat. Cancer Inst., 1979—87, rsch. chemist, 1987—88; pres. Carnegie Inst. Washington, 1988—2002, pres. emeritus, 2002—. Regents vis. lectr. U. Calif., Berkeley, 1981. Mem. editl. bd.: Jour. Biol. Chemistry, 1968—74, Sci. mag, 1972—82, chmn. editl. bd.: Procs. of NAS, 1985—88; co-author (with Paul Berg): 3 books on molecular biology and a sci. biog.; contbr. articles to scholarly jours. Chmn. Smithsonian Coun., 1992—93; trustee Wesleyan U., Middletown, Conn., 1972—75, Yale Corp., New Haven, 1975—90, Carnegie Inst. Wash., 2002—; bd. govs. Weizmann Inst. Sci., Rehovot, Israel, 1978—2011; bd. dirs. Whitehead Inst., 1985—94, chmn. bd., 2003—04. Recipient award for achievement in biol. scis., Washington Acad. Scis., 1969, award for rsch. in biol. scis., Yale Sci. and Engring. Assn., 1974, Superior Svc. Honor award, HEW, 1975, Dirs. award, NIH, 1977, DSM, HHS, 1983, Presdl. Disting. Exec. Rank award, 1987, U.S. Disting. Exec. Rank award, 1987, Mory's Cup, Bd. Govs. Mory's Assn., 1991, Wilbur Lucius Cross Medal for Honor, Yale Grad. Sch. Assn., 1991, Nat. Medal Sci., NSF, 1992, Pub. Svc. award, NIH Alumni Assn., 1995, Vannevar Bush award, Nat. Sci. Bd., 1999, Pub. Welfare award, NAS, 2007; named to Washington D.C. Hall of Fame, 2000. Fellow: Am. Acad. Arts and Scis.; mem.: AAAS (Sci. Freedom and Responsibility award 1982, Philip Hauge Abelson prize 2004), NAS (coun. 1982—85, com. sci., engring. and pub. policy 1989—91, chmn. 1999—2005, Pub. Welfare medal 2007), Am. Soc. Cell Biology, Pontifical Acad. of Scis., Inst. Medicine of NAS, Am. Philos. Soc.,

Am. Chem. Soc., Am. Soc. Microbiologists, Am. Soc. Biol. Chemists. Home: 5410 39th St NW Washington DC 20015-2902 Office: Carnegie Inst Washington 1530 P St NW Washington DC 20005-1933

SINGER, PAUL RICHARD, retired ophthalmologist; b. NYC, Feb. 1, 1947; m. Katherine W. Singer, June 13, 1970; children: Amy E., Evan P. BA with honors, U. Rochester, NYC, 1969, MD, 1973. Diplomate Am. Bd. Ophthalmology. Internal medicine intern U. N.C., Chapel Hill, 1973-74, resident in neurology, 1974-75; resident in ophthalmology Washington U. Sch. Medicine, St. Louis, 1975-78, Fight for Sight postdoctoral rsch. fellow dept ophthalmology, 1978-79; pres. Hartford (Conn.) Eye Physicians, 1980—; sr. staff dept. ophthalmology Hartford Hosp., 1980—2008; ret., 2008. Chmn. bd. dirs. Prevent Blindness Conn., Middletown, 1990-92, Combined Health Appeal, Hartford, 1993-95. Recipient Cmty. Svc. award Hartford County Med. Assn., 1993, Robert Polk award for outstanding vol. svc. Prevent Blindness Conn., 1993. Office: Hartford Eye Physicians 55 Nye Rd Ste 103 Glastonbury CT 06033-4394

SINGER, PETER ALEXANDER, biomedical researcher, educator; MD, U. Toronto, 1984; MPH, Yale U., 1990. Intern and resident, dept. medicine Toronto Western Hosp., 1984—86; resident, dept. medicine Toronto Gen. Hosp., 1986—87; fellow, Clin. Med. Ethics U. Chgo., 1987—88; Robert Wood Johnson clin. scholar Yale U. Sch. Medicine, 1988—90; asst. prof. medicine U. Toronto, 1989—94, assoc. mem. Sch. Grad. Studies, 1990—92, assoc. dir. Ctr. Bioethics, 1990—95, assoc. prof. medicine, 1994—99, dir. Joint Ctr. Bioethics, 1995—2006, Sun Life fin. chair in bioethics, 1997—, prof. medicine, 1999—, co-dir. and sr. sci. McLaughlin Rotman Ctr. Global Health, 2006—08, dir. McLaughlin Rotman Ctr. Global Health, 2008—, spl. to the dean of medicine, 2008—; staff physician U. Health Network, 1990—2006; co-dir. Can. Prog. on Genomics and Global Health, 2001—06; dir. PAHO/WHO Collab. Ctr. Bioethics, 2002—06. Fgn. sec., bd. dirs. Can Acad. Health Sciences, 2008—; bd. dirs. Branksome Hall Sch., 2003—. Recipient Nellie Westrman prize for Rsch. in Ethics, Am. Fedn. Clin. Rsch., 1988, Dr. W. Anderson Meml. award, Toronto Hosp., 1992, W. H. Anderson Tchg. award, 1995, Young Educators award, Assn. Can. Med. Colleges, 1995, award for excellence, Yale U. Sch. Pub. Health, 2005, Dales award, U. Toronto, 2005, Dept. Medicine Rsch. award, 2006, Michael Smith prize in Health Rsch., Can. Inst. Health Rsch., 2007; Med. scholar, Can. Life and Health Ins. Assn., 1990, Nat. Health Rsch. scholar, Nat. Health Rsch. and Devel. Prog., 1993. Fellow: ACP (George Morris Piersol Tchg. and Rsch. scholar 1992), Can. Acad. Health Sciences, Royal Coll. Physicians and Surgeons of Can., Royal Soc. Can.; mem.: Inst. Medicine (fgn. assoc.). Office: McLaughlin-Rotman Ctr Global Health Box 50 101 College St Toronto ON M5G 1L7 Canada Office Phone: 416-673-6567. Office Fax: 416-978-6826. E-mail: peter.singer@mrcglobal.org.

SINGER, ROBERT, plastic surgeon; b. Buffalo, Oct. 22, 1942; s. Murray and Fay Singer; m. Judith Harris. Student, SUNY, Buffalo, 1960-63; MD, SUNY, 1967. Lic. physician, Calif.; diplomate Am. Bd. Plastic and Reconstructive Surgery. Resident in gen. surgery Stanford Med. Ctr., Palo Alto, Calif., 1967-69, Santa Barbara Cottage and Gen. Hosp., 1972-74; resident in plastic surgery Vanderbilt U., 1974-76; pvt. practice specializing in emergency and trauma San Diego, 1971-72; pvt. practice plastic, reconstructive and aesthetic surgery La Jolla, Calif., 1976—. Clin. prof. plastic surgery U. Calif., San Diego; sr. staff, chief plastic surgery Scripps Meml. Hosp., La Jolla, 1980-86, vice chmn. dept. surgery, 1989-91; co-chmn. editl. adv. bd. New-Beauty Mag. Contbr. articles to profl. jours. Active San Diego Opera, San Diego Mus. of Man, La Jolla Playhouse, Voices for Children, San Diego Zoo, Mus. Photog. Arts, KPBS, others. Served, Vietnam, ret. lt. comdr. USNR, served in emergency dept., Balboa Naval Hosp., San Diego. Named one of Best Cosmetic Surgeons in Country, Town & Country Mag.; named to Best Doctors in America. Fellow ACS; mem. AMA, Calif. Med. Assn., San Diego County Med. Soc. (named to Best Plastic Surgeons in San Diego), San Diego Internat. Soc. Plastic Surgery (pres. 1988-89), Calif. Soc. Plastic Surgeons (pres. 1995-96), Am. Soc. Aesthetic Plastic Surgeons (pres. 1994-95, traveling vis. prof., Plastic Surgery Leadership award), Internat. Soc. Clin. Plastic Surgeons, Am. Soc. Plastic and Reconstructive Surgeons (trustee 1996—, chmn. bd. trustees 1998-99), J.B. Lynch Soc., Royal Soc. Medicine, Am. Assn. for Accreditation of Ambulatory Surgery Facilities (pres. 1991-2000), San Diego Plastic Surgery Soc. (pres. 1989-90), Aesthetic Surgery Edn. and Rsch. Found. (pres., 2000—) Avocations: tennis, travel, pre-columbian art. Office: 9834 Genesee Ave Ste 100 La Jolla CA 92037-1214 Office Phone: 866-660-0206, 858-455-0240.

SINGER, ROBERT H., biology professor; Prof. neuroscience Yeshiva U. Albert Einstein Coll. Medicine, prof. cell biology, prof. & co-chair anatomy & structural biology. Contbr. articles to profl. jours. Mem.: Am. Acad. Arts & Sciences. Achievements include patents in field. Office: Yeshiva Univ ASB AECOM Golding 601 1300 Morris Park Ave Bronx NY 10461 Office Phone: 718-430-8646 ext. 8647. Office Fax: 718-430-8697. Business E-Mail: rhsinger@aecom.yu.edu.

SINGH, AMARJIT, pharmacist, researcher; b. Shimla, Himachal Pradesh, India, June 19, 1958; s. Harbans Singh and Mehar Kaur; m. Jyoti Amarjit Uppal, Apr. 20, 1983; children: Divyapreet Kaur, Jasjit. B of Pharmacy, Panjab U., Chandigarh, 1978, M of Pharmacy, 1980; PhD, Panjab U., Chandigarh India, 1989. Product devel. chemist Warner Hindustan Ltd., Hyderabad, Andhra Pradesh, India, 1980—83; product devel. officer Ranbaxy Laboratories Ltd., New Delhi, New Delhi, 1983—85; rsch. assoc. Panjab U., 1985—89; dep. mgr. product devel. Nat. Inst. Of Immunology, New Delhi, 1989—91; sr. mgr. rsch. & devel. Max India Ltd, 1991—93; dir. rsch. & devel. Panacea Biotec Ltd, 1993—2003; chief sci. officer Sun Pharm. Industries Ltd., Mumbai, Maharashtra, 2003—05; pres. rsch. & devel. Panacea Biotec Ltd, 2005—. Editor: Jour. Pharm. Scis. & Tech.; contbr. articles to profl. jours. Senator Panjab U., Chandigarh, 1999—2003. Recipient G. P. Nair award, Indian Drug Mfrs. Assn., 1978, Meritorious Svc. award, Nat. Inst. Immunology, 1989, Meritorius Svc. award, Panacea Biotec Ltd, 2003; grantee, USAID, 1989—91. Fellow: Indian Pharm. Assn. (life); mem.: Indo French Ctr. Promotion Advanced Rsch. (advisor 1993—97), Tech. Export Devel. Orgn. (advisor 2001—05), All India Bd. Pharm. Edn. (bd. mem.

2001—05), Controlled Release Soc., Am. Assn. Pharm. Scis. Achievements include 10 US Patents, 10 European Patents, 9 Japanese Patents, 10 Indian Patents. Office: Panacea Biotec Ltd Samarpan N Link Rd Chkl Andheri E Mumbai 400 059 India Office Fax: 91-22-28303133. Personal E-mail: amarjit1821@hotmail.com. Business E-Mail: amarjitsingh@panaceabiotec.com.

SINGH, ANIL KUMAR, botanist; b. Varanasi, India, Oct. 30, 1952; MSc, India, PhD, 1970. Rsch. scientist Ctrl. Inst. Medicinal & Aromatic Plants, Lucknow, India, 1979—, scientist E II, 1998—2005, scientist F, 2005—. Avocations: music, reading. Home: Sector 25 House 06 Indira Nager Lucknow Uttar Pradesh 226016 India Home Fax: 91-522-2342666. Personal E-mail: dr_aksinghcimap@yahoo.co.in.

SINGH, ANIL KUMAR, neurosurgeon; MBBS, MS in Gen. Surgery, MCh in Neurology; diploma, World Fedn. Neurosurgical Soc. Dir. neurosciences Fortis Hosp., India; vis. neurosurgeon Madras Neuro Ctr., Chennai, India. Author numerous sci. articles, (books) Neurosurgery. Recipient Neurosurgery Excellence award, B.B Roy. Mem.: Delhi Neurological Assn. (pres.). Achievements include first to perform a successful Micro Vascular Decompression for Cranial Nerve Dysfunction (Trigeminal Neuralgia) due to Vascular Cross Compression in India; perform Median Corpectomy for Cervical Spondylosis in India; independently carry out a successful Transoral Decompression (Odontoidectomy) for Cranio Vertebral Junction Anomaly; start Direct Trans Nasal Trans Sphenoidal reomoval of Pituitary Tumours in India; was amongst the first persons to start using spinal instrumentation; was amongst the first persons to use Extra Cavitary approach to the Dorsolumbar Region; was amongst the first persons to implant an Artificial Cervical Disc (Bryan's Disc); was amongst the first to start using Steffie's method for fixing a Lumbar Spondylolisthesis. Office: Fortis Hospital B-22 Sector-62 Noida Uttar Pradesh 201301 India Office Phone: 911202400222. *

SINGH, BHUVANESH, otolaryngologist, educator; MD, SUNY, 1991; PhD, U. Amsterdam. Diplomate Am. Bd. Otolaryngology. Resident in otolaryngology SUNY Downstate Med. Ctr., 1991—97; assoc. prof. otolaryngology Cornell Univ.; fellow in head and neck surgery Meml. Sloan- kettering Cancer Ctr., 1997—99; instr. Meml. Sloan- Ketteriing Med. Cancer Ctr., physician. Office: Memorial Sloan- Kettering Cancer Center 1275 York Ave New York NY 10065 Office Phone: 212-639-2000. Office Fax: 212-639-3576.

SINGH, DIVYA, research scientist; b. Raebareilly, India, Mar. 21, 1975; MSc, Lucknow U., 1998; PhD, Jawahar Lal Nehru U., 2005. Scientist Ctrl. Drug Rsch. Inst., 2004—. Rschr. Ctrl. Drug Rsch. Inst., 2004. Mem.: Indian Soc. Bone and Mineral Rsch. Office: MG Marg PO Box No173 Uttar Pradesh Lucknow 226001 India Office Phone: +91-2612411. Business E-Mail: divya_singh@cdri.res.in.

SINGH, HARJIT, medical educator, artist; b. Shimla, Himachal Pradesh, India, Sept. 26, 1936; s. Achal Singh and Sunder Kaur; m. Cecilia Sepulveda, July 17, 1993; children: Namrita, Arshdeep. MB, BS, Govt. Med. Coll., Patiala, India, 1958; MD, Punjabi U., Patiala, 1964. Lic. Punjab Med. Coun., Ludhiana, India, 1958, cert. Ednl. Coun. for Fgn. Med. Grads., 1962, lic. pediat. specialist Dept. Health, Dubai, UAE, 1990. Sr. lectr. in pediat. Govt. Med. Coll., Patiala, Punjab, India, 1965—66, Med. Coll., Rohtak, Haryana, India, 1966—70, asst. prof. pediat., 1970—75, reader in pediat., 1975—76, assoc. prof. pediat., 1976—77, 1978—82, prof. pediat., 1977—78, 1982—84, Arab Med. U., Benghazi, Libya, 1984—88; cmty. pediatrician Am. Hosp., Dubai, United Arab Emirates, 1997—2000; CME program dir. Hackettstown Regional Med. Ctr., NJ, 2002—. Examiner in pediat. Arab Med. U., Benghazi, 1985—88; vis. prof. Sch. Tropical Medicine, Liverpool, 1986—95. Exhibitions include Dubai Internat. Art Ctr., 1991—99, Yolo County Art Coun., 2001, Sussex County Art & Heritage Coun., 2002, Warren County Art Coun., 2002, Triveni Art Gllery, New Delhi, 1970, Represented in permanent collections, India, Can., UK, UAE, US; contbr. scientific papers to profl. publs. Grantee, Indian Coun. Med. Rsch., New Delhi, 1975—88; fellowship in pediat. hematology, WHO, 1974-75. Fellow: RCP, Indian Acad. Pediat., Am. Acad. Pediat., Royal Coll. Pediats. & Child Health London; mem.: Alliance of CME (corr.), Indian Assn. Advancement Med. Edn. (life), Perinatology Forum (life). Office: Hackettstown Regional Med Ctr 651 Willow Grove St Hackettstown NJ 07840 Office Fax: 908-950-6815. E-mail: hsingh@hrmcnj.org.

SINGH, INDU, medical researcher, educator; b. Rohtak, Haryana, India, Feb. 12, 1961; d. Inder Pal Singh and Saroj Parmar; m. Dig Vijay Singh, July 7, 1984; 1 child, Karun Raghuvanshi. MS in Histopath, Kurukshetra U., Haryana, 1982; MS in Applied Scis., Charles Sturt U., Wagga Wagga, NSW, Australia, 2000; PhD, RMIT U., Bundoora, Victoria, Australia, 2008. Rsch. fellow Post Grad. Inst. Med. Edn. & Rsch., Chandigarh, Haryana, 1983—84; core lab. scientist Hong Kong Adventist Hosp., 1984—92, scientist in-charge-haematology & blood banking, 1992—98; part time med. scientist Melbourne Pathology, Victoria, 1999—; part time academic haematology, sch. of med. scis. RMIT U., 2001—08, unit leader & lectr. haematology, 2008—. Part time med. lab. scientist Cabrini Hosp., Malvern, Victoria, 2001—. Contbr. articles to profl. sci. publs. (Chris Francis Meml. award, 2007). Mem.: Inst. Bio Med. Scientists, Australian Inst. Med. Scientists. Home: 5 Dalray Close Mill Park Victoria 3082 Australia Office: RMIT Univ Plenty Rd 3083 Bundoora West Campus VIC Australia Office Phone: 61 3 99257590. Office Fax: 61 3 99257063. Business E-Mail: indu.singh@rmit.edu.au.

SINGH, JASVINDER, medical educator; b. India, July 26, 1971; MBBS, U. Coll. Med. Scis., 1993; MPH, U. Minn., 2003. Assoc. prof. Birmingham Vets. Affairs Med. Ctr. and U. Ala., 2009—. Steering com. mem. OMERACT, 2010—. Fellow: Am. Coll. Rheumatology. Avocation: birdwatching. Office: 510 20th St S FOT 805B Birmingham AL 35242 Business E-Mail: jasvinder.singh@va.gov.

SINGH, LAISHRAM RAKESH, research scientist; b. Imphal, India, May 28, 1979; PhD in Biochemistry, Molecular Biology, 2001. Rsch. assoc. U. Wis., 2008—; invited grad. rschr. Osaka U., Japan. Recipient Gold medal, Manipur U., 2001; fellowship, Am. Heart Assn., Jr. and Sr. Rsch. fellowship, CSIR, Summer Rsch. fellowship, Indian Inst.

Sci., Nat. Merit scholarship, India. Mem.: Sci. Congress Assn., Faculty 1000 Biology. Avocations: bicycling, reading, music. Office: 1300 University Ave MSC R-3720 Madison WI 53706 Business E-Mail: lsingh@wisc.edu.

SINGH, MANMOHAN, medical association administrator; b. India, Nov. 8, 1964; PhD, NII, Delhi, India, 1992. Global head, vaccine formulation sci. Novartis Vaccines, 1996—. Mem.: AAPS. Office: 45 Sidney St Mail Stop 3105D Cambridge MA 02139 Business E-Mail: manmohan.singh@novartis.com.

SINGH, NARENDRA, cardiologist, researcher, medical educator; b. Saraiya, Uttar Pradesh, India, June 10, 1963; Can., US; s. Rudra Prasad and Manorma Singh; m. Mitra Kumari Kandhal, June 26, 1993; children: Shailin Raj, Ishaan Vivek, Vrushali Kumari. BS in Biochemistry, Dalhousie U., Halifax, Can., 1983, MD, 1987. Diplomate Am. Bd. Internal Medicine, Am. Bd. Cardiovascular Disease, Cert. Bd. Nuclear Cardiology, NASPE Testamur. Rotating intern St. Michael's Hosp., U. Toronto, 1987—88, resident in internal medicine, 1988—91, cardiology fellow, 1991—93; cardiologist Centenary Cardiology Assocs., Toronto, Ont., Canada, 1994—2002, Northside Cardiology P.C., Atlanta, 2002—10, Atlanta Heart Specialists LLC, 2010—; dir. rsch. Northside Cardiology P.C., Atlanta, 2003—10; dir. Scarborough Cardiology Rsch., Toronto, 1996—2002; cardiology sect. chair Northside Hosp., Atlanta, 2003—06. Lectr. U. Toronto, 1994—2002; med. dir. Pacemaker/ICD Programme, 1995—2002, Cardiac Cath Lab., 1999—2001; co-founder Greater Toronto Area Cmty. Cardiologists, 1995—2001; clin. asst. prof. Emory U. Sch. Medicine, Atlanta, 2002—; mem. regional lipid adv. bd. Merck, Canada; mem. nat. adv. bd. Pfizer, Canada; regional spkrs. bur. Pfizer, GSK, Novartis, Sanofi Aventis, Boehringer Ingelheim; heart failure adv. bd. Saint Joseph's Hosp.; vice chair Saint Joseph's Rsch. Inst., 2009—; CME chairperson GA Am. Coll. Cardiology, 2006—10. Contbr. articles to profl. jours. Bd. dirs. Hosp. Found., Toronto, 1998—2002. Recipient award plaque in recognition for contbns., Greater Toronto Area Cmty. Cardiologists, Leadership award, Northside Hosp., 2006, Disting. Svc. award, Ga. chpt.-ACC, 2010; scholar, Dalhousie U., 1981, 1983, 1985; Rsch. fellow, U. Toronto, 1993. Fellow: Am. Coll. Cardiology (councillor, Atlanta region, Ga. chpt. 2008—, mem. nat. needs assessment working group), Royal Coll. Physicians and Surgeons Can. (cert. in cardiology/internal medicine), Am. Heart Assn. (bd. dirs. Atlanta 2008—09); mem.: Am. Soc. Nuc. Cardiology, Med. Assn. Ga., Can. Med. Assn., Med. Staff Soc. (bd. govs., mem. med. adv. com. 1995—97, pres. Centenary site, mem. strategic planning com. 1996), Can. Cardiovasc. Soc. (coun. mem. 1999—2002, nat. sec. 2000—02, coun., mem. exec. com., chairperson membership com. 2000—02). Avocations: travel, golf, theater. Office: Atlanta Heart Specialists LLC 1505 Northside Blvd Ste 2500 Cumming GA 30041 Home: 6350 Haddington Ln Johns Creek GA 30024 Office Phone: 678-679-6800. Office Fax: 678-679-6804. Business E-Mail: drsingh@ahsmed.com.

SINGH, RAJENDRA K., toxicologist; b. India, May 25, 1968; PhD, Avadh U., India, 2000. Postdoc. fellow U. ND, 2003—06; postdoc. assoc. U. Miami, 2006—. Recipient Excellence Rsch. award, Soc. Toxicology. Mem.: Soc. Toxicology, Am. Assn. Cancer Rsch. Office: 1011 NW 15th St Gauiter Res Bldg Miami FL 33136 Personal E-Mail: singhrtkbio@rediffmail.com.

SINGH, RAJENDRA PRATAP, surgeon; b. Allahabad, India, Sept. 16, 1939; arrived in U.S., 1973; m. Sushma Singh, 1971; children: Sonia, Jay D. MB, BChir, SN Med. Coll., Agra, India, 1963, MS, 1966. Diplomate Am. Bd. Surgery, 1978. Ho. surgeon SN Med. Coll., Agra, India, 1963—67; registrar gen. thoracic surgery England, 1968—72; surgical and chief resident Bronx, Lebanon, Barh, Beckley, W.Va., 1974—76; attending surgeon VA Hosp., Beckley, 1976—78, Barh and Raleigh Gen. Hosp., Beckley, 1978—; chief surgery Raleigh Gen. Hosp., Beckley, 2001—. Asst. clin. prof. Marshall and W.Va. U.; bd. trustees Raleigh Gen. Hosp. Bd. trustees Raleigh Gen. Hosp. Fellow: Am. Coll. Surgeons, Royal Coll. Surgeons Eng., Royal Coll. Surgeons Edinburgh; mem.: Raleigh County Med. Soc., W. Va. Med. Assn. Office: 201 Wooderest Dr Beckley WV 25801

SINGH, SAURABH, orthopedic surgeon; b. Gorakhpur, Uttar Pradesh, India, June 21, 1978; s. Rana Pratap and Shubhra Singh; m. Shaivya Singh, Nov. 27, 2004. MS in Orthop., NHL Med. Coll., Ahmedabad, 2005, MCh in Orthop., U. Seychelles, 2008. Registrar U.C.M.S, Delhi, India, 2005, A.I.I.M.S, New Delhi, 2005—07; cons. I.M.S, Varanasi, India, 2007—; lectr. Contbr. articles. Mem. IMA, Delhi. Wb Carell Shoulder fellowship, Carell Clinic, 2007, Travelling fellow, J.P.O.A, 2008. Mem.: IAS, IOA, AAOS. Achievements include research in bhu bicentric bipolar evaluation. Home: 4/59 Vishal Khand Gomti Nagar Lucknow 226010 India Office: IMS BHU Lanka Varanasi India Personal E-Mail: drsaurabhsinh@gmail.com.

SINGHAL, BHIM SEN, neurologist; b. Mt. Abu, India, Jan. 23, 1933; s. Ghisa Ram and Mohiribai Singhal; m. Asha Gupta, May 5, 1962; two children. MD, Bombay U., 1959. Neurologist Bombay Hosp., India, 1962—; prof., head dept. neurology Bombay Hosp. Inst., 1991—2009; dir. neurology Bombay Hosp., 2009—. From asst. prof. to prof. neurology Grant Med. Coll., Bombay, 1963-91; neurologist Sir J.J. Groups Hosps., Bombay, 1963-91. Fellow Royal Coll. Physicians (Edinburgh), Royal Coll. Physicians (London). Avocations: travel, reading, music. Office: Bombay Hosp Med Rsch Ctr 12 Marine Lines 400 020 Mumbai India Home Phone: 022-3630639; Office Phone: 022-22068787. Business E-Mail: bssingl@vsnl.com.

SINGHAL, SUNIL, thoracic surgeon, educator; b. Allentown, Pa., Feb. 18, 1973; BA, Dartmouth Coll., 1994; MD, U. Pa. Sch. Medicine, 1998. Asst. prof. surgery U. Pa. Sch. Medicine, 2008—; Chief, thoracic surgery Phila. Veterans Affairs Med. Ctr., 2008—11. Recipient Clin. Investigator award, Soc. Surg. Oncology, Clin. award, Soc. U. Surgeons. Mem.: AAAS, Soc. Thoracic Surgeons, Assn. Academic Surgery, Am. Assn. Cancer Rsch. Avocation: swimming. Office: 3400 Spruce St 6 White Bldg Philadelphia PA 19104 Office Fax: 215-573-4469. Personal E-Mail: sunil.x.singhal@gmail.com.

SINGH-DONCELL, JULIET, director; b. Guyana, Feb. 21, 1970; BA, Binghamton U., 1993; MA, LI U., 2009. CME program specialist Weill Cornell Med. Coll., 2005—10, asst. dir. continuing med. edn., 2010—. Home: 99-72 211th Pl Queens Village NY 11429 Business E-Mail: jsingh@med.cornell.edu.

SINGLETON, MARVIN AYERS, state legislator, otolaryngologist; b. Baytown, Tex., Oct. 7, 1939; s. Henry Marvin and Mary Ruth Singleton. BA, U. of the South, 1962; MD, U. Tenn., 1966. Diplomate Am. Bd. Otolaryngology. Intern City of Memphis Hosps., 1966-67; resident in surgery Highland Alameda City Hosp., Oakland, Calif., 1967-68; resident in otolaryngology U. Tenn. Hosp., Memphis, 1968-71; fellow in otolaryngic pathology Armed Forces Inst. Pathology, Washington, 1971; fellow in otologic surgery U. Colo. at Gallup (N.Mex.) Indian Med. Ctr., 1972; practice medicine specializing in otolaryngology/allergies Joplin, Mo., 1972—. Founder, operator Home and Farm Investments, Joplin, 1975—, staff mem. Freeman Hosp., Dameron Hosp. Stockton, St. John's Hosp., Joplin; cons. in otolaryngology Mo. Crippled Children's Service; pres. Ozark Mfg. Co., Inc., Joplin; mem. St. Joaquin Commn. on Aging, 2005—; dir. St. Mary's Interfaith Svcs., Stockton, 2007—; med. dir. Health Choice NW Mo. Mem. Internat. Arabian Racing Bd., 1983-88; mem. Mo. State Senate, 1990-2003; del. Rep. Nat. Conv., 1988, 92. Served with USNG, 1966-72. Fellow Am. Coll. Surgeons, Am. Acad. Otolaryngologic Allergy (past pres.), Am. Assn. Acad. Asthma, Allergy and Immunology; mem. AMA (Mo. del.), Mo. State Med. Assn., So. Med. Assn., Mo. State Allergy Assn., Ear Nose & Throat Soc. Mo. (past. pres.), Calif. Med. Assn. (trustee 2005—), San Joaquin Med. Soc. (pres. 2006-07), Masons (32d degree), Sigma Alpha Epsilon, Phi Theta Kappa, Phi Chi. Republican. Episcopalian. Office: 7373 W Ln Stockton CA 95210 Home: 1888 E Brookhaven Dr Fayetteville AR 72703-3781 Home Phone: 209-951-7273; Office Phone: 209-476-5623. Personal E-mail: senatorsingleton@hotmail.com.

SINGLETON, TANYA, nursing educator; b. Tuscaloosa, Ala., July 23, 1958; d. Crimpton and Inez Virginia (Powe) Singleton; children: David, Edward, Brittany Summerhill; m. Michael B. Brown, Nov. 2003. BS in Nursing, U. Ala., 1982; MPH in Maternal-Child Health, George Washington U., 1997; MA in Counseling, Liberty U., 2010. Cert. high risk perinatal nurse, childbirth educator Lamaze; cert. lactation cons. Commd. 2d lt. U.S. Army, 1986, advanced through grades to capt., 1988; staff nurse labor and delivery Druid City Hosp., Tuscaloosa, 1982—83, Huntsville (Ala.) Hosp., 1983—86; perinatal counselor Cen. North Ala. Health Svcs. Inc., Huntsville, 1984—86; staff nurse Tripler Army Med. Cu., Honolulu, 1986—90, asst. head nurse newborn nursery, staff nurse labor and delivery, childbirth counselor and inpatient lactation cons. DeWitt Army Hosp., Ft. Belvoir, Va., 1990—92; maternal infant health educator Providence Hosp., Washington, 1992—95; instr. Montgomery Coll. Sch. of Nursing, 1994; founder Sacred Conceptions Childbirth and Parenting Svcs., 1996—; exec. dir. Women's Wellness Ctr., Fredericksburg, Va., 1999—2000; tobacco cessation coord. MediCorp Health Sys., Fredericksburg, 2001—03; perinatal bereavement coord. Prince William Health Sys., 2002—04, nurse recruiter, 2004—, 2004—. Mem. low risk neonatal test com. Nat. Certification Corp., 1994—95; rsch. assoc. NIH-DC Initiative to Decrease Infant Mortality in D.C. Pride in Parenting Study, 1995—; pres. Rappahannock Teen Awareness Program; organizer Rappahannock Healthy Families Initiative Planning Bd., Ptnrs. in Prevention VA Planning Dist. XVI.; lactatian cons. child birth educator Mary Wash. Healthcare, 2000—; instr. Career Tng. Solutions Fredericksburg, Va., 2011—. Chair health com. Stafford County br. NAACP. Maj. USAR, 1995—2000, instr. 91C program 80th Tng. Divsn. USAR, res. comp. cmdr. 91W transition program USAR, 2001—04, Ft. Lee. Mem. ANA, Assn. Women's Health, Obstetric and Neonatal Nurses, Internat. Childbirth Edn. Assn., Sigma Theta Tau., Lamaze Internat. Home: 6917 Smith Station Rd Spotsylvania VA 22553-1808 Home Phone: 540-898-0560. Personal E-mail: singmo40@aol.com.

SINHA, AKHOURI A., cell and development biologist, researcher; b. Churamanpur, Bihar, India, Dec. 17, 1933; arrived in U.S., 1961; s. Akhouri Chandra B. and Bittan Devi Sinha; m. Dorothy Kay Pamer, Sept. 29, 1979. BSc, Allahabad U., India, 1954; MSc, Patna U., India, 1956; PhD, U. Mo., 1965. Lectr. Ranchi (India) U., 1956—61; asst. prof. U. Wis., Eau Claire, 1965—67; sr. scientist U. Minn., Mpls., 1967—69; rsch. scientist VA Med. Ctr., Mpls., 1969—. Prof. U. Minn., 1981—. Contbr. articles to profl. jours. Hindu. Avocations: cross country skiing, photography, travel, reading. Office: Rsch Svcs One Veterans Dr Minneapolis MN 55417 Office Phone: 612-467-2846. Business E-Mail: sinha001@tc.umn.edu.

SINHA, BINOD K., urologist, educator; b. India, June 10, 1951; MBBS, MD, Patna Med. Coll. India, 1976. Urology resident U. Minn., 1985; dir. Urology Care Ctrl. NJ, 1995—. Clin. asst. prof. surgery U. Medicine and Dentistry, 2008. Fellow: ACS. Avocations: golf, boating, travel. Office: 4 Progress St Edison NJ 08820 Office Fax: 908-754-9287. E-mail: drsinha007@yahoo.com.

SINHA, RENU, anesthesiologist, educator; b. Kanpur, India, Oct. 20, 1971; MBBS, BRD Med. Coll., Gorakhpur, India, 1994; MD in Anaesthesia, MLB Med. Coll., Jhansi, India, 2000. Rschr., physician All India Inst. Med. Scis., New Delhi, 2000, asst. prof., 2005—09, assoc. prof., 2009—. Mem.: Indian Soc. Ophthalmologist, Indian Soc. Anaesthesiologist. Office: S-6 1st Fl OPD Block RP Centre New Delhi 110029 India Office Fax: 91-11-26588911. Personal E-mail: renuagarwal4@rediffmail.com.

SINHA, RITESH KUMAR, physician; b. Birmingham, West Midlands, Dec. 13, 1976; s. Shailendra Kumar and Punam Sinha. MD in Medicine with honors, U. Latvia, 2003, PhD in Family Medicine, 2006; PhD in Pharmacology with honors, St. Regis U., 2003. Diploma in gen. medicine and surgery, geriat. medicine, ob-gyn., minor surgery, med. ethics, electrocardiography, occupl. medicine, pub. health, cardiology and med. edn. 2006. Cons. Nirvana Health Spa, Southport, England, 1998—2005, sr. mgr., 1999—2004; resident, sr. ho. officer P.Stradins U. Hosp., Riga, Latvia, 2003—05; resident P. Stradins U. Hosp., 2005—06. Adv. bd. Nirvana Health Spa, Southport, Lancashire, 1999—2003, dir., 2003—04. Active Sefton Cmty. Panel, England, 2006. Fellow: Royal Soc. Tropical Medicine and Hygiene (licentiate), Royal Soc. of Medicine (licentiate), Royal Soc. for the Promotion of Health (licentiate); mem.: U.K. Gen. Med. Coun. (licentiate), Latvian Med. Assn. (licentiate), Am. Coll. of Clin. Pharmacology (licentiate). Achievements include patents pending for advanced informative intra communications technology. Avocations: sailing, race cars, architectural design, interior decorating, travel. Home: Saroswati 15 Margaret Road Merseyside Liverpool L23 6TR England Office Phone: 44-0798-0192598. Personal E-mail: dr_rks@hotmail.com.

SINICI, EBRU, psychologist; b. Turkey, Mar. 12, 1973; MS, 1996. Psychologist Mil. Hosp., 1996—, EMDR CBT PPT. Office: Gata Ruh Sagligi Ad Etl&#304 Ankara 06100 Turkey Office Phone: 0 312 3044501. E-mail: esinici@gmail.com.

SINKFORD, JEANNE CRAIG, dental association administrator, retired dentist, dean, educator; b. Washington, Jan. 30, 1933; d. Richard E. and Geneva (Jefferson) Craig; m. Stanley M. Sinkford, Dec. 8, 1951; children: Dianne Sylvia, Janet Lynn, Stanley M. III. BS, Howard U., 1953, MS, 1962, DDS, 1958, PhD, 1963; DSc (hon.), Georgetown U., 1978, U. Med. and Dentistry of N.J., 1992, Detroit Mercy Med. Coll., 1996, Meharry Med. Coll., 2008. Instr. prosthodontics Sch. Dentistry Howard U., Washington, 1958—60, faculty dentistry, 1964—, rsch. coord., chmn. dept. restorative dentistry, assoc. dean, 1968—75, dean, 1975—91, prof. Prosthodontics Grad. Sch., 1977—91, dean emeritus, prof., 1991—; spl. asst. Am. Assn. Dental Schs., 1991—93, dir. office women and minority affairs, 1993—97, assoc. exec. dir., 1998—, Am. DEntal Edn. Assn. Instr. rsch. and crown and bridge Northwestern U. Sch. Dentistry, 1963—64; cons. prosthodontics and rsch. VA Hosp., Washington, 1965—; resident Children's Hosp. Nat. Med. Ctr., 1974—75; cons. St. Elizabeth's Hosp.; mem. attending staff Freedman's Hosp., Washington, 1964—; adv. bd. DC Gen. Hosp., 1975—; mem. nat. adv. dental rsch. coun. Nat. Bd. Dental Examiners; mem. ad hoc adv. panel Tuskegee Syphilis Study for HEW; sponsor DC Pub. Health Apprentice Program; mem. adv. coun. to dir. NIH; adv. com. NIH/NIDR/NIA Aging Rsch. Coun.; rschr. Advisory Com. Womans Health; mem. dental devices classification panel FDA; mem. select panel for promotion child health, 1979—80; mem. spl. med. adv. group VA; bd. overseers U. Pa. Dental Sch., Boston U. Dental Sch.; bd. advisors U. Pitts. Dental Sch.; mem. bd. visitors Temple U. Sch. Dentistry, Howard U Coll. Dentistry, Ind. U. Sch. Dentistry, W.Va. U. Health Ctr.; mem. anat. rev. bd. DC NRC Governing Bd.; cons. FDA; mem. Nat. Adv. Dental Rsch. Coun., 1993—96; active NRC Governing Bd. Mem. Mayor's Block Grant Adv. Com., 1982; mem. parents' coun. Sidwell Friends, 1983; adv. bd. United Negro Coll. Fund, Robert Wood Johnson Health Policy Fellowships; mem. women's health task force NIH; bd. dirs. Girl Scouts U.S.A., 1993—95; pres. NY Adv. Coun. NIH Office Rsch. Women's Health, 2008—; bd. visitors Temple U. Sch. Dentistry, W.Va. U. health Scis. Ctr., Howard U. Coll. Dentistry. Fellow Louise C. Ball fellow grad. tng., 1960—63. Fellow: Internat. Coll. Dentists (Merit award), Am. Coll. Dentists (mem. editl. bd. 1988—2006, sec.-treas. Wash. met. sect.); mem.: ADA (chmn. appeal bd. coun. on dental edn. 1975—82), Exec. Leadership Acad. Women (adv. bd.), RWJF, Soc. Am. Indian Dentists, Robert Wood Johnson Found., Nat. Adv. Coun. Rsch. Women's Health, Children's Dental Health Found. (mem. adv. bd.), Fedn. Dentistry Internat., Links Inc., Dean's Coun. (chair), Smithsonian Assocs., NY Acad. Scis., Am. Soc. Dentistry for Children, Inst. Medicine of NAS (coun.), Nat. Dental Assn., Fed. Prosthodontic Orgn., Am. Prosthodontic Soc., Am. Pedodontic Soc., Leadership in Acad. Medicine (adv. bd.), Health Professions Partnership Initiative (adv. bd.), Assn. Am. Women Dentists, Wash. Coun. Adminstrv. Women, So. Conf. Dental Deans (chmn.), Inst. Grad. Dentists (trustee), Am. Inst. Oral Biology, Dist. Dental Soc., Internat. Assn. Dental Rsch., Am. Soc. for Geriatric Dentistry (bd. dirs.), North Portal Civic League, Golden Key, Beta Kappa Chi, Psi Chi, Omicron Kappa Upsilon, Phi Beta Kappa, Sigma Xi (pres.). Achievements include first female dental dean at Howard U., and in the U.S.A.

SINNOTT, BRIDGET P., medical educator; b. Ireland, Feb. 21, 1975; MD, UCD, 1999. Asst. prof. medicine UTSW Dallas, 2009—. Office: 5161 Harry Hines Blvd 6th Fl Ste 10 Dallas TX 75390-8885 E-mail: bridgetsinnott@yahoo.com.

SINNOTT, DANIEL J., educational association administrator; Attended, Mt. St. Mary's Coll.; M in Health Care Adminstrn., Temple U. Sr. v.p., Ops. Cath. Health Initiatives, Denver; pres., CEO Nazareth Hosp., St. Agnes Med. Ctr., St. Francis Hospital, Wilmington, Del.; CEO, exec. dir. Temple U. Hosp., 2003; advisor, Access Leadership Ascension Health; pres. Sinnott Exec. Consulting; lectr. I.E.D.C. Bled Sch. Mgmt., Wharton Sch. Bus. Bd. dirs. Pa. Catholic Health Assn. Office: Wharton Business School 3700 Hamilton Walk Philadelphia PA 19104-6016 Office Phone: 215-898-5000. Office Fax: 215-573-2093. Business E-Mail: dsinnott@upenn.edu.

SINNOTT, JOHN THOMAS, internist, educator; b. Reading, Pa., May 16, 1948; s. John Thomas and Josephine (Mallon) S.; m. Barbara Ballentine, May 30, 1970. BA, Columbus Coll., Ga., 1971; MA, U. South Fla., 1973; MD, U. South Ala., 1978. Diplomate Am. Bd. Internal Medicine, Am. Bd. Infectious Diseases. Resident in internal medicine U. South Fla. Coll. Medicine, Tampa, 1978-81, infectious disease resident, 1981-83, asst. prof., 1983-87, assoc. prof., 1987-92, prof. and dir. infectious diseases, 1991—, James Cullison prof. medicine, 2000—, assoc. dean internat. affairs, 2005—; dir. epidemiology Tampa Gen. Healthcare, 1985—, mem. med. exec. bd., 1992—, vice chief staff, 1992-94, chief staff, 1994-96. Dir. S.W. Fla. Tissue Bank, 1987—, dir. epidemiology Shriners Hosp. for Children, 1987; co-founder CHART India, 1998-; mem. adv. bd. Lifelink Fla., 1988-; trustee Tampa Gen. Hosp. Found., 2000-, Hillsborough C.C. Found., 2003-; mem. bd. dirs. FoodTech, 2002- chmn. 2005- Editor jour. Infections in Medicine, 1994—. Recipient hon. alumnus award U. South Fla. Coll. Medicine, 1998, Outstanding Clin. Prof. award, 1986-92; Humanism in Medicine award NBI Healthcare Found., 1998, award For AIDS Care Today, 1998; John T. Sinnott Outstanding Clin Prof. award named in his honor U. So. Fla. Coll. Medicine, 1992. Fellow ACP, Infectious Disease Soc. Am. (fin. com. 1998—); mem. Soc. Hosp. Epidemiology (fin. com. 1998—), Alpha Omega Alpha. Avocations: fishing, flying. Home: 9666 Oak St NE Saint Petersburg FL 33702-2610 Office: Tampa Gen Hosp Dept Infectious Disease Tampa FL 33601-1289 *

SINSHEIMER, ROBERT LOUIS, retired academic administrator, educator; b. Washington, Feb. 5, 1920; s. Allen S. and Rose (Davidson) S.; m. Flora Joan Hirsch, Aug. 8, 1943 (div. 1972); children: Lois June (Mrs. Wickstrom), Kathy Jean (Mrs. Vandagriff), Roger Allen; m. Kathleen Mae Reynolds, Sept. 10, 1972 (div. 1980); m. Karen Current, Aug. 1, 1981. S.B., MIT, 1941, MS, 1942, PhD, 1948. Staff mem. radiation lab. MIT, Cambridge, 1942-46; assoc. prof. biophysics, physics dept. Iowa State Coll., Ames, 1949-55, prof., 1955-57; prof. biophysics Calif. Inst. Tech., Pasadena, 1957-77, chmn. div. biology, 1968-77; chancellor U. Calif., Santa Cruz, 1977-87, chancellor emeritus, 1987—, prof. Santa Barbara, 1988-90, prof. emeritus, 1990—. Editor: Jour. Molecular Biology, 1959-67, Ann. Rev. Biochemistry, 1966-72. Named Calif. Scientist of Year, 1968; recipient N.W. Beijerinck-Virologie medal Netherlands Acad. Sci., 1969 Fellow Am. Acad. Arts and Scis.; mem. Am. Soc. Biol. Chemists, Biophys. soc. (pres. 1970), AAAS, Nat. Acad. Scis. (mem. council 1970-73, chmn. bd. editors Proc. 1972-80), Inst. Medicine. Achievements include discovery of single-stranded DNA, circular DNA; research in first in vitro replication of infective DNA. Avocations: photography, travel. Office: U Calif MCD Biology Santa Barbara CA 93106 Business E-Mail: sinsheim@lifesci.ucsb.edu.

SINTON, CHRISTOPHER MICHAEL, neurophysiologist, educator; b. Beckenham, Kent, Eng., Sept. 10, 1946; came to U.S., 1983; s. Leslie George and Evelyn Mabel (Burn) S. BA, Cambridge U., Eng., 1968, MA, 1977; BSc, London U., 1978; PhD, U. Lyon, France, 1981. Rsch. fellow U. Lyon, 1980-83; rsch. assoc. Princeton (N.J.) U., 1983-84; sr. scientist Ciba-Geigy Corp., Summit, N.J., 1984-88; dir. electrophysiology Neurogen Corp., Branford, Conn., 1988-94; asst. prof. U. Tex. Southwestern Med. Ctr., Dallas, 1994—2007, assoc. prof., 2007—. Rsch. asst. prof. medicine NYU, N.Y.C., 1986-94; vis. asst. prof. Harvard U. Med. Sch., Boston, 1999-2007. Contbr. Scholar Med. Rsch. Coun. France vis. scholar, Princeton U., 1983. Mem. N.Y. Acad. Scis., Soc. Neurosci., European Sleep Rsch. Soc., Sleep Rsch. Soc. Achievements include research on genetic basis of narcolepsy, fetal effects of in-utero caffeine exposure, possible functional role of REM sleep and neuropeptide modulation of synaptic input. Office: U Tex SW Med Ctr Dept Internal Medicine 5323 Harry Hines Blvd Dallas TX 75390-8874 Office Phone: 214-648-8817. Business E-Mail: christopher.sinton@utsouthwestern.edu.

SINZ, ELIZABETH HYLTON, medical educator; b. Richmond, Va., Apr. 1, 1964; BS, Coll. William & Mary, 1986; MD, Va. Commonwealth U., 1991. Prof. anesthesiology and neurosurgery, assoc. dean clin. simulation Pa. State Hershey Med. Ctr., 2004—. Assoc. sci. editor Am. Heart Assn., 2009. Mem.: Assoc. U. Anesthesiologists, Am. Soc. Anesthesiologists, Soc. Simulation Healthcare (past pres. 2007—08). Home: 261 Elm Ave Hershey PA 17033 Home Fax: 717-531-7790. Business E-Mail: esinz@psu.edu.

SINZINGER, HELMUT FRANZ, physician, researcher; b. Vienna, May 6, 1948; s. Franz and Hedwig (Hummel) S.; m. Christa Pany; children: Alexandra, Thomas. MD, U. Vienna, 1973; Hon. diploma, Polish Acad. Scis., Cracow, 1993. Assoc. prof. U. Vienna, 1979, 1988; prof. U. Cracow, Poland, 1993, U. Barcelona, Spain, 1994, U. Perugia, Italy, 1994, Ekpomà, Nigeria, 1997; head Atherosclerosis Rsch. Group, Vienna, 1981-92; sec. Acad. Scis., Vienna, 1977-92; head Wilhelm Auerswald Atherosclerosis Rsch. Group, Vienna, 1992—; vice head dept. nuclear medicine U. Vienna, 1992—. Nat. rep. European Thrombosis Rsch. Orgn., Austria, 1991-95; pres. Internat. Soc. Radiolab. Cellular Blood Elements Austria, 1992-95, Austrian-Greek Atheroscl. Prevention Initiative, 1992—. Author, editor: Prostaglandine und Leukotriene bei Entzündung und Schmerz, 1984, PGE1 in Atherosclerosis, 1986, Prostaglandin E1, 1991, Radioactive Isotopes in Clinical Medicine and Research, 1990, 4th edit., 96, Radiolabelled Cellular Blood Elements, 1990, Atherogenesis, 1978, Prostaglandins in the Cardiovascular System, 1991, Prostaglandins in Clinical Research, 1987, 2nd edit. 1989; mem. editl. bd. various jours. Recipient more than 25 sci. awards from Kuner, 1979, Byk-Mallinckrodt for Nuclear Medicine, 1981, 91, Farbwerke Hoechst, 1984, Austro-Transplant, 1984, Austrian Cardiology Soc., Wiss. Förderungspreis d. Stdt. Wien, 1985, Denk-Price for Hematology, 1989, Unilever, 1989. Mem. Hungarian Atherosclerosis Soc. (hon.), Austrian Soc. Prostaglandin Rsch., Polish Soc. Atherosclerosis Rsch. Angiology, Polish Acad. Scis., N.Y. Acad. Sci. (life), Am. Heart Assn. (life), CIS-Jean Debiesse Nuclear Medicine, The Athenaeum. Home: Nadlergasse 1 A-1090 Vienna Austria Office: Währinger Gürtel 18-20 A-1090 Vienna Austria

SIO, JIMMY ONG, embryologist; b. Manila, Philippines, Mar. 9, 1954; arrived in U.S., 1973; s. Vicente and SiokBee (Ong) Sio. Biology major, U. Philippines, 1971—73; BS in Biology, Calif. State Coll. Bakersfield, 1976; PhD of Cell Biology, U. Tex. Health Sci. Ctr., Dallas, 1985; MD, Emory U., 1985. Diplomate Nat. Bd. Med. Examiners, Am. Bd. Hosp. Physicians, Am. Coll. Ethical Physicians. Resident in anat. pathology Emory U., Atlanta, 1985—86; resident in internal medicine Kern Med. Ctr., Bakersfield, Calif., 1990—93; physician Kaiser So. Calif. Permanente Med. Group, Bakersfield, 1993—, asst. area med. dir., 2006—. Pvt. Philippine Armed Forces, 1971—73. Recipient Businessman of Yr., NRCC, 2003, Man of Yr., IBC and ABI, 2004. Fellow: Am. Biog. Inst.; mem.: Internat. Biog. Assn., NY Acad. Scis., Order of Internat. Fellowship, InterNet Assocs. Avocation: reading. Home: 8604 Dinard Pl Bakersfield CA 93311 Office: Kaiser So Calif Permanente Med Group 8800 Ming Ave Bakersfield CA 93311 Office Phone: 661-664-3706. Personal E-mail: doctorsio@aol.com.

SIONOV, RONIT VOHT, immunologist, researcher; b. Oslo, Aug. 29, 1962; MSc in Pharmacy, U. Oslo, 1986; PhD in Immunology, Hebrew U. Jerusalem, 1993. Rsch. assoc., lab. mgr. Hebrew U. Jerusalem, 1993—. Office: Hebrew University Jerusalem Life Sci Inst Jerusalem 91904 Israel Office Fax: 972-2-6585660. Business E-Mail: sionov@cc.huji.ac.il.

SIPINEN, SEPPO ANTERO, obstetrician, gynecologist; b. Helsinki, Finland, Aug. 11, 1946; s. Uno Emil Rafael and Martta Liisa (Knuuttila) S.; m. Taru Katriina, Oct. 19, 1968; children: Samuel, Suzanne. MD, U. Freiburg, Germany, 1971, U. Helsinki, 1972, cert. specialist ob.-gyn., 1979, DMS, 1981, specialist in diving medicine, 1994; completed Nat. Defense Course, 1994, completed sr. officers course, 1998, completed first repetition course, 1999. Cert. diving medicine and hyperbaric oxygen treatment specialist. Resident in ob-gyn. and surgery U. Helsinki, State Maternity Hosp., Helsinki, 1973-80; sr. physician ob-gyn. State Maternity Hosp., Helsinki, 1981-83; commd. capt. Finnish Navy Med. Corps., 1997, surgeon gen., 1983—, rose through grades to capt., 1997; head naval dept. Rsch. Inst. Mil. Medicine, Helsinki, 1983-98, 2001—, head, 1998—2001; assoc. prof. diving and hyperbaric medicine U. Turku, 1996. Cons. ob-gyn. Finnish Def. Forces, 1983—, Subway in Helsinki, 1976-77; rsch. group Dept. Med. Chemistry, U. Helsinki, 1977-86; lectr. diving and hyperbaric physiology and medicine, 1977-82; cons. devel. group State Dept. Finland, 1984-86; head diving and hyperbaric med. treatment of State Salv. Edn. Inst., Finland, 1985-86; cons. devel. group of Profl. Diving Nat. Bd. Labor Protection, Finland, 1989-90, Compressed Air Work of Subway, 1976-77; mem., rep. for Finland European Diving Tech. Com., 1986—; mem. sci. bd. Diving Alert Network Europe, 1991; mem. European Commn. Hyperbaric Medicine, 1991-99; cons. Ministry Social Affairs and Health, Nat. Rsch. and Devel. Ctr. for Welfare and Health in Finland, 1994-2002; pres. XXI ann. meeting European Underwater and Baromed. Soc., Helsinki, 1995. Contbr. around 100 articles in endocrinology, bacteriology, serology, diving and hyperbaric medicine to profl. jours. Decorated knight 1st class Order of White Rose of Finland, comdr. Order of the Lion of Finland, 2001; recipient medal for Mil. Merit, 1988. Mem. Finnish Soc. Ob-Gyn., European Underwater and Baromed. Soc. (at-large exec. com., pres. XXIst ann. meeting, Helsinki 1995), Finnish Med. Assn., Finnish Soc. Perinatal Medicine, Finnish Soc. Diving and Hyperbaric Medicine (pres. 1977-99, exec. bd. 1999—), Undersea and Hyperbaric Med. Soc., Finnish Sport Divers Fedn. (safety com. 1976-79, pres. 1977-79, exec. bd. 1977-79, med. com. pres. 1980, Silver medal 1988, Diver of Yr. 1989, Gold medal 1999), Espoo Gymnastics Team, Finnish Gymnastics Fedn. (Silver medal 1993). Achievements include construction of diving support vessel; development of decompression tables for air diving, of oxygen-nitrogen mixed gas diving.

SIPPEL, SERRA, advocate; MA in religion. Internat. prog. dir. Catholics for a Free Choice; dep. dir. Ctr. Health and Gender Equity, Washington, 2006, pres. Office: Ctr Health and Gender Equity Ste 400 1317 F St NW Washington DC 20004 Office Phone: 202-393-5930. Office Fax: 202-393-5937. E-mail: change@genderhealth.org.

SIQUEIRA, LORENA M., pediatrician; d. Victor Frederick and Margaret Siqueira. MBBS, Seth GSMC & KEM Hosp., 1973; MSPH, U. Miami, 2005. Diplomate Am. Bd. of Pediat., 1981. Dir. adolescent medicne Mt Sinai City Svcs. Elmhurst, Queens, NY, 1987—96; dir. fellowship tng. Adolescent Medicine divsn. Mt Sinai Hosp., New York, 2000—02; dir. adolescent medicine Miami Children's Hosp., Fla., 2002—. Dir. stop nicotine addiction program Adolescent Medicine divsn. Mt Sinai Hosp., New York, 1996—2002. Contbr. articles to profl. jours. Recipient Clin. Scientist Rsch. award, NIH, 2002—; grantee Comprehensive HIV Svcs., N.Y. State Dept. Health., 1994—97; Primary Care Devel. Grant, 1991—94, Join Together Nat. Fellow, Boston U. funded by the RWJ Found., 1998—. Fellow: Am. Acad. Pediat. (life). Achievements include development of Adolescent Medicine Programs. Avocations: swimming, travel, music. Office: Miami Children's Hospital 3200 SW 60th Ct Ste 205 Miami FL 33155 E-mail: lorena.siqueira@mch.com.

SIRACUSANO, LUCA, medical educator; b. Messina, Feb. 23, 1948; MD, U. Messina, 1972. Prof., assoc. prof. U. Messina Sch. Medicine, 1978—. Avocation: reading. Home: Via Regina Margherita 28 Messina Sicily 98121 Italy Personal E-mail: lsiracusano@unime.it.

SIRBU, ADRIAN, forensic pathologist, physician; b. Ploiesti, Romania, Apr. 28, 1965; s. Victor and Floarea Sirbu; m. Dana Georgeta Spataru, Oct. 2, 1999. MD, Univ. Medicine, Craiova, 1984—90. Cert. Medical Doctor 1990. Family medicine, 1990—94; forensic pathologist Nat. Inst. Legal Medicine, Bucharest, Romania, 1994—2003. Cons. asst. Police Acad., Bucharest, Romania, 2001—03; presenter numerous sci. meetings. Author of several articles, studies, and communications. Pres. Ind. Union Forensic Pathologist, Bucharest, Romania, 2000—03. Orthodox. Avocations: travel, photography, gastronomy, sports, movies. Office: Nat Inst Legal Medicine Vitan-Barzesti # 9 75669 Bucharest Romania E-mail: cherysirbu@xnet.ro.

SIREGAR, ADIATMA YUDISTIRA MANOGAR, health economist; b. Bandung, West Java, Indonesia, Dec. 5, 1980; M in Econ. Studies, U. Queensland, 2006. Lectr., rschr. faculty economics, dept. economics U. Padjadjaran, 2006—; rschr. faculty pub. health U. Indonesia, Ctr. Health Economics and Policy Analysis, 2007—08. Mgmt. team, rschr. Integrated Mgmt. Prevention & Control and Treatment HIV-AIDS, 2007—11. Avocation: music. Home: Jl Progo 26 Bandung West Java 40115 Indonesia Personal E-mail: adiatma.siregar@fe.unpad.ac.id.

SIRETEANU, RUXANDRA, biophysicist, educator; b. Mediasch, Romania, Sept. 19, 1945; d. Modest Sireteanu and Eva Mathilde Sireteanu-Oberth; m. Dan Horia Constantinescu, Dec. 20, 1974; children: Laura Eva Constantinescu, Sorin Daniel Constantinescu. MSc, U. Bucharest, 1968; PhD, Scuola Normale Superiore, 1976; Venia legendi, Johannes Gutenberg U., 1989. Rschr. Ctr. for Molecular Biology and Radiobiology, Bucharest, Romania, 1968—69; asst. prof. Dept. Molecular Physics Inst. Oil, Gas and Geology, Bucharest, 1969—72; post-doctoral fellow Dept. Comparative Neurobiology U. Ulm, Germany, 1976—77; post-doctoral fellow Inst. d'Anatomie U. Lausanne, Switzerland, 1977—78; scientist Max-Planck-Inst. Psychiatry, Munich, 1978—84; sr. scientist Max-Planck-Inst. Brain Rsch., Frankfurt, Germany, 1984—; prof. biol. psychology Inst. Psychology Johann Wolfgang Goethe-U., Frankfurt, 1999—; vis. scholar Dept. Biomed. Engring. Boston U., 2002—. Dir. Inst. Psychology Johann Wolfgang Goethe-U., Frankfurt, 2003—. Author: (book) Development and plasticity of the visual function in human observers (Proze of the Heinz and Helene Adam-Foundation, 1991); contbr. to articles in jours. (Prize of "Bielschowsky"-Society for Research in Strabismus, 1994). Mem.: Rodin Remediation Soc., Bielschowsky Soc. for Rsch in Strabismus, Internat. Soc. Infant Studies, Assn. Rsch. in Vision and Ophthalmology, European Brain and Behaviour Soc. Office: Max-Planck-Institute for Brain Research Deutschordenstrasse 46 60528 Frankfurt Germany

SIRICA, ALPHONSE EUGENE, pathology educator; b. Waterbury, Conn., Jan. 16, 1944; s. Alphonse Eugene and Elena Virginia (Mascolo) S.; m. Annette Marie Murray, June 9, 1984; children: Gabrielle Theresa, Nicholas Steven. MS, Fordham U., 1968; PhD in Biomed. Sci., U. Conn., 1977. Asst. prof. U. Wis., Madison, 1979-84; assoc. prof. Med. Coll. Va., Va. Commonwealth U., Richmond, 1984-90, prof. of pathology, 1990—, divsn. chair exptl. pathology, 1992-99, divsn. chair cellular and molecular pathogenesis, 1999—. Organizer, chair FASEB Summer Rsch. Conf., 1999, 2001; vis. prof. Pa. State U. Coll. Medicine, 2000, Mayo Clinic, 2011; regular mem. sci. adv. com. on carcinogenesis and nutrition Am. Cancer Soc., Atlanta, 1989—92; metabolic pathology study sect. NIH, Bethesda, 1991—95, ad hoc mem. study sect., 1997—2006, 2008, 10; mem. bd. dir. CanLiv, Hepatobiliary Cancer Found., 2008—11. Editor, author: The Pathobiology of Neoplasia, 1989, The Role of Cell Types in Hepatocarcinogenesis, 1992, Cellular and Molecular Pathogenesis, 1996; co-editor, author: Biliary and Pancreatic Ductal Epithelia: Pathobiology and Pathophysiology, 1997; mem. editl. bd. Pathobiology, 1990-99, Hepatology, 1991-94, Exptl. and Molecular Pathology, 1999—, World Jour. Gastroenterology, 2006-09, Annals Clin. & Lab. Sci., 2010-; rev. bd. In Vitro Cellular and Devel. Biology-Animal, 1987—; contbr. articles to profl. jours. including Am. Jour. Pathology, Cancer Rsch., Hepatology, and other. Organizer, chair FASEB Summer Rsch. Conf. on Growth Factor Receptor Tyrosine Kinases in Mitogenesis, Morphogenesis, and Tumorigenesis, 1999, 2001. Recipient Rsch. Recognition award, Va. Commonwealth U. Sch. Medicine, 2002, 2007. Fellow: Am. Gastroent. Assn.; mem.: AAAS, Soc. Toxicology, Han. Popper Hepatopathology Soc., Soc. Exptl. Biology and Medicine, NY Acad. Scis., Am. Assn. Study Liver Diseases (chair conf. pathobiology of biliary epithelia and cholangiocarcinoma), Am. Soc. Investigative Pathology (chair program com. 1994—96), Assn. Clin. Scientists, Soc. for In Vitro Biology, Am. Assn. Cancer Rsch. (chmn. Va. state legis. com. 1992—95), Am. Soc. Cell Biology. Achievements include development of collagen gel-nylon mesh system for culturing hepatocytes; first establishment and characterization of hyperplastic bile ductular epithelial cells in culture; research in hepato- and biliary carcinogenesis, pathobiology of hepatocyte and biliary epithelial cells and molecular pathogenesis and experimental therapeutics of biliary cancer. Office: Med Coll Va Va Commonwealth U PO Box 980297 Richmond VA 23298-0297 Office Phone: 804-828-9549. Business E-Mail: asirica@mcvh-vcu.edu.

SIRIGU, ANGELA, neuropsychologist; b. Italy; PhD in psychology, U. Rome, 1983. Post-doctoral training in neuropsychology Centre Hospitalier Universitaire la Timone, Marseille, France, 1984—87; vis. fellow, Cognitive Neuroscience sect. Nat. Inst. Neurological Diseases and Stroke, NIH, Bethesda, Md., 1988—91; invited sci., exptl. medicine lab. la Salpetriere Hosp., Paris, 1992—96; rsch. sci. Centre Nat. de la Recherche Scientifique, Lyon, France, 1996—, dir. rsch., dir. neuropsychology group, Inst. Cognitive Sci. Recipient French Acad. Sci. award, 1999. Office: Centre de Neuroscience Cognitive Bron 67 boulevard Pinel 69675 Lyon France Office Phone: 0033.4.37911231. Office Fax: 0033.4.379110. E-mail: sirigu@isc.cnrs.fr.

SIRINATHSINGHJI, DALIP JAICARAN SASTRI, neuroscientist, researcher; b. Sangre Grande, Trinidad and Tobago, Mar. 26, 1947; s. Sirinath and Bhagmania Singhji; m. Montserrat Pla Puig, Aug. 6, 1977; children: Oriol Dalip, Eva Clare, Melanie Nuria. BSc (hon.), McGill U., Montreal, Canada, 1968; BSc (spl. hon.), U. WI, Jamaica, 1969; BA (hon.), Trinity Coll., Cambridge, England, 1972, MA, 1972; PhD, Wolfson Coll., Cambridge, England, 1977. Rsch. fellow in virology U. of the WI, Kingston, Jamaica, 1968—69; rsch. asst. exptl. surgery Inst. of Animal Physiology, Cambridge, England, 1970—71; rsch. fellow dept. med. U. Cambridge, England, 1973—77, post-doctoral fellow dept. med., 1977—78, vis. scientist dept. anatomy, 1979—80; royal soc. fellow U. Milan, 1978—79, ford found. fellow, 1978—79; royal soc. fellow Semmelweis U. Med. Sch., Budapest, Hungary, 1980—81; royal soc. travelling fellow Netherlands Inst. for Brain Rsch., Amsterdam, Netherlands, 1981, Semmelweis U. Med. Sch., Budapest, Hungary, 1982; sr. sci. officer, chief lab. of neuroendocrinology Agrl. & Food Rsch. Coun., Bristol, England, 1981—84; sr. staff scientist Inst. of Animal Physiology and Genetics, Cambridge, Cambridgeshire, England, 1990—92, 1985—89; visting sr. rsch. fellow Max-Planck Inst. of Psychiatry, Munich, 1988—89; vis. neuroscientist Lab. of Molecular Biology, Cambridge, Cambridgeshire, 1988—89; sr. investigator Merck Sharp& Dohme Rsch. Labs., Neuroscience Rsch. Centre, Harlow, Essex, England, 1992—96; disting. sr. scientist and dir. lab. of molecular neuropathology Merck Sharp & Dohme Rsch. Labs., Neuroscience Rsch. Ctr., Harlow, Essex, England, 1996—2004; ret., 2004. Sci. cons. Merck Rsch. Labs. and U. Cambridge Collaboration, 1999—; dir. acad. and indsl. rels. Merck Sharp & Dohme Rsch. Labs., 2003—04. Editor: (textbook) NMDA receptor antagonists as potential analgesic drugs; contbr. articles to profl. jours. Recipient Lectureship medal, Royal Coll. Physicians and Surgeons of Catalunya, 1989. Fellow: Cambridge U. Philos. Soc.; mem.: Internat. Brain Rsch. Org., Am. Soc. Neuroscience. Achievements include research in research into gene expression in brain, and novel strategies for treatment of Alzheimer's Disease; treatment of pain; treatment of Huntington's Disease and Parkinson's Disease. Home: 124 Duxford Road CB22 4NH Cambridge CB22 4NH England Personal E-mail: dalip_sirinathsinghji@bt.internet.com.

SIRIO, CARL ALEXANDER, internist, educator; b. Hoboken, NJ, June 28, 1958; m. Mary Beth Sirio; children: Alexander, Nicholas, James. AB, Columbia U., NYC, 1980; MD, U. Medicine & Dentisty NJ-Rutgers Med. Sch., 1984. Diplomate Nat. Bd. Med. Examiners, American Bd. Internal Medicine, cert. in critical care medicine, lic. Pa., Md., DC. Resident dept. medicine Milton S. Hershey Med. Ctr., Pa. State U., 1984—87; med. staff fellow critical care medicine NIH, Bethesda, Md., 1988—92; pulmonary fellow George Washington U. Med. Ctr., 1992; asst. prof. anesthesiology/critical care medicine U. Pitts. Sch. Medicine, 1993—2000, assoc. prof., 2000—02, assoc. prof. critical care medicine, 2002—07, prof., 2007—09, Drexel U. Coll. Medicine, Phila., 2009—. Asst. prof. medicine Pa. State U. Sch. Medicine, 1987—90; attending staff physician Milton S. Hershey Med. Ctr., 1987—90, Presbyn./Shadyside Hosp.-U. Pitts. Med. Ctr. Montefiore, 1990—2009, VA Med. Ctr., Pitts., 1994—2009, Magee-Womens Hosp., Pitts., 1998—2002, Allegheny Gen. Hosp., Pitts., 2009—; courtesy attending staff Washington County Hosp., Hagerstown, Md., 1989—98. Edtl. bd. mem. American Jour. Med. Quality; contbr. articles to med. jours. Vol. Jewish Healthcare Found., Pitts. Recipient Henry Christian award, Am. Fedn. Clin. Rsch., 1990, 1992. Fellow: ACP, American Coll. Critical Care Medicine, American Coll. Chest Physicians (DuPont Critical Care/Young Investigator award 1990, 1995); mem.: AMA (mem. House of Delegates 1985—92, mem.Coun. Med. Edn. 2000—09, bd. trustees 2010—), Allegheny County Med. Soc. (Frederick M. Jacob Outstanding Svc. award 2003), Soc. Critical Care Medicine, Pa. Med. Soc. (mem. House of Delegates 1984—89, 1993—98, 2003—09). Office: Allegheny Gen Hosp Divsn Surgical Critical Care 490 E North Ave Ste 309 Pittsburgh PA 15212 Office Phone: 412-359-6656. Office Fax: 412-359-6653. E-mail: csirio@wpahs.org, sirioca@live.com. *

SIRIVELLA, SRIKRISHNA, cardiologist, consultant; s. Hari and Lalitha Sirivella; m. Radhabai Bollineni, June 5, 1969; 1 child, Sudhama Srikrishna. MBBS, Guntur Med. coll., 1968. Diplomate in abdominal surgery Am. Bd. Med. Spltys., 1979, in surgery 1984, in thoracic surgery 1990, in surgery Nat. Acad. Med. Scis. India, 1981. Cons. Tamilnadu Hosps., Chennai, India, 1992—94; faculty SVIMS, Tirupati, Andhara Pradesh, India, 1993—. Attending surgeon Newark Beth Isreal Med. Ctr., Newark, 1989—2000. Contbr. articles to profl. jour. Trustee Animal Welfare, Chennai, 2007—08. Mem.: Soc. Thoracic Surgeons.

SIRKEN, MONROE GILBERT, statistician; b. NYC, Jan. 11, 1921; s. Irving and Henrietta (Oram) S.; m. Blanche Skalak Hurwitz (div. 1960); children: Robert, Philip. BA, UCLA, 1946, MA, 1947; PhD, U. Wash., 1950. Lectr. Med. Sch. U. Wash., Seattle, 1949; fellow Stats. Lab. U. Calif., Berkeley, 1950; statistician Census Bur., Suitland, Md., 1951-54, Pub. Health Svc., Washington, 1954-60, Nat. Ctr. Health Stats., Hyattsville, Md., 1961—. Cons. NIH, 1980-85, Nat. Inst. Drug Addiction, 1976-80, NSF, 1986—, Health Care Fin. Adminstrn., 1989-90. Contbr. articles to Jour. Am. Statis. Assn., Biometrics, Demography, Jour. APHA, Pub. Health Reports, also others. Home: 3114 Gracefield Rd Apt 405 Silver Spring MD 20904 Office Phone: 301-458-4505. Personal E-mail: mgsirken@aol.com. Business E-Mail: mgs2@cdc.gov.

SIRMALIS, GEORGE, medical association administrator; b. Sydney, Sept. 21, 1964; Diploma, East West Security Studies; MD, Calif., 1988, PhD, 1992. Pres. Antisoma PLC Bionuclear Group SA, 1995—2004; dir. UCB Pharma, 2007—09; exec. dir., med. affairs Solvay Abbot Innogenetics, 2009—10; head, med. affairs Sanofi Aventis, 2010—11; exec. chmn. Iqnovate Biopharma Consulting Group, 2010—. Educator cons. Gerson Lehrman Group, 2005—10. Decorated Royal Order Ministry of Interior. Fellow: AAPP, FRACNP; mem.: MASNM. Home: Yerong Pl Sydney NSW 2154 Australia Personal E-mail: gsyrmalis@gmail.com.

SIRMATEL, FATMA, physician; b. Sungurlu, Turkey, Jan. 1, 1955; Degree, Ankara U., 1978, degree, 1983. Rsch. prof., mgr. Abant Izzet Baysal U., 2004—. Mem.: KLIMIK, EKMUD. Avocation: movies. Office: Abant Izzet Baysal University Med Faculty Bolu 14286 Turkey Personal E-mail: sirmatel@yahoo.com.

SIROTIN, BORIS SALMANOVITCH, medical educator, department chairman; b. Ulan-Ude, Russia, Feb. 16, 1928; s. Salman Borisovitch Sirotin and Esphyr Grigoryevna Sirotina; m. Zinaida Vasilyevna Misteneva, July 21, 1963; children: Natalya, Olga. MD, Med. U., 1951, PhD in Med. Sci., 1966. Cert. internal medicine, cardiology, and rheumatology. Resident Dept. Internal Medicine Med. U., Khabarovsk, Russia, 1951—54, asst. prof. Dept. Internal Medicine, 1955—66, prof., 1966—, head Dept. Therapy, 1966—. Chmn. Regional Therapeutic Soc., Khabarovsk, 1967—2002; mem. sci. planning coun. Med. U., 1980—; mem. sci. bd. diabetes Health Dept., Khabarovsk, 2000—; mem. nephrology internal mgmt. med. bd. Russian Soc., 1982—. Author: Clinical Lectures on Therapy for Medical Students, 1995, Clinical Lectures on Therapy for Medical Students, 3d edit., 2003; contbr. articles to profl. jours. Lt. col. res. Russian Army. Named Honoured Man of Sci., Russian Govt., 1997; named to Order of People's Friendship, 1993. Mem.: Tchaykovsky Music Fan Club. Achievements include patents in field. Avocations: singing, gardening. Office: City Clinic N3 Pushkin St 54 680000 Khabarovsk Russia Home: App 9 ul. Volochayevskaya 153 680000 Khabarovsk Khabarovskiy Kray Russia

SIROTY, WILLIAM CHARLES, physician; s. Daniel Hirsch and Eileen (Gusman) S. BS, SUNY, Stony Brook, 1973; MD, Georgetown U., Washington, DC, 1977. Diplomate Am. Bd. Internal Medicine, Am. Bd. Allergy-Immunology. Intern in internal medicine Beth Israel Med. Ctr., NYC, 1977-78, resident in internal medicine, 1977-78; fellow allergy and immunology NY Hosp.-Cornell U. Med. Ctr., 1980-82; pvt. practice NYC, 1982-94; staff physician Nashua (NH) Med. Group, 1994—. Editor: NH News Links, 2000—08. Co-founder, first co-chair Gay People in Medicine Caucus Am. Med. Student Assn., 1976—77; active NH State Dem. Com., 1998—2006, Hillsborough County Dem. Com., NH, 1998—2006, vice-chmn., 2004—06; del. Dem. Nat. Conv., 2000, 2004; chair Dems. Amherst, 2002—06; bd. dirs. Democracy for NH, 2006—, Elizabeth Streb Ringside, Inc., NH Civil Liberties Union. Mem. Am. Acad. Allergy, Asthma and Immunology, NH Med. Soc. Office: Nashua Med Group 173 Daniel Webster Hwy Nashua NH 03060-5224

SIRTORI, CESARE R., pharmacologist, educator; b. Milan, Mar. 28, 1943; s. Carlo and Antonia (Biancardi) S.; m. Marina Bertoli, Dec. 20, 1975; 1 child, Carlo. MD, U. Milan, 1967; PhD in Pharmacology, U. Kans., 1972. Diplomate Bd. Cardiology and Clin. Pharmacology. From asst. prof. to prof. U. Milan, 1968-80, prof. chemotherapy, 1980-88, prof. clinical pharmacology, 1988—, dean. sch. pharmacy,

2006. Dir. Ctr. E. Grossi Paoletti, Milan, 1972; pres. XIV internat. symposium Atherosclerosis, Rome, 2006. Co-author: Arteriosclerosi, 1977, Farmacologia Clinica, 1993, Clinical Pharmacology, 2000; contbr. over 500 articles to sci. jours. Dist. councilor City of Milan, 1979-85; mem. bd. USL, Milan, 1985-90. Recipient Bezalip award, 1987, 92, Creasy award Wellcome Fund, 1985, Assitol award, 1994, Lombardia award, 2011. Mem. Am. Heart Assn., Brit. Pharmacol. Soc. Roman Catholic. Achievements include discovery of APO A-I Milano mutation, developed for human use by medco USA; research in the field of dietary proteins as cholesterol lowering agent. Avocation: exercise. Office: Dept Pharmacol Sci Via Balzaretti 9 20133 Milan Italy Home: Via Cino del Duca 8 20122 Milan MI Italy Home Phone: 0039-02-76013819; Office Phone: 0039-02-50318311. Business E-Mail: cesare.sirtori@unimi.it.

SISK, JANE ELIZABETH, economist, educator; b. West Reading, Pa., Sept. 23, 1942; 2 children. BA with honors, Brown U., 1963; MA, George Washington U., 1965; PhD, McGill U., Montreal, Que., Can., 1976. Cons. Nat. Planning Assn., Washington, 1976; scholar VA, Washington, 1978-81; rsch. dir. Office Tech. Assessment, U.S. Congress, Washington, 1976-78, sr. analyst, 1981-84, sr. assoc., 1984-91. Vis. prof. Columbia U. Sch. Pub. Health, N.Y.C., 1990-91, prof., 1992—99; prof. Mt. Sinai Sch. Medicine, N.Y.C., 1999—, dir. divsn. health care stats. Nat. Ctr. for Health Stats., Ctrs. for Disease Control, Hyattsville, Md., 2004—. Co-author: Toward Rational Technology in Medicine, 1981; mem. editl. bd. Internat. Jour. Tech. Assessment in Health Care, 1987—, vol. editor, 1990, 98; asst. editor Am. Jour. Pub. Health, 1990-91; mem. editl. bd. Health Svcs. Rsch., 1994—; contbr. articles to profl. jours. Pres. Internat Soc. Tech. Assessment in Health Care, 1991-93, bd. dirs., 1987-95; mem. N.Y. State Task Force on Clin. Guidelines & Med. Tech. Assessment, 1994-96; mem. study sect. on health care quality and effectiveness rsch. U.S. Agy. for Health Care Policy and Rsch., 1997-2001. Elisah Benjamin Andrews scholar Brown U., 1961, 63; Bronfman fellow McGill U., 1971. Fellow Assn. for Health Svcs. Rsch.; mem. Inst. of Medicine, NAS (mem. cancer policy bd. 1997-2000, inst. medicine, 2001—), Phi Beta Kappa. Office Phone: 301-458-4157.

SISLEY, NINA MAE, physician, public health service officer; b. Jacksonville, Fla., Aug. 19, 1924; d. Leonard Percy and Verna (Martin) S.; m. George W. Fischer, May 16, 1962 (dec. 1990). BA, Tex. State Coll. for Women, 1944; MD, U. Tex., Galveston, 1950; MPH, U. Mich., 1963. Intern City of Detroit Receiving Hosp., 1950-51; resident in gen. practice St. Mary's Infirmary, Galveston, Tex., 1951-52; sch. physician Galveston Ind. Sch. Dist., 1953-56; dir. med. svcs. San Antonio Health Dept., 1960-63, acting dir., 1963-64; resident in pub. health Tex. Dept. Pub. Health, San Antonio, 1963-65; dir. cmty. health svcs. Corpus Christi-Nueces County Dept. Health, Tex., 1964-67; dir. Tb control region 5 Tex. Dept. Health, Corpus Christi, 1967-73; chief chronic illness control City of Houston Health Dept., 1973-78; dir. pub. health region 11 Tex. Dept. Health, Rosenberg, 1978-87; dir. Corpus Christi-Nueces County Dept. Pub. Health, 1987—2002. Lectr. Incarnate Word Coll., San Antonio, 1963-64; adj. prof. U. Tex. Sch. Pub. Health, Houston, 1980—2002, adj. prof. Tex. A&M U., Corpus Christi, 1997—2002; pvt. practice Galveston, Stockdale, Hereford and Borger, Tex., 1952-59; mem. adv. bd. Cmty. Adv. Coun.; clin. instr. U. Tex. Health Sci. Ctr., San Antonio, 1997-2002 Mem. Nueces County Child Fatality REv. Com.; mem. adv. com. Nueces County Hosp. Dist.; mem. adv. bd. Alzheimers Assn.; mem. health adv. bd. Corpus Christi Ind. Sch. Dist.; bd. dirs. Coastal Bend chpt. ARC, Corpus Christi, 1990—94, 2003—07, pres., 1990—91; bd. dirs. United Way-Coastal Bend, Coastal Bend Coalition on AIDS, 1988—94, Charlie's Place Alcohol and Drug Rehab. Ctr. Fellow Am. Coll. Preventive Medicine; mem. Tex. Med. Assn., Nueces County Med. Soc. (pres. 1997-98), Tex. Assn. Pub. Health Physicians, Tex. Pub. Health Assn. (pres. 1991-92), Local Emergency Planning Assn., Long Term Health Assn., Asthma Coalition. Episcopalian. Avocations: fishing, crossword puzzles, raising african violets. Home: 62 Rock Creek Dr Corpus Christi TX 78412-4214 E-mail: nsisley@sbcglobal.org.

SISTO, DOMENICK J., orthopedist; b. Passaic, NJ, Jan. 17, 1953; MD, George Wash. Med. Sch., 1979. Sr. ptnr. LA Orthop. Inst., 1990—. Mem. Am. Jour. Sports Medicine. Named one of Top Drs. in Southern Calif., LA Mag. Mem.: Am. Orthop. Soc. Sports Medicine, Am. Acad. Orthop. Surgeons. Avocations: golf, tennis, skiing. Office: 4955 Van Nuys Blvd Ste 615 Sherman Oaks CA 91403 Office Fax: 818-905-8702. Personal E-mail: laortho1@yahoo.com.

SITARZ, ANNELIESE LOTTE, pediatrician, educator; b. Medellin, Colombia, Aug. 31, 1928; arrived in US, 1935; d. Hans and Elisabeth (Noll) Sitarz. BA cum laude, Bryn Mawr Coll., Pa., 1950; MD, Columbia U., 1954. Diplomate Nat. Bd. Med. Examiners, Am. Bd. Pediatrics, Am. Bd. Pediatric Hematology and Oncology. Intern Children's Med. Ctr., Boston, 1954—55; resident in pediat. Babies Hosp.-Columbia-Presbyn. Med. Ctr., NYC, 1955—57; mem. faculty Columbia U., NYC, 1957—74, assoc. prof. clin. pediat., 1974—83, prof., 1983—2000, prof. emerita, spl. lectr. in pediat., 2000—; attending in pediat. Babies and Children's Hosp., NYC, 1983—2007. Cons. pediatrics, hematology and oncology Harlem Hosp., NYC, 1967—72, Overlook Hosp., Summit, NJ, 1975—2001. Contbr. articles to profl. jours. Pres. Mt. Prospect Assn., Summit, 1987—. Fellow: Am. Acad. Pediat.; mem.: Internat. Soc. Hematology, Am. Soc. Hematology, Am. Soc. Clin. Oncology, Am. Assn. Cancer Rsch., Harvey Soc. Republican. Episcopalian. Avocations: gardening, sewing, hiking, stamp collecting/philately, photography. Office: Childrens Hosp of NY Presbyn Irving Pavilion 161 Ft Washington Ave New York NY 10032-3710 Business E-Mail: als4@columbia.edu. *

SITGES-SERRA, ANTONIO, surgeon, educator, researcher; b. Barcelona, July 29, 1951; s. Antonio Sitges and Ma Rita Serra; children: Francesc, Nora, David. MD with honors, U. Autonoma Barcelona, 1974, PhD, 1979. Resident in gen. surgery Hosp. Bellvitge, Barcelona, 1975-80, staff surgeon, 1980-85; prof. surgery U. Barcelona, 1982—; head gen. surgery Hosp. del Mar, Barcelona, 1985-89, head dept. surgery, 1989—. Dean sch. medicine U. Barcelona, 1990-92. Author: Parenteral Nutrition in the Surgical Patient, 1999, Endocrine Surgery, 1999, 2010, (poetry) Amor Roig, 1997 (Martí i Pol Poetry prize 1997); editor: Clinical Progress in Nutrition Research, 1988. Fellow Royal Coll. Surgeons (Edinburgh) (hon.); mem. European Soc. Endocrine Surgeons, Internat. Soc. Surgery, Catalan Soc. Surgery (pres.) Roman Catholic. Avocations: poetry, guitar, writing. Office: Hosp Del Mar Po Marítim 25-29 08003 Barcelona Spain

SITI-AISHAH, ALI, histologist, educator; d. Halimah; m. Abd-Razak Sulaiman; children: Yasmin Abd-Razak, Amera Abd-Razak. MBBCh, Cairo U., 1976. Houseman, Hosp. Pulau Pinang, Georgetown, Malaysia, 1977—78; med. officer Hosp. Kuala Lumpur, Malaysia, 1978—79. Cons. U. Kebangsaan, Kuala Lumpur, 1994—. Author: Patologi Trek Genital Wanita. Recipient Silver award, U. Putra Malaysia, 2002, Bronze award, U. Kebangsaan Malaysia, 2004, 2005; scholar, Malaysian Govt., 1970. Mem.: Acad. Medicine Malaysia (life). Achievements include patents in field. Office: UKM Dept of Pathology FM Jalan Yaakob Latif Bandar Tun Razak 56000 Cheras 56000 Malaysia Office Fax: 603-91737340. Business E-Mail: saishah@mail.hukm.ukm.my.

SITTE, HELLMUTH, retired medical educator; b. Innsbruck, Austria, May 6, 1928; arrived in Germany, 1958; s. Heinrich and Lisbeth Sitte; m. Gerda Hüttner, Sept. 11, 1956; children: Ingrid, Harald Hans. PhD, U. Innsbruck, 1956. Sci. asst. U. Innsbruck, 1952—57; med. student U. Heidelberg, 1958—62; dozent U. Saarland, Germany, 1962—67, prof., 1968—96, ret., 1996, rector Germany, 1968—73. Cons. Leica Microsystems (formerly Reichert Optical Works), Vienna, Austria, 1954—; active in co-operation. Fellow; (hon.) Royal Microscopical Soc. Achievements include invention of reichert-ultramicrotomes; of reichert cryo chamber; Leica freeze drying and freeze substitution system. Avocations: music, philosophy. Home: Reitherspitz St 166 Seefeld Tirol A-6100 Austria

SITTHIMONGKOL, YAJAI, nursing educator; b. Chachoengsao, Thailand, Dec. 15, 1958; PhD in Nursing, U. Ill., 1994. Project mgr. Thailand Health Promotion, 2003—07; assoc. dean grad. studies and internat. rels.; faculty nursing Mahidol U., 2007—. Bd. advanced practice nursing Thailand Nursing Coun., 2007—11. Mem.: Internat. Network Doctoral Edn. Nursing. Avocations: travel, singing, reading. Office: Faculty Nursing Madison University Banekoknoz Bankok 10700 Thailand Home Phone: 662-616-7296; Office Phone: 6624197466-80, 662 419 7466 850 ext 1414. Office Fax: 6624113258. Business E-Mail: nsyst@mahidol.ac.th.

SIU, MICHELLE KWAN YEE, pathologist, educator; b. Hong Kong, Feb. 16, 1977; Postgrad., Hong Kong U.; PhD, U. Hong Kong, 2002. Rsch. asst. prof. U. Hong Kong, 2007—. Named to Dean's Hon. List, U. Hong Kong, 1998—99. Mem.: Am. Assn. Cancer Rsch. (Avon Found.-AACR Internat. Scholar-in-Tng. grant). Office: Rm 515 University Pathology Bldg Hong Kong Hong Kong Personal E-mail: mkysiu@gmail.com.

SIU, WANDA LUEN WUN, medical educator; BS in Social Sci. with honors, Chinese U. Hong Kong, 1994, MPhil, 1996; PhD, U. Minn., Mpls., 2004. Cert. in ednl. stats. U. Minn., 2003. Asst. hosp. adminstr. Queen Mary Hosp., Hong Kong, 1996—99, clin. bus. mgr., ear, nose, throat, 1997—99; asst. pub. affairs mgr. Hosp. Authority, Hong Kong, 1999; asst. prof. Chinese U. Hong Kong, 2005—, investigator, food rsch. ctr., faculty sci., 2007—, adv. panel mem., investigator, Ctr. Chinese Studies, 2008—. Ad-hoc jour. reviewer Communication & Soc., Hong Kong, 2007—, Chinese Jour. Communication, Hong Kong, 2007—, Jour. Asian Pacific Communication, 2008—, Western Jour. Communication, 2008—; jury Hong Kong Govt., 2008—; external examiner Open U. Hong Kong, 2008—; conf. paper reviewer Internat. Communication Assn., Wash., 2008—; book reviewer Chinese U. Hong Kong Press, 2008—; advisor, cons. Hong Kong Fedn. Edn. Workers, 2008—. Contbr. scientific papers to presentations to numerous confs. (Top Conf. Paper award, 2003, 2005), articles to profl. jours., chapters to books. Mem. adv. panel film censorship Hong Kong TV and Entertainment Authority, 1993—97; lector Minn., 2003—04, Cath. Ch. Svc., Hong Kong, 2005—. Mem.: Assn. Lang. Awareness, Internat. Communication Assn. Office: Chinese Univ Hong Kong Shui Yan Yuen Tin Ha Rd Hong Kong New Territories Hong Kong Office Fax: (852)26035007. Business E-Mail: siuwanda@cuhk.edu.hk.

SIVA, SHANKAR, radiobiologist; b. Colombo, Sri Lanka, Apr. 23, 1980; MBBChir, U. Melbourne, 2002. Radiologist Peter MacCallum Cancer Ctr., 2007, clin. & rsch. fellow, 2011. Contbr. articles to profl. jours. Fellow: Royal Australian and New Zealand Coll. Radiology (Oncura Bourne and Langlands Prize). Achievements include first to introduce clinical trial of stereotactic lung radio surgery in Australia. Avocations: photography, guitar, running. Home: Peter MacCallum Ctr St Andrew Pl Melbourne Victoria 3003 Australia Personal E-mail: holidayshanks@yahoo.com.au.

SIVANANDAN, RANJIV, surgeon; MB and Surgery, Nat. U., Singapore, 1991, M of Medicine (Surgery), 1997. Cert. gen. surgeon. Fellowship Royal Coll. of Surgeons, Edinburgh, Am. Head and Neck Soc.; advance tng. in head and neck surg. oncology otolaryngology dept. Head and Neck Surgery Stanford Univ., Calif.; pvt. practice, 2009; sr. cons. and chief head and neck svc. surgery dept. Singapore Gen. Hosp. (SGH), co founded thyroid group, chmn. thyroid group, 2007—09, vis. cons., undergraduate and postgrad. tng.; prin. investigator head and neck cancer lab. Nat. Cancer Centre; clin. instr. advance trauma and life support program Singhealth and Singapore Armed Forces Med. Svcs.; surgeon Thyroid Head & Neck Surgery Centre, Singapore. Full time faculty mem. otolaryngology dept. Head and Neck Surgery Stanford Univ., asst. prof. surgery; sr. clin. lectr. Nat. Univ., Singapore. Recipient Resident Tchg. award, Stanford Univ., Svc. Quality award (Thrice), Singapore Gen. Hosp. Mem.: Nat. Transplant Ethics Com. Achievements include research in Head and Neck Cancer at the Stanford Inst. of Stem Cell Biology and Regenerative Medicine; The 1st worldwide to publish on Head and Neck Cancer Cells in 2007; 1st Robotic Thyroidectomy in Singapore. Office: Thyroid Head & Neck Surgery Centre Mt Elizabeth Medica Centre 3 Mt Elizabeth Number 15-10 Singapore 228510 Singapore Office Phone: 6567320710. Office Fax: 6567320112. Business E-Mail: ranjiv@thyroidheadandnecksurgery.com. *

SIVASUBRAMANIAN, KOLINJAVADI NAGARAJAN, neonatologist, educator; b. Coimbatore, Madras, India, May 9, 1945; came to U.S., 1971; s. Kolinjavadi Ramaswamy and Sukanthi (Subramanian) Nagarajan; m. Kalyani Hariharier, Feb. 5, 1975; children: Ramya, Rajeev, Ranjan. BSc, Madras U., 1964, MBBS, 1969. Diplomate Am. Bd. Pediatrics and Neonatal-Perinatal Medicine. Intern in pediat. Jewish Hosp. and Med. Ctr., Bklyn., 1971-72; resident in pediat. U. Md. Hosp., Balt., 1972-74; fellow in neonatology Georgetown U. Hosp., Washington, 1974-76, attending neonatologist, 1976—, dir. nurseries, chief neonatology, 1981—, vice chair pediat., 1988-98, prof. pediat. and ob-gyn. Co-chair rsch. com. Georgetown U. Med. Ctr., 2005—, co-chair children's health and devel., 2005—. Editor: Trace Elements/Mineral Metablolism During Development, 1993; editor pub. SIDS Series, 1985; editor jour. Current Concepts in Neonatology, India, 1990—; internat. editor Indian Jour. Pediat., India, 1988—. Chmn. Siva Vishnu Temple, Lanham, Md., 1981-91; mem. Fetus and New Born Com., Washington, 1988; founder, bd. dirs. Coun. of Hindu Temples U.S.A.; founder, coord. United Hindu Temples of Met. Washington; 1st v.p. Interfaith Conf., Washington; mem. D.C. bd. dirs. Nat. Youth Leadership Forum. Recipient "Preemies" cover article Newsweek, 1988, Interfaith Bridge Builder award, 2006, MAGIS Master Tchr. award, 2007, Clin. Tchr. of Yr. award, 2007; featured in "Washingtonian" jour., 1996, 2005, Georgetown U. Med. Ctr. Web Mag., 2003, 2007. Fellow Am. Coll. Nutrition, Am. Acad. Pediat.; mem. AAAS, N.Y. Acad. Scis., Internat. Soc. for Trace Element Rsch. in Humans, Soc. for Bioethics Consultation, Am. Soc. Law, Medicine and Ethics. Hindu. Achievements include research in neonatology, trace elements kinetics, reduction in infant mortality, neonatal immunology, and bioethics. Office Phone: 202-444-8709. Business E-Mail: sivasubk@georgetown.edu.

SIVIS, RAHSAN, counselor; b. Turkey, 1974; BS, Mid. East Tech. U., 1997, MS, 1999, PhD, 2005. Social Gerontology Programme United Nations Internat. Inst. on Aging, 2005, International Life-Link Seminar Life-Link Found., Sweden, 1992. Vis. rsch. scholar U. of Fla., Gainesville, Fla., 2002—03; rsch. asst. Mid. East Tech. U., Ankara, Turkey, 1998—2005. Exhibitions include in Ankara, Turkey. Joint Doctoral scholarship in Social Sciences, Turkish Acad. of Social Sciences. Home: Kukurtlu Mh Zubeyde Hanim Cd 46/10 Bursa Osmangazi 16080 Turkey Personal E-mail: rahsansivis@yahoo.com.

SJA'BANI, MOCHAMMAD, nephrologist, educator; b. Klaten, Central Java, Indonesia, June 29, 1947; MD, Gadjah Mada U., 1973, PhD, 2000. Prof. Gadjah Mada U., Yogyakarta, Indonesia, 2000—. Nephrology cons. Islamic Hosp., Gadjah Mada U., 1997, Panti Rapih Hosp., Gadjah Mada U., Yogyakarta, 2004; head Mlati rsch. Gadjah Mada U., 2005; guest prof. Juntendo U., Japan, 2009—. Recipient Bastian Trophy, Internat. Soc. Nephrology; Rsch. grant, Australia & New Zealand Nephrology. Master: Indonesian Nephrologist Assn.; fellow: Indonesian Internal Medicine; mem.: Indonesian Clin. Epidemiologist, Internat. Soc. Hypertension, ERA EDTA European Renal Assn., Internat. Soc. Nephrology, Am. Soc. Nephrology. Avocations: tennis, singing, travel. Home: Nandan Baru 19A Yogyakarta 55284 Indonesia Home Fax: 62274 625226. Personal E-mail: msbani_jogja@yahoo.com.

SJOBERG, STEFAN, physician; b. Stockholm, July 31, 1952; s. Sten Olof and Gyrid Ingeborg (Olsson) S.; m. Anna Birgitta Ståhl Christensen, Feb. 15, 1997; children: Sten, Kerstin. BM, Uppsala U., Sweden, 1974; MD, Karolinska Inst., Stockholm, 1977; PhD, Karolinska Inst., 1990. Intern Danderyds Hosp., Stockholm, 1978-79; resident Huddinge U. Hosp., Sweden, 1980-85, cons., 1985—, sr. cons. physician Ctr. for Metabolism and Endocrinology, 1994—, asst. head physician Acute Emergency Dept., 1994—2000, dir. grad. and postgrad. edn., 2002—04; assoc. prof. Karolinska Inst., Stockholm, 2001, Faculty Health Scis. U. Copenhagen, 2008; dir. residency program Karolinska U. Hosp., Stockholm, 2004—07; sr. cons., dept. medicine Halmstad County Hosp. Chmn. bd. Serafimer Kliniken AB, 1986—. Capt. med. corps Royal Swedish Life Guards, 1993—2010, mem., KLJ. With Lazarus Jerusalem. Fellow Arla Coldin, Swedish Soc. Medicine; mem. Swedish Med. Assn.(chmn.), Swedish Soc. Endocrinology (pres. 2011). Lutheran. Avocations: hunting, history, travel. Office: Halmstad Hosp Dept Medicine S 30185 Halmstad Sweden Office Phone: 4635131000. Business E-Mail: stefan.sjoberg@ki.se.

SJOLIE, ASTRID NORENG, physical therapist, researcher; b. Oslo, May 11, 1946; d. Harald and Alice Noreng; m. Olav Sjolie, May 15, 1971; children: Oystein, Harald died in 1980 Harald, Simen, Hanne. PhD, U. Bergen, Norway, 2002. Cert. physical therapist Norwegian Health Authority, 1970. Phys. therapist Peace Corps., Kampala, Uganda, 1971—72, Region Hosp., Elverum, Norway, 1974—82, Rendalen Municipality, Norway, 1989—2002, Amot Municipality, Rena, Norway, 2002—. Rschr. U. Bergen, 1999—2006, Hedmark U. Coll., Rena, 2006—. Contbr. articles to profl. jours. Recipient award, Spine Soc. Europe, 2001. Achievements include research in predictors of poor physical performance and low back pain in adolescents. Avocations: walking, skiing, travel, music. Home: Asta Ost Rena 2450 Norway Office: Amot Physiotherapy Clinic Wiborgs Gt 8 Rena 2450 Norway

SJOSTRAND, FRITIOF STIG, biologist, educator; b. Stockholm, Nov. 5, 1912; s. Nils Johan and Dagmar (Hansen) S.; m. Marta Bruhn-Fahraeus, Mar. 24, 1941 (dec. June 1954); 1 child, Rutger; m. Ebba Gyllenkrok, Mar. 28, 1955; 1 child, Johan; m. Birgitta Petterson, Jan. 23, 1969; 1 child, Peter. MD, Karolinska Institutet, Stockholm, 1941, PhD, 1945; PhD (hon.), U. Siena, 1974, North-East Hill U., Shillon, India, 1989. Asst. prof. anatomy Karolinska Institutet, 1945-48, assoc. prof., 1949-59, prof. histology, 1960-61; research assoc. MIT, 1947-48; vis. prof. UCLA, 1959, prof. zoology, 1960-82, prof. emeritus molecular biology, 1982—. Author: Über die Eigenfluoreszenz Tierischer Gewebe Mit Besonderer Berücksichtigung der Säugetierniere, 1944, Electron Microscopy of Cells and Tissues, Vol. I, 1967, Deducing Function from Structure, Vols. I and II, 1990; also numerous articles. Decorated North Star Orden Sweden; recipient Jubilee award Swedish Med. Soc., 1959, Anders Retzius gold medal, 1967; Paul Ehrlich-Ludwig Darmstaedter prize, 1971 Fellow Royal Micros. Soc. (hon., London), Am. Acad. Arts and Scis.; mem. Electron

Microscopy Soc. Am. (hon., Disting. Scientist award 1992), Japan Electron Microscopy Soc. (hon.), Scandinavian Electron Microscopy Soc. (hon.). Achievements include development technique for high resolution electron microscopy of cells, fluorescence microspectrography; inventor ultramicrotome. E-mail: fsjostra@ucla.edu.

SKAGGS, DAVID L., orthopedist, professor; BA in Neurosci. and Psychology, Amherst Coll., Mass., 1985; MD, Columbia U. Coll. of Physicians and Surgeons, NYC, 1989; Masters of Med. Mgmt., Marshal Sch. Bus., U. So. Calif., 2005—06. Diplomate Am. Bd. of Orthop. Surgery, 1998. Intern Columbia-Presbyterian Med. Ctr., NY, 1989—90, resident, 1990—94; Frank E. Stinchfield orthop. rsch. fellowship Columbia U., NY, 1991—92; pediatric orthop. fellowship U. So. Calif., Children's Hosp., LA, 1994—95; asst. prof., divsn. orthop. surgery U. Ala. Sch. Medicine, 1995—96; asst. prof. orthop. surgery U. of So. Calif.-Keck Sch. of Medicine, 1996—2002, assoc. prof. of orthop. surgery, 2002—; assoc. dir. Children's Orthop. Ctr., Children's Hosp. LA, endowed chair, pediat. spinal disorders, 2009—; chief orthop. surgery, Childrens Hosp., LA, 2009—; tenure prof. orthop. surgery U. Southen Calif. Cons. Stryker Spine, Allendale, NJ; instr. Am. Acad. of Orthop. Surgeons, Rosemont, Ill.; cons. Medtronics Sofamor Danek, Memphis. Author: (textbook) Staying Out of Trouble in Pediatric Orthopaedics; contbr. articles to profl. jours.; featured on Miracle Workers (ABC), 2006. Recipient Young Investigator Award, Pediatric Orthopaedic Soc. of N.Am., 2000, Sandoz award, Columbia U. of Coll. of Physicians and Surgeons, 1989; fellow Am., Brit., Can. Traveling Fellow, Am. Orthop. Assn., 2003, Traveling fellow, Pediatric Orthop. Soc. of N.Am., 2002. Mem.: Am. Acad. of Pediat., Sect. Orthopedic (exec. com.), Am. Acad. of Orthop. Surgeons, Pediatric Orthop.Soc. of N.Am. (bd. of directors, Young Investigators Award, Traveling Fellos 2000, 2002), Scoliosis Rsch. Soc. (program com.), LA Tennis Club, Salt Air Club. Achievements include design of Pediatric spinal instrumentation. Avocations: meditation, tennis, weightlifting, boogie boarding, yoga. Office: Childrens Hospital Los Angeles 4650 Sunset Blvd #69 Los Angeles CA 90027 Office Fax: 323-666-4409.

SKALSKA, ANNA BARBARA, medical educator, researcher; d. Bogdan Przewlocki and Zofia Przewlocka; m. Janusz Hieronim Skalski, July 7, 1977; children: Grzegorz Feliks Skalski, Barbara Malgorzata. MD, PhD, Jagiellonian U. Med. Coll., Kraków, Poland, 1979. Asst. Dept. Heart & Vessels Diseases Inst. Cardiology, Kraków, 1979—81; physician Residential Home for Aged, Kraków, 1981—83; asst. U. Hosp. Dept. Geriat., Kraków, 1983—2000; assoc. prof. U. Hosp. Dept. Internal Medicine & Gerontology, 2000—. Assoc. prof. Jagiellonian U. Med. Coll., 2003—. Contbr. scientific papers to profl. jours. Fellow: Polish Assn. Gerontology; mem.: Polish Assn. Hypertension, Polish Assn. Cardiology, European Acad. Medicine Ageing (Sion, Switzerland). Office: Dept Internal Medicine & Geriatrics Sniadeckich 10 Kraków 31-531 Poland

SKARO, ANTON I., surgeon, educator; b. Can., June 23, 1971; MD, U. Western Ont., 1998; PhD, Dalhousie U., 2003. Instr., surgery Comprehensive Transplant Ctr. Northwestern U. Feinberg Sch. Medicine, 2005—07, asst. prof., surgery, 2007—. Attending surgeon Northwestern Med. Faculty Found., 2007—11, Childrens Meml. Hosp., 2007—11. Recipient Young Investigator award, Can. Soc. Clin. Investigation. Fellow: ACS, Royal Coll. Physicians and Surgeons Can.; mem.: Transplantation Soc., Am. Soc. Transplant Surgeons, Assn. Academic Surgery. Avocations: soccer, hockey. Office: 676 N St Clair St Arkes Pavilion Chicago IL 60611 Office Fax: 312-695-9194. Business E-Mail: askaro@nmh.org.

SKATVEDT, OLAV, head and neck surgeon; b. Eidsvoli, Norway, Aug. 27, 1953; s. Knut and Dina (Kjos) S.; children: Helene, Marianne, Preben. Grad. in sociology, U. Oslo, 1975, MB, 1981, postgrad. in family medicine, 1990-95, postgrad. in otorhinolaryngology, 1991, PhD in Medicine, 1996. Gen. practice medicine, Eidsvoll, 1982-86; indsl. physician, 1982-86; sr. registrar, fellow Royal Nat. Throat, Nose and Ear Hosp., London, 1991-92; house officer, registrar, sr. registrar Ullevaal U. Hosp., Oslo, 1987-91, 92-94, cons., head sleep related breathing disorders unit, 1994, Omnia Hosp., Oslo, 2000—05; with pvt. clinic, 2006—; head Sovnspesialisten, Oslo, 2007—. Mem. editorial bd: Sleep and Breathing, 1996; mem. sci. bd. Jour. of Norwegian Med. Assn., 2005—; contbr. numerous articles on sleep pathology to med. jours. Grantee Norwegian SIDS Soc., 1991, Norwegian Rsch. Coun., 1992-94, 97, Norwegian Med. Assn., 1994, Ullevaal U. Hosp. Rsch. Found., 1995-96, Norwegian Rsch. Coun., 1997. Mem. Norwegian Otolaryn. Soc. (sec. bd. dirs. 1994-95, v.p. bd. dirs. 1996-97, pres. bd. dirs. 1998-99). Avocations: hunting, skiing, dog training. Home: Borgenveien 29B 0370 Oslo Norway Office: Ullensaker ENT 2050 Jessheim Norway Business E-Mail: olav.skatvedt@sovnspesialisten.no.

SKEBERDIS, VYTENIS ARVYDAS, research scientist; b. Kaunas, Lithuania, Nov. 26, 1959; M, Kaunas U. Tech., 1982; PhD, Kaunas U. Medicine, 1992. Postdoc. fellow U. Paris Faculty Pharmacy, 1995—97; rsch. assoc., dept. neurosci. Yeshiva U. Albert Einstein Coll. Medicine, 1999—2001; sr. scientist Kaunas U. Medicine, 2001—06; chief scientist, lab. head Lithuanian U. Health Scis. Inst. Cardiology, 2006—; prof., dept. physiology Lithuanian U. Health Scis., 2010. Bd. mem. Lithuanian Technol. Platform Nanomedicine, 2009, Lithuanian Sci., Inovations and Tech. Agy., 2011; expert Rsch. Coun. Lithuania, 2010. Recipient Lithuanian Sci. award, Rsch. Coun. Lithuania, 2008. Mem.: Lithuanian Physiol. Soc., Lithuanian Biochem. Soc. Avocations: jazz, basketball, literature. Office: 17 Sukileliu Ave Kaunas 50009 Lithuania

SKEHEL, SIR JOHN JAMES, research scientist; b. Feb. 27, 1941; m. Anita Varley; 2 children. BSc, U. Coll. Wales; PhD, U. Manchester, 1966; DSc (hon.), U. Coll. London, 2004. Postdoc. fellow dept. biol. chemistry Duke U. Med. Ctr., NC, 1965—69, U. Aberdeen, 1965—69; mem. sci. staff Med. Rsch. Coun., 1971—2007; fellow London divsn. virology MRC Nat. Inst. Med. Rsch., Mill Hill, England, 1969—; dir. London Nat. Inst. for Med. Rsch., London, 1987—2007; dir. WHO Collaborating Ctr. for Reference and Rsch. on Influenza, 1975—94; head divsn. virology and infections and immunity group. Vis. prof. U. Glasgow, Glasgow, Scotland, 1997—; bd. dir. Nat. Inst. Biol. Stds. and Control. Contbr. articles to profl. jours. Recipient Robert Koch prize, Jeantet Prix de Medicine prize, ICN Internat. prize in virology, Knighthood, 1996, Ernst Chain Prize, Imperial Coll. London, 2004, Stuart Mudd award for basic microbiology, 2005. Fellow: Acad. Med. Scis. (mem. coun. 2001, v.p. 2001), Royal Soc. (Royal medal 2004); mem.: Soc. Gen. Microbiology (hon.). Achievements include research in mechanisms of interferon induction by viruses, influenza virus genome struction, transcription and replication; influenza virus membrane protein structure and activities; three-dimensional structure of influenza virus haemagglutinin membrane glycoprotein; the mechanisms of its receptor binding and membrane fusion activities and the structural basis of its recognition by antibodies and its antigenic variation.

SKELTON, WILLIAM DOUGLAS, physician; MD, Emory U., 1963. Sr. v.p. rsch. and health affairs Mercer U., Macon, Ga., 1985—2004; dist health dir. Coastal Health Dist., Savannah, Ga., 2004—. Office: Coastal Health Dist 24 Oglethorpe Professional Blvd Savannah GA 31416 Home Phone: 912-598-0762; Office Phone: 912-356-2233, 912-644-5210. Business E-Mail: wdskelton@dhr.state.ga.com.

SKIDMORE, JULIAN ALEXANDRA, physiologist, researcher; b. Eastleigh, Eng., Oct. 3, 1963; d. Michael Alexander and Vivien Mary Skidmore. BS (hon.), U. London, 1985; PhD, U. Cambridge, Eng., 1994. Rsch. asst. Equine Fertility Unit, Newmarket, England, 1986—91; sci. dir. Camel Reproduction Ctr., Dubai, United Arab Emirates, 1994—. Mem.: Soc. of Reproduction and Fertility. Achievements include research in created the world's first Camas (camel x llama hybrids). Office: Camel Reproduction Ctr PO Box 11808 Dubai United Arab Emirates Office Fax: +971 4 3379030.

SKINNER, JON, rehabilitation hospital administrator; BBA, Hardin-Simmons U.; MBA, U. Colo. CPA. Dir. physician compensation and benefits Health Tex. Provider Network; exec. dir. Baylor Medical Ctr., Southwest Fort Worth; pres. Baylor Inst. Rehab.; interim pres. Baylor Specialty Health Centers and Our Children's House at Baylor. Mem.: Tex. State Soc. CPAs, Am. Inst. CPAs, Healthcare Financial Mgmt. Assn., American Coll. Healthcare Executives. Office: Baylor Inst Rehab 909 N Washington Dallas TX 75246

SKINNER, JONATHAN SNOWDEN, economics educator; b. Boston, Aug. 29, 1955; s. Walter Jay and Sylvia (H.) S.; m. Martha Amy McLafferty, Oct. 17, 1987; children: Owen, Lucy. BA, U. Rochester, 1977; MA, UCLA, 1978, PhD, 1983. Asst. prof. to prof. economics U. Va., Charlottesville, 1981—95; prof. economics Dartmouth Coll., Hanover, NH, 1995—, chair economics dept., 2004—06, John Sloan Dickey Third Century chair of economics, 2007—; prof. family and cmty. medicine Dartmouth Med. Sch., 1999—, Dartmouth Inst. Health Policy and Clin. Practice, 2007—. Rsch. assoc. Nat. Bur. Econ. Rsch., Cambridge, Mass., 1989—, rsch. fellow, 1991—93; health adv. panel Congl. Budget Office, 2007—. Mem.: Inst. Medicine, NAS. Office: Dartmouth Inst Health Policy & Clin Practice 35 Centerra Pkwy Lebanon NH 03766

SKINSTAD, ANNE HELENE, psychologist, researcher; b. Bergen, Hordaland, Norway, July 8, 1949; d. Alfhild (Hektoen) and Leif Sigurd Skinstad; m. Peter E. Nathan, 1993; 1 child, Siri Ødegaard. PhD in Psychology, U.of Bergen, Norway, 1977; PhD, U.of Bergen, 2001. Diplomate in Clin. Psychology Coll. Problems of Drug Dependence, 1985. Staff psychologist Hjellestad Clinic and Dr. Martens Clinic, Bergen, Norway, Hordaland, Norway, 1977—79; leading psychologist Blå-Kors Social Ctr., Bergen, Norway, 1979—83; facullty mem. U. Iowa, Iowa City, 1990—2001, assoc. clin. prof., Coll. Pub. Health, 2001—06. Rsch. fellow The U. of Bergen, Norway, 1983—87; leading psychologist treatment ctr. substance abusing women Hjellestad Clinic, Bergen, Norway, 1987—90; program dir. Prairielands Addiction Tech. Transfer Ctr., Iowa City, 1995—; asst. prof. Coll. Edn. U. Iowa, 1990—2001, asst. prof. dept. cmty. & behavioral health, 2001—06; clin. assoc. prof. dept. cmty. & behavioral health U. Iowa Coll. Pub. Health, 2006—. Contbr. articles to profl. jours. Recipient numerous grants, Norway, U.S. Mem.: APA, Nat. Assn. Lesbian, Gay, Addiction Prof. (bd. mem.), Am. Public Health Assn., Rsch. Soc. Alcoholism, European Roschach Assn. (founding mem. 1989), Nat. ATTC (chmn. liaison com., mem. curriculum com.), Norwegian Psychol. Assn. Avocations: owning Australian sheppards, piano. Office: U Iowa Coll Pub Health E239GH Iowa City IA 52242 Business E-Mail: anne-skinstad@uiowa.edu.

SKLADANOWSKI, ANDRZEJ C., medical researcher, educator; b. Gdynia, Poland, Oct. 27, 1951; MSc in Chemistry, Gdansk U. Tech., 1974; PhD, Med. U. Gdansk, 1980. Rsch. officer U. Wales Coll. Medicine, 1988—90; prof. med. biology Med. U. Gdansk, 2000—, vice dean intercollegiate faculty biotech., 2005—. Bd. dirs. Ctr. Excellence in Bio-safety and in Molecular Medicine, 2003—06; bd. pub. trustees Academic Hosps. Gdansk, 2005—08. Contbr. chapters to books to profl. publs. Recipient Outstanding Achievements award, Min. of Health, Poland; scholarship, Pres. of Republic of Poland. Mem.: Editl. Bd. Toxicology in Vitro, Polish Biochem. Soc. Avocations: literature, travel, bicycling. Office: 1 Debinki St Gdansk Pomerania PL-80-211 Poland Business E-Mail: acskla@gumed.edu.pl.

SKLAREW, ROBERT JAY, biomedical research educator, consultant; b. NYC, Nov. 25, 1941; s. Arthur and Jeanette (Laven) S.; m. Toby Willner, July 15, 1970; children: David Michael, Gary Richard. BA in Zoology, Cornell U., 1963; MS, NYU, 1965, PhD in Biology, 1970. Assoc. rsch. scientist NYU Sch. Medicine, NYC, 1965-70, rsch. scientist, 1971-73, sr. rsch. scientist, 1973-79; rsch. asst. prof. pathology Goldwater Meml. Hosp. Sch. Medicine, NYC, 1979-87, rsch. assoc. prof. pathology, 1987-88; dir. cytokinetics and imaging lab. NYU rsch. svc. Goldwater Meml. Hosp., NYC, 1980-88; prof. cell biology, anatomy and medicine N.Y. Med. Coll., Valhalla, 1988-98. Rsch. assoc. dept. pathology Lenox Hill Hosp., N.Y.C., 1981-88; pres., CEO R.J. Sklarew Imaging Assoc., Inc., Larchmont, N.Y., 1990—2003; chmn. consensus panel for diagnostic cancer imaging Nat. Cancer Inst., 1994. Author: Microscopic Imaging of Steroid Receptors, 1990; sr. author: Cytometry, Jour. Histochem. Cytochem., Cancer, Exptl. Cell Rsch. Group leader Boy Scouts Am., Larchmont, 1978—80; bd. dir. Pinelake Park Coop, 1998—2001, 2006—09, pres., 2007—09. Grantee Am. Cancer Soc., Nat. Cancer Inst./NIH Conc. for Tobacco Rsch., R.J. Reynolds Industries Found., NYU; recipient Shannon award Nat. Cancer Inst., 1991. Mem. AAAS, Cell Kinetics Soc. (sec. 1983-85, 85-87, v.p. 1987-88, pres. 1988-89, chmn. nominations 1991, 93), N.Y. Acad. Sci., Soc. for Analytic Cytology, Soc. for Cell Biology, Tissue Culture Assn., Union Concerned Scientists, Kappa Delta Rho. Democrat. Achievements include development of methodology, algorithms and Receptogram analytic software for application of microscopic imaging in medical research and in pathodiagnosis of cancer, imaging methods for simultaneous densitometry and autoradiographic analysis; research in diagnostic imaging of steroid receptors, oncogenes and DNA ploidy in cancer, proliferative patterns and cell cycle kinetics of human solid tumors. Home: 8 Vine Rd Larchmont NY 10538-1247 Office: RJ Sklarew Imaging Assoc Inc 8 Vine Rd Larchmont NY 10538-1247 Personal E-mail: rjsklarew@aol.com.

SKLOVSKY, ROBERT J., naturopathic physician, pharmacist, educator; b. NY; BS summa cum laude, Bklyn. Coll., 1975; MA in Sci. Edn., Columbia U., 1976; PharmD, U. Pacific, 1977; D in Naturopathic Medicine, Nat. Coll. Naturopathic Medicine, 1983. Intern Tripler Army Med. Ctr., Honolulu, 1977; pvt. practice Milwaukie, Oreg., 1983—. Recipient Bristol Labs. award Bklyn. Coll. Pharmacy, 1975, Coll. Gold medal, 1975, NYC Sci. Tchg. award Chemist's Club NY, 1976. Mem.: NY Acad. Sci. Avocations: classical and jazz music, art, gardening, painting. Office: 6910 SE Lake Rd Milwaukie OR 97267-2101 Office Phone: 503-654-3938.

SKLOWER BROOKS, SUSAN L., clinical geneticist, educator; Attended, Robert Wood Johnson Med. Sch., Piscataway, NJ, 1971—73, Mt. Sinai Sch. of Medicine, NY, NY, 1973—75. Diplomate Am. Bd. Pediatrics, 1979, Am. Bd. Med. Genetics-clin. genetics, 1982, Am. Bd. Med. Genetics-biochemical genetics, 1984. Resident pediatrician Mt. Sinai Med. Ctr., NYC, 1975—77, fellowship med. genetics, 1977—79; assoc. prof. pediat., obstetrics, gynecology and reproductive sciences Robert Wood Johnson Med. Sch., chief pediatric med. genetics divsn., chief perinatal genetics sect. Office: Robert Wood Johnson Medical School RWJ Professional Center 4th Fl 97 Paterson St New Brunswick NJ 08901 Office Phone: 732-235-9386. Office Fax: 732-235-7088.

SKOFFER, BIRGIT SØRENSEN, physiotherapist; d. Aksel Sørensen and Poula Pedersen Skoffer; m. Ole Kudsk Jensen, June 8, 1995; children: Esben Kudsk, Simon Kudsk, Jakob Kudsk. Degree in Physiotherapy, U. Holstebro, Denmark, 1977; MPH, U. Aarhus, Denmark, 2003. Phys. therapist Hosp. Horsens, Denmark, 1977—91, Hosp. Aarhus Cmty., 1992—94, U. Hosp. Aarhus, 2004—. Censor Assn. Danish Physiotherapists, Copenhagen, 2007—. Contbr. articles to profl. jours. Office: Univ Hosp Aarhus Tage Hansens Gade Aarhus C 8000 Denmark

SKOGSBERGH, JAMES H., health facility administrator; BS, Iowa State U.; M in health admin., U. Iowa. Exec. v.p. Iowa Health Sys., Des Moines; pres, CEO Iowa Meth. Med. Ctr., Iowa Luth. Hosp., Blank Children's Hosp.; admin. resident to exec. v.p., chief oper. officer Mem. Health Sys., South Bend, Ind., 1982—91; exec. v.p. Iowa Meth. Med. Ctr., 1991; chief operating officer Advocate Health Care, Oak Brook, Ill., 2001—02, pres., CEO, 2002—. Fellow: Am. Coll. Healthcare Exec.; mem.: Ill. Hosp. Assoc. Advocacy Coun., Metro. Chgo. Healthcare Coun., Young Pres. Organ., Chgo. Econ. Club. Office: Advocate Health Care 2025 Windsor Dr Oak Brook IL 60523-1586 *

SKOLNICK, LAWRENCE, neonatal physician, medical association administrator; b. NYC, July 29, 1947; s. Harry and Sylvia Skolnick; m. Tamar Tumarkin, Apr. 7, 1970; children: Daniel, Michael, Rachel. BS, CUNY, 1968; MD, NYU, 1972; MPH, U. N.C., 1980. Dir. newborn medicine Hosp. of Albert Einstein Coll. Medicine, Bronx, NY, 1977-80; dir. neonatology (N.J.), Morristown, NJ, 1980—, Overlook Hosp., Summit, NJ, 1999—, Atlantic Health Sys., 1999—; assoc. prof. med. pediat. UNDNJ-N.J.Sch. Medicine, 2001—. Business E-Mail: larry.skolnick@atlantichealth.org.

SKOLNIK, RICHARD ALAN, plastic surgeon; b. NYC, Jan. 7, 1951; BA in Biology summa cum laude, C.W. Post Coll., 1972; MD, Cornell U., 1976. Diplomate Am. Bd. Plastic Surgery. Resident gen. surgery Mt. Sinai Med. Ctr., NYC, 1976-79, resident plastic surgery, 1979-82, assoc. attending, 1982—; clin. instr. Mt. Sinai Sch. Medicine, NYC, 1982-84, asst. clin. prof., 1985—2005, assoc. clin. prof., 2005—; assoc. attending Beth Israel Med. Ctr., NYC, 1984—; courtesy staff Beth Israel North (Doctor's Hosp.), NYC, 1987—; plastic surgeon Madison Ave. Plastic Surgery, NYC. Fellow cleft lip and palate Children's Hosp., Lima, Peru, 1982; vis. prof. Reconstructive Surgery Found., Maceo, Brazil, 1990, Pune, India, 1994, Beijing, China, 1998; TV appearances Today Show, The View, Good Morning America, CNN, ABC, CBS, FOX News. Cons. editor: Breast Cancer the Complete Guide, Good Housekeeping's Illustrated Guide to Women's Health. Named one of Top 100 Doctors in NY, 1998—, The Best Beauty Docs, NY Mag., 2003. Fellow ACS; mem. AMA, Am. Soc. Plastic Surgeons, Am. Soc. Anesthetic Plastic Surgery, Med. Soc. State of NY, NY Regional Soc. Plastic and Reconstructive Surgeons, Barsky Soc. Avocations: ceramics, cooking, golf, tennis. Office: Madison Ave Plastic Surgery 21 E 87th St New York NY 10128-0506 Office Phone: 212-722-1977. Office Fax: 212-722-2283.

SKOOG, GERALD DUANE, science educator; b. Sioux City, Iowa, Feb. 27, 1936; s. Paul and Mary Ann Skoog; m. Elizabeth Ann Lee, Dec. 28, 1962; children: Jeffrey, John, Sarah. BS, U. Nebr., 1958. Tchr. various schs., Nebr., Ill., 1958-69; instr. U. Nebr., Lincoln, summer 1969; asst. prof. curriculum and instrn. Tex. Tech U., Lubbock, 1969-72, assoc. prof., coordinator program, 1972-74, assoc. prof., chmn. secondary edn., 1976-80, prof., chmn. secondary edn., 1980-90, prof., chmn. curriculum and instrn., 1990-97, Helen DeVitt Jones prof., 1997-2001, pres. faculty senate, 1986-87, dean Coll. Edn., 2002—03, Paul Whitfield Horn prof., 2000—04, prof. emeritus, 2005; dir. Ctr. Integration Sci. and Edn. Rsch., 2004—. Vis. prof. We. Ill. U., summer 1972; lectr. in field; participant, facilitator numerous workshops; cons. Contbr. numerous articles to profl. jours., also reviewer articles and papers; co-author secondary sch. science textbooks. Bd. dirs. Gloria Dei Luth. Ch., Lubbock, 1971-74, 92-93; bd. dirs. Luth. Coun. Cmty. Action, 1970-71, Good Neighbor Ministry, 1982-84;

leader Boy Scouts Am., 1978-79; foster parent Luth. Social Svcs. Tex.; bd. dirs. Triangle Coalition for Sci. and Tech., 1986-95. Recipient Pres.'s Faculty Achievement award Tex. Tech. U., 1986, Disting. Leadership award, 1996, Award of Excellence, U. Nebr., Lincoln Tchrs. Coll. Alumni Assn., 2003; named Notable Alumnus, U. Nebr., Lincoln, Tchrs. Coll., 1998; named to Tex. Sci. Hall of Fame, 2000. Fellow AAAS, AERA (inaugral fellow 2009); mem. ASCD, Friend Darwin, NCSE, NSTA (life, bd. dirs. 1977-79, pres. 1985-86, various coms., Disting. Svc. to Sci. Edn. award 1994, Robert H. Carleton award 2004), Nat. Assn. Rsch., Sci. Tchrs. Assn. Tex. (hon., past pres., Skoog Cup award), Nat. Assn. Biology Tchrs. Lutheran. Office: Tex Tech U Coll Edn Lubbock TX 79409 Home: 4709 116th St Lubbock TX 79424 Office Phone: 806-742-1997 x 259. E-mail: gerald.skoog@ttu.edu.

SKOOG, WILLIAM ARTHUR, retired oncologist; b. Culver City, Calif., Apr. 10, 1925; s. John Lundeen and Allis Rose (Gatz) Skoog; m. Ann Douglas, Sept. 17, 1949; children: Karen, William Arthur, James Douglas, Allison. AA, UCLA, 1944; BA with great distinction, Stanford U., 1946, MD, 1949. Intern in medicine Stanford Hosp., San Francisco, 1948-49, asst. resident in medicine, 1949-50, N.Y. Hosp., NYC, 1950-51; sr. resident in medicine Wadsworth VA Hosp., LA, 1951, attending specialist in internal medicine, 1962-68; pvt. practice internal medicine Los Altos, Calif., 1959-61; pvt. practice hematology and oncology, Santa Monica, Calif., 1971-72; pvt. practice med. oncology, San Bernardino, Calif., 1972-94; ret. Assoc. staff Palo Alto-Stanford Med. Ctr., 1959-61, U. Calif. Med. Ctr., San francisco, 1959-61; assoc. attending physician UCLA Hosp. and Clinics, 1961-78; vis. physician in internal medicine Harbor Gen. Hosp., Torrance, Calif., 1962-65, attending physician, 1965-71; cons. in chemistry Clin. Lab., UCLA Hosp., 1963-68; affiliate cons. staff St. John's Hosp., Santa Monica, 1967-71, courtesy staff, 1971-72; courtesy attending med. staff Santa Monica Hosp., 1967-72; staff physician St. Bernardine (Calif.) Hosp., 1972-94, hon. staff, 1994—; staff physician San Bernardino Cmty. Hosp., 1972-90, courtesy staff, 1990-94; chief sect. oncology San Bernardino County Hosp., 1972-76; cons. staff Redlands(Calf.) Cmty. Hosp., 1972-83, courtesy staff, 1983-94, hon. staff, 1994—; asst. in medicine Cornell U. Med. Coll., N.Y.C., 1950-51; jr. rsch. physician UCLA Atomic Energy Project, 1954-55; instr. medicine, asst. rsch. physician dept. medicine UCLA Med. Ctr., 1955-56, asst. prof. medicine, asst. rsch. physician, 1956-59; clin. assoc. in hematology VA Ctr., L.A., 1956-59; co-dir. metabolic rsch. unit UCLA Ctr. for Health Scis., 1955-59, 61-65; co-dir. Health Scis. Clin. Rsch. Ctr., 1965-68, dir., 1968-72; clin. instr. medicine Stanford U., 1959-61; asst. clin. prof. medicine, assoc. rsch. physician U. Calif. Med. Ctr., San Francisco, 1959-61, lectr. medicine UCLA Sch. Medicine, 1961-62, assoc. prof., 1962-72, assoc. clin. prof., 1973—2011. Contbr. articles to med. jours. Active duty USNR, 1943—46, lt. M.C. USNR, 1951—53. Fellow: ACP, Am Soc. Internal Medicine; mem.: AMA, San Bernardino County Med. Soc., Am. Soc Clin. Oncology, L.A. Acad. Medicine, Am. Fedn. Clin. Rsch., Western Soc. Clin. Rsch., So. Calif. Acad. Clin Oncology, Calif. Med. Assn., Redlands Country Club, Alpha Omega Alpha, Sigma Xi, Phi Beta Kappa, Alpha Kappa Kappa. Episcopalian (vestryman 1965-70). Home: 1119 Kimberly Pl Redlands CA 92373-6786 Home Phone: 909-798-7380. Home Fax: 909-798-5016. Personal E-mail: adsredarrow@aol.com.

SKORTON, DAVID JAN, academic administrator, medical educator; b. Milw., Nov. 22, 1949; s. Samuel and Pauline (Millstein) Skorton; 1 child, Joshua Samuel. BA in Psychology, Northwestern U., Evanston, Ill., 1970; MD, Northwestern U., Chgo., 1974. Diplomate Nat. Bd. Med. Examiners, American Bd. Internal Medicine, cert. in cardiovasc. disease. Intern, resident UCLA, 1974—77, cardiology fellowship, 1977—79, chief resident dept. medicine, 1978—79, adj. asst. prof., 1978—80; instr. dept. internal medicine U. Iowa, Iowa City, 1980—81, asst. prof., 1981—84, asst. prof. elec. and computer engring., 1982—84, dir. Cardiovasc. Image Processing Lab., Cardiovasc. Rsch. Ctr., Coll. Medicine, 1982—96, assoc. prof. internal medicine, elec. and computer engring., 1984—88, dir. divsn. gen. internal medicine, Coll. Medicine, 1985—89, prof. internal medicine, elec. and computer engring., 1988—2006, assoc. chair clin. programs, Coll. Medicine, 1989—92, v.p. rsch., 1992—2003, prof. biomedical engring., 1999—2006, v.p. external rels., 2000—03, pres., 2003—06; prof. dept. biomedical engring., pres. Cornell U., Ithaca, NY, 2006—, prof. dept. medicine and pediat., Weill Cornell Med. Coll. NYC, 2006—. Dir. echocardiology lab. VA Med. Ctr., Iowa City, 1980—89; co-founder, co-dir. Adolescent & Adult Congenital Heart Disease Clinic, U. Iowa Hospitals; mem. internat. and coop. projects Fogerty Ctr. study sect. NIH, 1988—92, chmn., 1990—92; mem. nat. adv. coun. Nat. Inst. Biomedical Imaging & Bioengineering; co-chair adv. bd. Africa-US Higher Edn. Initiative, Assn. Pub. & Land-Grant Universities; past chair Bus.-Higher Edn. Forum. Monthly columnist Cornell Daily Sun, mem. editl. bd. American Jour. Noninvasive Cardiology, Cardiovasc. Imaging, Echocardiography; contbr. numerous articles to profl. jours., chapters to books. Chair Task Force Diversifying NY State Economy Through Industry Higher Edn. Partnerships, 2009. Recipient Rsch. Career Devel. award, Nat. Heart Lung & Blood Inst., NIH, 1984—89, Disting. Achievement award, Roy J. & Lucille A. Carver Coll. Medicine, U. Iowa, 2003, Alumni Merit award, Feinberg Sch. Medicine, Northwestern U.; Regents' scholar, UCLA, 1967—68. Fellow: ACP, American Physiol. Soc., American Heart Assn., American Coll. Cardiology; mem.: AAAS, Inst. Medicine, Nat. Inst. Biomedical Imaging & Bioengring., Coun. Fgn. Rels. (life), Bus. Higher Edn., Internat. Soc. Adult Congenital Cardiac Disease, Assn. Univ. Cardiologists. Jewish. Office: Office of President Cornell University 300 Day Hall Ithaca NY 14853 Office Phone: 607-255-5201. Office Fax: 607-255-9924. E-mail: president@cornell.edu. *

SKOULAKIS, CHARALAMPOS E., medical educator; b. Chania, Greece, Jan. 13, 1960; s. Efstratios C. and Maria K. Skoulakis; m. Efthimia A. Petinaki; children: Efstratios C., Anargiros C., Klelia E. Pantelidi. PhD, Med. Sch. Crete, 1997. Diplomate Med. Sch. Patras, 1986. Lectr. ENT dept. U. Hosp. Crete, Heraklion, Greece, 1996—2000, U. Hosp. Thessaly, Larissa, Greece, 2000—04, Gen. Hosp. Volos, 2004—; assoc. prof. otolaryngology U. Thessaly, 2009. Office: University Hosp Larissa Larissa Greece Home: Mela Pavlou 13 383 33 Volos Greece Home Phone: 00302421034200. Home Fax: 00302421036870. Personal E-mail: skulakis@hotmail.com.

SKOUNTI, MARIA, special education educator; b. Rethymno, Crete, Greece, Apr. 1, 1980; BSc with honors, U. Crete, 2001, PhD, 2006. Spl. educator Ministry of Edn., 45th Primary Sch., Heraklion, Crete, 2002—. Adj. prof. Faculty Primary Edn., U. Crete, 2007—; instr. context introductory tng. tchrs. Greek Ministry of Edn., 2007—10; sci. assoc., dept. child & adolescent psychiatry U. Psychiat. Clinic, U. Gen. Hosp., Heraklion, 2010—. Recipient 2nd prize, Cultural Orgn. Municipality St. Nicholas, Greece. Master: Greek Fedn. Parent Children Learning Disabilities; mem.: Greek Sci. Assn. Spl. Edn., Greek ADHD Assn. Avocations: literature, music, squash. Home: Romanu Diogeni 9 Heraklion Crete 71305 Greece Personal E-mail: skountim@med.uoc.gr.

SKOURA, EVANGELIA, nuclear medicine physician; b. Athens, Greece, May 12, 1975; MD, Med. U. Patras, Greece, 2001; PhD, U. Athens. Cons., nuc. medicine dept. Evangelismos Gen. Hosp., Athens, 2009—. Mem.: Greek Soc. Nuc. Medicine, European Assn. Nuc. Medicine. Home: Bouziki 50 Athens 11524 Greece Personal E-mail: lskoura@yahoo.gr.

SKRICKOVA, JANA, pulmonologist, educator; b. Brno, Czech Republic, Feb. 18, 1952; d. Boris Bily and Eva Bila; children: Jan Skicka, Anna. MD, PhD, Masaryk U, Brno, 1976. Jr. physician Hosp. TB and Respiratory Diseases, Babice nad Svitavou, Czech Republic, 1976—83, registrar bronchology, 1983—85, asst. chair, 1985—90; head dept. respiratory diseases and TB U. Hosp. Brno, Brno, 1991—. Asst. prof. Masaryk U., Faculty of Medicine, Brno, 1993—. Contbr. chapter in book Pulmonary Infiltrates Aetiology in Leukemic Patients with Fever, 1995, articles to profl. jours. Mem.: European Assn. Bronchology and Interventional Pulmonology, European Soc. Bronchology, Czech Respiratory Soc. (bd. dirs. 1998—), World Assn. Sarkoidosis and Other Granulomatous Disordes, European Soc. Palliative Care, European Respiratory Soc. Avocations: skiing, volleyball, poetry, art. Home: Ondrouskova 20 Brno 635 00 Czech Republic Office: Univ Hosp Brno Bohunice Jihlavska 20 Brno 625 00 Czech Republic Office Fax: 00420-5-3223-2405. E-mail: jskric@fnbrno.cz.

SKRIP, CATHY LEE, psychologist; b. Berwyn, Ill., July 19, 1948; d. Raymond Joseph and Gladys Catherine (Mazanec) Jirsa; m. Paul Joseph Skrip, Aug. 29, 1970; children: Carrie Anne Ackerman, Christie Ellen, Jonathan Paul. AB in English, Miami U., Ohio, 1969; MS in Counseling, Calif. State U., LA, 1971. Cert. counselor, Calif.; lic. psychologist Minn. 1990. Counselor, instr. Rio Hondo Coll., Whittier, Calif., 1971-73; instr. N. Shore C.C., Beverly, Mass., 1974-75, counselor, dir. of placement, 1973-75; instr. Western Wis. Tech. Inst., La Crosse, Wis., 1975; asst. dir. Cmty. Care Orgn. of La Crosse County, Inc., Wis., 1976-79; planning analyst Dept. Health and Social Svcs., Madison, Wis., 1979-80; pvt. practice Hugo, Minn., 1992—98, Crystal, Minn., 1993—98, New Hope, Minn., 1998—2003, Forest Lake, Minn., 1998—. Charter trustee 621 Found., Shoreview, Minn., 1988-91, co-chair, 1990-91, chair, 1991-92, mem. 20th anniversary com.; sec. Rio Hondo Coll. Faculty Assn., Whittier Calif., 1972-73. Author: (with Kristin Kunzman) Women With Secrets: Dealing With Domestic Abuse and Childhood Sexual Abuse in Treatment, 1991. Vol. co-facilitator battered women's support group Alexandra House Circle Pines, 85-88, Treas. LWV, La Crosse, 1978-81, mem. Ramsey County Cmty. Initiative to End Family Violence, 1990—94, Family Violence Tng. Task Force, St. Paul, 1991, Mounds View Violence Prevention Coun., 1993—97, Anoka County Domestic Violence Coun., 1994—97, Forest Lake C. of C., 2003-; chair sch. adv. com. Chippewa Elem. Ctr., St. Paul, 1986-87; bd. dirs. YWCA, La Crosse, 1980-81; adv. com. Social Work Dept. U. Wis., La Crosse, 1981-82; bd. dirs. Ret. Sr. Vol. Program, La Crosse, 1980-82; founder, exec. dir. Abuse Resource Ctr., St. Paul, 1988-92; exec. dir. Abuse Resource Ctr. Hugo, 1992-93. Recipient Bertha Provine Oxford Coll. scholarship, Miami U., Oxford, Ohio, 1968, Alumni Assn. Departmental Honors award Calif. State U., LA, 1971. Mem. Minn. Women in Psychology (social action chair 1992-94, Greater Minn. co-chair 1993-94, steering com. 1992-98, vice-chair 1994-95, chair 1995-97, Founding Mother's award 2007, Profl. Devel.-Mentoring Com. 2008-), Minn. Psychol. Assn., Alpha Omicron Pi. Roman Catholic. Avocations: sewing, bicycling, crafts, running, canoeing. Office: 20 North Lake St Ste 308 Forest Lake MN 55025 Office Phone: 651-464-8918.

SKROCKI, EDMUND STANLEY, II, health fair promoter, executive; b. Schenectady, NY, Sept. 6, 1953; s. Edmund Stanley I and Lorraine (Nocian) S.; m. Diane Carolyn Sittig, Sept. 6, 1976 (div. 1992); children: Carolyn, Michelle, Edmund III, Johnathan Edmund; m. Deborrah Anne Allen, June 4, 1998 (div. Mar. 2000). AA, LaValley Coll., 1981; BA, Sonoma State U., 1982, MA, 1987; postgrad., Am. Inst. Hypnotherapy, 1988. Pres. Skrocki's Philos. Svc., Lakeview Terrace, Calif., 1971—81, Redding, Calif., 1982—; pres., CEO Skrocki's Superior Svc., Lakeview Terrace, 1971—76, Redding, 1976—; pres., CEO, promoter, prodr. Realife Expositions, 1991—; prodr. Realife Expo Stars Over Hollywood, 1997. Founder Realife Found., 2003. Prodr.: Superstars of Excellence, 2000—. Bd. govs., deacon Ch. of Universal Knowledge, 1991—; founder, exec. dir. Real Life Found., 2003; active Rep. Party, 1966-86, Young Ams. for Freedom, 1968-82, Nixon for Pres., 1968, 72, Regan for Gov., 1970, Murphy for Senate, 1970, Arklin for Assembly, 1970-72, Christian Anti Communist Crusade, 1970-72, Ford for Pres., 1976, Regan for Pres., 1980, 84, founder Chuslion Conf. Coalition, 2009 Named one of Outstanding Young Men Am., 1980. Mem. Shasta Submarine Soc. (pres. 1984—). Avocations: chess, basketball, reading, health, exercise. Office Phone: 530-241-1540. Personal E-mail: edskrocki2@hotmail.com.

SKROMNE-KADLUBIK, GREGORIO, nuclear medicine physician; b. Mex. City, Apr. 9, 1939; s. Benjamin and Ana (Kadlubik) Skromne; m. Blanca Sofia Castillo, Nov. 15, 1964; 1 child, Jorge David. MD, Nat. U., La Jolla, Calif., 1962, MSc, 1972. Prof. physiology Nat. U., Mexico City, 1965—; rschr. Fac. Medicine, Mexico City, 1972—; coord. Nuclear Medicine Nat. Polytech. Inst., 1978-88; head nuclear medicine ISSSTE, Mexico, 1974-88, Health Sec., 1969—. Cons. Nat. U., Chiapas, Mex., 1982—, Renal Ctr., Mexico City, 1988—. Recipient G. Soberon medal Health Sec. of Mex., 1994. Mem. AAAS, N.Y. Acad. Scis., Assn. Latino Am. Medicina Nucler. Achievements include invention of first inadiated vaccine against Hepatitis B; patent of visualization in vivo of steroid receptor in homono-dependence tumor. Office: Nat U Mexico Faculty Medicine Mexico City Mexico Office Phone: 55637568.

SKULSKI, LECH PIOTR, emeritus organic chemistry professor; b. Warsaw, June 29, 1931; s. Boleslaw and Kazimiera (Stodulska) S.; m. Elżbieta Maria Świerżewska, Dec. 4, 1955; children: Wojciech, Magdalena. MSChE, Poly. U., Warsaw, 1955; D in Tech. Sci., Poly. U., 1960, PhD, 1966. Sr. asst. dept. chemistry Poly. U., 1955-61, adj., 1961-66, asst. prof., 1966-68; asst. prof., head chair applied chemistry Tech. Mil. Acad., Warsaw, 1969-73; asst. prof., head phys. chemistry lab. dept. pharmacy Med. Univ., Warsaw, 1974-85, extraordinary prof., head chair, and lab. organic chemistry, 1985-93, ordinary prof., head chair and lab. organic chemistry, 1993—2002. Vis. prof. U. Egypt, 1993; head Main Polish Com. Chemistry Olympiad, 1974-81. Co-author 4 textbooks; contbr. over 200 articles to profl. jours. Mem. Solidarity, 1980—, Warsaw City Coun., 1990-98, 2001-02 Grantee Ford Found., 1962-63; recipient award Polish Acad. Scis., 1969, Ministerial awards Ministry Edn., Ministry Health and Social Welfare, 1979, 81, 92, Golden Cross of Merit, 1979, Cross of Polonia Restituta, 1984, Medal Nat. Edn., 1976. Mem. Polish Chem. Soc., Forum on Iodine Utilization Japan. Democrat. Avocation: history. Home: ul Zwyciezcow 3/5 St Apt 5 Warsaw 03-936 Poland Office: Med Univ Warsaw 1 Banacha St 02-097 Warsaw Poland Home Phone: (4822) 6176122. Personal E-mail: lechskulski@yahoo.com.

SKUPSKI, DANIEL, obstetrician-gynecologist, educator; AB, Albion Coll., 1980; MD, Univ. of Michi. Med. Sch., 1985. Diplomate Am. Bd. Ob-Gyn, cert. maternal and fetal medicine. Resident ob-gyn. Hurley Med. Ctr., Flint, Mich., 1985—89; fellow maternal and fetal medicine NY Hosp. Cornell. Med. Ctr., 1992—94; attending obstetrician and gynecologist NY-Presbyn. Hosp., NY Hosp. Med. Ctr. of Queens; prof. ob-gyn. Weill Cornell Med. Coll. Co-author: (peer reviewed publs.) Ethical issues in the management of pregnancies complicated by fetal anomalies., 2003, Intraobserver and interobserver reproducibility of fetal biometry., 2004, A randomized trial of septostomy versus amnioreduction in the treatment of twin olighydramnios-polyhydramnios sequence., 2005, Improving hospital systems for the care of women with major obstetric hemorrhage., 2006, and numerous others. Recipient Tchg. award, Chief Residents The NY Hosp.-Cornell Med. Ctr., 1994, Resident tchg. award, Coll. of Human Medicine Mich. State Univ., 1988, Top 10% of jour. reviewers, 2005, Best Poster presentation; named one of Top Doctors, NY Metro Area Castle-Connolly Med. Ltd., 2001—05. Office: NewYork-Presbyterian Hospital Weill Cornell 525 E 68th St New York NY 10021 Office Phone: 212-746-5454.

SKYLER, JAY S., medical educator, consultant; b. Phila., Feb. 14, 1947; m. Mercedes Armas Bach, Aug. 9, 2003; children: Jennifer Anne, Alexandria Regina Bach, Marcus Richard Bach. BS, Pa. State U., 1967; MD, Jefferson Med. Coll., 1969. Diplomate in internal medicine, also endocrinology, diabetes and metabolism Am. Bd. Internal Medicine. Intern, resident in internal medicine, fellow in endocrinology and metabolism Duke U., Durham, NC, 1969—73, assoc. then asst. prof., 1972—76; assoc. prof. then prof., medicine, pediatrics and psychology, divsn. endocrinology, diabetes, and metabolism, dept. medicine U. Miami, Fla., 1976—. Pres. Am. Diabetes Assn., Alexandria, Va., 1991—92, v.p. Internat. Diabetes Fedn., Brussels, 1994—2000; bd. dirs. Amylin Pharms., San Diego, DexCom, Inc, San Diego. Founding editor-in-chief (med. jour.) Diabetes Care, 1978—82, scientific editor Internat. Diabetes Monitor, 1989—, assoc. editor Diabetes Technology & Therapeutics, 2006—. With USPHS, 1973—75. Master: ACP (mem. bd. regents 1996—99, chmn., coun. of subspecialty societies); mem.: Internat. Diabetes Fedn. (past v.p.), So. Soc. for Clin. Investigation, Internat. Diabetes Immunotherapy Group, Am. Diabetes Assn. (past pres.). Independent. Achievements include research in multiple developments for treatment of diabetes. Office: Univ of Miami Diabetes Research Institut Ste 3054 1450 NW 10th Ave Miami FL 33136 Office Fax: 305-243-4484. Business E-Mail: jskyler@miami.edu.

SLACHTA, GREGORY ANDREW, urologist; b. Paterson, NJ, Mar. 17, 1946; s. Andrew Gregory and Mary Catherine (Shimko) S.; children: Gregory Andrew, Lara Ann, Andrea; m. Patricia A. Albano, Nov. 7, 1981. BS, Pa. State U., 1966; MD, Jefferson Med. Coll., 1968. Diplomate Am. Bd. Urology. Intern Lankenan Hosp., Phila., 1968—69; resident urology Temple U. Hosp., Phila., 1969—70, 1973—75; pvt. practice, Springfield, Mass., 1975—97, Hilton Head Med. Group, SC, 1997—99. Author: Inflammatory Diseases of the Male Genital Tract, 1982; contbr. chapter to books. Mem. City Coun. Com. for Health Ins., Springfield, 1984, Springfield Planning Bd., 1991; vice-chmn. UROPAC, 2003-08. Maj. US Army, 1971—73. Recipient Disting. Svc. award, 1994, Best Drs. in America, 1996—99, Presdl. citation, 2009. Fellow ACS; mem. AMA, Am. Urol. Assn. (chmn. socioecon. com. 1986-91, del. to AMA 1991-2008), Mass. Med. Soc. (alt. del. to AMA 1986-91, vice chmn. legis. and nat. legis. affairs com. 1987-89), Hampden Dist. Med. Soc. (pres. 1986-88), Mass. Assn. Practicing Urologists (pres. 1985-87), Beaufort County Med. Soc. (pres. 1998-2001). Republican. Roman Catholic.

SLADKY, JOHN THOMAS, physician, educator; b. Keshena, Wis., Sept. 21, 1950; BA, Yale U., 1972, MD, 1976. Prof. Emory U. Sch. Medicine, 1995—. Office: 2015 Uppergate Dr NW Atlanta GA 30322 Office Fax: 404-727-1981. Business E-Mail: jsladky@emory.edu.

SLÁMA, KAREL, biologist, zoologist; b. Tichá, Czechoslovakia, Czech Republic, Dec. 17, 1934; s. Vladimír Sláma and Marie (Michlová) Slámová; m. Věra Ležatková, June 25, 1960; children: Pavla, Martina, Tereza. MSc, Masaryk U., 1957, PhD, Czechoslovakian Acad. Scis., 1961. Rsch. asst. Czechoslovakian Acad Scis., Prague, 1961—64, rschr. Entomology Inst., 1965—85, rschr. Inst. Organic Chemistry, 1985—90; rsch. fellow Harvard U., Cambridge, Mass., 1964—65; dir. rsch. Lab. Ecol. Pharm. Intereco, Prague, 1990—92; dir Entomology Inst. Czech Acad Scis., 1993—95. Co-author: Insect Hormones and Bioanalogues, 1974; mng. dir. European

Jour. Entomology; contbr. over 180 sci. papers on insect hormones, chpt. to book. Achievements include discovery of paper factor with insect hormone activity in American paper products, use of insect hormones in medicine, antiviral 0-Phosphonyl-methyl deriatives of adenine used in AIDS therapy; 120 patents applied. Home: Evropska 674 160 00 Prague Czech Republic Office: Czech Acad Scis Drnovská 507 16100 Prague 6 Czech Republic Office Phone: +420 233 022 482. Business E-Mail: slama@entu.cas.cz.

SLAMON, DENNIS JOSEPH, research scientist; b. New Castle, Pa., Aug. 6, 1948; married; 2 children. BA, Washington & Jefferson Coll.; MD, U. Chgo. Pritzker Sch. Medicine, 1975, PhD in Cell Biology, 1975. Intern, medicine U. Chgo. Hosp., Ill., 1975—76, resident Ill., 1976—78; fellow, divsn. hematology-oncology, dept. medicine UCLA Sch. Medicine, 1979—81, assoc. chief divsn. hematology-oncology, 1989—91, chief divsn. hematology-oncology, 1991—, prof., dept. medicine, 1993—, exec. vice chair for rsch. Jonsson Comprehensive Cancer Ctr., 1994—, dir. clin./translational rsch.; dir. Revlon/UCLA Women's Cancer Rsch. Program Jonsson Comprehensive Cancer Ctr., UCLA Sch. Medicine, dir. Revlon/UCLA Women's Health Rsch. Program, dir. clin./translational rsch. Mem. sci. adv. bd. Coastview Capital Inc., New Biotics Inc.; named to Pres. Clinton's Cancer Panel, 2000; dir., med. adv. bd. Nat. Colorectal Cancer Rsch. Alliance. Contbr. articles to profl. jours. Recipient Outstanding Young Investigator award, Western Soc. Clin. Investigation, 1988, Salk Translational award, U. Calif., San Diego, 2000, Bristol-Myers Squibb Oncology Millennium award, 2000, Wadsworth Center's Brown-Hazen award for Excellence in the Basic Scis., 2001, Jeffrey A Gottlieb Meml. award, M.D. Anderson Cancer Ctr., Tex., 2002, Dorothy P. Landon Am. Assn. Cancer Rsch. prize for Translational Cancer Rsch., 2003, Medal of Honor for Clin. Rsch., Am. Cancer Soc., 2004, David A. Karnofsky Meml. award, Am. Soc. Clin. Oncology, 2006, European Inst. Oncology Breast Cancer award, Milan, Italy, 2006, Gairdner Found. Internat. award, 2007; named one of five Men for the Cure, GQ mag. and Concept:Cure, 1999. Achievements include development of the drug Herceptin for treating breast cancer. Office: UCLA Sch Medicine Divsn Hematology Oncology Factor Building 11-244 10833 Le Conte Los Angeles CA 90095 Address: UCLA Sch Medicine Jonsson Comprehensive Cancer Ctr 8-684 Factor Building Box 951781 Los Angeles CA 90095-1781 Office Phone: 310-825-5193. Business E-Mail: dslamon@mednet.ucla.edu. *

SLANKARD, MARJORIE LEE, allergist, immunologist; BA, U. Mo., Columbia, 1967, MD, 1971. Diplomate Am. Bd. Internal Medicine, Am. Bd. Allergy and Immunology, registered NY, 1973, lic. NJ, 1992. Intern Univ. of Mo. Hosp. and Clinics, Colombia, 1972; resident in internal medicine NY-Presbyn. Hosp./Cornell Univ. Med. Coll., 1974, Rockefeller Univ. Hosp., NY, 1974, fellow in immunology; fellow in allergy and immunology NY-Presbyn. Hosp./Cornell Univ. Med. Coll., 1976; hosp. affiliations include Valley Hosp., NY-Presbyn. Hosp./Colombia Univ. Med. Ctr. Co-author: (articles) Left and right ventricular pressures in mice, 1971, Studies on the control of antibody synthesis. XIII. Preferential depletion of precursors of high affinity antibody secreting cells by specific immunoadsorbents, 1979, Nucleotidase activity in permanent human lymphoid cell lines: implication for cell proliferation and aging in vitro, 1982, Cytotoxic effect of an autologous long term T cell line in a patient with malignant melanoma: adoptive autoimmunotherapy, 1984, various others. Named one of Top Doctors, NY Metro Area, America's Top-Rated Physicians, 1999, Leading Me. Specialists, Castle Connolly Med., 2001—05, Best Doctors, NY Mag., 2006, 2010. Fellow: Am. Coll. of Allergy, Asthma, and Immunology, Am. Acad. of Allergy, Asthma, and Immunology; mem.: Am. Acad. of Allergy, Asthma, and Immunology, Insect String Com., New York Allergy Soc., Alpha Omega Alpha, Pi Mu Epsilon. Office: New York-Presbyterian Hospital Columbia University Medical Center 16 E 60th St New York NY 10022 Office Phone: 212-326-8410. Office Fax: 212-326-5516.

SLATE, JOE HUTSON, psychologist, educator; b. Hartselle, Ala., Sept. 21, 1930; s. Murphy Edmund and Marie (Hutson) S.; m. Rachel Holladay, July 1, 1950; children: Marc Allan, John David, James Daryl. BS, Athens Coll., 1960; MA, U. Ala., 1965, PhD, 1970. Mem. faculty Athens (Ala.) State Coll., 1965-92, prof. psychology, 1974-92, chmn. behavioral scis., 1974-92; pvt. practice psychology Athens, 1970-92, Hartselle, 1992—; v.p. Slate Security Systems, Hartselle, Ala., 1984—. Author: Psychic Phenomena, 1988, Self-Empowerment, 1991, Psychic Empowerment, 1995, Psychic Empowerment for Health and Fitness, 1996, Astral Projection, 1998, Aura Energy for Health Healing, and Balance, 1999, Rejevenation: Strategies for Living Younger, Longer and Better, 2001, Psychic Vampires, 2002, Beyond Reincarnation, 2005, Connecting to the Power Nature, 2009, Self-empowerment for Everyone, 2009, Self-empowerment Through Self Hypnosis, 2010, Self Empowerment and Your Subconscious Mind, 2010, Doors to Past Lives and Future Lives, 2011. Named hon. prof. U. Montevallo, 1973, prof. emeritus Athens State U., 1992. Mem. APA, Am. Soc. Clin. Hypnosis, Inst. Parapsychol. Rsch. (founder), Coun. for Nat. Register Health Svc. Providers in Psychology, NEA, Ala. Edn. Assn., Delta Tau Delta, Phi Delta Kappa, Kappa Delta Pi. Home: 210 Main St West Hartselle AL 35640-4442 Office: 110 Sparkman St S Hartselle AL 35640 Office Phone: 256-773-0116. Personal E-mail: jhslate@aol.com.

SLATER, GORDON LESLIE, surgeon, consultant; b. Cessnock, Australia, Aug. 14, 1964; s. Edmund and Lynette Slater; m. Lisa Catherine Fendley; children: Campbell, Duncan, Adelaide. MB, BChir, U. NSW, 1987; grad., Hosp. Spl. Surgery, 1997, Royal Australian Coll., 1997. Cert. Advanced AO Course 1991. Sr. resident orthops., sr. resident surgery Ea. Health Svcs., Sydney, 1990—90; orthop. registrar Austrailian Orthop. Assn., 1992—96, St. George Hosp., 1995—96; orthop. cons. Alpine Orthosport, Albury, 1996—2003; orthop. registrar Wentworth Area Health, Penrith, 1991—92. Dir. Byron Bay Cookie Co., Byron Bay, Australia, 2001—03. Asst. editor Foot & Ankle Internat. Jour.; contbr. articles to profl. jours. Fellow: Royal Australian Coll. Surgeons; mem.: Australian Orthop. Assn. Avocations: tennis, skiing, surfing, squash. Office: Alpine Orthosport 1156 Padman Dr 2640 Albury NSW Australia

SLATER, JAMES MUNRO, radiation oncologist; b. Salt Lake City, Jan. 7, 1929; s. Donald Munro and Leone Forestine (Fehr) S.; m. JoAnn Strout, Dec. 28, 1948; children: James, Julie, Jan, Jerry, Jon. BS in Physics, U. Utah, Utah State U., 1954; MD, Loma Linda U., 1963; PhD (hon.), Andrews U., Berrien Springs, Mich., 1996. Diplomate Am. Bd. Radiology. Intern Latter Day Saints Hosp., Salt Lake City, 1963-64, resident in radiology, 1964-65; resident in radiotherapy Loma Linda U. Med. Ctr., White Meml. Med. Center, LA, fellow in radiotherapy, 1967-68, U. Tex.-M.D. Anderson Hosp. and Tumor Inst., Houston, 1968-69; dir. radiation oncology sect. Loma Linda U. Med. Ctr., Calif., 1970—79, dir. radiation sect. Calif., 1975—79, chmn. dept. radiation scis. Calif., 1978—90, chmn. dept. radiation medicine Calif., 1990—2001, dir. Cancer Inst., 1993—97, treas. Calif., 1995-96, exec. v.p. Calif., 1994—95; founder, dir. Loma Linda U./NASA Radiation Biology Lab., Calif., 1997—; vice chair radiation medicine Loma Linda U. Med. Ctr., 2003—. Co-dir. cmty. radiology oncology program L.A. County-U. So. Calif. Comprehensive Cancer Ctr., 1978-83; mem. cancer adv. coun. State of Calif., 1980-85; clin. prof. U. So. Calif., 1982—; founding mem. Proton Therapy Coop. Group, 1985—, chmn. 1987-91; cons. charged particle therapy program Lawrence Berkeley Lab., 1986-94; cons. R&D monoclonal antibodies Hybritech Inc., 1985-94, bd. dirs., 1985-94; cons. Berkeley lab., 1986-94; mem. panel cons. Internat. Atomic Energy Agy. UN, 1994-98; cons. Sci. Applications Internat. Corp., 1979, 89-91. Bd. dirs. Am. Cancer Soc., San Bernardino/Riverside, 1976-84, exec. com., 1976—; pres. Inland Empire chpt., 1981-83. NIH fellow, 1968-69; recipient exhbn. awards Radiol. Soc. N.Am., 1973, exhbn. awards European Assn. Radiology, 1975, exhbn. awards Am. Soc. Therapeutic Radiologists, 1978, Alumnus of Yr. award, 1993-94. Fellow Am. Coll. Radiology; mem. AAAS, AMA, ACS (liaison mem. to commn. on cancer 1976-84), Am. Radium Soc., Am. Soc. Clin. Oncology, Am. Soc. Therapeutics Radiologists, Assn. Univ. Radiologists, Soc. for Clinical Trials, N.Y. Acad. Scis., Calif. Med. Assn., Calif. Radiol. Soc., Gilbert H. Fletcher Soc. (pres. 1981-82), Loma Linda U. Med. Sch. Alumni Assn., Radiol. Soc. N.Am., Bernardino County Med Soc., Soc. Chairmen Of Acad. Radiation Oncology Programs, Alpha Omega Alpha. Achievements include development of proton accelerator system for treating patients with cancer and some benign diseases in a hospital environment; development of computer assisted radiation treatment planning system utilizing patient's digitized anatomic images with overlying radiation distribution images, Loma Linda U. Proton Facility renamed James M. Slater Proton Treatmant and Rsch. Ctr., 2007. Office: Loma Linda Univ Med Ctr 25590 Prospect Ave Apt 27c Loma Linda CA 92354-3150 Business E-Mail: jmslater@dominion.llumc.edu.

SLATER, JAMES PHILIP, cardiologist; b. Boston, July 25, 1960; BA, Franklin and Marshall Coll., 1982; MD, Case Western Res. Sch. Medicine, 1990. Attending cardiac surgeon Mid Atlantic Surg. Assocs., 1999—. Fellow: ACS; mem.: Soc. Thoracic Surgeons. Office: Mid Atlantic Surgical Associates 95 Madison Ave Morristown NJ 07960 Business E-Mail: james.slater@atlantichealth.org.

SLATER, JONATHAN, child and adolescent psychiatrist, educator; BA, Harvard U., 1981; MD, Columbia U., 1985. Diplomate Am. Bd. Psychiatry and Neurology. Pvt. practice specializing in pediatric psychopharmacology, Irvington, NY; resident in psychiatry NY State Psychiatric Inst., 1987—90, resident in child and adolescent psychiatry, 1990—92; dir. pediat. psychiatry cons.-lialson svc. NY-Presbyn. Hosp.; clin. prof. psychiatry Columbia Univ. Recipient Viola Bernard award, Departmental Research Grant, 1992—93, Medical Student Teacher of the Year award, 1997, Nancy C.A. Roeske Cert. of Recognition for Excellence, Am. Psychiatric Assn., 2003. Office: Columbia University One Bridge St Ste 24 Irvington NY 10533 Office Phone: 212-305-7102. Office Fax: 212-305-7102.

SLAUGHTER, DJUANIQUE NATÉ, healthcare analyst, project manager, consultant; BS in Criminal Justice, Grambling State U., La., 1993; MPA, Calif. State U., Dominiguez Hills, 1998. Med. clinic asst. Green Clinic, Ruston, La., 1993—97; pub. health intern Dept. Health and Human Svcs., Long Beach, Calif., 1997—98; project mgmt. specialist Scan Health Plan, Long Beach, 1998; adminstrv. asst. Salick Healthcare, LA, 1998—99, healthcare analyst, cons., project mgr., 1999; managed care report analyst Health Care Ptnrs., Torrance, Calif., 1999—2000; project mgr. Ops. Health Care Ptnrs., Torrance, 2000—03; mgr. claims adminstrn. Kaiser Permanent, Pasadena, Calif., 2003—04, cons. quality and risk mgmt., 2004—07, sr. cons. health plan regulatory svcs., 2007—; project mgr. Arlene M. Joyner A Dental Corp., 2006—. HIV/AIDS peer counselor Campus Awareness Prevention, Grambling, La., 1993; sr. cons. Health Plan Regulatory Svcs., 2007—. Mem. Reach 2010, Reach 2010 Project, 2001—. Am. scholar, Grambling State U. Personal E-mail: dedeaka@aol.com.

SLAUGHTER, FREEMAN CLUFF, retired dentist; b. Estes, Miss., Dec. 30, 1926; s. William Cluff and Vay (Fox) S.; m. Genevieve Anne Parks, July 30, 1948; children: Mary Anne, Thomas Freeman, James Hugh. Student, Wake Forest U., 1944, Emory U., 1946-47; DDS, Emory U. Sch. of Dentistry, 1951. Lic. real estate broker. Practice gen. dentistry, Kannapolis, N.C., 1951-89; ret. Mem. N.C. State Bd. Dental Examiners, 1966-75, pres., 1968-69, sec.-treas., 1971-74; chief dental staff Cabarrus Meml. Hosp. (now Carolinas Med. Ctr. NE), Concord, N.C., 1965-66, 75; mem. N.C. Adv. Com. for Edn. Dental Aux. Pers.-N.C. State Bd. Edn., 1967-70; advisor dental asst. program Rowan Cabarrus C.C., 1974-76; Duke Med. Ctr. Davison Century Club. Trustee N.C. Symphony Soc., 1962-68, pres. Kannapolis chpt., 1961; mem. Cabarrus County Bd. Health, 1977-83, chmn., 1981-83, acting health dir., 1981; vice chmn. Kannapolis Charter Commn., 1983-84; mem. City Coun. Kannapolis, 1984-85; Mayor protem, Kannapolis, 1984-85; past active Boy Scouts Am., Eagle scout with silver palm. QM2C asst. navigator on USS Xenia AKA 51, co-navigator on USS Gen. George O. Squier AP 130 with USN, 1944-46, WW II, ETO, MTO. Recipient Kannapolis Citizen of Yr. award, 1982. Fellow Am. Coll. Dentists (life); mem. ADA (life), Am. Legion, Kannapolis Jr. C. of C. (v.p. 1952), Toastmasters Internat. (pres. Kannapolis chpt. 1963-64), Am. Assn. Dental Examiners (Dentist Citizen of Yr. 1975, v.p. 1977-79, Recognition plaque, 1980), So. Conf. Dental Deans and Examiners (v.p. 1969), N.C. Dental Soc. (resolution of commendation 1975), N.C. Dental Soc. Anesthesiology (pres. 1964), Southeastern Acad. Prosthodontics, So. Acad. Oral Surgery, Am. Soc. Dentistry for Children (pres. N.C. unit 1957), Internat. Assn. Dental Rsch., Cabarrus County Dental Soc. (pres. 1953-54, 63-64, 69), N.C. Assn. Professions (dir. 1976-80), Kannapolis Music Club (pres. 1962-63), Emory U. Corpus Cordis Aureum (Emory U. disting. alumnus award 2006), Masons, Shriners, Rotary (dir. 1977-80), Omicron Kappa Upsilon, Alpha Epsilon Upsilon.

SLAUGHTER, THOMAS FREEMAN, anesthesiologist, educator, physician; s. Freeman Cluff and Genevieve Parks Slaughter; m. Janie C. Thomas, Aug. 3, 1996. Attended, Wake Forest U., Winston-Salem, NC, 1980—83; MD, Duke U. Sch. Medicine, Durham, NC, 1987; MHA, U. NC, Chapel Hill, 2009. Diplomate Nat. Bd. Med. Examiners, 1988, lic. NC Med. Bd., 1991, diplomate Am. Bd. Anesthesiology, 1992, testamur Nat. Bd. Echocardiography, 2002, lic. Va. Bd. Medicine, 2002, cert. in pub. health Nat. Bd. Pub. Health Examiners, 2010. Intern Emory U., Atlanta, 1987—88; resident Duke U. Health Sys., 1988—91, fellow cardiothoracic anesthesiology, 1990—92, assoc. in anesthesiology, 1992—93, asst. prof. anesthesiology, 1993—2000, assoc. prof. anesthesiology, 2000—02; attending anesthesiologist Durham VA Med. Ctr., 1992—2002; prof. anesthesiology, dir. cardiothoracic anesthesiology Va. Commonwealth U. Health Sys., Richmond, 2002—04; prof. anesthesiology Wake Forest U. Sch. Medicine, 2004, sect. head cardiothoracic anesthesia, 2006—, dir. cardiothoracic anesthesia fellowship tng. program, 2006—, mem. continuing med. edn. com., 2009—, mem. promotions and tenure com., 2010—. Chmn. transfusion rev. com. Durham VA Med. Ctr., Durham, NC, 1996—2002, inst. med. rsch., 1996—2002; diagnostic techs. com. Duke U. Health Sys., 1998—2002, human studies instl. rev. com., 1999—2002; sci. program com. Soc. Cardiovascular Anesthesiology, 1996—2000; dir. cardiothoracic anesthesia and fellowship tng. program Va. Commonwealth U. Health Sys., 2002—04, sci. program dir. anesthesiology grand rounds, 2002—04; dir. cardiothoracic anesthesiology Wake Forest U. Sch. of Medicine, Winston-Salem, NC, 2006. Contbr. chapters to books. Recipient Rsch. Career Devel. award, Found. Anesthesia Edn. and Rsch., 1992—94, Individual Clin. Investigator Devel. award, NIH, 1997—2002, Rsch. in Blood Conservation award, Bayer Pharm., 1998, 1999, Elected Hon. Mem., Assn. U. Anesthesiologists, 2001—, Faculty 1000 Medicine, 2009—. Mem.: AMA, Internat. Soc. on Thrombosis and Hemostasis, Soc. Cardiovasc. Anesthesiologists, Internat. Anesthesia Rsch. Soc., NC Soc. Anesthesiologists, Am. Soc. Anesthesiology, Assn. Univ. Anesthesiologists (hon.), Nat. Eagle Scout Assn. (Eagle Scout award 1979), Alpha Epsilon Delta Premed. Honor Soc., Beta Beta Beta Biol. Honor Soc. Achievements include patents for transglutaminase cell line and clones; research in perioperative hemostasis and thrombosis; perioperative blood conservation; transglutaminase biology. Office: Wake Forest Univ Sch Medicine Medical Center Blvd Winston Salem NC 27157-1009

SLAVIN, PETER L., hospital administrator; AB, Harvard U., 1979, MD, 1984, MBA, 1990. Sr. v.p., chief med. officer Mass. Gen. Hosp., Boston, 1994—97; pres. Barnes-Jewish Hosp., St. Louis, 1997-99; med. dir. Mass. Gen. Physicians Orgn., Boston, chair., CEO, 1999—2003; pres. Mass. Gen. Hosp., Boston, 2003—. Office: Mass Gen Hosp 55 Fruit St Boston MA 02114-2622 Office Phone: 617-724-9300. *

SLAVIN, RAYMOND GRANAM, allergist, immunologist; b. Cleve., June 29, 1930; s. Philip and Dinah (Baskind) S.; m. Alberta Cohrt, June 10, 1953; children: Philip, Stuart, David, Linda. AB, U. Mich., 1952; MD, St. Louis U., 1956; MS, Northwestern U., 1963. Diplomate Am. Bd. Internal Medicine, Am. Bd. Allergy and Immunology (treas.). Intern U. Mich. Hosp., Ann Arbor, 1956-57; resident St. Louis U. Hosp., 1959-61; fellow in allergy and immunology Northwestern U. Med. Sch., 1961-64; asst. prof. internal medicine and microbiology St. Louis U., 1965-70, assoc. prof., 1970-73, prof., 1973—, dir. divsn. allergy and immunology, 1965—2007. Mem. NIH study sect., 1985-89; cons. U.S. Army M.C. Contbr. numerous articles to med. publs.; editl. bd.: Jour. Allergy and Clin. Immunology, 1975-81. Chmn. bd. Asthma and Allergy Found. Am., 1985-88. With M.C., U.S. Army, 1957-59. Grantee NIH, 1967-70, 1984—2000, Nat. Inst. Occupl. Safety and Health, 1974-80. Master: ACP; fellow: Am. Acad. Allergy and Immunology (exec. bd., historian, pres. 1983—84, Disting. Svc. award 1995, Disting. Clinician award 2005); mem.: AAAS, Ctrl. Soc. Clin. Rsch., Am. Assn. Immunologists. Democrat. Jewish. Home: 631 E Polo Dr Saint Louis MO 63105-2629 Office: 1402 S Grand Blvd Saint Louis MO 63104-1004 Office Phone: 314-977-8829. Business E-Mail: slavinrg@slu.edu.

SLAVIN, SUMNER ANDREW, plastic surgeon; b. Boston, Aug. 19, 1947; MD, Univ. Vt. Coll. Med., 1973. Cert. Am. Bd. Plastic Surgery, 1983. Intern Beth Israel Deaconess Med. Ctr., Boston, 1973—74, resident in surgery, 1974—78; resident in plastic surgery NYU Med. Ctr., NYC, 1978—80, fellow in hand micro surgery, 1980—81; assoc. clin. prof. surgery Harvard Med. Sch., 1996; mem. Harvard Med. Faculty Physicians Beth Israel Deaconess Med. Ctr., Boston, chief Div. of Plastic & Reconstructive Surgery. Contbr. articles to profl. jours. Office: Beth Israel Deaconess Med Ctr 1101 Beacon St Brookline MA 02446 Office Phone: 617-277-7010. Office Fax: 617-734-5223.

SLAVIT, DAVID HAL, otolaryngologist; b. NYC, Sept. 5, 1960; s. Leonard S. and Barbara H. (Levine) S.; m. Robin E. Feldman, July 31, 1983; children: Danielle, Evan, Roni. BS, Cornell U., 1982; MD, Mt. Sinai U., 1986. Cert. in otolaryngology. Intern Mayo Clinic, Rochester, Minn., 1986-87, resident in otolaryngology, 1987-91; with Lenox Hill Hosp., NYC. Asst. prof. Health Sci. Ctr.-SUNY Downstate; cons. Juilliard Sch. Music, N.Y.C., 1994-99; dir. Ames Vocal Dynamics Lab., N.Y.C., 1998-2001. Author, editor: (book) Essentials of Otolaryngology, 1993; author: (books) Voice Disorders, 1995, Rhinologic Diagnosis and Treatment, 1996, Systemic Disease of the Nasal Airway, 1993; contbr. articles to profl. jours. Fellow ACS; mem. AMA, Am. Acad. Otolaryngology-Head and Neck Surgery, Am. Acad. Facial Plastic and Reconstructive Surgery, Am. Rhinologic Soc. Office Phone: 212-517-9177.

SLAVKIN, HAROLD CHARLES, dean, biologist; b. Chgo., Mar. 20, 1938; m. Lois S. Slavkin; children: Mark D., Todd P. BA in English lit., U. So. Calif., 1961, DDS, 1965; Doctorate (hon.),

Georgetown U., 1990, U. Paris, 1996, U. Md., 1997. Mem. faculty U. So. Calif. Sch. Dentistry, LA, 1968—, mem. faculty gerontology inst., 1969, chmn. dept. biochemistry and nutrition, 1969—75, prof., 1974—, chmn. grad. program in craniofacial molecular biology, 1975-85, founding dir. Ctr. for Craniofacial Molecular Biology, 1989-95, George & Mary Lou Boone prof. craniofacial molecular biology, 1989-95; dean U.Southern Calif. Sch. Dentistry, LA, 2000—; G. Donald and Marian James Montgomery Dean's Chair in Dentistry U. So. Calif. Sch. Dentistry, LA, 2000—; dir. Nat. Inst. Dental and Craniofacial Rsch., NIH, Bethesda, Md., 1995—2000. Vis. prof. Israel Inst. Tech., Haifa, 1987-88; cons. U.S. News and World Report, 1985-95, L.A. Edn. Partnership, 1983-95, Torstar Books, Inc., 1985-95. Contbr. articles to profl. jours. Mem. sci. adv. bd. Calif. Mus. Sci. and Tech., 1985-95. Rsch. scholar U. Coll. London, 1980. Mem. AAAS, Am. Assn. Anatomists, Am. Inst. Biol. Scis., Am. Soc. for Cell Biology, Am. Assn. for Dental Rsch. (pres. 1993-94), N.Y. Acad. Scis., Inst. Medicine of NAS, Internat. Coll. Dentistry, Am. Coll. Dentistry, Los Angeles County Art Mus. Assocs. Office: 925 W 34th St Los Angeles CA 90089 Office Phone: 213-740-2811. Office Fax: 213-740-1509. E-mail: slavkin@usc.edu. *

SLAYMAN, CAROLYN WALCH, geneticist, educator; b. Portland, Maine, Mar. 11, 1937; d. John Weston and Ruth Dyer (Sanborn) Walch; m. Clifford L. Slayman; children: Andrew, Rachel BA with highest honors, Swarthmore Coll., Pa., 1958; PhD, Rockefeller U., NYC, 1963; DSc (hon.), Bowdoin Coll., Brunswick, Maine, 1985. Instr., then asst. prof. Case Western Res. U., Cleve., 1967; from asst. prof. to prof. genetics Yale U. Sch. Medicine, New Haven, 1967—, Sterling prof. genetics, 1991—, chmn. dept. genetics, 1984-95, dep. dean acad. and sci. affairs, 1995—. Chmn. genetic basis of disease rev. commn. NIH, 1981—85, nat. adv. gen. med. scis. coun., 1989—93; bd. dirs. J. Weston Walch Pub., Portland, Maine, Applera Corp., 1995—2008; mem. sci. rev. bd. Howard Hughes Med. Inst., 1992—97. Mem. editl. bd. Jour. Biol. Chemistry, 1989-94; contbr. articles to sci. jours. Trustee Foote Sch., New Haven, 1983—89, Hopkins Sch., New Haven, 1988—93; bd. overseers Dartmouth Med. Sch., 1997—2003, Woods Hole Oceanographic Instn., Mass., 1997—2007, Bowdoin Coll., 1976—88, trustee, 1988—2001. Recipient Deborah Morton award Westbrook Coll., 1986. Mem. Am. Soc. Biol. Chemists, Genetics Soc. Am., Soc. Gen. Physiologists, Am. Soc. Microbiology, Inst. Medicine, Phi Beta Kappa Office Phone: 203-737-1770.

SLEBODZINSKI, ANDRZEJ BRUNO, retired endocrinologist; b. Gorlice, Poland, July 8, 1930; s. Antoni Józef Ślebodziński and Janina Petronela Bieniewska; m. Maria Ewa Suska-Brzezińska, July 1, 1971; children: Izabella Ślebodziński, Jacek Ślebodziński, Jerzy Ślebodziński. Degree in vet. surgery, U. Wrocław, Poland, 1953; PhD in Vet. Scis., U. Coll. Agr., Wroclaw, 1961. Tchr. vet. subjects Vet. Lyceum, Nowy Targ, Poland, 1953—55; rsch. asst. Polish Acad. Scis., Cracow, 1955—57; rsch. asst. dept. biochemistry Inst. Animal Husbandry, Cracow, 1957—65, adj. lectr. in environ. physiology, 1965—74, prof. vet. scis., 1974—76; prof. vet. scis. dept. exptl. pathology of animals Polish Acad. Scis., Poznań, 1976—88, prof. vet. scis. dept. devel. and exptl. endocrinology Inst. Animal Reprodn. and Food Rsch., Polish Acad. Scis., Olsztyn, 1988—2000. Head joint isotope and endocrinology lab. dept. biochemistry Inst. Animal Husbandry, Cracow, 1966—76; organizer, head dept. exptl. pathology of animals Polish Acad. Scis., Poznań, 1976—88, head dept. devel. and exptl. endocrinology, 1988—2000, initiator, chmn. com. Vet. Endocrinology of Domestic Animals, 1986—90; mem. sci. com., adv. bds. Inst. Animal Physiology and Nutrition and Inst. Animal Reprodn. and Food Rsch., Olsztyn, 1976—2000; cons. endocrinologist ENDO-CANIS Endocrine Rsch. and Diagnostics, Poznań, 2000—; chmn. sci. com. Pathophysiology of Adaptation and Non-Specific Resistance in Neonates, 1981—90; chmn. internat. French-Polish cooperative project Meat Prodn. Perinatal Mortality and Fertility Problems, 1982—90; head sponsored rsch. Internat. Atomic Energy Agy., Vienna, 1977—80; prin. investigator Influence of Energy Balance on Interaction Between Somatotropin, Thyroid Hormones and Cytokines U.S.-Poland Maria Skłodowska-Curie Joint Fund II, 1996—97; mem. internat. symposia organizing com. Slovak Acad. Scis., 1983, 85, 90, numerous others. Author: (textbook) Endocrinology of Domestic Animals, 1968, 2d edit.; co-author: (in Polish) Lexicon of Animal Reproduction, 1996; contbr. articles to profl. jours., chapters to books; editor-in-chief Annals of Animals Scis., Cracow, 1970—74, mem. editl. bd. Polish Endocrinology, 1978—90, Archivum Veterinarium Polonicum, 1989—99. Recipient award of merit and appreciation, Polish Endocrine Soc., 1962, 1972, individual award of II degree, Polish State Com. Atomic Energy, 1973, cert. appreciation, USDA, 1998; grantee, Brit. Coun., 1962—63, Commonwealth Sci. and Indsl. Rsch. Orgn., CSIRO Rockhampton, Australia, 1974—75, FAO/Internat. Atomic Energy Agy. Divsn. Isotope and Radiation Application of Atomic Energy for Food and Agrl. Devel., Vienna, 1976—78; fellow, PIDA,U.K., 1963—64, Wellcome Trust, 1983. Mem.: Polish Soc. Vet. Scis., Polish Soc. Endocrinology, Polish Soc. Physiology, Internat. Soc. Neuroendocrinology, European Soc. Nuc. Methods in Agr. and Vet. Medicine, European Soc. Comparative Endocrinology, Soc. Endocrinology. Achievements include contribution to development of thyroid-stimulating hormone-releasing factor activity in the hypothalamus during early ontogenesis; categorization of newborns across species into noradrenaline-type and thyroxine-type, based on evidence of importance of hormones for early adaptation to post-uterine life; developing evidence that enzyme extra-thyroidal conversion of thyroxine into tiiodothyronine plays a paracrine function in physiology of gonads and the mammary gland. Avocations: genealogy, art, gardening, fishing. Home: Ul. Promienista 166 A/34 60-157 Poznan Poland

SLEVIN, MARK ANTHONY, education educator, researcher; b. Manchester, England, Nov. 29, 1963; d. Peter Slevin and Jean Beaty; m. Vesna Ferlan-Slevin, Oct. 2, 1994. BSc with honors, Manchester Met. U., 1988, PhD, 1994. With Leighton Hosp., Cheshire, 1982—85; rsch. assoc. Manchester Med. Sch., 1992—94; sr. rsch. fellow Manchester Met. U., 1994—. Contbr. articles to profl. jours. Mem.: Am. Heart Assn., Am. Soc. for Biochemistry and Molecular Biology (assoc.). Avocations: golf, tennis, football, sports, gym. Office: Manchester Met Univ 6 Oxford Road M1 5GA Manchester England Home Phone: 0161 4567954; Office Phone: 0161 247 1172. E-mail: m.a.slevin@mmu.ac.uk.

SLIM, MICHEL S., surgeon, educator, health facility administrator; b. Nov. 18, 1929; s. Saliba and Julia Slim; m. Norma Gebara, Sept. 4, 1958; children: Julie, Lina, Nayla. MD, Am. U., Beirut, Lebanon, 1954. Diplomate Am. Bd. Surgery, Am. Bd. Pediatric Surgery, Am. Bd. Thoracic Surgery. Prof. surgery Am. U., Beirut, 1963-86, N.Y. Med. Coll., 1986—2006, prof. emeritus NY, 2006—; attending Westchester Med. Ctr., Valhalla, 1986—, chief pediatric trauma, 1991—2006, chief pediatric surgery, 1994—2002. Editl. cons. Pediatric Surg. Internat., 1985-2004; reviewer Ann. Thoracic Surgery, Jordan Med. Jour. Jour. Jordan Royal Med. Svcs.; contbr. articles to profl. jours Evarts Graham Traveling fellow Am. Assn. Thoracic Surgery, 1970-71. Fellow ACS, Am. Acad. Pediat., Am. Coll. Chest Physicians, Soc. Thoracic Surgeons, Soc. Critical Care Medicine; mem. Am. Pediatric Surgery Assn., Brit. Assn. Pediatric Surgery, Internat. Soc. Surgery, Eastern Assn. for Surgery of Trauma. Office Phone: 914-493-7620. Personal E-mail: normichslim@gmail.com. E-mail: mslimpedsurg@hotmail.com.

SLIPMAN, RONALD (SAMUEL SLIPMAN), hospital administrator; b. New Orleans, Aug. 24, 1939; s. Jake and Esther (Steinman) S.; m. Carole Marie Green, July 1, 1961 (div. Feb. 1982); children: Susan Rachel, Lawrence Jay; m. Marilyn Morais, Feb. 5, 1983 (dec. June 1985); m. Lelia Ruth Foster, Jan. 12, 1986; children: Ronald Andrew, Brian Edward. BS, Tulane U., 1961; cert. in supervision techniques, La. State U., 1984; postgrad., NE La. U., 1978-79, 80-81. Design progress estimator Boeing Co., New Orleans, 1964-66; interviewer Tex. Employment Commn., Tyler and Lufkin, 1977-78; pers. technician State of La., Baton Rouge, 1961-62, 63-64, 73-75, 81; rsch. statistician La. Ins. Commn., Baton Rouge, 1967-68; labor market analyst La. Dept. Labor, Baton Rouge, 1969-70, 77; pers. dir. Royal Orleans Hotel, New Orleans, 1966-67; mgmt. analyst for quality assurance Earl K. Long Hosp., Baton Rouge, 1981-84, dir. ancillary svcs., 1984-86; mgmt. analyst, spl. asst. to dir. for total quality mgmt. Dept. Vets. Affairs Med. Ctr., Alexandria, La., 1987-88, 89-90; mgmt. cons., 1990-91. Cubmaster pack 10 Boy Scouts Am., 1993-94, 96-98, asst. cubmaster, 1994-96, chmn. pack com., 1998-99, mem. pack com., 1999—2004; trustee Kent Plantation House, Inc., 2000-03; mem. Ann. Tom Peyton Meml. Arts Festival Com., 2003-05; mem. adminstrv. bd. 1st United Meth. Ch., 2003-05, chmn. presch. bd. Mem. La. Soc. Hosp. Pharmacists, Ctrl. La. Soc. for Human Resource Mgmt., S.W. La. Bridge Assn. (pres., bd. dirs.). Republican. Methodist. Avocations: duplicate bridge, tennis. Home and Office: 105 Foxfire Ln Alexandria LA 71302-8638 Personal E-mail: Rancher2000@aol.com.

SLOAN, ANDREW EDWARD, neurosurgeon, educator; b. Detroit; BS in Biology, Yale U., 1985; MD, Harvard U., 1990. Resident in neurosurgery UCLA, 1991-96, chief resident in neurosurgery, 1996-97; fellow in neurosurgery M.D. Anderson Cancer Inst., Houston, 1997-98; asst. prof. neurosurgery, neuro-oncology Wayne State U., Detroit, 1998—2004, assoc. prof., 2004—, Moffit Cancer Ctr., U. South Fla., Tampa, 2004—07, U. Hosps. Case Med. Ctr.; dir. Brain Tumor and Neuro Oncology Ctr.; dir. vice chair rsch. Seiderson Cancer Ctr. Recipient Clinician Investigator award Am. Brain Tumor Assn., 1999. Fellow ACS; mem. Am. Soc. Clin. Oncology (Clin. Rsch. Career Devel. award 2000), Am. Assn. Neurosurgery, Congress of Neurosurgery (mem. joint sect. tumors exec. com.). Office: Univ Hosp -Case Med Ctr Dept Neurosurgery 11100 Euclid Ave Cleveland OH 44106 Office Phone: 216-844-6054. Business E-Mail: andrew.sloan@uhhospitals.org.

SLOAN, HERBERT ELIAS, physician, surgeon; b. Clarksburg, W.Va., Oct. 10, 1914; s. Herbert Elias and Luella (Dye) S.; m. Doris Edwards, May 3, 1943; children: Herbert, Ann, Elizabeth, John, Robert. AB, Washington and Lee U., 1936; MD, Johns Hopkins U., 1940. Diplomate Am. Bd. Surgery, Am. Bd. Thoracic Surgery (bd. dirs. 1966-86, v.p. 1971-73, sec.-treas. 1973-86). Resident in surgery Johns Hopkins Hosp., 1941-44; instr. dept. surgery Johns Hopkins U., 1943-44; resident in thoracic surgery U. Mich. Hosp., Ann Arbor, 1947-49, instr. thoracic surgery, 1949-50; asst. prof. U. Mich., Ann Arbor, 1950-53, assoc. prof., 1953-62, prof. surgery, 1962-87, head sect. thoracic surgery, 1970-85; chief clin. affairs U. Mich. Hosps., Ann Arbor, 1982-86, med. dir. operating room, 1986-87, prof. emeritus surgery, 1987—; med. dir. managed health care U. Mich., Ann Arbor, 1989-96, Herbert Sloan Collegiate Professorship in cardiac surgery, 2003. Mem. staff VA Hosp., Ann Arbor, 1953—, cons., 1968—. Author: The American Board of Thoracic Surgery: A Fifty Year Perspective, 1998, (with Marvin M. Kirsh) Blunt Chest Trauma, General Principles of Management, 1977; editor Annals of Thoracic Surgery, 1969-85; contbr. (with Marvin M. Kirsh) chpts. to books, articles to profl. jours. Served to maj. M.C. U.S. Army, 1944-47. Recipient Bruce Douglas award in thoracic diseases, 1974, Med. Alumni Svc. award Johns Hopkins Sch. Medicine, 1973, Disting. Svc. award Johns Hopkins U. Sch. Medicine, 1983, Disting. Svc. award Mich. Med. Ctr. Alumni Soc., 1988, Herbert Sloan Collegiate Prof. Cardiac Surgery award, 2003; named to Hall of Honor, U. Mich. Med. Sch., 2006. Mem. ACS, Am. Surg. Assn., Am. Heart Assn., Am. Assn. Thoracic Surgery (pres. 1979-80), Soc. Thoracic Surgeons (pres. 1974-75, Disting. Svc. award 1981), Central Surg. Assn., Soc. Univ. Surgeons, So. Thoracic Surgery Assn. (hon.), Thoracic Soc. Gt. Britain (hon.), John Alexander Soc., Western Thoracic Surg. Assn. (hon.), Cardiovascular Surgeons Club, Detroit Heart Club, Am. Trudeau Soc., Mich. Heart Assn., Mich. Trudeau Soc., Am. Acad. Pediatrics, Soc. Vascular Surgery, Frederick A. Coller Surg. Soc., U. Mich. Med. Alumni Soc. (Disting. Svc. award 1988), U. Mich. James Angell Soc., Rsch. Club, Phi Beta Kappa, Alpha Omega Alpha, Omicron Delta Kappa, Sigma Xi. Clubs: Ann Arbor Figure Skating (pres. 1965-66). Home: 471 Barton North Dr Ann Arbor MI 48105-1017 Office: 1500 E Medical Center Dr Ann Arbor MI 48109 Business E-Mail: hsloan@umich.edu.

SLOAN, MICHAEL ALLAN, neurologist; b. Detroit, July 26, 1954; s. Eugene and Mildred Jody Sloan (Stepmother); children: Jessica Barry, Brittany Erin. MD, Wayne State U., 1980; MS, Rush U., 2003. Diplomate internal medicine Am. Bd. Internal Medicine, 1984, neurology Am. Bd. Psychiatry and Neurology, 1988, vascular neurology Am. Bd. Psychiatry and Neurology, 2005. Assoc. prof. neurology U. Md. Med. Ctr., Balt., 1993—97; neurologist Harbin Clinic, Rome, Ga., 1998—2000; assoc. prof. neurology U. Rush, Chgo., 2000—05; dir. stroke ctr. Carolinas Med. Ctr., Charlotte, NC, 2005—07; adj. prof. neurology U. NC, Chapel Hill, 2005—07; prof. neurology U. South Fla., Tampa, 2007—. AMA del. Am. Soc. Neuroimaging, 2001. Fellow: Am. Heart Assn., Am. Coll. Physicians, Am. Coll. Cardiology, Am. Acad. Neurology. Avocations: politics, music, performing arts, travel, sports. Business E-Mail: msloan@health.usf.edu.

SLOAN, TRISHA LYNNE, marriage and family therapist; b. Logan, Utah, July 14, 1956; BS, Brigham Young U., 1978; MFT, Ctrl. Conn. State U., 1999. Marriage and family therapist Cmty. Child Guidance Clinic Manchester, Conn., 1999—. Avocations: reading, swimming, hiking. Office: 317 North Main St Manchester CT 06040 Office Fax: 860-645-1470. Business E-Mail: tls@ccgcinc.org.

SLOCUM, ROSEMARIE R., retired physician services consultant; b. Port Arthur, Tex., Dec. 19, 1948; d. Edly and Ella (McNeely) Raccard; m. James Rubenstein; 1 child from previous marriage, Blair Ashton Slocum. BS in Secondary Edn., La. State U., Baton Rouge, 1971; MA in Bus. Comm., Jones Internat. U., Englewood, Colo., 1999. Cert. tchr. La. Edn. specialist La. Dept. Occupl. Stds., Baton Rouge, 1971—74; account exec. UARCO, Inc., 1974—77; owner, broker Rosemarie Slocum Real Estate, 1977—85; physician recruiter MSI, New Orleans, 1985—86; assoc. dir. physician recruitment Physician Svcs. Cons., Fairfax, Va., 1986-88; spl. cons. Caswell/Winters Inc.Physician Search Cons., Milw., 1988—89; v.p. U.S. Med. Search, Inc. subs. of Caswell/Winters Inc., 1988—89; dir. physician recruitment/mktg. East Range Clinics, Ltd., Virginia, Minn., 1989—91; pres. RSI Physician Svcs. Cons., Virginia, 1991—96, Mpls., 1996—2011.

SLONIM, ANTHONY DANIEL, pediatrician, internist; b. Newark, Apr. 14, 1964; s. Anthony Michael and Adelaide Eliz (Manara) S.; m. Teresa Ann Van Horn, Aug. 15, 1987; children: Michael, Samantha. BA, NYU, 1986; MD, N.Y. Med. Coll., 1991; MPH, DrPH, George Washington U. Diplomate Am. Bd. Pediat., Am. Bd. Internal Medicine, cert. in internal medicine, critical care, pediats., pediat. critical care, physician exec. Am. Bd. Pediats. Resident med.-pediatrics St. Joseph Hosp. and Med. Ctr., Paterson, N.J., 1991-95; fellow critical care NIH, Bethesda, Md., 1995-99, Children's Nat. Med. Ctr., 1996—99, attending physician in critical care medicine, 1999—, med. dir. performance improvement patient safety and clin. resource mgmt., 1999—. Surgeon gen. profl. adv. com. Public Health Svc., Rockville, 1997-99; asst. prof. internal medicine and pediats. George Washington U., 2003—. Mem. editl. bd.: Critical Care, CHEST; contbr. articles to profl. jours. Lt. comdr. USPHS, 1995-99. Mem. AMA, ACP, Am. Acad. Pediatrics, Soc. Critical Care Medicine, Am. Soc. of Internal Medicine. Office: Childrens Nat Med Ctr 111 Michigan Ave Washington DC 20010 Business E-Mail: aslonim@chmc.org.

SLY, RIDGE MICHAEL, pediatrician, allergist, immunologist, educator; b. Seattle, Nov. 3, 1933; s. Ridge Joseph and Eva Jean (Ruddell) S.; m. Ann Turner Jennings, June 12, 1957; children: Teresa Ann Perper, Cynthia Marie Schattenfield. AB, Kenyon Coll., Gambier, Ohio, 1956; MD, Washington U., St. Louis, 1960. Diplomate Am. Bd. Pediat., Am. Sub-Bd. Pediat. Allergy, Am. Bd. Allergy and Immunology. Intern, resident in pediat. St. Louis Children's Hosp, 1960—62; chief resident in pediat. U. Ky. Med. Ctr., Lexington, 1962—63; fellow in allergy and immunology UCLA Med. Ctr., 1965—67; from asst. prof. to prof. pediat. La. State U. Med. Ctr., New Orleans, 1967—78, head sect. allergy and immunology Children's Nat. Med. Ctr., Washington, 1978—2011; prof. pediat. George Washington U., Washington, 1978—. Author: Textbook of Pediatric Allergy, 1985; mem. editl. bd. Annals of Allergy, Asthma, & Immunology, 1982-98, 99-2002, Jour. Asthma, 1982-93, Clin. Revs. in Allergy, 1982-2001, Pediat. Asthma, Allergy, & Immunology, 1987—; assoc. editor Annals of Allergy, Asthma, & Immunology, 1989-90, editor, 1990-98; contbr. articles to profl. jours. Served to capt. USAF, 1963-65 Recipient La. plaque Am. Lung Assn. of La., 1978 Fellow Am. Acad. Allergy, Asthma & Immunology (chmn. com. on drugs 1981-87), Am. Acad. Pediats. (sect. on allergy com. 1972-75), Am. Coll. Allergy, Asthma, and Immunology (Disting. Fellow award 1993, Bela Schick award 1997, chmn. ethics com. 1997-99); mem. Assn. for Care of Asthma (pres. 1980-81, dir. postgrad. courses 1980—, Peshkin Meml. award 1983), AMA, Phi Beta Kappa. Republican. Baptist. Avocations: music, piano, organ. Office: Childrens Nat Med Ctr 9850 Key West Ave Rockville MD 20850

SMALL, DONALD, oncologist, educator; b. Washington, Jan. 25, 1956; BA, Johns Hopkins U., 1979; MD, Johns Hopkins U. Sch. Medicine, 1985, PhD. Kyle haydock prof. Johns Hopkins U. Sch. Medicine, 1990—. Dir., pediatric oncology Sidney Kimmel Cancer Ctr., Johns Hopkins, 2006. Mem.: Am. Soc. Hematology. Avocations: flying, skiing, mountain climbing. Office: 1650 Orleans St CRB1-251 Baltimore MD 21231 Office Fax: 410-955-8897. Business E-Mail: donsmall@jhmi.edu.

SMALL, ERIC, sports medicine physician; MD, U. Medicine & Dentistry of NJ. Diplomate Am. Bd. of Pediatrics. Resident Montefiore Med. Ctr.; fellow Children's Hosp., Pediatric Exercise Medicine; asst. clin. prof. pediatrics Mount Sinai Med. Ctr., asst. clin. prof. rehabilitation medicine, asst. clin. prof. orthopaedics. Office: Mount Sinai Medical Center 666 Lexington Ave Mount Kisco NY 10549 Office Phone: 914-666-7900. Office Fax: 914-666-7901.

SMALL, JUDITH A., dermatologist, educator; MD, U. Rochester. Diplomate Am. Bd. Dermatology. Intern Med. Coll. of Va.; resident Univ. Md. Med. System; practice ASPN Dermatology; adj. asst. prof. medicine Drexel Univ.; dir. divsn. of dermatology Allegheny Gen. Hosp. Named one of Top Doctors, Pitts. mag., 2011. Office: Allegheny General Hospital 320 E N Ave Pittsburgh PA 15212 Office Phone: 412-359-3131. Office Fax: 412-359-4108.

SMALL, LEIGH, nursing educator; b. Utica, NY, Feb. 18, 1958; MS, U. Rochester, 1993, PhD, 2003. Assoc. prof. Ariz. State U., 2004—. PNP program coord. Fellow: Nat. Academies Practice. Office: 500 North Third St Phoenix AZ 85004 Business E-Mail: leigh.small@asu.edu.

SMALL, MELVIN D., physician, educator; b. Somerville, Mass., May 22, 1925; s. Sidney J. and Ida (Gelbsman) Small; m. Judith Nogee, Dec. 23, 1962; children: Michael Dorian, Michele. AB, U. Wis., 1953; MD, Duke U., Durham, NC, 1959; studied under Dr. Gregory Pincus, Worcester Found. Exptl. Biol. and Medicine, 1950-53; studied under Prof. Brian Abel-Smith, London Sch. Econs, 1986-90, MPhil, 1988. Lic. physician Fla., Md., DC, Va. Intern Georgetown U. Med. Ctr., Washington, 1959-60, resident, 1960-61, chief gastrointestinal rsch., 1961-64, instr. medicine, 1961-66, asst. prof., 1966-67, asst. clin. prof., 1967—81, 1993; chief gastroenterology sect. Georgetown divsn. DC Gen. Hosp., Washington, 1964-68. Chief animal experimentation cancer rsch. under Dr. Sidney Farber Children's Med. Ctr., Boston, 1948—50; rsch. asst. Boston U. Sch. Medicine, 1956—57; lectr. hygiene and preventive medicine Peace Corps groups, Ethiopia, Turkey, Brazil, and Columbia Georgetown U., 1961—62; active staff Fairfax Hosp., Va., 1961—73, Arlington Hosp., Va., 1961—85, Cir. Terr. Hosp., Alexandria, 1965—85, Commonwealth Drs. Hosp., Fairfax, 1969—74, Mt. Vernon Hosp., Alexandria, 1976—85; attending physician DC Gen. Hosp., 1961—68, Georgetown U. Hosp., 1961—81, 1993—, Mt. Sinai Hosp., Miami Beach, Fla., 1992—; physician mem. presdl. appeals bd., under Pres. John F. Kennedy VA Adminstrn., 1961; cons. Children's Hosp., Washington, 1962—66; chmn. dept. medicine Alexandria Hosp., 1974—75, hon. staff mem., 1985—89, 1992—; founder, chmn. No. Va. Consortium Continuing Med. Edn., 1974—86; chmn. emeritus No. Va. Consotium Continuing Med. Edn., 1986; witness subcom. small bus. US Senate, 1967; founder, chmn. Nat. Coun. State Coms. Continuing Med. Edn., 1977—79; lectr. in field; cons. pain mgmt. and addiction treatment; med. dir. Advanced Med. Ctr., Melbourne, Fla. Author: publs. in field. Nominated candidate Palm Beach Town Coun., Fla., 1995—96; trustee Jefferson Meml. Hosp., 1965—74, mem. founding group, 1965, chmn. pharmacy com., 1965—76, co-chmn. tissue com., 1965—74. Fellow, Mallory Inst. Pathology, 1953—59, Gastroenterology Rsch., Evans Meml. Hosp., 1951—53. Mem.: ACP, AMA, Am. Acad. Addiction Psychiatry, Palm Beach County Med. Soc., Alexandria Med. Soc. (v.p. 1979—80), Med. Soc. Va. (chmn. commn. continuing med. edn. 1978—81), DC Med. Soc., Am. Soc. Gastrointestinal Endoscopy, Am. Physiol. Soc., Am. Soc. Nutrition, Am. Gastroent. Assn., Am. Coll. Gastroenterology. Personal E-mail: drmelv@comcast.net.

SMALL, PARKER ADAMS, JR., pediatrician, educator; b. Cin., July 5, 1932; s. Parker Adams and Grace (McMichael) S.; m. Natalie Settimelli, Aug. 26, 1956; children: Parker Adams, Peter McMichael, Carla Edmea. Student, Tufts U., 1950-53; MD, U. Cin., 1957; BS extraordinem, 1986. Med. intern Pa. Hosp., Phila., 1957-58; rsch. assoc. Nat. Heart Inst. NIH, Washington, 1958-60; rsch. fellow St. Mary's Hosp., London, 1960-61; sr. surgeon NIMH, Washington, 1961-66; prof. immunology and med. microbiology U. Fla., 1966-95, chmn. dept., 1966-75, prof. pediat., 1979—2003, prof. emeritus, 2003—, prof. pathology, 1995—2003, prof. emeritus, 2003—, adj. clin. prof. large animal sci., 1999—2003; pres. PigVax Inc., 2000—01. Dir. Ctr. for Coop. Learning for Health Sci. Edn., U. Fla., 1988-2003; vis. prof. U. Lausanne, Switzerland, 1972, U. Lagos, Nigeria, 1982, Al Hada Hosp., Saudi Arabia, 1983; vis. scholar Assn. Am. Med. Colls., Washington, 1973; assoc. life scis. panel Nat. Acad. Scis., 1981-88, co-chmn., 1982-83; bd. dirs. Biol. Sci. Curriculum Study, 1984-90, exec. bd., 1987-90; mem. edn. adv. com. Nat. Fund Med. Edn., 1984-87; mem. study com. Nat. Bd. Med. Examiners, 1983-85, mem. nat. vaccine adv. com., 1987-91, chmn. subcom. on new vaccines, 1987-91; v.p. smallgroupconsultants.com, 2003-; mem. Truro Shellfish Advisory Com.; cons. in field. Creator patient oriented problem solving system/POPS, for tchg. immunology and coop. learning to med. students and Team Packs for tchg. K-12 & coll. students health edn. and coop. learning; co-dir. Fla. Ptnrs. in Prevention of Substance Abuse, 1997-2003; editor: The Secretory Immunologic System, 1971; mem. editl. bd. Infection and Immunity, 1974-76, Jour. Med. Edn., 1978-80; cons. editor Microbios, Cytobios; patentee in field; contbr. more than 150 articles to profl. jours. Sec., treas. Oakmont, Md., 1964-65, mayor, 1965-66; chmn. Citizens for Pub. Schs. Gainesville, Fla., 1969-70; mem. Teen Pregnancy Prevention Action Com., 1998-2000, Truro Shellfish Adv. Com., 2004-. With USPHS, 1958-60, 61-66. Named Tchr. of Yr. U. Fla. Coll. Medicine, 1978-79, Disting. Lectr. AMA, 1986; recipient Presdl. medallion U. Fla., 1987, Nat. Basic Sci. Disting. Tchg. award Alpha Omega Alpha, 1993, Jacob Ehrenzeller award, 1995, Pres.'s Faculty Humanitarian award U. Fla., 1996, Pep award U. Fla., 1998, Lifetime Achievement award U. Fla. Coll. Medicine, 2003; NIH spl. fellow, 1960-61, rsch. grantee, 1966-91, U. Fla. Tchr./Scholar and commencement spkr., 1987; invited lectr. Assn. Am. Med. Colls., 1992. Mem. AAAS, Am. Assn. Immunologists (edn. com. 1983-86), Physicians for Social Responsibility, Fla. Med. Assn., Phi Beta Kappa, Sigma Xi, Alpha Omega Alpha, Theta Delta Chi. Office: U Fla Coll Med PO Box 100275 Gainesville FL 32610-0275 Personal E-mail: smallgroup2@aol.com. Business E-Mail: small@pathology.ufl.edu.

SMALLBONE, DAVID FRANK, physician, consultant; b. Birmingham, Eng., June 24, 1938; s. Samuel Frank and Kathleen Jessie Smallbone; m. Janet Sykes, Aug. 10, 1985; 1 stepchild, Jayne McCarthy. BChir, MB, Birmingham U., 1962. Med. cons., London, 1963—2008, Higher Nature PLC, Burwash Common, East Sussex, England, 1996—2008; med. advisor Irish Inst. Natural Health, 2008—. Regional med. adviser Brit. Motor Corp., Coventry, Warwickshire, England, 1964—80, Automobile Assn., Birmingham, West Midlands, England, 1968—81; med. adviser Coventry Radiator Ltd, Warwickshire, 1968—82. Author: (book) Healing, 1983. Fellow: Royal Soc. Medicine, Coll. Healing; mem.: Faculty of Homeopathy, Royal Coll. Physicians (licentiate), Royal Coll. Surgeons, NY Acad. Scis. Achievements include first to use natural Progesterone for various endocrine disorders. Avocations: travel, gardening, writing. Home: The Oak Coolgarrow Enniscorthy Co Wexford Ireland also: Willow Lodge Lordine Court Lordine Court Drive TN32 5TF East Sussex England Personal E-mail: d.smallbone@virgin.net. Business E-Mail: david@drdlavidsmallbone.com.

SMALLEY, WALTER E., physician, educator; b. Catoosa County, Ga., Aug. 22, 1959; BS, Emory & Henry Coll., 1981; MD, Duke U., 1985. Prof., medicine Vanderbilt U., 1991—. Office: 1030C MRB IV Nashville TN 37211 Office Fax: 615-343-6229. Business E-Mail: walter.smalley@vanderiblt.edu.

SMART, FRANK WILSON, physician; b. New Orleans, Apr. 12, 1956; s. Foch Mahlon and Laura Gladys Smart; m. Jaclyn Cutrone, Nov. 16, 1996; children: Daniel, Katherine, Michael. BS in Zoology, So. La. U., 1978; MD, La. State U., New Orleans, 1985. Diplomate Am. Bd. Internal Medicine, Am. Bd. Cardiovascular Disease. Intern Ochsner Found. Hosp., New Orleans, 1985-86, resident, 1986-88; fellow Baylor Coll. Medicine, Houston, 1988-90, fellow in transplant rsch., 1990-91; co-sect. head heart failure and cardiac transplantation Ochsner Med. Instn., New Orleans, 1991-97, dir. med. transplant svcs., multi-organ transplant ctr., 1994-97; dir. transplant Ochsner Clinic, New Orleans, 1991-97; prof. medicine, co-dir. to dir. cardiac transplant program Tulane U. Med. Ctr., New Orleans, 1997; med. dir., adv. heart failure, cardiac transplantation, Tex. Heart Inst. St. Luke's Episcopal Hosp., Houston; dir. cardiology Morristown (NJ) Meml. Hosp., 2006—, chmn., cardiology, vice chmn., cardiovascular medicine, 2006—. V.p., co-founder Rsch. Congestive Heart Failure, New Orleans, 1998—; rep. region 3 United Network Organ Sharing, Richmond, Va., 1999—; mem. adv. bd. Action Heart Failure, Parsippany, N.Y. Mem. editl. bd. Cardiology Today, 1996, Congestive Heart Failure, Jour. Heart & Lung Transplantation; author: The Transplantation & Replacement of Thoracic Organs, 1997, Primer on Transplantation, 1998; reviewer Am. Jour. Cardiology. Recipient Richard Van Reet award Baylor Coll. Medicine, Houston, 1991. Fellow ACP, Am. Coll. Cardiology (Syntex award 1990); mem. AMA, Internat. Soc. Heart or Lung Transplantation, Am. Soc. Transplantation, So. Med. Assn., Alpha Omega Alpha. Office: Morristown Meml Hosp 100 Madison Ave Morristown NJ 07962 Office Phone: 973-290-7316.

SMEAL, JANIS LEA, psychiatrist; b. Johnstown, Pa., Aug. 31, 1953; d. Charles Truman S. and Clara Belle (Smeal) Satterlee. RN, Mercy Hosp. Sch. Nursing, 1974; BS summa cum laude, U. Houston, 1996; DO, U. North Tex., 2001. bd. cert. in psychiatry and neurology, 2007. Staff, relief charge nurse emergency rm. Mercy Hosp., Altoona, Pa., 1974—85; staff nurse oper. rm. McAllen Med. Ctr., Tex., 1985—87, Rio Grande Regional Hosp., McAllen, 1987—88; co-owner Associated Hypnotherapy and Pain Mgmt. Svcs. Tex., Bellaire, 1991—97; staff nurse oper. rm. Meml. City Hosp., Houston, 1992—97; psychiatry resident U. Tex. Health Sci. Ctr., Houston, 2001—05, asst. prof. psychiatry, 2005—. Co-owner, cons. J.L. Med. Svcs., McAllen, Tex., 1988-94. Recognition Golden Key Nat. Honor Soc., 1993, Phi Kappa Phi, 1994, Natural Sci. and Math. Scholars and Fellows, 1995. Mem.: Tex. Med. Assn., Tex. Osteo. Med. Assn., Am. Psychiat. Assn., Golden Key, Phi Kappa Phi. Avocation: travel. Office: 2800 S MacGregor Ste 3D-08 Houston TX 77021

SMEAL, KEMP LESLIE, psychotherapist, musician; s. Ronald Leslie and Patricia Ann Smeal. MusB, Westminster Choir Coll., Princeton, NJ, 1981; MA in Clin. Psychology, Azusa Pacific U., Calif., 1994. Lic. marital and family therapist Bd. Behavioral Scis., Calif., 2000. Min. music Cmty. Presbyn. Ch., Danville, Calif., 1982—92; organist/pianist Glendale Presbyn. Ch., Calif., 1992—99, Glendale City Seventh-day Adventist Ch., 1997—, La Canada Presbyn. Ch., Calif., 1999—; assoc. prof. of accompanying Vanguard U., Costa Mesa, Calif., 2001—03; pvt. practice psychotherapy Long Beach, Calif., 2000—. Organist Welsh Choir So. Calif., North Hollywood, 2001—02; organist for the glory of easter Crystal Cathedral, Garden Grove, 2002—03, interim assoc. organist, 2003; recitalist Cathedral of Our Lady of the Angels, LA, 2003—07. Musician: (CD) Beside Still Waters, Hearts Afire, (featured pianist on time-life video) A Walk With Jesus: A Holy Land Journey With Hymns and Scripture. William and Mary Renneckar scholar, Westminster Choir Coll., 1978—79. Mem.: Calif. Assn. Marriage and Family Therapists (assoc.), Am. Guild Organists Orange County Chpt. (assoc.), Am. Guild Organists LA Chpt. (assoc.). Office: 5855 Naples Plz Ste 109 Long Beach CA 90802 Personal E-mail: ksmeal@aol.com. Business E-Mail: kempsmeal@aol.com.

SMEJKAL, PETR, hematologist; b. Brno, Czech Republic, Feb. 17, 1966; MD, Masaryk U. Brno, 1990, PhD, 2009. Physician, dept. internal medicine, hematooncology U. Hosp. Brno, 1990—93, physician, dept. hematology, 1993—, cons., 1997. Mem.: Czech Soc. Hematology. Avocation: hiking. Office: Jihlavska 20 Brno 625 00 Czech Republic Office Fax: 420 53223 3613. Business E-Mail: psmejkal@fnbrno.cz.

SMELLIE, JEAN MCILDOWIE, pediatrician; b. Liverpool, Eng., May 14, 1927; d. John McIldowie Hope and Mary Wilson (Clarkson) Smellie; m. Ian Colin Stuart Normand, June 30, 1961; children: Alison, Christopher, Caroline. BA, Oxford U., 1947, MA, 1957, BM BCh, 1950, DM, 1981. First asst. pediatrics U. Coll. Hosp., London, 1957—60, rsch. asst. cons., sr. lectr., 1961—92; lectr. pediatrics Radcliffe Infirmary, Oxford, 1960—61; fellow in pathology Johns Hopkins U., Balt., 1964—65; hon. sr. lectr. Cmty. Child Health, Southampton, 1978—92; hon. cons. paediatric nephrologist Guy's and Great Ormond St. Hosp., London, 1980—2000. Emeritus cons. U. Coll. Hosp., 1992—; mem. med. adv. com. Sir Jules Thorn Charitable Trust, London, 1985-97; chmn. Cmty. Child Health Group, Southampton, 1980-85; sci. adviser Internat. Reflux Study in Children, Essen, Germany, Albert Einstein, N.Y. Contbr. chapters to books, articles to profl. jours. Fellow Royal Coll. of Physicians, Royal Coll. Pediatrics and Child Health (hon.); mem. Internat. Pediatric Nephrol. Assn., European Soc. for Pediatric Nephrology, British Assn. for Paediatric Nephrology (hon. 1995), Am. Urol. Assn. (hon.), British Paediatric Assn. (hon.), European Soc. for Paediatric Urology (hon.). Mem. Ch. Eng. Avocations: music, photography, travel, gardening. Home and Office: 23 St. Thomas Street SO23 9HJ Winchester England Home Fax: 0-1962-852550.

SMETANA, KAREL FRANTISEK, cytologist, researcher; b. Prague, Czech Republic, Oct. 28, 1930; s. Karel Smetana and Marie Smetanova; m. Vlasta Krouzkova, Oct. 24, 1953; 1 child, Karel. MD, PhD, DSc, Charles U., Prague. Lic. internal medicine physician Inst. of Postgraduate Med. Studies, 1984. Lectr. dept. histology Charles U. Med. Faculty, Prague, 1955—62; dept. head Lab. Ultrastruct Rsch. Czechoslovak Acad. Scis., Prague, 1962—84; dir. Inst. Hematology and Blood Transfusion, Prague, 1984—90, sr. scientist, lab. cytology electron microscopy, 1990—2000, staff scientist, 2000—; head Chair Hematology Transfusion Svc. Inst. Postgrad. Med. Studies, Prague, 1985—93, lectr., 1993—2005; chmn. exam. bd. Lab. Methods Clinical Hematology, 1993—. Assoc. prof. Baylor Coll. Medicine, Houston, 1963—2004, prof., 1970, adj. prof., 99; chmn. Charles U. Bd. Postgrad. Sci. Studies Cell Biology and Pathology, 1994—2008, co-chmn., 2008—. Contbr. articles to profl. jours.; co-author: (monograph) The Nucleolus; contbr. chapters to books. Recipient Ministry Health Sci. prize, Czech Republic, 1974, State prize, 1986, State Purkynje medal, Ministry Health, Czech Republic, 1987, Hon. medal, Komenius U., 1980, Palacky U., Masaryk U., 1990, Slovak Med. Soc., Vet. Med. Sch., others, Babaks medal, Czechoslovak Biol. Soc., 2006, Purkynje medal, Czechhoslovak Biol. Soc., 1996, Chech Med. Soc., 2006, Bernhard medal, Internat. Workshop Cell Nucleus, 1995, Sci. prize, Czechoslovak Microscopy Soc., 2006. Fellow: Czech and Slovak Biol. Soc. (hon.), Czech Hematological Soc. (hon.; pres. 1985—90, Sci. prize); mem.: Soc. Clin. Cutology, Europe Cell Biology Orgn. (former gov.), Internat. Soc. Hemotology (former councelor), Soc. Clin. Cytology, Biorad Hematological Soc. (hon.), Czech Med. Soc. (hon.), Czech Histochem. Soc. (hon.; v.p. 1997—2008). Achievements include research in structural organization of the cell nucleus and nucleolus. Office: Inst Hematology Blood Transfusion U Nemocnice 1 128 00 Prague 2 Czech Republic Office Fax: 420 2 21977 249. Business E-Mail: karel.smetana@uhkt.cz.

SMIGEL, IRWIN, dentist; b. NYC, Oct. 9, 1924; m. Lucia Shvetz, Sept. 30, 1956; children: Bellanca Smigel Rutter, Robert. WSC, DDS, NYU, 1950. Diplomate Am. Bd. Aesthetic Dentistry. Dentist pvt. practice, NYC, 1950—. Vis. prof. Pitts. Dental Sch., 1980-83, Case Western U., 1990—; lectr. SUNY Buffalo, U. Mo., Kansas City, U. Minn.; cons., lectr. in field, with, Nat. Mus. Bentistiey Branch Smithsonian. Author: Dental Health, Dental Beauty, 1978; contbr. editor Dentistry Today, 1980-, dental adv. bd.; contbr. articles to dental jours. With INF., 1943-45. Irwin Smigel Chair in Aesthetic Dentistry established NYU Sch. Dentistry, 1996, Smigel Prize; recipient Outstanding Contbrn. to Aesthetic Dentistry award, Am. Acad. Cosmetic Dentistry, 1994 Fellow Am. Soc. Dental Aesthetics (founder, pres. 1976-2006); mem. Am. Dental Assn., Acad. Gen. Dentistry, Fedn. Dentaire, First Dist. Dental Soc. Achievements include invention of the Supersmile Whitening brand mouthrinse, toothpaste, floss and brush, tooth bonding technique, supersmile complete oral careline of products. Avocations: reading, tennis, racewalking, art, music. Office: 635 Madison Ave New York NY 10022-1009 Office Phone: 212-371-4575.

SMILEN, SCOTT W., obstetrician, gynecologist, educator; Attended, NYU, 1984—88. Diplomate Am. Bd. Ob-Gyn. Resident ob-gyn. NY Univ. Langone Med. Ctr., 1988—92, fellow urogynecology, physician; assoc. prof. ob-gyn. NY Univ. Sch. of Medicine; with Valley Hosp. Co-author: (publs.) Residency selection: should interviewers be given applicants' board scores?, 2001, Urinary incontinence in familial dysautonomia, 2003, Simple ultrasound evaluation of the anal sphincter in female patients using a transvaginal transducer, 2005, Vaginal delivery and serum markers of ischemia/reperfusion injury, and numerous other publications. Office: New York University Langone Medical Center 5th Fl 530 1st Ave New York NY 10016 Office Phone: 212-263-0395. Office Fax: 212-263-8250.

SMILEY, CAROL ANNE, retired health facility administrator, sculptor; b. Cedar Rapids, Iowa, Sept. 11, 1937; d. Ralph Derold and Mary C. Miller; m. Donald Victor Smiley, June 29, 1956 (div. Aug. 1970); children: Donald Victor Jr., Julie Ann, Joseph Charles, Thomas Wayne; m. Douglas Brewster Reed, Aug. 6, 1976 (div. Jan. 1988); 1 child, Brook (dec.). Co-founder, v.p., sec., treas. Anvic Enterprise, Cedar Rapids, 1963-70; co-founder, dir. Yankee Horse Trader, Bennington, Vt., 1974; organic farmer Solon, Iowa, Argyle, NY, 1970-86; fiber sculptor, 1970-86; tchr. Solon H.S., 1973-74; caregiver, coord. Home Health Care and Hospice, Brattleboro, Vt., 1986—2011; cons. in grassroots home health. Sculpture shows include Green Mt. Collaborative, Bennington, 1974-78, Woman Art Gallery, N.Y.C., 1977-78, Lincoln Ctr. Group Show, N.Y.C., 1978; exhbns. various group shows. Mem. GOP ctrl. com. for Johnson County, Iowa, 1971-72. Mem.: ACLU.

SMILOWICZ, MIROSLAW TADEUSZ, orthopedic surgeon, educator; b. Warsaw, July 10, 1934; s. Szymon Tadeusz and Maria Leokadia (Peczkowski) S.; m. Jolanta Staniszkis, Aug. 23, 1960; children: Piotr, Tomasz. Grad., Acad. Medicine, Warsaw, 1958, MD, 1960; PhD, Inst. Rheumatology, Warsaw, 1980. Pre-registration house officer Gen. Hosp., Acad. Medicine, Warsaw, 1959-60; house officer Children's Surg. Hosp., Warsaw, 1961-63; sr. house officer, registrar Omega Hosp., Warsaw, 1964-68; sr. registrar Inst. Rheumatology, Warsaw, 1969-70, sr. registrar, cons., 1972—; sr. house officer Inst. Orthop., Oswestry, England, 1971-72; assoc. prof. Inst. Rheumatology, 1998—2005; ret., 2005. Sr. cons. at med. ctrs. Contbr. author: A Gruca Chirurgia Orthopedyczna, 1993, author: instrnl. films on orthop. surgery; contbr. articles to profl. jours. Recipient Medal of State award, Poland, 1984, Gold Cross of Merit, 1985, Badge of the Sec. of State award, Poland, 1986. Mem. Polish Orthop. and Trumatological Soc., Polish Rheumatological Soc., European Rheumatism and Arthritis Surg. Soc. Roman Catholic. Avocations: photography, skiing, bicycling. Office: Inst Rheumatology Spartanska 1 02-637 Warsaw Poland Home: Ul. Dezyderego Adama Chlapowskiego 61 02-787 Warsaw Poland Office Phone: 022 8448724. E-mail: smilowicz@wp.pl, reumoortopedia@go2.pl.

SMIRNOV, SERGEY, research scientist; b. Moscow, Feb. 11, 1972; M, Nat. Rsch. Nuc. U. MEPhI, 1997. Lab. head Ajinomoto-Genetika Rsch. Inst., 1998—. Avocation: photography. Office: 1st Dorozhny pr 1-1 Moscow 117545 Russia

SMITH, ANDREW JOSEPH, cardiologist, educator; b. Somerset, NJ, Sept. 1, 1974; PharmD, UMKC Sch. Pharmacy, 2000. Primary care pharmacy resident VA Med. Ctr., Iowa City, 2000—01; cardiology clin. pharmacist KU Med. Ctr., 2001—08, Truman Med. Ctrs., 2008—. Pres. Greater Kans. City Soc. Health-Sys. Pharmacists, 2010—11; treas. Mo. Soc. Health-Sys. Pharmacists, 2009—11. Recipient Best Practice award, MSHP Rsch. & Edn. Found.; named Faculty of Yr., Rho Chi Pharmacy Honors Soc., UMKC. Mem.: Mo. Soc. Health-Sys. Pharmacists, Am. Assn. Coll. Pharmacy, Am. Coll. Clin. Pharmacy, Am. Coll. Cardiology, Phi Lambda Sigma Pharmacy Leadership Soc. Avocations: baseball, football, basketball. Office: 2464 Charlotte St HSB 3246 Kansas City MO 64108 Business E-Mail: smithandr@umkc.edu.

SMITH, ARLAN ROBERT, plastic and reconstructive surgeon; b. Surabaja, Indonesia, Aug. 3, 1948; arrived in Holland, 1954; m. Paulina Jacoba de Jong, May 25, 1990; children: Darryl Nathaniël, Beau Aurora Fabiana, Chloé Aphrodite Zoë. Student, St. Ignatius Coll., Amsterdam, The Netherlands, 1961-66; PhD, U. Amsterdam, The Netherlands, 1972, MD, 1974. Cert. plastic and reconstructive surgeon. Gen. surgery tng. dept gen. surgery U. Maastricht, The Netherlands, 1975-79; clin. and rsch. fellow Mass. Gen. Hosp., Harvard Med. Sch., Boston, 1977-79; specialist in plastic and reconstructive surgery dept. plastic surgery U. Hosp. Dijkzigt Rotterdam, The Netherlands, 1979-82, chef de clinique in microsurgery and hand surgery dept. plastic and reconstructive surgery, 1979-86; head dept. plastic and reconstructive surgery Holy Hosp. Vlaardingen, The Netherlands, 1985-96; vis. prof. plastic and reconstructive surgery U. Kristen Idonesia Jakarta, Indonesia, 1989-91; dir. and owner Clinic Holystaete Vlaardingen, Netherlands, 1991—. Contbr. articles to profl. jours. Mem. Dutch Soc. for Hand Surgery, Dutch Soc. Esthetic Surgery, Dutch Soc. Plastic and Reconstructive Surgery, Internat. Microsurg. Soc., Found. Moshe Yemin clinic Holystaete (chmn. bd.), the Netherlands. Avocations: gardening, pre-Columbian art, modern art, Egyptian and African art. Office: Clinic Holystaete Churchillsingel 480 3137XB Vlaardingen Netherlands Business E-Mail: info@kliniekholystaete.nl. E-mail: abr.smith@planet.nl.

SMITH, BARBARA RATH, medical association administrator; b. Washington, Oct. 22, 1946; d. Gunnar Emil and Mary (Faux) Rath; m. Stanley Sherrel Smith, Mar. 29, 1969; children: Trevor Eli, Whitney Marin, Kendall Risa Elisabeth. BA in Psychology, Fed. City Coll., 1970; postgrad., U. Md., 1976-77. Psychodramatist St. Elizabeth's Hosp., Washington, 1972-73; psychology technician VA Hosp., Washington, 1971-74; vol. Cedar Lane Unitarian Ch., Bethesda, Md., 1979-88; exec. adminstr. Am. Thyroid Assn., Washington, 1988-94, now exec. dir. Falls Church, Va., 2001—; assoc. dir. Nat. Assn. Hispanic Journalists, Washington, 1994-97; dir. found. and govt. rels. Assn. for Healthcare Philanthropy, Falls Church, Va., 1997—. Chair religious edn. coun. Cedar Lane Unitarian Ch., Bethesda, Md., 1987-89; v.p. ways and means Oakland Terr. Elem. Sch., Kensington, Md., 1982-84; pastoral caregiver St. Mark's Episcopal Ch., Washington. Mem. Am. Soc. Assn. Execs., Grtr. Washington Soc. Assn. Execs., Nat. Soc. Fundraising Execs. Democrat. Avocations: religious education leader, literacy and english teacher to speakers of other languages. Office: Am Thyroid Assn Ste 650 6066 Leesburg Pike Falls Church VA 22041 Office Phone: 703-998-8890. *

SMITH, BRADLEY E., anesthesiologist; b. Cedar Vale, Kans. MD, U. Okla., Norman, 1957. Diplomate Am. Bd. Anesthesiologists. Resident U.S. Naval Hosp., NYC, 1957-60; fellow Columbia Presbyn. Hosp., NYC, 1960—61; faculty Yale U., 1962-63, U. Miami, 1963-69; chmn., prof. dept. anesthesiology Vanderbilt U., Nashville, 1969-93, prof., 1993—, prof. emeritus, 2004—, prof. clin. anesthesiology, 2005—08; trustee Wood Libr. Mus. Anesthesiology, 2008—. Mem.: AMA, ACOG (assoc.), Am. Soc. Anesthesiologists. Office: Vandy Med Ctr Rm 209 Oxford House Nashville TN 37232-4245 Office Phone: 615-936-0718.

SMITH, BRENT J., facial plastic surgeon; BS in Biology, Stanford U., 1974—78; MD, Ind. U., Indpls., 1978—82. Lic. Colo., diplomate Am. Bd. Facial Plastic and Reconstructive Surgery, Am. Acad. Otalaryngology. Intern Univ. of Cin., Ohio, 1982—83, resident dept. of otalaryngology and maxillofacial surgery Coll. of Medicine Ohio, 1983—87; fellow The Facial Plastic and Cosmetic Surgery Ctr., Ky., 1987—88; cosmetic surgeon Smith Cosmetic Surgery. Co-author: chptrs. to texbooks pertaining to otoplasty (facial cosmetic and reconstructive surgery of the ears) and surg. principles for diseases of the inner ear and skull base; contbr. articles articles pub. in mags., pub. in Colo. Expression and People Mag.; featured in The Learning Channel. Fellow: ACS; mem.: Internat. Hyperbarics Assoc., Denver Med. Soc., Colo. Med. Soc., Colo. Ear. Nose and Throat Soc., Am. Bd. of Med. Specialists, Am. Acad. of Facial Plastic and Reconstructive Surgery, Am. Acad. of Otolaryngology/ Head and Neck Surgery. Office: Smith Cosmetic Surgery 5161 East Arapahoe Rd Ste. 350 Littleton CO 80122 Office Phone: 303-741-2211.

SMITH, BRIAN G., orthopedist, director; b. Balt., Apr. 27, 1956; BA, Williams Coll., 1978; MD, Georgetown U., 1982. Dir. pediatric orthopaedics Yale U. Sch. Medicine, 2007—, assoc. resident dir. dept. Orthopedics. Recipient Tchg. award, Orthop. Dept, Yale U. Sch. Medicine. Fellow: Am. Acad. Orthop. Surgeons. Avocations: reading, golf. Office: PO Box 208071 New Haven CT 06520 Office Phone: 203-737-1616. Office Fax: 203-785-7132. Business E-Mail: brian.g.smith@yale.edu.

SMITH, BRIAN PHILIP, statistician; b. Columbus, Ohio, May 13, 1966; BS in Math. and Physics, Ctr. Coll., 1988; PhD in Stats., U. Ky., 1994. Biostatistician U. Louisville, 1994—96; group leader, oncology, cardiovasc., muskoskelatal program phase stats. Eli Lilly and Co., 1996—2005; biostats. dir. Amgen, 2005—. Assoc. editor Clin. Pharmacology and Therapeutics, 2007; founding organizer Pacific Coast Statisticians and Pharmacometricians Innovation Conf., 2009. Mem.: Am. Soc. Clin. Pharmacology and Therapeutics. Home: 1141 Canyon Crest Ct Thousand Oaks CA 91360 Personal E-mail: brismith1313@yahoo.com.

SMITH, BRIAN R., surgeon, educator; b. Panorama City, Calif., June 25, 1973; BS, U. Calif., Santa Barbara, 1995; MD, NY Med. Coll., 2000. Asst. prof., surgery, assoc. residency program dir. U. Calif. Irvine Med. Ctr., 2008—. Chief, gen. surgery VA Long Beach Healthcare Sys., 2008—11. Fellow: ACS; mem.: Am. Soc. Metabolic and Bariatric Surgery, Pacific Coast Surg. Assn., Southern Calif. Chpt. of ACS, Assn. Program Dirs. Surgery. Office: 5901 East 7th St Box 12112 Long Beach CA 90822 Office Fax: 562-826-5666. Business E-Mail: brian.smith11@va.gov.

SMITH, BRIAN RICHARD, hematologist, oncologist, pathologist; b. Glen Cove, NY, May 7, 1952; s. Frank C. and Gloria R. S.; m. Keiren Donovan, Apr. 17, 1993. AB in Chemistry summa cum laude, Princeton U., 1972; MD, Harvard U., 1976; MA (hon.), Yale U., 1997. Diplomate Am. Bd. Internal Medicine, Hematology and Med. Oncology, Am. Bd. Pathology Hematopathology. Resident/fellow Harvard U., Brigham and Women's Hosp., 1976-80; instr. medicine Harvard Med. Sch., 1981—84; assoc. physician Brigham & Women's Hosp., Children's Hosp., Dana-Farber Cancer Ins, Boston, 1981-88; asst. prof. medicine Harvard Med. Sch., 1985-88; assoc. prof. medicine, lab. medicine & pediatrics sch. med. Yale U., New Haven, 1988-96, prof. medicine, lab medicine & pediatrics, 1996—, dir. immunohematology; vice chmn. dept. lab. medicine Yale Med. Sch.-Yale New Haven Hosp., 1997—2005, chmn. dept. lab. medicine, 2006—; DeCamp lectr. biomed. ethics Princeton U., NJ, 1992. Contbr. over 150 articles to med. publs. Trustee Richard D. Frisbee III Found.; chair study sect. Am. Heart Assn. Recipient George A. Howe prize Princeton U., 1976; Am. Cancer Soc. fellow, 1981-84, Leukemia Soc. fellow, 1982-88; Leukemia Soc. Am. scholar, 1989, Stohlman scholar, 1993, Nat. Blood Found. scholar, 1996. Fellow ACP, Coll. Am. Pathologists; mem. NIH (recombinant DNA adv. com. 1992-97), Acad. Clin. Lab. Physicians and Scientists (pres. 2006-), Phi Beta Kappa, Sigma Xi, Alpha Omega Alpha. Roman Catholic. Office: Yale U Sch Med PO Box 208035 333 Cedar St New Haven CT 06520-8035

SMITH, CAROLYN J(ANE) HOSTETTER, psychologist, educator; b. Indpls., Mar. 29, 1938; d. John Daniel and Louise Margaret (Reiber) Hostetter; m. Thomas Tomasian, June 18, 1988. BA, DePauw U., 1959; MS in Teaching-Guidance & Counseling, U. Chgo., 1962, PhD, 1981. Lic. psychologist, Mass. Guidance counselor Blue Island (Ill.) High Sch., 1962-63, Univ. Chgo. (Ill.) Lab. Schs., 1963-66; counseling dir. Upward Bound, Mundeline Coll., Chgo., 1966-68; assoc. prof. counseling Kennedy-King Coll., Chgo., 1968-82; psychotherapist Worcester County Counseling Assocs., Bolton, Mass., 1982-87; clin. supr. Valley Adult Counseling Svc., Bellingham, Mass., 1982-84; cons. psychologist Mass. Dept. Edn., Bur. of Instnl. Schs., Boston, 1984-90; dir., psychotherapist Ea. Shore Assocs., Shrewsbury, Mass., 1987—. Psychologist Dept. Pediatrics and Psychiatry, St. Vincent's Hosp., Worcester, 1986—; cons., educator various schs. and orgns., Mass., Ill., 1962—; workshop presenter. Bd. mem., chair children's com. Worcester (Mass.) Area Mental Health & Retardation Bd., 1984-87; bd. alumni affairs DePauw U., 2003-09; coord. Ctrl. Mass. disaster response network Mass. Psych Assoc., 1999 2005; mem. Local CISM Team, comm. on ministry Dioceses Western Mass., 1995-2005. Recipient Improvement Edn. grant Ford Found., Univ. Chgo., 1962, Cmty. Leadership award DePauw U., 2009. Fellow Am. Assn. Orthopsychiatry; mem. APA, Eye Movement Desensitization Reprocessing Internat. Assn., Mass. Psychol. Assn., New Eng. Soc. for Study Dissociative Disorders, Pi Lambda Theta, Psi Chi, Delta theta Chi, Episcopalian. Avocations: attending plays, jazz, swimming, travel. Office: Ea Shore Assocs 586 Main St Shrewsbury MA 01545-2920 Office Phone: 508-842-3100 14. *

SMITH, CONNIE, hospital administrator; d. Phillip and Betty (McSparin) Warrick. Diploma, Moline Pub. Sch. Nursing, 1969; BSN, U. Iowa, 1975; MSN, Rush U., 1981. Cert. nurse operating rm. Staff nurse operating rm. Moline (Ill.) Pub. Hosp., 1969-70; head nurse operating rm./recovery Resurrection Hosp., Chgo., 1970-72; staff nurse operating rm. Mennonite Hosp., Bloomington, Ill., 1973-74; instr. Franciscan Hosp. Sch. Nursing, Rock Island, Ill., 1975-77; staff nurse intensive care unit Moline Luth. Hosp., 1977-79; MICU staff nurse, unit leader operating rm., univ. faculty mem. Rush Presbyn-St. Luke's Med. Ctr., Chgo., 1979-85; dir. operating rm. Albert Einstein Med. Ctr., Phila., 1985-88; dir. operating rm. svcs. St. Joseph Hosp., Houston, 1988-90; regional dir. surg. svcs. Sharp HealthCare, San Diego, 1990-93; surg. svcs. cons. Coast Assocs., 1993-99; dir. Fountain Valley (Calif.) Surgery Ctr., 1999—2003, interim mgr., cons. surg. svc., 2004—. Presenter in field; interim mgmt. cons. surg. svc., 2004—10; dir. surg. svc. Methodist Hosp., Aracadia, Calif., 2010—.

SMITH, CORINNE ROTH, psychologist; b. Reading, Pa., May 22, 1945; d. Zoltan and Elizabeth (Foldes) Roth; m. Lynn Helden Smith, June 9, 1968; children: Juliette Sarah, Rachael Eliza. BA in Psychology cum laude, Syracuse U., 1967, PhD, 1973; MA, Temple U., Phila., 1969. Lic. psychologist, NY. Psychologist experimental presch. program Syracuse City Schs., 1970-71; psychologist reading clinic Syracuse U., 1969-70, coord. lab. sch. and clinic, 1971—72, asst. prof., 1971—84, founder, dir. psychoednl. teaching lab., 1971—, founder, dir. comprehensive assessment ctr., 1981-83, psychologist Devel. Evaluation Ctr., 1984—96, assoc. dean edn., 1992—2000, prof., 1997—, dean, 2000—02, chair inclusive elem. and spl. edn. program, 2005—, chair inclusive spl. edn. 1-6 MS program, 2005—, chair tchg. and leadership programs, 2006—, chair inclusive presch. spl. edn., 2008—, chair, sexual harassment policies, 2005—, senate agenda com. mem., 2005—08. Mem. Coun. for Exceptional Children; reviewer Aspen, Ablex, Mc Graw Hill, Little Brown & Co., NY, Allyn & Bacon, Pergammon, 1985—; apptd. mem. Gov. NY Coun. for Youth, Albany, 1984-91; chair hon. degrees com., Meredith selection com., sexual harassment com., Coll. Human Svcs. and Health Professions Formation Com., Syracuse U., 1993-2009; spkr. in field. Author: Learning Disabilities: The Interaction of Learner, Task and Setting, 1983, 2d edit., 1991, 3rd edit, 1994, 4th edit., 1998, 5th edit., 2004, (retitled) Learning Disabilities: The Interaction of Students and Their Environments, The People's Guide to Drug Education, 1992, Learning Disabilities A to Z: The Complete Parent Guide to Learning Disabiltities from Preschool to Adulthood, 1997, 2nd edit., 2010, Learning Disabilities: A to Z the Complete Guide to Learning Disabilities From Preschol to Adulthood revised edit., 2010, reprinted in Portuguese, Latvian, Romanian, Korean; contbr. articles to profl. jours. and chpts. to books. Bd. dirs. Ctrl. NY United Way, 1987-93, leadership giving chair, 2003-06; pres. Jewish Comm. Ctr., Syracuse, 1978-81; bd. dirs., chair career womens network Syracuse Jewish Fedn., 1985-87, womens campaign chair, 1987-89, gen. campaign chair, 1990-92, Cmty. Found. of Ctrl., NY, 2009-, Literacy Vol. Greater Syracuse, 2009-. Recipient Disting. Svc. award Jewish Comm. Ctr., 1976, Comm. Leadership award Syracuse Jewish Fedn., 1986, 89, Jewish Family Svc. Humanitarian award, 1991, Roth Humanitarian award, 1992, Citizen of Yr. award, 2000, Hall of Fame, Jewish Cmty. Ctr., 2010; named Woman of Yr. Post Std., 1990, Hall Of Fame Garish Cmty. Ctr., 2010; grantee NY State Office Mental Retardation and Devel. Disabilities, 1985-93; Leadership award Coun. Jewish Women, 1999. Mem. Am. Psych. Assn., Nat. Assn. Sch. Psychologists, NY State Learning Disabilities Assn., Learning Disability Assn. Am., Winnick Hillel (pres. nat. bd. 2003-06, treas. 2007-), Parents Mag. (adv. bd. 2002-07). Avocations: tennis, gardening. Office: Syracuse U 136 Huntington Hl Syracuse NY 13244-0001 Office Phone: 315-443-1468.

SMITH, CRAIG R., health products executive; m. Cynthia Smith; 2 children. BA, Univ. So. Calif. With Owens & Minor, Inc., Glen Allen, Va., 1989—; divsn. v.p., group v.p., sr. v.p. distbn. and info. sys. Owens & Minor, Glen Allen, Va., 1989—95, exec. v.p., COO, 1995—99, pres., COO, 1999—2005; pres., CEO Owens & Minor, Inc., Glen Allen, Va., 2005—. Bd. mem. Inst. for Diversity in Health Mgmt., Health Ind. Dist. Assn.; mem. bd. vis. St. Gertrude High Sch., Richmond; mem. bus. council Va. Mus. Fine Arts; bd. dir. Greater Richmond YMCA. Office: Owens & Minor Inc 9120 Lockwood Blvd Mechanicsville VA 23116 *

SMITH, CRAIG RICHEY, cardiothoracic surgeon; b. Cleve., Nov. 17, 1948; m. Patricia M. Smith; 1 child, Emily Van Gorder. BA, Williams Coll., Williamstown, Mass., 1970; MD, Case Western Res. U. Sch. Med., Cleve., 1977. Diplomate Am. Bd. Thoracic Surgery, Am. Bd. Surgery, lic. NJ, NY. Intern U. Rochester Hosp., NY, 1977-78, resident, gen. surgery, 1978-82; fellow cardiothoracic surgery Columbia Presbyn. Med. Ctr., NYC, 1982-84, chief, divsn. cardiothoracic surgery, 1996—. Prof. surgery Columbia U. Coll. Physicians & Surgeons, 2001—, interim chmn., dept. surgery, 2007—; adjunct prof. cardiothoracic surgery Columbia Presbyn. Med. Ctr. Contbr. articles to profl. jours. Mem.: ACS, AMA, Internat. Soc. Heart Transplantation, NY Soc. Thoracic Surgery, Am. Coll. Cardiology, Am. Surgical Assn., Am. Heart Assn., Soc. Thoracic Surgeons, Internat. Soc. Minimally Invasive Cardiothoracic Surgery, Cardiothoracic Surgery Network, Am. Assn. Thoracic Surgery (officer, cons., edn. com.). Office: Columbia Presbyn Med Ctr Milstein Bldg 7GN 435 177 Fort Wash Ave New York NY 10032-3713 Office Phone: 212-305-8312. Office Fax: 212-305-0905. Business E-Mail: crs2@columbia.edu.

SMITH, DANIEL, oncologist, gynecologist; b. Cushing, Okla., Feb. 12, 1946; MD, Harvard Med. Sch., 1972. Diplomate Am. Bd. Surgery, Am. Bd. Obstetrics and Gynecology with subspecialty in gynecologic oncology. Intern Mass. Gen. Hosp., Boston, 1972—73, resident, 1973—75, 1978, L.A. County/U. So. Calif. Med. Ctr., LA, 1975—78; fellow Meml. Sloan-Kettering Cancer Ctr., 1979—81; oncologist, ob-gyn. Columbia Presbyn. Med. Ctr., NYC, 1981—2003; assoc. prof. ob-gyn. Columbia Coll. Physicians and Surgeons. Office: Holy Name Medical Center 718 Teaneck Rd Teaneck NJ 07666

SMITH, DARVIN SCOTT, internist; b. Houston, Jan. 4, 1963; AB in Biochemistry, Bowdoin Coll., 1985; MS, Harvard U., 1987; MD, U. Colo. Sch. Medicine, 1992. Diplomate Am. Bd. Internal Medicine. Intern U. Colo., Denver, 1992-93; resident in internal medicine Stanford U., Calif., 1993-95, fellow in infectious disease, 1996—98, faculty mem., 1998—; chief infectious disease & geographic medicine Kaiser Permanente, Redwood City, Calif. Mem. AMA, Am. Coll. Physicians.

SMITH, DAVID ENGLISH, pathologist, educator; b. San Francisco, June 9, 1920; s. David English and Myrtle (Goodin) S.; m. Margaret Elizabeth Bronson, June 9, 1948; children: Ann English Smith Elbert, David Bronson, Mary Margaret. AB, Central Coll. Mo., 1941; MD cum laude, Washington U., St. Louis, 1944. Intern, resident pathology Barnes Hosp., St. Louis, 1944-46; instr. pathology Washington U. Med. Sch., 1948-51, asst. prof., 1951-54, asst. head dept., 1953-54, assoc. prof., 1954-55; prof. pathology U. Va. Sch. Medicine, 1955-73, chmn. dept., 1958-73; dir. div. U. Va. Sch. Medicine (Cancer Studies), 1972-73; prof. pathology Northwestern U. Sch. Medicine, 1974-75, U. Pa. Sch. Medicine, 1976-80, Tulane U. Sch. Medicine, 1980-85, assoc. dean, 1980-85; prof. pathology U. Tex. Med. Br., 1986—. Assoc. dir. Am. Bd. Med. Spltys., 1974-75; v.p., sec., dir. undergrad. evaluation Nat. Bd. Med. Examiners, 1975-80; trustee Am. Bd. Pathology, 1966-73, v.p., 1973; mem. Nat. Bd. Med. Examiners, chmn. pathology test com., 1966-72; chmn. test com. Ednl. Commn. for Fgn. Med. Grads., 1979-91; eligibility & due process com. Nat. Commn. Cert. Physician Assts., 1990-2001. Editor: Survey of Pathology in Medicine and Surgery, 1966-70; contbr. articles to profl. publs. Pres. Va. div. Am. Cancer Soc., 1967-69. Served from 1st lt. to capt. M.C. AUS, 1946-48. Recipient Preclin. Tchr. award, U. Tex. Med. Br., 1999; named Disting. Alumnus, Wash. U. Med. Sch., 2004; Paul Brindley Disting. scholar, U. Tex. Med. Br., 1997. Mem. Va. Soc. Pathology (pres. 1960), Am. Assn. Pathologists, Internat. Acad. Pathology (council 1956-59, pres. 1964-65), Am. Soc. Clin. Pathologists (co-dir. self assessment program 1970-75, Path Educator award 2000), AMA, Am. Assn. Neuropathologists, AAAS, Sigma Xi, Alpha Omega Alpha, Phi Beta Pi, Alpha Epsilon Delta. Home: 59 Colony Park Cir Galveston TX 77551-1737 E-mail: descolpkga@aol.com.

SMITH, DAVID JOHN, JR., plastic surgeon; b. Indpls., Feb. 20, 1947; s. David John and Carolyn (Culp) S.; m. Nancy Loonsten, June 7, 1975; children: Matthew, Peter, Hadley. BA, Wesleyan U., 1969; MD, Ind. U., 1973. Diplomate Am. Bd. Plastic Surgery. Resident Emory U.-Grady Hosp., Atlanta, 1973-78; resident Ind. U. Med. Ctr., Indpls., 1978-80; Christine Kleinert fellow in hand surgery, 1979; asst. prof. surgery Ind. U. Sch. Medicine, 1980-84; assoc. prof. of surgery Wayne State U. Sch. Medicine, 1984-87; assoc. prof. plastic surgery, surgery sect. head U. Mich. Med. Ctr., Ann Arbor, 1987-92, prof. surgery sect. head, 1992—2001; prof. surgery Coll. Medicine U. South Fla., 2004—, Juan Bolivar chair in surg. oncology, dir. divsn. plastic and reconstructive surgery, 2004—; interim chair, dept. surgery USF. Mem. Residency Rev. Com. for Plastic Surgery, 1992-2000, vice chmn., 1994, chmn. 1996-99; vis. prof. Ctr. Cutaneous Rsch. Queen Mary U., London, Eng., 2004—, Anglia Polytech. U., Cambrige, Eng., 2004—. Mem. editl. bd. Jour. of Surg. Rsch., 1989-95, Annals of Plastic Surgery, 1992-2002, assoc. editor, 1994-2002, Yearbook of Hand Surgery, 1989—; guest reviewer Surgery, 1988—, Plastic and Reconstructive Surgery, 1988—; contbr. articles to profl. jours. Recipient numerous grants. Fellow ACS (com. mem.), Am. Assn. Plastic Surgeons, Am. Surg. Assn., Am. Bd. Plastic Surgeons (vice chmn. 1997-98, chair-elect 1998-99, chmn. oral exam 1995-97, chmn. 1999-2000), Ctrl. Surg. Assn., Am. Soc. for Surgery of the Hand, Am. Soc. Plastic Surgeons, Plastic Surgery Ednl. Found. (bd. dirs. 1988-99, treas. 1994, v.p., pres.-elec., pres., chair nominating com. 1997-98), Plastic Surgery Rsch. Coun., Am. Burn Assn. (chmn. com. on organization and delivery of burn care 1995-98), Am. Burn Life Support Nat. Faculty, Am. Assn. for Hand Surgeons (pres. 1994), Assn. Acad. Chmn. Plastic Surgery (pres.-elect 1997, pres. 1998-99, chmn. nominating com. 1999-2000). Home: 3107 Prospect Rd Tampa FL 33629 Office: Divsn Plastic Surgery 4 Columbia Dr Ste 650 Tampa FL 33606 Home Phone: 813-250-9160. Business E-Mail: dsmith3@health.usf.edu.

SMITH, DAVID WAYNE, retired psychologist, educator; b. Ind., Apr. 16, 1926; s. Lowell Wayne and Ruth Elizabeth (Westphal) S.; m. Marcene B. Leever, Oct. 20, 1948; children: David Wayne, Laurreen Lea. BS, Purdue U., 1949; MS, Ind. U., 1953, PhD, 1955. Diplomate Am. Bd. Psychol. Specialties. Prof. rehab., dir. Rehab. Ctr.; assoc. dean, later asst. v.p. acad. affairs Ariz. Health Scis. Ctr., U. Ariz., Tucson, 1955-80; rsch. prof. rehab., adj. prof. medicine, cons. in rsch. S.W. Arthritis Ctr., Coll. Medicine, 1980-87; prof. rehab. and rheumatology, dept. medicine U. Ariz., Tucson, 1987—, dir. disability assessment program, Ariz. Arthritis Ctr., Coll Medicine, 2007—. Pres. allied health professions sect. Nat. Arthritis Found.; bd. dirs. Nat. Arthritis Found. (S.W. chpt.); nat. vice chmn. bd. dirs.; mem. NIH Nat. Arthritis Adv. Bd., 1977-84; also chmn. subcom. community programs and rehab.; mem. staff Ariz. Legislature Health Welfare, 1972-73; Mem. Gov.'s Council Dept. Econ. Security, 1978-85; pres., bd. dirs. Tucson Assn. for Blind, 1974-86; chmn. Gov.'s Council on Blind and Visually Impaired, 1987—; active Gov.'s Coun. on Arthritis and Musculoskeletal Disease, 1987—, Gov.'s State wide Coun. on Rehab., 1998—, Am. Bd. Forensic Examiners, 1997—. Author: Worksamples; contbr. chpts. to books and articles to profl. jours. Mem. Gov.'s State Rehab. Coun., 1998—, commr. Commn. on Civil Rights, Az., 2002. Recipient Gov.'s awards for leadership in rehab., 1966, 69, 72, 73; awards for sci. and vol. services Nat. Arthritis Found., 1973, 75; 1st nat. Addie Thomas award Nat. Arthritis Found., 1983, Benson award, 1989, Govt. Affairs award, 1989; Arthritis Found. fellow, 1983. Fellow Am. Coll. Forensics; mem. Am. Psychol. Assn. (div. 17 counseling psychology), Assn. Schs. Allied Health Professions, Nat. Rehab. Assn., Ariz. Psychol. Assn. Home: 5765 N Camino Real Tucson AZ 85718-4213 Office: University Ariz Coll Medicine 1501 N Campbell Ave PO Box 245093 Tucson AZ 85724-5093 Personal E-mail: davesfolly@earthlink.net.

SMITH, DENNIS G., public health service officer, state official; m. Laurel Smith; 4 children. BA in Polit. Sci., Ill. State U.; MPA, George Mason U. Staff mem. US Senate Finance Com., Washington, 1996; dir. dept. med. assistance services Commonwealth of Va., Richmond, 1998—2001; chief liaison to Bush-Cheney Transition Team US Dept. Health & Human Services, Washington, 2000—01; dir. Ctr. for Medicaid & State Ops. (CMSO) Centers for Medicare & Medicaid Services, US Dept. Health & Human Services, Washington, 2001—08; mng. dir. Medicaid practice Leavitt Partners, LLC, Washington, 2008—11; sr. fellow The Heritage Found., Washington, 2008—11; sec. Wis. Dept. Health Services, Madison, 2011—. Office: Wisconsin Dept Health Services 1 West Wilson St Madison WI 53703 Office Phone: 608-266-1865. *

SMITH, DONALD FREDERICK, psychologist, neuropsychopharmacologist; b. Chgo., Jan. 30, 1945; s. Leonard and Gertrude (Sankstone) S.; m. Helle Birgitte Knudsen; children: Martin Smith, Bo (Smith) Stork. BSc in Psychology, Duke U., Durham, NC, 1967; MA in Physiological Psychology, McMaster U., Ontario, Canada, 1968; PhD in Biopsychology, U. Chgo., 1971; Lic. Medicine, Aarhus U., Denmark, 1974; DSc in Med. Sci., Copenhagen U., 1980. Sr. lectr. psychobiology and health psychology U. East London; with Ctr. Psychiat. Rsch.; med. faculty Aarhus U. Lectr. prins. sci. rsch. and sci. writing Nat. Censor Corps Med. Psychology. Editor: Handbook of Stereoisomers: Psychotropic Drugs, Handbook of Stereoisomers: Therapeutic Drugs; contbr. numerous scientific rsch. reports to profl. jours. Office: Psychiat Hosp Aarhus U Skovagervej 2 8240 Risskov Denmark Home: Skaering Sandager 56 8240 Egaa Denmark Personal E-mail: dfsmithdfsmith@gmail.com.

SMITH, EARL CHARLES, nephrologist, educator; b. Pitts., Mar. 1, 1936; s. Mose and Irene Smith. BS, Tufts U., 1957; MD, U. Pitts., 1961. Diplomate in internal medicine and nephrology Am. Bd. Internal Medicine. Intern UPMC Montefiore Hosp., Pitts., 1961—62; resident, fellow Cleve. Clinic, 1964-68; physician Cook County Hosp., Chgo., 1968-71; chief nephrology divsn. Mt. Sinai Hosp., Chgo., 1971—, pres. med. staff, 1985-87, vice chair medicine, 1987—, interim chair medicine, 1994—95, 2005—06; chief nephrology divsn. Chgo. Med. Sch., 1994—, prof. medicine, 1995—, interim program dir., 2007—08. Cons. Internat. Jour. Artificial Organs, Milan, 1986—2009; med. adv. bd. Kidney Found. Ill., Chgo., 1980—; bd. dirs. Hektoen Inst. Medicine. Co-author: Medical Exam Book-Nephrology, 1976, Self Assessment in Internal Medicine, 1980; assoc. editor Kidney jour., 1991—; contbr. articles to profl. jours. Chair hypertension com. Chgo. Heart Assn., 1973-75. Capt. USAF, 1962-64. Recipient Meritorious Svc. award, Chgo. Heart Assn., 1975. Fellow Am. Coll. Physicians, Am. Soc. Nephrology; mem. Am. Soc. Artificial Internal Organs, Am. Soc. Hypertension Specialist in Clin. Hypertension, Internat. Soc. Nephrology, Phi Beta Kappa, Alpha Omega Alpha, Sigma Xi. Office: Mount Sinai Hosp 15th and California Ave Chicago IL 60608 Business E-Mail: smie@sinai.org.

SMITH, EDWARD HERBERT, radiologist, educator; b. NYC, Feb. 18, 1936; s. Nathan Leon and Rebecca Ada (Brodsky) S.; m. Anne Chantler Oliphant, June 27, 1971; children: Peter Chantler, Jeffrey Martin. AB, Columbia Coll., 1956; MD, SUNY, 1960. Intern U. Calif. Hosp., San Francisco, 1960-61; resident in internal medicine Montefiore Hosp., NYC, 1961-62; resident in radiology Kings County Hosp. Ctr., Bklyn., 1964-67, radiologist, 1967-69; instr. SUNY-Bklyn., 1967-69; radiologist Children's Hosp. Med. Ctr., Boston, 1969-70, Peter Bent Brigham Hosp., Boston, 1969-80; dir. div. radiology Charles A. Dana Cancer Research Ctr., Boston, 1974-80; instr. Harvard Med. Sch., Boston, 1969-70, asst. prof., 1970-75, assoc. prof., 1975-80, lectr. radiology, 1980—; radiologist U. Mass. Med. Ctr., Worcester, 1980—2001, prof., chmmn. dept. radiology, 1980—2001; prof. U. Mass. Med. Sch., Worcester, 1980—, prof. dept. surgery in urology, 1983—2001; radiologist, dept. radiology St. Elizabeth Med. Ctr., Boston, 2002—10; prof. chair emeritus dept. Radiology U. Mass. Med. Ctr., Worcester, 2009—. Vis. radiologist Rambam Govt. Hosp., Haifa, Israel, 1972; vis. prof. dept. ultrasound U. Copenhagen, Herlev, Denmark, 1977-78, Shanghai Med. Ctr., Peoples Republic China, 1987; cons. Tng. Program in Diagnostic Ultrasound for Physicians and Technologists, Va., 1974-75; reviewer profl. jours. Author: (with others) Abdominal Ultrasound: Static and Dynamic Scanning, 1980; contbr. articles to profl. jours. Fogarty sr. internat. fellow John E. Fogarty Internat. Ctr. for Advanced Study in Health Scis., NIH, Copenhagen, 1977-78 Fellow Am. Coll. Radiology, Soc. Radiologists in Ultrasound (charter, emeritis); mem. Radiol. Soc. N.Am. Home Phone: 617-497-2640. Personal E-mail: smithe3618@comcast.net.

SMITH, ELDON, cardiologist, physiologist, educator; MD, Dalhousie U., Halifax, NS, Can., 1967. From asst. prof. to assoc. prof. medicine and physiology Dalhousie U., 1973—80; prof. medicine and physiology and biophysics U. Calgary, Canada, 1980—2004, prof. emeritus, 2004—, chief divsn. cardiology, 1980—86, chair dept. medicine, 1985—90, assoc. dean clin. affairs, 1990—92, dean faculty of medicine, 1992—97. Corp. dir. Can. Natural Resources, Ltd., 1997—, Vasogen, Inc., 1998—2009, Sernova Corp., 2000—09, Aston Hill Fin., Inc., 2005—; dir. Alberta Health Svcs., 2011—. Editor-in-chief: Can. Jour. Cardiology, 1997—2009. Bd. dirs., pres. Peter Lougheed Med. Rsch. Found., 1999—2007, Premier's adv. coun. health, 2000—02, health professions adv. bd., 2002—07; trustee Alta. Heritage Found. for Med. Rsch., Canada, 2000—07. Recipient officer Order of Can. Fellow; Can. Acad. Health Scis., Am. Heart Assn., Internat. Acad. Cardiovasc. Scis., Royal Coll. Physicians and Surgeons Can. Office: U Calgary Faculty Medicine 3330-3330 Hospital Dr NW Calgary AB Canada T2N 4N1 Home Phone: 403-286-6800; Office Phone: 403-220-5500. Business E-Mail: esmith@ucalgary.ca.

SMITH, FREDRICA EMRICH, rheumatologist, internist; b. Princeton, NJ, Apr. 28, 1945; d. Raymond Jay and Carolyn Sarah (Schleicher) Emrich; m. Paul David Smith, June 10, 1967. AB, Bryn Mawr Coll., Pa., 1967; MD, Duke U., Durham, NC, 1971. Intern, resident U. N.Mex. Affiliated Hosps., 1971-73; fellow U. Va. Hosp., Charlottesville, 1974-75; pvt. practice, Los Alamos, N.Mex., 1975—; practicing physicians Adv. Coun. CMS, 2008—10. Chmn. credentials com. Los Alamos Med. Ctr., 1983—, chief staff, 1990, 2003; bd. dirs. N.Mex. Physicians Mut. Liability Ins. Co., Albuquerque, 1988-97; regional adv. bd. Am. Physicians Assurance, 1997-; cons. PPAC, 2008-10. Contbr. articles to med. jours. Mem. bass sect. Los Alamos Symphony, 1975—; active Los Alamos County Parks and Recreation Bd., 1984-88, 92-96, 2007-10, Los Alamos County Med. Indigent Health Care Task Force, 1989—2003; ops. subcom. Aquatic Ctr., Los Alamos County, 1988—. Fellow ACP, Am. Coll. Rheumatology; mem. N.Mex. Soc. Internal Medicine (pres. 1993-96), Friends of Bandelier. Democrat. Avocations: swimming, music, reading, hiking. Office: Los Alamos Med Ctr 3917 West Rd Los Alamos NM 87544-2275 Office Phone: 505-662-9400.

SMITH, G. RICHARD, psychiatry educator; BS in Chem.-Biology, Rhodes Coll., Memphis, Tenn., 1973; MD, U. Ark. Coll. Medicine, Little Rock, 1977. Intern, resident psychiatry U. Hosp., Little Rock, 1977—80; fellow, instr., psychiatry and med., med./psych liaison group U. Rochester, NY, 1980—81; asst. prof., psychiatry and medicine U. Ark. Med. Sch., Little Rock, 1981—85, dir., residency tng., dept. psychiatry and behavioral sciences, 1982—86, assoc. prof., medicine, 1985—97, assoc. prof., psych, dept. psychiatry and behavioral sciences, 1985—2001, vice-chmn., dept. psychiatry and behavioral sciences, 1985—2001, prof., psychiatry, dept. psychiatry and behavioral sciences, 1991—2001, prof. medicine, 1997—, Marie Wilson Howells prof. & chair, dept. psychiatry and behavioral sciences, 2001—, dir., Ctrs. for Mental Healthcare Rsch., dept. psychiatry and behavioral sciences, 1989—2001, prof., dept. health policy and mgmt., Coll. Pub. Health, 2001—; vis. scholar LBJ Sch. Pub. Affairs, U. Tex., Austin, 1997—98; CEO Psychiatric Assessment Systems, 2004—. Mem. NIMH Initial Review Group Services Rsch., 1989—93, chair, 1991—93; mem. NIMH Nat. Mental Health Adv. Coun., 1995—98, coordinating mem., 1996—98. Contbr. several articles to profl. jours. Office: U Ark Coll Pub Health 4301 WMarkham # 820 Little Rock AR 72205

SMITH, GARY A., medical association administrator; Chmn. Nat. Commn. Certifying Agencies; CEO, exec. dir. Nat. Bd. Respiratory Care, Inc., 2002—; pres., CEO Applied Measurement Profls., Inc., 2002—; pres. Nat. Orgn. Competency Assurance, 2003—04. Office: Nat Bd Respiratory Care Inc 18000 W 105th St Olathe KS 66061-7543 Office Phone: 913-895-4900. Office Fax: 913-895-4650. *

SMITH, GEORGE FLOYD, medical educator; b. St. Paul, Dec. 13, 1947; s. George Floyd and Dorothy Charlene (Tator) Smith; m. Christine Ruth Meyer, June 7, 1972; children: Randall, Ryan, Kathryn. BA, Macalester Coll., St. Paul, 1969; BS, MD, U. Minn., Mpls., 1972. Recertified FABFP 2005. Residency, family medicine St. Paul Ramsey Hosp., 1972—75; physician Eastside Med. Ctr., St. Paul, 1975—2000; tchr. medicine U. Minn., Mpls., 2000—09; caq geriatrics, 1994; with Health East Med. Care Srs,, 2009—, Resume Clin. Appointment, U. Minn. Contbr. articles to profl. jours. Presbyterian. Office: 1700 University Ave W Saint Paul MN 55104-3727 Office Phone: 651-232-2002. Business E-Mail: georgesmith04@comcast.net.

SMITH, GERALD, public health service officer; b. Havre, Mont., Mar. 25, 1948; BA, U. Wash., 1974. COO NW Spine & Sports Physicians, P.C., 2002—. Mem.: AICPA, Wash. Soc. CPAs. Office: 1750 112th Ave NE Ste D258 Bellevue WA 98004 Office Fax: 425-451-1052. Business E-Mail: gsmith@nwssp.com.

SMITH, HAMILTON OTHANEL, microbiologist, educator; b. NYC, Aug. 23, 1931; s. Tommie Harkey and Bunnie Othanel Smith; m. Elizabeth Anne Bolton, May 25, 1957; children: Joel, Barry, Dirk, Bryan, Kirsten. AB in Math, U. Calif., Berkeley, 1952; MD, Johns Hopkins U., 1956. Intern Barnes Hosp., St. Louis, 1956-57; resident in medicine Henry Ford Hosp., Detroit, 1959-62; USPHS fellow dept. human genetics U. Mich., Ann Arbor, 1962-64, rsch. assoc., 1964-67; asst. prof. molecular biology and genetics Johns Hopkins U. Sch. Medicine, Balt., 1967-69, assoc. prof., 1969-73, prof., 1973—98; scientist Celera Genomics Corp., Rockville, Md., 1998—2002; scientific dir. synthetic biology & bioenergy J. Craig Venter Inst., Rockville, 2002—; co-founder, co-chief sci. officer Synthetic Genomics, Calif., 2005—. Rsch. assoc. Rsch. Inst. Molecular Pathology, Vienna, 1990—91. Contbr. articles to profl. jours. Recipient Nobel prize in physiology/medicine, 1978; fellow John Simon Guggenheim Meml. Found., 1975—76. Mem.: NAS, AAAS, Am. Soc. Biol. Chemists, Am. Soc. Microbiology. Office: Synthetic Genomics 11149 N Torrey Pines Rd La Jolla CA 92037 also: J Craig Venter Inst 9704 Medical Center Dr Rockville MD 20850 E-mail: hsmith@jcvi.org. *

SMITH, IAN, international organization administrator; MD, Leeds Med. Sch., UK, 1980; MPH, Nuffield Inst. Health, Leeds, 1994. Med. missionary in a remote rural hospital, Nepal, 1982—92; with Ministry Health Nat. Tuberculosis Program, Kathmandu, Nepal, 1992—98; joined WHO, Geneva, 1998, founder & mgr., Global TB Drug Facility, 2001—03, advisor to the dir. gen., 2003—. Office: WHO avenue Appia 20 1211 Geneva Switzerland *

SMITH, IAN CORMACK PALMER, biophysicist; b. Winnipeg, Man., Can., Sept. 23, 1939; s. Cormack and Grace Mary Smith; m. Eva Gunilla Landvik, Mar. 27, 1965; children: Brittmarie, Cormack, Duncan, Roderick. BS, U. Man., 1961, MS, 1962; PhD, Cambridge U., Eng., 1965; PhD (hon.), U. Stockholm, 1986; DSc (hon.), U. Winnipeg, 1990, Brandon U., 2001, Cracow Polish Acad. Sci., 2006; diploma in tech. (hon.), Red River Coll., 1996. Fellow Stanford U., 1965-66; mem. rsch. staff Bell Tel. Labs., Murray Hill, NJ, 1966-67; rsch. officer divsn. biol. scis. NRC, Ottawa, Canada, 1967-87, dir. gen., 1987-91, Inst. Biodiagnostics, Winnipeg, Canada, 1992—. Adj. prof. chemistry and biochemistry Carleton U., 1973—90, U. Ottawa, 1976—92; adj. prof. biophysics U. Ill., Chgo., 1974—80; adj. prof. chemistry, radiology, physics and anatomy U. Man., 1992—; allied scientist Ottawa Civic Hosp., 1985—98, Ottawa Gen. Hosp., 1989—98, Ont. Cancer Found., 1989—91, St. Boniface Hosp., 1992—, Health Scis. Ctr., 1993—; exec. com. Man. Health Rsch. Coun., 1996—98, Econ. Tech. Innovation Coun., Man., 1994—98; chmn. Man. Health Rsch. Coun., 1998—2002, mem. exec. bd., 2007—; mem. adv. bd. Loeb Inst., Ottawa, 1999—2001, Keystone Ventures, 1999—2002, Western LIfe Scis. Fund, 2002—08, Novadaq, 2004—06, St. Boniface Hosp. Rsch. Enterprise, 2006—, Cancer Care Man., 2007—; bd. govs. U. Manitoba, Canada, 2000—06; bd. dirs. ENSIS Growth Fund, DIASPEC Holdings, IMRIS Inc., Magnetic Resonance Vets., Photonics Rsch. Ont., Spectex Pty., Biomed. Commercialization Can., Cognosis Canada Inc., Ontario Centres of Excellence, Genome Prairie, Man. Inst. Cell Biology, Biovantage Alberta Cimtec Ont. Contbr. chapters to books, articles to profl. jours. Mem. adv. bd. Smart Winnipeg, 2000—03; mem. Premier's Econ. Adv. Bd., Man., 2001—, exec. com. Man., 2004—. Decorated Order of the Star of Romania; recipient Barringer award, Can. Spectroscopy Soc., 1979, Herzberg award, 1986, Organon Teknika award, Can. Soc. Clin. Chemists, 1987, Sr. Scientist award, Sigma Xi, 1995, Queen's Jubilee medal, 2003, Paul Harris award, Rotary Club, 2006, Distingushed Alumni award, U. Manitoba, 2007, Outstanding Achievement award, Govt. of Can., 2008, Officer Order of Can., 2009. Fellow: Soc. Magnetic Resonance Medicine (mem. exec. com. 1989—94), Royal Soc. Can. (Flavelle medal 1996), Chem. Inst. Can. (Merck award 1978, Labatt award 1984); mem.: Biovantage, Ont. Ctrs. Excellence (dir. 2002—10, adv. bd. advanced health techs. 2011—), Ont. Ctr. Photonics (chmn. bd. mgmt. 2002—10, mem. adv. bd. chmn. 2011—), Internat. Union Pure and Applied Biophysics (mem. coun. 1993—, v.p. 1996—99, 2002—05, pres. 2005—08), Biophys. Soc. Can. (pres. 1992—94), Can. Biochem. Soc., Biophysical Soc., Internat. Coun. Sci. Unions (mem. gen. com. 1989—94), U. Man. Alumni Assn. (bd. dirs. 1994—2000, v.p. 1997—98, pres. 1998—99). Office: Inst Biodiagnostics Winnipeg MB Canada R3B 1Y6 Home Phone: 204-897-0650; Office Phone: 204-983-7526. Business E-Mail: ian.smith@nrc-cnrc.gc.ca.

SMITH, IAN EDWARD, physician; b. Bexleyheath, Kent, Eng., Oct. 23, 1961; s. Trevor Clasby and Edith (Crilley) Sponse; m. Susan Johnson, Apr. 1, 1991; children: Barton, Henry, Finlay. MA in Med. Sci., Cambridge U., Eng., 1984, MD, 1997; MBBS, London Hosp. Med. Sch., 1987. House officer London Hosp., 1987-88; sr. house officer Broomfield Hosp., Chelmsford, Eng., 1988-89, Charing Cross Hosp., London, 1989-90; registrar Addenbrooke's Hosp., Cambridge, Eng., 1990-91, Newmarket Hosp., Suffolk, Eng., 1991-92; sr. clin. fellow Papworth Hosp., Cambridge, 1992-96, cons. chest physician, 1996—, clin. dir., thoracic svcs., 2004—09, rsch. dir., 2011—; program dir. Respiratory Medicine East Eng. Deanery, 2008—. Contbr. articles to profl. jours. Mem. Royal Coll. Physicians, Brit. Thoracic Soc. Avocations: musical composition, cinema, food. Office: Respiratory Support & Sleep Ctr Papworth Hosp Huntingdon CB3 8RE England

SMITH, IAN K., writer, columnist, physician; b. Danbury, Conn., July 15, 1969; AB, Harvard U., 1992; MS in Edn., Teachers Coll., Columbia U., 1993; attended, Dartmouth Coll., Hanover, NH; MD, U. Chgo. Pritzker Sch. Medicine, 1997. Former med. corr. NewsChannel 4, NBC News Network; med. corr. VH1 Celebrity Fit Club; host HealthWatch (nat. syndicated radio show) American Urban Radio Networks; med. contbr. Rachael Ray Show. Founder, creator 50 Million Pound Challenge nat. health initiative, 2007; apptd. mem. President's Coun. Fitness, Sports & Nutrition, 2010—. Author: Dr. Ian Smith's Guide to Medical Websites, 2001, The Blackbird Papers,

2004 (Black Caucus ALA Fiction Hon. Book award, 2005), The Take-Control Diet, 2005, The Fat Smash Diet, 2006 (#1 NY Times bestseller), The Extreme Fat Smash Diet, 2007 (#1 NY Times bestseller), The 4 Day Diet, 2009 (NY Times bestseller), Happy: Simple Steps to Get the Most Out of Life, 2010, EAT: The Effortless Weight Loss Solution, 2011; contbr. numerous articles to profl. pubs.; appearances include The View, Tyra Banks Show, Larry King Live, Anderson Cooper 3600, Showbiz Tonight, others. Bd. dirs. NYC Mission Soc., American Coun. Exercise, NY Coun. Humanities. Office: PO Box 765 FDR Station New York NY 10150 Business E-Mail: ian@doctoriansmith.com.

SMITH, JAMES WARREN, pathologist, educator, microbiologist, parasitologist; b. Logan, Utah, July 5, 1934; s. Kenneth Warren and Nina Lou (Sykes) S.; m. Nancy Chesterman, July 19, 1958; children: Warren, Scott. BS, U. Iowa, 1956, MD, 1959. Diplomate Am. Bd. Pathology. Intern Colo. Gen. Hosp., Denver, 1959—60; resident U. Iowa Hosps., Iowa City, 1960—65; asst. prof. pathology U. Vt., Burlington, 1967—70; prof. pathology Ind. U., Indpls., 1970—98, chmn. dept. pathology and lab. medicine, 1992—98, Nordshow prof. of lab. medicine, 1997—98, prof. emeritus, 1998—. Contbr. articles to profl. jours. Served to lt. comdr. USN, 1965-67. Recipient Outstanding Contbn. to Clin. Microbiology award South Ctrl. Assn. Clin. Microbiology, 1977. Fellow Coll. Am. Pathologists (chmn. microbiology resource com. 1981-85); mem. AMA, Infectious Disease Soc. Am., Am. Soc. Investigative Pathology, Royal Soc. Tropical Medicine and Hygiene, Am. Soc. Clin. Pathology, Am. Soc. Microbiology, Am. Soc. Tropical Medicine and Hygiene, U.S.-Can. Acad. Pathology, Assn. Pathology Chairs, Binford Dammin Soc. Infectious Disease Pathologists, Soc. Protozoologists. Home: 4375 Cold Spring Rd Indianapolis IN 46228-3327 Office: Ind U Med Ctr 635 Barnhill Dr Rm A128 Indianapolis IN 46202-5126

SMITH, JASON, pharmacist; b. Lynwood, Calif., Apr. 23, 1972; BS, Calif. State U., San Francisco, 1997; PharmD, Ohio State U., 2000. Clin. pharmacy specialist Dept. Vets. Affairs, 2004—. Office: 11301 Wilshire Blvd 111C Los Angeles CA 90073 Business E-Mail: jason.smith2@va.gov.

SMITH, JESSE E., facial plastic surgeon; b. Fort Worth, Tex. BA in Biology minor in Chemistry, magna cum laude, Baylor U., Waco, Tex., 1990—94; MD, U. Tex. Southwestern Med. Ctr., Dallas, Tex., 1994—98. Lic. physician Calif. State Bd. Med. Examiners, Tex. State Bd. Med. Examiners, diplomate Am. Bd. Head & Neck Surgery, Am. Bd. Facial Plastic Surgery. Intern in gen. surgery Univ. Tex. Southwestern Med. Ctr., Dallas, 1998—99, resident in otolaryngology head & neck surgery, 2000—04, asst. clin. prof. otolaryngology dept.; fellow in facial plastic & reconstructive surgery Univ. Calif. Los Angeles Med. Ctr., Calif., 2004—05, Santa Barbara, 2004—05; joined Tex. Health Network, Fort Worth, 2005. Plastic surgeon CRISP Found. Recipient Disting. Chemist award, Baylor Univ., 1990, Academic Scholar Athlete, 1990—94, Outstanding Sr. in Biology, 1993—94, Outstanding Sr. Man, 1994, Golden Key, Nat. Honor Soc., Resident Tchg. award, Univ. Tex. Southwestern Med. Ctr., 2006, Outstanding Dr. award, Fortworth Tex. Mag., 2009. Avocations: bicycling, running, travel. Office: Jesse E Smith M D FACS 923 PA Ave Fort Worth TX 76104 Office Phone: 817-920-0484. Office Fax: 817-920-0068.

SMITH, JIM, medical research association administrator; Grad., Cambridge U., Eng.; PhD, Middlesex Hosp. Med. Sch., London U. Postdoc. rschr. Harvard U.; various positions including head divsn. devel. biology, head genes & cellular controls group Nat. Inst. Med. Rsch., London, 1984—2000, dir., 2009—; faculty Cambridge U., 2000, John Humphrey Plummer prof. devel. biology, 2001—, dir. Wellcome Trust/Cancer Rsch. UK Gurdon Inst., 2001—. Recipient Feldberg Found. award. Fellow: Acad. Med. Scis., Royal Soc.; mem.: European Molecular Biology Orgn., Academia Europaea. Office: Gurdon Inst Henry Williams Bldg U Cambridge Tennis Ct Rd Cambridge CB2 1QN England also: NIMR The Ridgeway Mill Hill NW7 1AA London England *

SMITH, JOAN H., retired women's health nurse, educator; b. Akron, Ohio; d. Joseph A. and Troynette M. (Lower) McDonald; m. William G. Smith; children: Sue Ann, Priscilla, Timothy. Diploma, Akron City Hosp., 1948; BSN in Edn., U. Akron, 1972, MA in Family Devel., 1980. Cert. in inpatient obstetric nursing. Mem. faculty Akron Gen. Med. Ctr. Sch. Nursing, 1964; former dir. obstet. spl. procedures Speakers Bur., Women's Health Ctrs. Akron Gen. Med. Ctr., 1988; ret., 1990. Cons., speaker women's health care. Mem. Assn. Women's Health, Obstet. and Neonatal Nursing (charter, past sec.-treas., past vice chmn. Ohio sect., chmn. program various confs.). Home: 873 Kirkwall Dr Copley OH 44321-1751

SMITH, JOANNE C., medical products executive; b. 1962; m. Rory Repicky; 2 children. BS, Oakland U.; MD, Mich. State U.; MBA, U. Chgo. Cert. Physical Medicine and Rehabilitation. Chief residency Northwestern U. Med. Sch.; asst. prof., Physical Medicine and Rehabilitation Northwestern U. Feinberg Sch. of Medicine; founder, Women's Health Rehabilitation Program Rehabilitation Institute of Chicago, physician, 1992—94, med. dir., Day Rehabilitation Centers program, 1994—95, sr. v.p., COO, Corp. Partnerships, 1995—97, sr. v.p., Corp. Strategy and Bus. Devel., 1997—2002, pres., Nat. Divsn., 2005—06, pres., CEO, 2006—; vice chmn. Hill-Rom Holdings, Inc. (formerly Hillenbrand Industries, Inc.), 2005—. Bd. dirs. AptarGroup Inc., Hill-Rom Holdings, Inc. (formerly Hillenbrand Industries Inc.), 2003—. Named a Woman to Watch, Crain's Chgo. Bus., 2007; named one of Chicago's 'Top Doctors', Chgo. Mag., 2004, 2005, 2006. Mem.: The Chgo. Network. Office: Hill Rom Holdings Inc 1069 State Route 46 E Batesville IN 47006 Office Phone: 312-238-6044, 812-934-7777. Office Fax: 812-934-8189. E-mail: joanne.smith@hill-rom.com. *

SMITH, JOSEPH A., JR., urologic surgeon; b. Memphis, July 13, 1949; s. Joseph A. Smith and Virginia E. (Redd) Mulroy; m. Barbara Bradford, June 14, 1974; children: Carolyn, Bradford J., Christiane. BS, U. Tenn., Knoxville, 1971; MD, U. Tenn., Memphis, 1974. Diplomate Am. Bd. Urology. Intern Parkland Meml. Hosp./U. Tex. Southwestern Med. Sch., Dallas, 1974—75, resident surgery, 1975—76; resident urology U. Utah, Salt Lake City, 1976—79; urologic oncology fellow Meml. Sloan-Kettering Cancer Ctr., NYC, 1979—80; asst. prof. surgery U. Utah Health Scis. Ctr., 1980—83, assos. prof. surgery, 1983—88, prof. surgery, 1988—91; William L. Bray prof. surgery & chmn. dept. urol. surgery Vanderbilt U. Med. Ctr., Nashville, 1991—, vice-chmn. sect. surg. scis., 1992—93, interim chmn. sect. surg. scis., 1993—95, assoc. dir. sect. surg. scis., 2004—06. Oral examiner Am. Bd. Urology, 1993—, trustee, 1998—2005, pres., 2004—05; chmn Am. Found. Urologic Disease, 1995—2003. Assoc. editor Investigative Urology, 1989—92, Endourology, 1990—, Jour. Urology, 2006—, Jour. Robotic Surgery, 2006—, mem. editl. bd. Lasers in Surgery and Medicine, 1995—, Prostate Cancer and Prostatic Diseases, 1995—, Primary Care Update, 1996—, Jour. Evolution in Clin. Practice, 1997—, Current Urology Reports, 2000—; contbr. articles to profl. jours., chapters to books. Recipient Outstanding Alumnus award, U. Tenn. Coll. Medicine, 2003; named one of Best Doctors in America, Castle Connelly Med. Ltd., 1988—2007, Am. Health Mag., 1996, Woodward White, Inc., Best 400 Doctors in America, Good Housekeeping, Best Med. Specialists in N.Am., Town & Country mag., Top 10 Am. Surgeons, US News & World Report. Fellow: ACS; mem.: AMA (vice-chmn. 1996, chmn. 1998—2000), Vanderbilt Urology Soc., Nashville Surg. Soc., Soc. Univ. Urologists (mem. exec. com. 2001—04), Tenn. Urologic Assn. (pres. 1999—2001), Nashville Acad. Medicine, Clin. Soc. Genitourology Surgeons, Am. Cancer Soc., Soc. Basic Urologic Rsch., Am. Assn. Clin. Urologists, Internat. Soc. Laser Surgery, Utah Urologic Soc. (pres. 1981—83), Am. Soc. Lasers in Medicine & Surgery, James Ewing Soc. Surg. Oncology, Soc. Urologic Oncology (sec. 1995—98, pres. 2001—03), Am. Assn. Genitourology Surgeons, Am. Soc. Clin. Oncology, Am. Urol. Assn. (pres. Southeastern sect. 2004—05, Disting. Contbn. award 2004), Alpha Omega Alpha. Office: Vanderbilt U A 1302 Med Ctr N Nashville TN 37232-0001 Office Phone: 615-343-0234. *

SMITH, KELLY M., pharmacist, educator, researcher; b. Statesboro, Ga. d. Kenneth P. and Janice A. Smith. BS, PharmD, U. Ga., Athens, 1993. Cert. BCPS, 2008; registered pharmacist Ga., 1993, Ky., 1995. Clin. asst. prof. U. Ky. Coll. Pharmacy, Lexington, 1996—2001, clin. assoc. prof., 2001, assoc. prof., 2002—, dir. residency program advancement, 2007—, asst. dean, 2008—09, assoc. dean, 2009—; dir. PGY1 pharmacy residency U. Ky. HealthCare, Lexington, 1998—2007, dir. drug info. ctr., 2001—05, clin. specialist medication use policy, 2005—. Presenter in field. Contbr. articles to profl. jours. Fellow: Am. Coll. Clin. Pharmacy (past chair drug info. PRN, chair residency task force), Am. Soc. Health Sys. Pharmacists (past chair commn. on credentialing, past chair clin. specialists and scientists sect., Pharmacy Residency Excellence award 2007); mem.: Univ. HealthSystem Consortium Pharmacy Coun. (past chair rsch. and edn. com.), Am. Assn. Colls. of Pharmacy (fin. com., Innovations in Tchg. award 2004, Leadership fellow 2007), Zeta Tau Alpha.

SMITH, KENNETH RUPERT, JR., neurosurgeon, educator; b. St. Louis, Sept. 23, 1932; s. Kenneth R. and Jocelyn (Ulmet) S.; m. Marjorie R. Sandin, 1956; children: Sue, Sally, Kenneth III, Nancy, Carol, Joanne, Patricia. Student, Greenville Coll., Ill., 1950-53; MD, Washington U., St. Louis, 1957. Diplomate Am. Bd. Neurol. Surgery. Intern in medicine Johns Hopkins Hosp., Balt., 1957-58; asst. resident surgery Washington U., St. Louis, 1958-59, resident neurosurgery, 1960-63, instr. neurosurgery and anatomy, 1964-66; asst. prof. surgery St. Louis U., 1966-67, assoc. prof., 1967-71, prof., 1971—2008, prof. emeritus, 2009. Contbr. articles to profl. jours. Cons. Bd. Police Commrs., St. Louis, 1967; chmn. Mayor's Health Task Force, St. Louis, 1977-81; mem. bd. commrs. St. Louis Mus. Sci. and Natural History, 1979-85. Named Disting. Alumnus Greenville (Ill.) Coll., 1983. Mem. AAAS, Am. Assn. Anatomists, Soc. Neurosci., Am. Assn. Neurol. Surgeons (nominating com. 1992-94), Soc. Univ. Neurosurgeons (pres. 1986), Soc. Neurol. Neurosurgeons (pres. 1986), Soc. Neurol. Surgeons (pres. 1995-96), St. Louis Med. Soc. (pres. 1983), St. Louis Soc. Neurol. Scis. (pres. 1975-77), Alpha Omega Alpha. Democrat. Avocations: hunting, music. Office: St Louis U Sch Medicine 3635 Vista Ave Saint Louis MO 63110-2539 Office Phone: 314-577-8796. *

SMITH, KENT ASHTON, information scientist, consultant; b. Boston, Sept. 3, 1938; s. Kent Wooliscroft and Dorothy Patten Smith; m. Mary Margaret Gaffney; children: Holly L. Smith, Kent W. BA, Hobart Coll., 1960; MBA, Cornell U., 1962; postgrad., Am. U., 1978-79. Mgmt. analyst Office of Sec., HEW, Washington, 1962-65; adminstrv. officer divsn. rsch. facilities and resources NIH, Bethesda, Md., 1965-67, asst. exec. officer divsn. rsch. facilities and resources, 1967-68, exec. officer divsn. rsch. resources, 1968-71, asst. dir. adminstrn. Nat. Libr. Medicine, 1971-78, dep. dir., 1978—2004, PHS spl. expert-info. scientist, 2000—02; cons. Nat. Ctr. for Biotechnology Info., 2004—, Computercraft Corp., 2004—, Office Sci. and tech. Info. Dept. Energy, 2005—. Mem. exec. bd. and bur. Internat. Coun. Sci. and Tech. Info., Paris, 1983—2001; v.p. U.S. Nat. Com. of UNESCO-PGI, Washington, 1983—85; mem. exec. adv. bd. Fed. Libr. and Info. Ctr. Com., Washington, 1984—89; exec. com. CENDI-Info. Consortia, Washington, 1985—; treas. Internat. Coun. Sci. and Tech. Info., Paris, 1986—89; pres. Nat. Fed. Abstracting and Info. Sci., Phila., 1988—89, v.p., 1987—88; chmn. Info. Policy Com., 1988—89, CENDI-Info. Consortia, Washington, 2001—04; mem. US Nat. Commn. for CODATA, 1990—2001, Science.gov Alliance, 2002—04, NISO Blue Ribbon Panel, 2004; pres. Internat. Coun. Sci. and Tech. Info., Paris, 1990—94; mem. panel US Dept. Energy info. infrastructure NAS, 2000, 07; reviewer study digital strategy for Libr. Congress NRC, 2000; mem. panel on Nat. Tech. Info. Svc. Nat. Commn. Libr. and Info. Sci., 2000; long-range planning panel mem. Nat. Libr. Medicine, 2005—07; bd. mem. Nat. Tech. Info. Svc. Adv. Bd., 2006—10; mem. Dept. Energy panel on accelerating knowledge diffusion NAS, 2007. Contbr. articles to profl. jours., chpt. to book: Management of Federally Sponsored Libraries, 1995. Mem. Citizens Com. for Pub. Libr. Montgomery County, Bethesda, 1981-82; fin. dir. Christ Ch., Rockville, Md., 1990-91. Recipient Asst. Sec. for Health Exceptional Achievement award USPHS, 1978, Sr. Exec. Svc. award, 1996, 97, 98, 99, HEW Superior Svc. medal 1974, Nat. Fedn. Abstracting Info. Sci., 1998, Miles Conrad hon. lectureship, Hammer award V.P. US, 1999, sponsor of MLA Govt. Rels. award, 2009. Fellow Nat. Fedn. Abstracting and Info. Svcs., Med. Libr. Assn. (hon.; Pres. award 1997, ICSTI Disting. Svc. award 2001, Joseph Leiter Hon. Lectureship, 2007, sponsor, Funk award for Govtl. Relations); mem. ASPA (vice chmn. 1971-72), AAAS, Int. Assn. Sci. Tech. and Med. Pubs., Am. Mgmt. Assn., Am. Soc. Info. Svc., Assn. Rsch. Librs. (Alfred Zipf fellow com. chair 2001-04), Cosmos Club. Episcopalian. Avocations: golf, baseball, genealogy, theater, birdwatching, antiques. Home and Office: 17517 Hidden Garden Ln Ashton MD 20861 Office Phone: 301-496-5359.

SMITH, KEVIN L., forensic psychiatrist, medical technology executive; s. Jerry and Patricia Smith. MD with honors, U. Colo., Denver, 1981. Bd. cert. in gen. psychiatry Am. Bd. Psychiatry and Neurology, 1986, bd. cert. in forensic psychiatry Am. Bd. Psychiatry and Neurology, 1999. Chief resident Walter Reed Army Med. Ctr., Washington, 1984—85; asst. divsn. surgeon, chief mental health Third Inf. Divsn., US Army, Wuerzburg, Bavaria, Germany, 1985—88; chmn. dept. psychiatry Catskill Regional Med. Ctr., Harris, NY, 1988—93, Benedictien Hosp., Kingston, 1993—2000; CEO Prism Med. Sys., Saugerties, NY, 2000—. Clin. faculty Boston U. Overseas Program, Beckenheim, Bavaria, Germany, 1985—88; clin. faculty dept. family Ppactice NY Med. Coll., Valhalla, 1989—94, asst clin. prof. psychiatry, 1995—; v.p. Catskill Regional Med. Ctr. Med. Staff, Harris, 1991—93; pres. Hudson Valley Psychiat. Assoc., Kingston, 1997—2000; mem. managed care com. Ulster County Bd. Health, 1999—2002; mem., v.p. med. staff Benedictine Hosp., Kingston, 2000—02. Chmn. Hist. Landmarks Commn., Kingston, NY, 1996—97, Law Enforcement Task Force, 1997—2000. Capt. US Army, 1978—88, Wuerzburg, Germany. Decorated Meritorious Svc. medal US Army; recipient Kenneth Artiss award, Walter Reed Army Med. Ctr., 1985, Meritorious Citizenship for Justice, NY State Senate, 2000. Fellow: Am. Psychiat. Assn. (hon.; chpt. pres. 2000—02, mem. managed care com. 2000—06); mem.: Am. Acad. Psychiatry and Law (assoc.; mem. 1998—2007). Democrat. Achievements include invention of prism electronic health record. Avocations: travel, photography, writing, skiing, fly fishing. Office: PO Box 159 Glasco NY 12432-0159

SMITH, LAWRENCE GERARD, dean, medical educator, health facility administrator; b. NYC, New York, Nov. 2, 1949; s. Gerald Joseph and Marion Margaret (Pfeiffer) Smith; m. Deborah Anne Smith, June 26, 1971; children: Kristofer, Kevin, Matthew, Patrick. BS in Physics, Fordham Sch. U., 1971; MD, NYU, 1976. Diplomate Am. Bd. Med. Examiners, Am. Bd. Internal Medicine and Critical Care. Resident physician U. Rochester, NY, 1976-79; staff physician Fitzsimmons Army Med. Ctr., Denver, 1979-81; gen. internist Northshore Med. Group, Huntington, NY, 1981-89; dir. edn., program dir. residency program internal medicine Stony Brook U. Hosp., SUNY, asst. prof. medicine, 1982—89, assoc. prof. medicine, 1989—93; vice chmn. Dept. Medicine, residency program dir. Mount Sinai Sch. of Medicine, NYC, 1994, prof. medicine, 1993—2005, dean med. edn., 2002—05; chief academic officer, sr. v.p. academic affairs North Shore-LI Jewish Health Sys. (North Shore-LIJ), 2005—06, chief med. officer, 2006—; founding dean Hofstra U. Sch. Med., 2008—. Team physician NY Islanders, Uniondale, 1982—90; adv. bd. Hazelton Found., NYC, 1994; profl. cons. Women's First Healthcare, NYC, 1997. Editor: International Medical Graduates in US Hospitals-A Guide for Program Directors and Applicants, 1995; contbr. articles to profl. jours. Capt. US Army, 1979—81. Recipient Alpha Omega Alpha, NY U. Sch. of Medicine, Mastership, ACP, Solomon Berson Award, NYU Sch. of Medicine, Dema C. Daley Founders Award, Assoc of Program Directors in Internal Medicine, Castle Connolly Top Doctors NY Metro Area, Castle Connolly LTD. Fellow: ACP; mem.: Orgn. Program Dirs. Assn. (exec. com. mem.), Assn. Program Dir. in Internal Med. (former pres.), Soc. of Med. Decision Making, Soc. of Gen. Internal Medicine, Phi Beta Kappa. Avocations: reading, wine-tasting, golf. Office: Hofstra North Shore LIJ School Medicine Mineola NY 11501 Office Phone: 516-465-3194. Office Fax: 516-465-8144. E-mail: lawrence.smith@nshs.edu.

SMITH, LEE ELTON, surgery educator, retired military officer; b. Ventura, Calif., July 19, 1937; s. Raymond Elroy and Edith Irene (Jordan) S.; m. Carole Sue Smith; children: Justine Diane, Alexander Loren. BS, U. Calif., Berkeley, 1959; MD, U. Calif., San Francisco, 1962. Diplomate Am. Bd. Surgery, Am. Bd. Colon and Rectal Surgery (pres. 1992-93). Commd. ens. USN, 1960, advanced through grades to capt., 1977; intern U. Utah, Salt Lake City, 1962-63; resident USN, San Diego, 1966-70, staff surgeon Bremerton, Wash., 1970-72; resident colorectal surgery U. Minn., Mpls., 1972-73; dir. colorectal surgery Nat. Naval Med. Ctr. USN, Bethesda, Md., 1973-82, ret., 1983, Seattle, 1982; clin. prof. surgery Uniformed Svcs. U., Bethesda, 1976—; prof. surgery George Washington U., Washington, 1983-96, Georgetown U., Washington, 2001—; dir. sect. of colon and rectal surgery Washington Hosp. Ctr., 1996—. Pres. Am. Bd. Colon and Rectal Surgery, 1993-94. Editor: Practical Guide to Anorectal Physiology, 1990, 2d edit., 1995; assoc. editor Diseases of the Colon and Rectum, 1984-96, Perspectives in Colon and Rectal Surgery, 1989-2000. Mem. ACS (pres. Met. Washington chpt. 1993-94), Soc. Am. Gastrointestinal Endoscopic Surgeons (pres. 1989-90), Am. Cancer Soc. (v.p. D.C. chpt. 1985-93), Am. Soc. Colon & Rectal Surgeons (pres. 1998-99). Home: 7512 16th St NW Washington DC 20012 Office: Washington Hosp Ctr 106 Irving St NW Washington DC 20010-2975 Office Phone: 202-877-8484. E-mail: lee.e.smith@medstar.net.

SMITH, LINDA B., psychology professor, department chairman; BS, Univ. Wis., Madison, 1973; PhD, Univ. Pa., 1977. Asst. prof., psychology Univ. Ind., Bloomington, 1977—81, assoc. prof., 1981—85, prof., 1985—97, chancellor's prof., 1997—, chair, dept. psychol. and brain sciences. Contbr. articles to profl. jours. Recipient Rsch. Career Devel. award, NIH, 1984—89, Award for Early Career Contribution, APA, 1985, James McKeen Cattell Sabbatical award, 1985. Fellow: Am. Acad. Arts & Scis.; mem.: Soc. Exptl. Psychologists, Cognitive Sci. Soc. (governing bd.), Phi Beta Kappa. Office: Psychological & Brain Sci Indiana Univ 1101 E Tenth St Bloomington IN 47405 Office Phone: 812-855-6052. Business E-Mail: Smith4@indiana.edu.

SMITH, LLOYD HOLLINGSWORTH, physician; b. Easley, SC, Mar. 27, 1924; s. Lloyd H. and Phyllis (Page) S.; m. Margaret Constance Avery, Feb. 27, 1954; children— Virginia Constance,

Christopher Avery, Rebecca Anne, Charlotte Page, Elizabeth Hollingsworth, Jeffrey Hollingsworth. AB, Washington and Lee U., 1944, D.Sc., 1969; MD, Harvard, 1948. Intern, then resident Mass. Gen. Hosp., Boston, 1948-50, chief resident physician, 1955-56; mem. Harvard Soc. Fellows, 1952-54; asst. prof. Harvard Soc. Fellows (Med. Sch.), 1956-63; vis. investigator Karolinska Inst., Stockholm, 1954-55, Oxford (Eng.) U., 1963-64; prof. medicine, chmn. dept. U. Calif. Med. Sch., San Francisco, 1964-85, assoc dean, 1985-2000. Mem. Pres.'s Sci. Adv. Com., 1970-73 Bd. overseers Harvard, 1974-80. Served to capt., M.C. AUS, 1950-52. Mem. Am. Acad. Arts and Scis., Am. Soc. Clin. Investigation (pres. 1969-70), Western Soc. Clin. Rsch. (pres. 1969-70), Assn. Am. Physicians (pres. 1974-75), Am. Fedn. Clin. Rsch. Achievements include special research genetic and metabolic diseases. Home: 309 Evergreen Dr Kentfield CA 94904-2709 Office: U Calif San Francisco Med Ctr San Francisco CA 94143-0001 E-mail: lloydhsmith@aol.com.

SMITH, M(AHLON) BREWSTER, retired psychologist, educator; b. Syracuse, NY, June 26, 1919; s. Mahlon Ellwood and Blanche Alice (Hinman) S.; m. Jean Dresden Schwartz, June 1942 (div. 1945); m. Deborah Anderson, June, 1947; children: Joshua H., T. Daniel, Rebecca M., J. Torquil. Student, Reed Coll., Portland, Oreg., 1935-38; AB, Stanford U., 1939, AM, 1940; PhD, Harvard U., 1947. Jr. analyst Office Coordinator of Info., U.S. Govt., 1941; Rantoul scholar Harvard U., 1940-41, Social Sci. Research Council fellow, 1946-47, asst. prof. social psychology, dept. social rels., 1947-49; prof. psychology, chmn. dept. Vassar Coll., 1949-52; staff Social Sci. Rsch. Coun., 1952-56; prof. psychology NYU, 1956-59, U. Calif. at Berkeley, 1959-68, dir. Inst. Human Devel., 1965-68; prof., chmn. dept. psychology U. Chgo., 1968-70; prof. psychology U. Calif. at Santa Cruz, 1970-88, prof. emeritus, 1988—2011, vice chancellor social scis., 1970-75, ret., 1988. Fellow Ctr. Advanced Studies Behavioral Scis., 1964-65; v.p. Joint Commn. Mental Illness and Health, 1955-61. Author: Social Psychology and Human Values, 1969, Humanizing Social Psychology, 1974, Values, Self and Society, 1991, For a Significant Social Psychology, 2003; co-author: The American Soldier, vol. 2, 1949, Opinions and Personality, 1956; editor: Jour. Social Issues, 1951-55, Jour. Abnormal Soc. Psychology, 1956-61; contbr. articles to profl. jours. Rsch. officer Info. and Edn. divsn. War Dept., 1943-46; rsch. assoc. spl. com. on soldier attitudes Social Sci. Rsch. Coun. 1946. Maj. AUS, 1942-46 Decorated Bronze Star medal; NIMH fellow, 1964-65, NEH fellow, 1975-76; Belding scholar Found. for Child Devel., 1982-83; Gold medal award Am. Psychol. Found., 1992 Fellow AAAS, APA (pres. 1978, Disting. Contbn. to Pub. Interest award 1988, Henry A. Murray award 1993); mem. Soc. Psychol. Study Social Issues (pres. 1959, Kurt Lewin Meml. award 1986, Presdl. citation 2004), Western Psychol. Assn. (pres. 1986, Lifetime Contbn. award 1996), Psychologists for Social Responsibility (pres. 1987-90), Internat. Soc. Polit. Psychology (Harold Lasswell award 1993), Internat. Assn. Applied Psychology (pres. divsn. polit. psychology 1994-98), Soc. Peace, Conflict and Violence (Lifetime Contbn. to Peace Psychology award 1999), Phi Beta Kappa, Sigma Xi. Democrat. Home: Dominican Oaks Apt B-203 3400 Paul Sweet Rd Santa Cruz CA 95065

SMITH, MARIE F., lobbyist, former association executive; b. East St. Louis, Ill., Mar. 12, 1939; d. David and Christina Ford; m. Richard Stanley Smith, Dec. 13, 1986; stepchildren: Jeffrey, Reginald, Laurie Debrotz. BA, Fisk U., Nashville, 1961. Dir. manpower mgmt. & orgn. planning Social Security Adminstrn.; commr. Status of Women; chair Nat. Legis. Coun., Am. Assn. Retired Persons (AARP), Washington, spokesperson Women's Initiative Prog., mem. audit & fin. com., exec. dir. search com., 2000—02, treas. found. bd. dirs., 2000—02, pres. elect, 2002—04, pres., 2004—08. Bd. dirs. Exploritas (formerly Elderhostel); owner Aina Anuhea Tropical Garden. Active Interfaith Vol. Caregivers; sec. bd. dirs. Maui Adult Day Care Ctr.; pres. bd. dirs. Maui Vol. Ctr. Recipient Woman of Excellence award, Commn. Status of Women, Circle of Women award, County Commn. Status of Women; named one of America's 100 Most Influential African Am. Leaders, Ebony mag. Mem.: Nat. Assn. Ret. Fed. Employees (pres., v.p., Hawaii), African Am. Heritage Found. Maui (pres.), Zonta Internat. Avocations: writing, travel, golf. Office: African American Heritage Foundation PO Box 2055 Kihei HI 96753 E-mail: mfsmith@aarp.org.

SMITH, MARTIN JAY, physician, biomedical research scientist; b. Bklyn., May 21, 1934; s. I. Richard and Marilyn (Bernard) S.; m. Joyce Ellen Gleason, June 26, 1960 (div. Nov. 1968); children: Danielle, Robert, Alexander; m. Ruby Helen Rhodes, Apr. 7, 1972. BA, Hofstra Coll., 1955; MD, Columbia U., 1959. Diplomate Am. Bd. Internal Medicine, Am. Bd. Internal Medicine in Hematology, Am. Bd. Pathology in Clin. Pathology, Am. Bd. Pathology in Immunopathology. Intern Meth. Hosp., NYC, 1959-60, resident in medicine, 1960-61, Montefiore Hosp., NYC, 1963-64; rsch. fellow in medicine Harvard Coll., Cambridge, Mass., 1964-66; clin. and rsch. fellow in medicine Mass. Gen. Hosp., Boston, 1964-66; physician Gundersen Clinic and Luth. Hosp., La Crosse, Wis., 1966-99, chmn. dept. internal medicine, 1971-73; dir. spl. hematology lab. Gundersen Clinic, La Crosse, 1967-99, chmn. dept. lab. medicine, 1973-96; dir. lab. medicine Luth. Hosp., La Crosse, 1973-96. Dir. rsch. Gundersen Med. Found., 1975-88; med. dir. Med. Lab. Tech. Program Western Wis. Tech. Inst., 1978-99. Contbr. articles to New Eng. Jour Medicine, Jour. Lab. Clin. Medicine, Blood, Ann. Internal Medicine, Biochim, Biophys. Acta, Jour. Infectious Diseases, Thrombosis and Haemostasis, Clin. Chemistry. Capt. USNR, ret. Fellow ACP, Coll. Am. Pathologists (inspector labs. 1983-99); mem. Am. Assn. for Cancer Rsch., Am. Soc. Hematology, Phi Beta Kappa. Home: 1428 Main St La Crosse WI 54601-4225

SMITH, MICHAEL W., physician, medical editor; MD, Mercer U. Sch. Medicine, Macon, Ga., 1994. Cert. Am. Bd. Internal Medicine. Intern Med. Ctr. Central Ga.; chief resident Ga. Baptist Med. Ctr.; chief med. editor WebMD Health; pvt. practice. Mem.: AMA, Am. Coll. Physicians. Office: 111 8th Ave 7th Fl New York NY 10011 Office Phone: 212-624-3700.

SMITH, MIRIAM ANN, epidemiologist; b. NYC, Apr. 13, 1953; MD, U. Cin., 1979; MBA, Hofstra U., 2010. Full-time faculty, infectious disease North Shore, LI Jewish Health Sys., 1987—2009; chair, medicine and residency program dir. North Shore U. Hosp. Forest Hills, 2009—. Adv. bd. mem. Eye Bank Sight Restoration, 2009. Recipient Samuel M. Rosen Outstanding Tchr. award, Albert Einstein Coll. Medicine, Bronx, NY. Fellow: ACP, Infectious Disease Soc. America; mem.: Leo Davidoff Soc., Zarb Sch. Bus., Hofstra U., Alpha Omega Alpha, Beta Gamma Sigma. Avocations: tennis, golf. Office: 102-01 66th Rd Forest Hills NY 11375 Office Fax: 718-830-1015. Business E-Mail: msmith@nshs.edu.

SMITH, MORTON EDWARD, ophthalmology educator, dean; b. Balt., Oct. 17, 1934; m. Paula Smith; 3 children. BS, U. Md., 1956, MD, 1960. Bd. cert. Ophthalmology Bd.; lic. physician Mo., Md., Wis. Rotating intern Denver Gen. Hosp., 1960-61; resident, nat. inst. of neurol. diseases and blindness fellow in ophthalmology Washington U. Sch. Medicine-Barnes Hosp., 1961-63; NIH spl. fellow in ophthalmic pathology Armed Forces Inst. of Pathology, Washington, 1964; chief resident, instr. ophthalmology Washington U. Sch. Medicine, St. Louis, 1965-66, instr. ophthalmology, 1966-67, asst. prof. ophthalmology and pathology, 1967-69, assoc. prof. ophthalmology and pathology, 1969-75, prof. ophthalmology and pathology, 1975—, asst. dean, 1978-91, assoc. dean, 1991-96, prof. emeritus, assoc. dean emeritus, 1996—; prof. ophthalmology U. Wis., Madison, 1995-2001. Vis. scholar Eye Inst., Columbia Presbyn. Med. Ctr., N.Y.C., 1966; prof./lectr. Montefiore Hosp., Pitts., 1969, U. Ark., 1970, 77, 80, 82, 84, 86, 88, U. Fla., 1972, 81, U. Tex. and Lackland AFB, San Antonio, 1973, U. Colo., 1974, 82, U. Mo., 1974, 79, 80, 88, So. Ill. U., Springfield, 1974, U. Md., 1975, Montreal (Can.) Gen. Hosp., 1975, U. Wis., 1976, 87, 93, U. Pitts., 1977, 83, 87, U. Iowa, 1977, 87, Cleve. Clinic, 1978, Colo. Ophthalmol. Soc., 1978, Brooke Army Hosp., San Antonio, 1979, Wills Eye Hosp., Phila., 1980, USPHS Hosp., San Francisco, 1981, U. Calif., Davis, 1981, Sinai Hosp., Balt., 1985, 89, 94, U. Calif., San Diego, 1985, Tufts U., Boston, 1985, Cornell U., N.Y.C., 1988, U. Wash., Seattle, 1990, Brown U., Providence, 1990, Vanderbilt U., Nashville, 1991, Duke U., Durham, N.C., 1992; Chandler lectr. Harvard U., 1988; The Lois A. Young-Thomas Meml. lectr. U. Md., 1991; Braley lectr. U. Iowa, 1993; Havener Meml. lectr. Ohio State, 1994. Editor pathology sect.: Perspectives in Ophthalmology, 1977; mem. editl. bd. Ophthalmic Plastic & Reconstructive Surgery, 1986-90; contbr. articles to profl. jours. With USAR M.C., 1958-66. Scholar U. Md., 1958, 59; Founder's Day award Wash. U., St. Louis; Grand Marshall Wash. U., 2007; recepient Samuel Goldstein Leadership award Wash. U. St. Louis, Sch. Medicine., 2009, Second Century award, Wash. U. St. Louis, Sch. Medicine, 2011. Fellow Am. Acad. Ophthalmology (ophthalmic pathology com. 1977-83, chmn. ophthalmic com. 1979-83, Honor award for svc. 1981, Sr. Honor award 1992); mem. AMA, Am. Bd. Ophthalmology (diplomate, bd. dirs. 1992—), Assn. for Rsch. in Vision and Ophthalmology (chmn. sect. pathology ann. meeting 1971), Am. Assn. Ophthalmic Pathologists (pres. 1977-80), Assn. Am. Med. Colls. (group med. edn. 1985—), Mo. Med. Assn., Mo. Ophthalmol. Soc., Verhoeff Soc., Theobald Soc., St. Louis Med. Soc., St. Louis Ophthalmol. Soc., Soc. Med. Coll. Dirs. for Continuing Med. Edn., Alpha Omega Alpha (sec.-treas. chpt. 1993-95, councillor 2003—). Home: 1275 Castle Gate Dr Saint Louis MO 63132 Office: Campus Box 8096 660 S Euclid Ave Saint Louis MO 63110-1093 Office Phone: 314-747-5559. Business E-Mail: smithm@vision.wustl.edu.

SMITH, NADINE BARRIE, biomedical engineer, educator; life ptnr. Andrew Webb. PhD, U. Ill., 1996. Radiology Brigham & Women's Hosp., Boston, 1996—99. Mem.: Am. Inst. Ultrasound in Medicine. Office: Pa State Univ 219 Hallowell Bldg University Park PA 16802 E-mail: nbs@engr.psu.edu.

SMITH, PAMELA LATRICE, school psychologist; b. Monroe, La., Jan. 11, 1975; d. Tommy Lee Smith and Lovely Marie Bams. BA, N.E. La. U., Monroe, 1997, MS, 1999. Cert. specialist in sch. psychology 2000, supr. sch. psychol. svcs. 2004, cert. trainer CPI's Non-Violent Phys. Crisis Intervention. Sch. psychologist Westside Alternative Sch., Tallulah, La., 1999—2000; sch. psychologist, divsn. student support svcs. Monroe City Schs., 2000—. Instr. psychology U. La., Monroe, 2002—. Founding mem. Wall of Tolerance, Montgomery, Ala., 2002—; mem. Southern Poverty Law Ctr., 2005—. Recipient Outstanding Academic Achievement, 1992—93; scholar La. Honor's Scholarship award, 1993. Mem.: AAUW, La. Sch. Psychol. Assn., Cooking Club of Am. (life), Mortar Bd. Honor Soc., Phi Kappa Phi, Psi Chi Nat. Honor Soc., Delta Sigma Theta Sorority Inc. Democrat. Avocations: travel, reading, music, cooking, baking. Office: Divsn Student Support Svcs PO Box 4180 Monroe LA 71211 Home: 98 Nelson Rd Monroe LA 71203 Home Phone: 318-342-8340; Office Phone: 318-388-3747 ext. 5230. Personal E-mail: psmith2002@bellsouth.net. Business E-Mail: pamela.smith@mcschools.net.

SMITH, PATRICIA V., medical association administrator; Grad., Monmouth U., NJ. V.p. polit. affairs Internat. Lyme and Associated Diseases Soc., Bethesda, Md.; pres. Lyme Disease Assn., Jackson, NJ. Former chair Gov. Lyme Disease Adv. Coun., NJ. Guest appearance: (TV series) Good Day New York, FOX-TV; contbr. articles. Co-creator LymeAid 4 kids; mem. Wall Twp. Bd. Edn., NJ, past. pres. Office: Lyme Disease Assn Inc PO Box 1438 Jackson NJ 08527 Office Fax: 732-938-7215. *

SMITH, PAUL JOHN, plastic and reconstructive surgeon, consultant; MBBS, Newcastle U., Eng., 1968. Lectr. in anatomy Glasgow U., Scotland, 1969-71; surg. trainee Western Infirmary, Glasgow, 1971-76; rsch. asst. Dept. Microsurgery, U. Louisville, 1978; Christine Kleinert Fellow in hand surgery U. Louisville, 1978-79; resident and clin. instr. in plastic surgery Duke U., Durham, NC, 1979-80; sr. registrar in plastic surgery Mt. Vernon Hosp., London, 1980-82, cons. plastic surgeon, 1982—, The Hosp. for Sick Children, Great Ormond St., London, 1988—. Sec. Royal Soc. of Medicine, London, 1988; editl. com. Jour. Hand Surgery (Brit. vol.), London, 1987-91. Author: Principles of Hand Surgery, 1989, Lister's The Hand, 2002; contbr. articles to profl. jours. Mem. rsch. com. Restoration of Appearance and Function Trust Found. Recipient 1st prize resident competition, Am. Assn. Hand Surgery, Toronto, 1979. Fellow Royal Coll. Surgeons; mem. Brit. Assn. Plastic Surgeons (organizing com. advanced courses plastic surgery, Hayward found. scholarship 1978), Brit. Soc. for Surgery of the Hand (Pulvertaft prize, 1986), Brit. Assn. Aesthetic Plastic Surgeons. Office: Mt Vernon Hosp Rickmansworth Rd Northwood HA6 2RN England also: Bishops Wood Hosp Rickmansworth Road HA6 2JW Northwood England Office Phone: 01923 828100.

SMITH, PETER K., cardiothoracic surgeon; b. Cleve., Ohio, Aug. 20, 1951; MD, Duke U. Sch. Medicine, 1977. Cert. Am. Bd. Thoracic Surgery, Am. Bd. Surgery. Intern Duke U. Med. Ctr., Durham, NC, resident, cardiovascular rsch., 1987, divsn. chief; asst. prof., surgery Duke U., Durham, NC, 1987, prof. surgery, thoracic and cardiovascular surgery. Contbr. several articles to profl. jours. Tchg. Scholar, Am. Heart Assn. Clinician Scientist Awardee, Duke U. Med. Ctr., NC, 1980—83. Office: Duke U Med Ctr Box 3442 Durham NC 27710 Office Phone: 910-684-2890. Office Fax: 919-681-7905.

SMITH, RAYMOND LEIGH, plastic surgeon; b. Norristown, Pa., Sept. 27, 1940; s. Walter Joseph and Pauline C. (Wolfskill) Smith; m. Coralynn Elder Smith, Jan. 8, 1966; children: Susan, Elizabeth, Christine. BS, Ursinus Coll., 1962; MD, Temple U., 1966. Diplomate Nat. Bd. Med. Examiners, Am. Bd. Plastic Surgery. Active staff Reading Hosp., Pa., 1976—2005, chief sect. of plastic surgery, 1994—2000, ret, 2005. Assoc. physician Reading Hosp. Med. Ctr. Wound Care & Hyperbaric Ctr.; mem. Republican Majority Found. Mem.: ACS, Berks County Med. Soc., Lipoplasty Soc. N.America, Pa. Med. Soc., Northeastern Soc. Plastic Surgeons, Am. Assn. Hand Surgery, Robert H. Ivy Soc., Am. Soc. Plastic Surgeons. Lutheran. Office Phone: 610-568-3949.

SMITH, REGINALD BRIAN FURNESS, retired anesthesiologist, educator; b. Warrington, Eng., Feb. 7, 1931; s. Reginald and Betty (Bell) S.; m. Margarete Groppe, July 18, 1963; children: Corinne, Malcolm. MB, BS, U. London, 1955; DTM and H, Liverpool Sch. Tropical Medicine, 1959. Intern Poole Gen. Hosp., Dorset, England, 1955-56, Wilson Meml. Hosp., Johnson City, NY, 1962-63; resident in anesthesiology Med. Coll. Va., Richmond, 1963-64, U. Pitts., 1964-65, from clin. instr. to prof., 1965-78, acting chmn. dept. anesthesiology, 1977-78; anesthesiologist in chief Presbyn. Univ. Hosp., Pitts., 1976-78; dir. anesthesiology Eye and Ear Hosp., Pitts., 1971-76; prof., chmn. dept. U. Tex. Health Sci. Ctr., San Antonio, 1978-98, anesthesiologist in chief hosps., 1978-98, clin. prof. anesthesiology, 1999—2007, clin. prof. rehab. medicine, 2003—07, med. dir. hyperbaric medicine and woundcare unit Univ. Hosp., 1993-2000, mem. med. staff Univ. Hosp., 2003—07; ret., 2000. Contbg. editor: Internat. Ophthalmology Clinics, 1973, Internat. Anesthesiology Clinics, 1983; contbr. articles to profl. jours. Served to capt. Brit. Army, 1957—59. Fellow ACP, Am. Coll. Anesthesiologists, Am. Coll. Chest Physicians; mem. AMA, Internat. Anesthesia Rsch. Soc., Am. Soc. Anesthesiologists (pres. Western Pa. 1974-75), Tex. Soc. Anesthesiologists, San Antonio Soc. Anesthesiologists (pres. 1990), Tex. Med. Assn., Bexar County Med. Soc. Home: 9 Bristol Green San Antonio TX 78209-1104 Personal E-mail: reginaldbriansmith@yahoo.com, reginaldbriansmith@aol.com.

SMITH, RICHARD V., otolaryngologist, educator; MD, Vt. U., 1990; attended Otolaryngology training, Georgetown U. Diplomate Am. Bd. Otolaryngology. Chair of the residents and fellows in Training Comm. Acad. of Otolaryngology, chair of the residents and fellows in Young Physicians Comm.; resident in otolaryngology Georgetown Univ. Hosp., Washington, 1991—95; clin. prof. surgery Yeshiva Univ.; chief of divsn. of otolaryngology North Ctrl. Bronx Hosp.; interim chair dept. of otolaryngology Yeshiva Univ., Montefiore Med. Ctr., co-dir. of head and neck svc., dir. of head and neck svc., 2005—. Author: (books) The Larynx, Two-Volume Set, The Larynx, Volume I, The Larynx, Volume II. Recipient Recent Alumni award, Univ. Vt., 2000, Honor award, Am. Acad. of Otolaryngology, 2001, Byers award, Am. Head and Neck Soc., 2003; named one of Best Doctors in America, Best Doctors in NY, Castle Connolly Med. Ltd., Top Doctor:NY Metro Area. Office: Montefiore Medical Center 111 E 210th St Bronx NY 10467 Office Phone: 718-920-4321. Office Fax: 718-920-6321.

SMITH, ROBERT A., medical association administrator; Dir. breast cancer screening Am. Cancer Soc. Office: 250 Williams St NW Atlanta GA 30303

SMITH, ROBERT B., geophysicist, educator; BS, Utah State U., 1960; MS, Utah State U., 1965; PhD, U. Utah, 1967. Emeritus rsch. prof. geology & geophysics U. Utah. Office: University of Utah Dept Geology & Geophysics 135 S 1460 E Rm 719 Salt Lake City UT 84112-0111 Office Phone: 801-581-7129. E-mail: robert.b.smith@utah.edu.

SMITH, RONALD EDWARD, ophthalmologist; b. Walkersville, Md., Oct. 7, 1942; s. Harry Otto and Marjorie Lee Smith; m. Sara Gutelius Watt, Sept. 4, 1965 (div. Oct. 1977); children: Kelly, Matt; m. Suzette Edith Le Blanc, Sept. 6, 1980. BA, Johns Hopkins U., 1964, MD, 1967. Diplomate Am. Bd. Ophthalmology. Intern Johns Hopkins Hospital, Baltimore, Md., 1967—68; resident opthalmology Johns Hopkin's Hosp., Baltimore, Md., 1968—72; asst. prof. U. So. Calif., LA, 1975—78, assoc. prof., 1978—81, prof., 1981—95, prof., chmn. dept. ophthalmology, 1995—. Co-author: Intraocular Inflammation, 1980, Vitrectomy Techniques, 1983, Uveitis: A Clinical Approach, 1986. Lt. comdr. USPHS, 1973—78. Recipient gold medal, Internat. Uveitis Study Group, 1998, Light award, Braille Inst., 1998. Mem.: Am. Acad. Ophthalmology (pres. 1994—95, 1998—, chmn. found. 1998—99). Avocations: golf, skiing, tennis. Office: USC Dept Ophthalmology 2617 E Chapman No 301 Orange CA 92829 *

SMITH, SIDNEY CRAWLE, JR., cardiologist, educator; b. Wilmington, Del., 1941; MD, Yale U., 1967. Diplomate Nat. Bd. Med. Examiners, 1969, Am. Bd. Internal Medicine, 1972, Cardiovascular Disease, 1973. Intern Peter Bent Brigham Hosp., Boston, 1967—68, resident cardiology, 1968—69, fellowship, 1969—71, Harvard Med. Sch., Boston, 1969—71; dir. cardiovascular labs. U. Colo. Health Sci. Ctr., 1973—77; dir. San Diego Cardiac Ctr. at Sharp Healthcare, 1977—94; chief cardiology U. NC, Chapel Hill, 1994—2001, dir. Ctr. Cardiovascular Sci. and Medicine, 1996—. Asst. prof. U. Colo., Denver, 1973—77; asst. clin. prof. medicine U. San Diego, 1977—85, assoc. clin. prof., 1985—90, clin. prof., 1990—94; prof. U. NC Sch. Medicine, 1994—. Contbr. articles to med. jours. Recipient Eugene

Drake Award, 2003, Award Spl. Recognition, Nat. Heart, Lung, and Blood Inst., NIH, 2003. Mem.: Am. Coll. Cardiology, Am. Heart Assn. (chief sci. officer 2001—03, nat. pres. 1995—96, Physician of Yr. Award 1993, Disting. Nat. Leadership Award 1996, Gold Heart Award 2000), Inter Am. Soc. Cardiology (v.p.), World Heart Fedn. (exec. com. mem.), World Heart Forum (chmn.). Office: U NC / Divsn Cardiology CB #7075 160 Dental Circle Chapel Hill NC 27599-7075 Office Phone: 919-966-0732. Office Fax: 919-966-1743. E-mail: scs@med.unc.edu.

SMITH, SIDNEY TALBERT, biomedical engineer; b. Decatur, Ill., Oct. 30, 1954; s. Sidney Paulsen and Patricia Louise (Talbert) Smith. BS, Millikin U., 1976; postgrad., Washington U., St. Louis, 1976-78; MBA with honors, Lake Forest Sch. Mgmt., Ill., 1985. Rsch. asst. Baxter Travenol, Morton Grove, Ill., 1980-82; devel. engr. Fenwal divsn. Travenol Labs., Round Lake, Ill., 1982-83, sr. devel. engr., 1983-84; prin. engr. Fenwal divsn. Baxter Healthcare, Round Lake, 1984-88; project mgr. biotech. systems Baxter Healthcare, Round Lake, 1988-89; dir. devel. Applied Immune Scis., Menlo Park, Calif., 1990-91; prin. Smith Engring., Lake Forest, Ill., 1989—95, mgr. container devel. Advanced Engr. Deerfield, Ill., 1995—98; sr. engring. specialist Advanced Engring. Design Ctr., Baxter Healthcare Corp., Deerfield, Ill., 1998—2005; sr. mgr. Manufacturing Global Tech., 2005—08; dir. Brand Integrity, 2008—. Patentee in field. Mem. Lake Forest/Lake Bluff Running Club. Home: 1326 W Everett Rd Lake Forest IL 60045-2610 Business E-Mail: sid_smith@baxter.com. E-mail: bio.engr@comcast.net.

SMITH, STEPHEN J., gynecologist, obstetrician; BS in Chem. Engring., Lafayette Coll., 1984; MD, U. Medicine and Dentistry of NJ-Sch. Health Related Prof, 1988. Diplomate Am. Bd. Ob-Gyn.-maternal-fetal medicine, Am. Bd. Ob-Gyn. Fellow in maternal-fetal medicine Pa. Hosp., 1988—92; intern ob-gyn. Abington Meml. Hosp., resident in ob-gyn.; fellow in maternal-fetal medicine Pa. Hosp.; assoc. dir. Abington Meml. Hosp. Recipient Gynecology Nat. Faculty award, 1996, Abington Meml. Hosp. Distinguished Faculty award, 2001; named one of Top Doctors, Phila. mag., 2011. Mem.: Pa. Med. Soc., ACOG, AMA. Office: Abington Memorial Hospital 1200 Old Tork Rd Abington PA 19001 Office Phone: 215-481-2000.

SMITH, STEPHEN MARK, medical association administrator; b. Nottingham, Eng., Oct. 3, 1962; PhD, U. Newcastle upon Tyne, 1988, MBBS, 1990. Assoc. prof. Oreg. Health & Sci. U., 2000. Dir. critical care medicine fellowship OHSU, 2010. Rsch. grant, NIDA. Fellow: Coll. Intensive Care Medicine. Office: 3181 Sw Sam Jackson Pk Rd Portland OR 97239 Business E Mail: smisteph@ohsu.edu.

SMITH, STEPHEN ROSS, endocrinologist; b. Iowa City, Mar. 5, 1938; s. Wendell Ross and Ruth Anne (Frudenfeld) S.; m. Elaine Cashman Frazier, July 4, 1964 (div. Dec. 1990); children: Julia Helene, Stuart Ross; m. Regina Alilada Clarito, Dec. 26, 1990; 1 child, Alexander Ross. AB, Princeton U., 1959; MD, Harvard U., 1963. Instr. medicine Johns Hopkins U. Sch. Medicine, Balt., 1970-72, asst. prof. medicine, 1972-73, 82—; chief endocrinology Kern County Hosp., Bakersfield, Calif., 1973-76; assoc. prof. medicine Tex. Tech. U. Sch. Medicine, El Paso, 1977-80; chief medicine Thomason Gen. Hosp., El Paso, 1977-80, Bon Secours Hosp., Balt., 1980-83, Security Forces Hosp., Riyadh, Saudi Arabia, 1984-88; pvt. practice Balt., 1988—; med. dir. Nat. Clin. Rsch. Ctrs., Bethesda, Md., 1988-93. Pres. med. staff Univ. Specialty Hosp., Balt., 1996—2010; rsch. assoc. Johns Hopkins Ctr. Med. Rsch. and Tng., Calcutta, India, 1970—72; cons. Liberty Med. Ctr. Diabetes Mgmt. Ctr., Balt., 1991—98, pharm. industry, 1993—; bd. dirs. El Paso Diabetes Assn., 1978—80, U. Splty. Hosp., Baltimore, 2008—10. Contbr. articles to profl. jours. Capt. USAF, 1965-67. Fellow ACP; mem. Am. Diabetes Assn., Princeton Club Md., Hampton Swim Club, Bodie Island Beach Club (pres. 2002-07, bd. dirs. 2000-07, nags. head, NC). Republican. Avocations: swimming, travel, history. Office: 8709 Harford Rd Baltimore MD 21234-4607

SMITH, STEVE, pharmaceutical executive; s. Robert and Evelyn Smith. Pres., CEO Tec Labs., Albany, Oreg., 1998—. Speaker Oregon State U. Entrepreneurship Soc. Meeting. Mem. Portland Bus. Alliance. Office: Tec Laboratories Inc 7100 Tec Labs Way SW Albany OR 97321 *

SMITH, STEVEN SIDNEY, molecular biologist; b. Idaho Falls, Idaho, Feb. 11, 1946; s. Sidney Ervin and Hermie Phyllis (Robertson) Smith; m. Nancy Louise Turner, Dec. 20, 1974. BS, U. Idaho, 1968; PhD, UCLA, 1974. Asst. rsch. scientist Beckman Rsch. Inst. City of Hope Nat. Med. Ctr., Duarte, Calif., 1982-84, staff Cancer Ctr., 1983—, asst. rsch. scientist depts. Thoracic Surgery and Molecular Biology, 1985-87, assoc. rsch. scientist, 1987-95; rsch. scientist City of Hope Nat. Med. Ctr., Duarte, 1995-00, prof. molecular sci., 2000—; dir. dept. cell and tumor biology City of Hope, Duarte, Calif., 1990—2002, assoc. dir. rsch. Prostate Cancer Program, 2003—. Vis. prof. in basic med. scis. Okla. State U., 1995—96; cons. Molecular Biosystems Inc., San Diego, 1981—84, Am. Inst. Biol. Scis., Washington, 1994, Okla. Ctr. for Advancement of Sci. and Tech., 2001—. Editl. bd. mem. Analytical Biochemistry, 1997—2000, exec. editor, 2000—, editl. bd. mem. Inscight Acad. Press., 1998—, Cancer Genomics and Proteomics, 2003; contbr. articles to profl. jours. Named Honors Laureate, Computer World, 2001; fellow Swiss Nat. Sci. Found. fellow, U. Bern, 1974—77, fellow, Scripps Clinic and Rsch. Found., 1978—82, NIH, 1979—81. Mem.: IEEE Computer Soc., Am. Urological Assn., Am. Math. Soc., Am. Chem. Soc., Am. Assn. Cancer Rsch., Am. Soc. Cell Biology, Phi Beta Kappa. Achievements include 5 U.S. patents. Avocations: backpacking, fishing, weightlifting. Office: Familian Science Bldg Rm 1102 City of Hope 1500 E Duarte Rd Duarte CA 91010-3011 Home Phone: 323-913-0418; Office Phone: 626-301-8316. Business E-Mail: ssmith@coh.org.

SMITH, STUART LYON, psychiatrist, corporate financial executive; b. Montreal, Que., Can., May 7, 1938; s. Moe Samuel and Nettie (Krainer) S.; m. Patricia Ann Springate, Jan. 2, 1964; children: Tanya, Craig. BSc, McGill U., 1958, MD, CM, 1962, diploma in psychiatry, 1967; LLD (hon.), Mt. Allison U., 1992, Royal Rds. U., 2000; B.Ap.Sc. (hon.), Humber Coll., 2005. Intern. Montreal Gen. Hosp., 1962-63, resident in psychiatry, 1963-67; from asst. prof. to assoc. prof. medicine McMaster U., Hamilton, Ont., Canada, 1967-75; leader Ont. Liberal Party Ont. Legislature, 1976-82, leader of the opposition, 1977-82; chmn. Sci. Coun. Can., Ottawa, 1982-87; pres. RockCliffe Rsch. and Tech., Inc., 1987—, Philip Utilities Mgmt. Corp., Toronto, Ont., 1994-97. Chmn. com. inquiry Can. U. Edn., 1989—91; chmn. Ensyn Tech. Inc., 1990—; sr. adv. ICF Cons., 2002; chmn. Nat. Round Table on Environment and Economy, Ottawa, 1995—2002; chmn. bd. dirs. Humber Coll., 2002—04, Esna Tech., Inc., 2004—. Decorated knight Nat. Order of Merit (France); McLaughlin travel fellow, 1964-65. Fellow Royal Coll. Physicians and Surgeons of Can. Personal E-mail: smithstuart@rogers.com.

SMITH, THURSTON SINCLAIR, behavioral healthcare consultant, community activist; b. NY, Aug. 7, 1962; s. Thurston Sinclair and Alethia Helena Smith; children: Jermaine Sinclair, Na'eema Iman. Attending, Graceland U., 2008—. Cert. addictions counselor, nationally cert. compulsive gambling counselor, cert. alcohol and drug counselor Ga., clin. counselor S.C.; instr. trainer U.S. Army Res., clin. supr., coach, mentor. Dir. client and prevention svcs. ACCESS Network, Beaufort, SC, 1996—98; resident Graceland U., Independence, Mo., 1997—2001; mental health care coord., addictions therapist, chem. dependency program coord. Vet. Health Adminstrn., Charleston, SC, 1998—. Addictions therapist Clark Ctr.-Meml. Med. Ctr., Savannah, Ga., 1996; cons. S.C. Dept. Alcohol and Other Drug Abuse Svcs., Columbia, SC, 1997—2004; adminstrv. program surveyor CARF: The Accreditation Commn., Tucson, 1999—; counter drug team S.C. Army Nat. Guard, Columbia, 1999—2000; chmn. NAADAC Southeast Regional Leadership Conf., Jekyll Island, 2000; presenter in field; Webinar presenter CARF Internat., 2011. Co-author: Masculintiy: Identity Issues in Addictions Treatment, 1999, Compulsive Gambling, The Hidden Addiction, 1997—, Substance Abuse Use Disroders and The Vererans Population, 2004; contbg. author: Advocates: A Publication of the South Carolina Governor's Office Division of Foster Care Review, 2001; reviewer A Provider's Guide to Substance Abuse Treatment, U.S. Dept. Health & Human Svc., Ctr. for Substance Abuse Treatment, 2001, Seeking Solace: Accessing Recovery for the Veteran Population, 2008; contbr. articles to profl. publs. Foster care rev. bd. mem. S.C. Gov.'s Office, Columbia, 2001—, chmn. First Foster Care Legislative Luncheon, 2001; bd. dirs. Father to Father Project, Charleston, SC, 2002—04; planning com. Ga. Conf. on HIV and AIDS, Augusta, 2000; EEO adv. com. Dept. Vet. Affairs, Charleston, 1999—2001; del. to Columbia, S. Am. S.C. Ptnrs. Am./U.S. Dept. State-Office Ednl. and Cultural Affairs, Washington, 2000; co-chmn. Beaufort (S.C.) and Jasper County HIV Prevention Collaboration, Beaufort, 1997—98; chmn. Evaluation com. Beaufort County EEO Commission, 1997; region IV rep. S.C. Assn. Alcoholism and Drug Abuse Counselors, Columbia, 1996—98; chmn. Charleston County Foster Care Rev. Bd., 2000—04; bd. mem. Charleston Dorchester Mental Health Com., 2004—06; del. S.C. Dem. Party, Columbia, 2000—01; candidate Charleston City Coun., SC, 2005; candidate del. Presidl. Candidate Barack Obama Congressional Dist. 7 Ala.; bd. dirs. Crisis Ministries, Charleston, SC, 2001—03. Sgt. USARNG, 1981. Recipient Leadership Beaufort Cert. of Achievement, Beaufort County C. of C., 1998, Cert. of Honor, U. Del Valle Sede Buga, Colombia, 2000, SATTC Svc. award, Morehouse Sch Medicine, 2003, Key to City, Mayor of Clemson, S.C., 2004, Vets. Integrated Svc. Network 7 Recognition, Lora Roe Meml. Alcoholism and Drug Abuse Counselor of Yr., 2004, Carey award, Bd. Examiners Vets. Health Adminstrn., 2006, Network 7 Leadership Achievement Award, 2006; named Nat. Counselor of the Yr., NAADAC, 2003, Counselor of the Yr., Vets. Integrated Svc., 2004, Counselor of Yr., S.C. Assn. Alcoholism and Drug Abuse Counselors, 1997. Mem.: Vets. Integrated Svc. Network, Assn. Addiction Profls. (Exec. Com. Svc. award 2004, Fla. Svc. award 2005, Ralph H. Johnson VA Med. Ctr. Pub. Safety Recognition 2005), Nat. Assn. Alcoholism and Drug Abuse Counselors (officer, membership chmn. 1998—2000, conf. chmn. 1999, S.E. regional v.p. 2000—04, legis. luncheon chmn. 2001, One to One Membership Campaign award 1996, Ralph H. Johnson VA Med. Ctr. Merit award 2002, named Lora Roe Meml. Alcoholism and Drug Abuse Counselor of Yr. 2003, Ralph H. Johnson VA Med. Ctr. Merit award 2004), S.C. Ptnrs. Am. (com. chmn. 2000, S.C. liaison to S.E. Addiction Tech. Transfer Ctr. 2002—03). Methodist. Avocations: music, travel. Office: Vets Health Adminstrn PO. Box 610033 Birmingham AL 35261 Office Phone: 383-324-9608. Office Fax: 901-825-4492. Personal E-mail: teesmith1@hotmail.com. E-mail: thurston.smith@va.gov.

SMITH, WAYNE THOMAS, healthcare company executive; b. Jan. 29, 1946; BS, Auburn Univ, 1968, MS, 1969; M in Hosp. Adminstrn., Trinity U.; postgrad., King's Fund Coll. Hosp. Adminstrn. With Trinity Univ, 1971-73, Humana Inc, Louisville, 1973-96, v.p. ctrl. hosp. region, 1978-80, sr. v.p., 1980-85, exec. v.p., 1985-86, pres., COO group health divsn., 1986-96, also bd. dirs.; exec. v.p. Humana Health Care Ops., Louisville, 1991-96; ret. Humana, Inc., 1996; pres. CEO Community Health Systems, Brentwood, Tenn., 1996—, chmn. bd., 2001—. Exec. v.p. health plan ops., bd. dirs. Humana Health Plan, Inc., Louisville; pres. Humana Health Ins. Nev., Inc., Humana Health Plan Fla., Inc., Humana Health Plan Ohio, Inc., Humana Health Chgo. Ins. Co., Humana Kansas City, Inc.; pres., COO Humana Health Plan Tex., Prime Health Mgmt. Svcs.; pres., bd. dirs. HMPK, Inc.; bd. dirs. Praxair, Inc.; chmn. bd. Fedn. Am.'s Hosps. Bd. dirs. Gov.'s Scholars Program, Ky., Actors Theatre of Louisville, Ky. Ctr. for the Arts, The Louisville Orchestra; bd. overseers U. Louisville; mem. exec. com. Greater Louisville Fund for the Arts; past chair bd. dirs. Louisville Collegiate Sch. With U.S. Army, 1969-73, capt., 1973. Mem. Group Health Assn. Am. (bd. dirs.), Health Ins. Assn. Am. (bd. dirs.). Office: Community Health Sys 4000 Meridian Blvd Franklin TN 37067 *

SMITH, WILLARD GRANT, psychologist; b. Sidney, NY, June 29, 1934; s. Frank Charles and Myrtle Belle (Empet) S.; m. Ruth Ann Dissly, Sept. 14, 1957; children: Deborah Sue Henri, Cynthia Lynn Koster, Andrea Kay Richards, John Charles. BS, U. Md., 1976; MS, U. Utah, 1978, PhD, 1981. Diplomate Am. Bd. Forensic Examiners, Am. Bd. Psychol. Specialities, Am. Bd. Disability Analysts, cert. forensic cons.; lic. psychologist Utah. Tchg. asst. dept. ednl. psychology U. Utah; rsch. asst. U. Utah Med. Ctr., 1976-78; rsch. cons. Utah Dept. Edn., 1977; program evaluator Salt Lake City Sch. Dist.; program evaluator, auditor Utah State Bd. Edn., 1978; sch. psychologist Jordan Sch. Dist., Sandy, Utah, 1978-82, tchr., 1979-80; exec. dir. Utah Ind. Living Ctr., Salt Lake City, 1982-83; spl. edn. cons. Southeastern Edn. Svc. Ctr., Price, Utah, 1983-85; sch. psychologist Jordan Sch. Dist., Sandy, Utah, 1985-96; assoc. psychologist Don W. McBride & Assocs., Bountiful, Utah, 1989-91; pvt. practice Sandy, Utah, 1991—. Master sgt. USAF, 1953-76. Decorated Air Force Commendation medal with 2 clusters. Fellow Am. Coll. Forensic Examiners (life); mem. APA (life), Nat. Assn. Sch. Psychologists, Air Force Assn. (life), Air Force Sgts. Assn. (life), Ret. Enlisted Assn. (life), Am. Legion (life), VFW (life), Phi Kappa Phi, Alpha Sigma Lambda. Home: 8955 Quail Hollow Dr Sandy UT 84093-1903 Office Phone: 801-942-5356. E-mail: dr_bill5@msn.com.

SMITHERAM, MARGARET ETHERIDGE, health facility administrator, director; d. Philip Fitzgerald and Mary Catharine (Dwyer) E.; m. Roy Charles McCracken, May 5, 1975; m. William Bertram Smitheram, Aug. 17, 1985. BA, Emory U., 1960; M in Health Adminstrn., Washington U., St. Louis, 1973. Registered record administr., 1960-71; spl. asst. to dir. VA Med. Ctr., Roseburg, Oreg., 1973-74; hosp. administrn, specialist VA Central Office, Washington, 1974-75; asst. dir. trainee VA Med. Ctr., Phila., 1976, assoc. dir. Hampton, Va., 1976--80, Buffalo, 1980-81; presdl. exchange exec. Kimberly Clark Corp., Neenah, Wis., 1981-82, Roswell, Ga., 1981-82; dir. VA Med. Ctr., Grand Island, Nebr., 1982-94; interim dir. Grand Island-Hall County Health Dept., 1996-97; instr. Cerritos Coll., 1969-70. Bd. dirs. Project 2M Coordinating Coun., Inc., Grand Island, 1985-87, Hall County Leadership Unlimited, Inc., 1990. Bd. dirs. Grand Island Area United Way, 1987-90, pres., 1989; bd. dirs. Grand Island Concert Assn, 1987-92, Ctrl. Nebr. Goodwill Industries, Inc., 1987-93, pres. 1991-92; hon. adm. Gt. Navy State of Nebr., 1987. Named Woman of Yr., Beta Sigma Phi Woman's Profl. Sorority, 1988, Bus. and Profl. Women's Club, Grand Island, Nebr. chpt., 1990, Grand Island, NE Ind. Newspaper, 1991. Fellow Am. Coll. Healthcare Execs. (life); mem. rev. bd. State of Nebr. Foster Care, Am. Hosp. Assn., Fed. Exec. Assn. (pres. Grand Island chpt. 1987), Nebr. Hosp. Assn., Grand Island C. of C. (bd. dirs. 1988-92, legis. affairs com 1984-85, priorities com. 1984-85, govtl. affairs com. 1984-88, nominating com. 1991-92, 94-95, audit com. 1992-93, pres. club 1993-94), Rotary Internat. Club #1485 (v.p. 1998-2000, pres. 2000-2001, District 5630 Group Study Exchange Team Leader to South Korea District 3710, 1999, Paul Harris fellow). Home: 221 Trail of the Flowers Georgetown TX 78633

SMITHERMAN, TODD A., psychologist, researcher; BA, Samford U., Ala., 2000; MS, Auburn U., Ala., 2002, PhD, 2006. Clinician Auburn U., Ala., 2000—06; resident U. Miss. Med. Ctr., Jackson, 2005—, postdoctoral psychology fellow, 2006—08; asst. prof. U. Miss., Dept. Psychology, 2008—. Contbr. articles to profl. jours. Charles V. Lair Fellowship Meml. award, Harry Merriwether fellowship. Mem.: APA, Soc. Behavioral Medicine, Assn. Behavioral Cognitive Therapies.

SMITHIES, OLIVER, geneticist, educator; b. Halifax, Eng., June 23, 1925; naturalized; m. Nobuyo Maeda. MA, PhD in Biochemistry, Balliol Coll., Oxford U., Eng., 1951; DSc (hon.), U. Chgo., 1991, Duke U., Durham, NC, 2004, U. São Paulo, 2008. Postdoc. fellow in phys. chemistry U. Wis., Madison, 1951—53, asst. prof. genetics, 1960—61, assoc. prof., 1961—63, prof., 1963—71, Leon J. Cole prof. genetics & med. genetics, 1971—80, Hilldale prof. genetics & med. genetics, 1980—88; Excellence prof. pathology and lab. medicine U. NC Sch. Medicine, Chapel Hill, 1988—. Rsch. asst., assoc. Connaught Med. Rsch. Lab., Toronto, Canada, 1953—60; mem. nat. adv. med. scis. coun. NIH, 1985—90. Contbr. articles to profl. jours. Recipient William Allen Meml. award, Am. Soc. Human Genetics, 1964, Karl Landsteiner Meml. award, Am. Assn. Blood Banks, 1984, Gairdner Found. Internat. award, 1990, 1993, NC award for sci., 1993, Alfred P. Sloan award, GM Found. Cancer Rsch. Found., 1994, CIBA award, Am. Heart Assn., 1996, Bristol-Meyers Squibb award for disting. achievement in cardiovasc./metabolic disease rsch., 1997, Internat. Okamoto award, Japan Vascular Disease Rsch. Found., 2000, Albert Lasker award for basic med. rsch., 2001, Oliver Max Gardner award, U. NC, 2002, Massry prize, 2002, Wolf prize in medicine, Israel, 2003, Nobel prize in physiology/medicine, 2007. Fellow: AAAS; mem.: NAS, Royal Soc. London (fgn.), Inst. Medicine, Genetics Soc. America (v.p. 1974, pres. 1975), Am. Acad. Arts & Scis. Office: U NC Dept Pathology & Lab Medicine CB #7525 Brinkhous Bullitt Bldg Chapel Hill NC 27599-0001 Office Phone: 919-966-6913. E-mail: oliver.smithies@pathology.unc.edu. *

SMITS, HELEN LIDA, administrator; b. Long Beach, Calif., Dec. 3, 1936; d. Theodore Richard Smits and Anna Mary Wells; m. Roger LeCompte, Aug. 28, 1976; 1 child, Theodore. BA with honors, Swarthmore Coll., 1958; MA, Yale U., 1961, MD cum laude, 1967. Intern, asst. resident Hosp. U. Pa., 1967—69; fellow Beth Israel Hosp., Boston, 1969-70; chief resident Hosp. U. Pa., 1970-71; chief med. clinic U. Pa., 1971-75; assoc. adminstr. for patient care svcs. U. Pa. Hosp., 1975-77; v.p. med. affairs Community Health Plan Georgetown U., Washington, 1977; dir. health standards and quality bur. Health Care Financing Adminstrn., HHS, Washington, 1977-80; sr. rsch. assoc. The Urban Inst., Washington, 1980-81; assoc. prof. Yale U. Med. Sch., New Haven, 1981-85; assoc. v.p. for health affairs U. Conn. Health Ctr., Farmington, 1985-87; prof. community medicine U. Conn. Sch. Medicine, Farmington, 1985-93; hosp. dir. John Dempsey Hosp., Farmington, 1987-93; dep. adminstr. Health Care Financing Adminstrn., Washington, 1993-96; pres., chmn. Health Right, Inc., Meriden, Conn., 1996-99; vis. prof. Robert F. Wagner Grad. Sch. Pub. Svc., NYU, 1999—2001. Commr. Joint Com. on Accreditation Hosps., Chgo., 1989-93, chair, 1991-92; mem., co-chair strategic framework bd. Nat. Forum on Health Care Quality Measurement and Reporting, 2000—01; Fulbright lectr. faculty medicine Eduardo Mondlane U., Maputo, Mozambique, 2001-04. Contbr. numerous articles to profl. jours. Bd. dirs. The Ivoryton Playhouse Fedn., Inc., 1990-92, The Connecticut River Mus., 1990-93, Hartford Stage, 1990-93; mem. Dem. Town Com., Essex, Conn., 1982-89; vol. The William J. Clinton Found., Mozambique, 2000-04. Recipient Superior Svc. award HHS, Washington, 1982; Royal Soc. Medicine Found. fellow, London, 1973; Fulbright scholar, 1959-60. Mem. ACP (master, regent 1984-90), Inst. Medicine (vice chmn. com. for evaluation of PEPPAR implementation 2005—), Nat. Acad. Scis., Phi Beta Kappa, Alpha Omega Alpha. Episcopalian. Avocations: sailing, cooking, gardening.

SMOAK, RANDOLPH DUNCAN, JR., surgeon; b. Bamberg, SC, May 5, 1933; MD, Med. Coll. S.C., 1959. Diplomate Am. Bd. Surgery. Intern Grady Meml. Hosp., Atlanta, 1959-60; resident surgery Med. U. S.C.-Teaching Hosps., 1962-65, resident, tchg. fellow, 1965-66; fellow surgery MD Anderson Cancer Ctr., Houston, 1966-67; surg. staff Orangeburg (S.C.) Calhoun Regional Hosp., 1967-87, emeritus staff, 1987; clin. prof. surgery Med. U. S.C., Charleston, 1987—, U.S.C. Sch. Medicine, Columbia, 86—. Fellow ACS; mem. AMA (pres. 2000-01), So. Med. Assn., Soc. Head and Neck Surgeons, So. Soc. Clin. Surgeons, Soc. Clin. Oncology. Office: 112 Cloister Cove Orangeburg SC 29115 Personal E-mail: randysmoak@earthlink.net. Business E-Mail: smoak@ama-assn.org.

SMOLENSKI, LISABETH ANN, physician; b. Pitts., Oct. 1, 1950; d. Anthony Edward and Betty Jean (Gross) S.; m. William Ward Daniels, May 24, 1980; 1 child, Kathryn Elizabeth. BA, Carlow Coll., Pitts., 1972; MD, Hahnemann U., Phila., 1982. Diplomate Am. Bd. Family Practice. Resident in family practice West Jersey Health Sys., Voorhees, N.J., 1982-85; pvt. practice, Somerville, Tenn., 1985-90, Memphis, 1990—2003; with Spectrum Pain Clinics, Franklin-Nashville, Tenn., 2003—04, Cumberland Back Pain Clinic PC, Cookeville, Tenn., 2005—, Clarksville, Tenn., 2005—. Sec. exec. com. med. staff Meth. Hosp. Somerville, 1988-90. Fellow: Am. Acad. Family Physicians. Republican. Avocation: reading. Office: Cumberland Back Pain Clinic PC 271 Med Park Dr Clarksville TN 37043-6310 also: Cumberland Back Pain Clinic PC 120 Walnut Commons Ln Ste D Cookeville TN 38501-6037 Office Phone: 931-520-8104, 931-647-5747. Business E-Mail: lsmolenski@painmgmtcenters.com.

SMOLIANSKIENE, GRAŽINA, chemist, researcher; b. Vilnius, Lithuania, Sept. 15, 1968; d. Antanas Valužis and Božena Valužiene; m. Genadijus Smolanskis (div.); 1 child, Martynas Smolianskis. M, Vilnius U., 1991; D, Vilnius Gediminas Tech. U., 1999. Specialist Inst. Hygiene, Vilnius, 1991—2000, rschr., 2000—05; sr. rschr. Vilnius U., 2005—11. Lectr. Vilnius U., 2002—; mem. sci. bd. Inst. Hygiene, 2004—09; convenor 4th Lithuanian Women's Congress, Vilnius, 2005. Contbr. articles to profl. jours. Vol. Vilnius Women's Ho., 1997—99, bd. dirs., 2004—08, Lithuanian Sci. Soc., Vilnius, 2002—03, Lithuanian Soc. Young Rschrs., Vilnius, 2002—03. Recipient Silver medal, Ministry Edn., Vilnius, 1986. Roman Catholic. Avocations: reading, travel. Home: Tuju 7-57 LT 05116 Lithuania Personal E-mail: gina@post.skynet.lt.

SMOLLER, BRUCE MELVYN, psychiatrist; b. Chgo., Sept. 19, 1944; s. Norman and Beatrice Betty (Janows) Smoller; m. Cosette Nieporent, Aug. 20, 1967; children: Jamie, Lauren. AB, Cornell U., 1965; MD, Tulane U., 1969. Diplomate Am. Bd. Psychiatry and Neurology. Intern Maimonides Med. Ctr., NYC, 1969-70; resident in orthopedic surgery Einstein Med. Ctr., NYC, 1970-73; resident in psychiatry Cornell Med. Ctr., NYC, 1973-76; pvt. practice in psychiatry with emphasis on clin. and rsch. aspects of pain Bethesda, Md., 1976—; chmn. dept. psychiatry Holy Cross Hosp., Silver Spring, Md., 1980-83; assoc. clin. prof. psychiatry George Washington U., 1977-91, clin. prof. psychiatry, 1991—. Cons. NIH, 1979—2001. Co-author: Pain Control: The Bethesda Program; editor: Md. Medicine, The State Med. Soc.'s Jour. With Med. Corps USAR, 1970—78. Mem.: Md. State Med. Soc. (pres. 2007—08), Montgomery County Med. Soc. (pres. 2004—05). Office: 5530 Wisconsin Ave Bethesda MD 20815-4404 Office Phone: 301-951-4466. E-mail: bsmoller@radix.net.

SMOOT, JOHN D., plastic surgeon; MD, U. Utah. Diplomate Am. Bd. Plastic Surgery. Chief plastic surgery Scripps Meml. Hosp.; plastic surgeon San Diego Plastic Surgery Ctr., Calif. Fellow: ACS; mem.: Calif. Soc. of Plastic Surgeons, Am. Soc. for Aesthetic Plastic Surgery, Am. Soc. of Plastic Surgeons. Office: San Diego Plastic Surgery Center Ste 300 and 380 9850 Genesee Ave La Jolla CA 92037 Office Phone: 858-587-9850. Home Fax: 858-622-2066.

SMOOT, WENDELL MCMEANS, III, plastic surgeon, educator; MD, U. UT, 1970. Diplomate Am. Bd. Surgery, 1977, Am. Bd. Plastic Surgery. Intern Univ. UT, 1970—71, asst. clin. prof. Sch. of Medicine; hosp. affiliations include Mercy Hosp., Children's Hosp. LA; plastic surgeon Scripps Meml. Hosp. La Jolla, Sharp Coronado Hosp. and Health Care Ctr., Sharp Meml. Hosp., San Diego Plastic Surgery Ctr. Recipient MD Nationwide Top Doctor award. Mem.: ACS, Am. Soc. of Plastic Surgeons, Am. Soc. for Aesthetic Plastic Surgery, Am. Soc. for Plastic and Reconstructive Surgeons. Office: Scripps Memorial-Hospital La Jolla Ste 28 9888 Genesee Ave La Jolla CA 92037 Office Phone: 858-626-4123.

SMULIAN, JOHN C., obstetrician; MD, Tulane U. Sch. Medicine Sch., New Orleans, LA, 1985; MPH, Tulane U. Pub. Health and Tropical Medicine, New Orleans, LA, 1985. Diplomate Am. Bd. Obstetrics Gynecology, 1991, cert. maternal fetal medicine Am. Bd. Obstetrics Gynecology, 1997. Prof., dept. obstetrics, gynecology reproductive scis. UMDNJ-Robert Wood Johnson Med. Sch., New Brunswick, NJ, 1994—2007; vice chairman, dept ob-gyn, chief-divsn. maternal fetal medicine Lehigh Valley Health Network, Allentown, Pa., 2008—; prof. dept. ob-gyn. Pa. State U. Coll. Medicine, 2008—. Author more than 120 rsch. articles in maternal fetal medicine. Named one of NJ. Top Dr., NJ. Mag., 2006—07. Office: Lehigh Valley Hosp Cedar Crest & I-78 Allentown PA 18105 *

SMYTHE, CHEVES MCCORD, internist, geriatrician, educator, dean; b. May 25, 1924; Student, Yale Coll., 1942—43; MD cum laude, Harvard, 1947. Diplomate Am. Bd. Internal Medicine, Am. Bd. Geriatrics. Intern, asst. resident Harvard Med. Svc., Boston City Hosp., 1947—49, chief resident, 1954—55; resident chest svc. Bellevue, 1949—50; rsch. fellow Presbyn. Hosp., NYC, 1950—52; assoc. medicine Med. Coll. S.C. Sch. Medicine, 1956—58, asst. prof. medicine, 1958—60, assoc. prof. medicine, 1960—66, dean, 1963—65; attending physician Wesley Meml., Cook County North Side VA Hosps., Chgo., 1967—70; with Aga Khan U. Hosp., Karachi, Pakistan, 1990—91; dean faculty health scis., prof. medicine Aga Khan U., Karachi, Pakistan, 1982—85, prof., chmn. dept. medicine, 1990—91; chief Med. Svcs. at LBJ Hosp., Houston, 1991—95; prof. divsn. gen. medicine dept. internal medicine U. Tex. Med. Sch., Houston, 1970—, dean, 1970—75, dean pro tem, 1995—96. Assoc. med. dir. Hermann Hosp., 1996—. Bd. dirs. Assn. Am. Assoc. Med. Colls., Office: U Tex Med Sch 6431 Fannin St 1-108 Houston TX 77030-1501

SNAREY, JOHN ROBERT, psychologist, educator; BS, Geneva Coll., Beaver Falls, Pa., 1969; MA, Wheaton Coll., Ill., 1973; EdD, Harvard U., Cambridge, Mass., 1982. Postdoctoral rsch. fellow dept. psychiatry Harvard U., Cambridge, Mass., 1982-84; assoc. rsch. psychologist Wellesley Coll., 1984-85; assoc. prof. human devel. and edn. Northwestern U., Evanston, Ill., 1985-87; prof. human devel. and ethics Sch. Theology and dept. psychology Emory U., Atlanta, 1987—. Mem. senate Emory U., 2001—05, pres., 2003—04, dir. moral cognition and devel. lab., 2005—. Author: How Fathers Care for the Next Generation, 1993; contbr. articles to profl. jours.; editor: Conflict and Continuity: A History of Ideas on Social Equality and Human Development, 1981, Remembrance of Lawrence Kohlberg, 1988, Race-ing Moral Formation: African Am. Perspectives on Care and Justice, 2004; mem. editl. bd. Harvard Ednl. Rev., 1979—81, Jour. Psychology and Theology, 1986—90, Jour. Moral Edn., 1998—, Am. Ednl. Rsch. Jour., 2001—04, mem. editl. adv. bd. Lawrence Erlbaum Assocs., 1988—90. Recipient Exemplary Dissertation award, Nat. Coun. Social Studies, 1982, Kuhmereker Dissertation award, Assn. Moral Edn., 1983, Outstanding Human Devel. Rsch. award, Am. Ednl. Rsch. Assn., 1988, James D. Moran Book award, Assn. Family and Consumer Sci., 1994, Marie C. Keel, Excellence in Mentoring award, 2003, Albert Levy Sci. Rsch. award, 2007. Fellow: APA, Am. Ednl. Rsch. Assn. (divsn. E exec. bd. 1990—2000, moral devel. and edn. spl. interest group co-chair 1994—96, sec. divsn. E 1997—99, Moral Devel. and Edn. Book award 2006); mem.: Assn. Moral Edn. (exec. bd. 1986—2007, program chair 1997, treas. 2001—04, pres. 2004—07). Office: Emory University Candler and Ethics Bldg 1531 Dickey Dr Ste 354 Atlanta GA 30322-0001 Office Phone: 404-727-4185. Business E-Mail: jsnarey@emory.edu.

SNASHALL, DAVID CHARLES, physician; b. Buckhurst Hill, England, Feb. 3, 1943; s. Cyril Francis and Phyllis Mary (Hibbitt) S.; children: Lesley, Rebecca, Corinna. MB ChB, U. Edinburgh, 1968; MSc, U. London, 1979; LLM, U. Cardiff, 1996. Resident various hosps., England, Can., France, 1968-75; chief med. officer Majes Project, Peru, 1975-77, Mufindi Project, Tanzania, 1981-82; sr. lectr. United Med. Schs., London, 1982—; clin. dir. occupl. health dept. Guy's and St. Thomas Hosp. Trust, 1993—; chief med. advisor Fgn. & Commonwealth Office, England, 1989-98, U.K. Health and Safety Exec., 1998—2003, chair rsch. ethics com., 2003—. Mem. Internat. Com. Occupl. Health, 1980, Gen. Med. Coun., England, 1989—96, 1999—2003; mem. Ct. of Govs. London Sch. Hygiene, 1995—99; chmn. Internat. Com. Andean Aid, England, 1992—2000; prof. occupl. medicine Kings Coll., London, 2011—. Fellow: Faculty Occupl. Medicine (pres. 2005—08), Royal Coll. Physicians; mem.: British Med. Assn. Office: St Thomas Hosp Dept Occupational Health London SE1 7EH England E-mail: david.snashall@gstt.nhs.uk.

SNELL, RICHARD SAXON, anatomist; b. Richmond, Surrey, Eng., May 3, 1925; came to U.S., 1963; s. Claude Saxon and Daisy Lilian S.; m. Maureen Cashin, June 4, 1949; children: Georgina Sara, Nicola Ann, Melanie Jane, Richard Robin, Charles Edward. MB, BS, Kings Coll., U. London, 1949, PhD, 1955, MD, 1961. House surgeon Sir Cecil P.G. Wakeley, Kings Coll. Hosp. and Belgrave Hosp. for Children, London, 1948-49; lectr. anatomy Kings Coll., U. London, 1949-59, U. Durham, Eng., 1959-63; asst. prof. anatomy and medicine Yale U., 1963-65, assoc. prof., 1965-67, vis. prof. anatomy, 1969; prof., chmn. dept. anatomy N.J. Coll. Medicine and Dentistry, Jersey City, 1967-69; vis. prof. anatomy Harvard U., 1970, 71, 80, 86; prof. anatomy Coll. Medicine, U. Ariz., Tucson, 1970; prof., chmn. dept. anatomy George Washington U. Med. Ctr., Washington, 1972-88, prof. emeritus, 1988—. Author: Clinical Embryology for Medical Students, 1972, 3d edit., 1983, Clinical Anatomy for Medical Students, 1973, 6th edit., 2000, Clinical Anatomy, 7th edit., 2003, Clinical Anatomy By Regions, 8th edit., 2007, Atlas of Normal Radiographic Anatomy, 1976, Atlas of Clinical Anatomy, 1978, Gross Anatomy Dissector, 1978, Clinical Neuroanatomy, 1980, 7th edit., 2009, Student's Aid to Gross Anatomy, 1986, Clinical Anatomy for Anesthesiologists, 1988, Clinical Anatomy of the Eye, 1989, 2d edit., 1997, Gross Anatomy: A Review with Questions and Explanations, 1990, Neuroanatomy: A Review with questions and Explanations, 1992, Clinical Anatomy for Emergency Medicine, 1993, Clinical Neuroanatomy: An Illustrated Review with Questions and Explanations, 3d edit., 2001, Clinical Anatomy: An Illustrated Review with Questions and Explanations, 4th edit., 2003 Clinical Anatomy by Systems, 2006; contbr. articles to med. jours. Med. Rsch. Coun. grantee, 1959; NIH grantee, 1963-65 Mem. Anat. Soc. Gt. Britain, Am. Soc. Anatomists, Am. Assn. Clin. Anatomists Cleave. (Hon. Mem. award, 2009), Alpha Omega Alpha. Home: 518 Boston Post Rd Madison CT 06443-2930

SNIDER, JAMES RHODES, radiologist; b. Pawnee, Okla., May 16, 1931; s. John Henry and Gladys Opal (Rhodes) S.; m. Lynadell Vivion, Dec. 27, 1954; children: Jon, Jan. BS, U. Okla., 1953, MD, 1956. Intern Edward Meyer Meml. Hosp., Buffalo, 1956—57; resident radiology U. Okla. Med. Ctr., 1959—62; radiologist Holt-Krock Clinic and Sparks Regional Med. Ctr., Ft. Smith, Ark., 1962—66; dir. Fairfield Comty. Land Co., Little Rock, 1968—87, Fairfield Comtys., Inc., 1968—87. Assoc. editor: Computerized Tomography, 1976—88. Mem. Ark. Bd. Pub. Welfare, 1969—71; bd. visitors U. Okla.; bd. dirs. U. Okla. Assn., 1967—70, U. Okla. Alumni Devel. Fund, 1970—74. Lt. comdr. USNR, 1957—62. Mem.: AMA, Am. Roentgen Ray Soc., Radiol. Soc. N.Am., Am. Coll. Radiology, Phi Beta Kappa, Alpha Epsilon Delta, Beta Theta Pi. Home: 5814 Cliff Dr Fort Smith AR 72903-3845 Office: 1500 Dodson Ave Fort Smith AR 72901-5128

SNIFFEN, MICHAEL JOSEPH, hospital administrator; b. Ossining, NY, June 16, 1949; s. John Francis and Mary Agnes (Madden) S.; m. Anne Marie Gillick; children: Kevin, Kristina. BS, Fordham U., 1971; MBA in Hosp. Adminstrn., Baruch Coll., 1977. Dir. of fin. planning Westchester div. N.Y. Hosp., White Plains, N.Y., 1971-74, assoc. dir. NYC, 1974-80, sr. assoc. dir., assoc. dean Cornell Med. Ctr., 1980-87; pres., CEO Overlook Hosp., Summit, NJ, 1987-96; exec. v.p., COO Atlantic Health Sys., Florham Park, NJ, 1996—2000; pres., CEO BSCPC, Hoboken, NJ, 2001—05; mng. ptnr. The Manchester Group, Hoboken, 2005—. Exec. dir. Cornell Health Policy Program, N.Y.C., 1984-87; adminstr. program Commonwealth Fund, N.Y.C., 1978-81; adv. bd. Robert Wood Johnson Found.-Teaching Nursing Home Program, Princeton, N.J., 1980-86. Vol. March of Dimes, Tarrytown, N.Y., 1984-88; bd. dirs. St. Columbans Sch., Peekskill, N.Y., 1981-84; mem. various svc. clubs, Westchester County, N.Y., 1976-91. Fellow Am. Coll. Healthcare Execs.; mem. Hosp. Fin. Mgmt. Assn. (advanced mem.), Echo Lake Country Club (Westfield, N.J.), Baltusrol Country Club (Springfield, N.J.). Roman Catholic. Avocations: golf, college basketball. Home: 47 Murray Hill Sq New Providence NJ 07974-1531 Home Phone: 201-798-7396; Office Phone: 732-887-4012. Personal E-mail: michael_sniffen@hotmail.com.

SNODGRASS, ALISON MARION, pediatrician; MRCPCH, Nat. U. Singapore, MMed in Pediat. Medicine, MBBS. Med. officer Singapore Health Svcs., 2002—06, registrar, pediat. medicine, 2006—10, assoc. cons., 2010—. Contbr. scientific papers to profl. jours. Mem. Cath. Med. Guild, Singapore, 2001—. Recipient Nat. Youth Achievement award, MCYS Singapore, 1994, Excellence award, Eurasian Assn. Singapore, 1995, 2001, Prime Ministers Book prize, Singapore, 1996, Deans List award, Faculty Medicine, Nat. U. Singapore, 1997, 1999, 2001, Acad. Medicine Silver medal, Nat. U. Singapore, 1997, Oliveiro Meml. Gold medal, 1997, Obstetrics and Gynaecology Book prize, 2000, Gibbs Gold medal, 2001, Nestle Book prize, 2001, Wong Hock Boon Gold medal, 2006. Mem.: Singapore Pediat. Soc., MENSA.

SNODGRASS, CHRISTINE AVERIL, retired obstetrician; b. Staines, Middlesex, Eng., Dec. 19, 1933; d. Sidney Cyril Poole and Violet E. Joscelyne Barnes; m. Graeme J. A. Inglis Snodgrass, Sept. 4, 1958 (div. 1963). MBChB, Edinburgh U., Scotland, 1958, MD with high commendation, 1968, MA in Archaeology with honors, 1994. Rsch. asst., hon. sr. registrar Hammersmith Hosp., London, 1964—69; lectr., sr. registrar Univ. Coll. Hosp., London; cons., lectr. Newcastle (Eng.) U. Hosps., 1971—93; dir. med. Newcastle Gen. Hosp., 1977—93, clin. dept. ob-gyn, 1987—93; ret., 1993. Mem. faculty bd. Newcastle U. Med. Sch., 1975—90. Contbr. articles to profl. jours. Grantee, Med. Rsch. Coun., 1965—68. Fellow: Royal Coll. Ob-gyn. Avocations: travel, photography, botany, archaeology.

SNOW, DAVID B., JR., pharmaceutical executive; b. Manchester, NH, Nov. 30, 1954; BS in Sci. & Econs., Bates Coll., 1976; MS in Healthcare Adminstrn., Duke U., 1978. Sr. v.p. Am. Internat. Healthcare, Rockville, Md., 1988—89; pres., CEO Managed Healthcare Systems, Reston, Va., 1989—93; exec. v.p. Oxford Health Plans, Norwalk, Conn., 1993—98, WellChoice, Inc. (formerly Empire Blue-Cross & BlueShield), NYC, 1999—2001, pres., CEO, 2001—03; pres. Medco Health Solutions, Inc., Franklin Lakes, NJ, 2003—06, chmn., CEO, 2003—. Office: Medco Health 100 Parsons Pond Franklin Lakes NJ 07417 *

SNOW, JAMES BYRON, JR., otolaryngologist, research administrator, educator; b. Oklahoma City, Mar. 12, 1932; s. James B. and Charlotte Louise (Andersen) S.; m. Sallie Lee Ricker, July 16, 1954; children: James B., John Andrew, Sallie Lee Louise. BS, U. Okla., Norman, 1953; MD cum laude, Harvard U., Cambridge, Mass., 1956; MA (hon.), U. Pa., Phila., 1973. Diplomate Am. Bd. Otolaryngology (dir. 1972-90). Intern Johns Hopkins Hosp., Balt., 1956-57; resident Mass. Eye and Ear Infirmary, Boston, 1957-60; prof., head dept. otorhinolaryngology Sch. Medicine U. Okla., Oklahoma City, 1962-72; prof., chmn. dept. otorhinolaryngology and human communication U. Pa., 1972-90; dir. Nat. Inst. on Deafness and Other Comm. Disorders, NIH, Bethesda, Md., 1990-97; convener, corr. Tinnitus Rsch. Consortium, 1998—. Mem. nat. adv. coun. neurol. and communicative disorders and stroke NIH, 1972-76, 82-86; chmn. Nat. Com. Rsch. Neurol. and Communicative Disorders, 1979-80. Editor: Am. Jour. Otolaryngology, 1979-83; Contbr. articles to sci. and profl. jours. Officer, M.C., U.S, Army, 1960-62. Recipient Regents award for superior tchg. U. Okla., 1970, Golden award Internat. Fedn. Otorhinolaryngological Socs., 1989, Disting. Achievement award Deafness Rsch. Found., 1993, Presdl. Meritorious Exec. Rank award, 1994; named to Soc. Scholars Johns Hopkins U., 1991. Fellow Japan Broncho-Esophagological Soc. (hon.), Am. Laryngological Assn. (hon.); mem. ACS (regent 1982-90), AMA (coun. on sci. affairs 1975-86), Soc. Univ. Otolaryngologists (pres. 1975), Am. Acad. Otolaryngology-Head and Neck Surgery, Assn. Acad. Depts. Otolaryngology (pres. 1981-82), Am. Laryngol., Rhinol. and Otol. Soc., Am. Otol. Soc. (merit award 2003), Am. Laryngol. Assn. (editor 1983-89, pres. 1990-91), Am. Broncho-Esophagol. Assn. (editor trans. 1973-77, pres. 1979), Collegium Otorhinolaryngologicum (pres. 2000-02), Phi Beta Kappa, Alpha Omega Alpha. Home: 327 Greenbriar Ln West Grove PA 19390-9490 Personal E-mail: jandssnow@comcast.net.

SNOWDON, JOHN AMBLER, psychiatrist; b. Warlingham, Eng., Apr. 30, 1940; arrived in Australia, 1977; s. Edward Walter and Barbara Joan (Smart) S.; m. Elizabeth Joan Ascott, June 16, 1979; children: David, Michael, Carolyn. MA, MB, BChir, Cambridge U., Eng., 1964; MPhil, U. London, 1975; MD, U NSW, 1998. House officer St. Thomas' Hosp., London, 1965-66; registrar Maudsley Hosp., London, 1971-75; med. supt. psychiat. unit Prince of Wales Hosp., Sydney, 1977-83; dir. cmty. health Eastern Sydney, 1983-89; psychogeriatrician Eastern Sydney Health Svc., 1989-92; dir. psychogeriat. svcs. Ctrl. Sydney, 1992—2008; clin. assoc. prof. U. Sydney, 1992—2003, clin. prof., 2003—; old age psychiatrist Sydney South West Area Health Svc., 2008—. Contbr. articles to profl. jours., chpts. to books. Chmn. Alzheimer's Assn. NSW, Sydney, 1981-82, sect. Psychiatry of Old Age, 1995-98; faculty psych. of Old Age, Australia, New Zealand, 1999-2001. Fellow Royal Australian Coll. Physicians, Royal Coll. Psychiatrists, Royal Australian and New Zealand Coll. Psychiatrists; mem. Psychiat. Rehab. Assn. Sydney (vice chmn. 1996—2008), Order of Australia (AM). Avocations: tennis, theater. Office: Concord Hosp Sydney NSW 2139 Australia Business E-Mail: jsnowdon@mail.usyd.edu.au.

SNUSTAD, DONALD PETER, geneticist, educator; b. Bemidji, Minn., Apr. 6, 1940; s. Ole Snustad and Vera Grife; m. Judy Adams; 1 child, Eric. PhD, U. Calif., Davis, 1965. Prof. genetics U. Minn., St. Paul, 1965—2008. Author: (textbook) Principles of Genetics. Recipient Horse T. Morse-Amoco award, U. Minn., 1984, Stanley Dagley Meml. Tchg. award, 1990; NSF Coop. Grad. fellowship, 1963, NIH Predoc. Trainee fellowship, 1964—65, NSF & NIH Rsch. grants, 1967—2001. Fellow: AAAS (Elected Fellow Soc. 2005). Achievements include research in bacteriophage and plant genetics. Office: Univ Minnesota 1445 Gortner Ave Saint Paul MN 55108

SNYDER, DENISE, nutritionist, researcher; MS in Nutrition, U. Pa., 1997. Clinical trials mgr. Duke U. Sch. Nursing, 2000—. Office: Duke University School of Nursing Clipp Bldg Rm 1057 Durham NC 27710 Office Phone: 919-660-7580. E-mail: snyde023@mc.duke.edu.

SNYDER, EDWARD L., medical researcher; BA, SUNY, Binghamton, 1967, MA, 1969; MD, NY Med. Coll., 1973. Cert. internal medicine. Fellowship, hematology, transfusion medicine Montefiore Hosp.; pres. Am. Assn. Blood Banks; med. dir. Frisbee Lab.; cons. food drug adminstrn. med. devices adv. com. Hematology and Pathology Devices Panel; chmn. Be The Match Found.; chmn. vol. bd. Nat Marrow Donor Program; dir., blood bank, apheresis svc. Yale-New Haven Hosp., asst. chief, assoc. chmn. clin. affairs dept.; prof. lab. medicine Yale U. Sch. Medicine, assoc. chair clin. affairs, dept. lab. medicine. Mem. bd. dirs. Pall Corp., East Hills, NY, 2000—. Office: Yale University School of Medicine CB 459 789 Howard Ave New Haven CT 06519-1304 Office Phone: 203-688-2441. Office Fax: 203-688-2748. Business E-Mail: edward.snyder@yale.edu. *

SNYDER, EVAN, stem cell biologist, neuroscientist, physician, educator; MD in Neuroscience & Linguistics, PhD in Neuroscience & Linguistics, U. Pa., 1980. Resident & fellow in pediatrics, neurology & newborn intensive care, Children's Hosp. Harvard Medical School, Boston, postdoctoral rsch., faculty, Children's Hosp., 1980—2003, instr. neurology, 1992—96, asst. prof. neurology, 1996—2003; dir. stem cell & regeneration program Burnham Inst., La Jolla, Calif., 2003, prof. Contbr. articles in high profl. jours. Office: Burnham Inst Mail Stop 7261 10901 N Torrey Pines Rd La Jolla CA 92037 Fax: 858-646-3199. Business E-Mail: esnyder@burnham.org.

SNYDER, PETER J., endocrinologist, educator; MD, Harvard Coll. Cert. endocrinology 1972. Intern Beth Israel Hosp., Boston, resident; fellow Hosp. of The Univ. of Pa.; med. dir. Penn Pituitary Ctr.; prof. medicine Penn Medicine. Named an The Top Docs, Phila. Mag., 2010—11; named one of The Best Doctors in Am., 2003—10, The Top Docs, Phila. Mag., 2004—08, America's Top Doctor, 2008, 2010. Office: Penn Pituitary Center Perelman Center for Advanced Medicine West Pavilion 4th Fl 3400 Civic Ctr Blvd Philadelphia PA 19104

SNYDER, RICHARD W., pulmonologist; Attended, U. Pa.; MD, Temple U. Diplomate Am. Bd. Internal Medicine, Am. Bd. Internal Medicine-pulmonary disease, Am. Bd. Internal Medicine-critical care medicine. Med. dir. critical care Abington Meml. Hosp. Office: Abington Memorial Hospital Pulmonary and Critical Care 1235 Old York Rd Ste G12 Abington PA 19001 Office Phone: 215-517-1200. Office Fax: 215-517-1219.

SNYDER, SOLOMON HALBERT, neuroscientist, educator; b. Washington, Dec. 26, 1938, s. Samuel Simon and Patricia (Yakerson) Snyder; m. Elaine Borko, June 10, 1962; children: Judith Rhea, Deborah Lynn. B, Georgetown U., Washington, 1958, DSc (hon.), 1986; MD cum laude, Georgetown U. Med. Sch., 1962; PhD (hon.), Ben Gurion U., Israel, 1990; DSc (hon.), Northwestern U., 1981, Technion Inst., Israel, 2002, Mt. Sinai Med. Sch., 2004, U. Md., 2006, Charles U., Prague, 2008; DPhil (hon.), Albany Med. Coll., 1998, Ohio State U., 2011. Intern Kaiser Found. Hosp., San Francisco, 1962-63; rsch. assoc. Nat. Inst. Mental Health, NIH, Bethesda, Md., 1963-65; asst. resident dept. psychiatry Johns Hopkins Hosp., Balt., 1965-68; assoc. prof. pharmacology/experimental therapeutics, assoc. prof. psychiatry Johns Hopkins Sch. Medicine, 1968-70, prof., 1970-77, disting. svc. prof. psychiatry/pharmacology, 1977-80, disting. svc. prof. psychiatry, pharmacology & neurosci., dir. dept. neurosci., 1980—; dir. dept. neurosci. Johns Hopkins Med. Sch., 1980—2006. Wellcome disting. prof. U. Wash., 1999. Author: (books) Uses of Marijuana, 1971, Madness and the Brain, 1973, The Troubled Mind, 1976, Biologic Aspects of Mental Disorder, 1980, Drugs and the Brain, 1986, Brainstorming, 1989, Science and Psychiatry, 2008; mem. editl bd. Molecular Medicine, FASEB Jour., Neurosci., Jour. Molecular Neurosci., Molecular Psychiatry, Jour. Nervous & Mental Diseases, Nitric Oxide Biology & Chemistry; contbr. articles to profl. jours. Recipient Outstanding Scientist award, Md. Acad. Scis., 1969, A.E. Bennett award, Soc. Biol. Psychiatry, 1970, Gaddum award, Brit. Pharm. Soc., 1974, F.O. Schmitt award in neuroscis., MIT, 1974, Rennebohm award, U. Wis., 1976, Stanley Dean award, Am. Coll. Psychiatrists, 1978, Lasker award for clin. med. rsch., 1978, Wolf Found. prize in medicine, Israel, 1983, Dickson prize, U. Pitts., 1983, Sci. Achievement award, AMA, 1985, Ciba-Giegy-Drew award in biomed. rsch., 1985, Edward J. Sachar Meml. award, Columbia U., 1986, Sense of Smell award, Fragrance Rsch. Found., 1987, J. Allyn Taylor prize, 1990, Pasarow Found. award for biomed. rsch., 1991, Bower award, Franklin Inst., 1991, Joseph Priestley prize, Dickinson Coll., 1992, Baxter award, Am. Assn. Med. Colleges, 1995, Bristol-Myers-Squibb award for disting. achievement in neurosci., 1996, Gerard prize, Soc. Neurosci., 2000, Salmon prize, NY Acad. Medicine, 2001, Lieber prize, Nat. Alliance Rsch. Schizophrenia & Depression, 2001, Goldman-Rakic prize, 2003, Nat. Medal of Sci., 2003, Edward Perl award, U. NC, 2007, Albany Med. Ctr. prize in medicine & biomed. rsch., 2007. Fellow: Am. Philos. Soc., Am. Acad. Arts & Scis., Am. Coll. Neuropsychopharmacology (Daniel Efron award 1974), Am. Psychiat. Assn. (Hofheimer award 1972, Disting. Svc. award 1989, Judd Marmor award 2000); mem.: NAS (Sarnat prize in mental health 2001), Inst. Medicine, Am. Pharmacology Soc. (John Jacob Abel award 1970), Am. Soc. Biol. Chemists, Soc. Neurosci. (pres. 1979—80, Presdl. lectr. 2000). Office: Johns Hopkins U Sch Medicine Dept Neurosci 725 N Wolfe St Rm 813 WBSB Baltimore MD 21205-2105 Office Phone: 410-955-3024. Office Fax: 410-955-3623. Business E-Mail: ssnyder@jhmi.edu.

SNYDER, STEPHEN JOSEPH, surgeon, director; b. Ellensberg, Washington, Aug. 19, 1947; MD, U. Oreg., 1969. Cert. orthop. surgeon U. So. Calif., 1981. Surgeon, dir. So. Calif. Orthop. Inst., 1981—. Inventor, rschr., product developer cons. REDYNS Med., 1981; founder & dir. SCOI, 1991. Mem.: Western Orthop. Assn., Twentieth Century Orthop. Assn., Am. Acad. Orthop. Surgeons, Arthroscopy Assn. N. America (Recipient Outstanding Tchg. award), Am. Shoulder & Elbow Surgeons. Avocations: bicycling, golf, fly fishing. Office: 6815 Noble Ave Ste 300 Van Nuys CA 91405 Office Fax: 818-901-6685. Personal E-mail: sjsscoi@yahoo.com.

SNYDERMAN, NANCY, broadcast journalist, physician; b. St. Louis, 1952; m. Doug Snyderman; 3 children. BA in Microbiology, Ind. U.; MD, U. Nebr. Coll. Medicine, 1977, PhD in Medicine. Diplomate American Bd. Otolaryngology. Resident pediat./ear, nose & throat surgery U. Pitts. Med. Ctr.; dir. head and neck surgery U. Ark. for Med. Scis., Little Rock, 1983—87; surg. practice Calif. Pacific Med. Ctr., San Francisco; med. corr. ABC News, 1987—2003; v.p. med. affairs corp. staff Johnson & Johnson, 2003—06; chief med. editor NBC News, 2006—. Author: Dr. Nancy Snyderman's Guide to Good Health for Women Over Forty, 1996, Necessary Journeys: Letting Ourselves Learn from Life, 2001, Medical Myths That Can Kill You And the 101 Truths That Will Save, Extend and Improve Your Life, 2008; co-author: Girl in the Mirror: Mothers and Daughters in the Years of Adolescence, 2003; monthly columnist Good Housekeeping mag. Mem.: American Acad. Otolaryngology-Head & Neck Surgery (bd. dirs.). Office: NBC 30 Rockefeller Plz New York NY 10112 *

SNYDERMAN, RALPH, medical educator, physician; b. Bklyn., Mar. 13, 1940; 1 child, Theodore Benjamin. BS, Washington Coll., Chestertown, Md., 1961; MD magna cum laude, SUNY, Bklyn., 1965, DSc (hon.) Health Sci. Ctr., 1996. Diplomate Am. Bd. Internal Medicine, Am. Bd. Allergy and Immunology. Intern Duke U. Hosp., Durham, 1965-66, med. resident, 1966-67; public health officer NIH, 1967-72; Howard Hughes med. investigator, asst. prof. medicine and immunology Duke U. Hosp., Durham, N.C., 1972-74, assoc. prof., 1974-77, chief divsn. rheumatology and immunology, 1975-87, prof. medicine and immunology, 1980-87, Frederic M. Hanes prof. medicine and immunology, 1984-87, adj. prof. medicine, 1987-89; surgeon USPHS, NIH, Bethesda, Md., 1967-69; sr. staff fellow Nat. Inst. Dental Rsch., NIH, Bethesda, Md., 1969-70, sr. investigator immunology sect. lab. microbiology and immunology, 1970-72, chief divsn. rheumatology Durham VA Hosp., Bethesda, Md., 1972-75; v.p. med. rsch. and devel. Genentech, Inc., South San Francisco, Calif., 1987-88, sr. v.p. med. rsch. and devel., 1988-89; chancellor for health affairs, dean Sch. Medicine Duke University, Durham, NC, 1989—2004, James B. Duke prof. medicine, 1989—2004; pres., CEO Duke U. Health Sys., Durham, 1998—2004. Howard Hughes med. investigator, Durham, 1972-77; dir. Lab Immune Effector Function, Howard Hughes Med. Inst., Durham, 1977-87; adj. prof. medicine U. Calif., San Francisco, 1987-89; bd. dirs. The Procter & Gamble Co., 1995-. Editor: Contemporary Topics in Immunobiology, 1979, Inflammation: Basic Concepts and Clinical Correlates, 1988, 2nd edit., 1992, Medical Clinics of North America, 1997, Journ. Integrated Med., 1997, Proceedings of Amer. Physician, 1997; contbr. articles to profl. jours. Recipient McLaughlin award, 1978, Alexander von Humboldt award Fed. Republic Germany, 1985, award for lifetime achievements in inflammation rsch. Ciba-Geigy Morris Ziff, 1992, Bonazinga award Soc. for Leukocyte Biology, 1993, Disting. Alumni Achievement award SUNY Bklyn., 1995, Disting. Alumni achievement award Washington Coll., 1995, Disting. Alumni citation, 1996, Lifetime Achievement award Arthritis Found., Eastern Reg., 1997, Lifetime Achievement award Argentine Nat. Acad. Medicine, 1998, others. Mem.: NAS, Am. Acad. Arts and Scis., Soc. for Med. Adminstrs., Assn. Am. Med. Colls. (chair task force on clin. rsch. 1998, chmn. coun. deans 1999—2000, chmn. 2001—02), Am. Coll. Rheumatology, Assn. Acad. Health Ctrs., Am. Soc. for Biochemistry and Molecular Biology, Assn. Am. Physicians, Am. Fedn. Clin. Rsch., Soc. for Leukocyte Biology, Am. Assn. Cancer Rsch., Am. Acad. Allergy, Am. Soc. Clin. Investigation, Am. Assn. Immunologists, Assn. Am. Physicians (pres. 2003—04), Inst. Medicine, Sigma Xi. Office: The Procter & Gamble Co One Procter & Gamble Plz Cincinnati OH 45202 Office Phone: 513-983-1100. Business E-Mail: snyderman.r@pg.com.

SNYDERS, DIRK JOHAN, electrophysiologist and biophysicist educator; b. Wilrijk, Antwerpen, Belgium, July 18, 1955; arrived in U.S., 1984; s. Godlief Stefaan and Mariette L. Snyders. BS in Med. Sci., U. Antwerp, Belgium, 1976, MD with great honor, 1980. Lic. physician, cert. cardiologist Belgium. Resident then fellow in internal medicine and cardiology Univ. Hosp. Antwerp, 1980—84; postdoctoral fellow U. Calif., San Francisco, 1984—85; instr. medicine Vanderbilt U., Nashville, 1986—87, asst. prof., 1987—95, assoc. prof. medicine and pharmacology, 1995—. With V.I.B. dept. biophysics and pharmacology Antwerp U., 1998—2003; prof. biochemistry U. Antwerp, 1998—, vice-chair dept. biochemistry, 1999—2001, chair dept. biomed. scis., 2001—, prof. biomed. scis., 2001—, vice chair rsch. coun., 2004—. Co-author: The Heart and the Cardiovascular System, 1991; mem. editorial bd. Circulation Rsch.; reviewer Jour. Gen. Physiology, Cardiovascular Rsch., Jour. Molecular and Cellular Cardiology, Molecular Pharmacology, European Jour. Pharmacology, Biophys. Jour., Jour. Biol. Chemistry; contbr. articles to profl. jours. Lt. Med. Svc. Belgian Army, 1987—88. Recipient Specia award Specia NV., Belgium, 1980; hon. fellow Belgian Am. Ednl. Found., NATO rsch. fellow, 1984, med. rsch. fellow Alta. Heritage Found., 1984; rsch. grantee NIH, Am. Heart Assn. Fellow Am. Heart Assn. (basic sci. coun.); mem. AAAS, Biophys. Soc., Soc. Gen. Physiologists, European Working Group (cardiac cellular electropmysiology bd. mem.) Achievements include research on mechanism of action of "specific bradycardiac agents", use-dependent unblocking and voltage clamp validation of modulated receptor theory (cardiac sodium channels and antiarrhythmic agents), electrophysiology and pharmacology of cloned channels molecular localisation of antiarrhythmic drug binding sites, cardiac potassium channels (including human), molecular ion channel structure-function relationships, molecular basis of congenital excitability disorders. Office: Antwerp U Dept Biomed Scis Universiteitsplein 1 T4 2160 Antwerp Belgium Address: Fazantenlaan 6 2610 Antwerp Belgium Home Phone: 011-32-3-449-4374; Office Phone: 011-32-3-820-2335. E-mail: dirk.snyders@ua.ac.be.

SOBEL, BURTON ELIAS, cardiologist, educator; b. NYC, Oct. 21, 1937; s. Lawrence J. and Ruth (Schoen) Sobel; m. Susan Konheim, June 19, 1958; children: Jonathan, Elizabeth. AB, Cornell U., 1958; MD magna cum laude, Harvard U., 1962. Intern Peter Bent Brigham Hosp., Boston, 1962-63, resident, 1963-64, 66-67; clin. asso., cardiology br. NIH, Bethesda, Md., 1964-66, 67-68; asst. prof. medicine U. Calif. at San Diego, La Jolla, 1968-71, asso. prof. medicine, dir. myocardial infarction research unit, dir. coronary care, 1971-73; asso. prof. medicine Barnes Hosp.-Washington U., St. Louis, 1973-75; adj. prof. chemistry Washington U., St. Louis, 1979-94; prof. medicine Barnes Hosp.-Washington U., 1975—, Tobias & Hortense Lewin prof. medicine, dir. cardiovascular div., 1973—, program dir. specialized ctr. rsch. ischemic heart disease, 1975-89, program dir. specialized ctr. rsch. in coronary and vascular diseases, 1990-94, program dir. principles in cardiovascular rsch., 1975-94; chmn. and E.L. Amidon prof. medicine, prof. biochemistry U. Vt., Burlington, 1994—2005, faculty mem. grad. coll., 2008—; physician-in-chief Med. Cr. Hosp. Vt., Burlington, 1994—2005, Fletcher Allen Health Care, Burlington, 1995—2005; prof. medicine, dir. Cardiovasc. Rsch. Inst. U. Vt., Burlington, 2005—; faculty mem. cell and molecular biology program U. Vt., Burlington, 2008—, univ. disting. prof. medicine, 2009—. Program dir. Collaborative Clin. Trial Therapy to Protect Ischemic Myocardium Washington U., 1977, prin. investigator Specialized Ctr. of Rsch. in Ischemic Heart Disease, 1975—95, program dir. Principles in Cardiovasc. Rsch., 1975—95, program dir. Nat. Rsch. and Demonstration Ctr. in Ischemic Heart Disease, 1985—95; chmn. cardio renal drugs US Pharmacopeial Conv., 1990—; prin. investigator BARI, II, NIH Fibrinalysis and Coagulation Core U. Vt., 2000; program dir. Cardiovascular Rsch. Inst./ Medtronic Corp./ U. Vt., 2006—, Disting. Rsch. Alliance / Medtronic Corp./ U. Vt., 2006—, Disting Rsch. Alliance/ Takeda Pharm./ U. Vt., 2008—; bd. dir. Scios Corp., Corvas Corp., Ariad Corp., Bristol Myers Squibb Corp., Fletcher Allen Health Care, New River Pharm., Inc, Nuvelo Corp., Clin. Data, Inc., Intrexon Corp., Area Biopharma, Inc.; scientific adv. bd. CV Therapeutics, Inc.; sci. adv. bd. Epix Med., Inc., New River Pharm., Inc.; chmn. HaptoGuiard, Inc; co-prin. investigator NIH Regional Heart Failure Network Ctr., U. Vt., 2007—. Assoc. med. editor: Heart Bull, 1971—72; editor: Clin. Cardiology, 1971—74; mem. circulation bd. Clin. Guides to Med. Mgmt., 1971—; editor: Coronary Artery Disease, 1989—, Clin. Guides to Med. Mgmt., 1996—, Circulation, 1983—88; cons. editor Circulation; mem. editl. bd.: Circulation Rsch., 1974—, Annals Internal Medicine, 1976—, Am. Jour. Cardiology, 1976—, Cardiology Digest, 1976—77, Jour. Clin. Investigation, 1977—, Jour. Continuing Edn. Cardiology, 1978—, Am. Jour. Physiology: Heart and Circulatory Physiology, 1978—, Cardiology in Elderly, 1991—, Current Med. Lit., —, Churchill Livingstone edtl. adv. bd.: Internat. Seminars Cardiovascular Medicine, 1978—, Cardiology in Rev., 1992—; mem. editl. bd. Internat. Jour. Cardiology, Fibrinolysis, 1986; assoc. editor: Internat. Jour. Cardiology, Fibrinolysis, 1990—, mem. editl. bd.: Current Opinion in Cardiology, —; editor, 1989—; mem. editl. bd. Can. Jour. Cardiology, 1995—, Arteriosclerosis, Thrombosis, and Vascular Biology, 1996—, Clin. Therapeutics, 1996, Clin. Insights in Diabetes, 1999, Heart Disease, 2000, Diabetes Treatment Today, 2000, Am. Jour. Geriatric Cardiology, 2000, Diabetes Care, 2002—, Current Diabetes Revs., 2004—. Served to lt. comdr. USPHS, 1964—68. Recipient Career Rsch. Devel. award, USPHS, 1972, Internat. Recognition award, Heart Rsch. Found., 1981, Disting. Achievement award, Am. Heart Assn. Sci. Couns., 1984, award, Robert J. and Claire Posatow Found., 1988, Va. Heart Ctr., 1991, Drake award, Maine Heart Assn., 1992, E.L. Amidon Excellence in Tchg. award, U. Vt., 2007. Master: ACP, ASIM; fellow: AAAS (councilor 1997—), Am. Coll Angiology, Am. Coll. Cardiology (Disting. Scientist award 1987), Am. Heart Assn. (coun. on basic cardiovasc. scis., clin. coun., circulation and arteriosclerosis, thrombosis and vascular biology, James B. Herrick award 1992, Spl. Recognition award coun. on arteriosclerosis, thrombosis and vascular biology 1999), Molecular Medicine Soc., Royal Soc. Medicine; mem.: Inst. Biomed. Scis. and Tech., Internat. Acad. Cardiovascular Scis., Internat. Soc. Applied Cardiovasc. Biology, Soc. Exptl. Biology and Medicine (councilor 1998—, pres. bd. govs. 2002—, pres.-elect 2005—, pres. 2007—, Disting. Scientist award 2010), Assn. Profs. Cardiology (pres.-elect 1992), Internat. Soc. Fibrinolysis and Thrombolysic (councilor), Western Soc. Clin. Rsch., Cardiac Muscle Soc., Am. Physiol. Soc., Assn. Am. Physicians, Am. Soc. Clin. Investigation (councilor, instnl. rep. 1997—), Assn. Univ. Cardiologists, Am. Fedn. Clin. Rsch. (councilor), Alpha Omega Alpha. Avocations: skiing, sailing. Home: 171 Lost Cove Rd Colchester VT 05446-7473 Office: U Vermont Colchester Rsch Facility 208 S Park Dr Colchester VT 05446

SOBEL, HOWARD D., dermatologist; b. 1950; MD, Albert Einstein Coll. of Medicine, Bronx, NY, 1973. Cert. in Dermatologic and Cosmetic Surgery. Residency in dermatology and dermatologic surgery Emory U. Sch. Medicine, Atlanta; clin. attending physician in dermatology and dermatologic surgery Lenox Hill Hosp., Beth Israel Hosp., and Cabrini Med. Ctr.; dir. Skin and Spa Cosmetic Surgery Ctr., NY. Editor-in-chief Internat. Jour. of Cosmetic Surgery and Aesthetic Dermatology, appeared on numerous television and radio programs (including: Sally Jesse Raphael Show, Home Show, Good Day NY, CNBC, MSNBC, New York 1, and Channels 2, 4, 5, and 7 News programs). Fellow: Am. Acad. Cosmetic Surgery; mem.: Am. Soc. Laser Surgery, Am. Soc. Hair Restoration Surgery, Am. Soc. Liposuction Surgery, Am. Acad. Dermatological Surgery, Am. Acad. Dermatology. Achievements include helping to pioneer the union of dermaology with cosmetic surgery; the first surgeon in 1986 to perform liposuction using the tumescent solution purely under local anesthesia; founder and chmn. of HDS Labs, the manufacturer if DDF (Doctor's Dermatologic Formula). Avocations: skiing, tennis. Office: Skin and Spa Cosmetic Surgery Ctr 960A Park Ave New York NY 10028 Office Phone: 212-288-0060. E-mail: hdsobel-md@nyc.rr.com.

SOBEL, JACK D., epidemiologist, educator; b. Krugersdorp, South Africa, Oct. 3, 1942; MD, Witwatersrand U., 1965. Prof., medicine Wayne State U., 1985—. Home: 6829 Knollwood Cir East West Bloomfield MI 48322 Home Fax: 313-993-0302. E-mail: jsobel@med.wayne.edu.

SOBEL, MARK ESAR, pathologist, researcher; b. NYC, Apr. 14, 1949; s. Abraham David and Selma Etta (Spitzer) S. BA, Brandeis U., 1970; MD, Mt. Sinai Sch. Medicine, NYC, 1975; PhD in Biomed. Scis., CUNY, 1975. Diplomate Nat. Bd. Med. Examiners. Med. intern, clin. fellow in pediatrics Children's Hosp. Med. Ctr./Harvard U. Med. Sch., Boston, 1975-76; rsch. assoc. NIH, Bethesda, Md., 1976-79, 80-83; sr. investigator Nat. Cancer Inst., Bethesda, 1983-92, chief molecular pathology sect., 1992-2001; sr. exec. dir. Am. Soc. Investigative Pathology, Bethesda, 2001—. Vis. scientist Max Planck Inst. for Biochemistry, Martinsried bei Munchen, Germany, 1979-80; dir. Concepts in Molecular Biology course Am. Soc. Investigative Pathology, Rockville, Md., 1987-99. Contbr. more than 100 articles to profl. jours.; patentee in field. Capt. USPHS, 1975-2001. Recipient Commendation medal USPHS, 1989, other awards. Mem. Am. Soc. for Biochemistry and Molecular Biology, Am. Soc. Investigative Pathology (councilor 1995-97, vice pres.-elect 1997-98, v.p. 1998-99, pres. 1999-2000), Assn. for Molecular Pathology (sec.-treas. 1995-97, pres.-elect 1998, pres. 1999), Assn. Accreditation Human Rsch. Protections Programs (bd. dirs. 2001-08), Fedn. of Am. Soc. Exptl. Biology Minority Access Rsch. Careers (adv. bd. 2006-), PubMed Ctrl. (nat. adv. com. mem. 2007-11), Phi Beta Kappa, Alpha Omega Alpha, Sigma Xi. Jewish. Avocations: classical music, history. Office: Am Soc Investigative Pathology 9650 Rockville Pike Bethesda MD 20814-3993 Business E-Mail: mesobel@asip.org.

SOBEL, RICHARD M., psychiatrist; BS, MIT, 1976, MS, 1977; MD, Pa. State U., 1981. Diplomate Am. Bd. Psychiatry and Neurology. Pvt. practice, 1988—. Clin. asst. prof., dept. psychiatry Jefferson Med. Coll., 1988—2011. Recipient Robert P. Waelder Tchg. award, Thomas Jefferson U. Hosp. Dept. Psychiatry; Disting. fellowship, Am. Psychiat. Soc. Fellow: Am. Psychiat. Assn.; mem.: Greater Phila. Pain Soc. (bd. dirs.), Am. Pain Soc. Avocations: singing, bicycling, woodworking. Office: 1500 Walnut St Ste 902 Philadelphia PA 19102 Office Phone: 215-731-1901.

SOBKOWICZ, HANNA MARIA, retired neurologist; b. Warsaw, Jan. 1, 1931; arrived in U.S., 1963; d. Stanislaw and Jadwiga (Ignaczak) S.; m. Jerzy E. Rose, Mar. 12, 1972. BA, Girls State Lyceum, Gilwice, Poland, 1949; M.D, Med. Acad., Warsaw, 1954, PhD, 1962. Intern. 1st Internal Med. Clinic Med. Acad., Warsaw, 1954-55; resident 1st Internal Med. Clinic, Med. Acad., Warsaw, 1955-59, Neurol. Clinic, Med. Acad., 1959, jr. asst., 1959-61, sr. asst., 1961-63; research fellow neurology Mt. Sinai Hosp., NYC, 1963-65; Nat. Multiple Sclerosis Soc. fellow Columbia U., NYC, 1965-66; asst. prof. neurology U. Wis., Madison, 1966-72, assoc. prof., 1972-79, prof., 1979—2006, prof. emerita, 2006—. Contbr. articles to profl. jours. NIH rsch. grantee, 1968—2002. Mem. Internat. Brain Rsch. Orgn., Soc. Neurosci., Internat. Soc. Devel. Neurosci. (editl. bd. 1984—).

SOBOL, STEVEN E., otolaryngologist; MD, McGill U., Can., 1997. Cert. Pediat. Otolaryngology, 2003. Intern McGill U., Canada, 2001, resident, 2002; fellow Children's Hosp. Phila., Pa., 2004; asst. prof., dir. pediat. otolaryngology Emory U. Hosp., 2004—. Contbr. several articles to profl. jours. Recipient James H. Birkett Meml. Scholarship (excellence in the field of otolaryngology, 1997, Glaxo Traveling Scholarship, best scientific paper presented at a nat. meeting, 2000, First prize resident rsch. competition, Assn. Otorhinolaryngology and Maxillofacial Surgery Quebec, 2001, William P. Potsic Basic Sci. Rsch. prize, Am. Soc. Pediat. Otolaryngology. Mem.: Royal Coll. Physicians and Surgeons of Canada, Am. Coll. Physician Executives, Soc. for Ear, Nose and Throat Advances in Children, Am. Acad. Otolaryngology-Head and Neck Surgery, AMA, Am. Acad. Pediat. Office: Emory Childrens Center 2015 Uppergate Dr Atlanta GA 30322 Address: Emory Childrens Center 2040 Ridgewood Drive NE Atlanta GA 30322 Office Phone: 404-727-1368.

SOBRINO SERRANO, FRANCISCO JOSÉ, physician; s. Francisco Sobrino and Anna Lucia Serrano; m. Beatriz Colorado, Apr. 20, 1991; children: Laura, Beatriz, Sofia. Med. Degree in Clin. Hosp., Complutense U., Madrid, 1985. Med. specialty in traumatology and orthopaedics. Surgery Clin. Hosp., Gregorio Maranon Hosp., Mapfre-Fremap Laboral Accidents Med. Group, 1985—2001; ergonomy specialist Complutense U., 1994—96, MD, 2004—08; mem. traumatology and orthopaedics surgery dept. Fremap, Madrid, 1992; mem. Madrid Coun. Med. Svc., 1986, divsn. chief, 1996—2001, traumatology and ergonomy specialist advisor, 2001—06, head dept., 2008—. Contbr. articles to more than 50 pubs., oral and free paper sci. presentation in traumatology and musculoskeletal disorders, prevention and treatment. Recipient Four Rsch. prizes in Traumatology and Musculoskeletal Disorders, Prevention and Treatment. Mem.: Spanish Laboral Traumatology Assn., Spanish Traumatology and Orthopaedic Surgery Assn., Spain Ergonomy Assn., Spanish Sport Traumatology Assn. Avocations: sports, golf, bicycling, football, travel. Office: Fremap C/ Capitan Haya n 39 28020 Madrid Spain Business E-Mail: francisco_sobrino@fremap.es.

SOBUE, ITSURO, internist, neurologist, educator; b. Konan, Aichi, Japan, Mar. 19, 1921; s. Tei-itsu and Sute Sobue; m. Shigeko, May 17, 1949; children: Gen, Kyoko Fukuzumi. MD, Nagoya U., 1943, PhD, 1951. Asst. prof. internal medicine Nagoya U. Sch. Medicine, 1952-67, assoc. prof., 1967-75, prof., 1975-84, prof. emeritus, 1984—; pres. Nat Chubu Hosp., 1984-87, Aichi Med. U., 1991-2000. Chmn. rsch. com. spinocerebellar degeneration Ministery of Health and Welfare, 1975-80, chmn. rsch. com. muscular dystrophy, 1978-84, chmn. rsch. com. new drug for spinocerebellar degeneration, 1979-85, chmn. rsch. com. neuropeptide for neuropsychiat. disorders, 1985-91; chmn. SMON, 1976-82. Author, editor: Spinocerebellar Degenerations, 1980, Peripheral Neuropathy, 1984, TRH and Spinocerebellar Degeneration, 1986; editor Clin. Neurology Jour., 1960-76. Chmn. Com. on Welfare in Nagoya, 1998—; chmn. Com. on Intractable Disease, Aichi-Ken, 1973—. Served with Japanese Navy, 1943-45. Mem. Japanese Soc. Neurology (emeritus), Japanese Soc. Psychosomatic Medicine (emeritus), Japanese Soc. Internal Medicine (emeritus), Japanese Soc. Rehab. Medicine (emeritus). Japanese Soc. Clin. Neurophysiology (emeritus), Japanese Soc. Peripheral Nerve (emeritus). Home: 603-1-311-1 Shinjuku Meito-ku Aichi-ken Nagoya 465-0063 Japan Office: Aichi Med U 21 Karimata Yasago Nagakute Aichi 480-1195 Japan

SOCKALINGAM, ANBAZHAGAN, pharmacist, educator; b. Paranam, June 5, 1970; PharmM, Jadavpur U., 1997, PhD, 2006. With Indian Assn. Pharm. Scientists and Tech.; prof. C.l. Baid Metha Coll. Pharmacy, 1999—2008; prin. cum prof. Vikas Coll. B Pharmacy, 2008—09, Chilkur Balaji Coll. Pharmacy, 2009—10, Karuna Coll. Pharmacy, 2010. Rsch. supr. Acharya Nagarjuna U., 2009, Indian Assn. Pharm. Scientists and Technologist. JRF scholarship, HRD Govt. India. Mem.: Indian Assn. Biomedical Scientists, Indian Sci. Congress, Indian Pharm. Assn., Assn. Pharm. Tchrs. India. Avocations: surfing, music, yoga. Office: Iringuttoor Near-Pattambi Thirumittacode Kerala 679533 India Office Fax: 91-4662258101.

SOCKOLOW, ROBBYN ELLEN, pediatrician; d. Harry Sockolow; m. Brian Keith Maier, Nov. 18, 1989. BA, Emory U., Atlanta, 1978, BA, 1982; MD, NY Med. Coll., Valhalla, 1986. Cert. in pediat. 2005, in pediatric gastroenterology and nutrition 2003, physician nutrition specialist. Internship in pediat. Montefiore Med. Ctr., Bronx, NY, 1986—87, residency in pediat., 1987—89, fellowship in gastroenterology, asst. attending pediatrician, 1990—92; fellowship in gastroenterology Mt. Sinai Hosp., NYC, 1989—90; attending pediatrician North Ctrl. Bronx Med. Ctr., Bronx Mcpl. Med. Ctr.; cons. attending pediat. South Nassau Cmtys. Hosp., Oceanside, NY; asst. prof. pediat. Albert Einstein Coll. Medicine, Bronx, Stony Brook U. Coll. Medicine, NY, Weill Cornell Med. Coll., NYC, 2004—, sect. chief, divsn. pediatric gastroenterology and nutrition, 2004—, assoc. prof. clin. pediat., assoc. attending pediatrician. Contbr. articles to profl. jours., chapters to books. Profl. adv. bd. David Ctr.; bd. trustees LI Chpt., Crohn's and Colitis Found. America. Recipient Chmn.'s Recognition award, 1989; named to America's Top Doctors, Castle Connolly Med., Ltd., 1999—. Mem.: Am. Acad. Pediat., Am. Coll. Gastroenterology, Bockus Soc., Am. Gastroenterol. Assn., N.Am. Soc. Pediatric Gastroenterology, Hepatology, and Nutrition.

SOCOL, MICHAEL LEE, obstetrician, gynecologist, educator; b. Chgo., Oct. 3, 1949; s. Joseph and Bernice (Bofman) S.; m. Donna Kaner, Dec. 17, 1972. BS, U. Ill., 1970; MD, U. Ill., Chgo., 1974. Diplomate Am. Bd. Ob-Gyn., Am. Bd. Maternal-Fetal Medicine. Resident obstetrics and gynecology U. Ill. Hosp., Chgo., 1974-77; clin. rsch. fellow dept. obstetrics and gynecology L.A. County-U. So. Calif. Med. Ctr., 1977-79; assoc. attending physician Northwestern Meml. Hosp., Chgo., 1980-86, attending physician dept. ob-gyn., 1986—; co-dir. Northwestern Perinatal Ctr., Chgo., 1987—; chief obstetrics Northwestern Meml. Hosp., Chgo., 1987—, dir. maternal-fetal medicine fellowship program, 1987-99, asst. prof. obstetrics and gynecology, 1979-84, assoc. prof., 1984-92, prof., 1992—. Vice chmn. dept. ob-gyn Northwestern Meml. Hosp., Chgo., 1992—. Author: (with others) Clinical Obstetrics and Gynecology, 1982, 1984, Diagnostic Ultrasound Applied to Obstetrics and Gynecology, 1987, Principles and Practice of Medical Therapy in Pregnancy, 1992; peer reviewer Am. Jour. Obstetrics and Gynecology, 1980—, Obstetrics and Gynecology, 1984—; contbr. numerous articles to profl. jours. Fellow Am. Coll. Ob-Gyn., Soc. Maternal-Fetal Medicine, Soc. for Gynecol. Investigation, Am. Gynecol. and Obstet. Soc.; mem. Assn. Profs. Gynecology and Obstetrics. Avocation: marathon running. Home: 30 W Oak St Apt 20 B Chicago IL 60610 Office: 250 E Superior St Ste 3-2307 Chicago IL 60611-3015

SODARO, EDWARD RICHARD, psychiatrist; b. Glen Cove, NY, Oct. 3, 1947; s. Edward Richard and Mae Florence Sodaro; 2 children. BS, Siena Coll., Loudonville, NY, 1969; MD, Georgetown U., 1973; MA, Grad. Faculty New Sch., NYC, 1976. Diplomate Am. Bd. Psychiatry & Neurology, Am. Bd. Adolescent Psychiatry, Am. Bd. Quality Assurance Utilization Rev. Physicians, Am. Soc. Addiction Medicine, Am. Forensic Psychiatry, Am. Bd. Geriatric Psychiatry, Am. Bd. Addiction Psychiatry, bd. cert. psychosomatic medicine Am. Bd. Psychosomatic Medicine, 2005. Resident in psychiatry LI Jewish Hosp., New Hyde Park, NY, 1973-76; staff psychiatrist NY Hosp./Cornell Med. Ctr., White Plains, NY, 1979—81, faculty, 1979-81; quality assurance dir. Suffolk Psychiat. Svcs., Stony Brook, 1996—. Clin. asst. prof. SUNY Sch. Medicine, Stony Brook; cons. Ct. Intervention Project; consulting psychiatrist Brunswick Hosp. Ctr., 1978—. Mem.: SAR, Am. Acad. Psychiatry and Law, Am. Soc. Addiction Medicine, Med. Soc. State NY (mem. com. physcians, mem. com. health), Am. Psychiat. Assn. Roman Catholic. Office: 137 Broadway Ste E Amityville NY 11701 Office Phone: 631-691-0807.

SODEN, JASON, medical educator; b. Atlanta, Feb. 18, 1973; BA, U. Mich., 1995; MD, Emory U., 1999. Asst. prof., pediat. U. Colo. Sch. Medicine, 2003—. Office: 13123 E 16th Ave B290 Aurora CO 80045 Business E-Mail: jason.soden@childrenscolorado.org.

SODERBERG, MARTEN, physician; b. Stockholm, June 3, 1961; MD, Karolinska Inst., 1989, PhD, 2008. Sr. clin. physician Sodersjukhuset, 1989—. Mem.: Swedish Med. Orgn. Avocations: mountain climbing, sailing, music. Office: Sodersjukhuset Dept Internal Medicine Stockholm SE 118 83 Sweden Office Fax: 46 8 6163146. E-mail: marten.soderberg@ki.se.

SODROSKI, JOSEPH G., medical educator; b. Coaldale, Pa. BS, Allentown Coll., 1976; MD, Jefferson Med. Coll., 1980. Intern in medicine New Eng. Deaconess Hosp., Boston, 1980—81; rsch. fellow in microbiology Dana-Farber Cancer Inst., Sch. Pub. Health Harvard U., Boston, 1981—84, from instr. to assoc. prof. div. human retrovirology Dana-Farber Cancer Inst., 1984—96, prof. div. human retrovirology Dana-Farber Cancer Inst., 1996—97, from instr. assoc. prof. dept. pathology Med. Sch., 1984—96, prof. dept. pathology Med. Sch., 1996—, assoc. prof. dept. cancer biology Sch. Pub. Health, 1992—96, prof. dept. cancer biology Sch. Pub. Health, 1996—97, prof. dept. cancer immunology and AIDS Dana-Farber Cancer Inst., 1997—, prof. dept. immunology and infectious diseases Sch. Pub. Health, 1997—. Chief div. human retrovirology Dana-Farber Cancer Inst. Harvard U., Boston, 1993—97; dir. Ctr. AIDS rsch. Dana-Farbert Inst. Beth Israel Deaconess Med. Ctr./Children's Hosp., Boston, 1994—; mem. sci. adv. bd. Ariel Project for prevention on HIV transmission from mother to infant, 1992—; mem. various coms. confs. in field; mem. external sci. adv. com. div. infectious diseases Mass. Gen. Hosp., 2000; mem. various coms. NIH; mem. sci. adv. bd. Aaron Diamond AIDS Rsch. Ctr. City N.Y., 1989—; mem. sci. adv. bd. Ctr. Human Retrovirology Thomas Jefferson U., 1995. Editor: Jour. Virology, 1993—98; editor: (assoc. editor) AIDS Scis., 1995—; reviewing editor AIDS, 1987—90, Jour. AIDS, 1988— (Howard Temin award for basic sci., 1993), AIDS Rsch. and Human Retroviruses, 1990—, Virology, 1991—, Jour. Virology, 1998—. Recipient David Gottlieb Meml. Lectureship, U. Ill., 1993, Best of What's New award, Popular Sci. mag., 1998, Harvey Lectr., 2005, Retrovirology prize, 2006; grantee, NIH, 1986—2005, Dept. Army, 1987—90, Am. Found. AIDS Rsch., 1987—88; fellow, Damon Runyon-Walter Winchell Found., 1982, Am. Found. AIDS Rsch., 1986; scholar, Leukemia Soc. Am., 1986; postdoctoral fellow, NIH, 1981, Spl. fellow, Leukemia Soc. Am., 1985, Stohlman Meml. scholar, 1991. Mem.: AAAS, Clin. Immunology Soc., Am. Soc. Virology, Am. Soc. Microbiology, Delta Epsilon Sigma, Alpha Omega Alpha, Sigma Xi. Office: Dana-Farber Cancer Inst Dept Cancer Immunology and AIDS 44 Binney St Ctr Life Scis Bldg Rm 1009 Boston MA 02115 Office Phone: 617-632-3371. Business E-Mail: joseph_sodroski@dfci.harvard.edu.

SOEJIMA, KAZUTAKA, medical educator; b. Shinagawa, Tokyo, Japan, Feb. 27, 1964; s. Hiroaki and Yoko Soejima; m. Haruna Ozaki, Apr. 19, 1997; 1 child, Hanaka. MD, Tsukuba U., Japan, 1988; PhD, Tokyo Women's U., 2000. Diplomate Japanese Soc. Plastic and Reconstructive Surgery, 1995. Resident Tokyo Women's U., 1988—90, Fuchu Met. Hosp., 1990—92; clin. instr. Tokyo Women's U., 1995; rsch. fellow U. Tex., Galveston, Tex., 1998—2000; asst. prof. Tokyo Women's Med. U., Shinjuku, Tokyo, Japan, 2004—. Contbr. articles to profl. jours. Mem.: Japanese Soc. Burn Injuries, Japan Surg. Soc. Home: Japan Office: Tokyo Women's Medical University 8-1 Kawadacho Tokyo Shinjuku-ku 162-8666 Japan

SOENARTO, YATI, pediatrician, educator; b. Sukamandi, Feb. 5, 1944; MD, U. Gadjah Mada, 1970; PhD, Vrije U., 1997. Chair child health dept. Faculty Medicine, U. Gadjah Mada, Sardjito Tchg. Hosp., 2002—06, chair Pediat. rsch. Office, dept. child health, 2006—, chair clin. epidemiology & biostatistics unit, 2007—10; chair health & med. rschr. cluster U. Gadjah Mada, 2004—; chair Unit Rsch. Mgmt. Clin. Epidemiology & Biostatistics, Sardjito Tchg. Hosp., Jogjakarta, 2009—. Mem. data and safety monitoring bd. SE Asia Infectious Disease Clin. Rsch. Network, 2008—; cons., host IMCI, Computer Adapted Tng. Tools, WHO, Geneva, 2009—10, USAID, Afghanistan, 2010; chair WHO-SEARO Tng. Med. Drs. on Rotavirus Surveillance, 2010; coord., 11. Recipient Achmad Bakrie award, Freedom Inst., Jakarta, Indonesia, 2010, R. Sutedjo award, Indonesian Pediat. Soc.; fellow, Dept. Social Medicine, Harvard Med. Sch. Mem.: Indonesian Task Force Group, Asian Pacific Pediat. Assn. (Outstanding Asian Pediatrician award). Avocations: dance, swimming. Office: Jl Kesehatan 1 Sleman Jogjakarta 55221 Indonesia Office Fax: 62 274 555455. E-mail: yatisoenarto@yahoo.com.

SOERGEL, KONRAD HERMANN, retired physician; b. Coburg, Germany, July 27, 1929; came to U.S., 1954, naturalized, 1962; s. Konrad Daniel and Erna Henrietta (Schilling) S.; m. Rosina Klara Rudin, June 24, 1955; children: Elizabeth Ann, Karen Theresa, Marilyn Virginia, Kenneth Thomas. MD, U. Erlangen, Germany, 1954, Dr. med., 1958. Intern Bergen Pines County Hosp., Paramus, NJ, 1954-55; resident in pathology West Pa. Hosp., Pitts., 1955-56; rsch. asst. U. Erlangen, Germany, 1956-57; resident in medicine Mass. Meml. Hosp., Boston, 1957-58; fellow in gastroenterology Boston U. Med. Sch., 1958-60, instr., 1960-61; mem. faculty Med. Coll. Wis., Milw., 1961—, prof. medicine, 1969—2002, prof. medicine emeritus, 2003—, prof. physiology, 1993—2002, chief sect. gastroenterology, 1961-93; ret., 2001. Chmn. gastroenterology and clin. nutrition study sect. NIH, 1979-80 Contbr. articles to profl. jours., chpts. to books. Recipient Rsch. Career Devel. award USPHS, 1963-72; Alexander von Humboldt Found. sr. fellow, 1973-74 Mem. Am. Gastroenterol. Assn., Am. Soc. Clin. Investigation, Am. Assn. Physicians, German Soc. for Digestive and Metabolic Disorders (hon.), Ger. Soc. Internal Medicine (hon.). Home: 14245 Hillside Rd Elm Grove WI 53122-1677

SOFFRITTI, MORANDO, medical researcher; b. Bologna, Italy, Mar. 6, 1946; s. Rossano Soffritti and Aurora Sambri; m. Maria Grazia Nanni, Apr. 29, 1973; children: Silvia, Federico. MD, U. Bologna, 1974, specialization in gastroenterology, 1977, specialization in oncology, 1984. Asst. physician gastroenterology Bellaria Hosp., Bologna, Italy, 1977—79; with Inst. Oncology U. Hosp. S. Orsola, Bologna, 1978—97; vis. scientist NIH, 1979—81; dep. sci. dir. Ramazini Found., Bologna, 1992—2001, sci. dir., 2001—. Sec. gen. Collegium Ramazzini, Bologna, 2001—; lectr. Sch. Oncology, U. Turin and Bologna; adj. prof. dept. cmty. preventive medicine Mt. Sinai Sch. Medicine. Co-editor 4 sci. vols.; contbr. articles to more than 160 sci. publs. Recipient Irving Selikoff award, 2007. Achievements include research in the causes of tumors of industrial and environmental origin. Office: European Found Oncology and Environ Scis Via Saliceto No 3 40010 Bentivoglio BO Italy Office Fax: 39 051/6640223. Business E-Mail: crcfr@ramazzini.it.

SOFMAN, MICHAEL S., dermatologist; b. Newark, Mar. 3, 1959; s. Howard and Harriet Sofman; m. Susan Abano, Sept. 20, 1987; children: Sarah, Andrew. BS in Biology, Georgetown U., Washington, 1981; MD, U. Med. and Dentistry NJ, 1985. Diplomate Am. Bd. Dermatology. Intern U. Pitts., 1985—86; resident SUNY Downtown Med. Ctr., 1986—88, chief resident NY, 1988—89; physician Sobel and Sofman, MD, PA, Hollywood, Fla., 1989—. Fellow: Am. Acad. Dermatology. Office: Sobel and Sofman MD PA 4340 Sheridan St Hollywood FL 33021 Business E-Mail: msofman@sobelandsofmanderm.com.

SOFOS, APOSTOLOS-GEORGIOS, surgeon; b. Corfou, Greece, Jan. 1, 1957; s. Ioannis Sofos and Elpiniki Sofou; m. Loukia Calovoulou, Feb. 4, 1984; children: Veroniki Sofou, Ioanna Sofou. MD, U. Pavia, Italy, 1982; PhD, U. Athens, 1992. Rural physician Prefecture of Chalkidiki, Riza, Greece, 1984—85; resident in surgery

Pammakaristos Hosp., Athens, 1985—90; registrar b Gen. Hosp. Karpenisi, Greece, 1991—2000, registrar a, 2000—. Contbr. articles to profl. jours. Physician Greek Army, 1983—84. Recipient First award, Hellenic Surg. Soc., 1989. Avocation: chess. Office: Gen Hosp Karpenisi P Mpakoyanni 2 Evritania Karpenisi 361 00 Greece Office Fax: +0302237080684; Home Fax: +302237025707. Personal E-mail: sofcal@otenet.gr. E-mail: gnnk100@otenet.gr.

SOFTNESS, BARNEY, pediatrician, educator; b. Coral Gables, Fla., 1954; BA, Amherst Coll., Mass.; MD, Columbia U., NYC. Cert. in pediat. Am. Bd. Med. Specialties, 1986, in pediatric endocrinology Am. Bd. Med. Specialties, 1986. Intern in pediat. Babies Hosp., NYC, 1980—81, resident in pediatric endocrinology & metabolism, 1981—83; fellow NY Hosp.-Cornell, NYC, 1983—85; asst. clinical prof. pediatric endocrinology Columbia U. Coll. Physicians and Surgeons; pediatric endocrinologist Naomi Berrie Diabetes Ctr. NY Presbyn. Hosp., Columbia U. Med. Ctr. Named to America's Top Doctors, 2006, NY Mag. Best Doctors, 2006. Office: Naomi Berrie Diabetes Ctr Columbia U 1150 St Nicholas Ave New York NY 10032 also: NY Presbyn Hosp 450 W End Ave New York NY 10024 Office Phone: 212-851-5494. Office Fax: 212-851-5493.

SOGA, JUN, surgeon, educator; b. Takao City, Taiwan, Mar. 15, 1934; m. Etsuko Seino, May 4, 1962; children: Satoru, Ryoko, Shun. DMSci, Niigata U., 1967. Diplomate Am. Bd. Pathology. Resident in pathology U. Utah, Salt Lake City, 1961-62; resident, resident fellow in pathology U. Kans. Med. Ctr., 1962-65; surg. prof. Coll. Biomed. Tech., Niigata U., Japan, 1975—99, prof. emeritus, 1999; intern Nagaoka Red Cross Hosp., Japan, 1958—59; surg. prof. Niigata Seiryo U., 1999—2005. Asia-Pacific regional editor: Jour. Exptl. Clin. Cancer Rsch. (JECCR), 1995—2002; editor (cons.), 2003—. Recipient award for Carcinoid Rsch., Niigata Pref., Japan, 1972, award for Mastomys Tumor Rsch., Niigata Pref., Japan, 1981, Eminent Scientist of Yr. award, Internat Rsch. Promotion Coun., 2004, 5th ENETS Paris, ENETS Life Achievement award, IPSEN Oberndorfer prize, 2008. Home and Office: Masago-1-21-26 Niigata City Nishi-ku 950-2074 Japan Office Phone: 81-25-266-9230. Personal E-mail: soga-j@ma.tip.ne.jp.

SOH, EUY YOUNG, surgeon, educator; b. Iksan-si, Republic Of Korea, Sept. 12, 1954; s. Chin Thack Soh and Moon Ae Rho; m. Hye Sook Kim; children: Byung Woo, Hye Ri. PhD, Yonsei U., Seoul, Republic Of Korea, 1992. Cert. physician Ministry Health and Welfare, 1979. Resident Yonsei U. Hosp., 1982—87; rsch. fellow U. Calif., San Francisco, 1994—96; prof. Ajou U. Sch. Medicine, Suwon, 1991—, chief med. divsn., 1999—2000, pres., 2003—; dir. Ajou U. Hosp., 2005—10; pres. Ajou U. Med. Ctr., 2010—; v.p. Ajou U. Dir. Dept. Planning, Suwon, Republic of Korea, 2002—05. Contbr. scientific papers. Trustee Korean Assn. Endocrine Surgery, Seoul, 2000—, Assn. Korean Hwad and Neck Oncology, Seoul, 2001—, Korean Hosp. Assn., Seoul, 2005—; mem. Daewoo Med. Found., Seoul, 2005—; chief sci. sect. Korean Thyroid Assn., Seoul, 2007—. Capt. 21st divsn. Korean Army, 1979—82, Kyungki-do. Mem.: Korean Surg. Assn. Office: Dept Surgery Ajou Univ Hosp 5 Woncheon-dong Yeongtong-gu Suwon 443-721 Republic of Korea Office Fax: 82-31-216-6657. Business E-Mail: sohey@ajou.ac.kr.

SOH, OK CHA, psychologist, educator; b. Seoul, Republic of Korea, d. Young Ha Soh and Im Soon Lee. BA in Ch. Edn., Wash. Bible Coll., Lanham, Md., 1990; MA in Counseling Psychology, Bowie StateU., Md., 1993; MA in Theology Missions, Capital Bible Seminary, Lanham, 1994; PhD in Social Psychology, Union Inst. & U., Cin., 2000. Sr. sales exec. Grant Hyatt Internat., Seoul, 1978—86; vis. prof. U. Sci. & Tech., YanBian, China, 1994—98; assoc. prof. Wash. Bible Coll., 1994—, Pres. Wash. Coalition Com. Women Issues, Inc., Annandale, Va., 2001—08. Democrat. Christian Ch. Achievements include contributed to the human rights comfort women world war II Sexual Slaves, passing house resolution. Avocations: swimming, travel. Office: Wash Bible Coll 6511 Princess Garden Pky Lanham MD 20706 Office Fax: 301-552-2775. Business E-Mail: osoh@bible.edu.

SOHN, DAE KYUNG, surgeon; MD, Seoul Nat. U., Korea. Rsch. fellow Mass. Gen. Hosp., Boston, 2008; staff surgeon Nat. Cancer Ctr., Goyang, Gyeonggi, Republic of Korea, 2003—. Office: Nat Cancer Ctr Madu 1 Dong Ilsan Dong-Gu 809 411-769 Goyang Gyeonggi Republic of Korea

SOHN, DAE-WON, cardiologist, educator; b. Seoul, Republic of Korea, Aug. 21, 1955; s. Suk-Chang Sohn and Hyun-Soon Choi; m. Eui-Kyung Kim, June 7, 1960; children: Jang-Hun, Jang-Jae. MD, Seoul Nat. U. Coll. Med., 1980; PhD, Seoul Nat. U., 1991. Intern Seoul Nat. U. Hosp., 1980—81, resident, 1985—88, fellow divsn. cardio., 1988—, dir. echocariography lab., 1991—; fellow divsn. cardio. Mayo Clinic, Rochester, Minn., 1992—93; chief coronary care unit Seoul Nat. U. Hosp., 1998—2002; chief. divsn. cardiology Seoul Nat. U. Hosp, 2007—. Med. dir. Clin. Trial Ctr., Seoul, 1998-02; chmn., bd. dirs. Korean Soc. Echocardiography, Seoul, 2004-06. Author: Echocariographic Case Studies, 1998, (e-book) Echo Education Program; contbr. articles to profl. jours. Capt. Korean Army, 1982—85. Home: Na-dong 102 Sinsamho Apt Bangbae-dong Seoul 137-069 Republic of Korea Office: Seoul Nat University Hosp 101 Daehak-ro Chongno-gu Seoul 110-744 Republic of Korea Home Phone: 82-2-536-8116; Office Phone: 82-2-2072-2855. Office Fax: 82-2-764-4281. Business E-Mail: dwsohn@snu.ac.kr.

SOHN, DONG HUN, pharmacist, educator; b. Bukcheong, Ham Nam, Korea, Apr. 8, 1930; s. Sung Hoo and Keum Sun (Lee) S.; m. Myo Hee Kim, Mar. 30, 1958; children: Soo Young Sohn Kim, Soo Jung Sohn Song. B in Pharmacy, Chung-Ang U., 1957, M in Pharmacy, 1959, PhD, 1970; diploma, Inst. Pub. Health, Tokyo, 1974. Rschr. Warner-Lambert Rsch., NJ, 1959-60; prof. Chung-Ang U., Seoul, 1960-95, prof. emeritus, 1995—, dean coll. pharmacy, 1980-82, dir. Pharm. Rsch. Inst., 1991-93, dir. cen. libr., 1993-95. Head environ. hygiene dept. Pharmacal Rsch. Inst., Seoul, 1987-95; cons. Ministry of Health and Social Affairs, Seoul, 1976-95, Ministry of Environ., Seoul, 1980—. Author: Modern Hygienic Pharmacy, 1993; contbr. articles to profl. jours. Commr. Ctrl. Coun. Pharmacal Affairs, Seoul, 1986—, Environ. Ctr. Han River, Seoul, 1994-97; chmn. Bukcheon County, Ham Nam province, Republic of Korea, 2004-08. Recipient Pharmacy award The Yak-up-Shin-Moon, Seoul, 1991, Nat. Decoration of Dong-Baek award the Pres., Korea, 1991. Mem. Pharm. Soc. Korea (sec. gen., Acad. award 1971), Pharm. Soc. Kapan, Japanese Soc. Air Pollution, Korea Air Pollution Rsch. Assn. (chmn.), Internat. Union Air Pollution Prevention and Environ. Protection Assns. (exec. mem., v.p., 1995-98), Seoul Eco Club (chmn. 2004-08). Avocations: golf, mountain climbing, Go. Home: 1327-1403 Mokdong Apt 158-773 Sinjung-dong Yongchun-ku Seoul Republic of Korea E-mail: sohndh@dreamwiz.com.

SOHN, HYUNG-SUN, medical educator; b. Seoul, Republic of Korea, Feb. 1, 1954; s. Woon-Chang and Ok-Soon Kim Sohn; m. Yong-Suk Kim, Dec. 27, 1980; children: Charles, Soo-Yeon. BA, Cath. U., Seoul, 1977, MA, 1980, PhD, 1990. From instr. to assoc. prof. Cath. U., Seoul, 1985—2001, prof., 2001—. Exhbn. com. chmn. World Fedn. Nuc. Medicine and Biology, 2002—. Contbr. articles to profl. jours. Capt. Republic of Korea Army, 1982—85. Mem.: Korean Soc. Family Medicine, Korean Soc. Diagnostic Radiology, Korean Soc. Nuc. Medicine (dir. gen. affairs 1993—96, dir. fin. affairs 1996—99, fin. audit com. 1999—). Avocations: mountain climbing, golf, fishing, reading, tennis. Home: Ichon 1-dong Hyundai Apt 33-508 140-031 Seoul Republic of Korea Office: St Marys Hosp Youido-dong Nuclear Medicine Dept 150-713 Seoul Republic of Korea

SOHN, IL SUK, medical educator; b. Nonsan, Republic of Korea, July 4, 1970; m. Hee Sun Kim, Nov. 4, 2001. PhD, Kyung Hee U., Seoul, Republic of Korea, 2005. Cert. Ministry for Health and Welfare, 1995. Fellow cardiology Kyung Hee U. Med. Ctr., Seoul, 1999—2002; asst. prof. medicine Kyung Hee U. East-West Neo Med. Ctr., Seoul, 2006—. Contbr. articles to profl. jours. (Academic award, Korean Soc. Hypertension, 2005). Capt. Suwon Airbase Korean Army, 1997—99, Republic of Korea. Mem.: Korean Soc. Circulation, Korean Soc. Echocardiography, Korean Soc. Hypertension. Achievements include research in cardiovascular disease and non-invasive imaging. Office: Kyung Hee University Hosp at Gangdong # 149 Sangil-dong Gangdong-gu Seoul 134-727 Republic of Korea Office Fax: 82-2-440-7242. Business E-Mail: issohn@khu.ac.kr.

SOHN, JIN-HUN, medical educator, researcher; b. Busan, Republic of Korea, Oct. 16, 1954; s. Soo-Jin Sohn and Kwi-Soon Cha; m. Sook-Hee Kim; children: Sunju, Ho-Ik. PhD, Korea U., Seoul, 1988. Asst. prof. Hyosung Cath. U., Daegoo, Republic of Korea, 1982—87, vis. prof. UCLA, Dept. Psychology, 1986—88, U. Miami Med. Sch., Fla., 1991—92, Cin. Children's Hosp., 2002—03, Kyushu U., Fukuoka, Japan, 2004—09; prof. Chungnam Nat. U., Daejeon, Republic of Korea, 1989—. Dir. Brain Rsch. Inst., Chungam Nat. U., 2000—02; exec. mem., pres. Korean Soc. Emotion & Sensibility, Seoul, 2004—05; exec. Korea Rsch. Coun. Pub. Sci. and Tech., Seoul, 2005—08. Contbr. scientific papers (Best Sci. Paper award, 1998). Recipient Commendation award, 1992, Appreciation award, Korean Soc. Emotion & Sensibility; named Disting. Lectr., 1999; numerous rsch. grants, 1998—2001, 2004—. Mem.: Internat. Assn. Physiol. Anthropology, Orgn. Human Brain Mapping. Achievements include research in Discovery Channel, NHK program in Japan, Korea TV channels in Korea. Home: Hanwool Apt# 110-806 Sinsung-dong Yusung Daejeon 305-764 Republic of Korea Office: Chungnam Nat Univ Psychology Dept Koong-Dong Yusung-Ku 220 305-764 Daejeon Daejeon Republic of Korea Office Phone: 82-42-821-6369. Office Fax: 82-42-821-8875. Business E-Mail: jhsohn@cnu.ac.kr.

SOHN, JU-TAE, anesthesiologist, educator; m. Mun-Jeong Choi Sohn, Mar. 1, 1993; children: Dong-Jin children: Jin-Young, Ji-Eun. MD, Pusan Nat. U., Korea, 1987, PhD in Medicine, 2002; MSc in Medicine, Seoul Nat. U., 1996. Lic. physician Ministry Health and Welfare, 1987, diplomate Korean Bd. Anesthesiology, 1991. Residency Dept. Anesthesiology Seoul Nat. U. Hosp., Republic of Korea, 1988—91; army surgeon Ministry Nat. Def., Wontong, Gangwon, Republic of Korea, 1991—94; instr. Coll. Medicine Gyeongsang Nat. U., Jinju, Republic of Korea, 1994—96, asst. prof. Coll. Medicine, 1996—2000, assoc. prof. Dept. Anesthesiology and Pain Medicine Coll. Medicine, 2000—06, prof. dept. anesthesiology and pain medicine, 2006—; rsch. fellow Ctr. Anesthesiology Rsch. Dept. Anesthesiology Cleve. Clinic Found., 1999—2001; rsch. fellow Dept. Anethesiology Kyushu U. Hosp., Japan, 1996. H. Contbr. articles to profl. jours. Capt. Korean Army, 1991—94. Mem.: Dongsung Academic Found. (scholar award 2006), Japanese Soc. Anesthesiologists (1st prize), Korean Soc. Anesthesiologists (reviewer jour. 2001—, scholar award 2004, Excellent Reviewer award 2006, Abbott scholar award 2006), Am. Soc. Anesthesiologists. Buddhist. Business E-Mail: jtsohn@nongae.gsnu.ac.kr.

SOHN, SEJUNG, pediatrician; b. Seoul, Republic of Korea, Jan. 19, 1955; children: Jina, Chang-Il. PhD, Seoul Nat. U., 1992. Cert. in pediat. Korean Pediatric Soc., 1987, in pediat. cardiology Korean Med. Assn. Clin. fellow Divsn. Pediat. Cardiology, U. Calif. San Diego Med. Ctr., 1992—93; prof. Dept. Pediat., Ewha Womans U. Sch. Medicine, Seoul, 1998—. Contbr. articles to profl. jours. Fin. sponsor Ae Kwang Won, Kerje Island, Republic of Korea, 2007. Capt., prof. Korean Mil. Physicians Sch., 1980—82, Daegu, South Korea. Recipient Alumni Assn. award, Seoul Nat. U., 1999. Mem.: Korean Pediat. Heart Assn. (mem., editl. com., ins. consulting dir., bd. dirs. 1997—2005). Achievements include research in acute and follow-up intravascular ultrasound findings after balloon dilation of coarctation of the aorta; multidetector row computed tomography for follow-up of patients with coronary artery aneurysms due to Kawasaki disease; accelerated thrombotic occlusion of a medium-sized coronary aneurysm in Kawasaki disease by the inhibitory effect of ibuprofen on aspirin. Office: Ewha Womans Univ Sch Medicine 911-1 Mokdong Yangchon-gu Seoul 158-710 Republic of Korea Office Fax: 82-2-2653-3718. Business E-Mail: sohn@ewha.ac.kr.

SOHN, UY DONG, pharmacist, education educator, researcher; b. Daega, Republic of Korea, July 5, 1956; s. Young Kwon Sohn and San Ran Kim; m. Kiock Kim; children: Heeju, Minji. BA, Coll. of Pharmmacy Chung Ang Univ., Seoul, republic of Korea, 1978; MA, Coll. of Pharmacy Pusan Univ., Pusan, Republic of Korea, 1989; PhD, Coll. Pharmacy Chung Ang Univ, Seoul, Republic of Korea, 1989. Tchg. asst. Pusan Med. Sch., Pusan, Republic of Korea, 1982—85; asst. lectr. Kyungpock Med. Sch., Tangu, Republic of Korea, 1986—90; rsch. assoc. Brown Med. Sch., Providence, 1994—95, asst. prof., 1994—95, Yeungnam Med. Sch., Taegu, Republic of Korea, 1995—96; assoc., full prof. Coll. of Pharmacy Chung Ang Univ., Seoul, Republic of Korea, 1997—. Vis, prof. Harvard Med. Sch., Boston, 2000. Editl. bd. (jour.) Anotomic Autacoid Pharmacology, 2003—; contbr. scientific papers pub. to profl. jour. Gen. affair Pharml. Soc. of Korea, Seoul, Republic of Korea, 1999—2000; assoc. editor Korean Pharmacology Soc., Seoul, Republic of Korea, 1999—2003; exec. com. KFDA, Seoul, Republic of Korea, 1999—, Korean Biology Soc., Seoul, Republic of Korea, 1999. 1st lt. US Army, 1978—80. Recipient Young Investigator award, Am. Molity Soc., 1992, 1993, Best Scientist award, Korean Soc. of Korea, 1999. Mem.: Am. Soc. of Pharm., Am. Gastroent. Assn. Achievements include international leader in the field of smooth muscle signaling of the gut; utilized a variety of advanced molecular and biochemical techniques, but maintained focus on signal tranduction mechanism of smooth muscle motility function after inflammation. Avocations: jogging, baseball. Office: Chung Ang Univ Coll of Pharmacy 201 Heasukdong Dongjakun 156 756 Seoul Republic of Korea Home: 10-802 Kyungnam Apt Banpo-dong Seochoya Seoul Republic of Korea Home Phone: 82-2-6247-3832; Office Phone: 82-2-820-5614. Business E-Mail: udsohn@cau.ac.kr.

SOHN, WONYEONG, medical researcher; b. Republic of Korea, Apr. 6, 1972; PhD, Rutgers U., NJ, 2004. Rsch. scientist Kimberly-Clark Corp., 2010. Office: 461-1 GongSe-dong GiHeung-gu YongIn-si GyeongGi-do 446-902 Republic of Korea Personal E-mail: wysohn@gmail.com.

SOIFER, SCOTT JAY, pediatrician; b. 1952; MD, SUNY Upstate Med. Ctr., Syracuse, 1977. Cert. in pediat. 1981, in pediatric cardiology 1981, in pediatric critical care medicine 2002. Residency in pediat. Yale U., New Haven; fellowship in pediatric cardiology U. Calif. Med. Ctr., San Francisco, program and clin. med. dir., pediatric intensive care unit, vice chair clin. affairs, dept. pediat. Contbr. articles to profl. jours. Office: Univ Calif Med Ctr Pediatric Critical Care Medicine 505 Parnassus Ave Box 0106 San Francisco CA 94143 Office Phone: 415-476-5153. Office Fax: 415-476-6083. Business E-Mail: SoiferS@peds.ucsf.edu.

SOIFER, TODD BARRETT, orthopedist, surgeon; MD, Mt. Sinai Sch. of Medicine, 1989. Diplomate Am. Bd. Orthopaedic Surgery, 1996. Intern State Univ. of NY Health Sci. Ctr.; resident Beth Israel Med. Ctr., 1990—94, attending physician dept. of orthopaedic surgery, resident orthopedic surgery Kingsbrook Jewish Med. Ctr. Named one of Best Doctors, NY Mag., 2011, Top Doctors NY Metro Area, Castle Connolly, 2011. Office: Beth Israel Medical Center Ste C11 3131 Kings Hwy Brooklyn NY 11234 Office Phone: 718-258-2588. Office Fax: 718-258-4138.

SOJKA, GARY ALLAN, biologist, educator, academic administrator; b. Cedar Rapids, Iowa, July 15, 1940; s. Marvin F. and Ruth Ann (Waddington) Sojka Green; m. Sandra Kay Smith, Aug 5, 1962; children. Lisa Kay, Dirk Allan. BS, Coe Coll., 1962; MS, Purdue U., 1965; PhD, Purdue U., Lycoming Coll., 1987; DL (hon.), Purdue U., 2002; DSc (hon.), Lycoming Coll. Bucknell U., 1995; DHL (hon.), 2009. Rsch. assoc. Ind. U., Bloomington, 1967-69, asst. prof., 1969-73, assoc. prof., 1973-79, prof., 1979-84, assoc. chmn. biology, 1977-79, chmn. biology, 1979-81, dean arts and scis., 1981-84; pres. Bucknell U., Lewisburg, Pa., 1984-95, prof. biology, 1984—2006, prof., pres. emeritus, 2006; interim pres. Assn. Coll. & Univs., Pa., 1995—97; commr. Pa. Gaming Control Bd., 2007—. Mem. higher edn. commn. Mid. States Assn. Colls. and Schs., 1992-96, chmn. task force on instnl. effectiveness, 1999-2000; chmn. tax policy subcom. Nat. Assn. Ind. Colls. and Univs., 1991-93; mem. study group on internat. edn. Am. Coun. Edn., 1992-94. Mem. So. Ind. Health Sys. Agy., Bedford; emeritus bd. dir. Geisinger Health Sys.; vice-chair Am. Livestock Conservancy, 2003—05, chmn. bd., 2005—07; bd. trustee Coe Coll., 2009—; chmn. bd. dirs. Stone Belt Coun. Ret. Citizens, Bloomington, 1977—78; mem. nominating com. Ind. Assn. Ret. Citizens, Indpls., 1979; bd. dirs. Geisinger Med. Found., Danville, Pa., 1985—97, 2003—06, mem. regional bd., 1997—2003; chmn. Pa. Assn. Ind. Colls. and Univs., 1989—90; mem. pres.'s commn. NCAA, 1993—95; mem. planning adv. com. Snyder County, Pa., 1996—98, mem. planning commn., 2001—10; bd. dirs. Bethesda Found., Lewisburg, 1996—98; trustee, bd. dirs. Am. Livestock Conservancy, 2001—08, vice chair, 2003—05, chair bd., 2006—08; dir. WITF Public Broadcasting, Harrisburg, bd. trustees, 2003—06; commr. Pa. Gaming Control Bd., 2007; gov. Inst. European Studies, 0989—1994, Citizen for the Future of Pa., 1999—. Recipient Ind. U. Sr. Class Tchg. award, 1975, Frederick B. Lieber award, 1977, Coe Coll. Alumni award of merit, 1982, Gary A. Sojka award Bucknell U., 1992, Cmty. Leadership award Susquahanna Valley Boy Scouts, 1994, Sheepskin award for Disting. Svc. to Higher Edn. Pa. Assn. Colls. and Univs., 2000, ECAC Appreciation award, Bucknell U., 2003, Adam Smith award Econ. Pa., 2003, Disting. Svc. medal Reading (Pa.) Ind. Day Coms., 2004; named to Coe Coll. Athletic Hall of Fame, 1988, Bucknell U. Athletic Hall of Fame, 2006; Gary A. Sojka Pavillion named in his honor, 2003. Mem.: AAAS, Pa. Assn. Coll. and Univs. (interim pres. 1997—98, exec. com., pres., Sheepskin award 1999), Phila. Soc. Promotion of Agriculture (pres. 2006—07), Am. Coun. Edn. (study group on internat. edn. 1992—94), Nat. Assn. Independent Colls. and Univs. (subcom. chmn. 1991—93), Am. Soc. Biol. Chemists, Am. Acad. Microbiology, Am. Soc. Microbiology, Phi Beta Kappa (hon.; pres. 2007—), Omicron Delta Kappa, Sigma Nu, Sigma Xi. Baptist. Business E-Mail: gsojka@bucknell.edu.

SOJKA, PETER, medical educator; b. Ostrava, Czech Republic, Jan. 20, 1950; came to the Sweden, 1969; s. Antonín and Marie (Neuwirthová) S.; m. Birgitta Karin Nilsson, Apr. 15, 1988; children: Daniel, Anna. MD, Umeå (Sweden) U., 1975, PhD, 1985. Cert. specialist in clin. physiology, rehab. and nuclear medicine. Intern Umeå U. Hosp., 1975-77; rsch. asst. Umeå U., 1977-85, acting prof., 1986, lectr., 1987-90; resident Umeå U. Hosp., 1991-94, lectr., 1995, assoc. prof. Neuroctr., 1996—97, 2001—, assoc. prof. Heart Ctr., 1998—2000, assoc. prof. Rehab. Ctr., 2001—07; prof. rehab. medicine Mid Sweden U., 2008—. Office: Östersund Rehab Ctr S-83102 Östersund Sweden Home Phone: 469014350l; Office Phone: 4663154915. Business E-Mail: peter.sojka@jll.se.

SOKOL, ERIC RUSSELL, urogynecologist, reconstructive surgeon, educator, inventor; b. Rapid City, SD, Jan. 18, 1972; s. Robert James and Roberta Sue Sokol; m. Karin Nicole Stitt, Aug. 25, 2001; children: Aria Helene, Zachary Eli. MD, Wayne State U., Detroit, 1998. Diplomate Am. Bd. Ob-Gyn. Ob-gyn resident Northwestern U., Chgo., 2002, resident physician, 1998—2002; tchg. fellow, urogynecology & reconstructive pelvic surgery Brown U. Sch. Medicine, Providence, 2002—05; asst. prof. ob-gyn, co-dir. urogynecology & pelvic reconstructive surgery Stanford (Calif.) U. Sch. Medicine, 2005—. Mem. grad. med. edn. com. Med. Sch. Brown U., Providence, 2003—05, instr. surg. skills course, 2003; dir. gyn. clinics Stanford Hosps. and Clinics, 2006—. Editor: The Requisites - Gynecology. Vol. physician Hosp. Maternidad, Dominican Republic, 2003. Recipient Alpha Omega Alpha, Wayne State U. Sch. of Medicine, 1998, Undergraduate Med. Edn. Rsch. Award, APGO/Ortho-McNeil, 2004. Mem.: ACOG (assoc.), Am. Assn. Gynecologic Laparoscopists (assoc.), Assn. Profs. Gynecology and Obstetrics (assoc.), Am. Urogynecologic Soc. (assoc.; lectr. 2004—), Phi Beta Kappa. Achievements include research exploring novel minimally invasive surgical treatment options for incontinence and prolapse; invention of anal sling system for fecal incontinence. Avocations: travel, gourmet cooking, art, hockey. Office: Stanford U Sch Medicine 300 Pasteur Dr Rm HH333 MC: 5317 Stanford CA 94305 Office Fax: 650-723-7737. Business E-Mail: esokol@stanford.edu.

SOKOL, MARIAN, medical association administrator; PhD in Early Childhood Spl. Edn., Univ. Tex., Austin; postdoctoral M in Pub. Health, Univ. Tex. Health Sci. Ctr., Houston. Founding dir. Any Baby Can Inc., 1982—2003; pres. First Candle/SIDS Alliance, 2003—. Vice chair Gov. Commn. for Women, Tex., 1991—93; commr. Nat. Adv. Comn. on Childhood Vaccines, 1995, chair, 97, 98; bd. chair Nat. SIDS Alliance. Founding chair Tex. Network for Medically Fragile and Chronically Ill Children. Recipient Imagineeer award, Mind Sci. Found., 1987, Excellence 90 Health Care Profl. award, Women's Coalition, Prudential HealthCare's Salute to San Antonio's Good Health award, 1996, San Antonio Cmty. of Churches award, 2001; named to San Antonio Women's Hall of Fame. Office: First Candle/SIDS Alliance Ste 210 1314 Bedford Ave Pikesville MD 21208 Office Phone: 800-221-7437. Business E-Mail: marian.sokol@firstcandle.org. *

SOKOL, ROBERT JAMES, obstetrician, gynecologist, educator; b. Rochester, NY, Nov. 18, 1941; s. Eli and Mildred (Levine) S.; m. Roberta Sue Kahn, July 26, 1964; children: Melissa Anne, Eric Russell, Andrew Ian. BA in Philosophy with highest distinction, U. Rochester, 1963, MD with honors, 1966. Diplomate Am. Bd. Ob-gyn. (assoc. examiner 1984-86), Sub-Bd. Maternal-Fetal Medicine. Intern Barnes Hosp., Washington U., St. Louis, 1966—67, resident in ob-gyn., 1967—70, asst. in ob-gyn., 1966—70, rsch. asst., 1967—68, instr. clin. ob-gyn., 1970; Buswell fellow in maternal fetal medicine Strong Meml. Hosp.-U. Rochester, 1972—73; fellow in maternal-fetal medicine Cleve. Met. Gen. Hosp.-Case Western Res. U., 1974—75, assoc. obstetrician and gynecologist, 1973—83, asst. prof. ob-gyn., 1973—77; asst. program dir. Perinatal Clin. Rsch. Ctr., 1973—78, co-program dir., 1978—82, program dir., 1982—83, acting dir. obstetrics, 1974—75, co-dir., 1977—83, assoc. prof., 1977—81, prof., 1981—83, assoc. dir. dept. ob-gyn., 1981—83; chair dept. ob-gyn. Hutzel Hosp., Detroit, 1983—89; prof. ob-gyn. Wayne State U., Detroit, 1983—2000, dist. prof. ob-gyn., 2000—, mem. grad. faculty dept. physiology, 1984—, interim dean Med. Sch., 1988—89, dean, 1989—99, pres. Fund for Med. Rsch. and Edn., 1988—99, interim dir. Applied Genomics Ctr., 2004—; interim chmn. med. bd. Detroit Med. Ctr., 1988—89, chmn. med. bd., 1989—99, sr. v.p. med. affairs, 1992—99, trustee, 1990—99; past pres. med. staff Cuyahoga County Hosps.; mem. profl. adv. bd. Educated Childbirth Inc., 1976—80; dir. C.S. Mott Ctr. for Human Growth and Devel., 1999—, John M. Malone Jr. MD endowed chair & dir, 2009—; chair WSU Dept. Clin. & Translational Sci., 2010. Sr. obstet. cons. Symposia Medicus; cons. Grant Planning Task Force Robert Wood Johnson Found., Nat. Inst. Child Health and Human Devel., Nat. Inst. Alcohol Abuse and Alcoholism, Ctr. for Disease Control, NIH, Health Resources and Svcs. Adminstrn., Nat. Clearinghouse for Alcohol Info., APA; mem. alcohol psychosocial rsch. rev. com. Nat. Inst. Alcohol Abuse and Alcoholism, 1982-86; mem. ob-gyn. adv. panel U.S. Pharmacopial Conv., 1985-90, adv. com. on policy Am. Jour. Ob-gyn., 1999-2001, internat. adv. bd. Karmanos Cancer Inst., Detroit, Mich., 2002-04; mem. clin. rsch. task force Assn. Am. Med. Colls., 1998-2000; mem. WSU Faculty Devel. Coun., 2003—. mem. at large Am. Med. Assn. Sect. Med. Schs. Governing Coun., 2009-, mem. WSU Clin. Translational Sci., chair, 2010, CISA SCi. ADv. Com., 2007- Mem. internat. editl. bd. Israel Jour. Obstetrics and Gynecology; reviewer med. jours.; mem. editl. bd. Jour. Perinatal Medicine; editor-in-chief Interactions: Programs in Clinical Decision-Making, 1987-90; rschr. computer applications in perinatal medicine, alcohol-related birth defects, perinatal risk and neurobehavioral devel.; contbr. chpts. to books and articles to profl. jours. Mem. Pres.'s leadership coun. U. Rochester, 1976—80, permanent trustee, 1986—; mem. exec. com. bd. trustees Southeast Mich. Ctr. Med. Edn., 1987—2000; chmn. Friends of the Grand Theatre, 2005—; mem. rsch. adv. com. Wayne State U., 2005—; mem. fetal alcohol spectrum disorders prevention adv. com. CDC and Prevention, 2005—07, mem. sci. review group, 2007; mem. WSU Clin. & Transcational Sci. Awards Sci. Adv. Com., 2007—; bd. dirs. Am. U. Caribbean, 2001—, vice chair, 2007—, chair, 2010—; trustee Stratford Am., 2004—, pres., 2007—, Grand Theatre, London, Ont., Canada, 2007, bd. dirs., 2002—. Maj. M.C. USAF, 1970—72. Recipient 15 sci. rsch. awards, 1986—, Disting. Svc. award, Wayne State U., Sch. Medicine, 2004. Mem.: APHA, ACOG (chmn. steering com. drug and alcohol abuse contract 1986—87, rep. ctr. for disease control & prevention task force 2000—07, editor-in-chief ACOG Update 2001—, Outstanding Dist. Svc. Excellence award 2006), NAS (Inst. of Medicine, com. to study fetal alcohol syndrome 1994—96), AMA (mem.-at-large sect. governing coun. 2009—, founding chair, liason com. 2010—), Am. Bd. Addiction Medicine Found. and ABAM (founding mem. 2007—), Am. Bd. Addiction Medicine, Soc. Maternal-Fetal Medicine Found. (found. bd. chmn. 2003—06, founding chair, liason com. Addiction Medicine 2010—, Dedication and Leadership award 2007), Soc. Physicians Reproductive Choice and Health, World Assn. Perinatal Medicine, Internat. Soc. Computers in Obstetrics, Neonatology, Gynecology (v.p. 1987—89, pres. 1989—92), Soc. for Neurosci. (Mich. chpt.), Am. Med. Soc. on Alcoholism and Other Drug Dependencies, Am. Gynecol. and Obstet. Soc., Neurobehavioral Teratology Soc., Soc. Perinatal Obstetricians (pres.-elect 1987—88, pres. 1988—89, v.p., Achievement award 1995), Rsch. Soc. Alcoholism, Ctrl. Assn. Obstetricians-Gynecologists (pres.-elect 1997—99, pres. 1999—2000), Detroit Acad. Medicine (pres.-elect 1999—2001, pres. 2001—02), Wayne County Med. Soc., Mich. Med. Soc., Royal Soc. Medicine, Assn. Profs. Ob-gyn., Perinatal Rsch. Soc., Soc. Gynecologic Investigation, Am. Med. Informatics Assn., Chgo. Gynecol. Soc. (hon.), Detroit Physiol. Soc. (hon.), Wayne State U. Acad. Scholars (pres. 2006—07), Alpha Omega Alpha, Sigma Xi, Phi Beta Kappa. Republican. Jewish. Achievements include named chair of molecular obstetrics and gynecology, WSU. Home: 7921 Danbury Dr West Bloomfield MI 48322-3581 Office: Wayne State U CS Mott Ctr for Human Growth and Devel Detroit MI 48201 Office Phone: 313-577-1337. Business E-Mail: rsokol@moose.med.wayne.edu.

SOKOL, THOMAS P., colon and rectal surgeon, educator; B in Physiology, U. Calif., Davis; MD, U. Health Sciences, 1980. Diplomate Am. Bd. Surgery, Am. Bd. Colon and Rectal Surgery. Intern in gen. surgery Harbor/UCLA Med. Ctr., resident in gen. surgery; felow in colorectal surgery Carle Clinic/Univ. Ill., Urbana; assoc. clin. prof. David Geffen sch. medicine UCLA; attending surgeon colorectal surgery divsn. Cedars-Sinai Med. Ctr. Co-author (with A. B. Sokol): How much lift in a facelift?, 1981, Transblepharoplasty brow suspension, 1982; co-author: The intracolonic bypass tube for left colon and rectal trauma. The avoidance of a colostomy, 1990, Laparoscopic removal of an intrauterine device perforating the sigmoid colon: a case report and review of the literature, 2005, Should HIV status alter indications for hemorrhoidectomy?, 1996, Colorectal cancer: comparison of laparoscopic with open approaches, 1998, Does HIV status influence the anatomy of anal fistulas?, 1998. Fellow: ACS, Am. Soc. of Colon and Rectal Surgeons. Office: Cedars-Sinai Medical Center Colorectal Surgery Division 8700 Beverly Blvd Los Angeles CA 90048 Office Phone: 800-233-2771.

SOKOLOFF, LEON, pathology educator; b. Bklyn., May 9, 1919; s. Barnet and Ray (Cohen) Sokoloff; m. Barbara Snow, June 1950 (dec. 1960); children: Michael D., Naomi B. Sokoloff Berry; m. Beverly Beinfeld Trachtenberg, July 18, 1971. BA, NYU, 1938, MD, 1944; postgrad., Columbia U., 1938—39. Diplomate Am. Bd. Pathology. Resident Bellevue Hosp., NYC, 1948—52; chief sect. on rheumatic diseases Lab. Exptl. Pathology, NIH, Bethesda, Md., 1953—73; prof. pathology SUNY, Stony Brook, 1973—91, emeritus, 1991—. Vis. prof. Royal Soc. Medicine, England, 1985. Author: Biology of Degenerative Joint Disease, 1969; editor: The Joints and Synovial Tissue, 1978; contbr. articles to profl. jours. Served to capt. USPHS, 1953—73. Recipient J. van Breemen medal, Dutch Rheumatism Assn., 1967, Disting. Alumnus award, NYU, 1975; grantee, NIH, 1973—87. Master: Am. Coll. Rheumatology; mem.: Am. Soc. Investigative Pathology, Am. Coll. Vet. Pathologists (hon.). Jewish. Avocation: medical history. Office: SUNY Dept Pathology Health Sci Ctr Stony Brook NY 11794-8691 E-mail: leobevsok@optonline.net.

SOKOLOFF, LOUIS, retired physiologist, neuroscientist; b. Phila., Oct. 14, 1921; married; 2 children. BA, U. Pa., 1943, MD, 1946; MD (hon.), U. Lund, Sweden, 1980; ScD (hon.), Yeshiva U, NY, 1982, U. Glasgow, UK, 1989, Philipps U. Marburg, Germany, 1990; MD (hon.), U. Rome, 1992; ScD (hon.), Georgetown U., Washington, 1992, Mich. State U., Lansing, 1993, U. Pa., Phila., 1997. Intern Phila. Gen. Hosp., 1946-47; rsch. fellow in physiology U. Pa. Grad. Sch. Medicine, 1949-51, instr., then assoc., 1951-56; assoc. chief, then chief sect. cerebral metabolism NIMH, Bethesda, Md., 1953-68, chief lab. cerebral metabolism, 1968—2004, emeritus scientist, 2004—. Chief editor Jour. Neurochemistry, 1974-78. Pvt. 1st class US Army, 1943—46, capt. MC US Army, 1947—49. Recipient F.O. Schmitt medal in neurosci., 1980, Albert Lasker clin. med. research award, 1981, Karl Spencer Lashley award Am. Philos. Soc., 1987, Disting. Grad. award U. Pa., 1987, Nat. Acad. Scis. award in Neurosci., 1988, Georg Charles de Hevesy Nuclear Medicine Pioneer award Soc. Nuclear Medicine, 1988, Mihara Cerebrovascular Disorder Rsch. Promotion award, 1988, Ralph Gerard award Soc. Neuroscience, 1996, Lifetime Achievement award Internat. Soc. Cereb and Mental Health, 1999. Mem. NAS, Inst. Medicine (sr.), Am. Physiol. Soc., Assn. Rsch. Nervous and Mental Diseases, Am. Biophys. Soc., Am. Neurol. Assn., Am. Philos. Soc., Am. Acad. Arts & Sci., Am. Soc. Biol. Chemists, Am. Soc. Neurochemistry, Internat. Soc. Neurochemistry, Internat. Soc. Cereb Blood Flow & Metab. Independent. Jewish. Achievements include development of methods for measurement of cerebral blood flow, metabolism and imaging of local functional activity in the brains of animals and man, and application of this for functional imaging in the brains of animals and man. Office: NIMH/NIH Bldg 49 Rm 1B80 9000 Rockville Pike Bethesda MD 20892-4030 Office Phone: 301-496-1371. Business E-Mail: louissokoloff@mail.nih.gov.

SOKOLSKI, KENNETH NEIL, psychiatrist, educator; b. LA, May 16, 1955; s. Edward Alter and Renee T Sokolski; m. Debra Jane Krachman, Dec. 23, 1984; children: Eleasa Ariel, Aaron David. BA, Occidental Coll., LA, 1977; MS, U. Calif., San Diego, 1981; MD, U. Calif., Irvine, 1987. Pvt. practice, Newport Beach, Calif., 1991—; chief mood disorder clinic Long Beach Vets. Affairs Health Care Sys., Long Beach, Calif., 1991—; med. dir. Clin. Innovations, Costa Mesa, Calif., 2002—. Assoc. adj. prof. dept., psychiatry and human behavior U. Calif. Irvine, 1991—. Contbr. scientific papers. Lead physician developing protocols to treat autistic children. Defeat Autism Now, Dallas, 1995—2000; asst. combat vets., treatment and claims VFW, Long Beach, 1991—. Recipient Vincent Carroll Rsch. award; named VFW Physician of the Yr., VFW Nat. Physician of the Yr.; Rsch. Adv. grant, Veterans Affairs Health Care Sys., 1993—96, At Large Marshall Scholarship. Fellow: Thomas J. Watson FOund.; mem.: Am. Psychiat. Assn., West Coast Coll. Biol. Psychiatry, Alpha Omega Alpah, Phi Beta Kappa. Avocations: photography, creative writing, guitar, travel. Office: Pvt Practice 1101 Dove St Ste 250 Newport Beach CA 92660 Office Phone: 949-222-3277. Office Fax: 949-863-1029; Home Fax: 949-863-0129. Business E-Mail: kksokolski@aol.com.

SOLAINI, LUCIANO, thoracic surgeon, consultant; b. Russi, Ravenna, Italy, Dec. 12, 1953; m. Bruna Spada, Sept. 30, 1978; 1 child, Leonardo. Degree, Med. Sch., Bologna, 1978. Asst. gen. surgeon ASL Ravenna, 1981—89, dep. chief, Dept. of Gen. and Thoracic Surgery S. Maria Delle Croci Hosp., 1989—99, cons. thoracic surgeon, 1999—2001. Med. surgeon vol. Rekko7, Yepocapa, Guatemala, 2002—07. Mem.: CTSnet. Office: ASL Ravenna Vle Randi 5 Ravenna 48100 Italy Home: Via Montesanto 19 48121 Ravenna RA Italy Office Phone: 390545217586. Personal E-mail: lsolaini@libero.it. Business E-Mail: lsolaini@gvm-vme.it.

SOLANKI, PUNITA VASANT, occupational therapist, educator; b. Mumbai, Sept. 17, 1974; BSc in Occupl. Therapy, Seth G.S. Med. Coll. and K.E.M. Hosp., 1995, MSc in Orthop. Condition Occupl. Therapy, 1998. Clin. & tchg. fellow Seth G.S. Med. Coll. and K.E.M. Hosp., 1998—, asst. prof., 2001—. Mem.: Indian Assn. Sports Medicine, Paediatric Orthop. Soc. India, All India Occupl. Therapist's Assn. Avocations: reading, writing, computers. Home: C/48 Bhanu Jyoti CH Soc Ltd Kishanlal Nivetia Rd Malad East Mumbai Maharashtra 400097 India Personal E-mail: therapistindia@gmail.com.

SOLDINI, MAURIZIO, educator, writer, poet; b. Rome, May 8, 1959; s. Sergio Soldini and Elena Filippone; life ptnr. Filomena Ciullo. MD, U. La Sapienza, Rome, 1984; PhD, U. Roma Tre, Rome, 2002; Specialist in Internal Medicine, U. La Sapienza, Rome, 1984—89. Cert. specialist internal medicine U. La Sapienza, Rome, 1989. Cardiologist, specialist internal medicine U. La Sapienza, Rome, 1989—, prof. bioethics, 2001—. Author: Issues of Bioethics, 1999, 2d edit., 2006, Philosophy and Medicine. For a practical philosophy of medicine, 2006; editor: Bioethics of Rising Life, 2001, Bioethics and Old Age, 1999, Wittgenstein e il Libro Blu, 2009;: In Controluce, 2009, Vono. Poemetto Di Bioetica, 2010, La Porta Sul Mondo, 2011. Recipient prize, Segni, Rome, 2008, Colleferrs, Rome, 2008. Mem.: Italian Philos. Soc. (corr.), Italian Soc. Internal Medicine (corr.). Roman Catholic. Office: Univ Rome La Sapienza Viale del Policlinico 155 Rome 00161 Italy Home: Via Pienza 243 139 Rome RM Italy Office Phone: 39649975362. Home Fax: 3968862799. Personal E-mail: soldini.maurizio@libero.it. Business E-Mail: maurizio.soldini@uniroma1.it.

SOLÉ, FRANCESC, physician; b. Barcelona, May 6, 1961; Degree in Biology, UAB, 1984, PhD, 1988. Chief, sect. Hosp. del Mar, 2000—. Adj. prof. UAB, 2000. Contbr. articles to profl. publs. Mem.: European Cytogenetic Assn., Spanish Genetic Assn., ASH, AEHH (award 1994, 1996). Office: Passeig Maritim 25-29 Barcelona 08003 Spain Office Fax: 34932483131.

SOLE, MICHAEL JOSEPH, cardiologist; b. Timmins, Ont., Can., Mar. 5, 1940; s. Fred and Lillian Sole; m. Susan Karen Samuels, May 26, 1964; children: David Frederick, Leslie Meredith. BSc, U. Toronto, Ont., Can., 1962, MD, 1966. Cert. Coll. Physicians and Surgeons Ont.; diplomate Am. Bd. Internal Medicine. Rotating intern, jr. asst. resident, sr. asst. resident in internal medicine Toronto Gen. Hosp., 1966-69; cardiology fellow Cardiovasc. Rsch. Inst., U. Calif., San Francisco, 1969-71; cardiology fellow Peter Bent Brigham Hosp., Boston, 1971-73, jr. assoc. medicine, 1973-74; rsch. assoc. MIT, Cambridge, 1973-74; instr. medicine Harvard Med. Sch., 1973-74; from asst. to assoc. prof. medicine U. Toronto, 1974-83, prof. medicine and physiology, 1983—, mem. staff inst. med. sci., 1978—, dir. cardiology rsch., 1987-89, dir. centre cardiovasc. rsch., 1989-99, Searle chair cardiovasc. rsch., 1998—; staff cardiologist Toronto Hosp., 1974-89, dir. non-invasive cardiology, 1974-79, dir. cardiology rsch., 1979-89, dir. divsn. cardiology, 1989-98, dir. cardiovasc. program, 1992—97, dir. Peter Munk Cardiac Ctr., 1992-97. Vis. prof. Harvard U., 1975, NIH, Bethesda, Md., 1981, U. B.C., 1982, 91, 92, Capital Med. Sch. and Beijing Hosp., 1985, U. Tokyo, 1992, others; mem. Can. Govt. Task Force Diagnostic Ultrasound, 1976-78; vice-chmn. econs. com. dept. medicine Toronto Gen. Hosp., 1977, chmn., 1978, 79, chmn. emeritus, 1980, mem. various coms., 1981-98, chmn. cardiology rsch. com., 1988-89, mem. cardiovasc. collaborative practice group, 1989-92; rsch. assoc. Ont. Heart Found., 1979-89; assoc. rsch. inst. pediat. Hosp. Sick Children, Toronto, 1979—05; mem. med. staff Mt. Sinai Hosp., Toronto, 1979—; mem. adv. bd. Merck Pharms., 1983—00, Boots Pharms., 1992-93; mem. Health Rsch. and Devel. Coun., Province of Ont., 1983-86, mem. exec. com., 1984-86; Levesque lectr. Montreal Heart Inst., 1984; mem. cardiovasc. panel Med. Rsch. Coun. Can., 1985-87; mem. heart and blood vessel rsch. adv. com. Toronto Hosp., 1986-89; chmn. cardiovasc. rsch. adv. com. faculty medicine U. Toronto, 1986-87, mem. various coms., 1987—, chmn. rsch. com. dept. medicine, 1987-88, mem. rsch. adv. bd., 1989-97, chair life scis. com., 1990-92, chair decanal promotions com. faculty medicine, 1992-94; mem. exec. com. Centre Cardiovasc. Rsch., 1998-99, chmn. sci. com., 1989-99, mem. exec. com. cardiovasc. clin. rsch. lab., 1992-99, chmn. rsch. com., 1992-99; Pfizer vis. fellow Clin. Rsch. Inst., Montreal, 1988; mem. sr. adv. com. Toronto Western Hosp., 1989-90; Katz vis. prof. U. Chgo., 1989; mem. provincial working group cardiovasc. svcs. Ministry of Health, 1990-91, mem. ctrl. east region cardiovasc. patient care mgmt. group, 1990-91; mem. trial devel. com. diabetes atherosclerosis intervention study WHO and Fournier Pharms., 1991-93, mem. trial exec. com., 1993-2000; mem. Joint Med. Rsch. Coun. Can./Pharm. Mfrs. Assn. Can. Adv. Com. Sci., 1993; mem. organizing coms. various sci. meetings; presenter in field, presdl. symposium lectr. Soc. Rsch. Biol. Rhythms, 2008. Mem. editl. bd. Can. Jour. Cardiology, 1988—07, Index and Revs. Congestive Heart Failure, 1988-90, Hypertension Can., 1988-90, European Jour. Pharmacology, 1992-96, Cardiosci., 1993, Jour. Heart Failure, 1994—09, Circulation, 1996—07, Jour. Molecular Medicine, 1996—05, Jour. Molecular Cell Cardiology, 1999-2001; mem. internat. editl. bd. Cardiology Digest, 1992—09; contbr. chpts. to books and articles to profl. jours.; patentee in field. Recipient Robert Beamish Leadership award, Inst. CV Sci., U. Man., 2001; grantee Grantee, Heart & Stroke Found. Ont., 1969—2007, Med. Rsch. Coun. Can., 1982—92, 1994—97; fellow Ivan Smith Rsch. fellow, U. Toronto, 1964, Hunter fellow, Ont. Heart Found., 1973; scholar Walter Watkins scholar, U. Toronto, 1962. Fellow Am.

Coll. Cardiology (abstract reviewer 1989, 91), Royal Coll. Physicians and Surgeons, Can. Acad. Health Sci.; mem. Am. Soc. Clin. Investigation, Assn. Am. Physicians, Am. Heart Assn. (fellow couns. clin. cardiology, hypertension, circulation and basic sci., mem. exec., basic sci. coun. 1986-89, mem. Katz prize selection com. 1988-90), Can. Inst. Acad. Medicine, Can. Soc. Clin. Investigation, Can. Cardiovasc. Soc. (mem. young investigators award panel 1982-84, mem. student presentation award com. 1988-90, mem. nat. task force cardiovasc. sci. 1992-93, Ann. Rsch. award 1975, Rsch. Achievement award 1989), Heart and Stroke Found. Can. (mem. sci. rev. bd. 1976-79, vice-chmn. 1980-83, chmn. hypertension and cardiovasc. pharmacology panel 1982-83, chmn. molecular biology, biochemistry, pathology panel 1989-90), Can. Med. Assn. (mem. coun. 1982-87), Am. Fedn. Clin. Rsch., Ont. Med. Assn. (alt. del. Toronto Gen. Hosp. bd. 1988-90), Heart and Stroke Found. Ont. (mem. med. rsch. com. 1978-81, bd. dirs. 1986-92, 96—02, mem. fin. com. 1986-90, 96-97, mem. corp. rels. com. 1990-92, mem. rsch. policy com. 1991-93, 96-97, chmn. 1997-99, mem. exec. com. 1997-99, nomination com. 1997-99, chmn. 50th anniversary com., mem. audit com., Disting. Rsch. prof. 1989-96, Murray Robertson Meml. lectr. 1989), Internat. Soc. Heart Rsch. (exec. Am. sect. 1979-88, lectr. Latin Am. sect. 1995), Banting Rsch. Found. (hon. sec.-treas. 1979-81), Gairdner Found. (mem. rev. panel 1979-94), Heart Failure Soc. Am. (publs. com. 2000-03, nominating com. 2001-04), Maple Downs Golf and Country Club (Toronto; bd. dirs. 2001-06, exec. bd. 2003-06), Alpha Omega Alpha. Office: Toronto Gen Hosp 585 University Ave Rm 4N488 Toronto ON Canada M5G 2N2 Office Phone: 416-340-3471. Business E-Mail: michael.sole@uhn.on.ca.

SOLENOV, EVGENIY IVANOVICH, medical educator; b. Nizhniy Novgorod, Nov. 25, 1949; PhD, 1968, DSc. Assoc. prof. Inst. Cytology & Genetics SB RAS, 1991—. Recipient Orbely prize, Russian Acad. Scis. Mem.: Russian Physiol. Soc. Avocations: skiing, bicycling. Office: AcadLavrentev Av Novosibirsk 630090 Russia Business E-Mail: eugsol@bionet.nsc.ru.

SOLEY, ROBERT LAWRENCE, plastic surgeon; b. NYC, Feb. 26, 1935; s. Max and Saide (Leader) S.; m. Judy Wasserman, June 16, 1963; children: John, Jill. BS, Yale U., 1956; MD, NYU, 1959. Diplomate Am. Bd. Surgery, Am. Bd. PLastic Surgery. Intern Bellevue Hosp., NYC, 1955—60; resident in gen. surgery Mt. Sinai Hosp., NYC, 1960—65; resident in plastic surgery Hosp. U. Pa., Phila., 1967—69; practice medicine specializing in plastic surgery White Plains, NY, 1969—. Mem. staff, mem. med. bd. White Plains Hosp., 1985—88, chief sect. plastic surgery, 1988—94. Contbr. articles to profl. jours. Capt. M.C., USAF, 1965-67. Grantee USPHS, 1968-69. Fellow ACS; mem. Am. Soc. Plastic Reconstructive Surgery, Am. Soc. Aesthetic Surgery, N.Y. State Med. Soc. (ho. of dels.), Westchester County Med. Soc. (pres. 1996 97, bd. dirs.), Rotary (bd. dirs. White Plains chpt. 1982-85). Home: 30 Griffin Ave Scarsdale NY 10583-7661 Office: Associated Plastic Surgeons Westchester PC 30 Griffen Ave Scarsdale NY 10583-7661

SOLFRIZZI, VINCENZO, geriatrician, researcher; b. Bari, Italy, Feb. 24, 1961; s. Francesco Solfrizzi and Antonietta Patrissi; m. Laura Fano; 1 child, Davide. Degree in Medicine, U. Bari, 1991, PhD, 2002. Rschr. U. Bari, 2002—. Roman Catholic. Achievements include research in role of mono unsaturated fatty acids on cognitive decline; role of alcohol consumption on mild cognitive impairment and dementia. Avocations: travel, movies, piano. Office: Univ Bari Pzza G Cesare 11 Bari 70124 Italy Home: Via Salvatore Cognetti 31 70121 Bari BA Italy Office Fax: 390805478633. Personal E-mail: sistat@tin.it. Business E-Mail: v.solfrizzi@geriatria.uniba.it.

SOLIMAN, ABDALLA MAHMOUD, psychology educator, researcher; b. Edfou, Egypt, Jan. 19, 1933; s. Mahmoud Mohammad Soliman and Amna Aly Mahmoud; m. Nagat Ahmad Awad, 1 child, Amel Abdalla. BA, Cairo U., 1955; MA, U. Minn., 1964, PhD, 1967. Counseling psychologist, cons. Am. U., Cairo, 1969-74; asst. to assoc. prof. psychology Faculty Arts, Cairo U., 1973-78; prof., cons. Inst. Edn., Cairo U., 2000—; assoc. prof. to prof. psychology Kuwait U., Kuwait City, 1974-91; prof. psychology United Arab Emirates U., Al-Ain, 1991—2000, chmn. dept. psychology, 1992-96; prof., cons. Amman Arab U., 2002—03. Vis. scholar Torrance Ctr., U. Ga., Atlanta, 1985-86; acad. coord. faculty humanities and social sci., United Arab Emirates U., 1994-95; counselor Psychology Edn. Clinic, Ain Shams U., Egypt, 1959-61. Mem. editl. bd., adviser Internat. Jour. Advnacement of Counseling, 1978—, Jour. Edn., United Arab Emirates, 1992-94, Jour. Humanities and Social Scis., 1995-97; contbr. articles to profl. jours. Mem. APA, ACA, Internat. Assn. Counseling (exec. coun. 1974-85), Maadi Club (Cairo). Avocation: writing for cultural media on psychological topics. Office: 31 85th St Maadi Cairo Egypt Home: 31-85th St MAADI Cairo 11431 Egypt Home Phone: 202 23597 370. Personal E-mail: soliman002@hotmail.com.

SOLIMAN, AHMED, surgeon; b. Tanta, Egypt, June 14, 1973; D, Tanta Med. Sch., 1998. Neurosurgery Tanta Med. Sch., 2000—. Home: Kornish St Tanta Gharbia 22 Egypt Business E-Mail: ahmed.soliman@med.lu.se.

SOLIMAN, HANI, geneticist, educational consultant; b. Egypt, Sept. 3, 1938; arrived in Can., 1964, Australia, 1975; m. Izabel Kapros, Aug. 5, 1970. BSc with honors, U. Alexandria, Egypt, 1960, MSc in Evolutionary Genetics, 1963; MSc in Animal Genetics, U. Alta., Can., 1968, PhD in Radiation Genetics, 1972. Tchg. fellow McGill U., Montreal, Canada, 1964-65; grad. tchg. asst., rsch. assoc. U. Alta., Edmonton, 1965-74; asst. prof. U. Louvain, Belgium, 1974-75; tchg. fellow, lectr. U. New Eng., Armidale, Australia, 1975-84; from assoc. prof. to prof. U. Gar Unis, Bengazi, Libya, 1984-86; mng. dir. Hi-Educonsult, Armidale, 1987—. Cons. Planning Authority, No. Ter. U., Darwin, Australia, 1982; vis. prof. U. Louvain, 1986-87. Coauthor: Staff Perception of Teaching Effectiveness, 1984; co-editor: Drosophila as a Model Organism of Aging Studies, 1988; contbr. numerous articles to profl. jours., chpts. to books. Australian Inst. Nuc. Sci. grantee, 1978. Fellow Am. Human Biology Coun.; mem. AAAS, Genetics Soc. Am., Am. Soc. for Study of Evolution, Australasia Soc. Human Genetics, Internat. Assn. Human Biologists, NY Acad. Sci. Office: HI-Educonsult PO Box 1182 Armidale 2350 Australia Home Phone: 612-6771-2252. Personal E-mail: soliman.hani@gmail.com.

SOLIMAN, NEVEEN A., medical educator; b. Cairo, Oct. 6, 1961; MBBCh, Kasr Al Aini Sch. Medicine Cairo U., 1984, PhD, 1993. Prof. Cairo U., 2003—. Founder, dir. Egyptian Group Orphan Renal Diseases; bd. dirs. Egyptian Soc. Pediatric Nephrology & Transplantation, 2007. Mem.: Internat. Pediatric Nephrology Assn. Avocations: reading, travel. Office: 99 Manial St Cairo 11451 Egypt Business E-Mail: nsoliman@kasralainy.edu.eg.

SOLITAR, BRUCE M., rheumatologist, educator; MD, NYU, 1988. Diplomate Am. Bd. Internal Medicine, 2001, Am. Bd. Internal Medicine-rheumatology, 2004. Resident internal medicine NYU Med. Ctr., 1988—92, fellow rheumatology, 1992—94; clin. assoc. prof. dept. of medicine NYU Langone Med. Ctr. Office: Lagone Medical Center Ste 1C 333 E 34 St New York NY 10016 Office Phone: 212-889-7217. Office Fax: 212-545-0174.

SOLOMON, BARRY J., human services administrator, consultant; b. Boston, May 16, 1934; s. Samuel and Ethel (Fleishman) Solomon; m. C. Priscilla Fugate, June 29, 1958; children: R. Stephen, Jon, Julie Ellen. BS in Biology and Chemistry, Tufts U., Medford, Mass., 1955; MBA in Health Care Adminstrn., Xavier U., Cin., 1960; MPH in Health Care Adminstrn., U. NC, 1989. Chief med. record adminstr. USPHS Hosp., Lexington, Ky., 1956-59; asst. dir. Union Meml. Hosp., Balt., 1960-61; asst. adminstr. James Lawrence Kernan Hosp., Balt., 1961-67; asst. to dean, lectr. health edn. and med. care sects. Yale U. Sch. Medicine, New Haven, 1967-70; dir. health svcs., clin. asst. prof. pharmacy adminstrn. U. RI, Kingston, 1970-76; assoc. dir. for adminstrn. USPHS Hosp., Norfolk, Va., 1976-81; dir., COO, sr. fellow in social medicine Montefiore Hosp., Bronx, NY, 1981-84; assoc. v.p. for med. affairs, mem. exec. coun. of Med. Sch. U. South Fla., Tampa, 1984-89; assoc. prof., acting chmn. dept. comprehensive medicine U. So. Fla., Tampa, 1984-89, assoc. prof. Coll. Pub. Health, 1984-89; cons. in health adminstrn., Columbia, Md., 1989-93; v.p. for acad. affairs North Broward Hosp. Dist., Ft. Lauderdale, Fla., 1993-96; chmn. bd. dirs. Sr. Benefit Ctrs. Am., Inc., 1998-2000; cmty. rep., mem. safety com. North Broward Med. Ctr., 2007—. 1st v.p. bd. trustees, CEO Count and Countess de Hoernle Alzheimer's Pavillion, 2000—06, cons. to bd. dirs., 2006—; pres. Villa D'Este Condominium, Inc., 1999—2001; exec. com., nominating com. Vis. Nurse Assn. Tampa Bay, 1987—90; planning com. bd. trustees Hillsborough County Hosp. Authority, 1986—88; profl. affairs com. bd. trustees H. Lee Moffitt Cancer Ctr. and Rsch. Inst., 1986—88; affiliation com. S.W. Fla. Blood Bank, 1988—89; instr. hosp. adminstrn. Xavier U., 1960; course asst., instr. Am. Med. Record Assn., 1962—72; instr. Howard U. Coll. Continuing Edn., Washington, 1993; cons. St. Elizabeth Hosp., Covington, Ky., 1959, City Hosp. Ctr. Elmhurst, 1965, Hall-Brooke Hosp., Westport, Conn., 1968—69, Conn. Mental Health Ctr., New Haven, 1969—70, South County Hosp., Wakefield, RI, 1970—76, Centurion Hosp., Tampa, 1989, Primary Care Svcs., Tampa, 1991, Holland & Knight, Tampa, 1991, NCC Internat., Colchester, England, 1991, F. W. Assocs., Tampa, 1989—92, Decking Design, Norfolk, 1986—93, SMinc., Columbia, 1993, Internat. Flooring & Protective Coatings, Inc., Norfolk, 1993—; sr. cons. Meisel Assocs., Inc., NYC, 1983—, bd. dirs. Care Source, Inc., 2007—; patient safety strategic team North Broward Med. Ctr., 2007—. Contbr. articles to profl. jours. Mem. Nat. Com. Religion and Health, 1982—84; mem., vice chmn. Chariho Sch. Bd., Richmond, RI, 1974—76; mem. Broward Econ. Devel. Coun., Inc.; trustee Montefiore-Mosholu Cmty. Ctr., 1981—84. Lt. USPHS, 1956—59, capt. USPHS, 1976—81. Recipient citation, Suncoast chp. Am. Heart Assn., 1988. Fellow: Am. Coll. Healthcare Execs.; mem.: APHA. Avocation: tennis. Home: 2863 Via Venezia Deerfield Beach FL 33442-8633 Personal E-mail: prisandbj@bellsouth.net.

SOLOMON, DANIEL, rheumatologist; b. Biloxi, Miss., Nov. 19, 1964; MD, Yale U., 1992—; MPH, Harvard U., 1998. Chief, sect. clin. scis. Brigham & Women's Hosp., Divsn. Rheumatology, 2007—. Office: Brigham & Women's Hosp 75 Francis Boston MA 02115 Business E-Mail: dsolomon@partners.org.

SOLOMON, DAVID ARTHUS, psychiatrist, educator; b. Mpls., Mar. 22, 1955; BA, Carleton Coll., 1978; MD, Boston U., 1986. Dep. editor psychiatry UpToDate Inc., 2009—. Clin. assoc. prof. dept. psychiatry and human behavior Warren Alpert Med. Sch. Brown U., 1999. Recipient Outstanding Tchg. award, Dept. Psychiatry and Human Behavior, Warren Alpert Med. Sch. Brown U. Mem.: AMA, Am. Psychiat. Assn. Avocations: skiing, hiking. Office: 95 Sawyer Rd Waltham MA 02453-3471 Business E-Mail: dasolomon@lifespan.org.

SOLOMON, DAVID HARRIS, geriatrician, educator; b. Cambridge, Mass., Mar. 7, 1923; s. Frank and Rose (Roud) Solomon; m. Ronda L. Markson, June 23, 1946; children: Patti Jean Sinaiko, Nancy Ellen. AB, Brown U., 1944; MD, Harvard U., 1946. Intern Peter Bent Brigham Hosp., Boston, 1946—47, resident, 1947—48, 1950—51; fellow endocrinology New Eng. Center Hosp., Boston, 1951—52; faculty UCLA Sch. Medicine, 1952—, prof. medicine, 1966—93, vice chmn. dept. medicine, 1968—71, chmn. dept., 1971—81, assoc. dir. geriatrics, 1982—89; dir. UCLA Ctr. on Aging, 1991—96; prof. emeritus UCLA, 1993—. Chief med. svc. Harbor Gen. Hosp., Torrance, Calif., 1966—71; cons. Wadsworth VA Hosp., LA, 1952—93, Sepulveda VA Hosp., 1971—93; cons. metabolism tng. com. USPHS, 1960—64, endocrinology study sect., 1970—73; cons. RAND Corp., 1997—. Editor: Jour. Am. Geriatric Soc., 1988—93; contbr. numerous articles to profl. jours. Recipient Ollie Randall award, Nat. Coun. on the Aging, 2004. Master: ACP (John Phillips Meml. award 2002); mem.: AAAS, Gerontol. Soc. Am. (Freeman award 1997), Am. Geriatrics Soc. (bd. dir. 1985—93, Milo Leavitt award 1992, Disting. Svc. award 1993, Edward Henderson award 1999, David H. Solomon Disting. Svc. award named in his honor), Am. Fedn. Aging Rsch. (Irving S. Wright award 1990), Western Assn. Physicians (councillor 1972—75, pres. 1983—84), Inst. Medicine Nat. Acad. Sci., Am. Thyroid Assn. (pres. 1973—74, Disting. Svc. award 1986), Endocrine Soc. (Robert H. Williams award 1989), We. Soc. Clin. Rsch. (councillor 1963—65, Mayo Soley award 1986), Am. Soc. Clin. Investigation, Assn. Am. Physicians, UCLA Med. Alumni Assn. (Extraordinary Merit award 2002), Assn. Profs. of Medicine (pres. 1980—81), Alpha Omega Alpha, Sigma Xi, Phi Beta Kappa. Achievements include The Parlow-Solomon Chair on Aging named in his honor at UCLA School of Medicine. Home: 3640 Dragonfly Dr Apt 202 Thousand Oaks CA 91360-8445 Home Phone: 805-241-4789. Personal E-mail: dsolomon1@earthlink.net.

SOLOMON, DENIS EON, research scientist; b. Georgetown, British Guiana, Sept. 8, 1949; BSc, U. Lancaster, MSc, 1976, PhD, 1981. Cons. Gehrson Lehman Inc., 2000—. Achievements include surgical medical dressing for the treatment of body burns and for wound healing. Office: 96 Standishgate Wigan Greater Manchester WN1 1XA England

SOLOMON, GAIL ELLEN, physician; b. Bklyn., May 26, 1938; d. Samuel and Estelle (Suffin) S.; m. Harvey Hecht, Oct. 28, 1962; children: Daniel, Jonathan, Elizabeth. AB, Smith Coll., 1958; MD, Albert Einstein Coll. Medicine, 1962. Diplomate Am. Bd. Pediats., Am. Bd. Psychiatry and Neurology (assoc. examiner), Am. Bd. Electroencephalography, Am. Bd. Electroencephalography and Neurophysiology, Am. Bd. Clin. Neurophysiology. Intern in pediat. Bronx Mcpl. Hosp. Ctr., 1962—63, resident in pediat., 1963—64, N.Y. Hosp.-Cornell U. Med. Coll., NYC, 1964—65; NIH vis. fellow in neurology and child neurology Columbia-Presbyn. Med. Ctr., NYC, 1965—68, NIH vis. fellow in clin. neurophysiology and electroenceph.; instr. neurology Columbia U. Coll. of Physicians and Surgeons, NYC, 1968—69, asst. prof. neurology and pediat., 1970—76, assoc. prof. clin. neurology and pediat., 1976—2004, prof. clin. neurology and pediat., 2004—; asst. prof. Cornell U. Med. Coll., 1969—70, prof. clin. neurology and and pediat., 2004—; asst. attending in neurology and pediat. N.Y. Hosp., NYC, 1969—76, dir. electroencephalography, 1969—, assoc. attending in neurology and pediat., 1976—, assoc. attending neurologist in psychiatry, 1983—. Mem. joint com. for stroke facilities NIH; mem. FDA Peripheral and CNS Adv. Com., 1979-83, chmn., 1983, cons., 1983-84; mem. med. audit com. N.Y. Hosp., mem. utilization rev. com.; mem. profl. adv. bd. N.Y. State Epilepsy Assn.; adj. attending physician in neurology Meml.-Sloan Kettering Cancer Ctr., 1982-93; assoc. attending pediatrician Hosp. Spl. Surgery, 1987—; neurology cons. Blythedale Children's Hosp., Valhalla, N.Y., 1991—, Meml.-Sloan Kettering Cancer Ctr., 1993—. Author: (with F. Plum) Clinical Management of Seizures: A Guide for the Physician, 1976, (with Plum and Kutt) 2d edit., 1983; editor: (with Kaufman and Pfeffer) Child and Adolescent Neurology for Psychiatrists, 1992, Neurologic Disorders: Developmental and Behavioral Sequelae, 1999; contbr. articles to profl. jours., chpts. to med. books. Fellow: Am. Acad. Neurology, Am. Acad. Pediats., Am. Electroencephalographic Soc.; mem.: AMA (Physician's Recognition award in Continuing Med. Edn.)), NY State Med. Soc., NY County Med. Soc., Am. Med. Women's Assn., Am. Epilepsy Soc., Am. Acad. Clin. Neurophysiology, Eastern EEG Soc., Am. Med. EEG Assn., Child Neurology Soc., Internat. Child Neurology Assn., Tristate Child Neurology Soc., Assn. for Rsch. in Nervous and Mental Diseases, NY Acad. Sci. Avocations: art, reading, languages, travel. Office: NY Presbyn Hosp Cornell U Med Coll 525 E 68th St New York NY 10021-4870 Home Phone: 914-472-5608. *

SOLOMON, HOWARD, pharmaceutical executive; b. Aug. 12, 1927; s. David and Faye (Gussow) Solomon; m. Carolyn Ruth Bower, Dec. 17, 1961 (dec. 1991); children: Andrew Wallace, David Frederick; m. Sarah Durie Billinghurst, Aug. 27, 2003. BA, CCNY, 1949; LLB, Yale U., New Haven, Conn., 1952. Bar: NY 1952. Atty. Moses & Singer, NYC, 1952-55, Kay Scholer, Fierman Hays & Handler, NYC, 1956-60; pres. Hildred Mgmt. Corp., NYC, 1967-83; dir. Forest Laboratories, Inc., NYC, 1964—, CEO, 1977—98, chmn., CEO, pres., 1998—. Bd. trustees NY-Presbyn. Hosp. Bd. dirs. Met. Opera, Lincoln Ctr. for Performing Arts; exec. com. mem., chmn. emeritus NYC Ballet; mem. Sch. AM. Ballet. Mem. NY State Bar Assn., Yale Club, Harmonie Club of NY. Office: Forest Labs Inc 909 3rd Ave New York NY 10022-4731 *

SOLOMON, KERRY D., ophthalmologist, surgeon, consultant; s. Alan M. and Sheila M. Solomon; m. Cynthia Loiacano Solomon, June 12, 1992; children: Brandon, Coleman. BA in Psychology, U. Vt., 1983, MD, 1987. Diplomate Am. Bd. Ophthalmology, 1993, lic. ophthalmologist SC, 1993. Felow in ophthalmic pathology U. Utah, Salt Lake City, 1987—88; intern Yale U. Hosp. St. Raphael, New Haven, 1988—89; resident in ophthalmology U. Ky., Lexington, 1989—92; fellow in cornea, external disease, anterior segment surgery Wilmer Inst. Johns Hopkins Hosp., Balt., 1992—93; staff Med. U. SC, 1993—, from asst. prof. to assoc. prof. ophthalmology, 1993—2002, prof. ophthalmology, 2002—. Dir. Magill Laser Ctr., SC, 1994—, ophthalmology ambulatory care com. liaison, 1994—99; chmn. hosp. laser com. Med. U. SC, 1999—, dir. cornea/refractive surgery svc., SC, 2000—; co-med. dir. SC Lions Eye Bank, 1996—2001, Magill Rsch. Ctr., SC, 2000—; lectr., presenter in field. Editor: Refractive Surgery Quar.; mem. editl. bd.: Ocular Surgery News, Phaco and Foldables, Ocular Therapeutics, Ophthalmic Practice, Cataract and Refractive Surgery Today; contbr. articles to profl. jours. Ednl. com. Internat. Soc. Refractive Surgery. Recipient Pierre Guatier Jenkins award, Med. U. SC, 2006—07; grantee, Allergan, 1994—95, 1998—2001, Chiron Vision, 1994—97, Akorn, Inc., 1997—99, Alcon Labs., 1997—, Pharmacia and Upjohn, 1997—98, Pharmacia, 1999—2000, JAEB Ctr. for Health Rsch., 1999—2004, Otsuka Md. Rsch. Inst., 2004—05, Advanced Med. Optics, 2004—; fellow, Heed Ophthalmic Found., Wilmer Eye Inst., Johns Hopkins Hosp., 1992; Rsch. grant, Nat. Soc. to Prevent Blindness, Wilmer Eye Inst., Johns Hopkins Hosp., 1992. Fellow: Am. Acad. Ophthalmology (Honor award 1998, Sr. Achievement award 2005); mem.: Charleston County Med. Soc., Charleston Ophthalmol. Soc., SC Soc. Ophthalmology, SC Med. Assn., Wilmer Resident Assn., Refractive Surgery Interest Group, Johns Hopkins Univ. Sch. Medicine Alumnae, Internat. Soc. Refractive Keratoplasty, Heed Ophthalmic Found., Eye Bank Assn. Am., Assn. for Rsch. in Vision and Ophthalmology, Am. Soc. Cataract and Refractive Surgery (program com., practice mgmt. com., FDA com., Best Paper award 1995, Grand prize 1997, Video award 1998, Best Paper award 2000, Lee T. Nordan Achievement award 2006). Avocations: golf, travel. Office: Storm Eye Inst 167 Ashley Ave Charleston SC 29403-5836

SOLOMON, LEIGH, oncologist, educator; b. June 7, 1973; MD, U. Miami Sch. Medicine, 1999. Gynecologic oncologist St. John Providence Health, 2008. Asst. prof. Wayne State U., 2009. Mem.: AMA, ACOG, SGO, ASCO. Office: 19229 Mack Ave Ste 39 Grosse Pointe Woods MI 48236 E-mail: leighsolomon@me.com.

SOLOMON, LINCOLN JOHN, pediatrician; b. Johannesburg, Aug. 16, 1965; MBChB, UCT, 1990; MS in Pediat., Medicine, UFS, 1998. Head, clin. unit PICU Dept. Pediat. and Child Health, 2008—. Fellow: Coll. Medicine Pediat. Critical Care South Africa; mem.: Critical Care Soc. South Africa. Avocations: running, photography. Office: Faculty Health Scis UFS Nelson Mandela Bloemfontein Free State 9300 South Africa Business E-Mail: solomonlj@ufs.ac.za.

SOLOMON, PHYLLIS LINDA, social work educator, researcher; b. Hartford, Conn., Dec. 6, 1945; d. Louis Calvin and Annabell Lee (Nitzberg) S. BA in Sociology, Russell Sage Coll., 1968; MA in Sociology, Case Western Res. U., 1970, PhD in Social Welfare, 1978. Lic. social worker Pa. Rsch. assoc. Inst. Urban Studies Cleve. State U., 1970-71; program evaluator Cleve. State Hosp., 1971-74; project dir. Ohio Mental Health and Mental Retardation Rsch. Ctr., Cleve., 1974-75; rsch. assoc. Psychiat. Rsch. Found. of Cleve., 1975; project dir. Ohio Mental Health and Mental Retardation Rsch. Ctr., 1977-78; rsch. assoc. dirs. rsch. and mental health planning Fedn. for Cmty. Planning, 1978-88; prof. dept. mental health scis., dir. sect. mental health svcs. and systems rsch. Hahnemann U., Phila., 1988-94; prof. Sch. Social Work U. Pa., Phila., 1994—. Secondary appointment Prof. Social Work in Psychiatry U. Pa. Sch. Medicine, 1994—; adj. prof. dept. psychiatry Allegheny U., 1994—97. Author (with others): Community Services to Discharged Psychiatric Patients, 1984, Principles and Practice of Psychiatric Rehabilitation: An Empirical Approach, 2008, Randomized Controlled Trials: Design and Implementation for Community Based Psychosocial Interventions, 2009; co-editor: New Developments in Psychiatric Rehabilitation, 1990, Psychiatric Rehabilitation in Practice, 1993, Research Process in the Human Services, 2005; mem. editl. adv. bd. Community Mental Health Jour., 1988—, mem. editl. bd. Jour. Rsch. in Social Work Practice, 1997—2000, Social Work Forum, 1997—, Health and Social Work, 1998—2000, Psychiat. Rehab. Jour., 1999—2008, Mental Health Svcs. Rsch. Jour., 2001—08, Brief Treatment and Crisis Intervention, 2001—08, Social Work, 2003—, Am. Psychiat. Rehab. Jour., 2006—; contbr. articles to profl. jours. Trustee Cleve. Rape Crisis Ctr., 1981-84, CIT Mental Health Svcs., Cleve., 1985-88; mem. citizen's adv. bd. Sagamore Hills (Ohio) Children's Psychiat. Hosp., 1984-88; bd. dirs. Plan of Pa., 2004—. Named Evaluator of the Yr., Ohio Program Evaluators Group, 1987; recipient Ann. award Cuyahoga County Cmty. Mental Health Bd., 1988, Armin Loeb award Internat. Assn. Psychosocial Rehab. Svcs., 1999, Outstanding Non-Psychiatrist award Am. Assn. Cmty. Psychiatrists, 2002, Knee/Wittman Outstanding Lifetime Achievement award Nat. Assn. Social Workers Found., 2005, Tchg. & Mentoring award, U. Provost, 2009, Excellence Psychiatric Rehab. Theory and Practice award CareLink Cmty. Support Svcs., 2010. Mem. NASW, U.S. Psychiat. Rehab. Assn., Soc. for Social Work and Rsch. (1st place award for pub. article 1997), Am. Acad. Social Work & Social Welfare. Jewish. Home: 205 Governor's Ct Philadelphia PA 19146 Office: U Pa Sch Social Policy & Practice 3701 Locust Walk Philadelphia PA 19104-6214

SOLOMON, ROBERT B., geriatrician; Grad., State U. of NY. Diplomate Am. Bd. of Internal Medicine, Am. Bd. of Internal Medicine-geriatrics medicine. Internship Westchester County Med. Ctr., resident, 1978—80; med. dir. acute care for the elderly Trinitas Regional Med. Ctr. Named Top Dr., NY Mag., 1999—2003, NJ Mag., 2001—03. Office: Trinitas Regional Medical Center 225 Williamson St Elizabeth NJ 07207 Office Phone: 908-994-5000.

SOLOMON, STEVEN L., federal agency administrator, physician; b. NYC, Jan. 13, 1951; BA, Rutgers U., 1971; MD, Tufts U., 1975. Diplomate Am. Bd. Internal Medicine, Am. Bd. Infectious Disease, Am. Bd. Preventive Medicine. EIS officer Ctr. for Disease Control, Atlanta, 1981—83, epidemiologist hosp. infections program, 1983—85, dep. chief epidemiology br., 1985—87, acting chief, epidemiology br., 1987, asst. dir. tng. and lab. program, 1987—89, assoc. dir. Nat. Ctr. for Infectious Disease, 1989—93, chief spl. studies, 1993—2001; attending physician Atlanta VA Med. Ctr., 1989—; acting dir. Healthcare Quality Promotion divsn., Atlanta, 2001—03; assoc. dir. Health Sys., Atlanta, 2003—04; acting dir. Nat. Ctr. Health Mktg., Atlanta, 2004—05; dir. coordinating ctr. for health info. and service Centers for Disease Control and Prevention, Atlanta; dep. dir. Office Healthcare Quality US Dept. Health and Human Services, Washington. Capt. USPHS, 1981—. Office: Office Healthcare Quality US Dept Health and Human Services 200 Independence Ave SW Rm 739H Washington DC 20201 Office Phone: 404-498-0123. Business E-Mail: sls1@cdc.gov. *

SOLOMON, ZAHAVA HAELION, social sciences educator; b. Israel, May 31, 1950; PhD, Sch. Pub. Health, U. Pitts., 1980. Prof. Tel Aviv U., 1992—. Recipient prize, Israel, Laufer award, Internat. Assn. Traumatic Stress. Office: Tel Aviv University Ramat Aviv Tel Aviv 69978 Israel Business E-Mail: solomon@post.tau.ac.il.

SOLON, LEONARD R(AYMOND), retired physicist, educator, consultant; b. White Plains, NY, Sept. 11, 1925; s. Morris and Rebecca (Bobrov) S.; m. Charlotte Rothman, June 30, 1946; children: Miriam Solon Weintraub, Matthew Benjamin, Emily Solon Bader. BA, Hamilton Coll., 1947; MSc, Rutgers U., 1949; PhD, NYU, 1960. Cert. Am. Bd. Health Physics. Physicist Nuc. Devel. Assocs., Inc., White Plains, 1950-52; asst. chief, then chief radiation br. AEC, NYC, 1952-60; dir. applied nuc. tech. Tech. Rsch. Group, Inc., Syosset, N.Y., 1960-62; cons. Burns & Roe, NYC, 1962-64, Servo Corp. Am., Hicksville, N.Y., 1962-64; mgr. R&D Del Electronics Corp., Mt. Vernon, N.Y., 1964-67; founder, exec. v.p., tech. dir. Hadron, Inc., Yonkers, N.Y., 1967-75; dir. bur. radiation control N.Y.C. Dept. Health, 1975-91; ret., 1991—2008. Lectr., then adj. assoc. prof. N.Y.U. Inst. Environ. Medicine, 1955-93; environ. & radiol. health cons.; prof. health physics U.S. Mcht. Marine Acad., 1963. Contbr.: Dictionary of American Biography, 1995, The Scribner Encyclopedia of American Lives, vol. 1, 2, 3, 4, 5, 1998-2002; contbr. articles to profl. jours. Served with inf. U.S. Army, 1944-46, ETO. Decorated Combat Inf. badge, Bronze Star; named Chevalier French Legion Honor, Pres. Republic, 2008. Mem. AAAS, Am. Nuc. Soc., Health Physics Soc., Am. Phys. Soc., N.Y. Acad. Scis., Conf. Radiation Control Program Dirs., Radiol. and Med. Physics Soc. N.Y., Phi Beta Kappa, Sigma Xi. Achievements include co-patentee for laser photocauterizer used in treatment of detached retina; powering lasers using nuclear sources.

SOLOVAN, CAIUS SILVIU, dermatologist; b. Timisoara, Timis, Romania, Jan. 1, 1958; s. Petru Solovan and Maria Hermina Molnar; m. Mirela Adriana Popa, Aug. 26, 1983 (div. Apr. 13, 1992); 1 child, Mark Christopher. MD, U. Medicine and Pharmacy Victor Babes, Timisoara, 1983, PhD, 1997. Cert. in dermatology and venereology Dept. of Health, 1994. Gen. practitioner County Hosp., Timisoara, 1983—90; asst. prof. U. Medicine and Pharmacy Victor Babes, Timisoara, 1991—98, assoc. prof., 1998—2007, prof., 2007—. Mem. cert. bd. dermatology and venereology Dept. of Edn. and Rsch., Timisoara, 1993—; organizer mtgs. New Trends in Dermatologic Therapy. Author: (book) Pathology of the Oral Muccosa, (guide) Guide of Dermatopathology; dir.: DEBRA.Ro; author: (guide) Textbook of Dermatology for Dentistry. Polit. guidance Civic Alliance, Timisoara, 1993—97; mem. Nat. Bd. Dermatology, 2007—. Grantee, Com. Tricontinental Mtg., Japan, 1992, Internat. Immunology Soc., 1997. Fellow: Am. Acad. Dermatology (AAD award for EADV mem. 2005); mem.: Internat. Soc. Cytokine, European Acad. Dermatology and Venereology. Roman Catholic. Achievements include research in oligoelements of the nails in normal humans and pemphigus vulgaris patients, implication for forensic medicine, and environment study and effects on humans; types of antibody in various forms of collagenosis; development of national program for psoriasis patients regarding their accesse to new biological treatments; research in photooxidative stress in porphyria cutanea tarda patients. Avocations: swimming, music. Office: Univ Clinic Dermatology Marasesti 5 Timis Timisoara 300077 Romania Office Fax: 0040256202619; Home Fax: 0040256493725. Personal E-mail: solovan99c@hotmail.com.

SOLOWAY, MARK STEPHEN, urologist, urologic oncologist; b. Balt., Jan. 24, 1943; s. Louis and Ada (Yoffee) S.; m. Cynthia T. Teper, May 30, 1966; children: Scott, Deanna. Student, Northwestern U.; MD, Case Western Reserve U., 1968. Diplomate Am. Bd. Urology; lic. MD, Ohio, Tenn., Mo., Fla. Clin. assoc. surgery br. Nat. Cancer Inst., 1970-72; resident in urology Univ. Hosps., Cleve., 1972-75; asst. prof. urology U. Tenn., Memphis, 1975-78, assoc. prof. urology, 1978-91; prof., chair dept. urology U. Miami (Fla.) Sch. Medicine, 1991—. Mem. med. staff U. Tenn./William F. Bowld Hosp., Memphis, 1975-91, mem. med. staff Cedars Med. Ctr., Miami, 1991—, mem. operating room com., 1991—, acad. affairs com., 1991—; mem. med. staff Jackson Meml. Hosp., Miami, 1991—, VA Hosp., Miami, 1991—; vis. prof. various univs. in U.S. and internat.; presenter and spkr. over 350 confs. and lectures in field. Editor Current Urology Reports; mem. editl. bd. Urology, Organo Ufficiale Suicmi (Italy); mem. internat. adv. bd. Progres en Urologie; reviewer Jour. Urology, Investigative Urology, 1978—, Cancer, Jour. Am. Med. Assn.; contbr. over 425 articles to profl. jours., over 35 chpts. to books in field. Lt. comdr. USPHS, 1970-72. Grantee NIH, 1975-87; Clin. fellow Am. Cancer Soc., 1973-74, Jr. Facility Clin. fellow, 1976-79; recipient 1st prize Cleve. Urol. Soc. Essay Contest, 1974. Mem. ACS, Am. Urol. Assn. (Southeastern sect., Gold Cystoscope award 1984, North Ctrl. Sect. Traveling fellow 1972-73), Am. Soc. Clin. Oncology, Am. Assn. Cancer Rsch., Soc. Surg. Oncology, Urol. Rsch. Soc., Soc. Urol. Oncology, Greater Miami Urol. Soc., Dutch Urol. Soc. (hon.), Buffalo Urol. Soc. (hon.), Phi Beta Kappa. Home: 9601 Collins Ave Apt 1410 Miami FL 33154-2213 Office: PO Box 16960 Miami FL 33101-6960 Office Phone: 305-243-8090. *

SOLOWAY, ROSE ANN GOULD, clinical toxicologist; b. Plainfield, NJ, Apr. 19, 1949; d. George Spencer Jr. and Rose Emma (Frank) Gould; m. Irving H. Soloway, Dec. 13, 1979. BSN, Villanova U., 1971; MS in Edn., U. Pa., 1976. Diplomate Am. Bd. Applied Toxicology. Staff nurse Hosp. of U. Pa., Phila., 1971-73; asst. clin. instr. Hosp. of U. Pa. Sch. Nursing, Phila., 1973-77; staff devel. instr. Hosp. of Med. Coll. Pa., Phila., 1977-78; dir. emergency nurse tng. program Ctr. for Study of Emergency Health Svcs., U. Pa., Phila., 1979-80; edn./comms. coord. Nat. Capital Poison Ctr. Georgetown U. Hosp., Washington, 1980-94; clin. toxicologist Nat. Capital Poison Ctr. George Washington U. Med. Ctr., Washington, 1994—; adminstr. Am. Assn. Poison Control Ctrs., Washington, 1994-99, assoc. dir., 1999—2005. Mem. clin. toxicology and substance abuse adv. panel U.S. Pharmacopeial Conv., Inc., Washington, 1990—2000, mem. expert panel clin. toxicology and substance abuse, 2000—05; bd. dirs., mem. Am. Bd. Applied Toxicology, 2000—05; mem. exec. com. Va. Injury Cmty. Planning Group, 2008—11. Contbr. articles to profl. jours. Vice-chair Poison Prevention Week Coun., 1988—91, 2001—03, chair, 1991—93, 2003—05. Mem.: Am. Acad. Clin. Toxicology (edn. com. 2000—08), Am. Assn. Poison Control Ctrs. (co-chmn. pub. edn. com. 1985—90). Avocations: reading, cooking, knitting, jewelry making. Office: Nat Capital Poison Ctr Ste 310 3201 New Mexico Ave NW Washington DC 20016-2756

SOLOWAY, STEPHEN, rheumatologist; MD, Am. U. Caribbean Sch. of Medicine, 1988. Diplomate Am. Bd. Internal Medicine-internal medicine, rheumatology, lic. to practice Fla., 1989, NJ, 1993. Fellow Hosp. Univ. Pa.; hosp. affiliation includes South Jersey Healthcare Regional Med. Ctr.; rheumatology tng. Med. Coll. Pa. Hosp.; internal medicine tng. Mercy Hosp. Pa. Office: South Jersey Healthcare Regional Medical Center 1505 W Sherman Ave Vineland NJ 08360 Office Phone: 856-641-8000.

SOLOWEY, CARL, dermatologist, educator; AB, NYU, Bronx, 1953; MD, SUNY, Bklyn., 1957. Diplomate Am. Bd. Dermatology. Intern Kings County Hosp., Bklyn., 1957—58; resident NYU, NYC, 1958—59, 1960—61, Bellevue Hosp., NYC, 1959—60; attending physician Univ. Hosp. Bklyn., 1962—, NY Hosp., Queens, 1962—, LI Jewish Hosp., New Hyde Park, NY, 1962—. Clin. asst. prof. dermatology Med. Sch. SUNY, Bklyn., 1982—. Fellow: ACP, NY Acad. Medicine, Am. Acad. Dermatology. Office: 98-05 63 Rd Rego Park NY 11374

SOLTERO-HARRINGTON, LUIS RUBÉN, retired surgeon, educator; b. San Juan, Sept. 4, 1925; s. Augusto Rafael Soltero and Anna Lila Harrington; m. Alice Joyce Carpenter, Apr. 24, 1958; children: Luis Ruben, Kathleen Ann, Susan Joyce, Robert Richard, Sharon Theresa. BS in Agr., U. P.R., Rio Piedras, 1945; BM, MD, Northwestern U., Chgo., 1949. Diplomate Am. Bd. Surgery, Nat. Be. Med. Examiners, P.R. Rd. Med. Examiners. Intern Michael Reese Hosp., Chgo., 1949-50; resident in gen. surgery Aguadilla (P.R.) Dist. Hosp., 1950-51; resident in gen. surgery, instr. Baylor U. Coll. Medicine and Affiliated Hosps., Houston, 1954-59; resident in gen. surgery Jefferson Davis, VA and M.D. Anderson Hosps., Houston, 1954-57; resident in pediatric, thoracic and cardiovasc. surgery St. Luke's-Tex. Children's Hosp., Houston, 1957-59; asst. prof. surgery U. P.R. Sch. Medicine, 1960-64, assoc. clin. prof., 1972-73, assoc. clin prof., 1973—, in charge devel. heart surgery program, 1960-64, dir. surgery residency tng. program, 1961-64; pvt. practice San Juan, 1959—2003; ret., 2003; prof. San June Bautisa Sch. Medicine, 2006—. Prof. surgery U. del Caribe Sch. Medicine, Cayey, P.R., 1981—, San Juan Bautista Sch. Med., 2006-; cons. in cardiovasc. and thoracic surgery Med. Examing Bd. P.R., San Juan, 1989; chief thoracic and cardiovasc. surgery Tchrs. Hosp., San Juan, from 1959; dir. surgery residency tng. program Univ. Hosp., Rio Piedras, from 1961; cons. in thoracic and cardiovasc. surgery San Juan City Hosp., 1962—, cons. in surgery, 1964—; cons. in surgery Presbyn. Hosp., 1972—, Mimiya's Hosp., 1987—; cons. in thoracic and cardiovasc. surgery Indsl. Hosp., San Juan, 1975—, Hosp. Met., 1982—, Clinic Fernández García, 1983—; chief surgery Ruiz Arnau Hosp., Bayamon, P.R., 1978—; asst. dir. ICU, Hosp. del Maestro, 1987—; bd. dirs. Rsch. Found. Cardiovasc. Surgery Tex., 1984—, Am. Cancer Soc., 1974; mem. Nat. Adv. Cun. Mended Hearts, Inc., 1969. Author: (textbook) The Management of the Acutely Ill Patient, 2002; contbr. articles to med. jours.; patentee partial occlusion vascular clamp to be used in small blood vessels; inventor respirator for infants based on electronic equipment. Capt., M.C., USAF, 1953-54. Recipient award for outstanding work in cardiovasc. surgery Lions Club, Hato Rey, 1961. Fellow Am. Acad. Pediat., Am. Coll. Legal Medicine (assoc.); mem. AMA (physician recognition award 1986); mem. Denton A. Cooley Cardiovasc. Surg. Soc., Michael E. De Bakey Internat. Cardiovasc. Soc., Pan Am. Med. Assn. (coun. pediatric surgery), P.R. Soc. Cardiology, Am. Heart Assn., P.R. Hear Assn., Phi Chi. Avocations: travel, horticulture, bridge.

SOLYOM, ANTAL ENDRE, retired psychiatrist; arrived in US, 1966, naturalized, 1972; s. Antal Solyom and Ilona Molnar; m. Gwen Ellen Cattle, Oct. 30, 1971; 1 child, Alexander Istvan. MD summa cum laude, Med. U. Szeged, Hungary, 1960; PhD in Biochemistry, U. Okla., Norman, 1970; MA in Bioethics, U. Va., Charlottesville, 2003. Diplomate in psychiatry Am. Bd. Psychiatry and Neurology, 1976, in child psychiatry Am. Bd. Psychiatry and Neurology, 1978, cert. in addiction medicine Am. Soc. Addiction Medicine, 1988. Rsch. assoc. dept. pharmacology Rsch. Inst. Pharm. Industry, Budapest, Hungary, 1960—64; vis. scientist inst. pharmacology and therapy U. Milano, Italy, 1964—66; postdoctoral fellow Okla. Med. Rsch. Found., Okla. City, 1966—70; rsch. fellow, neurochemistry NIH, Bethesda, Md., 1970—72; dir., children's outpatient svc. Detroit Psychiat. Inst., 1975—77; asst. prof. psychiatry sch. medicine Wayne State U., 1975—77; dir. infant study and infant psychiatry program med. sch. U. Mich., Ann Arbor, 1977—85, asst. prof. psychiatry med. sch., 1977—85; co-dir. Eleonore Hutzel recovery ctr. sch. medicine Wayne State U., Detroit, 1985—87, assoc. prof. psychiatry sch. medicine, 1985—89; dir. child-adolescent psychiatry edn. Fairlawn Ctr. Child/Adolescent Psychiat. Svcs., Pontiac, Mich., 1987—89; clin. prof. family medicine sch. medicine U. Va., 1989—2002; med. dir. bridges child-adolescent treatment ctr. Centra Health, Inc., Lynchburg, Va., 1989—2002, ret., 2002. Adj. affiliate ctr. biomedical ethics and humanities U. Va. Health Sys., Charlottesville, Va., 2003—; locum tenens psychiatrist Staff Care, Inc., Irving, Tex., 2004—. Contbr. more than 40 articles to profl. jours. Fellow: Am. Acad. Child and Adolescent Psychiatry (life); mem.: AMA (life), Am. Soc. Bioethics and Humanities, World Fedn. Mental Health, Am. Psychiat. Assn. (life). Achievements include research in pharmacological and hormonal regulation of lipid metabolism, particularly the effect of androgens on serum lipoproteins; research on the development and regulation of affects in infants and toddlers; postulated the affect-balance principle to understand the attachment to pecific persons or objects, and conceptualized the disease of addiction as a maladaptive/pathological attachment; the ethical challenges to the integrity of physicians regarding financial conflicts of interest in clinical research and in the use of assisted reproductive technologies; proposed special bioethical sonsiderations regarding clinical research in children/adolescents with psychiatric disorders, and in people with decisional impairments needing surrogate decision makers. Avocations: chess, classical music, travel, reading, swimming. Home: Po Box 3620 Lynchburg VA 24503

SOLZ, HERMANN, plastic surgeon; b. São Paulo, Brazil, May 5, 1952; s. Hermann and Hilde (Sihler) Solz; m. Jeanette Solz, Feb. 29, 1980; children: Sandra, Alex. MD, U. Sul Fluminense, Rio de Janeiro, 1976. Resident in internal medicine Hosp. Matarazzo, São Paulo, 1976; resident in plastic surgery BG Unfallklinik, Ludwigshafen, Germany, 1977—79, Marienhosp. Stuttgart, Germany, 1979—80, St. Markus Krankenhaus, Frankfurt, Germany, 1980; prof. plastic surgery U. Santa Cecilia, Santos, Brazil, 1983—88; plastic surgeon Hosp. Beneficencia Portuguese, Santos, 1983—88; chief plastic surgeon Mannheimer Clinic Plastic Surgery, Germany, 1989—. Fellow: Brazilian Soc. for Plastic Surgery, German Assn. Aesthetic Surgery, German Soc. Plastic Surgery. Avocations: diving, snowboarding, motorsports, languages. Office: Mannheimer Klinik für Plastische Chirurgie Mollstrasse 45 Mannheim D-68165 Germany Office Phone: +49-621-14740/152800. Office Fax: 0621 14849. Business E-Mail: info@beautyclinic.de. E-mail: drsolz@aol.com.

SOMASHEKAR, KALEGOWDA RAYA, science educator, researcher; b. Mysore, Apr. 4, 1957; MSc, U. Mysore, 1976, PhD, 1981. Rschr., cons. Bangalore U., 1981—, prof., 2002—. Recipient Young Scientist award, Govt. of Karnataka, CV Ramaan award, Dr. APJ Abdul Kalam award. Fellow: Nat. Environ. Sci. Assn. Avocations:

music, cricket, football. Home: 1492 Chandra Layout I Stage II Phase Bangalore Karnataka 560040 India Home Fax: 91 80 23213218. Personal E-mail: rksmadhu@rediffmail.com.

SOMASUNDARAM, JAYAPRAKASH, medical association administrator, educator; b. India, May 11, 1966; PharmM, 1993, PhD, 2009. Prin., prof. K.M. Coll. Pharmacy, 2005—, adminstr., 2010—. Mem.: Assn. Pharm. Tchrs. India, Tamil Nadu Dr. M. G. R. Med. U., Indian Pharmacy Coun. Home: 2 Old Chokkanathar Koil St Madurai Tamil Nadu 625001 India Personal E-mail: jpkmcp@yahoo.com.

SOMMER, ALFRED, ophthalmologist, medical educator, researcher; b. NYC, Oct. 2, 1942; s. Joseph and Natalie Sommer; m. Jill Abramson Sommer, Sept. 1, 1963; children: Charles Andrew, Marni Jane. BS summa cum laude, Union Coll., 1963; MD, Harvard U., 1967; MHS in Epidemiology, Johns Hopkins U., 1973. Diplomate Am. Bd. Ophthalmology, Nat. Bd. Med. Examiners. Tchg. fellow in medicine Harvard U. Med. Sch., Boston, 1968—69; dir. Nutritional Blindness Prevention Rsch. Program, Bandung, Indonesia, 1976—79; vis. fellow Inst. Ophthalmology U. London, 1979—80; founding dir., Dana Ctr. for Preventive Ophthalmology Johns Hopkins Med. Insts., Balt., 1980—90; assoc. prof. Johns Hopkins University, Balt., 1981—85, prof. ophthalmology, epidemiology and internat. health, 1985—2010, dean Johns Hopkins Sch. Hygiene and Pub. Health, 1990—2005, dean emeritus, 2005—, Gilman scholar, univ. disting. svc. prof., 2010—. Vis. prof. ophthalmology U. Padjadjaran, Indonesia, 1976—79; cons., advisor Helen Keller Internat., NYC, 1973—; cons., chmn. com. NIH, Bethesda, Md., 1981—; bd. dirs. Internat. Agy. for the Prevention of Blindness, Geneva; cons., com. mem. NAS, Washington, 1989; chmn. program adv. group on blindness prevention WHO, Geneva, 1989—90, com. mem., 1978—90, expert com., 1990—2010; chmn. steering com. Internat. Vitamin A Cons. Group Micronutrient Forum, Washington, 1975—2010; pres. Internat. Fedn. of Tissue Banks; chmn. sci. adv. bd. Edna McConnell Clark Found.; mem. & dir. Internat. Coun. Ophthalmology; dir. Becton Dickenson Corp., 1998—, T. Rowe Price Group, 2003—, Internat. Trachoma Initiative Found., 2004—09, chmn.; dir. Lasker Found., 2004—, chmn., 2008—; chair expect cmty. health global governance initiative World Econ. Forum; lectr. in field; dir. Bloomberg Family Found., 2010—. Author: Epidemiology and Statistics for the Ophthalmologist, 1980, Nutritional Blindness: Xerophthalmia and Keratomalacia, 1982, Vitamin A Deficiency: Health, Survival and Vision, 1995, Detection and Control of Vitamin A Deficiency and Xerophthalmia, 1978, 1982, 1995, Getting What We Diseases: Health and Medical Care in America, 2009; chmn. bd. overseers Am. Jours. Epidemiology and Epidemiologic Revs., 1990—2005, also bd. dirs., —; contbr. articles to profl. jours. Recipient Charles A. Dana Found. award for Pioneering Achievement in Health, 1988, Disting. Svc. award for Contbn. to Vision Care, APHA, 1988, E.V. McCollum Internat. Lectureship in Nutrition, Am. Inst. Nutrition, 1988, Second Ann. Am. Coll. Advancement in Medicine Achievement award in Preventative Medicine, 1990, Disting. Contbn. to World Ophthalmology award, Internat. Fedn. Ophthal. Socs., 1990, Smadel award, Infectious Diseases Soc. Am., 1990, Doyne Meml. medal, Oxford, 1995, Albert Lasker award Clin. Rsch., 1997, Helmut Horten Rsch. award, 1997, Gold medal, Singapore Ophthalmology Soc., 1997, Duke Elder Gold medal, Internat. Coun. Ophthalmology, 1998, Prince Mahidol award for contbns. to pub. health, 1998, Bristol-Meyers Nutrition Rsch. award, 2001, Danone Internat. award in nutrition rsch., 2001, Warren Alpert Found. prize, Harvard Med. Sch., 2003, Howe medal, Am. Opthal. Soc., 2003, Pollin prize, Columbia U., 2004, Helen Keller Rsch. Found prize, 2006, Gonin medal, Internat. Coun. Oph., 2007, First prize, Contbn. to Health, 2009, Thomas Francis medal, U. Mich., 2010; named to Ophthalmology Hall of Fame, ASCRS, 2011. Mem.: IOM, NAS, Inst. Medicine, Internat. Coun. Ophthalmology, Chgo. Ophthal. Soc., Assn. Schs. of Pub. Health (pres.), Internat. Assn. to Prevent Blindness (bd. dirs. 1978—2005), Nat. Soc. to Prevent Blindness (bd. dirs. 1984—94), Am. Acad. Ophthalmology (chmn. pub. health com. 1982—88, chmn. Quality of Care/Clin. Guidelines 1986—90, Laureate award 2011). Achievements include first to detail and publish epidemiologic approach disaster assessment; nutritional indices predict subsequent mortality in children, surveillance and containment is effective intervention strategy for controlling smallpox vaccenation effective 5 days after exposure; vitamin A deficiency increases childhood mortality and vitamin A supplementation decreases childhood mortality; nerve fiber layer is valuable diagnostic and prognostic sign of early glaucoma; routine preventive services cost-effective in eye disease; clinical guideline development and importance of outcome assessment; research in epidemiologic and public health approaches to ophthalmology, blindness prevention, and improved health and survival. Office: Johns Hopkins U Bloomberg Sch Pub Health 615 N Wolfe St Rm 1041 Baltimore MD 21205-2103 Office Phone: 410-502-4167. Office Fax: 410-502-4169. Business E-Mail: asommer@jhsph.edu.

SOMMER, MICHAEL, anesthesiologist, consultant; married. Diploma, Free U., Amsterdam, 1990. Cons. Ernst Moritz Arndt U., Greifswald, Germany, 1994—2002, U. Hosp., Maastricht, Netherlands, 2002—08. Mem.: Deutsche Gesellschaft Anesthesiologie und Intensivmedizin. Office: Dept Anesthesiology Prof Debeyelaan 25 6202 AZ Maastricht Netherlands

SOMMER, OSKAR HEINZ, psychiatrist, consultant; b. Vienna, Aug. 13, 1948; s. Richard Heinz and Elisabeth Höchenberger Sommer; m. Marita Trost, June 8, 1973; children: Kathrin Alice Dello Russo, Stefanie Metonou, Christina Suboh. Matura, Bundesgymnasium, Hollabrunn, 1967; MD, U. Innsbruck, Austria, 1976; PhD, U. Oslo. Cert. specialist in psychiatry Med. Assn. Norway, 2006. Cons. family medicine, Skotselv, Norway, 1997—2000; sr. cons. Sykehuset Innlandet HF, Reinsvoll, Norway, 2006—. Pres. Springs og Hope Norway, Raufoss, Norway, 2009—. Contbr. articles to med. jours. Elder Seventh Day Adventist Ch. Home: Storgata 73 B Raufoss 2830 Norway Office: Sykehuset Innlandet HF University Oslo Reinsvoll 2840 Norway Personal E-mail: oskarsommer@gmail.com.

SOMMER, ROBERT J., pediatric cardiologist, educator; MD, NYU, 1985. Diplomate Am. Bd. Pediatrics-pediatric cardiology, 2006. Pediatric cardiology St. Joseph's Med. Ctr., Paterson, NJ; assoc. prof. pediatrics Columbia Univ. Coll. Physicians and Surgeons; resident pediat. Mt. Sinai Med. Ctr., NYC, 1986—88, fellow pediatric cardiology, 1988—91; fellow interventional cardiology Childrens Hosp. Boston, Mass., 1991. Office: NewYork-Presbyterian Morgan Stanley Children's Hospital Columbia University Medical Center 630 W 168th St New York NY 10032 Office Phone: 212-305-2862.

SOMOGYI, PETER, neurobiology educator, health facility administrator; PhD in Cell Biology, Eötvös Loràand U., Budapest, Hungary; rsch. tng. in Neurocytology, Neuroanatomy, Semmelweis Med. Sch., Budapest; rsch. tng. in Biochemistry, U. Oxford, rsch. tng. in Immunocyto-chemistry; doctorate (hon.), Attila Jozsef U., Szeged, Hungary, 1990. Postdoctoral fellow Flinders Med. Ctr., South Australia, Australia; assoc., then co-dir. Med. Rsch. Coun. Anatomical Neuropharmacology Unit U. Oxford, England, 1985—98, prof. neurobiology, 1996—, dir. Med. Rsch. Coun. Neuropharmacology Unit, 1998—. Prof. neurobiology U. Oxford, Oxford, 1996; 9th Moruzzi Meml. lectr. European Neurosci. Assn., 1990; Jerzy Olszewski lectr. Montreal Neurol. Inst., 2001; Tobias meml. lectr. U. Chgo., 1995; Janos Szentagothai meml. lectr. U. Calif., 2005; Quastel lectr. Otto Loewi Conf., 2006; Hans Kosterlitz lectr. U. Aberdeen. Recipient Herrick prize, Am. Assn. Anatomists, 1984, Krieg Cortical Cortical Discoverer award, Cajal Club, Am. Anat. Soc., 1991, Yngve Zotterman prize, Swedish Physiol. Soc., 1995, Wenner-Gren Distiting. Lectr., 2003, Segerfalk Lectr. award, U. Lund, 2003, Feldberg Lectrs. prize, Feldberg Found., London, 2009, S.I. Palay prize, 2010, The Brain prize, Lundbeck Found., 2011. Fellow: Med. Acad. Scis. London, Hungarian Acad. Scis. (Janos Arany medal 2006), Royal Soc. London; mem.: Acad. Europea, Gen. German Nat. Acad. Scis. Achievements include research in synaptic organization of complex neural systems in the brain including the neocortex, hippocampus, thalamus, cerebellum, and the basal ganglia; molecular dissection of chemical synapses; physiological basis and pharmacological characterization of synaptic interaction between cortical neurones. Office: U Oxford MRC Anatom Neuropharmacology Unit Mansfield Road OX1 3TH Oxford England Office Phone: 44 1865 271898. Business E-Mail: peter.somogyi@pharm.ox.ac.uk.

SON, BYONG KWAN, pediatrician, educator; b. Chongwon-Gun, Korea, Apr. 29, 1949; m. Shin Ho Kang, Nov. 12, 1977; children: Eung Jung, Jun Bae, Eun Yong. Grad., Seoul Nat. U., Republic of Korea, 1975, D, 1979. Cert. specialist in pediats. Korean Med. Assn. Intern, resident pediat. Seoul Nat. U. Hosp., 1975—80; prof. Inha U. Med. Coll., Incheon, Republic of Korea, 2000—; vice-dir. Inha U. Hosp., 2002—. Vis. scholar Dept. Pediatric Allergy and Immunology UCLA, 1993—94. Co-author (in Korean): Allergic Plants in Korea, 2001, Textbook of Pediatrics, Textbook of Childhood Allergy and Respiratory Disease, Sports Medicine, 1st edit., 2001; co-author: Asthma and Allergic Disease, 2002, Guideline of Pediatric Asthma Management, 2003, Pediatric Asthma: Know Correctly and Treat Correctly, 2003; contbr. scientific papers. Mem.: Korean Soc. Allergology (auditing mem. 2003—05), Korean Pediatric Assn. (mem. bd. 2000—), Korean Acad. Pediatric Allergy and Respiratory Disease (v.p. 2005—). Home: #351-813 Apt Jamwon-Dong Seocho-Ku Seoul 137-951 Republic of Korea Office: Inha U Hosp Dept Pediats 7-206 3-Ga Shinheung-Dong Choong-Ku 400-711 Incheon Incheon Republic of Korea Office Fax: 82-32-890-2844. Business E-Mail: sonbk@inha.ac.kr.

SON, BYUNG CHUL, neurosurgeon, educator; b. Daegu, Republic of Korea, Mar. 4, 1964; s. Myung Gil Son and Jung Sook Ryu; m. Hye Jung Wi, Aug. 12, 1993; children: Juno, Joon Gee. MD, Cath. U. Korea, 1988, PhD, 2001. Instr., asst. prof. Dept. Neurosurgery Kangnam St. Mary's Hosp., Cath. U. Korea, Seoul, 1997—2003; asst. prof. neurosurgery St. Vincent's Hosp., Cath. U. Korea, Suwon, 2003—; clin. and rsch. fellow Dept. Neurosurgery Toronto We. Hosp., U. Korea, Ont., Canada, 2001—02. Cons. Hospice Ctr. St. Vincent's Hosp., Cath. U. Korea, Suwon, 2003—, dir. Stereotactic and Functional Neurosurgery, 2003—. Author: (academic award) MRS-guided stereotactic biopsy (The Academic Award from Korean Brain Tumor Soc., 2001); contbr. articles to profl. jours. Mng. dir. of web site St. Vincent's Hosp., Suwon, 2003. Capt. Med. Corps, 1994—97, Changnyung, Gyeongsangnam-do. Mem.: Korean Med. Assn., Korean Neurosurg. Soc. (cert. 1993), Korean Brain Tumor Soc., Korean Soc. Neurotraumatology, Korean Soc. Stereotactic and Functional Neurosurgery, Movement Disorder Soc., Asian Soc. Stereotactic and Functional and Computer-assisted Neurosurgery. Roman Catholic. Avocations: reading, cooking, drawing. Home: 1-1302 Ganbyun Apt Jamwon-dong Seocho-gu Seoul 137-794 Republic of Korea Office: St Vincent's Hosp Dept Neurosurgery 93 Chi-dong Paldal-gu Gyeonggi-do Suwon 442-723 Republic of Korea Office Fax: 82-31-245-5208. Business E-Mail: sbc@catholic.ac.kr. E-mail: sbc@vincent.cuk.ac.kr.

SON, BYUNG-HO, breast surgeon, researcher, educator; b. Pohang, Republic of Korea, Apr. 5, 1967; s. Kwang-Ik Son and Keum-Sun Park; m. Hyun-Hye Choi, Aug. 19, 1971; children: Sung-Eun, Juhee. MD, Coll. Medicine Kyungpook Nat. U., Korea, 1990; MS, Grad. Sch. Kyemyung U., Korea, 1997; PhD, Grad. Sch. U. Ulsan, Korea, 2002. Diplomate Ministry of Health and Welfare, Seoul, 1990, Korean Bd. of Surgery Ministry of Health and Welfare, Seoul, 1998. Internship Kyungpook Nat. U. Hosp., Taegu, Republic of Korea, 1993—94; resident in surgery Kyemyung U. Dongsan Med. Ctr., Taegu, Republic of Korea, 1994—98; fellowship in breast surgery Dept. Surgery, Coll. Medicine, U. Ulsan, Asan Med. Ctr., Seoul, Republic of Korea, 1998—2000; chief breast clinic Dept. Surgery, Sung Ae Hosp., Seoul, Republic of Korea, 2000—02; clin. dir. breast divsn. Dept. Surgery, Coll. Medicine, U. Ulsan, Asan Med. Ctr., 2002—03, asst. prof. breast clinic, dept. surgery, 2003—08, assoc. prof. breast clinic, dept. surgery, 2008. Author: (books) The Breast, 2005, Treatment Guide for Breast Cancer Patients, 2005 (Dong-A's Academic award, 2007, 2008). Recipient Roche's Achademic award, The Korean Breast Cancer Soc., Seoul, 2003, Novartis Endocrine Therapy award, 2005; grantee Granted Rsch., Asan Life Sci. Inst., Seoul, 2004, 2006. Mem.: The Korean Assn. of Endocrine Surgeons, The Korean Breast Cancer Soc., The Korean Surg. Soc. Presbyterian. Achievements include research in survivals, recurrence patterns and BRCA mutation in Korean breast cancer; tissue microarray of breast cancer. Avocations: tennis, choir. Office: Asan Med Ctr 388-1 Pungnap-dong Songpa-gu Seoul 138-736 Republic of Korea Office Fax: 82 2 474 9027. Business E-Mail: brdrson@korea.com.

SON, CHOONHEE, medical educator; b. Seoul, Republic of Korea, Mar. 27, 1962; PhD, Pusan U., 1986. Prof. Dong-A U., 1996—. Mem.: Korean Acad. Tb and Respiratory Diseases. Avocation: mountain climbing. Office: Dong-A University Hosp Pl Dept Busan 602-715 Republic of Korea

SON, HYO-SUNG, dermatologist; s. Young-Gil Son and Gang-Ock Kim; m. Hyun-Jung Lee, Feb. 28, 2005; 1 child, Gwan-Young. MD, Pusan Nat. U., Busan, Republic of Korea, 1997, M, 2003. With Coll. Natural Scis., Busan, 1991—93; intern Pusan Nat. U. Hosp., Busan, 1997—98, resident, 2001—05; dir. Kims Skin and Laser Clinic, Seoul, 2006—. Contbr. articles to profl. jours. 1st lt. Korean Army, 1998—2001. Fellow, Seoul Nat. U. Bundang Hosp., 2005—06. Fellow: Am. Acad. Dermatology (assoc.); mem.: Korean Med. Assn. (assoc.), Internat. Soc. Hair Restoration Surger (assoc.), Soc. Investigative Dermatology (assoc.), Am. Soc. Dermatologic Surgery (assoc.). Achievements include research in laser & IPL; intralesional injections. Avocations: painting, golf, swimming, travel, skiing. Office: Starmi Skin and Laser Clinic 5F Cheung Woo Yeonsan d-dong Yeonje-gu Busan 611822 Republic of Korea

SON, JAE-SUNG, pediatric cardiologist, educator; b. Chungnam, Korea, Nov. 1, 1971; MS, Seoul Nat. U., 1996. Assoc. prof. Konkuk U., 2011—. Mem.: Korean Pediat. Heart Assn., Korean Pediat. Soc. Office: 4-12 Hwayang-dong Gwangjin-gu Seoul 143-729 Republic of Korea Business E-Mail: drsonped@kuh.ac.kr.

SON, NGUYEN THAI, surgeon, director; s. Nguyen Luong Khan and Nguyen Thi Kham; m. Nguyen Thi Bich Huong, Dec. 2, 1984; children: Nguyen Thi Thai Ha, Nguyen Phu Hai. MD in Surgery, Hanoi Med. Sch., Vietnam, 1981. Cert. philosopist Hanoi Army Med. Sch., 2002, registered assoc. prof. Vietnam, 2007, lic. dr. 2003. Vice dir. St. Paul Hosp., Hanoi, 2000—; dir. Forensic Medicine Ctr., Hanoi, 2007—. Cons. Hanoi Health Dept., 2002—, cons. emergency med. svcs. and trauma care, 2002—. Contbr. articles to numerous profl. jours. Master: Vietnam Chidren Orthop. Assn.; mem.: Forensic Med. Assn., Hanoi Med. Sch. and Army Med. Sch. (mem. orthop. faculty), Vietnam Orthop. Assn. Office: Saint Paul Hospital 12 Chu Van An St 10000 Hanoi Vietnam E-mail: ntsonsp@gmail.com.

SON, SANG WOOK, dermatologist, educator; b. Seoul, Republic of Korea, July 12, 1970; s. Eu Mok Son and Jung Ran Jung. MD, Korea U., 1995, PhD, 2002. Lic. in dermatology Korean, 2000. Intern Guro Hosp Korea U., Seoul, 1995—96, resident dept. dermatology Guro Hosp, 1996—2000, clin. fellow dept. dermatology Ansan Hosp, 2000—02, asst. prof. Coll. of Medicine, 2003—. Active Jogey-Jong Seoul. Simon Greenberg Found. scholarship, World Congress Noninvasive Studies of Skin, 2005. Fellow: Am. Acad. Dermatology; mem.: Internat. Soc. Bioengineering and the Skin, Korean Soc. Dermatology (licentiate). Avocations: golf, tennis. Home: 6-3 Ewha Dong Jongro Gu Seoul 110 500 Republic of Korea Office: Korea Univ Ansan Hosp Gojan Dong Danwon Gu 516 426 707 Ansan Kyungki do Republic of Korea Office Fax: 82-31-412-5184. Business E-Mail: skin4u@korea.ac.kr.

SON, SEOK-MAN, medical educator; b. Busan, Republic Of Korea, Jan. 12, 1967, s. Byung-Chae Son and Won-Gui Jeong, m. You-Jin Han; 1 child, Bo-Young. MD, Pusan Nat. U. Med. Sch., Busan, 1994; PhD. Cert. in endocrinology and metabolism Korean Med. Assn., 1999. Clin. and rsch. fellowship Pusan Nat. U. Hosp., 1998—2000; asst. prof. medicine Pusan Nat. U. Sch. Medicine, 2000—03, assoc. prof. medicine, 2004—; postdoc. fellowship Emory U. Sch. Medicine, Atlanta, 2003—04. Mem.: Korean Med. Assn., Korean Diabetes Assn., Am. Diabetes Assn., Am. Endocrine Soc. Office: Diabetes Ctr Pusan Nat Univ Yangsan Hosp Beomeo-Ri Mulgum-Eup 626-770 Yangsan Gyeongsangnam-do Republic of Korea Office Fax: 82-55-360-1565. Business E-Mail: sonsm@pusan.ac.kr.

SON, SOOK-JA, dermatologist; b. Seoul, Nowon-gu, Republic Of Korea, Apr. 25, 1945; d. Dae-Shik Son and Myung-Ok Lee; m. Myung Kim, Sept. 24, 1982; 1 child, Hee-Joo Kim. PhD, Korea U., Seoul, 1986. Cert. dermatologist Min. Health and Welfare, 1969. Prof., dept. dermatology Eulji Hosp., Eulji Med. Coll., Seoul, 2005—08, vice dir., 2008. Contbr. articles to profl. jours. Home: 411-12 Pyungchang-dong Chongro-gu Seoul 110-848 Republic of Korea Office: Eulji Hosp Eulji Med Coll 280-1 Hagye 1-dong Nowon-gu Seoul 139-711 Republic of Korea Office Fax: 82-2-974-1577; Home Fax: 82-2-391-1004. Personal E-mail: ssjmdderma@hanmail.net. Business E-Mail: ssjmdderma@eulji.ac.kr.

SON, SOOK-MEE, legislative staff member; b. Geoje Island, Gyeongsangnam-do, Republic of Korea, Sept. 10, 1954; BA in Food Sci. & Nutrition, Seoul U., Republic of Korea, 1977; MS in Nutrition, Seoul Nat. U., Republic of Korea, 1979; PhD in Nutrition, U. NC, 1984. Registered dietitian Nat. Health Pers. Licensing Exam. bd., lic. tchr. Ministry Edn. Sci. & Tech. Prof. dept. food sci. & nutrition Cath. U. Korea, 1986—2008, chair sch. human ecology, 2000—01, dir. Inst. Life Sci., 2004—05; coun. mem. gyeonggi province vice chmn. Health, Welfare and Women's Policies Gyeonggi Coun., Republic of Korea, 2006—07; com. mem. Health, Welfare and Family Affaires Com., 2008—; rcom. mem. Gender Equality Com., Republic of Korea, 2008—; mem. nat. assembly Nat. Assembly Republic of Korear, 2008—; vis. prof. Cornell. Com. mem., assn. healthy life style practice Bucheon City Korea, 1998—2008; com. mem. sci. program com. Korean Soc. Obesity, 1999—2000; pres. Korean Assn. U. Prof. Food & Nutrition, 2002—03; chmn., com. dietitians nat. exam. Nat. Health Pers. Licensing Exam. Bd., 2003—05; com. mem., advertisement deliberation coms. Korea Advt. Rev. Bd., 2003—05; chmn. sci. program com. Korean Dietetic Assn., 2004—05; v.p. Korea Soc. Cmty. Nutrition, 2006—07; com. mem. team low salt intake project Ministry Health and Welfare, 2006—08; joint rep. forum Women's Non-smoking Movement, 2008; joint rep. fedn. Living Environ. Movement, 2008; dir. Korea Nat. Coun. Women, 2008; pres. Korean Dietetic Assn., 2008. Contbr. scientific papers. Dir. Korea Nat. Coun. Women, 2008; coun. mem. gyeonggi province Health, Welfare and

Women's Policies Gyeonggi Coun., 2006—07. Grantee Nutrition Edn. in CAPD patients, Ministry Health & Welfare Korea, 2003, 2004, 2005. Mem.: Korean Nutrition Soc., 2nd Asian Congress Dietetics. Roman Catholic.

SONDEL, PAUL MARK, pediatric oncologist, educator; b. Milw., Aug. 14, 1950; s. Robert F. and Audrey J. (Dworkus) S.; m. Sherie Ann Katz, Jan. 1, 1973; children: Jesse Adam, Beth Leah, Elana Rose, Jodi Zipporah. BS with honors, U. Wis., Madison, 1971, PhD in Genetics, 1975; MD magna cum laude, Harvard Med. Sch., Boston, 1977. Diplomate Nat. Bd. Med. Examiners, Am. Bd. Pediatrics; lic. physician, Wis. Postdoctoral rsch. fellow Harvard Med. Sch., Boston, 1975-77; intern in pediatrics U. Minn. Hosp., Mpls., 1977-78; resident in pediatris U. Wis. Hosp. and Clinics, Madison, 1978-80; asst. prof. pediatrics, human oncology and genetics U. Wis., Madison, 1980-84, assoc. prof., 1984-86, prof. pediatrics, human oncology and genetics, 1987—, head divsn. pediatric hematology/oncology, program leader, 1990—; assoc. dir. U Wisc. Cancer Ctr., 1996-99, U. Wis. Cancer Ctr., 2006—; vice chair rsch. dept. pediatrics U. Wis., Madison, 2006—. Sub-fellow pediat. oncology; Midwest Children's Cancer Ctr., Milw., 1980; vis. scientist dept. cell biology Weizmann Inst. Sci., Rehovot, Israel, 1987, 2000; chmn. immunology com. Children's Cancer Group 1990-2001; cancer ctr. rev. com. Nat. Cancer Inst., 1997-2000, bd. sci. counselors, 2005— Sr. editor Clin. Cancer Rsch., 1996-99; mem. editl. bd. Jour. Immunology, 1985-87, Jour. Nat. Cancer Inst., 1987—, Jour. Biol. Response Modifiers, 1990—, BLOOD, 1992—, Natural Immunity, 1992—; contbr. articles to Jour. Exptl. Medicine, Jour. Immunology, Cellular Immunology, Immunol. Revs., Med. Pediatric Oncology, Wis. State Med. Jour., Jour. Biol. Response Modifiers, Jour. Pediatrics, Jour. Clin. Oncology, Jour. Clin. Investigation, others State of Wis. Regents scholar, 1968; J.A. and G.L. Hartford Found. fellow, 1981-84. Mem. Am. Assn. Immunologists, Am. Assn. Clin. Histocompatibility Typing, Am. Fedn. Clin. Rsch., Am. Soc. Pediatric Hematology/Oncology, Am. Assn. Cancer Rsch., Am. Soc. Transplant Physicians, Am. Soc. Clin. Oncology, Am. Acad. Pediatrics, Leukemia Soc. Am. (bd. dirs. Wis. chpt. 1987-90 Achievements include patent for Typing Leukocyte Antigens; research on clinical and immunological effects of human recombinant Interleukin-2 and monoclonal antibodies. Home: 1114 Winston Dr Madison WI 53711-3161 Office: U Wis K4/448 Clin Sci Ctr 600 Highland Ave Madison WI 53792-3284 Business E-Mail: pmsondel@humonc.wisc.edu.

SONDHEIMER, STEVEN J., obstetrician, gynecologist, educator, reproductive endocrinologist; MD, U. Pa., Phila. Diplomate Am. Bd. Ob-Gyn-reproductive endocrinology, 1982, Am. Bd. Ob-Gyn, 1994. Intern Phila. Gen. Hosp.; resident Hosp. of the Univ. Pa., fellow, prof. ob-gyn., assoc. chief Penn Fertility Care. Named one of Best Doctors in America, 2003—04, 2005—06, 2007—08, 2009—10, America's Top Doctors, 2007—08, 2010, Top Docs, Phila. Mag., 2005, 2011. Mem.: Family Planning Coun. Southeastern Pa., Phila. Endocrine Soc., Obstetric Soc. Phila., Assn. Reproductive Health Professionals, Soc. Reproductive Endocrinologists. Office: Hospital of the University of Pennsylvania 8th Fl Market St Philadelphia PA 19104 Office Phone: 215-662-6100.

SONDIK, EDWARD J., health science administrator; BEE, MEE, U. Conn.; PhD in Elec. Engring., Stanford U. Faculty dept. engring econ. sys. Stanford U.; acting dir. Nat. Cancer Inst., 1982, acting dept. dir., dept. dir. divsn. cancer prevention and control, 1989, assoc. dir. surveillance program; dir. Nat. Ctr. Health Stats. Ctrs. Disease Control Prevention, Hyattsville, Md., 1996—. Sr. adv. health stats. Sec. Health Human Svcs. Office: National Ctr for Health Statistics 3311 Toledo Rd Hyattsville MD 20782 *

SONE, MICHIHIKO, otolaryngologist, educator; b. Morioka, Japan, Dec. 14, 1960; MD, Nagoya U., 1987, PhD, 1995. Assoc. prof. Nagoya U. Grad. Sch. Medicine, 2004—. Recipient Astrazeneca GERD Rsch. award. Mem.: Assn. Rsch. Otolaryngology. Office: 65 Tsurumai-cho Showa-ku Nagoya Aichi 466-8550 Japan Office Fax: 81-52-744-2325. Business E-Mail: michsone@med.nagoya-u.ac.jp.

SONENBERG, NAHUM, biomedical researcher, educator; b. Israel; married; 2 children. BSc in Microbiology and Immunology, MSc in Microbiology and Immunology, Tel-Aviv U., Israel; PhD in Biochemistry, Weizmann Inst. Scis., Rechovot, Israel, 1976. Chaim Weizmann postdoctoral fellow Roche Inst. Molecular Biology, Nutley, NJ; with McGill U., Montreal, Quebec, Canada, 1979—, James McGill prof., dept. biochemistry and McGill Cancer Centre. Internat. rsch. scholar Howard Hughes Med. Inst. Contbr. several articles to profl. jours. Recipient Rsch. Scholar award, Howard Hughes Med. Inst., 1997, David Thompson award, McGill U., 1994, Robert L. Noble prize, Nat. Cancer Inst. Can., 2002, Killam prize health sciences, 2005, Gairdner Found. Internat. award, 2008; named a Disting. Scientist, Can. Inst. Health Rsch. Fellow: Royal Soc. Can.; mem.: Am. Acad. Arts and Sciences (hon.; fgn. mem. 2006). Achievements include first to in cellular translation of genetic information. Office: Dept Biochemistry McGill Univ McIntyre Medical Bldg Rm 802 3655 Promenade Sir William Osler Montreal PQ Canada H3G 1Y6 Office Phone: 514-398-7262. Office Fax: 514-398-7384. E-mail: nahum.sonenberg@mcgill.ca. *

SONG, BONG GUN, cardiologist, educator; s. Tae Yeol Song and Keng Mei Sun; m. Jin Soo Choi, Sept. 23, 1978. MD, Sungkyunkwan U., Gangnam-gu, Seoul. Intern Inha U. Hosp., Incheon, Republic of Korea, 1999—2000; resident Sungkyunkwan U. Samsung Med. Ctr., Republic of Korea, 2000—04, rsch. fellow, 2007—08, clin. prof., 2008—09; tchg. prof. Inje U. Seoul Paik Hosp., 2009, Sungkyunkwan U., Samsung Changwan Hosp., 2009—10. Contbr. articles to profl. jours. Maj. US Army. Mem.: Am. Clin. Cardiology, Am. Heart assn., Am. Soc. Echocardiography, Korena Soc. Echocardiography (dir. 2010—), Korean Soc. Circulation. Office: Sungkyunkwan University Samsung Changwon Hospital 50 Hapseong-dong, masanwhaeweon-gu 630-723 KyungSangNamDo Republic of Korea Office Fax: 82-2-2278-0792. Business E-Mail: aerok111@hanmail.net.

SONG, CHANG-WOO, biologist; b. Choongnam, Republic of Korea, July 17, 1959; s. Keun-Seop Song and Ok-Nim Jang; m. Young-Ran Park; children: Seok-Moo, Yi-Sun. PhD, Osaka Prefecture U., Japan, 1998. Rschr. Korea Rsch. Inst. Chem. Tech., Daejeon, 1988—, prin. rschr., 2002—, sr. rschr., 1994—2002, v.p., 2011—; sr. rschr. Korea Inst. Toxicology. Mgr. treasure Korean Soc. Toxicology, Seoul, 2007—10; mgr. devel. Korean Assn. Lab. Animal Sci., Cheongju, 2007—09. Cell leader Urim Bapt. Ch., Daejeon, Republic of Korea, 1999—, elder, 2007—; bd. dirs. Frontier Project, Seoul, Republic of Korea, 2007—. Sgt. Korean Army, 1981—83, Seoul. Home: 408-601 EXPO Apt Jeonmindong Daejeon 305-762 Republic of Korea Office: Korea Inst Toxicology Shinsongno Tuseong Daejeon 305-343 Republic of Korea Office Fax: 82-42-610-8015.

SONG, CHENGLI, medical educator; b. Shandong, China, Feb. 28, 1968; PhD, U. Wales, Cardiff, 2000. Prof. U. Shanghai Sci. and Tech., 2009—. Recipient Med. Sci. Photography award, U. Dundee. Mem.: UK Chinese Life Scientists Soc., Soc. Med. Innovation and Tech. Avocations: calligraphy, travel, sports. Office: 516 Jun Gong Rd Shanghai 200093 China Business E-Mail: csong@usst.edu.cn.

SONG, EUN KYEUNG, medical educator; b. Daejeon, Republic of Korea, Jan. 27, 1977; PhD, Yonsei U., 2006. Asst. prof. U. Ulsan, 2010—. Recipient Nursing Rsch. Investigator award, Heart Failure Soc. America. Office: University Ulsan Daehakro 93 Nam-gu Ulsan 680-749 Republic of Korea Business E-Mail: gracesong@ulsan.ac.kr.

SONG, GEUNA, gynecologist; b. Pusan, Republic of Korea, July 20, 1971; MD, Dong-A U., 1997. Physician Dong-A Med. Hosp., 2004—05. Mem.: Korean Ob-Gyn. Home: Young-Ho 1 Lg Metrocity 209-303 Nam-Gu Pusan 608-100 Republic of Korea Personal E-mail: root-i@hanmail.net.

SONG, HONG SHICK, plastic surgeon; Grad., Seoul Nat. Univ. Med. Coll.; PhD, Seoul Nat. Univ. Bd. cert. tng. plastic surgery dept. Seoul Nat. Univ. Hosp., fellowship plastic surgery dept.; chief dir. plastic surgery dept. Hanil Hosp.; chmn. plastic surgery Seoul Hosp.; surgeon Dream Plastic Surgery Clinic. Clin. prof. Seoul Nat. Univ. Hosp. Mem.: Japan Soc. Aesthetic Surgery, Internat. Confederation Plastic Reconstructive and Aesthetic Surgery, Korean Cleft Palate-Craniofacial Assn., Korean Microsurgical Soc., Korean Soc. reconstructive Hand Surgery, Korean Med. Assn., Korean Soc. Aesthetic Plastic Surgery, Korean Soc. Plastic and Reconstructive Surgeons. Office: Dream Plastic Surgery Clinic Apkujung Subway Sta Seoul Republic of Korea Office Phone: 8225461616. Office Fax: 8225461614. *

SONG, HYUN SEOK, orthopedist, educator; b. Gyunsangnam-do, June 5, 1970; MD, Cath. U. Korea, PhD, 1994. Rsch. fellow Rothman Inst., Thomas-Jefferson U., 2007—08; assoc. prof. Cath. U. Korea, 2009—. V.p. IRB St. Paul's Hosp., 2009—; reviewer Jour. Arthroscopic & Related Surgery, 2009—. Mem.: Korean Soc. Sports Medicine, Korean Orthop. Ultrasound Soc. (editl. bd. mem. 2011), Korean Arthroscopy Soc. (editl. bd. mem. 2009—), Korean Orthop. Assn., Korean Shoulder Elbow Soc. Avocation: martial arts. Office: Saint Pauls Hosp Jeonnong-2-dong Dongdaemun-gu Seoul 130-709 Republic of Korea Office Fax: 82-2-965-1456. E-mail: hssongmd@yahoo.com.

SONG, JONG-MIN, cardiologist, educator; b. Seoul, Republic of Korea, Aug. 31, 1965; s. Yung-Bae Song and Sin-Ja Rho; m. Joo-Hyun Yoo; children: Ji-Won, Ji-Yoon. MD (hon.), Seoul Nat. U. Coll. Medicine, 1990; MS, Seoul Nat. U., 1994, PhD, 2000. Cert. internal medicine Ministry Health & Welfare, 1995, ECFMG, 1997, Cardiology Korean Assn. Internal Medicine, 2001. Internal medicine residency Seoul Nat. U. Hosp., 1991—95, clin. fellowship cardiology, 1998—2000, Asan Med. Ctr., Seoul, 2000—01, instr., 2001—03, asst. prof., 2003—08, assoc. prof., 2008—; rsch. fellow Cleve. Clinic Found., 2003—05. Contbr. articles to profl. jours. Capt. Republic of Korea Army, 1995—98, South Korea. Recipient Young Investigator's award, Korean Soc. Circulation, 1998, Yuhan Med. award, Seoul Med. Assn., 2008. Mem.: Korean Soc. Echocardiography, Korean Soc. Cardiology. Presbyterian. Office: Asan Med Ctr 388-1 Poongnap2-dong Songpa-gu 138-736 Seoul Republic of Korea Office Fax: 82-2-486-5918. Business E-Mail: jmsong@amc.seoul.kr.

SONG, JOSEPH, pathologist, educator; b. Pyong Yang, Korea, May 11, 1927; s. Ha Ju and Hwa Soon (Koh) S.; m. Kumsan Ryu, Apr. 12, 1958; children: Patricia, Michael, Jeff. MD, Seoul U. Sch. Medicine, 1950; MS in Pathology, U. Tenn., Memphis, 1956; MD, U. Ark. Med. Sch., 1965. Diplomate Am. Bd. Pathology. Pathologist in charge State Cancer Detection Survey, Providence, 1956—59; assoc. pathologist Providence Lying-In Hosp., 1958—61; assoc. prof. pathology U. Ark. Med. Ctr., Little Rock, 1961—64; dir. lab. Mercy Hosp., Des Moines, 1965—92, rschr. cancer, 1993—95; clin. prof. pathology Creighton U. Sch. Medicine, Omaha, 1968—95; med. dir. Corning Clin. Labs., Des Moines, 1995—97; ret., 1997. Cons. EPA, Washington, 1975-85; pres. med. staff Mercy Hosp., Des Moines, 1981 Author: (book) The Human Uterus, 1964, Pathology of Sickle Cell Anemia, 1971 (award 1975), Beyond the Horizon, 1995. Elder Winsdor Presbyn. Ch., Des Moines, 1964; com. mem. Aldersgate Meth. Ch., Des Moines, 1995. Major Med. Corps, 1950-52, Korea. Recipient Martin Luther King Med. Achievement award, So. Christian Leadership Conf., Statesmanship award Am. Assn. Med. Adminstrs., Las Vegas, Nev., 1987. Fellow ACP, Coll. Am. Pathologists, Am. Soc. Clin. Pathology, Am. Assn. Cancer Rsch. Methodist. Avocation: classical music. Home: 2345 Park Ave Des Moines IA 50321-1505 Home Phone: 515-243-7748.

SONG, JUN-HYEOK, neurosurgeon; b. Busan, Republic Of Korea, Nov. 17, 1964; s. Byung-Kyun Song and Myung-Suk Yeom; m. Yu-Seon Min, Feb. 1, 1994; children: Hae-Ryoung, Hae-Won. PhD in Neurosurgery, Korea U., Seoul, 1995. Lic. Korean Med. Assn., 1989. Neurosurgeon Korea U. Hosp., Republic of Korea, 1989—94, instr., 1994—96, Ewha Womans U. Hosp., Seoul, 1996—97, asst. prof., 1997—2001, assoc. prof., 2001—02; chmn. Wooshinhyang Hosp., Seoul, 2002—06; pres., CEO Barunsesang Hosp., Seong-Nam, Republic of Korea, 2007—. Author: (book) Essential Knowledge for Your Healthy Spine; contbr. articles to profl. jours. Mem.: Am. Assn. Neurol. Surgeons (assoc.), Korean Neurosurgical Soc. (life). Office: Samsung Tower Palace Dong 3702 Dogok 2 Dong Gangnam Gu Seoul 135-533 Republic of Korea Office Fax: 031 709 2075. Business E-Mail: neurosurgeon@naver.com.

SONG, KI-HOON, medical educator; b. Busan, Republic of Korea, July 14, 1967; s. Keun-Ho Song and Jong-Moon Jung; m. Young-Ah Sohn, Nov. 16, 1994; children: Yoo-Kyung, Hyung-Geun. BS in Medicine, Dong-A U. Coll. Medicine, Busan, 1993, MS, 1996, PhD, 1998. Diplomate Dong-A U. Coll. Medicine, 1998, cert. Korean Bd. Dermatology, 1998. Asst. prof. Dong-A U. Coll. Medicine, 2001—04, clin. assoc. prof., 2005—. Mem. bd. dir. Korean Soc. Phlebology, Busan, 2004—, Korean Soc. Aesthetic and Dermatologic Sugery, 2004—; editl. bd. Jour. Korean Soc. Phlebology, Busan, 2010—. Author: (text book) Aesthetic Dermatologic Surgery; contbr. articles to profl. jours. Recipient award, Congress 54th Korean Dermatol. Assn., 2002. Mem.: Assn. Korean Dermatologists (bd. mem. 2009—10). Office: Dong A University Hosp 3GA-1 Dongdaeshin-Dong Seo-gu Busan Republic of Korea Office Fax: 82-51-818-6882. Personal E-mail: tatabox7@nate.com. Business E-Mail: tatabox@hananet.net.

SONG, KWANG SOON, surgeon, educator; b. Daegu, Republic of Korea, Feb. 13, 1955; s. Suk Hee Song and Doo Nam Suh; m. Hye Young Jeong, Dec. 7, 1980; children: Byung Wook, Byung Chul. Vis. prof., U. of South Fla., Shriner Hosp. for Crippled Children, Tampa, 1992—93; MD, Kyungpook Nat. U., Daegu, Korea (south), 1989; PhD Philosophy, Kyungpook Nat. U. Medical License The Health-Social Affairs Ministry of Korea, 1979, Korean Board of Orthopedic Surgery The Health-Social Affairs Ministry of Korea, 1984. Vis. prof. Shriner Hosp. for Children, U. So. Fla., Tampa, 1992—93; chief of staff dept. orthop. surgery Keimyung U., Daegu, Republic of Korea, 2000—04, dir. dept. edn. and rsch. Dongsan Med. Ctr., 2005—. Dir. dept. edn. and rsch. Dongsan Med. Ctr., Keimyung U., Daegu, 2005—. Author: The Ilizarov Method for Treatment of Complex Fracture Orthopedics; contbr. articles to profl. jours. Maj. Korean Air Force, 1986—89, Daegu. Recipient New Investigator's Recognition Award, The Korean Orthop. Assn., 1986, 2003, New Investigator's Recognition Award, The Korean Pediatric Soc., 2002, Hon. Mention, Ann. meetng of Japanese Pediatric Orthop. Assn., 2002, award, Korean Med. Assn., 2004, Best award of Achievement, The Korean Orthopedic Assn., 2007; named one of 5th Boastful Person of Yr, Dosan Med. Ctr., Keimyung U., 2010; fellow Exchanged fellowship, The Korean Pediatric Orthop. Soc.- The Japanese Pediatric Orthop. Assn., 2002, Dept. of Orthopedics, Kyoto U., 1992. Mem.: Korean Assn. for Study and Application of Method of Ilizarov (bd. dirs. 2000—02, auditor 2004—06, pres. 2009), Korean Pediat. Orthop. Assn. (bd. dirs. 2002—), Korean Pediat. Orthop. Soc. (pres. 2007—), Korean Orthop. Assn. (com. for bd. exam. 1996—2000, bd. dirs. 2002—), Pediatric Orthop. Soc. N.Am. (corr.). Home: Manchondong Metro Palace 201-402 Daegu Republic of Korea Office: Dongsan Med Ctr Dept of Orthopedic Surgery Dongsandong 194 700-712 Daegu Daegu Republic of Korea Office Fax: 82 53 250 7205. Business E-Mail: skspos@dsmc.or.kr.

SONG, KYOUNGJUN, emergency physician, director; b. Seoul, Republic of Korea, Oct. 17, 1971; MS in Medicine, Seoul Nat. U. Med. Sch., 2006. Dir., dept. emergency medicine Seoul Nat. U. Boramae Med. Ctr., 2008—. Sec. gen. Korean Soc. Disaster Medicine, 2009. Mem.: Korean Coun. EMS Physician, Nat. Assn. EMS Physician, Korean Soc. Emergency Medicine. Avocation: mountain climbing. Office: Boramae-gil 39 Seoul 156-707 Republic of Korea Business E-Mail: doctorsong@paran.com.

SONG, MI-YEON, education educator, physician; b. Seoul, Republic of Korea, Dec. 21, 1971; d. Young-Ho Song and Jung-Hee Park; m. Sang-Hyun Moon; children: Chai-ho Moon children: Chai-jung Lim, Chai-hyun Lim. MD (Korean Medicine), KyungHee U., Seoul, 1996, PhD, 2001. Diplomate Nat. Cert. Commn. for Accupuncture and Oriental Medicine. Intern KyungHee Med. Ctr., Seoul, 1996—97, resident, 1998—2000; postdoc. fellow Columbia U., NY, 2001—03; instr. KyungHee U., Seoul, 2003—05, asst. prof., 2005—; postdoc. fellow John's Hopkins U., Balt. Contbr. chapters to books. KyungHee Rsch. Fund grantee, KyungHee U. Mem.: Soc. for Korean Med. Study of Obesity (life), Acad. Oriental Rehab. Medicine (life). Achievements include research in obesity and body composition, complementary and alternative medicine. Home: 41554 Bostonian Pl Aldie VA 20105 Office: Kyung Hee University Hosp 149 Sangil-Dong Gangdong-Gu Seoul 134-727 Republic of Korea Personal E-mail: mysong@khmc.or.kr.

SONG, SANG WOOK, physician, educator; b. Youngju, Republic of Korea, Oct. 16, 1964; MD, Cath. U. Korea, 1989, PhD, 1999. Prof., dept. family medicine, Cath. U. Korea St. Vincent's Hosp., 2000—, dir., Health Promotion Ctr., 2005. Mem.: Korean Soc. Health Promotion and Disease Prevention, Korean Acad. Family Medicine. Avocations: photography, computers. Office: 93-6 Ji-dong Paldal-gu Suwon Gyeonggi 42-723 Republic of Korea Office Fax: 82-31-248-7404. Business E-Mail: sswkoj@unitel.co.kr.

SONG, SUK-WON, medical educator; b. Seoul, Republic of Korea, Nov. 15, 1973; MD, Yonsei U., PhD, 1998. Prof. Yonsei U. Coll. Medicine, 1998—. Office: 612 Eonjuro Gangnam-gu Seoul 135-720 Republic of Korea Business E-Mail: sevraphd@yuhs.ac.

SONG, SUN UK, biomedical researcher, consultant; b. Daejeon, Chungnam, Republic of Korea, Mar. 2, 1963; s. Tae-Hyun Song and Ok-Soon Kim; m. Kee Ryoung Lee, Feb. 6, 1990; children: Seung Hyun, Seunghoon. BS, Evergreen State Coll., 1986; MS, U. Md., 1989; PhD, Johns Hopkins U., 1995. Rsch. assoc. Dana-Farber Cancer Inst., Boston, 1995—97, Mass. Gen. Hosp., Boston, 1997—99; rsch. dir. TissueGene Inc., Gaithersberg, Md., 1999—2000; prof. Inha U., Inchon, Republic of Korea, 2000—. Dir. TissueGene, Inc., Gaithersberg, Md., 2000. Author: (book) Gene Targeting Protocols. Recipient, Ctr. for AIDS Rsch., 1995, Rsch. Svc. award, NIH, 1997—99; Rsch. grant, Korean Ministry of Health and Welfare, 2002—. Mem.: Am. Assn. Cancer Rsch. Achievements include patents pending for mixed-cell gene therapy; bio-adhesive directed somatic cell therapy. Avocations: soccer, golf, travel, hiking, reading. Home: Yangchon-Gu Mokdong Apt # 705-1502 Seoul Republic of Korea Office: Inha Univ Hosp 7-206 3-Ga Shinheung-Dong Chung-Gu Inchon 400-711 Republic of Korea Office Fax: +82-32-890-2462. E-mail: sunuksong@inha.ac.kr.

SONG, WONKEUN, microbiologist; b. Seoul, Republic Of Korea, July 15, 1961; s. Young Goo Song and Bok Soon Kim; m. Hyun Sook Kwak, May 5, 1991; children: Joo Hyun, Joo Whan, Sun Joo. MD, Yonsei U., Wonju, Republic of Korea, 1987; MS, Hallym U., Chuncheon, Republic of Korea, 1998; PhD, Chung-Ang U., Seoul, 2000. Lic. MD Ministry Health and Welfare, Korea, 1987, lab. medicine Ministry Health and Welfare, Korea, 1995. Intern Yonsei U. Severance Hosp., Seoul, Republic of Korea, 1987—88; resident Yonsei U. Wonju Coll. Med. Christian Hosp., Republic of Korea, 1991—95; assoc. prof. dept. lab. medicine Hallym U. Coll. Medicine, Choonchun, Republic of Korea, 2002—07, asst. prof. dept. lab. medicine, 1998—2002, prof., 2007—; dir. Kangnam Sacred Heart Hosp., Seoul, 2000—; rsch. scholar Creighton U. Sch. Medicine, 2003—04. Lt. med. corp Korean Militar, 1988—91. Mem.: Korean Soc. Chemotherapy, Korean Soc. Infectious Diseases, Korean Assn. Quality Assurance Clin. Lab., Korean Soc. Nosocomial Infection Control, Korean Soc. Clin. Microbiology (rsch. award 2006), Korean Soc. Lab. Medicine, European Soc. Clin. Microbiology and Infectious Diseases, Am. Soc. Microbiology. Achievements include research in laboratory strategy to control antimicrobial resistance. Home: Shinjung-2 dong Yangcheon-gu Seoul 158-764 Republic of Korea Office: Kangnam Sacred Heart Hosp 948-1 Daelim-1 dong Youngdeungpo-gu Seoul 150-950 Republic of Korea Office Fax: 822-847-2403. Personal E-mail: swonkeun@naver.com. Business E-Mail: swonkeun@hallym.or.kr.

SONG, WOOHYUK, cardiologist; b. Busan, Republic of Korea, May 18, 1963; s. Byungkyoon Song and Myungsook Yeom; m. Jinhee Park; children: Nakyum, Taehun. MD, Korea U., Seoul, 1997; PhD. Med. dr. Ministry Health and Welfare Republic of Korea, 1988. Asst. prof. Coll. Medicine Korea U., Seoul, 1998—2001, assoc. prof. Coll. Medicine, 2001—07, dir. cardiology Ansan Hosp. Ansan, Republic of Korea, 2004—, prof. Coll. Medicine, 2007—. Capt. Korean Mil., 1992—95. Rsch. scholar, Weill Med. Coll., Cornell U., 2002—04. Mem.: Korean Assn. Internal Medicine, Korean Soc. Lipidology and Artherosclerosis (life), Korean Soc. Echocardiography (life), Korean Soc. Circulation (life), Korean Med. Assn. (life). Office: Korea Univ Ansan Hospital Kojan 1 dong Ansan Kyunggi-do 425-707 Republic of Korea Office Fax: 82-31-412-5594.

SONG, YO HAN, dentist; b. Jeonju, Jeonbuk, Republic of Korea, Jan. 18, 1961; s. Ho Joon Song and Hyun Ho Yoon; m. Hee Jeong Oh, May 29, 1994; children: Keun Hwi, Keun Ha. BS in Dental Surgery, Chonbuk Nat. U., Jeonju, 1985; MS, Seoul Nat. U., Republic of Korea, 1987, PhD, 1993. Cert. dentist Ministry health, welfare, family affairs, Republic of Korea, 1985. Faculty mem. Sch. Dentistry, Chonbuk Nat. U., 1992—2005, vice dean, 1998; vis. scientist Coll. Dentistry, U. Fla., Gainesville, 1999—2003; clin. dentist Song Yo Han Dental Clinic, Gunsan, Jeonbuk, Republic of Korea, 2005—; pvt. dentist. Contbr. articles to profl. jours. Chmn. Assn. fencing, Gunsan, Jeonbuk, 2007—. Grant, Korea Sci. Engring. Found., 1992, Ministry Edn., Republic of Korea, 1993, Korea Rsch. Found., 1993, 1995, Chonbuk Nat. U., 2001. Mem.: Acad. Osseointegration. Avocation: hiking. Home: Booyoung Apt 605-703 918-1 Inhoo-Dong Duckjin-Gu Jeonju Jeonbuk 561-735 Republic of Korea Office: Song Yo Han Dental Clinic Sekyung Bldg 2nd Fl 155 Nawoon-Dong 573-871 Gunsan Jeollabuk-do Republic of Korea Office Fax: 82-63-471-5204. Business E-Mail: ysong91@gmail.com.

SONG, YONG SANG, medical educator; s. Heui Bin Song and Pal Hee Kwon; m. Inhee Oh, Oct. 20, 1988; children: Eunji, Yaeji. MD, Seoul Nat. U., 1983, MS, 1987, PhD, 1994. Lic. dr. Korean Med. Assn., 1983, in obstetrics and gynecology Korean Soc. Obstetrics and Gynecology, 1987. Instr. Seoul Nat. U., 1993—95, asst. prof., 1995—2000, assoc. prof., 2001—05, prof. med., 2006—, assoc. dean rsch. affairs, 2006—08; affiliated prof. Guangdong Med. Coll., China, 2010—. Mem. editl. bd. Cancer Letters, 2009—, Cancer Rsch. & Treatment, 2007—, Jour. Women's Medicine, 2009—, ISRN, Obstetrics & Gynecology, 2010—; dir. Gynecologic Oncology Cancer Ctr., Seoul Nat. U. Hosp., 2009—, Cancer Rsch. Inst.; chmn. Gard. Sch. Cancer Biology, Seoul Nat. U., 2009—. Recipient 1st Prize Paper award, Korean Soc. Obstetrics and Gynecology, 2002, Sci. Paper prize, Korean Sci. Assn., 2004, Grand prize, Korean Soc. Colposcopy and Gynecologic Oncology, 2005, Acac. award, Internat. Conf. Ovarian Cancer, 2006, Clin. Rsch. Inst., Seoul Nat. U. Hosp., 2010; named Prof. of Superiority in Acad., 2008. Master: Korean Soc. Urogynecology; mem.: MSD (cons. to ovarian extl. tumor-specific strategy com. 2010—), Internat. Conf. NAPA (organizer 2009—), Asian Soc. Gynecologic Oncology (chair sci. com. 2010—), Korean Med. Assn., Korean Soc. Gynecologic Endoscopy, Korean Soc. Menopause, Korean Soc. Colposcopy and Gynecologic Oncology, Am. Assn. Cancer Rsch., Asian Clin. Oncology Soc., Korean Soc. Psychosomatic Obstetrics and Gynecology, Korean Soc. Obstetrics and Gynecology, Korean Cancer Soc. Achievements include research in gynecologic cancer. Home Phone: 82207082312845; Office Phone: 82-2-2072-2822. Business E-Mail: yssong@snu.ac.kr.

SONG, YUN SEOB, urologist, educator; b. Seoul, Republic Of Korea, Nov. 1, 1961; MD, Yonsei U. Sch. Medicine, Seoul, 1987, PhD, 1996. Diplomate urology Yonsei U. Sch. Medicine, Korea, 1992, cert. prof. 1997. Urologist Yonsei Mical Ctr., Seoul, 1988—92; dir., dept. urology Soonchunhyang U. Sch. Medicine, 2004—. Lectr. in fields. Contbr. scientific papers to profl. jours. Recipient award Best Article, Korean Urol. Assn., 2005, 2007, Korean Incontinence Soc., 2006, 2007, Korean Andrology Soc., 2000, 2002, 2007, 2008; Rsch. grant, Korean Continence Soc., 2006, Korean Urologic Oncology Soc., 2007, Korean Rsch. Found., 2008, Nat. Rsch. Found. Korea, 2010—. Achievements include research in urology and stem cell. Office: Dept Urology Soonchunhyang Univ Hosp 657 Hannam-Dong Yongsan-Gu Seoul 140-743 Republic of Korea Office Phone: 82-2-709-9375. Office Fax: 82-2-790-2468. Business E-Mail: yssong@hosp.sch.ac.kr.

SONGOK, MARTIM ELIJAH, virologist, researcher; s. Kipsongok Francis Getwo and Jerop Rosebella Songok; m. Jemisik Elizabeth Saina, May 6, 1989; children: Kipkemboi Denis, Chepchirchir Caroline, Chepkosgei Charity, Kibet Collins. BS in Life Scis., U. Nairobi, Kenya, 1985, MS in Biochemistry, 1996; PhD in Medicine, Kanazawa U., Japan, 2003. Cert. Med. Virologist Ministry Of Health, Kenya, 1998, Counsellor Kenya Red Cross Soc., 1994, Virology Inst. Of Tropical Medicine, Antwerp, Belgium, 1989, HIV Genotyping Kyoto Prefectural U. Of Medicine, Japan, 1997, Molecular Immunology WHO/ICRO, Weizmann Inst. Sci., Rehovot Israel, 1994, Blood Safety Japan Internat. Cooperation Agy., 1995. Asst. parasitologist Ministry of Health, Nairobi, Kenya, 1986—87, asst. microbiologist, 1988—89; asst. rsch. officer (virologist) Kenya Med. Rsch. Inst., Nairobi, Kenya, 1990—96, rsch. officer (virologist), 1997—. Supr., HIV/AIDS lab. Kenya Med. Rsch. Inst., Nairobi, Kenya, 1996—; vis. lectr. Shiga Med. U., Otsu, Japan, 2001—; advisor, HIV/AIDS Kenya Nat. AIDS Control Program, Nairobi, Kenya, 1996—; advisor/resource person, HIV/AIDS Kenya Ngo AIDS Consortium, Nairobi, Kenya, 1996—; coord. Terik Cmty. Program, Kisumu, Kenya, 2001—; editor, Kemri HIV/AIDS Update Jour. Kenya Med. Rsch. Inst., Nairobi, Kenya; participant various internat. profl. confs. Contbr. articles to profl. jours., including Lancet (Rsch. GRANTS, 2002). Fundraising coord. for edn. of socially disadvantaged children Terik cmty. program, Nandi, Kenya, 2001—03; creation of awareness for support of edn. of socially disadvantaged children in africa Hokuriku(Japan)-Africa Assn., Kanazawa, Japan, 2002—03. Grantee Rsch. grantee, Nat. Coun. Of Sci. And Tech., 1987—89;, Honjin Found., Japan, 2001, Toyota Found., Japan, 2002, Third World Acad. Of Scis., Trieste Italy, 1997, 2000. Mem.: Japan AIDS Soc. (assoc.; mem. 2000—03), Internat. AIDS Socity (life; mem.), Kenya AIDS Soc. (assoc.; mem. 1996—2003). Office: Kenya Med Rsch Inst Mbagathi Rd PO Box 54840 Nairobi Kenya

SONI, CHETAN, ophthalmologist; b. India, May 11, 1972; MD, Baroda Med. Coll., 2009; MS, U. Mo., Columbia, MHA, 2005. With dept. neurology, 2006—09; assoc. physician Mason Eye Inst., U. Mo., Columbia, 2009—. Recipient Ernst and Young award, Dept. Health Mgmt. and Informatics, U. Mo.; named Resident of the Month, U. Mo. Hosp. and Clinics, 2010, Resident of the Yr., Dept. Health Mgmt. and Informatics, U. Mo.; ASCRS Rsch. grant. Mem.: Mo. Soc. Eye Physicians & Surgeons, Internat. Soc. Cataract and Refractive Surgery, Am. Soc. Cataract and Refractive Surgery, Am. Acad. Ophthalmology. Office: University Mo Mason Eye Inst 1 Hosp Dr Columbia MO 65203 Business E-Mail: sonic@health.missouri.edu.

SONI, VIJAY KUMAR, physician, researcher; b. Bikaner, India, Jan. 5, 1970; MBBS, Sarder Patel Med. Coll., Bikaner, 1996. Dir. Reviewarticle.net, 2007—. Achievements include propounded a novel theory for male pattern baldness androgenic alopecia: a counter productive outcome of the anabolic effect of androgens. Avocation: astrology. Office: RAR Mansion Royan Cir Chamrajpet Bangalore Karnataka 560018 India Office Fax: 918042035322. Business E-Mail: drsonivijay@reviewarticle.net.

SONNEDECKER, GLENN ALLEN, pharmaceutical historian, educator; b. Creston, Ohio, Dec. 11, 1917; s. Ira Elmer and Leta (Linter) S.; m. Cleo Bell, Apr. 3, 1943; 1 child, Stuart Bruce. BS, Ohio State U., 1942, DSc honoris causa, 1964; MS, U Wis., 1950, PhD, 1952; DSc honoris causa, Phila. Coll. Pharmacy and Sci., 1989; PharmD honoris causa, Mass. Coll. Pharmacy, 1974. Lic. pharmacist. Mem. editorial staff Sci. Service, Washington, 1942-43; editor Jour. Am. Pharm. Assn. (practical pharmacy edit.), Washington, 1943-48; asst. prof. U. Wis., 1952-56, asso. prof., 1956-60, prof., 1960-81, Edward Kremers prof., 1981-86; sec. Am. Inst. History of Pharmacy, 1949-57; dir. Am. Inst. History Pharmacy, 1957—73, 1981—86, hon. dir. life, chmn. bd., 1988-89; editor-in-chief RPh, 1978-80. Sec., bd. dirs. Friends of Hist. Pharmacy, 1945-49; chmn. Joint Com. on Pharmacy Coll. Librs., 1960-61; US del. Internat. Pharm. Fedn., 1953, 55, 62; US rep. to Mid. East Pharm. Congress, Beirut, 1956; sec. sect. history of pharmacy and biochemistry Pan-Am. Congress Pharmacy and Biochemistry, 1957. Co-author books; contbr. to pharm. and hist. publs. Recipient Edward Kremers award (for writings), 1964, Nat. award Rho Chi, 1967, Schelenz plaquette Internat. Soc. for History of Pharmacy, 1971, Remington honor medal Am. Pharm. Assn., 1972, Urdang medal, 1976, Folch Andreu prize, Spain, 1985, Profile award Am. Found. Pharm. Edn., 1994; Am. Found. fellow, 1948-52, Guggenheim fellow, 1955, Fulbright Rsch. scholar, Germany, 1955-56. Mem. Am. Pharm. Assn. (life; sec. sect. history of pharmacy 1949-50, vice chmn. 1950-51, chmn. 1951-52, rsch. assoc. 1964-65, chmn. joint task force with Acad. Pharm Scis. 1985, hon. chmn. bd. trustees 1985), Internat. Acad. History Pharmacy (1st v.p. 1970-81, pres. 1983-91, hon. pres. 1991—), Am. Assn. History of Medicine (exec. coun. 1966-69), Internat. Gesellschaft fur Geschichte der Pharmazie (exec. bd. 1965-89), hon. mem. socs. for history of pharmacy of Italy, Benelux, Spain; mem. Rho Chi (mem. nat. exec. coun. 1957-59), Phi Delta Chi. Unitarian. Home: Apt 113 6205 Mineral Point Rd Madison WI 53705-4577

SONNENFELD, GERALD, microbiology and immunology educator; b. NYC, Oct. 14, 1949; s. Otto Arthur and Ann (Perelman) S.; m. Elizabeth; 3 children, Jennifer, Jessica, Susan. BS, CCNY, 1970; PhD, U. Pitts., 1975. Postdoctoral fellow Stanford (Calif.) U. Sch. Medicine, 1976-78; assoc. guest worker Ames Rsch. Ctr. NASA, Moffett Field, Calif., 1976-78; asst. prof. microbiology and immunology U. Louisville, 1978-83, from assoc. prof. to prof. microbiology and immunology, 1983-93; dir. rsch. immunology Carolinas Med. Ctr., Charlotte, NC, 1994—98. Prof., chair dept. microbiology and immunology, assoc. dean basic scis. & grad. studies Morehouse Sch. Med., Atlanta, 1999-2004; v.p. rsch. Binghamton U., SUNY, 2004-10, Clemson U., 2010-. Assoc. editor Jour. Interferon Cytokine Rsch., 1981—; contbr. over 150 articles to profl. jours. Grantee NASA, 1978—2008, Environ. Protection Agy., 1980-82, U.S. Army, 1983-87, NIH, 1984-87. Mem. Internat. Soc. for Interferon Rsch. (pubs. com. 1988—), Am. Assn. Immunologists (Lifetime Svc. award, 2010), Am. Soc. Microbiology, Am. Soc. Gravitational and Space Biology (governing bd. 1992-95, pres.-elect 1996-97, pres. 1997-1998), Sigma Xi. Avocation: railroading. Office: Clemson University 300 Brackett Hall Clemson SC 29634-5701

SONNENSCHEIN, RALPH ROBERT, physiologist; b. Chgo., Aug. 14, 1923; s. Robert and Flora (Kieferstein) S.; m. Patricia W. Niddrie, June 21, 1952; children— David, Lisa, Ann. Student, Swarthmore Coll., 1940—42, U. Chgo., 1942—43; BS, Northwestern U., 1943, BM, MS, Northwestern U., 1946, MD, 1947; PhD, U. Ill., 1950. Research asst. in physiology Northwestern U. Med. Sch., 1944-46; intern Michael Reese Hosp., Chgo., 1946-47; successively research fellow clin. sci., research asst. psychiatry, research asso. psychiatry U. Ill. Med. Sch., Chgo., 1947-51; mem. faculty U. Calif. Med. Sch., Los Angeles, 1951-88, prof. physiology, 1962-88, prof. emeritus, 1988—; liaison scientist Office Naval Research, London, 1971-72. Author papers on pain, innervation of skin, peripheral circulation. Served with AUS, 1943-46. Spl. research fellow USPHS, 1957-58; fellow Swedish Med. Research Council, 1964-65; grantee USAF; grantee Office Naval Research; grantee NIH; grantee NSF. Mem. Am. Physiol. Soc., Microcirculatory Soc., Soc. Exptl. Biology and Medicine, AAAS, Hungarian Physiol. Soc. (hon.). Home: 18212 Kingsport Dr Malibu CA 90265-5636 Office: U Calif Sch Medicine Dept Physiology Los Angeles CA 90095-1751

SONTAG, JAMES MITCHELL, oncologist, researcher; b. Denver, Dec. 8, 1939; s. Samuel Henry and Rose Hazel (Silverman) S.; m. Elizabeth Crockett Tunis; children: Ariella, Eythan. BS, Lamar State Coll. Tech., Beaumont, Tex.; MS, U. Ill., 1967; PhD, Weizmann Inst. Sci., Rehovot, Israel, 1971; MPH, Harvard U., 1982. Postdoctoral fellow Damon Runyon Meml. Fund Cancer Rsch., 1971-72; guest worker Nat. Cancer Inst., NIH, Bethesda, Md., 1972-73, staff fellow, 1973-74, exptl. oncologist, 1973-76, mgr. carcinogen bioassay program, 1973-76, asst. to divsn. dir. cancer cause and prevention, 1976-80; exec. sec. Clearinghouse on Environ. Carcinogens, 1976-80, asst. dir. for interagy. affairs Office of Dir., 1980-82, spl. asst. epidemiology and biostatistics program, 1982-96; chief office divsn. ops. & analysis divsn. cancer epidemiology and genetics Nat. Cancer Inst., 1996-99; vol. Grassroots Artisans, Med. Mission, L.Am., 1999—. Author, editor in field. ESL tchr. 2004-; Served with AUS, 1956-59. Beaumont LWV scholar, 1963-65 Mem. Beta Beta Beta.

SOO, BORSON, geriatrician, psychiatrist, educator; MD, Stanford U., 1969. Diplomate Am. Bd. Psychiatry and Neurology, 1985, Am. Bd. Psychiatry and Neurology-geriatric psychiatry, 2000. Intern beth Israel Hosp., 1970; resident psychiatry Univ. Wash. Med. Ctr., 1977—79, fellow geriatric psychiatry, 1979—81; prof. psychiatry Univ. Wash. Office: University of Washington Medical Center Box 356151 1959 NE Pacific St Seattle WA 98195-6151 Office Phone: 206-598-3300.

SOOD, ANIL K., oncologist, researcher; MD, U. N.C., 1991. Diplomate Am. Bd. Obstetrics and Gynecology 1999. Intern in ob-gyn. U. Fla., Gainesville, Fla., 1991—93, resident in ob-gyn., 1993—95; fellow in gynecol. oncology U. Iowa, Iowa City, 1995—98; asst. prof. U. of Iowa, 1998—2002; assoc. prof. gynecologic oncology and cancer biology M.D. Anderson Cancer Ctr., U. Tex., Houston, 2002—06, dir. ovarian cancer rsch., 2005—, prof. gynelogic oncology and cancer biology, 2006—. Editl. adv. bd. Cancer, 2003—; editl. bd. Current Cancer Therapy Reviews, 2003—, Cancer Biology and Therapy, 2005—, Obstetrics and Gynecology, 2006—. Recipient Reproductive Scientist Devel. award, NIH, 1999—2001, Rsch. award, Gynecologic Cancer Found., 2001, Am. Cancer Soc./U. Iowa, 1998, phase 2 RSDP award, Gynecologic Cancer Found., 2001, James F. Nolan award, Western Assn. Gynecologic Oncologists, 2002, 2004, Charles A. Hunter Jr. prize, Am. Gynecological and Obstetrical Soc., 2003, Faculty Scholar award, M.D. Anderson Cancer Ctr., 2006—09. Mem.: ACOG, Am. Soc. Clin. Investigation, Am. Soc. Clin. Oncology, Soc. of Gynecologic Oncologists, Am. Assn. for Cancer Rsch. Office: UTMD Anderson Cancer Ctr Dept Gyn Oncology 1515 Holcombe Blvd 440 Houston TX 77030

SOOMETS, URSEL, medical educator; b. Viljandi, Estonia, July 18, 1962; s. Vello Soomets and Heidi Bergmann; m. Tiina Soosaar, May 10, 2000; children: Krõõt, Risse. BS, U. Tartu, Estonia, 1985, MS in Organic Chemistry, 1994; PhD, U. Stockholm, 2000. Sr. lectr. dept. biochemistry, faculty medicine U. Tartu, 1991—2000, assoc. prof., sr. rschr. dept. biochemistry, faculty medicine, 2000—, prof. med. metabolomics, head bd. biomed. scis., med. faculty, mem. bd. neuroscis., 2010—. Mem. expert-commn. health Estonian Sci. Found., Tartu, 2010—. Recipient Nat. Sci. award, Govt. Estonia, 2009; grants, Estonian Sci. Found., 2001—02, Marie Curie Mobility grant, European Union, 2005—09, Project grant, Enterprise Estonia, 2009. Mem.: European Peptide Soc., Am. Peptide Soc., Estonian Biochem. Soc., Korporatsioon Ugala. Avocations: travel, reading, sports. Office: University Tartu 19 Ravila St Tartu 50411 Estonia Office Fax: 372 7 374 312. Business E-Mail: ursel.soomets@ut.ee.

SOONG-RYONG, JUNG, dentist; b. Republic of Korea, May 26, 1964; PhD, Chonnam Nat. U. Sch. Dentistry, 1989, M in Dentistry, 1995. Staff prosthodontist John D Dingell VA Med. Ctr., 2008—, co-dir. grad. prosthodontics program, 2009—. Adj. clin. lectr. U. Mich. Sch. Dentistry, 2009—11. Fellow: Am. Acad. Implant Dentistry, Am. Coll. Prosthodontics; mem.: ADA, Mich. Dental Assn., Korean Dental Assn. Avocations: golf, Judo. Home: 4478 Lake Forest Dr E Ann Arbor MI 48108 Personal E-mail: dr.srjung@gmail.com.

SOORIYAARACHCHI, GAMINI SARATHCHANDRA, oncologist, hematologist, educator; b. Kosgama, Sri Lanka; m. Chandrika Senerath; children: Jasmine, Marcus. MBBS with honors, U. Ceylon, Colombo, Sri Lanka, 1970; diploma in child health, Conjoint Bd. Examiners, London, 1975; diploma in obstetrics, Royal Coll. Ob-Gyn Gt. Britain, 1975; MBA, U. Tenn., Knoxville, 2004. Diplomate Am. Bd. Internal Medicine, Am. Bd. Geriatric Medicine, Am. Bd. Med. Oncology, Am. Bd. Hematology, cert. physician exec. Cert. Commn. Med. Mgmt., 2005. Intern U. Ceylon Tchg. Hosps., 1970-71; sr. house officer Guildford Hosps., England, 1971-73; registrar St. Helens Hosp., England, 1974-75; sr. house officer Royal Marsden Hosp. and Inst. Cancer Rsch., Sutton, England, 1973-74; fellow in med. oncology and hematology U. Wis. Comprehensive Cancer Ctr., Madison, 1975-77; cons. med. oncologist and hematologist Rockford Clinic and Rockford Meml. Hosp., Ill., 1977-83, Oncology Hematology West and Alegent Bergan Mercy Cancer Ctr., Omaha, 1983—; med. dir. Alegent Bergan Mercy Cancer Ctr., Omaha, 1984—; co-dir. bone marrow transplantation program Oncology Hematology West and Alegent Bergan Mercy Med. Ctr., Omaha, 1993—. Asst. clin. prof. medicine U. Ill. Sch. Medicine, Rockford, 1977—83; bd. dirs. Cancer Biotherapy Rsch. Group, Franklin, Tenn.; mem. at-large med. exec. com. Alegent Bergan Mercy Med. Ctr., 2002—03, pres.-elect, vice chmn., 2003—04; pres., chief med. staff Alegent Bergan Mercy Med.

Ctr, 2005—07; bd. dirs. Missouri Valley Cancer Consortium, Omaha, pres., 1999—2001, prin. investigator, 2006—; assoc. clin. prof. medicine Creighton U. Sch. Medicine, Omaha, 1984—96, clin. prof., 1996—; chmn. prof. edn. Am. Cancer Soc., 1986, Nebr. divsn., 87, bd. dirs. Douglas and Sarpy Counties, Neb., 86, Nebr. divsn., 87; med. dir., founding mem. No. Ill. Hospice Assn., Rockford, 1980—83; mem. exec. com., novel therapeutics com., audit com., ethnic diversity com., by-law com. North Ctrl. Cancer Treatment Group, Mayo Clin., Rochester, Minn.; mem. head and neck cancer steering com., alt. mem. breast cancer steering com. Nat. Cancer Inst., Bethesda, Md.; chmn. Am. Med. Assn. Sec. of Internat. Med. Graduates, 2007—; alt. rep. AMA Commn. to End Healthcare Disparities; mem. Coun. Long Range Planning & Devel, AMA. Contbg. author: Cancer Genetics in Women, 1987; contbr. over 60 articles and astracts to med. jours., including Jour. Clin. Oncology, Blood, Archives Surgery, Jour. Immunotherapy, Cancer Investigation, Annals Pharmacotherapy, Jour. Am. Acad. Dermatology, Jour. Clin. Pathology. Recipient Spirit Mission award, Alegent Health System, 2005, Leadership award (Internat. Med. Grad. Physician), AMA Found., 2006, Candle Light award, Alegent Bergan Mercy Med. Ctr., 2007. Fellow ACP, Royal Coll. Physicians (London), Soc. for Biol. Therapy; mem. AMA (alt. del. to House of Dels. 2006-, alt. rep. Commn. to End Healthcare Disparities 2006-), Royal Coll. Surgeons (Eng.), Am. Soc. Clin. Oncology, Am. Soc. Hematology (com. on practice), Am. Soc. for Blood and Marrow Transplantation, Nebr. Med. Assn., Am. Soc. Hematology(practise com.), Am. Soc. Clin. Oncology(by-law com. mem.), Am. Hosp. Pharmacists Assn.(oncology expert panel mem.) Office: Alegent Health Bergan Mercy Cancer Ctr 7710 Mercy Rd Ste 122 Omaha NE 68124-2346

SOOUDI, MATTHEW M., retired surgeon; b. Iran, Oct. 24, 1934; came to U.S., 1962; s. Yahya and Iran (Nicknejad) S.; m. Joyce J. Sooudi, Oct. 2, 1965; 2 children. MD, U. Iran, 1962. Diplomate Am. Bd. Surgery, Am. Bd. Colon and Rectal Surgery, Internat. Bd. Proctology. Intern. Bon Secours Hosp., Grosse Pointe, Mich., 1962-63; resident Grace Hosp., Detroit, 1963-67, Ferguson Clinic, Grand Rapids, Mich., 1967-68; pvt. practice St. Elizabeth Hosp., Tex., Beaumont (Tex.) Med. Hosp., Bapt. Hosp., Tex.; ret., 1996. Fellow ACS, Am. Soc. Colon and Rectal Surgeons, Internat. Assn. Proctologists; mem. AMA, Am. Assn. Phys. Surgeons, So. Med. Assn., Tex. Med. Assn., Tex. Soc. Colon and Rectal Surgeons. Address: 980 Thomas Rd Beaumont TX 77706-4621

SORBERA, CARMINE A., cardiac electrophysiologist; MD, NY Med. Coll. Diplomate Am. Bd. Internal Medicine, Am. Bd. of Internal Medicine-cardiovasc. disease, Am. Bd. of Internal Medicine-clin. electrophysiology. With Westchester Med. Ctr., resident internal medicine Valhalla, NY, 1984—87, fellow cardiovasc. disease, 1987—89, fellow interventional cardiology, 1989—90; assoc. prof. NY Med. Coll.; with Kingston Hosp. Office: Westchester Medical Center 19 Bradhurst Ave Suite 700 Hawthorne NY 10532 Office Phone: 914-593-7800. Office Fax: 914-593-7857.

SORDIA HERNANDEZ, LUIS HUMBERTO, physician, educator; b. Monterrey, Nuevo Leon, Mex., Mar. 9, 1960; MD, U. Autónoma Nuevo León, 1983; PhD, U. Barcelona, 2010. Prof. U. Autónoma Nuevo León, 1990—, dept. chief, svcs. med., 1998—2011. Recipient Best Resident award in Biology, U. Autónoma Nuevo León, 1st Pl. Clin. Investigation, Congreso Nat. Investigacion Biomedicauanl. Mem.: Am. Soc. Reconstructive Microsurgery. Avocation: golf. Office: Hidalgo 2534 Pte Monterrey Nuevo Leon 640160 Mexico

SORENSEN, ALMA GREGORY, neuroradiologist; b. Salt Lake City, Mar. 31, 1963; BS in Biology, Calif. Inst. Tech., 1984; MS in Computer Sci., Brigham Young U., 1987; MD, Harvard Med. Sch., 1989. Diplomate Am. Bd. Radiology, cert. in diagnostic radiology. Intern diagnostic radiology New Eng. Deaconess Hosp., Boston, 1989—90; resident neurol. radiology Mass. Gen. Hosp., Boston, 1990—93, fellow, 1993—95, dir. Ctr. Biomarkers in Imaging; assoc. prof. radiology Harvard Med. Sch., 1994—. Assoc. prof. health scis. & tech. Harvard-MIT, co-dir. Athinoula A. Martinos Ctr. Biomedical Imaging. Contbr. articles to profl. jours. Mem.: AAAS, Am. Coll. Radiology, Assn. Univ. Radiologists. Office: Mass Gen Hosp NMR Ctr Ste 2301 149 Thirteenth St Charlestown MA 02129 E-mail: sorensen@ieee.org, asorensen@partners.org, sorensen@nmr.mgh.harvard.edu. *

SØRENSEN, HOLGER JELLING, psychiatrist, educator; b. Kalundborg, Denmark, Apr. 29, 1959; s. Verner and Jytte Sørensen. MD, Copenhaben U., 1986; PhD, Copenhagen U., 1997; MS in Epidemiology, Netherlands Inst. Health Sci., Rotterdam, Netherlands, 1994. Resident neurology Rigs Hosp., Copenhagen U., 1987—88; resident psychiatry Bispebjerg, Copenhagen U., 1990—91; specialization in psychiatry Copenhagen U. Hosp., 1996—2001; chief physician psychiatry Amager, Copenhagen, 2003—. Home: Hostrups Have 18 5th Frederiksberg Copenhagen 1954 Denmark Office: Dept Psychiatry Amager Copenhagen Univ Hosp Digevej 110 Copenhagen 2300 Denmark Personal E-mail: holgerjs@dadlnet.dk.

SORENSEN, JOHN B., surgeon; s. Bruce F. and Suzanne B. Sorensen. MD, Temple U., 1986. Cert. surgery Am. Bd. Surgery, 1992, critical care Am. Bd. Surgery, 1995, transplantation surgery U. Pitts., 1993. Dir. transplantation LDS Hosp., Salt Lake City, 1993—2005; chief sect. transplantation dept. surgery U. Utah, Salt Lake City, 2005—. Med. dir. Intermountain Donor Services, Salt Lake City, 2004—. Col. US Army, 2002. Decorated Combat Med. Badge, Bronze Star U.S. Army. Fellow: ACS; mem.: Am. Soc. Transplant Surgeons, Sigma Chi. Mem. Lds Ch. Office: Univ Utah Dept Surgery 30 North 1900 East Salt Lake City UT 84132

SØRENSEN, TORBEN LYKKE, medical educator; b. Sønderborg, Denmark, Mar. 20, 1972; MD, U. Copenhagen, Denmark, 1999, DMS, 2004. Clin. assoc. rsch. prof. U. Copenhagen, 2009—. Recipient Foghs award, Part Danish Neurol. Soc. Mem.: Danish Ophthal. Soc. Office: Køgevej 7-13 Roskilde Zealand 4000 Denmark Business E-Mail: torbenls@dadlnet.dk.

SORENSON, CHARLES W., health system administrator, surgeon; BA, U. Utah, Salt Lake City, 1973; MD, Cornell U. Med. Ctr., NY, 1977. Cert. in urologic surgery. Clin. practice in urologic surgery LDS Hosp., Salt Lake City, ednl. dir. urologic residency program, vice chmn. dept. surgery, pres. med. staff; surgeon in urologic oncology Intermountain Med. Ctr., Salt Lake City; exec. v.p., COO Intermountain Healthcare, 1998—2009, pres., CEO, 2009—. Adj. prof. surgery U. Utah; bd. trustees LDS Hosp., Intermountain Healthcare, 1994—, chmn., 1995—98. Named one of Most Influential Physician Executives, Modern Healthcare, 2011. Fellow: American Coll. Surgeons; mem.: AMA, American Urol. Assn., Utah Med. Assn. (bd. trustees, spkr. house of dels.), Utah Urol. Soc. (past pres.). Office: Intermountain Healthcare 36 S State St Salt Lake City UT 84111 Office Phone: 801-442-2000. *

SORIA-MERCADO, IRMA ESTHELA, biology professor, researcher; b. Ensenada, Méx., Feb. 7, 1956; DSc, U. Autonoma de Baja Calif., 2004. Rschr., prof. Facultad de Ciencias Marinas, 1980—. Postgrad. coord. UABC, 2005—08. Recipient Hononific Mention award, PhD Def. Mem.: Soc. Química de Méx., Am. Chem. Soc. Avocation: skiing. Office: Km 103 Carretera Tijuana-Ensenada Ensenada Baja Calif 22830 Mexico Office Fax: 52-646-1744103. Business E-Mail: iesoria@uabc.edu.mx.

SORIAN, RICHARD MARK, federal agency administrator; b. 1958; BS in Polit. Sci. and Journalism, George Washington U., 1980. Journalist, 1980—93; sr. advisor for health policy comm. US Dept. Health & Human Services, 1993—98, asst. sec. for pub. affairs, 2010—; project dir. Inst. Health Care Rsch. & Policy, Georgetown U., 1998—2002; dir. pub. affairs Ctr. Studying Health System Change, 2002—03; v.p. pub. policy & external rels. Nat. Com. Quality Assurance (NCQA), 2003—10. Dep. dir. President's Adv. Commn. Consumer Protection & Quality in Health Care Industry, 1997—98. Author: The Health Care 500, 1988, The Bitter Pill: Tough Choices in America's Health Policy, 1989, A New Deal for American Health Care, 1993; editor: Jour. American Health Policy, Medicine & Health. Advanced Studies in Pub. Health fellowship, Harvard Sch. Pub. Health, 1989. Office: US Dept Health & Human Services 200 Independence Ave SW Washington DC 20201 Office Phone: 202-690-7850. E-mail: Media@hhs.gov. *

SORIOT, PASCAL, pharmaceutical executive; MBA, HEC, Paris, 1986. Fin. contr. Asia Pacific region Roussel Uclaf, 1986—87; dist. sales mgr. Roussel New Zealand, 1987—89; sales and mktg. mgr. Roussel Australia, 1989—94; divsn. global mktg. dir. Roussel Uclaf Pharmaceuticals, 1994—96; gen. mgr. Hoechst Marion Roussel Australia, 1996—97; regional v.p. Asia Pacific Hoechst Marion Roussel Tokyo, 1997—2000; sr. v.p., head global mktg. and med. affairs Aventis Bridgewater, 2000—02; COO Aventis US, 2002—06; head strategic mktg. F. Hoffman-La Roche Ltd., 2006, head. comml. ops., mem. enlarged corp. exec. com., 2007—09, COO pharm. divsn., mem. corp. exec. com., 2010—; CEO Genetech, Inc., 2009—10. Office: F Hoffman La Roche Ltd Konzern Hauptsitz Grenzacherstrasse 124 4070 Basel Switzerland *

SOROKIN, EVAN S., plastic surgeon; BA in Biology magna cum laude distinction in all subjects, Cornell U., NY; MD, Hahnemann U., Phila. Cert. NJ, diplomate Am. Bd. Plastic Surgery. Intern gen. surgery The Univ. of Tex. Southwestern Med. Ctr., resident gen. surgery, resident plastic surgery; dir. hyperbaric medicine Virtua Health-Wound Healing Ctr., hosp. affiliations include, Virtua Health- West Jersey Hosp., Voorhees, NJ, Virtua Hosp.- West Jersey Hosp., Marlton, NJ, Virtua Hosp., Berlin, NJ, Camden, NJ, Kennedy Meml. Hosp., Cherry Hill, NJ, Stratford, NJ, Washington Township, NJ; plastic surgeon Del. Valley Plastic Surgery. Co-author: (publs.) Recurrent Mammary Hyperplasia Current Concepts CME., 1993, Lessons from the University of Texas Southwestern Medical Center experience with ultrasound assisted liposuction., 2002, Is the Umbilicus Truly Midline?, 2003, numerous publs. Recipient Academic Excellence award, Univ. of Tex. Southwestern Med. Ctr., 2000, 2001, Super Star award, Virtua Health System, 2004; named Patients' Choice award, 2008, Top Doc for Kids, SJ Mag., 2009, 2011, numerous awards. Fellow: ACS; mem.: AMA, Camden County Med. Soc., NJ Soc. of Plastic Surgeons, Am. Soc. of Aesthetic Plastic Surgery, Am. Soc. of Plastic Surgeons. Office: Delaware Valley Plastic Surgery 1734 Route 70 East Cherry Hill NJ 08003 Office Phone: 856-872-4158. Office Fax: 856-751-7700.

SOROKULOVA, IRYNA, microbiologist, educator; b. Kiev, Ukraine, June 3, 1949; d. Boris Kalmanovsky and Varvara Khomenko; m. Valeriy Sorokulov, Aug. 10, 1973; 1 child, Volodymyr Sorokulov. Degree summa cum laude, Kiev U., 1971; PhD, Inst. Microbiology and Virology, Kiev, 1983, DSc, 1999. Cert. WHO, 1998. Asst. prof. Inst. Microbiology and Virology, 1974—91, assoc. prof., 1991—2000, prof., 2000—02; vis. prof. Auburn U., Ala., 2002—07, rsch. prof., 2007—. Head dept. Com. Biol. Products, Kiev, 1996—2002. Author; (book) Guide for Isolation and Identification of Bacteria of the Bacillus Genus from Human and Animals, Probiotic Subalin — New Approach to Treatment of Bacterial and Viral Infections; contbr. articles to numerous profl. jours. Recipient State prize, Ukraine Sci. and Tech., Govt. of Ukraine, 1995, Cert. of Recognition, Ministry of Health Ukraine, 2001, Mechnikov's prize, NAS Ukraine, 2002; grantee, Ukrainian Ministry of Sci. and Tech., 1997—98, NIH, 2003—05. Russian Orthodox. Achievements include patents for biosporin for prophylaxis and treatment of human enteric diseases; method of correction of vaginal microflora; method of eubiotic Biosporin production; probiotic preparation with complex activity; bacillus licheniformis strain with antiviral and antibacterial activity; souche bacillus subtilis CU1, son utilization comme agent immunomodulateur du systeme immunitaire et vaccin vivant recombinant contre Helicobacter pylori la contenant; method for enhancing the efficacy of antitumor vaccine; phage ligand sensor devices and uses theirof; strain of bacillus subtilis exhibiting the antiviral and antibacterial activity. Avocation: travel. Office: Auburn Univ 109 Greene Hall Auburn AL 36849 Business E-Mail: sorokib@auburn.edu.

SORRENTINO, ROBERT ANGELO, medical educator; b. Bklyn., Sept. 17, 1955; s. Umberto A. and Theresa (Ercolano) S.; m. Rebecca Lai-Kwan Leung, May 18, 1985; children: Theresa Ann, Katherine Marie, Natalie Rose. BA, NYU, 1977; MS, Wagner Coll., 1978; MD, Albany Med. Coll., 1985. Diplomate Am. Bd. Internal Medicine, Am. Bd. Cardiovascular Diseases, Am. Bd. Clin. Cardiac Electrophysiology. Intern, resident Duke U. Med. Ctr., Durham, N.C., 1985-88, fellow in cardiology, 1988-91, assoc. medicine, 1991-94, asst. prof. medicine, 1994—. Fellow Am. Coll. Cardiology; mem. N.Am. Soc. Pacing and Electrophysiology (exam. testamur 1999), Nat. Bd. Med. Examiners (cert.), Alpha Omega Alpha. Office: Duke U Med Ctr PO Box 3330 Durham NC 27702-3330 E-mail: sorre001@mc.duke.edu.

SORRIENTO, DANIELA, medical researcher; b. Naples, Italy, Mar. 30, 1976; d. Rita e Lucio Sorriento; m. Emilio Galli, July 4, 2009; 1 child, Ruggero. Degree in Biology, Federico II U. Naples, 2001, degree in Clin. Pathology, 2007, PhD, 2010. Early career scientist Federico II U. Naples, 2010—. Mem.: WG Myocardial Function, ESC. Office: Via Pansini 5 Naples 80131 Italy Business E-Mail: danisor@libero.it.

SOSLOW, ROBERT, pathologist, educator; b. Sept. 11, 1964; MD, U. Pa., 1991. Prof. Meml. Sloan-Kettering Cancer Ctr., 2000—, dir. gynecologic pathology, 2010—11. Office: 1275 York Ave Dept Pathology New York NY 10065 Business E-Mail: soslowr@mskcc.org.

SOSNOW, LAWRENCE IRA, health care company executive; b. Newark, Mar. 7, 1935; s. Emanuel and Edith (Grunt) S.; m. Ellen N. Rosenthal, May 30, 1965; children: Peter, Meg. BBA, Upsala Coll., East Orange, NJ, 1957; postgrad., NYU Grad. Sch. Bus., 1958. Pres. Sosnow & Co., Inc., Newark, 1960-66; chmn., pres. Spade & Archer, NYC, 1966-69; chmn. Gilbert Youth Research, NYC, 1968-69; pres. MIND, Inc., NYC, 1969-74, vice chmn., 1974-75; chmn. Patient Care Inc., West Orange, NJ, 1975-95, vice-chmn., 1995; dir. Home Health Agy. Assembly of N.J., 1985-88; chmn. I.V. Therapy Products, Inc., 1989-92; founder, chmn. SeniorBridge, NYC, 2000—, pres., CEO, 2000—07. Mem. N.Y. State Dept. Health Adv. Com. on Licensure, 1985-86, Home Care Assn. N.Y. Legis. Commn., 1992—. Bd. govs. Boy's Athletic League, N.Y.C., 1969-85, United Cerebral Palsy No. N.J., 1983-86, McBurney Sch., 1985-86. Served with AUS, 1957, 61-62. Mem. Nat. Assn. Home Care (dir. 1979-82) Office: 845 Third Ave New York NY 10022 Office Phone: 212-994-6100.

SOSSAI, PAOLO, gastroenterologist, internist; b. Feltre, Belluno, Italy, May 6, 1959; s. Silvio and Rosita (Manto) S. MD cum laude, Cath. U. Rome, 1985. Med. diplomate with specialization in gastroenterology cum laude. Intern Inst. Med. Pathology-Cath. U., Rome, 1980-84, resident, 1985; rschr. Italian League Against Cancer, Belluno, 1987, Nat. Inst. Nuc. Physics, Padua, Italy, 1990; physician dept. medicine Gen. Hosp., Feltre, 1988—; physician dept. oncology S. Giovanni Hosp., Bellinzona, Switzerland, 1996. Lectr. in field. Coauthor: Principles of Medical Pathology, 1994; contbr. publs. to profl. jours. including Endoscopy, Internat. Jour. Cardiology, Postgrad. Med. Jour., Pathology Rsch. and Practice, Am. Jour. Gastroenterology, Jour. Clin. Pathology, European Jour. Gastroenterology and Hepatology, Jour. Clin. Gastroenterology, Gastroenterology, Scandinavian Jour. Gastroenterology, Digestive Diseases and Scis., Digestion. Italian League Against Cancer grantee, 1987. Mem. European Soc. Oncology, N.Y. Acad. Scis., Italian Soc. Gastroenterology, Amnesty Internat. Home: Via Antonio Bettio 11 32100 Belluno Italy Office: Dept Medicine General Hospital 32032 Feltre Italy

SOSTMAN, DIRK, physician, clinical researcher, medical educator; b. NYC, Nov. 20, 1948; s. Henry and Theodora (Slokker) S.; m. Maria Preka, Sept. 1, 2003; 1 child Erik Alexandros. MD, Yale University, New Haven, 1977. Diplomate Am. Bd. Radiology, Nat. Bd. Med. Examiners. Intern and resident Yale-New Haven Hosp., 1977—82; prof., chair Weill Med. Coll. Cornell U., NYC, 1995—2005, exec. vice dean, 2003—; exec. v.p The Meth. Hosp., Houston, 2005—; CEO Meth. Physician Orgn., 2006—. Mem. lung scan interpretation panel and nuclear medicine working group Prospective Investigation of Pulmonary Embolism Diagnosis Study, Nat. Heart, Lung and Blood Inst., 1984-88; cons. Fluoromed Pharms, 1988, Am. Cancer Soc., 1992; mem. Duke Comprehensive Cancer Ctr., 1993—; program dir. Duke Winter Imaging Course, 1993-94; vis. prof. U. Pisa, 1993, U. Milan, 1993; dir. Imaging Rsch. Lab. Yale U. Sch. Medicine, 1981-84, dir. MR Imaging, 1983-87; mem. numerous adv. panels. Assoc. editor: Yearbook of Nuclear Medicine, 1984-92; mem. editorial bd.: Investigative Radiology, 1984—, Magnetic Resonance Imaging, 1985—, Jour. Thoracic Imaging, 1985—; manuscript referee; contbr. chpts. to books and numerous articles to profl. jours. Recipient Fales prize Rutgers U., 1972, Dolgan Meml. award Yale U., 1972; Yale U. summer fellowship, 1975, Lamport Biomed. Rsch. award, 1976; Winchester Chest fellow in radiology; grantee in field. Fellow Am. Coll. Chest Physicians, Am. Coll. Radiology; mMem. Fleischner Soc. (George Simon Meml. award 1982, exec. com. 1987-90, mem. Simon award com. 1991—), Soc. MRI (edn. com. 1984-86), Assn. Univ. Radiologists (Pres. 2001, Stauffer award 1988, Stauffer award com. 1983), Radiol. Soc. N.Am., Soc. Thoracic Radiology (founding mem.), Sigma Xi, Phi Beta Kappa, others. leadership in major clinical trials of venous thromboembolism diagnosis. Office: Dunn 200 6565 Fannin St Houston TX 77030 Office Phone: 713-441-2192. Business E-Mail: dsostman@tmhs.org.

SOTEREANOS, DEAN G., orthopaedic surgeon, educator; MD, MCP Hahnemann U. Cert. orthopaedic surgery, hand surgery. Resident Univ. Pitts. Med. Ctr.; fellow Duke Univ. Med. Ctr.; prof. orthopaedic surgery Drexel Univ.; pratice orthopaedic assocs. Allegheny Gen. Hosp., vice chmn. dept. orthopaedic surgery. Named one of Top Doctors, Pitts. mag., 2011. Office: Allegheny General Hospital 320 E N Ave Pittsburgh PA 15212 Office Phone: 412-359-3131. Office Fax: 412-359-4108.

SOTO, ARMANDO, plastic surgeon; MD, Johns Hopkins Sch. of Medicine. Diplomate Am. Bd. of Plastic Surgeon. Tng. gen. and plastic surgery The Barnes-Jewish Hosp. of Wash. Univ.; tng. advanced techniques for breast enhancement and reconstruction The Harry and Jeanette Weinberg Ctr. for Women's Health and Medicine, Baltimore; fellow Am. Coll. of Surgeons. Named one of Top 40 under 40, Baltimore Bus. Jour. Mem.: Am. Soc. for Aesthetic Plastic Surgery, Am. Soc. of Plastic Surgeons. Office: Aesthetic Enhancement Suite 100 7009 Dr. Phillips Blvd Orlando FL 32819 Office Phone: 407-218-4550.

SOTO, ELIZABETH, hospital administrator; b. Bayamon, Jan. 31, 1965; d. Beatriz Roman and Luis Soto. Student, John Jay Coll. Criminal Justice, 2004—. Adminstrv. asst. Columbia-Presbyn. Med Ctr., NYC, 1991—94; corp. dir., dermatology Beth Israel & St. Luke's-Roosevelt Hosp. Ctrs., NYC, 1994—. Instr. med. asst. program, NYC, 2003. Mem.: Med. Group Mgmt. Assn., Assn. Dermatology Administrs./Mgrs., Am. Acad. Med. Mgmt., Phi Theta Kappa, Latino Honor Soc. Democrat. Roman Catholic. Avocations: travel, swimming. Office: Beth Israel & St Luke's-Roosevelt Hosp 10 Union Sq East Ste 3C New York NY 10003 Business E-Mail: esoto@bethisraelny.org.

SOTOMORA-VON AHN, RICARDO FEDERICO, pediatrician, educator; b. Guatemala City, Guatemala, Oct. 22, 1947; s. Ricardo and Evelyn (von Ahn) S.; m. Eileen Marie Holcomb, May 9, 1990; m. Victoria Monzon, Nov. 26, 1971; children: Marisol, Clarisa, Ricardo III, Charlotte Marie. MD, San Carlos U., 1972; MS in Physiology, U. Minn., 1978. Diplomate Am. Bd. Pediats., Am. Bd. Pediat. Cardiology, Am. Bd. Neonatology-Perinatal Medicine. Rotating intern Gen. Hosp., Guatemala, 1971-72; pediat. intern U. Ark., 1972-73, resident, 1973-75; fellow in pediat. cardiology U. Minn., 1975-78; rsch. assoc. in cardiovasc. pathology United Hosps., St. Paul, 1976; fellow in neonatal-perinatal medicine St. Paul's Children's Hosp., 1977-78, U. Ark., 1981-82; instr. pediats. U. Minn., 1978-79; pediat. cardiologist, unit cardiovasc. surg. Roosevelt Hosp., Guatemala City, 1979-81; asst. prof. pediats. cardiology and neonatology U. Ark., Little Rock, 1981-83; pvt. practice Little Rock, 1983—. Fellow: Am. Coll. Angiology, Am. Coll. Chest Physicians, Am. Coll. Cardiology, Am. Acad. Pediat.; mem.: AAAS, ABA, Soc. Critical Care Medicine, So. Soc. Pediat. Rsch., Ctrl. Ark. Pediat. Soc., Guatemala Coll. Physicians and Surgeons, Soc. Pediat. Echocardiology, Am. Heart Assn., NY Acad. Scis., Ark. Med. Soc., Soc. Genealogists London, Guatemala Acad. Genealogy, Heraldry and Hist. Studies (corr.), The Country Club of Little Rock. Home: 3 River Ridge Ct Little Rock AR 72227-1523 Office: Evergreen Pl 1100 N Univ Ste 142 Little Rock AR 72207 E-mail: rfsotomora@aol.com.

SOTOS, JOHN GEORGE, cardiologist, writer; b. Homer, Alaska, Feb. 11, 1955; s. Luigi Vito and Bettina (Squalidozzi) S. B in Chemistry and Math., Dartmouth Coll.; M in Computer Sci. (artificial intelligence), Stanford U.; MD, John Hopkins U., 1980. Intern cardiology John Hopkins Hosp., Balt., 1983—84, resident, 1984—86, fellow transplantation cardiology and gen. cardiology, 1988—92; co-founding mem. to chief med. engr. Healtheon (now called WebMD); prin. scientist DNA Sciences; CEO Apneos Corp. Author: Zebra Cards: An Aid to Obscure Diagnoses, 1989, (web encyclopedia) The Medical History of American Presidents, The Physical Lincoln, 2008; technical advisor (TV series) House, MD. Lt. col. U.S. Air N.G., 1984—. Fellow RACC, Am. Coll. Cardiology; mem. Am. Acad. Sleep Medicine, American Sleep Apnea Assn. (bd. dirs.) In 2003 established that President William Howard Taft had severe obstructive sleep apnea during his Presidency. In 2008 requested President Abraham Lincoln's DNA to prove that Lincoln had a rare genetic cancer syndrome called MEN2B.

SOU, BELAMRI, medical researcher; b. Alger, Nov. 18, 1961; PhD, Medicine U., 1988, degree in Epidemiology, 1992. Mem. med. info. Pub. Health, 1995—2011. Office: El Biar Algiers 16000 Algeria Business E-Mail: belamrisou@yahoo.fr.

SOUAYA, EGLAL MYRIAM RAYMOND, chemistry professor, research scientist; d. Raymond Joseph and Simone Souaya; m. Shawky Ibrahim Abol El Malak, July 14, 1974; children: Nevine Shawki Abdel Malak, Raouf Shawki Abdel Malak. BSc in Spl. Chemistry with distinction, Ain Shams U., Cairo, Egypt, 1967, M in Chemistry, 1970, PhD in Inorganic Chemistry, 1974. Demonstrator, chemistry dept., faculty of sci. Ain Shams U., 1967—70, lectr. asst. chemistry, faculty of sci., 1970—73, lectr., chemistry dept., faculty of sci., 1974—80, asst. prof., 1981—89, prof. inorganic chemistry, 1989—, mem. ctrl. office of exams, mem. control higher studies, faculty of sci. Rschr. Belgium U., Leuven, Belgium, 1984—85, Surrey (Eng.) U., 1987, Inst. Inorganic Chemistry, Munich, 1994; mem. numerous coms. Contbr. over 40 articles to profl. jours. Fellow, Belgium U.Leuven, 1984—85, Brit. Coun., Surrey U., Eng., 1987, DFG, Munich U., 1994; scholar, Brit. Coun., 1987, Ain Shams U., 1994. Mem.: Chem. Soc. U.A.R., Royal Chem. Soc. London, Egyptian Chem. Soc., Gezira Sporting Club, Rowing Club, Lions, Gezira Sporting Club Egypt (life). Achievements include research in In Analytical And Inorganic Chemistry. Avocations: reading, museums, classical music, walking, languages. Home: 164A26 July St Sphinx Sq Mohandessin, Guiza 11111 Egypt Office: Ain Shams U Faculty of Sci Abbassiya Cairo 11566 Egypt Office Fax: 002-02-4831836. Personal E-mail: eglals@yahoo.com.

SOUBA, WILEY WILLIAM, JR., medical educator, researcher, dean; b. Caracas, Venezuela, May 17, 1953; came to the U.S., 1968; s. Wiley William and Phyllis (Rowe) S.; m. Lynne Hayes, Mar. 26, 1983; children: Matthew, Julia. BS in Chemistry, Muskingum Coll., New Concord, Ohio, 1975; MD, U. Tex., 1978; ScD in Nutritional Biochemistry, Harvard U., 1984, MS, 1994; MBA, Boston U., 1998. Assoc. prof. physiology U. Fla. Coll. Medicine, Gainesville, 1991-92, assoc. prof. biochemistry/molecular biology, 1991-92, prof. surgery, 1993, prof. biochemistry/molecular biology/physiology, 1993; prof. surgery Harvard U., Boston, 1993—99, prof. nutrition, 1996—99; assoc. dir. cancer ctr. Mass. Gen. Hosp., Boston, 1993—, dir. nutrition support svcs., 1993—99, dir. surg. oncology rsch. labs., 1993—99, chief Divsn. Surg. Oncology, 1993—99, chair Dept. Surgery Practice Coun., 1999; adj. prof. mgmt. policy Boston U., 1999; Waldhausen prof. chmn. Dept. Surgery Pa. State U. Coll. Medicine, University Park, 1999—2006, interim chair Dept. Ophthalmology, 2001—02, interim dir. Pa. State Cancer Inst., 2001—03, dir. Hershey Ctr. for Leadership Devel., 2002—06, prof. cellular and molecular physiology, 2002—06; dean, chief academic officer Ohio State U. Coll. Medicine, Columbus, 2006—10, prof. surgery, 2006—10; v.p. health affairs, prof. surgery, dean Dartmouth Med. Sch., NH, 2010—. Bd. dirs. Mass. Gen. Hosp. Cancer Ctr. Contbr. 160 articles to profl. jours.; author: 40 book chpts. Eagle Scout, Boy Scouts Am., 1967; named one of Top Drs. Am., 1992—; recipient NIH rsch. grants, 1990-95, 94-99, Shriners Burn Inst. (Boston Unit) rsch. grant, 1995-97. Fellow ACS; mem. AMA, Assn. Acad. Surgery (pres. 1994), Am. Soc. Parenteral and Enteral Nutrition, Surg. Infection Soc., Soc. Univ. Surgeons, Am. Soc. Clin. Oncology, Soc. Surg. Oncology, Collegium Internationale Chirurgiae Digestivae, Am. Coll. Nutrition, Am. Physiol. Soc., Am. Soc. for Clin. Nutrition, Am. Fedn. for Clin. Rsch., Soc. for Surgery of the Alimentary Tract, Am. Assn. for the Surgery of Trauma, Soc. Clin. Surgery, So. Surg. Assn., Ea. Assn. for Surgery of Trauma, Am. Surg. Assn., Alpha Omega Alpha. Achievements include rsch. in molecular regulation of the altered glutamine transport and metabolism that occurs during critical illness. Office: Dartmouth Med Sch Deans Office HB 7060 1 Rope Ferry Rd Hanover NH 03755-1404 Office Phone: 603-650-1200. E-mail: wiley.e.souba.jr@dartmouth.edu. *

SOULE, HOWARD R., medical association administrator; PhD in Virology & Epidemiology, Baylor Coll. Medicine. Fellow in immunology & vascular biology Scripps Rsch. Inst.; sr. rsch. & devel. exec. Corvas Internat.; mng. dir. Knowledge Universe Health & Wellness Group; exec. vice pres. & chief science officer Prostate Cancer Found., 1997—2004, exec. vice pres. discovery & translation, 2007—. Office: 1250 Fourth St Santa Monica CA 90401 Office Phone: 310-570-4700. Office Fax: 310-570-4701. E-mail: info@pcf.org.

SOULIOTI, ZOI, drug safety manager, researcher; d. Dimitrios Souliotis and Styliani Soulioti. Degree, U. Athens, Greece, 2000, MSc in Clin. Pharmacy, 2002. Clin. rsch. assoc. Boehringer-Ingelheim Ellas S.A, Athens, 2002—05, drug safety mgr., 2005—. Vol. Olympics Games Athens Olympic Pharmacy Polyclinic, 2004. Scholar, U. Athens, 2000-2002. Mem.: European Soc. Clin. Pharmacy (assoc.), European Respiratory Soc. (assoc.), Hellenic Soc. Pharmacy and Medicine (assoc.), Pan-Hellenic Soc. Pharmacy (assoc.). Achievements include research in determination of ropivacaine level in blood after epidural infusion. Avocations: travel, reading, cycling, mountaining, swimming. Personal E-mail: zoisoulioti@gmail.com.

SOUNEY, PAUL FREDERICK, pharmacist; b. Bristol, Conn., Mar. 29, 1947; s. Frederick Raymond and Julia Yvonne (Weeks) S.; m. Billie Lorraine Petersen, Apr. 7, 1972; children: Jared Paul, Jeremy Christian. BS, Northeastern U., 1971, MS, 1984. Drug info. pharmacist Hartford (Conn.) Hosp., 1971-77; pharmacy supervisor Boston Hosp. for Women, 1977-81; clin. rsch. pharmacist Channing Labs./Harvard Med. Sch., Boston, 1981-92; dir. drug info. Brigham and Women's Hosp., Boston, 1981—90, dir. clin. pharmacy, 1985—92; med. info. scientist Astra Merck Inc., Providence, 1992-97; field sci. ptnr. N.E. Customer Ctr. Astra Pharms., L.P., Providence, 1997-99; med. mktg. scientific leader AstraZeneca Pharms., Wayne, Pa., 1999-2000, group dir. med. mktg., 2000, nat. sci. dir. GI, 2000—03, sr. dir. med. affairs, 2003—04; prin. Sci. Commercialization LLC, Kennett Square, Pa., 2004—06; nat. dir. med. affairs Berlex Labs., Kennett Square, 2006—07, nat. dir. med. affairs, Neurosci. Bayer Healthcare Pharmaceuticals, 2007, exec. dir. med. affairs Prism Pharmaceuticals, 2007—. Cons. in field. Editor: Comprehensive Pharmacy Review, 7th edit., 2009; contbr. articles to profl. jours.; editl. adv. panelist Internat. Pharm. Abstracts, Pharmacy Practice News, Am. Jour. Gastroenterology. Treas. men's club First Congl. Ch., 1993-2000; vol. Mansfield (Mass.) Animal Shelter, 1990-94. Mem. Am. Coll. Clin. Pharmacy, Am. Soc. Health Sys. Pharmacists, Am. Pharmaceutical Assn., Acad. Managed Case Pharmacy, New Eng. Coun. Hosp. Pharmacists, Northeastern Univ. Alumnae Assn. Office: Prism Pharmaceuticasls 1150 First Ave King Of Prussia PA 19406 Office Phone: 484-734-0221. Business E-Mail: pfsjarjerm.pa@gmail.com.

SOUNTOULIDES, PETROS, urologist, researcher; b. Thessaloniki, Greece, Sept. 6, 1972; s. George and Marina Sountoulides; m. Irene Asouhidou, Oct. 8, 2004. MD, Aristotle U. Thessaloniki, 1996. Attending urologist U. Hosp. Alexandroupolis, Greece, 2005—07; clin. fellow Academic Med. Ctr., Amsterdam, 2007; attending urologist, urology dept. Gen. Hosp. Veria, Greece, 2007—08; rsch. endourology fellow U. Calif. Irvine, Orange, 2008—. Editor Archivos Espanoles Urologia. Contbr. chapters to books, articles to numerous med. jours. Fellow: Endourological Soc., European Bd. Urology, European Assn. Urology.

SOURIAL, ALFY SAIF, surgeon; b. Tanta, Egypt, Jan. 10, 1928; s. Saif and Erada Atiah (El-Sanady) S.; m. Elizabeth Ann Siebert, 1960; children: Edward S., Wynn Heather; m. Shirley Ann Maniscalco, Oct. 7, 1971; children: Dean Michael, Jill Soraya. MD, Cairo U., 1950. Diplomate Am. Bd. Surgery. Intern Doctors Hosp., Cleve., 1955-56, resident in surgery, 1956-57, Huron Rd. Hosp., Cleve., 1957-60; fellow in surgery Case Western Res. U., Cleve., 1960-61; surgeon Valley Hosp., Pomona, Calif., 1962-72; pvt practice Thousand Oaks, Calif., 1970-93; active staff Los Robles Hosp., Thousand Oaks, 1968-92, hon. staff, 1992—. Author: Beyond Mathematics, A Standard Physical Particle and the Unified Field of Energy. Lt. col. USAF, 1982-87. Fellow ACS; mem. AMA. Home: PO Box 4312 Blue Jay CA 92317-4312 Office Phone: 909-336-7240. Personal E-mail: asourial@aol.com. *

SOUSSA, ESSAM FAROUK, dentist, educator; b. Alexandria, Mar. 24, 1957; BDS in Dental Surgery and Medicine, Alexandria U., 1980, MSc, PhD in Oral Biology, 1989. Prof., head, dept. oral biology, vice dean, postgrad. rsch. Coll. Dentistry, Mansoura U., 1982—2002; prof., oral biology, BDS dept. U. Dammam (formerly King Faisal U.) Coll. Dentistry., 2002—. Master: Egyptian Salivary Glands Soc.; mem.: Assn. Medicines Franco-Phones, Egyptian Dental Assn. Avocations: stamp collecting/philately, drawing, painting. Home: Coll Dentistry University Dammam PO Box 1982 Al Dammam Eastern Province Saudi Arabia Home Fax: 966038572624. Personal E-mail: esoussa24@hotmail.com.

SOUTH, FRANK EDWIN, physiologist, educator; b. Norfolk, Nebr., Sept. 20, 1924; s. Frank Edwin and Gladys (Brinkman) S.; m. Berna Deane Phyllis Casebolt, June 23, 1946; children: Frank Edwin, Robert Christopher. AB, U. Calif., Berkeley, 1949, PhD, 1952. Asst. prof. physiology U. P.R. Sch. Medicine, 1953-54, U. Ill. Coll. Medicine, 1954-61; assoc. prof. Colo. State U., 1961-62, prof., 1962-65, U. Mo., 1965-76; prof., dir. Sch. Life and Health Scis., U. Del., Newark, 1976-82; prof. emeritus U. Del., Newark, 1989, Sch. Life and Health Scis., U. Del., Newark, 1989—. Mem. governing bd., dir. Hibernation Info. Exchange, 1959— Mem. editorial bd. Cryobiology, 1989; contbr. numerous articles on physiology of hibernation, temperature regulation, renal function, marine mammals, artificial atmospheres, and sleep to profl. jours. Bd. dirs. Del. Lung Assn., 1976-82, Del. Cancer Network, 1977-82; mem. research com. Del. Heart Assn., 1977-82; mem. N.E. regional research com. Am. Heart Assn.; mem. med. adv. bd. A.I. DuPont Inst., Wilmington, Del., 1978-83. Served with AUS, 1943-45. Decorated Purple Heart with oak leaf cluster, Bronze Star with oak leaf cluster, Pres. unit citation, Croix de Guerre (unit); NIH career devel. awardee, 1961-65; recipient European African Mid East campaign medal with bronze spear head and silver star, World War II victory medal, Army of Occupation medal with Germany clasp, combat med. badge. Fellow AAAS, Sigma Xi; mem. Am. Physiol. Soc.; Clubs: Ranger Bns. Assn. World War II (pres. 2005-06, 2008-), Haven Yacht Club. Episcopalian. Business E-Mail: fsouth@udel.edu.

SOUTHBY, RICHARD MCKELLAR FAIRFAX, health services educator, consultant; b. Melbourne, Victoria, Australia, Feb. 3, 1940; arrived in U.S., 1979, naturalized, 1985; s. Robert and Marie Heywood (Whyte) Southby; m. Janet Sue Rexrode, June 9, 1979. B.Com., U. Melbourne, 1965; M.P.A. Cornell U., 1967; PhD, Monash U., Clayton, Victoria, Australia, 1973. Rsch. asst. Inst. Applied Econ. Research U. Melbourne, 1965; Sloan scholar in hosp. and med. care adminstrn. Cornell U., Ithaca, NY, 1965—67; tchg. fellow Monash U., 1967—70, sr. tchg. fellow dept. social and preventive medicine Faculty of Medicine, 1970, lectr. in social and preventive medicine, 1971—75, sr. lectr., 1975—78; commr. Australian Hosps. and Health Services Commn., Canberra, Australian Capital Territory, 1975; dir. pub. health services research and tchg. Sch. Pub. Health and Tropical Medicine U. Sydney, New South Wales, Australia, 1978—79; from assoc. prof. to prof., chmn. dept. health svcs., mgmt. and policy The George Washington U. Med. Sch., Washington, 1979—97, assoc. dean health svcs., Friesen prof. internat. health and health policy, prof. health care sics., 1997—2001; dean, Ross prof. internat. health, sch. pub. health and health svcs. The George Washington U. Med. Ctr., Washington, 2001—03, exec. dean, disting. prof. global health, 2003—. Adj. prof. dept. preventive medicine and biometrics Sch. Medicine Uniformed Services U. Health Scis. Dept. Def., Bethesda, Md., 1979—; dir. Interag.-Inst. for Fed. Health Care Execs., 1984—; cons. in hosp. adminstrn. Walter Reed Army Med. Ctr., Washington, 1983—. Author (with E. Chesterman): Australia: Health Facts, 1979; editor (with others): Health Care Technology Under Financial Constraints, 1987, Health Care Law and Ethics, 1989, AIDS and Long Term Care: A New Dimension, 1989; contbr. articles to profl. jours. Decorated knight of grace Order St. Lazarus of Jerusalem, officer brother Order Hosp. of St. John of Jerusalem. Fellow: Royal Inst. Pub. Health, Royal Soc. Medicine (U.K.), Australian Coll. Health Svc. Execs., Am. Coll. Legal Medicine (hon.); mem.: APHA, Assn. Mil. Surgeons U.S, Internat. Epidemiol. Assn., Cosmos Club (Washington), Wallaby Club. Anglican. Avocations: tennis, gardening, hiking. Office: George Washington U Med Center 5325 MacArthur Blvd NW Washington DC 20016 2521 Home Phone: 202 966 6251; Office Phone: 202-416-0429.

SOUTHERN, SIR EDWIN, biochemist, researcher; BSc, U. Manchester, Eng., 1958; PhD, U. Glasgow, Scotland, 1962. With MRC Mammalian Genome Unit Western General Hosp., Edinburgh, 1967—79; assoc. dir. MRC Clin. and Population Cytogenetics Unit Western Gen. Hosp., Edinburgh, 1979; Whitley prof. biochemistry Univ. Oxford, 1985—, prof. emeritus; founder, chief sci. officer, mem. bd. dirs. Oxford Gene Technology IP Ltd., Oxford, England, 1995—. Dir. Cancer Rsch. Campaign Chromosome Moleular Biology Group; founder, trust chmn. The Kirkhouse Trust, 2000—. Contbr. articles to profl. jours. Recipient Lasker-DeBakey Clin. Med. Rsch. award, Lasker Found., 2005; named a Knighted Bachelor for services to the develop. of DNA microarray techniques., 2003. Achievements include devising a standard lab technique called the Southern Blot, that allows scientists to detect specific bits of genetic code within an organism's overall DNA. Office: Oxford Gene Technology IP Ltd Begbroke Business & Science Park Sandy Lane Yarton Oxford OX5 1PF England Address: Dept Biochemistry Univ Oxford Smith Parks Rd Oxford OX1 3 QU England Office Phone: 44 1865 856 340, 44 0 1865 275282. Office Fax: 44 1865 379 433, 44 0 1865 275283. Business E-Mail: ed.southern@bioch.ox.ac.uk. *

SOUTHWELL, DONALD G., insurance company executive; Grad., We. Mich. U. Mgmt. positions through pres. ins. & fin. svcs. Prudential Ins. Co. Am., 1974—96; pres. life & health ins. group Kemper Corp. (formerly Unitrin Corp.), Chgo., 1996—99, v.p., 1998—99, sr. v.p., pres. ins. ops., 1999—2002, pres., COO, 2002—06, pres., CEO, 2006—09, chmn., pres., CEO, 2010—. Bd. dirs. Kemper Corp., 2002—. Office: Kemper Corp One E Wacker Dr Chicago IL 60601 Office Phone: 312-661-4600. *

SOUZA, ALEX SANDRO ROLLAND, physician; b. Serra Talhada, Pernambuco, Brazil, Dec. 30, 1974; s. Antonio Ildefonso De Souza and Risvanilda Maria Souza; m. Erica Fonseca De Albuquerque Souza; children: Gustavo Fonseca DeAlbuquerque, Gabriela Fonseca De Albuquerque. D, U. Fed. de Pernambuco, Recife, 1997. Cert. in medicine UFPE, 1997. Fetal medicine coord. Inst. Medicina Integral, Recife, Brazil, 2002; prof. Fernando Figueira Inst., Med., Recife, 2002—. Contbr. scientific papers. Office: IMIP Rua dos Coelhos 300 Boa Vista Recife Pernambuco 50070-550 Brazil Office Phone: 558121224100. Business E-Mail: alexrolland@uol.com.br.

SOUZA, RENATO APARECIDO, engineering educator; b. Passos, Minas Gerais, Brazil, Mar. 19, 1981; PhD, Inst. R&D, U. Vale Paraíba, 2009. Prof. Inst. Fed. Educação, Ciência e Tech. Sul Minas Gerais., 2004. Home: Elisa 173 Muzambinho Minas Gerais 37890-000 Brazil Personal E-mail: tatosouza2004@yahoo.com.br.

SOUZA-TALARICO, JULIANA NERY, nursing educator; b. São Paulo, Brazil, Mar. 29, 1978; Degree in Nursing, U. São Paulo, 2003, PhD, 2009. Adj. prof. Sch. Nursing, U. São Paulo, 2010, prof. rsch. scientist, 2010—. Fellow, Conselho Nat. Pesquisa, 2001, 2006, grant, Fundação Amparo Pesquisa do Estado São Paulo, 2009. Mem.: Soc. Neurosci. Office: Av Dr Enéas De Carvalho Aguiar 419 São Paulo 05403000 Brazil Business E-Mail: junery@usp.br.

SOVERI, INGA, physician; b. Tartu, Estonia, Mar. 10, 1978; d. Jaan and Aive Eha; m. Tommi Heikki Soveri, July 7, 2001. MD, Tartu U., Estonia, 2002; PhD, Uppsala U., Sweden, 2006. Lic. physician Health Care Bd., Estonia, Nat. Bd. of Health and Welfare, Sweden. Med. intern Tartu U., 2002—03; jr. physician in internal medicine and nephrology Univ. Hosp., Uppsala, 2006—. Contbr. articles to profl. jours. Mem.: Swedish Med. Assn., Swedish Soc. of Nephrology, Swedish Soc. of Medicine. Avocations: badminton, theater, tour-skating.

SOWELL, JOSEPH A., III, hospital administrator, lawyer; b. Sept. 20, 1956; m. Joanne Sowell; children: Jacob Sowell, Joseph Sowell. B, U. Ala., 1978, JD, 1981; LLM, U. Fla., 1982. Co-mgr., corp., comml. transactions practice Waller Lansden Dortch & Davis, ptnr., 1987—96, 1999—2009; COO Arcon Healthcare; with Arcon Healthcare (Devel.), 1996—99; sr. v.p., chief devel. officer HCA, Inc., 2009—. Active Room In the Inn-Campus for Human Devel., St. Luke's Cmty. House. Mem.: ABA, Nashville Bar Assn. (health law comm.), Tenn. Bar Assn. Office: HCA Inc 1 Park Plz Nashville TN 37203 Office Phone: 615-344-9551. Office Fax: 615-344-2266. Business E-Mail: joseph.sowell@hcahealthcare.com. *

SOWERS, MARYFRAN, epidemiologist, gynecologist, educator; BA in Nutrition, Emporia State U., 1968; MS in Nutrition, Okla. State U., 1973; PhD in Epidemiology, U. Iowa, 1984. Fellow U. Iowa, 1985, rsch. coord. in pediatric cardiology, 1978—80; asst. prof. divsn. nutritional sciences Cornell U., 1986—87; asst. prof. dept. epidemiology U. Mich. Sch. Pub. Health, 1987—92, assoc. prof. dept. epidemiology, 1992—96, prof. dept. epidemiology, 1996—; adj. prof. obstetrics & gynecology UMDNJ, 1995—; adj. assoc. prof. obstetrics & gynecology U. Mich., 1995—99, adj. prof. obstetrics & gynecology, 1999—, adj. prof. internal medicine, 1999—. Mem.: Soc. Epidemiologic Rsch., Osteoarthritis Rsch. Soc., Endocrine Soc., Am. Soc. for Clinical Nutrition, Am. Soc. Bone & Mineral Rsch., Am. Pub. Health Assn., Am. Inst. Nutrition. Office: 1846 SPH I 109 Observatory St Ann Arbor MI 48109-2029 Office Phone: 734-936-3892. Office Fax: 734-763-4552. E-mail: mfsowers@umich.edu.

SOX, HAROLD CARLETON, JR., physician, educator, editor; b. Palo Alto, Calif., Aug. 18, 1939; s. Harold Carleton and Mary (Griffiths) Sox; m. Carol Helen Hill, Aug. 26, 1962; children: Colin Montgomery, Lara Katherine. BS, Stanford U., 1961; MD cum laude, Harvard U., 1966. Diplomate Am. Bd. Internal Medicine. Intern and resident Mass. Gen. Hosp., Boston, 1966—68; clin. assoc. Nat. Cancer Inst., Bethesda, Md., 1968—70; instr. Dartmouth Med. Sch., Hanover, NH, 1970—73; asst. prof. medicine to prof. clin. medicine Stanford U. Sch. Medicine, Calif., 1973—88; Joseph Huber prof., chmn. dept. medicine Dartmouth Med. Sch., 1988—2001; editor, Annals Internal Medicine ACP, Phila., 2001—09; emeritus prof. medicine Dartmouth Med. Sch. Pretest writing com. Am. Bd. Internal Medicine, 1992—94; panel mem. Nat. Bd. Med. Examiners, Physician Assts. Nat. Certifying Exam., 1973—76; chair com. on priority-setting for health tech. assessment Inst. Medicine, 1990—91, US preventive svcs. task force chair, 1990—95, chair IOM com. HIV & US blood supply, 1994—95, chair IOM com. health effects Persian Gulf War svc., 1998—2000, mem. complementary and alternative medicine IOM com., 2003—04, vice chmn. IOM com. high value health svcs., 2006—07, mem. IOM com. evidence framework obesity prevention, 2008—10, co-chair IOM com. priority-setting comparative effectiveness rsch., 2009, IOM com. stds. systematic revs., 2009—; chair task force to revise internal medicine residency curriculum Federated Coun. Internal Medicine, 1993—97; nat. adv. com. generalist physician Scholars Program Robert Wood Johnson Found., 1992—2008, chmn., nat. adv. com. physician Faculty Scholar Program, 2005—; physician Leaders Nat. Drug Policy, 1997—; founding chair exec. com. Medicare Coverage Adv. Com., 1999—2003; report rev. com. NRC, 2000—05. Author: Medical Decision Making, 1988; editor: Common Diagnostic Tests, 1987, 2d edit., 1990; mem. editl. bd.: Med. Decision Making, 1980—87, Jour. Gen. Internal Medicine, 1985—87, New Eng. Jour. Medicine, 1990—97, cons. assoc. editor: Am. Jour. Medicine, 1988—95, assoc. editor: Sci. Am. Medicine, 1995—2001; contbr. chapters to books, articles to profl. jours. Bd. dirs. Found. Informed Med. Decision Making, 2002—; internat. adv. bd. Clin. Trial Registration Platform program WHO, 2005—08. Master: ACP (clin. efficacy assessment subcom. 1985—92, bd. regents 1991—2000, chmn. ednl. policy com. 1994—97, pres. 1998—99); fellow: AAAS, Coll. Physicians Phila. (bd. trustees 2006—09), Royal Australasian Coll. Physicians (hon.); mem.: Internat. Com. Med. Jour. Editors, Inst. Medicine Nat. Acads., Assn. Am. Physicians, Soc. Med. Decision Making (trustee 1980—83, pres. 1983—84, Career Achievement award 1998, John Eisenberg award 2007), Soc. Gen. Internal Medicine (coun. 1980—83, Robert J. Glaser Career Achievement award 2000), Alpha Omega Alpha. Home: 31 Faraway Ln West Lebanon NH 03784

SOYOGUL GÜRER, ÜMRAN, pharmacy microbiology professor; b. Eskisehir, Sept. 26, 1956; Student, Istanbul U., 1978—82; MS in Biology, Marmara U., 1987, grad. student, 1987—89, PhD, 1994. Lab. asst., biologist Tchg. Hosp. Marmara U., 1982—85; lectr. Marmara U., Faculty Pharmacy, 1993—97, asst. prof., 1997—2009, assoc. prof. dept. pharm. microbiology, 2009—, dept. chair adj., Study Grant Com. mem., governing coun. mem. Avocations: walking, reading. Office: Tibbiye Cad 49 Haydarpasa Sta Üsküdar Istanbul 34668 Turkey Office Phone: 216-4142962 ext. 1190. Office Fax: 0216 -3452952. Business E-Mail: umran.gurer@superonline.com.

SPACKMAN, THOMAS JAMES, radiologist; b. Oak Park, Ill., Apr. 24, 1937; s. Thomas Frederick and Louise Mary (Kaiser) Spackman; m. Donna S. Stewart, June 25, 1960; children: Kirsten, Thomas James, Victoria. BA, DePauw U., 1959; MD, Western Res. U., 1964; diploma in bus. studies, London Sch. Econs., 1987. Intern, then resident in internal medicine Yale-New Haven Med. Ctr., 1964-66, resident in diagnostic radiology, 1966-68, fellow clin. rsch. tng. unit, 1968-69; instr., then asst. prof. radiology Yale U. Med. Sch., New Haven, 1969-74; assoc. prof. U. Pa. Med. Sch., 1974-78; prof. radiology U. Conn. Med. Sch., Farmington, 1978—, head dept., 1978-90; dir. radiology St. Francis Hosp. and Med. Ctr., Hartford, Conn., 1992-93; pres. Elscint, Inc., Hackensack, NJ, 1993-97; sr. v.p. Elscint, Ltd., Haifa, Israel, 1993-97; pres. Spackman Assocs., Vero Beach, Fla., 1997—; chmn. Xicon Technologies LLC, Vero Beach, 1997-98; v.p. physician affairs Quorum Health Resources, 2000—02, Cambio Health Solutions LLC, 2002—05; chmn. Navix Diagnostix, Inc., 2002—; mng. dir. FTI Cabmrio Health Solutions, 2005—07. Mem. Conn. Med. Exam. Bd., 1980—86; bd. dirs. Elscint, Inc. Mem. editl. adv. bd. Diagnostic Imaging, 1989—92; contbr. articles to profl. jours., chapters to books. Fellow: Am. Coll. Radiology; mem.: Indian River County Hosp. Dist. (Fla.) (trustee 2009—), Environ. Learning Ctr. (trustee 2007—), Soc. Pediatric Radiology, Assn. U. Radiolgoists. Office Phone: 772-388-4631. Business E-Mail: tspackman@bellsouth.net.

SPAETH, GEORGE LINK, ophthalmologist, educator, writer; b. Phila., Mar. 3, 1932; s. Edmund Benjamin and Lena Marie (Link) S.; m. Ann Ward, May 17, 1958; children: Kristin Lea Crowley, George Link Jr., Eric Edmund. BA magna cum laude, Yale U., 1954; MD cum laude, Harvard U., 1959; postgrad., U. Mich., 1960, U. Pa., 1961. Resident surgeon Wills Eye Hosp., Phila., 1961-63, attending surgeon, 1970—, dir. glaucoma svc., 1968—2007, dir. emeritus, 2007—; clin. fellow NIH, Bethesda, Md., 1963-65; instr. U. Pa., Phila., 1965-68; pvt. practice Phila., 1965-68; prof. ophthalmology Temple U. Med. Sch., Phila., 1968-75, Jefferson Med. Coll., Phila., 1975—, Louis Esposito glaucoma rsch. prof., 2000—; lectr. in fields. Ophthalmologist Chestnut Hill Hosp., Phila., 1975—; attending surgeon, Graduate Hosp.; cons., Bryn Mawr Hosp., Wills Eye Hosp., Hosp. Jefferson Med. Coll. Author: 19 books in ophthalmology, surgery, and med. ethics, 1970—, Poetry and Essays; contbr. over 600 articles to profl. jours.; editor Ophthalmic Surgery jour., 1985-96; editl. editor Ophthalmic Surgery and Lasers; mem. editl. bd. Jour., Ocular Surgery News, Jour. Glaucoma, Jour. Evidence-Based Ophthalmology, Glaucoma Abstracts; manuscript reviewer, New Eng. Jour. Medicine, Med. Letter Drugs and Therapy, others; patentee differometer, tonometer tip cover, construct sentiments test. Pres. Chestnut Hill Cmty. Assn., Phila., 1970-72; founder, CEO Internat. Soc. Spaeth Fellows, 1975—; trustee, founder, pres. E.B. Spaeth and Glaucoma Svcs. Found., 1978—, Profls. for Nuclear Army Control, 1985-88; trustee, treas. Thomas Skelton Harrison Found., Inc., 1984—; interviewer Yale Alumni Schs. Com., Phila., 1965—; Yale Class coun., 1968—, Yale Assn. Alumni Reps., 1996-2002; trustee Recording for the Blind and Dyslexia, 1996-2002, Internat. Arts-Medicine Assn., emeritus bd. mem. Pa. Ballet, 2002—, Bach Festival of Phila., 2002-2005, Squirrel Island Chapel, Maine; curriculum com. Jefferson Med. Coll., 1987-90; institutional review bd. Jefferson Med. Coll., 1990-95; pres. Phila. Glaucoma Inst., 1997—. Lt. comdr. USPHS, 1963-68. NIH grantee, 1968—; recipient Pub. Svc. medal Chestnut Hill Coll., 1972, Sir Stuart Duke Elder Glaucoma award Internat. Glaucoma Soc., 1986, Newberg award Lawyers Alliance for World Security, 1995, Derrick Vail award Internat. Soc. Prevention Blindness, 1996, Trantas award Greek Ophthalmol. Soc., 2000, Frominopolous prize Greek Glaucoma Soc., 2003, Large Flower and Vegetable Garden 1st Pl. award Pa. Horticultural Soc., 2004, Nizankowska award Polish Glaucoma Soc., 2006, Mildred Weisenfeld award, Assn. Rsch. Vision Ophthalmology, 2010, Pres.'s award Am. Glucoma Soc., 2010, Fransichetti award U. Geneva, 2011, Mc Lean award Cornell U. med. Sch., 2011; named Ophthalmic Visionary, Ocular Surgery News, 2003, Bausch & Lomb, 2005, Goldmann medal, Internat. Glaucoma Rsch. Soc., 2007, Silver fellowship, Assn. Rsch. Vision Ophthamology, 2009, Fransecletti award, U. Geneva. Fellow Am. Acad. Ophthalmology (chmn. ethics com. San Francisco 1987-95, coun. 1980-93, vice chmn. residency rev. com. Chgo. 1982-88, Sr. honor award 1988, life time achievement award 1999), Am. Assn. Rsch. in Vision and Ophthalmology, Royal Coll. Ophthalmologists U.K., Danish Ophthalmol. Soc., Ind. Soc. of Ophthalmology; mem. Ethiopeon Ophthal. Soc., Am. Glaucoma Soc. (pres. 1983-85), Coll. Physicians Phila. (sec. 1976-84), Phila. County Med. Soc., Pa. Acad. Ophthalmology (pres. coun.), German Ophthalmol. Congress, Physicians for Social Responsibility (pres. emeritus Phila. chpt.), ACS (bd. govs. emeritus, chmn. emeritus adv. coun. for ophthalmology), Phila. Club, Phila. Cricket Club, Phi Beta Kappa, Alpha Omega Alpha. Democrat. Avocations: composing music, piano, sports, photography, gardening. Office: Wills Eye Hosp 11th Fl 840 Walnut St Philadelphia PA 19107-5109 Office Phone: 215-928-3960. Business E-Mail: gspaeth@willseye.org.

SPAGNOLO, SAMUEL VINCENT, internist, pulmonary specialist, educator; b. Pitts., Sept. 3, 1939; s. Vincent Anthony and Mary Grace (Culotta) S.; children: Samuel, Brad, Gregg; m. Dorcas R. Hardy, Sept. 29, 1996. BA, Washington & Jefferson Coll., 1961; MD, Temple U., 1965. Diplomate Am. Bd. Internal Medicine, Bd. Pulmonary Disease, lic. physician Fla., Calif., Md., D.C., Va., Ariz., Pa., Mass. Sr. resident in medicine VA Med. Ctr., Boston, 1969-70, chief resident in medicine, 1970-71; Harvard Clin. and Rsch. fellow in pulmonary diseases Mass. Gen. Hosp., Boston, 1971-72; asst. chief med. svc. VA Med. Ctr., Washington, 1972-75, acting chief med. svc., 1975-76, chief pulmonary disease sect., 1976-94, chief of staff, 1998-99, dir. respiratory care and sr. attending in pulmonary diseases, 1999—; instr. in medicine Boston U. Sch. of Medicine, Tufts U. Sch. Medicine, Boston, 1970-71; clin. and rsch. fellow in pulmonary diseases Harvard U. Sch. of Medicine, Mass. Gen. Hosp., Boston, 1971-72; attending physician George Washington U. Med. Ctr., 1972—; clin. asst. prof. medicine Georgetown U., Washington, 1975-77; asst. prof. medicine George Washington U. Sch. of Medicine and Health Scis., Washington, 1972-75, assoc. prof., 1975-81, prof. medicine, 1981—, dir. divsn. pulmonary diseases and allergy, 1978-93; assoc. chmn. dept. medicine George Washington U. Med. Ctr., Washington, 1986-89. Cons. in pulmonary diseases The Washington Hosp. Ctr., Washington, DC, 1977—, Will Rogers Inst., White Plains, NY, 1980—, US Dept. Labor, Washington, 1980—, Walter Reed Army Med. Ctr., Washington, 1987-90; rep. Am. Coll. Chest Physicians to Am. Registry Pathology, Washington, 1981-92; radio tv appearances on Health Oriented Programs; invited lectr. in U.S., Russia, Jordan; med. chest cons. in attempted assasination of former Pres. Reagan; presenter in field. Author: Clinical Assessment of Patients with Pulmonary Disease, 1986; co-author: (with A.E. Medinger) Handbook of Pulmonary Emergencies, 1986, Handbook of Pulmonary Drug Therapy, 1993, (with Witorsch, P.) Air Pollution and Lung Disease in Adults, 1994; mem. editl. bd. CHEST Jour., 2002-06; mem. editl. bd. Chest, 2006—; contbr. numerous articles to profl jours. including Med. Clin. N.Am., Chest, So. Med. Jour., Am. Jour. Cardiology, Jour. Am. Med. Assn., Clin. Rsch., Am. Rev. Respiratory Disease, Am. Lung Assn. Bull., Clin. Notes on Respiratory Diseases, Jour. Nuc. Medicine, Drug Therapy. Pres., chmn. Found. Vets. Health Care, 1998—. Lt. comdr. USPHS, 1966-68. Decorated cavaliere Order of Merit, Republic of Italy; nominated for Golden Apple award by med. students George Washington Sch. Medicine, Phila., 1977; recipient cert. appreciation D.C. Lung Assn., 1983. Fellow ACP (coun. critical care 1983-85), Am. Coll. Chest Physicians (gov. DC, coun. of govs. 1989-96); mem. Am. Thoracic Soc. (exec. com. DC chpt. 1978, 85, 89, mem. adv. com. Tb control, 1978-84, pres. DC chpt. 1981-83), Nat. Assn. VA Physicians (sec. 1987-89, v.p. 1989-91, pres. 1992-98), Internat. Lung Found. (pres. 1991—). Achievements include first major review of patient outcome during early history of intensive care units; an analysis of mechanisms of hypoxemia in patients with chronic liver disease; first report of Pneumocystis Carinii Pneumonitis in patients with lung cancer; first prospective evaluation of short course therapy reported in U.S. using Isoniazid and Rifampin; first American report using laser through fiberoptic bronchoscope to treat lung cancer; first report to evaluate continuous intravenous morphine to control pain in cancer patients; description of a simple technique to measure the total lung volume non-invasively using the routing chest x-ray. Office: Medical Faculty Assoc Suite 5-425 2150 Pennsylvania Ave NW Washington DC 20037-3201 Office Phone: 202-741-2237.

SPAGNUOLO, MARK MARIO, retired dentist; b. Midland, Mich., July 24, 1928; s. Anthony and Rose Spagnuolo; m. Sarah Frances Novello, Aug. 7, 1954; children: Christina Marie, Anthony Mark, Natalie Louise. BS, Ctrl. Mich. U., Mt. Pleasant, 1951; MS, U. Detroit, 1952, DDS, 1956. Lab. asst. Ctr. Mich. U., 1949—51; instr. U. Detroit, 1951—53; dentist pvt. practice, Ferndale, 1956—57, Lansing, 1959—92; ret., 1992. Pres. Ceatnal Supply Co., Spagnulo Builders, 1982—. Contbr. articles to profl. jours. Co-chair Mich. Com. for Re-election of Nixon, 1972; chmn. Mich. Dentists for Reagan, 1980, 1984; pres. Anthony Apts., 1959—, Park Laynes Gardens Apt., 1993—. Capt. US Dental Corps., 1957—59, cmdr. Army Mobile Dental Svc. Recipient Eagle Scout, 56 merit badges, 3 palms. Fellow: Am. Acad. Gen. Dentistry, Royal Soc. Health, London (pres.); mem.: Nat. Italian-Am. Found., Internat. Platform Assn., Nat. Acupuncture Rsch. Soc., Acad. Gen. Dentistry, Internat. Acad. Orthodontice, Fedn. Dentare Internationale, Assn. Mil. Surgeons US, Mich. Soc. Dentistry Children, Am. Dental Assn. (produced, directed, wrote ednl. film), Mich. Dental Assn., Ctrl. Dist. Dental Soc., Chgo. Dental Soc., Detroit Dist. Dental Soc., Mich. Fedn. Physicians and Dentists (chmn. peer rev. com. 1974—92, bd. dirs. 1975—92, chmn. legis. com. 1975—92, chmn. travel sem. 1976—92), Century Club (founder), Rotary. Republican. Roman Catholic. Home: 1724 Old Mill Rd East Lansing MI 48823

SPAHN, THOMAS WERNER, internist, researcher; s. Günter E and Margret Spahn; m. Louisa Sarkissian, Nov. 1, 1996; children: Helena Maria, Jacqueline Emilia Maria. MD, Mainz U. Sch. Medicine, Mainz, Germany, 1993; Internat. Baccalaureate, Goethe Gymnasium, Frankfurt am Main, 1985. Cert. in internal medicine Med. Assn. Westphalia, Lippe, Germany, 2003, in gastroenterology Med. Assn. Westphalia, Lippe, Germany, 2004, in emergency medicine Med. Assn. Lower Saxonia, Germany, 2005, in proctology Med. Assn. Lower Saxonia, Germany, 2007, in diabetology Med. Assn. Lower Saxonia, Germany, 2007. Intern Dept. Gastroenterology, Mainz U. Hosp., Mainz, Germany, 1993—95; rsch. fellow Ctr. Neurologic Diseases, Brigham and Women's Hosp. and Harvard Med. Sch., Boston, 1995—98; resident, dept. medicine, Gastroenterology, Hepatology, Endocrinology, Rheumatology Muenster U. Hosp., Germany, 1998—2004; attending physician, cons., dept. gen. internal medicine / gastroenterology, Marienhospital Osnabrueck, Academic Tchg. Hosp. U. Hanover Med. Sch., Osnabrueck, Germany, 2004—08; chmn. dept. internal medicine Marienkrankenhaus Schwerte, 2008—. Investigator med. study with novartis, Germany, 2006—08; cons. essex pharmaceuticals adv. bd., Germany, 2007. Author: (medical textbook) The Nature of Oral Gastrointestinal Tolerance; In: Inflammatory Bowel Disease; contbr. articles to profl. sci. jours., chapters to books. With Army, 1986—87, Homberg/ Efze, Germany. Recipient Rsch. award, U. Mainz Med. Sch., 1992, Travel award, Fedn. Clin. Immunology Soc., 2001; Rsch. fellowship, German Rsch. Coun., 1995—97, Found. Neurologic Diseases, 1997—98, Rsch. Funding grant, Friends U. Muenster, 2003, Emerging Leaders in Gastroenterology fellow, AstraZeneca, 2004—05, Rsch. grant, U. Muenster, Faculty, Inovative Med. Rsch., 1999—2000, 2004—05. Mem.: German Diabetes Assn. (DDG), German Gastroent. Assn. (DGVS). Roman Catholic. Avocations: swimming, sailing, literature, classical music. Office: Marienkrankenhaus Schwerte Goethestrasse 19 Schwerte 58239 Germany Office Fax: 49-2304-109572. Business E-Mail: t.spahn@marien-kh.de.

SPALDING, STEVEN, rheumatologist; b. Akon, Ohio, Sept. 23, 1975; BA, Miami U., 1997; MD, Wright State U. Sch. Medicine, 2001. Head ctr. pediat. rheumatology Cleve. Clinic, 2009—. Fellow: Am. Coll. Rheumatology, Am. Acad. Pediat.; mem.: Pediat. Rheumatology Collaborative Study Group, Childhood Arthritis & Rheumatology Rsch. Alliance. Avocation: running. Office: 9500 Euclid Ave A111 Cleveland OH 44195 Office Fax: 216-445-7569. Business E-Mail: spaldis@ccf.org.

SPANGLER, ARTHUR STEPHENSON, JR., psychologist; b. Boston, June 20, 1949; s. Arthur Stephenson and Barbara Louise (Fellows) Spangler; m. Deborah A. Kauders, Nov. 27, 1971; children: Heather Anita, Rebecca Haley. BS, Hobart Coll., 1971; MEd, Boston Coll., 1974; ScD, Boston U., 1985. lic. psychologist, Mass., clin. social worker, Mass. Mass. counselor Met. State Hosp., Waltham, 1971-73; rehab. counselor J.T. Berry Rehab. Ctr., North Reading, Mass., 1974-75; program coord. Shore Collaborative, Medford, Mass., 1975-76; dir. instl. sch. programs South Shore Collaborative, North Weymouth, Mass., 1976-79; dir. mental retardation program South Shore Mental Health Ctr., Quincy, Mass., 1979-85; coord. outpatient clinic Boston Pain Ctr., Spaulding Rehab. Hosp., 1985-86; v.p., dir. behavioral medicine svcs. Mass. Bay Counseling, Quincy, 1985—; dir. indsl. disability mgmt. svcs., psychologist chronic pain program Miriam Hosp., Providence, 1987-88; psychologist John Graham Headache Ctr. Faulkner Hosp., Boston, 1992-94. Adj. prof. Sargent Coll., Boston U., 1990—99; med. cons. Social Security Adminstrn., Disability Determination Services, Boston, 2006—. Vol.

counselor Multi-Svc. Ctr., Newton, Mass., 1973-75; bd. dirs. Newton-Wellesley-Weston-Needham Cmty. Mental Health and Mental Retardation Ctr., Newton, 1976-80, pres. 1979-80; mem. Boston Symphony Assn. Vols. Recipient award Nat. Assn. Retarded Citizens, 1974. Mem.: ACA, APA (assoc.), New Eng. Pain Assn., Assn. for Study of Pain. Episcopalian. Home: 151 Tremont St # 11P Boston MA 02111-1110 Office: 234 Copeland St 3rd Fl Quincy MA 02169 Office Phone: 617-786-0137. Business E-Mail: sspangler.mbc@comcast.net.

SPANGLER, EDRA MILDRED, psychologist; b. Webbville, Ky., Sept. 6, 1941; d. Chester A. and Laura B. (Webb) Sawyer; m. Robert Noel Spangler, Sept. 6, 1959; children: Robert Mark Spangler, Kendra Lynn Lovett. AS in Bus. Adminstrn., Franklin U., 1975; BA in Social Psychology, Park Coll., 1979; MA in Mgmt. and Supervision, Ctrl. Mich. U., 1980; D in Psychology, Wright State U., 1989. Lic. psychologist Ohio, Fla, Nat. Register Health Svc. Providers Psychology. With adminstrn., mgmt., fin. and computer sys. design various pvt. and govt. orgns., 1958-85; psychology assoc. Stonegate Psychol. Assocs., Columbus, Ohio, 1989-91; dir. pain & stress program The Rehab. Ctr., Columbus, 1991-94; pvt. practice, 1991—; mem. med. staff Riverside Meth. Hosps., Columbus, 1992—; health psychologist Mind/Body Med. Inst., 1993-95; mem. med. staff Grady Meml. Hosp., Delaware, Ohio, 1997—2004. Fellow Biofeedback Cert. Inst. America (sr.), Am. Coll. Forensic Examiners, Nat. Bd. Cert. Clin. Hypnotherapists; mem. Ohio Psychol. Assn., Fla. Psychol. Assn. Avocations: reading, travel.

SPARBERG, MARSHALL STUART, gastroenterologist, educator; b. Chgo., May 20, 1936; s. Max Shane and Mildred Rose (Haffron) S.; m. Eve Gaymont Enda, Mar. 15, 1987. BA, Northwestern U., 1957, MD, 1960. Intern Evanston Hosp., Ill., 1960-61; resident in internal medicine Barnes Hosp., St. Louis, 1961-63; fellow U. Chgo., 1963-65; practice medicine specializing in gastroenterolgy Chgo., 1967—; asst. prof. medicine Northwestern U., 1967-72, assoc. prof., 1972-80, prof. medicine, 1980—; instr. Wash. U., St. Louis, 1961-63, U. Chgo., 1963-65. Author: Ileostomy Care, 1969, Primer of Clinical Diagnosis, 1972, Ulcerative Colitis, 1978, Inflammatory Bowel Disease, 1982; contbr. numerous articles to profl. jours. Pres. Fine Arts Music Found., 1974-76, Crohn's Disease and Colitis Found. of Am., pres. Ill. chpt., 1994-97; bd. dirs. Lyric Opera Guild, 1974-94, Chamber Music Soc. North Shore Chgo., 1984—; physician to Chgo. Symphony Orch., 1981-97. With USAF, 1965-67. Named Outstanding Tchr. Northwestern U. Med. Sch., 1972 Mem. AMA, ACP, Am. Gastroent. Assn., Am. Coll. Gastroent. (bd. govs.), Chgo. Med. Soc., Chgo. Soc. Internal Medicine, Chgo. Soc. Gastroenterology (pres.), Chgo. Soc. Gastrointestinal Endoscopy (pres.) Office: 676 N Saint Clair St Ste 1525 Chicago IL 60611-2862 Office Phone: 312-944-7080.

SPARKS, CHARLES EDWARD, pathologist, educator; b. Peoria, Ill., July 29, 1940; s. William Joseph and Meredith (Pleasants) S.; m. Janet Lindsay Dehoff, Aug. 18, 1977; children: William, Debra, Robert. BS in Biology, MIT, 1963; MD, Thomas Jefferson U., 1968. Diplomate Am. Bd. Pathology, Am. Bd. Clin. Chemistry. Rsch. asst. Mass. Gen. Hosp., Boston, 1963; intern NY Hosp., Cornell Naval Hosp., St. Albans, 1968-69; resident in clin. pathology Hosp. of U. Pa., 1972-75; fellow in cardiopulmonary medicine U. Pa., Phila., 1975-76, asst. instr., 1972-75; fellow in biochemistry Med. Coll. Pa., Phila., 1976-77, instr., 1976-77, asst. to assoc. prof. biochemistry and physiology, 1977-82; assoc. prof. pathology U. Rochester (NY), 1982-88, prof. pathology, 1988—. Advisor med. scientist tng. program U. Rochester, 1984-92; attending pathologist, dir. clin. chemistry unit Strong Meml. Hosp., 1982—, chair rsc. adv. com., assoc. chair pathology, 1994—, dir. grad. studies in Integrative Biomed. Scis., 1998—. Contbr. articles to profl. jours.; patentee in field. Chairperson Endocrinology VA Merit Rev. Study Sect., 2000—. Lt. comdr. USN, 1969—72. Postdoctoral fellow NIH, 1975-77. Mem. AAAS, Am. Diabetes Assn. (co-chmn. nat. symposium meeting 1988), Acad. Clin. Lab. Physicians and Scientists, Am. Heart Assn. (fellow coun. on arteriosclerosis, mem. nominating com.). Office: Dept Pathology U Rochester 601 Elmwood Ave Rochester NY 14642-0001 Home Phone: 585-381-9549; Office Phone: 585-275-8236.

SPARKS, DALE BOYD, allergist, health facility administrator; b. Springfield, Mo., July 14, 1929; s. Roscoe R. and Ruby V. (Boyd) S.; children: Susan L., Laura A., Lisa M., Jennifer G.; m. Leeanna M. Molccyk Priboy, Apr. 21, 2001. AB, BS, Southwest Mo. State U., 1951; BS in Medicine, U. Mo., 1953; MD, St. Louis U., 1955. Diplomate Am. Bd. Allergy and Immunology. Intern Kansas City (Mo.) Gen. Hosp. U. Med. Ctr., 1955-56; resident U. Mo. Hosp., 1958-60; fellow in allergy and immunology Northwestern U., 1960-61; mem. cons. staff Parkview Cmty. Hosp., 1961—; mem. med. staff Riverside County Regional Med. Ctr., 1961-2000, dir. respiratory therapy, 1968-85, dir. respiratory therapy and diagnostic svcs., 1965—, chmn. dept. medicine, 1978-98, chief med. staff, 1990-98; acting dir., health officer Riverside Pub. Health Dept., 1991-93; ret., 1993. Clin. prof. medicine Loma Linda U. Mem. editl. bd. Immunology and Allergy in Practice, 1980—. Lt. USNR. Fellow ACP (coun. subsplty. socs. 1988—), Am. Coll. Allergy and Immunology (disting., bd. regents 1989-93, pres. 1990-91, chmn. fin. com., treas. 1990-93, recert. com.), Coll. Allergy, Asthma and Immunology; mem. AMA, Am. Lung Assn. (bd. dirs. 1990-95), Am. Heart Assn. (bd. dirs. 1964-70, pres. 1966), Joint Coun. Am. Allergy and Immunology (bd. dirs. 1985-90), Calif. Med. Assn., Calif. Soc. Allergy, Inland Soc. Internal Medicine, Riverside County Med. Assn. (bd. councilors 1980-99, del. CMA 1988-99), Riverside County Found. Med. Care (sec., past pres.). Home and Office: 29368 Big Range Rd Canyon Lake CA 92587 Personal E-mail: dsparksmd@aol.com.

SPARKS, JANET LINDSAY DEHOFF, pathologist, educator; b. Lawrence, Mass., Sept. 13, 1950; d. Ronald and Barbara DeHoff; m. Charles Sparks, Aug. 18, 1977; 1 child, Robert. BA in Biology, BS in Med. Tech., U. Pa., 1972, PhD in Pathology, 1980. Cert. med. technologist Am. Soc. Clin. Pathologists. Instr. clin. chemistry U. Pa., Phila., 1974-76; fellow Wistar Inst. Anatomy and Biology, Phila., 1975-80; postdoctoral fellow U. Rochester (N.Y.), 1983-85, scientist, 1985-94, asst. prof. pathology and lab. medicine, 1994-96, assoc. prof. pathology and lab. medicine, 1996—2008, prof. pathology and lab. medicine, 2008—. Cons. NIH, Indpls., 1994-96. Contbr. numerous articles to profl. jours.; patentee in field. Nat. NIDDK RO1 grantee, 1995—. Fellow Coun. on Arteriosclerosis Thrombosis and Vascular Biology; mem. AAAS, Am. Soc. Clin. Pathologists, Am. Diabetes Assn., Am. Heart Assn. (coun. on arteriosclerosis, coun. on clin. cardiology), N.Y. Acad. Scis., Am. Physiol. Soc. Office: U Rochester Dept Pathology 601 Elmwood Ave # 626 Rochester NY 14642-0001 Business E-Mail: janet_sparks@urmc.rochester.edu.

SPARKS, LILLIAN AZALEA, federal agency administrator; b. Towson, Md., Oct. 16, 1975; BA in Polit. Sci., Morgan State U., Balt., 1998; JD, Georgetown U. Law Ctr., Washington, 2001. Monitoring specialist Amerix Corp., Balt., 1996—98; law clk., environ. law & litig. Air Force Legal Services Agy., Rosslyn, Va., 1999; law clk. Nat. Indian Gaming Commn., Washington, 2000; staff atty. Nat. Congress American Indians, 2001—04; exec. dir. Nat. Indian Edn. Assn., 2004—10; commr. Adminstrn. Native Americans, US Dept. Health & Human Services, 2010—. Mem. Miss Indian world com. Gathering of Nations, Albuquerque, 2003—. Mem.: Md. Bar Assn., Nat. Congress Am. Indians (life), Delta Sigma Theta. Mailing: Administration for Native Americans 2nd Fl W Aerospace Ctr 370 L Enfant Promenade SW Washington DC 20447 *

SPARKS, ROBERT DEAN, medical administrator, gastroenterologist; b. Newton, Iowa, May 6, 1932; s. Albert John and Josephine Emma (Kleinendorst) S.; children: Steven Robert, Ann Louise, John James. BA, U. Iowa, 1955, MD, 1957; D of Humanitarian Svc. (hon.), Creighton U., 1978. Diplomate Am. Bd. Internal Medicine. Intern Charity Hosp. of La., New Orleans, 1957-58, resident in internal medicine, 1958-59, asst. in medicine, 1958-59; fellow in gen. medicine and gastroenterology Tulane U. Sch. Medicine, 1959-62, instr. medicine, 1959-63, asst. prof., 1963-64, assoc. prof., 1964-68, prof., 1968-72, asst. dean, 1964-67, assoc. dean, acting dean, 1967-68, vice dean, 1968-69, dean, 1969-72, chief sect. gastroenterology, 1968-72; chancellor Med. Ctr. U. Nebr., 1972-76, prof. medicine, 1972-76; v.p. U. Nebr. System, 1972-76; health program dir. W.K. Kellogg Found., Battle Creek, Mich., 1976-81, v.p. programming, 1981-82, sr. v.p., 1982, pres., chief programming officer, 1982—88, trustee, 1988, pres. emeritus, cons., 1988-92; pres., CEO, Calif. Med. Assn. Found., Sacramento, 1995-98, sr. assoc., 1998—; dir. OMNI Med., Waban, Md., 2000—; with Great Plains Pub. Health Leadership Inst. Adv. Coun., 2002; dean coun. Tulane U. Sch. Medicine; hon. mem. Centro de Estudios en Medicina Familiar " Ian Mc Whinney", Buenos Aires, 2007. Cons. U. Tenn. Health Sci. Ctr., 1988-90, Boston U. Health Policy Inst., 1989-90; mem. sci., compensation and trust rev. coms. Syntex Corp., Palo Alto, Calif., 1987-91, v.p. product safety and compliance, 1991-93, mem. overseers com. to visit Harvard U. Med. and Dental Schs., 1984-90; mem. vis. com. U. Miami Sch. Medicine, 1982-86; assoc. med. dir. for addiction treatment svcs., dir. for edn. and rsch., Battle Creek Adventist Hosp., 1990-91; v.p. Howe-Lewis Internat Inc., Menlo Park, N.Y., 1993-94, cons., 1994-95; mem. adv. coun. to dean Tulane U. Sch. Medicine, 2004—. Mem. editl. bd. Alcoholism Treatment Quar., 1985--; contbr. articles to profl. jours. Bd. dirs. Nat. Coun. on Alcoholism and Drug Dependence, NYC, 1982-93, treas., 1986-88, chmn., 1989-90, past chmn., 1991-92; bd. dirs. Battle Creek Symphony Orch., 1981-88, Lakeview Sch. Dist., Battle Creek, 1979-83, 88-91, Omni Med, 2001-; trustee Monsour Med. Found., Jeannette, Pa., 1976-90, interim pres. 1989, chmn. bd., pres., 1989-90; mem. President's Adv. Bd. on Pvt. Sector Initiatives, Washington, 1986-89; chmn. bd. dirs. Bard Coll. Health Policy and Practice Inst., 1988-96, Consumer Health Info. Rsch. Inst., 1990-95, Chelsea-Arbor Treatment Ctr., 1990-91; bd. dirs. Calhoun County Bd. Health, 1988-91, chmn., 1989-91; mem., bd. dirs. Mental Health and Addictions Found. Mich., Battle Creek, 1991-93; mem. adv. coun. CMA Found., 2004-07; mem. cmty. adv. com., Taser Found., Scottsdale, Ariz., 2005—06, bd. dirs. 2006—10, chair, 2006—09, co-chair 2009-10. Recipient Harvard Dental award Harvard U. Sch. Dental Medicine, 1992, Disting. Alumni award for achievement U. Iowa Coll. Medicine, 1998, U. Iowa Alumni Assn, 2009, Disting. Alumni Achievement award, annual Robert D. Sparks Cmty. Health Leadership Achievement award CMA Found., 1997— Master ACP; mem. AMA, Nat. Acad. Scis. Inst. Medicine (com. study of treatment and rehab. svcs. for alcoholism and alcohol abuse, bd. mental health and behavioral medicine), Coun. Mich. Founds. (trustee 1986-88), Assn. Am. Med. Colls. (disting. svc. mem. 1975—), Phi Eta Sigma, Alpha Omega Alpha, Phi Kappa Psi. Republican. Methodist. Avocations: tennis, bridge, reading, travel. Home and Office: 5004 Gresham Dr El Dorado Hills CA 95762-7703 Office Phone: 916-605-6454. Personal E-mail: rdsparksmd1@earthlink.net.

SPARLE CHRISTENSEN, KAJ, physician, educator; b. Christiansfeld, Jan. 13, 1963; MD, Aarhus U., 1991, PhD, 2004. Asst. prof. Rsch. Unit Gen. Practice, 2004—. Office: Bartholins Allé 2 Aarhus Central Region 8000 Denmark Business E-Mail: kasc@alm.au.dk.

SPARROW, JOSHUA D., child psychiatrist; MD, Yale Med. Sch. Asst. prof. psychiatry Harvard Med. Sch., Boston; assoc. dir. Brazelton Touchpoints Ctr., dir. spl. initiatives. Cons. Harlem Children's Zone, NYC, Am. Indian Early Head Start Programs. Co-author (with Dr. T. Berry Brazelton): (NY Times syndicated column) Families Today, 1999—, (books) Touchpoints: Three to Six, 2001, Brazelton Way book series, 2004—; cons. (TV series) Brazelton on Parenting, 2000, Ready, Set, Learn, 2005—; contbg. editor: Parent & Child Mag. Office: Children's Hospital Ste 320 1295 Boylston St Boston MA 02215 also: Children's Hospital 300 Longwood Ave Boston MA 02215 also: NY Times Syndication Sales Corp 14th Fl 122 E 42nd St New York NY 10168 Office Phone: 617-355-7639. Office Fax: 617-859-7215, 212-499-3382. E-mail: joshua.sparrow@tch.harvard.edu, nytsyn-families@nytimes.com.

SPARROW, MARGARET JUNE, pharmaceutical executive, retired physician; b. Inglewood, New Zealand, June 26, 1935; d. Daniel James and Jessie Isabel Muir; m. Peter Sparrow, Jan. 7, 1956 (dec. June 6, 1982); children: Graeme, Beryl Sparrow Roche. BSc, Victoria U. of Wellington, New Zealand, 1955; MB, BChir, U. Otago, Dunedin, New Zealand, 1963—63; diploma in venereology, U. London and Soc. Apothecaries, 1977. Brit. joint cert.of family planning Royal Colls. Ob-gyn. and Gen. Practitioners and Family Planning Assn. Ho. surgeon Stratford (New Zealand) Pub. Hosp., 1964, Hawera (New Zealand) Pub. Hosp., 1964; med. officer child health Health Dept., New Plymouth, New Zealand, 1965—69; med. officer Student Health Svc., Victoria U. of Wellington, 1969—81; med. tng. officer, vasectomist New Zealand Family Planning Assn., Wellington, 1971—2005; sexual health physician Wellington Sexual Health Svc., 1977—2004; sr. lectr. dept. ob-gyn. Wellington Clin. Sch. Medicine, 1978—2004; abortion oper. dr. Parkview Clinic, Wellington Hosp., 1980—98; co-dir. Istar Ltd, Wellington, 1999—. Author (with Penny Kane): Consumer Guide to Birth Control, 1986; author: Choosing the Right Contraceptive, 1990; author: (with Lesley Bond) Vasectomy: Practical Information & Advice, 1999; author: Milestones in New Zealand Sexual Health, 2003, Abortion Then and Now, 2010; contbr. articles to profl. jours. Trust bd. mem. Intersex Trust Aotearoa New Zealand, Wellington, 1997—, New Zealand Sexual & Reproductive Health Ednl. Charitable Trust, Wellington, 1998—; mem. com., censor, past chair New Zealand Chpt. Sexual Health Medicine, 1994—2005; mem. of govt. del. to UN population conf., Bucharest, Romania New Zealand Govt., New Zealand, 1974—74; mem./chairperson iucd adv. com. Min. of Health, Wellington, New Zealand, 1986—90; pres. Abortion Law Reform Assn. of New Zealand, Wellington, 1975—2011. Decorated Mem. Brit. Empire Queen's Birthday Honor, Disting. Companion New Zealand Order of Merit, Order of Merit DNZM Dame Comdr. New Zealand; recipient New Zealand Centennial Suffrage medal, New Zealand Govt., 1993. Mem.: New Zealand Family Planning Assn. (hon.; hon. v.p. 1977, hon. life, cert.), New Zealand Venereological Soc. (life; pres. 1986—89, hon. life), Zonta Internat. (life; past pres. 1975, Dist. 16 award 2003). Achievements include first to promote use of emergency contraception in New Zealand; establish vasectomy clinic; help establish abortion service in Wellington. Avocations: Scottish country dancing, photography. Office: Abortion Law Reform Assn New Zealand P O Box 28008 Kelburn 6150 Wellington New Zealand

SPEAR, SCOTT LAWRENCE, plastic surgeon; b. Chgo., Aug. 25, 1948; s. Louis and Esther Spear; m. Cynthia Staley Spear; children: Alexandra, Geri, Louis. BA with honors, U. Mich., Ann Arbor, 1968; MD, U. Chgo.Pritzker Sch. Medicine, 1972. Diplomate Nat. Bd. Med. Examiners, Am. Bd. Med. Examiners, Am. Bd. Plastic Surgery, lic. DC, Md., Va. Intern surgery Beth Israel Hosp., Boston, 1972-73, jr. gen. surgery residency, 1974-75, sr. gen. surgery residency, 1976—77; jr. gen. surgery residency San Francisco Gen. Hosp., 1973-74; gen. surgery fellowship Guy's Hosp., London, 1975—76; plastic surgery residency U. Miami, 1979; craniofacial fellowship L'Hopital Enfants Malades, Paris, 1980; asst. prof. plastic surgery U. Fla., Gainesville, 1980-81, Georgetown U. Sch. Medicine, Washington, 1981-86, assoc. prof. plastic surgery, 1986—90, prof. plastic surgery, 1990—, chief divsn. plastic and reconstructive surgery, Georgetown U. Hosp., 1992—. Dir. plastic surgery training prog. Georgetown U. Hosp., 1992—; vis. prof. Med. Coll. Wis., 1994, U. Toronto, 1999, U. Calif., San Francisco, 1999, Monash U., Clayton, Australia, 2000, Ohio State U., 2001, Yale U., 2003. Mem. editl. bd. Annals of Plastic Surgery, 1992—95, Jour. Plastic & Reconstructive Surgery, 1998—, Perspectives in Plastic Surgery, 1998—; contbr. articles to profl. jours., chapters to books. Named one of Best Doctors in America, Washingtonian mag., 1986—. Fellow: ACS; mem.: Northeastern Soc. Plastic & Reconstructive Surgeons (bd. dirs. 1996—2000, pres. 1998—99), Am. Soc. Maxillofacial Sugeons (bd. trustees 1987—90), Am. Soc. Aesthetic Plastic Surgery, Am. Assn. Plastic Surgeons, Am. Soc. Plastic Surgeons (mem. exec. com. 1994—96, bd. trustees 1997—99, mem. exec. com. 1999, v.p. 2001), Plastic Surgery Ednl. Found. (bd. dirs. 1991—94). Office: Georgetown University Hosp 3800 Reservoir Rd NW 1 PHC Washington DC 20007-2113 Office Phone: 202-444-8612. Office Fax: 202-444-7204. Business E-Mail: spears@gunet.georgetown.edu. *

SPECK, EUGENE LEWIS, internist; b. Boston, Dec. 17, 1936; s. Robert A. and Anne (Rosenberg) S.; m. Rachel Shoshana; children: Michael Robert, Keren Sara. AB, Brandeis U., Waltham, Mass., 1958; MS, U. Mass., 1961; PhD, George Washington U., 1966, MD, 1969. Diplomate Am. Bd. Internal Medicine with subspecialty in infectious diseases. Intern N.Y. Hosp.-Cornell, 1969-70; rsch. assoc. NIH, Bethesda, Md., 1970-72; resident Barnes Hosp.-Washington U., 1972-73; instr. medicine Washington U., St. Louis, 1972-73; fellow Strong Meml. Hosp.-U. Rochester, 1973-75; instr. medicine U. Rochester, N.Y., 1973-75, asst. prof. medicine N.Y., 1975-80, U. Nev., Las Vegas, 1980-85, assoc. prof., 1985-95, prof. medicine, 1995—; dir./co-dir. infectious disease unit U. Med. Ctr. of So. Nev., Las Vegas, 1980—; ptnr. Infectious Diseases Consultants, 1983—. Cons. Clark County Health Dept., Las Vegas, 1980—, U. Med. Ctr. So. Nev., Las Vegas, 1980—, Sunrise Hosp., Las Vegas, 1980—, Valley Hosp., Las Vegas, 1980—; Am. coll. physicians gov., State Nev., 2007-11. Contbr. articles to profl. jours., chpts. to books. Recipient Disting. Physician award, State of Nev., 2002, Laureate award, ACP Nev. Chpt. Fellow ACP (Nev. gov. 2007-11, Laureate award 2011), Infectious Disease Soc. America; mem. Am. Soc. Microbiology, Alpha Omega Alpha. Avocations: tennis, skiing, racquetball. Home: 2228 Chatsworth Ct Henderson NV 89074-5309 Office: Infectious Diseases Cons 3006 S Maryland Pkwy Ste 780 Las Vegas NV 89109-2292 Office Phone: 702-737-0740.

SPECTOR, GERSHON JERRY, otolaryngologist, educator, researcher; b. Rovno, Poland, Oct. 20, 1937; came to U.S., 1949; naturalized, 1956; m. Patsy Carol Tanenbaum, Aug. 28, 1965. BA, Johns Hopkins U., 1960; MD cum laude, U. Md., 1964. Intern Beth Israel Hosp., Boston, 1964-65; resident in surgery Sinai Hosp., Balt., 1965-66; resident in otolaryngology Mass. Eye and Ear Infirmary, Boston, 1966-69, Peter Bent Brigham Hosp., Boston, 1968-69; teaching fellow in otolaryngology Harvard U. Med. Sch., Boston, 1968-69; assoc. physician Ill. Crippled Children's Svc., Carbondale, 1971; mem. faculty Washington U. Med. Sch., St. Louis, 1971—, assoc. prof. otolaryngology, 1974-76, prof., 1976—; chief dept. otolaryngology St. Louis County Hosp., 1971-77. Mem. staff Washington U. Med. Ctr., Barnes Hosp.; dir. temporal bone bank, 1971-81; guest examiner Am. Bd. Otolaryngology, 1975-77; rsch. cons. neurosci. group, G.D. Searle Pharm. Corp. Mem. editl. bd. Laryngoscope, 1978, editor-in-chief, 1984-94; contbr. articles to med. jours. With U.S. Army, 1969-71. Hancock scholar, 1962. Fellow ACS; mem. AAAS, AMA, Am. Acad. Ophthalmology and Otolaryngology (Honor award 1979), St. Louis Med. Soc., St. Louis County Med. Soc., Am. Coun. Otolarygology, St. Louis Ear, Nose and Throat Club (pres. 1986), So. Med. Assn., Deafness Rsch. Found., Pan. Am. Assn.

Otorhinolaryngology and Broncho Esophagology, Am. Soc. Head and Neck Surgery, Soc. Univ. Otolaryngologists, Am. Laryngol., Rhinol. and Otol. Soc. (Edmund Prince Fowler award 1974), Am. Soc. Cell Biology, Electron Microscopy Soc., N.Y. Acad. Scis., Am. Assn. Anatomists, Am. Acad. Facial Plastic and Reconstructive Surgery, Am. Neuro-Otology Soc., Gesellschaft fur Neurootologie und Aequilibrimoetrie A.V., Barany Soc., Am. Radium Soc., Assn. Acad. Surgery, Am. Fedn. Clin. Oncologic Socs., Am Otol. Soc., Acoustical Soc. Am., Soc. for Neurosci., Internat. Skull Base Soc. (founding), Brazilian Skull Base Soc. (hon.), Centurion Club, Alpha Omega Alpha, Psi Chi. Home: 7365 Westmoreland Dr Saint Louis MO 63130-4241 Office: Washington U Med Sch Saint Louis MO 63110 Office Phone: 314-362-7252. Business E-Mail: spectng@wustl.edu.

SPECTOR, JASON A., plastic surgeon, educator; b. NYC, Jan. 24, 1970; s. Bernard Robert Spector and Evelyn Rose Jefferies, Bryan Reginald Jefferies (Stepfather); m. Beth Chartoff, Nov. 21, 1998; children: Joshua Andrew, Samuel Benjamin. Grad., Cornell U., 1991; MD, NY U. Sch. Medicine, 1996. Diplomate Am. Bd. Plastic Surgery, 2007. Intern, resident & fellow NYU Med. Ctr., rsch. fellow Lab. Devel. Biology & Repair; asst. prof. Weill Cornell Med. Coll., NYC, 2006—; asst. attending surgeon NY Presbyterian Hosp. Mem.: Plastic Surgery Rsch. Coun., NY Regional Soc. Plastic Surgeons (Best Rsch. Presentation award 2003), Northeastern Soc. Plastic Surgeons (Best Resident Rsch. Presentation award 1999), Alpha Omega Alpha. Office: Weill Cornell Medical Coll 525 East 68th St Payson 709-A New York NY 10065 Office Fax: 212-746-8952. Business E-Mail: jas2037@med.cornell.edu.

SPEEDIE, MARILYN KAY, microbiologist, dean, educator; b. Salem, Oreg., Nov. 13, 1947; d. Arthur Alexander and Eleanor Ruth (Todd) Wilson; m. Stuart Mitchell Speedie, July 18, 1968; children: Andrea Elizabeth, Christopher Todd. BS in Pharmacy, Purdue U., West Lafayette, Ind., 1970, PhD, 1973. Asst. prof. Oreg. State U., Corvallis, 1973-75; asst. prof. then prof., dept. chmn. U. Md., Balt., 1975-91, prof. Sch. Pharmacy, 1991—96; prof. dept. medicinal chemistry, dean U. Minn. Coll. Pharmacy, Mpls., 1996—. Contbr. articles to profl. jours. Mem.: US Pharmacopoeia (bd. trustees mem. 2010—), Am. Pharm. Assn., Am. Soc. Health Sys. Pharmacists, Am. Chem. Soc., Am. Assn. Colleges of Pharmacy (pres. 2006—07, bd. dirs.), Am. Soc. Pharmacognosy (exec. com. 1987—89, 1999—2000), Soc. Indsl. Microbiology, Am. Soc. Microbiology, Rho Chi. Office: U Minn Coll Pharmacy 5 130 Weaver Densford Hall 308 Harvard St SE Minneapolis MN 55455-1142 Office Phone: 612-624-1900. Business E-Mail: speed001@umn.edu.

SPEER, KEVIN PAUL, surgeon; b. Evansville, Ind., June 8, 1959; m. Marcy Carlson Speer, Mar. 24, 1984; children: Casey, Kira. MD, Johns Hopkins U., 1985. Lic. physician N.C., 1992. Assoc. prof. orthopedics Duke U. Med. Ctr., Durham, NC, 1992—2000; pvt. practice Southeastern Orthopedics, Raleigh, NC, 2000—. Fellow, Am. Orthop. Assn., 1992. Fellow: AAOS. Office: Southeastern Orthopedics 3404 Wake Forest Rd Ste 201 Raleigh NC 27609 Business E-Mail: kspeer@nc.rr.com.

SPEICHER, CARL EUGENE, pathologist; b. Carbondale, Pa., Mar. 21, 1933; s. William Joseph and Elizabeth Marcella (Connolly) S.; m. Mary Louise Walsh, June 21, 1958; children: Carl E. Jr., Gregory, Erik. BS in Biology, King's Coll., 1954; MD, U. Pa., 1958; student, Sch. of Aerospace Medicine, Brooks AFB, Tex., 1969. Diplomate Am. Bd. Pathology. Intern U. Pa. Hosp., Phila., 1958-59, resident, 1959-63; chief lab. svcs. USAF Hosp., London, Eng., 1963-66, USAF Med. Ctr. Wright Patterson, Dayton, Ohio, 1966-70; dir. clin. labs. and chmn. dept. pathology Wilford Hall USAF Med. Ctr., San Antonio, 1971-77; prof. dept. pathology Ohio State U., Columbus, 1977—2000, vice chair dept. pathology, 1992—2000, prof. emeritus dept. pathology, 2000—; dir. clin. svcs. Ohio State U. Med. Ctr., Columbus, 1977—2000; dir. clin. lab. Stoneridge Med. Ctr., Ohio State U., 2000—11. Co-author: Choosing Effective Laboratory Tests, 1983; author: The Right Test, 1990, 3d edit., 1998. Col. USAF, 1956-77. Decorated Legion of Merit; fellow in med. chemistry SUNY, Syracuse, 1970-71. Mem. AMA, Ohio Soc. Pathologists, Ctrl. Ohio Soc. Pathologists, Am. Assn. for Clin. Chemistry, Assn. Clin. Scientists, Coll. Am. Pathologists, Am. Soc. Clin. Pathologists, Alpha Omega Alpha.

SPEISER, PHYLLIS WITZEL, pediatric endocrinologist, educator; m. Mark A. Speiser; 3 children. BA, Brandeis U., Waltham, Mass., 1975; MD, Columbia U. Coll. Physicians & Surgeons, 1979. Diplomate Am. Bd. Pediat., cert. in pediatric endocrinology. Intern, resident Bronx Mcpl. Hosp., Albert Einstein Coll. Medicine, NYC, 1979-82; fellow in pediatric endocrinology NY Hosp.-Cornell U. Med. Coll., NYC, 1982-84; asst. prof. Cornell U. Med. Coll., 1984-90, assoc. prof., 1990-99; prof. pediat. NYU Sch. Medicine, 1999—2010, Hofstra U. Sch. Medicine, 2010—. Med. advisor Nat. Adrenal Disease Found., 1993—; chief pediatric endocrinology Steven and Alexandra Cohen Childrens Med. Ctr., New Hyde Park, NY, 1993—; assoc. investigator Feinstein Inst. Med. Rsch. Contbr. articles to profl. jours. Mem. physician's adv. bd. CARES Found., Inc. Fellow: Am. Coll. Endocrinology; mem.: Pediatric Endocrinology Soc., Endocrine Soc., Soc. Pediatric Rsch., Am. Assn. Clin. Endocrinologists. Office: Cohen Childrens Med Ctr NY 269-01 76th Ave New Hyde Park NY 11040 Office Phone: 718-470-3290. Office Fax: 718-470-4565. *

SPELBRING, TAMMY SUE, ultrasonographer; b. Indianapolis, Ind., July 5, 1961; AS in Radiologic Tech., Ivy Tech. State Coll., 1984; BS in Sci., U. St. Francis, 1991, MS in Health Svcs. Adminstrn., 2004. Staff ultrasonographer Wishard Hosp., Indianapolis, 1987—91, IU Hosp., 1991—97; tech. specialist II St. Vincent Hosp., 1997—2001, mgr. maternal fetal medicine, 2001—05, dir. maternal fetal medicine and genetics ctr., 2005—. Recipient D.J. Angus Sciencetech. award, Sciencetech. Club of Indpls., 1982. Mem.: Soc. Diagnostic Med. Sonography, Am. Inst. Ultrasound in Medicine. Republican. Office: St Vincent Women's Hosp Maternal Fetal Medicine MOB 1 Ste 108 8091 Townshipline Rd Indianapolis IN 46260 Home Phone: 317-569-8108; Office Phone: 317-415-7744. E-mail: tsspellbr@stvincent.org, tspellbring@indy.rr.com.

SPELLACY, WILLIAM NELSON, obstetrician, gynecologist, educator; b. St. Paul, May 10, 1934; s. Jack F. and Elmyra L. (Nelson) Spellacy; m. Lynn Larsen; children: Kathleen Ann, Kimberly Joan, William Nelson. BA, U. Minn., 1955, BS, 1956, MD, 1959. Diplomate subsplty. cert. in maternal and fetal medicine Am. Bd. Ob-Gyn. Intern Hennepin County Gen. Hosp., Mpls., 1959—60; resident U. Minn., Mpls., 1960—63; practice medicine specializing in ob-gyn. Mpls., 1963—67, Miami, Fla., 1967—73, Gainesville, Fla., 1973—79, Chgo., 1979—88; prof., dept. head U. Ill. Coll. Medicine, Chgo., 1979—88; dept. chmn. U. So. Fla. Coll. Medicine, Tampa, 1988—2002, prof., 1988—. Prof. dept. ob-gyn. U. Miami, 1967—73; prof., chmn. dept. U. Fla., 1973—79. Contbr. articles to med. jours. Mem.: ACOG, AMA, Inst. Medicine, Ill. Med. Soc., Soc. Perinatal Obstetricians, Ctrl. Assn. Obstetrics and Gynecology, South Atlantic Soc. Obstetrics and Gynecology, Perinatal Rsch. Soc., Am. Diabetes Assn., Assn. Profs. Gynecology and Obstetrics, Am. Fertility Soc., Endocrine Soc., Am. Assn. Obstetricians and Gynecologists, Soc. Gynecol. Investigation, Am. Gynecol. and Obstet. Soc., Am. Gynecol. Soc., Rotary. Episcopalian. Office: Univ South Fla Coll Medicine Dept OBGYN 2A Tampa General Cir Tampa FL 33606-3589 Home: 516 Mirabay Blvd Apollo Beach FL 33572 Office Phone: 813-259-8542.

SPENCER, HEIDI HONNOLD, psychotherapist, writer, educator; b. Washington, June 30, 1943; d. John Otis and Annamarie (Kunz) Honnold; m. Charles David Spencer; children: Hans Steven, Jason John, Tanya Anna. BA, U. Pa., 1965; MA, Columbia U., 1966; MSW, Cath. U., 1982; PhD Adult and Family Psychology, Union Inst., Cin., 1990. LCSW, lic. clin. social worker DC, social worker Md., W.Va., Mass.; cert. Nat. Bd. Addictions Examiners. Tchr. h.s. Peace Corps, Yap Island, 1966—68; faculty instr. Ctrl. Wash. State Coll., Ellensburg, 1972—75; parent group facilitator Individual Psychology Assocs., Chevy Chase, Md., 1975—79; group facilitator Georgetown U. Med. Sch., Washington, 1977—80; staff clinician D.C. Inst. Mental Health, 1980—86; pvt. practice in adult psychotherapy Bethesda, Md., 1985—; faculty Cath. U. Psychoanalytic Found., 1989—91; bd. dirs., cons., faculty, supr. Clin. Social Work Inst.; pvt. practice Portland, Maine, 2006—. Mem. bd. doctoral program clin. social workers; counselor, tchr. Spl. Sch. Pregnant Teenagers, Seattle, 1969—71; crisis intervention counselor Montgomery County Hotline, Md., 1975—79; mental health intern No. Va. Mental Health Inst., Falls Church, 1979—80; faculty Cath. U., Washington, 1991; cons., counselor Christ Child Soc., Rockville, Md., 1985—86; cons. Billingual Project/Project BUILD, Yakima, Wash., 1973—75, Jewish Cmty. Ctr., Rockville, 1992, Brooklane Psychiat. Ctr., Hagerstown, Md., 1992, AmeriCorps, Washington, 1996, Affiliated Cmty. Counselors, Inc., Rockville, 1996—; instr. insvc. psychol. and learning ctr. Am. U., Washington, 1990—; chair Conf. Washington Psychoanalytic Found., 1989—90; mem. curriculum com. Clin. Social Work Inst., 1991—94; with recovery work Charles Town Race Traces Office Chaplain; clinician Shenandoah Valley Free Clinic, Charles Tocon, W.Va.; cons., primary clinician HIV/AIDS Network Tristate, Martinsburg, W.Va.; behavioural health specialist Canyon Ranch, Lenox, Mass., cons., primary clinician, 2007—, Brian Ctr. Substance Abuse and Mental Health, Pittsfield, Mass.; spkr., presenter in field. Author: Our Valley-Our Song, 1974, Did I Do Something Wrong? A Supportive Guide for Parnsets and Loved Ones or People in Psychotherapy, 1995; columnist: Family Therapy Acad., 1996—97. Trainer, cons. cmty.-based overflow shelters for homeless, Bethesda, 1989—94; active dr.-lawyer anti-drug program Fairfax Bar Assn., 1997; vice chair bd. social concerns Cedar Ln. Unitarian Ch., 1986—87. Mem.: Greater Washington Soc. Clin. Social Work (v.p. edn. 1992—94, at-large 1994—96, mem. membership task force 1995—96). Avocations: violin, piano, accordion, gardening, writing. Office: 30 Whipple Farm Ln Falmouth ME 04105 also: Integrated Behavioral Healthcare 200 Profl Dr Scarborough ME 04074 Office Phone: 413-358-2888. Business E-Mail: heidispencer@me.com.

SPENCER, MELVIN JOE, retired health facility administrator, lawyer, consultant; b. Buffalo Center, Iowa, Jan. 2, 1923; s. Kenos W. and Jennie (Michaelson) S.; m. Dena Joyce Butterfield, Mar. 1, 1952; children: Dennis Norman, Gregory Melvin, Shelly Lynn Spencer Goodnight. AB, U. Mich., 1948, JD, 1950. Bar: Iowa 1950, Mo. 1950, Okla. 1961. Practiced in, Kansas City, Mo., 1950-61, Oklahoma City, 1961—; assoc., then ptnr. Watson, Ess, Marshall & Enggas, 1950-61; ptnr. Miller & Spencer (and predecessor firm), 1961-75, of counsel, 1975-80; adminstr. Deaconess Hosp., 1975-92, cons., 1992-93; ret., 1993. Dir. Union Bank & Trust Co., Oklahoma City, 1977-88, 89-96, adv. dir., 1996-99; dir., sec. Hosp. Casualty Co., 1977-92; dir., treas. VHA Okla., Inc., 1986-92 Assoc. editor Mich. Law Rev., 1949-50. Mcpl. judge City of Roeland Park, Kans., 1952, city coun., 1954; area Rep. precinct chmn., 1968-69; del. Rep. State Conv., 1968, 96; bd. dir. Deaconess Hosp., Oklahoma City, 1966-2005, Christian Counseling Ctr., 1973-75, Witteman Corp., 2005-07, Butterfield Meml. Found., 2005—; chmn. Butterfield Meml. Found., 2010-; trustee Okla. Hosp. Assn., 1978-84, chmn. bd. trustees, 1983, trustee Okla. Co. Med. Soc. Found., 2002—; trustee, vice chmn. bd. dir. Ctrl. Coll., McPherson, Kans., 1972-86; trustee Okla. Ambulance Trust, 1984-87; adv. bd. Okla. State U. Tech. Inst., 1980-92; bd. dir. Emergency Med. Svcs. Ctrl. Okla., 1975-78, FMC Ministries, Inc.; const. coun. Free Meth. Ch. World Fellowship, 1975-95; chmn. Free Meth. Found., 1988-99; gen. counsel Free Meth. Ch. N.Am., 1969-95, bd. adminstrn., 1969-99, sec., 1985-95, investment com., 1976-88, chmn. investment com., 1986-88. Capt. USAAF, 1943-46 Named Layman of Yr., Free Meth. Ch. N.Am., 1984; recipient W. Cleveland Rodgers Disting. Svc. award Okla. Hosp. Assn., 1985; fellow Cen. Coll. Acad. of Achievers, 1990. Mem. Okla. Bar Assn., Oklahoma County Bar Assn., Order of Coif, Phi Beta Kappa, Phi Kappa Phi Home: 5910 N Shawnee Ave Oklahoma City OK 73112-1627

SPENCER, RICHARD THOMAS, III, health products executive; b. Oak Park, Ill., Mar. 18, 1936; s. Richard Thomas Spencer Jr. and Lois Anne (Pollock) Spencer; m. Andrea B. Schlickeiser, June 26, 1962; 1 child, Richard Thomas IV. BA, U. Mich., 1959; postgrad., U. Pa., 1976, Stanford U., 1984, Clemson U., 1985. Mktg. group Mobil Oil Co., Detroit, 1962; internat. trade specialist U.S. Dept. Commerce, Detroit, 1963—64; account exec. J. Walter Thompson Co., Detroit, 1965—66; sales mgr. Sarns Inc., Ann Arbor, Mich., 1967—69; v.p. mktg. Cordis Dow Corp., Miami, Fla., 1970—81; pres. mktg. divsn. Cordis Corp., Miami, 1982—87; pres., CEO Uni-Med Internat. Corp., Miami, 1988—2000; exec. v.p., COO, bd. dirs. World Med. Mfg. Corp., Sunrise, Fla., 1995—2000. Bd. dirs. Viacor Corp., Wilmington, Mass., Bioheart, Inc., Weston, Fla., Oxira Med., Inc., Boca Raton, Fla.; cons. in field. Contbr. articles to profl. jours. With CIC US Army, 1959—61. Republican. Avocations: skiing, golf, running, stereo equipment, geopolits. Home and Office: 3641 N 47th Ave Hollywood FL 33021-2211 Home: 811 E Hill Rd North Troy VT 05859 Office Phone: 954-558-3689. Personal E-mail: richardtspencer@yahoo.com.

SPENCER, ROGER FELIX, psychiatrist, educator; b. Apr. 19, 1934; came to U.S., 1941; s. Eugene S. Spitzer and Santa Spencer; m. Barbara Ann Houser, Aug. 18, 1958; children: Geoffrey, Jennifer, Rebecca. BS, Yale Coll., 1956; MD, Harvard Med. Sch., 1959. Diplomate Am. Bd. Psychiatry. Intern N.C. Meml. Hosp., Chapel Hill, 1959-60, resident in psychiatry, 1960-63; instr. U. N.C. Sch. Medicine, Chapel Hill, 1963-66, asst. prof., 1966-69, assoc. prof., 1969-76, prof., 1976—. Dir. of liaison and cons., U. N.C., 1967-77, dir. out patient psychiatry, 1977-95. Contbr. articles to profl. jours.;, author short stories. Recipient Career Tchr. award NIMH, 1965-67. Fellow Am. Psychiat. Assn. (life), Am. Psychoanalytic Assn.; mem. N.C. Psychoanalytic Soc. (past pres.), N.C. Psychiat. Assn. (past pres.). Office: UNC Hosps Dept Psychiatry CB 7160 Chapel Hill NC 27599-7160 Home Phone: 919-929-6192; Office Phone: 919-966-5772. Office Fax: 919-843-6102. Business E-Mail: roger_spencer@med.unc.edu.

SPENGLER, JOHN O., law educator; b. Mich., Jan. 8, 1963; BS, Wake Forest U., 1985; JD, U. Toledo; PhD, Ind. U., 1991. Assoc. prof. U. Fla., Coll. Health and Human Performance, 1999—. Named one of Tchr. of Yr., U. Fla.; Rsch. grants, Robert Wood Johnson Found. Fellow: AAHPERD Rsch. Consortium. Achievements include research in risk management and liability issues in sport and recreation, and policy issues relevant to physical activity and health promotion in school and park settings. Avocations: reading, sports. Office: University Fla PO Box 118208 Gainesville FL 32611 Office Fax: 352-392-7588. Business E-Mail: spengler@hhp.ufl.edu.

SPERANDIO, FELIPE FORNIAS, dentist, researcher; b. São Paulo, Brazil, Dec. 6, 1984; s. Walter Luiz Sperandio and Roseli Fornias. DDS, U. São Paulo, 2007, MS, PhD student, U. São Paulo, 2009—. Assoc. rschr. dermatology Harvard Med. Sch., 2011. Sci. jour. referee Jour. Lasers in Med. Sci., 2008, Jour. Gen. Dentistry, 2009, Jour. Photomedicine and Laser Surgery, 2009, Jour. Photochemistry and Photobiology-B, Biology, 2010, European Jour. Wound & Burns Mgmt., 2010, Jour. European Surg. Rsch., 2011. Grant, FAPESP, CAPES. Mem.: Mensa Brazil. Avocations: bass, model building. Office: Cidade Universitária Prof Lineu Prestes Ave 2227 São Paulo Brazil Personal E-mail: sperandio@usp.br.

SPERBER, ALAN B., urologist; s. Fred and Liselotte Sperber; m. Elizabeth Ann Pinck, June 6, 1982. BA, NYU, NYC, 1963, MD, 1967. Diplomate Am. Bd. Urology, 1977. Surg. intern Albert Einstein Coll. Medicine, Bronx, 1967—68, surg. resident, 1968—69; urology resident NYU Med. Ctr., 1971—75; attending physician Bellevue Hosp., 1975—78; asst. attending urologist NYU Med. Ctr., 1978—2008, vis. staff physician, dept. urology, 2008—; clin. assoc. prof. urology NYU Sch. Medicine, 1992—2010. Contbr. articles to profl. jours. Maj. US Army, 1969—71, Vietnam. Fellow: ACS; mem.: Am. Urol. Assn. Avocations: classical music, skiing, hiking, sports, reading. Home: 250 W 94th St Apt 7-B New York NY 10025

SPERELAKIS, NICHOLAS, SR., retired physiology and biophysics educator, researcher; b. Joliet, Ill., Mar. 3, 1930; s. James and Aristea (Kayaidakis) S.; m. Dolores Martinis, Jan. 28, 1960; children: Nicholas Jr., Mark (dec.), Christine, Sophia, Thomas, Anthony. BS in Chemistry, U. Ill., 1951, MS in Physiology, 1955, PhD in Physiology, 1957. Cert. in electronics, radio and radar US Navy & Marine Corps Electronics Sch., 1952. Tchg. asst. U. Ill., Urbana, 1954-57; instr. Case Western Res. U., Cleve., 1957-59, asst. prof., 1959-66, assoc. prof., 1966; prof. U. Va., Charlottesville, 1966-83; Joseph Eichberg prof. physiology Coll. Medicine U. Cin., 1983-96, chmn. dept., 1983-93, Eichberg prof. emeritus, 1996—. Cons. NPS Pharm., Inc., Salt Lake City, 1988-95, Carter Wallace, Inc. Cranbury, N.J., 1988-91; vis. prof. U. St. Andrews, Scotland, 1972-73, U. San Luis Potosi, Mex., 1986, U. Athens, Greece, 1994; Rosenblueth prof. Centro de Investigacion y Avanzades, Mex., 1972; mem. sci. adv. com. several internat. meetings, editl. bds. numerous sci. jours. Co-editor: Handbook of Physiology: Heart, 1979; editor: Physiology and Pathophysiology of the Heart, 1984, 2d edit., 1988, 3rd edit., 1994, 4th edit., 2000, Calcium Antagonists: Mechanisms of Action on Cardiac Muscle and Vascular Smooth Muscle, 1984, Cell Interactions and Gap Junctions, vols. I and II, 1989, Frontiers in Smooth Muscle Research, 1990, Ion Channels in Vascular Smooth Muscle and Endothelial Cells, 1991, Essentials of Physiology, 1993, 2d edit., 1996, Cell Physiology Source Book, 1995 (Outstanding Acad. Book, Choice Am. Libr. Assn. 1996, 98), 3d edit., 2001, 4th edit., 2011, Electrogenesis of Biopotentials, 1995; assoc. editor Circulation Rsch., 1970-75, 75-80, Molecular Cellular Cardiology; regional editor Current Drug Targets, 2000-02; contbr. more than 500 articles to profl. jours. Lectr. Project Hope, Peru, 1962. Sgt. USMC, 1951—53, Korean War, with USMCR, 1953—59. Recipient Disting. Alumnus award Rockdale (Ill.) Pub. Schs., 1958, Rsch. Excellence award Am. Heart Assn. Ohio, 1995, Visionary award Am. Heart Assn., S.W. Ohio, 1996; U. Cin. Grad. fellow, 1989; NIH grantee, 1959-99. Mem. IEEE, Engring. in Medicine and Biology, Am. Physiol. Soc. (chair steering com. sect. 1981-82), Biophys. Soc. (coun. 1990-93), Am. Soc. Pharmacology and Exptl. Therapeutics, Internat. Soc. Heart Rsch. (coun. 1980-89, 92-98), Am. Hellenic Ednl. Progressive Assn. (pres. Charlottesville chpt. 1980-82), Ohio Physiol. Soc. (pres. 1990-91), Phi Kappa Phi. Independent. Greek Orthodox. Avocations: stamp collecting/philately, coin collecting/numismatics. Personal E-mail: nicksperel@aol.com.

SPERGEL, JONATHAN MICHAEL, pediatrician, allergist, immunologist, researcher; married. MD, PhD, Mt. Sinai Sch. Medicine, NYC, 1992; BA in Chemistry, magna cum laude, Princeton U., 1985. Diplomate Am. Bd. Pediatrics, Am. Bd. Allergy and Immunology. Asst. prof. U. Pa. Sch. Medicine, Phila., 1998—; assoc. prof. U. Penn. Sch. Medicine. Chief allergy Children's Hosp. Phila., 2006—. Contbr. articles to profl. jours. Recipient Disting. Accomplishment NIH Biomed. Sci. Rsch. award, 1993, Glaxo Wellcome Allergy Tng.

award, 1997, Child Health Rsch. Ctr. award, NIH, 1997, Ethel Brown Foederer Excellence award, 2000, Penn. Allergy and Asthma Rsch. award, 2000, Top Docs award, 2009, Top Doctors in America, 2009—10; named Charles A. Janeway scholarship. Fellow: Am. Acad. Allergy, Asthma and Immunology, Am. Acad. Pediatrics, Am. Coll. Allergy. *

SPERLICH, DIETHER, biology educator; b. Vienna, Jan. 15, 1929; s. Karl and Maria (Sperlich) S.; m. Eva Sebek, June 26, 1957; children: Guenther, Monika, Martin, Klaus. PhD, U. Vienna, 1952; doctoral degree (hon.), U. Oulu, Finland, 1994. Asst. prof. biology U. Vienna, 1955-63; guest investigator The Rockefeller Inst., NYC, 1964; assoc. prof. biology U. Tuebingen, Germany, 1971-75, prof., head dept. population genetics, 1976-97; hon. prof. U. Salzburg, Austria, 1982—. Author: Populationsgenetik, 1973, 2d edit., 1988; co-author: Beiträge zur Evolutionstheorie, 1980, Biologie fuer Mediziner, 1995. Recipient Th. Koerner award Koerner Found., 1960, 64, Kardinal Innitzer Preis, Archdiocese of Vienna, 1967. Fellow: Soc. for Genetics, German Soc. Zoology; mem.: Finnish Acad. Sci. (corr.). Roman Catholic. Avocations: music, mountains. Home: Goesstrasse 82 Tübingen D7207 Germany Office: Biologisches Inst U Tübingen Auf der Morgenstelle 28 Tübingen D72076 Germany Home Phone: 49707145677. Business E-Mail: diether.sperlich@uni-tuebingen.de.

SPERLING, GEORGE, psychologist, educator; s. Otto and Melitta Sperling BS in Math., U. Mich., 1955; MA in Psychology, Columbia U., 1956; PhD in Psychology, Harvard U., 1959. Rsch. asst. in biophysics Brookhaven Nat. Labs., Upton, NY, summer 1955; rsch. asst. in psychology Harvard U., Cambridge, Mass., 1957-59; mem. tech. rsch. staff Acoustical and Behavioral Rsch. Ctr., AT&T Bell Labs., Murray Hill, NJ, 1958-86; prof. psychology and neural sci. NYU, NYC, 1970-92; disting. prof. cognitive scis., neurobiology and behavior U. Calif., Irvine, 1992—. Instr. psychology Washington Sq. Coll., NYU, 1962-63; vis. assoc. prof. psychology Duke U., spring 1964; adj. assoc. prof. psychology Columbia U., 1964-65; acting assoc. prof. psychology UCLA, 1967-68; hon. rsch. assoc. Univ. Coll., U. London, 1969-70; vis. prof. psychology U. Western Australia, Perth, 1972, U. Wash., Seattle, 1977; vis. scholar Stanford (Calif.) U., 1984; mem. sci. adv. bd. USAF, 1988-92. Recipient Meritorious Civilian Svc. medal USAF, 1993; Gomberg scholar U. Mich., 1953-54; Guggenheim fellow, 1969-70, APS fellow. Fellow: APA (Disting. Sci. Contbn. award 1988), AAAS, Am. Psychol. Soc. (William James fellow), Optical Soc. Am. (Tillyer award 2002), Am. Acad. Arts and Sci.; mem.: NAS, Internat. Neural Network Soc. (founding mem., mem. governing bd. 1987—91, Helmholtz award 2004), Soc. Math. Psychology (exec. bd. 1979—85, chmn. 1983—84), Soc. Exptl. Psychologists (Warren medal 1996), Psychonomic Soc., Soc. Computers in Psychology (steering com. 1974—78), Eastern Psychol. Assn. (bd. dirs. 1982—85), Ann. Interdisciplinary Conf. (organizer 1975—, founder), Assn. Rsch. in Vision and Ophthalmology, Sigma Xi, Phi Beta Kappa. Office: U Calif SS Plz A Dept Cognitive Scis Irvine CA 92697-5100 E-mail: sperling@uci.edu.

SPERLING, REISA A., neurologist, researcher; MD, Harvard U., 1991. Cert. Neurology, 2007. Intern Brigham and Women's Hosp., Boston, 1992, now neurologist; chief resident Longwood Residency Program, Boston; fellowship Harvard Longwood Neurology Training Program, Boston, 1997; dir. clin. rsch., staff physician Memory Disorders Unit Brigham Behavioral Neurology Group, Boston. Recipient award, AAN, Memory Ride award, Alzheimer's Assn.; grantee Am. Acad. Neurology Clin. Rsch. Training Fellowship; fellow Harvard/MIT Clin. Investigator Training Program; scholarship, AFAR Beeson. Office: Brigham Behavioral Neurology Group 221 Longwood Ave Boston MA 02115 Office Phone: 617-732-8060. Office Fax: 617-738-9122. E-mail: rasperling@bics.bwh.harvard.edu.

SPERLING, SILKE, biomedical researcher; b. Chemnitz, Saxony, Germany, Mar. 31, 1971; d. Fritz Bettermann and Martina Uhlmann. MD, Free U. of Berlin, 1997; MD in Cardiac Physiology suma cum laude, Free U. Berlin, 1999. Physician pediatric cardiology German Heart Ctr., Berlin, 1997—99; post doc. Max Planck Inst. Molecular Genetics, Berlin, 1999—2000, head rsch. group, 2001—, Hansen Gary prof., 2010—, Heisenberg prof., 2011—. Bd. mem. European Soc. of Human Genetics & Cardio Net, workpackage coord. European Integrated Project Heart Repair. Grantee, European Commn., 2005—. Fellow: European Soc. Cardiology; mem.: German Soc. Human Genetics, European Soc. of Human Genetics. Achievements include research in identification of DPF3; cardiac transcription networks; analysis of combinatorial roles of histone modifications in transcription; genomic organization of transcriptomes; patents for visualization of complex dataset. Office: Exptl and Clin Rsch Ctr Lindenberger Weg 80 Berlin 13125 Germany Office Fax: 43-30-84131699.

SPERRY, LEN THOMAS, psychiatrist and preventive medicine educator; b. Milw., Dec. 1, 1943; s. Leonard V. and Wanda R. (Sadowski) S.; m. Patricia L. Garcia, June 11, 1977; children: Tracey, Christen, L. Timothy, Steven, Jonathon. BA, St. Mary's U. Minn., Winona, Minn., 1966; PhD, Northwestern U., 1970; MD, CETEC U., 1981; MA, Loyola U., 1984; D in Ministry, Barry U., 2001. Diplomate Am. Bd. Profl. Psychology, Am. Bd. Psychiatry and Neurology, Am. Bd. Preventive Medicine. Asst. prof. Marquette U., Milw., 1971-74; assoc. prof. U. Wis., Milw., 1974-75, U.S. Internat. U., San Diego, 1976-78; resident in psychiatry and preventive medicine Med. Coll. Wis., Milw., 1982-85; fellow in behavioral medicine U. Wis. Med. Sch., Milw., 1984-85; assoc. prof. psychiatry, preventive medicine Med. Coll. Wis., Milw., 1986-92, prof., 1992-2000, prof. cmty. and family medicine, 1998-2000, vice chair dept. psychiatry, 1997-2000, clin. prof. psychiatry, 2000—; prof. health adminstrn., prof. psychology Barry U., Miami Shores, Fla., 2000—02, dir. doctoral program in counseling, 2003; prof. Fla. Atlantic U., 2003—. Author: Learning Performance and Individual Differences, 1972, Contract Counseling, 1974, You Can Make It Happen: Self-Actualization and Organization, 1977, Together Experience, 1978, Aderian Counseling and Psychotherapy, 1987, Psychiatric Case Formulations, 1992, Psychopathology and Psychotherapy, 1993, 2d edit., 1996, Psychiatric Consultation in the Workplace, 1993, Handbook of Diagnosis and Treatment of DSM-IV Personality Disorders, 1995, Psychopharmacology and Psychotherapy, 1995, Treatment Outcomes in Psychotherapy and Psychiatric Interventions, 1996, Aging in the 21st Century, 1996, Family Therapy: Ensuring Treatment Efficacy, 1997, The Disordered Couple, 1997, The Intimate Couple, 1998, Brief Therapy Strategies with Individuals and Couples, 2000, Ministry and Community, 2000, Integrative and Biopsychosocial Therapies, 2000, Spirituality in Clinical Practice, 2001, Transforming Self and Community, 2002, Effective Leader, 2002, Becoming an Effective Therapist, 2003, Becoming an Effective Health Care Manager, 2003, Sex, Priestly Ministry and the Church, 2003, Executive Coaching, 2004, Spiritually-Oriented Psychotherapy, 2005, Couple and Family Assessment, 2005, Health Promotion and Health Counseling, Couples Therapy (2d edit.), 2005, Family Therapy Techniques, 2005, Cognitive Behavior Therapy of DSM-TR Pesonality Disorders, 2006, Psychological Treatment of Chronic Illness, 2006, The Ethical and Professional Practice of Counseling and Psychotherapy, 2007, Dictionary of Ethical and Legal Terms and Issues, 2007, Treatment Chronic Med. Conditions, 2008, Highly Effective Therapy Developing Essential Clinical Conptency, 2010, Recovery of Intimacy, 2011, Core Competency in Counseling and Psychotherapy, 2010, Spirituality in Clinical Practice, 2nd edit., 2011; contbr. articles to profl. jours. Bd. dirs. Am. Coun. on Sci. and Health, Nat. Acad. for Certified Family Therapists, St. Camillus Health Ctr., 1996-2000, Cath. Health Svcs., 2001—; cons. dir. Staff Devel. Am. Appraisal Assn., Milw., 1972-76. Northwestern U. fellow, 1969, Med. Coll. Wis. grantee, 1981. Fellow APA (Harry Levinson award 1998), Am. Psychiat. Assn. (chair com. on psychiatry in workplace 1998—, fellow, 1987-2001, distinguished fellow, 2001-), Am. Coll. Preventive Medicine, Am. Coll. Psychiatrists, Am. Bd. Profl. Psychology, Am. Bd. Psychiatry and Neurology, Acad. Orgnl. and Occupational Psychiatry (v.p. 1993-96, Alan McLean lifetime achievement award 2000), Group for Advancement of Psychiatry, Coalition for Family Diagnosis. Avocations: reading, racquet sports, music. Office: Fla Atlantic U 777 Glades Rd Boca Raton FL 33431 Business E-Mail: lsperry@fau.edu.

SPETZGER, UWE, neurosurgeon; b. Karlsruhe, Germany, June 9, 1962; s. Hans and Elisabeth (Richter) Spetzger; m. Martina Karoline Scheurer, Aug. 26, 1994; children: Jan-Christian, Caroline Marlen, Susann Martine. PhD, Rheinisch Westfaelisch Technische Hochschule, 2000. Cert. foreign med. grad. examination in the med. scis. Ednl. Commn. Foreign Med. Grads., 1990. Intern Dept. Neurosurgery, Aachen, Germany, 1990—94, sr., 1994—96, asst. prof., 1996—99; prof., vice chmn. Dept. Neurosurgery U. Freiburg, Germany, 1999—; chmn. dept. neurosurgery Klinikum Karlsruhe, Germany, 2002. Examination of neurosurgery, Düsseldorf, 1997; European exam of neurosurgery, Brussels, 99. Editor: Navigated Brain Surgery; contbr. articles to profl. jours. Mem. German Soc. Neurosurgery, European Spine Soc., Congress of Neurosurgeons. Roman Catholic. Office: Dept Neurosurgery Klinikum Karlsruhe 76133 Karlsruhe Germany Office Phone: 497219743500. Personal E-mail: spetzge@web.de. Business E-Mail: uwe.spetzger@klinikum-karlsruhe.de.

SPHIRE, RAYMOND DANIEL, anesthesiologist, educator; b. Detroit, Feb. 12, 1927; s. Samuel Raymond and Nora Mae (Allen) S.; m. Joan Lois Baker, Sept. 5, 1953; children: Suzanne M., Raymond Daniel, Catherine J. BS, U. Detroit, 1948; MD, Loyola U., Chgo., 1952. Diplomate Am. Bd. Anesthesiology. Intern Grace Hosp., Detroit, 1952-53; resident Harvard Anesthesia Lab.-Mass. Gen. Hosp., 1953-55; attending anesthesiologist Grace Hosp., Detroit, 1955-72, dir. dept. inhalation therapy, 1968-70; sr. attending anesthesiologist, dir. dept., dir. dept. respiratory therapy Detroit-Macomb Hosps. Assn., 1970—, trustee, 1978—, chief of staff, 1980—. Clin. asst. prof. Wayne State U. Sch. Medicine, 1967—; clin. prof. respiratory therapy Macomb Community Coll., Mount Clemens, Mich., 1971—; examiner Am. Registry Respiratory Therapists, 1972—; insp. Joint Rev. Com. Respiratory Therapy Edn., 1972— Co-author: Operative Neurosurgery, 1970, First Aid Guide for the Small Business or Industry, 1978 With AUS, 1944-45; 1st lt. M.C., USAF, 1952 Fellow Am. Coll. Anesthesiologists, Am. Coll. Chest Physicians; mem. AMA, Am. Soc. Anesthesiologists, Wayne County Soc. Anesthesiologists (pres. 1967-69), Am. Assn. Respiratory Therapists, Soc. Critical Care Medicine, Country Club of Detroit, Grosse Pointe Club, Cumberland Club (Portland, Maine), Severance Lodge. Roman Catholic. Home and Office: 36 Sunningdale Dr Grosse Pointe Shores MI 48236

SPICHER, CLAUDE J., occupational therapist; b. Lausanne, Switzerland, Mar. 31, 1963; s. Louis Auguste and Lotti Golay; m. Pascale Spicher; children: Meloe Anne Cesarine, Pacome Luc Louis. BS, Belvedere Gymnase, Lausanne, 1980. Cert. hand therapist SSRM Swiss Soc. Hand Therapist, 2003. Head occupl. therapist State Friburgh Hosp., Switzerland, 1989—2002; dir. and founder Somatsensory Rehab. Ctr., Fribourg, 2004—. Editor-in-chief Swiss Soc. Hand Therapy, Basel, Switzerland, 2000—02. Office: Somatosensory Rehab Ctr rue Hans-Geiler 6 1700 Fribourg Switzerland Office Phone: 41 26 350 06 12. Office Fax: 41 26 350 06 35. Personal E-mail: claude.spicher@unifr.ch. Business E-Mail: reeducation.sensitive@cliniquegenerale.ch.

SPIECHOWICZ, EUGENIUSZ, dental educator; s. Kazimierz and Eugenia Westman Spiechowicz; m. Leokadia Zmyslowska, Sept. 15, 1951; children: Mira Weber, Grazyna Spiechowicz Kristensen. Dr. hab. med., DDS, PhD, Warsaw Med. U., Poland, 1952. Prof. head dept. prosthetics dentistry Warsaw Med. U., 1973—99, dep. rector, 1972—78. Mem.: European Prosthodontics Assn., Polish Dental Assn., Polish Assn. Oral Implant Slovene Dental Assn. (hon.), German Prosthodontics and Dental Material Assn. (hon.). Office: Warsaw Med Univ Nowogrodzka 59 Warsaw 02 006 Poland Office Fax: 48 22 5022145. Business E-Mail: eugeniusz.spiechowicz@am.edu.pl.

SPIEGEL, ALLEN MICHAEL, dean, internist; b. Lundsberg, Germany, May 18, 1946; BA summa cum laude, Columbia U., NYC, 1967; MD cum laude, Harvard U., Boston, 1971. Intern/resident internal medicine Mass. Gen. Hosp., Boston, 1971—73; mem. endocrinology rsch. tng. prog., Nat. Inst. Diabetes & Digestive & Kidney Disease (NIDDK) NIH, 1973—76, sr. investigator metabolic diseases br., 1977—84, chief molecular pathophysiology sect., 1985—88, chief metabolic diseases br., 1988, sci. dir. NIDDK, 1990—99, dir., 1999—2006; Marilyn and Stanley M. Katz dean Yeshiva U. Albert Einstein Coll. Medicine, NYC, 2006—, prof. departments medicine and molecular biology, 2006—. Recipient Jacobaeus prize, Novo Nordisk Insulin Found., 1990, Komrower Meml. Lecture award, Soc. Study of Inborn Errors of Metabolism, 1996, Edwin B. Astwood Lecture award, Endocrine Soc., 1998. Mem.: Inst. Medicine, Assn. Am. Physicians, Am. Soc. Clin. Investigation. Office: Albert Einstein Coll Medicine Jack & Pearl Resnick Campus 1300 Morris Park Ave Belfer Bldg Rm 312 Bronx NY 10461 Office Phone: 718-430-2801. Business E-Mail: allen.spiegel@einstein.yu.edu. *

SPIEGEL, DAVID, psychiatrist; b. NYC, Dec. 11, 1945; s. Herbert Spiegel and Natalie Shainess; m. Helen Margaret Blau, July 25, 1976; children: Daniel, Julia. BA, Yale Coll., 1967; MD, Harvard Med. Sch., 1971. Lic. psychiatrist Calif., diplomate Am. Bd. Med. Examiners, Am. Bd. Psychiatry and Neurology. Resident Mass. Mental Health Ctr. and Cambridge Hosp., 1971-74; resident tutor, premedical advisor Winthrop House Harvard Coll., Cambridge, Mass., 1972-74; clin. instr. Stanford (Calif.) U. Sch. Med., 1974-75; staff psychiatrist San Mateo (Calif.) County Mental Health Program, 1974-75; acting asst. prof. to prof. psychiatry, behavioral scis., Sch. Med. Stanford U., 1975—94, Jack, Lulu and Sam Willson prof., 2002—, chair, faculty senate, 2010—11. Chief brief treatment inpatient unit Palo Alto Vets. Adminstrn. Med. Ctr., Calif., 1975-76; dir. social psychiatry cmty. svcs. Palo Alto Vets. Adminstrn., 1976-80; dir. psychiatry clinic Stanford U. Med. Ctr., 1980-89, assoc. dir. psychiat inpatient therapeutic cmty. 1981-83, assoc. chair psychiatry, 2000-, med. dir. Ctr. for Integrative Medicine, 1997—; med. dir. Stanford U. Clinic, 1986-87; assoc. rsch. psychiatrist U. Calif., San Francisco, 1986-91; dir. Ctr. on Stress and Health Stanford U. Med. Ctr., 2001—. Editor: Progress in Psychiatry Series, 1984—2002, mem. editl. bd., 1986-89; med. co-editor: Internat. Jour. Clin. Exptl. Hypnosis, 1988-95; assoc. editor: Am. Jour. Clin. Hypnosis, 1985—, Am. Jour. Psychiatry, 1991-95, The Breast, 1994—; consulting editor: Health Psychology, 1990-91; mem. editl. bd.: Jour. of Psychosocial Oncology, 1983—88, Jour. Traumatic Stress, 1986-90, Dissociation, 1988—1990, Psycho Oncology, 1991, Consciousness and Cognition, 1991—, Health Psychology, 1992, Columbia U. Sch. Pub. Health Newsletter, 1994—1996. Mem. data processing policy com. Dept. Mental Health, Mass., 1972-73, bd. dirs. No. Calif. Burn Coun., 1976-84; pub. mem. Chief Justice's Spl. Com. to Study Appellate Practices in First Appellate Dist., 1977-81. Recipient Treya Killam Wilber award Cancer Support Cmty, 1993, Pierre Janet Wrting award Internat. Soc. for Study Dissociation, 1994, Edward A. Strecker, M.D. award The Inst. of Pa. Hosp. and Jefferson Med. Coll., 1995, 8th Annual Chrysalis Gala honoree CHEMOcare, 1993, Arthur M. Sutherland award Internat. Soc. Psych-Oncology. Fellow Am. Coll. Psychiatist(pres., 2005), Am. Psychiat. Assn. (Marmor award, 2004), Am. Soc. Clin. Hypnosis, Am. Psychiat. Assn., Assn. for Clin. Psychosocial Rsch., Soc. for Clin. and Exptl. Hypnosis (pres. 1995-97, Schneck award 1996), Am. Coll. Neuropsychopharmacology, Urgent Action Network, Amnesty Internat, Am. Coll. Psychiatrists (pres. 2005-06); mem. DSM5 Work Group Anxiety, PTSD, Dissoc Disorders Am. Psychiat. Assn. Office: Stanford U Sch Med 401 Quarry Rd Stanford CA 94305-5718

SPIEGEL, MELVIN, retired biology professor; s. Philip Edward and Sadie (Friedman) S.; m. Evelyn Schafer, Apr. 16, 1955; children: Judith Ellen, Rebecca Ann. BS, U. Ill., 1948; PhD, U. Rochester, 1952, MA (hon.), Dartmouth Coll. Research fellow U. Rochester, 1952-53, Calif. Inst. Tech., 1953-55, 64-65; asst. prof. Colby Coll., 1955-59; mem. faculty Dartmouth Coll., Hanover, NH, 1959—, prof. biology, 1966-93; prof. emeritus Dartmouth Coll, Hanover, NH; chmn. dept. biol. scis. Dartmouth Coll., Hanover, NH, 1972-74. Summer investigator Marine Biol. Lab., Woods Hole, Mass., 1954—; sr. rsch. biologist U. Calif.-San Diego, 1970-71; vis. prof. biochemistry Nat. Inst. Med. Rsch., Mill Hill, London, 1971; vis. prof. Biocenter, U. Basel, 1979-82, 85; Wilson Meml. lectr. U. N.C., 1975; program dir. developmental biology NSF, 1975-76; mem. cell biology study sect. NIH, 1966-70 Editl. bd.: Biol. Bull., 1966-70, 71-75, Cell Differentiation, 1979-88; contbr. articles to profl. jours. Trustee Marine Biol. Lab. Corp.; mem. exec. com., trustee Marine Biol. Lab., 1976-80. Fellow AAAS; mem. Am. Soc. Cell Biology, Am. Soc. Devel. Biology, Internat. Soc. Devel. Biologists (sec.-treas. 1977-81, bd. dirs. 1981-85). Home Phone: 603-643-4353. E-mail: melvin.spiegel@dartmouth.edu.

SPIELBERG, STEPHEN PAUL, pediatrician, medical educator, former dean; b. 1945; m. Laurel A. Spielbery. AB, Princeton U., 1966; PhD in pharmacology, U. Chgo., 1971; MD, U. Chgo. Pritzker Sch. Medicine, 1973. Pediat. resident Children's Hosp. Med. Ctr., Boston, 1974—75; instr. to asst. prof. pediat. & pharmacology Johns Hopkins U. Sch. Medicine, 1971—81; assoc. prof. to prof. pediat. & pharmacology U. Toronto, 1981—92, dir. Ctr. for Drug Safety Rsch., 1988—92; sr. scientist rsch. inst. Hosp. for Sick Children, Toronto, established & headed div. pediat. clin. pharmacology and toxicology, 1987—92; exec. dir. exploratory biochemical toxicology and clin. and regulatory develop. Merck Labs., 1992—97; v.p. pediat. drug develop. Johnson & Johnson Pharm. Rsch. & Develop., Titusville, NJ, 1997—2003, established dept. of pediat. drug develop.; v.p. health affairs Dartmouth Coll., 2003; dean & prof. pediat. and pharmacology and taxicology Dartmouth Med. Sch., 2003—08, prof. pediat., pharmacology and toxicology; prin. investigator Inst. Pediatric Innovation, Hanover, NH, 2007; dir. Ctr. Personalized Medicine and Therapeutic Innovation, Children's Mercy Hosp., Kansas City, Mo., 2009—; Marion Merrell Dow chair in Pediatric Pharmacogenomics U. Mo.-Kansas City Sch. Medicine. Adj. prof. pediat., medicine and pharmacology Thomas Jefferson U.; adj. prof. pediat. Robert Wood Johnson Med. Sch.; mem. adv. bd. PediaLink; mem. Fed. Adv. Com., Nat. Children's Study, Nat. Inst. of Child Health and Human Develop.; chair Pediat. Task Force, Pharm. Rsch. and Mfr. of Am.; bd. dirs. Found. for NIH; mem. panel on ethics and pediat. clin. trials Inst. Medicine; mem. pediat. adv. subcom. FDA; mem. sci. adv. bd. Elizabeth Glaser Pediat. Rsch. Network. Recipient Rawls-Palmer Award, Am. Soc. for Clin. Pharmacology and Therapeutics, 1992, Werner Kalow Award for Pharmacogenetics and Drug Safety, 1995, William B. Abrams Award and Lectureship, FDA & Am. Soc. for Clin. Pharmacology and Therapeutics, 2001, Exceptional Service Award, Pharm. Rsch. and Mfr. of Am., 2003. Fellow: Nat. Inst. of Child Health and Human Develop. (mem. of month 2008); mem.: Am. Soc. Clin. Pharmacology and Therapeutics. Office: Children's Mercy Hospitals & Clinics 2401 Gillham Rd Kansas City MO 64108 Office Phone: 816-234-3059.

SPIELER, JEFF, public health service officer; BS in zoology, U. Fla., 1967, PhD (hon.) in pub. svc., 2002; MS in zoological sciences and reproductive biology, Rutgers U., 1971. Scientist Lederle Labs. Pharm. Co., Pearl River, NY, WHO, Geneva; sr. biomedical rsch. advisor in pop. Office Pop. and Reproductive Health, US Agy. Internat. Devel., 1983—93, chief rsch., tech. and utilization divsn., 1993—2007, sr. sci. advisor, 2007—. Office: US Agy Internat Devel Off Pop and Reproductive Health 1300 Pennsylvania Ave NW Washington DC 20523

SPIELMANN, ANNETTE, ophthalmologist; b. Epinal, France, Aug. 10, 1933; d. Georges Barthelemy and Charlotte Jeandel; m. Claude Spielmann, June 22, 1959; children: Daniele, Agnes, Alain, Line. Grad., Coll. Luneville, U. Nancy. Ophthalmologist. Author: Chirurgie Du Strabisme, 1984, Les Strabismes Analyse Clinique Synthese Chirurgicale, 1991, Nystagmus Congenital-Nystagmus Acquis, 2005. Mem.: Soc. Ophtalmologie Est De France (pres. 1999—2001), Assn. Francaise Strabologie (pres. 1997—99), European Strabismological Assn. (pres. 1995—97), Internat. Strabismological Assn. (v.p. 1994—95). Home and Office: 11 Rue de la Ravinelle 54000 Nancy France Home Phone: 0383 32 2026; Office Phone: 03 83 32 94 98.

SPIERER, ROBERT, family practice physician; b. S.I., NY, June 26, 1945; s. Efram and Regina (Stern) Spierer; m. Marilyn J Borak, July 7, 1968; children: Sharon, Henry, Eric. BA, Columbia U., 1967; MD, Albert Einstein Coll. Medicine, 1971. Diplomate Am Bd. Family Medicine, Am. Bd. Pediatrics, Am. Bd. Emergency Medicine, Am. Bd. Internal Medicine, cert. added qualification in geriatrics Am. Bd. Internal Medicine. Intern Montefiore Med. Ctr., Bronx, NY, 1971-72, resident in pediatrics, 1972-73, 1975-76; resident in internal medicine U. Medicine and Dentistry of N.J., Newark, 1976-77; physician Edison (N.J.) Med. Group, 1977-98, Monroe Medical Group, 1999—. With USPHS, 1973—75. Office: Monroe Med Group 369 Applegarth Rd Monroe Township NJ 08831-3732 Office Phone: 609-395-1900.

SPIERS, ALEXANDER STEWART D., medical educator; b. Melbourne, Australia, Jan. 31, 1936; came to U.S., 1976; s. Alexander Donaldson and Joan (Patterson) S.; m. Margaret Overend, Dec. 20, 1960; children: Alexander, Ronald, Deborah, Gordon, James. MBBS, U. Melbourne, 1960, PhD, 1968, MD, 1975. Cert. in internal medicine, hematology and oncology. Sr. lectr. in medicine Hammersmith Hosp., London, 1970-75; assoc. prof. Boston U., 1976-80; prof. medicine Albany (N.Y.) Med. Coll., 1980-87, U. South Fla., Tampa, from 1987; ret., 1996. Editor: Chemotherapy and Urological Malignancy, 1982; contbr.over 400 articles and papers to profl. jours Trustee Leukemia Soc. Am., Albany, 1980-87, Tampa, 1987, chmn. edn. com., 1988. Lt. col. Royal Army M.C., 1987. Recipient Territorial decoration Queen Elizabeth, 1981; traveling fellow The Nuffield Found., 1968, Nat. Svc. medal. Fellow Royal Coll. Pathologists Australasia, Royal Soc. Medicine, ACP, Royal Australasian Coll. Physicians, Royal Coll. Physicians Edinburgh; mem. Brit. Officers Club New Eng., Treasure Island Tennis & Yacht Club. Presbyterian. Avocations: boating, history, travel, antiques, theater, gardening, chess, reading. Personal E-mail: spiersuk@thamesinternet.com.

SPIESS, HEINZ, pediatrician; b. Muelhausen, Fed. Republic Germany, Apr. 13, 1920; s. Richard and Hedwig (Rossner) S.; m. Anne Giehl; 1 child, Eva. MD, U. Goettingen, 1945, habil., 1952. Mem. med. faculty U. Goettingen, 1952—; prof. medicine Munich U., 1968—; chmn. Children's Policlinic, L.M.U. Author: Schutzimpfungen, 2d edit., 1966, Impfkompendium, 7th edit., 2011. Office: Pettenkoferstrasse 8A 80336 Munich Germany Office Phone: 0049 89 2180 75828. Business E-Mail: prof.spiess@lrz.uni-muenchen.de.

SPIESS, PAGE, medical researcher; b. Maine, Oct. 27, 1981; BS, Eckerd Coll., 2004; MS, U. Calif., Davis, PhD, 2008. Postdoc. fellow U. Vt., 2008—. Recipient NIEHS Regional Conf. Outstanding Poster award, U. Calif., Davis; Ines McMillan fellowship, NIEHS Superfund Basic Rsch. Program fellowship. Mem.: Soc. Toxicology, Soc. Free Radical Biology Medicine, Am. Chem. Soc., Omicron Delta Kappa Leadership Honor Soc., Sigma Xi. Office: 89 Beaumont Ave Given C264 Burlington VT 05405 Business E-Mail: pspiess@uvm.edu.

SPIGEL, DAVID R., oncologist, director; b. San Antonio, Jan. 22, 1970; BS, Tulane U., New Orleans, 1992; MD, U. Tenn., Memphis, 1996. Bd. cert. in internal medicine & med. oncology. Chief resident, internal medicine Ind. U. Med. Ctr.; fellow in hematology and oncology Dana-Farber Cancer Inst., Boston; dir., Lung Cancer Rsch. Program Sarah Cannon Rsch. Inst., Tenn. Oncology PLLC, 2006—. Mem.: Centennial Med. Ctr. Oncology Leadership Team, Centennial Med. Ctr. Cancer Com., Centennial Med. Ctr. Credentials Com., Am. Soc. Clin. Oncology, Am. Cancer Soc. Meml. Found. Hope Lodge (Nashville). Office: 250 25th Ave N Ste 110 Nashville TN 37203

SPIGELMAN, ALLAN DAVID, surgeon; b. Sydney, Mar. 6, 1953; s. Majloch and Gucia S.; m. Ruth Eliana Winfield, Dec. 23, 1989; children: Joshua, Naomi, Isaac. MBBS, U. Sydney, 1977, MD, 1996. Surg. rsch. fellow St. Mark's Hosp., London, 1988-89, hon. sr. rsch. fellow, 1990—; sr. lectr. Ctrl. Middlesex Hosp., St. Mary's Hosp., London, 1990-97, surgeon, 1994-97; hon. cons. surgeon St. Mary's Hosp., London, 1994-97; prof. surg. sci. U. Newcastle, Australia, 1997—2006; dir. clin. governance Hunter Health, New South Wales, Australia, 1999—2006; dir. cancer svcs. Hunter New Eng. Health, 2003—06; prof. surgery St. Vincent Hosp. Clin. Sch. U. NSW, Sydney, 2006—; dir. cancer svcs. St. Vincents and Mater Health, Sydney, 2006—. Chmn. adv. com. Hereditary Cancer Registers, New South Wales, Australia, 1997-2010; dir. Hunter Family Cancer Svc.; clin. assoc. dean U. NSW, 2007—. Co-author: Australian Colorectal Cancer Cure Survey, 2002; editor: FAP & Other Polyposis Syndromes, 1994; authored papers in field Recipient Nat. Health and Med. Rsch. Coun. award, 1998, 2004, Ramaciotti Found. award, 1998-99, Nat. Cancer Control Initiative award, 1999, Hunter Med. Rsch. Inst. award, 1998—. Fellow Royal Australasian Coll. Surgeons, Royal Coll. Surgeons Eng. and Wales; mem. Surg. Rsch. Soc., Leeds Castle Polyposis Group (coun. 1999—), Internat. Soc. for Gastrointestinal Hereditary Tumors (governing coun. 2005-, chair 2011-). Avocations: reading, swimming, skiing. Office: St Vincents Hosp Profl Ste Level 5 DeLacy Bldg Victoria St Darlinghurst 2010 Australia Office Fax: 61 2 83822328. Business E-Mail: aspigelman@stvincents.com.au.

SPIKES, PATRICIA WHITE, medical technologist; b. Houston, Nov. 30, 1951; d. Albert Carr and Willie Mae (Sneed) White; m. Herbert Charles Pete, May 24, 1980 (div.); 1 child, Sheatri Denise; m. John Ray Spikes, Sept. 7, 1991; 1 child, John Ray II. BS, Tex. Christian U., Ft. Worth, 1974. Cert. vols. in pub. sch. spl. svc. 1994. Med. technologist, edn. coord. Riverside Gen. Hosp., Houston, 1974—76; chief lab. technologist Almeda Med. Lab., Houston, 1976—80; med. technologist Jefferson Davis Hosp., Harris County Hosp. Dist., Houston, 1980, Lyndon B. Johnson Hosp., Harris City Hosp. Dist. Founder Coalition of Pre-Sch. Dirs., 1982—; dir. Parents Calling Parents, Houston, 1980—; 3d v.p. Vols. in Pub. Sch. Adv. Bd., Houston, 1981, 2d v.p., 1983, pres., 1986—89, v.p. tng. chair, 1990—92, v.p. cmty. coalitions, 1993; mem. Tex. State Bd. for Vols. in Pub. Sch, 1982—, sec., 1988—, 1st v.p., 1985, pres., 1986, sec., 1987—. Chairperson Bucks for Belts Coalition for Sch. Bus Seat Belts, 1985; chair awards com. Salute to Sch. Vols.; mem. Mayor's Task Force on Edn., Houston, Mayor's Com. on Child Abuse Prevention; panelist Regional IV Svc. Ctr. State Seminar; mem. adv. bd. Blueridge Health Dept., Attucks CC; pres. Reynolds Elem. Parent Tchr. Orgn., 1982, treas., 84; sec. Pershing Middle Sch., PTO, 1985, Class of 1969 Worthing High Sch. Reunion; candidate Houston Ind. Sch. Dist. Bd. Edn., 1989; pres. Kings Row Child Care Parent Tchrs. Orgn., 1978; mem. Nat. Sch. Vol. Program, 1982—, Mo. City Space; panelist Houston Area Black Sch. Educators, 1987; bd. dirs. Women in Action, 1984—85; mediator Dispute Resolution Ctr., 1984—, Women of Vision, Chs. Interested in Premature Parentage; city wide adv. com. Houston Ind. Sch. Dist., 1988; edn. adv. com. Family Life; pres. adv. com. Inner City 4-H, 1989—; chmn. adult leaders adv. bd. Harris County 4-H, 1989—91; treas. 1890 program, 1991—93; chmn. Northeast Adolescent Program, 1990—92; computer maintenance adv. com. Reagan HS, 1988—; chair Salute to Sch. Vols., 1984—86; spkr. career day Houston Ind. Sch. Dist., 1989—; chmn. adv. bd. Sunnyside Multi-Svc. Ctr., Health Ctr., 1991—; mem. steering com. Tex. Cancer Coun., 1992—; spkr., active Teen Health Symposium Prairie View Adminstrn 1980 4-H Program, 1992—93; coord. baby buddy program Sunnyside Clinic City of Houston Health Dept., 1989—; mem. S.E. br. adv. bd. ARC, 2000—, chair, 2004—06; membership com. Greater Houston Coun., 2004—; mem. membership com. Nat. Healthy Start Assn., 1974—; consortium chmn. Sunny Futures Healthy Start Program, Houston, 1998—2003; coord. Girls Rite of Passage, 2000—02; chmn. Prairie View A&M Coll. Coop. Extension Project H.O.P.E., 2001—; cons. Families Under Urban & Social Attack Non Profit Devel., 2002—; CEO, founder S&J Literary Works, 2003; mem. Syphilis Elimination Adv. Task Force, 2003—; chair Syphilis Elimination Bd., ARC, 2004—06; mem. Sunnyside Pride, 2005, Healthy Minority Marriage Initiative, 2006, City of Houston HIV/AIDS Task Force, 2003—; workshop trainer Families Under Urban and Social Attack, 2004—; presenter, cons., spkr. in field; pres. SE Br. America Red Cross Bd.; vol. Com. Houston Am. Red Cros Bd.; founder S & J Literary Works. Author: Band Aids for Peace. Recipient Cert. of Appreciation, Vols. Am., 1980, Vols. in Pub. Schs., 1986—87, Pres. award, 1986—95, Outstanding Service award, Reynolds Sch., Neighborhood Ctrs. Crystal House Cmty. Svc. award, 2005, Vol. award, Prairie View A&M U. Project H.O.P.E.; named to Top Ladies of Distinction. Mem.: NAACP, Delta Sigma Theta. Democrat. Baptist. Home: 3134 Sunbeam St Houston TX 77051-3526 Personal E-mail: pspikes30@aol.com.

SPILIOPOULOS, STAVROS, physician, researcher; b. Athens, Greece, Mar. 26, 1975; Degree in Medicine and Surgery, U. Turin, 2002; PhD, U. Patras, 2011. Gen. physician Mesologi Peripheral Gen. Hosp., 2004—06; radiology specialist Parts U. Hosp., 2007—11; clin. fellow Guy's and St. Thomas Hosps. NHS Found. Trust, London, 2011—. Mem.: CIRSE. Avocations: music, reading. Office: Westminster Bridge Rd London SE1 7EH England Business E-Mail: stavspiliop@upatras.gr.

SPINATO, SERGIO, dentist; b. Modena, Italy, Mar. 12, 1966; DDS, U. Modena, 1990. Pvt. practice, 1991—. Vis. prof. U. Modena, 2002—03, U. Bologna, 2011. Mem.: Italian Soc. Oral Implantology. Avocation: history. Office: Via Cavallotti 140 Sassuolo 41049 Italy Business E-Mail: albispina@tiscali.it.

SPINELLA, JUDY LYNN, health facility administrator; b. Ft. Worth, Apr. 8, 1948; d. Gettis Breon and Velrea Inez (Webb) Prothro; children: Scott Slater, Jennifer. BS, U. Tex., 1971; MS, Tex. Woman's U., 1973; MBA, Vanderbilt U., 1993. RN, Tex. Asst. prof. U. Tex., Arlington, 1976-81; dir. emergency svcs. San Francisco Gen. Hosp., 1981-84, assoc. adminstr. for clin. svcs., 1984-88; exec. dir. for nursing svcs. Vanderbilt U. Med. Ctr., Nashville, 1988-93, dir. patient care svcs., 1993-94; dir., COO Vanderbilt U. Hosp., Nashville, 1994-96; healthcare cons. APM, Inc., NYC, 1996—98; health care cons. The Meth. Hosp., Houston, 1998—2001, v.p. ops., 2001—04; pres., CEO Gunnison Valley Hosp., Colo., 2004—05; chief nursing officer U. N. Mex. Hosp., 2005—08; prin. cons. Houston Healthcare Ops. LLC, 2009—. Wharton fellow Johnson & Johnson, 1987. Mem. Am. Orgn. Nurse Execs.; fellow Am. Coll. Healthcare Execs., Emergency Nurses Assn. (bd. dirs., treas. 1979-86), Sigma Theta Tau. Avocations: hiking, travel. Office Phone: 832-382-1557. E-mail: jlspinella@aol.com.

SPINELLI, HENRY MICHAEL, plastic surgeon; b. NYC, Mar. 21, 1956; B, Johns Hopkins Univ.; MD, NYU Sch. Med., 1981. Cert. Am. Bd. Ophthalmology, 1987, Am. Bd. Plastic Surgery, 1993. Intern in ophthalmology NYU Med. Ctr., 1981—82; resident in surgery Manhattan Eye Ear & Throat Hosp., 1982—85; resident in plastic reconstructive surgery Columbia Presbyterian Hosp., NYC, 1985—88; resident in craniofacial surgery NYU Med. Ctr., 1988—90, fellow in plastic surgery, 1990—91; asst. prof. surgery, dir. craniofacial surgery Yale Univ., 1991—96; attending surgeon Lenox Hill Hosp., 2000; clin. assoc. prof. surgery Cornell Univ. Med. Ctr.; staff mem. NY Eye & Ear Infirmary, Manhattan Eye Ear & Throat Hosp., NY Hosp. Cornell Med. Ctr.; private practice in plastic surgery NYC. Editor-in-chief Jour. Internat. Soc. Aesthetic Plastic Surgery. Contbr. articles to profl. jours. Mem.: Am. Soc. Plastic Surgeons & other profl. societies. Office: 875 5th Ave New York NY 10065 Office Phone: 212-570-6235. Office Fax: 212-570-4168. Business E-Mail: hmspinelli@aol.com.

SPINNER, ROBERT JAY, orthopedic surgeon; b. NYC, Dec. 8, 1961; s. Morton and Paula (Lerner) S.; m. Alexandra Wolanskyj SB, MIT, 1984; M of Studies, Oxford U., Eng., 1985; MD, Mayo Clinic, 1989. Rsch. fellow, Luce scholar Prince of Wales Hosp., Hong Kong, 1989-90; intern in surgery Duke U., Durham, NC, 1990-91, jr. resident in surgery, 1991-92, resident in orthopaedic surgery, 1992-96; resident in neurosurgery Mayo Clinic, Rochester, Minn., 1996—2000, asst. prof. neurologic surgery and orthopedics, 2001—; asst. prof. anatomy Mayo Med. Sch., 2003—04, assoc. prof. neurologic surgery, orthopedics and anatomy, 2004—07, prof. neurologic surgery, orthopedics and anatomy, 2007—; chair neurosurgery Burton M. Onofrio, 2011—. Co-editor: Clinical Anatomy; mem. editl. bd. Mayo Clinic Procs., Practical Revs. in Neurosurgery, Microsurgery, Jour. Reconstructive Microsurgery, Jour. So. Orthop. Assn., Chinese Jour. Clin. Anatomy, World Neurosurgery. Recipient Davison Tchg. award Duke U. Med. Sch., 1993, Goldner Rsch. award in Orthopaedic Surgery Duke U. Med. Ctr., 1996, Mayo Bros. Disting. Fellowship award, 2000, Karis award, 2001; Schilling scholar Mayo Found., 1985-87; Cushing award Congress Neurol. Surgery, 2001, Presdl. award Am. Assn. Clin. Anatomists, 2005; Mayo Found. scholar, 2001. Mem.: ACS, Soc. Nuerological Surgeons, Am. Acad. Neurological Surgeons, Am. Orthop. Assn., Am. Acad. Orthop. Surgery, Alpha Chi Sigma, Sigma Xi, Phi Beta Kappa. Avocations: travel, reading. Office Phone: 507-284-2376. Business E-Mail: spinner.robert@mayo.edu.

SPINOLA, STANLEY M., medical researcher; b. Bklyn., Dec. 9, 1952; BA, Brown U., 1974; MD, Georgetown U., 1978. Asst. prof., divsn. infectious diseases SUNY, Buffalo, 1987—93; assoc. prof., divsn. infectious diseases Ind. U. Sch. Medicine, 1993—95, David H. Jacobs prof., dir., divsn. infectious diseases, 1995—2010, chair, dept. microbiology and immunology, 2010—. Fellow: Am. Acad. Microbiology, Infectious Diseases Soc. Am.; mem.: Am. Soc. Clin. Investigation. Office: 635 Barnhill Dr Indianapolis IN 46202 Business E-Mail: sspinola@iupui.edu.

SPIRI, WILZA CARLA, nursing educator; b. Brazil, Nov. 15, 1961; PhD, Sao Paulo State U., 2001. Asst. prof. Nursing Dept., 2000—. Office: Distrito de Rubiao Jr Botucatu Sao Paulo 18618-000 Brazil Business E-Mail: wilza@fmb.unesp.br.

SPIRITO, ANTHONY, clinical psychologist, psychiatry educator; b. Elizabeth, NJ, Mar. 25, 1953; s. Anthony L. and Ernestine (DeCabia) S.; m. Susan Gayle Baybutt, Aug. 20, 1977; children: Emilia, Evan. BA, Cornell U., 1975; PhD, Va. Commonwealth U., 1981; MA (hon.), Brown U., 1991. Cert. RI Bd. Registration in Psychology, 1985, American Bd. Clin. Child and Adolescent Psychology, 2003. Staff psychologist Dana Farber Cancer Inst. and Children's Hosp. Med. Ctr., Boston, 1982-84; instr. psychiatry Harvard Med. Sch., Boston, 1982—85; allied staff pediat. Dana Farber Cancer Inst., Boston, 1984—86; clin. asst. prof. dept. psychiatry and human behavior Brown U., Providence, 1984—87, asst. prof. dept. psychiatry and human behavior, 1987—90, assoc. prof. dept. psychiatry and human behavior, 1990—98, affiliated faculty Ctr. Alcohol and Addiction Studies, 1994—2001, prof. dept. psychiatry and human behavior, 1998—, assoc. dir. Ctr. Alcohol and Addiction Studies, 2001—10, dir. divsn. clin. psychology, dept. psychiatry and human behavior, 2010—; coord. pediatric psychology services RI Hosp., Providence, 1984—89, dir. psychology, 1989—96, dir. psychology child divsn., 1996—2001, affiliated staff, 2001—; allied health staff Women and Infants Hosp., 1985—2002. Mem. academic exec. com. child psychiatry RI Hosp., 1996—; cons. med. staff Bradley Hosp., 2004—, med. staff exec. com., 2005—09. Contbr. articles to profl. jours., chpts. to books. Nat. Inst. Child Health and Human Devel. grantee, 1985-90, R.I. Dept. Health grantee, 1987-89. Mem. Am. Psychol. Assn. (pres. Divsn. 53 Soc. Clin. Child & Adolescent Psychology, 2010), Assn. Advancement of Behavior Therapy, Soc. Behavioral Medicine. Avocations: sailing, skiing. Office: Ctr Alcohol and Addiction Studies Brown University Box G S121-4 Providence RI 02912 Office Phone: 401-863-6644. Office Fax: 401-863-6647. Business E-Mail: anthony_spirito@brown.edu. *

SPIRO, RICHARD MARC, physician; b. Camden, NJ, May 13, 1971; BS, Johns Hopkins U., 1994; MD, U. South Ala., 1998. Chief, spinal surgery UPMC Neurol. Surgery, 2004—. Named one of 100 Best Spine Surgeons in America, Becketts Orthops. Fellow: ACS, Internat. Coll. Surgeons; mem.: Am. Assn. Neurol. Surgeons, Congress Neurol. Surgeons, N.Am. Spine Soc. Avocations: sailing, photography. Home: 15 Darlington Ct Pittsburgh PA 15217 Business E-Mail: spirorm@upmc.edu.

SPITZER, ADRIAN, pediatrician, educator; b. Bucharest, Rumania, Dec. 21, 1927; came to U.S., 1963, naturalized, 1968; s. Osias and Sophia S. S.; m. Carole Zelter, Oct. 31, 1951; 1 son, Vlad. BS, Matei Basarab Lyceum, Bucharest, 1946; MD, Med. Sch. Bucharest, 1952. Diplomate: Am. Bd. Pediat., Am. Bd. Pediats./Nephrology. Intern White Plains (N.Y.) Hosp., 1964; resident Hosp. Med. Coll. Pa., 1965-66; postdoctoral fellow pediatric nephrology Albert Einstein Coll. Medicine, 1966-67; postdoctoral fellow in renal physiology Cornell U. Med. Sch., 1967-68; practice medicine specializing in pediatric nephrology Bronx, NY, 1968—; asst. prof. pediatrics Albert Einstein Coll. Medicine, 1968-72, assoc. prof., 1972-76, prof., 1976—2009, prof. emeritus, 2009—, dir. div. nephrology, 1973-99; mem. staff Bronx Mcpl. Hosp. Ctr., Hosp. Albert Einstein Coll. Medicine/Montefore Med. Ctr.; mem. Medicine B Study sect.-NIH, 1976-80. Prof. C. Donders rotating chmn. U. Utrecht, The Netherlands, 1990-91; Christiansen vis. fellow St. Catherine's Coll.; vis. fellow dept. biochemistry Oxford U., 1981-82; coord. Internat. Study Kidney Disease in Children; chmn. organizing com. 1st-7th Internat. Workshop on Devel. Renal Physiology, 1980-98, pres., 2001; mem. renal adv. com. N.Y.C. Dept. Health; sci. adv. bd. rsch. and grant com. Nat. Kidney Found., 1982; chmn. pediatric nephrology bd. Am. Bd. Pediat., 1982-83. Mem. editorial bd.: Pediatric Nephrology, Seminars in Nephrology; assoc. editor: Pediatric Renal Disease, 1979, 2d edit., 1992; editor: The Kidney Development, 1982. NIH spl fellow, 1967; John E. Fogarty Sr. Internat. fellow, 1981-82; grantee NIH, N.Y. State Health Research Council, Nat. Kidney Found.; recipient Bela Schick medal for extraordinary achievements in acad. and clin. pediatrics; The Scientific Advancement award of the Internat. Pediatr. Nephrol. Assn. Mem.: Intersoc. Coun. for Kidney and Urinary Tract Rsch.

(sec.-treas. 1984—89), Am. Pediat. Soc., Am. Acad. Pediat. (Henry L. Barnett award 2005), Soc. Pediatric Rsch., Am. Physiol. Soc., Am. Fedn. Clin. Rsch., Am. Soc. Pediatric Nephrology (coun. 1977—80, pres. 1981—82, Founder's award 2006), Am. Soc. Nephrology (com. on govtl. rels. 1999—2001). Office: Albert Einstein Coll Medicine Montefiore Med Ctr 111 E 210th St Bronx NY 10467-2401 Office Phone: 718-655-1120. Business E-Mail: adrian.spitzer@einstein.yu.edu.

SPITZER, PETER G., internist; MD, La. State U. Diplomate Am. Bd. Internal Medicine, 1984. Intern Deaconess Hosp., resident, fellow; hosps. affiliation includes Bryn Mawr Hosp., 1989, Lankenau Med. Ctr., 1997, Paoli Hosp., 1996; attending physician medicine and infectious disease dept.; mem. infectious control com., med. com. and morbidity conf. com. Bryn Mawr Hosp. Author: (publs.) Outbreak of acute pulmonary histoplasmosis in college students following spring break in Mexico: preliminary lessons and a modest proposal, 2001, A Large Outbreak Of Histoplasmosis Among American Travelers Associated With A Hotel In Acapulco, Mexico, Spring 2001, 2003. Named one of the Top Doctor, Main Line Today Mag., 2001, Consumers Checkbook Mag., 2003, Phila. Mag., 1994—96, 2004, 2011. Mem.: AMA, Infectious Disease Soc. of Am. Office: Bryn Mawr Hospital Bryn Mawr Personal Healthcare 933 Haverford Rd Lynn MA 01901 Office Phone: 610-527-8118. Office Fax: 610-526-3296.

SPITZGO, REBECCA H., federal agency administrator; BS in Info. Tech., U. Phoenix. Mem. Grant.gov presdl. mgmt. initiative US Dept. Health and Human Services, 2002—04, program mgr. Grants.gov, 2004—06, assoc. adminstr. office performance rev., 2006—08, assoc. adminstr. office fed. assistance mgmt., 2008—09, assoc. adminstr. bur. clinician recruitment and svc., health and resources and svc. adminstrn., 2009—, dir. Nat. Health Svc. Corps, 2009—. Office: US Dept Health and Human Resources Health Resources and Services Adminstrn 5600 Fishers Ln Rockville MD 20857 Office Phone: 301-594-4130. *

SPITZNAGEL, JOHN KEITH, retired microbiologist, immunologist, physician; b. Peoria, Ill., Apr. 11, 1923; s. Elmer Florian and Anna S. (Kolb) S.; m. Anne Moulton Sirch, Feb. 2, 1947, children: John, Jean, Margaret, Elizabeth, Paul. BA, Columbia U., 1943, MD, 1946. Diplomate Nat. Bd. Med. Examiners, Am. Bd. Internal Medicine. Intern Johns Hopkins Hosp., Balt., 1946-47; resident in internal medicine Barnes Hosp., St. Louis, 1949-51; vis. investigator Rockefeller Inst., NYC, 1952-53, Nat. Inst. Med. Research, London, 1967-68; mem. faculty U. N.C., Chapel Hill, 1957-79, prof. microbiology and infectious diseases, prof. medicine, 1957-79; cons. N.C. Meml. Hosp., Chapel Hill, 1974-79; ad hoc adviser NIH, 1971—; prof. microbiology and immunology, chmn. dept. Emory U., Atlanta, 1979-93, prof. emeritus microbiology and immunology, 1993—, assoc. dean rsch., 1997-98; attending physician, vol. and co founder Good Samaritan Health and Wellness Ctr., Jasper, Ga., 2001—, chmn. exec. bd., CEO, 2004—06. Mem. study sect. bacteriology and mycology NIH, 1975-79, 85-89, chmn., 1977-79. Editor: Infection and Immunity, 1970-80, Jour. Immunology, 1973-80, Jour. Reticuloendothelial Soc, 1973-80. Served with M.C. AUS, 1947-57. Recipient Research Career Devel. award USPHS, 1957-67, Disting. Service award Sch. Medicine U. N.C., Chapel Hill, 1987; USPHS postdoctoral fellow, 1968; USPHS and AEC grantee; lectureship named in his honor, Spitznagel Lectureship on Host Antimicrobial Def., Emory U., 1998. Fellow ACP, Infectious Disease Soc.; mem. AAAS (life), Am. Soc. Microbiology (div. group councilor 1977-79), Am. Assn. Immunologists, Reticuloendothelial Soc. (pres. 1982), Infectious Disease Soc., So. Soc. Clin. Rsch., Assn. Am. Med. Sch. Microbiology and Immunology Chmn. (pres. 1990-91), Sigma Xi. Achievements include research on cell biology of human neutrophil polymorphonuclear leukocytes, and oxygen ind. mechanisms of antimicrobial phagocytoses; first to demonstrate cationic antimicrobial proteins of polymorphonuclear leukocytes granules; co-discoverer of a cationic protein of polymorph granules with antimicrobial action and a powerful attractant for mononuclear phagocytes. Home: 95 Starcross Ln # 20804 Jasper GA 30143-7883 Office: 1510 Clifton Rd NE Atlanta GA 30322-4218

SPIVACK, FRIEDA KUGLER, psychologist, administrator, educator, researcher; b. NYC, Aug. 21, 1932; d. David and Anna (Steir) Kugler; married; children: Alizah Brozgold, Ely. MA with honors, Hunter Coll., 1963; PhD, NYU, 1971. Cert. graphologist. Prof. Manhattan Coll., NYC, 1971-74, Queens Coll., Flushing, NY, 1974-76, Lehman Coll., NYC, 1976-92; exec. dir. Hosp. Clinics Home Ctr. Instrnl. Programs, 1980—; project dir. Bushwick Even Start Program, NYC, 2001—04; prof. Touro Coll., 2003—. Bd. dir., pres. HCHC, Inc., Bklyn.; keynote spkr. NY State Edn. Conf., NYC, 1996, NY Divsn. Early Childhood Conf., 1997; spkr. NY Bklyn. Marriott Yearly Interagency Early Childhood Profl. Devel. Inst., 1998—; developer universal pre-kindergarten classes for Dist. 32, NYC; presenter in field. Contbr. articles to profl. jours., chpts. to textbooks; author family guidance program curriculum in field, infant abecedary program, children's devel. assessments; editor, author: Learning to Function in Life, 1996; author: Perspective of Conductive Education, Infants and Young Children, Young Children's Journal. Mem. exec. bd. NY State Divsn. Early Childhood, 1981—; del. Coun. for Exceptional Children, 1981—88; chmn. Empire State Consortium of Early Childhood Grants, 1990—91; exec. dir. Hosp. Clinic Home Ctr. Instrnl. Corp., 1976—; cmty. orgn. liaison ACE Integration Head Start; project dir. Danforth Found. Grant Transitions and Tracking of Presch. Children in the Pub. Sch., NYC Reggio Emilia program Parent Svcs. Project, Parent and Children Play and Project Enrichment and Coordination programs; chairperson N. Bklyn. Child Care Network, N. Bklyn. Child Health Care Adv. Coun.; project dir., author Bushwick Even Start Program, 2001—; chairperson No. Bklyn. Child Care Health Coun., 1997—, Bushwick Child Care Network, 1998—; chair cmty. partnership grant Child Care Partners, 1998—2006; regional rep. Raising a Reader, 2006—; bd. dirs., pres. Inter-Am. Conductive Edn. for Motor Disabled, Bklyn.; bd. dirs. ACE Integration Head Start, 1994—2005, exec. dir., 1994—; bd. dirs. sponsoring bd. coun. NYC Head Start; bd. dirs. Parent and Child Diagnostic Ctr., 1998—; grant project dir. Parent Access Points, 2003—, United Way, 2003—. Recipient PhD Founders Day award; grantee, United Way, 2003—; Fed. grantee, 2000—02. Mem.: AAUP, Curriculum Devel. Edn., Am. Soc. Profl. Graphologists, Nat. Assn. Young Children (accreditation), Nat. Even Start Assn., Internat. Coll. Pediat. (mem. exec. bd. 1986—), Assn. Edn. Young Children, Am. Fedn. Tchrs.-Profl. Staff Congress, Coun. Exceptional Children (lectr., keynoter 1994—98), Internat. Coun. Psychologists, Nat. Assn. Sch. Psychologists. Avocations: sculpture, writing, travel. Office: ACE Integration Head Start 1419-1423 Broadway Brooklyn NY 11221-4202 Address: HCHC Inc at Kingsbrook Jewish Med Ctr Leviton Bldg 595 Schenectady Ave Rm 413 Brooklyn NY 11203 Office: ACE Preschool 1441 Broadway Brooklyn NY 11221-3907 Office Phone: 718-604-5284, 718-604-5283. E-mail: FSpivack997@earthlink.net.

SPIVAK, JEFFREY M., orthopedist, surgeon, educator; MD, Cornell U., 1982—86. Cert. orthopedic surgery 2001. Intern gen. surgery Mt. Sinai Med. Ctr., 1986—87; resident orthopaedics NY Univ. Hosp. For Joint Diseases, 1987—92, dir., clin. fellow bioengineering, 1988—89; clin. fellow Thomas Jefferson Univ Hosp., 1992—93; asst. prof. NY Univ. Sch. of Medicine; with NY Univ. Langone Med. Ctr. Co-author: (publs.) Thoracolumbar Spine Trauma: II Principles of Management, 1995, Optimal selection and preparation of fresh frozen corticocancellous allografts for anterior interbody lumbar spinal fusion, 1997, Internal fixation of cervical trauma following corpectomy and reconstruction. The effects of posterior element injury, 2000, Somatosensory evoked potential monitoring of lumbar pedicle screw placement for in situ posterior spinal fusion, 2003, and other numerous publications. Office: New York University Hospital for Joint Diseases Ste 400 301 E 17th St New York NY 10003-3804 Office Phone: 212-598-6696. Office Fax: 212-598-6723.

SPIVAK, WILLIAM, pediatric gastroenterologist, educator; Grad., Albert Einstein Coll., 1976. Diplomate Am. Bd. Pediatrics, Am. Bd. Pediatrics-pediatric gastroenterology. Resident Albert Einstein Med. Ctr., 1979; fellow in pediatric gastroenterologist Children's Hosp., Boston, 1982; rsch. fellow The Brigham and Women's Hosp., Harvard Med. Sch.; chief of pediatric gastroenterology and nutrition NY Hosp.- Cornell Med. Ctr., 1982—89, Montefiore Med. Ctr., 1990—2003; clin. prof. of pediat. Cornell Univ. Med. Coll.; attending physician NY Presbyn. Hosp.; staff Lenox Hill Hosp., Children's Hosp. at Montefiore, Montefiore. Named Best Doctors of NY, NY Mag.; named one of Best Doctors in the NY Metro Area, Castle Connaly. Office: New York Presbyterian/ Weill Cornell Medical Center 525 East 68th St New York NY 10006 Office Phone: 212-746-5454. Business E-Mail: wspivak@earthlink.net.

SPIVEY, BRUCE E., ophthalmologist, educator, health facility administrator; b. Cedar Rapids, Iowa, Aug. 29, 1934; s. William Loranzy and Grace Loretta (Barber) S.; children: Lisa, Eric; m. Patti Amanda Birge, Dec. 20, 1987. BA, Coe Coll., 1956; MD, U. Iowa, 1959, MS, 1964; MEd, U. Ill., 1969; DSc (hon.), Coe Coll., 1978. Diplomate Am. Bd. Ophthalmology (fellow, bd. dirs. 1975-83, chmn. oral exam 1976-81). Asst. prof. U. Iowa Coll. Medicine, Iowa City, 1966, assoc. prof., 1968—71; dean Sch. Med. Scis. U. Pacific, San Francisco, 1971—76; prof., chmn. dept. ophthalmology Pacific Med. Ctr. (now Calif. Pacific Med. Ctr.), San Francisco, 1971—87; pres., CEO, dir. Calif. Pacific Med. Ctr., San Francisco, 1976—91; exec. v.p., CEO Am. Acad. Ophthalmology, San Francisco, 1977—93; pres., CEO Calif. Healthcare Sys., Bay area, 1986—92; CEO Northwestern Healthcare Network, Chgo., 1992—97, Columbia Cornell Care, NYC, 1997—2000, Columbia Cornell Network Physicians, NYC, 1998—2000. Bd. dirs. Reliance Group Holdings Inc., NYC; trustee, bd. dirs., sec. bd. MedEx, Balt., 1999—; v.p. Am. Bd. Med. Spltys., 1978—80, pres., 1980—82, Coun. Med. Splty. Socs., 2000—02, 1975—2008, dep. exec. v.p., 2002—08; chmn. bd. dirs. Vol. Hosps. of Am.-No. Calif., 1985—87, nat. bd. dirs., 1991—96; nat. adv. coun. NEI/NIH, 1987—92; spl. med. adv. group Dept. Vets Affairs, 1987—93; trustee, bd. dirs., sec. bd. Ophthal. Mut. Ins. Co., 1988—2007; trustee, sec. bd. PrimeSight, San Francisco, 1996—99. Contbr. over 120 articles to profl. jours.; inventor instruments for eye surgery. Bd. dirs. US-China Ednl. Inst., 1979—; trustee Coe Coll., 1985—, Found. AAO, 1981—, Internat. Coun. Ophthalmology, 1985—, Helen Keller Internat., 1999—; trustee Medbiquitous, 2000-07, chmn, 2001—07. Served to capt. U.S. Army, 1964-66, 85th Duke Hosp., Vietnam, 1965-66. Decorated Bronze Star; recipient Emile Javal Gold medal Internat. Contact Lens Council, San Francisco, 1982, Gradle medal Pan-Am. Assn. Ophthalmol., Disting. Alumni award U. Iowa, 2003, others. Fellow ACS, Am. Acad. Ophthalmology (Disting. Svc. award 1972, Sr. Honor award 1986, Guest of Honor 1996, Lifetime Achievement award, 2002, Internat. Blindness Prevention award, 2007); mem. AMA, Am. Ophthal. Soc. (Howe medal 1993, bd. dirs. 1986-91, pres. 1994-95), Academia Ophthal. Internat. (Bernardo Streiff Gold medal 2002), Soc. Med. Adminstrs. (pres. 1999-2001), Internat. Congress Ophthalmology (sec.-gen. 1978-82), Internat. Coun. Ophthalmology (sec.-gen. 1994—2006, trustee 1985—, pres. 2006—, Jules Francois Gold medal 2006, Jose Rizal Internat. Gold medal 2009), Asia Pacific Acad. Ophthalmology (Sir John Wilson award 2007), Pacific Vision Found. (bd. dirs. 1978-, chmn., San Francisco 2007-), Pacific-Union Club, Chevy Chase Club, Knickerbocker Club, Cosmos Club. Presbyterian. Office: 945 Green St San Francisco CA 94133 Business E-Mail: bruce@spivey.org.

SPODAK, MICHAEL KENNETH, forensic psychiatrist; b. Bklyn., Nov. 5, 1944; s. Harry and Betty (Rahn) S.; children: Lisa Beth, Brett David. BS, Union Coll., 1966; MD, SUNY-Syracuse, 1970. Diplomate: Nat. Bd. Med. Examiners, Am. Bd. Neurology and Psychiatry. Intern Mary Imogene Bassett Hosp., Cooperstown, NY, 1970-71; resident John Hopkins Hosp., Balt., 1974-77; practice medicine specializing in civil and criminal forensic psychiatry Towson, Md., 1977—; chief dept. psychiatry Balt. County Gen. Hosp., Randallstown, 1978-85; mem. staff Clifton T. Perkins Hosp. Ctr., Jessup, Md., 1977-92; clin. asst. prof. psychiatry U. Md. Hosp., Balt., 1983-97; psychiat. cons. Bur. Disability Ins., Social Security Adminstrn., Workmen's compensation Commn., Balt., 1981—; dir. community forensic services Mental Hygiene Adminstrn., Md., 1982-92; faculty Nat. Jud. Coll., 1988—. Mem. Md. Task Force on Somatic Therapies Contbr. numerous articles on forensic psychiatry to profl. jours., chpt. to book. Served with M.C. USN, 1972-74. Mem. Am. Acad. Psychiatry and Law, Am. Psychiat. Assn., Md. Psychiat. Soc. (chmn. peer rev. com. 2001), Md. Med. Soc. (chmn. occupational health com. 1983-90), Baltimore County Med. Soc. Office: 26 W Pennsylvania Ave Towson MD 21204-5001 Office Phone: 410-337-0343. E-mail: mkspodak@yahoo.com.

SPODICK, PEARL BLEGEN, retired counselor, medical psychotherapist; b. Mpls., June 4, 1927; d. Harry Cornelius and Vera Maude (Kidder) Blegen; m. Robert Casper Spodick, Nov. 1, 1955; children: Michael, Peter, Russell, Edward, Rebecca. BA, Albertus Magnus Coll., 1978; MA in Psychology and Art Therapy, Goddard Coll., 1980; postgrad., Simmon's Coll., 1977. Cert. Am. Bd. Behavioral Therapists; cert. med. psychotherapist, clin. mental health counselor; nat. cert. counselor; CHAMPUS (Civilian Health and Med. Program for Uniformed Svcs.) authorized marriage and family therapist, Conn.; lic. mental health counselor, R.I.; lic. profl. counselor, Conn., nat. cert. addictions prevention specialist; diplomate Nat. Bd. Cert. Clin. Hypnotherapists. Cons., art psychotherapist Conn. D.C.Y.S., 1978—2007, Conn. Sexual Trauma Trtatment Program, 1978-79, Arden House Long Term Care Facility, Hamden, Conn., 1979-82, Ctr. for Study of Normative Behavior, Hamden, 1982-85, Curtis Home Children's Residential Treatment Ctr., Meriden, Conn., 1982-93; instr. psychology Albertus Magnus Coll., Hamden, 1988-90; med. psychotherapist, counselor The Psychotherapy Ctr., Woodbridge, Conn., 1980-93, Hamden, Conn., 1993—2007, Art Psychotherapy and Counseling Ctr., Woodbridge, 1980-93, Hamden, 1993—2007; ret., 2007. Cons. in field. Fellow Am. Bd. Med. Psychotherapists (diplomate); mem. ACA (cert.), Am. Art Therapy Assn. (ATR, legis. rep. 1983-89), Am. Assn. Study Mental Imagery, Am. Assn. Cert. Clin. Mental Health Counselors (cert.), Am. Mental Health Counselors Assn., Conn. Assn. Marriage and Family Counselors (pres. 1997-99, treas. 1999-2002). Democrat. Jewish. Avocations: painting, drawing, sculpture, crocheting, reading. Home: Oronoque Village 108B Seminole Ln Stratford CT 06614-8147 Business E-Mail: pb.spodick@optonline.net.

SPOERI, RANDALL KEITH, healthcare company executive; b. Cleve., June 12, 1946; s. Theodore Warren and Marion (Barrick) S.; m. Kathleen Loma Bryden Hayes, Aug. 31, 1968 (div. Mar. 1981); 1 child, Jennifer Anne; m. Deborah Jean Hammett, June 20, 1981 (div. Nov. 1998); 1 child, Jason Randall; m. Laura Joan Lenhardt, Apr. 24, 1999. BS, Calif. Polytech. State U., 1968; MS, Tex. A&M U., 1970, PhD, 1976. Math. statistician U.S. Bur. of the Census, Suitland, Md., 1976-80; assoc. prof. U.S. Naval Acad., Annapolis, 1980-83; assoc. exec. dir. Am. Statis. Assn., Alexandria, Va., 1983-88; sr. corp. statistician Humana, Inc., Louisville, 1988-92; chief program coord. info. branch Health Care Fin. Adminstrn., Balt., 1993; asst. v.p. Nat. Com. for Quality Assurance, Washington, 1994-95; adminstrv. v.p. health care analysis NYLCare Health Plans, Inc., NYC, 1995-98; v.p. med. and quality information HIP Health Plans, NYC, 1998—2001; dir. Health Analytics, Cerner Corp., Kans. City, Mo., 2005—11. Author: Quantitative Methods In Quality Management, 1991; contbr. articles to profl. jours. Mem. adv. com. Health Care Fin. Adminstrn., Balt., 1990-92, bur. dir. citation, 1993, adv. bd. Juran Inst., Wilton, Conn., 1995-98. 1st lt. U.S. Army, 1970-72. Recipient Svc. award Am. Statis. Assoc., Alexandria, 1994. Fellow AAAS, Am. Soc. for Quality (health care divsn. chair 1995-96), mem. Am. Statis Assn., Inst. Indsl. Engring., Inst. for Ops. Rsch. and the Mgmt. Scis. Avocations: sports, music. Home: 148 Top Of The World Way Green Brook NJ 08812-1839

SPOONER, SHARON NAU, pediatric ophthalmologist; b. Melrose, Mass., Apr. 15, 1952; BA in Molecular Biology, San Diego State Coll., 1972, San Jose State U., Calif., 1975, MD, UCLA Sch. Medicine, 1980. Cert. in ophthalmology 1986. Internship in internal medicine Hosp. the Good Samaritan, LA, 1980—81; residency in ophthalmology UCLA Jules Stein Eye Inst., 1981—84, fellowship in pediatric ophthalmology, 1984—86, hosp. appointment, clin. instr.; pvt. practice in pediatric ophthalmology and strabismus surgery Santa Monica, Calif. Grantee Rosalind Alcott fellowship, 1984. Mem.: AMA, Am. Acad. Ophthalmology, Am. Assn. Pediatric Ophthalmology and Strabismus. Office: 2222 Santa Monica Blvd Ste 401 Santa Monica CA 90404 Office Phone: 310-453-0471. Office Fax: 310-453-0473. Business E-Mail: info@sharonspoonermd.com.

SPOOV, JOHAN, retired psychiatrist; b. Helsinki, Finland, Nov. 23, 1948; s. Eric Fredrik and Sirkka Ihalempi Spoof; m. Tuuli Kristiina Nuorvala, Aug. 18, 1972; 1 child, Henrik. MD, U. Helsinki, 1976, PhD, 1991. Gen. practice medicine Health Care Ctr., Heinola and Helsinki, Finland, 1977-78; pvt. practice Vantaa (Finland) Med. Ctr., 1979-80; resident in medicine Bronx (N.Y.) VA Hosp., 1980-81; resident in psychiatry Univ. Hosp., Helsinki, 1981-85, staff psychiatrist, 1986-90; psychiatrist Diacor Med. Ctr., Helsinki, 1990—2010, 1995—2010. Cons. specialist Finnish Patient Ins. Assn., Helsinki, 1995—. Contbr. articles to profl. jours. Med. lt. Finnish Army, 1968-69, 82. Avocation: photography. Office: Diacor Med Ctr Keskuskatu 7 00100 Helsinki Finland Home: Vironkatu 3 B 30B Heisinki 00170 Finland Personal E-mail: johan.spoov@fonet.fi.

SPORER, SCOTT M., orthopedist, surgeon; b. Davenport, Iowa, June 3, 1971; m. Alissa Lynn Swearingen, June 29, 1996; children: Andrew Daniel children: Emma Kathryn, Claire Elizabeth. BS in Biomed. Engring., U. Iowa, Iowa City, 1993; MD, U. Iowa Coll. Medicine, 1997; MS in Clin. Outcomes Rsch., Dartmouth Coll., Hanover, NH, 2001. Diplomate Am. Acad. Orthopaedic Surgery, cert. Am. Bd. Orthopaedic Surgery, 2005, lic. Ill. Resident Dartmouth Hitchcock Med. Ctr., 1997—2002; resident in children's orthopaedic surgery Conn. Children's Med. Ctr., 1999—2000; fellow in orthopaedic adult reconstruction Rush Presbyn. St. Luke's Med. Ctr., Chgo., 2002—03; staff mem. Rush U. Med. Ctr., 2002—, asst. prof. orthopaedic surgery, Midwest Orthopaedics, 2003—; staff mem. Ctrl. Dupage Hosp., Winfield, Ill., 2002—, Oak Park Hosp., Ill., 2003—. Contbr. articles to profl. jours., chapters to books. Recipient James Kary award, outstanding orthopaedic rsch. Fellow: Assn. Arthritic Hip and Knee Surgery; mem.: Mid-America Orthopaedic Assn. Office: Midwest Orthopaedics at Rush ASP Ste 505 25 North Winfield Rd Winfield IL 60190 Office Phone: 630-682-5653. Office Fax: 630-682-8946.

SPORN, AARON ADOLPH, physician, educator; b. NYC, Nov. 5, 1953; s. Herbert and Eunice (Aron) S.; m. Beverly Sporn; children: Hunter, Melanie. BS, SUNY, Stony Brook, 1974; MD, Columbia U., 1978. Diplomate Am. Bd. Orthopaedic Surgery. Intern. gen. surgery Roosevelt Hosp., NYC, 1978-79, resident gen. surgery, 1979-80; resident, chief resident in orthopaedic surgery NYU and Bellevue Hosp., NYC, 1980-83; fellow Midwest Inst. for Orthopaedics, Cin., 1983-84; v.p. medical affairs Inst. for Medicine in Sports, Trenton, NJ, 1984-85; clin. sr. instr. Hahnemann U. Med. Sch., Phila., 1986—; 1991clin. instr. Rutgers U. Med. Sch., New Brunswick, NJ, 1986—91; chief, dept. orthopaedic surgery Robert Wood Johnson U. Hosp., Hamilton, 1994—2004, vice chmn., dept. surgery, 1993—95, chmn. dept. surgery, 1995—98, chmn. surg. peer review com., chmn. operating room com. Vis. clin. fellow Columbia U., N.Y.C., 1978-80, teaching asst. NYU, N.Y.C., 1982-83; com. mem. Arthroscopy Bd. N.Am. Exam Com., 1989-90; cons. N.J. State Police, Trenton, 1987-92, NJ State Bd. Examiners; fundraising com. orthopaedics wing Hamilton Hosp., Trenton, 1989. Contbr. articles to profl. jours. Ind. Rsch. Project grantee NIMH, 1975, 88. Fellow Am. Acad. Orthopaedic Surgery, Arthroscopy Bd. N.Am.; mem. Phi Beta Kappa. Office: Med Arts Bldg 8 Quakerbridge Plz Hamilton NJ 08619-1255 Office Phone: 609-587-4600. *

SPORTY, LAWRENCE DOUGLAS, psychiatrist; b. June 17, 1943; BA in Chemistry and Biology, Queens Coll., CUNY, 1964; MD, SUNY, Bklyn., 1968. Diplomate Am. Bd. Psychiatry and Neurology. Attending psychiatrist SUNY, Bklyn., 1972—74; adminstrv. and clin. dir. South Beach Psychol. Ctr., NY, 1972—74, chief of svc. NY, 1974—75; asst. clin. prof. SUNY-Downstate Med. Ctr., Bklyn., 1975—76; med. dir. Met. State Hosp., Norwalk, Calif., 1978—79; assoc. prof. clin. psychiatry U. So. Calif., LA, 1978—79, chief adult in-patient svcs., 1979; acting chmn. dept. psychiatry U. Calif.-Irvine Med. Ctr., Orange, 1979—82, vice chmn. clin. svcs., 1982—87, assoc. clin. prof., 1979, clin. prof., 1979—83, prof. clin. psychiatry, 1983—. Cons., lectr. in field. Contbr. articles to profl. jours. Fellow: Am. Psychiat. Assn. (disting. life); mem.: So. Calif. Psychiat. Soc. (exec. coun. 1982—84), Alpha Omega Alpha. Office: 2021 E 4th St Ste 118 Santa Ana CA 92705 Office Phone: 714-285-0870.

SPOSI, NADIA MARIA, molecular biologist, researcher; b. Segni, Roma, Sept. 18, 1955; d. Carlo Sposi and Vincenzina Biancone; m. Maurizio Occhetti, Sept. 20, 1990; 1 child, Andrea Occhetti. Degree in Biol. Sci., La sapienza U., Roma, 1980; degree in Med. Genetics, La Sapienza U., Roma, 1983. Cert. specialist in medical genetics La Sapioenza U., 1983. Rschr. Inst. Superiore Sanità, Roma, 1986—. Mem.: Internat. BioIron Soc. Office: Inst Superiore Sanita Viale Regina Elena 299 161 Rome RM Italy Business E-Mail: nadia.sposi@iss.it.

SPOTNITZ, ALAN JEFFREY, cardiothoracic surgeon; b. NYC, May 31, 1944; s. Hyman and Miriam (Berkman) S. BA, Harvard U., 1966; MD, Columbia U., 1970; MPA, Harvard Kennedy Sch. Govt., 2002. Intern gen. surgery Beth Israel Hosp., Boston, 1970-71; rsch. fellow Columbia U., NYC, 1973-74; resident gen. surgery Beth Israel Hosp., Boston, 1971-75; thoracic resident thoracic surgery Presbyn., NYC, 1978-79; assoc. prof. clin. surgery Robert Wood Johnson Med. Sch., New Brunswick, NJ, 1982—87, chief sect. cardiac surgery, 1988—2001, med. dir., 2008—. Dir. surg. clerkship program Robert Wood Johnson Med. Sch., New Brunswick, 1982—, assoc. dir. thoracic surgery residency program U. Medicine and Dentistry N.J., 1991-2001, 03-. Author: (with others) Homograft Valve Durability: Host or Donor Influence, Heart Vessels, 1990; contbr. articles to profl. jours. Maj. USAF, 1975—77. Office: Robert Wood Johnson Med Sch 125 Paterson St New Brunswick NJ 08901 Home Phone: 732-828-2217; Office Phone: 908-235-7805. Business E-Mail: spotnitz@umdnj.edu.

SPRANG, MILTON LEROY, obstetrician, gynecologist, educator; b. Chgo., Jan. 15, 1944; s. Eugene and Carmella (Bruno) S.; m. Sandra Lee Karabelas, July 16, 1966; children: David, Christina, Michael. Student, St. Mary's Coll., 1962-65; MD, Loyola U., 1969. Diplomate Am. Bd. Ob-gyn; Nat. Bd. Med. Examiners; CME accreditation. Intern St. Francis Hosp., Evanston, Ill., 1969-70, resident, 1972-75, sr. attending physician, 1985—; assoc. attending phsycian Evanston Hosp., 1975-79, attending physician, 1980-84, sr. attending physician, 1985—, v.p. med. staff, 1990-91, pres.-elect, 1991-92, pres., 1992-93; also bd. dirs., 1991-94; sec. exec. com. Evanston Hosp., 1993-94; chmn. ob-gyn Cook County Grad. Sch. Medicine, Chgo., 1983-91. Instr. Northwestern U. Med. Sch., Chgo., 1975-78, asst. prof., 1984-95, assoc. prof., 1995-04, prof., 2004—; pres. Northwestern Healthcare Network Physician Leadership, 1994; lectr. acad. and civic groups Ob-Gyn. Nat. Ctr. Advanced Med. Edn., 1991—; bd. dirs. Ill. Found. Med. Rev.; bd. trustees Ill. State Ins. Svcs., 1992—2010, chair, 1998-00, chair rates and res., 2002—; bd. govs. Ill. State Med. Inter-Inst. Exch., 1987-92; adv. bd. practicing physicians Sec. Health and Human Svc. and Ctr. for Medicare Svcs., 2005—2010, Ctrs. Medicare and Medicaid. Editor: Profl. Staff News, 1992-93; chmn. editorial bd. Jour. Chgo. Medicine, 1986-91; contbr. articles to profl. jours. Bd. dirs. Am. Cancer Soc., chmn. profl. edn. com. North Shore unit, 1982-85; bd. dirs. Chgo. Community Info. Network, 1994-95; mem. Nat. Rep. Congrl. Com., 1981—, Ill. Med. Polit. Action Com.; bd. advisors Nat. Youth Leadership Forum on Medicine, Chgo., 1998—; trustee Midwest Ctr. Women's Healthcare, 2002—, pres. and chmn. bd. trustees, 2002—; adv. patients and med. profession. With USN, 1970-72. Fellow: ACOG (chmn. Ill. sect. 1975—76), ACS, Inst. Medicine Chgo.; mem.: AMA (com. to select pub. mem. 2003—, Physician Recognition award 1977, 1980, 1983), Gt. Lakes States Coalition of Dels. to AMA (chmn. 2003—04), Orgn. State Med. Assn. Presidents (steering com. 2003—, sec. 2006—, v.p. 2007, pres. 2008—09), Chgo. Found. Med. Care (med. care evaluation and edn. com. 1980—83, nominating com. 1980—84, practice guidelines com. 1984), Ednl. and Scientific Found. (bd. dirs. 1994—98), Chgo. Med. Soc. (adv. com. advt. stds. 1978—84, physician's rev. com. 1980—85, trustee ins. bd. 1982—, nominating com. 1985—, treas. 1986—89, chmn. fin. com. 1986—89, trustee 1986—92, sec. 1989—90, pres.-elect 1990—91, chmn. bd. trustees 1990—91, pres. 1991—92, chmn. ethical rels. com. 1994—), Ill. Med. Soc. (del. to AMA 1987—, govt. affairs com. 1988—, chmn. reference com. 1989, chmn. fin. com. 1992—94, sec.-treas. 1994—96, chmn. bd. trustees 1996—98, chmn. bylaws com. 1998—99, pres. 2000—01, vice speaker HOD 2007—09, spkr. ISMS HOD 2009—11), Physician Benefit Trust (chmn. fin. com. 1993—2004, chmn. and pres. 2004—). Roman Catholic. Avocations: reading, swimming. Home: 4442 Concord Ln Skokie IL 60076-2606 Office: AGSO 1000 Central St Evanston IL 60201-1777 Home Phone: 847-677-5890; Office Phone: 847-869-3300. E-mail: sprangml@aol.com.

SPRATT, BRIAN GEOFFREY, microbiologist, educator, researcher; b. Margate, Kent, Eng., Mar. 21, 1947; s. Clarence Albert and Marjory Alice (Jeffreys) S.; m. Jennifer Broome-Smith (div.); 1 child, Timothy Peter; m. Jiaji Zhou; 1 child, Henry Jestyn. BSc, London U., 1968, PhD, 1972. Rsch. assoc. Princeton U., NJ, 1973-75; rsch. fellow Leicester U., England, 1975-80; lectr. Sussex U., Brighton, England, 1980-87, reader, 1987-89, prof., 1990-97; prin. rsch. fellow Wellcome Trust, England, 1989—; prof. Wellcome Ctr. Epidemiology of Infectious Disease Oxford U., England, 1997-2001; prof., head dept. infectious disease epidemiology Imperial Coll., London, 2001—. Hon. prof. London Sch. Hygiene and Tropical Medicine. Contbr. numerous articles to profl. jours. Recipient Fleming award Soc. Gen. Microbiology, 1982, Hoechst-Roussel award Am. Soc. Microbiology, 1993. Fellow: Am. Acad. Microbiology, Acad. Med. Sci. (London), Royal Soc. London (Leeuwenhoek award 2003). Achievements include research on mechanisms of action and mechanisms of resistance to antibiotics, bacterial population genetics, molecular epidemiology and the evolution of bacterial pathogens. Office: Dept Infectious Disease Epidemiology Imperial Coll St Mary's Norfolk Pl London W2 1PG England Business E-Mail: b.spratt@imperial.ac.uk.

SPRAY, PAUL ELLSWORTH, retired surgeon; b. Wilkinsburg, Pa., Apr. 9, 1921; s. Lester E. and Phoebe Gertrude (Hull) S.; m. Mary Louise Conover, Nov. 28, 1943 (dec. Jun 12, 2008); children: David C., Thomas L., Mary Lynn (Mrs. Thomas Branham). BS, U. Pitts., 1942; MD, George Washington U., Washington, DC, 1944; MS, U. Minn., 1950. Diplomate Am. Bd. Orthop. Surgery. Intern U.S. Marine Hosp., SI, 1944-45; resident Mayo Found., Rochester, Minn., 1945-46, 48-50; practice medicine specializing in orthop. surgery Oak Ridge, Tenn., 1950-98; ret., 1998; vol. physician Knoxville Interfaith Clinic, 1998—2008. Mem. active staff Oak Ridge Hosp., 1950-98, hon. staff, 98-; courtesy staff Harriman Hosp., Tenn., ret., 1998; vol. vis. cons. CARE Medico, Jordan, 1959, Nigeria, 1962, 65, Algeria, 1963, Afghanistan, 1970, Bangladesh, 1975, 77, 79, Peru, 1980, U. Ghana, 1982; AMA vol. physician, Vietnam, 1967, 72; vis. assoc. prof. U. Nairobi, 1973; mem. tchg. team Internat. Coll. Surgeons to Peru, 1979, 84; vis. prof. orthop. surgery U. Khartoum, 1976; hon. prof. San Luis Gonzaga U., Ica, Peru, 1979; AmDoc vol. cons. U. Biafra Tchg. Hosp., 1969; vis. prof. Mayo Clinic, 1988; sec. orthops. overseas divsn. CARE Medico, 1971-76, sec. Medico adv. bd., 1974-76, vice chmn., 1976, chmn., 1977-79, v.p. CARE, Inc., 1977-79, pub. mem. CARE bd. dirs., 1980-90, mem. bd. overseers, 1991-99; chmn. Orthops. Overseas, Inc., 1982-86, treas., 1986-88, emeritus mem., 1994; mem. U.S. organizing com. 1st Internat. Acad. Symposium on Orthops., Tianjin, China, 1983; mem. CUPP Internat. Adv. Coun., 1986-99; invited guest spkr. Japan Orthop. Assn., 1994; mem. curriculum com. Oak Ridge Inst. Continual Learning, 1999-2007; bd. dirs. MMC Oak Ridge Found., chmn., 2003-04, emeritus, 2007. Mem. editl. bd. Contemporary Orthopedics, 1984-96. Pres. Anderson County Health Coun., 1976—77, v.p., 1975, hon. bd. dirs.; pres. health commn. Coun. So. Mountains, 1958—65, sec., bd. dirs., 1965—66; Tenn. pres. UN Assn., 1966—67; vice-chmn. bd. Camelot Care Ctr., Tenn., 1979—82, chmn. Tenn., 1982—86; hon. mem. World Orthopedic Concern, 1990; with del. to Vietnam People to People, citizen amb. to Vietnam, 1993; del. to Oak Ridge's Sister City, Obninsk, Russia Obninsk, Russia, 1993; trustee Vietnam Am. Scholarship Fund, 1992—95; Rotary vol. orthopaedic surgeon Kikuyu Hosp. Rehab. Ctr. of East Africa Presbyn. Ch., 1998; vol. Habitat for Humanity, 2004; bd. dirs. Hope of East Tenn., 2002—06, Clinch River Home Health Assn., 2005—08. Capt. USMC, 1946—48. Recipient Svc. to Mankind award, Serotoma, 1967, Humanitarian award, Lions Club, 1968, Freedom Citation, Sertoma, 1978, award, Amb. Goodwill Lions Club, 1979, Medico Disting. Svc. award, 1990, 1st Ann. Vocat. Svc. award, Oak Ridge Rotary, 1979, Tech. Comm. award, East Tenn. chpt. Soc. for Tech. Comm., 1983, Individual Achievement award, Meth. Med. Ctr. of Oak Ridge, 1991, Humanitarian award, Orthopaedics Overseas, 1992, Biographic Exhibit recognition, Mus. Appalachia Hall of Fame, Norris, Tenn.; named to Anderson County Hall of Fame for Philanthropy, 2007; fellow Melvin Jones fellow, Lions Club, 1993. Fellow Internat. Coll. Surgeons (Tenn. regent 1976-80, bd. councilors 1980-84, hon. chmn. bd. trustees 1981-83, trustee 1983-84, v.p. US sect. 1982-83, mem. surg. teams com. 1983-90, Humanitarian award 1992); mem. AMA (Humanitarian Svc. award 1967, 72), Socièté International Chirugie Orthopèdique et de Traumuatologie, So. Orthop. Assn., Western Pacific Orthop. Assn., Am. Fracture Assn., Am. Acad. Orthop. Surgeons (mem. com. on injuries 1980-86), Tenn. Med. Assn. (com. on emergency med. svcs. 1978-97), Peru Acad. Surgery (corr.), Peruvian Soc. Orthop. Surgery and Traumatology (corr.), Clin. Orthop. Soc., Mid-Am. Orthop. Soc., Rotary Club (Oak Ridge chpt., chmn. cmty. and world svc. com. 2000-04, Paul Harris fellow). Home: 507 Delaware Ave Oak Ridge TN 37830-3902 Home Phone: 865-483-9936. Personal E-mail: spray507@aol.com.

SPREHN, GWEN CAROL, psychology professor, researcher; b. Washington, Apr. 4, 1945; PhD, Emory U., 1973. Asst. prof., dir. clin. svcs., dept. neurology Ind. U. Sch. Medicine, 2007—. Mem.: APA, Am. Bd. Clin. Neuropsychology, Nat. Acad. Neuropsychology, Internat. Neuropsychological Soc., Am. Bd. Profl. Psychology. Avocations: gardening, travel. Office: 541 Clinical Dr CL-285 Indianapolis IN 46202 Office Fax: 317-274-1337. Business E-Mail: gsprehn@iupui.edu.

SPRIESTERSBACH, DUANE CARYL, academic administrator, speech pathology/audiology services professional, educator; b. Pine Island, Minn., Sept. 5, 1916; s. Merle Lee and Esther Lucille (Stucky) Spriestersbach; m. Bette Rae Bartell, Aug. 31, 1946; children: Michael Lee, Ann. BEd, Winona State Tchrs. Coll., 1939; MA, U. Iowa, 1940, PhD, 1948. Asst. dir. pers. rels. Pacific Portland Cement Co., San Francisco, 1946-47; prof. speech pathology U. Iowa, Iowa City, 1948-89, prof. emeritus, 1989—, dean. Grad. Coll., v.p. ednl. devel. and rsch., 1965-89, v. pres. and dean emeritus, 1989—, acting pres., 1981-82; v.p. ops. Breakthrough, Inc., Oakdale, Iowa, 1993-94; freelance cons., 1994—2006. Com. mem. Nat. Inst. Neurol. Disease and Blindess; chmn. dental tng. com. Nat. Inst. Dental Rsch., 1967—72, chmn. spl. grants rev., 1978—82; chmn. bd. dirs. Midwest Univs. Cons. Internat. Activities, Columbus, 1978—87. Author: (book) Psychosocial Aspects of Cleft Palate, 1973; author: (with others) Diagnostic Methods in Speech Pathology, 1978; co-editor: Cleft Palate and Communication, 1968, Diagnosis in Speech Language Pathology, rev. edit., 1999, The Way It Was: The University of Iowa 1964-1989, 1999. Pres. Iowa City Cmty. Theater, 1964, 1977, 1983. Served to lt. col. US Army, 1941—46, ETO. Decorated Bronze Star; fellow Nat. Inst. Dental Rsch., 1971. Fellow: AAAS; mem.: Midwestern Assn. Grad. Schs. (chmn. 1979—80), Am. Cleft Palate Assn. (pres. 1961—62, disting. svc. award), Am. Speech and Hearing Assn. (pres. 1965, honor award), Assn. Grad. Schs. (pres. 1979—80), Cosmos Clug (Washington), Mortar Bd., Sigma Xi. Home: 2 Longview Knoll NE Iowa City IA 52240-9148 Office: Univ Iowa M212 Oakdale Hall Iowa City IA 52242-5000 Home Phone: 319-351-8756; Office Phone: 319-335-4012. Business E-Mail: duane-spriestersbach@uiowa.edu.

SPRIGGS, DAVID RANDALL, healthcare administrator, educator; b. Chgo., May 12, 1950; s. Randall and Mary Spriggs; m. Nancy J. Gerlach, Jan. 22, 1973. BS, U. Wis., 1973, MD, 1977. Cert. Am. Bd. Internal Medicine; lic., N.Y. Fellow Dana Farber Cancer Inst., Boston, 1982-85; from instr. to assst. prof. Harvard U., Boston, 1985-89; asst. prof. U. Wis., Madison, 1989-93; mem., chief devel. chemotherapy, Winthrop Rockefeller chair med. oncology Meml. Sloan-Kettering Cancer Ctr., NYC, 1993—. Sr. editor: (jour.) Clin. Cancer Rsch., 1996. Grantee Nat. Cancer Inst., 1994—. Mem. AAAS, Am. Assn. for Cancer Rsch., Am. Soc. Clin. Oncology. Avocations: golf, science fiction. Office: Meml Sloan Kettering Hosp 1275 York Ave New York NY 10021-6094 Home Phone: 212-717-6438; Office Phone: 212-639-2203.

SPRINGER, TIMOTHY ALAN, health researcher, immunology educator; b. Ft. Benning, Ga., Feb. 23, 1948; BA in Biochemistry, U. Calif., Berkeley, 1971; PhD in Biochemistry & Molecular Biology, Harvard U., 1976. NIH rsch. fellow U. Cambridge (Eng.)/MRC Lab. Molecular Biology, 1976-77; asst. prof. Med. Sch., Harvard U., 1977-83, assoc. prof., 1983-89, Latham family prof., 1989—. Chief lab. membrane immunochemistry Dana-Farber Cancer Inst., Boston, 1981-88; v.p. Ctr. Blood Rsch. Inst. Biomed. Rsch., Boston, 1988—; organizer Juan March Found. Workshop, Madrid, 1991. Assoc. editor Jour. Immunology, 1981-85; adv. editor Jour. Exptl. Medicine, 1981-85; mem. editl. bd. Hybridoma, 1981-, Jour. Clin. Immunology, 1988-92, Cellular Immunology, 1988-93, Cell Regulation, 1989-92, New Biologist, 1989—; contbr. numerous articles to profl. jours. NIH grantee, 1988, basic Rsch. prize, Am. Heart Assn., 1993, William B. Coley Medal for Disting. Rsch. in Fundamental Immunology, Cancer Rsch. Inst., 1995, Marie T. Bonazinga award for Excellence in Leukocyte Biology Rsch, Society for Leukocyte Biology, 1995, Crafoord prize in Polyarthritis, Royal Swedish Acad. Sciences, 2004. Mem. Am. Assn. Immunologists, Reticuloendothelial Soc. (membership chair 1986—, chair 1989), Am. Soc. Biol. Chemists, Am. Assn. Immunologists (block chmn. macrophages and natural killer cells 1985-86), Am. Assn. Pathologists, Nat. Acad. Scis. (chair biophysics and computational biology sect. 29 2004-), Am. Acad. Arts and Sciences, Phi Beta Kappa. Achievements include mapping a different group of adhesion molecules in the cell membrane of the blood cells, termed integrins. Office: Ctr for Blood Rsch Inst for Biomedical Rsch Harvard Med Sch Warren Alpert Bldg Rm251 200 Longwood Ave Boston MA 02115 Office Fax: 617-278-3200, 617-278-3232. Business E-Mail: springer@cbr.med.harvard.edu.

SPRINGER, WAYNE RICHARD, safety consultant, research biochemist; b. Milw., Nov. 16, 1946; s. Richard Andrew and Irma Edna (Richter) S.; m. Jane Bradley, Aug. 19, 1972; chldren: Matthew Bradley, Katherine Jane. BA, Northwestern U., 1968; PhD, U. Calif., Berkeley, 1977. Vol. Peace Corps, Somalia, Antigua, 1969-72; post-doctoral fellow U. Calif., San Diego, 1977-79, rsch. biochemist, 1979-92, assoc. project biochemist, 1992-99; rsch. biochemist VA Healthcare Sys., San Diego, 1979-99; chem. hygiene officer VA Med. Ctr., San Diego, 1992-94, biosafety officer, 1992—2007, chief environ. health and safety, 1994—2006; rsch. safety cons., 2007—. Avocations: travel, gardening. Personal E-mail: sdressafco@hotmail.com.

SPRINGFIELD, SANYA A., federal agency administrator; BS in Zoology, Howard U., PhD in Physiology and Biophysics. Fellow Dept. Pharmacology Robert Wood Johnson Sch. Medicine, Piscataway, NJ; asst. prof. to assoc. prof. Dept. Biology CCNY, 1985—95; program dir. Divsn. Integrative Biology and Neurosiences NSF; participant NIH Grants Assoc. Program; sci. rev. adminstr. Grants Rev. Br. Nat. Cancer Inst., dir. Comprehensive Minority Biomedical Br., 1999—, acting dir. Ctr. to Reduce Cancer Health Disparities. Office: Comprehensive Minority Biomedical Br Nat Cancer Inst 6116 Executive Blvd Ste 7028 Bethesda MD 20892-8350 also: Ctr to Reduce Cancer Health Disparities Nat Cancer Inst 6116 Executive Blvd Ste 602 MSC 8341 Bethesda MD 20892 Office Phone: 301-496-7344. Office Fax: 301-402-4551. E-mail: springfs@mail.nih.gov.

SPRINKLE, ROBERT LEE, JR., podiatrist; b. Winston-Salem, NC, July 13, 1932; s. Robert Lee and Elton Elizabeth Sprinkle; children: Robert III, Karen, Ralph, Richard, Roy, Randy, Drouin; m. Nancy House Dixon. Student, Salem Coll., 1952; BS, Ohio Coll. Podiatry, 1956; DPM, Pa. Coll. Podiatry, 1970. Diplomate Am. Bd. Disability Analysts, Am. Coun. Cert. Podiatric Phys. and Surgeons, Sr. Acad. Ambulatory Podiatric Surgeons. Pvt. practice, Winston-Salem, 1957—. Chmn. N.C. Bd. Podiatry Examiners, 1968-74; clin. assoc. prof. Dr. William M. School Coll. Podiatric Medicine; researcher reconstructive surgery human foot and ankle; bd. dirs. Cmty. Gen. Hosp. Found., Thomasville, N.C.; bd. dirs. Am. Coun. Cert. Podiatric Phys. and Surgeons. Chmn. Mayor's Com. on Hiring the Handicapped, 1963-64; commr. Old Hickory Coun., Boy Scouts Am., 1970-71, v.p., 1973-74, Silver Beaver award, 1969, mem. adv. bd. Old North State Coun.; pres. St. Leo's Parochial Sch. PTA, 1969-70; dir. Halfway House, 1965-66; chmn. Bishop McGuiness PTA, 1976.

Recipient St. George medal Charlotte Diocese, Roman Cath. Ch., 1971, Order of the Long Leaf Pine, State of NC, 2006; Schering grantee, 1972-74. Mem. APHA, Am. Podiatric Med. Assn. (life mem.), N.C. Podiatry Assn. (past pres., Podiatrist of Yr. 1976), Piedmont Podiatry Assn., Acad. Ambulatory Podiatric Surgeons (life mem.), Internat. Analgesia Soc., Forsyth Country Club, Colonial Country Club, Twin City Club, KC (4th degree), SAR (life; N.C. state registrar, past pres. Bethabara chpt., N.C. state pres. 2002—, mem. George Washington Found.), SCV, NRA (life), Rotary (Paul Harris fellow, dist. gov. 1976-77), St. Andrew's Soc., Sons of the Revolution (life; state chpt. sec. pres. NCSSR). Republican. Roman Catholic. Home: 10 Mock St Thomasville NC 27360-4622 Office: Abc Family Foot Ankle 10 Mock St Thomasville NC 27360-4622 Office Phone: 336-848-2240. Business E-Mail: foot1@northstate.net.

SPRINTHALL, NORMAN ARTHUR, psychology educator; b. Attleboro, Mass., Aug. 19, 1931; s. William Archie and Edith Jarvis (Clark) S.; m. Barbara Weller (div. 1974); children: Douglas, Jayne, Carolyn; m. Lois May Thies. AB magna cum laude, Brown U., 1954, MA, 1959; EdD, Harvard U., 1963. Dir. fin. aid Brown U., 1955-60; asst. prof., then asso. prof. psychology, program chmn. counseling Harvard U., 1963-72; mem. faculty U. Minn., Mpls., 1972-82, prof. ednl. psychology, 1973-82, program chmn. counseling, 1972-74; prof. psychology, head counselor edn. program N.C. State U., Raleigh, 1982-87, prof., counselor, 1987-95, prof. emeritus, 1995—. Co-dir. Ethical Reasoning Project in Pub. Adminstrn., U.S. and Poland, 1993-95, Russia, 1998-99. Author: Educational Psychology: Readings, 1969, Guidance for Human Growth, 1971, Educational Psychology: A Developmental Approach, 7th edit., 1998, Value Development as the Aim of Education, 2d edit., 1981, Adolescent Psychology: A Developmental View, 1984, 2d rev. edit., 1988, 3d edit., 1995; co-author: Stewart-Sprinthall Management Survey (SSMS) Ethics and Public Administration, others; mem. editl. bd. profl. jours. Bd. dirs. Josephson Inst. Advancement of Ethics, 1986-90, mem. bd. advisors Character Counts Coalition, 1994—2004. Co-recipient Kuhmerker Career Rsch. award, Assn. Moral Edn., 2005. Fellow APA (Disting. Sr. Contbr. award); mem. Phi Beta Kappa. E-mail: nlsprint@aol.com.

SPRITZLER, JOHN G., medical researcher; b. LA, 1947; ScD, Harvard Sch. Pub. Health, 1992. Sr. rsch. assoc. Harvard Sch. Pub. Health, 1992—. Home: 114 Strathmore Rd #101 Brighton MA 02135 Business E-Mail: spritz@sdac.harvard.edu.

SPUNT, AVERY L., pharmacist; b. Chgo. m. Janet Spunt, Sept. 2, 1984; children: Marc, Sarah, Kate. BS in Pharmacy, U. Ill., Chgo., 1970, MEd, 1984. Lic. pharmacist Ill. Staff pharmacist U. Ill. Chgo., 1973—74, mem. staff Eye and Ear Infirmary, 1974—76, clin. asst. prof. dept. neurology, 1978—2002, asst. head acad. programs, clin. assoc. prof. dept. pharmacy practice, 1992—2002, pharmacy supr., clin. specialist Coll. Medicine, 1976—84; competency assessment dir. Nat. Assn. Bds. Pharmacy, Park Ridge, Ill., 2002—05; asst. dean Midwestern U. Chgo. Coll. Pharmacy, Downers Grove, Ill., 2005—07, prof., assoc. dean, 2007—. Cons. in field; v.p. Clin. Pharmacy Cons., Inc., 1975—90; lectr. at confs. in field. Contbr. articles to profl. jours., chpts. to books. Sgt. USMC, 1970—72. Fellow, Buehler Ctr. on Aging, McGaw Med. Ctr. of Northwestern U., 1990. Fellow: Am. Soc. Health Sys. Pharmacists (mem. student adv. panel 1985—96, ednl. programming assoc. 1989, resident 2008—09, Pharmacist of Yr. 2007), mem.. ASCD, No. Ill. Soc. Hosp. Pharmacists, Ill. Coun. Health-Sys. Pharmacists (mem. edn. com. 1996—), Ill. Pharmacists Assn. (ho. del. 1983—88, mem. pub. rels. com. 1984—88, mem. continuing edn. com. 1985—89, bd. dirs. 1988—89, Pharmacist of Yr. 1991), Am. Coll. Clin. Pharmacy, Am. Assn. Colls. Pharmacy (chmn. spl. interest group on exptl. edn. 1985—86, ho. dels. 1989, 1991, 1994), Am. Pharmacists Assn., U. Ill. Coll. Pharmacy Alumni Assn. (v.p. 1988—89, pres. 1989—90, pres. bd. dirs. 1989—90), Rho Pi Phi (1st vice chancellor 1974—76). Avocation: photography. Home: 1724 Mundelein Rd Naperville IL 60565 Office Phone: 630-515-6100. Business E-Mail: aspunt@midwestern.edu.

SQUADRITO, GIOVANNI, internist, educator; b. Messina, Italy, Dec. 26, 1967; MD, U. Messina, 1992. Asst. prof. internal medicine Policlinico U. G Martino, 1998—2011, assoc. prof. internal medicine, 2011—. Mem.: AISF. Home: Via S Pelagia 3 Messina Sicily 98122 Italy Home Fax: 39902213594. Personal E-mail: gsquadrito@unime.it.

SQUILLACI, SALVATORE, pathologist; b. Messina, Italy, Feb. 8, 1962; s. Giuseppe Squillaci and Concetta Tamburini; m. Fiorina Ottelli Zoletti, July 19, 1997; 1 child, Gabriele. Degree in Medicine and Surgery, U. Studies, Messina, 1988. Lic. medicochirurgical Italy, 1988, specialty Milan U., Italy, 1994. Specialist Dept. Anat. Pathology, Hosp. Vallecamonica, Esine, Italy, 1993—2009. Contbr. scientific papers to profl. publs. Mem.: SIAPEC. Achievements include research in ebv associated epithelial and soft tissue tumors. Office: Hosp Vallecamonica Via Alessandro Manzoni 142 25040 Esine BS Italy Personal E-mail: salvatore14@hotmail.com. Business E-Mail: anapat@ospedalevallecamonica.it.

SQUIRE, LARRY RYAN, neuroscientist, psychologist, educator; b. Cherokee, Iowa, May 4, 1941; s. Harold Walter and Jean (Ryan) Squire; children: Ryan, Luke, Charls, Caroline. BA, Oberlin Coll., Ohio, 1963; PhD in Psychology, MIT, 1968. Postdooc. fellow Albert Einstein Coll. Medicine, NYC, 1968—70; faculty dept. psychiatry U. Calif., San Diego, 1970—, prof. psychiatry, 1981—, prof. neuroscis., 1993—, prof. psychology, 1996—. Rsch. career scientist VA Med. Ctr., San Diego, 1980—; faculty Ctr. Neurobiology of Learning & Memory, U. Calif., Irvine. Author: Memory and Brain, 1987, (with Eric Kandel) Memory: From Mind to Molecules, 1999; sr. editor (textbook) Fundamental Neuroscience, 2008, editor-in-chief Encyclopedia of Neuroscience, 2008; contbr. articles to profl. jours. Recipient Charles A. Dana award for pioneering achievements in health, 1993, William Middleton award, US Dept. Vets. Affairs, Herbert Crosby Warren medal, Soc. Exptl. Psychologists, Met. Life Found. award for med. rsch. Mem.: AAAS (chair neurosci. sect. 2001, McGovern award), NAS (coun. mem. 2009—), Am. Psychol. Soc. (William James fellow, Disting. Sci. Contbn. award), Am. Acad. Arts & Scis., Inst. Medicine, Am. Philos. Soc. (Karl Lashley prize), Soc. Neurosci. (sec. 1988—90, pres. 1993—94). Office: VA Med Ctr 116A 3350 La Jolla Village Dr San Diego CA 92161 Office Fax: 858-552-7457. E-mail: lsquire@ucsd.edu.

SQUIRES, NANCY, psychology professor, department chairman; PhD, U. Calif., San Diego, 1972. Prof. biopsychology SUNY, Stony Brook, chair dept. psychology. Contbr. articles to profl. jours. Office: Dept Psychology SUNY Stony Brook Psychology B154 Stony Brook NY 11794-2500 Office Phone: 631-632-7808. E-mail: nancy.squires@stonybrook.edu.

SQUIZZATO, ALESSANDRO, internist; b. Tradate, Varese, Italy, Aug. 21, 1975; s. Giovanni Squizzato and Claudia Bernardoni. MD, U. Insubria, Varese, Italy, 2000, degree in internal medicine, 2005, PhD in Medicine, 2010. Rsch. fellow Acad. Med. Ctr., Amsterdam, Netherlands, 2003—04; rschr. internal medicine U. Insubria, 2006—. Named Young Rschr., Italian Soc. Internal Medicine, 2005. Roman Catholic. Office Phone: 00390332278831. E-mail: alexsquizzo@libero.it.

SRAMEK, JIRI, surgeon; b. Praha, Nov. 1, 1978; MD, Charles U., Praha, 2004; degree in Orthop. Surgery, IPVZ, 2009. Surgeon ProSpine, 2010—. Mem.: Czech Spine Surgery Soc. Office: Mussinanstrasse 6 Bogen Bayern 94327 Germany Business E-Mail: jiri.sramek@spinesurgery.cz.

SREENIVASAN, SRIRANGARAJ, medical educator; b. Mysore, India, June 5, 1980; MBBS, Sri Siddartha Med. Coll., Tumkur, 2002; MD, Mysore Med. Coll. and Rsch. Inst., 2008. Asst. prof. Mahathma Gandhi Med. Coll. & Rsch. Inst., 2008—. Dep. contr. examinations Sri Balaji Vidyapeeth U., 2011. Recipient prize, Indian Assn. Med. Microbiologists. Mem.: Indian Assn. Med. Microbiologists. Avocations: music, painting, travel. Home: 5-E Type-2 Staff Quarters MGMC &RI Pondicherry 607402 India Home Phone: 0413-2615996. Personal E-mail: rangaraj1980@indiatimes.com.

SRIDHAR, SESHAIAH KRISHNAN, pharmacist, educator; b. Chennai, India, July 6, 1970; s. Pogula Seshaiah Krishnan and Kuppuswamy Rukmani; m. Jagannathan Dhannalakshmi, Mar. 5, 1995; 1 child, Sridhar Aishwarya. BS in Pharmacy, The Tamilnadu Dr.MGR Med. U., 1992; PharmM, Banaras Hindu U., 1995; PhD in Pharmacy, The Tamilnadu Dr.MGR Med. U., 2002. Lectr. pharm. chemistry Vel's Coll. Pharmacy, Chennai, India, 1992—93, vice prin., head pharm. chemistry, 1995—2002; asst. prof. pharm. chemistry C. L. Baid Metha Coll. Pharmacy, Chennnai, 2002—03; lectr. pharm. chemistry Pharmacy Dept. Higher Coll. Tech., Muscat, Oman, 2003—05, head in-charge Pharmacy Dept., 2005—. Contbr. articles to profl. jours. (Best Paper award Indian Drugs, 2004). Recipient Gold Medal award, Banaras Hindu U., 1995, fellow, Ministry Human Resources Devel., Govt. India, 1993—93. Fellow: Indian Chemical Assn. (life); mem.: The Royal Soc. Chemistry, India Assn. Biomedical Scientists. (life). Achievements include patents for synthesis of 1 diphenylamino methyl 3 (4 bromo phenylimino) 5 chloro 1, 3-dihydro-indol-3-one as potential non-steroidal anti-inflammatory agent. Home: 19 First Street Balaji Nagar Chennai 600014 India Personal E-mail: sksridhar67@yahoo.com.

SRINIVASA, RAVI, radiologist; b. Houston, Apr. 9, 1982; MD, Tex. Tech U., 2006. Radiology resident William Beaumont Hosp., 2006—11; interventional radiology fellow U. Pa., 2011—. Mem.: ARRS, AUR, SIR, RSNA, ACR. Home: 437 E 14 Mile Rd Birmingham MI 48009 Business E-Mail: ravi.srinivasa@beaumont.edu.

SRINIVASAN, K.G., radiologist; b. Madurai, India, Aug. 24, 1969; MBBS, Madurai Med. Coll., 1991; MD, Nagpur U., 1994. Cons., propr. KGS Advanced MRI and CT Scan Ctr., 2002—. MRI tng. PD Hinduja Nat. Hosp., Mumbai, 1995; cons. radiologist Vita Diagnostic Ctr., Madurai, 1996—98, Indian MRI and Diagnostic & Rsch. Ctr., 1998—2002. Recipient Best Radiologist award, Indian Med. Assn., Madurai Br., Dr. Padmanur Ramarao Oration award, Indian Med. Assn. Mem.: European Sch. Radiology, Indian Radiol. Soc. Office: 766 Anna Nagar Madurai Tamilnadu 625020 India Personal E-mail: kgsscans@gmail.com.

SRINIVASAN, RANGASWAMY, chemical physicist; b. Madras, India, Feb. 28, 1929; came to U.S., 1953; s. K. Rangaswamy. BSc with honors, Madras U., India, 1949; PhD, U. So. Calif., 1956. Mgr., rsch. T.J. Watson Rsch. Ctr. IBM, Yorktown Heights, NY, 1961-90; chief exec. officer UV Tech Assocs., Ossining, NY, 1990—. Vis. rsch. prof. chemistry Ohio State U., Columbus, 1966-67, Wellman Lab., Mass. Gen. Hosp., Boston, 1987-89, Columbia-Presbyn. Med. Ctr., N.Y.C., 1984-90. Editor: (books) Organic Photochemical Syntheses, Vol. 1., 1972, Vol. 2, 1976; contbr. over 200 articles to profl. jours. Guggenheim fellow, 1966; recipient award for creative invention Am. Chem. Soc., 1997, Essalen award for chemistry in the pub. interest, 1997, prize Rank Found., 2009. Fellow AAAS, Am. Physical Soc. (Biol. Physics prize 1998), NY Acad. Scis., Am. Soc. Laser Medicine and Surgery; mem. Nat. Acad. Engring. (Inventor's Hall of Fame 2002), Am. Inst. Physics (Indsl. Applications prize 2003), Optical Soc. Am. (Wood prize 2004). Achievements include invention of Ablative Photodecomposition, a laser technique for removal of microscopic thickness of organic matter such as plastics (of use in microelectronics) or tissue (of use in LASIK eye surgery).

SRINIVASAN, UDDANAPALLI SREERAMULU, neurosurgeon; b. Hosur, Tamil Nadu, India, June 8, 1964; s. Uddanapalli Subbarayappa Sreeramulu and Hosur Seshagiri Rao Rajamani; m. Sellaratnam Sumathi Ratnam, Mar. 1, 1992; children: Srinivasan Sanjana Smruthi, Srinivasan Sadhana Smruthi. MBBS, Madurai Med. Coll., India, 1981—87, MCh in Neurosurgery, 1988—93. Asst. prof. dept. neurosurgery P. S. Govindaswamy Inst. Med. Scis., Coimbatore, India, 1994—97; assoc. prof. & head P. S. Govindaswamy Hosps. & P. S. Govindaswamy Inst. Med. Scis. & Rsch., Coimbatore, 1997—2002; chief neurosurgeon & head dept. neurosurgery Miot Hosps., Chennai, India, 2003—. Contbr. articles to profl. jours. Project helmet team leader Rotary Coimbatore Manchester, Coimbatore, 2001—03. Recipient 356th Shinshu Meml. Seminar award, Shinshu U., 2000, Rashtriya Ratna Shiromani award for contribution in field, Modern India Interaction Soc., 2003, Rashtriya Pratibha award, Integrated Coun. Socio-Economic Progress, 2004; grantee Advanced Spinal fellowship, Inselspital Hosp., U. Berne, 2005. Mem.: Congress Neurol. Surgeons(US), Internat. Assn. Orthopaedicians Spine Soc. (corr.), Skull Base Soc. India (life), Asian Congress Neurol. Surgeons (life), Neurotrauma Soc. India (life; organizing sec. 2001—02), Indian Med. Assn. (life), Neurol. Soc. India (life). Hindu. Avocations: photography, painting. Home: 3a 4th St Srinagar Colony Pnpudur Po Tamil Nadu Coimbatore 641 041 India Office: Miot Hosps 4/112 Mount Poonamale Road Manapakkam Tamil Nadu Chennai 600089 India Office Fax: 91 44 2249 1188. Business E-Mail: miot@vsnl.com.

SRIVASTAVA, ANJANA, agricultural studies educator; b. Kanpur, India, Apr. 14, 1961; PhD, Kanpur U., 1981. Assoc. prof. G.B.Pant U. Agr. & Tech., 1999—. Office: Coll Basic Sci & Humanities Pantnagar Uttarakhand 263145 India Personal E-mail: anj612003@yahoo.co.in.

SRIVASTAVA, SANJEEVA, engineering educator, researcher; b. Uttar Pradesh, India, Aug. 2, 1977; PhD, U. Alta., Can., 2006. Postdoc. Harvard Med. Sch., 2008; PI & group leader, Proteomics Rsch. Lab. Indian Inst. Tech., 2009, asst. prof., 2009—. Recipient Young Scientist Footstep award, Coun. Biotech. Info., Can., Apple Rsch. Tech. award, Eng., Young Scientist award, Dept. Atomic Energy-BRNS, India; SERC Fast Track Young Scientists grant, Dept. Sci. & Tech. Mem.: US HUPO. Office: Indian Inst Tech Mumbai Powai Mumbai Maharshtra 400076 India Office Phone: 91-22-25767779. Business E-Mail: sanjeeva@iitb.ac.in.

STAAS, WILLIAM E., JR., hospital administrator, physiatrist; b. Phila., 1936; BS, Phila. Coll. Pharmacy and Sci.; MD, Jefferson Med. Coll., 1962. Cert. in physical medicine and rehab. 1970. Intern Mercy Hosp., Darby, Pa., 1962-63; resident in phys. medicine and rehab. U. Pa. Hosp., 1965-68; attending physiatrist Magee Rehab. Hosp., Phila., pres., CEO, med. dir., 1977—2006; co-associate dir. ongoing care, regional spinal cord injury ctr. Delaware Valley Jefferson U. Hosp., Phila. Prof. rehab. medicine Jefferson Med. Coll; dir. med. advisory bd. Bayada Nursing Contbr. articles to profl. jours. Named one of Top docs, Phila. mag. Mem.: ACP, AMA, Am. Spinal Injury Assn. Office: Magee Rehab Hosp 1513 Race St Philadelphia PA 19102-1177

STAATS, ARTHUR W., psychology professor; b. Jan. 17, 1924; BA in Psychology, UCLA, 1949, MA in Psychology, 1953, PhD in Gen. Exptl. and Clin. Psychology, 1956. Psychologist UCLA Counseling Ctr., Los Angeles, 1950-53; clin. trainee VA Hosps., Los Angeles, 1953-55; instr. psychology Ariz. State U., Tempe, 1955-56, asst. prof., 1956-58, assoc. prof., 1958-60, prof., 1960-64; NSF faculty fellow U. London, 1961-62; vis. prof. U. Calif., Berkeley, 1964 65; prof. ednl. psychology and research U. Wis. Research and Devel. Ctr. Cognitive Learning, Madison, 1965-67; vis. prof. U. Hawaii, Honolulu, 1966-67, prof. psychology and ednl. psychology, 1967—. Author Complex Human Behavior, 1963, Learning, Language and Cognition, 1968, Child Learning, Intelligence, and Personality: A Behavioral Interaction Approach, 1971, Social Behaviorism, 1975, Psychology's Crisis of Disunity: Philosophy and Method for a Unified Science, 1983, Behavior and Personality: Psychological Behaviorism, 1996; editor Human Learning, 1964, Current Issues in Theoretical Psychology, 1987, Annals of Theoretical Psychology, Vol. 5, 1987; contbr. over 80 articles to profl. jours. and 61 chpts. to books; editl. bd. 9 Am. and internat. jours. Named in his honor, Arthur W. Staats Unifying Psychology lectr. (annually); named one of 20 People Who Changed Childhood, CHILD, 2006. Fellow AAAS, Am. Psychol. Soc., APA (gen. psychology divsn., exptl. psychology divsn., devel. psychology divsn., personality and social psychology divs., clin. psychology divsn., ednl. psychology divsn., theoretical and philos. psychology divsn., exptl. analysis of behavior divsn.); mem. Sociedad Interamericana de Psicologia, Psychonomic Soc., Assn. Latinoamericana del Analisis y Modificacion del Comportamiento, Soc. for Exptl. Social Psychology. Home: 1460 Kamole St Honolulu HI 96821-1422 Office: U Hawaii Dept Psychology Honolulu HI 96822 Home Phone: 808-373-4630; Office Phone: 808-377-3195, 8083773184. Business E-Mail: staats@aloha.com.

STAATS, THOMAS ELWYN, neuropsychologist; s. Percy Anderson and Julia (Bourmorck) S.; m. Debra R.; children: Lauren Malu, Kara Kristyn, Stacy Rhnea, Ronald Derek. BA cum laude, Emory U., 1970; MA, U. Ala., 1972, PhD, 1974; postgrad., U. Tex., Tyler, 1992. Diplomate Am. Bd. Profl. Disability Cons.; lic. psychologist. Dir., chief psychologist Caddo Parish Diagnostic Ctr., Shreveport, La., 1974-81; exec. dir. Doctors Psychol. Ctr., Shreveport, 1979-91, Comprehensive Assessments, 1991—. Cons. to Charter Forest Hosp., 1989-2000, Shreveport Impairment and Disability Evaluation Ctr., 1993—; clin. assoc. prof. psychology La. State U., Shreveport, 1977-1990; clin. assoc. prof. psychiatry La. State U. Sch. Medicine, Shreveport, 1980-92, 2003—; neuropsychol. cons. to dept. psychiatry, 1992-2002; mem. faculty Am. Acad. Disability Evaluating Physicians, 1986—, Health South Impairment Evaluation Lectr. Series, 1998—. Author: Manual for the Stress Vector Analysis Test Series, 1983, The Doctors Guide to Instant Stress Relief, 1987, Stress Management and Relaxation Training System Handbook; contbr. articles to profl. jours. and popular mags. Mem. Gov.'s Com. of 1000, La., 1979. Recipient AADEP award, 1991; Grad. Rsch. Coun. fellow, 1974. Fellow Am. Inst. Stress; mem. APA, Nat. Acad. Neuropsychology, Nat. Register of Health Svc. Providers, Am. Acad. Neuropsychology. Episcopalian. Avocations: scuba diving, gun collecting, camping, boating, paintball competition. Home: 4 Beaux Rivages Dr Shreveport LA 71106 Office: 4300 Youree Dr Ste 200 Shreveport LA 71105 Office Phone: 318-861-0194. Personal E-mail: drtomstaats@bellsouth.net.

STABELL, ULF, psychologist, educator; b. Ålesund, Norway, July 31, 1938; s. Rolf and Reidun (Christensen) S.; m. Kari Berg, June 21, 1963; children: Sindre, Njål. Psychology, Univ. Oslo, Oslo, Norway, 1966. Rsch. scholar Norwegian Coun. for Social Sci. and the Humanities, Oslo, 1967-75; researcher Nansen Found., Oslo, 1975-86; govt. scholarship Norway, 1986—. Contbr. articles to profl. jours. Recipient Rsch. grant Norwegian Coun. Social Sci. and Humanities, 1967-75, Nansen Found., 1975-86. Avocations: skiing, mountain climbing, philosophy study. Office: U Oslo Inst Psychology PO Box 1094 N-0317 Blindern Norway

STABILE, BRUCE EDWARD, surgeon; b. Monterey Park, California, Apr. 14, 1944; s. Edward Emilio and Angela (Tramantozzi) S.; m.

Caroline Graston, Sept. 18, 1967; children: Jessica, Drew. BA, UCLA, 1966; MD, U. Calif., San Francisco, 1970. Diplomate Am. Bd. Surgery. From assoc. prof. to prof. vice chmn. dept. surgery Sch. Medicine U. Calif., San Diego, 1985—93; from asst. prof. to assoc. prof. Sch. Medicine UCLA, 1977—85, vice chmn. dept. surgery Sch. Medicine, 1993—. Chmn. dept. surgery Harbor UCLA Med. Ctr., Torrance, 1993—, acting med. dir., 1997-98; interim assoc. dean UCLA Sch. Medicine, 1997-98; med. expert Med. Bd. Calif., 1980—; bd. dirs. Am. Bd. Surgery, 1998-2004. Mem. editl. bd.: Jour. Surg. Rsch., 1993—97, Archives of Surgery, 1991—2004. Fellow, ACS (gov. 2001-07, pres. So. Calif. chpt. 2005-06), Am. Surg. Assn.; mem. Soc. Univ. Surgeons, Assn. Acad. Surgery, Am. Gastroenterol. Assn., San Diego Soc. Gen. Surgeons (pres. 1992-93), L.A. Surg. Soc. (pres. 2000-01), Pacific Coast Surg. Assn. (pres. 2007-08). Office: Harbor U Calif at L A Med Ctr 1000 W Carson St Torrance CA 90502-2004 Office Phone: 310-222-2701. Business E-Mail: bstabile@ucla.edu.

STABILE, JOHN R., ophthalmologist, educator; MD, NY Med. Coll., 1976. Diplomate Am. Bd. of Ophthalmology, lic. NJ, 1979. Intern Lincoln Med. & Mental Health Ctr., 1977; resident St. Luke's Roosevelt Hosp., 1980; fellow Columbia Univ. Coll. of Physicians & Surgeons, 1981; clin. prof. ophthalmology Columbia P&S; with Holy Name Med. Ctr. Office: Englewood Hospital and Medical Center 350 Engle St Englewood NJ 07631 Office Phone: 201-894-3000.

STACEY, RULON F., health facility administrator; m. Linda Stacey; children: Laura, Maria, Jennifer, Catherine. BS in Economics, Brigham Young U., 1984, MHA, 1986; PhD in Pub. Adminstrn., U. Colo., 2000. CEO St. Vincent Gen. Hosp., Leadville, Colo., Summit Med. Ctr., Frisco, Colo.; asst. adminstr. Ninth Strategic Hosp., Beale AFB, Calif.; exec. v.p., COO St. Francis Hosp. and Health Sys., Chgo., 1994—96; pres., CEO Poudre Valley Health System, 1996—. Dir. Poudre Valley Health Sys. Host of blog, visionary.pvhs.org (visionary healthcare); author: Over Our Heads. Bd. dirs. Fort Collins C. of C., Poudre Sch. Dist. Found., Fort Collins Better Bus. Bur.; mem. exec. adv. bd. U. Colo. Grad. Sch. of Bus.; mem. Nat. Eagle Scout Assn.; mem. President's adv. com. Colo. State U. Named Northern Colorado Bus. Leader of the Yr., Fort Collins Coloradoan, 2005, Entrepreneur of the Yr., The Northern Colorado Bus. Report; named one of 12 Young Rising Stars of the healthcare adminstrn. profession in the country "up and comer", Modern Healthcare Mag., 1992, 100 Most Influential People in Healthcare, Modern Healthcare, 2011; Milstein Scholar, U. Colorado-Denver, 2000. Mem.: American Hosp. Assn. (mem. of regent for Colo., Colo. delegate, regional policy bd. region 8 2003—06, bd. trustee com. on governance 2004—07), Colo. Health & Hosp. Assn. (bd. dirs.), Colo. Bioscience Assn. (bd. dirs.), American Coll. Healthcare Executives (gov. 2007, chmn. governing bd. 2011—12, regent, Robert S. Hudgens award as Young Healthcare Exec. of Yr. 1999). Office: Poudre Valley Health System 2315 E Harmony Rd Ste 200 Fort Collins CO 80528

STACHON, AXEL, physician, researcher; b. Luenen, Germany, Jan. 1, 1968; s. Peter Stachon and Beate Loeer-Jargolla; m. Andrea Stachon, Oct. 15, 1993 (div. June 2004); children: Lucas, Felix. MD, Westfalen U., 1995. Cert. lab medicine Med. Assn. Westfalen-Lippe, Germany, in transfusion sys. Med. Assn. Westfalen-Lippe, Germany, med. specialist lab. medicine Med. Assn. Westfalen-Lippe, Germany. Asst. physician Clinic Internal Medicine Westfaelische-Wilhelms-University of Munster, Germany, 1995—97; asst. dir. Inst. Clin. Chemistry, Transfusion and Lab. Medicine Ruhr-U. Bochum, Germany, 1997—2001, asst. med. dir. Inst. Clin. Chemistry, Transfusion and Lab. Medicine, 2002—, supr. of the prodn. of blood preparations, 2002—. Cons. in lab. medicine, Bochum, 2002; tchr. Sch. for Med./Tech. Assts., Bochum, 1997—. Scholar, German Pub., 1990—91. Mem.: German Soc. for Lab. Medicine (assoc.). Roman Catholic. Achievements include the first successful isolation and primary culture of microvascular endothelial cells from the human prostate; research in analytical investigation of nucleated red blood cells in adults. Office: Inst Clin Chem Transf Lab Med Buerkle-de-la-Camp-Platz 1 44789 Bochum Germany Office Fax: xx49-234-302-6614. E-mail: axel.stachon@rub.de.

STACHOWIAK, MICHAL KACPER, science educator; b. Suwalki, Poland, Jan. 5, 1950; PhD, Gdans Med. Sch., 1980. Prof. SUNY, Buffalo, 1998—. Grant, NYSTEM. Mem.: Am. Soc. Neuroscis. Avocation: music. Office: SUNY 206A Farber Hall Buffalo NY 14214 Office Fax: 716-829-2911. Business E-Mail: mks4@buffalo.edu.

STACK, STEVEN JOSEPH, emergency physician; b. Cleve. m. Tracie Stack; 1 child. Grad. magna cum laude, Coll. Holy Cross, Worcester, Mass.; MD, Ohio State U., Columbus, 1998. Diplomate American Bd. Emergency Medicine. Intern, resident Ohio State U. Hosp., 1998—2001; emergency physician, med. dir. emergency dept. Baptist Meml. Hosp., Memphis, 2001—06; emergency medicine physician St. Joseph Hosp. East, Lexington, Ky., 2006—, chair, med. dir. Dept. Emergency Medicine, 2006—10. Mem.: AMA (bd. trustees 2006—, sec. 2010—11, chair-elect 2011—), Ohio State Med. Assn., Emergency Medicine Residents' Assn. Office: St Joseph Hosp East Dept Emergency Medicine 150 N Eagle Creek Dr Lexington KY 40509 Office Phone: 859-967-5176. Office Fax: 859-967-5784. *

STACY, MARK ALLEN, neurologist; b. Cape Girardeau, Mo., May 4, 1959; s. Billy Wayn and Jane Cooper S.; m. Tina Estrada, June 26, 1982; children: Bryan, Andrea. BS, S.E. Mo. State, 1981; MD, U. Mo., 1986. Diplomate Am. Bd. Neurology and Psychiatry. Intern in internal medicine St. Mary's Hosp., St. Louis, 1986-87; resident in neurology Hahnemann U., Phila., 1987-90, chief resident, 1989-90, clin. instr., 1989-90; asst. prof. neurology U. Mo., 1991-96, dir. Parkinson's Disease Clinic and Movement Disorders Ctr., 1992-96; neurologist Barrow Neurol. Inst., St. Joseph's Hosp., 1996, dir. Muhammad Ali Parkinson Rsch. Ctr., 1997; assoc. prof. neurology, dir. movement disorders prog. Duke U., Durham, NC, dir. Neurology Clin. Rsch. Ctr. Cons. neurology Harry S. Truman Meml. Vet. Hosp., 1991-96; adv. bd. DuPont Pharma, 1996—, Athena Pharm., 1997—; SmithKline Beecham, 1999, Elan Pharm., 1999; assoc. med. dir. Nat. Parkinson Found., 1997—; mem. Dystonia Study Group 1996—, Parkinson Study Group, 1997—, WeMove, LME, adv. com., 1998—.

Author: (chpt.) Current Pediatric Therapy, Vol. 16, 1999; co-author: (chpt.) Current Therapy in Neurologic Disease-3, 1990, Pathology of the Aging Nervous System, 1991, Neurobehavioral Aspects of Parkinson's Disease, 1992, Movement and Allied Disorders in Childhood, 1995, Adult Neurology, 1997, Textbook of Clinical Neurology, 1998; ed.: The Handbook of Dystonia; mem. editl. bd. Neurology Network Commentary, 1996—, Movement Disorders, 1997—; editl. bd. Southern Medical Jour. ad hoc reviewer, 1999—; contbr. articles to profl. jours. Mem. counseling staff Mo. Boys State, 1979—, dean of counselors, 1993—, bd. dirs., 1993—; mem. adv. bd. Physician's Home Health & Hospice Network, 1993-95, WE Move, 1998—; advisor Greater Mo. Tourette Syndrome Chpt., 1991-96, Am. Parkinson's Disease Assn., Columbia, Mo., 1992-96, bd. dirs. Fight Night Found., 1999—, Dystonia Med. Rsch. Found., 1993-96, Multiple Sclerosis Inst., 1993-96, Benign Essential Blepharospasm Found., 1997—; bd. deacons First Bapt. Ch., Columbia, 1995-96; mem. Internation Congress of Parkinsons Disease. 1999. Recipient Outstanding Young Alumni award S.E. Mo. State U., 1995, Caregivers award Nat. Parkinson Found.; Movement Disorders fellow Baylor Coll. Medicine, 1990-91; grantee DuPont Pharma, 1992, 93, Childrens Miracle Network Telethon, 1993, Sandoz Pharm., 1993, Berlex Pharm., 1994, Allergan, Inc., 1995-96, MDS Harris and Scherer DDS, 1997, Eli Lilly Pharm., 1997-98, Amgen, Inc., 1997, 98, Smith Kline Beecham, 1998—, NIH, 1998—, Pentech Pharm., Inc., 1999, Teva Pharm. USA, 1999, Roberts Pharm., 1999, others. Mem. Am. Acad. Neurology (movement disorders sect. 1995—, liaison com. 1995—), Movement Disorders Soc., Ariz. State Med. Assn., Maricopa County Med. Soc. Office: DUMC 3333 Durham NC 27710 Office Phone: 919-668-7600, 919-668-2493. Office Fax: 919-681-4935.

STADDON, ARTHUR P., oncologist, educator; MD, U. Pa. Diplomate Am. Bd. Internal Medicine, 1975, Am. Bd. Internal Medicine-hematology, 1979, Am. Bd. Internal Medicine-med. oncology, 1979. Intern Hosp. of Univ. Pa., resident, fellow; dir., Joan Karnell cancer ctr. Pa. Hosp., dir., sarcoma program; clin. prof., Univ. Pa. Univ. Pa. Named one of Best Doctors in America, 2005—06, 2007—08, 2009—10, Top Docs, Phila. Mag., 2008, 2011, Top Physicians, Suburban Life Mag., 2010. Mem.: ACP, Sarcoma Alliance for Rsch. through Collaboration (SARC), Connective Tissue Oncology Soc. (CTOS), Am. Soc. of Clin. Oncology. Office: Joan Karnell Cancer Center at Pennsylvania Hospital Farm Journal Bldg First Fl 230 W WA Sq Philadelphia PA 19106 Office Phone: 215-829-6466.

STADELMANN, WAYNE KARL, plastic surgeon; b. Milw., Wis., July 17, 1964; MD (with honors), U. Chgo.-Pritzker Sch. Medicine, 1990. Cert. Am. Bd. Plastic Surgery. Intern, gen. surgery U. Chgo. Hosp. & Clinics, 1990—91, resident, gen. surgery, 1991—94; resident, plastic surgery South Fla. Coll. Medicine, Tampa, Fla., 1994—97; joined staff Concord Hosp., NH, 2003—, New London Hosp., 2005—; private practice Stadelmann Plastic Surgery, PC, NH. Named one of Top Doctor, NH Mag. Mem.: Phi Beta Kappa. Office: Stadelmann Plastic Surgery PC 246 Pleasant St Ste 210 Concord NH 03301-2548 Office Phone: 603-224-5200. Office Fax: 603-224-5091.

STADING, JULIE A., pharmacist, educator; b. Omaha, Nov. 4, 1964; d. Jerry Dean Mathers and Phyllis Ann Garvey; m. Jeffrey Stading, June 21, 1986; children: Kelly, Michelle, Zac, T.J. DPharm, Creighton U., 1991. Registered pharmacist, cert. diabetes educator. Fellow cardiac rsch. Creighton Cardiac Ctr., Omaha, 1991—92, asst. clin. rschr., 1992—94, adminstrv. dir. clin. rsch., 1994—96; mgr. med. edn. cardio rschr. Bayer Pharm., West Haven, Conn., 1996—98; asst. prof. pharmacy practice Creighton U., Omaha, 1998—2005, assoc. prof. pharmacy practice, 2005—. Clin. coord. studies Creighton Cardiac Ctr., 1992—96. Contbr. articles to profl. jours.; reviewer: Am. Coll. Clin. Pharmacy, reviewer: Am. Jour. Pharm. Edn., reviewer: Am. Soc. Health-Sys. Pharmacists, reviewer: Am. Hosp. Formulary Svc. Mem. Eagle-Waverly PTA, 1999—2006; Sunday sch. tchr. Meth. Ch., Waverly, Nebr., 1999—, Edn. Dist. #145, Nebr., 2005—10. Grantee, Upjogn Co., 1993—94, Mass. Vet. Epidemiology Rsch., 2000—03, Bristol-Meyers-Squibb, 2001; CEgGrant, Glaxo-Smith-Kline, 2004, Rsch. grant, 2008—09. Mem.: Am. Coll. Clin. Pharmacy, Am. Assn. Coll. Pharmacy, Am. Soc. Health-Sys. Pharmacists. Methodist. Avocations: painting, horseback riding, himalayan persian cats, sports. Office: Creighton Univ 2500 California Plaza Omaha NE 68178 Office Phone: 402-280-3143. Business E-Mail: juliestading@creighton.edu.

STADLER, SELISE MCNEILL, laboratory and x-ray technician, medical assistant; b. Portsmouth, Va., Dec. 27, 1960; d. William M. and Jorja Lee (Rigg) Gaidos; m. Stephen Michael McNeill, Feb. 29, 1988 (div. July 1993); 1 child, Stephen Michael Jr.; m. David Robert Stadler, June 15, 1996. Cert. chiropractic asst., Practice Mgmt. Assn., 1983; student, Tarrant County Coll., 2000—01. Cert. limited radiologic technologist, instr. cert. World Modeling Assn. Chiropractic asst. Dr. Brad Hayes, DC, Tulsa, Okla., 1982-84; adminstrv. asst. Dr. Wallace Gauntner, MD, Pitts., 1984; traffic mgr., office mgr. WVBS-AM/FM, Wilmington, NC, 1985-87; med. asst. Dr. J. Bailey Bland, DC, Wilmington, 1988-90; therapy/radiology supr. Dr. Roy L. Creasy Jr., DC, Wilmington, 1990-91; med. asst., radiologist Westside Clinic, Dallas, 1991-94; model, exec. instr. Aleksaundra's Prodns., Ft. Worth, 1994-96; med. asst., radiologist Dr. Wayne R. English Jr., DO, Ft. Worth, 1994-2000; lab/x-ray technician, med. asst. Care Now, Ft. Worth, 2001—02; x-ray/bone scan technician Kaner Med. Group, Bedford, Tex., 2001—02; med. asst., x-ray tech. Premier Orthopedics, Dr. Craig Saunders, MD and Dr. Marvin Van Hal, MD, 2002—07; x-ray tech., med. asst. HEB Bone & Joint Surgeons, Dr. Daniel Foster & Dr. Frank Swords, 2007—. Author published poetry. Vol. Holy Family Cath. Ch., Ft. Worth, 1997-99. Recipient Employee Excellence award, Aleksaundra's Prodns., 1996. Mem. Tex. Soc. Radiologic Technologists (cert. in CPR and automated external defibrillation program), Am. Soc. Radiologic Technologists, Fort Worth Astronomy Club. Episcopalian. Avocations: scuba diving, tennis, rollerblading, photography. Home Phone: 817-304-9713; Office Phone: 817-540-1185.

STAFANOUS, SABAH NAEM, ophthalmologist, consultant; b. Dongla, Sudan, May 15, 1958; arrived in Eng., 1987; d. Naem Stafanous and Nagia Musad; m. Kameel Fawzi Sorial; children: George, Rozita, Marita, Antony. MBBS with distinction, U. Khar-

toum, 1978; DO, U. Glasgow, 1988. Specialist tng. Gen. Med. Coun., 1999. House officer Khartoum (Sudan) Tchg. Hosp., 1978—79; gen. practitioner Security Forces Clinic, Libya, 1979—81; med. officer and registrar Khartoum (Sudan) Eye Hosp., 1981—84; gen. practitioner Security Forces Hosp., Saudi Arabia, 1985—87; sr. resident Dammam Ctrl. Hosp., Saudi Arabia, 1988—91; house officer and registrar Paisley, Wakefield & Sidcup, Kent, England, 1991—94; specialist registrar No. Deanery, Newcastle, England, 1994—99; fellow in oculoplastics Cardiff (Wales) U., 1999; cons. ophthalmologist Sheffield Royal Hallamshire Hosp., England, 1999—2004, Chesterfield Royal Hosp., 1999—. Fellow: Royal Coll. Ophthalmologists; mem.: Hosp. Cons. and Specialists Assn., Brit. Occuloplastic Soc., Medica Def. Union. Coptic Orthodox. Avocations: cooking, sewing, reading. Office: Calow S44 5BL Chesterfield England Office Phone: 441246513709.

STAFFA, ROBERT, surgeon; married. MD, Palacký U., Olomouc, Czech Republic, 1987; PhD, Masaryk U., Brno, Czech Republic, 1999. Postgrad. diploma in general surgery Ministry of Health, Czech Republic, 1990, 1997, postgrad. diploma in vascular surgery 2000. Prof. surgery faculty medicine Masaryk U., mem. bd. tech. devel. faculty medicine, head, 2nd dept. surgery St. Anne's U. Hosp., Faculty Medicine, 2009—. Contbr. articles to profl. jour. Recipient Masaryk U. Chancellor award, 2006; fellowship, U. Vienna, 1993, 1998, Southwestern Med. Ctr., Dallas, 2003. Mem.: Czech Soc. Hepatic, Pancreatic and Biliary Surgery, Czech Soc. Angiology, Czech Surgery Assn., Czech Soc. Cardiovasc. Surgery (award 2005—06), European Soc. Vascular Surgery. Office: St Anne's Univ Hosp Pekarská 53 Brno 656 91 Czech Republic Office Phone: 420 604 585 969. Business E-Mail: robert.staffa@fnusa.cz.

STAFFEN, WOLFGANG, neurologist; b. Zell a See, Salzburg, Austria, Nov. 8, 1959; s. Alfred and Gudrun (Heiss) Staffen. MD, U. Vienna, 1986; cert. med. specialist in neurology, Christian Doppler Klinik, Salzburg, 1994. Neurologist Christian Doppler Klinik, 1988—; univ. docent. Contbr. articles to profl. jours. Recipient prize, Wilfried-Haslauer-Solidaritaetsfond, 1995, Med. Rsch. award, Salzburg-Cultural-Found., 1997. Mem.: Austrian Soc. Clin. Neurophysiology (Best Paper award 2002), Austrian Soc. Functional MRT. Avocations: neuroscience, bicycling. Office: Christian Doppler Klinik Ignaz Harrerstrasse 79 5020 Salzburg Austria Home Phone: 0043-664-3811369; Office Phone: 0043-662-44830. Business E-Mail: w.staffen@salk.at.

STAFFIER, PAMELA MOORMAN, psychologist; b. Passaic, NJ, Dec. 7, 1942; d. Wynant Clair and Jeannette Frances (Rentzsch) Moorman; m. John Staffier, Jr., Apr. 5, 1975; children: M. Anthony, C. Matthew. BA, Bucknell U., 1964; MA in Psychology, Assumption Coll., Worcester, Mass., 1970, CAGS, 1977; PhD, Union U., 1978. Psychologist Westboro (Mass.) State Hosp., 1965, prin. psychologist, dir. program planning & devel., 1973—76; rsch. psychologist Wrentham (Mass.) State Sch., 1966, Cushing Hosp., Framingham, Mass., 1967; prin. psychologist, dir. program planning & devel. Grafton (Mass.) State Hosp., 1967—72; dir. Staffier Clinic, 1978—2008; clin. dir. Moriarty Mental Health Clinic, 1975—78; cons. & sup. Agents of Change Counseling, 2009—. Mem.: APA, Nat. Register Health Svc. Providers Psychology, Mass. Psychol. Assn., Am. Psychol. Practitioners Assn. (founding mem.). Achievements include research in state hospital closings; biochemical basis of schizophrenia. Home: 68 Adams St Westborough MA 01581 Office: 45 Lyman St Westborough MA 01581-1464 Office Phone: 508-366-2300. Personal E-mail: johnstaffier@verizon.net.

STAFFORD, ARTHUR CHARLES, medical association administrator, insurance agent; b. Cleve., May 10, 1947; s. Charles Arthur and Florence Mildred (Hovey) S.; m. Patricia Anne Cz, Dec. 20, 1991. BS, Kent State U., 1977; MBA, Lake Erie Coll., 1984. Med. tech. VA, Cleve., 1977-81, supr. med. tech., 1981-97; lab. mgr. Univ. Hosps. Health System Meml. Hosp. of Geneva, Ohio, 1998-99; instr. Lake Erie Coll., Painesville, Ohio, 1980-82; mgr. customer svc. Giant Eagle Supermarket, Madison, Ohio, 2001—02; instr. Cuyahoga C.C., Cleve., 1988-91, 2003—05; preferred team Progressive Ins. Co., Highland Heights, 2004—. Pres. Kent State U. Veterans Assn., 1974, mem. Kent State U Budget Review Com., 1975. Contbr. articles to profl. jour. Mem. Am. Legion, 1974, VFW, 1973. With USN, 1968-72. Mem.: Rock and Roll Hall of Fame, Founders Club. Republican. Avocations: genealogy, antiques, chess, cooking, computers. Home: 2193 Chimney Ridge Dr Madison OH 44057-2588 Personal E-mail: czstafford@gmail.com.

STAGE, GINGER ROOKS, psychologist; b. Allentown, Pa., Sept. 23, 1946; d. John Myers Rooks and Catherine Estelle (Graser) Rooks Bistritz; m. Robert Roy Stage, Aug. 23, 1969; 1 child, Stephen. BA in Psychology magna cum laude, Moravian Coll., Bethlehem, Pa., 1968; MA in Psychology, Temple U., Phila., 1969. Lic. psychologist, Pa.; cert. clin. hypnotherapist Nat. Bd. Clin. Hypnotherapists; cons. Group I Host, 2005-. Instr. Beaver campus Pa. State U., Monaca, 1969-74; staff psychologist St. Francis Cmty. Mental Health Ctr., Pitts., 1974-83; pvt. practice family therapy Coraopolis, Pa., 1977—. Mem. Greenstein Family Therapy Consultation Group, Pitts., 1981-2000; mem., spkr. Human Sexuality Alliance, Pitts., 1989-91; spkr. in field. Mem. Greater Pitts. Psychol. Assn., Western Pa. Family Ctr. Anglican. Avocations: needlecrafts, guitar, walking, horseback riding, exercise. Home: 112 Wessex Hills Dr Coraopolis PA 15108-1021 Office: 409 Mill St Coraopolis PA 15108-1607

STAGER, SHEILA VEITCH, speech pathology/audiology services professional, director; b. Oakville, Ont., Can., Nov. 20, 1956; PhD, U. Tex., Dallas, 1985. IRTA postdoc. fellow, sr. fellow Nat. Inst. Deafness and Other Communication Disorders, 1988—95; dir. rsch. Voice Treatment Ctr., Med. Faculty Assocs., 1998—. Adj. prof., dept. surgery George Wash. U. Med. Sch., 2007. Mem.: Am. Speech-Lang.-Hearing Assn. Avocations: singing, exercise, reading. Home: 12103 Quick Fox Ln Bowie MD 20720 Business E-Mail: sstager@mfa.gwu.edu.

STAGGERS, BARBARA C., pediatrician; MD, U. Calif., San Francisco, 1980. Diplomate Am. Bd. Pediatrics-adolescent medicine, 2003. Fellow adolescent medicine Univ. of Calif., San Francisco, 1983—85; resident pediat. Children's Hosp. and Rsch. Ctr., Oakland,

1982—83, pediatrician. Named one of the Best Doctors in America, Best Doctors Inc., 2007. Office: Children's Hospital and Research Center 400 Telegraph Ave Oakland CA 94609 Office Phone: 510-428-3387. Office Fax: 510-428-3710.

STAGNARO-GREEN, ALEX, medical educator; MD, Mt. Sinai Sch. Medicine, 1983; MHPE, U. Ill., Chgo., 2005. Dean student affairs & med. edn. Mt. Sinai Sch. Medicine, acting chmn. dept. med. edn.; prof. obstetrics, gynecology & women's health NJ Med. Sch., assoc. dean for curriculum & faculty devel., sr. assoc. dean for edn.; sr. assoc. dean academic affairs Touro U. Coll. Medicine. Mem.: Assn. Am. Med. Coll., Nat. Bd. Med. Examiners, Acad. Med. Educators (chmn.). Office: Touro University College of Medicine PO Box 633 New York NY 10159-0633 Office Phone: 201-883-9320 ext. 2010. E-mail: alex.stagnaro-green@touro.edu.

STAGNI, GRAZIA, medical educator; b. Molinella, Italy, Oct. 11, 1956; PhD, U. Tex., Austin, 1994. Assoc. prof. LI U., 2000—. Pharmacy Faculty New Investigator grant, AACP-Am. Found. Pharm. Edn. Mem.: Am. Assn. Pharm. Scientists. Office: 75 DeKalb Ave Brooklyn NY 11231 Business E-Mail: gstagni@liu.edu.

STAHL, RICHARD SHELDON, surgeon; b. Chattanooga, Tenn., Dec. 8, 1950; s. Paul and Alena S. BA in Physics, Emory U., 1972; MD, Vanderbilt U., 1976; MBA, U. New Haven, 1994. Diplomate Nat. Bd. Med. Examiners, Am. Bd. Surgery, Am. Bd. Plastic Surgery. Intern, asst. resident dept. surgery Yale U. Sch. Medicine, New Haven, 1976-80, chief resident, 1980-81; resident plastic and reconstructive surgery Emory U. Sch. Medicine, 1981-82, chief resident, 1982-83; instr. surgery Yale U. Sch. Medicine, 1980-81, asst. prof. plastic surgery, 1983-89, assoc. prof. plastic surgery, 1989-90, assoc. clin. prof. plastic surgery, 1991-95, clin. prof. plastic surgery, 1995—, attending physician Yale Vascular Ctr., 1986-90, chmn. telemedicine com., 1998—2001; attending physician dept. surgery Yale-New Haven Hosp., 1980-81, 83—, asst. med. dir. surgery emergency svcs., 1983-90, attending physician surg. ICU, 1986-88, dir. internat. ops. dept. surgery, 1995—99, assoc. chief dept. surgery, 1994—2006, exec. dir., perioperative svc., 2002—06, v.p., ambulatory svcs., 2006—; attending physician Hosp. St. Raphael, 1983—; ptnr., pvt. practice Thoracic Healing Solutions, Guilford, Conn. Founding co-dir. Yale Breast Care Ctr., 1989-90; cons. physicians assoc. surg. residency program Yale U.-Norwalk Hosp., 1978-81; resident surgeon Hospital Albert Schweitzer, Deschapelles, Haiti, 1980; med. mgmt. cons. Yale-New Haven Health Sys., 1997-98; program dir. of clin. telemedicine of NASA Comml. Space Ctr. at yale, 1997-2000; spkr. in field. Sports reporter The Chattanooga Times, 1967-69; contbr. over 40 articles to profl. jours. Pres. Kingswood Homeowner's Assn., 1987-93; mem. Charter Oak Bassett Hound Club, 1981-90. Recipient Rsch. grant Charles W. Olise Fund, Rsch. grant Smith Kline and French Labs., Rsch. grant Kendall Co.; named one of Top Doctors in NY Met. area, NY mag., 2007, Redbook, McCall's., Martin Luther King Dream Builders award, Yale-New Haver Hosp., 2006 Fellow Am. Coll. Surgeons (mem. Conn. chpt.); mem. Am. Coll. Health Care Execs., AMA, Am. Assn. Plastic Surgeons, Am. Soc. Plastic and Reconstructive Surgeons, Am. Coll. Physician Execs., Am. Coll. Med. Quality, New Eng. Soc. Plastic and Reconstructive Surgeons (v.p. 1998-99, pres. 1999-2000), New Haven County Med. Soc., Conn. State Med. Soc. Office: Ambulatory Svcs Divsn #5B 60 Temple St New Haven CT 06510 also: 5 Durham Rd Guilford CT 06437 Office Phone: 203-458-4440.

STAIKOU, CHRYSSOULA, anesthesiologist, educator; b. Ioannina, Greece, Jan. 3, 1973; MD, Med. Sch., U. Thessaloniki, 1997; PhD, U. Athens. Gen. physician Health Ctr, Aitolikou, 1997—98; trainee Laiko Hosp., 1998—2003; staff anesthesiologist Aretaieio Hosp., U. Athens, 2003—04, instr. med. sch., 2005—. Avocations: reading, movies, exercise. Office: Vass Sophias 76 Athens Attiki 11528 Greece E-mail: c_staikou@yahoo.gr.

STAIR, THOMAS OSBORNE, physician, educator; b. Richmond, Va., Jan. 10, 1950; s. Frederick Rogers Jr. and Martha (Osborne) S.; m. Lucy Caldwell, Dec. 28, 1973; children: Rebecca Caldwell, Peter Caldwell. AB, U. N.C., 1971; MD, Harvard U., 1975. Diplomate Am. Bd. Emergency Medicine (examiner 1982-88). Residency dir. emergency dept. Georgetown U. Sch. Medicine, Washington, 1979-85, asst. dir. emergency dept., 1979-89, asst. dean for continuing med. edn., 1985-89, chair dept. emergency medicine, 1989-95; prof. U. Md., Balt., 1995-98; assoc. prof. Harvard Med. Sch., 1998—; attending emergency physician Brigham and Women's Hosp., Boston, 1998—. Co-author: Common Simple Emergencies, 1985, Emergency Medicine, 1997, Minor Emergencies, 1999. Recipient Excellence in Teaching award Emergency Medicine Residents Assn., 1986. Fellow Am. Coll. Emergency Physicians, Am. Acad. Emergency Medicine; mem. Soc. Acad. Emergency Medicine. Home: 46 Woodcliff Rd Newton MA 02461-1825 Office: 75 Francis St Boston MA 02115-6110 Home Phone: 617-928-3375; Office Phone: 617-732-5640. Business E-Mail: tstair@partners.org.

STAJCIC, ZORAN, surgeon; b. Belgrade, Serbia, Apr. 21, 1954; s. Zivota and Ljubica (Licina) S.; m. Dragoslava Mihailovic, Oct. 14, 1979 (div.); children: Nevena, Mina; m. Ljiljana Stojcev, Oct. 2000. D Stomatology, Faculty of Stomatology, Belgrade, 1979; MS, Faculty of Stomatology, 1983, PhD, 1990. Specialist oral and maxillofacial surgeon. Clin./rsch. asst. Faculty of Stomatology, 1979-83, lectr., 1983-87, sr. lectr., 1987-92, assoc. prof., 1992—2000; locum prof. Bristol Dental Hosp., England, 1994-95; asst. gen. dir. export-import Galenika a.d., 2001—03; prof. maxillofacial surgery Faculty of Medicine, Banja Luka BIH, 2000—07. Prof. oral implantology Faculty of Medicine, Novi Sad, 2001—07. Author: Anaesthesia in Stomatology, 1990, Glycerol and Streptomycin in the Treatment of Trigeminal Neuralgia, 1991, Maxillary Sinus in Surgery of Oro-Facial Region, 1992, Atlas of Oral Implantology, 2001; editor: Danubius Dental Jour., 2000-07; mem. editl. bd. Med. Sci. Monitor, Balkan Jour. Stomatology, Serbian Jour. Stomatology, Dentalart; contbr. articles to profl. jours. Fellow: Internat. Team Implantology, Alexander von Humboldt Found.; mem. European Assn. for Cranio-Maxillo-Facial Surgery (councillor), Internat. Assn. Oral and Maxillofacial Surgeons, Internat. Team for Implantology, Brit. Assn. of Oral and Maxillofacial Surgeons, European Assn. Osteointegration, European Acad. for Facial Plastic Surgery, Serbian Assn. Self-employed Physicians Dentists (pres. 2002-07), Serbian Med. Assn. (bd. dirs. 2001-04), Serbian Dental Chambre (dir. 2007-), Dental Implants Found., NY Acad. Scis. Office Phone: 381 113610651. Business E-Mail: beogradcentar@sbb.co.yu.

STALLONE, GEORGE R., neurophysiologist; b. Camden, NJ, Aug. 22, 1963; s. George Ralph and Rose Marie Anne Stallone. BS in Zoology, U. Md., 1989; D of Chiropractic, We. States Chirpractic Coll., 1994; postgrad. in clin. neurology, Logan Coll. Chiropractic, 1998. Cert. intraoperative neurophysiologic monitoring. Resident Triad Family Health, Hanover, Pa., 1995—96; intern Banister Chiropractic, Jacksonville, Fla., 1996—97; chiropractor pvt. practice, Nephi, Utah, 1998—2003; intraoperative neurophysiologist Teaneck, NJ, 2004—. Instr., rschr. Triad Family Health, 1995—96; rschr., lectr. Mind/Body Inst., Jacksonville, 1996—97. Sec. Ch. Men's Group, Mona, Utah, 2000—01. Mem.: Am. Soc. Electrophysiologists, Masons. Avocations: flying, scuba diving, skiing, martial arts. Home: PO BOX 4 Harrisonville NJ 08039-0004 E-mail: stallone@nebonet.com.

STALLONES, LORANN, epidemiologist, educator; b. San Francisco, May 6, 1952; MPH, U. Tex., 1975, PhD, 1982. Prof. Colo. State U., 1990—, dir. Colo. Injury Control Rsch. Ctr., 1995—, dir. Inst. Applied Prevention Rsch., dir. grad. degree program pub. health Colo. Sch. Pub. Health, 2007—. Recipient Prof. Laureate award, Coll. Natural Scis., Colo. State U., Faculty Excellence Rsch. award, Colo. Sch. Pub. Health. Fellow: Am. Coll. Epidemiology; mem.: APHA, Internat. Congress Occupl. and Environ. Epidemiology. Avocation: knitting. Office: Dept Psychology Sage Hall MS 1 Fort Collins CO 80523-1876 Office Fax: 970-491-0527. Business E-Mail: lorann@colostate.edu.

STALLWORTH, CHARLES DEROTHA, JR., psychologist; b. Riderwood, Ala., July 4, 1940; s. Charles D. and Annie (Horn) S. BS, Tenn. State U., Nashville, 1963, MS, 1966; postgrad., Calif. Sch. Profl. Psychology, 1977-79, U. South Ala., Mobile, 1967, Tuskegee Inst., 1968, U. Ky., Lexington, 1980; PhD in Psychology, Internat. Coll., 1983; cert. in mental disability law, N.Y. Law Sch., 2001. Diplomate Am. Bd. Psychotherapy, Am. Psychotherapy Assn., Am. Coll. Mental Health Practitioners, Am. Coll., Forensic Counselors, Acad. Cert. Neurotherapists. Psychiat. asst. Hubbard Hosp., Nashville, 1964-66; counselor, tchr. North Ctrl. H.S., Chatom, Ala., 1966-68; tchr. Washington County H.S., 1968—70; supr. adult edn. Washington County Bd. Edn., Chatom, 1968-70; dir. counseling ctr. Albany State Coll., Ga., 1970—91; pvt. practice, 1993—. Mem. staff Auburn U., summer 1969; counselor Spl. Svc. program Albany State Coll., 1992-93; cons. Peace Corps, 1979-81; dep. dir. gen. Internat. Biographical Ctr., Cambridge, Eng., 2004-. Contbr. articles to profl. jours. Bd. dirs. Dougherty County CODAC, Inc., Albany, 1973-77; hon. mem. Ga. Sheriff's Assn, citizen amb. People to People Internat., Kansas City, Mo. Recipient Eagle Scout award, Boy Scouts America, 1955, Internat. Poet of Merit award, 2003, Internat. Peace prize, United Cultural Consortium, 2002, Poet of Merit award, 2002—04, 2006, 2008; named Most Admired Man of Decade 90's, Bd. Internal Rsch., Am. Biog. Inst., 1992, Shield of Valor, Am. Biog. Inst., 1992; named one of Best Poems & Poets, Internat. Libr. Poetry, 2002; named to Hall of Fame, Am. Biog. Inst., 1985; grantee, HEW, 1970—77, US Office Edn., 1972. Mem. APA, Am. Psychotherapy Assn., Nat. Assn. Forensic. Counselors, Alpha Phi Alpha, Order of Arrow, Boy Scouts America. Achievements include research on impact of affective domain on learning outcomes and on application of cognitive therapies as a means of controlling negative effects. Home: 805 E 4th Ave Albany GA 31705-1203 Personal E-mail: charlesd260@yahoo.com.

STAMATELOU, KIRIAKI, nephrologist, director; d. Konstantinos Stamatelos and Marina Stamatelou; m. Konstantinos Sitaras, June 24, 1995. MD, Athens Med. Sch., Athens U., 1982—89; MS, MBA, Dept. of Health Planning and Mgmt., Keele U., UK, 1992; Splty. in Nephrology, Athens Med. Sch., 1992—96; PhD in Medicine, Athens Med. Sch., Athens U., 1996—2001. MD Hellenic Med. Assn., 1989, Nephrology Specialty Hellenic Nephrology Assn., 1996. MD Chania Gen. Hosp., Chania Crete, Greece, 1989—92; asst., nephrology dept. Veterans Hosp., Athens, Greece, 1992—96; rsch. assoc., divsn. of kidney, urologic and hematologic diseases NIH, Bethesda, Md., 1996—97; vis. assoc. nephrologist, spl. med. services The Royal Melbourne Hosp., Australia, 1998—99; assoc. nephrologist /quality assurance mgr., nephrology and dialysis unit Hygeia Hosp., Athens, 1999—2001; dir., nephrology/dialysis unit Kyanous Stavros Hosp., Athens, 2001—. Dir. Standing Com. profl. Exch., Internat. Fedn. of Med. Students Associations (IFMSA), Athens, 1987—89; quality assurance mgr. Nephrology Dept HYGEIA Hosp., Athens, 1999—2001; hon. pres. Internat. Fedn. of Med. Students Associations, Amsterdam, 1988—; devel. and tng. cons., Brit. Coun. Devel. and Tng. Services, London, 1998—; evaluator Hellenic Quality Accreditation Body, Athens, 2000—. Author: (sci. pub.) Jour.: Kidney Internat., NEPHRON, Contributions Nephrology; contbr. to several sci. pubs. Scholar WHO Scholarship for med. students, WHO, Geneva Hdqs., 1987, Brit. Fgn. and Commonwealth Office (FCO) Scholarship for studies in the UK., Brit. Fgn. and Commonwealth Office (FCO) London UK, 1992—93; Hellenic Soc. of Nephrology Fellowship for post grad. studies in the USA, 1996—97. Mem.: Internat. Soc. of Nephrology (assoc.), Hellenic Soc. for Med. Studies (assoc.), Hellenic Nephrology Assn. (assoc.), European Renal Assn. and the European Dialysis and Transplant Assn. (ERA-EDTA) (assoc.), Am. Soc. of Nephrology (assoc.), Mem. of the Internat. Brit. Graduates Soc. (assoc.), Keele U. Alumni Assn. (assoc.). Achievements include development of Quality Assurance Sys. cert. with ISO 9001 for the dialysis unit of HYGEIA Hosp. Office: Blue Cross Hosp 102 Vas Sofias Av Greece Athens 11528 Greece Office Fax: 30-210-7774304; Home Fax: 30-210-8040900. Personal E-mail: stamatelos@tee.gr.

STAMATIOU, KONSTANTINOS NIKOLAOS, urologist; b. Pireas, Greece, Mar. 31, 1968; Diploma, U. Athens, 1996; PhD in Urology, U. Crete, 2006. Cons. urologist Tzaneio Hosp., 2008—. Scholarship, Nat. scholarships Found. Fellow: Parnassus Lit. Soc., Hellenic Urologic Assn.; mem.: Med. Assn. Athens, EAU. Avocations: painting, sculpting. Home: Salepoula 2 Pireas Attica 18536 Greece Personal E-mail: stamatiouk@yahoo.com.

STAMLER, JEREMIAH, medical professor, researcher; b. NYC, Oct. 27, 1919; s. George and Rose (Baras) Stamler; m. Rose Steinberg, 1942; 1 child, Paul J. AB, Columbia U., NYC, 1940; MD, SUNY, Bklyn., 1943. Cert. specialist in clin. nutrition. Intern LI Coll. Medicine, Kings County Hosp., Bklyn., 1944, fellow pathology, 1947; rsch. fellow cardiovasc. dept. Med. Research Inst., Michael Reese Hosp., Chgo., 1948, rsch. assoc., 1949-55, asst. dir. dept., 1955-58; dir. heart disease control prog. Chgo. Bd. Health, 1958-74, dir. chronic disease control divsn., 1961-63, dir. adult health & aging divsn., 1963-74; assoc. dept. medicine Northwestern U. Feinberg Sch. Medicine, Evanston, Ill., 1958-59, asst. prof., 1959—65, assoc. prof., 1965-71, prof., dept. cmty. health & preventive medicine, 1972—90, chair dept., 1972—86, Harry W. Dingman prof. cardiology, 1973—90, prof. emeritus, 1990—, founder Master in Pub. Health prog. Exec. dir. Chgo. Health Rsch. Found., 1963—72; cons. medicine St. Joseph Hosp., Chgo., 1964—, Rush-Presbyn.-St. Luke's Hosp., Chgo., 1966—, vis. prof. internal medicine, 1972—; attending physician Northwestern Meml. Hosp., 1973—89, chmn. dept. cmty. health & preventive medicine, 1973—85; profl. lectr. dept. medicine U. Chgo. Pritzker Sch. Medicine. Author: (with L. N. Katz) Experimental Atheroscleroses, 1953, (with A. Blakeslee) Your Heart Has Nine Lives-Nine Steps to Heart Health, 1963, Four Keys to a Healthy Heart, 1976; co-author: Nutrition and Atherosclerosis, 1958, Epidemiology of Hypertension, 1967, Lectures on Preventive Cardiology, 1967; contbr. articles to profl. jours., chapters to books. Served in US Army, 1944—46. Recipient Howard W. Blakeslee award, 1964, Albert & Mary Lasker Med. Journalism award, 1965, Conrad Elvehjem award, Wis. Med. Soc., 1967, Albert Lasker Spl. Svc. award, 1980, Donald Reid medal, London Sch. Hygiene & Tropical Medicine/Royal Coll. Physicians, 1988, John Jay award, Columbia U., 1990; named to Nutrition Hall of Fame, Ctr. for Sci. in Pub. Interest. Fellow: AAAS, Am. Pub. Health Assn. (John M. Snow award 1986), Am. Coll. Cardiology (Disting. Svc. award 1985); mem.: Chgo. Inst. Medicine (Coleman award 1987), Internat. Soc. & Fedn. Cardiology (chmn. sci. bd., mem. exec. com.), Chgo. Acad. Scis., Chgo. Nutrition Assn., Am. Inst. Nutrition, Soc. Exptl. Biology & Medicine (sec. Ill. chpt.), Diabetes Assn. Greater Chgo., Ill. Acad. Scis., Ill. Pub. Health Assn. (mem. exec. com.), Chgo. Heart Assn. (Coeur d'Or award 1979, Gold Heart award 1992), Ctrl. Soc. Clin. Rsch., Middle States Pub. Health Assn., Assn. Clin. Scientists, Am. Soc. Study Arteriosclerosis (past bd. dirs., past chmn. prog. com., past sec.-treas.), Am. Soc. Clin. Nutrition, Am. Soc. Clin. Investigation, Am. Physiol. Soc., Am. Heart Assn. (bd. dirs., past vice-chmn. exec. com., fellow coun. arteriosclerosis, chmn. coun epidemiology & prevention, Outstanding Efforts in Heart Rsch. award 1964, Merit award 1967, Svc. award 1981, Disting. Rsch. Achievement award 1981, Achievement award 1987), Am. Fedn. Clin. Rsch., Phi Beta Kappa. Office: Northwestern U Feinberg Sch Dept Preventative Medicine 680 N Lake Shore Dr Ste 1102 Chicago IL 60611 Office Phone: 312-908-7914.

STAMM, CAROL ANN, obstetrician, gynecologist; b. Denver, Aug. 8, 1959; d. Robert L. and Mary Ellen Stamm. BA in Biology cum laude, U. Colo., 1981; MD with honors, U. Colo., Denver, 1991. Diplomate Am. Bd. Ob-Gyn; cert. in elem. tchg. U. Colo., 1986. Bilingual elem. tchr. Denver Pub. Schs., 1986—87; intern in ob-gyn U. Colo. Sch. Medicine, Denver, 1991—92, resident in ob-gyn, 1992—95, asst. prof., 1997—2003; staff ob-gyn, asst. prof. Denver Health Med. Ctr., 1995—2003; dir. women's health rotation Colo. Health Found. (formerly High St. Primary Care Clinic), Denver, 2003—, asst. prof. clin. medicine, 2003—, dir. women's svcs., 2004—. Mem. Patient and Family Edn. Work Group, 1996—97; mem. ob-gyn edn. com. U. Colo. Health Scis. Ctr., 1997—2003; dir. ob-gyn Grand Rounds, 1997—2001; provider design team Lifetime Clin. Record Project, 1998—2001; alt. mem. Colo. Multiple Instl. Rev. Bd., 1998—2003; presenter in field. Co-author: (book) Management of High-Risk Pregnancy, 4th edit., 1999, Medical Care of the Pregnant Patient, 2000, The Female Athlete, 2002, Contemporary Therapy in Obstetrics and Gynecology, 2002; contbr. articles to profl. jours.; peer reviewer Jour. Obstetrics and Gynecology, 1999—, Am. Jour. Obstetrics and Gynecology, 1999—. Recipient Richard Whitehead award, Phi Rho Sigma, 1989; grantee, March of Dimes, 2000—01; Trust fellow, Am. Cancer Soc. Brooks, 1988, Acad. Enrichment grantee, U. Colo. Health Scis. Ctr., 1993—95, NIH subcontract grantee, U. Pitts., 2000—03, NIH grantee, IBBEX, 2002. Fellow: ACOG (History fellow 2006); mem.: N.Am. Menopause Soc, Golden Key, Phi Beta Kappa (mem. mortar bd.). Avocations: reading, running, pilates, symphony, opera. Home: 155 S Jackson St Unit C Denver CO 80209 Office: Colorado Health Found 1801 High St Denver CO 80218 Office Phone: 303-869-2158. Business E-Mail: cstamm@coloradohealth.org.

STAMPER, ROBERT LEWIS, ophthalmologist, educator; b. NYC, July 27, 1939; m. Naomi T. Belson, June 23, 1963; children: Juliet, Marjorie, Alison. BA, Cornell U., 1961; MD, SUNY-Downstate, 1965. Diplomate Am. Bd. Ophthalmology (assoc. examiner 1976-92, bd. dirs. 1992-99). Intern Mt. Sinai Hosp., NYC, 1965-66; resident in ophthalmology Washington U.-Barnes Hosp., St. Louis, 1968-71; Nat. Eye Inst.-NIH fellow dept. ophthalmology Washington U., St. Louis, 1971-72, from instr. ophthalmology to asst. prof. dept. ophthalmology, 1971-72; asst. prof. dept. ophthalmology Pacific Presbyn. Med. Ctr., San Francisco, 1972-76, assoc. prof. ophthalmology, 1976-87; chmn. dept. ophthalmology Calif. Pacific Med. Ctr. (formerly Pacific Presbyn. Med. Ctr.), San Francisco, 1987-96; vice-chmn. dept. ophthalmology U. Calif., San Francisco, 1999—2003, prof. clin. ophthalmology, dir. glaucoma, 1999—. Asst. ophthalmologist Barnes Hosp., St. Louis, 1971-72, Harkness Hosp., San Francisco, 1973-74; dir. ophthalmic photography and fluorescin angiography, dept. ophthalmology Washington U., St. Louis, 1969-72; dir. resident tng. Pacific Presbyn. Med. Ctr., 1972-89, dir. glaucoma svc., vice-chmn. dept. ophthalmology, 1974-87; chief ophthalmology svc. Highland Hosp., Oakland, Calif., 1974-76; clin. instr. dept. ophthalmology U. Calif., San Francisco, 1974-77, prof. clin. ophthalmology, 1998—; clin. asst. prof. ophthalmology U. Calif., Berkeley, 1974-78, asst. clin. prof. ophthalmology, 1978-85; sr. rsch. assoc. Smith-Kettlewell Inst. Visual Scis., San Francisco, 1972-89; project co-dir. ophthalmic curriculum for med. students Nat. Libr. Medicine, 1973-75; commr. Joint Commn. on Allied Health Pers. in Ophthalmology, 1975-87, bd. dirs., 1978-88, sec., 1980, v.p., 1982-83, pres., 1984-85; provisional asst.

chief dept. ophthalmology Mt. Zion Hosp., San Francisco, 1976-87, assoc. chief dept. ophthalmology, 1982-86; ophthalmic cons. Ft. Ord, Calif., 1976-1984, Oakland Naval Hosp., 1978-83; instr. Stanford U., Calif., 1977—1992; glaucoma cons. U. Calif., Davis, 1978-84; vis. lectr. dept. ophthalmology Hadassah Hebrew U. Med. Ctr., Jerusalem, 1978, Oxford U. Eye Hosp., Eng., 1986; ind. med. examiner State of Calif., 1979—; mem. appeals hearing panel Accreditation Coun. for Grad. Med. Edn., 1986-93, mem. residency rev. com. for ophthalmology, 1993-98; mem. provisional courtesy staff Peralta Hosp., Oakland, 1988-92; mem. ophthalmic devices adv. panel USFDA, 1989-92; presenter, lectr. in field. Co-author: Update in Glaucoma, 2004, 2d edit., 2006; editor Ophthalmology Clinics of North Am., 1988-2004, 06; mem. editl. adv. com. Ophthalmology, 1982-89, mem. editl. bd., 1983-94; co-author: Becker and Shaffer's Diagnosis and Management of the Glaucomas, 7th edit., 1999, 8th edit., 2009; co-editor Essentials in Ophthalmology: Glaucoma, 2007, 2009; contbr. articles to profl. jours. Chmn. bd. Agy. Jewish Edn., Oakland, 1986-89; bd. dirs. Jewish Fedn. Greater East Bay, Oakland, 1992-94; bd. dirs. Found. Glaucoma Rsch.; mem. glaucoma adv. com. Nat. Soc. to Prevent Blindness, 1981-2004; mem. Am. Diabetes Assn. Surgeon USPHS, 1966-68. Recipient Self-Instrnl. Material in Ophthalmology award Nat. Soc. for Performance and Instrn., 1975, Honor award Am. Acad. Ophthalmology, 1982, Sr. Honor award, 1992, lifetime Achievement award, 2008, Am. Acad. Ophthalmology, 2008, Statesmanship award Joint Commn. on Allied Health Pers. in Ophthalmology, 1989, Disting. Alumnus award Wash. U. Sch. Medicine, 2004; named Troutman Master Tchr. in Ophthalmology, 2000; Regents scholar NY State, 1961, scholar NY State, 1965; Blalock fellow UCLA Sch. Medicine, 1961, Fight for Sight fellow Dept. Ophthalmology NY Hosp. and Cornell Med. Ctr., 1962, 63, 64. Fellow Am. Acad. Ophthalmology and Otolaryngology (rep. to joint commn. on allied health pers., faculty home study course sect. X, chmn. sect. VIII 1983-85, bd. councilors, editl. adv. com. Opthalmology jour. 1982-89, editl. bd. Ophthalmology jour. 1983-94, and many others), ACS; mem. AMA (Physician's Recognition award 1989), Am. Ophthalmologic Soc., Assn. for Rsch. in Vision and Ophthalmology, Calif. Med. Assn. (asst. sec. sect. ophthalmology, chmn., sci. bd. rep. adv. panel on ophthalmology 1985-91), Nat. Soc. Prevent Blindness (mem. glaucoma adv. com. 1981-2004), No. Calif. Soc. Prevent Blindness (bd. dirs. 1986-, pres. 2008-11), Calif. Assn. Ophthalmology, Pan Am. Ophthal. (bd. dirs. 1992—), Soc., NY Acad. Scis., Las Vegas Ophthal. Soc. (hon.), Am. Glaucoma Soc. (v.p. 1997-99, pres. 1999-2000), Glaucoma Rsch. Found. (bd. dirs.). Office: Dept Opht UCSF Med Ctr 8 Koret Way San Francisco CA 94143-0730 Business E-Mail: stamperr@vision.ucsf.edu.

STAMPER MADDOX, EWA, psychologist; b. Warsaw, Sept. 8, 1954; came to U.S., 1984; d. Tadeusz and Regina S.Szumotalska MA in Clin. Psychology, U. Warsaw, Poland, 1978; PhD in Psychology, New Sch. U., NYC, 1992. Staff therapist Marital Therapy Counseling Ctr., Warsaw, 1978—79, Ctr. for Psychotherapy and Personality Growth, Warsaw, 1978—80; sr. staff therapist Lab. for Psychoedn. Polish Psychol. Assn., Warsaw, 1981—85; postgrad. affiliate Washington Sq. Inst. for Psychotherapy, NYC, 1990—92; police psychologist Honolulu Police Dept., 1993—98; pvt. practice, Honolulu, 1994—. With Tng. Ctr. for Family Therapy, Warsaw, 1976—78, Stuyvesant Poly., NYC, 1988—89, North Ctrl. Bronx (N.Y.) Hosp., 1988—89, Yale Psychiat. Inst., 1989—90, Castle Med. Ctr., Kailua, Hawaii, 1993—94; co-chmn. Crystal Methampetamine Forum, Honolulu, 1996—99. Mem. APA, Hawaii Psychol. Assn. (clin. divsn. rep. 1998-99, coord. for Disaster Response Network 2005-09). Avocations: horseback riding, raising German Shorthaired Pointers and Siamese cats, gardening, running. Office: 41-019 Hihimanu St Waimanalo HI 96795-1607 Office Phone: 808-259-5256. Personal E-mail: neimaddox@aol.com.

STAN, CRISTIAN ADRIAN, forensic pathologist, physician; b. Vâlenii De Munte, Romania, June 5, 1968; s. Pantilimon and Florica Stan; m. Carmen Ioana Stan, Aug. 27, 1994; 1 child, Mihai-Cristian. BA, MD, Ovidius U., 1990—95; PhD in Med. Sci., C. Davila Medicine and Pharmacy U., 2004. Lic. forensic expert Ministry Justice and Ministry Mental Health. Resident forensics Nat. Inst. Legal Medicine, Bucharest, Romania, 1996—2000, jr. forensic pathologist, physician, 2000—04, head Dept. Profl. Risks, 2002—, sr. forensic pathologist, physician, 2004—. Bd. dirs. Medicoo-Legal Expert Co., Bucharest; legal adv. Coltea Clin. Hosp., Bucharest, 2005; expert in field. Contbr. articles to profl. jours. Mem.: I.G. Duca Found. Avocation: tennis. Office: Inst Nat De Medicina Legala Mina Minovici Vitan Bârzesti 9 75669 Sector 4 Bucharest Romania also: Ion Berindei 3 Bl OD21A Sc B Et 10 Ap 85 Sector 2 Bucharest Romania Office Phone: (+4) 0722 214 889. Office Fax: (+4) 021 327 11 65. Personal E-mail: crististan@xnet.ro. Business E-Mail: crististan@medicolegalexpert.ro.

STAN, STÉPHAN, orthopedic surgeon; b. Bucharest, Romania, Dec. 20, 1937; s. Dumitru and Elena (Zamfirescu) S.; m. Florentina Mosora, Jan. 22, 1977; 1 child, Guy-Bart. MD with highest honors, U. Bucharest, 1961, PhD, 1970; M. Appraisive Medicine with distinction, U. Liege, Belgium, 1993. Asst. lectr. Faculty of Medicine, U. Bucharest, 1963-66, chief asst. lectr., 1966-74; asst. lectr. Cath. U. Leuven, Belgium, 1974-76; orthopaedic surgeon Clinique St. Elisabeth, Liege, 1977-87; chief dept. orthopaedic surgery Centre Hospitalier J. Wauters, Waremme, Belgium, 1971, sr. hosp. lectr., 1986, pres. med. coun., 1981-86, med. dir., 1986-92. Author: Electric Stimulation of Bone Growth and Repair, 1978, A New Approach of Biomechanics of Vertebral Unit by Finite Elements, 1989, Effect of Piroxicam on Wound Healing after Orthopaedic Surgery, 1994; contbr. articles to profl. jours. Med. appraiser Ct. of Justice, Belgium, 1992. Recipient Shield of Valor, Am. Biog. Inst., 1992, also Medal of Honor, 1999, Golden Acad. award, 1995, Medal Amici del Cervino, casa della guide Breuil Italia, 1982. Mem. European Soc. Biomechanics, N.Y. Acad. Scis., Union Professionnelle Medicale Belge Orthopedie, Belgian Soc. Orthopedic Surgery and Traumatology. Roman Catholic. Avocations: swimming, mountain climbing, tennis, chess, music. Home: Residence Verdi Ave Blonden 7 4000 Liège Belgium

STANDLEY, JOHN T., retail executive; b. 1963; married; 2 children. BS in Acctg., Pepperdine U., 1985. Audit mgr. retail and fin. industry groups Arthur Andersen LLP, LA; v.p. fin. Food 4 Less Supermarkets, Inc., Compton, Calif., 1991—94; CFO Smitty's Super-valu, Inc., Phoenix, 1994—96; sr. v.p. admin. Smith's Food & Drug Stores, Inc., Salt Lake City, 1996—97; sr. v.p., CFO Ralphs Grocery Co., 1997—98, Fred Meyer, Inc., Portland, Oreg., 1998—99; exec. v.p., CFO Fleming Co. Inc., Oklahoma City, 1999, Rite Aid Corp., Camp Hill, Pa., 1999—2002, sr. exec. v.p., chief adminstrv. officer, 2002, CFO, 2003—05; CEO Pathmark Stores, Inc., 2005—08; pres., COO Rite Aid Corp., Camp Hill, Pa., 2008—10, pres., CEO, 2010—. Bd. dirs. Pathmark Stores, Inc., 2005—07, Rite Aid Corp., 2009—. Office: Rite Aid Corp 30 Hunter Lane Camp Hill PA 17011 *

STANEK, ROBERT V., hospital administrator; Former pres. and CEO Catholic Health East, chairperson bd. of trustees, 2011—; trustee St. Michael's Med. Ctr. Office: Catholic Health East Ste 100 3805 West Chester Pike Newtown Square PA 19073 Office Phone: 610-355-2000. Office Fax: 610-271-9600.

STANESCU, DAN CONSTANTIN, medical educator, researcher; b. Bucharest, Romania, Dec. 21, 1935; s. Constantin and Olympia (Heliotis) Stanescu; m. Bianca Segall, Apr. 14, 1961; 1 child, Dinu-Michel. MD, Bucharest Sch. Medicine, 1961; PhD, U. Cath. Louvain, Brussels, 1975. Cert. Bd. specialist in pneumology Brussels. Rsch. fellow Inst. Endocrinology, Bucharest, 1962-63; established investigator dept. occupl. diseases Inst. Hygiene, Bucharest, 1963-70; rsch. assoc. Cath. U. Louvain, 1970-72, maitre de conf., 1972-79, assoc. prof., 1979-87, prof., 1987—2001, prof. emeritus, 2001—. In charge Pulmonary Lab. Cliniques St. Luc, Brussels, 1975—2001; mem. Belgian Bd. Pneumology, Brussels, 1985—91; pres. pneumology contact group Belgian Nat. Found. Sci. Rsch., Brussels, 1992—96; mem. Hosp. du Monde, Brussels, 1990—99. Editor: European Respiratory Jour., 1991—95; mem. editl. bd.: Pediatric Pulmonology, 1986—95, CHEST, 2003—06, Pneumologia, 2006—; contbr. Decorated Officer Order Leopold II, Comdr. Order of the Crown Belgium; recipient Medaille Civique de 1st Classe; grantee rsch. grant, Belgian Nat. Found. Sci. Rsch., 1973—76, Steel and Coal European Cmty., 1971—74, 1977—81, 1982—87, 1990—96. Fellow: Am. Coll. Chest Physicians; mem.: Romanian Acad. Medicine (fgn. corr.), European Learning Resource Ctr. (coord. 1986—96), European Sch. Respiratory Medicine, Lung Mechanics Group (pres. 1984—88), European Respiratory Soc. (exec. com. 1985—89, expert), NY Acad. Scis., Am. Physiol. Soc., Am. Thoracic Soc. Liberal. Orthodox. Avocations: painting, literature. Personal E-mail: dcstanescu@gmail.com.

STANFILL, AMY BOBIS, pediatric surgeon; b. Ill., Nov. 20, 1973; BS, U. Iowa, 1995; MD, U. Iowa Coll. Medicine, 2000. Clin. asst. prof. surgey, pediat. OSF St. Francis Hosp., Childrens Hosp. Ill., U. Ill. Coll. Medicine, Peoria, 2007—. Recipient Tchg. Excellence award, U. Ill. Coll. Medicine at Peoria, 2010; named Outstanding Tchr. of Yr., 2009. Fellow: ACS; mem.: Internat. Pediatric Endosurgery Group, Assn. Women Surgeons, Midwest Surg. Assn., Ctrl. Surg. Assn. Office: 420 NE Glen Oak Ave Ste 201 Peoria IL 61603 E-mail: amybobis@gmail.com.

STANFORD, PAULETTE DENISE, pediatrician, educator; Grad., U. Medicine and Dentistry of NJ, 1975. Diplomate Am. Bd. Pediatrics, Am. Bd. Pediatrics-adolescent medicine. Pediat. resident Univ. of Medicine and Dentistry of NJ Hosp., 1976—77, fellow adolescent medicine, 1977—79; prof. pediat. Univ. of Medicine and Dentistry of NJ; assoc. dir. divsn. of adolescent and young adult medicine NJ Medical Sch. Office: New Jersey Medical School 185 South Orange Ave Rm F580 Newark NJ 07101-1709 Office Phone: 973-972-0361. Office Fax: 973-972-6433.

STANGER, ROBERT HENRY, retired psychiatrist, educator; b. NYC, May 19, 1937; s. Sidney and Mary (Strassner) S.; m. Andrea Rogin, Aug. 28, 1960; children: Lee Ann, David Neal. AB, Guilford Coll., 1959; MD, Emory U., 1964. Intern in internal medicine Wake Forest U., 1964-65; resident in gen. psychiatry U. Pitts., Western Psychiat. Inst. and Clinic, 1967-70; pvt. practice gen. psychiatry Monroeville, Pa., 1970-2001; med. dir. Allegheny Valley Mental Health-Mental Retardation Ctr., New Kensington, Pa., 1970-76; dir. psychiat. svcs. Allegheny Valley Hosp., Natrona Heights, Pa., 1983-96, chmn. dept. psychiatry and behavioral medicine, 1983-96; pvt. practice Natrona Heights, 1984-97; cons. psychiatrist, 1999—2010; ret., 2011. Clin. instr. psychiatry U. Pitts. Sch. Medicine, 1970-79, clin. asst. prof., 1980-2002, asst. prof. emeritus, 2002—; cons. Westinghouse Elec. Corp., East Pitts., 1977-87; ethics com. human rsch. Allegheny Valley Hosp., 1976-97; chmn. dept. psychiatry Citizens Gen. Hosp., 1978-88. Capt. M.C., U.S. Army, 1965-67, Vietnam. Mem. AMA, Am. Psychiat. Assn. (del. 1986-88), Pa. Psychiat. Soc. (councilor 1976-79, treas. 1979-80, sec. 1980-81, v.p. 1981-82, pres.-elect 1982-83, pres. 1983-84), Pitts. Psychiat. Soc. (councilor 1974-76, sec. 1977-78, pres.-elect 1978-79, pres. 1979-80), Allegheny County Med. Soc. Home and Office: 3910 Old William Penn Hwy Pittsburgh PA 15235-4837

STANICKA, SONA, endocrinologist, researcher; b. Kosice, Slovak Republic, May 13, 1974; d. Anton Stanicky and Sona Stanicka. MD, Charles U., Prague, 1998, PhD, 2005. Diplomate Bd. Internal Medicine, Prague, 2002, Bd. Endocrinology, Prague, 2005. Physician, rschr. Inst. Endocrinology, Prague, 1998—; rsch. assoc. divsn. endocrinology, metabolism and molecular medicine Northwestern U., Feinberg Sch. Medicine, Chgo., 2005—07. Contbr. articles to profl. jours. Mem.: Czech Endocrine Soc. (assoc.), Czech Med. Assn. (assoc.). Avocations: bicycling, swimming, travel, puzzles.

STANISLAO, JOSEPH, engineering educator, consultant; b. Manchester, Conn., Nov. 21, 1928; s. Eduardo and Rose (Zaccaro) S.; m. Bettie Chloe Carter, Sept. 6, 1960. BS, Tex. Tech. U., Lubbock, 1957; MS, Pa. State U., Univ. Park, 1959; DSc in Industrial Engring, Columbia U., NYC, 1970. Registered profl. engr., Mass., Mont. Asst. engr. Naval Ordnance Research, University Park, Pa., 1958-59; asst. prof. NC State U., Raleigh, 1959-61; dir. rsch. Darlington Fabrics Corp., Pawtucket, RI, 1961-62; from asst. prof. to prof. U. RI, Kingston, 1962-71; prof., chmn. dept. Cleve. State U., 1971-75; prof., dean ND State U., Fargo, 1975-94, acting v.p. agrl. affairs, 1983-85; asst. to pres. N.D. State U., Fargo, 1983—, dir. Engring. Computer Ctr., 1984—, prof. emeritus indsl. engring. and mgmt. Fargo, 1994—; pres. XOX Corp., 1984-90; chmn. bd., CEO ATSCO, 1989-94, chief engr., 1993—; prof. emeritus ND State U., 1994—2010. Adj. prof. Mont. State U., 1994-2010, dir. indsl. and mgmt. engring. program, 1996—, mfg. rsch., sponsored by Nat. Sci. Found. 1997—; pres., CEO J&B Inc., 1996-; v.p., co-owner, bd. dirs. D.T.&J., Inc., Fargo, ND, 1999-2006, London, 1999—; v.p. engring. Roll-A-Ramp, Rolla-A-Latter, and Rolla-A-conveyor, 2000-05; cons. to healthcare sys., 1999-2005, Handicap Lift. Contbr. chpts. to books, articles to profl. jours. Served to sgt. USMC, 1948-51. Recipient Sigma Xi award, 1968; Order of the Iron Ring award N.D. State U., 1972, Econ. Devel. award, 1991; named Best Tchr., Alpha Pi Mu, 2005; USAF recognition award, 1979, ROTC appreciation award, 1982. Mem. Am. Inst. Indsl. Engrs. (sr.; v.p. 1964-65), ASME, Order of the Engr., Am. Soc. Engring. Edn. (campus coord. 1979-81), Acad. Indsl. Engrs. Tex. Tech U., Lions, Elks, Am. Legion, Phi Kappa Phi, Tau Beta Pi (advisor 1978-79). Roman Catholic. Achievements include patents for pump apparatus, pump fluid housing, roll-conveyer, rotating vertical lift, gas-less engine, and handicap loading dock; roll-a-ramp; invention of telescopic sliding ramp, USA patents, Canadian patents European union registration thermal-brick, gas less engine; patents in field. Avocations: pool, billiards. Home: 8 Park Plaza Dr Bozeman MT 59715-9343 Office: Mont State U M&IE Dept 304 Roberts Hall Bozeman MT 59717-3800 Office Phone: 406-585-5416. Personal E-mail: bstanislao2314@msn.com, joseph&bettie1928@gmail.com. Business E-Mail: jstanslo@ie.montana.edu, drjoe1928@qwestoffice.net, jstanislao1928@qwestoffice.net.

STANKOVIC, KONSTANTINA M., otolaryngologist; b. Zagreb, Croatia, Nov. 3, 1969; PhD, MIT, 1998; MD, Harvard Coll., Cambridge, Mass., 1999. Asst. prof. Harvard Med. Sch., 2008; exec. bd. mem. Am. Auditory Soc., 2008—. Prin. investigator Eaton Peabody Labs. Mass. Eye and Ear Infirmary, 2008. Recipient Alumnae Ann. award, MIT, Henry Asbury Christian award, Harvard Med. Sch., Burt Evans Young Investigator award, Nat. Orgn. Hearing Rsch.; Rsch. fellowship, Howard Hughes Med. Inst., Rsch. grant, NIH. Mem.: ACS, Am. Acad. Otolaryngology Head and Neck Surgery, Am. Neurotology Soc., Phi Beta Kappa, Sigma Xi. Avocations: piano, swimming. Office: Mass Eye and Ear Infirmary 243 Charles St Boston MA 02114 Business E-Mail: konstantina_stankovic@meei.harvard.edu.

STANKUNAS, MINDAUGAS, public health educator; b. Kaunas, Lithuania, May 22, 1978; s. Alvydas Stankunas and Zita Stankuniene; m. Aurima Kripaityte, Aug. 16, 2002; children: Aine children: Matas. B in Pub. Health, Kaunas U. Medicine, Lithuania, 2000, M in Pub. Health Mgmt., 2002; M in Pub. Health, Nordic Sch. Pub. Health, Gothenburg, Sweden, 2004; DSc, Kaunas U. Medicine, Lithuania, 2007. Cert. pub. health leadership Imperial Coll., London, 2005. Asst. prof. Klaipeda U., Lithuania, 2000—02, Kaunas U. Medicine, 2002—05, sr. lectr., 2006—. Project coord. Kaunas U. Medicine, 2000—. Author: (book) Physician Planning in Lithuania in 1990-2015, 2003. Mem.: Lithuanian Health Mgmt. Assn. (EUPHA Ferenc Bojan Meml. Abstract prize 2007). Roman Catholic. Avocation: 17-19 century European fine art collecting. Office: Kaunas Univ Medicine A Mickeviciaus 9 Kaunas LT-44307 Lithuania Home Phone: 370-615-64242; Office Phone: 370-37-327373. Office Fax: 370-37-327325. Business E-Mail: stankuna@takas.lt.

STANLEY, JAMES CHARLES, vascular surgeon; b. Detroit, Sept. 18, 1938; s. Joseph Dean and Jeannette Stanley; m. Nancy Marion Norville, Aug. 5, 1961; children: Timothy James, Jeffrey John, Sarah Anne. MD, U. Mich., Ann Arbor, 1964; DSc (hon.), U. Toledo, 2010. Diplomate in vascular surgery Am. Bd. Surgery, Phila., 1983. Handleman prof. surgery U. Mich. Med. Sch., Ann Arbor, 2005—, dir., cardiovasc. ctr., 2008—. Contbr. articles to profl. jours., chapters to books. Chmn. U. Musical Soc., Ann Arbor, 2009—11. Capt., m.c. US Army, 1965—67, Fort Sam Houston, San Antonio. Fellow: Royal Coll. Surgeons (hon.); mem.: Royal Australasian Coll. Surgeon, Sect. Vascular Surgery, Nat. Academy Medicine Columbia, Soc. Vascular Surgery (pres. 1996—97). Episcopalian. Achievements include research in Aortic, cerebrovascular and renal disease. Avocations: classical music, jazz. Office: Univ Michigan 1500 East Med Ctr Dr Ann Arbor MI 48109 Office Phone: 734-936-5786. Business E-Mail: jstanley@umich.edu.

STANLEY, JOHN R., dermatologist, educator; BA, Cornell U., 1970; MD, Harvard Coll., 1974. Intern Univ. of Wash.; resident NYU Med. Ctr.; fellow Nat. Institutes of Health; prof. dermatology Univ. of Pa. Health System. Co-author: (publs.) Antibodies to the desmoglein I precursor proprotein but not to the mature cell surface protein cloned from individuals without pemphigus, 2009, Homologous regions of autoantibody heavy chain complementarity-determing region 3 (H-CDR3) in patients with pemphigus cause pathogenicity, 2010, and numerous others. Named one of Top Docs, Phila. Mag., 2004—08, 2010—11, Best Doctors in America, 2003—10, America's Top Doctors, 2007—10. Mem.: Assn. of Am. Physicians, Am. Soc. for Clin. Investigation, Soc. for Investigative Dermatology, Am. Acad. of Dermatology. Office: Perelman Center for Advanced Medicine S Pavilion 1st Fl 3400 Civic Center Blvd Philadelphia PA 19104 Office Phone: 800-789-7366.

STANNER, SARA, nutritionist; b. Hertfordshire, Eng., Mar. 4, 1969; BSc, U. Coll. Wales, 1990; MSc, London Sch. Hygiene and Tropical Medicine, 1999. Rsch. coord. U. Coll. London Med. Sch., 1991—99; sci. programme mgr. Brit. Nutrition Found., 1999—. Mem.: Nutrition Soc. (hon. pub. officer 2011—, pub. engagement theme leader 2004—10). Office: British Nutrition Found 52-54 High Holborn London WC1V 6RQ England Business E-Mail: s.stanner@nutrition.org.uk.

STANTON, M(ORRIS) DUNCAN, psychologist, researcher, dean; b. Lockport, NY; BA in Psychology, Alfred U., 1962; MA in Clin. Psychology, George Washington U., 1964; PhD in Clin. and Cmty. Psychology, U. Md., 1968. Lic. psychologist NY, Ky., bd. cert. diplomate in clin. psychology Am. Bd. Profl. Psychology, bd. cert. diplomate in family psychology Am. Bd. Profl. Psychology, approved supr. Am. Assn. Marriage Family Therapy, cert. in treatment of alcohol and other psychoactive substance abuse disorders APA. Commd. 2d lt. US Army, 1962, advanced through grades to capt., 1966; intern Walter Reed Gen. Hosp., Washington, 1966—67, asst.

chief, dir. tng. psychology svc., 1971—72; chief psychologist Ft. Dix, NJ, 1968—69, 98th Med. Detachment Vietnam, 1969—70, Ft. Meade, Md., 1970—71; lectr. U. Md., 1969—72; from asst. prof. to assoc. prof. psychology in psychiatry U. Pa. Sch. Medicine, Phila., 1972—83; assoc. clin. dir. Penn Psychiatry Phila. Gen. Hosp., 1972—74; dir. addicts and families prog. Phila. Child Guidance Clinic, 1974—83; dir. family therapy tng. program Drug Dependence Treatment Ctr., Phila. VA Med. Ctr., 1974—79; faculty mem. family therapy tng. ctr. Phila. Child Guidance Clinic, 1977—83; tchg. faculty Family Inst. of Phila., 1977—83; instr. Wilmington Med. Ctr., Del., 1978—79; dir. rsch. Phila. Child Guidance Clinic, Pa., 1982—83; prof., psychiatry (psychology) U. Rochester Sch. Medicine and Dentistry, 1983—97; dir. div. family programs, dept. psychiatry U. Rochester Med. Ctr., 1983—93; vis. faculty dept. continuing edn. Harvard Med. Sch., 1989; dir. rsch. div. family programs, dept. of psychiatry U. of Rochester Med. Ctr., 1993—97; prof., dean Sch. Profl. Psychology and Social Work Spalding U., Louisville, 1997—99, v.p., acad. rsch., 1999, prof. emeritus psychology, 1999—. Vis. scholar Fulbright Found., USIA, Argentina, 1991; cons. White House Office of Drug Abuse Policy, 1977—81, USIA, 1987—96, Inst. Medicine Nat. Acad. Scis., 1988, 1991—92; chair, mem. various rev. comms., task forces, site visit teams NIDA, NIMH, NIAAA, 1975—; mem. 16 editl. bds., including Am. Jour. Drug Alcohol Abuse, Family Process, Psychosocial Stress, 1980—; bd Family Process Press, NYC, 1982—99; spkr., presenter of over 520 invited lectrs., workshops in 27 countries. Contbr. more than 150 works to sci., profl. publs.; author: monographs and books in field, 1968—. Mem. dept. def. task group on alcoholism The Pentagon, Washington, 1971—72; ad hoc com. mem. special action office on drug abuse policy The White House, Washington, 1974; mem. advisory group family therapy prevention rsch. project Nat. Inst. Drug Abuse, 1981—82; chair, moderator family rsch. conf. Alcohol, Drug Abuse and Mental Health Adminstrn., 1981; cons. Family Health Plan, 1985—88; cons., sponsor, supr. Fulbright Commn., 1987—92. Decorated Bronze Star Medal; recipient Plaque of Appreciation, Found. for Parents in Action (Argentina), 1991, Shield of Police of Salta Province (Argentina), 1991, Cert. of Appreciation for Svc. on Mayor's Drug, Alcohol Planning Com., City of Louisville, 1998; named to Hall of Fame, Schenectady City Sch. Dist., 2008; grantee, NIH (NIDA/NIAAA), 1974—84, 1995—; Ann. Disting. fellow, Pikes Peak Mental Health Ctr., 1980. Fellow: APA (Pres. Citation 2001), Acad. Family Psychology, Nat. Coun. Family Rels. (Award Appreciation for dedication to the enhancement of family life 1988, Recognition cert. for longstanding svc. 1988, Legacy Circle award 1999), Am. Assoc. Marriage and Family Therapy (Outstanding Rsch. Contbn. in Marital and Family Therapy 1980, Cumulative Contbn. Family Therapy Rsch. award 2003, Ky. Divsn. award of Appreciation 2004); mem.: Internat. Family Therapy Assn., Am. Family Therapy Acad. (chair alcohol and drug interest group 1982—87, Disting. Contbn. Family Systems Rsch. 1997), Associacion Sistemica de Buenos Aires (hon.), South African Inst. Marital and Family Therapy (hon.). Office: The Morton Center 1028 Barret Ave Louisville KY 40204

STANTON, ROBERT ALAN, orthopaedic surgeon; b. NYC, June 28, 1946; s. Jay and Shirley (Rader) S.; m. Debby Ellen Beach, June 16, 1973; 1 child, Jim. BA, Williams Coll., 1968; MD, Coll. Physicians and Surgeons, 1972. Intern Columbia-Presbyn. Med. Ctr., NYC, 1972-73, resident in surgery, 1973-74; resident in orthopaedics Yale U., 1974-77; chmn., dir. Orthopaedic Specialty Group, P.C., Fairfield, Conn., 1981—; clin. instr., orthopaedics, rehabilitation Yale Univ. Med. Sch. Chmn. Alumni Fund of Williams Coll., Williamstown, Mass., 1993-96; bd. dirs. Bridgeport Hosp. Found., 1988-95; bd. investors Bridgeport Hosp., 1995-2007. Edward John Noble Found. fellow Columbia U., 1969 70. Fellow ACS, Am. Acad. Orthop. Surgeons; mem. Am. Orthop. Soc. Sports Medicine (pres.), Arthrascopy Assn. N.Am., Internat. Soc. for Arthroscopy, Knee Surgery and Orthop. Sports Medicine, Williams Club N.Y., Nantucket Yacht Club, Fairfield County Hunt Club (pres.), Internat. Polo Club (Palm Beach), Aiken Polo Club, Green Boundary Club (Aiken, SC), Wharf Rat Club, Nantucket Anglers Club. Avocations: skiing, polo, tennis, running, gardening. Office: Orthopaedic Specialty Group PC 75 Kings Highway Cutoff Fairfield CT 06824-5340 Office Phone: 203-337-2600.

STANTON-HICKS, MICHAEL D'ARCY, anesthesiologist, pain medicine specialist; b. Adelaide, Australia, June 3, 1931; arrived in U.S., 1972; s. Cedric Stanton-Hicks and Florence (Haggett) Perrin; m. Kristina Litsmark, Aug. 4, 1969 (div. Aug. 1984); children: Erik Michael, Leif Neal; m. Ursula Koch, Aug. 27, 1985. MB, BChir, Adelaide U., 1962; Dr. med., U. Dusseldorf, 1984. Bd. equivalent Am. Bd. Anesthesiology; diplomate Am. Bd. Pain Medicine, Interventional Pain Practice, 2002. Intern Queen Elizabeth Hosp., Adelaide, 1961-62, tutor, staff anesthesiologist, 1970-72; resident Royal Postgrad. Med. Sch., London and Lasarettet Köping, 1966-68; asst. dir. anesthesiology intensive care Södersjükhuset, Stockholm, 1968-69; instr. anesthesiology U. Wash. Med. Sch., Seattle, 1969-70, asst. prof., 1972-75; prof., chmn. dept. U. Mass. Med. Sch., Worcester, 1975-83; prof. U. Colo. Health Scis. Ctr., Denver, 1983-86, vice chmn. dept., 1983-85, acting chmn., 1985-86; prof., dir. pain clinic and rsch. Johannes Gutenberg U., Mainz, Germany, 1986-88, prof., 1986—97; dir. pain mgmt. ctr. Cleve. Clinic Found., 1988-98, vice chmn. pain mgmt. and rsch. divsn. anesthesia, 1998—; prof. Lerner Coll. Medicine, Case Western Res. U., Cleve., 2004—; staff physician Shaker Pediat. Pain Program, 2008—; with Dept. Functional Neurosurgery, 2009—. Med. examiner Indsl. Commn. Ohio; mem. Ohio Pain Adv. Com., Dept. Health; mem. liaison com. med. bd. Ohio Pain Com.; advisor Am. Acad. Disability Evaluating Physicians, 2000-02; appt. to gov.'s task force on compassionate care, Dept. of Health, Ohio; bd. dirs. World Inst. Pain; sci. advisor Reflex Sympathetic Dystrophy Assn., 2006, mem. Com. Pharmacy & Therapeutic Bureau Workers Compensation, 2005-; cons. Neurological Devices Panel Med. Devices Adv. Com., Ctr. Devices & Radiol. Health, Fed. Drug Adminstrn. Author, editor Regional Anesthesia: Advances and Selected Topics, 1978, (with Boas) Chronic Low Back Pain, 1982; author, editor: (with Wilson and Harden) CRPS: Current Diagnosis and Therapy, 2005; co-author: (with Raj and Nolte) Illustrated Manual of Regional Anesthesia, 1988 (Most Beautiful Book of Yr. award Frankfurt, Fed. Republic Germany Pubs. Book Conv., 1989), (with Janig and Boas) Reflex Sympathetic Dystrophy, 1989, (with Janig) Reflex Sympathetic Dystrophy: A Reappraisal, 1996; author: Pain and Sympathetic Nervous System, 1990; exec. editor Pain Practice Jour., 2001—, sect. editor Complex Regional Pain Syndrome, 2002, mem. editl. bd. Pain Physician, 2002—; author: Pain Management: A Cleveland Clinic Guide, 2009. Squadron leader res. Royal Australian Air Force, 1962-65., with Pharmacy & Therapeutic Com., Bureau Workers Compensation, Ohio, 2008 Named Scientist of Yr., Am. Herschel Soc., 1991-92, named one of Best Drs. in America, 2010-, 10 Best Pain Mgmt. Physicians, Beckers ASC Rev.; recipient Disting. Scientist award Reflex Sympathetic Dystrophy Assn., 2002, Disting. Svc. award European Soc. Regional Anesthesia, 2003, Lifetime Achievement award, Am. Soc. Interventional Pain Physicians, 2007; Australian Univs. Commn. mature age scholar, 1953-60, Lifetime Achievement award, North Am. Neuromodulation Soc., 2010, Best Pain Mgmt. Physician, Beakers Assn. Review, Best Doctors in America, 2010-. Fellow Royal Coll. Surgeons (faculty anesthetists), Royal Coll. Anesthetists, Am. Acad. Pain Medicine, Interventional Pain Practice; mem. Internat. Assn. Study Pain (chmn. spl. interest group pain and sympathetic nervous sys. 1990-2008), World Inst. Pain (bd. dirs. 1995—), Am. Soc. Regional Anesthesia (bd. dirs. 1979-91, pres. 1989-90, Disting. Svc. award, 1998), Assn. Anesthetists Gt. Britain and Ireland, Ohio State Med. Assn., Cleve. Acad. Medicine, Am. Acad. Med. Infrared Imaging (bd. dirs. 1991-95, pres. 1994-95, William Hobbins Rsch. award 1993), Am. Acad. Disability Evaluating Physicians (adv. com. mem. complex regional pain syndrome 2000—02), Am. Pain Soc., Am. Acad. Pain Medicine, Am. Neuromodulation Soc. (pres. 1994-98, bd. dirs. 1998-2000), Reflex Sympathetic Dystrophy Assn. (sci. adv. bd. 2000-05), Army-Navy-Air Force Club. Republican. Anglican. Avocations: skiing, photography, travel, flying. Home: 11405 Clearfield Lane Chardon OH 44024 Office: Cleve Clinic Found 9500 Euclid Ave Cleveland OH 44195-0001 Office Phone: 216-445-9559. Business E-Mail: stantom@ccf.org.

STAPLETON, F. BRUDER, pediatric nephrologist, academic administrator; b. Lawrence, Kans., Dec. 19, 1946; s. Harold Jack and Hazel Maria Stapleton; m. Barbara R. Stapleton, Sept. 16, 1969; children: Hillary J., F. Reed. BA, U. Kans., 1968, MD, 1972. Cert. Am. Bd. Pediat., in pediatric nephrology. Residency U. Kans. Med. Ctr., Kansas City, fellowship; residency U. Wash. Sch. Medicine, Seattle, Ford/Morgan Prof. and Chair, dept. pediat., 1996—; prof. pediat. U. Tenn. Coll. Medicine, Memphis, 1979—89; pediatrician Children's Hosp. Buffalo, 1989—96; chair dept. pediat. SUNY, 1989 96; pediatrician in chief Children's Hosp. and Med. Ctr., Seattle, 1996—, sr. v.p., chief academic officer, dir., dept. medicine. Contbr. articles to profl. jours.; founding editor-in-chief: Jour. Watch Pediat. and Adolescent Medicine, 2002—. Bd. dirs. Seattle Cancer Care Alliance, Ronald McDonald Children's Home, Buffalo, 1993—95, Seattle, 2000—. Lt. comdr. USN, 1977—79. Fellow pediatric nephrology, U. Kans., Kansas City, 1974—77. Mem.: Am. Bd. Pediat. (bd. dirs. 1998—2004, chair subspecialties com.), Am. Soc. Pediatric Nephrology (pres. 1995—96), Assn. Med. Sch. Dept. Chairs (pres. 2005—07), Internat. Pediatric Nephrology Assn. (treas. 2001—04). Home: 4693 NE 89th St Seattle WA 98115 Office: Childrens Hosp Dept Pediatrics CH-65 4800 Sand Point Way NE T-0211 Seattle WA 98105 Business E-Mail: bruder.stapleton@seattlechildrens.org. E-mail: bstaplet@u.washington.edu.

STARCHMAN, DALE EDWARD, medical educator; b. Wallace, Idaho, Apr. 16, 1941; s. Hubert V. and Lottie M. (Alford) Starchman; m. Erlinda Socrates Starchman, Dec. 13, 1969; children: Ann, Cindy, Julie, Mark. Student, Rockhurst Coll., 1959—61; BS in Physics, Pitts. State U., 1963; MS in Radiation Biophysics, U. Kans., 1965, PhD in Radiation Biophysics, 1968. Cert. Radiol. Physicist, Health Physicist, Med. Physicist. Chief health physicist IIT Rsch. Inst., Chgo., 1968—71; radiol. physicist Mercy Hosp. Inst. of Radiation Therapy, Chgo., 1968—71; prof., head radiation biophysics Northeast Ohio U. Coll. of Medicine, Rootstown, 1971—; pres. Med. Physics Svcs., Inc., Canton, Ohio, 1971—. Author: (with Wayne R. Hedrick and David L. Hykes) Ultrasound Physics and Instrumentation, 4th edit., 2005; contbr. numerous articles in profl. jours., chpts. in books, monographs. Fellow Am. Coll. Radiology; mem. Am. Assn. Physicists in Medicine (bd. mem. at large 1984-86, pres. Penn-Ohio chpt. 1975-76, rec. sec. midwest chpt. 1970, edn. coun. 1980-83, chmn. Am. assn. med. dosimetrists task group 1976-78, physics curriculum diagnostic residents task group 2003—, numerous other coms. 1975-83), Health Physics Soc. (chmn. summer sch. sub. com. 1977-78), Radiol. Soc. N.Am. (assoc. scis. com. 1976-86, task force chmn. 1983-86), Sigma Xi, Kappa Mu Epsilon. Achievements include research areas including selection, quality assurance and acceptance testing of diagnostic x-ray units, design of radiology facilities; effects of tissue inhomogeneities on electron therapy, radiation atrophy in bone, large field therapy swing technique, polymer dosimetry, photon spectra through thick shields, fetal effects, ultrasound, mammography. Office: 5942 Easy Pace Cir NW Canton OH 44718-2216

STAREK, ANDRZEJ, toxicologist, educator, research scientist; b. Cracow, Poland, Aug. 25, 1939; s. Andrzej and Maria; m. Bozena Janina Kawalec, Feb. 15, 1964; children: Beata, Vaud Krysztof. MSc, Med. Sch. Faculty Pharmacy, Cracow, Poland, 1963, DSc, 1970. Prof. Coll. Medicum Jagiellonian U., 1993. Asst. adj. Med. Acad., Cracow, Poland, 1963—83; asst. prof. Jagiellonian U., 1983—93, prof., 1993—. Head Dept. Indsl. Toxicology Jagiellonian U., Cracow, Poland, 1983—92, Dept. Biochem. Toxicology Jagiellonian U., 1992—; expert Interdepartmental Com. Maximum Admissable Concentrations, Lodz, 1984—. Author: Organ Taxicology, 2007, Dictionary of the Terms Applied in Toxicology, 1994; contbr. chapters to books, scientific papers to profl. jours. Recipient Sci. awards, Ministry of Nat. Edn. and Sport, 2003, Ministry of Health, 2009. Mem.: Polish Soc. Toxicology (hon.; pres. 1993—2002, exec. com. 2002—08). Achievements include patents in field. Office: Dept Biochem Toxicology Ul. Medyczna 9 30-688 Cracow Poland Business E-Mail: mfstarek@cyf-kr.edu.pl.

STARK, PATRICIA ANN, psychologist; b. Ames, Iowa, Apr. 21, 1937; d. Keith C. and Mary L. (Johnston) Moore. BS, So. Ill. U., Edwardsville, 1970, MS, 1972; PhD, St. Louis U., 1976. Counselor to alcoholics Bapt. Rescue Mission, East St. Louis, Ill., 1969; rschr. alcoholics Gateway Rehab. Ctr., East St. Louis, 1972; psychologist intern Henry-Stark Counties Spl. Edn. Dist. and Galesburg State Rsch. Hosp., Ill., 1972—73; instr. Lewis and Clark C.C., Godfrey, Ill., 1973—76, asst. prof., 1976—84, assoc. prof., 1994, coord. child care svcs., 1974—84; mem. staff dept. psychiatry Meml. Hosp., St. Elizabeth's Hosp., 1979—2001; supr. students interns, 1974—94. Dir. child and family svc. Collinsville Counseling Ctr., 1977-82; clin. dir., owner Empas-Complete Family Psychol. and Hypnosis Svcs., Collinsville, 1982—; cons. cmty. agys., 1974—; mem. adv. bd. Madison County Coun. on Alcoholism and Drug Dependency, 1977-80. Mem. APA, Ill. Psychol. Assn., Midwestern Psychol. Assn., Am. Soc. Clin. Hypnosis, Internat. Soc. Hypnosis. Office: 2802 Maryville Rd Maryville IL 62062 Office Phone: 618-345-6632.

STARKS, DANIEL J., medical technology and services executive; BA, Shimer Coll., Waukegan, Ill.; JD magna cum laude, U. Minn. Law Sch., 1979. Comml. litigation atty. Nichols, Starks, Carruthers and Kaster, 1979—85; gen. counsel to pres., CEO Daig Corp. (bought by St. Jude Medical Inc.), 1985—96; pres., CEO, Daig Corp. St. Jude Medical Inc., St. Paul, 1996—98; dir. St. Jude Medical, Inc., St. Paul, 1996—; pres., CEO Cardiac Rhythm Mgmt. div. St. Jude Medical Inc., St. Paul, 1998—2001, pres., COO, 2001—04; chmn., pres., CEO St. Jude Medical, Inc., St. Paul, 2004—. Bd. dir. Urologix Inc. Office: St Jude Medical Inc 1 Lillehei Plz Saint Paul MN 55117-9913 *

STARLING, RANDALL CARSON, cardiologist, educator; b. Pitts., Pa., Aug. 1, 1951; BS, MPH, U. Pitts.; MD, Temple U., 1981. Cert. Internal Medicine, Cardiovascular Disease, Bd. Med. Examiners. Intern U. Pitts. Med. Ctr., Pa., resident, internal medicine Pa., 1981—85, chief med. resident Pa., instr. medicine Pa., med. dir., cardiac transplant program Pa.; fellow, cardiology Ohio State U. Hospitals, Columbus, 1985—88, staff; asst. to assoc. prof., medicine Ohio State U., Columbus, med. dir., Cardiac Transplant Program; staff cardiologist, cardiovascular disease Cleve. Clinic, Ohio, 1995—, dir., heart transplant med. svcs. Ohio, 1995, sect. head, heart failure and cardiac transplant medicine Ohio, staff physician, Multi-Organ Transplant Ctr. Ohio, med. dir., Kaufman Ctr. for Heart Failure Ohio. Contbr. articles to profl. jours.; editl. bd. mem. Jour. Am. Coll. Cardiology, reviewer, editl. cons. for numerous jours.; editor: (chapter) Heart Failure in the Am. Coll. Cardiology Self-Assessment Program; editl. cons. 20/20, CNN Heroes In Medicine & PBS Specials. Fellow: Am. Coll. Cardiology; mem.: Internat. Soc. for Heart and Lung Transplantation, Heart Failure Soc. Am., Am. Soc. Transplantation, Am. Heart Assn. (mem. Coun. on Clin. Cardiology), Alpha Omega Alpha. Office: Cleveland Clinic Mail Stop F25 9500 Euclid Ave Cleveland OH 44195 Office Phone: 216-444-2268.

STARLINGER, ROLAND, microbiologist; b. Salzburg, Sept. 13, 1968; PhD, U. Innsbruck, 1996. Rsch. scientist Biochemie Gmbh, 1998—99; sales mgr. western Europe Ebewe Pharma, 1999—2002, product mgr., 2003—09; sales mgr. Proceryon Bioscis., 2002—03; internat. product mgr. Sandoz, 2009—. Mem.: ISOPP, ESMO. Avocations: golf, skiing, singing. Office: Mondseest 11 Unterach Upper Austria 4866 Austria Business E-Mail: roland.starlinger@sandoz.com.

STARNES, KATIE GERARD, retired community health nurse; b. Corpus Christi, Tex., Mar. 3, 1940; d. James Robert Gerard and Lillie Myrtle Henderson-Gerard; m. Lawrence Edwin Starnes, June 30, 1962; children: Nelvia LaVoy Starnes-Terrell, Ann Starnes-Adams, Nina Faye. BSN, Prairie View A&M, Tex., 1963; MSN Cmty Health Focus in Adminstrn./Mgmt., Tex. Womens U., Denton/Houston, 1978. Cert. in gerontology nursing, ANA, 2008, in Anger Mgmt., 2008. Staff charge nurse Hermann Hosp., Tex. Med. Ctr., Houston, 1964—67, cons., 2002—; staff and nurse supr. Vis. Nurse Assn., Houston, 1967—69, patient care mgr., 1969—74, br. office mgr. Rosenberg, Tex., 1978—83; dir. nursing/patient care facilitator United Home Health, Houston, 1976—78; auditing specialist Blue Cross/Blue Shield Medicare Intermediary, Dallas, 1983—84; home care nurse mgr. Houston Veterans Affairs Med. Ctr., Houston, 1985—2002, spinal cord home care, 1994—2002, intermediate care nurse mgr., 2001—02; home care cons., svc. edn, 2002—. Bd. dirs. United Home Health, Houston, 1976—79, Planned Parenthood, Fort Bend County, Tex., 1979—83; sub-com. chairperson ARC, Fort Bend County Chpt., Houston, 1978—85; chairperson disaster nursing svcs. ARC, Houston Chpt., 1985—87, mem., 2002—; organizer, bd. dirs. Ft. Bend County Health Coun., Richmond/Rosenburg, 1980—84; home care cons. Greater Houston Health Care, 1985; organizer, co-leader caregivers support group Houston Vet. Med. Ctr., Hosp. Based Home Care, 1987—2002; adj. clin. prof. U. Tex. Health Sci. Ctr., Houston, 1987—2005; adj. clin. prof., adv. bd. Alvin Jr. Coll., Tex., 1990—2002; profl. nurse std. bd. Houston Vet. Affairs Med. Ctr. Nursing Svc., 1988—2002; co-leader, vol. Alzheimer's Assn., 1988; mem. Gero-Education Com., Huffington Ctr. Aging, Baylor Coll. Medicine, Houston, 1996—2002; nursing cons. In-svc. Edn., 2002—. Active vol. Am. Heart Assn., Alzheimer's Disease Assn., Am. Red Cross Greater Houston Chpt.; instr., CPR & babysitting courses Tchg., Edn., Enrichment, Recreation, Outreach Ctr., bd. pres. & mentorship program, chair, fundraising & health svcs. com.; sec. Nurse Alumni Prairie View A&M U.; leader Alzheimers Support Group; mem., edn. com. Am. Orgn. Nurse Execs., 1995; coord. Annual Collaborative Cmty. Health Summit, 2006—11. Recipient Nat. Sec.'s award, VSN 16, Houston VAMC, 1999; named one of Top Twenty Nurses, Growth of Profession, Tex. Nurses Assn. Dist. 9, 1992. Mem.: AARP, Internat. Hon. Soc. Nursing, Wellness Comm. (co-chair), Black Nurses Assn., Fed. Employees Assn., Prairie View A&M Nurse Alumni Assn. (life; sec.), Alzheimer's Assn., A. Phillip Randolph Assn., Jack and Jill America, Inc. (assoc.; charter mem. and past pres. Fort Bend Co. chpt.), Eta Delta Chpt., Sigma Theta Tau, Delta Sigma Theta Sorority, Inc. (Houston Met. Chpt.) (life; chair youth acad. & GEMS 2009—). Church Of Christ. Avocations: writing, travel. Home: 15031 Chaseridge Dr Missouri City TX 77489 Personal E-mail: k.gerard-starnes@sbcglobal.net.

STARODUB, NIKOLAJ FEDOROVICH, biophysicist; b. Ivanovka, Dnipropetrovsk, Ukraine, Oct. 15, 1941; s. Fedir Vasilovich Starodub and Fedosija Ivanivna (Janghula) S.; m. Marija Ivanivna Dibko, Sept. 4, 1970; children: Olexander, Valentyna. Asst. of Vet. Doctor, Coll. Novomoskovsk, Ukraine, 1960; Biophysicist, U. Dhipropetrovsk, Ukraine, 1965; Cand. Biol. Sci., Inst. Biochemistry,

Kiev, Ukraine, 1969; D Biol. Sci., Moscow U., 1982; Docent, Inst. Molecular Biol. and, Genetics, Kiev, 1974; Prof., Inst. Biochemistry, Kiev, 1994. Investigator Inst. Physiology, Kiev, 1965-67; jr. rsch. worker Inst. Molecular Biology and Genetics, Kiev, 1967-69, sr. rsch. worker, 1969-86, leader scientist, 1986-88, chief scientific worker, 1988-93, Inst. Biochemistry, Kiev, 1993-98, head dept. biochemistry of sensoric and regulatoric sys., 1998—. Editl. bd. Ukrainian Biochem. Zhurnal, 1990—; contbr. articles to profl. jours. Mem. scientific bd. Inst. of Biochemistry, Kiev, 1985—, Ukraine Scientific Ctr. of Gygiene, Kiev, 1994—, Ukrainian Med. Inst. of Non-Traditional Medicine, Kiev, 1993-99; mem. com. New Med. Techniques, Ukraine Ministry of Pub. Health, Kiev, 1992-98; mem. Anti-AIDS com. at Pres. of Ukraine, 1992-97. Recipient A.V. Palladin's prize laureate Ukraine Nat. Acad. Sci., 1988; grantee NATO, Brussels, 1996, 97, 99, others. Mem. N.Y. Acad. Scis., Ukrainian Acad. of Scis. of Nat. Progress, Ukrainian Biochem. Soc., Internat. Electrochem. Soc., Ukrainian Biochem. Soc., Soc. Nexus. Avocations: chess, gardening. Home: Apt 7 7 Erevanskaya Str 03087 Kyiv Ukraine Office: AV Palladin Inst Biochemist 9 Leontovicha Str 01030 Kyiv Ukraine E-mail: prof@progress.freenet.kiev.ua, Starodub@paladin.biochem.kiev.ua.

STARR, ALBERT, thoracic surgeon, educator, research scientist; b. NYC, June 1, 1926; MD, Columbia Coll. Physicians & Surgeons, 1949; HHD, Lewis and Clark Coll., 1968; PhD (hon.), U. London, 1986. Cert. Surgery, Thoracic Surgery. Intern John Hopkins Hosp., Balt., 1949—50; resident Bellevue Hosp. & Presbyn. Hosp., 1950—57; asst. in surgery Columbia U., 1957; hosp. appointment Heart Inst., St Vincent, Portland, Oreg.; prof. surgery, head heart surgery prog. Oreg. Health Sci. U., 1957—64, spl. advisor to the dean and pres., disting. prof. cardiovascular medicine, sch. medicine, 2011—; pediatric staff mem. Starr-Wood Children's Cardiac Ctr.; med. dir., dir. emeritus Providence Heart and Vascular Inst., Portland, Oreg., 1964—2011; dir. biosci. R&D Providence Health Sys., Oreg.; chair holder Albert Starr Academic Ctr. for Cardiac Surgery, Oreg. Recipient Oreg. Heart Assn. award for Scientific Achievement, 1964, Modern Medicine award, 1971, Golden Plate award, Am. Acad. Achievement, 1973, Internat. Heart Pioneer award, Societe de Chirurgie Thoracique Cardio-Vasculaire de Langue Francaise, 2000; co-recipient (with Alain Carpentier) Lasker-DeBakey Clin. Med. Rsch. award, Lasker Found., 2007. Mem.: ACS (chmn. thoracic adv. bd.), Am. Coll. Chest Physicians (past trustee), Western Thoracic Surgical Assn., Assn. Thoracic and Cardiovascular Surgeons of Asia, Soc. U. Surgeons, Soc. Thoracic Surgeons (pres. 1985—86), Pan Pacific Surgical Assn., Internat. Cardiovascular Soc., Am. Surgical Assn., AMA, Am. Coll. Cardiology (Disting. Scientist award 1988), Am. Assn. for Thoracic Surgery (past coun. mem.), Pan Hellenic Surgical Soc. (hon.). Achievements include co-inventing of the first artificial heart valve, successfully implanted in 1960; joined Dr. Alain Carpentier in Paris for one of the world's first computer-assisted robotic surgeries in 1998. Office: Oreg Health Sci University 3181 SW Sam Jackson Park Rd Portland OR 97239-3098 Office Phone: 503-296-4027. Business E-Mail: starra@ohsu.edu. *

STARR, DOROTHY ANNE, retired psychiatrist; b. NYC, July 17, 1922; d. James Edward and Eileen Lillian (Gorman) S.; m. Charles O. Olsen, Aug. 29 1953; children: Margrete. Therese, Sara, Marie. BS, NYU, 1943; MD, SUNY, 1950. Intern St. Johns Episcopal Hosp., Bklyn., 1950-51; resident in ob-gyn St. Albans Naval Hosp., N.Y., 1951-52; resident psychiatrist Bethesda (Md.) Naval Hosp., 1953-54, St. Elizabeth's Hosp., Washington, 1954-56; pvt. practice psychiatry Washington, 1957—2004. Chief adult mental health Dept. Pub. Health, Washington, 1960-64; cons. St. Elizabeth's Hosp., Washington, 1965-73; physician mem. Mental Health Commn., Washington, 1969-73;/ asst. clin. prof. Georgetown U., Washington, 1975-81; assy. rep. Am. Psychiatric Assn., 1981-87, asys. recorder, 1987-88; bd. dirs. Nat. Capital Underwriters, Inc., Washington, 1980-97, Legal Resources Fund, Washington, 1982-84; psychiat. cons. Christ House Health Care for the Homeless, 1995-2005. With U.S. Army, 1943-45, USN, 1950-54. Mem. AMA (mem. adv. panel on women in medicine 1989-91, chmn. adv. panel 1991-92), Am. Med. Women's Assn., Washington Psychiatry Soc. (mem. coun. 1965-67, 71-72, asst. del. 1981-87, sec. 1972-73), Med. Soc. D.C. (pres. 1980, mem. exec. bd. 1974-92, chmn. exec. bd. 1981, alt. del. 1983-87, del. 1988-92), Am. Psychiat. Assn. (fellow, recorder assembly 1987-88). Home: 700 New Hampshire Ave Nw Washington DC 20037-2407

STARZ, TERENCE W., rheumatologist, internist; MD, Thomas Jefferson U., Phila. Diplomate Am. Bd. Internal Medicine, Am. Bd. Internal Medicine-rheumatology. Resident Univ. Pitts. Med. Sch., fellow; hospital affiliations include Magee-Womens Hosp. Univ. Pitts. Med. Ctr., Univ. Pitts. Med. Ctr. Presbyn., Univ. Pitts. Med. Ctr. Shadyside. Office: University of Pittsburgh Medical Center 3500 Fifth Ave 4th Fl Pittsburgh PA 15213 Office Phone: 412-682-2434.

STARZL, THOMAS EARL, physician, educator; b. Le Mars, Iowa, Mar. 11, 1926; s. Roman F. and Anna Laura (Fitzgerald) S.; m. Barbara Brothers, Nov. 27, 1954 (div.); children: Timothy, Rebecca, Thomas; m. Joy D. Conger, Aug. 1, 1981. BA in Biology, Westminster Coll., Fulton, Mo., 1947, DSc (hon.), 1965; MA in Anatomy, Northwestern U., Chgo., 1950, MD with distinction, 1952, PhD in Neurophysiology, 1952; DSc (hon.), N.Y. Med. Coll., 1970, Westmar Coll., 1974, Med. Coll. Wis., 1981, Northwestern U., 1982, Bucknell U., 1985, Muhlenberg Coll., 1985, Mt. Sinai Sch. Medicine, 1988; MD (hon.), U. Louvain, Belgium, 1985, U. Genova, 1988, U. Rennes, 1988; LLD (hon.), U. Wyo., 1971; LHD (hon.), LaRoche Coll., 1988. Intern Johns Hopkins U. Hosp., Balt., 1952-53, fellow, surg., 1953-54, resident, 1955-56; mem. faculty Northwestern U. Med. Sch., Evanston, Ill., 1958-61; assoc. prof. surgery U. Colo. Med. Sch., Denver, 1962-80, prof. surgery, 1964-80, chmn. dept. surgery, 1972-80; prof. surgery U. Pitts. Sch. Med., 1981—; dir. U. Pitts. Transplantation Inst., 1991—96; dir. emeritus U. Pitts. Transplantation Inst. (now called the Thomas E. Starzl Transplantation Inst.), 1996—. Mem. staff Presbyn. Univ. Hosp., Univ. Hosp., Children's Hosp. of Pitts., Pitts. VA Hosp; spkr. in field. Author: Experience in Renal Transplantation, 1964, Experience in Hepatic Transplantation, 1969, (autobiography) The Puzzle People: Memoirs of a Transplant Surgeon, 1992; mem. of several editl. bds.; contbr. articles to profl. jours. Recipient award Westminster Coll., 1965, Achievement award Lund U., 1965, Eppinger award Soc. Internat. de Chirurgie, 1965, Eppinger prize, Freiburg, 1970, William S. Middleton award for outstanding research in VA system, 1968, Merit award Northwestern U., 1969, Disting. Achievement award Modern Medicine, 1969, Creative Council award U. Colo., 1971, Colo. Man of Yr. award, 1967, Brookdale award in Medicine, AMA Bd. Trustees and Brookdale Found., 1974, David M. Hume Meml. award Nat. Kidney Found., 1978, Pitts. Man of Yr. award, 1981, Bigelow medal, Boston Surgical Soc., the City of Medicine award, Disting. Svc. award, Am. Liver Found., 1991, Willam Beaumont prize, Am. Gastroenterological Assn., Peter Medawar prize, Transplant Soc., Jacobson Innovation award, Am. Coll. Surgeons, 1998 Lannelongue Internat. medal, Nat. Acad. Surgery, France, 2001 King Faisal Internat. prize for Medicine, Nat. Medal of Science for Biol. Sciences, 2004; Markle scholar, 1958. Fellow ACS (Sheen award 1982), Am. Acad. Arts and Scis.; mem. Soc. Univ. Surgeons, Soc. Vascular Surgery, Am. Surg. Assn., Internat. Transplantation Soc.(past pres.), Deutsche Gesellschaft für Chirurgie, founding pres., Am. Soc. of Transplant Surgeons and Transplant Recipients Internat. Orgn., Nat. French Acad. Medicine, and numerous others. Achievements include performing transplantation on dogs, 1958-1960; the world's first liver transplant in 1963; the performing six baboon kidney transplants in 1963 and 1964; first successful liver transplant in 1967; the world's first chimpanzee liver transplant in three children between 1969 and 1974; first multiple organ transplant in 1983; the first heart and liver transplant in 1984; announcing the first-time use of a new, more effective anti-rejection agent, FK506 (tacrlimus) in 1989, approved for clinical use by FDA in 1994; made medical history with team in 1992 and 1993, when surgeons performed two baboon-to-human liver transplants; established chimerism theory in 1992; most cited scientist in clinical medicine in 1999. Office: Thomas E Starzl Transplant Inst Ste 729 Montefiore Hosp 3459 Fifth Ave Pittsburgh PA 15213-3403 Office Phone: 412-624-0112.

STASH, SUSAN MICHELE, critical care nurse; b. Inglewood, Calif., Mar. 28, 1965; d. Michael Paul and JoAnn Patricia (Margan) S. BSN, Westminster Coll., Salt Lake City, 1987. RN, Calif.; cert. med.-surg. nurse ANCC. Staff nurse gen. surg. unit St. Joseph Hosp., Orange, Calif., 1987-91; staff nurse gen. med. surg. unit Castle Med. Ctr., Kailua, Hawaii, 1992-94; staff nurse renal/pulmonary/telemetry unit Mary Washington Hosp., Fredericksburg, Va., 1994-95; intermediate med. care unit staff nurse Onslow Meml. Hosp., Jacksonville, NC, 1995-97; staff nurse progressive care unit Swedish Med. Ctr., Englewood, Colo., 1998—; staff nurse subacute ICU Hoag Meml. Hosp. Presbyn., Newport Beach, Calif., 1999—. Mem. ANA, AACN, Am. Assn. Cert. Nurses, Sigma Theta Tau.

STASON, WILLIAM BOAZ, medical educator, researcher, physician; b. Ann Arbor, Aug. 24, 1931; s. Edwin Blythe and Adeline Boaz Stason; m. Susan Burrowes Burrowes, June 15, 1968; children: William Burrowes, Thomas Boaz, Amanda Blythe, Suzannah Margaret. BS, U. Mich., Ann Arbor, 1953; MD, Harvard Med. Sch., Boston, 1960; MS, Harvard Sch. Pub. Health, 1975. Faculty medicine Cornell U. Med. Coll., NYC, 1968—70, Harvard Med. Sch., 1970—90; chief health svcs. rsch. svc. Veterans Adminstrn., West Roxbury, Mass., 1984—90; faculty Harvard Sch. Pub. Health, Boston, 1973—; sr. scientist Brandeis U., Waltham, Mass., 2000—. Author: (book) Hypertension:a Policy Perspective; contbr. numerous articles to profl. jours. Leadership town bds., Lincoln, 1973—2010. Lt. j.g. USN, 1953—56. Home: 29 Sandy Pond Rd Lincoln MA 01773 Office: Heller Sch Brandeis University 415 South St Waltham MA 02451 Personal E-mail: wbstason@verizon.net. Business E-Mail: stason@brandeis.edu.

STATE, MATTHEW W., cell biologist, neuroscientist, educator; BA, Stanford U., 1984, MD, 1991; PhD, Yale U., 2001. Dir. program on neurogenetics Yale Sch. Medicine, co-dir. med. genomics program, assoc. prof. child psychiatry & genetics. Office: Child Study Center 230 South Frontage Rd PO Box 207900 New Haven CT 06520-7900 Office Phone: 203-785-4659. Office Fax: 203-785-7560. E-mail: matthew.state@yale.edu.

STAUB, MARIA, medical biochemistry professor, medical educator; b. Városlõd, Hungary, Jan. 9, 1936; d. Vendel and Etelka Staub; m. Vilmos Stenger, 1956; 1 child, Annamaria. MD, Semmelweis U., Budapest, Hungary, 1960; PhD, Acad. Scis., Budapest, Hungary, 1974, DSc, 1984. Prof. dept. med. chemistry and pathobiochemistry Semmelweis U., Budapest, Hungary, 1984—. Tchr., med. biochemistry in Hungarian, English and German langs. Contbr. scientific papers, articles to profl. jours. Office: Semmelweis University Dept Med Biochemistry and Pathobiochemis Tuzoltó u 37-47 Budapest 1094 Hungary Office Phone: 36-1-4591500 ext.60157. Business E-Mail: staub@eok.sote.hu, staub@eok.sote.puskin.hu.

STAUB, W. ARTHUR, health care products executive; b. Detroit, Dec. 25, 1923; s. Edward Elmer and Emma Josephine (Fleury) S.; m. Alla Elizabeth Edwards, June 26, 1948; children: James Randall, Sally Ann, David Scott. BS, Dartmouth Coll., 1944; MD, Temple U., 1947. Intern Muhlenberg Hosp., Plainfield, NJ, 1947-48; resident in pediatrics Abington (Pa.) Meml. Hosp., 1950-51; practice medicine specializing in pediatrics Westfield (N.J.) Med. Group, 1948-63; assoc. med. dir. Ciba Pharm. Co., Summit, NJ, 1963-66; med. dir., v.p. life sci. div. Becton-Dickinson and Co., Rutherford, NJ, 1966-70; v.p. med. affairs C. R. Bard Co., Murray Hill, NJ, 1970-88, also bd. dirs. Bd. dirs. Crestmont Fed. Savs. and Loan Assn., Edison, N.J., Colonial Trust Nat. Bank, North Palm Beach, Fla.; cons. Children's Specialized Hosp., Westfield, 1948-88, Overlook Hosp., Summit, 1948-88. Contbr. articles to profl. jours. Deacon Presbyn. Ch., Westfield, 1959—. Ensign USNR, 1944—50, to capt. USAF, 1950—53. Fellow Am. Coll. Physician Execs.; mem. AAAS, Assn. Advancement Med. Instrumentation, Health Industry Mfrs. Assn. (chmn. med. and sci. steering com.). Clubs: Echo Lake Country (Westfield) (bd. trustees 1984-88); Lost Tree (North Palm Beach, Fla., bd. govs. 1989-94, sec. 1989-94); Skytop (Pa.). Republican. Presbyterian. Avocations: golf, physical fitness, reading, sailing, travel. Home: 3330 Devonshire Way Palm Beach Gardens FL 33418 E-mail: DoctorWAS@aol.com.

STAUSBERG, JÜRGEN, medical educator, researcher; MD, U. Düsseldorf, Germany, 1989; PhD in Med. Sci., U. Essen, 2001. Cert. med. informatics Med. Assn. Bavaria, 1995, quality mgmt. Med. Assn. North Rhine-Westphalia, 2007. Physician Mcpl. Hosp., Solingen, Germany, 1990—92; postdoctoral rsch. fellow GSF, Nat. Rsch. Ctr. Environment & Health, Neuherberg, Germany, 1992—94; lectr. U. Duisburg, Essen, 1994—2007; prof. U. München, 2008—. Contbr. articles to profl. jours. Mem.: German Assn. Surgery, German Assn. Med. Informatics, Biometry and Epidemiology. Home: Kordulastr 13 Essen 45131 Germany Personal E-mail: stausberg@ekmed.de.

STAV, ANATOLI OVSEI, anesthesiologist; b. Tchernoviz, Ukraine, Russia, Sept. 23, 1952; arrived in Israel, 1978; s. Ovsei Isaak and Zilia Aba (Zibenberg) Podstavkin; m. Inna Leon Schmulevitz, Aug. 10, 1974; children: Alexandra, Ilana, Anat, Michael. MD, Med. Inst. No. 1, Leningrad, Russia, 1976. Jr. anesthesiologist, Rovno, Russia, 1976-78, Hillel Jaffe Meml. Hosp., Hadera, Israel, 1978-80, 81-83, Beilinson Med. Ctr., Petah Tiqva, Israel, 1983-86; sr. anesthesiologist Hillel Jaffe Med. Ctr., 1986-94, work in Pain Clinic, 1987-91, chief postoperative care unit, 1994—. Anesthesiologist Hertzlia (Israel) Med. Ctr., 1989-93, Ramat Marpe Hosp., Ramat Gan, Israel, 1989-93, Elisha Hosp., Haifa, 1990—, Am. Med. Ctr., Rishon Lezion, Israel, 1989-94; lectr. postgrad. anesthesiology U. Tel-Aviv, 1986, 89, 90, 94—, anesthesiology immigrant physicians Hillel Jaffe Med. Ctr., 1991, 92, 95, 96, Nursing Med. Sch., 1991, 92, 94; presenter papers in field. Contbr. articles to profl. jours. Maj. Israeli Med. Force, 1980-81. Mem. Israel Med. Assn., Israel Soc. Anesthesiologists, Internat. Soc. Study of Pain, Israelian Soc. Study of Pain, Internat. Soc. Study of Lumbar Spine, World Soc. Pain Clinicians, European Soc. Regional Anesthesia. Office: Hillel Jaffe Med Ctr Dept Anesthesiology 38100 Hadera Israel Home: Ayasmin Str 15 PO Box 5730 Hadera 38506 Israel Home Phone: 972-4-6338-412; Office Phone: 972-4-6304-687. Business E-Mail: stav@hy.health.gov.il.

STAVITSKY, ABRAM BENJAMIN, immunologist, educator; b. Newark, May 14, 1919; s. Nathan and Ida (Novak) S.; m. Ruth Bernice Okney, Dec. 6, 1942; children: Ellen Barbara, Gail Beth. AB, U. Mich., 1939, MSPH, 1940; PhD, U. Minn., 1943; VMD, U. Pa., 1946. Research fellow Calif. Inst. Tech., 1946-47; faculty Case Western Res. U., 1947—, prof. microbiology, 1962—, prof. molecular biology and microbiology, 1983—89; emeritus, 1989; mem. expert com. immunochemistry WHO, 1963-83; mem. microbiology fellowship com. NIH, 1963-66; mem. microbiology test com. Nat. Bd. Med. Examiners, 1970-73; chmn. microbiology test com. Nat. Bd. Podiatry Examiners, 1978-82; adj. staff in pathobiology Lerner Rsch. Inst., Cleve. Clinic Found., 2006—. Mem. editl. bd. Jour. Immunological Methods, 1979-88, Immunopharmacology, 1983-96. Vice pres. Ludlow Community Assn., 1964-66. Fellow AAAS; mem. Am. Assn. Immunologists, Am. Soc. Microbiology, Sigma Xi. Home: 14604 Onaway Rd Shaker Heights OH 44120-2845 Office: 2119 Abington Rd Cleveland OH 44106-2333 Home Phone: 216-752-8631. Business E-Mail: abs7@case.edu.

STAW, BARRY MARTIN, business and psychology educator; b. Los Angeles, Sept. 13, 1945; s. Harold Paul and Shirley C. (Posner) S.; m. Adrienne McDonnell; 1 child, Jonah Martin. BS, U. Oreg., 1967; MBA, U. Mich., 1968; PhD, Northwestern U., 1972. Asst. prof. bus. adminstrn. U. Ill., Urbana, 1972-75; assoc. prof. Northwestern U., Evanston, Ill., 1975-77, prof., 1977-80, U. Calif., Berkeley, 1980—, Mitchell prof. Leadership and communication, 1986—. Researcher in organizational psychology. Editor: Psychological Dimensions of Organizational Behavior; co-editor: New Directions in Organizational Behavior, (book series) Research in Organizational Behavior; mem. editl. bd. Adminstrv. Sci. Quar., Organizational Behavior and Human Decision Processes, 1974—, Basic and Applied Social Psychology, Motivation & Emotion; contbr. numerous articles to profl. jours. Fellow APA, Am. Psychol. Soc., Acad. Mgmt. Soc. for Organizational Behavior. Democrat. Jewish. Avocations: basketball, tennis, skiing. Office: Univ of Calif Haas Sch Bus Adminstrn Berkeley CA 94720-0001 Business E-Mail: staw@haas.berkeley.edu. *

STAYTON, WILLIAM RALPH, retired psychologist, educator; b. Kelso, Wash., Dec. 25, 1933; s. Ralph Willard and Marguerite (Hunter) S.; m. Kathleen Boucher, Sept. 4, 1954; children: Mark, John, Cheryl, Paul. BA, U. Redlands, 1956; MDiv, Andover Newton Theol. Sem., 1960; ThD, Boston U., 1967; PhD, Inst. Advanced Study of Human Sexuality, 2002. Ordained to ministry Am. Bapt. Ch., 1959. Assoc. min. 1st Bapt. Ch. in Newton, Mass., 1956-61; min. 1st Bapt. Ch., Gloucester, Mass., 1961-68; chaplain New Eng. Bapt. Hosp., Boston, 1968-71; asst. prof. U. Pa. Sch. Medicine, Phila., 1971—78; adj. assoc. prof. U. Pa. Grad. Sch. Edn., Phila., lectr., faculty, 1982—2004; asst. prof. Jefferson Med. Coll./Thomas Jefferson U., 1978-83; marriage and family therapist Wm R. Stayton & Assocs., Ltd., P.C., Phila., 1978—2008. Mem. faculty La Salle U., Phila., 1983-2002; prof. and coord., human sexuality program Widener U., Chester, Pa., 1999-2006, prof./scholar-in-residence, 2006—; exec. dir. Ctr. for Sexuality and Religion, 2006-08; prof. sexuality & religion Morehouse Sch. Medicine, Atlanta, 2008-; adj. prof. program in human sexuality U. Minn. Med. Sch., 2011-. Editor spl. issue Topics in Clin. Nursing, 1980; contbr. articles to profl. jours., chpts. to books. Pres. Cmty. Svcs. for Human Growth, Paoli, Pa., 1989-91, bd. dirs., 1981-97. Named Man of Yr., B'nai B'rith, Gloucester, Mass., 1968; recipient Outstanding Svc. award Community Svcs. for Human Growth, 1990, Richard J. Cross award U. Medicine and Dentistry N.J., 1997, Dean's award Sch Human Svc. Professions Widener U., 2002, Tchr. Excellence award Kappa Delta Pi, 2006. Mem. APA, Am. Assn. Marriage and Family Therapists, Am. Assn. Sex Educators, Counselors and Therapists (bd. dirs. 1982-86, 88-90, chmn. dist. VI 1982-86, pres. 1996-98, Outstanding Svc. award 1978-87, Disting. Svc. award 2000, Profl. Standard of Excellence award 2006), World Assn. Sexual Health (Gold Medal award 2011), Sex Info. and Edn. Coun. U.S. (pres. 1985-87, sec. 1990-92), Soc. for Sci. Study Sex (chmn. ann. meeting 1983), Pa. Assn. Marriage and Family Therapists (continuing edn. com. 1985-90), Planned Parenthood Southeastern Pa. (bd. dirs. 1999—2006, 1st vice chmn. 2001-04, chmn. 2004-06), Phi Kappa Phi. Democrat. Home: 226 Highlands Ridge Pl SE Smyrna GA 30082 Business E-Mail: wmstayton@cs.com.

STEAD, MATT, neurologist, educator; b. Fiji Islands, May 30, 1968; BS in Biochemistry, SUNY, Binghamton, 1990; MD, SUNY, Downstate, PhD, 2001. Asst. prof., neurology Mayo Clinic, Rochester, Minn., 2006—. Mem.: Am. Epilepsy Soc. Avocations: skiing, scuba diving, skydiving. Home: 820 8th Ave SW Pine Island MN 55963 Business E-Mail: stead.squire@mayo.edu.

STECKEL, JULIE RASKIN, psychotherapist, lecturer, consultant; b. LA, Jan. 3, 1940; d. Edward M. and Selma (Romm-Rosby) Raskin; m. Richard Jay Steckel, June 16, 1960; children: Jan Marie, David Matthew. BA, UCLA, 1960, MSW, 1975; MA in Teaching., Harvard U., 1961. Lic. clin. social worker; Bd. Cert. Diplomate in Clin. Social Work, 1975; cert. in archeology UCLA, 1995, 96. Music tchr., Los Angeles, Beverly Hills and Santa Monica, Calif., 1968-70; psychol. cons. BMA Dialysis Units, Torrance, Calif., 1976—2008; pvt. practice Santa Monica, Calif., 2000—11, Santa Barbara, Calif., 2000—10. Lectr., cons. UCLA Dental Sch., 1984—95; lectr. social welfare UCLA Grad. Sch., 1985-90, Clin. Soc. Work MANN Ctr. Women With Cancer, UCLA Cancer Ctr., 1996-98; mem. Soc. Clin. Soc. Work, 1973-2010. Mem. editl. bd. Contemporary Dialysis and Nephrology Jour.; contbr. articles to profl. jours. Bd. dirs. Palisades Dem. Hdqrs., Pacific Palisades, Calif., 1972; credentials currier Dem. Conv., Miami, Fla., 1972; mem. LA Women's Commn. Task Force on Child Abuse, 1990—. Fellow Soc. Clin. Social Workers, Nat. Acad. Traumatic Stress; mem. Nat. Assn. Social Workers, Acad. Psychosomatic Medicine. Home and Office: 1126 Bel Air Dr Santa Barbara CA 93105-4642 Office Phone: 805-898-1044. Personal E-mail: listenr2@cox.net.

STECKER, MICHAEL S., interventional radiologist; s. Enid M. and Arthur Stecker; m. Jennifer A. Deaton, June 14, 1992; children: Maxwell S., Morrissa S. BS, Wright State U., Dayton, Ohio, 1988; MD, SUNY, Stony Brook, 1992. Diplomate in diagnostic radiology bd. Cert. Am. Bd. Radiology, 1988, in vascular and interventional radiology CAQ 2002, diplomate in med. Nat. Bd. Med. Examiners, 1993. Surgery resident Mary Imogene Bassett Hosp., Cooperstown, NY, 1992—94; radiology resident Nassau County Med. Ctr., East Meadow, NY, 1994—98, radiology chief resident, 1997—98; vascular and interventional radiology fellow U. Iowa Hosps. and Clinics, Iowa City, 1998—99; attending physician Ind. U. Radiology Assocs., Indpls., 1999—2005; asst. prof. Ind. U. Sch. Medicine, Indpls., 1999—2005; attending physician Brigham and Women's Hosp., Boston, 2005—, interventional radiology inventory mgr., 2007—; asst. prof. Harvard Med. Sch., Boston, 2005—. Interventional radiology site dir. Veteran's Adminstrn. Med. Ctr., Indpls., 1999—2005; assoc. editor, CME editor Jour. Vascular & Internat. Radiology, 2009—. Recipient Eagle Scout, Boy Scouts Am., 1982, Disting. Reviewer, Jour. Vascular and Interventional Radiology, 1999, 2000, 2006. Mem.: AMA (Physician's Recognition awards 1995—), New England Soc. Interventional Radiology (pres. 2006—07, sec. 2006—08, treas. 2006—), Am. Heart Assn., Soc. Interventional Radiology, Am. Roentgen Ray Soc., Radiol. Soc. N.Am., Am. Coll. Radiology, Tau Beta Pi, Beta Theta Pi. Office: Brigham and Women's Hosp 75 Francis St Boston MA 02115

STECKLER, ROBERT E., urologist, educator; Grad., Brandeis U., 1981; MD, Albany Med. Coll., NY, 1985. Diplomate Am. Bd. Urology, lic. NJ, Pa. Intern NY Hosp.-Cornell Med. Ctr., 1986, resident, 1991; fellow Hosp. for Sick Chidren, Canada; clin. asst. prof. Urology Weill Med. Coll. Cornell Univ.; asst. prof. surgery and pediat. dept. Drexel Univ.; urologist Abington and Wash. Township St. Chris Care; attending urologist St. Christopher's Hosp. for Children. Named Recognized Dr., HealthGrades; named one of th Top Doctors, Phila. Mag. Office: Saint Christopher's Hospital for Chidren 3601 A St Philadelphia PA 19134 Office Phone: 215 427 5434.

STEELE, CLAUDE MASON, academic administrator, psychology professor; b. Chgo., Jan. 1, 1946; s. Shelby and Ruth (Hootman) Steele; married, Aug. 27, 1967; children: Jory, Claude Benjamin. BA in Psychology, Hiram Coll., 1967; MA in Social Psychology, Ohio State U., 1969, PhD in Social Psychology, minor in Statistical Psychology, 1971; PhD (hon.), Yale U., 2002, Princeton U., 2003. Asst. prof. U. Utah, Salt Lake City, 1971-73; from asst. to prof. U. Washington, Seattle, 1978-87, prof. psychology, 1985—87; prof. U. Mich., Ann Arbor, 1987-91, rsch. scientist Inst. Social Rsch., 1989—91; prof. psychology Stanford U., Calif., 1991—2009, fellow Ctr. Advanced Study in Behavioral Sciences, 1994—95, chmn. Dept. Psychology, 1997—2000, Lucie Stern prof. social sciences, 1997—2009, co-dir. Ctr. Comparative Studies in Race and Ethnicity, 1999—2002, dir. Ctr. Comparative Studies in Race and Ethnicity, 2002—09, dir. Ctr. for Advanced Study in the Behavioral Scis., dean Sch. Edn., 2011—; provost, prof. psychology Columbia U., NYC, 2009—11. Mem. psychosocial rsch. study sect. Nat. Inst. Alcohol Abuse and Alcoholism, 1984—88; mem. rev. panel and mental health rsch. edn. rev. panel Nat. Inst. Mental Health, 1979—83. Assoc. editor Personality and Social Psychology Bull., 1984—87, consulting editor Jour. of Social Issues, 1983—90, Jour. Personality and Social Psychology, 1990—, Attitudes and Social Cognition, 1990—, Psychol. Rev., 1990—, Motivation and Emotion, 1990—, Basic and Applied Social Psychology, 1990—, Jour. Exptl. Social Psychology, 1990—; author: Whistling Vivaldi: And Other Clues to How Stereotypes Affect Us and What We Can Do, 2010. Mem. King County Alcoholism and Drug Abuse Adminstrv. Bd., 1980—85. Recipient Dean's Teaching award, Stanford U., Gordon Allport prize in Social Psychology, The Soc. for the Psychological Study of Social Issues, 1997, Kurt Lewin Meml. award, 1998. Fellow: American Psychol. Assn. (Disting. Scientific Contribution award 1998, Cattell Fellowship, Sr. award for Disting. Contribution to Psychology in the Pub. Interest & the), American Psychol. Soc. (bd. dirs. 1991—96, William James Fellow award for Disting. Scientific Career Contribution 2000); mem.: NAS, Nat. Acad. Edn., American Acad. Arts & Sciences, Soc. Personality & Social Psychology (pres. 2002—03, Donald Campbell award 2001), Soc. Exptl. Social Psychology (sec.-treas. 1987—88, chmn. 1988—89). Office: Stanford University Sch Education Office of Dean 485 Lausen Mall Stanford CA 94305-3096 Office Phone: 650-723-2109. Office Fax: 650-725-7412. *

STEELE, GLENN D., JR., healthcare educator, health products executive; BA in Literature, Harvard U.; MD, NYU; PhD in Microbiology, Lund U. Pres., CEO Deaconess Profl. Practice Group New England Deaconess Hosp., chmn. dept. surgery; William V. McDermott surgery prof. Harvard Medical School; Richard T. Crane prof., dept. surgery University of Chicago, v.p. medical affairs, dean divsn. biological sci. divsn. and Pritzker Sch. Medicine; pres., CEO Geisinger Health System, 2001—. Vice chmn. Am. Hosp. Assn., Wellcare Health Plans Inc., Weis Markets, Inc., 2009—; bd. dirs. Bucknell U., Temple U. Sch. Medicine, Premier Inc., Hosp. and Healthsystem Assn., Pa., Harvard Med. Faculty Physicians Beth Israel Deaconess Med. Ctr. Contbr. articles to profl. jours. Fellow: ACS, Am. Cancer Soc., Healthcare Exec. Network, Am. Soc. Clin. Oncology, Am. Surg. Assn.; mem.: New England Surg. Soc. Office: Geisinger Health System 100 N Academy Ave Danville PA 17822 Office Phone: 570-286-4571. Office Fax: 570-286-3286. Business E-Mail: gsteele@weismarkets.com. *

STEELE, MARK A., pediatric ophthalmologist; b. NYC, May 12, 1960; MD, NYU, 1986. Cert. in ophthalmology 1991. Internship in medicine Lenox Hill Hosp., NYC, 1986—87, hosp. appointment; residency in ophthalmology NYU Med. Ctr., 1987—90, clin assoc. prof., dept. ophthalmology, dir., pediatric ophthalmology and strabismus divsn.; clin. fellowship in pediatric ophthalmology & stabismus Willis Eye Hosp., Phila., 1990—91; attending surgeon NY Eye & Ear Infirmary, NYC; founder Pediatric Ophthalmic Consultants, NYC. Former pres. Greater NY Soc. Pediatric Ophthalmology and Strabismus; complex strabismus cons. NYU Ctr. Craniofacial Anomalies. Contbr. articles to profl. jours. Named to America's Top Doctors, Castle and Connolly Med., Ltd., NY Metro Top Doctors, New York Mag. Office: Pediatric Ophthalmic Consultants 40 W 72nd St New York NY 10023 Office Phone: 212-981-9800. Office Fax: 212-981-9818.

STEELE, ROBERT JAMES CAMPBELL, surgeon, educator; b. Edinburgh, Mar. 5, 1952; s. Robert Steele; m. Annie Scott Anderson, June 21, 2008; children: Mary, Peter, Katy. BSc, MBChB, MD, Edinburgh U. Prof. surgery Ninewells Hosp. & Med. Sch., Dundee, Scotland, 1996—. Dir Scottish Bowel Screening Programme, Edinburgh; head divsn. surgery Ninewells Hosp. & Med. Sch., Dundee. Contbr. chapters to books, articles to profl. jours. Fellow: CSHK, Royal Coll. Surgeons (UK), Royal Coll. Surgeons (Edinburgh). Office: Univ Dundee Ninewells Ave Dundee DD1 9SY Scotland Home Fax: +44 (0) 1382 496361. Personal E-mail: r.j.c.steele@dundee.ac.uk.

STEEN-HINDERLIE, DIANE EVELYN, social worker, musician; b. Duluth, Minn., June 13, 1947; d. Julian Sem and Evelyn Synnove (Helgaas) Steen; m. John Peter Hinderlie, June 27, 1971 (div. Sept. 1987); children: Peder Donald, Erik Steen; m. John Richard Olson, July 21, 1989. BA in Asian Studies/Social Psychology cum laude, St. Olaf Coll., 1969; MusB, U. Minn. and other instns., 1991; postgrad., Hamline U., 1989—91. Lic. social worker, Minn.; cert. music tchr. Music Tchrs. Nat. Assn. Social worker child care licensing Hennepin County Welfare Dept., Mpls., 1970—73; mem. clergy team exch. program Luth. World Fedn., Göppingen, Germany, 1973—77; mem. clergy team, music dir. Jubilation Singers Bethel Luth. Ch., Rochester, Minn., 1978—83; mem. clergy team, music dir. youth choir First Luth. Ch., St. Louis Park, Minn., 1983—86; adminstr. Family Child Care facility, St. Louis Park, 1986—90; faculty, tchr. Stenson Suzuki Studios and Home Studio, St. Louis Park, 1988—92; small group leader, tchr. vol. Mt. Olive Ch., Children's Hosp., Mpls., 1993, 1996—98; workshop and children's ministry Augsburg Coll. Youth and Family Inst., Trinity Cong., 1998—2006, 2009; founding dir. Fair Pay Inst., Mpls., 1995—2009; trainer United for a Fair Economy, 1997—. Founder orgn. and curriculum Early Childhood Orgn. for Edn. with Singing, 1993—, co-leader German-Am. youth group exch., 1979-82; co-founder Family DayCare Cert. Program and Babygarten (B-12 edn.) classes, 1970-73; bd. dirs. Midwest Coun., Nat. Peace Inst. Found., Grinnell, Iowa, 1991; presenter in field.; root causes of violence action team Initiative for Violence-Free Families, 4th Jud. Dist., Minn., 1997—; cons. Concordia Lang. Villages, 2005—2009. Author: (tng. manual) Mother Tongue Singing/Voice Method, 1988, (study packet) School Start Time/Teen Sleep Deprivation, 1996-97, A+=Baby Church School, 2002; rec. artist, mem. ensemble record/cassettes Nowell Sing We, 1986; performer Nordic Am. Psalmodikon Forbundet, 1997—. Vol. People of Faith Peacemakers, Feminists in Faith/ReImagining and Jewish Cmty. Rels. Coun., 1992-2003, Muslim-Christian Rels. Coun., Joint Religious Legis. Coalition; founder People for Reforming Early Start Time for Teens Orgn., Mpls., 1993—; mem. steering com. Progressive Cmty. and FairVote, Minn., 1994-99; local host youth com. NAACP Conv., Mpls., 1995; vol. Common Cause, St. Paul and Washington; charter mem. US Holocaust Mus., 1993; co-founder antitorture com. Women Against Mil. Madness, 2005-. Recipient appreciation plaque Christian Boy/Girl Scouts Germany; Svc. pin Am. Luth. Ch. Women; listed in Minn. Profiles, Minn. Hist. Soc. A Tribute to Outstanding Minn. Women by Marilyn Chelstrom, 2001; named Asset Builder of Month, St. Louis Park Children First Initiative, 1997; named to Honor Roll, Mendota Mdewakanton Dakota Cmty., 1999. Mem.: MADD, Minn. Music Tchrs. Assn. (first early childhood music chair 2001—03), Assn. Pre- and Perinatal Psychology and Health, Wash. Nat. Cathedral, Soc. for Psychol. Studies of Social Issues, Nat. Luth. Choir Acad., Suzuki Assn. Americas (study area co-organizer, editl. adviser), Internat. Suzuki Assn., Nat. Assn. Tchrs. Singing and Voice-Care Network, UN Assn., Sojourner Project, Inc., Am.'s Jr. Miss. Coun., World Wildlife Fund, Ctr. for Victims of Torture, Amnesty Internat., Nat. Peace Found., Germanic-Am. Inst., Sons of Norway (lodge trustee 1991—), Phi Beta Kappa, Am. Mensa. Green. Lutheran. Avocations: reading, travel, politics.

STEERE, ALLEN CARUTHERS, JR., physician, educator; b. Apr. 11, 1943; m. Margaret Mercer, 1969; children: Allen Caruthers III, Margaret Hamilton, Samuel Mercer, John Summers. BA, Columbia U., 1965, MD, 1969; DSc. (hon.), Indiana U., 1992, SUNY, 1997; DSc (hon.), Ohio Wesleyan U., 2008; M (hon.), Harvard Med. Sch., 2002. Diplomate Am. Bd. Internal Medicine; lic. rheumatologist, N.Y., Ga., Ct., Mass. Intern St. Luke's Hosp., NYC, 1969-70, asst., sr. resident, 1970-72, chief resident, instr. medicine, 1972-73; chief resident, instr. medicine Coll. Physicians and Surgeons Columbia U., NYC, 1972-73; clin. fellow in rheumatology Yale U., New Haven, 1975-77, asst. prof. medicine, epidemiology and pub. health, 1977-81, assoc. prof. medicine, 1981-87; prof. medicine, chief rheumatology and immunology New Eng. Med. Ctr. Tufts U., Boston, 1987—2002, Natalie V. & Milton O. Zucker prof. rheumatology/immunology, 1998—2002; prof. medicine Harvard Med. Sch., Boston, 2002—; dir. rheumatology Mass. Gen. Hosp., 2002—06, dir. clin. rsch. in rheumatology, 2006—. With USPHS, 1973-75. Recipient Citation for Elucidation of Lyme disease, Infectious Diseases Soc. Am., 1984, Ciba-Geigy Rheumatology prize, Internat. League Against Rheumatism, 1985, award for discovery of Lyme disease, Nat. Inst. Arthritis and Musculoskeletal Skin Diseases, 1988, Richard and Hinda Rosenthal award, ACP, 1990, Joseph Mather Smith prize, Coll. Physicians and Surgeons, Columbia U., 1990, Zucker Faculty prize, Tufts U., 1990, award for studies Lyme disease, Nat. Health Coun., 1990, Lee C. Howley Sr. prize, Arthritis Found., 1993, Gold medal, Albert Sabin Vaccine Inst., 1998, Astute Clinician award, NIH, 1999, award, Am. Lyme Disease Found., 2000, Columbia Coll. of Phys. and Surgeon's Alumni award for Disting. Acad. Accomplishment, 2001, Physician Achievement award, Artist Found.(Mass. Chapt.), 2006. Master Am. Coll. Rheumatology (Howard and Martha Holley rsch. prize in rheumatology 1995, Clin. Invest award, 2008); mem. Am. Soc. Clin. Investigation, Am. Fedn. Clin. Rsch., Assn. Am. Physicians, Clin. Immunology Soc. Office: Mass Gen Hosp 55 Fruit St CNY 149/8301 Boston MA 02114

STEFANADIS, CHRISTODOULOS, cardiologist; b. Eudilos, Ikaria, Greece, May 31, 1947; MD, Athens Med. Sch., 1971, PhD, 1981. Prof. cardiology Med. Sch. U. Athens, 2002—. Vis. prof. Hahnemann U., Phila., 1993, Ohio State U., 1997; dir. 1st dept. cardiology Athens Med. Sch., 2003, dean, 2007—11; clin. prof. medicine Emory U., Atlanta, 2005. Recipient Simon Dack award, Am. Coll. Cardiology; grant, Hellenic Heart Found., Hellenic Soc. Cardiology. Fellow: Soc. Cardiac Angiography and Interventions, European Soc. Cardiology, Am. Coll. Cardiology; mem.: Internat. Andreas Gruentzig Soc., Vulnerable Plaque Org. (mem. com. Detection of Vulnerable Plaques). Avocation: sailing. Home: Tepeleniou 9 Paleo Psychico Athens Attiki 15452 Greece Personal E-mail: chstefan@med.uoa.gr.

STEFANO, SCABINI, oncologist; b. Genoa, Jan. 5, 1972; Postgrad, U. Genoa, 1996. Oncologic surgeon AOU St Martino Hosp. Genoa, Italy, 2004. Grant, Soc. Ligure Gastroenterologia. Fellow: SLC; mem.: SIUCP, SICCR, ACOI, SIC. Office: Largo R Benzi 8 Genoa 16100 Italy Office Fax: 39 0106727. Business E-Mail: stefanoscabini@libero.it.

STEFANOPOULOS, PANAGIOTIS K., oral and maxillofacial surgeon; b. Tripolis, Greece, May 19, 1967; s. Konstantinos Stefanopoulos and Vassiliki Makri. Grad., Med. Mil. Acad., 1991; DDS, Aristotle U., 1991, MD, 2011. Resident gen surgery Army Hosp., Thessaloniki, 1994—95; trainee oral and maxillofacial surgery G. Papanicolaou Gen. Hosp., Thessaloniki, 2000—03. Cons. in field. Contbr. articles to profl. jours. Ret. col. Hellenic Army. Mem.: Assn. Mil. Surgeons US, Brit. Assn. Oral & Maxillofacial Surgeons, Am. Assn. Oral & Maxillofacial Surgeons (affiliate mem.), AO/ASIF(CMF), Hellenic Assn. Oral and Maxillofacial Surgeons (assoc.). Home Phone: 30210-7713894. Personal E-mail: pan.stefanopoulos@gmail.com.

STEFÁNSSON, EINAR, ophthalmology educator; b. Reykjavík, Iceland, May 19, 1952; s. Stefán Pétursson and Bryndis Alda Einarsdóttir; m. Bryndis Thórárdóttir; children: Arnar, Margrét, Stefán, Katrín Ólöf, Anna Bryndís. MD, U. Iceland, Reykjavík, 1978; PhD, Duke U., 1981. Diplomate Am. Bd. Ophthalmology, cert. specialist in ophthalmology Govt. Iceland, 1985. Rsch. assoc. Duke U., Durham, NC, 1979-81; resident in ophthalmology Duke U. Med. Ctr., Durham, 1982-85, asst. prof. ophthalmology, 1986-89; vis. scientist Nat. Eye Inst., Bethesda, Md., 1985-86; prof. ophthalmology U. Iceland, Reykjavík, 1987—, dean Sch. Medicine, 1996-98. Dir. Icelandic Pharm., Reykjavik, 1994—97, Cyclops ehf, Reykjavik, 1996—2000; v.p. Decode Genetics Inc., Reykjavik, 2000—02; mem. editl. bd. European Jour. Ophthalmology, Progress in Retinal and Eye Rsch. Author: Ocular Oxygenation and Neovascularization, 1981; co-editor: Icelandic Med. Jour., 1991—94, Acta Ophthalmologica Scandinavica, 1996—; editor, 2005—; co-editor: Diabetes Mellitus in Iceland, 1992; contbr. numerous articles and abstracts to profl. jours. Decorated knight Falcon Order Iceland; recipient Synoptic Found. Hon. award, 2006, Synoptik Fonden award, 2006, Pohl award, 2006; Melvin Jones fellow, Lions Internat. Found., 1994. Fellow: Am. Acad. Ophthalmology; mem.: Icelandic Ophthalmol. Soc., Icelandic Med. ASsn., Assn. Rsch. and Vision in Ophthalmology, Club Jules Gonin. Avocations: bridge, volleyball, fishing. Home: Fjardarás 13 110 Reykjavik Iceland Office: U Iceland Dept Ophthalmolog Landspítalinn 101 Reykjavik Iceland Home Phone: +354 577 9433; Office Phone: +354 543 7217. Business E-Mail: einarste@landspitali.is.

STEFÁNSSON, KÁRI, neurologist, educator, genomics company executive; b. Reykjavik, Iceland, Apr. 6, 1949; MD, U. Iceland. Cert. Neuropathology, 1983, Neurology, 1984. Tng. in neurology and neuropathology U. Chgo., faculty positions in neurology, neuropathology, and neurosciences, 1983—93; prof. neurology, neuropathology and neurosciences Harvard U., 1993—97; dir., neuropathology Beth Israel Hosp., Boston, 1993—96; co-founder, pres., CEO, dir. deCODE Genetics, Reykjavik, Iceland, 1996—, also chmn. bd. dir., 1999—. Named one of The World's Most Influential People, TIME mag., 2007. Achievements include opening the NASDAQ Stock Market on July 20, 2005, after deCode's 5 year anniversary on the NASDAQ Market. Office: deCODE Genetics Sturlugata 8 IS-101 Reykjavik Iceland Office Phone: 354-570-1900. Office Fax: 354-570-1903.

STEFFAN, JUDY MAE, medical/surgical nurse; b. Beatrice, Nebr., Apr. 6, 1949; d. Wilke J. and Mary Elizabeth (Shultz) Duitsman; m. William Arthur Steffan, Apr. 22, 1967; 1 child, Rodney Alan. RN, Lincoln Gen. Hosp. Sch. Nursing, 1973. Nurse Beatrice (Nebr.) Cmty. Hosp., 1973—80, Luth. Hosp., Beatice, 1980—83; pvt. duty nurse various nursing agencies, Omaha. Bus. adviser to Frank Sinatra; polit. advisor to Sen. Ted Kennedy, 1988—96, Pres. Bill Clinton, 1992—96. Author: A Presidential Story, 1996. Mem. St. Joseph's Cath. Ch.,

Beatrice. Recipient Bausch and Lomb Honoary Sci. award, 1966, Lifetime Achievements award, Am. Biog. Inst. Raleigh, NC. Democrat. Roman Catholic. Achievements include discovery of re-creation and the partitioning effect. Avocations: piano, reading. Home: 420 N 86th St Lincoln NE 68505 Office Phone: 402-488-7776.

STEFFENSEN, INGER-LISE, biologist, toxicologist; b. Oslo, Apr. 26, 1961; Cert. tchr., U. Oslo, 1989, PhD, 1994. Registered toxicologist Eurotox, 2002. Scientist Nat. Inst. Pub. Health (name now Norwegian Inst. Pub. Health), Oslo, 1993—98, sr. scientist, 1998—. Expert group on European Acceptance Scheme European Commn., 2006—; tchr. Akershus U. Coll., 2007—; mem. Core Group Experts, Joint FAO/WHO Project, 2007—09; mem. sci. panel Norwegian Sci. Com. Food Safety, 2004—, chair sci. panel 4, mem. sci. steering com., 2010—; with Rsch. Coun. Norway, 2010—; Norwegian expert European Food Safety Authority, 2011. Recipient travel award, Rhone-Poulenc, 1996; grantee, Scandinavian=Japan Sasahawa Found., 2001; postdoctoral fellow, Rsch. Coun. Norway, 1996—98, Travel grant, Norweign Govt., Rsch. Coun. Norway, 2009. Mem.: Am. Assn. Cancer Rsch., Norwegian Soc. Pharmacy and Toxicology. Office: Norwegian Inst Pub Health Divsn Environ Medicine Dept Food Safety and Nutrition POBox4404 Nydalen Lovisenberggata 8 Oslo NO-0403 Norway Office Phone: 47 21076530. Business E-Mail: inger-lise.steffensen@fhi.ho.

STEFFENSEN, KARINA DAHL, oncologist; b. Denmark, Jan. 1972; MD, U. Aarhus, 1999; PhD, U. Southern Denmark, 2008. Physician dept. clin. oncology Vejle Hosp., 2004—. Elite Rsch. scholarship, Danish Ministry Sci., Tech. and Innovation., grant, U. Southern Denmark, Danish Coun. Ind. Rsch.- Med. Scis. Mem.: NSGO, ENYGO, ESGO, ASCO, Danish Gynecol. Cancer Group. Office: Kabbeltoft 25 Vejle DK-7100 Denmark Business E-Mail: karina.dahl.steffensen@slb.regionsyddanmark.dk.

STEFOS, THEODOR, obstetrics-gynecology educator; b. Ioannina, Greece, Sept. 18, 1955; s. Ioannis and Marina (Sozou) S.; m. Ioanna Litou, Jan. 1, 1980; children: Marina, Spyros. Diploma, U. Athens, 1979; MD, U. Joannina, Greece, 1984. Fellowship on obstetrics Baylor Coll. of Medicine, Tex., 1987-88; ob-gyn. tng. U. Joannina, 1979-84, lectr. of ob-gyn., 1986-89, asst. prof., 1989-99, assoc. prof., 1999—. Dir. maternal-fetal medicine U. Joannina, 1989—. Author: Perinatal Care, 1994; contbr. articles to profl. jours. Mem. Am. Inst. Ultrasound in Medicine, Hellenic Ob-Gyn. Inst., Perinatal Soc. of Greece. Avocations: ping pong/table tennis, football. Home: N Papadopoulou 3 45444 Joannina Greece Office: U Joannina Panepistimiou 45000 Joannina Greece

STEGAROIU, ROXANA, dentistry professor; b. Bucharest, Dec. 17, 1967; d. Mihail and Irina Leontina (Codrea) S.; m. Yasunori Katagiri, July 6, 1998 DDS, U. Medicine and Pharmacy, Bucharest, 1991; PhD, Niigata U., Japan, 1998. Dental surgeon U. Hosp., Bucharest, 1991—92; asst. prof. Grad. Sch. Med. and Dental Scis. Niigata U., Japan, 1998—2004, assoc. prof. Grad. Sch. Med. and Dental Scis., 2004—06, assoc. prof. Faculty Dentistry, 2006—, assoc. prof. grad. sch. med. and dental scis., 2008—. Contbr. articles to profl. jours Mem. Internat. Assn. for Dental Rsch., Japan Prosthodontic Soc., Niigata Dental Soc., Japan Dental Edn. Assn., Internat. Coll. Prosthodontists. Avocations: reading, hiking, classical music, skiing. Office: Niigata U Faculty Dentistry Dept Oral Health and Welfare Gakkocho Dori 2-5274 951-8514 Niigata Japan Business E-Mail: roxana@dent.niigata-u.ac.jp.

STEGMANN, BARBARA JEAN, medical educator, researcher; b. St. Louis, Sept. 22, 1962; MD, U. Mo., Kansas City, 1986; MPH, U. NC, Chapel Hill, 2005. Asst. prof., scientist U. Iowa Hosp. and Clins., 2008—. Recipient Woman's Reproductive Health Rsch. Career Devel. award, NIH and U. Iowa; Tng. Epidemiology and Women's Health Rsch. grant, NIH and U. NC. Fellow: Am. Soc. Reproductiv Medicine, Aerospace Med. Assn., Am. Coll. Ob-Gyn. Avocation: horseback riding. Office: 200 Hawkins Dr 31324 PFP Iowa City IA 52242 Office Fax: 319-384-9367. Business E-Mail: barbara-stegmann@uiowa.edu.

STEIGBIGEL, ROY THEODORE, epidemiologist, educator, research scientist; b. Bklyn., Nov. 23, 1941; s. Samuel and Lillian I. (Parker) S.; m. Julia Ann Enterline, June 10, 1967 (div. 1983), children: Keith D., Glenn N.; m. Sidonie Ann Morrison, Oct. 15, 1985; 1 child, Andrew M. BA, Carleton Coll., 1962; MD, U. Rochester, 1966. Diplomate Am. Bd. Internal Medicine, Am. Bd. Infectious Disease. Resident U. Rochester, NY, 1966-68, Stanford U., Palo Alto, Calif., 1970-71, fellow, 1971-73; from asst. to assoc. prof. U. Rochester, NY, 1973-83; prof. SUNY, Stony Brook, 1983—. Mem. adv. panels NIH, Bethesda, Md., 1985-87. Contbr. over 20 chpts. to books and over 125 articles to profl. jours. Served in USPHS, 1968-70. Fellow NIH, 1971-73, grantee, 1985—. Fellow ACP, Infectious Disease Soc. Am. Office: SUNY Stony Brook Sch Medicine Hsc T 15 080 Stony Brook NY 11794-8153 Office Phone: 631-444-3497. Business E-Mail: roy.steigbigel@stonybrook.edu.

STEIGER, DAVID J., pulmonologist, educator; Attended, Leeds Med. Sch., UK, 1981. Diplomate Am. Bd. Internal Medicine, 2001, Am. Bd. Internal Medicine-pulmonary disease, 2002, Am. Bd. Internal Medicine-critical care medicine, 2005. Resident internal medicine St. Luke's Roosevelt Hosp., 1984—87, clin. fellow in emergency medicine, 1987—88, resident in internal medicine, 1988—89; clin. fellow in pulmonary medicine Univ. Calif., San Francisco, 1989—90, clin. fellow in critical care medicine, 1993—94; asst. prof. NYU Sch. Medicine; dir. ICU dept. NYU Langone Med. Ctr., NYU Hosp. for Joint Diseases. Office: New York University Langone Medical Center 305 2nd Ave Ste 16 New York NY 10003 Office Phone: 212-598-6091. Office Fax: 212-598-6212.

STEIGER, WILLIAM R. (BILL STEIGER), former federal agency administrator; BA history, Yale U., New Haven, CT; PhD Latin American History, U. Calif. LA. Edn. policy advisor to Gov. Tommy G. Thompson, Wis.; spl. asst. sec. internat. affairs U.S. Dept. Health and Human Services, 2001, dir. Office of Global Health Affairs, 2001—09. U.S. mem. exec. bd. World Health Org.; pres. exec. com. Pam Am. Health Org.; alternative U.S. mem. bd. dirs. Global Fund to Fight HIV/AIDS, Tuberculosis and Malaria.

STEIN, ARTHUR OSCAR, retired pediatrician; b. Bklyn., Apr. 3, 1932; s. Irving I. and Sadie (Brander) S.; m. Judith Lenore Hurwitz, Aug. 27, 1955; children: Susan, Jeffrey, Benjamin. AB, Harvard U., 1953; MD, Tufts U., 1957; postgrad., U. Chgo., 1963—66; BFA, San Jose State U., 1998. Intern U. Chgo. Hosps., 1957-58, resident, 1958-59, NY Hosp.-Cornell U. Med. Ctr., 1959-61; pediatrician, 1963-70, Healthguard Med. Group, San Jose, Calif., 1970-72, Permanente Med. Group, San Jose, 1972-95; ret., 1995; owner Artform Photography, 2001—05. Instr. pediat. Cornell U. Med. Sch., 1960-61, U. Chgo. Sch. Medicine, 1963-66, asst. prof., 1966-70; tchg. asst. photography San Jose State U., 1995—. Author: (CD) The Sketch Class. V.p. Jewish congregation 1969-70, pres. 1972-73. Capt., M.C., AUS, 1961-63. USPHS Postdoctoral fellow, 1963-66. Fellow Am. Acad. Pediat., Santa Clara County Med. Assn., Calif. Med. Assn.; mem. Light and Shadow Camera Club (pres. San Jose 1978-80), Ctrl. Coast Counties Camera Club (v.p. 1980-81, pres. 1981-82), Santa Clara Camera Club (pres. 1991), Villages Camera Club (pres. 2007-08). Achievements include co-discovery (with Glyn Dawson) of genetic disease lactosylceramidosis. Home: 8656 Solera Dr San Jose CA 95135 E-mail: artform2@pacbell.net.

STEIN, BARRY B., pediatrician, educator; MD, U. Witwatersrand, 1980. Diplomate Am. Bd. Pediatrics. Resident in emergency dept. Johannesburg Hosp.; rotating resident Groote Schurr Hosp.; resident in pediat. Mt. Sinai Hosp., NY, 1983—86; asst. clin. prof. pediat. Mt. Sinai Sch. Medicine; pediatrician Mt. Sinai Med. Ctr.; with Lenox Hill Hosp. Office: Mount Sinai Medical Center 1125 Pk Ave New York NY 10128 Office Phone: 212-289-1400. Office Fax: 212-289-5714.

STEIN, BARRY EDWARD, medical educator; BA, CUNY, Queens, 1966, MA, 1969; PhD, CUNY, 1971. Prof. dept. physiology Med. Coll. Va.-Va. Commonwealth U., Richmond, 1982-94, affil. prof., 1994—; prof., chair dept. neurobiology and anatomy Wake Forest U Sch. Medicine, Winston-Salem, NC, 1994—. Bd. trustees The Gwendolyn Hardy Williams and Oliver Williams Found., Inc., 1992—; lectr. in field. Co-author: The Merging of the Senses, 1993; contbr. chpts. to books including The Cognitive Neurosciences, 1995, 99, Electrophysiology of Vision, 1991, The Development of Intersensory Perception: Comparative Perspectives, 1994, others; co-editor: The Handbook of Multisensory Processes, 2004; mem. editl. bd. Jour. Cognitive Neuroscience, The Behavioral and Brain Sciences; contbr. numerous articles to profl. pubs. including Jour. Neurophysiology, Jour. Neurosci., Sci., Jour. Comparative Neurology, others. Home: 1825 Georgia Ave Winston Salem NC 27104-3101 Office: Wake Forest Sch Medicine Med Ctr Blvd Winston Salem NC 27157-0001 Business E-Mail: bestein@wfubmc.edu.

STEIN, CY AARON, oncologist, pharmacologist; b. NYC, Nov. 1, 1952; s. Herbert and Ruth (Schiffenbauer) S.; m. Myra Levine, Aug. 15, 1976; children: Allison, Lauren. BA magna cum laude, Brown U., 1974; PhD in Organic Chemistry, Stanford U., 1978; MD, Albert Einstein Coll. Medicine, 1982. Diplomate Am. Bd. Internal Medicine, 1986, Am. Bd. Oncology, 1987, lic. Md., NY. Intern N.Y. Hosp.-Cornell Med. Ctr., NYC, 1982-83, resident in internal medicine, 1983-85; clin. assoc. Nat. Cancer Inst., Bethesda, Md., 1985-88, sr. staff fellow, 1988-90; asst. prof. medicine and pharmacology Columbia U., Coll. of Physicians and Surgeons, NYC, 1990-93, Irving asst. prof. medicine and pharmacology, 1993-95, assoc. prof. medicine and pharmacology, 1996—2003; prof., medicine and molecular pharmacology, dir. Med. Genitourinary Oncology, Bronx, NY; attending physician Montefiore Med. Ctr., Bronx, NY. Former cons. chief med. officer, Tokai Pharm., Cambridge, Mass., mem. editl. bd., Clin. Cancer Rsch. Molecular Cancer Therapeutics Molecular Therapy. Co-editor: Oligonuclotides, contbr. numerous articles to profl. jours. Recipient Clin. Career Devel. award Am. Cancer Soc., 1992-95; named one of Best Drs. NY Metro Area, Castle Connolly Med. Ltd., 2004-11, NY Mag., 2008-09, NY's Super Drs., NY Times Mag., 2008-09, 11. Mem. Am. Assn. for Cancer Rsch., Am. Soc. Clin. Oncology, Am. Soc. for Gene Therapy (Oligonucleotide Com. 2005-08), Salus Therapeutics (Salt Lake City) (bd. dirs. 2003), Oligonucleotide Therapeutics Soc. (founder 2004, treas. 2004-08, ex-officer 2009) Alpha Omega Alpha. Achievements include development of medical genitourinary oncology program at Albert Einstein College of Medicine. Home: 11 Dolphin Rd New City NY 10956-6306 Office: Montefiore Med Ctr 111 E 210th St Bronx NY 10467 Office Phone: 718-920-8980. Home Fax: 718-652-4027. Personal E-mail: cstein@montefiore.org.

STEIN, DANIEL EVAN, obstetrician, gynecologist, educator; MD, NY Med. Coll., 1989. Diplomate Am. Bd. Ob-Gyn, Am. Bd. Ob-Gyn-reproductive endocrinology/infertility, registered NY, 1990. Intern St. Vincents Med. Ctr., 1990; resident in ob-gyn. Thomas Jefferson Univ. Hosp., 1995; fellow in reproductive endocrinology and infertility Univ. Medicine and Dentistry NJ, 1997; hosp. affiliations include LI Coll. Hosp., St. Luke's Cornwall Hosp.; tchg. faculty med. sch. Columbia Univ. Med. Ctr.; med. dir. in vitro fertilization program Continuum Reproductive Ctr.; faculty mem. reproductive endocrinology divsn. St. Luke's-Roosevelt Hosp. Ctr., NY, 2000—. Mem.: Olycystic Ovarian Syndrome Assn., Soc. for Assisted Reproductive Technologies, Am. Soc. for Reproductive Medicine, ACOG, AMA, Alpha Omega Alpha. Office: St Lukes Roosevelt Hospital Center Roosevelt Hospital 1000 Tenth Ave New York NY 10019 Office Phone: 212-523-4000.

STEIN, DAVID E., colon and rectal surgeon, educator; BA in Biology, Rutgers U., 1990; MD, SUNY, 1997. Diplomate Am. Bd. Surgery, Am. Bd. Colon and Rectal Surgery. Intern in gen. surgery Thomas Jefferson Univ. Hosp., Pa., 1997—98, resident in gen. surgery, 1998—2002; fellow Cleve. Clinic Found., 2002—03; assoc. prof. coll. medicine Drexel Univ.; chief colorectal surgery divsn. Hahnemann Univ. Hosp. Recipient Physician of the Yr., Crohn's & Colitis Found., 2011; named Top Doctor, Phila. Mag., 2011. Office: Hahnemann University Hospital 230 N Broad St Philadelphia PA 19102 Office Phone: 215-762-1750.

STEIN, DEAN K., health science association administrator; b. Cleve., Dec. 21, 1955; s. Martin Louis and Anita (Wolf) S. BA, Washington U., St. Louis, 1978; MBA, NYU, 1980. Bus. mgr. Manhattan Theatre Club, NYC, 1978-80; dir. adminstrn. Opera Am., Washington, 1980-83; exec. dir. Chamber Music Am., NYC, 1985—2000; asst. executive dir. Dyson Found., 2000—03; exec. dir. American Psychoanalytic Assn., 2003—. Ind. cons., Washington, 1983-85. Office: American Psychoanalytic Assn 309 E 49th St New York NY 10017-1601 Office Phone: 212-752-0450. Business E-Mail: deankstein@apsa.org. *

STEIN, ELLIOTT M., geriatric psychiatrist, educator; BS in Psychology, Pa. State U., 1969; MD, U. Miami, 1973. Diplomate Am. Bd. Psychiatry and Neurology-general psychiatry, 1979, Am. Bd. Psychiatry and Neurology-geriatric psychiatry, 1991, recertification 2001. Intern/resident Herrick Meml. Hosp., 1973—76; hosp. affiliation includes: Mt. Sinai Med. Ctr.; assoc. clin. prof. psychiatry Univ. Miami Sch. of Medicine; dir. geriatric psychiatry Jewish Home of San Francisco. Recipient Founder's award, Am. Assn. for Geriatric Psychiatry, 1997, Clinician of the Year award, 2003, Jack Weinberg Meml. award, Am. Psychiatric Assn., 2001, Disting. Alumnus award, Univ. Miami Sch. of Medicine, 2004; named one of Best Doctors in America, 1992. Fellow: Am. Psychiatric Assn. (life); mem.: Geriatric Psychiatry Alliance (bd. dirs. 1996—98), Dade County Alzheimer's Assn. (bd. dirs. and co-chair med. scientific adv. bd. 1988—95), South Fla. Psychiatric Soc. (v.p. 1988—89), Am. Psychiatric Assn. Coun. (cons. 1984—93), Internat. PsychoGeriatric Assn. (treas. 1989—93, bd. dirs. 1993—97), Gerontologic Soc. of Fla. (pres. 1989—90), Am. Assn. for Geriatric Psychiatry (bd. dirs. 1982—85, pres. 1985—87). Office: Jewish Home of San Francisco 302 Silver Ave San Francisco CA 94112 Office Phone: 415-406-1516. E-mail: estein@jhsf.org.

STEIN, ERIC J., intervention radiologist, educator; MD, U. Pa. Diplomate Am. Bd. Radiology. Intern Allentown Hosp., Lehigh Valley; resident Hosp. of the Univ. of Pa., fellow; hosp. affiliations include Lankenau Med. Ctr., 1997—, Paoli Hosp., 1997—; clin. asst. prof. radiology Jefferson Univ. Hosp.; with radiology assocs. Bryn Mawr Hosp., hosp. affiliations include, 1985—, attending phycician. Co-author: (publ.) Critical Issues in Cardiovascular and Interventional Radiology, Quality Improvement Guidelines for Adult Percutaneous Abscess and Fluid Drainage, (jour.) Jour. of Vascular and Interventional Radiology, 1995. Mem.: Soc. of Cardiovasc. and Interventional Radiology, Radiol. Soc. of North America, Pa. Angiography and Interventional Radiology Soc., Am. Heart Assn., Am. Coll. of Radiology, Soc. for Minimally Invasive Therapy, Soc. of Cardiovasc. and Interventional Radiology, Pa. Radiologic Soc. Office: Bryn Mawr Hospital 130 S Bryn Mawr Ave Bryn Mawr PA 19010 Office Phone: 484-337-4115.

STEIN, FRANKLIN JOSEPH, music educator; b. Eau Claire, Wis., Mar. 26, 1945; s. Herbert Charles Stein and Gwenn Marie Lassek. BS in Secondary Edn., U. Wis., Eau Claire, 1968; BS in Computer Sci., Coleman Coll., La Mesa, Calif., 1989, MIS in Info. Sys., 1995. Cert. tchr. Wis. Biology, sci., Spanish tchr. Stanley-Boyd HS, Stanley, Wis., 1968-71; salesman Jerry's Hammond Organ & Piano Studios, Eau Claire, Wis., 1971—72; dept. mgr. Day Music Co., Eau Claire, 1973—74; store mgr. Tropic Waters Pet Store, Eau Claire, 1975-76, Thearle Music Co., San Diego, 1977—82; 6th grade tchr. St. Paul's Luth. Sch., Pacific Beach, Calif., 1977-78; profl. theatre organist Organ Power Pizza Restaurants, San Diego, 1977-85; store mgr. Organ Stop Inc., San Diego, 1982—89; computer programmer analyst Health Examinetics, Rancho Bernardo, Calif., 1989-91; clin. computer systems specialist SHARP Health Care, San Diego, 1991—97; systems programmer/clin. analyst U. Calif., San Diego, 1997—2002; counselor emotionally disturbed youth New Alternatives, Inc. Comprehensive Adolescent Treatment Ctr., San Diego, 2003—04. Profl. musician, 1965—. Author: Technician's Manual of Thermography, 1987, IDXrad User's Manual & Annual Updates, 1991-97; editor: Manual of Thermography, 1988. Music dir., organist, Miramar, Calif., 1996—2007; sponsor PLAN USA/Childreach, 2000—07; minister music All Saints Luth. Ch., San Diego, 2005—. Recipient Silver medal Piano Performance Wis. Music Educators, 1962, 63, Cert. of Merit for Excellence in Sci., Wis. Jr. Acad. of Sci., 1963. Democrat. Buddhist. Avocations: classical music, reading, travel. Home and Office: 10227 Kamwood Pl San Diego CA 92126-5139 Personal E-mail: fjstein@msn.com.

STEIN, JAMES HOWARD, medical educator, researcher; b. Milw., Aug. 17, 1964; Bachelor's degree with honors, U. Wis.; MD, Yale U., 1990. Diplomate Am. Bd. Echocardiography in Comprehensive Adult Echocardiography, cert. Internal Medicine, 1993, Cardiovascular Disease, 1997. Intern, internal medicine U. Chgo. Pritzker Sch. Med. Ctr., 1990—91, resident, cardiology, 1991—93; fellow in cardiology Rush-Presbyterian-St. Luke Med. Ctr., Chgo., 1994—96; assoc. prof. cardiovascular medicine U. Wis. Med. Sch., Madison, Wis., 1996, prof. cardiovascular medicine, dir. Atherosclerosis Imaging Rsch. Prog., dir. preventive cardiology, assoc. dir. adult echocardiography. Dir., atherosclerosis imaging rsch. program U. Wis.; assoc. dir., preventative cardiology program U. Wis. Hosp. and Clinics, dir., vascular health screening program, dir., preventive cardiology; dir. Outpatient Cardiovascular Medicine Svcs.; assoc. dir. Adult Echocardiography Lab.; mem. Complications of HIV Therapy Subcommittee Rsch. Adv. Com., Adult AIDS Clin. Trial Group Divsn. AIDS, Nat. Inst. Allergy and Infectious Diseases; ad hoc reviewer for two NIH study sessions. Co-author: Am. Soc. Echocardiography Recommendations for Use Echocardiography in Clinical Trials; contbr. articles to peer-reviewed jours. Named one of Top Docs in Cardiology, Madison Mag., 2000—, 20 Best Cardiologists, Men's Health Mag., 2007, Women's Health Mag., 2008. Fellow: Am. Coll. Cardiology (cochmn. ann. scientific sessions 2006, rep. to Nat. Cholesterol Edn. program, mem. clin. expert and consensus documents task force, W. Proctor Harvey Young Tchr. award for Excellence in Tchg. 2001); mem.: ACP, Am. Soc. Echocardiography (mem. Carotid IMT task force), Am. Heart Assn., Alpha Omega Alpha. Office: U Wis Dept Medicine Mail Code 3248 600 Highland Avenue Madison WI 53792-3248 Office Phone: 608-263-9648. Office Fax: 608-263-0405. Business E-Mail: jhs@medicine.wisc.edu.

STEIN, JOEL, physiatrist; BS, Columbia U.; MD, Albert Einstein Coll. Medicine, 1986. Intern Montefiore Hosp., Bronx, NY, 1987, resident, 1989, Columbia-Presbyterian Medical Ctr., 1992; medical staff Spaulding Rehab. Hosp., Boston, 1992—2008, chief medical officer, 2000—08, medical dir. stroke rehab program; faculty mem. Harvard Medical Sch., 1993—2008; physiatrist-in-chief NewYork-

Presbyterian Hosp., 2008—; Simon Baruch Prof., chair dept. rehab. medicine Columbia U. Coll. Physicians and Surgeons, 2008—; prof., chief rehab. medicine Weill Cornell Medical Coll., 2008—. Office: Rehab Medicine Associates Harkness Pavilion 180 Fort Washington Ave Ste 1-199 New York NY 10032 Office Phone: 212-305-3535.

STEIN, KARL N., plastic and reconstructive surgeon; b. Phila., July 1, 1940; BA in Chemistry, Temple U., 1962, MD, 1966. Diplomate Am. Bd. Plastic Surgery. Intern U. Pa. Grad. Hosp., 1966-67; resident in surgery Abington Meml. Hosp., 1967-68, SUNY Up-State Med. Ctr., 1970-71, instr. in surgery, 1970—; resident in plastic surgery Hosp. Albert Einstein Coll. Medicine, Bronx Mcpl. Hosp. Ctr., 1971-74, asst. instr. plastic surgery and hand surgery, 1974; pvt. practice in plastic surgery, 1974—. Surgeon Sherman Oaks (Calif.) Burn Ctr., 1975—; cons. L.A. Dept. Water and Power; med. legal expert for burns and plastic surgery; med. legal cons. Author (patent) Treatment of Tar Burns, 1980. Capt. USAF, 1969-71. Fellow Am. Coll. Surgeons; mem. AMA, Am. Soc. Plastic and Reconstructive Surgeons, Am. Burn Assn., Am. Soc. Aesthetic Plastic Surgery, Calif. Soc. Plastic Surgeons, Calif. Med. Assn., L.A. County Med. Assn. Office: PO Box 220340 Newhall CA 91322-0340 Office Phone: 661-255-5451. Business E-Mail: ksteinmd@sbcgloba.net.

STEIN, KEITH LANCE, health system administrator; Diploma, Rensselaer Poly. Inst.; MD, Albany Med. Coll., 1980. Diplomate in anesthesiology and critical care medicine Am. Bd. Anesthesiology. Intern, resident, fellow U. Mass. Med. Ctr., 1980—85; chief med. officer, sr. v.p. Bapt. Health, Jacksonville, Fla., 1999—. Fellow: Am. Coll. Chest Physicians, Am. Coll. Critical Care Medicine. Office: Bapt Health 800 Prudential Dr Jacksonville FL 32207 Business E-Mail: keith.steinmd@bmcjax.com.

STEIN, KIRA D., psychiatrist; d. David H. and Vivien Y. Burt; m. Michel R. Stein, Aug. 18, 1996. BA in Polit. Sci., UCLA, 1991; MD, U. Rochester, NYC, 1997. Post-baccalaureate pre-med. cert. Bryn Mawr Coll., Pa., 1993, cert. in cognitive behavioral therapy UCLA Anxiety Disorders Clinic, 2000, in interpersonal psychotherapy UCLA Interpersonal Psychotherapy Clinic, 2001, in psychiatry Am. Bd. Psychiatry and Neurology, 2003, registered Drug Enforcement Agy., 1999, in transcranial magnetic stimulation. Intern internal medicine Huntington Meml. Hosp., LA, 1997—98; resident adult psychiatry program UCLA Neuropsychiatric Inst., 1998—2001, clin. instr., David Geffen Sch. Medicine, 2001—; dir. owner West Coast TMS Inst., 2011 . Pvt. practice, Sherman Oaks, Calif., 2001 . Contbr. chapters to books, articles to profl. jours. Mem.: UCLA Vol. Channel Faculty, LA Psychiatris Soc., Postpartum Support Internat., Am. Psychiat. Assn. Achievements include research in psychotherapy, psychopharmacology and Transcranial magnetic Stimulation. Avocations: travel, camping, hiking, swimming, theater. Office: 5170 Sepulveda Blvd Ste 300 Sherman Oaks CA 91403 Office Phone: 818-990-5901. Personal E-mail: kirasteinmd@gmail.com.

STEIN, MARK RODGER, allergist; b. Phila., Apr. 24, 1943; s. Eli and Norma Stein; m. Phyllis Feinstein, Dec. 27, 1964; children: Amy Lynn, Philip Warren. BA, LaSalle Coll., Phila., 1964; MD, Jefferson Med. Coll., Phila., 1968. Diplomate Nat. Bd. Med. Examiners, Am. Bd. Internal Medicine, Am. Bd. Allergy and Immunology. Intern Abington Meml. Hosp., Pa., 1968-69; resident internal medicine Letterman Army Med. Ctr., San Francisco, 1972-75; fellow allergy and clin. immunology Fitzsimons Army Med. Ctr., Denver, 1975-77; pvt. practice West Palm Beach, Fla., 1979—. Asst. prof. depts. medicine and pediatrics Uniformed Svcs. U. Health Scis. Sch. Medicine, Bethesda, Md., 1978—79; clin. asst. prof. dept. internal medicine U. South Fla. Coll. Medicine, Tampa, 1979—83, Tampa, 1997—2000; clin. care cons. Clin. Ctr., NIH, Bethesda, 1978—79; mem. active staff Good Samaritan Hosp., West Palm Beach, Fla., chief svc. dept. allergy, 1990—98, chief svc. allergy, 2001—; chief dept. allergy St. Mary's Hosp., West Palm Beach, 1985—98; mem. active staff Palm Beach Gardens Med Ctr.; chief allergy svc. Intracostal Health Sys., 2000—01. Editor Gastroesophageal Reflux Disease and Airway Disease, 1999; contbr. articles to profl. jours. Trustee Am. Lung Assn., West Palm Beach, 1984-93, 95-2007. Fellow ACP, Am. Acad. Allergy, Asthma and Immunology, Am. Coll. Allergy, Asthma and Immunology (chmn. geriat. com. 1988-90), Am. Assn. Cert. Allergists, Am. Coll. Chest Physicians; mem. Am. Thoracic Soc., Mil. Allergists, Fla. Med. Assn., Palm Beach County Med. Assn., Asthma and Allergy Found. Am., Fla. Allergy and Immunology Soc. (pres. 1987-88), Southeastern Allergy Assn. Jewish. Avocations: tennis, golf. Office: 840 Us Highway 1 North Palm Beach FL 33408-3830 Home Phone: 561-622-2728; Office Phone: 561-626-2006. Personal E-mail: latallergy@aol.com.

STEIN, PAUL DAVID, cardiologist; b. Cin., Apr. 13, 1934; s. Simon and Sadie (Friedman) S.; m. Janet Louise Tucker, Aug. 14, 1966; children: Simon, Douglas, Rebecca. BS, U. Cin., 1955, MD, 1959. Intern Jewish Hosp., Cin., 1959-60, med. resident, 1961-62, Gorgas Hosp., C.Z., 1960-61; fellow in cardiology U. Cin., 1962-63, Mt. Sinai Hosp., NYC, 1963-64; rsch. fellow Harvard Med. Sch., Boston, 1964-66; asst. dir. cardiac catheterization lab. Baylor U. Med. Ctr., Dallas, 1966-67; asst. prof. medicine Creighton U., Omaha, 1967-69; assoc. prof. medicine U. Okla., Oklahoma City, 1969-73; prof. rsch. medicine U. Okla. Coll. Medicine, Oklahoma City, 1973-76; dir. cardiovascular rsch. Henry Ford Hosp., Detroit, 1976-94, med. dir. cardiovascular rehab., 1994-2000; dir. rsch. St. Joseph Mercy Oakland Hosp., Pontiac, Mich., 2000—04, dir. rsch. edn., 2005—09; prof. medicine, Henry Ford Case Western Res. U., Cleve., 1994—2000; prof. medicine Wayne State U., Detroit, 2003—; vis. prof. dept. internal med. Mich. State U. Coll. Osteopathic Med., 2009—11; rsch. dir. St. Mary & Mercy Hosp., Mich., 2010—. Adj. prof. physics Oakland U., Rochester, Mich., 1985— Author: A Physical and Physiological Basis for the Interpretation of Cardiac Auscultation: Evaluations Based Primarily on Second Sound and Ejection Murmurs, 1981, Pulmonary Embolism, 1996, 2d edit., 2007; contbr. articles to profl. jours. Coun. on Clin. Cardiology fellow Am. Heart Assn., 1971, Coun. on Circulation fellow, 1972. Ret. capt. USAFR. Recipient Aristotle Gold medal, Aristotle U. Thessaloniki, 1993, Lifetime Achievement award, Am. Heart Assn., Mich. chpt., 2002, Plaque Recognition, St. Joseph Mercy Hosp., 2007, Daniel Drake award, U. Cin. Coll. Med., 2009; named to Hon. Order Ky. Cols., 1997. Master Fellow: Am. Coll. Chest Physicians (pres. 1993, medal recognition outstanding contbns. coll.); fellow ACP (Laureate award, Mich. chpt. 2003), ASME, Am. Coll. Cardiology, Am. Heart Assn. Office: St Mary Mercy Hosp 36475 Five Mile Rd Livonia MI 48154 Office Phone: 734-655-2753. Office Fax: 734-655-8430. Business E-Mail: steinp@trinity-health.org. *

STEIN, RENATO T., pediatrician, educator; b. Porto Alegre, Aug. 30, 1955; MD, Pontifícia U. Rio Grande do Sul, 1979; PhD, U. Fed. Rio Grande do Sul, 1996; MPH, U. Ariz. Adj. prof. pediat. Sch. Medicine, Pontifícia U. Cath. Rio Grande do Sul, 1982—. Postdoc. fellowship, Conselho Nat. Pesquisa, Brazil, Agència Gestió d'Ajuts U. i Recerca, Spain. Avocations: jogging, hiking, travel. Home: R Barão de Ubá 708/401 Porto Alegre Rio Grande do Sul 90450-090 Brazil Home Fax: 555133364211. Business E-Mail: rstein@pucrs.br.

STEIN, RICHARD ALAN, cardiologist, educator; b. NYC, Apr. 7, 1942; BA, Columbia Coll., 1963; MD, NYU, 1967. Diplomate in internal medicine, cardiovascular diseases, geriatrics and sports medicine Am. Bd. Internal Medicine; lic. physician, N.Y., Conn.; lic. handler radioactive materials, N.Y.C. Intern, then resident in medicine Downstate Med. Ctr.-Kings County Hosp., Bklyn., 1967—69, cardiology fellow, 1972—74; chief resident in medicine Kings County Hosp., 1971—72, attending physician; prof. medicine, chief cardiology divsn. dept. medicine SUNY-Health Sci. Ctr., Bklyn., 1985—95; chief preventive and rehab. cardiology Lenox Hill Hosp., NYC, 1995—99; attending physician SUNY Hosp., Bklyn.; chief cardiology dept. Bklyn. Hosp. Ctr., 1999—2003; assoc. chair dept. medicine, chief medicine Beth Israel Hosp. - Singer Divsn., NYC, 2003—05; dir. preventive cardiology Beth Israel Med. Ctr., NYC, 2005—07, dir. Cardiology Fellowship Program, 2005—07; prof. medicine, dir. urban cardiology program NYU Sch. Medicine, NYC, 2007—. Mem. vis. faculty Yale-New Haven Hosp., 1982; dir. cardiology fellowship program Bklyn. VA Hosp., Brookdale Hosp., S.I. U. Hosp., 1985—95; dir. cardiac rehab. program 92d St. YM-YWHA, NYC; prof. clin. medicine Weill-Cornell Med. Ctr., 1999—2003, Albert Einstein Coll. Medicine, NYC, 2003—. Co-editor: Complementary and Alternative Medicine in Cardiovascular Disease, 2004; mem. editl. bd. Preventive Cardiology, Jour. Cmty. Health; sect. editor Heart Disease: A Jour. of Cardiovasc. Disease; editor: (textbook) Cardiovascular Alternative and Complementary Medicine, 2004, Outliving Heart Disease - Winning By the New Rules, 2006; contbr. chpt. to: Coronary Rehabilitation for the Practicing Physician, 1979, Sports Medicine for the Primary Care Physician, 1984, Anesthesia as Co Existing Heart Disease, 1993, (with others) Diabetic Renal-Retinal Syndrome, 1980; contbr. articles to profl. jours. Maj. USAF, 1969-71. Recipient Acad. Career award, Preventive Cardiology Acad. award NIH, 1985-90. Fellow ACS, Am. Coll. Cardiology, Am. Coll. Chest Physicians, Am. Coll. Sports Medicine, N.Y. Cardiol. Soc. (bd. dirs.), N.Y. Acad. Medicine, mem. Am. Heart Assn. (fellow coun. on clin. cardiology, pres. Heritage affiliate, grantee in aid 1979-81), Assn. Profs. Cardiology, Am. Fedn. for Clin. Rsch., Sigma Xi. Office: NYU Med Ctr 550 1st Ave New York NY 10016 Office Phone: 212-263-7751. Personal E-mail: rastein@msn.com.

STEIN, RUTH ELIZABETH KLEIN, physician; b. NYC, Nov. 2, 1941; d. Theodore and Mimi (Foges) Klein; m. H. David Stein, June 9, 1963; children: Lynn Andrea Stein Melnick, Sharon Lisa, Deborah Michelle. AB, Barnard Coll., NYC, 1962; MD, Albert Einstein Coll. Medicine, Bronx, NY, 1966. Diplomate Am. Bd. Pediat., Devel. Behavioral Pediat. Intern, then resident Bronx Mcpl. Hosp. Ctr., 1966—68; sr. resident, fellow; instr. dept. pediats. George Washington U., Washington, 1968—70; with Albert Einstein Coll. of Medicine, Bronx, 1970—77, assoc. prof. pediats., 1977—83, prof., 1983—, vice-chmn. dept. pediats. Albert Einstein Coll., 1992—2002, dir. office of acad. affairs, dept. pediats., 1997—2002; pediatrician-in-chief, dir. pediats. Jacobi Med. Ctr. (formerly Bronx Mcpl. Hosp. Ctr.), 1992—97. Vis. prof. pub. health dept. epidemiology Yale U. Sch. Medicine, New Haven, 1986-87; scholar-in-residence United Hosp. Fund, NY, 1995-97; dir., prin. investigator Preventive Intervention Rsch. Ctr. for Child Health, NY, 1983-94, Nat. Child Health Assessment Planning Project, NY, Behavioral Pediatric Tng. Program, NY; dir. gen. pediatrics Pediat. Divsn., NY, 1992-97; apptd. to Montefiore Med. Ctr., North Ctrl. Bronx Hosp., Jacobi Med. Ctr.; bd. dirs. Ctr. for Child Health Rsch. of Am. Acad. Pediatrics, mem. exec. com., 1999-2004; co-chmn. com. on evaluation of child health 2002-04, NRC/Inst. Medicine, 1999-2005; bd. sci. advisors Nat. Inst. Arthritis and Musculoskelatal and Skin Diseases, 2005—; bd. sci. counselors Nat. Ctr. Health Stats. of CDC, 2006—10, mem., Steering Comm. DBPNe, 2010-, 10M Standing Comm. Experts & Social Sec., 2010; cons., Nat. Children's Study, Nat. Inst. Child Health & Human Devel., NIH, 2008-09. Editor: Caring for Children with Chronic Illness: Issues and Strategies, 1989, Health Care for Children: What's Right, What's Wrong, What's Next, 1997; mem. editorial bd. Jour. Behavioral and Devel. Pediatrics, 1993-2006, Ambulatory Pediatrics, 1998-2005; contbr. articles to profl. jours. Fellow Am. Acad. Pediats.; mem. APHA, Am. Pediatric Soc., Soc. for Pediat. Rsch., Ambulatory Pediat. Assn. (bd. dirs. 1982-89, pres. 1987-88, rsch. award 1995, Ray Helfer award 1999), NY Acad. Medicine (chmn. NY forum on child health 2001-05), Soc. for Devel. and Behavioral Pediats., Alpha Omega Alpha. Jewish. Home: 91 Larchmont Ave Larchmont NY 10538-3748 Office: Albert Einstein Coll Med Montefiore Med Ctr Dept Pediat 111 E 210 St Bronx NY 10467-2804 Office Phone: 718-920-7932. Business E-Mail: rstein@aecom.yu.edu, ruth.stein@einstein.yu.edu.

STEIN, YECHEZKIEL, retired physician, researcher; s. Mina Blum and Yehoshuah Stein; m. Olga Stein. MD, Hebrew Univ.-Hadassah Med. Sch., Jerusalem, 1952. Lic. MD Hebrew Univ.-Hadassah Med. Sch., 1953. Prof. of medicine Hebrew Univ.-Hadassah Med. Sch., Jerusalem, 1969—94; chmn., dept. of medicine Hadassah U. Hosp., Jerusalem, 1969—94; adj. faculty Rockefeller U., NY, 1993—2005, guest investigator, 1960—61; assoc. prof. of medicine Hebrew Univ.-Hadassah Med. Sch., Jerusalem, 1963—65; dir. lipid rsch. lab. Hadassah U. Hosp., Jerusalem, 1965—94; prof. of medicine Hebrew Univ.-Hadassah Med. Sch., Jerusalem, 1969—94; ret. Contbr. scientific papers pub. to profl. jour. Recipient Heinrich Wieland Prize (jointly with Dr. Olga Stein), Germany, 1978, R. R. Match Disting. Scholar Award, Rockefeller, NY, 1988, Humboldt Rsch. Award (jointly with Dr. Olga Stein), Humboldt Found., Germany, 1993, Dr. Rainer Wild Prize (jointly with Dr. Olga Stein), Germany, 1995, Israel Prize for Medicine, Govt. of Israel, 1996, Doljanski Prize for Outstanding Doctoral Thesis, Hebrew Univ.-Hadassah Med. sch., 1953; fellow Post-doctoral Magnes Fellowship, Hebrew U., Jerusalem, 1959-1960, Sr. Scientist Award, Am. Heart Assn., 1967-1968. Mem.: Fondation Cardiologique Princess Liliane, Argenteuil, Belgium (sci. adv. bd. 1976—88), Minerva Fellowship Com., European Atherosclerosis Soc. (chmn. 1990—93), The Jour. of Atherosclerosis (editl. bd. 1976—99), European Atherosclerosis Soc. (hon.), Polish Soc. for Atherosclerosis Rsch. (hon.), Japanese Assn. for Med. Sci. (hon.). Avocations: swimming, travel, opera, theater.

STEINBACH, LYNNE SUSAN, radiologist, educator; b. San Francisco, Dec. 28, 1953; d. Howard Lynne and Ilse (Rosengarten) S.; m. Eric Franklin Tepper, Aug. 14, 1977; 1 child, Mark Evan. Student, Vassar Coll.; BA, Stanford U., 1975; MD, Med. Coll. Pa., 1979. Cert. Am. Bd. Radiology, 1983. Intern Coll. Medicine and Dentistry N.J., Newark, 1979—80; resident radiology N.Y. Hosp.-Cornell Med. Ctr., NYC, 1980—83; fellow musculoskeletal radiology Hosp. Spl. Surgery Cornell Med. Ctr., NYC, 1983—84; asst. prof. radiology U. Calif., San Francisco, 1984—92, assoc. prof., 1992—98, prof., 1998—. Chief musculoskeletal imaging U. Calif. San Francisco, 1998—2007. Editor 4 books; contbr. articles 145 on radiology, 35 chpts. on musculoskeletal radiology to profl. publs. Fellow Am. Coll. Radiology; mem. Internat. Skeletal Soc. (mem.-at-large 2002-03, asst. sec. 2003-04, bd. dirs., 2006-, sec., 2008-, Pres. medal, 1996), Internat. Soc. Mag. Res. Med. (bd. dirs., 2007-10, elected fellow, 2010), San Francisco Radiol. Soc. (sec. treas. 1994, pres. 1996), Radiol. Soc. N.Am., Am. Assn. Women Radiologists (mem.-at-large 1987-88, sec. 1989-91, v.p. 1991-92, pres.-elect 1992-93, pres. 1993-94), Am. Roentgen Ray Soc., Assn. U. Radiologists, Soc. Skeletal Radiology. Avocations: swimming, travel, music, art. Home Phone: 415-388-7840. E-mail: lynne.steinbach@radiology.ucsf.edu.

STEINBERG, AMY WISHNER, dermatologist; b. NYC, Nov. 19, 1959; d. Arnold Blaine and Sylvia Fay (Biernoff) Wishner; m. Alan Lloyd Steinberg, June 15, 1986; children: Joshua Darren, Arielle Dana, Natalie Tara. BS, Northwestern U., Evanston, Ill., 1981; MD, Northwestern U., Chgo., 1983. Clin. instr. Univ. Hosp., Stony Brook, N.Y., 1987—; pvt. practice Stony Brook, 1987—. Fellow Am. Acad. Dermatology; mem. Suffolk Dermatology Soc., Internat. Soc. Dermatology, N.Y. State Dermatology Soc. Office: 2500 Route 347 Bldg 5 Stony Brook NY 11790 2555 Office Phone: 631 689 7683.

STEINBERG, DANIEL, biomedical scientist; b. Windsor, Ont., Can., July 21, 1922; came to US, 1922. s. Maxwell Robert and Bess (Krupp) S.; m. Sara Murdock, Nov. 30, 1946 (dec. July 1986); children: Jonathan Henry, Ann Ballard, David Ethan; m. Mary Ellen Strathaus, Aug. 11, 1991; 1 stepchild: Katrin Seifert. BS with highest distinction, Wayne State U., Detroit, 1941, MD with highest distinction, 1944; PhD with distinction, Harvard U., Boston, 1951; MD (hon.), U. Gothenburg, Sweden, 1991. Intern Boston City Hosp., 1944-45; physician Detroit Receiving Hosp., 1945-46; instr. physiology Boston U. Sch. Medicine, 1947-48; joined USPHS, 1951, med. dir., 1959; research staff lab. cellular physiology and metabolism Nat. Heart Inst., 1951-53, chief sect. metabolism, 1956-61, chief of lab. metabolism, 1962-68, lectr. grad. program NIH, 1955, mem. sci. adv. com. ednl. activities, 1955-61, com. chmn., 1955-60; mem. metabolism study sect. USPHS, 1959-61; chmn. heart and lung research rev. com. B Nat. Heart, Lung and Blood Inst., 1977-79; vis. scientist Carlsberg Labs., Copenhagen, 1952-53, Nat. Inst. Med. Research, London, 1960-61, Rockefeller U., 1981; pres. Lipid Research Inc., 1961-64, adv. bd., 1964-73; prof. medicine Sch. Medicine, U. Calif., San Diego, 1968—2000, prof. emeritus, 2000—. Former editor Jour. Lipid Research; mem. editorial bd. Jour Clin. Investigation, 1969-74, Jour. Biol. Chemistry, 1980-84, Arteriosclerosis, 1980—; exec. editor Analytical Biochemistry, 1978-80; contbr. articles to profl. jours. Bd. dirs. Found. Advanced Edn. in Scis., 1959-68, pres., 1956-62, 65-67. Served to capt. M.C. AUS, World War II. Fellow, Am. Cancer Soc., 1950—51. Mem. Nat. Acad. Scis., AAAS, Am. Acad. Arts and Scis., Am. Heart Assn. (mem. exec. com. coun. on arteriosclerosis 1960-63, 65-73, chmn. coun. arteriosclerosis 1967-69), Fedn. Am. Scientists (exec. com. 1957-58), Am. Soc. Biol. Chemists, Am. Soc. Clin. Investigation, Assn. Am. Physicians, Am. Fedn. Clin. Rsch., Inst. Medicine, European Atherosclerosis Discussion Group, Alpha Omega Alpha. Home: 7742 Whitefield Pl La Jolla CA 92037-3810 Office: U Calif San Diego Dept Medicine 9500 Gilman Dr La Jolla CA 92093-0682 Personal E-mail: dsteinb1@san.rr.com. Business E-Mail: dsteinberg@ucsd.edu.

STEINBERG, DANIEL HOWARD, cardiologist; b. Jan. 9, 1975; MD, UMDNJ NJ Med. Sch., 2001. Interventional cardiologist Med. U. SC, 2008—. Fellow: SCAI, ACC. Office: 25 Courtenay Dr ART7058 Charleston SC 29425 Business E-Mail: steinbe@musc.edu.

STEINBERG, HOWARD R., psychologist; b. NYC, Nov. 13, 1970; BA, U. Albany, 1988; PhD, U. South Fla., 2003. Psychologist VA Conn. Healthcare System, 2006—. Asst. prof., psychiatry Yale U. Sch. Medicine, 2006. Office: 950 Campbell Ave West Haven CT 06516 Business E-Mail: howard.steinberg@va.gov.

STEINBERG, JAMES PAUL, infectious diseases physician, educator; b. Omaha, June 12, 1954; s. Maurice M. and Muriel Naomi (Frank) S.; m. Shari Chaya Wasser, May 22, 1994; children: Eva Rose, Jonathan Alexander. BA, Cornell U., 1976; MD, U. Nebr., 1979. Med. resident Emory U., Atlanta, 1979-83; infectious diseases fellow Northwestern U., Chgo., 1985-87, assoc. in medicine, 1987-89; asst. prof. medicine Emory U., Atlanta, 1989-96, assoc. prof. medicine, 1997, prof. medicine; hosp. epidemiologist Crawford Long Hosp., Atlanta, 1991—, assoc. chief of medicine, 1993—. Fellow Infectious Diseases Soc. Am.; mem. ACP, AAAS, Am. Soc. Microbiology, Soc. for Healthcare Epidemiology of Am., Infectious Diseases Soc. Ga. (pres. 1995—). Office: Emory U Hosp Midtown 550 Peachtree St NE Atlanta GA 30308 Office Phone: 404-686-8114. E-mail: james.steinberg@emory.edu.

STEINBERG, MARVIN EDWARD, orthopaedic surgeon, educator; b. New Brunswick, NJ, Aug. 31, 1933; s. David and Fannie (Karshmer) S.; m. Delores Gusky White, Nov. 22, 1956; children: David,

James, Susan, Julie. BA, Princeton U., 1954; MD, U. Pa., 1958; MA (status pro tem), U. Oxford, Eng., 1964. Cert. Am. Bd. Orthop. Surgery, re-cert.; lic. Pa., NJ. Asst. prof. orthop. surgery U. Pa., Phila., 1968-73, assoc. prof., 1973-80, vice chmn., 1977-2000, prof. orthop. surgery, 1980—2002, prof. orthop. surgery in medicine, 1988—2002, interim chmn., 1994-95, prof. emeritus, 2002—. Dir. Joint Reconstrn. Ctr., Hosp. U. of Pa., Phila., 1987-97; examiner Am. Bd. Orthop. Surgeons, Chgo., 1977-97. Editor, author: The Hip and Its Disorders, 1991, Revision Total Hip Arthroplasty, 1998; guest editor, author: Seminars in Arthroplasty, 1998; guest editor: Orthop. Clinics of N.Am., 1982, (jour.) Seminars in Arthroplasty, 1991, Techniques in Orthopaedics, 2008; editl. cons. Clin. Orthop. and Related Rsch., 1987; assoc. editor Jour. Bone & Joint Surgery, 1992-2000; contbr. numerous articles to jours. and textbooks. Named one of The Best Drs. in Phila., Phila. Mag., 1984, 87, 94, 96, Best Drs. in America, 1996-98, 2001-02; Fulbright scholar, U. Oxford, 1963-64; fellow Arthritis Found., U. Oxford, 1963-64. Fellow ACS, Am. Acad. Orthop. Surgeons; mem. AMA, Assn. for Acad. Surgery, Ea. Orthop. Assn. (pres. 1975-76), Orthop. Rsch. Soc., Internat. Soc. for Orthop. Surgery and Traumatology (sec.-treas. 1997-2000, chmn. elect 2000-02, chmn. 2002-04), Am. Orthop. Assn., Hip Soc., Girdlestone Orthop. Soc. (chmn. elect 2011-), Assn. Rsch. Circulation Osseous, Lupus Found. Jewish. Avocations: travel, sailing, boating, photography. Home: 221 Winding Way Merion Station PA 19066-1217 Office: Hosp of U of Pa 3400 Spruce St Philadelphia PA 19104-4206 Office Phone: 215-349-3340. Business E-Mail: marvin.steinberg@uphs.upenn.edu. *

STEINBERG, RUSSELL MAX, behavioral pediatrician, educator; b. Salinas, Calif., Aug. 18, 1941; s. Martin and Eve S. AB in Zoology, UCLA, 1963, MA in Zoology and Endocrinology, 1964, PhD in Zoology and Endocrinology with distinction, 1969; MD, Med. Coll. Ohio, Toledo, 1972. Diplomate Nat. Bd. Med. Examiners. Intern in pediatrics U. Calif. Irvine Affiliated Hosps., 1972—73, resident in pediatrics, 1973—74; chief resident in pediatrics then mem. staff Childrens Hosp. of Orange County and U. Calif. Irvine Affiliated Hosps.; fellow in behavioral pediatrics and learning disabilities UCLA, 1975-76; behavioral pediatrician Childrens Med. Group, Anaheim, Calif., 1976-79; physician in child devel. program Fairview Devel. Ctr., Costa Mesa, 1979—81, physician behavior adjustment program, 1981—2004, chief med. staff, 1985, 1994—95; asst. clin. prof. pediatrics U. Calif., Irvine, 1990—94. Adj. asst. prof. zoology UCLA, 1969, instr. pediatrics, 1976; adj. asst. prof. pharmacy, U. Toledo, 1970-71; vis. lectr. Tchr. Edn. U. Calif., Irvine, 1980-93; lectr. and presenter in field. Contbr. articles to profl. jours. Rsch. fellow Ford Found., 1966, US Pub. Health Svc., 1965-69. Mem. Am. Acad. Pediats. (assoc.), Am. Coll. Sports Medicine, Soc. Devel. and Behavioral Pediatrics, Orange County Pediatric Soc., Sigma Xi.

STEINBRÜCK, KLAUS, surgeon; b. Rio De Janeiro, July 5, 1977; MD, U. Fed. Rio de Janeiro, 2003; MS, UFF, 2011. Surgeon Hosp. Fed. Bonsucesso, 2009—. Home: Rua Gustavo Sampaio 390/702 Leme Rio De Janeiro 22010-010 Brazil Personal E-mail: drsteinbruck@yahoo.com.br.

STEINBUCH, ROBERT, medical educator; b. NYC, Nov. 11, 1969; BA, U. Penn., 1985; JD, Columbia U., 1989. Prof. U. Ark., Little Rock, 2005—. Office: 1201 McMath Ave Little Rock AR 72202 Business E-Mail: resteinbuch@ualr.edu.

STEINBUECHEL-RHEINWALL, NICOLE VON, psychologist, human biologist; b. Hessen, Germany, Sept. 14, 1955; d. Rambald von and Eva von Steinbuechel-Rheinwall. Abitur, Bettina Realgymnasium, Frankfurt, 1965; PhD in human Biology, Ludwig-Maximilian-U., Munich. Cert. psychologist. Leader dept. neurogerontopsychology Genf U., Switzerland, 2001—04; dir., leader dept. med. psychology & med. sociology Goettingen U., Lower Saxony, Germany, 2004—. Recipient Dorothea-Erxleben Rsch. award, 1999. Master: Quality Life After Traumatic Brain Injury (leader steering com.). Office: Dept Med Psychology & Med Sociology Waldweg 37 Goettingen Lower Saxony 37073 Germany Office Fax: 49 5 51 39-1 81 89. Business E-Mail: nvsteinbuechel@med.uni-goettingen.de.

STEINDORF, KAREN, epidemiologist, biostatistician, researcher; b. Bonn, Germany, Mar. 20, 1966; d. Gerhard and Gisela Steindorf; m. Carsten Heuer; children: Patrick Heuer, Julius Heuer. Diploma in stats., U. Dortmund, Germany, 1991, PhD in Stats., 1994. Rsch. asst. U. Dortmund, Germany, 1991—92, German Cancer Rsch. Ctr., Heidelberg, 1992—95, post doctoral position, 1995—97; guest rschr. Nat. Cancer Inst., Bethesda, Md., 1993—94; project biostatistician Knoll AG, Pharm. Co., Ludwigshafen, Germany, 1997—99; rschr., unit dept. head German Cancer Rsch. Ctr., Heidelberg, 1999—2011; assoc. prof., epidemiology and med. biometry U. Heidelberg, Germany, 2011—. Author: (book) Epidemiologic methods for the risk assessment of carcinogenic substances in the environment, 1995; contbr. articles to profl. jours. Mem.: German Soc. Epidemiology (bd. dirs. 2004—08), German Soc. Med. Informatics, Biometry and Epidemiology (Johann-Peter-Süßmilch medal 1997), Internat. Biometric Soc. Office: DKFZ Im Neuenheimer Feld 280 Heidelberg D-69120 Germany Office Fax: +49 6221 42-2229. Business E-Mail: k.steindorf@dkfz.de.

STEINEMANN, THOMAS L., ophthalmologist, educator; MD, Med. Coll. Ohio, Toledo, 1985. Diplomate Am. Bd. Ophthalmology, 1990. Prof. ophthalmology Case Western Res. U., Cleve., 1999—; media corr. Am. Acad. Ophthalmology, San Francisco, 2003—09. Cons. US Food & Drug Adminstrn., Silver Spring, Md., 2006—. Contbr. articles to profl. jours. Dir. Contact Lens Assn. Ophthalmologists, St. Paul, 2004—09; cons. Cleve. Sight Ctr. Fellow: Am. Acad. Ophthalmolgy (councilor 2008—09, Secretariat award 2006, 2008). Achievements include patents for ophthalmic uses of activated protein c. Office: MetroHealth Med Ctr 2500 MetroHealth Dr Cleveland OH 44109-1998

STEINER, ANDREAS KONRAD, surgeon, writer, philosopher; b. Zurich, Switzerland, Jan. 29, 1937; s. Albert Henry and Margrit Olga (Stockar) S.; m. Katina Kokkinidhi, July 20, 1966; children: Irina, Mattheo, Francisca; m. Tshabu Cećile Mbombo, Dec. 10, 1985; children: Frédéric, Albert. MD, U. Zurich, 1961, M in Philosophy, 2003. Asst. Krankenhaus, Wald, Switzerland, 1962-63; med. officer Internat. Com. Red Cross, Yemenwar, 1964; intern, resident Buffalo Gen. Hosp., 1965—67; asst. U. Basle Hosp., Switzerland, 1968-73; head surgeon Kreisspital, Maennedorf, Switzerland, 1973-76; med. supt. Albert Schweitzer Hosp., Gabon, 1976-80; project dir. Hosp. Andino, Coina, Peru, 1980-84; dir. Integrated Health Project, Manono, Zaire, 1984—91; assoc. prof. Addis Ababa U., Ethiopia, 1992-95. Author: Doctor in the Bush, A Challenge, 1990, Stories From the Bush, Encounters of a Doctor in Africa, 1993, Africa and We, About Our Interventions in Africa, 1996, Signs of Flames, 2001, Life, Our Biggest Good. Albert Schweitzer's Ethics in the 21st Century, 2006, Translucent Reality, 2010; contbr. articles to profl. jours. Capt. health corps. Swiss Army, 1957—75. Mem. Swiss Med. Orgn., Swiss Surg. Soc., German Soc. Tropical Surgery, Authors of Switzerland, Philos. Soc. Zurich. Home: Hanfroosenweg 13 CH-8615 Wermatswil Switzerland Office: Olgastrasse 8 8001 Zurich Switzerland

STEINER, DONALD FREDERICK, biochemist, physician, educator; b. Lima, Ohio, July 15, 1930; s. Willis A. and Katherine (Hoegner) Steiner. BS in Chemistry and Zoology, U. Cin., 1952; MS in Biochemistry, U. Chgo., 1956, MD, 1956; DMS (hon.), U. Umea, Sweden, 1973, U. Ill., 1984, U. Uppsala, Sweden, 1993, Mt. Sinai Sch. Medicine, NYC, 1998. Intern King County Hosp., Seattle, 1956-57; USPHS postdoc. rsch. fellow, asst. medicine U. Wash. Med. Sch., 1957-60; faculty U. Chgo. Pritzker Sch. Medicine, 1960—, chmn. dept. biochemistry, 1973-79, A.N. Pritzker prof. biochemistry, molecular biology & medicine, 1985—. Sr. investigator Howard Hughes Med. Inst., Chevy Chase, Md., 1986—. Co-editor: The Endocrine Pancreas, 1972; contbr. articles to profl. jours. Recipient Lilly award, 1969, Ernst Oppenheimer award, 1970, Hans Christian Hagedorn medal, Steensen Meml. Hosp., Copenhagen, 1970, Gairdner award, Toronto, 1971, Diaz-Cristobal award, Internat. Diabetes Fedn., 1973, Passano award, 1979, Banting medal, Brit. Diabetes Assn., 1981, Wolf Found. prize in medicine, Israel, 1985, Frederick Conrad Koch award, Endocrine Soc., 1990, Manpei Suzuki award, Tokyo, 2010. Mem.: NAS, AAAS, Am. Acad. Arts & Scis., Am. Diabetes Assn. (Albert Renold award 2007), Am. Philos. Soc., Am. Soc. Biochemists & Molecular Biologists, European Assn. Study Diabetes (hon.), Alpha Omega Alpha, Sigma Xi. Office: Pritzker Sch Medicine 5841 S Maryland Ave AMB N216 Chicago IL 60637 Office Phone: 773-702-1334. Office Fax: 773-702-4292. Business E-Mail: dfsteine@uchicago.edu. *

STEINER, HEINZ, science professor, researcher; b. Birrwil, Aargau, Switzerland, July 1, 1956; Diploma, Swiss Fed. Inst. Tech., Zuerich, 1980; PhD, U. Duesseldorf, Germany, 1989. Postdoctoral rschr. NIMH, Bethesda, Md., 1990—95; rsch. asst. prof. U. Tenn. Coll. Medicine, Memphis, 1995—2000; assoc. prof. molecular and cellular pharmacology Rosalind Franklin U. Medicine & Sci./Chgo. Med. Sch., North Chgo., 2000—. Rsch. grant, NIH, 1998—. Business E-Mail: heinz.steiner@rosalindfranklin.edu.

STEINER, LUZIUS A., anesthesiologist; b. Basel, Switzerland, Jan. 25, 1966; married. MD, U. Basel, 1992; PhD, U. Cambridge, UK, 2003; diploma in anesthesiology intensive care, European Soc., 1998. Cert. anesthesiologist Swiss Med. Assn., 1999, intensive care physician Swiss Med. Assn., 2001. Cons. U. Hosp. Lausanne, Dept. Anesthesia, 2009—; faculty mem., anesthesiology pain mgmt. neurosurgical care 1000 Medicine, 2007—. Mem.: Swiss Soc. Intensive Care Medicine, Swiss Soc. Anesthesiologists (congress com. 2006, pre. 2009), European Soc. Intensive Care Medicine, European Soc. Anesthesiology. Office: Univ Hosp Lausanne Dept Anesthesia 1011 Lausanne Switzerland

STEINFELD, PHILIP SHELDON, pediatrician; b. Bronx, Mar. 4, 1932; s. Samuel and Sarah (Frishman) S.; m. Ruth L. Hyman, Aug., 1961 (div. June 1977); children: Andrea, Melissa, David; m. Sherry Lynn Rubinroit, Jan. 15, 1978; 1 child, Sara. BS, Queens Coll., 1953; MD, U. Basle, Switzerland, 1960. Diplomate Am. Bd. Pediats., 1965. Rotating intern Kings County Hosp. Ctr., Bklyn., 1960-61; resident pediatrics Mt. Sinai Hosp., NYC, 1961-63, jr. clin. asst. pediatrics, 1963-65, sr. clin. asst., 1965—; attending pediatrician L.I. Jewish Hosp., 1968—, North Shore U. Hosp., 1970—; clin. instr. pediatrics Cornell U., NYC, 1986-90, clin. asst. prof. pediats., 1991—, Hofstra North Shore-LIJ Health Sys. U. Med. Sch., 2011. Mem. adv. bd. TEMPO, Woodmere, N.Y., 1975-92, Five Town Adolescent Ctr., Woodmere, 1975-93. Fellow Am. Acad. Pediatrics. Office: 1573 Broadway Hewlett NY 11557-1428 Home Phone: 516-374-6356; Office Phone: 516-374-3322. Business E-Mail: philsteinfeld@pol.net.

STEINGART, RICHARD M., cardiologist, educator; MD, Mt. Sinai Sch. Medicine, 1974. Diplomate Am. Bd. Cardiology-cardiovascular disease, Am. Bd. Cardiology-nuc. cardiology, Am. Bd. Internal Medicine. Resident in internal medicine Yale New Haven Hosp., 1975—77; fellow in cardiovascular disease Mt. Sinai Med. Ctr., NY, 1977—79; prof. medicine Cornell Univ. - Weill Med. Coll.; chief cardiology svc. Meml. Sloan-Kettering Cancer Ctr., 2003. Office: Memorial Sloan-Kettering Cancer Center 1275 York Ave New York NY 10065 Office Phone: 212-639-8488.

STEINGLASS, PETER JOSEPH, psychiatrist, educator; b. NYC, Mar. 1, 1939; s. Sam and Bella Sarah (Bernstein) S.; m. Abbe Stahl, July 1, 1962; children: Matthew Aaron, Joanna Eowyn. AB, Union Coll., 1960; MD, Harvard U., 1965. Diplomate Am. Bd. Psychiatry and Neurology. Head clin. rsch. program Nat. Inst. Alcohol Abuse and Alcoholism, Washington, 1971-74; asst. prof. psychiatry George Washington U., Washington, 1974-77, assoc. prof. psychiatry, 1977-81, prof. psychiatry and behavioral sci., 1981-90; exec. dir. Ackerman Inst. for the Family, NYC, 1990—2004, pres., CEO, 2004—05, pres. emeritus, 2005—. Vis. prof. psychiatry Hebrew U., Jerusalem, 1981-82; clin. prof. psychiatry Cornell U. Med. Coll., 1993—. Author: The Alcoholic Family, 1987; contbr. articles to sci. publs. Lt. comdr. USPHS, 1969-71. Fellow Am. Psychiat. Assn., Am. Assn. Marriage and Family Therapy (cumulative contbn. award 1992), Assn. Clin. Psychosocial Rsch.; mem. Am. Family Therapy Acad. (charter, bd. dirs. 1987-89, v.p. 1989-91, Disting. Contbn. award 1987), Aesculapian Soc., Phi Beta Kappa. Democrat. Jewish. Avocations: photography, classical music. Office: 286 5th Ave Fl 7 New York NY 10001 Office Phone: 212-481-1860. Business E-Mail: psteinglass@ackerman.org.

STEINHAUS, JOHN EDWARD, retired anesthesiologist, educator; b. Omaha, Feb. 23, 1917; s. Emil F. and Pearl (Haynie) S.; m. Mila Jean Pinkerton, Feb. 21, 1943; children: Kathryn, Carolyn, Barbara, William, Elizabeth. BA, U. Neb., Lincoln, 1940, MA, 1941; MD, U. Wis., Madison, 1945, PhD, 1950. Diplomate Am. Bd. Anesthesiologists. Pvt. practice specializing in anesthesiology, Madison, Wis., 1951-58, Atlanta, 1958—; faculty U. Wis., 1951-58; mem. faculty Emory U., Atlanta, 1958—, prof. anesthesiology, 1959-87, prof. emeritus, 1987—, chmn. dept., 1959-85; chief anesthesiology service Grady Meml. Hosp., 1959-77, Emory U. Hosp., 1958-85; ret., 1987. Author: Medical Care Divided; contbr. articles to profl. jours. Past pres. Anesthesia Found. Mem. Am. Soc. Anesthesiologists (past pres., Disting. Service award 1982), So. Soc. Anesthesiologists (past pres.), AMA, AAAS, Assn. U. Anesthetists (past pres.), Anesthesiology History Assn. (past pres.), Soc. Pharm. Exptl. Therapeutics, Phi Beta Kappa, Sigma Xi, Alpha Omega Alpha. Home and Office: 836 Castle Falls Dr NE Atlanta GA 30329-4114 Office Phone: 404-741-5325.

STEINHAUSER, EMIL WALTER, maxillofacial surgeon, educator; b. Wurzburg, Bavaria, Germany, Sept. 24, 1926; s. Maximilian and Katharina Steinhauser; m. Miriam V. Balagtas, July 17, 1984; children: Stefanie, Katharina. DDS, U. Wurzburg, 1949, MD, 1952. Asst. U. Zurich Dental Sch., 1958—63, sr. staff, 1965—69; rsch. fellow U. Galveston Med. Sch., Tex., 1964; assoc. prof. U. Mpls. Dental Sch., 1969—72; prof. U. Erlangen, Germany, 1973—95, dir. dental sch., 1980—88, prof. emeritus, 1996—. Editor-in-chief: Jour. Cranio-Maxillofacial Surgery, 1993—99. Achievements include design of surgical instruments; osteosynthesis set for facial fractures. Avocations: sports, languages, literature. Home: Hindenburgstr 67 Erlangen 91054 Germany Office: Univ Erlangen Dental Sch Glueckstr 11 Erlangen 91054 Germany Office Phone: 0049 9131 21288. E-mail: ews-ms@t-online.de.

STEINHERZ, LAUREL JUDITH, pediatric cardiologist; b. NYC, Jan. 5, 1947; d. Bernard and Adeline Weinberger; m. Peter Gustav Steinherz, July 4, 1967; children: Jennifer, Jonathan, Daniel, David. Student, Hebrew U., Jersualem, 1966; BA with distinction, U. Rochester, 1967; MD, Albert Einstein Coll. Medicine, 1970. Diplomate Am. Bd. Pediatrics, sub-bd. pediatric cardiology. Intern in pediatrics N.Y. Hosp.-Cornell Med. Ctr., NYC, 1970-71; pediatric cardiology fellow N.Y. Presbyn. Hosp.-N.Y. Weill Cornell Med. Ctr. (formerly N.Y. Hosp. Cornell U. Med. Ctr.), NYC, 1973-75, asst. attending pediatrician, 1978-85, assoc. attending pediatrician, 1985—2007, attending pediatrician, 2008—; resident in pediatrics St. Louis Children's Hosp., 1971-72; attending pediatrician State U. Hosp. and King County Med. Ctr., Bklyn., 1975-77; asst. prof. pediatrics SUNY Downstate, 1975-77, Cornell U. Med. Coll., NYC, 1977-85, assoc. prof. pediatrics, 1985—2007, prof. pediat., 2008—; from asst. to attending pediatrician Meml. Sloan Kettering Cancer Ctr., NYC, 1977—, dir. pediatric cardiology, 1977—, asst. clin. mem., 1984-92, assoc. mem., 1997—2006, mem., 2006—. Contbg. author Adolescent Medicine II, 1976, Principles and Practice of Oncology, 1992, 1996, 2001, Supportive Care of Children With Cancer, 1993, 1997, Cardiac Toxicity After Treatment for Childhood Cancer, 1993, Progress in Pediat. Cardiology, 1998; contbr. articles to profl. jours. Hutzler Found. grantee, 1987. Fellow: Am. Coll. Cardiology, Am. Acad. Pediatrics; mem.: Children's Oncology Group, Am. Heart Assn. Avocations: photography, swimming, science fiction. Office: Meml Sloan Kettering Cancer Ctr 1275 York Ave New York NY 10021-6094 Office Phone: 212-639-8103.

STEINMAN, RALPH M., medical educator; b. Montreal, Can., Jan. 14, 1943; m. Claudia Hoeffel; children: Adam, Alexis, Lesley. BSc with honors, McGill U., 1963; MD magna cum laude, Harvard Med. Sch., 1968; degree (hon.), U. Innsbruck, 1998, Free U., Brussels, 1999, Erlangen U. Intern and resident Mass. Gen. Hosp.; postdoctoral fellow, cellular physiology and immunology lab Rockefeller U., NYC, 1970—72, asst. prof., 1972—76, assoc. prof., 1976—88, prof., 1988—95, Henry G. Kunkel prof., 1995—, dir., Chris Brown Ctr. for Immunology and Immune Diseases, 1998—, head, cellular physiology and immunology lab.; sr. physician Rockefeller U. Hosp., NYC, 1995—. Scientific advisor Charles A. Dana Found., Campbell Family Inst. Breast Cancer Rsch., Toronto, Canada, M.D. Anderson Cancer for Immunology Rsch., Houston, RIKEN Ctr. for Allergy and Immunology Rsch., Yokohama, Japan, CHAVI Ctr. for HIV AIDS Vaccine Immunology, Durham, NC. Editor: Jour. Exptl. Medicine; adv. editor Human Immunology, Jour. Clin. Immunology, Jour. Immunological Methods, Proceedings NAS. Trustee Trudeau Inst., Saranac Lake, NY. Recipient Emil von Behring prize, 1996, Freidrich-Sasse prize, 1996, Rudolf Virchow medal, 1997, Max Planck award, 1998, Coley medal, 1998, Robert Koch prize, 1999, Gairdner Found. Internat. award, 2003, Mayor's award in Biol. & Med. Scis., NY Acad. Scis., 2004, Debrecen prize in Molecular Medicine, U. Debrecen, Hungary, 2007, Albert Lasker award for Basic Med. Rsch., Lasker Found., 2007. Fellow: Royal Soc. Edinburgh (corr.); mem.: NAS, Soc. Leukocyte Biology, Am. Assn. Immunologists, Am. Soc. Cell Biology, Am. Acad. Microbiologists, Am. Soc. Clin. Investigation, Inst. Medicine, Kunkel and Practitioner's Societies, Harvey. Achievements include discovery of dendritic cells, the preeminent component of the immune system that initiates and regulates the body's response to foreign antibodies. Office: Lab Cellular Physiology and Immunology Rockefeller Univ 1230 York Ave New York NY 10021 Office Phone: 212-327-8000. E-mail: steinma@rockefeller.edu. *

STEINMETZ, SEYMOUR, pediatrician; b. Czechoslovakia, Oct. 6, 1934; arrived in U.S., 1947; s. Nathan and Gisela S. Steinmetz. BA, Yeshiva U., NYC, 1956; MD, Albert Einstein Coll. Medicine, Bronx, NY, 1960. Diplomate Am. Bd. Pediat. Intern UCLA Hosp., 1960-61, resident in pediat., 1961-62; chief resident in pediat. Montefiore Hosp., Bronx, 1964-65; fellow in child psychiatry Jacobi Hosp., Bronx, 1965-66; pvt. practice Great Neck, NY, 1966-74, Fremont

(Calif.) Pediatric Med. Group, 1974—, pres., 1984—. With M.C. USAF, 1962—64. Fellow: Am. Acad. Pediat. Office: Kaiser Permanente 43971 Boscell Rd Fremont CA 94538 Office Phone: 510-354-3200.

STEINORTH, CHRISTINA ENNI, psychotherapist, author; m. Matthew E. Steinorth, Apr. 3, 1999. BA, Calif. State U., Northridge, 1990; MA in Marriage and Family Therapy, Phillips Grad. Inst., 1995. Cert. in profl. counselling Internat. Assn. Behavioral Medicine, Counseling & Psychotherapy. Pvt. practice, Santa Barbara, Calif., 2000—. Monthly columnist Inland Empire Mag., 2000—02; former newspaper advice columnist. Mem.: Calif. Assn. Marriage & Family Therapists (Santa Barbara chpt. & Ventura County chpt. clin. mem.), Am. Assn. Marriage & Family Therapists (clin. mem.). Avocations: writing, reading, art, painting. Office: 510 State St Suite 220 Santa Barbara CA 93101 Office Phone: 805-320-6624. Office Fax: 805-984-4462. Business E-Mail: SteinorthC@aol.com.

STEINSSON, STEFAN, physician, writer; b. Seydisfjordur, Iceland, Jan. 18, 1958; s. Steinn Josua Stefansson and Arnthrudur Ingolfsdottir; m. Birna Norddahl, June 22, 1991; children: Robert Valur Stefansson, Steinunn Arnbjorg Stefansdottir, Elisabet Yr Norddahl, Jon Erlingur Stefansson. Degree in Medicine and Surgery, U. Iceland, 1984. Lic. physician Ministry Health, Iceland, 1985, psychiatrist Ministry Health, Iceland, 1998. Houseman Akranes Hosp., Iceland, 1984—85; sr. ho. officer ob-gyn. U. Hosp., Reykjavik, Iceland, 1985—87; gen. practitioner Med. Ctrs., Thingeyri and Budardalur, Iceland, 1987—93; psychiatry registrar South London Hosps., 1993—98; cons. psychiatrist U. Hosp., Reykjavik, 1998—2002, emergency physician, 2002—05; gen. practitioner Med. Ctr., Rangarthing, Iceland, 2005—. Translator: The Epic of Gilgamesh, 1996, Menander's Dyskolos, 2007. Mem.: Am. Coll. Emergency Physicians, Royal Coll. Psychiatrists. Avocations: the classics, music, literature, history, languages.

STEINWACHS, MATTHIAS REINHARD, orthopedist, sports medicine physician; b. Tuebingen, Germany, June 13, 1958; s. Friederich and Anneliese Steinwachs; m. Ute Guhlke-Steinwachs, Aug. 16, 1991; 1 child, Ann-Catherine. Student, U. Konstanz, Germany, 1980—83; MD, U. Heidelberg and Goettingen, Germany, 1990; D, U. Goettingen, 1992; Habil, U. Freiburg, 2004. Intern in surgery Bernward-Hosp., Hildesheim, Germany, 1991—92; intern in orthopaedics U. Freiburg, Germany, 1992—97, asst. prof. dept. orthop. surgery, 1997—, pvt. docent orthop. surgery, 2004. Mem. steering com. Valley-Tissue-Engrg. Ctr. U. Freiburg, 1997—, leader cartilage rsch. group, 1998—, dir. cartilage transplantation unit, 2003; privat dozent U Freiburg, 2004; hon. prof. Inst. Sports Medicine Peking U., 2006; mem. expert group German Ministry of Edn. and Sci., 2005; expert European Med. Agency, 2007; dir. Ctr. Orthobiologics & Cartilage Repair Schulthess Klinik, 2007. Author: Autologous Chondrocytes Transplantation Condrocytes Culturing and Clinical Aspects, 1998, Cellbiological Aspects in the ACT-Therapy Attachments in Genetic Engineering, 2000; editor: Joint Cartilage Defects, 2001; contbr. articles to profl. jours. Grantee Cartilage Engrng. grantee, Min. of Sci., Govt. of Germany, 1998—2001. Mem.: Internat. Cartilage Repair Soc. (chmn. outcome com., bd. dirs.), European Tissue Engrng. Soc. Office: Chefarzt Orthobiologie und Knorpelregeneration Schulthess Klinik Lengghalde 2 CH 8008 Zurich Switzerland Office Phone: 0041443857490.

STEITZ, JOAN ARGETSINGER, biochemistry professor; b. Mpls., Jan. 26, 1941; d. Glenn D. and Elaine (Magnusson) Argetsinger; m. Thomas A. Steitz, Aug. 20, 1966; 1 child, Jon. BS, Antioch Coll., 1963; PhD, Harvard U., 1967; DSc (hon.), Lawrence U., Appleton, Wis., 1981, Rochester U. Sch. Medicine, 1984, Mt. Sinai Sch. Medicine, 1989, Bates Coll., 1990, Trinity Coll., 1992, Harvard U., 1992, Brandeis U., 2002, Brown U., 2003, Princeton U., 2003, Watson Sch. Biol. Sciences, Cold Spring Harbor Lab., 2004. NSF postdoctoral fellow, Andorra, 1967—69; Jane Coffin Childs Meml. Fund Fellow, Divsn. Cell Biology Med. Rsch. Coun. Lab. Molecular Biology, Cambridge, England, 1967—70; asst. prof. molecular biophysics and biochemistry Yale U., New Haven, 1970-74, assoc. prof., molecular biophysics and biochemistry, 1974-78, prof., molecular biophysics and biochemistry, 1978—92, Henry Ford II prof. molecular biophysics and biochemistry, 1992—98, chmn. dept. molecular biophysics and biochemistry, 1996—99, dir. molecular genetics program Boyer Ctr. Molecular Medicine, Sterling prof. molecular biophysics and biochemistry, 1998—. Josiah Macy Scholar Max Planck Inst. fur Biophysikalische Chemie (Göttingen), Germany and Med. Coun. Ctr., Lab. of Molecular Biology, Cambridge, England, 1976—77; Fairchild Disting. Fellow Calif. Inst. Technology, Pasadena, Calif., 1984—85; investigator Howard Hughes Med. Inst, Yale Univ., 1986—; scientific dir. Jane Coffin Child Fund for Med. Rsch., 1991—2002; dir., molecular genetics program Boyer Center for Molecular Medicine; mem. vis. com. for biology divsn. Caltech, Calif. Inst. Technology, 1999—; mem. basic sciences scientific adv. bd. Fred Hutchinson Cancer Ctr., 2001—; mem. scientific adv. bd., biology divsn. Molecular Biology Dept., Princeton Univ., Max Planck Inst. for Biophysical Chemistry (Göttingen), 1999—; mem. Lasker Awards Jury, 2001—, Jury for L'Oréal UNESCO award, 2001—; mem. scientific adv. com. Sci. Found. Ireland, 2002—. Mem. editl. bd. Genes and Development, 1994—, assoc. editor RNA, 1994—, bd. reviewing editors Science, 2004—. Bd. overseers Harvard Univ., 2003—. Recipient Young Scientist award, Passano Found., 1975, Eli Lilly award in Biol. Chemistry, 1976, US Steel Found. award in Molecular Biology, 1982, Lee Hawley, Sr. award for Arthritis Rsch., 1983, Nat. Medal Sci., 1986, Radcliffe Grad. Soc. Medal for Disting. Achievement, 1987, Dickson Prize for Sci., Carnegie-Mellon U., 1988, Christopher Columbus Discovery Award in Biomed. Rsch., 1992, Rebecca Rice award for Disting. Achievement, Antioch Coll. Alumni Assn., 1993, Weizmann Women and Sci. Award, 1994, City of Medicine Award, 1996, Disting. Svc. award, Miami Bio/Technology Winter Symposium, 1996, Novartis Drew Award in Biomed. Rsch., 1999, UNESCO-L'Oreal Women in Sci. Award, 2001, Lewis S. Rosenstiel for Distinguished Work in Basic Medical Rsch. Award, 2002, FASEB Excellence in Sci. Award, 2003, Howard Taylor Ricketts Award, U. Chgo., 2004, Caledonian Rsch. Found. Prize Lectureship, Royal Soc. Edinburgh, 2004, The RNA Soc. Lifetime Achievement Award, 2004, E.B. Wilson medal, Am. Soc. Cell Biology, 2005, Gairdner Found. Internat. award, 2006, Rosalind E. Franklin award for Women in Sci., Nat. Cancer Inst., 2006; co-recipient (with Thomas R. Cech) Warren Triennial Prize, Mass. Gen. Hosp., 1989, Albany Med. Ctr. Prize in Medicine & Biomedical Rsch., 2008; named Fritz Lipmann Lectr., Am. Soc. for Biochemistry and Molecular Biology, 1989, 11th Ann. Keith Porter Lectr. on Cell Biology, Am. Soc. for Cell Biology, 1992. Fellow: AAAS, Am. Acad. Microbiology; mem.: NAS, Inst. Medicine, Academia Europaea, Japanese Biochemical Soc. (hon.), European Molecular Biology Orgn. (assoc.), Conn. Acad. Sciences and Engring., Am. Philos. Soc., Am. Acad. Arts and Sciences. Achievements include discovering and defining the function of small nuclear ribonucleoproteins in pre-messenger RNA which play a key role in recognizing and eliminating introns; research which has improved diagnosis and treatment of autoimmune diseases. Office: Molecular Biophysics and Biochemistry Dept Yale Univ PO Box 208024 333 Cedar St New Haven CT 06520-8024 Office Phone: 203-737-4418. Business E-Mail: joan.steitz@yale.edu. *

STEITZ, THOMAS ARTHUR, biophysicist; b. Milw., Aug. 23, 1940; BA, Lawrence U., Appleton, Wis., 1962, DSc (hon.), 1981; PhD, Harvard U., 1966. Postdoc. fellow Harvard U., 1966—67; Jane Coffin Childs postdoc. fellow MRC Lab. Molecular Biology, Cambridge, England, 1967—70; faculty Yale U., New Haven, 1970—, Sterling prof. molecular biophysics and biochemistry. Investigator Howard Hughes Med. Inst., Chevy Chase, Md., 1986—; vis. prof. U. Colo., Boulder, 1992—93. Contbr. articles to profl. jours. Recipient Pfizer award in enzyme chemistry, Am. Chem. Soc., 1980, Rosenstiel award for disting. work in basic med. rsch., 2001, Keio Med. Sci. prize, 2006, Gairdner Found. Internat. award, 2007, Nobel prize in chemistry, 2009, Lucia R. Briggs Disting. Achievement award, Lawrence U.; Macy Fellow, Göttingen, Germany, 1976—77, Fairchild Scholar, Calif. Inst. Tech., 1984—85. Fellow: Am. Acad. Arts & Scis. (Newcomb Cleveland prize 2001); mem.: NAS. Office: Yale U Dept Molecular Biophysics & Biochemistry Bass Center Room 418 PO Box 208114 266 Whitney Ave New Haven CT 06520-8114 Office Phone: 203-432-5619, 203-432-5617. Office Fax: 203-432-3282. Business E-Mail: thomas.steitz@yale.edu. *

STELLMAN, STEVEN DALE, epidemiologist; b. Toronto, May 7, 1945; s. Samuel David and Lillian (Mandlsohn) S.; m. Jeanne Esther Mager, Sept. 10, 1967; children: Andrew, Emma. BSc in Chemistry, Ohio State U., 1966; PhD in Phys. Chemistry, NYU, 1971; MPH in Health Policy and Mgmt., Columbia U., 1992. Rsch. assoc. biochem. sci. Princeton (N.J.) U., 1971-73; lectr. in chemistry U. Colo., Denver, 1973-74; chief div. computing and biostats. Am. Health Found., NYC, 1975-80, chief divsn. epidemiology, 1991—2003; asst. v.p. epidemiology Am. Cancer Soc., NYC, 1980-88; asst. commr. biostat. and epidemiol. rsch. N.Y.C. Dept. Health, 1988-91; adj. assoc. prof. dept. cmty. medicine Mt. Sinai Sch. Medicine, NYC, 1981-99; res. dir., dept. health and mental hygiene World Trade Ctr. Health Registry, NYC, 2007—. Sci. cons. agt. orange vet. payment program U.S. Dist. Ct., Bklyn., 1985-94; mem. adv. bd. pub. health grad. program Robert Wood Johnson Sch. Medicine, Piscataway, N.J., 1986-98; cons. in epidemiology and biostats. Meml. Sloan-Kettering Cancer Ctr., N.Y.C., 1993-2002; prof. clin. epidemiology Mailman Sch. Pub. Health, Columbia U., 2001—; dir. rsch. World Trade Ctr. Health Registry, NYC Dept. Health, 2007-. Author Women and Cancer, 1986; editor Vital Stats. Summaries, N.Y.C., 1988-91; assoc. editor Women and Health, 1991—, Preventive Medicine, 2005—, BMC Cancer, 2007-; contbr. articles to profl. publs. Condr. DeRossi singers Kane St. Synagogue, 1985-2004; mem. Dessoff Choirs, N.Y.C., 2002—, bd. mem., 2005—, treas., 2006—. Fogarty Sr. Internat. fellow NIH, 1992-93; recipient Disting. Svc. medal, The Am. Legion, 2003. Mem. APHA, Am. Coll. Epidemiology, Soc. for Epidemiologic Rsch., Am. Chem. Soc. Democrat. Jewish. Achievements include study of health effects of agent orange, cancer prevention study of 1.2 million Ams., health of world, Trade Ctr, 9/11 supr. Home: 117 Saint Johns Pl Brooklyn NY 11217-3401 Office: Dept Epidemiology Mailman Sch Pub Health Columbia U 722 W 168th St New York NY 10032 Home Phone: 718-789-2634.

STELLWAAG, MICHAEL KARL, cardiologist; b. Landau Pfalz, Germany, Mar. 8, 1951; s. Friedrich and Ursula Stellwaag; m. Ute Schmidt, Feb. 25, 1962; 1 child, Lars. Diplom Chemiker, U. Göttingen, Germany, 1976, MD, 1985. Intern Städtische Kliniken Oldenburg, Germany, 1980—81; resident radiology, oncology and surgery Pius Hosp. Oldenburg, Germany, 1982—85; resident in internal medicine U. Marburg, Germany, 1986—92, chief resident, 1992—93; cons. cardiology Deutsche Klinik für Diagnostik, Wiesbaden, Germany, 1993—99, pvt. practice, 2000—. Mem.: European Soc. Cardiology, Deutsche Gesellschaft fuer Kardiologie, Bund niedergelassener Kardiologen. Avocations: painting, photography. Office: Kardiologische Gemeinschaftspraxis Burgstrasse 6-8 Wiesbaden D65183 Germany Office Fax: 0049 611 39932.

STELWAGON, JENNIFER COOPER, psychiatrist; b. Valdosta, Ga., Jan. 18, 1973; d. Michael Thomas and Margaret Ann (Sorensen) Cooper; m. William Mantz Stelwagon, Apr. 28, 2007; children: William Cooper, John Michael. BA magna cum laude, DePauw U., Greencastle, Ind., 1995; MD, Johns Hopkins U., Balt., 1999. Lic. physician NY, diplomate Am. Bd. Psychiatry and Neurology, Am. Bd. Addiction Psychiatry. Resident in psychiatry NY Presbyn. Hosp./Weill Cornell Med. Ctr./Payne Whitney Clinic, NYC, 1999—2003; fellow in addiction psychiatry Weill Med. Coll. of Cornell U., NYC, 2003—04; staff psychiatrist Bridge Back to Life, NYC, 2004—05, med. dir., 2009—; pvt. practice psychiatry NYC, 2004—; med. dir. drug treatment Exponents, NYC, 2004—07. Clin. instr. psychiatry Weill Med. Coll. of Cornell U., 2006—; mem. adv. bd. David Dawes Nee II Found., 2007—. Ordained elder First Presbyn. Ch. NYC. Recipient Alumni award for resident tchg., Payne Whitney Clinic, 2003; named Career Directions Resident of the Yr., Pfizer Inc., 2002. Mem.: Presbyterian Church (ordained elder), Dave Nee Found. (mem. adv. bd. 2007—), Am. Acad. Addiction Psychiatry, Am. Psychiat. Assn. Avocations: skiing, scuba diving. Home: 1175 York Ave 7E New York NY 10065 Office: 420 East 51st St Ste C New York NY 10022

STELZER, PAUL, thoracic surgeon, educator; Attended, U. Nebr., Lincoln, 1964—65; BA summa cum laude, Abilene Christian U., 1968; MD, Columbia U., 1972. Diplomate Am. Bd. Surgery, Am. Bd. Thoracic Surgery. Intern, resident gen. surgery Roosevelt Hosp., NYC, 1972-77; resident cardiothoracic surgery NY Hosp.-Cornell Med. Ctr., 1979—81, staff cardiothoracic surgeon, asst. prof. surgery, 1981—85; chief thoracic surgery Okla. Meml. Hosp.; assoc. prof. surgery U. Okla. Health Scis. Ctr., Oklahoma City, 1985—89; staff cardiothoracic surgeon Lenox Hill Hospital, NYC, 1989—96; chief divsn. cardiothoracic surgery St. Luke's/Roosevelt Hosp. Ctr., 1999—2000; sr. cardiothoracic surgeon Beth Israel Med. Ctr., 1996—2007; co-dir. valve surgery Mt. Sinai Med. Ctr., 2007—. Office: Mt Sinai Hosp Dept Cardiothoracic Surgery 1190 Fifth Ave, Box 1028 New York NY 10029 Home Phone: 212-737-8103; Office Phone: 212-659-6871. Office Fax: 212-659-6818. Business E-Mail: pstelzer@bethisraelny.org. E-mail: Paul.Stelzer@mountsinai.org.

STELZNER, JOERG GERHARD HANS, anesthesiologist, educator; b. Magdeburg, Germany, Apr. 1, 1942; s. Otto and Erna (Theuerkauf) S.; m. Barbara Lina Maria Mueller, June 28, 1968; children: Matthias, Mark, Martin. MD, Georg-August U., 1968. Physician surgery, anesthesiology Hosp. Verden, Aller, Germany, 1968-72; anesthesiologist U. Goettingen, Germany, 1972-78; dir. dept. anesthesiology, ICU Dist. Hosp. Grossburgwedel, Germany, 1978—. Lectr. anesthesiology Medizinische Hochschule Hannover, 1979—. Contbr. articles to profl. jours. Mem. Berufsverband Deutscher Anaesthesisten, Deutsche Gesellschaft fuer Anaesthesiologie und Intensivmedizin, Deutsche Gesellschaft fuer Internistische Intensivmedizin und Notfallmedizin. Home: Gerstensteige 21 30938 Burgwedel Germany Office: Dist Hosp Grossburgwedel Fuhrberger Str 8 30938 Burgwedel Germany Home Phone: 49 5139 1375; Office Phone: 49 5139 8011. E-mail: dr.joerg.stelzner@t-online.de.

STEMERMAN, DAVID H., radiologist; b. Elmira, NY, Aug. 2, 1966; BA, Emory U., 1988; MD, Boston U., 1992. Diplomate Nat. Bd. Med. Examiners; bd. cert. Am. Bd. Radiology. Intern Mass. Gen. Hosp., Boston, 1992-93; resident Temple U., Phila., 1993-97; fellow NYU, NYC, 1997-98; assoc. radiologist Abington Meml. Hosp., Pa., 1998-99, St. Joseph's Med. Ctr., 1999—2000, St. Barnabas Hosp., 2000—01; med. dir. Open High-Field MRI and CT, Westchester and Fordham Radiology. Office Fax: 914-833-9641.

STEMMLER, EDWARD JOSEPH, physician, retired health facility administrator, dean; b. Phila., Feb. 15, 1929; s. Edward C. and Josephine (Heitzmann) Stemmler; m. Joan C. Koster, Dec. 27, 1958; children: Elizabeth, Margaret, Edward C., Catherine, Joan. BA, La Salle Coll., Phila., 1950, ScD (hon.), 1983; MD, U. Pa., 1960; ScD (hon.), Ursinus Coll., 1977, Phila. Coll. Pharmacy and Sci., 1989; LHD (hon.), Rush U., 1986, Med. Coll. Pa., 1994; ScD (hon.), SUNY, Syracuse, 1994; ScD, Georgetown U., 1998. Diplomate Am. Bd. Internal Medicine. Intern U. Pa. Hosp., 1960—61, resident in internal medicine, 1961—63, fellow in cardiology, 1963—64, chief med. resident, 1964—65, chief med. outpatient dept., 1966—67; chief of medicine U. Pa. Med. Svc., VA Hosp., Phila., 1967—73; deans com. VA Hosp., 1974—88; instr. medicine grad. divsn. medicine U. Pa., 1964—66, NIH postdoctoral rsch. trainee, dept. physiology, grad. divsn. medicine, 1965—67, assoc. in medicine grad. divsn. medicine, 1966—67; assoc. in physiology Grad. Div. Medicine, 1967—72, from asst. prof. medicine to prof., 1967—91, Robert G. Dunlop prof., 1981—91; prof. emeritus, 1991—; assoc. dean Univ. Hosp. Sch. Medicine, 1973, assoc. dean student affairs, 1973—75, from acting dean to dean, 1974—88, dean emeritus, 1989—; exec. v.p. U. Pa. Med. Ctr., 1986—89, Assn. Am. Med. Colls., 1990—94, sr. adv. to pres., 1994—95. Nominating and ad hoc governance coms. Nat. Bd. Med. Examiners, 1985, exec. com., 1986—99, vice-chmn., 1987—89, treas., 1989—91, chmn., 1991—95; ednl. policy com. Nat. Fund for Med. Edn., 1975—77; deans com. VA Hosp., 1974—89; chmn. Pa. Deans Com., 1976—87, Mid-Ea. Regional Med. Libr. Svcs., 1978—81; adv. com. dept. medicine U. Ala., Birmingham, 1985—89; vis. com. Tufts U. Sch. Medicine, 1990—94, Med. U. S.C., 1990—99, U. Calif., Davis, 1993—2008. Contbr. articles to profl. jours. Trustee Dorothy Rider Pool Healthcare Trust, 1991—2000, Ursinus Coll., 1991—2006, Wintergreen Nature Found., 1996—2001, Saw Cmty. Found., 2000—04, AHC Cmty. Found., 2002—08; mem. oper. bd. U. Va. Med. Ctr., 2004—; chair Quality Soc. Com. Recipient Frederick A. Packard award, 1960, Albert Einstein Med. Ctr. staff award, 1960, Roche award, 1960, Disting. Svc. award, Nat. Bd. Med. Examiners, 1999. Master: ACP (treas., chmn. investment com. 1975—80, Laureate award Ea. Pa. region 1986, Disting. Svc. award); mem.: AMA, Am. Clin. and Climatological Soc. (pres. 1997—98), Coll. Physicians Phila. (bd. censors, coun. 1979—85, coun. 1990—92), Assn. Am. Med. Colls. (ad hoc external exam. rev. com. 1980—82, exec. coun., coun. of deans adminstrv. bd. 1980—85, chmn. 1983—85, nat. chmn.-elect 1985—86, chmn. assembly 1986—87), Inst. Medicine, Alpha Omega Alpha. Republican. Home: RR 1 Box 676 Roseland VA 22967-9209

STENCHEVER, MORTON ALBERT, obstetrician, gynecologist; b. Paterson, NJ, Jan. 25, 1931; s. Harold and Lena (Suresky) Stenchever; m. Diane Bilsky, June 19, 1955 (dec. 1999); children: Michael A., Marc R., Douglas A.; m. Luba Kane, Sept. 8, 2001. AB, NYU, 1951; MD, U. Buffalo, 1956. Diplomate Am. Bd. Ob-gyn., 1965, recertified 1986. Intern Mt. Sinai Hosp., 1956-57; resident obstetrics and gynecology Columbia-Presbyn. Med. Center, NYC, 1957-60; asst. prof., Oglebey research fellow Case-Western Res. U., Cleve., 1962-66, asso. prof. dept. reproductive biology, 1967-70, dir. Tissue Culture Lab., 1965-70, coordinator Phase II Med. Sch. program, 1969-70; prof., chmn. dept. obstetrics-gynecology U. Utah Med. Sch., Salt Lake City, 1970-77; prof. ob-gyn. U. Wash. Sch. Medicine, Seattle, 1977-98; prof. emeritus, 1998—; chmn. dept. U. Wash. Sch. Medicine, Seattle, 1977-96. Chmn. test com. for ob-gyn. Nat. Bd. Med. Examiners, 1979-82; cons. in urogynecology Fedn. Internat. for Gynecology & Obstetrics, 1998—. Author: Labor: Workbook in Obstetrics, 1968, Labor: Workbook in Obstetrics, 2d edit., 1993, Human Sexual Behavior: A Workbook in Reproductive Biology, 1970, Human Cytogenics: A Workbook in Reproductive Biology, 1973, Introductory Gynecology: A Workbook in Reproductive Biology, 1974; co-author: Comprehensive Gynecology, 1987, Comprehensive Gynecology, 4th edit., 2001, Caring for the Older

Woman, 1991, Health Care for the Older Woman, 1996, Office Gynecology, 1992, Office Gynecology, 2d edit., 1996, Good Health, Great Sex After 40: A Woman's Guide, 1997; sr. editor: Atlas of Gynecology, 5 vols., 1997—99, assoc. editor: Ob-Gyn., 1986—2001, Ob-Gyn. Survey; editor: Clinical Updates in Women's Health Care, 2001—, ACOG Clin. Review, 2001—; mem. editl. bd.: Western Jour. Medicine; contbr. articles to profl. jours. Served to capt. USAF, 1960-62. Fellow Am. Coll. Obstetricians and Gynecologists (com. on residency edn. 1974-80, learning resource commn. 1980-86, vice chmn. 1982-83, chmn. prolog self-assessment program 1982-86, vice chair com. health care for the underserved women 1995-97), Am. Assn. Obstetricians and Gynecologists, Am. Gynecol. Soc., Am. Gyencol. and Obstetrical Soc., Pacific Coast Ob-Gyn. Soc.; mem. AAAS, AMA, Am. Bd. Ob-Gyn. (bd. dir. 1988-2004, v.p. 1990-92, treas. 1992-96, chmn. 1996-98, mem. resident rev. com. 1993-97, chmn. divsn. female pelvic medicine/reconstructive surgery), Assn. Profs. Gynecology and Obstetrics (chmn. steering com. teaching methods in ob-gyn. 1970-79, v.p. 1975-76, pres. 1983-84, v.p. Found. 1986-87, pres. Found. 1987-91), Pacific N.W. Ob-Gyn. Soc., Wash. State Med. Assn., Seattle Gynec. Soc. (v.p. 1981, pres.-elect 1982, pres. 1982-83), Am. Soc. Human Genetics, Ctrl. Assn. Ob-Gyn., Soc. Gynecologic Investigation, Wash. State Obstet. Soc., Tissue Culture Assn., N.Y. Acad. Sci., Utah Ob-Gyn. Soc., Utah Med. Assn., Teratology Soc., Am. Fertility Soc., Internat. Pelvic Floor Dysfunction Soc. Home: 8301 SE 83rd St Mercer Island WA 98040-5644 Office: Ob-Gyn 130 Knickerson St Ste 211 Seattle WA 98109 Office Phone: 206-286-1775. Business E-Mail: mstenchever@acog.org.

STENGAARD-PEDERSEN, KRISTIAN, medical educator, clinical scientist physician; b. Aarhus, Denmark, June 18, 1946; s. Frede Pedersen and Emmy Norsgaard Stengaard; m. Ulrikke Sorensen, Dec. 27, 1970; children: Kirsten, Erik, Eva. MD of Medicine, U. Aarhus, Denmark, 1973, DMSc, 1990. Cert. in internal medicine & rheumatology Nat. Bd. Health, Denmark, 1984. Resident Aarhus County Hosps., Aarhus, 1973—79; lt. Royal Navy, Denmark, 1975—76, res. officer, 1976—2006; postdoctoral rsch. assoc. U. Aarhus, Aarhus, 1979—83; sr. registrar Aarhus U. Hosp., Aarhus, 1983—89, chief physician, 1989—, prof., 1998—. Bd. mem. Danish Soc. Rheumatology, 1990—93, sec., 1993—96, pres., 1996—99. Mem. editl. bd.: Scandinavian Jour. Rheumatology, 1998—, editor-in-chief:, 2003—; contbr. more than 200 articles to profl. jours. & textbooks. Pres. Scandinavian Soc. for Rheumatology, 1996—98; advisor Expert Coun. Nat. Bd. Health, Copenhagen, 1991—, Medico-Legal Coun., Copenhagen, 1991—; chmn. Expert Coun. Rheumatology, Aarhus, 1998—; pres., rsch. com. Danish Rheumatism Assn., 2007—. Recipient Tordenskjold prize, Tordenskjold Found., Copenhagen, 1976, Morso Fron Foundry award, 1966, Ole Romers award, U. Arhus, 1969, Quin Ingrid's Rsch. award, 2006; named Bert Reynolds fellow, Rockefeller Found., 1977, Tchr. of Yr., U. Aarhus, 1997. Mem.: Am. Coll. Rheumatology, Internat. Assn. for Study of Pain, Danish Soc. Internal Medicine, Danish Soc. Rheumatology. Avocations: bicycling, windsurfing, swimming, skiing. Home: Sejrs Alle 17 DK-8240 Risskov Denmark Office: Aarhus U Hosp Dept Rheumatology Norrebrogade 44 DK-8000 Aarhus Denmark Home Phone: 0045 86176612; Office Phone: 0045 8949 4225. Fax: +45 8949 4210. Business E-Mail: stengaard@rheum.dk.

STENKLEV, NIELS CHRISTIAN, surgeon, educator; b. Oslo, Aug. 17, 1964; s. Tom and Inger Anette Stenklev. MD, U. Oslo, 1992; PhD, U. Tromsø, Norway, 2004. Intern Med./Surg. Dept. Graudal Sykehus, Lofoten, Norway, 1992—93; GP intern Kommunelegen, Vestvågøy, Lofoten, 1993—94; resident, ENT Dept. Nordland Sentral Sykehus, Bodø, Norway, 1995—96, U. Hosp. No. Norway, Tromsø, 1997—2000, cons. ENT surgery, 2000—; family practice Bjørnemyr Legekontor, Nesodden, Norway, 1996—97; assoc. prof. U. Tromsø, 2005—. Mem. adv. com. in audiology Norwegian ENT Assn., 2003—. Editor: (jour.) Helsetjenesten/Medisinsk teknitek, 1991. Lt. Norwegian Spl. Forces, 1994—95. Achievements include research in brain stem audiometry in the Atlantic cod; audiometry and hearing outcome after middle ear surgery for otosclerosis and tympanic membrane perforations; hearing in the elderly - a cross sectional study of presbycusis. Office: Univ Hosp Northern Norway Breivika 9038 Tromso Norway Office Fax: +4777627369. Business E-Mail: niels.christian.stenklev@unn.no.

STENSON, WILLIAM FREDERICK, gastroenterologist; b. Rome, NY, Dec. 2, 1945; s. Frederick Vincent and Mary Catherine (Tucker) S.; m. Janet Marie Breaugh, Dec. 28, 1968; children: Catherine, Karen, Thomas. BS, Providence Coll., 1967; MD, Washington U., 1971. Diplomate Am. Bd. Internal Medicine and Gastroenterology. Intern Barnes Hosp., St. Louis, 1971—72, resident in medicine, 1972—73, resident medicine, 1975—76; chief gastroenterology Jewish Hosp. of St. Louis, 1981—98; assoc. prof. medicine Washington U., St. Louis, 1985—91, prof. medicine, 1991—. Co-author: Manual of Nutritional Therapeutics, 1st edit., 1983, 2d edit., 1988, 4th edit., 2002, 5th edit., 2008; editor: (book) Inflammatory Bowel Disease, 1991, Gastrointestinal Pharmacology, 1992. Maj. USAF, 1973-75. Named Nicholas V. Costrini Prof. Gastroenterology & Inflammatory Bowel Disease, 2007—. Office: Washington U Sch Medicine PO Box 8124 Saint Louis MO 63110 Office Phone: 314-362-8952.

STENWICK, MICHAEL WILLIAM, retired internist, geriatrician, consultant; b. Red Wing, Minn., Nov. 12, 1941; s. Vincent Ferdinand and Geraldine Frances (Veith) S.; m. Judith Ann Nelson, June 10, 1961; children: Scott Michael, Gregg William. BS cum laude, Hamline U., 1963; MD, U. Minn., 1969. Diplomate Am. Bd. Internal Medicine. Fellow dept. pharmacology U. Minn., Mpls., 1966-68; intern in internal medicine Northwestern Hosp., Mpls., 1969-70, resident in internal medicine, 1970-73; sr. internist internal medicine sect. Bloomington Lake Clinic, Mpls., 1973—2000; ret., 2000. Bd. dirs. Bloomington Lake Clinic, Mpls., pres. 1977, v.p. 1989-97, fin. com., 1987—, chmn. properties, 1984—, chmn. trustees profit sharing; med. adviser Kimberly Quality Care, St. Paul, 1990-94; internal medicine cons. Fairview Multiple Sclerosis Ctr. and Rehab. Unit, Mpls., 1986-91; informal adviser internal medicine sect. Minn. Relative Value Index, Mpls., 1971; mem. task force Riverside Med. Ctr., Mpls., 1988-91, chmn. critical care com., 1986-91, reviewer quality assurance subcom., 1989-90. Contbr. articles to profl. jours. Mem., co-organizer, 1st pres. Cyrus Barnum Soc., U. Minn. Med. Sch., Mpls.; bd. dirs. Signal Inn Beach and Racquetball Club, Sanibel Island, Fla., 1983-84, 89-98, Signal Inn Condominium Assn., Sanibel Island, 1983-84, 89-98; co-emcee Nursing Talent Show, Northwestern Hosp., Mpls., 1969; 1st med. dir. Beltrami Health Ctr., Mpls., 1970-72. Recipient scholarship Charles and Alora Allis Found., 1960-63, Walter Kenyon award, 1963, grant U. Minn., 1963; named to Wall Honor, Red Wing HS, 2005. Fellow ACP; mem. AMA, Am. Soc. Internal Medicine, Minn. Med. Assn., Hennepin County Med. Assn., West Metro Med. Soc., Minn. Acad. Medicine. Republican. Lutheran. Achievements include research in drug specificity that could be defined even in an alkylating agent; providing evidence for an active role of the choroid plexus in distributing and concentrating morphine in the brain.

STEP, EUGENE LEE, retired pharmaceutical executive; b. Sioux City, Iowa, Feb. 19, 1929; s. Harry and Ann (Keiser) S.; m. Hannah Scheuermann, Dec. 27, 1953; children: Steven Harry, Michael David, Jonathan Allen. BA in Econs., U. Nebr., 1951; MS in Acctg. and Fin., U. Ill., 1952. With Eli Lilly Internat. Corp., London and Paris, 1964-69, dir. Elanco Internat. Indpls., 1969-70, v.p. marketing, 1970-72, v.p. Europe, 1972; v.p. mktg. Eli Lilly and Co., Indpls., 1972-73, pres. pharm. div., 1973-86, exec. v.p., 1986—. 1st lt. U.S. Army, 1953-56. Mem. Pharm. Mfrs. Assn. (bd. dirs. 1980-92, chmn. 1989-90), Internat. Pharm. Mfrs. Assn. (pres. 1991-92). Home: PO Box 8997 Rancho Santa Fe CA 92067-8997 Office Phone: 858-759-8958.

STEPANIAK, PIETER SZYMON, medical researcher; b. Breda, Netherlands, Apr. 19, 1967; s. Adam Stepaniak and Dzidka Biatogtowska. MSc, Erasmus U., Rotterdam, Netherlands, 1992, PhD, 2010. Mgmt. cons. Erasmus U., Pricewaterhouse Coopers, Utrecht, Netherlands, 1994—2000; mgr. KPN, Den Haag, Netherlands, 2000—03; mgr. oper. rms. St Fransicus Hosp., Rotterdam, 2004—07, Catharina Hosp., Eindhoven, 2010—; dir. Tweesteden Hosp., Tilburg, Netherlands, 2007—09. Lt. Spl. Forces, 1992—93. Personal E-mail: pieter.stepaniak@gmail.com.

STEPANYAN, LUSINE SAMVEL, research scientist; b. Armenia, Jan. 30, 1977; Diploma in Biology, YSU, 1998; PhD, Inst. Physiology Acad. Scis. RAS, 2009. Asst., rsch. scientist YSU, 1998—; tchr. biology Base Sch. ASPU, 2007—11; asst. ASIFC, 2008. Grant, Goulbenkian Found. Mem.: SPR, FENS (grant state com. sci.), IBRO. Avocations: gardening, jazz, reading. Office: Alex Manoogian 1 Yerevan 0025 Armenia Business E-Mail: slusine7@rambler.ru.

STEPENSKY, DAVID, pharmacologist, educator; b. Moscow, Aug. 17, 1972; PhD, Hebrew U. Jerusalem, 2002. Asst. prof. Ben-Gurion U. Negev, 2007—. Office: Dept Pharmacology Beer-Sheva 84105 Israel Business E-Mail: davidst@bgu.ac.il.

STEPHEN, JOSHUA, cell biologist, educator; b. Trivandrum, Kerala, India, Oct. 5, 1940; s. Joshua Manas and Harriet Joshua; m. Pamela Pansy Thangadas; children: Ruth, Sam, Sarah. BSc, U. Coll., Trivandrum, 1960; MSc, Fatima Coll., Quilon, India, 1963; PhD, U. Kerala, Trivandrum, 1974. Lectr. in cytogenetics U. Kerala, Trivandrum, 1969-79, reader, 1979-82, sr. grade reader, 1986-93, prof., 1997-2000; assoc. prof. Regional Cancer Ctr., Trivandrum, 1982-86, head divsn. Ethnopharmacology, 1993-97. In vitro autoradiographic predictive test for cancer chemotherapy; referee divsn. med. biotechnology Govt. India, New Delhi, 1990—. Author: Genetics, 1974, The Nucleus, 1983; contbr. articles to profl. jours. Sr. Rsch. fellow Govt. India, 1964-67; Commonwealth Acad. Staff scholar Assn. Commonwealth Univs. Chester Beatty, 1973-74; Internat. Cancer Rsch. Tech. Transfer fellow Union Internat. Contre le Cancer, 1990. Mem. European Assn. Cancer Rsch., Am. Assn. Cancer Rsch., Assn. Brit. Scholars. Avocations: reading, writing, gardening, church music, nature photography. Home: Bains Compound Nanthencode Beth-Shalom TC 11/1326 Trivandrum 695003 India Office: Ittyavirah Genetic Rsch Med Coll Chalakkughi Road Trivandrum 695011 India Home Phone: 91-471-2319893; Office Phone: 91-471-2444609. Personal E-mail: joshuastephen.tvm@gmail.com.

STEPHENS, FREDERICK OSCAR, surgeon, educator; b. Sydney, N.S.W., Australia, Aug. 7, 1927; s. Hedley Loxton and Dorys Louise (Reed) S.; m. Alison Barclay Lipp, Dec. 24, 1959 (div.); children: Jennifer Louise, Robert Bruce Henry, Gillian Dorys Janet, Frederick William Peter, Katriona Alison; m. Sheilagh Kelly. MB BS, U. Sydney, 1951, MD, MS in Surgery, 1970. Med. and surg. intern U. Sydney Hosps., 1951—53; surg. resident Met. Hosp., London, 1954-55; prosector in anatomy Royal Coll. Surgeons, London, 1955-56; registrar, sr. registrar in surgery profl. unit Royal Infirmary, Aberdeen, Scotland, 1957-60; Welcome traveling fellow, Joyce rsch. fellow U. Oreg. Med. Sch., Portland, 1960-61; assoc. prof. surgery U. Sydney Teaching Hosps., 1961-88, prof. and head dept. surgery, 1988-94, prof. emeritus; cons. emeritus in surg. oncology Royal Prince Alfred Hosp./Sydney Hosp., 1994—. Fulbright fellow and vis. prof. surgery U. Calif., San Francisco, 1969-70; past bd. dirs. Sydney Hosp., Sydney Hosp.; past chmn. Kanematsu Rsch. Labs., Sydney Hosp.; surgeon to H.M. The Queen, The Prince of Wales, The Duke of Edinburgh, U.S. Pres. Johnson, Shah of Persia, The Crown Prince of Japan, The King and Queen of Nepal during their visits to Australia, 1966, 71, 73, 77; vis. prof./vis. lectr. numerous internat. and nat. meetings throughout the world; dir., chmn. The Sporting Chance Found. for Cancer Rsch., 1997-2004. Mng. editor Internat. Jour. Regional Cancer Treatment, 1988—96; author: Cancer Explained, 1st edit., 1997, 2nd edit., 2009, Cancer Explanation and Prevention, 1998, All About Prostate Cancer, 2000, All About Breast Cancer, 2001, The Cancer Prevention Manual, 2002, Cancer Explained, 2nd edit., 2009, Basics of Oncology, 2009; contbr. over 200 articles to profl. jours.; author: From Kurmond Kid to Cancer Crusader, 2011. Decorated Order of Australia; recipient Queen's Silver Jubilee medal, 1978. Fellow ACS, Royal Coll. Surgeons of Edinburgh, Royal Australiasian Coll. Surgeons, (found. pres.), Internat. Soc. Regional Cancer Therapy (pres. 1991-95); mem. Surg. Rsch. Soc. Australasia (pres. 1971-72), Clin. Oncology Soc. Australia (founding mem. 1971), Sydney Hospitallers (pres. 1977-78). Mem. Uniting Ch. of Australia. Avocations: horseback riding and sports, long-distance running, carpentry, inventing, skiing. Home: 16 Inkerman St Mosman Sydney NSW 2088 Australia Office: Univ Sydney Dept Surgery Sydney NSW 2006 Australia Office Phone: 61 0 2 9960 1387. Personal E-mail: fredstephens@optusnet.com.au.

STEPHENS, MICHAEL MASSY, orthopaedic surgeon; b. Dublin, Feb. 8, 1951; s. Patrick Horace and Audrey (Pim) S.; m. Juliet Kathleen Ensor, June 6, 1977; children: Linda, Wendy, Nigel. Student, St. Columbas Coll., Dublin, Ireland, 1964-69, De La Salle Coll., Waterford, 1969-70, Royal Coll. Surgeons in Ireland, 1970—76; MSc, U. Strathclyde, Glasgow, Scotland, 1984; diploma in obstetrics, Royal Coll. Physicians, Dublin, 1981. Sr. registrar Dublin Scheme, 1984-87; sr. lectr. Hong Kong U., 1987; fellow in foot surgery U. Cin., 1988; cons. Dublin, 1989—; assoc. clin. prof. U. Coll. Dublin, 2008—. Cons., dir. foot clinic Mater Misericordae Univ. Hosp., Cappagh Nat. Orthopaedic Hosp., Children's Univ. Hosp., Ctrl. Remedial Clinic, Dublin, 1989—, assoc. clin. prof. orthop. surgery U. Coll. Dublin Author: Atlas of Foot and Ankle Surgery, 1998, 2d edit., 2006, Foot in Diabetes, 1991, Foot and Ankle Manual, 1991; asst. editor: Foot and Ankle Internat.; sr. editor Foot and Ankle Surgery. Fellow Robert Jones and Agneshunt Hosp., Shropshire, U.K., 1981-82. Fellow: Brit. Orthop. Assn., Brit. Assn. Clin. Anatomists, Royal Coll. Surgeons (Ireland); mem.: European Foot and Ankle Soc. (pres. 2000—03), Am. Orthop. Foot and Ankle Soc., Irish Orthop. Assn. (sec. 1990—98, pres.-elect 2001—03, pres. 2003—05), European Soc. Foot and Ankle Surgeons (founder, v.p. 1992—96, v.p. 2008). Avocation: equestrian activities. Office: Mater Pvt Hosp Eccles St Ste 1 Dublin 7 Ireland

STEPHENS, RALPH RENNE, massage therapy educator; b. Vinton, Iowa, Apr. 19, 1948; s. E.O. and Carrie D. S.; m. Sara Ann Pumphrey; children: Christian, Natalie. BS in Indsl. Edn., Iowa State U., 1971; degree in Natural Therapeutics, N.Mex. Sch. Natural Therapeutics, Albuquerque, 1986. Lic. massage therapist Iowa, N.Mex., massage therapy instr. N.Mex., cert. therapeutic massage and bodywork Nat. Cert. Bd. Therapeutic Massage and Bodywork, St. John method neuromuscular therapy. Pvt. practice Helping Hands Body Therapy Ctr., Iowa City, 1986-92; staff instr. Carlson Coll. Massage Therapy, Cedar Rapids, Iowa, 1987-92; instr. St. John Neuromuscular Therapy Seminars, 1991-99; pvt. practice Ralph Stephens Seminars, Cedar Rapids, 1992—; mem. tchg. staff Himalayan Inst. Yoga Sci. and Philosophy of U.S.A., Honesdale, Pa., 2001—. Dir. sports massage Iowa City Annual Hospice Road Race Com., 1986-88; cons., sys. engr., equipment supplier to workshop and seminar presenters Helping Hands Audio/Video, 1989-94; chairperson Iowa Bd. Examiners Massage Therapy, Des Moines, 1995-2000; sec. Iowa Bd. Examiners Massage Therapy, Des Moines, 1992-95; presenter in field, nat. bd. dirs., Alliance Massage Therapy Edn., 2010, edn. projector rep., 2011. Author: Massage Therapy Principles and Practice, 1999, 2d edit., 2003, 3rd edit., 2007, Therapeutic Chair Massage, 2005; contbr. articles to profl. jours.; prodr. videos Seated Therapeutic Massage, Vol. 1, Back and Neck, 1995, Vol. 2, Shoulder, 1996, Vol. 3, Forearm, Wrist and Hand, 1996, Feel Great Hands on Health Series (4 tapes) Feel Great Every Day, Posture Yourself and Move Right, Massage Made Easy, Stretching that Works, 1998, Event Sports Massage, 1998, Side-Lying Therapeutic Massage, 1999, Therapeutic Sports Massage for the Lower Extremity, 1999, Anatomy of the Lower Extreminty, 1999, Medical Massage for the Cervical Region, 2001, Medical Massage for the Lumbar Region, 2002, Golf-Flexology, 2003, Medical Massage for the Abdominal Wall, 2006, Medical Massage for the Shoulder Girdle, 2007, How to Grow a Successful Massage Therapy Business, 2009; monthly editl. columnist Massage Today, 2000-, quar. columnist Up Close and Personal Newsletter, 2002-07. Trustee Am. Massage Therapy Assn. Found., 1990-93, 95-96; chairperson Walford (Iowa) Disaster Preparedness Com., 1999. Named to Iowa Rock'n Roll Hall of Fame Rural, 2006, Massage Therapy Hall of Fame, 2008, The Dep. Dawgl Band, 2009. Mem. Am. Massage Therapy Assn. (cert. sports massage therapist, registered massage therapist cert., organizer, chair Iowa sports massage team 1986-88, 1st v.p., convention coord. Iowa chpt. 1988-89, edn. chair Iowa chpt. 1988-89, pres. Iowa chpt. 1989, ctrl. dist. rep. nat. bd. dirs. 1990-93, media spokesperson nat. media rels. team 1991-96, nat. nominating com. 1994, mem.-at-large nat. bd. dirs. 1995-96, nat. nominating commn. 1998-99, Disting. Nat. Officer award 1993, 96, Meritorious award Iowa chpt. 1997, Nat. Meritorious award 1997), Himalayan Inst. Yoga Sci. and Philosophy (tchg. staff 2000), Alliance for Massage Therapy Edn. (bd. dirs. 2010-). Independent. Avocations: golf, yoga, meditation. Home: PO Box 8267 Cedar Rapids IA 52408-8267 Office: Ralph Stephens Seminars LLC PO Box 8267 Cedar Rapids IA 52408-8267 Office Phone: 319-337-6277. Business E-Mail: ralph@ralphstephens.com.

STEPHENS, SHERYL LYNNE, physician; b. Huntington, W.Va., Dec. 11, 1949; d. William Clayton Stephens and Virginia Eleanor (Hætten) Stephens Terry; 1 child, William Earl Hicks III (dec.); m. Lannie Dale Rowe, Jan. 17, 1981; 1 child, Seton Christopher. BA, U. Ky., 1972; MA, Marshall U., 1982, MD, 1988. Tchr. Wayne County Bd. Edn., Ceredo, W.Va., 1973—83; real estate developer Huntington, 1981—88; resident in family practice Grant Med. Ctr., Columbus, Ohio, 1988—91; gen. practice indigent care physician Columbus (Ohio) Health Dept., 1991—2009; med. dir. St. Stephens Health Care Ctr., Columbus, 1995—98, Billie Brown Jones Family Health Care Ctr., Columbus, 1993—2003, lead physician, 1998—2002; staff physician East Ctrl. Family Health Ctr., Columbus, 2003—04, Health Care for the Homeless, 2004—07, John Maloney Health Ctr., 2004—08; med. dir. Health Care for the Homeless, 2005—07, Faith Mission Health Care Homeless, 2009—. Chair Coll. Health Dept. Com. on Pharmacy and Therapeutics, 1994-2000; rschr., 1976-81. Counselor, instr. Contact of Huntington, 1975-88; polit. activist pro choice movement and ratification of equal rights amemdment, 1976-81. Recipient Leadership award Marshall U., 1985. Mem. Am. Assn. Family Practitioners (pres. 1984-85, Leadership award 1985), Am. Med. Women's Assn. (sec. 1985-86), NOW (pres. 1976-78, 79-81, v.p. Huntington 1978-79, sec. 1981-82), Nat. Abortion Rights Action League. Democrat. Avocations: horseback riding, reading, boating, skiing (snow and water), travel. Home: 9323 Mccord Rd Orient OH 43146-9518 Office: John Malony South Side Health Ctr 1833 Parsons Ave Columbus OH 43207

STEPHENSON, HUGH EDWARD, JR., retired surgeon; b. Columbia, Mo., June 1, 1922; s. Hugh Edward and Doris (Pryor) S.; m. Sarah Norfleet Dickinson, Aug. 15, 1964; children: Hugh Edward III, Ann Dunlop. AB, BS, U. Mo., Columbia, 1943; MD, Washington U., St. Louis, 1945. Diplomate Am. Bd. Surgery, Am. Bd. Thoracic Surgery. Mem. faculty U. Mo. Sch. Medicine, Columbia, 1953—; prof. surgery U. Mo. Hugh E. Stephenson Jr. Dept. Surgery, Columbia, 1956—, chmn. dept. surgery, 1956—60, chief div. gen. surgery, 1976—87, chief staff, 1982—94; John Growdon Disting. prof. surgery emeritus U. Mo. Sch. Medicine, Columbia, 1987—, interim dean, 1988—89, assoc. dean, 1989—92, dist. prof. surgery emeritus, 1993; curator U. Mo. System, 1996—. Pres. bd. curators U. Mo., 2000; Markle scholar acad. medicine, 1954-60. Author: Immediate Care of the Acutely Ill and Injured, 2d edit, 1974, Cardiac Arrest and Resuscitation, 4th edit., 1975, The Kicks That Count; Contbr. articles to profl. jours. Named one of Outstanding Young Men of Nation, Nat. Jr. C. of C., 1956, James IV Surg. Traveler Gt. Britain, 1962, Dist. Faculty award, 1989. Mem. ACS, AMA (del., chmn. coun. on med. edn. 1994-95, co-chmn. liaison com. on med. edn. 1995, pres. surgical caucus 1996, Stephenson Endowed chair of Surgery), Vascular Surgery Soc., Soc. Thoracic Surgeons, So. Thoracic Surgery Assn., So. Med. Assn. (coun., pres. 2001), Mo. Med. Assn. (chmn. jud. coun. 1986-, v.p. 1986-), Beta Theta Pi (trustees, pres. gen. frat. 1978-81) Baptist. Home: 5 Danforth Cir Columbia MO 65201-3509 Office: University of Missouri Hugh E Stephenson Jr Dept Surgery 1 Hospital Dr Columbia MO 65201-5276 Home Phone: 573-442-3834; Office Phone: 573-882-5645.

STEPHENSON, PATRICIA ANN, public health researcher, educator; b. Washington, July 21, 1954; arrived in Sweden, 1990; d. Stanley Edwin and Mary Virginia (Brenneman) S.; m. Marsden Grigg Wagner, Dec. 14, 1990. BS, Calif. State U., Hayward, 1979; ScD, Johns Hopkins U., 1986. RN. Asst. prof. Sch. Pub. Health U. Wash., Seattle, 1986-90, adj. asst. prof. Sch. Nursing, 1987-90; sr. rschr. Ctr. for Pub. Health Rsch., Karlstad, Sweden, 1990-94; cons. health policy analyst, ops. rschr. Copenhagen, 1990-97; sr. advisor health and research USAID, Washington, 1998—. Vis. assoc. prof. Sch. Pub. Health U. Mich., Ann Arbor, 1995-96; cons. WHO, 1989, UNICEF, 1990—, World Bank, 1995-96. Mng. editor, co-founder European Jour. Pub. Health, 1991-94; author, editor: Tough Choices - InVitro Fertilization and the New Reproductive Technologies, 1993; contbr. articles to profl. publs. Women's health policy fellow John D. and Catherine T. MacArthur Found., 1995; recipient Commendation for work in fertility U.K. Parliament/House of Commons, 1989. Mem. APHA, Global Health Council, Delta Omega. Avocation: dog agility training, obedience and tracking. Home: PO Box 1222 Shepherdstown WV 25443-1222 Business E-Mail: pstephenson@usaid.gov.

STERMAN, DANIEL, pulmonologist, educator; AB in European History, Brown U., 1985; MD, Cornell U., 1989. Diplomate Am. Bd. Internal Medicine, Am. Bd. Internal Medicine-pulmonary medicine, Am. Bd. Internal Medicine-critical care medicine. Intern and resident internal medicine Hosp. of the Univ. of Pa., 1989—92, instr. emergency medicine, 1992—93, with Dr. Larry Kaiser gen. thoracic surgery divsn.; fellow pulmonary and critical care medicine Univ. of Pa. Med. Ctr., 1993—97, postdoc. rsch. fellow thoracic oncology rsch. lab.; advanced tng. with Dr. Michael Unger Pa. Hosp.; assoc. prof. medicine Univ. of Pa., assoc. prof. medicine in surgery, dir. interventional pulmonology, clin. dir. thoracic oncology gene therapy program. Co-author: (publs.) Adenovirus-mediated herpes simplex virus thymidine kinase gene delivery in patients with localized malignancy: Results of a phase 1 clinical trial in malignant mesothelioma, 1998, Humoral and cellular immune responses induced by adenoviral-based gene therapy for localized malignancy: Results of a phase 1 clinical trial for malignant mesothelioma, 1998, Advances in the treatment of malignant pleural mesothelioma, 1999, Interventional Pulmonology, 2001, Phase I trial of intravenous administration of PV701, an oncolytic virus, in patients with advanced solid cancers, 2002, Granulocyte-macrophage colony-stimulating factor gene-modified autologous tumor vaccines in non-small-cell lung cancer, 2004, and numerous others. Office: University of Pennsylvania 833 West Gates Bldg 3400 Spruce St Philadelphia PA 19104-4283 Office Phone: 215-614-0984. Office Fax: 215-662-3226. Business E-Mail: sterman@mail.med.upenn.edu.

STERN, DAVID MARK, dean, medical educator; b. Great Neck, NY; s. Robert and Florence Stern; m. Kathleen Shirley Stern; children: Eric David, Alan Robert. BS, Yale U., 1973; MD, Harvard U., 1978. Mem. faculty Coll. Physicians and Surgeons, Columbia U., NYC, 1983—2002, named Gerald & Janet Carrus Prof. of Surg. Sci., 1998, dir. Ctr. Vascular and Lung Pathobiology, dir. Juvenile Diabetes Rsch. Ctr.; dean sch. medicine, sr. v.p. clin. activities Med. Coll. Ga., Augusta, 2002—05, prof. medicine, physiology and grad. studies, 2002—05; Christian R. Holmes prof. medicine U. Cin. Coll. Medicine, 2005—10, dean, 2005—10, v.p. health affairs, 2008—10; exec. dean, prof. physiology U. Tenn. Coll. Medicine, Memphis, 2011—; vice chancellor clin. affairs U. Tenn. Health Sci. Ctr., Memphis, 2011—. Mem.: Am. Assn. Physicians, Am. Soc. Clin. Investigation. Office: University Tenn Health Sci Ctr 910 Madison Ave #1048 Memphis TN 38163 Office Phone: 901-448-5529. Business E-Mail: dstern@uthsc.edu. *

STERN, JOHN J., infectious disease physician, educator; MD, NYU. Diplomate Am. Bd. Internal Medicine, Am. Bd. Internal Medicine-infectious disease. Intern Univ. of Tex., resident; fellow NY Hosp.- Cornell Med. Ctr.; clin. assoc. prof. medicine dept. Univ. of Pa. Named one of Top Docs, Phila. Mag., 2002, 2008, 2010, 2011, Best Doctors in America, 2003—04, 2005—06, 2007—08, 2009—10. Office: Pennsylvania Hospital Duncan Building Ste 1 B 301 S 8th St Philadelphia PA 19107 Office Phone: 800-789-7366.

STERN, JUDITH SCHNEIDER, nutritionist, researcher, educator; b. Bklyn. d. Sidney and Lillian (Rosen) Schneider; m. Richard C. Stern; 1 child, Daniel Arthur. BS, Cornell U., 1964; MS, Harvard U. Sch. Pub. Health, 1966, ScD, 1970. Rsch. asst., dept. food sci. and nutrition MIT, Cambridge, 1964—65; rsch. assoc. dept. human behavior and metabolism The Rockefeller U., NYC, 1968—72, asst. prof. dept. human behavior and metabolism, 1972—74; contbg. editor Vogue Mag., Conde Nast Publs., NYC, 1974; asst. prof. nutrition U. Calif., Davis, 1975—77, assoc. prof. dept. nutrition, 1977—82, dir. food intake lab. group, 1980—2001, prof. dept. nutrition, 1982—, prof. divsn. endocrinology, clin. nutrition and vascular biology, 1988—, disting. prof., 2003—. Mem. editl. bd. Internat. Jour. Obesity, 1976-85, Appetite, 1990, Obesity Rsch., 1993—2002, Nutrition Today, 1999—. Bd. sci. advisors Am. Coun. Sci. and Health, 1980—; mem. U.S. Dept. Agr. Dietary Guidelines Adv. Com., 1983—85; mem. obesity task force NIDDK, 1996—2002; mem. expert com. U.S. Pharmacopeia Bioavailability and Nutrient Absorption, 2000—03; mem. adv. bd. USDA Nat. Agrl. Rsch. Ext., Edn. and Econs., 2000—03. Recipient Sec.'s Honor award USDA, 2004; NIH tng. grantee, 1979-2006. Fellow AAAS (mem. obesity task force), Am. Heart Assn.; mem. Am. Soc. Clin. Nutirition (pres. 1995-96), Am. Dietetic Assn., Am. Diabetes Assn., Am. Obesity Assn. (co-founder, v.p. 1995-2006), N.Am. Assn. for Study of Obesity (pres. 1992-93), Inst. Medicine of NAS, Inst. Food Technologists, Am. Soc. Nutrition Sci. (chair pub. info. com. 1992-94), Sigma Xi, Delta Omega. Office: U Calif Dept Nutrition 1 Shields Ave Davis CA 95616-5271 Office Phone: 530-752-6575. Business E-Mail: jsstern@ucdavis.edu.

STERN, LEONARD, physician; b. Buffalo, Apr. 7, 1950; s. Henry and Sarah S.; m. Joan Stern, Sept. 8, 1974; children: Rebecca, Jeffrey. BA, CUNY, Bklyn., 1972; MD, N.Y. Med. Coll., 1975. Diplomate Am. Bd. Internal Medicine, Am. Bd. Nephrology. Intern and resident Albert Einstein Coll. of Medicine, Bronx, N.Y., 1975-78; fellowship in nephrology Montefiore Hosp. and Med. Ctr., Bronx, N.Y., 1978-79, Yale New Haven (Conn.) Hosp., 1979-81; dir. Dialysis Ctr. Columbia U., NYC, 1995—, dir. peritoneal dialysis, 1985—; assoc. clin. prof. medicine Columbia U. Coll. Physicians and Surgeons, NYC. Contbr. articles to profl. jours. Fellow ACP, Am. Soc. Nephrology; mem. Internat. Soc. Nephrology, Internat. Soc. for Peritoneal Dialysis. Avocations: outdoor activities, hiking, skiing, sailing. Office: NY Presbyn Hosp Columbia Presbyn Campus 622 W 168th St New York NY 10032-3720 Office Phone: 212-305-0515.

STERN, NATHALIE M., pediatrician; b. Tourcoing, France, Sept. 1, 1964; MD, Lille U. Medicine & Pharmacy, Nord, France, 1993. Diplomate Am. Bd. Pediat. Internship in pediat. NY Hosp. Cornell Med. Ctr., NYC, 1994—95, residency in pediat., 1995—97, attending physician, 1998, clin. instr. pediat., 1998, Lenox Hill Hosp., NYC, 1998; pediatrcian The Continuum Ctr. Health and Healing, NYC; pvt. practice in pediatric homeopathy France. Contbr. articles to profl. jours. Mem.: French Homeopathic Ednl. Ctr. Office: c/o The Continuum Ctr Health and Healing 245 Fifth Ave 2nd Fl New York NY 10016 Office Phone: 646-935-2220.

STERN, PHYLLIS NOERAGER, nursing educator; b. San Mateo, Calif., Sept. 2, 1925; d. Philip Julius and Grace Ann (Zoellen) Noerager; m. David Arthur Hungerford, May 20, 1949 (div. Sept. 1950); 1 child, Paula Ann; m. Milton Stern, July 3, 1960 (dec. Jan. 2001). AA, Coll. San Mateo, 1968; BS magna cum laude, San Francisco State U., 1970; MS, U. Calif., San Francisco, 1971, D of Nursing Sci., 1976; LLD (hon.), Dalhousie U., Can., 2003. Asst. prof. Calif. State U., Hayward, 1971-76, U. Calif., San Francisco, 1976-80; prof. Northwestern State U. La., Shreveport, 1980-82; prof., dir. Dalhousie U., Halifax, N.S., Can., 1983-87, prof., 1987-91; prof. emeritus Ind. U., Indpls., 1991-96, prof., 1996—. Editor, author: Women Health and Culture, 1986; editor: Childbirth and Childcare, 1988, Lesbian Health Care, 1991, Grounded Theory: The Second Generation, 2009; co-author: (with Caroline Pour) Essentials of Grounded Accessible Theory, 2011; editor-in-chief: Health Care for Women Internat., 1983-2001; co-editor: (with R.S. Schreiber) Grounded Theory for Nurses (Am. Jour. Nursng Book of Yr. award 2001), 2001. Health educator Battered Women's Shelter, Indpls., Salvation Army, Indpls., 1994-96. Named Disting. Alumna U. Calif., San Francisco, 1995, named to Hall of Fame; rsch. grantee Ind. U., 1995; Glenn W. Irwin Jr. Rsch. scholar, 1999; recipient Lifetime Achievement award for contbns. to women's health internationally Internat. Soc. Qualitative Rschrs. Fellow Am. Acad. Nursing (mem. expert panel 1989-96, Living Legend 2008), Am. Acad. Practice Coun. (Disting. Practitioner 1992), Coun. Gen. Internat. on Women's Health Issues (co-founder 1984, coun. gen. emeritus 2002—, Biennial Phyllis Stern lectr. to Internat. Congress on Women's Health Issues 2004—), Sigma Theta Tau. Avocations: films, reading, mentoring. Office: Ind U 1111 Middle Dr Indianapolis IN 46202-5243 Home Phone: 317-872-7363; Office Phone: 317-274-0032. Personal E-mail: pnstern@comcast.net. Business E-Mail: pstern@iupui.edu. *

STERN, ROBERT, psychiatrist; b. Aug. 12, 1928; Diploma in Chem. Engring., Swiss Fed. Inst. Tech., Zurich, 1951; MS, Yale U., 1953, PhD, 1956; MD, Case Western Res. U., 1966. Diplomate Am. Bd. Psychiatry and Neurology; lic. physician, Conn. Asst. prof. chemistry Wesleyan U., Middletown, Conn., 1957—58, Conn. Coll., New London, 1959-60; supr. bio-organic chem. rsch. Arthur D. Little, Inc., Cambridge, Mass., 1960-62; vis. fellow medicine Mass. Gen. Hosp., 1964; rsch. assoc. biol. chemistry Harvard Med. sch., Boston, 1964, tchg. fellow psychiatry, 1967-68; intern medicine King County Hosp./U. Wash., Seattle, 1966-67; resident in psychiatry McLean Hosp., Belmont, Mass., 1967-68; jr./sr. asst. resident internal medicine Yale-New Haven Hosp., 1968-70, clin. fellow medicine, 1970-71; postdoctoral fellow psychiatry Yale U. Sch. Medicine, 1971-73, asst. clin. prof. psychiatry, 1974-86, assoc. clin. prof. psychiatry, 1986—; pvt. practice New Haven, 1973—. Cons. Child Guidance Clinic of Southeastern Conn., New London, 1973-82; cons. CHAMPUS peer reviewer Qualidigm, Inc., Middletown, 1994—; lectr. in field. Contbr. articles to profl. jours. Fellow Am. Psychiat. Assn. (Disting. life fellow); mem. New Haven Individual Practice Assn. (co-chmn. psychiatry panel 1985-98, quality assurance com. 1989-98, bd. dirs. 1986-89), Conn. Psychiatric Soc. (councilor-at-large 2001—06, councilor 2000-01, pres. New Haven/Middlesex chpt. 1999-2000, treas. 1996-99). Conn. State Med. Soc., New Haven County Med. Assn. Office: 340 Whitney Ave New Haven CT 06511-2317 Office Phone: 203-562-9110.

STERN, ROBERT ANDREW, neuropsychologist, medical educator; b. Brookline, Mass., Nov. 24, 1958; BA in Psychology, Wesleyan U., Middletown, Conn., 1980; MA in Psychology, U. RI, 1984, PhD in Clin. Psychology, 1988; MA (hon.), Brown U., Providence, 1997. Diplomate Am. Bd. Profl. Psychology, lic. psychologist RI, Mass. Intern psychology Boston VA Med. Ctr., 1986—87; postdoc. fellow, dept. psychiatry, Brain & Devel. Rsch. Ctr. U. NC Sch. Medicine, Chapel Hill, 1988—90, asst. prof. dept. psychiatry, 1990—93; adj. asst. prof., divsn. grad. med. scis. Boston U. Sch. Medicine, 1994—2004, assoc. prof., dept. neurology, 2004—, co-dir. Alzheimer's Disease Clin. & Rsch. Program. Asst. in neuropsychology McLean Hosp., Belmont, Mass., 1986—88; asst. prof., dept. clin. neuroscis., dept. psychiatry & human behavior Brown Med. Sch., 1993—96, assoc. prof., 1996—2003; clin. neuropsychologist Women's & Infants Hosp., Providence, 1993—2003; grad. faculty U. RI, Kingston, 1997—; clin. neuropsychologist Boston Med. Ctr., 2004—. Assoc. editor Jour. Neuropsychiatry & Clin. Neuroscis., 1998—, consulting editor Assessment, 2001—03, mem. editl. bd. Archives Clin. Neuropsychology, 2008—; contbr. articles to profl. jours. Recipient Ind. Investigator award, Nat. Alliance Rsch. Schizophrenia & Depression, 1997. Fellow: Nat. Acad. Neuropsychology, Am. Neuropsychiatric Assn.; mem.: Mass. Neuropsychological Soc., Am. Psychological Asn., Internat. Soc. Advance Alzheimer Rsch. & Treatment, Internat. Neuropsychological Soc. Office: Boston Univ Sch Medicine Robinson Complex Ste 7800 715 Albany St Boston MA 02118 Office Phone: 617-638-5678, 617-638-7100. Office Fax: 617-414-1197. Business E-Mail: bobstern@bu.edu. *

STERN, ROBERT MORRIS, psychologist, gastroenterology researcher; b. NYC, June 18, 1937; s. Irving Dan and Nellie (Wachstetter) S.; m. Wilma Olch, June 19, 1960; children: Jessica Leigh, Alison Rachel. AB, Franklin and Marshall Coll., 1958; MS, Tufts U., 1960; PhD, Ind. U., 1963. Research assoc. dept. psychology Ind. U., 1963-65; asst. prof. psychology Pa. State U., 1965-68, assoc. prof., 1968-73, prof., 1973—92, disting. prof., 1992—2005, emeritus prof., 2005—, head dept., 1978-87. Co-author (with W.J. Ray): Biofeedback, 1977; co-author: (with W.J. Ray and C.M. Davis) Psychophysiological Recording, 1980; co-author: (with K.L. Koch) Electrogastrography, 1985; co-author: (with W.J. Ray and K.S. Quigley) Psychophysiological Recording, 2nd edit., 2001; co-author: (with K.L. Koch) Handbook of Electrogastrography, 2004; co-author: (with K.L. Koch and P.L.R. Andrews) Nausea: Mechanisms and Management, 2011; contbr. Recipient Nat. Media award Am. Psychol. Found., 1978 Mem. Soc. Psychophysiol. Rsch. Home: 1360 Greenwood Cir State College PA 16803-3232 Office: Pa State U Moore Bldg University Park PA 16802-3105 Home Phone: 814-238-7063. Business E-Mail: rs3@psu.edu.

STERN, S(EESA) BEATRICE, executive secretary, medical/surgical nurse; b. Atlantic City, Feb. 13, 1919; d. Max and Gussie (Thierman) Rosen; m. Francis H. Stern, June 29, 1958 (dec. Feb. 1973); m. Bernard N. Abelson, Dec. 5, 1973 (div. Feb. 1992). AA, Miami-Dade C.C., Fla., 1982, AS in Nursing with highest honors, 1982, grad. with highest honors. RN Fla., NJ, Nev. Profl. dancer, 1928—32; sec. N.J. State Highway Dept., Trenton, 1938-41; columnist N.J. Herald, Trenton, 1939-41; sec. U.S. Army, various locations, 1941-46; legal sec. Gus Feuer, Atty. at Law, Miami, 1946-47; exec. sec. to pres. Pharmo., Inc., NYC, 1947-58; med. sec. Phila., 1958-72; nurse Mt. Sinai Med. Ctr., Miami Beach, Fla., 1982-83, Atlantic City Med. Ctr., 1983-84. Vol. Hollywood Med. Ctr., 1992-96, Aventura Hosp and Med. Ctr., 1992—; mem. Bd. Govs. Brith Sholom, 1970—. Mem. Brith Sholom Women (nat. pres. 1970-72), Four Chaplains Legion of Hon., Phi Theta Kappa. Achievements include competitive scholastic swimming with Olympic (1936) tryout 1934-36. Avocations: swimming, handcrafts, reading, crossword puzzles. Home: 3939 Conshohocken Ave Apt 1020 Philadelphia PA 19131

STERN, STANLEY, psychiatrist; b. NYC, Apr. 5, 1933; s. Frank and Gussie S.; children: Marcus F., David S. BA cum laude, NYU, 1953; MD, SUNY, 1957. Intern Ohio State U. Hosp., Columbus, 1957-58; resident in psychiatry Inst. Living, Hartford, Conn., 1958-60, Austen Riggs Ctr., Stockbridge, Mass., 1960-61; psychoanalytic tng. We. New Eng. Inst. for Psychoanalysis, New Haven, 1965-73; asst. clin. prof. psychiatry Yale U., New Haven, 1975-81; assoc. clin. prof. psychiatry U. Calif., San Diego, 1982-84; pvt. practice New Haven, 1965-82, La Jolla, Calif., 1982-84, Phoenix, 1984—. Mem. faculty San Diego Psychoanalytic Inst., 1980-84; pres. Ariz. Psychoanalytic Study Group, Phoenix, 1986-88, Phoenix Psychoanalytic Study Group, 1986-88; tng. and supervising analyst So. Calif. Psychoanalytic Inst., 1989; chmn. edn. com. Ariz. Psychoanalytic New Tng. Facility, 1990-91; lectr., presenter, participant seminars and confs. in field. Author: My Experience of Analysis with Loewald, 2009, The Psychoanalytic Quarterly; contbr. article to profl. jours. Trustee, Gesell Inst., New Haven, 1986-88, Ctr. for the Exceptional Patient, New Haven; bd. dirs. ACLU. Capt. USAF, 1961-63. Mem. Am. Coll. Psychoanalysts, Am. Psychoanalytic Assn. (cert.), Am. Psychiat. Assn., Am. Acad. Psychoanalysts, Irene Josselyn Group Advancement of Psychoanalysis, So. Calif. Psychoanalytic Inst and Soc. (faculty), San Diego Psychoanalytic Inst., Council for the Advancement of Psychoanalysis (treas. 1972-73, pres.-elect 1973-74, pres. 1974-75, councillor 1975-80), Phi Beta Kappa, Beta Lambda Sigma, Psi Chi. Home and Office: 3104 E Camelback Rd # 601 Phoenix AZ 85016 Office Phone: 602-840-5614.

STERN, WALTER EUGENE, neurosurgeon, educator; b. Portland, Oreg., Jan. 1, 1920; s. Walter Eugene and Ida May (McCoy) S.; m. Elizabeth Naffziger, May 24, 1946; children: Geoffrey Alexander, Howard Christian, Eugenia Louise, Walter Eugene III. AB cum laude, U. Calif., MD, 1943. Diplomate Am. Bd. Neurol. Surgery (vice chmn. 1975-80). Surg. intern, asst. resident surgery and neurol. surgery U. Calif. Hosp., 1943-46, asst. resident neurol. surgery and neuropathology, 1948; clin. clk. Nat. Hosp. Paralyzed and Epileptic, London, 1948-49; Nat. Rsch. fellow med. sci. Johns Hopkins, Balt., 1949-50; asst. resident, resident U. Calif. Svc., 1951; clin. instr. U. Calif., 1951; asst. prof. neurosurgery UCLA, 1952-56, assoc. prof., 1956-59, prof., 1959—87, prof. emeritus, 1987—, chief divsn. neurosurgery, 1952-85, chmn. dept. surgery, 1981-87; NIH spl. fellow univ. lab. physiology Oxford (Eng.) U., 1961-62. Cons. neurosurgery Wadsworth VA Hosp. Former mem., chmn. editl. bd. Jour. Neurosurgery; contbr. articles to sci. jours., chpts. to books. Lt. to capt. M.C. AUS, 1946-48. Fellow ACS (sec.); mem. AMA, Am. Surg. Assn., Pacific Coast Surg. Assn., L.A. Surg. Soc. (pres. 1978), Am. Assn. Neurol. Surgeons (pres. 1979-80, Cushing medalist, 1992), James IV Assn. Surgeons, Western Neurosurg. Soc. (past pres.), Soc. Neurol. Surgeons (past pres., Disting. Svc. award 1999), Neurosurg. Soc. Am., Am. Neurol. Assn., Soc. Univ. Surgeons, Soc. Brit. Neurol. Surgeons (hon.), Calif. Assn. Neurol. Surgery (Disting. Svc. award 2004), Phi Beta Kappa, Sigma Xi, Alpha Omega Alpha. Epsicopalian. Home: 435 Georgina Ave Santa Monica CA 90402-1909

STERN, YAAKOV, neuroscientist; BA in psychology, Touro Coll., 1975; PhD, CUNY, 1983. Prof. Columbia U., NYC, 1996—; prof. clin. neuropsychology Taub Inst. Rsch. on Alzheimer's Disease and the Aging Brain and Gertrude H. Sergievsky Ctr., Columbia U. Coll. Physicians and Surgeons, NYC; leader cognitive neuroscience divsn., Gertrude H. Sergievsky Ctr. Columbia U. Coll. Physicians and Surgeons, NYC; dir. neuropsychology, Memory Disorders Clinic NY State Psychiat. Inst. Office: Taub Inst 630 W 168th St New York NY 10032 Office Phone: 212-342-1350. Office Fax: 212-342-1838. E-mail: ys11@columbia.edu.

STERNBERG, ROBERT JEFFREY, provost, senior vice president, regents psychology and education professor, researcher; b. Newark, Dec. 8, 1949; s. Joseph Sternberg and Lillian Myriam (Politzer) Weingast; m. Karin Sternberg; children: Seth, Sara, Samuel, Brittary, Melody. BA summa cum laude, Yale U., 1972; PhD in Psychology, Stanford U., 1975; D honoris causa (hon.), Complutense U., Madrid, 1994, U. Cyprus, 2000, U. Paris, 2000, U. Leuven, Belgium, 2001, Constantine the Philosopher U., Nitra, Slovakia, 2004; DSc, U. Durham, Eng., 2006, St. Petersburg U., Russia, 2006, U. Tilburg, Netherlands, 2007, Ricardo Palma U., 2008, Eureka Coll., 2008, U. Conn., 2009. Mem. faculty dept. psychology Yale U., New Haven, 1975—2005, asst. prof., 1975—80, assoc. prof., 1980—83, prof. psychology, 1983-86, dir. grad. studies, 1983—88, IBM prof. psychology and edn., 1986—2005, acting chmn. dept. psychology, 1992, dir. Yale Ctr. Psychology of Abilities, Competencies and Expertise, 2000—05, prof. Sch. Mgmt., 2003—10; dean Sch. Arts and Scis. Tufts U., Medford, Mass., 2005—10, prof. psychology & edn., 2005—10; hon. prof. U. Heidelberg, 2007—; sr. scholar Ctr. for Pub. Leadership, Kennedy Sch. Govt., Harvard U., 2006—10; provost & sr. v.p. Okla. State U., 2010—; prof. psychology, 2010—. Disting. assoc. Psychometrics Ctr., Cambridge, England, 2007—. Editor-in-chief Ency. of Human Intelligence, Psychol. Bull., 1991-96, Contemporary Psychology, 1999-2004; cons. editor Learning and Individual Differences, 1992—, Intelligence, 1977—, Devel. Rev., 1987-91, Jour. Personality and Social Psychology, 1989-91, Psychol. Rev., 1989-91; assoc. ed. Ann. Rev. of Psychology, 2008-; author: Intelligence, Information Processing and Analogical Reasoning, 1977, Beyond IQ, 1985, The Triarchic Mind, 1988, Metaphors of Mind, 1990, In Search of the Human Mind, 1995, 98, (with T. Lubart) Defying the Crowd, 1995, Successful Intelligence, 1997, Pathways to Psychology, 1997, Thinking Styles, 1997, Intelligence, Heredity and Environment, 1997, Love is a Story, 1998, Cupid's Arrow, 1998, Handbook of Intelligence, 2000, Psychology 101-1/2, 2002, Wisdom, Intelligence, and Creativity Synthesized, 2003; co-author (with Karin Sternberg): The Nature of Hate, 2008, College Admissions for the 21st Century, 2010. Recipient award for Excellence Mensa Edn. and Rsch. Found., 1989, Disting. Lifetime Contbn. to Psychology Conn. Psychology Assn., 1999, Disting. Scientist and Scholar award Positive Psychology Network, 2002, Anton Jurovsky award, Slovak Psychol. Soc., 2004, Interam. Psychologist award Interam. Psychol. Soc., 2005, E. Paul Torrance award, 2006, Sir Francis Galton award Internat. Assn. Empirical Aesthetics, 2008; Guggenheim Found. fellow, 1985-86. Fellow AAAS, APA (bd. dirs. 2002-04, pres. 2003, past pres. divsns. 1, 10, 15, 24, trustee ins. trust 2004, McCandless Young Scientist award divsn. devel. psychology 1982, Disting. Sci. award for early career contbn. 1981, pres. 2003, Farnsworth award, Arthur W. Staats award, E.L. Thorndike award 2003, Arnheim award, 2005, Disting. Lifetime Contribution to Pub. U. Psychology award, 2008), Nat. Acad. Edn., East Psychol. Assn. (bd. dirs.2007-2009, pres. 2007—2008), Am. Psychol. Found. (trustee 2005—07), Internat. Assn. Cognitive Edn. and Psychology (pres. 2009-11), Fedn. Behavioral & Brain Scis.(pres. elect 2010-2010), Assn. of Am. Coll. & Univ. (bd. dir. 2007-2013, treas, 2011-2013), Am. Acad. Arts and Scis., Am. Psychol. Soc., Soc. Exptl. Psychologists; mem. Am. Edml. Rsch. Assn. (Rsch. Rev. award 1986, Outstanding Book award 1987, Sylvia Scribner award 1996, James McKeen Cattell award 1999), Soc. Multivariate Exptl. Psychology (Cattell award 1982), Nat. Assn. Gifted Children (Disting. Scholar award 1985, E. Paul Torrance award 2006), Phi Beta Kappa, Kappa Delta Pi (Laureate chpt. 2003). Achievements include theory of successful intelligence; balance theory of wisdom; theory of mental self government; investment theory of creativity; triangular theory of love; duplex theory of hate; wics theory of leadership. Avocations: exercise, travel, reading, cello. Office: Okla State University Whitehurst 101 Stillwater OK 74078 Office Phone: 405-744-5627. Business E-Mail: robert.sternberg@okstate.edu.

STERNER, BERTIL, optometrist, researcher; b. Uddevalla, Sweden, Mar. 8, 1959; s. Nils and Lena Sterner; m. Ulrica Sterner, July 12, 2003; children: Elvira children: Ebba. OD, PhD, Göteborg U., Sweden. Optometrist Low vision clinic at Sahlgrens U. Hosp., Göteborg, 1989—. Contbr. scientific papers. Fellow: SHT (assoc.; Göteborg 1994). Home: Ankarljusvägen 8 Torslanda 423 40 Sweden Personal E-mail: sterner@oft.gu.se.

STERNSON, JEREMY KEVIN, dentist; b. Scotland, Nov. 10, 1973; BDSc, Melbourne U., 1995. Dental surgeon Dr. Jeremy Sternson, 1995—. Hon. fellow, U. Melbourne, 2010—11. Fellow: Royal Australasian Coll. Dental Surgeons (com. mem. 2005—11); mem.: Evident (com. mem. 2009—11), Australian Ctrl. Assn. Dentists (exec. mem. 2002—11), Australasian Osseointegration Soc. (pres. 2010—11). Avocation: outdoor sports. Office: Ste 2 Level 10 20 Collins St Melbourne Victoria 3000 Australia Office Fax: 0396541411. Business E-Mail: drsternson@bigpond.com.

STERODIMAS, ARIS, plastic surgeon; b. Athens, Attica, Greece, Oct. 7, 1974; s. Konstantinos Sterodimas and Aikaterini Eleftheriou. MD, Semmelweis U., Budapest, Hungary, 1999; MSc, Imperial Coll. London, 2005; PhD student, Athens Kapodistrian U., 2007—. Gen. surgeon Mt. Vernon Hosp., London, 2002—05; chief plastic surgeon resident Ivo Pitanguy Inst., Rio de Janeiro, 2005—07, cons. plastic surgeon, 2007—. Cons. DHI Group, London, 2003—04. Contbr. scientific papers to profl. jours. Fellow: RCS; mem.: Nat. Sec. Illouz Assn. (Paris), Ivo Pitanguy (Brazil), Postgrad. Assn. Harvard Med. Sch. (Boston), EX Alumni Semmelweis U. (Budapest), Ex Alumni Imperial Coll. (London), Athens Med. Assn. Achievements include research in botulinum toxin use for blushing treatment; stem cells application in the field of plastic surgery. Office: Ivo Pitanguy Inst 65 Rua Dona Mariana Rio de Janeiro 22280-020 Brazil Home: Dhimosthenus 5 153 43 Athens Greece Office Phone: 00306937437637. Personal E-mail: steroaris@yahoo.com. Business E-Mail: aris@sterodimas.com.

STETLER-STEVENSON, WILLIAM GEORGE, pathologist; b. Trenton, NJ, Nov. 27, 1953; BS in Biochemistry cum laude, Albright Coll., 1975; PhD in Biochemistry & Molecular Biology, Northwestern U., 1983, MD, 1984. Diplomate Am. Bd. Pathology. Mem. house staff anatomic pathology McGaw Med. Ctr., 1984-87; sr. staff fellow NIH, 1987-91, med. officer, rschr., 1991—, chief extracellular matrix pathology sect., 1993—. Editl. bd. Cancer Rsch. Found. Am. Socs. Exptl. Biology Jour., Am. Jour. Pathology, Invasion & Metastasis; contbr. articles to profl. jours. Kemper Found. Med. scholar, 1978-79. Mem. Am. Soc. Biochemistry and Molecular Biology, Am. Soc. Investigative Pathology (Warner-Lambert/Parke-Davis award 1996), RCP (Watson Smith lectr. 2002), Biomed. Rsch. Svcs., NIH (sr.; investigator). Office: Nat Cancer Inst Radiation Oncology Br Extracellular Matrix Pathology Sect Advanced Tech Ctr 81147 Grovemont Cir Bethesda MD 20892-4605

STETTER, KARL OTTO, microbiologist, educator; b. Munich, July 16, 1941; s. Josef and Elisabeth (Huebner) S.; m. Heidi Zahradnik, Dec. 20, 1969; children: Sabine, Florian, Claudia. Abitur, Staatl. Luitpold-Oberrealschule, Munich, 1960; diploma in Biology, Tech. U., Munich, 1969, D (hon.), 1973, Ludwig-Maximilians U., 1977. Asst. Ludwig-Maximilians U., 1969-73; post doctoral fellow Max-Planck Inst. Biochemistry, Martinsried, Germany, 1974-75; asst. lectr. Ludwig-Maximilians U., 1975-77, lectr., 1977-80; prof. microbiology U. Regensburg, Germany, 1980—; vis. prof., faculty UCLA, 1989—; co-founder Diversa Corp., San Diego, 1994. Dir. Inst. Microbiology U. Regensburg, Germany, 1980. Mem. editl. bd.: Systematic and Applied Microbiology, Extremophiles, Astrobiology. Recipient Deutsche Ges. Hygiene award U. Microbiology, 1985, Gottfried-Wilhelm-Leibniz-Preis Deutsche Forschungsgemeinschaft, Germany, 1988, medal Lectr. The Internat. Inst. Biotech., London, 1994, Bergey medal, 1999, Leeuwenhoek medal, 2003. Fellow Am. Acad. Microbiology; mem. Am. Soc. Microbiology, Deutsche Akademie der Naturforscher Leopoldina, Royal Netherlands Acad. Arts and Scis., Bayerische Akademie der Wissenschaften, Vereinigung f. Allg. U. Angew. Mikrobiologie, Deutsche Gesellschaft f. Hygiene und Mikrobiologie, Gesellschaft Deutscher Naturforscher und Ärzte, Gesellschaft Deutscher Chemiker, Gesellschaft f. Biologische Chemie, The Internat. Inst. Biotech. Avocations: life sciences, orchid cultivation. Office: U Regensburg Abt Mikrobiologie Universitätsstrasse 31 D-93053 Regensburg Germany Office Phone: 499419431821. Business E-Mail: karl.stetter@biologie.uni-regensburg.de.

STEUER, JOHNNY, surgeon, researcher; b. Stockholm, Dec. 18, 1970; s. Maximilian and Edda Steuer. MD, Karolinska Inst., Stockholm, Sweden, 1995; PhD, Uppsala U., Uppsala, Sweden, 2004. Bd. cert. specialist of cardiothoracic surgery Swedish nat. bd. of health and welfare, 2002. Internship Skaraborg Hosp., Skövde, Sweden, 1995—97; resident Dept. of Cardiothoracic Surgery, Karolinska Hosp., Stockholm, 1997—98, Dept. of Cardiothoracic Surgery, U. Hosp., Uppsala, Sweden, 1998—2002; fellowship Dept. of Pediatric Cardiac Surgery, U. Hosp., Lund, Sweden, 2003; surgeon Dept. of Surgery, U. Hosp., Uppsala, Sweden, 2005—. Grantee, Swedish Heart Lung Found., 2002, 2003. Mem.: Scandinavian Assn. for Cardiothoracic Surgery, Swedish Assn. for Cardiothoracic Surgery. Achievements include research in Thesis on perioperative myocardial damage in association with coronary artery bypass grafting. Office: Dept Surgery Univ Hosp Uppsala 751 85 Sweden E-mail: johnny.steuer@surgsci.uu.se.

STEVANOVIC, RANKO, physician, health science association administrator; b. Apr. 11, 1957; s. Milutin and Jelica Stevanovic; m. Mirjana Svigir, Apr. 5, 1966; children: Stjepko Svigir Stevanovic, Eva Svigir Stevanovic. MD, PhD, Med. Faculty, Zagreb. Head primary health care dept. Nat. Inst. Pub. Health, Zagreb, Croatia, 1997—. Cons. Ministry of Health, Zagreb, 2001—06. Editor: Croatian Pub. Health Jour. Achievements include development of integral health informatic system. Home: D Stipca 10 Zagreb 10090 Croatia Office: Croatian Inst Public Health Rockefellerova Ulica 7 10-000 Zagreb Croatia Office Fax: +385 1 4683 011. Business E-Mail: ranko.stevanovic@hzjz.hr.

STEVEN, JAMES M., anesthesiologist; b. Hartford, Conn., July 12, 1953; AB, Columbia Coll., 1975; MD, U. Cin., 1981. Sr. anesthesiologist Children's Hosp. Phila., 1987—. Office: Children's Hosp Phila Philadelphia PA 19104 Business E-Mail: steven@email.chop.edu.

STEVENS, DAVID D., board member; Pres., COO Southern Health Sys., Inc., 1983—96; chmn., CEO Accredo Health (subs. of Medco Health Solutions, Inc.), 1996—2005; bd. dirs. Medco Health Solutions, Inc., 2006—. Mem. bd. dir. Thomas & Betts Corp., 2004—, Wright Medical Group, Inc., 2004—. Office: Thomas & Betts Corp Bd directors 8155 T&B Blvd Memphis TN 38125 Office Phone: 901-252-8000. Office Fax: 901-252-1354. Business E-Mail: david.stevens@tnb.com. *

STEVENS, JOSEPH CHARLES, psychology professor; b. Grand Rapids, Mich., Feb. 28, 1929; s. Joseph, Jr. and Anne Katheryn Stevens. AB, Calvin Coll., Grand Rapids, 1950; MA, Mich. State U., 1953; PhD, Harvard U., 1957. Instr., asst. prof. psychology Harvard U., 1957-66; fellow emeritus John B. Pierce Found. Lab., sr. rsch. scientist Yale U., 1966—. Cons. in field. Author: Laboratory Experiments in Psychology, 1965; co-editor: Sensation and Measurement, 1974; mem. editl. bds. profl. jours.; contbr. numerous articles to profl. jours. Grantee NSF; Grantee NIH, Air Force Office Sci. Rsch. Fellow AAAS, Am. Psychol. Soc., NY Acad. Scis.; mem. Acoustical Soc. Am., Optical Soc. Am., Soc. Neuroscience, Ea. Psychol. Assn., Gerontol. Soc. Am. Office: 290 Congress Ave New Haven CT 06519-1403 Business E-Mail: jstevens@jbpierce.org.

STEVENS, JUDY A., epidemiologist; PhD in epidemiology, Emory U. With Nat. Ctr. Injury Prevention and Control, CDC, Atlanta, 1996—, sr. epidemiologist, divsn. unintentional injury prevention. Office: CDC NCIPC MS F-63 4770 Buford Hwy NE Atlanta GA 30341-3717

STEVENS, JULIA L., pediatric ophthalmologist, educator; b. Florida, Nov. 7, 1958; MD, Duke U., Durham, NC, 1983. Diplomate in ophthalmology Am. Bd. Ophthalmology, 1988. Clin. instr. Wash. U., St. Louis, 1987—92; assoc. prof. U. Ky., Lexington, 1992—. U. of Ky.: U. of Ky. Office: Univ Kentucky Dept Ophthal E302 Kentucky Clinic Lexington KY 40536

STEVENS, LESLIE HOWARD, plastic surgeon, skier; b. LA; married; 1 child. Grad., U. Colo.; MD, Chgo. Med. Sch., 1981. Diplomate Am. Bd. Plastic Surgery. Fellow Am. Coll. of Surgeons; resident gen. surgery Cedars Sinai Med. Ctr.; resident plastic and reconstructive surgery Boston Univ. Affiliated Hosps.; plastic surgeon Lasky Clinic Beverly Hills. Mem.: LA Orgn. for Ednl. Resources and Technol. Tng. Coll. (bd. mem.), Am. Soc. Aesthetic Plastic Surgeons, Am. Soc. of Plastic Surgeons. Office: The Lasky Clinic Beverly Hills 201 S Lasky Dr Beverly Hills CA 90212 Office Phone: 310-556-1003. *

STEVENS, ROSEMARY ANNE, medicine and public health historian, artist; b. Bourne, Eng. came to U.S., 1961, naturalized, 1968; d. William Edward and Mary Agnes (Tricks) Wallace; m. Robert B. Stevens, Jan. 28, 1961 (div. 1983); children: Carey, Richard; m. Jack D. Barchas, Aug. 9, 1994. BA, Oxford U., Eng., 1957; Diploma in Social Adminstrn., Manchester U., Eng., 1959; MPH, Yale U., 1963, PhD, 1968; LHD (hon.), Hahnemann U., 1988; DSc (hon.), Northeastern Ohio U. Coll. Medicine, 1995; DSc, Rutgers U., 1995. Various hosp. adminstrv. positions, Eng., 1959-61; rsch. assoc. Med. Sch. Yale U., 1962-68, asst. prof. Med. Sch., 1968-71, assoc. prof. Med. Sch., 1971-74, prof. pub. health Med. Sch., 1974-76; master Jonathan Edwards Coll., 1974-75; prof. dept. health systems mgmt. and polit. sci. Tulane U., New Orleans, 1976-78, chmn. dept. health systems mgmt., 1977-78; prof. history and sociology of sci. U. Pa., Phila., 1979—2002, chmn. dept., 1980-83, 86-91, UPS Found. prof., 1990-91, dean Sch. Arts and Scis., Thomas S. Gates prof., 1991-96, Stanley I. Sheerr prof., 1997—2001, prof. emeritus, 2002—. Prof. emeritus U. Pa., Phila., 2002-; vis. lectr. Johns Hopkins U., 1967-68; guest scholar Brookings Instn., Washington, 1967-68; acad. visitor London Sch. Econs., 1962-64, 1973-74; DeWitt Wallace disting. scholar social medicine and pub. policy, dept. psychiatry Weill Cornell Med. Coll., 2005—. Author: Medical Practice in Modern England: The Impact of Specialization and State Medicine, 1966, new edit., 2003, American Medicine and the Public Interest, 1971, rev. edit., 1998, In Sickness and in Wealth: American Hospitals in the Twentieth Century, 1989, rev. edit., 1999, (with others) Foreign Trained Physicians and American Medicine, 1972, Welfare Medicine in America, 1974, new edit., 2003, Alien-Doctors: Foreign Medical Graduates in American Hospitals, 1978, The Public-Private Health Care State, 2007; editor: (with others) History and Health Policy in the United States: Putting the Past Back In. Bd. dirs. Milbank Meml. Fund. Rockefeller Humanities fellow, 1982-83, Guggenheim fellow, 1984-85; Bellagio Study and Conf. scholar, 1984; recipient Frohlich medal Royal Soc. Medicine, London, 1986, Baxter Found. prize distinction in health svcs. rsch., 1990, James A. Hamilton Book award Am. Coll. Healthcare Execs. best book, 1990, Welch medal distinction in history of medicine Am. Assn. History Medicine, 1990, Arthur Viseltear award history pub. health Am. Pub. Health Assn., 1990, Nicholas E. Davies award Piedmont Hosp., Atlanta, 1997, Investigator award in health policy rsch. Robert Wood Johnson Found., 1998-2003, Carlson award for extraordinary contbns. to history of medicine Cornell U., Weill Med. Coll, 2000., Lifetime Achievement award Am. Assn. History Medicine, 2002. Fellow Am. Acad. Arts and Scis.; mem. AAAS (chmn. sect. history and philosophy of sci., 2002-03), Inst. Medicine of Nat. Acad. Sci., Am. Sociol. Assn., Am. Assn. for History of Medicine, Coll. Physicians Phila. Home: 500 E 77th St Apt 419 New York NY 10162 Business E-Mail: ras2023@med.cornell.edu.

STEVENS, ROY W., microbiologist, researcher, photographer; BS, SUNY, Albany, 1956, MS, 1958; PhD, Albany Med. Coll., 1965. Diplomate Am. Bd. Med. Microbiology, cert. emeritus Am. Bd. Med. Microbiology, 2002. Rsch. scientist Wadsworth Ctr., N.Y. State Dept. Health, Albany, 1967—70, assoc. rsch. scientist, 1970—73, prin. rsch. scientist, 1973—79, dir. lab. diagnostic immunology, 1979—85, dir. retrovirology and immunology lab., 1985—91; adj. prof. microbiology and immunology Albany Med. Coll., 1982—92; assoc. prof. sch. pub. health State Univ. N.Y., Albany, 1988—98; pres. Bio-med. Resource Group, Albany, 1991—2001. Trustee Bender Sci., Albany, 1986-98; chair Bender Sci. Fund Cmty., Albany, 2002—; mem. libr. devel. com. U. at Albany, 2001—06, chair 2003-06. Fellow Am. Acad. Microbiology (emeritus 2002), Assn. Med. Lab. Immunologists (pres. 1989), Am. Soc. Microbiology (chmn. clin. and diagnostic immunology divsn. 1997-98), Nat. Assn. Photoshop Profls., Saratoga Arts, (Saratoga Springs, NY). Home: 507 Acre Dr Schenectady NY 12303-5226

STEVENS, WILLIAM GRANT (GRANT STEVENS), plastic surgeon; b. Orange, Calif., Nov. 13, 1953; s. William Raymond Stevens and Donna Lynn (Stabbert) Watson; m. Sheri Diane Eagle, Aug. 13, 1977; 1 child, Catherine Eagle. BS in Psychology, U. Oreg., 1976; MD, Washington U. Med. Sch., St. Louis, 1980. Lic. Calif., 1981, Idaho, 1994, diplomate Nat. Bd. Med. Examiners, 1981, Am. Bd. Plastic Surgery, 1989. Intern Harbor UCLA Med. Ctr., Torrance, 1980-81, resident, 1981-83; hand surgery fellow Washington U. Sch. Medicine, St. Louis, 1983-84, fellow plastic surgery, 1984-85, chief resident, 1985-86; med. dir. Marina Plastic Surgery Associates (Marina Outpatient Surgery Ctr.), Marina del Rey, 1988—; med. dir. hand therapy svcs. Washington Hosp., 1988—93; chmn. dept. surgery, mem. med. exec. com. Daniel Freeman Marina Hosp., Marina del Rey, Calif., 1989—96, assoc. med. dir. Marina Breast Ctr., 1991—92, physician advisor, Skin Care POD, 1995—98. Attending cons. surgeon, plastic surgery sect. UCLA, Olive View Med. Ctr., 1992, UCLA, Wadsworth Vet. Adminstrn., 1992—2000; clin. prof. Liposuction U.; clin. instr., dept. surgery, divsn. plastic & reconstructive surgery UCLA Sch. Medicine; assoc. clin. prof., dept. surgery, divsn.

plastic & reconstructive surgery U. So. Calif. Sch. Medicine; plastic surgery expert cons. Med. Bd. Calif., 1988—, mem., 11th dist. med. quality review com., 1990—94; clin. evaluator Dow-Corning M.S.I. Breast Implant, 1991—93; mentor clin. investigator adj. gel mammary study, 1992—; mentor investigator, saline mammary prosthesis prospective study, 1992—; facility inspector Am. Assn. for Accreditation Ambulatory Plastic Surgical Facilities, Inc., 1992—; McGhan clin. investigator adj. gel mammary study, 1998—; mentor clin. investigator adj. gel mammary study, 1998—; ebdotine endoscope brow investigator, 2001—; Silimed clin. investigator cohesive gel mammary implant study, 2003—; vis. plastic surgery professorships U. Herlev Hosp., Copenhagen, 1998, U. Switzerland, Luzon, Switzerland, 1997, Loma Linda U., 1997, U. So. Calif., 2002; lectr. in field; presenter in field; clin. investigator for several studies. Mem. editl. bd. Wounds: A Compendium of Clin. Rsch. & Practice, 1988, mem. editl. adv. bd. Plastic Surgery Products, 1998—2006, Cosmetic Surgery Times, 1998—2006, frequent TV appearances include Personal Story, TLC, Hard Copy, Plastic Surgery Before & After, Discovery Health, The Perfect Cut, frequently featured in The Argonaut, Glamour, LA Times Mag., Plastic Surgery News, Longevity, LA Times, LA Mag., Daily Breeze, Cosmetic Plastic Surgery Times, Cosmetic Plastic Surgery Mag., Cosmetic Surgery Mag.; contbr. articles to profl. journals. Pres. Native Sons of the Golden West, Santa Monica, 1989—; active Boys and Girls Club Marina Del Rey; plastic surgeon Ice Dog Hockey Team, 1995-98 Recipient Kovitz sr. prize in Surgery, 1980, County of LA Commendation, 1996, Disting. Svc. Citation, Med. Bd. Calif., 1984, cert. of tribute, City of LA, 1996, GTE Cmty. Spirit award, 1996, cert. of recognition, Calif. State Assembly, 1997, cert. of Spl. Congl. Recognition, 1997, cert. of recognition, Calif. State Senate, 1997; Louis & Dorothy Kovitz fellowship in Surg. Rsch., 1979. Fellow: Am. Soc. for Laser Medicine & Surgery, Internat. Coll. Surgeons, ACS; mem.: AMA (Physician Recognition award, Physician Recognition award), Calif. Soc. Plastic Surgeons, Inc. (mem. legis. com. 1992—96, med. bd. Calif., liaison com. 1992—93), Internat. Soc. Aesthetic Plastic Surgery, Internat. Confederation for Plastic, Reconstructive and Aesthetic Surgery, LA County Med. Assn., ACS, Southern Calif. ch., Calif. Med. Assn. (adv. panel on plastic surgery sect. asst. sec. 1991—92, adv. panel on plastic surgery sect. sec. 1992—93, adv. panel on plastic surgery chmn. 1993—94, past chmn., adv. panel), Lipoplasty Soc. N.Am., Barnes Hosp. Plastic Surg. Soc., Plastic Surgery Ednl. Found., LA Society of Plastic Surgeons, Inc., Am. Soc. for Aesthetic Plastic Surgery, Inc., Am. Soc. Plastic Surgeons, Am. Soc. Plastic & Reconstructive Surgeons, Inc. (young plastic surgeons com. 1991—93, CPT com. 1992—93, practice devel. com. 1992—93, govt. rels. com. 1992—95), Phi Beta Kappa. Republican. Office: 4644 Lincoln Blvd Ste 552 Marina Del Rey CA 90292 Office Phone: 866-588-7507.

STEVENSON, BENJAMIN JAMES, psychologist; b. Duncan, Miss., June 2, 1937; s. Samuel Stevenson and Anna Caldwell; m. Sandra Ann Stilling, Jan. 1, 1970 (div. June 1976); 1 child, Rhonda. BA, Pitzer Coll., 1978; MS, U. Beverly Hills, 1983, PhD, 1985. Cert. ombudsman Calif. Adminstr. State of Calif., Claremont, 1975—80, group therapist Corona, 1976—87; dir. dist. Am. Assn. Ret. Persons, Redding, Calif., 1992—98; ombudsman Sr. Adv. Ctr., Redding, 2000—. V.p. African Sch. Found., LA, 1965—67; adminstr. Dept. Pub. Health, Claremont, 1968—70, mem. adv. bd. Shasta County Art Coun., Redding, 1990—92. Election officer City of Redding, 1992—. Specialist 5 USAR, 1953—65. Mem.: Carl Sagan Planetary Soc. Avocation: tennis. Home: 275 Hilltop Dr Apt 16 Redding CA 96003

STEVENSON, EDWARD WARD, retired otolaryngologist, surgeon; b. Chester, SC, Jan. 9, 1926; s. Thomas M. and Annie Lu (Ward) S.; m. Dorothy Giles, Sept. 2, 1947; children: Sally Anne Stevenson Yeilding, Laura Stevenson Healy, Nancy Stevenson Shoneberger-(dec.), Molly Stevenson Walker. MD, U. Md., Balt., 1949. Cert. Am. Bd. Otolaryngology, 1959. Intern Bapt. Meml. Hosp., Memphis, 1949-50; resident Med. Coll. Va. Hosp., Richmond, 1953-55; fellow Ochsner Found. Hosp., New Orleans, 1955-56; staff otolaryngologist Ochsner Clinic, 1956—57; staff otolaryngology Ochsner Found. Hosp. New Orleans, 1956—57; pvt. practice Birmingham, 1957-60, 65-94, 1965—94; instr., clin. asst. prof. surgery U. Ala., 1957-94; pvt. practice Decatur, 1960-65; ret., 1994. Faculty Tulane U. Sch. Medicine, 1956-57; staff St. Vincents Hosp & U. Hosp., Birmingham, 1957-60, 65-94; staff Decatur Gen. Hosp., Ala., 1960-65; staff Carraway Meth. Hosp., 1965-68; clin. asst. prof otolaryngology U. Ala. Sch. Medicine, 1957-94, staff Bapt. Med. Ctr. Montclair, Birmingham, chief otolaryngology, head & neck surgery, bd. dirs., Birmingham History Ctr. Contbr. articles to profl. jours. Bd. dirs. So. Mus. Flight, Birmingham, 1989—, vice chmn. Ala. Aviation Hall Fame, chmn., bd. dirs., 2003—, vice-chmn. 2006—; pres. Birmingham Aero Club, 1996; bd. dirs., past pres. Birmingham-Jefferson Hist. Soc.; bd dir. Jefferson County History Assoc., Rotary Club Birmingham; mem., Sons the Revolution Ala. With V-12 Program USN, 1943—46, Lt. M.C. USNR, 1949—53. Fellow ACS; mem. AMA, Am. Laryngol., Rhinol. and Otol. Soc. (sec.- treas. so. sect. 1990-93, v.p. so. sect. 1993-94), Am. Soc. Head and Neck Surgery, Am. Acad. Otolaryn., Jefferson County Med. Soc., Ala. Otolaryn. Soc. (founder, pres. 1971), Med. Assn. State Ala., Morgan County Med. Soc. (Ala.) (pres. 1964-65), Tri-State Otolaryn. Assembly (co-founder), Birmngham Otolaryn. Soc. (pres. 1984), Newcomen Soc., Birmingham-Jefferson Hist. Soc. (pres. 2007-09), Birmingham Downtown Rotary Club, Sons Revolution, Alb., United Flying Octogenerians, Ala. Civil War Round Table. Methodist. Avocations: world travel, reading, history. Home: 3850 Galleria Woods Dr Apt 241 Birmingham AL 35244 Personal E-mail: edstevenson@charter.net.

STEVENSON, JAMES P., oncologist, educator; BA in English/Pre-Prof. Studies, U. Notre Dame, 1988; MD, Thomas Jefferson U., 1992. Lic. Nat. Bd. Med. Examiners, 1993, diplomate Am. Bd. Internal Medicine, 1995, Am. Bd. Internal Medicine-med. oncology, 1998. Intern medicine Univ. Fla. Hosps, Gainesville, 1992—93; resident medicine Thomas Jefferson Univ. Hosp., Phila., 1993—95, fellow hematology and medic. oncology, 1995—98; assoc. prof. clin. medicine Univ. Pa.; staff physician, hematology-oncology Penn Presbyterian Med. Ctr.-UPHS. Co-author: (publs.) Phase Ib trial of combretastatin A-4 phosphate (CA4P) in combination with carboplatin in patients with advanced cancer, 2003, Phase I trial of the antivascular agent Combretastatin A4 phosphate on a five-day schedule to patients with cancer: MRI evidence for altered tumor blood flow, 2003, Phase I Combination Trial of Gemcitabine, Paclitaxel, and Carboplatin in Patients with Advanced Malignancy, 2003, Phase II clinical/pharmacodynamic trial of the proteasome inhibitor PS-341 in advanced non-small cell lung cancer, 2003, A Phase I, Dose Escalation Trial of ZD0473, a Novel Platinum Analogue, in Combination with Gemcitabine, 2004, and numerous other publs. Mem.: ACP, Am. Coll. of Surgeons Oncology Group, Eastern Coop. Oncology Group, Internat. Assn. for the Study of Lung Cancer, Am. Soc. of Clin. Oncology. Office: Penn Presbyterian Medical Center 103-A Medical Arts Bldg Philadelphia PA 19104 Office Phone: 215-662-9801. E-mail: james.stevenson@uphs.upenn.edu.

STEVENSON, LYNNE W. (LYNNE LESLIE WARNER STEVENSON), cardiologist, educator; b. Joplin, Mo., June 15, 1954; AB summa cum laude, Princeton U., 1975; MD, Stanford U., 1979. Cert. Internal Medicine, 1982, Cardiovascular Disease, 1985. Intern Stanford U. Hosp., Calif., 1979—80; resident UCLA Ctr. for Health Scis., 1980—82, fellow cardiology, 1982—84, attending staff physician, 1984—93; med. dir. Heart Transplantation Program UCLA Med. Ctr., 1983—93, dir. UCLA Heart Failure Program, 1983—88, dir. Ahmanson-UCLA Cardiomyopathy Ctr., 1988—93; physician Brigham and Women's Hosp., Boston, 1993—, clin. dir. Cardiomyopathy and Heart Failure Program, 1993—, supr. 12ACT (Advanced Cardiomyopathy Therapies) Nursing Unit, 1994—, cardiology rep. Heart Failure Divsn. Mgmt. Devel. Team, 1998—2002, cons., 2002—. Adj. instr. cardiology UCLA Sch. Medicine, 1984—85, adj. asst. prof., 1985—87, asst. prof. medicine in residence, 1987—90, asst. prof. medicine, 1990—91, assoc. prof., 1991—93, Harvard Med. Sch., Boston, 1993—94, prof., 1994—; mem. Review Com. Clin. Programs of Cardiac Transplantation Health Care Financing Adminstrn., 1994—. Guest editor Jour. Am. Coll. Cardiology, 1992—, Am. Heart Jour.; contbr. articles to med. jours. Recipient Eugene Braunwald Tchg. Award, 1998. Fellow: Am. Heart Assn., Am. Coll. Cardiology; mem.: US Transplant Cardiology Rsch. Database Group (exec. com. mem.), Am. Coll. Physicians, Am. Fedn. Clin. Rsch., Internat. Soc. Heart and Lung Transplantation. Office: Brigham and Women's Hosp Cardiovascular Divsn 75 Francis St, PBB-1 Boston MA 02115 Office Phone: 617-732-7141. Office Fax: 617-278-6931. E-mail: lstevenson@partners.org.

STEVENSON, ROBERT BENJAMIN, III, prosthodontist, writer; b. Topeka, Feb. 13, 1950; s. Robert Benjamin and Martha (McClelland) S.; m. Barbara Jean Sulick, June 6, 1975; children: Jody Ann, Robert Woodrow. BS, U. Miami, Coral Gables, Fla., 1972; DDS, Ohio State U., 1975, MS, MA, 1980, cert. in prosthodontics splty. tng., 1980. Practice dentistry specializing in prosthodontics, Columbus, Ohio, 1981—; clin. assoc. prof. Ohio State U., Columbus, 1981-87, 98—. Chmn. oral cancer com. Columbus Dental Soc., 1981-85, Am. Cancer Soc., Columbus, 1985-97; trustee Ohio Divsn, 1997-2000; vol. dentist Provodencialis Ctr., Turks and Caicos Islands, Brit. West Indies, 1982-87; mem., adv. com. Ohio State U. Med. Heritage Ctr. Editor Columbus Dental Soc. Bull., 1981-87, 89-92; assoc. editor Ohio State U. Dental Alumni Quar., 1982-2008, Am. Med. Writer's Assn. Ohio Newsletter, 1983-86, Ohio State Journalism Alumni Assn. Newsletter, 1986-88, alumni spotlight editor, 1995-2004; assoc. editor Jour. Prosthetic Dentistry, 1987-92; mem. editl. coun. Jour. Prosthetic Dentistry, 2002—05; inventor intraoral measuring device; contbg. writer Gridison Greats, the Digest of North American Football History, 2004-. Vol. Am. Cancer Soc., Columbus, 1982-2001. Served to capt. USAF, 1975-78. Fellow Am. Coll. Dentists; mem. ACS, ADA, Am. Coll. Prosthodontists, Ohio Dental Assn. (alt. del. 1982-89, del. 1990-92, 97-2003, editor new products newsletter 1988-97), Carl Boucher Prosthodontic Conf. (editor 1987-92, sec. 1992-98, treas. 1998—2008), Procrastinator's Club America, Columbus Downtown Quarterback Club. Avocations: playing electric organ, golf, music, reading. Home: 1300 Southport Cir Columbus OH 43235-7642 Office: Riverview Profl Village 3600 Olentangy River Rd Columbus OH 43214 E-mail: lesgobucks@aol.com.

STEVENSON, THOMAS RAY, plastic surgeon; b. Kansas City, Mo., Jan. 22, 1946; s. John Adolph and Helen Ray (Clarke) S.; m. Judith Ann Hunter, Aug. 17, 1968; children: Anne Hunter, Andrew Thomas. BA, U. Kans., 1968, MD. Diplomate Am. Bd. Plastic and Reconstructive Surgery, Am. Bd. Surgery. Resident in gen. surgery U. Va., Charlottesville, 1972-78; resident in plastic surgery Emory U., Atlanta, 1980-82; asst. prof. surgery U. Mich., 1982-88, assoc. prof. surgery, 1988-89. Chief plastic surgery Ann Arbor VA Hosp., 1982—, U. Calif., Davis, 1989—. Served to maj. USAR, 1978-80. Fellow ACS; mem. Am. Soc. Plastic and Reconstructive Surgery, Am. Bd. Plastic Surgery, chair-elect 2006. Office: UC Davis Divsn Plastic Surg 2221 Stockton Blvd Ste E Sacramento CA 95817-2214

STEVENSON, WILLIAM GREGORY, cardiac electrophysiologist, educator; MD, Tulane U., 1979. Diplomate Am. Bd. Internal Medicine, 1982, Am. Bd. Internal Medicine-cardiovasc. disease, 1985, Am. Bd. Internal Medicine-clin. cardiac electrophysiology, 1992. Resident internal medicine UCLA Med. Ctr., 1982, chief med. resident, 1984, fellow cardiovasc. disease, 1985; fellow electrpohysiology Univ. of Limburg, Netherlands, 1985; dir. Clin. Cardiac Electrophysiology Program Brigham and Women's Hosp.; prof. medicine Harvard Univ. Office: Brigham and Women's Hospital Cardiovascular Division 75 Francis St Boston MA 02115 Office Phone: 857-307-1948. Office Fax: 857-307-1944.

STEWARD, DAVID JOHN, anesthesiologist, educator, researcher; b. Luton, England, Feb. 2, 1934; arrived in US, 1991; s. William John and Kathleen (Waterhouse) S.; m. Mary Alexandra Traquair, Nov. 1, 1958 (div. Feb. 1988); children: Jennifer, Nigel; m. Mary Louise Roberts, Mar. 17, 1988. MB BS, U. London, 1958. Diplomate Am. Bd. Anesthesiology. Resident anesthesia U. Toronto, Canada, 1964—65, resident internal medicine, 1966—67, sr. resident anesthesia, 1967—68, prof. anesthesiology, 1978—84; registrar anesthesia Southampton Gen. Hosp., England, 1965—66; chief of anesthesiology Hosp. for Sick Children, Toronto, Canada, 1972—84; chief anaesthesia BC Children's Hosp., Vancouver, Canada, 1984—91; prof. anesthesiology U. BC, Vancouver, 1984—91, hon. prof. anaesthesia, 2005—; prof. anesthesiology U. So. Calif., LA, 1991—2001; dir. anesthesiology Childrens Hosp. LA, 1991—2001. Chmn. pediat. com. World Fedn. Socs. Anesthesiologists, 1982-90; cons. Can. China Child Health Found., Vancouver, Can., 1986—. Author: (book) Manual of Pediatric Anesthesia, 1979, 6th edit. 2009; co-editor: (books) Anesthesia and Uncommon Pediatric Diseases, Pediatrics for Anesthesiologists, 1994. Flight lt. Royal Can. Air Force, 1960—65. Recipient Robert M. Smith award, Am. Acad. Pediat., 2000. Mem. Am. Soc. Anesthesiologists, Calif. Soc. Anesthesiologists. Avocations: sailing, photography, travel. Home: 5396 Goldfinch Way Blaine WA 98230 Personal E-mail: davidjsteward@comcast.net.

STEWART, COLIN L., biologist, researcher; DPhil, U. Oxford. Staff scientist European Molecular Biology Lab. (EMBL); mem. Roche Inst. Molecular Biology; chief Cancer and Devel. Biology Lab. Ctr. Cancer Rsch., Nat. Cancer Inst., head Mammalian Devel. Biology Sect., Cancer and Devel. Biology Lab.; now prin. investigator Devel. and Regenerative Biology Inst. Med. Biology, Singapore. Office: Inst Med Biology 8A Biomedical Grove #06-06 Immunos 138648 Immunos Singapore 138648 E-mail: colin.stewart@imb.a-star.edu.sg.

STEWART, ELIZABETH ANNELLA, gynecologist, researcher; b. Atlanta, Apr. 24, 1959; married. BA molecular biology magna cum laude, Vanderbilt U., 1980; MD, Harvard U., 1985. Cert. Nat. Bd. Med. Examiners 1986, Mass. License Registration 1988, Am. Bd. Ob-Gyn. 1993, diplomate in ob-gyn. and reproductive endocrinology Am. Bd. Ob-gyn., 1995, cert. Am. Bd. Ob-Gyn., Annual Recertification 2003. Intern Obstetrics & Gynecology, Magee Women's Hosp., Pitts., 1985—86; resident Obstetrics & Gynecology, Brigham & Women's Hosp., 1986—89, fellow, Reproductive Endocrinology Boston, 1990—92; clin. dir., Ctr. Uterine Fibroids, Brigham and Women's Hosp., Boston, 1998—; asst. prof. ob-gyn and reproductive biology Harvard Med. Sch., 1995—2003, assoc. prof., 2003—; assoc. ob-gyn. Brigham and Women's Hosp., Boston, 1989—; asst. gynecologist Mass. General Hosp., Boston, 1989—90; assoc. in ob-gyn. Mass. Inst. Tech. Med. Dept., Cambridge, 1989—90; clinical dir., Ctr. for Uterine Fibroids Brigham and Women's Hosp., 1998—; assoc. gynecologist Faulkner Hosp., Boston, 2005—. Rsch. asst., Dept. of Surgery Vanderbilt U. Sch. of Medicine, 1981, summer fellow, Diabetes Ctr., 82; clinical assoc. Nat. Institutes of Health (NIH), Clinical Elective in Endocrinology and Metabolism, 1984; med. dir., Quality Assurance Com. Fertility and Endocrinology Unit, Brigham and Women's Hosp., Boston, 1993—95; assoc. dir., Lab. of Cell Biology, Dept. of Obstetrics, Gynecology and Reproductive Biology Brigham and Women's Hosp., Harvard Med. Sch., 1995—99; cons., Reproductive Sciences Program U. Mich., 2000; visiting prof. of ob-gyn. Kuwait U., Kuwait, 2000; cons. for Women's Health Care Emirates Palomar Med. Tech. Services, Abu Dhabi, United Arab Emirates, 2000; assoc. dir., Reproductive Endocrinology Fellowship Program Brigham and Women's Hosp., 2002—04; ad hoc mem. Bd. of Sci. Counselors, Review of Epidemiology Br. Nat. Inst. of Environ. Health Sciences, Nat. Institutes of Health, 2005. Recipient First Prize, Boston Fertility Soc. Prize Paper Competition, 1991, Berlex Scholar Award, 1993, First Prize, Boston Obstetrical Soc. Prize Paper Competition, 1994, Second Prize, Boston Fertility Soc. Prize Paper Competition, 1996, Partners in Excellence Award, Partners HealthCare System, 1996, Bear and Eagle Feather Mentoring Award, Four Directions Summer Rsch. Program, Harvard Med. Sch., 2000, Partners in Excellence Award, Partner's Health Care System, 2000, Residency Teaching Award in Reproductive Endocrinology, Brigham and Women's Hospital, 2004, Leadership Award for Clinical Innovation, Brigham and Women's Physician's Org., 2004. Fellow: Am. Coll. Ob-Gyn.; mem.: Soc. for Gynecologic Investigation, Soc. of Reproductive Endocrinologists, Am. Soc. for Reproductive Medicine, Mortar Bd. Hon. Soc., Phi Beta Kappa. Achievements include U.S. Patent 6440445: Methods and Compounds for Treatment of Abnormal Uterine Bleeding. Office: Mayo Clinic 200 First St SW Rochester MN 55905 Office Fax: 507-284-1774.

STEWART, MICHAEL GLENN, otolaryngologist, educator; b. Bowling Green, Ky., Sept. 17, 1962; s. Michael Joseph and Barbara (Weisser) S. B in Engring. summa cum laude, Vanderbilt U., 1984; MD, Johns Hopkins U., 1988; MPH, U. Tex., 1996; Gen. Surgery, Baylor Coll. Medicine, 1990, Otolaryngology, 1994. Diplomate Am. Bd. Otolaryngology. Asst. prof. Baylor Coll. Medicine, Houston, 1994-99, assoc. prof., 1999—2005, dir. residency edn. dept. otolaryngology, 1996—2005, asst. dean clin. affairs, 1998-2000, gen. dir. affil. med. svc., 1999—2005, assoc. dean clin. affairs, 2000—05; prof., chmn. Dept. Otorhinolaryngology Weill Cornell Med. Coll., NYC, 2005—, sr. assoc. dean clin. affairs, 2010—; otorhinolaryngologist-in-chief NY Presbyn. Hosp., 2005—. Chief otolaryngology Ben Taub Gen. Hosp., 1994-2005; chmn. med. bd. Harris County Hosp. Dist., Houston, 1999-2000; sr. examiner Am. Bd. Otolaryngology, 2007-08, dir. 2008-, editl. bd. mem. ENToday, editor in chief, Thelarygoscope, 2011-; assoc. editor, editl. bd. mem. Allergy and Rhinology, 2010-11. Editor Rev. Head and Neck, 1994—; reviewer Archive Otolaryngology-Head and Neck, 1997—, Jour. Trauma, 1998—, Otolaryngology-Head and Neck Surgery, 1998—, Cancer, 2001—; assoc. editor, mem. editl. bd. Am. Jour. Rhinology, 2003—10; mem. editl. bd. Archives of Otolaryngology-Head and Neck Surgery, 2005—11. Recipient Outstanding Clin. Rsch. award Kelsey-Seybold Found., 1992, 93, Houston Disting. Surgeon award Assn. Perioperative Nurses, 2005. Fellow: ACS, Am. Rhinologic Soc. (bd. dirs. 2011—), Am. Laryngol., Rhinol. and Otol. Soc., Am. Acad. Otolaryngology Head and Neck Surgery (chair rsch. adv. bd. 2008—10, Disting. Svc. award 2004, Presdl. Citation award 2010); mem.: Triological Soc. (v.p., eastern sect.), Assn. Acad. Depts. Otolaryngology (pres., bd. dirs. 2011—), Soc. Univ. Otolaryngologists (pres. 2007—08). Office Phone: 646-962-4777. Business E-Mail: mgs2002@med.cornell.edu.

STEWART, MICHAEL IAN, orthodontist; b. Yonkers, NY, May 22, 1955; s. William Bernard and Bernice Barbara (Friedman) S.; m. Vicki Lynn Sapperstein, Mar. 26, 1988. BA cum laude, U. Miami, 1978; DDS, Emory U., 1984; cert. in orthodontics, Yeshiva U., 1990. Cert. Nat. Bd. Dental Examiners, diplomate Am. Bd. Orthodontics. Pvt. practice gen. dentistry, Tampa, Clearwater, Fla., 1985; pvt. practice children's dentistry, Clearwater, New Port Richey, Plant City, Fla., 1985-88; fellow in orthodontics Montefiore Med. Ctr.-Albert Einstein Coll. Medicine, Bronx, N.Y., 1988-90; pvt. practice orthodontics, Clearwater, Plant City, New Port Richey, 1990—. Provider dental svcs. Fla. Dept. Health, Clearwater, New Port Richey, Plant City, 1985—, Head Start, Clearwater, New Port Richey, 1985-88; cons. Health South Rehab. Hosp., 1996—. Illustrator: Mandibular Surgery and Sleep Apnea, 1990. Cons. LaSertoma, New Port Richey, 1986—; vol. VA Med. Ctr., Miami, Fla., 1978; cons., lectr. Apple program Pasco County Assn. for Retarded Citizens, 1987. Rsch.grantee Northeastern Soc. Orthodontists, 1989. Mem. ADA, Am. Assn. Orthodontists, So. Assn. Orthodontists, Fla. Dental Assn., Fla. Assn. Orthodontists, West Coast Dental Assn., Upper Pinellas County Dental Assn., Am. Soc. Dentistry for Children, Am. Assn. Orthodontists Rsch. Family, Ctrl. Fla. Orthodontic Study Group, Acad. Alumni and Friends U. Fla. Coll. Dentistry, Alpha Omega, Alpha Epsilon Delta. Avocations: automobiles and restoration, reading, sailing, landscaping, bicycling. Home: 2063 Swan Ln Palm Harbor FL 34683-6274 Office: 718 Lakeview Rd Clearwater FL 33756

STEWART, PAUL ARTHUR, pharmaceutical company executive; b. Greensburg, Ind., Sept. 28, 1955; s. John Arthur and Alberta Jeannette (Densford) S.; m. Susan Rhodes, Dec. 20, 1975; children: John Rhodes, Daniel Robbins. BS, Purdue U., 1976; MBA, Harvard U., 1987. Lic. prof. cert. 2007. Grad. asst. Purdue U., West Lafayette, Ind., 1977; asst. treas. Stewart Seeds Inc., Greensburg, 1997-82, sec., treas., 1982-84; cons. The Boston Cons. Group Inc., Chgo., 1986; founder, owner PASCO Group, mgmt. and computer cons., aircraft leasing, 1979-87; mgr. bus. planning agrichems. Eli Lilly & Co., Indpls., 1987-88, dist. sales mgr. agrichems., 1989-90, tech. acquisition mgr. med. devices and diagnostics divsn., 1990-92; dir. mktg. info. and bus. devel. IVAC Corp. subs. Eli Lilly & Co., 1992-94, advisor corp. fin. and investment banking, 1994-96; mgr. global bus. devel. (animal health) Eli Lilly & Co., 1996—. Author: (nonfiction) A Harvard MBA's Advice to His Sons, 2005. Mem. Greensburg-Decatur County Bd. Airport Commrs., 1980-85, pres., 1980-81, 83; mem. Decatur County Data Processing Bd., 1982-85; deacon 2d Presbyn. Ch. Indpls., 1991-92, elder, 1996-99; bd. dirs. Friends of Nat. Inst. Nursing Rsch., NIH, 1995-98, Park Tudor Sch., Indpls., 1997-2003; bd. govs. Cert. Licensing Profls. Orgn., 2010-, v.p., vice chair bd. govs., 2011-. Mem.: Indpls. Legal Aid Soc. (bd. dirs. 2004—10), Harvard Bus. Sch. Alumni Assn. (bd. dirs. 1999—2003, v.p. 2001—03), Alpha Gamma Rho. Republican. Presbyterian. Office: Eli Lilly & Co Lilly Corp Ctr Indianapolis IN 46285-0001 Office Phone: 317-277-6120. Personal E-mail: pstewart@mba1987.hbs.edu.

STEWART, RICHARD DONALD, internist, educator, writer; b. Lakeland, Fla., Dec. 26, 1926; s. LeRoy Hepburn and Zoa Irene (Hachet) S.; m. Mary Leeuw, June 14, 1952; children: R. Scot, Gregory D., Mary E. AB, U. Mich., 1951, MD, 1955, MPH, 1962; MA, U. Wis. Milw., 1979; PhD in English, U. Wis., Milw., 1997. Diplomate Am. Bd. Internal Medicine, Am. Bd. Med. Toxicology, Acad. Toxicol. Scis. Intern Saginaw (Mich.) Gen. Hosp., 1955-56; resident in internal medicine U. Mich. Med. Ctr., Ann Arbor, 1959-62; dir. med. rsch. sect. Dow Chem. Co., Midland, Mich., 1962-66; staff physician Midland Hosp., 1962-66; assoc. prof. preventive medicine Med. Coll. Wis., Milw., 1966-68, prof., chmn. dept. environ. medicine, 1968—78, prof. emergency med., 1989—91, adj. prof. dept. pharmacology and toxicology, 1978—. Cons. Children's Hosp. Wis., 1989-93, Internal Medicine St. Mary's Hosp., Racine, Wis., 1983-93; prof., dir. med. toxicology fellowship Dept. Emergency Medicine Milw. Regional Med. Ctr., 1989-91; sr. attending staff, 1967-90; staff Internal Medicine St. Luke's Hosp., Racine, 1983-93; med. dir. Poison Control Ctr. Southeastern Wis., 1989-93; corp. med. advisor S.C. Johnson & Son, Inc., Racine, 1971-78, corp. med. dir., 1978-89. Author: (med. biography) Leper Priest of Molokai, 2000, Flight for Life, 2011; contbr. 150 scientific papers. Mem. adv. med. staff Milw. Fire Dept., 1975—. Cadet USAF, 1945-46. Fellow ACP, Am. Coll. Occupl. Medicine, Am. Acad. Clin. Toxicology, Acad. Toxicological Scis.; mem. AMA, Soc. Toxicology, Wis. State Med. Soc., Racine Acad. Medicine, Rotary Internat., Phi Theta Kappa, Phi Kappa Phi, Sigma Tau Delta. Achievements include invention of medical devices including the hollow fiber artificial kidney and capillary artificial lung; being leader of team that performed first human dialyses with Hollow Fiber Artificial Kidney, beginning Aug. 4, 1967; leading the research term that studied teh Human Absorption, metabolism, excretion, physiologic responses to 32 toxic agents both acute and chronic exposure in the controlled atmosphere of 5 environmental chambers. Avocations: hiking, creative writing. Home and Office: 5337 Wind Point Rd Racine WI 53402-2322 Office Phone: 262-639-6483. Personal E-mail: rdstew@att.net.

STEWART, ROSALYN W., physician, educator; b. Houston, June 5, 1968; MS, U. Tex. Med. Br., 1993, MD, 1997. Asst. prof. Johns Hopkins U., 2004—. Office: 601 N Carolilne St Baltimore MD 21287 Office Fax: 410-614-1195. Business E-Mail: rstewar6@jhmi.edu.

STEWART, WILLIAM JAMES, cardiologist; b. Cleve., Aug. 17, 1951; s. James B. and Virginia Stewart; m. Denise Elizabeth Balk, Dec. 30, 1972; children: Emily, Travis. AB in Biology cum laude, Harvard U., 1973; MD, U. Cin., 1977. Diplomate Am. Bd. Internal Medicine with subspecialty in cardiovascular disease; lic. physician, Ohio. Intern/resident U. Mich. Affiliated Hosps., Ann Arbor, 1977-80; clin. fellow dept. cardiology Boston U. Hosp., 1980-82; clin./rsch. fellow Cardiac Ultrasound Lab. Mass. Gen. Hosp./Harvard Med. Sch., Boston, 1982-84; staff physician Cleve. Clinic, 1984—, dir. Echo Lab, 1992—. Clin. assoc. in medicine Boston U., 1980-82; rsch. fellow in medicine Harvard Med. Sch., 1982-84; asst. prof. medicine Ohio State U., Cleve. Clinic Health Scis. Campus, 1992-94, assoc. prof., 1995—. Contbr. numerous articles and abstracts to profl. jours., chpts. to books; reviewer Circulation, Jour. Am. Coll. Cardiology, Jour. Am. Soc. Echocardiography, Echocardiography, Am. Heart Jour., Am. Jour. Cardology, Brit. Heart Jour., Annals of Thoracic Surgery, Jour. Thoracic and Cardiovascular Surgery, Am. Jour. Cardiac Imaging; editl. bd. Echocardiography, 1992-96, Jour. Am. Soc. Echocardiography, 1991—. Christian youth leader. Fellow Am. Coll. Cardiology (Ohio chpt. adv. expert team in echocardiography 1995—), chmn. task force tng. in echocardiography 1994, mem. echocardiography com. 1991-96); mem. Am. Heart Assn. (mem. edn. com. N.E. Ohio chpt. 1985-88), Am. Soc. Echocardiography (chmn. com. on echocardiography in emergency medicine 1997, chmn. sci. sessions 1996, abstract chmn. sci. sessions 1994, mem. physicians' edn. and tng. com. 1993—, abstract vice chmn. 1993, bd. dirs. 1989-92), Internat. Soc. Ultrasound in Cardiac Surgery (pres. 1994—), Greater Cleve. Soc. Echocardiography (founder, bd. dirs. 1985—). Episcopalian. Avocations: jogging, sailing, skiing, music. Office: Cleveland Clinic Found Dept Cardiology F-15 9500 Euclid Ave Dept Cleveland OH 44195-0002

STICKLER, GUNNAR BRYNOLF, pediatrician; b. Peterskirchen, Germany, June 13, 1925; came to U.S., 1951, naturalized, 1958; s. Fritz and Astrid (Wennerberg) S.; m. Duci M. Kronenbitter, Aug. 30, 1956; children: Katarina Anna, George David. MD, U. Munich, Germany, 1949; PhD, U. Minn., Mpls., 1957. Diplomate Am. Bd. Pediatrics, ofcl. examiner and mem., 1965-95. Resident in clin. pathology Krankenhaus III Orden, Munich, 1950; resident in pathology U. Munich, 1950-51; intern Mountainside Hosp., Montclair, NJ, 1951-52; fellow in pediatrics Mayo Grad. Sch., Rochester, Minn., 1953-56; sr. cancer research scientist Roswell Park Meml. Inst., Buffalo, 1956-57; asst. to staff Mayo Clinic, Rochester, 1957-58, cons. in pediatrics, 1959-89, head sect. pediatrics, 1969-74; prof. pediatrics, chmn. dept. pediatrics Mayo Clinic and Mayo Med. Sch., 1974-80. Mem. test com. III Nat. Bd. Med. Examiners, 1973-75; vis. prof. at various univs and instns., including U. Dusseldorf (Germany) and U. Munich, 1971, Pahlavi U., Iran, 1975, Olga Hosp., Stuttgart, Germany, 1978, Martin Luther King Hosp., Los Angeles, 1979, U. Man., 1981; mem. emeritus staff Mayo Clinic, 1989. Mem. editl. bd. Clin. Pediatrics, 1968-76, 79-97, European Jour. Pediatrics, 1976-84, Pediatrics, 1983-89; contbr. more than 290 articles to med. publs. Active parent support groups in field of cyclic vomiting syndrome; life pres. Stickler Syndrome support group, 1997—. Recipient Humanitarian award Chgo. region chpt. Nat. Found. Ileitis and Colitis, 1978, award for excellence of subject matter and presentation So. Minn. Med. Assn., 1978 Mem. Am. Acad. Pediatrics (Disting. Svc. award Minn. chpt. 1999), Soc. Pediatric Rsch., Am. Pediatric Soc., Nat. Coun. Reliable Health Info., Midwest Soc. Pediatric Rsch. (coun. 1967-69, pres. 1970-71, Founders award 1996), N.W. Pediatric Soc. (pres. 1973-74) Achievements include description of hereditary progressive arthropthalmopathy in 1965, now called Stickler syndrome; and the treatment otitis media, hypophosphatemic rickets, renal disease; research in areas of parents' fears and the need of routine physical examinations in adolescents, and the excesses of alternative medicine. Office: Mayo Clinic Emeritus Ctr Rochester MN 55905

STIEFVATER, PAMELA JEAN, chiropractor; b. Utica, NY, Oct. 16, 1956; d. Kenneth Carl and Henriette Ramona (Billick) S. BS cum laude, SUNY, Oswego, 1977; D of Chiropractic cum laude, Palmer Coll., 1984. Lic. chiropractor, N.Y., Mass.; diplomate Nat. Bd. Chiropractic Examiners. Tchr. sci. Altmar, Parish, Williamstown H.S., Parish, NY, 1978—80; chiropractor, owner Bayside Chiropractic, South Dennis, Mass., 1986—. Mem. Am. Chiropractic Soc., Mass. Chiropractic Soc., Cape Cod Chiropractic Soc. Office: Bayside Chiropractic 430 Old Bass River Rd South Dennis MA 02660-2724

STIEG, PHILIP, neurosurgeon; b. Milw., July 30, 1952; BS, U. Wis., Madison, 1974; PhD in anatomy and neuroscience, Albany Med. Coll., Union U., 1980; MD, Med. Coll. Wis., 1983. Intern, resident U. Tex. Southwestern Med. Sch., Dallas, 1983—84, chief resident, 1988—89; fellow Karolinska Inst., Stockholm, 1987—88; instr. surgery Harvard Med. Sch., Boston, 1989—92, assoc. neurosurgery, 1989—, asst. prof. surgery, 1992—96, assoc. prof. surgery, 1996—; prof., chmn. neurological surgery Weill Cornell Med. Coll., NYC, 2000—; neurosurgeon-in-chief NY-Presbyn. Hosp., NYC, 2000—. Mem. Mem. Sloan Kettering Cancer Ctr., NYC, 2007—. Recipient Time, Feeling and Focus award, Am. Heart Assn., 1999, The Best Doctors in New York, NY Mag., 2008; named one of The Best Doctors, Boston Mag., 1997, The Best Doctors in New York, NY Mag., 2001—03, 2007. Fellow: ACS, NY Acad. Medicine, N.Am. Skull Base Soc.; mem.: AAAS, AMA, Med. Soc. of the State of NY, NY Soc. Neurosurgery (sec./treas. 2004, pres. 2006), Am. Acad. Neurological Surgery, Neurological Soc. America, Nat. Stroke Assn., Soc. U. Neurosurgeons (v.p. 1999—2000, pres. 2001—04), Am. Assn. Neurological Surgeons, Soc. for Neuroscience, Boston Soc. Neurology and Psychiatry, Am. Heart Assn., Am. Cleft-Palate-Craniofacial Assn., NY Acad. Sciences, New England Neurosurgical Soc., Congress of Neurological Surgeons, Boston Stroke Soc. Office: Starr Pavilion 651 525 E 68th St New York NY 10065 Office Phone: 212-746-4684. Office Fax: 212-746-6607.

STIEHM, E. RICHARD, pediatrician, educator; b. Milw., Jan. 22, 1933; s. Reuben Harold and Marie Dueno S.; m. Judith Hicks, July 12, 1958; children: Jamie Elizabeth, Carrie Eleanor, Meredith Ellen. BS, U. Wis., 1954, MD, 1957. Diplomate Am. Bd. Pediat., Am. Bd. Allergy and Clin. Immunology (bd. dirs. 1977-83), Am. Bd. Diagnostic Lab. Immunology. Intern Phila. Gen. Hosp., 1957-58; fellow in physiol. chemistry U. Wis., 1959-61, asst. prof. pediat., 1965—68, assoc. prof., 1968—69; med. officer USNR, Johnsville, Pa., 1961-63; resident in pediat. Babies Hosp., NYC, 1963-65; rsch. fellow in pediat. immunology U. Calif., San Francisco, 1965-68; assoc. prof. UCLA, 1969—72, chief divsn. immunology, allergy and rheumatology, 1969—2003, prof., 1972—, assoc. dir. Ctr. for Interdisciplinary Rsch. in Immunologic Diseases, 1981-82, co-dir. Cystic Fibrosis Ctr., 1988—95, vice chair acad. affairs dept. pediat., 1989—99; vis. scientist metabolism br. Nat. Cancer Inst., Bethesda, Md., 1982-88. Vis. prof. Yale U., Mayo Clinic, U. Cin., Great Ormond St. Hosp., U.K., U. Wis.; bd. sci. dirs. Immune Deficiency Found., 1981—, Eczema Found., 1988—, Pediat. AIDS Found., 1989-99; task force on pediatric allergy NIH, 1977; mem. gen. clin. rsch. ctr. study sect. NIH, 1978-82, 84-88; adv. com. Hartford Fellowship, 1984-88; co-dir. LA Pediatric AIDS Consortium, 1988—. Editor: Immunologic Disorders in Infants and Children, 1972, 80, 89, 96, 2004; Am. editor: Pediatric Rsch., 1984-89; assoc. editor: Pediat. Update, 2003-; mem. editl. bd. Pediat., 1972-78, Pediat. in Rev., 1978-81, Jour. Allergy and Clin. Immunology, 1976-80, Jour. Clin. Immunology, 1985-89, Jour. Asthma Pediatric Allergy and Immunology, 1987-91, Am. Jour. Diseases of Children, 1987-97, Contemporary Pediat., 1991-96, Am. Jour. Clin. Nutrition, 1992-97; contbr. articles to profl. jours. Commr. HHS Commn. on Childhood Vaccines, 1988-90; mem. clin. rsch. adv. com. Nat. Found. March of Dimes, 1992-97, 2004-09. Recipient Career Devel. award Nat. Inst. Allergy and Infectious Diseases, 1967-69, E. Mead Johnson award for Pediat. Rsch., 1974, Alumni Citation award U. Wis. Med. Sch., 1988, Lifetime Achievement award Immune Deficiency Found., 1995, Med. Sci. award UCLA Med. Alumni, 1999, Disting. Alumni award Babies and Children's Hosp. Alumni Assn., N.Y., 1999, Abbott Labs. award, Clin. and Diagnostic Immunology Am. Soc. Microbiology, 2007; Markle scholar, 1967-72. Fellow AAAS; mem. Am. Assn. Immunologists, Western Soc. Pediat. Rsch. (coun. 1977-80, pres. 1983, Ross Rsch. award 1971), Soc. Pediat. Rsch., Am. Pediat. Soc., Am. Acad. Allergy, Asthma and Clin. Immunology, Am. Acad. Pediat. (infectious diseases com. 1971-77), Am. Soc. Clin. Investigation, Clin. Immunology Soc., Phi Beta Kappa, Alpha Omega Alpha. Office: UCLA Dept Peds Divsn Immunology 10833 Le Conte Ave Los Angeles CA 90095-3075 Office Phone: 310-825-6481. Business E-Mail: estiehm@mednet.ucla.edu.

STIFANESE, ROBERTO, biologist; b. Varazze, SV, Italy, July 27, 1973; Degree in Biol. Scis., U. Genoa, 2001, PhD in Neurochemistry, Neurobiology, 2005. Cert. specialist in clin. pathology U. Genoa. Cons. Aquarium Genoa, 1992—94; sr. scientist dept. exptl. medicine-sect. biochemistry U. Genoa, 2005—, adj. prof. faculty medicine, 2009. Translator u.-level biochemistry text books, 2009; referee Internat. Jour. Biochemistry & Cell Biology, 2009. Mem.: Italian Soc. Exptl. Biology, Italian Soc. Biochemistry. Avocations: soccer, skiing, fishing. Office: Viale Benedetto XV 1 Genoa 16132 Italy Business E-Mail: stifanese@unige.it.

STIFF, PATRICK JOSEPH, internist, hematologist, oncologist, educator; b. Toledo, Nov. 27, 1950; BS, U. Toledo, 1972; MD, Loyola U., 1975. Intern Cleve. Clinic, 1975-76, resident in medicine, 1976-78; fellow in hematology and oncology Meml. Sloan-Kettering Med. Ctr., NYC, 1978-81; asst. prof. medicine Sch. Medicine So. Ill. U., 1981-86; asst. prof. medicine Loyola U. Med. Ctr., Maywood, Ill., 1986-92; assoc. prof. medicine Loyola U. Med. Ctr.-Stritch Sch. Medicine, Maywood, Ill., 1992-96; prof. medicine and pathology Loyola U. Med. Ctr., Maywood, Ill., 1996—, dir. Cardinal Bernardin Cancer Ctr., 2003—, dir. divsn. hematology and oncology, 2003—, assoc. chair dept. medicine, 2009—. Chair transplant subcom. Ill. State Med. Adv. Com., 1999—2004. Mem. Internat. Soc. Exptl. Hematology, Internat. Soc. Hematotherapy and Graft Engrs., SW Oncology Group (co-chair blood and marrow transplant com., 1996-), Am. Soc. Clin. Oncology, Am. Soc. Hematology. Office: Loyola Univ Med Ctr 2160 S 1st Ave Maywood IL 60153-3304 Office Phone: 708-327-3148. Business E-Mail: pstiff@lumc.edu.

STILL, CHARLES NEAL, retired neurologist, medical educator, consultant; b. Richmond, Va., Apr. 15, 1929; s. Charles Wright and Ruth (Kemp) S.; m. Dorothy Lee Varn, Dec. 27, 1958; children: Charles Herbert, Carl Nelson, Sara Alice. BS in Chemistry, Clemson U., 1949; MS in Biochemistry, Purdue U., 1951; MD, Med. U. SC, 1959; MA in Religion, Luth. Theol. So. Sem., Columbia, SC, 2007. Diplomate Am. Bd. Psychiatry and Neurology. Instr. chemistry Clemson (S.C.) U., 1951-52, US Mil. Acad., West Point, NY, 1953—55; rotating intern U. Chgo. Clinics, 1959-60; neurology fellow Sch. Medicine Johns Hopkins U., Balt., 1960-63; resident in neurology Johns Hopkins-Balt. City Hosp., 1960-63; NIH rsch. fellow Harvard U.-McLean Hosp., Belmont, Mass., 1963-65; chief neurology svcs. William S. Hall. Psychiat. Inst., Columbia, S.C., 1965-81, assoc. dir. gen. psychiatry and neurology, 1989-92; dir. C. M. Tucker Human Resources Ctr., Columbia, 1981-88; clin. prof. neuropsychiatry USC Sch. Medicine, Columbia, S.C., 1981-88, prof. neuropsychiatry, 1989—2004, clin. prof. neuropsychiatry and behavioral sci. Sch. Medicine, 2004; ret., 2004. Assoc. clin. prof. neurology Med. U. S.C., Charleston, 1973-92; assoc. prof. neuropsychiatry U. S.C. Sch. Medicine, Columbia, 1976-78, prof. neuropsychiatry, 1978-81, 88-2004, prof. neuropsychiatry emeritus, 2004-. Author: (with others) Handbook of Clinical Neurology, 1976, Neurologic Clinics, 1984, Movement Disorders, 1986; editor The Recorder Columbia Med. Soc., 1991-2003, editor emeritus, 2003—; mem. editl. bd. Jour. S.C. Med. Assn., 1980-2006, Jour. Applied Gerontology, 1983-88; contbr. articles to profl. jours. Chmn. grants rev. bd. S.C. Dept. Mental Health, Columbia, 1973-78; mem. exec. bd. Alzheimer's Assn. Columbia, 1985-93, pres. Mid-State chpt. Alzheimer's Assn., 1991-92; med. dir. Alzheimer's Disease Registry, Columbia, 1989-92, Alzheimer's Daycare Ctr., Columbia, 1989-92; mem. Gov.'s Adv. Coun. to Alzheimer's Disease and Related Disorders Resource Coordination Ctr., 1995-99. 1st lt. U.S. Army, 1952-55. Fellow: Am. Geriatrics Soc. (emeritus), Am. Acad. Neurology (emeritus), Am. Inst. Chemists (life), Gerontol. Soc. Am. (emeritus); mem.: AMA (life), Am. Men & Women Sci., John Hopkins Med. & Surg. Assn., Am. Chem. Soc. (emeritus). Baptist. Avocations: writing, photography. Home: 2 Culpepper Cir Columbia SC 29209-2234 Personal E-mail: cndstill@aol.com.

STILLINGS, DENNIS OTTO, retired non profit executive consultant; b. Valley City, ND, Oct. 30, 1942; s. Harlow Cecil and Ruth Alice (Wolff) S. BA, U. Minn., 1965. Tchr. Henry (S.D.) Pub. Schs., 1965-66, Darby (Mont.) Pub. Schs., 1966-68; tech. rsch. libr., then mgr. hist. dept. Medtronic, Inc., Mpls., 1968-79; instr. humanities U. Minn., Mpls., 1970-72; founding dir., then curator Bakken Libr., Mpls., 1976-80; ind. antiquarian hist. cons. Mpls., 1979-81; sole proprietor Archaeus Project, Kamuela, Hawaii, 1981—2006; exec. dir. Five Mountain Med. Cmty., 1996-97, also bd. dirs., 1996—2006; ret., 2006. Cons. Ctr. for Sci. Anomalies Rsch., Ann Arbor, Mich., 1993—97; bd. mem. Kohala Ctr., 2001—06; bd. dirs. Dan Carlson Enterprises, Mpls., Barnes County Hist. Soc. Columnist Med. Progress Through Technology, 1974-76; columnist Med. Instrumentation, 1973-76, Valley City Tennis Record, 2008-, guest editor, 1975; editor: Cyberphysiology: The Science of Self-Regulation, 1988, Cyberbiological Studies of the Imaginal Component in the UFO Contact Experience, 1989, The Theology of Electricity: On the Encounter and Explanation of Theology and Science in the 17th and 18th Centuries, 1990, Project 2010: On the Current Crisis in Health and Its Implications of the Hospital for the Future, 1992; founding editor: (jours.) Artifex, 1981-93, Archaeus, 1982-84, Healing Island. Fellow Am. Inst. Stress; mem. Soc. Sci. Exploration. Avocations: jungian psychology, golf, fishing, travel. Home: 116 5th Ave SW Valley City ND 58072 Personal E-mail: stillings@gmail.com.

STILLMAN, BRUCE, molecular biologist; b. Melbourne, Australia, Oct. 16, 1953; came to US, 1979; s. Graham and Jessie (England) S.; m. Grace Begley, Mar. 21, 1981; children: Keith, Jessica. BSc with honors, U. Sydney, 1975; PhD, Australian Nat. U., 1979. Staff investigator Cold Spring Harbor Lab., NY, 1981-83, sr. staff investigator, 1984-85, sr. scientist, 1985-90, asst. dir., 1990-93, dir. cancer ctr., 1992—, dir., 1994—2003, pres., CEO, 2003—. Former chair, exptl. virology study section NIH; mem. med. adv. bd. Howard Hughes Med. Inst.; bd. dirs. AMDeC; past co-chair bd. scientific councilors Nat. Cancer Inst.; past vice-chair Nat. Cancer Policy Bd.; bd. mem. life sciences Nat. Rsch. Council. Contbr. scientific papers to profl. publs. Apptd. to Order of Australia, 1999; Rita Allen Found. scholar, 1981-85; Cancer Rsch. fellow Damon Runyon-Walter Winchell, 1979-80; Julian Wells medal (Australia), 1994, Am. Cancer Soc. Basic Sci. award, Soc. Surgical Oncology, 2006, Curtin medal, Australian Nat. U., 2007; co-recipient Alfred P. Sloan, Jr. GM Cancer Rsch. Found., 2004, Louisa Gross Horwitz prize, Columbia U., 2010; appointed Officer of the Order of Australia, 1999. Fellow Royal Soc. London, Am. Acad. Arts and Scis.; mem. NAS, AAAS, Am. Soc. Microbiology, Am. Soc. Biochem. and Molecular Biology, Am. Assn. Cancer Rsch., NY Biotechnology Assn. (bd. dirs.). Office: Cold Spring Harbor Lab PO Box 100 One Bungtown Rd Cold Spring Harbor NY 11724-0100 Office Phone: 516-367-8383. Office Fax: 516-367-8879. *

STILLMAN, MICHAEL ALLEN, dermatologist; b. NYC, Apr. 12, 1943; s. Aaron and Anne (Turansky) S.; m. Susan Fuchs, July 8, 1973; children: Julie, Jeremy. BA, Clark U., 1963; MD, SUNY, 1967. Diplomate Am. Acad. Dermatology. Med. intern Maimonides Hosp., Bklyn., 1967—68; dermatology resident NYU Med. Ctr. and Bellevue Hosp., NYC, 1970—73; pvt. practice Mt. Kisco, NY, 1973—. Cons. dermatology U.S. Mil. Acad., West Point, N.Y., 1973-75 Contbr. essays and articles to profl. jours. and newspapers Bd. trustees South Salem (NY) Libr., 1990-98; boys varsity tennis coach John Jay H.S., Katonah, NY, 1996. Capt. USAF, 1968-70, Vietnam Decorated Combat Inf. badge Fellow Am. Soc. Dermatol. Surgeons, Am. Acad. Dermatology; mem. N.Y. State Med. Soc., Noah Worcester Dermatology Soc Avocations: tennis, jogging, writing. Home: 33 Mead St Waccabuc NY 10597-1107 Office: Mt Kisco Med Group 111 Bedford Rd Katonah NY 10536 Office Phone: 914-232-3135. Personal E-mail: stillie39@aol.com.

STILLWAGON, GARY BOULDIN, radiation oncologist; b. Memphis, Dec. 30, 1951; s. Jack Wright and Ida Jean (Bouldin) S. BS in Physics, Ga. Inst. Tech., 1974, MS in Nuclear Engring., 1975, PhD, 1978; MD, U. Tenn., 1983. Diplomate Nat. Bd. Med. Examiners, Am. Bd. Radiology in Radiation Oncology; cert. FLEX, 1983. Med. physicist Meth. Hosp., Memphis, 1974; rsch. asst. Ga. Inst. Tech., Atlanta, 1975-78; radiation safety officer, physicist VA Med. Ctr., Memphis, 1978-80, cons. radiation safety, 1980-83; fellow in radiation oncology Johns Hopkins U. and Hosp., Balt., 1983-87; asst. prof. oncology and radiology Johns Hopkins U. Sch. Medicine, Balt., 1987—; pres. house staff John Hopkins Hosp., 1986—87. Vis. rschr. radiobiology lab. U. Utah, 1978; com. mem., site visitor, radiation therapy oncology group, coop. group Nat. Cancer Inst., 1989—; cons. in field. Contbr. articles to profl. jours. CEO & founder charity Struggling Kids Inc., Boy Scouts Am., Bapt. Ch. Dept. of Energy fellow, 1976-78, Clin. fellow Am. Cancer Soc., 1986-87. Fellow Am. Coll. Radiology, mem. Health Physics Soc., Am. Assn. Physicists in Medicine, Am. Soc. Therapeutic Radiology and Oncology, Am. Soc. Clin. Oncology, Sigma Xi. Republican. Home: 655 River Chase Rdg NW Atlanta GA 30328 3568 Office: 320 Parkway NE Atlanta GA 30312

STIMMEL, BARRY, cardiologist, internist, dean, educator, b. Bklyn., Oct. 8, 1939; s. Abraham and Mabel (Bovit) S.; m. Barbara Barovick, June 6, 1970; children: Alexander, Matthew. BS, Bklyn. Coll., 1960; MD, SUNY, Bklyn., 1964. Diplomate: Nat. Bd. Med. Examiners, Am. Bd. Internal Medicine. Resident Mt. Sinai Hosp., NYC, 1964—65; asst. dean admissions and student affairs Mt. Sinai Sch. Medicine, CUNY, 1970—71, assoc. dean, 1971—81, asst. prof. medicine, 1972—75, assoc. prof., 1975—83, prof. medicine and med. edn., 1984—, assoc. dean acad. affairs, 1975—81, assoc. attending physician, 1975—83, acting chmn. dept. med. edn., 1979—94, dean admissions, acad. affairs and student affairs, 1981—94, dean grad. med. edn., 1994—2008, attending physician, 1984—, Katherine and Clifford Goldsmith prof. medicine (cardiology), 1998—, dean emeritus, med. edn., 2008—, Ombudsman Sch., 2008—. Mem. com. planning, priorities and evaluation N.Y. Met. Regional Med. Program, 1971-73; adv. com. Nat. Ctr. Urban Problems CUNY, 1970-71; adv. com. methadone maintenance Office of Drug Abuse Svcs. State N.Y., 1976-79; sci. adv. bd. Nat. Coun. Drug Abuse, 1978-84, N.Y. State Bd. Profl. Med. Conduct, 1983-97; bd. dirs. Am. Soc. Addiction Medicine, N.Y. State Coun. on Grad. Med. Edn., Greater N.Y. Hosp. Assn. Task Force on Health Manpower. Author: Heroin Dependency: Medical Social and Economic Aspects, 1975, Cardiovascular Effects Mood Altering Drugs, 1979, Pain, Analgesia, Addiction, 1984, Ambulatory Care, 1983, The Facts about Drug Use, 1993, Drugs Abuse and Social Policy in America: The War That Must Be Won, 1996, Pain and Its Relief Without Addiction, 1997, Alcoholism, Drug Addiction and the Road to Recovery: Life on the Edge, 2002; editor Advances in Alcohol and Substance Abuse, 1980-91, Jour. Addictive Diseases, 1991—; assoc. editor Am. Jour. Drug and Alcohol Abuse, 1979-85; contbr. chpts. to books, articles to profl. jours. With M.C. USNR, 1965—67. Mem. AAUP, Am. Assn. Physicians Assts. (adv. bd. 1972-73), Am. Assn. Higher Edn., Soc. Study of Addiction to Alcohol and Other Drugs, Assn. Med. Edn. and Rsch. Substance Abuse, Inst. Study of Drug Addiction, Am., N.Y. heart assns., Am., N.Y. State socs. internal medicine, Soc. Internal Medicine County of N.Y. (dir.), Am. Coll. Cardiology, Greater N.Y. Coalition on Drug Abuse, NYS Coun. on Grad. Medical Edn., N.Y. Acad. Medicine, Nat. Coun. Alcoholism, Rsch. Soc. on Alcoholism, Am. Ednl. Research Assn., Am. Fedn. Clin. Rsch., Am. Soc. Addiction Medicine (hon. bd. mem. 2007-08). Office: Mt Sinai Sch Med 5 E 98th St Fl 3 New York NY 10029-6501 Office Phone: 212-241-6694. E-mail: barry.stimmel@mssm.edu.

STINE, ROBERT HOWARD, retired pediatrician, allergist; b. Nov. 1, 1929; s. Harry Raymond and Mabel Eva (Newhard) S.; m. Lois Elaine Kihlgren, Oct. 22, 1960; children: Robert E., Karen E. Burnham, Jonathan N. BS in Biology, Moravian Coll., 1952. Diplomate in pediatrics and in pediatric allergy Am. Bd. Pediatrics, Am. Bd. Allergy and Immunology. Intern St. Luke's Hosp., Bethlehem, Pa., 1960-61, resident in surgery, 1961-62; physician Jefferson Med. Coll., Phila., 1956-60; resident in pediatrics U. N.Y., Syracuse, 1962-64; resident in allergy Robert A. Cooke Inst. Allergy Roosevelt Hosp., NYC, 1964-65; clin. instr. pediatrics U. Ill., Chgo., 1965-71; mem. courtesy staff Proctor Community Hosp., Peoria, Ill., 1966-77, mem. active staff, 1977—, chmn. dept. medicine, 1988—89; pres. elect. med. staff, 1990-91; pres. med. staff, 1991-92; mem. teaching staff St. Francis Hosp., Peoria, 1969—2002; clin. instr. pediatrics Rush-Presbyn. St. Luke's Hosp., Chgo., 1971—2002; ret. Bd. mem. Great Oaks Camping and Urban Youth Ministries, 2008—. Vol. Heartland Cmty. Health Clinic, Peoria, Ill., 2002—04. Lt. (j.g.) USN, 1953—56. Fellow Am. Acad. Pediatrics (emeritus), Am. Acad. Allergy Asthma and Immunology, Am. Coll. Allergy and Asthma, Am. Assn. Cert. Allergists Am. Coll. Chest Physicians (emeritus); mem. Ill. Soc. Allergy and Clin. Immunology, Peoria Med. Soc. (pres.-elect 1993, pres. 1994), Christian Med. and Dental Soc. Home: 105 Hollands Grove Ln Washington IL 61571-9623

STINNER, BENNO, surgeon; b. Kirchen, Germany, Feb. 11, 1958; s. Alban and Margarete S.; m. Gabi Horn, Aug. 8, 1987; children: Maria Rita, Heiner. Dr.med., Johannes-Gutenberg U., Mainz, Germany, 1985. Rschr. Inst. Physiology, Gottingen U., Germany, 1985-87; resident Marburg U., Germany, 1987-93, staff mem. dept. theoretical surgery, 1988—, cons. surgeon, 1993-98, substitute head dept., 1998-2000, prof. surgery; head dept. visceral-thoracic-vascular surgery Elbe Klinikum Stade, 2000—, prof. surgery, 2002—; med. hosp. dir., 2008. Cons. in field. Co-author: Lancet, 1994, Langenbecks Archiv Surgery, 1998. Fin. grantee Deutsche Forschungsgemeinschaft, Bonn, Germany, 1997, 99. Mem. Deutsche Gesellschaft Chirurgie, Internat. Soc. Colon and Rectal Surgeon, Working Group Surg. Oncology. Home: Bremervoerderstr 111 D-21682 Stade Germany Office: Dept Visceral-Thoracic-Vasc Bremervoerderstr 111 D-21682 Stade Germany Home Phone: 0494141 660700; Office Phone: 0494141 971200. Business E-Mail: benno.stinner@elbekliniken.de.

STISKAL, JOSEPH ALEXANDER, neonatologist; b. Elizabeth, NJ, June 13, 1962; s. Joseph and Matilda Stiskal; m. Helen D. Stiskal, June 18, 1988; 1 child, Alexander. BA, U. Pa., 1984; MD, Rutgers U., 1988. Cert. bd. cert. pediat., neonatology. Resident Georgetown U., Wash., 1988—91; fellow U. Toronto, Canada, 1991—94; neonatologist Main Line Neonatology, Bryn Mawr, Pa., 1994—99, Mid-Atlantic Neonatology, Morristown, NJ, 1999—. Reviewer articles to profl. jours., 1999—2003. Contbr. articles various profl. jours. Fellow: Am. Acad. Pediat. Democrat. Presbyterian. Achievements include publications and lectures on effects of maternal antidepressants on newborn babies. Avocation: long distance running. Home: 17 Harwich Rd Morristown NJ 07960 Office: Morristown Meml Hosp NICU 100 Madison Ave Morristown NJ 07962 Home Phone: 973-656-0313; Office Phone: 973-971-5488.

STITTICH, ELEANOR MARYANN, retired nursing educator; b. Blawnox, Pa. d. Joseph John and Mary T. Stittich. BS in Nursing Ed., U. Pitts., 1951, M.Litt., 1954; postgrad., Johns Hopkins U., 1958-60, Humphrey's Sch. Law, Fresno, Calif., 1973-74. Staff nurse Sinai Hosp., Balt., 1947, U. Hosps., Cleve., 1947-48; staff nurse, clin. instr. St. Francis Med. Ctr., Pitts., 1948-51, med.-surg. instr., 1951-56; lectr. fundamentals, asst. in charge fundamentals U. Mich. Sch. Nursing, Ann Arbor, 1956-57; assoc. dir. nursing edn. Sinai Hosp. Sch. Nursing, Balt., 1957-64; prof. dept. nursing Calif. State U., Fresno, 1964—92; trustee NSM, 1986—94; ret., 1992; guest prof. emeritus. Western region cons. Neuman Systems Model, 1986—; prof. emerita, Calif. Nurses Assn., 1993; trustee, exec. com., 1988-94; rschr. program for RN, Calif. State U., Fresno, 1982, programs for BSN degree students, 1988, mem. steering com. Ctrl. Calif. Ctr. for Excellence in Nursing, 2006-. Author: (with others) Neuman Systems Model, 1989, 95. Educator program planning Alpha Tau Delta, 1975, mem. Cen. Valley chpt. Am. Heart Assn., Fresno, 1978-87, chairperson, 1982-85; mem., chairperson Cen. Valley Cancer Soc., Fresno, 1980-86; chairperson, vol. hospice com. St. Agnes Med. Ctr., Fresno, 1978-80, task force for pastoral care, hospice com., 1978-79; mem. exec. com. regional med. program UCLA, 1977-82. Scholar Sinai Hosp. Sch. Nursing, Balt., 1947; recipient Cert. of Merit, Am. Heart Assn., 1986, Meritorious Performance & Profl. Promise award, 1987, 90, Nurse of Yr. award Calif. Nurses Assn., 1991; named to Calif. State U. Sch. Edn. Wall of Fame, Fresno, 1999; named to Nursing Hall of Fame, 2005. Mem. AACN (bd. dirs. 1979-90, pres. 1982-83, corr. sec. 1984-86), Sigma Theta Tau (faculty advisor, bd. dirs., pres.-elect Mu Nu chpt. 1991-92, pres. 1992-94, parliamentarian 1994-96), Delta Kappa Gamma (Eta Tau chpt., Chi state 1991-95, chair legis. com. 1992-93). Roman Catholic. Avocations: swimming, golf, painting, gardening.

STIVER, JAMES FREDERICK, retired pharmacist, health physicist, administrator, scientist; b. Elkhart, Ind., Jan. 27, 1943; s. Melvin Hugh and Pauline Anna (Schrock) S.; m. Joan Louise Trindle, Aug. 14, 1965; children: Gregory James, Richard Frederick, Kristin Louise, Elizabeth Ann. BS in Pharmacy and Pharm. Scis., Purdue U., 1966, MS, 1968, PhD, 1970. Lic. pharmacist, Ind., N.D. From asst. prof. to assoc. prof., radiol. safety officer ND State U., Fargo, 1969—76; radiation safety officer KMS Fusion Inc., Ann Arbor, Mich., 1976—80; mgr., pharmacist Kroger Sav-On Pharmacy Co., Elkhart, Ind., 1980—81; pharmacist Elkhart Gen. Hosp., 1981; environ. regulatory affairs adminstr. Upjohn Co., Kalamazoo, 1981—88, patent liaison scientist, 1988—92, sr. patent liaison scientist, 1992—94; pharmacist, asst. mgr. Judd Drugs, Elkhart, 1994—95; pharmacist Meijer Pharmacy, Goshen, Ind., 1995—99; pharmacist, asst. mgr. Wal-Mart Pharmacy, Elkhart, 1999—2000, mgr., 2000, K-Mart Pharmacy, Elkhart, 2000—02, Plymouth, Ind., 2002—04, K-Mart North, 2004—08, pharmacist, 2004—08; ret., 2008. Cons., lectr. Contbr. articles, abstracts to publs. Named to Hon. Fellow Am. Inst. Chemists; mem. Am. Pharm. Assn., Am. Chem. Soc., Health Physics Soc., Internat. Radiation Protection Assn., Ind. Pharmacists Assn., N.D. Pharm. Assn., Order Ky. Cols., Kappa Psi, Rho Chi, Phi Lambda Upsilon, Sigma Xi. Home: 505 Skyview Dr Middlebury IN 46540-9427

STJERNSWARD, JAN ERIC EYVIND, oncologist; b. Copenhagen, June 2, 1936; s. Carl Adam Nolcken Stjernsward and Anne Marie Monrad-Aas; m. Gunilla Dinkelspiel, 1960; m. Jayanthi Ramanathan, 1985; children: Birremie, Ladde, Lykke, Sigrid, Carl Fredrik, Jan Carl. BS, Lidingo Laroverk, Sweden, 1956; MD, Karolinska Inst., Stockholm, 1962, PhD in Tumorbiology, 1967. Cert. specialist in radiotherapy, oncology Karolinska Inst., 1972. Rsch. fellow, dept. tumorbiology Karolinska Inst., Stockholm, 1960—72; fellowship Elenore Roosevelt, Am. Cancer Soc. & UIGC, Geneva, 1966—67; physician Kenyatta Nat. Hosp., Nairobi, Kenya, 1966—67, Radiumhemmet, Karolinska Hosp., Stockholm, 1967—72; prof. assoc. Ctr. Hosp. U. Vaudouis; clin. head Ludwig Inst. Cancer Rsch., Lausanne, Switzerland, 1973—78; dir. Bern Br., 1978—80; prof. radiotherapy-oncology Stellanbosch U., South Africa, 1976; sabbatical Wis. Cancer Ctr., Madison, 1977—78, Finsen Inst., Copenhagen, 1977—78; chief, cancer WHO, Geneva, 1980—96; bd. mem. Internat. Assn. Hospice & Palliative Care, 1997—2002; advisor, cons. WHO and Ministries of Health, 1999—; exec. bd. mem. WHOCC Pub. Health Palliative Care Programmes, Barcelona, 2008—. Internat. dir. WHOCC Palliative Care, Oxford, 1977—2003; med. dir. Global Cancer Concern, London, 1997—2002; steering com. mem. Diana Palliative Care Initiative, Diana Princess of Wales Meml. Fund, London, 2000—05; advisor Palliative Care Pub. Health, Open Soc. Inst., NYC, 2002—08. Contbr. scientific papers including cancer control, palliative care, pain control. Recipient Sir Dorabji Tata award, India, Homenot Internat. prize, Catalonia, Am. Acad. Hospice and Palliative Medicine award, USA Sertumer prize, Germany. Fellow: Royal Soc. Physicians (Edinburgh) (hon.); mem.: WHO Med. Soc. (pres.), WHO Staff Assn. (former pres.), Indian Assn. Palliative Care, European Assn. Palliative Care (founding mem., 1st Internat. prize), Royal Physiographic Soc. (Lund, Scania). Office: WHO Collaborating Ctr Pub Health Inst Catala d'Oncologia Avda Granvi Barcelona 08907 Spain Home: Borringekloster 233 91 Svedala Sweden Office Phone: 46708488229. Personal E-mail: janstjernsward@hotmail.com. Business E-Mail: janstjernsward.whocc@iconcologia.net.

STOB, MARTIN, retired physiology educator; b. Chgo., Feb. 20, 1926; s. Cornelius and Theodora (Sluis) S BS, Purdue U., 1949, MS, 1951, PhD, 1953. Mem. faculty Purdue U., Lafayette, Ind., 1953—, assoc. prof. animal scis., 1958-63, prof., 1963-92; ret., 1992. Contbr. articles to profl. jours. Patentee prodn. of fermentation estrogen Served with USN, 1944-46; ETO, PTO Name Best Tchr. Sch. Agr., 1970, Best Counselor Sch. Agr., 1977, Best Counselor Purdue U., 1977 Fellow AAAS Episcopalian. Home: 6218 W Rd 75 N West Lafayette IN 47906

STOBO, JOHN DAVID, academic administrator, physician; b. Somerville, Mass., Sept. 1, 1941; BA, Dartmouth Coll., 1963; MD, SUNY, Buffalo, 1968. Intern Osler Med. Services, Johns Hopkins, Balt., 1968-69, asst. med. resident, 1969-70, chief med. resident, 1972-73; research assoc. NIH, Bethesda, 1970-72; asst. prof. Mayo Clinic and Research Found., Rochester, Minn., 1973-76; assoc. prof. Moffitt Hosp., San Francisco, 1976-82, prof., head section rheumatology, clin. immunology, 1982-85; William Osler prof. medicine, chmn. dept. medicine John Hopkins Hosp. and Univ., Balt., 1985-94, vice dean clin. sci., assoc. v.p. medicine, 1994—97; v.p. Johns Hopkins Health System, Balt., 1994—97; chmn., CEO Johns Hopkins Healthcare LLC, Balt.; pres. U. Tex. Med. Br., Galveston, 1997—. Mem. transp. and immunobiology adv. com. NIAID, 1976—81; vice chmn. rsch. com. Arthritis Found., 1982—84, chmn. rsch. com., 1984—86, sr. investigator, 1974—77; mem. bd. sci. counselors Nat. Cancer Inst., 1982; mem. sci. adv. bd. exec. com. Lupus Rsch. Inst.; mem. rsch. adv. bd. DuPont Co., 1987—94. Mem. editl. bd.: Jour. Immunology, 1981—86, Jour. Lab. and Clin. Investigation, 1977—82, Arthritis and Rheumatism, 1980—85, Jour. Reticuloendothelial Soc., 1982—84, Jour. Clin. Investigation, 1981—86, Jour. Clin. Immunology, 1982—87, Jour. Molecular and Cellular Immunology, 1984—86, Rheumatology Internat., 1984—86, Jour. Immunology, 1875—1987; contbr. numerous articles to profl. jours. Recipient Merck award, 1967, Maimonides Med. Soc. award, 1968. Fellow: ACP, Am. Clin. and Climatol. Assn.; mem.: AAAS, Assn. Profs. Medicine (sec.-treas. 1991—92, pres. 1994—95), Am. Soc. Clin. Investigation, Am. Fedn. Clin. Rsch., Assn. Am. Physicians, Am. Assn. Immunologists, Am. Rheumatism Assn. (sec., treas., 1st v.p. 1985—89), Am. Coll. Rheumatology (pres. 1989—90), Inst. Medicine, Md. Soc. Internal Medicine, Interurban Clin. Club, Balt. City Med. Soc., Alpha Omega Alpha. Office: U Texas Med Br Pres Office 301 University Blvd Galveston TX 77555-5302

STOCK, JEFFRY BENTON, molecular biology educator; b. LA, Dec. 27, 1946; s. Gene and Jane S.; m. Regina Hackenbeck. BA, Johns Hopkins U., 1967, PhD, 1975. Rsch. assoc. Johns Hopkins Univ., Balt., 1975-77; cystic fibrosis fellow Univ. Calif., Berkeley, 1977-79, rsch. assoc., 1979-82; assoc. mem., asst. prof. Princeton (N.J.) Univ., 1982-88, mem. molecular biophysiology, assoc. mem., assoc. prof., 1988-92, prof. molecular biology, 1992—. Lectr. Sigma Xi, 1979; vis. scholar Inst. Pasteur, 1995-96. Named Predoctoral fellow NIH, 1967-75; recipient fellowship Cystic Fibrosis, 1977-80, Wilson Coll. Faculty, 1986. Mem. AAAS, Am. Soc. for Biochemistry and Molecular Biology, Am. Soc. for Microbiology, Am. Chem. Soc., N.Y. Acad. Sci., Theabald Smith Soc. Office: Princeton Univ Dept Molecular Biology Princeton NJ 08544-0001

STOCK, MATT STEVEN, research scientist; b. Miami, Fla., Jan. 5, 1984; PhD student, U. Okla. Grad. rsch. asst. U. Okla., 2008—. Recipient Rsch. Award, U. Okla. Mem.: Nat. Strength and Conditioning Assn. Home: 3700 12th Ave SE Apt 514 Norman OK 73072 Business E-Mail: mattstock@ou.edu.

STOCK, RICHARD G., radiation oncologist, educator; MD Mt. Sinai Sch. of Medicine, 1988. Cert. Nat. Med. Bds., 1989, diplomate Am. Bd. Radiology, 1993, lic. NY, 1990, PA, 1992. Bd. mem. Am. Coll. of Radiology Testing, Am. Brachytherapy Soc., program dir., 1998; resident in radiation oncology Meml. Sloan-Kettering Cancer Ctr., 1989—91, chief resident in radiation oncology, 1991—92; intern Beth Israel Med. Ctr., 1988—89; asst. prof. sch. of medicine Pitts. U., 1992—93; asst. attendant dept. of radiation oncology Pitts. U, 1992—93; steering com. Queens Hosp., 1999; guest editor Spl. Brachytherapy Issue of Techniques in Urology, 2000; asst. prof. Mt. Sinai Sch. of Medicine, 1993—97, assoc. prof., 1997—, acting chmn. dept. of radiation oncology, 1998—2001, prof. radiation oncology, 2002—; clin. asst. attendant dept. of radiation oncology The Mt. Sinai

Hosp., 1993—97, clin. assoc. attendant dept. of radiation oncology, 1997—. Office: Mount Sinai Medical Center 1 Gustave L. Levy Place New York NY 10029 Office Phone: 212-241-6500.

STOCK, RICHARD JOHN, retired cardiologist; b. Newark, Feb. 19, 1923; s. Archie Frank and Marie (Lergenmiller) S.; m. Eleanor Marguerite Schwarz, Sept. 1, 1945; children: Hilary Ann, Alan Constable; m. Martha Rusk Sutphen, Nov. 27, 2007. BS, Yale U., 1944; MD, Columbia U., 1947. Diplomate Am. Bd. Internal Medicine. Intern Presbyn. Hosp., NYC, 1947-48, resident in internal medicine, 1948-49, trainee Nat. Heart Inst., 1949-50; asst. physician in cardiology Columbia U. Hosp., NYC, 1949-50, asst. physician in medicine, 1951-61, asst. attending physician, 1961-64, assoc. attending physician, 1981—, attending physician; vis. fellow Nat. Heart Inst. Coll. Physicians and Surgeons Columbia U., NYC, 1949-50, asst. in medicine, 1951-56, instr. medicine, 1956-61, assoc. in medicine, 1961-64, asst. clin. prof., 1964-71, assoc. clin. prof., 1971-81, clin. prof., 1981-97, clin. prof. emeritus, spl. lectr., 1997—. Clin. prof. emeritus, spl. lectr. Coll. Physicians and Surgeons Columbia U., N.Y.C., 1997—. Author: Columbia Presbyterian Therapeutic Talks, 1963, 2nd edit., 1964; contbr. articles to profl. jours. Bd. dirs. N.Y. Heart Assn., 1979-85, mem. dir.'s coun., 1985—. Recipient Conspicuous Svc. medal Columbia U. Alumni Fedn., 1976; 2 Richard J. Stock Professorships in dept. of medicine Columbia U., endowed, 1986. Fellow Am. Coll. Cardiology; mem. P & S Alumni Assn. (mem. admissions com. 1973-79, 81—, treas. 1973-81, mem. exec. com. 1973—, chmn. Alumni Day 1971-75, pres.-elect 1981-83, pres. 1983-85, chmn. capital campaign 1985—, Silver medal 1975, Gold medal 2004). Avocations: sculpture, music, skiing, tennis. Home: 155 E 72d St New York NY 10021-4371 Office: 755 Park Ave New York NY 10021-4255 E-mail: saggsodder@yahoo.com.

STOCKDALE, FRANK EDWARD, internist, educator; b. Long Beach, Calif., Mar. 15, 1936; s. Frank Parsons and Iza (McGuffin) Stockdale; m. Elizabeth Stanton, Sept. 8, 1978; children: Jonathan, Susan, Gregory. AB, Yale U., 1958; MD, PhD, U. Pa., 1963. Fellow dept. anatomy U. Pa. Sch. Medicine, 1958—63; intern dept. medicine U. Hosps., Cleve., Case Western Res. U., 1963—64; staff assoc. biochemistry lab. sect. intermediary metabolism Nat. Inst. Arthritis and Metabolic Diseases, 1964—66; sr. resident dept. medicine Stanford U. Sch. Medicine, 1966—67; instr. dept. medicine, div. oncology Std. U. Sch. Medicine, 1967—68, asst. prof. medicine dept. medicine, div. oncology, 1968—74, prof., 1982—, asst. prof. biology dept. biol. scis., 1971—74, assoc. prof. medicine and biol. scis., 1974—81. Contbr. articles to profl. jours. Lt. comdr. USPHS, 1964—66. Recipient Career Devel. award, USPHS, 1967—72; Guggenheim Found. fellowship, NYC, 1983, grantee NIH. Mem.: Western Assn. Physicians, Soc. Devel. Biology Northern Calif. Oncology Group, Western Soc. Clin. Investigation, Am. Soc. Clin. Oncology, Am. Soc. Clin. Investigation, Am. Soc. Cell Biology, Am. Soc. Clin. Rsch., Am. Assn. Cancer Rsch., Internat. Soc. Devel. Biology. Office: Stanford Sch Medicine 875 Blake Wilbor Dr Stanford CA 94305-5826

STOCKER, KEVIN DEAN, obstetrician, gynecologist; MD, U. Va., 1989. Intern Univ. Pitts. Med. Ctr., 1990; resident Magee Women's Hosp., 1993; physician The Washington Hosp. Group mem. Ob-Gyn. Assocs. Named one of the Top Doctors, Pitts. Mag., 2011. Fellow: Am. Congress of Obstetricians and Gynecologists. Office: Washington Hospital 2001 Waterdam Plz Washington PA 15301 Office Phone: 742-225-3640.

STOCKER, MICHAEL AUBREY, municipal healthcare company executive; b. Mpls., 1942; m. Louise Stocker; 1 child, Luke. Grad., U. Notre Dame; MD, Med. Coll. Wis., 1968; MPH, U. Mich., 1987. Intern Milw. County Gen. Hosp.; resident Mayo Clinic, U. Calif., San Joaquin Gen. Hosp.; assoc. chmn. dept. family practice Cook County Hosp., Chgo., 1975—80; med. dir. ANCHOR Rush Presbyn. St. Luke's Med Ctr., Chgo., 1980—85; exec. v.p., gen. mgr. NY area market US Healthcare, 1985—92; pres. CIGNA Health Plans, 1993—94; pres., CEO Empire Blue Cross and Blue Shield (subs. WellChoice Inc.), NYC, 1994—2005; CEO WellChoice Inc., NYC, 2002—05, pres., 2003—05; pres., CEO ea. region WellPoint Inc., Indpls., 2005—07; chmn. NYC Health and Hospitals Corp., 2008—. Bd. dirs. Nat. Quality Forum, Am. Assn. Health Plans, Coun. Affordable Quality Healthcare, Sec.'s Coun. for Pub. Health Preparedness, HHS, 2002—, Coventry Health Care, 2009—. Bd. dirs. Arthur Ashe Inst. Urban Health, United Hosp. Fund. Served US Army. Office: NYC Health and Hosp Corp 125 Worth St New York NY 10013 *

STOCKMAN, JAMES ANTHONY, III, medical association administrator, pediatrician; b. Phila., 1943; MD, Jefferson Med. Coll., 1969. Diplomate Am. Bd. Pediat. Intern Childrens Hosp., Phila., 1969—70, resident, 1970—71, chief resident in pediat., instr. dept. pediat., 1971—72, vis. fellow divsn. oncology, 1972; fellow in pediatric hematology/oncology SUNY, Syracuse, 1972—74, asst. prof. pediat., 1974—77, assoc. prof., vice-chmn. pediat., 1977—81, prof. pediat., 1981—84; prof., chair dept. pediat. Northwestern Med. Sch., Chgo., 1984—92; chair medicine, physician-in-chief and Women's Bd. Centennial chair in pediat. Children's Meml. Hosp., Chgo., 1984—92; chief pediat., assoc. dean hosp. academic affairs McGaw Med. Ctr., Chgo., 1984—92; pres., CEO American Bd. Pediat., 1992—; clin. prof. pediat. Duke U. Sch. Medicine, Durham, NC, U. NC, Chapel Hill. Author: Clinical Facts and Curios; editor: Year Book of Pediatrics, The Child's Doctor; editor-in-chief: Current Problems in Pediatrics, Focus and Opinion: Pediatrics; contbr. articles to profl. jours., chapters to books. Office: Office of the Pres Am Bd Pediatrics 111 Silver Cedar Ct Chapel Hill NC 27514-1512 Office Phone: 919-929-0461. *

STOCKWELL, DAVID CHRISTOPHER, medical association administrator; b. Tulsa, Okla., Sept. 26, 1967; MD, U. Okla. Sch. Medicine, 1999; MBA, George Washington U., 2009. Med. dir., patient safety Children's Nat. Med. Ctr., 2007—11, med. dir., pediatric ICU, 2008—11, exec. dir., improvement sci., 2009—. Named one of Leading Physicians of World, Internat. Assn. Pediatricians, Best Dr. in America, Americas Top Pediatrician, Consumers Rsch. Coun. America; Dr. David Lewis Meml. Outstanding fellow, Children's Nat. Med. Ctr. Fellow: Am. Acad. Pediat.; mem.: Am. Coll. Physician Execs., Soc. Critical Care Medicine, Beta Gamma Sigma. Avocations: fly fishing, baseball, computers. Home: 111 Mich Ave NW Ste M4800 Washington DC 20010 Business E-Mail: dstockwe@cnmc.org.

STOCKWELL, JANA ALHART, pediatrician; b. Houston, Mar. 28, 1959; BS, Tex. A&M U., 1980; MD, U. Tex. Southwestern Med. Sch., 1986. Pediat. intensivist Children's Healthcare Atlanta, 1996—, dir. children's sedation svcs., 2003—10; chief, divsn. pediat. critical care medicine Emory U. Sch. Medicine, 2010—, assoc. prof. pediat. Device resolution panel Food & Drug Adminstrn., 2011—. Fellow: Am. Acad. Pediat., Am. Coll. Critical Care Medicine; mem.: Soc. Pediat. Sedation (bd. dirs. 2008—), Soc. Critical Care Medicine. Office: NE Critical Care Medicine 1405 Clifton Rd Atlanta GA 30322 Office Fax: 404-785-6233. Business E-Mail: jana.stockwell@choa.org.

STODDARD, PATRICIA FLORENCE COULTER, retired psychologist; b. Detroit, Oct. 13, 1923; d. Glenn Monroe and Doris Carlyle (McDonald) Coulter; m. Charles Hatch Stoddard, June 30, 1956 (div. 1991); children: Glenn, Jeffrey. BA, U. Mich., 1945; MA, George Washington U., 1953; MA in Gerontology, Coll. of Scholastica, Duluth, Minn., 1987. Asst. to dir. personnel Dewey & Almy Chem. Co., Cambridge, Mass., 1946-48; asst. dir. mgmt. tng. program Radcliffe Coll., Cambridge, 1948-49; tng. rep. Woodward Lothrop, Washington, 1949; personnel assoc. Hot Shoppes, Inc., Washington, 1950-53; placement officer George Washington U., Washington, 1953-58; placement asst. U. Minn., Duluth, 1967; psychiat. social worker Northwood Children's Home, Duluth, 1968-80; coord. adult day svcs. Benedictine Health Ctr., Duluth, 1980-98; ret. Adv. com. on aging Regional Area Redevel. Agy., Duluth, 1992—; apptd. State Commn. on Aging, Minn., 1997. Author: Wolf Springs 100 Years: A Century of Life on One Piece of Land, 1991; contbr. articles to profl. jours. Pres. Maple Crest Village Homeowners Assn., Duluth, 1997; vol. recruiter Am. Reads Project. Mem. LWV, Area Aging Network, Algonquin Club. Avocations: tennis, elderhostels, reading, aerobics. Home: Apt 255 70 St Marie St Duluth MN 55803

STOFF, ALEXANDER, plastic surgeon, researcher; s. Fatemeh and Rainer Stoff; m. Mariam Alexandra Khalili-Araghi, Oct. 1, 2002; children: Maximilian Alexander, Julian Alexander. MD, Friedrich-Wilhelm Gymnasium, Germany, 1994. Diplomate Ärztekammer Nordrhein, 2002. Rschr. Gene Therapy Ctr., Birmingham, Ala., 2004—06; chief resident Dreifaltigkeits-Hosp., Wesseling, Germany, 2003—. Cons. Ethicon Endo Surgery, Hamburg, Germany, 2006—. Contbr. scientific papers. Achievements include development of an adenoviral vector overexpressing an scar reducing molecule. Home: Marienburger Strasse 64 Cologne 50968 Germany Home Phone: 49 221 7608128; Office Phone: 49 2236 77894. Office Fax: 49 2236 77380. Personal E-mail: dr.alexander.stoff@t-online.de. Business E-Mail: astoff@krankenhaus-wesseling.de.

STOFMAN, GUY M., plastic surgeon, otolaryngologist; BS, Villanova U., 1979; MD, Jefferson Med. Coll. Thomas Jefferson U., 1984. Diplomate Am. Bd. of Plastic Surgery, Am. Bd. of Otolaryngology. Intern gen. surgery Thomas Jefferson Univ. Hosp., 1985, resident gen. surgery, 1986, resident otolaryngology, 1989; fellow plastic surgery Univ. of Pitts. Med. Ctr. Mercy, 1991; pres. Pa. State Plastic Surgery Soc., 2004—05; with Univ. of Pitts. Med. Ctr. Fellow: ACS; mem.: Am. Acad. of Otolaryngology - Head and Neck Surgery, Am. Soc. of Aesthetic Plastic Surgery, Am. Soc. of Plastic Surgeons. Office: Mercy Hospital of Pittsburgh 13050 Locust St Ste G103 Pittsburgh PA 15219 Office Phone: 412-232-5616.

STOIBER, SUSANNE A., health science association administrator; m. Carlton R. Stoiber. BA, MPA, U. Colo.; MSc, London Sch. Econs. Principal analyst for health care fin. programs Congressional Budget Office; adminstr. clin. rsch. hosp. Nat. Inst. Health; dir. divsn. soc. and econ. studies Nat. Rsch. Coun., 1990-94; dep. asst. sec. for health, planning and evaluation US Dept. HHS, 1979, 1995—96, dep. asst. sec. for health, health promotion and disease prevention, 1996, dep. asst. sec. for planning and evaluation, program sys., 1997—98; exec. officer Inst. Medicine, 1998—2007; prin. Stoiber Health Policy, LLC, Washington. Spkr. in field. Contbr. several articles to profl. jours. Recipient Secretary's Disting. Svc. award, 1979, 1981, 1997, Dirs. award, NIH, 1985, Presdl. Rank Award for lifetime achievement in Senior Exec. Svc., 1998. Office Phone: 202-966-7793. E-mail: s.stoiber@earthlink.net.

STOICA, ADINA LILIANA, cardiologist; b. Creteni, Romania, Sept. 21, 1969; MD, U. Medicina si Farmacie Carol Davila, Bucuresti, 1996. Sr. cardiologist Inst. Urgenta Pentru Boli Cardiovasculare Prof. Dr. C.C. Iliescu, 2000—. Recipient Mitri Naaman's prize, Medicophonie, 2003. Mem.: Working Group on Peripheral Circulation European Soc. Cardiology, Heart Failure Assn. European Soc. Cardiology, European Soc. Cardiology, Heart Failure Working Group Romanian Soc. Cardiology, Romanian Soc. Cardiology (Poster prizes 2009, Excellence prize 2010). Avocations: movies, music, travel. Home: Sos Pantelimon Bucharest 021602 Romania Personal E-mail: adistoica1@yahoo.com.

STOKER, DAVID ALLEN, plastic surgeon; b. Miami, Fla., July 6, 1969; BA/BS in Biology and Polit. Sci. (grad. with honors), Stanford U., 1991; MD, U. Calif. Sch. Medicine, San Francisco, 1995. Diplomate Am. Bd. Plastic Surgery, lic. Calif. and NY. Intern, plastic surgery NYU Med. Ctr., 1995—96, resident, general surgery, 1996—99, resident, plastic surgery, Inst. Reconstructive Plastic Surgery, 1999—2000, chief resident, plastic surgery, Inst. Reconstructive Plastic Surgery, 2000—01; med. staff St. Johns Health Ctr., Santa Monica, Calif., 2001—, UCLA Med. Ctr., Calif., 2001—, Centinela Hosp. Med. Ctr., 2001—, Marina Outpatient Surgery Ctr., 2001—, Daniel Freeman Marina Hosp., 2001—; plastic surgeon in private practice Marina Plastic Surgery Associates, Marina Del Ray, Calif., 2001—; clin. asst. prof. surgery Keck Sch. Medicine, U. So. Calif., 2006—. Teaches course: Liposuction: Comprehensive and Integrated Am. Soc. Plastic Surgeons, 2006, Am. Soc. for Aesthetic Plastic Surgery, 2007; rsch. experience at various institutions, 1985—2006; presenter in field. Contbr. articles to profl. jours.; author: (textbook) Chpt. on Liposuction and Body Contouring; plastic surgery expert Dr. Phil, featured on Learning Channel and Discovery Health Channel. Recipient 1st Place, Plastic Surgery Educational Found., 1993, British Journal Surgery award, 1999; named one of Top Plastic Surgeons in the nation with spl. mention about experience in liposuction, tummy tucks and breast surgery, NY Times, NY Times Style Mag., 2005; Howard Hughes Med. Inst. Major Grant for Undergrad. Rsch., 1991. Fellow: Am. Coll. Surgeons; mem.: Am. Soc. for Anesthetic Plastic Surgery, Am. Soc. Plastic Surgeons, Alpha Omega. Achievements include being nationally recognized for research in power-assisted liposuctionand anatomy of the facial nerve as it relates to facelifts; pioneering research with power-assisted liposuction, the safest and most effective lipoplasty method available, contributed to a major advance in the field of body contouring. Office: 4644 Lincoln Blvd Ste 552 Marina Del Rey CA 90292 Office Phone: 310-827-2653. Office Fax: 310-823-1984.

STOKES, JOHN B., medical educator; m. Jacqueline Stokes. MD, Temple U., 1971. Diplomate Am. Bd. Internal Medicine. Asst. prof. medicine U. Iowa, Iowa City, 1978—82, assoc. prof. medicine, 1982—86, prof. medicine, 1986—. Cons. VA Med. Ctr., Iowa City, 1978—80, staff physician, 1991—; dir. divsn. nephrology U. Iowa, Iowa City, 1982—, assoc. chmn. for academic programs dept. internal medicine, 1994—2002, vice chmn. for rsch. dept internal medicine, 2002—04, sr. rsch. advisor to chmn. dept. internal medicine, 2004—. Contbr. articles to profl. jours. Recipient Alexander vonHumboldt prize, Alexander vonHumboldt Found., 1985—86; grantee, NIH, 1978—, Veterans Adminstrn., 1990—, NIH/NIDDK, 1997—. Fellow: ACP, Am. Heart Assn. (coun. for high blood pressure rsch. 1991); mem.: AAAS, Am. Soc. for Clin. Investigation, Ctrl. Soc. for Clin. Rsch. (chmn., kidney coun. 1987—88), Internat. Soc. Nephrology, Am. Heart Assn. (exec. com. 1984—89), Am. Soc. Nephrology (sec.-treas. 1997—2003, Pres. medal 2003), Am. Fedn. for Clin. Rsch. (councilor midwest sect. 1981—84), Assn. Subspecialty Prof., Assn. Am. Physicians, Mt. Desert Island Biol. Lab. (bd. trustees 1987—89), Am. Physiol. Soc., NY Acad. Sciences. Achievements include patents for copolyester/phenol-modified cumarone-indene blend compositions. Office: Univ Iowa 200 Hawkins Dr E300 GH Iowa City IA 52242-1009 Office Fax: 319-356-2999. Business E-Mail: john-stokes@uiowa.edu.

STOLAR, CHARLES J.H., pediatrician, surgeon, educator; BA cum laude, Washington U., St. Louis, 1970; MD, Georgetown U., 1974. Cert. Am. Bd. Surgery Gen. Surgery, 1982, Pediat. Surgery, 1986. Instr. biology Washington U., St. Louis, 1969—70; intern U. Ill. Hosp., Chgo., 1974—75, asst. resident, 1975—79, chief resident, 1979—80; pediat. surgery clin. fellow, rsch. assoc. Children's Hosp. Nat. Med. Ctr., George Washington U., Washington, 1976—77, 1980—82, instr. surgery, 1980—82, asst. attending Divsn. Pediat. Surgery, 1982—89; staff mem. Babies & Children's Hosp. of NY, NYC, 1982—; assoc. attending surgeon Divsn. Pediat. Surgery Morgan Stanley Children's Hosp. of NY-Presbyn., 1982—89, dir. Ctr. Extracorporeal Membrane Oxygenation, 1982—, surgeon-in-chief, 1982—, chief Divsn. Pediat. Surgery, 2000—, assoc. dir. Fellowship Training Program in pediat. surgery., co-dir. Ctr. for Prenatal Pediatrics, 2002—; asst. prof. divsn. pediat. surgery Columbia U. Coll. Physicians & Surgeons, 1982—89, assoc. prof., 1989—93, Rudolph N. Schullinger, MD, prof. surgery and pediats., 2000—. Disting. overseas lectr. Chilean Assn. Pediatric Surgery, 1995; William Kiesewetter meml. lectr. U. Pitts., Pittsburgh Children's Hosp., 1997; Arvin I. Philippart, invited lectr. Children's Hosp., Detroit; vis. prof., keynote spkr. Royal Coll.Surgeons of Thailand, 1998; vis. prof. Alder Hey Children's Hosp., Liverpool, England, 1999, U. Minn., 1999; cons. surgeon Wildlife Conservation Society, 1999—2002. Contbr. articles to profl. jours. Recipient Ray and Joan Kroc Award for Academic Surgery, U. Ill., 1980, Physician of Yr. Award, Pediat. Cancer Found., Scout of Yr. Award, Boy Scouts of Am., 2005; named Disting. Overseas Lecturer, Chilean Assn. of Pediat. Surgery, 1995; grantee NIH Training Grant Award, 1976—77. Mem.: AAAS, Am. Acad. Pediat., Am. Coll. Surgeons, Am. Heart Assn.-Cardiopulmonary Coun., Am. Pediat. Soc., Am. Pediat. Surgical Assn., Am. Soc. Artificial Internal Organs, Am. Soc. Clin. Oncology, Am. Soc. for Parenteral & Enteral Nutrition, Am. Surgical Assn., Assn. Academic Surgery, British Assn. Pediat. Surgeons, Extracorporeal Life Support Orgn., NY Acad. Scis., NY Soc. Pediat. Surgery, Societe Internat. De Chirugie, Soc. Pediat. Rsch., Soc. Univ. Surgeons. Office: Morgan Stanley Children's Hosp of NY-Presbyn Babies & Children's Hosp N Rm 212 3959 Broadway New York NY 10032 Office Phone: 212-305-2305. Office Fax: 212-305-5971. E-mail: cjs3@columbia.edu.

STOLL, JANET A., health science association administrator; Grad., Georgetown U., 1994. Acct. Chandler Products Corp., 1973—74; personnel adminstr. Velsicol Chemical Corp., 1975—81; dir., office fin. & adminstrn. Inst. of Medicine, 1981—. Office: Institute of Medicine 500 Fifth St NW Keck 845 Washington DC 20001 Office Phone: 202-334-2374.

STOLLAR, BERNARD DAVID, biochemist, educator; b. Saskatoon, Sask., Aug. 11, 1936; came to US, 1960. s. Percy and Rose (Direnfeld) S.; m. Carol A. Singer, Oct. 7, 1956; children: Lawrence, Michael, Suzanne. BA, U. Sask., Saskatoon, 1958, MD, 1959. Intern U. Sask. Hosp., 1959-60; postdoctoral fellow Brandeis U., Waltham, Mass., 1960-62; asst. prof. dept. pharmacology Tufts U. Schs. Medicine and Dental Medicine, Boston, 1964-67, asst. prof. dept. biochemistry, 1967-68, assoc. prof. biochemistry/pharmacology, 1968-74, prof., 1974—2005, prof. emeritus, 2005—, acting chmn. dept. biochemistry and pharmacology, 1984-86, chmn. dept. biochemistry, 1986-2001; interim dean Sackler Sch. Grad. Biomed Sci., Tufts U., 2002—04. Vis. prof. internat. course in immunology and immunochemistry Mexico City, 1971; sr. fellow Weizmann Inst. Sci., Rehovot, Israel, 1971-72; vis. prof. chemistry Wellesley Coll., Mass., 1976, U. Tromsö, Norway, 1981; Dozor vis. prof. Ben-Gurion U. Sch. Medicine, Beer Sheva, Israel, 1986; cons. USAF Office Sci. Rsch., 1966-69, Seragen, Inc., 1983-88, 1982-85, Gene-Trak, 1986-89, Alkermes, Inc., 1989-94, Catalytic Antibodies, Inc., 1993-98; 3d ann. alumni lectr. U. Sask. Coll. Medicine, 1989; mem. allergy/transplantation rsch. com. NIH/NIAID, 1990-94; mem. sci. vis. com. Okla. Med. Rsch. Found., 1996-98; mem. panel Israel Cancer Rsch. Found., 1996-2000. Contbr. over 200 articles to profl. jours., chpts. to books; exec. editl. bd. Analytical Biochemistry, 1988—; editl. bd. Jour. Immunology, 1981-85, Molecular Immunology, 1980-95, Arthritis and Rheumatism, 1986-89, Jour. Immunological Methods, 1988—. Mem. adult edn. com. Temple Reyim, Newton, Mass., v.p., 2001-04, 1st v.p. 2004-05, pres. 2005-07. Capt. USAF, 1962—64. Recipient (with Carol Stollar) 2d Century award Jewish Theol. Sem. and Temple Reyim, 1997; rsch. grantee NSF, NIH, 1964-2005; sr. fellow Weizmann Inst. Sci., 1971-72. Mem. Am. Assn. Immunologists. Office: Tufts Univ Sch Medicine Dept Biochemistry 136 Harrison Ave Boston MA 02111-1800 Home Phone: 617-965-0226; Office Phone: 617-636-2948. Business E-Mail: david.stollar@tufts.edu.

STOLLERMAN, GENE HOWARD, internist, educator; b. NYC, Dec. 6, 1920; s. Maurice William and Sarah Dorothy (Mezz) S.; m. Corynne Miller, Jan. 21, 1945 (dec. Mar. 1997); children: Lee Denise Stollerman Meyburg, Anne Barbara Stollerman DiZio, John Eliot; m. Vita Mark, Nov. 9, 1997. AB summa cum laude, Dartmouth Coll., 1941; MD, Columbia U., 1944. Diplomate Am. Bd. Internal Medicine. Clin. tng. Mt. Sinai Hosp., NYC, 1944-46, chief med. resident, 1948; Dazian research fellow microbiology NYU Med. Sch., 1949-50, mem. dept. medicine, 1951-55; med. dir. Irvington House for Cardiac Children, 1951-55; prin. investigator Sackett Found. Research in Rheumatic Diseases, 1955-64; asst. prof. medicine Northwestern U., 1955-57, assoc. prof., 1957-61, prof. medicine, 1961-65; prof., chmn. dept. medicine U. Tenn., 1965-81, Goodman prof., 1977-81; physician-in-chief City of Memphis Hosps., 1965-81; prof. medicine Boston U. Sch. Medicine, 1981-95, prof. pub. health, 1991-95, prof. medicine and pub. health emeritus, 1996—. Chief sect. gen. internal medicine Univ. Hosp., Boston U. Med. Ctr., 1983-86; Disting. physician VA Med. Ctr., Bedford, Mass., 1986-89; assoc. chief of staff Geriatrics and Extended Care, 1989-92; clin. dir. Bedford div. Geriatric Rsch., Ednl. and Clin. Ctr., 1989-92; dir. VA Health Svcs. Rsch. Field, 1990-93; chmn. research career program com. NIAMD-NIH, 1967-70; mem. commn. streptococcal and staphylococcal diseases U.S. Armed Forces Epidemiol. Bd., 1956-74; adv. bd. immunization practices Center for Disease Control, 1968-71; expert adv. panel cardiovascular disease WHO, 1966—; mem. Am. Bd. Internal Medicine, 1967-73, chmn. cert. exam. com., 1969-73, mem. exec. com., 1971-73; chmn. Panel on Bacterial Vaccines, FDA, 1973-80; mem. nat. adv. council Nat. Inst. Allergy and Infectious Diseases, NIH, 1978-82; mem. Dept. Health & Human Services nat. vaccine adv. com. Editor-in-chief Advances in Internal Medicine, 1968-93, Jour. Am. Geriatric Soc., 1984-88; co-editor Hosp. Practice, 1990—, editor, 1998—; contbr. chpts. to Braunwald's Textbook of Cardiology, Harrison's Textbook of Medicine, Cecil & Loeb Textbook of Medicine, others; contbr. articles to profl. jours. Served as capt. M.C., AUS, 1946-48. Cpt. Med. Corps. US Army, 1945—47. Recipient Bicentennial award in internal medicine Columbia U., 1967, Disting. Alumnus award Mt. Sinai Hosp., 1989, Thewlis award Am. Geriatric Soc., 1990, Mentor award Infectious Disease Soc. Am., 2004. Bruce medal medicine, Am Coll. Physicians 1985 Master ACP (bd. regents 1978, v.p. 1984, Bruce medal for preventive medicine 1985), Am. Coll. Rheumatology; mem. Am. Heart Assn. (mem. exec. com., pres. coun. on rheumatic fever and congenital disease 1965-67), Am. Fedn. Clin. Rsch., Am. Rheumatism Assn., Am. Soc. Clin. Investigation, Cen. Soc. Clin. Rsch. (v.p. 1973-74, pres. 1974-75), Assn. Profs. Medicine (pres. 1975-76), Am. Assn. Immunologists, Assn. Am. Physicians, Infectious Disease Soc. Am. (coun. 1968-70), Phi Beta Kappa, Alpha Omega Alpha. Personal E-mail: gstollerman2@comcast.net.

STOLLEY, PAUL DAVID, medical educator, researcher; b. Pawling, NY, June 17, 1937; s. Herman and Rosalie (Chertock) Stolley; m. Jo Ann Goldenberg, June 13, 1959; children: Jonathan, Dorie, Anna. BA, Lafayette Coll., 1957; MD, Cornell U., 1962; MPH, Johns Hopkins U., 1968; MA (hon.), U. Pa., 1976. Diplomate Am. Coll. Preventive Medicine, Am. Coll. Epidemiology. Intern U. Wis. Med. Ctr., 1962—63, resident in medicine, 1963—64; med. officer USPHS, Washington, 1964—67; asst. prof. Johns Hopkins Sch. Pub. Health, Balt., 1968—71, assoc. prof., 1971—76; Herbert C. Rorer prof. medicine U. Pa. Sch. Medicine, Phila., 1976—91; prof. dept. epidemiology U. Md. Sch. Medicine, Balt., 1991—2002; staff epidemiologist Public Citizen Health Rsch. Group, 2002—04. Co-author: Foundations of Epidemiology, 3d edit., 1995, Epidemiology: Investigating Disease, 1995 (Am. Med. Writers Assn. award, 1996); contbg. author: Case-Control Studies, 1982, mem. editl. bd.: New Eng. Jour. Medicine, 1989—93, Millbank Quar., Health and Soc., 1986—, assoc. editor: Clin. Pharmacology and Therapeutics, 1987—93; contbr. articles to med. jours. Charter mem. Physicians for Social Responsibility, 1961—. Lt. comdr. USPHS, 1964—67. Fellow: ACP; mem.: Johns Hopkins Soc. Scholars, Internat. Epidemiol. Assn. (treas. 1982—84), Am. Epidemiol. Soc. (pres. 1994—), Soc. Epidemiol. Rsch. (pres. 1982—84), Inst. Medicine of NAS, Am. Coll. Epidemiology (pres. 1987—89). Office Phone: 410-706-3610. Personal E-mail: pstolley@aol.com, pstolley@yahoo.com.

STOLL-KELLER, FRANÇOISE, biologist, educator; b. Strasbourg, Bas-Rhin, France, Oct. 15, 1951; d. Georges and Monique (Hollender) Stoll; m. Daniel Keller (div. oct. 1992); children: Nathalie, Pierre, Laetitia. MD, Sch. Medicine, Strasbourg, 1978. Asst. Sch. Medicine, Strasbourg, 1980-87; maitre de conf., assoc. prof. Praticien Hosp., Strasbourg, 1987-97, prof. Inst. Virologie, 1997—. Mem. Rotary. Office: Inst of Virologie 3 rue Koeberle 67000 Strasbourg France Office Phone: 33369551435. Business E-Mail: francoise.stoll@unistra.fr.

STOLOV, WALTER CHARLES, medicine physiatrist, educator; b. NYC, Jan. 6, 1928; s. Arthur and Rose F. (Gordon) S.; m. Anita Carvel Noodelman, Aug. 9, 1953; children: Nancy, Amy, Lynne. BS in Physics, CCNY, 1948; MA in Physics, U. Minn., 1951, MD, 1956. Diplomate Am. Bd. Phys. Med. and Rehab., Am. Bd. Electrodiagnostic Medicine. Physicist U.S. Naval Gun Factory, Nat. Bur. Stds., Washington, 1948-49; teaching and rsch. asst. U. Minn., Mpls., 1950-54; from instr. to assoc. prof. U. Wash., Seattle, 1960-70, prof., 1970-99, prof. emeritus, 1999—, also chmn., 1987-99, prof. emeritus, 1999—. Editl. bd. Archives Phys. Medicine and Rehab., 1967-78, Muscle and Nerve, 1983-89, 92-95; cons. Social Security Adminstrn., Seattle, 1975—; sec. Am. Bd. Electrodiagnostic Medicine, 1995—. Co-editor: Handbook of Severe Disability, 1981; contbr. articles to profl. jours. Surgeon USPHS, 1956-57. Recipient Townsend Harris medal CCNY, 1990. Fellow: AAAS, Am. Heart Assn.; mem.: Am. Spinal Cord Injry Assn., Am. Assn. Electrodiagnostic Medicine (pres. 1987—88, Lifetime Achievement award 2001), Assn. Acad. Physiatrists, Am. Congress Rehab. Medicine (Essay award 1959), Am. Acad. Phys. Medicine and Rehab. (Disting. Clinician award 1987). Avocations: dance, singing. Office: U Wash Box 356490 1959 NE Pacific St Seattle WA 98195-0001 Home Phone: 425-454-8346; Office Phone: 206-543-7065.

STOLOW, WILLIAM, foundation administrator; m. Carol Stolow; children: Kimberly, Jodi, Jenifer. Founder, pres. The Lyme Disease Network NJ, Inc., East Brunswick, NJ, 1991—. Office: Lyme Disease Network NJ Inc 43 Winton Rd East Brunswick NJ 08816 Business E-Mail: bstolow@lymenet.org. *

STOLTENBERG, MEREDIN, medical educator, medical safety advisor, researcher; b. Grenaa, Denmark, Feb. 20, 1968; s. Boerge Jorgensen and Tonna Stoltenberg Joergensen; m. Saloma I. Gardastovu; children: Una I. Gardastovu, Jonas I. Gardastovu. MD, U. Aarhus, Denmark, 1996, DMS, 2004, PhD, 1998. Asst. prof. U. Aarhus, 1999—2002, assoc. prof., 2002—08; med. safety advisor H. Lundbeck A/S. Internat. Pharm. Co., Copenhagen, Valby, 2008—. Contbr. articles to numerous peer-reviewed jours. Mem.: Internat. Soc. Zinc Biology (bd. mem. 2008—09). Personal E-mail: meredinstoltenberg@hotmail.com.

STOLZ, ERWIN P., neurologist; b. Bleckhausen, Germany, Nov. 15, 1964; s. Werner and Maria Stolz; m. Anousha Rahimi; 1 child, Florian A. Abitur, Geschwister-Scholl-Gymnasium, Daun, 1984. MD Univ. of Bonn, Germany, Manchester Univ., UK, 1992. Prof. Justus-Liebig-Univ., Giessen, Germany, 1994—. Recipient Ultrasound prize, German Soc. of Clin. Neurophysiology, 2001. Fellow: German Soc. of Ultrasound in Medicine (life); mem.: Neurosonology Rsch. Group of the World Fedn. of Neurology (assoc.), European Soc. of Neurosonology and Cerebral Hemodynamics (assoc.), German Soc. of Clin. Neurophysiology (assoc.), German Soc. of Neurology (assoc.). Achievements include research in neurovascular diseases. Office: Justus-Liebig-Univ Am Steg 14 35392 Giessen 35385 Germany Office Fax: 00496419945309.

STOLZBERG, MARK ELLIOTT, psychologist; b. NYC, Apr. 30, 1944; s. Seymour and Ruth (Petesky) S.; m. Marilyn Goldberg, Mar. 18, 1972; children: Susan Beth Swinkin, David Jonathan, Daniel Jason. BA, Hofstra U., Hempstead, NY, 1966, PhD; MA in Exptl. Psychology, C.W. Post Coll., Greenvale, NY, 1970; postgrad. in clin. psychology, SUNY, Albany, 1973. Diplomate in clin. psychology Am. Bd. Profl. Psychology. Intern in clin. psychology Maimonides Hosp., Bklyn., 1972-73; pres. Stolzberg Rsch., LLC, Stony Brook, NY, 1976—. Adj. lectr. Bklyn. Coll., 1973; faculty Coll. Optometry, SUNY, 1985-86; cons. psychologist in numerous clinical and business settings, 1994—. Contbr. articles to profl. jours. Co-pres. North Shore SEPTA, 1999-2001; founder, past pres. Ind. Practitioners Geropsychology. Grad. fellow SUNY, Albany, 1970-72, N.Y. State War Svc. scholar; recipient Disting. Achievement award for Rsch., NY State Optometric Assn. Mem. NY State Psychol. Assn. (pres., adult devel. & aging divsn. 2004), Nat. Aeronautics Assn. Achievements include two US transcontinental speed records for piston-engine aircraft. Home and Office: 6759 Shamrock Trail Boynton Beach FL 33437

STONE, ANNE, medical educator; b. New Hyde Park, NY, Dec. 17, 1973; AB, Dartmouth Coll., 1996; MD, NYU, 2002. Asst. prof. pediat. Weill Cornell Med. Coll., 2008— Office: 505 E 70th St HT 3 Box 378 New York NY 10065 Business E-Mail: ans9079@med.cornell.edu.

STONE, JAMES ROBERT, surgeon; b. Greeley, Colo., Jan. 8, 1948; s. Anthony Joseph and Dolores Concetta (Pietrafeso) S.; children: Jeffrey, Marisa, Erin; m. Monica Sry-Tucker, Nov. 2005. BA, U. Colo., 1970; MD, U. Guadalajara, Mex., 1976; MBA, Madison U., 2002. Diplomate Am. Bd. Surgery, Am. Bd. Surg. Critical Care, Am. Bd. Forensic Medicine; cert. Med. Investigation LTC. With LTC, Army Res.; intern Md. Gen. Hosp., Balt., 1978-79; resident in surgery St. Joseph Hosp., Denver, 1979-83; pvt. practice Grand Junction, Colo., 1983-87; staff surgeon, dir. critical care Va. Med. Ctr., Grand Junction, 1987-88; dir. trauma surgery and critical care, chief surgery St. Francis Hosp., Colorado Springs, Colo., 1988-91; pvt. practice Kodiak, Alaska, 1991-92; with Summit Surg. Assocs., 1992-96; asst. dir. trauma Tristate Trauma System, Erie, Pa., 1996-99; med. dir. LifeStar Aeromed, Erie, Pa., 1997-99; dir. trauma, sr. assoc. physician, med. dir. emergency svcs. ISJ Mayo Health, 1999—2001; clin. prof. surgery U. Minn. Med. Sch., Mpls., 1999—2001, dir. trauma/EMS med. dir., sr. assoc.; gen., thoracic and vascular surgery Caylor-Nickel Clinic, Bluffton, Ind., 2001—02, Emergency Medicine of Ind., Ft. Wayne, Ind., 2002—04; CEO Guymon Surg. Cons., Okla., 2004, 2007, SW Iowa Surgery, 2008—10, Clarinda Regional Health Ctr., 2010—; med. dir. surg. EMS ED Trauma. Asst. clin. prof. surgery U. Colo. Health Sci. Ctr., Denver, 1984-96; pres. Stone Aire Cons., Grand Junction, 1988—; owner, operator Jjnka Ranch and Stuno Ranch, Flourissant, Colo.; spl. advisor CAP, wing med. officer, 1992-96; advisor med. com. unit, 1990-92; advisor Colo. Ground Team Search and Rescue, 1994-96; cons. Am. Med. Forensic Specialists, Berkeley, Ca., 2002-. Contbr. articles to profl. jours.; inventor in field. Bd. dirs. Mesa County Cancer Soc., 1988-89, Colo. Trauma Inst., 1988-91; chmn. Guymon Pioneer Days Rodeo. Colo. Speaks out on Health grantee, 1988; recipient Bronze medal of Valor Civil Air Patrol; named one of Am.'s Top Surgeons, 2007-11. Fellow Denver Acad. Surgery, Southwestern Surg. Congress, Am. Coll. Chest Physicians, Am. Coll. Surgeons (trauma com. Colo. chpt.), Am. Coll. Critical Care; mem. Am. Coll. Physician Execs., Soc. Critical Care (task force 1988—), Assn. Air Med. Physicians. Roman Catholic. Avocations: horse breeding, hunting, fishing. Office Phone: 712-249-8143, 712-243-7535. Business E-Mail: stuno@q.com.

STONE, MARVIN JULES, hematologist, oncologist, educator; b. Columbus, Ohio, Aug. 3, 1937; s. Roy J. and Lillian (Bedwinek) S.; m. Jill Feinstein, June 29, 1958; children: Nancy Lillian, Robert Howard. Student, Ohio State U., 1955-58; SM in Pathology, U. Chgo., 1962, MD with honors, 1963. Diplomate Am. Bd. Internal Medicine, (Hematology, Med. Oncology). Intern ward med. svc. Barnes Hosp., St. Louis, 1963-64, asst. resident, 1964-65; clin. assoc. arthritis and rheumatism br. Nat. Inst. Arthritis and Metabolic Diseases, NIH, Bethesda, Md., 1965-68; resident in medicine, ACP scholar Parkland Meml. Hosp., Dallas, 1968-69; fellow in hematology-oncology, dept. internal medicine U. Tex. Southwestern Med. Sch., Dallas, 1969-70, instr. dept. internal medicine, 1970-71, asst. prof., 1971-73, assoc. prof., 1974-76, clin. prof., 1976—, chmn. bioethics com., 1979-81; mem. faculty & steering com. Immunology Grad. Program, Grad. Sch. Biomed. Scis., U. Tex. Health Sci. Ctr., Dallas, 1975, adj. mem., 1976—2008; dir. oncology med. edn., quality & safety, assoc. dir. Cancer Ctr., 2008—. Dir. Charles A. Sammons Cancer Ctr., chief oncology, dir. immunology, co-dir. divsn. hematology-oncology, attending physician Baylor U. Med. Ctr., Dallas, 1976—; v.p. med. staff Parkland Meml. Hosp., Dallas, 1982, dir. Oncology Med. Edn. Quality and Safety, 2008-, assoc. dir., Baylor Charles A. Sammon Cancer Ctr. Contbr. chpts. to books, articles to profl. jours. Chmn. com. patient-aid Greater Dallas/Ft. Worth chpt. Leukemia Soc. Am., 1971-76, chmn. med. adv. com., 1978-80, bd. dirs., 1971-80; mem. v.p. Dallas unit Am. Cancer Soc., 1977-78, pres., 1978—; mem. adv. bd. Baylor U. Med. Ctr. Found., Marvin J. Stone Libr., Baylor Inst. Immunology Rsch., 1999. With USPHS, 1965-68. Recipient Wings of Eagles award, Baylor Health Care Sys., 2001, Disting. Svc. award, U. Chgo., 2002, Lifetime Achievement award, Internat. Soc. Study of Waldenstrom's Macroglobulinemia, 2004. Master ACP (gov. No. Tex. 1993-97, laureate Tex. chpt. 2000); fellow Royal Soc. Medicine (London); mem. AMA, Am. Assn. Immunologists, Am. Soc. Hematology, Internat. Soc. Hematology, Coun. Thrombosis, Am. Heart Assn. (established investigator 1970-75), Am. Soc. Clin. Oncology (edn. com. 2002-05, career devel. com. 2002-05), Am. Osler Soc. (bd. govs. 1997-2000, 2005—, v.p. 2001-03, pres. 2003-04), Am. Assn. for Cancer Rsch., So. Soc. Clin. Investigation, Tex. Med. Assn., Dallas County Med. Soc., Clin. Immunology Soc., Phi Beta Kappa, Sigma Xi, Alpha Omega Alpha. Office: Baylor U Med Ctr Charles A Sammons Cancer Ctr 3500 Gaston Ave Dallas TX 75246-2096 Business E-Mail: marvins@baylorhealth.edu.

STONE, MICHAEL HOWARD, psychiatry educator; b. Syracuse, NY, Oct. 27, 1933; s. Moses Howard and Corinne (Gittleman) S.; m. Clarice Joan Kestenbaum, (div. 1979); children: David, John; m. Beth Janine Eichstaedt. BA, Cornell U., 1954, MD, 1958. Diplomate Am. Bd. Psychiatry and Neurology. Residency in psychiatry Columbia Coll. of Physicians & Surgeons, NYC, 1963-66; asst. prof. psychiatry Columbia Coll. Physicians and Surgeons, NYC, 1973-77; assoc. prof. Cornell Med. Coll., NYC, 1977-80; prof. psychiatry U. Conn., Farmington, 1980-84; clin. dir. U. Conn. Dept. Psychiatry, Farmington, 1980-84; prof. clin. psychiatry Mt. Sinai Sch. Medicine, NYC, 1984-85, Cornell Med. Coll., NYC, 1985-88, Columbia Coll. Physicians and Surgeons, NYC, 1988—; dir. research Middletown Psychiat. Ctr., NY; med. dir. addiction clinic Orange Regional Med. Hosp., Middletown, NY; cons. Personal Disorder Inst., NYC. Visiting prof. psychiatry Albert Einstein Med. Ctr., NYC, 1987—; lectr. in field, 1987-; prof. clin. psychiatry Columbia Coll. Physicians and Surgeons, bd. mem. Musica Sacra. Author: The Borderline Syndromes, 1980, The Fate of Borderline Patients, 1990; editor: Borderline Disorders, 1981, Treating Schizophrenic Patients, 1983, Essential Papers on Borderline, 1985, Personality Disorders. Treatable and Untreatable, 2006, The Anatomy of Evil, 2009; host (TV show) Most Evil, 2006-07, (radio show) Sanfrancisco Phil Hendrie, 2009, Frequent Appearances on Radio and TV-Discussing Current Forensic Topics, 2010-11; contbr. over 200 articles to profl. jours. Patron Metropolitan Opera. Recipient Hematology Fellowship NIH, 1961-63. Fellow Am. Psychiat. Assn.; mem. Am. Pschopathol. Assn., Am. Coll. Psychiatrists, Musica Sacra (bd. mem.) Republican. Jewish. Avocations: piano, collecting rare books, languages. Home and Office: 225 Central Park W New York NY 10024-6027 Office Phone: 212-758-2000. Personal E-mail: mhstonemd@yahoo.com.

STONE, NEIL JOSEPH, cardiologist, educator; b. Chgo., Jewish, Dec. 17, 1944; s. Milton J. and Margery Stone; m. Karla Saxon, May 4, 1975; children: Scott, Adam, Lauren. BS in Medicine, Northwestern U., 1966, MD with honors (summa cum laude), 1968. Diplomate Am. Bd. Internal Medicine, Am. Bd. Cardiovascular Diseases, Am. Bd. Clin. Lipidology. Intern to resident Peter Bent Brigham Hosp. at Harvard U. (now Brigham and Women's Hosp.), Boston, 1968—70; staff assoc. Nat. Heart, Lung, Blood Inst., NIH, Bethesda, Md., 1970—73; chief resident Northwestern Meml. Hosp., Chgo., 1973—74, adj. staff, 1975—76, assoc. attending staff, 1976—81, attending staff, 1981—, internist, cardiologist, lipidologist, 1975—, med. dir. Vascular Ctr., Bluhm Cardiovascular Inst., 2005—, Suzanne and Milton Davidson Disting. Physician, 2006—; fellow cardiology Feinberg Sch. Medicine, Northwestern U., Chgo., 1974—75, asst. prof., 1975—80, assoc. prof. medicine, 1981—96, prof. clin. medicine, cardiology, 1996—. Lectr. Cook County Grad. Sch., Chgo., 1976—; mem. NHLBI adult treatment guidelines panels, ATP I, III Nat. Cholesterol Edn. Program, 1986—87; mem. NHLBI Clin. Guidelines Leadership Group for Cardiovascular Risk Reduction; co-chmn. ATP IV guidelines com. Author: Fat Chance, 1980; co-author: Cholesterol: Your Guide for a Healthy Heart, 1993; co-author: (with Conrad Blum) Management of Lipids in Clinical Practice, 6th edit., 2006; contbr. articles to med. jours.; participated in the writing groups that published Am. Heart Assn. Guidelines for Primary Prevention of Cardiovascular Disease and Stroke, 2002, writing group mem. for revision 2004 Evidence-Based Guidelines for Cardiovascular Disease Prevention in Women for Am. Heart Assn. Coun. on Nutrition, Physical Activity, and Metabolism., writing group mem. Am. Heart Assn./Am. Dental Assn. Statement on Primary Prevention of CVD in Diabetes, assoc. editor Am. Heart Assn. Learning Library as editor for Metabolic Syndrome and Lipid Community Websites, Journal of Clinical Lipidology. Recipient Award of Yr., Chgo. Dietetic Assn., 1978, Teaching Attending of Yr. award, Northwestern Med. Sch., 1979, Jacques Smith Disting. Physician in Medicine award, 1993, NJ Healthcare Found. Humanism in Medicine award, Feinberg Sch. Medicine, Northwestern U., 2002. Master: ACP (Outstanding Vol. Clin. Tchr. award 2001); fellow: Inst. Medicine, Coun. Clin. Cardiology, Am. Coll. Cardiology, Am. Heart Assn. (mem. Couns. Arteriosclerosis and Clin. Cardiology, mem-at-large Coun. on Nutrition, Physical Activity and Metabolism, past chmn. nutrition com. and clin. affairs com., mem. expert panel on population and prevention sci., chair, com. on clin. lipidology, lipoprotein metabolism and thrombosis); mem.: Nat. Lipid Assn. (first pres. Midwest Lipid Assn. Chap., bd. dirs.), Am. Soc. Internal Medicine, Am. Fedn. Clin. Rsch., Chgo. Heart Assn. (nutrition sub com.), Northwestern Med. Sch.

Alumni Coun. (pres. 1981—83). Avocations: golf, stamp collecting/philately. Office: 211 E Chicago Ave Ste 1050 Chicago IL 60611 Address: Feinberg Sch Med Northwestern U 303 E Chicago Ave Chicago IL 60611-3008 Office Phone: 312-944-6677. Office Fax: 312-944-3346. E-mail: n-stone@northwestern.edu.

STONE, RICHARD ALAN, medical educator; b. Cambridge, Mass., Nov. 21, 1945; s. Jack David and Abigail Stone; children: Chelsea, Jordan, Lisa, Caroline. BA, Brown U., Providence, 1964; attended, Columbia U., NY, 1966; MD, Tufts U., Boston, 1970. Cert. Nat. Bd. Med. Examiners, 1971, diplomate Am. Bd. Internal Medicine, 1973, Am. Bd. Nephrology, 1976, lic. Calif., 1975. Intern medicine Montefiore Hosp., Bronx, 1970—71, asst. resident medicine, 1971—72; fellow nephrology Duke U. Med. Ctr. Dept Biochemistry, Durham, NC, 1972—74; asst. prof. medicine U. Calif. Sch. Medicine, La Jolla, 1974—78, assoc. prof. medicine, 1978—79; dir. Vets. Adminstrn. Hosp. Hemodialysis Unit, San Diego, 1974—79; chmn. nephrology section. Eisenhower Med. Ctr., Rancho Mirage, Calif., 1979—, chmn. dept. medicine, 1982—84, sr. attending physician, 1985—; ASH specialist clin. hypertension, 1999—. Contbr. over 100 articles to profl. jours. Mem.: Riverside County Heart Assn., Internat. Soc. Nephrology, Am. Soc. Artificial Internal Organs, Southern Calif. Kidney Found., Nat. Kidney Found., Am. Assn. Advancement Scis., Am. Heart Assn., Am. Fed. Clin. Rsch., Am. Soc. Nephrology. Office: Eisenhower Medical Ctr 39000 Bob Hope Dr Ste 316 Rancho Mirage CA 92270-3221 Office Phone: 760-568-0383.

STONE, VOYE LYNNE, women's health nurse practitioner; b. Grandfield, Okla., Apr. 17, 1941; d. Clint Voy and Mattie Evelyn (Averyt) Wynn; m. Don Dale Stone, Dec. 19, 1964; children: Melinda Anne Stone Phelps, Tari Elisabeth Stone Newhouse. Student, Bapt. Hosp. Sch. Nursing, Oklahoma City, 1965; diploma in nursing, U. Okla., Oklahoma City, 1965; BS, St. Joseph's Coll., North Windham, Maine, 1985; grad. women health care nursing program, U. Tex., Dallas, 1990; MS, U. Okla., 1996. Cert. women's health nurse; cert. legal nurse cons. Dietary cons. Frederick Meml. Hosp., 1967; pub. health nurse Dept. Health, State of Okla., Frederick, 1985; insvc. educator Frederick Meml. Hosp.; women's health nurse practitioner Dept. Health, State of Okla., Oklahoma City, 1990. Vol., unit pres. Am. Cancer Soc.; vol. ARC; pres. adv. coun. 4-H Club; pres. local PTA. Named one of Outstanding Young Women of Am., 1970. Mem. AWHONN, Am. Acad. Nurse Practitioners, ANA, Okla. State Nurses Assn., Okla. Pub. Health Assn., Okla. Mental Health Assn., PEO, Beta Sigma Phi (various offices, Girl of Yr. 1976, 77, 78), Sigma Theta Tau, Phi Kappa Phi, First United Methodist Ch. Home: 21918 CR EW 184 Frederick OK 73542-9721

STONER, MICHAEL J., emergency physician; b. Fla., Nov. 21, 1968; BS, U. South Fla., 1990, MD, 1995. Resident, pediat. UC Davis Med. Ctr., 1995—98; pediatrician USAF, 1998—2001; attending physician Hasbro Children's Hosp., 2001—03, Nationwide Children's Hosp., 2006, fellow, pediatric emergency medicine, 2003—06. Decorated Hon. Discharge US Air Force. Fellow: ACEP, AAP. Office: 700 Children's Dr Columbus OH 43205 Personal E-mail: stonermj@yahoo.com.

STOOPLER, MARK BENJAMIN, physician; b. NYC, Sept. 29, 1950; s. Alex and Blanche Sylvia (Kappel) S.; m. Lynn Sara Fruchter, Jan. 10, 1982; children: David Andrew, Emily Rachel, Jesse Bryan. BS, Tulane U., 1971; MD, Cornell U., 1975. Diplomate Am. Bd. Internal Medicine, Am. Bd. Oncology. Intern and resident in internal medicine North Shore U. Hosp., Manhasset, N.Y., 1975-78, Meml. Sloan-Kettering Cancer Ctr., NYC, 1975-78, asst. chief resident in medicine, 1978, fellow in med. oncology, 1978-80; asst. attending physician Presbyn. Hosp., NYC, 1980-93, assoc. attending physician, 1993—; asst. clin. prof. medicine Columbia U. Coll. of Physicians and Surgeons, NYC, 1980-93; assoc. clin. prof. medicine, 1993—. Contbr. articles to profl. jours. Named one of Am.'s Top Drs. Castle Connolly Guide, 2003-11, Best Drs. NY Mag., 2006-11; Tulane U. scholar, 1970-71. Fellow ACP; mem. Am. Soc. of Clin. Oncology, Am. Fedn. for Clin. Research, Internat. Assn. for the Study of Lung Cancer, Phi Beta Kappa. Office: Columbia-Presbyn Med Ctr 161 Fort Washington Ave New York NY 10032-3713

STOOPS, JAMES KING, biochemistry researcher; b. Charleston, W.Va., Sept. 15, 1937; s. William Nelson and Mary Alice (Duncan) S.; m. Pamela Ann Moore, Aug. 18, 1962; children: Timothy, Mary. BS, Duke U., 1960; PhD, Northwestern U., 1966. Adj. prof. Baylor Coll. of Medicine, Houston, 1990—2007; prof. U. Tex. Health Sci. Ctr. Med. Sch., Houston, 1990—. Contbr. articles to profl. jours. Grantee NIH, 1990, 91, 94. Mem. AAAS, Am. Chem. Soc., Am. Soc. for Biochemistry and Molecular Biology. Presbyterian. Achievements include contbn. to understanding of structure-function relationships of the enzymes involved in lipid metabolism; determination of three-dimensional structures of human alpha-2-macroglobulins, pyruvate dehydrogenase, Cam kinases and the fatty acid synthase which indicate how these macromolecules function, propose novel therapy for pulmonary TB. Home: 10310 Cliffwood Dr Houston TX 77035-3610 Office: U Tex Health Sci Ctr 6431 Fannin St Houston TX 77030-1501 Office Phone: 713-500-5345. Business E-Mail: james.k.stoops@uth.tmc.edu.

STOPLER, TRAIAN IOSEF, microbiologist, researcher; b. Bacau, Moldavia, Romania, Mar. 30, 1924; s. Iosef and Jenny (Moscovici) S.; m. Sonia Kant, 1953 (div. 1957); 1 child, Mihaela; m. Ana Negreanu, 1962 (dec. May, 1985). MD, U. Bucharest, 1953. Sci. rschr. Inst. Hygiene, Bucharest, 1953-62; lab. chief infectious diseases Hosp. Colentina, Bucharest, 1962-72; lab. chief mycoplasma-pertussis Govt. Ctrl. Labs., Jerusalem, 1972-94. Contbr. articles to profl. jours. Recipient, Dipl. of Recognition, Internat. Congress of the Internat. Orgn. for Mycoplasmology, 1998. Achievements include first to describe antigenic variation following contact of antigen with its own antigen; describe the microbe as part of evolutionary biology; the conflict between microb and its host suggests a mechanism of natural selection within th eframe of evolutionary biology; the contamination of the patient with microorganisms is followed by contact of antigen with its own antibodies an antigenic variant appears; the new variant is unable to develop specific antibidies to the host, resulting in a aggrevating patient condition and death, antibodies can be induced by administration to the patients of a heat inactivated suspension of the microorganism, the clinical signs of the disease are stopping. Home: Etzel 2/12 32427 Jerusalem 91323 Israel Office: Govt Ctrl Labs PO Box 6115 Jerusalem Israel

STORK, TRAVIS LANE, emergency physician; b. Fort Collins, Colo., Mar. 9, 1972; Grad. magna cum laude, Duke U.; MD with honors, U. Va. Resident Vanderbilt U., Nashville; faulty physician Emergency Dept. Vanderbilt Med. Ctr., Nashville; host The Doctors, 2008—. Co-author: Don't Be That Girl: A Guide to Finding the Confident, Rational Girl Within, 2008. Avocations: hiking, kayaking. Office: Dept Emergency Medicine 1313 21st Ave S 703 Oxford House Nashville TN 37232-4700 *

STORY, MARY T., epidemiologist, medical educator; PhD in Human Nutrition Sci., Fla. State U., Tallahassee. Prof. divsn. epidemiology & cmty. health Sch. Pub. Health, U. Minn., Mpls., 1998—, assoc. dean student affairs, 2001—04, assoc. dean academic & student affairs, 2004—05, assoc. dean student life, 2009—. Dir. Healthy Eating Rsch. nat. program Robert Wood Johnson Found., 2005—. Co-editor: Health and Welfare for Families in the 21st Century, 1999 (Outstanding Book award, American Coll. Nurse-Midwives, 2000, Book of Yr. award, American Jour. Nursing, 2000); bd. editors Jour. American Dietetic Assn., 2001—, Jour. Adolescent Health, 2004—, Nutrition Today, 2004—; contbr. articles to profl. jours. Pres. Assn. Faculties Grad. Programs in Pub. Health Nutrition, 1995—97; adv. mem. USDA Team Nutrition-Adolescent Project, 1999—2001; com. mem. Minn. Task Force Childhood Obesity, 2006—07; mem. childhood obesity prevention steering com. Minn. Dept. Health, 2008; mem. steering com. Healthy Kids, Healthy Future Conf., 2009—. Recipient Betty Hubbard Maternal & Child Health Leadership award, Minn. Dept. Health, 2003. Mem.: APHA (pres. food & nutrition sect. 2002, counselor food & nutrition sect. 2004—07, Mary C. Egan award 1998), American Dietetic Assn. (chair pub. health nutrition practice group 1992—93, mem. governing coun., food & nutrition sect. 1995—98, Excellence in Dietetic Rsch. award 2000, Medallion award 2009), American Soc. Clin. Nutrition (membership com. 1999—2002), Inst. Medicine. Achievements include research in child and adolescent nutrition, obesity prevention, eating behaviors and environmental and policy change related to healthy eating. Office: Univ Minn Divsn Epidemiology & Cmty Health 1300 S 2nd St Ste 300 Minneapolis MN 55454 Office Phone: 612-626-8801. Business E-Mail: story001@umn.edu. *

STOSSEL, THOMAS PETER, medical educator, researcher, director; b. Chgo., Sept. 10, 1941; m. Kerry Maguire, 1997. AB, Princeton U., NJ, 1963; MD, Harvard U., Cambridge, Mass., 1967; MD (hon.), U. Linkoping, Sweden, 1989, U. Geneva, 2004. Diplomate Am. Bd. Internal Medicine. Ho. staff medicine Mass. Gen. Hosp., Boston, 1967-69, chief hematology-oncology, 1976-90; staff assoc. NIH, Bethesda, Md., 1967-71; fellow to sr. assoc. Med. Ctr. Children's Hosp., Boston, 1971-76; prof. medicine Harvard Med. Sch., Boston, 1982—; chief divsn. exptl. medicine Brigham Women's Hosp., Boston, 1991—97, co-dir. hematology divsn., 1998—2006, dir. translational medicine div., 2006—; sr. fellow Manhattan Inst. Policy Rsch., 2008—10. Sci. bd. Biogen Corp., 1987—2002, Dyax Corp., 1996—2002; clin. rsch. prof. Am. Cancer Soc., 1987—; bd. dirs. Velico Med. (former Zymequest, Inc.), Critical Biologics Corp. Author (with B. Babior): (book) 2d edit., 1984, Hematology, A Pathophysiological Approach, 1994; editor (with R. Handin and S. Lux): Blood, Principles & Practice of Hematology, 1995, 2d edit., 2003; contbr. articles to profl. jours. Bd. dirs. Am. Coun. Sci. and Health, 2006—. Lt. comdr. USPHS, 1969—71. Mem.: NAS, Am. Acad. Arts and Scis., Assn. Am. Physicians, Am. Soc. Hematology (pres. 1997, Damashek prize 1983, Thomas prize 1993), Am. Soc. Clin. Investigation (pres. 1987), Inst. Medicine (Lasker awards Jury 1997—2009). Achievements include patents in field. Office: Brigham & Womens Hosp Karp 625 1 Blackfan Cir Boston MA 02115 Home Phone: 617-489-1299; Office Phone: 617-355-9001. Business E-Mail: tstossel@partners.org.

STOTZKY, GUENTHER, microbiologist, educator; b. Leipzig, Germany, May 24, 1931; arrived in US, 1939; s. Moritz Stotzky and Erna (Angres) Kester; m. Kayla Baker, Mar. 17, 1958; children: Jay, Martha, Deborah. BS, Calif. Poly. State U., 1952; MS, Ohio State U., 1954, PhD, 1956. Spl. sci. employee Argonne Nat. Lab. USAEC, Lemont, Ill., 1955; rsch. assoc. dept. botany U. Mich., Ann Arbor, 1956-58; head soil microbiology Ctrl. Rsch. Labs. United Fruit Co., Norwood, Mass., 1958-63; chmn., microbiologist Kitchawan Rsch. Labs. Bklyn. Botanic Garden, Ossining, NY, 1963-68; assoc. prof. dept. biology NYU, 1967-70, prof. dept. biology, 1970—2008, chmn. dept. biology, 1970-77, prof. emeritus, 2008—. Editor: Soil Biochemistry, 1990-2000; series editor Marcel Dekker, Inc., 1986-92; contbr. over 300 articles to profl. jours., chpts. to books. With USCG, 1957. Recipient Selman A. Waksman Hon. Lecture award Theobald Smith Soc., 1989, Honored Alumnus of Yr. award Calif. Poly. State U., 1992, fellowship Japanese Soc. for Promotion of Sci., 1996; named Disting. Vis. Scientist, U.S. EPA, 1986-89. Fellow AAAS, Am. Soc. Agronomy, Soil Sci. Soc. Am., Internat. Union Pure and Applied Chemistry, Internat. Symposia on Environ. Biogeochemistry; mem. Am. Acad. Microbiology, Am. Soc. Microbiology (Fisher Co. award for applied and environ. microbiology 1990, Excellence in Tchg. award N.Y.C. br. 1994). Jewish. Avocations: gardening, reading, music. Home: PO Box 411 East Marion NY 11939 Home Phone: 631-477-1429. Business E-Mail: gs5@nyu.edu.

STOUDT, HOWARD WEBSTER, biological anthropologist, consultant; b. Pitts., May 13, 1925; s. Howard Webster and Harriet Catharine (Powers) S.; m. Jean Gorey Henderson, Feb. 14, 1953; children: Katharine Webster, Roberta Henderson. AB, Harvard Coll., 1949; MA, U. Pa., 1953, PhD, 1959; SM in Hygiene, Harvard U., 1963. Rsch. asst. Harvard Sch. Pub. Health, Boston, 1952-55; rsch. specialist Air U., U.S. Air Force, Montgomery, Ala., 1955-57; rsch. assoc. Harvard Sch. Pub. Health, Boston, 1957-66, asst. prof., 1966-73; prof. community medicine Mich. State U., East Lansing, 1973-88, chmn. dept., 1973-78, prof. emeritus, 1988—; cons. Stoudt Assocs., Bath, Maine, 1988—. Cons. U.S. Army, USAF, NASA, USPHS, VA, NRC, NAS, pvt. industry, 1952—. Author: Physical Anthropology of Ceylon, 1961; co-author: Human Body in Equipment Design, 1971; contbr. over 40 articles to profl. jours. Sgt. U.S. Army, 1943-46, Europe. Harrison fellow U. Pa., Phila., 1951-52, USPHS fellow, Boston, 1961-62. Fellow Human Biology Coun.; mem. AAAS, Am. Assn. Phys. Anthropologists, Human Factors and Ergonomics Soc. Democrat. Home: 4 Schooner Ridge Rd Apt 4 Bath ME 04530-1662 Office Phone: 207-400-7660. Personal E-mail: hjstoudt@gmail.com.

STOUFFER, CHADWICK W., surgeon; b. St. Joseph, Mich., May 3, 1977; BS, U. Mich., 1999; MD, Mich. State U., 2003. Cardiothoracic surgeon East Tenn. Cardiovasc. Surgery Group, 2010—. Gen. surgery resident Mich. State U., Grand Rapids, 2003—08; cardiothoracic surgery fellow U. Fla., 2008—10. Fellow: ACS; mem.: Soc. Thoracic Surgeons, Alpha Omega Alpha. Avocations: golf, bicycling, running. Office: 9125 Cross Park Dr Ste 200 Knoxville TN 37923 Office Phone: 865-632-5900. Office Fax: 865-637-2114. Business E-Mail: c.stouffer@etcvsg.com.

STOUPEL, ELIJAH, medical educator; b. Kaunas, Lithuania, June 20, 1929; arrived in Israel, 1974; s. Gregory and Ester (Lan) S.; m. Sophia Danguole Nugaraite; children: Jannet, Ylana. MD, Vilnius U., Lithuania, 1952, PhD in Medicine, 1960, D of Med. Sci., 1967. Dir. Dist. Dept. Health and Dept. Internal Medicine, Nementzine, Lithuania, 1952-55; faculty appointment, family physician Vilnius U. Hosp., 1955-58, cardiologist dept. thoracic surgery, 1958-62, asst. prof. faculty for postgrad. med. studies, 1962-66, assoc. prof., 1966-70, full prof. medicine, 1970-74; chief cons. in cardiology Heart Inst. Beilinson Med. Ctr. (now Rabin Med. Ctr.), Petah-Tiqva, Israel, 1975—; prof. cardiology Tel Aviv U., 1994—. Author: Prognosis in Cardiology, 1971, Mitral Valve Disease After Comissurotomy, 1973, Forecasting in Cardiology, 1976, Studies in Clinical Cosmobiology, 1968—. Pres. Israeli br. Internat. Physicians for Prevention of Nuclear War, 1984-91. Fellow: European Soc. Cardiology (emeritus 2011); mem.: Israel Heart Soc., Lithuanian Heart Soc. (hon.). Office: Rabin Med Ctr Beilinson Campus Petah Tiqwa 49100 Israel Home: 27, Habanim 45100 Hod HaSharon Israel Personal E-mail: stoupel@inter.net.il.

STOUT, DAVID, academic administrator; b. Calif., Sept. 03; BS in Biology, UCI, 1986; PhD in Biomedical Physics, UCLA, 1999. Dir., preclin. tech. ctr. UCLA Crump Inst. Molecular Imaging, 2001—. Cons., 2003—. Mem.: WMIC, SNM. Office: 570 Westwood Plz CNSI bldg Room 2151 Los Angeles CA 90095 Business E-Mail: dstout@mednet.ucla.edu.

STOUTENBURG, JANE SUE WILLIAMSON, nurse practitioner, fund raiser, medical legal consultant; b. Davenport, Iowa, Mar. 10, 1949; d. George Baker and Hazel Elaine (Kline) W.; m. Noel Wayne Stoutenburg, Aug. 25, 1979 (div. July 1996); 1 child, Karyn Elaine. AS with honors, Black Hawk Jr. Coll., East Moline, Ill., 1970; BA, BS, Augustana Coll., 1973-75; Cert. in Fire Sci. with honors, Harper Coll., Palatine, Ill., 1982; AS in Nursing with high honors, Elgin Community Coll., 1987. EMT; cert. paramedic; cert. medicalegist Rescue Tech., rescue technician, Ill. Med. technologist Rush-Presbyn. St. Luke's Med. Ctr., Chgo., 1974-75; acct. supr., pvt. investigator Per Mar Security Inc., Davenport, Iowa, 1975—76; pre-trial release investigator 7th Jud. Ct. Dist., Davenport, Iowa, 0976—1978; pharm. rep. Bristol Labs., Syracuse, 1977—81; dir. safety tng. Zee Med., Irvine, Calif., 1981-83; tng. specialist ARC, Chgo., 1983-86, Lake County Fire Rescue, Ill., 1981—2003; nurse practitioner Boy Scouts of Am., St. Charles, Ill., 1990—; nurse trainer Buehler YMCA, Palatine, Ill., 1990-94; rsch. technologist Northwestern U. Emergency med. svc. coord. Robbins (Ill.) Fire Dept., 1985—2003; bd. dirs. Barrington Area Devel. Coun., 1981-90; EMS coord. Lake Counte Fire Rescue, 1980-2001, owner, Snail's Pace Gifts, Barrington, IL, 1997-2006, pres. Karyn Etcetera Inc., 1997—. Author: Academy of Science, 1967, (poetry), 1970, actress: 1997—2003, ER Earl U Edition, Backdraft, A Normal Life, Relic, My Best Friends Wedding. Camp nurse Boy Scouts Am., Camp Big Timber, Ill., YMCA Camp Duncan, Fox Lake, Ill.; pageant judge Miss Am. System, 1995—2002, bd. dirs. Elgin C.C., 1998—2002, NW Suburb Chgo. Vol. Bur., 1998—. Recipient Ill. EMT of the Yr. award, 1989-90, Disting. Svc. award ARC, 1989, Disting. Svc. key Alpha Phi Omega, 1989, Key, Phi Theta Kappa, 1989, Vol. of the Yr. award Chgo. Vol. Bur., 1993, J.C. Penney Golden Flame award, 1993. Mem. Am. Soc. Safety Engrs., Am. Trauma Soc., Am. Acad. Sci., Internat. Soc. Fire Sci. Instrs., Prehosp. Care Providers of Ill., Alpha Phi Omega (mem. bd. dirs. 1995—, publicity com.), P.E.O. Sisterhood, Delta Zeta. Episcopalian. Avocations: poetry, camping, firefighting, dixieland jazz, glass blowing.

STOVER, DIANE E., pulmonologist, educator; MD, Albert Einstein Coll. Medicine, 1970. Diplomate Am. Bd. Internal Medicine-pulmonary disease, Am. Bd. Internal Medicine. Resident in internal medicine Harlem Hosp. Ctr., NY, 1971—72, NY Hosp. - Cornell Med. Ctr., 1974—75; fellow in pulmonary disease Montefiore Med. Ctr., Bronx, NY, 1975—77; prof. medicine Cornell Univ. - Weill Med. Coll.; head gen. medicine divsn. Meml. Sloan-Kettering Cancer Ctr., chief pulmonary svc. Office: Memorial Sloan-Kettering Cancer Center 1275 York Ave New York NY 10065 Office Phone: 212-639-8380.

STOVER, ELLEN L., health scientist, former federal agency administrator; b. Bklyn., Nov. 21, 1950; d. Ralph and Charlotte (Tulchin) Simon; m. Alan B. Stover, June 3, 1973; children: Elena Randall Simon, Randall Alan Simon, Samantha Anne Simon. BA with honors, U. Wis., 1972; PhD, Catholic U., Washington, 1978. Cons. Nat. Inst. Mental Health (NIMH), Rockville, Md., 1972-74, exec. sec. drug abuse rsch. review com., 1974-76, spl. asst. to assoc. dir. extramural programs, 1976-77, chief small grants program, 1977-79, asst. then acting chief rsch. resources br., 1980-85, dep. dir. Divsn. Basic Scis., 1985-88, dir. office AIDS, 1988—2010, dir. divsn. AIDS, health and behavioral rsch., 1997—2010, spl. advisor office AIDS rsch., 2010—. Dir. divsn. AIDS, health, behavior NIMH. Recipient Superior Svc. award, USPHS, 1992, 1993, NIH Dir.'s award, 1996, Presdl. Rank award, 2001. Mem.: APA. Avocations: gardening, dance. Office: Nat Inst Mental Health DAHBR Neuro Sci Ctr 8228 6001 Executive Blvd Bethesda MD 20892 Office Phone: 301-451-9410. Business E-Mail: ellen.stover@nih.gov. *

STOVER, KAYLA RENAY, pharmacist, educator; b. Franklin, Pa., Mar. 3, 1983; PharmD, Ohio Northern U., 2007. PGY1 pharmacy resident, adj. prof. W.Va. U., 2007—08; PGY 2 infectious diseases resident U. Miss. Med. Ctr., 2008—09; asst. prof. pharmacy U. Miss., 2009—. Mem.: Miss. Coll. Clin. Pharmacy, Am. Coll. Clin. Pharmacy, Am. Soc. Microbiology, Soc. Infectious Diseases Pharmacists, Infectious Diseases Soc. America. Office: 2500 North State St Jackson MS 39216 Office Fax: 601-984-2618. E-mail: kstover@umc.edu.

STOVER, MICHAEL DAVID, surgeon, educator; b. Austin, Minn. married. BS in Biochemistry, U. Iowa, MD. Orthopaedic trauma surgeon Carolinas Med. Ctr., Charlotte, NC, 1996—97; pelvic and acetabular reconstruction surgeon Hosp. of Good Samaritan, LA, 1997—98; dir. orthop. traumatology, surg. preservation hip Loyola U. Med. Ctr., Marywood, Ill., 1998—. Office: Loyola U Med Ctr 2160 South First Ave Maywood IL 60153

STOWE, ZACHARY NEIL, psychiatrist, researcher; MD, U. Tex. Med. Branch, Galveston. Resident in psychiatry Duke U. Med. Ctr.; fellow in psychopharmacology Emory U. Sch. Medicine, prof. dept. psychiatry & behavioral sciences, 1992—, asst. prof. dept. gynecology & obstetrics, 1998—, founder & dir., Women's Mental Health Program. Recipient Young Investigator award, Nat. Depressive & Manic Depressive Assn. Mem.: Nat. Inst. Health, Nat. Alliance Mentally Ill, Am. Psychiatric Assn. (SmithKline Beecham Young Faculty award). Office: Emory University School of Medicine Emory Clinic Bldg B 1365 Clifton Rd NE Ste 6100 Atlanta GA 30322 Office Phone: 404-778-2524. Office Fax: 404-778-2535. E-mail: wmhp@emory.edu, zstowe@emory.edu.

STOZICKY, FRANTISEK VACLAV, pediatrician; b. Budyne, Czech Republic, Aug. 8, 1941; s. Frantisek and Paulina (Mackova) S.; m. Olga Vera Vahalova, June 21, 1975; children: Frantisek, Jan, Jana. MD, Charles U., 1966, D of Med. Scis., 1990. Pediatrician Regional Hosp., Ústí, Czech Republic, 1966—75; asst. to assoc. prof. pediat. Charles U., Prague, Czech Republic, 1975—2003, head dept. pediat., 2001—07, prof. pediat., 2007—. Cons. in field. Author: Apolipoproteins-Biochemistry and Clinical Significance, 1990, Dyslipidemias in Childhood, 2002, Prevention of Cardiovascular Diseases in Childhood, 2003, textbook of Pediatrics; inventor in field. Mem. Czech Med. Soc., Czech Pediat. Soc., Czech Atherosclerosis Group (pres. 1992-96) Avocation: lawn tennis. Home: Horomyslicka 16 31200 Plzen Czech Republic Office: Charles Univ Dept Pediatrics Husova 3 306 05 Plzen Czech Republic Office Phone: 377 104 664. Business E-Mail: stozicky@fnplzen.cz.

STRAATSMA, BRADLEY RALPH, ophthalmologist, educator; b. Grand Rapids, Mich., Dec. 29, 1927; s. Clarence Ralph and Lucretia Marie (Nicholson) S.; m. Ruth Campbell, June 16, 1951; children: Cary Ewing, Derek Green. Student, U. Mich., 1947, MD cum laude, Yale U., New Haven, Conn., 1951; DSc (hon.), Columbia U., NYC, 1984, JD cum laude, U. West LA, 2002. Diplomate Am. Bd. Ophthalmology (vice chmn. 1979, chmn. 1980). Intern New Haven Hosp., Yale U., 1951-52; resident in ophthalmology Columbia U., NYC, 1955-58; spl. clin. trainee Nat. Inst. Neurol. Diseases and Blindness, Bethesda, Md., 1958-59; assoc. prof. surgery/ophthalmology UCLA Sch. Medicine, 1959-63, chief div. ophthalmology, dept. surgery, 1959-68, prof. surgery/ophthalmology, 1963-68, prof. ophthalmology, 1968—2001, dir. Jules Stein Eye Inst., 1964-94, chmn. dept. ophthalmology, 1968-94, prof. emeritus, 2001—; ophthalmologist in chief UCLA Med. Ctr., 1968-94. Lectr. numerous univs. and profl. socs. 1971—; cons. to surgeon gen. USPHS, mem. Vision Research Tng. Com., Nat. Inst. Neurol. Diseases and Blindness, NIH, 1959-63, mem. neurol. and sensory disease program project com., 1964-68; chmn. Vision Rsch. Program Planning Com., Nat. Adv. Eye Coun., Nat. Eye Inst., NIH, 1973-75, 75-77, 85-89; mem. med. adv. bd. Internat. Eye Found., 1970-79; mem. adv. com. on basic clin. rsch. Nat. Soc. to Prevent Blindness, 1971-87; mem. med. adv. com. Fight for Sight, 1960-83; bd. dirs. So. Calif. Soc. to Prevent Blindness, 1967-77, Ophthalmic Pub. Co., 1975-93, v.p. 1990-93, Pan-Am. Ophthalmol. Found., 1985-95; chmn. sci. adv. bd. Ctr. for Partially Sighted, 1984-87; mem. nat. adv. panel Found. for Eye Rsch., Inc., 1984-94; mem. cons. com. Palestra Oftalmologica Panamericana, 1976-81; coord. com. Nat. Eye Health Edn. Program, 1989; mem. sci. adv. bd. Rsch. to Prevent Blindness, Inc., 1993—2003. Editor-in-chief Am. Jour. Ophthalmology, 1993-2002; mem. editorial bd. UCLA Forum in Med. Scis., 1974-82, Am. Jour. Ophthalmology, 1974-91, Am. Intra-Ocular Implant Soc. Jour., 1978-79, EYE-SAT Satellite-Relayed Profl. Edn. in Ophthalmology, 1982-86; mng. editor von Graefe's Archive for Clin. and Exptl. Ophthalmology, 1976-88; contbr. over 550 articles to med. jours. Trustee John Thomas Dye Sch., LA, 1967-72. Lt. USNR, 1952-54. Recipient William Warren Hoppin award NY Acad. Medicine, 1956, Univ. Service award UCLA Alumni Assn., 1982, Miguel Aleman Found. medal, 1992, Benjamin Boyd Humanitarian award Pan Am. Assn. Ophthalmology, 1991, Lucian Howe medal, Am. Ophthalmological Soc., 1992, Internat. Gold Medal award 3rd Singapore Nat. Eye Ctr. Internat. Meeting and 11th Internat. Meeting on Cataract, Implant, Microsurgery and Refractive Keratoplasty, 1998, award of merit in retinal rsch. Retina Rsch. Found., 2002, Jose Rizal gold medal Asia-Pacific Acad. Ophthalmology, 2003, Gold medal Barraquer Inst., 2005. Fellow Royal Australian and New Zealand Coll. Ophthalmologists (hon.); mem. Academia Ophthalmologica Internationales (pres. 1998-2002), Am. Acad. Ophthalmology (bd. councillors 1981, Life Achievement award 1999, Laureate award 2010), Found. of Am. Acad. Ophthalmology (trustee 1989, chmn. bd. trustees 1989-92), Am. Acad. Ophthalmology and Otolaryngology (pres. 1977), Am. Soc. Cataract and Refractive Surgery, AMA (asst. sec. ophthalmology sect. 1962-63, sec. 1963-66, chmn. 1966-67, coun. 1970-74), Am. Ophthalmol. Soc. (coun. 1985-90, v.p. 1992, pres. 1993), Assn. Rsch. in Vision and Ophthalmology (Mildred Weisenfeld award 1991), Assn. U. Profs. of Ophthalmology (trustee 1969-75, pres.-elect 1973-74, pres. 1974-75), Assn. VA Ophthalmologists, Calif. Med. Assn. (mem. ophthalmology adv. panel 1972-94, chmn. 1974-79, sci. bd. 1973-79, ho. of dels. 1974, 77, 79), Chilean Soc. Ophthalmology (hon.), Columbian Soc. Ophthalmology (hon.), Glaucoma Soc. Internat. Congress of Ophthalmology (hon.), Heed Ophthalmic Found. (chmn., bd. dirs. 1990-98), Hellenic Ophthalmol. Soc. (hon.), Internat. Coun. Ophthalmology (bd. dirs. 1993-2008, hon. life trustee 2008-, Jules Francois medal 2002, Internat. Duke-Elder medal 2006), LA County Med. Assn., LA Soc. Ophthalmology, Pan-Am. Assn. Ophthalmology (coun. 1972—, pres. elect 1985-87, pres. 1987-89, Harry S. Gradle Tchg. award 2007), Peruvian Soc. Ophthalmology (hon.), Retina Soc., Barraquer Inst. Ophthalmology (pres. 1996-05), Academia Ophthalmol. Internat. (pres. 1998-02), Internat. Coun. Ophthalmology Found.(pres. 2002-08, 10, dir. 2009-; Philip M. Corboy award 2005, Internat. Duke-Elder medal 2006, Middle East African Coun. Opthamology, Prince Abdul Aziz Ahmed Al-Saud Prevention of Blindness award, 2007), The Jules Gonin Club. Republican. Presbyterian. Avocation: music. Home: 3031 Elvido Dr Los Angeles CA 90049-1107 Office: UCLA 100 Stein Plz Los Angeles CA 90095-7065 Office Phone: 310-825-5051. Business E-Mail: straatsma@jsei.ucla.edu.

STRACK, ALISON MERWIN, neurobiologist; b. Midland, Mich., Apr. 19, 1963; d. William James and Alice (Armstrong) S. BS, U. Mich., 1985; PhD, Washington U., St. Louis, 1990. Asst. rsch. physiologist U. Calif. Sch. Medicine, San Francisco, 1990-97; rsch. fellow Merck Pharms., Rahway, NJ, 1997—2005, sr. rsch. fellow, 2005—07, atherosclerosis in vivo lead, 2008, dir. atherosclerosis lead optimization, dept. cardiovasc. diseases, 2009—. Contbr. articles to profl. jours. Grantee Am. Heart Assn., Calif. affiliate, 1993. Mem. Soc. Neurosci. Office: Merck Rsch Labs Dept Pharmacology R80Y-145 PO Box 2000 Rahway NJ 07065 Office Phone: 732-594-8367.

STRADA, SAMUEL J., dean, pharmacologist, educator; Attended, Rockhurst Coll., Kansas City, 1959—60; BSc in Pharmacy with distinction, U. Mo., Kansas City, 1964, MSc in Pharmacology, 1966; PhD in Pharmacology, Vanderbilt U., Nashville, 1970. Post-grad. tng. lab. pre-clinical pharmacology St. Elizabeth's Hosp., Nat. Institutes Mental Health, Washington, 1970—72; grad. faculty mem. U. Tex. Grad. Sch. Biomed. Sciences, 1972—83; asst. prof. pharmacology U. Tex. Med. Sch., Houston, 1972—75, assoc. prof. pharmacology, 1975—81, prof. pharmacology, 1981—83, acting chmn. dept. pharmacology, 1982; sabbatical dept. biochemistry U. Dundee Med. Sciences Inst., Scotland, 1979—80; prof. pharmacology U. South Ala. Coll. Medicine, Mobile, 1983—, chmn. designate dept. pharmacology, 1983, chmn. dept. pharmacology, 1983—94, acting dir. grad. program in basic med. sciences, 1990—92, acting head dept. psychiatry, 1992, sr. assoc. dean, 1993—2005, acting dean, 2005—07, dean, 2007—. Cons. in biology rsch., pharmacology divsn. Ciba-Geigy Corp., Summitt, NJ, 1984—86. Mem. editl. bd.: Jour. cyclic Nucleotide and Protein Phosphorylation Rsch., 1974—85, Second Messengers and Phosphoproteins, 1985—94, Substance and Alcohol Actions/Misuse, 1980—84, Patient Oriented Problem-Solving System in Pharmacology, 1993—98, CNS Drug Reviews, 1994—; contbr. articles to profl. jours., chapters to books. Mem.: AAAS, Ala. Acad. Sci., American Soc. Pharmacology and Expt. Therapeutics, Assn. Med. Sch. Pharmacology, Assn. Univ. Tech. Managers, Basic Sci. Edn. Forum, Found. Advanced Edn. in the Sciences, Internat. Assn. Med. Sci. Educators, NY Acad. Sci., Soc. Neurosciences, Tissue Culture Assn., Southeastern Pharmacology Soc. (life), Sigma Xi. Office: University South Ala Sch Medicine 2015 Med Sciences Bldg 5851 USA Dr N Mobile AL 36688 Office Phone: 251-460-6041. Office Fax: 251-460-6073. Business E-Mail: sstrada@jaguar1.usouthal.edu. *

STRAHLMAN, RICHARD SCOTT, pediatrician; s. Richard and Carol Ann Strahlman; m. Teresa Flores, May 11, 1996; children: John Wesley, Stephanie Leigh, Matthew Scott, Michael Allen. MD, Johns Hopkins U., Balt., 1978. Diplomate Am. Bd. Pediats. Instr. in pediats. Johns Hopkins U. Sch. of Medicine, Balt., 1985—; chief of pediats. Patuxent Med. Group, Columbia, Md., 1997—2004; pediatrician Columbia Med. Practice, Md., 2004—. Cons. in field, Columbia, 1995—. Author: (chpts. in med. textbooks) Primary Pediatric Care. Named Top Doc, Balt. Mag., 2002. Fellow: Am. Acad. Pediats. Office: Columbia Med Practice 5500 Knoll N Dr Columbia MD 21045 Home: 11838 Vineyard Path New Market MD 21774 Office Fax: 410-964-6227. *

STRAIGHT ARROW, JANET, holistic professional, educator; b. Orange, NJ, Aug. 3, 1952; d. John Paul and Martha Ann (Gallik) Bachmann; m. Steven Scott Zwiren, Sept. 25, 1971 (div. Feb. 1986); children: Paula Marie, Lisa Michelle. AA in Home Econs., Centenary Coll., Hackettstown, NJ, 1975; BA in Psychology, Coll. St. Elizabeth, Convent Station, NJ, 1987; Reiki master, Unltd. Potential, West Orange. NJ, 1994; grad., Realtors Inst., Edison, NJ, 1994. Cert. residential specialist. Title searcher Chelsea Title, New Brusnwick, NJ, 1972, Stewart Title, Morristown, NJ, 1973—75; title searcher, officer Heritage Abstract, Morristown, 1976—84; mortgage banker Fin. Investment Resources, Morristown, 1987—88, Greater Metro, Wayne, NJ, 1988; realtor residential sales Weichert Realtors, Succasunna, NJ, 1988—91, Re/Max Renown Realty, Randolph, NJ, 1991—99; Reiki Master, Shamanic practitioner Universal Life Energy Healing Ctr., Succasunna, 1994—97; dir., Shaman, Reiki master Oasis for the Soul, 1997—2003; woman of medicine, Shaman Succasunna, 2003—06; woman of medicine, Shaman, writer, spkr. Woodstock, NY, 2006—; author spkr., tchr. Bethe Med., Morris Town, NJ, 2007—; woman of medicine Med. Info. Live. Pvt. cons. Bus. Mktg. and Mgmt., Succasunna, 1995—. Leader Girl Scouts U.S.A., Succasunna, 1993, 1985, 88, Denville, N.J., 1981, 84; town coun. reporter League Women Voters, Randolph, 1975. Mem. Nat. Assn. Realtors, N.J. Assn. Realtors (Million Dollar Club bronze and silver awards 1988-98, Remax Internat. Hall of Fame, 1997), Morris County Bd. Realtors, Residential Spl. Coun., Grad. Realtors Inst., Remax Internat. 100 Club. Democrat. Avocations: sailing, reading, hiking, writing, travel. Office: Be The Medicine 18 Bank St Ste 300 Morristown NJ 07960 Office Phone: 973-647-2500. Personal E-mail: jstraightarrow@aol.com. Business E-Mail: janetoasis@aol.com, janet@bethemedicine.com.

STRAIN, ERIC CAMERON, psychiatrist, educator; BA in Chemistry, Amherst Coll., Mass., 1980; MD, Ohio State U., 1984. Diplomate Am. Bd. Psychiatry and Neurology-psychiatry, 1989, Am. Bd. Psychiatry and Neurology-addiction psychiatry, 2002. Intern medicine/psychiatry Johns Hopkins Univ., 1984—85, resident gen. psychiatry, 1985—88, fellow behavioral pharmacology/addiction psychology sch. medicine, 1988—90, asst. prof. dept. psychiatry and behavioral sciences sch. medicine, 1990—94, assoc. prof. dept. psychiatry and behavioral sciences sch. medicine, 1995—; resident psychiatry Johns Hopkins Hosp., Balt., 1985—88; dir. ctr. for substance abuse Johns Hopkins Medicine Bayview Med Ctr., Balt. Mem. drug adv. com. FDA, 1996—2000, chmn. drug adv. com., 1997—2000; mem. data monitoring bd. Nat. Inst. on Drug Abuse/Dept. of Veterans Affairs Coop. Studies Program, 1997. Co-author: (publs.) Chronic Pain and Depression, 1989, Intravenous Drug Abusers with Antisocial Personality Disorder: Increased HIV Risk Behavior, 1990, Intravenous Cocaine: Subjective and Physiologic Effects and Desire for Cocaine, 1990, The Early Treatment Time Course of Depressive Symptoms in Opiate Addicts, 1991, Clustering of Multiple Substance use and Psychiatric Diagnoses in Opiate Addicts, 1991, and numerous others. Office: Johns Hopkins Medicine Bayview Medical Center 4940 Eastern Ave Baltimore MD 21224 Office Phone: 410-550-1191. Office Fax: 410-550-0030.

STRAIN, JAMES ELLSWORTH, pediatrician, educator, retired medical association administrator; b. Lincoln, Nebr., Apr. 23, 1923; s. Elmer Ellsworth and Tessa Elizabeth (Stevens) Strain; m. Ruby Lee Shepard; children: James A., John D., Janet M. Strain McKinney, Jeffrey Lee Phillips-Strain. AB, Phillips U., Enid, Okla., 1945; MD, U. Colo., Denver, 1947. Diplomate Am. Bd. Pediat. (examiner 1984-89, mem. 1989-93, emeritus mem. 1993—). Intern Mpls. Gen. Hosp., 1947—48; resident in pediat. Denver Children's Hosp., 1948—50, pres. med. staff, 1964, dir. genetic unit, 1982—86; pvt. practice specializing in pediat. Denver, 1950—86; exec. dir. Am. Acad. Pediat., Elk Grove Village, Ill., 1986—93, ret., 1993. Pres. med. bd. Colo. Gen. Hosp., 1969—70; clin. prof. pediat. U. Colo. Med. Ctr., 1969—86, 1993—, U. Chgo., 1987—93; mem. Colo. Med. Adv. Coun. for Title 19, 1968—75, chmn., 1968—71; mem. Task Force on Iowa Health Care Stds. Project, 1984—85; presenter numerous profl. confs. Editl. bd. Pediat. in Rev., reviewer Jour. Pediat.; contbr. articles to profl. publs. Mem. Colo. Commn. on Children and Youth, 1971—75; trustee Phillips U., 1974—. Capt. US Army, 1953—55. Recipient Disting. Alumnus award, Phillips U., 1974, Florence Sabin award, U. Colo., 1984, Excellence in Pub. Svc. award, U.S. Surgeon Gen., 1988, Abraham Jacobi award, AMA and Am. Acad. Pediat., 1994, James E. Strain Child Advocacy award established in his name, Denver Children's Hosp., 1983. Fellow: Am. Acad. Pediat. (Clifford Grulee award 1985); mem.: AMA, APHA, Inst. Medicine NAS, Ambulatory Pediatric Assn., Can. Pediatric Soc., Denver Med. Soc., Colo. Med. Soc., Alpha Omega Alpha. Republican. Mem. Christian Ch. (Disciples Of Christ). Avocations: fishing, sports, reading. Personal E-mail: jstrain121@aol.com.

STRAMBI, MIRELLA, pediatrician; b. Colle Val d' Elsa, Siena, Nov. 27, 1947; MD, 1972. Assoc. prof. Dept. Pediat., Obstetric and Reproduction Medicine, 1984—, bd. dir. preventive pediat. Hosp. ' Santa Maria alle Scotte', 1997—. Vice dir. Ctr. Prevention Neurohandicap U., 1997—. Mem.: Italian Soc. Preventive Pediat., Italian Soc. Pediat. Avocations: gardening, walking, reading. Office: Viale Bracci Siena Tuscany 53100 Italy Office Fax: 390577586182. Business E-Mail: strambi@unisi.it.

STRAMETZ-JURANEK, JEANETTE, medical educator; b. Vienna, Sept. 15, 1964; Degree, Med. U. Vienna, 1991. Prof. Med. U. Vienna, 1991— Bd. mem. dirs. Internat. Soc. Gender Medicine, 2007; founder, head Austrian Soc. Gender Specific Medicine, 2007, Task Force Gender Cardiology Austrian Soc. Cardiology, 2008. Grants, FemTech FTI. Avocations: meditation, sports. Office: Währinger Gürtel 18-20 Vienna 1090 Austria Business E-Mail: jeanette.strametz-juranek@meduniwien.ac.at.

STRAMPEL, WILLIAM DERKEY, dean, medical educator; b. Saugatuck, Mich., Feb. 8, 1948; married; 3 children. BA, Hope Coll., 1970; DO, Chgo. Coll. Osteopathic Medicine, 1976. Intern Madigan Army Med. Ctr., Fort Lewis, Wash., 1976—77, resident in medicine, 1977—79; fellow in pulmonary disease Fitzsimons Army Med. Ctr., Aurora, 1980—82; staff internal medicine svc. and dir. intensive care 121 Evacuation Hosp., Seoul; pulmonary staff and dir. intensive care Fitzsimons Army Med. Ctr., Aurora, Colo.; divsn. surgeon First Infantry Divsn. Irwin Army Cmty. Hosp., Fort Riley, Kans., dep. comdr., dir. med. edn., Evans Army Cmty. Hosp., Fort Carson, Colo.; chief Quality Assurance Divsn., Dept. of Army, Office Surgeon Gen., 1991—94; dir. med. edn. Brooke Army Med. Ctr., 1994—96; comdr. Brooke Army Med. Ctr. and Great Plains Med. Command, 1996—97; dir. quality mgmt. Office Sec. Def.; chief med. officer Tricare Mgmt. Activity; spl. asst. for ops. and readiness to U.S. surgeon gen.; leader Mich. State U. Health Team; sr. assoc. dean Mich. State U. Coll. Osteo. Medicine, 1999—2002, prof. internal medicine, 2001—, acting dean, 2001—02, dean, 2002—. Served to col. US Army. Office: Mich State U Coll Osteo Medicine A308A E Free Hall East Lansing MI 48824-1316 Office Phone: 517-355-9616. Office Fax: 517-432-2125.

STRANG, RUTH HANCOCK, pediatrician, cardiologist, educator, retired priest; b. Bridgeport, Conn., Mar. 11, 1923; d. Robert H.W. and Ruth (Hancock) Strang. BA, Wellesley Coll., 1944, postgrad., 1944—45; MD, N.Y. Med. Coll., 1949; MDiv, Seabury We. Theol. Sem., 1993. Diplomate Am. Bd. Pediat.; ordained deacon Episc. Ch., 1993, priest Episc. Ch., 1994. Intern Flower and Fifth Ave. Hosp., NYC, 1949—50, resident in pediat., 1950—52; mem. faculty N.Y. Med. Coll., NYC, 1952—57; fellow cardiology Babies Hosp., NYC, 1956—57, Harriet Lane Cardiac Clinic, Johns Hopkins Hosp., Balt., 1957—59, Children's Hosp., Boston, 1959—62; mem. faculty U. Mich. Hosp., Ann Arbor, 1962—89, prof. pediat., 1970—89, prof. emeritus, 1989—; priest-in-charge St. Johns Episcopal Ch., Howell, Mich., 1994—2009. Dir. pediat. Wayne County Gen. Hosp., Westland, Mich, 1965-85; mem. staff U. Mich. Hosps., 1962-89; mem. med. adv. com. Wayne County chpt. Nat. Cystic Fibrosis Rsch. Found., 1966-80, chmn. med. adv. com. nat. found., Detroit, 1971-78; cons. cardiology Plymouth (Mich.) State Home and Tng. Sch., 1970-81; diocesan coun. Diocese Mich., 2003-05, mem. com. on nominations and elections Diocesan Conv., 2003, chmn. com., 2004. Author: Clinical Aspects of Operable Heart Disease, 1968; contbr. numerous articles to profl. jours. Mem. citizen's adv. coun. Juvenile Ct., Ann Arbor, 1968—76; mem. med. adv. bd. Ann Arbor Continuing Edn. Dept., 1968—77; v.p. Am. Heart Assn. Mich., 1989, pres., 1991; bd. dirs. Livingston Cmty. Hospice, 1995—99; bd. mgrs. Emrich Episcopal Retreat Ctr.,

1998—2008; mem. Diocesan Com. for World Relief, Detroit, 1970—72; trustee Episcopal Med. Chaplaincy, Ann Arbor, 1971—96; mem. bishop's com. St. Aidan's Episc. Ch., 1966—69, sec., 1966—68, vestry, 1973—76, 1978—80, 1984—86, 1990—91, sr. warden, 1975—76, 1978, 1986, 1990; del. Episc. Diocesan Conv., 1980, 1991; mem. Congl. Life Circle Episcopal Diocese Mich., 1995—2001, mem. loans and grants com., 1995—99, mem. com. on reference ann. diocesan conv., 1995-98, chmn., 1996; mem. Diocese Mich. Clergy Family Project, 1996—98; co-dean Huron Valley area coun. Diocese Mich., 1998—2000; bd. trustees Ecumenical Theol. Sem., Detroit, 1996—2008, chair acad. affairs com., 2000—08; mem. Congl. Devel. Commn., 2001—03; bd. dirs. Livingston County Cath. Social Svcs., 2004—07. Recipient Alumnae Life Achievement award, Baldwin Sch., 2005, Disting. Svc. award, Ecumenical Theol. Sem., Detroit, 2008. Mem. AMA, Am. Acad. Pediat., Am. Coll. Cardiology, Mich. Med. Soc., Washtenaw County Med. Soc., N.Y. Acad. Medicine, Am. Heart Assn., Women's Rsch. Club (membership sec. 1966-67), Ambulatory Pediat. Assn., Am. Assn. Child Care in Hosps., Am. Assn. Med. Colls., Assn. Faculties of Pediat. Nurse Assn./Practitioners Programs (pres. 1978-81, exec. com. 1981-84), Episc. Clergy Assn. Mich., Northside Assn. Ministries (pres. 1975, 76, 79-80), Soc. Companions of Holy Cross. Home: 4500 E Huron River Dr Ann Arbor MI 48105-9335 *

STRANGE, CHARLTON BELL, III, pulmonologist, educator; b. Fairbanks, Alaska, Mar. 3, 1956; s. Charlton Bell, Jr. and Carol Linda (Everett) Strange; m. Pamela Elaine Neagley, June 18, 1983; children: Robert Charlton, Alexandra Elizabeth. BS, Davidson Coll., 1978; MD, Med. Coll. Va., 1982. Diplomate Am. Bd. Internal Medicine, Am. Bd. Pulmonary Medicine, Am. Bd. Critical Care Medicine. Intern and resident in internal medicine Med. U. S.C., Charleston, 1982-85, fellow div. pulmonary and critical care medicine, 1986-87, instr. medicine div. pulmonary and critical care medicine, 1987-88, asst. prof., 1988—93, assoc. prof., 1993—2003, prof., 2003—, dir. Pulmonary Function Lab., 1991—. Dir. Alpha-1 Found. Rsch. Registry. Contbr. articles to profl. jours., chapters to books. Fellow: Am. Coll. Chest Physicians; mem.: Am. Thoracic Soc. Home: 17 Bull St Charleston SC 29401-1317 Office: Med University SC Pulmonary Medicine Unit 96 Jonathan Lucas St Charleston SC 29425-6300

STRANGE, DONALD ERNEST, healthcare company executive; b. Ann Arbor, Mich., Aug. 13, 1944; s. Carl Britton and Donna Ernestine (Tenney) Strange; m. Lyn Marie Purdy, Aug. 3, 1968 (div. Mar. 2001); children: Laurel Lyn, Chadwick Donald. BA, Mich. State U., 1966, MBA, 1968. Asst. dir. Holland (Mich.) City Hosp., 1968-72, assoc. dir., 1972-74; exec. dir. Bascom Palmer Eye Inst./Anne Bates Leach Eye Hosp., U. Miami, Fla., 1974-77; v.p. strategic planning and rsch. Hosp. Corp. Am., Nashville, 1977-80, group v.p. Boston, 1980-82, regional v.p., 1982-87; chmn., chief exec. officer HCA Healthcare Can., Toronto, 1985-87; exec. v.p. Avon Products, Inc., NYC, 1987-89; chmn. Sigecom, Ltd., Greenwich, Conn., 1989-94, U.S. Home-Care Corp., 1990-91; exec. v.p., COO, dir. EPIC Healthcare Group, Dallas, 1991-93; chmn, CEO TransCare Corp., Dallas, 1993-95; chmn., CEO First New Eng. Dental Ctrs., Inc., Boston, 1996-98; pres., CEO Behavorial Healthcare Ptnrs., Inc., Quincy, Mass., 2000; sr. v.p. Bon Secours Health Sys. Inc., Mariottsville, Md., 2001—06, COO, 2006—08. Dir. Altoona (Pa.) Regional Health Sys., 2004—08, Bon Secours Cottage Health Sys., Grosse Pointe, Mich., 2002—07. Trustee Boston Ballet, 1998—2001, chmn. bd. overseers, 1999—2001. Mem. Harvard Club (Boston), Nat. Arts Club (N.Y.). Episcopalian. Personal E-mail: don413@mac.com.

STRANGE, THEODORE, internist, educator; m. Valerie Panataleone; children: Elizabeth, Victoria, Marc, John. Grad. magna cum laude, Manhattan Coll.; MD, Suny Downstate, 1985. Cert. geriatic medicine, diplomate Am. Bd. Internal Medicine. Resident tng. Staten Island Univ. Hosp., chief resident, assoc. dir. medicine South, v.p. med. ops. South, med. dir. Geriatric Psychiatry South divsn., pres. med. and dental staff; assoc. clin. prof. medicine SUNY Downstate; co-founder and exec. v.p. Univ. Physicians Group. Bd. dirs. dept. health, NY; bd. dirs. Hosp. Coun. Corp., NY; assoc. bd. trustee Staten Island Univ. Hosp.; bd. trustee Xaverian High Sch. Bd. trustee Heartshare Human Svcs. Orgn.; actively involved Our Lady Star of the Sea. Recipient Louis R. Miller Leadership award, 2007, Ellis Island medal of honor award, 2008. Fellow: ACP; mem.: Gov. Health Care Adv. Coun., Am. Bd. of Quality Assurance and Utilization Rev. (diplomat). Avocation: travel. Office: Staten Island University Hospital 68 Seguine Ave Staten Island NY 10309 Office Phone: 718-356-6500. Office Fax: 718-356-0348.

STRASBURGER, VICTOR C., pediatrician; b. Balt., Oct. 7, 1949; s. Arthur Charles and Marjorie (Cohen) S.; m. Alison Reeve, Aug. 18, 1984; children: Max, Katya. BA summa cum laude in English, Yale U., New Haven, 1971; MD, Harvard U., 1975. Intern Children's Hosp.- U. Wash., Seattle, 1975-76, resident, 1976-77; residency Boston Children's Hosp., 1977-78; dir. adolescent medicine Bridgeport Hosp., Conn., 1979-86; vis. lectr. St. Mary's Hosp. Med. Sch., London, 1986-87; chief div. adolescent medicine sch. medicine U. N.Mex., Albuquerque, 1987—, prof. pediats., 1997—. Cons. Nat. PTA, Washington and Chgo., 1978-86; SAHM Adele Hofmann vis. prof., 2007. Author: Rounding Third and Heading Home, 1974, Adolescent Medicine: A Practical Guide, 1991, 2d edit., 1998, Getting Your Kids to Say No in the '90's When You Said Yes in the '60's, 1993, (with B. Wilson & A. Jordon) Children, Adolescents, and the Media, 2nd edit., 2009, (with R. Brown, P. Braverman, C. Holland, P. Rogers and S. Coupey) Care of the Adolescent: A Handbook for Primary Care, 2006; editor: Basic Adolescent Gynecology, 1990; editor-in-chief Adolescent Medicine: State of the Art Revs., 1989—. Recipient Adele Hofmann award, 2000, Outstanding Achievement award, Holroyd-Sherry award, 2000, Hofmann Vis. Prof. award, 2007, Vis. Professorship, U. Otago, New Zealand, 2010. Fellow Am. Acad. Pediatrics, Soc. for Adolescent Medicine; mem. Phi Beta Kappa. Office: University N Mex Sch Medicine Dept Pediats MSC10 5590 1 Univ New Mex Albuquerque NM 87131-0001 Home Phone: 505-856-7943; Office Phone: 505-272-0338. Business E-Mail: vstrasburger@salud.unm.edu.

STRASNICK, BARRY, otolaryngologist, health facility administrator, educator; b. Malden, Mass., Nov. 16, 1958; m. Victoria S. Strasnick; children: Evan, Ryan. BA in Biology summa cum laude, Boston U., 1980; MD, Baylor U., 1985. Diplomate Am. Bd. Otolaryngology. Intern Baylor Coll. Medicine, Houston, 1985—86, resident, 1986—87, UCLA Sch. Medicine, 1987—90; clin. prof. Vanderbilt U., 1991—92; from asst. prof. to assoc. prof. Ea. Va. Med. Sch., Norfolk, 1993—99, prof., 2000—, chmn., 1999—; dir. Hearing & Balance Ctr. DePaul Med. Ctr., Norfolk, 1993—; dir. pediatric otology divsn. Children's Hosp. King's Daus., Norfolk, 1993—. Co-author: (book) English Textbook of Otolaryngology, 1994, Ololaryngology, 1997, Pediatric Otolaryngology - H/N Surgery, 1998, The Ear: A Textbook of Otology, 2000. Chmn. Va. State Adv. Commn. Universal Newborn Hearing Screening, Richmond, 1998—; bd. dirs. Ear Ctr., Norfolk, 2000—. Fellow, Head/neck Surgery Found., 1997—. Fellow: Am. Acad. Otolaryngology; mem.: Norfolk Acad. Medicine, Tidewater Otolaryngology & Ophthalmology Soc., Va. Soc. Otolaryngologists (bd. dirs. 1997—), Va. Med. Soc. (Dr. Clarence A. Holland award 2001), Soc. Univ. Otolaryngologist. Office: Ea Va Med Sch 600 Gresnam Dr 1100 Norfolk VA 23507 Office Phone: 757-388-6200. Business E-Mail: strasnb@evms.edu. *

STRASSBERG, BARBARA ESTHER, pediatrician, educator; b. Monticello, NY, 1946; d. Irving Strassberg; m. Harold Enten, Nov. 18, 1984. Grad. magna cum laude, Bklyn. Coll.; grad. cum laude, Upstate Med. Coll.; MD in Edn., SUNY Syracuse, 1981. Cert. in pediat. Am. Bd. Med. Specialties, 1986. Intern in pediat. NY Presbyn. Hosp., 1981—82, resident, 1982—84, St. Lukes Roosevelt Hosp., attending pediatrician; assoc. prof. clinical pediat. Columbia U. Coll. Physicians and Surgeons; pediatrician Riverdale Pediat., NY. Named to America's Top Doctors, 2006. Office: Riverdale Pediat 2600 Netherland Ave Bronx NY 10463 Office Phone: 718-796-3580. Office Fax: 718-796-3987.

STRASSLER, MARC A., lawyer, retail executive; b. 1948; m. Meryl Strassler. BA, Bklyn. Coll., CUNY; JD, George Washington U. Bar: 1973. Joined Pathmark Stores Inc., Carteret, NJ, 1974, v.p., gen. counsel, sec., sr. v.p., gen. counsel, sec., 1998—2007; exec. v.p., gen. counsel, sec. Rite Aid Corp., 2009—. Office: Rite Aid Corp 30 Hunter Lane Camp Hill PA 17001 Office Phone: 732-499-3000. *

STRATHEARN, LANE, developmental pediatrician, neuroscientist; b. Redcliffe, Queensland, Australia, Apr. 4, 1967; s. Alan Inglis and Lucy Elizabeth Strathearn; m. Sonja Kay Hardman, Dec. 18, 1990; children: Lana Rose, Olivia Kay, Adam Inglis, Camilla Jane, Jacob Lane, Samuel Reginald, Sophia Elizabeth. MBBS, U. Queensland, 1992, PhD in Medicine, 2009. Pediatric chief resident Mater Misericordiae Childrens Hosp., Brisbane, 2000; assoc. lectr. U. Queensland, 2000; instr. Baylor Coll. Medicine, Houston, 2002—04, asst. prof., 2004—. Bd. mem. Internat. Assn. Study Attachment, 2008—. Contbr. articles to profl. jours. Recipient United Med. Protection Conf. prize, Australasian Conf. Child Abuse and Neglect, 1999, New Investigator award, Perinatal Soc. Australia and New Zealand, 2000; grant, Nat. Inst. Child Health and Human Devel., 2004—08, 2010—, Nat. Insts. Health RO1, 2010. Fellow: Royal Australasian Coll. Physicians (Pediat. Travelling fellowship 1999); mem.: Soc. Neuroscience. Mem. Lds Ch. Office: Tex Children's Hosp 6701 Fannin St Ste 1530 Houston TX 77030-2399 Business E-Mail: lanes@bcm.edu.

STRATHERN, JEFFREY N., medical researcher; PhD, U. Oreg., 1977. Sr. staff mem. Yeast Genetics Lab. Cold Spring Harbor Lab.; joined ABL-Basic Rsch. Program Nat. Cancer Inst., NIH, Frederick, 1984, joined Divsn. Basic Sciences (now Ctr. Cancer Rsch.), 1999; chief Gene Regulation and Chromosome Biology Lab. Ctr. Cancer Rsch., Nat. Cancer Inst., NIH, Frederick, head Genome Recombination and Regulation Sect., dep. dir. Office: Gene Regulation and Chromosome Biology Lab Nat Cancer Inst at Frederick PO Box B Bldg 539 Rm 152 Frederick MD 21701-1201 Office Phone: 301-846-1274. Office Fax: 301-846-6911. E-mail: strather@mail.ncifcrf.gov, strathej@mail.nih.gov. *

STRATTON, MARIANN, retired military nursing executive; b. Houston, Apr. 6, 1945; d. Max Millard and Beatrice Agnes (Roemer) S.; m. Lawrence Mallory Stickney, nov. 15, 1977 (dec.). BSN, BA in English, Sacred Heart Dominican Coll., 1966; MA in Mgmt., Webster Coll., 1977; MSN, U. Va., 1981. Cert. adult nurse practitioner. Ensign USN, 1966, advanced through grades to rear adm., 1991; patient care coord. Naval Regional Med. Ctr., Charleston, SC, 1981-83; nurse corps plans officer Naval Med. Command, Washington, 1983-86; dir. nursing svcs. U.S. Naval Hosp., Naples, Italy, 1986-89, Naval Hosp., San Diego, 1989-91; chief pers. mgmt. Bur. Medicine & Surgery, Washington, 1991-94; dir. USN Nurse Corps, Washington, 1991-94; ret. USN, 1994. Decorated Disting. Svc. medal, Meritorious Svc. medal with two stars, Naval Achievement medal, Navy Commendation medal. Mem. Interagy. Inst. Fed. Health Care Execs., Am. Volksporting Assn., Tex. Wanders, U. Va. Raven Soc., Fiber Artists San Antonio.

STRAUB, DIANE MARIE, physician, educator; b. Akron, Ohio, June 6, 1968; BS, Ohio State U., 1991; MD, Johns Hopkins U., 1995. Chief, divsn. adolescent medicine, assoc. prof. U. South Fla., 2002—. Mem.: Soc. Adolescent Health and Medicine. Office: University South Fla Dept Pediat 2 Tampa General Cir Tampa FL 33606 Office Fax: 813-259-8792. Business E-Mail: dstraub@health.usf.edu.

STRAUCH, BERISH, plastic surgeon, hand and cosmetic surgeon; b. NYC, Sept. 19, 1933; m. Rena (Feuerstein), June 12, 1955; children: Robert, Laurie. BA, Columbia U., 1955, MD, 1959. Diplomate Am. Bd. Surgery, Am. Bd. Plastic Surgery, qualification in hand surgery. Intern Bellevue Hosp., NYC, 1959—60; resident gen. surgery Montefiore Med. Ctr., Bronx, NY, 1960—64; hand surgery fellow Roosvelt Hosp., NYC, 1961; resident plastic surgery Stanford U., Palo Alto, Calif., 1966—67, chief resident, 1967—68; asst. prof. plastic surgery Albert Einstein Coll. Medicine, Bronx, NY, 1968—76, assoc. prof., 1976—81; chief plastic surgery svc. Montefiore Med. Ctr. and Albert Einstein Coll. Medicine, Bronx, NY, 1978—87; prof. plastic surgery Albert Einstein Coll. Medicine and Montefiore Med. Ctr., Bronx, NY, 1981—; acting chmn. dept. plastic surgery Montefiore Med. Ctr. and Albert Einstein Coll. Medicine, Bronx, NY, 1987—89, chmn., 1988—2007. Instr. Stanford U., 1967-68; vis. plastic surgeon Sing Sing Prison, N.Y., 1968-75; pres. World Soc. Reconstructive Microsurgery, 2007—,mktg. cons. Berish Strauch Ltd., 2009-; chair med. adv. bd. Ivivi-Health Scis. Inc., 2010-. Co-author: (with others) Atlas of Microvascular Surgery: Anatomy and Operative Approaches, 1993 (Best Healt Sci. Book, Doody's Rating Svc. 1993), 2nd edit., 2006; co-editor: (textbook) Course on Microsurgery, 1976, (with others) Grabb's Encyclopedia of Flaps, 3 vols., 1990, (Outstanding Publ. in Clin. Medicine, Assn. Am. Pub. 1990), 2nd edit. 1997, 3rd edit. 2008, Anatomy of the Hand and the Surgical Implications, 2005, Encyclopedia of Body Sculpting After Massive Weight Loss, 2010; contbr. articles to profl. jours. and 20 chpts. to sci. books and ency.; assoc. editor Plastic and Reconstructive Surgery, 1982-88; founder, editor-in-chief Jour. Reconstructive Microsurgery, 1983-2008, Mktg. editor JRM, 2008-, contbr. to ency. Capt. Med. Corp. U.S. Army, 1964-66, Mem. AAAS, ACS, Am. Soc. for Reconstructive Microsurgery (founder, past sec., treas., pres., chmn. Founder's Lectr. 1988), Am. Assn. Plastic Surgeons, Am. Soc. Reconstructive Microsurgery (chmn. founding coun. 1983-84, pres. 1984-85). Med. Soc. State of N.Y., Am. Trauma Soc. (founding mem.), N.Y. Acad. Sci., Am. Soc. for Peripheral Nerve Surgery (pres. 1993-94), World Soc. Reconstruction Microsurgery (pres. 2008-), Rhinoplasty Soc. (pres. 2008) and others. Home Phone: 914-967-9019; Office Phone: 914-282-4987. Business E-Mail: berishstrauch@gmail.com.

STRAUCHEN, JAMES ARTHUR, medical educator, pathologist; b. NYC, July 11, 1948; s. Murray and Helen Strauchen; m. Vivienne Sari Gold, May 27, 1972; children: Jennifer Mia, Katherine Sinead. BA magna cum laude, Columbia Coll., NYC, 1968; MD with honors, NY U., NYC, 1972. Diplomate Am. Bd. Pathology, 1978, cert. hematology Am. Bd. Pathology, 1981, diplomate Am. Bd. Internal Medicine, 1975, cert. med. oncology Am. Bd. Internal Medicine, 1977, hematology Am. Bd. Internal Medicine, 1978. Asst. prof. pathology Stanford U., Sch. Medicine, Palo Alto, Calif., 1978—81; assoc. prof. pathology U. Rochester, Sch. Medicine, NY, 1982—83; prof. pathology and neoplastic diseases Mt. Sinai Sch. Medicine, NYC, 1983—, vice chair dept. pathology, 2005—. Pres. NY Cancer Soc., NYC, 2006—07. Lt. comdr. USPHS, 1974—78. Mem.: Soc. for Study of Blood, NY Path. Soc., Arkadi M. Rywlin Pathology Club, Assn. Dirs. Anatomic and Surg. Pathology, Am. Soc. Hematology (assoc.), Phi Beta Kappa, Alpha Omega Alpha (pres. 1971—72). Office: Mt Sinai Sch Medicine 1 Gustave Levy Pl New York NY 10029 Office Phone: 212-241-9142. Office Fax: 212-289-2899. Business E-Mail: james.strauchen@mssm.edu.

STRAUMAN, TIMOTHY J., psychology professor, department chairman; b. Nov. 5, 1956; m. Janice Johnstone; children: Anne Jacqueline, Katherine Janice. BA in Psychology and Comm., magna cum laude, Duquesne U., Pitts., 1978; MA in Psychology and Human Devel., U. Chgo., 1979; PhD in Clin. and Social/Personality Psychology, NYU, 1987. Lic. clin. psychologist NC. Rsch. asst. stress and illness project Dept. Behavioral Sci. U. Chgo., 1978—79; sr. clin. data coord. Lederle Laboratories, Pearl River, NY, 1980—82, clin. rsch. cons., 1982—84; adj. faculty mem. Dept. Social Sciences Rockland CC, Suffern, NY, 1981—83; sr. systems analyst ORI Inc., Bethesda, Md., 1983; tchg. asst. Dept. Psychology NYU, 1982—84, statistical cons. clin. and devel. area groups Dept. Psychology, 1983—86; rsch. asst. Anxiety Disorders Clinic NY State Psychiatric Inst., 1984—87; asst. prof. clin. psychology area group Dept. Psychology U. Wis., Madison, 1987—92, assoc. prof. Depts. Psychology and Psychiatry, 1992—2000, dir. psychology tng. Dept. Psychiatry, 1992—2000, co-dir. depression treatment program, 1994—2000; prof. Dept. Psychology & Neurosci., Dept. Psychiatry and Behavioral Sci. Duke U., Durham, NC, 2000—, chmn. Dept. Psychology & Neurosci., 2002—. Crisis intervention svc. Rockland Cmty. Coll. Mental Health Ctr., Pomona, NY, 1980—82; clin. psychology intern Albert Einstein Med. Coll., Montefiore Med. Ctr., Bronx, NY, 1986—87; pvt. practice Mental Health Resources, Madison, Wis., 1988—92; clin. asst. prof. Ctr. for Affective Disorders Dept. Psychiatry U. Wis., Madison, 1990—92. Mem. editl. bd. Jour. Abnormal Psychology, 1998—, Jour. Personality and Social Psychology, 2002—, Personality and Social Psychology Bulletin, 2002—, Psychology Rev., 2003—, Self and Identity, 2002—, Jour. of Personality, 1991—98, assoc. editor, 1994—97. Fellow: Acad. Cognitive Therapy; mem.: Beck Inst. Cognitive Therapy and Rsch. (Van Ameringen fellow), Soc. Rsch. in Psychopathology, Soc. Psychotherapy Rsch., Am. Assn. for Behavior Therapy, Soc. Experimental Social Psychology, Soc. for Sci. of Clin. Psychology, Am. Assn. for Applied and Preventive Psychology, Am. Psychological Soc., APA, Acad. Psychological Clin. Sci. (co-chmn. internship com. 1998—2001, chmn. membership com. 2003—, treas. 2004—). Office: Dept Psychology & Neurosci Box 90086 Duke Univ 9 Flowers Dr Durham NC 27708 Office Phone: 919-660-5709. Office Fax: 919-660-5726. E-mail: tjstraum@duke.edu.

STRAUS, LORNA PUTTKAMMER, biology professor; b. Chgo., Feb. 15, 1933; d. Ernst Wilfred and Helen Louise (Monroe) Puttkammer; m. Francis Howe Straus II, June 11, 1955; children: Francis, Helen, Christopher, Michael. BA magna cum laude, Radcliffe Coll., 1955; MS, U. Chgo., 1960, PhD, 1962. Rsch. assoc. dept. anatomy U. Chgo., 1962—64, instr., 1964—67, asst. prof., 1967—73, assoc. prof., 1973—87, prof., 1987—, asst. dean, then dean students, 1967—82, dean admissions, 1975—80, marshal, 1999—. Trustee Radcliffe Coll., Cambridge, Mass., 1973-83; chmn. Cmty. Found., Mackinac Island, Mich., 1994—. Recipient silver medal Coun. for Advancement and Support Edn., 1987. Mem.: North Ctrl. Assn. (commr. 1998—, pres.-elect 2001—02, pres. 2002—04), Harvard U. Alumni Assn. (bd. dirs. 1980—83), Phi Beta Kappa. Avocations: travel, gardening. Home: 5642 S Kimbark Ave Chicago IL 60637-1606 Office: U Chgo 5845 S Ellis Ave Chicago IL 60637-1476 Office Phone: 773-702-7384. Business E-Mail: hlps@uchicago.edu.

STRAUS, ROBERT, behavioral sciences educator; b. New Haven, Jan. 9, 1923; s. Samuel Hirsh and Alma (Fleischner) Straus; m. Ruth Elisabeth Dawson, Sept. 8, 1945; children: Robert James, Carol Martin, Margaret Dawson, John William. BA, Yale U., 1943, MA, 1945, PhD, 1947. Asst. prof. Yale U., 1948—51, rsch. assoc. applied physiology, 1951—53; acting dir. Conn. Child Study and Treatment Home, New Haven, 1952—53; assoc. prof. preventive medicine SUNY Upstate Med. Ctr., 1953—56; prof. med. sociology U. Ky., Lexington, 1956—59, prof. dept. behavioral sci. Coll. Medicine, also chmn. dept., 1959—87; dir. for sci. devel. Med. Rsch. Inst. San Francisco, 1991—93. Vis. fellow Yale U., 1968—69; vis. prof. U. Calif., Berkeley, 1978, 86; sec. Com. Med. Sociology, 1955—57; chmn. Coop. Com. Study Alcoholism, 1961—63, Nat. Adv. Com. on Alcoholism, 1966—69; mem. Nat. Adv. Coun. on Alcohol Abuse and Alcoholism, 1984—87; trustee Med. Rsch. Inst. San Francisco, 1988—93; mem. Calif. Pacific Med. Ctr. Rsch. Coun., 1993. Author: Medical Care for Seamen, 1950; author: (with S.D. Bacon) Drinking in College, 1953; author: Alcohol and Society, 1973, Escape From Custody, 1974, A Medical School is Born, 1996; co-editor: Medicine and Society, 1963; mem. editl. bd.: Jour. Studies on Alcohol, 1950—2000. Pres. Bluegrass R.R. Mus., 1980. Mem.: Inst. Medicine NAS, Acad. Behavioral Medicine Rsch., Am. Pub. Health Assn. (lifetime achievement award sect. on alcohol, tobacco and other drugs 1993), Assn. Behavioral Scis. and Med. Edn. (pres. 1974), Am. Sociol. Assn. (chmn. med. sociology sect. 1967—68, Leo G. Reeder award Disting. Contbn. to Med. Sociology 1998), Sigma Xi, Phi Beta Kappa. Home: 656 Raintree Rd Lexington KY 40502-2874

STRAUSER, DAVID ROSS, healthcare educator, director; b. Sept. 4, 1968; m. Mary Ellen Chryst, Apr. 7, 1990; children: Matthew, David, John. MS, U. Wis., 1990, PhD, 1995. Asst. prof. U. Memphis, 1995-2001, dir. rehab. studies, 1998-2000, assoc. prof., 2001—05, U. Ill., Champaign, 2005—06, assoc. dir. Disability Rsch. Inst., 2006—08. Dir. cmty. based job readiness program U. Memphis, 1997—2001; dir. Ctr. Rehab. and Employment Rsch., 2000—05; owner Vocat. Consulting Svcs.; presenter in field; commr. Commn. Rehab. Counselors Cert., 2001—06, rsch. cons. Contbr. articles to nat. and internat. jours.; mem. editl. rev. bd.: leading jours. in field; co-editor (editor in chief): Jour. of Rehabilitation, 2001—07; editor in chief Rehab. Rsch. Policy & Educator. Recipient New Faculty Rsch. award Nat. Coun. on Rehab. Edn., Rsch. award Am. Counseling Rehab. Assn., 2002, 03, Dean's Excellence award for rsch. and scholarship, 2004, Rehab. Svcs. Adminstrn. Commn. award, 2004, James Garrett Disting. Rsch. award, Am. Rehab. Coun. Assn., 2011, Named Rschr. of Yr. Nat. Coun. Rehab. EDn, 2011 Mem. APA, Am. Rehab. Counseling Assn. (com. on rsch. and knowledge, Rsch. award 2002). Roman Catholic. Office: Univ Ill Dept Cmty Health 213A Huff Hall 1206 S 4th St Champaign IL 61820 Home Phone: 217-355-8714; Office Phone: 217-244-3936. Personal E-mail: drstrauser@insight.bb.com. Business E-Mail: strauser@uiuc.edu, strauser@illinois.edu.

STRAUSS, ARNOLD WILBUR, pediatrician, educator; b. Benton Harbor, Mich., Mar. 31, 1945; m. Patricia Tylisz, Mar. 14, 1970; children: Natasha Tanya, Lara Katyana. BA, Stanford U., 1966; MD, Washington U., St. Louis, Mo., 1970. Diplomate Am. Bd. Pediatrics. Resident in pediatrics St. Louis Childrens Hosp., St. Louis, 1970-72, fellow in pediatric cardiology, 1972-75; postdoctoral rsch. fellow Merck Sharp & Dohme Rsch. Labs., Rahway, NJ, 1975-77; asst. prof. pediatrics Washington U., St. Louis, 1977-79, asst. prof. biol. chemistry, 1977-80, assoc. prof. pediatrics, 1979-82, assoc. prof. biol. chemistry, 1980-82, dir. divsn. pediatric cardiology dept. pediatrics, 1981—2000, prof. pediatrics, 1982—2000, prof. biol. chemistry, 1983-89, prof. biochemistry and molecular physics, 1989-92, prof. molecular biology and pharmacology, 1992—2000, adj. prof. pediatrics, 2000—07; prof. molecular physiology and biophysics Vanderbilt U. Sch. Medicine, Nashville, 2000—07, James C. Overall prof. pediatrics, chair pediatrics, 2000—07, investigator, Kennedy Ctr. for Rsch. in Human Devel., 2000—07, investigator, human genetics prog., 2001—07, med. dir. Monroe Carell Jr. Children's Hosp., 2000—07; B.K. Rachford prof. and chair pediatrics U. Cin. Coll. Medicine, 2007—; med. dir., dir. rsch. found. Cin. Children's Hosp. Med. Ctr., 2007—. Investigator Am. Heart Assn., 1979-1984. Contbr. articles, chapters to books. NIH program grantee, 1989, prin. investigator, 1994; recipient E. Mead Johnson award for excellence in pediatric rsch., 1991, Alumni Faculty award, Washington U., 1995, Basic Sci. award, Am. Heart Assn., 2006. Fellow Am. Acad. Pediatrics; mem. AAAS, Inst. Medicine, Soc. for Pediatric Rsch. (mem. cardiovascular coun. 1987-90), Am. Coll. Cardiology (coun. Mo. chpt. 1992-94), Am. Heart Assn., Am. Soc. Clin. Investigation, Am. Pediatric Soc., Am. Assn. Physicians, Am. Physiol. Soc., Internat. Pediatric Rsch. Found. (trustee, sec. 1995—), Phi Beta Kappa, Alpha Omega Alpha. Roman Catholic. Office: Cin Childrens Hosp Med Ctr 3333 Burnet Ave Cincinnati OH 45229-3039 Office Phone: 513-636-2942. E-mail: arnold.strauss@cchmc.org.

STRAUSS, JEROME FRANK, III, medical researcher, educator; b. Chgo., May 2, 1947; s. Jerome Frank (Jr.) and Josephine (Newberger) Strauss; m. Catherine Blumlein, June 20, 1970; children: Jordan L., Elizabeth J. BA, Brown U., 1969; MD, U. Pa., 1974, PhD, 1975. Asst. prof. U. Pa. Sch. Medicine, Phila., 1976—83, assoc. prof., 1983—85, prof., 1985—, assoc. chair, 1987—, assoc. dean, 1990—98; Luigi Mastroianni jr. prof. and founding dir. Ctr. Rsch. on Women's Health and Reproduction, Phila., 1990—94; prof. Inst. Medicine NAS, 1994—; dean, exec. v.p. med. affairs, prof. ob-gyn. Va. Commonwealth U. Sch. Medicine, Richmond, 2005—. Biochem. endocrinology study sect. NIH, 1983—87, Nat. Adv. Child Health and Human Devel. Coun., 2002—06; chmn. population rsch. com. NICHHD, 1989—92; chair Reproductive Scientist of the Ams. Network, 1995—; dir. Ctr. Excellence in Women's Health, 1996—2002; co-chair Indo-U.S. Joint Working Grp. on Reproductive Sci. and Contraceptive Tech., 1999—; bd. dirs. Burroughs Wellcome Fund, 2003—; trustee Berlex Found., 2005—; Cheung Kong lectr., prof. Heilongjiang U. Chinese Medicine, 2006—08; clin. rsch. adv. com. NIEHS, 2009—. Editor: Lipoprotein and Cholesterol Metabolism in Sterodogenic Tissues, 1985, Current Topics in Membrane Research, 1987, Uterine and Embryonic Factors in Early Pregnancy, 1991, New Achievements in Research of Ovarian Function, 1995, Cell Death in Reproductive Physiology, 1997, Molecular Biology in Reproductive Medicine, 1999, Ovarian Function Research: Present and Future, 1999, Reproductive Medicine Molecular, Cellular and Genetic Fundamentals, 2002, New Frontiers in Contraceptive Research, 2004, Yen and Jaffe's Reproductive Endocrinology, 2004, Preterm Birth, 2007, Steroids jour., 1993—; assoc. editor Ency. of Reproduction, 1998—, assoc. editor, mem. editl. bd. Jour. Lipid Rsch., 1982—90, corr. editor Jour. Steroid Biochem. and Molecular Biology, 1990—99, mem. editl. bd. Endocrinology, 1986—90, 1997—2000, Biology of Reprodn., 1986—90, 1999—2003, Jour. of Women's Health, 1991—, Jour. Soc. Gynecologic Investigation, 1993—, Placenta, 1995—98, Trends in Endocrinology and Metabolism, 1999—2008, Reference en Gynecologie Obstetrique, 1999—, Seminars in Reproductive Endocrinology, 2000—, Jour. Endocrinology, 2000—06, Human Reproduction Update, 2001—05, Science, 2004—, assoc. editor Molecular Human Reproduction, 2007—. Recipient Transatlantic medal, Brit. Endocrine Soc., 1998, Disting. Grad. award, U. Pa., 2005, NAS Inst. Medicine, 2005, Rectoral medal, U. Chile, 2009. Fellow: Internat. Acad. Human Reproduction; mem.: Perinatal Rsch. Soc., Am. Soc. for Reproductive Medicine, Soc. for Study of Reproduction (bd. dirs. 1989—91, Rsch. award 1992), Endocrine Soc., Soc. Gynecologic Investigation (pres. 2003, Pres.'s Achievement award 1990, Disting. Scientist award 2006). Home: 2808 Monument Ave Unit 3 Richmond VA 23221 Office: Va Commonwealth U Dean's Office Sch Medicine 1101 E Marshall St Rm 1-070 Richmond VA 23298 Business E-Mail: jfstrauss@vcu.edu. *

STRAUSS, NANCY E., physiatrist, educator; MD, SUNY, Syracuse, 1988. Diplomate Am. Bd. Physical Medicine and Rehab., 2003, Am. Bd. Pediatrics, cert. electrodiagnostic medicine. Intern Nassau County Med. Ctr., East Meadow, NY, resident physical medicine & rehab., 1989—92; clin. prof. physical medicine & rehab. Coll. of Physicians and Surgeons Columbia Univ., NYC; attending physician NY-Presbyn. Hosp. Columbia Univ. Med. Ctr., NYC, Weill Cornell Med. Ctr. Office: New York-Presbyterian Hospital Baker Pavilion 16th Fl 525 E 68th St New York NY 10065 Office Phone: 212-746-1500. Office Fax: 212-746-8303.

STREETEN, BARBARA WIARD, ophthalmologist, medical educator; b. Candia, NH, Mar. 3, 1925; d. Robert Campbell Wiard and Gertrude Sarah Matheson; m. David Henry Palmer Streeten, Aug. 2, 1952; children: Robert Duncan, Elizabeth Anne, John Palmer. AB magna cum laude, Tufts U., 1945, MD cum laude, 1950. Diplomate Am. Bd. Ophthalmology. Jr. resident in gen. pathology Mallory Inst., Boston City Hosp., 1951-52; fellow in ophthalmic pathology Mass. Eye and Ear Infirmary, Boston, 1952-53; resident in ophthalmology Wayne County Gen. Hosp., Eloise, Mich., 1953-56; from jr. to sr. clin. instr. ophthalmology U. Mich. Med. Sch., Ann Arbor, 1956-60; from asst. prof. to prof. ophthalmology SUNY Health Sci. Ctr. (now called SUNY Upstate Med. U.), Syracuse, 1964—, dir. eye pathology lab., 1966—; from asst. prof. to prof. pathology SUNY Health Sci. Ctr., Syracuse, 1968—. Contbr. more than 120 articles to profl. jours., chapters to books. Mem. vision study sect. Nat. Eye Inst., NIH, Bethesda, Md., 1977-80, mem. bd. sci. counselors, 1982-86; mem. editl. bd., mem. editl. adv. com. Ophthalmology jour., 1982-94; gen. editor Investigative Ophthalmology and Visual Sci., 1979-82, mem. editl. bd., 1987-92. Grantee Nat. Eye Inst., NIH, 1975—2002. Mem. Am. Assn. Ophthalmic Pathologists (charter, past pres., bd. dirs., Zimmerman medal 1997), Am. Acad. Ophthalmology (honor award 1990), Verhoeff Ophthalmic Pathology Soc. (past pres.), Assn. for Rsch. in Vision and Ophthalmology (past sect. chmn.), Internat. Soc. Ophthalmic Pathology (co-v.p. N.Am. 1990-92), Phi Beta Kappa, Alpha Omega Alpha. Episcopalian. Achievements include establishment of elastic system nature of the suspensory ligament of the ocular lens; ultrastructural and immunopathologic contributions to diseases of the ocular connective tissue matrix, particularly those related to cataract and glaucoma. Office: SUNY Upstate Med Univ WH Rm 2107 766 Irving Ave Syracuse NY 13210-1602 Home: 177 Field St Corning NY 14830-2304

STREETER, OSCAR EDWARD, JR., radiation oncologist; b. Roanoke, Va., May 20, 1955; s. Oscar Edward Sr. and Betty (Richardson) S.; m. Paulette Y. Saddler; 1 child, Rebecca. BS in Biology, USC; MD, Howard U., 1982. Diplomate Am. Bd. Med. Examiners. Intern U. Calif., Irvine, 1983-85; resident Howard U. Med. Ctr., Washington, 1986-89; resident tng. program dir. dept. radiation oncology U. So. Calif. Sch. Medicine, LA, 1990-94, asst. prof. radiation oncology, 1990-95, asst. prof. clin. radiation oncology, 1995-97, assoc. prof. clin. radiation oncology, 1997—; dept. radiation oncology chief physician LAC, U. So. Calif. Med. Ctr., 1992-94, U. So. Calif. Norris Cancer Ctr., 1994—. Chair cancer com. U. So. Calif. Sch. Medicine, LA, 1997, med. exec., 1995—, acad. tech. adv. com., 1997; mem. leadership coun. U. So. Calif. Cancer Ctr., 1995—. Contbr. articles to profl. jours. Chmn. NBLIC/Western Region, LA, 1995—; adv. bd. Wellness Com. Foothills, Pasadena, Calif., 1995—; bd. dirs. Real Men Cook Found., LA, 1993—, Women of Color Breast Cancer Survivors Project, L.A., 1995—; mem. Real Men Cook Found., 1994; mem. Maxine Waters-35th Dist. Com. Svc., Mem. of Congress; mem. health svcs. Office of Willie Brown Jr. Spkr. of Assembly 13 Dist. Grantee U. So. Calif., 1993, 93-96, U. Calif., 1993-95, Biotech. Comms., LA, 1995; named one of Top 100 Black Physicians in Am., Black Enterprise Mag., 2001; named to America's Top Doctors, 2001-06, Best Doctors in Am., 2003-06. Business E-Mail: ostreeter@aol.com.

STREIFF, MICHAEL BLAKE, medical educator; b. Cambridge, Mass., 1961; BS, Wash. and Lee U., 1983; MD, Johns Hopkins U., 1988. Assoc. prof. medicine Johns Hopkins U. Sch. Medicine, 2008—. Chmn., venous thromboembolism guideline com. Nat. Comprehensive Cancer Ctr. Network, 2009—11. Fellow: ACP; mem.: Internat. Soc. Thrombosis and Haemostasis, Am. Soc. Hematology. Office: 1830 E Monument St Ste 7300 Baltimore MD 21205 Office Fax: 410-614-8601. Business E-Mail: mstreif@jhmi.edu.

STREIM, JOEL E., geriatric psychiatry, educator; BA in Philosophy, Haverford Coll., 1973; MD, U. Rochester, 1978. Diplomate Am. Bd. Psychiatry and Neurology, 1988, Am. Bd. Psychiatry and Neurology-geriatric psychology, 2001. Resident internal medicine Rochester Gen. Hosp. Univ. of Rochester, NY, 1978—81, chief resident internal medicine Rochester Gen. Hosp., 1981—82, fellow med.-psychiat. liaison Strong Meml. Hosp., 1981—82; resident psychiatry Univ. of Wis. Hosp. & Clinics Madison, Wis., 1982—85; fellow geriatric psychiatry William S. Middleton Meml. Veterans Hosp., Madison, Wis., 1985—87, rsch. fellow geriatric psychiatry, 1987—88; prof. psychiatry Hosp. of th Univ. of Pa. Author: (publs.) Safer Drug Trials, for Young and Old Alike, 2002, The need to include geriatric patients in drug trials (letter to the editor), 2002; co-author (presenter): Policy and politics: health care priorities for the 107th Congress, 2002, Randomized clinical trial of venlafaxine versus sertraline for depressed nursing home residents, 2002, Depressive symptoms in the nursing home setting: evolving ideas, 2002, Diabetic control among veterans with severe mental illness, 2003, Quality of diabetes care for aging U.S. veterans with serious mental illness, 2003; co-author: Pharmacological treatment of depression in nursing home residents: a mental health services perspective, Regulatory oversight, payment policy, and quality improvement in mental health care in nursing homes, Psychiatric services in long term care, 2002. Office: University of Pennsylvania Section on Geriatric Psychiatry 3535 Market St Rm 3053 Philadelphia PA 19104-3309 Office Phone: 215-615-3086. Business E-Mail: jstreim@mail.med.upenn.edu.

STRENGTH, CATHERINE BUSH, nursing educator; b. New Orleans, Dec. 7, 1955; d. Joseph Ernest Jr. and Patsy Ruth (Johnson) Bush; m. Steven Cole Strength, Aug. 18, 1984. BSN, Southeastern La. U., 1977; M of Nursing, La. State U., 1981. RN, La.; cert. med.-surg. nurse, clin. nurse specialist, instr. BLS. Nurse emergency rm. East Jefferson Gen. Hosp., Metairie, La., 1977—81; dir. edn. and tng. St. Jude Hosp., Kenner, La., 1982—85; asst. prof. Charity Hosp. Sch. Nursing/Delgado C.C., New Orleans, 1990—94; assoc. prof. Charity Hosp. Sch. Nursing, New Orleans, 1994—2010; prof. Charity Delgado Sch. Nursings., 2010, NSS Charity Sch., 2010. Recipient Adult Svc. award, St. Martha Ch., Harvey, LA, 2009. Mem. Nat. League Nursing, Sigma Theta Tau (hon.), Epsilon Nu. Home: 3905 Lake Des Allemands Dr Harvey LA 70058-5502 Office: Charity Delgado Nursing Sch 450 S Claiborne Ave New Orleans LA 70112-1310 Office Phone: 504-571-1346. Business E-Mail: cstren@dcc.edu.

STRENJA-LINIC, INES, neurologist; b. Rijeka, Sept. 4, 1965; MD, Med. Sch., 1988; M, 1994. Neurologist Neurology Dept Clin. Hosp. Rijeka, 2002—. Mem.: Croatian Ultrasound Soc., Croatian Neurologist Soc. Avocation: politics. Office: Neurology Dept Clin Hosp Rijeka Rijeka Primorsko-Goranska 51000 Croatia Personal E-mail: medines4@yahoo.com.

STREUR, WILLIAM J. (BILL STREUR), state official, public health service officer; b. 1947; BS in Pre-Medicine, Northern Mich. U. Pres., CEO Upper Peninsula Health Plan, Mich.; sr. dir. First Health Services Alaska; dep. commr. for medicaid & health care policy Alaska Dept. Health & Social Services, Juneau, acting commr., 2010—11, commr., 2011—. Recipient Bronze Star, Meritorious Svc. Medal. Office: Alaska Department Health & Social Services Office Commissioner 350 Main St Room 404 PO Box 110601 Juneau AK 99811-0601 Office Phone: 907-465-3030. Office Fax: 907-465-3068. *

STREVENS, HELENA INGRID, obstetrician; b. Bromley, Kent, Eng., July 12, 1963; 1 child, Victor Strevens Bolmgren. MD, Gothenburg U., 1988, PhD, 2002. Cert. Physician 1990, Specialist In Ob-Gyn 1996. Obstetrics-gynecologist Dept. Ob Gyn Lund U. Hosps., Lund, Skåne, Sweden, 1996—. Home: Fjelievägen 15 B Lund S-22736 Sweden Office: University Hospital Dept Obstetrics-Gynecology 221 85 Lund S-22185 Sweden Home Phone: +46 46 145824; Office Phone: +46 46 172544. Office Fax: +46 46 157868. Personal E-mail: helena.strevens@med.lu.se. Business E-Mail: helena.strevens@skane.se.

STRICK, SADIE ELAINE, psychologist; d. Michael and Mary (Oziemblowski) Wierzbicki; m. John Mackovjak, Dec. 31, 1947 (dec. Mar. 1972); children: Deborah, Susan (dec.); m. Ellis Strick, Aug. 11, 1974 (dec Jan. 2005). BSW, U. Pitts., 1975, MEd, 1977, PhD, 1981. Lic. psychologist; diplomate Am. Bd. Med. Psychotherapists and Psychodiagnosticians. Psychologist I Mayview State Hosp., Bridgeville, Pa., 1984-87; owner Counseling & Behavior Specialists, P.C., Pitts., 1981—. Mem. C.G. Jung Ednl. Ctr., Pitts., 1980-99; guest speaker Compassionate Friends, Pitts., 1986—, Womens Career Conv., Pitts., 1982. Author: Troubling Dreams-Opening the Door to Self Awareness, 2011. Bd. dirs. OAR/Allegheny, Pitts., 1981-82. Fellow Pa. Psychol. Assn.; mem. APA. Avocations: writing, walking, travel, gourmet cooking, reading, music. Office: Counseling and Behavior Specialists PC 429 Forbes Ave Ste 1614 Pittsburgh PA 15219-1604 Office Phone: 412-765-1665. Personal E-mail: sadiestrick@verizon.net.

STRICKLAND, BONNIE RUTH, psychologist, educator; b. Louisville, Nov. 24, 1936; d. Roy E. and Billie P. (Whitfield) S. BS, Ala. Coll., 1958; MS, Ohio State U., 1960, PhD (USPHS fellow), 1962. Diplomate: clin. psychology Am. Bd. Examiners in Profl. Psychology. From asst. to asso. prof. psychology Emory U., Atlanta, 1962—73, dean of women, 1964—67; prof. psychology U. Mass., Amherst, 1973—2003, prof. emeritus, 2003—, chmn. dept. psychology, 1976—77, 1978—82, assoc. to chancellor, 1983—84. Mem. adv. coun. NIMH, 1984-87; Sigma Xi nat. lectr., 1991-93. Adv. editor numerous psychology jours., acad. pub. houses; contbg. author texts personality theory.; contbr. of numerous articles on social personality and clin. psychology to profl. jours.; contbg. author of two citation classics. Recipient Outstanding Faculty award Emory U., 1968-69; Chancellor's medal disting. service U. Mass., 1983. Fellow APA (pres. divsn. clin. psychology 1983, pres. divsn. gen. psychology 2005, chmn. bd. profl. affairs 1980-83, chmn. policy and planning bd. 1983-85, pres. 1987, bd. dirs. 1986-87, Outstanding Leadership award 1992, Disting. Contbns. and Psychology in the Pub. Interest award 1999, Presdl. Citation 2001), Am. Psychol. Soc. (founder 1988, bd. dirs. 1989-93), New Eng. Psychol. Assn. (Disting. Contbns. award 2002), Am. Assn. Applied and Preventive Psychology (founder 1990, bd. dirs. 1990-94, pres. 1992-94). Home: 558 Federal St Belchertown MA 01007-9754 Office: U Mass Dept Psychology Amherst MA 01003-7710

STRICKLER, HOWARD MARTIN, physician, director; b. New Haven, Oct. 26, 1950; s. Thomas David and Mildred Laing (Martin) S.; m. Susan Hunter, May 2, 1982; children: Hunter Gregory, Howard Martin Jr. BA, Berea Coll., 1975; MD, Univ. Louisville, 1979. Cert. Am. Assn. Med. Rev. Officers, 1993, diplomate Am. Bd. Addiction Medicine. Resident Anniston (Ala.) Family Practice Residency, 1979-82; pvt. practice Monteagle, Tenn., 1982-85; fellow in addictive diseases Willingway Hosp., Statesboro, Ga., 1985-86; faculty devel. fellow Univ. N.C., Chapel Hill, 1985-86; pvt. practice Birmingham, Ala., 1986-90; pres. Employers Drug Program Mgmt., Inc., Birmingham, 1990—; med. dir. Am. Health Svcs., Inc., 1993—2007. Med. dir.

Bradford Facilities, Birmingham, 1987-90, New Life Clinic, Bessemer, Ala., Physicians Smoke Free Clinic, Birmingham, 1988-90, Am. Health Svcs., Inc., 1993-2008; chmn. dept. family practice and emergency medicine Bessemer Carraway Med. Ctr., 1993-95. Mem. tennis anti-doping appeals com. ATP Tour, Inc., 1997; bd. dirs. Ala. Vets. Meml. Found. With U.S. Army, 1969-72, Vietnam. Decorated Bronze Star, Vietnam Campaign medal, Vietnam Svc. medal 3 Stars; Named Small Bus. Person of Yr., Birmingham Regional C. of C., 2007. Fellow Am. Acad. Family Physicians; mem. Am. Soc. Addiction Medicine (cert.), Am. Assn. Med. Rev. Officers (cert.), Med. Assn. State of Ala., Phi Kappa Phi. Methodist. Avocations: flying, tennis, golf. Home: 868 Tulip Poplar Dr Birmingham AL 35244-1633 Office: Howard M Strickler Md 505 20th St N Ste 1200 Birmingham AL 35203-4610 Home Phone: 205-985-9928; Office Phone: 205-326-3100. Business E-Mail: drs@edpm.com.

STRICKLER, JEFFREY HAROLD, pediatrician; b. Mpls., Oct. 14, 1943; s. Jacob Harold and Helen Cecelia (Mitchell) S.; m. Karen Anne Stewart, June 18, 1966; children: Hans Stewart, Liesl Ann. BA, Carleton Coll., 1965; MD, U. Minn., 1969. Diplomate Am. Bd. Pediatrics. Resident in pediatrics Stanford U., Calif., 1969-73; pvt. practice Helena, Mont., 1975—2005; chief staff Shodair Children's Hosp., Helena, 1984-86; consulting ptnr. Strickler Enterprises, 2006—. Dir. maternal-child health Lewis and Clark County, Helena, 1978-88; chief of staff St. Peters Hosp., Helena, 1994-96; bd.chmn. Helena Health Alliance, 1996-99; founding mem., bd. dirs. Caring Found. Mont., 1992-2005; bd. mem. Intermountain Opera Assn., 2007-. Author: Big Sky Names, An Amble Through Western History and Ecology on the Roads, Streams, and Developments of Big Sky Montana, 2008, The Skier's Guide to the Biggest Skiing in America, 2011. Mem. Mont. Gov.'s Task Force on Child Abuse, 1978-79; mem. steering com. Region VIII Child Abuse Prevention, Denver, 1979-82; bd. dirs. Helena Dist. 1 Sch. Bd., 1982-88, vice chmn., 1985-87. Maj. MC USAF, 1973—75. Fellow: Am. Acad. Pediatrics (vice chmn. Mont. chpt. 1981—84, chmn. 1984—87, mem. nat. nominating com. 1987—90, chmn. 1989—90, coun. on govt. affairs 1990—96, future of pediatric edn. II 1996—2000, Wyeth award 1987); mem.: Am. Bd. Pediatrics (PMCP-G practice performance com. 2001—09), Rotary (youth exch. chmn. dist. 539 1984—88, pres. Helena 1988—89, polio plus chair dist. 5390 1996—, asst. gov. dist. 5390 2002—04, dist. gov. elect 2005—06, gov. 2006—07). Avocations: skiing, hiking. Home: PO Box 161815 2125 Yellowtail Rd Big Sky MT 59716-1815 Office Phone: 406-431-4331. Personal E-mail: j.strickler@3rivers.net.

STRICKLIN, GEORGE PUTNAM, dermatologist, educator; b. Marietta, Ga., July 11, 1949; MD, PhD, Wash. U., St. Louis, 1977. Asst. prof. medicine Wash. U. Sch. Medicine, 1982—84; assoc. prof. medicine U. Tenn. Health Scis. Ctr., 1984—88; prof. dermatology Vanderbilt U., 1988—, dir. divsn. dermatology Sch. Medicine, 2002. Chief sect. dermatology Tenn. Valley Healthcare Sys., Nashville Campus, 1988. Fellow: Am. Acad. Dermatology; mem.: Tenn. Dermatology Soc., Am. Dermatol. Assn., Soc. Investigative Dermatology. Office: 719 Thompson Ln Ste 26300 Nashville TN 37204 Business E-Mail: george.stricklin@vanderbilt.edu.

STRIK, HERWIG MATTHIAS, neurologist; b. Wurzburg, Germany, Sept. 21, 1964; s. Werner Otmar and Gretl S.; m. Claudia Barbara Burek, Oct. 20, 1989; children: Andreas, Laura, Michael, Lorenz, Mario MD, Julius Maximilians U., 1990. Cert. specialist neurology 1995, intensive care 1998, tumor therapy 2007; rehabilitation 2007. Resident in neurology U. Wurzburg, 1990-92, resident in neurosurgery, 1993; resident in psychiatry Regional Hosp., Lohr, Germany, 1994; sr. resident Klinik Bavaria Kreischa, Dresden, Germany, 1994-97; resident Inst. Brain Rsch., Tubingen, Germany, 1998-2000; resident Dept. Neurology U. Tuebingen, Tubingen, Germany, 2001, U. Goettingen, Germany, 2001—08; sr. resident, cons U. Marburg, Germany, 2009—. Scientific reviewer Cancer, 2000—. Mem. European Assn. Neuro-Oncology, German Cancer Soc., German Neurol. Soc. Office: University Marburg Dept Neurology Med Sch Baldingerstaße Marburg D-35043 Germany

STRIKER, PAUL S., plastic surgeon, educator; b. Denver; s. Irwin and Elizabeth Striker; m. Ursula Hautle Striker; children: Oliver, Clarissa. AB, Harvard Coll., 1959; MD, U. Colo., 1963. Diplomate Am. Bd. Plastic Surgery. Intern in gen. surgery Columbia-Presbyn. Hosp., NYC, 1963—64, resident in surgery, 1964—69, resident in plastic surgery, chief resident, 1969—71; instr. surgery Columbia Coll. Physicians and Surgeons, NYC, 1971—; sr. attending physician plastic surgery New York Eye and Ear Inst., NYC, 2005—. Office: 50 East 69th St New York NY 10021

STRINGER, MARILYN, nursing educator; b. Mar. 17, 1950; MSN, U. Pa., 1991, PhD, 1995. Prof., women's health nursing U. Pa., 1991—. Office: 418 Curie Blvd Philadelphia PA 19104 Business E-Mail: stringer@nursing.upenn.edu.

STRITZLER, RONALD, dermatologist, educator; b. NYC, July 31, 1931; s. Conrad Stritzler and Annette Beck; m. Helen N. Schenker, June 14, 1953; children: Jan, Nina, Suzanne. BA, U. Vt., 1953; MD, U. Lausanne, Switzerland, 1960. Diplomate Am. Coll. Dermatology. Asst. prof. dermatology NYU Sch. Med., NYC; dermatologist pvt. practice, 1964—. Pres. Physicians Social Responsibility, Nassau County, NY, 1980—82. Fellow: Am. Acad. Dermatology; mem.: NY State Med. Soc. Office: 193-03 Union Turnpike Fresh Meadows NY 11366 Office Phone: 718-740-8392.

STROBAUGH, TERENCE PHILIP, JR., molecular biologist, microbiologist; b. Altoona, Pa., Dec. 19, 1958; s. Terence Philip Strobaugh, Sr. and Lois Ann Strobaugh; m. Shelly L. Kamp, Aug. 3, 2007. BA in Psychology, Pa. State U., University Park, 1988, BS in Life Sci., 1992. Molecular biologist, microbiologist USDA, Agrl. Rsch. Svc., Ea. Regional Rsch. Ctr., Wyndmoor, Pa., 1994—. Presenter in field. Contbr. articles to profl. jours. Mentor Mentornet, San Jose, Calif., 2000—06; parish rep. Malvern Laymen's Retreat League, Pa., 1985—2006. Recipient Cert. of Merit for Outstanding Performance rating, USDA, 1997, Silver medal for Achievement in Recognition of Outstanding Pub. Svc., Fed. Exec. Bd. Excellence in Govt. Awards Program, 1999. Mem.: Nittany Lion Club, Suburban Cyclists Unlimited (ride coord. 2001—02, Most Improved Male Cyclist 2001), Internat. Soc. for Philos. Enquiry (assoc.). Roman Catholic. Avocations: bicycling, photography, genealogy, chess. Home: 1272 Quakertown Ave Pennsburg PA 18073 Office: USAD-ARS-ERRC 600 E Mermaid Ln Wyndmoor PA 19038 Office Fax: 215-233-6581; Home Fax: 215-541-4001. Personal E-mail: terence.strobaugh1989@psualum.com. Business E-Mail: terence.strobaugh@ars.usda.gov.

STROBER, SAMUEL, immunologist, educator; b. NYC, May 8, 1940; s. Julius and Lee (Lander) S.; m. Linda Carol Higgins, July 6, 1991; children: William, Jesse; children from a previous marriage: Jason, Elizabeth. AB in Liberal Arts, Columbia U., 1961; MD magna cum laude, Harvard U., 1966. Intern Mass. Gen. Hosp., Boston, 1966-67; resident in internal medicine Stanford U. Hosp., Calif., 1970-71; rsch. fellow Peter Bent Brigham Hosp., Boston, 1962-63, 65-66, Oxford U., England, 1963-64; rsch. assoc. Lab. Cell Biology Nat. Cancer Inst. NIH, Bethesda, Md., 1967-70; instr. medicine Stanford U., 1971-72, asst. prof., 1972-78, assoc. prof. medicine, 1978-82, prof. medicine, 1982—, Diane Goldstone Meml. lectr., 1978-97, John Putnam Merrill Meml. lectr., chief div. immunology & rheumatology, 1978-97. Investigator Howard Hughes Med. Inst., Miami, Fla., 1976-81; chmn., bd. dirs. La Jolla Inst. for Allergy and Immunology; founder Dendreon, Inc. Assoc. editor: Jour. Immunology, 1981-84, Transplantation, 1981-85, 99—, Internat. Jour. Immunotherapy, 1985—, Transplant Immunology, 1992—, Biol. Bone Marrow Transplantation, 1999—; contbr. articles to profl. jours. Served with USPHS, 1967-70. Recipient Leon Reznick Meml. Rsch. prize, Harvard U., 1966. Mem. Am. Assn. Immunology, Am. Soc. Clin. Investigation, Am. Coll. Rheumatology, Transplantation Soc. (councilor 1986-89), Am. Soc. Tranplantation Physicians, Western Soc. Medicine, Am. Assn. Physicians, Clin. Immunology Soc. (pres. 1996), Alpha Omega. Office: Stanford U Sch Medicine 300 Pasteur Dr Palo Alto CA 94304-2203

STROHECKER, LEON HARRY, JR., orthodontist; b. Schuylkill Have, Pa., Aug. 14, 1932; s. Leon Harry and Anna (Fabian) S.; m. Juanita Mary Puyoou, Apr. 13, 1957; children: Sandra Lee Strohecker Beckett, Leon Harry III. Student, U. Pa., 1950-53, DDS, 1957, orthodontic cert., 1960. Bd. cert. Am. Bd. Orthodontics. Pres., pvt. practice, Lansdale, Pa., 1961—; dir. Face Head & Neck Pain and Trauma Ctr., Lansdale, 1987-99. Bd. dirs. Artman Home Retirement Ctr., Ambler; treas., bd. dirs. Valley Ctr. Mental Health Clinic, Lansdale, 1984—2002; pres. Strohecker's Profl. Consulting Co.; guest lectr. in field. Pres. Lansdale Rotary Club, 1967-68; coun. mem. Trinity Luth. Ch., Lansdale, 1977-85, chmn. fin. com., 1980-85. Lt. (j.g.) USN, 1957-59. Recipient Spoke award, Jr. C. of C., 1963, Spark Plug award, 1963, Widsom award of Honor, Best Orthodontist vote, 2 Lansdale area newspapers, One Thousand Great Ams. award, Internat. Biographical Ctr., 2001, 2002; named Internat. Health Profl. of Yr., 2003. Mem. ADA, Internat. Acad. Head, Neck and Facial Pain, Internat. Coll. Cranio-Mandibular Orthopedics, Am. Acad. Pain Mgmt. (diplomate), Am. Assn. for Functional Orthodontics, Am. Profl. Practice Assn., Am. Soc. Dentistry for Children, Am. Acad. Oral Medicine, Am. Assn. Orthodontists, Am. Assn. Stomatologists, Am. Acad. Oral Medicine, Middle Atlantic Orthodontic Soc., Pa. Orthod ontic Soc., Phila. Orthodontic Soc., Pa. Dental Assn., Second Dist. Dental Assn., Montgomery-Bucks Dental Soc., Alpha Omega, Omicron Kappa Epsilon. Avocations: tennis, travel, bridge, water sports. Home: 709 Radcliff Ct Lansdale PA 19446-5895 Office: Strohecker's Professional Consulting Co 4822 Fallcrest Cir Sarasota FL 34233 Office Phone: 215-855-7717, 215-808-8731. Personal E-mail: lstroheckr@hotmail.com.

STROLLO, PATRICK J., JR., medical educator, researcher; BS, Wash. Coll., 1976; MS, Wagner Coll., 1977; MD, Uniformed Services U. Health Sciences, 1981. Intern internal medicine Wright Patterson Med. Ctr., 1982; resident internal medicine Wilford Hall USAF Med. Ctr., 1984, fellow pulmonary, 1985—87; assoc. prof. medicine U. Pittsburgh, clin. dir., sleep disorder program. Mem. Nat. Football League Cardiovascular Health Com. Recipient Air Force Achievement medal, 1985, Meritorious Svc. medal, 1993; named to Doctors in America, 2001—. Fellow: Am. Acad. Sleep Medicine (bd. dirs.), Am. Coll. Chest Physicians; mem.: Sleep Rsch. Soc., Am. Thoracic Soc. (chmn., planning com., respiratory neurobiology and sleep assembly), Am. Coll. Physicians. Office: 628 NW UPMC-Montefiore 3459 Fifth Ave Pittsburgh PA 15213 Office Phone: 412-692-2880. Office Fax: 412-692-2888. Business E-Mail: strollopj@upmc.edu.

STROM, BRIAN LESLIE, internist, educator; b. NYC, Dec. 8, 1949; s. Martin and Edith (Singer) S.; m. Elaine Marilyn Moskowitz, June 4, 1978; children: Shayna Lee, Jordan Blair. BS, Yale U., 1971; MD, Johns Hopkins U., 1975; MPH, U. Calif., Berkeley, 1980. Diplomate Am. Bd. Internal Medicine, Am. Bd. Epidemiology. Intern in medicine U. Calif., San Francisco, 1975-76, resident in medicine, 1976-78, research fellow in clinical pharmacology, 1978-80; from asst. prof. to assoc. prof. medicine and pharmacology U. Pa., Phila., 1980-93, prof. medicine, 1993—, prof. biostatistics & epidemiology, 1995—. Adj. asst. prof. clin. pharmacy Phila. Coll. of Pharmacy and Sci., 1981-90, adj. assoc. prof., 1990-93, adj. prof., 1993—; mem. U. Pa. Cancer Ctr., 1981—; attending staff Hosp. U. Pa., 1980—, co-dir Clin. Epidemiology Unit, 1980-91, dir., 1991-2001; dir. Clin. Pharmacology Cons. Svc., 1981-82; dir. Ctr. for Clin. Epidemiology and Biostats., 1993—, chair dept. biostats. and epidemiology, 1995—; lectr. in field; George S. prod. pub. health and preventive medicine, 2002—; cons. CDC, 1981, Coun. for Internat. Orgn. of Med. Scis., Geneva, Switzerland, 1981-83, Office of Tech. Assessment, Congress of U.S., 1980-81, Aging Rev. Com., Nat. Inst. Aging, 1982, Ministry of Pub. Health, State of Kuwait, 1982, Royal Tropical Inst., Amsterdam, 1983, others. Editl. cons. Johns Hopkins U. Press, J.B. Lippincott; referee Annals of Internal Medicine, Archives of Internal Medicine, Clin. Pharmacology and Therapeutics, Digestive Diseases and Sci., Internat. Jour. Cardiology, Internat. Jour. Epidemiology, Jour. AMA, Jour. Gen. Internal Medicine, Med. Care, Primary Care Tech., Sci.; editor Pharmaepidemiology and Drug Safety; mem. editl. bd. 7 jours.; contbr. numerous articles to profl. jours. Nat. Acad. Scis. grantee, Rockefeller Found. grantee, NIH grantee, many others. Fellow ACP, Am. Coll. Epidemiology, Am. Epidemiology Soc.; mem. Am. Fedn. Med. Rsch., Am. Pub. Health Assn., Am. Soc. Clin. Pharmacology and Therapeutics, Am. Soc. Clin. Investigation, Am. Assn. Physicians, Internat. Soc. Pharmacoepidemiology, Internat. Epideliol. Assn., Soc. for Epidemiologic Rsch., Soc. Gen. Internal Medicine, Inst. Medicine, Inst. Medicine. Democrat. Jewish. Avocations: hiking, bicycling, camping, skiing. Home: 332 Hidden River Rd Narberth PA 19072-1111 Office Phone: 215-898-2368. Business E-Mail: bstrom@mail.med.upenn.edu.

STROME, SCOTT ERIC, otolaryngologist; b. Detroit, Mich., Aug. 10, 1965; s. Marshall Strome, Deena Strome; m. Strome Beth Wertheim; children: Maxwell children: Arianna, Sophie. MD, Harvard Med. Sch., 1991. Cert. Am. Bd. Otolaryngology, 1998. Cons. Mayo Clinic, Rochester, Minn., 1998—2002.

STROMINGER, JACK LEONARD, biochemist; b. NYC, Aug. 7, 1925; AB, Harvard U., 1944; MD, Yale U., 1948; DSc (hon.), Trinity Coll., Dublin, 1975, Washington U., 1988. From asst. prof. to prof. pharmacology sch. med. Washington U., St. Louis, 1955-61, prof. pharmacology and microbiology, 1961-64; prof. pharmacology and chem. microbiology med. sch. U. Wis., Madison, 1964-68; prof. biochemistry Harvard U., 1968-83, chmn. dept. biochemistry and molecular biology, 1970-73, Higgins prof. biochemistry, 1983—; head tumor virol. divsn. Dana-Farber Cancer Inst., Boston, 1977—. Recipient John J. Abel award, 1960, Paul-Lewis Lab award, 1962, Rose Payne award Am. Soc. Histocompat. & Immunogen., 1986, Hoechst-Roussel award, 1990, Pasteur medal, 1990, Albert Lasker Award for Basic Med. Rsch., Lasker Found., 1995; named Passano Found. laureate, 1993. Mem. NAS (mem. inst. medicine, Microbiology award 1968, Selman Waxman award 1968), AAAS, Am. Soc. Biol. Chemists, Am. Soc. Pharmacology & Exptl. Therapeutics, Am. Assn. Immunologists, Am. Soc. Microbiologists, Am. Chem. Soc., Am. Acad. Arts & Sci., European Molecular Biol. Orgn., Sigma Xi. Office: Dana Farber Cancer Inst Dept Biochem 44 Binney St Boston MA 02115-6084 Address: Harvard University Dept Molecular & Cellular Biology 52 Oxford St NW 249 50 Cambridge MA 02138 Office Phone: 617-495-2733. Business E-Mail: jlstrom@fas.harvard.edu. *

STRONG, DOUGLAS L., health facility administrator; MA, U. Pa., MBA in Health Care Adminstrn. Various positions U. Pa. Sch. Medicine; assoc. dean planning and ops. St. Louis U. Sch. Medicine; assoc. dean adminstrn. and fin. sch. medicine State U. NY Stony Brook; assoc. dean Pritzker Sch. medicine and biol. scis. divsn. U. Chgo.; assoc. v.p. health system fin. and strategy U. Mich. Health Sys., 1998—, interim CFO, 2002—04, COO, 2004; interim CEO U. Mich. Hosps. and Health Ctrs., 2005—06, CEO, 2006—. Office: Univ Mich Health Sys 1500 E Med Ctr Dr Ann Arbor MI 48109 *

STRONG, JOHN OLIVER, plastic surgeon, educator; b. Montclair, NJ, Feb. 1, 1930; s. George Joseph and Olivia (LeBrun) S.; m. Helen Louise Vrooman, July 19, 1958 (dec. Mar. 1973); m. Deborah Sperberg, May 20, 1978; children: John Jr., Jean LeB., Andrew D. BS, Yale U., 1952; MD, U. Pa., 1957. Cert. vol. paleontologist Calif. Practice medicine specializing in plastic and reconstructive surgery, Santa Ana, Calif., 1964-97; asst. clin. prof. plastic and reconstructive surgery U. Calif., Irvine, 1970—. Chief of staff Western Med. Ctr., Santa Ana, 1996-97, interim chmn. bd., 1996-97, bd. dirs.; bd. dirs. United Western Med. Ctrs., Healthcare Found. Orange County, chmn.; vol. Anza Borrego Desert State Pk., steering com., 1998-2003. Vol. Anza -Borrego Desert State Pk. Fellow ACS; mem. Calif. Med. Assn. (chmn. sci. adv. panel 1983-89), Calif. Soc. Plastic Surgeons (pres. 1991-92). Republican. Office: PO Box 94 Borrego Springs CA 92004-0094 Address: 511 Seaward Rd Corona Del Mar CA 92625-2600

STRONGIN, JONATHAN DAVID, physician; b. Kingston, NY, June 19, 1951; s. Jack and Thelma (Kaufman) S.; m. Ellen Wells Seely, June 11, 1983; children: Jessica, Matthew. BA, Columbia Coll., 1973; PhD, MD, Columbia U., 1982. Diplomate Am. Bd. Internal Medicine, Am. Bd. Pulmonary Disease, Am. Bd. Critical Care Medicine. Intern, resident Cambridge (Mass.) Hosp., 1982-84; med. resident Beth Israel Hosp., Boston, 1984-85; pulmonary fellow Mass. Gen. Hosp., Boston, 1985-97; physician Pulmonary Assocs. of Greater Boston, 1994—96. Pres. med. staff Whidden Meml. Hosp., Everett, Mass., 1995-97; trustee Melrose Wakefield Health Care Corp., 1996-98; med. dir. respiratory care, pres. med. staff Cambridge Health Alliance. Fulbright scholar, 1976-77. Fellow Am. Coll. Physicians, Am. Coll. Chest Physicians. Avocation: running.

STROSAKER, ROBYN HEATHER, pediatrician, educator; b. Oct. 28, 1973; MD, Case Western Reserve U., 2000. Cert. Am. Bd. Pediat., 2003. Resident in pediat. U. Hospitals Cleve., 2003—04, chief resident in pediat.; asst. prof. gen. acad. pediat. Case Western Reserve U., Cleve.; pediatrician Rainbow Babies & Children's Hosp., Cleve. Office: UH Rainbow Babies & Childrens Hosp 11100 Euclid Ave Cleveland OH 44106 Office Phone: 216-844-8260, 216-844-8716. Office Fax: 216-844-8444. Business E-Mail: robyn.breen@case.edu.

STROTHER, ALLEN, biochemical pharmacologist, researcher; b. Nolan County, Tex., Feb. 20, 1928; s. Henry Allen and Minnie Etta (Taylor) S.; m. Julia Ann Gutch, Feb. 7, 1957; children: Wesley Allen, Lori Ann. BS, Tex. Tech U., 1955; MS, U. Calif., 1957; PhD, Tex. A&M U., 1963. Rsch. asst. Tex. A&M, Coll. Sta., 1959-63; rsch. biochemist FDA, Washington, 1963-65; asst. prof. pharmacology Loma Linda (Calif.) U., 1965-70, assoc. prof., 1970-75, prof., 1975-95, retired, vol. faculty, 1995—, prof. emeritus Physiology and Pharmacology, 1997—. Cons. WHO, Geneva, 1982-86. Contbr. numerous articles to profl. jours.; chpt. to WHO Bull. Pilot CAP/USAF Search and Rescue San Bernardino, Calif., 1967-95; pilot examiner CAP Air Force Aux., Norton AFB, 1970-86. Named Investigator of Yr. Walter E. McPherson Soc., Loma Linda U., 1984, Basic Sci. Fellow of Yr., 1986, Outstanding Faculty Rschr. of Yr. award, 1997. Mem. Am. Soc. Pharmacology and Exptl. Therapeutics, Am. Chem. Soc., Xzenobiotic Soc. Avocations: flying, golf. Home: 74448 Nevada Cir E Palm Desert CA 92260-2269 Office: Loma Linda U Sch Medicine Dept Physiology and Pharmacology Loma Linda CA 92354

STRUNK, JULIE ANN, nursing educator; b. Harrisonburg, Va., Sept. 22, 1957; MSN, James Madison U., 2008; PhD, Va. Commonwealth U., 2011. Asst. prof. Ea. Mennonite U., 2011—. Adj. prof. Va. Commonwealth U., 2009, ednl. cons., 11. Recipient Vida Huber Spirit of Nursing award, James Madison U. Dept. Nursing. Mem.: ANA,

Nat. League Nurses, Nat. Assn. Sch. Nurses, Southern Nursing Rsch. Soc., Sigma Theta Tau Honor Soc. Avocations: quilting, knitting, reading. Home: 855 Wild Cherry Ln Harrisonburg VA 22801 Personal E-mail: strunkja@jmu.edu.

STRUNK, ROBERT CHARLES, physician; b. Evanston, Ill., May 29, 1942; s. Norman Wesley and Marion Mildred (Ree) S.; m. Juanita; children: Christopher Robert, Alix Elizabeth. BA in Chemistry, Northwestern U., 1964, MS in Biochemistry, 1968, MD, 1968. Lic. MD, Ariz., Colo., Mass., Mo. Resident in pediatrics Cin. Children's Hosp., 1968-70; pediatrician Newport (R.I.) Naval Hosp., 1970-72; rsch. fellow in pediatrics Harvard Med. Sch., Boston, 1972-74; asst. prof. pediatrics U. Ariz. Health Sci. Ctr., Tucson, 1974-78; dir. clin. svcs. Nat. Jewish Ctr. for Immunology and Respiratory Med., Denver, 1978-87; sabbatical leave Boston Children's Hosp., 1984-85; dir. divsn. allergy and pulmonary medicine Children's Hosp., St. Louis, 1987-98; pediatrician Barnes and Allied Hosp., St. Louis, 1987—; prof. pediatrics Washington U. Sch. Medicine, St. Louis, 1987—, Strominger prof., 2002—. Recipient Allergic Disease Acad. award Nat. Inst. Allergy and Infectious Disease of NIH. Mem. Am. Acad. Allergy and Immunology, Am. Thoracic Soc. Office: Washington U Sch Med Dept Pediatrics 1 Childrens Pl Saint Louis MO 63110-1002 Business E-Mail: strunk@kids.wustl.edu.

STRYGLER, BERNARDO, physician, researcher; b. Mexico, Jan. 31, 1959; came to U.S., 1988; s. Marcos and Lily (Zagursky) S.; m. Sandra Sommer; children: Michelle, Alan. BS in Biol. Chemistry Sci., Israelite Coll. of Mex., 1979; MD, Nat. Autonomous U. Mex., 1985. Intern in internal medicine Am. Brit. Cowdray Hosp., Mexico, 1983-84, asst. resident in internal medicine, 1984-87; instr. in internal medicine Donald McKenzie Clinic, Mexico, 1986-88; fellow in internal medicine and gastroenterology Baylor U. Med. Ctr., Dallas, 1988-89; fellow in geriatric medicine U. Calif., Sacramento, 1989-92; geriatrician in pvt. practice Mexico City, 1992—; mem. staff A.B.C. Hosp., Mexico City, 1992—. Prin. investigator memory disorders clinic for the Spanish speaking population U. Calif. at Davis Med. Ctr., Sacramento, 1989—. Mem. Nat. Hispanic Coun. on Aging, Washington, 1989, Alzheimer's Disease Internat., Chgo., 1989. Fellow InterAm. Coll. of Physicians and Surgeons; mem. ACPE, Am. Med. Dirs. Assn., Am. Geriatric Soc., N.Y. Acad. Scis., So. Med. Assn., Calif. Med. Assn., Gerontol. Soc. Am. Avocations: diving, swimming, water polo, reading, music. Office: #650-503 Ave Ejercito Nacional Mexico City 11560 Mexico E-mail: stryb@hotmail.com.

STRYKER, JOAN COPELAND, retired obstetrician, gynecologist, educator; b. Swayzee, Ind., Apr. 17, 1918; d. Kenneth Bayard and Elsie Weser Copeland; m. Walter Stryker (dec.); children: Sara Gill, Peter, David; m. Dawson James Lewis. BS, U. Ill., Urbana, 1939; MD, U. Ill., Chgo., 1943. Resident U. Mich., Ann Arbor, 1943—46, fellow, 1946—47; asst. prof. Wayne State U., Detroit, 1965—85, prof., 1985—2001, prof. emeritus, 2001—. Chief menopausal clinic Hutzel Hosp., Detroit, 1992—2001. Chief investigator (book) Addicted Neonatals. Med. dir. Planned Parenthood, Detroit, 1965—70, treas., 1970; staff mem. WHO, 1958—61. Recipient Disting. Svc. award, Wayne State U. Sch. Medicine, 1988, Pathfinders award in medicine, 1991; named Tchr. of Yr., 1990. Mem.: ACOG (pres., Cmty. Svc. award, Gynecologist of Yr. 1994), Am. Menopausal Soc., Alpha Omega Alpha, Sigma Xi. Avocations: sailing, skiing. Home: 403 Sunrise Dr Nokomis FL 34275-3140

STUART, ROBERT KENNETH, internist, hematologist, oncologist, educator; b. Baton Rouge, July 6, 1948; s. Walter Bynum and Rita Bess (Kleinpeter) S.; m. Gail Elaine Wiscarz, June 12, 1971 (div. Dec. 1988); children: R. Morgan, Elaine C.; m. F. Charlene Gates, Nov. 2, 1991. BS, Georgetown U., 1970; MD, Johns Hopkins U., Balt., 1974. Diplomate Am. Bd. Internal Medicine. Resident in medicine Johns Hopkins Hosp., Balt., 1974-76, oncology fellow Oncology Ctr., 1976-78; rsch. fellow Sloan-Kettering Inst., NYC, 1978-79; asst. prof. Johns Hopkins U., Balt., 1979-84, assoc. prof., 1984-85; prof. medicine Med. U. S.C., Charleston, 1985—; assoc. dir. Hollings Cancer Ctr., Charleston, 1993-97; chmn. dept. oncology King Faisal Specialist Hosp and Rsch. Ctr., Riyadh, Saudi Arabia, 1997-2001; prof. medicine Med.U. S.C., Charleston, 2001—. Bd. dirs. Aplastic Anemia Found., Balt., 1982-93, med. adv. bd., 1993-98; mem. nat. team Tour of Hope, 2004. Recipient Champions Advocacy award, Am. Soc. Hematology, 2004, Partners in Progress award, Leukemia and Lymphoma Soc., 2004, Physician Healthcare Hero award, Charleston Regional Bus. Jour., 2007; named one of Best Dr. Am., 2007—. Democrat. Roman Catholic. Office: Medical Univ of South Carolina 171 Ashley Ave Charleston SC 29425-0100 E-mail: stuartrk@musc.edu.

STUBBE, RAY WILLIAM, minister, writer; b. Milw., Aug. 15, 1938; s. Clarence Arnold and Ruby Otillie (Mueller) Stubbe. BA, St. Olaf Coll., 1962; MDiv, Northwestern Luth. Theol. Sem., 1965; postgrad., U. Chgo., 1967. Ordained to ministry Evang. Luth. Ch. Am., 1965. Mission devel. bd. Am. missions Luth Ch. in Am., Oak Creek, Wis., 1965-66; organizer, pastor All Saints Luth Ch., Oak Creek, 1966-67; enlisted USN, 1955; commd. ensign USNR, 1963, advanced through grades to lt., comdr. chaplain corps, 1971; augmented to USN, 1971; chaplain, 1967-85; ret. USN, 1985. Interviews on national televised programs including Vietnam: A Soldier's Story, 1998, War Stories With Oliver North: Khe Sanh, 2001, Atmospheres: War and Weather, 2002, R. Lee Ermey's Mail Call: Back to Vietnam, 2005, Inside: The Vietnam War, 2008. Author: Inside Force Recon, 1989, Khe Sanh Chaplain, 1970, Paddles, Parachutes, Patrols, 1979, Aarugha, 1989, Valley of Decision, 1991; The Final Formation, 1995, Khe Sanh and the Mongol Prince, 2002, Battalion of Kings, 2005, revised edit., 2008, B5-T8 in 48 QXD: The Secret Official History of the North Vietnamese Army of the Siege at Khe Sanh, Vietnam, Spring, 1968, 2006, numerous poems; editor: Khe Sanh Veteran/Red Clay, 1996—98; contbr. articles to profl. jours.; author: Pebbles in My Boots, 2011. Founder, pres. emeritus Khe Sanh Vets., Inc., 1988—; spkr. numerous vet. assemblies; chaplain Wis. Vietnam Vets, Milw., 1984—, Wis. Vietnam Vets., Milw., 1984—, 3d Marine Divsn. Assn., 1988. Decorated Bronze Star with combat V; recipient Legion of Honor award, Chapel Four Chaplains. Mem.: DAV (life), VFW (life), Soc. Bibucol Lt., UDT-Seal Assn. (life), Am. Legion (life), 3rd Recon Assn. (life), Mil. Chaplains Assn. of USA (life), Wis. Acad. Scis., Arts and Letters (life), Spl. Ops. Assn. (life), 3d Marine Divsn. Assn. (life), Spl. Forces Assn. (life), Force Reconnaissance Assn. (life), Mil. Chaplains Assn. (life), Mil. Officers Assn. Am. (life), Wis. Vietnam Vets. (life), Vietnam Vets. Am. (life), Marine Corps Hist. Found. (life), Pi Kappa Delta. Lutheran. Avocation: boxing. Home: 8766 Parkview Ct Wauwatosa WI 53226-2729 Office Phone: 414-771-9987.

STUBBLEFIELD, MICHAEL D., physiatrist, educator; AB, Brown U., 1992; MD, Columbia U., 1996. Diplomate Am. Bd. Internal Medicine, 2001, Am. Bd. Physical Medicine and Rehab., cert. electrodiagnostic medicine. Resident internal medicine Columbia Presbyn. Med. Ctr., NYC, 1996—2001, resident physical medicine & rehab., 1997—2001; asst. prof. physical medicine & rehab. Weill Cornell Med. Coll., NYC; attending phycisian Meml. Sloan-Kettering Cancer Ctr., NYC. Office: Memorial Sloan-Kettering Cancer Center 1275 York Ave New York NY 10021 Office Phone: 212-639-2000.

STUBER, CHARLES WILLIAM, retired genetics educator, researcher, director; b. St. Michael, Nebr., Sept. 19, 1931; s. Harvey John and Minnie Augusta (Wilks) S.; m. Marilyn Martha Cook, May 28, 1953; 1 child, Charles William Jr. BS, U. Nebr., 1952, MS, 1961; PhD, N.C. State U., 1965. Vet., agrl. instr. Broken Bow HS, 1956-59; rsch. asst. U. Nebr., Lincoln, 1959-61; rsch. geneticist Agrl. Rsch. Svc., USDA, Raleigh, NC, 1962-75, supervisory rsrch. geneticist, rsch. leader, 1975-98, collaborator, 1998—; prof. genetics & crop sci. NC State U., Raleigh, 1975-98, prof. emeritus, 1998—, dir. Ctr. Plant Breeding and Applied Plant Genomics, 2006—. Assoc. editor Crop Sci. Jour., 1979-82, tech. editor, 1984-86, editor, 1987-89; contbr. over 200 articles to profl. jour., chpt. to books. Chmn. coun. on ministries and numerous offices Highland United Meth Ch., Raleigh. Lt. USN, 1952-56. Named Outstanding Sci. of Yr., USDA-ARS, 1989; recipient Genetics and Plant Breeding award Nat. Coun. Comml. Plant Breeders, 1995, Award of Merit, U. Nebr. Alumni Assn., 1997, Outstanding Alumnus award Coll. Agr. & Life Scis., NC State U., 2010; inductee USDA-Agrl. Rsch. Svc. Sci. Hall of Fame, 1999; Vol. 45 of MAYDICA dedicated to Charles W. Stuber, 2000. Fellow: Crop Sci. Soc. Am. (editor-in-chief 1987—91, pres. 1992—93, Crop Sci. Rsch. award 1995, DeKalb Genetics Crop Sci. Disting. Career award 1999), Fellow Am. Soc. Agronomy (pres. 2002); mem.: Am. Genetic Assn. (sec. 1984—86), Genetics Soc. Am., Phi Kappa Phi, Sigma Xi. Avocations: windsurfing, water-skiing. Home: 1800 Manuel St Raleigh NC 27612-5510 Office: NC State University NC Agril Res Svc 4124 A Williams Hall Raleigh NC 27695-7620 Office Phone: 919-515-5834. Office Fax: 919-515-7959. Personal E-mail: cstuber2@aol.com.

STÜBGEN, JOERG-PATRICK, neurologist; b. Tripoli, Libya, Sept. 7, 1959; s. Fritz Hans Georg and Marie-Louise Hildegard Stubgen; m. Dana Annenberg; 1 child, Charlotte. MD, U. Pretoria, South Africa, 1983. Diplomate Am. Bd. Psychiatry and Neurology. Intern Grey's Hosp., Pietermaritzburg, South Africa; neurology resident U. Pretoria, South Africa, 1984—89, neuromuscular fellow, asst. prof. dept. neurology, 1990—91, assoc. prof., 1991—92; asst. prof. Cornell U., NYC, 1995—99, assoc. prof. dept. neurology, 2000—08, prof. clin. neurology, 2008—. Contbr. articles to profl. jours., chapters to books. Recipient Patients' Choice award, 2010; named one of Best Doctors in Am., 2003—04, America's Top Physicians, Consumer's Rsch. Coun. Am., 2005, Top Doctors N.Y. Metro Area, Castle Connelly Med. Ltd., 2006. Fellow: South Africa Coll. Medicine, Am. Bd. Electrodiagnostic Medicine, Royal Coll. Physicians and Surgeons Can., Coll. Physicians South Africa, Am. Assn. Electro-Diagnostic Medicine; mem.: AMA, Am. Neurological Assn., Med. Soc. State N.Y., N.Y. Med. Soc., Am. Acad. Neurology. Lutheran. Avocations: road running, travel. Office: Cornell Univ Med College 525 E 68th St New York NY 10021 Office Phone: 212-746-2334, 212-746-8742. Business E-Mail: pstuebge@med.cornell.edu.

STUDAHL, MARIE KRISTINA, epidemiologist, educator; b. Stockholm, May 31, 1957; MD, Göteborg U., 1984, PhD, 1999. Assoc. prof. Sahlgrenska U. Hosp., Göteborg, Västra Götaland, Sweden, 2009—. Cons. pediatric infectious diseases Queen Silvias Children Hosp., 2004. Elion grant. Mem.: Swedish Orgn. Infectious Specialists. Avocations: sailing, travel, literature. Office: Sahlgrenska University Hosp Göteborg Västra Götaland 416 85 Sweden Office Fax: 46 31 84 78 13. Business E-Mail: marie.studahl@vgregion.se.

STUDENSKI, STEPHANIE ANNE, internist, educator; BSN, U. Kans., 1976, MD, 1979; MPH, U. NC, 1986. Diplomate Am. Bd. Internal Medicine, Am. Bd. Internal Medicine-rheumatology, Am. Bd. Family Practice-geriatric medicine. Intern, dept. medicine Duke Univ. Med. Ctr., 1980, resident, dept. medicine, 1982, fellow, divsn. rheumatic/genetic disease, 1983, fellow, geriatrics divsn., 1986; dir. clin. rsch. Univ. of Pitts. Inst. on Aging; prof. divsn. geriatric medicine Univ. of Pitts., prof. sch. of health and rehab. sciences, prof. sch. Nursing, dir. Claude D. Pepper Older Americans Independence Ctr.; hosp. affiliations include Inst. on Aging, UPMC Presbyterian. Mem.: Am. Geriatrics Soc. (chair). Office: University of Pittsburgh Medical Center 4th Fl 3459 Fifth Ave Pittsburgh PA 15213 Office Phone: 412-692-4200.

STUHLMANN, HEIDI, medical educator, researcher; b. Hamburg, Germany, Dec. 28, 1952; Diploma, U. Hamburg, 1979, PhD, 1983. Postdoc. fellow Whitehead Inst. and MIT, 1983—87, Stanford U. Sch. Medicine, 1987—91; asst. prof. Mt. Sinai Sch. Medicine, 1991—99; assoc. prof. Scripps Rsch. Inst., 1999—2006; prof. Weill Cornell Med. Coll., 2006—. German postdoc. fellowship, Deutsche Forschungsgemeinschaft, Postdoc. fellowship, Multiple Sclerosis Soc., Cystic Fibrosis Found. Mem.: Harvey Soc. (NY), Am. Soc. Investigative Pathology, Soc. Devel. Biology, Am. Heart Assn., N. Am. Vascular Biology Orgn. Office: Weill Cornell Med Coll 1300 York Ave New York NY 10029 Business E-Mail: hes2011@med.cornell.edu.

STUKLOV, NIKOLAY IGOREVICH, hematologist; b. Moscow, Mar. 30, 1976; MD, PhD, Russian State Med. U., 1999. Physician Moscow Regional Rsch. Clin. Inst., 2009—. Employee Dept. Obgyn., Inst. Advanced Studies Fed. Med.-Biol. Agy., 2009—11. Home: Novoyasenevskiy Prospect 13-1-590 Moscow 117588 Russia Personal E-mail: stuklovn@mail.ru.

STULBERG, BERNARD NATHAN, orthopaedic surgeon, research scientist; b. Kalamazoo, Aug. 2, 1948; s. Julius and Esther (Lieberman) S.; m. Carolyn Sue McComish, Oct. 16, 1976; children: Jonah James, Benjamin L., Micah Adam, John Samuel. BA, U. Mich., 1970, MD, 1974. Diplomate Am. Bd. Orthopaedic Surgery. Intern U. Chgo., 1974-75, resident in surgery, 1974-76; resident in orthop. surgery Hosp. for Spl. Surgery, NYC, 1979, fellow in orthop. rsch., 1980; staff surgeon in orthop. surgery Cleve. Clinic Found., 1980-90, staff scientist dept. musculoskeletal rsch., 1985-90; head divsn. arthritis surgery Case Western Res. U., Cleve., 1990-92; dir. Cleve. Ctr. Joint Reconstrn., 1992—2008, Cleve. Clinic, 2008—, staff surgeon; prof. surgery, orthop. surgery CCLCM-CWRU. Cons. Johnson & Johnson Orthopaedic Divsn., Inc., New Brunswick, N.J., 1983-89, Techmedia Corp., 1986-94, Implex Corp., 1994-2004, Wright Med., 1994-99, Collaborative Clin. Rsch. Sci. Adv. Bd., 1995-97. Contbr. orthopaedic articles to profl. jours.; patentee in field. ABC Exch. fellow Am. Orthopaedic Assn., 1987. Mem. AMA, Am. Acad. Orthop. Surgeons (chmn. FDA device adv. bd. 1996-2007), Orthop. Rsch. Soc. (bd. dirs. 1988-89), Am. Orthop. Assn., Mid-Am. Orthop. Assn., The Hip Soc., The Knee Soc., Ohio Orthop. Soc., Cleve. Orthop. Club, Internat. Soc. Tech. in Arthroplasty (pres. 1994-95), Phi Beta Kappa, Phi Kappa Phi, Pi Sigma Alpha. Jewish. Avocations: music, violin, tennis, golf, long distance running. Home: 7470 Water Fall Trl Chagrin Falls OH 44022-3967 Office: Cleve Clinic Orthop & Rheumatology Inst 1730 W 25th St Ste 4E Cleveland OH 44113 Office Phone: 216-363-3300. Business E-Mail: stulbeb@ccf.org.

STULTING, ANDRIES ANDRIESSEN, ophthalmologist; b. Cape Town, South Africa, Aug. 29, 1948; s. Andries Andriessen and Magdalena (Van Huyssteen) Stulting; m. Lemainé Fouché, Dec. 15, 1973; children: Lizette, Liesl. MB ChB, U. Pretoria, 1973, MMed in Ophthalmology, 1981. Intern S.A. Def. Force, Pretoria, 1974; sr. houseman H.F. Verwoerd and Kalafong Hosps., Pretoria, 1975-76, med. officer, 1976, sr. med. officer, 1976-77, sr. med. officer, registrar dept. ophthalmology, 1977-81, sr. specialist, 1982; head dept. ophthalmology U. of the Free State, 1982—. V.p. Colls. of Medicine of South Africa, 1998—2007. Chmn. Bloemfontein Children's choir, 1992-97; chmn. Free State Govern Sch. Bodies, 1993-97; vice chmn. South African Schs. Governing Bodies, 1993-97; chmn. Ctrl. H.S., 1992-97. Recipient Bloemfonteiner of Yr., Publicity Com. of Bloemfontein, 1996. Fellow ACS, Am. Acad. of Ophthalmology; mem. Ophthalmol. Soc. of South Africa (pres. 1989-91, 97-99), Health Professions Coun. of South Africa, South African Med. Assn. (past vice chmn., past pres. free state br.). Dutch Reformed Ch. Avocations: reading, writing, light classical music, sport photography. Office: Dept Ophthalmology PO Box 339 Bloemfontein South Africa Home: 50 Gascony Crescent 9301 Bloemfontein South Africa Office Phone: 27514052151, 27825541994. Personal E-mail: aaseyedoc@lantic.net. Business E-Mail: stultinga@fshealth.gov.za.

STUMP, JOHN LEE, medical association administrator; b. Welch, W.Va., Aug. 29, 1946; BS, U. Md., 1969; PhD, US Sports Acad., EdD, 1998. Coun. pres. Am. Chiropractic Assn., 1990—. Sports chiropractor, acupuncturist, nutritionist World Olympic Com., 1986—2006. Contbr. articles to profl. jours. Named Chiropractor of Yr., Del., Ala. Fellow: Ala. Acupuncture Coun. Avocations: martial arts, writing. Home: 14 Audubon Pl Fairhope AL 36532 Home Fax: 251-990-8159. Personal E-mail: bamashogun@aol.com.

STUMPF, DAVID ALLEN, medical executive pediatric neurologist; b. LA, May 8, 1945; s. Herman A. and Dorothy F. (Davis) S.; children: Jennifer F., Kaitrin E.; m. Elizabeth Dusenbery, Feb. 2, 1989; children: Todd Coleman, Shilo Walker. BA, Lewis and Clark Coll., 1966; MD cum laude, U. Colo., 1972, PhD, 1972. Diplomate Am. Bd. Pediat., Am. Bd. Psychiatry and Neurology, lic. MD State of Ill. Pediatric intern Strong Meml. Hosp., Rochester, NY, 1972-73, resident, 1973-74; resident in neurology Harvard Med. Sch., Boston, 1974-77; dir. pediatric neurology U. Colo. Health Sci. Ctr., Denver, 1977-85; chief neurology Children's Meml. Hosp., Chgo., 1985-89; chmn. neurology, Benjamin and Virginia T. Boshes prof. Northwestern U., 1989-98, prof. neurology and pediatrics, 1999—2001; pres. and CEO Oyxis, LLC, 1999—2001; med. dir. United Healthcare, Chgo., 2005—08, SVP Clin. Data Strategies. UnitedHealth Group, Chgo., 2008—10, SVP Innovation & Transformation, OptumInsight (formerly Ingenix), Chgo., 2010—. Mem. sci. adv. com. Muscular Dystrophy Assn., 1981-87; bd. dirs. Northwestern Meml. Corp., Chgo., Health Information Technology Adv Comm, National Quality Forum, Wash, DC. Mem. editl. bd. Neurology, 1982-87; contbr. articles to sci. jours. Recipient Lewis and Clark Coll. Disting. Alumni award, 1991; NIH grantee, 1979-84; Muscular Dystrophy Assn. grantee, 1977-89; March of Dimes grantee, 1983-85. Fellow Am. Acad. Neurology (treas. 2005-07); mem. Child Neurology Soc. (counsellor 1982-84, pres. 1985-87), Am. Neurol. Assn., Am. Pediatric Soc., Soc. Pediatric Rsch., Internat. Child Neurology Assn. (sec. 2002-04); Am Med Informatics Assoc., Am. Acad. Pediat., Am. Med. Assoc., Health Info. Mgmt. Sys. Soc. (HIMSS), Health Level 7. Presbyterian. Home: 540 Judson Ave Evanston IL 60202-3084 also: 1101 Alpine Ln Woodstock IL 60098 Office Phone: 312-424-6905. Personal E-mail: david@stumpf.org. Business E-Mail: david.a.stumpf@optum.com.

STUNKARD, ALBERT JAMES, psychiatrist, educator; b. NYC, Feb. 7, 1922; s. Horace Wesley and Frances (Klank) Stunkard. BS, Yale U., 1943; MD, Columbia U., 1945; MD (hon.), U. Edinburgh, 1992, La. State U., 2006. Intern in medicine Mass. Gen. Hosp., Boston, 1945—46; resident physician psychiatry Johns Hopkins Hosp., 1948—51, rsch. fellow psychiatry, 1951—52; 1rsch. fellow medicine Columbia U. Svc., Goldwater Meml. Hosp., NYC, 1952—53; Commonwealth rsch. fellow, then asst. prof. medicine Cornell U. Med. Coll., 1953—57; mem. faculty U. Pa., 1957—73, 1976—, prof. psychiatry, 1962—73, 1976—, Kenneth Appel prof. psychiatry, 1968—73, chmn. dept., 1962—73; prof. psychiatry Med. Sch., Stanford U., 1973—76. Contbr. 500 articles on psychol., physiol., sociol., therapeutic and genetic aspects of obesity to profl. jours. Capt. M.C. AUS, 1946—48. Recipient Disting. Svc. award, Am. Psychiat. Assn., 1994, Goldberger award, AMA, 1990, Willendorf award, Internat. Assn. Study of Obesity, 1998, Sarnat award mental health, NAS Inst. Medicine, 2004, Disting. Achievement medal medicine, Columbia U. Coll. Physicians and Surgeons, 2005;

fellow, Ctr. Advanced Study in Behavioral Scis., 1971—72. Mem.: Soc. Behavioral Medicine (past pres.), Assn. Rsch. Nervous and Mental Diseases (past pres.), Am. Psychosomatic Soc. (past pres.), Acad. Behavioral Medicine Rsch. (past pres.), Am. Assn. Chmn. Depts. Psychiatry (past pres.), Inst. Medicine of NAS. Achievements include contributions to the behavioral, pharmacological, community and surgical treatment of obesity and to understanding of sociological, physiological, psychological and genetic aspects of the disorder; contributions also to nosology and treatment of the eating disorders. Office: U Pa Sch Medicine Dept Psychiatry 3535 Market St 3rd Flr Philadelphia PA 19104-2641

STURGES, SIDNEY JAMES, pharmacist, educator, investment and development company executive; b. Kansas City, Mo., Sept. 29, 1936; s. Sidney Alexander and Lenore Caroline (Lemley) Sturges; m. Martha Grace Leonard, Nov. 29, 1957 (div. 1979); 1 child, Grace Caroline; m. Gloria June Kitch, Sept. 17, 1983. BS in Pharmacy, U. Mo., 1957, postgrad.; MBA in Pharmacy Adminstrn., U. Kans., 1980; PhD in Bus. Adminstrn., Pacific Western U., 1980. Cert. vocat. tchr. Mo.; in gerentology Avila Coll., 1986, registered pharmacist Mo., Kans., nursing home adminstr. Mo. Pharmacist, mgr. Crown Drugs, Kansas City, Mo., 1957—60; pharmacist, owner Sav-On-Drugs and Pharmacy, Kansas City, 1960—62; ptnr. Sam's Bargain Town Drugs, Raytown, Mo., 1961—62; pharmacist, owner Sturges Drugs DBA Barnard Pharmacy, Independence, Mo., 1962—; pres., owner Sturges Med. Corp., Independence, 1967—77, Sturgess Investment Corp., Independence, 1967—78, Sturwood Investment Corp., Independence, 1968—, Sturges Agri-Bus. Co., Independence, 1977—, Sturges Devel. Co., 1984—; bd. dirs. Comprehensive Mental Health Corp., Truman Med. Ctr., 1992. Instr. pharmacology Penn Valley C.C., 1976—92; instr., lectr. Various Clubs and Groups. Contbr. articles to profl. jours. Bd. dirs. Independence House, 1981—83; mem. Criminal Justice Adv. Commn., Independence, 1982—. Recipient Outstanding award, Kans. City Alcohol and Drug Abuse Coun., 1982. Mem.: U. Mo. Alumni Assn., Mo. Found. Pharm. Care, Mo. Pharm. Assn. (pharmacy dr. 1981, Pharmacists Against Drug Abuse award 1989), Mo. Sheriffs Assn. Home and Office: Sturges Co 16805 E Cogan Rd Ste B Independence MO 64055-2815 Office Phone: 816-478-0764.

STURTEVANT, RUTHANN PATTERSON, anatomist, educator; b. Rockford, Ill., Feb. 7, 1927; d. Joseph Hyelmun and Virginia (Wharton) Patterson; m. Frank Milton Sturtevant Jr., Mar. 18, 1950 (dec.); children: Jill Sturtevant Rovani, Jan Sturtevant Cassidy; m. Richard Kiegler, Aug. 8, 2010. BS, Northwestern U., Evanston, Ill., 1949; MS, Northwestern U., 1950; PhD, U. Ark., Little Rock, 1972. Instr. life scis. Ind. State U., Evansville, Ind., 1965—72, asst. prof., 1972—74; asst. prof. anatomy Ind. U. Sch. Medicine, Evansville, 1972—74, U. Evansville, 1972—74; lectr. anatomy Northwestern U., Chgo., 1974—75; asst. prof. anatomy and surgery Loyola U., Maywood, 1975—81; assoc. prof. Loyola U. Sch. Medicine, Maywood, 1981—88, prof., 1988—90, prof. emerita, 1990—. Contbr. articles to profl. jours.; mem. editl. bd. Chronobiology Internat., 1988-90; reviewer numerous profl. jours. Active Mayor's Task Force on High Tech. Devel., Chgo., 1983-85; exec. bd. Anatomical Gifts Assn. Ill., Chgo., 1981-90, docent, instr. Mote Marine Labs; vol. many cmty. svcs.; docent Mote Rsch. Aquarium. Grantee Pott's Found., NIH, others, 1978—. Mem. Am. Assn. Anatomists, So. Soc. Anatomists (councillor 1978-80), Internat. Soc. Chronobiologists, Am. Soc. Pharmacology and Exptl. Therapeutics, Soc. for Exptl. Biology and Medicine, Am. Assn. Clin. Anatomists, League of Underwater Photographers, Sarasota Scuba Club, Sigma Xi. Avocations: photography, scuba diving, flying, community volunteering. Address: 5760 Midnight Pass Rd Unit 610-D Sarasota FL 34242 Personal E-mail: patty5760@verizon.net.

STURTZ, DONALD LEE, surgeon, military officer, educator; b. Coshocton, Ohio, Apr. 18, 1933; s. Walter Raymond and Helene Josephine (Kubic) S.; m. Alice Marie McGuire, June 11, 1955; children: Jimalee, Janel. BS, US Naval Acad., Annapolis, Md., 1955; MD, U. Pa., Phila., 1965; diploma med. care catastrophe, Soc. Apothecaries London, 1996. Diplomate Am. Bd. Surgery. Surg. resident USN, Phila., 1965-70, ship's surgeon, 1970-71; staff surgeon Bethesda Naval Hosp., USN, 1971-80; chief of surgery San Diego Naval Hosp., USN, 1980-84; exec. officer Oakland Naval Hosp., USN, Calif., 1984-85; prof. clin. surgery USN, Bethesda, Md., 1985-87, commd. Naval Med. Command, 1987-88, Atlantic fleet surgeon, Supreme Allied Command surgeon Norfolk, Va., 1989-91; prof. surgery USUHS, Bethesda, Md., 1991—. Contbr. articles to profl. jours. Mem. nat. adv. cabinet Guideposts, 1980—. Recipient B.D. Larrey award for Surgical Excellence, Surgical Dept. USUHS, Bethesda, 1988, Exceptional Svc. medal, Uniformed Svcs. U., 1998. Fellow ACS (gov. 1985-88); mem. Am. Assn. for Surgery of Trauma, Assn. Mil. Surgeons, USN Inst. Republican. Presbyterian. Avocations: travel, gardening, antiques, music, reading. Office: USUHS Dept Surgery 4301 Jones Bridge Rd Bethesda MD 20814-4799 Office Phone: 301-295-9825. Personal E-mail: sturtzd@aol.com.

STUZIN, JAMES M., plastic surgeon; b. Miami, Fla., June 1, 1952; BA, U. Fla., Gainesville, 1974, MD, 1978. Cert. in gen. surgery 1985, in plastic surgery 1989. Intern, gen. surgery U. Wash. Hosps., Seattle, 1978—79, resident, gen. surgery, 1979—83; fellow, plastic surgery NYU Hosps., NYC, 1984—86; craniofacial fellow U. Miami Hosps., Fla., 1986, UCLA Sch. Medicine, 1987, asst. clin. prof., plastic surgery, 1987; clin. instr., dept. plastic surgery U. Miami Sch. Medicine, Fla., 1989—95, clin. asst. prof., plastic surgery, 1995—. Chmn. Am. Bd. Plastic Surgery, 2008—. Mem. editl. bd. Annals of Plastic Surgery, 1993—; co-editor: Jour. of Plastic and Reconstructive Surgery; co-author: Facial Skin Resurfacing, 1998. Mem.: Am. Soc. for Aesthetic Plastic Surgery (pres. 2006), Alpha Omega Alpha, Phi Beta Kappa. Office: 3225 Aviation Ave Ste 100 Coconut Grove FL 33133 Office Phone: 305-854-8828.

STYER, DENISE MARIE, psychologist; d. Kenneth James and Mary Ellen Styer; 1 child, James Kenneth Marketti. BA, U. Wis., Milw., 1990; MA, Alfred Adler Inst. Minn., 1995; PsyD, Adler Sch. Profl. Psychology, 2001. Lic. Profl. Counselor Ill., 2001. Therapist, intake coord. SAFE Alternatives, Naperville, Ill., 2000—01; clin. coord. Self Injury Recovery Svcs. Alexian Bros. Behavioral Hosp., Hoffman Estates, Ill., 2001—. Mem.: APA (prevention rschr. adv. bd. 2005). Home: 537 E Constitution Dr Apt 2 Palatine IL 60074-1911 Personal E-mail: drdenisestyer@comcast.net.

SU, CHENG-CHUAN, pathologist, director; b. Kaohsiung, Taiwan, Sept. 4, 1960; MD, Chung Shan Med. U., 1985. Dir., dept. clin. pathology Chi Mei Found. Hosp., 2002—04, Buddhist Dalin Tzu Chi Gen. Hosp., 2005—. Office: 2 Minsheng Rd Dalin Town Chiayi 622 Taiwan Personal E-mail: sucpo@yahoo.com.tw.

SU, CHIH YING, physician, researcher; b. Kaohsiung, Taiwan, June 22, 1953; s. Ping Yu and Su Chin (Hsu) S.; m. Ching Wei Wang; children: Wei-Wei, Wei-Han, Wei-Fan. MD, Kaohsiung Med. Coll., Taiwan, 1979. Chief resident doctor Kaohsiung (Taiwan) Med. Coll. Hosp., 1986; attending physician Chang Gung Meml. Hosp., Kaohsiung, Taiwan, 1985-89, chief of otolaryngology, 1990—, from assoc. prof. to prof., 1993—. Mem. com. Nat. Health Rsch. Inst., Taipei, Taiwan, 1997; editor Chang Gung MEd. Jour., Taipei, Taiwan, 1997. Contbr. articles to profl. jours. 2nd lt. Army of ROC, 1979-80, Taiwan. Grantee Nat. Sci. Coun. of ROC, Taipei, 1993-95, 97; recipient Outstanding Rsch. award Tu S-M Found., Taipei, 1993. Mem. AAAS, Taiwan Otolaryngology Soc. (editor jour. 1998-2001, bd. dirs. 1996-1998), Am. Acad. Otolaryngology Head and Neck Surgery. Avocations: swimming, tennis, badminton, music, travel. Home: 123-2 Ta-Pei Rd Niao Sung Hsiang Kaohsiung Hsien 833 Taiwan Office: Chang Gung Meml Hosp 123TA-Pei Rd Niao Sung Hsiang Kaohsiung Hsien 833 Taiwan Office Phone: 886-7-7317123 ext 2533. Personal E-mail: wbhwbj@yahoo.com.tw, voicebeautysu@gmail.com. Business E-Mail: usgniy@adm.cgmh.org.tw.

SU, EDWIN, orthopedist; s. Philip and Wen-Huey Su; m. Karen Lin, Nov. 7, 1998; children: Justin, Steven. MD, Cornell U. Med. Coll., NYC, 1997. Lic. NY, 1997. Attending orthopedic surgeon Hosp. Spl. Surgery, NYC, 2003—. Active contbr. Hosp. Spl. Surgery Charitable found., NYC, 2003—07. Fellow: Am. Acad. Orthopedic Surgeons. Achievements include research in hip and knee surgery. Office: Hosp Spl Surgery 535 E 70th St New York NY 10021

SU, JIING-YUAN, medical educator, researcher; b. Taiwan, Taiwan, Feb. 15, 1949; MD, Kaohsuing Med. U., 1975. Assoc. prof. Kaohsiung Med. U. Hosp., 1975—. Office: Kaohsiung Medical U Hosp 100 Tzyou 1st Rd Kaohsiung City 817 Taiwan Office Fax: 886-7-3119544; Home Fax: 886-7-3119544. Personal E-mail: jiing.su@msa.hinet.net.

SU, MING-JAI, physiologist, educator; b. Pindong, Taiwan, Nov. 3, 1948; PhD, Nat. Taiwan U., 1980. Rsch. asst. prof. dept. physiology U. Pa., 1983—85; prof. Nat. Taiwan U., 1994—. Office: 1 Sec 1 Jen-Ai Rd Taipei 10051 Taiwan Business E-Mail: mingja@ntu.edu.tw.

SU, PING, research scientist; arrived in US, 1989; d. Hexiang and Zhu Luan (Guo) Su; m. Fuzu Zhang, Jan. 1, 1978; 1 child, Luke Le John. MSc, Fudan U., Shanghai, 1984; PhD, U. NSW, Sydney, 1989. Rsch. fellow U. Pa., Phila., 1989—90; sr. rsch. scientist DSM Food Specialties, Sydney, 1990—2004, U. NSW, Sydney, 2004—. Recipient Food Microbiologist award, Australian Inst. Food Sci. and Tech., Sydney, 2001, 1st Prize oral presentation, 13th Internat. Conf. on Campylobacter, Helicobacter and Related Organisms, Gold Coast, Australia, 2005; Cooperative Rsch. Centre Food Industry Innovation grant, Australian govt., Sydney, 1995—2002. Mem.: Australian Assn. Biotech., Am. Soc. Microbiology. Achievements include invention of plasmids encoding phage resistance; LIaFI, a type IIIR/M system in L. lactis; food-grade cloning vector for S. thermophilus, probiotics and prebiotics. Avocations: travel, table tennis, swimming. Office: U NSW Sch Biotech and Biomolecular Scis 2052 Sydney Australia Office Phone: 612 9385 3514. Office Fax: 612 9313 6710. Business E-Mail: p.su@unsw.edu.au.

SU, SHIH-BIN, medical educator, director; b. Tainan, Taiwan, Oct. 29, 1959; s. Chun-Chieh and Bai-Lu Su; m. Alison Ko, Sept. 5, 1986; children: Edward, Tina. BS, Nat. Taiwan U., Taipei, 1982, MD, 1989; MS, Nat. Cheng Kung U., Tainan, 2002; PhD, Nat. Cheng Kung U. Cert. chem. engring., Yuan Test, Taiwan, 1982; lic. dr. Dept. Health, Taiwan, 1989, cert. family medicine 1994, occupl. medicine 2002. Med. dir. and adminstr. Hsing-Yin City Health Adminstrn., Tainan, 1991—97; med. dir. Tainan Sci. Based Indsl. Pk. Clinic Chimei Med. Ctr., 1999—; asst. prof. Chang Jung Christian U., Tainan county, 2004—07, So. Taiwan U., 2007—, assoc. prof., 2009—. Supr. Taiwan Med. Assn., Taipei, 2004—07; bd. dirs. Taiwan Assn. Family Medicine, Taipei, 2006—08; dir. Tainan Med. Assn., 1995—2008. 2nd lt. Army, 1982—84, Taoyuan, Taiwan. Recipient Rsch. award, Urbani Found., 2006, 2007, Spl. Svcs. award, CDC, Taiwan, 2007. Mem.: Taiwan Occupl. Med. Soc., Taiwan Family Medicine Soc. Office: Tainan Sci Pk Clinic Chi-Mei Hosp 1F No 7 Nan-Ke 3rd Rd Tainan Sci Tainan 74147 Taiwan Office Fax: 886-6-5050227. Business E-Mail: shihbin.su@msa.hinet.net.

SU, SHU-JEM, medical educator; b. Kaohsiung, Sept. 25, 1968; PhD, Nat. Cheng Kung U., 2000. Assoc. prof. Fooyin U., 2000—. Office: 151 Jinxue Rd Daliao Dist Kaohsiung 83102 Taiwan Business E-Mail: sc096@mail.fy.edu.tw.

SU, YI, ophthalmologist, otolaryngologist; m. Shaoyuan Li, June 6, 1991; 1 child, Yan Li. Prin. physician Ophthalmology and Otolaryngology Hosp., Shanghai, 1999—.

SU, YU-JANG, physician; MD, China Med. Coll., Taichung, Taiwan, 1997. Diplomate in specialist emergency medicine Taiwan Soc. Emergency Medicine, 2002, in specialist geriatric emergency and critical care medicine Taiwan Soc. Geriatric Emergency and Critical Care Medicine, 2006. Residency Dept. Internal Medicine, Shin-Kong Wu Ho-Su Meml. Hosp., Taipei, Taiwan, 1999—2000, Dept. Emergency Medicine, Mackay Meml. Hosp., Taipei, 2000—03, attending physician, 2003—; lectr. Univs. and Colls., 2007—. Contbr. articles to profl. sci. jours. Recipient Best Tchr. award, Mackay Meml. Hosp., 2003—05, 2007—09. Office: Mackay Memorial Hosp Emergency Dept No 92 Sec 2 N Chung Shan Rd Taipei 10449 Taiwan Office Phone: 886-2-25433535 ext. 3126. Personal E-mail: pioneermd@gmail.com. Business E-Mail: yjsu@ms1.mmh.org.tw.

SUAMI, HIROO, plastic surgeon, researcher; MD, Shinshu U., Nagano, Japan, 1991; PhD, Keio U., Tokyo, 1998. Lic. physician Ministry of Health and Welfare, Japan, 1991. Oncological trainee Nat. Cancer Ctr., Tokyo, 1993—96; resident Keio U., 1991—93, instr. plastic surg., 1996—97, Kyorin U., Tokyo, 1997—2003; rsch. fellow Royal Melbourne Hosp., Parkville, Victoria, Australia, 2003—05, U. Melbourne, Parkville, 2005—08; vis. prof. Okayama U., Japan, 2008—; clin. rsch. program coord., dept. plastic surgery U. Tex., MD Anderson Cancer Ctr., Houston, 2009—; asst. prof., dept. plastic surgery U. Tex., Md. Cancer Ctr., Houston, 2010—. Overseas Rsch. grant, Promotion Mut. Aid Corp. Pvt. Sch. Japan, 2001, 2002, 2010, Project grant, Nat. Health and Med. Rsch. Coun., 2005, 2006, 2007, Kyte grant, Kyre Found., 2009—, Instl. Rsch. grant, 2011—, grant, Sister Instnl. Network Fund, 2011—. Mem.: Am. Assn. Clin. Anatomists, Japanese Soc. Lymphology, Internat. Sentinel Node Soc., Internat. Soc. Lymphology, Internat. Confederation for Plastic and Reconstructive Surg., Japan Soc. Plastic and Reconstructive Surg. (bd. plastic surg. 1999). Achievements include research in developing a new protocol for investigating the lymphatic system. Office: Univ Tex M D Anderson Cancer Ctr Dept Plastic Surgery 1515 Holcombe Blvd Unit 1488 Houston TX 77030-4009 Office Phone: 713-794-1247. Personal E-mail: hsuami@hotmail.com. Business E-Mail: hsuami@mdanderson.org.

SUAREZ, MARIA C., health care plan company executive; BA in Math. and Computer Sci., Queens Coll., CUNY; MBA in Quantitative Analysis and Computer Info. Sys., St. John's U. Applications developer Coopers & Lybrand; tech. lead managed care project North Shore U. Hosp.; dir. internet/intranet Empire BlueCross BlueShield, privacy officer, now asst. v.p. security assurance. Named one of Premier 100 IT Leaders, Computerworld, 2005.

SUAREZ, SALLY ANN TEVIS, health facility administrator, nurse, consultant; b. Jersey City, Jan. 23, 1944; d. Paul John and Gertrude Marie (Clancey) Tevis; 1 child, Maria E. Diploma, St. Mary Hosp. Sch. Nursing, 1965; BA in Health Edn. and Nursing, Jersey City State Coll., 1966, MA in Health Sci., 1977. Staff nurse St. Mary Hosp., Hoboken, N.J., 1965, Bayonne (N.J.) Hosp., 1966, Jersey City Med. Ctr., 1965-66; adminstr. Hoboken Med. Arts Family Health Ctr., 1969-75; adj. faculty Jersey City State Coll., 1976-77; adminstrv. supr. St. Mary Hosp., Hoboken, 1977-80; dir. North Hudson Commn. Action Corp. Clinic, West New York, N.J., 1979-88; nursing clin. dir. St. Mary Hosp., Hoboken, 1988-89; corp. dir. nursing Francisan Health System N.J., 1989-92; dir. maternal child health svcs. St. James Hosp., Newark, 1992-93, dir. Family Care Ctr., Cathedral Healthcare Sys., 1993-97, dir. nursing, 1992—97; ind. cons., 1995—; v.p., COO Med. Resource Network, 1997—2003; med. case mgr. MCR, 2000—03, Corvel Corp., 2003—04; coord. family health ctr. North Hudson Cmty. Action Corp., 2004—06; coord. case mgmt. U. Medicine and Dentistry N.J. Univ. Hosp., 2006—. Instr. nursing St. Mary Hosp. Sch. Nursing; cons. Creative Concepts in Counseling, Rutherford, N.J., 1979-82, Com. for Cytogenetics, Newark, 1986-88; cons. in health svcs., 1996—; case mgr. workers' compensation, critical care MCR, 2000-2003; case mgr. workers' compensation CorVel Corp., 2003-2004; health ctr. coord. North Hudson Cmty. Action Corp. Health Ctr., 2004-2006; case mgr. and coord UMDNJ, 2006—. Hudson County ARC, 1984-88, United Way, 1984-94; mem. Hudson County Perinatal Consortium Bd., 1987-92, Gateway Consortium, 1993-96; mem. adv. bd. Health Start, 1995-97, N.J. Assn. Women Bus. Owners, 1996-98; bd. dirs. Passaic Head Start; mem. adv. bd. Harrison Care Inst., 2005—. Mem. U.S. Assn. Women Bus. Owners, Am. Cancer Soc., N.J. Family Planning Forum (exec. com. 1980-86), Family Planning Assn. N.J. (exec. com. 1986-88). Roman Catholic. Home: 113 Wilson Ave Rutherford NJ 07070-2726 Office Phone: 973-972-4655. Personal E-mail: nursesrch@aol.com. Business E-Mail: suarezst@umdnj.edu.

SUAREZ DE LA TORRE, RAUL SERGIO, dermatologist; s. Jose Suarez and Irene de la Torre; m. Isabel Fernandez, Mar. 6, 1980; children: Pablo Suarez, Sergio Suarez. Grad. in dermatology, Nat. U. Mexico, 1979. Dermatologist Centro Med. Nat., Mexico City, 1979—85, Hosp. Gen. Social Security, Celaya, Mexico, 1985—2003; pvt. practice Celaya, 1985—. Contbr. articles to profl. jours. Pres. Amigos Filarmonica del Bajio, Guanajuato, 1988—92. Fellow: ACP; mem.: Coll. Dermatology Guanajuato (pres. 1994—95), Am. Acad. Dermatology. Avocations: music, trains. Office: Centro de Especialidades Med Madero 104-210 38000 Celaya Mexico Personal E-mail: isaferpos@hotmail.com.

SUBASI, FERYAL, physical therapist, educator; b. Ankara, Turkey, June 12, 1965; d. Hayrettin Gur and Zeynep Bolukbasi; m. Levent Subasi, June 29, 1990; 1 child, Yaprak. Degree in Phys. Therapy and Rehab., U. Hacettepe, Ankara, Turkey, 1987; PhD, Istanbul U., Turkey, 1999. Phys. therapist Ankara U., 1987—90; rschr. Istanbul U., 1990—93; lectr. Sch. Phys. Therapy and Rehab. Abant Izzet Baysal U., Bolu, Turkey, 1993—96; asst. prof. Faculty Health Edn. Marmara U., Istanbul, 1999—. Prin. of project Marmara U., Istanbul, 2002—. Mem.: Turkish Phys. Therapy Assn., Internat. Coun. Health Phys. Edn. Recreation Sports and Dance (assoc.).

SUBBIAH, VIVEK, oncologist, researcher; b. India, Dec. 1, 1978; MD, Sri Ramachandra Med. Coll., 2003. Internat. vis. scholar Stanford U. Med. Ctr., 2003; resident-combined internal medicine and pediat. Case Western Res. U., Metro Health Med. Ctr., 2004—08; fellow-pediat. hematology-oncology U. Tex. MD Anderson Cancer Ctr., 2008—11, fellow-med. oncology, 2011—, grad. med. edn.-adminstrv. fellow, 2011—. Recipient Rsch. award, Bayer Healthcare Pharms., Inc. and U. Tex. MD Anderson Cancer Ctr., Pfizer Rsch. Excellence award, 2004, Rsch. Excellence award, Case Western Res. U., 2008, Metro Health Med. Ctr. 1st prize, 2008; Daniel Gazen Benedict fellowship, U. Tex. MD Anderson Cancer Ctr. Mem.: Am. Soc. Pediat. Hematology Oncology, Am. Soc. Hematology, Am. Soc. Clin. Oncology. Avocations: photography, violin, poetry. Office: 1515 Holcombe Blvd Houston TX 77054 Business E-Mail: vsubbiah@mdanderson.org.

SUBHAS, GOKULAKKRISHNA, physician; b. Salem, India, June 15, 1977; MBBS, Govt. Med. Coll., Nagpur, India, 1999. Resident Providence Hosp. and Med. Ctrs., 2007—. Office: 16001 W Nine Mile Rd Southfield MI 48075 Personal E-mail: drsgokul@gmail.com.

SUBLETT, JAMES LEE, allergist, pediatrician, educator; b. Campbellsville, Ky., 1948; BA, U. Louisville, MD, 1975. Diplomate American Bd. Allergy and Immunology, American Bd. Pediat. Intern U. Louisville, 1975-76, resident in pediat., 1976-77; fellow allergy and immunology, dept. pediat. Children's Hosp., U. Louisville Sch. of Medicine, 1977-79; with Kosair Children's Hosp., U. Louisville Sch. of Medicine, Louisville, chief allergy sect.; mng. ptnr. Family Allergy & Asthma, Louisville; founder, chmn. AllergyZone, LLC. Assoc. clin. prof. to clin. prof. U. Louisville; sect. chief pediat. allergy dept., U. Louisville Sch. of Medicine; nat. med. dir. Vivva Asthma Allergy Care America; clin. investigator, Family Allergy & Asthma Rsch. Inst., mem. bd. dirs. and exec. com. Joint Coun. of Allergy, Asthma, & Immunology; spkr. in the field. Editl. bd. mem. Annals of Allergy, Asthma, and Immunology; contbr. of several articles to peer-reviewed jours.; editor of several spl. articles. Fellow American Acad. Allergy, Asthma, and Immunology (mem. Indoor Allergen Com.), American Coll. Allergy, Asthma and Immunology (bd. regent, mem. Indoor Allergen Com.), American Acad. Pediat.; mem. Ky. Med. Assn., Ky. Allergy Soc. (past pres.), American Soc. of Heating, Refrigeration, and Air-Conditioning Engineers (mem. Indoor Allergen Com.)., Drug Info. Assn., American Coll. of Physician Executives Achievements include developer of the Fantastic Filter by AllergyZone Physicians Group. Office: Family Allergy and Asthma 9800 Shelbyville Rd Ste 220 Louisville KY 40223 also: Family Allergy and Asthma Research Inst 1700 Bluegrass Ave Ste 400 Louisville KY 40215 Office Phone: 502-429-8585. *

SUBRAMANIAM, VIJAYALAKSHMI, otolaryngologist, educator; b. Bangalore, Aug. 16, 1972; MBBS, Dr BR Ambedkar Med. Coll., Bangalore U., 1995; DLO, KMC, Mangalore; DNB, NBE, Ministry H & FW, Govt. of India, 2004. Med. officer MRPL Hosp. MRPL ONGC Janseva Trust, Mangalore, 1998—2000; postgrad. resident Kasturba Med. Coll., Mangalore, 2000—02, sr. resident Yenepoya U., 2002—04, lectr., 2004—06, asst. prof., 2006—. Mem., quality assurance & audit com. Yenepoya Med. Coll., Mangalore, 2005—08; academic coord. Dept. Otorhinolaryngology Head & Neck Surgery, Yenepoya Med. Coll., Mangalore, 2005—; mem. gov. coun. Yenepoya Rsch. Ctr., Yenepoya U., Mangalore, 2008—. Contbr. articles to profl. jours. Mem.: Assn. Otorhinolaryngologists India, Indian Soc. Otology, Nat. Acad. Med. Scis., New Delhi. Avocations: dance, swimming, classical music, badminton, reading. Home: 205 Preethi Towers Urwa Market Mangalore Karnataka 575006 India Personal E-mail: vijisubbu@gmail.com.

SUBRAMANIAN, KAVIARASAN, research scientist; b. Cuddalore, Aug. 15, 1978; PhD in Biochemistry, Annamalai U., 2008. Postdoc. fellow U. Malaya Med. Ctr., 2008—09, Nagoya U. Grad. Sch. Medicine, 2009—. Sr. Rsch. fellowship, Indian Coun. Med. Rsch. Fellow, Japan Soc. Promotion Sci.; mem.: Soc. Free Radical Rsch. Avocations: singing, cricket, reading. Home: 5 Sowrashtra St Keezh Bhuvanagiri Chidambaram Tamil Nadu 608601 India Personal E-mail: kavi_sing@yahoo.com.

SUBRAMANIAN, TAMIL SELVAN, research scientist; b. Madurai, Tamil Nadu, India, June 2, 1965; PhD, Madurai Kamaraj U., 1992. Prin. rsch. scientist, project leader, supervision students Inst. Bioengring. & Nanotechn. Singapore, 2003—08; rsch. scientist Inst. Materials Rsch. and Engring., 2008—. Recipient Best Mentor award, Inst. Bioengring. & Nanotech. Singapore; grant, JCO A STAR Singapore. Mem.: Materials Rsch. Soc. Singapore. Avocations: reading, movies, yoga, swimming. Office: Inst Materials Rsch and Engineering Singapore 117602 Singapore Office Fax: (65) 6774 4657. Business E-Mail: subramaniant@imre.a-star.edu.sg.

SUBTIL, DAMIEN, gynecologist; b. Troyes, France, Feb. 10, 1960; PhD, Lille U., 1990. Hôpital jeanne de flandre Ctr. Hospitalier Regional U., 1996—. Chief dept., ob-gyn. Neonatology, 2010. Office: 1 rue Eugène Avinée Lille Nord Pas de Calais 59037 France Office Fax: 33 3 20 44 63 11. Business E-Mail: damien.subtil@chru-lille.fr.

SUCATO, DANIEL J., orthopaedic surgeon; s. Justin and Ilde Sucato; m. Lisa Sucato; children: Daniel, Emma, Matthew. BA magna cum laude, Canisius Coll., Buffalo, 1987; MD, U. Buffalo, 1991, MS in Biophysics, 1997. Orthopaedic resident U. Buffalo, 1991—97, basic sci. rsch. fellow, 1992—93; pediatric orthopaedic surgery fellow Tex. Scottish Rite Hosp., Dallas, 1997—98, prof. orthop. surgery, U. Tex. at Southwestern Med. Ctr., Dallas, 1998—. Active staff mem. Children's Med. Ctr. Dallas. Contbr. articles to profl. jours., including Jour. Bone and Joint Surgery; cons. reviewer Spine, Jour. of Spinal Cord Medicine, Jour. of Bone and Joint Surgery, Jour. Pediat. Orthop., mem. editl. bd. Spine Universe. Active smem. Recipient Dr. William Beaumont award, AMA, 2005; Hip Preserving fellowship, Bern, Switzerland, 1998, SRS Internat. Traveling Fellow, 2003. Mem.: N.Am. Spine Soc., Tex. Med. Assn., Pediatric Orthopaedic Soc. N.Am., Am. Acad. Orthopaedic Surgeons, Scoliosis Rsch. Soc. Office: Texas Scottish Rite Hosp 2222 Welborn St Dallas TX 75219 Office Fax: 214-559-7570. Business E-Mail: dan.sucato@tsrh.org.

SUCHANEK, JAKUB, dentist; b. Litomerice, Czech Republic, Dec. 19, 1981; MUDr, Charles U. Prague, Hradec Kralove, Czech Republic, 2005, PhD, 2011. Asst. Charles U. Prague, Faculty Medicine Hradec Kralove, 2005—. Office: Charles Univerzity Prague Simkova 870 Hradec Kralove 50038 Czech Republic Business E-Mail: suchanekj@lfhk.cuni.cz.

SUCHY, FREDERICK JOSEPH, pediatrician; b. Bridgeport, Conn., Apr. 4, 1947; AB, Columbia U., 1970; MD, U. Cin., 1974. Prof., chair pediat. Mt. Sinai Sch. Medicine, 1996—2009; dir., Children's Hosp. Rsch. Inst., assoc. dean child health rsch. Children's Hosp., Colo., 2010—. Recipient Rsch. Excellence award, Am. Acad. Pediat., Andrew Sass-Kortsak award, Can. Liver Found., Shwachman award, N.Am. Soc. Pediat. Gastroenterology, Hepatology and Nutrition, Pediat. Rsch. prize, Am. Liver Found. Mem.: Assn. Am. Physicians, Am. Pediat. Soc., Soc. Pediat. Rsch., Am. Soc. Clin. Investigation, Am. Gastroent. Assn. Office: Children's Hosp Colo 13123 E 16th Ave Aurora CO 80045 Business E-Mail: suchy.frederick@tchden.org.

SUCIU, CRISTIAN SILVIU, medical educator; b. Lupeni, Romania, Mar. 25, 1972; s. Tiberiu and Iagusa Suciu; m. Oana Bereteu, Oct. 13, 2007; 1 child, Bianca. Degree, U. Medicine & Pharmacy, Timisoara, 1997, degree in Pathology, 2003. Diplomate UMFT, Romania, 1997. Physician, dept. pathology Emergency County Hosp., 2004; lectr. U. Medicine & Pharmacy, Romania, 2009—. Contbr. articles to profl. jours. Grant, Lab. Molecular Diagnosis Breast Cancer, 2007—, Molecular Characterization Breast Cancer & Identifying New Therapeutic Targets, 2008—. Mem.: Romanian Soc. Morphology. Office: Piata Eftimie Murgu Nr 2 Timisoara 300041 Romania Business E-Mail: cristian_suciu@umft.ro.

SUDHIVORASETH, NIPHON, pediatrician, immunologist, allergist; b. Bangkok, 1940; MD, Chulalongkorn Hosp. U., Bangkok, 1966. Diplomate Am. Bd. Pediatrics, Am. Bd. Allergy and Immunology. Intern Ch. Home Hosp., Balt., 1967-68; resident in pediatrics St. Lukes Hosp., NYC, 1968-69, Beth Israel Hosp., NYC, 1969-70; fellow in allergy Metro Hosp., N.Y. Med. Coll., NYC, 1970-72; staff Marshall Meml. Hosp., Tex., 1978—; pvt. practice. Mem. AMA, Am. Acad. Allergy, Asthma, and Immunology, Am. Acad. Pediats., Am. Coll. Allergy and Immunology. Office: PO Box 2087 705 S Grove St Marshall TX 75670-5220 Personal E-mail: drniphonsudhi@yahoo.com. *

SÜDHOF, THOMAS CHRISTIAN, molecular genetics educator; b. Göttingen, Germany, Dec. 22, 1955; Degree in medicine, RWTH, Aachen, Germany, 1977; MD, Georgia Augusta U., Göttingen, Germany, 1982. Postdoctoral fellow Max-Planck-Inst. Biophysikallsche Chemie, Göttingen, 1982-83; postdoctoral fellow dept. molecular genetics U. Tex. Southwestern Med. Ctr., Dallas, 1983-85, asst. prof. dept. molecular genetics, 1987-89; asst. investigator U. Tex. Southwestern Med. Ctr., Howard Hughes Med. Inst., Dallas, 1986-89, investigator, 1991—, assoc. prof. dept. molecular genetics, 1989-91, prof. dept. molecular genetics, 1991—2008, Gill disting. chair neurosci. rsch., 1995—2008, dir. center for neuroscience, 1997—2006, adj. prof. neurosci., 2008—; Avram Goldstein prof. molecular and cellular physiology Stanford U. Sch. Medicine, 2008—. Loyd B. Sands disting. chair in neurosci.; mem. molecular, cellular and devel. neurobiology rev. com. NIMH, 1995—. Mem. editl. bd. Jour. Biol. Chemistry and of Neuron; contbr. numerous articles to profl. publs. Recipient W. Alden Spencer award Columbia U., 1993, Wilhelm Feldberg award, 1994, MetLife award for Alzheimers Rsch. MetLife Found., 2004, Freedom to Discover Achievement award for Neuro-Science, Bristol-Myers Squibb, 2004, Passano Found. award, 2008; co-recipient Bernhard Katz award, Biophysical Soc., 2008, Kavli prize, Norwegian Acad. Sci. and Letters, Kavli Found. and Norway's Ministry of Edn. and Rsch., 2010. Fellow: Am. Acad. Arts & Sciences; mem.: NAS (Molecular Biology award 1997), Inst. Medicine. Office: Howard Hughes Med Inst Stanford Sch Medicine 1050 Arastradero Rd B249F Palo Alto CA 94304-5543 Office Phone: 650-721-1418, 650-721-1421. Office Fax: 650-498-4585. E-mail: tcs1@stanford.edu.

SUDIKOFF, STEPHANIE N., pediatrician, educator; b. May 27, 1966; BA, Columbia U., 1988; MD, Mt. Sinai Sch. Medicine, 1992. Asst. prof., pediat. critical care, dir. simulation Yale SOM, Yale-New Haven Health Sys., 2008—. Office: 730 Howard Ave New Haven CT 06520 Business E-Mail: stephanie.sudikoff@ynhh.org.

SUD'INA, GALINA FEDOROVNA, research scientist; b. Pskovskaya oblast, Russia, May 8, 1952; PhD, Moscow State U., 1974. Prin. rsch. scientist A.N. Belozersky Inst., Moscow State U., 1997—. Mem.: Soc. Leukocyte Biology. Home: Universitetsky Prosp 4-337 Moscow 119333 Russia Personal E-mail: sudina@genebee.msu.ru.

SUE, MICHAEL ALVIN, allergist; b. LA, Apr. 15, 1956; MD, U. Chgo., 1980. Diplomate Am. Bd. Internal Medicine, Am. Bd. Allergy and Immunology. Intern, resident and fellow West Los Angeles VA Med. Ctr., LA, 1980-86; allergist Kaiser Permanente, Panorama City, Calif., 1986—. Fellow Am. Coll. Allergy, Asthma, and Immunology; mem. Am. Acad. Allergy, Asthma, and Immunology. Office: Kaiser Permanente 13652 Cantara St Panorama City CA 91402-5497 Office Phone: 818-375-1720.

SUEBNUKARN, SIRIWAN, biomedical researcher; d. Vinai and Somsri Suebnukarn. DDS, Prince of Songkhla U., Thailand, 1992; degree in Endodontology, Chulalongkorn U., Thailand, 1994; MSc in Engring. and Tech. (hon.), Asian Inst. Tech., Thailand, 2001, PhD in Engring. and Tech., 2005. Asst. prof. Thammasat U., Thailand. Developer (software) COMET: A Collaborative Medical Tutor (Inventors Award, 2007); contbr. articles to profl. jours. Recipient James A. Linen III prize, Asian Inst. Tech., 2001; Thammasat U. Rsch. fellow, 2000—01, Royal Thai Govt. Rsch. fellow, 2002—05. Master: Global Network Systematic Health Care (assoc.); mem.: Asian Inst. Tech. Alumni Assn. (fin. officer 2006). Home: Banggrui-sainoi Road 101/38 Soi 9A Moo 4 Chonlada Nonthaburi Bangbuathong 11110 Thailand Office: Thammasat U Dental Sch Paholyothin Pathumthani Khlongluang 12121 Thailand Business E-Mail: ssiriwan@tu.ac.th.

SUEDFELD, PETER, psychologist, educator; b. Budapest, Hungary, Aug. 30, 1935; emigrated to US, 1948, naturalized, 1952; s. Leslie John and Jolan (Eichenbaum) Field; m. Gabrielle Debra Guterman, June 11, 1961 (div. 1980); children: Michael Thomas, Joanne Ruth, David Lee; m. Phyllis Jean Johnson, Oct. 19, 1991. Student, U. Philippines, 1956-57; BA, Queens Coll., 1960; MA, Princeton U., 1962, PhD, 1963. Rsch. assoc. Princeton U.; lectr. Trenton State Coll., 1963-64; vis. asst. prof. psychology U. Ill., 1964-65; asst. prof. psychology Univ. Coll. Rutgers U., 1965-67, assoc. prof., 1967-71, prof., 1971-72, chmn. dept., 1967-72; prof. psychology U. B.C., Vancouver, 1972-2001, head dept., 1972-84, dean faculty grad. studies, 1984-90, disting. scholar-in-residence, P. Wall Inst. Adv. Studies, 2000, dean and prof. emeritus, 2001—. Chmn. Can. Antarctic Rsch. Program, 1994—98; Disting. vis. scholar Ohio State U., 2000—03; affiliated prof. U. Haifa, 2005—; cons., lectr. in field. Author: Restricted Environmental Stimulation: Research and Clinical Applications, 1980; editor: Attitude Change: The Competing Views, 1971, Personality Theory and Information Processing, 1971, The Behavioral Basis of Design, 1976, Psychology and Torture, 1990, Restricted Environmental Stimulation: Theoretical and Empirical Developments in Flotation REST, 1990, Psychology and Social Policy, 1991, Light from the Ashes, 2001, Understanding the Bush Doctrine, 2007; editor Jour. Applied Social Psychology, 1975-82; assoc. editor Environment and Behavior, 1992—; contbr. articles to profl. jours. Served with US Army, 1955-58. Recipient Antarctica svc. medal, NSF, US Navy, 1994, Zachor award, Parliament of Can., 2000; grantee, NIMH, 1970—72, Can. Coun., 1973—2006, Nat. Rsch. Coun. Can., 1973—90, NIH, 1980—84, Can. Space Agy., 2003—, Def. Rsch. and Dev. Can., 2007—. Fellow Royal Soc. Can., Can. Psychol. Assn. (pres. 1998-99, Donald O. Hebb award 2001, Lifetime Achievement Gold medal 2011), APA, Am. Psychol. Soc., Acad. Behavioral Medicine Resch., Soc. Behavioral Medicine, NY Acad. Sci., Royal Can. Geog. Soc.(hon.); mem. Internat. Soc. Polit. Psychol. (v.p. 1999-2001, Harold D. Lasswell award 2001, Roberta Sigel award 2005), Internat. Acad. Astronautics, Soc. Exptl. Social Psychology, Phi Beta Kappa, Sigma Xi. Office: U BC Dept Psychology Vancouver BC Canada V6T 1Z4 Home Phone: 604-687-8886; Office Phone: 604-822-5713. Business E-Mail: psuedfeld@psych.ubc.ca.

SUEI, YOSHIKAZU, oral and maxillofacial radiologist, educator, researcher; b. Mukaihara-chyo, Hiroshima, Japan, Dec. 16, 1962; s. Syougo and Toyoko Suei; m. Ryouko Yamasaki, Feb. 14, 1997; 1 child, Hiroaki. DDS, Hiroshima U., 1988, PhD, 1996. Rsch. aassoc. Hiroshima U., 1988—99; asst. prof. Hiroshima U. Hosp., 1999—. Asst. editor Japanese Soc. for Oral and Maxillofacial Radiology, Koto-ku, Tokyo, 2004—10; assoc. editor Oral Radiology, 2010—. Contbr. articles to sci. jours. Recipient Incentive award, Japanese Soc. Oral and Maxillofacial Radiology, 1996. Liberal. Avocation: fishing. Office: Hiroshima Univ Hosp 1-2-3 Kasumi Minami-ku Hiroshima 734-8553 Japan Home: 5-10-2-304 Ujimakanda Minami-ku Hiroshima 734-0004 Japan Office Fax: 81 82 257 5692. Business E-Mail: suei@hiroshima-u.ac.jp.

SUEN, LORNA KWAI PING, nursing educator; d. Wing Kit Suen and Ching Tuen Law; m. Yue Hon Hong; 1 child, Prisca Christina Yue. B in Nursing, U. Sydney, Australia, 1994; MPH, U. Sydney, 1996; PhD, Hong Kong Poly. U., 2002; diploma in clin. acupuncture, U. Hong Kong, 2003. RN Nursing Bd. of Hong Kong, Calif., Commn. on Grads. of Fgn. Nursing Schs., US, UK Ctrl. Coun. Nursing, NSW Nurses Registration Bd., Australia, registered midwife, Midwives Bd. of Hong Kong; cert. Auriculotherapy Cert. Inst., Inc., USA. RN United Christian Hosp., Hong Kong, 1985—91; vice-supt. Lau Mui Hin Home for Elderly, Hong Kong, 1991—92; RN Dept. of Health, Hong Kong, 1992—93; asst. health tng. officer Hong Kong Red Cross Assn., 1996; lectr. Hong Kong Poly. U., 1996—97, asst. prof., 1997—2004; assoc. prof. Chinese U. of Hong Kong, 2004—. Contbr. articles to profl. jours.; hon. reviewer Hong Kong Nursing Jour., 1995—; editor: Hong Kong Nursing Jour., 2005—; mem. editl. bd. Asian Jour. Nursing Studies. Recipient Tchg. award, Hong Kong Poly. U., 1999, 2002; scholar U. Sydney, 1993—94. Mem.: Hong Kong Epidemiol. Assn., Assn. Hong Kong Nursing Staff (life), Sigma Theta Tau, Golden Key. Office: Nethersole Sch Nursing Esther Lee Bldg Chinese University Hong Kong Hong Kong E-mail: lornasuen@cuhk.edu.hk.

SUESS, JAMES FRANCIS, retired clinical psychologist; b. Evanston, Ill., Aug. 8, 1950; s. James Francis and Rae Love (Miller) S.; m. Linda Grace Powell, July 31, 1976; 1 child, Misty Lynne. BS, U. So. Miss., 1974, MS, 1978, PhD, 1982. Lic. psychologist, NY, Ala.; diplomate Am. Bd. Profl. Psychology, Am. Bd. Med. Psychotherapists, Profl. Assn. Custody Evaluators, Am. Coll. Forensic Examiners, Am. Bd. Forensic Medicine. Assoc. psychologist State of Miss., Ellisville, 1978-80; clin. psychologist SUNY Med. Sch./Erie County Med. Ctr., Buffalo, 1982-84, supervising clin. psychologist, 1984-87, assoc. dir., 1987—2005; prof. dept. psychology Clinic South Ala., 2001—05; prof. emeritus SUNY, 2005—. Dir. practica SUNY Med. Sch., 1982-90, faculty counsel, 1988—; cons. Buffalo Dept. Social Svcs., 1985—; mem. spkrs. bur. Erie Alliance for Mentally Ill, 1986—; vis. prof. U. Guadalajara Sch. Medicine, 1985—; clin. dir. Stickney Adolescent Ctr. Mobile MHC, 1993-97; clin. dir. Physicians' Psychiat. Clinic, 1997—; CEO Stillwood Clin. Group, 1998—; adj. prof. dept. psychology U. South Ala., 2000—; clin. dir. Adm. Mc Collough Inst. of Rejuvenology. Author: Annotated Bibliography of Sex Roles, 1972, Personality Disorder and Self Psychology, 1991, (textbook) Enduring My Journey Throug Life: The Borderline Personality Disorders, 2005; contbr. chpts. to books, numerous articles to refereed jours. including Perceptual and Motor Skills, Jour. Clin. and Consulting Psychology, Am. Annals of Deaf, Assessment of Children. Mem. small bus. adv. coun. Nat. Congl. Com., 2005-, life mem. Am. Legion, 2009-, USAR Speca OPS- Weapons Psy Recon, 2009- With USAR, 1969—76. Fellow Am. Orthopsychiat. Assn. (life, diplomate), Soc. Personality Assessment; mem. APA, Am. Bd. Forensic Exam (life), Ala. Lic. Psychol. (pres.), Mobile Assn. Psychol. (pres.). Home: 507 Evergreen Rd Mobile AL 36608-3845 Office: The Stillwood Clin Grp 717 Executive Park Dr Ste B Mobile AL 36606-2843 Office Fax: 251-342-8599. Personal E-mail: drjfsuess@comcast.net, drjfsuess@ymail.com.

SUESS, JOCHEN RICHARD, gynecologist, obstetrician, quality manager; b. Nuremberg, Bavaria, Germany, July 3, 1959; s. Georg Johann and Ingeborg Maria Anna (Roscher) S. MD magna cum laude, U. Friedrich-Alexander, Erlangen-Nuremberg, 1986; MBA, U. Lueneberg, 2007. Cert. in sports medicine, emergency medicine, human genetics, quality mgmt., visitor KTQ/PCC, auditor PIN EN ISO 9001:2008; specialist in reproductive medicine. Asst. dept. human genetics U. Friedrich-Alexander, Erlangen-Nuremberg, 1988-91; asst. dept. ob-gyn. Klinikum St. Marien, Amberg/Oberpfalz, Bavaria, 1987-88, 91-98, sr. physician, 1998—2010, genetic counselor, 2000—, quality mgr., 2010—; ptnr. Office of Dr. Krieg, 1997—; assoc. Office of Dr. Juergen Krieg, 2007—. Contbr. articles to profl. jours. Capt. Med. Corps German Army, 1986-87. Mem. Fedn. Med. Genetics, German Soc. Med. Ultrasound (DEGUM). Roman Catholic. Avocations: collecting semi-precious stones, literature, movies, music, science. Home: Laufamholzer Kirchensteig 28 90482 Nuremberg Bavaria Germany Office: Klinikum St Marien Amberg Mariahilfberg-weg 7 92224 Amberg Oberpfalz Bavaria Germany Business E-Mail: suessjochen@web.de.

SUGAHARA, SHINJI, radiation oncologist, educator; s. Nobuyuki and Ikuko Sugahara; m. Kuniko Ogura; children: Atsunobu, Mizuki. MD, U. Tsukuba, Japan, 1985; PhD, U. Tsukuba, 1999. Diplomate Japanese Bd. Radiology, Japanese Bd. Radiation Oncology. Resident in radiation oncology Tsukuba U. Hosp., 1985—90; asst. prof. Inst. Clin. Medicine, U. Tsukuba, 2000—08; chief radiation oncologist Hitachi (Japan) Gen. Hosp., 1991—99, Nat. Inst. Radiol. Sci., Japan, 2009; assoc. prof. Ibaraki Med. Ctr., Tokyo Med. U., 2010—. Contbr. articles to profl. jours. Pres. The Yurigaoka Self-Govt.Assn., Mito, Japan, 2000—01. Grantee Japanese Ministry Edn., Sci., Sports and Culture, 2001—02. Mem.: Japan Radiol. Soc. (licentiate), Japanese Soc. Therapeutic Radiology and Oncology (licentiate), Am. Soc. Therapeutic Radiology and Oncology (licentiate). Achievements include development of proton beam therapy for digestive organ cancers. Office: Ibaraki Med Ctr Tokyo Med University 3-20-1 Ami-machi Chuo Ibaraki 300-0395 Japan Office Fax: 81-29-887-1512. Business E-Mail: ssuga@tokyo.med.ac.jp.

SUGARMAN, JEREMY, medical educator; b. Jan. 23, 1960; BA, Duke U., Durham, NC, 1982; MD, Duke U. Sch. Medicine, 1986; MPH, Johns Hopkins U., Balt., 1992; MA, Georgetown U., Washington, 1993. Diplomate American Bd. Internal Medicine. Resident internal medicine Duke U., 1986-89; fellow internal medicine Johns Hopkins U., 1990-93; formerly prof. medicine and philosophy, founding dir. Ctr. Study Med. Ethics & Humanities Duke U.; Harvey M. Meyerhoff prof. bioethics & medicine Johns Hopkins U., dep. dir. medicine Berman Inst. Bioethics, prof. dept. health policy & mgmt., Bloomberg Sch. Pub. Health. Sr. policy & rsch. analyst White House Adv. Com. Human Radiation Experiments, 1994—95; sr. advisor Presidl. Commn. Study of Bioethical Issues, 2011—; faculty affiliate Kennedy Inst. Ethics, Georgetown U.; mem. Md. Stem Cell Research Commn. Author: 20 Common Problems: Ethics in Primary Care, 2000; co-editor: Beyond Consent: Seeking Justice in Research, 1998, Ethics of Research with Human Subjects: Selected Policies and Resources, 1998, Methods in Medical Ethics, 2001; contbr. articles to profl. jours., chapters to books. Mem. sci. & rsch. adv. bd. Can. Blood Svc.; chair ethics working group HIV Prevention Trials Network; ethics officer Resuscitation Outcomes Consortium; bd. dirs. Pub. Responsibility in Medicine & Rsch. (PRIM&R). Fellow: AAAS, ACP; mem.: Internat. Soc. Stem Cell Rsch. (mem. ethics & pub. policy com.), Inst. Medicine, American Soc. Clin. Investigation. Achievements include recognition as leader in the field of biomedical ethics with particular expertise in the application of empirical methods and evidence-based standards for the evaluation and analysis of bioethical issues. Office: Berman Inst Bioethics Deering Hall 203 1809 Ashland Ave Baltimore MD 21205 Office Phone: 410-614-5634. Office Fax: 410-614-5360. E-mail: jsugarman@jhu.edu. *

SUGARMAN, MICHAEL, physician, rheumatologist; b. Galveston, Tex., May 26, 1945; s. Harold and Amelia Sugarman; m. Hilda Roberta Krug, Aug. 26, 1967; children: Jason, Steven. BS, U. Calif., Berkeley, 1966; MD, U. Calif., San Francisco, 1970. Diplomate Am. Coll. Physicians, Am. Coll. Rheumatology. Rheumatologist Fullerton (Calif.) Internal Medicine Ctr., Fullerton, Calif., 1976-94. Pres. St. Jude Heritage Med. Group, 1996—. Bd. trustees St. Jude Hosp. Fellow Am. Coll. Rheumatology, Orange County Rheumatism Soc.; mem. AMA, Orange County Med. Assn. Office: 2141 N Harbor Blvd Ste 25000 Fullerton CA 92835 Home Phone: 714-525-4422.

SUGAWA, MAKOTO, physiologist; married. PhD, Tohoku U., Sendai, Japan, 1992. Diplomate Physiological Soc. Japan, 1996. Guest investigator Tokyo Met. Inst. Gerontology, Itabashi-Ku, 1999—2006. Grant, Ministry Edn., 2000. Achievements include research in role of EPO in neural development, cGMP function in cerebral vasodilation. Business E-Mail: sugawamkt@chugai-pharm.co.jp.

SUGAWARA, JUN, research scientist; b. Miyagi, Japan, Aug. 21, 1973; PhD, U. Tsukuba, 2000. Sr. rschr. Nat. Inst. Advanced Indsl. Sci. and Tech., 2002—. Office: 1-1-1 Higashi Tsukuba Ibaraki 305-8566 Japan E-mail: juns0821@gmail.com.

SUGAYA, EIICHI, health facility administrator, educator; b. Tokyo, Mar. 25, 1929; s. Tsuneshino and Huchi (Yamada) S.; m. Aiko Sugaya, May 3, 1967. MD, Keio U., Tokyo, 1953, PhD, 1958. Asst. dept. physiology Keio U., Tokyo, 1954-58; boursier (French govt.) dept. physiology Sorbonne, Paris, 1956-58, Neurophysiology Lab. Musee Oceanographique, Monaco, 1958; asst. dept. surgery Keio U., Tokyo, 1958-64; gen. surgeon Ichikawa Hosp., Tokyo Dental Coll., Japan, 1959-60; surgeon neurosurgery 2d Tokyo Nat. Hosp., 1960-64; rsch. fellow div. neurol. surgery Washington U., St. Louis, 1962-63; prof. physiology dept. physiology Kanagawa Dental Coll., Yokosuka, Japan, 1964-96; prof. divsn. oriental medicine Sch. Medicine Tokyo. Hosp. Tokai U., Tokyo, 1996—2001; dir. Aieido Clinic, Tokyo, 2001—. Cons. Tsumura (Pharm.) Co., Tokyo, 1983-2000; specialist doctor Rappongi Hosp. (Oriental medicine), Tokyo, 1964-96; vis. prof. Inst. for Oriental medicine Sch. of Medicine, Keio U., Tokyo, 1992-96; chief rschr. lab. molecular & devel. medicine Inst. Exptl. Animals, Kawasaki, 1996-99;. Mem. Japan Soc. Oriental Medicine (specialist), Japan Autonomic Nerve Soc. (councilor, editing exec. 1964-99), Japan Physiol. Soc. (councilor 1964-99). Avocation: violin. Fax: 81-422-42-0532.

SUGERMAN, DAVID EDWARD, physician; b. Fayetteville, NC, Apr. 26, 1976; MPH, Johns Hopkins Bloomberg Sch. Pub. Health, 2003; MD, Jefferson Med. Sch., 2004. Med. officer Ctr. Disease Control and Prevention, 2007—. Emergency medicine physician Emory U. Hosp., 2010. Decorated Achievement medal US Pub. Health Svc. Office: 1600 Clifton Rd MS F62 Atlanta GA 30333 Business E-Mail: ggi4@cdc.gov.

SUGIE, KAZUMA, physician, educator; b. Kyoto, Dec. 22, 1970; MD, PhD, Nara Med. U., 1995. Lectr. Nara Med. U., 2006—. Grant, Kanae Found. Mem.: World Muscle Soc., Japanese Soc. Neurology. Office: 840 Shijo-cho Kashihara Nara 634-8521 Japan Business E-Mail: ksugie@naramed-u.ac.jp.

SUGIKI, SHIGEMI, ophthalmologist, educator; b. Wailuku, Hawaii, May 12, 1936; s. Sentaro and Kameno (Matoba) Sugiki; m. Bernice T. Murakami, Dec. 29, 1958; children: Kevin S., Boyd R. AB, Washington U., St. Louis, 1957, MD, 1961. Intern St. Luke's Hosp., St. Louis, 1961-62; resident in ophthalmology Washington U., 1962-65; chmn. dept. ophthalmology Straub Clinic, Honolulu, 1965-70, Queens Med. Ctr., Honolulu, 1970-73, 80-83, 88-90, 93-2000; clin. prof. ophthalmology Sch. Medicine U. Hawaii, 1997. Maj. M.C., AUS, 1968-70. Decorated Hawaiian N.G. Commendation medal, 1968. Fellow ACS; mem. AMA, Hawaii Med. Assn., Honolulu County Med. Soc., Am. Acad. Ophthalmology, Contact Lens Assn. Ophthalmologists, Pacific Coast Oto-Ophthal. Soc., Am. Soc. Cataract and Refractive Surgery, Am. Glaucoma Soc., Internat. Assn. Ocular Surgeons, Am. Soc. Contemporary Ophthalmology, Washington U. Eye Alumni Assn., Hawaii Ophthal. Soc., Rsch. To Prevent Blindness. Home: 2398 Aina Lani Pl Honolulu HI 96822-2024 Office: 1380 Lusitana St Ste 714 Honolulu HI 96813-2443 Office Phone: 808-528-5333. Personal E-mail: vision2damax@yahoo.com.

SUGIMOTO, MITSUSHIGE, medical association administrator, researcher; b. Numazu, Shizuoka, Japan, Aug. 21, 1970; s. Hiroshi and Tomie Sugimoto; m. Yoko Yanagino; children: Masataka, Tatsuya. MD, Hamamatsu U. Sch. Medicine, Japan, PhD, 2006. Diplomate Japanese Govt., 1998. Resident internal medicine Hamamatsu U. Sch. Medicine, Shizuoka, 1996—, med. staff and asst. prof., 2001—08; med. staff gastroenterology Seirei Hamamatsu Gen. Hosp., 1997—2001; fellow Michael E. DeBakey Veterans Affairs Med. Ctr. and Baylor Coll. Medicine, Houston, 2008—. Councilor Japanese Soc. Gastroenterology, Tokyo, 2006—, Japan Gastroent. Endoscopy Soc., Tokyo, 2006—, Japanese Gastroent. Assn., Tokyo, 2008—; editl. bd. gastrointestinal cancer rev. letters Gastrointestinal Cancer Rev. Letters, Beijing, 2009—. Contbr. articles to profl. jours. (award Japanese Soc. Clin. Pharmacology and Therapeutics, 2006). Grant, Japanese Govt., 2007. Mem.: Japanese Soc. Gastrointestinal Endoscopy, Japanese Soc. Clin. Pharmacology, Japanese Soc. Gastroenterology, Japanese Soc. Internal Medicine, Japanese Gastroent. Assn., Japanese Soc. Clin. Oncology, Japanese Soc. Helicobacter. Office Fax: 713-794-7280. Business E-Mail: sugimoto@bcm.edu.

SUGIMURA, YOSHIHISA, physician; b. Aichi, Japan, Mar. 14, 1962; MD, Nagoya U. Grad. Sch. Medicine, PhD, 2007. Physician Nagoya U. Grad. Sch. Medicine, 2007—. Office: 65 Tsurumai-cho Showa-ku Nagoya Aichi 466-8550 Japan Office Fax: 81-52-744-2212. Business E-Mail: sugiyosi@med.nagoya-u.ac.jp.

SUGITA, SHOEI, agricultural studies educator, researcher; b. Iwate Prefecture, June 26, 1952; MS, Utsunomiya U., 1978; PhD in Medicine, Agr., Chiba U., 1982. Asst. prof. Chiba U., Sch. Medicine, 1982—90; assoc. rschr. Ind. U., Sch. Optometry, 1990—92; assoc. prof. Utsunomiya U., Sch. Agr., 1993—95, prof., 1995—, vice dean, 2009—, dir. Satoyama Sci. Ctr., 2011—. Recipient Zool. Sci. award, Japanese Zool. Sci. Assn., 2010, Best Tchr. award, Utsunomiya U. Avocations: walking, swimming, photography. Office: 350-Minemachi Utsunomiya Tochigi 321-8505 Japan Office Fax: 81-28-649-5436. Business E-Mail: sugita@cc.utsunomiya-u.ac.jp.

SUGITA, TAKAHISA, pharmaceutical executive; b. Osaka, Mar. 21, 1959; PhD, Osaka U., 1983. Gen. mgr. Mitsubishi Tanabe Pharma Corp., Pharmacology Rsch. Labs. I, 1983—. Office: 1000 Kamoshida-cho Aoba-ku Yokohama Kanagawa 227-0033 Japan Business E-Mail: sugita.takahisa@mp.mt-pharma.co.jp.

SUGIU, KENJI, neurosurgeon and team doctor; b. Soja, Okayama, Japan, Feb. 27, 1963; s. Ryosuke and Fumiko Sugiu; m. Etsuko Sugiu; children: Michiko, Maiko. Degree, Kurume U. Med. Sch., Fukuoka, 1987. Cert. dr. Okayama U. Med. Sch., 1994. Rsch. fellow Geneva U., 1997—99; asst. prof. Dept. Neurol. Surgery, Okayama U. Med. Sch., 1999—; team dr. Fagiano Okayama Football Club. Recipient Sunada prize, Okayama U., 1996, Spl. prize, Japan Neurosurgical Soc., 1996, Exhibit award, Swiss Soc. Radiology, 1999. Office: Okayama Univ Med Sch 2-5-1 Shikata-cho Okayama 700-8558 Japan Office Phone: 81-86-235-7336. Business E-Mail: ksugiu@md.okayama-u.ac.jp.

SUGIYAMA, KENJI, research scientist; b. Hokkaido, Japan, Sept. 9, 1950; PhD, Tokyo Met. U., Grad. Sch. Sci., 1979. Rsch. assoc., dept. chemistry Sasaki Inst., 1979—91; head, Exptl. Animal Lab. Nat. Cancer Ctr. Hosp. East, Rsch. Ctr. Innovative Oncology, 1991—2011, rsch. assoc., 2011—. Guest prof. Chiba U., Grad. Sch. Advanced Integration Sci., 2005—. Recipient Tamiya prizes, Found. Promotion Cancer Rsch. Mem.: Japanese Cancer Assn. Avocations: sports, photography, badminton. Home: Nishimabashi-Hirotecho 29 Mastudo Chiba 271-0048 Japan Office Phone: 81-4-7133-1111. Business E-Mail: nature-photos@nifty.com.

SUGIYAMA, YOSHIO, psychology professor; BS, Kyoto U., 1988; MEd, Tsukuba U., 1990, PhD in Health and Sport Scis., 1995. Asst. prof. Nat. Inst. Fitness and Sports, Kanoya, Japan, 1996—2003; assoc. prof. Inst. Health Sci. Kyushu U., Kasuga, Japan, 2003—. Office: Inst Health Science Kyushu Univ 6-1 Kasuga-koen Kasuga Fukuoka 816-8580 Japan Business E-Mail: sugiyama@ihs.kyushu-u.ac.jp.

SUGWAN, KIM, dental educator; b. Haenam, Republic of Korea, Aug. 23, 1964; s. WanSik and Jeonglm Kim; m. SunMi Kim; children: YuJeong Kim, YuMin Kim. DDS, Chosun U., 1989, MSD, 1992; PhD, Chonnam U., Gwangju, Korea, 1998. Diplomate in dental Ministry Health Welfare, South Korea, 1989. Chmn. dept. oral maxillofacial surgery Chosun U. Dental Hosp., Gwangju, 1999—, capt. edn., 2001—04, capt. diagnosis, 2007, dean Sch. Dentistry, 2009—. Editor-in-chief: Jour. Korean Implant Dentistry, 2007—; contbr. articles to profl. med. jours. Chmn. ChildFund, Gwangju, 2005—. Capt. army, 1993—96. Recipient Key of Success, Am. Biog. Inst., 2007, Achievement award, Internat. Biog. Ctr., 2008. Fellow: Internat. Assn. Oral Maxillofacial Surgeons; mem.: William R. Laney Award Com., European Assn. Osseointegration, Internat. Congress Oral Implantologists, Acad. Osseointegration, Am. Assn. Oral Maxillofacial Surgeons. Achievements include research in restorative and grafting material for hard tissue defects prepared from animal teeth and design the sinus lift. Office: Chosun Univ Sch Dentistry Seosukdong Donggu 375 501-759 Gwangju Republic of Korea Office Phone: 82 62 220 3819. Office Fax: 82 62 228 7316. Business E-Mail: sgckim@chosun.ac.kr.

SUH, BYUNGSE, medical educator; b. Ansung, Republic of Korea, Mar. 6, 1941; came to U.S., 1964; s. Sang Keun and Chong Sang (Lee) S.; m. Youngjoo Lee, Dec. 21, 1974; children: Jason, Jessica, Janice. BS, Chungang U., Seoul, Korea, 1962; MA, U. Kans., 1967, PhD, 1969; MD, U. Miami, 1973. Diplomate Am. Bd. Internal Medicine; diplomate Am. Bd. Infectious Diseases. Asst. prof. medicine Temple U. Sch. Medicine, Phila., 1978-83, assoc. prof. medicine, 1983-90, prof. medicine, 1990—. Contbr. articles to profl. jours. Pres. Korea Ilsan Handicapped Children Support Assn., 1983—. Recipient Presdl. award, Republic of Korea, 1994. Fellow Infectious Diseases Soc. Am., Am. Coll. Physicians, Coll. Physicians Phila.; mem. Am. Soc. Microbiology, Alpha Omega Alpha. Republican. Roman Catholic. Office: Temple U Sch Medicine Sect Infectious Diseases 3401 N Broad St Philadelphia PA 19140 Office Phone: 215-707-1982. Business E-Mail: bingsuh@temple.edu.

SUH, JEFFREY D., otolaryngologist, educator; b. Santa Monica, Calif., June 21, 1976; BS, UCLA, 1999, MD, 2003. Clin. faculty U. Pa., 2009—10; asst. prof. UCLA, 2010—. Fellow: Am. Bd. Otolaryngology; mem.: Am. Rhinologic Soc. Office: 200 UCLA Med Plz Ste 550 Los Angeles CA 90095 Business E-Mail: jsuh@ucla.edu.

SUH, JEONG-YUL, geochemist, consultant; b. Daegu, Republic of Korea, Nov. 15, 1965; s. Youngsang Suh and Kyungsool Cho; m. Juyoung Lee, May 14, 1997; children: Hyunsoo, Hayeon. PhD, U. Sydney, Australia, 2003. Cert. applied geological eng., Ministry Edn., Republic of Korea, 1992. Rschr. Olympic Co-ordination Authority, Sydney, 1999—2001; CEO Geoenvirotec. Co., Daegu, Republic of Korea, 2002—. Rschr. Korea Inst. Constrn. & Tech., Seoul, 1994—97. Contbr. articles to profl. jours. With Korean mil., 1987—88. Scholar, Ministry of Edn., 1990—92. Mem.: Geol. Soc. Australia (life). Achievements include research in environ. geochemistry. Avocations: soccer, travel. Office: GeoenvirotecCoKr 904Ho BeomeTower Beomedong 45-4 SoosungGu Daegu 706-010 Republic of Korea Office Fax: 82 53 752 1754. Personal E-mail: jysuh2000@yahoo.com.

SUH, KUEN TAK, orthopedist, educator, surgeon; b. Pusan, Republic of Korea, Jan. 13, 1955; s. Suk Soo Suh and Keong Ja Jang; m. Bu Yong Han, May 21, 1983; children: Su Bin, Su Youn. MD, Pusan Nat. U., 1979, MS, 1982, PhD, 1988. Diplomate Ministry of Health and Welfare, 1984. Intern Pusan Nat. U., 1979—80, resident in orthop. surgery, 1980—84, instr., 1987—89, asst. prof., 1989—93; fellow Wayne State U., Detroit, 1991—92; assoc. prof. Pusan Nat. U., 1993—98, prof., 1998—; exch. prof. Case Western Res. U., Cleve., 1999. Chmn. dept. orthop. surgery Pusan Nat. U. Hosp., 2002—08; dean Pusan Nat. U. Sch. Medicine, 2009—. Lt. Korean Navy, 1984—87. Recipient Unbong Med. Achievement award, Coll. Medicine Pusan Nat. U., 2004, Med. Rsch. Inst. Acad. award, Pusan Nat. U., 2007. Mem.: Korean Orthop. Assn. (editl. bd. 2002—, Rsch. award 2003, Acad. award 2006), Korean Hip Soc. (editl. bd. 1996—, councilor 2000—, pres. 2007—08), Am. Assn. Hip and Knee Surgeons, Internat. Soc. Orthop. Surgery and Traumatology. Avocation: golf. Office: Pusan Nat Univ Hosp 1-10 Ami-Dong Seo-Gu Pusan 602-739 Republic of Korea Office Fax: 82-55-360-2155. Business E-Mail: kuentak@pusan.ac.kr.

SUH, KWANG WOOK, medical educator; s. Okbong Kim; m. Hee Kyung Cho, Jan. 17, 1987; children: Inho, Ingun. MD, Yonsei U. Coll. Medicine, Seoul, 1985; PhD, Yonsei U., Seoul, 1995. Bd. cert. surgeon Dept. Health and Social Affair, Republic of Korea. Instr. Yonsei U. Coll. Medicine, Seoul, 1991—93; prof. Ajou U. Sch. Medicine, Suwon, Republic of Korea, 2003—. Postdoctoral fellow Johns Hopkins U. Sch. Medicine, Balt., 1996—98. Fellow: Soc. Surg. Oncology (licentiate). Home: 331-16 Hagal Li Yong In 449-906 Republic of Korea Office: Surgery Ajou U Sch Medicine San 5 Woncheon Dong Young Tong Ku 442-749 Suwon Republic of Korea Office Fax: 82-31-219-5755. Business E-Mail: suhkw@ajou.ac.kr.

SUH, MOO KYU, dermatologist, educator; b. Daegu, Republic of Korea, Feb. 3, 1958; s. Sun Tae Kim; m. Won Hee Jun, Feb. 10, 1985; 1 child, Min Ji. MD, Kyungpook Nat. U., Daegu, Korea, 1982, M, 1985, PhD, 1993. Lic. dermatologist Korean Dermatol. Assn., 1986. Resident in dermatology Kyungpook Nat. U. Hosp., Daegu, 1983—86; instr. then prof. dept. dermatology Coll. Medicine Dongguk U., Kyongju, Republic of Korea, 1991—, chmn. dept. dermatology Kyongju Hosp., 1991—. Contbr. articles to profl. jours. With Navy, 1986—89, Republic of Korea. Mem.: Korean Soc. Med. Mycology (assoc. Best Paper award 2002, 2004), Korean Dermatol. Assn. (assoc.), Internat. Soc. Human and Animal Mycology (assoc.), Japanese Soc. Med. Mycology (assoc.). Home: 101-1706 Dong-A apt 372-3 Chimsan-dong Daegu 702-780 Republic of Korea Office: Dept Dermatology Kyongju Hospital Coll of Medicine Dongguk University Kyungbuk Kyongju 780-350 Republic of Korea Office Fax: +82-54-773-1581. Business E-Mail: mksuhmd@hanmail.net.

SUH, TAE SUK, biomedical engineer, educator; b. Seoul, Republic of Korea, Mar. 13, 1957; s. Kwang Rok and Sun Tae Suh; m. Myung Hae Bae, Dec. 26, 1986; children: Susie, Jun Ho. BA in Nuc. Engring., Seoul Nat. U., 1980; MS in Health Physics, U. Fla., 1986, PhD in Med. Physics, 1990. Cert. Korea Soc. Med. Physics, Seoul, 1992. Rsch. asst. dept. nuc. sci. U. Fla., Gainsvile, 1984—86, grad. asst. dept. radiology, 1986—90; asst. prof. dept. biomed. engring. Cath. U. Korea, Coll. Medicine, Seoul, 1990—96, assoc. prof. dept. biomed. engring., 1996—, dir. rsch. Inst. Biomed. Engring., 1996—, chair dept. biomed. engring., 1999—2005, dir. rsch. Inst. MRI, 1999—, prof. dept. biomed. engring., 2001—. Exec. com. Korean Assn. Radiation Protection, Seoul, 1994—98, Korean Soc. Magnetic Resonance Medicine, 1996—98; pres. World Congress Med. Physics and Biomed. Engring., 2003—. Contbr. scientific papers. Com. chair rsch. evaluation Ministry Health & Welfare, Seoul, 1996—2000; com. mem. rsch. evaluation Ministry Commerce, Industry and Energy, 1998—2002; com. chair long-term rsch. plan Ministry Sci. & Tech.,

1998—2005. Staff sgt. Korean Mil., 1980—82. Recipient First Prize award Excellent Paper, Korean Assn. Radiation Protection, 1996, Korean Fedn. Sci. and Tech. Socs., 1997, Young Investigator's award, The 14th Internat. Conf. Use Computers Radiation Therapy, 2004, Superior Prof. award, Cath. U. Korea, 2005, Poster award, 4th Japan-Korea Joint Meeting Med. Physics and 5th Asia-Oceania Congress Med. Physics, 2005. Mem.: Korean Soc. Med. Physics (v.p. 1998—2002), Asia-Oceania Fedn. Orgns. Med. Physics (sci. com. chair 2002—04, sec. gen. 2003—), Internat. Orgn. Med. Physics (sci. com. 2003—, nomitating com. 2003—), Korean Soc. Med. Physics Radiosurgery (pres. 2002—), Am. Assn. Physicists Medicine. Achievements include development of Radiation Therapy Planning System; 3T Magnetic Resonance Image; patents for Reference Plate for X-ray Exposure and Reference Plate Holder; Measuring Instrument for Absorbed Dose; Stereotactic Whole-body Frame; Inhomogeneous Phantom for Absorbed Dose Measurement; Phantom for evaluating image registration accuracy; Brain Stereotacitc Radiation therapy frame; Phantom and Phantom equipment for evaluating accuracy of the planning of High dose rate Brachytherapy; Collimator, Collimator adaptor, and Holder for Radiation Therapy. Avocations: climbing, travel, jogging, tennis, fishing. Home: Dongsong Park Village B-301 Suyu4-dong Seoul 142-070 Republic of Korea Office: Cath U Korea Banpo-Dong 505 Seocho-Gu Seoul 137-040 Republic of Korea Office Fax: 82-2-532-1779; Home Fax: 82-2-594-0419. Personal E-mail: suhsanta@catholic.ac.kr.

SUH, WONSUK WARREN, radiation oncologist; s. Chai-Pill and Myung-Hi Suh; m. Jeewon Park, Nov. 22, 2000; children: Ryan Joonwon, Sidney Chaewon. BA, Cornell U., 1991; MD, U. Chgo., 1996; MPH, Harvard U., 1996. Diplomate internal medicine and radiation oncology. Resident internal medicine Mayo Clinic, Rochester, Minn., 1996—99; from radiation oncology resident to chief resident U. Mich., Ann Arbor, 2000—04; faculty radiation oncologist Dana-Farber/Brigham & Women's Cancer Ctr., Boston, 2004—. Contbr. articles to profl. jours. Recipient H. Hughes award, 1990; named Eminent Scientist Yr. in Radiation Oncology, Internat. Rsch. Prom Coun., 2006—07. Mem.: Am. Coll. Radiology (mem. appropriateness criteria expert panel, rectal and anal cancers 2006—), Am. Soc. Therapeutic Radiation and Oncology (health svcs. outcome rsch. leadership com. 2004—, adj. prostate radiation panel chair 2007—), Am. Soc. Clin. Oncology (mem. new tech. com., PET evaluation 2002—, Merit award 2003). Office: Cancer Ctr Santa Barbara 300 W Pueblo St Santa Barbara CA 93105 Home: 2275 Feather Hill Rd Santa Barbara CA 93108 Office Phone: 805-682-7300. Business E-Mail: wsuh@ccsb.org.

SUH, YOO-HUN, molecular neurobiology educator, administrator; b. Kimchun, Kyungbook, South Korea, Feb. 8, 1948; s. Kyung-Duk and Yoon-Soo (Kim) S.; m. Sook-Hee Lee, Apr. 6, 1974; children: Won-Hyuk, Jee-Kyung. MD, Seoul Nat. U. Med. Coll., 1973, PhD, 1980. Intern Seoul Nat. U. Hosp., 1973-74, resident, 1974-76; rschr. Army Def. Devel. Inst., Seoul, 1976-79; instr. pharmacology Seoul Nat. U. Med. Coll., 1979-82, asst. prof., 1983-84, vis. prof. Cornell Med. Coll., NYC, 1984-86; assoc. prof. Seoul Nat. U. Med. Coll., 1986-92; exch. prof. Ctr. for Molecular Biology U. Heidelberg, Germany, 1989-90; chmn. dept. molecular biology Neurosci. Rsch. Ctr., Seoul, 1990—, prof. Seoul Nat. U. Med. Coll., 1992—; dean Kangwon Nat. U. Coll. Medicine, 1997—99; dir. Biomed. Brain Rsch. Ctr., NIH, 1998—, Neurosci. Rsch. Ctr., 1999—, Nat. Creative Initiative Rsch. Ctr. for Alzheimers Disease, 2000—. Vis. prof. Imperial Coll., 1996—. Author: Neurotransmitter, 1990, Mystery of the Brain, 1994, Pharmacology, 1994, Amazing Brain, 1995, Know the Brain and Use the Brain, 1996, The Brain and Longevity, 1996, The Brain Scape, 1997, The Brain World, 1997, Awake Sleeping Brain, 2000, Brain Brased Learning, 2001; editor: Jour. Neurochemistry, 1994, Jour. Molecular Neurosci., Jour. Neurosci. Rsch., 1998, editl. bd. mem., Neurochem. Rsch., 2002-, editl. bd. mem., Neurosci. Rsch., 2002-, assoc. editor, Jour. Pharmacol. Scis., 2011-. Maj. Korean Army, 1976. Recipient Excellent Achievement award Korean Engring. and Sci. Found., 1991, Med. Achievement award Yuhan Pharm. Co., 1992, Drug Devel. award Ministry Sci. and Tech., 1992, Kwang Hae prize, 1995, Sejong Cultural award, 1997, Korean Publ. award, 1997, Yu Han Grand prize, 2002, Nat. Govt. medal, Wong Bie medal, 2002, Eui Dang Med. award, 2004, 5.16 Nat. award, 2004; named one of 20 Outstanding Med. Scientists, 2002, one of 21 outstanding Korean Scholars of 21st Century, 2001, Excellent SCI award, 2007, Ho Sup Shi Med. award, 2008, SNU Excellent Rsch. award, 2008, Koreas Most Disting. Scientist award, 2009. Mem. Am. Soc. Neurosci., Internat. Soc. Neurchemistry, Internat. Brain Rsch. Orgn., Asian Pacific Soc. Neurochemistry (pres. 1996—), Korean Brain Soc. (pres. 1998—). Achievements include patents in field. Office: Seoul Nat U Coll Med Dept Pharm 28 Yeongeondong Jongno-gu Seoul 110-799 Republic of Korea Business E-Mail: yhsuh@snu.ac.kr.

SUH, YOUNG-GER, dean; b. Gochang, Republic of Korea, May 30, 1952; M, Seoul Nat. U., 1980; PhD, U. Pitts., 1987. Dean, prof. Seoul Nat. U., Coll. Pharmacy, 2007—. Editor-in-chief Pharm. Soc. Korea, 2003—04; pres. Korean Assn. Coll. Pharmacy, 2007—09. Recipient award, Pharm. Soc. Korea, Ministry of Health and Welfare, King, Sae-Jong award, Chungang Press, 2005. Mem.: Korean Healthcare Tech. Policy, Korean Fedn. Sci. and Tech. Soc. (Outstanding Work award), Pharm. Soc. Korea. Avocations: tennis, mountain climbing. Office: Seoul Nat University Coll Pharmacy Seoul 151-742 Republic of Korea Office Fax: 82 2 888 0649. Business E-Mail: ygsuh@snu.ac.kr.

SUH, YOUNG-SUNG, professor; s. Jeong-Sik Suh and Jae-Yeon Koh; m. Mi-Yeon Kim, Jan. 26, 1992; children: Jun-Woo, Seung-dong. BS in Medicine, Keimyung U., Daegu, 1989; MS in Med. Sci., Keimyung U., 1992; MD, Jeonbuk U., Jeonju, Republic of Korea, 2001. Lic. Health and Welfare, Republic of Korea, 1989. Internship Dongsan Med. Ctr., Daegu, 1989—90, residency, dept. family medicine, 1990—92, fellowship, dept. family medicine, 1995—97; vis. scholar, dept. endocrinology unit Penington Biomed. Rsch. Ctr., Baton Rouge, La., 2003—04; assoc. prof. Keimyung U. Sch. Medicine, Daegu, Republic of Korea, 2010—; dir. dept. family medicine Dongsan Med. Ctr., Daegu, 2004—08. Mem. editl. bd. Korean Jour. Family Medicine, 2010—. Contbr. articles to profl. jours. Mem. Newlite, Daegu, Republic of Korea, 2005—. Capt. Korean Army, 1992—95, Republic of Korea. Mem.: Korean Obesity Soc. Family Medicine (pres. 2009—), Korean Obesity Soc. (bd. dir. 2009—), Korean Med. Assn. (Meritorious Svc. prize 2007), Korean Soc. Obesity (sci. com. 2005—06), Korea Family Medicine (Seoul) (licentiate; sec. gen. 2005—, bd. exam. com. 2005—). Office: Dongsan Med Ctr Dongsan-Dong Jung-Gu 194 700-712 Daegu Daegu Republic of Korea Business E-Mail: ysseo@dsmc.or.kr.

SUH, ZUNG-SHIK, engineering educator; b. Taegu, Kyungpook, Republic of Korea, Feb. 1, 1960; s. Yeon-Hee Kim and Jong-Cheol Suh; m. Zung-Souk Lee, Feb. 3, 1997; 1 child, Yung. PhD, Korea Advanced Inst. Sci. and Tech., 2002. Rschr. Gold Star Ctrl. Rsch. Inst., Seoul, Republic of Korea, 1988—91; tchr. Kyungpook Nat. U., Taegu, 1991—93; assoc. prof. Kumi Coll., Kyungpook, 1996—. Achievements include research in effects of initial interaction and leaky mode phase-matching in the evolution of Cerenkov optical second-harmonic generation in a nonlinear dielectric waveguide; analysis of the effects of initial interaction and leaky made pinose matching; in the evolution of the length dependence in the Cerenkov Optical Second-Harmonic generation in a nonlinear dialectric waveguide. Office: Kumi Coll Bukok-Dong 407 730-711 Kumi Gyeongsangbuk-do Republic of Korea Business E-Mail: zssuh@kumi.ac.kr.

SUHLER, ERIC BARTON, ophthalmologist, educator; b. Calif., Dec. 7, 1968; MD, UT Southwestern, 1995; MPH, OHSU, 2007. Assoc. prof., chief ophthalmology OHSU, Portland Va. Med. Ctr., 2002. Fellow: Am. Acad. Ophthalmology. Office: 3375 SW Terwilliger Blvd Portland OR 97239 Office Fax: 503-494-6875. Business E-Mail: suhlere@ohsu.edu.

SUHR, KI-BEOM, dermatologist; b. Daejeon, Republic of Korea, June 16, 1959; s. Myung-Won Suhr and Kye-Young Song; m. Kyung-Woon Jun, Dec. 28, 1960; children: Kang-Hyuk, Kang-Yoon. MD, Chungnam Nat. U., Daejeon, 1984, PhD, 1991. Bd. cert. diplomate Korean Dermatol. Assn., 1989, Atopic Dermatitis Member Korean Atopic Dermatitis Rsch. Soc., 2001. Intern, resident Chungnam Nat. U. Hosp., Daejeon, 1984—89; asst. prof. dept. dermatology Chungnam Nat. Univ., Daejeon, 1995—99, assoc. prof. dept. dermatology, 1999—2002; CEO CnU Skin Rsch. Ctr., Daejeon, 2003—; rep. dr. CnU Med. Skin Hosp., Daejeon, 2003—. Mem.: Korean Health Ins. Assessment Assn., Korean Atopic Dermatitis Rsch. Soc. (corr.), Japanese Soc. Investigative Dermatology (corr.), Korean Dermatol. Assn. (assoc.). Home: Kwanjo-Dong 990 Daejeon Seo-Ku 301-153 Republic of Korea Office: CnU Skin Hospital Eunhaeng-Dong 139-1 Jung-Ku Daejeon 301-050 Republic of Korea Office Fax: 042-0505-254-9200; Home Fax: 042-0505-254-9200. Business E-Mail: seokb@cnu.ac.kr.

SUI, HONG-JIN, anatomist, educator; married. MD, Dalian Med. U., China, 1999. Prof. Dalian Med. U., 2001, dir. dept. anatomy, 2006—. Gen. mgr., exhbn. designer Dalian Hoffen Bio-Tech. Co. Ltd., Dalian, 2004—. Contbr. articles to publ. Achievements include to be designer of exhibitions with plastic human bodies & comparative anatomy exhibitions.

SUINN, RICHARD MICHAEL, psychologist; b. Honolulu, May 8, 1933; s. Maurice and Edith (Wong) S.; m. Grace D. Toy, July 26, 1958; children: Susan, Randall, Staci, Bradley. Student, U. Hawaii, 1951-53; BA summa cum laude, Ohio State U., 1955; MA in Clin. Psychology, Stanford U., 1957, PhD in Clin. Psychology, 1959, Doctorate (hon.), Calif. Sch. Profl. Psychology, 1999. Lic. psychologist, Colo.; diplomate Am. Bd. Profl. Psychology. Counselor Stanford U., Calif., 1958-59, rsch. assoc. Med. Sch., 1964-66; asst. prof. psychology Whitman Coll., Walla Walla, Wash., 1959-64; assoc. prof. U. Hawaii, Honolulu, 1966-68; prof. Colo. State U., Ft. Collins, 1968-99, head dept. psychology, 1972-93, emeritus prof., 2000—. Cons. in field; psychologist US Ski Teams, 1976, Olympic Games, US Women's Track and Field, 1980 Olympic Games, US Ski Jumping Team, 1988, US Shooting Team, 1994; mem. sports psychology adv. com. US Olympic Com., 1983-89; reviewer NIMH, 1977-80, 94-98. Author: The Predictive Validity of Projective Measures, 1969, Fundamentals of Behavior Pathology, 1970, The Innovative Psychological Therapies, 1975, The Innovative Medical-Psychiatric Therapies, 1976, Psychology in Sport: Methods and Applications, 1980, Fundamentals of Abnormal Psychology, 1984, 88, Seven Steps to Peak Performance, 1986, Anxiety Management Training, 1990; editorial bd.: Jour. Cons. and Clin. Psychology, 1973-86, Jour. Counseling Psychology, 1974-91, Behavior Therapy, 1977-80, Behavior Modification, 1977-78, Jour. Behavioral Medicine, 1978-83, Behavior Counseling Quar., 1979-83, Jour. Sports Psychology, 1980-91, Clin. Psychology: Science and Practice, 1994-97, Professional Psychology, 1994-97; author: tests Math. Anxiety Rating Scale, Suinn Test Anxiety Behavior Scale, Suinn-Lew Asian Self-identity Acculturation Scale. Mem. City Coun., Ft. Collins, 1975-79, mayor, 1978-79; mem. Gov.'s Mental Health Adv. Coun., 1983, Colo. Bd. Psychologist Examiners, 1983-86. Recipient cert. merit US Ski Team, 1976, APA Career Contbn. to Edn. award, 1995, Lifetime Contbn. to Ethnic Minority Issues award, 2004, Raymond D. Fowler award, 2005; NIMH grantee, 1963-64; Office Edn. grantee, 1970-71. Fellow APA (chmn. bd. ethnic minority affairs 1982-83, chmn. edn. and tng. bd. 1986-87, policy and planning bd. 1987-89, publs. bd. 1993-97, bd. dirs. 1990-93, pres.-elect 1998, pres. 1999, chmn. membership com. 2005, chmn. presdl. task force on enhancing diversity, 2005, coun. of rep., chmn. bd. convention affaires), Behavior Therapy and Rsch. Soc. (charter); mem. Am. Psychol. Found. (trustee 2000-04), Assn. for Advancement Psychology (trustee 1983-86), Assn. for Advancement Behavior Therapy (sec.-treas. 1986-89, pres. 1992-93), Asian Am. Psychol. Assn. (bd. dirs. 1983-88), Am. Bd. Behavior Therapy (bd. dirs. 1987-2000), Phi Beta Kappa, Sigma Xi. Home: 808 Cheyenne Dr Fort Collins CO 80525-1560 Office: Colo State U Dept Psychology Fort Collins CO 80523-0001 Office Phone: 970-491-1351. Business E-Mail: suinn@lamar.colostate.edu.

SUIT, HERMAN DAY, radiation oncologist, medical educator; b. Houston, Feb. 8, 1929; BA, U. Houston, 1948; MSc in Biochemistry, Baylor U., MD, 1952; PhD, Oxford U., Eng., 1956. Cert. Radiation Oncology (England), 1956, Radiation Oncology, US, 1957. Intern Jefferson Davis Hosp., Houston, 1952-53; resident in radiation oncology Jefferson David Hosp., Houston, 1953; postdoctoral tng., radiation oncology Oxford United Hosp., England, 1954—; sr. asst. surgeon radiation br. Nat. Cancer Inst., 1957-59; asst. radiotherapist U. Tex. M.D. Anderson Hosp. and Tumor Inst., Houston, 1959-63, assoc. radiotherapist, 1963-68, radiotherapist, 1968-71, chief sect. exptl. radiotherapy, 1959—70; Andres Soriano prof. radiation oncology Harvard Med. Sch., 1970—; head dept. radiation oncology Mass. Gen. Hosp., Boston, 1970—2000, radiologist, oncologist. Recipient Charles F. Kettering prize, GM Cancer Rsch. Found., 1997, Gray medal, Internat. Comm. on Radiation Units and Measurments, Inc., 2001; named Disting. Alumnus, Baylor College of Medicine, 1978, Janeway Lectr., Am. Radium Soc., 1987; named a Disting. Alumnus, U. Houston, 2005. Mem. Am. Soc. Therapeutic Radiology and Oncology (pres. 1980-81, recipient Gold medal, 1990). Office: Mass Gen Hosp Cancer Ctr Dept Radiation Therapy 55 Fruit St Boston MA 02114 Office Phone: 617-724-1155. Office Fax: 617-726-4805.

SUK, KYUNG-SOO, surgeon; b. Seoul, Republic Of Korea, Aug. 29, 1964; s. Seil Suk and In-Sook Kim; m. Sookjean Lee, Feb. 19, 1969; children: Jee-Young, Jae-Hyun. MD, Yonsei U. Coll. Medicine, Seoul, 1990; MS, Yonsei U. Grad. Sch., Seoul, 1995, PhD, 2002. Cert. orthopaedic surgeon Ministry Health Welfare and Family Affairs, Korea, 1995, spine surgeoon Korean Soc. Spine Surgery, Korea, 1999. Rsch. instr., spine fellow Dept. Orthopaedic Surgery, Yonsei U. Med. Coll., Seoul, 1998—2000; spine and rsch. fellow Dept. Orthopedic Surgery, Johns Hopkins Med. Inst., Baltimore, 2000—01; assoc. prof. Dept. Orthopaedic Surgery Kyung Hee U. Coll. Medicine, Seoul, orthopaedic & spine surgeon, chief divsn. spine. Com. mem. computer com. Korean Soc. Spine Surgeon, Seoul, 2003—; rsch. com. mem. Korean Orthopaedic Rsch. Soc., Seoul, 2004—; com. mem. info. and computer com. Korean Orthopedic Assn., Seoul, 2004—; com. mem. cervical spine rsch. com. Korean Soc. Spine Surgeon, Seoul, 2005—; reviewer jour. Jour. Korean Orthopedic Assn., Seoul, 2005—, Jour. Korean Soc. of Spine Surgeon, Seoul, 2004—; cons. Nat. Pension Svc., Sepi;, 2006—; chief case conf. com. Korean Orthopedic Ciber Soc., Seoul, 2006—; com. mem. exam. prep. com. Korean Orthopedic Assn., Seoul, 2006—; editl. mem. Clinics Orthopaedic Surgery, Seoul, 2008—; cons. Gen. ins. assn. Korea, Seoul, Republic of Korea, 2008—; mem. academic com. Korean Soc. Spine Surgeon, Seoul. Contbr. articles to profl. jours. Capt. Seoul Dist. Hosp., 1995—98, Seoul. Recipient Academic award, Korean soc. Spine Surgery, 2002, SICOT 93 Seoul, 2002, 2003, Best sci. award, PASMISS, 2004, Academic award, Korean Soc. Spine Surgery, 2005, Korean soc. spine surgery, 2005, Manre found., Korean Orthopaedic Assn., 1999; grantee, R & D fund health and med. tech. supported, 1989—99, LINKS Rsch. Fund, 1999—2000, rsch. fund faculty Yonsei U., 1999—2000, Health Ins. Rev. & Assessment Svc., 2008—, Korea Food & Drug Adminstrn., 2008—09, Yonsei U. Coll. Medicine, 1998, Yonsei U., 1998—99. Mem.: Asia-Pacific Cervical Spine Rsch. Soc., Spine Arthoplasty Soc., North Am. Spine Soc., Korean Orthopaedic Rsch. Soc., SICOT, Korean Soc. Spine Surgery, Korean Orthopaedic Assn., Korean Med. Assn. Avocations: skiing, golf, travel. Office: Dept Orthop Surg KHMC 1 Hoekidong Dondamunku Seoul 130-702 Republic of Korea Office Fax: 822-964-3865; Home Fax: 822-964-3865. Business E-Mail: sks111@khmc.or.kr.

SUKBONG, KOH, gynecoligic oncologist and medical educator; b. Daegu, Republic of Korea, Nov. 3, 1961; MD, Youngnam U., 1987, PhD, 2002. Asst. prof. Dept. Ob-Gyn., Cath. U. Daegu, 2006—10, prof., 2010—, vice dean, 2011, chief instr. dept. ob-gyn., 2011. Recipient Best Edn. award, Dept. Ob-Gyn., Cath. U. Daegu. Avocation: hiking. Office: 3056-6 Deamyung-4 dong Namgu Daegu 705-718 Republic of Korea Office Phone: 010-5567-8424, 82-053-650-4074. Business E-Mail: sbko@cu.ac.kr.

SUKHOVA, GALINA K., medical educator; arrived in U.S., 1992; d. Konstantin Stepanovich Sukhov and Tamara Sergeevna Alekseeva; m. Alexander Golger, Aug. 23, 1969; 1 child, Igor Golger. BS, Moscow State U., 1969, MS, 1971, PhD, 1978. Rsch. scientist The First Moscow Med. Inst., Moscow, 1978—86; sr. staff scientist Cardiology Rsch. Ctr., Moscow, 1986—91; rsch. asst. Brigham and Women's Hosp., Boston, 1992—93, dir. morphology lab., 1994—98, instr. medicine Harvard Med. Sch., 1999—. Contbr. articles to profl. jours. Fellow: Am. Heart Assn. Avocations: literature, music, travel. Office: Brigham and Women's Hosp 77 Avenue Louis Pasteur Boston MA 02215

SUKI, SAMER SAID, oncologist; b. Beirut, May 1, 1961; s. Said Amine and Afife Elsouki; m. Rihab Aref Abdul Hosn; children: Sarah, Zeins, Omar. BS in Biology, Am. U. Beirut, 1982, MD, 1986. Diplomate Am. Bd. Internal Medicine, Am. Bd. Hematology, Am. Bd. Med. Oncology. Intern Am. U. Beirut, 1986—87; internal medicine resident St. Agnes Hosp., Balt., 1986—87; fellow in oncology/hematology M.D. Anderson Cancer Ctr., Houston, 1990—93, bone marrow transplant trainee, 1991—92; adj. asst. prof. M.D. Adnerson Cancer Ctr., Houston, 1995—96; pvt. practice physician W.Va., 1993—95; ptnr. Houston Physicians Med. Assn., PLLC, dba Houston Cancer Clinics, 1995—. Admitting/consulting staff Houston Northwest Med. Ctr., Northeast Med. Ctr. Hosp., Houston, Columbia Kingwood (Tex.) Med. Ctr., Tomball (Tex.) Regional Hosp., Cypress Fairbanks Med. Ctr., Houston; presenter in field. Contbr. articles to profl. med. jours. Mem.: AMA, ACP, So. Med. Assn. Office: Houston Cancer Clinic 800 Peakwood # 6F Houston TX 77090 Office Phone: 281-397-6555. Personal E-mail: samersuki@hotmail.com.

SUKIASYAN, SAMVEL HRANT (GRANT), psychiatrist, director; b. Yerevan, Armenia, Nov. 24, 1957; MD, Yerevan State Med. Inst., 1981, PhD, DSc in Medicine, 1996. Head dept. Psycho Neurological Hosp. Japan, 1983—84; aspirant, postgrad. edn. mem. Sci. Rsch. Inst. Clin. Psychiatry Sci. Ctr. Mental Health Acad. Med. Sci., Moscow, 1984—87; dep. dir. Rep. Hosp. Neorosis, 1987—93, Ctr. Mental Health Stress, 1993—2000, dir., 2000—11. Dir. sci. project Sci. Project Creation Post Stress Somatized Mental Disorders Devel. Model & Elaboration Early Diagnosis Methods, 2000—01; mem. pub. coun. Med. Jour. Psychiatry Moscow Russian Fedn., 2003—10; prof. chair Stressology Nat. Inst. Health MH RA, 2004—11; dir. sci. project Sci. Project Affective & Stress Disorders, Elaboration Early Diagnosis & Profl. Assistance Methods Gen. Med., 2005—07; prof. Chair

Psychology Yerevan State U., 2007—11. Contbr. scientific papers. Master: Sci. Sec. Exec. Com. Armenian Psychiat. Assn.; mem.: NY Acad. Scis., World Fedn. Socs. Biol. Psychiatry, Internat. Early Psychosis Assn., Russian Soc. BioPsychiatry. Avocations: drawing, photography. Home: 9 th May Str 13 14 Yerevan Marz of Yerevan 0006 Armenia Office Phone: 374 10 628997. Personal E-mail: samsu57@yahoo.com.

SUKUMARAN, PRABHU, lecturer, researcher; b. Palghat City, Kerala, India, Feb. 21, 1971; s. Sukumaran Nair Kizhakancheri Thonakoatai and Subhadra Amma Naanathae. PhD, 2006. Lectr. Jaya Arts and Sci. Coll., Chennai, Tamil Nadu, India, 1995—, Sivet Coll., Gowrivakkam, Chennai, 1996—2005; sr. lectr. Bharath U., Chennai, 2005—07; sr. lectr., dept. biotech. SVCE Coll., Pennalur, Sriperumbudur, Tamilnadu, 2007—. Guest lectr. Balaji Nursing Coll., Chennai, 1998—2002. Contbr. articles to profl. jours. Mem.: Indian Inst. Sci. (Bangalore, India) (life), Biol. Chem. Soc. (India) (life). Home: Guruswamy Nagar Extension Gowrivakkam #6/2 S S Bhavanam Saraswathy St Chennai Tamilnadu 600073 India Office: Univ Madras Guindy Campus Chennai Tamilnadu 600025 India Office Phone: 9840180535. Personal E-mail: prabhubio2k@yahoo.co.in. Business E-Mail: prabhussb2008@gmail.com.

SUL, YI CHUL, neurologist; b. Seoul, May 5, 1947; arrived in US, 1976; s. Tae Woon Sul and Jung Sook Suh; m. Kyu Won, Nov. 21, 1976; children: Caroline, Douglas, Joseph. MD, Yonsei U., Seoul, 1972. Diplomate Am. Bd. Psychiatry and Neurology, Am. Bd. Neurophysiology. Clin. instr. Vanderbilt U., Nashville, 1981-82; v.p. Lakeside Neurology, PC, Grosse Pointe Woods, Mich., 1985—; asst. clin. prof. Mich. State U., Lansing, 1995—. Adj. clin. asst. prof. U. Osteo. Medicine and Health Sci., 1998—99; clin. asst. prof. Coll. Osteo. Medicine U. Health Sci., 2000—; chief neurology sect. St. John N.E. Cmty. Hosp., Detroit, 2002—03; mem. neurosci. adv. group St. John Health Sys., 2004—06. Pres. Lakside Neurology, 2005—; sec. Christian Assn. Med. Mission, Detroit, 1991—95, pres., 1999—2001; med. mission Thailand, 1994, China, 1997; chairperson adminstrv. bd. Korean United Meth. Ch., Detroit, 1997—98, chairperson bd. trustees, 2001; pres. Severance Alumni Assn. Mich., 2008—09. Capt. Republic of Korea Army, 1972—75. Grantee, Muscular Dystrophy Assn., 1981—82. Fellow: Am. Assn. Electrodiagnostic Medicine; mem.: AMA, Korean Am. Med. Assn. Mich. (pres. 2009), Mich. State Med. Soc., Am. Clin. Neurophysiology Soc., Am. Acad. Neurology. Home: 20720 Green Ct Grosse Pointe Woods MI 48236-1459 Office: Lakeside Neurology PC 20867 Mack Ave Ste 6 Grosse Pointe Woods MI 48236-1356 Office Phone: 313-882-2922.

SULAIMAN, NABIL DAWOOD, physician, educator; s. Dawood Sulaiman Al-Rawachy and Gharbia Ismail Kharoofa; m. Imtithal Shakir Jawad, July 19, 1979; children: Saif Nabil, Taif Nabil, Ahmad Nabil. MB ChB, Coll. Medicine, Mosul, 1976; MPH, Dundee U., Scotland, 1984, PhD, 1988; diploma in Child Health, Trinity Coll., Dublin, 1989. Iraqi Med. Assn. 1976, Health Ministry UAE, 2006. Acting dir. U. Melbourne Gen. Practice, Australia, 2000—05; head family and cmty. med. U. Sharjah, United Arab Emirates, 2005—, head behaviorial scis., 2005—. Vice chmn. Australian Arabic Coun., Melbourne, 1996—2006, gulf rep., 2005—; founding mem. Australian Iraqi Forum, Melbourne, 2003—; clin. skills coord. Sharjah U., 2005—; mem. nat. polio eradication program Ministry of Health, Abu Dhabi, United Arab Emirates, 2006—. Vice chmn. Australian Arabic Coun., ria, 1996—2005. Physician Army Res., 1980—82, Iraq. Grantee, Nat. Health Med. Rsch. Coun., 2005—08; fellow, Glaxowelcome Trust, 2002—05. Mem.: Austrailan Assn. Academic Gen. Practitioners. Islam. Avocation: travel. Office: Univ Melbourne 200 Berekley St Victoria a Melbourne 3050 Australia Home: 14/90 Edgars Rd Thomastown Victoria 3074 Australia Personal E-mail: nsulaiman@sharjah.ac.ae. Business E-Mail: n.sulaiman@unimelb.edu.au.

SULAMANIDZE, MARLEN ANDREEVICH, plastic surgeon; b. Kutaisi, Georgia, Oct. 8, 1947; s. Andro Mikhailovich Sulamanidze and Nina Konstantinovna Kachkachishvili; m. Tatiana Georgievna Paikidze, Nov. 15, 1978; children: George Marlenovich, Constantin Marlenovich. BS, State Med. U. Irkutsk, 1972; degree in Maxillofacial Surgery, 1984. Ship dr., Sakhalin, Russia, 1972—73; maxillofacial surgeon Rep. Hosp. Ga., Kutaisi, 1973—82, plastic surgeon, 1982—93, Ctr. Aesthetic Correction, Moscow, 1993—2000, Clin. Plastic and Aesthetic Surgery Total Charm, Moscow, 2000—07, Tbilisi, Georgia, 2007. Protection dissertation. receptions status md. Vishnevski Acad. Surgery, Moscow, 1998. Sr. lt. med. svc. Georgion Army, 1974—77, Kutaisi. Master: Japan Soc. Lipoplasty; mem.: Internat. Soc. Plastic Reonstructive and Aesthetic Surgery, Am. Soc. Dermatologic Surgery, French Soc. Aesthetic Surgery. Achievements include patents for aptos needle - suggested methods of nose alar base width diminution with L-dissection; aptos needle - suggested methods of excessive skin removal from the end of the nose; dual needle and a new design of protrusions on the thread, also suggested appropriate methods of surgical wounds and drooping tissues suturing; development of original technique of autolypofilling; original brassiere for a big female breast and for the mammary fixation after mammaplasty; patents for aptos spring and suggested techniques of "grief wrinkles" elastic lifting; aptos needle - facial and neck soft tissues ptosis. Home and Office: Aptos Orbeliani 18 Tbilisi 0105 Georgia Office Fax: 99532920371. Personal E-mail: gracia@aptos.ru. Business E-Mail: info@aptos.ge.

SULEK, ANNA MARZENA, molecular geneticist; b. Warsaw, Nov. 21, 1969; d. Kazimierz and Zoja Sulek; 1 child, Julia. MS, U. Warsaw, 1994; MSc, Warsaw Sch. Trade, 1998; PhD, Inst. Exptl. Clin. Medicine, Warsaw, 2003. Asst. Child's Meml. Health Inst., Warsaw, 1995—98; sr. asst. Inst. Psychiatry and Neurology, Warsaw, 1998—. Mem.: Polish Soc. Human Genetics, European Soc. Human Genetics. Avocations: literature, skiing. Office: Inst Psychiatry and Neurology Sobieskiego 9 02-857 Warsaw Poland Business E-Mail: suleka@ipin.edu.pl.

SULEYMAN, HALIS, medical educator; b. Namangan, Uzbekistan, June 30, 1956; s. Ensar and Muhabbet Suleyman; m. Zulfiye Habibova, May 9, 1981; children: Bahadir, Kahraman, Suna Yaman, Bahtiyar. MD, Tashkent Med. U., Uzbekistan, 1981, PhD in Pharmacology, 1989. Assoc. prof., faculty medicine, dept. pharmacology Ataturk U., Erzurum, Turkey, 2004—. Contbr. scientific papers to numerous rsch. publs. Mem.: Turkish Soc. Pharmacology. Achievements include patents for drug activity. Office: Ataturk Univ Faculty Medicine Erzurum 25240 Turkey Office Phone: 904422316558. Office Fax: 904422360968. Business E-Mail: halis.suleyman@gmail.com.

SULLEBARGER, JOHN THOMPSON, internist, cardiologist, educator; b. Plainfield, NJ, May 2, 1957; s. Franklyn Jackson and Joanne Abbott (Aspinall) S.; m. Lorrie Jeanne Miller, June 14, 1980; children: Jeffrey Franklyn, Melissa Jeanne. Student, U. Mainz, 1977; AB, Dartmouth Coll., 1979; MD, Johns Hopkins U., 1983. Intern U. Rochester, NY, 1983-84, resident in medicine, 1984-86, fellow in cardiology, 1986-89, from sr. instr. to asst. prof., 1989-92; asst. prof. U. South Fla., Tampa, 1992-96, assoc. prof., 1997-99; dir. CCU Tampa Gen. Hosp., 1997—; clin. assoc. prof. U. South Fla., Tampa, 2004—. Dir. Cardiac Catheterization Lab. James Haley VA Hosp., Tampa, 1992—99; dir. interventional cardiology U. South Fla., 1994—99; attending physician Strong Meml. Hosp., Rochester, 1989—92; pres. Fla. Cardiovascular Inst., 2004—; chief cardiology Tampa Gen. Hosp., 2008—. Author: (with others) book chapters; contrb. articles to profl. jours. Chmn. Bd. Christian Svc., 1st Bapt. Ch., Rochester, 1991-92. Fellow ACP, 1992, Am. Coll. of Cardiology, 1991, Counc. on Clin. Cardiology of Am. Heart Assn., 1991, N.Y. Cardiological Soc., 1992. Fellow ACP, Soc. Cardiac Angiography and Interventions, Am. Coll. Cardiology, N.Y. Cardiol. Soc.; mem. Am. Heart Assn. (fellow coun. on clin. cardiology), Tampa Internat. Heart Found. (founder 2004-). Avocation: music. Office: 509 S Armenia Ste 200 Tampa FL 33609 Office Phone: 813-353-1515.

SULLIVAN, LOUIS WADE, medical educator, former United States Secretary of Health & Human Services; b. Atlanta, Nov. 3, 1933; s. Walter Wade and Lubirda Elizabeth (Priester) S.; m. Eve Williamson, Sept. 30, 1955; children: Paul, Shanta, Halsted. BS magna cum laude, Morehouse Coll., Atlanta, 1954; MD cum laude, Boston U., 1958. Diplomate: Am. Bd. Internal Medicine. Intern N.Y. Hosp.-Cornell Med. Ctr., NYC, 1958-59, resident in internal medicine, 1959-60; fellow in pathology Mass. Gen. Hosp., Boston, 1960-61; rsch. fellow Thorndike Meml. Lab. Harvard Med. Sch., Boston, 1961-63; instr. medicine Harvard Med. Sch., 1963-64; asst. prof. medicine N.J. Coll. Medicine, 1964-66; co-dir. hematology Boston U. Med. Ctr., 1966; assoc. prof. medicine Boston U., 1968—73; dir. hematology Boston City Hosp., 1973-75; prof. medicine & physiology Boston U., 1973—75; dean Sch. Medicine, Morehouse Coll., Atlanta, 1975—83; pres. Morehouse Sch. Medicine, Morehouse Coll., Atlanta, 1981—89, 1993—2002, pres. emeritus, 2002—; sec. US Dept. Health & Human Services, Washington, 1989-93. Non-exec. dir. GM, 1993-2002; bd. dirs. 3M Co., Henry Schein Inc., Bristol-Myers Squibb Co., CIGNA Corp., Equifax Inc., Georgia-Pacific Corp., United Therapeutics Corp., Emergent Biosolutions, BioSante Pharm.; mem. sickle cell anemia adv. com. NIH, 1974-75; ad hoc panel on blood diseases Nat. Heart, Lung Blood Disease Bur., 1973, Nat. Adv. Rsch. Coun., 1977; mem. med. adv. bd. Nat. Leukemia Assn., 1968-70, chmn., 1970, Pres. Commn. on HIV and AIDS, 2001-06, Pres. Commn. on Hist. Black Colleges and Universities, 2002-09, Nat. Health Mus., Atlanta, Sullivan Alliance to Transform America's Health Professionals, Washington; mem. Sec. of Edn.'s Commn. on Future of Edn., 2005. John Hay Whitney Found. Opportunity fellow, 1960-61; recipient Honor medal Am. Cancer Soc., 1991. Mem. Assn. Am. Physicians, Am. Soc. Hematology, Am. Soc. Clin. Investigation, Clin. and Climatological Soc., Inst. Medicine, Phi Beta Kappa, Alpha Omega Alpha. Episcopalian. Achievements include research in suppression of hematopoiesis by ethanol, pernicious anemia in childhood, folates in human nutrition. Office: Morehouse Sch Medicine Office of the Pres Emeritus 133 Peachtree St Ste 4040 Atlanta GA 30303 Office Phone: 404-752-1933.

SULLIVAN, MARGARET M., biologist, educator; d. Charles Watson and Ann McGee McKay; m. Jacob Edwin Sullivan, May 17, 1974 (dec. June 14, 2003); children: Margaret-Ann, Mary-Katherine, Jacob Edwin III. BS, MS, U. Ala., 1973; MEd, Ala. State U., 1991. Cert. tchr. Ala., 1991. Adj. prof. Huntingdon Coll., Montgomery, Ala., 1975—84; tchr. Montgomery Pub. Sch., 1993—2003; adj. prof. Troy U. Montgomery, 1999—; tchr. Elmore County Sch., Millbrook, Ala., 2003—05; environ. scientist Ala. Dept. Environ. Mgmt., Montgomery, 2005—. Dist. trainer Montgomery County Sch., 1997—2002; cons. Ala. Wildlife Fedn., Montgomery, Ala., 2001, Dallas County Sch., Selma, Ala., 2002. Leader Girl Scouts Am., Montgomery, Ala., 1987—97; co-chair Ala. Dance Theatre Com., Montgomery, 1990—2000; v.p. Montgomery Zoo, Ala., 1990—92. Recipient Outstanding Environ. Program award, Legacy, Ptnrs. in Environ. Edn., 1998, NSTA/FDA Profl. Devel. Program participant, Nat. Sci. Tchr. Assn., 2003, edn. grant, Ala. Electric Coop., 2004, 2005; named Toyota Internat. Tchr., Toyota, USA, 2002, Outstanding Svc. Team leader, Girl Scouts Am., 1992, Outstanding Svc. Team Vol., 1995; finalist Outstanding Tchr., State Farm, 1999; grantee, Cmty. Found. of Montgomery, 1998—2000, Legacy, Ptnrs. in Environ. Edn., 1999, 2002, America's Unsung Heroes, Star Ins., 2000, Alagasco, 2000, Ala. Power Co., 2001; fellow Operation Pathfinder, Ala., Miss. Sea Grant, 1995; Eleanor Roosevelt fellow, AAUW, 2002. Mem.: SE Water Pollution Biologist Assn., Ala. Sci. Tchr. Assn., Nat. Marine Edn. Assn., Nat. Sci. Tchr. Assn., Delta Kappa Gamma. Office: Ala Dept Environ Mgmt 1350 Coliseum Blvd Montgomery AL 36109

SULLIVAN, ROBERT EMMETT, pediatric dentist, educator; b. Sioux City, Iowa, May 28, 1932; s. Joseph A. and Daisy B. (Stanieforth) S.; m. Mary Ann Haerer, Sept. 22, 1961. BA, Morningside Coll., 1954; DDS, U. Nebr., 1961, MSD, 1963. Diplomate Am. Bd. Pediat. Dentistry. Prof., chair pediat. dentistry U. Nebr. Coll. Dentistry, Lincoln, 1963—; prof. pediats. U. Nebr. Coll. Medicine, Omaha, 1969—. Contbr. articles to profl. jours. With U.S. Army. Fellow Am. Acad. Pediat. Dentistry, Am. Coll. Dentists, Internat. Coll. Dentistry; mem. ADA, VFW, Am. Soc. Dentistry for Children, N.E. Nebr. Dental Assn., Lincoln Dist. Dental Assn. Democrat. Avocation: music. Home: 2530 Ridge Rd Lincoln NE 68512-2418 *

SULLIVAN, SCOTT J., radiologist; MD, Georgetown U., 1991. Diplomate Am. Bd. Radiology-diagnostic radiology, Am. Bd. Radiology-neuroradiology. Intern Winthrop Univ. Hosp., NYC; resident radiology Yale-New Haven Hosp., New Haven, 1992—95, fellow neuroradiology, 1995—96; diagnostic radiology Greenwich Hosp., Conn. Office: Greenwich Hospital Department of Radiology 5 Perryridge Rd Greenwich CT 06830 Office Phone: 203-869-6220. Office Fax: 203-863-4712.

SULLIVAN, STEPHEN GENE, psychiatrist, pharmacologist, health facility administrator; b. Manchester, NH, Feb. 27, 1947; BS, Georgetown U., 1970; MS, NYU, 1976, PhD, 1977, MD, 1984. Assoc. research scientist NYU Sch. Med., 1978-81, rsch. asst. prof. pharmacology, 1981-82, adj. asst. prof. pharmacology, 1984-91; intern Beth Israel Med. Ctr., NYC, 1984, resident in psychiatry, 1984-88, physician-in-charge Clin. Psychopharmacology Lab., 1988-90; sci. dir. The Corp. for Clin. Psychopharmacology Research, NYC, 1988-99; pvt. practice NYC, 1986—. Instr. psychiatry Mt. Sinai Sch. Med. CUNY, 1986-88, asst. clin. prof. psychiatry, 1988-90. Author, adminstr.: (Web site) speciesaccounts.org, 2001—; contbr. numerous articles to profl. jours., author ten book chpts., 1976—. Med. scientist tng. program fellow NIH, 1970-76, 82-83, postdoctoral fellow, 1976-77. Mem. AAAS, AMA, Am. Psychiat. Assn., N.Y. Acad. Scis. Avocation: composing music. Office: 533 E 13th St New York NY 10009-3508 Office Phone: 212-979-9145.

SULLIVAN, STUART FRANCIS, anesthesiologist, educator; b. Buffalo, July 15, 1928; s. Charles S. and Kathryn (Duggan) S.; m. Dorothy Elizabeth Faytol, Apr. 18, 1959; children: John, Irene, Paul, Kathryn. BS, Canisius Coll., 1950; MD, SUNY, Syracuse, 1955. Diplomate Am. Bd. Anesthesiology. Intern Ohio State U. Hosp., Columbus, 1955—56; resident Columbia Presbyn. Med. Ctr., 1958—60; fellow Columbia-Bellevue Hosp. Ctr., NYC, 1960—61; instr. anesthesiology Columbia U. Coll. Physicians and Surgeons, NYC, 1961—62, assoc., 1962—64, asst. prof., 1964—69, assoc. prof., 1969—73; prof. dept. anesthesiology UCLA, 1973—91, vice chair anesthesiology, 1974—77, exec. vice chair, 1977—90, acting chmn., 1983—84, 1987—88, 1990—91, prof. emeritus, 1991—. Capt. M.C., USAR, 1956-58. Fellow NIH, 1960-61; recipient research career devel. award NIH, 1966-69. Mem. Assn. Univ. Anesthetists, Am. Physiol. Soc., Am. Soc. Anesthesiologists. Home: 101 Foxtail Dr Santa Monica CA 90402-2047 Office: UCLA Sch Medicine Dept Anesthesiology Los Angeles CA 90095-0001

SULLIVAN, THEODORE R., JR., vascular surgeon; BA in Geology and German Minor, St. Lawrence U., 1977; pre-med, Villanova U., 1983; MD, Temple U., 1988. Diplomate Am. Bd. Surgery-vascular surgery, Am. Bd. Surgery-gen. surgery. Resident gen. surgery Temple Univ. Hosp., Phila., 1988—94, fellow researched gastrointestinal physiology, 1990—91, chief surg. resident and clin. instr. surgery, 1993—94; fellow vascular surgery Sch. of Medicine Tufts Univ., Boston, 1994—96; dir. vascular surgery svcs. Abington Meml. Hosp., gen. surgeon blank vascular ctr. Author: (publs.) The effect of estrogen on vascular smooth muscle cell proliferation, Restenosis after carotid and peripheral vascular surgery. Recipient Excellence in Teaching award, Abington Meml. Hosp.; named one of the Top Doctor, Phila. Mag., 2011. Fellow: ACS; mem.: Phila. Coll. of Physicians, Assn. for Academic Surgery, Soc. for Vascular Surgery, Soc. for Clin. Vascular Surgery (mem. volunteers program), Peripheral Vascular Surgery Soc., Pa. Med. Soc., Eastern Vascular Soc., Deterling Surg. Soc. Office: Abington Memorial Hospital The Blank Vascular Ctr 1200 Old York Rd Abington PA 19001 Office Phone: 215-887-5935. Office Fax: 215-481-3481.

SULLIVAN, TIMOTHY JOHN, allergist, immunologist, educator; MD, U. Miami, 1966. Diplomate Am. Bd. Allergy and Immunology, 1979. Intern Univ. of Miami Jackson Health System, 1967; resident internal medicine Barnes Hosp., 1971—73, fellow allergy & immunology, 1971—73; assoc. clin. prof. pediat. Med. Coll. of Ga.; hosp. affiliations include Atlanta Med. Ctr., Children's Healthcare of Atlanta, DeKalb Med. Ctr., Northside Hosp., Wellstar Kennestone Hosp., St. Joseph's Hosp. Office: Northside Hospital NE 1000 Johnson Ferry Rd Atlanta GA 30342-1611 Office Phone: 404-851-8000.

SULLIVAN, WILLIAM JOHN, osteopath; b. Pittsburg, Kans., Nov. 5, 1963; s. William Leroy and Joan Elizabeth (Prete) S; div.; 1 child, Lauren Marie. BS in Biology, Pittsburg State U., 1986; DO, U. Health Scis., Kansas City, Mo., 1990. Diplomate Nat. Bd. Osteo. Med. Examiners, Am. Bd. Internal Medicine, Am. Assn. Med. Rev. Officers. Intern Riverside Hosp., Wichita, Kans., 1990-91; resident Deaconess Hosp., St. Louis, 1991-94; pvt. practice Med. Cons. of Pitts., LLC, Kans., 1994—; active staff Mt. Carmel Med. Ctr., 1994—, med. dir. occupl. health, med. dir. employee health, 1995—2002, med. dir. cardiomyopathy clinic, 1997—, med. dir. pulmonary rehab., 2008—, chief medicine, 1998—, chief-of-staff-elect, 1999—, pres. med. staff, 2001—. Mem. adv. bd. dirs. Cmty. Nat. Bank, Pittsburg; med. staff sec. Mt. Carmel Med. Ctr., Pittsburg, 1999; clin. instr. Pittsburg State U. Sch. Nursing; participating physician Pittsburg Free Clinic; clin. adv. Pittsburg State U. Pre-Med Club; mem. health occupations adv. bd. Unified Sch. Dist. #250; physician Congl. Health Ministries; cons. physician Cmty. Health Clinic SE Kans., 2006—09. Mem. exec. bd. dirs. Pitts. Family YMCA, pres.-elect, 2003, pres., 2004—, chief internal medicine, 1995—; bd. dirs. Pitts. State U. Alumni Assn., 2001-07, nat. 2d v.p., 2003-04. Lt. col. Kans. Army N.G., 1988—2008. Recipient Outstanding Alumni award, Pitts. State U., 2009; named America's Top Physician's List, Consumers Rsch. Coun., 2009—10. Fellow ACP; mem. VFW, Kans. Med. Soc., Am. Assn. Med. Rev. Officers, N.G. Assn. U.S., KC, Crawford County Med. Soc. (pres. 2000), Am. Legion, Sigma Chi (life loyal Sig program), Am. Legion Riders, Kansas Patriot Guard. Republican. Roman Catholic. Avocations: music, golf, stamp collecting/philately. Office: Med Consultants Pitts LLC 1015 Mt Carmel Pl Pittsburg KS 66762 Home: 1502 Woodland Terr Pittsburg KS 66762 Office Phone: 620-231-8849. Personal E-mail: wsullivan21@cox.net.

SULLOWAY, FRANK JONES, social sciences educator, historian; b. Concord, NH, Feb. 2, 1947; s. Alvah Woodbury and Alison (Green) Sulloway; 1 child, Ryan. AB summa cum laude, Harvard U., Cambridge, Mass., 1969, AM in History Sci., 1971, PhD in History Sci., 1978. Jr. fellow Harvard U. Soc. Fellows, 1974-77; mem. Sch. Social Sci. Inst. Advanced Study, Princeton, NJ, 1977-78; rsch. fellow Miller Inst. Basic Rsch. Sci. U. Calif., Berkeley, 1978-80, vis. Miller rsch. prof., 1999—2000, vis. prof., 2000—; rsch. fellow MIT, Cambridge, 1980-81, vis. scholar, 1989-98; postdoctoral fellow Harvard U., Cambridge, 1981-82, vis. scholar, 1984-89; rsch. fellow U. Coll., London, 1982-84; Vernon prof. biography Dartmouth Coll., Hanover, NH, 1986. Author: (book) Freud, Biologist of the Mind, 1979 (Pfizer award History Sci. Soc., 1980), Born to Rebel, 1996; contbr. articles to profl. jours. Recipient Randi award, Skeptics Soc., 1997, Golden Plate award, Am. Acad. Achievement, 1997; fellow, NEH, 1980—81, NSF, 1981—82, John Simon Guggenheim Meml. Found., 1982—83, MacArthur Found., 1984—89, Dibner Inst., MIT, 1993—94, Ctr. Advanced Study Behavioral Scis., Stanford, Calif., 1998—99. Fellow: AAAS (mem. electorate nominating com. sect. L 1988—91, 1994—97), Assn. Psychol. Sci., Linnean Soc. London; mem.: History Sci. Soc. (mem. fin. com. 1987—92, mem. com. devel. 1988—92), Human Behavior and Evolution Soc., Am. Psychol. Soc. Home: 1709 Shattuck Ave Apt 205 Berkeley CA 94709-1753 Office: U Calif Dept Psychology IPSR 4125 Tolman Hall Berkeley CA 94720-1603 Home Phone: 510-540-9336; Office Phone: 510-642-7139. Business E-Mail: sulloway@berkeley.edu.

SULSTON, SIR JOHN EDWARD, research scientist; b. Buckinghamshire, Eng., Mar. 27, 1942; married; 2 children. BA in Organic Chemistry, U. Cambridge, 1963, PhD, 1966; DSc (hon.), Trinity Coll., Dublin. Postdoc. fellow Salk Inst. Biol. Studies, San Diego, 1966—69; staff scientist Lab. Molecular Biology, Cambridge U., 1969—92; dir. Wellcome Trust Sanger Inst., Cambridgeshire, England, 1992—2000. Mem. Human Genetics Commn. Co-author (with Georgina Ferry): The Common Thread: A Story of Science, Politics, Ethics and the Human Genome, 2002. Recipient W. Alden Spencer award, Columbia U., 1986, Gairdner Found. Internat. award, 1991, 2002, Lewis S. Rosenstiel award, Brandeis U., 1998, Pfizer prize for innovative sci., 2000, George W. Beadle medal, Genetics Soc. America, 2000, Sir Frederick Gowland Hopkins medal, Biochemical Soc., 2000, Edinburgh medal, 2001, Prince of Asturias award, 2001, Nobel prize for physiology/medicine, 2002, Alfred P. Sloan Jr. prize, GM Cancer Rsch. Found., 2003, Golden Plate award, Acad. Achievement, 2004. Mem.: European Molecular Biology Orgn., Royal Soc. (Darwin medal 1996). Office: Human Genetics Commn Dept Health Area 652C Skipton House 80 London Rd London SE1 6LH England Address: The Wellcome Trust Sanger Inst Campus Hinxton Cambridge CB10 1SA England *

SULTAN, MARK R., plastic surgeon; b. NJ; BS, Brandeis U.; MD, Columbia U. Coll. Physicians and Surgeons, 1982. Diplomate rgery, Am. Bd. Plastic Surgery. Resident in gen. surgery Columbia-Presbyn. Med. Ctr., NYC, 1983—87, resident in plastic surgery, 1987—88, 1989—90; fellow in head and neck surgery/microvascular reconstrn. Emory U. Affiliated Hosps., Atlanta, 1988—89; attending physician dept. plastic surgery St. Luke's Roosevelt Hosp., NYC, 1998—, chief divsn. plastic and reconstructive surgery, Beth Israel Hosp., NYC; pvt. practice plastic surgery NYC. Assoc. prof. clin. surgery Columbia U. Coll. Physicians and Surgeons, NYC. Recipient Allen O. Whipple award for Outstanding Performance in Surgery, named one of NY's Top Doctors, NY mag. Mem.: Am. Assn. Plastic Surgery, Soc. Reconstructive Microsurgery, NY Head and Neck Soc., Northeast Regional Soc. Plastic and Reconstructive Surgeons, Am. Soc. Reconstructive Microsurgery, Am. Soc. Plastic and Reconstructive Surgeons, Am. Soc. Aesthetic Plastic Surgery, Alpha Omega Alpha Soc., Phi Beta Kappa. Office: 1100 Park Ave New York NY 10128 Business E-Mail: samson@slrsurgery.org, msultan@chpnet.org.

SULTAN, SHERIF AH, consultant endovascular surgeon; b. Cairo, Heliopolis, Egypt, Sept. 4, 1964; arrived in Ireland, 1993; s. Abdel Hamid and Zieneb Sultan; m. Basma Homosany, Aug. 14, 1988; children: Ahmed, Mohamed. Gen. Cert. Edn., English Mission Coll., Cairo, 1981; MBBCh, Ain-Shams U., 1987, MCh in Surgery, 1991, MD in Surgery, 1995; MD, Trinity Coll., 2003. Resident in surgery Ain Shams U. Hosp., Cairo, 1989; chief resident in surgery Aim Shams U. Hosp., Cairo; sr. registrar St. James Hosp., Dublin, 1995; lectr. in vascular surgery Trinity Coll., Dublin, 1999; sr. lectr. in vascular surgery Galway (Ireland) U. Hosp., 2001, cons. vascular surgeon, 2002—. Fellow in radiology, Paris, 1998; fellow in vascular and endovascular surgery, Phoenix, 99. Contbr. articles to profl. jours. Fellow Royal Coll. Surgeons; mem. Am. Coll. Angiology (pres. Irish chpt., 2007). Home: Stoneyacre, Corcullen Bushypark Galway Ireland Office: Dept Vascular/Endovas Surg Galway Univ Hosp Galway Ireland Home Phone: 0035391-555764; Office Phone: 00353 91720122. E-mail: vascularsultan@galwayclinic.com, sherif.sultan@whb.ie.

SULTZER, BARNET MARTIN, microbiologist, immunologist, researcher; b. Union City, NJ, Mar. 24, 1929; s. Moses Joseph and Florence Gertrude (Fischer) Sultzer; m. Judith Ray Moreinis, Aug. 26, 1956; 1 child, Steven Bennett. BS, Rutgers U., 1950; MS, Mich. State U., 1951, PhD, 1958. Rsch. assoc. Princeton (N.J.) Labs., Inc., 1958-64; from asst. prof. to prof. microbiology SUNY, Bklyn., 1964-94, prof. emeritus, 1994—, interim chmn. dept. microbiology, 1980-82. Vis. scientist Karolinska Inst., Stockholm, 1971—72; vis. prof. Pasteur Inst., Paris, 1979—80; adj. prof. Fels Inst. Cancer Rsch. and Molecular Biology Temple U., Phila., 1995—2004; v.p. rsch. Stem Cell Therapeutics, King of Prussia, Pa., 1995—2000. Assoc. editor: Jour. Immunology, 1983—86; mem. editl. bd. Infection and Immunity, 1980—94; contbr. chapters to books, articles to profl. jours. Mem. Cmty. Bd. #1, NYC, 1989—94; pres. Tenants Assn. Gateway Plz., NYC, 1990—92. 1st lt. USMC, 1952—55. Grantee, USPHS, NIH, Office of Naval Rsch., 1967—94. Mem.: AAAS, Internat. Endotoxin & Innate Immunity Soc., NY Acad. Sci., Am. Assn. Immunologists, Am. Soc. Microbiology (Pres.'s fellow 1957), Harvey Soc., Sigma Xi. Achievements include patents for chemical detoxification of endotoxins and discovery of the genetic basis for mammalian responses to endotoxins including immunological and pathophysiological effects; co-discoverer of a signal transduction gene controlling mammalian cellular responses to lipopolysaccharide endotoxin; development of first commercial immunological pregnancy test; research in microbiology and immunology. Personal E-mail: bsultzer@aol.com.

SUMICHIKA, HIROSHI, research scientist; s. Shouzou Sumichika; m. Keiko Sumichika, Nov. 19, 1967. PhD, Kyushu U., Fukuoka. Rsch. scientist Mitsubishi Tanabe Pharma Corp., Yokohama. Author: (pharmaceutics) Identification of a potent and orally active non-peptide C5a receptor antagonist (11th nat. Conf., Inflammation Rsch. Assn., 2002); contbr. articles to profl. jours. Achievements include invention of Orally active non-peptide C5a receptor antagonists. Office: Mitsubishi Tanabe Pharma Corp 2-2-6 Nihonbashi-Honcho Chuo Ku Tokyo 103-8405 Japan Business E-Mail: sumichika.hiroshi@mg.m-pharma.co.jp.

SUMIYOSHI, TOMIKI, psychiatrist, researcher; b. Tokyo, Dec. 18, 1964; s. Hiroshi and Fusako (Naganuma) S.; m. Sawako Suemasa, Apr. 4, 1993. MB, MD, Kanazawa U., Japan, 1989, PhD, 1993. Med. diplomate. Resident Fukui Prefectural Psychiat. Hosp., Japan, 1990; ward adminstr., dir. neurochemistry rsch. Kanazawa U. Hosp., Japan, 1991—93; rsch. assoc. dept. psychiatry Case Western Res. U., Cleve., 1993-95; asst. prof. dept. psychiatry, dir. psychopharmacology rsch. Saitama Med. Sch., Japan, 1995—96; asst. prof. dept. neuropsychiatry, dir. neurochemistry rsch. Toyama Med. and Pharm. U., Japan, 1996—2000; assoc. prof. dept. neuropsychiatry U. Toyama, Grad. Sch. Medicine and Pharm. Sci., 2000—; apptd. psychiatrist Health and Welfare Ministry Japan, 1996—, clin. prof., 2009—; cert. dr. Japanese Soc. Clin. Neuropsychopharmacology, 2005—, Japanese Soc. Psychiatry and Neurology, 2007—. Vis. prof. dept. psychiatry Vanderbilt U., Nashville, 2000—02; rsch. bd. adv. Am. Biog. Inst., Inc., 2005—; cons. in field. Author: Clinical Perspective of the New Antipsychotic Drugs, 2001, Relapse in Schizophrenia, 2002, Electrophysiological Imaging Evaluation of Schizophrenia and Treatment Response, 2011; contbr. articles to profl. jours. Rep. athlete The Nat. Athletic Meeting, Hachinohe, Japan, 1993; mem. TIME Opinion Leader's Panel, 2007-. Recipient Psychiat Rsch. award, Saburo Matsubara Meml. Fund, Kanazawa, Japan, 1993, Young Investigator award, Nat. Alliance for Rsch. on Schizophrenia and Depression, Chgo., 1995, NY, 2001, Meml. Travel award, Am. Coll. Neuropsychopharmacology, 2001, prize, Japanese Soc. Biol. Psychiatry, 1996, award, Japanese Soc. Clin. Neuropsychopharmacolgy Rsch. Encouragement, 2008; fellow Rsch. fellow, Min. Edn. and Sci., Japan, 2000—02; scholar, Rotary, 1994—95. Mem. Soc. Neurosci., NY Acad. Scis., World Fedn. Socs. Biol. Psychiatry, Coll. Internat. Neuropsychopharmacologicum, Schizophrenia Internat. Rsch. Soc., Internat. Pharmaco-EEG Group, EEG and Clin. Neurosci. Soc., Japanese Soc. Psychiatry and Neurology, Japanese Soc. Biol. Psychiatry, Japanese Soc. Neuropsychopharmacology, Japanese Soc. Clin. Neuropsychopharmacology, Japanese Soc. for Brain Scis., Japanese Soc. Clin. Neurophysiology, Japan Soc. Psychiat. Diagnosis, Japanese Soc. Prevention in Psychiat. Disorders, Japanese Soc. Schizophrenia Rsch. Avocations: foreign languages, classical music, figure skating, foreign travel. Home: 144-14-B2 Nishiaraya Toyama 939-8251 Japan Office: Univ Toyama Grad Sch Medicine Pharmaceutical Sci Dept Neuropsychiatry 2630 Sugitani Toyama 930-0194 Japan Office Phone: +81-76-434-7323. Personal E-mail: tomikisumiyoshi840@yahoo.co.jp. Business E-Mail: tomikisumiyoshi840@hotmail.com.

SUMME, GREGORY LOUIS, construction executive; b. Ft. Mitchell, Ky., Nov. 25, 1956; s. James Augustine and Mary Elizabeth (McQueen) S.; m. Susan Louise Stevie, Aug. 1, 1981; children: Heather, Erin. BSEE, U. Ky., 1978, MSEE, U. Cin., 1980; MBA with distinction, U. Pa., 1983. Mng. dir., vice chmn., global buyout Carlyle Group; design engr. Mostek Corp., Dallas, 1980—81; mktg. specialist Gen. Electric Plastics Europe, Netherlands, 1982; ptnr. McKinsey & Co. Inc., Atlanta and Hong Kong, 1983—92; gen. mgr., comml. motors General Electric Co., 1992—93; pres. automotive products group, aerospace engines, gen. aviation avionics Allied Signal Inc., 1993—98; pres., COO PerkinElmer, Inc., Wellesley, Mass., 1998—2007, chmn., CEO, 1999—2008; sr. adv. Goldman Sachs Capital Ptnrs., 2008—09. Bd. dirs. Biomet Sports Medicine Inc., Freescale Semiconductor, Inc., Veyance Corp., State St. Bank and Trust Co., State St. Corp., 2001—, TRW Aero. Sys., 2001—02, Automatic Data Processing Inc., 2007—, Biomet, Inc., 2008—09. Contbr. articles to profl. jours. Alex Proudfoot fellow Wharton Sch., U. Pa., 1981-83; named to Univ. Ky. Coll. Engring. Hall of Distinction. Mem. IEEE, Eta Kappa Nu. Roman Catholic. Avocations: running, squash, golf. Office: Carlyle Group 9073 Nemo St Ste 100 West Hollywood CA 90069-5544 Office Phone: 310-550-8656. Business E-Mail: gregory.summe@carlyle.com. *

SUMMERS, ADAM N., plastic surgeon; Grad. with dean's honor roll, U. Mo., 1985; MD with honors and distinction in rsch., St. Louis U., 1989. Diplomate Am. Bd. Plastic Surgery. Resident gen. surgery Med. Coll. of Wis., Milw., 1993, fellow plastic surgery, 1996, fellow microsurgery and hand surgery, 1998; fellow cosmetic surgery Aesthetic and Reconstructive Surgery Assocs., Milw., 1999; clin. assst. prof., surgery U. Md.; dir. Md. Plastic Surgery. Contbr. articles Balt. Sun, Wash. Post; co-author: (jours.) Computer-based multimedia in plastic surgery educatio, 1994, Teaching surgical knot tying and suturing by interactive compact disc (CD-I), 1996, The microarterial anatomy of the lateral arm fascial free flap, 2000, Decontamination of the oral cavity - CME article, 2001, The mid-face sling: A new technique to rejuvenate the midface, 2002, numerous other jours. Recipient Best Sci. Exhibit, Am. Assn. for Hand Surgery, 1991, Am. Soc. of Plastic and Reconstructive Surgeons, 1991, Spl. Tech. award, Alpha Omega Alpha Student Rsch. Forum, 1992, First prize in Sr. Rsch, Midwestern Assn. of Plastic Surgeons, 1992, Best Presenter award, Multimedia Applications for Med. Practice, 1993, Best Sci. Paper, Am. Assn. for Hand Surgery, 1999, Best Maxillofacial Paper, Internat. Conf. on Oral and Maxillofacial Surgery, 1999; named Physician of the Year Honoree, Nat. Rep. Congl. Com., 2003, 2005, 2006, 2007; named one of American's Top Physicians, Nat. Consumer Rsch. Coun., 2002, 2003, 2004, 2005. Mem.: Am. Soc. of Plastic Surgeons. Office: Maryland Plastic Surgery Ste E 7704 Quarterfield Rd Glen Burnie MD 21061 Office Phone: 410-553-9444.

SUMMERS, WILLIAM COFIELD, science educator; b. Janesville, Wis., Apr. 17, 1939; s. Crosby Hungerford and Rebecca Delores (Cofield) S.; m. Wilma Jean Poos, July 24, 1965; 1 child, Emily Alexandra. BS, U. Wis., 1961, MS, 1963, Phd, MD, 1967; MAH, Yale U., 1977. Post-doctoral fellow MIT, Cambridge, Mass., 1967-68; asst. prof. Yale U., New Haven, 1968-70, assoc. prof., 1970-77, prof., 1977—. Cons. NIH, Bethesda, Md., 1976—. Editor Nucleic Acids Research Jour., 1977-79, Gene jour., 1984-91; contbr. articles to profl. jours. Cons. Anna Fuller Fund, New Haven, 1973-88, Searle Scholars Program, Chgo., 1980-84; trustee Leukemia Soc. Am., N.Y.C., 1981-85, Yale-China Assn., New Haven, 1982-88, 94-98. Mem. Am. Soc. for Microbiology, History Sci. Soc., Am. Assn. History of Medicine. Office: Yale U Box 208114 New Haven CT 06520-8114 E-mail: william.summers@yale.edu.

SUMMERS, WILLIAM KOOPMANS, psychiatrist, internist, entrepreneur, researcher; b. Jefferson City, Mo., Apr. 14, 1944; s. Joseph S. and Amy Lydia (Koopmans) Summers; m. Angela Forbes McGonigle, Oct. 2, 1972 (div. Apr. 1985). Student, Westminster Coll., Fulton, Mo., 1962-64; BS, U. Mo., 1966; MD, Washington U., St. Louis, 1971. Internal medicine intern Barnes Hosp-Washington U., St. Louis, 1971—72; resident in internal medicine Jewish Hosp., St. Louis, 1972—73; resident in psychiatry Washington U. Sch. Medicine, St. Louis, 1973—76; asst. prof. U. Pitts., 1976—78, U. So. Calif., LA, 1978—82; asst. clin. prof. rsch. UCLA, 1982—88; rschr. Arcadia, Calif., 1988—92, Albuquerque, 1992—; pres., CEO Alzheimers Corp., Albuquerque, 1999—. Mem.: ACP, AMA, Am. Fedn. Clin. Rsch., Soc. Neurosci., N.Y. Acad. Scis., Am. Psychiat. Assn. Episcopalian. Achievements include holder of 8 patents in neuropharmacology and neuroceuticals; invention of Tacrine (Cognex), the first FDA approved drug to treat Alzheimers disease; formulator for Memory reVITALIZER. Avocation: gardening. Office: Alzheimers Corp 6000 Uptown NE Ste 308 Albuquerque NM 87110 Business E-Mail: md@wksummers.com.

SUN, ANDY, dentist; b. Ping-Dong, Taiwan, Nov. 23, 1953; s. Shi-Kia Sun and Su-Ju Chen; m. Shu-Yun Hsiung, Mar. 11, 1978; children: Han-Wei, Wan-Lin. DDS, Nat. Taiwan U., Taipei, 1978, PhD in Immunology, 1992. Attending physician Nat. Taiwan U., 1989—; assoc. prof. Fu-jen Cath. U., Taipei, 1993-94, Shih Hsin U., Taipei, 1996—2003, prof., 2003—. Vis. prof. Tianjin Med. U., China, 1999—, Hu-Bei Traditional Chinese Med. Coll., China, 1999—; vis. assoc. prof. Shanghai Traditional Chinese Med. U., China, 1999-2003, prof., 2003—. Contbr. articles to profl. jours. Mem. ctrl. com. KMT, Taipei, 1995-98. Lt. Taiwan armed forces, 1978-80. Recipient Outstanding in Immunology Rsch. award Found. Immunology Rsch., 1987. Mem.: Formosan Med. Assn., NY Sci. Coun., Chinese Soc. Immunology, Straits Acad. and Cultural Exch. Assn. (v.p. 1997—2001, pres. 2001—), Univ. and Coll. Lectrs. Assn. (pres. 1998—). Roman Catholic. Avocations: speech, singing, meditation, qigong. Office: Nat Taiwan U Hosp No 1 Chang te St Taipei 100 Taiwan Office Phone: 886-2-23123456 ext. 67702. Personal E-mail: andysun.sun@msa.hinet.net. Business E-Mail: andysun7702@yahoo.com.tw.

SUN, CHI CHIN, ophthalmologist; b. Kaohsiung, Taiwan, Mar. 12, 1969. MD, Kaohsiung Med. U., 1994; PhD, Grad. Inst. Clin. Med. Scis., Chang Gung U., 2006. Chmn., dept. ophthalmology Chang Gung Meml. Hosp., Keelung, Taiwan, 2008—, dir., Med. Rsch. Ctr., 2009. Assoc. prof. Chang Gung U., 2011. Contbr. articles to numerous profl. jours. Mem.: Assn. Rsch. Vision and Ophthalmology, European Soc. Cataract and Refractive Surgeons, Am. Acad. Ophthalmology, Taiwan Soc. Cataract and Refractive Surgeons (bd. trustee 2006), Ophthal. Soc. Taiwan (dep. sec. gen. 2010). Avocations: classical music, badminton, travel. Office: 6F 222 Maijin Rd Anle Dist Keelung 204 Taiwan Office Fax: 886-2-24311190. Business E-Mail: aarvin.sun@msa.hinet.net.

SUN, DEMING, immunology researcher; b. Shanghai, People's Republic of China, Jan. 30, 1947; parents Liantai Sun and Yüxian Lü; m. Feb. 1, 1972; 1 child, Shu. MD, Shanghai 1st Med. Coll., 1971; Rsch. MD, Albert-Ludwig U., Freiburg, Fed. Republic of Germany, 1982. Sr. rsch. staff Max-Planek Rsch. Unit for Multiple Sclerosis, Würzburg, Fed. Republic of Germany, 1986-88; rsch. assoc. St. Jude Children's Rsch. Hosp., Memphis, 1988, asst. mem., 1989—. Contbr. articles to Nature. Grantee Nat. Multiple Sclerosis Soc., 1991; NIH First award. Mem. Am. Assn. Immunologists, Internat. Soc. Neuroimmunology. Office: St Jude Childrens Rsch Hosp 332 N Lauderdale St Memphis TN 38105-2729

SUN, HUI MIN, research scientist; b. Wuhan, Sept. 7, 1968; PhD, Wuhan U., 2010. With Zhongnan Hosp., Wuhan U., 2006—. Office: 169 Donghu Rd Wuchang Dist Wuhan Hubei 430071 China

SUN, JIAN, food scientist, director; b. Hami, China, Mar. 6, 1978; PhD, Chinese Acad. Scis., 2008. Rsch. fellow Guelph Food Rsch. Ctr., Agr. and Agri-Food Can., Canada, 2007—08; dir. Inst. Agro-food Sci. & Tech., Guangxi Acad. Agrl. Scis., 2008—, adj. prof., 2009—11. Recipient Excellent award, Chinese Acad. Scis., award, Guangxi Acad. Agrl. Scis., Guangxi Govt.; scholarship, China scholarship Coun. Fellow: Chinese Soc. Hort. Sci.; mem.: Supervisory Com. Grad. Studies Com. U. Putra Malaysia, Am. Chem. Soc. Avocations: painting, music. Office: 174# Daxue East Rd Nanning Guangxi 530007 China Office Fax: 86 771 3240232. Personal E-mail: jiansun@yahoo.cn.

SUN, JIANLI, medical educator; b. China, Oct. 6, 1970; PhD, Fudan U., 2005. Instr. U. Va., 2005—. Mem.: Soc. Neurosci. Office: Jefferson Park Ave Charlottesville VA 22908 Business E-Mail: js5ce@virginia.edu.

SUN, KAINAN, medical researcher; b. Fushun, China, May 9, 1979; MS, U. Iowa, 2007, PhD, 2008. Rsch. scientist Health Rsch. Inc., 2008—. Recipient New Investigator's award, Am. Stats. Assn., 2008, Occupl. Epidemiology Trainee award, NIOSH Heartland Ctr. Occupl. Health and Safety; Presdl. fellowship, U. Iowa. Mem.: Delta Omega Hon. Pub. Health Soc., Alpha Phi. Home: 2 Mallard Dr Rexford NY 12148 Personal E-mail: kxs26@health.state.ny.us.

SUN, LIANGZHONG, pediatrician, educator; b. Hunan, China, Aug. 30, 1970; PhD, Sun Yat-sen U., 2005. Lector, chief physician First Affiliated Hosp., Sun Yat-sen U., 1999—2007, assoc. prof., cons., 2007—. Grant, Ministry Edn. China, Natural Sci. Found. Guangdong Com., Guangdong Health Dept., China. Mem.: Guang Dong Med. Assn. (China), Chinese Med. Assn. Office: 58 Courtyard Zhongshan Rd 2 Guangzhou Guangdong 510080 China Business E-Mail: sunlzh@mail.sysu.edu.cn.

SUN, LINGYUN, rheumatologist, educator; b. Nanjing, Aug. 4, 1962; MD, PhD, Nanjing Med. U., 1990. Dean, prof. rheumatology and immunology Nanjing Drum Tower Hosp., Nanjing U. Med. Sch., 1993—. Grant, Jiangsu Province Govt. Mem.: Jiangsu Rheumatology Assn., Chinese Rheumatology Assn. Avocations: swimming, fishing, ping pong/table tennis. Office: Drum Tower Hosp 321 Zhongshan Rd Nanjing Jiangsu 210008 China Office Fax: 86-25-83105209. E-mail: lingyunsun2001@yahoo.com.cn.

SUN, NANXIONG, medical educator; b. Nanjjing, China, July 10, 1943; Degree, Nanjing Med. Coll., 1966, M in Medicine, 1982. Asst. lectr. Nanjing Med. U., 1982—83, lectr., 1983—92, asst. lectr., 1992—93, assoc. prof., 1992—2000, prof., 2000—. Dep. chmn. Jiangsu Soc. Tropical Diseases & Parasitic Diseases, 1997—2004, chmn., 2004—10; dep. chmn. Chinese Soc. Tropical Diseases & Parasitic Diseases, Chinese Med. Assn., 2007—10. Mem.: Nat. Com. Chinese People's Polit. Consultative Conf. Office: 300 Guanzhou Rd JPH Nanjing Jiangsu 210029 China Office Phone: 18913820914. Office Fax: 02583190852. E-mail: s9876@vip.163.com.

SUN, NORA CHI-JUN, pathologist, educator; b. Shanghai, June 16, 1937; came to U.S., 1966; d. K.F. and S.W. Sun; m. David T. Sung; children: Thomas C.K. Lee, Anthony D. Sung. MD, Shanghai 2d Med. Coll., 1960; MS in Pathology, U. Minn., 1973. Demonstrator U. Hong Kong, 1964-66; rsch. biologist A.H. Robins Co., Richmond, Va., 1966-67; resident Med. Coll. Va., 1967—68; clin. teaching asst. Boston U. Sch. Medicine, 1968-70; resident Mallaory Inst. Pathology, 1968—70; fellow Mayo Clinic and Grad. Sch., 1970—73; asst. prof. pathology U. So. Calif., LA, 1973-76; staff pathologist John Wesley Hosp., LA, 1973-76; asst. prof. UCLA Sch. Medicine, LA, 1976-82; staff pathologist, head hematopathology Harbor-UCLA Med. Ctr., Torrance, Calif., 1976—2002; assoc. prof. UCLA Sch. Medicine, LA, 1982-88, prof. pathology, 1988—2002, prof. emeritus, 2002—. Recipient Women Achievement award Delta Kappa Gamma, Rochester, Minn., 1972, Disting. Svc. award Am. Soc. Clin. Pathologists, 1996, Lifetime Achievement award, LA Soc. Pathologists, 2008. Mem. Internat. Assn. Chinese Pathologists (pres.-elect 1991-93, pres. 1993-95), Harbor-UCLA Med. Ctr. Faculty Soc. (pres.-elect 1990-91, pres. 1991-92). Office: Harbor UCLA Med Ctr 1000 W Carson St Torrance CA 90502-2004

SUN, SHUJUAN, pharmacist; b. Shandong, China, June 11, 1961; PhD, Shandong U., 2004. Sr. pharmacist, vice leader, pharmacy dept. Shandong Provincial Qianfoshan Hosp., 2004—. Office: 16766 Jingshi Rd Jinan Shandong 250014 China Personal E-mail: sunshujuan888@163.com.

SUN, WEIJING, oncologist, educator; MD, Shanghai Med. U., 1982; MS, U. Nebr., 1991. Diplomate Am. Bd. Internal Medicine, 1998, Am. Bd. Internal Medicine-med. oncology, 2001. Staff Shanghai Med. Univ., 1983—87; intern medicine Loyola Univ. Med. Ctr., Maywood, Ill., 1995—96, resident medicine, 1996—98; postdoc. rschr. Univ. Pa., 1991—95, fellow hematology/oncology, 1998—2001, assoc. prof. medicine, dir. gastrointestinal med. oncology, divsn. hematology-oncology dept. medicine, Abramson cancer ctr. Co-author: (publs.) Cancer of large bowel and hepatobiliary tract. Cancer Chemotherapy & Biological Response Modifiers, 2003, Phase I trial of the antivascular agent combretastain A4 phosephate on a five-day schedule to patients with cancer: MRI evidence for altered tumor blood flow, 2003, Two Phase I Combined Modality Studies of Concurrent Radiotherapy (XRT) With Continuous Infusion 5-FU, Epirubicin and Cisplatin (ECF) or Irinotecan (EIF) for Locally Advanced Upper GI Adenocarcinoma, 2004, Cancer of large bowel and hepatobiliary tract. Cancer Chemotherapy & Biological Response Modifiers, 2005. Named one of Top Docs, Phila. Mag., 2009—11, America's Top Doctors, 2010. Mem.: APC, Am. Assn. for Cancer Rsch., Am. Med. Assn., Am. Soc. of Hematology, Am. Soc. of Clin. Oncology, Am. Soc. of Internal Medicine. Office: Hospital of the University of Pennsylvania 16 Penn Tower 3400 Spruce St Philadelphia PA 19104 Office Phone: 215-662-7964. Office Fax: 215-662-2432. E-mail: weijing.sun@uphs.upenn.edu.

SUN, XIN, parasitologist, educator; b. Anhui, China, July 21, 1955; MD, Bengbu Med. Coll., 1983; M in Parasitology, Nanjing Med. U., 1992. Vis. rschr. U. Lyon I Claude Bernard, 1992—93, U. Paris V René Descartes, 1999—2000; dean faculty basic medicine Bengbu Med. Coll., 1998—2001, prof., 1998—, dean sci. rsch. affair sect., 2001—11. Standing mem. editl. bd. Jour. Bengbu Med. Coll., 2003—; cons. edtl. bd. Jour. Pathogen Biology, 2006—, Jour. Tropical Medicine and Parasitology, 2003—, Jour. International Med. Parasitic Diseases, 2006—. Contbr. chapters to books. Recipient Sci. and Tech. award, Anhui provincial Govt., China; scholarship, China Scholarship Coun., rsch. grant, Nat. Natural Sci. Found. China, Nat. S & T Academic Book Pub. Found. Master: Anhui Provincial Med. Parasitology Assn. (vice dir.); mem.: China Zool. Soc., Chinese Preventive Med. Assn., Chinese Med. Assn. Avocations: chinese handwriting, ping pong/table tennis, bicycling. Office: 312 Bldg E Bengbu Med Coll 2600 Donghai Dadao Bengbu Anhui 233030 China Office Fax: 0086 552 317 1333. Personal E-mail: bengbusx@yahoo.com.cn.

SUN, XIWEN, medical educator, director; b. Qiqihaer, China, Dec. 29, 1968; D, Shanghai Med. Sch., 1997. Dir., dept. radiology Shanghai Pulmonary Hosp., 2004—; prof. Tongji U., 2004—. Office: 507 Rd Zhengmin Shanhai 200433 China E-mail: xwsun@citiz.net.

SUN, YU, medical association administrator; b. Hsin-Chu City, China, Apr. 10, 1966; PhD, Nat. Taiwan U., 2010. Dir. En Chu Kong Hosp., 1998—. Office: 399 Fuxin Rd Sansia Dist New Taipei 100 Taiwan Personal E-mail: sunyu.jj.lu@gmail.com.

SUNDAR, UMA, medical educator; b. Kerala, Mar. 30, 1961; MBBS, CMC, Vellore, 1984, MD, 1989. Prof Lokmanya Tilak Mun Med. Coll. and Hosp., 2009—. Recipient Hargobind Khorana award, Nat. Trust, 2005. Mem.: Indian Stroke Assn., Assn. Physicians, Neurol. Soc. India. Avocations: reading, music. Office: Lokmanya Tilak Mun Hosp Sion Mumbai Maharashtra 400022 India E-mail: umasundar2@rediffmail.com.

SUNDARAM, CHANDRU P., urologist; arrived in US, 1992; MS, Madras Med. Coll., India, 1985; MS in Gen. Surgery, Bangalore U., India, 1988; FRCS, Royal Coll. Surgeons, England, 1989. Diplomate Am. Bd. Urology, lic. Ind., Mo. Urology residency U. Minn., Mpls., 1997; asst. prof. surgery Washington U., St. Louis, 1998—2002; assoc. prof. urology Ind. U., 2002—10, prof. urology, 2010—, dir. minimally invasive urologic surgery, 2002—; urology residency program dir., 2008—; endourology fellowship Harvard Med. Sch., Boston, 1998. Dir. fellowship in minimally invasive urology Ind. U., 2002—; pres. Ind. Urologic Assn., 2009—11. Contbr. articles various profl. jours., chapters to books. Recipient Resident Tchg. award, Washington U., 2002, Trustee Tchg. award, Ind. U., 2009. Mem.: Endourological Soc., Soc. Laparoendoscopic Surgeons (Best Urology Video award 2005), Am. Urological Assn. (mem. leadership program 2009, chair laparoscopy & robotic surgery com. 2011—, pres. elect 2011—). Office: Ind U Sch Medicine 535 N Barnhill Dr Indianapolis IN 46202 Business E-Mail: sundaramc@netscape.net.

SUNDARAM, KRISHNAMURTHI, medical educator; b. Chennai, India, June 5, 1949; MBBS, Madras Med. Coll., 1973. Clin. prof., vice-chmn. SUNY Downstate Med. Ctr., LICH, 2007—. Recipient Tchg. awrad, SUNY Downstate Med. Ctr. Otolaryngology. Fellow: ACS. Office: 339 Hicks St Brooklyn NY 11201 Office Phone: 718-780-1498. Office Fax: 718-780-2819. Business E-Mail: krishnamurthi.sundaram@downstate.edu. E-mail: krishsun@aol.com.

SUNDBERG, MARSHALL DAVID, biology professor; b. Apr. 18, 1949; m. Sara Jane Brooks, Aug. 1, 1977; children: Marshall Isaac, Adam, Emma. BA in Biology, Carleton Coll., 1971; MA in Botany, U. Minn., 1973, PhD in Botany, 1978. Lab. technician Carleton Coll., Minn., 1973-74; teaching asst. U. Minn., Mpls., 1974-76, rsch. asst., 1976-77; adj. asst. prof. Biology U. Wis., Eau Claire, 1978-85, mem. faculty summer sci. inst., 1982-85; instr. La. State U., Baton Rouge, 1985-88, asst. prof. Biology, 1988-91, coord. dept. Biology, 1988-93, assoc. prof. Biology, 1991-97; prof., chair dept. biol. scis. Emporia State U., 1997—. Author: General Botany Laboratory Workbook, 5th revision, 1984, General Botany 1001 Laboratory Manual, 1986, General Botany 1002 Laboratory Manual, 1987, Biology 1002 Correspondence Study Guide, 1987, Boty 1202: General Botany Laboratory Manual, 1988, Biol 1208: Biology for Science Majors Laboratory Manual, 1988, 2d edit., 1989, Instructor's Manual for J. Mauseth, Introductory Botany, 1991; contbr. articles to profl. jours. Brand fellow U. Minn., 1976-77, Faculty Grants scholar U. Wis., 1984-85. Fellow Linnaean Soc. London; mem. NSTA, AAAS, Am. Inst. Biol. Scis. (coun. mem. at large 1992-95, edn. com. 1994-95, 98-2002), Nat. Sci. Tchrs. Assn., Assn. Biology Lab. Edn., Bot. Soc. Am. (chmn. tchg. sect. 1985-86, workshop com. tchg. sect. 1983-84, slide exch./lab. exch. tchg. sect. 1980-89, edn. com. 1991, 92, editor Plant Sci. Bull. 2000—, Charles H. Bessey award 1992, Centennial award 2006), Internat. Soc. Plant Morphologists, Nat. Assn. Biology Tchrs. (Outstanding 4-Yr. Coll. Tchr. award 1997, 2003), Soc. Econ. Botany, The Nature Conservancy, Sigma Xi (chpt. sec. 1982-84, 93-95, 2000-02, v.p. 1984-85, 96-97, pres. 1996, 99, 2005). Home: 1912 Briarcliff Ln Emporia KS 66801-5404 Office: Emporia State U Dept Biol Scis 1200 Commercial St Emporia KS 66801-5087

SUNDBERG, RUTH DOROTHY, hematologist, educator; b. Chgo., July 29, 1915; d. Carl William and Ruth (Chalbeck) S.; m. Robert H. Reiff, Dec. 24, 1941 (div. 1945). Student, U. Chgo., 1932-34; BS, U. Minn., 1937, MA, 1939, PhD, 1943, MD, 1953. Diplomate: Am. Bd. Pathology. Instr., asst. prof. anatomy U. Minn., 1939-53, assoc. prof., 1953-60, prof., 1960-63, prof. of lab. medicine and anatomy, 1963-73, prof. lab. medicine, pathology and anatomy, 1973-84, emeritus prof., 1984—; hematologist, dir. Hematology Labs., 1945-74, hematologist, co. dir., 1974-84. Editorial bd.: Soc. Exptl. Biology and Medicine, until 1975; mem. editorial bd.: Blood, 1960-67; assoc. editor, 1967-69. Recipient Lucretia Wilder award for research in anatomy, 1939 Mem.: Sigma Xi. Home (Winter): 12558 Shanandoah Ct Marco Island FL 34145-5023 Home: 6690 Morgans Run Rd Loveland OH 45140-7205

SUNDE, DOUGLAS, plastic surgeon; b. Evanston, Ill., May 18, 1960; s. Edward Albert and Marilyn S.; m. Linda Neff, 1989. AB, Stanford U., 1982; MD, U. Calif., San Francisco, 1986. Diplomate Am. Bd. Plastic Surgery. Resident in plastic surgery Stanford (Calif.) U., 1986-92, clin. instr., 1992; fellow in aesthetic surgery Manhattan Eye Ear and Throat Hosp., NYC, 1990; fellow in hand, microsurgery Davies Med. Ctr., San Francisco, 1993; pvt. practice Monterey, Calif., 1994—. Clin. asst. prof. Stanford Med. Ctr., 1998—. Contbr. articles to profl. jours. Named Nat. Merit scholar 1977. Fellow ACS; mem. Am. Bd. Plastic Surgery, Am. Soc. Plastic Reconstructive Surgery, Calif. Soc. Plastic Surgery, Alpha Omega Alpha. Office Phone: 831-372-0200.

SUNDEL, MARTIN, management consultant, psychologist, educator; b. Bronx, NY, Sept. 22, 1940; s. Louis and Pauline (Brotman) S.; m. Sandra Stone, Aug. 22, 1971; children: Adam Daniel, Jenny Rebecca, Ariel Pauline. BA cum laude, St. Mary's U., 1961; MSW., Our Lady of the Lake Univ., 1963; MA, PhD, U. Mich., 1968. Social group work supr. Valley Cities Jewish Cmty. Ctr., Van Nuys, Calif., 1963-65; asst. prof. U. Mich. Sch. Social Work, Ann Arbor, 1968-71; dir. rsch. and evaluation River Region Mental Health-Mental Retardation Bd., Louisville, 1972-77; assoc. clin. prof. dept. psychiatry and behavioral sci., adj. prof. Kent. Sch. Social Work, U. Louisville, 1974—77; sr. research assoc. The Urban Inst., Washington, 1977-80; pvt. practice psychology Dallas, 1980-95; Dulak Disting. prof. U. Tex., Arlington, 1980-89, prof., 1980-95, Fla. Internat. U., Miami, Fla., 1995-2000; faculty assoc. S.E. Fla. Ctr. on Aging, 1996-2000; pres. Sundel Cons. Group, 2000—. Mental health cons. UN High Commn. for Refugees in Cyprus, 1993-95; profl. adv. coun. Dallas Geriatric Rsch. Inst., 1980-89; long-range planning com. Dallas Jewish Coalition for the Homeless, 1986-95; coordinating com. Arlington Human Svcs. Project, 1981-90, Mayor's Forum on Human Svc. Needs Assessment, Ft. Worth, 1983-86; vis. prof. U. So. Calif. Sch. Social Work, spring 1985, mem., Gen. Sys. Theory rsch. Group, Neuropsychatric Inst., UCLA, 1985; sr. consortium rsch. fellow, Dept. Def., 1996-99. Author: (with Sandra Stone Sundel) Behavior Change in the Human Services, 1975, 5th edit., 2005; Be Assertive, 1980; co-author: Women at Midlife, 2002; co-editor: Assessing Health and Human Service Needs, 1983, Individual Change Through Small Groups, 2d edit., 1985, Midlife Myths, 1989; mem. editl. bds. and cons. to profl. jours. Named Nat. Table Tennis Champion, U1600 Round Robin Age Group of 40 Yrs. and Older, 2005; fellow, Harvard U. Lab. Cmty. Psychiatry, Boston, 1971—72. Fellow Prescribing Psychologists Register (diplomate), Internat. Coun. Prescribing Psychology (diplomate in psychopharmacology); mem. Behavior Therapy and Rsch. Soc. (charter clin. fellow). Home: 3804 Barbados Ave Hollywood FL 33026-4659 Personal E-mail: sundelm@bellsouth.net.

SUNDLOF, STEPHEN FREDERICK, federal agency administrator, veterinarian; b. Peoria, Ill., May 4, 1951; m. Sandra Linden Sundlof; children: Christofer Linden, Thomas Michael. BS in Zoology/Chemistry with honors, So. Ill. Univ., Carbondale, Ill., 1973; MS in Veterinary Toxicology, U. Ill., Coll. Veterinary Med. Sciences, Urbana, Ill., 1976, BS in Veterinary Medicine with honors, 1977, DVM in Veterinary Medicine with honors, 1980, PhD in Veterinary Toxicology, 1980. Diplomate Am. Bd. Vet. Toxicology. Rsch. asst., dept. physiology and pharmacology U. Ill., Coll. Vet. Medicine, Urbana, Ill., 1973—76, rsch. asst., dept. veterinary biosciences, 1976—80; asst. prof., dept. preventative medicine Coll. Vet. Medicine, U. Fla., Gainesville, Fla., 1980—86, prof., dept. physiological sciences, 1995, assoc. prof., dept. physiological sciences, 1986—95; dir. Ctr. for Vet. Medicine FDA, Rockville, 1994—2008, Ctr. for Food Safety & Applied Nutrition College Park, Md., 2008—. Chmn., drug abuse com., Fla. Vet. Med. Assn., 1982-85; divsn. leader, divsn. toxicology and pathophysiology, dept. preventative medicine, 1982-83; animal drug coordinator, So. Region IR-4 Project, 1982-94; vice-chair, Ineragency Coordinating Com. for Animal Production Food Safety, 1995-; rep., Fla. Prescription Abuse Data Synthesis Com, Coll. Vet. Medicine and Fla. Vet. Med. Assn., 1984-86; courtesy prof., dept. physiological sciences, Coll. Vet. Medicine, U. Fla., Gainesville, Fla., 1996; mem. US Pub. Health Svc. spl. oversight com. to review allegations of mismanagement and abuse of authority by the US FDA, Ctr. for Vet. Medicine, 1986-87; Am. Vet. Med. Assn. delegate to the WHO/FAO Codes Alimentarius Com. on Residues of Vet. Drugs in Foods, 1986-94; Inst. Food Technologists delegate to the Food Safety Workshop, 1989; mem., vet. medicine adv. com., US FDA, 1991-94, chmn. 1993-94; chmn., WHO/FAO Codes Alimentarius Com. on Residue of Vet. Drugs in Foods, 1994-; temporary advisor, WHO/FAO Joint Expert Com. on Food Additives, 1995-; mem. steering com. on Internat. Cooperation on Harminization of Tech. Requirements for Registration of Vet. Medicinal Products, Office of Internat. Epizootics, 1995-; mem. external adv. bd., Inst. Food Sci. and Engring, Tex. A7M U., 1996-97; mem., USDA Food Safety and Inspection Svc., Food Rsch. Working Group, 1996-97; US Delegate to the Codex Alimentarius Internat. Ad Hoc Task Force on Animal Feeding, 1999-2004; mem., WHO/FAO, Office of Internat. Epizootics expert consultation on non-human antimicrobial usage and antimicrobial resistence, 2004; US delegation to Japan to discuss trade implications following finding of BSE-positive cow in US, 2004-; presenter in field. Editoral reviewer, Journal Veterinary Pharmacology and Therapeutics, 1988-; contbr. articles to profl. jours. Recipient Presidential Exec. Rank award Meritorious Exec. Rank, 1999; named Hon. Diplomate, Am. Vet. Epidemiology Soc., 1996, Disting. Practitioner in the Nat. Acad. Practice in Vet. Medicine, Nat. Acad. Practices, 1997. Mem. Am. Acad. Vet. Pharmacology and Therapeutics (pres.-elect 1993-95, pres. 1995-97), Am. Acad. Vet. and Comparative Toxicologists, Am. Vet. Med. Assn. (President's award, 1997), Am. Bd. Veterinary Toxicology. Office: Ctr Food Safety & Applied Nutrition FDA 5100 Pain Branch Pkwy College Park MD 20740

SUNDNES, KNUT OLE, physician, consultant; b. Oslo, Oct. 18, 1946; s. Jon Sigurd and Marte (Westre) S.; m. Sissel Koller, Apr. 19, 1969; children: Ane Kristin, Jon Erlend. Student, U. Basel, Switzerland, 1972, Ednl. Coun. Fgn. Med. Grads., 1972, Nat. Def. Coll., Norway, 1986, Staff Officers Course, UN, Sweden, 1994. Lic. physician, Norway, 1974, specialist in anesthesiology and intensive care, 1981. Med. registrar Akershus Cen. Hosp., Norway, 1972-73; surg. registrar Oslo City Hosp., Norway, 1974-76; anesthesiology registrar Baerum County Hosp., Norway, 1976-78, Akershus Cen. Hosp., Norway, 1978-79, sr. registrar anesthesiology, 1979-82, Nat. Hosp., Oslo, 1982-87; cons. Dept. Anesthesiology Baerum County Hosp., Norway, 1987-96; head Anaesthetic Svcs. Norway Def. Forces, 1996—, dir. Ctr. for War Surgery and Emergency Medicine, 1999—2005. Med. officer UNIFIL, South Lebanon, 1979; med. del. Internat. Com. Red Cross, Thailand, 1983-84, Kabul, Afghanistan, 1990, 92, med. coord., Mekele, Ethiopia, 1991; force med. ops. and planning officer UNPF, Zagreb, 1994-95; guest lectr. U. Bergen, Norway, 1991—, U. Oslo, 1992—, European Ctr. Disaster Medicine; chmn. Task Force on Quality Control of Disaster Mgmt., 1994—, head civilian mil.capacity bldg. on anaethesia for civilian Afghan hosp., 2006-. Co-author, editor: Health Disaster Management: Evaluation and Research in the Utstein Style, 2003; contbr. numerous articles to profl. jours. Union rep. Akershus Cen. Hosp., Norway Med. Assn., 1981-82, National Hosp., 1985-86; chmn. Physicians Adv. Bd., Baerum County Hosp., 1993-96. Lt. col. UNPF, Zagreb, 1994-95. Recipient UNIFIL medal UN, 1979, UNPF medal UN, 1995. Mem. Norwegian Assn. for Disaster Medicine (pres. 1993-94), Nordic Soc. for Disaster Medicine (mem. bd. dirs. 1993—, pres. 1998-2002), Rotary Internat., Norwegian Med. Assn., World Assn. Disaster and Emergency Medicine (bd. dirs. 1995-2001, pres.-elect World Assn. Disaster and Emergency Medicine 1999-2001, pres. 2001-05). Avocations: hunting, sailing, veteran cars. Office: Joint Med Commd Norwegian Defense Forces 2058 Sessvollmoen Norway Office Phone: +47-48010672. E-mail: kosundnes@c2i.net.

SUNDT, THORALF MAURITZ, III, cardiothoracic surgeon; b. Memphis, Tenn., Oct. 14, 1957; s. Thoralf Mauritz Jr. and Lois Ethelwyn (Baker) Sundt; m. Kathleen Suzan McDonald, Sept. 19,

1987; 1 child, Harald Thorsten. BA in Biochemistry, Princeton U., NJ, 1979; MD, Johns Hopkins U. Sch. Medicine, Balt., 1984. Diplomate Am. Bd. Surgery, Am. Bd. Thoracic Surgery. Surgery intern, resident Mass. Gen. Hosp., Boston, 1984—87, cardiothoracic surgery residency, 1989—91; med. staff fellow NIH, Bethesda, Md., 1987—89; resident Washington U., St. Louis, 1991—93; sr. registrar Herefield Hosp., England, 1993-94; hon. sr. lectr. Nat. Heart & Lung Inst., London U., 1994; faculty Washington U. Sch. Medicine, 1994—2001; prof. divsn. cardiovasc. surgery Mayo Clinic Transplant Ctr., Rochester, Minn., 2001—, vice chair dept. surgery. Contbr. articles to profl. jours. Mem.: AMA, Am. Assn. Thoracic Surgery (sec. 2007, Robert Gross scholar 1994), Internat. Soc. Heart & Lung Transplantation, Soc. Transplant Surgeons, Assn. Academic Surgery. Office: Mayo Clinic 200 First St SW Rochester MN 55905 Office Phone: 507-255-7064. Fax: 507-255-7378. Business E-Mail: sundt.thoralf@mayo.edu. *

SUNDWALL, DAVID NIELSEN, medical educator; b. Murray, Utah, May 22, 1941; m. Catherine Sundwall; 3 children. MD, U. Utah, 1969. Adminstr. Health Resources & Services Adminstrn.; v.p., med. dir. American Healthcare Sys., 1988—94; pres. American Clinical Laboratory Assn., 1994—2003; asst. surgeon gen. USPHS, Washington, 2003—05; exec. dir. Utah Dept. Health, Salt Lake City, 2005—11; prof. family & preventitive medicine U. Utah Sch. Medicine, 2011—. Vol. physician HealthCare for the Homeless Project, Washington; clinical assoc. prof. family med. Georgetown Univ.; assoc. prof. Univ. Utah Sch. Med. Contbr. articles to profl. jours. Trustee Spelman Coll., Atlanta. Mem.: AMA, American Acad. Family Physicians. Office: University Utah School of Medicine 375 Chipeta Way Ste A SLC Salt Lake City UT 84108 Office Phone: 801-581-7234. E-mail: David.Sundwall@hsc.utah.edu. *

SUNG, A-YOUNG, optometrist, educator; d. Ki-Tae Sung and Kum-Ri Ryu. BS, Chonnam Nat. U., Kwangju, 1992; MS, Chonnam Nat. U., 1994, PhD, 1998. Cert. tchr. sci. South Korea. Prof. Daebul U., 1999—, chmn. dept. optometry, 2001—02, chmn. grad. sch., 2005—. Adv. bd. Optinews, Seoul, 2006—; mem. organizing com. Daegu Internat. Optical Show, 2005, mem. acting com., 04; vis. rsch. prof. Cambridge U., England, 1999—2000, Oxford U., England, 2000, U. Calif., Berkeley, 2001—02, Harvard U., Boston, 2002—03, Sydney U., 2002—03. Author: Introduction of Contact Lens, 2004; chief editor Jour. Korean Ophthalmic Optics Soc., 2006—; contbr. articles to profl. jours. Chmn. expert com. Korean Ministry of Commerce, Industry and Energy, 2004—, mem. coun., 2004—. Named Internat. Profl. of the Yr., Internat. Biog. Ctr., Cambridge, 2005. Mem.: Joennam Techno Pk. (pres. 2008—), Korean Women Scientists and Engrs. (dir. 2004—), Korean Ophthalmic Optics Soc. (pres. 2006—, chief editor 2006—, Acad. Achievement award 2004, Excellent Presentation award 2006), Internat. Assn. Contact Lens Educators (coord.). Achievements include patents for on polymerization of contact lens including quartary ammonium; hydrophilic contact lens and manufacturing method with unethane and silicone. Avocations: piano, violin, radio broadcasting announcer. Office: Daebul University Samho-Eup Sanho Ri 72 Youngam-Gun Chonnam 526-702 Republic of Korea Personal E-mail: angel123sg@yahoo.com.

SUNG, DEUK JAE, radiologist, educator; b. Busan, Republic of Korea, Feb. 1, 1967; MD, Korea U. Coll. Medicine, 1992; PhD, Korea U. Grad. Sch., 2000. Assoc. prof., dept. radiology Anam Hosp., Korea U. Coll. Medicine, 2008—. Chmn., dept. urology & radiology Uiwang Sun Hosp., 2001—03; editor genitourinary imaging Korean Jour. Radiology, 2007. Mem.: Korean Soc. Urogenital Radiology, Korean Urologic Assn., Korean Soc. Radiology. Avocations: travel, opera, movies. Office: 126-1 5-Ka Anam-dong Sungbuk ku Seoul 136-705 Republic of Korea Business E-Mail: urorad@korea.ac.kr.

SUNG, GYUNG TAK, urologist, department chairman; b. Daegu, Republic of Korea, Aug. 15, 1958; s. Ui Joon Sung and Won Ok Rho; m. Sung Jong Kyung, Feb. 7, 1989; children: Seh-Rin, Catherine, Christine. Degree, State U. NJ, 1981, Busan Coll. Medicine, Republic of Korea, 1987, Busan Nat. Grad. Sch., 1990. Resident neurology Pusan Nat. U. Hosp., Busan, 1988—92; asst. prof. Coll. Medicine Dong-N U., Busan, 1995—98, chmn. dept. urology Coll. Medicine, 2002—; rsch. fellow dept. urology Cleve. Clinic Found., 1999, co-dir. laparoscopic rsch., 1999—2001, mem. staff Urol. Inst., 2001—02. Cons. in field. Co-editor: Robotic Surgery In Urology, 2003; co-author: Laparoscopic Prestatertomy, 2003, Retropa-Floneoscope Adrenarectomy: Lateral Approach, 2003. Recipient Video award, World Congress Endourology and Shockwave, 2001. Mem.: The Korean Urol. Assn., World Endourology and Shockwave Soc. (Academic Paper 2d prize 2002), Am. Urol. Assn. (Best Video 1st prize 1999, Best Video hon. mention 2001, Best Video 2d prize 2002). Avocations: jazz, golf. Office: Dept Urology Dong A Univ Hosp 3Ga1 Dongdaesin dong Seo gu Busan Republic of Korea 602 715 Home: PO Box 181578 Cleveland OH 44118-7578 Office Phone: 82 51-240-5446. Personal E-mail: sunggt@daunet.donga.ac.kr.

SUNG, JAEKYU, gastroenterologist, medical educator; b. Daejeo, Republic of Korea, May 16, 1969; m. Sukyung Chung, May 1998; children: Seungjoo Sung, Minyoung Sung. MD in medicine, Chungnam Nat. U., Daejeon, 1994, PhD in internal medicine, 2003. Cert. Korean Bd. Internal Medicine, gastroenterology specialist Korean Assn. Internal Medicine, gastrointestinal endoscopy specialist Korean Soc. Gastrointestinal Endoscopy. Asst. prof., internal medicine Chungnam Nat. U., Daejeon, Republic of Korea, 2006—. Editl. bd. mem. World Jour. Gastrointestinal Endoscopy, 2010—; mem. com., computerization & information Korean Soc. Neurogastroenterology & Motility, 2007—09; mem. com. scholarship Korean Coll. Helicobacter & Upper Gastrointestinal Rsch., 2007—08. Mem.: Korean Soc. Gastrointestinal Cancer, Korean Assn. Study Intestinal Diseases, The Korean Soc. Gastrointestinal Endoscopy, The Korean Soc. Gastroenterology, Korean Coll. Helicobacter & Upper Gastrointestinal Rsch., The Korean Soc. Neurogastroenterology & Motility, The Korean Assn. Internal Medicine. Avocation: classical music. Office: Chungnam Nat University Hosp Internal Medicine Dept 33 Munhwa-ro Jung-gu Daejeon Chungnam 301-721 Republic of Korea Office Phone: 82-42-280-7163. Office Fax: 82-42-254-4553. Business E-Mail: jksung69@gmail.com, jksung69@cnuh.co.kr.

SUNG, KI-SUN, medical educator; b. Pohang, Gyungsangbuk-do, Republic of Korea, Nov. 29, 1969; MD, Seoul Nat. U. Sch. Medicine, PhD, 1994. Assoc. prof. Sungkyunkwan U. Sch. Medicine Samsung Med. Ctr., 2004—. Mem.: Korean Bone and Joint Tumor Soc., Korean Foot and Ankle Soc., Korean Orthop. Assn., Am. Orthop. Foot and Ankle Soc. Office: Ilwon-dong 50 Gangnam-gu Seoul 135-710 Republic of Korea Office Fax: 82-2-3410-0061. Personal E-mail: kissung@empal.com.

SUNG, KIWOL, nursing educator, researcher; b. Daegu, Republic Of Korea, Sept. 17, 1955; d. Moonkyung Sung and Jinseek Chung; m. Sangkeun Bae, Oct. 25, 1980; children: Jisun Bae, Jihye Bae, Jio Bae. PhD, Kyungpook Nat. U., Deagu, 1993. RN Korean Nurses Assn., 1978. Staff RN Cath. U. St. Mary Hosp., Seoul, Republic of Korea, 1978—80; part time lectr. Kyungpook Nat. U., Daegu, 1985—93; asst. prof. Daegu Sci. Coll., 1993—98; lectr. Cath. U. Daegu, 1998—2000, asst. prof., 2000—04, assoc. prof., 2004—10, prof., 2011—. Dean Dept. Nursing, Deagu, 2002—03, head mgr., 2004—05, mem. curriculum com., 2006—07; faculty mem. Korean U. Assn., Daegu, 1993—. Contbr. articles to profl. journals. Mem. health promotion com. Jung-Gu Health Ctr., Daegu, 2005—09. Grant, Nat. Rsch. Found. Korea, 2004—09, Daegu, Jung-Gu Health Ctr., 2006. Master: Korean Acad. Cmty. Health Nursing; fellow: Korean Acad. Nursing; mem.: Korean Gerontol. Nurses Assn. (pres. 2009—), Am. Heart Assn., Korean Gerontol. Soc., Korean Acad. Soc. Cmty. Health Nursing, Korean Acad. Soc. Nursing. Liberal. Roman Catholic. Achievements include research in the influencing factors on wisdom in the elderly; influencing variables on life satisfaction of Korean elders in institutions; scale development on health conservation of the institutionalized elderly; comparison of health conservation for the elders in assisted living facilities and nursing homes; effects of regular walking exercise on health behaviour with diabetic elders; effects of 16-week group exercise program on physical function and mental health of elderly korean women in long term assisted living facility; self care behaviors and depressive symptoms with hypertension in the low income women elderly; influencing factors on constipation of the elderly in nursing homes; effects environmental education using newspapers in education on environmental concern and practice; exploring wisdom in the Korean elderly; relation of successful aging and wisdom in Korean older adults; factors associated with depressive symptoms in low-income Korean older women with hypertension; relationship of daily activity and biochemical variables in the elderly with DM. Avocations: mountain climbing, travel. Home: Jukgok-ri Dasa-myeon Daegu Dalseong-gun 711-782 Republic of Korea Office: Catholic University Daegu Daemyung 4dong Nam-Gu 705-718 Daegu Daegu Republic of Korea Office Fax: 82-53-650-4392. Business E-Mail: kwseng@cu.ac.kr.

SUNG, KYUNG MI, nursing educator; b. Yeju, Korea, Mar. 20, 1965; PhD, Yonsei U., Seoul, Republic of Korea, 2003. Postdoc. U. Pitts., 2005; asst. prof. Gyeongsang Nat. U., 2008—. Tchr., rschr. Coll. Nursing, 2008. Mem.: Korean Soc. Nursing Sci. Office: 816-15 Jinju-Daero Jinju Gyeongsangnam 660-751 Republic of Korea Office Fax: 82-55-772-8222. E-mail: skmpark@yahoo.co.kr.

SUNG, PEI-KUN, physician; b. Wu Ren, AnKao, China, Sept. 10, 1928; s. Han-Chung Sung and Cheng-Lan King; m. Yun Sung Wang; children: Dai-Lun, Ting-Lun, Dan-Lun. MD, Nat. Def. Med. Ctr., Taipei, Taiwan, 1956. Bd. cert. in cardiology Taiwan. Dep. dir. Tri-Svc. Gen. Hosp., Taipei, 1983—85, dir. (mayor gen.), 1985—88; dep. dir. Cheng-Hsin Med. Ctr. Hosp., Taipei, 1988—93, dir. in chief MJ Health Screening Ctr., Taipei, 1993—. Cons., mem. adv. bd. Internat. Jour. Japan Ningen Dock, Tokyo, 2000—. Author: Distribution and Familiar Aggregation of Risk Factors, 1998, Physical Activity and Cardiovascular Risk Factors, 1999, Health Evaluation - MJ View Point, 2nd edit., 2003, The Guide Book for Health Care, 2004. Fellow: Am. Coll. Cardiology; mem.: Health Evaluation and Promotion Assn., Internat. Health Evaluation Assn. Home: 12F No 2 Ln 78 An-Ho Rd Sect 1 Taipei 106 Taiwan Office: MJ Health Screening Ctr 86-B1 Hsin-Sheng N Rd Sect 1 Taipei 104 Taiwan E-mail: pk_sung@mjlife.com.

SUNG, SANG HYUN, pharmacologist, educator; b. Jinju, Republic of Korea, Sept. 1, 1968; PhD, Seoul Nat. U., 1998. Adj. prof. Seoul Nat. U. Sci. and Tech., 2000—02; R & D dir. Elcom Sci., 2003—05; rschr. Kanazawa U., 2005—06; lectr. Seoul Nat. U., 2006—08, asst. prof., 2008—. Recipient Disting. Sci. and Tech. award, Korean Fedn. Sci. and Tech. Socs. Fellow: Korean Soc. Pharmacognosy; mem.: Korea Plant Conservation Soc., Pharm. Soc. Korea, Am. Soc. Chemistry. Office: 21-214 Gwanak_1 Gwanak-ro Gwanak-gu Seoul 151-742 Republic of Korea Business E-Mail: shsung@snu.ac.kr.

SUNG YEUN, YANG, medical educator; b. Busan, May 15, 1967; PhD, Inje U., 1993. Assoc. prof. Haeundae Paik Hosp., 2002—. Office: Jwa-Dong Haeundae-Gu Busan 611722 Republic of Korea

SUNIL ROY, THOTTUVELIL NARAYANAN, medical educator; b. Cochin, Kerala, India, May 15, 1969; s. Thottuvelil Untan Narayanan and Nalukandathil Narayanan Manohari; m. Sukumaran Rekha Sukumaran, Oct. 29, 2001. MD, Jawaharlal Inst. Postgrad. Med. Edn. and Rsch., Pondicherry, 1998; DM, Maulana Azad Med. Coll. and GB Pant Hosp., New Delhi, 2005. Sr. lectr. cardiology Govt. Med. Coll., Calicut, Kerala, India, 1998—2006; specialist cardiologist Belhoul Speciality Hosp., Dubai, United Arab Emirates, 2006—. Sr. resident, cardiology GB Pant Hosp., New Delhi, 2002—05. Mem.: Cardiology Soc. India. Home: Thottuvelil House Edacochin Cochin Kerala 682006 India Office: Belhoul Speciality Hosp Al Khaleej Rd Dubai 5527 United Arab Emirates Personal E-mail: sunilroytn@hotmail.com. Business E-Mail: sroy@belhoulspeciality.com.

SUNTRA, CHARLES RATAPOL, surgeon, educator; b. Detroit, Dec. 4, 1968; s. Sathien and Malee Suntra. BA summa cum laude, St. Louis U., 1991, MD cum laude, 1995. Diplomate Am. Bd. Otolaryngology, bd. eligible Am. Bd. Facial Plastic and Reconstructive Surgery. Intern gen. surgery Boston U. Sch. Medicine/Boston Med. Ctr., 1995—96; resident otolaryngology-head and neck surgery Boston U. Sch. Medicine, 1996—2000; chief resident Boston Med. Ctr./Boston U., 1999—2000; fellow facial plastic and reconstructive surgery Park Ctrl. Inst./Forest Park Hosp., St. Louis, 2000—01; med. staff Forest Pk. Hosp., St. Louis, 2000—01, Sutter Gould Med. Found., Modesto, Calif., 2001—, Doctors Med. Ctr., Modesto, 2001; asst. clin. prof. Sch. Medicine U. Calif., Davis. Presenter in field. Contbr. articles to profl. jours. Fellow: ACS, Am. Bd. Otolaryngology; mem.: Thai Physicians Assn. Am., Am. Rhinologic Soc., Am. Acad. Facial Plastic and Reconstructive Surgery, Am. Acad. Otolaryngology-Head and Neck Surgery, Phi Eta Sigma, Alpha Epsilon Delta, Beta Beta Beta, Alpha Sigma Nu, Phi Beta Kappa, Alpha Omega Alpha. Office: Gould Med Group 600 Coffee Rd Modesto CA 95355 Office Phone: 209-550-4770. Personal E-mail: csuntra@yahoo.com. Business E-Mail: suntrac@sutterhealth.org.

SUPANICH, BARBARA ANN, physician; b. Detroit, Sept. 24, 1952; d. Donald George. BS in Chemistry, Mercy Coll. Detroit, 1974; MD, Mich. State U., 1980. Diplomate Am. Bd. Family Practice, Am. Bd. Hospice and Palliative Medicine, 2006, lic. physician Mich., Fla., Md.; joined Sisters of Mercy, 1973. Resident in family practice Creighton U. Affiliated Hosps., Omaha, 1980—83; pvt. practice Eaton Rapids, Mich., 1983—86, Houghton Lake, Mich., 1986—92; fellow in clin. ethics Ctr. Ethics Mich. State U., East Lansing, 1992—93, asst. prof. family practice, 1993—97, assoc. prof., 1998, assoc. chair clin. svcs., dept. family practice, 1995—99, assoc. residency dir. family practice residency Munson, 1999—2005; fellow palliative medicine and hospice care Mayo Clinic, Jacksonville, Fla., 2005—06; med. dir. palliative medicine, sr. svcs. Holy Cross Hosp., Silver Spring, Md., 2006—. Cons. Mich. Dept. Cmty. Health, Lansing, 1996—99. Contbr. chapters to books, articles to profl. jours. Recipient Teacher-Scholar award, Mich. State U., Coll. Human Medicine, 1998, Two Thousand Notable American Women award, 2003, Palliative Care Program award, Greater Wash. Partnership, 2009; named Am.'s Top Family Dr., Palliative Medicine Dr., 2007. Fellow: Am. Acad. Hospice and Palliative Medicine (Outstanding award 2009), Am. Acad. Family Physicians (bd. dirs., regional dir. 2000—04, 2d v.p. 2004—05); mem.: Md. Acad. Family Physicians. Democrat. Roman Catholic. Avocations: swimming, bicycling, walking, mystery and science fiction novels, movies. Home: 4013 Postgate Terr Apt 201 Silver Spring MD 20906 Office: Holy Cross Hosp 1500 Forest Glen Rd Silver Spring MD 20910 Home Phone: 301-828-0748; Office Phone: 301-754-7910.

SUPERNEAU, DUANE WILLIAM, geneticist, physician; b. Ogden, Utah, Dec. 31, 1950; s. Richard Edwin and Mary Ellen Superneau; children: Adam, Ashley, Allison. BA, Carroll Coll., 1973; MD, U. Wash., 1977. Diplomate Am. Bd. Pediat., Am. Bd. Med. Genetics. Asst. prof. dept. med. genetics U. So. Ala., Mobile, 1982-87, assoc. prof. dept. med. genetics, 1987-91; chief sect. med. genetics Ochsner Clinic, New Orleans, 1991—2005; dir. Genetic Svcs. La., Baton Rouge, 2005—10, Our Lady of the lake Genetics Svcs., Baton Rouge, 2010—. Clin. asst. prof. La. State U., New Orleans, 1992—. Bd. dirs. The ARC Greater New Orleans, 1991—, pres. 1994-96; bd. dirs. ARC of La., 1994—, pres., 1999-2001; bd. dirs. Jefferson Parish Human Svcs. Authority, Jefferson Parish, La., 1992-99. Roman Catholic. Office: Olol Genetics Svcs 8415 Goodwood Blvd Ste 202 Baton Rouge LA 70806-7851 Home: 981 Tifton De Baton Rouge LA 70815 Office Phone: 225-231-5381. Business E-Mail: duane.superneau@womans.org.

SUPINO, PHYLLIS GAIL, medical researcher, educator; m. Rene Patrick Supino, June 7, 1980; children: Lisa Michelle, Christopher Duvieu. BS in Biol. Scis., CCNY, 1964; EdD in Sci. Edn., Rutgers U., New Brunswick, NJ, 1976. Instr. psychology, rsch. assoc. in cognitive psychology Princeton U., 1975—77; dir. rsch. and evaluation The Ednl. Improvement Ctr. divsn. NJ. State Dept. Edn., West Orange, 1977—79; adj. instr. environ. and cmty. medicine, adj. instr. family medicine Robert Wood Johnson Med. Sch./U. Medicine and Dentistry NJ, Piscataway, 1979—90; asst. prof. pub. health in medicine, dir. data mgmt. Cornell U. Med. Coll., NYC, 1990—95; rsch. assoc. prof. emergency medicine, rsch. assoc. prof. med. edn., dir. rsch. in emergency medicine Mt. Sinai Sch. Medicine, NYC, 1996—99; assoc. rsch. prof. pub. health in medicine, dir. data mgmt., epidemiology and ednl. programs Weill Cornell Med. Coll., NYC, 1999—2008; prof. medicine, dir. clin. epidemiology & clin. rsch., divsn. cardiovasc. medicine SUNY Downstate Coll. Medicine, Bklyn., 2008—. Mem. editl. bd.: Cardiology, reviewer: Med. Edn.; contbr. chapters to books, articles to profl. jours. Vol. Morocco VI US Peace Corps, Washington; mem. sci. adv. bd. 15th World Congress Heart Diseases. Recipient Phi Delta Kappa award, Rutgers U., 1976, The Howard Gilman award, The Howard Gilman Found., 1995, Best Mentor of the Yr. award, Mt. Sinai Sch. Medicine, 1998, Best Nat. Sci. Abstract award, Am. Soc. Nuc. Cardiology and Internat. Affiliates, 2001; grantee Pilot Rsch. award, Weill Med. Coll. of Cornell U. Fellow: NY Acad. Medicine; mem.: Internat. Acad. Cardiology (sci. adv. bd.), Heart Valve Soc. Am., Am. Soc. Nuc. Cardiology, Am. Heart Assn., Am. Statis. Assn., Cardiology (editl. bd. Cardiology), Am. Fedn. for Med. Rsch., Kappa Delta Pi (life). Achievements include development of first comprehensive approved course on clinical research methodology for physicians at Weill Medical College, Mount Sinai School of Medicine and SUNY Downstate College of Medicine; first course on hypothesis and protocol design for physicians at WMC; research mentor to more than 100 medical students residents, fellows and junior faculty in medicine. Avocations: theater, vocal music. Business E-Mail: phyllis.supino@downstate.edu.

SUR, TAPAS KUMAR, medical researcher; b. Kolkata, Apr. 28, 1968; MSc, PhD, U. Calcutta, 1989. Jr. rsch. fellow U. Coll. Medicine, 1990—95, sr. rsch. fellow, 1995—99, rsch. assocs., 2000—03, Inst. Postgrad. Med. Edn. & Rsch., 2003—10; scientist Isha Natural & Herbal Products Pvt. Ltd., 2011—. Rsch. investigator Sci. & Tech., 2004—06, Union Drug Ltd., 2007—09, Health Reactive, 2009—10. Recipient Young Scientist award, Indian Sci. Congress Assn., B. R. Sengupta Internat. Gold medal, UNESCO, ASOMPS; scholarship, Indian Coun. Med. Rsch., Govt. of India, fellowship, U. Student Found., Bassel, Geneva. Mem.: K. M. Health & Rural Welfare Soc., Indian Sci. Congress Assn., Indian Pharmacological Soc. (P. C. Dandiya award). Avocations: writing, gardening. Home: 16a Durga Charan Mukherjee St Kolkata West Bengal 700003 India Personal E-mail: drtapassur@rediffmail.com.

SURACE, DARIO, ophthalmologist, director; b. Padua, Italy, Jan. 29, 1961; MD, Padova's U., 1987, degree in Ophthalmologist, 1992. Dir. dept. ophthalmology Ospedale S.Maria del Carmine, Rovereto, Italy, 2006—. Mem.: Am. Acad. Ophthalmology Internat., European Soc. Ophthalmic Plastic and Reconstructive Surgery, Italian Soc. Ophthalmology. Avocations: skiing, jazz. Home: Piazza Mercato 25 Mira 30034 Italy Personal E-mail: mail@dariosurace.it.

SURACI, PATRICK JOSEPH, clinical psychologist; b. Rochester, NY, May 31, 1936; s. Frank and Josephine Rosalie (Marino) S. PhD in Psychology, New. Sch. for Social Rsch., NYC, 1981. Cert. clin. psychologist, N.Y. Intern in clin. psychology Morrisania Neighborhood Family Care Ctr., Montefiore Hosp., NYC, 1979-80; staff psychologist N.Y. Police Dept., 1981-83; pvt. practice NYC, 1982—. Adj. lectr. N.Y. Inst. Tech., N.Y.C., 1975-78, John Jay Coll. Criminal Justice, CUNY, 1973-81; adj. asst. prof. dept. psychology Baruch Coll., CUNY, 1983-92; vol. Manhattan Ctr. for Living, 1994-96, Police Orgn. Providing Peer Assistance, 2001—. Author: Male Sexual Armor. Erotic Fantasies and Sexual Realities of the Cop on the Beat and the Man in the Street, 1992, Sybil In her Own Words: The Untold story of Shirley Muson, Her Multiple Personalities and Paintings, 2011 Mem. The Nat. Arts Club. With U.S. Army, 1959-62. Mem. Actors Equity. Office Phone: 212-473-5966. Personal E-mail: drsuraci@aol.com.

SURAWICZ, BORYS, physician, educator; b. Moscow, Feb. 11, 1917; came to U.S., 1951, naturalized, 1956; s. Josef and Mathilda (Soloweczyk) S.; m. Frida G. Van Klaveren, July 19, 1946; children: Christina M., Nina M., Tanya S., Serge J. MD, Stefan Batory U., Wilno, Poland, 1939. Mem. staffs hosps., Germany, Norway, 1945-49; staff De Goesbriand Meml. Hosp., Burlington, Vt., 1951-53, Phila. Gen. Hosp., 1953-55; instr. cardiology U. Pa., Phila., 1954-55; instr. U. Vt., Burlington, 1955-57, asst. prof. clin. and expt. medicine, 1957-62; chief div. cardiology U. Ky. Coll. Medicine, Lexington, 1962-81, assoc. prof. medicine, 1962-66, prof., 1966-81; prof. medicine Ind. U. Sch. Medicine, Indpls., 1981—. Cons. VA Hosp., Indpls. Editor: (with E.D. Pellegrino) Sudden Cardiac Death, 1964, (with C. Fisch) Digitalis, 1969; (with E. Prystowsky, C.P. Reddy) Tachycardias, 1985, Electrophysiologic Basis of ECG and Cardiac Arrhythmics, 1995, Chou's Electrocardiography in Clinical Practice, 2001, 2008, Doctors in Fiction Lessons from Literature, 2009; mem. editl. bds. profl. jours. Recipient award, U. Ky. Rsch. Found., 1971, Cummings Humanitarian award, 1975, NASPE Disting. Scientist award, 1992, Merit award, Hungarian Cardiac Soc., 1995, award, Cardiac Electrophysiology Soc., 2006. Mem. AMA, ACP, Am. Heart Assn., Assn. Univ. Cardiologists (pres. 1978), Am. Coll. Cardiology (master; pres. 1979), Am. Physiol. Soc., Sigma Xi. Office Phone: 317-338-6227. Personal E-mail: bsurawic@yahoo.com.

SUREKA, RAJENDRA KUMAR, neurologist, educator; b. Nohar, Rajasthan, Dec. 6, 1953; MBBS, Sms Med. Coll., Jaipur, India, 1981, MD; DNB in Neurology, Nat. Bd. Examinations, New Delhi, 2002. Assoc. prof. Sms Med. Coll. & Hosp., Jaipur, 1987—. Recipient award, State Govt. Mem.: Nat. Acad. Med. Sci. Home: 47 Sanjay Marg Hathroi Scheme Gopal B Jaipur Rajasthan 302011 India Personal E-mail: rsureka@rediffmail.com.

SURH, YOUNG-JOON, medical educator; b. Seoul, Korea, Sept. 26, 1957; came to the U.S., 1985; s. Jung-Chun and Kyung-Ok (Yoon) S.; m. Young-Kyu Lee, Jan. 10, 1983; 1 child, Jee-Hyuk. BS, Seoul U., Republic of, 1981, MS, 1983; PhD, U. Wis., 1990. Tchg. staff Seoul (Korea) Nat. U., 1983-85; rsch. asst. U. Wis., Madison, 1985-90, tchg. asst., 1988; rsch. assoc. Harvard Med. Sch., Boston, 1990; postdoctoral assoc. MIT, Cambridge, Mass., 1991-92; asst. prof. Yale Sch. Medicine, New Haven, 1992-96; prof. Seoul Nat. U., 1996—. Adv. bd. Soc. Biomed. Rsch., Rockville, Md., 1994-95; editl. bd. mem. Mutation Rsch. (Elsevier Sci.), 1997—. Author: Adv. Exp. Medicine Biol., 1991, Advances in Pharmacology, 1994, Handbook Exp. Pharmacol., 1994; assoc. editor Jour. Environ. Pathology, Toxicology and Oncology, 2000—, Asia Pacific Jour. Cancer Prevention, 2000—; mem. editl. bd. Mutation Rsch., 1997—; mem. editl. bd. Jour. Biochemistry and Molecular Biology, 1998-2000, mng. editor, 2001-02. 2d lt., 1983-84, Korea. Recipient Best Paper award U. Ill., Urbana, 1989, Spl. Interest Rsch. award Am. Cancer Soc., 1992, Ochi Young Scholar's award Japan Inst. Aging, 1995. Mem. Internat. Assoc. of Environmental Mutagen Soc. (councilor, 1997-), Internat. Soc. for the Study Xenobiotics, Am. Assn. for Cancer Rsch., N.Y. Acad. Scis. (acting), Sigma Xi. Achievements include first demonstration of formation of a covalently bound adduct between vitamin C and an ultimate electrophilic and carcinogenic metabolite; first demonstration of DNA adduct formation in vivo from electrophilic sulfate esters. Office: Seoul Nat U Coll Pharmacy Shinlim-dong Kwanak-gu Seoul 151-742 Republic of Korea E-mail: surh@plaza.snu.ac.kr.

SURI, JASJIT S., research scientist; BS in Computer Engring., Regional Engring. Coll., Bhopal, India, 1988; MS, U. Ill., Chgo., 1991; PhD in Elec. Engring., U. Wash., 1997. Lectr. dept. electronic and computer engring. Regional Engring. Coll., Bhopal, 1988-89; rsch. asst. biomed. visualization dept. U. Ill., Chgo., 1989-90; rsch. programmer image sci. group IBM Palo Alto (Calif.) Sci. Ctr., summer 1990-91; rsch. assoc. U. Wash., Seattle, 1992-97; rsch. software engr. radiation treatment planning group Siemens Med. Sys., Calif., 1991-92; rsch. scientist Gammex Inc., Middleton, Wis., 1997, Sch. Medicine, U. Wis., Madison, 1997; rsch. scientist software devel. TSI, N.Y., 1997; rsch. staff scientist image guided surgery dept. Image Processing & Computer Graphics Picker Internat., Cleve., 1999—, Eigen, Robotic surgery, 2005—09. With Bharat Heavy Elec. Ltd., Bhopal, 1986, Larson & Tubro Ltd., Bombay, India, 1987, Nat. Info. Tech. Ltd., Bhopal, 1987; presenter in field; mem. Mayo Clinic Procs., Rochester, Minn.; rev. com. Internat. Conf. in Pattern Analysis and Applications, Plymouth, Eng., 1998. Author: (with others) Model Based Segmentation, 2d. rev. edit., 2000; mem. editl. bd. Radiology, Jour. Computer Assisted Tomography, Internat. Jour. Pattern Analysis and Applications, Internat. Conf. Pattern Analysis and Applications; contbr. over 300 articles. to profl. jours.; patentee in field. Scholar Regional Engring. Coll., 1985-88; fellow AIMBE. Mem. IEEE, Assn. Computing Machinery, Artificial Intelligence, Optical Engring. Soc. Am., Engring. in Medicine and Biology Soc. (mem. editl. bd.), Am. Assn. Artificial Int., USENIX-Tcl/Tk. Office: GBTI Roseville CA 95661 Home Phone: 916-797-4942. Personal E-mail: jsuri@comcast.net.

SUROW, JASON B., otolaryngologist, educator; MD, U. Pa., 1982. Diplomate Am. Bd. Otolaryngology. Resident in surgery Univ. Pa. Hosp., 1983—84, resident in otolaryngology, 1984—87; mem. bd. govs. NJ Acad. of Otolaryngology; otolaryngologist Good Samaritan Hosp., Valley Hosp. Mem.: Soc. for Ear, Nose and Throat Advances in Children, Bergen County Soc. of Otolaryngology, Am. Acad. of Otolaryngology- Head and Neck Surgery. Office: Valley Hospital 223 N Van Dien Ave Ridgewood NJ 07450 Office Phone: 201-447-8000.

SURPRISE, JUANEE, chiropractor, nutrition consultant; b. Gary, Ind., Apr. 28, 1944; d. Glenn Mark and Willia Ross (Vasser) Surprise; m. Peter E. Coakley, Feb. 12, 1966 (div. Jan. 1976); children: Thaddeus, Mariah, Darius; m. Robert T.Howell, Feb. 24, 1984. RN, Phila. Gen. Hosp. Sch. Nursing, 1965; D of Chiropractic summa cum laude, Life Chiropractic Coll., Marietta, Ga., 1981. Diplomate Am. Acad. Pain Mgmt., Coll. Clin. Nutrition, Chiropractic Bd. Clin. Nutrition, Thompson tech., Nimmo receptor tonus tech.; cert. acupuncturist. Staff nurse Children's Hosp., Balt., 1966-67; charge nurse Melrose-Wakefield Hosp., Mass., 1967-68; hosp. adminstr. Animal Hosp. of Wakefield, Mass., 1967-79; chiropractor Chiropractic Clinic of Greenville, NC, 1982-84, Family Chiropractic Clinic, Denton, Tex., 1984—; dean Sch. Nutrition Quantum-Veritis Internat. Univ. Sys., 2003—09; dir. Ctr. Clin. Sci., Parker Coll. Chiropractic, Dallas, 1996-97, dir. diplomate and certification programs, 1997-2000. Post-grad. faculty Northwestern U. Health Scis., 2000—. Mem., chmn. Cmty. Planning Commn., North Reading, Mass., 1976-79; chmn. bldg. com. Immaculate Conception Ch., Denton, 1987-90, parish coun., 1990-92; v.p. Property Owners Assn., 2000-02. Fellow Am. Acad. Integrated Medicine; mem. Am. Assn. Pain Mgmt., Am. Chiropractic Assn., Am. Chiropractic Bd. on Nutrition (past pres.), Tex. Chiropractic Assn. (past chair), Chiropractic Bd. Nutrition (sec.), Pi Tau Delta. Republican. Roman Catholic. Avocation: health education. Office: Family Chiropactic Clinic 400 N Loop 288 Ste 120 Denton TX 76209 Office Phone: 940-566-0000.

SURREY, MARK WAYNE, reproductive endocrinologist; b. Washington, Jan. 15, 1947; BS, U. Pitts., 1968; MD, George Washington U. Sch. Medicine, 1972. Diplomate American Bd. Ob-Gyn. Intern ob-gyn. UCLA Med. Ctr., 1972—73, resident, 1973—76; reproductive endocrinology & infertility fellowship Hammersmith Hosp., U. London, 1976; co-founder, med. dir. Southern Calif. Reproductive Ctr. (formerly Reproductive Medicine & Surgery Associates), Beverly Hills, 1983—. Staff Cedars-Sinai Med. Ctr., LA, 1986—, dir. advanced technologies, Ctr. Fertility & Reproductive Medicine; assoc. clin. prof. dept. ob-gyn. UCLA David Geffen Sch. Medicine. Contbr. articles to profl. jours. Fellow: ACS, ACOG; mem.: AMA, American Soc. Reproductive Medicine, Calif. Ob-Gyn. Soc., Calif. Med. Assn., LA County Med. Assn., American Assn. Gynecologic Laparoscopists (past pres.), Pacific Coast Fertility Soc. (past pres.), Soc. Reproductive Surgeons. Achievements include rigorous training in pelvic reconstructive surgery, microsurgery and laparoscopic surgery, IVF and preimplantation genetic diagnosis; research to improve embryo implantation, reduce the risk of multiple pregnancies and advance the success of embryo transfer. Office: Southern California Reproductive Center 450 N Roxbury Dr Ste 500 Beverly Hills CA 90210 Office Phone: 866-989-4083. Office Fax: 310-274-5112. *

SURRUN, SOONDAL KOOMAR, internist, senior consultant; s. Seewoodoth Madho Surrun and Anne Marie Bhica; m. Roopmatee Rani Jeeawock, May 15, 1980; children: Sonia Devi, Vidya Kumari, Poonam Sandya. BS in Medicine and Surgery, St. John's Med. Coll., Bangalore, India, 1975. Diplomate Bangalore Med. Coun., India, 1976. Dir. med. rsch. inst. U. Mauritius, Reduit, 1994—99; cons. physician All-Jahra hosp. Ministry Health Kuwait., 2000—04; cons. internal medicine Singapore Gen. Hosp., 2004—, acting head, sr. cons. internal medicine, 2008—; adj. asst. prof. Duke-Nus Grad. Med. Sch. Presenter in field. Author: (book) Handbook of the Cardiac Patient, 1995; editor: (e-publication) Al-Jahra Hospital Bull. Kuwait, 2002—04; contbr. articles to profl. jours. Recipient Best Player Musical Instrument award, Cath. Club Musical Contest, 1970. Mem.: Indo-Mauritian Cath. Assn. (pres. 1996—97), Giants of Mauritius (asst. pres. 1997—98). Home: Ave de Marly Roches-Brunes Beau-Bassin Mauritius Personal E-mail: sksurrun@yahoo.com.

SUSCOVICH, DAVID J., neuropsychologist, marriage and family therapist; b. Mt. Pleasant, Pa., Sept. 20, 1952; s. Joseph Anthony and Helen G. Suscovich; m. Edith P. Suscovich, May 23, 1980 (div. Sept. 15, 2001); children: Joseph Alfred, John David, Mark Andrew. BS/BA in Psychology and Sociology, U. Pitts., 1973, postgrad., 1974; MA in Marriage and Family Therapy, U. Conn., 1977; PsyD in Clin. Psychology, Antioch New Eng., 1997. Cert. marriage family therapist Conn., diplomate Am. Coll. Forensic Examiners, Nat. Bd. Addiction Examiners; lic. marriage and family therapist Am. Assn. Marriage and Family Therapists, Conn. Psychiat. clinician psychiatry dept. Waterby (Conn.) Hosp., 1974—80; pvt. practice individual and marriage and family therapy Naugatuck, Conn., 1987—. Clin. cons. Waterby Youth Svcs., Inc., 1988—, Salvation Army Youth Shelter, Waterby, 1995—, Conn. Dept. children and Familites, 2001—03; clin. neuropsychology examiner Conn. Resource Group, LLC, Waterby, 1988—, Conn. Edn. Svcs., Middletown, 2001—; mental health cons. Danby (Conn.) Head Start, Conn., 1994—97; adj. faculty So. Conn. State U., New Haven, 1992—, Yale U. Sch. Medicine, New Haven, 2002—; full adj. prof., adj. Ctrl. Conn. State U., New Britain, Conn., 1994—; presenter in field; co-facilitater G.R.A.S.P. parent advocacy and support group. Weeblos Cub Scout leader Boy Scouts Am. Pack 110, Naugatuck, 1989—98; troop com. mem. Boy Scouts Am. Troop 109, Naugatuck, 1997—. Mem.: Electroencephalography and Clin. Neurosci. Soc., Conn. Assn. Marriage and Family Therapy (chair state election com. 2002—), Phi Kappa Phi. Democrat. Roman Catholic. Achievements include research in negative neurophysiological effects of stress on children and teens delaying development of executive brain functions; neurofeed back training for brain disorders. Avocations: camping, canoeing, fishing, woodworking, music. Home: 23 May St Naugatuck CT 06770 Office: Dr David Suscovich 984 Southford Rd Ste 2 Middlebury CT 06762-3234 Office Phone: 203-758-7400 ext 205. Personal E-mail: dsuscovich@yahoo.com.

SUSHRUTA, KOPPULA, pharmacologist, educator; s. Koppula Hemadri and Koppula Krishna veni; m. Kopalli Rajendra Spandana, Feb. 18, 2005; 1 child, Koppula Samhith. PhD, U. Coll. Pharm. Scis., Andhra U., India, 2005. Registered pharmacist Andhra Pradesh, 2004. Pharmacologist M/S Laila Impex, R & D Ctr., Mfr.'s Medicinal and Herbal Plant Extracts, Vijayawada, Andhra Pradesh, 1999—2000; sr. rsch. fellow Andhra U., U. Coll. Pharm. Scis., Visakhapatnam, 2000—05; asst. prof. Elrazi Coll. Med. and Technol. Scis., Khartoum U., Sudan, 2005—06; postdoc. fellow, dept. pharmacology Seoul Nat. U., 2006—09; asst. prof. Biomed. and Health Scis. Konkuk U., Chungju, Chungju-si, Republic of Korea, 2009—. Sr. Rsch. fellowship, Coun. Sci. and Indsl. Rsch., 2000—05. Mem.: Soc. Neuro Sci. Avocations: travel, sports, swimming. Office: Biomed and Health Sci Konkuk University Danwol Dong Chungju-Si Chungbuk-do 322 380-701 Chungju Chungcheongbuk-do Republic of Korea Home Phone: 821093563193; Office Phone: 82438403609, +821058310448. Business E-Mail: koppula@kku.ac.kr.

SUSLOV, KONSTANTIN, medical researcher; b. Vologda, Russia, Nov. 26, 1979; MSc in Chemistry, Moscow State U., 2002; student, U. Oxford, 2003—. Rschr. NIH, Bethesda, Md., 2002—03, Mechnikov Inst. Vaccines & Sera, Moscow, 2006—09, Russian State Med. U., 2009—. Contbr. chapters to books, articles to med. journals. Home: Yunich Lenincev 3 Apt 300 Moscow 109 390 Russia Office: Russian State Med University ul Ostrovityanova 1 117997 Moscow Russia Office Fax: +7(495) 434-61-29. Business E-Mail: suslov_kv@mail.ru.

SUSMAN, JEFFREY L., dean, medical educator; m. Linda Susman; 5 children. B cum laude, Dartmouth Coll., Hanover, NH, MD. Various positions including rsch. dir. dept. family medicine, assoc. dean primary care and faculty devel., and med. dir. for primary care network U. Nebr. Med. Ctr., 1987—99; prof. & chmn. dept. family medicine, mem. health sys. bd., chmn. physician orgn. and exec. com. mem. of practice group U. Cin., 1999—2010; dean medicine, prof. family medicine Northeastern Ohio Universities Coll. Medicine, 2010—. Chmn. commn. on quality and practice American Acad. Family Physicians, co-chmn. nat. quality forum mental health outcomes com.; mem. case simulation com. Nat. Bd. Med. Examiners; mem. mental health SAM devel. group American Bd. Family Medicine. Editor: Jour. Family Practice. Curator Ctr. for History Family Medicine; mem. steering com RWJ Aligning Forces for Quality Initiative, Cin.; bd. mem. Soc. Teachers of Family Medicine; bd. mem., sec. Assn. Departments of Family Medicine; bd. mem. Aultman Coll. Nursing; bd. trustees Goldman Found., Ohio Acad. Family Physicians. Scholar Nat. Health Svc. Corps, Wahoo, Nebr. Office: Northeastern Ohio Universities Coll Medicine 4209 St Route 44 PO Box 95 Rootstown OH 44272-0095 Office Phone: 330-325-6254. Business E-Mail: jsusman@neoucom.edu. *

SUSMAN, MILLARD, geneticist, educator; b. St. Louis, Sept. 1, 1934; s. Albert and Patsy Ruth S.; m. Barbara Beth Fretwell, Aug. 18, 1957; children: Michael K., David L. AB, Washington U., St. Louis, 1956; PhD, Calif. Inst. Tech., 1962. With microbial genetics research unit Hammersmith Hosp., London, 1961-62; asst. prof. genetics U. Wis., Madison, 1962-66, assoc. prof., 1966-72, prof., 1972—2002, prof. emeritus, 2002—, chmn. lab. genetics, 1971-75, 77-86, assoc. dean med. sch., 1986-95, acting dean Sch. Allied Health Professions, 1988-90, vice dean med. sch., 1994-95, spl. advisor to the dean med. sch., 1995; dir. Ctr. for Biology Edn., Madison, 1996—2002. Phage course instr., Cold Spring Harbor, N.Y., 1965; v.p. scis., Wis. Acad. Scis., Arts and Letters, 2000—11, pres.-elect, 2011-. Co-author: Life on Earth, 2d edit., 1978, Human Chromosomes: Structure, Behavior, Effects, 3d edit., 1992; contbr. articles to sci. jours. Mem Genetics Soc. Am., AAAS, UW-Madison Retirement Assn. (pres. 2011-), Sigma Xi, Phi Beta Kappa, Phi Eta Sigma, Omicron Delta Kapp. Home: 2707 Colgate Rd Madison WI 53705-2234 Office: 2432 Genetics/Biotech Ctr Bldg Madison WI 53706 Office Phone: 608-263-5075. Business E-Mail: msusman@wisc.edu.

SUSSMAN, MICHAEL DAVID, orthopedic surgeon; b. Balt., Feb. 20, 1943; s. Sidney and Leonora H. (Applebaum) S.; m. Nancy Evans Whiteley, Aug. 13, 1971; children: Evans (dec.), Tovah. AB, Washington and Lee U., 1963; MD, U. Md., Balt., 1967. Diplomate Am. Bd. Orthopaedic Surgery. Intern, jr. resident surgery Med. Coll. Va., Richmond, 1967-69; rsch. assoc. NIH, Bethesda, Md., 1969-71; resident orthopaedic surgery Johns Hopkins Hosp., Balt., 1971-75; fellow pediatric orthopaedic surgery Childrens Hosp. Med. Ctr., Boston, 1975-76; from asst. prof. to prof. dept. orthopaedic surgery and dept. pediat. U. Va., Charlottesville, 1976—92, head div. pediatric orthopaedics, 1985—92; chief med. staff Shriners Hosps. for Children, Portland, Oreg., 1992—99, staff surgeon, 1999—. Mem. rsch. adv. bd. Shrine Hosp., 1984—92; mem. grant rev. bd. Orthopaedic Rsch. Edn. Found., 1985—86. Mem. editl. bd.: Jour. Pediatric Orthopedics, Jour. Pediatric Orthopedics B, Childrens Orthopedics; contbr. articles to profl. jours., chapters to books. Bd. dirs. Bloomfield Inc., Ivy, Va., 1979-83, Dyslexia Ctr., Charlottesville, 1987-92. Served to lt. commdr. USPHS, 1969-71. Frank Ober fellow, 1976, Gianestras-Schmerge Traveling fellow, 1978. Fellow Am. Acad. Orthopaedic Surgery (com. on pediatric orthopaedics 1986—89), Am. Acad. Cerebral Palsy and Devel. Medicine (sci. program com. 1986—, membership com. 1986—, pres. 2001-03), Am. Acad. Pediat., Scoliosis Rsch. Soc.; mem. Pediatric Orthopaedic Soc. (Arthur H. Huene award, 2000). Democrat. Jewish. Office: Shriners Hospitals Children 3101 SW Sam Jackson Park Rd Portland OR 97239-5090 Office Phone: 503-221-3424. Office Fax: 503-221-3490. Business E-Mail: msussman@shrinenet.org.

SUSTKOVA, MAGDALENA, pharmacologist, educator; b. Prague, Mar. 14, 1963; PharmD, Charles U. Prague, 1987, PhD in Pharmacology, 1992. Rschr. dept. pharmacology Rsch. Inst. Pharmacy Prague, 1987—92; dept. pharmacology, 3rd Faculty Medicine Charles U. Prague, 1993—. Mem. European Monitoring Ctr. Drugs and Drug Addiction, 2002; mem. editl. bd. Addictology Jour., 2001—. Mem.: Soc. Addictive Diseases of Czech Med. Soc. J.E.P, Czech Neuropsychopharmacol. Soc. (award 1995), Czech Soc. Clin. and Exptl.

Pharmacology and Toxicology of Czech Med. Soc. J.E. Purkyne. Avocations: skiing, singing, painting, ceramics. Office: Charles University Prague 3rd Faculty Medicine Ruska 87 Prague 10000 Czech Republic Business E-Mail: magdalena.sustkova@lf3.cuni.cz.

SUTER, LUDWIG HERMANN, retired dermatologist, educator; b. Berlin, May 24, 1938; s. Emil Otto Hermann and Margarete Johanne Luise (Paul) S.; m. Jacoba-Johanna Braaksma, Nov. 12, 1971; children: Margrit, Elke. Student, Free U., Berlin, 1957-63; med. state exam., U. Würzburg, Germany, 1964. Approbation for physicians; diploma for dermatology. Intern Evangelisches Krankenhaus, Holzminden, Germany, 1965-66; rsch. fellow Max-Planck-Inst., Göttingen, Germany, 1966-70; rsch. assoc. Albert Einstein Coll. Medicine, NYC, 1970-72; asst. dept. dermatology U. Münster, Germany, 1972-78, asst. med. dir. dept. dermatology, 1978-80; med. dir. Fachklinik Hornheide, Münster, 1980—2001, ret., 2001. Contbr. articles to biochem., immunol., and derm. jours. Rsch. grantee Deutsche Forschungsgemeinschaft, 1971-72, 72-80, Deutsche Krebshilfe, 1987-90. Mem. Deutsche Dermatologische Gesellschaft Avocation: hiking. Home: In der Stroth 37 D-48157 Münster Germany Home Phone: 0049-251-325778. E-mail: l.suter@t-online.de.

SUTER, ROBERT EDUARD, emergency physician, educator; b. Decatur, Ill., Aug. 29, 1961; s. Robert Koester and Erika Ilse Suter; children: Robert E. Jr., Joseph E., Jennifer E. B, Washington U., 1982; M in Healthcare Adminstrn., Des Moines U., 1989, D of Osteopathy, 1989. Diplomate Am. Bd. Emergency Medicine. Chmn. Emergency Svcs. Eisenhower Army Med. Ctr., Ft. Stewart, Ga., 1993—95; chmn. emergency svcs. Providence Hosp. and Med. Ctrs., Detroit, 1995—97; regional med. dir. Questcare Med. Svcs., Dallas, 1997—2001; chmn. emergency dept. Spring Br. Med. Ctr., Houston, 2001—06; dir. emergency med. practice mgmt. and health policy U. Tex. Southwestern. Pres. Tex. Emergency Physicians; prof. Med. Coll. Ga., U. Tex. S.W. Bd. dirs. alumni assn. Des Moines U. Col. US Army, 1978—. Recipient Founders award, Continuing Edn. Coord. Bd. for EMS, 2004, Wackerle Founders award, Emergency Medicine Residents Assn., 1998, Alumnus of the Yr., Des Moines U., 2005, Order of IFEM, 2008. Fellow: Am. Coll. Osteopathic Emergency Physicians, Am. Coll. Emergency Physicians (pres. bd. dirs. 2001—06); mem.: Emergency Medicine Found. (chair 2006), Internat. Fed. Emergency Medicine (pres. 2006), Soc. for Academic Emergency Medicine. Cath. Home: 5926 St Marks Cir Dallas TX 75230

SUTER, STEVEN E., veterinarian, educator; MS in Biochemistry, NY Med. Coll.; PhD in Molecular Biology, U. Pa., VMD. Diplomate oncology Am. Coll. Veterinary Internal Medicine. Intern U. Pa. Mathew J. Ryan Veterinary Teaching Hosp., 2000—01; resident U. Calif. Veterinary Med. Training Hosp., 2001—03, lectr in med. oncology, 2003—05, med. oncologist Sacramento Animal Med. Group, 2005; asst. prof. oncology NC State U. Coll. Veterinary Medicine, 2006—, med. dir. Canine Bone Marrow Transplant Unit. Office: 4700 Hillsborough St Raleigh NC 27606 Office Phone: 919-513-0813. Office Fax: 919-513-7301. E-mail: steven_suter@ncsu.edu.

SUTHERLAND, DONALD WOOD, retired cardiologist; b. Kansas City, Mo., July 29, 1932; s. Donald Redeker and Mary Frances (Wood) S.; m. Margaret Sutherland, Sept. 11, 1954 (div. 1994); children: Kathleen Sutherland, Ellen Baltus, Richard, Ann, Julia McMurchie; m. Roslyn Ruggiero Elms, Mar. 31, 1995. BA, Amherst Coll., 1953; MD, Harvard U., 1957. Intern, resident Mass. Gen. Hosp., Boston, 1957-60; fellow in cardiology U. Oreg., Portland, 1961-63; pvt. practice Portland, 1963—2006; ret. Assoc. clin. prof. medicine Oreg. Health Sci. U., Portland, 1967—; chief of staff St. Vincent Hosp. and Med. Ctr., Portland, 1971-72. Contbr. articles to profl. jours. Fellow Am. Heart Assn., Am. Coll. Cardiology (pres. Oreg. chpt. 1972); mem. Multnomah Athletic Club, North Pacific Soc. Internal Medicine (pres. 1985), Pacific Interurban Clin. Club (pres. 2000). Avocations: flying, scuba diving. Home: 4405 SW Council Crest Dr Portland OR 97239 Home Phone: 503-243-2535. Personal E-mail: dwscardio@comcast.net.

SUTHERLAND, TOM, radiologist; b. Melbourne, Australia, June 15, 1977; MBBS with honors, Monash U., 2002; M in Medicine, Melbourne U., 2010. Radiologist St. Vincents Hosp. Med. Imaging Dept., 2010—. Fellow: Royal Australian and New Zealand Coll. Radiologists, Royal Australiasian Coll. Radiologists; mem.: Australiasian Soc. Ultrasound in Medicine (mem., ann. sci. meeting organising com. 2011), European Soc. Radiology, Radiol. Soc. N.Am., Abdominal Radiology Group Australia and New Zealand. Office: Saint Vincents Hosp 55 Victoria Parade Fitzroy Victoria 3065 Australia Business E-Mail: tom.sutherland@svhm.org.au.

SUTHERS, HANNAH LOUISE BONSEY, biologist, consultant; b. Lorain, Ohio, Oct. 4, 1931; d. William Edwin and Hannah Elisabeth Bonell B.; m. Derwent Albert Suthers, June 20, 1953 (div. Oct. 1968); children: Daniel Derwent, Hannah Marie Suthers McCabe, Edwin Bonsey. BA, Oberlin Coll., 1953, MS equivalent in biology, 1998, MA equivalent in theology, 1998. Cert. avian rehabilitator Fish and Wildlife Svc. U.S. Dept. Interior, master permitee bird banding Migratory Bird Mgmt. U.S. Geologic Survey Dept. Interior. Sec., clk. Union Theol. Sem., NYC, 1953-54; nursery sch. tchr. Berkeley (Calif.) Unified Sch. Dist., 1954-55; sec./clk. Ch. Div. Sch. of Pacific, Berkeley, 1955; nursery sch. tchr. Edgewood People's Ch., East Lansing, Mich., 1964-65; overseas missionary Protestant Episcopal Ch., Brazil, 1965-68; lab. tech. Princeton (NJ) Labs., Inc., 1968; profl. rsch. staff Princeton U., 1968-89, profl. tech. staff, 1989-96. Reviewer Am. Jour. Botany, 1971—73, 1983, N.Am. Bird Bander, 1977—; area rep. Princeton U., 1978—80, 1982—89; coord. com. Princeton U. Women's Orgn., 1982—89; cons. Bracco Rsch. USA, Inc., Princeton, 1996—2009, Williams Transcontinental Gas Pipeline Corp., Lawrenceville, NJ, 1996—2003, FMC Corp., Princeton, 1997—2001, Allelix Neurosci., Inc., Cranbury, NJ, 1997—99, Johnson & Johnson Consumer Products, Inc., Skillman, NJ, 1998—2008, Purdue Pharma LP, Cranbury, 1999—2004. Author: (novel) Not By Force But By Good Will: The Odyssey Of A Runaway Slave At The Time Of Constantine The Great, 2006; contbr. articles to profl. jours. Bird bander U.S. Geol. Survey, 1953—; leader Bits and Boots 4-H Horse Club, Mercer County, NJ, 1969—75; county coach Mercer County 4-H Competitive Trail Ride and Mercer County 4-H Horse Judging Team, 1973—75; rep. Mercer County Horse Coun., 1970—75; mem. Migratory Bird Rehab. Policy and Permit Rev. Com.,, NJ, 1988—90, others; participant N.J. Audubon Breeding Bird Atlas, 1980—85, 1991—95; trainer N.Am. Banding Coun., 1998—; vol. cons. Woodrow Wilson Nat. Fellowship Found., Princeton, 1997; vol. State of N.J. Wildlife Conservation Corps, NJ, 2000—. Recipient Outstanding Layperson award Diocese of Mich. Bishop's award 1955, Frank M. Chapman Meml. award Am. Mus. Natural History, 1986, Paul A. Stewart award Wilson Ornithol. Soc., 1986, 87, Jack Gleeson Meml. Environ. award Friends Hopewell Valley Open Space, 2004; grantee Audubon/Washington Crossing Chpt., 1986-88, 94—, Women and Wildlife award Conserve Wildlife Found. N.J., 2006, others. Mem. Sigma Xi. Democrat. Episcopalian. Achievements include finding near-extinct Hawaiian ferns Diellia spp on Maui; Hawaiian Petrel, Petrodroma phaeopygia sandwichensis, colonies in Haleakala Crater, Maui; reporting appearance of Band-winged Nightjars, Caprimulgus longirostris in Leblon, Rio de Janeiro, Brazil; discovery of day-length sensitivity of Xanthium seedlings, allowing aseptic culture of sprouts for plant hormone bioassays; developed aseptic culture techniques of Xanthium hypocotyl tissue for bioassays; teammate in discovery of the chemoattractant in the cellular slime mold Polysphondylium violaceum and in the discovery of the role of ammonia in chemotaxis; discovered the transcontinental transport of cellular slime molds (Dictyostelids) by migratory songbirds; longest operating independent bird banding and research station in New Jersey.

SUTIONO, AGUNG BUDI, neurosurgeon, educator; b. Jakarta, July 12, 1974; MD, Padjadjaran U., 2000; PhD, U. Electro-Comm., 2010. Vis. prof. med. social informatics U. Electro-Comm.; vis. prof., skull base neurosurgery Keio U., Tokyo, 2010—. Grant, Japan Soc. Promotion Sci., Matsushita Found. Japan, Asia Pacific Advanced Network, Asia Pacific Telecmty., Clin. fellowship, Ministry of Edn., Culture, Sport, Sci. and Tech. Fellow: World Fedn. Neurosurg. Soc., Skull Base Com.; mem.: Internat. Med. Informatics Assn., Japan Neurosurg. Soc., Japan Assn. Social Informatics. Avocations: travel, reading, photography. Office: 1-5-1 Chofugaoka Chofushi Tokyo 182-8585 Japan also: Keio University Hosp Dept Neurosurgery 35 Shinanomachi Shinjuku-ku Tokyo 160-8582 Japan Business E-Mail: agungbudis@ohta.is.uec.ac.jp. E-mail: agungbudis@z2.keio.jp.

SUTKER, WILLIAM LEVIN, internist; b. Chgo., July 9, 1948; s. Robert H. and Carol (Levin) S.; m. Helen E. Horowitz, Dec. 20, 1970; children: Tara, Nikki, Cory. BS, U. Ill., 1970; MD, Chgo. Med. Sch., 1974. Diplomate Am. Bd. Internal Medicine, Infectious Diseases. Intern, resident internal medicine Baylor U. Med. Ctr., Dallas, 1974-77, fellow infectious diseases, 1977-79, attending physician, 1979—. Dir. med. edn. Baylor U. Med. Ctr., Dallas, 1979-, chief infectious diseases, 1990—. Contbr. articles to profl. jours. Fellow ACP; mem. AMA, Am. Soc. Microbiology, Infectious Diseases Soc. Am., Assn. Program Dirs. Internal Medicine. Avocations: basketball, tennis. Office: N Tex Infectious Dis Cons 3409 Worth St Ste 710 Dallas TX 75246-2043

SUTNICK, ALTON IVAN, internist, dean, educator, researcher, consultant; b. Trenton, NJ, July 6, 1928; s. Michael and Rose (Horwitz) S.; m. Mona Reidenberg, Aug. 17, 1958; children: Amy Sutnick Plotch, Gary Benjamin Sutnick. AB, U. Pa., 1950, MD, 1954; student in Biomed. Math., Drexel U., 1961—62; student in Biometrics, Temple U., 1969—70. Diplomate Am. Bd. Internal Medicine. Rotating intern Hosp. U. Pa., 1954—55, resident in anesthesiology, 1955—56, resident in medicine, 1956, USPHS postdoctoral research fellow, 1956—57; asst. instr. anesthesiology, then asst. instr. medicine U. Pa. Sch. Medicine, 1955—57; resident in medicine Wishard Meml. Hosp., Indpls., 1957—58, chief resident in medicine, 1960—61; resident instr. medicine Ind. U. Sch. Medicine, Indpls., 1957—58; USPHS postdoctoral research fellow Temple U. Hosp., 1961—63; instr., then assoc. in medicine Temple U. Sch. Medicine, 1962—65; mem. faculty U. Pa. Sch. Medicine, 1965—75, assoc. prof. medicine, 1971—75; clin. asst. physician Pa. Hosp., 1966—71; research physician, then assoc. dir. Inst. Cancer Research (now Fox Chase Cancer Ctr.), Phila., 1965—75; vis. prof. medicine Med. Coll. Pa., Phila., 1971—74; prof. medicine Drexel U. Coll. Medicine (formerly Med. Coll. Pa.), 1975—; dean Med. Coll. Pa., 1975—89, sr. v.p., 1976—89; v.p. Ednl. Commn. Fgn. Med. Grads, 1989—95; dir. internat. med. edn. Carelift Internat., 1997—2005. Dir. clin. devel. Am. Oncologic Hosp., Phila., 1973-75; attending physician Phila. VA Hosp., 1967-89, Allegheny U. Hosps., 1971-95; cons. in field; mem. U.S. nat. com. Internat. Union Against Cancer, 1969-72; mem. Nat. Conf. Cancer Prevention and Detection, 1973, Nat. Cancer Control Planning Conf., 1973; vice chmn. Gov. Pa. Task Force Cancer Control, 1974-76, chmn. com. cancer detection, 1974-76; mem. health rsch. adv. bd. Commonwealth of Pa., 1976-78; mem. diagnostic rsch. adv. group Nat. Cancer Inst., 1974-78; chmn. coord. com., comprehensive cancer ctr. program Fox Chase Cancer Ctr., U. Pa. Cancer Ctr., 1975; cons. WHO, Govt. of India, 1979, Govt. of Indonesia, 1980, entire S.E. Asia region, 1981, U. Zimbabwe, 1989, Minister of Health of Poland, 1992, Israel Sci. Coun., 1992, U. Autonoma de Guadalajara, Mex., 1993, Generalitat de Catalunya, Spain, 1993, Ministry of Health Russian Fedn., 1993, Inst. de Pos-Graduacae Medica Carlos Chagas, Brazil, 1993, Fondazione Smith Kline, Italy, 1995, Assn. Med. Schs. Europe, 1995-99, U. Jordan, 1995, U.S.-China Ednl. Inst., 1996, Georgian Postgrad. Med. Found., 1996, Instituto Universitario de Ciencias Biomedicas, Argentina, 1996, faculty of medicine U. Saarland, Germany, 1996, Ctr. for Med. Edn., Ben Gurion U., Israel, 1996-, Hungarian Nat. Health Ins. Fund, 1996, Carelift Internat., 1997, Intercoll., Cyprus, 1997, Open Soc. Inst., 1997-99, Aieti Med. Sch., Republic of Georgia, 1997-2001, Tartu U., Estonia, 1998-99, WHO European Office, 1998, Vilnius U. and Kaunas Med. U., Lithuania, 1998-99, U. Zagreb, Croatia, 1998-99, Larnaca Hosp., Cyprus, 1998, Netherlands and Russian med. schs., Temple U., Govt. of Republic of Georgia, others; faculty of medicine Moldova State Med. and Pharm. U., 1997-, vis. prof., 2002, prof. assoc., 2003-; rep. for internat. med. and health scis. edn. MCP Hahnemann U. of the Health Scis., 1996-99; adv. com. Open Soc. Inst. Muskie Fellowship Program, 1997, working group on implementation of presdl. policy on internat. edn., 2000, selection comm. Internat. Consortium for the Advancement of Med. Edn., 2001-05; mem. adv. com. internat. health program Temple U., 2005—. Author numerous articles in field.; asst. editor: Annals Internal Medicine, 1972-75; mem. editl. bd. other med. jours. Bd. dirs. Israel Cancer Rsch. Fund, 1975—95, Am. Assocs. for Democracy in Georgia, 2000—; nat. bd. dirs. Am. Assocs. Ben Gurion U., 1991—; bd. Internat. Med. Scholar Program, 1988—89, Sight Savers Internat., 1988—91; adv. commn. Internat. Participation Phila. '76, 1973—76; bd. dirs. Phila. Coun. Internat. Visitors, 1972—77; nat. bd. dirs. Phila. divsn. Am. Assocs. Ben Gurion U., 1986—, assoc. chair, 1993—95, 2000—. Capt. M.C. US Army, 1958—60. Recipient Torch of Learning award Am. Friends of Hebrew U., 1981, medal Ben Gurion U. of Negev, Israel, 1985, medal U. Cath. de Lille, France, 1987, medal U. Belgrade, Yugoslavia, 1988, Founder's award and medal Med. Coll. Pa., 1989, St. Thomas Aquinas award Santo Tomas U. Med. Alumni Assn., The Philippines, 1989, medal Kiev Med. Inst., Ukraine, 1991, Benjamin Albagli medal Inst. de Pos-Graduacao Medica Carlos Chagas, Brazil, 1993, shield Coll. Physicians and Surgeons, Pakistan, 1993, medal Ukrainian State Med. U., 1994, medal Universidad de Cantabria, Spain, 1999, medal Hadassah-Hebrew U. Dental Sch., 1999, Negev award Am. Assocs., Ben Gurion U., 2000. Fellow ACP (internat. adv. network), Coll. Physicians Phila. (censor 1977-86, councillor 1977-86); mem. AMA (Arnold and Marie Schwartz award in medicine, 1976, Dr. William Beaumont award), AAAS, Am. Fedn. Clin. Rsch. (pres. Temple U. chpt. 1964-65), Am. Assn. Cancer Rsch., Am. Soc. Clin. Oncology, Am. Dermatoglyphics Assn., Assn. Am. Cancer Insts., Assn. Am. Med. Colls., Northeast Consortium on Med. Edn. (treas. 1983-89, chmn. 1986-87), Coun. of Deans of Pvt. Free-Standing Med. Schs. (co-founder, nat. chmn. 1983-85), Pa. Coun. Deans (chmn. 1987-89), Am. Cancer Soc. (vice chmn. service com. Phila. div. 1974-76, bd. dirs. 1974-80, chmn. awards com. 1976), Am. Lung Assn., Am. Heart Assn., NAFSA-Assn. Internat. Educators, Pan Am. Med. Assn., Phila. Coop. Cancer Assn., N.Y. Acad. Scis., Pa. Heart Assn., Heart Assn. Southeastern Pa., Pa. Med. Soc., Phila. County Med. Soc. (chmn. com. internat. med. affairs 1964-72, Strittmatter award 2006), Pa. Lung Assn., Phila. Assn. for Clin. Trials (bd. dirs. 1980-81), Health Systems Agy. Southeastern Pa. (gov. bd., exec. com. 1983-87, sec. 1985-87), Am. Assn. Ben Gurion U. (bd. dirs. 1986—), Soc. des Medecins Militaires Français, Assn. Med. Edn. in Europe, Soc. Española de Educacion Medica, Internat. Med. Sch. Affiliates Consortium (co-founder, vice chmn. 1985-87), Phi Beta Kappa, Sigma Xi, Alpha Omega Alpha (councillor 1963-65). Achievements include discovery of association of hepatitis B surface antigen with hepatitis; performed 1st studies of pulmonary surfactant in adult human lung disease; developed cancer screening system based on risk status; pioneer in describing non-A non-B hepatitis C, pioneer in showing relationship of body iron stores to cancer susceptibility and life expectancy; organized first symposium on problems of foreign medical graduates; coined word "ergasteric" for lab.-contracted disease; responsible for advances in assessment of clinical competence; demonstrated validity of clinical competence assessment using standardized patients; demonstrated reliability of clinical competence assessment across six different languages and cultures; medical education advisor to over 50 countries, with a measurable impact on health care delivery system. Personal E-mail: altonsutnick@msn.com.

SUTOO, DEN'ETSU, neuroscientist, researcher; b. Tendo, Yamagata, Japan, May 29, 1952; s. Den'ichiro and Kikue (Shinohara) S.; m. Sumi Inoue, Mar. 20, 1976; children: Lemi, Ken'etsu. B of Hygienic Sci., Kitasato U., Tokyo, 1975, PhD, 1989. Rschr. U. Tsukuba, Japan, 1975—, expert officer, 1990—92, head officer, 1992—. Cons. Tosoh Corp., Tokyo, 1977-90, Jeol Ltd., Tokyo, 1978-97, Nikon Corp., Tokyo, 1983-2010, Taisho Pharm. Co. Ltd., Tokyo, 1996-2010, Yamato Sci. Co., Ltd., Tokyo, 1999—. Author: The Vulnerable Brain and Environmental Risks, 1994, Trends in Exercise and Health Research, 2005; contbr. articles to profl. jours. Fellow Japanese Sci. Jamboree, Tokyo, 1970-2010; exec. mem. Tsukuba Children's Art Contest, Tokyo, 1984-2010; adviser preservation of stickleback, Yamagata, Japan, 1998—; spl. judge Intel Internat. Sci. and Engring. Fair, Phoenix, 2005. Recipient Spl. award U.S. Patent Office, 1969, Prime Min. award Japanese Govt., 1969; Grant award Toyota Found., Tokyo, 1987, Yamaha Music Found., Tokyo, 2005. Fellow Japanese Pharmacological Soc., Japanese Finalist Club; mem. NY Acad. Scis. Buddhist. Avocations: classical music, bicycling, photography, gardening, fishing. Home: 3-22-13 Namiki Tsukuba 305-0044 Japan Office: U Tsukuba Inst Med Sci Tsukuba 305-8575 Japan Home Phone: 81-29-851-0125; Office Phone: 81-29-853-3113. Office Fax: 81-29-854-9817. Personal E-mail: den@sutoo.jp.

SUTPHEN, JAMES L., pediatrician; b. Aug. 9, 1946; MD, Columbia U., NYC, 1972. Cert. in pediat., in pediatric gastroenterology 2005. Residency in pediat. Johns Hopkins U., Balt.; fellowship in clin. nutrition, pediatric gastroenterology Harvard Med. Sch. Boston Children's Hosp.; prof., dept. pediat. U. Va. Health Sys., Charlottesville, head, divsn. pediatric gastroenterology, nutrition. Contbr. articles to profl. jours. Named to Best Doctors in America, Best Doctors, Inc. Office: Univ Va Health Sys Divsn Pediat Gastroenterology Nutrition PO Box 800386 Charlottesville VA 22908-0386 Office Phone: 434-924-2457. Office Fax: 434-924-8798. Business E-Mail: jls5z@virginia.edu.

SUTTON, BEVERLY JEWELL, psychiatrist; b. Rockford, Mich., May 27, 1932; d. Beryl Dewey and Cora Belle (Potes) Jewell; m. Harry Eldon Sutton, July 7, 1962; children: Susan, Caroline. MD, U. Mich., 1957. Diplomate Am. Bd. Pediat., Am. Bd. Psychiatry and Neurology. Rotating intern St. Joseph Mercy Hosp., Ann Arbor, Mich., 1958; resident in child psychiatry Hawthorne Ctr., Northville, Mich., 1958-62; resident in pediat. U. Hosp./U. Mich. Med. Ctr., Ann Arbor, 1959-61; resident in psychiatry Austin (Tex.) State Hosp., 1962-64, dir. children's svc., 1964-89, dir. psychiat. residency program, 1989—, dir. tng. and rsch., 1993-98. Cons. in field. Contbr. articles to profl. jours. Active numerous civic orgns. Recipient Outstanding Achievement award, YWCA, 1989, Jackson Day award, Tex. Soc. Child and Adolescent Psychiatry, 1989, Showcase award, Tex. Dept. Mental Health/Mental Retardation, 1990. Fellow Am. Acad. Child and Adolescent Psychiatry (life), Am. Psychiat. Assn. (Disting. fellow), Am. Pediatric Assn.; mem. Group for Advancement Psychiatry, Tex. Soc. Child and Adolescent Psychiatry (pres. 1979-80,

Jackson Day award), Tex. Soc. Psychiat. Physicians (Disting. Svc. award 1990), AMA, Tex. Med. Soc., Am. Genetics Soc. Office: Seton Shoal Creek Hosp 3501 Mills Ave Austin TX 78731 Business E-Mail: bsutton@seton.org.

SUTTON, DOUGLAS HOYT, nursing educator; b. McHenry, Ill., Oct. 27, 1962; s. Hoyt Douglas and Barbara Sutton. Cert. in emergency med. tech., Polk C.C., Winter Haven, Fla., 1985; ADN, SUNY, Albany, 1990, BS in Psychology, 1993; MSN, U. Fla., 1995; MPA, Troy State U., 1998; EdD, Fla. Internat. U., 2004, master's cert., 2003. RN Calif., cert. adult health nurse practitioner, adult clin. nurse specialist. Paramedic Polk County Emergency Med. Svcs., Bartow, Fla., 1984—88; edn. cons. Moore Pubs., 1990—94; mgr. orthopedics and skilled care programs Columbia Healthcare, Inc., Gainesville, Fla., 1995—97; dir. med. surg. nursing U. Cmty. Hosp., Tampa, Fla., 1997—98; dir. patient svcs. Bethesda Meml. Hosp., Fla., 1998—2000; asst. prof. nursing Broward C.C., Ft. Lauderdale, Fla., 2000—02, Barry U., Miami, Fla., 2002—05; posdoctoral fellow Wash. State U., Spokane, 2003; assoc. prof. nursing Fla. Atlantic U., Boca Raton, Fla., 2005—06, DON programs Broward campus, 2006—07. Mem.: Nat. Assn. Bariatric Nurses, Am. Acad. Nurse Practitioners (cert. adult health nurse practioner 2004—), Nat. League of Nursery (cert. nurse educator), Sigma Theta Tau. Home: 1747 NE 45 St Fort Lauderdale FL 33334 Office Phone: 561-297-2872. Business E-Mail: dsutton@fau.edu.

SUTTON, GREGORY PAUL, obstetrician, gynecologist; b. Tokyo, Dec. 12, 1948; (parents Am. citizens); s. Vernon S. And Vonna Lou (Streeter) S.; m. Judith Craigie Holt, June 26, 1977; children: Anne Craigie, James Streeter. BS in Chemistry with honors, Ind. U., 1970; MD, U. Mich., 1976. Diplomate Am. Bd. of Ob/Gyn. Prof. gynecol. oncology Ind. U. Sch. Medicine, Indpls., 1986-97; Mary Fendrich Hulman prof. Gynecologic Oncology Ind. U. Sch. Med., Indpls., 1997-2000; dir., gynecologic oncology St. Vincent Hosp. and Health Svcs., 2000—01. Cancer Clin. fellow Am. Cancer Soc., Phila., 1981-83; recipient Career Devel. award Am. Cancer Soc., 1986-89. Fellow: Am. Coll. Obstetrics and Gynecology (chair Ind. sect. 2000—03); mem.: ACS (com. on cancer, Ind. state liaison), Nat. Cancer Inst. (grampian cancer steering com. mem. 2008—), Hoosier Oncology Group, Soc. of Gynecologic Oncologists, Bayard Carter Soc., Ind. State Med. Soc., Marion County Med. Soc., Gynecologic Oncology Group (cert. Spl. Competence in Gynecologic Oncology 1985). Avocations: swimming, bicycling, woodworking, sailing, crossword puzzles. Office: 8301 Harcourt Rd Ste 202 Indianapolis IN 46260-1453 Office Phone: 317-415-6740. E-mail: gsutton@stvincent.org.

SUTTON, HARRY ELDON, geneticist, educator; b. Cameron, Tex., Mar. 5, 1927; s. Grant Edwin and Myrtle Dovie (Fowler) S.; m. Beverly Earlene Jewell, July 7, 1962; children: Susan Elaine, Caroline Virginia. BS in Chemistry, U. Tex., Austin, 1948, MA, 1949; PhD in Biochemistry, U. Tex., 1953. Biologist U. Mich., 1952-56, instr., 1956-57, asst. prof. human genetics, 1957-60; assoc. prof. zoology U. Tex., Austin, 1960-64, prof., 1964-99, chmn. dept. zoology, 1970-73, asso. dean Grad. Sch., 1967-70, 73-75, v.p. for research, 1975-79, Ashbel Smith prof. emeritus molecular genetics and microbiology, 2000—. Mem. adv. council Nat. Inst. Environ. Health Scis., 1968-72, council sci. advs., 1972-76; mem. various coms. Nat. Acad. Scis.-NRC; cons. in field; bd. dirs. Associated Univs. for Research in Astronomy, 1975-79, Argonne Univs. Assn., 1975-79, Univ. Corp. for Atmospheric Research, 1975-79, Associated Western Univs., 1978-79 Author: Genes, Enzymes, and Inherited Disease, 1961, An Introduction to Human Genetics, 1988, Genetics: A Human Concern, 1985; editor: First Macy Conference on Genetics, 1960, Mutagenic Effects of Environmental Contaminants, 1972, Am. Jour. Human Genetics, 1964-69. Trustee S.W. Tex. Corp. Public Broadcasting, 1977-80, sec., 1979-80; bd. dirs. Ballet Austin, 1978-84, 98-2004; mem. Austin Arts Commn., 1991-95. Served with U.S. Army, 1945-46. Mem. AAAS, Am. Soc. Human Genetics (dir. 1961-69, pres. 1979), Genetics Soc. Am., Am. Soc. Biochem. and Molecular Biology, Am. Chem. Soc., Tex. Genetics Soc. (pres. 1979), Am. Genetic Assn., Headliners Club (Austin), Town and Gown Club. Achievements include research and publications in human genetics. Home: 1103 Gaston Ave Austin TX 78703-2507 Office: Univ Tex Sect Molecular Genetics & Microbiology Austin TX 78712 Business E-Mail: eldon.sutton@mail.utexas.edu.

SUTTON, JEFFREY PAUL, physician, scientist, administrator; b. NYC, July 6, 1958; MD, U. Toronto, Ontario, Can., 1982, MSc in Med. Sci., 1985, PhD in Physics, 1988. Resident Harvard Med. Sch., Boston, 1988-91; vis. scientist brain & cognitive scis. MIT, Cambridge, 1988-95; facaulty Harvard Med. Sch., Boston, 1991—2002; founder. dir. neural sys. grp. Mass. Gen. Hosp., 1995—2002; pres., inst. dir. Nat. Space Biomed. Rsch. Inst., Houston, 2001—. Recipient Career Rsch. Scientist award, NIH, Presidents Citation, Soc. NASA Flight Surgeons. Office: National Space Biomedical Research Institute One Baylor Plaza NA 425 Houston TX 77030 Office Phone: 743-798-7412. Office Fax: 743-798-7413. *

SUTTON, PHILIP D(IETRICH), psychologist, educator; b. June 20, 1952; s. Clifton C. and Ida-Lois (Dietrich) S.; m. Kathleen E. Duffy, June 17, 1973; children: Heather, Shivonne. BA, So. Ill. U., 1974; MA, U. Chgo., 1975; PhD, U. Utah, 1979. Lic. psychologist, Colo. Psychologist VA Hosp., Salt Lake City, 1975-76; psychology intern Salt Lake Cmty. Mental Health Ctr., 1976-78; counselor, instr. Counseling Ctr. U. Utah, 1976-78; counselor, acting dir. spl. svcs. program Met. State Coll., Denver, 1978-80; staff psychologist Kaiser-Permanente Health Plan, 1980—83; pvt. practice Boulder, 1983—. Adj. prof. U. Colo., 1979-83; cons. spl. program for disacvantaged students in higher edn. HEW, 1980. Mem. APA, Biofeedback Soc., Am. Soc. Behavioral Medicine. Office: Box 1781 Nederland CO 80466 Office Phone: 720-406-0400. Personal E-mail: pdsphd@aol.com.

SUVAG, NAZIM, ophthalmologist; b. Mardin, Turkey, Feb. 3, 1945; s. Vedat and Zehra Suvag; m. Zehra Gunduzalp Suvag, Jan. 4, 1972; children: Ipek, Nazimcan. Degree, Med. Sch. Hacettepe U., 1971. Resident Med. Sch. Hacettepe U., Ankara, Turkey, 1971—77; ophthalmologist pvt. practice, 1977—; cons. surgeon, Oculoplastic Dept. Ophthalmology Ankara Ednl. Tng. and Rsch. Hosp., 1990—, chief prosthesis labs. Performer (founder, conductor, singer): Turkish Classical Music Chorus Hacettepe U., 1964—2009. Mem.: European Soc. Ophthalmolic Plastic and Reconstructive Surgery, Turkish Ophthalmology Assn., Turkish Med. Assn. Avocations: music, photography, drawing, skiing, water-skiing. Home: 35 sok No 97 Bahçelievler Ankara Turkey Office: Ziya Gokalp Cad 22/19 6420 Ankara Ankara Turkey Office Phone: 90-312-431-4412. E-mail: nazimsuvag@superonline.com.

SUWA, MICHIHIRO, hospital administrator; b. Osaka, Japan, Mar. 15, 1949; MD, Osaka Med. Coll., 1974, PhD. Assoc. prof. Osaka Med. Coll., 1993—2008; v.p. Hokusetsu Gen. Hosp., 2008—. Recipient Young Investigator's award, Japanese Circulation Soc. Fellow: Japanese Coll. Cardiology. Office: 6-27 Kitayanagawa-cho Takatsuki Osaka 569-8585 Japan Office Fax: 81-72-694-2657. Business E-Mail: suwa-mic@hokusetsu-hp.jp.

SUXING, WANG, research scientist; b. China, Nov. 20, 1960; MD, Norman Bethune Med. U., China, 1987; MSc in Microbiology, Nat. U. Singapore, 1995. Sr. sci. officer Ctrl. Tb Lab. Dept. Pathology Singapore Gen. Hosp., 1995—2000, lab. scientist, lab. supr., 1995—2011, prin. sci. officer, 2001—05, sr. prin. sci. officer, 2006—. Avocation: travel. Office: Ctrl Tuberculosis Lab Dept Pathology Singapore 169608 Singapore Office Fax: 6562245057. Personal E-mail: wangsuxing@gmail.com.

SUZAKI, YOSHIKA, nursing educator; b. Nakama, Fukuoka Prefecture, Japan, Nov. 15, 1967; BSN, Seinan Jo Gakuin U., 1998; PhD, Tokyo Women's Med. U., 2008. Asst. prof. Japanese Red Cross Kyushu Internat. Coll. Nursing, 2010—. Office: 1-1 Asty Munakata Fukuoka Prefecture 811-4157 Japan Office Fax: 81-940-35-7045. Business E-Mail: yoshika_suzaki@ybb.ne.jp.

SUZER, CUNEYT, zoologist, educator; b. Izmir, Turkey, Mar. 24, 1970; PhD, Ege U., 2003. Assoc. prof., rschr., faculty fisheries Ege U., 1995—. Office: Ege University Faculty Fisheries Aqu Izmir 35100 Turkey Office Fax: 902323883685. Business E-Mail: cuneyt.suzer@ege.edu.tr.

SUZEWITS, JEFFREY A., dean, physician, educator; DO, AT Still U. Kirksville Coll. Osteo Medicine, Mo., 1988; MPH, U. Ill., Springfield, 2001. Cert. American Bd. Family Practice, 1994, American Bd. Osteo. Family Physicians, 2003. Internship Normandy Hospitals, St. Louis, 1988—89; residency in family practice So. Ill. U. Sch. Medicine, Springfield, 1989—91, chief resident, 1990—91; assoc. prof. dept. family medicine, preventive medicine and cmty. health A.T. Still U. Health Sciences, assoc. dean clin. ednl. affairs and OPTIK, interim dean Kirksville Coll. Osteo. Medicine, 2011—. Office: AT Still University Health Sciences Kirksville Coll Osteo Medicine 800 W Jefferson St Kirksville MO 63501 Office Phone: 660-626-2354. Office Fax: 660-626-2080. Business E-Mail: jsuzewits@atsu.edu. *

SUZUKI, ATSUSHI, endocrinologist, educator; b. Nagoya, Aichi, Japan, July 13, 1963; s. Hideo and Hiroyo Suzuki; m. Yasuko Kano, Apr. 18, 1993; children: Hiroko, Atsuko. MD, Nagoya U., 1988, PhD, 1996. Diplomate Japanese Bd. Internal Medicine, 1991. Resident and fellow in internal medicine Japanese Red Cross Nagoya First Hosp., 1988—91; fellow divsn. endocrinology and metabolism Shizuoka (Japan) Saiseikai Hosp., 1991—92; instr. divsn. clin. pathophysiology U. Hosp. Geneva, 1996—98; clin. rschr. divsn. endocrinology and metabolism Nagoya U., 1999—2001; asst. prof. Fujita Health U., Toyoake, Aichi, Japan, 2000—05, assoc. prof., 2005—. Recipient Preclinical Rsch. award, Swiss Bone and Mineral Soc., 1999, 2006. Fellow: Japanese Soc. Internal Medicine, Japan Diabetes Soc., Japan Endocrine Soc.; mem.: Am. Coll. Physicians, Japan Gerontol. Soc., Japan Osteoporosis Soc., Japan Thyroid Assn., Internat. Bone and Mineral Soc., Endocrine Soc., Am. Soc. Bone and Mineral Rsch., Japanese Soc. Bone and Mineral Metabolism. Office: Fujita Health U 1-98 Dengakugakubo Kutsukake Aichi Toyoake 470-1192 Japan Office Fax: +81562951879. E-mail: aslapin@fujita-hu.ac.jp.

SUZUKI, HIDEKAZU, medical educator; b. Konosu, Japan, Dec. 1, 1963; s. Kazuo and Kazuko (Mimaru) Suzuki; m. Kimiko Kino, Apr. 29, 1998; children: Kieko, Risako. MD, Keio U., Tokyo, 1989, PhD, 1994. Instr. Keio U. Sch. Medicine, Tokyo, 1995—2003, asst. prof., 2003—06, assoc. prof. dept. internal medicine, 2006—; head dept. gastroenterology Kitasato Inst. Hosp., 2005; head outpatient clinic dept. gastroenterology Keio U. Hosp., Tokyo, 2007—. Edtl. mem. Neurogastroenterology and Motility, Gastric Cancer; exec., editor jour. Clin. Biochemistry & Nutrition Soc. Free Radical Rsch. Japan; editor neurogastroenterology & motility; assoc. editor Am. Jour. Gastroenterology. Recipient Young Investigator award, Asian Microcirculatory Soc., 1997, Gasric Mucosal Bioregulation award, 2003, Rokuzo Kobayashi Meml. Helicobacter prize, 2004, Kitajima award, Keio U. Med. Sch., 2007, SFPR Japan Young Scientist award, 2002, Gastroenterology High Citation award, 2011, SFRR Sci. Excellence award, 2011; Rsch. fellow, Am. Heart Assn., 1993, U. Calif., San Diego, 1993—95, Faculty and Alumni grantee, Keio U. Med. Sch., 2001. Mem.: Japanese Gastric Cancer Assn. (editor), Japanese Gastroent. Assn. (exec.), Am. Coll. Gastroenterology, Am. Gastroent. Assn., Soc. Free Radical Rsch. Japan (exec., Young Investigator award 2002), Japanese Soc. Gastroenterological Endoscopy (exec.), Japanese Soc. Gastroenterology (exec.), Japanese Soc. Ulcer Rsch. (exec.), Japanese Soc. Autonomic Nervous Systems (exec.), Japanese Soc. Microcirculation (exec., assoc. editor Microvascular Comm. and Rev.), Japanese Soc. Helicobacter Rsch. (exec.), Am. Assn. Study of Liver Disease. Avocations: reading, skiing. Office: Keio U Sch Medicine Dept Internal Med 35 Shinanomachi Shinjuku-ku Tokyo 160-8582 Japan Home: 1-5 Naitomachi Shinjuku-ku Tokyo 160-0014 Japan Office Phone: 81-3-5363-3914. Business E-Mail: hsuzuki@a6.keio.jp.

SUZUKI, HIDEO, psychologist; b. Sapporo, Hokkaido, Japan, Aug. 13, 1979; s. Kazuaki and Michiko Suzuki. BA, Vanderbilt U., Nashville, 2002; MA, Loyola U., Chgo., 2005, PhD, 2009. Evaluation intern Chgo. Pub. Schs., 2006; lectr. Loyola U., 2006—08, postdoc. fellow, 2009—10; postdoc. rsch. assoc. Wash. U. Sch. Medicine, 2010—. Contbr. articles to numerous sci. profl. jours. Recipient Rsch. Asst. award, Loyola U., 2006; Travel grant, 2007. Mem.: APA (Washington), Orgn. Human Brain Mapping(Mpls.), Assn. Psychol. Sci. (Washington) (rev. bd. mem. 2006, 2008), Soc. Neurosci. (Washington), Psi Chi (Chattanooga), Phi Beta Delta (Washington). Achievements include research in animal neurobiological studies and human neuroimaging studies in relation to emotional behaviour and stress. Avocations: skiing, art, travel, calligraphy. Home: 3267 January Ave Apt #3 Saint Louis MO 63139

SUZUKI, HIROSHI, medical educator, researcher; b. Tokyo, Japan, July 6, 1962; MD, Showa U. Sch. Medicine, Tokyo, PhD, 1988. Fellow Showa U., Tokyo, 1988—94, 1996—2003, lectr., 2003—07, assoc. prof. Fujigaoka Hosp. Yokohama, Kanagawa, Japan, 2007—; fellow Huntington Med. Rsch. Inst., Pasadena, Calif., 1994—96. Office: Showa Univ Fujigaoka Hosp 1-30 Fujigaoka Aoba-ku Yokohama Kanagawa 227-8501 Japan Office Phone: 81-45-971-1151.

SUZUKI, HITOSHI, biology professor; b. Kakegawa, Shizuoka, Japan, Mar. 5, 1975; PhD, Nara Advanced Inst. Sci. & Tech., Sch. Biol. Sci., 2002. Asst. prof. Japan Advanced Inst. Sci. & Tech., 2006—11. Office: 1-1 Asahidai Nomi Ishikawa 923-1292 Japan Business E-Mail: suzuki-h@jaist.ac.jp.

SUZUKI, HOWARD KAZURO, retired anatomist, educator; b. Ketchikan, Alaska, Apr. 3, 1927; s. Goerge K. and Tsuya S.; m. Tetsuko Fujita, Sept. 12, 1952; children: Georganne, Joan, James, Stanley. BS, Marquette U., 1949, MS, 1951; PhD, Tulane U., 1955. Instr. anatomy Yale U. Sch. Medicine, 1955-58; asst. prof. anatomy U. Ark. Med. Center, Little Rock, 1958-62, asso. prof., 1962-67, prof., 1967-70; prof. anatomy, asso. dean health related professions U. Fla., Gainesville, 1970-71; prof. anatomy U. Fla. (Coll. Medicine), 1970-71; dean U. Fla. (Coll. Health Related Professions), 1971-79; prof. anatomy U. Fla. (Coll. Medicine and Health Related Professions), 1979-90, ret., 1990. Cons. NIH, VA, NASA; vis. research prof. U. Utah Sch. Medicine, 1962 Contbr. articles to profl. jours. Bd. dirs. Civitan Regional Blood Bank, 1977—; regional v.p. Fla. Retarded Citizens Assn., 1974-76; mem. Fla. Adv. Council on Vocat. Edn., 1978-86, chmn., 1981; active United Way. Fellow AAAS; mem. Soc. Exptl. Biol. Medicine, Am Assn. Anatomists, Am. Soc. Allied Health Professions, Am. Soc. Marine Artists, Sigma Xi. Episcopalian. Home: 4331 NW 20th Pl Gainesville FL 32605-3436 E-mail: hksuzuki@aol.com.

SUZUKI, JON BYRON, medical educator, periodontist, microbiologist; s. George K. and Ruby Suzuki. BA in Biology, Ill. Wesleyan U., 1968; PhD in Microbiology magna cum laude, Ill. Inst. Tech., 1971; DDS magna cum laude, Loyola U., 1978; MBA, Katz Grad. Sch. Bus., U. Pitts., 2001. Diplomate Am. Bd. Periodontology; lic. lab. dir. Hawaii Dept. Health. Med. technologist Ill. Masonic Hosp. and Med. Ctr., Chgo., 1966—67; instr. lab. in histology and parasitology Ill. Wesleyan U., Bloomington, 1967—68; med. technologist Augustana Hosp., Chgo., 1968—69; rsch. assoc., instr. microbiology Ill. Inst. Tech., Chgo., 1968—71; clin. rsch. assoc. U, Chgo. Hosps., 1970—71; clin. microbiologist St. Luke's Hosp., Columbia Coll., Physicians and Surgeons, NYC, 1971—73; assoc. med. dir. Paramed Tng. and Registry, Vancouver, BC, Canada, 1973—74; dir. clin. labs. Registry of Hawaii, 1973—74; chmn. clin. labs. edn. Kapiolany C.C., U. Hawaii, Honolulu, 1974; lectr. periodontics, oral pathology Loyola U. Med. Ctr., Maywood, Ill., 1974—90; lectr. stomatology Northwestern U. Dental Sch., Chgo., 1982—90; NIH rsch. fellow depts. pathology and periodontics Ctr. for Rsch. in Oral Biology, U. Wash., Seattle, 1978—80; prof. dept. periodontics and microbiology U. Md. Coll. Dental Surgery, Balt., 1980—90; attending faculty divsn. dentistry and oral and maxillofacial surgery Johns Hopkins Med. Inst., Balt., 1985—96; practice specializing in periodontics Balt. and Pitts.; prof., dean, Sch. Dental Medicine U. Pitts., 1989—2000, prof., dir. periodontics residency program, 2002—04; hosp. chief dentistry UPMC-Presbyn. U. Hosp.; prof., dir. grad. periodontics, assoc. dean, grad. edn. and internat. affairs Grad. Periodontology and Oral Implantology, Temple U., Phila., 2004—. Cons. Dentsply Internat., York, Pa., U.S. Army, Walter Reed Med. Ctr., Washington, U.S. Army, Ft. Gordon, Ga., USN, Nat. Naval Med. Command, Bethesda, The NutraSweet Col, Chgo., FDA, Rockville, Md., 1995—, Phillips Oral Health Care, Snoqualmie, Wash.; oral biology/medicine study sect. NIH, Bethesda, 1985-90; nat. adv. dental rsch. coun. NIH/NIDCR, Bethesda, 1994-98; vis. scientist Moscow State U., USSR, 1972, NASA, Houston, 1976-92; lectr. Internat. Congress allergology, Tokyo, 1973; immediate past-chmn. Food and Drug Adminstrn. Dental Products Panel, Wheaton, Md. Author: Clinical Laboratory Methods for the Medical Assistant, 1974; mem. editl. bd. Jour. Clinical Dentistry, Jour. Practical Hygiene, Jour. Acad. Gen. Dentistry; contbr. articles on rsch. in microbiology, immunology and dentistry to profl. jours. Instr. water safety ARC, Honolulu, 1973—90. Faculty USN, Bethesda, Md. Recipient Pres.'s medallion Loyola U., Chgo., 1977; named Alumnus of Yr., Ill. Wesleyan U., 1977, Loyola U., Chgo., 1997, Faculty of Yr., U. Md.; NIH Immunology fellowship, U. Washington. Fellow Acad. Dentistry Internat., Am. Coll. Dentists, Internat. Coll. Dentists, Am. Coll. Stomatognathic Surgeons; mem. ADA (chair coun. sci. affairs 1998, sci. coun. cons.), AAUP, Am. Acad. Periodontology (diplomate), Am. Dental Edn. Assn., Am. Inst. Biol. Scis., Internat. Soc. Biophysics, Internat. Soc. Endocrinologists, Ill. Acad. Sci., Am. Internat. Assn. Dental Rsch. (pres. Md. chpt.), Am. Coll. Microbiology (diplomate, examiner), Am. Soc. Clin. Pathology (specialist microbiology), N.Y. Acad. Scis., Sigma Xi, Omicron Kappa Upsilon (past nat. pres., exec. sec.-treas., supreme chpt. 1989—, treas. 2006—), Beta Beta Beta. Office: Temple Univ Dentistry Office of the Dean 3223 N Broad St Philadelphia PA 19140 Office Phone: 215-707-7667. Business E-Mail: jon.suzuki@temple.edu. E-mail: jsuzuki@temple.edu.

SUZUKI, KENJI, thoracic surgeon; b. Tokyo, Feb. 10, 1965; s. Toshio and Naoko Suzuki; m. Mayumi Akiyama, Aug. 4, 1991; children: Humino, Yukina, Ayako, Yoko. MD, Nat. Def. Med. Coll., Japan, 1990. Bd. cert. thoracic surgeon. Resident Nat. Def. Med. Coll., Tokorozawa, Saitama, Japan, 1990—92; surgeon Maritime Self-Def. Force Yokosuka (Japan) Hosp., Kanagawa, 1992—95; specialist in diving medicine USN, Groton, Conn., 1993—94; resident in thoracic surgery Nat. Cancer Ctr. Hosp. E., Kashiwa, Chiba, Japan, 1995—99; attending surgeon Nat. Cancer Ctr. Hosp., Chuo-ku, Tokyo, 1999—. Contbr. articles to profl. jours. Lt. j.g. Maritime Self Def. Force,

1990—95, Japan. Recipient Shinoi-Kawai Award, Japan Lung Cancer Assn., 2000. Mem.: Am. Soc. Clin. Oncology. Avocations: kendo, scuba diving. Home: RH102 5-28 Higashigaoka 2 cho-me Tokyo Megoru-ku 152-0021 Japan Office: Nat Cancer Ctr Hosp 1-1 Tsukiji 5-chome Tokyo Chuo-ku 104-0045 Japan Home Phone: +81-3-5430-2586; Office Phone: +81-3-3542-2511. Office Fax: +81-3-3542-3815. E-mail: kjsuzuki@ncc.go.jp.

SUZUKI, KUNIHIKO, biomedical educator, researcher; b. Tokyo, Feb. 5, 1932; arrived in U.S., 1960; s. Nobuo and Teiko (Suzuki) Suzuki; m. Kinuko Ikeda, Dec. 20, 1960; 1 child, Jun. BA in History and Philosophy of Sci., Tokyo U., 1955, MD, 1959; MA (hon.), U. Pa., 1971. Diplomate Nat. Bd. Med. Licensure Japan. Rotating intern USAF Hosp. Tachikawa, Tokyo, 1959-60; asst. resident in neurology Bronx (N.Y.) Mcpl. Hosp. Ctr.-Albert Einstein Coll. Medicine, 1960-61, resident in neurology, 1961-62, clin. fellow in neurology, 1962-64; instr. in neurology Albert Einstein Coll. Medicine, Bronx, 1964, asst. prof., 1965-68; assoc. prof. U. Pa. Sch. Medicine, Phila., 1969-71, prof. neurology and pediatrics, 1971-72; prof. neurology Albert Einstein Coll. Medicine, 1972-86, prof. neurosci., 1974-86; prof. neurology and psychiatry, faculty curriculum in neurobiology U. N.C. Sch. Medicine, Chapel Hill, 1986—2002, prof. emeritus neurology and psychiatry, 2002—; dir. UNC Neurosci. Ctr., Chapel Hill, 1986-99, dir. emeritus, 1999—; prof. Future Sci. and Tech. Joint Rsch. Ctr. Tokai U., Japan, 2003—, dir. Inst. Glycotechnology, 2003—. Staff dept. neuropsychiatry Tokyo U. Faculty Medicine, 1960, U. Pa. Inst. Neurol. Scis., 1969—72; attending physician Bronx Mcpl. Hosp. Ctr., 1976—86, Hosp. Albert Einstein Coll. Medicine, 1977—86; vis. prof. fellowship Japan Soc. for Promotion Sci., 1980, Yamada Sci. Found., 1981; mem. neurology B study sect. NIH, 1971—75, guest scientist, 1984—85, program com. mental retardation and devel. disabilities, 1989—92; mem. basic neurosci. task force Nat. Inst. Neurol. and Communicative Disorders and Stroke, 1978, adv. panel directions and opportunities for future rsch., 83; bd. sci. counselors NIH, 1980—84; mem. adv. com. on fellowships Nat. Multiple Sclerosis Soc., 1974—77; jury St. Vincent Internat. award for Med. Sci., 1979; mem. adv. com. Eunice Kennedy Shriver Ctr., Waltham, Mass., 1974—84; mem. U.S. Nat. Com. for Internat. Brain Rsch. Orgn., 1985—89. Editor: Ganglioside Structure and Function, 1984; editor: (chief) Jour. Neurochemistry, 1977—82; dep. chief editor Jour. Neurochemistry, 1975—77, mem. editl. bd. Jour. Neuropathology and Exptl. Neurology, 1981—83, Neurosci., 1975—, Molecular Chem. Neuropathology, 1983—, Neurochem. Rsch., 1985—89, Metabolic Brain Disease, 1985—87, Molecular Brain Rsch., 1985—, Jour. Molecular Neurosci., 1987—, Devel. Neurosci., 1987—, Jour. Neurosci. Rsch., 1993—97; contbr. Mem. Nat. Adv. Commn. on Multiple Sclerosis, 1973—74; mem. med. adv. bd. United Leukodystrophy Found., 1982—86, 1997—, Nat. Tay-Sachs and Allied Diseases Assn., 1971—2001, Canavan Found., 1992—. Recipient A. Weil award, Am. Assn. Neuropathologists, 1970, Saul R. Korey Lecturship, 1993, M. Moore award, 1975, Jacob K. Javits Neurosci. Investigator award, NIH, 1985, 1992, Humboldt Sr. Rsch. award, Humboldt Found., 1990, Eminent Scientist award, Inst. Phys. Chem. Rsch., Japan, 1995, Japan Acad. prize, 2002. Mem.: AAAS, Japan Soc. Inherited Metabolic Disease (hon.), Am. Soc. Human Genetics, Internat. Brain Rsch. Orgn., Japanese Neurochem. Soc., Japanese Med. Soc. Am. (Disting. Scientist award 1985), Am. Acad. Neurology, Am. Soc. Biochemistry and Molecular Biology, Soc. for Neurosci., Internat. Soc. for Neurochemistry (coun. 1987—89, treas. 1989—93, pres. 1993—95), Am. Soc. for Neurochemistry (pres. 1985—87, coun. 1973—77, 1987—91, Basic Neurochemistry Lectureship 1995), Inst. Medicine NAS. Avocations: piano, photography, birdwatching, skiing.

SUZUKI, MAKOTO, cardiologist; b. Ehime, Japan, Jan. 7, 1964; s. Miyoko Suzuki; m. Mayumi Murakami; children: Haruka, Yuya. MD, Ehime U. Sch. Medicine, 1994. Asst. prof. 2d dept. internal medicine Ehime U., Japan, 1998—2000; dir. cardiology Ehime Prefectural Ctrl. Hosp., Matsuyama, 2000—10; assoc. prof. dept. cmty. emergency medicine Ehime U. Grad. Sch. Medicine, 2010—. Office: Dept Cmty Emergency Medicine Toon Ehime 791=0295 Japan Office Phone: 81 89 960 5525. Home Fax: 81 89 975 6164. Business E-Mail: suzuki-m@mail.netwave.or.jp.

SUZUKI, MASANORI, biologist, educator; b. Miyazaki, Japan, Feb. 7, 1948; BS in Agrl. Scis., Hokkaido U., Sapporo, Japan, 1970, MS in Agrl. Scis., 1972, PhD in Pharmacology, 1975. Postdoctoral fellow Calif. Inst. Tech., Pasadena, 1975—77, Cornell U., Ithaca, NY, 1977—78; postdoc fellow City of Hope Nat. Med. Ctr., Duarte, Calif., 1978—79; chief rschr. ctrl. rsch. lab. Wakunaga Pharm. Co. Ltd., Koda-Cho, Japan, 1978—85; chief rschr., head genetic engring. group lab. basic rsch. Tonen Corp., Iruma-Gun, Japan, 1985—90, prin. rschr., head genetic and protein engring. group lab. basic rsch., 1991—93; head lab. biorefining process lab. basic rsch. lab. Petroleum Energy Ctr., Shimizu, Japan, 1993—99; sr. scientist Genomic Scis. Ctr. Inst. Phys. and Chem. Rsch., Yokohama, Japan, 2000—05; team leader Gene Transcriptional Regulation Rsch. Team, 2005—08; unit leader Omics Regulation Rsch. Unit, 2008—. Adj. instr. grad. sch. agrl. scis. Hiroshima U., Fukuyama, Japan, 1984—85; vis. assoc. prof. Grad. Sch. Nanosci., dept. supramolecular biology Yokohama City U., Japan, 2001—. Author: (book) Challenges of Biotechnology, 1982. Achievements include patents for peptidyl cis-trans isomerase; thermophilic biodesulfurization. Office: Riken 1-7-22 Suehiro-Cho Tsurumi-Ku Yokohama 230-0045 Japan Kanagawa Office Fax: 81-045-508-7370. Business E-Mail: msuzuki@gsc.riken.jp, msuzuki@tsurumi.yokohama-cu.ac.jp.

SUZUKI, NORIHIRO, neurologist; b. Tokyo, Dec. 16, 1952; s. Tadao and Sumiko (Kajitani) S.; m. Hiroko Furukawa, Mar. 31, 1979; 1 child, Shota. MD, Keio U., 1977, DMSc, 1981; PhD, Lund U., 1989. Instr. medicine Keio U. Hosp., Tokyo, 1981—82, 1982—86, Tokyo, 1989—91; vice dir. neurology Shizuoka Red Cross Hosp., Japan, 1982; rsch. fellow neurobiology U. Lund, Sweden, 1986—89; dir. medicine and neurology Mito Red Cross Hosp., Japan, 1991—98. Asst. prof. medicine Keio U., 1992—, Tsukuba (Japan) U., 1993-98; v.p. Mito (Japan) Red Cross Hosp., 1997-98; asst. prof. medicine Kitasato U., Kanagawa, 1998-99, assoc. prof., 1999-2003, prof., 2003-04; prof. medicine Keio U. 2004—, v.p. Keio U. Hosp. 2007-09. Contbr. articles and procs. to profl. jours. Fellow ACP, Japanese Soc. Internal Medicine; mem. Internat. Soc. Cerebral Blood Flow and Metabolism, World Fedn. Neurology, Internat. Neurology, Internat. Soc. Stroke, Internat. Headache Soc., Japanese Mozart Soc., Japanese Flute Soc., Japan-Sweden Soc., Japan-Sweden Sci. Club. Avocations: playing the flute, research on mozart's music. Home: 7-23-8 Higashi Rinkan Minami-ku Sagamihara Kanagawa 252-0311 Japan Office: Dept Neurology Sch Med Keio Univ 35 Shinanomachi Shinjuku ku Tokyo 160 8582 Japan Business E-Mail: nrsuzuki@sc.itc.keio.ac.jp.

SUZUKI, NORIYASU, physician, psychologist, journalist; b. Sanjo, Niigataken, Japan, Oct. 20, 1947; s. Souroku and Haru Suzuki. Degree in physics, Nihon U.; degree in journalism, Tokyo U. With USHHSC, San Chico, Japan; mathematician Army Coll. U. Home: 1-7-4 Cinema House Sanchiku Sanjo 955-0041 Japan Office: 1-7-6 USHHSC San Chico Santo Niigata Japan

SUZUKI, SHIGENORI, medical educator; b. Sapporo, Japan, July 17, 1936; m. Shigenori Suzuki. MD, PhD, Hokkaido U., Japan, 1968. Lic. physician Health Ministry, Japan, 1964. Prof. Coll. of Med. Tech. Hokkaido (Japan) U., Sapporo, Japan, 1983—2000; prof. Grad. Sch. Human Svcs. Hokusho U., Ebetsu-City, Japan, 2004—. Grantee, Ednl. Ministry Japan, 1979, 1980, 1983, 1986, 1987, 1990, 1991, 1992, 1993, 1994, 1995, 1995, 1996. Mem.: Japanese German Soc. (dir. Japanese chpt. 2004—). Home: Kita21-jo Nishi7-chome 2-17 Sapporo Hokkaido 001-0021 Japan Office: Hokusho Univ Bunkyodai 23 Hokkaido 069-8511 Japan Ebetsu Office Fax: 0081-11-387-3640; Home Fax: 0081-11-728-6144. Personal E-mail: 10toh.s@sapporo.email.ne.jp.

SUZUKI, TORU, cardiologist, educator; b. Kamakura, Kanagawa, Japan, May 12, 1967; married. MD, PhD, U. Tokyo, 1992. Resident dept. cardiology Sakakibara Heart Inst., Tokyo; intern dept. internal medicine U. Tokyo, instr. cardiovascular medicine, instr. dept. clin. bioinformatics, assoc. prof. dept. ubiquitous preventitive medicine. Recipient Young Investigator award, Am. Heart Assn., 1995, IFCC/AVL award, Internat. Fedn. of Clin. Chemistry, 1996. Achievements include research in in biomedical clinical and basic research; biochemical diagnosis of aortic dissection. Office: U Tokyo Dept Ubiquitous Preventitive Medicine 7-3-1 Hongo Bunkyo 113-8655 Japan Office Phone: 81-3-5800-9846. Business E Mail: torusuzu tky@umin.ac.jp.

SUZUKI, YOSHIHISA, engineering educator; b. Miyagi, Japan, Jan. 20, 1970; PhD, Tohoku U., 1997. Assoc. prof. U. Tokushima, 2000. Avocations: swimming, woodworking. Office: 2-1 Minamijosanjima Tokushima 770-8506 Japan Office Fax: 81-88-655-7025. Business E-Mail: suzuki@chem.tokushima-u.ac.jp.

SUZUKI, YOSHIO, pharmaceutical executive, educator; b. Tokyo, June 23, 1962; B in Agrl. Chemistry, U. Tokyo, 1985, PhD, 2003; M in Med. Sci. Rsch., Osaka U., Japan, 1991. Cert. Profl. Engr., Ministry Edn., Culture, Sports, Sci., Tech., Japan; Nutrition Rep. Nat. Inst. Health and Nutrition, Japan. Mgr. Nisshin Flour Milling Co. Ltd., Chiyoda, Japan, 1985—2001, Nisshin Pharma Inc., Chiyoda, 2001 . Vis assoc prof. Juntendo U., 2007—. Reviewer Jour. Agrl. Food Chemistry, Am. Chem. Soc., 2001—. Mem.: Japan Health Food and Nutrition Food Assn. Achievements include development of enteral nutrition, functional food and ingredients. Office: Nisshin Pharma Inc Kanda-Nishiki cho 1 25 Chiyoda Tokyo 101 8441 Japan Office Fax: 81-3-5282-6151. Business E-Mail: suzukiyo@mail.ni-net.co.jp.

SVABE, VIJA, medical educator; b. Riga, Latvia, June 15, 1943; MD, Riga Stradins U., 1985. Asst. prof. Riga Stradins U., 1993 . Mem.: Latvian Pediatrician Allergologists & Pneumonologists Assn., Latvian Pneumonologists Assn., Latvian Pediatricians Assn., ECFS, ERS. Home: Dzirnavu 31 - 41 Riga LV 1010 Latvia Home Fax: 37167622791. Personal E-mail: vija.svabe@rsu.lv.

SVARDSUDD, KURT FOLKE, internist, educator; b. Pitea, Sweden, Sept. 7, 1942; s. Ernst Folke and Karin Cecilia (Lundmark) S.; m. Gudrun Katharina Elisabeth Sundberg, Oct. 16, 1965; children: Charlotte, Ulf, Mats. MB, Göteborg U., Gothenburg, Sweden, 1964; MD, Umea U., Sweden, 1968; PhD, Göteborg U., Gothenburg, Sweden, 1978. Intern, resident, Boden, Sweden, 1968-80; intern Gothenburg, 1968—80; rsch. assoc. U. Minn., 1980-81; lectr. internal medicine Göteburg U., Gothenburg, Sweden, 1982-87; lectr. family medicine Uppsala U., 1987-90, prof. epidemiology, 1990-95, prof., chmn. dept. family medicine, 1995-97, chmn. dept. pub. health, caring scis., 1998—2002, chmn. family medicine, clin. epidemiology, 2002—. Contbr. more than 350 sci. papers internat. jours. Med. capt. Swedish Army, 1970—89. Rsch. grantee various orgns., 1980—. Fellow Swedish Med. Soc. (bd. dirs. 1995-97), Swedish Med. Assn.; mem. Swedish Epidemiology Assn. (chmn. 1993-95), Internat. Soc. and Fedn. Cardiology. Avocation: sailing. Home: Kronparksv 5 S 75752 Uppsala Sweden Home Phone: 46 18 421814; Office Phone: +46 708 574 395. E-mail: kurt.svardsudd@pubcare.uu.se.

SVARTENGREN, MAGNUS ULF, physician; b. Stockholm, Aug. 12, 1957; s. Tage Ingemar and Aina Ragnhild (Lilja) S.; m. Katharina Birgitta Ohman, May 21, 1983. MB, Karolinska Inst., Stockholm, 1978, MD, 1983, PhD, 1986. Rsch. asst. Karolinska Inst., 1978, rschr., 1979-86, asst. prof., 1986-89, assoc. prof., 1989, sr. lectr., 1989, qualified specialist occupl. & environ. medicine, 1995; expert in environ. medicine Swedish Nat. Bd. Health and Welfare. Mem. Internat. Soc. Aerosol Medicine (bd. dirs.), Swedish Twin Registry (bd. mem. steering com.). Avocations: art, music, long distance running, computers. Office: Dept Pub Health Scis Karolinska Inst Norrbacka S-1776 Stockholm Sweden

SVEDRUZIC, ZELJKO MIJO, biochemist; b. Croatia, Mar. 16, 1969; Diploma in Natural Scis., U. Zagreb, 1993; PhD in Biochemistry, Okla. State U., 1998. Lab leader faculty medicine U. Rijeka, 2010. Office: Dept Med Biochemistry Faculty Med Rab 51208 Croatia Business E-Mail: zeljko@wsu.edu.

SVEHLAK, STEVEN ANDREW, plastic surgeon; b. Derby, Conn., Oct. 14, 1966; BS in Biology, U. Conn., Storrs, Conn.; MD, NY Med. Coll., Valhalla NY, 1994. Cert. Am. Bd. Surgery, 2001, Am. Bd. Plastic Surgery, 2003, lic. Calif. Bd. Medicine, DC Bd. Medicine. Surg. intern, gen. surgery Stamford Hosp., Columbia U. Coll. Physicians and Surgeons, Stamford, Conn., 1994—99; resident, gen. surgery Columbia Presbyn. Med. Ctr. Program in Surgery, Stamford, Conn.; resident, plastic surgery George Wash. U. Med. Ctr., Washington, 1999—2001, fellow, plastic surgery, 2001, Children's Nat. Med. Ctr., Washington; hosp. appt. plastic surgery Midway Hosp., West LA, Calif., Cedars Sinai Hosp., LA; advanced cosmetic surgery tng. fellowship Dr. Richard Ellenbogen, Beverly Hills, Calif., 2002; plastic surgeon Sunset Cosmetic Surgery, LA. Lectr. and presenter in field. Contbr. articles to profl. jours.; featured on Dr. 90210. Fellow: Am. Coll. Surgeons; mem.: AMA, Calif. Med. Assn., Am. Soc. Plastic Surgeons (candidate assoc.), Northeastern Soc. Plastic Surgery. Office: Sunset Cosmetic Surgery 9201 Sunset Blvd Ste 805 Los Angeles CA 90069 Office Phone: 310-858-9100. E-mail: drssvehlak@yahoo.com.

SVENSSON, CRAIG KARL, pharmaceutical sciences educator, dean; b. Balt., Feb. 6, 1957; s. Emil Leonard and Teresa Jane (Nugent) Svensson; m. Susan Jane Morey, July 7, 1984; children: Kate Marie, Eric David. BS, U. Md. Sch. Pharmacy, 1979, PharmD, 1981; PhD, SUNY, Buffalo, 1984. Poison info. specialist Md. Poison Ctr., U. Md., 1979—81; cons. clin. pharmacokinetics lab. Buffalo Gen. Hosp., 1981—82; postdoc. fellow dept. pharmaceutics SUNY, Buffalo, 1984-85; asst. prof. dept. pharm. scis. Wayne State U. Coll. Pharmacy, Detroit, 1985-91, assoc. prof., 1991—98, prof., 1998—2003, assoc. chmn. dept. pharm. scis., 1999—2003; Lynn & Sharon Bighley prof. pharm. scis. U. Iowa Coll. Pharmacy, Coralville, 2003—06, head divsn. pharmaceutics, 2003—06; prof. medicinal chemistry/molecular pharmacology Purdue U. Coll. Pharmacy, Nursing & Health Scis., West Lafayette, Ind., 2006—, dean, 2006—. Mem. Barbara Ann Karmanos Cancer Inst., Wayne State U., 1992—2003; mem. exec. coun., adv. coun. U. Iowa Coll. Pharmacy, 2003—06; cons. Warner Lambert/Parke-Davis, Ann Arbor, Mich., Pyro Pharm., Inc., Costa Mesa, Calif., 2001, Oxford Biomed. Rsch., Mich., 2002, Pfizer Global Rsch. & Devel., 2004. Rep. US Pharmacopeial Conv., 1996—2003. Recipient Meritorious Rsch. award, Am. Fedn. Clin. Rsch., 1982, James A. Shannon Dir.'s award, NIH, 1992; named Tchr. of Yr., Wayne State U. Coll. Pharmacy, 2003, U. Iowa Coll. Pharmacy, 2005. Mem.: AAAS, Soc. Toxicology, Soc. Investigative Dermatology, Internat. Soc. Study of Xenobiotics, Am. Soc. Pharmacology & Experimental Therapeutics (sec.-treas. drug metabolism divsn. 2003—06), Am. Assn. Colleges of Pharmacy, Am. Assn. Pharmaceutical Scientists, Rho Chi. Office: Purdue U Heine Pharmacy Bldg Rm RHPH 108 575 Stadium Mall Dr West Lafayette IN 47907 Office Phone: 765-494-1368. Office Fax: 765-494-7880. Business E-Mail: svensson@purdue.edu.

SVENTEK, JEFF, medical association administrator, retired military officer; MS, Rutgers U., NJ, 1985. Cert. in aerospace physiology. Officer through the grades to col. USAF, 1978—2006, aerospace physiologist holding various operational and staff positions of increasing responsibility, 1985—96, chief aerospace physiology, 1996—99, squadron & group comdr., chief biomed. sciences corps, 1999—2006, ret., 2006; def. contractor for USAF and Dept. Def. med. ops., 2006—09, exec. dir. Aerospace Med Assn., 2010—. Mem.: Aerospace Physiology Soc. (former pres.), Aerospace Med. Assn. Office: Aerospace Med Assn 320 S Henry St Alexandria VA 22314-3579 Office Phone: 703-739-2240 ext. 105. Office Fax: 703-739-9652. Business E-Mail: jsventek@asma.org. *

SVERZICKIS, RODRIGO, neurosurgeon; b. Riga, Latvia, Aug. 13, 1970; m. Evita Sverzicka, Aug. 8, 2008. MD, Latvian Med. Acad., Riga, 1994; PhD, U. Latvia, Riga, 2008. Registered neurosurgeon Latvian Neurosurgical Soc., 2000. Neurosurgeon P. Stradins Clin. U. Hosp., Riga. Contbr. articles. Mem.: World Fedn. Neurol. Soc., European Assn. Neurol. Soc., Latvian Neurosurgical Soc. Lutheran. Achievements include research in PhD, Treatment effectiveness of brain astrocytomas and metastases by neuronavigation. Office: P Stradins Clin Univ Hosp Pilsonu 13 Riga LV 1002 Latvia Office Phone: 37167069230. Business E-Mail: sverzickis@gmail.com.

SVETKEY, LAURA PAT, nephrologist; b. Carlisle, Pa., Sept. 19, 1951; d. Edward Robert and Marcia Tuchman (Wallace) S.; m. Charles Michael van der Horst, May 17, 1980; children: Anna Svetkey. Student, Barnard Coll., 1969-70; BA, Sarah Lawrence Coll., 1974; MD, Harvard U., 1979; postgrad., Duke U., 1988—. Diplomate Nat. Bd. Internal Medicine, Am. Bd. Internal Medicine; lic. physician, N.C., N.Y. Intern internal medicine Montefiore Hosp. and Med. Ctr., Bronx, NY, 1979-80, resident, 1980-82; fellow divsn. gen. internal medicine Duke U. Med. Ctr., Durham, NC, 1982-83, assoc. medicine divsns. nephrology & gen. internal medicine, 1983-86, co-dir., dir. Duke Hypertension Ctr., 1985—, asst. prof. medicine divsn. nephrology, 1986-93, sr. fellow Ctr. for Study Aging and Human Devel., 1990—, assoc. prof., 1994—, mem. Stedman Nutriton Ctr., 1992—; staff physician dept. medicine Lincoln Community Health Ctr., Durham, NC, 1983-84. Cons. NC Commr. Agr.; ad hoc rev. com. NIDDK, NIH, 1990; adv. com. on status of women dept. medicine Duke U. Med. Ctr., 1987—; mem. spl. emphasis panel NHLBI, NIH, 1993; instr., moderator, speaker, presenter various organizations, 1984-93. Contbr. articles to profl. jours., chpts. to books. Mem. Am. Soc. Hypertension, Am. Soc. Nephrology, Internat. Soc. Hypertension in Blacks, Am. Heart Assn. (Kidney Coun.). Office: Duke U Med Ctr PO Box 3075 Durham NC 27715-3075 Office Phone: 919-419-5840, 919-668-7630. Office Fax: 919-419-5841. E-mail: svetk001@mc.duke.edu.

SVINTRADZE, DAVID V., research scientist; b. Tbilisi, Georgia, Nov. 14, 1981; s. Vasili O. Svintradze and Darejan V. Apridonidze; life ptnr. Diploma in Biophysics, Georgian Acad. Scis., 2002; diploma in Physics, G. Soros Found. Young Scientists, 2002, diploma in Physics, 2003, Tbilisi State U., 2002, PhD, 2006; attended in Phys. & Math. Scis., El Andronikashvili Inst. Physics, 2006. Rschr. Tbilisi State U., Faculty Exact and Natural Scis., 2005—07; prin. investigator, dept. gen. chemistry N. Copernicus U., Torun, Poland, 2006; invited lectr., dept. physics II. Chavchavadze State U., Tbilisi, 2007; rsch. assoc. Va. Commonwealth U., Dept. of Mech. Engring., Richmond, 2007—08; postdoc. fellow Va. Commonwealth U. OCMB Philips Inst., Richmond, 2008—. Mem. Biophys. Soc., 2006—. Contbr. articles to sci. jours. Recipient Internat. Travel award, Biophys. Soc., 2006, 2008; scholarship, Pres. Ga., 2005—06, Collaborative Linkage grant, NATO, 2006—08. Mem.: Am. Chem. Soc. Achievements include first to make molecular model of Collagen-DNA/siRNA complexes; development of topological similarities of gene delivery systems, application to gene therapy; hypothetic non-equilibrium systems and entropy; biomacromolecular topology and geometry of hydrogen bonds in water mechanism of self assembly of biomacromolecules; equation of conformational motion fundamental principals of energetic fluctuations in non equilibrium systems; time profile of entropy in non equilibrium systems; modification of fundamental principals of classical physics; theory of conformational motion; description of hydrophobic and hydrophilic interactions. Office: VA Commonwealth Univ OCMB Philips Inst, Schl Dentistry 521 N 11th St Richmond VA 23298-0566 Home: 4600 Forest Hill Ave Richmond VA 23225 Business E-Mail: dsvintradze@vcu.edu.

SVOBODA, JAN, cell and microbiology scientist, educator; b. Prague, Czech Republic, Aug. 14, 1934; s. Karel and Antonie (Kojzarová) S.; m. Ingrid Gröhe, Oct. 27, 1962; children: Jan, Václav. MS, Charles U., Prague, 1957; PhD, Inst. Exptl. Biol. Genetics, Prague, 1960, DS, 1966; prof., Charles U. Rsch. scientist Inst. Exptl. Biol. Genetics, Acad. Sci. Czech Republic, Prague, 1957—76, Inst. Molecular Genetics, Prague, 1976—, dir., 1991—99. Rschr. ITCC, ICRETT Project, Geneva, 1976—; mem. adv. coun., GM Cancer Rsch. Found. Co-author: (chpts.) Advances in Cancer Research, 1970, 2003, 2008, Portraits of Viruses, 1988. Mem. Club Friends of Nature, 1995—. Am. Cancer Soc. fellow, 1993-94; recipient Jane Coffin Child Meml. award, 1967. Mem. Am. Assn. Cancer Rsch., Internat. Assn. Comparative Rsch. Leukemia and Related Diseases, European Molecular Biology Orgn. Avocation: nature preservation. Office: Inst Molecular Genetics Acad Scis Czech Republic Videnvská 1083 142 20 Prague 4 Czech Republic Home: Rozvojovß 250/12 165 00 Prague 6 Czech Republic Business E-Mail: svoboda@img.cas.cz.

SWAIM, JOHN FRANKLIN, physician, health care executive; b. Bloomingdale, Ind., Dec. 24, 1935; s. Max DeBaun and Edna Marie (Whitely) S.; m. Joan Dooley, Sept. 19, 1957 (div. Apr. 1979); children: John Franklin, Parke Allen, Pamela Ann; m. Peggy Lou Sankey, May 30, 1979; one child, Anne-Marie. BS cum laude, Ind. State U., 1959; MD, Ind. U., Indpls., 1963. Diplomate Am. Bd. Family Practice with added cert. in geriatrics; Lic. Health Facility Admin. Med. dir. Newport (Ind.) Chem. Depot, 1968—, Parke Clinic, Rockville, Ind., 1969—, Rockville Correctional Facility, 1970—98; pres. Swaim Investment Corp., 2001—, Parke Investments Inc., Rockville, 1972—, Vermillion Health Care Corp., Clinton, Ind., 1977—2003, Parke County Coroner, 1980, Swaim Farm Corp., 1998—, Parke County Health Officer, 1999—. Med. dir. Lee Alan Bryant Health Facility, 1980-, Parke County Jail and Vermillion County Jail, 1990-2000. Author: One Year and Eternity, 1978; contbr. articles to profl. jours. Coroner, Parke County, Ind., 1972-82. Capt. USAF, 1963-67, Vietnam. Decorated Bronze Star. Mem. Am. Acad. Family Physicians, AMA, Ind. Med. Assn. (dist. pres. 1986—), Hoosiers Assocs. Club, Elks, Masons, Shriners. Republican. Avocation: reading and investing. Home and Office: Parke Clinic PO Box 185 Rockville IN 47872-0185 Office Phone: 765-569-3182.

SWAIM, MARK WENDELL, physician, molecular biologist, hepatologist, essayist, gastroenterologist, photographer; b. Winston-Salem, NC, Dec. 4, 1960; s. Donnie Lee and Bernice Earline (Brown) S. BA summa cum laude, U. N.C., 1983; MD, Duke U., 1990, PhD with honors, 1990. Diplomate Am. Bd. Internal Medicine, Am. Bd. Gastroenterology and Hepatology. Resident dept. medicine Duke U. Med. Ctr., Durham, NC, 1990-93; postdoc. fellow, dept. pharmacology Nat. Taiwan U., Taipei, 1992; fellow gastroenterology Duke U. Med. Ctr., Durham, NC, 1993-97, clin. med. instr., 1994-2000, fellow in advanced hepatology and transplant hepatology, 1997-98, attending physician, 1998-2000, Durham VA Med. Ctr., 1998-2000; asst. prof. medicine Gastrointestinal Ctr., U. Tex.-M.D. Anderson Cancer Ctr., Houston, 2000—02; dir., prin. investigator, med. dir. Regional Rsch. Inst., Jackson, Tenn., 2002—; founder Southeastern Liver Inst., Jackson, 2002—; hepatologist, gastroenterologist Ctr. Liver Diseases, Laurea McKennan U. Med. Ctr., Sioux Falls, SD, 2009. Assoc. dept. medicine Duke U., 1998-2000; instr. clin. medicine Duke U. Sch. Medicine, 1994-2000, mem. admissions com.; instr. U. Tenn. Sch. Medicine, 2004—; asst. prof. medicine Gastrointestinal Ctr., U. Tex. M.D. Anderson Cancer Ctr., Houston; vis. med. resident Nat. Taiwan U., Taipei, 1991, 92; vis. physician Saratov (Russia) Med. U., 1995; faculty senator U. Tex. M.D. Anderson Cancer Ctr., 2000-02; book rev. panelist The Pharos of Alpha Omega Alpha; cons. physician Al-Jazeira Hosp., Abu Dhabi, United Arab Emirates; mem. med. adv. bd. Axium Pharms., Inc.; cons. Intermune Pharms, Forest Pharms., Three River Pharms., Coley Pharms. Axcan Pharms. Contbr. articles to profl. jours., Ency. Brit. Great Ideas Today, 1996; photography pub. in Am. Photo. Advisor. Protech Pharma Svcs. Corp., Paipei, Taiwan. Recipient Brody award for history of medicine, 1998, Davison award for tchg. excellence, 2000; NIH Med. Sci. Tng. Program fellow, 1983-90, numerous acad. scholarships and grants. Fellow: ACP (winner assocs. competition 1994), Am. Coll. Forensic Examiners; mem.: Internat. Liver Cancer Assn., European Assn. for Study of Liver, Houston Acad. Medicine, Tex. Med. Assn., Am. Liver Found. (bd. dirs. Tex. chpt.), Engel Soc., Reticuloendothelial Soc., Am. Assn. for Study Liver Diseases, Am. Soc. for Gastrointestinal Endoscopy, Am. Coll. Gastroenterology, Sigma Pi Sigma, Phi Lambda Upsilon, Sigma Xi, Phi Beta Kappa, Alpha Omega Alpha (pres. Duke chpt. 1989). Avocations: photography, chamber music, writing, travel. Home: 61 Valley Oak Loop Jackson TN 38305 Office: 45 Physicians Dr Jackson TN 38305 Personal E-mail: markswaim@msn.com. *

SWAIMAN, KENNETH FRED, pediatric neurologist, educator; b. St. Paul, Nov. 19, 1931; s. Lester J. and Shirley (Ryan) S.; m. Phyllis Kammerman Sher, Oct. 1985; children: Lisa, Jerrold, Barbara, Dana. BA magna cum laude, U. Minn., 1952, BS, 1953, MD, 1955; postgrad., 1956-58. Diplomate Am. Bd. Psychiatry and Neurology, Am. Bd. Pediatrics, Am. Bd. Psychiatry and Neurology with Spl. Competence in Child Neurology. Intern Mpls. Gen. Hosp., 1955-56; resident in pediatrics, fellow in pediatrics to chief resident U. Minn. Hosp., 1956-58, spl. fellow in pediatric neurology, 1960-63, dir. pediatric neurology tng. program, 1968-94, various to interim head dept. neurology, 1994-96; chief pediatrics U.S. Army Hosp., Ft. McPherson, Ga., 1958-60; asst. prof. pediatrics, neurology U. Minn. Med. Sch., Mpls., 1963-66, prof., dir. pediatric neurology, 1969-96, mem. internship adv. coun. exec. faculty, 1966-70, interim head dept. neurology, 1994-96; postgrad. fellow pediatric neurology Nat. Inst. Neurologic Diseases and Blindness, 1960-63, assoc. prof., 1966-69. Cons. pediatric neurology Hennepin County Gen. Hosp., 1963—, Mpls., St. Paul-Ramsey Hosp., St. Paul Children's Hosp., Mpls. Children's Hosp.; vis. prof. numerous univs. including Loyola U., 1982, U. N.Mex., 1982, U. Ind. Med. Sch., 1983, U. Kyushu, Shiga, Nagoya, Tokyo, 1985, Driscoll Children's Hosp., Corpus Christi, Tex., 1986, Inst. Nacional de Pediatria, Mexico City, 1986, U. de Concepion, Chile, 1989, Beijing U. Med. Sch., 1989, Xian Med. U., China, 1989, Children's Hosp. of Mich., Detroit, 1990, Hong Kong Child Neurology Soc., 1995, Tartu, Estonia, 1997, Krem, Austria, 1997, Santiago, Chile, 1997, Kaunas, Lithuania, 1998, ICNA Ednl. Seminar, Tartu, 1998, Montevideo, Uruguay, 1999, others; lectr. in field; guest worker NIH, NICHD, Bethesda, Md., 1978-79, 79-81. Author: (with Francis S. Wright) Neuromuscular Diseases in Infancy and Childhood, 1969, Pediatric Neuromuscular Diseases, 1979, (with Stephen Ashwal) Pediatric Neurology Case Studies, 1978, 2d edit., 1984, Pediatric Neurology: Principles and Practice, 1989, 4th edit., 2006; editor: (with John A. Anderson) Phenylketonuria and Allied Metabolic Diseases, 1966, (with Francis S. Wright) Practice Pediatric Neurology, 1975, 2d edit., 1982, Pediatric Neurology: Principles and Practice, 4th edit., 2006; mem. editl. bd. Annals of Neurology, 1977-83, Neurology Update, 1977-82, Pediatric Update, 1977-85, Brain and Devel. (Jour. Japanese Soc. Child Neurology), 1980—, Neuropediatrics (Stuttgart), 1982-92, Chinese Jour. Pediat., 2009; editor-in-chief: Pediatric Neurology, 1984—; contbr. articles to sci. jours. Chmn. Minn. Gov.'s Bd. for Handicapped, Exceptional and Gifted Children, 1972-76; mem. human devel. study sect. NIH, 1976-79, guest worker, 1978-81. Served to capt. M.C. U.S. Army, 1958-60. Recipient Hon. award, Ann. Child Neurology Found., 2009. Fellow Am. Acad. Pediatrics, Am. Acad. Neurology (rep. to nat. coun. Nat. Soc. Med. Rsch., A.B. Baker Neurol. Edn. Lifetime Achievement award 2005); mem. Soc. Pediatric Rsch., Ctrl. Soc. Clin. Rsch., Ctrl. Soc. Neurol. Rsch., Internat. Soc. Neurochemistry, Am. Neurol. Assn., Minn. Neurol. Soc., AAAS, Midwest Pediatric Soc., Am. Soc. Neurochemistry, Child Neurology Soc. (1st pres. 1972-73, Hower award 1981, Founder's award 1996, chmn. internat. affairs com., 1991-96, mem. long range planning com. 1991-97, chmn. fin. com. 1995—), Internat. Assn. Child Neurologists (exec. com. 1975-79, chmn. global edn. com. 1996-99), Profs. of Child Neurology (1st pres. 1978-80, mem. nominating com. 1986-92), Japanese Child Neurology Soc. (Segawa award 1986, mem. nominating com. 1986-92, chair internat. affairs com. 1991—, mem. long range planning com. 1991-98), Soc. de Psiquiatria y Neurologia de la Infancia y Adolescencia, Internat. Child Neurology Assn. (chair internat. edn. com. 1996-99), Lithuanian Child Neurology Soc. (hon., mem. 2000—), Child Neurology Found. (pres. 2000-03), Phi Beta Kappa, Sigma Xi. Office: Pediatric Neurology 1821 University Ave W Saint Paul MN 55104-2801 Business E-Mail: swaim001@umn.edu. E-mail: pncomm@qwestoffice.net.

SWAIN, JUDITH LEA, cardiologist, educator; b. Long Beach, Calif., Sept. 24, 1948; m. Edward W. Holmes. BS in Chemistry with deptl. honors, UCLA, 1970; MD, U. Calif., San Diego, 1974. Diplomate Am. Bd. Internal Medicine, cardiovasc. disease; lic. physician Calif., Pa., N.C. Intern in medicine Duke U. Med. Ctr., 1974-75, resident in medicine, 1975-76, fellow in cardiology, 1976-80, assoc. in medicine, 1979-81, from asst. prof. medicine to assoc. prof. medicine, 1981-91, asst. prof. physiology, 1981-88, assoc. prof. microbiology & immunology, 1988-91, Herbert C. Rorer prof. med. scis., prof. genetics, 1991-92, mem. molecular biology grad. group, 1991-92, chief cardiovasc. divsn., 1991-92; chair dept. medicine Stanford (Calif.) U., 1996—2006; dir. Coll. Integrated Life Scis. U. Calif., San Diego, 2004—06; exec. dir. Singapore Inst. Clinical Sciences Agy. for Sci. Tech., & Rsch. (A*STAR), 2006—; Lie Ying Chow prof. medicine Nat. U. Singapore, 2006—. Vis. asst. prof. dept. genetics Harvard Med. Sch., Boston, 1985-86; mem. search com. for dir. Ctr. for Aging, Duke U. Med. Ctr., 1991—, mem. exec. com. deptl. awards selection, 1992—, chmn. combined degree dir. search com., 1993, mem. clin. rsch. ctr. adv. com., 1993-94, mem. grad. student admissions com., 1993, mem. search com. for chief cardiovasc. surgery, 1992, dept. medicine intern selection com., 1992—; mem. instnl. rev. com. Pa. Muscle Inst., 1993; cardiology adv. com. Nat. Heart, Lung, & Blood Inst., 1989-93; dir. USA-Russia Cardiovasc. Rsch. Program, 1992—; mem. NIH Task Force on Heart Failure, 1992-93, dirs. standing com. on clin. rsch. NIH, 1995—; cons. Netherlands Rsch. Initiative in Molecular Cardiology, 1993; external adv. com. Ctr. for Prevention of Cardiovasc. Disease, Harvard Sch. Pub. Health, 1993—; adv. coun. NHLBI, 1995—, Friends of NHLBI com., 1996—, lectr. in field.; bd. dirs, Lexico Pharmaceuticals Inc., 2007- Exec. editor: Trends in Cardiovascular Medicine, 1990-93; mem. editl. bd. Circulation Rsch., 1991—, Circulation, 1991—, Jour. Clin. Investigation, 1992—; cons. editor: Circulation, 1993—; contbr. articles to med. jours. Mem. exec. com. Coun. on Basic Sci., Am. Heart Assn., 1986-93, chmn. Katz Prize Award Com., 1989-92, rsch. rev. com., 1990-93, fellowship rsch. com., 1992—, program com., 1992—, mem. Levine Young Investigator Awards Com., Coun. on Clin. Cardiology, 1994—, mem. Basic Sci. Coun.; bd. dirs. Southeastern Pa. Heart Assn., 1992—. Recipient Bristol-Myers Squibb Cardiovasc. Achievement award, 1992, also numerous rsch. grants. Fellow Am. Coll. Cardiology (internat. edn. com. 1994—, chair cardiovasc. rsch. com. 1996—), Coll. Physicians of Phila.; mem. Assn. Univ. Cardiologists, Assn. Am. Physicians, Assn. Prof. of Cardiology, Am. Soc. Cell Biology, Am. Fedn. Clin. Rsch., Am. Soc. Clin. Investigation (pres.-elect 1994—, councilor 1991—), Internat. Soc. Heart Rsch. (councilor 1988—), Interurban Clin. Club, Clin. and Climitol. Soc., John Morgan Soc, Inst. Medicine (coun. mem.). Office: Nat U Hosp Main Bldg Level 3 5 Lower Kent Ridge Rd 119074 Singapore Singapore also: Singapore Inst Clinical Sciences 30 Medical Drive 117609 Singapore Singapore E-mail: judith_swain@sics.a-star.edu.sg.

SWAISLAND, HELEN CHRISTINE, pharmacologist; b. Thirsk, North Yorkshire, Eng., July 27, 1960; BSc with honors in Biochemistry, U. Surrey, 1982. Pharmacokineticist Beecham Pharms., 1982—89; sr. clin. pharmacology scientist AstraZeneca Pharms., 1989—. Avocation: ballroom dancing. Office: Alderley Pk Macclesfield Cheshire SK10 4TG England Office Fax: 44 (0)1625 516904. Business E-Mail: helen.swaisland@astrazeneca.com.

SWAMI, HARI MOHAN, hospital administrator; b. Shimla, India, Oct. 12, 1949; s. Sukhdev and Kalawati Swami; m. Madhu Swami, Nov. 14, 1979; 1 child, Arjun. MBBS, Indira Gandhi Med. Coll., Shimla, 1972; MD in Cmty. Medicine, Inst. Med. Sciences, Varanasi, India, 1979. Med. officer Med. Coll. Shimala, Urban Health Training Ctr., Shimala, India, 1973—76; jr. resident inst. bed. sciences Banaras Hindu U., Varanasi, India, 1976—77, sr. resident inst. bed. sciences, 1977—78; med. officer I.G Med. Coll., Shimala, India, 1976—81, med. officer, rural health ctr., 1981—82, registrar, 1982, lectr., 1982—92; reader, head Govt. Med. Coll. & Hosp., Chandigarh, India, 1992—96, prof., head, cmty. medicine, 1996—, dir., prin., 2003—. Contbr. articles to profl. jours., chapters to books. Zonal cum nodal officer Polio Immunization Campaign, India, 1996—2003; trainer on HIV/AIDS State AIDS Control Soc.; nodal officer HIV surveillance NIH, 1998—; chmn. purchase com. Govt. Med. Coll. Hosp., India, 1999—2002, chmn. libr. com., 1999—2002, chmn. sports com., 1999—2001; task force vector borne diseases. Fellow, WHO, 1990, Indian Assn. Preventive and Social Medicine, 2001. Mem.: AAAS, State Health Mission. Office: Government Medical College & Hospital Sector 32 Chandigarh 160030 India Office Phone: 011911722662000. Office Fax: 0119101722609360. Personal E-mail: dpgmcc@yahoo.com.

SWAMY, GEETA K., obstetrician, gynecologist; MD, U NC Sch. Medicine, Chapel Hill, 1997. Resident ob-gyn U. Pitts., 2001; fellow in maternal-fetal medicine Duke U. Med. Ctr., 2004; ob-gyn Duke Perinatal Durham-Fetal Diagnostic Ctr. Office: 2608 Erwin Rd Ste 200 Durham NC 27705 Office Phone: 919-681-5220. Office Fax: 919-681-7861.

SWAMY, MANJUNATH NARASIMHA, medical educator; b. Karnataka, India, Nov. 1, 1953; MD, All India Inst. Med. Scis., 1980. Prof. Tex. Tech U. Health Scis. Ctr., 2008—11. Home: 6305 Camino Alegre El Paso TX 79912 Business E-Mail: manjunath.swamy@ttuhsc.edu.

SWAN, BARBARA E., medical director; MD, Jefferson Med. Coll. Cert. electrodiagnostics medicine, diplomate Am. Bd. Physical Medicine and Rehab. Practice Choice Care Physicians; resident Univ. Cin. Med. Ctr., Phila.; dir. physical medicine and rehab. Western Pa. Hosp., med. dir. inpatient acute rehab. unit; dir. physical medicine and rehab. Allegheny Gen. Hosp. Named one of Top Doctors, Pitts. mag., 2011. Office: Allegheny General Hospital 320 E N Ave Pittsburgh PA 15212 Office Phone: 412-359-3131. Office Fax: 412-359-4108.

SWANGER, RONALD SCOTT, medical educator; b. Northridge, Calif., Dec. 12, 1973; Degree in Biology & Psychology, U. Calif., San Diego, 1996; degree in Medicine, NY Med. Coll., 2004. Asst. prof., radiology Westchester Med. Ctr., 2009—. Rsch. manuscript reviewer Archives Gynecology and Obstetrics, 2009—10. Recipient Radiology award, NY Med. Coll., 2009, Outstanding Performance award, Westchester Med. Ctr., 2004, 2005; Roentgen Resident fellow, Radiol. Soc. N.Am. Rsch. & Edn. Found. Mem.: Radiol. Soc. N.Am., Am. Coll. Radiology, Am. Soc. Neuroradiology. Avocations: travel, hiking, baseball. Office: 100 Woods Rd Valhalla NY 10595 Office Fax: 914-493-1820. Business E-Mail: swangerr@wcmc.com.

SWANN, NAT HENDERSON, JR., physician; b. Danville, Va, Nov. 2, 1927; s. Nat Henderson, Sr. and Mary Stokes S.; m. Sarah Hayes, Aug. 7, 1952; children: Nat H. III, Wayland Hayes. AB in Chemistry, U. N.C., Chapel Hill, 1950, MD, 1954. Fellow Royal Soc. Medicine, London. Resident in internal medicine Med. Coll., Va., 1954-56, Boston VA Hosp., 1956-57, Cleve. VA (Crile) Hosp., 1957-58; specialist internal medicine Chattanooga, 1958—. Med. dir. Chattem, Inc., Chattanooga, 1960—; cons. rheumatic heart clin. Children's Hosp., Chattanooga, 1959-63; chief of staff Downtown Gen. Hosp., Chattanooga, 1986-90. Author: Harbinger; Contbr. articles to profl. jours. Dir. Physician's Giving, United Way, Chattanooga, 1980; mem. Chattanooga Met. Coun., 1961; bd. spkr. Air Pollution Control Bd., Chattanooga, 1962; bd. dirs. The Salvation Army. With U.S. Army Med. Corps, 1946-47. Recipient Disting. Achievement award Am. Heart Assn. Fellow: ACP, Internat. Coll. Angiology, Royal Soc. Medicine, Am. Coll. Angiology, Am. Coll. Chest Physicians (assoc.); mem.: AMA, Am. Coll. Cardiology, Athenians Club (Chattanooga), Torch Club (Chattanooga), Mountain City Club (bd. dir.), Rotary (bd. dir.). Avocations: short story and novel writer, golf, tennis. Home: 412 Brady Point Rd Signal Mountain TN 37377-2206

SWANSBURG, RUSSELL CHESTER, retired nursing educator, writer, consultant; b. Cambridge, Mass., Aug. 6, 1928; s. William W. and Mary A. (Pierce) S.; m. Laurel Clark, Sept. 1951; children: Philip Wayne, Michael Gary, Richard Jeffrey. Diploma, N.S. Hosp. Sch. Nursing, 1950; BSN, Western Res. U., Cleve, 1952; MA in Nursing Edn., Columbia U., NYC, 1961; PhD, U. Miss., University, 1984. CNAA. Asst. adminstr. U. South Ala. Med. Ctr., Mobile, 1980—85, prof., 1981—86, v.p., 1984—86; prof. Auburn U., Montgomery, 1986—88, Med. Coll. Ga., Augusta, 1989—90; vis. prof. La. State U. Sch. Nursing, New Orleans, 1990—92; instr. U. of Incarnate Word, San Antonio, 1993—2003; ret., 2006. Mil. cons. USAF Surgeon Gen., 1972; sr. med. svc. cons., 1973-76; nurse cons. VA Med. Ctr., Tuskegee, Ala., 1987-88; mem. editl. adv. bd. Nursing Adminstrn. Manual, 1980, 86, 90. Author: Team Nursing: A Programmed Learning Experience, 1968, Inservice Education, 1968, The Measurement of Vital Signs, 1970, The Team Plan, 1971, Management of Patient Care Services, 1976, Strategic Career Planning and Development, 1984, The Nurse Manager's Guide to Financial Management, 1988, Management and Leadership for Nurse Managers, 1990 (Book of Yr. Selection, Am. Jour. Nursing 1990), 3d edit., 2002 (Book of Yr. Selection, Am. Jour. Nursing 2002), 4th edit., 2006, Management and Leadership for Nurse Administrators 5th edit., 2009, Am. Jour. Nursing (Book of Yr. award 2009), Introductory Management and Leadership for Clinical Nurses, 1993, 2d edit., 1999 (Book of the Yr. Selection, Am. Jour. Nursing 1999), Staff Development: A Component of Human Resource Development, 1994, Budgeting and Financial Management for Nurse Managers, 1997, (audiovisual course) Nurses & Patients: An Introduction to Nursing Management, 1980; contbr.

articles to profl. publs Bd. dir. Air Force Village Found., Alzheimer's Care and Rsch. Found. Col. USAF, 1956-76. Decorated Air Medal with oak leaf clusters, Legion of Merit, Air Force commendation medal with oak leaf cluster, Meritorious Svc. medal with oak leaf cluster, Vietnam Svc. medal, Am. Expeditionary medal, Republic of Vietnam Svc. medal; recipient award for outstanding work in hosp. adminstrn. Ala. State Nurses' Assn., 1985, Outstanding Nursing Svc. Adminstrn. award, 1981, Outstanding Nurse Rschr. 1984, Disting. Svc. award Air Force Village Found., 1999, Disting. Alumnus award Frances Payne Bolton Sch. Nursing Case Western Res. U., 2006, Vol. Achievement award Air Force Village Tex. Assn. Homes and Svcs. for Aging, 2007, 11. Fellow AONE, Ala. Orgn. Nurse Execs. (past state pres.); mem. Coun. Grad. Edn. Adminstrn. in Nursing (sec.), Ala. Acad. Sci., Sigma Xi, Phi Kappa Phi, Sigma Theta Tau. Home and Office: 4917 Ravenswood Dr Apt HCC14 San Antonio TX 78227-4356 Office Phone: 210-673-9475. Personal E-mail: swansburg@sbcglobal.net.

SWANSON, JACQUELINE V., academic administrator, women's health nurse practitioner, educator; b. Houston, Feb. 12, 1944; d. Ivan Jack and Edith Wilson; m. James Swanson, Aug. 21, 1965; children: Jim, Charlotte, Robert, Guy, Danny. BS, Tex. Woman's U., 1967, MS, 1974; PhD, U. North Tex., Denton, 1989. Cert. clin. nurse specialist, in maternal-newborn health, women's health nurse practitioner Planned Parenthood of Rocky Mountains, sexual assault nurse examiner. Various clin. nursing positions, Tex., Kans., Montana, Okla., Tex., 1967-73; supr. obstet. and nursery Harris County Hosp. Dist., Houston, 1970-73; instr. Prairie View (Tex.) A&M U., 1973-75; asst. prof. Tex. Woman's U., Denton, 1975-85; labor and delivery nurse Tarrant County Hosp. Dist., Ft. Worth, 1987-89; assoc. prof., chmn. dept. nursing Ft. Hays State U., Hays, Kans., 1989-94; dir. BS nursing program Lamar U., Beaumont, Tex., 1994-95; prof., dean Coll. Nursing, Mont. State U. No., Havre, 1995—98, prof. nursing, 1998-2000; assoc. prof. nursing Tarleton State U., 2000—03, women's health nurse practioner Student Health Clinic, 2003—04; clin. instr. Tex. Christian U., 2005; dean Sch. Nursing Bacone Coll., 2005—07, Hometown Hosp., 2007—08, North Tex. VA Healthcare, 2008—. Contbr. articles to profl. jours.; presenter U.S. and internat. Mem. Denton Area War on Drugs. Mem. AAUP, ANA, Nat. Assn. Nurse Practioners Women's Health, Assn. Women's Health, Obstetric and Neonatal Nurses, Kans. State Nurses Assn., Tex. Nurses Assn., Tex. Nurse Practioner's Assn., Mont. Nurses Assn., Internat. Coun. on Women's Health Issues, Internat. Soc. for Univ. Nurses, Sigma Theta Tau. Home: 315E 9th Bonham TX 75418

SWANSON, STEPHEN OLNEY, minister, retired English educator; b. Mpls., Aug. 31, 1932; s. Carl R. and Dorothy Olney Swanson; m. Judith Seleen Swanson, June 10, 1956; children: Scott, Shelley, Noel, Kim, Brian. BA, St. Olaf Coll., 1954; grad. in theology, Luther Theol. Sem., St. Paul, 1958, BD, 1960; MA, U. Oreg., 1964, ArtsD, 1970. Ordained to ministry Evang. Luth. Ch. Am., 1958. Instr. theology Augustana Coll., Sioux Falls, SD, 1957; instr. writing U. Oreg., Eugene, 1964—66, asst. prof. English and writing Tex. Luth. Coll., Seguin, 1966—70; assoc. prof. English and writing Camrose (Alta.) Univ. Coll., 1970—73; prof. writing St. Olaf Coll., Northfield, Minn., 1976—99; adj. prof. writing Waldorf Coll. Forest City, Iowa, 2005—08. Parish pastor Luth. congregations, Minn., 1958-61, Oreg., 1962-65, Sask., 1973-74; interim pastor 40 congregations, Minn., Iowa, Wis., Alta., Sask., 1956—; dir. creative writing Tex. Luth. Coll., 1966-70, Camrose Univ. Coll., 1970-73; coach wrestling, football, volleyball, hockey, Tex., Can., Minn.; coowner Nine-Ten Press, Northfield, 1997—; adj. prof. Waldorf Coll., Forest City, Iowa, 2004-07; v.p., Friends of Third World Found., Kenyon, Minn., 2007-, Human Rights Commn., Northfield, 2008-11. Author 27 books for adults, teens and children, including Is There Life After High Sch., 1991, The Earthkeeper Mystery Series, 4 vols., 1994, Moving Out on Your Own, 1995, The First Fall: Ytterboe Hall, 1946, 1997, One Couple's Gift, 2009; playwright 6 plays; contbr. articles to jours.; columnist Now and Then, 1998-99, centennial hymn texts, Our Savior's, Faribault, Minn., 2005, Bethel, Northfield, 2008; metal sculpture exhbns. include Luth. Brotherhood Corp. Gallery, Mpls., 1992, 94, 98, Waldorf Coll., Forest City, Iowa, 1999, Luther Coll., Decorah, Iowa, 2002, Art Ctr. of St. Peter, Minn., 2003, Thrivent Fin. Corp. Gallery, Mpls., 2003, St. Olaf Coll., Northfield, Minn., 2003, Am. Swedish Inst., Mpls., Minn., 2004, Edge Gallery, Big Fork, Minn., 2005, Jacques Art Ctr., Aitkin, Minn., 2007. Recipient award Minn. Arts Bd., 1987, Blandin Found., Grand Rapids, Minn., 1988-89; fellow NDEA, Washington, 1968-69. Mem.: Blue Key (hon.), Am. Swedish Inst. Avocations: metal sculpture, fishing, Volvo repair. Home: 910 St Olaf Ave Northfield MN 55057

SWARTZ, JON DAVID, psychologist, educator; b. Houston, Dec. 28, 1934; s. Orville Elmo and Nina June (Baker) S.; m. Carol Joseph Hampton, Oct. 20, 1966; children: Eric Jason McFarland, Sally Katherine Baker, Edward Joseph Bryson. BA, U. Tex., Austin, 1956, MA, 1961, PhD, 1969, postgrad., 1973-74. Rsch. and tng. asst. dept. psychology U. Tex., 1956-62, asst. prof. dept. ednl. psychology, 1969-72; assoc. prof. psychology, chmn. U. Tex.-Permian Basin, 1974-78, chmn. anthropology and sociology, 1975-78, field dir., 1962-65; asst. dir. Austin Longitudinal Rsch. project, 1965-69, co-dir., 1969-74; research scientist Hogg Found. for Mental Health, 1972-74; prof. edn. and psychology Southwestern U., Georgetown, Tex., 1978-90, vis. prof. psychology, 1991, dir. testing and guidance, 1978-81, holder Brown vis. chair, 1978-82, assoc. dean for libss. and learning resources, 1981-90; coord., adminstrv. head Killeen office Cen. Counties Ctr. for MHMR Svcs., Temple, Tex., 1990-91; chief psychol. svcs. Temple, Tex., 1991-99; pvt. practice Tex., 2000—. Lectr. Nat. U., Mexico, 1962, U. Ctrl. Tex., 1994, Temple Coll., 1994. Author: (with W.H. Holtzman) Inkblot Perception and Personality, 1961, (with C.C. Cleland) Mental Retardation: Approaches to Institutional Change, 1969, Administrative Issues in Institutions for the Mentally Retarded, 1972, Exceptionalities Through the Lifespan: An Introduction, 1982, Multihandicapped Mentally Retarded, 1973, (with W.H. Holtzman, R. Diaz-Guerrero) Personality Development in Two Cultures, 1975; editor: (with C.C. Cleland, L.W. Talkington) Profoundly Mentally Retarded, 1976, (with R.K. Eyman, C.C. Cleland) Research with the Profoundly Retarded, 1978, Holtzman Inkblot Technique: An Annotated Bibliography (supplement), 1988, (with R.C. Reinehr, W.H. Holtzman) Holtzman Inkblot Technique: An Annotated Bibliography 1956-1982, 1983, (with R.C. Reinehr) Handbook of Old-Time Radio, 1993, Holtzman Inkblot Technique: Research Guide and Bibliography, 1999, Southwestern University Bibliographic Series, 1986-1990, Historical Dictionary of Old-Time Radio, 2008, A To Z of Old Time Radio, 2010, Pseudonyms of Science Fiction, Fantasy and Horror Authors, 2010; contbr.: Handbook of Texas, 1996; editl. assoc. Current Anthropology, 1971-77; assoc. editor: Am. Corrective Therapy Jour., 1971-81, Exceptional Children, 1982-84; mem. editl. bd. Tex. Psychologist, 1979-83, Phi Kappa Phi Jour./Nat. Forum, 1976-80; editl. cons. Mental Retardation, 1972-77; rev. editor Jour. Biol. Psychology, 1972-80, Revista Interamericana de Psicologia, 1983-89; reviewer Sci. Books, Films, 1978—; cons. editor Jour. Personality Assessment, 1981-90; spl. features editor: Scientifiction: The First Fandom Report, 2002—; rev. editor The National Fantasy Fan, 2003-10; frequent contbr. Paperback Parade, 2004—;contbr. Big Little Times, 2008-, contbg. editor Fan Dominion, 2008-; contbr. over 500 articles to profl. jours. Mem. Mayor's Drug Abuse Panel, Odessa, Tex., 1975-78; chmn. adv. bd. Human Potentials Ctr., Permian Basin Cmty. Ctrs. for Mental Health and Mental Retardation, Odessa and Midland, Tex., 1975-78; bd. govs. Mood-Heritage Mus., 1984-90. US Office Edn. fellow, 1964-66, U. Tex. fellow, 1973-74; recipient Franklin Gilliam prize Humanities Rsch. Ctr. U. Tex., 1965, Spencer Rsch. award Nat. Acad. Edn., 1972, Faculty Fellowship award Southwestern U., 1981. Fellow AAAS, Am. Psychol. Soc., Soc. Personality Assessment (life); mem. Western Rsch. Conf. on Mental Retardation, Am. Acad. Mental Retardation, Southwestern Psychol. Assn., Bell County Psychol. Assn., Sigma Xi, Psi Chi, Mu Alpha Nu, Delta Tau Kappa, Phi Kappa Phi, Phi Delta Kappa, Nat. Fantasy Fan Fedn.: Club Historian (mem. directorate, 2007-10, pres. 2010-; Franson award 2005, 07), First Fandom. Personal E-mail: jon_swartz@hotmail.com.

SWARTZ, KATHERINE (B. KATHERINE SWARTZ), economist, educator; m. Frank Levy; 2 children. BS, MIT, 1972; MS, U. Wis., Madison, 1974, PhD, 1976. Lectr. Goldman Sch. Pub. Policy, U. Calif., Berkeley, 1976—77; asst. prof. economics U. Md., College Park, 1977—82; rsch. assoc. health policy Urban Inst., 1982—85, sr. rsch. assoc. health policy Washington, 1986—92; assoc. prof. pub. policy Brown U., 1989—90; assoc. prof. health policy and mgmt. Harvard Sch. Pub. Health, Boston, 1992—2000, prof. health economics and policy, 2001; dir. Robert Wood Johnson Scholars in Health Policy Rsch. Prog. Harvard U., 2005—. Editor Inquiry, 1995—2007; vis. scholar Russell Sage Found., NYC, 2000—01. Author: Reinsuring Health: Why More Middle-Class People are Uninsured and What Government Can Do, 2006. Mem.: Inst. Medicine, Nat. Acad. Social Ins., Assn. Pub. Policy Analysis and Mgmt. (sec. 1991—93, v.p. 2002—04, pres. 2007—, David Kershaw award 1991). Office: Harvard Sch Pub Health Kresge Bldg 404 677 Huntington Ave Boston MA 02115 Office Phone: 617-423-4325. Office Fax: 617-432-4494. E-mail: kswartz@hsph.harvard.edu.

SWARTZ, MORTON NORMAN, medical educator; b. Boston, Nov. 11, 1923, s. Jacob H. and Janet (Heller) Swartz; m. Cesla Rosenberg, Sept. 18, 1956; children: Mark David, Caroline Joan. BA, Harvard Coll., 1945; MD, Harvard U., 1947; MD (hon.), U. Geneva, Switzerland, 1988. Diplomate Am. Bd. Internal Medicine. Med. intern and resident Mass. Gen. Hosp., Boston, 1947—50, chief resident in medicine, 1953—54, chief infectious disease unit, 1956—90, chief James Jackson Firm, med. svcs., 1990—; USPHS postdoctoral rsch. fellow Johns Hopkins U., McCollum-Pratt Inst. Enzymology, Balt., 1954—56, assoc. prof. medicine Harvard Med. Sch., Boston, 1967—73, prof., 1973—, prof. medicine, 2007. Vis. assoc. prof. biochemistry Stanford Med. Sch., Palo Alto, Calif., 1969—70; chmn. Nat. Inst. Child Health and Devel., 1995—97, bd. sci. counselors. Co-author: Osteomyelitis, 1971; editor: Current Clinical Topics in Infectious Diseases, 1980—2002; assoc. editor: New Eng. Jour. Medicine, 1981—2002; contbr. articles to profl. jours. 1st lt. US Army, 1950—52. Mem.: ACP (Disting. Tchr. award 1989), Inst. Medicine, Infectious Diseases Soc. Am. (Bristol award 1984, Feldman award 1989, Soc. Citation award 2003), Assn. Am. Physicians, Am. Soc. for Clin. Investigation, Am. Soc. Biochemistry and Molecular Biology. Jewish. Avocations: biology, birdwatching, cosmology. Office: Mass Gen Hosp Dept Medicine Bulfinch Bldg #127 Boston MA 02114-2696 Home: 101 Monmouth St Apt 917 Brookline MA 02446-5637 Business E-Mail: mswartz@partners.org.

SWAZEY, JUDITH POUND, academic administrator, science educator; b. Bronxville, NY, Apr. 21, 1939; d. Robert Earl and Louise Titus (Hanson) Pound; m. Peter Woodman Swazey, Nov. 28, 1964; children: Elizabeth, Peter. AB, Wellesley Coll., 1961; PhD, Harvard U., 1966. Rsch. assoc. Harvard U., 1966-71, lectr., 1969-71, rsch. fellow, 1971-72; cons. com. brain scis. NRC, 1971-73; staff scientist neurosciences rsch. program MIT, Cambridge, 1973-74; assoc. prof. dept. socio-med. scis. and cmty. medicine Boston U., 1974-77, prof., 1977-80, adj. prof. Schs. Medicine and Pub. Health, 1980—; exec. dir. Medicine in the Pub. Interest, Inc., Boston and Washington, 1979-82, 89-93; pres. Coll. of the Atlantic, Bar Harbor, Maine, 1982-84, Acadia Inst., Bar Harbor, 1984-2001, founding pres., sr. scholar, 2001—07. Mem. Army Sci. Bd., 1987-92. Author: Reflexes and Motor Integration, the Development of Sherrington's Integrative Action Concept, 1969, (with others) Human Aspects of Biomedical Innovation, 1971, (with R.C. Fox) The Courage to Fail, a Social View of Organ Transplants and Hemodialysis, 1975, rev. edit., 1978, 02 (hon. mention Am. Med. Writers Assn., C. Wright Mills award Am. Sociol. Assn.), Chlorpromazine in Psychiatry, a Study of Therapeutic Innovation, 1974, (with K. Reeds) Today's Medicine, Tomorrow's Science, Essays on Paths of Discovery in the Biomedical Sciences, 1978; editor: (with C. Wong) Dilemmas of Dying, Policies and Procedures for Decisions Not to Treat, 1981, (with F. Worden and G. Adelman) The Neurosciences: Paths of Discovery, 1975, (with R.C. Fox) Spare Parts, Organ Replacement in American Society, 1992, Japanese transl., 1999, (with C. Messikomer and A. Glicksman) Society and Medicine. Essays in Honor of Renée Fox, 2002, (with R.C.Fox) Observing Bioethics, 2008; assoc. editor IRB: A Jour. of Human Subjects Rsch., 1979-00; mem. editl. bd. Sci. and Engring. Ethics, 1994—; contbr. articles to profl. jours. Mem. Maine Dept. Human Svcs. Bioethics Adv. Com. (chair 1991-94); mem. Commn. on Rsch. Integrity, 1994-95; bd. dirs. Maine Bioethics Network, 1994-99. Wellesley Coll. scholar, 1961; Wellesley Coll. Alumnae fellow Harvard U., 1966, NIH predoctoral fellow, 1966, Radcliffe Coll. Coll. grad. fellow, 1966. Fellow AAAS (sci. freedom and responsibility com. 1986-89, nominations com. 2003-2004), Inst. Medicine of NAS (mem. health scis. policy bd. 1986-89), Grad. Record Exam. (bd. dirs. 1987-91), Phi Beta Kappa, Sigma Xi (mem. ethics com. 2004-). Office: PO Box 243 Bar Harbor ME 04609-0243 Office Phone: 207-288-3295. Personal E-mail: swazey.jp@gmail.com.

SWEDISH, JOSEPH R., healthcare company executive; b. Richmond, Va. BS, U. NC, Charlotte, 1973; M in Health Adminstrn., Duke U., 1979. Pres., CEO, Ctrl. Fla. and East Fla. Divsns. Hosp. Corp. of America, 1994—98; pres., CEO Centura Health, Colo., 1999—2004, Trinity Health, Novi, Mich., 2005—, chief diversity officer Mich., 2006. Bd. dirs. Cross Country Healthcare, Fla., 2001—, Coventry Health Care, Inc., 2010—; vice chair/chair elect Catholic Health Assn. Bd., chmn., 2012—13; mem. Nat. Quality Forum Bd.; chmn. inst. for diversity in health mgmt. American Hosp. Assn., mem. health rsch. and edn. trust, mem. spl. adv. group on improving hosp. care for minorities, mem. nonprofit system CEO group, mem. long range policy com., mem. ad hoc com. on payment for health svcs., mem. regional policy bd.; chmn. Colo. Hosp. Assn. Bd. dirs. Am. Hosp. Assn; mem. bd. Colo. Concern, Colo. Forum; chmn. Colo. Hosp. Assn; mem. econ. devel. coun. Metro Denver C. of C.; mem. bd. Metro Denver Boy Scouts. Recipient Univ. Medal, Bd. Regents U. Colo., CEO Diversity Leadership award, Diversity Best Practices, 2009; named Entrepreneur of Yr., Rocky Mountain Region, Ernst & Young, 2003; named one of Top 100 Most Powerful Leaders in Healthcare, Modern Healthcare, 2006—. Fellow: American Coll. Healthcare Executives (Career Achievement Regents award 2004). Avocations: fly fishing, golf, skiing. Office: Trinity Health 27870 Cabot Dr Novi MI 48377-2920 Office Phone: 248-489-6000. Business E-Mail: joseph.swedish@trinity-health.org. *

SWEE, DAVID ETHAN, physician; b. NYC, Sept. 3, 1947; s. Eugene and Joan (Shalit) S.; m. Karen Virginia Hermanson, Dec. 30, 1971; children: Kendra Olivia, Julia Elizabeth. BA, Grinnell Coll., 1969; MD, Dalhousie U., 1975. Diplomate Am. Bd. Family Practice. Dir. premed. programs dept. family medicine U. Medicine and Dentistry NJ-Robert Wood Johnson Med. Sch., Piscataway, NJ, 1977-85, dir. fellowship program, 1985-87, med. dir. family practice ctr., vice chair dept. New Brunswick, 1987-91, prof., chmn. dept. family medicine, 1991—2005, acting sr. assoc. dean. edn., 2005—06, assoc. dean. edn., 2006—. Chief dept. family medicine Robert Wood Johnson U. Hosp., New Brunswick, 1991-05; mem., liaison com. on med. edn., 2008-, mem. coun. on med. edn. AMA, 2006-, chair, 2011-. Editor, main author: Teaching Family Medicine in Medical School: A Companion to Predoctoral Education in Family Medicine, 1991. Grantee Prudential Ins. Co., 1987-89, US Dept. HHS, 1984-87, 91-04, 93-96, 96-99, 99-02, 02-05; Bishop fellow Am. Coun. Edn., 2002-03. Fellow Am. Acad. Family Physicians; mem. Soc. Tchrs. Family Medicine (bd. dirs. 1985-89, group on predocotoral edn. 1984—, group on faculty devel. 1985—). Avocations: music (piano), writing. Home: 259 Lawrence Ave Highland Park NJ 08904-1837 Office: 675 Hoes Ln Rm N 112 Piscataway NJ 08854 Office Phone: 732-235-4578. Business E-Mail: swee@umdnj.edu.

SWEENEY, H. LEE, physiologist, educator; b. New Orleans, La., Apr. 18, 1953; BS, MIT, 1975; PhD, Harvard U., 1984. Prof., chmn. physiology Perleman Sch. Medicine U. Pa., 1989—. Sci. dir. parent project muscular dystrophy Parent Project Muscular Dystrophy, 2000—11; cons. in field, 2003—11; gene doping adv. com. mem. World Anti-Doping Assn., 2005—11; adv. coun. mem. Nat. Inst. Arthritus and Musclo-Skeletal and Skin Diseases, 2008—; scientifc advisor Assn. Française Contre les Myopathies, 2009—11. Recipient Hamdan award, Sheikh Hamdan Dubai Awards Com., Stanley N. Cohen Biomedical Rsch. award, Pereleman Sch. Medicine. Fellow: Am. Heart Assn.; mem.: Assn. Chairs Dept. Physiology, Am. Physiol. Soc., Am. Soc. Cell Biology, Biophysical Soc. Avocation: winemaking. Office: Dept Physiology B400 Richards Bldg Philadelphia PA 19104-6085 Office Fax: 215-573-2273. Business E-Mail: lsweeney@mail.med.upenn.edu.

SWEET, JAMES BROOKS, oral and maxillofacial surgeon; b. Darlington, Pa., Mar. 28, 1934; s. Lufay Anderson and Margaret Jean (Brooks) S.; m. N. Gayle Laird, Oct. 11, 1958; children: James Brooks II, Laird Anderson, Bradley Stephen. BA, Lafayette Coll., 1956; DDS, U. Pitts., 1964, DMD, 1974; MS in Dentistry, NYU, 1975. Aviation flight officer USNR, 1957; advanced through grades to dir. USPHS; rotating intern USPHS Hosp., Staten Island, N.Y., 1964-65, resident oral and maxillofacial surgery, 1970-73; chief dept. dentistry Fed. Correctional Inst. Hosp., Ashland, Ky., 1965-67, Terminal Island, Calif., 1967-70; chief oral and maxillofacial surgery Clin. Ctr. NIH, Bethesda, Md., 1973-80; chief dept. dentistry and oral and maxillofacial surgery USPHS Hosp., Nassau Bay, Tex., 1980-81; ret. USPHS, 1981; assoc. prof. dept. oral and maxillofacial surgery Health Sci. Ctr. U. Tex., Houston, 1981-84, prof., 1984—95, prof. emeritus, 2002—. Asst. clin. prof. med. br. U. Tex., Galveston, 1980-2002, prof. emeritus, 2002--; assoc. attending physicianBen Taub Gen. Hosp., Houston, 1984-95; cons. oral and maxillofacial surgery self study guides, Stoma Press, Seattle, 1983-; cons. VA Hosp., Houston, 1986-. Contbr. articles to profl. jours.; editorial reviewer: Annals of Internal Medicine, 1977-. Coach basketball Olney (Md.) Boys Club, 1975-80; mem. aim rev. Tex. area USCG, 1981-82. Lt. USNR, 1957-64. Fellow Am. Assn. Oral and Maxillofacial Surgeons; mem. Tex. Soc. Oral and Maxillofacial Surgeons, Houston Soc. Oral and Maxillofacial Surgeons, Am. Assn. Dental Schs., USPHS Profl. Assn., NIH Sailing Club, Omicron Kappa Upslion (pres. Mu Mu chpt. 1993-94). Presbyterian. Avocations: sailing, swimming, real estate, travel. Home: 2013 Sweet St Navarre FL 32566-3042 Office: U Tex Health Sci Ctr 6516 John Freeman St Houston TX 77030-3402 Business E-Mail: jamesbsweet@mediacombb.net.

SWEIGARD, KEITH W., internist; Grad., Lehigh U.; MD, Hahnemann U. Diplomate Am. Bd. Internal Medicine. Dir. Abington Health Physicians Abington Meml. Hosp., chief internal medicine divsn. Named one of the Top Doctor, Phila. Mag., 2011. Office: Abington Memorial Hospital Ste 203 Rydal Sq 500 Old York Rd Jenkintown PA 19046 Office Phone: 215-886-0174. Office Fax: 215-886-9217.

SWEIS, ILIANA, plastic surgeon, educator; MD, Northwestern U., Chgo. Diplomate Am. Bd. Medical Examiners, Am. Bd. Plastic Surgery. Appointments in hosps. and surg. centers in Chgo. area; faculty mem. Allergan's Physicians Network for Botox Cosmetic; resident gen. surgery Case Western Reserve Univ., Cleveland; resident plastic and reconstructive surgery Nothwestern Univ., Chgo.; clin. asst. prof. surgery Univ. Ill., Chgo.; dir. North Shore Ctr. for Plastic Surgery Ltd., Northbrook, Ill. Contbr. articles Plastic and Reconstructive Surgery, Aesthetic Jour. Quar., Am. Surgeon, various others. Recipient Jordan's award of Highest Distinction; named one of Top Plastic Surgeons America, Consumers Rsch. Coun. America. Fellow: Am. Coll. Surgeons; mem.: AMA, Am. Soc. Plastic Surgeons, Nat. Coun. Leaders in Breast Aesthetics. Office: NorthShore Center For Plastic Surgery 680 North Lake Shore Dr Ste 930 Chicago IL 60611 Office Phone: 312-932-9900.

SWEITZER, MICHAEL COOK, healthcare product executive; b. Cin., July 29, 1961; s. Charles Samuel and Louise (Cook) S. BS in Biomedical Engring., Rensselaer Poly. Inst., 1983, M in Engring., 1985. Product specialist Siemens Med. Sys., Iselin, N.J., 1985-89, tech. mgr, 1989-90, nat. sales mgr., 1993-94, product mgr., 1994-96, cons., 1996-98, product specialist San Francisco, 1990-92; product mgr. Toshiba Am. Med. Sys., S. San Francisco, 1992-93, Varian Med. Sys., Palo Alto, Calif., 1998—2001, bus. unit mgr., 2001—03, mgr. emerging techs., 2003—06, dir., rsch. collaborations, 2006—. Contbr. chpt. to MRI Guide for Technologists, 1994. Mem. Am. Healthcare Radiology Adminstrs., Inst. for Indsl. Engrs. Office: Varian Med Sys Inc MS E 263 3100 Hansen Way Palo Alto CA 94304-1129

SWENSEN, CLIFFORD HENRIK, JR., psychologist, educator; b. Welch, W.Va., Nov. 25, 1926; s. Clifford Henrik and Cora Edith (Clovis) S.; m. Doris Ann Gaines, June 6, 1948; children: Betsy, Susan, Lisa, Timothy, Barbara BS, U. Pitts., 1949, MS, 1950, PhD, 1952. Diplomate Am. Bd. Profl. Psychology. Instr. U. Pitts., 1951-52; clin. psychologist VA, 1952-54; from asst. prof. to assoc. prof. U. Tenn., Knoxville, 1954-62; assoc. prof. psychology Purdue U., West Lafayette, Ind., 1962-65, prof., 1965—99, prof. emeritus, 1999—, dir. clin. tng., 1975-85; vice chair U. Senate, 1994-95. Vis. prof. U. Fla., 1968-69, U. Bergen, Norway, 1976-77, 83-84; cons. VA, 1981 White House Conf. on Aging, others; Am. Psychol. Assn.-NSF Disting. Sci. lectr., 1968-69; Fulbright-Hays lectr., Norway, 1976-77 Author: An Approach to Case Conceptualization, 1968; Introduction to Interpersonal Relations, 1973; contbr. chpts. to books, articles to profl. jours. Mem. Ind. Gov.'s Task Force Alzheimer's Disease and Related Senile Dementia, 1998—; bd. dirs. Ind. Assn. Homes and Svcs. Aging, 2007-. Served with USN, 1944-46 Recipient Gordon A. Barrows Meml. award for disting. contributions to psychology, 1990; named to Hall of Fame, Brentwood Pa. H.S., 2001. Fellow APA (pres divsn. cons. psychology 1976-77, Presdl. citation 1999, Cert. achievement 2000), Assn. for Psychol. Sci., Soc. Personality Assessment, Am. Assn. Applied and Preventive Psychology, Acad. Clin. Psychology; mem. Midwestern Psychol. Assn., Southeastern Psychol. Assn., Ind. Psychol. Assn., Gerontol. Soc., Sigma Xi, Psi Chi. Republican. Mem. Ch. of Christ Home: 1700 Lindberg Rd 229 West Lafayette IN 47906 Office: Purdue U Dept Psychol Scis West Lafayette IN 47907 Office Phone: 765-494-6977. Business E-Mail: cswensen@psych.purdue.edu.

SWENSON, SUE, federal agency administrator; married; 3 children. BA, MA, U. Chgo.; MBA, U. Minn. Mktg. mgr. Barr Engring., Minn. Heart and Lund Inst., U. Minn.; commr. Adminstrn. on Developmental Disabilities, 1998—2001; exec. dir. Joseph P. Kennedy Jr. Found., Washington, 2001—03, The ARC US, 2003—07; disability cons., 2008—10; dep. asst. sec. Office Spl. Edn. and Rehab. Services US Dept. Edn., Washington, 2010—, acting dir. Nat. Inst. on Disability and Rehab. Rsch., 2010—. Cons. subcom. on disability policy U.S. Senate, Washington. Fellow Joseph P. Kennedy Jr. Found., 1996. Office: Office Spl Edn and Rehab Services US Dept Edn 400 Maryland Ave SW Washington DC 20202-7100 Office Phone: 202-245-7468. *

SWERDLOFF, RONALD S., physician, educator, researcher; b. Pomona, Calif., Feb. 18, 1938; s. Julius Lewis and Eva (Kelman) S.; m. Christina Wang; children: Jonathan Nicolai, Peter Loren, Paul Im, Michael Im. BS, U. Calif., 1959, MD, 1962. Diplomate Am. Bd. Internal Medicine, Am. Bd. Endocrinology. Intern U. Wash., Seattle, 1962-63, resident, 1963-64; rsch. assoc. NIH, Bethesda, Md., 1964-66; resident UCLA Sch. Medicine, 1966-67; rsch. fellow Harbor-UCLA Med. Ctr., Torrance, Calif., 1967-69, asst. prof., 1969-72, assoc. prof. divsn. Endocrinology, 1972-78, chief divsn. Endocrinology, 1973—, prof., 1978—, assoc. chair dept. medicine, 1997—; dir. UCLA Population Rsch. Ctr., Torrance, 1986-92, Mellon Found. Ctr. in Reproductive Medicine, 1997—. Dir. WHO Collaborating Ctr. Reproduction, Torrance, NIH Contraceptive Clin. Trials Ctr., 2005—, Torrance; cons. WHO Geneva, 1982-90, NIH, Bethesda, 1982—, UN Fertility Planning Assn., Geneva, 1983—, Am. Bd. Internal Medicine, Phila., 1989—; inaugural lectr. Australian Soc. Reproductive Biology, Perth, 1990; mem. tech. adv. com. Contraceptive R & D Agy. (CONRAD, AID), 1992—. Editor: 3 books; contbr. chapters to books 100, articles 250 to profl. jours. Bd. dirs., vice chair Harbor-UCLA Rsch. and Edn. Inst; bd. dirs. Scaplanes Corp. Recipient Sherman Mellinkoff award, UCLA, 1998. Fellow: ACP; mem.: We. Soc. Clin. Rsch. (pres. 1983—84, Sherman Mellinkoff award UCLA, Mayo Soley award 2000), Endocrinology Soc., Pacific Coast Fertility (pres. 1984, Outstanding Rsch. award 1976, 1984, Wyeth award 1984, Squibb award), Am. Soc. Clin. Rsch. (pres. we. sect. 1972—73), Am. Assn. Physicians, Am. Soc. Andrology (pres. 1992—93, Serono award 1986, Disting. Andrologist award 2004). Office: Harbor UCLA Med Ctr Divsn Endocrinology 1000 W Carson St Torrance CA 90502-2004 Office Phone: 310-222-1867. Business E-Mail: swerdloff@labiomed.org.

SWERDLOW, MARTIN ABRAHAM, retired pathologist, educator; b. Chgo., July 7, 1923; s. Sol Hyman and Rose (Lasky) Swerdlow; m. Marion Levin, May 19, 1945; children: Steven Howard, Gary Bruce. Student, Herzl Jr. Coll., 1941—42; BS, U. Ill., 1945; MD, U. Ill., Chgo., 1947. Diplomate Am Bd Pathology. Intern Michael Reese Hosp. and Med. Center, Chgo., 1947-48, resident, 1948-50, 51-52, mem. staff, 1974—2008, chmn. dept. pathology, v.p. acad. affairs, 1974-90; pathologist Menorah Med Ctr, Kansas City, Mo., 1954—57. Asst prof, pathologist Univ Ill Col Med, Chicago, 1957—59, assoc prof, 1959—60, clin prof, 1960—64, prof, pathologist, 1966—72, assoc dean, prof pathology, 1970—72; prof pathology, chmn Univ Mo, Kansas City, 1972—74; prof pathology Univ Chicago, 1975—89, Geever prof, head pathology emeritus, 1993—; mem comt standards Chicago Health Sys Agency, 1976—. With MC US Army, 1944—45. Recipient Alumnus of the Yr Award, Univ Ill Col Med, 1973, Instructorship Award, Univ Ill, 1960, 1965, 1968, 1971, 1972. Mem.: Inst. of Medicine, Am. Soc. Dermatopathology, Internat. Acad. Pathology, Coll. Am. Pathologists, Am. Soc. Clin. Pathologists, Chgo. Pathology Soc. (pres 1980—). Jewish. Business E-Mail: maswerdl@uic.edu.

SWETLIK, WILLIAM PHILIP, orthodontist; b. Manitowoc, Wis., Jan. 31, 1950; s. Leonard Alvin and Lillian Julia (Knipp) S.; m. Cheryl Jean Klein, June 30, 1973 (div.); children: Alison Elizabeth, Lindsey Ann, Adam William; m. Joyce M. Caris, Mar. 10, 1995. Student, Luther Coll., Decorah, Iowa, 1968-70; DDS, Marquette U., 1974; MS in Dentistry, St. Louis U., 1977. Diplomate Am. Bd. Orthodontics. Resident in gen. dentistry USPHS, Norfolk, Va., 1974-75; practice dentistry specializing in orthodontics Green Bay, Wis., 1977—. Instr. oral pathology NE Wis. Tech. Coll., Green Bay, 1979-86. Author: (with others) Orthodontic Headgear, 1977. Mem. Prevention Walking Club, Family Crisis Ctr. of Green Bay. Served as lt. USPHS, 1974-75. Fellow Coll. Diplomates Am. Bd. Orthodontics; mem. ADA, Am. Assn. Orthodontists, Wis. Dental Assn. (Continuing Edn. award 1986), Wis. Soc. Orthodontists, Orthodontic Edn. and Research Found., Brown Door Kewaunee Dental Soc. (program chmn. 1985-86, sec., treas. 1986-87, v.p. 1987-88, pres. 1988-89), Shawano County Dental Soc. (sec.-treas. 2005-06, pres. 2006—07), St. Louis U. Orthodontic Alumni Assn. (pres. 1988-89), Acad. Gen. Dentistry, Violet Club of Am. Roman Catholic. Avocations: skiing, running, fitness training, raising violets, bicycling. Home: 2160 Greenleaf Rd De Pere WI 54115-8621 Office: 115 Alpine Ct Shawano WI 54166-2041 Home: 10040 Scull Creek Dr Austin TX 78730 Office Phone: 715-526-2544. Personal E-mail: wswetlik@earthlink.net, wswetlik@gmail.com.

SWIBINSKI, EDWARD THOMAS, internist, endocrinologist, educator; b. Jersey City, Jan. 26, 1950; s. Stanley Adolph and Celina Frances (Szymanski) S. BA, Rutgers U., 1972; MD, N.Y. Med. Coll., 1975. Diplomate Am. Bd. Internal Medicine, Am. Bd. Endocrinology and Metabolism. Resident in medicine N.Y. Med. Coll., NYC, 1975-78; gen. internist Nat. Health Svcs. Corp., Camden, NJ, 1978-79; fellow in endocrinology Hosp. of U. Pa., Phila., 1979-80; fellow in endocrinology -R.W. Johnson Med. Sch. U. Medicine and Dentistry N.J., Piscataway, NJ, 1980-81, clin. prof. medicine R.W. Johnson Med. Sch.; clin. prof. medicine Cooper Med. Sch. at Rowan U., Cooper U. Hosp. Med. Sch. Rowan U. Mem. ACP, Phila. Endocrinology Soc. (v.p. 1993-94, bd. dirs. 1991-96, pres. 1994-95), Camden County Med. Soc., Phi Beta Kappa, Alpha Omega Alpha, Am. Diabetes Assn., Endocrine Soc., Am. Assn. Clin. Endrocrinologists. Roman Catholic. Office: 1210 Brace Rd Cherry Hill NJ 08034-3213 Home Phone: 856-424-2052; Office Phone: 856-795-3597.

SWIFT, MICHAEL RONALD, internist, educator; b. NYC, Feb. 5, 1935; s. Herbert Allen and Estelle (Clafter) S.; m. Ronnie Elaine Gorman, Nov. 27, 1971; children— Melissa, Amy, Laura. BA, Swarthmore Coll., 1955; MA in Math., U. Calif.-Berkeley, 1958; MD, NYU Sch. Med., 1962. bd. cert. Am. Bd. Internal Medicine, 1969, Am. Bd. Med. Genetics, 1987. Intern med. Coll. Physicians and Surgeons, NY, 1962—63; asst. resident med. NYU Bellevue Hosp., 1963—64; Instr., then asst. prof. NYU Sch. Medicine, NYC, 1966-70; asst. prof. med., 1970; assoc. prof., then prof. U. N.C., Chapel Hill, 1972-92, also chief genetics div.; prof. pediatrics, dir. Inst. for Genetic Analysis Diseases N.Y. Med. Coll., NYC, 1992—2001, prof. med., pathology, 1998. Dir. Inst. Genetic Analysis Common Diseases, 1994—2001, Disease Insight Rsch. Found., 2004—; CEO Sci. dir. Life Testing LLC (now GenDex LLC), 2001—. Author: Malignant Neoplasms in the Families of Patients with Ataxia Telangiectasia, 1976, Breast Cancer and other Cancers in Ataxia-Telangiectasia Families, 1987, Incidence of Cancer in 161 Families affected by Ataxia-Telangiectasia, 1991, Molecular Genotyping shows that Ataxia Telangiectasia Heterozygotes are Predisposed to Breas Cancer, 1996. Mem. AAAS, Am. Soc. Human Genetics, Alpha Omega Alpha. Achievements include discovery of Mutations in the A-T gene predispose carriers in the general population to cancer, particularly female breast cancer. Avocations: hiking, fishing, travel, theater. Personal E-mail: msuriftmd@gmail.com.

SWILLER, RANDOLPH JACOB, internist; b. NYC, Jan. 21, 1946; s. Abraham Irving and Helen (Emmer) S.; m. Florence Tena Davis, Sept. 3, 1967; children: Jeremy Adam, Rebecca Susan, Steven Eric. BA in Biology cum laude, Hofstra U., 1968; MD, Chgo. Med. Sch., 1972. Diplomate Am. Bd. Psychiatry and Neurology, Am. Bd. Med. Examiners. Intern L.I. Jewish-Hillside Med. Ctr., New Hyde Park, NY, 1972—73; psychiatrist SUNY Downstate Med. Ctr., Bklyn., 1973—76, resident in psychiatry, 1973—76; supervising psychiatrist for psychiatry residents, clin. instr. Maimonides Med. Ctr., Bklyn., 1976—78; med. resident, mem. med. ethics com. Jewish Hosp. Med. Ctr. Bklyn., 1978—80; chief med. resident Greenpont Hosp., 1979—80; fellow in hematology and oncology North Shore U. Hosp., Manhasset, NY, 1980—81; attending physician in internal medicine Fla. Med. Ctr., Lauderdale Lakes, 1982—, mem. credentials and qualifications com., 1986—96; attending physician in internal medicine Coral Springs Med. Ctr., Fla., 1987—. Cons. in internal medicine HealthSouth-Sunrise Rehab. Hosp., 2004—. Co-author: (book) Prognosis Disaster, 2010; asst. editor CMS Quar., 1971—72. Mem. Alpha Epsilon Delta Internat. Premedical Soc., 1966—68, Beta Beta Beta Internat. Biology Soc., 1966—68, Am. Clin. Soc., 1966—68, Am. Cancer Soc., 1980—81. Fellow ACP; mem. AMA, Am. Soc. Internal Medicine, Am. Acad. Psychiatry and the Law, Am. Psychiat. Assn., Am. Cancer Soc. Psychiatry, Fla. Med. Assn., Fla. Psychiat. Soc., Broward County Med. Assn., So. Poverty Law Ctr. Democrat. Jewish. Achievements include research in disseminated intravascular coagulation in obstetrical practice, angioimmunoblatic lymphadenopathy syndrome. Office Phone: 954-340-3775. Office Fax: 954-340-1404. Personal E-mail: rjswillermd@yahoo.com.

SWINKER, MARIAN LEA, public health service officer, state official; b. Phila., Jan. 10, 1951; d. Robert J. and Margaret P. Swinker; m. Allen C. Schlobohm, Dec. 11, 1981. BS, U. Pitts., 1971, MPH, 1972; MD, Pa. State U., 1978. Diplomate American Bd. Preventive Medicine, American Bd. Family Medicine. Chem. technologist Pa. Dept. Environ. Rsch., Pitts., 1973-74; intern W.Va. U. Hosp., Morgantown, 1978-79, resident, 1981-83; physician Nat. Health Svc. Corps, Burton, W.Va., 1979-81; prof. medicine W.Va. U., Morgantown, 1983-94, East Carolina U., Greenville, NC, 1994—2011; commr. W.Va. Dept. Pub. Health, Charleston, 2011—. Hysterectomy panelist RAND, Santa Monica, Calif., 1993-95; bd. dirs. Eastern region N.C. Dept. Labor Safety Sch., Greenville, 1995-97. Contbr. chpt. to book. Mem. American Coll. Occup. & Environ. Medicine (occup. infection com. 1998—), American Acad. Family Physicians, N.C. Med. Soc. (occup. and environ. med. com. 1996—), N.C. Spine Soc., N.C. Occupl. Medicine Assn., Pitt County Med. Soc. Avocations: horseback riding, golf, gardening. Office: West Virginia Department Public Health Room 702 350 Capitol St Charleston WV 25301 Office Phone: 304-558-2971. Office Fax: 304-558-1035. *

SWIONTKOWSKI, MARC FRANCIS, orthopedist; b. Elizabeth, NJ, Sept. 15, 1951; s. William Robert and Agnes Eileen (Baker) S.; m. Beth Ellen, Sept. 2, 1972. BA, Calif. State U., 1973; MD, U. So. Calif., 1979. Gen. surgeon U. Wash., Seattle, 1979-80, resident orthop., 1980-84, assoc. prof., 1988-91, prof., 1991-97; orthopedic cons. KIlimanjoro Christian Med. Ctr., Moshi, Tanzania, 1984; rsch. assoc. Lab. for Experiment, Davos, Switzerland; asst. prof. surgery Vanderbilt U., Nashville, 1985-86, assoc prof., 1986-88; prof., chair dept. orthop. surgery U. Minn., Mpls., 1997—2007, prof. dept. orthop. surgery, 2007—. Fellow Am. Acad. Orthopaedic Surgery, Soc. Internat. Chgo., Chirurgie Orthopaedic Traumatology, Am. Coll. Surgery, Am. Bd. Orthopaedic Surgery (bd. dirs. 1999-2007), Am. Bd. Med. Specialties (bd. dirs. 2007-08). Democrat. Avocations: carpentry, bicycling. Office: U Minn Dept Ortho Surgery 2450 Riverside Ave Minneapolis MN 55454 *

SWISTEL, ALEXANDER JULIAN, surgeon, researcher, educator; b. Munich, Jan. 18, 1949; arrived in US, 1950; s. George and Irene Swistel; m. Patricia Lois Myskowski, July 31, 1976; children: Emily, Christopher(dec.), Gregory. AB, Harvard U., Lawrenceville Sch., 1971; MS in Med. Sci., Rutgers U., NJ, 1973; MD, Brown U. Sch. Medicine, Providence, 1975. Diplomate Am. Bd. Surgery. Intern surgery, then resident surg. oncology St. Luke's-Roosevelt Hosp., NYC, 1975-81; fellow surg. oncology Meml. Sloan-Kettering Cancer Ctr., NYC, 1981-83; asst. clin. prof. surgery Columbia U. Coll. Physicans & Surgeons, NYC, 1984—; asst. to assoc. prof. clin. surgery Cornell U. Weill Med. Coll., NYC, 1996—, also chief Breast Surgery, dir. Weill Cornell Breast Ctr. Sr. attending surg. staff St. Luke's-Roosevelt Hosp., 1984—; attending surg. staff Beth Israel Med. Ctr., NYC, 1984—, NY Presbyn. Hosp./Weill Cornell Med. Ctr., 1996—. Contbr. articles to profl. jours. Named one of Top Drs. for NY Metro Area, Castle Connolly Med. Ltd., 1998—2011, Top Drs. for Cancer, 2007—11, America's Top Doctors, 2008—11. Mem.: ACS, NY Met. Breast Cancer Group (past pres.), Soc. Surg. Oncology, Am. Soc. Breast Surgeons, Am. Soc. Breast Diseases, NY Met. Mammography Soc., Am. Soc. Clin. Oncology, Soc. Head & Neck Surgeons, NY County Med. Soc., Brown Med. Alumni Assn., Union Club (NY).

SYAM, PADMANABHA PILLAI, ophthalmologist, surgeon; s. Padmanabha Pillai and Vijyalekshmi Amma; m. Asha Ambika Nair, Nov. 9, 1995; children: Sharan Pillai, Kaushal Pillai. Degree, Arts Coll., Trivandrum, Kerala, India, 1984; MBBS, U. Kerala, 1991; MS in Ophthalmology, U. Sambalpur, Orissa, India, 1995. Sr. ho. officer Leighton Hosp., Crewe, Cheshire, 1997—98, Eastbourne Dist. Gen. Hosp., East Sussex, 1998—2000; clin. rsch. fellowship in anterior segment surgery Sussex Eye Hosp., Brighton, East Sussex, 2000—02; specialist registrar Calder Royal Hosp., Halifax, Yorkshire, 2002—03, Scarborough Hosp., Yorkhire, 2003—04; staff grade Peterborough Dist. Gen. Hosp., Cambridghsire, 2004—. Staff grade Peterborough Dist. Gen. Hosp., 2004—. Contbr. articles to profl. jours. Recipient Math. Sci. award, U. Kerala, 1982, Sci. Math. award, 1984, Sanskrit award, Goverment Model H.S., 1982. Fellow: Royal Coll. Surgeons; mem.: Internat. Assn. Keratoprosthesis (life). Achievements include research in calcification of intraocular lens. Avocations: swimming, travel, bicycling.

SYED, ELIZABETH CHANCE, health facility administrator, critical care nurse; b. Clermont, Fla., Oct. 18, 1958; d. Brooker Lawson and Beulah Catharine (Lord) Chance; m. Mohsin M. Syed, Dec. 30, 1993; children: Adam, Jibran. B in Gen. Studies, Howard Payne U., 1981; MA in Comm. without thesis, SW Bapt. Theol. Sem., 1985; ADN, Ea. N.Mex. U., 1988. Cert. CCRN, program nurse sr. options, med. office mgr. Critical care nurse Meml. Hosp. & Med. Ctr., Midland, Tex., 1990—94, Angelo Cmty. Med. Ctr., San Angelo, Tex., 1992; staff nurse ICU Med. Ctr. Hosp., Odessa, Tex., 1998; mental health nurse Glenwood Hosp., Midland, Tex., 1998—99; practice adminstr. Family Care Clinic and Med. Spa of Midland, 1998—, MIdland Odessa Symphony Chorale. Instr. ACLS. Mem. Cmty. Chorale, Farmington, N.Mex., 1981, Roswell, N.Mex., 1989-90. Mem. AACN (rsch. assoc. Thunder Project 1991-92). Avocation: music. Home: 100 Bayberry Pkwy Midland TX 79705-3040 Office Phone: 432-689-6818. Business E-Mail: elizabeth@medicalspaofmidland.com.

SYED, IBRAHIM BIJLI, medical educator, physicist, founder evidence based religion; b. Bellary, India, Mar. 16, 1939; came to US, 1969, naturalized, 1975; s. Syed Ahmed Bijli and Mumtaz Begum (Maniyar) S.; m. Sajida Shariff, Nov. 29, 1964; children: Mubin, Zafrin. BS with honors, Veerasaiva Coll., Bellary U., Mysore, 1960; MS with honors and distinction, Bangalore U., Mysore, 1962; diploma, U. Bombay, 1964; DSc, Johns Hopkins U., Balt., 1972; PhD (hon.), Malta, 1985. Cert. hazard control officer, 1980, internat. health care safety profl., 1980; diplomate Am. Bd. Radiology, Am. Bd. Health Physics. Lectr. physics Veerasaiva Coll., Bellary U., Mysore, 1962-63; med. physicist, radiation safety officer Victoria Hosp., India, 1964-67, Bowring and Lady Curz on Hosp. & Postgrad. Med. Rsch. Inst., Bangalore, India, 1964-67; cons. med. physicist, radiation safety officer Ministry of Health, Govt. of Karnataka, India, 1964-67, Bangalore Nursing Home, India, 1964-67; med. physicist, radiation safety officer Baystate Med. Ctr., Springfield, Mass., 1973-79; assoc. prof. Springfield Tech. C.C.; also adj. prof. radiology Holyoke C.C., Mass., 1973-79; asst. clin. prof. nuclear medicine U. Conn. Sch. Medicine, Farmington, 1975-79; cons. med. physicist Mercy Hosp., Springfield, 1973-79, Wing Meml. Hosp., Palmer, Mass., 1973-79; med. physicist, radiation safety officer VAMC, Louisville, 1979—, exec. officer radiation safety com., 1979—; prof. medicine U. Louisville Sch. Medicine, 1979—, dir. nuclear med. scis., 1980—; mem. Instl. Review Bd. Veterans Admin. Medical Ctr., Louisville, 2000—. Guest lectr. religious studies program U. Louisville, 1979—; vis. prof. Bangalore U., 1987—88, Gulbarga U., India, 1987—88; vis. scientist Bhabha Atomic Rsch. Ctr., Bombay; invited spkr. Veerasaiva Coll., Bellary, India, 1996, Vijayanagar Coll., Hospet, 1996, Vajayanagar Inst. Med. Scis., Bellary, 1996, Deccan Coll. Med. Scis., Hyderabad, India, Bhabha Atomic Rsch. Ctr., Bombay, 1997, 15th Ann. Islamic Conf. New Eng., Islamic Coun. New Eng., 1999, Coun. for a Parliament of the World's Religions, Cape Town, South Africa, 1999, Garden City Coll. Bangalore, 2000, Veerasaiva Coll., Bellary, 2000, Islamic Rsch. Found., Mumbai, India, 2001, Islamic Assn. of Essex, England, 2001, Assn. Muslim Social Scientists, Detroit, 2001, Darus Salam, Bangalore, India, 2005; invited faculty Assn. Muslim Social Scientists, Dallas, 2005; invited spkr. Islamic Orgn. Med. Scis., Cairo, 2002; PhD thesis examiner Allahabad U., 1996—; course dir. licensing for nuclear cardiologists U. Louisville, 1980—, mem. admissions com. nuclear medicine program, 1980—; guest relief examiner Am. Bd. Radiology, 1991, 2005; examiner in radiol physics, 1995, 97, 98, 2000; examiner in radiol. physics, 03, 05, 06; mem. panel of examiners Am. Bd. Health Physics; PhD thesis examiner U. Delhi, Internat. Inst. for Advanced Study, Clayton, Mo., 1985—, Allahabad (India) U., 1996—2005; faculty mem. Med. Physicists of India Ann. Meeting, 1987; IAEA tchr. expert in nuclear medicine on mission to People's Republic of Bangladesh, 86; to Guatemala, 94; founder, pres. Islamic Rsch. Found. Internat., Louisville, 1988—; convener Internat. Conf. on Islamic Renaissance: Action Plan for the 21st Century, Chgo., 1995; cons. Coun. Sci. and Indsl. Rsch., Govt. India, 0809—, Am. Coun. Sci. and Health, 1980—; cons. gastroenterology and urology divsn. FDA, HHS, 1988—, cons. radiopharm. divsn., 1989—; cons. Govt. India in nuclear medicine, diagnostic radiol. physics, therapeutic radiol. physics and radiation safety, 1992; cons. radiol. and med. nuc. physics Govt. India, Un Devel. Program, 1992; convenor Internat. Conf. on Islamic Renaissance, Chgo., 1995; guest spkr. Muslim Cmty. Ctr., Chgo., 1988; invited spkr. objective studies and Islamic voice, Bangalore, 96, Parliament of World Religions, Chgo., 1993, Cape Town, South Africa, 99, Cooper Mosque, Mississauga, Ont., Canada, 2002; invited faculty Assn. of Muslim Social Scientists, Dallas, 2005; invited spkr. Internat. Conf. on Alternative Medicine, Cairo, 2002, Darus Salam, Bangalore, India, 2005, Internat. Conf. on Alternative Med., Cairo, 2002. Author: Radiation Safety for Allied Health Professionals, Radiation Safety Manual, 1979, Intellectual Achievements of Muslims, 2002, Qur'anic Inspirations, 2007, contbg. editor Jour. of Islamic Food and Nutrition Coun. of Am., 1986—, health and sci. column Muslim Jour., 1989—; freelance writer Minaret Biweekly, NYC, 1975—, Islamic Voice, India, 1988—, Al-Balaagh, Lenasia, South Africa, 1989—, AL'FURQAN Internat., Norcross, Ga., 1990, Message Internat., Jamaica, NY, 1990, Minaret Monthly Mag., LA, 1995—, The Message, London, 1998—, The Minaret, Botswana, 1998—; editor: Science and Technology for the Developing World, 1988; mem. editl. bd. Jour. Islamic Med. Assn., 1981—; regular contbr. Pres.'s Page; manuscript reviewer for sci. and med. jours., 1973; assoc. editor AAlim, 1998—; contbr. more than 100 articles to sci. jours.; pub. internat. more than 400 articles on various topics of Islam in jours. and mags. Moderator fgn. policy workshop U.S. Dept. State, Louisville, 2000; spkr. Dayton Islamic Ctr., Dayton, 2000, Muslim Student Assn. U. Cin., 2000, Muslim Cmty. Ctr., Chgo., 2001; invited spkr. Muslim Assn. of Cleve. East, 2002, Biotech. Conf., Kuala Lumpur, Malaysia, 2007; adv. bd. Partnership to Prevent Child Abuse, Louisville, 2007—; bd. dir. Nur Islamic Sch., Louisville, 2003, Am. Muslim Assn. Louisville, 2003—; commr. Human Rels. Commn. Metro Louisville Ky. Govt., 2010; bd. dirs. Islamic Ctr. of Louisville, 1992—; founder, mgr., trustee Bijli Found. Charitable Trust, Bellary, India, 2005—. Recipient Disting. Cmty. Svc. award India Cmty. Found., 1982, Hind Rattan Jewel of India Title award Govt. India, 1994, Disting. Svc. award, Am. Bd. radiology, 2008, Mus. Jour. Muslim Civilization Advancement award, 2010; WHO fellow, Govt. India scholar Bhabha Atomic Rsch. Ctr., Bombay, 1963-64; USPHS fellow Johns Hopkins U., 1969-72. Fellow Inst. Physics (UK), Am. Inst. Chemists, Royal Soc. Health, Am. Coll. Radiology, Internat. Acad. Med. Physics; mem. Am. Assn. Physicists in Medicine, Am. Coll. Nuclear Medicine, Health Physics Soc., Am. Acad. Health Physics, Soc. Nuclear Medicine (faculty mem. ann. meeting 1987, convenor internat. conf. 1995), Nat. Assn. Ams. of Asian Indian Descent (chmn. state pub. rels. com. 1982—), Islamic Med. Assn. N.Am. (life, faculty 1994, 96, 98), Internat. Inst. Islamic Medicine (faculty Orlando, Fla. 1996, 97, Birmingham, UK 1998), Islamic Soc. N.Am. (faculty Chgo. 1998), Islamic Soc. Balt. (founding mem.), Islamic Cultural Ctr.(sec. 1999-), Louisville, Islamic Assn. Maritime Provinces Can., Halifax, N.S. (asst. sec. 1967-69), Health Physics Soc. (chmn. med. health physics com. 1989—, affirmative action com. 1984—), Am. Assn. Physicists in Medicine (biol. effects com.), Assn. Muslim Scientists and Engrs. N.Am. (program chmn. ann. conf. 1987, treas. 1987-88, sec. 1988—), AAUP, Soc. Nuc. Medicine India (life, faculty mem. ann. meeting 1987, invited spkr. and faculty ann. meeting 1996), Assn. Med. Physicists India (life, invited spkr. and faculty ann. meeting Madras 1996), Med. and Biol. Physics (divsn. Can.) Assn. Physicists, Hosp. Physicists Assn., NY Acad. Scis., Islamic Assn. Maritime Provinces of Can., Ky. Med. Assn., Jefferson County Med. Soc. (assoc.), Am. Muslim Assn. Louisville (bd. dirs. 2003—), Assn. Muslim Social Scientists, Sigma Xi Islamic. Home: 7102 W Shefford Ln Louisville KY 40242-4642 Office: 800 Zorn Ave Louisville KY 40206-1499 Office Phone: 502-287-6262.

SYED, MUBIN ISAAC, interventional radiologist, neuroradiologist; s. Ibrahim Bijli and Sajida Syed; m. 3 children. BA summa cum laude, Boston U.; MD, Boston U. Sch. Medicine, 1989. Bd. cert. in diagnostic radiology Am. Bd. Radiology, 1994, cert. of added qualifications in vascular and interventional radiology Am. Bd. Radiology, 1998, 2008, of added qualifications in neuroradiology Am. Bd. Radiology, 1999, 2009, diplomate Am. Bd. Interventional Pain Physicians. Resident in medicine U. Louisville Affiliated Hosps., 1989—90, Ind. U. Med. Ctr., Indpls., 1990, resident in radiology, 1990—94, fellow in neuroradiology, 1994—95, fellow in vascular and interventional radiology, 1995—96; vis. fellow Miami Vascular Inst., 1996; ptnr. Diagnostic Imaging Assocs. Ohio, Springfield, 1996—2001, Radiology Physicians Springfield, 2001—06; pres. Dayton Interventional Radiology, 2005—, Elizabeth Pl. interventional cons., ptnr., 2007—; ptnr. Pure M.D., 2011—; clin. assoc. prof. radiol. scis. Wright State U. Sch. Medicine, Dayton, Ohio, 2006—; summer rsch. fellow NIH, Bethesda, Md., 2007. Faculty, spkr. Otsuka Pharms., 1999—2004; spkr., moderator Genentech, 2000—01; faculty, keynote spkr., cons. Stryker Interventional Pain, 2002—; faculty, spkr. Arthrocare Inc., 2004—08; med. dir. MedScan Middletown Open MRI, 2004—08; spkr. Possis Inc., 2006—08; faculty, spkr. Bacchus Vascular, 2006—08, Am. Soc. Internat. Pain Physicians, 2007—. Author: (book) Radiology of Non Spinal Pain Procedures, 2010; Contbr. articles to profl. jours., chapters to books, presenter in field,. Chmn. movie com. Coll. of Liberal Arts Forum, Boston U., 1984-85, del., 1983-84. NIH Summer Rsch. fellow, 1987; Nat. Merit scholar, 1983, William Marshall Warren scholar Boston U., 1985; recipient Silver medal U.S. Acad. Decathlon, 1983, named Practice Leader CME Tchg. Vertebroplasty to Physicians; Nominee Physician of Yr., Cmty. Mercy Health Ptnrs., 2006. Fellow: Am. Coll. Radiology, Soc. Interventional Radiology (faculty, instr. 2003-08, Cert. Recognition for Disting. Faculty 2005), AMA; Mem. Montgomery County Med. Soc., Ohio State Med. Assn., Ohio State Radiol. Soc., Am. Soc. Spine Radiology, Radiol. Soc. N.Am., Am. Roentgen Ray Soc., Vascular Access Soc. America, Am. Soc. Interventional Pain Physicians, Am. Soc. Neuroradiology (sr.), Islamic Med. Assn. N.Am., Assn. Physicians Indian Origin, Assn. Physicians Pakistani Decent N. Am., Nat. Geographic Soc. (life), Islamic Rsch. Found. (bd. trustees), Endovascular Com., Good Samaritan Hosp., Phi Beta Kappa. Muslim. Avocations: music composition, chess, tennis, table tennis, running. Home: 3108 Henderson Ct Springfield OH 45503-1307 Office: Dayton Interventional Radiology 3075 Governors Pl Blvd Ste 120 Dayton OH 45409 Office Phone: 937-424-2580. Office Fax: 937-424-2581. Business E-Mail: mubinsyed@aol.com.

SYED, MUSHABBAR A., cardiologist; b. Gujrat, Punjab, Pakistan, May 24, 1962; s. Muzaffar A. and Rashida Syed; m. Humaira Syed, May 28, 1988; children: Daneyal, Ameena, Aleena. MD, King Edward Med. Coll., Lahore, Pakistan, 1987. Diplomate in cardiovasc. diseases Am. Bd. Internal Medicine, 2002, Am. Bd. Internal Medicine, 1997, Am. Bd. Internal Medicine, 2009, cert. Ednl. Comm. Fgn. Med. Graduates, 1994. Resident Sheikh Zayed Hosp., Lahore, 1988—89; house officer Mayo Hosp., Lahore, 1988, med. officer, 1989—90; resident Blackburn Royal Infirmary, England, 1991—94, Henry Ford Hosp., Detroit, 1994—97, attending physician, 1997—99, chief fellow cardiology, 1999—2002; fellow cardiovasc. MRI NIH, Bethesda, Md., 2002—04; dir. cardiac imaging Emory U. Sch. Medicine, Atlanta, 2004—06, dir., advanced cardiovasc. imaging U. Ky., Lexington, 2006—10; dir. cardiovascular imaging Loyola U. Med. Ctr., Maywood, Ill. Contbr. articles to rsch. papers (ACCP Young Investigator award, 1997). Fellow: Am. Coll. Cardiology (sci. sessions planning com. mem. 2008—); mem.: Soc. Cardiovasc. MRI, Assn. Pakistani Cardiologists N. America (chair sci. com. 2007—08), Soc. Cardiovasc. CT (regional dir. 2007—08). Avocations: travel, reading. Home: 2160 S First Ave Maywood IL 60153

SYKES, NIGEL PHILIP, palliative medicine physician, consultant; b. London, Oct. 10, 1954; s. Basil and Margaret (Knee) S.; m. Anne Charlotte Lloyd, Aug. 11, 1984; children: Catherine, Rachel, Peter. BA, Oxford U., Eng., 1977, BM, BCh, 1980, MA, 1981. Macmillan lectr. palliative medicine U. Leeds, Eng., 1987-91; registrar, sr. registrar in palliative medicine St. Christopher's Hospice, London, 1985 87, cons. in palliative medicine, 1991—. Chmn. palliative care working group Yorkshire (Eng.) Cancer Orgn., 1988-91; hon. cons. St. Thomas' Hosp., London, 1991—, Guy's Hosp., London, 1991—; sr. lectr. King's Coll., U. London; mem. Nat. Coun. Palliative Care Strategy, Group On Neurological Palliative care, 2004-; chmn. Help the Hospices Internat. Palliative Care Reference Group; spkr. in field. Contbg. author: Oxford Textbook of Palliative Medicine, 1993, 3d edit., 2004; co-editor: The Management of Terminal Malignant Disease, 1993, Cancer Pain, 2003, 2d edit. 2008, Management of Advanced Disease, 2004; mem. editl. adv. com. Hospice Jour., 1995-99, Jour. Palliative Medicine, 1998—, Clin. Oncology, 2006—, Jour. Pain Symptom Mgmt., 2008-; contbr. numerous articles to med. jours., including Lancet, Palliative Medicine, Jour. Pain and Symptom Mgmt., Geriatric Medicine, also chpts. to books. Spkr. all-party hospice com. Houses of Parliament, London and many Nat. and Internat. Conf. Fellow Royal Coll. Physicians, Royal Coll. Gen. Practitioners, Royal Soc. Arts; n Higher Edn. Acad., mem. Assn. for Palliative Medicine Gt. Britain and Ireland (treas., exec. com. 1988-92, mem. ethics com. 1995-2001, Evans prize for rsch. 1991), European Assn. for Palliative Medicine, Brit. Med. Assn., Oxford Med. Grads. Soc. Anglican. Office: St Christopher's Hospice Lawrie Park Rd London SE26 6DZ England Business E-Mail: n.skykes@stchristopher.org.uk.

SYKES, ROBIN ALEXIS, plastic surgeon; b. McKeesport, Pa., May 17, 1954; d. Robert T. and Joyce P. Sykes; m. Thomas Richard Rowe, Aug. 12, 1989; children: Galen, Alexis. BA in Biology, Wells Coll., 1976; MD, Johns Hopkins U., 1980; postgrad., U. Miami, 1983, U. Kans., 1985. Diplomate Am. Bd. Med. Specialties. Pvt. practice, Jupiter, Fla., 1985—. Reporter Healthvision TV Sta. WPBF, 2001—02; spkr. in field. Mem.: Palm Beach County Plastic Surgeons, Am. Soc. for Laser and Medicine and Surgery, Am. Med. Womens Assn., Fla. Soc. Plastic Surgeons, Am. Soc. Plastic Surgeons, Fla. Med. Assn. Avocations: music, reading, travel, theater, movies. Office: Jupiter Plastic Surgery Ctr 2055 Military Tr Ste 305 Jupiter FL 33458 Office Phone: 561-746-9400. Personal E-mail: drrasplastic@aol.com.

SYKIOTIS, GERASIMOS, biomedical researcher, geneticist; US, 2003; MD, U. Patras, 1997, PhD, 2003. Resident internal medicine Patras U. Hosp., 1998—2000; postdoctoral rsch. assoc. U. Rochester Med. Ctr., NY, 2003—07; investigator Novartis Insts. for Biomed. Rsch., Cambridge, Mass., 2007—09; clin. rsch. fellow Reproductive Endocrinology Mass. Gen. Hosp., Harvard Med. Sch., 2009—. Contbr. articles to 20 scholarly rsch. jours., med. textbooks. Mem.: AAAS, Endocrine Soc., Hellenic Bioscientific Assn. USA, Hellenic Med. Assn., Nat. Postdoctoral Assn., Soc. Free Radical Biology and Medicine, Genetics Soc. Am., Am. Assn. Cancer Rsch. Home: 144 Sherman Rd Chestnut Hill MA 02467-3179

SYMEONIDES, PHIVOS KOSTAS, cardiologist; b. Nicosia, Cyprus, Sept. 5, 1971; s. Kostas Nikolaos Symeonides and Despoina Kostas Symeonidou; 1 child, Despoina Phivos Symeonidou. Med. diploma, Athens Med. Sch., Greece, 1996. US med. lic. Ednl. Commn. Fgn. Med. Grad., 1998, diplomate cardiologist Athens, 2003, cert. in ALS provider course European Resuscitation Coun., 2006. Pre-registration tng. Nicosia Gen. Hosp., Cyprus, 1996—97; cardiology resindency program Internal Medicine, Arta Dist. Gen. Hosp., Greece, 1997—99, Evangelismos Hosp., Athens, 1999—2003; cardiologist Euroclinic, Athens, 2003—05; cons. cardiologist Mitera Clinic, Athens, 2003—05; cardiologist Nicosia Gen. Hosp., 2005—07, Hippocrateon Pvt. Hosp., Nicosia, 2007—. Contbr. articles to profl. jours. & med. mags., chapters to books. With Cyprus Army, 1988—90. Recipient award, Greek Diabetes Soc.; Greek Found. scholarships, 1990—96. Mem.: Greek Soc. Cardiology, Cyprus Resuscitation Coun., Cyprus Soc. Cardiology, Greek Heart Failure Soc., Greek Med. Soc., Cyprus Med. Soc., Am. Soc. Angiology. Achievements include research in comparison of the effects of ramipril vs telmisartan in reducing serum levels of high sensitivity c-reactive protein and oxidized low-density lipoprotein-cholesterol in patients with type II diabetes; acute changes in N-terminal pro-brain natriuretic peptide induced by dobutamine stress echo cardiography. Avocations: travel, music, reading. Office: Hippocrateon Pvt Hosp Psaron 6-12 Engomi Nicosia 2408 Cyprus Home: Markou Drakou 2650 Nicosia Cyprus Office Fax: 35722351938. Personal E-mail: phisym@hotmail.com. Business E-Mail: drphisym@gmail.com.

SYMONDS, ERIN LEIGH, research scientist; b. Adelaide, May 20, 1977; BS (hon.), U. Adelaide, 1998, PhD, 2003. Med. scientist Gastroenterology Dept., Womens & Childrens Hosp., 2002—05; postdoc. fellow Elementary Pharmabiotic Ctr., U. Coll. Cork, 2005—08, Nutrigenomics & Nutrigenetics Lab., CSIRO Food & Nutritional Sc, 2008—10; sr. rsch. officer Nerve-Gut Rsch. Lab., Royal Adelaide Hosp., 2010—. Recipient Outreach award, NASPGN soc., Internat. Travel award, Internat. Congress Nutrition Internat. Union Nutritional Scis. & Nutrition Assn. Thailand; named Young South Austlralian of Yr., SA Gt.; CJ Martin fellowship, NHMRC Australia, Travel grant, Australian Gastroenterology Week. Mem.: Nutrition Soc. Australia. Home: 16 Ellen St Nailsworth SA 5083 Australia Personal E-mail: erinsymonds@yahoo.com.

SYN, WING-KIN, gastroenterologist, hepatologist, researcher; b. Singapore, 1972; s. Y. and W. Syn. MBChB with honors, U. Sheffield, 1998. Intern Royal Hallamshire Hosp., Sheffield, England, 1998—99; sr. ho. officer in medicine U. Hosp. Birmingham, West Midlands, England, 1999—2001; sr. ho. officer in hepatology King's Coll. Liver Unit, London, 2001—02; gastroenterology and hepatology specialist registrar Liver and Hepatobiliary Unit, 2002—07, advanced hepatology specialist registrar, 2006—07, hepatologist, 2007—; rschr. divsn. gastroenterology Duke U., Durham, NC, 2007—, U. Birmingham, England, 2008—; hon. prof. Dept. Physiology, U. Basque County, Bilbao, Spain, U. Basque County, Bilbao, Clinician Nat. Health Svc., 1998—; rschr. Duke U., 2007—; hon. prof. dept. physiology U. Basque Country Bikao, Serbia. Recipient Bronze Medal, U. Sheffield, 1994, Travel Fellowship award, Midlands Gastroenterology Soc., EASL Sheila Sterlock award. Mem.: Brit. Assn. Study of Liver, Med. Rsch. Soc., ACP, Brit. Soc. Gastroenterology, European Assn. Study of Liver, Royal Coll. Physicians. Office: Duke Univ GSRB-1 DUMC 3256 595 LaSalle Street Durham NC 27710

SYNDER, MICHAEL, pediatric cardiologist, educator; BA with honors, Williams Coll., Williamstown, Mass., 1975; MD, Cornell U., Ithaca, NY, 1979. Diplomate Am. Bd. Pediatrics, 1984, Am. Bd. Pediatrics-pediatric cardiology. Intern pediat. Cornell Med. Hosp., NYC, 1979—80, resident pediat., 1980—82, fellow pediatric cardiology, 1982—84; assoc. clin. prof. pediat. Columbia Univ. Med. Ctr.; pediatric cardiologist Stamford Hosp. Co-author: (articles) A five-year clinical experience with 112 Blalock-Taussig shunts, 1993, Right and left ventricular performance 10 years after Mustard repair of transposition of the great arteries, 1994, Nature of heart failure in patients with ventricular septal defect, 1995, Regional functional depression immediately after ventricular septal defect closure, 2004, Expression of gastric pyloric mucin, MUC6, in colorectal serrated polyps, 2010, various others. Office: Stamford Hospital 30 Shelburne Rd Stamford CT 06904 Office Phone: 203-276-1000.

SZABO, ATTILA, medical researcher; BS, McGill U., 1968; PhD, Harvard U., 1973. Chief theoretical biophysical chemistry sect. Lab. of Chem. Physics Nat. Inst. Diabetes and Digestive and Kidney Diseases, NIH, Bethesda, Md. Contbr. articles to profl. jours. Mem.: NAS, Biophysical Soc. (Founders Award). Office: National Institue of Health NIDDK Bldg 5, Rm 138 5 Memorial Dr Bethesda MD 20892 Office Phone: 301-496-2650. Office Fax: 301-496-0825. E-mail: attilas@mail.nih.gov. *

SZAKACS, GERGELY, medical researcher; b. Budapest, Hungary, Mar. 20, 1970; MD, Semmelweis Med. U., 1996, PhD, 2001. Lab. head Hungarian Acad. Scis., 2006—. ERC Starting grant, European Union, Marie Curie fellowship, Young Rschr.s' Program grant, Hungarian Acad. Scis., Bolyai fellowship, SDIG fellowship, European Molecular Biology Orgn. Avocation: classical music. Office: Karolina ut 29 Budapest Pest 1026 Hungary Business E-Mail: kagyek@freemail.hu.

SZAKAL, ANDRAS KALMAN, immunologist, anatomist, educator; s. Andor Viktor and Maria Szakal; m. Norma Elisabeth Skinner; children: Andras Robert, Tamas Kalman. BA in Zoology, U. Colo., 1961, MA in Biology, 1963; PhD, U. Tenn., 1972. Rsch. biologist for immunology of carcinogenesis group divsn. biology Oak Ridge (Tenn.) Nat. Labs., 1972—74; prin. scientist Meloy Labs., Springfield, Va., 1974—79; assoc. prof. dept. anatomy, divsn. immunobiology Va. Commonwealth Univ./Med Sch., Richmond, 1979—91, prof. dept. anatomy and neurobiology and The Immunology Group, 1991—2005. Cons. electron microscopist in exptl. biology Oak Ridge Nat. Lab., 1969—70; cons. electron microscopist Lunar Receiving Lab., NASA Manned Spacecraft Ctr., Houston, 1969; cons. on electron micros.

autoradiography Nat. Cancer Inst., NIH, Bethesda, Md., 1974. Contbr. articles to profl. jours. Grantee, NIH, Nat. Inst. on Aging, 1985—88, 1991—94, 1999—2004. Mem.: AAAS, Va. Acad. Sci., Am. Assn. Immunologists, Am. Assn. Anatomists. Achievements include discovery of Antigen Transport Cell; ICCOSOMEs and the role of follicular dendritic cells (FDCs) in aging; demonstrated periodicity of immune complex finding on FDCs.

SZÁLLÁSI, JÁNOS, retired oncologist; b. Budapest, Hungary, June 28, 1941; s. Sándor Szállási and Rózsa Novák; m. Ilona Boross, July 1, 1965; 1 child, Zoltán. MD, Med. U., Budapest, 1966. Cert. Registration Ministry Health, 1967. Surgeon, anaesthesiologist 3rd Surg. Clinic, Budapest, 1966—71, Polyclinic of the 18th Dist., Budapest, 1971—80, Jahn Ferenc Hosp., Budapest, 1980—91, clin. oncologist, 1991—2005, Oncological Welfare Ctr. 18th Dist., 1991—2009. Med. advisor CD of the 18th Dist., Budapest, 1968—95. Editor: Hungarian Ostomy Organizations about Themselves, 1993, (book) 10 Years of the Ostomy Club of South Pest, 1997, 15 Years of the Ostomy Club of South Pest, 2003, Ostomy Jour. South Pest, 1997—2004; co-author: (book) Treatment and Care of Abdominal Stoma, 1997. Lt. med. Hungarian Army, 1967—68. Recipient medal, Hungarian Govt., 1978, 1983, 1988, Bronze medal, Hungarian Red Cross, 1981, Solicitude for the Human award, Local Govt. of the 18th Dist. of Budapest, 1996, Hon. Diploma, Min. of Health, 2003. Mem.: Hungarian Ostomy Assn. (cons. 1987—2004), Ostomy Club South Pest (med. dir. 1987—2004), Hungarian Soc. Clin. Oncology, Hungarian Surg. Soc., Hungarian Soc. Anaesthesiology. Roman Catholic. Personal E-mail: janos@szallasi.hu.

SZASZ, THOMAS STEPHEN, psychiatrist, educator, writer; b. Budapest, Hungary, Apr. 15, 1920; came to U.S., 1938, naturalized, 1944; s. Julius and Lily (Wellisch) S.; m. Rosine Loshkajian, Oct. 19, 1951 (div. 1970); children: Margot Szasz Peters, Susan Marie Szasz Palmer. AB, U. Cin., 1941, MD, 1944; DSc (hon.), Allegheny Coll., 1975, U. Francisco Marroquin, Guatemala, 1979; LHD (hon.), Towson U., 1999; D Sc(hon.), SUNY, 2001. Diplomate: Nat. Bd. Med. Examiners, Am. Bd. Psychiatry and Neurology. Intern 4th Med. Service Harvard, Boston City Hosp., 1944-45; asst. resident medicine Cin. Gen. Hosp., 1945-46, asst. clinician internal medicine div. out-patient dispensary, 1946; asst. resident psychiatry U. Chgo. Clinics, 1946-47; tng. research fellow Inst. Psychoanalysis, Chgo., 1947-48, rsch. asst., 1949-50, staff mem., 1951-56; practice medicine, specializing in psychiatry, psychoanalysis Chgo., 1949-54, Bethesda, Md., 1954-56, Syracuse, NY, 1956—; prof. psychiatry SUNY Health Sci. Ctr., Syracuse, 1956-90, prof. psychiatry emeritus, 1990—. Vis. prof. dept. psychiatry U. Wis., Madison, 1962, Marquette U. Sch. Medicine, Milw., 1968, U. N.Mex., 1981; holder numerous lectureships, including C.P. Snow lectr. Ithaca Coll., 1970; E.S. Meyer Meml. lectr. U. Queensland Med. Sch.; Lambie-Dew orator Sydney U., 1977; Mem. nat. adv. com. bd. Tort and Med. Yearbook; cons. com. mental hygiene N.Y. State Bar Assn.; mem. research adv. panel Inst. Study Drug Addiction; adv. bd. Corp. Econ. Edn., 1977— Author: Pain and Pleasure, 1957, The Myth of Mental Illness, 1961, Law, Liberty and Psychiatry, 1963, Psychiatric Justice, 1965, The Ethics of Psychoanalysis, 1965, Ideology and Insanity, 1970, The Manufacture of Madness, 1970, The Second Sin, 1973, Ceremonial Chemistry, 1974, Heresies, 1976, Karl Kraus and the Soul-Doctors, 1976, Schizophrenia: The Sacred Symbol of Psychiatry, 1976, Psychiatric Slavery, 1977, The Theology of Medicine, 1977, The Myth of Psychotherapy, 1978, Sex by Prescription, 1980, The Therapeutic State, 1984, Insanity: The Idea and its Consequences, 1987, The Untamed Tongue: A Dissenting Dictionary, 1990, Our Right to Drugs: The Case for a Free Market, 1992, A Lexicon of Lunacy, 1993, Cruel Compassion, 1994, The Meaning of Mind, 1996, Fatal Freedom, 1999, Pharmacracy: Medicine and Politics in America, 2001, Liberation By Oppression: A Comparative Study of Slavery and Psychiatry, 2002, Words to the Wise: A Medical-Philosophical Dictionary, 2004, Faith in Freedom: Libertarian Principles and Psychiatric Practices, 2004, Szasz Under Fire: The Psychiatric Abolitionist Answers His Critics, 2004, My Madness Saved Me: The Madness and Mariage of Virginia Woolf, 2006, Coercion as Cure: A Critical History of Psychiatry, 2007, The Medicalization of Everyday Life, 2007, Psychiatry: The Science of Lies, 2008, Antipsychiatry: Quackery Squared, 2009, Suicide Prohibition: The Shame of Medicine, 2011; editor: The Age of Madness, 1973; cons. editor of Psychiatry and Psychology: Stedman's Medical Dictionary, 22d edit, 1973; contbg. editor: Reason, 1974—, Libertarian Rev., 1986—; mem. editl. bd. Psychoanalytic Rev, 1965—, Jour. Contemporary Psychotherapy, 1968—, Law and Human Behavior, 1977—, Jour. Libertarian Studies, 1977—, Children and Youth Services Rev, 1978—, Am. Jour. Forensic Psychiatry, 1980—, Free Inquiry, 1980—. Comdr. M.C., USNR, 1954-56. Recipient Stella Feiss Hofheimer award U. Cin., 1944, Holmes-Munsterberg award Internat. Acad. Forensic Psychology, 1969; Wisdom award honor, 1970; Acad. prize Institutum atque Academia Auctorum Internationalis, Andorra, 1972; Distinguished Service award Am. Inst. Pub. Service, 1974; Martin Buber award Midway Counseling Center, 1974, Thomas S. Szasz award Ctr. Ind. Thought, 1990, Alfred R. Lindesmith award for achievement in field of scholarship and writing Drug Policy Found., 1991, Rollo May award APA, 1998; others; named Humanist of Year Am. Humanist Assn., 1973; Hon. fellow Postgrad. Center for Mental Health, 1961, Mencken award, 1981, Humanist Laureate, 1984, Statue of Liberty-Ellis Island Found. Archives Roster, 1986, George Washington award Am. Hungarian Found., 2003. Fellow Am. Psychiat. Assn. (life), Am. Psychoanalytic Assn., Internat. Psychoanalytic Soc., Western N.Y. Psychoanalytic Soc. Home: 4739 Limberlost Ln Manlius NY 13104-1405 Office: 750 E Adams St Syracuse NY 13210-2306 Personal E-mail: tszasz@aol.com.

SZEBENI, AGNES, internist; d. Miklós and Miklósné Szebeni; m. Imre Szentpétery, July 14, 1955; children: Mária Szentpétery, Julia Szentpétery. MD, Semmelweis Med. U., Budapest, Hungary, 1956, PhD, 1988, DSc, 1999. Internist Péterfy S. Hosp., Postgrad. Med. U., Budapest, 1956—79; chief ultrasound lab. MI Ctrl. Hosp., Budapest, 1979—2007; ret. Dr., pvt. docent Semmelweis Med. U., 1998—. Author: (monography) Ultrasonography in Internal Medicine, 1988, 2d edit., 2003; contbr. chapters to books, to profl. publs. Mem.: Hungarian Radiol. Soc., Hungarian Oncological Soc., Hungarian Gastroent. Soc. (pres. ultrasound sect. 1975—93), Hungarian Ultrasound Soc., European Union Med. Specialists, Internat. Soc. Prevention Clin. Medicine, Am. Inst. Ultrasound in Medicine, NY Acad. Scis., World Fedn. Ultrasound in Medicine and Biology, European Fedn. Ultrasound in Medicine and Biology, Hungarian Soc. Internal Medicine, Hungarian Biophysical Soc. (pres. ultrasound sect. 1972—2011), Deutsche Gesellschaft Ultraschall and Medicine (corr.), Internat. Gastrosurg. Club. Personal E-mail: szebenius@t-online.hu.

SZEGO, CLARA MARIAN, cell biologist, educator; b. Budapest, Hungary, Mar. 23, 1916; arrived in U.S., 1921, naturalized, 1927; d. Paul S. and Helen (Elek) S.; m. Sidney Roberts, Sept. 14, 1943. AB, Hunter Coll., 1937; MS, U. Minn., 1939, PhD, 1942; DSc (hon.), CUNY, 2007. Instr. physiology U. Minn., 1942-43; Minn. Cancer Rsch. Found. fellow, 1943—44; rsch. assoc. OSRD, Nat. Bur. Stds., 1944-45, Worcester Found. Exptl. Biology, 1945-47; rsch. instr. physiol. chemistry Yale U. Sch. Medicine, 1947-48; mem. faculty UCLA, 1948—, prof. biology, 1960—. Contbr. articles to profl. jours., book chapters and revs. Garvan fellow U. Minn., 1939; Guggenheim fellow, 1956; named Woman of Year in Sci. Los Angeles Times, 1957-58; named to Hunter Coll. Hall of Fame, 1987. Fellow AAAS; mem. Am. Physiol. Soc., Am. Soc. Cell Biology, Endocrine Soc. (CIBA award 1953), Soc. for Endocrinology (Gt. Britain), Biochem. Soc. (Gt. Britain), Internat. Soc. Rsch. Reproduction, Phi Beta Kappa (pres. UCLA chpt. 1973-74), Sigma Xi (pres. UCLA chpt. 1976-77). Home: 1371 Marinette Rd Pacific Palisades CA 90272-2627 Office: U Calif Dept Molecular Cell & Devel Biology Los Angeles CA 90095-1606 Business E-Mail: cmszego@ucla.edu.

SZEREMETA-BROWAR, TAISA LYDIA, endodontist; b. Geneva, NY, Mar. 21, 1957; d. Swiatoslaw Bohdan and Stefania (Melnyk) Szeremeta; m. Andrew Wolodymyr Browar, Sept. 19, 1981. BS in Dentistry, Case Western Res. U., 1978, DDS, 1980; cert. specialty endodontics magna cum laude, U. Ill., Chgo., 1982. Pvt. practice Hinsdale (Ill.) Periodontics and Endodontics, 1982—; asst. clin. prof. Northwestern U. Dental Sch., Chgo., 1986—97. Adminstr. Ukrainian Sch. Dance, 2001—08. Counselor, mem. Plast-Ukrainian Scouting, 1963—; presenting team Worldwide Marriage Encounter, Chgo., 1985-94; mem. parish coun. Sts. Volodymyr and Olha, Chgo., 1985-94. E. Wach rsch. grantee U. Ill., Chgo., 1980. Mem. ADA, Am. Assn. Endodontists, Am. Coll. Stomatologic Surgeons, Ukrainian Med. Assn. (chair membership 1983-88), Ill. Assn. Endodontists (pres. 1990-91), Ill. State Dental Soc., Chgo. Dental Soc. (sec. table clinic 1990, vice chair 1991, chair 1992, sec. dental benefits com. 2002, 05, 08, vice chmn., 2003, 06, 09, chmn. 2004, 07, 10), Hinsdale C. of C. Ukrainian Catholic. Avocations: embroidery, marriage enrichment, marriage preparation, theology. Office: Hinsdale Periodontics & Endodontics 40 S Clay St Ste 111W Hinsdale IL 60521-3280 Office Phone: 630-655-3737. Personal E-mail: healthysmile@msn.com.

SZERLAG, CHESTER THEODORE, health care executive; MBA, U. Chgo., 1984. Exec. dir. U. Chgo., 1980—. Contbr. articles to profl. jours.; mem. editl. bd.: Enterprise Imaging and Radiation Oncology Management Jour. Pres. Chgo. Health Exec. Forum, 2010, past pres., 2011; bd. trustee Village of Woodridge, Ill., 1997—2005; vice chmn. U. Chgo. Credit Union, Ill., 2001—. Recipient Gold medal, Soc. Radiation Oncology Adminstrs., 1991. Fellow: Am. Coll. Healthcare Execs.; mem.: Healthcare Fin. Mgmt. Assn., Radiol. Soc. N.Am. (chair assoc. sci. consortium), Am. Coll. Med. Practice Execs. (cert. med. practice exec. 2004), Soc. Radiation Oncology Adminstrs. (pub. chair, past treas., past. pres., past chmn.), Woodrige Club (pres. 2005—06), Rotary Internat. (asst. dist. gov. 2008—). Office: Univ Chgo 5758 S Maryland Ave MC 9006 Chicago IL 60637 Business E-Mail: cszerlag@radonc.uchicago.edu.

SZIGETI, NÓRA, gastroenterologist, educator; b. Szombathely, County Vas, Hungary, Feb. 4, 1972; d. Lajos Szigeti and Hilda Huber. Physician U. Pécs, County Baranya, Hungary, 1996—2001, asst. lectr., 2001—10, asst. prof., 2010—. Home: 58 Surányi u Pécs County Baranya 7625 Hungary Office: Univ Pécs 1 Pacsirta u Pécs Baranya County 7624 Hungary Business E-Mail: nora.szigeti@aok.pte.hu.

SZILAGYI, GEORGE, microbiologist, physician; b. Carei, Romania, Dec. 30, 1916; s. Adolph Szilagyi and Lotte Kepecs; m. Magdalena Virag, Aug. 11, 1945; children: Edith, Andrew. MD, Franz Joseph U., 1942. Lab. physician, microbiologist Lab. Hygiene, Oradea, Romania, 1942-49; chief dept. of labs. Anti-Epidemic Ctr., Satu-Mare, Romania, 1949-62; rsch. assoc. Montefiore Hosp., Bronx, N.Y., 1963-69; dir. microbiology Albert Einstein Hosp., Bronx, 1969-96, asst. prof. microbiology and immunology, 1971-79, assoc. prof. microbiology, immunology and lab. medicine, 1979-93, assoc. prof. microbiology, immunology and pathology, 1993-96; assoc. prof. emeritus Albert Einstein Coll. Medicine, Bronx, 1996—. Contbr. articles to sci. and profl. jours. Fellow Am. Acad. Microbiology. Avocations: photography, hiking, travel. Home: 67-71 Yellowstone Blvd Forest Hills NY 11375 Office: Jack D Weiler Hosp 1825 Eastchester Rd Bronx NY 10461-2301 Office Phone: 718-794-1359. E-mail: gszilagy@montefiore.org.

SZNAJDERMAN, MAREK, retired physician, researcher, educator; b. Warsaw, Aug. 28, 1929; s. Ignacy and Amelia (Rozenberg) S.; m. Malgorzata Ciswicka, Mar. 23, 1958 (dec. Sept. 1988); 1 child, Monika; m. Teresa Wasowska, Aug. 31, 1991. MD, Med. Acad., Warsaw, 1959. Asst., sr. asst. Med. Acad., Warsaw, 1952-70, assoc. prof., 1971-80, prof., 1980—. Head dept. hypertension Nat. Inst. Cardiology, Warsaw, 1981-99. Co-author: Arterial Hypertension, 5 edits., 1983-90; editor: Polish Cardiology; author or co-author of numerous sci. papers in Polish and fgn. med. jours. Recipient State Prize for Sci. Achievements, 1980. Mem. Polish Soc. Cardiology, Polish Soc. Internal Medicine, Polish Soc. Hypertension (v.p. 1992-94), Polish Soc. Atherosclerosis Rsch. Avocations: tourism, classical music, literature. Home: Okolnik 11a Apt 6 Warsaw 00-368 Poland E-mail: marek.sznajderman@neostrada.pl.

SZNAJER, YVES, pediatrician, educator; b. Brussels, Aug. 6, 1967; s. Jozef Sznajer and Fanny Rosenblum; m. Caroline Anne Zalcman, Aug. 5, 2003. MD, U. Libre Bruxelles, Brussels, 1985; MSc in Biomedical Scis., U. Montréal, 2000; PhD student, U. Libre Bruxelles, 2006—, diploma, 2003. Cert. Belgian Ministry Health, 1999, pediatrician Belgian Ministry Health, 2000, intensivist Belgian Ministry Health, 2001. Resident pediat. U. Libre Bruxelles, 1994—99, pediatric and prenatal genetics, cons., 2002—; fellowship pediatric intensive care U. Montréal, Quebec, Canada, 1998—2000; registrar clin. genetics Hôsp. Robert Debré, Paris, 2002. Translator: (book) New Clinical Genetics - Génétique Médicale: de la biologie à la clinique; co-author: Pediatric Emergency handbook: Urgences en Pédiatrie; contbr. articles to profl. jours. Com. mem. Belgian Soc. Human Genetics, Brussels, 2004—, 2008—. Mem.: European Soc. Human Genetics, Am. Soc. Human Genetics. Home: Nekkersgat ave 3 1180 Brussels Belgium Office: Ctr Genetique Tour R Franklin Ave Mounier 52 B1200 Brussels Belgium Office Fax: 3227646936. Business E-Mail: yves.sznajer@uclouvain.be.

SZODORAY, PETER, physician, researcher; b. Debrecen, Hungary, Feb. 17, 1973; m. Britt Nakken. MD, U. Debrecen, 1998; PhD, Broegelmann Rsch. Lab., U. Bergen, Norway, 2005. Chief physician, 3rd dept. medicine Med. and Health Sci. Ctr., U. Debrecen, 1998—2008. Postdoc. rsch. scientist Okla. Med. Rsch. Found., Okla. City, 2003—05. Achievements include discovery of pathogenesis of systemic autoimmune diseases.

SZOMSTEIN, SAMUEL, medical association administrator; b. NYC, Jan. 16, 1968; MD, Ctrl. U. Venezuela, 1993. Assoc. dir. bariatris, metabolic inst. Cleve. Clinic Fla., 2001—. Assoc. clin. prof. surgery NOVA Sutheastern U., 2009—11, Fla. Internat. U., 2011; asst. prof. surgery Fla. Atlantic U., 2011. Named Dr. of Yr., Cleve. Clinic Fla.; named one of America's Top Surgeon, Consumer Rsch. Coun. Am., 2004—06, Top Dr., Gold Coast/Boca Life Mag., 2010, Castle Connolly, 2010, 2011. Fellow: ACS, Am. Soc. Metabolic and Bariatric Surgery. Avocation: baseball. Office: 2950 Cleveland Clinic Blvd Weston FL 33331 Office Fax: 954-659-5256. Business E-Mail: szomsts@ccf.org.

SZOSTAK, JACK WILLIAM, molecular biologist, educator; b. London, Nov. 9, 1952; s. William J. and Viola (Munford) Szostak. BS in Cell Biology, McGill U., Montreal, Can., 1972; PhD in Biochemistry, Cornell U., Ithaca, NY, 1977. Rsch. assoc. in biochemistry Cornell U., 1977-79; asst. prof. dept. biol. chemistry Harvard Med. Sch., Boston, 1979-83, assoc. prof. dept. biol. chemistry, 1983-84, assoc. prof. dept. genetics, 1984-87, prof. dept. genetics, 1988—. Assoc. molecular biologist Mass. Gen. Hosp., 1984—87, molecular biologist, 1988—, Alex Rich disting. investigator dept. molecular biology, 2000—; Jean Weigle lectr. U. Geneva, 1994; William Rauscher meml. lectr. Rensselaer Poly. Inst., Troy, NY, 1995; Susan Swerling meml. lectr. Dana Farber Cancer Inst., Boston, 1997; Proctor & Gamble lectr. U. Ill., Urbana-Champaigne, 1998; investigator Howard Hughes Med. Inst., 1998—; Capital Sci. lectr. Carnegie Instn. Washington, 2001; vis. fellow Brasenose Coll., Oxford U., 2005. Mem. editl. bd. Chemistry and Biology, 1994—, RNA, 1995—98; contbr. articles to profl. jours. Recipient Louis Vuitton-Moet Hennesey 'Vinci of Excellence' award, 1996, Hans Sigrist prize, U. Bern, Switzerland, 1997, Genetics Society of America medal, 2000, Harrison Howe award, Am. Chem. Soc., 2003, Albert Lasker award for basic med. rsch., 2006, H.P. Heineken prize, Royal Netherlands Acad. Arts & Scis., 2008, Nobel prize in physiology/medicine, 2009. Fellow: NY Acad. Scis.; mem.: NAS (Award in molecular biology 1994), Am. Acad. Arts & Scis. Achievements include research in origin, early evolution and laboratory synthesis of life; patents in field. Office: Mass Gen Hosp Simches Rsch Ctr CPZN 7250 185 Cambridge St Boston MA 02114 Office Fax: 617-726-6893. Business E-Mail: szostak@molbio.mgh.harvard.edu. *

SZUMLINSKI, KAREN KATHLEEN, psychology professor; b. Toronto, Ont., Can., May 19, 1972; PhD, Albany Med. Coll., 2000. Assoc. prof. U. Calif., Santa Barbara, 2005—. Recipient Young Scientist award, Internat. Soc. Neurochemistry, Young Investigator award, Internat. Behavioural & Neural Genetics Soc. Mem.: Coll. Problems Drug Dependence, Rsch. Soc. Alcoholism (Young Investigator award), European Behavioural Pharmacology Soc., Am. Coll. Neuropsychopharmacology (Bristol-Meyers Squibb award), Soc. Neurosci. Office: Dept Psychological & Brain Scis Santa Barbara CA 93106-9660 Office Fax: 805-893-4303. Business E-Mail: szumlinski@psych.ucsb.edu.

SÝKORA, JOSEF, pediatrician, gastroenterologist; b. Pilsen, Czech Republic, Oct. 3, 1957; s. Josef Sýkora and Olga Sýkorová; m. Jarmila Formánková, Aug. 21, 1962; 1 child, Josef. Academic, Sch. of Medicine Charles U. Prague, Pilsen, 1976—82; PhD, Charles U., 2002. Diplomate Charles U. Sch. of Medicine, Prague, Czech Republic, 1982. Physician, dept. of pediat. Charles U. Hosp., Pilsen, 1982—, gastroent., cons., dept. of pediat., 1990—96, asst. prof., pediatric gastroent., dept. of pediat., 1996—. Asst. prof., consulting, rschr., dept. of pediat. Charles U. Hosp., 1996—, assoc. prof. Author: (monograph) Gastroduodenal disorders in childhood (Book of the yr. in pediatric gastroent., Czech Republic, 2002); contbr. numerous articles in var. med. jours. Grantee, Ministry of Health Czech Republic, 2003-2008. Mem.: Inst. Damome, European Helicobacter Study Group, Pediat. Task Force, European Cystic Fibrosis Working Group, Internationale Geselschaft fur Preventive Medizine (assoc.). Achievements include research in helicobacter (H.pylori, H.heilmannii) studies in childhood and inflammatory bowel disease, autoimmunily in H pylori u infection; stress and DNA repair capacity in diabetes mellitus and inflammatory bowel disease; autoimmunity in H.pylori infection biological masters of diseases in childhood. Avocations: football, travel. Home: Vojanova 27 Plzen 318 00 Czech Republic Office: Dept of Paediatrics/Faculty Hosp Alej Svobody 80 323 00 Plzen Czech Republic Home Phone: 420 377380331; Office Phone: 42 377104679, 420 377 104 678. Office Fax: 420 377104694. Business E-Mail: sykorajo@fnplzen.cz.

TAALAS, JAAKKO ADOLF, retired neurologist, consultant; b. Helsinki, Finland, Apr. 15, 1939; s. Boris Adolf and Elli Eveliina (Lauri) T.; m. Leena Kauhanen, Jan. 1963 (dec. Feb. 1977); children: Jukka Petteri, Peppi Johanna, Sami Johannes; m. Sirkka-Liisa Hakuni, Jan. 1979 (dec. Feb. 1997); children: Siri Eveliina, Tuulia Adolfiina, Jere Mikael. MD, U. Helsinki, 1966, specialist in neurology, 1972. Communal gen. practicioner Jyväskylä County, Finland, 1967; intern U. Hosps., Helsinki, 1968-72; neurologist in chief Mikkeli Ctrl. Hosp., Finland, 1972—2002; ret., 2002. Cons., tchr., 1972—2006; chmn. bd. dirs. Finn-Neuro Co., Saint Michel; cons. indsl. medicine

Olavi Räsänen Co., Saint Michel, 1978—2006; authorized pilot examiner Finnish Civil Aviation Authority, Saint Michel, 1970—. Trustee of colleagues Akava, Saint Michel, 1976-86; bd. mem. Epilepsy Assn. of Saint Michel, 1980-90. Mem. Finnish Med. Assn., Finnish Neurol. Assn., Finnish Neurologists (chmn. bd. dirs. 1972-81), Finnish Hosp. Physicians (bd. dirs. 1973-86). Avocation: outdoor activities.

TABACHNICK, NORMAN DONALD, psychiatrist, educator; b. Toronto, Ont., Can., Feb. 21, 1927; BS, U. Ill., 1947, MD, 1949; PhD in Psychoanalysis, So. Calif. Psychoanalytic Inst., 1977. Diplomate Am. Bd. Med. Examiners, Am. Bd. Psychiatry and Neurology. Intern Michael Reese Hosp., 1949-50; resident in psychiatry U.S. VA Hosp., Bedford, Mass., 1950-51, U.S. AFB, Biloxi, Miss., 1951-52, L.A. County Gen. Hosp., 1953-54; staff psychiatrist Sepulveda VA Hosp., 1976-78; pvt. practice LA; mem. staff Resthaven Sanitarium, U. So. Calif. Med. Ctr., L.A. County, Westwood Hosp., Edgemont Hosp., Cedars-Sinai Med. Ctr.; mem. staff Neuropsychiatric Inst. UCLA; clin. prof. psychiatry U. So. Calif., LA, 1970-75, UCLA, 1975—2008, disting. clin. prof. psychiatry, 2008—. Hon. mem. med. staf. Resthaven Cmty. Med. Health Ctr., 1973; guest lectr. Cedars-Sinai Med. Ctr., 1985; mem. adv. bd. divsn. psychoanalysis Nassau County Med. Ctr.; mem. faculty Calif. Sch. Profl. Psychology, L.A. Ctr. Group Psychotherapy, Grad. Ctr. Child Devel. and Psychotherapy; cons. L.A. County Coroner's Office, 1963-70, Bur. Vocat. Rehab., Jewish Family Svc., profl. adv. bd. Resthaven Sanitarium, Marianne Frostig Sch. Ednl. Therapy, W. Valley Ctr. Edl. Therapy. Author: Accident or Suicide?, 1973; mem. edtl. bd. Jour. Acad. Psychoanalysis, book rev. editor, 1978; mem. edtl. bd. Internat. Jour. Psycho-analytic Psychotherapy, 1979-83; reviewer Am. Jour. Psychiatry, 1983—, Jour. Neuropsychiatry and Clin. Neuro Scis., 1988-90; contbr. articles to profl. jours.; cons. (film) Suicide Prevention: The Physician's Role, 1967, Highlights of the 1964 American Psychiatric Association; cons., participant The Thin Edge--Guilt., 1975; author book revs. Assoc. chief psychiatrist L.A. Suicide Prevention Ctr., 1968-76, prin. investigator; adv. com. Walter Briehl Human Rights Found., 1984; v.p., bd. dirs. Suicide Prevention Ctr., Inc.; bd. dirs. Inst. Suicide Prevention, L.A., 1996, chmn. funding a crisis line com., 1997; bd. dirs. We. divsn. Am. Found. Suicide Prevention, 1998, chair program com., 1999-2002. Recipient award for disting. creativity and leadership, Am. Found. for Suicide Prevention, 2003; rsch. grantee, Founds. Fund Rsch. Psychiatry, 1963, NIMH, 1970. Fellow Am. Psychiatric Assn. (life), Am. Acad. Psychoanalysis (pres. 1974, chmn. nominating com. 1975, trustee, chmn. com. on rsch., mem. editl. bd. The Acad., presdl. citation 1975); mem. Internat. Psychoanalytic Assn., Internat. Assn. Suicide Prevention, Am. Psychoanalytic Assn. (cert., mem. com. liason with AAAS 1977-80), Am. Assn. Suicidology, (founder, mem. editl. bd. Life-Threatening Behavior, cert. recognition 1996) Inst. Contemporary Psychoanalysis (founding mem., trustee 1990-93), So. Calif. Psychoanalytic Inst. (pres., tng. and supervising analyst, selection rsch. clin. assocs. com., dir. rsch. divsn. 1970-81, chief investigator 1976-88, chmn. com. rsch. award stds. 1979, pres.-elect 1980, 86, pres. 1981, 87-90, mem. tng. and supr. analyst, new ctr. for psychoanalysis), Am. Coll. Psychiatrists, Med. Rsch. Assn. So. Calif., So. Calif. Psychiat. Soc. (consultation and violence panel), L.A. County Med. Assn. Office: 865 Comstock Ave Los Angeles CA 90024 Office Phone: 310-270-4420. Personal E-mail: ndtmd@aol.com.

TABACOF, JACQUES, physician; b. Salvador Bahia, Brazil, July 3, 1962; MD, FMUSP, 1985. Physician Ctr. Paulista Oncologia, 1990—, dir., 2000. Mem.: ASCO. Avocation: surfing. Office: Avenida Europa 105 Sao Paulo 01449-001 Brazil Office Fax: 55 11 30646108. Business E-Mail: jataba@uol.com.br.

TABAK, LAWRENCE A., federal agency administrator; b. Bklyn., Dec. 15, 1951; BS in Biology and Chemistry, CUNY City Coll., 1972; DDS, Columbia U., NYC, 1977; PhD in Oral Biology, SUNY, Buffalo, 1981. Cert. in Endodontics SUNY, Buffalo, 1985. Asst. prof. oral biology SUNY, Buffalo, 1980—81, asst. prof. endodontics and oral biology, 1981—85, assoc. prof., 1985—86; assoc. prof. dental rsch. & biochemistry U. Rochester Sch. Medicine & Dentistry, NY, 1986—92, prof., 1992—96, chair dept. dental rsch., 1995—97, prof. dental rsch., biochemistry & biophysics, 1996—97, prof. dentistry, biochemistry & biophysics, 1998—2000, sr. assoc. dean rsch., 1998—2000; sr. investigator Nat. Inst. Diabetes, Digestive & Kidney Diseases, Bethesda, Md., 2000; dir. Nat. Inst. Dental & Craniofacial Rsch., 2000—10, acting dir. divsn. Program Coordination, Planning & Strategic Initiatives, 2010; acting prin. dep. dir. NIH, 2008—09, prin. dep. dir., 2010—. Vis. scientist Nat. Inst. Dental Rsch., 1982—83. Contbr. articles to profl. jours. Named Alumnus of Yr., Columbia U. Sch. Dental & Oral Surgery, 1997. Fellow: AAAS; mem.: Inst. Medicine, Soc. Glycobiology, American Assn. Dental Rsch., Internat. Assn. Dental Rsch. (Disting. Scientist award 1996). Office: National Institutes of Health Bldg 1, Shannon Bldg, 126 1 Center Dr Bethesda MD 20892 Office Phone: 301-496-2433. E-mail: lawrence.tabak@nih.gov. *

TABAK, STEVEN WILLIAM, cardiologist; b. LA, May 7, 1952; MD, Johns Hopkins U., 1977. Intern Cedars-Sinai Med. Ctr., LA, 1977-78, resident in internal medicine, 1978-81, fellow in cardiovascular disease, 1981-83; assoc. clin. prof. medicine UCLA; clin. chief of cardiology, chmn. cardiac catheterization com. Cedars-Sinai Med. Ctr., 1996-98. Pvt. practice., interventional cardiologist, Cardiovascular Med. Group So. Calif. Fellow Am. Coll. Cardiology; mem. AMA, ACP Office: 414 N Camden Dr Ste 1100 Beverly Hills CA 90210-4532 Office Phone: 310-278-3400. E-mail: tabak@cvmg.com.

TABAQCHALI, SOAD, medical microbiology educator, consultant; b. Baghdad, Iraq, Dec. 15, 1934; naturalized Brit. citizen, 1962; d. Mahmoud Nadim and Munira (Kadri) T.; m. Peter Shiakallis, 1959 (div. 1968); m. Christopher Charles Booth, (div. 1999); 1 child, Nadya Christina. MB, BChir, St. Andrew's U., Scotland, 1958. House physician Maryfield Hosp., Dundee, Scotland, 1959; rsch. fellow med. unit Royal Free Hosp., London, 1959-62; asst. lectr. Royal Postgrad. Med. Sch., London, 1965-70; from lectr. to reader St. Bartholomew's Hosp., London, 1973-86, prof. med. microbiology, head dept., 1986-98, St. Bartholomew's & Royal London Sch. Medicine and Dentistry, 1995-98; prof. emeritus Queen Mary Coll., London U., 1998—. Hon. cons. N.E. Thames Regional Health Authority, London, 1974-94, Royal Hosp. Nat. Health Svc. Trust, London, 1994-98, former mem. com. for pathogenic organisms; adv. bd. Priz Galien Awards, 1994-99; expert panelist Inco-Copernicus Programme, 1997-2001; adv. bd. Med. Rsch. Coun., 1997-2002, past mem., Wolfson Inst Preventive Med Charterhouse, 1999- 2006. Contbr. over 250 articles to sci. jours., chpts. to books; patentee in field. Fellow Royal Coll. Pathologists (London), Royal Coll. Physicians (London). Avocations: opera, music, travel, charity work. Home: 29 Chartwell House 12 Ladbroke Ter London W113PG England Home Phone: 44 020 7589 2504. E-mail: soadtabachali@yahoo.com.

TABATZNIK, BERNARD, retired cardiologist; b. Mir, Poland, Jan. 8, 1927; arrived in US, 1959, naturalized, 1966; s. Max and Fay (Ginsberg) T.; m. Marjorie Turner, Jan. 8, 1956; children: Darron Mark, Keith Donald, Ilana Wendy; m. Charline Edwards Harmon, Aug. 7, 1992. BSc, U. Witwatersrand, South Africa, 1945, MB, BChir, U. Witwatersrand, South Africa, 1949. Intern Baragwanath Hosp., Johannesburg, 1950-51, Hillingdon Hosp., Ashford Hosp., also rsch. unit Can. Red Cross Meml. Hosp., Taplow, England, 1951-54; med. registrar Ashford Hosp., 1954-56, Johannesburg Gen. Hosp., 1956-58; physician Baragwanath Hosp., 1958-59; fellow in medicine Sch. Medicine Johns Hopkins U., Balt., 1959-60, fellow in cardiology, 1960-61, asst. prof. medicine, 1966-97, ret., 1997; head cardiopulmonary divsn. Sinai Hosp., Balt., 1961-72, assoc. chief medicine, 1964-72; chief cardiology dept. North Charles Gen. Hosp., Balt., 1972; also dir. med. edn., dir. Postgrad. Inst., coord. ambulatory svcs.; med. dir. Nurse Practitioner-Physician Asst. Program Ch. Hosp., Balt., 1987-90. Contbr. articles to profl. jours. Recipient Save-A-Heart Humanitarian award, 1977, Maimonides award, 1983, Shaarei Zion Humanitarian award, 1987. Fellow Royal Coll. Physicians (London); mem. South African Cardiac Soc., Am. Heart Assn., Md. Heart Assn. (chmn. health careers 1964-66), Am. Coll. Cardiology. Home: 63 Oakridge Dr Monterey VA 24465-2350 Personal E-mail: btabatznik@aol.com.

TABB, WALLER CROCKETT, retired allergist, immunologist; b. Richmond, Va., 1935; MD, U. Va., 1959. Diplomate Am. Bd. Internal Medicine, Am. Bd. Allergy and Immunology. Intern U. Va. Hosp., Charlottesville, 1959-60, resident in internal medicine, 1964-66, fellow in allergy/immunology and pulmonary medicine, 1966-67; mem. staff Lakeland (Fla.) Regional Med. Ctr., 1967—; pvt. practice Watson Clinic, Lakeland, ret., 1997. Fellow ACP, Am. Acad. Allergy and Immunology, Am. Coll. Chest Physicians; mem. Alpha Omega Alpha. Address: PO Box 178 Ware Neck VA 23178-0178 Home: 6102 WAre Neck Rd Ware Neck VA 23178 Personal E-mail: aroca2@earthlink.net.

TABBAL, NICOLAS G., plastic surgeon; b. Beirut, July 14, 1946; MD, Am. U., Beirut, 1972. Diplomate Am. Bd. Plastic Surgery, Am. Bd. Surgery. Intern Am. U. Med. Ctr., Beirut, 1971—72, resident in surgery, 1972—76; resident in plastic surgery Akron City Hosp., Ohio, 1977—79; fellow in gen. surgery Upstate Med. Ctr., Syracuse, NY, 1976—77; fellow in aesthetic surgery Manhattan Eye, Ear & Throat Hosp., 1979—80; fellow in plastic reconstructive surgery NYU Med. Ctr., 1980; pvt. practice plastic surgery NYC, 1980—; attending plastic surgeon Manhattan Eye, Ear, and Throat Hosp. Clin. instr. plastic surgery NYU Med. Ctr. Office: 521 Park Ave New York NY 10021-1840 Office Phone: 212-644-5800. Office Fax: 212-644-5828. Business E-Mail: mail@tabbal.us.

TABEI, ISAO, surgeon, researcher; b. Iwatsuki, Japan, Mar. 11, 1963; s. Toru and Hiroko Tabei; m. Aya Tabei, May 23, 1999; children: Yuta, Eri, Kenta. MD, Jikei U. Sch. Medicine, 1988. Surgical Medical Specialist Japn Surg. Soc., 2002. Staff dept. of surgery Jikei U. Sch. of Surgery, Tokyo, 1997—; vis. asst. prof. U. Nebr. Med. Ctr., Omaha, 1995—97. Recipient rsch. Fellowship Award, Japan Soc. of Parenteral and Enteral Nutrition, 2000, Academic Award, Japan Human Cell Soc., 2002, Prize for Encouragement, Jikei Doctors Soc., 2003, Internat. Exch. Encouragement Award, Japanese Jour. of Gastroent. Surgery, 2004. Mem.: Am. Soc. of Parenteral and Enteral Nutrition (assoc.), Am. Soc. of Clin. Oncology (assoc.), Japanese Soc. of Surg. Metabolism and Nutrition (assoc.), Japanese Breast Cancer Soc. (assoc.), Japanese Jour. of Gastroent. Surgery (assoc.), Japan Surg. Soc. (assoc.). Office: Jikei Univ Sch of Medicine 3 25 8 Nishishinbashi Minatoku Tokyo 105 8461 Japan Office Fax: 03-5472-4140. Personal E-mail: tabei@jikei.ac.jp.

TABER, DAVID O., urological surgeon; b. Panama City, Panama, June 30, 1938; s. Alden Pugh and Virginia (Kresler) Taber; m. Rebecca M.; children: Sharon Taber Silverman, Jeffrey, Andrew, Richard; m. Rebecca M. Taber, Dec. 20, 1987. BA, Syracuse U., 1959; MD, George Washington U., 1963. Diplomate Am. Bd. Urology. Urologic surgeon in pvt. practice, El Paso, Tex., 1973—; pres. El Paso County Med. Soc., 2008—; intern. Walter Reed Gen. Hosp., 1968—69, urological resident, 1965—69; chief urology 130th Gen. Hosp., Nurnberg, 1969—73. Chief med. staff Columbia West Hosp., El Paso, 1975-76, chief of urology, 1998-99; chief of surgery Sierra Med. Ctr., El Paso, 1977-78, chief of urology, 1995-97; prof. urology Tex. Tech Sch. Medicine, El Paso, 1998—. Mem. state com. on prostate cancer Am. Cancer Soc., Austin, 1998-99, bd. dirs. El Paso unit, 1999; mem. Tex. Rangers Found., Waco, 1998-2005; judge Santa Fe Indian Market; med. exec. com. El Paso County; founder Am. Mus. Served to lt. U.S. Army, 1963-72. Lt. col. US Army. Named one of Best Doctors in Tex., 2010. Fellow ACS; mem. AMA, Urol. Soc. Internat., Urostomy Assn. (adv.), Tex. Urol. Soc., Am. Urol. Assn., Tex. Med. Assn. (del. 2009), Am. Fertility Soc., Am. Lithotripsy Soc., El Paso Med. Soc. (exec. com. 2004- sec. 2006-, pres. elect, 2007, pres., 2008-, named in Best Doctors in Am., Best Doctors in Tex.), Mason (32 degree), Elmaida Shrine, Rotary, Alpha Epsilon Delta, Pi Sigma. Episcopalian. Avocations: photography, diving instructor. Office: 2201 N Stanton St El Paso TX 79902 Office Phone: 915-533-0800. Personal E-mail: dotabermd@yahoo.com.

TABOR, EDWARD, medical researcher; BA, Harvard U., Cambridge, Mass., 1969; MD, Columbia U., NYC, 1973. Intern and resident Columbia-Presbyn. Med. Ctr., NYC, 1973-75; rsch. investigator Bur. Biologics, Bethesda, Md., 1975-83; dir. divsn. anti-infective drug products FDA, Rockville, Md., 1983-88; assoc. dir. for biol. carcinogenesis Nat. Cancer Inst./NIH, Bethesda, 1988-95; dir. divsn. transfusion transmitted diseases FDA, Bethesda and Rockville, Md., 1995-99; assoc. dir. med. affairs Office Blood Rsch. and Rev., FDA, Rockville, 1999—2005; exec. dir. Regulatory Consulting, Quintiles, Inc., Rockville, 2005—06; head regulatory affairs Am. Quintiles, Inc., Rockville, 2006—08; v.p. Quintiles, Inc., 2008—, head global regulatory strategy, 2008—. Author: Infectious Complications of Blood Transfusion, 1982; editor: Viruses and Liver Cancer, 2002, Emerging Viruses in Human Populations, 2007,(with others) Etiology, Pathology, and Treatment of Hepatocellular Carcinoma in North America, 1991, Hepatitis C Virus and its Involvement in the Development of Hepatocellular Carcinoma, 1995, Liver Cancer, 1997; contbr. more than 300 articles to profl. jours. Capt. USPHS, 1975-05. Achievements include formulation of US regulatory policy on antibiotics, anti-viral drugs, and blood transfusion safety, research in hepatitis viruses, hepatocellular carcinoma. Office: Quintiles Inc 1801 Rockville Pike Ste 300 Rockville MD 20852 Business E-Mail: edward.tabor@quintiles.com.

TÁBORSKÝ, MILOŠ, cardiologist, educator; b. Suice, Oct. 5, 1962; Degree, Charles U., Prague, 1986, PhD, 2001; MBA, UJAK Prague, 2008. Faculty gen. medicine Charles U., 1987—89; head arrhythmiological operating theater and outpatients dept. Na Homolce Hosp., 1992—2007, faculty gen. medicine, 1989—; head internal cardiology clinic U. Hosp. Olomouc, 2009—. Mem., bd. EHRA devel. emerging countries electrophysiology and pacing European Heart Rhythm Assn., 2010. Mem.: Heart Rhythm Soc., Cardiac Electrophysiology Soc., Deutsche Kardiologische Gesellschaft, Czech Cardiological Assn. (chmn. 2001—06). Avocation: architecture. Office: University Hosp Olomouc 1st Internal Cardiology Clin Olomouc Czech Republic Business E-Mail: milos.taborsky@fnol.cz.

TACAL, JOSE VEGA, JR., retired public health official, veterinarian; b. Ilocos Sur, Philippines, Sept. 5, 1933; arrived in US, 1969; s. Jose Sr. and Cristina (Vega) T.; m. Lilia Caccam, 1959; children: Joyce, Jasmin, Jose III. DVM, U. Philippines, Quezon City, 1956; diploma, U. Toronto, 1964. Diplomate emeritus Am. Coll. Vet. Preventive Medicine; lic. vet., Calif. Provincial veterinarian Philippine Bur. Animal Industry, Manila, 1956-57; instr. vet. medicine U. Philippines, Quezon City, 1957-64, asst. prof., chmn. dept. vet. microbiology, pathology and pub. health, 1965-69; pub. health veterinarian San Bernardino (Calif.) County Dept. Pub. Health, 1970-83, sr. pub. health veterinarian, program mgr., sect. chief, 1984-2000. Zoonotic diseases lectr. Calif. State U., San Bernardino, 1984; lectr. U. Calif. Ext., Riverside, 1985, vis. prof. vet. pub. health U. Philippines at Los Banos, Laguna, 1988; participant 1st Internat. Conf. on Emerging Zoonoses, Jerusalem, 1996; presenter 4th Internat. Symposium on Ectoparasites of Pets, U. Calif., Riverside, 1997; presenter 8th Ann. Rabies in the Ams. Conf., Kingston, Ont., Can., 1997; rabies and ferret adv. group Calif. Dept. Health Svcs., 1998; presenter 48th Western Poultry Disease Conf., Vancouver, B.C., Can., 1999, 10th Rabies in Ams. Meeting, San Diego, 1999. Columnist LA Free Press, 1991, Filipinas Times, 1993, Mabuhay Times, 1994-95; panelist Filipino-Ams. TV series The Many Faces of San Bernardino, California, contbr. more than 30 articles to profl. jours. Pres. Filipino Assn. of San Bernardino County, Highland, Calif., 1979; charter mem. Greater Inland Empire Filipino Assn., Highland, 1986—; del. First Filipino Media Conf. N.Am., LA, 1993; active San Bernardino County Africanized Honey Bee Task Force, 1993-2000, City of Highland Historic and Cultural Preservation Bd., 2006-08; v.p. Friends of the Highland Libr., 2006-09. Recipient Donald T. Fraser Meml. medal, U. Toronto, 1964, cert. of merit, Philippine Vet. Med. Assn., 1965, cert. of appreciation, Calif. State Bd. Examiners in Vet. Medicine, 1979, 1984, cert. of recognition, Congressman George E. Brown Jr., 42d Congl. Dist. Calif., 1994, Assemblyman Joe Baca, 62d Assembly Dist., Calif. State Legis., 1994, Vet. Medicine/Journalism award, Greater Inland Empire Filipino Assn., 1999, Cert. of Appreciation award, San Bernardino County Libr., Highland Br., 2005—06, Cert. of Recognition award, City of Highand, Calif., 2007—08, Proclamation, City Highland, Calif., 2008, Recognition award, Highland Calif., 2009; named Vol. of Yr., Friends of Highland Libr., 2007; Colombo Plan Study fellow, Can./Philippine Govts., 1963—64, hon. fellow, Philippine Coll. Vet. Pub. Health, 2002. Mem.: ACLU, Highland Area Hist. Soc. (bd. mem. 2009, 2011—), Soc. for Advancement of Rsch., Western Poultry Disease Conf., Am. Vet. Med. History Soc., U. Philippines Alumni Assn. (life), Phi Sigma, Phi Kappa Phi. Office: PO Box 1023 Highland CA 92346-1023

TACHDJIAN, RAFFI, pediatrician; b. July 8, 1969; BS, UCLA, 1992; MPH, Univ. Ala., Birmingham, 1994; MD, Morehouse Sch. Med., Atlanta, 2001. Cert. Am. Bd. Pediatrics, 2007. Epidemiologist in diphtheria surveillance Centers for Disease Control & Prevention, 1995—97; intern & resident in pediatrics Harvard Med. Sch., Mass. Gen. Hosp., 2001—04; fellow in pediatric immunology & rheumatology Mattel Children;s Hosp., UCLA, 2004—07. Vis. prof. Berklee Coll., Boston, 2004—; Chrysalis Mentor Am. Acad. of Allergy, Asthhma & Immunology, 2006. Contbr. articles to profl. jours. Mem.: Am. Acad. of Allergy, Asthma & Immunology, Am. Coll. of Allergy, Asthma & Immunology, Am. Acad. Pediatrics. Office: Mattel Children's Hosp MDCC 22-464 10833 LeConte Ave Los Angeles CA 90095-1752 Office Phone: 310-825-0731. Business E-Mail: rtachdjian@mednet.ucla.edu.

TACHIHARA, MOTOKO, medical educator; b. Japan, Mar. 18, 1975; MD, Fukushima Med. U. Sch. Medicine, PhD, 2000. Asst. prof. Kobe U. Grad. Sch. Medicine, 2011, Fukushima Med. U. Sch. Medicine, 2006—. Grant, Asian Pacific Soc., 2008. Mem.: Kobe U. Grad. Sch. Medicine. Office: 7-5-1 Kusunoki-cho Chuo-ku Kobe 650-0017 Japan Personal E-mail: lovelovemotoko@hotmail.com.

TACHMES, LEONARD, plastic surgeon; BS, Duke U.; MD, Jefferson Med. Coll. Diplomate Am. Bd. of Plastic Surgery, 1997, recertification 2008. Fellow Meml. Sloan Kettering Cancer Ctr., Manhattan; resident plastic and reconstructive surgery Univ. Chgo. Hosps.; resident gen. surgery Brookdale Hosp. Med. Ctr., Bklyn.; internship surgery Mary Imogene Bassett Hosp., Cooperstown, NY; hosp. affiliations include Jackson North Med. Ctr., Fla. Med. Ctr., North Shore

Hosp. Med. Ctr. Mem.: Am. Soc. of Plastic Surgeons. Office: Miami Beach Plastic Surgery Center and MedSpa Suite 204 1674 Meridian Ave Miami Beach FL 33139 Office Phone: 305-531-9800. Office Fax: 305-531-9801.

TACK, THERESA ROSE, women's health nurse; b. Lunenburg, Vt., Nov. 10, 1940; d. Gustave L. and Blanche Rose Fournier; m. Dennis M. Tack, Sept. 2, 1961; children: Lynelle Scullard, Karyn Terry, LeAnn Gomez. Diploma, Cen. Maine Gen. Hosp., 1961. Cert. ACLS, neonatal resuscitation Am. Heart Assn. Staff nurse neurosurgery unit Hillcrest Med. Ctr., Tulsa, 1961-62; staff nurse cardiovascular unit Meth. Hosp., Houston, 1962-65; staff nurse St. John's Hosp., Red Wing, Minn., 1979-85, Wasatch County Hosp., Heber City, Utah, 1985-97. Columnist, Nurses Notes in Wasatch Wave, Heber City, Utah, 1990-97.

TADA, HITOSHI, pharmacist, educator; b. Shizugawa, Miyagi, Japan, Jan. 15, 1958; s. Kunio and Michiko Tada; life ptnr. Tetsuko Maeda, June 8, 1985; 1 child, Yayoi. PhD, Hokkaido Pharm. U., 1982. Chief pharmacist Akita U. Hosp., 1998—2005, assoc. prof., 2005—06. Office: OHU Univ 31-1 Misumido Tomita-Machi Koriyama Fukushima 963-8611 Japan Office Phone: 81-24-932-9159.

TADEUSZ, IZBICKI, oncologist, pediatric surgeon, researcher; b. 1955; MD, Med. Acad., Wroclaw, Poland, 1973—79; PhD, Inst. Mother and Child, Warsaw, 1986—90. Diplomate Bd. cert. 1st degree pediatric surgery Poland, 1983, Bd. cert. 2nd degree oncologic surgery Poland, 1993. Asst. Regional Hosp., Opole, Poland, 1979—83; sr. asst. Inst. Mother and Child, Warsaw, 1983—90; rsch. fellow, dept. pediatric surgery U. Clinic, Fukuoka, Japan, 1987—88; ultrasonography trainee Stiftsbogen Clinic, Munich, 1985; adj. Inst. Mother and Child, Warsaw, 1990—. Grant directorship Nat. Commn. Sci. Rsch., Warsaw, 1995—98. Author: (rsch. papers on neuroblastoma) Anticancer Rsch., Jour. of Pediatric Surgery, Annals of N.Y. Acad. Scis., Procs. of Am. Assn. Cancer Rsch., Pediatra Polska. Recipient Brown Iron Cross Medal, Polish Ministry Health, 1987. Mem.: Internat. Soc. Pediatric Oncology (assoc.), Japanese Oncological Soc. (assoc.), Polish Soc. Pediatric Oncologists (assoc.; sec.), Polish Soc. Pediatric Surgeons (assoc.). Avocations: hiking, philosophy of science, linguistics (Japanese).

TADORI, YOSHIHIRO, research scientist; b. Japan, May 25, 1968; MS, Saitama U., 1993. Rschr. Qs' Rsch. Inst., Otsuka Pharm. Co., Ltd., 1993—. Office: 463-10 Kagasuno Kawauchi-cho Tokushima 771-0192 Japan Business E-Mail: y_tadori@research.otsuka.co.jp.

TAEKMAN, MICHAEL SEYMOUR, neurological surgeon; b. Chgo., June 30, 1937; s. Harry Joseph and Rose Anne (Sturner) T.; m. Ilene Roberta Erlich, Dec. 18, 1960; children: Jeffrey Marc, Jennifer Lynn, Jessica Beth. MD, U. Ill., Chgo., 1962. Diplomate Am. Bd. Neurol. Surgery. Intern U. Ill., Chgo., 1962—63, resident in gen. surgery, 1963—64, 1971; resident in neurosurgery U. Ill. Neuropsychiat. Hosp., Chgo., 1964—67; fellow U. Edinburgh, Scotland, 1967; attending neurosurgeon Chgo. Mcpl. Contagious Disease Hosp., 1967; pres. East Bay Med. Group, Berkeley, Calif., 1969—99. Asst. clin. prof. U. Calif., San Francisco, 1990-99, assoc. clin. prof., 1999—; instr. U. Ill., Chgo., 1963-67; lectr. U. Calif., Berkeley, 1975—1992; chmn. dept. surgery Childrens Hosp. Med. Ctr., Oakland, Calif., 1980-90; assoc. clin. prof., Stanford U., 1999—; assoc. prof. pediatric neurosurgery Leland Packard Childrens Hosp. Contbr. articles to profl. jours. Adv. mem. San Rafael Sch. Bd., 1976-77; med. examiner State Calif., Berkeley, 1976—, docent, chmn. acad. sci. Served to capt. USAF, 1964-71. Scholar Internat. Coll. Surgeons, 1967, Med. Rsch. Coun. Great Britain, 1967. Fellow ACS, Am. Assn. Neurol. Surgeons, Am. Assn. Pediatric Neurol. Surgeons; mem. Calif. Acad. Medicine, Alameda Contra Costa Med. Assn., Rafael Racket Club, Phi Eta Sigma. Republican. Jewish. Office: 4350 Clement St San Francisco CA 94121 Office Phone: 415-459-3616. Personal E-mail: michaeltaekman@gmail.com.

TAEKO, SASAI, medical educator; b. Kyoto, Oct. 10, 1979; MT, Tokyo Med. and Dental U., 2003, PhD, 2010. Rschr. Japan Somnology Ctr., 2004; asst. prof. Tokyo Med. and Dental U., 2010, Tokyo Med. U., 2010. Office: 1-17-7 Yoyogi Shibuya Tokyo 151-0053 Japan E-mail: taeko_ssi@yahoo.co.jp.

TAFANI, JEAN-PIERRE J., physiologist; b. Creteil, France, Feb. 20, 1957; s. Jean M.J. and Lucette M. (Sollier) Tafani; 1 child, Marion A.L. Vet. medicine cert., Maisons-Alfort, France, 1979; MS in Physiology, U. Paris VI, 1981; DVM, U. Creteil, France, 1982. Diplomate European Coll. Vet. Pharmacology and Toxicology. Product mgr. Pioneer-France-Mais, Paris, 1982-83; project leader Pioneer Overseas Corp., Paris, 1983-85; dir. R&D nutrition Brit. Petroleum, Paris, 1985-89; pres., CEO S.A. APCIS, Maisons-Alfort, France, 1990—. Expert pharmaco-toxicologist New Drug Applications, France, 1990—; expert pharmacologist Ct. Appeals, Reims, France, 1995—2002; vis. lectr. Inst. Nat. Agronomique, Paris, 1995. Founder Marta's Coop. for Contemporary Art, 1996—. Recipient Siemens Trophy of Innovation for neuropharmacology work, 2006. Mem.: Controlled Release Soc., Wildlife Photographers Assn. Achievements include invention of pulsatile liquid drug dispenser; pulsatile delivery sys. electrochemically driven; new feed additive using membrane stabilization properties of silybinine; new beta-carbolines, new pyrrolo-oxyquinoleines. Office: SA APCIS 14 avenue du General Leclerc 94700 Maisons-Alfort France E-mail: tafanijp@club_internet.fr.

TAFT, TIMOTHY NED, orthopedist, surgeon, sports medicine physician; s. Samuel Milton and Helen Taft; m. Judith Ann Huffman, Sept. 13, 1971; children: Todd Daniel, Rebecca Lynn Fecher. AB, Princeton U., NJ, 1964; MD, U. Mo., Columbia, Mo., 1969. Diplomate Am. Bd. Orthopaedic Surgery, 1978, lic. physician N.C., 1978. Intern, resident in orthopedics U. N.C., NC, 1969—74, prof., 1974—, dir. sports medicine, 1991—. Mem.: Spl. Olympics N.C. (chmn., bd. dirs.). Office: University of North Carolina 3154 Bioinformatics CB 7055 Chapel Hill NC 27599 Office Fax: 919-966-6750; Home Fax: 919-967-6750. Business E-Mail: ttaft@med.unc.edu. *

TAGAMI, TETSUYA, endocrinologist, educator; MD, Kyoto U., 1984, PhD, 1993. Cert. internal medicine Japan, 1987, endocrinology Japan, 2004, thyroidology Japan, 2004. Physician Mcpl. Shizuoka Hosp., Japan, 1987, Kyoto U., 1988—92, Kyoto Nat. Hosp., 1998—2003; chief physician Nat. Hosp. Orgn., Kyoto Med. Ctr., 2003—, head lab., 2003—, head divsn. endocrinology and metabolism, 2007—; postdoc. fellow Kyoto U., 1993—94; rsch. fellow Northwestern U., Chgo., 1995—98; asst. prof. Kyoto U., 1994—98, attending instr., 1999—2003, clin. assoc. prof., 2003—05, clin. prof., 2005—. Judge screening com. remumeration Social Ins. Med. Fee Payment Fund, Kyoto, 1999—. Recipient Thyroid Rsch. award, Endocrine Soc., 1998, Young Investigator award, 1999, Shichijo award, Japan Thyroid Assn., 2003, Rsch. award Growth and Devel., Novo Nordisk, 2008, 2010; Clin. Rsch. grant Nat. Hosp. Orgn., Ministry of Health, Labour and Welfare, 1999, 2003, Travel grant, Astellas Found. Rsch. Metabolic Disorders, 1995, grant, Found. Growth Sci., 2000, Sci. Rsch. grant, Japanese Soc. Promotion Sci., 1993, 1999, 2005, 2008, Rsch. grant, Yamaguchi Endocrine Rsch. Found., 2007, All Japan Coffee Assn., 2009. Mem.: Japan Diabetes Soc., Japan Thyroid Assn., Japan Endocrine Soc., Japanese Soc. Internal Medicine, Endocrine Soc.

TAGATZ, GEORGE ELMO, retired obstetrician, gynecologist, educator; b. Milw., Sept. 21, 1935; s. George Herman and Beth Elinore (Blain) T.; m. Susan Trunnell, Oct. 28, 1967; children: Jennifer Lynn, Kirsten Susan, Kathryn Elizabeth. AB, Oberlin Coll., 1957; MD, U. Chgo., 1961. Diplomate Am. Bd. Obstetricians and Gynecologists, Am. Bd. Reproductive Endocrinology (examiner, bd. reproductive endocrinology 1976-79). Rotating intern Univ. Hosps. of Cleve., 1961-62, resident in internal medicine, 1962-63; resident in ob-gyn U. Iowa, 1965-68; sr. research fellow in endocrinology U. Wash. dept. obstetrics and gynecology, 1968-70; prof. emeritus Med. Sch. U. Minn., 1970—96, 1996—. Fertility and maternal health adv. com. FDA, USPHS, HHS, 1982-86; cons. in field. Ad hoc editor: Am. Jour. Ob-Gyn, Fertility and Sterility; contbr. articles to profl. publs. Served with M.C. U.S. Army, 1963-65. Mem. AMA, Minn., West Metro med. socs., Minn. Obstet. and Gynecol. Soc., Am. Coll. Ob-Gyn (subcom. on reproductive endocrinology 1979-82), Endocrine Soc., Am. Fertility Soc., Central Assn. Obstetricians and Gynecologists, U. Iowa Ob-Gyn Alumni Soc., Am. Soc. Reproductive Endocrinology & Infertility, Am. Soc. Reproductive Medicine. Home: 5828 Long Brake Trl Edina MN 55439-2622 Home Phone: 952-941-7930. Personal E-mail: george.tagatz@comcast.net.

TAGAWA, MINORU, cardiologist; married. Chief cardiology Nagaoka Chuo Gen. Hosp., Niigata, Japan, 2001—.

TAGGART, LINDA DIANE, retired women's health nurse; b. Balt., June 14, 1940; d. Louis and Annie Helena (Heertje) Glick; divorced; 1 child, Keri Anne. AS in Nursing, Pensacola Jr. Coll., 1967; BA, U. West Fla., 1970; postgrad., St. Joseph's Coll., 1976-78. RN, Fla., Ala. Staff nurse Bapt. Hosp., Pensacola, Fla., 1967-70, head nurse, 1970-72; dir. in-svc. edn. Baycrest, Inc. Extended Care Facility, Pensacola, 1973, DON, 1973-74, Medica Media, Pensacola, 1974; clinic adminstr. Cmty. Healthcare Ctr. (formerly Medica Media), Pensacola, 1974—2006; ret., 2006. Dir. sex and health edn. Cmty. Healthcare Ctr., Pensacola, 1974—; regional dir. Medica Media, ea. U.S., 1990; testified before Jud. com. U.S. Ho. of Reps., 1994. Contbr. project The Gideon Project, 1993, project Wrath of Angels, 1998, articles to profl. jours.; appeared on (documentaries) Dateline NBC, 48 Hours, Nightline, Turning Point, ABC, CNN, (HBO documentaries) Soldiers in the Army of God, 2000, Keeping It Real, Program of RCRC, South Africa, 2002; contbr. documentary I, Witness, 1998, documentary AGB "I Witness" Addy & Goldwater, 1999. Bd. dirs. Rape Crisis Ctr., Pensacola, 1976-91, chair, 1980, 84, 89 (Addie Brooks award 1984); mem. exec. com. Lakeview Community Mental Health Ctr., Pensacola, 1989 (Expression of Appreciation award 1980-91). Recipient Pioneer/Heroe award Fla. Abortion Coun., 1989, Woman of Yr. award NOW, 1995, Women's Equity Day award 1986. Mem.: ACLU, Am. Assn. Sex Educators, Counselors and Therapists (cert. sex educator), Planned Parenthood Fedn. Am., So. Poverty Law Ctr., People for Am. Way, Religious Coalition for Reproductive Choice (bd. dirs. 2000—), Feminist Majority Found. Democrat. Presbyterian. Avocations: skiing, jewelry design, cross-stitch, reading, ballroom dancing.

TAGIURI, CONSUELO KELLER, child psychiatrist, educator; b. San Francisco; d. Cornelius H. and Adela (Rios) Keller; m. Renato Tagiuri; children: Robert, Peter, John. BA, U. Calif.-Berkeley; MD, U. Calif.-San Francisco. Diplomate Am. Bd. Psychiatry and Neurology. Resident psychiatry Mass. Gen. Hosp., Boston; staff psychiatrist Children's Hosp., Boston, 1951-59; med. dir. Gifford Sch., Weston, Mass., 1965-85; chief psychiatrist Cambridge (Mass.) Guidance Ctr., 1961-84; mem. faculty dept. psychiatry Harvard Med. Sch., 1965—2002; cons. early childhood program Children's Hosp., 1985—. Contbr. articles in field to books. Fellow Am. Orth. Psychiat. Assn., Mass. Med. Soc., New Eng. Coun. Child Psychiatry.

TAGLI, HUGO, JR., lawyer, insurance company executive; b. 1942; BS, Loyola U., Chgo.; JD, John Marshall Law Sch., Chgo. Various positions with Health Care Svc. Corp., Chgo., 1965—, sr. v.p., chief legal counsel, corp. sec., 2002; chmn. Ill. Life and Health Insurance Guaranty. Mem. bd. Ill. C. of C. Mem.: Chgo. Bar Assn., Ill. Bar Assn., Am. Bar Assn., Justinian Soc. Lawyers, Ill. HMO Guaranty Assn. (chmn.), Ill. Life & Health Ins. Guaranty Assn. Office: Ill Life & Health Insurance Guaranty Assn 8420 W Bryn Mawr Ave Ste 550 Chicago IL 60631

TAGUCHI, FUMIHIRO, virologist, educator; b. Gero, Gifu, Aug. 16, 1950; PhD, U. Tokyo, 1974. Prof. lab. virology and viral infections Nippon Vet. and Life Sci. U., 2010—. Mem.: Am. Soc. Virology, Virology Soc. Japan. Avocations: fishing, birdwatching, walking. Office: 1-7-1 Kyounan Musashino Tokyo 180-8602 Japan Business E-Mail: ftaguchi@nvlu.ac.jp.

TAHA, ASSAD M., surgeon; b. Nabatieh, Lebanon, Dec. 12, 1955; came to U.S. 1980; s. Muhyddin S. and Hind (Jaber) T. BS, Am. U. Beirut, 1976, MD, 1980; PhD, Med. Coll. Ohio, Toledo, 1992. Diplomate Am. Bd. Surgery, Am. Bd. Surg. Critical Care. Surgery resident Good Samaritan Hosp., Cin., 1980-82, Med. Coll. Ohio, Toledo, 1982-85, attending surgeon, 1985-94, Am. U. of Beirut, 1994—, assoc. prof. surgery and physiology, 1994—. Dir. hyperbaric medicine Med. Coll. Hosp., Toledo, 1987—94, dir. surg. intensive care, 1988—94, assoc. prof. surgery; vis. surgeon surg. critical care Brigham & Women's Hosp., Harvard Med. Sch., Boston, 2000—01; vis. assoc. prof. Harvard U., 2000—01; vis. scholar trauma Ryder Trauma Ctr., U. Miami Sch. Medicine, Fla., 2003—04. Mem. editl. bd. European Jour. Emergency Surgery and Intensive Care; contbr. articles to profl. jours. Recipient AMA Physician Recognition award, 1987, 1991, 1997, 2000; grantee, Ohio Lions, 1987—92, Am. U.-Beirut U. Rsch. Bd., 1993—2000. Fellow ACS, AMA, Am. Heart Assn., Am. Physiologic Soc., Am. Soc. Gastrointestinal Endoscopy, European Assn. Trauma and Emergency Surgery, Royal Coll. Surgeons Can., Soc. Critical Care Medicine, Undersea and Hyperbaric Med. Soc., Am. Soc. Laser Medicine and Surgery, Am. Coll. Nutrition, Internat. Coll. Surgeons, Assn. Acad. Surgery, Shock Soc., European Soc. Intensive Care Medicine, World Assn. Disaster and Emergency Medicine, Soc. Am. GI Endoscopic Surgeons, World Med. Assn., Laser Inst. Am., Royal Soc. Medicine, Am. U. Beirut Alumni Assn., Am. Trauma Soc., Crit. Care Club, Disaster Med. Asst. Team; mem. AMA, AAUP. Avocations: chess, bridge. Office: Am U Beirut 3 Dag Hammarskjold Plz 8th Fl New York NY 10017-2303 Home Phone: 0119611735105; Office Phone: 0119613628627. Office Fax: 0119611363291. Personal E-mail: assadtaha@gmail.com.

TAHA, SAFWAN ABDUL-RAHMAN, surgeon, consultant; b. Abul-Khaseeb, Basrah, Iraq, Apr. 29, 1960; s. Abdul-Rahman Taha Al-Maatoq and Zekiya Abdul-Qadir Al-Doal; m. Farkad Kamil Al-Doregi, Apr. 7, 1988; children: Ali Safwan, Zaineb Safwan, Hala Safwan. MBChB, Basrah U., 1983. Cert. Arab League Bd. Surgery, 1992. Prof. gastrointestinal and laparoscopic surgery Basrah Coll. Medicine, 2000—08; dean Thi-Qar Coll. Medicine, Nasiriyah, Thi-Qar, Iraq, 2002—03; med. dir., chief surgeon Al Noor Hosp., Abu Dhabi, United Arab Emirates, 2008—. Cons. gastrointestinal and laparoscopic surgeon Basrah Tchg. Hosp., 1994—2007, Nasiriyah Gen. Hosp., 2002—03; mem. bd. examiners Arab Bd. Surgery, Arab League, Damascus, Syria, 2006—; cons. laparoscopic and bariatric surgeon Al Noor Hosp., 2007—. Founding editor: Basrah Jour. Surgery, 1995; contbr. scientific papers in field. Master: European Assn. Transluminal Surgery; fellow: ACS; mem.: Iraqi Soc. Gastroenterology and Hepatology, Soc. Iraqi Surgeons, Endoscopic and Laparoscopic Surgeons Asia, European Digestive Surgery, Soc. Am. Gastrointestinal and Endoscopic Surgeons (Internat. Fellowship award 2006—07). Office: Al Noor Hosp Air Port Rd Abu Dhabi 971 United Arab Emirates Office Fax: 971 2 444199. Personal E-mail: safwanat@yahoo.com.

TAHBOUB, REF'AT S., lab administrator; b. Hebron, West Bank, Palestine, May 15, 1951; s. Salah O. and Nafeesa T. Tahboub; m. Amina A. Tahboub; children: Hamdi, Su'ad, Moh'd, Nour, Iman. BSc, U. of Jordan, Amman, Jordan, 1973—77; M Med. Adminstrn., Hebron U., Hebron, 1997—2000. Lab. technician Ramallah Hosp., Ramallah, West Bank, Palestine, 1977—79; labs regional dir. Governmental Hosp. Directorate, Hebron, West Bank, Palestine, 1979—84; med. lab. and blood bank dir. Alia Governmental Hosp., Hebron, West Bank, Palestine, 1984—; adj. lectr. AlRahama Cmty. Coll., Hebron, West Bank, Palestine, 1992—97. Cons. Palestine the Future for Thalasimia, Hebron, West Bank, Palestine, 1999—. Elected council mem. U. Graduates Union, Hebron, West Bank, Palestine, 1991—2004; sec. Palestinian Med. Technology Union, Ramallah, West Bank, Palestine, 1996—99; mem. Red Crescent Soc., Hebron, West Bank, Palestine, 1985—2004, Patients' Friends Soc., Hebron, West Bank, Palestine, 1982—2004; bd. mem. Al Ihsan Charitable Soc. for Aged and Hadicapped, Hebron, West Bank, Palestine, 1987—94; mem. bd. trustees Palestine Polytechnic U., Hebron, West Bank, Palestine, 1999—2004. Recipient Honor Degree, Hebron U., 2000. Mem.: Palestinian Med. Technology Union. Muslim. Avocations: travel, chess, football. Home: PO Box 131 West Bank Hebron Palestine Office: Alia Hosp Faisal St West Bank Hebron Palestine Home Phone: 972 2 2292232; Office Phone: 972 2 2228 126.

TAHK, SEUNG-JEA, cardiologist, educator; b. Seoul, Republic of Korea, May 25, 1956; s. Yeon-Tack Tahk and Hae-Sun Jang; m. Eun-Ju Moon, Dec. 1, 1984; 1 child, Young-Min. MD, 1981; PhD, Yonsei U., Seoul, 1998. Dir. Ajou U. Med. Ctr. Interventional Cardiology, Suwon, Republic of Korea, 1994—; prof. Ajou U. Sch. Medicine, 2000—; chief Ajou U. Med. Ctr. Dept. Cardiology, 2003—, Ajou U. Med. Ctr. Dept. Internal Medicine, 2007—. Dir. Beyond Angiography Korea, Seoul, 1998—2000; co-dir. Angioplasty Summit, Seoul, 1997—; internat. faculty Complex Catheter Therapeutics, Japan, 1998—, Beyond Angiography Japan, 1999—, Interventional Cardiology, Aspen, Colo., 2000—, China Interventional Therapeutics, 2002—; course dir. Coronary Physiology and Imaging Summit, Seoul, 2007—. Author: (medical book) Mannual of Interventional Cardiology (Best Author prize, 2004). Capt. Korean Army, 1985—88. Mem.: Korean Soc. Interventional Cardiology, Korean Soc. Circulation, Korean Assn. Internal Medicine, Korean Med. Assn., Cardiovasc. Rsch. Found. Achievements include research in cardiovascular Intervention and Hemodynamics. Office: Ajou University Medical Center 5 Wonchundong Yeongtong-gu Suwon 443-721 Republic of Korea Office Phone: 82 31 219 5723. Office Fax: 82 31 219 5708. E-mail: sjtahk@ajou.ac.kr.

TÄHTELÄ, RIITTA KRISTINA, chemist; b. Stockholm, June 13, 1948; MSc, Helsinki U., 1986, PhD, 2004. Chemist United Labs. Ltd, 1987—92, Mehiläinen Oy, 2003—; chemist, head dept. United Labs. Ltd, 1992—99; sr. med. writer Schering Finland, 1999—2003. Lectr. Metropolia U. Applied Scis., Helsinki U., 1989; cons. Novartis, 2006—09. Mem.: Finnish Soc. Clin. Chemistry, Finnish Bone Soc. Office: P Hesperiankatu 17 C Helsinki Uusimaa 00260 Finland Office Fax: 358104144231. Business E-Mail: riitta.tahtela@mehilainen.fi.

TAI, JOHN JEN, biostatistician; b. Taipei, Taiwan, Oct. 15, 1953; s. Hong-Wen and Ya-Fang (Yao) Tai; m. Szu-Hua Kuo; children: Albert Hua, Ting-Yu. PhD, Med. U. S.C., 1984. Assoc. rsch. fellow Academia Sinica, Taipei, Taiwan, 1984-90; assoc. prof. Nat. Taiwan U., Taipei, 1989-90; prof. Fu-Jen Catholic U., Taipei, 1990-98, Nat. Yang-Ming U., Taipei, 1990-98; rsch. fellow Academia Sinica, Taipei, 1990-98; prof. Nat. Taiwan U., 1998—. Protocol statistician Nat.

Health Rsch. Insts., Taipei, 1986—; dep. exec. sec. gen. academic adv. com. Academia Sinica, Taiwan, 1990-94, dir. secretariat, 1992-94; cons. Taipei Vet. Gen. Hosp., Taipei, 1996—. Author (with others): Biomedical Statistics, 2000, Genetic Epidemiology-Genetic Design and Analysis Methods for Gene Mapping, 2002; contbr. articles to profl. jours.; edit. bd. Science, 1996. Mem. Internat. Statistical Soc. Home: F 3 no 6 alley 441 ln 150 Hsin Yi Rd Sec 5 Taipei 110 Taiwan Office: Inst Epid Nat Taiwan U 17 Xu Zhou Rd Taipei 100 Taiwan Office Phone: 886-2-33668038. Business E-Mail: jjtai@ntu.edu.tw.

TAI, MING-CHENG, physician, educator; b. Taiwan, Apr. 3, 1966; MD, Nat. Def. Med. Sch., 1991. Attending physician, chief corneal sect. Dept. Ophthalmology, 2009—. Asst. prof. Nat. Def. Med. Ctr., 2009. Mem.: Taiwan Ophthalmology Soc. (sec. gen.). Avocations: sports, photography, travel. Home: Fl 13 1 Ln 20 Alley 123 Sec Taipei 114 Taiwan Home Fax: (02)87927164. Personal E-mail: mingtai1966@yahoo.com.tw.

TAIEB, JULIEN, medical educator, researcher; b. Châtenay-Malabry, France, Sept. 1, 1969; MD, U. Paris, 1998, PhD, 2002. Prof., head oncology dept. Asst. Publique des Hopitaux de Paris, Faculté Paris Descartes, 2007—. Rsch. scientist INSERM, 2002—11. Mem.: ESMO, ASCO. Office: Georges Pompidou European Hospital 20 r Paris 75015 France Business E-Mail: julien.taieb@egp.aphp.fr.

TAILLIBERT, SOPHIE MARIA-EMMA, physician; b. Feb. 24, 1969; d. Roger and Béatrice (Pfister) Taillibert. MS in Microbiology, U. René Descartes Paris V, 1993; postgrad in Neurosci. Marie Curie, U. Paris, 1997; diploma in Applied Statistics Medicine, U. Pierre Et Marie Curie Paris VI, 1997; MD, U. Descartes, Paris, 2000. Neuro oncologist, staff physician Ctr. Hosp. U. Pitié-Salpêtrière Marie Curie Paris VI, 2002—. Asst. prof. Hospitalo-U., 2002; residency neurology U. Paris V, 1994—2000, fellow clin. oncology, 2000—02, Hôsp. Pitié-Salpêtrière, U. Paris. Recipient Yr. Nomination award, Interne des Hôpitaux de Paris, 1994. Mem.: Assn. Neuro-Oncologues d'Expression Française, Soc. Française Neurologie, Soc. Neuro-Oncology, Am. Soc. Clin. Oncology, European Orgn. Rsch. & Treatment Cancer (brain tumor group mem.). Achievements include research in brain metastases and leptomeningeal metastases, neurological complications of cancer's treatments. Avocations: photography, painting, architecture, art. Office: Ctr Hospitalo-Universitaire Pitié-Salpêtrière Svc Neurologie Mazarin 47 Bd De l'hôpital Paris 75013 France Office Fax: 33142160418. Business E-Mail: sophie.taillibert@psl.aphp.fr.

TAISHI, YOSHIDA, pharmacologist; b. Tokyo, Apr. 27, 1974; MSc, U. Tokyo, 1999. Assoc. sr. rschr. Daiichi Sankyo Co., Ltd., 2010—. Office: 1-2-58 Hiromchi Shinagawa-ku Tokyo 140-8710 Japan Business E-Mail: yoshida.taishi.bc@daiichisankyo.co.jp.

TAJIMA, TSUYOSHI, medical educator; b. Hitoyoshi, Japan, Oct. 3, 1965; s. Noboru and Kinuyo Tajima; m. Yumi Tajima, Apr. 11, 1993; children: Hajime, Akira. MD, Kyushu U., 1990, PhD, 2002. Resident Kyushu U., Fukuoka, Japan, 1990—91; med. staff Kokura Meml. Hosp., Kita Kyushu, 1991—92, Yamagachi Red Cross Hosp, 1992—93, Saga Prefectural Hosp., 1993—94, Aso Iizuka Hosp, 1994—95, Kyushu U., 1996—99, Kyushu Cancer Ctr., 1999—2001; teaching asst. Kyushu U., 2001—. Cons. Med. Sci. Monitor, NY, 2003—. Contbr. articles to profl. jours. Recipient Irie award, Alumni Soc. Dept. Clin. Radiology, 2002. Mem.: Japanese Radiol. Soc., Japanese Soc. Angiography and Interventional Radiology. Avocation: reading. Office: Kyushu U Dept Clin Radiology 3-1-1 Maidashi Higashi-ku Fukuoka 812-8582 Japan Office Fax: +81-92 642-5708. E-mail: ttajima@dr.hosp.kyushu-u.ac.jp.

TAK, TAHIR, cardiologist, researcher; b. Lahore, Punjab, Pakistan, July 18, 1951; arrived in US, 1985, naturalized, 2000; s. E. Tak. BS, Govt. Coll. Lahore, 1971; MD, U. Nijmegen, 1980; PhD, U. Maastricht, 1989. Diplomate in internal medicine and cardiovascular diseases 2000, Am. Bd. Internal Medicine, 2010. Cardiology fellow U. Amsterdam, 1982—85; resident in internal medicine U. So. Calif., LA, 1988—89, asst. prof. medicine, 1989—96; assoc. prof. medicine U. Nev., Las Vegas, 1996—98; cardiologist Scott and White Clinic, Temple, Tex., 1998—2001; assoc. prof. Tex. A&M U. HSC, Temple, 1998—2001; cardiologist Marshfield Clinic, Wis., 2001—04; clin. prof. medicine U. Madison Sch. Medicine, Wis., 2001—04; prof. medicine U. North Tex., Ft. Worth, 2004—07; cardiologist cons. Mayo Clinic, Rochester, Minn., 2007—. Fellow: ACP, Am. Coll. Cardiology, Am. Heart Assn., European Soc. Cardiology. Office: Mayo Clinic 200 First St SW Rochester MN 55905 Home: 510 Stonebridge Ave Onalaska WI 54650 Business E-Mail: tak.tahir@mayo.edu.

TAKAAKI, FUJII, medical educator; b. Japan, May 21, 1974; MD, Gunma U., PhD, 2000. Asst. prof. Dept. Gen. Surg. Sci. Grad. Sch. Medicine, Gunma U., 2008—. Office: 3-39-22 Showa-Machi Maebashi Gunma 371-8511 Japan Business E-Mail: ftakaaki@med.gunma-u.ac.jp.

TAKABAYASHI, SHIN, surgeon, cardiologist, medical educator, researcher; b. Nagoya, Aichi, Japan, Mar. 29, 1970; s. Masa Takabayashi; m. Harumi Tanaka, Nov. 22, 1997; children: Hina, Yuzu. MD, Mie U., 1996, PhD, 2005. Lic. Ministry of Health, Labor and Welfare, Japan, 1996, Cardiovas. Surgery Japanese Bd. of Cardiovasc. Surgery, Japan, 2003. Trainee Mie U. Dept. of Thorac. and Cardiovasc. Sugery, Tsu, Mie, Japan, 1996—97; resident Mie U. Dept. of Thorac. and Cardiovasc. Surgery, Tsu, Mie, Japan, 1998—2000; clin. fellow Fukuoka Children's Hosp., Fukuoka, Japan, 2000—02; staff surgeon Mie U. Dept. of Thorac. and Cardiovasc. Surgery, Tsu, Mie, Japan, 2002—. Med. tchr. Dept. Thoracic and Cardiovasc. Surgery, Mie U. Sch. Medicine, Tsu, Mie, Japan, 2002—, asst. prof., 2006—. Recipient Young Investigator award, 31st meeting Japanese Soc. for Cardiovasc. Surgery, Ube, Yamaguchi, 2001. Fellow: Japanese Soc. of Pediatr. Cardiology and Cardiac Surgery (42nd Ann. Young Investigator's award 2006); mem.: Japanese Soc. Cardiovasc. Surgery, Japanese Assn. Thoracic Surgery, Japan Surg. Soc. Avocations: fishing, motorcycling, exploration, computers. Office: Mie U Dept Thorac and Cardiovasc Surgery 2-174 Edobashi Mie Tsu 514-8507 Japan Office Fax: 81-59231-2845. Business E-Mail: shin1111@clin.medic.mie-u.ac.jp.

TAKAFUMI, ITO, nephrologist, educator; b. Japan, Mar. 1, 1968; MD, Hiroshima U., 1992, PhD, 2001. Asst. prof., dir. divsn. nephrology Shimane U. Faculty Medicine, 2008—. Grant, Baxter PD Fund. Fellow: ACP, Japan Soc. Healing Environment, Japanese Soc. Nephrology, Japanese Soc. Dialysis Therapy, Japanese Soc. Internal Medicine. Avocation: ping pong/table tennis. Office: 89-1 Enya-cho Izumo-City Shimane Prefecture 693-8501 Japan Office Fax: 81-853-20-2201. Business E-Mail: tito@med.shimane-u.ac.jp.

TAKAGAKI, MASAO, neurosurgeon, researcher; b. Wakayama, Japan, Mar. 3, 1953; s. Hideichi and Momoyo Takagaki; m. Yoshiko Takagaki, Sept. 22, 1951; children: Tomoko, Keiko. MD, PhD, Kyoto U., Japan, 2001. Lic. physician Japan, 1982. Asst. prof. Kyoto (Japan) U., 1990—2001; prof. Aino Coll., Ibaraki, Japan, 2001—. Rschr. No. Ill. U., Dekalb, Ill., 2000—. Contbr. articles to profl. jours. Mem.: Japanese Neurosurgical Soc. (assoc.). Home: 1-14-7 Sakuragaoka Seika 619-0232 Japan Office: Aino College 4-5-4 Higashioda Ibaraki 567-0012 Japan Office Fax: +81-726-21-3706. Personal E-mail: takagaki@bnct.jp.

TAKAHAMA, MAKOTO, thoracic surgeon, director; b. Osaka, Japan, Nov. 29, 1966; MD, Nara Med. U., 1991, PhD, 1997. Dep. dir., dept. gen. thoracic surgery Osaka City Gen. Hosp., 2006—. Assoc. prof., dept. thoracic and cardiovasc. surgery Nara Med. U., 2005—06. Avocations: golf, jazz. Office: 2-13-22 Miyakojima-hondoori Miyakojima Osaka 534-0021 Japan Office Fax: 81-6-6929-1090. Personal E-mail: mktkhm@yahoo.co.jp.

TAKAHARA, RYOJI, public health service officer, educator, economist; b. Okayama, Japan, May 16, 1947; s. Michiharu and Michiko (Ukida) T.; m. Yuko Takahara, Aug. 1, 1972; children: Nogusa, Sion. AA, Okayama U., 1968, MD, 1972; MPH, U. Tex., Houston, 1980. Resident Toshima Met. Hosp., Tokyo, 1972-74; chief health statistician Ministry of Health, Tokyo, 1976-77, dep. dir. Health Econs., 1976-82; 1st sec. embassy of Japan Ministry of Fgn. Affairs, Manila, 1982-85; dir. divsn. Ministry of Health and Welfare, 1989-91; dir., dir. gen. Ministry of Health and Environment, Okayama, 1991-93, dir. food sanitation, 1993-95, dir. nat. hosp. adminstrn., 1995-97, dir. cmty. health, health promotion disease prevention and nutrition, 1997-98, dir. divsn. health sci. policy, 1998-99; dir. gen. health med. affairs Japan Def. Agy., Tokyo, 1999—2001; dir. gen. health and welfare svcs. for disabled Ministry of Health Labor and Welfare, Tokyo, 2001—02, dir. gen. Bur. Health Svc., 2002—04; vice chair exec. bd., mng. exec. dir. Japan Coun. for Quality Health Care, 2004—; prof. health and welfare policy Sophia U., 2005—. Cons. WHO, Geneva, 1989; mem. mgmt. bd. Nat. Okayama U. Inc. Contbr. more than 50 articles to profl. jours. Fellow Royal Soc. Health (London); mem. APHA. United Ch. of Christ. Avocations: art, travel, music. Office: Japan Coun for Quality Health Care Mitsui-Sumitomo Bldg 7A 3-11 Kansa-Surugadai, Chiyodaky Tokyo 101-0062 Japan Office Phone: 81-3-5217-2320. E-mail: takahara@post.nifty.jp.

TAKAHASHI, AKIRA, pharmacologist, educator; b. Tokyo, Nov. 9, 1949; s. Masaji and Hisako Fumiko Takahashi; m. Junko Sekiguchi, May 11, 1974; children: Akitaka, Nobutaka. PhD (hon.), Tokyo Coll. Pharmacy, 1973. Rsch. scientist Psychiat. Rsch. Inst. Tokyo, Tokyo, 1973—84; asst. prof. Ehime U. Sch. Medicine, Shigenobu, 1984—90; asst. prof., mgr. Gunma Sch. Medicine, Maebashi, 1990—2000; sr. mgr. Tsumura Rsch. Inst. Tsumura & Co., Inashiki gun Ami, 2000—07, sr. mgr., 2007—10. Achievements include research in hypothalamic control of energy metabolism. Business E-Mail: taka1109@mail2.accsnet.ne.jp.

TAKAHASHI, CHIAKI, physician, educator; b. Takamatsu, Japan, Oct. 16, 1964; MD, Kyoto U. Sch. Medicine, PhD, 1990. Prof. Kanazawa U. Cancer Rsch. Inst., Ishikawa, Japan, 2009—. Fellow: Japan Cancer Assn. (Young Investigator's award); mem.: Am. Soc. Biochemistry and Molecular Biology, Japan Soc. Cell Biology, The Japanese Biochemical Soc., Molecular Biology Soc. Japan. Avocation: piano. Office: Kanazawa University Kakuma-machi Kanazawa Ishikawa 920-1192 Japan Office Fax: 81-76-234-4521. Business E-Mail: chtakaha@staff.kanazawa-u.ac.jp.

TAKAHASHI, HIROSHI, health facility administrator, researcher; b. Iwatsuki, Saitama, Japan, Aug. 17, 1951; s. Taketeru and Kimiko Takahashi; m. Chisato Asahara, July 23, 1989; children: Midori, Anna children: Kentaro John, Erika Ingrid, Erika Ingrid. MD, Jikei U., Tokyo, 1977; PhD, Jikei U., 1981. Lic. physician Ministry of Health, 1977, diplomate Japan Assn. of Internal Medicine, Japan Assn. of Gastroenterology. Instr. in medicine Jikei U., Tokyo, 1984—93, Harvard Med. Sch., Boston, 1989—93, asst. prof. of medicine, 1993—2000, assoc. prof. of medicine, 2000—02; prof. of medicine Jikei U. Sch. of Medicine, Tokyo, 2001—; dir. Inst. of Clin. Medicine/Rsch., Kashiwa, Chiba, Japan, 2001—04, Winchester Inst Clin. Medicine Rsch., Tokyo, 2005—. Grantee First Award/RO-1, NIH, 1992—2001. Mem.: Am. Assn. for the Study of Liver Diseases (assoc.). Achievements include research in cancer research. Office: Winchester Inst Clin Medicine Rsch 1-3-8-504 Shirokane Minato-Ku Tokyo 108-0072 Japan Home: No 5 Ln 408 Wunzih Rd Kaohsiung 813 Taiwan Personal E-mail: topjournal@mac.com.

TAKAHASHI, ICHIRO, orthodontist; s. Saiichi and Keiko Takahashi; m. Toshiko Okamoto, Sept. 29, 1986; children: Kazuhisa, Fumiko. D in Dentistry, Osaka Dental U., Japan, 1979. Orthodontic specialist Japanese Orthodontic Soc., 2008. Lectr. Osaka Dental U., 1996—2008; office dir., 2008—. Contbr. articles to profl. jours. Mem. Nara Dental Assn., Japan, 1985—2008. Mem.: Am. Assn. Orthodontists. Office: Saidaiji Takahashi Orthodontic Office Saidaiji-Higashi-machi 2-1-55-6F Nara 631-0821 Japan Office Fax: 81-742-35-3521. Business E-Mail: ichiro-t@nn.iij4u.or.jp.

TAKAHASHI, KENTARO, obstetrician, gynecologist; b. Oita, Japan, Feb. 26, 1952; s. Sadami and Chiyo Takahashi; m. Yayoe Anjiki; children: Yumie children: Kanae, Marie. PhD, Nat. Tottori U., Tottori, Japan, 1982. Asst. prof. Shimane Med. U., Izumo City, Shimane Pref., Japan, 1985—94; assoc. prof. Shimane Med. U. Gynecology, Nat. Shimane Med. U., Izumo City, Shimane Pref., Japan, 1994—2004; assoc. prof. dept. obstetrics and gynecology Shiga U. Med. Sci., 2004—07, prof. dept. cmty. med. sys., 2007—10, prof. dept. cmty. perinatal medicine, 2010—. Chief female pelvic surgery & reproductive medicine Shiga Med. Sci. Hosp., Otsu City, Shiga Pref., 2006—. Contbr. articles to profl. jours. Shinto. Avocation: travel. Office: Shiga University Med Sci Dept Cmty Perinatal Medicine Seta-Tsukinowa-cho Otsu Shiga 520-2192 Japan Home: 2-8-19 Matsumoto Otsu City 5200807 Japan Office Phone: 81-0-77-548-2447. Business E-Mail: taka27@belle.shiga-med.ac.jp.

TAKAHASHI, KYOICHI, ophthalmologist, researcher; b. Takasaki, Gunma, Japan, Jan. 5, 1961; s. Zenichi and Ayako Takahashi; m. Yuriko Kurumazuka, Mar. 6, 1994; children: Takuya, Kento, Yuto. MD (hon.), Gunma U., Maebashi, Japan, 2005. Lic. Japan, 1985. Resident Gunma U., 1985—87, assoc. prof. Sch. Medicine, 2003—; ophthalmology practice Gunma U. Hosp., 1988—98; rsch. assoc. Wilmer Eye Inst., Balt., 2000—02. Asst. prof. Gunma U., 1998—2002. Contbr. articles to profl. jours. Grantee, Japanese Ministry, 1997. Achievements include research in remodelling of choroidal circulation in pathologic condition and mechanism of serous macular detachment in retinal vascular disorders. E-mail: kyotaka@showa.gunma-u.ac.jp.

TAKAHASHI, MASAKI, orthopedist, surgeon; s. Takahashi Tetsuo and Takahashi Keiko; m. Reiko Denma, Sept. 1, 1994 (div. July 11, 2002). MD, Juntendo U., Tokyo, 1990, PhD, 2003. Asst. Juntendo Urayasu Hosp., Urayasu, Japan, 1997—99; chief asst. Juntendo U., Tokyo, 1999—. Co. exec. Fromcradle, Ichikawa, Japan, 1997—. Recipient award, Japan Spine Rsch. Soc., 2003. Fellow: Matsubayashi Kenkou Club (corr.); mem.: Soc. Matsubokkuri (bd. dirs. 1997—2003). Achievements include invention of health food. Home: Sanbancho 12-3 Chiyodaku Tokyo 102-0075 Japan Office: Juntendo U Sch Medicine Hongo 2-1-1 Bunkyo 113-0033 Japan Office Fax: 03-3813-3428. Business E-Mail: mastk@med.juntendo.ac.jp.

TAKAHASHI, MASAO, psychiatrist, researcher, educator; b. Misato-cho, Japan, May 22, 1954; s. Masami and Eiko Takahashi; m. Michiko Takahashi, Feb. 22, 1987; 1 child, Saori. MB, U. Tokyo, 1979, MD, 1996. Physician U. Tokyo Hosp., 1979—80, 1982—84, Saku Ctrl. Hosp., Usuda, Japan, 1980—82; chief Tokyo Met. Govt., 1985—89; instr. U. Tokyo, 1989—96; asst. prof. U. Tsukuba, Japan, 1996—2003, prof., 2003—. Contbr. articles to profl. jours. Mem.: Japan Acad. for Comprehensive Rehab., Japanese Assn. Pathography (award 1999). Office: Univ Tsukuba 3-29-1 Otsuka Bunkyo-ku Tokyo 112-0012 Japan

TAKAHASHI, MASATO, pediatric cardiologist, educator; b. Tokyo, Feb. 10, 1933; came to U.S., 1952; s. Noboru and Fujiko (Tarumoto) T.; m. Marcia Parnell, Jan. 16, 1966; children; Rumi Anne, Yuki Lynn. AB, Wabash U., 1956; MD, Ind. U., 1960. Attending physician Children's Hosp., LA, 1968—; prof. pediatrics,, Keck Sch. Medicine U. So. Calif., LA, 1986—2005, prof. pediat. emeritus, 2005—. Chmn. 4th Internat. Kawasaki Disease Symposium, 1991. Vol. Habitat for Humanity, San Fernando Valley, Calif., 1993-94, Am. Heart Assn. L.A., 1982-85, com. mem. 1991-93 (Disting. Achievement award 1983). Mem. Am. Acad. Pediatrics, Am. Coll. Cardiology, Meth. Avocations: long distance running, wood working. Office: Divsn Cardiology Children's Hosp LA MS#34 4650 Sunset Blvd Los Angeles CA 90027 Office Phone: 323-361-4634. Business E-Mail: mtakahashi@chla.usc.edu.

TAKAHASHI, MASATO, medical educator; b. Meguro, Tokyo, Aug. 29, 1959; s. Takahashi Akiko; m. Takahashi Kayo. Cert. masato takahashi Interant. Budo U., Japan. Prof. Internat. Budo U., Katsuura, Chiba, Japan, 1994—. Office: Internat Budo Univ 841 Shinkan Katsuura Chiba 299-9295 Japan Office Phone: 81-470-73-4111. Office Fax: 81-470-73-4148. Business E-Mail: t-masato@budo-u.ac.jp.

TAKAHASHI, MUTSUMASA, radiologist, educator; b. Miya konojo, Miyazaki, Japan, Aug. 26, 1935; s. Katsumasa and Midori (Kawabata) T.; m. Sayoko Hirata, June 8, 1962; children: Eri, Naoki, Tomoki. BSc, Chiba U., Japan, 1956; MD, Kyushu U., Fukuoka, Japan, 1960. Resident Kyushu U., Fukuoka, 1961-62, asst., 1967-69, asst. prof., 1969-72; resident U. Mich., 1962-65; fellow Stanford U., 1965-66, UCLA, 1966-67; prof., chmn. Akita (Japan) U., 1972-80, Kumamoto (Japan) U., 1980-2001; dir. Internat. Imaging Ctr., Kumamoto, 2001—07, Imaging Ctr., Ugadake Hosp., 2007—10, Nishinihon Hosp. Instr. Stanford U., 1965-66; acting asst. prof. UCLA, 1966-67, vis. prof., 1977-78; cons. VA Hosp., L.A., 1966-67, 77-78. Editor-in-chief Neuroradiology, 1982—2005, sect. editor, 2005-07. Mem. Japan Radiol. Soc. (bd. dirs. 1994—), Internat. Soc. Magnetic Resonance in Medicine (bd. trustees 1997-2000), Radiol. Soc. N.Am. (hon.), European Soc. Radiology (hon.), Am. Soc. Neuroradiology (hon.), Am. Coll. Radiology (hon.), French Soc. Radiology (hon.), Royal Coll. Radiology (hon.). Avocations: tennis, travel, baseball, golf. Office Phone: 81-96-380-1111. Office Fax: 81-96-380-0539. Business E-Mail: sm.takahashi@hog.ocn.ne.jp.

TAKAHASHI, RYOTA, physician; b. Osaka, Japan, Mar. 6, 1978; MD, Nat. Def. Med. Coll., 2002. Physician, internal medicine Self Def. Force Ctrl. Hosp., 2009. Home: Shimouma 5-29-14-205 Setagaya City Tokyo 154-0002 Japan Personal E-mail: ryotaka@fb3.so-net.ne.jp.

TAKAHASHI, SHINICHIRO, medical educator; b. Sendai, Japan, Feb. 16, 1969; MD, Hirosaki U. Sch. Med., 1994; PhD, Tohoku U. Grad. Sch. Med., 2000. Prof. Kitasato U. Sch. Allied Health Sci., 2007—. Councilor Japanese Soc. Hematology, 2007. Recipient Young Investigator Encouragement award, Japan Leukaemia Rsch. Found.; grant, Takeda Sci. Found., Rsch. Encouragement grant, Nakayama Found. Human Sci. Mem.: Japanese Assn. Clin. Lab. Physicians, Japanese Soc. Lab. Medicine, Japanese Soc. Internal Medicine, Am. Soc. Hematology, Japanese Soc. Hematology. Office: 1-15-1 Kitasato Minami-ku Sagamihara Kanagawa 252-0373 Japan Business E-Mail: shin@kitasato-u.ac.jp.

TAKAHASHI, SUSUMU, internist, educator; b. Namerikawa, Toyama, Japan, June 23, 1937; MD, Nihon U., Tokyo, 1964, PhD, 1969. Prof. Sch. Medicine Nihon U., Tokyo, 1992, prof. Grad. Sch. Bus., 1999—; dir. Nishi-Kof-U Nat. Hosp., Japan, 1992-98, Yokosuka Nat. Hosp., Japan, 1998-99. Recipient Oshima award Kidney Found. Japan, 1990. Office: Nihon U Grad Sch Bus 8-24 Kudan-Minami

4-Chome Chiyoda-ku Tokyo 102-8275 Japan Home Phone: 81-3-3449-9610; Office Phone: 81-3-5275-9448. Fax: 81-3-5275-9460. Business E-Mail: takahasi@gsb.nihon-u.ac.jp.

TAKAHASHI, TAKEO, retired anesthesiology educator; b. Otaru-city, Japan, Mar. 4, 1922; s. Chokichi and Sumi (Nemoto) T.; m. Tamiko Hiraki, Oct. 17, 1951; children: Masako, Hiroo, Muneo, Arihiro, Makio. MD, Hokkaido U. Sch. Medicine, 1945, PhD, 1950. Assoc. prof. surgery Sapporo Med. Coll. and Hosp., Japan, 1955—57, prof. dept. anesthesiology, 1957—87; prof. emeritus Sch. Medicine Sapporo Med. U., 1987—; pres. Noboribetsu Gen. Hosp., Japan, 1987—89. Chair bd. dirs. Sapporo Med. U. Found. Promotion of Med. Sci., 1997—2002. Recipient Fulbright scholarship, N.Y. Postgrad. Sch. at Bellevue Hosp., 1953—55. Mem.: Japan Soc. Circulation Control (hon.), Japan Soc. Pain Clinicians (hon.), Japan Soc. Anesthesiology (hon.). Avocations: music, ceramic art, drawing. Home: 3-7 1-jyo 7-chome Yamanote Nishi-ku 063-0001 Sapporo Hokkaido Japan E-mail: takeo-takahashi@hokkaido.med.or.jp.

TAKAHASHI, TOHRU, hematologist; b. Asahikawa, Hokkaido, Japan, July 11, 1959; s. Tadashi and Kyoko Takahashi; m. Naoko Toki, May 8, 1960; children: Makoto, Eriko. MD, Sapporo Med. U., Japan, 1985, PhD, 1989. Rsch. fellow Sloan-Kettering Cancer Ctr., NYC, 1988—90; clin. fellow Sapporo Med. U., Sapporo, Hokkaido, Japan, 1990—92; physician-in-chief Hokkaido Kitano Hosp., Sapporo, Hokkaido, Japan, 1992—94; instr. Sapporo Med. U., Sapporo, Hokkaido, Japan, 1994—98; dir. internal medicine Mikasa City Hosp., Hokkaido, Japan, 1998—2000; dept. of hematology chief Tenshi Hosp., Sapporo, Hokkaido, Japan, 2000—. Fellow: Japanese Soc. Clin. Hematology, Japanese Soc. Hematology, Japanese Soc. Internal Medicine (Young Investigator's award 1998). Home: Makomanai Minamimachi 2 Chome Hokkaido Sapporo 005-0016 Japan Office: Tenshi Hospital Higashi-ku kita 12 Higashi 3 Hokkaido Sapporo 065-0012 Japan Personal E-mail: tohrut@cocoa.ocn.ne.jp.

TAKAHASHI, TOMOKO, pharmacologist, educator; d. Kan and Yukiko Takahashi; m. Hideki Sabata, Mar. 27, 1971 (div. Jan. 7, 1974); 1 child, Keita. BS, U. Tokyo, 1961, MS, 1963, PhD, 1966. Cert. Pharmacist The Ministry of Health and Welfare of Japan, 1961. Chief rschr. Nat. Inst. of Infectious Diseases, Shinagawa-ku, Tokyo, Japan, 1966—74; asst. prof. Hoshi U., Shinagawa-ku, Tokyo, Japan, 1974—86, prof., 1986—. Author: Animal, Plant and Microbial Toxins, 1976, Toxins: Animal, Plant and Microbial, 1978, Methods in Enzymology, 1981; contbr. articles to profl. jours. Grantee High Technique Rsch. Ctr. Promotion Fund, Ministry of Edn., Sci., Sports, and Culture of Japan, 1997—2001. Fellow: Pharm. Soc. of Japan, Japanese Soc. for Sexually Transmitted Diseases, Japanese Biochemical Soc. Office: Hoshi U 2-4-41 Ebara Tokyo Shinagawa 142-8501 Japan Office Fax: +81(3)5498-5794. E-mail: t-tomoko@hoshi.ac.jp.

TAKAHASHI, YOSHIHISA, pathologist, researcher; b. Sendai, Japan, July 8, 1971; s. Masatake and Keiko Takahashi. MD, Tokyo U., 2000; grad., Tokyo U. Sch. Medicine, 1996. Clin. rschr. Tokyo Med. U., 2000—01; asst. Tokyo U. Hosp., 2001—03; instr. Teikyo U., Sch. Medicine, 2003—. Contbr. articles to profl. jours. Grantee, Mitsui Norin Co., Ltd., 2005. Mem.: Japanese Soc. Hepatology, Japanese Cancer Assn., Japanese Soc. Clin. Cytology (cytological specialist 2002—), Japanese Soc. Pathology (path. specialist 2001—, acad. councilor 2004—). Home: 6-4-28-201 Kawaguchi Kawaguchi Saitama 332-0015 Japan Office: Teikyo U Sch Medicine 2-11-1 Kaga Itabashi-ku Tokyo 173-8605 Japan Office Fax: 81-3-3964-9622. Personal E-mail: ytakaha-tky@umin.ac.jp.

TAKAHASHI, YUSUKE, dentist, educator; b. Japan, July 16, 1973; DDS, Osaka U., 1998, PhD, 2002. Asst. prof. Osaka U. Grad. Sch. Dentistry, 2006—. Office: 1-8 Yamadaoka Suita Osaka 565-0871 Japan Business E-Mail: takahasi@dent.osaka-u.ac.jp.

TAKAHASHI, YUTAKA, medical educator; b. Osaka, Japan, May 29, 1963; MD, Kobe U. Grad. Sch. Medicine, PhD, 1996. Assoc. prof., divsn. diabetes and endocrinology dept. internal medicine Kobe U. Grad. Sch. Medicine, 2004—. Recipient Rsch. award, Japan Endocrine Soc., Japan Hypothalamic and Pituitary Disease Soc. Mem.: Endocrine Soc. Office: 7-5-1 Kusunoki-cho Chuo-ku Kobe Hyogo 650-0017 Japan Business E-Mail: takahash@med.kobe-u.ac.jp.

TAKAHASHI, YUUICHI, physician, director; b. Oosaki, Miyagi, Japan, Oct. 25, 1964; s. Eko Takahashi; m. Kiyomi Miyazato, Nov. 22, 1996; children: Nayu, Noa. BA, U.Electro-Comm., Tokyo, 1988; MD, U. Ryukyus, Okinawa, Japan, 1995. Resident Tokyo Med. and Dental U., 1995—96, Chubu Tokushukai Hosp. and Tokushukai Groups Hosp., 1996—2001; staff gastroenterology Naha City Hosp., 2001—02, Tomishiro Chuo Hosp., 2002—05; dir. Takahashi Clinic, 2006—, physician. Achievements include research in sedation-free colonoscopy. Office: Takahashi Clinic 8-15 Yone Tomishiro 901-0224 Japan Office Fax: +81-098-851-2462. Business E-Mail: takahashi@takaclinic.jp.

TAKAHIKO, SHIMIZU, medical researcher; b. Hiroshima, Japan, July 27, 1967; PhD, Hiroshima U., 1995. Rsch. Tokyo Met. Inst. Gerontology, 1997—. Office: 35-2 Sakae-cho Itabashi-ku Tokyo 173-0015 Japan Business E-Mail: shimizut@tmig.or.jp.

TAKAHIRO, ARIMA, medical educator; b. Hukuoka, Japan, Apr. 6, 1957; MD, Kyusyu U., PhD, 1986. Prof. Tohoku U. Grad. Sch. Medicine, 2010—. Office: 2-1 Seiryo-cho Aoba-ku Sendai Miyagi 980-8575 Japan Office Fax: 81 22-717-7063. Business E-Mail: tarima@med.tohoku.ac.jp.

TAKAMI, YOJI, surgeon; b. Japan, Apr. 12, 1969; D, Chiba U. Sch. Medicine, 1996, D, 2005. Gen. surgeon Nat. Hosp. Orgn. Chiba Med. Ctr., 2008—. Mem.: Internat. Assn. Surgeons, Gastroenterologist and Oncologist. Avocation: soccer. Office: 4-1-2 Tsubakimori Chuo-ku Chiba 260-8606 Japan Office Fax: 81-43-251-1675. Business E-Mail: yoji-t@kd5.so-net.ne.jp.

TAKAMI, YOSHIHIRO, surgeon, researcher; b. Hokkaido, Japan, Jan. 13, 1956; s. Yataro and Yoshiko Takami; m. Atsuko Tan; children: Kiyo, Kana. MD, Sapporo Med. U., Japan, 1982, PhD, 1987. Assoc. prof. Kyorin U., Sch. Medicine, Mitaka, Tokyo, 2001—05; dir. Seibu Gen. Hosp., Saitama City, Japan, 2005—. Vis. prof. Shanghai Jiao Tong U. Sch. Medicine, 2000—, Nippon Med. Sch., Tokyo, 2007—. Contbr. articles to profl. jours. Grant, Ministry Edn., Japan, 1999—2006, Saitama City Govt., Japan, 2005, 2007. Mem.: Japanese Soc. Dermatology (cert.), Japanese Soc. Burn Injuries (cert.), Japanese Soc. Plastic Surgery (cert.). Achievements include patents for skin decellularization method, acellular dermal matrix. Office Fax: 81-3-5685-3076. Business E-Mail: takamiyo@nms.ac.jp.

TAKAMINE, YUJI, surgeon; b. Maebashi, Japan, Dec. 23, 1970; s. Kazuo and Kyoko Takamine; m. Chinatsu Hasegawa, Mar. 26, 2000; children: Yuta, Hinako. MS in Medicine; MD, Nagoya U., 2002. Lic. Japan, 1996. Resident Okazaki Mcpl. Hosp., Japan, 1996—98, dr., 1996—98; rschr. Cedars Sinai Med. Ctr., LA, 2002—03; orthop. surgeon Ctrl. Hosp. Aichi Welfare Ctr., Kasugai, Japan, 2003—. Achievements include research in distraction osteogenesis enhanced by osteoblastlike cells and collagen gel; mutations in the EVC1 gene as not being a common finding in the ellis-van creveld and short rib-polydactyly type III syndromes; occipital projections in the skeletal dysplasias; patellar dislocation in achondroplasia. Home: 3-51 Asaoka-cho Chikusa-ku Nagoya 464-0811 Japan Office: Shikenya Orthop Clinic 2-8-7 Shonan-cho Owariasahi City Aich 488-0823 Japan Office Phone: 81 52 777 1222. Office Fax: 81321111200. Business E-Mail: yujitaka@sannet.ne.jp.

TAKAMIZAWA, SHIGERU, pediatric surgeon; b. Nagano, Japan, Apr. 1, 1967; s. Kiyoshi and Sachiko Takamizawa; m. Taemi Akahane, Feb. 11, 2000; 1 child, Haruna. MD (hon.), Juntendo U., Hongo, Japan, PhD, 1991. Cert. pediat. surgeon Hyogo, 2004. Staff physician Kobe Children's Hosp., Kobe, Japan, 2004—08, pediatric surg. resident, 2000—04; intern and surg. resident Okinawa Chubu Hosp., 1991—93; pediatric surg. resident Dept. Pediatric Surgery, Juntendo U. Sch. Medicine, 1993—94, 1996—97, rsch. fellow, 1999—2000; pediatric surg. resident Shizuoka Children's Hosp., 1994—96; rsch. fellow Dept. Surgery, Iowa U., 1997—99; surgeon-in-chief Dept. Surgery, Nagano Children's Hosp., 2008—. Office: Nagano Children's Hosp 3100 Toyoshina Azumino Nagano 399-8288 Japan Office Phone: 0263-73-6700. Office Fax: 0263-73-5432; Home Fax: 0263-46-8046. Business E-Mail: takamizawa@naganoch.gr.jp.

TAKANO, SUSUMU, gastroenterologist; b. Mitaka, Japan, May 4, 1957; parents Atsuto and Mieko Takano; children: Satoru, Yutaka. MD, Chiba U., 1982. Physician Chiba (Japan) U. Hosp., 1982-92; dir. home medicine, med. record mgr. Kawasaki (Japan) Social Ins. Hosp., 1992—. Author: Viral Hepatitis and Liver Diseases, 1994; contbr. articles to profl. jours. Avocations: playing violin, travel. Office: Kawasaki Social Ins Hosp Tamachi 2-9-1 Kawasaki 210-0822 Japan Home Phone: 81-422-48-3875; Office Phone: 81-44-266-2801. Business E-Mail: wombats@kawasakihp.jp.

TAKAO, TOSHIKO, medical researcher; b. Tokyo, Jan. 9, 1962; MD, Toho U., PhD, 1987. Sr. rschr. Inst. Adult Diseases, Asahi Life Found., 2005—. Office: 1-6-1 Marunouchi Chiyoda-ku Tokyo 100-0005 Japan Office Fax: 03-3201-6881.

TAKAOKA, AKINORI, medical educator, researcher; b. Wassam-cho,Kamikawa-gun, Hokkaido, Japan, July 29, 1967; MD, 1996; PhD, Sapporo Med. U., Japan, 1995. Rsch. assoc. U. Tokyo, 1997—2000, asst. prof., 2000—02, lectr., 2002—. Recipient Kanahara Meml. Found. award, 2000, Young Investigator award, Internat. Cytokine Soc., 2000, Rsch. award, Japanese Cancer Assn., 2001, Young Investigator award, Internat. Soc. Interferon & Cytokine Rsch., 2003, Sumito Fund, 2004, Nakajima Fund, 2004, Princess Takamatsu Cancer Rsch. Fund, 2004, Mitsubishi Chem. award, 2005; grantee, Yamanouchi Found. for Rsch. on Metabolic Disorders, 1999, Mochida Meml. Found. for Med. and Pharm. Rsch., 2000, Welfide Medicinal Rsch. Found., 2001, Kanae Found. for Life & Socio-Med. Sci., 2001, Senri Life Sci. Found., 2001; fellow, Japan Soc. for Promotion of Sci., 1999. Achievements include research in cytokine signal transductions; cancer. Avocations: piano, skiing, music, ken-do. Office: Univ Tokyo Dept Immunology Grad Sch Medicine Hongo 7-3-1 Bunkyo-ku Tokyo 113-0033 Japan Office Fax: 81-(0)3-5841-3450. Personal E-mail: takaoka9@yahoo.co.jp. E-mail: takaoka9@m.u-tokyo.ac.jp.

TAKAOKA, YUTAKA, medical educator; b. Osaka, Japan, Mar. 22, 1966; LAc, 1988; B in Acupuncture, Meiji U. Integrative Medicine, 1989; PhD in Medicine, U. Tokyo, 1999. Postdoc. rsch. fellow Human Genome Ctr. Inst. Med. Sci. U. Tokyo, 1997—98, RIKEN Inst., 1998—2001; asst. prof., dept. biochemistry Iwate Med. U. Sch. Dentistry, 2002—04; assoc. prof., divsn. applied genome sci. & bioinformatics Kobe U. Grad. Sch. Medicine, 2005—11; assoc. prof., divsn. med. informatics & bioinformatics Kobe U. Hosp., 2011—. Dir. Soc. Rsch. Nano-bio Sys., 2009—; assoc. prof. Life Sci. Ctr. Kobe Tokiwa U., 2011—. Recipient Universal Design award, Hyogo Prefecture Hyogo Indsl. Assn., 2009, Good Design award, Japan Inst. Design Promotion, 2010. Mem.: Japan Soc. Oriental Medicine, Inst. Electronics, Info. and Communication Engrs., Japan Assn. Med. Informatics, Molecular Biology Soc. Japan, Japanese Biochem. Soc. Office: niversity Hosp Kusunoki-cho 7-5-2 Chuo-ku Kobe Hyogo 650-0017 Japan Business E-Mail: ytakaoka@med.kobe-u.ac.jp.

TAKASHI, KITA, anesthesiologist; Anesthesiologist Osaka Med. Ctr.Cancer and Cardiovasc. diseases, Osaka, 1997—2001, Osaka Police Hosp., 2001—. Office: Osaka Police Hosp 10-31 Kitayamacho Tennoji Osaka 543-8502 Japan

TAKATA, JIRO, pharmacologist, educator; b. Hiroshima, Japan, Feb. 12, 1952; s. Takumi and Shizuko Takata; m. Reiko Nakagawa, Oct. 27, 1952; children: Fuyuko, Sosuke. PhD, U. Tokyo, 1997. Assoc. prof. Fukuoka U., Japan, 2000—, asst. prof., 1977—2000. Achievements include patents for Tocotrienol derivative, process for producing the same and gammma-CEHC delivering agent. Avocations: travel, golf, tennis. Office: Fukuoka Univ 8-19-1 Nanakuma Johnan-ku Fukuoka 814-0180 Japan Office Fax: 092-801-5102. E-mail: jtakata@fukuoka-u.ac.jp.

TAKATSUGU, KAWASE, physician, educator; b. Gifu, Japan, Aug. 10, 1971; MD, Keio U., 1996, PhD, 2008. Instr. Keio U. Sch. Medicine, 1996—2000; attending physician Nat. Tokyo Med. Ctr. Hosp., 2000—02; asst. prof. Keio U. Sch. Medicine, 2002—08; lectr. with tenure Nat. Def. Med. Coll., 2008—09; assoc. prof. Internat. U. Health and Welfare Mita Hosp., 2009—. Mem.: Japanese Soc. Nuc. Medicine, Japan Radiol. Soc., Japanese Soc. Therapeutic Radiology and Oncology (Umegaki award 2010), Am. Soc. Clin. Oncology, Am. Soc. Radiation Oncology. Office: 1-4-3 Mita Minato-ku Tokyo 108-8329 Japan Office Fax: 81-3-3454-0067. Business E-Mail: kawase@proof.ocn.ne.jp.

TAKAYAMA, KIYOSHIGE, neurophysiologist; b. Isesaki, Japan, Oct. 27, 1948; B, Gunma U., 1971, M, 1973, PhD, 1977. Asst. Gunma U., Maebashi, Japan, 1980, asst. prof., 1980—91, assoc. prof., 1991—97, prof., 1997—. Contbr. articles to profl. jours. Mem.: Japan Neurosci. Soc., Physiol. Soc. Japan. Office: Gunma University Grad Sch Health Sci 3 39 22 Showa Maebashi 371 8514 Japan Office Phone: 81 27 220 8943. Business E-Mail: takayama@health.gunma-u.ac.jp.

TAKAYAMA, TATSUYA, physician, educator; b. Japan, Apr. 17, 1967; MD, Hamamatsu U. Sch. Medicine, Shizuoka, Japan, 1993. Sr. asst. prof. Hamamatsu U. Sch. Medicine, 2010—. Office: Hamamatsu University Sch Medicine 1-20-1 Higashi-ku Handayama Hamamatsu Shizuoka 431-3192 Japan Office Fax: 81-53-435-2305. Business E-Mail: ttakayam@hama-med.ac.jp.

TAKAYAMA, YOSHIHARU, biochemist, researcher; b. Hiroshima, Japan, June 13, 1969; s. Noboru and Yoshiko Takayama. MD, Osaka U., Japan, 1999. Rschr. Nat. Inst. Animal Industry, Tsukuba, Japan, 1999—2001, Nat. Inst. Livestock and Grassland Sci., Tsukuba, 2001—03, sr. rschr., 2005—; postdoctoral fellow Southwestern Med. Ctr. U. Tex., Dallas, 2003—05. Scholar, The Takenaka Scholarships Found., 1990—99. Mem.: Am. Soc. Biochemistry and Molecular Biology. Achievements include research in functional analysis of lipoprotein receptors. Office: Natl Inst Livestock and Grassland Sci 2 Ikenodai Ibaraki Tsukuba 305-0901 Japan Business E-Mail: takay@affrc.go.jp.

TAKAYANAGI, MASARU, physician; b. Japan, July 8, 1961; MD, PhD, Tohoku U., 1987. Physician Sendai City Hosp., 1996—. Avocation: fishing. Office: 3-1 Shimizukoji Wakabayashi-ku Sendai Miyagi 984-8501 Japan E-mail: masarutakayanagi@hotmail.com.

TAKAZAWA, KENJI, cardiologist, researcher; b. Tsurugashima, Saitama-ken, Japan, Mar. 7, 1952; s. Genzaburou and Nagako Takazawa; m. Yoshie Orihata, Nov. 17, 1954; children: Shinya, Yayoi, Ikuo. MD, PhD, Tokyo Med. U., 1983. Prof. medicine Tokyo Med. U., Shinjyuku, 2003—06, prof., 2006—; v.p., dir. cardiology Tokyo Med. U. Hachioji Med. Ctr., Hachioji, 2004—. Vis. prof. Tokyo U. Pharmacy, Tokyo, 2004—. Fellow, Japanese Coll. Cardiology, 1996. Mem.: Japanese Soc. Med. Ultrasound, Am. Heart Assn., Japanese Soc. Interventional Cardiology, Japanese Coll. Cardiology, Japanese Circulation Soc., Japanese Soc. Internal Medicine (assoc.). Achievements include research in vasucular age, pulse wave analyses. Home: 6-18-7 Tsurugashima 350-2211 Japan Office: Tokyo Med Univ Hachioji Med Ctr 1163 Tate-machi Tokyo Hachioji 193-0998 Japan Office Fax: 0426-67-7506; Home Fax: 049-286-0917. Business E-Mail: takazawa@tokyo-med.ac.jp.

TAKECHI, MAKIKO, researcher, surgeon, director; MD, PhD, Hyogo Med. Coll., Japan, 1995; postgrad., Hyogo Med. Coll., 1990—95. Dr. in 2nd surgery dept. Hyogo Med. Coll. Hosp., Nishinomiya City, Hyogo Pref., Japan, 1987—90; clin. dr., rschr. European Acad. Dermatology and Veneology; prof. Kochi U. Med. Sch. Mem.: European Acad. Dermatology and Venereology (endorser). Achievements include discovery of treatment of pollinosis with COX-2 inhibitor, treatment of atopic dermatitis with itraconazole. Office: Tsuchibashi Shinryosho Clinic 1-6-28 Honmachi Kochi 780-0870 Japan Office Phone: 81-88-872-8238. Office Fax: 81-88-822-0058. Business E-Mail: takechi@tcbs.jp.

TAKEDA, SHINHIRO, medical educator; b. Kyoto, Mar. 30, 1960; s. Eitaro and Yuko Takeda; m. Koko Suzuki, Aug. 20, 1996; children: Tomona, Fujina. MD, PhD, Nippon Med. Sch., Tokyo, 1986. Assoc. prof., head surg. sect. ICU Nippon Med. Sch., Bunkyo-Ku, Tokyo, Japan, 2000—. Recipient Tokyo Med. Assn. award, 2003; Rsch. fellow, Karolinska Inst., 1996—97. Office: Nippon Med Sch 1-1-5 Sendagi Bunkyo 113-8603 Japan E-mail: shinhiro@nms.ac.jp.

TAKEDA, TADASHI, physician; b. Osaka, Japan, July 3, 1958; s. Shigeo and Toshiko Takeda; m. Yukie Yamanaka; children: Kazuma, Takayoshi. MD, PhD, Osaka City U., Grad. Sch. Medicine, 1991. Diplomate Ministry Health and Welfare, 1984. Lectr. Osaka City U., Grad. Sch. Medicine, 1992—2007; dir. Takeda Internal Medicine Clinic, 2008. Office: Takeda Internal Medicine Clinic 2-9-5 Matsuzaki-cho Abeno-ku Osaka 545-0053 Japan Office Fax: 81-6-6480-9502.

TAKEDA, YOSHITSUGU, orthopedist; b. Tokushima, Japan, Feb. 25, 1959; MD, U. Tokushima, PhD, 1983. Asst. prof. U. Tokushima, 1999—2001; chief, dept. orthop. surgery Tokushima Red Cross Hosp., 2001—. Grant, Western Pacific Orthopaedic Assn. Knee and Sports Medicine Sect., ESSKA. Mem.: Orthop. Magellan Soc., Internat. Soc. Arthroscopy, Knee Surgery and Orthop. Sports Medicine. Avocations: jogging, reading. Office: 103 Irinokuchi Komatsushima-cho Komatsushima Tokushima 773-8502 Japan Office Fax: 81-885-32-3800. Business E-Mail: ytakeda@tokushima-med.jrc.or.jp.

TAKEMURA, HIROSHI, anesthesiologist; b. Komagane, Nagano, Japan, June 23, 1962; s. Tadashi and Michiko Takemura; m. Yoshiko Takemura, Jan. 14, 1990; children: Haruka, Kaoru. MD, Showa U., Shinagawa-ku, Tokyo, Japan, 1988, PhD, 1998. Resident dept. anesthesiology Showa U. Hosp., Shinagawa-ku, Tokyo, 1988—90; med. staff Sempo Tokyo Takanawa Hosp., Minato-ku, Tokyo, 1990—91; asst. dept. anesthesiology Showa U. Toyosu Hosp., Koutou-ku, Tokyo, 1991—93, Showa U. Hosp., Shinagawa-ku, Tokyo, 1993—93; med. expert (tech. cooperation) Cairo U. Pediatric Hosp., Cairo, 1993—94; asst. dept. anesthesiology Showa U. Hosp., Shinagawa-ku, Tokyo, 1994—2003; med. practitioner Pain Mgmt. Office TA, Yokohama, Kanagawa, Japan, 2003—. Author: (clinical investigation) Correlation of cleft type with incidence of perioperative respiratory complications in infants with cleft lip and palate. Paediatric Anaesthesia 2002;12:585-588., (case report) Mandibular nerve block treatment for trismus associated with hypoxic-ischemic encephalopathy. Regional Anesthesia and Pain Medicine 2002;27:313-315. Mem.: Am. Soc. of Regional Anesthesia & Pain Medicine, Japan Soc. of Pain Clinicians, Japanese Soc. of Anesthesiologist. Avocations: sport, gardening. Home and Office: Pain Mgmt Office TA 13-74 Kakinokidai Aoba-ku Yokohama 227-0048 Japan Office Phone: 81-45-971-9635.

TAKEMURA, KAZUHISA, psychologist, educator; b. Kyoto, Oct. 8, 1960; s. Osamu and Kiyoko (Kitagawa) Takemura. BA, Doshisha U., Kyoto, 1983, MA, 1985; PhD, Tokyo Inst. Tech., 1994. Asst. prof. Koka Women's Jr. Coll., Kyoto, 1989-92, U. Tsukuba, 1992-95, assoc. prof., 1995—2002; prof. dept. psychology Waseda U., Tokyo, 2002—, dir., Ctr. Decision Rsch., 2002—. Fulbright Sr. rschr. social and decision scis. dept. Carnegie Mellon U., Pitts., 1999-2000; chief editor Japanese Jour. Behaviormetrics, 2009-. Author: Behavioral Decision-Making, 2009; editor: Social Psychology of Consumer Behavior, 2000, Social Psychology, 2004; editl. bd. Asian Jour. Social Psychology, 1997-98, Japanese Jour. Social Psych.; chief editor Japanese Jour. Behaviormetrics, 1998—, Jour. Japan Soc. for Fuzzy Theory and Intelligent Informatics, 2001-06, Jour. Japan Soc. Kansei Enging., 2006—; contbr. articles to profl. jours. Recipient award for encouragement of young scientists Ministry of Edn., 1993-98, Hayashi Award, Behaviormetric Soc. Japan, 2002, Disting. Paper award Japan Soc. Kansei Engring., 2003, Japan Soc. Social Psychol., 2010, Disting. Book award; grantee for Sci., Ministry of Edn., 1999-. Mem. Japanese Psychol. Assn., Japanese Group Dynamics Assn., Japanese Social Psychol. Assn., Soc. for Judgment and Decision Making, European Assn. Decision Making. Avocation: swimming. Office: Waseda Univ Dept Psychology 1-24-1 Toyama Shinjuku-ku Tokyo 162-8644 Japan Office Phone: 81 35286 3549. Business E-Mail: kazupsy@waseda.jp.

TAKENOBU, MURAKAMI, neurologist, researcher; b. Tsuwano, Shimane, Japan, Aug. 12, 1977; s. Murakami Tatsuo and Murakami Toshiko; married. MD, Tottori U., Yonago, Japan, 2002; PhD, Grad. Sch. Tottori U., Yonago, Japan, 2008. Cert. Neurologist Soc. Neurologica Japonica, 2008. Staff physician Shimane Prefectural Ctrl. Hosp., Japan, 2008; postdoc fellow J.W. Goethe U., Frankfurt am Main, Germany, 2009—. Fellow Postdoc. Rsch. fellowship, Alexander von Humboldt Found., 2008; Grant, Ministry Edn., Culture, Sports, Sci. and Tech. Japan, 2007. Office: JW Goethe University Schleusenweg 2-16 Frankfurt 60528 Germany Personal E-mail: maaboubou@gmail.com. Business E-Mail: t.murakami@med.uni-frankfurt.de.

TAKENORI, YAO, physician; b. Japan, Sept. 16, 1974; MD, Shiga U. Med. Sci., 2000; PhD, Grad. Sch. Shiga U. Med. Sci., 2005. Staff physician Okamura Meml. Hosp., 2009—. Clin. fellow Shiga U. Med. Sci. Hosp., 2005—09. Mem.: Japanese Circulation Soc., Asia Pasific Heart Rhythm Soc., Japanese Heart Rhythm Soc. Avocation: computers. Office: 293-1 Kakida Shimizu-cho Sunto-gun Shizuoka 411-0904 Japan Office Fax: 81-55-973-3404. Business E-Mail: yao@voyage.shiga-med.ac.jp.

TAKEOKA, HIROYA, nephrologist; b. Japan, Apr. 20, 1960; MD, Shimane Med. U., 1988; PhD, Kyoto U., 1999. Physician divsn. nephrology and dialysis Hyogo Prefectural Amagasaki Hosp., 1997—, dir. nephrology, 2005. Mem.: ACP, Japanese Soc. Internal Medicine, Japanese Soc. Nephrology, Internat. Soc. Nephrology, Am. Soc. Nephrology. Avocations: music, travel. Office: 1-1-1 Higashidaimotsucho Amagasaki Hyogo 660-0828 Japan Business E-Mail: htakeoka@ares.eonet.ne.jp.

TAKETANI, SHGIERU, medical educator; b. Nara, Japan, July 16, 1949; PhD, Kyoto U., 1978. Assoc. prof. Kansai Med. U., 1994—2000; prof. Kyoto Inst. Tech., 2000—. Mem.: Japan Biochemical Soc. Avocation: mountain climbing. Office: Sakyo-ku Matsugasaki Kyoto 606-8585 Japan Office Fax: 81-75-724-7789. Business E-Mail: taketani@kit.ac.jp.

TAKEUCHI, AKIRA, neurophysiologist, educator; b. Tokyo, May 5, 1927; parents Naohiko and Toshi (Sawabe) T.; m. Noriko Tanaka, Apr. 25, 1954; 1 child, Keiko. MD, U. Tokyo, 1951, PhD, 1958. From assoc. prof. to prof. Juntendo U., Tokyo, 1956-93, prof. emeritus, 1993—. Dep. dir. City of Hope Med. Ctr., Duarte, 1966-68; dean Juntendo U., 1988-91. Decorated Purple Ribbon Govt. Japan. Mem.: AAAS, Japan Physiol. Soc. Home: 1-11-10 Wakamiya Nakanoku Tokyo 165-0033 Japan

TAKEUCHI, HIDEYUKI, biology professor; b. Saitama, Japan, Apr. 17, 1972; PhD, U. Tokyo, 2001. Asst. prof. U. Tokyo, 2003—09; rsch. asst. prof. Stony Brook U., 2008—. Mem.: Soc. Glycobiology. Avocations: baseball, travel. Office: 474 Life Sciences Bldg Stony Brook NY 11794-5215 Office Fax: 631-632-8575. Business E-Mail: htakeuchi@ms.cc.sunysb.edu.

TAKEUCHI, KAZUHISA, nephrologist, educator; b. Sirakawa, Fukushima, Japan, Jan. 1, 1956; s. Katsuo and Hisako Takeuchi; m. Yuriko Takeuchi, Nov. 12, 1952; children: Maho, Shiho. MD, PhD, Tohoku U., Sendai, 1989. Rsch. fellow Brigham and Women's Hosp., Harvard U., Boston, 1989—90, Falk Cardiovasc. Inst., Stanford U., Palo Alto, Calif., 1990—91; rsch. fellow cardiology Emory U., Atlanta, 1991—93; asst. prof. Tohoku U. Sch. Medicine, Sendai, 1993—2000; assoc. prof. Tohoku U. Grad. Sch. Medicine, Sendai, 2000—. Mem.: Japanese Hypertension Soc. Achievements include research in molecular biology of blood pressure regulatory genes, Gitelman's syndrome. Avocations: tennis, golf, swimming. Office Fax: 81-22-717-7168. E-mail: hek293@mail.tains.tohoku.ac.jp.

TAKEUCHI, KAZUO, neurosurgeon, educator; b. Tokyo, Sept. 29, 1923; s. Suematsu and Toshie (Saito) T.; m. Michiko Ohsuga, Feb. 3, 1959; children: Seiko, Numata. MD, U. Tokyo, 1946, PhD, 1955. Cert. spl. qualification in neurosurgery. Lectr. in neurosurgery U. Tokyo, Japan, 1953-58; chief neurosurgeon Toranomon Hosp., Tokyo, 1958-73; prof. neurosurgery Kyorin U., Mitaka/Tokyo, 1973-98, dean Sch. Medicine, 1983-92, pres., 1988-98, emeritus prof., 1998—, emeritus pres., 2011—. Editor: (textbook) Standard Neurosurgery, 1979; author of monographs. Recipient Medal with Purple Ribbon Japanese Govt., 1991, Prize of Extreme Merit, Japan Med. Assn., Tokyo, 1993, Kesatria Mangku Negara Malaysian Govt., 1994, Pegawai Bintang Sarawak Govt. of Sarawak State, Malaysia, 1994, Order of Sacred Treasure, Gold and Silver Star Japanese Govt., 1998. Mem. Japanese Epilepsy Soc. (hon. pres. 1985-86), Japan Neurosurg. Soc. (hon. pres. 1985-86), Japanese Soc. Surgery Cerebral Stroke (hon. pres. 1983-84), Japanese Neuroradiol. Soc. (hon. pres. 1986-87), Soc. Interventional Neuroradiology (hon. pres. 1988-89), Kyorin Med. Soc. (hon. pres. 1993-98), Japan Assn. Bioethics (pres. 1995-96), Japanese Soc. Chemotherapy (hon. mem.). Home: Minamiaoyama 5-4-43 Minatoku Tokyo 107-0062 Japan Office: Kyorin Univ Sch Medicine Shinkawa 6-20-2 Tokyo 181-8611 Japan E-mail: ktake929@jeans.ocn.ne.jp.

TAKEUCHI, MAKOTO, hematologist; b. Kurashiki, Japan, Jan. 1, 1959; s. Minoru and Sadami Takeuchi; m. Miyoko Shinozaki, May 3, 1988; children: Mari, Yuki. MD, Okayama U. Med. Sch., Japan, 1983, D in Physiology, 1993. Resident Chugoku Ctrl. Hosp., Fukuyama, Japan, 1983—84, Kochi Koseinenkin Hosp., Japan, 1984—85, Kochi Prefectural Hosp., Japan, 1985—86; rsch. resident Okayama U. Med. Sch., Japan, 1986—90; physician internal medicine Nat. Minami Okayama Hosp., Tsukubo Gun, Japan, 1990—2000, chief hematology dept., 2000—. Attending hematologist Japanese Soc. of Hematology, Kyoto, 1995—; councilor Japanese Soc. of Clin. Hematology, Tokyo, 1998—, Japanese Soc. of Hematology, Br. of Chugoku-Shikoku, Okayama, Japan, 1999—. Author: (jour. article) Brit. Jour. of Hematology, (book) Resent Rsearch Developments in Hematology. Mem.: Leukemia Study Group of the Ministry of Health, Labor and Welfare. Office: Nat Minami Okayama Med Ctr 4066 Hayashima Cho Tsukuba 701-0304 Japan Office Fax: 81-86-483-2110. Business E-Mail: takeuchim@s-okayama.hops.go.jp.

TAKIMOTO, EIKI, cardiologist, educator; b. Liverpool, Eng., Dec. 23, 1966; s. Akio and Masako Takimoto; m. Sachiko Takimoto, Dec. 29, 1995; children: Yuki, Miyu Nancy. MD, U. Tokyo, 1992, PhD, 2001. Med. lic. Ministry Health, Labor and Welfare, Japan, 1992. Resident U. Tokyo Hosp., 1992—93, Cancer Inst. Hosp., Tokyo, 1993—94; clin. fellow Toranomon Hosp., Tokyo, 1994—97; rsch. fellow cardiology Johns Hopkins Med. Inst., Balt., 2001—05, rsch. assoc., 2006, asst. prof. medicine, 2007—. Rsch. fellowship, Uehara Meml. Found., 2002—03, Grant, NIH, 2009—. Fellow: Japanese Soc. Internal Medicine; mem.: Japanese Circulation Soc., Am. Heart Assn. (grant 2004—09). Achievements include research in clarification of cyclic GMP & oxidative stress in cardiac disease; patents for PDE5 inhibitor compositions and methods for treating cardiac indications; use of a nitric oxide synthase modulator for the treatment of cardiac indications. Office: Johns Hopkins Med Insts 720 Rutland Ave Ross 830 Baltimore MD 21205 Business E-Mail: etakimo1@jhmi.edu.

TAKIZAWA, HIDEAKI, gastroenterologist; b. Saitama, Japan, July 17, 1960; s. Eiichi and Youko Takizawa; m. Kyoko Kimura, Nov. 10, 1991; children: Hiroki, Naoki. MD, Niigata U., Japan, 1985, DPhil, 1992. Resident Niigata U. Hosp., 1985, physician, 1988-90; rsch. fellow gastroenterology Niigata U., 1986-87; physician Kouseiren Murakami Hosp., Murakami, Japan, 1991; asst. chief gastroenterology Nagaoka Red Cross Hosp., Japan, 1992-96; chief gastroenterology Kido Hosp., Niigata, 1997-2000; dir. Endo Clinic, Niigata, 2001—. Author: Digestion, 1995; contbr. articles to profl. jours. Mem. Japanese Soc. Gastroenterology, Japanese Soc. Internal Medicine, Japan Gastroenterol. Endoscopy Soc. Office: Endo Clinic 1-4-11 Minami-Sasaguchi Niigata 950-0912 Japan

TAKLIKAR, SHRIPAD M., medical educator; b. Aurangabad, Nov. 7, 1977; MBBS, Lokmanya Tilak Mcpl. Med. Coll., MD, 2000; PGDHM, Symbiosis, 2005. Asst. prof. Lokmanya Tilak Mcpl. Med. Coll., 2005—. Recipient C. K. Deshpande Gold medal, Mumbai U. Office: Tilak Municipal Med Coll 4th Fl College Bldg Mumbai Maharashtra 400022 India E-mail: drshripadt@rediffmail.com.

TAKOOSHIAN, HAROLD, social psychology educator; b. NYC, Nov. 21, 1949; s. Alfred C. and Dorothy H. T. BA, CCNY, 1971; PhD in Social Psychology, CUNY, 1979. Lic. psychologist, N.Y. Prof. div. social scis. Fordham U., NYC, 1975—, dir., orgnl. leadership program, 2003—. Vis. prof. U. Talca, Chile, 1983, U. Atacama, Copiapo, Chile, 1984, 85; U.S. Fulbright scholar USSR, 1987-88; cons. projects for indsl. and govtl. orgn., 1979—. Editor: Bull. and Directory of Armenian Behavioral Scientists, 1988—, Feminism Survey, 1990—; (with W.M. Verdi) Short-Form Scale of Attitudes toward Terrorism, 1989, (with T.D. Guzewicz) Public Attitudes toward Homeless, 1991. Nat. bd. dirs. Alliance Guardian Angels, 1982-. Recipient Apple Polisher award WOR-TV, N.Y.C., 1981, Denmark Faculty Adv. award Psi Chi, 1988, 2010, Kurt Lewin award N.Y. State Psychol. Assn., 1990, Denmark Award, 2010. Fellow APA (mem. coun. reps. 2011-), Soc. Psychol. Study Social Issues (chmn. N.Y.C. regional group 1991—), Soc. Tchg. Psychology; Am. Psychol. Assn. (pres., divsn. 52, internat. psychology 2003, pres., divsn. 1, gen. psychology 2006-07, APA coun. rep., 2011-), Psi Chi (v.p. ea. region 1993-97, pres. 1998-99), Psi Beta (hon., distinguished mem.) (Wolman award, 2006), Psi Chi. Developer standardized scales, use of field experiment to study social issues. Office Phone: 212-636-6393. Business E-Mail: takoosh@aol.com.

TAKU, OKAZAKI, medical educator; b. Kyoto, July 5, 1974; MD, Kyoto U., PhD, 2003. Prof. U. Tokushima, 2008—. Recipient Young Investigator award, Japanese Soc. Immunology. Fellow: Japanese Biochemical Soc., Japanese Soc. Immunology. Office: 3-18-15 Kuramoto Tokushima 770-8503 Japan Business E-Mail: tokazaki@genome.tokushima-u.ac.jp.

TAKUMI, NAKANO, surgeon; b. Kochi, Japan, May 14, 1960; MD, Kochi Med. Sch., PhD, 1987. Staff dept. surgery Tano Hosp., 1993—97, Noichi Ctrl. Hosp., 1997—99, Inan Hosp., 1999—2001, Chiba Aiyu-kai Kinen Hosp., 2007—; asst. dept. surgery 1 Kochi U., 2001—07. Mem.: Japan Soc. Clin. Oncology, Japan Cancer Assn., Japanese Soc. Gastroent. Surgery, Japan Surg. Soc. Office: Hiregasaki 1-1 Nagareyama Chiba 273-0161 Japan Office Fax: 81 4 7159 6056. Business E-Mail: ntaku@qc4.so-net.ne.jp.

TAKURO, MURAKAMI, anatomist, physician, educator; b. Fukunaga, Japan, Mar. 4, 1939; s. Rikuro and Fumie Murakami; m. Yoriko Murakami, Apr. 30, 1967; children: Kyoko Murakami, Shinichiro Murakami, Tetsuro Murakami. MD, Okayama U., Japan, 1969, PhD in Philosophy, 1974. Asst. prof. Okayama U., 1974—80, prof., 1980—2004, prof. emeritus, rsch. fellow dept. anatomy, 2004—. Vis. prof. U. Calif., San Francisco, 1979; hon. prof. U. Harbin, China, 1991; exch. prof. U. Rome, 1999. Editor: Application of SEM, 1996. Dir. Okayama Med. Found., 2003—. Recipient award, Sanyo Newspaper Ltd., 2001. Home: 1-10-2 Gakunan-Cho Okayama 700-0011 Japan Office: Okayama Univ Human Morphology Dept Shikata-Cho Okayama 700-8558 Japan Office Phone: +81-086-234-0864. Home Fax: 086 254-1224. Business E-Mail: em2hai@md.okayama-u.ac.jp. E-mail: yoriko@wk9.so.net.ne.jp.

TAKURO, TOMITA, psychologist; b. Bunkyo, Tokyo, Japan, Aug. 15, 1968; s. Koji and Eiko. PhD, Waseda U., Tokyo. Cert. clin. psychologist Japanese Certification Bd. Clin. Psychologist, 2001. Rsch. fellow NIMH, Ichikawa, Chiba, Japan, 1997—2001, sr. rsch. fellow Kodaira, Tokyo, 2006—09; sch. psychologist Tokyo Met. Bd. Edn., 2002—06; assoc. prof. Kansai U., Suita, Osaka, Japan, 2009—11, prof., 2011—. Contbr. articles to profl. jours. Mem.: APA. Office: Dept Psychology Fac of Soc Kansai Univ 3-3-35 Yamate cho Suita Osaka 564-8680 Japan Business E-Mail: tomitat@pop01.odn.ne.jp, tomitat@kansai-u.ac.jp.

TALALAY, PAUL, pharmacologist, educator; b. Berlin, Mar. 31, 1923; arrived in U.S., 1940, naturalized, 1946; s. Joseph Anton and Sophie (Brosterman) Talalay; m. Pamela Judith Samuels, Jan. 11, 1953; children: Antony, Susan, Rachel, Sarah. SB, MIT, 1944; student, U. Chgo. Sch. Medicine, 1944—46; MD, Yale U., 1948; DSc (hon.), Acadia U., 1974. House officer, asst. resident surg. services Mass. Gen. Hosp., Boston, 1948—50; asst. prof. surgery U. Chgo., 1950—51, asst. prof. biochemistry, 1955—57, assoc. prof., then prof., 1957—63; asst. prof. Ben May Lab. Cancer Research, 1951—57, assoc. prof., then prof., 1957—63; John Jacob Abel prof., dir. dept., pharmacology and exptl. therapeutics Johns Hopkins Sch. Medicine, 1963—75, John Jacob Abel Distinguished Service prof., 1975—, Am. Cancer Soc. prof., 1958—63, 1977—. Sr. asst. surgeon USPHS, 1951—53; vis. prof. Guy's Hosp. Med. Sch., London, 1970, London, 1974—76; nat. adv. cancer coun. USPHS, 1967—71; vis. com. dept. biology MIT, 1964—67; bd. sci. advisers Jane Coffin Childs Meml. Fund for Cancer Rsch., 1971—80; bd. sci. consultants Sloan Kettering Inst. Cancer Rsch., 1971—81. Hon. editl. adv. bd. Biochem. Pharmacology, 1963—68, editl. bd. Jour. Biol. Chemistry, 1961—66, Molecular Pharmacology, 1965—68, 1971—80, editor-in-chief, 1968—71. Recipient Premio Internationale la Madonnina Milan, 1978, Med. Alumni Disting. Svc. award, U. Chgo., 1978; fellow Guggenheim Meml., 1973—74; scholar Am. Cancer Soc., 1954—58. Fellow: Am. Acad. Arts and Scis.; mem.: NAS, AAAS (Theobald Smith award med. scis. 1957), Am. Soc. Pharm. and Exptl. Therpeutics, Am. Chem. Soc., Biochem. Soc., Am. Soc. Clin. Investigation, Am. Soc. Biochem. Molecular Biology, Am. Philos. Soc., Alpha Omega Alpha, Sigma Xi, Phi Beta Kappa. Home: 5512 Boxhill Ln Baltimore MD 21210-2039 Office: Johns Hopkins U Sch Medicine 725 N Wolfe St Baltimore MD 21205 Office Phone: 410-955-3499. Fax: 410-502-6818. Business E-Mail: ptalalay@jhmi.edu.

TALAMINI, MARK A., surgeon, department chairman; BA in Natural Sciences, Johns Hopkins U., 1978; MD, Johns Hopkins U. Sch. Medicine, 1981. Lic. Md., 1987, Calif., 2005, cert. Am. Bd. Surgery, 1988, Critical Care Bd., 1990. Intern Johns Hopkins Hosp., 1981—82, jr. asst. resident, 1982—83, sr. asst. resident, 1983—86, chief resident, 1986—87, asst. chief svc., 1987—88, dir. minimally invasive surgery, 1992—2004, dir. nutrition support svc., 1995—2005; fellow in surgical nutrition U. Cin. Sch. Medicine, 1984—85; instr. dept. surgery Johns Hopkins U. Sch. Medicine, 1987—88, asst. prof. dept. surgery, 1988—95, assoc. prof. dept. surgery, 1995—2001, prof. dept. surgery, 2001—05; prof. & chmn. dept. surgery U. Calif. Sch. Medicine, San Diego, 2005—; surgeon-in-chief U. Calif. Med. Ctr., 2005—. Editorial bd. mem. Surgical Laparoscopy & Endoscopy, 1990—, INSIGHTS, 1991—94, Jour. Gastrointestinal Surgery, 2003—; co-editor Jour. Laparoscopy, 1991—93; editor-in-chief Jour. Laparoendoscopic & Advanced Surgical Techniques, 2002—. Fellow: Am. Surgical Assn., Am. Coll. Surgeons; mem.: Western Surgical Assn., San Diego County Med. Soc., Baltimore Acad. Surgery, Southern Surgical Assn., Soc. U. Surgeons, Soc. Am. Gastrointestinal Endoscopic Surgeons, Soc. for Surgery of Alimentary Tract, Soc. for Laparoendoscopic Surgeons, Am. Soc. Clinical Nutrition, Assn. for Academic Surgery, Am. Soc. Parenteral & Enteral Nutrition, Halsted Soc., Crohn's & Colitis Found. Office: UCSD Medical Center Dept of Surgery 200 W Arbor Dr #8400 San Diego CA 92103-8400 Office Phone: 619-543-6453. Office Fax: 619-543-3763. E-mail: talamini@ucsd.edu.

TALAMO, JONATHAN HASKELL, ophthalmologist, educator; b. Boston, Sept. 25, 1960; Student, Cornell U., Ithaca, NY, 1978-80; AB, Johns Hopkins U., Balt., Md., 1982, MD, 1986. Diplomate Am. Bd. Ophthalmology. Intern in medicine Children's Hosp. San Francisco-U. Calif., 1986—87; resident in ophthalmology Wilmer Ophthal. Inst., Johns Hopkins Hosp., Balt., 1987—90; clin. fellow ophthalmology, cornea and external disease Mass. Eye and Ear Infirmary-Harvard U. Med. Sch., Boston, 1990—91, asst. surgeon, 1992—95, sr. surgeon, 1995—, dir. gen. eye and cataract consultation svc., 1992—94, dir. keratorefractive surgery unit, 1992—95, acting dir. cornea svc., 1994—95, dir. cornea and external disease fellowship program, 1994—95; pvt. practice Providence, 1991—92, Boston, 1995—. Rsch. fellow in ophthalmology Harvard U. Med. Sch., 1984-85, clin. fellow in ophthalmology, 1990-91, instr. ophthalmology, 1992-94, asst. prof., 1994-95, asst. clin. prof., 1995-2005, assoc. clin. prof., 2005—, med. dir. Surgisite Boston, 2011-; clin. fellow in ophthalmology Johns Hopkins U. Med. Sch., 1987-90; asst. clin. prof. dept. surgery Brown U. Sch. Medicine, Providence, 1991-93; attending surgeon Miriam Hosp., Providence, 1991-93, R.I. Hosp., Providence, 1991-93; med. adv. bd. Intralase Corp., 2003—06, Optimedical Corp., 2008-, Nexis Vision, 2011-. Author: The Excimer Manual: A Clincians Guide to Excimer Laser Surgery,1996; asst. editor jour. Refractive Surgery, 1994-99; mem. editl. bd. Ophthalmology Times, 1995—; contbr. 70 articles to profl. jours., chpts. to books. Tng.

grantee USPHS, 1984, travel grantee Assn. for Rsch. in Vision and Ophthalmology, 1985, N.E. Corneal Transplant Rsch. Fund, 1993-94, Coherent Med., Inc., 1994-95; fellow Fight for Sight, 1985, Heed Ophthalmic Found., 1990. Mem. Am. Acad. Ophthalmology (Honor award 1998, 2009), Internat. Soc. Refractive Surgery (bd. dirs. 1995-2001), Am. Soc. Cataract and Refractive Surgery, Soc. Heed Fellows, New Eng. Ophthal. Soc., Mass. Soc. Eye Physiciand and Surgeons. Home Phone: 617-899-7233; Office Phone: 781-890-1023.

TALAVERA-ADAME, DODANIM, research scientist; b. Mex., Apr. 2, 1961; MD, Sch. Medicine Nat. Poly. Inst., 1985; PhD, Ctr. Rsch. & Advanced Studies, 2003. Rsch. scientist Cedras Sinai Med. Ctr., 2006—, instr., 2011. Recipient Disting. Rsch. award, Rachmiel Levine Sci. Achievement award. Mem.: Internat. Soc. Stem Cell Rsch., Am. Soc. Transplantation. Avocations: weightlifting, reading, movies. Office: 8700 Beverly Blvd SSB319B Los Angeles CA 90048 Office Fax: 310-248-8066. Business E-Mail: talaverad@cshs.org.

TALBOT, MARTHA HAYNE, conservationist, biologist; b. San Francisco, Aug. 3, 1932; d. Francis Bourn and Anna (Walcott) Hayne; m. Lee Merriam Talbot, May 16, 1959; children: Lawrence Hayne, Russell Merriam. BA, Vassar Coll., 1954. Co-founder, asst. dir. student conservation program U.S. Nat. Parks, 1955-59; co-dir. East African Ecol. Rsch. Project, Kenya and Tanzania, 1959-63; asst. dir. S.E. Asia Project, Internat. Union for Conservation of Nature/Natural Resources, 1964-65; asst. coord. Internat. Biol. Programme, London, 1966; rsch. assoc. Smithsonian Instn., Washington, 1966-75; mem., treas. Fairfax County Park Authority, Fairfax, Va., 1973-77; sec.-treas. Talbot Racing Assocs., McLean, Va., 1983—; owner, dir. Talbot Hayne Vineyard, St. Helena, Calif., 1988—; sec.-treas. Lee Talbot Assocs. Internat., McLean, 1991—. Bd. dir. Student Conservation Assn., 1966-78, 83-87, hon. dir., 1987— (Svc. Honor award), Defenders of Wildlife, 1974-77, Audubon Naturalist Soc., 1975-78, Rachel Carson Coun., 1975-94, treas., 1994-98, v.p., 1998—. Co-author: Introduction to the Landscape, East Africa, 1961; co-editor: Conservation in Tropical South East Asia, 1968; contbr. articles to profl. jours. Leader Boy Scouts Am., Geneva, 1978-83, transp. coord., McLean, 1989-95; mem. adv. coun. State of the Pks. Program, Nat. Pks. Conservation Assn., 2010-. Recipient Outstanding Pub. award The Wildlife Soc., 1963, Cinema Golden Eagle award Documentary Film, 1968, Disting. Alumna award Katharine Branson Sch., 1981, Conservation Svc. award U.S. Dept. Interior, 1986, Bd. Tribute to co-founder, Student Conservation Assn., 1984, Resolution of Honor, 1999; N.Y. Zool. Soc. grantee, 1961; co-recipient World Comm. on Protected Areas East Asia award, 2005, Hon. award Explorers Club Celebratory, 2009. Mem. Soc. Woman Geographers (bd. dir. 1972-75, treas. 1984-89, treas. Washington group 1990-96, pres. 2008-11, Flag award 2007, 11, Outstanding Achievement award 2008, Award of Appreciation 2011), Napa Valley Grape Growers Assn., Rachels Network, Explorers Club (Flag award 2007, 11), Woman's Nat. Dem. Club. Avocations: backpacking, hiking, bicycling, travel, swimming. Home: 6656 Chilton Ct Mc Lean VA 22101-4422

TALBOT, NYNA LUCILLE, clinical psychologist; b. Warrington, Eng., May 24, 1954; d. John Robert Talbot and Lois June Snow. MA, Calif. Inst. Integral Studies, 1997, PhD, 2000; BA, Elmhurst Coll., 1976. Sr. tech. writer Hitachi Data Sys., Santa Clara, Calif., 1986—2006; clinical psychologist Royal Cornhill Hosp., Aberdeen, Scotland, 2007—08; pvt. practice Scotland, 2009—. Clin. psychology intern San Mateo County Emergency Response Team, 1990—91, San Mateo County Mental Health Svcs., Half Moon Bay, 2000—01. Clin. psychology intern mem. Red Cross, San Mateo, 1990—91. Mem.: Internat. Coun. Psychologists, Brit. Psychol. Soc., APA. Achievements include research in the relationship of companionship coupling in two significant populations. Avocations: painting, poetry. Home: Dogshillock AB54 7PS Aberchirder Scotland Office Phone: 07928 338119. Personal E-mail: drnyna@yahoo.com.

TALCOTT, JAMES AUSTIN, internist, oncologist, educator; b. Gt. Falls, Mont., Aug. 27, 1951; s. James Grant and Doris Duane (Austin) T.; m. Nancy Stanton Knox, Dec. 01, 2007; children: Wesley John, Nicholas James, William Austin. BS, Stanford U., 1973; BA, Oxford U., 1976; MD, Yale U., 1980; SM in Epidemiology, Harvard U. Diplomate Am. Bd. Internal Medicine, Am. Bd. Med. Oncology. Intern and resident in internal medicine U. Wash. Affiliated Hosps., Seattle, 1980-83; chief resident Harborview Med. Ctr., Seattle, 1983-84; fellow in med. oncology Dana-Farber Cancer Inst.-Harvard U. Med. Sch., Boston, 1984-87, instr., 1987-92, asst. prof., 1992—2004, assoc. prof., 2004—09; dir. Ctr. Outcomes Rsch. Mass. Gen. Hosp. Cancer Ctr., Boston, 1997—; dir. Ctr. Health Care Quality & Outcomes Rsch. County Cancer Ctrs. NY, Boston, 1997—2011. Contbr. articles to med. jours. HEW Presdl. scholar, 1969, Rhodes scholar, 1974. Democrat. Methodist. Avocations: outdoor activities, art. Home: 54 E 91st St # 3 New York NY 10128-1350 Office: 325 W 15th St New York NY 10011

TALL, ALAN R., molecular biologist, educator; MB, BS, U. Sydney, 1970. Intern Royal Prince Alfred Hosp., 1971, resident, 1972; sr. resident Boston City Hosp., 1973—74, chief resident, 1975—76, asst. visiting physician, 1976—77; fellow in gastroenterology Boston U. Hosp, 1974—75; asst. prof. medicine Boston U., 1977, Columbia U. College Physicians & Surgeons, 1978—81, assoc. prof. medicine, 1982—89, prof. medicine, 1989, dir. Specialized Ctr. Rsch in Atherosclerosis, 1990—96, dir. Specialized Ctr. Rsch. in Molecular Medicine & Atherosclerosis, 1997—; attending physician Presbyterian Hosp., 1989. Scienctific adv. bd. Gladstone Rsch. Found., 1992—; bd. scientific counselors NHLBI. Mem.: Assn. Am. Physicians, Am. Heart Assn. (program com. 1985—86, Arteriosclerosis coun. 1987—89, rsch. com. 1999—2000), Am. Soc. Clinical Investigation. Office: Columbia University Division of Molecular Medicine 630 W 168th St P&S 8-401 New York NY 10032 Office Phone: 212-305-9418. Office Fax: 212-305-5052.

TALLAJ, JOSE A., medical educator, director; b. Santiago, Chile, Mar. 10, 1969; MD, Pontificia U. Catolica Madre y Maestra, 1992. Assoc. prof., med. dir., heart transplant program U. Ala., Birmingham, 2008—. Reviewer Multiple Peer-review Jour., 2005—11. Recipient H. Cecil Coghlan award, UAB Divsn. Cardiology, Clin. Excellence award, UAB Dept. Medicine; named one of Top Ten Tchrs. Fellow: Am. Coll. Cardiology; mem.: Internat. Soc. Heart and Lung Transplantation, Am. Heart Assn. Office: THT-321 1900 University Blvd Birmingham AL 35294 Office Fax: 205-975-9320. Business E-Mail: jtallaj@uab.edu.

TALLEDO, OSCAR EDUARDO, medical educator; b. Sullana, Piura, Peru, Aug. 1, 1929; s. Jorge Antonio and Flora Natividad (Cordova) T.; m. Jeanette McCarley, June 8, 1959; children: Roy Anthony, Paul Frederick, Linda Jeanette. BS, San Marcos U., 1948, MD, 1955. Diplomate Am. Bd. Ob-Gyn., Am. Bd. Laser Surgery. Intern Crawford W. Long Hosp., Atlanta, 1956-57, resident, 1957-58, Med. Coll. Ga., Augusta, 1958-60, fellow in gynecology, 1960-61, chief gynecologic oncology, 1961—, prof. ob-gyn, 1970—, instr., 1961-63, asst. prof., 1963-68, assoc. prof., 1968-71, prof., 1971—, acting chmn., 1981-82. Nat. Heart Inst. grantee, 1965 Fellow Am. Coll. Ob-Gyn, ACS, Gynecologic Oncology Soc.; mem. Soc. Gynecologic Investigation, AMA, Am. Fertility Soc., Richmond County Med. Soc., Ga. Ob-Gyn Soc., So. Med. Assn., S. Atlantic Assn. Ob-Gyn, Gyn-Urology Soc., Ga. Med. Assn. Clubs: Augusta Country. Lodges: Rotary (chmn. world community service com., Augusta 1983). Presbyterian. Home: 817 Aumond Pl W Augusta GA 30909-3106 Office: Med Coll Ga Dept Gyn Oncology Dept Ob Gyn Augusta GA 30912 Personal E-mail: cordoba@comcast.net. Business E-Mail: ctalledo@mail.mcg.edu. *

TALLETT, ELIZABETH EDITH, biopharmaceutical company executive; b. London, Apr. 2, 1949; d. Edward and Edith May (Vickers) Symons; m. James Edward Wavle Jr.; children: James Edward Tallett, Alexander Martin Tallett, Christopher Andrew Wavle. BS with honors, Nottingham U., Eng., 1970. Ops. rsch. analyst So. Gas Bd., 1970-73; mgmt. svcs. mgr. Warner-Lamber (UK), Eastleigh, England, 1973-77, strategic planning mgr., 1977-81; internat. dir. strategic planning Warner-Lambert, Morris Plains, NJ, 1981-82, corp. dir. strategic planning, 1982-84; head mktg. ops./exec. com. mem. Parke-Davis, Morris Plains, 1984-87; exec. v.p. therapeutic products Centocor, Malvern, Pa., 1987-89, pres. pharms. div., 1989-92; pres., CEO Transcell Techs., Inc., Monmouth Junction, NJ, 1992-96, Dioscor, Inc., Stockton, 1996—2003; prin. Hunter Partners, LLC, 2002—. Bd. dirs. Prin. Fin. Group, Inc., Coventry Health Care, Inc., IntegraMed Am. Inc., Meredith Corp. Inc., Qiagen, Inc. Contbr. articles to profl. jours. Trustee Solebury Sch., Pa. Avocations: acting, badminton, travel, skiing.

TALLEY, JOSEPH EUGENE, psychologist; b. Springfield, Mass., May 27, 1949; s. Joseph Addison and Miriam Louise (Ayers) T.; m. Vibeke Absalon, Jan. 3, 1981; children: Kirsten, David, Jonathan. BA, U. Richmond, 1971; MA, Radford Coll., 1973; PhD, U. Va., 1978. Diplomate in counseling psychology Am. Bd. Profl. Psychology, 1986, in clin. psychology, 2002; lic. psychologist, NC; cert. health svc. provider, NC. Faculty Duke U. Med. Ctr., Durham, NC, 1977—, prof. med. psychology, dept. psychiatry, 2005—, with counseling and psychol. svcs., 1977—, asst. dir., 2006—; gen. practice psychotherapy Durham, 1980—. Author: Study Skills, 1981, Performance Prediciton of Law Enforcement Personnel, 1990, The Predictors of Successful Very Brief Psychotherapy, 1992, Seeking Something Sacred: Managing Our Frustrations, Losses and Fears, 2001; author, editor: Counseling and Psychotherapy Services, 1985, Counseling and Psychotherapy with College Students: A Guide to Treatment, 1986, Multicultural Needs Assessment with College and University Populations, 1995; contbr. articles to profl. jours. Bd. deacons Hillsborough Presbyn. Ch., NC, 1983-85, chmn., 1985, bd. elders, 1987-94, 2002-07, v.p. bd. trustees, 1992-94; bd. dirs. Orange County Mental Health Assn., Chapel Hill, NC, 1982-83, mem. legis. com., 1983, APA site visitor for accreditation. Recipient Disting. Contbn. award, ABPP, 2002; named Disting. Practitioner, Nat. Acads. Practice, 2009. Fellow APA (awards com. divsn. 17, 2002-05, chair awards com. 2006-07, chair Leona Tyler lifetime achievement award com., 2007-08, mem. external interface bd. 2009-), Am. Acad. Clin. Psychology, Am. Acad. Counseling Psychology, Am. Acad. Counseling Psychology (pres. 1995-97, pres. emeritus 2007, Disting. Svc. award 2002); mem. Am. Bd. Profl. Psychology (sec., treas. coun. of pres.'s psychology splty. acads. 1997-98, chmn., CEO 2000-03, spl. liaison to related groups 2003—, past chmn., CEO 2003-05, exec. bd. and spl. liaison to congress and related profl. groups, 2005—, Disting. Contbns. award 2002, chair and CEO emeritus, 2008-), NC Psychol. Assn., Nat. Soc. Clin. Hypnosis (cert. and approved cons., supr. and practitioner, ethics com. 1995-97), Phi Kappa Phi, Omicron Delta Kappa, Psi Chi, Phi Kappa Sigma. Democrat. Presbyterian. Home: 134 E Tryon St Hillsborough NC 27278-2550 Office: Duke U Counseling & Psychol Svcs PO Box 90955 214 Page Bldg Durham NC 27708-0955 Office Phone: 919-660-1000. Business E-Mail: jtalley@duke.edu.

TALLEY, NICHOLAS JOSEPH, medical educator, research scientist, physician; b. Perth, Australia, Jan. 9, 1956; arrived in U.S., 2002, naturalized, 2010; s. Nicholas Alexander and Irene Mary Talley; m. Catherine Elizabeth Davies, Dec. 30, 2004; children: Nicholas Stephen, Matthew Jonathon, Nicole Sarah, Luke James. MB, BS, U. NSW, 1979; PhD, U. Sydney, 1987; MD, U. NSW, 1993, M in Med. Sci., 2003. Resident med. officer/registrar Prince of Wales Hosp., Sydney, 1979—83; rsch. fellow, prof. registrar Royal North Shore Hosp., Sydney, 1983—87; rsch. fellow Mayo Clinic, Rochester, Minn., 1987—88, asst. prof. medicine, 1988—91, assoc. prof., 1991—93; head divsn. medicine, prof. medicine Nepean Hosp., Sydney, 1993—2001; area dir. medicine Westworth Area Health Svc., Nepean Hosp., Sydney, 2001—02; prof. medicine, cons. Mayo Clinic Coll. Medicine, Rochester, 2003—10, prof. epidemiology, 2007—10; chair dept. internal medicine Mayo Clinic, Jacksonville, 2007—10, adj. prof. medicine, 2010—; pro vice chancellor, prof., faculty health U. Newcastle, Australia, 2010—. Adj. prof. Karolinska Inst., Stockholm, 2010—. Author: Examination Medicine, 1985, 6th edit., 2010, Clinical Examination, 1988, 6th edit., 2010, Internal Medicine, 1990, 2d edit., 2000, Clinical Gastroenterology, 1996, 3rd edit., 2010, Multiple Choice Questions in Clinical Examination, 1996, Pocket Clinical Examination, 1998, 3d edit., 2009, Conquering Irritable Bowel Syndrome, 2006, GI Epidemiology, 2007, Handbook of Gastroenterology, 2007; asst. editor Am. Jour. Gastroenterology, 1992-97; co-editor-in-chief, Am. Jour. Gastroenterology, 2004-09; mem. editl. bd. Gastroenterology, 1993-98, Jour. Clin. Gstroenterology, 1994-2008, Alimentary Pharmacology and Therapeutics, 1995-03, editor-in-chief, 2009-, Jour. Gastroenterology and Hepatology, 1996-98, editor, 1998-03; contbr. articles and revs. to profl. jours., chpts. to books. Pres. Miranda br. Young Liberals, Sydney, 1976; wing comdr. Royal Australia Air Force, 2000. Postgrad. rsch. scholar Nat. Health and Med. Rsch. Coun., Australia, 1984-85. Fellow ACP, Royal Australasian Coll. Physicians, Am. Coll. Gastroent., Australian Faculty Pub. Health Medicine (founding mem.), Royal Coll. Physicians (London and Edinburgh); fellow Am. Gastroent. Assn., Gastroent. Soc. Australia, Brit. Soc. Gastroenterology, Functional Brain Gut Rsch. Group (pres.). Avocations: tennis, writing, travel, jogging, martial arts. Office: Mayo Clinic 4500 San Pablo Rd Jacksonville FL 32224 Personal E-mail: talley5173@msn.com. Business E-Mail: talley.nicholas@mayo.edu, nicholas.talley@newcastle.edu.au.

TALLEY, ROBERT COCHRAN, academic administrator, cardiologist; b. May 26, 1936; m. Katherine Ann Plocar; children: Andrew, Katherine, David. BS, U. Mich., 1958; MD, U. Chgo., 1962. Diplomate Nat. Bd. Med. Examiners (mem. medicine com. 1984-88, com. chair 1988-93). Asst. prof., dept. physiology and medicine U. Tex. Med. Sch., San Antonio, 1969—71, head, sect. cardiovascular diseases, 1971—75, assoc. prof., dept. medicine, 1971—75; acting chief medicine VA Hosp., San Antonio, 1974, chief cardiology svc., 1973—75; chmn. dept. internal medicine U. SD Sch. Medicine, Sioux Falls, 1975—87, Freeman prof. medicine, 1984—87, interim v.p., dean, 1986—87, v.p., dean, 1987—2004, dir. residency program, 2004—. Mem. liaison com. med. edn., 1998—. Contbr. articles to med. jours. Surgeon USPHS, 1966—68. Tchg. scholar, Am. Heart Assn. U. Chgo., 1972—75. Fellow: ACP, Am. Coll. Cardiology; mem.: AMA, Liaison Com. on Med. Edn., Assn. Am. Med. Coll. (mem. coun. deans new dean mentoring program, mem. adminstrn. bd. coun. deans 1999—2004), Am. Fedn. Clin. Rsch., Am. Heart Assn. (bd. dirs. Dakota affiliate). Home: 1305 Cedar Ln Sioux Falls SD 57103-4512 Office: U SD Sch Medicine 1400 W 22nd St Sioux Falls SD 57105-1505

TALLMER, MARGOT SALLOP, psychologist, gerontologist, psychoanalyst; b. NYC, Sept. 8, 1925; d. Harry and Mildred (Schifrin) Sallop; m. Jonathan Tallmer, Apr. 12, 1949 (dec.); children: Mary, Megan, Jill, Andrew. MS, NYU, 1948; MA, Yeshiva U., 1962, PhD, 1967; cert. in psychotherapy and psychoanalysis, NYU, 1976. Faculty dept. psychol. founds. Hunter Coll., NYC, 1969-76, assoc. prof., 1976-79, prof., 1979—94, prof. emeritus; staff psychologist Mt. Sinai Hosp., NY, 1967-68; pvt. practice NYC, 1979—; faculty NY Ctr. for Psychoanalytic Tng., NY. Lectr. N.Y. Ctr. Psychoanalytic Tng. Author: Sex in Later Life, 1996; editor: Sex and Life Threatening Illness, HIV Testing Positive, The Child and Death, Sexuality and the Older Adult; co-author: Suicide in the Elderly; mem. editl. bd. in Psychoanalysis, Psychoanalytic Rev.; contbr. chpts. to textbooks, articles to profl jours. Mem. APA, N.Y. State Psychol. Assn. (past pres. divsn. adult devel. and aging), Nat. Psychol. Assn. for Psychoanalysis (trustee 1972-2005, bd. dir. 1972—). Address: 515 E 85th St New York NY 10028-0246 Personal E-mail: mamadoc4@n.y.c.rr.om. E-mail: mamadoc4@gmail.com. *

TALLROTH, KAJ ARVID, radiologist, educator; b. Helsinki, Finland, Apr. 24, 1940; s. Paul and Märtha (Lilius) T.; m. Alexandrine Elisabeth Gummerus, Dec. 2, 1970; 1 child, Karin. B Medicine, Helsinki U., Finland, 1964, MD, 1967, D Medicine and Surgery, 1976. Lic. medicine in Finland, specialist in radiology, musculoskeletal radiology, nuc. medicine. Resident in surgery U. Hosp. Helsinki, Finland, 1967-68; resident in radiology ORTON Orthop. Hosp., Helsinki, 1969, head dept. radiology, 1982—2004; resident in radiology U. Hosp., Helsinki, 1970-74, sr. radiologist, 1974-82; CEO Diagno-Soft, 1998—2004. Vis. assoc. prof. U. Mich., 1989-90; sr. lectr. in radiology Helsinki U., Finland, 1980—; assoc. prof. and vice chmn. Dept. Radiology U. Hosp. Helsinki, 1984; divsn. dir. Dept Radiology U. Mich., 1989-90. Exec. com. Helsinki Reserve Officers Soc., 1961-64. Maj. U.N. Forces, 1968. Decorated knight 1 class Order of White Rose of Finland, Nat. Def. medal; recipient UNFICYP medal U.N., 1968, P. Vuoria hon. lectr. Radiological Soc. Finland, 1993, P. Vuoria hon. prof., 2008, Gold medal of merit Ctrl. C. of C. of Finland, 1999; C. Wegelius hon. lectr. Radiol. Soc. Finland. Fellow: Internat. Coll. Angiology; mem.: European Soc. Musculoskeletal Radiology (exec. com. 1996—98), Internat. Skeletal Soc., Finnish Soc. Musculoskeletal Radiology (hon.; exec. com. 1999—2004), Internat. Soc. Lymphology (exec. com. 1981—87), Finnish Med. Doctor Soc. (treas. 1983—90). Lutheran. Avocations: golf, skiing, woodworking. Home: Mellstenintie 17 B 14 2170 Esbo Finland

TALMAGE, DAVID WILSON, retired microbiologist, educator, dean; b. Kwangju, Korea, Sept. 15, 1919; s. John Van Talmage and Eliza (Emerson) Talmage; m. LaVeryn Marie Hunicke, June 23, 1944; children: Janet, Marilyn, David, Mark, Carol. Student, Maryville Coll., Tenn., 1937—38; BS, Davidson Coll., NC, 1941; MD, Washington U., St. Louis, 1944. Intern Ga. Baptist Hosp., 1944—45; resident medicine Barnes Hosp., St. Louis, 1948—50, fellow medicine, 1950—51; asst. prof. pathology U. Pitts., 1951—52; asst. prof., then assoc. prof. medicine U. Chgo., 1952—59; prof. medicine U. Colo., 1959—, prof. microbiology, 1960—86, disting. prof., 1986—, chmn. dept., 1963—65, assoc. dean, 1966—68, dean, 1969—71; dir. Webb-Waring Lung Inst., 1973—83, assoc. dean for rsch., 1983—86. Mem. nat. council Nat. Inst. Allergy and Infectious Diseases, NIH, 1963—66, 1973—77. Author (with John Cann): Chemistry of Immunity in Health and Disease; editor: Jour. Allergy, 1963—67; editor: (with M. Samter) Immunological Diseases. With M.C. AUS, 1945—48. Scholar Markle, 1955—60. Mem.: Am. Assn. Immunologists, Am. Acad. Allergy, Inst. Medicine, NAS, Alpha Omega Alpha, Phi Beta Kappa. Home Phone: 303-388-1898.

TALMAGE, LANCE ALLEN, obstetrician, gynecologist, military officer; b. Vandergrift, Pa., Feb. 23, 1938; s. Guy Wesley and Martha Lois (Bradstock) T.; m. Diana Elizabeth Heywood, June 23, 1962; children: Tamara, Lance Jr., Tenley. BS in Chem. Engring., U. Toledo, Ohio, 1960; MD, U. Mich., 1964. Flight surgeon 24th Infantry Divsn. US Army, 1966-69; resident U. Mich. Med. Ctr., Ann Arbor, 1969-73; clin. prof. U. Toledo Coll. Medicine, 1987—; med. dir. Ctr. for Women's Health, Toledo, 1987—2003. Brigadier gen. 112th Med. Brigade Ohio Army Nat. Guard, Columbus, 1995-97; pres. med. staff Toledo Hosp., 1989-91, chair dept. Ob-gyn., 1979-86; pres. Toledo

Lucas County Acad. Medicine, 1994-95; mem. Toledo Hosp. Found. Bd., 2000-05, Ohio State Med. Bd., 1999—, supervising sec., 2003-, bd. dirs., Fedn. State Med. Bds., 2008-, chair-elect, bd. dirs., 2011. Cabinet mem. United Way, Toledo, 1994-96; hon. chmn. March of Dimes Mothers-March, Toledo, 1989; pres. Ottawa Hills Athletic Boosters, Ohio, 1986-88, team physician, 1981-2003; trustee U. Toledo Found., 1999—. Decorated Legion of Merit; recipient Disting. Alumni award, Waite H.S., 1996, Garde Nationale Trophy, N.G. Assn. U.S., 1998, Outstanding Team Physician, Ohio H.S. Athletic Assn., 2002, Gold T award, U. Toledo, 2009, Blue T award, 2002, Outstanding Chem. Engr. Grad. award, 2002—03; named to, Ohio Vets. Hall Fame, 2001. Fellow ACS, ACOG (dist. chair 1996-99, v.p. 2000-01, Disting. Dist. Svc. award, 2004), Fedn. State Med. Bds. (editl. com. 2007-08, bd. dirs. 2008-11, chair elect 2011); mem. AMA (mem. ho. of dels. 1998-2010), Am. Soc. Reproductive Medicine, Ohio State Med. Assn. (pres. 1998-99), Pi Kappa Phi Alumni Assn. (found. bd. mem. 2010-, Beta Iota chpt. Hall of Fame), U. Toledo Alumni Assn. (trustee 1996-2002, pres. 2000-01, athletic com., 2005—09), Res. Officers Assn., Soc. Med. Cons. to Armed Forces, Am. Legion Post 335, Mil. Officers Assn. Am. (life), Assn. Mil. Surgeons US (life), Nat. Guard Assn. US (life), Pi Kappa Phi Found. (bd. trustees 2010). Republican. Lutheran. Office: The Toledo Hosp 2150 W Ctrl Ave Toledo OH 43606 Office Phone: 419-291-2192, 419-291-1426, 419-291-3020. Personal E-mail: latalmage@bex.net.

TALPAZ, MOSHE, oncologist, educator; b. Poland, Mar. 17, 1947; MD, Hebrew U., Jerusalem, 1971. Prof., medicine dept. exptl. therapeutics MD Anderson Cancer Ctr., 1981—2006; prof., medicine U. Mich. Comprehensive Cancer Ctr., 2006—. Recipient Janet R. Rowley award, European Soc. Hematology, Gerald. R. Bodey award, MD Anderson, prize, European Interferon Soc., John J. Kenny award, Leukemia and Lymphoma Soc., Mankind award, Janet Rowly award, ESH Gerald Bodly Professorship MD Anderson. Mem.: Internat. Cytokine Soc., Internat. Soc. Interferon and Cytokine Rsch. (Milstein award), Am. Assn. Cancer Rsch., Am. Soc. Hematology, Am. Soc. Clin. Oncology. Office: University Mich Cancer Ctr 15 Ann Arbor MI 48109-5936 Office Fax: 734-647-9654. Business E-Mail: mtalpaz@umich.edu.

TAM, ALISON, dermatologist; MD, Western U. Health Sciences, 2001. Diplomate Am. Bd. Dermatology, Am. Bd. Family Medicine, 2004. Chief resident in family medicine Mesa Gen. Hosp.-Midwestern Univ.; resident in dermatology and dermatol. surgery Kingman Regional Med. Ctr.-Midwestern Univ.; dermatologist Western Wyoming Dermatology and Surgery; lead physician in cosmetic laser and hair transplant depts. Dr Anson and Dr Higgins Plastic Surgery Assocs., 2010—. Author: various publs. Fellow: Am. Soc. for Mohs Surgery, Am. Osteopathic Coll. of Dermatology; mem.: Am. Coll. of Osteopathic Family Medicine, Am. Osteopathic Assn., Am. Acad. of Dermatology. Office: Dr Anson & Dr Higgins Plastic Surgery Associates 8530 W Sunset Ste 130 Las Vegas NV 89113 Office Phone: 702-822-2100. Office Fax: 702-822-2105.

TAM, CONSTANTINE SI LUN, hematologist; b. Hong Kong, Feb. 17, 1975; MBBS with honor, U. Melbourne, Victoria, Australia, 1998, MD, 2009. Leukemia fellow U. Tex. MD Anderson Cancer Ctr., 2006—08; sr. fellow U. Melbourne, 2009—11; cons. hematologist St Vincent's Hosp., 2008—. Specialist rev. coun. mem. Dept. Vet. Affairs, 2009—; sci. adv. bd. mem. Australasian Leukaemia and Lymphoma Group, 2010—. Recipient Merit award, ASCO Found., Young Investigator award, HSANZ, Junior Davis Singletary fellowship, U. Tex. MD Anderson Cancer Ctr.; fellowship, Sylvia and Charles Viertel Charitable Found. Mem.: Haematology Soc. Australia and New Zealand, Am. Assn. Cancer Rsch., European Hematology Assn., Am. Soc. Clin. Oncology, Am. Soc. Hematology. Avocations: gardening, running, Ju Jitsu. Office: Ste 514 100 Victoria Parade Melbourne Victoria 3002 Australia Office Fax: 61392884068. Business E-Mail: ctam@tpg.com.au.

TAM, KA-WAI, surgeon; b. Hong Kong, Feb. 3, 1967; MS, Grad. Inst. Med. Scis., Taipei Med. U., 2004. Dir., evidence-based medicine ctr. Taipei Med. U. Hosp., 2008—, vice dir., dept. edn. and rsch., 2010. Mem.: Taiwan Evidence-Based Medicine Assn., Chinese Oncology Soc., Taiwan Soc. Endoscopic Surgery, Taiwan Surg. Soc. Gastroenterology, Surg. Assn. Taiwan. Avocations: basketball, music, reading. Office: 252 Wuxing St Taipei 11031 Taiwan Business E-Mail: kelvintam@h.tmu.edu.tw.

TAM, PAUL KWONG HANG, pediatric surgeon, educator; b. Hong Kong, May 27, 1952; s. Shou Wa and Shui Chun (Tang) T.; m. Amy Yan Mi Chum, Dec. 26, 1981; children: Greta Chun Huen, Isabel Chun Yee. B Medicine and Sci., U. Hong Kong, 1976; M Surgery, U. Liverpool, Eng., 1984. Intern U. Hong Kong Queen Mary Hosp., 1976-77, med. officer dept. surgery, 1977-83; research fellow dept. pediatric surgery Alder Hey Children's Hosp., Liverpool, 1983-84; lectr. dept. surgery U. Hong Kong, 1984-86; sr. lectr. dept. child health U. Liverpool, 1987-90; reader Nuffield dept. surgery U. Oxford, Eng., 1990-96; prof., chair pediatric surgery, dept. surgery U. Hong Kong, 1996—, pro-vice chancellor, 2004—. Hon. cons. Royal Liverpool Children's Hosp., Alder Hey, 1987-90; hon. cons. John Radcliffe Hosp., U. Oxford; sr. Nuffield rsch. fellow Lincoln Coll., 1990-96; dep. chair Genome Rsch. Ctr., U. Hong Kong, 2002—. Author book chpts. and contbr. articles to profl. pubs. Mem. British Assn. Pediatric Surgeons, British Pediatric Assn. Surg. Rsch. Soc., British Soc. of Pediatric Gastroenterology and Nutrition (coun. mem.), U.K. Children's Cancer Study Group, Societe Internationale Chirugie, Assn. Surgeons of South Asia, Hong Kong Surg. Soc., Hong Kong Pediatric Soc., Asian Surg. Assn., Royal Automobile Club. Roman Catholic. Office Phone: 852-22554850. Office Fax: 852-28173155.

TAM, PO-CHOR, surgeon; Intercollegiate urology fellowship, 1991; higher urology tng. Commonwealth Med. Fellowship Award Scheme, England; chief urology divsn. Queen Mary Hosp., Hong Kong, dir. robotic surgery programme. Hon. assoc. prof. surgery dept. Univ. Hong Kong. Fellow: Coll. Surgeons Hong Kong (found. fellow, v.p., chmn. urology bd.), Hong Kong Acad. Medicine (found. fellow), Royal Australian Coll. Surgeons 1990, Royal Coll. Surgeons (Edinburgh 1988). Office: Queen Mary Hospital 102 Pokfulam Rd Hong Kong Office Phone: 85222553838. Office Fax: 85228175496. *

TAM, TERESA, gynecologist; b. Philippines, July 1, 1964; MD, Chgo. Med. Sch., 1994. Physician, ptnr. Lakeshore Women's Health Specialists, 1998—. Asst. prof. clin. ob-gyn. Northwestern U., Feinberg Sch. Medicine, 2000; ob-gyn. staff attending physician Northwestern Meml. Hosp., 2001; assoc. program dir., obstetrics, gynecology residency program Resurrection Healthcare, St. Joseph Hosp., 2004, quality assessment & improvement com., 04, nominating com., 11. Contbr. articles to profl. jours. Recipient Physician's Recognition award, AMA, 2005—07, St. Joseph Hosp. Med. Staff Com. Svc. award, Resurrection Healthcare, St. Joseph Hosp., 2009, Nat. Faculty award, Am. Coll. Ob-Gyn., 2001, 2004, 2009, 2010; named Mentor of Yr., ACOG Com., 2011. Fellow: Am. Congress Ob-Gyn.; mem.: Am. Assn. Gynecologic Laparoscopists, Am. Inst. Minimally Invasive Surgery, Soc. Laparoendoscopic Surgeons, Chgo. Gynecol. Soc. Avocations: running, travel, reading. Office: 1460 N Halsted Ste 503 Chicago IL 60642 Office Fax: 312-787-4424.

TAMAOKA, YUKOKU, obstetrician, gynecologist; b. Tokyo, Dec. 18, 1947; s. Akitaka and Chisen Tamaoka; m. Senki Im, Oct. 25, 1974; children: Keishou, Keita. BS of Mech. Engring., Chiba U., 1970; MD, Seoul Nat. U., 1979; PhD, Keio U., 1988. Intern Keio U. Hosp., Tokyo, 1980—81, resident, 1981—85; dir. dept. ob.-gyn. Saiseikai Ctrl. Hosp., Tokyo, 1998—, chair. instl. rev. bd., 1998—2003. Lic. physician healthcare industries. Japan Med. Assn., Tokyo, 2000—05, lic. physician maternal healthcare., 2002—05. Grantee, Nat. Inst. Infectious Disease, 1997—2005. Mem.: Japan Human Cell Soc. (assoc.), Japan Soc. Endocrinology (assoc.), Japan Soc. Fertility and Sterility (assoc.), Japan Soc. Gyn. and Obs. Endoscopy (assoc.), Japan Soc. Obs.-gyn. (assoc.). Achievements include showing Danazol has a direct effect on endometrial hyperplasia including atypical hyperplasia by the way of danazol-releasing intrauterine device; confirmed this effect by in vivo and in vitro study. Avocations: mountain climbing, travel. Home: 1 8 13 Takaban Meguro-ku Tokyo 152 0004 Japan Office: Saiseikai Ctrl Hosp 1 4 17 Mita Minato ku Tokyo 108 0073 Japan Office Fax: 03-3451-6102. Personal E-mail: yukoku@mac.com. E-mail: sanfu@saichu.jp.

TAMARGO, RAFAEL J., neurological surgeon, educator; b. Havana, Cuba, Mar. 22, 1958; AB magna cum laude, Princeton U., NJ, 1980; MD, Columbia U., NYC, 1984. Diplomate Am. Bd. Neurol. Surgery. Intern Columbia Coll. Physicians and Surgeons, NYC, 1984—85; resident in neurosurgery Johns Hopkins Hosp., Balt., 1985—92, active staff, 1992—, from assoc. prof. neurosurgery to Walter E. Dandy prof., 1998—2004, Walter E. Dandy prof., 2004—, assoc. prof. of otolaryngology, 2002—04, prof. otolaryngology, 2004—. Fellow ACS; mem. Am. Assn. Neurol. Surgeons. Office: Johns Hopkins Hosp 600 N Wolfe St Meyer 8-181 Baltimore MD 21287-0001 Office Phone: 410-614-1533. Business E-Mail: rtamarg@jhmi.edu. *

TAMAROFF, MARC ALLEN, allergist, immunologist, educator; MD, U. Ariz., 1974. Diplomate Am. Bd. Internal Medicine, 1979, Am. Bd. Allergy and Immunology, 1983, lic. Calif., 1977. Intern St. Mary Med. Ctr., 1975, resident internal medicine, 1975—77, fellow allergy and immunology Ronald Reagan Univ. of Calif. Med. Ctr., 1977—79; assoc. clin. prof. medicine Univ.of Calif., hosp. affiliations include Los Alamitos Med. Ctr., St. Mary Med. Ctr., Long Beach Mcml. Med. Ctr. Office: Long Beach Memorial Medical Center 2801 Atlantic Ave Long Beach CA 90806-1737 Office Phone: 562-933-2000.

TAMARU, JUN-ICHI, medical educator; b. Tokyo, Jan. 26, 1955; s. Shigeo and Etsu Tamaru; m. Kiyoe Shikama; 1 child, Gentarou. MD, Dokkyo Med. U., Tochigi, 1979; PhD, Chiba U., Japan, 1984. Cert. pathologist Japan, 1985, human autopsy Japan, 1986. With Chiba U. Sch. Medicine, 1986—95, asst. prof., 1995—99; assoc. prof. Saitama Med. U., Kawagoe, Japan, 1999—2007, prof., 2007—. Guest physician Free U. Berlin, 1992—94; mem. editl. bd. Japanese Jour. Clin. Oncology, Tokyo, 2005—, Pathology Internat., Tokyo, 2007—, Jour. Clin. and Exptl. Hematology, Tokyo, 2007—, Jour. Japanese Soc. Clin. Cytology, Tokyo, 2007—, Diagnostic Pathology, Tokyo, 2008—. Choreographer. Boardman Japanese Soc. Pathology, Tokyo, 1986—, Japanese Soc. Lymphoreticular Tissue Rsch., Nagoya, Aichi, Japan, 1988—, Japanese Soc. Clin. Cytology, Tokyo, 1995—. Grantee, Edn. Ministry, Japan, 1987, 1991, 1997—2000. Avocations: bicycling, travel, music, movies. Office: Saitama Med Univ 1981 Kawagoe kamotatsujido Saitama 350-8540 Japan Office Fax: 049-228-3522. Business E-Mail: jtamaru@saitama-med.ac.jp.

TAMBURRINI, GIANPIERO, neurosurgeon; b. Naples, Aug. 25, 1967; Degree in Neurosurgery, Cath. U., Rome, 1991. Asst. prof. pediat. neurosurgery Inst. Neurosurgery, Cath. U. Med. Sch., Rome, 1992—. Mem.: WFNS, ESPN, ISPN. Avocation: running. Office: Largo A. Gemelh 8 Rome Lazio 00168 Italy Business E-Mail: gianpiero.tamburrini@rm.unicatt.it.

TAMPAS, JOHN P., radiologist; married; children: Jessica, Peter, Andrea, Christiana. BS, U. Vt., 1951, MD, 1954. Diplomate Am. Bd. Radiology. Radiology resident U. Vt., Burlington, 1957—60; teaching fellow pediat. radiology L.A. Children's Hosp., 1960—61; NIH Nat. Heart Inst. resident fellow cardiovascular radiology U. Ind., Indpls., 1961—62; attending radiology Med. Ctr. Hosp. Vt., Burlington, 1962—; asst. prof. radiology Coll. Medicine U. Vt., 1962—70; prof. & chmn. dept. radiology Med. Ctr. Hosp. Vt., Burlington, 1970—96. Contbr. articles to profl. jours. Recipient Karl Jefferson Thompson Meml. Excellence in Tchg. award, 1969, 1975; scholar, James Picker Found./NRC, 1962—65. Fellow: Am. Coll. Radiology (pres. 1987—88, bd. chancellors, emergency radiology com., accreditation com., chmn. mem. ins. com., adminstrv. affairs commn., radiologic practice commn., Gold medal 1996); mem.: AMA, Vt. Med. Soc., Vt. Radiol. Soc., Assn. Univ. Radiologists, Soc. Chmn. Acad. Radiology Depts., New Eng. Roentgen Ray Soc., Radiol. Soc. N.Am., Am. Roentgen-Ray Soc. (pres. 1982—83, Gold medal 1992), Soc. Pediat. Radiology, Alpha Omega Alpha. Office: Fletcher Allen Health Ctr 111 Colchester Ave Burlington VT 05401-1416 also: Hosp Vt Med Ctr Dept Radiology Burlington VT 05401

TAMURA, TOSHIYO, engineering educator; b. Tokyo, Feb. 28, 1949; PhD, Tokyo Med. & Dental U., 1980. Dir. Nat. Inst. Longevity Scis., 1998—2004; prof. Chiba U., 2004—. Adj. prof. Kanazawa U., 1997—. Mem.: IEEE, Japanese Soc. Med. & Biol. Engring. Avocations: travel, music. Office: 1-33 Yayoi Chiba 263-8522 Japan Office Fax: 81432903050. Business E-Mail: tamurat@faculty.chiba-u.jp.

TAMVAKOPOULOS, SPIROS K., surgeon, educator; b. Athens, Greece, Sept. 7, 1935; s. Spiros Kostas Tamvakopoulos and Zoe Christina Hayou; m. Elli George Tsami, May 11, 1962; children: Zoe, Kostas, George. MD, Athens U. Med. Sch., Greece, 1959, PhD, 1961. Sr. resident surgeon Columbia Presbyn. Hosp., NYC, 1966—67; chief resident surgeon R.I. Hosp., Providence, 1967—70; cons. surgeon Evangelismos Hosp., Athens, Greece, 1970—76, Hygga Hosp., Athens, 1976—92, Athens Med. Ctr., Athens, Greece, 1992—; prof. surgery Athens U. Med. Sch., 1982—2005. Jr. resident surgeon Brigham Women's Hosp., Boston, 1962—66. Fellow: ACS, Hellenic Surgical Assn. Democrat. Greek Orthodox. Avocations: tennis, skiing, flying. Address: Praxitelus 1 105 62 Athens Greece

TAN, DENNIS CUNANAN, surgeon; b. Davao, July 25, 1971; MD, Davao Med. Sch. Found., 1998; degree in Cosmetic Plastic Surgery, King Chulalongkorn U. Hosp., 2005. Aesthetic cosmetic surgeon Asia Pacific Acad. Cosmetic Surgery, 2005—10. Med. dir., cons. Bethany Med. Group, 2005—10. Cosmetic Surgery Practitioner fellowship, APACS. Fellow: Philippine Soc. Cosmetic Surgery. Avocation: photography. Office: Bethany Med Group Unit 8 Level 2 Davao Mindanao 8000 Philippines Business E-Mail: dr.dennis.tan@gmail.com.

TAN, DONALD, surgeon; MBBS, Singapore, 1983; FRCS, Glasgow, 1988; FRC Opthalmology, UK, 1989; FAMS, 1994; FRCS, Edinburgh, 1998. Sci. expert adviser Tianjin eye ctr. Tianjin Med. Univ.; chmn. sci. adv. bd. NeuroVision Inc.; sr. cons. opthalmology dept. Nat. Univ. Hosp.; head opthalmology dept. Nat. Univ., Singapore; med. dr. Singapore Eye Bank; dir. Singapore Eye Rsch. Inst., chmn.; sr. cons. and head corneal svc. Singapore Nat. Eye Centre (SNEC). Mem. Asia Pacific Dry Eye Adv. Bd., Asia Pacific Soc. of Eye genetics; pres. Asia Cornea Soc.; country liason Tear Film & Ocular Surface Soc.; mem. Ocular Surgery New Europe/Asia-Pacific Edit. Bd.; mem. sci. adv. bd. Bausch & Lomb; bd. mem. Cornea Soc.; mem. expert panel opthamology Health Sci. Authority; mem. adv. com. transp. Ministry of Health; coun. mem. Nat. Med. Rsch. Coun.; prof. opthalmology Yonh Loo Lin Sch. of Medicine Nat. Univ., Singapore. Contbr. various publ. including "Optimized analytical method for cyclosporin A by high-performance liquid chromatography-electrospray ionization mass spectrometry", "Defensins HNP1 and HBD2 stimulation of wound-associated responses in human conjunctival fibroblasts" and "Outcomes of Femtosecond Laser-Assisted Penetrating Keratoplasty". Recipient Best Teaching Video award, Meeting Film Festival, Pacific Acad. of Opthalmology Disting. Svc. award, 1997, Asia-Pacific Acad. of Opthalmology De Ocampo award, 2001, Best Sci. Presentation award, Am. Soc. of Cataract and Refractive Surgery (ASCRS), 2004, 1st Prize Film Festival award, 2005, Best Sci. Presentation award, 2006, 1st Prize Meeting Film Festival award, 2008, Outstanding Performance in Pub. Health award, Ministry of Health, 2006, Disting. Achievement award, Am. Acad. of Opthalmology (AAO), 2006, Best Paper award, 2007, Nat. Outstanding Clinician Scientist award, Nat. Med. Rsch. Coun. Ministry of Health, Singapore, 2008. Mem.: Asia-Pacific Contact Lens Assn. of Opthalmologist (bd. mem.), Asia Cornea Found. (bd. mem.). Office: SINGLASIK Centre Singapore National Eye Centre (SNEC) 11 3rd Hospital Ave Singapore 168751 Singapore Office Phone: 6563228891. Office Fax: 6562263403. *

TAN, ENG MENG, immunologist, biomedical researcher; b. Seremban, Malaysia, Aug. 26, 1926; arrived in US, 1950; s. Ming Kee and Choon Eng (Ang) T.; m. Liselotte Filippi, June 30, 1962; children: Philip, Peter. BA, Johns Hopkins U., 1952, MD, 1956. Intern Duke U., Durham, NC, 1956-57; resident, fellow Case-Wc. Res. U., Cleve., 1957-62; rsch. assoc. Rockefeller U., NYC, 1962—65; asst. prof. Washington U. Sch. Medicine, St. Louis, 1965—67; assoc. mem. and mem. Scripps Rsch. Inst., LaJolla, Calif., 1967—77; prof. Scripps Rsch. Inst., LaJolla, Calif., 1982—2006, prof. emeritus, 2006—; prof. U. Colo. Sch. Medicine, Denver, 1977-82. Chmn. allergy & immunology rsch. com. NIH, Bethesda, Md., 1982-84; mem. nat. arthritis adv. bd. HHS, Washington, 1981-85; hon. prof. Shanghai Jiao Dong U., Zhengzhou U., China. Contbr. chapters to books, articles to profl. jours. Recipient US Sr. Scientist award, Humboldt Found., Germany, 1986, Ciba-Giegy-Internat. League against Rheumatism award, 1989, Carol Nachman award, Wiesbaden, Germany, 1989, Lee Howley Sr. award, Arthritis Found., 1989, Paul Klemperer award and medal, NY Acad. Medicine, 1993, City Medicine award, Duke U., Durham, NC, 1996, Disting. Med. Alumnus award, Duke U., 2000, Mayo Soley award, Western Soc. Clin. Investigation, 2002, Japan Rheumatism Found. Internat. prize, 2003, Meritorious Svc. award, European League Against Rheumatism, 2005, Lifetime Achievement award, 8th Internat. Lupus Congress, China, 2007; named to Nat. Lupus Hall Fame, 1984. Fellow AAAS; mem. Am. Coll. Rheumatology (pres. 1984-85, chmn. Blue Ribbon com. Future Acad. Rheumatology 1997-98, Disting. Investigator award 1991, Gold medal award 1998), Assn. Am. Physicians, Am. Soc. Clin. Investigation, Western Assn. Physicians (v.p. 1980-81), Am. Assn. Immunologists, Brazilian Soc. Rheumatology (hon.), Australian Rheumatism Assn. (hon.), Brit. Soc. Rheumatology (hon.), Mex. Nat. Acad. Medicine (hon.). Achievements include research on antibodies and antigens in cancer and in autoimmune diseases, systemic lupus erythematosus, scleroderma, Sjogren's syndrome, myositis and mixed connective tissue disease; relationship of autoantibodies to pathogenesis. Autoantibodies to tumor associated antigens as diagonastic biomakers in cancer. Home: 8303 Sugarman Dr La Jolla CA 92037-2224 Office: Scripps Rsch Inst 10550 N Torrey Pines Rd La Jolla CA 92037-1000 Office Phone: 858-784-8686. Business E-Mail: emtan@scripps.edu.

TAN, HOCK LIM, pediatric surgeon, educator; b. Kuala Lumpur, Malaysia, Jan. 7, 1949; arrived in Australia, 1964; s. Chye and Irene (Yong) T.; m. Evelyn Chong; children: Melanie, Alexander. MB BS, Adelaide U., 1971, MD, 2000. Resident Adelaide Children's & Royal Children's Hosp., Melbourne, Australia, intern; cons. surgeon Gleneagles Hosp., Singapore, 1995-97; assoc. prof. Chinese U. Hong Kong, 1997-98; cons. in minimally invasive surgery Great Ormond Street Hosp., London, 1998-99; chief Dept. Pediat. Surgery Adelaide

U., Australia, 2000—, prof., 2000—. Mem. exec. com. Red Cross, Singapore, 1997; bd. dirs. Werribee Hosp., Melbourne, 1993-94. Fellow Royal Australia Coll. Surgeons. E-mail: hockltan@yahoo.com.

TAN, JAMES, urologist; MBBS, Nat. U. of Singapore, 1989, basic med. degree, 1990, M in Medicine, 1995. Training Cleve. Clinic; course dir. Laparoscopic Urology, 2002; tchg. faculty XXXIII World Congress of the Internat. Coll. of Surgeons, Taiwan; faculty Soc. of Surgeons, Nepal; tchg. faculty Nat. Healthcare Group Annual Sci. Meeting, 2002—04, Asian Congress in Urology, Hong Kong, 2004; course dir. Laparoscopic Workshop, 2005; with Ministry of Health's Clin. Guideline Com.; mem. Chpt. of Urology Subspecialty Coms.; head of urology Tan Tock Seng Hosp., lead surgeon, dep. dir., TTSH's Clin. Rsch. Unit; sec. Urology Fair, 2003—04, tchg. faculty, 2005, sci. chmn., 2005, chmn. organizing com., 2006; treas. Singapore Urological Assn., 2004—06; mentor, supr. Advanced Surg. (Urology) Trainees; v.p. Singapore Coll. of Surgeons, 2007; cons. Urologist Mt. Elizabeth Medical Centre, Gleneagles Hosp., Mt. Alvernia Hosp. Vis. specialist Singapore Gen. Hosp.; clin. lectr. Nat. Univ. of Singapore. Author numerous pubs. and award wining videos. Reviewer Nat. Med. Rsch. Coun., Nat. Healthcare Group Rsch. Fund, Tan Tock Seng Hosp. Rsch. Fund. Recipient Best Oral Paper prize, 1999, Ministry of Health HMDP scholarship, 2000—01, Ann. Book prize, 2000, Acad. of Medicine Traveling Fellowship, 2002, Best in Knowledge prize, 2002, Best Video prize, First Nat. Healthcare Group Ann. Sci. Meeting, 2002. Fellow: Acad. of Medicine, Royal Coll. of Physicians and Surgeons of Glasgow, Royal Coll. of Surgeons of Edinburgh; mem.: Singapore Urological Assn. (hon. treas.). Office: Mount Elizabeth Medical 17-14 3 Mount Elizabeth 228510 Singapore Office Phone: 6567350369. Office Fax: 6567351317. *

TAN, JERRY, surgeon; MBBS, Singapore, 1981; FRCS, London UK, 1986. Sr. registrar; pvt. practice Singapore Gen. Hosp., Tan Tock Seng Hosp., Nat. Eye Centre, Singapore; cons. Alcon USA, Schwind Eye-Tech.-Solutions; cons. eye surgeon Jerry Tan Eye Surgery, Singapore. With editl. bd. W B Saunders Co. Contbr. chapters to books internat. opthalmic textbooks on LASIK surgery. Office: Jerry Tan Eye Surgery Camden Medical Centre 1 Orchard Blvd Number 10-06 Singapore 248649 Singapore Office Phone: 6567388122. Office Fax: 6567383822. *

TAN, KEVIN ENG KIAT, endocrinologist; b. Singapore, Nov. 19, 1962; MBBS, Nat. U. Singapore, 1987. Dir., cons. endocrinologist Kevin Tan Clinic Diabetes, Thyroid and Hormones Pte Ltd., 2000—. Vis. cons. endocrinologist Singapore Gen. Hosp., 2000—11; v.p. Diabetic Soc. Singapore, 2004—; vis. cons. endocrinologist Thomson Med. Ctr., 2000—. Fellow: Royal Coll. Physicians (Edinburgh), Acad. Medicine (Singapore). Avocations: reading, running. Office: #15-14 Mt Elizabeth Med Ctr Singapore 228510 Singapore Office Fax: 6567333808. E-mail: kektan@yahoo.com.

TAN, KIM LEONG, pediatrician, educator; b. Malaysia, Oct. 30, 1936; s. Chim Ean Tan and Siew Bo Yeoh, m. Kwok Yee Leng, June 15, 1963; children: Min-Li, Min-Ching, Wei-Liang. MBBS, U. Singapore, 1962; DCH, U. London, 1967. Cert. MRCP Edinburgh, 1966, FRCP Edinburgh, 1977, FRACP Australia, 1978. Med. officer Ministry of Health, Singapore, 1963—67; head neonatal unit Kandang Kerbau Hosp., 1968—89, Nat. U. Hosp., Singapore, 1985—98, chief dept. neonatology, 1990—98; lectr. U. Singapore, 1968-71, sr. lectr., 1971-75, assoc. prof., 1976-79; prof. Nat. U. Singapore, 1980—98; ret., 1999; pvt. practice Specialist Infant-Child Ctr. Mt. Elizabeth Med. Ctr.; cons. Mt. Elizabeth Hosp. Vis. prof. McGill U., Montreal, 1995. Co-editor: Procs. of 1st Asia Oceana Congress of Perinatology, 1979; mem. editl. bd. AMA (SEA), 1984—, referee various med. jours., —. Mem. panel of doctors Kim Seng Cmty. Ctr. Night Clinic, Singapore, 1981-2003; mem. exec. com. Children's Aid Soc., Singapore, 1981-91. Fellow Royal Coll. Physicians, Royal Coll. Physicians Edinburgh, Royal Australasian Coll. Physicians; mem. Singapore Pediat. Soc. (life, pres. 1972, 1975-77, chmn. rsch. fund 1975—, Haridas Meml. lectr. 1972, 77), Ob-gyn. Soc. Singapore (Benjamin Henry Sheares lectr. 1976), Brit. Med. Assn., Singapore Med. Assn., Acad. of Medicine. Home: The Tessarina 22 Wilby Road #09-20 the Tessarina 276306 Singapore Singapore Office Phone: 65-67359544. Personal E-mail: kl.drtan@gmail.com. Business E-Mail: ylkltan@singnet.com.sg.

TAN, MASAKI, surgeon, director; b. Akita, Japan, Feb. 13, 1946; s. Chiyoshi and Masae (Akahira) T.; m. Keiko Takahashi, Jan. 28, 1975; children: Hiroki, Chihiro. MB, Tohoku U., Sendai, Japan, 1971, MD, 1978; LLB, Kinki U., Osaka, Japan, 1985. Asst. prof. dept. surgery Tohoku U., Sendai, 1973-85; head dept. surgery Ohfunato Prefectural Hosp., Japan, 1985-88, Kitakami Prefectural Hosp., Japan, 1988-94, Isawa Prefectural Hosp., Mizusawa, Japan, 1994-98; vice dir. Wakayanagi Hosp., Kurihara, Japan, 1998—2011; dir. Kitakami Kiboen Geriatric Health & Welfare Facilities, 2011—. Author: Recent Advances in Chemotherapy, 1985, New Applications of OK-432, 1986. Mem. AAAS, Am. Chem. Soc., NY Acad. Sci. Avocations: reading, movies, music, travel. Office Phone: 0197637711. Personal E-mail: mtan@mve.biglobe.ne.jp. Business E-Mail: tan@kibouen.net.

TAN, SER KIAT, healthcare organization administrator; b. Singapore; MB, BChir, U. Singapore, 1971. Surg. tng. Thomson Rd. Gen. Hosp., Singapore; Colombo Plan fellowship advanced orthop. tng. Edinburgh, Birmingham, Derby, London, 1977—79; surgeon Singapore Gen. Hosp., 1979—84, head dept. orthop. & exptl. surgery, 1988—98, chmn. divsn. surgery, 1992—98, chmn. Med. Bd., 1998—2000, CEO, 2003—08; head dept. orthop. surgery Alexandra Hosp., Singapore, 1984—88; group CEO Singapore Health Svcs. (SingHealth), 2000—. Clin. prof. Faculty Medicine, Nat. U. Singapore, 2001—. Pres. Movement for Intellectually Disabled Singapore (MINDS), 1994—2003, Singapore Med. Coun., 2010; chmn. bd. govs. Raffles Instn., Singapore. Recipient Gold Pub. Adminstrn. medal, Prime Min. Singapore, 1999, May Day Medal of Commendation, 2004, Leading CEO award, Singapore Human Resources Inst., 2005, Pub. Svc. Medal, Singapore Nat. Day Awards, 2006, Svc. to Edn. award, Ministry Edn. Singapore, 2007. Fellow: Royal Coll. Physicians & Surgeons Glasgow; mem.: Acad. Medicine Singapore. Office: Singapore Health Services 31 Third Hospital Ave #03-03 Bowyer Block C Singapore 168753 Office Phone: 65574901. Office Fax: (65) 6557 2138. E-mail: tan.ser.kiat@singhealth.com.sg. *

TAN, TJIAUW-LING, psychiatrist, educator; b. Pemalang, Java, Indonesia, June 2, 1935; came to U.S., 1967; naturalized, 1972; s. Ping-Hoey and Liep-Nio (Liem) T.; m. Esther Joyce Kho, June 2, 1961; children: Paul Budiman, Robert Yuling, Alice Ayling. BS, U. Indonesia Faculty Medicine, 1957, MD, 1961; postgrad., U. Indonesia, Jakarta, 1961-65, UCLA, 1967-71, Pa. State U., 1971-72. Diplomate Am. Bd. Psychiatry and Neurology, Gen. Psychiatry, Bd.Psychiatry & Neurology, Geriat. Psychiatry. Lectr. psychiatry U. Indonesia, Jakarta, 1965-67; psychiat. cons. Ctrl. Gen. Hosp., Jakarta, 1965-67; postdoctoral fellow UCLA Brain Rsch. Inst., 1967-69; asst. rsch. psychiatrist, dept. psychiatry Neuropsychiat. Inst., UCLA, 1969-70; asst. prof. psychiatry Pa. State U., 1972-87, assoc. prof. psychiatry, 1987-99, prof. psychiatry, 1999—. Chief inpatient psychiatry Univ. Hosp. Milton S. Hershey Med. Ctr., 1972-2005, dir. Behavioral Medicine Clinic, co-dir. Biofeedback Lab., 1975—2005; cons. psychiatry Family and Children's Svc. Lebanon County, Lebanon, Pa., 1971-79. Contbr. articles to profl. jours. Bd. dir. Retarded Children's Assn. Dauphin County, Inc., 1971—73. Fellow Am. Psychiat. Assn. (disting. life), Pa. Psychiat. Soc.; mem. Ctrl. Pa. Psychiat. Soc., Assn. Behavioral & Cognitive Therapy, Assn. Applied Psychophysiology and Biofeedback, Soc. Behavioral Medicine, Assn. Psychophysiol. Study of Sleep, Am. Assn. for Geriat. Psychiatry, Internat Positive Psychology Assn. Democrat. Presbyterian. Home: 1478 Bradley Ave Hummelstown PA 17036-9143 Office: Pa State U Coll Medicine Dept Psychiatry 500 University Dr Hershey PA 17033-2390 Home Phone: 717-566-3009; Office Phone: 717-805-6082. Business E-Mail: lingtan@psu.edu.

TAN, WEN-SIANG, science educator, medical researcher; b. Kangar, Perlis, Malaysia, Jan. 22, 1968; s. Hooi-Sin Tan and Soo-Goh Lee; m. Bee-Kee Lim, May 14, 1994; children: Yee Herng children: Jean Yin. BSc with honors, U. Putra Malaysia, 1993, MSc, 1995; PhD, U. Edinburgh, 1998. Prof. Universiti Putra Malaysia, Serdang, Selangor, Malaysia, 2008—. Advisor Edn. Chamber of Selangor Citizen, Serdang, Selangor, Malaysia. Contbr. articles to profl. jours. (UPM Rsch. award, 2001). Recipient ICI Gold medal, 1993, Environ. award, Ministry of Sci., Tech. and Environment Malaysia, 1993, Internat. Invention Innovation Indsl. Design and Tech. Exhbn. Gold medal, Malaysian Invention and Design Soc., 2003, Sci. and Tech. Expo Gold medal, Malaysia Inst. Nuc. Tech., 2003, Ramrais and Ptnr. award, ITEX, 2006, Gold medal, Brussels Eureka, 2006; grantee, Third World Acad. Scis., 2001—03; scholar, Roseanne Campbell Trust Hepatitis Rsch., 1997; Norken Stiftung Rsch. fellowship, 2005. Mem.: Malaysian Soc. for Molecular Biology and Biotechnology (assoc.), Malaysian Soc. for Microbiology (assoc.), Malaysian Soc. for Biochemistry and Molecular Biology (assoc.). Achievements include invention of molecules that inhibit the propagation of hepatitis B virus. Home: 41 Jalan SP 8/12 47100 Puchong Malaysia Office: Univ Putra Malaysia/Faculty Biotech & Biomolec Scis Dept Microbiology 43400 Serdang 43400 Malaysia Office Phone: 603-89466715. Office Fax: 03-89430913. Personal E-mail: wensiangtan@yahoo.com. Business E-Mail: wstan@biotech.upm.edu.my.

TANABE, TOSHIZUMI, engineering educator, researcher; b. Osaka, Japan, Nov. 24, 1951; BS in Engring., Osaka City U., 1974, PhD, 1979. Prof. Osaka City U., Grad. Sch. Engring., 2005—. Office: 3-3-138 Sugimoto-cho Sumiyoshi-ku Osaka 558-8585 Japan Business E-Mail: tanabe@bioa.eng.osaka-cu.ac.jp.

TANAE, AYAKO, pediatrician, director; b. Yamagata, Japan, Sept. 28, 1934; 1 child, Mario. MS, Tohoku U., Sendai, 1956; PhD, Fukushima Med. U., 1960; MD, Tokyo U., 1966. Staff dr. Dept. Pediat. Tokyo U., 1961—69; dir. Dept. Pediat. Endocrinology Nat. Children's Hosp., 1969—2000, Shonan - Kamakura Gen. Hosp., Kamakura, 2002—. Author: (book) Precocious Puberty in Comprehensive Hand Book of Woman's Medicine, 2000; author & editor (book) The Treatment of Pediatric Endocrine Diseases by Medical Specialists new edit., 2007. Recipient prize, Nat. Children's Hosp., Min. Welfare, Tokyo, 1997. Mem.: Endocrine Soc., Md., Japanese Soc. Pediatric Endocrinology, Tokyo, Japan Pediatric Soc. Home: 1-11-7-1909 Tsukuda Tokyo Chuoh-Ku 1040051 Japan Office: Shonan - Kamakura Gen Hosp 1-1202 Yamazaki Kamakura Kanagawa Japan Office Phone: (0457) 46-1717. Home Fax: (03) 3532-5981. E-mail: han55031@rio.odn.ne.jp.

TANAKA, AKEMI, pediatrician, researcher; b. Osaka, Japan, Dec. 30, 1952; d. Ryoichi and Kotsuru Tanaka. MD, Osaka City U., 1977, PhD, 1981. Diplomate Nat. Bd. Med. Licensure, Japan. Asst. prof. dept. bacteriology Osaka City U. Sch. Medicine, 1981—82, asst. prof. dept. pediat., 1982—90, assoc. prof. dept. pediat., 1990—99, prof. dept. pediat. and clin. genetics, 1999—. Vis. rschr. Neurosci. Rsch. Ctr. U. N.C. Sch. Medicine, Chapel Hill, 1988—90; med. advisor Japanese Soc. Patients and Families with Mucopolysaccharidoses, 1987—. Contbr. articles to profl. jours. Recipient prize for med. rsch., Osaka City Mayor, 1984, 1991; grantee, Dept. Edn., Japan, 1979—84, 1983—86, 1987—99, 1999—, Ministry of Welfare, Japan, 1980—82, 1993—, 2001—. Mem.: Japanese Soc. for Genetic Counseling (councilor 2001—), Japanese Soc. Gene Therapy, Japanese Soc. Human Genetics (cert. clin. genetics specialist, cert. clin. genetics educator, councilor 1999—), Japanese Soc. Pediat. (councilor 2002—), Japanese Soc. Child Neurology (cert. clin. child neurology specialist), Japanese Soc. for Study of Inborn Errors of Metabolism (councilor 1999—), Am. Soc. Human Genetics, Internat. Soc. for Study of Inborn Errors of Metabolism. Office: Osaka City U Grad Sch Medicine 1-3-4 Asahi-machi Abeno-ku Osaka 545-8585 Japan Business E-Mail: akemi-chan@med.osaka-cu.ac.jp.

TANAKA, ATSUSHI, medical educator; b. Tokyo, Sept. 15, 1961; MD, Tokyo U., PhD, 1988. Assoc. prof. Teikyo U. Sch. Medicine, 2003—. Office: Teikyo University Sch Medicine 2 Tokyo 1738605 Japan Business E-Mail: a-tanaka@med.teikyo-u.ac.jp.

TANAKA, FUMIHIRO, medical educator; b. Japan, Oct. 21, 1960; MD, Kyoto U., PhD, 1986. Prof., dept. chest surgery U. Occupl. and Environ. Health, 2010—. Office: 1-1 Iseigaoka Yahata-nishi-ku Kitakyusyu Fukuoka 8078555 Japan Office Fax: 81-93-6924004. Business E-Mail: ftanaka@med.uoeh-u.ac.jp.

TANAKA, HIROHIKO, gynecologist; b. Japan, Sept. 23, 1961; PhD, Mie U., Japan, 1992. Staff dept. ob-gyn. Mie Prefectural Gen. Med. Ctr., 2006—. Fellow: Internat. Acad. Cytology. Office: Hinaga 5450-132 Yokkaichi Mie 510-8561 Japan Office Fax: 59-347-3500.

TANAKA, HIROMITSU, research scientist; b. Miyagi, Japan, Nov. 23, 1966; PhD in Agr., Tohoku U., 1994. Rschr. Nat. Inst. Agrobiol. Scis., 1999—2001, chief rschr., 2001—. Guest lectr. Tokyo U. Agr. & Tech., 2010. Mem.: Molecular Biology Soc. Japan, Japan Soc. Biosci., Biotech. & Agrochemistry, Japanese Soc. Sericultural Sci. (Encouragement prize 2006). Avocation: golf. Office: 1-2 Owashi Tsukuba Ibaraki 305-8634 Japan Office Fax: 81-29-838-6028. E-mail: htanaka1@nias.affrc.go.jp.

TANAKA, HIROSHI, research scientist; b. Aichi, Japan, Sept. 6, 1962; MS, Nagoya City U., 1987; PhD, Kyoto Prefectural U. Medicine, 1998. Sr. chief rschr. Rsch. Labs., Nippon Menard Cosmetic Co. Ltd., 1987—. Recipient 2nd prize, China Assn. Fragrance Flavor and Cosmetic Industries. Mem.: Japanese Cosmetic Sci. Soc. Avocations: soccer, bicycling. Office: 2-7 Torimi-cho Nishi-ku Nagoya Aichi 451-0071 Japan Business E-Mail: tanaka.hiroshi@menard.co.jp.

TANAKA, HIROYUKI, critical care physician; b. Yokohama, Kanagawa, Japan, Mar. 31, 1954; s. Kiyoyuki and Katsuko Tanaka; m. Hiroko Beppu, Dec. 20, 1981; children: Takeshi, Masashi. MD, PhD, Kitasato U., Sagamihara, Japan, 1990. Resident Kitasato U. Hosp., Sagamihara, 1978—79; fellow Sakakibara Heart Inst., Tokyo, 1979—81; investigator Kitasato U., Sagamihana, 1981—82; instr. Teikyo U. Med. Sch., 1983—98; assoc. prof. Akita U. Sch. Medicine, 1998—2004; dir. Emergency Med. Svc. Sys., Kishiwada City Hosp., Kishiwada, Osaka, Japan, 2004—06; prof. Kasumigaura Inst. Emergency Med. Svc. Sys., Tokyo Med. U., Ibaraki, Japan, 2006—09; dir. emergency divsn. JR Tokyo Gen. Hosp., 2009—. Author: Servo 900C, 2001, Servo-i, 2006, Benett 840, 2008, Savina, 2011. Recipient promotion for investigation, Japan Surg. Soc., 2002. Fellow: Japanese Soc. Intensive Care Medicine, Japanese Assn. for Acute Medicine; mem.: Japanese So. Emergency Medicine. Home: 5-10 Okusawa 2-chome Setagaya Tokyo 1580083 Japan Office: JR Tokyo Gen Hosp Emergency Divsn 1-3 Yoyogi 2-Chone Shibuya Tokyo 151-8528 Japan Office Phone: 81-3-3320-2200. Business E-Mail: hiroyukitanaka@jreast.co.jp.

TANAKA, KOUICHI ROBERT, hematologist, educator; b. Fresno, Calif., Dec. 15, 1926; s. Kenjiro and Teru (Arai) T.; m. Grace Mutsuko Sakaguchi, Oct. 23, 1965; children: Anne M., Nancy K., David K. BS, Wayne State U., 1949, MD, 1952. Cert. in internal medicine Am. Bd. Internal Medicine, 1961, recertified in internal medicine Am. Bd. Internal Medicine, 1974, cert. in hematology Am. Bd. Internal Medicine, 1972. Intern Los Angeles County Gen. Hosp., 1952—53; resident, fellow Detroit Receiving Hosp., 1953—57; instr. Sch. Medicine UCLA, 1957—59, asst. prof. medicine, 1959—61, assoc. prof. medicine, 1961—68, prof. Sch. Medicine, 1968—97, prof. emeritus, 1998—. Chief hematology divsn. Harbor-UCLA, Torrance, Calif., 1961—97, chief hematology, 1998—2000. Author 137 rsch. publs. Served US Army, 1946—48. Recipient Disting. Alumni Svc. award, Wayne St. U. Sch. Med. Alumni Assn., Med. Alumni Assn. Disting. Svc. award, UCLA. Master ACP (gov. So. Calif. region I 1993-97); mem. Am. Fedn. Med. Rsch., We. Soc. Clin. Investigation, Am. Soc. Hematology, Internat. Soc. Hematology, We. Assn. Physicians, Am. Soc. Clin. Investigation, Assn. Am. Physicians, Sigma Xi, Alpha Omega Alpha. Achievements include research on red cell metabolism. Home: 4 Cayuse Ln Rancho Palos Verdes CA 90275-5172 Office: LA Bio Med Res Inst Harber UCLA Med Ctr Torrance CA 90502 Home Phone: 310-377-7687; Office Phone: 310-222-3695.

TANAKA, MIDORI, psychology professor, researcher; b. Meguro, Japan, July 25, 1951; d. Seigo and Reiko Tanaka; m. Ryu Motogi, Apr. 21, 1979; 1 child, Taku Motogi. BA, Ochanomizu U., Tokyo, 1974, MA, 1977. Asst. Ochanomizu U., Tokyo, 1980—82; lectr. Chuo U., Tokyo, 1982—91, Edogawa U., Nagareyama, Japan, 1990—95, assoc. prof. psychology, 1995—2000, prof. psychology, 2000—02, Shukutoku U., Chiba, Japan, 2002—10; prof. Kagawa Nutrition U., Sakado, Saitama, Japan, 2010—. Acad. advisor Bd. Edn., Oimachi, Japan, 1990—2006; dir. planning com. Japan Soc. Devel. Psychol., Tokyo, 2005; councilor Japan Assn. Audio-Visual Edn., 2005. Coauthor: Psychology of Human Development, 1990, Development of Play, 1996, Psychological Way of Viewing Things, 1997; co-editor: Comparative Developmental Psychology (in Japanese), 2001, The Development of Joint Attention (in Japanese), 2004, Psychology of Communication (in Japanese), 2005; consulting ed.: Japanese Jour. Devel. Psychology, 2008. Mem.: Japan Soc. Ednl. Psychology, Japan Soc. Psychology, Soc. of Rsch. in Child Devel. Home: 3-11-16 Higashisugano Ichikawa Chiba 272-0823 Japan Office: Kagawa Nutrition University 3-9-21 Chiyoda Sakado Saitama 350-0288 Japan Office Phone: +81-49-282-3615. Personal E-mail: ghh07725@nifty.ne.jp. Business E-Mail: midorit@eiyo.ac.jp.

TANAKA, NOBUYUKI, rheumatologist; b. Fukagawa City, Japan, June 2, 1957; s. Koji and Takako Tanaka; m. Kumiko Shimada, Nov. 23, 1987. MD, Sapporo Med. U., 1983, PhD, 1987. Diplomate orthopedic surgery, bd. cert. instr. rheumatology, bd. cert. rheumatology, bd. cert. orthopedic surgery. Head orthop. surgery Kushiro Red Cross Gen. Hosp., Kushiro, Japan, 1989—90, Hakodate Goryoukaku Gen. Hosp., Hakodate, Japan, 1990—91; head orthop, surgery Asahikawa Kousei Gen. Hosp., Hadodate, 1991—92; resident N.Y. Med. Coll., NYC, 1992—95; assoc. prof. dept. orthop. surgery Sapporo Med. U., Sapporo, Japan, 1995—99; v.p. Sapporo Gorinbashi Orthop. Hosp., 1999—2006; dir. Motomachi Orthop. Clinic, Sapporo, 2006—. Contbr. articles to profl. jours. Mem.: Japanese Soc. Joint Diseases (councilor), Japan Coll. Rheumatology (councilor). Office: Motomachi Orthopedic Clinic 1-11 N 21 E 16 Higashi-ku Sapporo 065-0021 Japan Office Phone: 011-781-6151. Personal E-mail: nobuyuki.tanaka@ryumachi-jp.com.

TANAKA, YASUO, otorhinolaryngology educator; b. Kyoto, Kansai, Japan, Mar. 14, 1931; s. Shuichiro and Take (Kamio-Tanaka) T.; m. Reiko Nakagawa, Oct. 3, 1960; 1 child, Akio. MD, Kyoto Prefecture U. Medicine, 1956, PhD, 1964. Instr. otolaryngology Kyoto Prefecture U. Medicine, 1959-63, vis. assoc. prof., 1967-75; instr. physiology Tokyo Med. and Dental U., 1963-65; asst. rsch. scientist NYU, NYC, 1965-67; vis. assoc. prof. Tsurumi U. Sch. Dentistry, Yokohama, Japan, 1975-79; assoc. prof. Dokkyo U. Sch. Medicine, Tochigi, Japan, 1979-83, prof., 1983-96, prof. emeritus, 1996—; spl. prof. Himejv Dokkyou Faculty Healthcare Scis., Hyogo, Japan, 2006—. Head dept. otolaryngology Kaibara Red Cross Hosp., Hyogo Prefecture, Japan, 1961, Yodogawa Christian Hosp., Osaka, Japan, 1961-63, Dokkyo U. Koshigaya Hosp., 1983-96; dir. Nagokakyo City Med. Clinic, 1967-79. Contbr. articles to profl. jours. Grantee Ministry of Edn., Japan, 1985, 88, 89, 90, 91, 94, 95. Mem. Japan Audiol. Soc. (councilor 1993-, del. Otoacoustic Emission sect. 1993-96, 2002—, chmn. com. terminology 1998-2003), Japan Otological Soc. (councilor 1993-97), Soc. Practical Otolaryngology (com. mem. 1993-). Avocation: collecting wooden dharma images. Office: Tanaka ENT Clinic Nagaokakyoshi 4-5 Takenodai Kyoto fu 6170827 Japan E-mail: rya-tnk@blue.vecceed.ne.jp.

TANAKA, YUGO, physician; b. Kobe, June 11, 1977; MD, Kobe U., 2002; PhD, Kobe U. Grad. Sch., 2009. Med. staff Hyogo Cancer Ctr., 2009—. Office: 7-5-2 Kusunoki-cho Chuo-ku Kobe Hyogo 650-0017 Japan

TANAKA, YUICHIRO, medical researcher; b. Japan, June 4, 1965; PhD, U. Hawaii, 1998. Rsch. scientist Vets. Affairs Med. Ctr. U. Calif., 2004—. Asst. rschr. U. Calif., San Francisco, 2002. Mem.: Am. Assn. Cancer Rsch. Avocation: tennis. Office: 4150 Clement St 112F San Francisco CA 94121 Business E-Mail: yuichiro.tanaka@ucsf.edu.

TANAKA, YUMIKO OISHI, radiologist; d. Isamu and Fujie Tanaka; m. Mitsunobu Oishi, July 6, 1991. MD, U. Tsukuba, Japan, 1988, PhD, 1998. Cert. physician Health, Labor and Welfare Ministry/Japan, 1988, bd. radiology Japan Radiol. Soc., 1993. Resident U. Tsukuba, 1988—94; clin. fellow Tsukuba Med. Ctr., 1994—97; asst. prof. U. Tsukuba, 1997—. Presenter in field. Contbr. articles to profl. jours.; mem. editl. bd.: European Radiology, 2006—10. Recipient Cert. of Merit, Radiol. Soc. N.Am., 2003, 2009. Mem.: Radiol. Soc. N.Am. (corr.). Office: Univ Tsukuba 1-1-1 Tennodai Ibaraki 305 8575 Japan Office Phone: 81-29-853-3205. Office Fax: +81-29-853-3205. Personal E-mail: ytanaka@md.tsukuba.ac.jp.

TANAKA-AZUMA, YUKIMASA, pharmacologist, biochemist, microbiologist, researcher; b. Sakai, Osaka, Japan, Mar. 7, 1964; m. Hiromi Tanaka, Mar. 3, 1991; children: Miki Tanaka, Seiya Tanaka. BSc, Konan U., Kobe, Japan, 1986, MSc, 1988; PhD, Okayama U., Okayama, Japan, 2000. Rschr. Ctrl. Rsch. Inst. Nissin Food Products, Co., Ltd., Kusatsu, Shiga, Japan, 1988—95, supr., 1995—2000, asst. mgr., 2000—02, asst. mgr., Food Safety Rsch. Inst., 2002—08, Nissin Food Holdings, Co., Ltd., 2008—; rsch. student Japan Collection of Microorganisms, RIKEN, Wako, Saitama, Japan, 1999—2000. Mem.: The Japanese Soc. Food Sci. and Tech., The Japanese Pharmacol. Soc. Office: Food Safety Rsch Inst Nissin Food Holdings Co Ltd 7-4-1 Nojihigashi Kusatsu 525-0058 Japan Office Phone: 81-77-561-9114. Business E-Mail: y-azuma@nissinfoods-holdings.co.jp.

TANCREDI, LAURENCE RICHARD, medical educator, psychiatrist; b. Hershey, Pa., Oct. 15, 1940; s. Samuel N. and Alvesta (Pera) T. AB in English, Franklin and Marshall Coll., 1962; MD, U. Pa., 1966; JD, Yale U., 1972. Diplomate Am. Bd. Neurology and Psychiatry; Bar: N.Y. 1982. Sr. profl. assoc. Inst. Medicine, NAS, Washington, 1972-74; fellow in psychiatry Columbia U. Coll. Physicians and Surgeons, NYC, 1974-75; postdoctoral fellow in psychiatry Yale U. Med. Sch., New Haven, 1975-77; assoc. prof. psychiatry Med. Sch. NYU, NYC, 1977-84; Kraft Eidman prof. medicine and law U. Tex. Health Sci. Ctr., Houston, 1984-92, dir. health law program, 1983-92; clin. prof. psychiatry NYU, 1992—; clin. prof. health care scis. U. Calif., San Diego, 1993—2003; mem. staff Brookhaven Nat. Labs. Clin. Ctr., 1994-96; pvt. practice NYC, 1994—. V.p. bd. dirs. Internat. Acad. Law and Mental Health, 1987—95, bd. dirs., 2002—07, v.p., 2003—07; mem. adv. com. on transplantations Health Care Fin. Adminstrn., Dept. Health and Human Svcs., 1981—84; mem. nat. adv. bd. NIMH Ctr. Study of Pub. Mental Health N.Y. State Office Mental Health, 1994—99; cmty. svcs. bd. Dept. Mental Health, Mental Retardation and Alcohol Svcs., City of N.Y., 1995—2001; mem. sci. adv. com. Am. Suicide Found., 1995—; cons. Commn. on Med. Profl. Liability; co-prin., investigator study ABA, 1978—80; cons. in field. Fellow: Am. Coll. Psychiatry, N.Y. Acad. Med. Office: 129B E 71st St New York NY 10021-4201 Office Phone: 212-288-5197. Personal E-mail: lrtancredi@yahoo.com.

TANDLER, BERNARD, cell biology educator; b. Bklyn., Feb. 18, 1933; s. Arthur and Pauline (Solomon) T.; m. Helen Weisman, Dec. 25, 1955 (dec. Aug. 14, 1986); children: Janice Dena, Evan Charles. BS, Bklyn. Coll., 1955; AM, Columbia U., 1957; PhD, Cornell U., 1961; DMD (hon.), U. Cagliari, 1997. Instr. anatomy NYU, NYC, 1962-63; assoc. Sloan Kettering Inst., 1963-67; asst. prof. cell biology Cornell U., NYC, 1965-67; assoc. prof. Case Western Res. U., Cleve., 1967-72, prof. oral biology, 1972-91, acting chmn. dept. oral biology, 1987-89. Affiliate prof. oral biology U. Wash., Seattle, 1993—; vis. prof. U. Copenhagen, 1973, U. Cagliari, 1983, Kyushu Dental Coll., 1994-98, bio. sci. Case We. Res. U., 2003—; sr. rsch. scientist Tex. Tech U., Lubbock, 1999-01; cons. NIH, NSF, VA. Author: (with C.L. Hoppel) Mitochondria, 1972; assoc. editor: Anatomical Record, 1974-98; guest editor: Microscopy Rsch. and Technique, 1993-94, European Jour. Morphology, 1995-2000, 02—; contbr. chpts. to books, articles to profl. jours. Recipient Disting. Alumnus award Bklyn. Coll., 1981, Robert E. Kennedy award for Acad. Freedom, Ohio chpt. AAUP, 1992, Disting. Scientist award Am. Assn. Dental Rsch., 1999; USPHS fellow, 1957-62. Mem. Am. Assn. Anatomists, Am. Soc. Cell Biology, Electron Microscopy Soc. Am., Japanese Soc. Oral Biology, Japanese Assn. Anatomists, Internat. Assn. Dental Rsch. (Disting. Scientist award 1999) Am. Soc. Mammalogists, Italian Soc. Anatomy (hon.), Sigma Xi. Office Phone: 216-368-0563. Business E-Mail: bernard.tandler@case.edu.

TANDON, NITIN, neurosurgeon, educator; b. India, Sept. 1, 1970; MD, Armed Forces Med. Coll., 1992. Assoc. prof. UTHSCH, 2004—. Office: 6400 Fannin Ste 2800 Houston TX 77030 Office Fax: 713-500-5456. Business E-Mail: nitin.tandon@uth.tmc.edu.

TANEJA, SAMIR, urologist; Attended, Northwestern U. Med. Sch., 1986—90. Diplomate Am. Bd. Urology, 2009. Resident UCLA Med. Ctr., 1992—96; chief urology sect. Veterans Administrn. NY Harbor Healthcare System, Manhattan. Chair Am. Bd. Urology Exam Com.; assoc. prof. urologic oncology NYU Langone Med. Ctr., dir. divsn. of urologic oncology; program leader Genitourinary Oncology Program NYU Cancer Inst.; weekly host The Men Health show Sirius/XM satelite radio. Author over 110 articles, 20 book chpts. and 5 textbooks; editor: (books) 3rd Edit. Complications of Urologic Surgery: Prevention and Diagnosis, 4th Edit. Complications of Urologic Surgery: Prevention and Diagnosis. Mem.: Urologic Rsch. Soc. (sec. gen.), Soc. for Urologic Oncology (program chair and exec. com. mem.), Oncology Task Force. Office: New York Presbyterian Hospital 525 E 68th St New York NY 10021 Office Phone: 212-746-5454.

TANERI, SUPHI, ophthalmic surgeon, researcher; b. Nicosia, Cyprus, July 23, 1971; MD, Westfälische Wilhelms U., Münster, Germany, 1997. Facharzt für Augenheilkunde Germany, 2003. Trainee Mass. Eye and Ear Infirmary, Schepen's Eye Rsch. Inst., Harvard Med. Sch., Boston, 2002; mng. ptnr. Zentrum für Refraktive Chirurgie, Münster, 2003—; ptnr. Eye Dept. at St. Franziskus Hosp., Münster, 2003—. Asst. editor: Mid. East Jour. Ophthalmology; contbr. chapters to books, articles to profl. jours. Mem.: German Commn. for Refractive Surgery, German Ophthalmologic Soc., European Soc. Cataract and Refractive Surgery, Am. Soc. Cataract and Refractive Surgery. Achievements include patents pending for field of refractive eye surgery. Office: Zentrum für Refraktive Chirurgie Münster Hohenzollernring 57 48145 Münster Germany Office Fax: +492519877898. Business E-Mail: mail@refraktives-zentrum.de.

TANG, CHIH-HSIN, medical educator; s. Zhu-Kui Tang and Xue-Mei Lee; m. Yu-Ting Lin, Oct. 28, 2007. PhD, Nat. Taiwan U., Taipei, 2005. Cert. pharmacist Dept. Health, Taiwan, 1996. Tchg. asst. Nat. Taiwan U., 2003—05, postdoc. fellow, 2005—06; asst. prof. China Med. U., Taichung, Taiwan, 2006—. Recipient Outstanding Rsch. award, Coll. Medicine, Nat. Taiwan U., 2003, 2004, Taiwanese Osteoporosis Assn., 2004, 2005, 2006, Internat. award, Japanese Assn. Lab. Animal Sci., 2006, Rsch. Award, Taiwan Assn. Lab. Animal Sci., 2006, Best Rsch. Award, Tien-Te Lee Found., 2006; named Young Investigator award, Taiwan Pharmacological Soc., 2007. Office: China Med Univ 91 Hsueh-Shih Rd Taichung 404 Taiwan Office Phone: 886-4-22052121-7726.

TANG, GAUJUN-, hospital administrator; Clin. fellow Johns Hopkins Hosp., 1990—91; attending physician Veterans Gen. Hosp., Taipei, Taiwan, 1991—96; supt. I-Lan Hosp., Taiwan, 2001—07, Taipei city hosp., Zhongxiao, Taiwan, 2007—08, Nat. Yang-Ming Univ. Hosp., Taiwan, 2008—. Clin. fellow Univ. of Pitts., 1998; prof. Nat. Yang-Ming Univ., Taiwan, 1999—2001. Office: National Yang Ming University Hospital No. 152 Xin Min Rd I-Lan 26042 Taiwan Office Phone: 88639325192. *

TANG, HAO, preventive medicine physician, research scientist; m. Xiang Xu; 1 child, Grace Jiaming. MD, Shanghai Med. U., Shanghai, China, 1995; PhD, U. Ala. Birmingham, Birmingham, AL, 2001. Preventive physician Divsn. Health, Shanghai Rlwy. Bur., Shanghai, Shanghai, 1995—97; rsch. scientist Calif. Dept. Health Serivces, Sacramento, 2000—. Office: Calif Dept Health Svcs PO Box 997413 MS 7206 Sacramento CA 95899-7413

TANG, HUI, orthopedist; b. Chongqing, Aug. 3, 1979; MD, Third Mil. Med. U., 2009. Surgeon, orthop. dept. Kunming Gen. Hosp. Chengdu Mil. Command, 2003—. Office: Da Guan St Kunming Yunnan 650032 China Business E-Mail: tanghui9791@sina.com.

TANG, JIANMING (JAMES TANG), biology professor; b. Hunan, China, July 12, 1965; DVM, Beijing Agrl. U., 1986; PhD, U. Queensland, 1993. Asst. prof U. Ala., Birmingham, 1996—2004, assoc prof, 2004—. Editl. adv. bd. Jour. Infectious Diseases, 2005—10; editl. bd. Genes and Immunity (Nature Pub. Group), 2005—. Grant, Nat. Cancer Inst., Nat. Inst. Allergy and Infectious Diseases. Mem.: Am. Soc. Histocompatibility and Immunogenetics, Am. Soc. Microbiology. Avocations: reading, fishing, photography. Office: 1665 University Blvd Birmingham AL 35294 Office Fax: 205-934-8665. Business E-Mail: jtang@uab.edu.

TANG, JING-SHI, medical educator; b. Shaanxi, China, Nov. 7, 1937; MD, Xi'an Med. Coll., 1963. Prof. Xi'an Jiaotong U. Sch. Medicine, 1995—. Recipient award, Chinese Sci. Large Meeting, 1978, Shaanxi Province Govt., 2006, Chinese Med. Soc., 2008. Mem.: Pain Medicine Soc. China, Neuroscience Soc. China, Physiol. Sci. Soc. China. Avocations: theater, fishing. Office: Yanta St W 76 Xi'an Shaanxi 710061 China Office Fax: 029-82656364. Business E-Mail: jstang@mail.xjtu.edu.cn.

TANG, PAK-LAI, physiologist, researcher; b. Happy Valley, Hong Kong, Oct. 20, 1939; d. Kwok-Yip Tang and Yuk-Yin Tam. BSc in Chemistry and Biology with honors, U. Hong Kong, 1964, post grad. cert. in Sci. Edn., 1974, PhD in Med. Physiology, 1986. Cert. in neuro-linguistic programming 2003, in animal diseases affecting humans 2007, in electron microscopy U. Wales, 1991. Sr. grad. master pre-med. course Kau Yan Coll., Hong Kong, 1964—70, St. Joseph's Coll., Hong Kong, 1970—79; lectr. then sr. lectr. Hong Kong Polytechnic U., 1979—81, prin. lectr. physiology, 1981—85, assoc. dean and prof., 1993—99, prof. physiology and dir., 1999—2002, vis. prof. nursing, 2002—; bd. dir. Clark Inst. Psychiatry, U. Toronto, 1993—98; vis. prof. nursing, dir. centralised animal facilities Australian Cath. U., Melbourne; head cluster sci. tech. Coll. profl. and Continuing Edn., Hongkong Poly. U. Hon. prof. physiology Qingdao Med. Sch., China, 1992—, Hong Kong U., 1992—; external examiner Open U. Hong Kong, 1999—2005; tech. advisor traditional Chinese medicine Shan Xi U. Traditional Chinese Medicine, China, 2003—; dir. Centralized Animal Facilities, 2005—08. Co-author: Notes in Neuroscience I and II, 1990; co-editor: A Universal Photoperiodic Signal with Diverse Actions, 1996. Tourists amb. Hong Kong Tourism Bd., 1991—; mem. curriculum devel. coun. Hong Kong Govt., 1990—2000, mem. obscene articles tribunal, 1996—. Recipient Pres. award for outstanding svc., Hong Kong Polytechnic U., 1998; named Outstanding Biologist, Am. Optical Inc., 1974. Fellow: Royal Soc. Health, U.K. (local rep. 1982—2000); mem.: China Physiology Assn., Hong Kong Soc. Immunology, Hong Kong Soc. Neurosci., European Pineal and Biological Rhythms Soc., Inst. Biology, China Sleep Rsch. Assn., Asia Assn. Biology Edn. (chmn. exec. com. 1986—2002), N.Y. Acad. Scis., Asia & Oceania Soc. Comparative Endocrinology Australia (mem. exec. com. 1996—2008), Gastro-intestinal and Endocrinology Assn., China (mem. exec. com. 1994—), Internat. Brain Orgn. U.S. (local rep. 1980—2008). Avocations: swimming, basketball, soccer, horticulture, Chinese painting. Office: Sch Nursing Hong Kong Polytechnic Univ Faculty Health Social Scis Yuk Choi Rd Hunghom KIN Hong Kong Home: 6A Village Rd. Happy Valley Hong Kong Island Hong Kong Home Phone: 852 2572 1388; Office Phone: 852 2766 6683. Office Fax: 852 2364 9663. Business E-Mail: hspltang@inet.polyu.edu.hk.

TANG, PAUL C., medical administrator, educator; b. May 20, 1953; BS, Stanford U., Calif., 1975, MS, 1976; MD, U. Calif., San Francisco, 1981. Cert. in internal medicine Am. Bd. Internal Medicine, Pa., 1984. Program mgr. Hewlett-Packard Laboratories, Palo Alto, Calif., 1984—94; assoc. prof. medicine Northwestern U. Med. Sch., Chgo., 1994—98; med. dir., info. systems Northwestern Meml. Hosp., Chgo., 1994—98; v.p. Epic Rsch. Inst., Mountain View, Calif., 1998—2000; v.p., chief med. info. officer Palo Alto Med. Found., Mountain View, 1998—; consulting assoc. prof. medicine Stanford U. Sch. Medicine, 2007—. Chmn. Am. Med. Informatics Assn., Bethesda, Md., 2006—07. Fellow: ACP, Healthcare Info. Mgmt. Systems Soc., Coll. Healthcare Info. Mgmt. Execs., Am. Coll. Med. Informatics; mem.: Inst. Medicine. Achievements include research in electronic health records and decision support; personal health records and disease management; patents for clinical decision support. Avocation: photography. Office: Palo Alto Medical Found 2350 W El Camino Real Mountain View CA 94040 Business E-Mail: paultang@stanford.edu.

TANG, SHAOTAO, surgeon; b. Wuhan, Hubei, China, Dec. 9, 1964; MD, Tongji Med. Coll. Huazhong U. Sci. & Tech., 1998. Sect. leader pediat. surgery Wuhan Union Hosp., 1998—. Prof., dept. pediat. Surgery Wuhan Union Hosp., 1998—; standing bd. mem. Chinese Jour. Pediat. Surgery, 1998—; bd. mem. Jour. China Pediat. Blood and Cancer, 2003—, Chinese Jour. Minimally Invasive Surgery, 2004—. Recipient 1st prize, People's Govt. Hubei, Endoes Med. Sci. & Tech. award, World Endoscopy Orgn. Master: Funnel Chest Treatment Ctr. Hubei; fellow: Hubei Soc. Pediat. Surgery, Endoscopic Profl. Com. Chinese MD Assn.; mem.: Hubei Soc. Laparoscopic Surgery, Hubei Jiusan Soc. Office: JieFang Ave Wuhan Hubei 430022 China Personal E-mail: tshaotao83@yahoo.com.cn.

TANG, WEI, research scientist; PhD, U. BC, 1996. Rsch. fellow, sr. rsch. fellow Merck & Co., 1996—2005, dir., 2005—06, disting. sr. investigator, 2006—. Mem.: Internat. Soc. for Study of Xenobiotics. Office: RY 80 171 Merck & Co Rahway NJ 07065 Business E-Mail: wei_tang@merck.com.

TANG, XIAOLEI, immunologist; s. Hui Tang and Jiafen Yu; m. Yan Xie; m. Dongqin Zhang (div.); children: Wade X., Liyan. MD, Wannan Med. Coll., Wu Hu, An Hui Province, China, 1988, MS, Fudan Med. Sch. (formerly Shanghai Med. U.), China, 1993; PhD, U. Ariz., Tucson, 2001. Cert. in immunology Chinese Acad. Scis., 1996, methods in cell and molecular biology Adademia Sinica Max-Planck Guest Lab., 1996. Physician Huang-Shan City Hosp., An Hui Province, China, 1988—90; ms candidate in microbiology and immunology Fudan Med. Sch., Shanghai, 1990—93, lectr. and scientist, 1993—97; postdoc. fellow Torrey Pines Inst. for Molecular Studies, San Diego, 2002—06; rsch. fellow Harvard Med. Sch., Dana-Farber Cancer Inst., Boston, 2006—10; asst. prof. U. Tex., El Paso, 2010—. Recipient Outstanding Student, Shanghai Bur. Edn., 1991, Outstanding Student Shanghai Med. U., Fudan Med. Sch., 1992. Mem.: Reuters Insight. Achievements include research in Definition of pathogenic role of newly discovered soluble survival factors from accessory cells in autoimmune diseases; discovery and cloning of a new subset of regulatory CD8 T cells bearing CD8alphaalpha homodimer and cloning technology for studying Qa-1 restricted CD8 T cells; development of Qa-1 tetramer strategy for the study of Qa-1 restricted CD8+ T cells; definition of mechanisms leading to preferential killing of T helper 1 cells by Qa-1 restricted CD8+ T cells. Avocations: soccer, basketball, tennis. Office: University Tex El Paso Biol Sci Bldg Rm 4122 El Paso TX 79968 Office Fax: 617-632-4630. Personal E-mail: charles.x.l.tang@cheerful.com. Business E-Mail: xtang@utep.edu.

TANG, YAO LIANG, medical educator, researcher, surgeon; b. Shanghai, July 14, 1970; s. HaiChuan Tang and MeiJuan Liang; m. Yan Shen, Oct. 27, 2000; 1 child, SongTing. MD, Shanghai 2nd Med. U., 1993; PhD, Fudan U., Shanghai, 2002. Diplomate physician Ministry of Health P.R. China, 2000. Cardiac surgeon Shanghai Inst. of Cardiovasc. Diseases, Shanghai, Shanghai, 1997—2002; postdoctoral fellow Univeristy of South Fla., St. Petersburg, 2003—04; asst. prof. U. of South Fla., Tampa, 2004—; postdoctoral fellow U. of Fla., Gainesville. Ad hoc reviewer Can. Inst. of Health Rsch. (CIHR), Ottawa, Ont., 2005—, Nat. Med. Rsch. Coun. (NMRC), Singapore, 2005—. Contbr. articles to profl. jours. Recipient Outstanding Postdoctoral Fellow Rsch. award, Am. Heart Assn. (Fla./Puerto Rico Affiliate), 2003, Young Investigator award, Am. Coll. of Cardiology Found., 2004, Dr. Jeff Isner Young Investigator award, Mass. Gen. Hosp., 2004, Melvin L. Marcus award, Am. Heart Assn., 2004. Mem.: Am. Heart Assn., Sigma Xi (Outstanding Postdoctoral Fellow award 2004). Buddhism. Achievements include patents pending for vigilant cell system for enhancing grafted cell survial in ischemic myocardium; stem cell beacon system for targeting stem cells to ischemic myocardium for repair; vigilant vector for cardioprotection; invention of adult cardiac stem cells for heart repair. Avocations: swimming, travel. Office: Keck Grad Inst Applied Life Scis 535 Watson Dr Claremont CA 91711 Home: 6751 Dawson Rd Cincinnati OH 45243-2419 E-mail: tangyl888@hotmail.com.

TANGALOS, ERIC G., internist, geriatrician, educator; MD, Stritch Sch. Medicine. Cert. geriatric medicine Am. Bd. Internal Medicine. Fellow Mayo Grad. Sch. Medicine; med. dir. Bethany Samaritan Heights, 1981—; prof. medicine Mayo Clinic, chmn. dept. primary care internal medicine, 1997—2006. Fellow: Am. Coll. Physicians (former gov.); mem.: Alzheimer's Assn., Am. Med. Dirs. Assn. (former pres.). Office: 200 First St SW Rochester MN 55905

TANGJITGAMOL, SIRIWAN, obstetrician, gynecologist; b. Bangkok, Dec. 23, 1959; MD, Gullas Coll. Medicine, 1988; degree in Ob-gyn., Vajira Hosp., 1995. Physician, faculty medicine Vajira Hosp., U. Bangkok Metropolis, 1996—2011. Mem.: Royal Thai Coll. Obstetricians and Gynecologists. Office: 681 Samsen Rd Dusit Vajira Bangkok 10300 Thailand Office Fax: 66-2-2437907. Personal E-mail: siriwanonco@yahoo.com.

TANIGUCHI, KIKUYO, immunologist, educator; b. Kukachyo, Japan, Sept. 19, 1950; d. Tsuguo Yoshikawa and Takayuki Taniguchi (Stepfather), Kazuko Taniguchi (Stepmother); m. Kenji Taniguchi, June 2, 1974; children: Tetsuji, Takashi, Misato. B, Hiroshima U., 1974, PhD, 2000. Lectr. immunology Hirosha Coll. Med. Tech., 1974; rsch. fellow Hiroshima U., 1993—, chief sch. affairs, 2003—. Achievements include research in Production of neutrophil-specific monoclonal antibodies, TAG1, TAG2, TAG3, TAG4 and TAG5. Avocations: reading, movies. Office: Hiroshima Coll Med Tech 1-1 Honmachi Sagata Hatsukaichi 738-8504 Japan Office Fax: 0829-32-7242. E-mail: tkiku@mth.biglobe.ne.jp.

TANIMOTO, HITOSHI, medical researcher; s. Shigeyuki and Ikuko Tanimoto. MD, Kobe U., Japan, 1995. Cert. specialist Oto-Rhino-Laryngological Soc. Japan, Inc., 2001. Rsch. assoc. Kobe U., 2003—. Office Phone: 81-78-382-5111. Business E-Mail: tanimoto@med.kobe-u.ac.jp.

TANIMURA, SHINYA, surgeon; b. Kochi, Japan, Oct. 25, 1960; s. Shiro and Aiko Tanimura; m. Chieko Kaneyasu; children: Yuka, Misaki. PhD, Tokushima U., Japan, 1985. Dir., surgery Osaka City Gen. Hosp., Japan, 1993—2008; dir., endoscopic surgery Kariya Toyota Gen. Hosp., Aichi, Japan, 2008—. Office: Kariya Toyota Gen Hosp 5-15 Sumiyoshicho Kariya Aichi 448-8505 Japan Office Phone: 81-566-21-2450. Office Fax: 81-566-22-2493. Personal E-mail: stoghjpn@aol.com.

TANINO, HIROMASA, orthopedist; b. Japan, Nov. 5, 1969; MD, Asahikawa Med. U., 1996, PhD. Rsch. fellow Lab. Orthop. Rsch., Good Samaritan Med. Ctr., West Palm Beach, Fla., 2003—04; rsch. scholar Dept. Mech. & Aerospace Engring., U. Fla., 2004—05; asst. prof. Dept. Arthroplasty, Asahikawa Med. U., 2006—08, sr. asst. prof., 2008. Com. mem. Hokkaido Transnational Rsch., 2007, Eastern Japan Assn. Orthops. and Traumatology, 2010; editl. bd. mem. Jour. Arthroplasty, 2008. Mem.: Japan Orthop. Assn. Office: Midorigaoka-Higashi 2-1-1-1 Asahikawa Hokkaido 078-8510 Japan Office Phone: 81-166-68-2511. Office Fax: 81-166-68-2519. E-mail: taninohiromasa@hotmail.com.

TANIYAMA, KIYOMI, oncologist, director; b. Japan, Mar. 2, 1954; MD, Hiroshima U., PhD, 1978. Dir. Nat. Hosp. Orgn. Kure Med. Ctr., Chugoku Cancer Ctr., 2002—. Clin. prof. Hiroshima U. Sch. Medicine. Recipient award, Japanese Breast Cancer Soc., 2009. Office: 3-1 Aoyama-cho Kure Hiroshima 7370023 Japan Office Fax: 81-823-22-3273. Business E-Mail: taniyamak@kure-nh.go.jp.

TANK, ROD GAILLARD, orthopaedic physical therapist; b. Harlan, Iowa, Jan. 12, 1947; s. Gaillard B. and Irene B. (Thraen) T.; m. M. Sue Howard, Dec. 15, 1972; children: Karynn S., Brad S. BS, U. Nebr., 1970; grad. in phys. therapy, Mayo Clinic, Rochester, Minn., 1972; MPA, Tex. Tech U., 1979. Dir. phys. therapy VA Hosp., Big Spring, Tex., 1974-76, Tex. Tech U. Sch. Medicine, Lubbock, 1976-78; exec. dir. ambulatory clinics Tex. Tech U. Health Sci. Ctr., 1980-82; asst. hosp. adminstr. Rosewood Hosp., Houston, 1982-83; COO AMI Heights Hosp., Houston, 1983-90, Winona Meml. Hosp., Indpls., 1990-92; sr. phys. therapist Physiotherapy Assocs., Indpls., 1992-97; clin. dir. Replay Physical Therapy, Noblesville, Ind., 1997—2008; phys. therapist St. Vincent Hosp., Indpls., 2008—. Ch. lector, mem. parish coun. Our Lady of Mt. Carmel Cath. Ch., Carmel, Ind., 1993-95. Maj. USAR, 1976-86. Mem. Am. Phys. Therapy Assn. (cert. orthopaedic clin. specialist), Am. Coll. Healthcare Execs. (diplomate), Am. Acad. Orthop. Manual Phys. Therapists. Avocations: running, reading, Karate, martial arts. Home: 13772 Laredo Dr Carmel IN 46032-5257 Office: Saint Vincent Outpatient 9012 E 126th St Fishers IN 46038 Office Phone: 317-415-6510.

TANNA, ANGELO PETER, ophthalmologist, educator, researcher; BA, Johns Hopkins U., 1989; MD, Columbia U. Coll. of Physicians and Surgeons, 1994. Glaucoma Fellowship Johns Hopkins Hosp. / Md., 1999. Internship Grad. Hosp., Md., 1995; ophthalmology residency Wilmer Eye Inst., Md., 1998; attending ophthalmologist Johns Hopkins Bayview Med. Ctr., Baltimore, Md., 1998—99; dir., glaucoma svc. Northwestern Med. Faculty Found., Chicago, Ill., 1999—; asst. prof. of ophthalmology Northwestern U. Feinberg Sch. of Medicine, Chicago, Ill., 1999—; vice chmn. dept. ophthalmology Northwestern U. Feinberg Sch. Medicine. Dir., glaucoma svc. Northwestern Med. Faculty Found., Chicago, Ill., 1999—; editl. bd. mem. Survey of Ophthalmology, Brookline, Mass., 2000—. Contbr. articles various profl. jours. Recipient Frey prize in engring., Northwestern U., 2003, Achievement award, Am. Acad. Ophthal., 2009; named to Best Drs. in America, Best Drs., Inc., 2005—10. Fellow: Am. Acad. Ophthalmology; mem.: Ophthalmology Mgmt. (editl. bd. mem. 2007—), Am. Glaucoma Soc. (bd. dirs. 2010—), Alpha Omega Alpha. Office: NW Med Faculty Found 675 N Saint Clair Ste 15-150 Chicago IL 60611 Office Phone: 312-908-8152.

TANNEN, RICHARD LAURENCE, nephrology educator, clinical epidemiologist; b. NYC, Aug. 31, 1937; s. Harold and Fannie (Rosenberg) T.; m. Elizabeth Whitney Harriman, Aug. 8, 1964 (div. Apr. 1990); m. Vivien Baraban, Nov. 17, 1990; children: Bradford, Whitney, Jennifer, Alison, Julie. Student, Vanderbilt U., 1957; MD, U. Tenn., Memphis, 1960. Rsch. internist Walter Reed Inst. Rsch., Washington, 1966-69; assoc. prof., co-dir. nephrology unit U. Vt., Burlington, 1969-78; prof., chief nephrology divsn. U. Mich., Ann Arbor, 1978-88; prof., chmn. dept. medicine U. So. Calif., LA, 1988-95; vice dean for rsch. U. Pa., Phila., 1995-97, prof. medicine, 1995—, sr. vice-dean, 1997—2002. Established investigator Am. Heart Assn., 1971-76. Co-editor: Fluids and Electrolytes, 1986, 3d edit., 1996; contbr. more than 130 sci. articles to profl. jours. Maj. U.S. Army, 1966-69. Recipient Merit award NIH, 1986-94, Disting. Alumnus award U. Tenn., 1991. Fellow ACP; mem. Am. Soc. Nephrology (pres. 1991-92), Am. Soc. Clin. Investigation, Assn. Am. Physicians, Nat. Kidney Found. (regional v.p. 1984-87, Pres.'s award 1986). Jewish. Avocations: tennis, travel. Office: U Pa Sch of Med 295 John Morgan Bldg Philadelphia PA 19104 Office Phone: 215-898-2270. Business E-Mail: tannen@mail.med.upenn.edu.

TANNER, MARTIN ABBA, statistician, educator; b. Highland Park, Ill., Oct. 19, 1957; s. Meir and Esther Rose (Bauer) T.; m. Anat Talitman, Aug. 14, 1984; 1 child, Noam Ben. BA, U. Chgo., 1978, PhD, 1982. Asst. prof. stats. and human oncology U. Wis., Madison, 1982-87, assoc. prof., 1987-90; dir. lab., prof. and dept. chair biostatistics U. Rochester, 1990-94; prof. dept. statistics Northwestern U., 1994—. Cons. Kirkland & Ellis, 1980-82; mem. Nat. Inst. Allergy and Infectious diseases study sect., 1994-98; reviewer NIH, NSF, VA. Assoc. editor Jour. Am. Stat. Assn., 1987-99; editor Jour. Am. Statis. Assn., 1999-03, Chapman & Hall, 2002-; contbr. articles to profl. jours. Recipient New Investigator Rsch. award NIH, 1984, Mortimer Spiegelman award Am. Pub. Health Assn., 1993; NSF grantee, 1983, 95, NIH grantee, 1986—. Fellow Royal Statis. Soc., Am. Statis. Assn. (Continuing Edn. Excellence award); mem. AAAS, Mensa, Sigma Xi. Avocations: poetry, guitar. Office: Northwestern U 2006 Sheridan Rd Evanston IL 60208-0852 Home Phone: 847-491-2700; Office Phone: 847-491-2700. Business E-Mail: mat132@northwestern.edu.

TANODEKAEW, SIRIPORN, research scientist; b. Samutsakhon, Thailand, Dec. 13, 1969; PhD, U. Manchester, 1995. Prin. rschr. Nat. Metal and Materials Tech. Ctr., 1995—. Business E-Mail: siriporn@mtec.or.th.

TANOOKA, HIROSHI, retired research scientist; b. Tanabe, Wakatama, Japan, Jan. 26, 1931; MS, Nagoya U., 1955; PhD, U. Rochester, 1962. Chief radiobiology divsn. Nat. Cancer Ctr., 1970—93; rsch. advisor Ctrl. Rsch. Inst. Electric Power Industry, 1993—2001. Mem. bd. dirs. Radiation Effects Assn., 1993—2011. Home: 2-12-17 Sugano Ichikawa Chiba 272-0824 Japan Home Fax: 81-47-321-3712. E-mail: tanooka-h@wind.ocn.ne.jp.

TANPHAICHITR, KONGSAK, rheumatologist, allergist, immunologist, internist; b. Bangkok, Feb. 22, 1946; came to U.S., 1971; s. Boonchoo and Hong (Nayakovit) T.; m. Sirirat Tareesung, June 17, 1973; children: Saksiri Marc, Marisa. Student, Mahidol U., Bangkok, Thailand, 1964-66, MD cum laude, 1970; PhD in Sci. Communication (hon.), Rajapat Surin U., Thailand, 2010. Diplomate Am. Bd. Internal Medicine, Am. Bd. Rheumatology, Am. Bd. Allergy and Immunology; cert. Rheumatologist Royal Coll. Physicians Can. Straight med. intern Detroit Gen. Hosp.-Wayne State U., 1971-72; resident Barnes Hosp.-Washington U., St. Louis, 1972-74, fellow in rheumatology and immunology, 1974-76; instr. in medicine Washington U., 1976-77, asst. prof. medicine, 1977-97, assoc. prof. clin. medicine, 1997—2004, prof. clin. medicine, 2005—; attending physician Barnes Hosp., 1976—, Jewish Hosp. of St. Louis, 1981—. Dir. Allergy, Rheumatology & Immunology Specialists, St. Louis; cons. rheumatology Washington U., St. Louis, 1976—. Author: Amyloid Fibrils in Joint Fluid, 1976, Studies of Tolerance in NZB/NZW Mice, 1977, Vasculitis and Multiple Sclerosis, 1980, Buddhism and Science, 1987, Buddhism: Answers to Common Questions, 1990, Buddhism Answers Life, 1995, 2006, Mindfulness: The Key to Perfect One's Life, 1997, Mind and Universe, Mindfulness and Stress Management, 1998, Awakened Life for the New Millennium, 2000, Ethics and Morality, 2000, Parenting, 2000, Buddhism Beyond Non-Violence, 2001, Mom, 2001, The Best, the Worst and the Horrible of 9/11, 2001, Miracle of the Buddha's Wisdom, 2002, Mindfulness Amidst the Evolving World, 2003, Self-Awareness: The Neglected Essence of Life, 2003, Universal Language, Laws, and Community, 2004, Dharma In Action, 2006; editor: Vipassana 101, 2004, World Peace, 2004, Dependent Arising: Center of all Truths, 2004, Essence of Life: Mindfulness and Self-Awareness, 2005, Buddhism: The Ultimate Self-Improvement System, 2005, Science on Mind & Mindfulness, 2005, Buddhism and Qualia, 2006, Buddhism & Medicine, 2006, How Brain, Mind and Consciousness Work, 2007, PDR on Theravada Buddhism, 2007, The Buddha and Healthcare, 2008, Social Interaction with Mindfulness, 2010, How Buddhism Promotes Peace, Love and Harmony in Our Diverse Society, 2011, Buddhist View on World Religious Founders, 2011; author: Buddhist Genesis Thai, 2009, Mind Science, 2010. Dharma tchr., bd. dirs., sec. Wat Phrasriratanaram Buddhist Temple, St. Louis, 1983—; co-dir. Buddhist Coun., St. Louis, 1985-90; chmn. Buddhist Coun. Greater St. Louis, 1999—. Recipient Dharma Wheel Pillar award, Royal Thai Crown Princess Sirindhorn, 2008; named Am.'s Top Physician, Consumers' Rsch. Coun. Am., 2003—. Fellow: ACP, Royal Coll. Physicians Can., Am. Coll. Rheumatology, Am. Acad. Allergy, Asthma, and Immunology; mem.: Thai-Am. Physicians Found. (treas., bd. dirs. 2000—), Thai Physicians Assn. Am. (treas. Midwest chpt. 1994, sec. Midwest chpt. 1997, nat. treas. 1998, nat. bd. dirs. 1999—2001, nat. treas. 2000), UN Assn. Greater St. Louis (bd. dirs. 2004—07), UN Assn. U.S.A., Thai Assn. Greater St. Louis (pres.), Thai Temple Karate Shorinryu Club (Black Belt). Avocations: Karate, karaoke, insight meditation. Home: 12413 Ladue Rd Saint Louis MO 63141-8100 Office: Allergy Rheum & Immun Specs 11115 New Halls Ferry Rd Florissant MO 63033-7613 Home Phone: 314-878-1014; Office Phone: 314-839-4339. Personal E-mail: kongsakt@sbcglobal.net.

TANRIKUT, CIGDEM, researcher; b. Gainesville, Fla., Oct. 3, 1972; BA, U. Pa., 1993; MD, Georgetown U., 1999. Dir., male reproductive medicine Mass. Gen. Hosp., 2007—. Fellow, male reproductive medicine and microsurgery Weill Cornell Med. Coll., 2006—07, adj. asst. prof., urology and reproductive medicine, 2007; postdoc. fellow Population Coun., 2006—07; asst. prof., surgery Harvard Med. Sch., 2008. Fellow: ACS; mem.: Soc. for Study of Male Reproduction, Sexual Medicine Soc. N.Am., Am. Soc. Reproductive Medicine, Am. Urol. Assn. Office: 55 Fruit St YAW-10A MGH Fertility Ctr Boston MA 02114 Office Fax: 617-724-8882. Business E-Mail: ctanrikut@partners.org.

TANSER, PAUL HARRY, cardiologist, educator; arrived in New Zealand, 2003; s. Harry Ambrose and Isabella Grace Tanser; m. Catherine Lydia Weaver, Sept. 1, 1962; children: Christopher Paul, Carl Rodney. MD magna cum laude, U. Ottawa, 1962. Cert. specialist Royal Coll. Physicians Can., 1967, Quebec Coll., 1969. Intern Royal Victoria Hosp., 1962, resident, 1963—67; commd. lt. Canadian Army, 1984, advanced through grades to maj.; asst. prof. medicine McGill U., Montreal, Quebec, Canada, 1969—75; head of cardiology St. Joseph's Hosp., Hamilton, Canada, 1975—85; assoc. prof. medicine McMaster U., Hamilton, Ont., Canada, 1975—83, prof. medicine, 1983—2003, emeritus prof. medicine; head cardiology Palmerston North (New Zealand) Hosp. Head cardiology rsch. St. Joseph's Hosp., Hamilton, 1975—2003, chief of medicine, 1980—90; sr. cons. in cardiology Waitemata DHB, Auckland, New Zealand, 2005—; cons. in field. Editor (cardiology section): The Merck Manual, 1985—. Maj. Canadian Army, 1991—96, ret. Canadian Army, 1996. Fellow: Internat. Coll. Angiology, Royal Australasian Coll. Physicians, Am. Coll. Physicians (gov. Ont. Chpt. 1999—2003), Royal Coll. Physicians (Can., Glasgow), Am. Coll. Cardiology (gov. Ont. chpt. 2003). Avocations: violin, sailing, tennis, skiing, bicycling. Office: Waitamata District Health Bd North Shore City Auckland New Zealand Business E-Mail: paul.tanser@waitematadhb.govt.nz.

TANYI, RUTH A., family practice nurse practitioner, lifestyle diseases consultant; b. Cameroon, West Africa; arrived in US, 1987, naturalized; d. Johnson and Mercy Tanyi. BS in Journalism, U. Wis. River Falls, 1993; BSN, Met. State U., St. Paul, 1999; MSN, U. Wis. Eau-Claire, 2002; DrPH in Lifestyle Diseases & Prevention, Loma Linda U., Calif. Cert. nurse practitioner, Am. Acad. Nurse Practitioner & Am. Nurses Credentialing Ctr., 2002, health fitness specialist, Am. Coll. Sports Medicine, 2005, nutrition specialist, Am. Coll. Nutrition, 2007. Family nurse practitioner Preventive Care & Wellness Svcs., Loma Linda, Calif., 2002—, lifestyle & disease prevention cons., 2004—; TV exec. prodr. Lifestyle & Preventive Care TV Show, Loma Linda, 2005—. Guest spkr. Radio & Television Programs Lifestyle Related Diseases & Prevention, 2004—; reviewer Jour. Advanced Nursing, 2003—, Jour. Am. Acad. Nurse Practitioner, 2008; med. journalist, host exec. prodr., creator Lifestyle & Preventive Care Television Show, 2005—; key note & plenary spkr., creator Lifestyle & Disease Annual Conf., 2007—; creator Preventive Care Today-Television Show, 2007. Contbr. scientific papers, to numerous sci. poster presentations. Vol. health educator on lifestyle practices & diseases prevention Abundant Living Family Ch., Rancho Cucamonga, Calif., 2008. Recipient Student Rsch. award, U. Wis. Eau-Claire, 2002, Golden Lamp award for Bad Sugar, Television Series, Best Media Depictions Nurses Television, 2006, Glen Blix award Excellence Preventive Care, Loma Linda U., Sch. Public Health, 2009; Selma Andrews scholarship, 2008. Mem.: Am. Coll. Sports Medicine, Am. Coll. Nutrition, Sigma Theta Tau Internat. Honor Soc. of Nursing. Achievements include research in spirituality & health in various populations. Avocations: reading, dance.

TANZI, RUDOLPH EMILE (RUDY TANZI), neuroscientist, researcher, educator; b. Providence, Sept. 18, 1958; s. Rudolph Anthony and Anne Marie (Macari) Tanzi; m. Dora Marta Kovacs, May 24, 2002. BS in Microbiology, U. Rochester, 1980, BA in History, 1980; PhD in Neurobiology, Harvard U., 1990. Rsch. asst. genetics unit to prof. Mass. Gen. Hosp., Boston, 1980—99, prof. neurology, 1999—, dir. Genetics and Aging Unit, 1999—. Instr. neurology Harvard U. Med. Sch., 1990—92, asst. prof. to prof., 1992—; bd. sci. counselors Nat. Inst. Aging; chmn. sci. adv. bd. Blanchette Rockefeller Neurosciences Inst. Editl. bd. Neuron, 1994—; co-editor: Molecular Mechanisms of Dementia, 1997, Presenilins and Alzheimer's Disease, 1998, Alzheimer's Disease: Advances in Genetics, Molecular and Cellular Biology, 2006; co-author: Decoding Darkness: The Search for the Genetic Causes of Alzheimer's Disease, 2001; contbr. articles to profl. jours. Adv. bd. Lifeboat Found. Recipient Nathan Shock New Investigator award, Gerontology Soc. Am., 1993, Met. Life award, 1995, Potamkin prize, 1995; fellow French Found., 1991, Pew scholar in biomed. scis., 1993. Fellow: AAAS; mem.: Am. Soc. Human Genetics, Am. Soc. for Neurosci. Avocations: skiing, tennis, scuba diving, piano. Office: Mass Gen Hosp - East Genetics and Aging Rsch Unit 114 16th St Charlestown MA 02129 Office Phone: 617-726-6845. Office Fax: 617-724-1949. E-mail: tanzi@helix.mgh.harvard.edu.

TAO, STANLEY S., orthopedic surgeon; s. Eddie V. and Irene Y. Tao; m. Ann B. Tao, June 8, 1991; children: Andrew W., Hollyn G. MD, Case Western Res. U., Cleve., 1995, Med. Coll. Ohio, Toledo, 2000. Sports medicine and arthroscopic fellow Orthopedic Rsch. Va., Richmond, 2000—01; orthop. surgeon Scott Orthop. Ctr., Huntington, W.Va., 2001—. Bd. mem. United Way, Huntington, 2001—07. Named Am. Top Physicians. Avocation: sports. Office: Scott Orthopedic Center 2828 1st Ave Ste 400 Huntington WV 25702 Office Phone: 304-525-6905. Office Fax: 304-525-4316; Home Fax: 304-525-4316. Personal E-mail: totalsportscare@hotmail.com. Business E-Mail: socbecky@yahoo.com.

TAO, YUAN-XIANG, neuroscientist, educator; b. Dongtao, Jiangsu, China, July 25, 1963; MD, Nanjing Med. U., 1986; PhD, Shanghai Brain Rsch. Inst., Chinese Acad. Scis., 1997. Instr. Johns Hopkins U. Sch. Medicine, 1999—2000, asst. prof., 2001—04, assoc. prof., 2005—. Guest prof. Nanjing Med. U., 2009—. Recipient Young Scientist award, Beckman Instruments Corp. Mem.: Am. Pain Soc., Internat. Assn. Study Pain, Soc. Neurosci. Avocations: tennis, travel, swimming. Office: 1721 E Madison St 370 Ross Baltimore MD 21205 Office Fax: 410-502-5554. Business E-Mail: ytao1@jhmi.edu.

TARANTA, ANGELO (VISCA TARANTA), physician, educator; b. Rome, 1927; came to U.S., 1952, naturalized, 1956; MD, U. Rome, 1949. Diplomate Am. Bd. Internal Medicine, also sub-bd. Rheumatology. Intern, dept. internal medicine and pediatrics Univ. Hosp., Rome, 1949-50, resident, 1950-52; resident in medicine St. Mary's Hosp., Rochester, NY, 1952-53; resident in cardiology Irvington House, NY, 1953-54, research assoc., 1955-59, research dir., 1959-62;

assoc. dir. Irvington House Inst., NYC, 1965-71; research fellow in microbiology NYU Sch. Medicine, 1955-56, instr. in microbiology, 1955-58, adj. asst. prof. microbiology, 1958-60, asst. prof. medicine, 1960-65, assoc. prof., 1965-75, on leave of absence, 1975-79; dir. medicine Cabrini Health Care Ctr., NYC, 1973-93; prof. medicine, chief rheumatology and immunology div. N.Y. Med. Coll., 1979-85, chief div. humanities and ethics, 1985-88. Co-chmn. study group on heart disease in the young Inter-Soc. Commn. on Heart Disease Resources, 1972-78; bd. dirs. Am. Heart Assn., 1975-77; chmn. Council on Cardiovascular Disease in the Young, 1975-77; cons. in field. Author: (with M. Markowitz) Rheumatic Fever; editor (with E. Kaplan) Infectious Endocarditis; contbr. numerous articles to profl. publs. and textbooks. Fulbright travel grantee, 1952; recipient Terence Cardinal Cooke medal N.Y. Med. Coll., 1985. Master Am. Coll. Rheumatology; mem. Soc. Clin. Investigation, Am. Assn. Immunologists, N.Y. Acad. Medicine (chmn. sect. medicine 1980-87), Italian Rheumatology Soc. (hon.), Argentine Rheumatology Soc. (hon.). E-mail: angelissimo27@hotmail.com.

TARANTO, MARIA ANTOINETTE, psychology researcher, educator; b. Framingham, Mass., Dec. 28, 1941; d. Gaetano (Tom) Peter and Rose Marie (Busceme) T.; m. John Curtis Mahon, June 5, 1988. BA in Psychology, Bennington Coll., 1965; MA in Psychology, George Peabody Coll., 1968; M Philosophy in Psychology, Columbia U., 1981, PhD, 1985. Tchr. Head Start Pub Sch. System, Pitts., 1966-67; rsch. assoc. Hofstra U., Hempstead, NY, 1968-69, instr., 1969-72; co-dir. Inst. for Piagetian Studies, Hempstead, 1972-76; instr. Nassau C.C., Garden City, NY, 1976-78, asst. prof., 1978-85, assoc. prof. psychology, 1985-95, prof. emeritus, 1996—. Jour. reviewer Baywood Pub. Co., Long Island, N.Y., 1989, Karger, Basel, Switzerland, 1989. Contbr. articles to profl. jours. Mem. Union of Concerned Scientists, 1981—, Amnesty Internat.;hon. pres. Eoliano Mus. Emigrazione, Salina, Italy. Recipient Mellon fellowship CUNY, N.Y.C., 1987, Woman of Yr. award Sicilia Mondo Soc., 2004. Mem. APA, Jean Piaget Soc., Gerontol. Soc., New Eng. Psychol. Assn., Filicudi Assn. (pres. 2002-06, v.p. 2007-08) Avocations: hiking, gardening, picniking, cooking. Personal E-mail: minervasowl2@earthlink.net.

TARASENKO, OLGA, microbiologist, immunologist, educator; d. Elizaveta Grebenyuk; m. Pierre Alusta. MD, Kyrgyz State Med. Acad., Kyrgyzstan, 0190, PhD, 1998. Postoctoral rsch. assoc. Poly. Inst. NYU, NYC, 2001—05; asst. prof. U. Ark., Little Rock, 2005—11, assoc. prof., 2011—. Mentor Biology Club BioNanoTox Internat. U. Ark., 2005—; founder, co-chair BioNanoTox and Applications Internat. Rsch. Conf., 2006—. Recipient Med. Student Conf. First prize, Kyrgyz State Med. Acad., 1990, Appreciation cert., Polytechnic U., 2002; named Exceptional Inventions award, Govt. of Kyrgyz Republic, State Agy. of Sci. and Intellectual Properties, 2004; grantee, European Sch. Transfusion Medicine, 1993; fellow, Union Hematological Ctr., Moscow, Russia, 1991, Rsch. Inst. Hematology and Blood Transfusion, St. Petersburg, Russia, 1991, 1992; scholar, Asian Devel. Bank, 1999—2001. Mem.: BioNanoTox Internat. Soc., Am. Chem. Soc., MidSouth Computational Biology and Bioinformatics Soc., Kyrgyz Soc. Allergy and Immunology (assoc.), Am. Soc. Microbiology (assoc.). Achievements include research in phagocytosis and inhibition of bacterial spores using glycoconjugate polymers; patents for protective immunogenetics factors against tuberculosis; patents pending for inhibitors of sporeforming pathogens; destruction of spores through glycoconjugate enhanced phagocytosis. Office: University of Arkansas at Little Rock 2801 South University Little Rock AR 72204 Office Phone: 501-569-3504.

TARASZKIEWICZ, WALDEMAR, physician; b. Wilno, Poland, July 6, 1936; arrived in U.S., 1979, naturalized, 1984; s. Michal Taraszkiewicz-Sirocki and Nina Lutomska-Jurylowicz Dylla; m. Teresa Barbara Szwarc, Oct. 15, 1966. MD in Internal Medicine, Med. Acad., Gdansk, Poland, 1961, MD in Internal Medicine Specialty II, 1972. Diplomate Am. Bd. Family Practice. Family physician Out Patient Clinic, Sopot, Poland, 1962—64; resident U. Hosp., Gdansk, 1965—71; allergist Clinic of Allergy, Gdansk, 1965—75; physician Cardiology Dept., Gdansk, 1971—75, Hopital Civil, Telagh, Algeria, 1975—79; surg. asst. Hinsdale (Ill.) Hosp., 1979—82; resident physician St. Mary of Nazareth Hosp., Chgo., 1982—85, emergency room physician, 1984—85; family practice medicine Brookfield, Ill., 1985—88, Westmont, Ill., 1988—89, Chgo., 1987—; med. dir. Winston Manor Nursing Home, Chgo., 1989—90; clin. asst. prof. U. Ill. Med. Coll., 1994—. Sr. asst. dept. cardiology Univ. Hosp., Gdansk, 1971—75; mem. adminstrv. com., pres. med. staff Hopital Civil, Telagh, 1976—79; clin. asst. prof. U. Ill., Med. Coll. Chgo., 1994—. Contbr. articles to profl. jours. Recipient Bronze medal, Polski Zwiazek Wedkarski, 1970, cert. 3d pl., 1971. Fellow: Am. Acad. Family Practice; mem.: AMA (Continuing Edn. award), N.Y. Acad. Scis., Polish Med. Alliance, Am. Coll. Allergy and Immunology, Am. Acad. Allergy and Immunology, World Med. Assn., Chgo. Med. Soc. (mem. practice mgmt. com.), Ill. Med. Soc. Avocations: art collecting, fishing.

TARAWNEH, RAWAN, research scientist; b. Amman, Jordan, July 13, 1980; Degree in Medicine, U. Jordan, 2003. Diplomate Am. Bd. Neurology and Psychiatry, 2009. Mem. student coun. U. Jordan, 2000—03, resident Dept. Internal Medicine, 2003—05; intern PGY-1, dept. internal medicine, Washington U. Sch. Medicine, 2005—06, resident PGY2-4, Dept. Neurology, 2006—09, physician and rsch. fellow, Lab Dr David Holtzman Dept. Neurology Alzheimer Disease Rsch. Ctr. Student rep Com. for Ednl. Devel., Jordan, 1995—97; rep. Jordan in the Youth Adv. Group, World Health Orgn., 1995, First Youth Summit for Peace in the Middle East, 1998, Seeds Peace Orgn., 1996—98. Recipient Jubilee Sch. award, 1994—96, Med. Dean's award, U. Jordan, 2003, Ministry Health's award, 2003, The Patient's Choice award, Mdx Med. Inc., 2008—10. Mem.: Am. Bd. Med. Specialties. Achievements include research in Visinin-like protein 1: a novel biomarker for Alzheimer disease; identification and characterization novel brain biomarkers for neurodegenerative disorders, particularly Alzheimer disease, through the utilization genomics, proteomics, and bioinformatics. Office: Campus Box 8111 Dept Neurology Washington University Sch Medicine 660 S Euclid Ave Saint Louis MO 63110 Office Phone: 314-367-7512. Office Fax: 314-362-2244. Personal E-mail: rawantarawneh@gmail.com.

TARCEA, MONICA, medical educator; b. Blaj City, Alba, Romania, Aug. 24, 1967; MD, U. Targu Mures, 1992, PhD, 1999. Lectr. U. Medicine and Pharmacy Targu Mures, 2004—06, asst. prof., 2006—. Cons. NGO East Timor World Vision Internat., 2002. Mem.: European Soc. Clin. Microbiology and Infectious Diseases, Hygiene and Pub. Health Romanian Assn., Romanian Healthy Nutrition Found., Nutrition Soc. (Cambridge, Eng.), European Confederation Med. Mycology, EUPHA. Avocations: reading, music. Office: 38 Gh Marinescu 29/44 Aleea Carpati Targu Mures Transylvania 540139 Romania Office Fax: 0040265210407. Personal E-mail: monaumf2001@yahoo.com.

TARDIF, TWILA, psychology professor; b. Can., July 22, 1965; PhD, Yale U., 1993. Assoc. prof. to asst. prof. Chinese U Hong Kong, 1996—2001; prof., program dir. U. Mich., Ann Arbor, 2001—08, dir., Ctr. Human Growth and Devel., 2009—. Curriculum cons. Nickelodeon, 2006—08. Fellow: Am. Psychol. Soc.; mem.: Soc. Rsch. Child Devel. Office: University Mich Ctr Human Growth and Devel Ann Arbor MI 48109-5406 Office Fax: 734-936-9288. Business E-Mail: twila@umich.edu.

TARGHER, GIOVANNI, endocrinologist, consultant; b. Rovereto, Italy, Dec. 23, 1966; m. Paola Panizza, June 24, 2000; children: Elisa, Riccardo, Silvia. MD, U. Med. Sch., Verona, VR, Italy, 1991. Bd. cert. diplomate in endocrinology and diabetology Verona, 1996. Sr. cons. endocrinology Sacro Cuore Hosp., Negrar, VR, 1996—; asst. prof. U. Verona, Sect. Endocrinology, Verona, 2006—. Sr. cons. endocrinology Civil Hosp., Verona, 2006—. Office: Univ Verona Sec Endocrinology Piazzale Aristide Stefani 1 37126 Verona VR Italy Office Fax: 00390458027314. Business E-Mail: giovanni.targher@univr.it.

TARGOVNIK, SELMA E. KAPLAN, dermatologist; b. NYC, Apr. 22, 1936; d. Harry A. and Helen (Goodstein) Kaplan; m. Jerome H. Targovnik, Dec. 2, 1961; children: Nina Rebecca, Labe Eric (dec.), Diane Michelle. BA, NYU, 1957; MD, Albert Einstein Col. Medicine, 1961. Diplomate Am. Bd. Dermatology. Intern Kaiser Found. Hosp., San Francisco, 1961-62; resident in internal medicine Bellevue Hosp., NYU Med. Ctr., 1962-63, U. Colo. Med. Ctr., Denver, 1963-64; rsch. fellow, resident in dermatology Boston U. Med. Ctr., 1964-66, mem. staff, 1968-69, NYU Med. Ctr., 1966-68, St. Joseph's Hosp., Phoenix, 1969—98, Good Samaritan Hosp., Phoenix, 1969—, Carl Hayden VA Hosp., Phoenix, 1998—. Mem. staff St. Joseph's Hosp., Phoenix, St. Luke's Hosp., Phoenix; chief divsn. dermatology Good Samaritan Hosp., Phoenix, 1985-90; adj. assoc. prof. Midwestern U. Coll. Medicine, Glendale, Ariz., 1998—; clin. assoc. prof. dermatology Kirksville Coll. Osteopathic Medicine, 2000—, clin. assoc. prof. dermatology, 1998; physicians asst., PA studentship, 2011-, med. students, podiatry students, psychiatry students, 2011-, residents, family practice, internal medicine residents Carl Hayden VA Hosp., Phoenix, 1998-. Bd. dirs. ACLU, Ariz., 1973-78, 83-94, Congregation Beth El, Phoenix, 1971-75, 2011-, Flagstaff Festival of the Arts, 1984-86; active Jewish Nat. Fund; adv. bd., Lowell Obs. Flagstaff, Ariz., 2007-. Fellow Am. Acad. Dermatology, Assocs. for the Weizmann Inst. Sci., Assocs. for the Technion Inst.; mem. Am. Technion Soc. (bd. dirs. 1988-92, pres. Ariz. divsn. 1990-92), Dermatology Found., Sonoran Dermatologic Soc., Southwestern Dermatologic Soc., Pacific Dermatological Soc., Noah Worcester Dermatol. Soc., Phi Beta Kappa, Mu Chi Sigma, Pi Delta Phi, Beta Lambda Sigma. Democrat. Jewish. Home: 3706 E Rancho Dr Paradise Valley AZ 85253 Office Phone: 602-628-8117. Fax: 602-667-6813. Personal E-mail: selmaderm@cox.net.

TARHAN, OMER RIDVAN, surgeon, educator; b. Isparta, Oct. 24, 1971; PhD, Istanbul U., 1995. Assoc. prof. gen. surgery Suleyman Demirel U. Faculty Medicine, 2008—. Avocations: gardening, motorcycling, reading. Office: Suleyman Demirel University Med Sch Isparta 32900 Turkey E-mail: drtarhan@yahoo.com.

TARKOWSKI, ANDRZEJ K., embryologist; MSc, Warsaw U, 1955; PhD Warsaw U., 1959, DSc Warsaw U., 1964; D honoris causa, Jagiellonian U., Cracow, Med. U., Lodz. Assoc. prof. to prof. Warsaw U. Vis. prof. dept. zoology Royal Soc. / U. Oxford, England, 1984—85. Recipient Albert Brachet prize, Royal Acad. of Belgium, 1980, Polish Nat. award, 1980, Alfred Jurzykowski Found. (USA) award, 1984, Embryo Transfer Pioneer award, Internat. Embryo Transfer Soc., 1991, Japan prize, Sci. & Tech. Found. of Japan, 2002. Mem.: Academia Europaea, Polish Acad. Arts Scis., Fr. Acad. Scis., Polish Acad. Scis., NAS. Office: Warsaw Univ Ul. Miecznikowa 1 02-096 Warsaw Poland Office Phone: (48)(22)5541208. Business E-Mail: akt@biol.uw.edu.pl.

TARLOV, ALVIN RICHARD, foundation administrator, physician, educator; b. Norwalk, Conn., July 11, 1929; s. Charles and Mae (Shelinsky) T.; m. Joan Hylton, June 12, 1956 (div. 1976); children: Richard, Elizabeth, Jane, Suzanne, David. BA, Dartmouth Coll., 1951; MD, U. Chgo., 1956. Intern Phila. Gen. Hosp., 1956-57; resident in medicine U. Chgo. Hosps., 1957-58, 62-63, research assoc., 1958-61; asst. prof. medicine U. Chgo., 1963-68, assoc. prof., 1968-70, prof., 1970-84, prof. medicine, 2006—, chmn. dept. medicine, 1969-81; chmn. grad. med. edn. nat. adv. com. HHS, Washington, 1980; pres. Henry J. Kaiser Family Found., Menlo Park, Calif., 1984-90; sr. scientist New Eng. Med. Ctr., Boston, 1990-99, exec. dir. The Health Inst., 1995-99; prof. pub. health Harvard U., Boston, 1990-99; prof. of medicine Tufts U., 1990-99. Dir. Tex. Program for Soc. and Health, James Baker III Inst. for Pub. Policy, Rice U., 1999-2005. Pres. Med. Outcomes Trust, Inc., 1993-2000; chmn. bd., pres. Mass. Health Data Consortium, 1994-98. Served to capt. U.S. Army, 1958-61. Recipient Research Career Devel. award NIH, 1962-67; John and Mary Markle Found. scholar, 1966-71. Mem. ACP (master), Inst. Medicine of Nat. Acad. Scis. Home: 1024 E Camino Diestro Tucson AZ 85704-7695 Home Phone: 914-478-1868. Personal E-mail: atarlov@gmail.com.

TARNOVE, LORRAINE, medical association executive; b. Atlantic City, July 26, 1947; d. Leonard Robert Tarnove and Jeanne Tarnove Yudkin; m. Steven B. Friedman, July 1, 1969; 2 children. BA, U. Md., 1969. Pres. Lorraine Tarnove Consulting, Columbia, Md., 1985-93; exec. dir. Am. Med. Dirs. Assn., Columbia. Contbr. chapters to books. Office: AMDA 10840 Little Patuxent #760 Columbia MO 21044 Office Phone: 301-596-5774. E-mail: ltarnove@amda.com. *

TARRÉS, JOSEP, physician; b. Barcelona, Sept. 27, 1950; MD, U. Barcelona, 1973, degree in Pneumology, 1978. Physician ICS, 1973—. Recipient award, Jour. Bronconeurnology Files, 2009, Brit. Med. Coun., 2010; grant, Spain Health Dept., Rsch. grant, 2004, Jordi Goli Gorina Found., 2005, FIS grant, Health Inst. Carlos III, Health Min., 2006. Home: Anselm Clavé num 25 porta A Cerdanyola Del Valles Barcelona 08290 Spain Home Fax: 345863696. Business E-Mail: 7893jto@comb.cat.

TARRO, GIULIO, virologist; b. Messina, Italy, July 9, 1938; s. Emanuele and Emanuela (Iannello) Tarro; 1 adopted child, Giuseppe. MD, U. Naples, 1962, postgrad. in nervous diseases, 1968, PhD in Virology, 1971; postgrad. in med. and biol. scis., Roman Acad., 1979; degree in medicine (hon.), U. Pro Deo, Albany, NY, 1989; degree in immunology (hon.), St. Theodora Acad., NY, 1991; degree in bioethics (hon.), Constantinian U., Cranston, RI, 1996; MSc in Biomed. Techs. (hon.), ASAM U., Rome, 2008; degree in Social Scis. (hon.), Bonake U., Abidjan Cote DAvoize, 2010. Asst. in med. pathology Naples U., Italy, 1964-66; rsch. assoc. divsn. virology and cancer rsch. Children's Hosp., Cin., 1965-68; asst. prof. rsch. pediat. U. Cin. Coll. Medicine, 1968-69; rsch. fellow Nat. Rsch. Coun., Naples, 1966-74, rsch. chief, 1974; prof. oncologic virology Coll. Medicine U. Naples, 1971-85, prof. microbiology and immunology Sch. Specialization, 1972—2006; chief divsn. virology D. Cotugno Hosp. Infectious Diseases, Naples, 1973—2006, pres. ethic com., 1998—2007, head dept. diagnostic labs., 2003—06, emeritus, 2006—. Sr. scientist Nat. Cancer Inst. Frederick Ctr., Md., 1973; project dir. Nat. Cancer Inst., Bethesda, Md., 1971-75; edn. min. rep. Zool. Sta., Naples, 1975-79; cons. Italian Pharmacotherapic Inst., Rome, 1980-98, med. dir., 2006-07; nat. com. on bioethics, 1995-98; ethics com. Basilicata Oncologic Hosp., 2005-; pres. De Beaumont Bonelli Found. Cancer Rsch., Naples, 1978—, European Group Econ. Interest, Rsch. and Devel., Naples, 2003-07, Campania Tech. and Ecology Ctr., 2004-; dean faculty natural and phys. scis. Nobile Accademia di Santa Teodora Imperatrice, 1993-2003; dept. head medicine Naples People U., 2000-05; sci. coord. extracorporeal hyperthermia in HCV patients First Circle Med., Mpls., 2000-03; vice chmn., gen. sec. sci. adv. bd. Unihart Biotech Pharm., London, 2005-07; chmn. com. on biotechs. and virusphere World Acad. Biomed. Techs., UNESCO, Paris, 2007-; adj. prof. dept. biology Temple U. Coll. Sci. and Tech., Phila., 2007—, pres. sci. com. Moravia U. Gonzaga Inst. Naples, 2008-09, hon. pres. Norman Acad. Rome, 2009-. Author: Virologia Oncologica, 1979, Patologia dell'AIDS, 1991, Con il Cancro si Puó Vivere, 1992, AIDS Cosa Possiamo Fare Cosa Dobbiamo Sapere, 1994, Pocket File Research Collection, 1997, 6th edit., 2003, To Prevent Is To Win, 1998, Bioethics and Culture of Prevention, 2001, Health Without Borders, 2004, 4th edit., 2009, Safety No Limits, 2008; editor-in-chief: Internat. Jour. Clin. Investigation, 2000—, Cotugno News, 2003—, Fratres, 2004—; contbr. more than 470 articles to profl. jours. Pres. Sci. Cultural Com., Torre Annunziata, Italy, 1984, Tumor Prevention Assn., Rome, 1984; mem. acad. senate Constantinian U., Providence, 1990, U. Pro Deo, NY, 1994; hon. acad. U. Sancti Cyrilli, Valletta, Malta, 2001; mem. UNESCO-Hebrew U. Jerusalem Internat. Sch. Molecular Biology and Microbiology, hon. rector Ruggero II U., Fla., 2003. Maj. Italian Navy, 1982-84, lt. col., 1993-95, mem. UN Internat. Computing Sci. Acad., 1997, mem. Lions Found., 1990-91 Decorated comdr. Nat. Order of Merit, Star of Europe, knight grand cross Sovereign Constantinian Order St. George, gt. officer Italian Republic; recipient Internat. Lenghi award Lincei Acad., 1969, Gold Microscope award Italian Health Min., 1973, Knights of Humanity award Internat. Register of Chivalry, Malta, 1978, Gold medal of culture Pres. Italian Republic, 1975, Culture award, 1985, 1st prize in biomed. rsch., Italian Acad. Arts and Scis., 1987, Castello di Pietrarossa award, Italy, 1991, Gold Cesare award Padova, 1991, Gold Little Horse, Transnat. European Fedn., Rome 1996, King Manfredi award and Silverplate Pres. Italian rep. Manfredonia, 1999, Equestris Ordinis S. Sepulcri of Jerusalem, Rome, 1999, Gold medal of health Pres. Italian Republic, 1999, Saint Catherin award, Siena, 2003, Sorrento in the World award, 2004, Medal of Culture Ministry, 2005, Knight of Solidarity Internat. award Norman Acad., Rome, 2006, hon. pres. 2009-, St. Pio for Peace award City of Fiuggi, 2006, Tables of Law award Internat. Assn. Cath. Apostleship, Naples, 2006, 32nd Casentino Internat. award in medicine Poppi-Arezzo, 2007, Grand Cross Internat. Acad. State Wyo., 2008, award Pres. Italian Rep, Silver medal, 2004, 2008, Lifetime Achievement award, Sbarro Health Rsch. Orgn.Phila., 2009, Nat. award for solidarity Fratres St. Giovanni La Punta, 2010, Global Edn. Sanremo award, 2011, Internat. Peace award, 2011. Fellow: AAAS; mem.: Am. Chem. Soc., European Soc. Clin. Virology, NY Acad. Scis., Nat. Order Journalists, AIDS Soc. Asia and the Pacific, Assn. Res. Prevention of Cancer (sci. com. 1995), Italian Assn. Viral Study and Rsch. (pres. 1995—2008, hon. pres. 2009—), Italian Soc. Immuno-Oncology (v.p. 1975—, pres. 1990—2008), Internat. League Drs. for Abolition of Vivisection (pres. 1992—), Internat. Assn. Leukemias, Am. Assn. Cancer Rsch., Am. Soc. Microbiology (people to people amb. to South Africa 2010), Rotary, Lions (pres. Pompei chpt. 1987—89, pres. com. fight cancer 1989—90, vice gov. dist. 1991—92, pres. com. fight cancer 1992—94, pres. com. sci. and life 1994—95, pres. com. fight drug addiction and AIDS 1995—97, pres. com. transplant and donations 1998—99, pres. com. oncology 2000—02, pres. com. on stem cells 2002—03, dist. dir. operative area ethics and social solidarity 2003—04, pres. Pompei chpt. 2004—06, dist. dir. operative area health and rsch. 2006—, Melvin Jones fellow 1993, 2004, 2008, 2010). Roman Catholic. Achievements include patents in field of first link of viruses to human cervical cancer; discovery of RSV virus in infant deaths in Naples and of tumor liberated protein as a tumor associated antigen, 100 kilodalton protein overexpressed in lung tumors and other epithelial adenocarcinomas. Office Phone: 39-081-5463222. Personal E-mail: gitarro@teletu.it. E-mail: gitarro@tin.it.

TARTAGNI, FLAVIO MARCO, cardiologist; b. Meldola, Forli, Italy, Jan. 21, 1948; s. Pasquale and Olga (Tramonti) T.; m. Maria Grazia Frani, Sept. 2, 1979; 1 child, Elisa. MD, U. Bologna, 1973, degree in cardiology, 1977, degree in sport medicine, 1983, degree in nuclear medicine, 1987. Asst. cardiologist Heart Inst. Bologna (Italy), 1975-86, U. Bologna, 1986-90, chief of staff, 1996; chief cardiologist Cesena, 1996—; chief med. dept., 2001—. Prof. nuclear cardiology Bologna U., 1986-95; cons. working group on arteriosclerosis Am. Heart Assn., 1995—; presenter in field. Contbr. articles to profl. jours., chpts. to books. Am. Field Svc. scholar, 1965. Fellow: European Soc. Cardiology; mem.: Soc. Cardiovasc. Magnetic Resonance, European Working Group Nuc. Cardiology (founder), Am. Soc. Nuc. Medicine (founder). Roman Catholic. Avocations: Judo, saxophone. Home: Via Roselle 4 40138 Bologna Italy Office: Cardiology Dept Ospedale Bufalini Cesena Forli Italy

TARUMI, KIMIO, healthcare educator; s. Tarumi Shigehito and Tarumi Takako; m. Tarumi Yuriko. Grad., Kyoto Prefectural U. Medicine, 1982, PhD, 1989. Assoc. prof. U. Occupl. and Environ. Health, Kitakyushu, Fukuoka, Japan, 1990—2006; prof. Fukui Prefectural U., Eiheiji-cho, Japan, 2008—. Cons. Sumitomo Metal Industries, Osaka, Japan, 1994—2006. Contbr. articles to jours. Bd. mem. Ogata Pub. Office, Ogata-machi, Ouita Prefecture, Japan, 1999—2001. Grant, Japan Soc. for Promotion Sci., 2005, 2006. Mem.: Japan Soc. Hygiene. Office: Fukui Prefectural Univ Faculty Nursing & Social Welfare Sci 4-1-1 Kenjoujima Matsuoka Eiheiji-cho Fukui 910-1195 Japan Office Fax: 81-776-61-6016. Business E-Mail: tarumikm@fpu.ac.jp.

TARVESTAD, ANTHONY M., medical association administrator; BA magna cum laude, Winona State U., 1973; JD, William Mitchell Coll. of Law, 1977. Exec. dir. Am. Bd. Physical Medicine and Rehab. Named Super Lawyer Minn. Jour. Law and Politics, 1994. Mem. Am. Coll. Healthcare Execs., Am. Health Laywers Assn., ABA, Am. Arbitration Assn. (arbitrator), Minn. State Bar. Assn. Office: Am Bd Physical Medicine and Rehabilitation 3015 Allegro Park Lane SW Rochester MN 55902-4139 Office Phone: 507-282-1776. Office Fax: 507-282-9242. E-mail: tarvestad@abpmr.org. *

TASDEMIR, TAMER, vice dean; Attended, Ataturk U., 1994; PhD, Inst. of Health Sci., 2003. Dentist Kutahya Prison, 1997—98; res. officer Navy Warfare Command, 1995—96; rsch. asst. faculty of dentistry Karadeniz Tech. Univ., Trabzon, Turkey, assoc. dean faculty of dentistry, 2005—, mem. faculty of dentistry endodontics dept., 2005—, vice dean faculty of dentistry. Mem.: European Soc. of Endodontology, Turkish Endodontic Soc. Office: Karadeniz Technical University Gumushane Artvin Trabzon 61080 Turkey E-mail: tamer@ktu.edu.tr.

TASER, FIGEN, medical educator; b. Izmir, Turkey, June 15, 1975; MD, Dokuz Eylul U., 1998. Asst. prof. Dumlupinar U., 2007—. Office: Dumlupinar University Medical Faculty Kutahya 43100 Turkey Personal E-mail: figentaser@yahoo.com.

TASHIRO, TADASHI, cardiologist, thoracic surgeon, educator; b. Fukuoka, Japan, Feb. 28, 1951; MD, Kagoshima U. Sch. Medicine, 1969; PhD (hon.), Kurume U. Sch. Medicine, 1984. Resident Kurume U. Sch. Medicine, Japan, 1978—82; staff thoracic & cardiovas. surgeon St. Mary's Hosp., Japan, 1982—90; clin. fellow cardiovas. surgery Toronto Gen. Hosp., 1986—87; chief thoracic & cardiovasc surgeon St. Mary's Hosp., Kurume, 1990—94; assoc. prof. cardiovasc. surgery Fukuoka U. Sch. Medicine, 1994—2004, prof. cardiovasc. surgery, 2004—. Mem.: Japanese Soc. Cardiovas. Surgery, Japanese Assn. Thoracic Surgery, Boston Soc. Thoracic Surgeons. Office: Fukuoka U Medicine Dept Cardiovasc Surgery 7-45-1 Nanakuma Jonanku Fukuoka 814-018 Japan Office Phone: 81 92 801 1011.

TASHJIAN, ROBERT, physician, educator; b. Worcester, Mass., May 22, 1972; BA, Amherst Coll., 1994; MD, Tufts U. Sch. Medicine. Asst. prof. U. Utah Sch. Medicine, 2006—. Home: 590 Wakara Way Salt Lake City UT 84108 E-mail: robert.tashjian@hsc.utah.edu.

TASIAN, SARAH KATHLEEN TAYLOR, pediatric hematologist, oncologist; d. Henry Beverly and Nancy Oberle Taylor; m. Gregory Edward Tasian, Jan. 20, 2007. BS, BA, U. Notre Dame, Ind., 1999; MD, Baylor Coll. Medicine, Houston, 2004. Cert. Am. Bd. Pediat., 2007. Pediat. resident U. Wash., Seattle Children's Hosp., Seattle, 2004—07; pediatric hematology-oncology fellow U. Calif., San Francisco, 2007—. Fellowship, Howard Hughes Med. Inst., 2001—02. Mem.: Am. Soc. Pediat. Hematology - Oncology, Am. Soc. Clin. Oncology, Am. Assn. Cancer Rsch., Am. Soc. Hematology, Alpha Omega Alpha, Phi Beta Kappa. Office: The Childrens Hosp Phila Divsn Pediatric Oncology 34th St & Civic Ctr Blvd Philadelphia PA 19104 Business E-Mail: tasians@email.chop.edu.

TASKER, JEFFREY, biology professor; b. Jan. 28, 1958; BA, U. Colo., 1981; PhD, U. Bordeaux, 1986. Prof. Tulane U., 1991—. Mem.: Soc. Neurosci. Office: Dept Cell and Molecular Biology New Orleans LA 70118 Business E-Mail: tasker@tulane.edu.

TASKER, JOHN B., veterinary medical educator, dean; b. Concord, NH, Aug. 28, 1933; s. John Baker and Catherine Mabel (Baker) T.; m. Grace Ellen Elliott, June 17, 1961; children: Sybil Alice, Sarah Catherine, Sophia Ethel DVM, Cornell U., 1957, PhD, 1963. Instr. Cornell U., Ithaca, N.Y., 1960-61, from assoc. prof. to prof., 1967-78; from asst. prof. to assoc. prof. Colo. State U., Fort Collins, 1963-67; prof. vet. clin. pathology, assoc. dean La. State U., 1978-84; dean Coll. Vet. Medicine Mich. State U., East Lansing, 1984-94; prof. vet. pathology Coll. Vet. Medicine/Mich. State U., East Lansing, 1984-95; dean, prof. emeritus Mich. State U., East Lansing, 1995. Cons. Ralston-Purina Co., St. Louis, 1978, Universidad Nacional P. Urena, Dominican Republic, 1980, U. Nebr., Lincoln, 1982-83 Editor: Veterinary Clinics of North America, 1976, Author: Standing on the Shoulders of Giants - Foundations in Veterinary Medicine For the Advancement of Human Welfare, 2008 Served to lst lt. U.S. Army, 1958-60 Recipient Outstanding Instr. award Colo. State U. Vet. Coll., 1967; Norden Teaching award Cornell U. Vet. Coll., 1977 Mem. AVMA, Am. Coll. Vet. Pathologists (diplomate; examiner 1972-74), Am. Soc. Vet. Clin. Pathology (pres. 1971-72), Assn. Am. Vet. Med. Colls. (exec. com. 1986-91, pres. 1989-90). Avocations: reading, travel. Home: 101 Briny Ave #2305 Pompano Beach FL 33062 Personal E-mail: jtasker8@comcast.net.

TASMAN, ALLAN, psychiatry educator; b. Louisville, Feb. 8, 1947; s. Goodman and Zelda Tasman; m. Cathy Faye Goldstein, May 24, 1970. BA in Chemistry, Franklin and Marshall Coll., 1969; MD, U. Ky., 1973. Diplomate Am. Bd. Psychiatry and Neurology. Resident in psychiatry U. Ky. Med. Sch., Lexington, 1973—74, U. Cin. Med. Ctr., 1974—76; asst. prof. psychiatry U. Conn. Med. Sch., Farmington, 1976—82, assoc. prof. psychiatry and tenure, 1982—88, prof. psychiatry, 1988—91; prof. psychiatry and behavioral scis., tenure and chmn. U. Louisville Sch. Medicine, 1991—; dir. Cognitive Neurosci. Lab., 1991—. Editor: Annual Review of Psychiatry, 1989-92, Clinical Challenges in Psychiatry, 1993, Less Time to Do More, 1993; sr. editor: Textbook of Psychiatry, 1997, 2d edit., 2003, 3rd edit., 2008, assoc. editor Am. Jour. Psychotherapy, 2002-; founding dep. editor Jour. Psychotherapy Practice and Rsch., 1992-2001; founding editor Asia Pacific Psychiatry, 2009-. Recipient Alpha Omega Alpha Faculty award, 2002, Nat. Alliance Mental Illness Exemplary Psychiatrist award, 2002, Pres.'s Disting. Faculty award for svc. to the profession, U. Louisville, 2003, St. Clair award, Ky. Psychiat. Assn., 2007, Disting. Alumnus award, U. Ky. Coll. Medicine, 2008. Fellow RCP, Am. Psychiat. Assn. (disting. fellow, v.p. 1996-98, pres.-elect 1998-99, pres. 1999-2000, Nancy Roeske award for excellence in med. student edn. 1991, Irma Bland award for excellence in resident tchg. 2005), Royal Coll. Psychiatrists, Am. Assn. Dirs. Psychiat. Residency Tng. (pres. 1993-94), Assn. Acad. Psychiatry (pres. 1993-94, Educator of Yr. award 2000), Am. Assn. Chmn. Depts. Psychiatry (pres. 1996-97, 97-98), World Psychiat. Assn. (bd. dirs. 2002-11, sec. for edn. 2005-11), Pacific Rim Coll. Psychiatrists (pres. 2006—08).

TASMAN, WILLIAM SAMUEL, ophthalmologist, educator; b. Phila., 1929; MD, Temple U., 1955. Intern Phila. Gen. Hosp., 1955-56, 1957—59; resident in ophthalmology Wills Eye Hosp., Phila., 1959-61; fellow Mass. Eye and Ear Infirmary, Boston, 1961-62; prof., emeritus chmn. dept. ophthalmology Jefferson Med. Coll., Phila., 1985—2008, Wills Eye Hosp., 1985—2007, attending surgeon, 1974—, ophthalmologist-in-chief, 1985—2007; with USAF, Wiesbaden, Germany. Mem. AMA, Am. Acad. Ophthalmologists (sec. ann. meeting 1992-97, pres. elect. 1998, pres. 1999), Pa. Acad. Ophthalmologists, Am. Ophthal. Soc. (pres. 1999). Office: Wills Eye Hosp 840 Walnut St Ste 830 Philadelphia PA 19107-5109

TASSINARI, MELISSA SHERMAN, teratologist, developmental toxicologist; b. Lawrence, Mass., Sept. 26, 1953; m. R. Peter Tassinari; children: Michael, Emily, Sara. AB, Mt. Holyoke Coll., 1975; postgrad., U. St. Andrews, Scotland, 1973-74; PhD, Med. Coll. Wis., 1979. Diplomate Am. Bd. Toxicology, 1995. Rsch. asst. in orthopedic surgery., Lab. Human Biochemistry Children's Hosp. Med. Ctr., Boston, 1981-83; rsch. affiliate in toxicology Forsyth Dental Ctr., Boston, 1983-86, staff assoc. dept. toxicology, 1986-89; asst. prof. cell biology U. Mass. Med. Ctr., Worcester, 1989-91; head reproductive and developmental toxicology Pfizer Inc., Groton/New London, Conn., 1991—2000; group dir. worldwide safety scis. Pfizer Global R&D, Groton/New London, Conn., 2000—04, sr. dir. worldwide regulatory policy and intelligence, 2004—09; sr. staff fellow, pediatric and maternal health staff Office of New Drugs, CDER FDA, White Oak, Silver Spring, Md., 2009—. Rsch. fellow oral biology Harvard Sch. Dental Medicine, Boston, 1978-81, instr. oral biology and pathophysiology, 1981-83; asst. prof. biol. scis. Wellesley Coll., Mass., 1985-91, biology Simmons Coll., Boston, 1986-87. Contbr. abstracts, articles to profl. jours. Mem. Teratology Soc. (coun. mem. 2000-07, v.p. 2004, pres. 2005-06), Neurobehavioral Teratology Soc., Mid. Atlantic Reprodn. and Teratology Assn. (steering com. 1994), Midwest Teratology Assn., Soc. Toxicology, Orgn. Teratogen Info. Svcs., Drug Info. Assn.

TASSIOPOULOS, APOSTOLOS K., vascular surgeon; b. Trikala, Greece, Oct. 8, 1965; arrived in US, 1992; s. Konstantinos A. Tassiopoulos and Vasiliki D. Tassiopoulou; m. Yianna Darsinos-Tassiopoulos, Aug. 23, 2003; children: Vasia, Constantine. MD, Aristotle U., Thessaloniki, Greece, 1989. Resident gen. surgery Upstate Med. U., Syracuse, 1993—99; fellow vascular surgery Loyola U. Med. Ctr., Haywood, Ill., 1999—2001; sr. attending Cook County Hosp., Chgo., 2001—06; asst. prof., surgery Rush U. Med. Ctr., Chgo., 2002—06, SUNY, 2006—08, assoc. prof., surgery, 2008—, chief, divsn. vascular surgery, 2008—, program dir., vascular surgery residency, 2008—. Contbr. chapters to books and articles to profl. jours. Recipient Allastair Carmody award, 2002. Fellow: Am. Coll. Surgeons; mem.: Am. Assn. Vascular Surgery, European Soc. Vascular Surgeon (assoc.). Home: 5 Bayberry Ct Miller Place NY 11764 Office: SUNY Stony Brook Med Ctr Dept Surgery HSC Level T-19 Rm 090 Stony Brook NY 11794

TASSONE, J. CHANNING, pediatrician, orthopedist, educator; b. Youngstown, Ohio, Oct. 23, 1969; MD, U. Wash., Sch. Medicine, 1996. Asst. prof., pediat. orthops. Med. Coll. Wis., 2002—08, assoc. prof., pediat. orthops., 2008—. Bd. dirs. Children's Spity. Group, 2010. Mem.: Wis. Orthop. Soc. (pres. 2009—11), Am. Acad. Orthop. Surgeons, Scoliosis Rsch. Soc., Pediat. Orthop. Soc. N.Am. Office: 9000 W Wisconsin Ave Ste C360 Milwaukee WI 53201 Business E-Mail: ctassone@chw.org.

TATAR, ARNOLD MARSHALL, internist, educator; b. Chgo., June 26, 1933; s. Louis and Rose Goldberg Tatar; m. Marina Deull-Wirszup, Aug. 30, 1959; children: Carolyn Beth, Audrey Michelle, Lauren D. W. BA in Chemistry, U. Ill., 1954; BS in Medicine, U. Ill., Chgo., 1955, MD cum laude, 1957. Lic. physician, Ill.; cert., recert. Am. Bd. Internal Medicine. Resident in internal medicine Michael Reese Hosp. and Med. Ctr., Chgo., 1957-60, chief med. resident, 1960-61, attending physician, 1961—2001; pres. Drs. Tatar Tatar Buchanan Hunt Suh and Lavery, Chgo., 1961—; attending physician Northwestern Meml. Hosp., Chgo., 1991—. Assoc. prof. internal medicine U. Chgo., 1973-91; asst. prof. internal medicine Northwestern U., Evanston/Chgo., 1991—; dir. med. intensive care Michael Reese Hosp., Chgo., 1969-76, dir. investigative hypertension clinic, 1964-76, pres. med. staff, 1988-90, hosp. trustee, 1982-91. Contbr. rsch. articles to profl. jours. Pres. Parent-Tchr. Orgn., John F. Kennedy Sch., Highland Park, Ill., 1970-72. Lt. col. U.S. Army, 1967-69. Decorated Commendation medal US Army; named one of Chgo.'s Top Drs., Chgo. Mag., 1997, 2001, 2004, Outstanding Primary Care Physicians in U.S., Town and Country Mag., 1999. Fellow Am. Coll. Chest Physicians, Am. Coll. Angiology, Am. Heart Assn. (coun. on hypertension, coun. on clin. cardiology), Am. Soc. Internal Medicine. Avocations: music, theater, dance, bicycling, photography. Home: Apt 5-East 189 E Lake Shore Dr Chicago IL 60611 Office: Drs Tatar Tatar Buchanan Hunt Suh and Lavery Ste 1801 111 W Washington Chicago IL 60602

TATARA, MARCIN RAFAL, veterinarian, surgeon; b. Lublin, Poland, Mar. 4, 1977; s. Stanislaw Ryszard and Teodora Tatara. DVM, Agriculture U. Lublin, 2002, PhD, 2003; habil, U. Life Scis., Wroclaw, 2009. Asst. Agrl. U. Lublin, 2002—04, adj., 2004—; dir. rsch. project Polish Ministry Edn. and Sci., 2005—08. Young Scientist scholar, Found. Polish Sci., 2006—07. Mem.: Polish Acad. Sci. (POLAND2000PLUS com.). Roman Catholic. Achievements include research in effects of prenatal treatment with alpha-ketoglutarate and 3-hydroxy-3-methylbutyrate on programming of skeletal system development in mammals; investigations on effects of nutritional, physiological, and pharmacological factors on bone metabolism regulation, as well as osteoporosis prevention and treatment. Avocations: travel, sports. Office: Univ Life Scis Lublin Akademicka 12 20-950 Lublin Poland Home Phone: Ul. Teodora Leszetyckiego 5/20 20-861 Lublin Poland Home Phone: 48 81 7420342; Office Phone: +48 602199 337. Business E-Mail: marcinta@tlen.pl.

TATE, SHIN-ICHI, science educator; b. Japan, Dec. 24, 1961; PhD, U. Tokyo, 1985. Prof. Hiroshima U., 2006—. Office: 1-3-1 Kagamiyama Higashi Hiroshima 739-8526 Japan Business E-Mail: tate@hiroshima-u.ac.jp.

TATESHIMA, SATOSHI, neurosurgeon; b. Tokyo, Japan; MD, Jikei U., 1995, PhD in Med. Sci., 2004. Cert. US Med. Lic. Exam Ednl. Commn. Fgn. Med. Grad., 2001, in neurological surgery Japan Neurosurgical Soc., 2005, neuro-endovascular therapy specialist Japanese Soc. Neuro-endovascular Therapy, 2005. Asst. rschr. divsn. interventional neuroradiology UCLA Med. Ctr., 1999—2001, asst. clin. prof. divsn. interventional neuroradiology, 2005—; resident neurol. surgery Jikei U. Hosp., Nishi-shinbashi, Tokyo, Japan, 1995—99, resident, neurol. surgery, 2003—04; vis. asst. prof. Keio U. Grad. Sch. Sci. and Tech., Yokohama, Kanagawa, Japan, 2003—05; guest prof. dept. neurosurgery St Marianna Sch. Medicine, Kawasaki, Japan, 2005—. Adj. asst. prof. divsn. interventional neuroradiology UCLA Med. Ctr., 2001—03. Grantee, NIH, 2007—; Pilot Rsch. grant, Soc. Interventional Radiology Found., 2005. Mem.: Asia-Australacia Soc. Neurological Surgery, Japan Neurosurgical Soc. (councilor), World Fedn. Neurosurgical Socs., Am. Soc. Neuroradiology. Office: UCLA Med Ctr Radiology Dept 10833 Le Conte Ave Los Angeles CA 90095-1721

TATIYA, ANIL UTTAMCHAND, pharmacist; b. Jan. 12, 1970; PharmM, Kle Coll. Pharmacy, 1992, PhD. Pharmacist R.C. Patel Coll. Pharmacy, Shirpur, 2002—. Mem.: APTI. Home: Karwand Naka 59 Dadusing Colony Shirpur Maharashtra 425405 India Personal E-mail: aniltatiya@rediffmail.com.

TATSUO, YAGURA, cell biologist, educator; b. Hyogo-ken, Japan, Nov. 20, 1948; PhD, Hokkaido U., 1976. Rsch. staff Saitama Cancer Ctr. Rsch. Inst., 1977—88; prof. Kwansei Gakuin U., 1988—. Mem.: Japanese Cancer Assn. Avocation: yachting. Office: 2-1 Gakuen Sanda Hyogo 669-1337 Japan Office Fax: 81 79 565 8473. Business E-Mail: tyagura@kwansei.ac.jp.

TATSURO, BABA, health products executive, medical educator; b. Shimonoseki, Yamaguchi, Japan, Feb. 6, 1958; s. Shigeo and Asako Baba; m. Masako Baba, Nov. 29, 1990; 1 child, Yusuke Baba. BS in Precision Engring., Osaka U., Japan, 1981, MS in Precision Engring., 1983; DEng (hon.), Kobe U., Japan, 2006. Dep. mgr. ultrasound sys. devel. dept. Toshiba Med. Sys. Corp., Otawara, Japan, 1983—. Contbr. articles to profl. jours. Fellow: Japan Soc. Ultrasonics Medicine; mem.: IEEE, Acoustical Soc. Japan, Profl. Engrs. Assn. Japan. Avocations: movies, music, baseball, computers. Home: 1920-2 Usuba Otawara 324-0035 Japan Office: 1385 Shimoishigami Otawara 324-8550 Japan Business E-Mail: baba@us.nasu.toshiba.co.jp, ezdo03014@nifty.ne.jp.

TAUB, EDWARD, psychology researcher; b. Bklyn., Oct. 22, 1931; s. Samuel Hart and Ida Pearl (Kimmel) T.; m. Mildred Allen Taub, Aug. 13, 1959. BA, Bklyn. Coll., 1953; MA, Columbia U., 1959; PhD, NYU, 1969. Rsch. asst. Columbia U., NYC, 1956; rsch. asst. dept. exptl. neurology Jewish Chronic Disease Hosp., NYC, 1957-60, rsch. assoc., 1960-68; dir. Behavioral Biology Ctr., Inst. for Behavioral Rsch., 1968-83; assoc. dir. Inst. for Behavioral Rsch., 1978-83; univ. prof. psychology U. Ala., Birmingham, 1986—2000, 2000—; standing guest prof. U. Konstanz, Germany, 1995—2002; guest prof. U. Jena, Germany, 1996—2002. Asst. prof. dept. psychiatry Johns Hopkins U., Balt., 1972-82; vis. prof. grad. program dept. psychology CUNY, 1984-85; vis. prof. U. Tuebingen, U. Muenster, Humboldt U., Germany, 1993—2001. Contbr. articles to profl. jours. Recipient Pioneering Rsch. Contbn. award, 1989, Disting. Scientist of 1998 award, Assn. of Applied Psychophysiology and Biofeedback, Ireland prize for scholarly distinction, U. Ala., Birmingham, 1997, Humboldt Rsch. award, 2000; fellow Guggenheim Found., 1983—84. Fellow AAAS (pres. psychol. sect. 2009), APA (exec. com. divsn. 6, Disting. Sci. award for the applications of psychology 2004), Soc. for Behavioral Medicine, Am. Psychol. Soc. (charter, William James Fellow award 1997); mem. Soc. for Neurosci. (named one of 10 leading translational rsch. projects in neurosci. in the 20th Century 2003), Biofeedback Soc. Am. (pres. 1978-79, Outstanding Rsch. Contbn. award 1988), Am. Physiol. Soc. (exec. com. neurosci. sect. 1988-91). Achievements include invention of technique of thermal biofeedback; Constraint-Induced Movement therapy for rehabilitation for stroke, traumatic brain injury, spinal cord injury, cerebral palsy and other motor disorders due to neurological injury. Office: U Ala at Birmingham 712 CPM 1530 3d Ave S Birmingham AL 35294-0018 Office Phone: 205-934-2471. Business E-Mail: etaub@uab.edu.

TAUBER, CHANAN, orthopedist, surgeon; b. Kfar Saba, Israel, Feb. 5, 1944; s. Felix Schlomo and Ruth Louise (Schoenfeld) Tauber; m. Tsivia Deborah Herzberger, May 31, 1946; children: Amir, Elad, Yael. MD, Hebrew U., Jerusalem, 1968. Intern Meir Med. Ctr., Kfar Saba, Israel, 1968; resident in surgery Soroka Med. Ctr., Beer Sheba, Israel, 1972; resident in orthopedics Sheba Med. Ctr., Tel Hashomer, Israel, 1973—79, Hosp. Cochin, Paris, 1979—80; sr. surgeon orthopedics Kaplan Med. Ctr., Rehovot, Israel, 1981—89, dep. dir. hosp., 1989—94, head orthopedic dept., 1993—. Contbr. articles to profl. jours. Lt. col. Israeli Def. Forces, 1969—94. Mem.: Israeli Orthopedic

Assn. (pres. elect 2001—02, pres. 2002—06), Am. Orthopedic Assn. Jewish. Avocations: swimming, classical music, reading. Office Phone: 97289416023. E-mail: tauber_c@clalit.org.il.

TAUBMAN, MARK B., dean, cardiologist, educator; BA in Biochemistry, Columbia U., NYC, 1972; MS in Pre-Med., NYU Sch. Medicine, 1976, MD, 1978. Cert. in internal medicine American Bd. Internal Medicine, in cardiovasular disease American Bd. Internal Medicine. Internship in internal medicine Harvard U. Med. Sch. / Brigham & Women's Hosp., 1978—79, residency in internal medicine, 1979—81, fellowship in cardiovascular disease, 1981—83; cardiology rschr. Children's Hosp., Boston, 1984—89; vascular biology rschr., dir. cardiovascular rsch., NIH prin. investigator, dir. of med. scientist tng. program Mt. Sinai Sch. Medicine, 1989—2003; prof. cardiology U. Rochester Med. Ctr., NY, 2003—, chief cardiology unit, Paul N. Yu prof. medicine, 2003—07, prof. and former dir. Aab Cardiovascular Rsch. Inst., chmn. dept. medicine, Charles E. Dewey prof. medicine, 2007—09, former assoc. chmn. rsch., CFO medicine, interim CEO, 2009—10, dean sch. medicine and dentistry, univ. v.p. health sciences, 2010—. Editor-in-chief: Arteriosclerosis, Thrombosis and Vascular Biology; contbr. chapters to books, articles to profl. jours. Office: University Rochester Sch Medicine and Dentistry 601 Elmwood Ave Box 706 Rochester NY 14642 Office Phone: 585-275-0810. Office Fax: 585-442-9176. *

TAUBMAN, MARTIN ARNOLD, immunologist, educator; b. NYC, July 10, 1940; s. Herman and Betty (Berger) T.; m. Joan Petra Mikelbank, May 30, 1965; children: Benjamin Abby, Joel David. BS, Bklyn. Coll., 1961; DDS, Columbia U., 1965; PhD, SUNY, Buffalo, 1970; MA (hon.), Harvard U., 1997. Asst. mem. staff Forsyth Dental Ctr., Boston, 1970—, head immunology dept., 1972—, assoc. mem. staff, 1974-80; sr. staff mem. The Forsyth Inst., 1980—; asst. clin. prof. oral biology and pathophysiology Harvard U. Sch. Dental Medicine, 1976-79, assoc. clin. prof., 1979-97, prof. dept. oral and devel. biology, 1997—2005, prof. dept. devel. biology, 2005—. Mem. oral biology and medicine study sect. NIH, 1980-84. Editor: (with J. Slots) Contemporary Microbiology and Immunology; assoc. editor: Jour. Den Res., 2004-; contbr. articles to profl. jours, chpts. to books. Recipient Rsch. Career Devel. award, 1971-76, Fred Birnberg Alumni award for disting. dental rsch. Columbia U. Assn. Dental Alumni, Disting. Faculty award Harvard Sch. Dental Medicine, 1990, MERIT award NIH, 1991 2000; USPHS fellow, 1962 63; postdoctoral fellow, 1966-70. Mem. Am. Soc. Microbiology, Soc. Mucosal Immunology, Internat. Assn. Dental Rsch. (Oral Biology award 1991), Am. Assn. Immunologists, Am. Assn. Dental Rsch. (v.p. 1987—, pres.-elect 1988, pres. 1989). Office: The Forsyth Inst 245 1st St Cambridge MA 02142-1200 E-mail: mtaubman@forsyth.org.

TAUBØLL, ERIK, neurologist; b. Oslo, July 3, 1957; s. Gunnar and Oddrun (Solberg) T.; m. Tone-Marcelle Rudene, Aug. 14, 1983; children: Henrik, Elisabeth. MD, U. Oslo, 1983, PhD, 1994. Sr. registrar dept. neurology Rikshospitalet, The Nat. Hosp., Oslo, 1986-88; scientist Norwegian Rsch. Coun. for Sci. and Humanities, 1988-91; sr. registrar dept. neurology Rikshospitalet, The Nat. Hosp. and U. Oslo, 1991—2002, dep. head dept. neurology, prof. neurology, 2004—, head rsch. divsn. clin. neuroscience, 2006—07, sect. head dept. neurology, 2010—; head sect. for adult epileptology Nat. Epilepsy Ctr., Rikshospitalet Univ. Hosp., 2007—10. Contbr. over 80 articles to profl. jours. 1st lt. Royal Norwegian Air Force, 1987-88. Recipient Forsberg Legacy grant, 1988, Monrad-Krohns Neurology prize, 2000. Mem. N.Y. Acad. Scis. Office: Rikshospitalet Dept Neurology 0027 Oslo Norway Office Phone: +4723070000. E-mail: erik.tauboll@rikshospitalet.no.

TAULBEE, THOMAS LESTER, psychotherapist, educator; b. Normal, Ill., June 12, 1947; s. Marion L. and Marjorie S. T. BS, Ill. State U., 1970; MS, Tex. A&M U., 1971, EdD, 1973. Cert. marriage and family therapist; cert. sports counselor; ordained min. Psycotherapist Human Resource Devel. Ctr., Dallas, 1974-76; prof. psychology Richland Coll., Dallas, 1976—, prof. history, 1994—. North Tex. regl. dir. Nat. Inst. Sports, 2000-2003, nat. coord. of divsn. chmn., 2002-03; bd. advisors Revival Fires Ministries, Branson West, Mo., 1997-99, bd. dirs. Sports Sys. Internat., 2001-2003, mem. sports chaplaincy adv. com. U.S. Coun. for Sports Chaplaincy, 2002-2003, exec. dir., exec. v.p., chief orgnl. officer, 2003; pres., founder Internat. Escorted Tour Svc., 2004—; internat. tour guide, with nat. and internat. cos., 1980—. Co-author: Psychology from a Personal Perspective, 1992, rev. edit., 1997; editor, co -author: Personal Applications of Psychology, 1997. Dir. Superior Student Roundtable, Parker, Tex., 1993, 1996—; bd. dirs. U.S. Coun. for Sports Chaplaincy, 2003—. Recipient Nat. Inst. for Staff and Orgnl. Devel. excellence award U. Tex., 2004; Ctr. for Behavioral Studies U. North Tex., Denton, 1973-74; named Basketball All-Am., Ill. State U., 1969; named to Ill. State U. Athletic Hall of Fame. Mem. Tex. Jr. Coll. Teachers Assn., Nat. Assn. Scholars, Assn. Behavior Analysis. Avocations: world travel, scuba diving, cooking. Office: Richland Coll 12800 Abrams Rd Dallas TX 75243-2173 E-mail: ttaulbee@verizon.net.

TAUPIN, PHILIPPE JACQUES, neurobiologist, researcher; s. Daniel Marie Taupin and Jacqueline Suzanne Humbert. BSc in Biochemistry, U. Pierre et Marie Curie, 1989, M of Biochemistry, 1989, PhD in Neurosci., 1993. Post-doctoral rschr. Salk Inst. Biol. Studies U. Calif., San Diego, 1994—2003; head lab. Nat. Neurol. Inst., Singapore. Assoc. prof. Nat. U. Singapore, 2003—07; sci. dir. Fighting Blindness Mission Rsch. Inst., Dublin City U., Glasnevin, 2007—. Author: Adult Neurogenesis and Neural Stem Cells in Mammals, 2006, The Hippocampus, 2007, The Cystatin Superfamily of Protease Inhibitor, 2008; contbr. articles to profl. jours. Recipient France Parkinson award, 1994; grantee, Groupe Servier, 1989—93, Juvenile Diabetes Rsch. Found. Bio Med Res Coun., 2004—, Nat. Med. Rsch. Coun., 2004—, Bio Med. Rsch. Coun., 2005—; fellow, Found. Med. Rsch., 1993, French Assn. Myopathies, 1995, Cancer Ctr. NIH, 1997—2000; Pasarow scholar, 2002. Mem.: Soc. Neurosci. Achievements include patents for stimulation cell proliferation by glycosylated cystatin C; postmortem stem cells. Office: Fighting Blindness Mission Rsch Inst Dublin City Univ Glasnevin Dublin 9 Ireland Personal E-mail: philippesg@hotmail.com.

TAURA, NAOTA, preventive medicine physician; b. Nagasaki, Japan, July 18, 1968; s. Tadashi and Akiko Taura; m. Yukiko Haruta; 1 child, Yuka. MD in Philosophiae, Nagasaki U. Sch. Medicine, Sakamoto, 2006. Cert. Med. Dr. Health Labour and Welfare Ministry, Japan, 1996. Hepatologist Nagasaki U. Sch. Medicine, Japan, 2003—06, Nat. Nagasaki Med. Ctr., Omura, Nagasaki, 2006—08; hepatologist dept. gastroenterology & hepatology Nagasaki U. Sch. Med., Sakamoto, Nagasaki, Japan, 2009—. Office: Dept Gastroenterology & Hepatology Nagasaki Univ Sch Med Sakamoto Nagasaki 1-7-1 852-8501 Japan Office Phone: 81-(95)819-7482. Office Fax: 81-(95)819-7482.

TAUSER, ROXANA-GEORGIANA, pharmacist, educator; b. Roman, Neamt, Romania, Sept. 18, 1968; PhD in Pharmacy, U. Medicine and Pharmacy Gr.T.Popa, Iasi, Romania, 1998; MD, U. Medicine Iasi, 2002. Assoc. prof. pharmacogenomics and individualized therapy U. Medicine and Pharmacy Gr.T.Popa Iasi, 2004—, mem. bd., 2008; guest rschr. U. Medicine Vienna, 2008; vis. scientist U. Christian Albrechts, Kiel, Germany, 2008. Prof. Bologna Nat. Assn. Students from Romania. Avocations: classical music, art. Home: 4D Garii St 4 Iasi 700094 Romania Personal E-mail: georgiana.tauser@gmail.com.

TAUVERON, IGOR, endocrinologist, educator; b. France, Jan. 1, 1962; MD, U. Auvergne, 1991, PhD. Prof, head dept., 2009—. Prof., head med. dept. Auvergne U., Clermont Ferrand U. Hosp., 2009. Mem.: French Diabetes Soc., French Endocrine Soc. Office: Endocrinologie Diabetologie CHU Clermont Ferrand Auvergne F63000 France Business E-Mail: itauveron@chu-clermontferrand.fr.

TAVAKKOLI, JAHANGIR, biomedical engineer, researcher; b. Tehran, Iran, Mar. 27, 1963; arrived in Can., 1997; s. Ghodrat Tavakkoli and Ozra Khaleghi; married; children: Niki, Neda. BS, Sharif U. Tech., Tehran, 1988, MS, 1992; PhD, U. Claude Bernard, Lyon, France, 1997. Quality control engr. Ministry of Health, Tehran, Iran, 1991—93; rsch. engr. INSREM Unit 556, Lyon, France, 1993—97; rsch. assoc. U. Toronto, Ont., Canada, 1997—2000; assoc. faculty Purdue U., Indpls., 2002—; sr. R&D scientist Focus Surgery, Inc., Indpls., 2000—. Contbr. articles to profl. jours. Rsch. grantee, NIH, 1993—. Mem.: IEEE (assoc.), Am. Inst. Ultrasound in Medicine, Acoustical Soc. Am. (assoc.). Achievements include development of novel laparoscopic probe to treat cancer using ultrasound; design of novel computer model to simulate nonlinear ultrasound beam propagation in tissue. Avocations: soccer, playing cards. Office: Focus Surgery Inc 3940 Pendleton Way Indianapolis IN 46226

TAVARES, PURIFICAÇÃO VALENZUELA S., geneticist, educator; b. Porto, Portugal, June 15, 1953; d. Amandio Sampaio and Carmen Valenzuela (Simon) Tavares; children: Bruna, Daniel. MD, U. Porto, 1976, PhD in Med. Genetics, 1990. Lectr. Faculty of Medicine, Porto, 1973-78, 1978-85; genetic cons. N.Y. Infirmary Beekman Downtown Hosp., NYC, 1983-87; asst. prof. Faculty of Medicine, Porto, 1990-94; prof. Faculty of Dental Medicine, Porto, 1994—. Prof. med. genetics U. Lisbon, Portugal, 1991—; CEO and clin. dir. Centro Genetica Clinica genetica. Author: Repeated Pregnancy Loss in Medical Genetics, 1990, Medical Genetics Departments—Aspects of Culture and Society, 1990, (chpts. in books) Bioethics, 1995, Obstetrics and Gynecology, 1995. Mem.: European Soc. Human Genetics, Ibero-Am. Soc. Human Genetics of N.Am., Portuguese Soc. Human Genetics, Assn. Portuguese Prenatal Diagnosis, Am. Soc. Human Genetics, Portugal Med. Assn. (bd. med. genetics 1999—). Avocations: painting, travel, reading, golf. Office: Centro Genetica Clinica Genetics R Sa da Bandeira 706 1 4000 432 Porto Portugal Address: Centro Genetica Clinica Av Infante Santo 34 3 1350 179 Lisbon Portugal Office: Avemida Del General Peron 44 Madrid 28020 Spain Office Phone: 351 223 389 900.

TAVARES, SAMANTHA, psychologist, educator; b. Bahia, Brazil, Oct. 23, 1968; arrived in U.S., 1984; d. Jose and Clarice Maria Tavares; 1 adopted child, Satyana Lua 1 child, Titus Sol. BA in Chinese Lang. Studies, Taipei, 1988; BA in Asian Studies, UCLA, 1990; M in Psychology, Forest Inst. Profl. Psychology, 1993; MA in Ea. Religion, U. Hawaii, 2000; PhD in Clin. Psychology, Am. Schs. Profl. Psychology, 1995. Lic. psychologist Hawaii, 1996, cert. hypnotherapist 1994, level II cert. Eye Movement Desensitization and Reprocessing. 1998, cert. holistic therapist 2000. Sch. counselor Han Guan Inst., China, 1986—88; pvt. practice clin. psychology Honolulu, Kailua, Hawaii, 1995—; clin. psychologist Dept. Health, Honolulu, 1996—98; clin. supr. Alaka'I Na Keiki, Inc., 1996—; clin. psychologist evaluator Dept. Edn. Dist. Hawaii, 1997—2000; assoc. prof. Holos U. Grad. Seminary, 2000—; faculty staff Inst. for Sci. Med. Intuition, 2000—04. Co-founder Samba Axe Hawaii, 1993—; dance instr., performer, 1993—; project dir. Support Adoption Hawaii, 2005—; exec. dir. Hawaii Hearts Helping Adoptions, 2005. Author: (compact disk, cassette tape) Transformative Liberation, 2005. Avocations: dance, yoga, meditation, running, surfing. Office: 43 Oneawa St Kailua HI Office Phone: 808-261-3731. E-mail: dr.tavaressam@yahoo.com.

TAVLI, VEDIDE, pediatric cardiologist, educator; d. Çetin and Kanite Mergen; m. Talat Tavli, Mar. 5, 1988; children: Ahmet, Nur. Degree in Medicine, Dokuz Eylul U. Sch. Medicine, Izmir-Turkey, 1986. Cert. pediatric cardiologist Turkey, 1995. Assoc. prof. pediat. Dr.Behçet Uz Children's Hosp., Izmir, 2001—, dir., 2002—, clin. chief pediatric cardiology, 2003—; prof. pediat. faculty medicine Yeditepe U., 2009. Mem. Nat. Edn. Coun. Medicine, Ankara, Turkey, 2008. Fellow: European Soc. Cardiology and Pediatric Cardiology. Office Phone: 902324892301. Personal E-mail: vedidetavli@hotmail.com.

TAVOULARIS, MARJORIE OSTERWISE, psychiatrist; b. Mt. Pleasant, Pa., May 28, 1938; d. Robert Russell and Violet Jane (Watson) Osterwise; m. James Harry Tavoularis, Mar 23, 1962 (div. 1987); children: Laura, Suzanne, Diana, Patricia. BS, U. Pitts., 1961, MD, 1966; postgrad., Pitts. Psychoanalytic Inst., 1976-85; PhD, Calif. Psychoanalytic Inst., 1996. Rotating intern St. Francis Gen. Hosp., 1966-67; resident in psychiatry U. Pitts. Western Psychiat. Inst., 1967-70; staff psychiatrist St. Frances Med. Ctr., Pitts., 1972-85, Kern Med. Ctr., Bakersfield, Calif., 1986-89; sr. psychiatrist Calif. Correctional Inst., Teachapi, 1989-91, Calif. Parole OP Clinic, Bakersfield, 1991-96; psychiatrist pvt. practice, Pitts. & Bakersfield, 1972—2006; chief psychiatrist CPS-Corcoran, 1995-96, Pelican Bay State Prison, 1996. Chief mental health svcs. Calif. Dept Correction, 1996-97, Kern County MH 1997-2008; Vet.'s Adminstr. Outpatient Clinic, 2001-05, Chestnut Ridge Counselling, 2007-2009, Family Svc. West Pa., 2005-. Fellow. Am. Psychiat. Assn.(life); mem. Ctrl. Calif. Psychiat. Soc., Kern County Med. Soc., Pa. Psychiat. Soc. (pres. 1984-85), Pitts. Psychiat. Soc. (pres. 1981-82), Pa. Med. Soc. Avocation: bridge. Home: 1340 W Pittsburgh St Scottdale PA 15683 Home Phone: 724-220-2422. Personal E-mail: moojiet2@aol.com.

TAY, JOHN SIN HOCK, pediatrician, educator, dean; b. Tangkak, Johor, West Malaysia, Oct. 8, 1942; s. Seng Hoon Tay and Hoon Hock Loh; m. Ivy Kim Kee Goh, Aug. 10, 1968; children: Faith, Say Luan, David, Say Kong. MBBS with first class honors, U. Sydney, Australia, 1967; BD with honors, U. London, 1971; M of Medicine in Pediat., U. Singapore, 1973; MD, Nat. U. Singapore, 1977, PhD, 1985, Bethany Internat. U., 2007. House officer Gen. Hosp. Malacca, Malaysia, 1967-68; med. officer Ministry of Health, Johor, Malaysia, 1968-72; univ. trainee dept. pediatrics U. Singapore, 1972-73, lectr., 1973-76, sr. lectr., 1976-80; assoc. prof. dept. pediatrics Nat. U. Singapore, 1980-84, prof., 1985-95, prof., head dept., 1988-95. Editor: A Practical Manual on Acute Paediatrics, 1989; author: (book) God's Destiny for You, 2008, God's Destiny for Your Nation, 2008, Sudoku for Everyone, 2009, Discovering God in Mathematics, 2009, A Short History of Indigenous Mission in Singapore, 2010, Born Gay?, 2010, Ancient Paths Journeys Along The Ancient Trade Routes, 2010, Acts of The Apostles, 2010. Dean, faculty Bibilical studies Bethany Internat. U., 2007—; hon. priest Diocese of Singapore (Anglican), 1980—95; dean St. Andrew's Cathedral (Anglican), Singapore, 1996—2004, Covenant Vision Ctr. Sch. Bibl. Studies, 2004—06. Colombo Plan scholar, Med. U. Sydney, Australia, 1961—66. Fellow: Acad. Medicine Singapore (Young Investigator's award 1977), Royal Coll. Physicians Edinburgh, Am. Coll. Med. Genetics, Am. Coll. Cardiology, Royal Australasian Coll. Physicians; mem.: Assn. S.E. Asian Nations Pediat. Fedn. (v.p. 1983—86, pres. 1986—88), Singapore Pediat. Soc. (pres. 1983—85, 9th Haridas Meml. lectr. 1982). Avocations: music, reading, chess. Home: 21 Corporation Rise Singapore 618335 Singapore Home Phone: 65-6898-3180. Fax: 65-6262 1214. E-mail: stjh21@singnet.com.sg.

TAYAL, ASHIS H., neurologist, educator; MD, Tufts U. Diplomate Am. Bd. Psychiatry and Neurology-vascular neurology, Am. Bd. Psychiatry and Neurology-neurology, Am. Bd. Internal Medicine, Am. Soc. Neuroimaging-neurosonology. Intern Mt. Sinai Med. Ctr., NYC, resident, Univ. Pitts. Med. Ctr., Pa., fellow in vascular neurology; asst. prof. neurology Drexel Univ.; med. dir. comprehensive stroke ctr. Allegheny Gen. Hosp. Named one of Top Doctors, Pitts. mag., 2011. Office: Allegheny General Hospital 320 E N Ave Pittsburgh PA 15212 Office Phone: 412-359-3131. Office Fax: 412-359-4108.

TAYAR, RENE BENEDICT, radiologist, consultant; b. Sliema, Malta, Oct. 3, 1945; arrived in England, 1971. s. Oscar and Violetta (Riccardi) T.; m. Margaret Rose Tortell, Jan. 25, 1971; 1 child, Benjamin. MD, Royal U. Malta. Registrar Bristol Royal Infirmary, England, 1974—77, sr. registrar, 1977—81; cons. radiologist St. Helier Hosp., Carshalton, Surrey, England, 1981—2010, Parkside Hosp., Wimbledon, London, 1985—, St. Anthony's Hosp., Cheam, Surrey, 1995—, Royal Hosp. Neurodisability, London, 2009—. Hon. sr. lectr. St. George's Hosp. Med. Sch., U. London, 1985 2010; com. magnetic resonance British Standards Inst. Co-founder, organizer Sir Harry Secombe Ct. Scanner Pub. Appeal, 1985, Sir Harry Secombe M.R. Scanner Pub. Appeal, 1992. Fellow: Coll. Radiologists (London); mem.: Magnetic Resonance Radiologists Assn. (hon. sec.), Royal Automobile Club (Pall Mall). Avocations: tennis, motor vehicles, jazz. Personal E-mail: rene.tayar@epsom-sthelier.nhs.uk.

TAYLOE, DAVID T., JR., pediatrician; b. Phila., Mar. 24, 1949; MD, U. NC Sch. Medicine, 1974. Intern pediat. St. Christopher's Hosp. Children, Phila., 1974—75, resident pediat., 1975—76; resident NC Meml. Hosp., Chapel Hill, 1976—77; pvt. practice pediatrician Goldsboro, NC, 1977—. Contbr. articles to profl. jours. Fellow: Am. Acad. Pediat. (NC chpt. pres. 1993—95, nat. pres. 2008—09). Address: Goldsboro Pediat 2706 Medical Office Pl Goldsboro NC 27530 Office: AAP Nat Hdqs 141 Northwest Point Blvd Alden IL 60001 *

TAYLOR, ALLEN, nutritionist, educator; PhD in Organic Chemistry, Rutgers U. Dir. & sr. scientist Lab. Nutrition & Vision, Jean Mayer USDA Human Nutrition Rsch. Ctr. on Aging; prof. dept. biochemistry Sackler Sch. Grad. Biomedical Sciences; assoc. prof. dept. ophthalmology Tufts U. Sch. Medicine; prof. Friedman Sch. Nutrition Sci. & Policy Tufts. U. Office: Tufts University Jean Mayer USDA HNRCA 711 Washington St Boston MA 02111-1524 Office Phone: 617-556-3156. Office Fax: 617-556-3132. E-mail: allen.taylor@tufts.edu.

TAYLOR, ANDREA B., medical educator; b. Evanston, Ill., Apr. 18, 1961; BA, U. Calif., Berkeley, 1983; PhD, U. Pitts., 1992. Assoc. prof. Duke U. Sch. Medicine, Durham, NC, 2000—. Assoc. editor Jour. Human Evolution, 2006—. Recipient Master Clinician & Tchr. Award, Duke U. Sch. Medicine; grants, NSF, grant, NIH. Mem.: Am. Assn. Clin. Anatomists, Am. Assn. Anatomists, Am. Assn. Phys. Anthropologists (exec. com. mem. 2011—). Avocations: travel, reading, gardening. Office: Duke University Sch Medicine Doctor Physical Therapy Program Durham NC 27708 Business E-Mail: andrea.taylor@duke.edu.

TAYLOR, ANDREW T., JR., radiologist, educator; b. Jackson, Tenn., Jan. 14, 1942; MD, Duke U., 1968. Cert. nuclear medicine Splty. Bd. 1, internal medicine Splty. Bd. 2. Resident U. Hosp.-U.C.S.D., San Diego, 1970, 1972—74, intern, 1969; co-dir. nuc. medicine Emory U. Sch. Med., prof. radiology, 2002—. Mem.: Am. Bd. of Nuclear Medicine (past chair). Office: Emory U Sch of Medicine Radiology 1440 Clifton Rd Atlanta GA 30322

TAYLOR, AUBREY ELMO, physiologist, educator; b. El Paso, Tex., June 4, 1933; s. Virgil T. and Mildred (Maher) Taylor; m. Mary Jane Davis, Apr. 4, 1953; children: Audrey Jane Hildebrand, Lenda Sue Taylor Brown, Mary Ann. BA in Math. and Psychology, Tex. Christian U., 1960; PhD in Physiology, U. Miss., 1964. Fellow biophysics lab. Harvard U. Med. Sch., Boston, 1965-67; from asst.

prof. to prof. dept. physiology U. Miss. Coll. Medicine, Jackson, 1967-77; prof., chmn. dept. physiology U. South Ala. Coll. Medicine, Mobile, 1977—2002, Louise Lenoir Locke eminent scholar disting. prof. emeritus, 2002—. Pulmonary score com. mem. Nat. Heart, Lung and Blood Inst., 1976; with Surgery and Anesthesiology, 1979—82, Manpower Com., 1985—95; chmn. RAP, 1983; spl. lectr. Wu-Ho-Su Meml. Symposium. Mem. editl. bd.: Jour. Applied Physiology, 1994—, Critical Care Medicine, 1991—97, Circulation Rsch., Am. Jour. Physiology, Internat. Pathophysiology, Microcirculatory and Lymphatic Rsch., Chinese Jour. Physiology, Microcirculation, Jour. Biomed. Sci., Am. Rev. Resp. and Critical Care Jour., Internat. Soc. Pathology, author 9 books:; contbr. chapters to books, over 730 articles to profl. jours.; N.Am. editor: Clin. Scis., 1998—. With US Army, 1953—55. Recipient Lederle Faculty award, 1967—70, Philip Dow award, U. Ga., 1984, NIH Merit award, 1987—97, Lucian award, McGill U., 1988, John Whitney award, U. Ark., 1990, Gelen award, Intestinal Shock Soc., 1991, Arthur C. Guyton award, U. Miss Coll. Medicine, 1993, Myerson-De Luzio Lectr., Tulane Sch. Medicine, 1997, Disting. Lectr., La State U., Shreveport, 1997, Med. Student Rsch. Conf., U. Tex. Sch. Medicine, Galveston, 1998, Abreu Meml. Keynote Spkr., 1998, Disting. Alumnus award, Tex. Christian U., 1998, 1998, Disting Svc. award, USA med. Alumni Assn., 2000, Disting. Graduate award, Paschal H.S., 2002; named Disting. Physiologist, Am. Coll. Chest Physicians, 1994; grantee NIH, 1964—. Fellow: Royal Soc. Medicine (bd. dirs.), Am. Heart Assn. (So. regional rev. com. 1977—81, cardiopulmonary, critical care coun. 1977—, chmn. 1979—81, EIA Rev. Com. 1986—95, pulmonary and devel. rev. com. 1987—95, nat. rsch. com. 1990—95, del. assembly 1990—99, chmn. 1993—98, chmn. grant/rev.com 1994—95, coun. affairs com. 1994—98, nominating com. 1998—99, basic sci. com. 1998—, circulation coun., chmn., AALAC bd. trustees rep., Bronze award Miss. AHA 1976, Dickinson W. Richards award 1988, Outstanding Ala. AHA program 1993, Sci. Coun. Achievement award 1995, Disting. Svc. award 1995, Rsch. Achievement award 1997, So. Ala. Dist. Achievement award 2000, Gala honoree 2000, Hall of Fame Spring Hill Hosp. Heart Assn. 2001), AAAS; mem.: European Respiratory Soc. (sec. lung injury group), Am. Thoracic Soc., Fedn. Am. Socs. for Exptl. Biology (bd. dirs. 1988—90, reorganizing com.), Biophys. Soc., N.Y. Acad. Scis., Internat. Pathophysiology Soc. (v.p. 1991—99), N. Am. Soc. Lymphology (pres. 1988—90, Cecil Drinker Rsch. award 1988), Internat. Lymphology Soc., Ala. Acad. Scis. (Am. State Rsch. award 1988), Micro Circulatory Soc. (coun. 1977—81, pres. 1981—83, Eugene Landis Rsch. award 1985), Assn. Dept. Chairs of Physiology (exec. com. 1996—2001, sec. treas. 1998—2002), Am. Physiol. Soc. (coun. 1984—87, chmn. mem. com. 1985—87, pres. 1987—90, hon. com., chmn. 1993—96, chmn. Perkins fellow com. 1996—98, Cannon lectr. 1999, Wiggers award 1987, Achievement award 2002), NAS (com. for Internat. Union Physiol. Sci.), Sigma Xi, Alpha Omega Alpha. Democrat. Presbyterian. Achievements include research in in cardio-pulmonary physiology, fluid balance, edema, microcirculation and capillary exchange of solute and water and inflammatory processes in the lung. Home: 11 Audubon Pl Mobile AL 36606-1907

TAYLOR, BARRY LLEWELLYN, microbiologist, educator; b. Sydney, May 7, 1937; arrived in US, 1967; s. Fredrick Llewelyn and Vera Lavina (Clarke) T.; m. Desmyrna Ruth Tolhurst, Jan. 4, 1961; children: Lyndon, Nerida, Darrin. BA, Avondale Coll., Cooranbong, New South Wales, 1959; BSc with honors, U. New South Wales, Sydney, 1966; PhD, Case Western Res. U., 1973; postgrad., U. Calif., Berkeley, 1973-75. Vis. postdoctoral fellow Australian Nat. U., Canberra, 1975-76; asst. prof. biochemistry Loma Linda (Calif.) U., 1976-78, assoc. prof. biochemistry, 1978-83, prof. biochemistry, 1983—, prof., chmn. dept. microbiology and molecular genetics, 1988-2000, interim dir. Ctr. for Molecular Biology, 1989-94, 96-98, v.p. for rsch. affairs, 2000—06, prof. microbiology and molecular genetics, 2006—. Contbr. articles to profl. publs. Rsch. grantee Am. Heart Assn., 1978-85, NIH, 1981—. Mem. Am. Soc. Microbiology, Am. Soc. Biochemistry and Molecular Biology. Office: Divsn Microbiology and Molecular Genetics Loma Linda U Loma Linda CA 92350-0001 Office Phone: 909-558-4881. Business E-Mail: bltaylor@llu.edu.

TAYLOR, CARMEL THERESE, medical researcher; b. Goondiwindi, Queensland, Australia, July 24, 1965; BS, U. Queensland, 1986. Rsch. asst. dept. vet. pathology & pub. health U. Queensland, 1987, rsch. asst. dept. ob-gyn., 1988—89, rsch. asst. dept. microbiology, 1989—90; scientist Queensland Health Forensic and Sci. Svcs., 1990—2008, supervising scientist, diagnostic serology, pub. health virology, 2008—. Mem.: Australian Soc. Microbiology. Home: 36 Monash Rd Tarragindi Queensland 4121 Australia Business E-Mail: carmel_taylor@health.qld.gov.au.

TAYLOR, COLMAN BRIAN, research scientist; b. New Zealand, Mar. 17, 1982; BPE, U. Otago, 2003; M in Nutrition & Dietetics, U. Sydney, 2005. Rsch. fellow George Inst. Global Health, 2006—. Recipient Innovation award, U. Sydney, Coll. Health Scis. Office: PO Box M201 Missenden Rd Camperdown NSW 2050 Australia

TAYLOR, DORIS ANITA, molecular biology educator; b. San Francisco, Feb. 21, 1956; d. Benton and Julia P. (Williams) T. BS in Biology, Miss. U. for Women, 1977; PhD in Pharmacology, Southwestern Med. Sch., Dallas, 1988. Lab.instr. med. pharmacology U. Tex. Southwestern Med. Sch., Dallas, 1981-83, lectr. physician's assts. pharmacology course, 1981-86; molecular biology tng. dept. microbiology and immunology Albert Einstein Coll. Medicine, Bronx, NY, 1988-91; med. rsch. assoc. dept. medicine divsn. cardiology Duke U. Med. Ctr., Durham, NC, 1991-96, asst. rsch. prof. depts. medicine-surgery divsn. cardiology, 1996—, asst. rsch. prof. dept. biomed. engring., 1997; with U. Minn., 2003—, prof. medicine and physiology, Medtronic Bakken Chair in Cardiovascular Repair, dir., Ctr. for Cardiovascular Repair. Dir. molecular biology course immunologist fellowship tng. program Bronx-Lebanon Hosp., 1991; cons. drug utilization rev. program 1st Health Svcs. Corp., Chapel Hill, N.C., 1993-95; cons. Medtronic, Mpls. and Fridley, Minn., 1997-99; ad hoc reviewer surgery and bioengring. study sect. NIH, 1998-99; co-moderator Am. Heart Assn. 63rd Ann. Sci. Sessions, Dallas, 1998; mem. scientific committee and jury, Grand Prix Lefoulon-Delande Found., Inst. France; presenter in field, 1991—. Mem. editl. bd. Jour. MOlecular and Cellular Cardiology, 1997—; Assoc. editor Jour. Cardiac Vascular Regeneration, 1998—; contbr. several articles and abstracts to sci. jours., including Jour. Biol. Chemistry, Am. Jour. Med. Scis., Jour. Molecular Biology, Devel. Biology, Jour. Molecular Cell Cardiology, Egyptian Heart Jour., Molecular Cell Biochemistry, Am. Jour. Physiology, Nature Medicine. Bd. dirs. Our Own Place, cmty. ctr., Durham, 1994-96, N.C. Pride PAC, Raleigh, 1996-97; chpt. pres. People's Alliance, Durham, 1999-00. Profiled in Pitts. Tissue Engring. Initiative, 1997, Blackwell Corp. for Pub. Broadcasting, 1998; grantee Am. Cancer Soc., 1992-93, N.C. Heart Assn., 1995-97, Medtronic Inc., 1996-98, 99-00, Duke Heart Ctr., 1996-97, NIH, 1997-04, N.C. Biotech. Assn., 1998-99. Mem. AAAS, Am. Heart Assn. (coun. on basic sci.), Am. Assn. Engring. Eductors, Heart Failure Assn. Am., Tissue Culture Assn., Internat. Soc. for Heart Rsch., Internat. Soc. for Heart and Lung Transplantation (co-chair cell therapy tissue engring. coun.), Rsch. NC (spkr.'s bur.), N.C. Assn. for Biomed. Rsch. Democrat. Medical firsts with team members include: Repair of function in an injured heart with cell therapy in 1998; prevention and reversal of atherosclerosis with cells in 2003 and 2007; Robot-based cell delivery in heart (in animals) in 2007; found new stem cells in adult heart that can generate blood vessels and both left and right ventricular cardiocytes in 2007; showed male and female stem cells differ in their ability for repair in 2007; measured endogenous repair in heart disease in 2008; perfusion decellularization of whole organs in 2008; created a completely new beating rat heart in the laboratory on January 14, 2008. This breakthrough is expected to pave the way for future research to eventually create entire replacement organs based on the patient's own cells, which would eliminate the need for transplants or drugs to prevent rejection. Mailing: U Minn Biomedical Engring Inst 7-105 BSBE 1191 312 Church St SE Minneapolis MN 55455 Office: U Minn Biomedical Engring Inst 7-112 BSBE Minneapolis MN 55455 Office Phone: 612-626-1416.

TAYLOR, DUNCAN PAUL, pharmacologist, researcher; b. Bremerton, Wash., Feb. 4, 1949; s. Alan Earl and Barbara Eleanor (Thiel) T.; m. Jeanne Louise Damgaard, Apr. 8, 1972; 1 child, Jack Xander. BS in Chemistry, Calif. Inst. Tech., 1971; PhD in Biochemistry, Oreg. State U., 1978. Technician analytical svcs. Carnation Co. Rsch. Labs., Van Nuys, Calif., 1967-70; Peace Corps vol. Princess Margaret Secondary Sch., St. Johns, Antigua and Barbuda, 1971-73; grad. tchg. and rsch. asst. biochemistry and biophysics Oreg. State U., Corvallis, 1973-77; rsch. assoc. sect. biochemistry and pharmacology NIMH, Bethesda, Md., 1977-79; scientist, neuropharmacologist, rsch. assoc. Pharm. divsn. Mead Johnson & Co., Evansville, Ind., 1979-80; sr. scientist, group leader Pharm. div. Mead Johnson & Co., Evansville, Ind., 1980-82; sr. scientist, group leader, neuropharmacologist Pharm. R & D divsn. Bristol-Myers Co., Evansville, 1982-83, sr. rsch. scientist, mgr., 1983-85, rsch. fellow preclin. ctrl. nervous sys. rsch., 1985-89; sr. rsch. fellow preclin. ctrl. nervous sys. rsch. Pharm. Rsch. Inst. Bristol-Myers Squibb Co., Wallingford, Conn., 1989-94; dir. pharmacology Symphony Pharms., Malvern, Pa., 1994-95; cons., 1995-96; analyst bus. devel. Pharmacia & Upjohn, Kalamazoo, 1996-98, dir. strategic rsch. assessment, 1998—2003, Pharmacia Corp., Kalamazoo, Biovail Techs., Ltd., Bridgewater, NJ, 2004—05; sr. dir. strategic intelligence Biovail Pharms., Inc., Bridgewater, 2005—07; prin. MT Enterprises, Flemington, NJ, 2007—08; sr. dir. bus. devel. SK Life Sci., Fair Lawn, NJ, 2008—. Mem. external adv. bd. dept. chemistry U. So. Miss.; grant reviewer NSF, 1981, 82, Med. Rsch. Coun. Can., 1987, 88; frequent presenter to profl. confs.; cons. in field. Contbr. numerous articles and abstracts to profl. jours. Bd. dirs. Posey County chpt. Am. Cancer Soc., 1983—85; mem. Tri-State Cursillo Cmty.; mentor Horizons Leadership Acad., Evansville-Vanderburgh Sch. Corp., 1985; cons. Project Bus. Jr. Achievement, 1988; mem. chancel choir 1st United Meth. Ch., Mt. Vernon, Ind., 1979—86; mem. adult choir South Congl. Ch., Middletown, Conn., 1986—96, deacon, 1987—90, 1995—96, co-chmn., 1989—90, 1996, mem. coun., 1989—90, mem. task force on long-range planning, 1989—90; mem. adult choir 2d Reformed Ch., Kalamazoo, 1997—2004, mem. handbell choir, 1997—2004, mem. worship coun., 1997—99, elder, 1998—2001, consistory mem., 1998—2001, ch. outreach coun., 2000—01; mem. Grace United Ch. of Christ, Flemington, NJ, 2005—, trustee, 2006—11, coun. moderator, 2006—10. Scholar Carnation Co., 1967-70, Calif. State scholar, 1967-68, 70; rsch. fellow NSF, 1970, Cold Spring Harbor Labs., 1974. Fellow: Am. Inst. Chemists; mem.: Lic. Exec. Soc., Am. Acad. Neurology, Internat. Brain Rsch. Orgn.-World Fedn. Neuroscientists, Fedn. Am. Socs. for Exptl. Biology, European Brain and Behavior Soc., Brit. Brain Rsch. Assn, Soc. for Neurosci. (v.p. Conn. chpt. 1989—93), Am. Soc. for Pharmacology and Exptl. Therapeutics, Am. Chem. Soc., Phi Lambda Upsilon, Sigma Xi. Democrat. Achievements include patent for method and treatment of ischemia in the brain; made significant efforts in identification and development of new antipsychotics and antidepressants; identification of potential mechanism of action of the antipsychotic BMY14802; research in receptors, in etiology, expression and pharmacotherapy of psychiatric disorders. Home: 11 Jockey Ln Flemington NJ 08822-1599 Business E-Mail: dtaylor@sklsi.com.

TAYLOR, EDNA JANE, retired employment program counselor; b. Flint, Mich., May 16, 1934; d. Leonard Lee and Wynona Ruth (Davis) Harvey; children: Wynona Jane MacDonald, Cynthia Lee Zellmer. BS, No. Ariz. U., 1963; MEd, U. Ariz., 1967. Tchr. h.s. Sunnyside Sch. Dist., Tucson, 1963—68; employment program counselor employment devel. State of Calif., Canoga Park, 1968—98; ret., 1998. Mem. adv. coun. Van Nuys Cmty. Adult Sch., Calif., 1983-96, steering com., 1989-91, leadership coun., 1991-92; mem. adv. coun. Pierce CC, Woodland Hills, Calif., 1979-81; first aid instr., recreational leader ARC. Mem. AARP, NAFE, Internat. Assn. of Pers. in Employment Security, Calif. Employment Counselors Assn. (state treas. 1978-79, state sec. 1980), Delta Psi Kappa (life). Avocations: writing, tennis, health and fitness, gardening.

TAYLOR, EDWARD STEWART, obstetrician, educator; b. Hecla, SD, Aug. 20, 1911; s. Robert Stewart and Sylvia Frances (Dewey) T.; m. Ruth Fatherson, June 15, 1940; children: Edward Stewart, Elizabeth Dewey Taylor Bryant, Catherine Wells Taylor. BA, U. Iowa, 1933, MD, 1936. Diplomate Am. Bd. Ob-Gyn (dir. 1962-69). Intern, Hurley Hosp., Flint, Mich., 1936-37; splty. tng. ob-gyn L.I. Coll. Hosp., 1937-41; prof. ob-gyn, chmn. dept. Sch. Medicine, U. Colo., 1947-76, clin. prof., 1976-81, prof., chmn. emeritus, 1981—. Nat. cons. ob-gyn to surg. gen. USAF, 1958-62. Author: Manual of Gynecology, 1952, Essentials of Gynecology, 4th edit.; editor: Beck's Obstetrical Practice, 10th edit.; editor-in-chief for obstetrics: Obstetrical and Gynecol. Survey, 1967-92. Trustee Denver Symphony Orch., 1979-85. Served to lt. col. AUS, 1942-45. Endowed ob-gyn. chair U. Colo., 1999. Fellow ACS, Am. Coll. Obstetricians and Gynecologists (Disting. Svc. award 1984); mem. AMA, Am. Gynecol. Soc. (v.p. 1974-75), Am. Assn. Obstetricians and Gynecologists (pres. 1970-71), Ctrl. Assn. Obstetricians and Gynecologists, S.W. Obstet. and Gynecol. Soc. (hon.), Am. Gynecol. and Obstet. Soc., Assn. Profs. Ob-Gyn (pres. 1974-75), Western Surg. Soc., Finnish Gynecol. Soc. (hon.), University Club, Alpha Omega Alpha. Congregationalist. Home: 80 S Dexter St Denver CO 80246-1051

TAYLOR, GEORGE PEACH, JR., aerospace transportation executive, retired military officer; b. Birmingham, Ala. BA in Physics and Russian Language, Rice U., Houston, Tex., 1975; MD, Baylor Coll. Medicine, 1978; MPH, Harvard Sch. Pub. Health, Boston, Mass., 1984; attended, Nat. War Coll., Fort Lesley J. McNair, Washingron, DC, 1992—93. Lic. Tex. Advanced through grades to gen. USAF, 2002; resident USAF Sch. of Aerospace Medicine, Brooks AFB, Tex., 1984—85; chief flight medicine, squadron flight surgeon USAF Clinic, Kadena AFB, Japan, 1979—81; chief aerospace medicine Detachment 3 Air Force Flight Test Ctr., Henderson, Nev., 1981—83; chief aerospace medicine, comdr. air transportable hosp. USAF Hosp., Torrejon AFB, Spain, 1985—88; med. inspector active duty forces Air Force Inspection and Safety Ctr., Norton AFB, Calif., 1988—90; chief aerospace medicine USAF Hosp., Air Force Flight Test Ctr., Edwards AFB, Calif., 1990—92; comdr. and dir. base med. svcs. 75th med. group Ogden Air Logistics Ctr., Hill AFB, Utah, 1993—95; chief aerospace med. divsn., later dep. dir. Air Force Med. Ops. Agy., Bolling AFB, Washington, 1995—96; assoc. dir. to dir. med. programs and resources USAF, 1996—97, command surgeon Ramstein AFB, Germany, 1997—2000, Air Combat Command, Langley AFB, Va., 2000—02; asst. surgeon gen. expeditionary ops., sci. & tech. USAF, Washington, 2002, spl. asst. to surgeon gen. Air Force, 2002, surgeon gen., 2002—06; sr. mng. dir. fed. practice PriceWaterhouseCoopers, LLP, Washington, 2006—09; v.p. health & human services info. tech. divsn. Northrop Grumman Corp., McLean, Va., 2009—. Chmn., base realignment and closure Joint Med. Cross Svc. Group, 2002—05; disting. prof. mil./emergency medicine Uniformed Svcs. U. Health Svcs. Decorated DSM, Def. Superior Svc. medal, Legion of Merit with oak leaf cluster, Bronze Star medal, Meritorious Svc. medal with four oak leaf clusters, Air Force Commendation medal, Air Force Achievement medal, Air Force Recognition Ribbon, Gold Cross of Honor of the Bundeswehr Germany; recipient Malcom C. Grow award for Air Force Flight Surgeon of Yr. Fellow: Aerospace Med. Assn. (former coun. mem.), Am. Coll. Preventive Medicine; mem.: AMA (Air Force delegate), Soc. US Air Force Flight Surgeons (former pres.), Assn. Military Surgeons of U.S. (life Founders Medal), Am. Soc. Aerospace Medicine Specialists (former pres.). Office: Northrop Grumann Information Technology 7575 Colshire Dr Mc Lean VA 22102 Office Phone: 703-713-4000.

TAYLOR, HARRIS C., endocrinologist, consultant; b. Bklyn., Apr. 30, 1940; s. William and Florence Ruth T.; m. Diana Kahn, Sept. 3, 1962; children: Brian David, Rebecca Lynn. BS, Queens Coll., 1961; MD, U. Chgo., 1965. Diplomate Am. Bd. Internal Medicine, Am. Bd. Endocrinology and Metabolism. Cons. endocrinologist Kaiser Found., Cleve., 1972-86; chief divsn. endocrinology Luth. Med. Ctr., Cleve., 1977-96, dir. endocrinology & radioimmunoassay lab., 1978-96, dir. internal medicine residency, 1985-94, dir. rsch., internal medicine residency program Fairview Health Sys., 1996—. Sr. clin. instr. Case Western Res. U. Sch. Medicine, Cleve., 1977-81, clin. asst. prof., 1981-88, clin. assoc. prof. medicine in endocrinology, 1988-2003, clin. prof., 2003—11; site prin. investigator NIH, 2006-08, co-prin. investigator, 2008-2009. Contbr. articles to profl. jours. Chmn. program com. Diabetes Assn. Cleve., 1976-81, exec. com., 1978-85, pres.-elect, 1981-82, pres., 1982-84. Sr. asst. surgeon USPHS, 1966-68. Named One of Best Drs. in Cleve., Cleve. Mag., 1998, 2002, 2004. Fellow: ACP (reviewer Annals of Internal Medicine 1986—2008, Master Tchr. award 2001), Am. Coll. Endocrinology (editl. bd. Endocrine Practice 1997—2004); mem.: Endocrine Soc., Am. Assn. Clin. Endocrinologists, Phi Beta Kappa. Jewish. Avocations: stamp collecting/philately, classical music. Office: Fairview Gen Hosp Dept Medicine 18101 Lorain Ave Cleveland OH 44111 Office Phone: 216-476-7369. Personal E-mail: dkthct62@sbcglobal.net.

TAYLOR, IAN LOGAN, dean; b. Eng. MD, PhD, Liverpool Med. Sch. Fellow in gastrointestinal rsch. UCLA, mem. Wadsworth V.A. Tng. Program, various positions, prof. medicine; chief of gastroenterology Duke U., 1986—89, dir. Sarah W. Stedman Ctr. for Nutritional Studies, 1989—90, prof. physiology, dept. cell biology, 1990—93; prof. and chmn. dept. medicine Med. U. S.C., 1993—2001, pres. U. Med. Assocs., 1999—2001; dean Sch. Medicine Tulane U., 2001—05; dean Coll. Medicine SUNY Health Sci. Ctr., Bklyn., 2006—. Office: Coll Medicine SUNY Health Sci Ctr 470 Clarkson Ave Brooklyn NY 11203 *

TAYLOR, JILL BOLTE, neuroanatomist; b. 1959; BA in Biology and Physiol. Psychology, Ind. U., Bloomington, 1982; PhD in Neuroanatomy, Ind. U., 1991. Rsch. asst. Ind. U., Terre Haute Ctr. Med. Edn., Med. Gross Anatomy Lab., Neurosci. Lab., Med. Histology Lab., 1983—91; postdoctoral fellow, Dept. Neurobiology, Lab. Visual Physiology Harvard Med. Sch., Boston, 1991—93; rsch. assoc., asst. neuroanatomist, Lab. Structural Neurosci. McLean Hosp., Dept. Psychiatry, Harvard Med. Sch., 1993—97; cons. neuroanatomist, brain cancer Midwest Proton Radiotherapy Inst. Tchg. asst., instr. Ind. U., 1985—89; tchg. asst., vis. lectr. Terre Haute Ctr. Med. Edn., 1985—91; vis. lectr. DePauw Coll., 1990—91; brain bank assoc., spokesperson McLean Brain Tissue Resource Ctr., 1993—95; instr. Harvard Sch. Dental Med., 1993—96; course dir. Rose Hulman Inst. Tech., Dept. Applied Biology, Biomedical Engring., 1999, Ind. U., Dept. Kinesiology, 2004—06; vol. lab. instr. Ind. U. Sch. Medicine, 2004—06, adjunct instr., Bloomington Med. Sci. Prog., 2005—; mem. planning com. Crisis Intervention Trainingprog., 2006—; founder Bloomington Brain Tumor Support Grp., 2007—; nat. spokesperson, psychiat. disorders Harvard Brain Tissue Resource

Ctr. Author: My Stroke of Insight: A Brain Scientist's Personal Journey, 2006 (Publishers Weekly bestseller); contbr. articles to profl. jours. Vol. Am. Heart Assn., Am. Stroke Assn., 2000—02; singer for inmates Monroe County Jail, 2006, instr. drug awareness prog., 2006—; mentor to Eagle Scouts Bloomington, Terre Haute, Columbus, 2006—; mentor women's basketball team Ind. U., 2007—. Recipient Excellence award for contribution in advocacy, Mass. Alliance Mental Illness, 1995, Indpls. Mini-Marathon Celebration of Life award, Nat. Alliance Mental Illness, 2007, Distinguished Alumni award, Ind. U., 2007; named Mem. of Yr., Nat. Alliance Mental Illness, 2003; named one of The 100 Most Influential People in the World, TIME mag., 2008. Mem.: Nat. Alliance Mental Illness (bd. dirs. 1996—97, pres. greater Bloomington area 2005—). Achievements include design of anatomically correct stained glass brains. Office: Jill Bolte Taylor PhD PO Box 1181 Bloomington IN 47402 Personal E-mail: drjill@drjilltaylor.com.

TAYLOR, JIMMY LYNN, retired family practice physician, administrator; b. Franklin County, NC, May 11, 1936; s. Herman Benjamin and Ruby Lynn (Perry) T.; m. Dorothy Keenum, Sept. 4, 1960; children: Gregory Scott, Sonya Lynn Taylor Loper. AA, Mars Hill Coll., 1956; BS, Wake Forest U., 1958; MD, Wake Forest U. Sch. Medicine, 1962. Postdoctoral fellow Greenville (S.C.) Gen. Hosp., 1962-63; staff physician USPHS Indian Hosp., Pine Ridge, SD, 1963-65, chief of obstetrics, 1964-65; family physician, co-founder Monroe (N.C.) Family Med. Ctr., 1965, family physician, ptnr., 1965-95; student physician Wingate (N.C.) U., 1987-94; med. dir. Brian Ctr. Nursing Facility, Monroe, 1992-95. H.S. team physician, 1965—75. Lt. comdr. USPHS, 1963-65. Recipient Head Start Child Care Achievement award N.C. Head Start Assn., 1990. Fellow Am. Acad. Family Physicians; mem. Am. Bd. Family Practice (diplomate), N.C. Acad. Family Physicians, N.C. Med. Soc., Union County Med. Soc. (pres. 1976-77). Republican. Baptist. Avocations: golf, fishing, gardening, bridge, collecting autographed first edition books. Home: 1657 Pageland Hwy Monroe NC 28112-8737 Office: Monroe Family Med Ctr 5231 John Tyler Hwy Williamsburg VA 23185-2553 Personal E-mail: jtaylor28112@yahoo.com, jtaylor6@carolina.rr.com.

TAYLOR, JOHN CALVIN, dentist; b. Cin., July 22, 1914; s. John Calvin Taylor V and Magdala Elizabeth Siehl; m. Adah Packard Boggs, Mar. 7, 1941; children: Sarah, Margaret, Virginia, John, Frederick, Alison, Carla. BSc, Muskingum Coll., 1937; BD, Cedarville Sem., 1939; DDS, U. Pitts., 1949; cert. excellence in Hindi and Urdu, Lang. Sch., Landour, India, 1940-41. Diploma Acad. Gen. Dentistry, Am. Biog. Inst., 2005; cert. in med. missions, wildlife and theology, Internat. Biog. Ctr., 2009. Missionary Reformed Presbyn. Synod, Roorkee, India, 1939-46; moderator Reformed Presbyn., Pitts., 1946—47; nat. missions missionary Presbyn. Bd. Home Missions, Pitts., Tyre, Pa., 1947-52; missionary dentist United Presbyn., Pitts., Seattle, 1953-59; dir. Meth. Mission Hosp. Dental Clinic, Bariely, India, 1954—55; founder Dental Clinic Landour Cmty. Hosp., Mussoorie, India, 1955-59; pres. Rotary Club Internat., Mount Union, Pa., 1964-65; pastor 3 chs. Mt. Union, Johnsonburg and St. Mary areas, 1964-68; founder Shanta Bhawan Hosp. Dental Clinic, Katmandu, Nepal, 1968, Missionary Dentist, Inc., 1977; dental missionary svc. E.L.W.A. Hosp., Liberia, 1977, Tank Hosp., Pakistan, 1980—81, Sahiwal Hosp., Pakistan, 1981, Shell Clinics, Ecuador, 1983; provider free dental care India, 1978—2001; founder Oral Clinic Ctr., Dera Dun, India, 1981—. Tchr. emergency dentistry Vellore (India) Med. Coll., 1958, dentist Youth With a Mission, Mercy Ship, Hawaii, 1985. Author: Wildlife in India's Tiger Kingdom, 1980, Face the Devil's Roar, 1995, God's Kingdom helps Animal Kingdoms, 2005, The Creator God Saves Lives- Some Eternally, 2009 Co-founder, life mem. Wildlife Preservation Soc., Dehra-Dun, India, 1954—, organizer, founder Rajpur Wildlife Cheetal Pk., 1954—. Recipient Cert. of Honor for 50 Yrs. of Dedicated Svc. to Dentistry, ADA, 1999. Mem. Herminie Lions Club (fgn. chmn., Lions Hat award), N.Am. Hunting Club, NRA. Republican. Presbyterian. Avocations: zoology, hunting, taxidermy, photography, music. Home Phone: 724-446-7732; Office Phone: 724-446-7732. Personal E-mail: tgrtlr@juno.com.

TAYLOR, LINDSAY DAVID, JR., health care executive, bank executive, federal agency administrator; b. Balt., Dec. 15, 1945; s. Lindsay David Sr. and Lillian Helen (Wagner) T.; children: Sarah Ruth, John David, Margaret Katherine. B in Mech. Engring., Rensselaer Poly. Inst., 1967; MBA, Dartmouth Coll., 1969. Bus. assoc. U.S. Steel Corp., Pitts., 1968-70; spl. asst. to asst. sec. for health HEW, Washington, 1970-71, mgr. operational planning, 1971-74, dep. asst. sec. mgmt., 1977-79; programming officer World Bank, Washington, 1974-76; dir. exams. and supervision Fed. Home Loan Bank Bd., Washington, 1979-81; exec. v.p. Perpetual Bank, Alexandria, Va., 1981-89; pres., CEO Columbia (Md.)-FreeState Health Sys., 1989-91, Preferred Health Network, 1992-96; CEO Alpha Health Plan, 1997-99; COO NPD, LLC, Bethesda, Md., 1999—, Nat. Assn. Cmty. Health Ctrs., Washington, 2001—. Cons. Nat. Acad. Pub. Adminstrn., Washington, 1985—86, Ctr. for Advancement of Health, Washington, 1988—89, Diabetex Corp., Balt., 1996—2003, Latin Am. Youth Ctr., 2003—04; trustee Md. Sci. Ctr., 1996—2000; co-chair Greater Balt. Health Care Coun., 1996—2001, Leadership Md., 1996; mem. bd. advisors Found. for Island Health, 2001—06; mem. adv. bd. WAMU Pub. Radio, 1985—88; bd. dirs. Hospice No. Va., 1984—88; chmn. Washington Employers Coalition on Day Care, 1983—90; chair CHC Funding, LLP, 2002—06; bd. dirs. Capital Link, 2003—08. Recipient Mgmt. Improvement award Pres. U.S., 1973, 77; Edward Tuck scholar, South Dakota Comm. Health Leadership award, 2008 Mem. Ctr. for Excellence in Govt. (prin. 1986-07), Washington Coun. Govts. (devel. policy com. 1986-89, mem. editl. adv. bd. Managed Care 1989-95), Tau Beta Pi, Pi Tau Sigma. Avocations: photography, folk music instruments, travel, wilderness, coaching youth baseball and basketball. Office: 4800 Montgomery Ln Ste 1000 Bethesda MD 20814-3472 also: Ste 210 7200 Wisconsin Ave Bethesda MD 20814 E-mail: LDavidTaylor@yahoo.com.

TAYLOR, MARJORIE, psychology professor; m. Bill Harbaugh; children: Sarah, Amber, Anna. BS, Acadia U., NS, Can., 1979, MS, 1981; PhD, Stanford U., Calif., 1985. Prof. psychology U. Oreg., former head, dept. psychology. Author: Imaginary Companions and the Children Who Create Them, 1999; contbr. articles to profl. jours. Office: Dept Psychology 1227 University of Oregon 395 Straub Hall Eugene OR 97403-1227 Office Phone: 541-346-4933. E-mail: mtaylor@uoregon.edu.

TAYLOR, MICHAEL R., federal agency administrator, lawyer; b. 1949; BA in Polit. Sci., Davidson Coll., NC, 1971; JD, U. Va., 1976. Atty. Office Gen. Counsel, FDA, 1976-80, exec. asst. to commr., 1980-81, dep. commr. policy, 1991—94, sr. adv. to commr., 2009—10, dep. commr. for foods, 2010—; assoc. King & Spalding LLP, Washington, 1981-84, ptnr., 1984-91; acting undersecretary for food safety USDA, 1994—96; v.p. pub. policy Monsanto Corp., 1998—2001; sr. fellow Resources for the Future; rsch. prof. Sch. Pub. Health & Health Services, George Washington U., 2007—09. Mem. editl. bd. Food Drug Cosmetic Law Jour., 1988—2001; contbr. articles to profl. jours. Served with US Army, 1971—73. Office: FDA 10903 New Hampshire Ave Silver Spring MD 20903 Office Phone: 202-994-4234. Office Fax: 202-296-0025. E-mail: mike.taylor@gwumc.edu. *

TAYLOR, NATHALEE BRITTON, retired nutritionist, freelance/self-employed writer; b. Lubbock, Tex., June 8, 1941; d. Nathaniel E. and Dessie Pauline (Moss) Britton; children by previous marriage: Clay H., Bret N. Courtney. BS in Home Econs., Tex. Tech U., 1963. Home economist Pioneer Gas, Lubbock, Tex., 1963-65; dietitian Tex. Tech U., Lubbock, 1966-71; home economist South Plains Electric Co-op., Lubbock, 1986; mgr. quality control Rip Griffins Enterprises, Lubbock, Tex., 1987; sales rep. Time Chem., Lubbock, 1987—2003; with Sentry, Lubbock; mktg. rep. Dodson Group Ins., Lubbock, Farmers Ins., Lubbock, Southwestern Bell Wireless; ret., 2003. Ranch Historian. Co-author: (cookbook) From Our House to Yours, 1975; columnist: Lubbock Lights (mag.) Ranch Record, Nat. Ranching; presenter: (TV show) Southwestern Cooking Sta. KTXT; contbr. articles to profl. publs. Bd. dirs. Am. Heart Assn., Lubbock, 1985-87; mem. Home Economist in Bus., pres. Lubbock chpt., 1985; culinary co-chmn. Lubbock C. of C. Arts Festival, 1982, 83, 84; mem. Write for Nat. Ranching Heritage Ctr., Lubbock., Womens Studies Cmty. Connection. Named Lincoln County Fair Queen. Mem. Tech. Home Econs. Alums (sec./treas.), Am. Home Econs. Assn. (v.p., sec./treas.), Bd.-Cove, Soroptomist (v.p. Lubbock club). Democrat. Achievements include competing in reining horse competition. Avocations: gardening, writing, cooking, horseback riding. Personal E-mail: nathaleet@ranch-horses.com.

TAYLOR, PEYTON TROY, JR., oncologist, educator; b. Tuscaloosa, Ala., July 21, 1941; s. Peyton Troy, Sr. and Frances (Sutter) Taylor; m. Helena Ström, Sept. 23, 1967; children: Annika, Karin, Sarah. BS, U. Ala., 1963, MS, 1968; MD, Med. Coll. Ala., 1968. Intern U. Va. Hosp., Charlottesville, 1968-69, resident, 1969-70, 72-75; asst. prof. ob-gyn. U. Va., Charlottesville, 1976-79, assoc. prof., dir. divsn. ob-gyn. Health Scis. Ctr., 1981-87, Richard N. and Louise R. Crockett prof., 1987—, med. dir. Cancer Ctr., 1996—2008, dep. med. dir. Cancer Ctr., 2008—; clin. assoc. surgery Nat. Cancer Inst., Bethesda, Md., 1970-72. Assoc. prof. U. Ala., Birmingham, 1979—81. Contbr. articles to profl. jours. With USPHS, 1970—72. Recipient Disting. Alumnus, U. Ala. Med. Alumni Assn., 2000. Fellow: ACS, Am. Coll. Obstetricians and Gynecologists; mem.: So. Surg. Assn., Internat. Gynecol. Cancer Soc., Am. Assn. Cancer Rsch., Am. Soc. Clin. Oncology, Soc. Surg. Oncology, Soc. Gynecol. Oncologists, Assn. Acad. Surgeons. Episcopalian. Avocations: sports, travel. Office Phone: 434-924-9933. Personal E-mail: pttivy@aol.com. Business E-Mail: peyton.taylor@virginia.edu.

TAYLOR, ROBERT BROWN, physician, educator, writer; b. Elmira, NY, May 31, 1936; s. Olaf C. Taylor and Elizabeth (Place) Brown; m. Anita Dopico; children: Diana Taylor Root, Sharon Taylor Oliverio. Student, Bucknell U., 1954-57; MD, Temple U., 1961. Diplomate Am. Bd. Family Medicine. Gen. practice medicine, New Paltz, NY, 1964-78; faculty physician Sch. Medicine Wake Forest U., Winston-Salem, NC, 1978-84; prof. dept. family medicine Oreg. Health Scis. U. Sch. Medicine, Portland, 1984—, chmn., 1984-98, prof. emeritus family medicine, 1998—. Mem. comprehensive part II com. Nat. Bd. Med. Examiners, Phila., 1986-91. Author: Common Problems in Office Practice, 1972, A Primer of Clinical Symptoms, 1973, The Practical Art of Medicine, 1974; editor: Family Medicine: Principles and Practice, 1978, 6th edit., 2003, Health Promotion: Principles and Clinical Applications, 1982, Difficult Diagnosis, 1985, Difficult Medical Management, 1991, Difficult Diagnosis II, 1992, Fundamentals of Family Medicine, 1996, 3rd edit, 2003, Manual of Family Practice, 1997, 2d edit., 2002, Taylor's Review of Family Medicine, 1998, Manual of Ten-Minute Diagnosis, 2000, The Clinician's Guide to Medical Writing, 2004, Taylor's Diagnostic and Therapeutic Challenges, 2005, Taylor's Cardiovascular Diseases, 2006, Academic Medicine: A Guide for Clinicians, 2006, Taylor's Musculoskeletal Problems and Injuries, 2006, White Coat Tales: Medicine's Heroes, Heritage and Misadventures, 2008, Medical Wisdom and Doctoring: The Art of 21st Century Practice, 2010, Essential Medical Facts Every Clinician Should Know, 2011; contbg. editor Physicians Mgmt. Mag., 1972-99; editl. bd. Family Practice Rsch. Jour., 1980-90, Female Patient, 1984-2006, Am. Family Physician, 1990-98, Jour. Family Practice, 1990-93, Med. Tribune, 1993-99. Served as surgeon USPHS, 1961-64. Recipient J. David Bristow MD award, Oreg. Health Scis. U., 1993, Continuing Med. Edn. Disting. Faculty award, 2010, F. Marian Bishop Leadership award, Soc. Tchrs. Family Medicine Found., 2007, Disting Faculty award, Oreg. Health Scis., 2010. Fellow Am. Acad. Family Physicians (sci. program com., Thomas W. Johnson award 1998, bd. curators found. archives, John G. Walsh Lifetime Achievement award 2003, Outstanding Sci. Paper award 1982); mem. Soc. Tchrs. Family Medicine (bd. dirs., Excellence cert. 1989), Assn. Am. Med. Colls., Am. Assn. for Study Headache, World Orgn. Family Doctors (chmn. sci. program com.), Portland City Club, Multnomah Athletic Club, Phi Beta Kappa (award 1957), Alpha Omega Alpha (award 1961). Home: 1414 SW 3rd Ave Apt 2904 Portland OR 97201-6629 Office: Oreg Health Sci U Sch Medicine Mail Code FM 3181 SW Sam Jackson Park Rd Portland OR 97239-3098 Home Phone: 503-241-1826; Office Phone: 503-494-6611.

TAYLOR, ROBERT E., dean, pharmacologist, educator; BS in Pharmacology, MS in Pharmacology, Butler U., Indpls.; PhD in Pharmacology / Toxicology, Purdue U., Ind.; MD, Vanderbilt U., Nashville. Chmn., prof. dept. pharmacology Howard U. Coll. Medicine, Washington, 1992—, dir. Alcohol Rsch. Inst., interim dean, 2005—08, dean, 2008—. Contbr. articles to profl. jours., chapters to books. Fellow: American Coll. Physicians; mem.: Rsch Soc. on Alcoholism, American Soc. Clin. Pharmacology and Therapeutics, American Soc. Hematology, Acad. Medicine DC, Med. Soc. of DC, Nat. Med. Assn., Medico-Chirurgical Soc. of DC, Alpha Omega Alpha. Office: Howard University Coll Medicine Office of Dean SG Mudd Bldg Rm 512 520 W St NW Washington DC 20059 Office Phone: 202-256-0691. Office Fax: 202-806-7934. Business E-Mail: rtaylor@howard.edu. *

TAYLOR, ROGER RALPH, cardiology educator; b. Tenterfield, Australia, May 27, 1935; s. Ralph and Mary Alexandra (Smith) T.; m. Lorraine Mary McGlynn, July 29, 1961; children: David Roger, Andrew James, Kylie Anne. MBBS, U. Sydney, Australia, 1957; DSc, U. Western Australia, Perth, 2006. Med. registrar Royal Prince Alfred Hosp., Sydney, 1960-61; vis. scientist cardiology br. Nat. Heart Inst., Bethesda, Md., 1967; physician, assoc. prof. U. Western Australia, Royal Perth Hosp., 1968-74; head, chmn. dept. cardiology Royal Perth Hosp., 1993-96; prof. cardiology U. Western Australia, Royal Perth Hosp., 1974-2000, prof. cardiology emeritus, 2000—. Contbr. articles to profl. jours. Recipient RT Hall prize Cardiac Soc., 1974, Outstanding Svcs. award Royal Perth Hosp., 1999, Nat. Pres.'s award Nat. Heart Found. Australia, 2000; fellow Hallstrom Inst. Cardiology, Royal Prince Alfred Hosp., 1962-64, Nat. Heart Inst., Bethesda, 1965-66. Mem. Royal Australasian Coll. Physicians, Cardiac Soc. Australia & New Zealand, Australian Atherosclerosis Soc., Internat. Soc. Heart Rsch, Nat. Heart Found., (overseas res. fellow). Avocations: fishing, swimming, gardening. Home: 21 Valencia Ave Churchlands WA 6018 Australia Business E-Mail: roger.taylor8@bigpond.com.

TAYLOR, RONALD FULFORD, physician; b. Bethesda, Md., Mar. 23, 1956; s. Harold Bernard and Evelyn (Stansbury) T.; m. Sharon Delyn Stevenson, Mar. 7, 1987. BS, Frostburg State U., Md., 1978; MD, Med. Coll. Va., 1982. Diplomate in internal medicine, pulmonary disease, critical care medicine & sleep medicine Am. Bd. Internal Medicine, Am. Bd. Sleep Medicine. Intern Vanderbilt U., Nashville, 1982-83, resident, 1983-85, fellow in pulmonary and critical care medicine, 1985-87; practice pulmonary and critical care medicine, sleep medicine Jackson (Tenn.) Clinic, 1987—. Contbr. articles to profl. jours. Bd. dirs. Am. Lung Assn. Tenn., Nashville, 1987-95. Fellow Am. Coll. Chest Physicians, Am. Acad. Sleep Medicine. Office: Jackson Clinic 700 W Forest Ave Jackson TN 38301-3966 Office Phone: 731-422-0230. E-mail: rftaylormd@yahoo.com.

TAYLOR, SARAH ANN, oncologist, educator; b. Wichita, Kans., July 2, 1950; Grad., Cornell Coll., Iowa; MD, U. Kansas Sch. Medicine, 1975. Cert. Internal Medicine, Med. Oncology. Intern, internal medicine U. Kansas Med. Ctr., 1975—76, resident, oncology, 1976—78, fellow, 1978—80, hosp. appointment, 1980—, med. dir., Palliative Care Svcs., 1987—; prof. internal medicine, divsn. hematology/oncology U. Kansas, med. dir., hematology, oncology fellowship program. Named one of Kansas City Super Doctor, Kansas City Mag. Mem.: FDA, CIRB. Office Phone: 913-588-6029. Office Fax: 913-588-4085.

TAYLOR, SHELLEY E., psychology researcher, educator; m. Mervyn Francis Fernandes, May 1, 1972; children: Sara F., Charles F. AB magna cum laude in Psychology, Conn. Coll., 1968; PhD in Social Psychology, Yale U., 1972. Asst. prof. psychology and social rels. Harvard U., Cambridge, Mass., 1972-77, assoc. prof., 1977-79; assoc. prof. psychology UCLA, 1979-81, prof., 1981—. Mem. vis. faculty dept. adminstrv. scis. Yale U., New Haven, 1971-72, vis. Sloane fellow, 1978; mem. basic sociocultural rsch. rev. com. NIH, 1979-83; Katz-Newcomb lectr. U. Mich., 1982; cons. to pub. houses and TV producers. Author: Social Cognition, 1986, 2d edit., 1991, Health Psychology, 1986, 3d edit., 1995, 5th edit., 2002. Positive Illusions: Creative Self-Deception and the Healthy Mind, 1989, The Tending Instinct: How Nurturing is Essential to Who We Are and How We Live, 2002; contbr. numerous articles to sci. publs. Active numerous charitable and fund-raising orgns. including Curtis Sch. PTA and U. So. Calif./Norris Cancer Ctr. Recipient Rsch. Scientist Devel. award NIMH, 1981-86, 86-91, MERIT award, 1987, Donald Campbell award for disting. sci. contbn. to sociology, 1995; numerous rsch. grants in field; Winthrop scholar, 1967; Woodrow Wilson fellow, 1968, NIMH fellow, 1968-72. Fellow APA (Sci. Weekend lectr. 1988, Disting. Sci. award 1980, Outstanding Sci.Contbn. award Divsn. 38, 1994), Brit. Psychol. Soc. (flying fellow), Acad. Behavioral Medicine Rsch., Soc. Psychol. Study Social Issues, Soc. Behavioral Medicine; mem. AAAS, Soc. Exptl. Social Psychology, Western Psychol. Assn. (pres. 1993-94), Inst. Medicine. Office: UCLA Dept Psychology PX 29 Franz 4611 Box 951563 Los Angeles CA 90095-1563

TAYLOR, STEPHEN LLOYD, toxicologist, food scientist, educator; b. Portland, Oreg., July 19, 1946; s. Lloyd Emerson and Frances Hattie (Hanson); m. Susan Annette Kerns, June 23, 1973; children: Amanda, Andrew. BS in Food Sci. Tech., Oreg. State U., 1968, MS in Food Sci. Tech., 1969; PhD in Biochemistry, U. Calif., Davis, 1973. Research assoc. U. Calif., Davis, 1973-74, research fellow, 1974-75; chief food toxicology Letterman Army Inst., San Francisco, 1975-78; asst. prof. food toxicology U. Wis., Madison, 1978-83, assoc. prof., 1983-87; head dept. food sci. technology, dir. Food Processing Ctr. U. Nebr., Lincoln, 1987—2004, prof. dept. food sci. tech., 2004—. Cons. in field. Contbr. articles to profl. jours. Fellow: Inst. Food Technologists (divsn. chmn. 1981—82, sect. chmn. 1984—85, exec. com. 1988—91); mem.: Soc. Toxicology, Am. Chem. Soc., Am. Acad. Allergy, Asthma and Immunology. Democrat. Presbyterian. Home: 941 Evergreen Dr Lincoln NE 68510-4131 Office: U Nebr Dept Food Sci Tech Lincoln NE 68583-0919 Home Phone: 402-488-6477; Office Phone: 402-472-2833. Business E-Mail: staylor2@unl.edu.

TAYLOR, SUSAN SEROTA, biochemist, researcher; b. Racine, Wis., June 20, 1942; d. Rudolph M. and Helen L. (Vohs) Serota; m. Palmer William Taylor, July 3, 1965; children: Tasha Katherine,

Ashton David, Palmer Andrew. BA in Chemistry, U. Wis., Madison, 1964; PhD in Physiol. Chemistry, Johns Hopkins U., Balt., 1968. Postdoc. fellow MRC Lab. Molecular Biology, Cambridge, England, 1969—70, U. Calif., San Diego, 1971-72, asst. prof. chemistry, 1972-79, assoc. prof., 1979-85, prof. chemistry and biochemistry, 1985—, prof. pharmacology, 2004—. Investigator Howard Hughes Med. Inst., 1997—; sr. fellow San Diego Supercomputer Ctr.; mem. adv. coun. GM Cancer Rsch. Found.; Edwin G. Krebs lectr. molecular pharmacology U. Wash. Sch. Medicine, Seattle; Hans Lindner meml. lectr. Weizmann Inst., Rehovot, Israel. Contbr. articles to profl. jours. Recipient Excellence in Sci. award, Fedn. Am. Societies Exptl. Biology, 2009, Vanderbilt prize in biomed. scis.; Fogarty Internat. fellowship, 1981—82. Fellow: AAAS, Am. Acad. Arts & Scis.; mem.: NAS (coun. mem. 2010—), Am. Soc. Biochemistry & Molecular Biology (coun. mem. 1989—92, pres. 1995—96, William C. Rose award), Inst. Medicine, Am. Chem. Soc. (Outstanding Scientist award 1998, Francis P. Garvan—John M. Olin medal 2001). Office: U Calif Taylor Lab Leichtag Biomed Rsch Bldg 4th Fl Rm 412 9500 Gilman Dr MC 0654 La Jolla CA 92093-0654 Business E-Mail: staylor@ucsd.edu.

TAYLOR, VICKY, physician, educator; b. Kent, Eng., July 28, 1955; MD, Nottingham U., 1978; MPH, U. Wash., 1989. Prof. divsn. pub. health scis. Fred Hutchinson Cancer Rsch. Ctr., 1990—. Rsch. prof. Dept. Health Svcs., U. Wash., 1996. Office: Fred Hutchinson Cancer Research Ctr Seattle WA 98109 Business E-Mail: vtaylor@fhcrc.org.

TAYLOR, WAYNE EMERY, medical educator, researcher; b. Yreka, Calif., Mar. 11, 1949; s. Leo Lloyd and Helen Louise Taylor; m. Linda Jean Vician, July 21, 1979; children: Wendy Heavilon, Laura, Katrina. BA, U. Oreg., 1973; MS, U. Wis., 1977, PhD, 1983. Sr. fellow biochemistry U. Wash., Seattle, 1984—89; asst. prof. biochemistry Calif. State U., Fullerton, 1989—93; vis. prof. ophthalmology Cedars Sinai Med. Ctr., LA, 1994—95; asst. prof. medicine, endocrinology Charles Drew U. Medicine & Sci., LA, 1995—, assoc. prof. biomedicine, Coll. Sci. and Health. Adj. assoc. prof. medicine UCLA, 2004—; DNA module dir. RCMI DNA Core Lab., Drew U., LA, 2000—04. Contbr. sci. papers to profl. jours. (Outstanding Svc. award, Cosh, 2008). Grantee, Rsch. Ctr. Minority Inst., NIH, 2000—. Mem.: Endocrine Soc. (Glenn Found. award 2001). Christian. Avocations: mountain climbing, genealogy, planetary science. Office: Charles Drew Univ Health and Life Sci Dept COSH 1731 E 120th St Los Angeles CA 90059 Home: 2518 E Balfour Ave Fullerton CA 92831 Office Phone: 323-563-5830. Business E-Mail: waynetaylor@cdrewu.edu. E-mail: wayneetaylor@yahoo.com.

TAYLOR, WILLIAM COLTON, physician, educator; b. Boston, Jan. 25, 1948; s. Manuel and Marjorie Taylor; m. Julia Katherine Landau, Dec. 4, 1983; children: Rachel, Hannah, Daniel, Benjamin, Jessica. BA, Yale U., New Haven, Conn., 1970; MD, U. Pa., Phila., 1974. Cert. bd. Am. Bd. of Internal Medicine, 1977. Sr. physician Beth Israel Deaconess Med. Ctr., Boston, 1996—; assoc. prof. population medicine Harvard Med. Sch., Boston, 1994—, assoc. prof. medicine; assoc. physician Brigham and Women's Hosp., Boston, 2006—. *

TCHERNEV, VELIZAR TZVETANOV, physician, research scientist; b. Sofia, Bulgaria, Oct. 29, 1969; arrived in US, 1994; s. Lilia Zaharieva Jeleva and Tzvetan Vasilev Tchernev; m. Ralitza Vladislavova Gueorguieva; children: Alexander Velizar, Liliana Velizar. Cert. in tropical medicine, Higher Med. Inst., Sofia, Bulgaria, 1992, MD, 1993; cert. in biotechnology, U. Fla., 1994, PhD, 1998. Rsch. asst. dept. pathology, immunology and lab. medicine U. Fla., Gainesville, 1994—98; rsch. scientist discovery dept. CuraGen Corp., Alachua Fla. and Branford, Conn., 1998—2001; rsch. scientist Molecular Staging Inc., New Haven, 2001—03, sr. rsch. scientist, 2003—04; dir. clin. rsch. Genomas Inc., Hartford, Conn., 2004—05; country mgr. PSI Pharma Support Internat., 2005—07; dir. Crossover, 2007—. Contbr. articles to profl. jours. Recipient award, Am. Fedn. for Clin. Rsch., 1996; Scholarship, Internat. Mammalian Genome Soc., 1998, Fellowship for Excellent Academic Performance, Higher Med. Inst. Sofia, Bulgaria, 1988—93. Mem.: AAAS. Achievements include diplomas for translations of med. lit. to Eng. lang. and German lang; 3 issued patents and more than 50 patents pending in field. Personal E-mail: vtchernev@hotmail.com.

TCHOUNWOU, PAUL BERNARD, environmental health specialist, toxicologist, educator; b. Bangou, Cameroon, Aug. 14, 1960; came to U.S., 1985; s. Maurice and Christine (Kouanang) Seumo; m. Martha Namondo Mondoa, Aug. 3, 1990; children: Christine K., Hervey M., Solange S. BSc, U. Yaounde, Cameroon, 1983, MSc, 1984; MS in Pub. Health, Tulane U., 1986, ScD, 1990. Cert. toxicologist Nat. Environ. Health Assn.; registered sanitarian La. State Bd. Examiners for Sanitarians. Tchg. asst. Tulane Sch. Pub. Health, New Orleans, 1988—90; med. rschr. Inst. Med. Rsch., Yaounde, 1991—94; asst. prof. Faculty Medicine, Yaounde, 1992—94; rsch. assoc. Xavier and Tulane Univs., New Orleans, 1994—96; assoc. prof., dir. environ. sci. PhD program Jackson State U., 1996—; adj. assoc. prof. sch. pub. health Tulane U., 1999—2005; prof., dir. environ. sci. doctoral program Jackson State U., 2001—, dep. dir. Ctr. for Environ. Health, 2003—06, chair dept. biology, 2004—, interim assoc. dean coll. sci., engring, and tech., 2006—07; assoc. dean Coll. Sci. Engring. and Tech., 2007—, interim dean, 2011—. Adj. prof. Tulane U. Sch. Pub. Health, 2005—; environ. health cons. Orstom & UNICEF, Yaounde, 1992-93, U.S. AID, Kaele, 1991-93; rsch. supr. Tulane Sch. Pub. Health, New Orleans, 1994—; tng. and rsch. fellow U.S. AID, Washington, 1985-90; adj. assoc. prof. environ. health scis. Tulane U. Sch. Pub. Health and Tropical Medicine, 1999—. Editor-in-chief: Internat. Jour. of Environ. Rsch. and Pub. Health, 2003—, mem. editl. bd.: Internat. Jour. Environ. Toxicology and Water Quality, 1994—2005, guest editor: Internat. Jour. Molecular Scis., 2002—, regional editor: USA-Environ. Toxicology, 2002—, mem. overseas editl. bd.: Jour. Environ. Biology, 2002—; contbr. articles to profl. jours.; editor-in-chief: Environmental Toxicology, 2006—, mem. editl. bd.: Revs. on Environ. Health, 2003—. Grantee, Internat. Devel. Rsch. Ctr., 1992—93, Nat. Aeronautics and Space Adminstrn., 1977—99, NIH, 1998—, Nat. Oceanic and Atmospheric Adminstrn., 2001—, Dept. Army, 2002—07; grant, Dept. Def., 2011—. Mem. APHA, AAUP, AAAS, Am. Assn. Cancer Rsch., Water Environ. Fedn., Cameroon Bioscis. Soc., Cameroon Assn. Epidemiology, Nat. Environ. Health Assn., N.Y. Acad. Scis., Miss. Acad. Sci., Soc. Environ. Toxicology and Chemistry, Soc. Toxicology, Delta Omega. Roman Catholic. Avocations: travel, playing tennis, watching tv sport programs. Home: 230 Clark Farms Rd Madison MS 39110-8112 Office: Jackson State U Coll Sci Engring and Tech PO Box 18540 Jackson MS 39217

TEAGUE, BRUCE WILLIAMS, chiropractor; b. Dayton, Ohio, Sept. 6, 1947; s. Bige Barnett and Lena Teague; m. Germaine Lee Mullican, Oct. 15, 1977; children: Deanna, Katrina, Bret, Travis, Krystal. BBA, Ea. Ky. U., 1970; D.Chiropractic, Palmer Coll. Chiropractic, 1977. Chiropractor, pres., dir. Teague Chiropractic Ctr., Anchorage, 1980—. Mem. L.A. Coll. Chiropractic Orthopedics, 1988—. Mem. Am. Chiropractic Assn. (mem. nutrition coun., coun. on sports injuries and phys. fitness), Coun. Diagnostic Imaging, Am. Coll. Chiropractic Edn. and Rsch., Alaska Chiropractic Soc., Internat. Chiropractors Assn., Palmer Coll. Alumni Assn., Moose, Rotary. Office: Teague Chiropractic Ctr 11435 Old Seward Hwy Anchorage AK 99515-3041 Business E-Mail: dcdoc@gci.net.

TEAGUE, ROBERT COLE, physician; b. Waxahachie, Tex., June 13, 1930; s. Isaac Lawson and Frances (Cole) Teague; m. Virginia M. Teague, Nov. 11, 1960 (dec. May 1, 2005); children: Patrick, Michael. BA in Chemistry, Baylor U., Waco, Tex., 1951; MD, U. Tex., Galveston, 1955. Lic. physician Ariz.; cert. ABFB, 2005. Intern McLaren Hosp., Flint, Mich., 1955—56; med. officer, active duty USNR, 1956—58; physician family practice LaJolla, Calif., 1958—63, Phoenix, 1963—. Med. dir., pres. Vis. Nurse Svc., Phoenix; chmn. Family Practice Humana Hosp., 1984—86, past chmn.; chmn. Family Practice Good Samaritan Hosp., 1990—91. Fellow Am. Acad. Family Physicians (charter); mem. Ariz. Acad. Family Physicians (pres. 1988-90). Republican. Episcopalian. Avocation: travel. *

TEBBETTS, JOHN BERYL, plastic surgeon; b. Ruston, La., Nov. 9, 1946; BS, Tulane Univ., 1968; MD, Univ. Tex. Med. Branch, Galveston, 1972. Cert. Am. Bd. Gen. Surgery, 1978, Am. Bd. Plastic Surgery, 1980, lic. Tex., 1972, Wyo., 1987. Intern LDS Hosp., Salt Lake City, 1972—73; resident in surgery Univ. Utah Affiliated Hospitals, 1973—77; resident in plastic surgery Southwestern Med. Sch., Dallas, 1977—79; asst. clin. prof. in plastic surgery Southwestern Univ.; attending staff plastic surgery Mary Shiels Hosp., Baylor Univ. Med. Ctr., Longview Regional Hosp.; plastic surgeon Board Certified Surgery-Dallas. Contbr. articles to profl. jours.; co-author (with Terrye B. Tebbetts): The Best Breast. Recipient Ralph Millard award, Canadian Soc. for Aesthetic Plastic Surgery, 1994. Mem.: AMA, Am. Assn. Plastic Surgeons, Am. Coll. Surgeons, Am. Coll. Emergency Physicians, Am. Soc. Plastic & Reconstructive Surgery, Am. Cleft Palate Assn., Am. Soc. Aesthetic Plastic Surgery (Walter Scott Brown award 1984, 1990, Simon Fredericks award 1990), Tex. Soc. Plastic Surgeons, Tex. Med. Assn., Dallas Soc. Plastic Surgeons, Dallas County Med. Soc. Office: Board Certified Surgery-Dallas Ste W-300 2801 Lemmon Ave Dallas TX 75204 Office Phone: 972-220-2712, 888-888-8769. Office Fax: 214-969-0933.

TECCA, KIMBERLY ANN, physician assistant; b. Detroit, Nov. 20, 1947; d. George Leonard and Jeanne (Austin) Wilkie; m. Joseph P. Tecca; children, Aaron Thomas Kunkel, stepchildren Kristyn Rouse, Sarah, Jonathan. AA, Pensacola Jr. Coll., 1971; BS in Medicine, physician's asst. cert. in medicine, U. Ala., Birmingham, 1976; cert. in mgmt., Am. Mgmt. Assn., 1989; postgrad., U. West Fla., 1995—. Cert. physician's asst. Asst. mgr. Christo's, Gulf Breeze, Fla., 1966-67; teller, bookkeeper loan dept. Bank Gulf Breeze, 1967-72; med. tech. aide USN Hosp., Pensacola, 1972, physician's asst., 1972-73, John Kingsley, MD, Pensacola, 1976, Mountain Comprehensive Health Corp., Whitesburg, Ky., 1976-78, N.W. Fla. Nephrology, Pensacola, 1978-87, med. adminstr., 1987-95, Nephrology Ctr. of Pensacola, Fla., 1987-95; COO Nephrology Ctr. Inc., Crestview, Pensacola, 1995—, Nephrology Ctr., Inc., Crestview, Pensacola, 1995-96, Nephrology Ctr. Assocs., Pensacola, 1995-96; regional COO, Renal Care Group Inc., Pensacola, Fla., 1996-98; COO Nephrology Ctr. Assoc. PA, 1998-99; area adminstr. Renal Care Group Inc., Houston, 1999—2002, clin. ops. cons., 2002, dir. clin. ops., 2002, 2002—; dir. regulatory affairs Fresenius Med. Care, 2006—. Fellow Am. Acad. Physician's Assts. (del. nat. meeting 1978—), Nat. Commn. on Cert. Physician's Assts., Nat. Renal Adminstrs., Nat. Renal Adminstrn. Assn. Fla. Acad. Physician's Assts. (jud. com. 1979-80), Natural Wildlife Assn., Assn. Practioners Infection Control. Republican. Roman Catholic. Avocations: photography, antiques, reading, wildlife preservation, wine. Office: Fresesnius Med Care 920 Winter St Waltham MA 02451 Personal E-mail: ktecca1@aol.com.

TEDALDI, ELLEN M., internist, educator; BA, Cornell U.; MD, SUNY, 1980. Diplomate Am. Bd. Internal Medicine. Intern Hennepin County Med. Ctr., 1981, resident Mpls., chief resident; prof. medicine dept. Temple Univ.; dir. HIV program. Co-author: (publs.) Prevalence of diabetes mellitus and dyslipidemia among naive patients co-infected with hepatitis C (HCV) and and HIV-1 compared to patients without co-infection, 2005, Effect of IL-2 on Hepatitis C Virus (HCV) levels in patients coinfected with Human Immunodeficiency Virus (HIV) receiving HAART, 2005, and numerous others. Named one of the Top Doctors, 2010—11. Office: Temple University School of Medicine Medicine Education and Research Bldg 3500 N Broad Str Philadelphia PA 19140 Office Phone: 215-707-1800. Office Fax: 215-707-3644. E-mail: ellen.tedaldi@temple.edu.

TEDDER, THOMAS FLETCHER, immunology educator, researcher; b. Chateauroux, France, May 14, 1956; came to U.S. 1959; s. Raymond Percy and Barbara (Hagemann) T. AA, Okaloosa-Walton C.C., Niceville, Fla., 1976; BS with honors, U. Fla., 1978, MS, 1980; PhD, U. Ala., Birmingham, 1984. Rsch. fellow in pathology Harvard Med. Sch., Boston, 1984-85, instr. pathology, 1986-88, asst. prof. pathology, 1988-93; assoc. prof. pathology Harvard U. Med. Sch., Boston, 1993; prof. immunology Duke U. Med. Ctr., Durham, NC, 1993—, chmn. dept. immunology, 1993—. Alter Geller prof. rsch. in immunology Duke U. Med. Ctr., 1997—, founder, Collective Therapeutics, Inc.; co-founder Angelica Therapeutics, Inc.; cons. in field. Assoc. editor Jour. Immunology, 1989-93, sect. editor, 1993-98, dep. editor, 2004-08; contbr. numerous articles to med. jours., including Jour. Immunology, Nature, Cell, Lancet, Immunity. Recipient LeRoy Collins Disting. Alumnus award Fla. Assn. C.C.'s; named 25th Anniversary Disting. Alumnus, Okaloosa-Walton C.C., 1989; Damon Runyon-Walter Winchell rsch. fellow, 1985-87; scholar Leukemia Soc. Am., 1991-96, Stohlman scholar, 1995-96. Mem. Am. Soc. for Microbiology (Pres. fellow 1982), Am. Assn. Immunologists, Sigma Xi, Phi Kappa Phi. Achievements include identification and determination of structure and function of many human B lymphocyte cell-surface molecules. Office: Duke U Med Ctr Dept Immunology PO Box 3010 Durham NC 27710-0001 Office Phone: 919-684-3681. E-mail: thomas.tedder@duke.edu.

TEDESCO, MARK J., career military officer, physician; BS, Tufts U., Medford, Mass., 1980, MD, 1986; MPH in in Health Care Mgmt., Harvard Sch. Pub. Health, 1994. Diplomate Am. Bd. Family Medicine, Am. Bd. Preventive Medicine. Family practice residency, Ft. Belvoir, Va., 1986—89; aerospace medicine residency Brooks Air Force Base, San Antonio, 1994—95; various assignments as Army physician including, treatment platoon leader 24th Inf. Divsn. Saudi Arabia & Iraq, flight surgeon 224th Army Mil. Intelligence Battalion, flight surgeon Air Station Savannah at Hunter Army Airfield Ga.; transfer to USCG, 1997, various positions including med. readiness br. chief, Coast Guard Hdqs. Washington, med. dir. ops. for disaster response teams World Trade Ctr. Disaster site, 2001, chief operational medicine & med. readiness divsn., Coast Guard Hdqs., comd. as rear adm., 2007—, asst. US surgeon gen., dir. health, safety & work-life, 2007—. Decorated Army Expert Field Medic Badge, Meritorious Svc. medal (3); named US Army Aerospace Medicine Specialist of Yr., 1997, USPHS Physician Exec. of Yr., 2005. Office: Coast Guard Hdqs 2100 Second St SW Washington DC 20593 Business E-Mail: mark.tedesco@uscg.mil. *

TEDJARATI, SEAN S., gynecologist, educator; b. Tehran, Iran, Sept. 27, 1967; MD, Spartan Health Scis. U., 1993; MPH, Johns Hopkins U., 2008. Resident, ob-gyn. Ohio State U., 1997—2000; fellow, gynecologic oncology U. Tex. MD Anderson Cancer Ctr., 2000—03; asst. prof. Moffitt Cancer Ctr., 2003—05; assoc. prof., assoc. residency dir. Tex. Tech. U., 2006—09; chief, assoc. prof., gynecologic oncology and robotic surgery NY Med. Coll. Westchester Med. Ctr., 2009—. Mem. Fla. Cancer Control and Rsch. Adv. Coun., 2002—03, Admissions Com. Tex. Tech. U. Sch. Medicine, 2007—09, Instl. Rev. Bd. Tex. Tech. U., 2007—09. Recipient Nat. Faculty award, Coun. Resident Edn. Ob-Gyn., Dean's Faculty Clin. Tchg. award, Tex. Tech. U. Health Scis. Ctr., Chairs award; named Outstanding Resident Tchr. of Yr., Ohio State U., Tennyson Williams Outstanding Resident of Yr. Mem.: Health Care Vols. Overseas, Internat. Gynecologic Cancer Soc., Am. Soc. Clin. Oncologists, Am. Coll. Ob-Gyn., Soc. Gynecologic Oncologist (mem., edn. com. 2010—). Avocations: hiking, travel, martial arts. Office: 19 Bradhurst Ave 2575 Hawthorne NY 10532 Office Fax: 914-493-2232. Business E-Mail: tedjaratis@wcmc.com.

TEE, AUGUSTINE, pulmonologist, intensivist; b. Singapore, Jan. 30, 1971; MBBS, Nat. U. Singapore, 1997, MMed in Internal Medicine, 2002. Med. officer, registrar Singhealth Svcs., 1998—2005; assoc. cons. Changi Gen. Hosp., 2005—08, cons. respiratory physician, 2008—. Adj. asst. prof. Yong Loo Lin Sch. Medicine, Singapore, 2009—. Recipient Commendation medal, Nat. Day Awards (SARS), 2003, Singapore Health Svc. Quality award, Singhealth Svcs., 2011, Excellent Svc. award, SPRING Singapore, Deans award, Yong Loo Lin Sch. Medicine, 2008—09; fellow Singhealth Health Manpower Devel. Program award, Singhealth-Ministry Health, Singapore, 2006. Fellow: Am. Coll. Chest Physicians, Acad. Medicine (Singapore); mem.: RCP. Office: Changi General Hosp Dept Respiratory Medicine Singapore 529889 Singapore Office Fax: 67816202. Business E-Mail: augustine_tee@cgh.com.sg.

TEESALU, REIN NONE, cardiologist, educator; b. Estonia, Saaremaa, June 19, 1939; MD, U. Tartu, 1964, MD, 1981. Head dept. cardiovasc. rsch. U. Tartu, 1984—86, head lab. clin. physiology, biochemistry, 1987—88, head chair internal medicine propedeutics, 1988—92, bd. mem. med. faculty, 1988—2004, head dept. cardiology, 1992—2004, prof. emeritus, cardiology, 2004—. Bd. mem. Tartu U. Hosp., 1992—2004; chmn. working group heart failure Estonian Cardiac Soc., 1999—2009; pres. Estonian Soc. Hypertension, 2000—05, Estonian Heart Assn., 2004—06. Recipient Sci. award, Estonian govt., 1985, 1998, award, Tartu U. Hosp., 2006. Fellow: Am. Coll. Angiology, European Soc. Cardiology; mem.: Estonian Soc. Hypertension, Estonian Cardiac Soc., European Heart Failure Assn. Avocations: gardening, hiking. Office: Puusepa Tartu 51014 Estonia Office Fax: 3727318402. E-mail: rein.teesalu@kliinikum.ee.

TEH, HUI SEONG, radiologist, consultant; s. Tat Sin Teh and Siew Kheng Wong; m. Wan Teng Koh; children: Rui-Qian, Rui-Kai. MB BS, Nat. U. Singapore, 1990. Cons. radiologist Changi Gen. Hosp., Singapore, 1997—. Rsch. grant, NMRC, 2004—05, Changi Gen. Hosp. Fellow: Royal Coll. Radiologists; mem.: Singapore Radiol. Soc. Achievements include research in MR cystography for detection of vesico-uretic reflux; MR renography as an alternative to radionuclide renography. Office: Changi General Hosp 2 Simei Street 3 Changi General Hospital 529889 Singapore Singapore Office Fax: 65-62601703. E-mail: cyber_xray@yahoo.com.

TEH, JAMES LIP ZE, radiologist, consultant; b. Kuala lumpur, Malaysia, Aug. 18, 1967; m. Jacqueline Cullen. BSc, Westminster Sch., London, 1984, degree in Medicine, 1984. Lic. Royal Coll. Radiologists, UK, 1997. Cons. musculoskeletal radiologist NOC NHS Trust, Oxford, England, 2000—. Exec. com. mem. BSSR; mem. Internat. Skeletal Soc.; clin. v.p. UK Radiol. Conf., 2011—. Fellow: Royal Coll. Radiologists; mem.: Royal Coll. Physicians. Office: Nuffield Orthop Ctr Nat Health Service Trust Windmill Rd Oxford OX3 7LD England

TEHRANI, KEVIN, aesthetic plastic surgeon, educator; m. Leontine Tehrani; children: Jude, Kaelin. MD, SUNY Downstate Med. Ctr. Diplomate Am. Bd. Plastic Surgery. Gen. surgery residency Beth Israel Med. Ctr., NYC, chief resident gen. surgery; postgrad. tng. plastic and reconstructive surgery Kans. Univ. Med. Ctr.; asst. clin. prof. surgery dept. SUNY Downstate Med. Ctr., chief plastic surgery divsn.; founder, dir. Aristocrat Plastic Surgery. Lt. comdr. Naval

Reserves Med. Corps. Fellow: Am. Coll. of Surgeons; mem.: Am. Soc. of Plastic Surgeons. Office: Aristocrat Plastic Surgery 521 Park Ave New York NY 10065 Mailing: SUNY Downstate Medical Center 1st Fl 760 Parkside Ave Brooklyn NY 11226 Office Phone: 212-439-9900, 718-221-5087. Office Fax: 718-270-8248. Business E-Mail: kevin.tehrani@downstate.edu.

TEHRANY, ARMIN M., orthopedic surgeon, educator; b. Phila., Mar. 4, 1970; s. Jamshid M. and Shala R. Tehrany; m. Valerie Laury, Oct. 27, 2002; children: Jacqueline, Natalie. BA, CUNY, Bklyn., 1991; MD, NYU, 1994. Orthopedic resident Lenox Hill Hosp., NYC, 1994—99; shoulder arthroscopy fellow Baylor Coll. Medicine, San Antonio, 1999—2000; orthopedic attending Richmond Orthopedic Assocs., SI, NY, 2000—; asst. clin. prof. dept. orthop. surgery Mt. Sinai Sch. Medicine, NY; attending orthop. surgeon Richmond Orthop. Assocs., 2000—07, Staten Island Med. Group, NY, 2000—07. Master instr. Arthroscopy Assn. N.Am., Rosemont, Ill., 2001—. Contbr. chapters to books, articles to publs. Bd. dir. NYS-SOS; with AANA Young Mems. Task Force, AANA Comm. Com.; adv. bd. NYCMS Young Physicians.; bd govs. Poly Prep Country Day Sch. Recipient 2d pl., Isakos, 2001. Mem.: NY U. Sch. Medicine Alumni Assn., Richmond County Med. Soc., NY County Med. Soc., Medical State Soc. NY, NY State Soc. Orthop. Surgeons, Am. Orthopedic Soc. Sports Medicine, Internat. Soc. Arthroscopy, Knee Surgery, and Orthopaedic Sprots Medicine, Arthroscopy Assn. N.Am., Am. Acad. Orthopedic Surgeons. Avocations: tennis, guitar. Office: 515 Madison Ave New York NY 10022 Business E-Mail: armin@tehrany.com.

TEICHHOLZ, LOUIS EVAN, cardiologist; b. Passaic, NJ, Jan. 31, 1942; AB, Harvard Coll., 1962; MD, Harvard Med. Sch., 1966. Assoc. chief cardiology, vice-chmn. medicine Mt. Sinai Med. Ctr., 1974—96; cardiology chief, med. dir. cardiac svcs. Hackensack U. Med. Ctr., 1996—. Prof. medicine Mt. Sinai Sch. Medicine, 1978, UMDNJ-NJ Med. Sch., 1996. Fellow: ACP, Am. Heart Assn., Am. Coll. Cardiology (pres., NJ chpt. 2009). Avocations: tennis, magic. Office: 30 Prospect Ave Hackensack NJ 07601 Office Fax: 201-489-6290. Business E-Mail: lteichholz@hume.com.

TEIGLAND, LILLIAN MCKAY, physician; b. Balt., Oct. 28, 1954; BA, Swarthmore Coll., 1976; MD, Duke U., 1980. Physician Novant Health, 1980, South Pk. Family Physicians, 2006—. Mem.: Am. Acad. Family Physicians. Office: 6324 Fairview Rd Ste 201 Charlotte NC 28210 Business E-Mail: lmteigland@novanthealth.org.

TEIRSTEIN, PAUL SHEPHERD, cardiologist, educator; b. NYC, July 5, 1955; s. Alvin Stanley and Alice Teirstein. BA in Biology, Vassar Coll., 1976; MD, CUNY, 1980. Diplomate Am. Bd. Internal Medicine and Cardiovascular Diseases. With Lab. of Vision Rsch. NIH, Bethesda, Md., 1977-79; intern and resident Brigham & Women's Hosp., Boston, 1980-83; fellow in cardiology Stanford U., Calif., 1983-86; fellow in advanced coronary angioplasty Mid-Am. Heart Inst., Kansas City, Mo., 1986-87; fellow in stents, artherectomy and lasers NIH, Bethesda, 1987; dir. interventional cardiology Scripps Clinic and Rsch. Found., La Jolla, Calif., 1987—, chief cardiology, 2006—; cardiologist Ctr. for Interventional Vascular Therapy, NY-Presbyn. Hosp.l/Columbia U. Med. Ctr. Prof. medicine Columbia Med. Ctr. NY Presbyn. Hosp., NYC, 2006—; presenter in field. Recipient Harold Lampert Rsch. Prize, 1980, Saul Horowitz, Jr. Meml. Award, Mt. Sinai Sch. Medicine, 1995, Spirit of Scripps Award, 1998, Erasmus Thoraxcenter Interventional Cardiology Award, 1998; named Skaggs Clin. Scholar, Scripps Rsch. Inst., 1998; named to Best Doctors in Am., 1994—97, Am.'s Top Doctors, Castle Connolly Medical LTD, 2001—05; grantee NSF, 1975. Fellow: Am. Coll. Cardiology; mem.: Assn. for Rsch. in Vision and Ophthalmol ogy, Alpha Omega Alpha, Beta Beta Beta. Office: Scripps Clinic & Rsch Found 10666 N Torrey Pines Rd S1-056 La Jolla CA 92037-1092 also: Ctr Interventional Vascular Therapy 161 Fort Washington Ave 5th FL New York NY 10032 Office Phone: 858-554-9905, 212-305-7060. Office Fax: 212-342-3660. E-mail: pteirstein@crf.org.

TEITELBAUM, PHILIP, psychologist; b. Bklyn., Oct. 9, 1928; s. Bernard and Betty (Schechter) T.; m. Osnat Boné; children: Benjamin, Daniel, David, Jonathan, Gideon. BS, CCNY, 1950; MA, Johns Hopkins U., 1952, PhD, 1954. Instr., asst. prof. physiol. psychology Harvard U., 1954-59; assoc. prof. psychology U. Pa., Phila., 1959-63, prof., 1963-73; prof. psychology U. Ill.-Urbana-Champaign, 1973-85, emeritus prof., 1985—, Disting. prof. Ctr. Advanced Studies, 1980-85; grad. research prof. U. Fla., Gainesville, 1984—. Author: Fundamental Principles of Physiological Psychology, 1967; editor: (with E. Satinoff) Motivation: Handbook Behavioral Neurobiology, 1983, (with Osnat Teitelbaum) Does Your Baby Have Autism, 2008; contbr. chpts. to books; contbr. articles to profl. jours. Fellow Ctr. for Advanced Study in Behavorial Scis., Stanford U., 1975-76, Fulbright fellow Tel Aviv U., 1978-79, Guggenheim fellow, 1984-85, Carnegie Found. fellow Inst. Neurol. Scis., U. Pa. Med. Sch., 1958-59. Fellow APA (pres. div. physiol. psychology, disting. sci. contbn. award 1978), Am. Psychol. Soc. (William James fellow); mem. NAS, AAAS, Am. Physiol. Soc., Soc. for Neurosci., Soc. Exptl. Psychology. Home: 2239 NW 17th Ave Gainesville FL 32605-3909 Office Phone: 352-392-0615, 352-392-2180. Personal E-mail: teitelb@hotmail.com. *

TEITELBAUM, STEVEN, plastic surgeon; b. LA, Aug. 22, 1962; AB, U. Calif. Berkeley; MD, UCLA, 1988. Lic. Mass., 1989, Calif., 1993, DEA, 1993, cert. Am. Bd. Plastic Surgery, 1997, Am. Bd. Plastic Surgery, 2006, Am. Bd. Surgery, 1995. Intern Harvard/Beth Israel Hosp., Boston, 1988—89, gen. surgery resident, chief resident, 1989—93; plastic & reconstructive surgery resident U. Southern Calif., 1993—95; at Santa Monica/ULCA Med. Ctr., 1995—2006, St. John's Hosp., Santa Monica, Calif., 1995—, UCLA Ctr. Health Sciences, 2006—; asst. clin. prof. plastic surgery UCLA David Geffen Sch. Medicine, 2006—; pvt. practice Santa Monica, Calif. Guest editor Aesthetic Surgery Jour., 2002—, Plastic & Reconstructive Surgery, 2006—. Chair new leadership div. Israel Bonds; state pres. Am. Jewish Congress; bd. mem. Maestro Found. U. Calif. Presdl. rsch. grant, 1982, Heart Assn. rsch. grant, 1985. Mem.: Internat. Soc. Aesthetic Plastic Surgeons, Internat. Ultrasonic Soc., Am. Coll. Surgeons, Calif. Soc. Plastic Surgeons, Bay Surg. Soc., LA Soc. Plastic Surgery (bd. dirs. 2005—, sec. 2005—), Calif. Soc. Plastic Surgery (ethics com. 2000—, co-chair exhibits com. 2001—04, co-chair legis. com. 2003—, exec. coun. 2006—), Calif. Med. Assn. (alt. del. 2004), Am. Soc. Plastic Surgeons (legis. com. 2002—04, exhibits com. 2004—06, performance metrics task force 2007—), Am. Soc. Aesthetic Plastic Surgery (govt. rels. com. 2001—03, electronic comms. com. 2003—, breast implant task force exhibits com. 2004, practice rels. com. 2004—, emerging trends task force & innovative procedures com. 2005—). Avocations: sailing, triathlon, photography, piano, scuba diving. Office: 1301 20th St Ste 350 Santa Monica CA 90404 Office Phone: 310-315-1121. Office Fax: 310-315-9921. Business E-Mail: steve@drteitelbaum.com.

TEITELBAUM, STEVEN LAZARUS, pathology educator; b. Bklyn., June 29, 1938; s. Hyman and Rose Leah (Harnick) T.; m. Marilyn Ruth Schaffner; children: Caren Beth, Aaron Michael, Rebecca Lee. BA, Columbia U., NYC, 1960; MD, Washington U., St. Louis, 1964; DSc (hon.), CUNY SI Coll., 2004. Intern Washington U. Sch. Medicine, St. Louis, 1964-65, 3d. yr. asst. resident, ACS clin. fellow, 1967-68; intern NYU, 1965-66, 2d yr. resident, 1966-67; assoc. pathologist Jewish Hosp. at Washington U. Med. Ctr., St. Louis, 1969-89, pathologist-in-chief, 1987-96; assoc. pathologist Barnes-Jewish Hosp., St. Louis, 1986—; pathologist St. Louis Shriners Hosp. for Crippled Children, 1986—; Wilma and Roswell Messing prof. pathology Washington U. Sch. Medicine, St. Louis, 1987—. Mem. Othopedics and Musculoskeletal Study Sect. NIH, 1983-87; adv. counsel NIH, 2003—. Contbr. numerous sci. articles to med. jours., 1965—, 12 chpts. to med. books and texts, 1976—; mem. editorial bd. Calcified Tissue Internat., 1980-85, 89-91, Human Pathology; mem. bd. assoc. editors Jour. Orthopaedic Rsch., Jour. Cellular Biochemistry. Recipient 2nd Century award, Washington U. Sch. Medicine, 2004, Rouse-Whipple award, Am. Soc. Investigative Pathology, 2006. Mem. Am. Soc. Clin. Investigation, Assn. Am. Physicians, Am. Acad. Orthopaedic Surgeons (Ann Doner Vaughan Kappa Delta award 1988), Paget's Disease Found. (adv. panel), Am. Soc. for Bone and Mineral Rsch. (pres. 1993, William F. Neuman award 1998), Fed. Am. Soc. Expl. Biology (bd. dirs. 1997—, pres. 2002—). Office: Washington U Sch Medicine 216 S Kingshighway Blvd Saint Louis MO 63110-1026

TEITELL, MICHAEL ALAN, cancer biologist and immunologist; s. Philip Lawrence and Phyllis Rita (Henkin) T. BS in Biochemistry magna cum laude, UCLA, 1985, MS in Biochemistry, 1985, MD, PhD, 1993. Cert. in clin. pathology Am. Bd. Pathology, 1997, in anatomic pathology 1997, in pediat. pathology 2001. Auto mechanic BMW Svc. Ctr., Woodland Hills, Calif., 1977-80, Bob Smith BMW, Canoga Park, Calif., 1980-81; chemistry lab. tech. L.A. Pierce Coll., Woodland Hills, Calif., 1978-80, UCLA, 1981-84, chief pediatric pathology, 1999—, prof. pathology and pediatrics, 2008—; intern, resident Brigham and Women's Hosp., Boston, 1993—; clin. rsch. fellow pathology Harvard Med. Sch., 1993—. Rsch. assoc. dept. medicine Brigham & Women's Hosp. Contbr. articles to profl. jours. Recipient FOCIS/Millenium Pharms. award, Genomics Rsch., 2001, Scholar award, Leukemia and Lymphoma Soc., 2003; Stohlman scholar, 2008. Mem. Am. Assn. Immunologists, Am. Soc. Biochemistry and Molecular Biology, Am. Assn. Cancer Rsch., Epigenetics Soc., Biophys. Soc., Sigma Xi, Phi Beta Kappa (UCLA Eta chpt.), Am. Soc. Clinical Investigators Avocations: running, baseball, travel, theater, food. Home: 5945 Beckford Ave Tarzana CA 91356-1104

TEITGE, ROBERT A., medical association administrator; b. LA, Oct. 18, 1942; s. Allan Bernhard and Barbara Hodges (Means) T.; m. Louise Janet Hirschmann, Dec. 28, 1968; children: Erika, Stefan, Shera, Mieke. AB, Stanford U., 1964; MS, U. Puget Sound, 1965; MD, U. So. Calif., 1969. Diplomate Am. Bd. Orthopedic Surgery. Intern RI Hosp., Providence, 1969-70, resident in orthopedic surgery LA County-U. So. Calif. Med. Ctr., 1970-74; postgrad. fellow in sports medicine Kaplan Jobe Clinic, Inglewood, Calif., 1976-77; orthopedic surgeon Tacoma Orthopedic and Fracture Clinic, 1977-79, Palo Alto Med. Clinic, Calif., 1979-80; dir. Ctr. for Athletic Medicine Henry Ford Hosp., Detroit, 1980-84; prin. Teitge Orthopedic Assocs., P.C., Warren, Mich., 1984—. Team physician Stanford U., 1979-80, Detroit Lions Profl. Football Team, 1980-84, Detroit Red Wings Profl. Hockey Team, 1982-88, Detroit Drive Profl. Football Team, 1987-88; orthopedic cons. Detroit Tigers Profl. Baseball Team, 1980-84, Detroit Pistons Profl. Basketball Team, 1984-94, 96—; chief med. officer sports medicine U.S. Figure Skating Championship, 1994, World Cup U.S.A., 1994; prof. Wayne State U. Sch. Medicine. Contbr. articles to profl. jours. Trustee AO Found., Berne, Switzerland, 1985-90; Maj. USAF, 1974-76. Mem. AMA, Am. Acad. Orthopedic Surgeons, Am. Orthopedic Soc. for Sports Medicine, Mid-Am. Orthopedic Assn., Mich. State Med. Soc., Acad. Orthopedic Soc., Wayne County Med. Soc., Detroit Acad. Orthopedics, Organ Procurement Agy. Mich.

TEIXEIRA, CASSIANO, physician; b. São Francisco de Paula, June 27, 1972; PhD, UFCSPA, 1995. With intensive care Moinhos de Vento Hosp., 2000. Office: Ramiro Barcelos Porto Alegre 90135-510 Brazil Business E-Mail: cassiano.rush@terra.com.br.

TEIXEIRA, JERÓNIMA MARIA ALVES, obstetrician; b. Paraiso, Castelo de Paiva, Portugal, Feb. 17, 1963; arrived in Eng., 1993; children: Sofia, Simao. MD, Oporto Med. Sch., Portugal, 1987, specialist in materno-fetal medicine, 1996; MPhil, Imperial Coll., London, 2000; PhD, Imperial Coll., 2005. Specialist tng. ob-gyn. Oporto Med. Sch., 1990-93; sr. clin. rschr. Imperial Coll., London, 1995-99, med. writer, 2000—. Contbr. articles to profl. jours. Avocations: reading, travel. Office: Chelsea & Westminster Hosp Acad Ob Fulham Rd London SW10 9WH England E-mail: jeronima.teixeira@fcm.unl.pt.

TEIXEIRA, MARCELO FONTES, dentist; b. Pirai, Brazil, Apr. 15, 1972; Degree in Dentistry, Unifoa U., 1993; degree in Implantodontist, SLMAndic, 2008. Dentistry Unifoa U., 2000—. Avocation: soccer. Office: Ave Evandro Lins e Silva 840 1205 Rio de Janeiro 22631470 Brazil Office Fax: 55 21 21782135. Business E-Mail: mfonttes@uol.com.br.

TEIXEIRA, SOLANGE PISTORI, dermatologist, researcher; d. Solon Teixeira Rezende and Stella Pistori Teixeira; m. Sergio Bortolai Libonati, Sept. 19, 1987; children: Raphael Teixeira Libonati, Thais Teixeira Libonati. Degree, Santos Faculty Med. Scis., São Paulo, 1981; MS in Dermatology, U. Fed. São Paulo, 1994. Bd. cert. diplomate in dermatology Brazilian Soc. Dermatology, 1984. Resident in dermatology U. Fed. São Paulo, 1982—83; gen. practitioner Teixeira Dairy Industry, São Paulo, 1982—88; dermatologist Sec. of Health, São Paulo, 1983—87; asst. prof. dermatology Sch. Medicine, Sao Francisco U., Braganca Paulista, Brazil, 1984—86; clin. dir., pvt. practice São Paulo, 1984—. Postgrad. fellow in advanced dermatology Paulista Sch. Medicine, Fed. U. São Paulo, 1997; reference dermatologist, collaborator dr. Pediat. Oncology Inst. - Grupo de Apoio ao Adolescente e a Crianca com Cancer, São Paulo, 2001—; trainee in dermatology Unidad Dermatologica del Hosp. Durand, Buenos Aires, 1983; clin. coord. lymphoma sect. dermatology dept. U. Fed. São Paulo, São Paulo, 1996—, clin. collaborator Unidade Cosmiatria, Cirurgia e Oncologia dept. dermatology, 2001—. Contbr. articles to profl. jours., chapters to books. Fellow: Am. Acad. Dermatology (assoc.); mem.: Brazilian Soc. Aesthetic Medicine (assoc.), Brazilian Soc. Dermatol. Surgery (assoc.), Internat. Acad. Cosmetic Dermatology (assoc.), Brazilian Melanoma Group (assoc.), Latin. Am. Acad. Dermatology (assoc.), Acad. of Medicine of Sao Paulo (assoc.), Brazilian Med. Assn. (assoc.), Brazilian Soc. Laser Medicine (assoc.; 2d treas. 2005—), São Paulo Regional Med. Coun. (assoc.), Paulista Med. Assn. (assoc.), Brazilian Dermatol. Soc. (assoc.). Office: R Joaquim Floriano 100 4th Fl 04534-000 São Paulo Brazil Office Fax: 55-11-3078-8668. Personal E-mail: solangeteixeira@clinderm.com.br. Business E-Mail: clinderm@clinderm.com.br.

TEJADA, FRANCISCO, physician, educator; b. Moyobamba, San Martin, Peru, July 25, 1942; arrived in US, 1969, naturalized; s. Francisco Tejada and Semiramis Reateqi; m. Barbara Ann Kotowski, Feb. 1, 1970; children: Anamaria, Semiramis, Barbara Lee, Francisco, James. BS, U. Nat. Mayor de San Marcos, Lima, Peru, 1961; MD, U. Peruana Cayetano Heredia, Lima, 1967. Diplomate Am. Bd. Internal Medicine, Am. Bd. Oncology. Resident in medicine Johns Hopkins U., Balt., 1969-72; sr. cancer rschr. Nat. Cancer Inst., NIH, Bethesda, Md., 1972-75; asst. clin. dir. Comprehensive Cancer Ctr. Fla., Miami, Fla., 1975-80; asst. prof. U. Miami, 1975-79, assoc. prof., 1979-85, prof., 1985—; vis. prof. U. Peruana Cayetano Heredia, Lima, 1994—; sr. ptnr. Oncology Assocs., Miami, 1980-85; chief cancer control Papanicolaou Cancer Ctr., Miami, 1984-86; assoc. dir., clin. dir. AMC Cancer Rsch. Ctr., Denver, 1986-87; pres. Am. Oncology Ctrs., Miami, 1985—2009; prof. U. San Agustin, Arequipa, Peru, 1992—, U. Peruana Cayetano Heredia, Lima, Peru, 1994—; clin. rsch. scientist UM/Sylvester Comprehensive Cancer Ctr., 2001—; investigator Lovelace Rsch. Svcs., Inc., 2002—05; hon. prof. Barcelo Found. Med. Schs., Buenos Aires, 2010—, Peruvian U. Cayetano Heredia, Lima, Peru, 2010—. Oncology expert Pan Am. Health Orgn., Washington, 1975-85, Nat. Cancer Inst., Bethesda, Md., 1984-86; dir. Miami Cancer Inst., 1980—; dir. Peruvian-Am. Endowment Inc., 1993-99, v.p., 1995-97; bd. dirs. Integrated Med. Svcs. Fla. Keys, Key West, 1997-2000; dir. oncology dept. Clinica Ricardo Palma, Lima, Peru, 1991-99; med. dir. Fla. Comprehensive Cancer Control Initiative, 2000 03; dir. CureMeDoctor Inc., 2002 2002, Precision Med. Devices, Inc., 2007—; dir. Precision Med. Devices, Inc, 2007-, v.p., 2009-. Editor Miami Health Letter, 1986—; inventor cancer risk assessment. Mem. Beacon Coun., Miami, 1984, Latin Am. Cancer Info., Washington, 1976, Hispanic Cancer Rsch. Network, Washington, 1990; chpt. pres. Peruvian Am. Med. Soc., Miami, 1986; trustee Miami-Dade County Pub. Health Trust, 2002-05; bd. dirs. Miami-Dade County Policy Health Authority, 2002-03, mem. strategic planing com., Peruvian Med. Soc., Inc. 2010. Lt. Peruvian Army, 1966-67. Decorated comendador Orden Sociedad, Peruvian U. Caytano Heredia; recipient Gold Medal Merit award Ministry of Edn., Lima, 1959, Hipolito Unanue award Hipolito Unanue Inst., Lima, 1968. Fellow ACP, Johns Hopkins U., Nat. Cancer Inst.; mem. Colegio Medico del Perú, Am. Assn. Cancer Rsch., Am. Soc. Clin. Oncology, Am. Soc. Hematology, Bolivian Cancer Soc. (hon.), Peruvian Cancer Soc. (hon.), Chilean Soc. Cancer (hon.), Argentinian Soc. Head and Neck Pathology (hon.). Roman Catholic. Avocations: hiking, photography, reading. Office: Dept Epidemiology and Pub Health Clin Rsch Bldg 1120 NW 14th St Rm 1042 Miami FL 33136 Office Phone: 305-251-4540. Personal E-mail: ftejadamd@gmail.com.

TEJA-ISAVADHARM, PAKTIYA, pharmacologist, researcher; d. Kasem and Tieng Tangtatsawasdi; m. Dhavajjai Teja-Isavadharm, Jan. 26, 1986; children: Ekkachat, Patcharin. Diploma in Analytical Chemistry Tng., Chulalongkorn U., Bangkok, Thailand, 1977; BSc, Towson State U., 1979; MSc, U. of Md., 1981; PhD, Mahidol U., Bangkok, Thailand, 1998. Lic. pharmacologist. Rsch. scientist U. of Md., Balt., 1981—82; supr. Armed Forces Rsch. Inst. of Med. Sci. U.S. Army, Bangkok, 1983—98, med. rsch. scientist Armed Forces Rsch. Inst. of Med. Sci., 1998—. Mem.: Rho Chi. Buddhist. Achievements include development of in vitro bioassay method for quantitative analysis of anti-malarial activity in plasma; research in studies of pharmacokinetic/pharmacodynamic of artemisinin anti-malarial compounds for the US Army Drug for Severe Malaria research program. Avocation: photography. Office: Inst of Med Scienc Armed Forces Rsch 315/6 Rajvithi Road 10400 Bangkok Bangkok Thailand Office Fax: 66-02-644-4784. E-mail: paktiyat@afrims.org.

TEKELIOGLU, MERAL, physician, educator; b. Ermenek, Konya, Turkey, Dec. 23, 1936; d. Sefik and Zeynep Tekelioglu; 1 child, Kaya Uysal. Grad., Ankara Med. Faculty, Turkey, 1961, specialist degree in histology-embryology, 1964, docent, 1969. Asst. in histology-embryology faculty medicine Ankara U., 1961—64, chief asst., 1964—69; docent dept. histology-embryology Hacettepe U., 1969—75, prof., dir. dept. histology-embryology, 1975, Anka U. Faculty Medicine, 1983—2004, prof. emeritus, 2004—. Cons. electron microscopy. Author (with others): The Cell: Fine Structure and Function, 1972; author: 4th edit., 1982, Medical Embryology, 1984, General Medical Histology, 1989, 3d edit., 1999, Sobotta, Atlas of Histology, 4th edit. (Turkish version, 1994, 5th edit., 1999, Human Reproduction and Development (Medical Embryology, 1995, articles on fine morphology of early pregnant and HCG and HMG treated human endometrium and brain morphology of slow-growing viral infectious, degenerative diseases of the human central nervous system, related topics; editor: Special Histology, 2002. Mem.: Cambridge U. Alumnus, European Microscopical Soc., Oxford, Am. Soc. Reprod.

Med. Birmingham, European Soc. Human Reproduction and Fertility (Belgium), Turkish Soc. Natural Protection Istanbul, European Pineal Soc. Strasburg, Cytochem. Soc., Royal Micros. Soc. (Oxford, Eng.), European Soc. Anatomy (Cambridge, Eng.), Clare Hall Cambridge (England) U. (assoc.), Turkish Electron Microscopy Soc. (life). Muslim. Home: Cinnah Caddesi Vali Dr Resit Sokak No 9/2 06550 Ankara Turkey Home Phone: 90 312 442 3429. Business E-Mail: mkuysal@politics.ankara.edu.tr.

TEKKOK, ISMAIL H., neurosurgeon, educator; b. Ankara, Turkey, Sept. 30, 1958; s. Yalcin and Gokcen Tekkok; m. Ebru Oncel Tekkok, June 11, 2000. MD, Hacettepe U., Ankara, 1983; Master of Surgery, Hecettepe U., Ankara, 1992. Fellow in epilepsy surgery Montreal Neurol. Inst., Que., Canada, 1994; fellow in trigeminal surgery Med. Coll. Ohio, Toledo, 1994—95; fellow in pediat. neurosurgery Children's Hosp. Ea. Ont., Ottawa, Ont., Canada, 1995—96, 1997; fellow in radiosurgery U. Va., Charlottesville, 1996; cons. neurosurgery Bayindir Med. Ctr., Ankara, 1997—2001; assoc. prof. neurosurgery Sch. Medicine Mersin U., Turkey, 2002—. Editor: Child's Nervous Sys., 1998—2002. Mem.: N.Y. Acad. Scis., Internat. Soc. Pediat. Neurosurgeons, Congress Neurol. Surgeons. Avocations: hiking, fishing, music. Office: MESA Hosp Neurosurgery Dept Sogutozu 06510 Ankara 06510 Turkey Business E-Mail: itekkok@mesa.com.tr.

TELANG, NITIN T., cancer biologist, educator; b. Bombay, July 3, 1943; came to U.S., 1976; s. Trimbak Pandharinath and Madhumalati (Kanitkar) T. BSc, U. Poona, India, 1963, MSc, 1966, PhD, 1974. Assoc. rsch. scientist Tata Meml. Hosp. Cancer Rsch. Inst., Bombay, 1974-76; rsch. assoc. U. Nebr., Lincoln, 1976-78; staff fellow Am. Health Found., Valhalla, NY, 1978-81; rsch. assoc. Sloan-Kettering Inst., NYC, 1981-85; attending biochemist Meml. Sloan-Ketering Cancer Ctr., NYC, 1985-91; assoc. prof. Cornell U. Med. Coll., NYC, 1991—2004; dir. divsn. carcinogenesis & prevention Strang-Cornell Cancer Rsch. Lab., NYC, 1991-95, dir. carcinogenesis and nutrition core lab., 1991—2003; dir. divsn. carcinogenesis and prevention Strang Cancer Prevention Ctr., NYC, 1995—2007, sr. scientist, head Julian H. Robertson Jr. Chemoprevention Rsch. Lab., 1998—2007. Vis. investigator The Rockefeller U., N.Y.C., 1985-89. Contbr. numerous articles to profl. jours. Mem. Am. Assn. Cancer Rsch., European Assn. Cancer Rsch. Office Phone: 201-476-0773. Business E-Mail: entitytoo@gmail.com.

TELEGRAFI, SHPETIM, physician, educator; b. Gjirokaster, Albania, June 4, 1948; MD, Tirana Faculty Medicine, 1971. Assoc. prof. Sch. Medicine, 1994—. Adj. assoc. prof. diagnostic med. sonography NYU-SCPS, 1994. Recipient Medal of Excellent Pub. Health Svc., Parlament Republic of Albania. Mem.: Kosova Ultrasound Assn., Albanian Imaging Assn., SDMS, ESR, AIUM, AUA. Avocation: fishing. Home: 350 Hollywood Ave Tuckahoe NY 10707 Business E-Mail: shpetim.telegrafi@nyumc.org.

TELEMAQUE, SABINE, medical educator; b. Can., Aug. 19, 1966; PhD, U. Sherbrooke, 1993. Asst. prof. U. Ark. Med. Scis., 2004—. Peer reviewer AHA, 2011. Recipient Doctoral Tng. award, Fonds Rsch. Santé Qué.; Parke-Davis Exch. fellowship, U. Cambridge, Postdoc. fellowship, Med. Rsch. Coun. Can., Can. Heart and Stroke Found. Mem.: Hypertension Can., Am. Physiol. Soc., Am. Heart Assn., Club Rschs. Cliniques Que. Avocations: travel, reading. Office: 4301 W Markham Slot # 839 Little Rock AR 72205 Business E-Mail: stelemaque@uams.edu.

TELFER, MARGARET CLARE, internist, hematologist, oncologist; b. Manila, Apr. 9, 1939; came to U.S., 1941; d. James Gavin and Margaret Adele (Baldwin) T. BA, Stanford U., 1961; MD, Washington U., St. Louis, 1965. Diplomate Am. Bd. Internal Medicine, Am. Bd. Hematology, Am. Bd. Oncology; lic. Ill., Mo. Resident in medicine Michael Reese Hosp., Chgo., 1968, fellow in hematology and oncology, 1970, assoc. attending physician, 1970-72, dir. Hemophilia Ctr., 1971—, interim dir. div. hematology and oncology, 1971—74, 1984—84, 1989—99, attending physician Chgo., 1972—2009, Rush-Presbyn. St. Luke's Hosp., 1999—2009, Olympia Fields (Ill.) Hosp., 1999—2006, Cook County Hosp., Chgo., 2000—, dir. hematology/oncology fellowship, 2004—; asst. prof. medicine U. Chgo., 1975-80, assoc. prof. medicine, 1980-85, assoc. prof. clin. medicine, 1985-89; assoc. prof. medicine U. Ill., Chgo., 1990-2001, Rush U., Chgo., 2001—. Mem. med. adv. bd. Hemophilia Found. Ill., 1971, chmn., 1972—83, lectr. annual symposium, 1978—84; mem. med. adv. bd. State of Ill. Hemophilia Program; dir. hematology-oncology fellowship program Michael Reese Hosp., 1971—75, 1981—84, 1989—2000, dir. Cook County Fellowship Program, 2004—, mem. numerous coms.; lectr. in field. Contbr. articles to profl. jours. Fellow ACP; mem. Am. Soc. Clin. Oncology, Am. Assn. Med. Colls., Am. Soc. Hematology, World Fedn. Hemophilia, Blood Club (Chgo.), Thrombosis Club (Chgo.). Office: Stroger Cook County Hosp Rm 750 Adminstrn Bldg 1900 W Polk Chicago IL 60612 Office Phone: 312-864-7250. Business E-Mail: mtelfer@ccbhs.org.

TELFORD, SAM ROUNTREE, JR., zoologist; b. Winter Haven, Fla., Aug. 25, 1932; s. Sam Rountree Telford and Ann Marion Frances Schiller; m. Michiko Miyazawa, Dec. 20, 1957; children: Sam Rountree III, Randolph Stuart, Robert Miyazawa. BA, U. Va., Charlottesville, 1955; MS, U. Fla., Gainesville, 1961; PhD, U. Calif., LA, 1964. NIH postdoc. fellow Inst. Infectious Diseases, U. Tokyo, 1965—67; vertebrate ecologist Gorgas Meml. Lab., Panama, 1967—70; asst. prof. U. Fla., 1970—73; med. zoologist WHO, Acarigua, Venezuela, 1973—74, Karachi, Pakistan, 1975—77, Geneva, 1977—78, Rangoon, Myanmar, 1978—80; project leader Danish Internat. Devel. Agy., Morogoro, Tanzania, 1981—85. Ecol. cons., Fla., 1985—98. Contbr. scientific papers. Sgt. US Army, 1956—59, Tokyo. Mem.: Am. Soc. Parasitologists. Democrat. Avocations: reading, gardening. Home Phone: 352-375-4214.

TELIS, SHERMAN, dentist; BA in Polit. Sci., Casa Western Res. Sch., DMD, 1976. Dentist Washington Ctr. for Dentistry. Mem.: ADA, DC Dental Soc., Internat. Congress of Oral Implantologists, Am. Acad. of Cosmetic Dentistry, Comprehensive Care Study Club. Office: Washington Ctr. for Dentistry 8th Fl 1430 K St NW Washington DC 20005 Office Phone: 202-223-6630.

TELLES, CYNTHIA ANN, psychologist; b. El Paso, Tex., Aug. 10, 1952; d. Raymond Lawrence and Delfina Telles; m. David Jimenez (div. Aug. 1991); 1 child, Raymond; m. Robert Myles Hertzberg. BA, Smith Coll., Northampton, Mass., 1974; PhD in Clin. Psychology, Boston U., 1982. Cert. psychologist Calif. Tchg. fellow Boston U. Sch. Medicine, 1975—78; psychologist Boston U. Med. Ctr., 1977-78; rsch. fellow dept. psychology UCLA School Medicine, 1978-79, lectr. dept. psychiatry, 1980—85, dir. Spanish-Speaking Psychosocial Clinic, Neuropsychiatric Inst. & Hosp., 1981—, asst. clin. prof. dept. psychiatry, 1986—96, assoc. clin. prof. dept. psychiatry, 1996—. Cons. LA County Dept. Mental Health, 1985—, Calif. Sch. Profl. Psychology, 1986—; nat. adv. coun., Substance Abuse & Mental Health Services Adminstrn. US Dept. Health & Human Services, 1993—98; bd. dirs. Calif. Endowment, 2001—, vice chair, 2002—04, chair, 2004—06; bd. dirs. Kaiser Found. Health Plan & Hospitals, 2004—, Calif. Cmty. Found., 2005—, United Calif. Bank, 1994—2002, Burlington Northern Santa Fe Corp., 2009—10, Gen. Motors Co., 2010—; mem. Mental Health Task Force, The Carter Ctr., Atlanta; bd. dirs. founding mem. Pub. Policy Inst. Calif., 1995—2005; ctr. bd. dirs. Performing Arts Ctr. LA, 2000—; apptd. White House Commn. Presdl. Scholars, 2010—. Author: Latino Mental Health: Cumnt Research and-Policy Perspeztives, 1994; contbr. articles to profl. jours. Founder, pres. Hispanic Health Found., 1988—98; commr. City of LA, 1990—2003, v.p. LA City Ethics Commn., 1991—94, pres. LA Commn. on Status of Women, 1994—99, mem. Commn. on Children, Youth & Their Families, 1999—2001, past v. p. LA Bd. Libr. Commissioners; bd. dirs. Coalition Pro-Salud Hispana, Boston, 1977—78, Nat. Hispanic Psychol. Assn., 1984—86, LA Police Found., 2010—, Nat. Alliance Hispanic Health, 1994—; past chair bd. dirs. Nat. Coalition Hispanic Health & Human Svc. Organizations, Washington; mem. bd. dirs. Pacific Coun. on Internat. Policy, 2010—; bd. mem. LA Police Meml. Found., 2010—. Recipient Humanitarian award, East LA Coll., 1988, Civic & Cmty. Leadership award, Nat. Network Hispanic Women, 1989, Crystal Eagle award, CORO Found., 2006, Pioneer for Justice award, LA Mex. Am. Found., 2006, Silver Achievement award, YWCA, 1994, Women of Couiage award, LA, 2010; named 100 Most Influential Hispanic in Nation, Hispanic Bus. Mag. Mem.: APA, Nat. Hispanic Psychol. Assn. Roman Catholic. Office: UCLA Dept Psychiatry 300 Ucla Medical Plz Los Angeles CA 90095-8346 Office Phone: 310-825-4568.

TELLEZ, CLAUDIA, hematologist, oncologist, educator; MD, U. Ill., Chgo., 1990. Cert. Internal Medicine, 1997, Oncology, 1997, Hematology, 1998. Residency in internal medicine Northwestern Meml. Hosp., 1990—93, fellowship in hematology and oncology, 1993—96; instr. clin. medicine Northwestern Med. Sch.; ptnr. Hematology Oncology Assoc. Ill. Prin. investigator for two clin. trials. Office: Hematology Oncology Associates Ill 676 N St Clair Ste 2140 Chicago IL 60611 *

TELLEZ, CORA M., healthcare company executive; b. 1949; BA, Mills Coll., 1972; MPA, Calif. State U. Various exec. positions to v.p., regional mgr. Hawaii Region Kaiser Found. Health Plan, 1978-94; sr. v.p., regional CEO Blue Shield, 1994-97; pres., chairwoman Prudential Health Care Plan of Calif., Inc., 1997-98; pres. CEO Health Net Foundation Health Systems, Inc., 1998—2002; founder, pres., CEO Sterling Health Services Adminstrn., Inc., 2003—, Sterling Self Insurance Adminstrn., 2010—. Mem. advisory bd. Practice Fusion, 2006—, bd. dirs., 2011—, Crescent Healthcare, Inc. V.p. S.H. Cowell Found.; bd. dirs. Inst. for Medical Quality. Mem. Phi Beta Kappa. Office: Sterling HSA 475 14th St Ste 650 Oakland CA 94612 Office Phone: 800-617-4729. Office Fax: 877-517-4729. *

TEMIZ, ABDULKERIM, physician, educator; b. Mersin, Jan. 1, 1974; Degree, Anakara U., 1997. Physician, asst. prof. dept. pediat. surgery Baskent U., 2007—. Mem.: Turkish Assn. Pediat. Surgery. Avocation: travel. Office: Baraj Yolu Adana 0901150 Turkey E-mail: aktemiz@yahoo.com.

TEMME, ACHIM, molecular biologist, researcher; b. Juelich, Germany, Jan. 16, 1966; s. Franz and Sibylle Temme; m. Annette Rothenberger, June 9, 1993; children: Julian Paul, Lea Louise, Hellen Lilith. PhD, U. Bonn, 1997. Sr. scientist Inst. for Genetics, Bonn, Germany, 1997—98; group leader Inst. of Immunology, Dresden, Germany, 1998—. Mem.: AACR (assoc.), ASCB (life), ELSO (life). Office: Inst Immunology MTZ TU Dresden Fetscherstrasse 74 01307 Dresden Germany Office Fax: +49-(0)351-4586316. Business E-Mail: temme@rcs.urz.tu-dresden.de.

TEMMIM, LABIBA, oncologist, director; d. Ibrahim Temmim and Aziza Ibrahim Bouchouk; MD, U. Rene Descartes, France, 1964; PhD in oncology, U. Rene Descartes, 1977. Diplome Doctorat Faculty of Medicine Broussais Hotel-Dieu, 1974. Lectr. Kuwait U., Kuwait, Kuwait, 1990—2005; cons. WHO, Geneva, 1982—2003; dir. dept. Kuwait Cancer Control Ctr., Kuwait, Kuwait, 1982—2004; dir. of dept. Saad Specialist Hosp., Al-Khobar, Saudi Arabia, 2004—. Recipient Chevalier Palmes Academiques, Ministry Foreign Affairs, France, 2005. Achievements include research in profile of breast cancer in the Middle East; profile of Lymphoid malignancies in the Middle East; cancer control and early prevention in breast cancer and malignancies in women; cancer control and early prevention in lung cancer and prostate. Office Fax: +966 3 882 11 38.

TEMNYALOV, NIKOLAI DIMITROV, pharmacologist, educator, researcher; b. Glogene, Lovetch, Bulgaria, Feb. 2, 1935; s. Dimitar Nenov and Penka Ivanova (Tzatcheva) T.; m. Mara Vassileva Shalapatova, Nov. 29, 1964; children: Pavlina Nikolaeva Temnyalova-Lozanova, Vladimir Nikolaev. MD, Univ. Med. Sch., Sofia, Bulgaria, 1959; diploma (hon.), Med. U., Varna, Bulgaria, 1961; PhD, Sofia Inst. Physiology, Varna, Bulgaria, 1994. Ordinator ward of internal diseases Regional Hosp., Ardino, Bulgaria, 1959-61; asst. prof. Med. U., Varna, 1961-65, sr. asst. prof., 1966-72, sr. lectr. dept. pharmacology, 1973-98, vis. assoc. prof., 1999—2000, cons. in pharmacotherapy, 2000—08. Cons. Bulgarian Movement for Sobriety, Varna, 1969-93, head ednl. commn., 1969—, v.p., 1975-93; head med. rsch. group for help in cessation of smoking, 1994—; cons. lectr. in field, 1966—; hon. lectr. in pharmacology Univ. Sch. for Nurses, Varna, 1961-2002. Author: Urea-Pharmacophysiological, Clinical and Therapeutic Aspects, 2004, Endogenous Betz, Endogenons Beta Advenergic Receptor Antag0nists, 2007, Gentamycin, 1971; co-author: Manual for Pharmacological Exercises, 1980, Psychosomatic Medicine, 1981; patentee in field. Lectr. Bulgarian Red Cross, 1961—; head med. sect. Dem. Alternative for Republic, Varna, 1994—; mem. med. sect. Alliance Francaise, Varna, 1989—99; mem. Party of Bulgarian Euroleft; v.p. Club Euro-Medic, 1998—99. Recipient diploma of ctrl. com. Bulgarian Red Cross, 1965, Hon. medal Ministry of Pub. Health, Bulgaria, 1981, Kliment Ohridsky medal Soc. for Dissemination of Sci. Knowledge, 1986; grantee in field. Mem. N.Y. Acad. Scis., Internat. Union Pharmacology, Internat. Union Angiology. Social Democratic Party. Avocations: chess, ping pong/table tennis, volleyball, swimming, travel. Home: Makedonia Str # 69A 9002 Varna Bulgaria Office: Med U Academician M Drinov St #55 9002 Varna Bulgaria

TEMPELIS, CONSTANTINE HARRY, immunologist, educator; b. Superior, Wis., Aug. 27, 1927; s. Harry and Thelma Marie (Hoff) T.; m. Nancy Louise Foster, Aug. 27, 1955; children: William H., Daniel S. BS, U. Wis.-Superior, 1950; MS, U. Wis.-Madison, 1953, PhD, 1955. Project assoc. immunology U. Wis., Madison, 1955-57; instr. immunology U. W.Va., Morgantown, 1957-58; asst. rsch. immunologist U. Calif., Berkeley, 1958-66, assoc. prof. immunology, 1966-72, prof., 1972-95, prof. emeritus, 1995—, prof. grad. sch., 1996—. Vis. scientist Wellcome Rsch. Labs., Beckenham, Kent, Eng., 1977-78, U. Innsbruck, Austria, 1985, 90, 91; cons. in field. Contbr. articles to profl. jours. Served with USNR, 1945-46. Recipient Rsch. Career Devel. award, 1965-70; Fogarty sr. internat. fellow NIH, 1977-78 Mem. AAAS, Am. Assn. Immunologists, Fedn. Am. Soc. Exptl. Biology, Sigma Xi. Office: U Calif Sch Pub Health Berkeley CA 94720-0001 Office Phone: 510-642-3744. Business E-Mail: chtemp@berkeley.edu, champ@berkeley.edu.

TEMPLE, DONALD, retired allergist, dermatologist; b. Chgo., May 21, 1933; s. Samuel Leonard and Matilda Eve (Riff) T.; m. Sarah Rachel Katz, Sept. 29, 1957; children: Michael A., Matthew D., Madeline B. AB in Biology cum laude, Harvard U., 1954; MD, U. Chgo., 1958. Diplomate Am. Bd. Allergy and Immunology, Am. Bd. Dermatology, Nat. Bd. Med. Examiners; lic. Intern Michael Reese Hosp., Chgo., 1958-59; resident in dermatology U. Chgo. Hosps., 1959-62; clin. asst., dept. dermatology Boston U., 1963-64; clin. instr., dermatology dept. Stanford U. Sch. Medicine, 1965; preceptee in allergy Offices of Leon Unger, M.D., and Donald Unger, M.D., Chgo., 1965-69; pvt. practice Des Plaines, Ill., 1969-76; with allergy dept. Glen Ellyn (Ill.) Clinic, 1972-97; ret., 1997. Dermatology and allergy staff Louis A. Weiss Hosp., Chgo., 1965-73, allergy sect. Loyola U. Med. Ctr., Maywood, Ill., 1977-80, exec. and contract medicine coms. Glen Ellyn; clin. asst. prof. dermatology Abraham Lincoln Sch. Medicine, U. Ill., 1972-75; clin. asst. prof. medicine sect. allergy and dermatology, Loyola U., 1977-85; mem. staff Cen. DuPage Hosp., Winfield, Ill., 1973-97, Glen Oaks Med. Ctr., Glendale Heights, Ill., Glendale Heights Cmty. Hosp., 1980-92. Contbr. articles to profl. jours. Bd. dirs. Am. Lung Assn., DuPage, McHenry counties, 1980-91; chmn. Contract Medicine, HMO Com., Glen Ellyn Clinic, 1985, mem. exec. com., 1988-92. Fellow Am. Coll. Chest Physicians, Am. Assn. Cert. Allergists, Am. Coll. Allergists, Am. Acad. Allergy, Ill. Soc. Allergy and Clin. Immunology, Chgo. Dermatol. Soc.; mem. AMA, Ill. State Med. Soc., DuPage County Med. Soc., Chgo. Med. Soc., Fla. Med. Assn. Collier County Med. Soc. Jewish. Avocations: sailing, investing. Home: 6585 Nicholas Blvd Ph 3 Naples FL 34108-7210 E-mail: don.temple@post.harvard.edu.

TEMPLETON, JOHN MARKS, JR., retired pediatric surgeon, professor, foundation administrator; b. NYC, Feb. 19, 1940; s. John Marks and Judith Dudley (Folk) T.; m. Josephine J. Gargiulo, Aug. 2, 1970; children: Heather Erin, Jennifer Ann. BA, Yale Coll., 1962; MD, Harvard U., 1968; degree (hon.), Beaver Coll., Buena Vista U., Va. Commonwealth U., Alvernia Coll. Intern Med. Coll. Va., Richmond, 1968-69, resident, 1969-73; dir. trauma program U. Pa. and Children's Hosp. Phila., 1989—95, adj. prof. pediat. surgery, 1995. Chmn. bd. Templeton Growth Fund, Ltd. Assoc. editor: Textbook of Pediatric Emergencies, 1993; pub. 6000 Name Geneology, 1997, A Searcher's Life, 1999, Thrift and Generosity, 2004. Chmn. health and safety, exec. bd. Cradle of Liberty coun. Boy Scouts Am.; mem. exec. bd. Eastern U., Fgn. Policy Rsch. Inst., Nat. Recreation Found., Coll. Physicians Phila., Melmark Charitable Found.; nat. bd. dirs., pres. Pa. divsn. Am. Trauma Soc.; bd. dirs. Nat. Bible Assn.; elder Proclamation Presbyn. Ch.; pres. John Templeton Found. With M.C., USNR, 1975-77; bd. mem. Am. Trauma Soc., Foreign Policy Rsch. Inst., Nat. Bible Assn., EAST Found., John Templeton Found., Session and Proclamation Presbyterian Ch. Barclay fellow Green Templeton Coll., Oxford U., fellow George H. Gallup Internat. Inst. Mem. ACS, Am. Pediat. Surg. Assn., Am. Assn. Surgery Trauma, Ea. Assn. Surgery Trauma, Phila. Coll. Physicians, Union League, Order Charlemagne, Lyford Cay Club, Merion Cricket Club, Athenaeum Club London, Rotary Internat., White's London, United Oxford and Cambridge U. Club (London). Republican. Evangelical. Office: 300 Conshohocken State Rd Ste 500 West Conshohocken PA 19428 Personal E-mail: templeton.pembroke@comcast.net.

TEMPLETON, LEAH, anesthesiologist, educator; b. Conover, NC, Jan. 17, 1973; BA, Barnard Coll. Columbia U., 1995; MD, Wake Forest U. Sch. Medicine, 1999. Asst. prof. pediatric anesthesiology Wake Forest U. Bapt. Health, 2004—. Recipient Funk award, Northwestern U. Dept. Anesthesiology. Mem.: Am. Soc. Anesthesiologist, Soc. Pediatric Anesthesia, Phi Beta Kappa. Avocations: reading, running. Office: Wake Forest University Baptist Health M Winston Salem NC 27157 Business E-Mail: ltemplet@wfubmc.edu.

TENENBAUM, ALEXANDER, cardiologist, educator; s. Moshe Monya Tenenbaum and Masha Maria Segal; m. Helena Pinkhasov; children: Ilan, Oren. MD, Kirhgiz State Med. Inst., 1978; PhD, VAK, Moscow, 1987. Diplomate Bd. Cardiology, Israel Sci. Soc., 1993. Dir. rsch. Chaim Sheba Med. Ctr., Ramat Gan, Israel, 2004—; dir. Heart Inst., Givataim, Israel, 2005—. Prof. cardiology Tel Aviv U., 2006—; editor-in-chief Cardiovasc. Diabetology, Biomed Ctrl., London, 2002—. Author (editor): (book) Cardiovascular Diabetology. Chmn. Israeli Working Group Cardiovasc. Pharmacology and Drug Therapy, Ramat Gan. Recipient Outstanding Publ. prize, Henry Neufeld Rsch.

Award Fund, 1997. Mem.: Israel Heart Soc. (Jan J. Kellermann Rsch. prize 1999). Achievements include research in bezafibrate in prevention of diabetes, myocardial infarction and colon cancer; mitral regurgitation in myocardial infarction; cardiac CT; diastolic dysfunction; coronary calcifications; aortic atheromas and calcifications; cardiac embolism; ACE-inhibitors cough and aspirin; Type 2 diabetes and heart diseases; metabolic syndrome; development of prevention of diabetes. Home: Shaul Hameleh 8 Kiriat Ono 55654 Israel Office: Cardiac Rehab Inst Chaim Sheba Med Ctr Tel Hashomer Ramat Gan 52621 Israel Office Fax: 97235735029. Personal E-mail: altenen@yahoo.com.

TENENBAUM, JOSEPH, cardiologist; b. Neptune, NJ, Feb. 11, 1946; s. Sol and Marilyn Tenenbaum; m. Marilou Faith Jones, May 19, 1978; 1 child, Mollie Rodriguez. BA, Brandeis U., 1968; MD, Harvard U., 1974. Diplomate Am. Bd. Internal Medicine, Am. Bd. Cardiology. Edgar Leifer clin. prof. medicine Columbia U., NYC, 1979—; attending physician, interim chair dept. medicine Presbyn. Hosp., NYC, 2001—03. Fellow Am. Coll. Cardiology; mem. Columbia Faculty Practice Orgn. (chmn. 2000-03)

TENENBAUM, JOSHUA BRETT, medical educator, researcher; BS in Physics (magna cum laude), Yale U., 1993; PhD in Brain and Cognitive Sciences, Mass. Inst. Tech., 1999. Asst. prof. Computer Sci. Stanford Univ., 2000—02, asst. prof., Psychology, 1999—2002; asst. ptof., Cognitive Sci. and Computation Mass. Inst. of Tech., 2002—07, Paul E. Newton career devel. pref, 2004—08, prin. investigator, Computer Sci. and Artificial Intelligence Lab. (CSAIL), 2003—, assoc prof., of Cognitive Sci. and Computation, 2007—. Editl. bd. mem. Cognitive Sci., 2004—08, assoc. editor, 2004—08; co-author: (jours.) Learning causal schemata, 2007 (Cognitive Sci. Computational Modeling prize, 2007), Learning grounded causal models, 2007 (Cognitive Sci. Computational Modeling prize, 2007), Bayesian models of cognition, 2008, Structured statistical models of inductive reasoning, 2009, A probabilistic model of theory formation, 2010, (jours) and numerous other jours. Recipient Early Investigator award, Soc. of Exptl. Psychologists, 2007, Disting. Lectr., Univ. of Brit. Columbia, 2007, Univ. of Calif., San Diego', 2007, Disting. Sci. award for Early Career Contbn. to Psychology, APA, 2008; co-recipient Troland Rsch. award, NAS, 2011; vis. scholar Symbolic Sys. Program, Stanford Univ., 2010. Fellow: Soc. of Exptl. Psychologists. Achievements include formulating a groundbreaking new Bayesian model of human inductive learning and for using this model to generate innovative empirical studies of human perception, language, and reasoning. Office: Massachusetts Institue of Technology Bldg 46-4015, 77 Massachusetts Ave Cambridge MA 02139 Office Phone: 617-452-2010. Office Fax: 617-253-8335. E-mail: jbt@mit.edu.

TENG, HAO-WEI, veterinarian; b. Taiwan, Oct. 23, 1971; D. Yang Ming U., 1987. Physician Vets. Gen. Hosp. Taipei, 2007—. Home: 9f-5 2 Lane 10 Shigyi Rd Taipei 112 Taiwan Personal E-mail: danny_teng@yahoo.com.tw.

TENGKU MUHAMMAD, TENGKU SIFZIZUL, molecular biologist, educator; b. Kuala Terengganu, Malaysia, Aug. 29, 1970, s. Tengku Muhammad Tengku Abdul Rahman and Tengku Azizah Tengku Musa; m. Hayatul Safrah Salleh, Apr. 30, 1994; children: Tengku Eikmal Aqil, Tengku Eideen Aiman, Tengku Elisa Najiha. BSc with honors, Cardiff U., Wales, 1993, PhD, 1998. Lectr., assoc. prof. U. Sains Malaysia, Penang, 1998—. Contbr. articles to profl. jours. Recipient Nat. Young Scientist award, Malaysia, Young Scientist and Technologist award, Assn. S.E. Asian Nations, 2005; grantee, Internat. Found. Sci., 1999, Ministry of Sci., Tech. and Environment, 1999 , Malaysian Toray Sci. Found., 1999—2005, FELDA Found., 2000—02, Fundamental Rsch. Grant Scheme, 2003—05, Sci. Advancement Grant Allocation, 2005—; fellow, Ministry of Sci., Tech. and the Environment, 1999—2000. Mem.: Malaysian Soc. Molecular Biology and Biotechnology (assoc.). Home: Fairway View Apt 21-1-6 Solok Bukit Jambul Penang 11950 Malaysia Office: Univ Sains Malaysia Sch Biol Sci Minden 11800 Penang Malaysia Office Fax: 04-6565125. Personal E-mail: sifzizul@time.net.my. E-mail: joe@usm.my.

TENKANEN, LEENA, epidemiologist, educator; b. Helsinki, Finland; d. Yrjö and Aune Kyllikki Kauko; m. Olli Ilmari Tenkanen; children: Tuija Katariina, Helena, Tuomas Juhani. MSc in Math. and Chemistry, Helsinki U., 1971; PhD in epidemiology, Tampere U., 1993. Asst. prof. epidemiology Sch. Pub. Health Tampere U., Finland, 1991—92, adj. prof. epidemiology, 1994—96, tutoring PhD students, 1998—; epidemiologist Helsinki Heart Study, Finland, 1988—; rsch. scientist Finnish Cancer Registry, Helsinki, 1983—87. Contbr. articles to profl. jours. Grantee, Various Orgns., 1997—2008. Avocation: sailing. Office: Helsinki Heart Study Kalliolinnantie 4 Helsinki FIN-00140 Finland Office Fax: 358-919124074. Business E-Mail: leena.tenkanen@uta.fi.

TENNAKOON, SAMPATH UDAYA BANDARA, medical educator; b. Kandy, Sri Lanka, Apr. 8, 1969; MBBS, U. Peradeniya, 1996; MPhil, U. Oslo, 2006. Med. officer Ministry Health, Sri Lanka, 1997—2001; lectr. Faculty Medicine, 2001—06, sr. lectr. Peradeniya, 2006—, dir. Health Emergency and Disaster Mgmt. Tng. Ctr., 2009—. Mem.: Nutrition Soc. Sri Lanka. Avocations: dance, reading. Home: 59 Nugegoda Katugastota 20800 Sri Lanka Personal E-mail: sampathte@yahoo.com.

TENOVUO, OLLI SAKARI, physician, researcher; b. Turku, Finland, July 31, 1956; s. Rauno and Kaarina Tenovuo; m. Tuula Pulli, June 5, 1985; children: Karno Henrik, Tuulianna Maria, Niklas Henrik, Juliana Henrika, Thomas Axel. MD, U. Turku, 1981, PhD, 1993. Cert. neurology specialist U. Turku, 1989, Finnish Med. Assn., 1989, pain medicine specialist 2000, rehab. specialist 2004. Rehab. cons. Turku U. Ctrl. Hosp., 1993—2002; sr. lectr. U. Turku, 2003—, leader, TBI rsch. group, 1996—; project chief Health Dist. Southwestern Finland, Turku, 2007—. Leader Duodecim, Specialist Group for TBI Recommendations, Helsinki, Finland, 1997—2005. Numerous grants. Mem.: Euroacademia Multidisciplinaria Neurotraumatologica, Nat. Neurotrauma Soc., Internat. Brain Injury Assn. (mem. editl. bd., profl. jour. 2007—). Avocations: photography, birdwatching. Office: Turku Univ Kiinamyllynkatu 4-8 Turku 20520 Finland Office Phone: 358504383802. Office Fax: 35823132737. Personal E-mail: olli.tenovuo@pp.inet.fi.

TEO, TERENCE, physician; b. Singapore, Mar. 5, 1974; MBBS, Nat. U. Singapore, 2000. Cons. Singapore Gen. Hosp., 2010—. Decorated Good Svc. medal Ministry of Def., Singapore; scholarship, Ministry of Health, Singapore. Fellow: Royal Coll. Radiologists (UK); mem.: Singapore Radiol. Soc., Singapore Med. Coun. Office: Singapore Gen Hosp Outram Rd Singapore 169608 Singapore E-mail: tkbteo@yahoo.com.sg.

TEPERMAN, LEWIS W., surgeon, educator; MD, Mt. Sinai Sch. Medicine, 1981. Diplomate Am. Bd. Surgery, 2007. Resident in surgery Columbia Presbyn. Med. Ctr., 1981—84, Long Island Jewish Med. Ctr., 1984—86; clin. fellow in transplant surgery Pitts. Univ., 1986—88; assoc. prof. surgery NYU, vice chair dept. surgery; divsn. chief transplant surgery NYU Langone Med. Ctr. Author: Improved arterial allograft preservation with the University of Wisconsin solution, 1991, Anatomic distribution of preservation solutions during canine hepatic procurement, 1991, Retrograde Caval Flush with Portal Venting in Orthotopic Liver Transplantation, 1993, Prolonged Abnormalities of Hemostasis Following Orthotopic Liver- Transplantation, 1993, Elevations of Platelet-Associated Antibodies During Orthotopic Liver- Transplant Rejections, 1994, Primary cutaneous infection by Aspergillus ustus in a 62-year-old liver transplant recipient, 1994, Changes in Platelet-Associated Antibodies with Orthotopic Liver-Transplantation, 1994, Use of Ribavirin for Recurrent Hepatitis C Virus (HCV) in Liver-Transplant Patients after Failure if Interferon, 1994, MRI Reliability Detects Macroregenerative Nodules and Small Hepatocellular-Carcinoma in Cirrhotic Livers, 1995, Chemoembolization of hepatocellular carcinoma induces capsule formation, 1996, various publs. Office: New York Langone Medical Center 403 E 34th St 3rd Fl New York NY 10016 Office Phone: 212-263-8134. Office Fax: 212-263-8157.

TEPPER, CLIFFORD, allergist, immunologist, educator; b. Schenectady, NY, Oct. 26, 1922; s. Solomon B. and Annette (Lifset) T.; m. Cynthia S. Tepper; children: Stewart, Nancy, Henry, Audrey. Chief allergy dept. Ellis Hosp., Schenectady, 1990—; allergist allergy asthma immunology ctr. Albany (N.Y.) Med. Coll., 1992—, prof. pediats., 1973—. Co-dir. Schenectady Vol. Physicians Free Clinic; cons. in field. Trustee Schenectady Mus., 1987-99, Schenectady Pub. Libr., 1985—; pres. Antismoking Acad. Schenectady County; co-dir. Vol. Physician Clinic, Shcenectady County. Mem. Coll. Allergy and Immunology, Am. Acad. Pediatrics, Am. Acad. Allergy and Immunology, New Eng. Soc. Allergy (pres. 1990-92), N.Y. State Allergy Soc. (treas. 1993-95), Eastern Allergy Soc. (exec. com.), Physicians for Social Responsibility. Avocations: bird watching, art history. Home: 2216 Stoneridge Rd Niskayuna NY 12309-5524 Office: Allergy Asthma Immunology Ctr Albany Med Coll 1201 Washihngton Ave Ext Albany NY 12205 Fax: 518 452 2683. E-mail: tepperc@mail.amc.edu.

TEPPER, HOWARD, academic administrator; b. Jan. 31, 1963; BA in Acctg. and Info. Sys, CUNY, 1984, MBA in Healthcare Adminstrn., 1988. Adminstr. Mt. Sinai Med. Ctr., NYC, 1984-87, Beth Israel Med. Ctr., NYC, 1989-91; adminstrv. dir. St. Vincent's Hosp. and Med. Ctr., NYC, 1991-93; adminstrn. dir. Univ. Medicine and Dentistry, Newark, 1993—2002; ptnr. Grassi Healthcare Consulting, 2002—03; vice chmn., CFO Mt. Sinai Sch. Medicine, NYC, 2003—06; assoc. dean Touro U. Coll. Medicine, 2009—; exec. dir. Hecterseck U. Med. Ctr. Contbg. chapters in books. Home Phone: 201-836-3451, Office Phone: 201-906-2508. E-mail: htepper@homed.com.

TEPPER, LYNN MARSHA, gerontologist, educator; b. NYC, Mar. 16, 1946; m. William Chester Tepper, Aug. 27, 1967; children: Sharon Joy, Michelle Dawn. BS, SUNY, Buffalo, 1967; MA, Wayne State U., 1971; MS, Columbia U., 1977, EdM, 1978, EdD, 1980. Instr. John F. Kennedy Sch., Berlin, 1967-68, ednl. counselor, 1968-69; ednl. coordinator Army Edn. Ctr., Berlin, 1969-71; psychologist U.S. Dept. Def., Berlin, 1971-73; prof. gerontology L.I. U., 1979—2000, Mercy Coll., Dobbs Ferry, 1979—, Columbia U., NYC, 1982—. Cons. NATO, Naples, Italy, 1969-71, SHAPE, Brussels, 1969-71, Found. for Long Term Care, 1992—, others; dir. Gerontology Resource Ctr., Ctr. for Geriatrics and Gerontology, Columbia U., NYC, 1980-85, dir. Behavioral Sci. Program, 1982—; del. White House Conf. on Aging, 1980; clin. prof. Columbia U., 1982— Author: (textbooks) Long Term Care, 1993, Respite Care, 1993, Multidisciplinary Perspectives on Aging, 2004; contbr. articles to profl. jours., chpts. to books. Advisor Office on Aging, State of N.Y., Albany, 1980-90; dir. Mercy Coll., Inst. Gerontology, 1990—; trustee, St. Cabrini Nursing Home, 1988-98, Morningside Nursing Home, 1998—; bd. dirs. Found. Long Term Care. Brookdale Inst. on Aging fellow, 1983; rsch. grantee NIH, Nat. Inst. on Aging, Nat. Inst. Gen. Med. Sci., U.S. Dept. Edn., U.S. Bur. Health Professions, interdisciplinary geriat. tng. U.S. Dept. Health Resources Svcs. Adminstrn. Fellow Gerontol. Soc. Am.; mem. Am. Psychol. Assn. Avocations: hiking, bicycling. Office: Columbia U Med Campus Box 20 630 W 168th St New York NY 10032-3702

TERAGAWA, HIROKI, cardiologist, educator; b. Hiroshima, Japan, July 1, 1964; s. Kiyoshi and Takako Teragawa; m. Mitsuko Kano; children: Yuki, Mayo. MD, Hiroshima U., Japan, 1990. Instr. Hiroshima (Japan) U. Hosp., 2002—04; instr. Grad. Sch. Biomed. Scis. Hiroshima (Japan) U., 2004—. Grantee, Japan Heart Found., 2002. Fellow: Am. Coll. of Cardiology (corr.). Office: Hiroshima Univeristy 1-2-3 Kasumi Minami-ku Hiroshima 734-8551 Japan Office Fax: 81-82-257-5194; Home Fax: 81-82-505-0181. Business E-Mail: hteraga@hiroshima-u.ac.jp.

TERAKI, YUICHI, dermatologist; b. Tokyo, Feb. 9, 1958; MD, Hamamatsu Med. U., 1984. Asst. prof. Kyorin U. Sch. Medicine, Tokyo, 1994—2005; assoc. prof. Saitama Med. U., Japan. Office: Saitama Medical University 1981 Kamoda Kawagoe Saitama 350-8550 Japan Office Phone: 81-49-228-3652. E-mail: teraki@saitama-med.ac.jp.

TERAMO, KARI ATLE, obstetrician, gynecologist, researcher; b. Helsinki, Finland, Jan. 12, 1938; s. Wadim W. and Ester O. (Sandström) T.; m. Arja H. Ritvala, Jan. 1, 1964 (div. 1989); children: Tuulikki, Elina; m. Anna K. Tefke, Jan. 27, 2001. Lic. in Medicine, U. Helsinki, Finland, 1965, PhD in Medicine, 1972, Docent (sr. lectr.), 1974. Diplomate Finnish Bd. Med. Examiners; specialist in ob.-gyn., specialist in maternal-fetal medicine. Asst. prof. dept. Ob.-Gyn. U. Helsinki, Finland, 1975-76; staff mem. dept. Ob.-Gyn. U. Ctrl. Hosp., Helsinki, 1977-90, chief obstetrics dept. Ob.-Gyn., 1991—2001. Rsch. fellow Cardiovascular Rsch. Inst. U. Calif.,San Francisco, 1971-73; vis. prof. Brown U., Providence, R.I., 1981-82, UCLA, 1988-89; acting dir. Divsn. Maternal -Fetal Medicine, Women & Infants' Hosp., Providence, 1981-82; staff mem. Dept. Ob.-Gyn., UCLA, 1988-89. Contbr. articles to profl. jours. including Pediatric Rsch., Brit. Med. Jour., Obstetrics and Gynecology, Am. Jour. Obstetrics and Gynecology. Lt. Finnish Army Med. Corps, 1960-61. Grantee: Bay Area Heart Assn. U. Calif. San Francisco, 1971-73, Sigrid Juselius Rsch. grant Helsinki, 1979-84, Finnish Med. Acad. Rsch. grant 1986-87. Mem. Fedn. Scandinavian Socs. Ob.-Gyn. (sec. gen. 1990-94), Diabetic Pregnancy Study Group (bd. dirs. 1994-97, treas. 2004-10), Finnish Perinatal Soc. (pres. 1981-89), Soc. for Gynecologic Investigation. Avocations: photography, outdoor activities. Office: U Ctrl Hosp Helsinki Dept Ob-Gyn 290 Helsinki Finland Personal E-mail: kari.teramo@hus.fi.

TERAO, TOSHIO, internist, educator; b. Jan. 18, 1930; s. Eiji and Mitsuko (Katagiri) Terao; m. Setsuko Nishigaki, Nov. 13, 1961; children: Toshiya, Yasuo, Yoshio. Diploma, U. Tokyo, 1953, MD, 1960. Intern Tokyo U. Hosp., 1953—54; sr. scientist Nat. Inst. Radiol. Sci., Chiba, Japan, 1963—67; rsch. assoc. Mayo Clinic, Rochester, Minn., 1970—72; asst. U. Tokyo, 1972—77, lectr. medicine, 1977—79; prof. medicine Teikyo U., Tokyo, 1980—91, prof. neurology, 1991—. Pres. Teikyo U. Med. Hosp., 1987—93, dean, 1993—95; pres. North Tokyo Jueien, 1995—. Author; editor in field:. Mem.: NY Acad. Sci., Japanese Soc. for Neuroinfectious Disease, Japanese Peripheral Nerve Soc., Japanese Soc. Cerebrovascular Disease, Japanese Soc. Neurology, Japanese Soc. Internal Medicine, Am. Acad. Neurology, Sigma Xi. Office: Teikyo U 2-11-1 Kaga Itabashiku Tokyo 173 Japan

TERASHIMA, MITSUYASU, physician; b. Fukuoka, Aug. 29, 1962; MD, Kobe U., 1987. Co-dir. cardiovasc. medicine Toyohashi Heart Ctr., 2005—. Avocation: tennis. Office: 21-1 Gobudori, Oyama-cho Toyohashi Aichi 441-8530 Japan Office Fax: 81-532-37-3366. Business E-Mail: mitsu.terashima@gmail.com.

TERENTIEV, ALEXANDER ALEXANDROVICH, biochemistry professor; b. Astrakhan, Russia, May 2, 1942; s. Alexander Petrovich Terentiev and Nina Georgievna Terentieva; m. Liudmila Michaylovna Skripnikova, children: Zlata Alexandrovna Terentieva, Alexey Alexandrovich. MD, Astrakhan Med. State Inst., PhD, 1966. Cert. physician Astrakhan State Med. Inst., 1966. Postgrad. asst., docent Astrakhan State Med. Inst., 1966—74; docent, full prof. Moscow State Med. U., 1974—2008, prof., 2000—08, head, biochemistry dept., 2000—08; scientist expert and assessor Russian State Med. U., Moscow, 1994—2008, head, dept. biochemistry and lab. bioactive compounds, 2008 . Contbr. scientific papers. Named Honoured Worker of Higher Sch., Honour Insignia, 2002. Mem.: ISOBM Internat. Soc. Oncology and BioMarkers, Russian Med. Sci. Acad. (corr.). Russian Orthodox. Achievements include research in physycal and chemical properties of alpha-fetoprotein, oncofetal and placental proteins. Avocations: swimming, chess, philosophy, history. Office: Russian State Med University ul Ostrovityanova 1 117997 Moscow Russia Office Fax: 8-495-434-03-29. Business E-Mail: aaterent@mtu-net.ru.

TERKELTAUB, ROBERT A., rheumatologist, medical educator; b. Montreal, Can., Jan. 22, 1952; DSc in Biology, McGill U., Montreal, 1972, MD, 1976. Diplomate Am. Bd. Internal Medicine, cert. in geriatric medicine. Internship, residency, fellowship internal medicine/rheumatology Montreal Gen. Hosp., 1976—81; postdoc. fellow, dept. immunology Scripps Rsch. Inst., La Jolla, Calif., 1981—84, sr. rsch. assoc. immunology, 1984—85; asst. prof. medicine in residence U. Calif. Sch. Medicine, San Diego, 1985—92, assoc. prof. medicine in residence, 1992—99, prof. medicine in residence, 1999—, assoc. dir. divsn. rheumatology, allergy & immunology, 2003—. Chief rheumatology sect. Vets Adminstrn. Med. Ctr. San Diego, 1985—, dir. rheumatology training program, 1998—; rsch. sci. Veterans Med. Rsch. Found., La Jolla, 1992—; mem. NIH Atherosclerosis & Inflammation of Cardiovasc. Sys. Study Sect., 2004—; chair NIH Crystal Arthropathy RFA Study Sect., 2005—. Mem. editl. bd. Arthritis & Rheumatism, 1993—97, assoc. editor, 2004—, Current Rheumatology Reports, 1998—; contbr. articles to profl. jours. Mem.: Am. Heart Assn., Arthritis Nat. Rsch. Found. (mem. sci. adv. bd. 2000—). Office: U Calif San Diego Med Ctr 9500 Gilman Dr Rm 3221 La Jolla CA 92093 Office Phone: 858-552-8585 ext. 3519. Office Fax: 858-552-7425. Business E-Mail: rterkeltaub@ucsd.edu. *

TERLETSKAIA-LADWIG, ELENA NIKOLAEVNA, research scientist; b. Moscow, Apr. 20, 1959; d. Nikolaj Alexandrovich Terletskij and Olga Sergejewna Terletskaia; m. Herbert Ladwig, Sept. 1, 1998; 1 child, Ekaterina Grizik. Diploma in Hygiene and Epidemiology, 1st I. U. Sechenov Moscow Med. Acad., 1984; MD, Inst. Poliomyelitis and Viral Encephalitis, Moscow, 1990. Rsch. scientist Inst. Poliomyelitis and Viral Incephalitis, Moscow, 1984—90; sr. rschr. D.I. Ivanovsky Inst. Virology, 1991—93; dep. head virology lab Lab. Prof. G. Enders and Ptnr., Stuttgart, Germany, 1997—. Contbr. articles to profl. jours. Avocations: sailing, skiing. Home: Forststrasse 139 Stuttgart BW 70 193 Germany Office: Labor Enders and Ptnr Rosenbergstr. 85 70193 Stuttgart G BW Germany Personal E-mail: elenaladwig@web.de.

TERNBERG, JESSIE LAMOIN, pediatric surgeon, educator; b. Corning, Calif., May 28, 1924; d. Eric G. and Alta M. (Jones) T. AB, Grinnell Coll., Iowa, 1946, ScD (hon.), 1970; PhD, U. Tex., Austin, 1950; MD, Washington U., St. Louis, 1953; ScD (hon.), U. Mo., St. Louis, 1981, ScD (hon.), 2008, Wash. U., 2008. Diplomate: Am. Bd. Surgery. Intern Boston City Hosp., 1953—54; asst. resident in surgery

Barnes Hosp., St. Louis, 1954-57, resident in surgery, 1958-59; rsch. fellow Washington U. Sch. Medicine, 1957-58; practice medicine specializing in pediatric surgery St. Louis, 1966—; instr., DGMS trainee in surgery Washington U., 1959-62, asst. prof. surgery, 1962-65, assoc. prof. surgery, prof., 1965-71, prof. surgery, 1971-96, chief divsn. pediatric surgery, 1972-90, prof. emeritus, 1996—; mem. staff Barnes Hosp., 1959—90; gen. surgeon in chief Children's Hosp. of St. Louis, 1974-90. Mem. staff Children's Hosp., dir. pediatric surgery, 1972-90. Contbr. numerous articles on pediatric surgery to profl. jours. Trustee Grinnell Coll., 1984—. Recipient Alumni award Grinnell Coll., 1966, Faculty/Alumni award Washington U. Sch. Medicine, 1991, 2nd Century award 2006, 1st Aphrodite Jannopaulo Hofsommer award, 1993, Local Legend Changing the Face of Medicine award AMWA. Fellow AAAS; mem. SIOP, Am. Pediatric Surg. Assn., We. Surg. Assn. (2d v.p. 1984-85), St. Louis Med. Soc., Soc. Surgery of the Alimentary Tract, Am. Acad. Pediatrics, Soc. Pelvic Surgeons (v.p. 1991-92), Brit. Assn. Paediatric Surgeons, Assn. Women Surgeons (disting. mem. 1995), Mo. State Surg. Soc., St. Louis Surg. Soc. (pres. 1980-81), St. Louis Pediatric Soc., Soc. Surg. Oncology, Pediatric Oncology Group (chmn. surg. discipline 1983-96), St. Louis Childrens Hosp. Soc. (pres. 1979-80), Acad. Sci. St. Louis (Trustees award 2002), St. Louis Met. Med. Soc. (hon., councilor, trustee), Barnes Hosp. Soc., Phi Beta Kappa, Sigma Xi, Iota Sigma Pi, Alpha Omega Alpha. Office: St Louis Childrens Hosp 1 Childrens Pl Saint Louis MO 63110-1002 Personal E-mail: ternbergj@earthlink.net.

TERPENING, CHRISTOPHER MILES, pharmacist, educator; b. Dallas, Aug. 20, 1962; PharmD, U. Colo. Health Scis. Ctr., 1999; PhD, U. Ariz., 1991. Clin. assoc. prof. W.Va. U., 2001—, vice-chair CAMC instl. rev. bd., 2002. Dir. pharmacotherapy clinic CAMC Family Medicine Ctr., 2001; mem. W.Va. Drug Utilization Rev. Bd., 2002. Recipient Faculty Recognition award, W.Va. U. Dept Family Medicine; named Tchr. of Yr., W.Va. U., 2004, 2006; grant, Nat. Inst. Gen. Medicine. Mem.: AACP, ASHP, ACCP. Avocation: theater. Office: 3110 MacCorkle Ave SE Charleston WV 25304 Business E-Mail: cterpening@hsc.wvu.edu.

TERPOS, EVANGELOS P., hematologist; b. Agrinion, Greece, Sept. 11, 1967; s. Paul E. and Sophia G. Terpos; m. Chrysoula K. Mourdoukouta, Dec. 3, 1994; children: Sophia, Elisabeth. MD, U. Salonica, Greece, 1990. Gen. practitioner, Kalamata, Greece, 1991-93; fellow in internal medicine 251 Air Force Gen. Hosp., Athens, 1993-95, fellow in hematology, 1995-99, cons. hematologist Athens, 1999—2001; hon. cons. haematologist dept. hematology Imperial Coll. Sci., Tech. and Medicine, Hammersmith Hosp., London, 2001—. Contbr. articles to profl. jours. Maj. Greek Air Force, 1997-2001. Recipient award for Best Creative Work in Hematology, Greek Soc. Hematology, 1997, 2000, 2001, Nat. award for univ. progress, U. Salonica, 1987, 1988. Mem.: Greek Soc. Haematology, Brit. Soc. Haematology, Internat. Soc. Thrombosis and Hemostasis, European Assn. for Cancer Rsch., European Hematology Assn., Internat. Soc. Hematology. Achievements include research in the role of bisphosphonates on multiple myeloma; treatment of myelodysplastic syndromes; paroxysmal nocturnal hemoglobinuria; bone marrow transplantation. Avocations: coin collecting/numismatics, reading, history. Office: 251 Air Force Gen Hosp 3 Kanellopoulou St 11525 Athens Greece also: Dept Hematology ICSTM Hammersmith Hosp DuCane Rd London W12 0NN England Home Phone: 44 0 781225 1483. Office Fax: 44 0 208-8963531. E-mail: eterpos@hotmail.com.

TERR, LENORE C., child and adolescent psychiatrist, educator; MD, U. Mich., Ann Arbor, 1961. Diplomate Am. Bd. Psychiatry and Neurology, 1968, Am. Bd. Psychiatry and Neurology-child and adolescent psychiatry, 1969. Resident psychiatry Univ. Mich. Med. Ctr., Ann Arbor, Mich., 1962—64, fellow child and adolescent psychiatry, 1964—66; clin. prof. Univ. Calif. San Francisco. Mem.: Am. Acad. Child and Adolescent Psychiatry (Norbert and Charlotte Rieger Psychodynamic Psychotherapy award 2009). Office: 450 Sutter St 2534 San Francisco CA 94108 Office Phone: 415-433-7800. Office Fax: 415-433-2130.

TERR, LENORE CAGEN, psychiatrist, writer; b. NYC, Mar. 27, 1936; d. Samuel Lawrence and Esther (Hirsch) Cagen; m. Abba I. Terr; children: David, Julia. AB magna cum laude, Case Western Res. U., 1957; MD with honors, U. Mich., 1961. Diplomate Am. Bd. Psychiatry and Neurology (subspecialty bd. child and adolescent psychiatry). Intern U. Mich. Med. Ctr., Ann Arbor, 1961-62; resident Neuropsychiat. Inst. U. Mich., Ann Arbor, 1962-64, fellow Children's Psychiat. Hosp., 1964-66; from instr. to asst. prof. Case Western Res. U. Med. Sch., Cleve., 1966-71; pvt. practice Terr Med. Corp., San Francisco, 1971—; from asst. clin. prof. to clin. prof. psychiatry Sch. Medicine U. Calif., San Francisco, 1971—. Lectr. law, psychiatry U. Calif., Berkeley, 1971—90, Davis, 1974—88; dir. Am. Bd. Psychiatry and Neurology, 1988—96, chair psychiatry coun., 1996. Author: Too Scared to Cry, 1990, Unchained Memories, 1994, Beyond Love and Work, 1999, Magical Moments of Change, 2008; contbr. articles to profl. jours.; exhibited works in art show at Canessa Gallery, San Francisco, 2002. Recipient Career Tchr. award, NIMH, 1967—69, Child Advocacy award, APA, 1994; named to Cleveland Heights H.S. Disting Alumni Hall of Fame, 2003; grantee project, Rosenberg Found., 1977, William T. Grant Found., 1986—87, Leon Lowenstein Found., 2002; scholar-in-residence, Rockefeller Found., Italy, 1981, 1988. Fellow: Am. Acad. Child and Adolescent Psychiatry (coun. 1984—87, Reiger award 2009), Am. Coll. Psychiatrists (program chair 1991—92, Bowis award 1993), Am. Psychiat. Assn. (Child Psychiatry Rsch. award 1984, Clin. Rsch. award 1987, Marmor Sci. award 2002); mem.: Phi Bet Kappa, Alpha Omega Alpha. Avocations: piano, walking, travel, gardening, needlepoint. Office: Terr Med Corp 450 Sutter St Rm 1336 San Francisco CA 94108-4204 Office Phone: 415-433-7800. Office Fax: 415-433-2130. Personal E-mail: scott.terrmd@sbcglobal.net.

TERRIQUEZ-KASEY, LAURA MARIE, emergency nurse; b. Bronx, NY, May 12, 1950; d. Gilbert Manuel and Elizabeth (Arevena) Terriquez; m. William Kasey, July 23, 1988 (dec. May 1995). AAS, SUNY, Morrisville, 1971; BSN, Long Island U., 1980; MSN, CUNY, 1985. RN, N.Y., Tex. Commd. 2d lt. AUS, 1974, advanced through grades to maj., 1993; staff nurse emergency svc. Bellevue Hosp. Ctr., NYC, 1971-73, head nurse emergency svc., 1973-81, nursing supr., 1981-84; clin. nurse coord. South Nassau Cmty. Hosp., Oceanside, N.Y., 1984-85; staff nurse Brooke Army Med.Ctr., San Antonio, 1985-86; head nurse vascular surg. ward Brooke Army Med. Ctr., San Antonio, 1987-89, charge nurse, EMT, head nurse PACU, 1987-89; staff nurse med. ICU William Beaumont Army Med. Ctr., Ft. Bliss/El Paso, Tex., 1985-90, staff nurse trauma unit, 1990-91, head nurse trauma unit, 1991-92, asst. chief nurse, 1992-93; nurse mgr. emergency/trauma svcs. Bassett Health Care Sys., Cooperstown, N.Y., 1993-2000, adminstr. emergency and svc. tng. program, 1997-98, co-chair network adv. group, nurse advisor emergency svcs.; asst. clin. prof. SUNY Sch Nursing, Binghamton, 2000; asst. coun. prof. Sch. Nursing, Binghamton U. Instr. U. El Paso, Tex., 1991-92; mem. com. nursing adv. Southwest Organbank, El Paso, 1992—; adj. instr. U. Tex. Dept. Nursing, El Paso, 1992; Advanced Emergency Med. Technic Critical Care, N.Y. State Dept. Health sponsor for EMS programs, 2000-02; dir. Binghamton Program Abroad, Internat. Dominican Republic, 2004-10, lectr. in field. With disaster med. assistance team Team Houston, Tex., 2001; with disaster med. assistance team team response Anthrax Postal Response, NYC, 2001; mem. disaster med. assistance team NY Dept. Health and Human Svcs., NY, 2001; Ground Zero med. team World Trade Ctr., 2001; mem. hurricane disaster med. assistance team N.Y. Disaster Med. Assistance Team, FEMA, Fla., 2004—05. Decorated Army Commendation medal with 3 oak leaf clusters, Army Achievement award; recipient Meritorious Svc. award San Antonio Police Dept., 1988, Svc. award ARC, 1980, Cert. Appreciation N.Y. Emergency Med. Svcs., 1984, Chancellors award for internat. edn. program on cmty. health in Dominican Republic, Tchg. Excellence Tyson award, Decker Sch Nursing, SUNY Binghamton U. Mem.: Red Cross So. Tier, Emergency Nurses Assn. (pres. rural nursing orgn. 2006), Am. Legion, Sigma Theta Tau. Achievements include development of disaster nursing courses. Avocations: swimming, biking. Home: 125 Park Dr Oneonta NY 13820 Office: Decker Sch Nursing Box 6000 SUNY Binghamton Binghamton NY 13902 Office Phone: 607-777-6033. Business E-Mail: kasey@binghamton.edu.

TERRIS, SUSAN, physician, cardiologist, researcher; b. Morristown, NJ, Sept. 5, 1944; d. Albert and Virginia Terris. BA in History, U. Chgo., 1967, PhD in Biochemistry, 1975, MD, 1976. Diplomate in internal medicine, endocrinology and metabolism, cardiovasc. disease Am. Bd. Internal Medicine. Resident in internal medicine Washington U., Barnes Hosp., St. Louis, 1976-78; fellow in endocrinology and metabolism U. Chgo., 1978-80, fellow cardiology, 1980-83, U. Mich., Ann Arbor, 1983-85, instr. cardiology, 1985-86; head cardiac catheterization lab., head cardiology Westland (Mich.) Med. Ctr., 1985. Contbr. articles to Jour. Biol. Chemistry, Am. Jour. Physiology, Am. Jour. Cardiology, Jour. Clin. Investigation, other profl. publs. Grantee Juvenile Diabetes Found., 1978-80, NIH, 1978-79. Mem. N.Y. Acad. Sci. Achievements include rsch. demonstrating dependence of intracellular degradation of insulin upon its prior binding to hepatic insulin receptors; studies on the electrophysiologic effect of cathecholamimes on sheep Parkinje fibers and on the hemodynamic effects of various drugs on the human circulatory system.

TERRITO, MARY C., health facility administrator, hematologist, educator; BS in Biology, Wayne State U., 1965, MD, 1968. Intern/resident in internal medicine Parkland Hosp., Dallas, 1971-73; fellow in hematology/oncology Harbor-U. Calif., LA, 1973-74, UCLA, 1974-75; rsch. assoc. Wadsworth VA Hosp., LA, 1975-81; asst. prof. dept. medicine UCLA, 1975-81, assoc. prof., 1981-96, prof., 1996—2007, dir. bone marrow transplant program Ctr. Health Scis., 1981—. Contbr. articles to profl. jours. Office: UCLA Bone Marrow Transplantation Program Ctr 42-121 CHS 10833 Le Conte Ave Los Angeles CA 90095-3075

TERRY, FRANCES JEFFERSON, retired psychiatric nurse practitioner; d. Walter Louis and Ruth Williams Jefferson; m. Robert Terry, Sept. 29, 1926; children: Deborah Ella Terry-Hays, Robert David, Michael Duane, William Brian, Walter Louis. BSN, Seattle U., 1951; MSN, U. Wash., Seattle, 1981. Lic. Advanced RN Practitioner, ANCC. Health enhancement-program nurse Ctrl. Area Sr. Ctr., Seattle; staff nurse Providence Hosp., Seattle; prescribing and consulting nurse Cmty. Ho. Mental Health Agy., Seattle; psychiat. mental health practitioner U. Wash.-Harborview Med. Ctr., Seattle; nursing instr. Shoreline CC, Seattle; nurse case mgr.-mental health U. Wash.; nursing instr. Seattle U.; dir. health svcs. NW Ctr. Developmentally Challenged, Seattle; sch. nurse Seattle Pub. Schs.; pub. health nurse Seattle King County Health Dept., Seattle. Diabetes support group vol. facilitator Joslin Diabetes Ctr., Seattle. Auditor, ch. coun. ImmaculateConception Ch., Seattle; mem. Seattle Ctrl. Cmty. Coll. Found. Recipient Cmty. Svc. award, Seattle U., 2004, honoree, Knights of Peter Claver Ladies, 2008, Black Heritage Soc. Wash. State, 2008, Wash. State Nurses Soc. Centennial Celebration, 2008; named Outstanding Nurse, U. Wash.-Harborview Med. Ctr., 1993; named to Hall of Fame, Wash. State Nurses Assn., 2000. Mem.: Cert. Ret. Nurse Amb. Cir., Am. Nurse Credentialing Ctr., Mary Mahoney Profl. Nurses Assn., Am. Nurses' Assn. (life), Alpha Kappa Alpha Sorority (life). Personal E-mail: bobfrater@comcast.net.

TERRY, PETER BROWNE, medical educator; b. Peoria, Ill., May 2, 1941; s. Charles and Frances Terry; m. Joan Salim; children: Michael, Norah Smith, Vanessa Smith. BSc, Loyola U., Chgo., 1964; MD, St. Louis U., 1968; MPhil, Georgetown U., 1993. Lic. Mo., 1968. Intern U. Conn., 1968—69, resident, 1969—70, Johns Hopkins U., Balt., 1972—73, fellow pulmonary medicine, 1973—74, Mayo Clin., 1974—75; from asst. prof. to prof. medicine Johns Hopkins U., 1975, prof. medicine, 1993—. Chmn. ethics com. Johns Hopkins Hosp., Balt., 1994—97. Contbr. articles to profl. jours. Vice chmn. sci. and med. adv. bd. Hereditary Hemmorhagic Telangetasia Found., Balt., 2003—07. Maj. US Army, 1970—72. Recipient Roger C. Bone Meml. Lectureship award, Am. Coll. Chest Physicians, 1999. Mem.: Am. Thoracic Soc. Achievements include development of treatment of for rare disease Hereditary Hemorrhagic Telangectasia. Office: The Johns Hopkins Univ 1830 East Monument St Baltimore MD 21210

TERRY, WAYNE GILBERT, healthcare educator, hospital administrator; b. Plymouth, Mass., Oct. 2, 1932; s. Lawrence Arthur and Betty Frances (Boutemain) Terry; m. Barbara Aileen Bromwell, Sept. 20, 1980; children: Karleton Wayne, Dale Duane, Kendrick Shane, Kristen Alayne, Tammye Van Clief, Wade Bromwell Delk. AA in Gen. Adminstrn., Allan Hancock Coll., Santa Maria Calif., 1960; BBA in Bus. Mgmt., U. Hawaii, Honolulu, 1966; MHA, Med. Coll. Va., Va. Commonwealth U., Richmond, 1973; PhD in Health Svcs. Mgmt., LaSalle U., 1999; PhD, Manderville, La., 1999. Commd. 2d lt. USAF Med. Svc. Corps, 1967, advanced through grades to maj., 1976; asst. adminstr. for registrar activities USAF Hosp., Orlando AFB, Fla., 1966-67; assoc. adminstr. aeromed. evacuation activities USAF, Hickam AFB, Hawaii, 1967-71; adminstrv. resident USAF Regional Hosp., Langley AFB, Va., 1972-73; CEO USAF Hosp., Columbus AFB, Miss., 1973-75; nat. health edn. and tng. program advisor Office of Surgeon Gen., Dept. of Air Force, Washington, 1975-78; dir. health professions pers. planning and policy divsn. Office of Asst. Sec. Def. for Health Affairs, The Pentagon, Washington, 1978-80; dep. project mgr./adminstrv. dir. King Faisal U. Teaching Hosp., Al-Khobar, Saudi Arabia, 1980-82; dep. project mgr., hosp. dir. North Yemen Healthcare Project, As-Salem Hosp., Sadah, Yemen Arab Republic, 1982-83; hosp. dir., CEO western area Armed Forces Hosps., Khamis Mushayt, Saudi Arabia, 1983-84; chief adminstr./commissioning team chief Orbit Summit Health, Ltd., Riyadh, Saudi Arabia, 1984-85; hosp. dir., adminstrv. dir. Truk State Dept. Health Svcs., Moen, Federated States of Micronesia, 1985-87; assoc. adminstr. support svcs. King Fahad Hosp., Saudi Arabian N.G., Riyadh, 1987-90; project mgr., CEO N.W. Armed Forces Hosps. Program, Tabuk, Saudi Arabia, 1990-98, cons. in health svcs. mgmt., 1998-99; cons., mediator in health svcs. mgmt. Crozet, Va., 1999-2000; exec. dir., CEO Southside Area Health Edn. Ctr. Longwood U., Farmville, Va., 2000—. Apptd. mil. cons. healthcare planning to the Air Force Surgeon Gen., 1979; apptd. preceptor program in healthcare adminstrn. U. Mich. for adminstrv. residents at N.W. Armed Forces Hosps. Programs, Tabuk, Saudi Arabia, 1993; supervisory bd. Royal Coll. Surgeons in Ireland, Dublin, 1990-98; cert. sr. grant specialist, reviewer, cons.; lectr., cons. in field. Contbr. articles to profl. jours. Warden to Am. Cmty. N.W. Region of Yemen Arab Republic to Am. Embassy in Sanaa, 1982-83, warden to Am. Cmty. N.W. Region of Saudi Arabia to Am. Embassy in Riyadh, 1990-99; mem. Internat. Sch. Sys. Coord. Com., Tabuk, 1990-99; bd. dirs. Taif Sch. Dist. Sys., Saudi Arabia, 1981-82; chmn., exec. com., bd. dirs. Ctrl. Va. Health Planning Agy., Richmond, Va., 2001-08; bd. dirs. Va. Tobacco Settlement Found., Regional Adv. Bd., Richmond, Va., 2001—09, Southside Area Health Edn. Ctr., Longwood U., Farmville, 2001—; leadership and planning group Nat. Area Health Edn. Ctr. Assn., Balt., 2003-04, Va. Dept. Health Commr's. Healthcare Workforce Devel. Authority, 2008-, chmn., program adv. group. Va. Statewide AHEC Program, 2008-. Decorated Def. Meritorious Svc. medal, Air Force Meritorious Svc. medal with 3 Oak Leaf Clusters, Air medal with 3 Oak Leaf Clusters, Air Force Commendation medal with 3 oak leaf clusters, Republic of Vietnam Gallantry Cross with palm, Republic of Vietnam Svc. medal with 11 svc. stars, Korean Def. Svc. medal, Sec. of Def. Svc. medal/badge, Air Staff Svc. Badge Dept. Air Force, Air Force Chief Med. Svc. Corps badge; recipient Citation of Appreciation Nat. Coun. Social Welfare, Seoul, Republic of Korea, 1963, Citation of Appreciation award Suchan Province Gov., Choong Nam, Republic of Korea, 1963, award of merit Pacific Air Forces Command, Hickam AFB, Hawaii, 1965, Outstanding Jr. Officer in 22nd Air Force, USAF, 1970, Outstanding Rsch. award Med. Coll. Va., 1973, Personality of the South award, 1975, Men of Achievement award, Cambridge, Eng., 1982, Citation of Appreciation Gov. Truk State, Federated States of Micronesia, 1987, Citation of Merit Internat. Red Cross Commn., Bern, Switzerland, 1991, N.W. Armed Forces Hosps., Ministry Def. and Aviation, Tabuk, 1991, Citation of Appreciation Presidency of Gen. Staff Hdqs., Ministry of Def. and Aviation, Tabuk, 1992-93, 95-99, Disting. Alumni award Allan Hancock Coll., Santa Maria, 2000, Citation of Appreciation Longwood U., Va., 2006, Cert. of Appreciation, Longwood U., 2010, Commitment to Excellence award, Air Force Surgeon Gen., Wash-.,Outstanding Svc. Med. Svc. Corps. Officer award, ACHE Congress Chgo., Washington, 2011. Fellow Am. Coll. Healthcare Execs. (life), Ctrl. Va. Assn. Healthcare Execs. Group (2007-), Royal Soc. Health; mem. Am. Hosp. Assn., Am. Mgmt. Assn. (life), Air Force Med. Svc. Corps Assn. (membership and awards com. 2003—, bd. dirs., newsletter editor 2005—), Assn. Mil. Surgeons of U.S., Air Force Assn; life mem., Vets. of Foreign Wars (2001-), The American Legion (2007-), Military Officer's Assn. of Am., Piedmont Region (2001-). Republican. Baptist. Avocations: tennis, coin collecting/numismatics, hiking. Office: Southside Area Health Edn Ctr Longwood Univ 201 High St Farmville VA 23909-1800 Home Phone: 434-392-3226; Office Phone: 434-395-2862. Business E-Mail: terrywg@longwood.edu.

TERSIGNI, ANTHONY, hospital administrator; b. Det., July 25, 1949; s. Andrea and Benedetta (D'Annunzio) T.; m. Flora Pelino Tersigni, June 12, 1977; children: Maria Teresa, John, Andrea. BA, U. Mich., 1971; MPA, Oakland U., Mich., 1983; EDD, We. Mich. U., 1988. Sr. v.p. St. Joseph Hosp., Ann Arbor, Mich., 1978-84; dir. ops. Detroit Med. Ctr., Mich., 1984-85; clin. prof. health and behavioral sciences Oakland U., Rochester, Mich., 1985—; pres., CEO Oakland Gen. Health Systems, Rochester, Mich., Huron Valley Hosl.- DMC, Mich., 1985-86; sr. leadership positions Sisters of Charity Health Care Systems, Cin., Hosp. Corp. America, Nashville; exec. v.p., COO St. John Health, Detroit, 1994—95, pres., CEO, 1995—2000; exec. v.p., COO Ascension Health, St. Louis, 2001—03, pres., CEO, 2004—. Dir. SE Mich. Hosp. Assn.-Fin. Planning Com. Southfield 1986; vice chmn. Mich. Hosp. Assn., Service Corp. Lansing 1985; bd. trustees Healthcare Leadership Coun. Dir. Orch. Hall, Detroit, 1985; bd. mem. Detroit Econ. Club, United Way Greater St. Louis, Inc., Coalition to Protect America's Healthcare; bd. mem., mem. exec. com. St. Louis Regional Chamber Growth Assn.; bd. chmn. Healthcare Leadership Coun.; bd. governors Legatus Internat., Nat. Cath. Bioethics Ctr., Cath. U. America. Served with Nat. Guard, 1969—75. Named one of 100 Most Powerful People in Healthcare, Modern Healthcare, 2006—10, Most Influential St. Louisans, St. Louis Bus. Jour., 2009—11. Mem. Am. Coll. Hosp. Administrs., Am. Pub. Health Assn., Am. Coll. Healthcare Execs., Cath. Health Assn. of US (past chmn.) Roman Catholic. Avocations: golf, tennis, racquetball. Office: Ascension Health 4600 Edmundson Rd Saint Louis MO 63134 Office Phone: 314-733-8000. *

TERUHIKO, BEPPU, retired microbiologist; b. Tokyo, Mar. 9, 1934; PhD, U. Tokyo, 1956. Prof. U. Tokyo, 1977—94, Nihon U., 1994—2010. Recipient Order of Sacred Treasure, Govt. of Japan, Medal with Purple Ribbon, award, Japan Acad., Arima award, Internat. Union Microbiol. Socs., Charles Tom award, Soc. Indsl. Microbiology. Fellow: Am. Soc. Microbiology; mem.: Japan Acad. Avocations: gardening, stamp collecting/philately. Home: Horinouchi 1-5-21 Suginami Tokyo 166-0013 Japan Business E-Mail: beppu@brs.nihon-u.ac.jp.

TERVO, TIMO MARTTI, ophthalmologist, educator; b. Helsinki, Finland, Mar. 9, 1950; s. Martti Vilho and Pirkko Kaarina (Tuhkanen) T.; m. Kaarina Maria Kesä, Aug. 13, 1977; children: Tomi, Markku. MB, U. Helsinki, 1972, MD, 1975, PhD, 1977. Diplomate in ophthalmology, traffic medicine. Asst. dept. anatomy U. Helsinki, 1972-79, resident dept. neurosurgery, 1980, resident dept. ophthalmology, 1980-83, asst. prof. dept. anatomy, 1978-83, asst. prof. dept. ophthalmology, 1986-2000, sr. ophthalmologist, 1983-89, prof. applied clin. ophthalmology, 2000—, chief physician dept. ophthalmology, 1989—, assoc. prof. ophthalmology, 1997; physician Helsinki Naval Sta., Kirkkonummi, Finland, 1979-80. Cons. Labsystems Co., Helsinki, 1986-90, Biohit Co., Helsinki, 1990-92. Lt. Finnish Navy, 1978-79. Mem. Assn. Rsch. in Vision and Ophthalmology, Finnish Soc. Traffic Medicine (chair 2005-09), Traffic Safety Fin. Bd. Avocations: cross country skiing, boating, vehicles. Home: Jatasalmentie 9 00830 Helsinki Finland Office: Haartmaninkatu 4C PO Box 220 00029 Helsinki Finland

TESHIMA, RYOTA, orthopedic surgeon; b. Matsue, Japan, Jan. 14, 1949; s. Hiroshi and Misao (Omura) T.; m. Yumiko Kubota, June 13, 1977; children: Masahiro, Takehiro, Kumi. MB, Tottori U., Yonago, Japan, 1973, DMS, 1978. Resident in orthopedic surgery Tottori U., Yonago, 1978-81, from asst. prof. to assoc. prof., 1982-99, prof., 1999—; rsch. fellow Mass. Gen. Hosp., Boston, 1981-82. Home: 8-5-24 Higashi Fukubara Yonago 6830802 Japan Office: Tottori U Dept Ortho Surg 36 Nishi Machi Yonago 6838504 Japan Home Phone: 81 859 324132; Office Phone: 81 859 386587. Business E Mail: ryota@med.tottori u.ac.jp.

TESHIMA, TERUKI, medical educator; b. Hiroshima, Japan, Nov. 27, 1955; s. Teruji and Kyoko Teshima; m. Junko Sakurai, Oct. 4, 1956; children: Karin, Yuri, Midoriko. MD, Hiroshima U., 1980; PhD, Osaka U., 1987. Cert. bd. radiation oncologist Japanese Soc. Therapeutic Radiology and Oncology, 1999, bd. radiologist Japan Radiol. Soc., 1993. Resident Hiroshima U. Hosp., 1980—81, Osaka U. Hosp., 1982—83; attending physician Osaka Med. Ctr. Cancer and Cardiovasc. Diseases, Osaka, 1983—90; asst. prof. Osaka U., 1990—95, assoc. prof. Suita, 1995 2003, prof., 2003—. Vis. scientist & prof. Fox Chase Cancer Ctr., Philadelphia, Pa., 1994—97. Contbr. articles to profl. jours. Grant-in-aid Cancer Rsch., Ministry Health, Labour and Welfare, Japan, 1996—2009, Grant-in-aid Sci. Rsch., Japanese Soc. Promotion Sci., 2001 02, 2004 09, Grant in aid Internat. Coop. Study, Pfizer Health Rsch. Found., 1997, Grant-in-aid Cancer Rsch., Found. Promotion Cancer Rsch., 1998, Found. Multidisciplinary Cancer Therapy, 1997—2010, fellowship, Am. Coll. Radiology, 2010. Fellow: Am. Coll. Radiology (hon.); mem.: Japanese Soc. Therapeutic Radiology and Oncology. Liberal. Buddhism. Achievements include research in Japanese national cancer database; high dose rate brachytherapy. Avocation: walking. Office: Osaka Univ 1-7 Yamadaoka Suita Osaka 565 0871 Japan Office Fax: 81-6-6879-2570. Business E-Mail: teshima@sahs.med.osaka-u.ac.jp.

TESK, JOHN ALOYSIUS, materials scientist; b. Chgo., Oct. 19, 1934; s. John August and Theresa Mary (Mattea) T.; m. Regina Sophia Budzyn, Dec. 10, 1966; 1 child, John A.W. BS in Engring. Sci., Northwestern U., 1957, MS in Metallurgy, 1960, PhD in Materials Sci., 1963. Asst. prof. U. Ill., Chgo., 1964-67; cons. Argonne (Ill.) Nat. Lab., 1964-67, asst. metallurgist, 1967-70; dir. rsch. Dental, Howmedica Inc., Chgo., 1970-77; dir. edn. svcs. Inst. Gas. Tech., Chgo., 1977-78; gen. phys. scientist, group leader, biomaterials coord. polymers divsn., sr. tech. advisor, indsl. liaison dir.'s office Nat. Inst. Stds. & Tech., Gaithersburg, Md., 1978—2005; cons. in biomed. materials and devices, 2005—. Mem. bioengineered materials applications bd. Nat. Acads., 2001-03; cons. Dentsply Internat., York, Pa., 1977-78; mem. review bd. Dental Sch. Case Western Res. U., Cleve., 1987-88, Biomaterials Program, Clemson U., 1972-74, Dental Sch., Tokushima U., Japan, 1997; mem. orthopaedic adv. bd. Clemson U., 1999-2001; mem. adv. bd. Industry/Univ. Ctr. of NSF, U. Buffalo, 2002-03; chmn. dental stds. ADA, Chgo., 1980-86; leader U.S. Del. Internat. Stds. Orgn., 1980-86; organizer confs. Holder 8 patents; mem. editl. bd. Jour. Dental Materials, 1988-91, Jour. Oral Implantology, 1984-2000, Biomaterials Forum, 1996—2005, Applied Biomaterials, 1998—; mem. editl. rev. bd. Nat. Inst. Stds. and Tech., 1996-2001; contbr. chpts. to books, articles to profl. jours. Mem. bldg. com. Divine Savior Parish, Downers Grove, Ill., 1971-72; chmn. troop 737 Cub Scouts, Highland, Md., 1980; adult supr. youth group Saint Louis Parish, Highland, 1982-83. Fellow Acad. Dental Materials (exec. com. 1987-94); mem. ASTM (exec. com. 2000—), Am. Phys. Soc., Am. Soc. Metals (exec. com. Chgo. chpt. 1964-67, 78), Biomaterials Soc. (founding mem., charter, nominating com. 1987, 96, editl. bd. Applied Biomaterials 1998—, stds. com. 1995—2004, contbg. editor Biomaterials Forum, co-chmn. reference materials/reference data com., coun. 1996-2003, liaison com. 1996-98, program com. 1999), Internat. Assn. Dental Rsch. (treas. dental materials group 1987-94), Tech. Materials Soc. (exec. com. Chgo chpt. 1965), Japanese Soc. for Dental Materials (hon.). Roman Catholic. Avocations: gardening, boating, travel, walking. Home: 6759 Cortina Dr Highland MD 20777-9501 Office: Nat Inst Stds & Tech Rm A143 Bldg 224 Gaithersburg MD 20899-0001 Home Phone: 301-854-9727; Office Phone: 301-854-9727. Personal E-mail: jatesk@erols.com. Business E-Mail: john.tesk@nist.gov.

TESSAROLO, FRANCESCO, research scientist; b. Bassano del Grappa, Nov. 4, 1977; Degree in Physics, U. Trento, 2002, PhD in Material Engring., 2006. Rschr. Interdepartmental Ctr. on Biomed. Techs., U. Trento, 2006—. Cons. Azienda provincial per i Servizi Sanitary, Trento, 2004—11. Grant, Italian Soc. Microscopic Scis., U. Porto, Portugal, Soc. Italiana Biofisica Pura e Applicata. Mem.: European Soc. Clin. Microbiology and Infectious Diseases, Health Tech. Assessment Internat., Soc. Italiana Biomatenali, Soc. Italiana di Biofisica. Office: via delle regole 101 Trento 38123 Italy Business E-Mail: tessaro@science.unitn.it.

TESSIER-LAVIGNE, MARC TREVOR, academic administrator, neurobiologist, researcher; b. Trenton, Ont., Canada, Dec. 18, 1959; arrived in US, 1987; s. Yves Jacques and Sheila Christine (Midgley) Tessier-L.; m. Mary Alanna Hynes, Feb. 4, 1989; children: Christian, Kyle, Ella. BSc, McGill U., 1980; BA, Oxford U., 1982; PhD, U. London, 1986. Exec. dir. Can. Student Pugwash Orgn., Ottawa, Ont., 1982-83; rsch. fellow devel. neurobiology unit Med. Rsch. Coun., London, 1986-87; rsch. fellow Ctr. for Neurobiology, Columbia U., NYC, 1987-91; asst. prof. dept. anatomy U. Calif., San Francisco, 1991-95, assoc. prof. dept. anatomy, 1995-97, prof. dept. anatomy and dept. biochemistry and biophysics, 1997—2000; Susan B. Ford prof. dept. biol. scis. Sch. Humanities and Scis. Stanford U., 2000—03; sr. v.p. rsch. drug discovery Genentech Inc., 2003—08, exec. v.p. rsch. drug discovery, 2008—09, exec. v.p. rsch. and chief sci. officer, 2009—11; pres. Rockefeller U., 2011—. Asst. investigator Howard Hughes Med. Inst., 1994-97; investigator Howard Hughes Med. Inst., 1997—. Contbr. articles on neurobiology to profl. jours. Recipient McKnight Investigator award, 1994, Karl Judson Herrick award for comparative neurology Am. Assn. Anatomists, 1994, Ameritec prize for significant contbn. in basic rsch. towards cure for paralysis, 1995, Ipsen prize for neuronal plasticity, 1996, Viktor Hamburger award in devel. neurobiology Internat. Jour. Devel. Neurosci., Young Investigator award Soc. for Neurosci., 1997, Wakeman award, 1998, Rober & Dow award, 2003, Rewe Irvine Rsch. medal, 2007; Rhodes scholar, 1980, Commonwealth scholar, 1983, Markey scholar, 1989, Searle scholar, 1991, McKnight scholar, 1991; Klingenstein fellow, 1992. Fellow: AAAS, Royal Soc. of Canada, Royal Soc. of London (Fermi prize 2007); mem.: Acad. Med. Scis. (UK), NAS, Soc. for Neuroscience (nominating com. 2000—02). Office: Rockefeller Univeristy Office of President 1230 York Ave New York NY 10065 Office Fax: 212-327-8000, 212-327-7974. E-mail: Marc.Tessier-Lavigne@rockefeller.edu. *

TESTA, DOMENICO MARIA, otolaryngologist, researcher; b. Caserta, Italy, Apr. 22, 1967; s. Benedetto Testa and Adele Ferrante; m. Isabella Ponzetta; children: Benedetto, Lilio. MD, U. Naples, Italy, 1992, Surgeon otolaryngology head and neck, 1997; PhD Otolaryngology, U. Catania, Italy, 2001. Specialized Otolaryngology, Naples, 1993—97; cons. Otolaryngology Head and Neck Surgery U. Naples, 2000—05; rschr. Otolaryngology 2d U. Naples, 2005—. Author: Emergency in Otolaryngology, 1997, Surgery of OSAS, 2003. Lt. Italian Mil. Medicine, 1995—96. Fellow: Italian Soc. Audiology, Italian Soc. Otolaryngologists (Sio award 2004); mem.: Italia U. Soc. Otolaryngology (Audio award 1999). Avocations: soccer, skiing, tennis, theater, classical music. Office: Univ Naples via Cotugno 3 80100 Naples Italy

TESTA, JOSEPH R., geneticist, researcher, biologist; PhD in Biology, Fordham U., Bronx, NY, 1976. Cancer cytogeneticist U. Chgo., 1976-80; rsch. scientist Nat. Cancer Inst., Balt., 1980—82, vis. scientist, 1987—89, mem. bd. sci. counselors, 2005—10; prof. U. Md., Balt., 1980 89; sr. mem. rsch. staff, dir. human genetics program Fox Chase Cancer Ctr., Phila., 1989—2008, Weg endowed chair human genetics, 1999—; co-leader Cancer Biology Program, Kidney Cancer Keystone Program, 2008—. Adj. lectr. Johns Hopkins U., Balt., 1983—87. Assoc. editor: Cancer Rsch., mem. editl. bd.: Cancer Genetics, Leukemia Rsch., Genes Chromosomes & Cancer, Genes & Cancer; contbr. articles to profl. jours., chapters to books. Recipient Selikoff Cancer Rsch. award, Ramazzini Inst., 1999, Disting. Alumnus award, Southern Conn. State U., 2006, Stohlman Meml. Scholar award, Leukemia Soc. Am., 1987, Reimann Honor medal, Fox Chase Cancer Ctr., 2011; co-recipient AACR Landon award, 2008; named SE, Pa Scientist of Yr., Am. Cancer Soc., 2009; scholar Leukemia Soc. Am., 1984—90; Spl. fellow, Leukemia Soc. Am., 1982—84. Mem. AAAS, ASHG, Am. Assn. Cancer Rsch., Am. Soc. Hematology, Am. Soc. Microbiology; founding fellow Am. Coll. Med. Genetics. Achievements include discovery of mutations associated with mesothelioma tumor formation; cloning of AKT2 and APPL1 genes; discovery of first alterations of AKT2 in human cancers; co discoverer of BAPI gene associated cancer susceptibility syndrome. Office: Fox Chase Cancer Ctr 333 Cottman Ave Philadelphia PA 19111-2497 Office Fax: 215-214-1623. Business E-Mail: Joseph.Testa@fccc.edu.

TESTORI, TIZIANO G., periodontologist, oral surgery educator; b. Como, Italy, Sept. 2, 1956; s. Ferdinando N. and Matilde A. (Spinelli) T.; m. Giovanna Perrotti, July 5, 1987; 1 child, Veronica Bapu. MD, U. Milan, 1981, DDS, 1984, PhD, 1986. Pvt. practice, Milan, 1986—; vis. prof. U. Milan, 1991—; head implantology sect., dept. periodontology U. Milan, Galeazzi Hosp., Milan, 1998—; chmn. R.L. Weinstein prof. U. Milan, 1998—. Scientific advisor Ctr. for Advanced Dental Studies in Milan, 1994—. Contbr. articles to profl. jours.; mem. edit'l bd.: Italian Jour. of Oral Surgery. Mem. Am. Acad. Osseointegration, Am. Acad. Implant Dentistry, N.Y. Acad. Sci., European Bd. Oral Surgery, Acad. Osseointegration, European Acad. Osseointegration, Italian Soc. Oral Surgery (v.p.), Knights of Malta, Rotary. Avocations: photography, travel, sports. Office: Via Giulio Rubini 22 22100 Como CO Italy

TÉTÉNYI, PÉTER, pharmacist; b. Budapest, Hungary, May 11, 1956; s. Péter Tétényi and Magdolna Erdosi; m. Éva Mária Kovács, Oct. 21, 1989; 1 child, Péter. M in Pharmacy, Semmelweis U., Budapest, 1979; PhD, Hungarian Acad. Scis., Budapest, 1982. Rsch. fellow Richter Pharm. Works, Budapest, 1979—90; postdoctoral fellow chem. dept. Marquette U., Milw., 1984—85; asst. prof. dept. organic chemistry Semmelweis U., Budapest, 1990—. Contbr. chapters to books. Mem.: Am. Chem. Soc., Assn. Hungarian Chemists, Hungarian Chamber Pharmacists. Achievements include patents for heterocyclic compounds and polymer supported synthesis. Home: Josef University 27 H-1161 Budapest Hungary Office: Semmelweis University Dept Org Chem Hogyes Endre Utca 5 7 1092 Budapest Hungary Office Phone: 361-476-3600 ext. 53025. Office Fax: 361-217-0851. Personal E-mail: peter.tetenyi2@invitel.hu. Business E-Mail: tetpet@szerves.sote.hu.

TETZ, VICTOR VENIAMIN, microbiology educator, researcher; b. Leningrad, Russia, Mar. 28, 1949; s. Veniamin I. and Gilda G. (Lozinskaya) T.; m. Rimma I. Achkinazi; 1 child, George. PhD, 1st Pavlov Med. Inst., Leningrad, 1975, MD, 1990. Rschr. 1st Pavlov Med. Inst., 1972-76, asst. prof., 1976-89, assoc. prof., 1989-91; prof. State Pavlov Med. U., Leningrad, 1991—. Head dept. microbiology, virology and immunology State Pavlov Med. U., St. Petersburg, Russia, 1991—, head sci. diagnostic complex, 1994—, mem. sci. coun., 1990—. Author: Self-regulation of Parasitogenic Systems, 1987, Manual of Clinical Microbiology, 1998, Microorganisms and Antibiotics, Pulmonary Diseases, 2002, Sepsis, 2003, Sexually Transmitted Diseases, 2004, Urinary Tract Infections, 2005, Infections of Skin, Soft Tissues, Bone and Joints, 2006, Nosocotrial infections, 2007, Infections in Otolaryngology, 2009; author, editor: textbook Medical Microbiology, Virology and Immunology, 2002; author, editor (textbook) Medical Microbiology, Virology and Immunology, 2010; editor: Cells Communities, 1998; author: Infections in Otolaryngology, Molecular Biology of Bacteria, 1998; contbr. articles to profl. jours. Recipient award Internat. Sci. Found., 1993. Mem. Russia Acad. Natural Scis., Russian Soc. Microbiology, Russian Soc. Clin. Microbiology (chmn. St. Petersburg br. 1997—), Am. Soc. Microbiology, N.Y. Acad. Scis. Avocations: sports, literature, music. Office: State Pavlov Med Univ L Tolstoy 6/8 197089 Saint Petersburg Russia Home: AP 95 ul. Lyensovyeta 27 196066 Saint Petersburg Sankt-Pyetyerburg Russia E-mail: vtetzv@yahoo.com.

TEUFACK, SONIA G., physician; b. Douala, Camerron, Apr. 21, 1983; BS, U. Bridgeport, 2004; MD, St. Louis U. Sch. Medicine, 2008. Neurosurgery resident Thomas Jefferson U. Hosp., 2008—. Office: 909 Walnut St Philadelphia PA 19107 Personal E-mail: sonigary@gmail.com.

TEWARI, SHIKHA, dentist; b. Meerut, India, Feb. 11, 1967; BDS, King George Med. Coll., 1992, MDS, 1996. Cons. Govt. Dental Coll., Rohtak, India, 1997—2011, assoc. prof., 2002—07, prof., 2007—. Avocation: music. Home: 6/6J Medical Campus Rohtak Haryana 124001 India Personal E-mail: drshildiatewari@gmail.com.

TEY, HONG LIANG, physician, dermatologist; MBBS, Nat. U. Singapore, 2001; diploma in Geriatric Medicine, Singapore; diploma in Skin Cancer Medicine, Australia. Cert. Edn. Commn. for Fgn. Graduates, splty. in dermatology RCP (UK). Cons. Nat. Skin Ctr., Singapore, 2011—. Contbr. articles to profl. jours.; author: The Black Book of Clinical Examination. Capt. Singapore Armed Forces. Fellow: Acad. Medicine Singapore; mem.: RCP, Internat. Forum for Study Itch, Dermatological Soc. Singapore. Roman Catholic. Business E-Mail: hltey@nsc.gov.sg.

THA, KHIN KHIN, radiologist, educator; b. Yangon, Myanmar, Dec. 27, 1971; MBBS, U. Yangon, 1997; PhD, Hokkaido U. Grad. Sch. Medicine, 2005. Postdoc. rschr. Hokkaido U. Grad. Sch. Medicine, 2005, asst. prof., 2010—. Travel fellowship, Symposium Neuroradiologicum, 2006, Grant-in-aid, Japan Soc. Promotion Sci., 2011— Mem.: Japanese Soc. Magnetic Resonance in Medicine (Presdl. Poster award 2010), Japanese Soc. Neuroradiology (Kato award 2010), Internat. Soc. Magnetic Resonance in Medicine, Japan Soc. Radiology, Radiol. Soc. N.Am. (award 2005). Avocations: cooking, music, sports. Office: Hokkaido University Grad Sch Medicine Sapporo Hokkaido 060-8638 Japan Office Fax: 81-11-706-7876. Business E-Mail: kktha@med.hokudai.ac.jp.

THACH, ROBERT EDWARDS, biology educator, former dean; b. Oklahoma City, Okla., Feb. 2, 1939; s. William Thomas and Mary Elizabeth (Edwards) T.; m. Carol Ann Schmidt, Sept. 23, 1959 (div. Aug. 1967); children: Catherine Anne, Robert Edwards Jr.; m. Sigrid Stumpp, Apr. 20, 1968; 1 child, Christopher Alexander. AB, Princeton U., NJ, 1961; PhD, Harvard U., 1964. Asst. prof. biochemistry and molecular biology Harvard U., Cambridge, Mass., 1966-69, assoc. prof. biochemistry and molecular biology, 1969-70; assoc. prof. biol. chemistry Wash. U., St. Louis, 1970-73, prof. biol. chemistry, 1973—, prof. biology, 1977—, chmn. biology, 1977-81, dean Grad. Sch. Arts and Scis., 1993—2008. Instl. biosafety com. mem. Monsanto Co., St. Louis, 1980-83; mem. Grad. Record Exam. Bd., 1998-2003, chair 2001-2002;mem. North Ctr. Assn. Grad. Adv. Group, 1996-1998, Coun. Grad. Sch. Bd., 1997-2000, Emory U. Grad. Adv. Coun. 1996-2003, Assn. Grad. Sch. Exec. Com., 1998-2000, Mid. States Commn. Higher Edn. Team, 2004, Woodrow Wilson Found. Adv. Coun. 2000-05, co chair, 2001-05; organizer Internat. Grad. Scholarship Confs. China, 2005-10. Mem. editorial bd. Jour. of Biol. Chemistry, 1984-89, Archives of Biochemistry and Biophysics, 1972-78; editor Enzyme, 1990-91; contbr. articles to profl. jours. including Sci., Nature, Cell, and Proc. Nat. Acad. Sci. Fellowship Woodrow Wilson Found., 1961-62, NSF, 1962-64, John Simon Guggenheim Meml. Found., 1969; grantee NSF, NIH Time For Lyme Inc., 1970-93. Fellow AAAS; mem. Am. Soc. of Biol. Chemists, Am. Soc. for Virology (Washington U. Arts & Sci. Dean's medal, 2008). Achievements include discovery of initiation codon "AUG" for mRNA translation, 5'-3' direction for mRNA translating, translational repressor for ferritin synthesis; devel. of methods for RNA synthesis. Office: Washington Univ 256 Busch Laboratory 1137 Saint Louis MO 63130 E-mail: thach@wustl.edu.

THACKER, STEPHEN BRADY, medical association administrator, epidemiologist; b. Independence, Mo., Dec. 30, 1947; m. 1976; 2 children. AB, Princeton U., 1969; MD, Mt. Sinai Sch. Medicine, 1973; MSc, London Sch. Hygiene and Tropical Medicine, 1984. Chief consolidated surveillance and commn. activity epidemiol. program office Ctrs. Disease Control and Prevention, Atlanta, 1978-83, dir. surveillance and epidemiol. studies, 1983-86, asst. dir. sci. Ctr. Environ. Health and Injury Control, 1986-89, dir. Epidemiol. Program Office, 1989—2004, acting dir. Nat. Ctr. Environ. Health, 1993-95, acting dep. dir., 1998, acting dir. Nat. Ctr. Injury Prevention and Control, 1999-2000, dir. Office Workforce and Career Devel., 2004—10, acting dir. Nat. Ctr. Pub. Health Informatics, 2009, dep. dir., 2010—, dir. Office Surveillance Epidemiology & Lab. Services, 2010—. Mem. steering com. Assn. Behavioral Sci. Med. Edn., 1971-74; assoc. Dept. Cmty. Medicine, Med. Ctr. Duke U., Durham, N.C., 1975-76; lectr. Cmty. Ctr. Mt. Sinai Sch. Medicine, N.Y.C., 1978—, Sch. Medicine Emory U., Atlanta, 1985-86; cons. epidemiology Arab Republic Egypt, 1979-91; clin. asst. prof. cmty. health Sch. Medicine Emory U., 1986-91; adj. prof. Emory U. Sch. Pub. Health, 1992—. Editor: Epidemiologic Revs., 1990-2003. Clin. scholar Robert Wood Johnson Found., 1974-75; recipient Mosby Book award for excellence, 1973, Pub. Health Svc. Outstanding Svc. medal, 1987, Pub. Health Svc. Meritorious Svc. medal, 1988, 2002, Saul Horowitz Jr. Meml. award, 1990, Supervisory award for contbr. advantage of women, 1991, Pub. Health Svc. Commendation medal, 1991, Pub. Health Svc. Disting. Svc. medal, 1993, 2006, Pub. Health Svc. Surgeon Gen.'s Exemplary Svc. medal, 1993, Pub. Health Svc. Disting. Svc. medal, 1997, Medal of Excellence William C. Watson, Jr., 1996, Ray E. Brown award Assn. Mil. Surgeons of U.S., 2003, Lifetime Sci. Achievement award CDC, 2009. Achievements include rsch. public health surveillance, infectious disease, environ. health, injury prevention, alcohol abuse, health care delivery, meta-analysis, technology assessment. Office: Ctrs for Disease Control and Prevention MS E94 1600 Clifton Rd NE Atlanta GA 30333 Business E-Mail: sbt1@cdc.gov. *

THAEN, LENNARD, surgeon; married; 3 children. MBChB, U. Leicester, 1990; FRCSEd (Ophth), FAMS. Cert. LASIK, PRK, Femtosecond Laser Surgery (Visumax) and the use of Phakic intraocular lenses including ICL. Trained in opthalmology, England; refractive laser surgery fellowship; sub splty. opthalmic fellowship on uveitis and glaucoma; clinician scientist Agy. for Sci. Tech and Rsch. (ASTAR), Singapore; head cataract, LASIK and refractive laser surgery svcs. Nat. Univ. Hosp. (NUH), Singapore, sr. cons. opthalmic surgeon. Asst. prof. of opthalmology Nat. Univ., Singapore. Avocations: running, mountain climbing, sailing. Office: National University Hospital (NUH) Lasik Centre 11 Biopolis Way Helios Number 01-06/07 Singapore Singapore Office Phone: 6567732015. Office Fax: 6564789712. *

THAI, HOANG, medical educator; b. Saigon, Vietnam, Apr. 21, 1966; BS, Ariz. State U., 1988; MD, U. Ariz., 1991. Assoc. prof., medicine U. Ariz., 1999—. Interventional cardiologist Southern Ariz. VA Health Care Sys., 1992. Fellow: Soc. Cardiac Angiography and Intervention, Am. Coll. Cardiology. Office: 3601 S 6th Ave Tucson AZ 85723 Office Fax: 520-629-4636. Personal E-mail: hoangthai@msn.com.

THALBERG, O. KYRRE, principal scientist, chemical engineer; b. Oslo, Sept. 13, 1957; arrived in Sweden, 1963; s. Bjorn T. and Margareth Thalberg; children: Olof, Joel. MChemE, Lund U., Sweden, 1982, PhD in Phys. Chemistry, 1990. Scientist Pharmacia AB, Uppsala, Sweden, 1983—86; rsch. scientist Astra AB, Lund, 1991—96; mgr. Astrazeneca AB, Lund, 1997—2006, prin. scientist, 2006—08. Achievements include invention of pyramidal phase diagram for polyelectrolyte-surfactant systems; research in mixing method for pharmaceutical powders for inhalation; development of dry powder granulation method for turbuhaler. Avocations: backpacking, skiing, running, writing. Office: Astrazeneca R&D Lund Scheelev 8 22187 Lund Sweden Home: Klang V 1 Lund 224 72 Sweden Business E-Mail: kyrre.thalberg@astrazeneca.com.

THALER, ARNULF R.G., retired ophthalmologist; b. Klagenfurt, Aug. 22, 1942; MD, Med. U. Vienna, 1968. Prof. Med. U. Vienna, 1978. Mem.: AAO. Office: Waehringer St 24 Vienna A-1090 Austria Business E-Mail: arnulf.thaler@meduniwien.ac.at.

THALLER, SETH RAY, plastic surgeon; b. NYC, June 22, 1949; m. Patricia Thaller; children: Cody, Lexi. BA, Lafayette Coll., 1971; MD, U. Louisville, 1975; DMD, Boston Sch. Dentistry, 1978; resident gen. surgery, St. Vincent's Hosp., 1978-80. Intern in internal medicine SUNY, Buffalo, 1975-76; resident in gen. surgery St. Vincent's Hosp., NYC, 1978-80; resident otalaryngology/head and neck surgery Mass. Eye and Ear Infirmary, 1980-83; resident in plastic surgery Albert Einstein Coll. Medicine Affiliated Hosps., 1983—85; craniofacial fellowship UCLA Sch. Medicine, 1986; clin. instr. NYU Sch. Dentistry, NYC, 1984-86; adj. asst. prof. plastic surgery U. Calif., LA, 1986, asst. prof. plastic surgery, 1987-93, acting chief divsn. plastic surgery, 1989, assoc. prof. plastic surgery Davis, 1993-95; prof. and chief divsn. plastic surgery U. Miami/Jackson Meml. Hosp. Mem.: ACS, Am. Assn Plastic Surgeons, Assn. Academic Chmn. Plastic Surgeons, Am. Soc. Maxillofacial Surgeons, Am Soc. Plastic & Reconstructive Surgeons, Am. Cleft Palate Craniofacial Assn., Am. Society for Aesthetic Plastic Surgery, AMA. Home: 11010 Paradela St Coral Gables FL 33156-4244 Office: Univ Miami Jackson Meml Hospital PO Box 16960 Miami FL 33101-6960 Office Phone: 305-585-5285.

THALLURI, JYOTHI, medical educator; b. Chennai, Apr. 1, 1955; MSc, Christian Med. Coll., 1980; PhD, John Curtin Sch. Med. Rsch., 1985. Sr. lectr. U. South Australia, 1987—. Recipient Australian Endeavour Exec. award, CommonWealth Govt., award, Australian Learning and Tchg. Coun. Mem.: Australian Endeavour Alumni Assn., Assn. Health Profl. Orgn. Avocation: travel. Office: Frome Rd City E Campus Adelaide South Australia 5066 Australia Office Fax: 61-8-302 2389. Business E-Mail: jyothi.thalluri@unisa.edu.au.

THAM, IVAN, oncologist; b. Singapore, May 2, 1974; MBBS, Nat. U. Singapore, 2000. Assoc. cons. Nat. Cancer Ctr., Singapore, 2006—08, vis. cons., 2010; cons. Nat. U. Cancer Inst., Singapore, 2009—. Recipient prize, Dermatology Soc. Singapore; named one of Top Drs., Nat. U. Singapore, 1999; named to Dean's List, 1996, 1999, 2000. Fellow: Royal Australian and New Zealand Coll. Radiologists, Royal Coll. Radiologists. Office: 1E Kent Ridge Rd Singapore 119228 Singapore E-mail: ivantham@yahoo.com.

THAM, TONY CHIEW KEONG, gastroenterologist; b. Batu Gajah, Perak, Malaysia, Feb. 8, 1962; s. Sek Cheong and Ik Ching (Lee) T.; m. Kathleen Rebecca Elizabeth Long, July 8, 1988; children: Jennifer, Alison, Caroline. MBBCh, Queen's U., Belfast, No. Ireland, 1985; MD, Queen's U., 1990. Intern, resident Belfast Tchg. Hosps., 1985-89; rsch. fellow dept. therapeutics Queen's U., 1989-90; fellow gastroenterology and internal medicine Royal Victoria Hosp., Belfast, 1991-95; vis. advanced endoscopy, gastroenterology fellow Brigham & Women's Hosp., Harvard Med. Sch., Boston, 1995-96; cons. physician, gastroenterologist Ulster Hosp., Belfast, 1997—; head sch. medicine Northern Ireland Deanery, 2008—. Sr. tutor Queen's U., Belfast, 1991-95; mem. com. Acute Hosps. Reorganization project, Belfast, 1995, Joint Royal Coll. Physicians Training Bd., 2009-; mem. com. on orgn. of Oesophegeal Cancer Svc. in No. Ireland. Co-author: Gastrointestinal Emergencies; contbr. articles to profl. jours. No. Ireland Coun. Postgrad. MEd. Edn. scholar, 1995, Robert Leathem scholar Queen's U., 1995; co-recipient Best Abstract award Am. Coll. Gastroenterology/Astra Merck, 1996. Fellow Royal Coll. Physicians (assoc. tutor 1994-95), Am. Soc. Gastrointestinal Endoscopy, Brit. Soc. Gastroenterology, Irish Soc. Gastroenterology (coun. mem. 2002-), Ulster Soc. Internal Medicine, Ulster Soc. Gastroenterology (treas. 1999-2003). Avocations: hi-fi, computers, hill walking, photography. Office: Ulster Hosp Dundonald Belfast BT16 0RH Northern Ireland Home: 43 Newforge Lane BT9 5NW Belfast Northern Ireland Office Phone: 2890 561 344. E-mail: ttham@utvinternet.com.

THANAPPRAPASR, DUANGMANI, physician; b. Bangkok, Sept. 1, 1975; MD, Mahidol U., 2000. Cert. gynecologic oncologist. Physician Mahidol U., 2006—. Office: Phayathai Bangkok 10400 Thailand E-mail: dmngynonc@gmail.com.

THANAVALA, YASMIN M., lab administrator, educator; b. India, Oct. 8, 1948; PhD, U. London, 1979. Prof., mem., lab head Roswell Pk. Cancer Inst., 1985—. Recipient Bharat Samman award, NRI Inst., Gov.'s award, NY State, Am. award, FEZANA Soc., Gold medal, Indian Coun. Med. Rsch. Office: Elm and Carlton St Buffalo NY 14221 Business E-Mail: yasmin.thanavala@roswellpark.org.

THANOPOULOU, ANASTASIA, internist, diabetologist educator; b. Indpls., Mar. 2, 1965; MD, Aristotelian U. Salonica, 1989, MD, 1998. Instr. Technol. Inst. Athens, 1999—2005; lectr. Diabetes Ctr., 2nd Dept. Internal Medicine, Nat. U. Athens, Hippokration Gen. Hosp., Greece, 2005—. Nat. scholarship, Greek Govt. Mem.: Mediterranean Group Study Diabetes, Diabetes and Nutrition Study Group European Diabetes Assn. (sec., Young Investigator's award 2002), Hellenic Diabetes Assn. Home: 82 Ioulianou Athens 14040 Greece Personal E-mail: athanopoulou@hotmail.com.

THARP, ROLAND GEORGE, psychology professor; b. Galveston, Tex., June 6, 1930; s. Oswald Roland and Berma Lucille (Keefer) T.; m. Stephanie Dalton; children: Donald Martin, Thomas Roland, David Michael, Julie. Student, Middlebury Coll., 1956-60; BA cum laude, U. Houston, 1957; MA, U. Mich., 1958, PhD, 1961. Cert. Am. Bd. Examiners in Profl. Psychology. Reporter Tex. City Sun, 1946-47; mgr. Tharp Lumber Co., LaMarque, Tex., 1949-54; intern VA Hosp., Menlo Park, Calif., 1960; asst. prof. U. Ariz., Tucson, 1961-65, assoc. prof., 1965-68; prof., dir. clin. studies, dir. multicultural ctr. for higher edn. U. Hawaii, Honolulu, 1968-87; provost and v.p. for acad. affairs U.S. Internat. U., San Diego, 1987-89; prof. edn., psychology U. Calif., Santa Cruz, 1990—, rsch. prof. Berkeley; dir. Nat. Rsch. Ctr. for Diversity, 1995—; prof. U. Greenland, 2006—. Dir. Ctr. for Rsch. on Edn., Diversity and Excellence, 1996—; prin. investigator Kamehameha Early Edn. Program, Honolulu, 1969-89; field selection officer Peace Corps, Washington, 1965-67. Author: (poetry) Highland Station, 1978; co-author: Behavior Modification in the Natural Environment, 1969, Self-Directed Behavior, 1980, Rousing Minds to Life, 1988, Teaching Transformed, 2000; writer, producer, dir. film Scenes from the Life, 1981 (Purchase prize The Contemporary Mus. 1981). Mem. Bd. Psychologist Examiners, Ariz., 1964-67; pres. Hawaii Literary Arts Coun., Honolulu, 1982. Robert Frost fellow Middlebury Coll., 1960; recipient Am. Film Mag. award for filmmaking Hawaii Internat. Film Festival, 1990, Grawemeyer award edn., 1993. Mem. Am. Ednl. Rsch. Assn., Am. Anthropol. Assn. Episcopalian. Avocations: tennis, painting. Office: 560 N St SW Apt N702 Washington DC 20024-4621 E-mail: tharp@ucsc.edu.

THASE, MICHAEL E., psychiatrist; BS in Psychology, Wright State U.; MD, Ohio State U., 1979. Resident & fellow Western Psychiatric Inst. & Clinic, dir. Depression Treatment & Rsch. Program, 1987—, chief adult psychiatry; prof. psychiatry U. Pitts. Med. Ctr. Editor-in-chief Psychopharmacology Bulletin. Mem.: Am. Psychiatric Assn. (Marie Eldredge award). Office: 3811 O'Hara St Pittsburgh PA 15213-2593 Office Phone: 412-624-1000.

THATTASSERY, EMIL GEORGE, cardiologist; b. Washington, Mar. 19, 1977; s. Pious and Jacie Thattassery. BS, Johns Hopkins U., 1997; MD, U. Md., 2003; MPH, Columbia U., 2006. Rsch. intern Walter Reed Army Inst. Rsch., Washington, 1993—97; software engr. Genesis Med. Tech., Balt., 1998—99, Trilogy Software, Austin, Tex., 1999; resident in internal medicine Northwestern Meml. Hosp., Chgo., 2003—06; mem. rapid response team Meml. Sloan Kettering Cancer Ctr., Chgo., 2006—07; cardiology fellow Emory Med. Ctr., Atlanta, 2007—10, Mid-Atlantic Permanente Greater Balt. Med. Ctr., Divsn. Cardiology, 2010—; asst. chief med. spltys. Balt. Contbr. articles to med. jours. Pres. Cir. K, Johns Hopkins U., Balt., 1996—97; pres. student coun. U. Md. Med. Sch., Balt., 2000—01. Mem.: AMA, Tau Beta Pi. Office: 6565 N Charles St Ste #615 PPE Baltimore MD 21204 Home: S129 Northern Focus Ln Columbia MD 21044 Personal E-mail: ethat001@hotmail.com.

THAVICHAIGARN, PARINYA, colon and rectal surgeon; b. Bangkok, Dec. 25, 1955; s. Sa-Ngium and Suree Thavichaigarn; m. Venika Kamlang-ek, Aug. 29, 1994; 1 child, Napasorn. MD, Mahidol U., Bangkok, 1978, BSc, 1976; postgrad., Edinburgh Postgrad. Bd. Medicine, Scotland, 1984; attended, War Coll., 2002—03. Diplomate Thai Bd. Surgery, Thai Gen. Med. Coun., 1983, Thai Sub-specialty Bd. in Colon and Rectal Surgery, Thai Gen. Med. Coun., 1998, Thai Sub-specialty Bd. in Surg. Oncology, Thai Gen. Med. Coun., 2005. Intern Siriraj Hosp., 1979, surg. resident, 1979—83; surg. registrar Chalmers' Hosp. Edinburgh, 1985—86; cons. surgeon Phramongkutklao Hosp., Bangkok, 1987—93, chief coloproctology, 1994—98; assoc. prof. surgery Pramongkutklao Coll. Medicine, 1996; vice chmn. Dept. Accidental and Emergency Medicine Phramongkutklao Hosp., 1999—2000, chmn. Dept. Surgery, 2002—. Anatomy demonstrator U. Newcastle Upon Tyne, England, 1983—84; vis. surgeon St. Marks's Hosp., England, 1986; cons. surgeon and sr. lectr. Dept. Surgery Pramongkutklao Hosp. and Coll. Medicine, 1987—93; vis. surgeon Divsn. Colon and Rectal Surgery Mayo Clinic, Rochester, Minn., 1997; cons. surgeon Phayathai Hosp., Bangkok, 2000—, Vichaiyuth Hosp., 2000—. Contbr. articles to profl. jours., chapters to books. Mem. adv. bd. Mil. Com. Senate of Thailand, Bangkok, 2002—05, Health Com. The Senate of Thailand, 2004—05. Sr. col. Thailand Mil., 2000. Fellow: ACS, Royal Coll. Surgeons Ireland, Internat. Coll. Surgeons, Royal Coll. Surgeons Thailand (coun. mem. 2005—), Royal Coll. Surgeons Edinburgh; mem.: Assn. Gen. Surgeons Thailand (coun. mem. 2001—), Assn. Surg. Oncologists Thailand (treas., chmn. orgn. com. 2002—), Soc. Colon and Rectal Surgeons Thailand (pres. 2005—), Coll. Family Medicine Thailand, The Royal Bangkok Sport Club. Buddism. Avocations: golf, tennis, badminton, reading, movies. Office: Dept Surgery Phramongkutklao Hospit 315 Rajavithi Rd Rajthavee Bangkok 10400 Thailand Home: Rama VI Rd Soi 20 Rajthavee 277 10400 Bangkok Bangkok Thailand Office Fax: +6623547707. Personal E-mail: pthavichaigarn@yahoo.com.

THAXTON, SHAD (COLBY SHAD THAXTON), biotechnology company executive, urologist; b. 1975; BA in Environ. Biology summa cum laude, U. Colo., Boulder, 1999; MD, Northwestern U., 2004, PhD, 2007. Asst. prof. urology Feinberg Sch. Medicine Northwestern U., Evanston, Ill., 2008—; co-founder AuraSense LLC, Evanston, Ill., 2010—. Recipient TR35 award, MIT Tech. Reviews; named Rschr. of the Yr., Bioscience Tech., 2009; named one of The 40 Under 40, Crain's Chgo. Bus., 2010. Mem.: Alpha Omega Alpha, Phi Beta Kappa. Office: AuraSense LLC 1801 Maple Ave Suite 4301 Evanston IL 60201 also: Feinberg School Medicine Tarry Bldg Rm 16-703 300 E Superior Chicago IL 60611 Office Phone: 847-467-2874, 312-908-8145. Office Fax: 847-556-6411. E-mail: cthaxton003@md.northwestern.edu. *

THAYER, EDNA LOUISE, health facility administrator; b. Madelia, Minn., May 21, 1936; d. Walter William Arthur and Hilda Engel Emily Ann (Geistfeld) Wilke; m. David LeRoy Thayer, Aug. 30, 1958; children: Scott, Tamara, Brenda. Diploma in nursing, Bethesda Luth., 1956; BS in Nursing Edn., U. Minn., 1960; MSN, Washington U., St. Louis, 1966; MS in Counseling, Mankato State U., Minn., 1972. Cert. nursing adminstr. advanced ANA. Nurse Bethesda Luth. Hosp., St. Paul, 1956-58, U. Minn. Hosp., Mpls., 1958; from nurse to asst. head nurse supr., edn. dir. Fairmont (Minn.) Community Hosp., 1959-63; instr. Alton (Ill.) Meml. Hosp., 1963-66; from nursing instr. to assoc. prof. and dean Sch. Nursing Mankato State U., 1966-77; asst. adminstr. Rice County Dist. One Hosp., Faribault, Minn., 1977-89; RN, adminstrv. supr. St. Peter (Minn.) Regional Treatment Ctr., 1990-96; spkr., 1996—. Nurse surveyor Minn. Dept. Tech. Edn., St. Paul, 1980-93; mem. adv. co. LPN and MA programs Tech. Inst., Faribault, 1977-2001. Co-author (with Mary Huntley and Linda Beer): Celebrating the First Fifty Years, 2003; co-author: (with Mary Huntley) A Mirthful Spirit: Embracing Laughter for Wellness, 2007; author: Feisty Lydia, Memoirs of a German War Bride, 2009. Mem. Rice County Ext. Bd., Faribault, 1986-91, adult leader 4-H Club, Rice County and St. Paul, 1971-97; advisor Med. Explorers, Faribault, 1977-89; mem. Rep. Rodosovich Health Com., Faribault, 1984-94; coun. mem. Our Savior's Luth. Ch., Faribault, 1984-87; mem. Rep. Boudreau Health Care Adv. Com., 1996-2001. Recipient Alumni award, Nat. 4-H Club, 1983, Disting. Friend of Nursing award, Mankato State U., 1995, Women of Distinction award, Girl Scouts, 2007. Mem. Minn. Orgn. Nurse Execs. (bd. dirs. 1987-89), Dist. F Nursing Svc. Adminstrs. (pres. 1980-82), Minn. Nurses Assn. (bd. dirs. 1982-87, Pres.'s award 1983, pres. 5th dist. 1974, 75, pres. 13th dist. 1984-86), AAUW, Sigma Theta Tau, Delta Kappa Gamma (pres. Pi chptr. 1982-84, Woman of Achievement award 1985, Golden Stipend award 2006), Hosp. Aux., Legion Aux. Republican. Avocations: crafts, volunteer work, theater, plays. Home: 7 Roots Beach Ln Elysian MN 56028-9731 Office Phone: 507-267-4588. Personal E-mail: dethayer@myclearwave.net.

THAYER, WALTER RAYMOND, retired internist; b. Providence, Apr. 16, 1929; s. Walter Raymond and Esther Veronica (Hulme) Thayer; m. Meredith Marks, 1998; children from previous marriage: Walter, Ida Marie, Peter. BS, Providence Coll., 1950; MD, Tufts U., 1954. Intern R.I. Hosp., Providence, 1955-57; sr. asst. surgeon USPHS/NIH, Bethesda, Md., 1956-58; resident Georgetown U. Hosp., Washington, 1958-59; fellow in gastroenterology Sch. Medicine Yale U., New Haven, 1959-61, rsch. fellow in internal medicine, 1961, from instr. to asst. prof. medicine, 1960-65; from assoc. prof. to prof. medicine Sch. Medicine Brown U., Providence, 1965—2004; prof. emeritus biol. and med. scis. Brown U. Sch. Medicine, Providence, 2005—; ret., 2005. Rschr. Wenner Glen Inst., Stockholm, 1972—73, Mayo Clinic, Rochester, Minn., 1980, Colo. State Coll., Ft. Collins, 1987; mem. Cancer Control Bd., RI, 1976—77; nat. sci. adv. bd. Crohn's and Colitis Found., Inc., 1978—83, rsch. and tgn. awards com., 1978—85, chmn., 1980—85, chmn. med. adv. bd. R.I. chpt., 1983; adv. bd. Nat. Coop. Crohn's Disease Study Group, 1981—83. Editl. reviewer: Gastroenterology, Digestive Disease and Scis.; contbr. articles to profl. jours. Sr. asst. surgeon USPHS, 1956—58. Recipient Humanitarian of Yr. award, New Eng. chpt. Crohn's and Colitis Found., Keen award, Brown U. Sch. Medicine, 2001; fellow NSF, 1972—73. Fellow: ACP (Hamolsky Achievement award, RI Chpt. 2007), Am. Coll. Gastroenterology (gov. R.I. 1996—98); mem.: Providence Med. Soc., R.I. Gastroenterology Soc., R.I. Med. Soc., Am. Fedn. Clin. Rsch., Am. Gastroenterol. Assn. (Clinician of the Yr. award 1999). Avocations: cross country skiing, birdwatching, gardening. Home: 65 Bullocks Point Ave Riverside RI 02915-5318

THEBNER, LISA ILENE, pediatrician; b. Oct. 1, 1971; BA in Internat. Rels., Tufts U., Medford, Mass.; MD, SUNY Buffalo, 1999. Cert. in pediat. Am. Bd. Med. Specialties. Resident Montefiore Med. Ctr., Bronx; pediatrician NY Presbyn./Weill Cornell, NYC, Montefiore Med. Ctr., Schneider Children's Hosp. at North Shore, Great Neck, NY, West End Pediatrics, NYC. Office: West End Pediatrics 450 West End Ave New York NY 10024 Office Phone: 212-769-3070.

THEIN, HLA-HLA, research scientist; d. Thein Maung and Khin Hla Myint. MBBS, Inst. Medicine, Yangon, 1980; MPH, U. Calif., Berkeley, 1997; postgrad., U. New South Wales. Med. officer Dept. of Health Svcs., Yangon, 1982—88, Ministry of Health, Labasa, Northern Division, Fiji, 1991—96, 1997—2000; rsch. asst. Nat. Ctr. HIV Epidemiol/Clin. Rch., Darlinghurst, Australia, 2001—. Fellow, Toronto Gen. Rsch. Inst., U. Health Network, 2005—; scholar, Nat. Centre in HIV Epidemiology and Clin. Rsch., U. New South Wales, 2003—; Population fellow, Internat. Sch. Pub. Health, U. Calif.,

Berkeley, 1996—97. Mem.: Australasian Soc. HIV Medicine (assoc. Jr. Rsch. award 2003—06). Office: Univ Health Network Toronto Gen Rsch Inst Critical Decision Making and Health Care 200 Elizabeth St Rm 13E 222A Toronto ON M5G 2C4 Canada E-mail: rthein@uhnres.utoronto.ca.

THEISS-ABENDROTH, PETER, psychiatrist; b. Berlin, Berlin, Germany, Mar. 14, 1964; s. Karl-Heinz Otto and Gisela Theiss; m. Marlies Abendroth, Sept. 3, 1999. MD, Freie U., Berlin, 1992. Cert. psychiatrist Ärztekammer Berlin, 2000, psychotherapist Ärztekammer Berlin, 2001. Head physician St. Joseph Hosp., Berlin, 2003—04; specialist pvt. practice, Berlin, Berlin, 2004—; psycho-analyst Berliner Inst. für Psychotherapie und Psychoanalyse, 2010. Contbr. articles to profl. jours. Grant, Senate Berlin, 1993. Home: Kanzlerweg 1 Berlin 12101 Germany Personal E-mail: theiss-abendroth@gmx.net.

THENG, JULIAN THIAM SIEW, surgeon; married. MBBS, Nat. U., Singapore, 1992; MMED (Ophth). Fellowship Royal Coll. Surgeons, Edinburgh, Royal Coll. Surgeons (Ophthalmology), London; rep. surgeon phase 4 clin. FDA Singapore; surgeon Eagle Eye Centre (EEC), Singapore. Deacon Prinsep st. Presbyterian Ch.; spkr. world Opthalmology Congress; editl. bd. Jour. of Cataract & Refractive Surgery Today (CRST) Europe; mem. hosp. bd. Mt. Alvernia Hosp., chmn. CME program. Author: (book) A Long Sighted Look at Presbyopia (Lau Hua Yan) Facts, Fiction and Hope. Achievements include Asia's rep. to implant the 1st pair of acrysof phakic IOL lens in Singapore; renowned in the areas of corneal transplants, LASIK & refractive surgery as well as cataract surgery; FIRST Breakthrough "tooth-in-eye" surgery and successfully restoring sight to a blind teenager. Avocations: sports, music, singing, fishing, oil and acrylic, cooking. Office: Eagle Eye Centre (EEC) Mt Alvernia Hosp 820 Thomson Rd Med Ctr Block B 02-11/17 Mt Alvernia 574623 Singapore Office Phone: 6564561000. Office Fax: 6564561006. *

THEODORESCU, DAN, urologic oncologist, molecular biologist; b. Bucharest, Romania, May 6, 1962; s. Radu Amza Serban and Ana Elena (Florescu) Theodorescu; m. Diane Louise Causier, June 1, 1991; children: Thomas William, Claire Ana. MD, Queen's U., Kingston, Ont., Can., 1986; PhD, U. Toronto, Ont., Can., 1993. Diplomate Am. Bd. Urology, cert. in urology Royal Coll. Physicians & Surgeons Can., lic. Va. Surg. intern U. Toronto, 1986-87, MRC rsch. fellow, Mt. Sinai Hosp. Rsch. Inst., 1988-91, urology resident, 1991-94; clin. fellow urology svc. Meml. Sloan Kettering Cancer Ctr., NYC, 1994—95; asst. prof. dept. urology U. Va., Charlottesville, 1995-98, asst. prof. dept. molecular physiology & biol. physics, 1995—2001, assoc. prof. urology, 1998—2001, assoc. prof. molecular physiology & biol. physics, 2001—02, Paul Mellon prof. & chair urologic oncology, 2001—10, prof. molecular physiology & biol. physics, 2002—10, dir. Paul Mellon Prostate Cancer Inst., 2003—10; dir., Paul Bunn chair cancer rsch. U. Colo. Cancer Ctr., 2010—. Atending urologic oncologist U. Va. Health Scis. Ctr., Charlottesville, 1995—2010. Mem. editl. bd. Cancer Letters, Prostate Cancer & Prostatic Diseases, reviewer Cancer Rsch., Cancer, Clin. Cancer Rsch., Am. Jour. Pathology, Jour. Urology; contbr. articles to profl. jours. Recipient Career Devel. award, Am. Cancer Soc., 1996, Edwin Beer award, NY Acad. Medicine, 1998. Fellow: Royal Coll. Physicians & Surgeons Can.; mem.: ACS, Am. Soc. Clin. Investigation, Soc. Urologic Oncology, Am. Urological Assn., Med. Soc. Va., Med. Coun. Can. (licentiate), Am. Soc. Clin. Oncology, Am. Assn. Cancer Rsch. (Sydney Kimmel award 2002), Soc. Basic Urologic Rsch. (Young Investigator award 1998). Achievements include research in cellular and molecular aspects of tumor invasion and metastasis with a special emphasis on prostate and bladder cancer. Office: U Colo Cancer Ctr Mail Stop F434 13001 E 17th Pl Aurora CO 80045 *

THEODORIDIS, THEODOROS, surgeon; MD, Heinrich Heine U., Duesseldorf, Germany, 1996. Asst. med. dir. St. Josef Hosp., Dept. Orthop., Med. Sch., Ruhr-U. Bochum, Nordrhein Westfalen, Germany, 2002—07; dir. dept. pain therapy and spinal surgery Viktoria Klinik Bochum, 2007—. Contbr. articles to med. publs. Mem.: German Assn. Orthop. and Orthop. Surgery, German Assn. Study Pain, IGOST-IMPS. Achievements include research in human medicine. Office: Viktoria Klinik Bochum Viktoriastr 66-70 Bochum Nordrhein-Westfalen 44787 Germany Business E-Mail: info@dr-theodoridis.de.

THEODOULOU, MARIA, physician; b. NYC, Jan. 14, 1949; MD, SUNY Buffalo Sch. Medicine, 1988. Attending physician Meml. Sloan-Kettering Cancer Ctr., 1988—. Mem. Komen Found. Adv. Bd., Hellenic Med. Soc. Recipient Clin. Excellence award, Brook Army Base, AXIOS award, AHEPA Cancer Found., Outstanding Physician award, Sass Found. Med. Rsch., Hally Yaccino Steiner Meml. award, 2009. Mem.: Am. Soc. Clin. Oncology. Office: 300 East 66th St 7th Fl Rm 73 New York NY 10065 Office Fax: 646-888-4555. Business E-Mail: theodoum@mskcc.org.

THEOFANIDIS, STYLIANOS N., neonatal-perinatal doctor, educator; Grad., U. Athens, Greece, 1980. Diplomate Am. Bd. Pediatrics-neonatal-perinatal medicine, Am. Bd. Pediatrics. Intern St. Luke's-Roosevelt Hosp., resident pediat., 1982—85; fellow neonatal-perinatal medicine NY Hosp.- Cornell Med. Ctr., 1985—87; asst. clin. prof. pediat. Yale Univ.; physician Greenwich Hosp. Office: Greenwich Hospital- Department of Neonatolgy 5 Perryidge Rd Greenwich CT 06830 Office Phone: 203-863-3816. Office Fax: 203-863-3816.

THEOHARIDES, THEOHARIS CONSTANTIN, pharmacologist, physician, educator; b. Thessaloniki, Macedonia, Greece, Feb. 11, 1950; s. Konstantinos A. and Marika (Krava) T.; m. Efthalia I. Triarhou, July 10, 1981; children: Niove, Konstantinos. Diploma with honors, Anatolia Coll., 1968; BA in Biology, History of Sci. and Med., Yale U., 1972, MS in Immunology, 1975, MPhil in Endocrinology, 1975, PhD in Pharmacology, 1978; postgrad., Tufts U., Harvard U. Asst. in rsch. biology Yale U., New Haven, 1968—71, asst. in rsch. pharmacology, 1973—78, spl. instr. modern Greek, 1974, 77, exec. sec. univ. senate, 1976—78, rsch. assoc. faculty clin. immunology, 1978—83; asst. prof. biochemistry and pharmacology Tufts U., Boston, 1983—88, co-dir. med. pharmacology curriculum, 1983—85, 1983—85, dir. med. pharmacology, 1985—93, assoc. prof. pharmacology, biochemistry and psychiatry, 1989—94, dir. grad. pharmacology, 1994—2000, prof. pharmacology and internal medicine, 1995—, prof. biochemistry, 2002—. Vis. faculty Aristotelian U. Sch. Medicine, Thessaloniki, 1979; trustee Anatolia Coll., 1984-85; clin. pharmacologist Commonwealth Mass. Drug Formulary Commn., 1985—; trainee internal medicine and allergy Tufts-New Eng. Med. Ctr., 1986-93; co-chmn. neuro-immunology 2d and 3d World Conf. on Inflammation, Monte Carlo, 1986, 89; mem. internat. adv. bd. 4th, 5th, 6th and 7th World Conf. on Inflammation, Geneva, 1991, 93, 95, 97; spl. cons. Min. of Health, Greece, 1993-95; mem. supreme spl. sci. health coun. Hellenic Republic, 1998—; chmn. Internat. Com. to Upgrade Med. Edn. in Greece, 1994; bd. dirs., spl. cons. Inst. Pharm. Rsch. & Tech., Athens, 1994-2002; mem. Supreme Health Bd.; mem. Nat. Pub. Health Coun. Hellenic Republic, 2003—; vis. prof. Athens U., 2006; spl. advisor Allergy Clin. Rsch. Ctr., Ahikon Hosp., Athens U., 2006—. Author books on pharmacology; mem. editorial bd. numerous jours.; contbr. articles to profl. jours.; patentee in field. Recipient Theodore Buyler award, Yale U., 1972, George Papanicoalou Grad. award, 1977, Med. award, Hellenic Med. Soc. N.Y., 1979, 1983, M.C. Winternitz prize in pathology, Yale U., 1980, Disting Svc. award, Tufts U. Alumni Assn., 1986, Spl. Faculty Recognition award, Tufts U. Med. Sch., 1987, 1988, Boston Mayor Menino Cmty. Svc. award, 1998, Oliver Smith award, 1999, Archon of Ecunemical Patriarchate of Christian Orthodox Ch., 2000, George Papnikolase award, 2003. Mem. AMA, AAUP, AAAS, European Acad. Allergology and Clin. Immunology, Am. Acad. Allergy, Asthma, Immunology, Hellenic Biochem. and Biophys. Soc., N.Y. Acad. Scis., Am. Inst. History Pharmacy, Soc. Health and Human Values, Am. Assn. History Medicine, Am. Soc. Cell Biology, Soc. Neurosci., Am. Fedn. Clin. Rsch., Conn. Acad. Arts and Scis., Am. Soc. Pharmacology and Exptl. Therapeutics, Hellenic Soc. Cancer Rsch., Hellenic Soc. Med. Chemistry, Internat. Soc. Immunopharmacology, Am. Soc. Microbiology, Am. Assn. Immunologists, Internat. Soc. History of Medicine, Mass. Med. Soc., N.E. Hellenic Med. Soc. (sec. 1984-85, v.p. 1985-86, 94-96, pres. 1986-87), Hellenic Sci. Assn. Boston (bd. dirs. 1985), Internat. Anatolia Alumni Assn. (sec. 1984-85), Alpha Omega Alpha, Sigma Xi. Achievements include research on mechanisms of release of secretory products: immunopharmacology, membrane functions of polyamines; pathophysiology of mast cells in neuroimmunoendocrine diseases exacerbated by stress such as irritable bowel syndrome, interstitial cystitis, psoriasis, migraines and multiple sclerosis. Home: 14 Parkman St Apt 2 Brookline MA 02446-3802 Office: Tufts U Sch Med 136 Harrison Ave Boston MA 02111-1817 Office Phone: 617-636-6866. Business E-Mail: theoharis.theoharides@tufts.edu.

THESLEFF, STEPHEN WILHELM, retired pharmacology educator; b. Helsinki, Jan. 6, 1924; arrived in Sweden, 1944; s. Wilhelm Alexander and Mary (af Schulten) Thesleff; m. Ulla Margareta Ericson, Apr. 7, 1951; children: Peter, Jan. MD, Karolinska Inst., Stockholm, 1950, PhD, 1951. Asst. prof. pharmacology Karolinska Inst., 1951-52; Rockfeller Found. fellow U. Ill., Urbana, 1953-54; rsch. fellow dept. biophysics U. Coll. London, 1956-57; assoc. prof. pharmacology U. Lund, Sweden, 1959-62, prof., 1963-89, ret., 1989. Vis. prof. Duke U., Durham, N.C., 1962-63; mem. Swedish Med. Rsch. Coun., 1980-86. Editor: Motor Innervation of Muscles, 1976; Aminopyridines and Similarly Acting Drugs, 1982, Neuromuscular Junction, 1989. Mem. Physiol. Soc., Brit. Pharm. Soc., Am. Soc. for Pharmacology and Exptl. Therapeutics, Academia Europea. Home: Karl XII gatan 20A S-222 20 Lund Sweden E-mail: Stephen.Thesleff@med.lu.se.

THIBAUDON, MICHEL, pharmacist; b. Paris, Dec. 9, 1951; s. Pierre and Xaviere Thibaudon; m. Marie Isabelle Puccinelli, May 28, 1976; children: Claire, Laurent. PharmD, Paris U. Pharmacist Instit. Pasteur, Paris, 1976—91; mgr. Axcell biotechnologies, Lyon, France, 1992—; sci. advisor Indicia Tech., St. Genis L'argentiere. Pres. RNSA, 1996—. Author: (book) Adjuvant for Allergy, 1986. Fellow: SFAIC, Internat. Assn. for Aerobiology; mem.: ASPEC. Office: Reseau Natl Surveillance Aerobiol 5 Genis 69610 L'Argentiere France Office Phone: 33474261948. Business E-Mail: michel.thibaudon@wanadoo.fr.

THIBAULT, GEORGE EDWIN, foundation administrator; b. Sept. 4, 1943; m. Barbara C. Thibault; children: Rebecca L., Adam. Grad. summa cum laude, Georgetown U., 1965; MD magna cum laude, Harvard Med. Sch., 1969. Diplomate American Bd. Internal Medicine. Cardiology tng. Nat. Heart & Lung Inst., Bethesda, Md., Guys Hosp., London; intern, resident internal medicine Mass. Gen. Hosp., Boston, 1971—74, cardiology fellow, 1975—76, dir. med. practices evaluation unit, dir. ICU/CCU, 1977, dir. med tng. program, asst. to assoc. chief Dept. Medicine, 1978—88; chief med. svcs. Brockton/West Roxbury VA Med. Ctr., Mass., 1988—90, dir. health svcs. rsch., 1990; vice chmn. medicine Brigham & Women's Hosp., Boston, 1988—95, chief med. officer, 1995—98; v.p. clin. affairs Partners HealthCare Sys. Inc., Boston, 1999—2007; founding dir. The Acad., Harvard Med. Sch., 2001—07, Daniel D. Federman prof. medicine & med. edn., dir. alumni rels., 2005—07, Federman prof. emeritus, 2008—; pres. Josiah Macy Jr. Found., NYC, 2008—. Chair spl. med. adv. group US Dept. Vets. Affairs; mem. adv. bd. NY Acad. Scis., Inst. Medicine as a Profession, Lebanese American U. Mem.: NAS, Inst. Medicine, Harvard Med. Alumni Assn. (past pres.). Office: Josiah Macy Jr Foundation 44 E 64th St New York NY 10065 E-mail: gthibault@macyfoundation.org. *

THIBODEAU, GARY A., academic administrator; b. Sioux City, Iowa, Sept. 26, 1938; m. Emogene J. McCarville, Aug. 1, 1964; children: Douglas James (dec.), Beth Ann. BS, Creighton U., 1962; MS, S.D. State U., 1967, MS, 1970, PhD, 1971. Profl. service rep. Baxter Lab., Inc., Deerfield, Ill., 1963-65; tchr., researcher dept. biology S.D. State U., Brookings, 1965-76, asst. to v.p. for acad. affairs, 1976-80, v.p. for adminstrn., 1980-85; chancellor U. Wis., River Falls, 1985-2000; sr. v.p. acad. affairs U. Wis. Sys., 2000—01. Mem. investment com. U. Wis., River Falls Found.; trustee W. Cen. Wis. Consortium U. Wis. System; bd. dirs. U. Wis. at River Falls Found.; mem. Phi Kappa Phi nat. budget rev. and adv. comm., Phi Kappa Phi Found. investment comm., comm. on Agrl. and Rural Devel., steering commn. Coun. of Rural Colls. and Univs., Joint Coun. on Food and Agrl. Scis., USDA. Author: Basic Concepts in Anatomy and Physiology, 1983, Athletic Injury Assessment, 2000, Structure and Function of the Body, 2011, The Human Body in Health & Disease, 2010, Anatomy and Physiology, 2010. Mem. AAAS, Am. Assn. Anatomists, Am. Assn. Clin. Anatomists, Human Anatomy and Physiology Soc., Sigma Xi, Phi Kappa Phi, Gamma Sigma Delta, Gamma Alpha. Office: U Wis 116 N Hall River Falls WI 54022

THIBODEAU, STEVEN R.J., technologist; b. Van Buren, Maine, Aug. 16, 1965; s. Roger Joseph and Irene Thibodeau. A, So. Maine Vocat. Inst., 1986; BS, U. So. Maine, 1990; cert. in MR spectroscopy, Huntington Meml. Rsch. Inst., Pasadena, Calif., 2002. Registered technologist. Chief MR tech. Brigham and Women's Hosp., Boston, 1999—2000, application specialist, 2000—. Cons. Medrad, Inc., Indianola, Pa., 1999—. Contbr. articles to profl. jours. Mem.: Soc. Cardiovasc. Magnetic Resonance, Am. Soc. Radiologic Tech.

THIEBAULD, CHARLES MARIE, physician; b. Brussels, Aug. 12, 1937; s. Emmanuel and Julienne (Ugeux) T.; m. Jacqueline Hermand; children: Anne, Emmanuel, Sandrine, Laurent. MD with distinction, U. Louvain, Belgium, 1963; postgrad., U. Brussels. Diplomate in sports medicine and electrocardiography. Asst. in surgery Clinique Ste. Anne, Brussels, 1963-66; pres. Commn. Medico-Sportive Fed. Belge Tennis, 1970-82; chief dept. sports medicine Hopital d'Ixelles, 1983-86; advisor dept. clin. rsch. Omnichem Pharm., Louvain, 1975-81; probation period's master U.C.L., 1977; conseiller dept. clin. rsch. Nippon Zoki Pharm., Osaka, Japan, 1984-91; pres. Centre Medecine Avancée, Brussels, 1983—. Pres. Mission Medicale Belge, Paris-Dakar, 1983, Internat. Meeting Crescendo, 1993, 95-97, 2005-; sci. adv. Consulting Nippon ZOKI Pharm. Co. Ltd., Osaka, Japan. Editor: L'Enfant et Le Sport, 1997, Le Sport Apres 50 Ans; contbr. articles to profl. jours. including Lancet, Clin. Chemistry, Fundamental Clin. Pharmacology, Methods and Findings, others Named Hon. Citizen, State of Okla., 1971. Fellow: Am. Coll. Sports Medicine; mem.: N.Y. Acad. Sci. Achievements include patents in field. Avocations: jogging, tennis, skiing, sailing. Office: Centre de Medecine et d'Etudes Victor Allard 120 1180 Brussels Belgium Office Phone: 32-2-3767072. E-mail: charlesthiebauld@skynet.be.

THIEDE, MEREDITH, marketing executive, director; b. Ohio, June 27, 1979; BFA, Bowling Green State U., 2001; degree, U. Toledo, 2008. Graphic designer U. Toledo, 2004—09, ProMedica Health Sys., 2007—09; dir. mktg., brand mgmt. Signature Med. Group, 2009—. Bd. dirs. Delta Gamma Ctr., 2010, Toledo Ballet, 2007—10. Recipient Healthcare Advt. award, HMR Publications Group, Inc., Crystal award, Assn. Women Communication, Am. Inhouse Design award, Editors Graphic Design USA Mag. Mem.: Am. Mktg. Assn. Avocations: travel, gardening, photography. Office: 633 Emerson Rd Ste 30 Saint Louis MO 63141 Business E-Mail: mthiede@siganturehealth.net.

THIEL, DAVID BRIAN, physician assistant; b. Cin., July 2, 1956; s. Joseph Lee and Mary Jane (Otting) T. BA, Wabash Coll., Crawfordsville, Ind., 1978; AS with honors, Kettering Coll. Med. Arts, 1980. Cert. physician asst. Resident Los Angeles County U. So. Calif. Med. Ctr., L.A., 1985-86; physician asst. in orthopedic surgery Ketchikan, Alaska, 1980-85; physician asst. in phys. medicine and electrodiagnostic medicine New Orleans, 1987—2004; physician asst. USCG, 2004—. In-svc. lectr. HealthSouth Rehab., Harahan, La., 1990—. Tannenbaum scholar, 1974-78; recipient Orchid award Paphiopedilum Mystic Jewel, David's Dream, Highly Commended Cert. Am. Orchid Soc., 2003. Fellow: Sigma Xi (numerous Orchid awards); mem.: Internat. High IQ Soc. Republican. Avocations: swimming, skiing, sailing, orchid growing, bicycling. Home: 2998 Sugartree Rd Bethel OH 45106-8214 E-mail: cynicno@hotmail.com.

THIELMAN, GREGORY T., physical therapist, educator; b. Meriden, Conn., Apr. 16, 1965; MSPT, Springfield Coll., 1991; EdD, Columbia U. Tchrs. Coll., 2005. With sr. level Nat. Rehab. Hosp., 1993—96; assoc. prof. Academia, 2005—. Subaward grant, NIH. Mem.: Nat. Athletic Tng. Assn., Am. Phys. Therapy Assn. Avocations: bicycling, basketball. Office: 600 S 43rd St Philadelphia PA 19104 Business E-Mail: g.thielm@usp.edu.

THIELMANN, MATTHIAS, cardiac surgeon; b. Mannheim, Baden-Württemberg, Germany, Dec. 25, 1967; s. Heinz-Walter Thielmann and Mechthild Thielmann-Grieger. MD, U. Heidelberg, Germany, 1996. Diplomate U. Heidelberg, 1996. Resident dept. cardiac surgery U. Heidelberg, Germany, 1996—99; resident dept. cardiovasc. surgery German Heart Ctr., Munich, 1999—2001; rsch. fellow U. Essen Inst. Pathophysiology, Germany, 2001—02; assoc. cardiac surgeon dept. thoracic and cardiovasc. surgery West-German Heart Ctr., 2002—. Recipient Young Investigator award, Am. Coll. Chest Physicians, 2005. Mem.: German Soc. Thoracic and Cardiovasc. Surgery (licentiate), European Assn. Cardiothoracic Surgeons (assoc.), Am. Coll. Chest Physicians (assoc.), Am. Heart Assn. (assoc.). Office Fax: 49-201-5451. E-mail: matthias.thielmann@uni-essen.de.

THIEMERMANN, CHRISTOPH, pharmacologist, educator; b. Cologne, Germany, June 14, 1960; Registration as physician, U. Cologne, 1986, MD, 1987; PhD, U. London, 1991. Rsch. scientist Inst. Pharmacology, Dusseldorf, Germany, 1986—87; vis. scientist William Harvey Rsch. Inst., London, 1987—88, vis. scientist (Thyssen Found.), 1989, sr. scientist, 1989—96, dir., 1995—, reader in pharmacology, 1996—98; prof. pharmacology (chair) William Harvey Rsch. Inst., U. London, 1998—; mem. exec. com. William Harvey Rsch. Inst., 2000—, CEO, 2003—. Vis. prof. pharmacology U. Florence, Italy, 1993—, U. Sunderland, England, 1995—2000; sr. fellow Brit. Heart Found., London, 1996—2001; vis. prof. exptl. medicine U. Messina, Italy, 2000—. Recipient Ann. prize for contbns. to vascular biology, German Soc. Angiology, 1991, John Vane award for contbns. to prosteglandin rsch., 1991, medal of Polish Physiol. Soc., Centennial Celebration, 1992, Sandoz prize for contbns. to pharmacology, Brit. Pharmacol. Soc., 1994, Young Investigator award, Korean Pharmacol. Soc., 1997, Surg. Infection Soc. Europe, 1997, Menarini award, 2001. Office: William Harvey Rsch Inst Translational Medicine Charterhouse Sq London EC1M 6BQ England Business E-Mail: c.thiemermann@qmul.ac.uk.

THIER, SAMUEL OSIAH, physician, educator; b. Bklyn., June 23, 1937; s. Sidney and May Henrietta Thier; m. Paula Dell Finkelstein, June 28, 1958; children: Audrey Lauren, Stephanie Ellen, Sara Leslie.

Student, Cornell U., 1953—56; MD, SUNY, Syracuse, 1960, DSc (hon.), 1987, Tufts U., 1988, George Washington U., 1988, Mt. Sinai Sch. Med., 1989, Hahnemann U., 1989; DSc (hon.), U. Pa., 1994, Dartmouth Coll., 1996; LHD (hon.), Rush U., 1988, Va. Commonwealth U., 1992, Med. Coll. Pa., 1992; LHD (hon.), Brandeis U., 1994. Diplomate Am. Bd. Internal Medicine. Intern Mass. Gen. Hosp., Boston, 1960—61, asst. resident, 1961—62, sr. resident, 1964—65, clin. and research fellow, 1965, chief resident, 1966; clin. asso. Nat. Inst. Arthritis and Metabolic Diseases, 1962—64; from instr. to asst. prof. medicine Harvard U. Med. Sch., 1967—69; prof. medicine, health care policy Harvard Med. Sch., 1994—2007; asst. in medicine, chief renal unit Mass. Gen. Hosp., Boston, 1967—69; asso. prof., then prof. medicine U. Pa. Med. Sch., 1969—72, vice chmn. dept., 1971—74; assoc. dir. med. svcs. Hosp. U. Pa., 1969—71; David Paige Smith prof. medicine Yale U. Sch. Medicine, 1978—81, Sterling prof. medicine, 1981—85, chmn. dept., 1975—85; pres. Inst. Medicine NAS, Washington, 1985—91; pres., Univ. prof. Brandeis U., Waltham, Mass., 1991—94; pres. Mass. Gen. Hosp., Boston, 1994—97, Ptnrs. HealthCare Sys., Inc., Boston, 1994—96, 1997—2002, CEO, 1996—2002; emeritus prof. Medicine Health Care Policy Harvard Med. Sch., 2008—. Chief medicine Yale-New Haven Hosp., 1975—85, trustee, 1978—85; bd. dirs. Conn. Hospice, Inc., 1976—82; dir. Am. Bd. Internal Medicine, 1977—85, exec. com., 1981—85, chmn., 1984—85. Mem. editl. bd.: New Eng. Jour. Medicine, 1978—81; contbr. articles to med. jours. Mem. adv. com. to the dir. NIH, 1980—85. With USPHS, 1962—64. Recipient Christian R. and Mary F. Lindback Found. Disting. Tchg. award, 1971. Mem.: ACP (bd. regents 1982—85), Interurban Clin. Club, Assn. Am. Physicians, Assn. Profs. Medicine, Internat. Soc. Nephrology, Am. Physiol. Soc., Am. Soc. Nephrology, Am. Fedn. Clin. Rsch. (pres. 1976—77), John Morgan Soc., Assn. Am. Med. Colls. (adminstrv. bd. coun. acad. socs.), Alpha Omega Alpha. Home: 99-20 Florence St # 8 Chestnut Hill MA 02467-1927

THIERER, MARK A., health products executive; MBA in Mktg., U. Minn. With IBM; v.p corp. accounts CaremarkRx, exec.; pres. Physicians Interactive Allscripts, Inc.; pres., COO SXC Health Solutions Corp., pres., CEO, bd. dirs., 2008—. Adv. bd. Scribe Healthcare Technologies. Office: SXC Health Solutions Corp 2441 Warrenville Rd, Ste 610 Lisle IL 60532-3642 Office Phone: 630-577-3100. *

THIERY, MICHEL, medical doctor; b. Ghent, Belgium, Nov. 14, 1924; s. Michel Leo and Marie-Augusta (de Taeye) T.; m. Huguette Descheemaeker, Aug. 28, 1957; 1 child, Dominique. MD, U. Ghent, 1949, PhD, 1962. Specialist in ob-gyn. Asst. State U. Ghent, 1949-63; postgrad. fellow Coll. Physicians and Surgeons Columbia U., NYC, 1952-53; postgrad. in oncology Radiumhemmet, Stockholm, 1955; asst. prof. State U. Ghent, 1963-64, full prof. and chmn. dept obstetrics, 1964-89, prof. emeritus, 1989—. Mem. Belgian royal Acad. of Med., Brussels, 1969—; pres. Belgian Royal Soc. Obstetrics and Gynecology, 1962-63; v.p. European Soc. Perinatal Med., 1983. Contbr. articles to profl. jours.; author: Experimental Carcinoma of Uterine Cervix, Textbook on Contraception; co-author: Monograph on Abortion. Fellow Royal Coll. Obstetricians and Gynaecologists (London). Avocations: history of medicine, hiking, botany, birdwatching. Home: 6 Aan de Bocht B-9000 Ghent Belgium

THIESEN, HENRIK, physician; b. Denmark, Aug. 20, 1960; m. Inga Christensen Bach; children: Lucas Lyst, Celina Lyst. MD, Copenhagen U., 1992. Cert. gen. practitioner specialist Danish Med. Assn., 1998, cmty. physician Danish Med. Assn., 2000. Mgr., staff specialist Health Team for Homeless, Copenhagen, 2005—. Bd. mem. Danish Ctr. Alcoholism and other Addiction Diseases, 2002—07. Recipient Schering-Plough award for med. rsch. in addiction, Danish Soc. for Addiction Medicine. Mem.: Internat. Drs. Healthy Drug Policies, Danish Soc. Clin. Neuropsychiatry, Danish Soc. Quality in Healthcare, Danish Assn. Cmty. Mental Health, Danish Coll. Gen. Practitioners, Danish Med. Assn., Street Medicine Inst. (Chgo.) (mem., bd. dirs. 2009—), Danish Assn. Addiction Medicine (bd. mem. 2002—), Coun. Socially Marginalised People, Danish Network Double Diagnosis (founding mem. 2008—), European Fedn. Nat. Orgns. Working with Homeless. Avocation: music. Home: Skovridergårdsvej 5 Virum 2830 Denmark Office Phone: 45 26758911. Personal E-mail: alkodoktor@dadlnet.dk.

THIESSEN, DELBERT DUANE, psychologist; b. Julesberg, Colo., Aug. 13, 1932; s. David and Eva Peters (Wetherby) T.; children: Trevor, Theron, Kendell Courtney. BA in Psychology with distinction, San Jose State Coll., Calif., 1958; PhD, U. Calif., Berkeley, 1963. Extension instr. U. Calif., La Jolla, fall 1964; asst. sect. med. psychology, divsn. psychiatry and neurology Scripps Clinic and Research Found., La Jolla, 1962-65; faculty U. Tex., Austin, 1965-2000, prof. psychology, 1971-2000, prof. emeritus Austin, 2000—. Rsch. cons. NIMH. Author: Gene Organization and Behavior, 1972, The Evolution and Biochemistry of Aggression, 1976, Bitter-Sweet Destiny: The Stormy Evolution of Human Behavior, 1996, Universal Desires and Fears: The Deep History of Sociobiology, 1997, Survival of the Fittest: The Darwinian Diet and Exercise Program, 1998, Night of the Dagger: A Historical Voodoo Novel, 2005; contbr. articles and chpts. to books. With AUS, 1952-54, Korea. Fellow USPHS, 1960-61; recipient Career Devel. award NIMH, 1967-72, grantee, 1967-78; grantee Russel Sage Found., NSF, U. Tex. Rsch. Inst. Fellow AAAS, APA; mem. Alumni Assn. Roscoe B. Jackson Meml. Lab., Am. Genetic Assn., Psychonomic Soc., Animal Behavior Soc., Southwestern Psychol. Assn., Behavior Genetics Assn., Sigma Xi, Phi Kappa Phi, Psi Chi.

THIGPEN, JAMES TATE, oncologist, educator; b. Columbia, Miss., June 8, 1944; m. Louisa Berdie Kessler, June 14, 1969; children: Monroe Tate, James Howard, Samuel Calvin, Richard Allen, David Albert. BS, U. Miss., 1964, MD, 1969. Cert. Am. Bd. Internal Medicine, Oncology Subspecialty Bd. Am. Bd. Internal Medicine, Hematology Subspecialty Bd. Am. Bd. Internal Medicine. Intern Strong Meml. Hosp., U. Rochester, NYC, 1969-70; resident U. Miss. Sch. Medicine, 1970-71, prof., dir. divsn. med. oncology dept. internal medicine, 1973—. Nat. med. del. from Miss. Am. Cancer Soc., 1983-85, nat. pub. issues com., 1983-85; cancer clin. investigations rev. com. Nat. Cancer Inst., 1990-95, chmn., 1993-95. Nat. bd. govs. ARC, 1981-87. Fellow divsn. hematology/oncology dept. medicine, 1971-73. Fellow ACP; mem. AMA, Miss. Med. Assn., Ctrl. Med. Soc., Jackson Acad. Medicine, Miss. Acad. Scis., SW Oncology Group, Gynecologic Oncology Group (group vice chmn. sci. 1988—), Am. Fedn. Clin. Rsch., Am. Assn. Cancer Edn., Am. Soc. Clin. Oncology, Am. Assn. cancer Rsch., Am. Soc. Hematology, Soc. Gynecologic Oncologists, Soc. Assn. Oncology (pres. 1988-90), Am. Radium Soc., Optimists (internat. v.p. 1983-84, internat. pres. 1990-91). Republican. Baptist. Home: 3601 Kings Hwy Jackson MS 39216-3322 Office: Univ Physicians 2500 N State St Jackson MS 39216-4500 Office Phone: 601-984-5590. Personal E-mail: jtthigpen@att.net.

THIPE-MOKHUANE, ESTHER MARGARET QUEEN, psychologist, educator; b. Johannesburg, Gauteng, South Africa, Apr. 28, 1949; d. Barbara Dikeledi Moeng; m. Patrick Leeto Mokhuane, July 3, 1976; children: Mokhuane Ofentse, Mokhuane Letshego, Mokhuane Obakeng. MA in Psychology, U. Natal, Kwa-Zulu Natal; PhD in Psychology, U. South Africa, Pretoria, Gauteng. Libr. U. Zululand, Kwa-Zulu Natal, South Africa, 1975—77; clin. psychologist Dr. George Mukhari Hosp., Pretoria, 1990—; chief clin. psychologist, prof. head dept. U. Limpopo, Medunsa Campus, Pretoria, 1990—; expert advisor, human rights United Com. Rights Children, Geneva, 1997—2001; pub. health fellow U. Wash., Seattle, 1998. Chairperson Profl. Bd. Psychology, Pretoria, 2005—; sec. Students Representative Coun. U. Zululand. Contbr. chapters to books. Mem. adv. com. Kellogg's Found. Cmty. Partnerships in Health Edn., 1993—95; advisor Medicos Sch., Soshanguve, Gauteng, South Africa, 1984—89; chairperson TSOSOLOTSA, Soshanguve, 1985—88. Grant, Sales House, 1968, Ernest Oppenheimer, 1995. Mem.: Gender Equity Com. (medunsa campus 1998—2004), Lesedi Women's Club (pretoria 1995—97). Roman Catholic. Avocations: gardening, interior decorating, reading, soccer, tennis, travel. Office: University Limpopo Medunsa Campus Box 110 Ga-Rankuwa Gauteng Province 0204 South Africa Home: 18 Dancing Duel Mooikloof Estate 81 Pretoria South Africa Office Fax: 2712 521 4632; Home Fax: 2712 322 5191. Business E-Mail: mokhuane@ul.ac.za. E-mail: tlhoki@worldonline.co.za.

THIRLBY, RICHARD COLLER, surgeon; b. Traverse City, Mich., Aug. 30, 1952; s. Richard Leeson Thirlby; m. Patricia Rosso, July 17, 1976; children: Marjorie Rose, David Ryan. BA, Dartmouth U., Hanover, NH, 1974; MD, U. Mich., Ann Arbor, 1978. Contbr. articles to profl. jours. Mem.: ACS (pres. Wash. State chpt. 2003—04), Am. Bd. Surgery (bd. dirs. 2006—), Western Surg. Assn. (pres. 2005—06). Office: Virginia Mason Med Ctr 1100 9th Ave Mailstop C6-GSUR Seattle WA 98111 *

THIRTHALLI, JAGADISHA, psychiatrist, educator; b. Karkala, Karnataka, Apr. 23, 1971; MD, NIMHANS, 1998. Prof. NIMH & Neuroscis. NIMHANS, 2009—. Recipient Jayaram award, Indian Psychiat. Soc., South Zone, 2006, Bombay Psychiat. Soc. award, Indian Psychiat. Soc., 2007, Best Poster award, Internat. Soc. Bipolar Disorder, 2008, Poona Psychiatrists Associations award, Indian Psychiat. Soc., 2010; Lilly Young Rschr. fellow, Internat. Soc. Bipolar Disorder, 2011. Mem.: Indian Psychiat. Soc. Office: Dept Psychiatry NIMHANS Bangalore Karnataka 560029 India Business E-Mail: jagatth@gmail.com.

THIRY, KENT J., health products executive; BA in Polit. Sci., Stanford U., 1978; MBA with honors, Harvard U., 1983. Sr. cons. Andersen Consulting, 1978-81; ptnr., v.p. Bain & Co., Inc., 1983—91; pres., COO Vivra, Inc., San Francisco, 1991-92, pres., CEO, 1992-97; chmn., CEO Vivra Holdings Inc., 1997—99, Da Vita, Inc., El Segundo, Calif., 1999—. Dir. Oxford Health Plans, 1998—2004, chmn., 2002—04. Bd. dirs. Vol. Ctr. San Mateo County. Mem. Phi Beta Kappa. Office: 601 Hawaii St El Segundo CA 90245-4814 *

THISTED, RONALD AARON, statistician, educator, consultant; b. LA, Mar. 2, 1951; s. Dale Owen and Barbara Jean (Walker) T.; m. Linda Jeane Soder, Dec. 30, 1972; 1 child, Walker. BA, Pomona Coll., 1972; PhD, Stanford U., 1977. Asst. prof. statistics U. Chgo., 1976-82, assoc. prof. statistics, 1982-92, assoc. prof. anesthesia and critical care, 1989-92, prof. stats. and anesthesia and critical care, 1992—, prof. health studies, 1996—, chmn. health studies, 1999—. Co-dir. Clin. Rsch. Training Program, 1999—. Author: Elements of Statistical Computing, 1988; contbr. more than 100 articles to profl. jours. Fellow AAAS, Am. Statis. Assn.; mem. Assn. for Computing Machinery, Inst. for Math. Stats. Office: U Chgo MC 2007 5841 S Maryland Ave Chicago IL 60637-1463 Home Phone: 773-947-9243; Office Phone: 773-834-1242. Business E-Mail: thisted@health.bsd.vchicago.edu.

THODER, JOSEPH, orthopaedic surgeon, educator; BS, Moravian Coll., Bethlehem, Pa., 1977; MD, Temple U., Phila., Pa., 1982. Diplomate Am. Bd. Orthopaedic Surgery, 1990, Am. Bd. Orthopaedic Surgery-hand surgery, 1995. Intern in gen. surgery Episcopal Hosp., Phila., 1983; resident in orthop. surgery Temple Univ. hosp., Phila., 1987; fellow hand and microsurgery Thomas Jefferson Univ. Hosp., Phila., 1988; John W. Lachman prof. Temple Univ.; chairperson orthop. surgery and sport medicine depts. Temple Univ. Hosp. Co-author: (med. publs.) Scaphoid fractures: dorsal versus volar approach, 2002, Upper extremity compartment syndrome secondary to acquired factor VIII inhibitor, 2005, "De quervain tenosynovitis of the wrist", Am. Acad. Orthop. Surgeon, 2007, CMC arthroplasty of the thumb, 2007, "Interposition arthroplasty options for carpometacarpal arthritis of the thumb", Hand Clinic, 2010, numerous other med. publs. Named one of the Top Doctors, Phila. Mag., 2011. Office: Temple University Hospital Outpatient Bldg 6th Fl 3401 N Broad St Philadelphia PA 19140 Office Phone: 215-707-8331. Office Fax: 215-707-2324. E-mail: joseph.thoder@temple.edu.

THOENEN, HANS, neuroscience researcher; b. 1928; MD, U. Bern; PhD in Pharmacology, U. Basel; MD (hon.), U. Zurich, Switzerland, 1992, U. Würzburg, Germany, 1997. Rsch. group leader biocenter U. Basel, 1972-78; with dept. exptl. medicine F. Hoffmann-LaRoche & Co. AG, Basel, 1962-68, 69-71; with lab. clin. scis. section on pharmacology Nat. Insts. Mental Health, Bethesda, Md., 1968-69; prof., head dept. neurochemistry Max-Planck Inst. für Psychiatrie, 1979-96, dir. emeritus, 1996. Hon. prof. U. Munich, 1981. Author of books; contbr. chpts. to books, articles to profl. jours.; mem. editl. bd. EMBO Jour., Neuron, Jour. Neurochemistry, Current Opinion Cell Biology, Neurosci. Rsch., Jour. Neurosci. Co-recipient Charles A. Dana award for pioneering achievements in health Inst. of Medicine/NAS, 1994; recipient Ralph W. Gerard prize in neurosci. for outstanding contbn. to field of neurosci., 1995, Cloetta prize U. Zurich, 1985, Wakeman award Duke U., Durham, 1988, Ipsen prize for Neuronalplasticity, 1994Bristol-Myers Squibb award, 1997, Gold medal Ernst Jung, 2007. Fellow AAAS; mem. Deutsche Akademie der Naturforscher Leopoldina, European Molecular Biology Orgn., Academia Europea, Nat. Acad. Sci. (assoc.), Swiss Acad. Med. Scis. (corr.). Office: Max Planck Inst Neurobio Am Klopferspitz 18 D-82152 Martinsried Germany

THOKCHOM, NANDAKISHORE SINGH, dermatologist, consultant; b. Imphal, Manipur, India, Mar. 1, 1961; s. Tolamu and Ahanbi Devi Thokchom; m. Bimola Devi Chingsubam, Mar. 6, 1995; children: Daniel, Nelson. MB, BChir, Regional Inst. Med. Scis., Imphal, India, 1983; MD, All India Institute Med. Scis., New Delhi, 1992. Cert. dermatologist AIIMS, 1992. Jr. dermatologist Directorate Health Svcs., Govt. Manipur, Imphal, 1993—2000; sr. resident dept. dermatology Regional Inst. Med. Scis., Imphal, 2000—05, asst. prof. dept. dermatology, 2005—. Cons. dermatologist Regional Inst. Med. Scis., Imphal, 2005—. Recipient Dr. KC Kandhari award for Best Resident in Dermatology, All India Inst. Med. Scis., Imphal, 1992. Mem.: Indian Med. Assn. (life), Cosmetology Soc. India (life), Indian Assn. Dermatologists, Venereologists and Leprologists (life). Achievements include research in dermatogical diseases. Home: Lamphel Imphal Manipur 795004 India Office: Regional Institute Medical Sciences Lamphel Imphal Manipur 795004 India Office Fax: 03852414625. Personal E-mail: nandathokchom@yahoo.com. Business E-Mail: rimsmanipur@yahoo.com.

THOMAN, MARK EDWARD, pediatrician, medical toxicologist; b. Chgo., Feb. 15, 1936; s. John Charles and Tasula Mark (Petrakis) T.; m. Theresa Thompson, 1984; children: Marlisa Rae, Susan Kay, Edward Kim, Nancy Lynn, Janet Lea, David Mark. AA, Graceland Coll., 1956; BA, U. Mo., 1958, MD, 1962. Diplomate Am. Bd. Pediat., 1967, Am. Coll. Toxicology, 1975. Intern U. Mo. at Columbia, 1962—63; resident in pediat. Blank Meml. Children's Hosp., Des Moines, 1963—65; cons. in toxicology USPHS, Washington, 1965—66; chief dept. pediat. Shiprock (N.Mex.) Navajo Indian Hosp., 1966—67; dir. N.D. Poison Info. Ctr.; also practice medicine specializing in pediat. Quain & Ramstad Clinic, Bismarck, ND, 1967—69; dir. Iowa Poison Info. Ctr., Des Moines, 1969—99; mem. pediat. exec. com. Broadlawns Med. Ctr., Des Moines, 1969—2000, pres. med. staff, 2000—02. Accident investigator FAA, 1976—2005, sr. aviation examiner, 1977—2000; lectr. aviation seminars, 1977—2007; mem. faculty Des Moines U., 1969—2005, dir. cystic fibrosis clin., 1973—82; dir. Mid-Iowa Drug Abuse Program, 1972—76; mem. med. adv. bd. La Leche League Internat., 1965—; chief med. officer Broadlawns Med. Ctr., Des Moines, 2000—02; sci. rev. panel Nat. Libr. Medicine, 2003—; med. cons., med. exam. Social Security Adminstrn., Office Disability Adjudication and Review, 2001—; cons. in field. Editor-in-chief AACTION, 1975-90; monthly columnist Aviation Medicine Twin and Turbine Mag., 2005-06. Bd. dirs. Polk County Pub. Health Nurses Assn., 1969-77, Des Moines Speech and Hearing Ctr., 1974-79, Ecumenical Coun. Iowa, 1990-99; bd. govs. Mo. U. Sch. Medicine Alumni, 1988-, pres. bd. govs.; pres. parish coun. Greek Orthodox Ch., 2007-09. With USMCR, 1954-59; lt. comdr. USPHS, 1965-67; capt. USNR, 1988-96, ret. 1996; dir. Dept. Health Svcs. USNR. Recipient N.D. Gov.'s award of merit, 1969, Cystic Fibrosis Rsch. Found. award, 1982, Am. Psychiat. Assn. Thesis award, 1962. Fellow Am. Coll. Med. Toxicology (diplomate 1996), Am. Acad. Clin. Toxicology (trustee 1969-90, pres. 1982-84); mem. AMA (del. 1970-88), APHA, NRA (life), Assn. Am. Physicians & Surgeons (chief of staff, pres. Broadlawns Polk County Med. Ctr. 2000-02), Polk County Med. Soc., Iowa State Med. Assn., Aerospace Med. Assn., Res. Officers Assn., Civil Aviation Med. Assn., Soc. Adolescent Medicine, Inst. Clin. Toxicology, Internat. Soc. Pediat., Am. Acad. Pediat. (chmn. accident prevention com. Iowa chpt. 1975-2000), Cystic Fibrosis Club, Am. Assn. Poison Control Ctrs., Am. Coll. Physician Execs., U.S. Naval Inst., Flying Physicians Club, Aircraft Owners and Pilots Assn, Nat. Pilots Assn. (Safe Pilot award), Aerospace Med. Assn. Republican. Greek Orthodox. Home: 5355 Crane Ave E Port Orchard WA 98366 Office Phone: 360-871-2219. Office Fax: 360-871-4436. Personal E-mail: paro1795@aol.com.

THOMAS, CHERYLL C., epidemiologist, federal agency administrator; BS in Biochemistry, UCLA, 1995; MPH, Emory U., Atlanta, 1999. Staff rsch. assoc. UCLA Med. Ctr., 1995—97; epidemiologist American Cancer Soc., 1999—2004; epidemiologist, divsn. cancer prevention & control US Centers Disease Control & Prevention, Atlanta, 2004—. Contbr. articles to profl. jours. Office: Centers Disease Control & Prevention 1600 Clifton Rd Atlanta GA 30333 Business E-Mail: zzg3@cdc.gov. *

THOMAS, CHRISTOPHER YANCEY, III, surgeon, educator; b. Kansas City, Mo., Oct. 27, 1923; s. Christopher Yancey and Dorothea Louise (Engel) Thomas; m. Barbara Ann Barcroft, June 27, 1946 (dec. Aug. 19, 2001); children: Christopher, Gregg, Jeffrey, Anne; m. Carol Joan Reynolds, Aug. 9, 2008. Student, U. Colo., 1942-44; MD, U. Kans., 1948. Diplomate Am. Bd. Surgery. Intern U. Utah Hosp., Salt Lake City, 1948-49; resident in surgery Cleve. Clinic Found., 1949-52; pvt. practice specializing in surgery Kansas City, Mo., 1954-89. Mem. staff St. Luke's Hosp., chief surgery, 1969-70; mem. staff Children's Mercy Hosp.; clin. prof. surgery U. Mo., Kansas City Med. Sch.; pres. St. Luke's Hosp. Edn. Found., 1977-83, Med. Plaza Corp., 1977-79; pres. Midwest Organ Bank, 1977-82. Editor IMTRAC investment adv. letter, 1978-2000. Served to capt. M.C., U.S. Army, 1952-54 Fellow ACS; mem. AMA, Southwestern Surg. Congress, Central Surg. Assn., Mo. State Med. Soc., Kansas City Surg. Soc. (pres. 1968), Jackson County Med. Soc. (pres. 1971) Clubs: Kansas City Country. Republican. Methodist. Home: 50 Coventry Ct Shawnee Mission KS 66208-5225 Personal E-mail: christhomas5452@sbcglobal.net.

THOMAS, CLAUDEWELL SIDNEY, psychiatrist, educator; b. NYC, Oct. 5, 1932; s. Humphrey Sidney and Frances Elizabeth (Collins) T.; m. Carolyn Pauline Rozansky, Sept. 6, 1958; children:

Jeffrey Evan, Julie-Anne Elizabeth, Jessica Edith (dec.). BA, Columbia U., 1952; MD, SUNY, Downstate Med. Ctr., 1956; MPH, Yale U., 1964. Diplomate Nat. Bd. Med. Examiners, Am. Bd. Psychiatry. From instr. to assoc. prof. Yale U., New Haven, 1963—70, dir. Yale tng. program in social community psychiatry, 1967-70; dir. div. mental health service programs NIMH, Washington, 1970-73; chmn. dept. psychiatry UMDNJ, Newark, 1973-83, vis. prof. psychiatry, 1983—; prof., chmn. dept. psychiatry Drew Med. Sch., 1983—93, chmn. dept. psychiatry, 1983-93; prof. dept. psychiatry UCLA, 1983-94, vice chmn. dept. psychiatry, 1983-93, prof. emeritus dept. psychiatry, 1994—; med. dir. Tokanui Hosp., TeAwamutu, N.Z., 1996. Cons. A.K. Rice Inst., Washington, 1978—80, SAMSA/PHS Cons., 1991—99; mem. LA County Superior Ct. Psychol. Panel, 1991—97; cons. psychiatrist L.A. County AB2034 Homeless Outreach Program (Skid Row Dual Diagnoses), 2001—04. Author: (with B. Bergen) Issues and Problems in Social Psychiatry, 1966, Your Personal Pouniip, 2010; editor (with R. Bryce LaPorte) Alienation in Contemporary Society, 1976, Your Peronal Power up, 2010, (with J. Lindenthal) Psychiatry and Mental Health Science Handbook, (with B. Fulleon), 2010; mem. editl. bd. Adminstrn. Mental Health, 2002-2009. Bd. dirs. Bay Area Found., 1987—; adv. bd. mem. Strokeshield Found. Served to capt. USAF, 1959-61. Fellow APHA, Am. Assn. Psychoanalytic Physicians (hon.), Am. Psychiat. Assn. (disting. life), NY Acad. Sci., NY Acad. Medicine; mem. Am. Sociol. Assn., Am. Coll. Mental Health Adminstrs., Am. Coll. Psychiatrists (emeritus), Sigma Xi. Avocations: tennis, racquetball, violin, piano. Office: 30676 Palos Verdes Dr E Palos Verdes Peninsula CA 90275-6354 Personal E-mail: cysid32@ucla.edu, cst240@columbia.edu.

THOMAS, COLIN GORDON, JR., surgeon, medical educator; b. Iowa City, July 25, 1918; s. Colin Goudenz and Eloise Kinzer (Brainerd) T.; m. Shirley Forbes, Sept. 14, 1946 (dec.); children: Karen, Barbara, James G., John F. BS, U. Chgo., 1940, MD, 1943. Diplomate Am. Bd. Surgery. Intern U. Iowa Hosp., 1943-44, resident surgery, 1944-45, 47-50; assoc. in surgery U. Iowa Med. Sch., 1950-51, asst. prof., 1951-52; mem. faculty U. N.C. Med. Sch., Chapel Hill, 1952—, prof. surgery, 1961—, Byah Thomason Doxey-Sanford Doxey prof. surgery, 1982—, chmn. dept., 1966-84, chief div. gen. surg., 1984-89, part-time prof., 1991—. Contbr. surg. texts, numerous articles to med. jours. Served to capt., M.C. AUS, 1945-47. Recipient Prof. award U. N.C. Sch. Medicine, 1964, Disting. Svc. award U. Chgo., 1982, Med. Alumni Disting. faculty award U. N.C., 1984; Berryhill lectr. U. N.C., 1989; recipient Fleming Fuller award U. N.C. Hosps., 1994, Disting. Alumnus award, Shattuck, St. Marys Sch., Minnesota, 2011. Mem. AMA, ACS (Disting. Leadership award N.C. chpt. 1990), AAUP, Am. Thyroid Assn., Am. Assn. Cancer Research, Am. Assn. Endocrine Surgeons (pres. 1989-90), Soc. Univ. Surgeons, So. Surg. Assn. (v.p. 1989-90), N.Y. Acad. Scis., Halsted Soc., Am. Surg. Assn., Womack Surg. Soc. (pres. 1981-83), Soc. Internationale de Chirurgie, Soc. Surgery Alimentary Tract, N.C. Surg. Assn., Internat. Assn. Endocrine Surgeons, Kiwanis (pres. Tarheel Golden Kiwanis 2004), Alpha Omega Alpha. Episcopalian (warden 1961-62). Home: 621 Cedars Club Cir Chapel Hill NC 27517 Office: Univ NC Chapel Hill 4005 Burnett-Womack CB 7228 Chapel Hill NC 27599-7228 Business E-Mail: cgt@med.unc.edu. *

THOMAS, DAVID LAMARR, surgeon, educator; b. Phila., Oct. 13, 1945; MD, U. Miami Sch. Medicine, 1970; JD, Stetson U. Coll. Law, 1995. Dep. sec., dir. health svcs., Fla., 1994—2003; prof., chair dept. surgery, divsn. correctional medicine Nova Southeastern U., 2003—, prof. pub. health. Mem. fla. ho. reps. Fla. Legislature, 1984—94; bd. govs. exec. com. Am. Correctional Assn., 2005. Recipient Better Life award, Fla. Health Care Assn., 1985, Disting. Svc. award, Am. Correctional Health Care Assn., 2002, Spl. Achievement award, Fla. Soc. Ophthalmology, award, Fla. Juvenile Justice Blueprint Commn., Outstanding Legislative Efforts award, Am. Lung Assn. Fellow: Am. Coll. Ophthalmology. Avocation: boating. Office: 3200 S University Dr Ste 1443 Fort Lauderdale FL 33328 Office Fax: 954-262-3271. Business E-Mail: davithom@nova.edu.

THOMAS, DAVID LLEWELLYN, physician; b. Clinton, Iowa, June 11, 1948; s. Marvin Llewellyn and Marjorie Emma (Mayer) Thomas; m. Sheryl L. Miller, 2002; children: Tana, Paige, Drew, Aleksandr. BA in Zoology, U. Iowa, 1970, MD, 1974. Diplomate Am. Bd. Family Practice, cert. added qualification in geriatric medicine. Resident in family medicine U. Ill., Rockford, 1977; pvt. practice Marshalltown, Iowa, 1977—; family physician McFarland Clinic, PC, Marshalltown, 1994, also bd. dirs., v.p., 1995—98, treas., 1999—. Clin. lectr. U. Iowa Coll. Medicine, Iowa City, 1981—2007, adj. clin. asst. prof., 2007—; med. dir. Iowa Found. Med. Ctr., 1992—. Bd. dirs. Iowa Found. Med. Care, Des Moines, 1986—2001, Iowa Ctrl. Agrl. Safety and Health, 1995—97, v.p., 2011—; trustee Marshalltown Med. and Surg. Ctr., 1998—2003. Mem.: Am. Health Quality Assn. (bd. dirs. 1995—2005, v.p. 1997—2000, pres. 2000—03). Republican. Episcopalian. Office: McFarland Clinic 303 Nicholas Dr Ste 1 Marshalltown IA 50158-4443 Office Phone: 641-752-0099. Business E-Mail: dthomas@mcfarlandclinic.com.

THOMAS, EDWARD DONNALL, hematologist; b. Mart, Tex., Mar. 15, 1920; m. Dorothy Martin; 3 children. BA, U. Tex., Austin, 1941, MA, 1943; MD, Harvard Med. Sch., Boston, 1946; MD, MD, U. Warsaw, Poland, 1996. Diplomate Am. Bd. Internal Medicine, lic. Mass., NY, Wash. Intern in medicine Peter Bent Brigham Hosp., Boston, 1946—47, rsch. fellow hematology, 1947—48, chief med. resident, sr. asst. resident, 1951—53, hematologist, 1953—55; NRC postdoc. fellow in medicine MIT, 1950—51; instr. medicine Harvard Med. Sch., Boston, 1953—55; assoc. clin. prof. medicine Columbia U. Coll. Physicians & Surgeons, NYC, 1955—63; prof. medicine U. Wash. Sch. Medicine, Seattle, 1963—90, head divsn. oncology, 1963—85, prof. emeritus, 1990—; dir. med. oncology Fred Hutchinson Cancer Rsch. Ctr., Seattle, 1974—89, assoc. dir. clin. rsch. programs, 1982—89, dir. emeritus clin. rsch. divsn., 1990—. Rsch. assoc. Cancer Rsch. Found., Children's Med. Ctr, Boston, 1953—55; physician-in-chief Mary Imogene Bassett Hosp., Cooperstown, NY, 1955—63; attending physician U. Wash. Hosp., Harborview Med. Ctr. & VA Hosp., Seattle, 1963—90, Providence Med. Ctr., Seattle, 1973—90; mem. hematology study sect. NIH, 1965—69; mem. med. sci. adv. com., bd. trustees Leukemia Soc. America, Inc., 1969—73; mem. clin. cancer investigation rev. com. Nat. Cancer Inst., 1970—74. Mem. editl. bd. Blood, 1962—75, 1977—82, Transplantation, 1970—76, Procs. Soc. Exptl. Biology & Medicine, 1974—81, Leukemia Rsch., 1977—87, Hematological Oncology, 1982—87, Jour. Clin. Immunology, 1982—87, Am. Jour. Hematology, 1985—, Bone Marrow Transplantation, 1986—; contbr. articles to profl. jours. With US Army, 1948—50. Recipient A. Ross McIntyre award, U. Nebr. Med. Ctr., 1975, Philip Levine award, Am. Soc. Clin. Pathologists, 1979, Disting. Svc. award, Am. Cancer Soc., 1980, Kettering prize, GM Cancer Rsch. Found., 1981, Spl. Keynote Address award, Am. Soc. Therapeutic Radiologists, 1981, Robert Roesler de Villiers award, Leukemia Soc. America, 1983, Karl Landsteiner Meml. award, Am. Assn. Blood Banks, 1987, Terry Fox award, Can., 1990, Gairdner Found. Internat. award, 1990, Hong Kong prize, N.Am. Med. Assn., 1990, Nobel prize in physiology/medicine, 1990, Nat. Medal Sci., 1990, Lifetime Achievement award, Am. Soc. Blood & Marrow Transplantation, 2004. Mem.: NAS, Transplantation Soc., Soc. Exptl. Biology & Medicine, Western Assn. Physicians, Swiss Soc. Hematology, Internat. Soc. Hematology, Internat. Soc. Exptl. Hematology, Am. Soc. Hematology (pres. 1987—88, Henry M. Stratton lectr. 1975), Am. Soc. Clin. Investigation, Am. Soc. Clin. Oncology (David A. Karnoksky Meml. lectr. 1983), Am. Fedn. Clin. Rsch., Assn. Am. Physicians (Kober medal 1992), Am. Assn. Cancer Rsch., Royal Acad. Medicine Belgium (corr.), Nat. Acad. Medicine Mex. (hon.), Royal Coll. Physicians & Surgeons Can. (hon.), Swedish Soc. Hematology (hon.). Office: Fred Hutchinson Cancer Ctr 1100 Fairview Ave N D5-100 PO Box 19024 Seattle WA 98109-1024 *

THOMAS, GARY, pain medicine physician; MD, Mt. Sinai Sch., 1991. Diplomate Am. Bd. Anesthesiology, Am. Bd Pain Medicine. Resident anesthesiology Mt. Sinai Med. Ctr., NY, 1992—95, fellow pain medicine, 1992—95; physician NY Meth. Hosp. Office: Comprehensive Pain Management 10 Union Square E Ste 4K New York NY 10003

THOMAS, HERBERT CUSHING, JR., physician, educator; b. Charlotte, NC, Oct. 6, 1941; s. Herbert Cushing and Doris (Roberts) T.; m. Laureen Thompson, June 9, 1961 (div. 1983); children: Steven, Michael; m. Catherine Anne Campbell, Feb. 11, 1989. BA, U. Colo., 1963, MD, 1967; MS, U. Wash., 1976. Resident in surgery Swedish Hosp., Med. Ctr., Seattle, 1972-73; resident in otolaryngology U. Wash., Seattle, 1973-77; fellowship in otology Ear Rsch. Inst., LA, 1977-78; pvt. practice Seattle, 1978—2007. Attending physician Seattle Children's Hosp. and Med. Ctr., Seattle, 1985—, pres. med. staff, 1991-92; pres. Surg. Specialists, Inc., Seattle, 1988-90; dir. Pacific Northwest Otolaryngology, 1978-2007. Capt. USN, 1963-86, USNR, ret. Mem. AMA, Am. Acad. Otolaryngology, Wash. State Med. Soc., King County Med. Soc., Seattle Surg. Soc., N.W. Acad. Otolaryngology, Old Antarctic Explorers Assoc. Avocations: travel, skiing, wine collecting, food and wine, photography. Office: 4800 Sand Point Way NE Seattle WA 98105 Office Phone: 206-987-2105. Personal E-mail: hct392@aol.com.

THOMAS, HUW FRANCIS, dean, dental educator; BDS, U. London, Guy's Hosp., 1975; MS in Dental Rsch., U. Rochester, 1978; PhD in Biomedical Sci., U. Conn., 1986. Cert. pediatric dentistry Eastman Dental Ctr., U. Rochester, 1978. Postdoctoral fellow. NIH, 1980—84; asst. prof. pediatric dentistry U. Tex. Health Sci. Ctr., San Antonio, 1978—80; assoc. prof. pediatric dentistry dept. U. Conn. Health Ctr., Conn., 1980—92; prof., chmn. dept. pediatric dentistry U. Tex. Health Sci. Ctr., San Antonio, 1992—2003, prof. dept. pediat. & cellular and structural biology, prof., dean Sch. Dentistry, U. Ala., Birmingham, 2004—. Sci. cons. ADA Commn. on Dental Accreditation. Reviewer: American Journal of Anatomy, Archives of Oral Biology, Journal of Dental Education. Recipient New Investigator Research award, NIH, 1985. Fellow: Internat. Coll. Dentists, Am. Coll. Dentists, Am. Acad. Pediat. Dentistry; mem.: AAAS (mem. at large sec. on dentistry and oral health sci.), Am. Assn. Dental Rsch. (mem. nominating com.), Am. Acad. Pediat. (mem. exec. com. pediat. dentistry sect.), Omicron Kappa Upsilon. Office: U Ala Birmingham Sch Dentistry SDB 406 1530 3rd Ave S Birmingham AL 35294-0007 Office Phone: 205-934-4720. Office Fax: 205-975-6544. Business E-Mail: hft@uab.edu.

THOMAS, J. GROVER, JR., insurance company executive; b. Kingman, Ariz. m. Cathy Thomas; 3 children. B, Briar Cliff U., Sioux City, Iowa; MBA, Ga. State U., Atlanta, 1985. Career ins. industry profl.; former v.p. American Fin. Co.; chmn. Fortis Health, 1982—2000, Assurant Health, 1995—2000, Trustmark Mutual Holding Co., 2000—, Crioestaminal-Saúde e Tecnologia SA, Cantanhede, Portugal, 2009—. Bd. dirs. America's Health Ins. Plans, US Health Group. Former pres. Ga. State U. Alumni Assn.; trustee Ga. state U. Found., Actuarial Found.; chmn. Freedom from Hunger, 2002—. Recipient Disting. Alumni Achievement award, Ga. State U. Office: Trustmark Companies 400 Field Dr Lake Forest IL 60045 Office Phone: 847-615-1500. Office Fax: 847-615-3910. *

THOMAS, J. REGAN, plastic surgeon, educator; B, Drury U., Springfield, Mo., 1968; MD, U. Mo. Sch. Medicine. Cert. Am. Bd. Facial Plastic/Reconstructive Surgery, Am. Bd. Otolaryngology. Intern Yale U. Med. Ctr.; residency in otolaryngology, head & neck surgery U. Missouri Sch. of Medicine, fellowship in facial plastic and reconstructive surgery; Francis Lederer prof. and dept. head, otolaryngology, head & neck surgery U. Ill. Med. Ctr., Chicago, 2004—; plastic surgeon Facial Plastic Surgery Ctr., 2004—. Fomer pres. Am. Bd. Facial Plastic/Reconstructive Surgery, Am. Acad. Facial Plastic and Reconstructive Surgery; mem. bd. dirs. Am. Acad. Otolaryngology-Head & Neck Surgery. Mem. editl. bd.: Archive Facial Plastic Surgery; editor: Facial Plastic Surgery Clinics; contbr. more than 100 articles to profl. jours. Recipient Schoenrock award, Am. Bd. Facial Plastic/Reconstructive Surgery, William Wright award, Am. Acad. Facial Plastic and Reconstructive Surgery, John Dickinson Teacher of Yr. award, Disting. Alumni award, Drury U., 1993; named one of Best Doctors in America. Office: Facial Plastic Surgery Ctr 60 E Delaware Pl Chicago IL 60611 also: U Ill Med Ctr Eye and Ear Inst 1855 W Taylor St 3d Fl Chicago IL 60612

THOMAS, JOAB LANGSTON, retired academic administrator, biologist, educator; b. Holt, Ala., Feb. 14, 1933; s. Ralph Cage and Chamintney Elizabeth (Stovall) Thomas; m. Marly A. Dukes, Dec. 22, 1954; children: Catherine, David, Jennifer, Frances. AB, Harvard U., 1955, MA, 1957, PhD, 1959; DSc (hon.), U. Ala., 1981; LLD (hon.), Stillman Coll., 1987; LHD (hon.), Tri-State U., 1994; LHD (hon.), N.C. State U., 1998. Cytotaxonomist Arnold Aboretum, Harvard, 1959—61; prof. biology U. Ala., University, 1966—76, 1988—91, asst. dean Coll. Arts and Scis., 1964—65, 1969, dean for student devel., 1969—74, v.p., 1974—76, dir. Herbarium, 1961—76, dir. Arboretum, 1964—69, pres. Tuscaloosa, 1981—88; chancellor N.C. State U., Raleigh, 1976—81; pres. Pa. State U., University Park, 1990—95, pres. emeritus, 1995. Intern acad. adminstrn. Am. Coun. on Edn., 1971. Author: A Monographic Study of the Cyrillaceae, 1960, Wildflowers of Alabama and Adjoining States, 1973, The Rising South, 1976, Poisonous Plants and Venomous Animals of Alabama and Adjoining States, 1990. Bd. dirs. Internat. Potato Ctr., 1977—83, chmn., 1982—83; bd. dirs. Internat. Svc. for Nat. Agrl. Rsch., 1985—91. Recipient Ala. Acad. Honor, 1983, Palmer Mus. Art medal, Coll. Pres.'s award, All-Am. Football Found., 1997, Spl. Recognition award, Assn. for Continuing Higher Edn., 1998; named Citizen of Yr., City of Tuscaloosa, 1987. Mem.: Golden Key, Phi Kappa Phi, Omicron Delta Kappa (Laurel Crowned Circle award 2001), Sigma Xi, Phi Beta Kappa. Office: Univ Ala 413 Sci Collections Bldg Tuscaloosa AL 35487-0001 Home Phone: 205-554-7875; Office Phone: 205-348-1850. Business E-Mail: jlthomas@dbtech.net.

THOMAS, JOHN ARLEN, pharmacologist, educator, science administrator; b. LaCrosse, Wis., Apr. 6, 1933; s. John M. and Eva Hazel (Nelson) T.; m. Barbara A. Fisler, June 22, 1957; children: Michael J., Jane L. BS in Sci. Edn., U. Wis., 1956; MA in Physiology, U. Iowa, 1958, PhD in Physiology, 1961. Diplomate Am. Acad. Toxicologic Sci. Instr. U. Iowa, Iowa City, 1961; asst. prof. U. Va., Charlottesville, 1961-64; assoc. prof. Creighton U., Omaha, 1964-67, W.Va. U., Morgantown, 1968-69, prof. pharmacology, 1970-80; asst. dean W.Va. Sch. Medicine, Morgantown, 1973-75, assoc. dean, 1973-80; v.p. corp. rsch. Baxter Internat. Travenol Labs., Round Lake, Ill., 1980-87; v.p. acad. svcs. U. Tex. Health Sci. Ctr., San Antonio, 1988-99, prof. emeritus pharmacology dept. toxicology, 1988—; prof. Ind. U. Sch. Medicine, 2005—. Chmn. expert adv. com. Can. Network Toxicol. Ctr., 1999-02; sci. adv. bd. USAF, 2002-05, FDA, 2003—08; adj. prof. pharmacology Ind. U. Sch. Medicine, Indpls., 2005; cons. to NIH, Inst. of Medicine, NRC, NAS. Author (with M.G. Mawhinney): Synopsis of Endocrine Pharmacology, 1978; author: (with E.J. Keenan) Principles of Endocrine Pharmacology, 1986; editor (with others): Basic and Clinical Toxicology of Lead, 1985; editor: Endocrine Toxicology, 1985, 1996, Drugs Athletes & Physical Performance, 1988, Biotechnology and Safety Assessment, 1993; editor: (with Laurie A. Myers) Biotechnology and Safety Assessment 2d edit., 1981; editor: (with Roy L. Fuchs) Biotechnology and Safety Assessment, 3d edit., 2002; editor: Endocrine Methods, 1996, Toxic Substances Mechanism Jour., contbr. articles to profl. jours. Sgt. U.S. Army, 1951-53. Recipient Cert. Svc. US EPA, 1977, Commn. Spl. citation FDA, 2006, Advis Commn. Svc. award FDA, 2007; named Outstanding Tchr., W.Va. U., 1971, 73, 79, Outstanding alumnus U. Wis., La Crosse, 1978, Disting. Alumni, U. Iowa, 1997, Adv. Com. Svc. award FDA, 2007; named to Hall of Excellence-LaCrosse, 2002. Fellow Acad. Toxicol. Sci. (pres. 2001); mem. Endocrine Soc., Soc. Toxicology (councilor, Merit award 1998), Am. Soc. Pharmacology and Exptl. Therapeutics, Am. Coll. Toxicology (councilor, pres., disting. fellow 2004, Disting. Svc. award), Teratology Soc., Am. Acad. Vet. Pharmacology, Am. Chem. Soc. (pres. chem. toxicology pathology), Tex. Soc. Biomed. Rsch. (bd. sci. advisors 1989-99, Disting. Svc. award 1996), Russian Acad. Med. Sci. (fgn. fellow-elect 1995). Home and Office: 7258 Pymbroke Cir Fishers IN 46038 Office Phone: 317-845-5224. Personal E-mail: jat-tox@sbcglobal.net.

THOMAS, JOSEPH, medical educator; b. 1956; BS in Pharmacy, U. La. at Monroe (formerly NE La. U.), 1978; PhD, Purdue U. Prof. Purdue U., 2002—. Academic Leadership fellow, Com. on Instl. Coop. Fellow: Am. Pharmacists Assn.; mem.: Internat. Soc. Outcomes Rsch. and Policy. Avocations: fishing, gardening. Office: Robert Heine Pharmacy Bldg 575 Stadium Mall Dr West Lafayette IN 47907-2091 Business E-Mail: jt3@purdue.edu.

THOMAS, KIMBERLY L., lawyer; b. Grand Rapids, Mich., July 8, 1973; d. Rob and Cheryl Thomas. BA, U. Mich., 1995; JD magna cum laude, Notre Dame U., South Bend, Ind., 1998. Bar: Mich. 1998. Assoc. Warner Norcross & Judd, Grand Rapids, 1995—2003; founding mem. Barnes & Thornburg LLP, Grand Rapids, assoc., 2003—07, mng. ptnr., 2008—10; gen. counsel Priority Health, 2010—. Mem. cert. com. Womens Bus. Enterprise; bd. dirs. Girl Scouts Mich. Trails, Grand Rapids, 2002—, Girls on the Run. Named one of 40 Bus. Leaders Under 40, Grand Rapids Bus. Journal, Grand Rapids Bus. Review. Mem.: Alliance Women Entrepreneurs (bd. dirs. 2003—06), Assn. Corp. Growth (mem. membership com. 2006—), Gilda's Club (bd. dirs. 2002—). Office: Priority Health MS 1260 1231 E Beltline NE Grand Rapids MI 49525 *

THOMAS, LINDSEY KAY, JR., research ecology biologist, educator, consultant; b. Salt Lake City, Apr. 16, 1931; s. Lindsey Kay and Naomi Lurie (Biesinger) T.; m. Nancy Ruth Van Dyke, Aug. 24, 1956; children: Elizabeth Nan Thomas Cardinale, David Lindsey, Wayne Hal, Dorothy Ann Thomas Brown. BS, Utah State Agrl. Coll., Logan, 1953; MS, Brigham Young U., Provo, Utah, 1958; PhD, Duke U., Durham, NC, 1974; grad, Utah State U. Park naturalist Nat. Capital Pks., Nat. Pk. Svc., Washington, 1957—62, pk. naturalist (rschr.) Region 6, 1962—63, rsch. pk. naturalist Nat. Capital Region, 1963—66; rsch. biologist S.E. Temperate Forest Pk. Areas, Washington, 1966, Durham, NC, 1966—67, Great Falls, Md., 1967—71, Nat. Capital Pks., Great Falls, 1971—74, Nat. Capital Region, Triangle, Va., 1974—93, Washington, 1985—93; rsch. biologist, Patuxent Environ. Sci. Ctr. Nat. Biol. Survey, 1993—94, Nat. Biol. Svc., Washington, Triangle, 1994—96; resource mgmt. specialist Balt.-Washington Pkwy., Greenbelt, Md., 1996, Nat. Capital Parks-East, 1996—98; rsch. ecologist emeritus and cons. Nat. Capital Region, Nat. Park Svc., 1998—. Bd. dirs. Prince William County Svc. Authority, Va., 1996-2004; adj. prof. George Mason U., Fairfax, Va., 1988—, George Washington U., Washington, 1992-98; instr. US Dept. Agr. Grad. Sch., 1964-66; aquatic ecol. cons. Fairfax County Fedn. Citizens Assns., Va., 1970-71; guest lectr. Washington Tech. Inst. (now U. DC), 1976. Contbr. articles to profl. jours. Wildlife mgmt.

cons. Girl Scouts Am., Loudoun County, Va., 1958; preservation and mgmt. cons. McAteean Magnolia Bogs, Save Araby, Mattawoman and Mason Springs in Charles County, Md., 2002-06, Nat. Resources Divsn., Arlington County, Va., 2004—; asst. scoutmaster, scoutmaster, merit badges counselor Boy Scouts Am., 1958—, Scouters Tng. award, 1961. Recipient Incentive awards Nat. Park Svc., 1962, Superior Performance award, 1989; rsch. grantee Washington Biologists' Field Club, 1977, 82. Mem.: AAAS, Md. Native Plant Soc., Nat. Trust for Historic Preservation, Washington Biologists' Field Club, So. Appalachian Bot. Soc., Soc. for Early Hist. Archaeology, The Nature Conservancy, George Wright Soc., Ecol. Soc. Am., Bot. Soc. Washington, Sigma Xi. Mem. Lds Ch. Home: 13854 Delaney Rd Woodbridge VA 22193-4654 Office: Prince William Forest Park 18100 Park Hdqrs Rd Triangle VA 22172

THOMAS, NANCY J., pathologist; b. Chgo., Dec. 4, 1948; BS, U. Calif., Berkeley, 1972; DVM, U. Calif., Davis, 1978; MS, U. Idaho, 1984. Diplomate Am. Coll. Vet. Pathologists, 1985. Endangered species specialist USGS, Nat. Wildlife Health Ctr., 1984—. Mem.: North Am. Crane Working Group, Am. Assn. Vet. Lab. Diagnosticians., Wildlife Disease Assn., Phi Zeta Vet., Phi Beta Kappa. Office: 6006 Schroeder Rd Madison WI 53711 Office Fax: 608-270-2415. Business E-Mail: nthomas@usgs.gov.

THOMAS, PATRICK ROBERT MAXWELL, oncologist, educator, academic administrator; b. Exmouth, Devon, Eng., Feb. 23, 1943; came to U.S., 1976; s. Christopher Codrington and Aileen Daphne (Gordon) T.; m. Linda Sharon Rich, June 23, 1986 (dec. 1987), m. Geraldine M. Jacobson, Mar. 2, 1996 (div. 1999); m. Frances Aquino, Feb. 19, 2005. Diploma in biochemistry, London U., 1965, MB, BS, 1968. Lectr. Inst. Cancer Rsch., London, 1974-76; assoc. chief clinician Roswell Park Meml. Inst., Buffalo, 1976-79; asst. prof. Washington U., St. Louis, 1979-83, assoc. prof., 1983-89, prof., 1989-90; prof., chmn. Temple U., Phila., 1991-98; radiation oncologist Pinellas (Fla.) Radiation Oncology Assocs., 1998—2003; prof. radiation oncology Pa. State U., Pa., 2006—. Extramural bd. PDQ, Bethesda, Md., 1989—; mem. in-svc. exam. com. Am. Coll. Radiology, Reston, Va., 1990-97; examiner Am. Bd. Radiology, Louisville, 1990—. Mem. editl. adv. bd.: Med. and Pediatric Oncology, 2002—. Fellow: Royal Coll. Physicians of London, Am. Soc. Radiation Oncologists, Am. Coll. Radiologists; mem.: Pediat. Radiation Oncology Soc. (founding sec.), Internat. Soc. Pediat. Oncology (sci. com. 2000—). Office: 500 University Dr MC H063 Hershey PA 17033 Business E-Mail: pthomas2@psu.edu.

THOMAS, RANDAL J., cardiologist; b. Salt Lake City, May 24, 1958; MD, George Washington U., 1986. Cert. Internal Medicine, 1989. Intern in internal medicine Ga. Bapt. Med. Ctr., Atlanta, 1986—87, resident, 1987—89; fellow in preventive cardiology, Robert Wood Johnson clin. scholar Stanford U.; assoc. prof. medicine Mayo Clinic, Rochester, Minn., dir. cardiovascular health clinic. Office: Mayo Clinic 200 First St SW Rochester MN 55905

THOMAS, SABU, biotechnologist, educator; b. Thalavoor, July 20, 1963; MSc, Mahatma Gandhi U., 1986; PhD, Kerala U., 1996. Scientist, adj. prof. Rajiv Gandhi Ctr. Biotech., 1994—2000, rschr., 2001—. Mem. Indian Arctic Expedition. Recipient Global Health Travel Award, Bill and Melinda Gates Found., 2009. Fellow: Internat. Soc. Biotech.; mem.: Global Lab. Network Cholera and Other Diarrhoea Infections, Freshwater Action Network South Asia. Office: Poojappura Trivandrum Kerala 695014 India

THOMAS, SEEMON, statistician, educator; b. Meenachil, Kerala, India, Sept. 30, 1970; PhD, A.K.J.M., 1991. Assoc. prof. St. Thomas Coll., Pala, 2009—. Office: St Thomas Coll Pala Arunapuram Kottayam Kerala 686 574 India Personal E-mail: seemonpala@rediffmail.com.

THOMAS, STEPHEN JAY, anesthesiologist; b. Washington, 1943; MD, Jefferson Med. Col., 1968. Intern San Francisco Gen. Hosp., 1968-69; resident in anesthesiology Mass. Gen. Hosp., Boston, 1971-73, fellow, 1973-74; assoc. prof. NYU Med. Ctr.; vice chmn., Topkins-Van Poznak prof. dept. anesthesiology N.Y. Presbyn. Weill Cornell Ctr., 1989—. Office: NY Presbyn Weill Cornell Ctr Dept Anesthesiology 525 E 68th St New York NY 10021-4870

THOMAS, TERESA ANN, retired microbiologist, educator; d. Sam Charles and Edna Thomas. BS cum laude, Coll. Misericordia, Dallas, Pa., 1961; MS in Biology, Am. U., Beirut, 1965; MS in Microbiology, U. So. Calif., LA, 1973; cert. in ednl. tech., U. Calif., San Diego, 1998. Cert. Special Dist. Leadership Acad. Calif. Special Dist. Assn., 2008. Tchr., sci. supr., curriculum coord. Meyers H.S., Wilkes-Barre, 1962-64, Wilkes-Barre Area Pub. Schs., 1961-66; rsch. assoc. Proctor Found. Rsch. in Ophthalmology U. Calif. Med. Ctr., San Francisco, 1966-68; instr. Robert Coll. of Istanbul, Turkey, 1968-71, Am. Edn. in Luxembourg, 1971-72, Bosco Tech. Inst., Rosemead, Calif., 1973-74, San Diego C.C. Dist., 1974-80; prof. microbiology and ecology Sch. Math Sci. and Engring. Southwestern Coll., Chula Vista, Calif., 1980—2005, prof. emeritus, 2005—. Pres. acad. senate, 1984-85, del., 1986-89; chmn., coord., steering com. project Cultural Rsch. Ednl. and Trade Exch., 1991-2000, Southwestern Coll.-Shanghai Inst. Fgn. Trade; coord. great tchg. seminar Southwestern Coll., 1987, 88, 89, coord. scholars program, 1988-90, mem. Vecinos Baja Studies Eco-Mundo team internat. program, mem. steering com.; steering com. mentor Bridges to the Future program Southwestern Coll. and San Diego, 1993-98, exec. com. Acad. Senate for Calif. C.C.s, 1985-86, Chancellor Calif. C.C.s Adv. and Rev. Coun. Fund for Instrnl. Improvement, 1984-86; co-project dir. statewide, coord. So. Calif. Biotech. Edn. Consortium, 1993-95, steering com., 1993-98; adj. asst. prof. Chapman Coll., San Diego, 1974-83, San Diego State U., 1977-79; chmn. Am. Colls. Istanbul Sci. Week, 1969-71; adv. bd. Chapman Coll. Cmty. Ctr., 1978-81; cons. sci. curriculum Calif. Dept. Edn., 1986-89; pres. Internat. Rels. Club, 1959-61; mem. San Francisco World Affairs Coun., 1966-68, San Diego World Affairs Coun., 1992—; v.p. Palomar Palace Estates Home Owners Assn., 1983-85, pres., 1994-99, 2003-2004, v.p., 1999—; mem. Rsch. Conf. on Undergrad. Microbiology Edn., Conn. Coll., 1999; bd. dirs. US Orgn. Med. Ednl. Needs, US Internat. Boundary and Water Commn. Citizens Forum Bd., 2001-08; mem. South Bay Networking Group, 2005-07; dir. South Bay Irrigation Dist., 2006—, v.p. 2007-08, pres. 2009-10; governing bd. dir. Sweetwater Authority, 2006—; appt. mem. water quality com. Assn. Calif. Water Agencies, 2008—, chmn. Sweetwater Authority Ops. Com., 2009-. Past emeritus mem. editl. rev. bd., adv. bd.: Jour. Coll. Sci. Tchg. Commr. Internat. Friendship Commn., Chula Vista, 1985-95, vice chmn., 1989-90, chmn., 1990-92; mem. US-Mex. Sister Cities Assn., nat. bd. dirs., 1992-94, gen. chair 30th nat. conv., 1993; founding pres. Chula Vista-Odawara Sister Cities Assn., 1992—; mem. City of Chula Vista Resource Conservation Commn., 1996-05, chmn. 2002-04; mem. Chula Vista Bd. Ethics, 1999-2000, County San Diego Solid Waste Hearing Panel, 2000-05; co-organizer Chula Vista People-to-People Sister City Dels. to Odawara City, Japan, 1991, 94, 99; cmty. adv. com. San Diego Mus. Man, 2000-03; steering com. Chula Vista Gen. Plan Update, 2002-05; mem. vision 20/20 com. Chula Vista Environ., Open Space & Sustainable Devel., 2002-05, Chula Vista Energy Generated Task Force, Ad Hoc Com., 2010-11; del. citizens adv. com. Port of San Diego & City Chula Vista Bayfront Master Plan, 2003—2008; mem. Calif. Local Govts. Commn., 2005—; vol. Bonita Mus. & Cultural Ctr., 2006—; mem. spl. dist. adv. bd. Local Agys. Formation Commn., San Diego County, 2009-; govs. bd. dirs. Chula Vista Charitable Found., 2009-. Grantee Pa. Heart Assn., 1962; Tchg. fellow NSF Am. U. Beirut, 1965, Rsch. fellow USPHS U. SC, 1972-73; recipient Nat. Tchg. Excellence award Nat. Inst. Staff and Orgnl. Devel., 1989; named Southwestern Coll. Woman of Distinction, 1987, Hon. Coach Southwestern Coll. Ladies Basketball Apaches, 2001, Jaguars Basketball Team, 2003, Chula Vista Environmentalist of Yr., 2005, 50th Anniversary Cir. Dist. Vol. award Sister Cities Internat., 2006. Mem.: NSTA (life; coord. internat. honors exch. lectr. competition 1986, internat. com.), NEA (life), Crossroads II, Endow Chula Vista Charitable Found. (founding bd. mem. 2008—), Japanese Coord. Coun. San Diego, Bonita Bus. Profl. Assn., Southwest Chula Vista Civic Assn. (founding steering com. mem. 2006—), Faculty Assn. Calif. CC's (state policy com. 2003—05), Am. Soc. Microbiology Southern Calif. (So. Calif. MicrobeDiscovery Team 1995—99, mem. emeritus 2007—), Northwest Chula Vista Civic Assn. (assoc.), Calif. Sci. Tchrs. Assn. (life), Calif. Tchrs. Assn. (life), Nat. Assn. Biology Tchrs. (life), Assn. Calif. Water Agys. (Water Quality Com.), Am.-Lebanese Assn. San Diego (1st v.p. 1984—91, pres. 1988—93, chmn. scholarship com. 2009—), Am. U. Beirut Alumni and Friends of San Diego (1st v.p. 1984—91), Chula Vista C. of C., South Bay Water Conservation Garden, San Diego Zool. Soc., Japan Soc. San Diego and Tijuana (life), Japanese Am. Hist. Soc. (life), Chula Vista Nature Ctr. (life), San Diego Yokohama Sister Cities Assn. (life), Congress History (life), Am. Lebanese Syrian Ladies Club (pres. 1982—83), Lions Internat. (Melvin Jones fellow for humanitarian svc. bull. editor 1991—93, 2d v.p. 1992—93, 1st v.p. 1993—94, editor Roaring Times Newsletter 1993—94, chmn. dist. internat. rels. and cooperations com. 1993—95, pub. rels. 1997—98, S.W. San Diego County v.p. 2006—07, Best Bull. award 1992—93, Southwest San Diego County Lion of Yr. award 2002, 2006), Delta Kappa Gamma (Gamma Omicron chpt. corr. sec. 2006—07, Outstanding Pub. Svc. award, Gamma Omicron chpt. 2003, liaison Learning Is For Everyone), Sigma Phi Sigma, Kappa Gamma Pi (pres. Wilkes-Barre chpt. 1963—64, pres. San Francisco chpt. 1967—68), Alpha Pi Epsilon (hon.; advisor Southwestern Coll. chpt. 1989—90, founder), Phi Theta Kappa (hon.). Office Phone: 619-425-4564. Personal E-mail: terrythomas4water@cox.net. Business E-Mail: tthomas@sweetwater.org.

THOMAS GORDON, LYNNE, medical association administrator; BS in Health Info. Mgmt., Med. Coll. Ga., 1978; MBA, Ga. State U., Atlanta, 1989. V.p., COO Children's Hosp. Mich.; dir. ops. Shands AGH, 1997—2004, Shands Healthcare, 1997—2006; faculty exec.-in-residence U. Fla.; adminstr. Houston Med. Ctr., 2008—10; assoc. v.p. hosp. ops. Rush U. Med. Ctr., 2010—11; dir. Rush Children's Hosp., 2010—11; CEO American Health Info. Mgmt. Assn., 2011—. Fellow: American Coll. Healthcare Executives (bd. governors, Early Career Healthcare Exec. Regent's award); mem.: American Health Info. Mgmt. Assn. (Achievement and Edn.-Practitioner awards), Ga. Health Info. Mgmt. Assn. (Disting. Mem. award). Office: American Health Info Mgmt Assn 233 N Michigan Ave 21st Fl Chicago IL 60601 Office Phone: 312-233-1100. Office Fax: 312-233-1500. *

THOMASHOW, BYRON MARTIN, pulmonary physician; b. Bklyn., Apr. 19, 1949; s. Alexander Irwin and Emma (Zaslow) T.; m. Laurie Jo Kasoff, July 2, 1972; children: Samantha, Michael. BA, Columbia U., 1970, MD, 1974. Diplomate Nat. Bd. Med. Examiners, Am. Bd. Internal Medicine, subspecialty in pulmonary medicine. Med. intern Roosevelt Hosp., NYC, 1974-75, med. resident, 1975-77, med. chief resident, pulmonary fellow, 1977-78; sr. pulmonary fellow Harlem Hosp., NYC, 1978-79; asst. attending physician Presbyn. Hosp., Columbia Presbyn. Med. Ctr., NYC, 1979-90, assoc. attending physician, 1991-99, attending physician, 1999—; physician in charge Tbc Clinic Presbyn. Hosp., NYC, 1983-90, attending physician Chest Clinic, 1979—; asst. prof. clin. medicine Columbia U., NYC, 1979-90, assoc. clin. prof. medicine, 1990-99, clin. prof. medicine, 1999—. Lectr. in field; mem. NY Presbyn. Hosp. Med. Bd., 1995-2004; med. co-dir. Jo-Ann LeBuhn Ctr Chest Disease. Columbia Presbyn. Med. Ctr., Medical Director Lung Volume Reduction Program NewYork-Presbyterian Hospital, chmn., bd. dirs. COPD Foundation,co-investigator, primary pulmonol. Columbia Ctr., Nat. Emphysema Treatment Trial, NIH; primary investigator Columbia Site COPP Found. Bronchiectasis Registry; co-chmn. NY State COPP Coalotion, 2010-, COOP's USA Meeting, 2011; chmn. respiratory coun., NY Presbyn. Hosp. Network; co-chmn. NY State COPD Coalition, 2010; mem. planning com. Nat. Conf. Coalition Meeting, 2011. Stony Wold-Herbert Fund fellowship grantee, 1978-79; Byron M. Thomashow endowed professorship at Columbia U. named in his honor, 2006. Fellow ACP, Am. Coll. Chest Physicians; mem. Am. Thoracic Soc., N.Y. Trudeau Soc. (exec. com. 1992-94, chmn. membership com. 1992-94), Soc. Practitioners (exec. com. 1994-, chmn. quality care com. 1995-2005). Office: 161 Fort Washington Ave New York NY 10032-3713 Office Phone: 212-305-5261. E-mail: bmt@columbia.edu.

THOMAS RATTAY, KARYL, state agency administrator, public health service officer; BA in Zoology and Premedicine, Ohio Wesleyan U., Delaware, Ohio, 1987; MD, Med. U. Ohio, 1992; MSc in Epidemiology, U. Md., 2001. Cert. in preventive medicine, pediatric preventive medicine physician, pediatrician. Residency in pediat. Georgetown U., Washington; resident U. Md.; pvt. practice pediatrician; sr. pub. health advisor to the surgeon gen. US Dept. Health and Human Services, Washington, asst. sec. health, Office Disease Prevention and Health Promotion, 2001—04; sr. policy and program analyst Nemours Health & Prevention Services, 2004—09; assoc. faculty, dept. population, family and reproductive health Johns Hopkins Bloomberg Sch. Pub. Health, Balt., 2007—; clin. care weight mgr. Alfred I. Dupont Hosp. for Children, Wilmington, Del., 2008—09; dir., divsn. pub. health Del. Dept. Health and Social Services, 2009—. Mem. USDA/HHS Dietary Guidelines Adv. Com.; faculty Del. Sch. Dist. Learning Collaborative. Contbr. articles to profl. jours. Active Pres. Healthier US Initiative; chairwoman Del. Primary Care Initiative on Childhood Overweight. Office: Del Divsn Pub Health Jesse Cooper Bldg 417 Federal St Dover DE 19901 Office Phone: 302-744-4700. Office Fax: 302-739-6659.

THOMASSEN, PAULINE FRANCES, medical and surgical nurse; b. Cleve., Jan. 19, 1939; d. Henry Clifford and Mabel Pauline (Hill) Nichols; m. Ruben Thomassen, Nov. 10, 1979; children: Rhonda, Terry, Diana, Philipp, Jody, Barbara. AA in Nursing, So. Colo. State Coll., 1974, BA in Psychology with distinction, 1975; BSN magna cum laude, Seattle Pacific U., 1986. RN Wash. Staff nurse III orthopedic unit, clin. spine educator Swedish Hosp. Med. Ctr., Seattle, 1975—, preceptor orientation of RNs and student RNs, 1975—, clin. spine educator, 1998—2002; ret., 2002. Mem. planning task force and faculty Nat. Nurses Conf., The Nurse and Spinal Surgery, Cleve.; lectr. Coll. of Nursing, Raleigh Fitkin Meml. Hosp., Manzini, Swaziland, South Africa, 1999, St. Petersburg, Russia, 2003; mem. med. mission to assist in clinic for street children, Satipo, Peru, 00, Honolulu Police Dept., 2001; mem. med. mission, Philippines, 04, 06, 2008—09, Mexico, 2006, Miss. Katrina Relief, 2006—07; med. mission ofcl. Camp Nurse Camp Li-WA, Fairbanks, Alaska, 2002, Fairbanks, 06, Mexico, 06; guest spkr. degenerative lumbar spinal techniques, cadaver workshop U. Wash., Seattle, 2001; guest spkr. Am. Acad. Orthop. Surgeons, Dallas, 2002, Dallas, 02. Author: Spinal Disease and Surgical Interventions, 1995; author: (contbg. author) Making Sense of Minimally Invasive Spine Surgery, 1998. Mem.: Nat. Assn. Orthop. Nurses. Office: Swedish Health Ctr 747 Broadway Seattle WA 98122-4379

THOMAS-VIRNIG, CHRISTINA, biologist; b. NC, June 11, 1974; PhD, U. Wis., 2003. Molecular and cell biology scientist Stratatech Corp., 2003—. Office: 505 S Rosa Rd Ste 169 Madison WI 53719 Business E-Mail: cthomas@stratatechcorp.com.

THOMPSON, CATHERINE RUSH, physical therapist, educator; b. Kansas City, Mo., Feb. 26, 1954; d. John Adams and Jacqueline (Richard) Rush; children: Richard Lathen, Eric Rush. BS in Phys. Therapy with distinction, U. Colo., Denver, 1976; MS in Spl. Edn. with distinction, U. Kans., 1981; PhD in Psychology and Edn., U. Mo.Kansas City, 2001. Cert. phys. therapist, Kans., Mo. Sch. phys. therapist Easter Seal Soc., Miami, Fla., 1976, Taylor Rehab. Ctr., Cedar Rapids, Iowa, 1977-79; cons. B.W. Shepard State Schs., Kansas City, Mo., 1979-86; pediatric phys. therapist Consol. Sch. Dist. 1, Kansas City, Mo., 1986-94, Spina Bifida Clinic-U. Kans. Med. Ctr., Kansas City, Kans., 1991-94; instr. phys. therapy U. Kans. Med. Ctr., Kansas City, Kans., 1990-96, Rockhurst U., 1997—. Phys. therapy cons. Lakemary Ctr., Paola, Kans., 1991—1995; pediat. phys. therapist, early intervention for Johnson Co. and Leavenworth Co., 2002-; mem. desegregation monitoring com. Kansas City (Mo.) Sch. Dist., 1991—1993; chair Kansas City (Mo.) Pediatric Alliance, 1981-84; adv. com. Ctr. for Devel. Disabled, Kansas City, Mo., 1982-85; pres. Rush Assocs., Inc., 1980-85; spkr. in field. Author: Prevention Practice: A Physical Therapist's Guide to Health, Fitness and Wellness, 2007. Festival chair Hyde Park Neighborhood Assn., Kansas City, Mo., 1985; parent rep. sch. adv. com. Faxon Montessori Sch., Kansas City, Mo., 1987; summer tchr. Trinity United Meth. Ch., Kansas City, Mo., 1991; grants chair sch. adv. com. Ecole Longan, Kansas City, Mo., 1991. Arthur Mag fellow U. Mo., 1989. Mem. Am. Phys. Therapy Assn. (abstract editor pediatric sect. 1981-83), Kans. Phys. Therapy Assn. (rsch. com. 1989-94), Spina Bifida Assn., Kansas City Soc. Neurosci., Ind. Therapy Svcs. (pres. 1982-86). Avocations: wellness, historic preservation, gardening, poetry. Home: 711 Manheim Rd Kansas City MO 64109-2633 Office: Rockhurst Univ Dept Phys Therapy Edn 108 Van Ackeran Kansas City MO 64110-2561 Business E-Mail: catherine.thompson@rockhurst.edu.

THOMPSON, CHARLOTTE ELLIS, pediatrician, educator, writer; d. Robert and Ann Ellis; divorced; children: Jennifer Ann, Geoffrey Graeme. BA, Stanford U., 1950, MD, 1954. Diplomate Am. Bd. Pediat. Intern Children's Hosp., San Francisco, 1953-54; resident UCLA, 1960-61, L.A. Children's Hosp., 1962-63; pvt. practice La Jolla, Calif., 1963-75; dir. Muscle Disease Clinic Univ. Hosp.-U. Calif. Sch. Medicine, San Diego, 1969-80, asst. clin. prof. pediat., 1969—; founder, dir. Ctr. for Handicapped Children and Teenagers, San Francisco, 1981—2004. Cons. U.S. Naval Hosp., San Diego, 1970-91; dep. dir. Santa Clara County Child Health and Disability, Santa Clara, Calif., 1974-75; dir. Ctr. for Multiple Handicaps, Oakland, Calif., 1976-81; co-dir. Muscle Clinic Children's Hosp., San Diego, 1963-69; dir. muscle program U. Rochester, 1957-60. Author: Raising a Handicapped Child: A Helpful Guide for Parents of the Physically Disabled, 1986, 4th edit., 1991, rev., expanded edit., 2000, Allein leben: Ein umfassendes Handbuch für Frauen, 1993, Making Wise Choices: A Guide for Women, 1993, Raising a Child with a Neuromuscular Disorder, 1999, Raising A Handicapped Child, 1999, 101 Ways To The Best Medical Care, 2006, Grandparenting a Child With Special Needs Jersica Kingsley, 2010; contbr. articles to med. jours., including Clin. Pediat., New Eng. Jour. Medicine, Neurology, Jour. Family Practice, Mothering, Jour. Pediatric Orthopedics, Pediatrician, Am. Baby, Pediatric News, Grandparenting a Child with Special Needs, 2009, also chpts. to books; editor The Everything Parent's Guide to Children with Autlsin-2e, 2010. Mem. Calif. Children's Svc. Com., 1977—2000. Fellow: Am. Acad. Pediat. Avocations: tennis, ice skating, opera. Office: 8070 La Jolla Shores Dr # 514 La Jolla CA 92037-3296 Office Phone: 858-456-2105. Personal E-mail: cetmd@earthlink.net.

THOMPSON, CHRISTOPHER C., gastroenterologist; b. Omaha, Nebr., Dec. 8, 1969; BS, SUNY, Binghamton, 1992; MD, Pa. State U. Coll. Medicine, 1996. Dir. bariatric endoscopy Brigham and Women's Hosp., 2003—05, dir. devel. endoscopy, 2005—11, dir. therapeutic endoscopy, 2011—. Instr. Harvard Med. Sch., 2003—07, asst. prof., 2007—11. Recipient 1st Pl. award, New Eng. Endoscopy Soc. Ann. Rsch. Symposium; grant, Brigham and Women's Physician Orgn. Fellow: Am. Coll. Gastroenterology, Am. Soc. Gastrointestinal Endoscopy (26th Ann. Audiovisual award, 23rd Ann. Audio Visual award); mem.: Soc. Am. Gastrointestinal and Endoscopic Surgeons, Am. Gastroent. Assn. Office: 75 Francis St Boston MA 02115 Office Fax: 614-264-6342. Business E-Mail: christopher_thompson@hms.harvard.edu.

THOMPSON, CRAIG BERNIE, hospital administrator, medical researcher, educator; b. Cambridge, Mass., Feb. 9, 1953; m. Tullia Lindsten; children: Kajsa, Nicklas. AB summa cum laude, Dartmouth Coll., 1973, BS with honors, 1975; MD, U. Pa., 1977. Sr. resident Boston U., 1979—81; asst. prof. Uniformed Svcs. U. Health Sciences, Bethesda, Md., 1982-87; asst. investigator Howard Hughes Med. Inst., Ann Arbor, Mich., 1987-89; asst. prof. U. Mich., Ann Arbor, 1987-89, assoc. prof., 1989-92; assoc. investigator Howard Hughes Med. Inst., Ann Arbor, 1989-93, investigator, 1993—99; prof. U. Chgo., 1993—99; prof. med. U. Pa., 1999—2010, sci. dir. Leonard & Madlyn Abramson Family Cancer Rsch. Inst., 1999—2006, dir. Abramson Cancer Ctr., 2006—10; assoc. v.p. cancer services U. Pa. Health Sys., 2006—10; pres., CEO Meml. Sloan-Kettering Cancer Ctr., NYC, 2010—. Bd. dirs. Assn. American Cancer Institutes, American Assn. Cancer Rsch.; mem. Lasker Prize Jury. Served in USN. Recipient Clinical Investigator award, Am. Soc. Clinical Investigation, 2003, Mosby Book award, Merck award, Med. Sci. award, Alpha Omega Alpha. Mem.: American Acad. Arts & Sciences, IOM, NAS. Office: Memorial Sloan-Kettering Cancer Center 1275 York Ave New York NY 10065

THOMPSON, DENNIS PETERS, plastic surgeon; b. Chgo., Mar. 18, 1937; s. David John and Ruth Dorothy (Peters) T.; m. Virginia Louise Williams, June 17, 1961; children: Laura Faye, Victoria Ruth, Elizabeth Jan. BS, U. Ill., 1957, BS in Medicine, 1959, MS in Physiology, 1961, MD, 1961. Diplomate Am. Bd. Surgery, Am. Bd. Plastic Surgery. Intern Presbyn.-St. Lukes Hosp., Chgo., 1961—62; fellow in gen. surgery Mayo Clinic, Rochester, Minn., 1964—66; resident in gen. surgery Harbor Gen. Hosp., LA, 1968—70; resident in plastic surgery UCLA, 1971—73, clin. instr. plastic surgery, 1975—82, asst. clin. prof. surgery, 1982—97, assoc. clin. prof. plastic surgery, 1998—2008; clin. prof. Plastic Surgery, 2009—. Practiced medicine specializing in plastic and reconstructive surgery, LA, 1974-78, Santa Monica, Calif., 1978—2008; chmn. plastic surgery sect. St. John's Hosp., 1986-91; staff Olive View Hosp., 1982—, St. John's Hosp., 1982-2008; chmn. dept. surgery Beverly Glen Hosp., 1978-79; pres. Coop. of Am. Physicians Credit Union, 1978-80; bd. dirs. Coop. Am. Physicians, 1980-97, chmn. membership devel. com., 1983-97, treas., 1985-97. Contbr. articles to med. jours. Moderator Congl. Ch. of Northridge (Calif.), 1975-76, chmn. bd. trustees, 1973-74, 80-82; bd. dirs. L.A. Bus. Coun., 1987-90. Am. Tobacco Inst. rsch. grantee, 1959-60. Fellow ACS; mem. AMA (Physicians Recognition award 1971, 74, 77, 81, 84, 87, 90, 93, 96, 99, 2002, 05), Calif. Med. Assn., L.A. County Med. Assn. (chmn. bylaws com. 1979-80, chmn. ethics com. 1980-81, 2000-01, sec.-treas. dist. 5 1982-83, program chmn. 1983-84, pres. 1985-86, councilor 1988-96, 2001-03, councilor-at-large 2004-08, v.p. 1999-2000), Pan-Pacific Surg. Assn., Am. Soc. Plastic Surgeons, Calif. Soc. Plastic Surgeons (chmn. bylaws com. 1982-83, chmn. liability com. 1983-85, councilor 1988-91, sec. 1993-95, v.p. 1995-96, pres.-elect 1996-97, pres. 1997-98), L.A. Soc. Plastic Surgeons (sec. 1980-82, pres. 1982-97), Lipoplasty Soc. N.Am., UCLA Plastic Surgery Soc. (treas. 1983-84, v.p. 1996-98, pres. 1998-2003, 2005), Am. Soc. Aesthetic Plastic Surgery, Internat. Soc. Clin. Plastic Surgeons (bd. dirs. 1999-2006, pres. 2004-06), Am. Assn. Accreditation of Ambulatory Surg. Facilities (bd. dirs. 1995-97, 2002-09, ofcl. observer to AMA ho. of dels. 1999-2009), Western L.A. Regional C. of C. (bd. dirs. 1981-84, 86-89, chmn. legis. action com. 1978-80), Phi Beta Kappa, Alpha Omega Alpha, Nu Sigma Nu, Phi Kappa Phi, Delta Sigma Delta, Omega Beta Pi, Phi Eta Sigma. Republican. Business E-Mail: dthompson@dslextreme.com.

THOMPSON, GERALDINE KELLEHER RICHTER, retired orthopedist; b. Tokyo, Aug. 22, 1948; (parents Am. citizens); d. Edward Elkins and Marguerite Geraldine Kelleher; m. Wayne Wray Thompson, Dec. 30, 2000; m. Paul S. Richter (div.); children: Karl Kelleher Richter, Brian Kelleher Richter, Kelly Kelleher Richter. BA with high honors, Wellesley Coll., Mass., 1969; MD, Georgetown U., Washington, 1973. Intern internal medicine Georgetown U. Hosp., Washington, 1973—74, residency orthop. surgery, 1974—78; pvt. practice orthop. surgery Fairfax and Manassas, Va., 1978—2002; assoc. prof. orthop. surgery Georgetown U., Washington, 1978—2002; fellow Am. Acad. Orthop. Surgery, 1981—2001. Pres. Prince William Med. Soc., 1999—2000. Parent leader Boy Scouts Am., 1990—99; mem. parents assn. St. Albans Sch., Washington, Nat. Cathedral Sch. Girls. Fellow: Am. Acad. Orthop. Surgeons; mem.: Wellesley Literary Cir., AOA, Sigma Xi, Phi Beta Kappa. Avocations: literature, history. Home: 908 Deer Road Bryn Mawr PA 19010

THOMPSON, HERBERT ALDEN, microbiologist, public health scientist; s. Otto Anous and Carmen Louise Thompson; m. Donna Rae Burrhus, June 13, 1964; 1 child, Bradley Alden. BA, Drake U., Des Moines, 1964; MA, Drake U., 1966; PhD, U. Kans., Lawrence, 1971. From asst. to full prof. W.Va. U., Morgantown, 1976—2000; microbiologist Ctrs. for Disease Control and Prevention, Atlanta, 2000—02, chief viral and rickettsial zoonoses br., 2002—06; retired, 2006. Contbr. articles to profl. jours. Pres., treas., newsletter editor Trout Unlimited, Morgantown, 1982—88. Recipient MacLachlan award, W.Va. U. Sch. Medicine; named Outstanding Tchr., W.Va. U., 1980; grantee, NIH, 1997—99, NSF, 1980—86. Mem.: Am. Biol. Safety Assn. (corr.), Am. Soc. Rickettsiology (corr.), Soc. Gen. Microbiology (corr.), Sigma Xi (corr.). Avocations: physical fitness, physical rehabilitation, fly fishing, carpentry, astronomy.

THOMPSON, IAN MURCHIE, JR., urologist, oncologist; b. Montgomery, Ala., May 18, 1954; m. BS, US Mil. Acad., West Point, NY, 1976; MD, Tulane U. Sch. Medicine, New Orleans, 1980. Diplomate Am. Bd. Urology. Intern surgery Brooke Army Med. Ctr., San Antonio, 1980—81, resident urology, 1982—85; clin. fellow urologic oncology Meml. Sloan-Kettering Cancer Ctr., NYC, 1985—88; clin. assoc. prof. Uniformed Svcs. U. Health Scis., Bethesda, Md., 1992—; prof. and chair dept. urology, Henry B. & Edna Smith Dielmann meml. chair urologic sci. U. Tex. Health Sci. Ctr., San Antonio, 1998—, also Glenda & Gary Woods disting. chair in genitourinary oncology, Cancer Therapy & Rsch. Ctr. Chmn. divsn. urology & dept. surgery Brooke Army Med. Ctr., 1992—98; chmn. GU task force Am. Joint Commn. on Cancer, Chgo., 1999—. Contbr. articles to profl. jours., chapters to books. Col. US Army, 1976—2000. Mem.: Soc. Urologic Oncology (pres. 2004, Huggins medal 2008), Am. Urol. Assn. (chmn. prostate cancer panel 1994—, Disting. Contbn. award 1997). Office: Univ Tex Health Science Ctr 7703 Floyd Curl Dr San Antonio TX 78229 Office Phone: 210-567-5643. Business E-Mail: thompsoni@uthscsa.edu. *

THOMPSON, JEROME WALTER, otolaryngologist; b. Blytheville, Ark., Jan. 8, 1950; MD, UCLA, 1976, MBA, 1994. Prof., chmn. ear, nose and throat dept. U. Tenn. Health Sci. Ctr., Memphis; pediat. ear, nose and throat surgeon LeBonhowe Children's Med. Ctr., Memphis; clin. lectr. U. Southern Calif., Sch. Medicine, LA, 1981—86, asst. clin. prof., 1986—94, assoc. clin. prof., 1994; assoc. prof. pediat. U. Tenn., Memphis, Sch. Medicine, 1994—; assoc. prof. Otolaryngology - head and neck surgery U. Tenn., 1994—2001; head UT div. Pediat. Otolaryngology, LeBonheur Children's Hosp., U. Tenn., 1994—; assoc. dean Grad. Med. Edn., U. Tenn., 1999—2002; interim chair Dept. Otolaryngology, U. Tenn., 2000—01; program dir. otolaryngology, head and neck surgury U. Tenn., 2006—, program dir. otolaryngology, head and neck surgery, 2001—03, prof. otolaryngology, head and neck surgery, 2001—, chair, otolaryngology, head and surgery, 2001—; faculty mem. Dept. Allergy & Immunology, U. Tenn., 2001—. Chmn. Meth. U. Hosps., Memphis, 2004—; adj. assoc. prof. U. Memphis, Dept. Hearing and Speech Pathology, 1998—; adj. clin. faculty mem. St. Jude Children's Rsch. Hosp., 2001—; cons. appointment Telemedicine Hosp. U. Tenn., 2008. Clin. faculty mem., vol. Vanderbilt U. Sch. Nursing, Nashville, 2004—. Fellow: Am. Acad. Pediat.; mem.: Am. Acad. Otolaryngology (mem. audit com. 2006—). Office: 910 Madison #430 Memphis TN 38163 Office Phone: 901-448-5885. *

THOMPSON, JOHN, medical association administrator; b. June 21, 1946; MBBS, U. Sydney, 1971, MD, 1997. Exec. dir. Melanoma Inst. Australia, 1999—. Prof., surgery, melanoma and surg. oncology U. Sydney, 1999. Fellow: ACS, Royal Australasian Coll. Surgeons. Office: 40 Rocklands Rd Sydney NSW 2060 Australia

THOMPSON, JOHN ALBERT, JR., dermatologist; b. Austin, Tex., June 5, 1942; s. J. Albert Sr. and Elizabeth (Brady) T. BA, Georgetown U., 1963; MD, Bowman Gray Sch. Medicine, 1967; Dermatology Fellowship, U. N.C., 1971-73. Diplomate Am. Bd. Dermatology. Resident in internal medicine N.C. Baptist Hosp., Winston-Salem, NC, 1967-69; resident in dermatology N.C. Meml. Hosp., Chapel Hill, NC, 1971-73; pvt. practice Charlotte, NC, 1974—; clin. prof. dermatology Dept. Dermatology, U. N.C. Sch. Medicine, Chapel Hill, 1974—. Author profl. papers. Lt. comdr. USNR, 1969-71, Vietnam. Mem. Am. Acad. Dermatology (chmn. subcom. for sch. health edn. 1976-79, task force nat. health ins.), Carolinas-Va. Dermatology Assn. (adv. bd. council rep. 1976-79), Charlotte Dermatology Assn., Mecklenburg County Med. Soc., N.C. Med. Soc., North Am. Clin. Dermatology Soc. Southern Med. Assn., Southeastern Consortium for Continuing Dermatol. Edn. (steering com. 1983—2003), South Cen. Dermatol. Congress (organizing com. 1982-86), Am. Soc. Dermatol. Surgery, Am. Dermatol. Soc. Allergy and Immunology, Am. Soc. Laser Medicine and Surgery, Inc. Democrat. Episcopalian. Home: 2633 Richardson Dr Apt 8A Charlotte NC 28211-3346 Office: Dermatol Laser Ctr Dermatologic Laser Ctr 2310 Randolph Rd Charlotte NC 28207-1526 Office Phone: 704-376-9849.

THOMPSON, JUDITH KASTRUP, nursing researcher; b. Marstal, Denmark, Oct. 1, 1933; arrived in US, 1951; d. Edward Kastrup and Anna Hansa (Knudsen) Pedersen; m. Richard Frederick Thompson, May 22, 1960; children: Kathryn Marr, Elizabeth Kastrup, Virginia St. Claire. BS, RN, U. Oreg., Corvallis, 1958; MSN, U. Oreg., 1963. RN Calif., Oreg. Staff nurse U. Oreg. Med. Sch., Eugene, 1957-58, Portland, 1958-61, head staff nurse, 1960-61; instr. psychiat. nursing U. Oreg. Sch. Nursing, Portland, 1963-64; rsch. asst. U. Oreg. Med. Sch., Portland, 1964-65, U. Calif., Irvine, 1971-72; rsch. assoc. Stanford (Calif.) U., 1982-87; rsch. asst. Harvard U., Cambridge, Mass., 1973-74; rsch. assoc. U. So. Calif., LA, 1987—. Contbg. author: Behavioral Control and Role of Sensory Biofeedback, 1976; contbr. articles to profl. jours. Treas. LWV, Newport Beach, Calif., 1970-74; scout leader Girl Scouts Am., Newport Beach, 1970-78. Named Citizen of Yr. State of Oreg., 1966. Mem. Soc. for Neurosci., Am. Psychol. Soc. (charter), ANA, Oreg. Nurses Assn. Republican. Lutheran. Avocations: travel, tennis. Office: U So Calif University Park Los Angeles CA 90089-0001 Home: 952 Jacqueline Pl Nipomo CA 93444-6605 Office Phone: 213-740-7350, 213-740-7339. Business E-Mail: judith@usc.edu.

THOMPSON, KIMBERLY M., non-profit organization executive, eductor; m. Kamran Badizadegan. BS in Chem. Engring., Harvard U. Sch. Pub. Health, 1988; DSc in Environ. Health, Harvard U. Sch. Pub. Health, Boston, 1995; MS in Chem. Engring. Practice, MIT, Cambridge, 1989. Asst. dir. chem. engring. practice sch. MIT, 1989; asst. prof. risk analysis and decision sci., dept. health policy and mgmt. Harvard Sch. Pub. Health, 1997—2002, creator, dir., Kids Risk Project, 2000—09, assoc. prof. risk analysis and decision sci., departments of health policy and mgmt. and soc., human develop. and health, 2002—08; assoc. prof. risk analysis and decision sci. (pediatrics), assoc. staff (adolescent medicine), co-founder, Ctr. on Media and Child Health Children's Hosp. Boston, Harvard Med. Sch., 2003—; founder, pres. Kid Risk, Inc., 2008—, AORM, LLC, 2008—. Mem. Harvard U.-wide Com. on the Environment, 1999—2009, Harvard U. Com. on Higher Degrees in Health Policy, 2000—07, Centers for Disease Control and Prevention Adv. Com. on Childhood Lead Poisoning Prevention, 2002—05; core mem., peer consultation panel EPA Voluntary Children's Chem. Evaluation Program, 2002—06; mem., Strategic Adv. Group of Experts (SAGE) Working Group on Polio WHO, 2008—; external examiner U. New South Wales, Sch. Information Tech. and Electrical Engring., Canberra, Australia, 2008; vis. assoc. prof. MIT, Sloan Sch. Mgmt., 2005—07; adj. assoc. prof. risk analysis and decision sci. Harvard Sch. Pub. Health, 2008—; bd. dirs. Am. Coun. on Sci. and Health, 2002—05, First Star, 2003—; mem. external adv. bd. Procter & Gamble, Ctrl. Safety Divsn., 2005—; mem. tech. adv. bd. Dow Chem. Co., 2006—; mem. energy and adv. coun. RAND, 2007—; several prof. svc. positions for NAS; invited presenter in the field; cons. in field. Co-author: Overkill:How Our Nation's Abuse of Antibiotics and Other Germ Killer is Hurting Your Health and What You Can Do About It, 2002; author: (book) Risk In Perspective: Insight and Humor Age Risk Management, 2004; refereed jour. articles, manuscript reviewer for several peer-reviewed jours., websites created and maintained www.health-insight.harvard.edu, 1999—, www.kidsrisk.harvard.edu, 2000—, www.pracourse.harvard.edu, 2000—, www.aorm.com, 2002—, www.voila.harvard.edu, 2007—, www.kidrisk.org, 2009—, software review editor and sr. editor for risk Comm. Human and Ecological Risk Assessment, 2002—05, assoc. editor Journal of Children's Health, 2002—05, mem. editl. bds. Risk Analysis, 2008—, Medical Decision Making, 2008—, interviewed by ABC World News Tonight, CBS Evening News, TODAY, CBS Morning Show, CNBC, CNN, ESPN, C-SPAN2, MSNBC, Canada Today, Australian Today Show, JAMA video news release, FETCH!, and all Boston local network news stations, (radio stations) NPR, BBC, Canadian Broadcasting Corp., CBS, ABC and numerous local radio stations around the world, featured in New York Times, Wall Street Journal, USA Today, LA Times, Chicago Times, Washington Post, Boston Globe, Boston Herald, Scotland on Sunday, AP, Reuters, US News & World Report, Newsweek, Time Mag., Harper's, Better Homes & Garden, Parents Mag., Child Mag., Reason Mag., Business Week, Nature, Discover Mag., Fitness Mag., Realtor Mag., American Way, Sports Illustrated, and Parents' Paper. Recipient Chauncey Star Disting. Young Risk Analyst award, Soc. Risk Analysis, 2004. Fellow: Soc. for Risk Analysis (pres. 2006—07, pres.-elect 2005—06, councilor 2002—05, historian 2003—05, chair, exposure assessment specialty group 1999, Chauncey Starr Disting. Young Risk Analyst award 2004); mem.: System Dynamics Soc. (World Champion, Beer Distribution Game 2007, Jay Wright Forrester award 2008), Internat. Soc. Exposure Analysis, INFORMS, Decision Analysis Soc. (co-chair of student paper competition 2007, Practice award finalist 2008), Am. Statistical Assn., Am. Pub. Health Assn., Am. Inst. Chem. Engineers, AAAS. Office: Harvard Sch Pub Health 677 Huntington Ave 3rd Fl Boston MA 02115 Address: Kid Risk Inc and AORM LLC PO Box 590129 Newton MA 02459 Office Phone: 617-432-4285, 617-680-2836. Office Fax: 617-432-3699. Business E-Mail: kimt@hsph.harvard.edu, kimt@kidrisk.org, kimt@aorm.com.

THOMPSON, MARI HILDENBRAND, medico-legal and administrative consultant; b. Washington, Apr. 26, 1951; d. Emil John Christopher Hildenbrand and Ada Lythe (Conklin) Hildenbrand-Kammer; m. R. Marshall Thompson, Sept. 27, 1970 (div. June 1981); 1 child, Jeremy Marshall. BA in Secondary Edn., Am. U., 1976, BA in Performing Arts, 1976. Cert. med. staff coord., cert. profl. credentialing specialist. Employment interviewer Scripps Meml. Hosp., La Jolla, Calif., 1977-81; office mgr. Jacksina & Freedman Press Office, NYC, 1982-83; staffing coord., med. staff asst. Am. Med. Internat. Clairemont Hosp., San Diego, 1983-85; adminstrv. asst. Am. Med. Internat. Valley Med. Ctr., El Cajon, Calif., 1985-88; med. staff coord. Sharp Meml. Hosp., San Diego, 1988-92; adminstrv. asst. Grossmont Hosp., La Mesa, Calif., 1992-93, coord. Sharp family practice residency program, 1993-94; mgr. Sharp Meml. Hosp. med. staff svcs., San Diego, 1994-96; cons. med. staff svcs. San Diego Rehab. Inst., 1997. Cons. and adminstrv. support for Legal Support, Inc., 1989—, St. Charles Med. Ctr., 1998—2004; cons. Legal Support N.W., LLC, 1999—; coord. Deschutes Ct. Defenders, 1999-2008; Bend Attorney Group (treas. 2008-), wardrobe mistress various cmty. theatres, San Diego, 1978-79, actress, San Diego, 1979-81. Co-founder N.Y.C. Playreaders Group, 1981-83, N.J. Shakespeare Theatre, Madison, 1982, Good Humor Improv Co., N.Y.C., 1982-83; contbg. writer to Poetry Revival: An Anthology, 1994. Active Dem. Nat. Com., 1996-2009, Pacific Green Party, 2010-; vol. Cascades Theatre Co., 1997-2005. Named one of Outstanding Young Women of Am., 1986. Mem. AFTRA. Buddhist. Avocations: poetry, swimming, gardening, fishing.

THOMPSON, NOREEN C., mental health nurse, educator; b. Phila., June 22, 1949; BSN, U. Pa., 1972, MSN, 1976. Nurse psychotherapist Cape May County Cmty. Mental Health Ctr., 1976—77; asst. prof. nursing Bishop Neumann Coll., 1977—79, Thomas Jefferson Coll. Allied Health Scis., 1980—82; psychiat. clin. nurse specialist Kans. Inst., 1988—89; psychiat. liaison clin. nurse specialist U. Kans. Med. Ctr., 1989—. Adj. faculty U. Kans. Sch. Nursing, 1989—; cons. U. Kans., 1990. Grant, Cerner/Am. Nurses Found., Dr. Carol Smith's NINR grant, U. Kans. Mem.: Internat. Soc. Psychiat. Mental Health Nurses (Clin. Excellence award), Sigma Theta Tau (Clin. Excellence award). Achievements include research in photovoice studies, diagnostic disclosure interventions for psychogenic symptoms or somatization and coping with chronic illness. Avocations: reading, art, music, movies. Home: 9959 Bluejacket Dr Overland Park KS 66214 Personal E-mail: noreencthompson@gmail.com. Business E-Mail: nthmpo2@kumc.edu.

THOMPSON, NORMAN WINSLOW, surgeon, educator; b. Boston, July 12, 1932; s. Herman Chandler and Evelyn Millicent (Palmer) T.; m. Marcia Ann Veldman, June 12, 1956; children: Robert, Karen, Susan, Jennifer. BA, Hope Coll., Holland, Mich., 1953; MD, U. Mich., 1957; MD (hon.), U. Linköping, Sweden, 1995. Diplomate Am. Bd. Surgery. From intern to prof. emeritus surgery U. Mich., Ann Arbor, Mich., 1957—2001, prof. emeritus surgery, 2001—. Contbr. articles to profl. jours. Trustee Hope Coll., 1973-88. Fellow Royal Australasian Coll. Surgeons (hon.), Royal Coll. Physicians and Surgeons of Glasgow; mem. ACS (gov. 1979-85), Ctrl. Surg. Assn., Western Surg. Assn. (1st v.p. 1992-93, pres. 1994-95), F.A. Coller Surg. Soc. (pres. 1986), Am. Surg. Assn., Am. Thyroid Assn., Soc. Surg. Alimentary Tract, Internat. Assn. Endocrine Surgeons (pres.

1989-91), Internat. Soc. Surgeons (v.p. 1995—), Am. Assn. Endocrine Surgeons (pres. 1980-81, 81-82), Royal Soc. Medicine, Brit. Assn. Endocrine Surgeons, Spanish Assn. Surgeons (hon.), Assn. French Endocrine Surgeons, Scandanvian Surg. Soc., Soc. Surg. Oncology, Turkish Assn. Endocrine Surgeons, European Soc. Endocrine Surgeons (hon.), Spanish Soc. Surgeons (hon.), European Surg. Assn-.(hon.), Alpha Omega Alpha. Home: 465 Hillspur Rd Ann Arbor MI 48105-1048 Office: Surgery Emeritus Faculty Taubhan Blvd 1500 E Med Ctr Dr Ann Arbor MI 48105 Office Phone: 734-936-9815. Office Fax: 734-998-0173. Business E-Mail: normant@med.umich.edu.

THOMPSON, RENEE J., psychologist; b. Peoria, Ill., Dec. 31, 1978; BS, U. Ill., Urbana-Champaign, 2001, PhD, 2007. Postdoc. scholar Stanford U., 2008—. Office: 450 Serra Mall Jordan Hall Bldg 420 Stanford CA 94305 Business E-Mail: reneet@stanford.edu.

THOMPSON, RICHARD PAUL HEPWORTH, retired physician; b. Esher, U.K., Apr. 14, 1940; s. Stanley Henry and Winifred Lilian (Collier) H.; m. Eleanor Mary Hughes, 1974. BA, Oxford U., Eng., 1961, MA, BM, Oxford U., Eng., 1964, DM, 1971. Rsch. fellow Mayo Clinic, Rochester, 1969—71; lectr. Kings Coll. Hosp., London, 1968—72; cons., physician St. Thomas Hosp., London, 1972—2005. Chmn. grants com. King Edward VII Fund, London, 1992-96; vice-chmn. coun. Brit. Heart Found., 2002-06. Author: Physical Signs in Medicine, 1980, Lecture Notes on the Liver, 1985. Fellow Royal Coll. Physicians (London) (treas. 2003—10, pres. 10-), Worcester Coll. (hon.). Home: 36 Dealtry Rd London SW15 6NL England Home Phone: 0208 789 3839. E-mail: richard@rpht.co.uk.

THOMPSON, THEODIS, retired healthcare executive, health management consultant; b. Palestine, Ark., Aug. 10, 1944; s. Percy and Grozellia Monroves (Weaver) T.; m. Patricia Holley, Sept. 16, 1964; children: Gwendolyn Ware, Theodis E., Omari P. BS, Tuskegee Inst., 1968; MPA, U. Mich., 1969, PhD, 1972. Asst. chemist John T. Stanley Co., NYC, 1964-66; news announcer, disc jockey KATZ Radio Sta., St. Louis, 1966-67; sr. rsch. assoc. U. Mich., Ann Arbor, 1969-71; asst. prof., chmn. Howard U., Washington, 1973-78; assoc. prof., dir. health planning U. So. Calif., LA, 1978-79; dir. planning and evaluation Memphis Health Ctr., 1979-87, chief oper. officer, 1987-88; CEO Bklyn. Plz. Med. Ctr., 1988—2005. Cons. Charles Mathis Assocs., Yonkers, N.Y., 1991-98, USPHS, Bethesda, Md., 1993—; mem. adv. bd. N.Y. Urban League, Bklyn., 1991-93; lectr. St. Joseph's Coll., Bklyn., 1998—. Author, editor: Health Policy and Planning, 1975; contbr. articles to profl. jours. Bd. dirs. CHCANYS, Inc., N.Y.C., 1994; vice chair Cmty. Assocs. Devel. Corp., Inc., Bklyn., 1989. Recipient Disting. Svc. award N.Y. State Assn. Black and Puerto Ricans, Inc., 1992; named Disting. Man of Yr., 18th Senatorial Dist., 1996. Mem. APHA. Office Phone: 901-292-9684. Personal E-mail: thadt29@aol.com.

THOMPSON, THEODORE ROBERT, pediatric educator; b. Dayton, Ohio, July 18, 1943; s. Theodore Roosevelt and Helen (Casey) J.; m. Lynette Joanne Shenk; 1 child, S. Beth. BS, Wittenberg U., 1965; MD, U. Pa., 1969. Diplomate Am. Bd. Pediatrics (Neonatal, Perinatal Medicine). Resident in pediat. U. Minn. Hosp., Mpls., 1969—72, chief resident in pediat., 1971—72, fellow neonatal, perinatal, 1974—75, asst. prof., 1975—80, dir. divsn. neonatology and newborn intensive care unit, 1977—91, assoc. prof., 1980—85, prof., 1985—, co-dir. Med. Outreach, 1988—91, med. dir. med. outreach, 1991—2000, assoc. chief pediat. svcs., 1988—2003, assoc. head pediat. edn. and cmty. programs, 2003—04, assoc. head cmty. affairs, 2004—; med. dir. outreach, bd. dirs. U. Minn. Physicians, 1992—2008. Med. exec. com., sec.-treas. U. Minn. Med. Ctr., Fairview, 2002—04, chief of staff elect, 2004—07, chief of staff, 2007—09, past chief staff, 2009—11. Editor: Newborn Intensive Care: A Practical Manual, 1983. Bd. dirs. Life Link III, St. Paul, 1987—; cons. Maternal and Child Health, Minn. Bd. Health, 1975-94; bd. dirs. Minn. Med. Found., 1995-99. With USPHS. 1972-74. Recipient Advocacy award, U. Minn. Med. Sch., Pres.'s award for outstanding svc., U. Minn., Alumni Catalogs award, Wittenberg U., 2005, Disting. Svc. award, Minn. Chpt. Acad. Pediat., 2009. Fellow: Am. Acad. Pediats.; mem.: Acad. Med. Educators, Gt. Plains Orgn. for Perinatal Health Care (Sioux Falls, SD Kunshe award 1989). Lutheran. Office: MMC 39 420 Delaware St SE Minneapolis MN 55455-0374 Business E-Mail: thomp005@umn.edu.

THOMPSON, TILLIAN, cardiologist; b. June 2, 1954; d. Andrea and Alex Milltel (Stepfather); m. Bobby Thompson; children: Michael, Kayla, Sarah. BA in Music, Temple Univ., 1976, MD, 1980. Cardiologist Thomas Jefferson Hosp., 1988—99; adj. prof. Thomas Jefferson Medical Sch., 1992—97, full prof., 2011—; cardiology dept. head Tucson Hearts Hosp., 2000—05; chief. of med. Meriks Hosp., Tucson, 2006—. Intern Temple Univ. Hosp., 1980—83, cardiology resident, 1983—88. Mem.: AMA (life; dist. rep. 2006—, Life Mem. award 2008). Independent. Achievements include research in in diet and exercise in obese versus healthy families. Avocations: Monopoly, movies. Office: Meriks Hosp 2509 N Campbell St #311 Tucson AZ 85719-3362

THOMPSON, TOMMY (THOMAS GEORGE THOMPSON), lawyer, former United States Secretary of Health and Human Services; b. Elroy, Wis., Nov. 19, 1941; s. Allan and Julia (Dutton) T.; m. Sue Ann Mashak, 1969; children: Kelli Sue, Tommi, Jason. BS in Polit. Sci. and History, U. Wis., 1963, JD, 1966. Polit. intern U.S. Rep. Thomson, 1963; legis. messenger Wis. State Senate, 1964-66; sole practice Elroy and Mauston, Wis., 1966-87; mem. Wis. State Assembly from Dist. 87, 1966-87, asst. minority leader, 1972-81, floor leader, 1981-87; self-employed real estate broker Mauston, 1970—; gov. State of Wis., 1987-2001; sec. US Dept. Health & Human Services, Washington, 2001—05; pres. Logistics Health, Inc., 2005—10, chmn., 2010—11; ptnr. Akin Gump Strauss Hauer & Feld, LLP, 2005—; ind. chmn, sr. adv. Deloitte Ctr, Health Solutions Deloitte & Touche USA, LLP, 2005—. Alt. del. Rep. Nat. Conv., 1976; chmn. Intergovtl. Policy Adv. Commn. to U.S. Trade Rep.; chmn. Nat. Govs. Assn., 1995-96, mem. nat. govs. assn. exec. com., AGA Med. Corp.; chmn. bd. dirs., Amtrak, 1998-2001; mem. bd. dirs. C.R. Bard, Inc., 2005-, Certere Corp., 2005-; nat. health policy adv. US Preventive Medicine, Dallas, 2008-. Served with USAR. Recipient med. award for Legis. Wis. Acad. Gen. Practice, Thomas Jefferson Freedon award Am. Legis. Exchange Coun., 1991, Most Valuable Pub. Official award City and State Mag., 1991, Governance award Free Congress Found., 1992, Governing Mag. Public Ofcl. of the Year, 1997, recipient Horatio Alger award, 1998, USA Mex. C of C, Good Neighbor award., 1999. Mem. ABA, Wis. Bar Assn., Rep. Govs. Assn., Phi Delta Phi. Republican. Roman Catholic. Office: Akin Gump Robert Stauss Bldg 1333 New Hampshire Ave NW Washington DC 20036-1564

THOMPSON, WILLIAM MOREAU, radiologist, educator; b. Phila., Oct. 20, 1943; s. Charles Moreau and Aileen (Haddon) T.; m. Thompson Coopon Saudraliez, Oct 20, 2007; children: Christopher Moreau, Thayer Haddon. BA, Colgate U., 1965; MD, U. Pa., 1969. Diplomate Am. Bd. Radiology. Intern Case Western Res. U., Cleve., 1969-70; resident in radiology Duke U., Durham, NC, 1972-75, from asst. prof. Med. Ctr. to prof., 1975—2001, prof. radiology Med. Ctr., 2001—10, The Reed and Martha Rice Disting. prof. radiology Med. Ctr., 2004—06; chmn. Dept. Radiology U. Minn. Hosp. and Clinic, Mpls., 1986-2000, Vilhelmina and Eugene Gedgared chair radiology, 1986—2001, prof. radiology, dir. imaging rsch., 2000-01; prof. & vice chair, dept. radiology, chief imaging svc. U. N.Mex., Albuquerque, 2010. Contbr. chpts. to books and articles to profl. jours. Served with USPHS, 1970-72. Recipient James Picker Found. Scholar in Acad. Medicine award, 1975-79, Disting. Scientist award, Armed Forces Inst. Pathology, Washington, 2001-02; R & D grantee VA, 1977-86. Fellow Am. Coll. Radiology; mem. AMA, Radiology Soc. N.Am. (program chmn. 1994-97), Minn. Med. Soc., Am. Roentgen Ray Soc., Assn. Univ. Radiologists (pres. 1989-90, Gold medal 2001), Soc. Gastrointestinal Radiology (pres. 1994-95, Cannon medal 2001), Assn. Program Dirs. (pres. 1995, Achievement award 2001), Soc. Chairs of Acad. Radiology Depts. (pres. 1997-98), Sigma Xi. Republican. Presbyterian. Office: NMex Health Care Sys Chief Imaging Svc 1301 San Pedro Albuquerque NM 87108 Home: 8809 3 Rio Grando Blvd Albuquerque NM 87114 Office Phone: 505-256-2768. Personal E-mail: thomps132@gmail.com. Business E-Mail: thomp132@nc.duke.edu.

THOMPSON, ZACHARY, city health department administrator; AS, El Centro Coll.; BS in Social Work, U. Tex., Arlington; MS, Amberton U., Garland, Tex. With W. Dallas Cmty. Ctr.; dep. dir. Dallas Co. Dept. Health and Human Svcs., Dallas, 1997—2004, dir., 2004—. Office: Dallas Co Dept Health and Human Svcs 2377 N Stemmons Fwy Dallas TX 75207-2710

THOMS, NORMAN WELLS, retired cardiovascular and thoracic surgeon; b. Bahrain, Nov. 5, 1934; (parents Am. citizens); S. Wm Wells & Ethel Scudder (Beth) Thoms; m. Anna J. Holmes, June 22, 1962; children Sharon, Alice, Galena BA, Oberlin Coll., 1955; MD, U. Mich., 1959. Diplomate Am. Bd. Surgery, Am. Bd. Thoracic Surgery. Intern Blodgett Meml. Hosp., Grand Rapids, Mich., 1959-60; resident in gen. surgery Detroit Gen. Hosp., 1960-62, 66-68, resident in thoracic surgery, 1968-70; instr. surgery Wayne State U. Sch. Medicine, Detroit, 1968-70, asst. prof., 1970-74, assoc. prof., 1974-75; pvt. practice Topeka, 1975—2003; active staff Lawrence Meml. Hosp., 2003—06; ret., 2006. Contbr. articles to profl. jours. Med. missionary, Muscat, Oman, 1964-65. Officer M.C., U.S. Army, 1962-64. Recipient Regents' award for best sci. exhibit Am. Coll. Chest Physicians, 1972, Bal Jeffrey award Stormont-Vail Found., 1995, Heart of St. Francis award, 2010. Fellow ACS, AMA; mem. Kans. Med. Soc., Shawnee County Med. Soc., Soc. Thoracic Surgeons, Wayne State Surg. Soc.

THOMSEN, HENRIK SEGELCKE, radiologist; b. Copenhagen, Apr. 29, 1953; s. Gregers Segelcke and Else Lutz (Jørgensen) T.; m. Pia Lauritzen, Jan. 5, 1980; children: Jannick, Michael, Ulrik. MD, U. Copenhagen, 1979. Cert. radiologist Be. Nat. Health Denmark, 1993. Postdoctoral scholr U. Calif., San Diego, 1980; rschr. U. Copenhagen, 1981-83; jr., sr. resident Hosps. in Copenhagen, 1981-95; cons. radiologist Copenhagen Univ. Hosp., Herlev, 1995—, lectr. in radiology, 1993—96, prof. radiology, 1997—, chmn. dept. diagnostic radiology, 2002—08; dir. dept. diagnostic scis. Faculy Health Scis., U. Copenhagen, 2007—. Cons. Bd. Nat. Health, Denmark, 1992—, Arbejdsskadestyrelsen, Denmark, 1994—2004. Editor: Uroradiology, Copenhagen '90, 1990, European Uroradiology '92, 1992, European Uroradiology '94, 1994, Internat. Uroradiology '96, 1996, Radionuclides in Nephrology, 1997, Trends in Contrast Media, 1999, Radionuclides in Nephrourology, 1998, Contrast Media Safety Issues and ESUR Guidelines, 1st edit., 2006, 2nd edit., 2009; mem. editl. bd. Acad. Radiology, Abdominal Imaging, Acta Radiologica, Urogenital Imaging, 2009, European Radiology, Roentgenologia and Radiology, Jour. Radiologie, Annals of Medicine. Named hon. mem. The Pacific N.W. Radiol. Soc., 1995. Fellow Soc. Uroradiology (Pres.'s award 1990, Lifetime Achievement award 2010); mem. European Soc. Urogenital Radiology (hon., sec., treas. 1990-96, pres.-elect 1996-98, pres. 1998-2000, 2000-02), Radiol. Soc. N.Am. Avocations: swimming, travel. Home: Olaf Poulsens Vej 5A DK-2920 Charlottenlund Denmark Office: Copenhagen University Herlev Hosp Herlev Ringvej 75 Herlev DK 2730 Denmark Office Phone: 45 44883212, 45 4488 4488. Office Fax: 45 4491 0480. Business E-Mail: hentho01@heh.regionh.dk.

THOMSON, GERALD EDMUND, physician, educator; b. NYC, 1932; s. Lloyd and Sybil (Gilbourne) T.; m. Carolyn Webber; children: Gregory, Karen. MD, Howard U., 1959; DSc (hon.), Morehouse Med. Coll., 1997. Diplomate Am. Bd. Internal Medicine (bd. govs. 1985-92, exec. com. 1988-91, chmn.-elect 1990-91, chmn. 1991-92). Resident in medicine SUNY-Kings County Hosp. Center, 1959-62, chief resident, 1962-63, NY Heart Assn. fellow in nephrology, 1964-65, asst. vis. physician, 1963-70, clin. dir. dialysis unit, 1965-67; practice medicine specializing in internal medicine NYC, 1963-64; attending physician SUNY Med. Bklyn. Hosp., 1966-70; instr. in medicine SUNY, Bklyn., 1963-68, clin. asst. prof. medicine, 1968-70; asso. chief med. services Coney Island Hosp., Bklyn., 1967-70; attending physician Presbyn. Hosp., 1970—; dir. nephrology Harlem Hosp. Center, NYC, 1970-71, dir. med. services, 1971-85, pres. med. bd., 1976-78; assoc. prof. medicine Columbia Coll. Physicians and Surgeons, 1970-72, prof., 1972—, Samuel Lambert prof. medicine, 1980—, Robert Sonneborn prof. medicine, 1997—; exec. v.p. for profl. affairs, chief of staff Columbia-Presbyn. Med. Ctr., 1985-90; sr. assoc. dean Coll. Physicians and Surgeons, Columbia U., NYC, 1990—2003. Mem. Health Rsch. Coun. City NY, 1972-75; mem. med. adv. bd. NY Kidney Found., 1971-82; mem. Health Rsch. Coun., State NY, 1975-81; mem. hypertension info. and edn. adv. com. NIH, 1973-74, NY State Adv. Com. on Hypertension, 1977-80; com. on non-pharm. treatment of hypertension Inst. of Medicine, Nat. Acad. Scis., 1980; mem. med. adv. bd. Nat. Assn. Patients on Hemodialysis and Transplantation, 1973-83; mem. adv. bd. Sch. Biomed. Edn., CUNY, 1979-83, Med. News Network, 1993-95; mem. com. on mild hypertension Nat. Heart and Lung Inst., 1976, mem. clin. trials rev. com., 1980-85, mem. rev. panel, 1979; bd. dirs. NY Heart Assn., 1973-81, chmn. com. high blood pressure, 1976-81; bd. dirs. Primary Care Devel. Corp.; chmn. com. hypertension NY Met. Regional Med. Program, 1974-76; mem. adv. com. Heart and Hypertension Inst. of NY State, 1984; mem. NY Gov.'s Health Adv. Coun., 1981-84, pub. Health Coun., NY, 1983-95, Joint Nat. Com. High Blood Pressure NIH, 1983-84, 87-88, mem. rev. panel hypertension detection and monitoring bd. study cardiovasc. risk factors in young Nat. Heart, Lung and Blood Inst., 1984-90; mem. panel on receiving and withholding med. treatment ACLU, 1984-88; mem. Grad. Med. Edn. Commn., State of NY, 1984-86, mem. Commn. on End-State Renal Disease, 1985, 89-90; pres. Washington Heights-Inwood Ambulatory Care Network Corp., 1986-91; bd. dirs. Primary Care Devel. Corp., 1993-98. Mem. adv. bd. Jour. Urban Health, 1974-80, Med. News Network, 1993-94. Chmn. ad hoc com. on access to nursing homes Pub. Health Coun. State of NY, 1982-96; pres. Washington Heights-Inwood Ambulatory Care Network Corp., 1986-91; mem. Mayor's Commn. Health and Hosps. Corp.; dir. Harlem Ctr. for Health Promotion and Disease Prevention, 1993-95. Recipient Nat. Med. award Nat. Kidney Found., NY, 1984, Outstanding Alumnus award Howard U., 1987, Disting. Alumnus award, 1998, Dean's Outstanding Tchg. award Coll. Physicians and Surgeons Columbia U., 1986, Columbia U. Pres. award Outstanding Tchg., 2002, Nickens award, Soc. General Internal Med., 2004. Mem: AAAS, ACP (master, Gov.'s coun. downstate region 1982-89, chmn. com. health pub. policy NY chpt. 1982-89, health care professions com. 1987-90, bd. regents 1990-97, chmn. nat. health and pub. policy com. 1993-94, pres.-elect 1994-95, pres. 1995-96), NY Acad. Medicine (mem. com. medicine in soc. 1974-76, chmn. com. medicine in soc. 1997-98, bd. trustees, 2000-2007, sec., 2003-07), NY Soc. Nephrology (pres. 1973-74), Am. Fedn. Clin. Rsch., Federated Coun. for Internal Medicine (chmn. 1991-92, 95-96), Soc. Urban Physicians (pres. 1972-73), Am. Soc. Artificial Internal Organs (adv. bd., 1998-2002, chmn. bd. trustees, 2002-), Assn. Program Dirs. in Internal Medicine, Pub. Health Assn. NYC (dir. 1983-86), Inst. Medicine (chmn., bd. dirs., 2003-), Physicians for Social Responsibility of NY (dir. 1983), Physicians Human Rights (bd. trustees, 2005-) Assn. Acad. Minority Physicians (pres. 1988-90), Inst. Medicine, Nat. Acad. Scis. (chmn. com. on review of NIH strategic plan on health disparities, 2004-06). Home and Office: Premium Pt New Rochelle NY 10801-5327 Business E-Mail: get1@columbia.edu.

THOMSON, J. GRANT, orthopedist, surgeon, educator; MD, McGill U., 1983. Diplomate Am. Bd. of Orthopaedic Surgery-hand surgery, 2004, Am. Bd. Plastic Surgery, 2004. Resident surgery Montreal Gen. Hosp., Canada, 1983—88, resident plastic surgery, 1988—90; rsch. fellow Royal Victoria Hosp., Montreal, Canada, 1985; fellow hand surgery Barnes Hosp., St. Louis, 1990—91; assoc. prof. plastic surgery Yale Univ.; with Yale Medical Group, Yale-New Haven Hosp. Office: Yale Plastic Surgery Yale Physicians Bldg 4th Fl 800 Howard Ave New Haven CT 06519 Office Phone: 203-737-5130. Office Fax: 203-785-5714.

THOMSON, JAMES ALEXANDER, molecular biologist, educator; b. Oak Park, Ill., Dec. 20, 1958; married; 2 children. BSc in Biophysics, U. Ill., Champaign, 1981; DVM magna cum laude, U.Pa., 1985, DS in Molecular Biology, 1988. Diplomate Am. Coll. Veterinary Pathologists. Postdoctoral rsch. fellow, Nonhuman Primate In Vitro Fertilization and Exptl. Embryology Oreg. Regional Primate Ctr., 1989—91; joined U. Wis., Madison, 1991, resident, veterinary pathology, Wis. Regional Primate Ctr., 1991—94, assoc. veterinarian, asst. scientist, Wis. Regional Primate Ctr., 1992—95, chief pathologist, Wis. Regional Primate Rsch. Ctr., 1995—; asst. prof., dept. anatomy U. Wis. Med. Sch., 1999—2001; scientific dir. WiCell Rsch. Inst., Madison, Wis., 1999—; John D. McArthur Prof., dept. anatomy U. Wis. Sch. Med. and Pub. Health, Madison, 2002—. Adj. prof., molecular, cellular, and develop. biology dept. U. Calif., Santa Barbara, 2007—; dir., regenerative biology Morgridge Inst. for Rsch. Contbr. articles to profl. sci. jours. Recipient Ill. Gen. Assembly award, 1978, Eastman Kodak award in biol. scis., 1979, C.L. Davis award for Student Scholarship in Veterinary Pathology, 1994, Golden Plate award, Am. Acad. Achievement, 1999, Hall of Fame award for Scientific Achievement, 15th Ann. Conf. Biotechnology CEO's, 2001, World Tech. award, 2002, LIFE Internat. Rsch. award, 2002, Frank Annunzio award, Christopher Columbus Fellowship Found., 2003, Outstanding Achievement award, Am. Coll. Veterinary Pathologists, 2003, Disting. Service award for enhancing edn. through biol. rsch., Nat. Assn. Biology Tchrs., Inc., 2005, Nathan R. Brewer Sci. Achievement award, Am. Assn. Lab. Animal Sci., 2006, Lois Pope award Ann. LIFE Internat. Rsch. award, 2002; named Man of Yr., Madison Mag., 2001; named a Nat. Merit Scholar, 1977, finalist for World Tech. award in health and medicine, The Economist, London, 1999; named one of The Most Intriguing People, People Mag., 2001, 18 Scientists representing America's Best in Science and Medicine, TIME Mag., 2001, The 100 Most Influential People in the World, TIME mag., 2008; fellow Wis. Acad. Scis., Arts, and Letters, 2002; NSF Undergraduate Rsch. Participation Fellow, Princeton U., 1979, Summer Fellow, Friedrich Miescher Inst., Basel, Switzerland, 1981, Veterinary Med. Scientist Tng. Program Fellow, U. Pa. Sch. Veterinary Medicine, 1981—87. Mem.: Soc. for Devel. Biology, Internat. Soc. for Stem Cell Rsch., Am. Coll. of Veterinary Pathologists, Phi Zeta, Phi Beta Kappa. Achievements include first to isolate and culture nonhuman primate embryonic stem cells in 1995, and human ES cells in 1998; lab had reported determining a method to modify human skin cells in such a way that they appear to be embryonic stem cells without using a human embryo in 2007. Office: Univ Wisconsin Genome Ctr of WI 425 Henry Mall Rm 4420 Madison WI 53715 Office Phone: 608-263-3585. Office Fax: 608-265-8984, 608-263-3517. E-mail: thomson@primate.wisc.edu.

THOMSON, KEITH STEWART, biologist, author; b. Heanor, Eng., July 29, 1938; s. Ronald William and Marian Adelaide (Coster) T.; m. Linda Gailbreath Price, Sept. 27, 1963; children: Jessica Adelaide, Elizabeth Rose. B.Sc. with honors, U. Birmingham, Eng., 1960; A.M., Harvard U., 1961, PhD (NATO fellow), 1963. NATO postdoctoral fellow Univ. Coll., London U., 1963-65; asst. prof. to prof. biology Yale U., 1965-87, dean Grad. Sch., 1979-87; dir. Peabody Mus. Natural History, 1976-79; pres. Acad. Natural Scis., Phila., 1987-95; disting. scientist-in-residence New Sch Social Rsch., NYC, 1996-98; prof., dir. Mus. Natural History Oxford U., 1998—2003, prof. emeritus, 2003—; sr. rsch. fellow Am. Philos. Soc., Phila., 2003—. Dir. Sears Found. Marine Rsch. and Oceanographic History; hon. rsch. fellow Australian Nat. U., 1967; trustee, mem. corp. Woods Hole Oceanographic Inst.; bd. dirs. Wistar Inst., Ctrl. Phila. Devel. Corp., Wetlands Inst., Phila. Cultural Alliance, Charles Darwin Trust; rschr. in vertebrate evolution. Mem. editl. bd. Paleobiology, Jour. Morphology, 1988, Aspects of Lower Vertebrate Evolution, 1968, Origin of Terrestrial Vertebrates, 1968, Saltwater Fishes of Conn., 1971, 88, Priorities and Needs in Systematic Biology, 1981, Morphogenesis and Evolution, 1988, Living Fossil, 1991, The Common But Less Frequent Loon and Other Essays, 1993, HMS Beagle, 1995, 2003, Treasures on Earth, 2002, Before Darwin: Reconciling Science and Religion, 2005, Fossils, A Very Short Introduction, 2005, The Legacy of the Mastodon, 2008, Passion for Nature: Thomas Jefferson and Natural History, 2008, The Young Charles Darwin, 2009. Fellow Linnean Soc. London, Zool. Soc. London; mem. Soc. Vertebrate Palaeontology, Sigma Xi.

THORELL, EVA ELISABETH, genealogist; b. Stockholm, May 19, 1956; MD, 1994; PhD, Örebro U., 2004. Avocations: golf, genealogy. Office: Götgatan 5 Kumla Närke SE-69231 Sweden Business E-Mail: eva@fopro.se.

THORGEIRSSON, SNORRI SVEINN, medical researcher; b. Iceland, Dec. 1, 1941; arrived in US, 1972, naturalized, 1980; d. Thorgeir Jonsson and Sigurlina Sigujonsdottir Thorgeirsson; m. Unnur Thorgeirsson Thorgeirsson, Sept. 5, 1969; children: Sif, Christian. MD, U. Iceland, 1968; PhD, U. London, 1971. Intern U. Hosp., Reykjavik, Iceland, 1968—69; registrar, rsch. fellow dept. clin. pharmacology Royal Postgrad. Med. Sch., London, 1969—71. Vis. fellow Lab. Chem. Pharmacology, Nat. Heart and Lung Inst., NIH, Bethesda, Md., 1972—73; vis. scientist sect. devel. pharmacology Neonatal & Pediatric Medicine Br. Nat. Inst. Child Health & Human Devel., 1974—75; chief sect. on molecular toxicology devel. pharmacology br., 1975—76; head biochem. pharmacology sect. Lab. Chem. Pharmacology, Nat. Cancer Inst., 1976—81; chief Lab. Exptl. Carcinogenesis, 1981—; head Cellular & Molecular Biology Sect.; mem. Chem. Selection Working Group, 1978—, Com. Occupl. Carcinogenesis, 1979, mem. com. on amines Nat. Acad. Scis., 1979—80; co-chmn. Internat. Conf. on Carcinogenic and Mutagenic N-Substituted Aryl Compounds, NIH, Bethesda, 1979; preceptor Pharmacology Rsch. Assoc. Program, Nat. Inst. Gen. Med. Scis., 1977—; mem. biol. response modifiers decision network com. Nat. Cancer Inst., 1980; lectr. in field. Contbr. articles to profl. jours. Mem.: AAAS, European Assn. Cancer Rsch., Soc. Toxicology, Environ. Mutagen Soc., NY Acad. Scis., Am. Chem. Soc., Am. Soc. Exptl. Pharmacology & Exptl. Therapeutics, Am. Assn. Cancer Rsch. Achievements include research in in mechanisms of chem. carcinogenesis, control of differentiation in neo-plastic cells. Office: Nat Cancer Inst Lab Exptl Carcinogenesis Bldg 37 Rm 4146A1 37 Convent Dr Bethesda MD 20892 4262 Office Phone: 301-496-1935. Office Fax: 301-496-0734. E-mail: snorri_thorgeirsson@nih.gov. *

THORNBURG, COURTNEY D., medical educator; b. Mich., 1972; AB, Duke U., 1994, MD, 1998. Lectr. U. Mich., 2004—05; asst. prof. Duke U., 2005—09, assoc. prof., 2010—. Mem.: Internat. Soc. Thrombosis & Hemostasis, Am. Soc. Pediat. Hematology, Oncology, Am. Soc. Hematology. Office: 315 Trent Dr DUMC PO Box 102382 Durham NC 27710 Business E-Mail: thorn006@mc.duke.edu.

THORNBURY, JOHN ROUSSEAU, radiologist, physician; b. Cleve., Mar. 16, 1929; s. Purla Lee and Gertrude (Glidden) T.; m. Julia Lee McGregor, Mar. 20, 1955; children: Lee Allison, John McGregor. AB cum laude, Miami U., Oxford, Ohio, 1950; MD, Ohio State U., 1955. Diplomate: Am. Bd. Radiology. Intern Hurley Hosp., Flint, Mich., 1955-56; resident U. Iowa Hosps., Iowa City, 1958-61; instr., asst. prof. radiology U. Colo. Med. Center, Denver, 1962-63; practice medicine specializing in radiology Denver, 1962-63, Iowa City, 1963-66, Seattle, 1966-68, Ann Arbor, Mich., 1968-79, Albuquerque, 1979-84, Rochester, NY, 1984-89, Madison, Wis., 1989-94. Mem. staff U. Wis. Hosp., Madison; prof. radiology, chief sect. body imaging, U. Wis. Med. Sch., 1989-94, prof. emeritus, 1994—; asst. prof. radiology U. Iowa Hosps., 1963-66, U. Wash. Hosp., Seattle, 1966-68; assoc. prof. radiology U. Mich. Med. Ctr., 1968-71, prof., 1971-79, chief uroradiology sect., 1971-79; prof. radiology, chief divsn. diagnostic radiology Sch. Medicine, U. N.Mex., 1979-84; prof. radiology U. Rochester Sch. Medicine, 1984-89, acting chmn., 1985-87; chmn. sci. com. on efficacy studies Nat. Coun. on Radiation Protection, 1980-95; rapporteur/mem. sci. group on indications/limitations of x-ray diagnostic procedures WHO, 1983; cons. com. on efficacy of magnetic resonance nat. health tech. adv. panel Australian Inst. Health, 1986; invited U.S. cons. MRI program, U. Med. Ctr., Nijmegen, The Netherlands, 1992; mem. planning group Low Back Pain Collaboratives and Nat. Congress, Inst. for Health Care Improvement, 1997-98; mem. methodologic rsch. issues working group NIH and Pub. Health Svc.-Office of Women's Health, 1998; cons., spkr. Royal Australasian Coll. Radiologists, Melbourne, Australia, 1997; cons. tech. assessment and outcomes rsch., 1994—; cons. in tech. assessment and outcomes rsch. to dept. neuroradiology Loma Linda Med. Ctr., 2002-; cons. to Am. Soc. Neuroradiology, 1995-2000; lectr. in field. Co-author/cons. Clin. Efficacy Assessment Project, Am. Coll. Physicians, 1986-89; assoc. editor: Yearbook of Radiology, 1971-82; mem. editl. bd.: Contemporary Diagnostic Radiology, 1977-84, Urologic Radiology, 1977-84 Bd. dirs. Sally Jobe Found., Denver, 1996—. Capt., M.C. USAF, 1956-58. Recipient Dist. Svc. award Am. Bd. Radiology, 2000, Alumni Achievement award Ohio State U. Coll. Medicine, 2000, Gold medal Assn. Univ. Radiologists, 2002, Gold medal Soc. Uroradiology, 2005; grantee Agy. Health Care Policy and Rsch., 1986-91, U. Rochester, 1986-89, U. Wis., Madison, 1989-91 Fellow Am. Coll. Radiology (mem. emeritus); mem. Am. Coll. Radiology Imaging Network (outcomes and quality of life subcom., urology com., NIH, 1999-2002), Soc. Uroradiology (pres. 1976-77, dir. 1977-79, gold medal 2005), Assn. Univ. Radiologists (pres. 1980-81), Radiol. Soc. N.Am., Am. Roentgen Ray Soc. (Caldwell medal 1993), Soc. for Health Svcs. Rsch. in Radiology (adv. com. to bd. dirs. 1998—), Colo. Radiol. Soc., Phi Beta Kappa, Delta Tau Delta, Omicron Delta Kappa, Phi Chi. Episcopalian. Home: 2310 9th Ave Unit 217 Longmont CO 80503-4089

THORNE, CHARLES HEDGES MCKINSTRY, plastic surgeon; b. Oakland, Calif., Oct. 27, 1952; BA in Biophysics and Biochemistry, Yale Coll., 1974; MD, UCLA Sch. Medicine, 1976—81. Cert. Am. Bd. Surgery, 1987, Am. Bd. Plastic Surgery, 1991. Peace Corps volunteer, Ghana, 1974—76; intern Mass. Gen. Hosp., 1981—82, resident in plastic surgery, 1982—86, NYU Med. Ctr., 1986—88, fellow in craniofacial surgery, 1988—89, dir., Plastic Surgery Residency Prog., 1989—98, dir., Ctr. for Ear Anomalies, 1990—; exec. chief resident Inst. Reconstructive Plastic Surgery, 1987—88; co-dir. Ctr. for Craniofacial Prosthetics, 1992—; chief, Plastic Surgery Svc. Bellevue Hosp., 1992—2003; prog. dir., Cosmetic Surgery Manhattan Eye and Ear Hosp., 1998—99; assoc. prof., Dept. Surgery NYU Sch. Medicine; private practice in plastic surgery NYC; assoc. attending surgeon NYU Med. Ctr., Bellevue Hosp. Ctr., Manhattan Eye Ear & Throat Hosp. Mem. exec. com., NYU Med. Bd., 1994—96, Surgical House Staff Com., 1989—97, Oper. Rm. Com., NYU, 1990—98, Oper. Rm. Com., Bellevue Hosp., NYU, 1993—98, Exec. Com., NYU Assn. Attending M.D.'s, 1995—98; mem., Credentials Com. Manhattan Eye, Ear and Throat Hosp., 1998—99, mem., Quality Assurance Com., 1998—99, bd. mem., Surgeon Directors, 2000—; mem. LCME Faculty Com., NYU Sch. Medicine, 1999, Curriculum Com., NYU Sch. Medicine, 2002, Adv. Bd., Forward Face; sr. examiner Am. Bd. Plastic Surgery, 2002—. Assoc. editor (journals) Journal of Cranio-Maxillofacial Trauma, 1995—2001, Journal of Plastic and Reconstructive Surgery, 2000—. Vol. Peace Corps, Ghana, 1974—76. Recipient First prize, Am. Soc. Maxillofacial Surgeons, 1990, 1992, NY Regional Soc. Plastic Surgery, 1990, Tchr. of Yr. award, Inst. Reconstructive Plastic Surgery, NYU Med. Ctr., 1993—94, 1997—98, 1999—2000. Mem.: Northeastern Soc. Plastic Surgeons (trustee 2004—07, parliamentarian 2000—01, bd. mem.-at-large 2001—03, pres. 2002—03), Internat. Soc. Craniomaxillofacial Surgeons, Forum for Academic Plastic Surgeons (pres. 1996—97), Am. Soc. Plastic Surgeons, Am. Soc. Craniofacial Surgery, Am. Soc. Aesthetic Plastic Surgery (bd. dir. 2007—, parliamentarian 2006—07), AMA, Am. Coll. Surgeons, Am. Cleft Palate Assn., Am. Assn. Plastic Surgeons. Office: 812 Park Ave New York NY 10021 also: NYU Med Ctr 550 First Ave New York NY 10016 Office Phone: 212-794-0044. Office Fax: 212-772-1326. Business E-Mail: thornc01@popmail.med.nyu.edu.

THORNE, JOHN CARL, speech educator; b. Albuquerque, June 9, 1965; PhD, U. Wash., 2010. Instr. U. Wash., 2010—. Mem.: Am. Speech-Language Hearing Assn. Avocation: music. Office: 1417 NE 42nd St Box 354875 Seattle WA 98102 Personal E-mail: cncmicsnet@yahoo.com.

THORNER, MICHAEL OLIVER, medical educator; b. Beaconsfield, Eng., Jan. 14, 1945; came to U.S., 1977; s. Hans and Ilse T.; m. Prudence Maria Ross, July 7, 1966; children: Benjamin Bruno, Anna Rosa MB, BChir, U. London, 1970. Intern, resident Middlesex Hosp., St. Bartholomew's Hosp., London; lectr. chem. pathology St. Bartholomews Hosp., London, 1974, research fellow, 1974-75, lectr. medicine, 1975-77; assoc. prof. medicine U. Va., Charlottesville, 1977-82, prof. medicine, 1982-90, head div. endocrinology and metabolism, 1986-98, dir. Clin. Research Ctr., 1984-97, assoc. dir. CRC, 1981-84, Kenneth R. Crispell prof. in internal medicine, 1990-98, chmn. dept. internal medicine, 1998—2006, Henry B. Mulholland prof. internal medicine, 1998—2006, David C. Harrison prof. internal medicine, 2006—. Contbr. articles to profl. jours. Recipient Albion O. Bernstein award, 1984, Virginia Scientist of Yr. award, 1985, Gen. Clin. Rsch. Ctrs. program award, 1995, The Pituitary Soc. Annual award for contbns. to understanding pituitary disease, 1995, Theodore E. Woodward Award 1996. Master Am. Coll. Physicians; fellow ACP (John Phillips Meml. award 1999), AAAS, Royal Coll. Physicians, Soc. Endocrinology (Dale medal 2009), Endocrine Soc. (Edwin B. Astwood award 1992), Assn. Am. Physicians, Am. Soc. Clin. Investigations; fellow: Am. Acad. Arts & Scis. Office: U Va Health Sys Dept Internal Medicine Endocrinology PO Box 801411 Charlottesville VA 22908 Home: 906 Fendall Terr Charlottesville VA 22903 Fax: 434-982-0147. E-mail: mot@virginia.edu.

THORNSBERRY, CLYDE, microbiologist; b. Pippa Passes, Ky., June 20, 1930; s. Columbus B. and Ollie Mae (Sparkman) T.; m. Glenda L. Martin, May 13, 1952; children: Teresa, David, Robert. BS, U. Ky., Lexington, 1958, PhD, 1966. Chief Antimicrobial Investigations Br. Ctrs. for Disease Control, Atlanta, 1966-89; dir. Inst. for Microbiol. Rsch., Franklin, Tenn., 1989-93, Focus BioInova, Inc., Franklin, 1993—; dirt. Eurofins Medinet, Inc., Franklin. Lectr. in field; chmn., vice-chmn. Intersci. Conf. Anti-Agts., Washington, 1989-94; adv. bd. several pharm. cos., 1980—. Contbr. articles to profl. jours. Recipient awards USPHS, Washington, 1982, 87. Fellow Infectious Disease Soc. of Am.; mem. Am. Soc. Microbiology (BD award for Rsch. in Clin. Microbiology 2003), Am. Acad. Microbiology, NY Acad. Scis., WHO Coms. on Antibiotics, Nat. Com. Clin. Lab. Stds. Democrat. Achievements include patent-use of antimicrobial agts. to sterilize tissue for implanting; study of antimicrobials, antimicrobial resistance, and in vitro testing of antimicrobial activity; lab. was designated a WHO lab. for antimicrobial agts. Home: 5182 Waddell Hollow Rd Franklin TN 37064-9436 Office: Eurofin Medinet Inc 5182 Waddell Hollow Rd Franklin TN 37064 Personal E-mail: clyde.thornsberry@gmail.com. Business E-Mail: clyde.thornsberry@eurofinsmedinet.com.

THORNTON, CHARLES A., neurologist, educator; b. Missoula, Mont., July 23, 1955; BS, U. Iowa, 1981; MD, U. Iowa Coll. Medicine, 1981. Instr. U. Rochester Med. Ctr., Dept. Neurology, 1989—91, sr. instr., 1991—92, asst. prof., 1992—97, assoc. prof., 1997—2006, prof., 2006—. Rsch. fellowship, Muscular Dystrophy Assn., Exptl. Therapeutics fellowship, NRSA, Clin. Investigator Devel. grant, NIH-NINDS. Fellow: Am. Acad. Neurology. Office: University Rochester Med Ctr Rochester NY 14642 Office Fax: 585-276-1126. Business E-Mail: adele_cook@urmc.rochester.edu.

THORNTON, JAMES F., plastic surgeon, former military officer; b. Orange, NC, Jan. 4, 1961; m. Katherine Thornton; 5 children. BA, Austin Coll., 1982; MD, Univ. Tex. Southwestern Med. Ctr., 1989. Cert. Am. Bd. Plastic Surgery, 2000. Intern Univ. Tex. Southwestern Med. Ctr., 1989—90, resident in surgery, 1993—97; fellow in plastic surgery Emory Univ., 1997—99; assoc. prof. Univ. Tex. Southwestern Med. Ctr., Dallas, 2000—; staff mem. Parkland Meml. Hosp., Zale Lipshy Univ. Hosp., Children's Med. Ctr., St. Paul Med. Ctr. Comdr., flight surgeon Air Training Wing USN, & USNR. Decorated Navy & Marine Corps Commendation Medal, Nat. Defense Medal Dept. of the Navy; recipient Armed Forces Reserve Medal with M device, 2003; named a Top Doctor - Plastic Surgery, Redbook Mag., 2001. Fellow: Am. Coll. Surgeons; mem.: AMA, Tex. Med. Assn., Dallas County Med. Soc., Am. Soc. Plastic Surgeons, AO No. Am. Maxillofacial Faculty, Am. Soc. Maxillofacial Surgeons, Jurkiewicz Soc., Parkland Surgical Soc. Office Phone: 214-645-3113. Office Fax: 214-645-3140. Business E-Mail: james.thornton@utsouthwestern.edu.

THORNTON, SPENCER P., ophthalmologist, educator; b. West Palm Beach, Fla., Sept. 16, 1929; s. Ray Spencer and Mae (Phillips) T.; m. Annie Glenn Cooper, Oct. 6, 1956; children: Steven Pitts, David Spencer, Ray Cooper, Beth Ellen. BS, Wake Forest Coll., 1951, MD, 1954. Diplomate: Am. Bd. Ophthalmology. Intern Ga. Bapt. Hosp., Atlanta, 1954-55; resident gen. surgery U. Ala. Med. Center, 1955-56; resident ophthalmology Vanderbilt U. Sch. Medicine, 1960-63; practice medicine specializing in ophthalmic surgery Nashville, 1960—; med. dir. Thornton Eye Ctr., 1995-99; clin. prof. ophthalmology U. Tenn., Memphis, 2002. Disting. vis. prof. dept. ophthalmology U. Tenn., Memphis 2001, Ridley medal lectr., 2001; mem. staff Bapt. Hosp., chief ophthalmology svc., 1982-87; guest prof., vis. lectr. U. Toronto, 1990-92, U. Paris, 1989, Rothchilds Inst., Paris, 1992, 94, U. Pretoria, 1991, 93, others; instr. Moscow Inst. Eye Microsurgery, 1981; instr. ophthalmic surgery Am. Acad. Ophthalmology Ann. Courses; lectr. lens implant symposiums Eng., Spain, Australia, Switzerland, Can., Sweden, Greece, Germany, France, Republic of South Africa, Japan; Berzelius lectr. U. Lund, Sweden, 1992; P.J. Hay Gold medal lectr. North of Eng. Ophthal. Soc., Scarborough, 1992; pres. Biosyntrx Inc., 2002—. King Features syndicated newspaper columnist, 1959-60, feature writer, NBC radio and TV, 1958-60; author, co-author textbooks on cataract and refractive surgery; mem. editl. bd. Jour. Refractive and Corneal Surgery, Jour. Cataract and Refractive Surgery, Video Jour. Ophthalmology, Ocular Surgery News (Ophthalmologist of Yr. 1996), Ophthalmic Practice (Can.), Eye Care Tech. Mag. (Lifetime Achievement award 1996); contbr. articles to profl. jours.; inventor instruments and devices for refractive and lens implant surgery. Named one of 100 Best Ophthalmologists in Am., Ophthalmology Times mag., 1996; recipient Honor award Can. Implant Assn., 1993, Outstanding Achievement award Bowman Gray Sch. Medicine, 1995, Ridley medal U. Tenn., Memphis, Tenn., 2001, Epstein medal lectr. Durban S. Africa, 2005. Fellow: ACS (life), Am. Coll. Nutritional Medicine (pres. 2000—), Am. Acad. Ophthalmology (honor award 1995); mem.: Am. Soc. Cataract and Refractive Surgery (pres. 1997—99), Can. Implant Soc. (life), South African Intraocular Implant Soc. (life), Am. Med. Soc. Vienna (life), Delta Kappa Alpha, Phi Rho Sigma. Baptist. Home and Office: 5070 Villa Crest Dr Nashville TN 37220-1425 Business E-Mail: sthornton@biosyntrx.com.

THORNTON, YVONNE SHIRLEY, obstetrician, author, musician; b. NYC, Nov. 21, 1947; d. Donald E. and Itasker F. (Edmonds) T.; m. Shearwood McClelland, June 8, 1974; children: Shearwood III, Kimberly Itaska. BS in Biology, Monmouth Coll., 1969; MD, Columbia U., 1973, MPH, 1996; DSc (hon.), Tuskegee U., 2003. Diplomate Am. Bd. Ob-gyn. Resident in ob-gyn Roosevelt Hosp., NYC, 1973-77; fellow maternal-fetal medicine Columbia-Presbyn. Med. Center, NYC, 1977-79; commd. lt. comdr. M.C. USN, 1979; asst. prof. ob-gyn Uniformed Svcs. U. Health Scis., 1979-82; assoc. prof. Cornell U. Med. Coll., NYC, 1989-92; dir. clin. svcs. dept. ob-gyn N.Y. Hosp.-Cornell Med. Center, 1982-88; asst. attending N.Y. Lying-In Hosp., 1982-89; assoc. clin. prof. ob-gyn. Columbia P&S, 1995-98, assoc. clin. prof., 2001—02; clin. prof. ob-gyn. U. Medicine and Dentistry N.J., 1998-2000, Med. Coll. Cornell U., 2003—05, NY Med. Coll., 2008—. Dir. Chorionic Villus Sampling Program, 1984-92; dir. perinatal diagnostic testing ctr. Morristown Meml. Hosp., 1992-2000, divsn. maternal-fetal medicine St. Luke's Roosevelt Hosp. Ctr., 2000-02; vice chair ob-gyn, dir. maternal-fetal medicine, Jamaica Hosp. Med. Ctr., 2002-05; staff Nat. Naval Med. Ctr., Bethesda, Md.; saxophonist Thornton Sisters ensemble, 1955-76; vis. assoc. physician The Rockefeller U. Hosp., 1986-96; prof. clinical OB/GYN Cornell U. Med. Coll., 2003-05; examiner Am. Bd. Ob-Gyn, 1997—2010; Med. Ctr.; bd. dirs. Integra Med Am., 2006, perinatal cons. Westchester Med. Ctr., Valhalla, NY, 2007-. Author: The Ditchdigger's Daughters, 1995, (named best books for young adults ALA, Excellence in Lit. award, NJ Edn. Assn., One Book NJ, NJ Libr. Assn., 2006, nominated Pulitzer Prize 1995) Primary Care for the Obstetrician and Gynecologist, 1997, Woman to Woman, 1997, Something to Prove, 2010, Inside Information for Women, 2011 Bd. dirs. Fair Housing Coun. Northern NJ, 1985—. Recipient Excellence in Literature award, NJ Edn. Assn., 1996, winner Daniel Webster Oratorical Competition, Internat. Platform Assn., 1996, named Grand prize, NY Book Festival, 2011; nominated Pulitzer Prize, 1995. Fellow: ACOG, ACS; mem.: AMA, Am. Fedn. Musicians, Soc. Maternal-Fetal Medicine, Assn. Women Surgeons, NY Acad. Medicine. Democrat. Baptist. Office Phone: 201-570-8181. Business E-Mail: thornton@carroll.com.

THORP, JOHN MERCER, JR., physician; b. Rocky Mountain, NC, Aug. 31, 1957; BA in Zoology, U. NC, Chapel Hill, 1979; MD, East Carolina Univ., 1983. Intern Univ. NC Sch. Medicine, Chapel Hill, 1983, resident ob-gyn., 1983-87, fellow maternal-fetal medicine, 1987-89, clin. asst. prof., divsn. maternal-fetal medicine, dept. ob-gyn., 1989—90, asst. prof., divsn. maternal-fetal medicine, dept. ob-gyn., 1990—95, assoc. chair, dept. ob-gyn., 1995—99, assoc. prof., divsn. maternal-fetal medicine, dept. ob-gyn., 1995—2000, co-dir., Inst. Generalist Physician, 1999—2000, sr. rsch. fellow, Cecil G. Sheps Ctr. for Health, Svcs. Rsch., 1999—, co-dir., NC program for women's health rsch., Cecil G. Sheps Ctr. for Health Svcs. Rsch., 1999—2004, prof., dept. ob-gyn., 2000—, Hugh McAllister Disting. prof. ob-gyn, dept. ob-gyn., 2001—, interim and dep. dir., Ctr. for Women's Health Rsch., Cecil G. Ships Ctr. for Health Svc. Rsch., Dept. Epidemiology, Sch. Pub. Health, Dept. Ob-gyn, 2004—. Med. dir., HORIZONS Perinatal Substance Abuse Program U. NC, Chapel Hill, 1993—; adj. prof., dept. epidemiology, sch. pub. health and tropical medicine Tulane U., 2003—; adj. prof., dept. epidemiology, sch. pub. health U. NC, Chapel Hill, 1999—2004, Chapel Hill, 2004—, fellow, Carolina Population Ctr., 2003—, dir., biomedical core, Carolina Population Ctr., 2004—. Contbr. several articles to profl. jours. Recipient NC Divsn. Mental Health Develop. Disabilities and Substance Abuse Recogntion award for Outstanding Svc. to Women and Children, 1999, Perinatal Health Model of Excellence NC Dept. Health and Human Svcs. in Conjunction with the March of Dimes, 1999; named Mcallister Disting. Prof. Ob-gyn., 2002. Fellow: Am. Gynecological and Obstetrical Soc.; mem.: Soc. for Maternal-Fetal Medicine, Assn. Professors Gynecology and Obstetrics, Soc. Gynecologic Investigation, South Atlantic Assn. Ob-gyn., Am. Fertility Soc., Am. Coll. Ob-gyn. Office: Dept Ob-Gyn 4012 Old Clinic Bldg CB #7570 Chapel Hill NC 27599-7570 Office Phone: 919-843-7850. Office Fax: 919-843-6938. Business E-Mail: thorp@med.unc.edu.

THORPE, JOHN ELTON, research biologist, educator, consultant; b. Wolverhampton, Eng., Jan. 24, 1935; s. William Edward and Sophie Grace (Chell) T.; m. Judith Anne Johnson, Mar. 9, 1963; children: Michael, Peter. BA, U. Cambridge, Eng., 1959; PhD, U. Cambridge, 1979. Leader expedition to Brit. Honduras U. Cambridge, 1959-60; agronomist Shell Internat. Chem. Co., Eng., 1960-62; exptl., sr. sci., prin. sci. officer Freshwater Fisheries Lab., Pitlochry, Scotland, 1963-81, sr. prin. sci. officer, 1981-95; prof. II U. Bergen, Norway, 1995—2000. Vis. prof. U. Glasgow, Scotland, 1995—; disting. lectr. Dept. Fisheries and Oceans, Halifax, N.S., 1988; tech. advisor Overseas Devel. Adminstrn., Falkland Islands, 1978-79, 83-84; cons. Fundacion Chile, 1996, chmn. Internat. Adv. Bd. U. Hokkaido, Japan, 2007-2009. Co-author: (travelog) From the Cam to the Cays, 1961; editor Jour. Fish Biology, 1991-2000, Salmon Ranching, 1980; mem. editl. bd. Jour. Animal Ecology, 1989-97, Fisheries Mgmt., 1979-94, Aquaculture Rsch., 1995—, Revs. in Fish Biology and Fisheries, 1991-98, Folia Zoologica, 1992—2009, Sarsia, 1996-2004; contbr. over 270 papers to profl. jours. Chmn. cmty. coun. Killiecrankie, Scotland, 1978-80; mem. com. Scottish Wildlife Trust, Perth, 1966-71., treas. Scottish Wildlife Trust Pitlochry, 2010-, With Brit. Army med. corps, 1954-56. Recipient spl. medal for svcs. to sci. U. Lodz, Poland, 1992; emeritus fellow Leverhulme Trust, London, 1995-97, Am. Inst. Fishery Rsch. Biologists. Mem. Am. Fisheries Soc., Brit. Ecol. Soc. (editl. bd. 1988-97), Fisheries Soc. of Brit. Isles (hon.; coun. 1972-74, 76-78, 80-82, 84-86, v.p. 1988-91, pres. 2005-07, Beverton medal 2002), World Coun. Fisheries Socs. (bd. dirs. 2005-2007). Avocations: hiking, travel, music, art. Office: Inst Biomed and Life Scis U Glasgow Glasgow G12 8QQ Scotland Home: Pipers Croft PH16 5LW Killiecrankie Scotland Office Phone: 44-0-1796-47-3886. Personal E-mail: johnethorpe@btinternet.com.

THORPE, PAUL LAWRENCE, surgeon; b. Gt Driffield, Yorkshire, Eng., Sept. 15, 1967; s. Anthony Arnold Paul and Oonagh Patricia (Nee Egan) Thorpe; m. Joanna Nee Barlow, Mar. 23, 1994; children: Joseph Benedict, Patrick Jonathan, Dominic Paul, Clodagh Mary Jane. MB ChB, U. Leicester, 1991. FRCS anatomy demonstrator U. London, 1992—93; A&E officer Royal Hallamshire Hosp., Sheffield, England, 1993—94; surg. SHO North Bristol Rotation, England, 1994—97; orthop. registrar Bristol Rotation, 1997—2003; spine fellow Frenchay Hosp., Bristol, 2002—03, AO Spine Ctr., Brisbane, Australia, 2003—04; cons. spinal surgeon Somerset Spinal Surgery Svc., Taunton, England, 2004—. Faculty AO Spine, Switzerland, 2004—; founding ptnr. Blackdown Orthop. and spinal Svc., Taunton, England, 2006—; instr. ATLS-RCSEng, London, 2007—. Contbr. scientific papers. Chmn. Jr. Dr. Forum, Brit. Med. Assn., Bristol, 2000, Jr. Dr. Cmty., Brit. Med. Assn., London, 2002—03. Flying officer Royal Air Force, 1988—91, Eng. Decorated Garth Manning Trophy East Midlands U. Air Squadron, Nottingham, Eng., Aims award; recipient Gold award, Duke Edinburgh award Ctr., London, 1985. Fellow: Royal Coll. Surgeons Edinburg; mem.: Brit. Assn. Spinal Surgeons, Brit. Scoliosis Soc. Roman Catholic. Avocations: aviation, football, skiing, diving, crossword puzzles. Office: Somerset Spinal Surgery Svc Level 1 Queens Bldg Musgrove Park Hosp Taunton Somerset TA15DA England Office Phone: 01823 344825. Office Fax: 01823 343444. Business E-Mail: plpjt@doctors.org.uk.

THORSEN, MARIE KRISTIN, radiologist, educator; b. Milw., Aug. 1, 1947; d. Charles Christian and Margaret Josephine (Little) T.; M. James Lawrence Troy, Jan. 7, 1978; children: Katherine Marie, Megan Elizabeth. BA, U. Wis., Madison, 1969; MBA, George Washington U., Washington, 1971; MD, Columbia Coll. Physicians and Surgeons, 1977. Diplomate Am. Bd. Radiology. Intern. Columbia-Presbyn. Med. Ctr., NYC, 1977-78, resident dept. radiology, 1978-81; asst. prof. radiology Med. Coll. Wis., 1982-84, assoc. prof., 1984-89, prof., 1989-94; dir. computed tomography Waukesha Meml. Hosp., 1994—, Oconomowoc Meml. Hosp., 1994—. Contbr. articles to profl. jours. Fellow, Med. Coll. Wisc., Milw., 1981—82. Fellow Am. Coll. Radiology, Radiol. Soc. N. Am., Wis. Radiologic Assn. (v.p., 2005, pres., 2007). Office Phone: 262-928-2400.

THORSON, ALAN GLEN, surgeon; b. Omaha, June 20, 1952; s. E. Wallace and Vendela Marie (Havenstein) T.; m. Nancy Lois Maricle, Apr. 18, 1981; children: Alicia Marie, Scott Alan, Katherine Elizabeth. BS in Agrl. Econs., U. Nebr., 1974, BA in Internat. Rels., 1976; MD, U. Nebr., Omaha, 1979, cert. gen. surgery, 1984. Diplomate Am. Bd. Med. Examiners, Am. Bd. Surgery, Am. Bd. Colon and Rectal Surgery. Intern gen. surgery U. Nebr. Hosp., Omaha, 1979-80, resident gen. surgery, 1980-84; fellow colon and rectal surgery U. Minn., Mpls., 1984-85; sec. Colon and Rectal Surgery, Inc., Omaha, 1987-89, v.p., 1989—2008, pres., 2008; clin. asst. prof. surgery U. Nebr. Coll. Medicine, Omaha, 1985-93, clin. assoc. prof., surgery, 1993—2009, clin. prof. surgery, 2009—; clin. asst. prof. surgery Creighton U. Sch. Medicine, Omaha, 1986-88, asst. prof. surgery, 1989-92, assoc. prof. surgery, 1992—2002, program dir. sect. colon and rectal surgery, 1988—, clin. assoc. prof. surgery, 2002—09, clin. prof., 2009—. V.p. Todd Valley Farms, Inc., Mead, Nebr., 1988—; med. advisor United Ostomy Assn., Omaha chpt., 1986—; assoc. examiner Am. Bd. Colon and Rectal Surgery, 1993-96, mem 1998-2005, pres. 2004-05, CARES, chair, Nebr., 2003-10. Contbr. articles to profl. jours., chapters to medical textbooks. Trustee Nebr. satellite Crohn's Colitis Found. of Am., 1992—93, med. adv. bd. Nebr. satellite, Rocky Mt. chpt., 2007—08, med. adv. bd. Nebr. chpt., 2008—; pres. Met. Omaha Med. Soc., 1999—2000, Nebr. Med. Assn., 2003—04, Met. Omaha Med. Assn., 2006—; 1st v.p. St. Andrews United Meth. Ch., 2008; pres. elect Am. Cancer Soc., 2009; mem. adminstrv. bd. Faith Westwood United Meth. Ch., Omaha, 1988—92; active health ministries St. Andrews United Meth. Ch., Omaha, 2006—09; bd. dirs. Nebr. divsn. Am. Cancer Soc., 1991—96, pres. Nebr. divsn., 1995—96, sec. Heartland divsn., 1998—99, vice chair Heartland divsn., 1999—2000, chmn. Heartland divsn., 2000—03, chief med. office High Plains divsn., 2005—07, pres. Cancer Action Network, 2004—06, 2d v.p. Nat. Bd., 2007—, 1st v.p. Nat. Bd., 2008, nat. bd. pres., 2009—10, past pres., 2010—. Fellow ACS, Am. Soc. Colon and Rectal Surgeons (treas. 2007—), Southwestern Surg. Congress (sec.-treas. 1999-2005, v.p 2005-06, pres. elect., 2006-07, pres. 2007-08), Soc. Surg. Oncology; mem. AMA, Am. Soc. Colon Rectal Surgeons (treas. Rsch. Found. 2007-11), Rsch. Found. Am. Soc. Colon & Rectal Surg. (treas. 2007-11), Am. Soc. Gastrointestinal Endoscopy, Soc. Surgery Alimentary Tract, Soc. Am. Gastrointestinal Endoscopic Surgeons, Wilderness Med. Soc., Nebr. Med. Assn. (pres. 2003-04), Omaha Midwest Clin. Soc., Assn. Program Dirs. for Colon and Rectal Surgery (pres. 1996-99), Am. Assn. Clin. Anatomists, Met. Omaha Midwest Soc. (pres. 1999-2000, sec., treas. found. 2005—), Nebr. Cancer Coalition (chair 2010-). Avocations: swimming, backpacking, landscape painting in oil. Office: Colon and Rectal Surgery 9850 Nicholas St Ste 100 Omaha NE 68114 Office Phone: 402-343-1122.

THORSTEINSSON, GUDNI, physiatrist; b. Vestmannaeyjar, Iceland, Aug. 5, 1941; came to U.S., 1971; s. Thorsteinn and A. G. Einarsson; m. Elin Klein, Apr. 10, 1965; children: Arnar Karl, Asdis Thora. BS, Reykjavik (Iceland) Coll., 1961; candidatus med. et chirurg., U. Iceland, Reykjavik, 1968; MS, U. Minn., 1976. Diplomate Am. Bd. Phys. Medicine and Rehab. Dist physician Icelandic Govt., Djupivogur, 1970-71; resident dept. phys. medicine and rehab. Mayo Found., Rochester, Minn., 1972-75, mem. consulting staff, 1975-80; chair dept. Nat. Hosp., Reykjavik, 1980-81; dir. rehab. Mayo Clinic/St. Mary's Hosp., Rochester, 1981-85; dir. out-patient rehab. Mayo Clinic, Rochester, 1985-88, chair dept., 1987-91, chair dept. phys. medicine and rehab. Jacksonville, Fla., 1991-99. Physiatrist cons. Mayo Clinic, Rochester, 81-91, Jacksonville, 1991—. Author: (with others) Efficacy of Transcountaneous Electrical Stimulation, 1977, Placebo Effect of Transcountaneous Electrical Stimulation, 1978, Electrical Stimulation for Anagesia, 1983, Management of Post Polio Syndrome, 1997. Mem. Am. Acad. Phys. Medicine and Rehab. Office: Mayo Clinic Jacksonville 4500 San Pablo Rd S Jacksonville FL 32224-1865

THOTATHIL, ZIAD, oncologist; b. Alwaye, Kerala, India, Nov. 7, 1969; s. Said Mohammed Thotathil and Suhara Mohammed; m. Fouzia Abdul Kader, May 20, 1993; children: Nabeel, Aliyah. MBBS, Calicut Med. Coll., India, 1994; MD, Kidwai Meml. Inst. Oncology, Bangalore, India, 1998. Diplomate in radiotherapy Nat. Bd. Exams. India, 1999. Registrar radiation oncology Tata Meml. Hosp., Mumbai, 1998—2000; registrar oncology Kuwait Cancer Control Ctr., 2000—05; registrar med. oncology Waikato Hosp., Hamilton, New Zealand, 2005—07, cons. oncologist, 2007—. Contbr. articles to profl. jours. Fellow: Royal Coll. Radiologists; mem.: Nat. Acad. Med. Sciences, Indian Soc. Oncology, Indian Assn. Palliative Care, European Soc. Therapeutic Radiology Oncology, Am. Soc. Clin. Oncology (mem. internat. adv. group 2005—08). Avocations: soccer, travel, photography. Office: Waikato Hosp Pembroke St 3204 Hamilton New Zealand Office Fax: 6478398778. Business E-Mail: thotathz@waikatodhb.govt.nz.

THRALL, JAMES HUNTER, radiologist, educator; b. Ann Arbor, Mich., 1943; BA, U. Mich., Ann Arbor, 1964, MD, 1968. Intern Walter Reed Army Med. Ctr., Washington, 1968-69, resident in radiology, 1969-72, fellow in nuclear medicine, 1972-73, asst. chief nuclear med. svc. dept. radiology, 1973-75; asst. prof. radiology and nuclear medicine U. Mich., Ann Arbor, 1975-78, assoc. prof., 1978-81, prof., 1981-83; chmn. radiology dept. Henry Ford Hosp., Detroit, 1983; Juan M. Taveras prof. radiology Harvard Med. Sch., Cambridge, Mass., 1988—, chmn. dept. radiology; radiologist-in-chief Mass. Gen. Hosp., Boston, 1988—. Cons. nuclear medicine Ann Arbor VA Hosp.; chmn. bd. dirs. Mobile Aspects; co-founder, bd. chmn. WorldCare Ltd., 1992; chair exec. com. Harvard Depts. Radiology; hon. lectr. European Soc. Radiology, 2008. Contbr. articles to profl. jours.; mem. editl. bd.: Jour. Nuc. Medicine, Internat. Jour. Cardiac Imaging, Investigative Radiology, Jour. the Am. Coll. Radiology. Bd. trustees Mass. Gen. Physicians Orgn., Rsch. and Edn. Found. the Radiol. Soc. North America; bd. councilors Soc. Chiefs Academic Radiology Depts.; chair internat. medicine com. Mass. Gen. Hosp.; mem. Am. Coll. Radiology Found. Maj. M.C. US Army, 1968—75. Recipient Excellence of Leadership award, Diagnostic Imaging mag. Fellow: Am. Coll. Radiology (chmn. bd. chancellors 2008—, mem. Web site adv. com., past chmn. commn. on molecular imaging); mem.: Radiol. Soc. North America (Gold medal 2007), Am. Roentgen Ray Soc. (past. pres., Gold medal 2007).

THRASHER, J. BRANTLEY, urologist; MD, Med. U. SC. Diplomate Am. Bd. Urology. Intern Walter Reed Army Med. Ctr.; resident Fitzsimons Army Med. Ctr.; fellow Duke U. Med. Ctr.; program dir. urology residency program Madigan Army Med. Ctr.; prof. & William L. Valk chair. urology. U. Kans. Med. Ctr., 1998—, co-dir. operative svcs. Presenter in field; prin. investigator on numerous clin. and lab. rsch. protocals; co-investigator or collaborator in rsch. funded by CDC and Dept. of Def. Assoc. editor The 5-Minute Urology Consult, coord. editor Prostate Cancer Journal, Prostate Diseases Journal, Practical Reviews in Urology, specialty editor Journal of Urology, mem. editl. adv. bd. Journal of American Family Physician, mem. editl. coun. Urology Times, sect. editor, Cancer Prevention Seminars in Urologic Oncology; contbr. several articles to peer-reviewed jours. Named one of America's Top Physicians in Urologic Oncology, Consumer's Rsch. Coun., 2003, 2006, 2007, Best Doctors in America, Best Doctors Consortium, 2002—06; named to Best Doctors list, Ingram's Bus. Mag., 2003, 2004, Best Doctors, Kansas City Mag., 2002, 2007. Fellow: ACS (chmn. metropolitan Kansas City com. on applicants); mem.: Soc. Urologic Oncology (exec. bd. and chmn. fellowship com.), Am. Urological Assn. (Kansas state rep. to bd. dirs. of the South Ctrl. sect.). Office: University of Kansas Medical Center 3901 Rainbow Blvd Kansas City KS 66160

THRASHER, ROSE MARIE, critical care and community health nurse; b. Urbana, Ohio, Jan. 19, 1948; d. Jesse and Anna Frances (Clark) T. Student, Mercy Med. Ctr. Sch. Med. Tech., 1966—67, Wittenberg U., Springfield, Ohio, 1969—70; BSN, Ohio State U., 1974, BA in Anthropology, 1994, BA in Art History, 1997, BA in Geography, 2002, MSN, 2009. RN, Ohio; bd. cert. cmty. health nurse ANA; cert. provider BCLS and ACLS, Am. Heart Assn., CCRN, AACN; cert. asthma mgmt. edn. Am. Lung Assn. Ohio. Critical care nurse Staff Builders Health Care Svc., Oakland, Calif., 1975—76, 1981—85; supr., case mgr. and home health nurse passport and intermittent care programs Interim Health Care (formerly Med. Pers. Pool), Columbus, Ohio, 1976—77, 1985—2004; pub. health nurse Columbus Health Dept., 1977—78, Vis. Nurse Assn., Atlanta, 1978, Planned Parenthood, Columbus, Ohio, 1979—80; critical care nurse VA Med. Ctr., San Francisco, 1981; chart reviewer Interim Health Care Support Svc., Columbus, 1996—98; IRP nurse Ohio State U. Hosps. East, 1999—2003; ind. home health nurse, provider med. svcs. State of Ohio Dept. Human Svcs., 1999—2005; home health nurse Interim Health Care, Newark and Pataskala, Ohio, 2004—11, case mgr., 2007—08; ind. contractor for people with disabilities WOHL Comm. Svcs. Inc., Gaithersburg, Md., 2007—08; RN Med. Health Sys., Ohio Jobs and Family Svc., Columbus, 2008—. Acad. scholar Wittenberg U., Ohio State U. Mem. AACN, ANA (coun. cmty. health nursing), AAUW, AAAS, Internat. Union Anthrop. and Ethnol. Scis., NY Acad. Scis., Ohio Nurses Assn., Intravenous Nurses Soc., Ohio State U. Alumni Assn., Am. Anthrop. Assn., Midwest Art History Soc., Coll. Art Assn., Nat. Mus. Women in Arts, Nat. Women's Hall of Fame, Ohio Acad. Sci., Ohio State U. Coll. of Nursing Alumni Soc., Nat. Women's History Mus. Business E-Mail: thrasher.2@osu.edu.

THREEFOOT, SAM ABRAHAM, physician, educator; b. Meridian, Miss., Apr. 10, 1921; s. Sam Abraham and Ruth Frances (Lilienthal) Threefoot; m. Virginia Rush, Feb. 6, 1954; children: Barbara Jane Stockton Mattingly, Ginny Ruth Threefoot Lindberg, Tracyann Threefoot Esenstad, Shelley Ann Cowan. BS, Tulane U., New Orleans, 1943, MD, 1945. Diplomate: Am. Bd. Internal Medicine. Intern Michael Reese Hosp., Chgo., 1945-47; asst. vis. physician Charity Hosp. New Orleans, 1947-50, vis. physician, 1950-57, sr. vis. physician, 1957-69, cons., 1969-70, 76-91; clin. asst. dept. medicine Touro Infirmary, New Orleans, 1953-56, jr. asst., 1956-60, sr. asst., 1960-63, dir. med. edn., 1953-63, dir. research, 1953-70, sr. dept. medicine, 1963-70; fellow dept. medicine Tulane U., 1947-49, instr., 1948-53, asst. prof., 1953-59, asso. prof., 1959-63, prof., 1963-70, 76-91, prof. emeritus, 1991—, asst. dean, 1979-91, adj. prof. emeritus Sch. Pub. Health & Tropical Medicine, 1993—; chief of staff VA Hosp. (Forest Hills div.), Augusta, Ga., 1970-76; asso. chief staff VA Hosp., New Orleans, 1976-79, chief of staff, 1979-91, cons., 1991—97; asst. dean Med. Coll. Ga., 1970-76, prof. medicine, 1970-76. Cons. physician Lallie Kemp Charity Hosp., Independence, La., 1951-53 Editor: Lymphology, 1967-70, sr. mem. editl. bd.; Contbr. articles profl. jours. Served with AUS, 1943-45. La. Heart Assn. grantee, 1953-55; John A. Hartford Found. grantee, 1956-74; Am. Heart Assn. grantee, 1959-61; USPHS grantee, 1953-66 Fellow ACP, Am. Coll. Cardiology, NY Acad. Sci.; mem. Am. Heart Assn. (v.p. 1970, fellow council on circulation), Central Soc. Clin. Research, So. Soc. Clin. Investigation (pres. 1967), AAAS, Internat. Soc. Lymphology, Soc. Exptl. Biology and Medicine, Soc. Nuclear Medicine, Microcirculatory Conf., Inc., Am. Fedn. Clin. Research, La. Heart Assn. (pres. 1967), Nat. Assn. VA Chiefs of Staff (pres. 1987-88), Phi Beta Kappa, Sigma Xi. Jewish. Home: 1750 St Charles Ave Unit 616 New Orleans LA 70130 Office Phone: 504-524-3668. Personal E-mail: threefoot@bellsouth.net.

THRODAHL, MARK CRANDALL, medical products executive; b. Charleston, W.Va., Mar. 31, 1951; s. Monte Cordon and Josephine (Crandall) T.; m. Sudie Kenton, Oct. 21, 1978; children: Mary Elizabeth, Anne Katherine, Andrew Kenton. AB, Princeton U., 1973; MBA, Harvard U., Boston, 1975. Various positions Mallinckrodt, Inc., St. Louis, 1975-88; dir. corp. planning Becton Dickinson & Co., Franklin Lakes, NJ, 1988-91, pres. Nippon Becton Dickinson Tokyo, 1991-94, sector pres. Franklin Lakes, 1994-95, sr. v.p., 1995-2001; CEO Consort Medical, London, 2001—. Mem. Old Warson Country Club, Ivy Club. Republican. Episcopalian. Home: 38 Carteret Rd Allendale NJ 07401-1850 Office: PO Box 708 Warsaw IN 46581-0708 Business E-Mail: mark.throdahl@gmail.com.

THU ANH, NGUYEN, medical researcher; b. Hanoi, Vietnam, Jan. 3, 1975; MD, Hanoi Med. U., Vietnam, 1998; PhD in Social Sci., U. Amsterdam, 2009. Officer Textile and Garment Health Ctr., Vietnam, 1998—99; lectr. Hanoi Med. U., Vietnam, 1999—2008; chief Chemonics Internat., Vietnam, 2008—. Cons. in field, 2003—08. Scholarships, Ministry of Fgn. Affairs. Mem.: Vietnam Tech. Working Group HIV/AIDS. Home: 1502 262 Nguyen Huy Tuong Hanoi 10000 Vietnam Personal E-mail: anhstat@yahoo.com.

THUMBOO, JULIAN, rheumatologist, researcher; b. Singapore, Apr. 3, 1965; m. Lai-Fun Sum; 3 children. MB BChir, Nat. U. Singapore, 1988, M in Medicine, 1993. Intern Singapore Gen. Hosp., 1988—89; resident Singapore Gen. Hosp./Tan Tock Seng Hosp., 1991—93; registrar Tan Tock Seng Hosp., Singapore, 1994—96, sr. registrar, 1997—99, cons. rheumatologist, 1999—2000; fellow Mayo Clinic, Rochester, Minn., 1996—97; cons. rheumatologist Nat. U. Hosp., Singapore, 2000—03; head health svcs. rsch. unit. Singapore Gen. Hosp., 2009—, head dept. rheumotology; mem. Civil Aviation Med. Bd., 2011—. Asst. prof. Nat. U. Singapore, 2000—02, assoc. prof., 2003—09, adj. prof., 2009—; cons. rheumatologist Singapore Gen. Hosp., 2003, sr. cons. rheumatologist, 2004—, head dept.

rheumatology, 2007—, head, health svcs. rsch. unit, 2009—; mem. specialist tng. com. rheumatology Ministry Health; mem. Civil Aviation Med. Bd., 2011—. Mem. editl. bd.: Asia Pacific League Against Rheumatism Jour. Rheumatology, 1997—, assoc. editor:, 2003—05; contbr. chapters to books, articles to profl. jours.; editor: (Nat. Arthritis Found. patient newsletter) Arthritis Today, 2001—02. Vice chmn. Nat. Arthritis Found., Singapore, 2002. Maj. Singapore Armed Forces, 2000. Recipient Overseas Svc. medal, Singapore Armed Forces, 1990. Fellow: Royal Coll. Physicians; mem.: Coll. Physicians Singapore (hon. sec. 2005—06, treas. 2006—), Acad. Medicine Singapore (exec. com. mem. 2001—02, hon. sec. 2003—04, chpt. physicians, vice chmn., chpt. rheumatologists 2007—11, vice chmn. chapt. rheumatologists 2007—11), Singapore Soc. Immunology, Allergy and Rheumatology (sec. 1994—96). Office: Singapore General Hosp Outram Road Singapore 169608 Singapore Office Phone: 65-6326-6893. Office Fax: 65-6220-7765. Business E-Mail: julian.thumboo@sgh.com.sg.

THYE, CHAN HENG, orthopaedic surgeon; b. July 5, 1939; s. Chan Hoe Lum and Kan Hup Yee; m. Chan Seok Loo, Sept. 1969; children: Chan Ching Wan, Chan Lye Wan. MB BS, U. Singapore, 1966; MCH in Orthopedics, U. Liverpool, 1973. Sr. registrar Singapore Gen. Hosp., 1975; head cons. Dept. accident and emergency medicine Tan Tock Seng Gen. Hosp., 1976—80, head and sr. cons. dept. orthop. surgery, 1976—80; dir. Chan Orthopedic Clinic Mt. Elizabeth Hosp., 1980—95, Gleneagles Med. Ctr., Singapore, 1995—. Surgeon St. John Ambulance, Singapore, 1975—; pres. Alumni Assn., Singapore, 1992—93, Coll. Pvt. Practitioners, Singapore, 1986—90. Fellow: Acad. Medicine, RACS; mem.: Western Pacific Orthop. Assn., Singapore Med. Assn. Avocations: swimming, golf, exercise. Office: Chan Orthopaedic Clinic 6 Napier Rd # 02-10/11 Singapore 258499 Singapore Home: 4 Namly Hill 267268 Singapore Singapore Office Phone: 64758011. Personal E-mail: hengthye@hotmail.com.

THYSEN, BENJAMIN, biochemist, health science facility administrator, researcher; b. NYC, July 27, 1932; s. Bernard and Clara (Linietsky) Tissenbaum; children: Julie Ann. BS, CCNY, 1954; MS, U. Mo., 1963; PhD, St. Louis U. Med. Sch., 1967. Instr. biochemistry and ob-gyn. depts. St. Louis U. Med. Sch., 1967-68; sr. rsch. scientist Technicon Instrument Corp., Ardsly, N.Y., 1968-69, group leader Tarrytown, N.Y., 1969-70; asst. prof. depts. ob-gyn. and lab. medicine Albert Einstein Coll. Medicine, Bronx, 1971-86, dir. endocrine labs., 1971-2001, assoc. prof. dept. ob-gyn., 1986—2001, dir. andrology labs., 1991—2001, assoc. clin. prof. depts. ob-gyn. and epidemiology, 2001—04, assoc. prof. emeritus dept. epidemiology, 2004; lab. dir. Park Ave. Fertility, NYC, 2001—09, Calif. Cryobank, 2009—. Cons. Technicon Instrument Corp., Tarrytown, 1979-81; mem. spl. study sect. Nat. Inst. Environ. Health Sci., 1986. Contbr. articles to profl. jours. Served with U.S. Army, 1956-58. Recipient Cancer Rsch. award St. Louis U., 1967-68; NIH fellow, 1963-66; E.A. Doisy, Sr. fellow, 1966-67. Mem. AAAS, Fed. Am. Soc. Exptl. Biology, Assn. Clin. Scientists, Soc. Study of Reprodn., Endocrine Soc., Sigma Xi., Am. Soc. Andrology. Office: California Cryobank 369 Lexington Ave New York NY 10017 Office Phone: 212-779-1608. Personal E-mail: bthysen@aol.com.

TIAGO, ROMUALDO SUZANO LOUZEIRO, otolaryngologist; b. Corrente, PI, Brazil, Jan. 13, 1970; s. José Tiago Nogueira and Maria Elsa Louzeiro Tiago; m. Raquel Paganini Louzeiro Pereira; 1 child, Carolina Paganini Louzeiro. Degree, Goiás Fed. U., Brazil, 1993; MS, São Paulo Fed. U., Brazil, 2001, PhD, 2005. Cert. Brazilian Assn. Otorhinolaryngology-Facial and Neck Surgery, 1997, Brazilian Soc. Head and Neck Surgery, 1999. Asst. physician Hosp. Servidor Púb. Mcpl. São Paulo, 1999—; postdoc. Fed. U. São Paulo, 2005—07. Mem.: Brazilian Assn. Otorhinolaryngology-Facial and Neck Surgery, Am. Acad. Otolaryngology-Head and Neck Surgery (V.P.'s award 2006). Achievements include research in age-related changes in human laryngeal nerves. Home: Rua Pio 12 439 - Apt 122 01322-030 São Paulo SP Brazil

TIAN, SHAOQI, surgeon; b. Shandong, China, Apr. 15, 1982; MD, Qingdao U. Med. Coll., PhD, 2009. Physician Affiliated Hosp. Med. Coll. Qingdao U., 2009—11. Office: 16 Jiangsu Rd Qingdao Shandong 266003 China Office Fax: 86532-82911840. Personal E-mail: shaoqi99@yahoo.com.cn.

TIAN, XINRONG, chemist; b. Liaocheng, China, Feb. 10, 1965; PhD, Va. Tech, 1995. Investigator GlaxoSmithKline, 2006. Mem.: Am. Chem. Soc., Phi Kappa Phi Honor Soc. Home: 2512 Condor Dr Audubon PA 19403 Personal E-mail: tian.x@hotmail.com.

TIAN, YA-CHUNG, nephrologist, educator; b. Kaohsiung, Taiwan, Apr. 10, 1968; MD, Med. Coll. Kaohsiung U., Taiwan, 1993; PhD, U. Cardiff, 2003. Chief clin. nephrology divsn. Dept. Nephrology, Lin-Kou Chang-Gung Meml. Hosp., Taiwan, 2008—, assoc. prof., 2008—11. Recipient Rsch. award, Chen Wan-Yu Scholar Found. Mem.: Taiwan Soc. Nephrology. Avocations: baseball, basketball, hiking. Office: 5 Fusing St Gueishan Twp Tao-yuan 333 Taiwan Office Fax: 00886-3-3282173. Business E-Mail: dryctian@yahoo.com.

TIAN, YONGPING, medical educator; b. Dingxi, Gansu, China, Jan. 24, 1969; B, Gansu TCM Coll., 1989. Assoc. prof. acupuncture and moxibustion Affiliated Hosp., Gansu TCM Coll., 1989—. Office: Affiliated Hospital Gansu TCM Coll Lanzhou Gansu 730020 China Office Fax: 0931-8635229. Business E-Mail: tianypw@126.com.

TIAN KANG, GUO, surgeon, educator; b. Lanzhou, Gansu, Mar. 19, 1959; MD, Lanzhou U., 2008. Prof., pres. Gansu Provincial Hosp., 2004. Office: Dong Gang West Rd 160 Lanzhou Gansu 730000 China Business E-Mail: gssyyb1883@126.com.

TICHÝ, MILON, toxicologist; b. Praha, Czech Republic, Apr. 28, 1937; s. Gustav Tichý and Jarmila (Pantucková) Tichá; m. Marie Karlová; 1 child, Zuzana Tichá (Lebedová). RNDr, Charles U., Faculty Natural Scis., Praha, 1961; PhD, Czechoslovak Acad. Scis., 1966; DSc, Charles U., Faculty Pharmacy, Hradec Králové, 1990. Natural Scientist Diplomate, Charles U., 1963. Head rsch. group Nat. Inst. Pub. Health, Rsch. Group Toxicological Analysis; Lab. Predictive Toxicology, Praha, Czech Republic, 1984—; cons. ctr. dir. Nat. Inst. Pub. Health, Ctr. Lab. Processes, Praha, 2008; assoc. Prof. Charles U., Faculty Natural Scis., Praha, Czech Republic, 1993. Contbr. scientific papers. Recipient Occupl. Medicine award, Czech Med. Soc., 1976, 1984, Czech Nat. Prize, 1989, prize, Saprik Chem. Soc., 2011. Mem.: Internat. QSAR Soc., Czech Chem. Soc. Sect. Analytical Toxicology (head 2003—09, head, sect. toxicology 2009—), Exptl. and Clin. Pharmacology and Toxicology, Toxicological Sect., Internat. Soc. Studies Xenobiotics, Soc. Environ. Toxicology and Chemistry, Am. Chem. Soc., Czech Med. Soc. (hon.). Achievements include research in quantitative structure-activity relationships; quantitative activity-activity relationships; chemical safety, alternative toxicity testing, toxicokinetics; predictive toxicology. Office: Nat Inst Public Health Šrobárova 48 Prague 10042 Czech Republic Business E-Mail: mtichy@szu.cz.

TICOZZI, NICOLA, neurologist; b. Milan, Feb. 25, 1979; MD, U. Milan Med. Sch., 2004. Cert. specialization in neurology U. Milan Med. Sch., 2009. Resident neurology IRCCS Inst. Auxologico Italiano, 2004—09, cons. neurologist, 2009—; postdoc. fellow day lab. neuromuscular rsch. Mass. Gen. Hosp., 2008; postdoc. fellow dept. neurology U. Mass. Med. Sch., 2008—09. Office: Ple Brescia 20 Milan 20149 Italy Office Fax: (39)02619112937. Business E-Mail: n.ticozzi@fastwebnet.it.

TIDBALL, M. ELIZABETH PETERS, physiologist, educator; b. Anderson, Ind., Oct. 15, 1929; d. John Winton and Beatrice (Ryan) Peters; m. Charles S. Tidball, Oct. 25, 1952. BA, Mt. Holyoke Coll., 1951, LHD, 1976; MS, U. Wis., 1955, PhD, 1959; MTS summa cum laude, Wesley Theol. Sem., 1990; DSc (hon.), Wilson Coll., 1973, Trinity Coll., 1974, Cedar Crest Coll., 1977, U. of South, 1978, Goucher Coll., 1979, St. Mary-of-The-Woods Coll., 1986; LittD (hon.), Regis Coll., 1980, Coll. St. Catherine, 1980, Alverno Coll., 1989; HHD (hon.), St. Mary's Coll., 1977, Hood Coll., 1982; LLD (hon.), St. Joseph Coll., 1983; LHD (hon.), Skidmore Coll., 1984, Marymount Coll., 1985, Converse Coll., 1985, Mt. Vernon Coll., 1986. Tchg. asst. physiology dept. U. Wis., 1952—55, rsch. asst. physiology dept., 1958—59; rsch. asst. anatomy dept. U. Chgo., 1955-56, rsch. asst. physiology dept., 1956-58; USPHS postdoctoral fellow NIH, Bethesda, Md., 1959-61; staff pharmacologist Hazleton Labs., Falls Church, Va., 1961, cons., 1962; assoc. in physiology George Washington U. Med. Ctr., 1960-62, asst. rsch. prof. dept. pharmacology, 1962-64, assoc. rsch. prof. dept. physiology, 1964-70, rsch. prof., 1970-71, prof., 1971-94, prof. emeritus, 1994—; asst. dir. M of Theol. Studies program Wesley Theol Sem., 1993-94; disting. rsch. scholar Hood Coll., Frederick, Md., 1994—, co-dir. Tidball Ctr. for Study of Ednl. Environments, 1994—. Lucie Stern Disting. vis. prof. natural scis. Mills Coll., 1980; scholar in residence Coll. Preachers, 1984, Salem Coll., 1985, Wesley Theol. Sem., 1992; Disting. scholar in residence So. Meth. U., 1985; vis. trustee prof. Skidmore Coll., 1995; cons. FDA, 1966-67, assoc. sci. coord. sci. assocs. tng. programs, 1966-67, com. on NIH tng. programs and fellowships NAS, 1972-75; faculty summer confs. Am. Youth Found., 1967-78; founder, dir. Summer Seminars Women Am. Youth Found., 1987-95; cons. for instl. rsch. Wellesley Coll., 1974-75; exec. sec. com. on edn. and employment women in sci. and engring. Commn. on Human Resources, NRC/NAS, 1974-75, vice-chmn., 1977-82; cons., staff officer NRC/NAS, 1974-75; cons. Woodrow Wilson Nat. Fellowship Found., 1975-99, NSF, 1974-91; cons. Middle State Assn. Colls. & Schs., 1986-94, bd. mentor Assn. Governing Bds. Univs. and Colls., 1991-2000, Gale Fund for the Study of Trusteeship Adv. Comm., 1992-98; cons. Women's Coll. Coalition Rsch. Adv. Com., 1992-2000; Single Gender Schooling Working Group, US Dept. Edn., 1992-94, Women's Colls. Roundtable, 1998; rep. to DC Commn. on Status of Women, 1972-75; nat. panelist Am. Coun. on Edn., 1983-90; panel mem. Congl. Office Tech. Assessment, 1986-87; fellows selection com., fellows mentor Coll. Preachers, 1992-05. Lead author: Taking Women Seriously: Lessons and Legacies for Educating the Majority, American Council on Education Higher Education Series, 1999; columnist Trusteeship, 1993-95; mem. editl. bd. Jour. Higher Edn., 1979-84, cons. editor, 1984—; mem. editl. bd. Religion and Intellectual Life, 1983—; contbr. articles to profl. jours. Trustee Mt. Holyoke Coll., 1968-73, vice chmn., 1972-73, trustee fellow, 1988—2010; trustee Hood Coll., 1972-84, 86-92, exec. com., 1974-84, 89-92, trustee emerita, 1997—; overseer Sweet Briar Coll., 1978-85, dir. emerita, 2003—; trustee Cathedral Choral Soc., 1976-90, pres. bd. trustees, 1982-84, hon. trustee, 1991—; trustee Skidmore Coll., 1988—11, exec. com., 1993—2009, trustee emeritus, 2011-; trustee Bishop Claggett Ctr., 2003-; governing bd. Cathedral Coll. of Preachers, 1979-85, chmn., 1983-85; governing bd. Protestant Episcopal Cathedral Found., 1983-85, exec. com., 1983-85; bd. vis. Salem Coll., 1986-93; ctr. assoc. Nat. Resource Ctr., Girls Club Am., 1983-90; governing bd. Buckinham's Choice Residents' Assn., 1999-2002; cathedral vol. coun. Washington Nat. Cathedral, 2006-09. Recipient Alumnae medal Honor, Mt. Holyoke Coll., 1971, Outstanding Svc. award, Am. Youth Found., 1975, Valuable Contbns. Gen. Alumni Assn. award, George Washington U., 1982, 1987, Pres.'s medal, 1999, medal Outstanding Achievement, Chestnut Hill Coll., 1987, Lifetime Svc. and Scholarship award, Bd. Women's Coll. Coalition and Nation's Women's Coll. Presidents, 1998, Order of Merit, Cathedral Choral Soc., 2000, Kemball-Cook Trustee award, Skidmore Coll., 2008; named Outstanding Grad., The Penn Hall Sch., 1988; Shattuck fellow, 1955—56, Mary E. Woolley fellow, Mt. Holyoke Coll., 1958—59, postdoctoral fellow, USPHS, 1959—61. Mem. AAAS, Am. Physiol. Soc. (chmn. task force on women in physiology 1973-80, com. on coms. 1977-80, mem. emeritus 1994—), Am. Assn. Higher Edn., Mt. Holyoke Alumnae Assn. (dir. 1966-70, 76-77), Histamine Club, Sigma Delta Epsilon, Sigma Xi. Episcopalian.

TIEFENBRUN, JONATHAN, surgeon; b. NYC, Feb. 5, 1943; s. Joseph and Helen (Henkin) Tiefenbrun; m. Susan Kissil, June 19, 1966; children: Michele, Jeremy, Gregory. MD, SUNY, Bklyn., 1966. Diplomate Am. Bd. Surgery. Med. intern Kings County Hosp., Bklyn., 1966—67; resident in surgery Mt. Sinai Hosp., NYC, 1967—73, chief resident in surgery, 1972—73, attending surgeon, 1973, Beth Israel Hosp., NYC, 1981; sr. attending surgeon St. Luke's Roosevelt Hosp., NYC, 1981; dir. clin. rsch. Lifescore Global Network, San Diego, 2001—03; dir. Balboa Nephrology Ultrasound Lab., San Diego, 2003—. Asst. prof. Mt. Sinai Sch. Medicine, NYC, 1973; clin. prof. surgery U. Calif., San Diego, 2003; mem. nat. ultrasound faculty Am. Coll. Surgeons. Contbr. articles to profl. journals. Fellow NIH, 1968—70. Fellow: Nat. Ultrasound Faculty of ACS (instr. clin. ultrasound, cons. dialysis access surgery); mem.: NY Cardiovasc. Soc. Achievements include patents in field; invention of catheters; endovascular grafts; ultrasonic and laser devices; gen. and vascular medicine and surgery diagnostic ultrasound. Avocation: classical guitar. Personal E-mail: susant@tjsl.edu.

TIEFENBRUNN, ALAN JAMES, medical educator; b. St. Louis, Aug. 26, 1948; s. Kenneth Sylvester and Margaret Ann (Smith) T.; m. Sharon Kay Frost, June 3, 1972; children: Theresa, Curtis. AB cum laude, Washington U., St. Louis, 1970, MD, 1974. Intern, resident U. Calif., San Diego, 1974-77; fellow in cardiology Washington U., St. Louis, 1977-79, asst. prof. medicine, 1980-86, assoc. prof. medicine, 1986—2008, prof. medicine, 2008—, asst. prof. radiology St. Louis, 1980—; physician Barnes Hosp., St. Louis, 1980—2008, phyisician, 2008—, prof. medicine, 2008—. Mem. adv. bd. Nat. Registry Myocardial Infarction, 1991—; cons. in field. Contbr. articles to profl. jours. Fellow Am. Coll. Cardiology, Am. Heart Assn. (coun. clin.cardiology), Alpha Omega Alpha. Avocations: skiing, scuba diving, shotgun sports. Home: 6255 Wydown Blvd Saint Louis MO 63105-2306 Office: Washington U Box 8086 660 S Euclid Ave Saint Louis MO 63110-1093 E-mail: atiefenb@im.wustl.edu.

TIEN, HWEI-FANG, hematologist, educator; b. Taipei, Taiwan, June 24, 1952; d. Yi-Ching and Kwei-Hsing (Huang) T.; m. Hsian-Fu Hung, Sept. 16, 1984; children: Kai-Lin, Kuang. MD, Nat. Taiwan U., 1977, PhD, 1990. Resident Nat. Taiwan U. Hosp., 1977-81, vis. staff, 1982—, assoc. prof. sch. medicine, 1990-95, prof., 1995—, head hematology sec., dept. internal medicine, 1995—. Guest rschr. Nat. Cancer Inst., Bethesda, Md., 1985; rsch. fellow, vis. scientist VA Med. Ctr., Louisville, 1984-85. Contbr. articles to profl. jours. Named Outstanding Rschr. Nat. Sci. Coun., 1992, 98, 2010, Disting. Prof., Nat. Taiwan U., 2008; recipient award for med. rsch. Prof. Chen's Found., 1993, Outstanding Med. Rsch. award in Oncology, Chinese Oncology Soc., 1995—, Med. award, Ching-Hsing Med Found., 1997, Outstanding Rsch. Excellence award, Nat. Taiwan U. Hosp., 2010. Mem. Hematology Soc. Taiwan, Am. Soc. of Hematology, Chinese Oncology Soc., Soc. Internal Medicine, Internat. Soc. Hematology. Office: Nat Taiwan U Hosp # 7 Chung-Shan S Rd Taipei 100 Taiwan Fax: 886-2-23959583. E-mail: hftien@ntu.edu.tw.

TIENBOON, PRASONG, pediatrician, nutritionist, researcher; b. Sukhothai, Thailand, July 31, 1952, s. Chaiheng and Thonglhaw Tienboon. BS, Chiang Mai U., Thailand, 1974, MD, 1976; MCN, U. Queensland, Australia, 1982; PhD, Deakin U., Australia, 1991. Cert. specialist in clin. nutrition. Assoc. prof. pediat. Chiang Mai U., 1993—, head divsn. nutrition dept. pediat. Faculty Medicine, 1993—, dir. nutrition rsch. ctr. Faculty Medicine, 1993—. Cons. divsn. catering Maharaj Nakorn Chiang Mai Hosp., 1993—; v.p. Soc. Parenteral and Enteral Nutrition Thailand, Bangkok, 1998—; mem. com. Pediatric Nutrition Soc. Thailand, Bangkok, 1998—; adj. prof. pediat. La. State U. Med. Ctr., New Orleans, 1997—98; editor in chief Thai Jour. Clin. Nutrition, 2008—. Editor: Parenteral and Enteral Nutrition, 1996, Nutrition and Metabolic Support in Clinical Practices, 1996, Nutrition for Children in the 21st Century, 2000, Nutrition support team in clinical nutrition, Bangkok, 2000, Nutrition support team in specific diseases: Role of the team, Bangkok, 2000, Fighting Against Malnutrition in the Hospital, 2001; prodr.: (computer program) Thai (Tienboon) Food Calculation, 2001; mem. editl. bd. Asia Pacific Jour. Clin. Nutrition, 1995—, Thai Jour. Parenteral and Enteral Nutrition, 1992—. Grantee Internat. Devel. Rsch. Ctr., Can. Govt., 2000—02. Fellow: Royal Coll. Pediatricians, Internat. Coll. Nutrition (life; hon. prof. clin. nutrition 1997—); mem.: Parenteral and Enteral Nutrition Soc. Asia (chmn. sci. program 1995—), Asia Pacific Clin. Nutrition Soc. (pres. 2005—). Buddhist. Avocations: travel, swimming, tennis, basketball, ping pong/table tennis. Office: Chiang Mai U Faculty Of Medicine/Dept Pediat 50200 Chiang Mai Thailand Office Phone: 66-53-895269. Fax: 66-53-214437. Business E-Mail: prasong@chiangmai.ac.th.

TIERNO, PHILIP MARIO, JR., microbiologist, educator, researcher; b. Bklyn., June 5, 1943; s. Philip M. and Phyllis (Tringone) T.; m. Josephine Martinez, Apr. 2, 1967; children: Alexandra Lorraine, Meredith Anne. BS, Bklyn. Coll. Pharmacy, 1965; MS, NYU, 1974, PhD, 1977. Microbiologist Luth. Med. Ctr., Bklyn., 1965-66; chief rsch. microbiologist hemodialysis unit VA Hosp., Bronx, NY, 1966-70; dir. microbiology divsn. NYU Med. Ctr. Goldwater Meml. Hosp., F.D. Roosevelt Island, 1970-81; assoc. and cons. microbiologist Maimonides Med. Ctr., Bklyn., 1970-79; dir. microbiology dept. Tisch-U. Hosp., NYU Langone Med. Ctr., 1981—. Adj. asst. prof. CUNY, 1974—76, Bloomfield (NJ) Coll., 1975—82; clin. prof. microbiology and pathology NYU Med. Sch., 1981—; cons. Office Atty. Gen. NY State, NIH, Coll. of Am. Pathologists, Dept. Health City of NY, 1981—; mem. Mayoral Task Force on Bioterrorism, NYC. Author: The Secret Life of Germs: Observations and Lessons from a Microbe Hunter, 2001, Protect Yourself Against Bioterrorism, 2002, Nuclear, Chemical and Biological Terrorism: Emergency Response and Public Protection, 2003, The Secret Life of Germs: What They Are, Why We Need Them, and How We Can Protect Ourselves Against Them, 2004; contbr. articles to profl. jours., chapters to books. Pres. Flushing Taxpayers Assn., 1973-77; bd. dirs. Comprehensive Health Planning Agy. City of NY, 1974-75, Norwood Bd. Adjustment, NJ, 1978-83, 86-98, Norwood Bd. Edn., 1983-86; chmn. Norwood Environ. Commn., 1986-98; co-founder, bd. dirs. Found. Sci. Rsch. in Pub. Interest, S.I., NY, 1985—. Recipient Leone de San Marcos award, 2005. Mem. AAAS, NY Acad. Scis., Am. Acad. Microbiology, APHA, Am. Soc. Microbiology, Am. Soc. for Clin. Pathology, Optimists (v.p. Norwood 1978-95), Knights of Malta (Knighthood). Office: Tisch Hosp-Microbiology Dept NYU Langone Med Ctr 560 1st Ave New York NY 10016-6402 Office Phone: 212-263-5905. Business E-Mail: philip.tierno@nyumc.org.

TIESENGA, MARVIN FRANCIS, surgeon; b. Slayton, Minn., Apr. 3, 1929; s. Edward Tiesenga and Sieka Drenth-Tiesenga; m. Ardythe Rae Noorlag, Aug. 19, 1955; children: Jane, Edward, Mary, Frederick, Anne. BS, Roosevelt U., 1950; MD, U. Ill., 1954. Diplomate Am. Bd. Surgery. Intern Cook County Hosp., Chgo., 1954, resident gen. surgery, 1957—61; pres. med. staff West Suburban Hosp., Oak Park,

Ill., 1986—88, chief surgery, 1989—. Contbr. articles to profl. jours. Mem. Elmhurst Christian Ref. Ch., 1971—. Capt. US Army, 1955—57, Korea. Recipient Number one Dr., Crane's Chgo. Mag., 2004, Ken Douglas award for excellence, Citizens of Oak Park, 2000; named Number one Dr., Crane's Chgo. Mag., 2000, 2001, 2002, 2003. Fellow: ACS; mem.: AMA, SAGES, Chgo. Med. Soc., Ill. Med. Soc., Am. Soc. Breast Surgeons, Am. Soc. Bariatric Surgery, Aux Planes Med. Soc., Christian Med. and Dental Assn. Avocations: boating, travel, history, collecting antique tractors. Office: 1950 N Harlem Ave Elmwood Park IL 60707

TIGARI, PRAKASH, medical educator; b. Mahajanadahalli, India, May 7, 1970; PharmM, KLE Coll. Pharmacy, Belgaum, 1999; PhD, Acharya Nagrjuna U., Guntur, 2011. Prof. SCS Coll. Pharmacy, 1999, Acharya B.M. Reddy Coll. Pharma, Bangalore, 2006—. Mem.: Indian Pharmacological Soc., Assn. Pharm. Tchr. India. Avocations: reading, music. Office: Soldevanahalli Hesaraghatta Rd Bangalore Karnataka 560090 India Personal E-mail: prakash_tigari@yhaoo.com.

TIGGEMANN, CARLOS LEANDRO, medical educator; b. Estrela, Rio Grande do Sul, Brazil, Jan. 25, 1974; MS, U. Fed. Rio Grande do Sul, 2007. Tchr. U. Santa Cruz do Sul, 2009, Faculdade Serra Gaúcha, 2010—. Tchr. CERTEL, 2003. Home: Gustavo Henrique Schuck 705 Teutônia RS 95890-000 Brazil Personal E-mail: cltiggemann@yahoo.com.br.

TIKK, ARVO, neurosurgeon; b. Tallinn, Estonia, Oct. 30, 1929; s. Aleksander Eduard and Melita Tikk; m. Mona Karus, Nov. 6, 1956; children: Tiina Vilimaa, Reet. MD, U. Tartu, Estonia, 1954. Cert. neurosurgeon. Prof. U. Tartu, 1975—95; chmn. Estonian Coun. Bioethics, Tallinn, 1998—2008. Consulting U. Clinics, Tartu, 1996—. Recipient award for Sci. Achievment, Suprema Coun. Sov. Estonia, 1965. Mem.: Coun. Europe (assoc.; mem. bioethics com.). Avocation: photography. Home: Riia 3-21 51010 Tartu Estonia Office: U Tartu Dept Neurosurgery Sepa 2 50113 Tartu Estonia Office Phone: 3727318538. Office Fax: 3727318509. Business E-Mail: arvo.tikk@kliinikum.ee.

TILGHMAN, SHIRLEY MARIE, academic administrator, biology professor; b. Toronto, Canada, Sept. 17, 1946; 2 children. BSc in Chemistry with honors, Queen's U., Kingston, Ont., 1968; PhD in Biochemistry, Temple U., Phila., 1975; DSc (hon.), Mt. Sinai Coll. Medicine of City Coll. NY, 1994, Queen's U., Kingston, Ont., 2002, Oxford U., 2002, Westminster Choir Coll. Rider U., 2002, Bard Coll., 2002, Dickinson Coll., 2002, Yale U., 2002, Queen's U., 2002, Simon Fraser U., 2002, U. BC, 2002, U. Western Ont., 2003, U. Toronto, 2003, Drew U., 2004, Harvard U., 2004, U. Medicine & Dentistry NJ, 2005, NYU, 2005, Columbia U., 2005, Rutgers U., 2006, Rockefeller U., 2006, Wash. U., 2007, Mills Coll., 2007, Mem. U. Newfoundland, 2007, Ryerson U., 2007, Rensselaer Poly. Inst., Amherst Coll., U. Md., Balt., 2008; postgrad., NIH. Secondary sch. tchr., West Africa, Sierra Leone, 1968—70; Fogarty internat. fellow NIH, Bethesda, Md., 1975—77; mem. Inst. Cancer Rsch., Phila., 1979—86; investigator Howard Hughes Med. Inst., Chevy Chase, 1988—2001; asst. prof., Fels Rsch Inst. Temple U., Phila., 1978—79; prof. molecular biology Princeton U., NJ, 1986—, Howard A. Prior prof. life scis., 1986—2001, chair Coun. Sci. and Tech., 1993—2000, pres., 2001—. Founding dir. Lewis-Sigler Inst. Integrative Genomics, 1998—2003; adj. assoc. prof. human genetics and biochemistry and biophysics U. Pa., 1980—86; adj. prof. Robert Wood Johnson Med. Sch., 1988—2001; mem. sci. adv. bd. Whitehead Inst. for Biomed. Scis., MIT, 1995—2001; founding mem. Nat. Adv. Coun. Human Genome Project Rsch. NIH, 1991—96, adv. coun. dir., 1997—2001; mem. Am. Soc. Cell Biology, Soc. Devel. Biology, Am. Soc. Biochemistry & Molecular Biology, Commn. Life Scis., Nat. Rsch. Coun., 1993—2001, Am. Acad. Arts Scis., 1990, Inst. Medicine, 1995, Foreign Assoc., US Nat. Acad. Scis., 1996, Am. Philos. Soc., 2000; fellow Royal Soc. London, 1995; editl. bd. mem. Genes & Development, 1990—2001, Journal Cell Biology, 1988—91, Molecular & Cellular Biology, 1985—94, editor; executive editor Nucleic Acids Rsch, 1983—91, bd. mem.; chair Nat. Acad. Com., Intellectual property Genomic & Protein Rsch. & Innovation, 2004—05; sci. adv. bd. Ctr. Advanced Biotechnology & Medicine, Rutgers U., 1993—2001; bd. mem. of sci. advisors Roche Inst. Molecular Biology, 1988—94; sci. adv. bd. Oak Ridge Nat. Labs., 1987—91; chair, mem. Molecular Biology Study Sec., NIH, 1983—87, Visiting Com. Cell & Devel. Biology, Harvard Coll., 1990—95; mem. U. Coun. Biol. Scis., Yale Coll., 1990—94; bd. trustees Cold Spring Harbor Lab., 1990—96. Trustee The Jackson Lab., 1994—, Carnegie Endowment Internat. Peace, 2005—, Google Inc., 2005, Rockefeller U., 1999—2001, Cold Spring Harbor Lab.; mem. Pew Charitable Trusts Scholars Prog., Biomedical Scis. Selection Com., Lucille P. Markey Charitable Trust Scholar Selection Com.; trustee King Abdullah U. Sci. & Tech., 2008—. Recipient Pres.'s award disting. tchg., Princeton U., 1996, L'Oréal-UNESCO Internat. Women in Sci. award, 2002, Lifetime Achievement award, Soc. Devel. Biology, 2003, Radcliffe Inst. medal, Harvard U., 2004, Presdl. Medal of Honor, Dillard U., 2006; named one of America's Best Leaders, US News & World Report, 2007. Mem.: NAS, Am. Acad. Arts and Scis., Royal Soc. London, Inst. Medicine, Am. Philos. Soc. Achievements include first to identify the H19 gene in mice, an early example of parental imprinting; research in cloning the first mammalian gene. Office: Princeton University Office of President One Nassau Hall Princeton NJ 08544-0001 Office Phone: 609-258-6101. Office Fax: 609-258-1615. *

TILL, JAMES EDGAR, medical educator, researcher; b. Lloydminster, Sask., Can., Aug. 25, 1931; s. William and Gertrude Ruth (Isaac) T.; m. Marion Joyce Sinclair, June 6, 1959; children: David William, Karen Sinclair, Susan Elizabeth. BA, U. Sask., 1952, MA, 1954; PhD, Yale U., 1957; DSc (hon.), U. Toronto, 2004, U. Lethbridge, Can., 2007, U. Saskatchewan, 2008. Mem. physics divsn. Ont. Cancer Inst., Toronto, 1957-67, mem. divsn. biol. rsch., 1967-89, divsn. head, 1969-82, scientist divsn. epidemiology and stats., 1989—; assoc. dean U. Toronto, 1981-84, univ. prof., 1984-97, univ. prof. emeritus, 1997—. Contbr. articles to profl. jours. Recipient Gairdner Found. Internat. award, 1969, Order of Can., 1994, Albert Lasker award for Basic Med. Rsch., Lasker Found., 2005; named to Canadian Med. Hall Fame, 2004, Canadian Sci. & Engring. Hall of Fame, 2010. Fellow: Royal Soc. London, Royal Soc. Can. Achievements include research in biophysics, cell biology and cancer control research. Office: Princess Margaret Hosp 9th Fl Rm 416 610 University Ave Toronto ON Canada M5G 2M9 Office Phone: 416-946-4501 ext. 2948. Business E-Mail: till@uhnres.utoronto.ca.

TILSON, M(ARTIN) DAVID, III, surgeon, scientist, educator; b. Texarkana, Tex., Aug. 25, 1941; s. M. David and Leta (Martin) Tilson; 3 children. BA, Rice U., 1963; MD, Yale U., 1967. Diplomate Am. Bd. Surgery, Nat. Bd. Med. Examiners. Surg. intern Yale U., New Haven, 1967-68; resident in surgery U. New Haven, 1968-72; asst. to assoc. prof. Yale U., New Haven, 1974-83, prof., 1983-89; Ailsa Mellon Bruce prof. surgery Columbia U., NYC, 1989—. Contbr. articles to profl. jours. Maj. USAF, 1972-74. Rsch. grantee, NIH, 1983—94, 1999—2003. Mem. ACS, Soc. Univ. Surgeons, Am. Surg. Assn., Soc. Vascular Surgery, Internat. Soc. Cadiovasc. Surgery, Halsted Soc. Home: 105 Garth Rd B2 Scarsdale NY 10583-2714 Office: St Lukes Roosevelt Hosp 1000 10th Ave New York NY 10019-1192 E-mail: mdt1@columbia.edu.

TIMMCKE, ALAN EDWARD, colon and rectal surgeon; b. Madison, Wis., July 7, 1949; s. Wesley Eugene Timmcke; m. Teresa Ann Watkins, Dec. 31, 1977; children: Gretchen Kristine, Alan Edward Jr. BS, Dickinson Coll., 1971; MD with honors, Temple U., 1975. Diplomate Am. Bd. Surgery, Am. Bd. Colon and Rectal Surgery; lic. physician, Pa., La., Fla. Intern in surgery Nat. Naval Med. Ctr., Bethesda, Md., 1975-76, resident in gen. surgery, 1976-79; rsch. fellow in colon and rectal surgery Jewish Hosp./Washington U. Med. Ctr., St. Louis, 1985-86, clin. fellow in colon and rectal surgery, 1986-87; asst. in surgery Washington U. Sch. Medicine, St. Louis, 1985-87; staff colon and rectal surgeon Ochsner Clinic, New Orleans, 1987—. Staff surgeon Nat. Naval Med. Ctr., Bethesda, 1979, Naval Regional Med. Ctr., Newport, R.I., 1979-82, dept. colon and rectal surgery Lahey Clinic Med. Ctr., Burlington, Mass., 1984-85; staff surgeon Rumford (Maine) Community Hosp., 1982-84, med. staff v.p., 1983-84; instr. surgery Uniformed Svcs. U. of Health Scis., Bethesda, 1978-79; lectr. in field. Assoc. editor Diseases of the Colon and Rectum, 2002—08; contbr. articles and abstracts to profl. jours. Lt. comdr. M.C., USN, 1975-82. Recipient Harry E. Bacon Found. award for best original paper, 1987; NIH Summer Rsch. fellow, 1972. Fellow ACS, Am. Soc. Colon and Rectal Surgeons; mem. New Orleans Surg. Soc., Surg. Assn. of La., Internat. Soc. Univ. Colon and Rectal Surgeons, Soc. of Am. Gastrointestinal Endoscopic Surgeons, Alpha Omega Alpha. Office: Ochsner Clinic Dept Colon/Rectal Surgery 1514 Jefferson Hwy New Orleans LA 70121-2483 Office Phone: 504-842-4060. Personal E-mail: atimmcke@aol.com.

TIMMONS-MITCHELL, JANE CHRISTINA, clinical psychologist, researcher, consultant, educator, entrepreneur; b. Indpls., Feb. 11, 1955; d. Gerald Dean and Janet Wilson Timmons; m. Robert Allan Mitchell, May 23, 1981; children: Clare Christina Mitchell, Stephen James Mitchell. PhD, Case Western Res. U., Cleve., 1982. Cert. in psychologist Ohio State Bd. Psychology, 1984. Psychologist, med. staff U. Hosps., Cleve., 1990—2001; assoc. prof. Case Sch. Medicine, Cleve., 2000—01, assoc. clin. prof. psychology dept. psychiatry, 2001—; assoc. dir. evaluation and rsch. Ctr. Innovative Practices, Inst. Study & Prevention Violence, Kent State U., 2006—11; adj. prof. Mandel Sch.; sr. rsch. assoc. Mandel Sch. Applied Social Scis., Case Western Res. U., 2011—. Pres., CEO Junction Psychol. Svcs. Corp., Cleveland Heights, Ohio, 2001—. Musician: Cleve. Orch. Chorus; singer (Regional Emmy, 2001). Spearhead Build it Now (campaign for the Recreation Ctr.), Cleveland Heights, 1997—99; head coach, speech and debate Cleve. Heights HS, 1999—2004; mem., choir Trinity Cathedral, Cleve., 2008—. Recipient Hon. Mention, SAMHSA, 2005; named Rschr. the Yr., MST, 2006; grantee, Cleveland Heights U., Heights Sch. Dist., 2003—06. Mem.: APA. Liberal. Avocations: music, gardening, baking. Home: 2995 E Overlook Rd Cleveland Heights OH 44118 Office: 11235 Bellflower Dr Cleveland OH 44106 Home Fax: 216-397-1107. Personal E-mail: jtm07@aol.com.

TIMPA, VICKI ANN, government health program administrator; b. Houston, Aug. 20, 1955; d. Edmund Burke and Helen Kanosky Huber; m. John Gerrard Fewel, May 27, 2000; children: Julie Marie Fecht, Anthony Alan. BSN, U. Tex., 1977; MSN in Edn. Adminstrn. and Rsch., Tex. Woman's U., 1990, advanced nurse practitioner, 1993. Cert. ACLS, domestic preparedness for biol.-radiol.-chem. VA, neurosurg. cert., cert. prevention inst. instr.; critical care nurse; cert. Covey trainer, antiques and collectibles appraiser. Team leader cardiopulmonary shock trauma emergency ctr., nurse Ben Taub Emergency Ctr., Harris County Hosp. Dist., Houston, 1977; peritoneal dialysis nurse Parkland Meml. Hosp., Dallas County Hosp. Dist.; emergency rm. and GI lab staff nurse Mesquite Hosp., Tex., 1978—80; nurse Baylor U. Med. Ctr. Hosp. Sys., Dallas, 1980—90; rsch. nurse coord. VA, Dallas, 1990—93; dept. of edn. mgr. Meth. Hosps. of Dallas, 1993; patient health and continuing med. edn. coord., chief ethics cons. VA North Tex. Health Care Sys., Dallas, 1993—2011, vet. health edn. coord., ethics team mem., 2010—. Coord. nat. rsch. studies VA, Dallas, 1990—92, nat. liaison for Nat. Ctr. for Health Promotion and Disease Prevention, Durham, NC, 2002—05, congl. legis. cons., Washington, 2000—; ICU mock code creator and trainer Baylor U. Hosp. Sys., Dallas, 1980—90; cardiopulmonary resuscitation instr. Am. Heart Assn., Dallas, 1989—94, 2009, continuing med. educator, 2007—, coord., 2009; Plain Lang. Act cons. Exec. Br., Washington, 1995—. Contbr. articles to profl. pubs. Sr. v.p. Miracle Wish Found., 2006—. Recipient Unsung Hero award, VA, 1993, Plank award, Nat. Ctr. Health Promotion, 2002—05, Customer Svc. award, VA North Tex. Healthcare Sys., 2007, 2009; named Most Valuable Person, VA Rsch., 1992; named one of Great 100 Nurses award, 1997; Pub. Health grant, VA North Tex. Healthcare Sys., 2007. Mem.: Sigma Theta Tau (fin. and fund raising com. 1993—2001, vice chairperson of bd. dir., Miracle Wish Found. 2006—, Academic Excellence and Rsch. Excellence awards 1993, 2001, Public Health Grant award 2007—). Roman Catholic. Avocation: travel. Home: 1307 High Ridge Dr Duncanville TX 75137 Home Fax: 972-572-5525. Personal E-mail: vickiern7@netzero.com.

TINAJERO, JO CARMEN, medical researcher; b. Mar. 22, 1955; MD, Med Sch., Leon, Guanajuato, 1980; MS in Chemistry, Guanajuato, Mex., 1983, PhD in Chemistry, 1997. Med. rschr. U. Guanajuato, Leon, Mexico; rschr. Nat. Inst. Health, Bethesda, vis. assoc.; academician Med. Sch. Leon. Contbr. articles to profl. med. publs. Recipient award, Nat. Investigator Mex., 1993; grant, Svcs. Health Guanajuato, 2000. Mem.: Endocrine Soc.(Chem Chase), Am. Soc. Reproductive Medicine. Office: Facultad Medicine de Leon Bioquimica Paseo de Los Quetzales 141 San Isidro Leon 37512 Mexico Office Phone: 477116206. Office Fax: 4777116206. Personal E-mail: tinajero_josec@yahoo.com. Business E-Mail: tinajerojosec@yahoo.com.

TINETTI, MARY E., geriatrician, educator; b. July 31, 1951; BA, U. Mich., Ann Arbor, 1973; MD, U. Mich. Med. Sch., 1978. Diplomate Am. Bd. Internal Medicine, Am. Bd. Geriatric Medicine. Resident U. Mich., Mpls., 1978—81; Kaiser gen. medicine and geriatrics fellow U. Rochester/Monroe Hosp., NY, 1981—84; assoc. prof. medicine Yale Sch. Medicine, New Haven, 1984, prin. investigator, Claude D. Pepper Older Americans Independence Ctr., 1992—, chief geriatrics divsn., 1994—, dir. Yale Prog. on Aging., 1995—, Gladys Phillips Crofoot prof. medicine, epidemiology & pub. health, 2000—. Recipient Herbert deVries rsch. award, Coun. Aging & Adult Devel., 2009; named a MacArthur Fellow, John T. & Catherine MacArthur Found., 2009; named one of Top Doctors in NY Metro Area, Castle Connolly Med. Ltd., 1999—2009, America's Top Doctors, 2002—09. Mem.: Inst. Medicine. Office: Adler Geriatric Assessment Ctr 874 Howard Ave New Haven CT 06510 also: Yale Sch Medicine Sect Geriatrics Dept Internal Medicine 20 York St New Haven CT 06510 Office Phone: 203-688-5238. Office Fax: 203-688-4209. E-mail: mary.tinetti@yale.edu. *

TINETTI, MARY ELIZABETH, geriatrician; MD, U. Mich., 1978. Diplomate Am. Bd. of Internal Medicine, 1981, Am. Bd. of Internal Medicine-geriatric medicine. Resident Univ. Minn., 1981; fellow Univ. of Rochester, Monroe Hosp. Prof. medicine Yale Univ. Mem.: Yale Med. Group. Office: Yale-New Haven Hospital 20 York St New Haven CT 06510 Office Phone: 203-688-4242.

TING, ALBERT CHIA, biomedical engineer, researcher; b. Hong Kong, Sept. 7, 1950; came to U.S., 1957; s. William Su and Katherine Sung T.; m. Shirley Roung Wang, July 30, 1988, (dec. Aug. 2003). BA, UCLA, 1973; MS, Calif. State U., LA, 1975, Calif. Inst. Tech., 1977; PhD, U. Calif., San Diego, 1983. Rsch. asst. Calif. Inst. Tech., Pasadena, 1975-77, U. Calif., San Diego, 1982-83; sr. staff engr. R&D Am. Med. Optics, Irvine, Calif., 1983-86; project engr., rsch. Allergan Med. Optics, Irvine, Calif., 1987-89, sr. project engr., rsch., 1989-92, sr. project engr., engring., 1993-94; bioengr. cons. Pharmacia Iovision, Inc., Irvine, Calif., 1995-97; sr. engr. D & E, 1997, sr. engr., project mgr., 1998-99; rsch. and devel. mgr., surg. Bausch & Lomb, Irvine, 1999—2001; R & D mgr. Visiogen, Inc., Irvine, 2001—02, sr. R & D mgr., 2002—10, R & D mgr., Abbott Med. Optics, 2010—. Contbr. articles to profl. jours. Mem. AAAS, Biomed. Engring. Soc., Assn. for Rsch. in Vision and Ophthalmology, Biomed. Optics Soc. Achievements include invention of med. and optical devices. Office: Visiogen Inc 2 Goodyear Ste B Irvine CA 92618 Office Phone: 949-900-3352. Business E-Mail: ating@visiogen.com, albert.ting@amo.abbott.com.

TING, JESS, plastic surgeon, educator; Grad., Juilliard Sch.; MD, Columbia U. Med. Ctr. Diplomate AM. Bd. Plastic Surgery, cert. hand surgery. Resident surgery Columbia-Presbyn. Med. Ctr.; resident plastic surgery Univ. of Pittsburgh; fellowship hand surgery Hosp of Special Surgery; asst prof. surgery and plastic surgery Mt. Sinai Med. Ctr. Co-author: (publs.) Commentary on Intrasynovial flexor tendon repair: an experimental study on low versus high levels of in vivo force rehabilitation in canines, 2001, Role of ancillary procedures in surgical management of carpal tunnel syndrome: epineurotomy, internal neurolysis, tenosynovectomy, and tendon transfers, Facial nerve monitoring parameters as a predictor of postoperative facial nerve outcomes after vestibular schwannoma resection, 2005. Recipient Robert F. Loeb award, 1995, Teacher of the Tear award, Mt. Sinai Med. Ctr., 2004, Attending of the Year award, 2004; named one of Top Doctors New York Metro Area, Castle Connolly, 2008—09, Best Doctors, NY Magazine, 2009, America's Top Doctors, Castle Connolly, 2010, numerous awards. Office: Mount Sinai Medical Center 14th Fl Suite B Box 1259 New York NY 10029 Office Phone: 212-241-4410. Office Fax: 212-241-5999.

TINGLEY, F. WARREN, retired internist; b. Charlotte, NC, Nov. 22, 1933; s. Floyd Warren Sr. and Janie (Suggs) T.; m. Sandra Carpenter, Aug. 20, 1955 (div. Dec. 1984); children: Sheryl Tingley Hagen, David Alan; m. Johnette Hill, Apr. 5, 1985. BA in English, Emory U., 1955, MD, 1959. Diplomate Am. Bd. Internal Medicine (bd. govs. 1986-92). Intern USAF Hosp., Lackland AFB, Tex., 1959-60; resident in internal medicine Parkland Meml. Hosp., Dallas, 1963-65, fellow in cardiology, 1965-66; pvt. practice specializing in internal medicine Arlington, Tex., 1966-88; med. dir. southwestern region Met. Life Ins. Co., Irving, Tex., 1988-90; regional practice leader William M. Mercer Inc., 1990-91; v.p., sr. med. dir. Provident Life and Accident Co., Chattanooga, 1991-92; v.p., nat. med. dir. Travelers Ins. Cos., Hartford, Conn., 1992-94; sr. v.p., chief med. officer Kemper Nat. Svcs., Plantation, Fla., 1995-2000; med. dir. Mednet Connect, 2005—07, Fairpay Solutions, 2007—09. Apptd. Tex. Commn. on Health Care Reimbursement Alternatives, 1987; bd. dirs. Riverside Nat. Bank, Grand Prairie, Tex. Contbr. articles to profl. jours. Pres. Arlington YMCA, 1971; chmn. budget com. Family Services, Ft. Worth, 1973; participant Health Policy Agenda for Am. People, Chgo., 1984-87; trustee Tex. Med. Liability Trust, Austin, 1987-88. Capt. USAF, 1958-63. Fellow ACP (pres. Tex. chpt. 1981); mem. AMA (chmn. sect. coun. internal medicine, 1979-88), Am. Soc. Internal Medicine (pres. 1986-87), Tex. Med. Assn. (treas. 1978-85, alt. del. to AMA 1985-91, commendation 1985), Tarrant County Med. Soc. (pres. Arlington br. 1974, del. to Tex. Med. Assn., Community Svc. award 1983). Presbyterian. Avocations: photography, sailing, gardening. Home: 1912 Channing Park Dr Arlington TX 76013

TINGUS, STEVEN JAMES, physiologist, researcher; b. Sacramento, Aug. 19, 1963; s. James George and Joanne Fotene (Kamilos) Tingus. BS in Biol. Sci., U. Calif., Davis, 1985, MS in Physiology,

1990, PhD in Physiology, 1994. Policy analyst Calif. Dept. Health Svcs., 1995—98; dir. resource devel./pub. policy Calif. Found. Ind. Living Centers, Inc., 1998—2001; dir. Nat. Inst. Disability & Rehab. Rsch., US Dept. Edn., Washington, 2001—07; dep. asst. sec. planning & evaluation for disability, aging & long term care policy, HHS, Washington, 2007—09; chief govt. & pub rels. officer Lao Amigos Rsch. & Edn. Inst., Inc., 2010—. Recipient Gil Moss award, Nat. Spinal Cord Injury Assn., 2003, Best New Freedom Individual award, Jim Mullen Found., 2003, Commr.'s Spl. Citation award, FDA, 2005, 2007, Isabelle & Leonard Goldenson Tech. and Rehab. award, United Cerebral Palsy Rsch. & Ednl. Found., 2006; named one of 40 Under 40, Sacramento Bus. Jour., 2000. Mem.: AAAS, Am. Assn. Polit. Cons. Republican. Greek Orthodox. Home: 1010 Wilshire Blvd Ste 911 Los Angeles CA 90017-5666 Personal E-mail: stingus@earthlink.net.

TINICA, GRIGORE, cardiac surgeon, professor of surgery; b. Cusmirca, Republic of Moldavia, Nov. 9, 1960; MD, U. Medicine and Pharmacy Nicolae Testemitanu Chisinau, 1984; PhD, U. Medicine and Pharmacy Carol Davila Bucuresti, 1996. Mgr. Inst. Cardiovasc. Diseases, 2005—. Prof. U. Medicine and Pharmacy Gr. T. Popa Iasi, 2006. Recipient Disting. Prof. award, Carolinas Heart Inst. and Heineman Med. Rsch. Mem.: Danubian Cardiovasc. Forum, Panhelenik Thoracic and Cardiovasc. Surgery Soc., European Assn. Cardio-Thoracic Surgery, Internat. Soc. Cardiovasc. Surgery, Euro-Asian Bridge Soc. Avocations: painting, music, travel. Office: B-dul Carol I 50 Iasi 700503 Romania Office Fax: 40232410280. E-mail: grigoretinica@yahoo.com.

TINO, GREGORY, pulmonologist, educator; MD, Mt. Sinai Sch. Medicine. Diplomate Am. Bd. Internal Medicine, 1989, Am. Bd. Internal Medicine-pulmonary disease, 1992, cert. critcal care 1995. Intern Hosp. of the Univ. of Pa., resident, fellow, dir. pulmonary outpatient practices; assoc. prof. medicine Univ. of Pa. Named one of the Top Docs, Phila. Mag., 2004—07, 2010—11, Best Doctors in America, 2003—04, 2005—06, 2007—08, 2009—10, America's Top Doctors, 2007, 2008, 2010. Mem.: ACP, Am. Thoracic Soc., Am. Coll. of Chest Physicians. Office: Perelman Center for Advanced Medicine West Pavilion 1st Fl 3400 Civic Center Blvd Philadelphia PA 19104 Office Phone: 800-789-7366.

TINOCO, EUGENIO, surgeon, educator; b. Brazil, Mar. 26, 1964; Grad., Campos Med. Sch., Brazil, 1984; M in Vascular Surgery, Rio de Janeiro Med. U., 2004. Resident gen. surgery, Rio de Janeiro, 1988—89; resident vascular surgery, 1989—91; chief vascular surgery Hosp. São Jose Avai, Itaperuna, Brazil, 1992—2005, prof. angiology and vascular surgery Campos Med. Sch., 1995—2000; prof. vascular surgery Brazil, 2000—. Mailing: Rua Dez de Maio 609/306 28300-000 Itapcruma Brazil

TINOCO, RENAM CATHARINA, surgeon; b. Itaperuna, Brazil, Mar. 5, 1938; s. Ruth Oliveira and Cordelia Catharina (Rezende) T.; m. Darcy Almeida, June 30, 1961; children: Eugenio, Augusto. MD, U. Fed. Fluminense, Rio de Janeiro, 1963. Med. diplomate. Gen. surgeon Hosp. São Jose, Itaperuna, 1964-68, 71—; gen. surgeon, asst. prof. U. Fed. Flumi, Niteroi, Brazil, 1968-70, rschr., 1991—; titular prof. surgery Faculty Med. Campos, Brazil, 1975—; dir. med. sch. U. Ignacu. Founder Hosp. São Jose do Avi, Rio de Janeiro, dir., 1980 95; cons. Clnica São Camil, Itaperuna, 1985 93, Hosp. Plantadores, Campos, 1988-95, Med. Coun., Rio de Janeiro, 1994—. Pioneer in video surgery, Rio de Janeiro; creator most productive svc. of cardiac surgery in Rio de Janeiro; author: Gastric Surgery, 1982, Esophageal Surgery, 1988, Endosurgery, 1994, Choledocoscopy Video Surgery, 1993. Fellow ACS, Internat. Coll. Surgeons, Brazilian Coll. Surgeons; mem. Am. Soc. Gastroendoscopy Surgery, European Assn. Endoscopy Sugery. Roman Catholic. Avocations: reading, fishing, soccer. Home: Rya Apolinario Cunha 115 28300000 Itaperuna Brazil Office: Hosp São Jose Rya Coronel Ferraz 397 28300000 Itaperuna Brazil

TINT, DIANA, cardiologist, educator; b. Brasov, Romania, June 8, 1969; MD, U. Medicine and Pharmacy Targu-Mures, Romania, 1994, PhD, 2005. Asst., internal medicine dept. Faculty Medicine Transilvania U., Brasov, 1996—2006, lectr., 2007—09, assoc. prof., sr. cardiologist, Clin. Emergency County Hosp. Brasov Cardiology Dept., 2009—; electrophysiology fellow Inst. Cardiology U. Debrecen Hungary, 2009—11. Fellow: European Soc. Cardiology; mem.: Hungarian Soc. Cardiology, Romanian Soc. Cardiology, ESC Acute Cardiac Care Working Group, European Heart Rythm Assn. (Rsch. fellowship). Office: Calea Bucuresti 25-27 Brasov 500326 Romania Office Fax: 0040-268333015. Personal E-mail: dianatint@yahoo.com.

TIRADO-SALDIVAR, ALEJANDRO, internal medicine physician, educator; b. Ciudad Victoria, Tamaulipas, Mex., May 8, 1946; s. Jose Manuel Tirado-Cortes and Lilia Saldivar-Morales; m. Patricia Hallam-Zurita, Dec. 20, 1970; children: Patricia, Ana Gabriela, Cecilia, Monica. MD, U. Nuevo Leon, Monterrey, Mex., 1970. Diplomate Am. Bd. Internal Medicine, Am. Bd. Endocrinology and Metabolism, Consejo Mexicano de Medicina Interna. Intern Providence Hosp., Washington, 1971-72, St. Louis U. Med. Ctr., 1972, med. resident, 1972-74; fellow in medicine U. Md. Hosp., Balt., 1974-76; med. cons. City Hosp., Ciudad Victoria, 1977-85; chief medicine, gen. dir. Hosp. Gen., Ciudad Victoria, 1985-99; prof. medicine U. Autonoma de Tamaulipas, Ciudad Victoria, 1987-99; pvt. practice Ciudad Victoria, 1999—. Fellow ACP, Mex. Nat. Acad. Bioethics; mem. AAAS, Am. Fertility Soc., Mexican Soc. Nutrition and Endocrinology, NY Acad. Scis., Endocrine Soc., Assn. Internal Medicine Avocations: walking, swimming, music, reading. Office: Gaspar de la Garza Sur 181-A 87000 Victoria Tamaulipas Mexico Home: Zacatecas 10 y 12 # 760 87020 Tamaulipas Tamaulipas Mexico Office Phone: 52-834-31-24863. E-mail: dr_atirado@hotmail.com.

TIRELLI, ALESSANDRA, obstetrician, gynecologist; b. Guastalla, Emilia-Romagna, Italy, Dec. 12, 1974; Degree in Medicine, U. Modena and Reggio Emilia, 1999, degree in Ob-Gyn., 2004. Obstetrician, delivery rm. Azienda Ospedaliero-U. Policlinico di Modena, 2001, gynecologic surgeon, 2001, cons. contraception, 2001, physician, 2004—08, cons., surgeon reproductive medicine, 2005, attending physician, 2008—. Pvt. practice, 2004. Mem.: Soc. Italiana di Contraccezione, European Soc. Human Reprodn. and Embriology, European Soc. Contraception. Avocations: horseback riding, piano, skiing. Office: Via Del Pozzo 71 Modena 41124 Italy Business E-Mail: alessandra.tirelli@unimore.it.

TIRONE, BARBARA JEAN, retired health insurance administrator; b. Celina, Ohio, Nov. 19, 1943; d. Vincent James and Theresa Barbara (Goettermoeller) G. BA, Miami U., 1965; MBA, U. Chgo., 1977. Asst. dir. for internat. trade State of Ill., Chgo., Brussels, Hongkong and Sao Paulo, Brazil, 1973-76; dir. office of mgmt. and planning Office Human Devel. Svcs., Chgo., 1976-79; dep. regional adminstr. Health Care Financing Adminstrn., Chgo., 1979-82, regional adminstr., 1982-87, dir. bur. of prog. ops. Balt., 1987-92; dir. health stds. and quality bur. Health Care Fin. Adminstrn., Balt., 1992-96; pres., CEO AdminaStar, Inc., Indpls., 1996-2001; ret., 2002. Recipient Presdl. Disting. Rank award 1988, 94, Presdl. Meritorious Rank award 1987, 92; named Fed. Exec. of Yr., 1987. Home: 11212 Appaloosa Dr Reisterstown MD 21136 Office Phone: 410-833-5570. Personal E-mail: bgtirone@yahoo.com.

TISCHENDORF, FRANK WALTER, internist, clinical chemist, immunologist; b. Gera, Thuringia, Germany, Oct. 12, 1936; s. Walter and Claire (Grimm) T.; children: Sven, Jens James. MD, U. Goettingen, Germany, 1963; Habil., U. Tuebingen, Germany, 1976, Diploma in Internal Medicine, 1972, Diploma in Lab. Medicine, 1979. Rsch. fellow Columbia U., NYC, 1965-67; sci. asst. in internal medicine U. Tuebingen, 1967-77; sr. physician Mcpl. Hosp. Esslingen of U. Tuebingen, 1977-80; head, physician in chief dept. clin. chemistry Bernhard Nocht-Inst. for Tropical Medicine, Hamburg, Germany, 1980—2001; docent Tech. Acad. Esslingen, 1975-80, U. Tuebingen, 1976-85, U. Hamburg, 1986—; dir. tropical medicine course Bernhard Nocht Inst., 1988-89. Mem. standardization com. on immunoglobulins of Internat. Union Immunol. Socs., 1977; mem. expert adv. panel on clin. chemistry Mcpl. Hosps. of Hamburg, 1980—2001; cons. Harbour Hosp., Hamburg, 1980-97; mem. expert adv. panel on lab. medicine Baden-Wüerttemberg Assn. Practitioners, 1976-86. Author: (atlas and text book) Prima Vista Diagnosis, 1995, 4th edit., 2010; editor: External Manifestations of Disease, 1973, 7th edit., 2008; co-editor (with C.H. Meyer and C.W. Spraul): The Eye in Systemic Diseases, 2004; assoc. editor Jour. Die Internistische Welt, 1976—86, mem. editl. bd. Haemostaseologie, 1992—, Natur-und Ganzheitsmedizin, 1993—94, Die Medizinische Welt, 1987—, Tieraerztliche Praxis, 1998—99; contbr. more than 100 articles to profl. jours. Mem. N.Y. Acad. Sci., German Soc. Tropical Medicine. Achievements include large scale crystallization of human fetal oxyhemoglobin (with L. Flohé and G. Stoeffler) and original contributions to immunochemistry and clinical significance of monoclonal immunoglobulins and lysosomal proteins of neutrophil and eosinophil granulocytes. Home: Kuulsbarg 17 Hamburg 22587 Blankenese Germany

TISCHLER, GARY LOWELL, psychiatrist, educator; b. NYC, Oct. 30, 1935; s. Louis and Dorothy (Green) T.; m. Judith Post, Aug. 18, 1957; children: Laurie Dee, Marc David, Rachel Mara. AB, Hamilton Coll., 1957; MD, U. Pa., 1961; MS, Yale U., 1975. Intern Kings County Hosp., Bklyn., 1961-62; resident in psychiatry Yale U. Sch. Medicine, New Haven, 1962-65, asst. prof., 1967-70, assoc. prof., 1970-75, prof. psychiatry, 1975-90, chmn. dept. psychiatry, 1986-87; prof., chmn. dept. psychiatry and biobehavioral scis., dir. Neuropsychiatric Inst. UCLA Sch. Medicine, 1990-95; dir. Yale Psychiat. Inst., New Haven, 1978-87; chief psychiatry Yale-New Haven Hosp., 1986-87; clin. dir. Hill-West Haven divsn. Conn. Mental Health Ctr., New Haven, 1968-70, dir., 1970-77; prof. psychiatry UCLA, 1990-95, prof. emeritus, 1996—; prof., exec. vice chair dept. psychiatry, dir. Cornell U. Med. Coll., 1994—2002; dir. Westchester divsn., dir. mental health programs N.Y. Hosp., 1994-99, dir. Payne Whitney Clinic, 1996-97. Study dir. Pres.'s Commn. on Mental Health, Washington, 1977-79; cons. Arthur D. Little Inc., Boston, 1973-75, IBM Corp., Armonk, N.Y., 1986-87; mem. profl. adv. com. Am. Med. Internat., L.A., 1984-86; mem. bd. mental health and behavioral medicine Inst. Medicine, Washington, 1986—, com. on clin. evaluation, 1990-94. Author: Quality Assurance Thru Utilization and Peer Review, 1982; editor: Patient Care Evaluation in Mental Health, 1985, Diagnosis and Classification in Psychiatry, 1987; contbr. articles to profl. jours. Mem. Gov.'s transition staff on mental health, Conn., 1975; vice chmn. Bd. Mental Health State of Conn., 1986. Served to capt. U.S. Army, 1965-67, Vietnam. Fellow Am. Psychiat. Assn., Am. Coll. Mental Health Adminstrn., Am. Assn. for Social Psychiatry, Am. Coll. Psychiatry. Home: 36 Rock Hill Rd Bedford NY 10506-1522 E-mail: glt35@netscape.net.

TISHER, CHARLES CRAIG, nephrologist, educator, former dean; MD, Wash. U., St. Louis, 1961. Resident Barnes Hosp., St. Louis, U. Wash. affiliated Hosps., Seattle; fellow in nephrology U. Wash., Seattle; positions at Walter Reed Hosp. and Walter Reed Army Inst. Rsch., Washington; joined faculty Duke U. Sch. Medicine, 1969; prof. medicine and pathology U. Fla. Coll. Medicine, Gainesville, Fla., 1980—, chief divsn. nephrology, hypertension and transplantation, 1980—87, named Ctr. Fla. Kidney Ctr. Eminent Scholar Chair in Nephrology, 1989, prof. anatomy and cell biology, sr. assoc. dean, 1998—2002, Folke H. Peterson Disting. Professorship, 1999—, dean, 2002—07, assoc. v.p. program devel., 2007—; dir. Ctr. Clin. Trials Rsch U. Fla. Founding asst. editor Kidney Internat. jour.; chmn. med. adv. board Bioavailability Systems Inc., Cocoa Beach, Fla. Recipient Faculty Rsch. Prize in Clin. Scis., U. Fla., 1985. Mem.: Internat. Soc. Nephrology, Am. Soc. Nephrology (pres. 1990—91, jour. editor 1996—2001, John P. Peters Award 2001). Office: U Fla Divsn Nephrology Box J224 JHMHC Gainesville FL 32610 also: U Fla PO Box 100215 Gainesville FL 32610-0215 Office Phone: 352-273-7508. Business E-Mail: tisher@ufl.edu.

TISHMAN, LYNN P., psychologist, psychoanalyst; b. Yonkers, NY, Apr. 3, 1951; d. Neal and Olga Petrucci; m. Peter V. Tishman, May 31, 1992; stepchildren: Steven, Linda, Anita. AAS in Acctg., Westchester CC, 1971; BA in Psychology summa cum laude, Hunter Coll., 1993; MSW, LCSW with honors, Hunter Sch. Social Work, 1995; PhD in Clin. Psychology, Columbia U., 2007. Lic. massage therapist Swedish Inst., NY, 1980, cert. biofeedback therapist BCIA, 1985, psychoanalyst, psychotherapist, and rschr., adult and child cert. psychoanalyst Psychoanalytic Inst. Postgrad. Ctr., NYC, 2002. Child devel. specialist and rschr. Pacella Parent Child Ctr., NY Psychoanalytic Inst. Mem.: NASW, APA, NY State Psychol. Assn., Assn. Applied Psychophysiology and Biofeedback, Postgrad. Psychoanalytic Soc. Avocations: running, weightlifting, bicycling, sailing.

TISSUE, MIKE, medical educator, respiratory therapist; b. Garfield, Wash., Aug. 24, 1941; s. Altha Lester and Fern Adeline (Willard) T.; m. Marjorie Lena Atkinson, Feb. 24, 1961 (div. June 1991); children: Sue Tipton, Pam Kromholtz, Paul, Donna Leach; m. Mary Emma Napier, Aug. 24, 1998. AAS (4 degrees) with honors, Spokane CC, Wash., 1985; BS in Respiratory Therapy cum laude, Loma Linda U., Calif., 1987; MS in Respiratory Care, Ga. State U., 1999. Registered cardiovasc. invasive specialist; registered cardiac sonographer; registered respiratory therapist-neonatal pediat. specialist; registered pulmonary function technologist, respiratory care practitioner; diplomate sr. disability analyst. Respiratory intern, NICU therapist Loma Linda (Calif.) U. Med. Ctr., 1985-87; educator, therapist Riyadh (Saudi Arabia) Armed Forces Hosp., 1987-91; head dept. respiratory care Security Forces Hosp., Riyadh, 1991-93; asst. prof., dir. clin. edn. respiratory therapy program Morehead (Ky.) State U., 1993-94; program dir. assoc. degree respiratory therapy Chattahoochee Tech. Coll., Marietta, Ga., 1994—98; clin. instr. Ga. State U., Atlanta, 1999-2001; dir. respiratory therapy program Nat. Inst. Tech., Atlanta, 2001—08. Pres., founder Riyadh Cardiorespiratory Soc., 1988-93; rschr. Loma Linda U., 1987, Riyadh Armed Forces Hosp., 1988; instr. and affil.various heart assns. at various times cons. ARC, Tacoma, 1984, instr. standard and advanced first aid, and CPR, Inland Empire chpt., Spokane, 1975-94; instr. first aid San Bernardino/Redlands Svc. Ctr., Loma Linda, 1985-87, Am. Cmty. Svcs. U.S. Embassy, Riyadh, 1987-93, U.S. Mil. Operation Desert Storm, Riyadh, 1991-93; instr. Freedom From Smoking Clinic Program Am. Lung Assn., Calif., 1985-87, Saudi Arabia, 1987-93, Smyrna, Ga., 1994-96; mem. several coms. Chattahoochee Tech. Coll., 1994-98. Contbr. articles to profl. jours. Bd. dirs. Am. Heart Assn., Spokane, 1976-83, chair fin. com., 1981-83; chair programming and spkrs. bur. Am. Lung Assn., Smyrna, Ga., 1994-98, chmn. bd. dirs., 1995-96; sec. Cobb County Cmty. Coun., Marietta, 1995-96, spkr., 1995, v.p., 1996, pres. 1997; vol. Ga. Internat. Cultural Exch., 1995; registry exam. sr. proctor Cardiovasc. Credentialing Internat./Nat. Bd. Cardiovasc. Technologists, Riyadh, 1987-90; commr. Boy Scouts Am., Spokane, 1973-82. Named Citizen of Day, KGA Radio, Spokane, 1983. Mem. AAUP (legis. com. Atlanta 1995-96), Am. Assn. Respiratory Care (therapist-driven protocol rev. com. 1994, ad hoc com. on patient-driven protocol rev. com. 1996, ad hoc com. for sects. rev. 1995-96, job analysis, neonatal pedit. specialist 2002), Applied Measurement Profls., Alliance of Cardiovasc. Profls., Ga. Soc. Respiratory Care (chmn. cardiopulmonary com. 1994-95, edn. com., smoking and health com.), Phi Delta Kappa (pub. rels. com. 1995-96). Avocations: photography, travel. Home: 1881 Arnold Dr SW Austell GA 30106-2907 Personal E-mail: miketissue@hotmail.com.

TITTON, ROSS LEWIS, radiologist; b. Phila., Jan. 13, 1973; m. Jennifer Lynn Dublirer; 1 child, Reese Whitney. BS, U. Miami, Coral Gables, Fla., 1992; MD, U. Miami, Fla., 1996. Bd. cert. Am. Bd. Radiology, 2001. Resident, diagnostic radiology NY Presbyn. Hosp., NY Cornell Med. Ctr., NYC, 1997—2001; fellow, abdominal imaging and intervention Mass. Gen. Hosp., Mass. Harvard Med. Sch., Boston, 2001—03; diagnostic radiologist Booth Radiology Assocs., Woodbury, NJ, 2003—. Contbr. articles to profl. jours. Vice chmn. Dept. Radiology Underwood Meml. Hosp. Mem.: med. Soc. NJ, Radiological Soc. North America, Am. Roentgen Ray Assn., Am. Bd. Radiology, Alpha Omega Alpha Nat. Med. Honor Soc. Home: 7 Shingle Oak Ct Voorhees NJ 08043 Office: Booth Radiology Assocs 748 Kings Hwy Woodbury NJ 08096 Business E-Mail: rltitton@comcast.net.

TIWARI, ASHOK KUMAR, biologist, researcher; b. Narahan Chandauli, Uttar Pradesh, India, July 4, 1963; s. Murahu and Sudama Tiwari; m. Usha Pandey, June 15, 1983; children: Divya, Ashutosh. BSc, Gorakhpur U., Varanasi, 1983, MSc in Zoology, 1985; PhD, Banaras Hindu U., Varanasi, 1992. Rsch. fellow Banaras Hindu U., Varanasi, Uttar Pradesh, India, 1986—92, post doctoral fellow, 1993—98; fellow council scientific and indsl. rsch. Indian Inst. of Chem. Tech., Hyderabad, Andhra Pradesh, India, 1998—2001; scientist Indian Inst. Of Chem. Tech., 2001—. Rschr. Indian Inst. of Chem. Tech., Hyderabad, 1998—; mem. editl. bd. 6 internat. jours. Contbr. scientific papers to profl. jours., over 82 rsch. papers to internat. jours. Engaged in bringing out traditional Indian med. knowledge ayurveda on internat. forum by explaining its philosophy and medicine Indian Inst. Chem. Tech., Hyderabad. Achievements include patents for antioxidants, antiatherosclerotic and alpha glucosidase inhibitors from traditional medicinal plants; research in drug discoveries from traditional medicinal plants and explaining traditional therapeutic knowledge in modern scientific terms. Home: 501 Sri Tirumala Residency Mallapur Andhra Pradesh Hyderabad 500076 India Office: Indian Inst Of Chem Tech Habsiguda Andhra Pradesh Hyderabad 500007 India Office Fax: 91-40-27193753. Personal E-mail: astiwari@yahoo.com. Business E-Mail: tiwari@iict.res.in.

TIWARI, MEENA, oncologist; b. Allahabad, Oct. 10, 1974; MBBS, NSCB Med. Coll., 1999; MD, Moti Lal Nehru Med. Coll., 2005. Cons. radiation oncologist Dr. Balabhai Nanavti Hosp., Mumbai, 2008—. Cons. BLK Walawalkar Hosp., 2008. Mem.: Soc.Thermal Medicine, Assn. Radiation Oncologist India. Office: Dr Balabhai Nanavati Hosp SV Rd Vile Parle W Mumbai Maharashtra 400056 India Personal E-mail: tiwarimeena@rediffmail.com.

TIWARI, RAJNARAYAN R., physician, researcher; b. Gwalior, India, Oct. 28, 1970; MBBS, Nagpur U., 1992, MD, 1997. Scientist D NIOH, 2009—. Office: NIOH Meghani Nagar Ahmedabad Gujarat 380016 India E-mail: rajtiwari2810@yahoo.co.in.

TIWARI, RUCHI, pharmacist; b. Lucknow, India, Sept. 23, 1981; PharmM, Rajeev Acad. Pharmacy, 2007; PhD, Jaipur Nat. U., 2011. Pharmacist Saroj Inst. Tech. and Mgmt., 2007—08, Pranveer Singh Inst. Tech., 2008—, asst. prof., 2008. Recipient Best Asst. Prof. award, Pranveer Singh Inst. Tech., 2009, 2010. Avocation: reading. Office: Kanpur Agra Hwy Kalpi Rd Bhauti Kanpur Uttar Pradesh 208020 India Personal E-mail: lda_mpharm@rediffmail.com.

TIWARI, SUDHANSHU, research scientist; b. India, July 7, 1978; PhD, Gorakhpur U., Uttar Pradesh, India, 2004. Sr. rsch. fellow

Gorakhpur U., 1998—2001. Sr. Rsch, fellowship, Indian Coun. Agrl. Rsch., New Delhi. Avocation: reading. Home: Betiahatya Gorakhpur Uttar Pradesh 273001 India Personal E-mail: sudhansh4@rediffmail.com.

TIWARI-WOODRUFF, SEEMA KAUSHALYA, medical educator; b. India, June 23, 1963; PhD, Southern Ill. U., 1994. Asst. prof. David Gefen Sch. Medicine, 2006—. Rsch. grant, Nat. Multiple Sclerosis Soc., NUH, Teva Pharms. Mem.: APS, ASN, SFN. Achievements include research in understanding sex differences in demyelination induced neurodegeneration in the CNS and finding neuroprotective agents that can halt and reverse this neurodegeration. Avocations: travel, cooking, exercise. Office: 635 Charles E Young Dr NRB1-475C Van Nuys CA 91411 Business E-Mail: seemaw@ucla.edu.

TJADEN, PATRICIA, researcher, director; b. Lakehurst, NJ, July 10, 1950; BA, U. Colo., 1972, PhD, 1983. Asst. prof. Loretto Heights Coll., 1979—83, U. NC, 1984—86; lectr. U. Canterbury, 1987; sr. rschr. Ctr. Policy Rsch., 1987—2001; dir. Tjaden Rsch. Corp., 2002—. Tech. peer reviewer Nat. Inst. Justice, 1994—; adv. bd. mem. Nat. Violence Against Women Prevention Rsch. Ctr., 1999—2001; rsch. cons. US Dept. Health and Human Svcs., Ctrs. Disease Control and Prevention, 2000—03, US Dept. Def., Def. Manpower Data Ctr., 2004—07; peer reviewer US Dept. Justice, Cmty. Oriented Policing Svcs., 2003. Mem.: Assn. Threat Assessment Profls., Am. Soc. Criminology. Avocations: skiing, hiking, sailing. Office: 208 S French St PO Box 3125 Breckenridge CO 80424 Business E-Mail: tjadenp@comcast.net.

TJANDRA, RAMA, health facility administrator, obstetrician, gynecologist; b. Surabaya, Indonesia, July 18, 1953; s. Ahmad Kannu and Rofiah; m. Sri Sundari, Nov. 4, 1979; children: Randi Novianto, Rangga Pranawa, Rando Pradika, Ranti Pratiwi. MD, Airlangga U., 1979, degree in Ob.-gyn., 1990. Chief health Ctr. Health Dept., Bangkalan, India, 1979—86, resident Ob-gyn. Surabaya, India, 1986—90; mem. staff Ob-gyn. Ctrl. Army Hosp., Jakarta, India, 1990—; chief Divsn. Fertility Gynecol. Endocrinology Indonesia U., 1997; med. dir. Medikaloka Health Care, Jakarta, 2000—. Mem.: Indonesian Menapause Soc. (chief organizing com. 1999—), Indonesian Ob-gyn. Soc. (fertility reproduction staff 1993—96). Office: Medikaloka Health CareGedung Graha Irama JL HR Rasuna Said Mezzanine & 2nd Fl Blok X-1 Kav 1-2 Kuningan Jakarta 12950 Indonesia

TJELL, CARSTEN, otolaryngologist; b. Dronninglund, Denmark, Sept. 12, 1947; arrived in Sweden, 1975; s. Hjalmar and Randi Tjell; m. Wenche Iglebekk, Sept. 17, 2007; Kirsten Wiese, Sept. 12, 1970 (div. June 2007); children: Lise, Mette MD, Arhus, 1975; PhD, Karolinska Inst., Stockholm, 1998. Asst. physician, Kiruna, Sweden, 1975-78; surgeon ENT dept. Ctrl. Hosp., Sundsvall, Sweden, 1978-82, Trondheim, Norway, 1982-84, med. dirs., chief ENT Dept. Visby, Sweden, 1984-88, cons. otolaryngologist Skovde, Sweden, 1988—2002, chief ENT dept., 2002—04; neurotologic and audiologic chief ENT dept. Sorlandet Sykehus, Arendal, Norway, 2004—. Instr. middle ear surgery, New Delhi, 1992; spkr. in field. Author: SADE: The Eustachian Tube, 1991, Diagnostic Considerations on Whiplash Associated Disorders, 1998, VERNON: The Cranio-cervical Syndrome, 2001; contbr. articles to profl. jours. Mem. AAAS, European Acad. Otology and Neuro-Otology, Swedish Soc. Otosurgery, Swedish Vestibular Soc., Movement Disorder Soc., Assn. Physicians Audiology, Internat. Assn. Physicians for Prevention of Nuclear War, Danish Traffic Accident Soc. (Rsch. prize 1999). Social Liberal. Avocations: philosophy, mountain tracking, classical music, gastronomy, politics. Office: Ent-Dept Sorlandet Sykehus PO Box 605 N-4809 Arendal Norway Home: Hoy Vei 12 N 4838 Arendal Norway Business E-Mail: carsten.tjell@sshf.no.

TJIAN, ROBERT TSE NAN, biochemistry educator, medical institution administrator; b. Hong Kong, Sept. 22, 1949; BA in Biochemistry, U. Calif., Berkeley, 1972; PhD in Biochemistry and Molecular Biology, Harvard U., 1976. Staff investigator molecular virology Cold Spring Harbor Lab., NY, 1976-79; asst. prof. biochemistry U. Calif., Berkeley, 1979—82, prof. biochemistry, 1982—, prof. molecular & cell biology. Investigator Howard Hughes Med. Inst., Chevy Chase, Md., 1987—, pres., 2009—; co-founder Tularik, Inc., Calif., 1991; adj. prof. biochemistry & biophysics U. Calif., San Francisco. Contbr. articles to profl. jours. Recipient Pfizer award for enzymology, 1983, Cancer Rsch. award, Milken Family Med. Found., 1988, Lewis S. Rosenstiel award for disting. work in basic med. sci., Brandeis U., 1995, Alfred P. Sloan Jr. prize, GM Cancer Rsch. Found., 1999, Louisa Gross Horwitz prize, Columbia U., 1999, MERIT award, Nat. Cancer Inst., 2004; named Calif. Scientist of Yr., 1994. Mem.: NAS (Monsanto award for molecular biology 1991), Academia Sinica (Taiwan), Am. Philos. Soc., Am. Acad. Arts & Scis. Office: U Calif Dept Molecular & Cell Biology Dept 142 LSA #3200 Berkeley CA 94720-3204 also: Howard Hughes Med Inst 4000 Jones Bridge Rd Chevy Chase MD 20815-6789 Office Phone: 510-642-8258, 301-215-8500. Office Fax: 510-642-0884. Business E-Mail: jmlim@berkeley.edu. *

TJONG, YUNG WUI, research scientist; b. Hong Kong, Aug. 9, 1978; PhD in Physiology, U. Hong Kong, 2007. Postdoc. fellow Chinese U. Hong Kong, 2008—. Office: Rm 215 2/F Run Run Shaw Sci Bldg Shatin Hong Kong Personal E-mail: jefftjong@yahoo.com.hk.

TKATCHENKO, ANDREI V., medical researcher, educator; b. Russia, Aug. 26, 1964; MD, Russian State Med. U., Moscow, 1988; PhD, Engelhardt Inst. Molecular Biology, Russian Acad. Scis., 1992. Rsch. fellow Inst. Nat. Sante Recherche Medicale, France, 1996—98, Med. U. SC, 1998—2000, asst. prof., 2003—06; rsch. fellow Harvard Med. Sch., 2000—03; asst. prof. Wayne State U., 2006—. Dana Mahoney Rsch. Fellow, Harvard Neurosci. Inst. Mem.: Soc. Neurosci., Assn. Rsch. Vision & Ophthalmology. Office: 540 E Canfield Ave 7133 Scott Hall Detroit MI 48201 Business E-Mail: atkatche@med.wayne.edu.

TOBIAS, EDWARD S., medical researcher; b. Paisley, Scotland, Dec. 13, 1965; BSc with hons., U. Glasgow, 1987, MBChB with commendation, 1990, PhD, 1997. Med. genetics specialist registrar Yorkhill Hosp., Glasgow, 1997—2001; post doctoral rschr. Beatson Inst. for Cancer Rsch., Glasgow, 1996—97; MRC tng. fellow U. Glasgow, 1993—96, GlaxoSmithKline clin. rsch. fellow Yorkhill Hosp., 2001—07. Sr. lectr. U. Glasgow, 2007—; hon. cons. clin. geneticist, 2001—. Fellow: Royal Coll. Physicians U.K.; mem.: Cancer Genetics Group U.K., European Assn. Cancer Rsch., Brit. Soc. Human Genetics, Brit. Assn. Cancer Rsch. Achievements include discovery of human TES gene. Office: Univ Glasgow Inst Medical Genetics/Yorkhill Hosp G3 8SJ Glasgow Scotland Business E-Mail: e.tobias@clinmed.gla.ac.uk.

TOBIAS, GEOFFREY, otolaryngologist, plastic surgeon; b. Paterson, NJ, Dec. 20, 1947; MD, Tufts U., 1973. Intern Tufts New England Med. Ctr., 1973—76; resident Mt. Sinai Hosp., NYC, 1976—78; attending surgeon and instr. Mt. Sinai Hosp. and Sch. Medicine, NYC; assoc. chief head and neck surgery Englewood Hosp., NJ. Mem. sci. adv. bd. Longevity mag. Named one of Top Doctors in NY, NY Mag., 2004. Mem.: Am. Acad. Otolaryngology - Head and Neck Surgery, Am. Acad. Facial Plastic Surgery. Office: 214 Engle St Englewood NJ 07631-2418 also: 815 Park Ave New York NY 10021-3276 Office Phone: 201-567-7966. Office Fax: 201-567-6770.

TOBIAS, JOSEPH DREW, pediatric anesthesiologist; b. St. Louis, Dec. 16, 1958; s. Sherwin Larue and Georgia Xenos Tobias; m. Julie Ann Turpin, Nov. 3, 2001. BA, U. Mo., Kansas City, 1981, MD, 1983. Diplomate Am. Bd. Pediat., Am. Bd. Anesthesiology, Am. Bd. Pediat. Critical Care, Am. Bd. Anesthesiology Critical Care Medicine, Am. Bd. Anesthesiology Pain Mgmt., cert. Am. Acad. Pain Mgmt. 1990. Chief pediatric anesthesiology, attending pediatric ICU St. Jude Children's Hosp., Memphis, 1990—91; assoc. dir., divsn. pediatric anesthesiology/critical care; assoc. prof. anesthesiology and pediat. Vanderbilt U., Nashville, 1991—95; chief, pediatric anesthesiology-pediat. critical care, prof. anesthesiology and pediat. U. Mo., Columbia, 1995—2010, vice-chmn., dept. anesthesiology, 2010—; chmn. Dept. Anesthesiology & Pain Medicine, Nationwide Childrens Hosp. Office: 700 Children's Dr Columbus OH 43205 Office Phone: 614-722-4200. Office Fax: 614-722-4203.

TOBIAS, RANDALL LEE, former federal agency administrator, retired pharmaceutical company executive; b. Lafayette, Ind., Mar. 20, 1942; m. Marilyn Jane Salyer, Sept. 2, 1966 (dec. May 1994); children: Paige Noelle, Todd Christopher; m. Marianne Williams, July 15, 1995; stepchildren: James Russell Ullyot, Kathryn Lee Ullyot. BS in Mktg., Ind. U., 1964; LLD (hon.), Galuedette U.; D of Engring. (hon.), Rose Hulman Inst. Tech., Sagamore of the Wabash, Ind.; LLD (hon.), Ind. U., 1997. Numerous positions Ind. Bell, 1964-77, Ill. Bell, 1977-81; v.p. residence mktg. sales and service AT&T, 1981-82, pres. Am. Bell Consumer Products, 1983, pres. Consumer Products, 1983-84, sr. v.p., 1984-85, vice chmn. NYC, 1986-93; chmn., CEO AT&T Comm., NYC, 1985-91, AT&T Internat., Basking Ridge, NJ, 1991-93, Eli Lilly & Co., Indpls., 1993-98, chmn. emeritus, 1999—; coord., US Govt. Activities to Combat AIDS Globally US Dept. State, Washington, 2003—06, dir. US Fgn. Assistance, 2006—07; adminstr. US Agy. Internat. Devel. (USAID), Washington, 2006—07. Bd. dirs. Kimberly-Clark, 1994-2003, ConocoPhillips Petroleum Co., 2002-03, Knight-Ridder, Inc. Co-Author: Put The Moose On The Table, 2003 Chmn. bd. trustees Duke U.; trustee Colonial Williamsburg Found.; bd. govs. Indpls. Mus. Art; bd. dirs. Indpls. Symphony Orch., Ind. U. Found. (hon.), Econ. Club Indpls. Named one of Top 25 Mgrs. of Yr., Bus. Week, 1997, Family Champion, Working Mothers Mag., 1997. Mem. Bus. Coun., Indpls. Corp. Cmty. Coun., Coun. Fgn. Rels., Meridian Hills Country Club (Indpls.), Woodstock Club (Indpls.), Columbia Club (Indpls.), Athletic Club (Indpls.), Univ. Club (Indpls.), Amwell Valley Conservancy (N.J.), Theta Chi. Avocations: skiing, fly fishing, shooting.

TOBIAS-MACHADO, MARCOS, urologic surgeon, researcher; b. São Caetano do Sul, São Paulo, Brazil, Sept. 23, 1969; s. Marcos Antônio and Olga Aparecida Roque Machado; m. Telma Murias Santos (div.); children: Dante dos Santos Machado, Luísa dos Santos Machado, Débora dos Santos Machado; m. Sonia Yara Nascimento, Sept. 22, 2006; children: Felipe Eduardo Samella, Mariana Samella, Maria Eduarda Nascimento Machado. MD, Santa Casa Faculty Medicine, São Paulo, 1992; MD in Gen. Surgery, U. São Paulo, 1995, MD in Urology, 1997, PhD in Med. Sci., 2008; postgrad. in Urologic Oncology, U. Miami, 2000; MBA in Laparoscopic Surgery, U. Paris, 2004. Cert. in urology Brazilian Med. Assn., 1999. Physician Brazilian Army, Itu, São Paulo, 1993—94; resident gen. surgery Hosp. das Clinicas, U. São Paulo, 1994—95; resident urology Hosp. Indianopolis, São Paulo, 1996—97; kidney transplantation staff ABC Med. Sch., Hosp. Dante Pazzanesse, Albert Einstein Jewish Hosp., São Paulo, 1998—2007; resident in chief, urology ABC Med. Sch., 1998—99, mem. rsch. ethics com., 1999—2001, head urologic oncology and minimally invasive surgery, 2001—, head molecular biology for urologic cancers lab., 2004—, chief divsn. rsch. and technol. devel., 2004—; vis. resident urologic oncology U. Miami, Fla., 2000. Cons. in field; observer dept. urology U. Miami, 2000; co-investigator various clin. trials, 2000—; prof. Superior Sch. Urology, 2002—, mem. staff Heart Hosp., 2002—; staff Brazilian Inst. Cancer Control, 2006—; postdoc. rschr. Inst. Edn. and Rsch., Albert Einstein Hosp., 2008—. Reviewer: various jours. in field; contbr. chapters to books. 2d lt. Brazilian Army, 1993, São Paulo. Grantee, Inst. Rsch. Edn., 2007—08. Mem.: Brazilian Soc. Urology (assoc.; prof. urology superior sch. 2002—, Best Clin. Rsch. award 2003, rsch. grantee 2004—06). Freedom. Achievements include development of endoscopic extraperitoneal access and new techniques in urology; video endoscopic inguinal lymphadenectomy for penile cancer; alternatives for minimally invasive urinary diversion in radiated patients. Avocations: travel, soccer, music, dance. Office: Rua Ramon Penharrubia 130 Sala 302 01340-140 Sao Paulo Brazil Business E-Mail: tobiasmachado@uol.com.br.

TOBIS, JEROME SANFORD, physician; b. Syracuse, NY, July 23, 1915; s. David George and Anna (Feinberg) T.; m. Hazel Weisbard, Sept. 18, 1938; children: David, Heather, Jonathan. BS, CCNY, 1936; MD, Chgo. Med. Sch., 1943. Diplomate Am. Bd. Phys. Medicine and Rehab. Intern Knickerbocker Hosp., 1943-44; resident Bronx VA Hosp., 1946-48; med. dir. state fever therapy unit USPHS, Brookhaven, Miss., 1944-46; practice medicine NYC, 1948-70; prof. dir. dept. phys. medicine and rehab. N.Y. Med. Coll., Flower and Fifth Av. Hosps., 1948-61; prof. rehab. medicine Albert Einstein Coll. of Medicine, 1963-70; chief div. rehab. medicine Montefiore Hosp., 1961-70; dir. vis. physician Met., Bird S. Coler hosps., 1952-61; prof., chmn. dept. phys. medicine and rehab. Calif. Coll. Medicine, U. Calif. at Irvine, 1970-82, prof., dir. program in geriatric medicine and gerontology, 1980-86; mem. adv. com. Acad. Geriatric Resource program, 1984-86, 95—. Expert med. com. Am. Rehab. Found., 1961-70; cons. Dept. Health, NYC, Long Beach VA Hosp., 1970—, Fairview State Devel. Ctr., 1976—; adv. coun. phys. medicine and rehab. for appeals com. Calif. Med. Assn., 1971-74, adv. com. U. Calif. Acad. Geriatric Resource Program, 1995—; NIH Internat. Fogarty fellow, hon. lectr., dept. geriat. medicine U. Birmingham, 1979-80; rev. panel musculoskeletal diseases NIH, 1996; rsch. prof. dept. phys. medicine & rehab. U. Calif., Irvine, 1986—, chair med. ethics com., 1986—; mem. Ctr. Health Policy Rsch. U. Calif., Davis, 1996—. Author: (book) Fundamentals of the Stem Cell Debate: The Sci., Religious, Ethical, and Polit. Issues Monroe, K. R., Miller, R. B. and Tobis, J., U. Calif. Press, 2008; mem. editorial bd.: Heart and Lung, 1973-76, Geriatrics, 1975-80, Archives of Phys. Medicine and Rehab, 1958-73. Named Physician of the Year, 1957; recipient Distinguished Alumnus award Chgo. Med. Sch., 1972, Acad. award Nat. Inst. on Aging, 1981-86; named hon. faculty mem. Calif. Zeta chpt. Alpha Omega Alpha, 1981; Leavitt Meml. lectureship Baylor Coll. Medicine, 1983, Griffith Meml. lectureship Am. Geriatric Soc., 1984; Australian Coll. Rehabilitation Medicine, 1984; Jerome S. Tobis Ann. Conf. on Geriatric Medicine established in his name, U. Calif. at Irvine, 1986. Fellow ACP, Am. Coll. Cardiology, Am. Congress Rehab. Medicine (hon.); mem. AMA (mem. residency rev. com. Coun. Med. Edn. 1973), AAAS, Am. Acad. Cerebral Palsy, Am. Acad. Phys. Medicine and Rehab. (Disting. Clinician award 1993), Am. Congress Rehab. Medicine (pres. 1962), Calif. Coun. Gerontology and Geriatrics (bd. dirs. 1980-86, pres. 1985), N.Y. Acad. Medicine, N.Y. Acad. Sci., Orange County Med. Soc., Assn. U. Calif. Irvine (chair emeritae/i 1996-97). Home: 1115 Goldenrod Ave Corona Del Mar CA 92625-1508 Office Phone: 714-456-5626. Personal E-mail: jstobis@uci.edu.

TOBITA, KOUJI, surgeon, researcher; b. Mito, Japan, Dec. 26, 1967; s. Katsuhiko and Katsu Tobita; m. Yoko Koga, Aug. 6, 1961; 1 child, Kazuhiro. MD, Chiba U., 2000. Contbr. articles (Award of the Japan Gastroent. Endoscopy Soc., 2001). Achievements include research in the minute surface structures of the depressed-type early gastric cancer with magnifying endoscopy. Office: Shimothuga General Hosp Fujimi-cho 5-32 Tochigi 328-8505 Japan Office Fax: 0282-24-1631. Personal E-mail: tobi@mbp.ocn.ne.jp.

TOCHIKURA, TATSUROKURO, applied microbiologist, home economics educator; b. Nagaoka, Niigata, Japan, Nov. 15, 1927; s. Tatsujiro and Fuji (Sato) T.; m. Kano Takako, Nov. 8, 1953; children: Momoyo, Tadafumi. BS in Agrl. Chemistry, Kyoto U., Japan, 1951, PhD, 1960. Cert. indsl. microbiology and microbial biochemistry. Rsch. assoc. dept. agrl. chemistry Kyoto (Japan) U., 1956-61, assoc. prof. dept. agrl. chemistry, 1961-68, prof. dept. food sci. and tech., 1968-91, prof. emeritus, 1991; prof. home econs. Kobe (Japan) Women's U., 1991—2002, prof. emeritus, 2002. Vis. asst. prof. Oreg. State U., 1964-65. Co-author: Microbial Production of Nucleic Acid-Related Substances, 1976, Methods in Carbohydrate Chemistry, 1980, Bioconversion of Waste Materials to Industrial Products, 1991. Mem. Japan Bioindustry Assn., Japan Soc. for Fermentation and Bioengring., Japan Soc. for Bioscience Biotech. and Agrochemistry. Home: 31-12 Nogamiyama Kamiueno-cho Muko-shi Kyoto 617-0006 Japan

TODD, GEORGE J., vascular surgeon, educator; Grad., Pa. State U. Coll. of Medicine, Hershey, PA, 1974. Diplomate Am. Bd. Surgery, 1989, recertified 2000, Am. Bd. Surgery-vascular surgery, 1986, recertified 1996. Residency tng. gen. surgery Columbia-Presbyterian Med. Ctr., NYC, 1975—79, fellowship vascular surgery, 1979—80; prof. surgery College of Physicians and Surgeons Columbia Univ.; chmn. surgery dept. St. Luke's Roosevelt Hosp. Named Best Doctors, NY Mag., 2008; named one of Top Doctors-NY Metro Area, 2009. Office: St. Luke's Roosevelt Hospital Ste 5G-77 1000 10th Ave New York NY 10019 Office Phone: 212-523-7481. Office Fax: 212-523-7483.

TODD, LINDA MARIE, singer, nutrition researcher, circulation facilitator, financial consultant, pilot; b. LA, Mar. 30, 1948; d. Ithel Everette and Janet Marie Fredricks; m. William MacKenzie Cook, Jan. 11, 1982 (div. Oct. 1989); m. Robert Oswald Todd, Apr. 8, 1990; 1 child, Jesse MacKenzie Todd. BA in Psychology and Sociology, U. Colo., 1969; student in Psychology, U. No. Colo., 1970; ins. and estate planning courses, 1990—2007, mgmt. tng. programs, 2001—11. Pilot lic., weather cert., FCC lic., Calif. life ins. lic., coll. teaching credential; registered with Nat. Assn. Securities Dealers. Counselor Jeffco Juvenile Detention Ctr., Golden, Colo., 1969-71; communications Elan Vital, Denver, 1971-81; legal sec. Fredman, Silverberg & Lewis, San Diego, 1980-82; escrow supr. Performance Mktg. Concepts, Olympic Valley, Calif., 1982-85; mgmt. commn. instr. Sierra Coll., Truckee, Calif., 1986-87; regional mgr. Primerica Fin. Svcs., Reno, 1987-91; air traffic, weather advisor Truckee Tahoe Airport Dist., Calif., 1986-96; circulation mgr. Sierra Sun and Tahoe World Newspapers, 2001—08. Student tour leader, air show organizer Truckee (Calif.) Tahoe Airport, 1986-96; fin. cons. Primerica Fin. Svcs., Truckee, 1987-91; gen. agt. TTS Fin., 1992—2007; co-founder Todd Nutrition, 1995—; co-owner Todd Aero, 1990—2011; bd. dirs. Pacific Crest Fin. Corp., 1996—. Editor: (newsletter) Communications, 1975; singer: Mountain Belles, 2011-. Chorus mem. operas and musicals, 1960s-70s; prodn. crew Lake Tahoe Summer Music Festivals, 2000-03; sec. gen. Arapahoe H.S. Model UN, Littleton, Colo., 1965; del. State Model UN, Colo., 1966; conv. del. Elan Vital, The Ninety-Nines, Inc.; pub. info. officer Civil Air Patrol. Univ. scholar Littleton (Colo.) Edn. Assn., 1966, flight scholar The Ninety-Nines Inc., Reno, 1990; named Recruiter of Month, Al Williams Primerica,

Reno, 1987. Mem. CAP (lt.), Mountain Belles, TPRF, Plane Talkers, EAA Avocations: hiking, skiing, swimming, flying, soaring, singing. Home and Office: PO Box 1303 Truckee CA 96160-1303 Personal E-mail: ltodd.1971@gmail.com.

TODD, MARY BETH, oncologist, researcher; b. Tulsa, Okla. BA, Okla. City U., 1972; postgrad., U. Tulsa, 1973-74; DO, Okla. State U., 1978. Assoc. rsch. scientist Yale Sch. Medicine, New Haven, 1984-86; dir. outpatient svc. Yale Medical Sch., New Haven, 1986-93; asst. prof. Sch. Medicine Yale U., New Haven, 1986-91, assoc. prof., 1991-93; assoc. prof. medicine UMDNJ-RWJMS, New Brunswick, 1993—2002, prof. medicine, 2002—; deputy dir. The Cancer Inst. N.J., New Brunswick, NJ, 1993—2005, chief med. officer, 2005—06, COO, 2005—. Scientific adv. panel for immunology svcs. Food & Drug Adminstrn., Washington, 1991-95; scientific adv. bd. HEM Pharmeceuticals Corp., 1991-93; external medical adv. bd. Conn. Hospice, 1990-92; co-chair N.J. Working Group to Improve Outcomes in Cancer Patients. Recipient grants Nat. Inst. Health, 1989-98. Mem. Am. Coll. Physicians, Am. Fedn. Clinical Rsch., Am. Soc. Clinical Oncology, Am. Assn. Cancer Rsch., Am. Soc. Hemetology, Internat. Soc. Interferon and Cytokine Rsch. Office: The Cancer Inst NJ 195 Little Albany St New Brunswick NJ 08903-2681 Office Phone: 732-235-7413. Business E-Mail: toddmb@umdnj.edu.

TODD, ROBERT FRANKLIN, III, oncologist, educator; b. Granville, Ohio, Apr. 16, 1948; m. Susan Erhard, 1977; children: Currier Nathaniel, Andrew Joseph. AB, Duke U., 1970, PhD, 1975, MD, 1976. Diplomate Am. Bd. Internal Medicine. Intern Peter Bent Brigham Hosp., Boston, 1976-77, resident, 1977-78; fellow in oncology Sidney Farber Cancer Inst., Boston, 1978-80; clin. fellow in medicine Harvard Med. Sch., Boston, 1978-81; postdoctoral fellow divsn. tumor immunology Sidney Farber Cancer Inst., Boston, 1979-81; asst. prof. medicine Harvard Med. Sch., Boston, 1981-84; assoc. prof. internal medicine U. Mich., Ann Arbor, 1984-88, assoc. prof. cellular and molecular biology, 1985-88, assoc. dir. divsn. hematology-oncology internal medicine, 1987-91, prof. internal medicine, 1988—, assoc. chair for rsch. dept. internal medicine, 1989-91, assoc. chair dept. internal medicine, 1991-93, chief divsn. hematology-oncology dept. internal medicine, 1993—2007, assoc. v.p. rsch., 1999—2005, Frances and Victor Ginsberg prof. hematology/oncology, 1999—, interim chair, dept. internal medicine, 2007—. Attending physician U. Mich. Hosps., 1984—. Contbr. numerous articles to profl. jours.; patentee in field. Mem.: Assn. Am. Physicians, Am. Soc. Clin. Investigation, S.W. Oncology Group, Ctrl. Soc. Clin. Rsch. (councilor 1997—, pres. 2001—02), Am. Fedn. Clin. Rsch. (councilor midwest chpt. 1986—89), Am. Soc. Hematology (councilor 2005—), Soc. Leukocyte Biology (councilor 1996—99), Am. Soc. Clin. Oncology, Am. Assn. Cancer Rsch., Am. Assn. Immunologists, ACP, Alpha Omega Alpha, Phi Beta Kappa. Business E-Mail: robtodd@umich.edu.

TODHUNTER, JOHN ANTHONY, toxicologist, consultant; b. Cali, Valle, Colombia, Oct. 9, 1949; s. John Arthur and Teresa Maria (Torres) T.; divorced, 1986; children: Jennifer, Julia; m. Holli Wilson, Apr. 19, 1986; 1 child, Jacqueline Rose. BSc, UCLA, 1971; MSc, Calif. State U., 1973; PhD, U. Calif., Santa Barbara, 1976. Diplomate Am. Bd. Toxicology, Am. Bd. Forensic Examiners. Instr. Calif. State U., LA, 1972-73; rsch. asst. U. Calif., Santa Barbara, 1973-76; fellow Roche Inst. Molecular Biology, Nutley, NJ, 1976-78; asst. prof. Cath. U. Am., Washington, 1978-81, chmn. Biochemistry Program, 1980-81; asst. adminstr. U.S. EPA, Washington, 1981-83; cons. Sci. Regulatory Svcs. Internat., Washington, 1983-91; pres. SRS Internat. Corp., 1991—2010, SRS Internat. Health Care Group, 1995—2010; CEO Assura Pharms., 2006—11; chief sci. officer, sr. v.p. R & D SinoFresh HealthCare, Inc., 2010—. Expert advisor European regional office WHO, Stockholm, 1984; mem. Hazardous Waste Siting Bd., Annapolis, Md., 1980-81. Contbr. articles to profl. jours. Bd. dirs. Reagan Alumni Assn., Washington, 1985—; vol. Am. Cancer Soc., Washington, 1988-93; mem. Presdl. Transition Team, Washington, 1980. U. Calif. Bd. Regents fellow, 1975, B.R. Baker Meml. fellow dept. chemistry U. Calif., Santa Barbara, 1976. Fellow Am. Inst. Chemists (dir. at large 1989-92, vice chmn. bd. 1992); mem. Soc. of Toxicology, Am. Chem. Soc., Soc. for Risk Analysis, N.Y. Acad. Sci. Business E-Mail: todhunter@svsinternational.com.

TODKAR, MANOJ SHANKARRAO, orthopedist; b. Pune, Maharashtra, India, Dec. 24, 1973; s. Shankarrao Mahadeorao and Prabhavati Shankarrao Todkar; m. Veena Manoj Rotte, May 21, 2002; 1 child, Aabha Manoj. MBBS, B. J. Med. Coll., Pune, 1995; MSc in Orthopaedic Surgery, Pune U., 2000; MCh, U. Dundee, Scotland, UK, 2006. Diplomate Nat. Bd., Delhi, 2001. Cons. Ruby Hall Clinic, Pune, 2006—; rsch. fellow U. Dundee, 2005—06; registrar NHS, UK, 2003—05; resident dr. Sassoon Gen. Hosp., Pune, 1997—2000, lectr., 2000—03. Hon. Dervan Charitable Hosp., Maharashtra, 2006—, Red Cross Assn., Pune, 2006—. Contbr. scientific papers. Dr. Red Cross Assn., 2001—. Nat. Merit scholarship, Indian Govt., 1989. Fellow: Shizuoka Hosp., Japan, Internat. Ctr. Orthopaedic Edn., Internat. Coll. Suregons, Indian Soc. Hip And Knee Surgeons; mem.: Nat. Acad. Med. Scis., Delhi, Royal Coll. Surgeons Glasgow, Indian Arthroscopy Soc. Hindu. Avocations: travel, swimming, reading, mountain climbing. Office: Dr Todkar Hosp 1-Aug 411 011 Pune India Office Fax: 91-20-26121552.

TODO, MITSUGU, medical educator; b. Saga, Japan, Feb. 27, 1963; PhD, Ohio State U., 1995. Assoc. prof. Kyushu U., 1995—. Avocation: biomaterials and biomechanics for regenerative medicine and orthopedic implants. Office: 6-1 Kasuga-koen Kasuga Fukuoka 816-8580 Japan Business E-Mail: todo@riam.kyushu-u.ac.jp.

TODOROVIC, VLADIMIR STOJAN, psychiatrist, director; b. Nova Gradiska, Croatia, May 8, 1949; s. Stojan Nedeljko and Ljubica Dusan Todorovic; m. Todorovic Mihailo Griva, Oct. 6, 1990; children: Jelena Aleksandar, Milan. MD, Med. Sch. Belgrade, Serbia, 1980. Forensic psychiatrist RDMHS, Rockhampton, Queensland, Australia, 2002—08, clin. dir., 2007—. Cons. Corrections, Rockhapton, 2002—. Fellow: SMA; mem.: ANZAPPL. Home: 2 Jolinda Way Rockhampton Queensland 4701 Australia Office: RDMHS C Quarry St Rockhampton Queensland 4700 Australia Office Fax: 61749211500. Personal E-mail: vavtod@hotmail.com.

TOENSHOFF, BURKHARD, pediatrician, nephrologist; b. Wuppertal, Germany, Mar. 4, 1958; s. Paul Rolf and Hildegard (Neuhaus) T.; m. Christianne Senghaas, May 27, 1989; children: Sebastian, Isabel. Grad., Albrecht-Dürer-Gymnasium, Hagen, 1976; habilitation, Ruprecht Karls U., Heidelberg, Germany, 1995. Diplomate Albert Ludwigs U., Freiburg, Germany, 1983. Resident pediat., fellow pediat. nephrology U. Children's Hosp., Heidelberg, Germany, 1985—92, prof., 1995—, dir. pediat. renal transplantation program, 1995—, vice chmn., dept. pediats. I, 2002; instr. Med. Sch. SUNY, Stony BJrook, NY, 1992—94. Contbr. numerous articles, revs. to profl. publs., chpts. to books. Councilor Internat. Pediat.Transplant Assn., Mt. Laurel, NJ, 2007—. Scholar German Govt., 1978, Deutsche Akademische Austauschdienst, 1979; Feodor-Lynen rsch. grantee Alexander von Humboldt Found., 1992, rsch. grantee Am. Heart Assn., 1993, Nat. Kidney Found., 1994. Mem.: others, European Soc. Pediat. Nephrology, Endocrine Soc. USA, Internat. Soc. Insulin-like Growth Factor Rsch., German Soc. Pediat. Nephrology (councilor 2001—05, Else Kröner Freseniu prize 1999), Am. Soc. Nephrology, Internat. Pediat.Transplant Assn. (coun. mem. 2007, Councilor 2007), Internat. Pediatric Nephrology Assn. Roman Catholic. Achievements include research in pediatrics and pediatric nephrology. Home: Weberstr 14 Heidelberg D-69120 Germany Office: Univ Childrens Hosp Im Neuenheimer Feld 430 69120 Heidelberg Germany Office Phone: 49-6221-568401, 49 6221 562396. Office Fax: 49-6221-564203. Business E-Mail: burkhard.toenshoff@med.uni-heidelberg.de.

TOFT, ANDERS DYHR, medical and clinical director; b. Copenhagen, Oct. 9, 1973; MD, PhD, U. Copenhagen, 2001. Med. dir. Novo Nordisk, 2003—. Office: Novo Nordisk Broadfield Pk Brighton RARO Crawley West Sussex RH11 9RT England Business E-Mail: adto@novonordisk.com.

TOFUKU, KATSUHIRO, orthopedist, surgeon, researcher; b. Soo, Japan, July 5, 1971; s. Katsuji and Kazue Tofuku; m. Yumiko Masuzaki, Dec. 24, 2002; children: Daiki, Takahiro, Mao, Kenya. MD, Hamamatsu U., Japan, 1997; PhD, Kagoshima Grad. Sch. Med. and Dental Scis., Japan, 2006. Orthopedic surgeon Kagoshima Grad. Sch. Med. and Dental Scis., 1997—. Contbr. articles to profl. jours. Mem.: Japan Soc. Spine Surgery and Related Rsch., Japanese Orthop. Assn. Avocations: kendo, yachting.

TOGASHI, KEN-ICHI, thoracic surgeon; b. Murakami-shi, Niigata-ken, Japan, Apr. 17, 1950; s. Ichiro and Yasui Togashi; m. Tomii Kazama, May 28, 1979; children: Kentaro, Tetsuya, Hideyo. DMS, Niigata U., Japan, 1983. Diplomate Japanese Nat. Bd. Med. Practitioners, 1976. Chief divsn. thoracic surgery Japanese Red Cross Nagaoka Hosp., 1997—2002, mgr. divsn. thoracic and cardiovasc. surgery, 2003—. Dist. welfare commr. Ministry of Health and Welfare, Nagaoka-shi, 1999—2002. Grantee, Ministry of Edn., 1992. Mem.: Japanese Assn. Thoracic Surgery (assoc.). Achievements include research in study of negative effect of cardiopulmonary bypass surgery on human immunity. Home: 1-13-3 Nakajima Niigata-ken Nagaoka-shi 940-0094 Japan Office: Japanese Red Cross Nagaoka Hosp 1-297-1 Senshu Niigata-ken Nagaoka-shi 940-2085 Japan Home Phone: 0258-36-1847; Office Phone: 0258-28-3600. Office Fax: 0258-28-9000. Business E-Mail: tgskn-ch@nagaoka.jrc.or.jp.

TOGLIA, MARC R., gynecologist, obstetrician; MD, Vanderbilt U. Diplomate Am. Bd. Ob-Gyn.-gynecology, Am. Bd. Ob-Gyn.-urogynecology, Am. Bd. Ob Gyn. Intern Univ. Mich. Hosp., resident; hosp. affiliations include Riddle Hosp., 1997—, Paoli Hosp., 2000—, Lankenau Med. Ctr., 2000—, Bryn Mawr Hosp., 2000—; assoc. prof. ob-gyn. Jefferson Med. Coll; chief urogynecology Main Line Healh System; assoc. clin. prof. Lankenau Inst. for Med. Rsch. Author numerous scientific publs.; co-author: (textbook) Office Urogynecology. Named one of Top Doctors, Phila. mag., 2011. Office: Riddle Hospital 1068 W Baltimore Pike Media PA 19063 Office Phone: 484-227-9400.

TOH, EIREN, orthopaedic surgeon; b. Tokyo, May 16, 1960; s. Shibun and Reiko Toh. MD, Tokai U., 1985, PhD, 1997. Resident Tokai U. Sch. Medicine, Isehara, Japan, 1985-90, staff, 1994—, asst. prof. dept. orthopaedic surgery, 2000—06, assoc. prof. dept. orthopaedic surgery, 2006—; rsch. fellow U. Calif.-Davis Med. Ctr., Sacramento, 1996-98. Mem. Japanese Orthopaedic Assn., Japan Spine Rsch. Soc., Japan Med. Soc. of Paraplegia. Office: Dept Ortho Surg Tokai U Sch Medicine Bohseidai Isehara 259-1193 Japan also: Tokai University Hachioji Hosp 1838 Ishika-machi Hachioji Tokyo 192-0032 Japan Office Fax: 81426391144.

TOH, SATOSHI, orthopedist, educator; b. Tono, Iwate Prefecture, Mar. 27, 1949; MD, Hirosaki U., 1975, PhD, 1988. Prof., chmn. Dept. Orthop. Surgery, Hirosaki U. Grad. Sch. Medicine, 2002—. Pres. Japanese Orthop. Soc. Sports Medicine, 2009—; ann. meeting chmn. Japanese Soc. Clin. Sports Medicine, 2010—, Japanese Soc. Surgery Hand, 2010—; pres. Am. Orthop. Soc. Sports Medicine, Japanese Orthop. Soc. Sports Medicine, 2010—. Avocations: skiing, jazz, winemaking. Office: Hirosaki University Sch Medicine Hirosaki Aomori 036-8562 Japan Office Fax: 81-172-36-3826. Business E-Mail: toh@cc.hirosaki-u.ac.jp.

TOH, UHI, oncologist, educator; b. China, Aug. 24, 1962; MD, Kurume U. Sch. Medicine, Fukuoka, Japan, 1990, PhD, 1994. Lectr. dept. surgery faculty medicine Kurume U., 2009—. Chief Divsn. Breast and Gen. Surgery, 2009. Japan Soc. Promotion Sci. fellowship, Japan Coop. Cancer Rsch. Program. Mem.: Japan Soc. Clin. Oncology, Japanese Breast Cancer Soc., Japan Soc. Surgery, Am. Assn. Cancer Rsch., Am. Soc. Clin. Oncology. Avocation: travel. Office: 67 Asahi-machi Kurume Fukuoka 830-0011 Japan Office Fax: 81-942-340709. Business E-Mail: utoh@med.kurume-u.ac.jp.

TOHRU, SHIMIZU, medical educator; b. Hokkaido, Japan, Sept. 1, 1957; MD, Kagawa Med. Sch., PhD, 1987. Prof. Med. Sch., Kanazawa U., 2004—. Recipient Kuroya Rsch. award, Japanese Soc. Bacteriology, Rokuzo-Kobayashi Meml. award. Mem.: Am. Soc. Microbiology, Japanese Soc. Bacteriology. Avocations: piano, guitar. Office: 13-1 Takara-machi Kanazawa Ishikawa 921-8036 Japan Business E-Mail: tshimizu@med.kanazawa-u.ac.jp.

TOIRAC-CAPOTE, MARIO, microbiologist; b. Havana, Cuba, Dec. 10, 1954; s. Samuel Toirac and Modesta Capote. Degree in Agrl. Engring., Havana U., 1979; B, St. Thomas U., Miami, 1983; AS, Miami Dade Coll., 1986. Cert. med. technologist Fla. Dept. Health, 1986, Am. Med. Technologist, agrl. engr. specialist in genetics. Med. technologist, microbiologist Miami Veterans Adminstrn., Fla., 1988—; faculty Miami Dade Coll., 1993—. Med. technologist, generalist, quality control coord. Palm Springs Gen. Hosp., 1988—. Fellow: Am. Assn. Med. Technologists. Home: 22 Madeira Ave Apt 1 Coral Gables FL 33134 E-mail: mtoirac@mdc.edu.

TOKIN, IVAN B., biologist, researcher; b. Moscow, June 5, 1932; s. Boris P. Tokin and Agnessa G. Filatova; m. Galina F. Filimonova, Sept. 22, 1967; children: Ivan, Anna. PhD, State U., Leningrad, Russia, 1954; D of Biology, Inst. Morphology Acad. Sci., Moscow, 1960; DSc, Inst. Devel. Biol. Acad. Sci., Moscow, 1973. Cert. excellent biol. diplomate. Scientist State U., Leningrad, 1959-63; head lab. electron microscopy Inst. Radiation Hygiene, Leningrad, 1963-72; dir. Inst. Marine Biology, Acad. Sci. USSR, Murmansk, 1972-80; head, prof. dept. math. biology State U., St. Petersburg, 1980—. Author: (books) Electron Microscopy of Germ and Somatic Cells of P. Equorum, 1961, Problems of Radiation Cytology, 1974, (with V. M. Schubik) Action of Radiation on Immunology Processes, 1972 (premium of Ministry of Health 1974), (with G. F. Filimonova) Intestinal Epithelium: Proliferation, Regulation, Apoptosis, 1997, Human Health and Environment, 2009; mem., chief sec., editl. coun. Jour. Anatomy, Histology, and Embryology, 1964-74. Dep. Chamber of Deps., Severomorsk, 1973. Recipient medal Soc. Anatomists of Italy, 1968; grantee Internat. Sci. Found., 1994, German Radiation Rsch. Soc., 1995. Mem. Soc. Anatomists, Histologists, and Embryologists (mem. supreme coun. 1969-73), Soc. Ecology and Ecotoxicology (pres. 1996—), Bodega Marine Sci. Assn., INTECOL. Avocations: chess, painting. Office: State U Fac Applied Math Library Sq 2 Saint Petersburg 198904 Russia Office Phone: 7-812-4287159. Fax: 7-812-4284677. Personal E-mail: Ivan.Tokin@rambler.ru. Business E-Mail: Ivan.Tokin@pobox.spbu.ru.

TOKUHATA, GEORGE K., retired medical educator, epidemiologist, consultant; b. Matsue, Japan, Aug. 25, 1924; arrived in U.S., 1951; s. Yujiro and Hama Tokuhata; m. Sumiko Matsui, June 10, 1949. BA, Keio U., 1950; MA, Miami U., Oxford, Ohio, 1952; PhD, U. Iowa, 1955; Dr.PH, Johns Hopkins U., 1962. Chief epidemiology chronic disease divsn. USPHS, Washington, 1961—64; assoc. prof. preventive medicine U. Tenn., Memphis, 1965—67; dir. rsch. Pa. Dept. Health, Harrisburg, 1968—89; prof. behavioral sci. Pa. State U. Coll. Medicine, Hershey, 1970—95; prof. epidemiology U. Pitts., 1970—90; ret., 1990. Cons. product safety U.S. FDA, Washington, 1970—73; cons. maternal child health rsch. U.S. Children's Bur., 1974—77, cons. rsch. grant svcs. Nat. Cancer Inst., 1982—86. Contbr. chapters to books, articles over 100 articles to profl. jours. Grantee, USPHS, U.S. FDA. Fellow: APHA, Am. Coll. Epidemiology; mem.: Fgn. Policy Assn. (bd.dirs. 1995—2000), Torch Club Internat. (bd.dirs. 1999—2002). Achievements include design of and execution of long-term cohort study of health effects of the Three Mile Island accident - first major episode among all commercial nuclear plants in the US; development of a new method of finding familial aggregation of chronic diseases, first to find genetic role played in lung cancer; research in radiation, stress and health. Avocations: classical music, landscape design, gardening. Home: 410 Rupley Rd Camp Hill PA 17011

TOKUMINE, JOHO, anesthesiologist, intensive care physician; b. Naha, Japan, Apr. 3, 1961; s. Chosho and Yukiko Tokumine. MD, U. of the Ryukyus, Okinawa, Japan, 1988; PhD, U. of the Ryukyus, 1992. Diplomate Japanese Soc. Anesthesiologists. Asst. prof. U. of the Ryukyus Hosp., Nishihara, Japan, 2002—. Vice-dir. ICU U. of the Ryukyus Hosp., 2002—. Home: Tsuboya 1-26-20-805 Naha 902-0065 Japan Office: U of the Ryukyus Hosp Uehara 207 Nishihara 903-0215 Japan Office Fax: 81-98-895-1430; Home Fax: 81-98-868-3102. Personal E-mail: tokumine2003@yahoo.co.jp. Business E-Mail: jtokumi@med.u-ryuky.ac.jp.

TOLAN, MARY ANN, health care services company executive; b. 1960; BBA, Loyola U., 1982; MBA, U. Chgo., 1992. Mng. ptnr. North American retail industry group Accenture Ltd., 1996—98, mng. ptnr. global retail industry group, 1998—99, mng. ptnr. growth & strategy, 1999—2000, group CEO Resources Operating Group, 2000—03; founder, pres., CEO Accretive Health, Inc., Chgo., 2003—. Bd. dirs. Accretive Health, Inc., 2003—, Best Buy Co., Inc., 2004—08. Trustee U. Chgo., Loyola U., Lyric Opera Chgo. Named E & Y Entrepreneur of the Yr.; named a Woman to Watch, Crain's Chgo. Bus., 2011, Disting. Alumni, U. Chgo. Office: Accretive Health Inc 401 N Michigan Ave Chicago IL 60611 Office Phone: 312-324-7820. *

TOLAN, ROBERT WARREN, pediatric infectious disease specialist; b. Bowling Green, Ohio, Nov. 20, 1960; s. Robert Warren Tolan and Margaret Delores (Petter) Cardwell; m. Judy Nishitani, Nov. 22, 2003. BA, Ind. U., 1982, MA, 1983; MD, Washington U., St. Louis, 1987. Diplomate Nat. Bd. Med. Examiners, Am. Bd. Pediatrics, sub-bd. of pediat. infectious diseases. Resident in pediat. Riley Hosp. for Children, Indpls., 1987-90; fellow in infectious diseases St. Louis Children's Hosp., 1990-94; pvt. practice pediatrics and pediatric infectious diseases, 1994—2004; clin. instr. pediat. Washington U. Sch. Medicine, 1994—98; clin. assoc. prof. pediat. Drexel U. Coll. Medicine, 2002—; chief divsn. allergy, immunology and infectious diseases Children's Hosp. at St. Peter's Univ. Hosp., New Brunswick, NJ, 2004—. Co-author: Fever of Unknown Origin in Children, 1991; contbr. articles to profl. jours. Pediatric Scientist Devel. Program fellow, 1990—94. Fellow: Infectious Diseases Soc. Am., Am. Acad. Pediatrics; mem.: AMA, Pediatric Infectious Diseases Soc., Am. Soc. Microbiology, Physicians for Social Responsibility, Soc. for Preservation and Encouragement of Barbershop Quartet Singing in Am. Democrat. Episcopalian. Achievements include patent for a cloned outer membrane protein from Haemophilus influenzae type b which is being developed as a vaccine candidate; reviews of surgical management of pediatric endocarditis and of toxic shock syndrome and influenza; description of systemic pseudomalignant form of cat-scratch disease in normal children, the cloning of an outer membrane protein from Haemophilus influenzae type b, the lack of epidemiologic utility of analysis of lipopolysaccharide from the same organism. Office: MOB 3110 254 Easton Ave New Brunswick NJ 08901 Office Phone: 732-339-7841. Personal E-mail: pedidbob@aol.com. Business E-Mail: RTolan@saintpetersuh.com.

TOLBERT, BERT MILLS, biochemist, educator; b. Twin Falls, Idaho, Jan. 15, 1921; s. Ed. and Helen (Mills) T.; m. Anne Grace Zweifler, July 20, 1959; children— Elizabeth Dawn, Margaret Anne, Caroline Joan, Sarah Helen. Student, Idaho State U., 1938-40; BS, U. Calif., Berkeley, 1942, PhD, 1945; postgrad., Fed. Inst. Tech., Zurich, Switzerland, 1952-53. Chemist Lawrence Radiation Lab., Berkeley, 1944-57; faculty U. Colo., Boulder, 1957-89, prof., 1961-89, prof. emeritus, 1989—, assoc. chmn. dept. chemistry and biochemistry, 1980-88. Bd. dirs. Hauser Chem. Rsch., Boulder, 1983-99; dirs. Hauser Inc., Boulder, 1983-99, vis. prof. IAEA, Buenos Aires, Argentina, 1961-62; Biophysicist U.S. AEC, Washington, 1967-68; cons. pvt. cos, govt. agys. Author: (with others) Isotopic Carbon, 1948; contbr. (with others) articles to profl. jours. Fellow AAAS; mem. Am. Chem. Soc., Am. Soc. Biochemistry and Molecular Biology, Radiation Rsch. Soc., Soc. for Exptl. Biology and Medicine. Achievements include rsch. on organic chemistry, including use of isotopes in chemistry and biochemistry, radiation chemistry, radiation effects in protein, intermediary metabolism, metabolism of ascorbic acid, nutritional biochemistry, instrumentation in radioactivity. Home: 444 Kalmia Ave Boulder CO 80304-1732 Personal E-mail: bert.tolbert@colorado.edu.

TOLCHIN, JOAN GUBIN, psychiatrist, educator; d. Harold and Bella (Newman) Gubin; m. Matthew Armin Tolchin; 1 child, Benjamin. AB, Vassar Coll.; MD, NYU, 1972. Diplomate Am. Bd. Gen. Psychiatry, Am. Bd. Child Psychiatry. Instr. psychiatry med. coll. Cornell U., NYC, 1977-78, clin. instr., 1978-86, clin. asst. prof., 1986—2004, clin. assoc. prof., 2004—. Contbr. articles to profl. jours., chapters to books. Fellow: Am. Acad. Psychoanalysis and Dynamic Psychiatry (sec. 1998—2001, pres. elect 2007—08, pres. 2008—10, past pres. 2010—11), Am. Acad. Child and Adolescent Psychiatry; mem.: AMA, Am. Coll. Psychiatrists, Am. Psychiatric Assn., N.Y. Coun. Child and Adolescent Psychiatry (bd. dirs. 1992—96, pres. 1994—95, bd. advisors 2001—), Alpha Omega Alpha. Office: 35 E 84th St New York NY 10028-0871

TOLCHINSKY, PAUL DEAN, organization design psychologist; b. Cleve., Sept. 30, 1946; s. Sanford Melvin and Frances (Klein) T.; m. Laurie S. Schermer, Nov. 3, 1968 (div. Jan. 1982); m. Kathy L. Dworkin, June 19, 1988; children: Heidi E., Dana M. BA, Bowling Green State U., 1971; PhD, Purdue U., 1978. Asst. br. mgr., tng. instr. Detroit Bank and Trust, 1971-73; mgr. tng. and devel. nuclear divsn. Babcock and Wilcox Co., Barberton, Ohio, 1973-75; internal cons. food products divsn. Gen. Foods Corp., West Lafayette, Ind., 1975-77; grad. tchg. asst. Krannert Grad. Sch. Mgmt. Purdue U., West Lafayette, 1975-78; asst. prof. mgmt. Coll. Bus. Adminstrn. Fla. State U., Tallahassee, 1978-79, U. Akron, Ohio, 1979-81; pres. Performance Devel. Assocs., Cleve., 1975—; ptnr. Dannemiller Tyson Assocs., Cleve., 1994-99; mng. ptnr. Performance Devel. Assocs., 2000—. Sr. lectr. Case Western Res. U., 2002—. Contbr. articles to profl. publs. Bd. dirs. Temple Tiferth Israel, Cleve., 195, Cleve. Jewish News, Jewish Family Svcs. Assn. Cleve. With U.S. Army, 1966-69, Vietnam. Mem. APA, Acad. Mgmt. Democrat. Jewish. Avocations: running, travel. Office: Performance Devel Assocs PO Box 809 Chagrin Falls OH 44022-0809 Home Phone: 440-349-1441; Office Phone: 440-349-1990. Personal E-mail: kdtpdt@aol.com. *

TOLEDO, LUIZ C., surgeon; Grad., U. State Sap Paulo (UNESP), 1971. Pvt. practice, 1975—; asst. plastic surgery Inst. Arnaldo Vieira de Carvalho, Santa Casa, chief plastic surgery; sr. cons. MedAesthetic Clinic, Munich; surgeon Internat. Modern Hosp., Dubai, United Arab Emirates. Med. expert Conselho Regional de Medicina; regional editor Aesthetic Plastic Surgery Jour., Brazil; prof. postgrad. edn. in aesthetic plastic surgery Internat. Soc. Aesthetic Plastic Surgery (ISAPS), chmn. pub. edn. com., course dir., 1994—2000. Mem.: Am. Soc. Plastic Surgery (ASPS), Med. Assn. Brazil (AMB) (specialist plastic surgeon), Brazilian Soc. Plastic Surgery (SBCP). Office: International Modern Hospital Sheik Rashid Rd / Al Mina Rd Dubai United Arab Emirates Office Phone: 97144063000. *

TOLEDO, RONALDO NUNES, surgeon; b. Goiania, Brazil, June 2, 1969; Degree in Medicine, UNIFESP, 1996. ENT surgeon AC Camargo Cancer Hosp., 2001. Home: Rua Afonso Celso 833 Apt 81 B São Paulo 04119060 Brazil Personal E-mail: rntoledo@uol.com.br.

TOLIA, VASUNDHARA K., pediatric gastroenterologist, educator; b. Kolkata, India; came to U.S., 1975; d. Rasiklal and Saroj (Kothari) Doshi; m. Kirit Tolia, May 30, 1975; children: Vinay, Sanjay. MBBS, Calcutta U., 1968-75. Intern, resident Children's Hosp. Mich., Detroit, 1976-79, fellow, 1979-81, dir. pediat. endoscopy unit, 1984-90, dir. pediat. gastroenterology and nutrition, 1990—2005. Instr. Wayne State U., Detroit, 1981—83, asst. prof., 1983—91, assoc. prof., 1991—97, prof., 1997—2005; adjunct prof. pediat. Mich. State U., 2008—. Mem. editl. bd. Inflammatory Bowel Diseases, 1999-2005, Am. Jour. Gastroenterology, 1999-2005, Rev. World Lit. in Pediatrics, 1999—, AAP Grand Rounds and Therapy, 2006—, Gastroenterology Rsch. and Practice, 2008-; contbr. articles to profl. jours. Named Woman of Distinction, Mich. chpt. Crohn's and Colitis Found. Am., 1991. Fellow Am. Coll. Gastroenterology (chair ad-hoc com. pediat. gastroenterology 1998-2000), Am. Acad. Pediats.; mem. Am. Gastroenterology Assn., N.Am. Soc. Pediat. Gastroenterology and Nutrition, Soc. Pediat. Rsch. Office Phone: 248-568-1500.

TOLICH, NIKOLAI, physicist, educator; MSc., U. Auckland; PhD, Stanford U. Fellow Lawrence Berkeley Nat. Lab.; asst. prof. dept. physics U. Wash. Office: University of Washington Dept Physics Box 351560 Seattle WA 98195 Office Phone: 206-543-4223. Office Fax: 206-543-1493. E-mail: ntolich@u.washington.edu.

TOLLEY, AUBREY GRANVILLE, psychiatrist, health facility administrator; b. Lynchburg, Va., Nov. 15, 1924; married. Student, Duke U., 1942—43, U. Va., 1946—48, MD, 1952. Diplomate Am. Bd. Psychiatry and Neurology. Intern St. Elizabeths Hosp., Washington, 1952-53; asst. resident psychiatry U. Va. Hosp., Charlottesville, 1953-54; resident psychiatry VA Hosp., Roanoke, Va., 1955-56; instr. U. NC Sch. Medicine, 1956—61, asst. prof., 1961—66, clin. asst. prof. psychiatry, 1966—72, clin. assoc. prof., 1972—76, clin. prof., 1976—2010, adj. prof. psychiatry, 2010—; dir. psychotherapy Dorothea Dix Hosp., Raleigh, NC, 1962-67, dir. hosp., 1973-88. Dir. resident tng. John Umstead Hosp., Butner, N.C., 1966-67; dir. profl. tng. and edn. N.C. Dept. Mental Health, Raleigh, 1967-72, asst. dir., 1972-73; prin. investigator USPHS grant, 1957-59; cons. VA Hosp., Fayetteville, N.C., 1957-78; sr. cons., supervising faculty, cmty. psychiatry sect. dept. psychiatry U. N.C. Sch. Medicine, 1971-88; exec. sec. Multiversity Group, 1968-73 Trustee Found. Hope, Raleigh, 1984—. Served with USNR, 1943-46. Recipient The Order of the Long Leaf Pine, State of N.C., 1982. Fellow Am. Psychiat. Assn. (disting. life; assembly rep. N.C. Dist. br. 1969-82, 86-2000, mem. joint commn. on pub. affairs 1984-87, mem. constl. membership com. 1990-96, mem. commn. on subspecialization 1990-94, Warren Williams award 1987), Am. Coll. Psychiatrists (life); mem. AMA, N.C. Med. Soc. (life), Durham-Orange County Med. Soc., N.C. Psychiat. Assn. (pres. 1984-85, Lifetime Disting. Svc. award 1999), N.C. Hosp. Assn. (life), George C. Ham Soc. (Disting. Alumni award 1992). Home and Office: 110 Laurel Hill Rd Chapel Hill NC 27514-4323

TOLOMIO, SILVIA, health fitness instructor; b. Camposampiero, July 10, 1979; PhD, U. Padua, 2011. Rschr. dept. med. and surg. scis., sports medicine unit U. Padua, 2004—. Recipient Young Investigators award, EUCAPA, Torino, Italy, 2008. Avocation: sports. Home: Pelosa 134/B Borgoricco 35010 Italy Personal E-mail: silvia.tolomio@unipd.it.

TOLOR, ALEXANDER, psychologist, educator; b. Vienna, Oct. 21, 1928; s. Stanley and Josephine (Kellner) T.; m. Belle Simon, Sept. 2, 1951; children: Karen Beth, Lori Ann, Diana Susan. BA, NYU, 1949, MA, 1950, PhD, 1954. Diplomate Am. Bd. Profl. Psychologists. Grad. asst. NYU, 1950-52; intern Neurol. Inst., NYC, 1952-53, clin. psychologist, 1953-55; sr. clin. psychologist Inst. of Living, Hartford, Conn., 1957-59; dir. psychol. services Fairfield Hills Hosp., Newtown, Conn., 1959-64; clinic dir. Kennedy Center, Bridgeport, Conn., 1964-65; dir. Inst. Human Devel., Fairfield U., 1965-77, assoc. prof. psychology, 1965-68, research prof. psychology, 1968-75, prof. psychology, 1975-89, dir. school psychology div., 1975-77, dir. sch. and applied psychology program, 1982-86, prof. emeritus, 1989—; practice psychology Danbury, Conn., 1960-96; clin. instr. psychology Yale U., 1963-67. Cons. West Haven VA Hosp., 1962-66, Bridgeport Bd. Edn., Silver Hill Found., 1972-75, Fairfield Hills Hosp., 1973-94, Hallbrooke Hosp., 1975-92. Author: (with H.C. Schulberg) An Evaluation of the Bender-Gestalt Test, 1963, (with G.G. Brannigan) Research and Clinical Applications of the Bender-Gestalt Test, 1980, (with M. Deignan) Adjustment Problems in Children, 1984; editor: Effective Interviewing, 1985; adv. editor Jour. Cons. and Clin. Psychology; cons. editor Personality: An Internat. Jour.; contbr. articles to profl. jours. Served to 1st lt. USAF, 1955-57. Fellow Am. Psychol. Assn., Soc. Personality Assessment, Conn. Psychol. Assn. (mem. council 1964, pres. 1984); mem. Eastern Psychol. Assn., Psi Chi, Delta Phi Alpha, Beta Lambda Sigma, Phi Delta Kappa Home: 6 Brittania Dr Danbury CT 06811-2606 Personal E-mail: atbt51@aol.com.

TOMANDL, JOSEF, biomedical researcher, educator; m. Marie Hyksová; children: David, Annette, Elisabeth. MA in Biochemistry, Masaryk U., Brno, Czech Republic, 1983; PhD in Med. Chemistry, Palacky U., Olomouc, Czech Republic, 1999. Cert. Coll. Prevention of Cruelty to Animals, 2006, bioanalyst for clinical biochemistry Ministry of Health, Czech Republic, 2007. Asst. prof. Masaryk U., Faculty Medicine, 1991—, clin. bioanalyst, 1996—. Editor 16 textbooks in med. chemistry and biochemistry. Fellow: Czech Soc. Clin. Biochemistry. Home: Brno 612 00 Czech Republic Office: Masaryk University Dept Biochemistry Faculty Medicine Kamenice 5 Brno 625 00 Czech Republic Personal E-mail: tomandl@gmail.com. Business E-Mail: tomandl@med.muni.cz.

TOMANOVIC, TATJANA K., audiologist; b. Negotin, Serbia, Nov. 1, 1963; D, U. Belgrade, 1990. Specialist Dept. Audiology and Neurootology, Stockholm, 2002—. Rsch. scientist Karolinska Inst., 2005. Mem.: Swedish Audiology Soc., Swedish Neurootology Soc. Avocations: motorcycling, skiing, running, painting. Office: University Hosp Karolinska Solna Stockholm 17176 Sweden Office Fax: 46851774041. Business E-Mail: tatjana.tomanovic@karolinska.se.

TOMAR, RUSSELL HERMAN, pathologist, educator, researcher; b. Phila., Oct. 19, 1937; s. Julius and Ethel (Weinreb) T.; m. Karen J. Kent, Aug. 29, 1965; children: Elizabeth, David. BA in Journalism, George Washington U., 1959, MD, 1963. Diplomate Am. Bd. Pathology, Am. Bd. Allergy and Immunology, Am. Bd. Pathology, Immunopathology. Intern Barnes Hosp., Washington U. Sch. Medicine, 1963-64, resident in medicine, 1964-65; asst. prof. medicine SUNY, Syracuse, 1971-79, assoc. prof., 1979-88, assoc. prof. microbiology, 1980-84, prof., 1984-88, asst. prof. pathology, 1974-76, assoc. prof., 1976-83, prof., 1983-88, dir. immunopathology, 1974-88, attending physician immunodeficiency clinic, 1982-88, acting dir. microbiology, 1977-78, 82-83, interim dir. clin. pathology, 1986-87; prof. pathology and lab. medicine U. Wis. Ctr. for Health Scis., Madison, 1988—2003; dir. div. lab medicine U. Wis., Madison, 1988-95, dir. immunopathology and diagnostic immunology, 1995-98, prof. population health scis., 1999—2003, vis. prof. population health scis., 2003—07; chair dept. pathology Stroger Hosp. Cook County, Chgo., 2009—; prof. pathology Rush U., 1999—2009. Past mem. numerous coms. SUNY, Syracuse, U. Wis., Madison; mem. exec. com., chair and med. cons. AIDS Task Force Cen. N.Y., 1983-88. Assoc. editor Jour. Clin. Lab. Analysis; contbr. articles, rev. to profl. jours. Mem. pub. health com. Onondaga County Med. Soc., 1987-88. Lt. comdr. USPHS, 1965-67. Allergy and Immunology Div. fellow U. Pa. Fellow Coll. Am. Pathologists (diagnostics immunology rsch. com. 1993-2003, stds. com. 1995-97, commn. on clin. pathology 1997-2003), Am. Soc. Clin. Pathology (com. on continuing edn. immunopathology 1985-91, pathology data presentation com. 1976-79, pathology rep. coun. med. subspecialty socs. 2004—), Am. Acad. Allergy (penicillin hypersensitivity com. 1973-77); mem. AAAS, Am. Assn. Immunologists, Am. Assn. Pathology (chmn. 2002—), Acad. Clin. Lab. Physicians and Scientists (com. on rsch. 1979-81, chairperson immunology 1979), Clin. Immunology Soc. (clin. lab. immunology com., chair coun. 1991-96, pathology rep. to Coun. Med. Subspecialty Socs. 2003—). Home: 3573 Richie Rd Verona WI 53593 Personal E-mail: rtomar@comcast.net. Business E-Mail: russell.tomar@hektoen.org.

TOMARU, TAKANOBU, cardiologist, physiologist, educator; b. Katsu-ura, Tokushima, Japan, Apr. 18, 1951; s. Chikahiro and Hanae Tomaru; m. Yasuko Takeyama, Apr. 26, 1981; children: Erika, Maya Toamru. MD, U. Tokyo, 1978, PhD, 1987. Dir. cardiology divsn. Japanese Red Cross Med. Ctr., Tokyo, 1998—2001; prof. medicine, dir. emergency and intensive ctr. and dept. physiology, cardiology divsn. Toho U. Med. Ctr. Sakura Hosp., Chiba, Japan, 2001—. Contbr. articles to med. jours. Pres., dir. E-Health Consorcium, Tokyo, 2004—08; coun. mem. Chiba Social and Med. Ins. Orgn., Japan, 2004—, Japan Internet Med. Assn., Tokyo, 2007—, Japan Circulation Soc., Kyoto, 2006—; exec. coun. Internat. Acad. Cardiology, Vancouver, Canada, 2007—. Grantee, Japan Found. Cardiovasc. Rsch., 1993; Laser Angioplasty grant, Japanese Ministry Edn. and Sci., 1993—94, Local Delivery grant, 1995—97, Neutron Capture Therapy grant, 2003. Fellow: Internat. Acad. Cardiology (LA). Office: Toho Univ Med Ctr Shimoshizu 564-1 Sakura 285-8741 Japan Office Phone: 81-43-462-8811. Office Fax: 81-43-462-8820. Business E-Mail: tomaru-t@sakura.med.toho-u.ac.jp.

TOMAS, TOMAS, surgeon; b. Brno, Czech Republic, Jan. 19, 1968; MD, Masaryk U., Brno, 1992, PhD, 2003. Surgeon Orthop. Dept., Masaryk U., Brno, 1993—2001, head septic unit, 2001—10, dep. head, 2010—. Head Johnson and Johnson Co., 2006—, revision total knee replacement cons., 2010—; total knee replacement cons. Zimmer Co., 2010—. Mem.: Slovak Soc. Orthop. and Traumatology, European Foot and Ankle Soc., European Hip Soc., Czech Soc. Orthrop. and Traumatology. Avocation: sports. Office: Pekarská 53 Brno 65691 Czech Republic Business E-Mail: tomas.tomas@fnusa.cz.

TOMAS BATLLE, XAVIER, radiologist, consultant; b. Barcelona, Nov. 20, 1961; s. Benedicto Tomas and Carmen Batlle; m. Alejandra Rodriguez, Oct. 6, 1989; children: Xavier Tomas Jr., Paula Tomas. MD, U. Barcelona, 1985, D in Medicine cum laude, 1999. Media Internet Master U. Oberta de Catalunya, 2003; Radiologist Hosp. Clinic. Barcelona, 1992. Med. radiologist resident Hosp. Clinic Radiology Dept., Barcelona, 1988—91; staff radiologist Hosp. Clinic. Radiology Dept., 1994—. Staff cons. skeletal radiology Hosp. Clinic, Barcelona, 2004—, webmaster radiology and nuc. medicine, 2005—. Editor (invited guest editor): (special issue in seminars in US) Diagnostic Imaging of TMJ (In press); contbr. chapters to books. Mem. Greenpeace, Barcelona, Spain, 1997—2005. Recipient Certifie of Merit, 1999. Mem.: European Soc. Skeletal Radiology, Spanish Soc. Muscular-Skeletal Radiology (corr.), Spanish Soc. Med. Radiology (assoc.), Am. Roentgent Ray Soc. (assoc.). Catholic. Office: Hosp Clinic Radiology Dept Villarroel 170 Barcelona 08036 Spain Office Fax: +34 932279323. Personal E-mail: 22812xtb@comb.es. E-mail: xtomas@clinic.ub.es.

TOMASELLI, GORDON FRANK, cardiologist, medical educator; b. Portland, Maine, Aug. 5, 1955; BS in Biochemistry and Chemistry, SUNY, Buffalo, 1977; MD, Albert Einstein Coll. Medicine of Yeshiva U., 1982. Resident internal medicine U. Calif., San Francisco, rsch. fellow Cardiovascular Rsch. Inst.; cardiology fellow Johns Hopkins U. Sch. Medicine, Balt., 1986, faculty mem., 1989—, vice-chair rsch. Dept. Medicine, David. J. Carver prof. medicine, Michel Mirowski, M.D. prof. cardiology, 2007—, co-dir. Donald W. Reynolds Cardiovascular Clin. Rsch. Ctr., dir. Divsn. Cardiology, 2009—, co-dir. Heart and Vascular Inst., 2009—. Dep. editor, assoc. editor Circulation Research: Jour. of the American Heart Assn., editl. bd. mem. Jour. of Cardiovascular Electrophysiology; contbr. articles to med. journals. Recipient David M. Levine Excellence in Mentoring Award, Johns Hopkins Dept. Medicine, 2004. Mem.: Cardiac Electrophysiology Soc. (pres. 2003—05), Heart Rhythm Soc. (bd. dirs.), American Coll. Cardiology, American Heart Assn. (program chair Scientific Sessions 2007, 2008, chmn. Strategic Planning Task Force 2010—, pres.-elect 2010—11, pres. 2011—). Office: Johns Hopkins School of Medicine 844 Ross Building 600 N Wolfe St Baltimore MD 21287 Office Phone: 410-955-2774. Office Fax: 410-955-7953. E-mail: gtomasel@jhmi.edu. *

TOMASIK, MARTIN J., psychologist; b. Wroclaw, Poland, Dec. 2, 1977; arrived in Germany, 1985; s. Krzysztof and Urszula Tomasik; m. Christiane Huff, Sept. 11, 2001; children: Jona, Leo, Carl. Diploma in psychology, Free U., Berlin, 2004; PhD in Psychology Fredrich Schiller U., Jena, Germany, 2008. Rsch. asst. Max Planck Inst. for Human Devel., Berlin, 1999—2002; tchg. asst. U. Tech., Berlin, 2001—04; rsch. assoc. Friedrich Schiller U., Jena, Germany, 2004—. Contbr. articles to profl. jours. Roman Catholic. Business E-Mail: martin.tomasik@uni-jena.de.

TOMASZEWSKI, JOHN E., pathologist, educator; MD, U. Pa., 1977. Diplomate American Bd. Pathology-anatomic pathology, 1982, American Bd. Pathology-immunopathology, 1983. Intern Hosp. Univ. Pa., 1978, resident pathology, 1978—82, fellow surg. pathology, 1982—83, vice-chmn. anatomic pathology hosp. svcs.; prof. pathology and lab. medicine Univ. Pa. Named one of Top Doctors, Phila. Mag., 2004—10, America's Top Doctors, 2007—08, 2010. Mem.: American Soc. Clin. Pathologists (pres. 2010—11). Office: Hospital of the University of Pennsylvania 3400 Spruce St Philadelphia PA 19104-4206 Office Phone: 215-662-4000. *

TOMBERG, TIIU, neurologist, researcher; b. Tartu, Estonia, Apr. 12, 1943; d. Aleksander and Heine Laas; m. Rein Tomberg; children: Karel, Erik, Jaak. MD, U. Tartu, 1967, PhD, 1977. Cert. neurologist U. Tartu, 1969, radiologist U. Tartu, 1982. Neurologist Jõgeva Dist. Hosp., Estonia, 1967—72; rschr., ctrl. med. lab. U. Tartu, 1972—79, sr. rschr., inst. gen. and molecular pathology, 1979—93, cons. clinics, 1983—, sr. rschr., dept. neurology and neurosurgery, 1993—. Contbr. articles to profl. jours. Creating mem. Commn. Estonian Med. Terminology, Tallinn, Estonia, 2003—08. Recipient medal, U. Tartu, 2008. Mem.: European Fedn. Neurol. Socs., Estonian Med. Assn., European Soc. Radiology, Estonian Soc. Radiology, Estonian Soc. Neurologists and Neurosurgeons. Home: 13 KAHermann Tartu 51005 Estonia Office: Univ Tartu L. Puusepa 8 51014 Tartu Estonia Office Fax: 372 7 318 509. E-mail: tiiu.tomberg@kliinikum.ee.

TOMBROS, PETER GEORGE, pharmaceutical executive; b. Oak Hill, W.Va., June 12, 1942; s. George P. and Mary Jane (Boliski) T.; m. Ann Riblett Cullen, June 12, 1965. BS, Pa. State U., 1964, MS, 1966; MBA, U. Pa., 1968. Mktg. asst. Pfizer Labs. div. Pfizer Inc., NYC, 1968; asst. product mgr. Pfizer Inc., NYC, 1969, product mgr., 1970-71, group product mgr., 1972-74, v.p. mktg., 1975-80; sr. v.p., gen. mgr. Roerig div. Pfizer Inc., NYC, 1980-86; exec. v.p. Pfizer Pharms. div. Pfizer Inc., NYC, 1986-90, v.p. corp. strategic planning, 1990-94; also corp. officer Pfizer Inc., NYC; ret. pres., CEO Enzon, Inc., Piscataway, 1994—2001, also bd. dirs.; chmn., CEO VivoQuest Inc., 2001—05; dir. Cambrex Corp., East Rutherford; prof., exec. in residence Pa. State U., 2005—. Alumni fellow Pa. State U., 1993; bd. dirs. Alpharma Inc., Bridgewater, NJ, 1995-2008; dir., non-exec. chmn. bd., NPS Pharm., Inc., Bedminster, NJ, bd. dirs. non exec. chmn.; Pharma Net Devel., Inc., 2007-09, PharmaNet's, 2007-09, non-exec. chmn. bd., 2006-09. Bd. dirs. Dendrite Internat., Bedminster, NJ, 2006-07, Am. Found. Pharm. Edn., North Plainfield, NJ, 1980-01, past chmn.; trustee Fisk U., Nashville, 1986-96, Dominican Coll., Orangeburg, NY, 1987-02; trustee Bklyn. Borough Hall Restoration, 1987-92; mem. corp. devel. com. Cen. Park Conservancy, NYC, 1986-94; bd. dirs. Vote America, 1990; bd. dirs. Cancer Care; chmn. bd. dirs. NJ Tech. Coun., 2001-03. Recipient Disting. Alumnus award, Pa. State U., 2006. Mem. Pharm. Mfrs. Assn. (past chmn. mktg. steering com., 1986-1992), Links Club, Blind Brook Club, Masons. Avocations: marathon running, golf, tennis, skiing, bridge. Business E-Mail: put10@psu.edu.

TOMER, BRITTA, orthodontist, educator; b. Denmark; undergraduate studies, DDS, Denmark. Cert. orthodontic specialty U. Calif. San Francisco, 1977. Rsch. fellow, dept. craniofacial anomalies Univ. Calif. San Francisco, 1971—76; pvt. practice in orthodontics San Francisco, 1978—; orthodontist OrthoWorks, San Francisco. Part-time assoc. prof. U. Calif. San Francisco, 1978—. Contbr. articles to numerous profl. jours. Mem.: European Orthodontics Soc., Am. Cleft Palate-Craniofacial Assn., Am. Assn. Orthodontics. Office: OrthoWorks 450 Sutter St Ste 2418 San Francisco CA 94108 Office Phone: 415-982-0990. Office Fax: 415-982-0909.

TOMER, YARON, internist, endocrinologist; b. Petah-Tikva, Israel, Jan. 3, 1959; s. Avner and Nitza (Rubinstein) Nachmias; m. Gitit Rosenbach, Feb. 7, 1991; children: Nir, Danielle. Student, Columbia U., 1976-77; MD magna cum laude, Tel-Aviv U., 1985. Intern Beilinson Med. Ctr., Petah-Tikvah, 1983-84; brigade physician Israel Def. Forces, 1984-89; resident, chief resident in internal medicine Sheba Med. Ctr., Tel Hashomer, Israel, 1989-93, attending in autoimmunology, 1989-93; endocrinologist Mt. Sinai Med. Ctr., NYC, 1995—; vice chair dept. medicine Mt. Sinai Sch. Medicine, 2010, prof. medicine NYC, 2010, chief divsn. endocrinology, 2011; chief, divsn. endocrinology, metabolism Mt. Sinai Hosp., 2011. Attending rsch. fellow in endocrinology, autoimmune thyroid diseases Mt. Sinai Med. Ctr., N.Y.C., 1993-02, assoc. prof., 2002—; prof. Cin. Coll. Medicine, 2005—; vis. scientist dept. cell biology Weizmann Inst. Sci., Rehovot, Israel, 1988-93; columnist Jour. Israeli Med. Assn., Tel Aviv. Mem. editl. bd.: jours. Endocrinology, Thyroid, Autoimmunity Revs.; contbr. chapters to books, articles to profl. jours. Recipient Rsch. award Al-Zohar Found., Tel Hashomer, 1991, rsch. award Ministry of Health, Jerusalem, Israel, 1993, Van Meter award Am. Endocrine Soc., 2003; named one of Top Drs. in USA, 2008-09; grantee NIH, 2000, 02, 04. Fellow ACP, Am. Coll. Endocrinology; mem. AAAS, ASCI, N.Y. Acad. Sci., Israeli Soc. Internal Medicine. Avocations: music, skiing, soccer, horseback riding. Home: 21 Kehilat Yassi St Tel Aviv 69512 Israel Office Phone: 212-241-6834, 800-637-4624. Business E-Mail: tomerdngy@pipeline.net, yaron.tomer@mssm.edu.

TOMESCU, DANA RODICA, anesthesiologist, educator; b. Bucarest, Romania, July 6, 1966; d. Misu and Aurora Floarea Tomescu; m. Cristian Nastase-Bejenariu, Feb. 14, 2002; 1 child, Alexandru Nastase-Bejenariu;. MD, Carol Davila U. Medicine and Pharmacy, 1990; MS in Mgmt., Politechnical Inst., 2000. Anesthesiologist Board of romanian anesthetists certified diplomate Bd. of Romanian anesthetists and intensivists, 1995, Grant Universite Paris VI Pierre Marie Curie/France, 1993, Israeli Soc. of anaesthesia and intensive care/Israel, 1996, Fellowship in anaesthesia for liver transplant romanian Soc. of anesthesiologists and intensive care/Romania, 2000. Intern Fundeni U. Hosp., Bucarest, 1990—91, resident, 1991—92, resident anesthesia and intensive care, 1992—93; chief resident anesthesia and intensive care Groupe Hosp. Pitie- Salpetriere, Paris, 1993—94; fellow in anesthesia and intensive care Fundeni Clin. Inst., Bucarest, 1994—95; fellow in cardiac anaesthesia C. C. Iliescu Heart Inst., Bucarest, 1995; asst. prof. Med. Sch. Carol Davila U., Bucarest, 1995—; staff sr. anesthetist and intensivist Fundeni Clin. Inst., 1998—. Cons. anesthetist for bone marrow transplant Fundeni Clin. Inst., 2001—, coord. adv. bd. for transfusions, 1999—2001; mem. Nat. Adv. Bd. Antimycotics, Bucarest; asst. prof. anaesthesia and intensive care Med. Sch. Carol Davila U., Bucarest, Romania, 1991—. Co-author: Le Desflurane, Arnette-Paris; editor: Romanian Jour. Anaesthesia Intensive Care; contbr. articles to profl. jours. Pres. Asklepios Student Humanitary Aid Orgn., Bucarest, 1989—92. Grantee, Carol Davila U. Med. Sch., 1993—94. Fellow: Romanian Soc. Anaesthesia and Intensive Care; mem.: Romanian Bd. Sepsis, European Soc. Enteral and Parenteral Nutrition, Romanian Soc. Pain, Romanian Soc. Enteral and Parenteral Nutrition, European Soc. Anaesthesia. Orthodox. Achievements include first to member of the team that performed the first bone marrow transplant in Romania; development of first CD-rom for anaesthesia and intensive care-problems in nutrition; first to member of the team that performed the first liver transplant in Romania. Avocations: travel, foreign languages, skiing, piano, jazz. Home: Calea Mosilor 133 etaj2 apt7 Bucharest 70314 Romania Office: Fundeni Clinical Institute Soseaua Fundeni 258 sector2 Bucharest 7000 Romania Office Fax: (40)-21-2410804. Personal E-mail: tomeasca@hotmail.com. E-mail: danaroto333@yahoo.com.

TOMIITA, MINAKO, pediatrician; b. Aichi, June 14, 1963; MD, Sch. Medicine, Chiba U., 1989; PhD, Chiba U. Assoc. prof. Dept. Pediat., Grad. Sch. Medicine, Chiba U., 2004—11; chief med. dir. Dept. Allergy and Rheumatology, Chiba Children's Hosp., 2011—. Bd. dirs. Japanese Soc. Sjögren's Syndrome, 2008, Pediat. Rheumatology Assn. Japan, 2010. Avocations: music, travel. Office: 579-1 Heta-cho Midori-ku Chiba 2660007 Japan Office Fax: 81 43 292 3815. Business E-Mail: m.tomiita@gmail.com.

TOMINAGA, MAKOTO, physiologist, educator; b. Osaka, Japan, Apr. 22, 1958; MD, Ehime U., 1984; PhD, Kyoto U., 1992. Prof. Mie U. Sch. Medicine, 2000—04, Okazaki Inst. Integrative Biosci., 2004—. Mem.: Internat. Assn. Study Pain, Neurosci. Soc. Office: Higashiyama 5-1 Myodaiji Okazaki Aichi 444-8787 Japan Office Fax: 81-564-59-5285. Business E-Mail: tominaga@nips.ac.jp.

TOMIOKA, KIYOSHI, chemistry professor; b. Tokyo, Jan. 14, 1948; s. Yoshiro and Aiko Tomioka; m. Makiko Tomioka, Nov. 23, 1974; children: Mari, Yuka, Aya. BA, U. Tokyo, 1971, PhD, 1976. Asst. prof. U. Tokyo, 1978-83, assoc. prof., 1983-92; prof. Osaka U., 1992-96, Kyoto U., 1996—2010. Advisor Ministry Pub. Welfare, Japan, 1986—. Author: Asymmetric Synthesis, 1983. Mem. Chem. Soc. Japan, Pharm. Soc. Japan (Award 1984), Am. Chem. Soc. Home: 3-8-6 Ushikubo-Nishi Tsuzuki Yokohama 224-0015 Japan Office: Doshisha Women's Coll Liberal Arts Faculty Pharmaceutical Scis Kyoto 610-0395 Japan Office Phone: 81 774 65 8676.

TOMIOKA, TOSHIYA, anesthesiologist, educator; b. Yono, Japan, Jan. 18, 1966; s. Tokuya and Yoshie Tomioka; m. Naoko Ohgaki, May 19, 1996; children: Seiko, Noriko, Tetsuya. MD, Toho U., Tokyo, 1992; PhD, Toho U., 1996. Fellow Toho U., Tokyo, 1996—98, Nagoya U., Japan, 1998; staff anesthesiologist Toranomon Hosp., Tokyo, 1999—2000; asst. prof. U. Tokyo, 2000—02, 2004—; postdoctoral rsch. fellow Yale U., Conn., 2002—04. Author: Handbook of Congenital Insensitivity to Pain and Anhidrosis, 1997, Paget Disease, 2001, Congenital Insensitivity to Pain and Anhidrosis, 2002. Mem.: Japan Soc. Anesthesiology (Young Investigator award 1995), Japan Assn. Patient with CIPA (sec.), Internat. Assn. Study Pain. Avocations: scuba diving, automobiles. Office: U Tokyo Bunkyo-ku 7-3-1 Hongo Tokyo 113-8655 Japan Personal E-mail: tomiokat@kb3.so-net.ne.jp.

TOMITA, SANDRA, pediatrician; b. Inglewood, Calif., Feb. 3, 1961; BS, Calif. State U., Dominguez Hills, 1984; MD, Northwestern U. Sch. Medicine, 1988. Gen. surgeon USN, 1994—96, pediatric surgeon, 1998—2009, NYU Med. Ctr., 2009—, asst. prof. surgery, 2009—11. Decorated Meritorious Svc. medal USN, 2 Navy Commendation medal, Navy Achievement medal, Nat. Def. Svc. medal; recipient Donald Sturtz Tchg. award, Naval Med. Ctr. Surgery Chief Residents, 2009. Fellow: ACS, Am. Acad. Pediat.; mem.: Pacific Assn. Pediatric Surgeons, Am. Pediatric Surg. Assn. Avocations: hiking, cooking, travel. Office: NYU Med Ctr 530 First Ave Ste 10W New York NY 10016 Business E-Mail: sandra.tomita@nyumc.org.

TOMLINSON, STEPHEN, academic administrator, medical educator; b. Farnworth, Eng., Dec. 20, 1944; s. Frank and Elsie Tomlinson; m. Christine Margaret Hope, 1970; children: Rebecca Claire Louise, Sarah Lucy Jane. MB ChB, U. Sheffield, 1968, MD, 1976. Sir Henry Wellcome fellow MIT, Cambridge, Mass., 1976—77; Wellcome Trust sr. rsch. fellow, sr. lectr. U. Sheffield, 1977—85, prof. medicine U. Manchester, England, 1985—2001, dean medicine dentistry and nursing, 1993—99; vice-chancellor Coll. Medicine U. Wales, 2001—04; provost Cardiff (Wales) U., 2004—10, emeritus prof. medicine. Contbr. articles to profl. jours. Fellow: Acad. Med. Scis., Royal Coll. Physicians London; mem.: Assn. Clin. Profs. Medicine U.K. (chmn. 1996—2000), Assn. Physicians Great Britain and Ireland (pres. 2002—03). Office: Rm 046 PVC Office Main Bldg Park Pl Cardiff CF103AT Wales Office Phone: 2920870651.

TOMOHIKO, SATO, medical researcher; b. Japan, Jan. 30, 1978; PhD, Tokyo Med. U., 2010. Med. staff Tokyo Med. U., 2006. Office: 6-7-1 Nishishinjuku Shinjuku-ku Tokyo 160-0023 Japan Office Fax: 81-3-3342-2305. E-mail: tomohiko@tokyo-med.ac.jp.

TOMOHIRO, ITOH, science educator; b. Aichi, Japan, Nov. 27, 1975; PhD, Nat. Fisheries U., 1998. Assoc. prof. Kinki U., 2011—. Office: 3327-204 Nakamachi Nara 631-8505 Japan Office Fax: 81-742-1316. Business E-Mail: titoh@giib.or.jp.

TOMOHISA, SHOKO, physician, educator; b. Yokohama, Japan, Feb. 19, 1967; MD, U. Occupl. and Environ. Health, Japan, 1991; PhD, Tokyo Med. and Dental U. Asst. prof. Shock Trauma and Emergency Med. Ctr., Tokyo Med. and Dental U. Hosp. Medicine, 2006—. Mem.: Japanese Soc. Acute Care Surgery, Japan Surg. Soc., Japanese Assn. Acute Medicine. Avocations: camping, sailing. Office: 1-5-45 Yushima Bunkyo-ku Tokyo 113-8519 Japan Business E-Mail: shouaccm@tmd.ac.jp.

TOMOUM, HODA YAHYA, pediatrician, educator; b. Cairo, June 15, 1968; d. Yahya Mahmoud Salem Tomoum and Hawaa Mohamed Hassanein Lotfy. MD, Ain Shams U., Abbasseya, Cairo, Egypt, 1999. Resident Children's Hosp. Ain Shams U., Cairo, 1993—96; asst. lectr. dept. pediat. Ain Shams U., Cairo, 1996—2000, lectr. pediat. dept. pediat., 2000—05, assoc. prof. dept. pediat., 2005—10, prof. dept. pediat., 2010—. Cons. Pediat. Neurology Outpatient Clinic, Ain Shams U. Hosps., Cairo, 1999—; active Eastern Mediterranean regional office WHO, Cairo, 2005—06. Reviewer: Jour. Epilepsia, Jour. Neurology, Neurosurgery and Psychiatry, Jour. Egyptian Soc. Child Neuropsychiatry. Named Exemplary Dr., Ain Shams U. Hosps., 1999. Mem.: Am. Acad. Pediats., Egyptian Pediat. Assn., Ain Shams Egyptian Pediat. Soc., Egyptian Soc. Child Neuropsychiatry, Internat. Child Neurology Assn. Muslim. Avocation: travel. Home: 10 El-Nagah 11361 Cairo El- Nozha Heliopolis Egypt Office Phone: 00 202 22588 012. Personal E-mail: tomoumh@yahoo.com.

TOMOV, SLAVCHO TOMOV, oncologist, researcher; b. Levski, Pleven, Bulgaria, Feb. 21, 1962; s. Milka Lozanova and Toma Vasilev Tomov; m. Vesela Dimcheva Dimova, Feb. 12, 1989; children: Momchil Slavchev, Mila Slavcheva. MA, Med. U., Pleven, 1989, MD, 2006. Gen. practitioner Hosp. Obnova, Pleven, Bulgaria, 1989—92; physician Emergency Ctr., Levski, 1992—94, Pleven, 1994—97; specialist in gynecology and oncology Clinic of Gynecologic Oncology Med. U., Pleven, Pleven, Bulgaria, 1997—. Author: Menopause, 2000; co-author: Lymph Node Disection, 2003, Cervical Cancer, 2003, Ovarian Cancer, 2003, Breast Cancer - Contemporary Surgical Therapy, 2005. Paleative care of patients with advanced cancer Hospice, Trastenik, Pleven, 2003—06; vol. Oncologic Ctr., Pleven, 2004—06. Grantee, Dreyfus Health Found., Pleven Regional Health Ctr., 1999, 2001, Med. U., Pleven, 2002—03. Mem.: Bulgarian Med. Assn., Bulgarian Assn. Gynecol. Endoscopy, Bulgarian Assn. Ob-Gyn. Achievements include research in modification of Radioligand binding assay for determination of epidermal growth factor receptor in ovarian tumors; prognostic model in ovarian cancer including the molecular marker EGFR. Avocations: dance, mountain climbing, accordion, guitar. Home: Grenaderska 40-V-12 Pleven 5800 Bulgaria Office: Clinic Gynecologic Oncology Georgi Kochev St 8A Pleven 5800 Bulgaria Office Fax: +35964801603; Home Fax: +35964834615. Personal E-mail: slavcho_tomov@yahoo.de.

TOMPKINS, RONALD K., retired surgeon, educator; b. Malta, Ohio, Oct. 14, 1934; s. Kenneth Steidley and Mildred Lillian (Loomis) T.; m. Suzanne Colbert, June 9, 1956; children: Gregory Alan, Teresa Susan, Geoffrey Stuart. BA, Ohio U., 1956; MD, Johns Hopkins U., 1960; MS, Ohio State U., 1968; DSc (hon.), U. Bordeaux, 1995. Diplomate Am. Bd. Surgery. Intern in surgery Ohio State U., 1960-61, resident in surgery, 1964-68, adminstrv. chief resident in surgery, 1968-69, NIH trainee in acad. surgery, instr. physiol. chemistry, 1966-69; asst. prof. surgery UCLA, 1969-73, assoc. prof., 1973-79, prof., 1979-2001, prof. emeritus, 2001—, chmn. basic surg. tng. program, 1970-79, asst. dean student affairs, 1979-82, chief divsn. gen. surgery, 1982-88, chief gastrointestinal surgery, 1986-97, assoc. dean, 1988-91, dir. surg. edn., 1996—2004; ret., 2004. Cons. VA Hosps. Editor-in-chief World Jour. Surgery, 1993-2004. With M.C. USAF, 1961-64. Recipient Disting Alumni award, Ohio U. Arts & Scis., 2001; grantee, NIH, 1968—70, John A. Hartford Found., 1970—79; fellow, Royal Soc. Medicine Eng., 1976—77. Fellow ACS (So. Calif. chpt. pres. 1987); mem. Am. Surg. Assn., Am. Gastroenterol. Assn., Am. Fedn. Clin. Rsch. Am. Inst. Nutrition, AMA, Assn. Acad. Surgery, Pacific Coast Surg. Assn. (recorder 1986-91, pres. 1995), Japan Surgical Soc. (hon.), French Surg. Assoc. (hon.), Soc. Clin. Surgery, Soc. Surgery Alimentary Tract (sec. 1982-85, pres.-elect 1985, pres. 1986, chmn. bd. trustees 1987), Soc. Univ. Surgeons, Societe Internationale de Chirurgie (U.S. chpt. sec. 1990-94, pres. 1996-98), Internat. Biliary Assn. (pres. 1979-81), Internat. HepatoPancreato-Biliary Assn. (hon.), Bay Surg. Soc., LA Surg. Soc. (pres. 1981), Robert M. Zollinger/Ohio State U. Surg. Soc. (pres. 1988-90), Longmire Surg. Soc. (pres. 1997-99), Phi Beta Kappa, Sigma Xi, Alpha Omega Alpha, Delta Tau Delta, Soc. Surg. Alimonary Tract (Founders medal, 2008). Achievements include numerous research publications in gastrointestinal surgery and gastrointestinal metabolism and biochemistry. Home: 309 20th St Santa Monica CA 90402

TONA, FRANCESCO, cardiologist, researcher; s. Renato Tona and Anna Abita; m. Michela Zandonà, June 15, 2002. MD, U. Padova Med. Sch., Italy, 1992; Cardiology fellowship, U. Padova Med. Sch., 2001, PhD, 2004. Cert. Medicine and Surgery Health Dept. of Italy, 1993. Cons. in cardiology U. Padova Med. Sch., Padova, Italy, 2000 , rsch., 2005. Contbr. articles various profl. jours. Tenent, 1994—95, Military Hospital Padova. Fellow: Italian Soc. of Cardiology (assoc.). Achievements include research in development of new noninvasive diagnostic tools in evaluating cardiac allograft function in heart transplantation; etiology of cardiac allograft vasculopathy; ethiopathogenesis of cardiomyopathies and myocarditis; determination of new prognostic indexes in heart failure; development of new diagnostic and prognostic tools in pulmonary hypertension and embolism. Office: Cardiology Univ Padua Via Giustiniani 2 35129 Padua Italy Office Fax: 09 876 1764. Personal E-mail: francescotona@hotmail.com.

TONE, ATSUHITO, physician; b. Katano, Osaka, Japan, Apr. 28, 1975; MD, Okayama U., 2000, PhD, 2005. Staff Dept. Diabetes and Metabolism, Nat. Hosp. Orgn., Okayama Med. Ctr., 2007—. Vis. scholar Dept. Medicine and Clin. Sci., Okayama U. Grad. Sch. Medicine, Dentistry and Pharm. Sci., 2007, clin. instr., 2008—09; mem. editl. bd. Jour. Diabetes & Metabolism, 2010. Office: 1711-1 Tamasu Kita-ku Okayama 701-1192 Japan Office Phone: 81-86-294-9911. Office Fax: 81-86-294-9255. Business E-Mail: aitone@okayama3.hosp.go.jp.

TONEGAWA, SUSUMU, biology professor; b. Nagoya, Japan, Sept. 6, 1939; arrived in U.S., 1963; s. Tsutoma and Miyoko T. (Masuko) Tonegawa; m. Mayumi Yoshinari, Sept. 28, 1985; children: Hidde, Hanna, Satto. BS in Chemistry, Kyoto U., Japan, 1963; PhD in Molecular Biology, U. Calif., San Diego, 1968. Rsch. asst. U. Calif., San Diego, 1963—64, tchg. asst., 1964—68; postdoc. fellow Salk Inst. Biol. Studies, San Diego, 1969—71; staff Basel Inst. Immunology, Switzerland, 1971—81; Whitehead prof. biology MIT, Cambridge, Mass., 1981—94, Picower prof. biology and neurosci., 1994—, dir. RIKEN-MIT Neurosci. Rsch. Ctr. Investigator Howard Hughes Med. Inst., Chevy Chase, Md., 1988—; founding dir. Picower Inst. Learning & Memory, MIT, 1994—2006; dir. RIKEN Brain Sci. Inst., Wako-shi, Japan, 2009—. Mem. editl. bd. Immunity; contbr. articles to profl. jours. Decorated Order of Culture Emperor of Japan; recipient Cloetta prize, Switzerland, 1978, Warren Triennial prize, Mass. Gen. Hosp., 1980, Genetics Grand prize, Genetics Promotion Found., Japan, 1981, Avery Landsteiner prize, Germany, 1981, Asahi prize, Tokyo, 1982, Louisa Gross Horwitz prize, Columbia U., 1982, V.D. Mattia award, Roche Inst. Molecular Biology, Nutley, NJ, 1983, Gardiner Found. Internat. award, 1983, Robert Koch Found. prize, Germany, 1986, Bristol-Myers award for disting. achievement in cancer rsch., 1986, Nobel prize in physiology/medicine, 1987, Albert Lasker award for basic med. rsch., 1987. Mem.: NAS (fgn. assoc.), Scandinavian Soc. Immunology (hon.), Am. Assn. Immunologists (hon.). Office: MIT Dept Biology Rm 46 5285 31 Ames St Cambridge MA 02139 Office Phone: 617-253-6459. E-mail: tonegawa@mit.edu. *

TONELLO, LUCIO, biomedical engineer, researcher, mathematician, educator; b. Montebelluna, Treviso, Italy, Apr. 25, 1972; s. Mario Tonello and Laura Binotto; m. Glenda Cappello, Nov. 26, 2001; 1 child, Claudia. MS in Biomed. Electronic Engring., U. Padova, Italy, 2001. Cert. profl. engr. Head informatics Brain Antiageing Rsch. Club, Bologna, Italy, 2000—05; lectr. informatics and automatic systems Liceo Scientifico, Montebelluna, Treviso, Italy, 2001—05;

head, Artificial Neural Network Imperial Coll. Lipid Neurosci. Group, 2007—09; full prof. bio-math. sci. Free U. of Human and Technol. Scis., U. Lugano, Switzerland, 2009—. Cons. U. Modena and Reggio Emilia, Italy, 2002—04, Villa Maria Found., Lugo di Romagna, Italy, 2005—06. Author: (software) ADAM - Analysis of Depression with Artificial Neural Network (awarded by Italian Soc. of Exptl. Biology, 2006), CAIN - Computer Aided Ischemic Diagnosis with Artificial Neural Network. Pres. Regional Fedn. Students, Treviso, 1989—91; mem. Italian Bd.r Paranormal Assertion Control, Padova, 2001. Lance cpl. Italian Air Force, 1994—95. Recipient Scientific Merit Declaration, Kary B. Mullis, 2006; grantee, Dept. Clin. Medicine and Applied Biotech., U. Bologna, 2005—07; fellow, 2005—07, Vet. Morpho-Physiology and Animal Production Dept., U. Bologna, 2007—. Fellow: Villa Maria Found. Sci. Bd. Mem. (hon.); mem.: Italian Soc. Exptl. Biology (assoc.), Engring. PA (assoc.). Achievements include discovery of artificial neural network research and application. Home: Via Alcide de Gasperi 44 31010 Maser TV Italy Personal E-mail: luciotonello@gmail.com.

TONETTI, DEBRA A., science educator; b. Chgo., Aug. 27, 1958; MS, Loyola U., 1985, PhD, 1990. Assoc. prof. U. Ill., Chgo., 2001—. Office: 833 S Wood St Chicago IL 60612 Office Fax: 312-996-1698. Business E-Mail: dtonetti@uic.edu.

TONG, H.Y. HENRY, pharmacist, educator; b. Hong Kong, China, July 12, 1975; s. Bo-Lin Ma. B in Pharmacy (hon.), Chinese U. Hong Kong, 1997; ADip in Health Svcs. Mgmt., Open U. Hong Kong, 1998; PhD, Chinese U. Hong Kong, 2003. Registered pharmacist Hong Kong and Macao. Pharmacist Tuen Mun Hosp., Hong Kong, 1998—99; cons. pharmacist Seaview Consultation Co., 2000—; assoc. prof. Sch. Health Scis. Macao Poly. Inst., 2003—, program coord., 2005—. Program coord. Sch. Health Sci. Macao Poly. Inst., China, 2005—. Home: Flat A1 4/F Nos 305 Chung On Bldg Sha Tsui Rd Hong Kong Tsuen Wan China Office: Macao Poly Inst Alameda Dr Carlos D' Assumpção No 335-341 Centro Hotline 5 Andar Macau China Office Fax: 853-753159. Personal E-mail: henry-tong@alumni.cuhk.net. E-mail: henrytong@ipm.edu.mo.

TONG, JOHN, ophthalmic plastic surgeon, pediatric ophthalmologist, educator; Bd. cert.; double fellowship trained. Faculty Jule Stein Eye Inst., LA, 2000; asst. clin. prof. Davis Med. Ctr., Sacramento, 2001—. Faculty mem. UCLA Jule Stein Eye Inst., 2000; lectr. in field. Contbr. chapters to books, articles to profl. jours. Fellow: ACS, Am. Acad. Ophthalmology, Am. Assn. Pediat. Ophthalmology and Strabismus, Am. Acad. Cosmetic Surgery, Am. Soc. Ophthalmic Plastic Surgery. Office: 1631 Lancaster Dr Ste 200 Grapevine TX 76051 Office Phone: 972-329-5433.

TONG, TERRY YOKE YIN, endocrinologist; b. Malaysia, Oct. 13, 1968; BSc (hon.), U. Adelaide, 1992; PhD, Nat. U. Singapore, 2004. Endocrine lab. mgr. & rschr. Nat. U. Health Sys., 2007—. Rsch. scholarships, Dept. Ob-Gyn., U. Adelaide, South Australia, 1991—92, Dept. Ob-Gyn., Nat. U. Singapore, 1993—95. Avocations: photography, travel, reading. Office: O&G Rsch Labs BLK S16 6 Sc Singapore 117546 Singapore Business E-Mail: terry_tong@nuhs.edu.sg.

TONG, TOMMY R., surgeon, pathologist; M.B., B.S.(HK), U. of Hong Kong Med. Sch., Pokfulam, Hong Kong, 1976—81; MD, SUNY. Diplomate Am. Bd. of Pathology. Surgeon St. Teresa's Hosp., Kowloon, Hong Kong, 1988—; sr. pathologist Princess Margaret Hosp., 1996—2006; with Alumnus Pathology Depts. U. Sask., Mt. Sinai Hosp., Meml. Sloan Kettering Cancer Ctr., NY; pathologist AW Pathology Med. Group, Bakersfield, Calif., 2006—08; attending pathologist Motefiore Med. Ctr., NY, 2008—, dir. pathology, north divsn., 2008—; assoc. prof. Albert Einstein Coll. Medicine, 2010—. Vis. prof. Mt. Sinai Pathology, 1999; invited spkr. Vanderbilt U. Pathology, 2004, HKUST, 2010; reviewer Med. Virology. Reviewer: Jour. Clin. Microbiology, Jour. Infectious Diseases; reviewer BMJ, JAMA, Lancet Infection Diseases, Lancet Neurology; reviewer: Open Microbiol. Jour.; mem. editl. bd. Jour. Clin. Microbiology; mem. editl. bd.: Open Microbiol. Jour., Internat. Jour. Bimed. Scis.; mem. editl. bd. Open Infection Diseases Jour., Recent Patents on Anti-Infective Drug Discovery; contbr. articles to profl. jours.; editor: J Cancer Res. Exp. Oncology; sect. editor Infectious Disorders Drug Targets. Grantee, Princess Margaret Hosp., 2001, 2001, Innovation and Tech. Commn., the Govt. of the Hong Kong Spl. Adminstrv. Region, 2001, 2003, 2004. Fellow: Am. Soc. of Clin. Pathologists, Coll. of Surgeons of Hong Kong, Royal Australasian Coll. of Surgeons, Coll. of Am. Pathology, Royal Coll. of Surgeons of Edinburgh; mem.: Am. Clin. Soc., Am. Soc. of Cytopathology, US and Can. Acad. of Pathology, NY Acad. of Sciences, Assn. for the Advancement of Sci., Papanicolaou Soc. of Cytopathology. Achievements include patents for electromolecular diagnosis; molecular diagnosis; cervical cancer screening; collection of upper respiratory clinical sample; novel biochip microarrays. Office: Montefiore Med Ctr Dept Pathology 600 E 233rd St Bronx NY 10466 Office Phone: 718-920-9150. Personal E-mail: tommy.tong@electrobiochip.com, tommyrtong@gmail.com.

TONG, WANGYU, research scientist, educator; b. Changde, July 10, 1963; PhD, Zhejiang U., 2001. Postdoc. rschr. Inha U., 2001; prof. East China U. Sci. and Tech., 2002; vis. asst. prof. Ohio State U., 2006; postdoc assoc. Cornell U., 2007; prof. Anhui U., 2008. Mem. editl. bd. Rsch. Jour. Biotech., 2010. Mem.: Sci. Adv. Bd. Office: 111 Jiulong Rd Hefei Anhui 230601 China Business E-Mail: tongwy@ecust.edu.cn.

TONG, YAO, medical educator; PhD, Shanghai U. Traditional Chinese Medicine, 1991. Dean, faculty, basic med. sci. Shanghai U. Traditional Chinese Medicine, 1995—98, v.p. and prof., 1998—2003; v.p. Shanghai Acad. Traditional Chinese Medicine, 1998—2003; dir. and chair prof. Sch. Chinese Medicine, U. Hong Kong, 2004—. Editor Chinese Jour. New Drugs and Clin. Remedies, 2004—08, Chinese Medicine Jour., Macao, 2007—; mem. bd. LKS faculty medicine U. Hong Kong, 2004—, mem. bd. dirs. Clin. Trials Ctr., 2004—; mem. Consortium Globalization Chinese Medicine Found. Ltd., 2004—; dep. chmn. profl. evaluation clin. effectiveness com. World Fedn. Chinese Medicine Socs., 2007—. Author: (lit.) Medicine and Philosophy; editor: (med. book) Clinical Case Collection - Ding Gan Ren (Shanghai Distinction Pub., 2000), Practical Hepatology in Chinese Medicine, (textbook) Experimental Chinese Medicine (21th Century Tchg. Material grant, Shanghai Edn. Com., 2000); chief editor (textbook for postgrad.) Research Approach and Methodology of Chinese Medicine; contbr. scientific papers to profl. jours. Advisor Alliance for Patients' Mut. Help Orgns., Hong Kong SAR, 2005—; com. mem. Chinese Assn. Higher Edn. Chinese Medicine, 2008—; mem. Chinese Medicine Practitioners Bd., Chinese Medicine Coun. Hong Kong, 2008—, mem. com. assessment of Chinese medicine degree courses, 2005—; mem. Use of Proprietary Chinese Medicine Steering Com., Hosp. Authority, Hong Kong, 2006—07, Endangered Species Adv. Com., Agr., Fisheries and Conservation Dept., Hong Kong, 2004—06. Recipient Tchg. Achievements prize, Nat. Edn. Ministry, China, 2001, Shanghai Edn. Com., 2001, Nat. Excellent Tchr., Assn. Internat. Higher Edn. Chinese Medicine, 1994; named Outstanding Woman, Shanghai Mcpl. Higher Ednl. Sys., 1994. Master: Assn. Higher Med. Edn. Shanghai; mem.: Cell Stress Soc. Internat., Am. Chem. Soc., Assn. Higher Med. Edn. China (dir. 2003—05), Hong Kong Assn. Integration of Chinese-Western Medicine, Hong Kong Acupuncture and Moxibustion Assn., Bd. Internat. Soc. Chinese Medicine. Avocations: opera, travel, movies. Office: Sch Chinese Medicine HKU 10 Sassoon Rd Pokfulam Hong Kong Island Hong Kong Office Phone: 852-25890436. Office Fax: 00852-28725476. Business E-Mail: tongyao@hkucc.hku.hk.

TONGE, BRUCE JOHN, psychiatrist; b. Melborne, Australia, May 9, 1947; s. JOhn Feltham and Joyce (Bates) Tonge; m. Gera Eleanore Degooijer-Tonge, Oct. 12, 1970 (div. June 1996); m. Avril Vaux Brereton, June 10, 1996; children: Jonathan, Rachel, Claire. MB BS, Monash U., Melbourne, 1970; DPM, Royal Coll. Physicians, London, 1974; MD, U. Melbourne, 1985. Cert. child psychiatrist Vic. Child psychiatrist Austin Hosp., Melbourne, 1976—80, dir. dept. child psychiatry, 1980—87; head dept. psychiatry, prof. child psychiatry Royal Alexandra Hosp. for Children, Sydney, NSW, 1987—89; med. dir., mental health program So. Health, Melbourne, 1990—, head ctr. for devel. psychiatry and psychology, 1990—2009; prof. and head, dept. psychiatry Monash U., Melbourne, 1992—2006, found. head Sch. Psychology and Psychiatry, 2000—11, emeritus prof., 2011. Chair child psychiatry and tng. com. RANZCP, Melbourne, 1986—91; bd. dirs. Autism Victoria, Melbourne, 1991—2001; mem. com. on mental health and ID WHO, London, 1997—; bd. dirs. Neurosci. Australia, Victoria, 2003—. Author (18 books on child psychiatry); editor: Handbook of Child Psychiatry, 1990; contbr. 58 chpts. to books, articles to profl. jours.; co-author: Developmental Behaviour Checklist; author: Self-Efficacy Questionnaire for Adolescents, Draw a Dream. Flight lt. RAAF, 1961—70. Recipient Rsch. Excellence prize, Monash U., 2001, Nat. Rsch. prize, Australian Soc. for Study of Learning Disabled, 1998, Julian Katz award, RANZCP, 1998, David De Kretjer medal, Monash U., 2010, ASPR Founders medal, 2010, Ranzep meritorious Svc. award, 2010; named Blake Marsh Lectr., Roy Coll. Psychiatrists of Edinburgh, 2005. Mem.: Royal Melbourne Tennis Club. Anglican. Office: Ctr for Developmental Psychiatry Monash Medical Ctr 246 Clayton Rd Clayton VIC 3168 Australia Home: PO Box 177 Mt Macedon Victoria 3441 Australia Office Phone: 61-39594-1354. Office Fax: 51-3-9594-6937. Business E-Mail: bruce.tonge@monash.edu.

TONGWEN, SUN, medical educator; b. Xinxiang, Henan, China, Sept. 15, 1969; MD, Zhengzhou U., 2010. Assoc. prof. First Affiliated Hosp. Zhengzhou U., 2006—. Office: Jianshe East Rd Zhengzhou Henan 450052 China Business E-Mail: suntongwen@163.com.

TONIETTE, SALLYE JEAN, physician; b. Sulphur, La., 1929; d. Eugene Augusta and Sallye (Tanner) T. Student, John McNeese Jr. Coll., 1946-47; BS, La. State U., 1949, tchrs. cert., 1950, MD, 1955. Intern Crawford W. Long Meml. Hosp., Emory U., Atlanta, 1955-56, resident in ob-gyn., jr., sr., chief residencies, 1956-59; practice in ob-gyn. Sulphur, La., 1959—. Mem. med. staff West Calcasieu Cameron Hosp., 1959—. Dir. Calcasieu Parish Cancer Soc., 1963-67. Named Woman of Distinction, Calcasieu Parish Police Jurors, also Bus. and Profl. Women's Club of West Calcasieu, 1969; Queen of Krewe of Cosmos, 1963, Mardi Gras. Fellow Am. Coll. Ob-Gyn.; mem. La. Med. Assn., Calcasieu Parish Med. Soc., La. Wildlife Fedn., Am. Quarter Horse Assn., Assn. Am. Physicians and Surgeons, Bayou Oaks Country Club (v.p., bd. dirs. 1974—), Krewe de Bon Coer, Krewe of Cosmos, Alpha Chi Omega, Beta Tau Mu, Iota Sigma Pi, Phi Theta Kappa, Beta Sigma Phi. Republican. Methodist. Home: 4917 La Paix Dr Sulphur LA 70665 Office: 521 Cypress St Sulphur LA 70663-5049 Home Phone: 337-583-7223; Office Phone: 337-527-7841.

TONIGAN, JEFFREY SCOTT, psychology professor; b. Arlington, Va., Nov. 21, 1955; PhD, U. N.Mex, 1989. Rsch. prof. Ctr. Alcoholism, Substance Abuse, & Addictions, 1989—. Cons. NIAAA, 1993—2010. Rsch. grant, NIH. Mem.: Rsch. Soc. Alcoholism. Avocation: skiing. Office: 2650 Yale SE Albuquerque NM 87106 Office Fax: 505-925-2301. Business E-Mail: jtonigan@unm.edu.

TONIOLO, ANTONIO QUIRINO, medical educator; b. Siena, Italy, Mar. 13, 1948; s. Giuseppe Toniolo and Silvia Majorana; m. Amelia Giuditta Tremolanti, Sept. 5, 1977; children: Giuseppe Sergio, Giovanni Paolo. MD, U. Pisa, 1972. Prof. med. microbiology U. Sassari, Italy, 1985—89; dir. lab. clin. microbiology Ospedale di Sassari, 1985—89; prof. med. microbiology U. Pisa, 1990—91, U. Pavia, 1991—98; dir. lab. clin. microbiology Ospedale Circolo Fondazione Macchi, Varese, 1994—2000, dir. clin. pathology dept., 2001—; prof. med. microbiology U. Insubria Med. Sch., Varese, 1998—. Cons. Inst. Pharm. Analysis, Ligornetto, Switzerland, 2000—; cons. virologist Ospedale Santa Chiara, Pisa, 1989—91; vis. assoc. NIH, Bethesda, Md., 1978—81. Sci. dir. Giornale Italiano Microbiologia Medica, Milano, 2001—03. Lt. Italian Army, 1975—76. Grantee Virus Rsch., Nat. Coun. Rsch., Rome, 1985—2001, Infectious Diseases, 1985—88, AIDS Rsch., Istituto Superiore Sanità, Roma, 1996—2000, Mechanisms Drug Resistance, Nat. Ministry U. and Rsch., Rome, 1998—2002, Antibiotic Resistance, Wyeth Co., 2000—01, Cultured Muscle Cells Cardiac Failure, Banca Monte Lombardia, Milano, 2001—03, Prion Infection and Viral Susceptibility, U. Tokyo, 2003; fellow, Istituto Nazionale Tumori, Milano, 1975, Fogarty Ctr., Bethesda, Md., 1978—81, Fellow, Nat. Coun. Rsch., Rome, 1978; scholar, Chester Beatty Inst. Cancer Rsch., London, 1970. Mem.: Italian Soc. Med., Dental, and Clin. Microbiology (pres. 2001—), NIH Alumni Assn. (corr.), Internat. AIDS Soc. (corr.), Am. Soc. Microbiology (corr.), Società Italiana Microbiologia (life), Rotary Club (pres. 1999—2000). Achievements include research in Demonstration that viruses and chemicals may synergize in causing type-1 diabetes; Demonstration that certain cytokines (IL6 and IL8) are produced by human epithelial cells of the mammary and thyroid glands; their production is lost in transformed (tumoral) cells; Demonstration that HIV-1 is capable of infecting mammary epithelial cells that may explain virus transmission through lactation; Demonstration that a DNA-based vaccine may protect against enteroviral infections; Finding of new drug-resistance enzymes in enteric bacteria (IMP-12, VIM-4, TEM-134); Demonstration that one of the foamy viruses can infect humans; Demonstration that HIV-1 is capable of infecting renal cells this may contribute to renal failure in HIV-infected patients; Demonstration that coxsackieviruses can produce diabetes in mice. Home: Via Casluncio 21 Varese 21100 Italy Office: Univ Insubria Med Sch Viale Luigi Borri 57 21100 Varese VA Italy Office Fax: 39-0332-260.517. Personal E-mail: a.toniolo@uninsubria.it. E-mail: antonio.toniolo@ospedale.varese.it.

TONKIN, INA LYNN DYER, physician, cardiovascular radiologist, educator; b. Louisville, Apr. 26, 1944; d. Robert S. and Nancy E. (Camp) Dyer; m. Allen K. Tonkin, June 29, 1968; children: Allison Elizabeth-Ann, Kieth Allen. BA, DePauw U., 1966; MD, U. Louisville, 1970. Diplomate Am. Bd. Radiology, 1974; Am. Bd. Vascular Interventional Radiology, 1994; Am. Bd. Pediatric Radiology, 1996. Pediatric intern U. Fla., Gainesville, 1970-71, resident in radiology, 1971-73, fellow in cardiovasc. radiology, 1974-75; asst. prof. U. Ariz. Health Sci. Ctr., Tucson, 1975-77, U. Ala.-Birmingham, 1977-79; assoc. prof. radiology U. Tenn., Memphis, 1979-84, prof., 1984—, prof. pediat., 1985—. Exec. com. LeBonheur Children's Med. Ctr., Memphis, 1981-85, chief med. staff, 1987; disting. scientist Armed Forces Inst. Radiologic Pathology, Washington, 1992-93; prof. radiology & pediat. U. Tenn. Hlth. Sci. Ctr., Memphis; lectr. nat. and internat. Editor: (book) Pediatric Cardiovascular Imaging, 1992; contbr. chpts. to books, rsch. articles to profl. jours. Recipient Disting. Alumnus award U. Louisville Med. Sch., 1999. Fellow Soc. Interventional Radiology, Am. Coll. Radiology, Cardiovasc. Coun. Am. Heart Assn.; mem. Soc. Pediat. Radiology (treas.), Jour. Rev. Club Memphis (sec. 1984, pres. 1985), Soc. Interventional Radiology, N.Am. Soc. Cardiac Imaging (pres. 1991). Methodist. Home: 3415 Chambers Chapel Rd Lakeland TN 38002-9573 Office: LeBonheur Children's Med Ctr 50 N Dunlap St Memphis TN 38103-4909 also: Univ Tenn Health Sci Ctr Prof Radiology and Pediat 50 N Dunlap St Memphis TN 38103-4909 Personal E-mail: drstonkin@mindspring.com.

TONKONOGY, JOSEPH MOSES, physician, neuropsychiatrist, researcher; b. Belaya Tserkov, Kiev, Ukraine, Oct. 22, 1925; came to U.S., 1979, naturalized, 1985; s. Moysey Iosifovich and Beyla (Gdalievna (Schvachkina) T.; married; children: Vitaly, Milla, Bella. MD, Military Med. Acad., Leningrad, USSR, 1947; PhD, All Union Acad. Med. Sci., Moscow, 1956; DSc, 1st Med. Inst., Leningrad, 1966. From asst. to prof. The Bechterev Inst., Leningrad, 1956-66, prof., chmn., 1966-78; assoc. Boston U. Sch. Medicine, 1980-81; physician VA Med. Ctr., Northampton, Mass., 1981-87; assoc. prof. U. Mass. Med. Ctr., Worcester, 1987-95, prof., 1995—. Dir. neuropsychiatry svc. Worcester State Hosp., Mass., 1989—. Author: Introduction to Clinical Neuropsychology, 1973, Vascular Aphasia, 1986, The Brief Neuropsychological Cognitive Examination, 1997; editor: Problems of Contemporary Psychoneurology, 1966, Psychological Experiment in Psychiatry and Neurology, 1969, Mathematical Methods in Psychiatry and Neurology, 1971, Current Problems of Clinical Psychology, 1975; cons. (book) Soviet Military Psychiatry, 1986; contbr. numerous articles to profl. jours. Capt. Med. Corps, Germany, 1947-48. Recipient The Bechterev Prize, All Union Acad. Med. Scis., Moscow, 1974. Fellow: The Royal Soc. Medicine (U.K.); mem.: Internet Psychogeriatric Soc., Soc. Neurosci., Internat. Neuropsychol. Soc., Am. Acad. Neurology, Am. Neuropsychiat. Assn. Jewish. Office: U Mass Med Ctr Dept Psychiatry 55 Lake Ave N Worcester MA 01655-0002

TONN, ELVERNE MERYL, pediatric dentist, dental benefits consultant, forensic odontologist; b. Stockton, Calif., Dec. 10, 1929; s. Emanuel M. and Lorna Darlene (Bryant) T.; m. Ann G. Richardson, Oct. 28, 1951; children: James Edward, Susan Elaine (dec.). AA, La Sierra U., Riverside, Calif., 1949; DDS, U. So. Calif., 1955; BS, Excelsior Coll., 1984; grad., Citizens Police Acad., Manteca, 2003, San Joaquin County Citizens Sheriff's Acad. Cert. lifetime cmty. coll. instr., tchg. credential Calif., 1982; lic. dentist Calif., 1955, diplomate Am. Bd. Quality Assurance and Utilization Rev. Physicians, Am. Bd. Forensic Dentistry, Am. Bd. Spl. Care Dentistry, Am. Bd. for Cert. in Homeland Security, cert. dental cons., forensic cons. Am. Coll. Forensic Examiners, 2004, med. investigator Am. Coll. Forensic Examiners, 2004. Pediat. dentistry intern Childrens Hosp. LA, 1957—59; pediatric dentist, assoc. Walker Dental Group, Long Beach, Calif., 1957-59, Children's Dental Clinic, Sunnyvale, Calif., 1959-61; pediatric dentist in pvt. practice Mountain View, Calif., 1961-72; pediatric dentist, ptrn. Pediatric Dentistry Assocs., Los Altos, Calif., 1972-83; pediatric dentist, ptnr. Valley Oak Dental Group, Manteca, Calif., 1987—2003; from clin. instr. to assoc. prof. Sch. Dentistry, U. Pacific, San Francisco, 1964-84; assoc. prof. Sch. Dentistry, U. Calif., San Francisco, 1984-86. 2pediat. dental cons. Delta Dental Plan, San Francisco, 1985—2002; chief dental staff El Camino Hosp., Mountain View, Calif., 1964—65, 1984—85; dental cons. Interplast program Stanford U. Sch. Medicine, 1973; cert. physician adv. Physicians' Review Network, Phoenix, 2004—; peer review cons. Broadspire Svcs. Inc., Fla., 2009—; forensic dental cons. San Joaquin County Sheriff/Coroner, 2007—; appt. Weekly columnist Manteca Bull., 1987-92; producer 2 teaching videos, 1986; contbr. articles to profl. jours. Extern, dentist for disabled Long Island Jewish Med. Ctr., 1970. Capt. US Army, 1955—63. Recipient Dr. Willard Fleming Meritorious Svcs. award, Am. Coll. Dentists, 2006. Fellow Am. Coll. Dentists, Internat. Coll. Dentists, Am. Acad. Pediatric Dentistry, Royal Soc. Health, Acad. of Dentistry for Handicapped, Pierre Fauchard Acad., Acad. Dental Materials, Am. Soc. Dentistry for Children (mastership award 2001), Am. Acad. Forensic Scis., Am. Coll. Forensic Examiners; mem. ADA, Internat. Assn. Pediatric Dentistry, Internat. Assn. Dental Rsch., Am. Soc. Forensic Odontology, Fedn. Dentaire Internationale, Am. Assn. Dental Cons., Calif.

Dental Assn., Calif. Soc. Dentistry for Children (pres. 1968), Calif. Soc. Pediatric Dentistry, NY Acad. Scis., Calif. Acad. Sci., Rotary Internat. (Paul Harris fellow 1990), Manteca Police Dept. (Badge 2003), Nat. Disaster Med. Svc., Disaster Mortuary Org. Response Team (DMORT region 9), Am. Coll. Med. Quality, Manteca Cert. Emergency Response Team, Calif. State Dental Identification Team, AMA (assoc.). Republican. Avocations: photography, travel, medieval history, anthropology. Home and Office: Tonn Forensic Cons Svcs 2420 Bellchase Dr Manteca CA 95336-5108 Personal E-mail: emtonn@comcast.net.

TONN, ROBERT JAMES, retired entomologist; b. Watertown, Wis., June 23, 1927; s. Harry James and Elise (Foogman) Tonn; m. Noemi C. Tonn; children: Sigrid M., Monica E. BS, Colo. State U., 1949, MS, 1950; MPH, Okla. Med. Sch., 1963; PhD, Okla. State U., 1959. Rsch. assoc La. State U., Costa Rica/New Orleans, 1961-63; dir. Taunton (Mass.) Field Sta., 1963-65; chief PMO unit WHO, various locations, 1965-87; ret., 1987. Adj. prof. parasitology U. Tex., El Paso, 1988—; cons. USAID/VBC, 1987—. Contbr. articles to profl. jours. Mem.: Royal Soc. Tropical Medicine and Hygiene, US/Mex. Border Health Assn., Am. Mosquito Control Assn., Soc. Vector Ecology (pres. 1984), Am. Soc. Tropical Medicine, Masons. Congregationalist. Home: 4247 E Winchester Rd Las Cruces NM 88011-7544 Personal E-mail: tonnapollo@aol.com.

TONTI-FILIPPINI, NICHOLAS ANTONY, medical ethicist, educator; b. Melbourne, Victoria, Australia, July 5, 1956; s. Michael Angelo Tonti-Filippini and Coralie Mary Mumford; m. Mary Dean Walsh, Mar. 17, 1954; children: Claire Therese, Lucianne Mary, Justin Antony, John Michael. MA, Monash U., Melbourne, 1981; PhD, U. Melbourne, 2001. Fellow HERDSA; hosp. ethicist St. Vincent's Hosp., Melbourne, 1982—89, dir. bioethics, 1985—89; assoc. dean, head bioethics John Paul II Inst., Melbourne, 2002—, assoc. dean, 2008—; lectr. U. Melbourne, 2003; appt. Knight Comdr. KCSG, 2009. Mem. Australian Health Ethics Com., Canberra, 2004—09; dir. rsch. Australian Cath. Bishop Conf., Canberra, Australia, 1990—92, bd. mem. Natural Family Planning, 1995—99; mem. Matercare, Sydney, 2000—04; chmn. Siena Coll. Ltd, Melbourne, 2000—05. Scholar, Monash U., 1981—84. Mem.: Internat. Bioethics Assn. Office: John Paul II Institute PO Box 146 East Melbourne VIC 3002 Australia Home Fax: 61 3 9848 3676. Business E-Mail: ntf-dsl@keypoint.com.au.

TOOKER, JOHN PHILLIP, internist, educator, medical association administrator; b. Denver; m. Nancy Tooker; 2 children. MD, U. Colo., 1970; MBA, Temple U. Diplomate Am. Bd. Internal Medicine, Am. Bd. Critical Care Medicine, Am. Bd. Pulmonary Disease. Intern Bellevue Hosp. Ctr., NYC, 1970—71, resident in medicine, 1971—72, U. Colo., 1972—73; fellow Maine Med. Ctr., Portland, 1975—76; fellow internal medicine U. Wash., Seattle, 1976—77; asst. chief dept. internal medicine, program dir. Maine Med. Ctr., Portland; dep. exec. v.p., COO ACP, Phila., 1995—2002, CEO, exec. v.p., 2002—10, assoc. exec. v.p., 2010—. Assoc. prof. medicine U. Vt.; adj. prof. U. Pa. Named one of 50 Most Powerful Physician Execs. in Healthcare, Modern Physician, 2005. Fellow: Coll. Physicians Phila., Am. Coll. Chest Physicians; mem.: AMA, Am. Thoracic Soc., Alpha Omega Alpha. Address: ACP 190 N Independence Mall W Philadelphia PA 19106-1572 Office Phone: 215 351 2800. *

TOOLE, JAMES FRANCIS, medical educator; b. Atlanta, Mar. 22, 1925; s. Walter O'Brien and Helen (Whitehurst) T.; m. Patricia Anne Wooldridge, Oct. 25, 1952; children: William, Anne, James, Douglas Sean, Lauren, James, Robert, Dean, Tyler, Kyle, Kaitlin, Grace. BA, Princeton U., 1947; MD, Cornell U., 1949; LLB, LaSalle Extension U., 1963; Dr. Honoris Causa, U. Targu Mures, Romania, 1998. Intern, then resident internal medicine and neurology U. Pa. Hosp., London, 1949—55, Nat. Hosp., London, 1955—56; mem. faculty U. Pa. Sch. Medicine, 1959—61; prof. neurology, chmn. dept. Sch. Medicine Wake Forest Bapt. Hosp., 1962—83, emeritus prof. neurology, 2011. Vis. prof. neuroscis. U. Calif., San Diego, 1969—70; vis. scholar Oxford U., 1989; mem. Nat. Bd. Med. Examiners, 1970—76; mem. task force arteriosclerosis Nat. Heart Lung & Blood Inst., 1970—81; chmn. 6th and 7th Princeton confs. cerebrovascular diseases; cons. epidemiology WHO, Japan, 1972, 73, 93, USSR, 68, Switzerland, 74, Côte d'Ivoire, 77; mem. Lasker Awards com., 1976—77; chmn. neuropharmacologic drugs com. FDA, 1979; chair Commn. on Presdl. Disability, 1994—97; cons. NASA, 1966. Author: Cerebrovascular Diseases, 6th edit., Translation into Chinese, Japanese, Portugese, Spanish, German, Russian., 1999; editor: Current Concepts in Cerebrovascular Disease, 1969—73, Jour. Neurol. Sci., 1990—97; mem. editl. bd. Annals Internal Medicine, 1968—75, Stroke, 1972—74; mem. editl. bd. Jour. AMA, 1975—77; mem. editl. bd. Ann. Neurology, 1980—86, Jour. of Neurology, 1985—89. Pres. N.C. Heart Assn., 1976-77. Served with AUS, 1950-51; flight surgeon USNR, 1951-53. Decorated Bronze Star with V, Combat Med. badge. Master: ACP (licentiate); fellow: AAAS (life), Royal Coll. Physicians; mem.: AMA, Greek Neurological Assn., Osler Soc., Am. Acad. Neurology Rsch. Found., Am. Chem. Soc., Soc. for Neurosci., Hungarian Neurol. Soc., Polish Neurol. Soc., N.C. Stroke Assn. (pres. 1999—2001), Nat. Stroke Assn. (bd. dirs. 1993—, exec. com. 1994—, chmn. Commn. on U.S. Presdl. Disability 1994—), Am. Clin. and Climatol Assn. (life), Assn. Brit. Neurologists (hon.), German Neurol. Soc. (hon.), Austrian Soc. Neurology (hon.), Irish Neurol. Assn. (hon.), Russian Acad. Neurology (hon.), Internat. Stroke Soc. (exec. com. 1989—97, program chmn. 1992, pres. 1999—2004), Am. Soc. Neuroimaging (pres. 1992—94), Am. Acad. Neurology (bd. mem. 2004—09), World Fedn. Neurology (sec.-treas. 1982—89, mgmt. com. 1990—98, pres. 1998—2001, chmn. Rsch. and Edn. Found. 1999—2004), Am. Neurol. Assn. (sec.-treas. 1978—82, pres. 1984—85, historian 1988—, archivist 2004), Am. Physiol. Soc., Am. Heart Assn. (chmn. com. ethics 1970—75), Bohemian Club. Office Phone: 336-716-2338. Business E-Mail: jtoole@wfubmc.edu.

TOOMEY, BERNADETTE A., foundation administrator; b. Bklyn. BA in Comm., Marymount Manhattan Coll., NY; M in Adult Edn., Am. U., Washington. Dir. pub. policy edn. programs Brookings Instn.; v.p. Cosmetic Toiletries and Fragrance Assn.; with Internat. Mgmt. Group; co-creator Nat. Acad. Found.; cons. Dept. Edn., Washington; exec. v.p. strategic partnerships and devel. Am. Legacy Found.; pres., CEO Am. Lung Assn., Washington, 2007—08; dir. northeast region Diabetes Rsch. Inst. Found., NYC, 2011—. Office: Diabetes Rsch Inst Found 381 Park Ave S Ste 1118 New York NY 10010 Office Phone: 212-888-2217. Office Fax: 212-888-2219. *

TOOMEY, KATHLEEN ELIZABETH, public health service officer; b. Aspinwall, Pa., Nov. 21, 1951; AB in biology cum laude, Smith Coll., 1973; MPH, MD, Harvard U., 1979. Diplomate Am. Bd. of Family Practice, Nat. Bd. of Med. Examiners. Resident dept. family medicine U. Wash., Seattle, 1979-82; clin. dir. Alaska Native Hosp., Kotzebue, 1982-85; Pew Health Policy fellow Inst. for Health Policy Studies, U. Calif. Sch. Medicine, San Francisco, 1985-87; Epidemic Intelligence Svc. officer Nat. Ctr. for Prevention Svcs., Ctrs. for Disease Control, Atlanta, 1987-89; legis. asst. on health issues to Senator John Chafee, U.S. Senate, Washington, 1991; asst. to dir. for external rels., 1989-90; state epidemiologist, dir. epidemiology and prevention br. Divsn. of Pub. Health, Ga. Dept. of Human Resources, 1993-97, dir. Atlanta, 1997—2005; dir. coordinating ctr. health promotion Ctr. for Disease Control and Prevention, Atlanta, 2005—09, dir. BOTUSA Botswana, 2009—. Adj. assoc. prof. in epidemiology Rollins Sch. of Pub. Health, Emory U.; clin. assoc. prof. Morehouse U. Sch. Medicine, Emory U.; mem. Statewide Child Fatality Rev. Panel, 1998; mem. Bd. Health Promotion and Disease Prevention, Inst. of Medicine, 1998—; mem. Tech. Adv. Group on Devolution and Federalism, Nat. Health Policy Forum, George Washington U., 1998—. Mem. task force The Nat. Campaign to Prevent Teen Pregnancy, 1996-99. Fulbright scholar, 1973-74; Public Health award, American Academy Family Physicians, 2003. Mem. Am. Acad. Family Physicians, Am. Pub. Health Assn. (governing coun. Ga. state chpt. rep. 1997-99), Am. Sexually Transmitted Diseases Assn., Assn. State and Territorial Health Ofcls. (exec. com. 1998—), Ga. Acad. Family Physicians, Ga. Pub. Health Assn., Med. Assn. Atlanta, Med. Assn. Ga. (pub. health and preventative health care com. 1997—). Office: BOTUSA Plot 14818 Lebatlane Rd Phase One PO Box 90 Gaborone Botswana *

TOP, FRANKLIN HENRY, JR., physician, researcher; b. Detroit, Mar. 1, 1936; s. Franklin Henry Sr. and Mary (Madden) T.; m. Lois Elizabeth Fritzell, Sept. 23, 1961; children: Franklin H. III, Brian N., Andrew M. BS, Yale U., 1957, MD cum laude, 1961. Diplomate Am. Bd. Pediatrics. Intern, resident, infectious diseases fellow U. Minn. Hosps., Mpls., 1961—66; commd. officer U.S. Army, advanced through grades to col.; med. officer, dept. virus diseases Walter Reed Army Inst. Research, Washington, 1966—70, chief dept. virus diseases, 1973—76; dir. divsn. communicable diseases and immunology Walter Reed Army Inst. Rsch., Washington, 1976—79, dep. dir., 1979—81, dir. and comdt., 1983—87; chief dept. virology Seato Med. Rsch. Lab., Bangkok, 1970—73; comdr. U.S.A. Med. Rsch. Inst. of Chem. Def., Aberdeen Proving Ground, Md., 1981—83; ret. U.S. Army, 1987; sr. v.p. Praxis Biologics Inc., Rochester, NY, 1987—88; exec. v.p. MedImmune, Inc., Gaithersburg, Md., 1988—2004; sr. v.p. MedImmune Ventures, Gaithersburg, Md., 2004—. Contbr. over 40 articles to med. jours. Decorated Legion of Merit with 2 oak leaf clusters. Fellow Am. Acad. Pediatrics(emeritus mem.), Infectious Diseases Soc. Am.; mem. AMA, Alpha Omega Alpha. Avocation: ornithology. Office Phone: 301-398-4251. Business E-Mail: topf@medimmune.com.

TOPHAM, NEAL, plastic surgeon. Grad., Case Western Res. U., 1994. Diplomate Am. Bd. Plastic Surgery, lic. Pa. Chief plastic and reconstructive surgery Fox Chase Cancer Ctr. Office: Fox Chase Cancer Center 333 Cottman Ave Philadelphia PA 19111-2497 Office Phone: 215-728-6900.

TOPLAK, HERMANN, medical educator; b. Graz, Austria, June 4, 1960; MD, U. Graz, 1984. Postdoc. rsch. fellow U. Berne, Switzerland, 1986—88; resident, internal medicine Med. U. Graz, 1988—93, specialisation, endocrinology, 1993—95, assoc. prof., internal medicine, 1995—2011, prof., internal medicine, 2011—. Recipient Grand Gold Decoration award, Styrian Drs. Coun., 2010, Congress award, City of Graz, 2011. Mem.: EASD, EASO. Avocations: classical music, singing, hiking. Office: Auenbruggerplatz 15 Graz Styria A-8036 Austria Office Fax: 4331538513812. Business E-Mail: hermann.toplak@medunigraz.at.

TOPOL, ERIC JEFFREY, academic administrator, cardiologist, educator, geneticist; b. NYC, June 26, 1954; s. Erwin and Susan (Lepp) T.; m. Susan Leah Merriman, May 5, 1979; children: Sarah, Evan. BA with highest distinction, U. Va., 1975; MD with honors, U. Rochester, 1979. Med. resident U. Calif., San Francisco, 1979-82; fellow Johns Hopkins U. Med. Ctr., Balt., 1982-85; asst. prof. U. Mich. Sch. Medicine, Ann Arbor, 1985-87, assoc. prof., 1987-90, prof., 1990; dir. cardiac catheterization labs. and interventional cardiology U. Mich. Med. Ctr., Ann Arbor, 1986-91; chmn. dept. cardiovasc. medicine Cleve. Clinic Found., dir. Ctr. for Thrombosis and Arterial Biology, 1991—2006; founder, provost, chief acad. officer Cleve. Clinic Lerner Coll. Medicine, Case Western Reserve Univ., 2002—05, prof. medicine, 2004—06; prof. genetics Case Western Reserve Univ. Sch. Medicine, 2006; dir., Scripps Translational Sci. Inst. The Scripps Rsch. Inst., 2007—, chief academic officer, Scripps Health, 2007—, sr. cons. divsn. cardiology, Scripps Clinic, 2007—, prof. molecular and exptl. medicine, 2007—, founding dean, Scripps Sch. Medicine, 2008—. Editor: Acute Coronary Intervention, 1988, Textbook of Interventional Cardiology, 1990, 4th edit., 2002, Textbook of Cardiovascular Medicine, 1st and 2d edits.; mem. editl. bd. Circulation, Circulation Rsch., Am. Jour. Cardiology, Coronary Art Disease, Jour. Am. Coll. Cardiology, Brit. Heart Jour.; mem. editl. bd. of several med. publs.; contbr. articles to profl. jours. Recipient Clin. Rsch. Innovator award, Doris Duke Charitable Found., 2003, Andres Gruentzig award, European Soc. Cardiology, 2004. Fellow ACP, Am. Coll. Cardiology (editor jour., Simon Dack award, 2005), Am. Soc. Clin. Investigation, Am. Heart Assn. (mem. coun. on clin. cardiology, coun. on circulation and thrombosis), European Soc. Cardiology; mem. Cen. Soc. Clin. Rsch., Am. Fedn. for Clin. Rsch. (councilor), Assn. Am. Physicians, AMA (Dr. William Beaumont award in Medicine 2002), IOM, NAS, John Hopkins Soc. Scholars. being one of the first scientists to raise doubts about the safety of Vioxx, and was a key witness in lawsuits against Merck & Co. Office: Scripps Translational Sci Inst 3344 N Torrey PInes Ct La Jolla CA 92037

TOPOLCAN, ONDREJ, immunologist, director; b. Plzen, Czech Republic, July 11, 1943; s. Ondrej Topolcan and Josefa Topolcanova; m. Jirina Stastna, Aug. 17, 2003; children: Marie Karlikova, Hana Vobrubova, Eva Scharf; m. Anna Skodova, Apr. 15, 1966 (div. Mar. 5, 1986). MD, Charles U. Prague, Med. Faculty, Plzen, 1967. Assoc. prof. internal medicine Charles U. Prague, Med. Faculty, 1967—96; head 2nd internal clinic U. Hosp., Plzen, 1996—2001, head immunoanalytical lab., 2001—, dep. dir. R & D, 2001—. Mem.: Immunoanalytic Soc. Czech Soc. Nuc. Medicine (head 2000—08), European Group Tumour Markers. Avocations: travel, music, theater. Office: Univ Hosp Pilsen Edvarda Benese 13 301 00 Plzen Czech Republic Office Fax: 42377402454. Personal E-mail: topolcan@seznam.cz. Business E-Mail: topolcan@fnplzen.cz.

TOPPING, KEITH JAMES, social sciences educator, psychologist, consultant; b. Manchester, Eng., Oct. 1, 1947; s. James Edward and Mabel Topping; children: Leigh, Ryan, Luke, John. BA, U. Sussex, Eng., 1969; MA in Child Devel., U. Nottingham, Eng., 1977; PhD in Ednl. Psychology, U. Sheffield, Eng., 1989. Chartered psychologist. Dir. Ctr. Peer Learning U. Dundee, Scotland, 1992—. Author: Educational Systems for Disruptive Adolescents, 1983, Parents as Educators: Training Parents to Teach Their Children, 1986, Thinking Reading Writing: A Practical Guide to Paired Learning with Peers, Parents and Volunteers, 2001, Inclusive Education, 2005. Office: Univ Dundee Sch Edn Nethergate DD1 4HN Dundee Scotland Office Phone: 44 (0)1382 383000.

TOPRAK, SELAMI KOÇAK, hematologist, educator; b. Ankara, Turkey, Sept. 13, 1970; MD, Ankara U., 1996. Fellow specialist dept. internal medicine Ankara U. Sch. Medicine, 1996—2001, resident specialist dept. hematology, 2002—05, Gaziantep State Hosp., 2006—08; vis. rschr. dépt. d'hématologie L'U. Paris VI, Hopital Hotel Dieu, 2001—02; asst. prof. dept. hematology Baskent U. Sch. Medicine, 2009—. Master: Assn. Academic Staff; mem.: European Hematology Assn., Ankara Med. Chamber, Turkish Soc. Hematology (grant). Avocations: sports, music, literature, politics. Office: Baskent University Hematology Dept Ankara 06490 Turkey E-mail: sktoprak@yahoo.com.

TOPTYGINA, ANNA PAVLOVNA, immunologist, researcher; b. Moscow, Dec. 1, 1959; d. Pavel Mezhnev and Inna Mezhneva; m. Serge Yu Toptygin, Nov. 14, 1987; children: Vasilii Toptygin, Ivan Toptygin. MD in Pediatrics, Russian State Med. U., 1984; PhD, Russian Inst. Med. Genetics, 1990; diploma in Immunology, Russian Inst. Immunology, 2000. Intern Morozoff Children's Hosp. No. 1, Moscow; jr. scientist Inst. Med. Genetics, Moscow, 1984—90; staff scientist Rsch. Ctr. Med. Genetics, Moscow, 1990—94, sr. scientist, 1994—2001; head group G.N. Gabrichevsky Inst. Epidemiology and Microbiology, Moscow, 2001—. Cons. Ctr. Med. Consultation Gabrichevsky Inst., Moscow, 1989—. Mem.: Russian Assn. Allergology and Clin. Immunology. Russian Orthodox. Avocations: travel, reading, growing of flowers. Office: Gabrichevsky Institute of Epidemiology a ul. Admirala Makarova 10 125212 Moscow Moskva Russia Home: Yartsevskaja 28-61 Moscow 121351 Russia Office Fax: +7 095 452 1830. Business E-Mail: toptyginaanna@rambler.ru.

TORAN-ALLERAND, C(LAUDE) DOMINIQUE, neuroscientist, neurologist, educator; arrived in USA, 1943, naturalized, 1948; d. Jean-Jacques Allerand and Georgette Elias; m. Edward Alexander Toran, Sept. 23, 1972. AB summa cum laude, Smith Coll., Northampton, Mass., 1955; MD, Albany Med. Coll., NY, 1959; ScD (hon.), Smith Coll., 1998. Diplomate Am. Bd. Neurology & Psychiatry, 1972. Internship Albany Med. Ctr. Hosp., 1959—60, asst. resident medicine, 1960—61; asst. resident neurology Columbia-Presbyterian Med. Ctr., New York Neurol. Inst., NYC, 1961—64; postdoctoral fellowship Columbia U., 1964—68, asst., 1968—69, instr., 1968—69; asst. prof. neurology NYU Med. Sch., NYC, 1969—73; rsch. assoc. Columbia U., 1973—74, asst. prof. neurology, 1974—81, assoc. prof. neurology, 1981—89, prof. neurology, pathology & cell biology, obstetrics & gynecology, 1989—. Contbr. articles to profl. jours. Recipient Otolaryngology prize, 1959, International Photomicroscopy award, Nikon, 1994. Mem.: Soc. Neurosci., Sigma Xi, Phi Beta Kappa. Achievements include research in the role and mechanisms of estrogen action in the developing brain; sexual differentiation of the brain; steroid growth factor interactions in the brain; estrogen signal transduction in the brain; novel estrogen hormones and receptor systems. Office: Columbia Univ 630 W 168th St New York NY 10032 Office Phone: 917-804-0783. Office Fax: 212-305-2134. Business E-Mail: cdt2@columbia.edu.

TORFFVIT, OLE JOHN, physician, researcher; b. Naestved, Denmark, Nov. 11, 1951; s. Jens Carl William and Annelise (Kristansen) Jensen; m. Annette Britta Petersen, Nov. 27, 1971 (div. Oct. 1991); children: Kasper, Nana; m. Eva Kerstin Maria Persson, Feb. 17, 1996; children: Felicia, Simon. MD, U. Copenhagen, 1977; diploma in internal and renal medicine, Sweden, 1985; diploma in Endocrinology & Family Medicine, U. Hosp., 1988; diploma in endocrinology, Sweden, 1998; PhD, U. Lund, Sweden, 1991. Resident Halmstad Hosp., Sweden, 1977—82, Univ. Hosp., Lund, Sweden, 1982—85, specialist, 1985—, tchr., 1988—91, specialist internal and renal medicine, 1985—, assoc. prof., 1995, chief staff, 2000—07; with primary care unit Höör, 2007. Author: Diabetic Nephropathy, 1991, and others; contbr. articles to profl. jours. Mem. European Assn. for the Study of Diabetes, European Diabetic Nephropathy Study Group (hon. sec. 2000-03), Am. Diabetes Assn. Business E-Mail: ole.torffvit@med.lu.se.

TORG, JOSEPH STEVEN, orthopaedic surgeon, educator; b. Phila., Oct. 25, 1934; m. Barbara Jane Groenendaal, May 23, 1959; children: Joseph Steven, Elisabeth, Jay Michael. AB, Haverford Coll., 1957; MD, Temple U., 1961. Diplomate: Am. Bd. Orthopaedic Surgeons. Intern San Francisco Gen. Hosp., 1961-62; resident in orthopaedic surgery Temple U. Hosp., Phila., 1964-68, Shriners Hosp. for Crippled Children, Phila., 1966-67; asst. surgeon Episcopal Hosp., Phila., 1968-70; surgeon Shriners Hosp. Crippled Children, 1970-78; mem.

staff Temple U. Hosp., 1970-78, instr. orthopaedic surgery, 1968-70, asst. prof., 1970-75, assoc. prof., 1976-78; dir. Center for Sports Medicine and Sci., 1974-78; chief orthopaedic sect. St. Christopher's Hosp. for Children, Phila., 1971-74, mem. staff, 1974—; active staff St. Joseph's Hosp., Phila., 1977—; prof. U. Pa., 1978—, active staff hosp., 1978—; dir. Sports Medicine Center, 1978—; prof. orthopaedic surgery Temple U., 1995. Mem. active staff Children's Hosp., Phila., 1978; med. cons. Pres.'s Coun. on Phys. Fitness and Sports Mem. editl. bd. Sports Medicine, Yearbook of Sports Medicine, Contemporary Orthopaedics, Jour. Clin. Sport Medicine, Am. Jour. Knee Surgery, Orthopaedic Rev.; contbr. articles to profl. jours. Served with M.C. US Army, 1962-64. Recipient Layman Honor award Pa. State Assn. Health, Phys. Edn. and Recreation, 1970, Grad. Honor award, 1975; Commendation of Merit Phila. Public HS Football Coaches, 1974 Fellow Am. Acad. Orthopaedic Surgeons, Am. Coll. Sports Medicine (trustee 1975-78), Phila. Coll. Physicians; mem. AMA, Eastern Orthopaedic Soc., Am. Orthopaedic Soc., Sports Medicine, Phila. County Med. Soc., Phila. Orthopaedic Soc., Pa. State Med. Soc., Pa. State Orthopaedic Soc. Home: 401 Conestoga Rd Wayne PA 19087-4811 Office: Temple U Hospital 6th Floor 3401 N Broad St Philadelphia PA 19140 Office Phone: 215-707-1321. Personal E-mail: torgmd@aol.com. Business E-Mail: joseph.torg@tuhs.temple.edu. *

TORIELLO, CONCHITA, microbiologist, researcher; arrived in Mexico, 1976; d. Lionel Saravia Toriello and Mimi Saravia Nájera; m. Alejo Vendrell Martínez; children: Gabriel Toriello Martínez, Adrián Toriello Martínez, Aldo Toriello Martínez. Degree, U. San Carlos de Guatemala, 1971; DSc, U. Paris XIII, Orsay, France, 1974. Assoc. prof. U. Nacional Autónoma México, Mexico City, 1976—92, prof., 1992—, chief lab. basic mycology faculty medicine dept. microbiology and parasitology, 1978—. Cons. Enterpise Productos Ecológicos, Guatemala City, 1994—95. Editor: Revista Mexicana de Micología; contbr. over 55 articles to profl. jours. Recipient Glaxo prize, 1993, award, Guatemalan Nat. Coun. Sci. and Tech., 2005, 2006; grantee, Mexican Nat. Coun. Sci. and Tech., 1981—2005, Office Support Academics, U. Nacional Autónoma México, 1994, 2004; scholar, French Govt., 1971—74. Fellow: Mexican Soc. Mycology (sec. coun. bd. 1981—82). Achievements include research in Mexican national research system; economic rewards for academic performance program; patents in field. Home: Grullas 124 Col Lomas de las Águilas Mexico City Delegac Álvaro Obregón 01730 Mexico Office: Univ Nacional Autónoma México Facultad de Medicina Mexico City 04510 Mexico Office Fax: +52 55 56232461. Business E-Mail: toriello@servidor.unam.mx.

TORII, KENGO, dentist, researcher; b. Imaichi, Tochigi, Japan, Oct. 5, 1945; s. Tomi Torii; 1 child, Daisuke. DDS, Nippon Dental U., Tokyo, 1969, postgrad., 1969—73. Postgrad. rschr. Nippon Dental U., Tokyo, 1969—73, lectr., 1975—95; asst. Nippon Dental U. Hosp., Tokyo, 1973—75; lectr. Shizuoka Dental Technician Sch., 1981—. Dir. dental ins. Shizuoka Prefecture Dental Assn., 2002—05. Mem.: Japan Prosthodontic Soc. Achievements include research in jaw position and temporomandibular joint sounds. Avocation: climbing. Home: 1-23-2 Ando Shizuoka 420-0882 Japan Office: Torii Dental Clinic 1-23-2 Ando Shizuoka 420-0882 Japan Home Fax: 054 248 2130. Personal E-mail: wbs89508@mail.wbs.ne.jp.

TORIUMI, DEAN MICHAEL, facial, plastic and reconstructive surgeon, educator; b. Chgo., Ill., 1958; Degree in biology, Knox Coll., 1980; grad., Norwestern U. Med. Ctr.; MD, Rush Med. Coll., 1981. Cert. otolaryngology 1988. Resident, gen. surgery U. Ill., Chgo., 1983—85; resident, otolaryngology Northwestern U. Med. Sch., Chgo., 1985—87; fellowship, facial plastic and reconstruction surgery Tulane Med. Sch., New Orleans, 1988, Va. Mason Med. Ctr., Seattle, 1989; prof., head Div. of Facial Plastic & Reconstructive Surgery U. Ill., Dept. Otolaryngology, Chgo. Co-author: Open Structure Rhinoplasty; contbr. articles various profl. papers, chapters to books. Mem.: Am. Acad. Facial Plastic and Reconstructive Surgery (pres.). Office: U Ill Chgo Coll Medicine Dept Otolaryngology 1855 W Taylor St Rm 242 Chicago IL 60612-7242 Office Phone: 312-996-8897. Office Fax: 312-996-1282.

TORKOS, ATTILA, surgeon, consultant; b. Kunszentmárton, Hungary, June 22, 1971; s. Béla Torkos and Gizella Herczeg; m. Ágnes Fekete, July 1, 2000; children: Adam Levente children: Dalma Regina. MD, Albert Szent-Györgyi Med. U., Szeged, Hungary, 1995, PhD, 2009. Cert. otorhinolaryngology specialist Imre Haynal U. Health Scis., Hungary, 1999, pediatric otorhinolaryngology specialist U. Szeged, Hungary, 2006. Ho. officer dept. otorhinolaryngology & head & neck surgery, U. Szeged, Hungary, 1995—96, cons., 1999—; ho. officer, dept. otorhinolaryngology Orosháza Hosp., Hungary, 1996—99; head otorhinolaryngology Dept. Pediat., U. Szeged, 2009; cons. dept. otorhinolaryngology Oasis Hosp. Al Ain, United Arab Emirates, 2009—. Contbr. articles to profl. jours., chapters to books. Grantee Rsch. scholarship, Hannover Med. U., 2004—06. Home: Bárka UTCA 15 Szeged 6721 Hungary Office Phone: 97137014274. Personal E-mail: a.torkos@freemail.hu, atorkos@oasishospital.org.

TORMOLLAN, GARY GORDON, health facility administrator, physical therapist; b. Plainfield, NJ, Feb. 23, 1954; s. Gordon William and Doris Evelyn (Palmer) T.; m. Stacey Lee Cole, Aug. 20, 1983; children: Brian, Kristin. BS in Health Edn., Trenton State Coll., 1976; cert. in phys. therapy, Hahnemann U., 1982; MEd, Trenton State Coll., 1987. Lic. phys. therapist, Maine, Pa. Athletic trainer Princeton H.S., NJ, 1976—81; phys. therapist Holy Redeemer Hosp., Huntington Valley, Pa., 1982—83, Phys. Therapy of Princeton, 1984—86; coord. sports medicine Omni-Fit, Mt. Laurel, NJ, 1986—87; dir. rehab. svcs. Med. Coll. of Pa., Phila., 1987—90; dir. phys. therapy Mid-Maine Med. Ctr., Waterville, 1990—92; pres., CEO Maine Phys. Therapy, Waterville, 1993—2009. Cons. Burnt Mill Med. Ctr., Cherry Hill, N.J., 1983; mem. clin. faculty Temple U., Phila., 1989-90; cons., mem. adv. bd. phys. therapy asst. program Kennebec Valley Tech. Coll., Fairfield, Maine, 1990-94. Deacon Ewing (N.J.) Presbyn. Ch., 1989; coach Waterville Little League, Waterville Youth Soccer Assn. Congregationalist. Avocation: golf. Home: 42 Messalonskee Ave Waterville ME 04901-5352 Office: Inland Hosp Rehab Works Lakewood Rd Madison ME 04950 Office Phone: 207-474-8847. Personal E-mail: tormollan@roadrunner.com.

TÖRNQUIST, ALBA LUCIA, optometrist; b. Cali, Colombia, Mar. 5, 1966; MSc, Pa. Coll. Optometry, 1997; PhD, Karolinska Inst., 2010. Optometrist U. La Salle. Optometrist, U. La Salle, 1990; optometrist Pvt. Clinic, Colombia, 1991—2000; optometrist, rsch. scientist Karolinska Inst., 2010—. Cons. Johnson & Johnson, 1993—95; translator, internat. program Pa. Coll. Optometrist, 1995; adj. tchr. Karolinska Inst., 2000, pres., bd. internat. program, 2003—09, linnaeus-palme program coord., 2005. Grant, Vision Rsch. Found., Mary Béves Found., Samariten Found., Karolinska Inst. Fund, Bernadotte Lab. Mem.: Am. Acad. Optometry, US Nat. Honor Soc. Avocations: reading, music, scrapbooks. Home: Sjökarbyvägen 23 Åkersberga Stockholm 18434 Sweden Home Fax: 468 672 3846. Personal E-mail: alba.lucia@tornquist.se.

TÖRÖK, TAMÁS LÁSZLÓ, pharmacologist, researcher; b. Budapest, Pest, Hungary, Jan. 23, 1944; s. Tibor Török and Eulália Fóris; m. Melinda Kontsek, Aug. 10, 1968; children: Melinda, Bettina. Diploma in Pharm., Semmelweis Med. U., Budapest, 1968, D, 1972; PhD, Hungarian Acad. Scis., Budapest, 1981, ScD, 1991. Asst. prof. dept. pharmacodynamics Semmelweis U., Budapest, 1980—81, adj. dept. pharmacodynamics, 1981—89, assoc. prof. dept. pharmacodynamics, 1989—94, prof. dept. pharmacodynamics, 1994—98, prof., chmn. dept. pharmacodynamics, 1998—2008. Brit. Coun. student dept. pharmacology Oxford (Eng.) U., 1978-79. Contbr. articles to sci. publs. 2d lt. Hungarian Med. Corps, 1968-69. Avocation: small railways. Office: Semmelweis U Nagyvárad tér 4 Budapest 1089 Hungary

TORQUATO, JAMILI ANBAR, physical therapist, educator; b. Santa Fé do Sul, Sao Paulo, Brazil, Mar. 25, 1968; PhD, U. São Paulo, 2005. Asst. prof. physiotherapy U. Cruzeiro do Sul, 2000, educator health scis., 2000—, prof. master's program health scis., 2005. Rsch. group leader CNPQ, 2008; dirs. FIBRA-Physiotherapy Brazil-EPP, 2009. Avocations: reading, walking. Office: Consolação 3563 São Paulo 01416001 Brazil E-mail: jamilianbar@yahoo.com.

TORRENCE, PAUL F., retired chemistry professor; b. New Brighton, Pa., Apr. 22, 1943; PhD, SUNY, Buffalo, 1969. Rsch. chemist, sect. chief NIH, 1969—99; prof., chair, chemistry Northern Ariz. U., 1999—2007. Instr. Found. Advanced Edn. in Scis., 1988—2009, academic dir., 1998—99; co-founding scientists, cons. Gemini Technologies & Ridgeway Biosys., 1995—2001; investigator Ariz. Cancer Ctr., 2003—07; prof., medicine U. Ariz., 2005—07. Recipient Acheivement award, Wash. Acad. Scis. Avocations: writing, hiking. Home: 16282 Watergap Rd Williams OR 97544 Business E-Mail: pft2@nau.edu.

TORRES, ANTONI, physician; b. Barcelona, June 9, 1954; D, U. Barcelona, 1977. Head Intensive Care Unit, Hosp. Clinic Barcelona, 2010; prof. U. Barcelona. Assoc. editor European Respiratory Jour. & Frontiers Pharmacotherapy Respiratory Diseases; mem. European Respiratory Jour., Jour. Respiratory and Critical Care Medicine, Thorax, Chest, Critical Care Medicine, Intensive Care Medicine, Clin. Pulmonary Medicine, Jour. Bronchology & Interventional Pulmonology, Archivos de Bronconeumologia, World Jour. Critical Infectious Diseases, World Jour. Respirology, Seminars in Respiratory and Critical Care Medicine. Contbr. articles to profl. jours. Recipient award, Found. Healthcare Scis., 2001, Found. award, Biomed. & Clin. rsch., 2007. Office: Villarroel 170 Catalunya 08036 Spain Business E-Mail: atorres@ub.edu.

TORRES, CARLOS MADAIL MANITTO, physician, consultant; b. Lisbon, Portugal, May 15, 1954; M.D., Faculty Med. Scis. Lisbon, 1981; M in Gerontology, U. Salamanca, Spain, 2002. Cert. psychotherapist Soc. Port. Psicoterapias Breves. Asst. grad. cons. Servico Nacional de Sade, Lisbon, 1995—. Mem.: NY Acad. Scis., Am. Counseling Assn., World Med. Assn. Home: Largo da Rep da Turquia n¦5-10¦ D 1750-250 Lisbon Portugal Personal E-mail: cmtorres@netcabo.pt.

TORRES, CATHERINE DIANE, public health service officer, state official; b. Albuquerque, N.Mex., 1962; BS, U. N.Mex., Albuquerque, 1985, MD, 1990. Pediatrician Rio Grande Med. Group, Las Cruces, N.Mex.; med. dir. First Step Pediat., Las Cruces, N.Mex., 2005—09; commr. US Mex. Border Health Commn., 1999—2006, Sonora Health Commn., N.Mex.; chairperson adv. com. N.Mex. Health Coun., 2008—10; chairperson med. adv. com. Doña Ana County Detention Ctr., 2008; sec. N.Mex. Dept. Health, Santa Fe, 2011—. Office: New Mexico Department of Health Office of the Secretary 1190 Saint Francis Dr N4100 Santa Fe NM 87502-6110 Office Phone: 505-827-2613. Office Fax: 505-827-2530. *

TORRES, CLARIVET, pediatrician, director; b. Colombia, Oct. 18, 1957; MD, Colegio Mayor de Nuestra Señora del Rosario, 1981; degree in Pediatric Gastroenterology Hepatology and Nutrition, Creighton Nebr. U. Health Found., 2001. Pediatric attending Police Clinic. Bogotá, Colombia, 1991—93, CAFAM Clinic, diatric Residency U. Javeriana, Bogotá, Colombia, 1991—96; pediatric gastroenterology, hepatology fellow Creighton Nebr. U. Health Found., 1998—2001; med. dir., intestinal rehab. program U. Nebr. Med. Ctr., 2002—07; dir., intestinal rehab. program, liver and small bowel transplant Children's Nat. Med. Ctr., George Wash. U., Georgetown U., 2007—. Named one of Best Drs. in America, 2011, Best Pediatric Plenum of Yr., Hosp. Infantil Lorencita Villegas de Santos. Mem.: Am. Soc. Transplantation, North Am. Soc. Pediatric Gastroenterology and Nutrition, Am. Gastroenterology Assn., Internat. Pediatric Transplantation Assn., Intestinal Transplant Assn. Avocations: swimming, reading. Office: 111 Michigan AV NW Washington DC 20010-2970 Office Fax: 202-476-4156. Business E-Mail: ctorres@cnmc.org.

TORRES, ESTHER A., gastroenterologist; b. San Juan, Feb. 26, 1949; MD, U. PR, 1972. Prof. medicine U. PR Sch. Medicine, 1976—, dir. GI rsch. unit, 1992, chair medicine, 1996—2011, dir. ctr. inflammatory bowel diseases. Assoc. med. dir. LifeLink of PR, 2001—; bd. dirs. LifeLink Found., 2006—. Recipient Disting. Faculty award, UPR Sch. Medicine Alumni Soc. Master: ACP, Am. Coll. Gastroenterology; fellow: Am. Gastroent. Assn.; mem.: Am. Assn. Study Liver Diseases, Alpha Omega Alpha. Avocations: tennis, reading. Home: 690 Cesar Gonzalez Apt 508 San Juan PR 00918-3903 Home Fax: 787-758-4613. Personal E-mail: etorres@pol.net.

TORRES, LUDGERIO DIOSOMITO, health facility administrator, thoracic surgeon, cardiologist; b. Mar. 26, 1940; s. Petronilo Lantin and Gertrudis Diosomito Torres; m. Veronica Karganilla Molina, Dec. 22; children: Anna Leticia, Lourdes Angela, Veronica Linda, Jose Rionilo, Jose Ludgerio, Jose Paulo Antonio. AA in pre-Medicine, U. Santo Tomas, Manila, 1957, MD magna cum laude, 1962. Diplomate thoracic and cardiovasc. surgery Philippine Bd. Thoracic and Cardiovasc. Surgery. Gen. surgery resident U. Santo Tomas Hosp., Manila, 1962—67; thoracic and cardiovasc. surgery resident Harvard Med. Sch., Boston, 1967—70, Peter Bent Brigham Hosp., Boston, 1967—70; chmn. dept. cardiovasc. surgery Philippine Heart Ctr., Quezon City, Philippines, 1975—86, St. Luke's Med. Ctr., Quezon City, Philippines, 1986—90; chief pediat. cardiac surgery Philippine Heart Ctr., Quezon City, Philippines, 1980—, med. dir., 1997—. Tng. fellow pediat. cardiac surgery U. Ala., Birmingham, 1978—79; exec. v.p. Heart Found. of Philippines, 1997—; chmn. Philippine Bd. Thoracic and Cardiovasc. Surgery, 2002—. Co-author: Surgery of Congenital Heart Disease, 1980; contbr. articles to profl. jours. Named one of Ten Outstanding Young Men, Philippine Jaycees, 1973; fellow, Harvard Med. Sch. and Peter Bent Brigham Hosp., 1967—70. Fellow: ACS, Am. Coll. Cardiology, Philippine Assn. Thoracic and Cardiovasc. Surgery, Philippine Coll. Cardiology, Am. Coll. Chest Physicians, Philippine Coll. Surgeons; mem.: Asian Thoracic and Cardiovasc. Surgeons of Asia (coun. mem. 1980), Rotary Club Manila (sr. active mem.). Roman Catholic. Avocations: piano, basketball, gardening, golf, bowling. Home: 106 Greenmeadows Ave Quezon City Philippines Office: Philippine Heart Ctr East Ave Quezon City Philippines Office Phone: 632-922-0551.

TORRES CORZO, JAIME G., neurosurgeon, consultant; b. San Luis Potosi, Mexico, Feb. 21, 1957; s. Teofilo Torres Diaz De Leon and M. (Del Socorro) Corzo; m. M. Otañez Del Socorro; children: Jessica Torres Felix, Jaime Torres Felix, Juan Carlos Torres Felix, Jose Antonio Torres Felix. Med. degree, U. Autonoma San Luis Potosi, 1979. Dir. neuroscience dept. Hosp. Nuestra Señora De La Salud, San Luis Potosi, 1993—2005, chief neurosurgery dept., 1993—; staff chief neurosurgery dept. Hosp. Ctrl., San Luis Potosi, 1995—. Tchr. U. Autonoma San Luis Potosi, 1990—. Mem.: WFNS (assoc.), Am. Assn. Neurol. Surgery (assoc.). Office: Hosp Nuestra Se±ora De La Salud Madreperla # 345 Fracc Industrias 78090 San Luis Potosi Mexico Office Fax: 52 444 813 7069. Personal E-mail: torrescjaime@gmail.com.mx. E-mail: torrescjaime@yahoo.com.mx.

TORRESE, DANTE MICHAEL, prosthodontist, educator; b. Yonkers, NY, Feb. 12, 1949; s. Dante Angelo and Matilda (Dal Lago) T.; m. Camille Patricia DiPaola, Aug. 7, 1982. BS in Biology, Manhattan Coll., 1971; DDS, Columbia U., 1975; prosthodontic cert., NYU, 1983. Resident in dentistry Presbyn. Hosp., NYC, 1975-76; clin. instr. dentistry Columbia U., NYC, 1976-78, asst. clin. prof. dentistry, 1978—; pvt. practice dentistry Yonkers, N.Y., 1976—. Attending dentist Presbyn. Hosp., N.Y.C., 1976-86; lectr. in field. Recipient Am. Acad. Oral Pathology Grad. award 1975, Densply Corp. award for removable prosthodontics, 1975, Psi Omega Scholastic Achievement award, 1975. Fellow Am. Coll. of Dentists, Royal Soc. Health; mem. NRA (life), Yonkers Dental Soc., 9th Dist. State Dental Soc., Invested Baker St. Irregular, Sherlock Holmes Wireless Soc., Single Action Shooting Soc. (life), Yonkers Amateur Radio Club, Westchester Astronomy Club, Exch. Club (sec. 1979—), Three Garridebs of Westchester, Priory Scholars of N.Y.C. Club, Montague Street Lodgers of Bklyn. Club, Omicron Kappa Upsilon. Office: 984 N Broadway Ste 503 Yonkers NY 10701-1308 Office Phone: 914-965-4004.

TORRES FILHO, IVO, medical educator; b. Belem, Pará, Brazil, Apr. 17, 1958; s. Ivo and Vilma Torres; m. Luciana Neves, Aug. 27, 2000;; children: Patricia Torres, Rodrigo Torres, Natasha Torres. MD, State U. of Rio de Janeiro, 1981; MSc, Fed. U. of Rio de Janeiro, 1984, PhD, 1988; postgrad., U. Calif.-San Diego, La Jolla, 1994. Lic. physician State U. of Rio de Janeiro, 1981. Instr. State U. Rio de Janeiro, 1982—84, asst. prof., 1984—88, assoc. prof., 1988—, Va. Commonwealth U., Richmond, 2003—11. Dir. Microcirculatory Lab, Va. Commonwealth U., Richmond, Va., 2003—11. Contbr. over 100 articles and abstracts to profl. jours. Recipient Innovative Instrumentation award, Microcirculatory Soc., Inc, Travel award, Radiation Rsch. Soc., 1993; fellow Postdoctoral fellow, The PEW Charitable Trusts, Fogarty Internat. Ctr. Mem.: European Soc. Microcirc (assoc.), Am. Physiol. Soc. (assoc.), Microcirculatory Soc., Inc (assoc.). Office: US Army Inst Surgical Rsch 3698 Chambers Pass Fort Sam Houston TX 78234 Personal E-mail: ivoptf@msn.com.

TORRES GÓMEZ, FRANCISCO JAVIER, pathologist; b. Sevilla, Spain, Oct. 27, 1975; Degree, San Francisco de Paula. Sevilla, 1993; degree in Medicine, U. Sevilla, 1999; student in Pathology, Vergen Macarena Hosp., 2000—04. Pathologist La Inmaculada Hosp., 2004, Gen. Hosp. Alcázar de San Juan. Ciudad Real. Spain, 2004—05, Gen. Hosp. Jerez de la Frontera, Cádiz. Spain, 2005—06, Punta de Europa Hosp. Algeciras, Cádiz, Spain, 2006, High Resolution Hosp. Utrera, Sevilla, 2006—. Mem.: Cytology Spanish Soc., Pathology Spanish Soc. Avocations: writing, painting, reading. Home: Matahacas 18 A 1B Sevilla 41003 Spain Personal E-mail: javiertorresgomez@yahoo.es.

TORREY, E. FULLER (EDWIN FULLER TORREY), psychiatrist, medical researcher; b. Utica, NY, Sept. 6, 1937; married; 2 children. BA magna cum laude, Princeton U.; MD, McGill U.; MA in Anthropology, Stanford U. Physician Peace Corps, Ethiopia; gen. medicine physician O.E.O. Health Ctr., Bronx, NY, Indian Health Svc., Alaska; spl. asst. to dir. Nat. Inst. Mental Health, 1970—75; clin. staff St. Elizabeth's Hosp., 1976—85, study dir., 1988—92; founder Treatment Advocacy Ctr., Arlington, Va.; assoc. dir. lab rsch. Stanley Med. Rsch. Inst., Chevy Chase, Md., co-dir. Brain Rsch. Lab., exec. dir. Prof. psychiatry Uniformed Svcs. U. of the Health Scis.; adj. prof. George Mason U. Sch. Law. Author: Out of the Shadows: Confronting America's Mental Illness Crisis, 1996, Freudian Fraud: The Malignant Effect of Freud's Theory on American Thought and Culture, 1992, Surviving Schizophrenia: A Manual for Families, Consumers and Providers, 2001, 2006, The Invisible Plague: The Rise of Mental Illness from 1750 to the Present, 2002, Surviving Manic-Depressive Illness, 2002, Beasts of the Earth: Animals, Humans, and Disease, 2005; contbr. articles to profl. jours. Recipient Commendation Medals, US Pub. Health Svc., Spl. Families Award, NAMI, 1984, Nat. Caring Award, 1991, rsch. award, Internat. Congress of Schizophrenia, 1999, humanitarian award, NARSAD. Office: Stanley Medical Research Institute 8401 Connecticut Ave, Ste 200 Chevy Chase MD 20815 also: Treatment Advocacy Center 200 N Glebe Rd, Ste 730 Arlington VA 22203 Office Phone: 301-571-2078. Office Fax: 301-571-0775. *

TORTAMANO, ISABEL PEIXOTO, dentist, educator; b. Araraquara, São Paulo, Brazil, Jan. 5, 1965; Degree in Dentistry, U São Paulo, 2007. Tenured prof. U. Sao Paulo, Sch. Dentistry, 1987—. Office: Ave Prof Lineu Prestes 2227 Cidade Universitária São Paulo 05508900 Brazil Office Fax: 30917813. Business E-Mail: iptortam@usp.br.

TORTI, FRANK MICHAEL, oncologist, medical educator, former federal agency administrator; b. 1947; BA, MA, Johns Hopkins U., Balt., 1969; MPH, Harvard U., 1973, MD, 1974. Diplomate American Bd. Internal Medicine, cert. in med. oncology. Intern, resident Beth Israel Hosp., Boston; fellow med. oncology Stanford U., Calif., asst. prof. medicine, 1979-84, clin. assoc. prof. medicine, 1984-86, assoc. prof. medicine, 1986-93; Charles L. Spurr prof. medicine Wake Forest U. Sch. Medicine, Winston-Salem, NC, 1993—2008, dir. Comprehensive Cancer Ctr., chmn. dept. cancer biology, 1993—2008, 2009—, v.p. strategic programs, 2009—; prin. dep. commr., chief scientist FDA, Rockville, Md., 2008—09, acting commr., 2009. Chmn. Gov.'s Commn. Cancer Coordination & Control, NC, 1993—2003. Recipient MERIT award, NIH. Fellow: ACP; mem.: Soc. Biol. Therapy, Internat. Soc. Interferon Rsch., American Soc. Cell Biology, American Soc. Clin. Oncology, American Assn. Cancer Rsch. Office: Wake Forest U Sch Medicine Medical Center Blvd Winston Salem NC 27157-1082 *

TORTOLANI, ANTHONY JOHN, surgeon, educator; b. Eastchester, NY, Oct. 15, 1943; s. Salvatore Paul and Yolanda (Vecciarelli) Tortolani; m. Beth Callahan, Dec. 15, 1967 (dec. Oct. 1993); children: Julia Sue, Paul Justin; m. Katherine Gormley, Sept. 25, 1999. BS, Fordham U., 1965; MD, George Washington Sch. Medicine, 1969. Diplomate Am. Bd. Surgery, Am. Bd. Thoracic Surgery. Chief divsn. cardiovascular & thoracic surgery North Shore U. Hosp., Manhasset, NY, 1978-90, chmn. dept. surgery, 1988-96, chmn. med. bd., 1994-96, chmn. dept. surgery Glen Cove, NY, 1990-96; John D. Mountain chair surgery North Shore U. Hosp.- Cornell U. Med. Coll., Manhasset, 1989-96, program dir. surg. residency program, 1992-96; prof. surgery Cornell U. Med. Coll., NYC, 1993 97, prof. cardiothoracic surgery, 1997-99, mem. staff N.Y. Hosp., NYC, 1997-99, dir., prof. cardiothoracic surgery Jack D. Weiler Hosp./Montefiore Med. Ctr. Albert Einstein Coll. of Medicine, NYC, 1999-2001; prof. clin. cardiothoracic surgery Weill Med. Coll. Cornell U., 2001—. Vice-chmn. NY Presbyn. Cornell Cardiothoracic Surgery Network; chmn. dept. cardiothoracic surgery, NY Meth. Hosp., 2004-, chmn. dept. surgery, 2007-. Active Columbus Citizens Found., N.Y.C. Maj. USAF, 1974-76. Roman Catholic. Avocation: breeding horses. Office: NY Presbyn Hosp 525 E 68th St Rm M-404 New York NY 10021 Business E-Mail: astoltol@meo.cornell.com.

TORTOLERO, SUSAN, medical association administrator, educator; b. Houston, May 18, 1963; MS, U. Tex. Sch. Pub. Health, 1989, PhD in Epidemiology, 1994. Dir., ctr. health promotion, prevention rsch. U. Tex. Houston Sch. Pub. Health, 2001—11, asst. prof., health promotion, behavioral sci. and epidemiology, 2002—07, assoc. prof., health promotion, behavioral sci. and epidemiology, 2007—11, Allan King prof. pub. health, 2010—11. Chief editor Jour. Primary Prevention, 2009—11; editl. bd. Jour. Applied Rsch. Children. Recipient Hannah G. Solomon award, Nat. Coun. Jewish Women, 2010, Pres's award, U. Tex. Health Sci. Ctr. Houston, 2000. Mem.: Tex. Campaign to Prevent Teen Pregnancy (vice chair). Avocation: bicycling. Office: 7000 Fannin Ste 2080 Houston TX 77030 Office Fax: 713-500-0369. Business E-Mail: susan.tortolero@uth.tmc.edu.

TORTORELLA, GAETANO, neurologist, educator; b. Messina, Italy, Oct. 11, 1948; MD, U. Messina, 1973; PhD, U. Pisa, 1976. Assoc. prof. U. Messina, 1995—. Head physician Azienda Ospedaliera U., Messina, 2009. Mem.: Italian League Against Epilepsy, Italian Soc. Child and Adolescent Neuropsychiatry. Office: Via Consolare Valeria Messina Sicily I-98123 Italy Office Fax: 390902930414. Business E-Mail: gaetano.tortorella@unime.it.

TORU, EGUCHI, microbiologist, researcher; b. Neyagawa, Osaka, Japan, Sept. 16, 1958; s. Haruo and Teruko E.; m. Emi Kameyama; children: Yui, Fumi. B in environ. health, Azabu U., 1982, PhD, 2007. Rschr. SLC Inc., Hamamastu, Japan, 1982; rschr. SUNSTAR Inc., Osaka, 1982-93, sr. rschr., 1993—; head Sunslar Shizuoka Rsch. Lab., 2007. Guest rschr. Osaka U. Faculty of Tech., 1985-87. Contbr. articles to profl. jours. Patentee in field. Avocation: fishing. E-mail. Office: SUNSTAR Inc 3 1 Asahi machi Tatatsuki 569 1195 Japan E-mail: tooru.eguchi@jp.sunstar.com.

TÕRU, INNAR, psychiatrist; b. Kuressaare, Estonia, Mar. 24, 1961; MD, Tartu U., 1995, MSc, 2007. Psychiatrist Psychiat. Clinic Tartu U. Hosp., 2001—. Rsch. fellow, sr. asst. Dept. Psychiatry,Tartu U., 2005. Mem.: World Fedn. Socs. Biol. Psychiatry (Travel grant). Achievements include research in mechanisms underlying panic attacks and panic disorder, CCK-4 induced experimental panic. Office: Raja 31 Tartu Tartumaa 50417 Estonia Office Fax: 3727318801. Business E-Mail: innar.toru@kliinikum.ee.

TORU, NAKAMURA, thoracic surgeon; b. Hamamatsu, Japan, June 26, 1969; MD, PhD, 1994. Surgeon, gen. thoracic surgery divsn. Seirei Hamamatsu Gen. Hosp., 2003—. Office: 2-12-12 Sumiyoshi Hamamatsu Shizuoka 430-8558 Japan Business E-Mail: tonakamu@nifty.ne.jp.

TORU, YAMADA, urologist; b. Japan, Apr. 26, 1969; MD, Gifu U. Sch. Medicine, 1995, PhD, 2010. Attending physician Advanced Critical Care Ctr., Gifu U. Hosp., 2005, clin. asst. prof., 2006; clin. asst. prof., dept. emergency & disaster medicine Grad. Sch. Medicine, Gifu U., Gifu, 2005—06; divsn. chief urology Chunou Kousei Hosp., Gifu, Japan, 2006—07, Kakegawa Mcpl. Gen. Hosp., Shizuoka, Japan, 2007—. Grant, Japan Soc. Promotion Sci., Japan. Fellow: Japan Soc. Clin. Oncology, Japanese Soc. Dialysis Therapy, Japanese Urol. Assn.; mem.: Japan Soc. Clin. Oncology, Japanese Urol. Assn. Avocation: football. Office: 1-1-1 Sugiya-minami Kakegawa Shizuoka 436-8502 Japan Office Fax: 81-537-24-2539. Business E-Mail: toruyama@aqua.ocn.ne.jp.

TOSATTO, SILVIO CARLO ERMANNO, bioinformatics educator, researcher; b. Bressanone, Bolzano, Italy, Dec. 21, 1974; s. Vittorio Tosatto and Vittorina Zung. M in Computer Sci., U. Mannheim, Germany, 1998, PhD, 2002. Postdoctoral rschr. U. Padova, Italy, 2002—03, asst. prof., 2003—07, assoc. prof., 2007—. Office: Univ Padova Viale G Colombo 3 35121 Padua Italy Business E-Mail: silvio.tosatto@unipd.it.

TOSCANO, JAMES VINCENT, medical foundation president; b. Passaic, NJ, Aug. 8, 1937; s. William V. and Mary A. (DeNigris) T.; m. Sharon Lee Bowers; children: Shawn Truelson, Lauren Bjorklund, David Brendan Toscano, Dania Toscano Miwa. AB summa cum laude, Rutgers Coll., 1959; MA, Yale U., 1960. Lectr. Wharton Sch., U. Pa., 1961-64; chief opinion analyst Pa. Opinion Poll, 1962-64; mng. dir. World Press Inst., St. Paul, 1964-68, exec. dir., 1968-72; dir. devel. Macalester Coll., St. Paul, 1972-74; v.p. resource devel. and pub. affairs Mpls. Soc. Fine Arts, 1974-79; pres. Minn. Mus. Art, 1979-81; exec. v.p. Park Nicollet Inst., 1981—2006; corp. sec. Park Nicollet Clinic, 1983-86; sr. v.p. Am. Med. Ctrs., Inc., 1985-87; pres. Mpls. Heart Inst. Found., 2006—; prin. Toscano Advisors, LLC. Adj. prof. sch. of mgmt. U. St. Thomas, 1989-01; co-chair prin. practices nonprofit excellence com. MCN, 1994-98, 2004—05; adj. prof. Sch. Bus., Hamline U., 2003. Author: The Chief Elected Official in the Penjerdel Region, 1964; co-author, co-editor: The Integration of Political Communities, 1964. Bd. dirs., exec. com., sec.-treas. World Press Ins., 1972-2007; bd. dirs., chmn. Southside Newspaper Mpls., 1975-79; chmn. com. to improve student behavior St. Paul Pub. Schs., 1977-79; bd. dirs. Planned Parenthood St. Paul, 1965-72, Mpls. Action Agy., 1976-79; emeritus dir. Help Enable Alcoholics Receive Treatment; mem. St. Paul Heritage Preservation Commn., 1979-82, vice chmn., 1981; mem. Citizens Adv. Com. on Cable Comm.; bd. dirs. Minn. Newspaper Found., 1987-92, Minn. Coun. Nonprofits, 1989-95, 1997-2003; bd. mem. Vocal Essence, 1993-96, alt. Minn. Healthcare Commn., 1993-95, mem. Minn. Healthcare Commn., 1995-97, chair task force med edn. rsch. costs, 1994-96. com. med. rsch. edn. costs, 1996-2003; chair, 1996-99; liason health tech adv. com., 1993-97; pres. 2000-03, bd. dirs. Summit Ave Residential Preservation Assn., 2000-06, bd. dirs. Citizens League, 1980, African-Am. Culture Ctr., 1979-82, Am. Composers Forum, 1981-85, St. Paul Chamber Orch., 1976-80, 83-89, United Theol. Sem., 1985-88; dir. emeritus Minn. Citizens for the Arts; mem. exec. com., chmn. Life Scis. Alley Assn., 1986-96, bd. dirs., 1986-96, task force on tech. assessment Life Scis. Alley, 1992-93; mem. health affairs adv. com. Acad. Health Ctr. U. Minn., 1988-95; bd. dirs. Mother Cabrini House, 1985-92, Minn. Civil Justice Coalition, 1987-91, also chmn.; chmn. Gov.'s Task Force on Health Care Promotion, 1985-86, mem. Gov.'s Com. Promotion Health Care Resources, 1986-87; chmn. bd. Minn. Fin. Counseling Svcs., Inc., 1990-93; mem. task force cost effectiveness Life Scis. Alley, 1994-95; bd. dirs. Meml. Blood Bank, 1995-2001, mem. exec. com., 1996-2001; bd. dirs. Bakken Mus., 1997-2003, Stevens Sq. Cmty. Orgn., 1997-99; bd. dirs. Rainbow Rsch., Inc., 2002—10, chmn. bd., 2004-07; bd. dirs. Friends of the St. Paul Libr., 2004-07, 11-; bd. dirs., treas. Pub. Arts St. Paul, 2004 2007, Minn. Charities Rev. Coun., 2004-009, chmn., 2007-08, mem. West Summit Neighborhood Adv. Coun., 2004-09; co-chair, 2004-07; mem., chair Alley Found., 2006-09, bd. mem. 515 Edn. Found., 2009. Woodrow Wilson Nat. fellow, 1960. Mem. Skylight Club, Informal Club, Korner Club, Fox and Hounds Club. Congregationalist. Address: 1982 Summit Ave Saint Paul MN 55105-1460 Office: Mpls Heart Inst Found 920 E 28th St Ste 100 Minneapolis MN 55407 Home Phone: 651-699-1765; Office Phone: 612-863-3978. Personal E-mail: jvt2@comcast.net. Business E-Mail: jtoscano@mhif.org.

TOSCANO, NICHOLAS, periodontist; b. NY, Jan. 1, 1969; DDS, Columbia U., 1998; MS in Periodontics, Naval Postgrad. Dental Sch., 2006. Dental officer USN, 1996—2009; pvt. practice, 2009. Co-editor-in-chief Jour. Implant and Advanced Clin. Dentistry, 2008—. Decorated Navy and Marine Corp Commendation medal USN, Naval Achievement medal. Office: 45 W 54th St Ste 1E New York NY 10019 E-mail: navygumdoc@aol.com.

TOSHIHIKO, KISHIMOTO, biology professor; b. Japan, Nov. 15, 1964; M, Osaka U., 1989; PhD, Chiba U., 1997. Rschr. Sumitomo Electric Industries Ltd., 1989—2001; asst. prof. Toho U., 2001—06, assoc. prof., 2006—. Tech. advisor LinkGenomics Inc., 2006—11. Mem.: Soc. Biotech. (Japan), Japan Soc. Cell Biology, Soc. Evolutionary Study (Japan), Japanese Biochem. Soc., Biophys. Soc. Japan. Avocations: reading, sports. Office: 2-2-1 Miyama Funabashi Chiba 274-8510 Japan Office Fax: 81-47-472-1836.

TOSHINORI, OKA, research scientist; b. Tara-cho, Saga, Japan, Oct. 27, 1959; B, Kyushu U., 1982; PhD, U. Tokushima, 1995. Dir. Postmarketing Rsch. Lab. Taiho Pharm. Co., Ltd., 2004—06, dir. Personalized Medicine Rsch. Lab., 2006—10, chief dept. human resources, 2010—. Guest adj. prof. Faculty Pharm. Scis., U. Tokushima, 2004—09, guest prof., 2010—11, Faculty Agr., Kagoshima U., 2006—10. Home: 14-17 Seicho Aizumi-cho Tokushima 771-1272 Japan Business E-Mail: t-oka@taiho.co.jp.

TOSHIO, MUNESUE, physician, educator; b. Tokyo, Dec. 6, 1954; MD, PhD, Kanazawa U., 1980. Prof. Kanazawa U., 1997. Mem.: Japan Brain Sci. Soc., Japanese Soc. Child and Adolescent Psychiatry, Japanese Soc. Biol. Psychiatry, Japanese Soc. Psychiatry and Neurology. Avocation: reading. Office: 13-1 Takara-machi Kanazawa Ishikawa 920-8640 Japan Office Fax: 81 76 234 4213. Business E-Mail: munesue@med.kanazawa-u.ac.jp.

TOSHITAKA, MATSUI, biochemist, educator; b. Osaka, Jan. 19, 1971; D, Grad. U. Adv. Studies, 1998. Sr. asst. prof. Tohoku U., 2006—. Office: Katahira 2-1-1 Sendai Miyagi 980-8577 Japan Business E-Mail: matsui@tagen.tohoku.ac.jp.

TOSKES, PHILLIP PAUL, gastroenterologist, educator, researcher; b. Balt., Jan. 4, 1940; s. John F. and Mary R. (Vonelli) T.; m. Patricia A. Sponsel, June 3, 1961; children: Tammy Lynn Price, Tracey Lynn, Steven D. BA, Johns Hopkins U., 1961; MD, U. Md., 1965. Diplomate Am. Bd. Internal Medicine (bd. dirs.), Am. Bd. Gastroenterology. Intern, resident U. Md. Hosp., Balt., 1965-68; fellow in gastroenterology Hosp. U. Pa., Phila., 1968-70; asst. prof. medicine U. Fla., Gainesville, 1973-75, assoc. prof. medicine, 1975-78, prof. medicine, 1978—, dir. divsn. gastro, hepatology, 1978-97, prof., chmn. dept. medicine, 1997—2002. Chief gastro sect. Gainesville VA Med. Ctr., 1973-92; chmn. Nat. Digestive Disease Adv. Bd., Washington, 1992-94. Author chpts. to books. Maj. U.S. Army, 1970-73. Recipient Disting. Achievement award Can. Gastroenterol. Assn., 1982. Fellow ACP (Meade Johnson scholar 1966-68); mem. Am. Soc. Clin. Investigation, Am. Fedn. Clin. Rsch., Am. Gastroenterol. Assn. (pres. 1997-98). Avocations: travel, swimming, boating. Office: U Fla Box 100214 1600 SW Archer Rd Gainesville FL 32610-3001 Home: 202 NW 114th Way Gainesville FL 32607-1122 Office Phone: 352-392-2877. Business E-Mail: toskepp@medicine.ufl.edu.

TOSUN, ZEYNEP, anesthesiologist, educator; b. Kayseri, Nov. 4, 1967; MD, Erciyes U. Med. Faculty, 1991; specialist, Hacettepe U. Med. Faculty Anesthesiology & Reanimation, 1998. Anesthesiology, reanimation, assoc. prof., 2007—. Office: Erciyes University Med Faculty Anes Kayseri 38039 Turkey Office Fax: 90 352 4377333. Business E-Mail: zeynept@erciyes.edu.tr.

TÓTH, GÉZA, chemist, educator; b. Köröstarcsa, Hungary, Oct. 25, 1944; Degree in Chemistry, U. Szeged, 1969, PhD, 1971. Sci. adviser Biol. Rsch. Ctr., Hungarian Acad. Scis., 1974—. Prof. U. Szeged, 2000. Mem.: Hungarian Chem. Soc. Avocations: gardening, travel. Office: Temesvari 62 Szeged Csongrad 6726 Hungary Office Fax: 36-62-433-566. Business E-Mail: geza@brc.hu.

TÓTH, PETER PAUL, physician, researcher; b. Torrington, Conn., May 5, 1959; s. John and Ilona Barbara (Bereczky) T.; m. Karen Faye Ireland, June 3, 1989. AB, Princeton U., 1981; PhD, Mich. State U., 1988; MD, Wayne State U., 1992. Cert. Am. Bd. Family Practice, Am. Bd. of Clin. Lipidology. Resident U. Iowa; dir. preventive cardiology Sterling Rock Falls Clinic, Ltd.; chief of medicine CGH Med. Ctr. Clin. prof. U. Ill. Coll. Medicine, Peoria; clin. assoc. prof. So. Ill. U. Sch. Medicine, Springfield; bd. dirs. Midwest Cardiovascular Rsch. Found. Co-author: (textbooks) Handbook of Family Practice, 1997, Comprehensive Management of High Risk Cardiovascular Patients, 2006, Clinical Challenges in Hypertension, Year in Lipid Disorders, 2010, Comprehensive Cardiovascular Medicine in the Primary Care Setting, 2010, Therapeutic Lipidology, 2007, Current Controversies in Dyslipidemia Management, 2007, Practical Lipid Management, 2007; editor in chief: Jour. Applied Rsch. Clin. and Exptl. Therapeutics, co-contbr. articles to Pediatrics Jour., Jour. Pediatrics Surgery, Jour. Biol. Chemistry, Arch. Biochem. Biophysics, Comp. Biochem. Physiol., Methods Enzymol., Nutrition, Circulation, Current Opinion in Cardiology, Am. Jour. Cardiology, Current Opinion in Lipidology, Family Practice Recertification, Clin. Therapeutics; sect. editor: Current Atherosclerosis Reports; mem. editl. bd. Future Lipidology, MosbyGenRx, Jour. Clin. Lipidology, Assoc. editor Yr. Book. Endocrinology(Elsevier) Recipient Searle-Donald F. Richardson Meml. Prize, Am. Coll. Ob-Gyn. Fellow: Am. Coll. Chest Physicians, Am. Coll. Cardiology (mem. coun. cardiovascular disease prevention), Internat. Coll. Angiology, Am. Acad. Family Physicians, Am. Heart Assn. (mem. clin. affairs com.); mem.: AMA, AAAS, Nat. Lipid Assn., Am. Bd. Clin. Lipidology (mem. bd. dirs.), Midwest Cardiovascular Rsch. Found. (bd. dirs.), Nat. Lipid Assn. (bd. dirs., bd. dirs. midwest chpt., pres. 2010), Sigma Xi, Alpha Omega Alpha. Roman Catholic. Achievements include research in mitochondrial respiration, carnitine metabolism, enzymology, spectroscopy, lipidology, heart disease prevention. Home: 17719 Grandview Dr Sterling IL 61081-8564 Office: Sterling Rock Falls Clinic 101 E Miller Rd Sterling IL 61081 Business E-Mail: peter.toth@srfc.com.

TOTTON, CARL ALLEN, II, psychologist; s. Carl Allen and Elva T. Student, Calif. State U., 1976, BS in Rehab. Counseling, 1978, MS in Counseling, 1980; PsyD in Clin. Psychology, Pepperdine U., Malibu, Calif., 1998. Cert. sch. psychologist, counselor, Calif.; lic. psychologist, Calif., Diagnostic Ctr. South, 2006-2008; ordained Taoist abbot, 1983. Sch. psychologist Alhambra (Calif.) Sch. Dist., LA, 1990—2006; dir. Taoist Inst., North Hollywood, Calif., 1981—; chair Sch. Psychology Phillips Grad. Inst., 2004—. Faculty mem. Calif. State U., Northridge, 1993-96, SAMRA U. Oriental Medicine, 1996-98; dir., counselor Rehab. Counseling Assocs., North Hollywood, 1981-83; stress mgmt. cons., hypnotherapist; bd. advisors Rancho San Antonio Home for Boys, Chatsworth, Calif., 1996—. Author: Comprehensive Guide to Chinese Medicine and Structural Tui Na, Martial Arts Chi Kung, 1997, Pediatric Tui Na, 1998; editor: Tui Na: Chinese Healing and Acupressure Massage, 1984; author, pub., prodr., The Core System for Martial Arts, Health, and Chi Kung, 2005; contbr. articles to mags. Recipient Presdl. Sports award, 1993, 95, 97; elected to US Martial Arts Hall Fame as Grandmaster, 2002. Mem. APA, Calif. Rehab. Counseling Assn. (pres. 1983-84), Soc. Existential Analysis, Nat. Assn. Sch. Psychologists, Calif. Assn. Sch. Psychologists (bd. dirs., 2001-2003, named Outstanding Sch. Psychologist 2000), Calif. Assn. Lic. Ednl. Psychologists (named Lic. Ednl. Psychologist of Yr. 1999), Calif. Assn. Marriage and Family Therapists. Office: Taoist Inst 10630 Burbank Blvd North Hollywood CA 91601-2511 Office Phone: 818-760-4219.

TOUEG, SAM, internist; b. Cairo, June 3, 1954; arrived in U.S., 1982; s. Maurice and Sarina (Sabbagh) Toueg; m. Rosalie Abitbol, Mar. 26, 1996. MD, U. Grenoble, France, 1979. Diplomate Am. Bd. Internal Medicine. Intern U. Grenoble Hosp., 1978—79, resident, 1979—83; fellow in tranplantation nephrology Washington Hosp. Ctr., 1983—84; fellow in nephrology U. Conn. Health Ctr., Farmington, 1984—86; resident Franklin Square Hosp., Balt., 1986—87; asst. chief resident in internal medicine VA Med. Ctr., Georgetown U. Hosp., Washington, 1987—89; physician Harford Meml. Hosp., Havre-de-Grace, Md., 1989—90; asst. attending physician Elmhurst (N.Y.) Hosp., 1990—. Frm instr. to clin. asst. prof. medicine Mt. Sinai Sch. Medicine. Contbr. articles to profl. jours. Mem.: AMA (Physician Recognition award), ACP, Renal Physicians Assn., Am. Soc. Nephrology, Am. Soc. Internal Medicine. Avocations: tennis, soccer. Home: 230 E 79th St Apt 6E New York NY 10021 Office: Elmhurst Hosp 79-01 Broadway Ave Elmhurst NY 11373

TOUMA, DANY J., dermatologist, surgeon; MD, Lebanese U., 1984—91. Diplomate Am. Bd. Dermatology, 2008, lic. Lebanese Order of Physician. Resident internal medicine Carney Hosp., Boston, 1992—94; resident dermatology Boston Univ./Tufts Univ., 1994—97; fellowship mohs micrographic and cosmetic surgery Boston Univ., 1997—98; dermatologist The Skin Clinic, Beirut. Co-author (with Demierre MF): (book) The Clinics Atlas of Office Procedures, 2002; author: (book chpts.) Photodynamic Therapy for Basal Cell Nevus Syndrome, Topical Photodynamic Therapy. In Skin Aging, Gilchrest and Krutmann, 2006, numerous articles. Mem.: Am. Soc. for Lasers in Medicine and Surgery, Am. Coll. of Mohs Micrographic Surgery and Cutaneous Oncology, Am. Soc. for Dermatologic Surgery, Am. Acad. of Dermatology, Lebanese Order of Physicians, Lebanese Dermatologic Soc. Office: The Skin Clinic 12th Fl Speciality Clinic Center 102 Maamary St Beirut Lebanon Office Phone: 9611347546. Office Fax: 9611740078. *

TOUMPAS, NICHOLAS A. (NICK TOUMPAS), public health service officer, state official; b. 1950; Grad., U. NH, 1972; MBA, U. NH Whittemore Sch. Bus. & Economics. Intergration & sales exec. Digital Equipment Corp., 1980—92; cons. DMR Group, 1992—94; pres. XNT Sys., 1994—99; v.p. Excel Switching Lucent Technologies, 1999—2001; adminstr. NH Dept. Health & Human Services, Concord, 2002—03, sys. specialist, 2003—05, dep. commr., 2005—07, acting commr., 2007—08, commr., 2008—. Office: New Hampshire Department of Health and Human Services 129 Pleasant St Concord NH 03301-3852 Office Phone: 603-271-4688. Office Fax: 603-271-4912. *

TOUNTAS, YANNIS, medical educator; b. Athens, Greece, Oct. 31, 1952; BS in Biology, Harvard U., 1974; PhD, U. Athens, 1981. Assoc. prof. social medicine Ctr. Health Svcs. Rsch., Med. Sch., U. Athens, 2002—. Pres. First Regional Health Care And Welfare Sys. Attica, 2003—04; nat. rep. health com. OECD, 2008—10; pres. Nat. Orgn. Medicines, 2010. Office: Alexandroupoleos 25 Athens 11527 Greece Business E-Mail: ytountas@med.uoa.gr.

TOURAINE, JEAN-LOUIS DIDIER, physician, medical researcher, educator; b. Lyon, France, Oct. 8, 1945; s. Yves and Suzanne (Barbier) T. MD, Claude Bernard U., 1972, PhD, 1975. Resident in nephrology Lyons Hosps., 1968-72, asst. prof., 1973-79; prof. C. Bernard U. and Hosp., 1979—; head dept. transplantation and clin. immunology Hopital E. Herriot, Lyon, 1986—. Immunologist, Edinburgh, Scotland, 1969, Mpls., 1972, NYC, 1973; pres. Haut Com. Med. Social Security, Paris, 1992-96, France Transplant, Paris, 1995—. Author: Hors de la Bulle, 1985; co-author 30 sci. books in field; contbr. over 1000 articles to profl. publs.; mem. editl. bd. Bone Marrow Transplantation, Fetal Diagnosis and Therapy, Human Reproduction, Jour. Immunology and Immunopharmacology, others; rschr. in field. Mayor 8th Dist. Lyon, 1995-01; v.p. Cmty. Urbaine de Lyon, 1995—; consciller Municipality of Lyon, 1989—, consciller communautaire, 1989—; first dep. mayor Lyon, 2001-; mem. French Parliament, 2007-. Recipient prize Found. Alexis Carrel, 1969, Delahautemaison de Nephrology, 1982, Soranos Sci. award, 1997. Mem. NY Acad. Scis., Internat. Soc. Nephrology, European Bone Marrow Transplantation, Internat. Soc. Transplantation. Achievements include discovering the disease Bare Lymphocyte Syndrome, then initiating the first fetal liver cell transplants, especially in human fetuses to treat inherited diseases. Home: 42 rue Villon 69008 Lyon France Office: Hopital E Herriot Dept Transplantation 69437 Lyon France Office Phone: 33 472110151. E-mail: jean-louis.touraine@chu-lyon.fr.

TOURLENTES, THOMAS THEODORE, retired psychiatrist; b. Chgo., Dec. 7, 1922; s. Theodore A. and Mary (Xenostathy) T.; m. Mona Belle Land, Sept. 9, 1956; children: Theodore W., Stephen C., Elizabeth A. BS, U. Chgo., 1945, MD, 1947. Diplomate Am. Bd. Psychiatry and Neurology (sr. examiner 1964-88, 90). Intern Cook County Hosp., Chgo., 1947-48; resident psychiatry Downey (Ill.) VA Hosp., 1948-51; practice medicine specializing in psychiatry Chgo., 1952, Camp Atterbury, Ind., 1953, Ft. Carson, Colo., 1954, Galesburg, Ill., 1955-71; staff psychiatrist Chgo. VA Clinic, 1952; clin. instr. psychiatry Med. Sch., Northwestern U., 1952; dir. mental hygiene consultation service Camp Atterbury, 1953-54, Ft. Carson, 1953-54; asst. supt. Galesburg State Research Hosp., 1954-58, supt., 1958-71; dir. Comprehensive Community Mental Health Ctr. Rock Island and Mercer Counties; dir. psychiat. services Franciscan Hosp., 1971-85; chief mental health services VA Outpatient Clinic, Peoria, Ill., 1985-88; clin. prof. psychiatry U. Ill., Chgo. and Peoria, 1955—96; preceptor in hosp. adminstrn. State U. Iowa, Iowa City, 1958-64; ret., 1996. Councilor, del. Ill. Psychiat. Soc.; chmn. liaison com. Am. Hosp. and Psychiat. Assns., 1978-79, chmn. Quality Care Bd., Ill. Dept. Mental Health, 1995-97. Contbr. articles profl. jours. Mem. Gov. Ill. Com. Employment Handicapped, 1962-64; zone dir. Ill. Dept. Mental Health, Peoria, 1964-71; mem. Spl. Survey Joint Commn. Accreditation Hosps.; chmn. Commn. Cert. Psychiat. Adminstrs., 1979-81; pres. Knox-Galesburg Symphony Soc., 1966-68; bd. dirs. Galesburg Civic Music Assn., pres., 1968-70; chair Knox county United Way Campaign, 1989; pres. Civic Art Ctr., 1990-92. Capt. M.C. AUS, 1952-54. Fellow AAAS, AMA, Am. Psychiat. Assn. (chair hosp. and cmty. psychiatry award bd. 1989-90, dist. life fellow, 2002), Am. Coll. Psychiatrists, Am. Coll. Mental Health Adminstrs.; mem. Ill. Med. Soc. (chmn. aging com. 1968-71, coun. on mental health and addictions 1987-89), chair mental health substance abuse com. 1987-89), Ill. Psychiat. Soc. (pres. 1969-70), Am. Pub. Health Assn., Soc. Biol. Psychiatry, Ill. Hosp. Assn. (trustee 1968-70), Am. Coll. Hosp. Adminstrs., Assn. for Rsch. Nervous and Mental, Am. Assn. Psychiat. Adminstrs. (pres. 1980), Ctrl. Neuropsychiat. Assn. (pres. 1988-89). Home and Office: 138 Valley View Rd Galesburg IL 61401-8524 Office Phone: 309-344-1177. E-mail: tourlentes@gallatinriver.net.

TOURLITSAS, JOHN CONSTANTINE, radiologist; b. Cavala, Greece, Oct. 4, 1926; came to U.S., 1956; s. Constantine Nacos and Marica Constantine (Athanasiou) T. MD, U. Athens, Greece, 1955. Diplomate Am. Bd. Radiology. Intern Sioux Valley Hosp., Sioux Falls, SD, 1956-57; resident Midway Hosp., Mpls.-St. Paul, 1957-59, New Eng. Deaconess Hosp./Harvard U., Boston, 1959-60, Mass. Meml. Hosps./Boston U., 1960-61, Toronto (Ont., Can.) Western Hosp.-U. Toronto, 1961-62; rsch. fellow in radiology Postgrad. Rsch. Inst. Hosp for Sick Children, U. Toronto, 1962; resident Sunnybrook VA Hosp.-U. Toronto, 1963, Royal Victoria Hosp., McGill U., Montreal, 1963-65; attending radiologist, vis. radiologist Maimonides Med. Ctr., Coney Island Hosp., Bklyn., 1966-68; attending, cons. radiologist Bronx (N.Y.)-Lebanon Hosp. Ctr.-Albert Einstein Coll. Med., 1968-95; ret., 1995. Instr. radiology Albert Einstein Coll. Medicine, 1972-77. Joslin Clinic fellow, Boston, 1959-60. Fellow Am. Coll. Chest Physicians; mem. AMA, Am. Coll. Radiology, Am. Roentgen Ray Soc., Radiol. Soc. N.Am., N.Y. State Med. Soc. Avocations: reading, walking, travel. Home: 372 Fifth Ave Apt 8C New York NY 10018-8109 *

TOURTELLOTTE, CHARLES DEE, internist, rheumatologist, educator; b. Kalamazoo, Aug. 28, 1931; s. Dee and Helen May (Lotz) T.; m. Barbara Richwine, June 25, 1955; children: Daniel DeWitt (dec.), Elizabeth Anne, William Charles, Scott David. AB, Johns Hopkins U., 1953; MS in Biochemistry, MD, Temple U., 1957. Diplomate Am. Bd. Internal Medicine. Intern, resident in medicine U. Mich. Hosp., Ann Arbor, 1957-60; fellow in rheumatology Temple U. Hosp., Phila., 1960-61; fellow in biochemistry Rockefeller U., NYC, 1961-63; faculty Sch. Medicine, Temple U., 1963—, prof. medicine, 1972-97, prof. emeritus, 1997—; chief rheumatology Temple U. Hosp., 1994-97, pres. med. staff, bd. govs., 1984-86. Dir. Greater Delaware Valley Arthritis Control Program, 1974-77; pres. Eastern Pa. chpt. Arthritis Found., 1972-74; mem. active/cons. staff 10 area and regional hosps. Contbr. chpts. to textbooks, articles to profl. jours.; mem. editl. bd.: Arthritis and Rheumatism, 1969-77, 19th-24th Rheumatism Revs, 1969-81. Mem. Haddonfield (N.J.) Bd. Edn., 1968-74, pres., 1974; mem. Borough of Haddonfield Environ. Comm., 1975-87, chmn., 1977-85; mem. Haddonfield Civic Assn., 1963—; South N.J. chmn. Johns Hopkins U. Alumni Schs. Com., 1975-90; trustee Bobby Fulton Meml. Fund, 1979-2008, 1st Presbyn. Ch. of Haddonfield, 1998-2000. With AUS, 1953-61. Helen Hay Whitney Found. fellow, 1962-63; Arthritis Found. fellow, 1963-66 Fellow ACP, Phila. Coll. Physicians, Am. Coll. Rheumatology (founding fellow); mem. Pa. Med. Soc., Phila. County Med. Soc.,(50 yr. mem. 2007) Babcock Surg. Soc., Phila. Rheumatism Soc. (pres. 1968-69), Pa. Rheumatology Soc. (founding pres. 1985-86), N.J. Soc. of Pa., Nat. Huguenot Soc. (surgeon gen. 2002-04), Huguenot Soc. Pa., Temple U. Med. Alumni Assn. (pres. 1997-99), Tavistock Country Club (N.J.), Little Egg Harbor Yacht Club, Med. Club of Phila. (bd. dirs., pres. 1998-99), Sixty-five Club of Haddonfield (dir. 2003—08), Interfaith Caregivers (trustee 2004-2007), Sigma Xi, Alpha Omega Alpha, Delta Upsilon, Phi Chi. Presbyterian. Home: 6 Lane Of Acres Haddonfield NJ 08033-3505 Office: Temple University Hosp Dept Rheumatology Philadelphia PA 19140-5192 Office Phone: 215-707-2000. E-mail: cdtourte@comcast.net.

TOURTELLOTTE, WALLACE WILLIAM, neurologist, educator; b. Great Falls, Mont., Sept. 13, 1924; B in Philosophy, Hutchin's Coll., U. Chgo., 1945; BS in Anatomy, U. Chgo., 1945, PhD in Neurochemical Pharmacology, 1948, MD, 1951. Instr. biochem Neuro pharmacology U. Chgo., 1948—49; intern Strong Meml. Hosp. Straight Medicine U. Rochester Sch. Medicine and Dentistry, NY, 1951—52; resident in neurology U. Mich. Med. Ctr., Ann Arbor, 1954-57, asst. prof., 1957-59, assoc. prof., 1959-66, prof., 1966-71; vice chmn. dept. neurology UCLA, 1971—99, emeritus vice chmn. dept. neurology, 1998; chief neurology svcs. VA Wadsworth, West LA, Calif., 1971-99, emeritus dir. chief dir. neurology tng. program, 1999—, staff neurologist, neuroscientist, 1999—, Inst. Sci. Info., 1981—; dir. neurology train program Va. Wadsworth Med. Ctr. Vis. assoc. prof. pharmacology Washington U., St. Louis, 1963-64; hon. mem. med. adv. bd. Nat. Multiple Sclerosis Soc., 1968—, So. Calif. Multiple Sclerosis Socs., 1972—; dir. Multiple Sclerosis Rsch. and Treatment Ctr., 1971-, Human Brain and Spinal Fluid Resource Ctr., 1961—; reviewer neuroscientist profl. jours. in field. Co-editor (with Cedric Raines, Henry McFarland): Multiple Sclerosis, Clinical and Pathogenetic Basis, 1997; The Wallace W. Tourtellotte Clin. and Neurosci. Libr., Va. Wadsworth, LA, 1999-; author Post-Lumbar Headache Book, 1967, Quantitative Examination Of human Neurologic Function, 2 vols., 1985. Lt. (j.g.) M.C., USNR, 1952-54. Recipient Disting. Alumni Service award U. Chgo., 1982. Fellow Am. Acad. Neurology (S. Weir Mitchell Neurology Reseach award 1959-); mem. Am. Neurol. Assn. (counselor 1982—, v.p. 1992-), World Fedn. Neurochemistry Commn. (founding mem. 1969), Am. Assn. Neuropathologists, Internat. Soc. Neurochemsitry (founding mem. 1959), Am. Soc. Pharmacology and Exptl. Therapeutics, Am. Soc. Neurochemistry (founding mem.), Soc. Neurosci., Confrerie de la Chaine des Rotisseur, Argentier du Baillage de Los Angeles (vice chanceller, comdr. 1971), Pasadena Wine and Food Soc., Physician Wine and Food Soc., Culinary Club French Cuisine LA. Home Phone: 310-480-7560, 310-480-7570; Office Phone: 310-268-4638. Fax: 310-454-7650. Business E-Mail: wtourtel@ucla.edu.

TOUSIMIS, ELENI, surgeon, educator; b. Washington, Jan. 21, 1970; MD, Albany Med. Coll., 1996. Attending surgeon, dept. surgery NY Presbyn. Hosp., 2003—11; asst. prof., dept. surgery Weill Cornell Med. Coll., 2003—09, asst. prof. clin. surgery, 2009—. Exec. com. NY Met. Breast Soc., 2009; bd. dirs. Am. Med. Women's Assn., 2011. Recipient Achievement award, Office NYC Comptr., William Thompson, Tchg. Excellence award, Weill Med. Coll. Cornell U.; named one of America's Top Surgeons, Best Drs. in Am.; grant, Leir Found. Mem.: AMA, ACS, NY Met. Breast Soc., Hellenic Med. Soc. (NY), Soc. Surg. Oncology. Office: 425 E 61st St 10th Fl New York NY 10065

TOUTOUZAS, KONSTANTINOS, physician, educator; b. Athens, Attica, Greece, Mar. 22, 1971; MD, 1987. Asst. prof. Athens Med. Sch., 2010. Office: Athens University Med Sch Hippokration Hosp 114 Vasilissis Sofias Athens Attica 15454 Greece Business E-Mail: ktoutouz@otenet.gr.

TOUYZ, STEPHEN WILLIAM, clinical psychologist, educator; b. Cape Town, South Africa, Aug. 29, 1950; s. Harry and Tilly (Woolfowitz) T.; m. Rennette Dawn Elk, Jan. 18, 1976; children: Justin Lawrence, Lauren Marissa. BS, U. Cape Town, 1972, PhD, 1976; BS with honors, U. Witwatersrand, 1974. Tutor U. Witwatersrand, 1974; sr. tutor U. Cape Town, 1974-75; sr. rsch. asst. Groote Schuur Hosp., Cape Town, 1974-75, intern clin. psychologist, 1976-78; staff psychologist Royal Prince Alfred Hosp., Sydney, Australia, 1978-80; clin. lectr. U. Sydney, 1979-91, clin. assoc. prof. psychiatry, 1991-94, clin. prof. psychiatry, 1994-96; dir. Ctr. for Study and Treatment of Dieting Disorders, 1994-95; prof., chmn. dept. psychology U. Sydney, 1996-98, prof. clin. psychology, 1999—. Head clin. psychology unit Royal Prince Alfred Hosp., Sydney, 1980-88; cons. psychologist anorexia nervosa unit Northside Clinic, Sydney, 1979-84, Royal Prince Alfred Hosp., 1983-88, Lynton Pvt. Hosp., 1984-97; head dept. med. psychology Westmead Hosp., 1988-96; hon. assoc. dept. psychology U. Sydney, 1979-96, prof.; hon. clin. assoc. dept. psychology Macquarie U., 1990-96; dep. chmn. divsn. psychol. medicine Westmead Hosp., 1993-94; NSW advisor on health psychol. dept. of vets affairs Commonwealth of Australia, 1994—; program dir. Peter Beumont Ctr. Eating Disorders, Wesley Pvt. Hosps., 2003—09, dir. Beumont Ctr. Eating Disorders, Hills Pvt. Hosp., 2009-; mem. Westmead Hosps. Sci. Coun., 1988-96; cons. practice guidelines com. eating disorders APA, 1990-93. Author: Handbook of Neuropsychological Assessment, 1984, Eating Disorders: Prevalence and Treatment, 1985, Managing Anorexia Nervosa: Clinical, Legal and Social Perspectives on Involuntary Treatment, 2006, Eating Disorders, 2008; editor Neuropsychology in Clinical Practice, 1994. Found. treas. Australian and New Zealand Acad. Eating Disorders. Rsch. grantee South African Coun. Sci. and Indsl. Rsch., 1973-76, Nat. Health and Med. Rsch. Coun. Australia, 1983-87, 1995-97, 2007-, Ramaciotti Found., 1983-84, Eli Lilly, 1991-93, Australian Rsch. Coun., 2001—. Fellow Internat. Coll. Psychosomatic Medicine (v.p. Australia and New Zealand chpt. 1993-99), Australian Psychol. Soc., Acad. Eating Disorders; mem. Australian Assn. Advancement Cognitive Behavior Therapy, Australian Soc., Psychiat. Rsch., Am. Psychol. Assn. (affiliate), Internat. Acad. Sci., Eating Disorders Rsch. Soc. (pres. 2005-06), Eating Disorders Found. NSW (exec. mem. 2003—09), Eating Disorders Rsch. Soc. (pres. 2005-06). Office: U Sydney Dept Psychology Sydney New South Wales 2006 Australia Business E-Mail: stephent@psych.usyd.edu.au.

TOWER, ALTON G., JR., pharmacist; b. Buffalo, Jan. 16, 1927; m. Nan R. Spinner, Aug. 15, 1953; children: Adrienne, Michele, Renee. BS in Pharmacy, U. Buffalo, 1953. Registered pharmacist. Pharmacist Woldmans Drug Store, Buffalo, 1946-53; med. svc. rep. Strasenburgh Lab., Rochester, N.Y., 1953-66; pharmacist, mgr. Eckerd Drugs, Clearwater, Fla., 1966—. Bd. dirs. Am. Cancer Soc. Pinellas County, Fla., 1976—, pres., 1988-89, Life Saver award, 1988, life mem., 1995—, dir. cmty. affairs Pinellas Pharmacist Soc.; charter mem. Smoke Free Class of 2000, Pinellas County, 1988—. Recipient Vol. of Yr. award Am. Cancer Soc. Pinellas County, 1987, 97, Willis G. Gregory award U. Buffalo Sch. Pharmacy, 2004, IPA Corrons Motivation & Inspiration award, 2010. Mem. Am. Cancer Soc. (life, Lifesaver award Pinellas County chpt. 1988, named Vol. of Yr. 1997), Am. Pharm. Assn., Fla. Pharmacy Assn. (bd. dirs. 1981-85, speaker ho. of dels. 1986, chmn. bd. trustees, R.Q. Richards award 1989, Bowl of Hygeia award 1990, Sid Simkowitz Involvement award 1991, named Pharmacist of Yr. 1992), Pasco Hernando Pharmacists Assn. (James Beal award 1992), Pinellas County Pharmacy Soc. (life; dir. 1968-73, 78-81, 89-91, pres. 1973, 88, Pharmacist of Yr. 1973), Fla. Pharmacy Found. (pres. 1999, Jean Lamberti Mentorship award 2003), Phi Lambda Sigma. Avocations: gardening, hiking, travel.

TOWNSEND, ALAIN, immunologist, educator; Med. grad., St. mary's Hospital, London, 1977. Joined Inst. Molecular Medicine, Oxford, 1984, Ad Hominem prof. molecular immunology, 1992; prof. molecular immunology New Coll, U. Oxford. Hon. cons., gen. internal medicine John Radcliffe Hosp.; internat. rsch. scholar Howard Hughes Med Inst. Recipient William B. Coley award, Cheadle medal, prize for Clin. Medicine, Louis Jeantet prize for Medicine, Gairdner Found. Internat. award, 2000. Fellow: Royal Soc. Office: New Coll Holywell Street OX1 3BN Oxford England *

TOWNSEND, COURTNEY M., surgeon; b. Lubbock, Tex., 1943; MD, U. Tex., Galveston, 1969. Specialty bd. 1 Surgery 1975. Intern U. Tex. Med. Br., 1969—70, resident surgery, 1970—74; fellow surg. oncology U. Calif., LA, 1974—76; staff surgeon, surg. dir. intensive care unit Nat. Naval Med. Ctr., Bethesda, 1976—78; assoc. prof. U. Tex. Med. Br., 1978—83; prof., 1983—95, chair, dept. surgery, 1995—. James IV Surg. Traveller U. Tex. Med. Br., 1986; pres. Am. Pancreatic Assn., 1992—93; mem. Tex. Cancer Coun., 1992—2008; dir. Am. Bd. Surgery, 2000—07. Editor-in-chief: Sabiston Textbook of Surgery: The Biological Basis of Modern Surgical Practice, 16th edit., 18th edit. Recipient Rsch. Career Devel. award, NIH, 1982, Ashbel Smith Disting. Alumnus, 1986. Fellow: ACS (exec. com. 1999—2003, chmn. bd. govs. 2004—05, sec. 2006—); mem.: AMA (residency rev. com. 1999—2003), Am. Surg. Assn. (pres. 2007—08), Am. Bd. Surgery (chair 2006—07), So. Surg. Assn. (sec. 1999—2003, pres. 2003—04). Office: 301 University Blvd Galveston TX 77555-0527

TOWNSEND, DAVID W., physicist, radiology professor; b. Jan. 13, 1945; BS in Physics, U. Bristol, Eng., 1966; PhD in Exptl. High Energy Physics, Westfield Coll., U. London, 1971. Docent in med. imaging U. Geneva, 1987. Rsch. assoc. Westfield Coll., 1969—70; sci. programmer, data handling divsn. European Orgn. Nuc. Rsch. (CERN), Geneva, 1970—78; vis. sci. cons., med. imaging processing group SUNY, Buffalo, 1978—79; physicist, computer analyst divsn. nuc. medicine Univ. Hosp. Geneva, 1979—93; assoc. prof. dept. radiology U. Pitts. Sch. Medicine, 1993—99, prof., 2000—03; prof. depts. medicine & radiology, dir. molecular imaging and translational rsch. program U. Tenn. Sch. Medicine, Knoxville, 2003—09, prof. dept. anesthesiology, 2006—09, adj. prof., 2009—; prof. radiology Yong Loo Lin Sch. Medicine, Nat. U. Singapore, 2009—, dir. Clin. Imaging Rsch. Ctr., 2010—. Hon. vis. scientist PET (positron emission tomography) group Hammersmith Hosp., London, 1987—2000; sr. scientist PET facility U. Pitts. Med. Ctr., 1993—2003, acting co-dir. PET facility, 1996—2001; head SPECT/PET devel. Singapore

Bioimaging Consortium, 2009—. Assoc. editor Transactions in Med. Imaging, Jour. Nuc. Medicine, mem. editl. bd. Current Med. Imaging Reviews, mem. internat. editl. bd. Annals Nuc. Medicine, Japan; contbr. articles to profl. jours. Named one of 100 Names You Need to Know, Health Imaging & IT, 2004. Fellow: IEEE (Medal for Innovations in Healthcare Tech. 2010); mem.: Acad. Molecular Imaging (bd. dirs., treas. 2004, Disting. Clin. Scientist of Yr. 2004), Soc. Nuc. Medicine, Swiss Soc. Radiology & Nuc. Medicine. Achievements include with electrical engineer Ronald Nutt, implementing design, commercial development and clinical implementation of hybrid PET/CT scanners, named TIME Magazine's Invention of the Year in 2000; patents in field. Mailing: Univ Tenn Sch Medicine 1924 Alcoa Hwy Box 93 Knoxville TN 37920 Office Phone: 865-305-6181. E-mail: DTownsend@mc.utmck.edu. *

TOWNSEND, JANE KALTENBACH, biologist, educator; b. Chgo., Dec. 21, 1922; BS, Beloit Coll., 1944; MA, U. Wis., 1946; PhD, U. Iowa, 1950. Asst. in zoology U. Wis., 1944-47, asst., project assoc. in pathology, 1950—53; asst., instr. U. Iowa, 1948-50; rsch. fellow Wenner-Grens Inst. Am. Cancer Soc., Stockholm, 1953—56; asst. prof. zoology Northwestern U., 1956-58; asst. prof. to assoc. prof. zoology Mt. Holyoke Coll., South Hadley, Mass., 1958-70, prof., 1970-93, chmn. biol. scis., 1980-86, prof. emeritus, 1993—; summer investigator Marine Biol. Lab., Woods Hole, Mass., 1993—. Contbr. articles to profl. sci. jours. Fellow AAAS (sec. sect. biol. sci. 1974-78); mem. Am. Assn. Anatomists, Am. Inst. Biol. Scis., Soc. Integrated Comparative Biology, Soc. Exptl. Biology and Medicine, Soc. Devel. Biology, Corp. of Marine Biol. Lab., Sigma Xi, Phi Beta Kappa. Achievements include research in amphibian metamorphosis and immune responses in marine sponges. Office: Mount Holyoke Coll Dept Bio Scis South Hadley MA 01075 Office Phone: 413-538-2124. Business E-Mail: jtownsen@mtholyoke.edu.

TOWNSEND, JOHN CUNNINGHAM, optometrist; s. Charles Eby and Marjorie Rhodes Townsend; m. Sheila Frances Anderson, May 26, 1990; children: Alicia, James. BS, U. Fla., 1975; OD, U. Houston, 1979. Lic. optometrist Calif., Fla., Mo., Okla., Tex., W.Va. Hosp.-based resident in optometry Kansas City (Mo.) VA Med. Ctr., 1979—80; chief ocular disease So. Calif. Coll. Optometry, Fullerton, 1980—83; optometrist Family Health Plan HMO, Long Beach, Calif., 1984—85; asst. chief optometry svc. West L.A. VA Med. Ctr., 1985—91, chief optometry svc., 1991—96; chief optometry VA Greater L.A. Healthcare, Santa Barbara, Calif., 1996—2000; dir. VHA optometry svc. VA, Washington, 2000—. Instr. So. Calif. Coll. Optometry, 1980—81, asst. prof., 1981—83, 1985—88, assoc. prof., 1988—94, tenured prof., 1994—2000; mem. Exec. Adv. Cmty. AMSUS, 2005—06, 2010—11; planning com. mem. Nat. Eye Health Edn. Program NEI NIH US DHHS, 2006—11; affiliated mem. Assn. Schs. & Colls. Optometry, 2000—; rep. ANSI Com. 280 Ophthalmic Standards, 2000—. Author: Visual Fields: Clinical Case Presentations, 1991; mem. editl. bd. Optometry and Vision Sci., 1998—2003, Jour. Rehab. R&D, 2001—; contbr. articles to profl. jours. Mem. therapeutic pharm. agt. adv. com. State of Calif. Dept. Consumer Affairs, Sacramento, 1996—2000; mem. therapeutic pharm. agt. study com. Calif. Optometric Assn., 1997—2000. Recipient Pres.'s award, Nat. Assn. VA Optometrists, 1993, Optometry award, Amsus, 2005, named Disting. Optometry Alumnus, U. Houston Coll. Optometry, 2001, Distin. Practitioner Optometry, Nat. Acad. Practice, 2003—. Fellow: Am. Acad. Optometry; mem.: Am. Optometric Assn. (chair clin. guidelines coordinating com. 2000—05), Armed Forces Optometric Soc. (exec. coun. 2001—08), Beta Sigma Kappa, Phi Kappa Phi. Office: VA 103 S Gay St Rm 714 Baltimore MD 21202 Office Phone: 410-779-1576. Business E-Mail: john.townsend@va.gov.

TOWNSEND, RAYMOND R., nephrologist, educator; BA, LaSalle U.; MD, Hahnemann Med. Coll. Diplomate Am. Bd. Internal Medicine, Am. Bd. Internal Medicine-clin. pharmacology, Am. Bd. Internal Medicine-renal/nephrology, Am. Bd. Internal Medicine-hypertension. Intern Allegheny gen Hosp., Pitts.; resident Allegheny Gen. Hosp., Pitts.; fellow Temple Univ., Phila.; prof. medicine Univ. Pa. Named Tops Docs, Phila. Mag., 2004, 2011, America's Top Doctors, 2007, 2008, 2010. Mem.: Am. Heart Assoc., Nat. High Blood Pressure Coun., Am. Soc. of Nephrology, Internat. Soc. of Nehphrogy. Office: Hospital of the University of Pennsylvania 3400 Spruce St Philadelphia PA 19104 Office Phone: 215-662-4000.

TOWNSON, GILLIAN ANNE, gastroenterologist; b. Liverpool, Eng., May 19, 1967; d. Sidney and Linda Moody; m. Paul John Townson, Aug. 29, 1998; children: Holly, Ella, Samuel. MB,ChB, Leicester Med. Sch., Eng., 1990; MD, Leicester U., 1996. Registrar Wessex Rotation, 1994—96; sr. registrar Leicester Hosp., 1996—; cons. physician, gastroenterologist Princess Royal Hosp., Telford, England, 1999—. Contbr. articles to profl. jours. Recipient, Stuart Halley Trust award. Fellow: Royal Coll. Physicians London. Avocations: reading, skiing, interior decorating, cooking. Office: Princess Royal Hosp Apley Castle TF6 6TF Telford England

TOWU, EMMANUEL, pediatric surgeon, consultant; b. Jakpa, Nigeria, June 25, 1955; s. Anthony and Janet Towu; children: Lillian, Anthonia. MBBS, U. of Benin Med. Sch., 1978. Specialist Registration in Pediatric Surgery Gen. Med. Coun., 2000. Cons. pediat. surgeon City and U. Hospitals, Nottingham, England, 1990—92, North West Armed Forces Hosp., Tabuk, Saudi Arabia, 1992—96; clin. rsch. fellow Royal Free Hosp., London, 1996—98; registrar in pediat. surgery Queen Mary's Hosp., Carshalton, England, 1986—88; sr. specialist registrar St. George's Hosp., London, 1998—99; sr. registrar in paediatric surgery Queen Mary's Hosp., 1988—90; cons. paediatric surgeon Royal Victoria Infirmary, Newcastle upon Tyne, England, 2005; clin. instr./sr. trauma fellow Children's Hosp., Pitts., 2001; cons. pediat. surgeon Leeds Tchg. Hospitals NHS Trust, Leeds, England, 2001—02; surg. fellow Gt. Ormond St. Hosp. for Sick Children, London, 2002—03; cons. paediatric surgeon King's Coll. Hosp. NHS Trust, London, 2003—04, Lewisham, Guys and St Thomas' Hospitals, London, 2003—04; cons. pediat. surgeon Southampton Gen. Hosp., 2005—; cons. paediatric surgeon Royal Alexandra Children's Hosp., Brighton, 2005. Recipient Barclay's Scholarship award, Barclay's Bank, 1973, Nigeria Nat. Scholarship award, Fed. Govt. of Nigeria, 1974, Nigeria Fed. Govt. Postgraduate award, 1982; fellowship, Stanley Thomas Johnson, 1997. Mem.: Brit. Med. Assn. (corr.). Achievements include research in targeted therapy of embryonal tumours including hepatoblastoma.

TOYAMA, HIDEO, biotechnologist; b. Miyazaki, Japan, Nov. 22, 1954; s. Nobuo and Keiko Toyama; m. Akiko Ohtsubo, Aug. 4, 1985; children: Akira, Makoto. BS, Miyazaki U., 1978, MS, 1980; PhD, Osaka U., Japan, 1984. Engr. Orgn. for Promotion of Indsl. Tech., Miyazaki, 1984-85, Info. Ctr. of Indsl. Tech, Miyazaki, 1985-88, chief engr., 1988-89; lectr. Minamikyushu U., Miyazaki, 1989-92, asst. prof., 1992-2000, prof., 2000—; dir. Tech. Leasing Org., Inc., Miyazaki, 2006—. Contbr. articles to profl. jours. Mem. Soc. for Biotech., Japan Soc. Biosci., Biotech. and Agrochemistry, Soc. for Antibacterial and Antifungal Agts. Japan. Achievements include breeding of cellulase hyper-producing mutants of fungus. Home: Maruyama 2-235 Miyazaki 880-0052 Japan Office: Utilization of Fermentation Lab Dept Food Sci for Health/Fac Health and Kirishima 5-1-2 Miyazaki 880-0032 Japan Office Phone: 81-985-83-3524. Office Fax: 81-985-83-3524. E-mail: toyama@nankyudai.ac.jp.

TOYAMA, HIROHIDE, agricultural studies educator; b. Shizuoka, Japan, Jan. 25, 1964; PhD, Kyoto U., 1992. Asst. prof. Yamaguchi U., 1991—2001, assoc. prof., 2001—07; prof. U. Ryukyus, 2007—. Office: 1 Senbaru Nishihara Okinawa 903-0213 Japan Business E-Mail: toyama@agr.u-ryukyu.ac.jp.

TOYAMA, HIROSHI, radiologist, educator; b. Nagoya, Aichi, Japan, Apr. 24, 1958; s. Naohiko and Teruko (Hibino) T.; m. Masako Suzumuru, Oct. 10, 1988; children: Yutaka, Yoko. BM, Fujita Health U., Toyoake, Japan, 1984, D Med. Sci., 1990. Resident Fujita Health U. Hosp., 1984-86, radiologist, 1986-90; postdoctoral fellow dept. radiology Fujita Health U., 1990-91, asst. prof. dept. radiology, 1992—2004, assoc. prof. dept. radiology, 2004—; rsch. fellow dept. radiology U. Toronto, 1991—92. Vis. scientist molecular imaging br. NIMH, NIH, 2001—03. Contbr. articles to profl. jours. Recipient, Japan Soc. Promotion Scis., 2006—08, Ctr. of Excellence award, 2004—07, Best Sci. Exhibit award, 7th Asia and Oceania Congress Nuclear Medicine and Biology, 4th Internat. Congress Nuclear Oncology, 2000; grantee, Yoshida Found. for Sci. and Tech., 1991, Suzuken Meml. Found., 2006—07. Fellow: Japan-N.Am. Med. Exch. Found. (grantee 1991); mem.: Japanese Soc. Nuc. Medicine (councilor), Japan Radiol. Soc. (councilor), Soc. Nuc. Medicine (bd. dirs, councilor brain imaging coun. 2001—03). Avocations: travel, art museums, baseball. Office: 1-98 Dengakugakubo Kutsukake Toyoake Aichi 470-1192 Japan Business E-Mail: htoyama@fujita-hu.ac.jp.

TOYOKAWA, TATSUYA, gastroenterologist; b. Japan, July 31, 1967; MD, Okayama U., 1992. With dept. gastroenterology Nat. Hosp. Orgn. Fukuyama Med. Ctr., 2008—. Office: 4-14-17 Okinogami-cho Fukuyama Hiroshima 720-8520 Japan Office Fax: 81849313969. E-mail: toyotatu@kmail.plala.or.jp.

TOYONE, TOMOAKI, spine surgeon, educator; b. Japan, Mar. 14, 1961; s. Tadaaki and Shigeko Toyone; m. Tomoko Goto; children: Konosuke, Noriko. MD, Chiba U., Japan, 1985, PhD, 1993. Diplomate Nat. Bd. Medicine Japan, Japanese Bd. Orthop. Surgery, Japanese Bd. Spinal Surgery. Dir. orthop. surgery Kimitsu Chuo Hosp., Kisarazu, Japan, 1997—2004; assoc. prof. orthop. surgery Teikyo U. Sch. Medicine Ichihara Hosp., Japan, 2005—06; prof. orthop. and spinal surgery Teikyo U. Chiba Med. Ctr., Chiba, 2006—. Recipient Lyman Smith Award, Internat. Intradiscal Therapy Soc., 1993, Poster award, Am. Acad. Orthopaedic Surgeons, 2008. Avocations: diving, classical music, travel, golf, horseback riding. Office: Teikyo U Chiba Med Ctr Orthop and Spinal Surgery 3426 3 Anesaki Chiba 299-0111 Japan Office Fax: 81-436-61-8690.

TOYOOKA, SHINICHI, thoracic surgeon; MD, PhD, Okayama U., Japan, 2001. Asst. prof. Okayama U., 2004—. Achievements include research in cancer. Home: 1-36-19-803 Nishifurumatsu Okayama 700-8558 Japan Office: Okayama Univ 2-5-1 Shikatacho Okayama 700-8558 Japan Office Phone: 81-86-235-7265. Office Fax: 81-86-235-7269. Business E-Mail: toyooka@md.okayama-u.ac.jp.

TRABER, PETER GEORGE, medical educator, former academic administrator; b. Johnstown, NY, Apr. 6, 1955; m. K. Bobbi Traber; 2 children. Grad., U. Mich., 1977; MD, Wayne State U. Med. Sch., 1981; completed Mgmt. Devel Program for Physician Exec., Wharton Sch. U. Pa. Resident in internal medicine Northwestern U. Med. Sch., Chgo., fellow in gastroenterology, U. Mich. Sch. Medicine, faculty mem. Ann Arbor, 1987—92; chief gastroenterology U. Pa. Sch. Medicine, 1992—97, T. Grier Miller prof. medicine, 1993—97, Frank Wistar Thomas prof. and chair dept. medicine, 1997—2000, interim dean Phila., 2000; interim CEO U. Pa. Health Sys., Phila., 2000; sr. v.p. clinical devel. & med. affairs & chief med. officer GlaxoSmith-Kline, 2000—03; pres., CEO, prof. medicine Baylor Coll. Medicine, Houston, 2003—08, exec. dean, 2008—, pres. emeritus, 2008—. Bd. dirs. Tanox Inc., 2004—. Bd. trustees Baylor Coll. Medicine; bd. dirs. Houston Branch Fed. Res. Bank Dallas. Recipient Disting. Alumni award, Wayne State U. Sch. Medicine. Mem.: Assn. Am. Physicians, Am. Soc. Clinical Rsch., Am. Gastroenterologic Assn. Office: Baylor Coll Medicine BCM100 One Baylor Plz Houston TX 77030 Office Phone: 713-798-6363. Office Fax: 713-798-6353. E-mail: pgtraber@bcm.tmc.edu.

TRACY, THOMAS MILES, international health organization official; b. Great Barrington, Mass., July 8, 1936; s. Thomas Paul and Marion (Miles) T.; m. June Betts, June 17, 1967; children: Miles Christopher, Keir Thomas John. BA, Colgate U., 1958; MA, Stanford U., 1959; MBA, Columbia U., 1973. Fgn. service officer Dept. State, Washington, 1960-84; counselor Am. Embassy, Moscow, 1975-78, Bonn, Germany, 1978-79; asst. sec. Dept. State, Washington, 1979-83; chief adminstrn. Pan Am./WHO, Washington, 1983-98; mgmt. cons. Dept. State, 2003—. V.p. Pan-Am. Health and Edn. Found., treas. Trustee, vice chmn. Chelsea Sch., 1988-2004. With U.S. Army, 1959-60. Recipient Superior Honor award Dept. State, 1978 Mem.: Am. Fgn. Svc. Protective Found. (sec., treas.), Am. Fgn. Svc. Protective Assn. (dir. 1988—, v.p. 1997—2005, pres. 2005—), Am. Fgn. Svc. Assn. (dir. 1970—72). Home: 5902 Devonshire Dr Bethesda MD 20816-3416

TRADER, JOSEPH EDGAR, orthopedic surgeon; b. Milw., Nov. 2, 1946; s. Edgar Joseph and Dorothy Elizabeth (Senzig) T.; m. Janet Louise Burzycki, Sept. 23, 1972 (div. Nov. 1987); children: James, Jonathan, Ann Elizabeth; m. Rhonda Sue Schultz, May 26, 1990. Student, Marquette U., 1964-67; MD, Med. Coll. Wis., 1971. Diplomate Am. Bd. Orthop. Surgery. Physician emergency rm. Columbia, St. Joseph's Hosps., Milw., 1972—76; orthop. surgeon, pres. Orthop. Assn., Manitowoc, Wis., 1979—. Mem. exec. com. Holy Family Meml. Med. Ctr., Manitowoc, 1985-96, chief-of-staff, 1994-96, ethics com., 1995—, chair instnl. rev. com., 1995-2009. Former pres., bd. dirs. Holy Innocents Mens Choir; county del. State Med. Soc. Charitable Sci. and Edn. Found.; bd. dirs. (trustee), mem. cobia com., pres. bd. dirs. Wis. Maritime Mus. Fellow ACS, Am. Acad. Orthopaedic Surgeons; mem. AMA, Wis. State Med. Soc., Wis. Orthop. Soc., Midwest Orthop. Soc., Am. Coll. Sports Medicine, Orthop. Assn. Manitonoc (pres.), Crown and Anchor, Wis. Maritime Mus. (cobia com. mem., bd. dirs.), Manitowoc Yacht Club, Phi Delta Epsilon, Psi Chi. Roman Catholic. Avocations: singing, tennis, skiing, sailing, golf. Home: 1021 Memorial Dr Manitowoc WI 54220-2242 Office: Orthopaedic Assocs 501 N 10th St Manitowoc WI 54220-4039 Office Phone: 920-682-6376.

TRAFIMOW, JORDAN HERMAN, retired orthopedist; b. Chgo., Nov. 4, 1935; s. Jack and Florence (Silver) Trafimow; m. Alice Emma Lewis, July 11, 1959; children: David, Alan, Janet. BS in Med., U. Ill., 1957, MD, 1958. Orthopedic surgeon Permanente Med. Group, LA, 1966-69, Elmhurst (Ill.) Clin., 1969-86; asst. prof. Rush St. Luke Presbyn. Med. Ctr., Chgo., 1986—. Contbr. articles to profl. jours. Capt. U.S. Army, 1960-62. Fellow: N.Am. Spine Soc., Am. Acad. Orthopedic Surgeons. Jewish. Avocation: chess.

TRAINI, TONINO, dental educator; b. Ripatransone, Italy, June 15, 1961; DDS, Ud'A U. Chieti, 1998, PhD, 2005. Prof. Ud'A U. Chieti, 2008—, adj. prof., 2008—11. Recipient Lobende Anerkennung award, Internat. Competition Das Goldene Parallelometer. Avocation: fishing. Office: Piazza Pericle Fazzini 8 San Benedetto del Tronto 63039 Italy Office Fax: 39073584183.

TRAISTER, MICHAEL, pediatrician, educator; Grad., Med. Coll., NY, 1975—78. Diplomate Am. Bd. Pediatrics, 1980. Tng. in pediat. Jacobe hosp. ctr. Albert Einstein Sch. Medicine; resident Bronx Mcpl. Hosp., 1978; fellow in ambulatory pediat. Bellevue Hosp., NY, 1978—79; asst. med. dir. Pediatric Clinic, Bellevue; med. advisor Grace Children's Found.; with Lenox Hill Hosp.; asst. clin. prof. pediat. NYU Sch. Medicine; pediatrician NYU Langone Med. Ctr. Co-author: (jour. articles) Health status of US adopted Chinese orphans , 1996, Cutaneous anthrax associated with microangiopathic hemolytic anemia and coagulopathy in a 7-month-old infant, 2000, (Book) Diagnostic Testing in the Emergency Department, 1984. Recipient Alpha Omega Alpha medal, Nat. Med. Honor Soc. Fellow: Am. Acad. Pediat. Office: NYU Langone Medical Center 390 W End Ave New York NY 10024 Office Phone: 212-787-1444. Office Fax: 212-799-8620.

TRAN, CHRISTIAN, pharmacist, researcher; b. Saigon, Vietnam, Nov. 7, 1975; s. Son Dan Tran and Hong Nhung Nguyen. M in Analytical Chemistry, U. Bourgogne, Dijon, France, 1997; dipl. in chemistry, U. Lyon, France, 1998, PhD, 2002. Pharmacist Hopitaux Universitaires de Geneve, 2002—. Contbr. chapters to books, articles to profl. jours. Achievements include invention of system to evaluate the efficiency of sunscreens; discovery of a new class of anti-inflammatory drugs; research in effects of ultraviolets radiation on skin, and cutaneous vitamin A; development of new anti-inflammatory drugs for skin. Office: Hopitaux Universitaires de Geneve 24 rue Micheli-du-Crest Geneve CH-1211 Switzerland Personal E mail: christian.tran@orange.fr.

TRAN, JUDITH THUHA, psychiatrist; arrived in US, 1975; d. Phuong Nguyen and Ailien Huynh; children: Christopher Baoquoc, STephen Anhkhoa. BS in Biology, Tex. U., San Antonio, 1990; MD, Temple U., Phila., 1994. Intern Pa. Hosp., Phila., 1995—96, resident, 1996—99, chief resident, 1998—99; asst. dir. Friends Hosp. Crisis Response Ctr., 1999—2000; med. dir. Friends Hosp., 2000—03, Mercy Hosp. Phila. Crisis Response Ctr., 2003—. Recipient Merit award, Pa. Hosp., 1998—99. Mem.: Phila. Psychiat. Soc. (com. mem. 1999), Am. Psychiat. Assn. Avocations: reading, dance, swimming. Office: Mercy Hosp Phila 501 S 54th St Philadelphia PA 19143 Office Phone: 215-748-9525.

TRANQUADA, ROBERT ERNEST, retired internist, educator; b. LA, Aug. 27, 1930; s. Ernest Alvro and Katharine (Jacobus) Tranquada; m. Janet Martin, Aug. 31, 1951; children: John Martin, Katherine Anne, James Robert. BA, Pomona Coll., 1951, DSc (hon.), 2007; MD, Stanford U., 1955; DSc. (hon.), Worcester Poly. Inst., 1985. Diplomate Am. Bd. Internal Medicine. Intern in medicine UCLA Med. Center, 1955—56, resident in medicine, 1956—57; resident Los Angeles VA Hosp., 1957—58; fellow in diabetes and metabolic diseases UCLA, 1958—59; fellow in diabetes U. So. Calif., 1959—60, asst. prof. medicine, 1960—63, assoc. prof., 1964—68, chmn. dept. community medicine, 1967—70; med. dir. Los Angeles County/U. So. Calif. Med. Center, 1969—74; assoc. dean U. So. Calif. Sch. Medicine, 1969—76; regional dir. Central Region, Los Angeles County Dept. Health Services, 1974—76; assoc. dean Sch. Medicine U. Calif., LA, 1976—79; chancellor and dean U. Mass. Med. Sch., 1979 86; dean Sch. Medicine U. So. Calif., 1986—91, prof. medicine, 1986—92, Norman Topping/Nat. Med. Enterprises prof. med./pub. policy, 1992—97; prof. emeritus, 1997—. Mem, chair L.A. County Task Force on Health Care Access, 1992—94. Corporator Worcester Art Mus., 1980—86; mem. Ind. Commn. on L.A. Police Dept., 1991—92; governing bd. LA County Local Initiative Health Authority, 1994—2007, chmn., 2001—05; bd trustees Pomona Coll., 1969—, vice chmn., 1971—79, chmn., 1991—2000, emeritus chmn., 2000—; bd. fellow Claremont U. Ct., 1971—79, 1991—2000; chmn. bd. overseers Claremont U. Consortium, 2000—06, emeritus chmn. bd. overseers, 2006—; vice-chmn., bd. trustees Keck Grad. Inst. Applied Life Scis., 1997—2000, emeritus, 2000—; bd. dirs. Nat. Med. Fellowships, Inc., 1973—2005, chmn., 1980—85; bd. trustees Charles Drew U. Med. and Sci., 1968—79, 1986—95, Orthopaedic Hosp., 1986—91, Barlow Hosp., 1987—89; bd. dirs. Worcester

Acad., 1984—86, U. So. Calif. Univ. Hosp., 1988—91, Alliance for Childrens Rights, 1991—95, Cmty. Health Coun., Inc., 1993—, Good Hope Med. Found, 1994—, chmn., 2006—; bd. dirs. Ralph M. Parsons Found., 2000—, vice chmn., 2008—; bd. dirs. Huntington Med. Rsch. Inst., 2006—, Congl. Homes, Inc., Mt. San Antonio Gardens, 2006—; mem. coun. pres. Assn. Governing Bodies Colls. and Univs., 2000—03, chair, 2002—03; bd. trustee Alta Med. Health Svc., 2008—. Fellow Milbank Found., 1967—72. Fellow: AAAS, Am. Antiquarian Soc.; mem.: Inst. Medicine of Nat. Acad. Scis., Calif. Med. Assn., L.A. Acad. Medicine, L.A. County Med. Assn., AMA, Alpha Omega Alpha, Sigma Xi, Phi Beta Kappa.

TRANQUILLI, ANDREA LUIGI, obstetrician, gynecologist; b. Rome, Oct. 19, 1955; s. Antonio and Maria (Albano-Leoni) T. MD, Cath. U. of the Sacred Heart, 1979, cert. ob-gyn., 1983. Med. ward asst. Rome Health Unit, 1981-83; asst. dept. ob-gyn. Ancona U., 1983-93, head asst. dept. ob-gyn., 1993—; contract prof. ob-gyn. Ancona U. Sch. Medicine, 1986—, Ancona U. Postgrad. Sch., 1985—; contract prof. gyn. Ancona U. Sch. Pediatrics, 1985—. Head perinatal medicine unit Salesi Hosp., Ancona U., 1994—. Author: Fetal Reactivity, 1984; editor: Experimental Models in Ob-Gyn., 1989; guest editor Clinical and Experimental Hypertension in Pregnancy, 1991. Scholarship Cath. U., 1981-82. Fellow Soc. Perinatal Obstetricians; mem. Italian Soc. Gynecology Obstetrics, Internat. Soc. Study Hypertnesion in Pregnancy (internat. com. 1988, exec. 1994), Rotary Club Rome Parioli (founder). Avocations: guitar, skiing, sea sports. Office: 3 Via E Tot 60123 Ancona Italy also: Ancona Salesi Hosp Dept Ob-Gyn U 11 Via F Corridoni 60123 Ancona Italy

TRAUBE, MORRIS, gastroenterologist, educator; b. NY, Mar. 20, 1953; MD, SUNY, Bklyn., 1978; JD, Quinnipiac U. Sch. Law, 2001. Prof., dir, GI porcedure ctr., YNHH Yale U. Sch. Medicine, 1984—2004, dir, clin. affairs, sect. dig diseases; adj. prof. law Quinnipiac U. Sch. Law, 2001—04; prof., assoc. chair clin. affairs, dept. medicine, sect. chief, gastro, tisch hosp. NYU Sch. Medicine, 2004—, dir, ctr esophageal disease. Office: NYU Sch Medicine 530 1st Ave New York NY 10016 Office Fax: 212-263-3096. Business E-Mail: morris.traube@nyumc.org.

TRAUTNER, CHRISTOPH, medical educator, consultant; s. Erich and Hanna Trautner. MD, Ludwig-Maximilian U., Munich, 1978; M in Polit. Sci., Free U. of Berlin, 1986; MPH, Harvard Sch. of Pub. Health, Boston, 1991. Public Health Physician Bd. of Physicians, Hamburg, Germany, 1989. Dist. health commr. Tiergarten Dist. Authority, Berlin, 1981—85; dir., sect. of prevention and rehab. Authority for Health, Employment and Social Affairs, Hamburg, 1986—90; rsch. assoc. Heinrich Heine U., Duesseldorf, 1992—97; dep. dir. rsch. Inst. Social Medicine, Occupl. Medicine and Epidemiology, Berlin, 1997—2001; privatdozent U. of Bielefeld, Sch. of Pub. Health, 2000—; prof. of medicine / pub. health U. of Applied Scis., Wolfsburg, Germany, 2002—. Bd. mem. Pub. Health Rsch. Network, North-Rhine Westfalia, Duesseldorf, Bielefeld, 1992—96; dep. chair, organizer World Diabetes Day, Conf. of the German Diabetes Union, Duesseldorf, 1996; chair Gesundheitsforschung e.V, Berlin, 1999—; chair, organizer Prevention - What is the Evidence, satellite symposium of the World Congress of Epidemiol., Montreal, Canada, 2002; cons. Nat. Assn. Statutory Health Ins. Physicians, Berlin, 2003—05; mem. departmental coun. U. Applied Scis. Dept. Pub. Health, Wolfsburg, Germany, 2003—05, mem. tchg. commn., 2003—05, mem. exam. commn., 2003—05; peer reviewer Diabetologia, Diabetic Medicine. Contbr. articles to profl. jours. Mem. fed. com. on health affairs Free Dem. Party, Bonn, Germany, 1989—91, chair, com. on health affairs Hamburg, Germany, 1987—90. Mem.: Soc. for Epidemiologic Rsch., European Assn. for the Study of Diabetes, Internat. Epidemiol. Assn., Harvard Club Berlin, Harvard Club Hamburg. Achievements include research in epidemiology of diabetic complications, blindness, obesity. Avocations: languages, philosophy, history. Home: Stephanstr 67 Berlin D-10559 Germany Home Fax: +49 30 39035122. Personal E-mail: ct@christoph-trautner.net.

TRAVERS, W. LAWRENCE, healthcare executive; b. Syracuse, NY, Nov. 1, 1943; s. Walter Roy and Elizabeth Laurene (Hicks) T. BS, Coll. of Emporia, Kans., 1965; MSW, Syracuse U., 1972. Diplomate in clin. social work N.Y.; cert. addictions counselor. Cons. alcoholism treatment Hutchings Psychiat. Ctr. N.Y. State, Office of Mental Health, Syracuse, 1972-73, program dir. alcoholism rehab. unit, 1973-76, program dir. psychogeriatric day treatment/outpatient svcs., 19976-80, mental health outpatient svc., 1980-86, program dir. mentally ill chem. abuse sr. adv. panel, 1986-91; rehab. coord. Capital Dist. Psychiat. Ctr., Albany, N.Y., 1991-94; edn. and tng. cons., 1994-97; cons. to med. dir. managed care N.Y. State/Office of Mental Health, Albany, 1997-98, dir. co-occurring psychiat. and addictive disorders, 1998-2000, dir. health systems transition, 2000—; cons. N.Y.C. Office of Mental Hlth., 2000—; pvt. practice Albany, N.Y. Dir. Health Systems Transition, Albany,NY, bd. dirs. Franklin Med. Lab. Sch., Westbury, N.Y., 1980. Dem. Party ofcl., 1974-76. Recipient Sci. Achievement award Chem. Rubber Co., 1965. Fellow Am. Orthopsychiat. Assn.; mem. NASW (clin. register), Acad. Cert. Social Workers (diplomate), Am. Coll. Addiction Treatment Adminstrs., Am. Bd. Examiners in Clin. Social Work, Nat. Assn. Drug Abuse and Alcoholism Commn. (master addiction counselor), Am. Coll. Health Care Execs. Presbyterian. Office: NY State Office Mental Health 44 Holland Ave Albany NY 12208-3411 Home: 6185 Leslieanne Path Cicero NY 13039-9392 Home Phone: 315-546-3376. Business E-Mail: lawrencetravers@care2.com.

TRAVIS, RANDALL HOWARD, retired physiologist, retired endocrinologist; b. Curdsville, Ky., July 11, 1924; s. Charles Spaulding and Celestine Frances Travis; m. Priscilla Beryl Korabeck, June 24, 1949 (div.); m. Ilona Marie Engel, June 14, 1974; children: Randall Howard, Laura Jane. BS, U. Chgo.; MD, Western Res. U., 1948—52. Assoc. prof. Case Western Res. U., Physiology Dept., Cleve., 1968—85; asst. prof. dept. medicine Case Western Res. U., 1963—85; physician dept. medicine Copley Hosp., Morrisville, Vt., 1985—97. Assoc. physician, medicine Cleve. Met. Gen. Hosp., 1974—85. Contbr. articles to biomed. jours. Adv. RSVP, Morrisville, Vt., 1996—2003, Sr. Companions Program, Barre, Vt., 2000—03. Sgt. USMC, 1943—46. Grantee Established Investigator, Am. Heart Assn., 1956-1959, Rsch. grants, NIH, 1959-1974. Mem.: AAAS, Endocrine Soc., Ctrl. Soc. for Clin. Rsch. (assoc.), Vt. Med. Soc. (life). Liberal. Avocations: boating, skiing, bicycling, hiking. Home: PO Box 553 Waterbury VT 05676

TRAVIS, THOMAS L., career military officer, physician; BS in Biology, Va. Polytechnic Inst. and State U., Blacksburg, 1976, MS in Physiology, 1980; MD, Uniformed Services U. of Health Sciences Sch. Medicine, Bethesda, Md., 1986; MPH, U. Tex. Health Sci. Ctr., San Antonio, 1991; attended, Air War Coll., 1996; MS in Nat. Resource Strategy, Nat. Def. U. Indsl. Coll. of Armed Forces, Ft. Leslie McNair, Washington, DC, 1999; attended, Georger Wash. U. Interagency Inst., Washington, 2003. Joined US Air Force, 1976, second lt., 1976—78, pilot tng. Williams AFB, Ariz., 1977—78, fighter tng. Holloman AFB, N.Mex., 1978, F-4 replacement tng. unit MacDill AFB, Fla., 1978—79, first lt., 1978—82, F-4 aircraft comdr. 334th Tactical Fighter Squadron Seymore Johnson AFB, NC, 1979—82, capt., 1982—88, intern Andrews AFB, Md., 1986—87, pilot physician Langley AFB, Va., 1987—90, maj., 1988—94, resident in aerospace medicine Brooks AFB, Tex., 1990—92, lt. col., 1994—98, chief med. ops., human systems program office, 1992—98, col., 1998—2004, dir. operational health support, chief aerospace medicine divsn., Air Force Med. Ops. Agency Washington, 1999—2001, comdr. USAF Sch. Aerospace Medicine Brooks AFB, 2001—03, comdr. 311th Human Systems Wing Brooks City-Base, Tex., 2003—05, brig. gen., 2004—07, comdr. 89th Med. Group Andrews AFB, 2005—06, command surgeon, Hdqs. Air Force Dist. Washington Bolling AFB, Washington, DC, 2006, comdr. 79th Med. Wing Andrews AFB, 2006, command surgeon Hdqs. Air Combat Command Langley AFB, 2006—07, maj. gen., 2007—, comdr. 59th Med. Wing Lackland AFB, Tex., 2007—10, dep. surgeon gen. Washington, 2010—. Sr. med. officer test pilot Royal Air Force Sch. Aviation Medicine, Farnborough, England, 1996—98. Decorated Disting. Svc. medal, Legion of Merit, Oak Leaf Cluster, Meritorious Svc. medal, Four Oak Leaf Clusters, Aerial Achievement medal, Air Force Commendation medal, Joint Svc. Achievement medal, Combat Readiness medal, Air Force Recognition Ribbon; recipient Paul W. Meyers award, Air Force Assn., 1995, Marie Marvingt award, French Soc. Aerospace Medicine, 2007, George E. Schafer award, Soc. USAF Flight Surgeons, 2007; named Stewart Lectr., Royal Aeronautical Soc., 2003. Fellow: Aerospace Med. Assn. (Julian E. Ward Meml. award 1994), American Coll. Preventative Medicine (former aerospace med. regent); mem.: Aerospace Med. Assn., Assn. Mil. Surgeons of US (life John D. Chase award 2008), Soc. US Air Force Flight Surgeons (former pres., Unger Literary award 1994), Internat. Assn. Mil. Flight Surgeon Pilots (former pres.), Order of Daedalians, Alpha Omega Alpha. Office: US Air Force Office of Surgeon General US Air Force Hdqs Washington DC 20032 *

TRAYHURN, PAUL, research biologist, educator; b. Exeter, England, May 6, 1948; s. William and Eileen (Morphew) T.; m. Deborah Gigg; four children. BSc, U. Reading, Eng., 1969; DPhil, U. Oxford, Eng., 1972, DSc, 1995. Rsch. staff Med. Rsch. Coun., Cambridge, Eng., 1975-86; prof., heritage scholar U. Alta., Edmonton, Can., 1986-88; head divsn. biochem. scis. Rowett Rsch. Inst., Aberdeen, 1988-97, asst. dir. acad. affairs, 1997-2000; prof. U. Aberdeen, 1992-2000; prof. Inst. Nutrition Rsch., U. Oslo, Norway, 2000-01; prof. nutritional biology U. Liverpool, England, 2001—. Co-editor: Brown Adipose Tissue, 1986; editor-in-chief Brit. Jour. Nutrition, 1999-2005; contbr. articles to profl. jours. Fellow Royal Soc. Edinburgh; mem. AAAS, Biochem. Soc., Nutrition Soc. Office: U Liverpool Sch Clin Sci Duncan Bldg Liverpool L69 3GA England E-mail: p.trayhum@liverpool.ac.uk.

TRC, TOMÁ, medical educator; b. Prague, Czech Republic, May 31, 1955; Docent, FVL UK Praha, 1981; MBA, PIBS Praha, 2006. Head, orthop. clinic 2nd Med. Sch., 1998, asst. prof., chief, clinic, 1998—. Recipient Chlumského Best Book award, 2008. Mem.: SSTA, ESSKA, CSOT, SICOT. Avocations: sports, music. Home: Korandova 28 Prague 147 00 Czech Republic Personal E-mail: tomas.trc@lfmotol.cuni.cz.

TREABA, DIANA OLGUTA, physician; b. Ludus, Romania, Nov. 20, 1966; arrived in US, 1999; d. Constantin and Eugenia Treaba; m. Zoltan Szabolcs Szilagyi, June 22, 2004. MD Summa cum laude, U. Medicine and Pharmacy, Targu-Mures, 1987—93. Diplomate Anatomic Pathology and Clin. Pathology Am. Bd. of Pathology, 2003, Hematology Am. Bd. of Pathology, 2004, Specialist in Anatomic Pathology Ministry of Health and Family/Romania, 1998. Intern dr. Clin. County Hosp., Targu-Mures, Romania, 1994—95; resident in anatomic pathology Dept. of Pathology, Clin. County Hosp., Targu-Mures, Romania, 1995—99; resident in anatomic pathology and clin. pathology Dept. of Pathology, Rush Presbyn. St. Luke's Med. Ctr., Chgo., 1999—2003; fellow in hematopathology Northwestern Meml. Hosp., Chgo., 2003—04; fellow in immunohistochemistry PhenoPath Laboratories, Seattle, 2004—. Fellow: US and Can. Acad. of Pathology; mem.: AMA, Am. Assn. of Clin. Pathologists (licentiate), Coll. of Am. Pathologists (licentiate). Christian Orthodox. Office: RI Hosp APC 1142 Dept Pathology Providence RI 02903 Business E-Mail: dtreaba@lifespan.org.

TREFFERT, DAROLD ALLEN, psychiatrist, writer, hospital administrator; b. Fond du Lac, Wis., Mar. 12, 1933; s. Walter O. and Emma (Leu) T.; m. Dorothy Marie Sorgatz, June 11, 1955; children: Jon, Joni, Jill, Jay. BS, U. Wis., 1955, MD, 1958. Diplomate Am. Bd. Psychiatry and Neurology. Resident in psychiatry U. Wis. Med. Sch., 1959-62, clin. prof. psychiatry, 1965—; chief children's unit Winnebago (Wis.) Mental Health Inst., 1962-64, supt., 1964-79, Ctrl. State Hosp., Waupun, Wis., 1977-78; dir. Dodge County Mental Health Ctr., Juneau, Wis., 1964-74; mem. staff St. Agnes Hosp., Fond du Lac, 1963—; exec. dir. Fond du Lac County Mental Health Ctr., 1979-92. Chmn. Controlled Substances Bd. Wis.; chmn. med. examining bd. State of Wis. Author: Extraordinary People: Understanding Savant Syndrome, 1989, 3d edit., 2006, edits. in U.S., U.K., Italy, Japan, Netherlands, Sweden, Korea, China, Mellowing: Lessons from Listening, 2006; autism cons. (movie) Rainman, 1988, Islands of Genius The Bountiful Mind of the Autistic, Acquired and Sudden Savant, 2010. Trustee Marian U., Fond du Lac, Wis. Fellow Am. Coll. Psychiatrists; mem. AMA, Wis. Med. Soc. (pres. 1979-80), Wis. Psychiat. Assn. (pres.), Am. Assn. Psychiat. Adminstrs. (pres.), Alpha Omega Alpha. Home: W 4065 Maplewood Ln Fond Du Lac WI 54937-9562 Office: 430 E Division St Fond Du Lac WI 54935-4560 Office Phone: 920-921-9381. Business E-Mail: daroldt@charter.net.

TREFNY, ZDENEK, cardiologist, educator, researcher; b. Prague, Czech Republic, July 1, 1926; s. Martin and Zdeňka (Straková) T.; m. Božena Švábová, Sept. 28, 1956; children: Martin, Zdenek, Pavel. MD, Charles U., Prague, 1950, postgrad. diploma pediatrics 1st grade, 1955, postgrad. diploma pediatrics 2d grade, 1961, Sci. Degree pediatrics, 1972. Physician, asst. med. faculty Charles U., Prague, 1951-60; pvt. practice Prague, 1961—. External coop. with faculty of phys. edn. Charles U. Prague, 1961—, assoc. prof., 1991—; sci. cons. Grant Agy., Prague, 1995—; med. councillor Dept. Health Instns., 1992-95; dir. hosp. with polyclinic, Prague, 1971-82. Author: Human Physiology, 1983, 1997, Physiology of Exercise, 1980, Physiology of the Child, 1958—61; contbr. articles to profl. jours. Mem.: Mil. and Hospitaller Order St. Lazarus of Jerusalem (knight comdr. 2003), European Soc. for Noninvasive Cardiovascular Dynamics (Burger award 1995), Am. Cardiovascular Sys. Dynamics Soc. (Golden Distinction 1985). Achievements include patentee in field; research in quantitative ballistu cardiography quantitative seismocardiography. Avocations: classical music, travel. Home: Šrobárova 1 130 00 Prague Czech Republic Office: U Pruhonu 52 17000 Prague Czech Republic Office Phone: 420220878403. Business E-Mail: z.m.trefny@grbox.cz.

TREFRY, ROBERT J., health facility administrator; b. Springfield, Vt., Mar. 29, 1947; married. Bachelors' degree, Ga. Inst. Tech., 1970; Masters' degree, George Washington U., 1974. With Greater Southeast Community Hosp., Washington, 1973, adminstrv. asst., 1973-74, asst. adminstr., 1974-79; sr. v.p. North Kansas City (Mo.) Community Hosp., 1979-83; exec. v.p., chief exec. officer St. Agnes Hosp., White Plains, NY, 1983-88; exec. v.p., chief operating officer Carle Found. Hosp., Urbana, Ill., 1988-91; exec. v.p., chief oper. officer Bridgeport (Conn.) Hosp., 1991-94, pres., CEO, 1994—; exec. v.p. Yale New Haven Health Sys., 1996—. With U.S. mil. 1970-71. Office: Bridgeport Hosp 267 Grant St Bridgeport CT 06610-2870

TREFZGER, RICHARD CHARLES, retired surgeon; b. Peoria, Ill., Jan. 27, 1948; s. John Dennis and Marilyn Lestilie (Wilson) Trefzger; m. Nancy Ellen Guy, Dec. 19, 1971; children: Emily Jean, Michael Guy. BS, U. Ill., 1970, MD, 1973. Diplomate Am Bd Surgery; lic. min. 2010. Intern in surgery Med. Coll. Wis., Milw., 1973-74, resident in surgery, 1974-75, Presbyn.-St. Luke's Hosp., Chgo., 1975-78; instr. surgery Rush Med. Coll., Chgo., 1977-78; med. dir. Westminster Village Retirement Ctr., Bloomington, Ill., 1980-84, St. Joseph's Trauma Ctr., Bloomington, 1986-96, BroMenn Regional Trauma Ctr., Normal, Ill., 1994-96; chief surgery Bromenn Regional Med. Ctr., Normal, Ill., 1987-88, 94-96, St. Joseph's Med. Ctr., Bloomington, 1989-91, pres. med. staff, 1991-92. Clin. instr. U. Ill. Coll. Medicine, 1980—2006, clin. asst. prof. surgery, 2006—; chmn. bd. dirs. BroMenn Physician Hosp. Orgn., 1995—96; sec. med. staff BroMenn Regional Med. Ctr., 1998, v.p., 99, bd. dirs., 1999—2002, pres. med. staff, 2000—02. Mem. Ill. State U. Civic Chorale, Normal, 1991—98; bd. dirs. Cmty. Cancer Ctr, Bloomington, 1996—2006, pres., 2000; lic. min., 2010—; v.p. ofcl. bd. First Christian Ch., Bloomington, 1981—82, 1999—2002, 2005—06, elder, 1980—, pastoral asst., 2009—; rector Cursillo Christianity, 2001; bd. dirs. Barton Stone Christian Home, Jacksonville, Ill., 1979—82. Fellow: ACS (councilor Ill. chpt. 1986—88, mem. Ill. chpt. com. trauma 1996—2003); mem.: AMA, Ill. Surg. Soc. (gov. 1990—94, v.p. elect 1997, v.p. 1998, pres. elect 1999, pres. 2000, trustee 2001—04), Danvers Cmty. Band-Saxophone, Scottish Rite, Rotary (dir. 1982—85, 1994—99, sec. 1995—96, v.p. 1996—97, pres. 1997—98, band-saxophone, Paul Harris fellow 1989), Masons, Alpha Omega Alpha. Avocations: music, travel. Home: 41 Pendleton Way Bloomington IL 61704-6243 Office: First Christian Ch 401 W Jefferson St Bloomington IL 61701 Office Phone: 309-829-9327. Personal E-mail: mendr2@comcast.net. E-mail: richard.trefzger@gmail.com.

TREGLIA, GIORGIO, nuclear medicine physician; b. Formia, Italy, Apr. 6, 1979; Postgrad., 2003. Physician Inst. Nuc. Medicine, Cath. U. Sacred Heart, Rome, 2009—. Mem.: European Assn. Nuc. Medicine. Office: Largo Gemelli 8 Rome 00168 Italy Business E-Mail: giorgiomednuc@libero.it.

TREHAN, RAM S., oncologist, hematologist; MD, Armed Forces Med. Coll., 1979. Diplomate Am. Bd. Internal Medicine, Am. Bd. Internal Medicine-med. oncology. Fellow in hematology and oncology The Wash. Hosp. Ctr.; pres. med. staff Holy Cross Hosp., sec. treas. bd. trustee. Named Washingtonians Top Doctors. Office: Washington Adventist Hospital 7600 Caroll Ave Takoma Park MD 20912 Office Phone: 301-891-7600.

TRENT, CALVIN R., city health department director; BA, MA Edn., Wayne State Univ.; MA, PhD, Univ. Detroit-Mercy. Adminstr. Detroit Pub. Sch. Sys. & Highland Park Cmty. Coll., 1976—92; addictions therapist Vet. Adminstrn. Hosp., Battle Creek; dir. Detroit Counseling Ctr.; dir. substance abuse prevention prog. Detroit Dept. Health & Wellness Promotion, 1998—2009, dir. spl. population health services, 2006, health officer & dir., 2009—. Office: Dept Health & Wellness Promotion Herman Kiefer Complex 1151 Taylor Detroit MI 48202 Office Phone: 313-876-4776.

TRENTO, ALFREDO A., thoracic surgeon, educator; b. Padua, Italy, July 3, 1950; MD, U. Padova, 1975. Cert. Am. Bd. Surgery, Am. Bd. Thoracic Surgery. Intern, internal medicine Cittadella Gen. Hosp., Padua, Italy; intern, gen. surgery U. Mass., Worcester, Mass., 1977, fellow, 1982; resident, thoracic surgery U. Mass. Med. Ctr., Worcester, Mass., 1977—82; resident, surgery U. Pitts. Sch. Medicine, Pa., 1983—85, faculty mem.; dir., ECMO Program Children's Hosp. Pitts.; dir., divsn. cardiothoracic surgery Cedars-Sinai Med. Ctr., LA, Estelle, Abe and Marjorie Sanders Endowed Chair, cardiac surgery; prof., surgery, David Geffen Sch. Medicine UCLA Sch. Medicine, Calif. Presenter in field. Contbr. articles to profl. jours., chapters to books. Fellow: ACS; mem.: Western Assn. Transplant Surgeons, Am. Assn. for Thoracic Surgery, Soc. Thoracic Surgeons, Internat. Soc. for Heart Transplantation. Office: Cedars Sinai Med Ctr 8700 Beverly Blvd Ste 6215 Los Angeles CA 90048 Office Phone: 310-423-3851. Office Fax: 310-423-0127. Business E-Mail: alfredo.trento@cshs.org.

TRETHOWAN, JONATHAN BRIAN, biomedical researcher, consultant; b. Truro, Cornwall, England, Aug. 31, 1971; s. John Treve and Janet Gaynor Trethowan; m. Sarah Jayne Morgan, Aug. 5, 1995; children: Erin Grace, Kieran John. BSc, U. Westminster, England, 1992; PhD, Royal Holloway U. London, 1998. Rsch. scientist GlaxoSmithKline, London, 1996—97; regulatory affairs advisor ML Labs., PLC, 1997—2001; regulatory affairs cons. Trac Svcs. Ltd., Truro, England, 2001—. Mem.: Orgn. Profls. in Regulatory Affairs. Avocations: golf, reading. Office: Trac Svcs Ltd 1 E Pool Tolvaddon Bus Pk TR14 0HX Camborne England Office Phone: 44 1209 612 650.

TRÉTON, JACQUES ALAIN, medical researcher; b. Boulogne-Billancourt, France, June 17, 1947; s. Roger Emile Tréton and Fernande Flora Verdier; m. Véronique Elisabeth Gauthier, Sept. 9, 1978; children: François Charles, Guillaume Victor, Anne-Laure Virginie. Bacalauréat (Sciences exp), Lycée La Fontaine, annexe Boulogne-Billancourt, 1967; ScD, U. Paris VII, 1981. Rschr. dir. Assn. Claude Bernard, Paris, 1989—2004; pres. Soc. Française Gérontologie et Gériatrie, Paris, 2004—06, v.p., 2006—10; chargé de mission AP-HP, Paris, 2004—. Fogarty fellow NIH/NIE, Bethesda, Md., 1993. Author: (book) Histoire de Montainville (1rst Price of the Yveline Dept., 1998). Mem.: Légion d'Honneur. Home: 101 Ave JB Clément Boulogne-Billancourt F-92100 France Office: INSERM U872 Institut des Cordeliers 15 Rue de L'Ecole de Médecine Paris 75006 France Business E-Mail: treton@infobiogen.fr.

TREUTING, EDNA GANNON, retired nursing administrator, educator; b. New Orleans, Dec. 16, 1925; d. Alphonse Joseph and Clara Josephine (David) Gannon; m. August Raymond Treuting, Sept. 4, 1948 (dec.); children: Keith, Karen Treuting Stein, Madeline Treuting LeBlanc, Jaime Treuting Gonzales, Jay (dec.). Diploma, Charity Hosp. Sch. Nursing, New Orleans, 1946; BS in Nursing Edn., La. State U., 1953; MPH, Tulane U., 1972, DPH, 1978. RN, La.; cert. family nurse practitioner Tulane U. Head nurse premature nursery Charity Hosp., New Orleans, 1946-47, head nurse pediatrics, 1947-49; instr. pediatrics Charity Hosp. Sch. Nursing, New Orleans, 1949-52, 54, instr. LPN, 1953; pvt. duty Touro, Hotel Dieu, New Orleans, 1957-59; instr. maternal and child health La. State U. Sch. Nursing, New Orleans, 1960, 65, 69-71; from instr. to prof., sect. head Tulane Sch. Pub. Health and Tropical Medicine, New Orleans, 1972-83; dean, prof. Our Lady Holy Cross Coll. Nursing Div., New Orleans, 1983-84; chief nurse Dept. Health and Hosp., New Orleans, 1987-94. Region IV nurse practitioner Baylor U., Health Edn. and Welfare, 1974-76; citizen amb. to South Am. People to People, 1979; presentor U. Hawaii Pub. Health and Nursing, 1977; planner, advisor, reviewer continuing edn. U. Tenn., Memphis, 1990-95. Author, editor: Occupation Health Nursing, 1979; sect. head, prin. investigator Practitioner Programs Family and Pediatric, 1973-83, item writer Nurse Practitioners, Community Health and Occupational Nursing, 1974-80; mem. editl. bd. to sci. jours. and Nurse Practitioner Jour., 1974-2005. Pres. Oti-Mrs Internat. New Orleans, 1955-68; sponsor bd. dirs. Holy Cross H.S. Treuting Scholarship, New Orleans, 1966—; hurricane and disaster nurse ARC, New Orleans, 1966-77; v.p. Pandora Carnival Club, New Orleans, 1968-78; alternate state health dept. Commn. Nursing Supply and Demand by Legislation, 1991-94, planner, presentor La. State Rsch. Day, 1990-92. Named outstanding woman in the mainstream world's fair women of achievement, 1984. Mem. AARP (chpt. 3086 pres. 1999-, sr. mem., chpt. pres. 2001—, Mandeville chpt. pres. 2001-, Cmty. Svc. award 2006), New Orleans Dist. Nurses Assn. (First J.B. Hickey Meml. Cmty. award 1985, Great 100 Nurse-First Yr. 1987), La. Pub. Health Assn. (Dr. C.B. White Merritorious Diligent Svc. 1990), La. Nurse Practitioners Assn.(Edna Treuting scholarship named in her honor), Tulane U. Alumni Assn. (past pres.), Tulane Med. Alumni Assn. (past pres.), New Image Club of Mandeville (chmn. 1986-2003), Mandeville Rep. Women, Mandeville Srs., New Image Club (chmn. line dance, co-chmn. trips and travel 1995-2004, Young at Heart, New Image Club (chmn. trips and travel, vice chmn.), Delta Omega (nat. and chpt. past pres.), Sigma Theta Tau, AARP(pres. chpt. 3086, 1999-) Republican. Roman Catholic. Avocations: travel, dance, swimming, photography, reading. Home: 1914 Marlin Dr Mandeville LA 70448-1069

TREVATHAN, EDWIN, dean, educator, neurologist; b. Louisville, Nov. 3, 1956; s. Norman Edwin, Jr. and Joyce Brent (Sawyer) Trevathan; m. Linda Scott, Dec. 31, 1977; children: Scott, Daniel, Luke. BS in Biochemistry and Math., Lipscomb U., 1977; MD, Emory U., 1982, MPH in Chronic Disease Epidemiology, 1982. Diplomate Am. Bd. Psychiatry and Neurology, Am. Bd. Pediat., Am. Bd. Clin. Neurophysiology. Resident in pediats. Yale U. Sch. Medicine, New Haven, 1982-84; resident and fellow in neurology/child neurology Mass. Gen. Hosp., Harvard Med. Sch., Boston, 1984-87; fellow in neurophysiology and epilepsy Boston Children's Hosp., 1986-87; epidemic intelligence officer Ctrs. for Disease Control & Prevention, Atlanta, 1987-89; dir. Children's Epilepsy Ctr., chief neurology Scottish Rite Children's Med. Ctr., Atlanta, 1989-95; ptnr. Child Neurology Assocs., P.C., Atlanta, 1989-95; dir. Comprehensive Epilepsy Ctr. U. Ky. Coll. Medicine, Lexington, 1995-98; dir. Pediat. Epilepsy Ctr. Washington U. Sch. Medicine, St. Louis Children's Hosp., 1998—2007, prof. neurology & pediatrics, 2004—07; neurologist in chief St. Louis Children's Hosp., 2004—07; dir. divsn. pediat. and devel. neurology Washington U. Sch. Medicine, 2004—07; dir. nat. ctr. birth defects and developmental disabilities Ctrs. Disease Control and Prevention, Atlanta, 2007—10; dean, prof. St. Louis U. Sch. Pub. Health, 2010—. Assoc. chief neurology svc. U. Ky. Coll. Medicine, Lexington, 1996—98. Contbr. articles to profl. jours. Bd. dirs., mem. Epilepsy Found. Am., Atlanta, 1991—95; mem. profl. adv. bd. Epilepsy Found. Greater St. Louis, 1999—2003. With USPHS, 1987—89. Fellow: Royal Soc. Medicine (London); mem.: Am. Acad. Neurology, Alpha Omega Alpha. Office: Office of Dean St Louis University Sch Pub Health 3545 Lafayette Ave Saint Louis MO 63104 Office Phone: 314-977-3240. Business E-Mail: etrevath@slu.edu. *

TRIADAFILOPOULOS, GEORGE, medical educator; b. Greece, Aug. 30, 1955; MD, Aristotelian U., 1979. Clin. prof. Stanford U. Sch. Medicine, 1992—. Office: 2490 Hosp Dr 211 Mountain View CA 94040 Office Fax: 650-988-7486. Business E-Mail: vagt@stanford.edu.

TRIANA, LINA M., plastic surgeon; b. Feb. 15, 1974; MD, U. Valle, 1999, degree in Plastic Surgery, 2005. Pres. Dr. Lina Triana Aesthetic Plastic Surgery, 2005—. Mem.: Laser Vaginal Rejuvenation Inst. America, Soc. Colombiana de Cirugia Plastica, Am. Soc. Aesthetic Plastic Sugery, Internat. Soc. Aesthetic Plastic Surgery (worldwide nat. secretaries chair). Avocations: horseback riding, reading. Office: Calle 3 Oeste # 34-96 Cali Valle del Cauca 99999 Colombia Office Fax: 5726604164. Personal E-mail: drlinatriana@gmail.com.

TRIANDIS, HARRY CHARALAMBOS, psychologist, educator; b. Patras, Greece, Oct. 16, 1926; s. Christos Charalambos and Louise J. (Nikokavouras) T.; m. Pola Fotitch, Dec. 23, 1966; 1 child, Louisa. B.Engring., McGill U., 1951; M.Commerce, U. Toronto, Ont., Can., 1954; PhD, Cornell U., 1958; Doctorate (hon.), U. Athens, Greece, 1987. Asst. prof. U. Ill., Champaign, 1958-61, assoc. prof., 1961-66, prof. psychology, 1966-97; cons. USIA, 1970-75, NSF, 1968-75; prof. emeritius, 1997—. Author: Attitudes and Attitude Change, 1971, The Analysis of Subjective Culture, 1972, Varieties of Black and White Perception of the Social Environment, 1975, Interpersonal Behavior, 1977, Culture and Social Behavior, 1994, Individualism and Collectivism, 1995, Fooling Ourselves: Self-deception in Politics, Religion and Terrorism, 2009; editor: Handbook of Cross-Cultural Psychology, Vol. 1-6, 1980-81, Handbook of Industrial and Organizational Psychology, Vol. 4, 1994; editorial cons.; Jour. Personality and social Psychology, 1963-71, Jour. Applied Psychology, 1970-79, Sociometry, 1971-74, Jour. Cross-Cultural Psychology, 1974—, others. Chmn. fgn. grants com. Am. Psychol. Found., 1968-90. Sr. fellow Ford Found., 1964-65; Guggenheim fellow, 1972-73; grantee USPHS, 1956-60, 62; grantee Office Naval Research, 1960-68, 80-85; grantee Social and Rehab. Service, HEW, 1968-73; grantee Ford Found., 1973-75; recipient award Interam. Soc. Psychology, 1981 Mem. Soc. for Psychol. Study of Social Issues (pres. 1975-76), Internat. Assn. Cross-Cultural Psychology (pres. 1974-76), Interam. Soc. Psychology (pres. 1985-87), Soc. for Exptl. Social Psychology (chmn. 1972-74), Soc. for Personality and Social Psychology (pres. 1976-77), Internat. Assn. Applied Psychology (pres. 1990-94). Office: 603 E Daniel St Champaign IL 61820-6232 Home: 2008 Eagle Ridge Ct Apt A Urbana IL 61802-8695 Business E-Mail: triandis@uiuc.edu, triands@illinois.edu.

TRIANTOPOULOU, CHARIKLEIA, radiologist; b. Athens, Greece, Feb. 29, 1964; d. Christos Triantopoulos and Kaliopi Triantopoulou; m. Efstathios Panagoulias, Sept. 20, 1989; children: Anastasios Panagoulias, Christos Panagoulias. MD, U. Athens, 1987, radiologist, 1992, PhD, 1993. Supr. radiology dept. Pvt. Med. Ctr., Athens, 1992—94; registrar CT and MRI dept. Social Security Orgn. - 1st Hosp., Athens, 1994—2000; subdirector CT dept. Gen. Hosp. Agia Olga, Athens, 2000—. Contbr. articles to profl. jours. Mem.: European Soc. Gastrointestinal and Abdominal Radiology, European Assn. Radiology, Hellenic Radiol. Soc. Office: Gen Hosp Agia Olga 3-5 Agias Olgas N Ionia Athens 14233 Greece Personal E-mail: chatri@mycosmos.gr.

TRICHE, ELIZABETH W., epidemiologist, educator; Asst. prof. med. svcs. Dept. Cmty. Health & Epidemiology Brown U., co-dir. epidemiology grad. program; affiliate Yale Ctr. for Perinatal, Pediatric & Environ. Epidemiology. Office: Dept of Community Health 121 S Main St Box G-S121 Providence RI 02912 Office Phone: 401-863-1987. Office Fax: 401-863-3713. E-mail: elizabeth_triche@brown.edu.

TRICKETT, GARY LEWIS, hospital administrator, management information systems consultant; b. St. John's, Nfld., Can., Jan. 13, 1959; s. Lewis George and Marion Louise (Locke) T.; m. Judith Ida Mosher, July 6, 1985; children: Gina Danielle, Mark Gary. B in Comm., Meml. U., St. John's, Nfld., 1981; postgrad., Ctrl. Mich. U. Cert. healthcare exec. V.p., owner NewCom Ltd., St. John's, Nfld., Can., 1981-83; data processing mgr. Western Meml. Hosp., Corner Brook, Nlfd., 1983-85; dir. MIS St. Clare's Hosp., St. John's, 1985-90; adminstr. Charlotte County Hosp., St. Stephen, N.B., Can., 1990-93, St. John Regional Hosp., Saint John, N.B., Can., 1993—. Mem. ACHE, Can. Coll. Health Svc. Execs., St. John Rotary Club, St. John Bd. Trade. Avocations: skiing, travel, woodworking, fishing, hunting. Home: 18 Weeden Ave Fairvale NB Canada E2E 3L7 Office: St John Regional Hosp Tucker Park Saint John NB Canada E2L 4L2 *

TRIER, JERRY STEVEN, gastroenterologist, educator; b. Frankfurt, Germany, Apr. 12, 1933; came to U.S., 1938, naturalized, 1943; s. Kurt J. and Alice L. (Cahn) T.; m. Laurel M. Bryan, June 8, 1957; children: Stanley, Jeryl, Stephen. MD, U. Wash., 1957; MA (hon.), Harvard U., 1973. Diplomate Am. Bd. Internal Medicine. Intern U. Rochester, NY, 1957-58, resident in medicine, 1958-59; clin. asso. Nat. Cancer Inst., Bethesda, Md., 1959-61; trainee in gastroenterology U. Wash., Seattle, 1961-63; asst. prof. medicine U. Wis., Madison, 1963-67; asso. prof. U. N.Mex., Albuquerque, 1967-69, Boston U., 1969-73, Harvard U. Med. Sch., Cambridge, Mass., 1973-76, prof., 1976—. Sr. physician Brigham and Women's Hosp.; cons. Dana Farber Cancer Ctr., Nat. Inst. Diabetes and Digestive and Kidney Disease; adv. coun. NIH, 1986-90. Editor: Internal Medicine; mem. editorial bd.; Anatomical Record, 1969-98, Gastroenterology, assoc. editor, 1971-77, mem. editorial bd., 1967-71, 78-83, 93-98, chmn., 1988-93, Am. Jour. Medicine, 1978-87, Current Opinion in Gastroenterology, 1990—; contbr. articles to profl. jours.; contbr. chpts. to books. Served as surgeon USPHS, 1959-61. Recipient Disting. Med. Alumnus award U. Wash., 2004, NIH Merit award, 1988-94, Silen Lifetime Mentoring Achievement award Harvard Med. Sch., 2008; USPHS/NIH grantee, 1963-94. Mem. Am. Soc. Clin. Investigation, Assn. Am. Physicians, Am. Gastroent. Assn. (pres. 1985-86, Julius Friedenwald medal 1999, Disting. Mentor award, 2009), Am. Soc. Cell Biology, Am. Fedn. Clin. Research. Office: Brigham and Women's Hosp 75 Francis St Boston MA 02115-6110

TRIGG, JACK WALDEN, JR., retired physician; b. Birmingham, Ala., Apr. 18, 1932; s. Jack Walden Sr. and Florine (Hagood) T.; m. Dorothy Wynne, June 3, 1958; 1 child, James Albert. BS, Va. Mil. Inst., 1953; MD, Med. Coll. of Ala., 1958. Diplomate Am. Bd. Internal Medicine. Cardiology fellowship U. Ala. Birmingham, 1956—57; intern in medicine Duke U. Hosp., Durham, NC, 1958-59; resident in medicine Univ. Hosp., Birmingham, 1959-62; physician So. Med. Group, Birmingham, 1964-98, pres., 1987—96. Pres. med. staff St. Vincent's Hosp., 1986, Southview Group, 1987-1996. Capt. USAF, 1962-64. Fellow ACP; mem. Jefferson County Med. Soc., Birmingham Rotary Club. Republican. Episcopalian. Home: 2006 Garden Pl Birmingham AL 35223-1156

TRIGGLE, DAVID JOHN, dean, pharmacist, consultant; b. Eng., Apr. 5, 1935; came to U.S., 1962; s. William John and Maud F. (Henderson) T.; m. Ann M. Jones, Sept. 22, 1959; children: Andrew B., Jocelyn A. BSc in Chemistry, U. Southampton, Eng., 1956; PhD, U. Hull, Eng., 1959. Sch. fellow U. Ottawa, Ont., Can., 1959-61; rsch. fellow U. London, 1961-62; asst. prof. SUNY Sch. of Pharmacy, Buffalo, 1962-65, assoc. prof., 1965-69, prof., 1985-95, chmn. dept., 1971-85, dean, 1985-95, Disting. prof., 1987—, vice-provost for grad. edn., 1995-2001, dean Grad. Sch., 1995-2001, provost, 2000-01, univ. prof., 2000—; pres. Ctr. for Inquiry, Inst. Buffalo. Cons. to pharm. industry, 1980—. Author: Chemical Aspects of Autonomic Nervous System, 1965, Neurotransmitter-Receptor Interactions, 1971, Chemical Pharmacology of the Synapse, 1976; editor: Comprehensive Medicinal Chemistry, 2006. Recipient Volwiler Rsch. Achievement award Am. Assn. Colls. Pharmacy, 1988, 89, George Koepf award Biomed. Rsch. Med. Found. Buffalo, 1994. Fellow AAAS; mem. Am. Chem. Soc., Am. Soc. Pharmacology and Therapeutics (Otto Krayer award 1995), Soc. Neurosci., Brit. Pharmacology Soc., Am. Pharm. Assn., Rho Chi (Rho Chi award 1998). Office: SUNY Sch Pharmacy 126 Cooke Buffalo NY 14260-0001 Business E-Mail: triggle@buffalo.edu.

TRIGIANO, LUCIEN LEWIS, physician; b. Easton, Pa., Feb. 9, 1926; s. Nicholas and Angeline (Lewis) T.; children: Lynn Anita, Glenn Larry, Robert Nicholas. Student, Tex. Christian U., 1944-45, Ohio U., 1943-44, 46-47, Milligan Coll., 1944, Northwestern U., 1945, Temple U., 1948-52. Diplomate Am. Bd. Phys. Medicine & Rehab. Intern Meml. Hosp., Johnstown, Pa., 1952-53; resident Lee Hosp., Johnstown, 1953-54; gen. practice Johnstown, 1953-59; med. dir. Pa. Rehab. Ctr., Johnstown, 1959-62, chief phys. medicine & rehab., 1964-70; fellow phys. medicine & rehab. N.Y. Inst. Phys. Medicine & Rehab., 1962—64; dir. rehab medicine Lee Hosp., 1964-71, Ralph K. Davies Med. Ctr., San Francisco, 1973-75, St. Joseph's Hosp., San Francisco, 1975-78, St. Francis Meml. Hosp., San Francisco, 1978-83, Rehab. Ctr. Nev., Las Vegas, 1998—2000; pvt. practice Las Vegas, 1998—. Asst. prof. phys. medicine and rehab. Temple U. Sch. Medicine; founder Disability Alert; bd. adv. Sch. Medicine Temple U., 2003—, bd. visitors, 2003; adj. prof. Touro U. Sch. Medicine, Las Vegas, 2005—. Served with USNR, 1944-46. Fellow ACP; mem. AMA, Pa. Med. Soc., San Francisco County Med. Soc., Am. Acad. Phys. Medicine and Rehab., Am. Congress Phys. Medicine, Calif. Acad. Phys. Medicine, Nat. Rehab. Assn., Babcock Surg. Soc. Home and Office: 20 Woodside Dr Easton PA 18042 Office Phone: 610-258-1509. Personal E-mail: lltmdmd@aol.com.

TRIMIS, GEORGIOS, pediatrician, director; b. Athens, Jan. 4, 1969; PhD, Athens Coll., 1988. Med. dir. Sanofi Pasteur MSD, 2005. Mem.: Am. Acad. Pediat. Home: Kifisias 32 Athens Attiki 11526 Greece Personal E-mail: gtrim@otenet.gr.

TRIN, YVES, orthodontist; b. Paris, June 3, 1949; PhD in Chirurgie Dentaire, U. Paris, 1974, PhD in Scis. Odobtologiques, 1994. Physician Cabinet Yves TRIN, 1978—. Master: Syndicat des Spécialistes Français en Orthpédie Dento Faciale, Soc. Française d'Orthopédie Dento-faciale, European Straigth Wire Soc., French Fedn. Orthodontits; fellow: World Fedn. Orthodontits. Avocation: scuba diving. Office: 34 Rue Du Plateau Paris IDF 75019 France Office Fax: 33-1-48-03-11-33. Personal E-mail: cabortho@me.com.

TRINCHIERI, GIORGIO, medical researcher; Rschr. Wistar Inst.; dir. Schering Plough Lab. Immunol. Rsch., Dardilly, France; NIH Fogarty scholar Lab. Parasitic Diseases, Nat. Inst. Allergy and Infectious Diseases; dir. Cancer and Inflammation Program, chief Lab. Exptl. Immunology Ctr. Cancer Rsch., Nat. Cancer Inst., NIH, Frederick, Md., 2006—. Office: Nat Cancer Inst at Fredrick Bldg 560, Rm 31-93 PO Box 8 Frederick MD 21701-1201 Office Phone: 301-846-1323. Office Fax: 301-846-1673. E-mail: trinchig@mail.nih.gov. *

TRINDADE, INGE ELLY KIEMLE, physiologist, educator, researcher; b. Sao Paulo, Brazil, Sept. 18, 1953; d. Heinrich and Hannelore Else Kiemle; m. Alceu Sergio Trindade, Dec. 13, 1975; children: Ivy Kiemle, Sergio Henrique Kiemle, Paulo Alceu Kiemle. BS, Sch. Medicine, U. Sao Paulo, Brazil, 1973—76, MS, 1977—80, PhD, 1985—90. Head, lab. physiology Hosp. for Rehab. of Craniofacial Anomalies, U. Sao Paulo, Bauru, Brazil, 1981—, pres., postgraduation com., 1997—, pres., rsch. com., 2001—; vice-head, dept. of biol. sciences Sch. Dentistry, U. Sao Paulo, Bauru, Brazil, 2002—; exchanges dir. Found. for the Study and Treatment of Craniofacial Deformities, Bauru, Brazil, 1999—2002, sci. dir., 2002—03; coord., internat. rsch. and edn. agreement U. Manchester, U. N.C., U. Sao Paulo, 1998—2003; coord., patient support agreement Smiletrain and Soc. Social Promotion Cleft Lip and Palate Individuals (PROFIS). Mem., adminstrv. bd. Hosp. for Rehab. of Craniofacial Anomalies, U. Sao Paulo, Bauru, Brazil, 1997—; rschr., cons. Brazilian Sci. and Tech. Ministry, Brasilia; cons. State of Sao Paulo Rsch. Found. (FAPESP), State Rsch. Agy., Sao Paulo, Brazil, Brazilian Edn. Ministry, Brasília, WHO, Geneva, 2000. Mem.: Brazilian Soc. Physiology, Am. Cleft Palate Craniofacial Assn. (assoc.). Office: Univ Sao Paulo HRAC Travessa Manoel Parentes 3-20 17043-900 Bauru SP Brazil Office Fax: 55(14)3224-1590. E-mail: ingetrin@usp.br.

TRINK, BARRY, otolaryngologist, educator; b. South Africa, Oct. 1, 1952; PhD, Bar Ilan U., 1992. Asst. prof. Johns Hopkins U., 2000—. Mem.: AACR (Young Investigator award). Office: 1550 Orleans St CRB2 Baltimore MD 21209 Business E-Mail: btrink@jhmi.edu.

TRIPATHI, RAMESH CHANDRA, ophthalmologist, researcher, educator; b. Jamira, India, July 1, 1936; came to U.S., 1977, naturalized, 1983; s. Arjun and G. Tripathi; m. Brenda Jennifer Lane, May 20, 1969; children: Anita, Paul. ISc, Lucknow Christian Coll., 1954; MD, Agra U. Med. Coll., 1959; M of Surgery in Ophthalmology, Lucknow U., 1963; PhD, U. London, 1970. Ophthalmic resident in surgery and demonstrator Lucknow U. Med. Coll., Kanpur, 1959—63; asst. surgeon, med. officer in charge casualty dept. Rly Hosp., Delhi, 1963; fellow Univ. Eye Clinic, Ghent, Belgium, 1964; ophthalmic registrar Southwest Middlesex Hosp., 1965-68; Hayward fellow, registrar, chief clin. asst. Inst. Opthalmology and Moorfields Eye Hosp., London, 1968-72; lectr. U. London Inst. Opthalmology, 1968-70; sr. lectr. U. London, 1970-77; cons. ophthalmologist and pathologist Moorfields Eye Hosp., London, 1972-77; prof. ophthalmology U. Chgo., 1977-93, The Coll. prof., 1979-93, sec. dept. ophthalmology, 1977-87, cons. pediatric tumor bd., 1978-80; attending ophthalmologist, attending ocular pathologist, mem. med. staff U. Chgo. Med. Ctr., 1977-93, dir. Eye Pathology Labs., 1977-93; prof. ophthalmology U. S.C., Columbia, 1993—2006, chmn., 1993—98, endowed chair ophthalmology Columbia, 2000—; dir. ophthalmology edn. Richland Mem. Hosp., SC, 1993—98; prof. The Graduate Sch., 1996—2006; adj. prof. pathology and microbiology, 2002—06; emeritus disting. prof., 2006—. Cons., attending ophthalmologist Oak Forest (Ill.) Hosp., 1986-93, dir. ophthalmology resident program, 1986-89, chmn. instnl. rev. bd., 1988; quality assurance com. U. Chgo. Hosp., 1979-93, med. curriculum com. U. Chgo., 1990-93; cons. Nat. Eye Inst. NIH, 1981—, Fight for Sight Rev. Bd., 1990-91; vis. prof. Yeshiva U., NYC, 1973, U. Wurzberg, Germany, 1974, U. Toronto, 1979, Jefferson U., Phila., 1979, Columbia U., NYC, 1981, U. Oxford, Eng., 1984, 86, 89, Nat. Autonomous U. Mex., Mexico City, 1981, Hotel Dieux de Paris, 1975, U. Tex. Med. Br., Galveston, 1990, Kresge Eye Inst. Wayne State U., Detroit, 1991, NY Eye and Ear Infirmary, NYC, 1991, Boston U. Dept. Ophthalmology, New Eng. Eye Ctr., Tufts U., Boston, 1991, Mayo Clinic Dept. Ophthalmology, Rochester, Minn., 1992, others; preceptor MS and PhD degree candidates in ophthalmology and visual sci., U. Chgo., 1977-93, U. SC, 1993—; mem. coun. Ill. Asian-Am. Adv. Com. to Gov. State of Ill., 1989-93; rep. to AMA & Chgo. Med. Soc. from Oak Forest Hosp./Cook County Hosp. Med. Staff, 1987-93, alt. del. Ill. State Med. Soc., 1991-93; del. Bd. Govs. Southeastern Chgo. Med. Soc. from U. Chgo. Hosp. & Clinics, 1991-93; faculty basic and clin. sci. course Am. Acad. Opthalmology, 1991-2003; attending ophthalmologist WBJ Dorn VA Hosp., 1993—2006; vis. prof. Harvard Med. Sch. Eye and Ear Infirmary, Boston, Mass., 1997-. Author: Wolff's Anatomy of the Eye and Orbit, 1997; exec. editor Exptl. Eye Rsch., 1973—2000, sect. editor, 1987—99, mem. editl. bd. Ophthalmic Literature, 1974—76, sect. editor, mem. editl. bd. Cornea, 1981—86, assoc. editor Afro-Asian Jour. Ophthalmology, 1981—93, Drug Devel. Rsch., 1988—92, Lens and Eye Toxicology Rsch., 1989—93, Sci. Rsch. Jour., 1990—; contbr. over 600 articles to profl. jours., over 60 chpts. to books and monographs. Chmn. Med. Coun. Assn. Indians in Am., Chgo., 1983-93, v.p., 1986-88; bd. dirs. Indo-Am. Ophthal. Soc. World Eye Found.; mem. Chgo. Found. for Med. Care, 1977-93; pres. Vision Rsch. Found., 1987—; mem. exec. bd. Assn. Scientists of Indian Origin in Am. Recipient Ophthalmology prize Royal Soc. Medicine London, 1971, Royal Eye London prize Ophthal. Soc. London, 1976, Resolutions Commendation, Ill. State Gen. Assembly, 1987, 88, Outstanding US Citizen award, 1984, Internat. prize Alcon Rsch. Inst., 1987; Med. Rsch. Coun. London grantee, 1972-75, Nat. Eye Inst. USPHS grantee, 1977—; named Litchfield endowed lectr. U. Oxford (Eng.), 1986, Ida Mann Gold medal U. Oxford, 1989, Disting. Physician of Am., 1990. Fellow: ACS (diplomate), Am. Acad. Ophthalmology (sect. 2 fundamentals and principles of ophthalmology 1991—2001, chair and past chair, basic and clin. sci. com., Honor award 1984, sr. honor award 1997), Internat. Coll. Surgeons (diplomate, vice regent U.S. 1984—), Royal Coll. Ophthalmologists London (diplomate), Royal Coll. Pathologists (diplomate), Nat. Acad. Scis. of India (life), Royal Soc. Medicine London (coun. 1973—76); mem.: AAUP, AMA, Ill. Med. Soc. (alternate del.), Internat. Soc. Ocular Toxicology (sec., treas. 1993—97, bd. dirs. 1993—, pres. 1998—2000, founder Hockwin-Green Meml. Endowment Fund 2002), Chgo. Ophthal. Soc., S.C. Ophthal. Soc., Glaucoma Soc., Electron Microscopical Soc. Am., Am. Assn. Ophthalmic Pathologists, Am. Assn. Pathologists, Internat. Acad. Pathologists, Contact Lens Assn. Ophthalmologist, Oxford Ophthal. Soc., Ophthal. Soc. U.S., Assn. for Rsch. Vision and Ophthalmology, Pan-Am. Assn. Ophthalmology, Royal Microscopical Soc., Assn. Eye Rsch. Europe (guest of honor 1974), Indian Med. Assn. U.S.A. (bd. dirs. 1984—85, Disting. Physician award 1987), Chgo. Med. Soc. (v.p. 1993, bd. dirs. Southea. br., pres. 1993), Assn. Indians in Am. (v.p. 1988—90, honor award 1986), Fedn. Am. Soc. Exptl. Biology, Physiol. Soc. London, Royal Coll. Physicians and Surgeons (diplomate, conjoin bd.). Achievements include research in pathophysiology, diagnosis and medical and surgical treatment of various ocular disorders including corneal diseases, glaucoma, cataract, vitreoretinopathy; optic nerve; orbital diseases & ocular toxicology; pioneer in the field of aqueous humor and cerebrospinal fluid dynamics, growth factors, contact lens spoilage and fibrinolytic therapy of the eye. Avocations: photography, swimming. Office: Univ South Carolina Sch Medicine Dept Opthalmology 4 Medical Pk Ste 300 Columbia SC 29203 Office Fax: 803-749-4554. Business E-Mail: ramesh.tripathi@uscmed.sc.edu.

TRIPATHY, SUJIT KUMAR, surgeon, researcher; b. Kubedega, India, June 28, 1980; MBBS, VSS Med. Coll., Burla, 2002; MS in Orthop., Postgrad. Inst. Med. Edn. and Rsch., Chandigarh, 2008. Jr. resident, orthops. PGIMER, Chandigarh, 2005—08, registrar, orthops., 2009—11; clin. rsch. fellow Friarage Hosp., Northallerton, England, 2011—. Mem.: Northzone IOA, Paediatric Orthop. Assn. India, Indian Orthop. Assn., SICOT, Nat. Acad. Med. Scis. (New Delhi). Avocation: singing. Home: Kubedega Bheden Bargarh Orissa 768104 India Personal E-mail: sujitortho@yahoo.co.in.

TRIPODI, TONY, retired social worker, dean, editor, writer; b. Sacramento, Nov. 30, 1932; s. Nicola and Christina (Grandinetti); m. Roni Roberts, Oct. 28, 1969 (div. 1986); children: Lee Anna, Anthony, David, Stephen; m. Miriam Potocky-Tripodi, July 25, 1998 (div. 2006). AB, U. Calif., Berkeley, 1954, MSW, 1958; D of Social Work, Columbia U., 1963. Rsch. tech. Calif. Dept. Mental Hygiene, Sacramento, 1958-59; rsch. analyst Calif. Youth Authority, Sacramento, 1959-60; from rsch. asst. to asst. prof. Columbia U., NYC, 1962-65; asst. prof. U. Calif., Berkeley, 1965-66; from assoc. prof. to prof. U. Mich. Sch. Social Work, Ann Arbor, 1966-87; assoc. dean prof. U. Pitts. Sch. Social Work, 1987—92; prof., assoc. dir., head doctoral program Fla. Internat. U., 1992—95; prof. Coll. Social Work Ohio State U., 1995—2005, dean Coll. Social Work, 1995—2005, dean and prof. emeritus, 2005—. Rsch. assoc. Bklyn. Coll., 1963-65; editor in chief Social Work Rsch. and Abstracts, NYC, 1980-84; interim assoc. dean U. Mich. Sch. Social Work, Ann Arbor, 1985, 1986, 1987; rsch. cons. Zancan Found., Padova, Italy, 1974-1992, NIMH, Silver Spring, Md., 1989-, Nat. Rsch. Adv. Com., Clinton, Mich., 1988-95; vis. Zellerbach prof. social welfare U. Calif., Berkeley, 2006, vis. Moses prof. social work Hunter Coll., NYC, 2006-07. Author: (with others) Clinical and Social Judgement, 1966, Requiem for Torchy, 2003, Tuscan Landscapes, 2005, International Social Work Research, 2006, Research Techniques for Clinical Social Workers, 2007, Eternal Love in St. Patrick's Cathedral, 2007, Love and Hope By the Sea, 2008, My Cane and I, 2009, Lifetime Expressions, 2011, 23 other books; co-editor: Jour. of Social Work Rsch. and Evaluation: An Internat. Pub., 1998-2005; series editor: Pocket Guides to Social Work Research Methods, Oxford U. Press, 2007-; contbr. articles to profl. jours. Bd. dirs. Parental Stress Ctr., Pitts., 1987-92, Comm, Rsch. Partners, 2000-05, Asian Am. Comm. Svc., 2000-05, Coun. Public Reps. Assoc., NIH, 2003-. With USNR, 1954-62. Doctoral rsch. fellow Sage Found., NYC, 1960-63; rsch. grantee NSF, 1965-66; Fulbright Hays scholar U.S. Govt., Italy, 1973-74; invited scholar Tilburg U., the Netherlands, 1977; vis. scholar U. Kent, Canterbury, Eng., 1980; named to Hall of Fame Columbia U. Sch. Social Work Alumni Assn. Mem. NASW, Acad. Cert. Social Workers, Coun. Social Work Edn., Soc. Social Work and Rsch. (pres. 1998-2000), Internat. Assoc. Sch. Social Work, WHO (World Health Orgn.), Mensa, Phi Kappa Phi. Home: 1401 Riverpl Blvd Apt 2207 Jacksonville FL 32207 Business E-Mail: tripodi.5@osu.edu.

TRITSCH, GEORGE LEOPOLD, retired biochemist, educator; BA, NYU, 1948; MS, U. Md., 1951; PhD, Purdue U., 1954. Rsch. assoc. Cornell Med. Coll., NYC, 1954—56, Rockefeller U., NYC, 1956—59; cancer rsch. scientist Roswell Pk. Cancer Inst., Buffalo, 1959—95, cancer. rsch. scientist emeritus, 1995—; from asst. rsch. prof. to prof. emeritus SUNY, Buffalo, 1961—; prof. biochemistry Niagara U., Niagara Falls, NY, 1961—; ret., 1995. Vis. prof. dept. biochemistry Dartmouth Med. Sch., 1968, Purdue Cancer Ctr., W. Lafayette, Ind., 1983; mem. grant rev. panel nat. prostatic cancer project NIH, Bethesda, Md., 1975—85; symposium organizer adenosine deaminase N.Y. Acad. Scis., 1984; invited spkr. in field. Editor, author Axenic Mammalian Cell Reactions, 1969, Adenosine Deaminase, 1985; contbr. articles to profl. jours. Bd. dirs. N.Y. State Health Rsch. Coun., Buffalo, 1975—80. Grantee, USPHS, 1960—90, Am. Cancer Soc., 1961—69. Mem.: Soc. Exptl. Biology, Am. Assn. Cancer Rsch., Am. Soc. Pharmacological and Exptl. Therapeutics, Am. Inst. Nutrition, Am. Soc. Biochemistry and Molecular Biology, Harvey Soc., Sigma Xi, Alpha Chi Sigma, Phi Lambda Upsilon. Avocations: playing piano, water sports. Office: Roswell Park Cancer Inst 666 Elm St Buffalo NY 14263-0001

TRITTON, THOMAS RICHARD, former academic administrator, biologist, educator; b. Lakewood, Ohio, Dec. 20, 1947; s. William Frank and Margie Jean (Galbraith) Tritton; m. Louise Meschter Tritton; children: Lara, Christiana. BA, Ohio Wesleyan U., 1969; PhD, Boston U., 1973. Asst. prof. Yale Med. Sch., New Haven, 1975—80; assoc. prof. Yale U., 1980—85; prof. U. Vt., Burlington, 1985—97, vice provost, 1991—97; pres. Haverford Coll., Pa., 1997—2007; pres. and CEO Chem. Heritage Found., 2007—; pres. sci. Kilford nonprofit. Mem. NIH Exptl. Therapeutics Study Sect., 1988—92; bd. dirs. Fox Chase Cancer Ctr., 1997—; bd. trustees Ohio Wesleyan U., 2007—. Editor books; mem. editl. bd.: various profl. jours.; contbr. scientific papers to profl. jours. Mem.: Am. Soc. Biol. Chemists, Am. Assn. Cancer Rsch. (com. mem.). Mem. Soc. Of Friends. Avocations: music, tennis, golf. Home: 316 S 2nd St Apt D Philadelphia PA 19106-4342 Home Phone: 267-324-5646; Office Phone: 215-873-8207, 215-873-8290. Business E-Mail: ttritton@chemheritage.org.

TRIVELLATO, MARIO, cardiologist; b. Apr. 4, 1942; s. Placido and Afra (Liviero) Trivellato; m. Grazia Sordina, Jan. 31, 1973; 1 child, Diego. MD in Medicine and Surgery, U. Padova, 1967, diploma in anaestesia and reanimation, 1970, diploma in cardiology and rheumatology, 1973, diploma in internal medicine, 1979. Cert. Edn. Commn. Fgn. Med. Grads. (U.S.). Asst. Surg. Pathology Inst. U. Padova, 1968—70; asst. dept. cardiology City Hosp., Padova, 1970—86, dep. chief dept. cardiology, 1986—96; chief cardiology svc. Geriatric Hosp., Padova, 1996—2007. Translator: Practical Electrocardiografy, 1975, The Heart, 1981; contbr. articles to profl. jours. Pres. Assn. Volontari Ospedalieri, Padova, 1997—. Named to Padovano Eccellente, 2009; scholar spl. scholar in cardiology, St. Luke's Episcopal Hosp., Houston, 1973—74, 1979—80; Fulbright-Hays, Bursary, 1973—74, 1979—80. Fellow: Am. Coll. Cardiology; mem.: Soc. Italiana Terapia Intensiva, Am. Heart Assn., Am. Soc. Echocardiography, Coun. Geriatric Cardiology, Tex. Heart Inst. Cardiac Soc., Soc. Italiana di Ecografia Cardiovascolare, Societa Triveneta Di Chirurgia, Grouppo Italiano Studi Emidinamici, Societa Italiana Di Cardiologia, European Soc. Cardiology, Assn. Nazionale Medici Cardiologi Ospedalieri, Denton A. Cooley Cardiovascular Surg. Soc., N.Y. Acad. Sci., Am. Med. Students Assn. Padova, Rotary Club Padova. Roman Catholic. Office: Ctr Medico Vesalio via Sorio 12 35100 Padua Italy Home: Via Cesare Pollini 9 35126 Padova PD Italy Office Phone: 39360466215. E-mail: mtrivellato@tin.it.

TRKSAK, PAUL M., orthopedist; MD, Loyola Univ. Stritch Med. Sch. Intern North Chgo. VA Hosp.; resident Great Lakes Naval Hosp., Loyola Univ. Med. Ctr., Chgo., Cook County Hosp., Ill.; staff physician Silver Cross Hosp., Joliet, Ill., past chmn., dept. orthopaedic surgery; staff physician Provena St. Joseph Med. Ctr., Hinsdale Hosp., Surg. Ctr., Ill.; pvt. orthopaedic practice Joliet, 1989—99; ptnr. Hinsdale Orthopaedic Associates, SC, 1999—. Mem.: Ill. State Med. Soc., Combine Orthopaedics Specialists. Office: Hinsdale Orthopaedic Assoc 550 W Ogden Ave Hinsdale IL 60521

TRNKA, LUDEK, physician, microbiologist; b. Trencin, Czechoslovakia, Dec. 18, 1925; s. Karel Trnka and Milada Trnkova; m. Miluse Trnkova; 1 child, Jan. MD, Charles U., Prague, Czech Republic, 1949, PhD, 1963, DrSc, 1985. Resident Regional Hosp., Strakovice, Czech Republic, 1950—54, TB Hosp., Kostelec, Czech Republic, 1954—55; clin. assoc. Rsch. Inst. TB, Prague, Czech Republic, 1955—63; vis. rschr. Internat. Children's Ctr., Paris, 1963; lab. rschr. Rsch. inst. TB, Prague, Czech Republic, 1964—67; vis. prof. dept. med. microbiology U. Wis., Madison, 1967—68; dep. dir. Rsch. Inst. Respiratory Disease, Prague, 1969—93; chief TB surveillance unit Czech Republic U. Hosp., Prague, 1994—, U. Hosp. Soc. prof. Charles U. Med. Sch., Prague, 1985; chief specialist in TB Ministry of Health, Czech Republic, 1986—91; expert cons. in TB, Czech Republic, 1994—; nat. coord. in TB WHO Ministry of Health, 2001—; resident Europe region Internat. Union Against TB, Paris, 1990—94. Author: (guidebook (in Czech) Chest Diseases, 1987; co-author: (handbook) Antituberculosis Drugs, 1988. Mem.: Czech Pneumological and Phtiseol. Soc. (hon.), Finnish Assn. Lung Health (hon.), Rotary (pres. 1994—95). Achievements include organizer TB control in Czech Republic. Home: Korunni St 127 13000 Prague Czech Republic Office: UNI Hosp Bulovka 18072 Prague Czech Republic Home Phone: 420-774962512, 420 774 692512; Office Phone: 420-283840513, 420-266082468. Business E-Mail: ludek.trnka@fnb.cz.

TRO, TEVI DAVID, former federal agency administrator; b. 1967; s. Bernard and Elaine Troy; m. Kami Tro; 4 children. BS Indsl. Design, Labor Rels., Cornell U.; MA in Am. Civilization, PhD in Am. Civilization, U. Tex., Austin. Rschr. Am. Enterprise Inst., Washington DC; sr. domestic policy adv. US House Policy Com., 1996—98, domestic policy dir., 1996—98; policy dir. to Senator John Ashcroft US Senate; dep. asst. sec. for policy US Dept. Labor, dir. Office Faith Based Initiatives; spl. asst. to Pres. The White House, 2003—04, liaison to Jewish Cmty., 2003—04, dep. asst. to Pres., 2005—07; dep. sec. US Dept Health & Human Services, Washington, 2007—09; vis. sr. fellow The Hudson Inst., Washington, 2009—. Author: Intellectuals and the American Presidency: Philosophers, Jesters, or Technicians?, 2002. Republican. Jewish. Office: The Hudson Institute 1015 15th St NW 6th Fl Washington DC 20005

TROCKI-VIDELL, CYLA, psychiatrist, healthcare administrator; d. Jack and Mira (Kiejdan) Trocki; m. Jared Steven Videll, Dec. 27, 1969; children: Haviv Elana, Mikhael Alon, Samara Pilar. BA, Temple U., 1968, MA, 1972; postgrad., U. Pa., 1972—74; DO, Phila. Coll. Osteo. Medicine, 1978. Diplomate in med. psychology Am. Bd. Psychol. Spltys., Am. Bd. Forensic Medicine. Pediat. intern Med. Coll. Pa., Phila., 1979—89, resident in psychiatry, 1991—93, fellow in child and adolescent psychiatry, 1993—95; pvt. practice Phila., 1983—91; med. dir., cons. Med-Psych Healthcare Assocs., NJ, 2000—; pvt. practice PR, 1995—. Cons. in field. Contbg. author Women's Future World's Future, 2000; contbr. chapters to books. Mem. Nat. Women's History Mus., Washington, 2005, Med. Women's Delegation to Russia, Latvia and Lithuania; mem. USA/China Joint Conf. on Women's Issues, Med. Women's Delegation, mem. World Conf. on Family Values Singapore, mem. NGO Forum-UN 4th World Conf. on Women Beijing; mem. Am. Med. Polit. Action Com., Washington, 1998—. Recipient Nat. Leadership award, Physicians Adv. Bd., Nat. Rep. Congl. Com., Washington, 2000; named to, Am. Biography Polit. Scientists. Mem.: AAUW, AMA, Phila. County Med. Soc., Am. Med. Women's Assn., Pa. Osteopathic Med. Assn., Med. Women's Internat. Assn., Am. Soc. Law, Medicine and Ethics, Am. Acad. Child and Adolescent Psychiatry, Am. Psychiat. Assn., Pa. Med. Soc. Republican. Jewish. Avocations: art, architecture, dance, politics. Office Phone: 609-823-1989. Office Fax: 609-823-1989.

TROITZSCH, DIRK, biophysicist, researcher; b. Dessau, Germany, Sept. 25, 1966; s. Guenter and Gisela Brigitte (Christall) Troitzsch; m. Grit Boettcher, Nov. 23, 2001. MS Physics, MLU-Univ., Halle, Germany, 1990. Fellow, registrar Univ. Hosp., Leipzig, 1988—94, cardiovascular surgery, 1994—2001, neurosurgery, 1995—97, cellular physiology and biophysics, 1998—; rsch. assoc. pediatric cardiology German Heart Inst., Berlin, 2001—; surgeon Univ. Hosp., Tuebingen, Germany, 2001—04, Marburg, Germany, 2004—05; biomed. rschr. Anhalt U. Applied Sci., Koethen, Germany, 2005—. Co-author: Cerebral Protection in Cerebrovascular and Aortic Surgery, 1997, Extrcorporeal Circulation in Theory and Practice, 1999, esp. edit.; contbr. articles to profl. jours.; mem. editl. staff Jour. Cardiovascular Engring. Mem.: Internat. Soc. Applied Cardiovascular Biology, Internat. Soc. Heart and Lung Transplantation, European Soc. Extracorporeal Techniques, European Soc. Organ Transplants, European Soc. Engring. Medicine. Avocations: sports, swimming, skin-diving, literature. Office: Anhalt U Applied Sci Ferdinand Schulz St 29 D-06366 Koethen Germany

TROJIAN, THOMAS, sports medicine physician; b. Md., Mar. 2, 1965; MD, Howard U., 1993; MMB, Drexel U., 1989. Assoc. prof. dept. family medicine and orthop. U. Conn. Health Ctr., 1998—. Team physician U. Conn., 1998; sect. editor Current Sports Medicine Reports, 2008. Named Hank Feder Tchr. of Yr., UCHC; grant, NIH. Fellow: Am. Coll. Sports Medicine; mem.: Soc. Tchrs. Family Medicine, Am. Med. Soc. Sports Medicine (bd. dirs. 2011). Avocations: hiking, soccer. Office: 236 Farmington Ave Farmington CT 06030 Business E-Mail: ttrojian@stfranciscare.org.

TROKHANOVA, OLGA VALENTINOVNA, gynecologist; b. Yaroslavl, Russia, Mar. 5, 1967; Degree, Yaroslavl State Med. Acad., 1991. Assoc. prof., dept. ob-gyn. Yaroslavl State Med. Acad., 1997. Office: Revoljutsionnaya St 5 Yaroslavl 150000 Russia Office Fax: 72-91-42, 30-50-13. Business E-Mail: trokhanova@yandex.ru.

TRONINA, OLGA, medical educator; b. Russia, Sept. 8, 1977; PhD, RSMU, 2006. Asst. prof., 2nd internal disease dept. RSMU, 2006—. Mem.: ERA, ESC. Home: Molodezhnaya Khimki Moscow 141407 Russia Personal E-mail: troninaoa@mail.ru.

TRONTZOS, CHRISTOS ANASTASIOS, nuclear medicine physician; b. Thessaloniki, Greece, Mar. 31, 1961; s. Anastasios Christos Trontzos and Ermina Psvlina Trontzou; m. Sonia Pinelope Asstof; children: Anastasios, Alexanderos, Ermina. MD, Aristotel U., 1989, PhD, 1996. Dir. Eurodiagnosi, Thessaloniki, Greece, 1997—2004, Iatriui Prolipsi, 2005—. Mem. WNF; active UNICEF. Mem.: Soc. Nuc. Medicine, European Assn. Nuc. Medicine. Avocations: chess, computers. Office: Iatriui Prolipsi Kosti Palama 33 55133 Thessaloniki Greece Home: Agias Theodhoras 8 546 23 Thessaloniki Greece E-mail: tromtes@hol.gr.

TROPÉ, CLAES, medical educator, researcher; b. Landskrona, Sweden, Feb. 21, 1943; MD, U. Lund Sweden, 1971, PhD, 1974. Pdocent anatomic inst U. Lund Sweden, 1965—97; head gynecol.

oncology dept. U. Hosp. Lund Sweden, 1977—86; prof., gynecol. oncology dept. U. Oslo, 1986—2006, prof., rschr., 1986—. Bd. dirs. Norwegian Radium Hosp., 1986—2006. Grant, Norwegian Soc. Gynecol. Oncology. Mem.: European Soc. Gynecol. Oncology, European Soc. Clin. Oncology, Soc. Gynecol. Oncologists, Am. Soc. Clin. Onciology, Soc. Surgeons. Avocations: soccer, tennis, golf. Home: Ris Skolevei 15a Oslo 0373 Norway Personal E-mail: c.g.trope@medisin.uio.no.

TROPEZ-SIMS, SUSANNE, pediatrician, educator; b. New Orleans, Apr. 13, 1949; d. Maxwell Sterling and Ethel (Ross) Tropez; m. James Carnell White, Apr. 10, 1971 (div. 1992); children: Lisa, Janifer, James Carnell; m. Michael Milroy Sims, Feb. 18, 1995. BS, Bennett Coll., 1971; MD, U. N.C., 1975, MPH, 1982. Diplomate Am. Bd. Pediatrics. Resident pediat. N.C. Meml. Hosp., Chapel Hill, 1975—76, 1977—79; pediatrician Darnell Army Hosp., Ft. Hood, Tex., 1976—77; acting dir. pediat. day clinic Wake County Med. Ctr., Raleigh, NC, 1979—82; dir. pediat. day clinic, asst. prof. U. N.C., Chapel Hill, 1982—88; assoc. prof. pediat. La. State U. Med. Ctr., New Orleans, 1988—97; dir. divsn. pediat. emergency rm. La. State U., New Orleans, 1988—89, chief divsn. ambulatory care, 1989—97; chmn. and prof. dept. pediat. Meharry Med. Coll., Nashville, 1997—2005; chair Meharry Med. Svc. Found., Nashville, 2000—02; chair curriculum com. Meharry Med. Coll., Nashville, 2003—, assoc. dean acad. support, 2005—06, assoc. dean clin. affiliation, 2006—, Joy McCann prof., 2006—10, pediatric clearkship dir., 2005—. Clin. dir. maternal and child health units New Orleans Health Dept., 1992-97, chief divsn. cmty. pediat. and adolescent medicine, 1992-97; pediatrician Shelly Child Devel. Ctr., Raleigh, 1981-88, child med. examiner program, 1979-88; chair sch. health com. local chpt. AAP, 1993-96; mem. Nat. Com. Sch. Health, 1992-99; chair health info. network bd. Nat. Edn. Assn., 2000-02, 2011-; vice chair pediat. sect., Nat. Med. Assn., 2009-11, chair pediat. sect., 2011-, Dom Com., 2011-, chair, Health Network Bd. NEA, 2011-, vice chair, Pediat. Sect. NMA, 2009-11, chair, 2011-. Contbr. articles to profl. jour. Chair adminstrv. bd. Cornerstone U.M.C., 1993-96, chair edn. com., 1991-92; mem. United Meth. Women, Walnut Terr. Child Devel. Ctr., Raleigh, 1981-83, chmn., 1982-83; chmn. pastor parish com. Long view Ch., Raleigh, 1982-84, 87-88, chmn. membership care com.; chair bd. trustees Clark Meml. United Meth. Ch., 2001-06, chair bldg. com., 2005-10; with L.D.M. Com., 2011-. Fellow preventive medicine, 1979 82, Faculty Devel. fellow U. NC Sch. Medicine, 1985-87; named America's Top Pedistrician Consumer Rsch. America, 2009. Fellow Am. Acad. Pediatrics (mem. sch. health com.); mem. N.C. Pediatric Soc. (com. child abuse and neglect, adolescent pregnancy), La. Pediatric Soc., Ambulatory Pediatric Assn., Adolescent Pregnancy Coalition United Way, Bennett Coll. Alumnae Assn. Democrat. Office Phone: 615 327 6925, 615 327 5915. Business E-Mail: stsims@mmc.edu.

TROTTA, FRANCESCO, rheumatologist; b. Udine, Italy, Aug. 9, 1943; s. Enrico Trotta and Vittoria Belardini; m. Sandra Manicardi. Diploma in medicine, U. Ferrara, Italy, 1968, postgrad., 1973, postgrad., 1975. Asst. in rheumatology St. Anna Hosp., Ferrara, 1971—86, head internal medicine, 1986—88, head rheumatology, 1988—2000; prof. rheumatology U. Ferrara, 2000—. Author: Digital Radiology in Rheumatology, 1999, Quality of LIfe in Rheumatic Diseases, 2001. Mem.: Italian Soc. Rheumatology, Am. Coll. Rheumatology. Home: Via Della Paglia 3 44100 Ferrara Italy Office: Ospedale S Anna Dept Rheumatology Corso Giovecca 203 44100 Ferrara Italy E-mail: trf@unife.it.

TROUILLIER, HANS-HEINRICH, orthopaedic surgeon; b. Berlin, Germany, Sept. 26, 1960; s. Hans-Karl and Henriette Trouillier; m. Karola Trouillier, Aug. 10, 1962; children: Philipp, Louis. MD, U. Munich, 1989; D, Tech. U. Munich, 1993. Registrar Traumatology Clinic U. Munich, Augsburg, Bavaria, Germany, 1990—93, sr. registrar Ortho. Surgery Clinic Bavaria, 1993—97; chief physician Franziskus Hosp. U. Hannover, Bielefeld, NRW, Germany, 2003—. Mem. sci. bd. Periodical Sports Ortho. and Traumatology, Jena, Germany, 2001—; cons. Traumatology and Ortho. Surgery Clinic U. Basel, Switzerland, 1998—99; cons. Ortho. Surgery Clinic U. Munich, 2000—03. Author: (book chpt. scuba diving medicine) Manual of Sportstraumatology; contbr. articles to profl. jours. Recipient Posterprize Traumatic Patellaluxation, GOTS Congress Munich, 1998. Mem.: Trauma Assn. Germany (assoc.), Swiss Soc. Surgery and Medicine of Foot (assoc.), Swiss Soc. Orthop. Surgery (assoc.), Assn. German Speaking Arthoscopists (assoc.), Assn. German Orthop. Surgery (assoc.), Assn. Orthop. and Trauma in Sports Medicine (assoc.), South-German Ortho. Soc. (assoc.). Achievements include research in Biomechanical and morphological aspects of disc replacement and non fusion technology in spine surgery; Biomechanical and morphological aspects of ankle prosthesis in orthopaedic surgery. Office: Franziskus Hospital Surgical Clinic II Kiskerstrasse 26 33615 Bielefeld NRW Germany Office Fax: +49 521 589 1304. E-mail: dr.trouillier@ws-chirurgie.com.

TROUNSON, ALAN OSBOURNE, state agency administrator, embryologist; b. Sydney, Feb. 16, 1946; MSc in Wool and Pastoral Sciences, U. New South Wales, 1971; PhD in Animal Embryology, Sydney U., 1974. Dalgety Research Fellow, ARC Inst. Animal Physiology and Biochemistry U. Cambridge, 1974—76; joined as sr. rsch. fellow by 1984 reader in the dept. of Obstetrics and Gynecology Monash U., 1977—84, dir. Centre Early Devel., 1985, Personal Chair in Obstetrics and Gynaecology/Paediatrics, 1991, Personal Chair as Professor of Stem Cell Sciences, 2003, Emeritus Professor, 2008—; pres. Calif. Inst. Regenerative Medicine, San Francisco, 2008—. Fellow: Royal Coll. Obstetricians and Gynaecologists, Australian and New Zealand Coll. Obstetricians and Gynaecologists (hon.). Achievements include pioneer of human in vitro fertilisation (IVF) and associated reproductive technologies; first IVF birth in Australia in 1980; diagnosis of inherited genetic disease in pre-implantation embryos; discovery and production of human embryonic stem cells and of their ability to be directed into neurones, prostate tissue and respiratory tissue. Office: Calif Inst Regnerative Medicine 210 King St San Francisco CA 94107

TROUT, MONROE EUGENE, health facility administrator; b. Harrisburg, Pa., Apr. 5, 1931; s. David Michael and Florence Margaret (Kashner) T.; m. Sandra Louise Lemke, June 11, 1960; children: Monroe Eugene, Timothy William. AB, U. Pa., 1953, MD, 1957; LLB, Dickinson Sch. of Law, 1964, JD, 1969; LLD (hon.), Dickinson Sch. Law, 1996, Bloomfield Coll., 1994, Cumberland Coll., 2003. Intern Great Lakes (Ill.) Naval Hosp., 1957-58; resident in internal medicine Portsmouth (Va.) Naval Hosp., 1959-61; chief med. dept. Harrisburg State Hosp., 1961-64; dir. drug regulatory affairs Pfizer, Inc., NYC, 1964-68; v.p., med. dir. Winthrop Labs., NYC, 1968-70; med. dir. Sterling Drug, Inc., NYC, 1970-74, v.p., dir. med. affairs, 1974-78, sr. v.p., dir. med. affairs, bd. dirs., mem. exec. com., 1978-86; pres., CEO Am. Healthcare Sys., Inc., 1986-95, chmn., 1987-95; also bd. dirs. Am. Healthcare Systems, Inc.; chmn. emeritus Am. Healthcare Sys., Inc., 1995—; interim CEO Cytran Inc., 1996. Chmn. bd. dirs. Cytyc Inc., 1998—2002, Ineed MD, Inc., Am. Excess Ins. Ltd., 1990—95; adj. assoc. prof. Bklyn. Coll. Pharmacy; spl. lectr. legal medicine, trustee Dickinson Sch. Law, 1970—93; trustee Ariz. State U. Sch. Health Adminstrn., 1988—91; mem. rsch. bd. Sterling Winthrop, 1977—86; mem. Joint Commn. Prescription Drug Use, 1976—80; sec. Commn. on Med. Malpractice, HEW, 1971—73, cons., 1974; co-chmn. San Diego County Health Commn., 1992—94. Author, Winter Galley, 2008; mem. editl. bd. Hosp. Formulary Mgmt., 1969-79, Forensic Sci., 1971—, Jour. Legal Medicine, 1973-79, Reg. Tox. and Pharmac, 1981-87, Med. Malpractice Prevention, 1985—; editl. reviewer Annals of Internal Medicine; contbr. articles to profl. jours. Exec. com. White House Mini Conf. on Aging, 1980; mem. Nat. Health Adv. Bd. AAA; chmn. bd. Am. Coll. Legal Medicine Found., 1983—87; mem. N.Y. State Commn. Substance Abuse, 1978—80, Town Coun., New Canaan, 1978—86, vice chmn., 1985—86; trustee Cleve. Clinic, 1971—87, Albany Med. Coll., 1977—86, St. Vincent DePaul Ctr. for the Homeless, 1987—90, U. Calif.-San Diego Thornton Hosp. and Med. Ctr., 1990—97, San Diego Mus. Art, 1996—98, Bapt. Health Sys. Found., Knoxville, 1999—2007; trustee, vice chmn. Morehouse Med. Sch., 1980—89; assoc. trustee U. Pa.; bd. visitors U. Pa. Sch. Nursing, 1988—92; pres. bd. trustees U. Calif. San Diego Found., 1994—97; vice chmn. Med. Commn. for Food and Shelter, Inc.; chmn. Internat. B'nai B'rith Dinner, 1989, 1994, Rep. dist. leader New Canaan, 1966—68; bd. dirs. New Canaan Interchurch Svc. Com., 1965—69, Athletes Kidney Found., Cir. in the Sq. Theatre Inc., 1984—86, Knoxville Symphony Soc., 2001—04, Knoxville Opera Co., 2001—04, East Tenn. Hist. Soc., 2003—04. Recipient Alumni award of merit U. Pa., 1953, Disting. Alumni award Dickinson Sch. Law, 1989, Nat. Healthcare award Internat. B'nai B'rith, 1991, Entrepreneur of Yr. award San Diego, 1994, Horatio Alger award, 1995, Salvation Army Tradition of Caring award, 1996, Cívis Universitatus award U. Calif. San Diego, 1997, Gold Medal award, Am. Coll. Legal Medicine, 1999, Bapt. Health Sys. Visionary award, 2002, Knoxville Philanthropist of Yr., 2004, Cumberland Coll. Caring Servant award, 2005; Monroe E. Trout Day named in his honor, Knox County, Tenn., Mar. 13, 2007, 2011. Master Bridge (life); fellow Am. Coll. Legal Medicine (v.p., pres., bd. govs.), mem. AMA (Physician's Recognition awards 1969, 72, 76, 82, 85, 88, 92), Med. Execs. (pres. 1975-76), Delta Tau Delta (Alumni Achievement award 1996, Named to 100 Most Influential Delts of Twentieth Century 2000). Lutheran. Achievements include Appleton Art Center, Wisconsin renamed Trout Museum of Art in honor of Sandra Louise Trout and Monroe Eugene Trout. Office: 2110 Cove View Way Knoxville TN 37919

TROUVÉ, RENAUD THEODORE, medical and consulting company executive, anesthesiology educator; b. Ham, Somme, France, June 23, 1954; s. Michel Albert and Colette Marie (Guilbert) T.; divorced; children: Helene, Claire, Vincent; m. Valerie Suzanne André, Aug. 4, 2006. BS in Biochemistry, U. Paris, 1980, MS in Physiology, Human Biology, 1980, PhD in Toxicology, 1982, MD, PhD in Biophysics, 1984, DSc in Pharmacology, 1991. Rsch. asst. U. Paris Toxicology Lab., 1980-82; rsch. assoc. U. Paris Biophysics, 1982-84; rsch. scientist Inst. Nat. de la Santé et de la Recherche Médicale, Paris, 1984-86; asst. prof. Columbia U., NYC, 1986-89; sr. project leader Ctr. Nat. de Transfusion Sanguine, Paris, 1989-91, dir. rsch., 1989-92; assoc. prof. anesthesiology U. Tex., Houston, 1991—; directing mgr. Transonic Sys. France, Angers, 1992-96; pres. and CEO Biocerom, Angers, France, 1992-97. Cons. pharmacology ASERC, Paris, 1983—92; cons. Rhone Poulenc, 1984—96; consulting scientist Nat. Inst. Drug Abuse, Balt., 1986—87; assoc. prof. U. Angers, 1994—2001; cons. in quality and health, 1998—2000; dir. R&D Virtual Functions Sys., Palos Verdes, Calif., 1998—2001; founder, adminstr. Serendi Internat. Cons., Luxembourg, 1999; prof. ISAB, Beauvais, 2001—05; assessor Luxemburg Price for Quality, 2004—06; expert Accreditation Com. OLAS, Grand Duchy Luxembourg, 2010—11, mem., 2011—. Author: (book) Toxicomanies, 1989; contbr. to publs. Proceedings Soc. Exptl. Biology and Medicine, 1983—, New Eng. Jour. Medicine, 1985; inventor antidotes to cocaine toxicity, 1986, antiaggregant properties of activated protein C, 1992. Gen. sec. Nat. League Against Toxicomania, Paris, 1992-96, Ctr. on Drugs, Paris, 1993-96; pres. French Rsch. Inst. on Toxicomania; v.p. Internat. League Against Toxicomania, 1996-2001; adminstr. Fedn. Nationale Assns. Prevention Toxicomanie, 1996-2001; patron Humanity Orgn. Entraide-Caraibes; accredited mentor Luxembourg C. of C., 2010-. Recipient Nat. Laureate French Assn. Ins. Cos., Paris, 1989, Nat. Laureate (for Biocerom) L'usine Nouvelle, Nantes, France, 1995. Mem. Am. Soc. Pharmacology and Exptl. Therapeutics, Am. Heart Assn., NY Acad. Scis., Brit. Pharm. Soc., European Soc. Microcirculation, French Toxicologists Soc. (Nat. Laureate award 1986). Achievements include patents for antidotes to cocaine toxicity, antiaggregant properties of activated protein C, calcium channels inhibitors in parasympathetic syndromes, cerebral amino acids carriers in newborns, improvement of cardiac ischemia using hemodilution, antidotes to organophosphoreous compounds, true flow measurement in .250 mm or micrometer vessels by a transit time technique, web-based quality management tools, zero paper approach, risk management by hahrdra method, health and health related institutions management by TOC, MBC II or HBC implementation of the TPS. Design of new cursus by QFD. Office: 5 ZAI Bourmicht L-8070 Bertrange Luxembourg Office Phone: 352-691-448760. Business E-Mail: rtrouve@serendi.lu. E-mail: trouve@mac.com.

TROWSDALE, JOHN, research scientist; b. Hull, England, Feb. 8, 1949; s. Roy Robinson and Doris (Graham) T.; m. Susan Price, July 17, 1971. BSc, U. Birmingham, England, 1970, PhD, 1973. Rschr. Imperial Cancer Rsch. Fund, London, 1980-97; prof. U. Cambridge, England, 1997—. Fellow Acad. of Med. Scis. Avocation: music. Office Phone: 01223-330248. Business E-Mail: jt233@cam.ac.uk.

TROXELL, MARY THERESA (TERRY TROXELL), geriatrics services professional; b. Syracuse, NY, Aug. 29, 1950; d. Henry and Mary (McDermott) Flynn; 1 child, Melissa Lee. BSN, U. Pa., 1971. Cert. quality improvement specialsit; cert. gerontol. nurse specialist; cert. case mgr. Supr. neonatal ICU St. Joe's, Syracuse, 1976-79; dir. nursing Hillhaven, Phoenix, 1979-81; quality assurance nurse long term care Maricopa County, Phoenix, 1981-83; dir. nursing Desert Haven Nursing Home, Phoenix, 1983-84; team leader, surveyor health care licensure State of Ariz., Phoenix, 1985-87, program mgr. long term care licensure and certification, 1987-89, program mgr. enforcement and compliance licensure and cert., 1989-91; dir. profl. svcs. Unison Healthcare, Phoenix, 1991-94; v.p. clin. ops. SunQuest Healthcare, Phoenix, 1994-96; sr. v.p. clin. and ancillary ops. Unison Healthcare, 1996-98, exec. v.p. opers., 1998—99, CEO, 1999—2000; COO, v.p. health ops., chief complaince officer Fountains Retirement Cmtys., Tucson, 2000—. Author: (manuals) Licensure Procedures, 1990, Quality Improvement, Restorative Nursing: A Key to Quality, 1992, Director of Nursing Manual, 1996, Clinical Operations Series, 1997. Developer legislation for adult care homes, health care licensure laws State of Ariz., 1990. Mem.: Am. Health Care (v.p. region XI), Gerontol. Nurses Assn., Quality Improvement Nurses Assn., Am. Health Care Assn. (nat. facilitu stds. com. 1992—96, nat. multifacility com. 1993—96, LTC nurses coun. 1995, nat. quality com. 1996—97, regional v.p. region XI adv. com., regional v.p. and bd. dirs.), Ariz. Health Care Assn. (chair legis. com. 1992—94, chair devel./revision nursing facility laws 1992—94). Home: 10224 E Sahavro Scottsdale AZ 85260-6331 Office: Fountains Retirement Cmtys 2020 W Rudasell Rd Tucson AZ 85704

TROY, FREDERIC ARTHUR, II, medical biochemistry professor; b. Evanston, Ill., Feb. 16, 1937; s. Charles McGregor and Virginia Lane (Minto) T.; m. Linda Ann Price, Mar. 23, 1959; children: Karen M., Janet R. BS, Washington U., St. Louis, 1961; PhD, Purdue U., 1966; postdoctoral, Johns Hopkins U., Balt., 1968. Asst. prof. U. Calif. Sch. Medicine, Davis, 1968-74, assoc. prof., 1974-80, prof., 1980—2006, chmn., 1991-94, 2006—; co-founder SialoGen Therapeutics, Inc., Davis, Calif., 2003—, pres., 2003—, CEO, 2003—; adj. prof. medicine Xiamen U. Sch. Medicine, Xiamen, China, 2008—. Cons. NIH, Bethesda, Md., 1974—, NSF, Washington, 1975—, Damon Runyon Cancer Found., NYC, 1980-81, VA, Washington, 1984-88, US Army Breast Cancer Study Sect., 1999—; vis. prof. Karolinska Inst. Med. Sch., Stockholm, Sweden, 1976-77. Mem. editl. bd. Jour. Biol. Chem., 1988—, Glycobiol., 1990—; contbr. articles to profl. jours. Recipient Research Cancer Devel. award Nat. Cancer Inst., 1975-80; Eleanor Roosevelt Internat. Cancer fellow Am. Cancer Soc., 1976-77. Mem. AAAS, Am. Soc. Biol. Chemistry and Molecular Biology, Am. Assn. Cancer Rsch., Am. Chem. Soc., Am. Soc. Enologists, Biochemistry Soc., Biophysics Soc., Am. Fedn. for Clin. Rsch., NY Acad. Scis., Soc. for Glycobiol. (pres. 1991-92), Am. Med. and Grad. Sch. Dept. Biochem. (pres. elect 1995—), Sigma Xi. Office: Sch Medicine Dept Biochem and Molecular Medicine U Calif Davis CA 95616 Business E-Mail: fatroy@ucdavis.edu.

TRPIS, MILAN, vector biologist, educator; b. Mojsova Lucka, Slovakia, Dec. 20, 1930; came to U.S., 1971, naturalized, 1977; s. Gaspar and Anna (Sevcikova) T.; m. Ludmila Tonkovic, Dec. 15, 1956; children: Martin, Peter, Katarina. MS, Comenius U., Bratislava, 1956; PhD, Charles U., Prague, 1960. Research asst. Slovak Acad. Sci., Bratislava, 1953-56, sci. asst., 1956-60, scientist, 1960-62, ind. scientist, 1962-69; ecologist-entomologist East Africa-Aedes Rsch. Unit WHO, Dar es Salaam, Tanzania, 1969-71; asst. faculty fellow dept. biology U. Notre Dame, 1971-73, assoc. faculty fellow, 1973-74; assoc. prof. med. entomology Johns Hopkins U. Sch. Hygiene and Pub. Health, 1974-78, prof., 1978—, dir. labs. med. entomology. Med. entomology, rsch. assoc. U. Ill., Urbana, 1966-67, Can. Dept. Agr., Lethbridge, Alta., 1967-68; dir. Biol. Rsch. Inst. Am., 1971-79; external dir. rsch. Liberiran Inst. Biomed. Rsch., 1981-89; dir. AID project on transmission of river blindness in areas of Liberia, Sierra Leone, and Cote d'Ivoire; dir. WHO rsch. grant; tech. adv. com. AID Vector Biology and Control Project, 1986-91; dir. Johns Hopkins U./Fed. U. Tech. Akure Onchocerciasis Project in Nigeria, 1991-94, Johns Hopkins U./Orgn. Coordination et de Cooperation pour la Lutte les Grandes Endemies-Pierre Richet Inst. Onchocerciasis Project, Bouakė, Ivory Coast, 1993-96; dir. Johns Hopkins U./Pierre Richet Inst./ORSTOM onchocerciasis project in Ivory Coast, 1993-96; prof.,advisor doctoral students, USA, Can., Africa, Asia, Cen. Am., 1979—. Editor: Jour. Biologia, 1956-71, Jour. Entomol. Problems, 1960-72; zool. sect.: Jour. Biol. Works, 1960-71; contbr. articles to profl. jours. Dir. WHO project on prophylactic drugs for river blindness, Liberia, 1985-87. Recipient Slovak Acad. Sci., 1st prize for research project. Mem. AAUP, AAAS, Am. Inst. Biol. Soci., Am. Mosquito Control Assn., Am. Soc. Parasitologists, Helminthol. Soc. Washington, Am. Soc. Tropical Medicine and Hygiene, Entomol. Soc. Am., Am. Genetic Assn., Soc. of Vector Ecology, N.Y. Acad. Scis., Johns Hopkins U. Tropical Medicine Club, Smithsonian Assocs., Royal Soc. Tropical Medicine and Hygiene, Royal Entomol. Soc. of London, Sigma Xi, Delta Omega (Alpha chpt.). Home: 1504 Ivy Hill Rd Cockeysville MD 21030-1418 Office: Johns Hopkins U 615 N Wolfe St Baltimore MD 21205-2103 Office Phone: 410-955-3475. Business E-Mail: mtrpis@jhsph.edu.

TRUANT, ALLAN L., medical educator, laboratory scientist, health science administrator; b. July 6, 1950; BS, U. Mich., 1971; PhD, U. Oreg., 1977. Fellow Ctrs. for Disease Control, Atlanta, 1977-79; assoc. prof., assoc. dir. Univ. Tex. Med. Br., Galveston, 1979-85; prof., dir. clin. microbiology, immunology and virology lab. Temple U. Hosp. and Sch. Medicine, Phila., 1985—. Inspector Coll. Am. Pathologists, Chgo., 1983—; mem. exam. bd. Am. Bd. Bioanalysis, St. Louis, 1996—. Editor: Manual of Commercial Methods in Clinical Microbiology, 2002. Recipient Rorer award for manuscript excellence

Am. Coll. Gastroenterology, 1983. Office: Temple U Hosp and Sch Medicine Broad Ontario Sts Philadelphia PA 19140 Office Phone: 215-707-3415. Business E-Mail: allan.truant@tuhs.temple.edu.

TRUCCO, MARCO, neurologist, researcher; b. Savona, Italy, Aug. 30, 1957; s. Giuseppe Trucco and Maria Grazia Savelli; MBBChir, U. Pavia, Italy, 1981, specialization in Neurology, 1985, specialization in Clin. Neurophysiology, 1990. Asst. in neurology Santa Corona Hosp., Pietra Ligure, Italy, 1987—93, cons. in neurology, 1993—94, med. dir. neurology, 1995—. Dir. Headache Ctr. Santa Corona Hosp., Pietra Ligure, Italy, 1987—; guest rschr. Söder Hosp., Stockholm, 1992, Bispebjerg Hosp., Copenhagen, 1999; advisory bd. Giornale delle Cefalee, Perugia, Italy, 2004—; referee Jour. Headache and Pain, Springer, Milan, Italy, 2005—, Headache, Blackwell, Oxford, England, 2006—. Contbr. chapters to books, articles to profl. jours.; website prodr. Recipient Cicladol award, U. Milan, 1990, Astra-Zeneca award, Italian Soc. Psychiatry, 2002. Mem.: Italian Soc. Study of Headache (mem. exec. bd., sec. NW sect.), Italian Soc. Neurology, Internat. Headache Soc., Amnesty Internat. Roman Catholic. Avocations: skiing, bicycling, mountaineering, reading, photography, movies. Home: Via Costa 7 A 17055 Toirano Italy Office: Ospedale S Corona Via Xxv Aprile 38 17027 Pietra Ligure SV Italy Office Phone: 39-019-6234001. Personal E-mail: truccom1@virgilio.it. Business E-Mail: m.trucco@asl2.liguria.it.

TRUITT, GARY R., lawyer, insurance company executive; b. 1950; BA, U. Pitts.; JD, Duquesne U., Pitts. Sr. v.p., gen. counsel, corp. sec. Highmark Inc., Pitts., exec. v.p. regulatory affairs, gen. counsel, corp. sec. Mem.: Allegheny County Bar Assn. Office: Highmark Inc Ste 3112 120 5th Ave Pittsburgh PA 15222-3099 Office Phone: 412-544-8190. Office Fax: 412-544-7583. E-mail: gary.truitt@highmark.com. *

TRUJILLO-CHAVEZ, ROMELL, pharmaceutical executive; b. Huanuco, Peru, May 13, 1972; s. Diego Trujillo-Quispe and Meri Chavez-Trujillo. BS in Pharmacy, U. Nac. Mayor San Marcos, Lima, Peru, 1995; MSc in Exptl. Pharmacology, U. Nac. Mayor San Marcos, 1999. R&d asst. Lab. Magma S.A., Lima, 1994; pharm. plant asst. Lab. Farmindustria S.A., Lima, 1995; r&d mgr. Corp. Infarmasa S.A., Lima, 1996—99; r&d asst. Alexander Von Humbolt - Tropical Medicinal Inst., Lima, 1999—2000; r&d mgr. Corp. Medco SAC, Lima, 2000—. Regente Drogueria Medco, Lima, 2000—. Mem.: Am. Assn. Pharm. Scientist (assoc.). Roman Catholic. Avocations: guitar, piano, drawing, reading, collecting ancient pharmacy bottles. Home: Jiron Ricardo Flores 355-A - La Victoria Lima 13 Peru Office: Corp Medco SAC Avevenezuela 5415 - San Miguel Lima Peru Office Fax: 511-4150520. Personal E-mail: romelltrujillo@gmail.com. Business E-Mail: rtrujillo@medco.com.pe.

TRULLAS, JOAN CARLES, physician; b. Barcelona, Dec. 30, 1975; MD, U. Autonoma de Barcelona, 1999. Sr. specialist. Internal Medicine Svc., Hosp. Sant Jaume Olot., 2005—. Assoc. prof. medicine U. de Girona, 2009—. Recipient Young Investigator award, CROI, San Francisco, 2010; named Best Young Internal Medicine Specialist, Spain, 2010. Office: Mulleras 15 Olot Girona 17800 Spain Office Fax: 0034+972275235. Business E-Mail: jctv5153@comg.cat.

TRUNNELL, THOMAS NEWTON, dermatologist; b. Waterloo, Iowa, May 7, 1942; s. Thomas Lyle and Vivian (Dahl) T.; m. Patricia Rautiala, Aug. 2, 1974; children: Suzanne, Thomas, Sarah. AB cum laude, Princeton U., 1964; MD, U. Iowa, 1968. Diplomate Am. Bd. Dermatology, 1973. Intern U. So. Calif., LA, 1969; resident NYU, 1969—72; pvt. practice dermatology Tampa, Fla., 1974—; asst. clin. prof. U. S. Fla., Tampa, 1975—. Contbr. articles to profl. jours. Maj. USAF, 1972—74. Mem.: AMA, Fla. Dermatology Soc., Fla. Soc. Dermatological Surgeons (pres. 1993), Fla. Med. Assn., Am. Acad. Dermatology. Republican. United Methodist. Avocations: fishing, hunting. Office: 13801 Bruce B Downs Blvd Tampa FL 33613-3939 Office Phone: 813-977-1024.

TRUOG, WILLIAM EDWARD, III, pediatrician, educator, researcher; b. Kans. City, Mo., Feb. 5, 1947; s. William E. and Virginia (Sylvester) Truog; m. Jill D. Jacobson, July 11, 1992. BA cum laude, Carleton Coll., 1969; MD, U. Chgo., 1973. Intern, resident pediat., chief resident Children's Orthop. Hosp.-U. Wash., Seattle, 1973—76, rsch. fellow neonatology, 1976—78; asst. prof., assoc. prof., prof. pediat. U. Wash., Seattle, 1978—93; prof. pediat. U. Mo. Kansas City Sch. Medicine, 1993—, assoc. chair faculty devel. dept. pediats., 2007—; dir. Ctr. Pulmonary Disorders Mercy Hosp., 2008—. Med. dir. infant ICU Children's Orthop. Hosp., Seattle, 1982—91. Author: Critical Care of the Newborn, 1983, 1988; contbr. articles to profl. jours. Recipient Sosland Endowed Chair Neonatal Rsch., 2001, Founders award, Midwest Soc. Pediat. Rsch., 2008; named First Physician Scientist, Children's Mercy Hosp., 1993, Best Drs. in America, 2005—; grantee, NIH, 1981, 1984, 1997, 2002, 2011. Mem.: Perinatal Rsch. Soc., We. Soc. Pediat. Rsch., Soc. Pediat. Rsch., Am. Pediat. Soc., Am. Thoracic Soc. (grantee 1978). Episcopalian. Office: Children's Mercy Hosp 2401 Gillham Rd Kansas City MO 64108-4619 *

TRYBA, MICHAEL, anesthesiologist, researcher; b. Walsum, Germany, July 21, 1950; s. Bernhard and Johanna Tryba; m. Jacoba Sperschneider, Dec. 31, 1975; children: Christiane, Carmen, Phillip. MD, U. Hannover, 1977. Resident U. Hannover, 1977-83, sr. physician, 1983-84, oberarzt, 1985-86, lectr., 1984-86; vice chmn. U. Hosp. Bergmannsheil, Bochum, 1987-96; chmn. Klinikum Kassel, 1997—. Lectr. Ruhr U., Bochum, 1987-90, prof., 1990—. Author: Prevention of Stress Bleeding--A New Concept, 1988; contbr. articles to profl. jours. Mem. European Acad. Anesthesiologists, European Soc. Anesthesiologists (Brussels, past bd. dirs.), European Soc. Regional Anesthesia (Hans Killian award 1987, past bd. dirs.), Am. Soc. Regional Anesthesia, European Soc. Intensive Care Medicine (Brussels), Internat. Assn. of the Study of Pain, Sertuerner Soc. (bd. dirs.). Roman Catholic. Avocations: music, enamel crafts, sports. Office: Klinikum Moenchebergstr 41-43 D-34125 Kassel Germany E-mail: tryba-michael@web.de.

TRYBUS, MAREK, plastic surgeon; b. Krakow, Poland, May 5, 1955; Diploma, Jagiellonian U., 1979, doctorate, 1987. Cert. specialist plastic surgery Med. Ctr. Postgrad. Edn., 1987. Plastic surgeon and hand surgeon 2nd Dept. Surgery, Krakow, 1987—, asst. prof., 2009—. Lectr. 2nd Chair Surgery Jagiellonian U., Krakow, 1987—. Contbr. articles to profl. jours. Mem.: Internat. Fedn. Socs. Surgery Hand, Internat. Confederation Plastic, Reconstructive and Aesthetic Surgery. Office: 2nd Dept Surgery Kopernika 21 Cracow 31-501 Poland Home: Ul. Wroclawska 52/4 30-011 Cracow Poland Office Fax: 48124213456. Personal E-mail: m_trybus@interia.pl.

TRZECIAK, HENRYK IRENEUSZ, pharmacologist, educator; b. Ruda Śląska, Poland, May 28, 1938; s. Bronislaw and Magdalena (Opielka) T.; m. Jadwiga Teresa Dubicka, Apr. 19, 1969; 1 child, Hanna Malgorzata. MSChE, Poly. High Sch., Gdansk, 1961; MD, DSc, Silesian Acad. Medicine, 1968, PhD, 1980. From asst. pharmacologist to asst. prof. Silesian Acad. Medicine, Katowice, Poland, 1961—85, assoc. prof., 1985—96; prof. Silesian Med. U., Katowice, Poland, 1996—2008, head dept. pharmacology, 2008—; head dept. pub. health The Cardinal August Hlond U. Edn., Myslowice, Poland, 2008—. Mem.: Polish Pharmacol. Soc. (pres. 1998—2001). Roman Catholic. Office: Powstańców 19 41-400 Mysyowice Poland Home: Ul Robotnicza 14/1 40-689 Katowicel Piotrowice Poland Office Phone: 48-32-225 39 05. E-mail: henryktrzeciak@onet.pl.

TSAI, CHIA-WEN, nutritionist, educator; b. Changhwa, Sept. 10, 1977; PhD, Chung Shan Med. U., 2006. Asst. prof. dept. nutrition China Med. U., 2006—. Office: 91 Hsueh-Shih Rd Taichung 404 Taiwan Business E-Mail: cwtsai@mail.cmu.edu.tw.

TSAI, CHIEH-CHIH, ophthalmologist, researcher; b. Taipei, Taiwan, Nov. 15, 1965; m. Hui-Chuan Kau; 1 child, Yuan-Ton. MD, Nat. Yang-Ming U., Taipei, 1992, postgrad., 2003. Cert. physician China, ophthalmologist Taiwan. Attending physician Taipei Vets. Gen. Hosp., Taipei, 1997—; clin. lectr. Nat. Def. Med. Coll., Taipei, 1998—; lectr. Nat. Yang-Ming U., Taipei, 2002—. Tai Chi instr.; Chikung instr. Scholar, Nat. Yang-Ming U., 1985—89. Mem.: Chinese Med. Assn., Ophthalmologic Soc. Republic of China, Am. Acad. Ophthalmology. Achievements include first to efficacy of probing the nasolacrimal duct with adjunctive Mitomycin-C for epiphora in adults; research in relationship between genetic polymorphism of hOGG1 and susceptibility to pterygium in Chinese; pulsatile ocular blood flow in patients with Graves' Ophthalmopathy; photo-oxidative DNA damage in human pterygium. Home and Office: No201 Shih-Pai Rd Sect 2 Taipei 11217 Taiwan Office Fax: 886-228213984; Home Fax: 886-228213984. E-mail: cctsai@vghtpe.gov.tw.

TSAI, HENRY, biotechnologist, educator; b. Taiwan, Feb. 6, 1962; PhD, Mich. State U., 1996. Sr. scientist Devel. Ctr. Biotech., Taiwan, 2003—07; asst. prof. Asia U., Taiwan, 2007—. Adj. asst. prof. China Med. U., Taiwan, 2005—. Avocation: mountain climbing. Office: 500 Lioufeng Rd Wufeng Dist Taichung 41354 Taiwan Office Fax: 886-4-2332-1126. E-mail: henry_j_tsai@yahoo.com.

TSAI, HORNG-DER, obstetrician, gynecologist, educator; b. Taichung, Taiwan, July 17, 1943; s. Mu and Chen-Chuan Tsai; m. Whei-Ju Chang, June 1, 1982; children: Ming-Ju, Ming-Shyun, Ming-Shiun. MD, China Med. U., Taichung, 1979; fellow, Keio Med. Sch., Tokyo, 1986. TSRM Dept. Health, Exec. Yuan, Taiwan, 1987. Chief dept. obstetrics China Med. U. Hosp., Taichung, 1987—91, chief dept. ob-gyn., 1991—2002, prof., 2000—. Referee Human Reproduction; contbr. articles to profl. jours. Recipient Prize paper, Nat. Sci. Coun., 1996, 2000. Mem.: Taiwan Assn. Ob-gyn. (assoc.; cons. physician 1994—2003, Best Paper award 2000), Taiwanese Soc. for Reproductive Medicine (assoc.; pres. 1998—2000, Best Paper award 1996). Achievements include research in recombinant human leukemia inhibitory factor enhances the development of preimplantation mouse embryo in vitro; subcutaneous low-dose leuprolide acetate depot injection may offer a useful alternative for pituitary suppression in ovarian stimulation for IVF. Avocations: tennis, travel, wine, hiking, music. Home: No 5 Lane 249 Da-Der St Taichung 404 Taiwan Office: China Med Univ Hosp 2 Yu Der Road Taichung 404 Taiwan Office Fax: 886-4-22052121 ext 3761; Home Fax: 886-4-22052121 ext 3761. Personal E-mail: hongte2000@yahoo.com. Business E-Mail: d0026@www.cmuh.org.tw.

TSAI, I-CHEN, radiologist; b. Taipei, Taiwan, Sept. 24, 1978; s. Yao-Jen Tsai and Hui-Jong Lin; m. Wan-Chun Liao, Oct. 22, 2005. MD, Nat. Yang Ming U., Taipei, 2002. Chief resident Taichung Vet. Gen. Hosp., 2006—, attending physician, 2007—. Rev. Am. Roentgen Ray Soc., Leesburg, Va., 2005—. Mem.: Radiologic Soc. Republic of China. Achievements include long term contribution to radiological society in MDCT field; invention of contrast-covening time concept for pediatric applications. Office: Dept Radiology No160 Sec 3 Taichung Harbor Rd Taichung 407 Taiwan Office Fax: 886-4-23592639. Personal E-mail: sillyduck.radiology@gmail.com.

TSAI, JAMES C., ophthalmologist, researcher; BA in Neurosci., Amherst Coll., 1985; MD, Stanford U., 1989; MBA, Vanderbilt U., 1998. Diplomate Am. Bd. Ophthalmology, Nat. Bd. Med. Examiners. Intern Cedars-Sinai Med. Ctr., LA, 1989—90; resident in ophthalmology U. So. Calif., Doheny Eye Inst., LA, 1990—93; fellow Bascom Palmer Eye Inst., Miami, Fla., 1993—94, Moorfields Eye Hosp., London, 1994—95; asst. prof. ophthalmology and visual scis. Vanderbilt U. Sch. Medicine, Nashville, 1995—2001; dir. glaucoma divsn., assoc. prof. ophthalmology Harkness Eye Inst., Columbia U. Coll. Physicians and Surgeons, NYC, 2001—06; Robert Young prof., chair dept. opthalmology and visual sci. Yale U. Sch. Medicine, New Haven, 2006—. Homer McK. Rees Glaucoma scholar, Columbia U., 2001—04. Fellow: ACS, Am. Acad. Ophthalmology (Achievement award). Office: Yale Eye Ctr 40 Temple St Ste1B New Haven CT 06510 Office Fax: 203-785-7694. Business E-Mail: james.tsai@yale.edu.

TSAI, JUI-YI, chemist, researcher; s. Yu-chen Tsai and Hui-Mei Chen; m. Tzu-Hui Liu, June 10, 2001; 1 child, Lawrence YinCheng. PhD, Auburn U., 1998. Postdoctoral fellow Harvard Med. Sch., Boston, 1999—2000; rsch. chemist PPG Industries Inc., Monroeville, Pa., 2000—. Editor: Current Medicinal Chemistry. Mem.: Am. Chemistry Soc. (assoc.). Achievements include discovery of therapeutic approaches on APP processing and Alzheimer's Disease. Avocation: swimming. Office: PPG Industries Inc 440 College Park Monroeville PA 15146 Home: 8 Candlewood Ct Newtown PA 18940-1411

TSAI, KUN-NAN, biomedical engineer, biologist; BS in Biology, Tung Hai U., 1999; MS in Basic Medicine Sci., Chang Gung U., 2001; PhD in Bioinformatics, Nat. Taiwan U., 2009. Postdoc. rschr. Rsch. Ctr. for Emerging Viral Infections, Chung Gung U., 2009—10, Biodiversity Rsch. Ctr., Academia Sinica, 2010—. Mem.: Taiwan Bioinformatics & Systems Biology Soc. Achievements include studying function of allophycocyanin in inhibition of enterovirus 71-induced apoptosis; deciphering pathways of enterovirus 71-infected cells; include breakthroughs in splice site prediction of RNA viruses; breakthroughs in cytotoxic effect of recombinant Mycobacterium tuberculosis; inferring genetic interactions in S. cerevisiae and pathways of pulmonary disease in human cell line; research in recent progress in influenza genome diversity and evolution and discussing newest applications of deep sequencing methods in influenza virology. Personal E-mail: freprose@gmail.com.

TSAI, LI-HUEI, pathologist, researcher; b. Taipei, Taiwan, Mar. 18, 1960; m. Lonarto Liong; 1 child, Jessica Liong. PhD, U. Tex. Southwestern, Dallas, 1990. Asst. prof. pathology Harvard Med. Sch., Cambridge, Mass., 1994—99, assoc. prof., 1999—2002, prof., 2002—06, asst. investigator pathology, 1997—2002; prof. Picower Ctr. Learning and Memory MIT, Cambridge, 2006—, assoc. mem. Broad Inst., 2006—; investigator RIKEN-MIT Neuroscience, Cambridge, 2006—, Howard Hughes Med. Inst., Cambridge, 2006—. Contbr. articles to profl. jours. Mem.: Soc. Neuroscience (assoc.). Office: 77 Massachusetts Ave 46-4235a Cambridge MA 02139 Office Fax: 617 324 1657; Home Fax: 617-324-1657. Business E-Mail: lhtsai@mit.edu.

TSAI, MING-HUNG, internist, researcher; s. Tseng-Li Tsai and Chieh-Min Tsai-Chuang; m. Yun-Shing Peng-Tsai; children: Sharon, Ann, Juan-Carlos. MD, Chung-Shan Med. U., Taichung, 1992. Cert. physician Adminstrn. Health, Taiwan, 1992, specialist internal medicine Adminstrn. Health, Taiwan, 1995, specialist gastroenterology Soc. Gastroenterology Taiwan, 1998, specialist gastroenterological endoscopy Soc. Gastroent. Endoscopy Taiwan, 1999, specialist for critical care medicine Taiwan Soc. Critical Care Medicine, 2008. Resident dept. internal medicine Chang Gung Meml. Hosp., Taipei, 1992—95, clin. fellow divsn. gastroenterology, 1995—97, attending physician divsn. gastroenterology, 2001—; rsch. fellow sect. digestive diseases Yale U., New Haven, 1999—2001; asst. prof. Chang Gung U., Taipei, 2005—; assoc. prof. Chang Gung Meml. Hosp., Taipei, 2010—, chief, divsn. digestive therapeutic endoscopy, 2010—. Contbr. chapters to books, articles to profl. jours. Recipient Med. Rsch. award, New Century Health Care Promotion Found., Taipei, 2007—08. Mem.: European Assn. Study Liver Disease, Soc. Gastroenterologic Endoscopy, Soc. Gastroenterology, Am. Assn. Study Liver Diease. Achievements include research in the mechanism behind nitric oxide overproduction in early stage of portal hypertension when hyperdynamic circulation is not fully established; the association between adrenal insufficiency and multiple organ failure in patients with liver cirrhosis and severe sepsis and the association between hypolipoproteinemia and severe sepsis in cirrhotic patients; critical care for cirrhotic patients; role of hypolipoproteinemia in patients with liver cirrhosis and severe sepsis. Office: Chang Gung Meml Hosp 199 Tung-Hwa North Rd Taipei 105 Taiwan Office Phone: 886-3-3281200 ext. 2110. Office Fax: 886-3-3288662. Business E-Mail: mhtsai@cgmh.org.tw.

TSAI, MING-LING, ophthalmologist, researcher; b. Tainan, Taiwan; s. Shi-Zen Tsai and Yue-Tao Wei. MD, Nat. Def. Med. Ctr., Taipei, Taiwan, 1990, PhD, 2002. Cert. ophthalmologist Taiwan, 1997. Vis. scholar Yale U., New Haven, 2005—06; chief ophthalmology dept. Tri-Svc. Gen. Hosp., Taipei, 2004—; assoc. prof. Nat. Def. Med. Ctr., 2004—. Contbr. scientific papers to profl. jours. Lt. col. Taiwan Army, 2004—. Recipient Jour. Golden award, Ophthal. Soc. Taiwan, 2002—04. Mem.: Tri-Svc. Med. Ctr. Achievements include patents for intraocular lens with photocatalytic coating; visual performance during aviation. Home and Office: Nat Defense Med Ctr 325 Sec 2 Chenggong Rd Neihu Dist Taipei 114 Taiwan Personal E-mail: doc30845@yahoo.com.tw.

TSAI, MING-TIEN, finance educator, consultant; b. Taipei, Taiwan, Mar. 20, 1953; s. Bing-Kuei Tsai and Eye-Jane Lee; m. Tina Hsu; children: Victor, Monica. EdD, Columbia U., NY, 1985. Bd. dirs. Shinih Enterprise Co., Ltd., Taipei, 2004—; CEO EMBA program Coll. Mgmt., Tainan City, Taiwan, 2005—. Cons. Sengda Medicine & Chem. Corp., Tainan, 1999—2001. Ind. outside bd. mem. Shnih Enterprise Co. Ltd., Taipei, 2004—08. With Taiwan Army, 1975—77, Taichung. Recipient Cert. of Best Author award, Jour. Am. Acad. Bus., 2005. Avocations: travel, hiking. Office: Nat Cheng-Kung Univ 1 Tashieh Rd Tainan City 701 Taiwan Office Fax: 8866-2755156. Business E-Mail: mingtien@mail.ncku.edu.tw.

TSAI, TSEN-FANG, dermatologist, educator; b. Taipei, Taiwan, July 13, 1963; s. Chun-Po Tsai and Show-Er Lin. MD, Taipei Med. U., 1988. Med. lic. Taiwan, 1988, cert. dermatologist specialist Taiwan, 1992. Resident Nat. Taiwan U. Hosp., Taipei, 1989—93, staff, 1993—. Cosmetic cons. Bur. of Health, Taipei, 1996—99, mem. new drugt application adv. com., 2001—; fellow Jefferson U., Phila., 1998, U. Calif., San Francisco, 1998—99; bd. dirs. Taiwancse Dermatologic Soc., Taipei, 1999—; cons. GABA, Taipei, 2001—, Procter & Gamble, Cin., 2002—; asst. prof. Nat. Taiwan U. Hosp., Taipei, 2003—. Author: Psoriasis Handbook, English-Chinese Dictionary of Dermatology, Care of Skin from Daily Life, Hair Care, Salon Care & Hair Regrowth, Understanding Psoriasis and Psoriatic Arthritis, Hair Care, Scalp Care, and Hair Regrowth, Understanding Psoriasis and Psoriatic Arthritis; internat. editor: Jour. Clin. Dermatology, 2003—, editor-in-chief: Dermatologica Sinica, 1999—; contbr. chpt. to book. Grantee, Nat. Soc. Sci., 2002; scholar, Dept. of Edn., 1998—99. Mem.: European Acad. Dermatolovenereology (assoc.), Am. Acad. Dermatolgy (assoc.). Achievements include research in among the first to identify the role of EBV in skin lymphoma. Home: F3 2 Alley 21 Ln 50 Wu-Shin St Taipei 10501 Taiwan Office: Nat Taiwan Univ Hosp 7 Chung-Shan South Rd Taipei 100 Taiwan Home Fax: 886-2-23934177. Personal E-mail: tftsai@yahoo.com.

TSAI, WEN-CHI, agricultural studies educator; b. Taiwan, Aug. 7, 1964; PhD, Imperial Coll. London, 1994. Tech. specialist, dept. health, exec. FDA, Yuan, Taiwan, 1988—95; assoc. prof. Grad. Inst. Biotech., Chinese Culture U., 1995—2010, prof., 2010—. Grants, Nat. Sci. Coun., Taiwan. Mem.: Agrl. Chem. Soc. Taiwan. Office: 55 Hwa-Kang Rd Taipei 111 Taiwan Business E-Mail: wctsai@faculty.pccu.edu.tw.

TSAI, YAO-CHOU, urologist; b. Taiwan, May 23, 1970; B, Taipei Med. U., 1997. Attending staff Buddhist Tzu Chi Gen. Hosp., Taipei Br., 2005—. Recipient Young Investigator award, World Congress Endoscopic Surgery, Japan, 2008. Office: Jianguo Rd Xindian 289 Taiwan E-mail: tsai1970523@yahoo.com.tw.

TSAKAYANNIS, DIMITRIS E., surgeon, researcher; b. Athens, Greece, Mar. 7, 1965; s. Elefterios and Kassiani Tsakayannis; m. Lia Kosmidou, Oct. 15, 1999; children: Elefterios, Kassiani. MD (hon.), U. Athens, 1989, PhD (hon.), 1993. Diplomate Am. Bd. of Surgery, Greek Bd. of Surgery. Rsch. fellow in surgery Harvard Med. Sch., Boston, 1990—91; resident, assoc. in surgery Tufts U. Med. Sch., Boston, 1991—93; assoc. in surgery Harvard Med. Sch., Boston, 1993—95, U. Mass. Med. Sch., Worcester, 1995—97, Hygeia Hosp. Med. Ctr., Athens, Greece, 1997—. Adv. bd. Hellenic-American Med. Assn., Athens, Greece, 2001—. Contbr. articles to profl. jours., chapters to books. V.p. internat. affairs Angiogenesis Found., Boston, 1993—2005, adv. bd., founding bd. dirs., 1993—. Fellow, Harvard Med. Sch., 1990—91, 1993—95, Harvard Coll., 1992—96; scholar, EEC, 1985—87, Greek Nat. Scholarship Found., 1984—87. Fellow: ACS, Soc. Am. Gastrointestinal Endoscopic Surgeons; mem.: Greek Med. Assn., U. Mass. Med. Alumni Assn., Tufts Med. Alumni Assn., Hellenic AMA (pres. 2001—03), Harvard Alumni Assn., Athens Coll. Alumni Assn. Achievements include research in angiogenesis and wound healing. Avocations: swimming, travel, hiking. Personal E-mail: dtsak@ath.forthnet.gr.

TSALIKIAN, EVA, physician, educator; b. Piraeus, Greece, June 22, 1949; came to U.S., 1974; d. Vartan and Arousiak (Kasparian) T.; m. Arthur Bonfield, Apr. 8, 2000. MD, U. Athens, 1973. Rsch. fellow U. Calif. Med. Sch., San Francisco, 1974—76; resident in pediats. Children's Hosp., Pitts., 1976-78, fellow in endocrinology, 1978-80; rsch. fellow Mayo Clinic, Rochester, Minn., 1980-83; asst. prof. U. Iowa, 1983—87, assoc. prof., 1987—2004, prof., 2004—, interim chmn., 2004, vice chmn. clin. affairs, 2005—; dir. pediat. endocrinology dept. pediats. U. Iowa Coll. Med., 1988—; chief staff U. Iowa, 2006—, U. Iowa Hosp. & Clinics. Recipient Young Physician award, AMA, 1977; fellow, Juvenile Diabetes Found., 1978—80, Heinz Nutrition Found., 1980—81. Mem. Am. Diabetes Assn. (bd. dirs. Mid-Am. sect.), Endocrine Soc., Soc. Pediat. Rsch., Am. Pediat. Soc., Lawson Wilkins Soc. for Pediat. Endocrinology, Internat. Soc. Pediat. and Adolescent Diabetes, Midwest Pediat. Endocrino Soc. (pres. 1996-99). Home: 206 Mahaska Dr Iowa City IA 52246-1606 Office: U Iowa Dept Pediatrics 2856 JPP Iowa City IA 52242 *

TSANG, TAT KIN, medical association administrator; b. Hong Kong, Mar. 10, 1949; MD, Northwestern U., 1978; MA, Trinity Evang. Div. Sch., 2001. Pres., ceo TZAM Diagnostics, LLC, 2008; clin. prof. medicine U. Chgo., 2009—. Prof. clin. medicine Northwestern U., 2005—10. Recipient Attending Physician Yr., NorthShore U. HealthSystem, 1986—87; named Am. Top Physicians, Consumers' Rsch. Coun. America; Rsch. grant, Am. Liver Found. Fellow: ACP, Am. Gastroenterology Assn. Avocations: fishing, basketball, bicycling, swimming, writing. Office: 1821 Wilmette Ave Wilmette IL 60091 Office Fax: 847-256-3371. E-mail: doctat@aol.com.

TSANGARIS, GEORGE THEODORE, biomedical researcher; married. PhD in Biochemistry, U. Ioannina, Greece, 1991. Rsch. scientist prof. Biomed. Rsch. Found., Acad. Athens, 2003—; group leader, project responcible U. Rsch. Inst. Study & Treatment Childhood Genetic & Malignant Diseases U. Athens, 1994—2002, rsch. assoc. Hematology Oncology Unit, A' Dept. Pediat., 1994—2002; rsch. fellow Roche Ctr. Med. Genetics, Basel, Switzerland, 2002; rsch. assoc. Inst. Nat. de la Santé et de la Rschr. Méd., Clamart, Paris, 1992—94. Sci. adv. bd. mem. Internat. Inst. Anticancer Rsch., Athens, 2000—; assoc. editor Cancer Genomics & Proteomics, Canada, 2003—; editl. bd. mem. Jour. Proteomics, Netherlands, 2006—. Contbr. articles to 65 rsch. papers. Achievements include patents for proteins with prognostic, diagnostic and therapeutic importance for trisomy 21 Down syndrome; chromosomal abnormalities as well as for the isolation and identification of naturally occuring peptides in biological materials; research in application of proteomics in human reproduction and pregnancy complications in neurology and cancer. Office Phone: 302106597075.

TSAO, ANNE, medical educator; b. Pa., Sept. 17, 1973; BS, MIT, 1994; MD, U. Chgo., 1998. Assoc. prof. U. Tex., Anderson Cancer Ctr., 2004—. Office: 1515 Holcombe Blvd Unit 432 Houston TX 77030 Business E-Mail: astsao@mdanderson.org.

TSAY, CHING SOW, retired anesthesiologist; b. Taipei, Taiwan, 1939; MD, Kaohsiung Med. Coll., Taiwan, 1964. Diplomate Am. Bd. Anesthesiology. Intern St. Vincent's Med. Ctr., Staten Island, NY, 1967-68; resident in anesthesiology St. Joseph Hosp., Joliet, Ill., 1968-69, Washington Hosp. Ctr., 1969-71; staff Cmty. Health Ctr. Branch County, Coldwater, Mich.; ret., 2006. Mem. Am. Soc. Anesthesiologists, Mich. Soc. Anesthesiologists, Internat. Anesthesia Rsch. Soc.

TSE, HARLEY Y., immunologist, educator; b. China, July 17, 1947; s. Ton-Cheuk and Hou-Ying (Choy) T.; m. Kwai-Fong Chui, Jan. 13, 1979; children: Kevin Y., Alan C., Leslie W. BS with honors, Calif. Inst. Tech., 1972; PhD, U. Calif., San Diego, 1977; MBA, Rutgers U., 1986. Fellow Arthritis Found., NIH, Bethesda, Md., 1977-80; sr. rsch. immunologist Merck Sharp & Dohme Rsch. Lab., Rahway, NJ, 1980-83, rsch. fellow, 1983-86; adj. asst. prof. Columbia U., 1981-84; assoc. prof. Wayne State U. Sch. Medicine, Detroit, 1986—, grad. officer dept. immunology and microbiology, 2003—. Mem. immunol. sci. study sect. NIH, 1995—99, mem. hypersensitivity, autoimmune and immune-mediated diseases study sect., 2005—08. Contbr. articles to profl. jours. Bd. dir. Chinese Social Svc. Ctr., San Diego, 1975. Recipient NIH Rsch. Career Devel. award, 1992-97; Calif. Biochem. Rsch. fellow, 1975; Arthritis Found. fellow, 1977-80; grantee NIH, 1988—, Nat. Multiple Sclerosis Soc., 1988—. Mem. Am. Assn. Immunologists, Chinese Student Assn. (pres. 1974-76), Soc. Chinese Bioscientists in Am., Detroit Immunol. Soc. (pres. 1989-91). Roman Catholic. Home: 5393 Tequesta Dr West Bloomfield MI 48323-2351 Office: Wayne State U Sch Medicine 540 E Canfield St Detroit MI 48201-1928 Home Phone: 248-681-6909; Office Phone: 313-577-1564. Business E-Mail: htse@wayne.edu.

TSEDEKE, AYELE TADDESE, medical educator; b. Addis Ababa, Ethiopia, Mar. 10, 1982; DVM, Addis Ababa U., Ethiopia, 2006; MS in Anatomy Tissue Engring., U. Putra Malaysia, 2010. Cert. AIDS Prevention and Support Orgn. Asst. prof. U. Gondar, 2006—, head, unit basic vet. scis., 2010—. Mem.: Ethiopian Vet. Assn. Avocations: reading, movies. Office: DR Ayele Taddese Tsedeke University Gondar Amhara 196 Ethiopia Office Fax: 251-0581141233. Personal E-mail: ayutadei@yahoo.com.

TSEKOURAS, PANAYOTIS, food microbiologist; b. Athens, Greece, July 4, 1952; s. Dimitrios and Akrivi T. BSc, U. Ill., 1977, BSc, 1979; MSc, So. Ill. U., 1981. Quality control supr. Bingo SA, Athens, 1983-88; head microbiology dept. Delta Dairy SA, Athens, 1989-95; lab. instr. TEI, Athens, 1996-98; microbiology dept. supr. Food Qualitec Lab., Athens, 1998—. Trainer Greek Food Adminstrn. Home: Agathupoleos 71 104 46 Athens Greece Personal E-mail: pantsek@otenet.gr.

TSELEPIS, ALEXANDROS, medical educator; b. Heraklion, Greece, Dec. 17, 1954; s. Dimitris A. and Maria J. Tselepis; m. Christine J. Theriou, July 18, 1982; children: Maria A., Dimitris A. BS in Pharmacy, Sch. Pharmacy, U. Thessaloniki, Greece, 1974—79; PhD in BioChemistry, U. Ioannina, Greece, 1980—86, MD, 1986—91. NIH postdoctoral fellow U. Tex., San Antonio, 1988—89; lectr. in biochemistry U. Ioannina, Greece, 1987—92, asst. prof., 1992—2000, assoc. prof., 2000—06, prof. clin. biochem., 2006—. Grantee, European Union, 1996—99; fellow, NIH, 1988—89. Office: Univ Ioannina Dourouti 451 10 Ioannina Greece Office Fax: +302651 047832. E-mail: atselep@uoi.gr.

TSENG, FRANK S.C., education educator, researcher; b. ChangHua, Taiwan, June 30, 1964; m. Annie Y.H. Chou; 1 child, Kevin C.J. BA, Nat. Chiao Tung U., HsinChu, TAIWAN, 1986, MS, 1988, PhD, 1992. Assoc. prof. and chmn. Dept. Info. Mgmt., Yen-Ze U., ChungLi, Taoyuan County, Taiwan, 1995—97; assoc. prof. Dept of Info. Mgmt., Nat'l Kaohsiung 1st Univ of Sci & Tech, YenChao, Kaohsiung County, Taiwan, 1997—2005, prof., 2005—. Cons. Netnifty Tech., Inc., Taipei, Taiwan, 1999—, Culture Bur. of Kaohsiung County Govt., FengSheng, Kaohsiung County, Taiwan, 1998—2001. Contbr. articles to profl. jour. Recipient One of the Outstanding PhD Dissertation Award, Acer Long Term Thesis Award, 1993. Achievements include development of Customer Relationship Management System of Jih-Sun Securities, TAIWAN. Office: Nat'l Kaohsiung 1st Univ Sci & Tech 1 Univ Rd Taiwan Yenchao 824 Taiwan Office Fax: +886-7-6011042; Home Fax: +886-7-7659541. Personal E-mail: imfrank@ccms.nkfust.edu.tw.

TSENG, HAN CHI, physician; b. Nantou County, Taiwan, Sept. 1, 1952; s. Chen Shen Tseng and Kwai Hsu; m. Fan Li Kung, Sept. 28, 1980; children: Felicia Ingtyng, Catherine Yuchen. MD, Taipei Med. Coll., Taiwan, 1978. Cert. specialist in digestive surgery and family medicine Dept. of Health, Taiwan. Coun. Taiwan Med. Assn., Taipei, 2001; vice sec. gen. Taiwan Med. Assn. for Study Of Obesity, Taipei, 2004; attending physician, resident dept. surgery Taipei Vets. Gen Hosp., 1978—85; supr. Tseng Han Chi Gen. Hosp., Taiwan, 1985—. Author: How to Maintain Long Term Weight Loss, 2001. Bd. dirs. Nantou County Jen-Ai Charitable Home, 1986. Recipient prize, Taiwan Provincial Govt., 1986. Mem.: Taiwan Digestive Surgery Assn. (licentiate), Collegium Internat. Chirurgiae Digestivae (corr.). Avocations: music, tennis. Office: Tseng Han Chi Gen Hosp 915 Hu-shan Rd Tsaotun Nantou 542 Taiwan Office Phone: 886-49-2314145. Office Fax: 886-49-2327603. Business E-Mail: chi-ch@umail.hinet.net.

TSENG, HSIANG-KUANG (ERIC H.K. TSENG), physician; b. Taipei, Taiwan, Oct. 14, 1966; s. Fan-Tung and Yueh-Hua (Wang); m. Yi-Huei (Huang), June 29, 1996; children: Ling-Yi, Ling-Cheng. MD, Kaohsiung Med. U., Taiwan, 1993; PhD student, Nat. Yang-Ming U., Inst. Clin. Medicine, 2007—. Bd. cert. medicine, 1993, lab. medicine, 1994, internal medicine, 2000, infectious disease, 2001, tuberculosis, 2004, clin. geriatric emergency and critical core medicine, 2007, geriatrician, 2008. Resident, dept. internal med. Mackay Meml. Hosp., Taipei, 1996—99, chief resident, sect. infectious diseases, 1999—2001, attending physician, sect. infectious diseases, 2001—, sr. attending physician, sect. infectious diseases, 2007. Co-tutor problem-based learning, 2005—06, 2009—; clin. lectr. Nat. Yang-Ming U., 2005—06. Co-author: BioMed Central Medical Genetics, 2003; contbr. articles to profl. jours. Responsible brother of district 8, Ch. in Taipei, Hall 4, 2000—. 2d lt. mil. surgeon, Taiwan, 1993-95. Named Best Tchr. Intern Dr., Mackay Meml. Hosp., 2005; vis. scholar, Duke U., NC. Mem. Taiwan Soc. Internal Medicine, Infectious Disease Soc. of Taiwan, Am. Soc. Microbiology. Christian. Achievements include conducting infection control during SARS epidemic in Taiwan, 2003. Office: Mackay Memorial Hospital No 92 Sec 2 Zhong Shan N Rd 10449 Taipei Taiwan

TSENG, SZU-WEN, oncologist; b. Kaohsiung, Taiwan, Sept. 23, 1961; MD, Chung Shan Med. U., 1988; PhD, U. Pa., 1996. Dir., divsn. med. oncology Chung Shan Med. U. Hosp., 2007—, CEO, 2007—. Recipient Best Tchg. Attending award, Chung Shan Med. U. Hosp., 2009—10. Mem.: Chinese Oncology Soc. Avocations: reading, sports, travel. Office: 110 Sec 1 Chien-Kuo N Rd Taichung 402 Taiwan E-mail: doc1952b@yahoo.com.tw.

TSIAOUSIS, PANAGIOTIS Z., general surgeon; b. Thessaloniki, Greece, Oct. 29, 1973; Degree in Medicine, Aristotle U. Thessaloniki Med. Sch., 2001, MSc in Med. Rsch. Methodology, 2006; MSc in Mgmt. Health Care Units, 2011; attending, Aristolle U. Thessaloniki. Med. dir. Balcan Med. Clinic Ikeda-Euromedica Group, Korce, Albania, 2010—. Instr. Advanced Life Support European Com.; sci. assoc. 2nd Surg. Clinic Aristotle U. Thessaloniki Med. Sch., 2010. Mem.: Greek Assn. Mgmt. Health Care Units, European Digestive Surgery Assn., Northern's Greece Assn. Surgery, European Assn. Surgery, European Assn. Endoscopic Surgery. Avocations: basketball, music. Office: 14A Athanasiou Diakou Str Kastoria Macedonia 52100 Greece

TSIAOUSSIS, JOHN YIANNIS, colon and rectal surgeon, consultant; b. Athens, Greece, June 10, 1965; s. Christos and Irene Tsiaoussis; m. Irene Micheloudaki, Jan. 10, 1993; children: Irilema, Christine, Danai. MD, Med. Sch., U. Crete, Heratlion, 1991, PhD, 1994. Trainee gen. surgery Tzanio Gen. Hosp., Piraeus, Greece, 1993—95, U. Hosp., Heraklion, Greece, 1995—98; clin. fellow, colorectal unit Royal Infirmary, Edinburgh, 1999—2000, rsch. fellow, liver unit, 2000; cons. surgeon Met. Hosp., Athens, 2001—. Vis. prof. anatomy Med. Sch., Heraklion, 2006—. Contbr. scientific papers to numerous med. jours., chapters to books. Fellow: European Soc. Coloproctology (Edinburgh); mem.: Hellenic Soc. Digestive Surgery (Athens) (bd. mem. 2004—, rsch. com. mem. 2004—), Greek Surg. Soc. (Athens). Avocations: football, swimming, music. Home: Platonos 34 Moschato Athens 18344 Greece Office: Metropolitan Hosp Ethn Makarioy 9 N Faliro 18547 Greece Office Phone: 30-210-4809921. Personal E-mail: jtsiaoussis@hotmail.com. Business E-Mail: jtsiaoussis@metropolitan-hospital.gr.

TSIBULSKY, VLADIMIR LVOVICH, psychologist, researcher; b. Moscow, Apr. 19, 1951; arrived in U.S., 1993; s. Lev Nikolaevich Tsibulsky and Anna Sergeevna Subbotovich; m. Svetlana Olegovna Dmitrieva, Feb. 15, 2005; children: Cyril, Veronica, Anastasia, Alice. BS, Moscow State U., 1972, MS, PhD, Moscow State U., 1973. Rsch. scientist Severtsov Inst. Evolutionary Morphology and Ecology Animals, USSR Acad. of Sciences, Moscow, 1973—82; sr. rsch. scientist Lab. Neuropharmacology, Ctrl. Sci. Lab. of USSR Ministry of Health, Moscow, 1982—85, All-Union Sci. Ctr. Narcology USSR Ministry of Health, Moscow, 1985—90; vis. scientist Ctr. Studies Behavioral Neurobiology Concordia U., Montreal, Que., Canada, 1990—92; rsch. asst. prof. U. Cin., 1993—. Grantee, Nat. Inst. Drug Abuse, 2001—05; scholar, Nat. Heart, Lung, and Blood Inst., 1998—2001. Mem.: N.Y. Acad. Scis., Soc. Neuroscience, Pavlovian Physiol. Soc. Orthodox Christian. Achievements include patents for 1 (Silatranyl) Metyl Derivate Lactams possessing Neurotropic activity and the method to produce them. Avocations: travel, reading. Office: U Cin 231 Albert Sabin Way Mail Location 559 Cincinnati OH 45267-0559 Business E-Mail: vladimir.tsibulsky@uc.edu.

TSIEN, ROGER YONCHIEN, chemist, cell biologist; b. NYC, Feb. 1, 1952; s. Hsue Chu and Yi Ying (Li) Tsien; m. Wendy M. Globe, July 30, 1982. AB in Chemistry and Physics, summa cum laude, Harvard Coll., 1972; PhD in Physiology, Churchill Coll., U. Cambridge, Eng., 1977; PhD (hon.), Cath. U., Leuven, Belgium, 1995. Rsch. asst. U. Cambridge, 1975-78, postdoc. rschr., 1978—81; asst. prof. dept. physiology-anatomy U. Calif., Berkeley, 1981-85, assoc. prof., 1985-87, prof., 1987-89; prof. dept. pharmacology and chemistry U. Calif., San Diego, 1989—. Investigator Howard Hughes Med. Inst., Chevy Chase, Md., 1989—; T.Y. Shen vis. prof. medicinal chemistry MIT, 1991; Todd vis. prof. chemistry U. Cambridge, 2003. Contbr. articles to profl. jours., chapters to books. Recipient Lamport prize, NY Acad. Scis., 1986, Javits Neurosci. Investigator award, Nat. Inst. Neurological Disorders & Stroke, 1989, Young Scientist award, Passano Found., 1991, W. Alden Spencer award in neurobiology, Columbia U., 1991, Artois-Baillet-Latour Health prize, Belgium, 1995, Gairdner Found. Internat. award, 1995, Am. Heart Assn. Rsch. prize, 1995, Pearse prize, Royal Microscopical Soc., 2000, Creative Invention award, Am. Chem. Soc., 2002, Christian B. Anfinsen award, Protein Soc., 2002, Heineken prize for biochemistry/biophysics, Royal Netherlands Acad. Scis., 2002, Max Delbrück Medal, Berlin, 2002, Wolf Found. prize in medicine, Israel, 2004, Keio Med. Sci. prize, Japan, 2004, Perl prize in neurosci., U. NC, 2005, J.Allyn Taylor Internat. prize in medicine, Robarts Inst., Canada, 2005, Lewis S. Rosenstiel award for disting. work in basic med. scis., Brandeis U., 2006, E.B. Wilson medal, Am. Soc. Cell Biology, 2008, Nobel prize in chemistry, 2008. Mem.: NAS, Inst. Medicine, Am. Acad. Arts & Scis., Phi Beta Kappa. Achievements include design of a green fluorescent protein; development of a biological application of molecules to measure and/or manipulate intracellular calcium, sodium, and hydrogen ions; new methods for microscopic imaging and pharmaceutical high-throughput screening. Office: U Calif Sch Medicine 9500 Gilman Dr 310 George Palade Labs La Jolla CA 92093-0647 Office Phone: 858-534-4891. Fax: 858-534-5270. E-mail: rtsien@ucsd.edu. *

TSIMTNTKAKIS, NIKOLAOS CONSTANTINOS, surgeon; b. Athens, Greece, May 17, 1964; MD, Med. Sch. U. Athens, 1989. Attending surgeon surg. dept. Dist. Hosp. Chania, 2001—. Mem.: Greek Trauma Soc., Greek Surg. Soc., European Assn. Endoscopic Surgeons. Avocations: sports, music, reading. Home: Demokratias St Daratso Kydonia 73100 Greece E-mail: nikotsim@otenet.gr.

TSIOUFIS, KONSTANTINOS PANAYIOTIS, cardiologist, consultant; b. Agrinio, Greece, Aug. 20, 1963; s. Panayiotis Efstathios Tsioufis and Stayroula Dimitrios Tsioufi; m. Despoina Georgios Tsoura, Dec. 30, 1991; 1 child, Panayiotis. MD, Med. Sch. Of Athens, Greece, 1987. Cardiologist Med. Sch. Of Athens, 1997. Cons. cardiologist Hippokration Hosp., Athens, Greece, 2003—, interventional cardiologist, 1997—. Chief, antihypertensive outpatient clinic Cardiology Dept., Hippokration Hosp., Athens, Greece, 1997—. Contbr. articles to profl. jours. Fellow: European Soc. Hypertension (Clin. HYPERTENSION SPECIALIST 2002), Am. Coll. Cardiology. Personal E-mail: ktsioufis@hippocratio.gr.

TSIRIDIS, ELEFTHERIOS, orthopedist, consultant; b. Kavala, Greece, Feb. 26, 1968; s. Emilios and Alice Tsiridis; m. Eva-Maria Tsapakis, Sept. 2, 2001. MD, Athens Kapodistrian U., 1992; MSc in Orthop., U. Coll. London Med. Sch., 2000. Board Certification in Trauma and Orthopaedic Surgery 2002, cert. Specialist Tng. Trauma & Orthop. Gen. Med. Coun. London, 2002. Resident gen. surgery Gen. Army Hosp., Athens, Greece, 1993—94; resident neurosurgery Dist. Gen. Hosp., Kavala, Greece, 1994—95; sr. ho. officer trauma and orthop. James Paget Hosp. NHS Trust, Norfolk, England, 1995—97, sr. ho. officer trauma & orthop. Royal Devon and Exeter Hosp. Exeter, England, 1997—99; clin. rsch. fellow trauma & orthop. Royal Nat.

Orthop. Hosp., Stanmore, 1999—2000; specialist registrar trauma & orthopaedics Royal Nat. Orthop., Stanmore Affiliated Hospitals, London, 2000—03; cons., trauma & orthopaedic surgeon Whittington Hosp. NHS Trust, London, 2003—, rsch. fellow Inst. Orthop., Royal Nat. Orthop. Hosp. Stanmore, 2001—; fellow trauma and orthop. Boston U. Sch. of Medicine, 2003—. Author: (book chpt.) Encyclopaedia of Biomaterials and Biomedical Engineering; medical researcher (post-doctoral studies (mphil/phd) (Alexander Onassis Internat. Scholarship, 2001), (post-doctoral studies) (Culyer Grant, 2002), research in clinical orthopaedics (fellowship at boston university) (Brit. Orthopaedic Assn. Travelling Fellowship, 2003), medical student (outstanding performance in medical studi) ('Papadakis' Scholarship, Inst. for Scholarships, Greece, 1988). Mem. Provincial Coun., Kavala, Greece, 1992—96. Lt. Greek Spl. Forces, 1992—94. Fellow: Royal Coll. Surgeons Edinburgh, Brit. Orthop. Assn.; mem.: Internat. Hippocratic Found. Greek Orthodox. Achievements include research in Bone, Cell, and Tissue Engineering. Avocations: water polo, opera, hiking, travel, swimming. E-mail: tsiridis@bu.edu.

TSIRIKOS, ATHANASIOS IOANNIS, orthopedist, spinal surgeon, educator; s. Ioannis Athanasios Tsirikos and Theodora Tsirikou; m. Victoria Maria Papageorge, June 9, 2001; children: Theodora, John, George. MD, U. Athens, 1994, PhD, 2007. Resident gen. surgery 411 Gen. Mil. Hosp., Dist. Gen. Hosp. Syros, Greece, 1994—96; resident orthopedics U. Hosp., Athens, 1996—2000; fellow pediat. orthopedics A.I. duPont Hosp. for Children, Wilmington, Del., 2001—02; fellow in spine surgery Gt. Ormond St. Hosp. for Children, Royal Nat. Orthopedic Hosp., Stanmore, England, 2002—03, Royal Infirmary, Royal Hosp. for Sick Children, Edinburgh, Scotland, 2004—05; cons. orthop. and spine surgeon Scottish Nat. Spine Deformity Ctr., Royal Hosp. for Sick Children, Edinburgh, 2005—. Clin. dir. Scottish Nat. Spine Deformity Ctr., Edinburgh, 2006—; hon. clin. sr. lectr. U. Edinburgh, 2006—; presenter in field. Contbr. articles to profl. jours., chapters to books. With Greek Army, 1994—95. Scholar, Greek Orthopedic Soc. Fellow: Royal Coll. Surgeons; mem.: Greek Spine Soc., Scoliosis Rsch. Soc. (Best Clin. Poster Presentation award 2003), European Soc. Sports Traumatology, Brit. Orthopedic Assn., Greek Orthopedic Soc., Brit. Scoliosis Soc. (Best Oral Paper Presentation award 2003, Best Clin. Poster Presentation award 2003, Best Oral Paper Presentation award 2005). Avocations: sports, music, literature, films, travel. Office: Scottish Nat Spine Deformity Ctr Royal Hosp Sick Children Sciennes Rd Edinburgh EH9 1LF Scotland

TSIRLIS, THEODORE, surgeon; b. Thessaloniki, Greece, July 29, 1971; s. Dimitrios Tsirlis and Athina Tsirli. MD, Kapodistrian U., Athens, Attica, Greece, 2000. Cert. gen. surgeon Greek Bds. Surgery, 2008. Resident surgeon Aegion Gen. Hosp., Achaia, 2002—05, resident surgeon, G.Gennimatas, 2005—08; staff surgeon Hygeia Hosp., Athens, 2008—09; sr. clin. fellow hepatobility & transplant surgery Freeman Hosp., Newcastle upon tyre, 2009—. Clin. asst. HPB Surgery, Hammersmith Hosp., Imperial Coll., London, 2006. Contbr. scientific papers. Achievements include research in Lymphangiogenic Growth Factors, Gastric Cancer.

TSIRONI, MARIA, internist, educator; b. Athens, Greece, June 14, 1968; d. Panagiotis Tsironis and Andromachi Tsironi; m. George Poulokefalos, June 21, 1997; 1 child, Panagiotis Poulokefalos. PhD, U. Athens Med. Sch. Cert. specialist in internal medicine Health Ministry Greece, 1999. Cons. internal medicine Nat. Health Sys. Sparta Gen. Hosp., Greece, 2000; asst. prof. pharmacology U. Peloponnese Nursing Sch., 2005—. Mem. and sci. cons. Laconia Thalassemia Patients Fedn., Sparta, Greece, 2003. Grantee, Internat. Atomic Energy Agy., Austria. Socialist. Greek Orthodox. Achievements include research in hemoglobinopathies. Avocations: reading, travel, cooking. Office: Gen Sparta Hosp Sparta 23100 Greece Home: Platanista 101 231 00 Sparta Greece Personal E-mail: tsironi@uop.gr. E-mail: gpoyl@otenet.gr.

TSIVIAN, ALEXANDER, urologist; b. St.Petersburg, Russia, Sept. 23, 1956; s. Lev M. and Marksena V. Tsivian; m. Tatiana Baranova, Mar. 17, 1978; children: Moty, Maria. MD, 1st Med. U., St.Petersburg, 1980. Staff surgeon Mcpl. Hosp. No 37, St. Petersburg, 1981—84; staff urologist Mcpl. Hosp. No 15, St.Petersburg, 1984—92, acting head, 1990—92, head urogyn. unit, 1991—92; fellow in tng. dept. urogyn. Med. Stomatological U., Moscow, 1989; resident in urology Wolfson Med. Ctr., Holon, Israel, 1994—2002; staff urologist Wolfson Med Ctr, Holon, Israel, 2002—; fellow laparoscopic urology U. Heilbronn, Germany, 2002. Contbr. articles to profl. jours. Mem.: St. Petersburg Urol. Soc., Israeli Med. Soc., Israeli Soc. Endoscopic Surgery, Israeli Urol. Soc., European Assn. Endoscopic Surgery. Avocations: boxing, volleyball, travel. Office: Dept Urologic Surgery Wolfson Med Ctr PO Box 5 Holon 58100 Israel Personal E-mail: atsivian@hotmail.com.

TSOTSOS, ATHANASIOS S., microbiologist, virologist, educator; b. Thessaloniki, Greece, Jan. 11, 1937; s. Sawas and Anthoula T.; m. Lucy Kerameos, Aug. 12, 1967; children: Sawas, Anthea. MD, Med. Sch., Thessaloniki, 1961; diploma in pub. health, Sch. Hygiene, Athens, Greece, 1964; diploma in bacteriology, Med. Sch., Manchester, Eng., 1971, PhD in Virology, 1973. Commd. Greek Army M.C., 1960, advanced through grades to gen., 1993; dir. microbiology lab. Gen. Mil. Hosp., Athens, 1983-86, gen. dir. Thessaloniki, 1990-91; dir. microbiology lab. Gen. Pension Officers Hosp., Athens, 1986-89; asst. prof. med. microbiology U. Athens, 1977—. Cons. virology lab. pasteur Inst., Athens, 1978; mem. Internat. Com. on Taxonomy Viruses, 1975—. Author: Taxonomy of Viruses, 1975, Medical Virology, 1992; editor: Hellenic Armed Forces Med. Rev., 1975-77, 83-85, Hellenic Virology, 1996-99. Decorated Knight of Order of Phoenix; recipient B class medal Mil. Valor. Mem. Hellenic Soc. Microbiology, Hellenic Soc. Virology (pres. 1999-2003), Hellenic Soc. Clin. Virology (pres. 1992-2004). Christian Orthodox. Home and Office: Papandreou Andrea St 11 Glyfada 166 75 Athens Greece Office Phone: +302108983196.

TSOU, MEI-YUNG, anesthesiologist; b. Taiwan, Oct. 1, 1959; MD, Nat. Def. Med. Ctr., 1986; PhD, Nat. Yang-ming U., 1993. Divsn. chief, neuro-anesthesia Dept. Anesthesiology Taipei Vets. Gen. Hosp., 2001—. Divsn. chief Divsn. Maternal and Pediatric Anesthesia, 1997—2001. Recipient Outstanding Rsch. award, Taipei Vets. Gen. Hosp., Taiwan, Outstanding Tutor award, Nat. Yang-Ming U. Med. Sch. Mem.: Taiwan Soc. Study of Pain, Taiwan Soc. Cardiovasc. Anesthesia, Taiwan Soc. Anesthesiologists. Avocation: travel. Office: 201 Pei-Tou 11211 Sect 2 Shi-pai Rd Taipei 11211 Taiwan Office Fax: 886-2-28751597. Personal E-mail: mytsou8095@gmail.com.

TSUBURA, AIRO, pathologist educator; b. Amagasaki, Hyogo, Japan, Feb. 24, 1950; s. Yoshihiko and Kazue (Wada) T.; m. Ryoko Momotani, Nov. 3, 1978; children: Aisaku, Junko. MD, Kansai Med. U., 1981. Cert. pathologist, toxicological pathologist. Rsch. assoc. Kansai Med. U., Osaka, Japan, 1975-76, 77-81, U. Chgo., 1976-77; instr., assoc. prof. Kansai Med. U., Osaka, 1981-93, prof., 1993—. Grantee Osaka Cancer Assn., 1981, 86, 87, Osaka Cancer Soc., 1992, Yasuda Meml. Found., 1990. Mem. Japan Soc. Pathology, Japan Assn. Histochemistry and Cytochemistry, Japan Breast Cancer Assn. Home: Amagasaki 33-21 Tsukaguchi-1 Hyogo 661-0002 Japan Office: Dept Pathology Kansai Med Univ Moriguchi Osaka 570-8506 Japan Business E-Mail: tsubura@takii.kmu.ac.jp.

TSUCHIYA, MASAHIKO, anesthesiologist, biochemist; b. Kofu, Yamanashi, Japan, Oct. 18, 1958; s. Kunio and Setsuko (Suzuki) T.; 4 children. MD, Kochi Med. Sch., Japan, 1984, PhD, 1988. Asst. prof. anesthesiology Kochi Med. Sch., 1993-94, assoc. prof., 1994-95; head physician Nat. Hosp. Tokyo Disaster Med. Ctr., 1995-98; vis. assoc. prof. biochemistry and anesthesiology Osaka City Univ. Med. Sch., Japan, 2000—05, asst. prof. anesthesiology and intensive care medicine, 2005—06, assoc. prof. anesthesiology and intensive care medicine, 2006—07, assoc. prof. anesthesiology, 2007—. Avocation: computers. Home: 5-6-16-304 Daido Tennoji-ku Osaka 543-0052 Japan Office: Osaka City Univ Med Sch Dept Anesthesiology 1-5-7 Asahi-machi Abene-ku Osaka 545-8586 Japan Office Phone: 81 6 6645 2186. Business E-Mail: oxymasa@ea.mbn.or.jp.

TSUI, KE HUNG, urologist; b. Taiwan, June 15, 1962; MD, Taipei Med. Coll., 1977. Physician Chang Gung Meml. Hosp., Taiwan. Contbr. articles to profl. jours. Med. Chang Gung, Taoyuan, Taiwan, 1970—77. Mid., Taipei. Mem.: Chang. Achievements include research in prostate cancer. Home: 5 Fu-Shing Taoyuan Kweishan 333 Taiwan Office: Chang Gung Meml Hosp 5 Fu-shing Kweishan Taoyuan 333 Taiwan Home Fax: 886-2-27358775. Business E-Mail: khtsui@yahoo.com.

TSUI, LAP-CHEE, academic administrator, molecular genetics educator; b. Shanghai, Dec. 21, 1950; arrived in Can., 1981; s. Jing Lue Hsue and Hui Ching Wang; m. Ellen Lan Fong, Feb. 11, 1977; children: Eugene, Felix. BS, Chinese U. Hong Kong, 1972, MPhil, 1974; PhD, U. Pitts., 1979; DSc (hon.), Chinese U. Hong Kong, 1991; DCL (hon.), U. King's Coll., Halifax, NS, Can., 1991; DSc (hon.), U. N.B., Can., 1991; DLL (hon.), U. St. Francis Xavier, Antigonish, NS, Can., 1994; DSc (hon.), York U., Can., 2001. Postdoctoral investigator Oak Ridge Nat. Lab., Tenn., 1979—80; postdoctoral fellow Hosp. for Sick Children, Toronto, Ont., Canada, 1981—83, geneticist-in-chief, 1996—2002; asst. prof. depts. genetics and med. genetics U. Toronto, Ont., Canada, 1983—88, assoc. prof., 1988—90, prof., 1990—2006, u. prof., 1994—2006, u. prof. emeritus, 2006—; H.E. Sellers chair in cystic fibrosis, 1998—2002; head genetics and genomic biology program, 1998—2002. Chmn. chromosome 7 subcom. Human Gene Mapping Workshop, 1986-97; mem. mammalian genetics study sect. NIH, Bethesda, Md., 1988-93; dir. Cystic Fibrosis Rsch. Ctr., Hosp. for Sick Children Spl. Rsch. Ctr., 1994-2002; scientist Med. Rsch. Coun. Can., 1989-2002; advisor European Jour. Human Genetics, 1992-96, Molecular Medicine Today, 1995—; adj. prof. U. New Brunswick, 2000-2002; vice-chancellor & pres. U. Hong Kong, 2002—. Editor: Cytogenetics and Cell Genetics, 1988-92, Internat. Jour. Genome Rsch., 1990—95, Biochimica et Biophysica Acta, 2002—; assoc. editor: Am. Jour. Human Genetics, 1990-93, Genomics, 1994—2010; mem. editl. bd. Mammalian Genome, 1990, Clin. Genetics, 1991—2005, Human Molecular Genetics, 1991-98; communicating editor: Human Mutation, 1991-2002, Molec. Medicine Today, sr. editor: Physiological Genomics, 2000-01; internat. adv. The Chinese Jour. of Medical Genetics, 2000—05; mem. editl. bd. Human Genetics, 2005-09; contbr. over 300 articles to sci. jours. Trustee Edn. Found., Fedn. Chinese Canadian Profls., Toronto, 1987-93; advisor, 1994-. Recipient Paul di Sant Agnese Disting. Achievement award Cystic Fibrosis Found., 1989, Zellers SR. Scientist award, 2001, Gold medal of honor Pharm. Mfrs. Assn. Can., 1989, award of excellence Genetics Soc. Can., 1990, Gairdner Internat. award 1990, Cresson medal Franklin Inst., 1992, E. Mead Johnson award, 1992, Disting. Scientist award The Canadian Soc. Clin. Investigators, 1992, Canadian Conf. medal 1992, Sarstedt Rsch. prize, 1993, Sanremo Internat. award for Genetic Rsch., 1993, J.P. Lecocq prize Inst. de France, 1994, Henry Friesen award The Canadian Soc. for Clin. Investigation and the Royal Coll. of Physicians and Surgeons of Can., 1995, Can. Med. Assn. award of honour, 1996, Jonas Salk award Ontario March of Dimes, 1997, Initiative Cmty. Svc. award Toronto Biotech., 1998, Disting. Scientist award Med. Rsch. Coun., 2000, Killam prize Can. Coun., 2002; named scholar Can. Cystic Fibrosis Found., 1984-86. Fellow Royal Soc. Can., Royal Soc. London, Academia Sinica, Royal Coll. Physicians U.K. (hon.); mem. Human Genome Orgn., Am. Soc. Human Genetics, NAS (fgn. assoc.), CAS (fgn. mem.). Achievements include co-discoverer of cystic fibrosis gene. Office: U Hong Kong Vice-Chancellor's Office Pokfulam Rd Hong Kong Hong Kong Office Phone: 852-2859-2100. Office Fax: 852-2858-9435.

TSUJI, KOH, radiation oncologist; b. Kozagawa, Wakayama, Japan, Jan. 18, 1958; s. Sohta and Misao (Nagano) T.; m. Keiko Misaki, Jan. 22, 1989. Diploma, Wakayama Med. U., 1982. Staff radiologist, radiation oncologist Wakayama Med. U. Hosp., 1989-92, intern, 1982-83; resident radiologist Osaka City Med. U. Hosp., 1983-84; radiologist Nat. Wakayama Hosp., Mihama, 1985-87; staff rschr. Fukui Med. U., Matsuoka, 1987-89; chief radiologist, radiation oncologist Minami-Wakayama Nat. Hosp., Tanabe, Japan, 1993—2003; vice dir. Nat. Hosp. Orgn. Minami-Wakayama Med. Ctr., 2004—. Recipient rsch. grants Ministry Edn., Culture and Sci., 1991, Ministry Health and Welfare, 1995-97, Ministry Health, Labor and Welfare, 2003-05. Mem. Japan Radiol. Soc., Japan Radiation Rsch. Soc., Japanese Soc. for Therapeutic Radiology, Japan Soc. for Cancer Therapy, Am. Soc. Therapeutic Radiology and Oncology. Avocations: playing flute, classical music. Office: Nat Hosp Orgn Minami Wakayama Med Ctr 27-1 Takinai Tanabe Wakayama 646-8558 Japan Home: Katada 2500-69 Shirahama Wakayama 649-2201 Japan Office Phone: 81739267050. Personal E-mail: tjk0118@yahoo.co.jp. Business E-Mail: k_tsuji@mwn.hosp.go.jp.

TSUJI, TAKASHI, medical educator, researcher; b. Mino, Gifu, Japan, Jan. 19, 1962; s. Kin-ichiro and Kimiko Tsuji; m. Chika Tsuji, 1992; 1 child, Masahito. BSc in Biology, Niigata U., Japan, 1984, MSc in Biology, 1986; PhD in Biology, Kyushu U., 1992. Rschr. Yamanouchi Pharm. Co., Ltd., Tokyo, 1986—89; rsch. fellow Japan Soc. Promotion Sci., Tokyo, 1991—92, Niigata U., Japan, 1992—94; sr. rschr. Japan Tobacco, Inc., Tokyo, 1994—2001; prof. Tokyo U. Sci., Noda, Chiba, Japan, 2001—. Advisor Otsuka Chem. Co., Ltd., 2004—, Yamachu Co., Ltd., Niigata, 2004—; vis. prof. U. Louis Pasteur, 2008; dir. Organ Techs. Inc., Tokyo, 2008—. Contbr. articles to profl. jours. Mem.: Japanese Soc. Carbohydrate Rsch., Molecular Biology Soc. Japan, Japan Soc. Hematology, Japanese Assn. Regenerative Dentistry (dir. 2007—), Japan Soc. Organ Preservation and Med. Biology (councilor 2006—), Japanese Soc. Regenerative Medicine (councilor 2002—). Achievements include research in the identification of a molecular mechanism of onset of adult T-cell leukemia/lymphoma; identification of TGFbeta-binging protein; development of in-vitro expansion system for human hematopoietic stem cells; a three-dimensinally cell processing method for future organ replacement regenerative therapy; technologies for glycoprotein engineering. Office: Tokyo Univ Sci 2641 Yamazaki Noda Chiba 278-8510 Japan Office Fax: 81 4 7122 1499. Business E-Mail: tsujilab@rs.noda.tus.ac.jp.

TSUJI, TATSUYA, surgeon; b. Kumamoto, Japan, Jan. 1, 1957; m. Youme Haraguchi, Dec. 23, 1982; children: Akira, Hikaru. MD, Kumamoto U., 1982, PhD, 1998. Transplant fellow Queensland Liver Transplant Svc., Brisbane, Queensland, Australia, 1994—96; asst. prof. Kumamoto U. Hosp., 2001—. Sr. asst. med. staff Kumamoto U. Hosp., 2001—. Mem.: Internat. Hepato Pancreato Biliary Assn. Achievements include invention of rational extent of hepatectomy for GB cancer. Office: Dept Surgery Kumamoto Univ 1-1-1 Honjo Kumamoto 860-0811 Japan E-mail: klatskin@mac.com.

TSUJI, TETSUYA, physician, educator; b. Tokyo, Jan. 8, 1966; D, Keio U. Sch. Medicine, 1990. Assoc. prof. Dept. Rehab. Medicine, Keio U. Sch. Medicine, 2005—, dir. Cancer Ctr., 2010. Grant, Ministry of Health, Labour and Welfare, Japanese Govt. Mem.: Japanese Soc. Palliative Medicine, Japanese Assn. Rehab. Medicine (chmn. clin. practice guidelines com. 2009). Avocations: horseback riding, baseball, bicycling. Office: Shinanomachi 35 Shinjuku Tokyo 160-8582 Japan Office Fax: 81-3-3225-6014. Business E-Mail: cxa01423@nifty.com.

TSUJI, TOSHIZO, hospital administrator, educator; b. Kyoto, Jan. 2, 1932; s. Yasujiro and Yuki (Nakamura) T.; m. Yoshiko Taniguchi, Mar. 21, 1977; children: Mari, Toshifumi. MD, Kyoto Prefectural U. Medicine, 1957; DMSc, Kyoto Prefectural U. Medicine, 1964. Intern Kyoto 1st Red Cross Hosp., 1957-58; clin. fellow Kyoto Prefectural U. Medicine, 1959-60, asst. prof., 1971-74, assoc. prof., 1974-97; clin. fellow U. Ala. Med. Ctr., Birmingham, 1964-67, instr. medicine, 1967-68; postdoctoral fellow in molecular biology U. Edinburgh, Scotland, 1968-70; v.p. Kyoto Prefectural Yosanoumi Hosp., Iwataki, 1983—97; pres. Kyoto Prefectural Yosanoumi Blood Ctr., Iwataki, 1974-83; prin. Kyoto Prefectural Nursing Sch., Iwataki, 1988-94; pres., med. juridical person Ohtha Found. Ohta Hosp., Kyoto, 1997—2006; pres., med. juridical person Miyazu Kosei Found., Miyazu Takeda Hospy Miyazu, Kyoto, 2006—; emeritus pres., med. juridical person WHO, Osaka, 2009. Mem. WHO, Osaka, 1983—. Contbr. articles to profl. jours. Recipient med. diploma Japanese Ministry Health and Welfare, 1958; fellow NIH, 1965, European Molecular Biology Orgn., 1968. Fellow Japanese Soc. Internal Medicine, Japanese Soc. Gastroenterology, Japanese Soc. Hepatology; mem. AAAS, NY Acad. Scis. Avocations: golf, tennis, stamp collecting/philately, gardening, music. Home: 988 Uoya Kyoto 626-0015 Japan Office Phone: 0 772-22-2157.

TSUKAMOTO, TAIJI, urologist, educator; b. Asahikawa, Hokkaido, Japan, Feb. 11, 1949; MD, Sapporo Med. U. Sch. Medicine, 1973. Prof., chairperson urology dept. Sapporo Med. U. Sch. Medicine, 1995—, dir., 2008—. Mem.: European Assn. Urology, Am. Urol. Assn., Japanese Urol. Assn. Office: Minami-1 Jo Nshi-16 Chome Chuo-Ku Sapporo Hokkaido 060-8543 Japan Office Fax: 81-11-612-2709. Business E-Mail: taijit@sapmed.ac.jp.

TSUKAMOTO, YUSUKE, nephrologist, director; b. Japan, Feb. 26, 1952; MD, Kitasato U. Sch. Medicine, 1976, PhD, 1985. Dep. dir. Itabashi Chuo Med. Ctr., 2011—. Exec. com. mem. Kidney Disease: Improving Global Outcome, 2008—11; chair internat. adv. coun. Asian Forum CKD Initiative, 2008—11. Recipient Internat. Disting. medal, Nat. Kidney Found. Mem.: Am. Soc. Nephrology, Japanese Soc. Nephrology, Internat. Soc. Nephrology. Office: 2-12-7 Azusawa Itabashi Tokyo 174-0051 Japan Office Fax: 81-3-3967-0572. Business E-Mail: tsukamoto@jinzou.net.

TSUKUI, KAZUO, medical researcher; b. Maebashi-shi, Gunma, Japan, Jan. 10, 1949; s. Seiichirou and Kou Tsukui; m. Hiroko Tamura, Mar. 16, 1975; children: Satoko Ehara, Hajime, Hideyuki. Degree in Pharmacy, Toyama U., Sch. Pharmaceutics, 1971; PhD, Kyoto U., Japan, 1976. Cert. pharmacist Ministry Health and Welfare, Japan, 1973. Rschr. Ctrl. Blood Ctr., Japanese Red Cross Soc., Hiroo, Tokyo, 1978—2002, Tokyo Met. Red Cross Blood Ctr., Hiroo, 2002—06; dir. Ctrl. Blood Inst., Japanese Red Cross Soc., Koto-ku, Tokyo, 2002—. Office: Japanese Red Cross Soc 2-1-67 Tatsumi Koto-ku Tokyo 135-8521 Japan

TSUNESHIROU, KAWASAKI, pharmaceutical executive; b. Nagasaki, Japan, Aug. 23, 1961; Grad., Kyushu U., 1984. Mgr. drug quality assurance dept. Asahi Kasei Pharma Corp., 1984—. Office: 1-105 Kanda Jinbocho Chiyodaku Tokyo 101-8101 Japan Business E-Mail: kawasaki.tb@om.asahi-kasei.co.jp.

TSURUDOME, MASATO, medical educator; b. Japan, Dec. 16, 1955; PhD, U. Tokyo, 1979. Assoc. prof. Mie U. Grad. Sch. Medicine, 1991—. Mem.: Am. Soc. Microbiology. Avocations: movies, reading. Home: 3028-11 Nagaoka-Cho Tsu Mie 514-0064 Japan Personal E-mail: turudome@doc.medic.mie-u.ac.jp.

TSURUI, HIROMICHI, medical educator; b. Utsunomiya, Japan, Apr. 10, 1955; s. Masaru and Yae Tsurui. MD, U. Tokyo, 1981, PhD, 1989. Asst. prof. Juntendo U. Sch. Medicine, Tokyo, 1989—. Contbr. articles to profl. jours. Mem.: Japanese Soc. Immunology, Internat. Soc. Optical Engring., Histochem. Soc. Achievements include development of hyper-multi-color fluoresce tissue imaging; application of solid-phased DNA probe to gene engineering. Avocations: photography, driving. Office: Juntendo U Sch Medicine 2-1-1 Hongo Bunkyo-ku Tokyo 113-8421 Japan Office Phone: 81-3-5802-1039, 81-3-5802-1671. Office Fax: 81-3-3813-3164. Business E-Mail: tsurui@med.juntendo.ac.jp, tsurui@juntendo.ac.jp.

TSURUTA, DAISUKE, dermatologist, researcher; b. Osaka, Japan, Jan. 30, 1967; s. Masaru and Jazuko (Ishii) T.; m. Sachiko Tsuta, Nov. 23, 1998. MD, Osaka City U. Grad. Sch., 1999, PhD. Board Certified Dermatologist Japanese Dermatol. Assn., 1998. Asst. prof. Osaka City U. Grad. Sch. of Medicine, Japan, 2005—. Recipient Osaka City Mayor's award, 1999. Mem. Japanese Soc. Dermatology. Avocation: French horn. Home: 2-13-17-1302 Seiiku Johtoh-ku Osaka 5360007 Japan Office: Osaka City U Grad Sch 1-4-3 Asahimachi Abeno-ku Osaka 5458585 Japan Office Fax: 81666453828. Business E-Mail: dtsuruta@med.osaka-cu.ac.jp.

TSUTOMU, KAWABE, physician, educator; b. Maibara, Shiga, Japan, June 17, 1961; MD, Nagoya U., 1987, PhD, 1994. Prof. Nagoya U. Sch. Med. Scis., 2009—. Office: 1-1-20 Daikou-minami Higashi-ku Nagoya Aichi 461-8673 Japan

TSUTSUI, HIDEMITSU, medical educator; b. Tokyo, Mar. 6, 1964; PhD, Tokyo Med. U., 1990. Assoc. prof., dept. surgery Tokyo Med. U., 2008—. Office: 6-7-1 Nishishinjuku Shinjuku-ku Tokyo 160-0023 Japan Business E-Mail: htsutsui@sd.dcns.ne.jp.

TSUTSUMIMOTO, TAKAHIRO, orthopedist; b. Iida, Nagano, Japan, Nov. 28, 1968; s. Chinobu and Miyoshi Tsutsumimoto; m. Reiko Nakajima, June 7, 1998; children: Ryo, Sou. MD, Jichi Med. Sch., Japan, 1993, PhD, Shinshu U. Grad. Sch., Japan, 2001. Diploma of Orthopaedic Surgery Japanese Bd. of Orthopaedic Surgery, 2000. Resident Shinshu U. Hosp., Matsumoto, Nagano, Japan, 1993—94, JA Nagano Saku Cul. Hosp., Saku, 1994—95, med. staff Tatsuno Gen. Hosp., 1995—96, Syowa Inan Gen. Hosp., Komagane, Nagano, Japan, 1996—97, Shinsyu U. Hosp., Matsumoto, 1997—99, Toumi City Hosp., 1999—2000, Yodakubo Hosp., Nagato, 2000—02; rsch. fellow U. of Tex. Health Sci. Ctr. at San Antonio, 2002—04; med. staff Yodakubo Hosp., Nagato, 2004—. Recipient Shinshu Orthopedic award, 2000; Lilly Rsch. grant Program for Bone & Mineral Rsch., Eli Lilly, 2005. Home: Japan Office: Yodakubo Hosp 2857 Furumachi Nagato Nagano Chiisagata-gun 386-0603 Japan E-mail: takatsutsumimoto@ybb.ne.jp.

TU, MING-SHIUM, medical researcher, educator; b. Hsin-Chu, Taiwan, Feb. 19, 1956; s. Ching Tseng and Tsa Mei (Su) Tu; m. Wei-Jen Yeh, Jan. 25, 1986; children: Yu-Fang, Yu-Ting, Ting-Yu. MB, Nat. Yang-Ming Med. Coll., Taipei, 1982. Diplomate Taiwan Assn. Family Medicine, 1989, Taiwan Assn. Internal Medicine, 1989, Taiwan Assn. Hospice Palliative Medicine, 2001. Resident Taipei Veterans Gen. Hosp., Taiwan, 1984—89, attending phsician, 1989—90; attending physician Kaohsiung Veterans Gen. Hosp., Taiwan, 1990—93, head, 1993—, exec. cmty. health promotion program, 2004—, exec. hosp. palliative shared care program, 2004—. Exec. gen., com. mem. Dept. Health, Nat. Med. Care Network Chia-I Region, Taiwan, 1990—97; adv. editor Assn. Family Medicine, Taipei, 1991—; com. mem. Assn. family medicine, Taipei, 1992—; editl. cons. Taiwan Assn. Hosp. Palliative Medicine, Taipei, 1996—; clin. assoc. prof. Sch. Medicine, Nat. Yang-Ming U., Taipei, 2001—02; clin. prof. Nat. Def. Med. Ctr., Taipei, 2005—; editl. bd. mem. Taiwan Coll. Family Physicians, Taipei, 2003—; med. auditorship Bur. Nat. Health Ins., Kao-Ping Regional Med. Svc., Kaohsiung, 1995—; asst. prof. Sch. Nursing, I-Shou U., Kaohsiung, Taiwan, 2003—; com. mem. Hosp. Med. Ethics, Hosp. Bioinformatics Promotion, Cmty. Health Promotion, Hosp. Quality Improvement, Med. Edn., Hosp. Labors' Safety and Health Promotion. Kaohsiung Veterans Gen. Hosp., 2005—. Contbr. articles to numerous jours. Bd. mem. to exec., Nat. Med. Care Network Program, Dept. Health, Chia-I, 1990—97, sec., Nat. Med. Care Network Program Taiwan, 1997—99; hosp. rep., exec. Rescue Program 921 Chi-Chi Earthquake, Mingjian Township, Taiwan, 1999. Lt. Army, 1982—84, Taiwan. Named People of Benevolence, Assn. Benevolent People Promotion, 2000, Exemplar Pub. Servant, Veterans Affairs Commn., Exec. Yuan, 1999, Outstanding Med. Treatise, 1992; vis. scholar Dept. Family and Cmty. Medicine, U. Ariz., 1996. Mem.: American Soc. Tchrs. Family Medicine, Taiwan Pub. Health Assn., Soc. Ultrasound Medicine, Taiwan Soc. Tchrs. Family Medicine, Taiwan Assn. Family Medicine, Taiwan Soc. Internal Medicine. Independent. Achievements include discovery to delineate the proper compass of spiritual care and uncover the distinction between spirituality, religion, and psyche; campaign to raise a charity fund to build up a 20 bed hospice ward. Avocations: tennis, travel. Office: Kaohsiung Vets Gen Hosp 386 Ta-Chung 1st Rd Tso-Ying Dist Kaohsiung 81362 Taiwan

TU, YOUYOU, medical researcher; b. Ningbo, Zhejiang Province, China, Dec. 30, 1930; Grad., Beijing Med. Coll. Rschr., prin. investigator Chinese Acad. Med. Sciences, Beijing, dir. rsch. and devel., 1980—, master instr., doctoral supr., 2001—. Recipient Lasker-DeBakey Clin. Med. Rsch. award, Lasker Found., 2011. Achievements include discovery of artemisinin and its utility for treating malaria. Office: China Acad Med Sciences Beijing China *

TUALLY, PETER JOHN, medical researcher, director; b. Sydney, Feb. 13, 1972; s. David Bruce and Janice Anne Tually; m. Gemma Louise Stabler, Feb. 21, 2009. M in Nuc. Medicine, U. Sydney, 1993; MAppSci in Nuc. Medicine, 2009, PhD in Nuc. Cardiology & Biomarkers, 2010. Dir. nuc. medicine, telemedicine & ICT Imaging South, Perth, Western Australia, Australia, 1997—; dir. TeleMed Pty Ltd., Perth, 2006—. Contbr. scientific papers. Pres. & com. mem. Rural Assn. Nuc. Scintigraphy, Sydney, 2007—10. Mem.: Australian & New Zealand Soc. Nuc. Medicine. Achievements include research in methodology in telemedicine, nuclear telemedicine. Office: Imaging The South Lot 800 Bussell Hwy Bunbury Leederville, 6230 Australia Office Fax: 61 0 897266900; Home Fax: 61 0 99218393. Personal E-mail: p.tually@telemed.net.au. Business E-Mail: p.tually@imagingthesouth.com.au.

TUCHMAN, MICHAEL, medical association administrator; b. Havana, Cuba, Nov. 17, 1948; MD, U. Fla., 1974. Pres., dir. clin. rsch. Palm Beach Neurol. Ctr., 1983—. Fellow: Am. Acad. Neurology. Office: 4520 Donal Ross Rd Ste 200 Palm Beach Gardens FL 33418 Office Phone: 561-694-1010.

TUCKER, N(IMROD) H(OLT), III, physician; b. Columbus, Ga., Nov. 22, 1947; s. Nimrod Holt Jr. and Sarah Elizabeth (King) T.; m. Kathryn Gail Waddle, June 6, 1976; children: Jennifer Leigh, Nimrod Holt IV. BS, Auburn U., Ala., 1969; MD, U. Ala., 1973. Diplomate Am. bd. Internal Medicine. Intern and resident ednl. program Jacksonville Hosp. U. Fla., 1973-76; pvt. practice Jacksonville, Fla., 1976—; mem. med. staff St. Vincent's Hosp., Jacksonville, 1976—. Bd. dirs. Profl. Found. for Health Care, Tampa, Fla. Bd. dirs. Fla. C.C. Found., Jacksonville, 1986—, St. Vincent's Hosp. Heart and Lung Inst., 1989—, Fla.-Ga. Blood Alliance, 1999—; chair bd. dirs., 2008. Fellow ACP (bd. dirs. Fla. chpt. 1988—); mem. Fla. Soc. Internal Medicine (bd. dirs. 1988-, v.p. 1998), AMA, Fla. Med. Assn. (del. 1987, 89), Duval County Med. Soc. (pres. 1999), Jacksonville C. of C. (bd. dirs. 1999), Timuquana Country Club, Fla. Yacht Club, River Club. Methodist. Avocations: racquetball, tennis, golf, poker, bridge. Office: 2149 St Johns Ave Jacksonville FL 32204-4418 Office Phone: 904-384-2525.

TUCKSON, REED V., physician, health insurance company executive; Grad., Howard U.; MD, Georgetown U. Residency & fellowship in internal med. Hosp. Univ. Pa.; commr. pub. health Washington, 1986—90; sr v.p. progs. March of Dimes Birth Defects Found., 1990—91; pres. Charles R. Drew U., LA, 1991—97; sr. v.p. profl. standards AMA, Chgo., 1998—2000; sr. v.p. consumer health and med. care advancement UnitedHealth Group, Inc., Mpls., 2000—06, exec. v.p., chief med. affairs, 2006—. Featured in (Black Enterprise mag.), 2009. Named one of Power 150: The Most Influential Blacks in Maerica, Ebony mag., 2008, Top 25 Minority Execs., Modern Healthcare, 2008, 50 Most Powerful Physician Execs. in Healthcare, Modern Healthcare/Modern Physician, 2009, 100 Most Powerful Execs. in Corp. America, 2009. Mem.: American Health Info. Cmty., Ambulatory Care Quality Alliance, Performance Measurement Workgroup, Certification Commn. on Health Info. Tech. (commr.), Inst. of Medicine of the Nat. Acad. of Sciences (chairperson quality chasm summit com., com. on the consequences of the uninsured). Office: UnitedHealth Group Inc PO Box 1459 Minneapolis MN 55440-1459 also: UnitedHealth Group Inc 9900 Bren Rd E Minnetonka MN 55343 Office Phone: 800-328-5979. *

TUFARO, ANTHONY PAUL, surgeon, educator; b. NYC, Dec. 1, 1954; DDS, NYU, 1979; MD, Hahnemann U., 1993. Diplomate Am. Bd. Plastic Surgery, Am. Bd. Oral and Maxillofacial Surgery, Nat. Bd. Med. Examiners. Assoc. prof., plastic surgery and oncology Johns Hopkins U. Sch. Medicine, 1998—, attending surgeon, 1998—. Fellow: ACS; mem.: Am. Soc. Plastic Surgeons, Am. Assn. Plastic Surgery, Soc. Surg. Oncology. Office: Dept Plastic Surgery 601 N Caroline St 8th Fl Baltimore MD 21287 Office Fax: 410-955-7060. Business E-Mail: aptufaro@jhmi.edu.

TUFTON, JANIE LEE (JANE TUFTON), dental hygienist, lobbyist; b. Allentown, Pa., Jan. 6, 1949; d. Robert Harry and Jean Lorraine (Seng) T. BS in Edn., Indiana U. Pa., 1979; postgrad. in English, 1979—82. Registered dental hygienist, Pa., N.J., Calif.; cert. tchr., Pa. Dental hygientist pvt. dental practices, Pa., N.J., Calif., 1976-90. Author bd. game for dental health edn., 1974. Lobbyist, activist for animal rights; bd. dirs. and pub. rels. Lehigh Valley Animal Rights Coalition, 1984-93; active civil rights movement, cultural events, literacy programs, detoxification units for drug and alcohol abuse, venereal disease clinics, practical-life workshops for the cognitively impaired, suicide hotlines, YWCA, Girl Scouts U.S. Recipient recognition Pa. Dental Hygienists Assn., 1974 Mem. Am. Anti-Vivisect. Soc., Nat. Humane Edn. Soc., The Fund for Animals, The Humane Soc. of the U.S., Nat. Alliance for Animals, Internat. Soc. for Animal Rights, Physicians Com. for Responsible Medicine, Culture and Animals Found., Animal Legal Def. Fund, People for the Ethical Treatment of Animals, Farm Animal Reform Movement, Farm Sanctuary, Com. to Abolish Sport Hunting, Animal Rights Mobilization, In Def. of Animals, United Animal Nations, Internat. Platform Assn., Internat. Network for Religion and Animals, Humane Religion, Performing Animal Welfare Socs., Disabled and Incurably Ill for Alternatives to Animal Rsch., United Poultry Concerns, Am. Soc. for Prevention of Cruelty to Animals. Avocations: photography, tennis, reading, environmental issues, women's studies.

TUGGLE, DAVID W., pediatric surgeon; b. Tex. BS with highest honors, Abilene Christian U., Tex., 1975; MD, U. Tex. Southwestern Med. Sch., 1979. Diplomate Am. Bd. Surgery, cert. Spl. Competence in Pediat. Surgery and Added Qualification in Surgical Critical Care, lic. Tex., 1979, Okla., 1985. Resident, gen. surgery Parkland Meml. Hosp., Dallas, 1979—82, 1983—84, chief resident, gen. surgery, 1984—85; surgical rsch. fellow U. Tex. Health Sci. Ctr., Dallas, 1982—83; chief resident, pediat. surgery Okla. Children's Meml. Hosp., 1985—87; coord., surgical critical care Children's Hosp. Okla., 1987—; clin. asst. prof., dept. pediat. U. Okla., 1987—, asst. prof. surgery, dept. surgery, sect. pediat. surgery, 1987—92, assoc. prof. surgery, dept. surgery, sect. pediat. surgery, 1992—99, chief, sect. pediat. surgery, dept. surgery, 1995—, prof. surgery, dept. surgery, sect. pediat. surgery, 1999—, Paula Milburn Miller, Children's Med. Rsch. Inst., chair pediat. surgery, 2001—, vice-chmn., dept. surgery, 2002—. Trauma med. dir. Okla. U. Med. Ctr., Level 1 Trauma Ctr., 1999—2001; dir., Extracorporeal Membrane Oxygenation Ctr. Children's Hosp. Okla., 1992—97. Peer-reviewer Archives of Surgery, Journal Pediatric Surgery; contbr. several articles to profl. jours. Recipient Weigelt-Wallace award for exemplary med. care for performing an on-site amputation to free a victim from the debris of the Olka. City bombing, 1995. Fellow: Am. Acad. Pediat. (Spl. Achievement award 1996), Am. Coll. Critical Care Medicine, ACS (com. on trauma 1997—2003, liaison to Am. Acad. Pediat. com. on pediat. emergency 2002—, Okla. Dist. #1 com. on applicants 1994—99, verification review com. 1995—2003); mem.: Okla. Chpt. ACS (vice-pres. 1995—96, pres.-elect 1996—97, pres. 1997—98, Spl. Achievement award 1996), Am. Assn. Surgery of Trauma, AMA, Am. Pediat. Surgical Assn. (critical care com. 1992—93, publications com. 1995—98, trauma com. 1998, chmn. 2004—05), Am. Soc. for Parenteral and Enteral Nutrition, Am. Trauma Soc., Assn. for Academic Surgery, Ctrl. Okla. Pediat. Soc., Okla. City Surgical Soc., Okla. County Med. Assn., Okla. Organ Sharing Network, Okla. State Med. Assn., Okla. Surgical Assn., Parkland Surgical Soc., Soc. for Critical Care Medicine (sec./treas., surgical sect. 1987—90, chmn. surgical sect. 1991—92), Southwestern Surgical Congress, So. Surgical Assn., Alpha Omega Alpha. Achievements include being part of surgical team who separated what is believed to be the first known American Indian conjoined twins in 2008. Office: U Okla Dept Surgery PO Box 26901 CHO 2B 2403 Oklahoma City OK 73126 Office Phone: 405-271-5922. Office Fax: 405-271-3278. Business E-Mail: David-Tuggle@ouhsc.edu.

TULLMAN, GLEN, management consultant; BA in Economics and Psychology, magna cum laude, Bucknell U., 1981; Masters in Social Anthrop., Oxford U., Eng. Pres., COO CCC Info. Svcs. Group, 1983—94; CEO Enterprise Sys., Inc., 1994—97; fellowship, social anthropology Oxford U.; joined, exec. office Pres., US, Wash., DC; CEO Allscripts Healthcare Solutions, Inc., Libertyville, Ill., 1997—. Capital campaign chmn. Juvenile Diabetes Rsch. Found. Ill. Chap.; mem., Internat. Bd. Juvenile Diabetes Rsch. Found.; bd. trustees Certification Commn. for Healthcare Info. Tech. (CCHIT). Recipient CEO of the Year, Il. Info. Tech. Assn., 2006. Office: Allscripts-Misys Healthcare Solutions Ste 2024 222 Merchandise Mart Plz Chicago IL 60654 Office Phone: 312-506-1200. Office Fax: 312-506-1201. Business E-Mail: glen.tullman@allscripts.com. *

TULVING, ENDEL, cognitive neuroscientist; b. Estonia, May 26, 1927; s. Johannes and Linda T.; m. Ruth Mikkelsaar, June 24, 1950; children: Elo Ann, Linda. BA, U. Toronto, Ont., Can., 1953, MA, 1954; PhD, Harvard U., 1957; MA (hon.), Yale U., 1969; FD (hon.), U. Umea, Sweden, 1982; DLitt (hon.), U. Waterloo, 1987, Laurentian U., 1988; D Psychology (hon.), U. Tartu, Estonia, 1991; ScD (hon.), Queen's U., Kingston, Can., 1996, U. Toronto, 2001, Columbia U., 2005; PhD (hon.), U. Haifa, 2003. Lectr. U. Toronto, 1956-59, asst. prof., 1959-62, assoc. prof., 1962-65; prof., 1965-70; prof. psychology Yale U., New Haven, 1970-75, U. Toronto, 1972-85, chmn. dept., 1974-80, univ. prof., 1985-92, Univ. prof. emeritus psychology, 1992—. Vis. scholar U. Calif., Berkeley, 1964-65; fellow Ctr. Advanced Study in Behavioral Scis., Stanford, Calif., 1972-73; Commonwealth vis. prof. Oxford (Eng.) U., 1977-78; Tanenbaum chair in cognitive neurosci. Rotman Rsch. Inst. of Baycrest Ctr., Can., 1992—; disting. prof. neurosci., disting. prof. psychology U. Calif., Davis, 1993-98; Clark Way Harrison disting. vis. prof. psychology and neurosci. Washington U., St. Louis, 1996-2006. Author: Elements of Episodic Memory, 1983; editor Jour. Verbal Leaning and Verbal Behavior, 1969-72, Psychol. Rsch., 1976-88, Memory, Consciousness and the Brain: The Tallinn Conference, 1999, The Oxford Handbook of Memory, 2000; co-editor: Organization of Memory, 1972, Memory Sys. 1994, 1994; mem. editl. bd. Oxford Psychology Series, 1979-95; contbr. numerous articles on memory to sci. jours. Decorated apptd. Officer of Order of Canada, 2006; recipient Izaak Walton Killam Meml. prize, Can. Coun., 1994, John P. McGovern award AAAS, Pasteur-Weizmann-Servier Internet. prize, 2009; Meml. scholar, 1976-77, Gold medal award for life achievemnt in psychol. sci. Am. Psychol. Found., 1994, Gairdner Found. Internat. award, 2005; Guggenheim fellow, 1987-88; named to Canadian Med. Hall of Fame, 2007. Fellow Can. Psychol. Assn. (disting. sci. contbn. award 1983), Am. Psychol. Soc. (disting. sci. contbn. award 1983, William James fellow), Royal Soc. Can., Am. Acad. Arts and Scis. (fgn. hon.), Soc. Exptl. Psychologists (Warren medal 1982), Royal Soc. London; mem. NAS (fgn. assoc.), Am. Psychol. Soc., Psychonomic Soc. (governing bd. 1974-80), Royal Swedish Acad. Scis. (fgn.), Cognitive Neurosci. Soc., Academia Europaea (fgn.), Estonian Acad. Scis. Office: Rotman Rsch Inst Baycrest 3560 Bathurst St 932 Toronto ON Canada M6A 2E1 Office Phone: 416-785-2500. Business E-Mail: tulving@psych.utoronto.ca.

TUMA, STANISLAV JOSEF, radiologist; b. Mělník, Czech Republic, Mar. 30, 1934; s. Josef and Marta (Panochová) T.; m. Vanda Langrová, May 10, 1954 (div. 1966); children: Zuzana, Ondřej, Magdalena; m. Jitka Fabichová, Nov. 2, 1990. MD, Charles U., Prague, Czech Republic, 1958, cert. pediat. I, 1962, cert. radiology I, 1964, CSc, 1970, cert. radiology II, 1971. Med. registrar Dist. Hosp., Šumperk, Czech Republic, 1958-60, Clinic of Pediat., Prague, 1960-64, X-Ray Dept., Prague, 1964-70; rsch.fellow Pediat. Cardiocenter, Prague, 1970-90; head Clinic Imaging Methods, Prague, 1990-99; head dept. rsch. and edn. Ministry Health Czech Republic, 2000—02. Prof. South Bohemian U., Ceske Budejovice, 2003. Editor: Congenital Anomalies, 1995, Dextrocardia, 1999; contbr. articles to profl. jours. Office: U Hosp Clinic Imaging Methods Motol V Uvalu 84 Prague Czech Republic Office Phone: 420-22-443-8101, 420-777-620-408. Business E-Mail: sttuma@volny.cz.

TUMLIN, JAMES ALAN, nephrologist, educator; b. Leesburg, Fla., Oct. 4, 1959; BA, U. South Fla., 1982, MD, 1986. Prof. medicine, nephrology U. Tenn. Coll. Medicine Chattanooga, 2008—. Prof. clin. investigator SE Renal Rsch. Inst., 1992—. Grantee, NIH. Fellow: Am. Soc. Nephrology. Avocation: woodworking. Office: 2300 E 3rd St Ste 100 Chattanooga TN 37403 Office Fax: 423-305-1544. Business E-Mail: jamestumlinmd@nephassociates.com.

TUMUSHIME-BUTURO, CHARLES GARDEN, surgeon, consultant; b. Kampala, Uganda, Apr. 15, 1953; s. Pheneas and Ellen Buturo; m. Beata Florence Tumushime, Jan. 23, 1981; children: David, Charlene, Arthur, Mary. MBChB, Makerere U., Kamapala, 1978, MMEd, 1982; MSc in Clin. Epidemiology, U. Zimbabwe, Harare, 2005. Sr. house officer Ministry Health, Kampala, 1979—82, registrar, 1982—83, sr. registrar Harare, Zimbabwe, 1984—86, cons.,

1986—; sr. registrar U. Pavia, Italy, 1983. Hon. lectr. U. Zimbabwe, 1986—. Fellow: Coll. Surgeons East Ctrl. & Southern Africa; mem.: Zimbabwe Soc. Otolaryngologists (pres. 2001—08). Avocations: golf, fishing. Home: 6 Morningside Dr Harare Mount Pleasant Zimbabwe Office: West End Clinic 13 Baines Ave CNR Baines Ave-Harare Str Harare Zimbabwe Office Fax: (263)4 700251. Business E-Mail: tumbut@africaonline.co.zw.

TUN, YUAN, engineering educator; b. Sichuan, China, Aug. 9, 1977; PhD, Sichuan U., Chengdu, 2010. Lectr. Engring. Rsch. Ctr. Biomaterials, Sichuan U., 2003—. Mem.: China Com. Biomaterials. Office: Sichuan University 29 Wangjiang Rd Chengdu Sichuan 610064 China Office Fax: 86 28 85412428. Business E-Mail: stalight@163.com.

TUNCA, FATIH, medical educator; b. Bursa, Turkey, June 10, 1975; Assoc. prof. Istanbul Faculty Medicine, 2010—. Avocations: tennis, scuba diving. Office: Istanbul Tip Fakültesi Genel C Istanbul 34390 Turkey E-mail: drfatihtunca@yahoo.com.

TUNGPRADABKUL, SUMALEE, biology professor; b. Bangkok, Sept. 29, 1956; PhD in Molecular Biology, Vrij U. Brussel, 1994. Assoc. prof. Faculty Sci. Mahidol U., 1990—. Cons. Higher Edn. Commn., 2006—11. Office: Rama VI Bangkok Phyatai 10400 Thailand Office Fax: 66-02-3547174. Business E-Mail: scstp@mahidol.ac.th.

TUOMISTO, JOUKO JUHANI, medical educator, researcher, author; b. Kurikka, Finland, Mar. 13, 1939; s. Eino A. and Aino M. (Saari) T.; m. Leena M. Vuorinen, Mar. 14, 1964; children: Hanna, Jouni, Paula. MD, U. Helsinki, Finland, 1965, Dr.Med.Sci., 1968; PhD, U. Kans., Kansas City, 1972; PhD (hon.), U. Kuopio, Finland, 2005. Instr. U. Helsinki, 1964-69, assoc. prof. pharmacology, 1977; postdoctoral rsch. fellow U. Kans., 1969-71; rschr. Acad. of Finland, 1971-76, acad. prof. Kuopio, 1991-96; prof. toxicology U. Kuopio, 1978-82; dept. dir., rsch. prof. Nat. Pub. Health Inst., Kuopio, 1983—2004, dir. Ctr. Excellence of Environ. Health Risk Analysis, 2002—04, cons., 2004—07; gov. Rotary Dist. 1430, 2008—09; prof. environ health U. Kuopic, 1998—2003. Coord. several European Commn. Rsch. Contracts, 1996-2004; cons. WHO, European Union. Author (editor): Farmakologia Ja Toksikologia, 1978, 8th edit., 2011, 20 books; contbr. articles to profl. jours.; author: Arsenic to Zoonoses: One Hundred Questions About The Environment and Health, 2010. Recipient Eurotox Merit award, 2006, several nat. awards & honors. Home: Niuvantie 10B FIN-70200 Kuopio Finland Office: Nat Inst Health Welfare PL 95 70701 Kuopio Finland Personal E-mail: j.tuomisto@drnainternet.net. Business E-Mail: jouko.tuomisto@thl.fi.

TURALE, SUE, nursing educator, consultant; b. Melbourne, Victoria, Australia, Jan. 15, 1951; d. Victor Prew and Florence Hilda Watt; m. Philip Stanley Turale, May 18, 1974 (div. 1993); m. Philip Robert Benson, Sept. 2, 1999; children: Megan Philippa children: Benjamin Donald. Diploma in Applied Sci. Advanced Psychiat. Nursing, Royal Melbourne Inst. Tech. U., Australia, 1983, BS in Applied Sci., 1987; MS in Nursing Studies, La. Trobe U., Melbourne, 1992; EdD, U. Melbourne, Victoria Australia, 1998. Cert. psychiatric nurse, Adelaide Australia, 1974, RN Tasmania Australia, 2007, commercial cert., Gosford Tech. Coll., Gosford NSW, 1968, cert. in gen. nursing, Queen Elizabeth Hosp. Sch. Nursing, Adelaide Australia, 1976, midwife, Queen Elizabeth Hosp. Sch. Nursing, Adelaide Australia, 1977. Vis. prof. Sun Yat Sen U. Med. Scis., Guangzhou, Guangdong, China, 1998—2001; head, Sch. Nursing U. Ballarat, Victoria, Australia, 1995—2001, dir. internat. programs, 1995—2001; dir. indigenous nursing & midwifery edn. project Congress Aboriginal & Torres Strait Islander Nurses, Bribie Island, Queensland, Australia, 2003—05; prof. internat. nursing Yamaguchi U., Ube Japan, Yamaguchi, Japan, 2005—, spl. advisor to v.p., internat. affairs, 2006—; editor-in-chief Nursing & Health Sci., Ube, Yamaguchi, 2006—. Vis. prof. Nara Med. U., Kyoto, Japan; mem. Internat. Network Doctoral Edn. Nursing, U. Mich.; Nara Found. fellow Australian Coll. Mental Health Nursing, Sydney, 1992—; chair Victorian & Tasmanian Deans Nursing, Melbourne, 1998—2001; inaugural gen. mgr. inst. cmty. health Royal Dist. Nursing Svc., Melbourne, 2001—03; don Medea Pk. Residential Care, St Helens, Tasmania, Australia, 2003—04; Soverino support mem. Australian Red Cross, Hobart, Tasmania, 2005—; vis. prof. Chiang Mai U. Faculty Nursing, Thailand, 2006—08, Khan Kaen Univ. Faculty Nursing, 2006—08, Silliman U., Philippines, 2008—; zfcsdcf Wuhan U., China, 2010—; mem. East Asian Forum Nursing Scholars, Hong Kong, 2006—, Japan Acad. Nursing, Tokyo, 2006—; secretariat Asia Pacific Alliance Health Leaders, Ube, Yamaguchi, Japan, 2006—; charter mem. and faculty counselor Sigma Theta Tau Internat. Tau Nu Chpt., Ube, 2006—10, pres., 2010—; mem., internat. svc. adv. coun. Sigma Theta Tau Internat. Honor Soc. Nursing, Indpls., 2008—. Contbr. articles to profl. jours., chapters to books. Recipient Vice Chancellor's award, U. Ballarat, 1997; Edn. Study scholarship, Victorian Govt., 1983, 1985—86. Fellow: Australian Coll. Mental Health Nurses, Royal Coll. Nursing Australia. Achievements include first to establish of nursing & health management programs in Hong Kong for University of Ballarat; establishment of collaborative midwifery program in western region of Victoria Australia; collaborative agreement Sun Yat Sen Medical University Guangzhou China and University of Ballarat Australia; development of collaborative agreements University College London and Yamaguchi University Japan; research in poverty of university students Victoria Australia; genetic nursing education, Japan; ethics education of nurses Australia. Office: Yamaguchi Univ Sch Medicine 1-1-1 Minami-Kogushi Yamaguchi Ube 755-8505 Japan Office Fax: 81836222130. Business E-Mail: sturale@yamaguchi-u.ac.jp.

TURAN, ARZU, pathologist; b. Ankara, May 10, 1972; MD, U. Istanbul, 1995; PhD, U. Marmara, 2009. Surg. and forensic pathologist Coun. Forensic Medicine, 2001—. Mem.: Turkish Soc. Pediat. Pathology, Turkish Soc. Thoracic Diseases, Turkish Soc. Pathology, European Assn. Cardiovasc. Pathology. Avocations: music, exercise, art. Office: Adalet Bakanligi Adli Tip Kurumu Yenib Istanbul 34000 Turkey E-mail: arzu_turantr@yahoo.com.

TURANO, SALVATORE, oncologist; b. Cosenza, Nov. 9, 1976; Degree in Medicine & Surgery, U. Catanzaro, Calabaria, Italy, 2002, degree in Oncology, 2006. Physician Cosenza's Hosp., 2007—. Med. dir. I level Cosenza's Hosp., 2007. Mem.: Italian Sarcoma Group, Italian Assn. Psychosocial Oncology, Italian Assn. Med. Oncology. Avocations: football, motorcycling. Home: Via G Mazzuca 1 Rovito Cosenza Calabria 87050 Italy Personal E-mail: galactus76@yahoo.it.

TURBINO, MÍRIAM LACALLE, dentist, educator; b. Bragança Paulista, São Paulo, Sept. 12, 1962; DDS, U. São Paulo, 1984, MSc, PhD, 1997. Assoc. prof. Faculdade Odontologia, U. São Paulo, 1989—, postgraduation program coord., 2009—. Mem.: Soc. Brasileira Pesquisa Odontológica. Office: Av Lineu Prestes 2227 São Paulo 05508-900 Brazil Office Fax: 11-3091-7839. Business E-Mail: miturbin@usp.br.

TURCOT, MARGUERITE HOGAN, medical researcher; b. White Plains, NY, May 19, 1934; d. Joseph William (dec.) and Marguerite Alice (dec.) Barrett) Hogan; children: Michael J., Susan A. Turcot, William R. Student, Syracuse U., 1951-54; BSN, U. Bridgeport, 1968. RN, Conn., N.C. Nurse Park City Hosp., Bridgeport, Conn., 1968-69, Meml. Mission Hosp., Asheville, N.C., 1969-70; instr. St. Joseph's Hosp., Asheville, 1970-71, oper. rm. nurse, 1973-77, charge nurse urology-cystoscopy, 1977-85; tchr. Asheville-Buncombe Tech. Coll., Asheville, 1971-72, Buncombe County Child Devel., Asheville, 1972-73; rschr. VA Med. Ctr., Asheville, 1988—; owner Reed House Bed & Breakfast, Asheville, 1985—2001. Bd. dirs. RiverLink, Quality Foreward. Charter mem. French Broad River Planning Com., Asheville, 1987—, Biltmore Village Hist. Mus.; mem. Asheville Bicentennial Commn., 1990-93; exec. dir. Preservation Soc. Asheville and Buncombe County. Recipient Griffin award, 1994, Friend of the River award, Land of Sky Regional Coun., 1995, Sondley award, Hist. Resources Commn. Asheville and Buncombe County, 1996, Vol. of Yr. award, RiverLink, 2001, Critical Link award, 2003; grantee U. Bridgeport, 1967—68; scholar Syracuse U. Faculty, 1951—54. Mem. Am. Urology Assn. (presenter VA urology workshop Asheville chpt. 1981, nat. meeting allied), Am. Bd. Urologic Allied Health Profls., Nat. Trust for Hist. Preservation, Preservation Found. N.C., Blue Ridge Pkwy. Assn., Preservation Soc. Asheville and Buncombe County (bd. dirs., past pres.), Asheville Newcomers Club (founder, 1st pres.), Earthwatch, Friends of Blue Ridge Pkwy. Inc. Republican. Roman Catholic. Avocations: preservation, history, architecture, sewing, hiking. Office: Preservation Soc Asheville & Buncombe County PO Box 2806 Asheville NC 28802

TURECKI, STANLEY, child and adolescent psychiatrist, educator; MD, U. of Cape Town, South Africa, 1961. Diplomate Am. Bd. Psychiatry and Neurology-child and adolescent psychiatry, Am. Bd. Psychiatry and Neurology. Pvt. practice, NYC; mem. bd. advisors Parents mag.; resident in psychiatry Tara Hosp., Johannesburg, 1965—71, Mt. Sinai Hosp., NY, 1969—71; staff Lenox Hill Hosp., Beth Israel Med. Ctr. Author: (books) The Difficult Child, Normal Children Have Problems, Too. Recipient Physician Recognition award, Am. Med. Assn., Castle Connolly Top Doctors: NY Metro Area, 2011, Castle Connolly America's Top Doctors, 2011; named one of Best Doctors in NY, NY mag. Office: Lenox Hills Hospital 136 E 64th St Ste 1B New York NY 10021-2137 Office Phone: 212-355-2535.

TURELL, MICHAEL J., entomologist; b. NYC, Feb. 19, 1948; BS, Cornell U., 1970; PhD, U. Calif., Berkeley, 1981. Rsch. entomologist Virology Divsn., USAMRIID, 1983—. Adj. assoc. prof. Uniformed Svcs. U. Health Scis., 2005—. Decorated Army Commendation medal US Army, Meritorious Civilian Svc. award. Mem.: Soc. Vector Ecology, Entomol. Soc. America, Am. Mosquito Control Assn., Am. Soc. Tropical Medicine and Hygiene. Avocation: tennis. Office: Virology Divsn USAMRIID 1425 Porter Fort Detrick MD 21702 Office Fax: 301-619-2290. Business E-Mail: michael.turell@amedd.army.mil.

TURINO, GERARD MICHAEL, internist, educator; b. NYC, May 16, 1924; s. Michael and Lucy (Arciero) T.; m. Dorothy Estes, Aug. 25, 1951; children: Peter, Phillip, James. AB, Princeton U., 1945; MD, Columbia U., 1948. Diplomate: Am. Bd. Internal Medicine. Intern Columbia U., Bellevue Hosp., 1948-49, asst. resident in medicine, 1949-50; resident in medicine New Haven Hosp., 1950-51; chief resident in medicine Columbia U. div. Bellevue Hosp., 1953-54; sr. fellow N.Y. Heart Assn., 1956-60; career investigator Health Research Council City of N.Y., 1961-71; asst. prof. medicine Columbia U., 1960-67, assoc. prof., 1967-72, prof. medicine, 1973-83, John H. Keating prof. medicine, 1983—; mem. staff Presbyn. Hosp., NYC, 1960—, attending physician, 1983—; dir. med. svcs. St. Lukes-Roosevelt Hosp., NYC, 1983-92; dir. St. Lukes-Roosevelt Hosp. James P. Mara Ctr, 1997. Cons. on sci. affairs Am. Thoracic Soc., 1992—; mem. sci. adv. com. Nat. Heart, Lung, and Blood Inst., Am. Lung Assn., Am. Heart Assn., N.Y. Lung Assn., N.Y. Heart Assn., Alpha, Antitrypsin Found.; mem. staff divsn. med. sci. Nat. Rsch. Coun., Washington; cons. VA Hosp., East Orange, N.J., 1962-67; cons. in medicine Englewood (N.J.) Hosp., Hackensack (N.J.) Hosp.; pres.-elect Am. Bur. Med. Advancement in China, 1994, pres., 1994-2001, chmn., 2001-; chmn. bd. dirs. Chronic Obstructive Pulmonary Disease Found., 2004; pres. East Hampton Health Found., 2005-. Contbr. articles to med. jours. Mem. Bd. Edn., Alpine, N.J., 1960-67; chmn. Chronic Obstructive Pulmonary Disease Found., 2004. Served to capt. USAF, 1951-53. Recipient Joseph Mather Smith prize Columbia U., 1965, Alumni medal, 1983, Silver medal Alumni Assn. Coll. Physicians and Surgeons Columbia U., 1979, gold medal, 1986, Edward Livingston Trudeau medal Am. Lung Assn., 2003, Lifetime Achievement award, Birmingham UK 7 Conf., 2010, Rsch. Achievement award, Copd Found., 2010. Fellow AAAS; mem. Assn. Am. Physicians, Am. Soc. Clin. Investigation, Harvey Soc., Am. Thoracic Soc. (pres. 1987-88, Edward Livingston Trudeau prize 2003), Am. Fedn. Clin. Rsch., Am. Physiol. Soc. (chmn. steering com. respiration sect.), Am. Heart Assn. (award of merit 1980, Disting. Achievement award 1989, bd. dirs.), N.Y. Heart Assn. (pres. 1981-83, dir.), N.Y. Lung Assn. (dir.), N.Y. Med.-Surg. Soc. (pres. 1995), N.Y. Clin. Soc., Princeton Club (N.Y.C.), Maidstone Club, Devon Yacht Club, Century Assn. Club. Home: 66 E 79th St New York NY 10021-0244 Office: St Lukes Roosevelt Hosp 1000 10th Ave New York NY 10019-1192 Business E-Mail: GMT1@Columbia.edu.

TURK, JON BRANDEN, plastic surgeon; b. Bklyn., Jan. 31, 1963; s. Stephen Noel and Sandra (Rich) T.; m. Carolyn Sue Gusoff, Sept. 21, 1991; children, Graham, Amanda BA, Amherst Coll., Mass., 1984; MD, SUNY, 1988. Med. diplomate Am. Bd. Facial Plastic and Reconstructive Surgery. Asst. prof. SUNY Health Sci. Ctr., 1994—; clin. asst. attending Mt. Sinai Hosp., NYC, 1997—; attending physician Lenox Hill & Manhattan Eye & Ear Hosp. Author: (chpt.) Otolarynlogical Clinics of North America, 1994. Fellow Am. Acad. Facial Plastic and Reconstructive Surgery, Am. Acad. otolaryngology Heal and Neck Surgery; mem. N.Y. Facial Plastic Surg. Soc. Office: Jon Turk MD 800 5th Ave New York NY 10065-7239 also: 173 Froehlich Farm Blvd Woodbury NY 11797 Office Phone: 516-921-8989.

TURK, RICHARD ERRINGTON, retired psychiatrist; b. Staten Island, NY, Oct. 6, 1925; s. Richard Jason and Marian (Errington) T.; m. Dec. 30, 1948 (widowed Dec. 23, 1978); children: Stephanie, Jeffrey, Alan. BA, Dartmouth Coll., 1945; MD, Johns Hopkins Med. Sch., 1948. Diplomate Am. Bd. Psychiatry. Intern Highland-Alameda County Hosp., Oakland, Calif., 1948-49; resident Herrick Meml. Hosp., Berkeley, Calif., 1949-50; fellow psychiatry Med. Sch. Harvard U., Boston, 1950-51, 53-54; clin. instr. Med. Sch. U. Calif., San Francisco, 1954—70; pvt. practice psychiatry Berkeley, 1954-85. Pvt. practice, Walnut Creek, Calif., 1972-88; staff Herrick Meml. Hosp., 1954-85, Walnut Creek Hosp., 1972-88, John Muir Meml. Hosp., Walnut Creek, 1972-88. Capt. USAF Res., 1951—53. Mem. AMA, Am. Psychiat. Assn., No. Calif. Psychiat. Assn., Calif. Med. Assn., Alameda-Contra Costa County Med. Assn. Avocations: travel, bicycling, boating, car camping.

TUR-KASPA, ILAN, obstetrician/gynecologist, infertility specialist, researcher; b. Hadera, Israel, Jan. 28, 1956; s. Chaim and Miriam Tur-Kaspa; m. Hana Tur-Kaspa, Aug. 21, 1986; children: Leeron, Adi. MD, Hebrew U., Jerusalem, 1981; diploma in ob-gyn. with distinction, Tel Aviv U., 1987, M in Ob-gyn., 1993; diploma in med. adminstrn., Galillee Coll., Tivon, Israel, 1995. Lic. physician, Israel, Ill. Intern Hadassah Med. Ctr., Jerusalem, 1980; maj. med. corps Israel Def. Forces, 1981-84, lt. col., head infertility clinic, 1993-95; resident in ob-gyn. Sheba Med. Ctr., Tel Hashomer, Israel, 1985-88, attending physician in vitro fertilization unit, 1991-98, dir. sperm bank, 1992-93; resident in ob-gyn. Mt. Sinai Med. Ctr., Chgo., 1988-91, attending physician in ob-gyn., 1991, Grant Hosp., Chgo., 1991-93; dir. infertility and in vitro fertiliation unit Barzilay Med. Ctr., Ashkelon, Israel, 1998—. Mem. organizing com. internat. symposium on signal transduction in health and disease, Tel Aviv, 1997, others; rsch. asst. in physiology and biophysics U. Ill., Chgo., 1991-94; chmn. Nat. Com. Hosp. Preparation for Toxicological Mass Casualties Event Israel Ministry of Health, 1995—; head R & D Sheba Med. Ctr., 1996-97; vis. scientist in biol.-chemistry Weizmann Inst. of Sci., Rehovot, Israel, 1997-99. Contbr. articles to profl. jours., chpts. to books; reviewer jour., 1989-96. Recipient Gen. Program Prize Paper award Am. Fertility Soc., 1989; grantee Israel Ministry of Health, 1995-96, Prize Paper award Israel Fertility Soc., 1998. Mem. ACOG, Israel Med. Assn., Israel Fertility Assn., Am. Soc. Reproductive Medicine, GynecoRadiology Soc. (councilor 1991-94, treas. 1994-96). Office: IVF Unit Dept Ob-gyn Barzilay Med Ctr Ashkelon 78306 Israel Fax: 972-8-9266066. E-mail: bmtur@wis.weizmann.ac.il.

TURKLE, JANET, plastic surgeon; MD, U. Kans. Diplomate Am. Bd. Surgery, Am. Bd. Plastic Surgery. Resident gen. surgery Univ. Kans. Sch. Medicine; resident plastic surgery Ind. Univ. Med. Ctr.; owner Turkle & Assocs. Named Top Doctor Cosmetic Surgery, Indpls. Mem.: An. Soc. Plastic Surgeons, Ohio Valley Soc. Plastic and Reconstructive Surgery, Ind. State Med. Assn., Indpls. Med. Soc. Office: Turkle & Associates 11455 N Meridian St Ste 150 Carmel IN 46032 Office Phone: 317-848-0001.

TURKMEN, ARIF, plastic surgeon; b. Islahiye, Turkey, Jan. 24, 1964; s. Mehmet and Meryem Turkmen. MD, Ankara U., Turkey, 1988. Cert. European Bd. Plastic Reconstructive and Aesthetic Surgey. Plastic surgeon South Manchester U. Hosp., Manchester, England, 2001—. Fellow: Royal Coll. Surgeons. Office: South Manchester Univ Hosp Southhmoore Rd Manchester M23 9LT England Personal E-mail: turkmenarif@yahoo.com.

TURMAN, ALI BULENT, neuroscientist, researcher, physiologist, researcher; b. Izmir, Turkey, Feb. 15, 1957; s. Mufit and Yelda Sevincer T.; m. Nicola Kay Davis, March 27, 1987, (div. Sept. 1999); children: Zoe and Lydia; m. Gonca (Tuzcu) Turman, Dec. 21, 1999; 1 child, Troy. MD, Ege Univ. Med. Fac., Izmir, Turkey, 1982; PhD, Univ. New South Wales, Sydney, Australia, 1992. Med. practitioner Ministry of Health, Tunceli, Turkey, 1983-85, Ministry of Defense, Agri, Turkey, 1986-87; doctoral stud. Univ. NSW, Sydney, 1988-92; lectr. Univ. Sydney, 1991-95, sr. lectr., 1996—2001, head Sch. Biomed. Sci., 2002—05; assoc. prof. Bond U., Queensland, Australia, 2005—07, prof., 2008—. Head Mother and Child Health and Family Planning Clinic, Tunceli, Turkey, 1983—85; mem. various rsch. and mgmt. coms. Sydney U., 1991—. Journalist, columnist, Dunya Newspaper, Sydney, Australia, 1999—. Lt., Turkish Military Forces, 1986-87. Recipient commendation, Ministry of Health, Turkey, 1985, Med. Postgrad. scholarship, Nat. Health Med. Rsch. Coun., Australia, 1990, various grants, Sydney U., Nat. Health and Med. Rsch. Coun., Australia, 1993—2005. Mem. Australian Neurosci. Soc., Soc. for Neurosci., NY Acad. of Scis., Applied Neurosci. Soc. Australasia. Avocations: computers, travel. Office: Faculty Health Sci and Med Bond Univ Gold Coast Queensland 4229 Australia Home Phone: 61755965593; Office Phone: 61755954431. Business E-Mail: b.turman@fhs.usyd.edu.au, bturman@bond.edu.au.

TURNBULL, H. RUTHERFORD, III, lawyer, educator; b. NYC, Sept. 22, 1937; s. Henry R. and Ruth (White) T.; m. Mary M. Slingluff, Apr. 4, 1964 (div. 1972); m. Ann Patterson, Mar. 23, 1974; children: Jay, Amy, Katherine. Grad., Kent (Conn.) Sch., 1955; BA, Johns Hopkins U., 1959; LLB with honors, U. Md., 1964; LLM, Harvard U., 1969. Bar: Md., N.C. Law clk. to Hon. Emory H. Niles Supreme Bench Balt. City, 1959-60; law clk. to Hon. Roszel C. Thomsen U.S. Dist. Ct. Md., 1962-63; assoc. Piper & Marbury (now LDA Piper), Balt., 1964-67; prof. Sch. Govt. U. N.C., Chapel Hill, 1969—80, U. Kans., Lawrence, 1980—. Disting. prof. spl. edn., courtesy prof. law U. Kans. Editor-in-chief Md. Law Rev. Cons., author, lectr., co-founder, co-dir. Beach Ctr. on Disability, U. Kans.; pres. Full Citizenship Inc., Lawrence, 1987-93; spl. staff-fellow U.S. Senate subcom. on disability policy, Washington, 1987-88; bd. dirs. Camphill Assn. N.Am., Inc., 1985-87; trustee Judge David L. Bazelon Ctr. Mental Health Law, 1993-2007, chmn., 2000-05. With US Army, 1960-65. Recipient Nat. Leadership award Nat. Assn. Pvt. Residential Resources, 1988, Internat. Coun. for Exceptional Children, 1996, Am. Assn. on Mental Retardation, 1997, Century award Nat. Trust for Hist. Preservation in Mental Retardation, 1999, Nat. Adv. award Am. Music Therapy Assn., 2002, Leadership award Camphill Assn. N.Am., 2004, Leadership award The Arc of the US, 2004, U. Kans. Gene A. Budig Disting. Tchg. Professorship award, 2005, Nat. award advocacy positive supports Assn. Persons with Severe Handicaps, 2005, Kans.U. Sch. of Edn. Disting. Leadership award, 2005, Burton Blatt award Coun. Exceptional Children, 2006; named Nat. Educator of Yr., The Arc of the U.S., 1982; Pub. Policy fellow Joseph P. Kennedy, Jr. Found., 1987-88. Fellow Am. Assn. on Mental Retardation (pres. 1985-86, bd. dirs. 1980-86); mem. ABA (chmn. disability law commn. 1991-95), U.S.A. Assn. for Retarded Citizens (sec. and dir. 1981-83), Assn. for Persons with Severe Handicaps (treas. 1988, bd. dirs. 1987-90), Nat. Assn. Rehab. Rsch. and Tng. Ctrs. (chair govt. affairs com. 1990-93), Internat. Assn. Sci. Study of Mental Deficiency, Internat. League of Assns. for Persons with Mental Handicaps, Johns Hopkins U. Alumni Assn. (pres. N.C. chpt. 1977-79). Democrat. Episcopalian. Office: U Kans 3111 Haworth Hall 1200 Sunnyside Ave Lawrence KS 66045-7534 Office Phone: 785-864-7600. Business E-Mail: Rud@ku.edu.

TURNDORF, HERMAN, anesthesiologist, educator; b. Paterson, NJ, Dec. 22, 1930; s. Charles R. and Ruth (Blumberg) T.; m. Sietske Huisman, Nov. 24, 1957; children: David, Michael Pieter. AB, Oberlin Coll., 1952; MD, U. Pa., 1956. Diplomate Am. Bd. Anesthesiology. Instr. anesthesiology U. Pa. Hosp., 1957-59; asst. anesthetist med. sch. Harvard U., Mass. Gen. Hosp., Boston, 1961-63; assoc. attending anesthesiologist, asst. dir. dept. anesthesiology Mt. Sinai Hosp., NYC, 1963-70, clin. prof. anesthesiology, 1966-70; prof., chmn. dept. anesthesiology W.Va. U. Sch. Medicine and Med. Ctr., Morgantown, 1970-74, NYU Sch. Medicine, 1974—2000; dir. anesthesiology NYU Tisch Hosp., Bellevue Hosp. Ctr., 1974—2000; pres. med. bd., med. dir. Bellevue Hosp. Med. Ctr., 1990—91, 1997; ret., 2000. Co-author: Anesthesia and Neurosurgery, 2nd edit., 1986, Trauma, Anesthesia and Intensive Care, 1990; contbr. over 200 articles to profl. jours. Lt. M.C., USNR, 1959-61. Fellow Am. Coll. Chest Physicians, Am. Coll. Anesthesiologists (mem. bd. govs. 1977-85, chmn. bd. govs. 1984), N.Y. Acad. Medicine; mem. AMA, Am. Soc. Anesthesiologists, Assn. Univ. Anesthetists, Internat. Soc. Study of Pain, Soc. Acad. Anesthesia Chairmen, Soc. Critical Care Medicine, Soc. Neurosurg. Anesthesia and Neurologic Supportive Care, N.Y. Acad. Scis., N.Y. State Soc. Anesthesiologists. Home: 898 Park Ave Apt 3 New York NY 10075 Personal E-mail: hermanturndorf@roadrunner.com.

TURNDORF, JAMIE, psychotherapist; b. Boston, July 12, 1958; d. Gary Owen and Sharon (Sandow) Turndorf; m. Emile Jean Pin, Jan. 2, 1988. AB in Am. Culture, Vassar Coll., Poughkeepsie, NY, 1980; MSW, Adelphi U., Garden City, NY, 1983; PhD, Calif. Coast U., 1994. Lic. clin. social worker N.Y. Pvt. practice psychotherapy, NYC and Millbrook, NY, 1981—. Lead creative movement and psychodrama program Lincoln Farms Work Camp, Roscoe, NY, 1976; with Astor Child Guidance Clinic, Poughkeepsie, NY, 1982—83; leader various groups Craig House Hosp., Beacon, NY, 1982—87, developer, dir. eating disorders program, 1984—86; founder, dir. INC.TIMACY, 1990—, J. T. Developers, Inc., Poughkeepsie, 1983—91; dir. Hudson Valley br. Ctr. Advancement Group Studies, Ctr. Emotional Comm., Millbrook, NY, 1990—. Author (with Emile Jean Pin): The Pleasure of Your Company: A Socio-Psychological Analysis of Modern Sociability, 1985; author: Till Death Do Us Part (Unless I Kill You First): A Step-by-Step Guide to Resolving Relationship Conflict, 2007; columnist: Dr. Love various newspapers and web-site (award); host Ask Dr. Love, Sta. WEVD, N.Y.C., 1992, creator, inventor LoveQuest: The Game of Finding Mr. Right, 1990 (One of the Best New Games award Fun and Games mag., 1991); author: Make Up Dont Break Up. Mem.: NASW. Avocations: house restoration, opera singing, antiques. Home and Office: PO Box 475 Millbrook NY 12545-0475 Office Phone: 845-677-3450. Personal E-mail: drlove@drlove.com.

TURNER, ANDREW L., healthcare management company executive; BA, Ohio State Univ. Adminstr skilled nursing facility, Springfield, Ohio, 1970-75; mgr. regional nursing home chain; sr. v.p. ops. Hillhaven Corp.; co-founder Horizon Healthcare Corp., 1986-89; founder, chmn.,CEO Sun Healthcare Group, Inc., Albuquerque, 1989—2000; chmn. Ballantrae Healthcare, 2000; founder, chmn. EnduraCare Therapy Mgmt., 2000, Code Blue Staffing Solutions, 2001; mem. bd. of directors Sports Clubs/L.A., Watson Pharmaceuticals.

TURNER, ANTHONY PETER FRANCIS, biotechnologist, educator; b. London, June 5, 1950; s. Thomas F.W. and Juliette M. (Frasca) T.; Ellen Katherine, Daniel Anthony John. BSc (hon.), U. East London; postgrad. cert. in edn., Christchurch Coll., 1973; MSc, U. Kent, Canterbury, Eng., 1977; PhD, Portsmouth U., Eng., 1980; DSc, U. Kent, 2002; DSc (hon.), U. Bedfordshire, 2008. Lectr. South Kent Coll. Tech., Folkstone, 1974-76; rsch. asst. U. Kent, 1976-77, rsch. fellow, 1980-81; rsch. asst. Portsmouth U., 1977-80; sr. fellow Cranfield U., Bedfordshire, England, 1981—87, prof., 1989—, head biotech. ctr., 1992—, head inst., 1996—, prin., 1999—2006, chmn. postgrad. med. sch., 2002, disting. prof., 2006—, comml. dir., 2007—, dir. Cranfield ventures, 2007—; project dir. MediSense, Inc., Mass., 1983-84; rsch. dir. Pena Biotech. Ltd., 1987-89; prof.; Linköping U., Sweden, 2010. Cons. Gloucestershire NHS Trust, 2004; bus. dir. Cranfield Biotech. Ltd., 1989-91; project leader European Concerted Actions, Brussels, 1988-2000; vis. prof. Tokyo Inst. Tech., 1989, U. Florence, 1993; bd. dirs. Can. Bioconcepts, Nat. Applied Scis., Internat. Adv. Bd., Thailand, 2005; chair sci. adv. bd., dir. Pelikan Techs. Inc., 2002—; chmn. bd. Real Time Sense (Europe); mng. dir. Cranfield Diagnostics, Silsoe Ventures, 1999—; hon. rschr. Bedford NHS Trust, 2004; presenter in field; editl. bd. mem. Jour. Nanosci., 2008. Acad. editor Elsevier Applied Sci., London, 1985—; editor: Biosensors: Fundamentals and Applications, 1987, 89, Advances in Biosensors, 1991, 92, 93, 95, 98; editor-in-chief Jour. Biosensors and Bioelectronics, 1985—; editor Jour. Instrumentation and Analytical Methods, 1995; mem. editl. bd. Jour. Anaerobe, 1994, Avanced Materials, Am. Jour. Biomrd. Sci., Open Nanosci. Jour.; contbr. over 600 papers to profl. publs. Recipient Energy prize Brit. Petroleum, 1982, Pers. Investigation award Royal Soc., London, 1982, Best Paper award Eurosensors, 1991, prize for measurement sci. Nat. Phys. Lab., 1994, Hewlett Packard award, 1995, ATB Milano award, 1995, Mid Bedfordshire Innovation award, 1998; Brit. Diabetic Assn. sr. fellow, 1982. Fellow Royal Soc. Chemistry, Inst. Biology, Inst. Physics, Higher Edn. Acad. (reg. practitoner 2007); mem. European Biosensor Group (founder, chmn. 1987), European Soc. for Engring. and Medicine, Romanian Soc. Clin. Engring. and Medicine (hon.), U.K. Sensor Group (exec. 1991); mem. NAE (fgn. assoc.), Inst. Learning & Tchg. Achievements include some patents in elucidation and application of synthetic receptor and biosensors; co-development of biosensor for blood glucose. Office: Cranfield Univ Cranfield MK4J OAL England Home: 1 Oakley Rise MK45 3FD Bedfordshire England Office Phone: 01236 758355, 44(0)1234 758355. E-mail: a.p.turner@cranfield.ac.uk.

TURNER, ANTHONY SIMON, veterinarian, director; b. Melbourne, Australia, Oct. 24, 1949; BVSc, Melbourne U., 1972; MS, Ohio State U., 1975; DVSc (hon.), U. Melbourne, 2011. Lab. dir. Comparative Orthop. Rsch., 1979—. Prof. Dept. Clin. Scis., 1977. Recipient Lifetime Excellence Rsch. award, AVMA, 2009, Disting. Alumnus award, Ohio State U., 2011. Mem.: Am. Coll. Vet. Surgeons. Avocations: cooking, gardening, cross country skiing. Office: Colo State University Dept Clinical Scis Fort Collins CO 80523 Office Fax: 970-297-0303. Business E-Mail: sturner@colostate.edu.

TURNER, CHRISTOPHER D., oncologist pediatrician, medical director; MD, U. Rochester Sch. Medicine, NY, 1994. Diplomate in pediat. 1997, in hematology oncology Am. Bd. Pediat., 2004. Dir., pediat. neuro oncology program Dana Farber Cancer Inst., Boston, 2001—08, attending, 2008—; med. dir. oncology ARIAD Pharm., Inc., Cambridge, 2008—. Editor: (med. book) Late Effects of Treatment for Brain Tumors. Vol. physician Mass. Med. Res. Corp, Boston, 2006—. Fellow: Am. Acad. Pediat.; mem.: Children's Oncology Group, Soc. Neuro Oncology, Am. Soc. Clin. Oncology. Office: Dana Farber Cancer Inst 44 Binney St Boston MA 02115 Office Fax: 617-632-4897. Business E-Mail: christopher_turner@dfci.harvard.edu.

TURNER, GILLIAN, retired medical geneticist; b. Welnyd Gdn, UK, Aug. 31, 1931; d. Ernest and Winifred Watkins; m. Brian B. Turner (dec.); children: David, Kate; m. Michael Partington, Oct. 12, 1989. B Medicine B Surgery, St. Andrews U., Scotland, 1956; DSc, U. NSW, Australia, 1990. Pediat. resident, chief resident U. Hosp., Edmonton, Canada, 1957—60; fellow mental handicap Johns Hopkins Hosp., Balt., 1964—65; rsch. fellow Children's Med. Rsch. Found., NSW, Australia, 1970—76; dir. clinic Sydney (Australia) Children's Hosp., 1976—93; prof. med. genetics, dir. Hunter Genetics, Newcastle, Australia, 1993—2000, dir. genetics learning disability, 2000—08. Cons. com. Dept. Vet Affairs, Australia. Contbr. articles to profl. publs. Recipient Sir Lorimer Dodds award for rsch. in autism, 1973, disting. achievement award, Internat. Assn. for Study of Mental Deficiency, 1992; named officer, Order of Australia, 1991. Fellow: Royal Coll. Physicians Can., Human Genetics Assn. Australasia (hon.); mem.: Royal Coll. Physicians Edinburgh. Achievements include identification of the importance of genes on the X chromosome as a major cause of mental retardation and for defining the fragile X syndrome. Avocation: planting trees. Home: 37/48 Zaara St 2300 Newcastle NSW Australia Personal E-mail: parturn@gmail.com. Business E-Mail: parturn@ozemail.com.au.

TURNER, GRACE-MARIE, non-profit organization executive; d. Nell Amelia and Will Seaton Arnett; m. Douglas Kearny Turner, May 19, 2001. BA, U. N.Mex, 1969. Exec. dir. Wash. Psychiat. Soc., Washington, 1982—84; pres. Arnett & Co., Washington, 1984—95; exec. dir. Nat. Commn. on Econ. Growth and Tax Reform, Washington, 1995—96; v.p. The Heritage Found., Washington, 1996—97; founder, pres., trustee Galen Inst., Inc., Alexandria, Va., 1997—. Facilitator Health Policy Consensus Group, Washington, 1993—. Dir. Ethics and Pub. Policy Ctr., Washington, 1998—99. Recipient Numerous Journalistic Writing awards, 1970—82, Outstanding Achievement award for Promotion of Consumer Driven Health Care, Consumer Health World, 2007. Roman Catholic. Avocations: piano, gardening, travel, theater. Office: Galen Institute Inc PO Box 320010 Alexandria VA 22320 E-mail: gracemarie@galen.org.

TURNER, HARRY SPENCER, preventive medicine physician, educator; b. Dayton, Ohio, July 25, 1938; s. Eli and Daphne (Cunagin) T.; m. Jan (Fairley) T.; children: Michael, Mary, Daniel. BA, Manchester Coll., North Manchester, Ind., 1960; MD summa cum laude, Ohio State U., 1963, MS in Preventive Medicine, 1968. Diplomate Am. Bd. Preventive Medicine. Resident in preventive (aerospace) medicine Ohio State U., Columbus, 1966-69, chief resident, 1968-69, clin. asst. prof. dept. preventive medicine, 1969-80, dir. Univ. Health Svc., 1970-80; pvt. practice Dayton, 1980-90; dir. Univ. Health Svc., head team physician U. Ky., Lexington, 1991—2003, prof. preventive medicine and environ. health, 1991—2003, prof. emeritus, 2003, dir. emeritus, 2003; med. dir. Sutton Pl. Behavioral Health, 2003—. Editor: (textbook) History and Practice of College Health, 2002; contbr. articles and papers to profl. jours. and meetings. Bd. dirs. Blue Shield, 1981-86; mem. Cin. Internat. Chorale, 1989-94; mem. Lexington Singers, 1992—2003, Island Chamber Singers, 2005-11. Capt. U.S. Army, 1964-66. Recipient Army Commendation medal. Fellow Am. Coll. Preventive Medicine, Am. Coll. Health Assn. (pres. 1980, Ruth Boynton award 1982, Edw. Hitchcock award 1996, Lifetime Achievement award 2003), Alpha Omega Alpha Avocation: music. Personal E-mail: hsturner904@comcast.net.

TURNER, HOLLY STULTS, human resources specialist; b. Memphis, Feb. 18, 1981; BEd, U. Tenn., Knoxville, 2003; MS in Health Adminstrn., U. Memphis, 2005. Human resources rep. Bapt. Meml. Hosp., Memphis, 2005—08, human resources mgr., 2008—. Office: 6019 Walnut Grove Rd Memphis TN 38120 Business E-Mail: holly.turner@bmhcc.org.

TURNER, HUGH MICHAEL, biology professor, researcher; b. Marianna, Fla., Sept. 20, 1942; BS, Ga. Southern U., 1965; PhD, La. State U., 1977. Prof. zoology McNeese State U., 1977—2001; sr. lectr. biology U. Tenn., 2001—. Cons. med. parasitologist W.O. Moss Regional Hosp., Lake Charles, La., 1985—2001. Decorated Navy Commendation medal with combat V Sec. of Navy, Dept. Def.; recipient Edon Byrd award, Southeastern Soc. Parasitologists; Rsch. grant, US Office of Coastal Zone Mgmt., La. Bd. Regents, Rsch. Instrumentation grant, NSF. Mem.: Tenn. Acad. Sci., Helminthological Soc. Wash., Am. Soc. Parasitologists, Soc. Sigma Xi. Avocations: gardening, exercise. Office: 544 University Dr Martin TN 38238-5041 Business E-Mail: hturner@tennessee.edu.

TURNER, JENNIFER JANE, pathologist, researcher; 2 children. MB, BChir, U. Sydney, 1970. Resident med. officer Royal Prince Alfred Hosp., Sydney, NSW, 1971—72; sr. house officer in pathology Royal Free Hosp., London, 1973; registrar in anat. pathology St. Vincent's Hosp., Sydney, 1974—78, Sydney Hosp., 1979, sr. staff specialist and dep. dir. anat. pathology, 1980—82; sr. staff specialist in anat. pathology St Vincent's Hosp., Sydney, 1983—2009; anatomical pathologist Douglas Hanly Moir Pathology, Sydney, 2009—; hon. clin. assoc. prof. Australian Sch. Advanced Medicine Macquarie U., Sydney, 2010—. Med. assessor NATA/RCPA Registration Scheme for Pathology Labs., Australia, 1990; internat. councillor Internat. Acad. Pathology, 1990—92; mem. med. bd. exec. St Vincent's Hosp., Sydney, 1990—91, mem. informatics steering com. Inst. Lab. Medicine, 1995—2000, mem. prostate cancer group mgmt. com., 2001—, sec. divsn. pathology, 2002—03; mem. histopathology panel Australian and New Zealand Lymphoma and Leukaemia Group, Australia, 1994—; mem. diagnostic working party for lymphoma Australian Cancer Network, 2001—; mem. pathology group InterLymph Internat. Collaborative Epidemiology Project for Non-Hodgkin Lymphoma, 2001—; mem. clin. reference group Australian Blood Cancer Registry, 2007—. Mem. editl. bd.: Jour. Pathology, 1983—97, mem. internat. editl. bd.: Jour. Hematopathology, 2007—; contbr. articles to profl. jours. Dir. found. Ascham Sch. for Girls, Sydney, 1995—2000, gov., 1993—2005. Fellow. Royal Coll. Pathologists Australasia (mem. NSW state com. 1983—84, examiner 1992—98); mem.: Cancer Inst. NSW (lymphoma expert), Internat. Soc. Urol. Path., Clin. Reference Group Australian Blood Cancer, European Hematology Assn., InterLymph Collaboration, European Assn. for Haematopathology, Australian Prostate Cancer Collaboration, Australasian Leukemia and Lymphoma Group, Internat. Acad. Pathology (internat. councillor 1990—92), Royal Sydney Golf Club, Nat. Parks Assn., Bush Club NSW. Achievements include research in epidemiology of non-Hodgkin lymphoma; mismatch repair deficiency in colorectal carcinoma; prognostic and molecular factors in prostate cancer; skull base pathology; lymphoproliferative disease in immunodeficiency; development of Australian ACN guidelines for diagnosis of lymphoma; consultation service for lymphoma classificaton; development of structured reporting protocol for pumours of haematopoietic and lymphoid tissue. Office: Douglass Hanly Moir Pathology 14 Giffnock Ave Macquarie Park 2113 Australia Personal E-mail: jtur8838@bigpond.net.au.

TURNER, JOHN RICHARD GEORGE, biologist, writer; b. Liverpool, Eng., Sept. 11, 1940; s. George Hugh and Elsie Ellen (Booth) Turner; m. Sandra Fordyce Millar, Apr. 3, 1967; children: Richard Douglas, Lois Jacqueline. BSc with distinction, U. Liverpool, 1961; BSc 1st class, U. Liverpool, 1962; DPhil, U. Oxford, 1968, DSc, 1987. Rsch. asst. N.Y. Zool. Soc., Trinidad and Tobago, 1964; lectr. U. York, England, 1965—72; assoc. prof. SUNY, Stony Brook, 1971—77; prin. sci. officer Rothamsted Exptl. Sta., Rothamsted, England, 1977—78; lectr. genetics U. Leeds, England, 1978—80, reader in evolutionary genetics, 1980—87, prof. evolutionary genetics, 1987—2000, rsch. prof. biology, 2000—03, hon. fellow, 2003—. Mem. animal procedures com. Home Office of U.K. Govt., London, 1997—2000; joint hon. sec. Coun. for Acad. Autonomy, London, 1987—88. Author: (poetry) Rimbaud Translations, 1989, Verlaine Translations, 2010—11; contbr. articles and book reviews to profl. jours. including N.Y. Times, Times Literary Supplement, chapters to books; mem. editl. bd. Evolution, 1978—91, Heredity, 1980—82, Evolutionary Ecology, 1987—90, Entomologist, 1980. Recipient prize, Liverpool Biol. Soc., 1961, Edward Forbes prize, U. Liverpool, 1962, John Dryden prize, 2009; nominee Stephen Spender prize for Poetry in Translation, 2005, 2009. Fellow: Royal Soc. of Arts, Royal Entomol. Soc. London; mem.: Coun. for Acad. Autonomy (joint hon. sec. 1987—88), Lepidopterists Soc. (life), Genetics Soc. Am. (com. on race and intelligence), Conservation Soc. (founder). Achievements include pioneer in the culture of free-living butterflies in glass-houses; in energy theory of biodiversity gradients; in evolution of mimicry; in puncuated equilibrium. Avocations: opera, wildlife, drawing, translating poetry. Office: Univ of Leeds Faculty of Biological Scis Leeds LS2 9JT England Office Phone: 44 1133 43 28 28. Business E-Mail: j.r.g.turner@leeds.ac.uk.

TURNER, JOHN SIDNEY, JR., retired otolaryngologist, educator; b. Bainbridge, Ga., July 25, 1930; s. John Sidney and Rose Lee (Rogers) T.; m. Betty Jane Tigner, June 5, 1955 (dec.); children: Elizabeth, Rebecca, Jan Marie; m. Nina Jones, June 16, 1999. BS, Emory U., 1952, MD, 1955. Diplomate Am. Bd. Otolaryngology. Intern U. Va. Hosp., 1955-56; resident in otolaryngology Duke U. Med. Ctr., 1958-61; prof. otolaryngology Emory U., Atlanta, 1961-95, chmn. divsn., 1961—95; ret. Ear specialist, chief otolaryngology Emory Clinic, 1961-95; area cons. in field U.S. 3d Army, 1962-69; assoc. dir. heart disease control program Fla. Bd. Health, 1956-58; Ga. state chmn. Deafness Rsch. Found., 1968-95; v.p. Clifton Casualty Ins. Co., Atlanta, 1975-95. Mem. internat. editl. bd. Drugs Jour., 1982-2004, Ethicals in Med. Progress, 1982—, Dialogue Jour., 1988-95; mem. editl. bd. Otolaryngolog—Head and Neck Surgery, 1991; contbr. chpts. to books, articles to profl. jours. With USPHS, 1956-58. Recipient Appreciation award Children of Fulton County and Fulton County Health Dept., 1975, Citation for Disting. Svc., Fla. divsn. Am. Cancer Soc., 1957, Lester A. Brown award Ga. Soc. Otolaryngology*Head and Neck Surgery, 1995. Mem. AMA, So. Med. Assn. (chmn. otolaryngology sect. 1974, cert. of appreciation 1974), Am. Acad. Otolaryngology--Head and Neck Surgery (Honor award 1994), Triological Soc. (v.p., chmn. so. sect. 1991—), Am. Acad. Otolaryngic Allergy, Ga. Soc. Otolaryngology (pres. 1973), Med. Assn. Ga., Med. Assn. Atlanta, Assn. Acad. Depts. Otolaryngology, Optimists (pres. Atlanta 1975), Alpha Omega Alpha. Democrat. Methodist.

TURNER, JOSEPH VERNON, medical educator, consultant, rural generalist; b. Armidale, NSW, Australia, Mar. 24, 1977; s. Vernon Joseph and Theresia Turner. BMedSc with honors, U. Sydney, Australia, 1998, PhD, 2004; MB BChir, U. Queensland, Brisbane, Australia, 2006. Lectr. U. Sydney, 2002; rsch. affiliate U. Queensland, Toowoomba, 2003—06, conjoint lectr., 2007—. Cons. artificial intelligence and data analysis, Toowoomba, Australia, 2002—; sec. Nat. Rural Health Network, Melbourne, Australia, 2005—06; mem. mgmt. com. Med. Rural Bonded Scholar Support Program, 2005—06. Editor: (conference proceedings) 8th National Undergraduate Rural Health Conference; contbr. chapters to books, articles to profl. jours. Recipient U. Gold, U. Sydney, 2002, Australian and New Zealand Soc. Occupl. Medicine prize, 2004, Karl Kessler Meml. prize, U. Queensland, 2006; scholar, Faculty Sci. Alumni U. Sydney, 1995—97, Faculty Pharmacy U. Sydney, 1999—2001; JG. Hunter Rsch. fellow, AMA, 2005. Mem.: Sydney U. Sport (v.p. 1997—2001, Gold medal 2002), Early Mgmt. Severe Trauma, Postgrad. Med. Coun. Queensland (JHO forum rep.), Gen. Practice Registrars Australia (bd. mem. 2007—), Australian Rural Health Edn. Network, Towards Rural & Outback Health Profls. Queensland (exec. 2005), GP Connections, Australian Med. Assn., Rural Doctors Assn. Queensland (Student prize 2005), Royal Australian Coll. Gen. Practitioners (Nat. Rural Faculty Bursary 2005), Australian Coll. Rural and Remote Medicine (registrar com. 2008, John Flynn scholar 2003—06), U. Sydney Union, Golden Key Internat., Johnsmen's Assn. (bd. mem. 2002—03). Business E-Mail: jvturner@catholic.org.

TURNER, KATHY ANN, special education services professional, director; b. Cinn., May 16, 1962; d. James Robert and Alice Louise Taylor; m. Michael Arcia Turner, Jr., June 1, 1985; children: Joseph Paul, Christopher James, Sarah Alyse. AA, Riverside C.C., 1998; BS in Edn., Lewis Clark State Coll., 2002. Spl. edn. asst. Corona-Norco Unified Sch. Dist., Norco, Calif., 1996—98; direct care provider devel. disabilities Inclusion North, Inc., Grangeville, Idaho, 1998—2000; tech. for tchrs. asst. Lewis Clark State Coll., Lewiston, Idaho, 2000—01; sub. tchr. Prairie Sch., Idaho, 2001—03; specialist devel. disabilities Opportunities Unltd., Inc., 2003—05; psycho social rehab provider Camas Profl. Counseling, 2005—06; spl. edn. tchr. lower Kuskokwim sch. dist. Bethel Regional High Sch., Ark., 2006—07; devel. disabilities dir. Yukon Kuskokwim Health Corp., 2007—. Psychol. social rehab. provider Frontier Journeys, Grangeville, Idaho, 2002—05, 2007—; counselor Hope Pregnancy Ctr., Grangeville, 2003—06, 2007—. Portrait, Liz (2nd pl. award Idaho County Art Competition, 1998). Daffodil days chmn. Am. Cancer Soc., Corona, Calif., 1995—98; com. mem. Relay for Life, 2005; chmn. Key Coalition. Named Life Woman of the Yr., Norco C. of C., 1995. Mem.: Bethel Art Guild, Coun. for Exceptional Children, Grangeville Elks, Kappa Delta Pi (pres. 2001—03). Republican. Avocations: baking, fishing, sewing, card playing, ballroom dancing. Home: PO Box 1901 Bethel AK 99559 Personal E-mail: imspcl2002@yahoo.com.

TURNER, RALPH JAMES, obstetrician, gynecologist; b. Waco, Tex., 1952; BS, McMurry U., 1974, BA, 1976; MD, U. Tex. Southwestern, Dallas, 1978. Cert. in med. mgmt. Am. Coll. Physician Exec., Tulane U., 1996, diplomate Am. Coll. Physician Execs.; diplomate Am. Bd. Ob-Gyn. Intern Tripler Army Med. Ctr., Honolulu, 1978-79, resident ob-gyn., 1979-82; ob-gyn. Darnall U.S. Army Cmty. Hosp., Ft. Hood, Tex., 1982-86, Presbyn. Hosp., Dallas, 1986—2009; asst. prof. surgery U. Tex. Health Sci. Ctr., Tyler, 2009—. Trustee Genesis Physicians Group, 1992-05, chmn. 1997-02; ob-gyn. Columbia Med. Ctr., Plano, Tex., 1994-05, Presbyn. Hosp., Plano, 1994—2009; med. adminstr., interim med. dir. Sys. Health Providers Inc., 1995-97, 99-01; bd. trustees McMurry Univ., Abilene, Tex., 2004—. Contbr. articles to profl. jours. Trustee Found. of Am. Assn. Gynecol. Laparoscopists, 1996—2001, exec. dir. Cypress, Calif., 2001—; trustee McMurry U., 2004—. Named Disting. Alumni, McMurry U., 2006. Mem. ACOG, Am. Assn. Gynecol. Laparoscopists (bd. trustees 2000-02), Am. Coll. Physician Execs., North Am. Menopause Soc. (cert. menopose practitioner 2010-). Methodist. Office: Univ Tex Health Sci Ctr at Tyler 11937 US Hwy 271 Tyler TX 75708 Office Phone: 972-312-1309.

TURNER-WARWICK, MARGARET, physician, educator; b. Nov. 19, 1924; d. William Harvey and Maud Kirkdale (Baden-Powell) Moore; m. Richard Trevor Turner-Warwick, Jan. 21, 1950; children: Gillian, Lynne. MA, BM, BCh, Oxford U., Eng., 1950, DM, 1956; PhD, London U., 1961; DSc (hon.), NYU, 1985, Exeter U., 1990, U. London, 1990, Hull U., 1991, U. Sussex, 1992, U. Oxford, 1992, U. Cambridge, 1993, U. Leicester, 1997. Clin. tng. U. Coll. Hosp., Brompton Hosp., 1950-61; cons. physician Elizabeth Garrett Anderson Hosp., 1961-67, Brompton and London Chest Hosps., 1967-72; prof. medicine Brompton and Cardio Thoracic Inst., London, 1972-87; dean Cardiothoracic Inst., London, 1984-87; pres. Royal Coll. Physicians, London, 1989-92. Chmn. UKCCCR, London. Author: (book) Immunology of Lung, 1979. Non-exec. mem. Royal Brompton Governing Body, London; chmn. Royal Devon Exeter Healthcare Trust, 1992-95. Decorated dame comdr. Brit. Empire, 1991; recipient Osler medal Oxford, 1996, Pres. award European Respiratory Soc., 1997. Fellow: ACP (hon.), Royal Coll. Radiology, Acad. Med. Sci. (founder fellow 1998), Royal Coll. Physicians Ireland, Royal Coll. Physicians and Surgeons Glasgow, U. Coll. London, Faculty Pub. Health Medicine, Faculty Occupl. Medicine, Royal Australian Coll. Physicians, Imperial Coll. London (hon.), Royal Coll. Physicians and Surgeons Can. (hon.), Royal Coll. Anaesthetists (hon.), Coll. Medicine South Africa (hon.), Royal Coll. Pathologists (hon.), Bencher Mid. Temple (hon.), Royal Coll. Surgeons England (hon.), Royal Coll. Gen. Practitioners (ad enundum), Royal Coll. Physicians Edinburgh, Royal Coll. Gen. Practitioners, Green Coll. Oxford (hon.), Lady Margaret Hall Oxford (hon.), Girton Coll. Cambridge (hon.); mem.: Brit. Thoracic Soc. (pres. 1982, President's medal 1999), Acad. Malaysia, South German and Australasian Thoracic Socs. (hon.), Assn. Physicians Gt. Britain and Ireland (hon.), Alpha Omega Alpha. Avocations: gardening, violin, painting. Home: Pynes House Thorverton Nr Exeter EX5 5LT Devon England

TUROCK, JANE PARSICK, nutritionist; b. Peckville, Pa., Apr. 15, 1947; d. Paul Charles and Elizabeth Dorothy (Mistysyn) Parsick; m. Michael John, July 12, 1968; children: Eric Matthew, Nathan Andrew, J. Seth, Melanie Kay. BS, Marywood Coll., Scranton, Pa., 1969, MS, 1982. Registered dietitian; cert. nutrition specialist. Registered dietitian Jane P. Turock, Scranton, Pa., 1985—; founder and chief dietitian Gastric Bubble, Scranton, Pa., 1986—; prof. Penn State Coll., Scranton, Pa., 1987—; dietitian & presenter WNEP TV Healthwatch, Avoca, Pa., 1988—; dir. & chief dietitian Vascular Inst. of Northeast Pa., Pa., 1989—; owner, mgr. Nutrition...Plus/Fitness Unlimited, Scranton, Pa., 1991—; owner Pauliz Profl. Plz., Olyphant, Pa., 2006—, Sonny's Patching, Inc., 2007. Cons. Home Health Care Assn., Clarks Summit, 1985—; dietitian Clarks Summit, 1985—; founder Nat. Nutrition Month Bakeoff; dir. Camp Jane. Treas. Lackawanna County Med. Soc. Aux., 1974-76, pres., 1979-80, bd. dirs., 1980-81; allocations com. United Way Lackawanna County, 1990—; bd. dirs. Lupus Found., 1995, St. Francis of Assissi Kitchen, 1995; coord. Gary DiBileo For Mayor Scranton Campaign, 2005. Mem. Am. Dietetic Assn., Northeast Dist. Pa. Dietic Diet Therapy, Consulting Nutritionists in Pvt. Practice, Am. Diabetic Assn., Northeast Womens Network, Allied Wedding Firm. Republican. Roman Catholic. Avocations: skiing, tennis, gourmet cooking, jogging, swimming. Office: 397 N 9th Ave Scranton PA 18504 Personal E-mail: janeturock@excite.com.

TUROW, JUDITH ANNE, pediatrician; MD, NY Med. Coll., 1976. Diplomate Am. Bd. Pediatrics, lic. to practice Pa., 1987, NJ, 1998. Intern St. Vincent's Hosp., 1977; resident Indiana Univ. Hosp., 1981, Methodist Hosp., 1982; hosp. affiliations include Children's Hosp. Pa., Pa. Hosp., Thomas Jefferson Univ. Hosp. Office: Pennsylvania Hospital 800 Spruce St Philadelphia PA 19107 Office Phone: 215-829-3000.

TURPIN, DAVID HOWARD, biologist, educator, university president; b. Duncan, BC, Can., July 14, 1956; s. George Howard and Marilyn Elizabeth (Jones) T.; m. Suromitra Sanatani, Nov. 4, 2006; children: Chantal, Joshua. BSc in Biology, U. BC, 1977, PhD in Botany and Oceanography, 1980. Postdoctoral rsch. fellow Natural Scis. Engring. Rsch. Coun., 1980—81; rsch. assoc. Simon Fraser U., 1980; v.p. Sigma Resource Cons., Vancouver, BC, 1980—81; from asst. prof. to assoc. prof. Queen's U., Kingston, Ont., Canada, 1981—90, prof. biology, 1990—91, dean arts and sci., 1993—95, vice prin. acad., 1995—2000; prof., head botany U. BC, 1991—93, dean, faculty arts and sci., 1993—95; pres., vice-chancellor U. Victoria, BC, 2000—. Invited spkr. profl. meetings univs. worldwide. Co-editor: Plant Physiology, Biochemistry and Molecular Biology, 1990, 2d edit., 1996; mem. editl. bd. Jour. Phycology, 1992-96, Plant Physiology, 1988-92, Plant Cell and Environ., 1994-96, Jour. Exptl. Botany, 1995-98; contbr. chpts. in books; author numerous articles, conf. procs. Kingston City rep. Cataraqui Regional Conservation Authority, 1984-86; v.p. Great Lakes Tomorrow, 1986-90; mem. program com. Great Lakes Course-Ont. Sci. Ctr., 1988; hon. adv. mem. Soong Ching Ling Children's Found. Ltd., 2001-; bd. govs. Bus. Coun. BC, 2008-; mem. chair Can. Rsch. Knowledge Network, 2006-09; mem. Order of Can., 2010. Recipient Excellence in Tchg. Alumni award Queen's U., 1989, Outstanding Alumni award U. B.C., 1990, Darbaker prize in phycology Am. Bot. Assn., 1991; Natural Scis. and Engring. Rsch. Coun. E.W.R. Stacie Meml. fellowship, 1989-90, Royal Soc. Can. fellow, 1998-; postgrad. scholar Natucral Scis. and Engring. Rsch. Coun., 1979-81, Edith Ashton Meml. scholar U. BC, 1979, NRC scholar, 1978-79, Capt. T.S. Byrne Meml. scholar U. BC, 1980; Natural Scis. and Engring. Rsch. Coun. grantee, 1979—81. Mem. Phycological Soc. Am., Am. Soc. Limnology and Oceanography, Can. Soc. Plant Physiologists (C.D. Nelson award 1989), Am. Soc. Plant Physiologists (cert. recognition 1992), Minister Nat. Def. Edn. (adv. bd. mem. 2003-06), Discovery Found. Bd., Assn. Univs. and Colls. Can. (mem. 2002-). Office: University Victoria Office of the Pres Ring Rd Victoria BC Canada V8W 2Y2 Business E-Mail: pres@uvic.ca.

TURPIN, GÉRARD CHRISTIAN, endocrinologist, educator, consultant; b. Nov. 11, 1939; s. Raymond Alexandre and Simone Henriette (Gaillochet) T.; m. Anne-Lise Colette Rambert, Nov. 24, 1964; children: Eric, Sylvie. MD, U. Paris, 1964. Extern Hosps. of Paris, 1960-64, intern, 1964-70; clin. specialist Hosps. and Acad. of Paris, 1970-80, prof. medicine, 1980—. Dir. Ctr. for Study and Rsch. for Endocrinological and Metabolic Disorders, 1984—. Author: Why, When, How to Treat Hyperlipoproteinemias, 1982, rev. edit., 1991, 97, Pediatric Hyperlipidemias, 1985, The Dyslipoproteinemias, 1989, rev. edit., 1991, 97; author numerous articles on endocrinology and metabolism. Served to lt. French Army, 1964-65. Decorated Officier de la Légion d'Honneur. Mem. French Endocrine Soc. (treas. 1979-84), Med. Soc. of Paris Hosps., Endocrine Soc. Avocations: classical music, piano. Office: Hopital la pitie-Salpetriere 83 Blvd de l'Hopital 75013 Paris Cedex 06 France Personal E-mail: alturp@free.fr.

TURRA, CHRISTIAN, agronomist; b. Marília, São Paulo, Brazil, Feb. 17, 1972; Degree in Agronomy, UNESP, Jaboticabal, Sao Paulo, 1995; PhD, Ctr. Energia Nuc. na Agricultura, U. Sao Paulo, 2010. Rschr. Ctr. Energia Nuc. na Agricultura, U. Sao Paulo, 2003—11. Avocations: reading, travel, running. Home: Rua Nove de Julho 1826 Araraquara São Paulo 14801-295 Brazil Personal E-mail: christian.turra@gmail.com.

TURRINI, FABRIZIO, cardiologist; b. Sassuolo, Italy, Mar. 31, 1969; MD, U. Modena, 1995, degree in Internal Medicine and Cardiology, 2000. Physician Nuovo Ospedale Sant'Agostino Estense-Medicina Cardiovasc., 2001—. Mem.: Italian Assn. Cardiology, Italian Assn. Internal Medicine, European Assn. Echocardiography. Office: Via Giardini 1355 Baggiovara Modena 41100 Italy Business E-Mail: turrini.it@tiscalinet.it.

TURTZ, ALAN R., neurosurgeon, educator; MD, Med. Coll. Pa., 1986. Diplomate Am. Bd. Neurol. Surgery, lic. Pa., 1987, NJ, 1996. Intern Lankenau Hosp.; resident Med. Coll. Pa.; assoc. prof. Cooper Univ. Hosp., NJ, dir. pituitary tumor and neuroendocrine program. Fellow: ACS; mem.: Am. Assn. of Neurol. Surgeons, Congress of Neurol. Surgeons, Eastern Assn. for the Surgery of Trauma. Office: Cooper University Hospital 3 Cooper Plz Ste 104 Camden NJ 08103 Office Phone: 856-968-7965. Office Fax: 856-968-8697.

TURZÓ, KINGA LACZKÓNÉ, biophysicist; b. Brasov, Romania, July 18, 1967; BSc in Physics, U. Bucharest, Romania, MSc in Physics, 1989; PhD in Physics, U. Szeged, Hungary, 2000. Asst. prof., dept. biophysics József Attila U., Szeged, 1991—99, U. Szeged, 2000—01, rsch. fellow, dept. dentistry and oral surgery, faculty medicine, 2001—04, sr. rsch. fellow, dept. prosthodontics and oral biology, faculty dentistry, 2004—, erasmus coord. faculty dentistry, 2008—. Mem.: Internat. Assn. Dental Rsch., Hungarian Biophysical Soc. Avocations: mountain climbing, skiing, music. Office: Tisza Lajos krt 64 Szeged Csongrád 6720 Hungary Office Phone: 36-62-545285. Office Fax: 36-62-545301. Personal E-mail: kturzo@yahoo.com. Business E-Mail: turzo@stoma.szote.u-szeged.hu.

TUSIIME, JAYNE BYAKIKA, pharmacist; b. Kampala, Uganda, June 14, 1971; PharmD, Makerere U. Kampala, 1996; PhD, U. Calif., Berkeley, 2010. Clin. pharmacist Mulago Tchg. and Referral Hosp., 1996—2002; project dir. Makerere U.-U. Calif. San Francisco Rsch. Collaboration, 2003—06; sr. behavioral scientist Ctrs. Disease Control and Prevention Uganda, 2010—. Lectr. Makerere U. Coll. Health Scis., 2003—05; peer reviewer Jour. AIDS and Behavior, 2006, AIDS Care, 2006, Internat. Jour. STIs & AIDS, 2006. Recipient Young Investigators award, Conf. on Retroviruses and Opportunistic Infections; Rsch. grant, Ctr. AIDS Rsch. UCSF, AIDS Care Rsch. in Africa, Travel grant, Conf. on Retroviruses and Opportunistic Infections. Mem.: Toastmasters Internat., Internat. Assn. Physicians in AIDS Care, Pharm. Soc. Uganda, Uganda Soc. Health Scientists (chairperson 2005—06), Internat. Clin. Epidemiology Network. Avocations: reading, swimming, cooking. Office: Plot 51/59 Nakiwogo Rd Entebbe Uganda Office Fax: 256 414 321 457. E-mail: tusjayne@hotmail.com.

TUTER, GULAY, medical educator; b. Antalya, Oct. 14, 1968; DDS, 1991, PhD in periodontology, 1997. Prof. Gazi U., 2008—. Office: Gazi Universitesi Dis Hek Fak Biskek Emek-Ankara 06510 Turkey Business E-Mail: gulay@gazi.edu.tr.

TUTHILL, OLIVER W., JR., psychologist, consultant, author, composer, independent film producer, director; b. Orange, NJ, Aug. 8, 1945; s. Oliver W. and Virginia Tuthill. BA in Sociology, Olivet Coll., 1968, BA in Psychology, 1968; MA in Psychology, Antioch U., 2002. Singer, songwriter, Chgo., 1955—72; actor Hollywood, Calif., 1972—84, Universal, Hollywood, 1973—84; pres., profl. spkr. Autumn Tree Prodns., Seattle, 1999—2005; pres. Blue Pony Trail Music, Seattle, 2005—. Pres. 140th St Promotions, Seattle, 1986—88, Blue Wood Films LLC, Seattle, 2003—; cons. Jr. Achievement, Seattle, 1996—2000; advisor, com. mem. Gov. Blue Ribbon Commn., Seattle, 2000—02; pres. Blue Wood Television, 2011—, Blue Wood Radio Productions, 2011—. Dir.: (films) Understanding 6 Forms of Emotional, 1999 (Bronze Telly award, 2000, 2003), Dysphoria, 2001 (Best Feature Film, 2001), Children's Rights: Why America Says No, 2004 (4 Bronze Telly awards, 2004); prodr.: (albums) Acoustic Concerto, 2005; prodr.(dir.): (films) Willatuk: The Legend of Seattle's Sea Serpent, featuring Graham Greene, 2006; prodr. (dir.): (films) Child Abuse (Silver telly awards); prodr.(dir.): (films) Wounded Heart: Pine Ridge Run and The Sioux Featuring Russell Means, 2005 (Bronze Telly award, 2005, Grand Goldie Film award, 2005); dir.: (documentary) Question For Crazy Horse Featuring Russell Means, (producer, writer): The Right To Bear Arms Starring John Savage, 2009; composer (writer, prodr.): Rappon Shadowyze, 2010; prodr.(writer, composer): What Would Crazy Rap Artist Jay, 2011. Recipient Media award, Gov. Wash. State, 2002, Horace Mann award, Antioch U., 2003, Silver Plaque, Music Intercom Video Competition, 2001, Silver Telly award for Complex: Life Inside a Section 8 Apt., 2006, Silver Telly award, Hon. Mention Black Lights, Mex. Internat. Film Festival, 2011; named Song of Yr., Semi Finalist Placement Constantine Great, 2011; nominee Screen Actors Guild award, Theoretical Motion Pictures, 2009. Mem.: APA (assoc.), Recording Acad. (Grammy awards 2011), Am. Screenwriters Assn., Internat. Documentary Assn., Screen Actors Guild, Broadcast Music Inc. Avocations: sports, swimming, singing, reading, politics. Home: 20044 Bagley Dr N Y304 Seattle WA 98133 Office Phone: 206-364-9202. Personal E-mail: owtuthi@earthlink.net.

TUTT, DOUGLAS CHARLES, health facility administrator, director; b. Nambour, Australia, Dec. 20, 1952; s. Charles William and Olive May (Reynolds) Tutt; m. Esmeralda Terese Branco; children: Alexander Douglas Tutt-Branco, Amelia Rachel Tutt-Branco. BSc, U. Ctrl. Queensland, 1973. Health surveyor Paroo Shire Coun., Cunnamulla, Australia, 1973—74; team leader, cmty. youth svcs. Ctrl. Coast Area Health Svc., Gosford, Australia, 1974—86; dir. Health Promotion Unit No. Sydney Ctrl. Coast Area Health Svc., Gosford, 1986—. Founding mem. and pres. Woy Woy (Australia) Youth Cottage Accommodation Svc., 1974—90; mem. mgmt. bd. Gosford (Australia) City Cmty. and Info. Svc., 1985—90; mem. tobacco legis. com. State Sydney, 2002—, mem. population health reference group, 2005—; adviser nat. tobacco sales to minors com., Canberra, Australia, 2001—; mem. NSW Health Alcohol and Drug Prevention Com., 2006—; adv. alcohol and minors Office of Min. for Gaming and Racing, Sydney, 2003—04; mem. adv. bd. Ctr. Phys. Activity and Health, Sydney, 2001—03. Author: (CD) Crackdown on Retail Sales of Cigarettes to Minors Cuts Teenage Smoking; prodr.: (advertisements, educational cd) Supply Means Supply, (various health advt. campaigns). Inaugural mgr. Erina HS Equestrian Team, Gosford, 2001; chmn. Gosford (Australia) City Cmty. Child Care Inc, 1989—94. Recipient Edn. Week award, NSW Dept of Edn. and Tng., 2000, Outstanding Contbn. to China Health Promotion Australian Tech. Assistance award, Ministry Health, People's Republic of China, 2000, Quality and Innovation Excellence award, No. Sydney Ctrl. Coast Health, 2004. Mem.: Erina HS Parents and Citizens Assn. (pres.

2001—), Suicide Safety Network, Matcham Valley Pony Club (v.p. 2004—06, instr. 2004—). Achievements include development of a model for health promotion success with certain drugs first presented at the 2nd Australasian conference on drugs strategy; a decade of success in supply side strategy for stopping juvenile uptake of tobacco, resulting in a 50% decline in teen smoking; first to one of the first large scale childhood obesity prevention programs in Australia; research in the emerging role of Cannabis in road trauma. Avocations: cricket, tennis, horseback riding, wooden boats. Office: Central Coast Health Promotion Unit No Sydney Ctrl Coast Area Health Svc PO Box 361 Gosford NSW 2250 Australia Office Fax: +61+2+43494866. Business E-Mail: dtutt@nsccahs.health.nsw.gov.au.

TUTTLE, GEORGIA A., dermatologist; b. Virginia Beach, Va. BA, U. Maine, Orono; MD, Tufts U. Sch. Medicine, Boston. Cert. American Acad. Dermatology, American Bd. Dermatology, Nat. Bd. Med. Examiners. Dermatology tng. Dartmouth-Hitchcock Med. Ctr., Lebanon, NH; pvt. practice dermatologist NH; pres. med. staff, mem. bd. trustees Alice Peck Day Meml. Hosp., Lebanon; councilwoman, Ward 1 Lebanon City Coun.; mayor City of Lebanon. Clin. instr. Dartmouth Med. Sch., Hanover, NH. Founding mem. bd. dirs. NH Endowment Health; past pres. New Eng. Coun. State Med. Societies. Recipient Disting. Alumnus award, Tufts U. Sch. Medicine, 2005. Mem.: AMA (chair coun. med. svc., chair New Eng. del., state chair organized med. staff sect., mem. dermatology sect. coun., bd. trustees 2011—), Atlantic Dermatol. Soc., New Eng. Dermatol. Soc., NH Dermatol. Soc., Grafton County Med. Soc., NH Med. Soc. (pres., Marjorie Parsons award), Phi Kappa Phi, Phi Beta Kappa. Office: 129 Mechanic St Lebanon NH 03766 Office Phone: 603-448-1071. *

TUTTLE, JEREMY BALLOU, neuroscientist; s. John Bauman and Charlotte Marion (Root) T.; m. Sara Jane Stasko, Mar. 23, 1971. AB, U. Rochester, 1969; PhD, Johns Hopkins U., 1977. Postdoctoral fellow U. Conn., Storrs, 1976-79, vis. asst. prof., 1980, asst. prof. in residence, 1981-84; asst. prof. physiology U. Va., Charlottesville, 1984-87, asst. prof. neuroscience, 1987-90, rsch. asst. prof., 1990-93, assoc. prof. urology neuroscience, 1993-98, prof., 1998—. Contbr. articles to Devel. Biology, Science, Jour. Neuroscience, others; mem. editl. bd. Investigative Urology, Jour. Urology, Jour. Hypertension. Chmn. mem. Common Area Planning Commn., 1984-87; pres. bd. Earlysville Forest Homeowner's Assn., 1986-89, Earlysville, Va.; chmn. urology spl. emphasis panel NIH, 1996-2001; chmn. spl. emphasis panel on female pelvic floor disorders Nat. Inst. Child Health and Human Devel., 1999; mem. promotion and tenure com. U. Va., 2004—. U. Rochester Hon. scholar, 1965-69, Regent's scholar for Medicine, 1969, NIH predoctoral fellow, 1971-75, Nat. Rsch. Svc. fellow, 1976-79, Nat. Spinal Cord Injury Found. rsch. fellow, 1979-80; recipient Rsch. Career Devel. award Nat. Inst. Neurol. Disease/NIH, Muscular Dystrophy Assn. Rsch. award, 1990—; Am. Heart Assn. grantee, 1987-89, 90—, fellowship, Fogarty Internat. Ctr. for Rsch. NIH, Japan, 1997. Mem.: AAAS, Am. Soc. Cell Biology, Biophys. Soc., Soc. Neuroscience, Sigma Xi. Achievements include research on NGF dynamics in hypertrophic disease, carbon dioxide transport and chemosensitivity, molecular mechanisms of quantal synaptic transmission, nerve growth factor synthesis by vascular smooth muscle, trophic regulation of motor neurons, neurodegenerative diseases. Office: U Va Med Sch PO Box 801392 Charlottesville VA 22908-1392 Office Phone: 434-924-5634. Business E-Mail: tuttle@virginia.edu.

TUTTLE, R. MICHAEL, endocrinologist; MD, U. Louisville. Diplomate Am. Bd. of Internal Medicine endocrinology & metabolism. Resident Dwight David Eisenhower Army Med. Ctr.; fellow Madigan Army Med. Ctr. Chmn. thyroid cancer panel Nat. Comprehensive Cancer Network; cons. endocrinologic & metabolic drugs adv. com. FDA; cons. Chernobyl Tissue Bank. Mem.: Endocrine Soc., Am. Thyroid Assn. Office: Memorial Sloan-Kettering Cancer Center 1275 York Ave New York NY 10065 Office Phone: 212-639-2000.

TUXHORN, INGRID E.B., pediatrician, educator; b. Cape Town, South Africa, Dec. 5, 1952; MBChB, U. Cape Town, 1976. Divsn. chief pediat. epilepsy U. Hosps. Cleve., 2010—. Prof. pediat. Case Western Res. U., 2009—. Named one of Best Physicians of America. Avocation: sailing. Office: 11100 Euclid Ave Cleveland OH 44106 Office Fax: 216-844-8966. Business E-Mail: ingrid.tuxhorn@uhhospitals.org.

TUZCU, EMIN MURAT, cardiologist, educator; b. Isparta, Turkey, July 5, 1953; came to U.S., 1985; s. Omer Lufti and Guzide T.; m. Füsun Tuzcu, Apr. 26, 1982; children: Omer C., Hande N. MD, Istanbul Med. Faculty, 1977. Diplomate Am. Bd. Internal Medicine. Intern, resident Istanbul U. Sch. Medicine, 1971—81; fellow in cardiology Cleve. Clinic Found., 1985—89, staff physician, cardiologist, 1992—, prof. medicine, 1992—, vice chmn. Dept. Cardiovascular Medicine; fellow Mass. Gen. Hosp., 1989—91. Contbr. articles to profl. jours. Fellow: ACP, Am. Coll. Cardiology; mem.: Turkish Soc. Cardiology, Soc. Cardiac Angiography and Interventions, Am. Heart Assn. Office: Cleveland Clinic Found 9500 Euclid Ave Cleveland OH 44195-0002 Office Phone: 216-444-8130.

TUZIMSKI, TOMASZ JERZY, pharmacist; b. Lublin, Poland, Dec. 17, 1971; s. Jerzy Stanislaw Tuzimski and Barbara Danuta Tuzimska. PhD, Faculty Pharmacy, Med. U. Lublin, 2002. Diplomate in pharm. Med. U. Lublin, 1995. Asst. rschr. Med. U. Lublin, 1995—2004, adj. rschr., 2004—. Contbr. articles to profl. jours. Recipient Team prize, Polish Ministry Health, 2001, Individual prize, 2003; grants, Polish Ministry Sci. and Higher Edn., 2005—08, 2009—11. Roman Catholic. Avocations: swimming, travel, mountain climbing, bicycling, diving. Home: Kaskadowa 11/68 Lublin 20 819 Poland Office: Medical University Lublin Ul Chodiki 4A Lubin 20 081 Poland Office Fax: (48)(81) 535 73 50. Business E-Mail: tomasz.tuzimski@umlub.pl.

TUZUNER, NUKHET NURIYE, medical educator; b. Istanbul, Turkey, May 1, 1953; Degree, U. Cerrahpasa, 1975, degree in Med. Pathology, 1978. Prof., pathology & hematopathology Istanbul U. Cerrahpasa Sch. Medicine, 1990—. Dir. Hematopathology and Molecular Oncology Rsch. Ctr., 1998—2006, Dept. Pathology, 2002—05. Grant, Istanbul U. Cerrahpasa Med. Faculty, U. Southern Calif. Mem.: Turkish Soc. Pathology, Turkish Soc. Hematology, European Soc. Hematopathology. Avocations: bicycling, mountain climbing, literature, writing, swimming. Office: Cerrahpasa Tip Fakultesi Patoloji Abd Istanbul Aksaray 43303 Turkey Office Fax: 02124143000-21850. Personal E-mail: tuzunern@yahoo.com.

TWEARDY, DAVID JOHN, physician, scientist, educator; b. Monessen, Pa., Feb. 12, 1952; s. John Tweardy Sr. and Helen Kotch Tweardy; m. Ruth Falik, Jan. 21, 1982; children: Samuel David, Benjamin John, Daniel James. AB in Chemistry, Princeton U., 1974; MD, Harvard U., 1978. Diplomate Am. Bd. Internal Medicine, 1983, Am. Bd. Infectious Diseases, 1984. Asst. prof. medicine U. Pitts. Sch. Medicine, 1987—93, assoc. prof. medicine, 1993—99; prof. medicine Baylor Coll. Medicine, Houston, 1999—, chief sect. infectious diseases, 1999—. Grantee, NIH, 1997—2005, 2002—, 2004—. Mem.: Am. Clin. and Climatalogical Assn., Assn. Am. Physicians. Home: 3769 Nottingham St Houston TX 77005 Office Phone: 713-798-8918. E-mail: dtweardy@bcm.edu.

TWISDALE, HAROLD WINFRED, dentist; b. Roanoke Rapids, NC, Apr. 28, 1933; s. James Robert and Elma (Smith) T.; m. Barbara Ann Edmonds, Aug. 2, 1958 (div. Apr. 1974); children: Harold Winfred, Leigh Ann.; m. Frances Jean Winstead, July 1983. BS in Dentistry, U. N.C., 1955, D.D.S., 1958. Individual practice dentistry, Charlotte, NC, 1961—; head, dept. dental prosthetics Meml. Hosp., 1964-66; lectr. dental subjects.; pres., gen. mgr. WCTU-TV, Charlotte Telecasters, Inc., 1967-69, WATU-TV, Augusta, Ga., Augusta Telecasters, Inc., 1968-69, Television Presentations, Inc., Charlotte, 1967-69; partner Twisdale and Steel Assos., Charlotte, 1965-70; propr. Twisdale Enterprises, Charlotte, 1965-70. Pres. Memphis Telecasters, Inc., 1966-76, Va. Telecasters, Inc., Richmond, 1966—, Durham-Raleigh Telecasters, Inc., Durham, N.C., 1966-70, Gentil Elite, Inc., 1979— Transp. chmn. Miss N.C. Pageant, 1965; v.p. N.C. Jaycees, 1963-64; Trustee Boys Home, Lake Waccomaw, N.C., 1966-67. Served to capt. USAF, 1958-60. Recipient various awards Charlotte Jaycees, 1962-66. Fellow Acad. Dentistry Internat.; mem. ADA, N.C. Dental Found., N.C. Dental Soc., Charlotte Dental Soc. (chmn. various coms. 1961—), Am. Analgesia Soc., Internat. Analgesic Soc. (dir. 1980 85), N.C. Dental Soc. Anesthesiology (v.p. 1983-84), Charlotte Analgesia Study Club (co founder 1970), N.C. 2d Dist. Dental Soc., Metrolina Dental Soc. (founder 1994, pres. 1994-95), U. N.C. Dental Alumni Assn., Southeastern Analgesia Soc. (founder 1972, pres. 1972-74), Lambda Chi Alpha, Delta Sigma Delta. Republican. Methodist. Office: 3104 Weddington Rd Ste 200 Matthews NC 28105 Home Phone: 704-841-3605; Office Phone: 704-849-2595. Personal E-mail: twisdds@aol.com.

TWU, NAE-FANG, gynecologist; b. Taiwan, Nov. 9, 1956; MD, Nat. Def. Med. Ctr., 1991; MBA, Nat. Chengchi U., 2007. Attending physician Taipei Vets. Gen. Hosp., 1992—. Mem.: Soc. Gynecol. Oncologist (Taiwan). Office: Dept Obstetrics-Gynecology Taipei Veterans Gen Hosp 201 SE Taipei 112 Taiwan Office Fax: 886-2-77232788. Business E-Mail: nftwu@vghtpe.gov.tw.

TYAGI, MANOJ GYANCHANDRA, pharmacologist; b. Delhi, India, Dec. 24, 1962; s. Gyanchandra Ramachandra and Rajanibala Raghuraj Tyagi; m. Nidhi Tyagi, May 15, 1991; 1 child, Vishakha. BSc in Biochemistry, Gujarat U., Ahmedabad, 1982; MSc in Medicine, BJ Med. Coll., Ahmedabad, 1986; PhD, Madras U., 1991. Demonstrator GSVM Meml. Med. Coll., Kanpur, 1986-87; doctoral rsch. fellow Christian Med. Coll., Vellore, 1987-90; sci. officer JIPMER, Pondicherry, 1991-92; postdoctoral fellow Med. Coll. Ga., Augusta, U. Tenn., Memphis, U. Ill., Chgo., 1992—96; sr. resident Inst. Human Behavior and Allied Scis., Delhi, 1997-98; reader Christian Med. Coll., Vellore, 1998—, sr. lectr., 2001—. Rsch. worker Nat. U. Singapore, 1989; rsch. assoc. Indian Inst. Sci., Bangalore, 1992; sci. referee Indian Jour. Exptl. Biology, Vellore, 1998—. Contbr. articles to profl. jours. Mem. Dr. P.C. Dandiya Endowment Trust, 1998—. Wellcome Trust Travel grantee, 2000, U. Tenn.-Memphis Neurosci. Ctr. grantee, 1995. Mem. Indian Soc. Hypertension (joint sec.), Indian Acad. Neurosci. (life), Indian Pharmacol. Soc. (life). Achievements include research in neuroendocrinology; mechanism of action of vasopressin; physiological role of vasopressin; a novel neurohumoral circuitry "The Pulmonary-Renal Cascade"; Aquaporin-1 and Caveolins in hemostasis; immunoglobulins modulate triple helix DNA formation. Avocations: international affairs, sports. Home: 514/A1 Palm Rd Vellore 632 002 India Office: Fleming Rsch Inst/Pharmacol Christian Med Coll Vellore 632 002 India Office Phone: 0416-228-4237. Office Fax: 0416 262788. Personal E-mail: tyagi243@yahoo.co.in, tyagi239@yahoo.co.in. Business E-Mail: tyagi237@indiatimes.com.

TYAN, YU-CHANG, medical educator; b. Taiwan, Dec. 12, 1973; PhD, Chung Yuan Christian U., 2002. Asst. prof., dept. med. imaging and radiol. scis. Kaohsiung Med. U., 2007—10, assoc. prof. dept. med. imaging & radiol. scis., 2010—. Office: 100 Shi-Chuan 1st Rd Kaohsiung 807 Taiwan Personal E-mail: yc_tyan@hotmail.com.

TYERS, ANTHONY GORDON, ophthalmologist, surgeon, consultant; s. Arthur and Marion Joan Tyers; m. Renee Constance de Waard, Oct. 7, 1983; children: Jonathan Richard, Richard Christopher, Johanna Rachel, Rebecca Louise. MB, Charing Cross Med. Sch., London, 1970. Lic. gen. surgery Royal Coll. Surgeons Eng., 1975, ophthalmologist Royal Coll. Surgeons Edinburgh, 1980, Royal Coll. Ophthalmologists, London, 1989. Cons. ophthalmologist, ophthalmic plastic surgeon Salisbury Health Care Found. Trust, England, 1986—; cons. ophthalmic surgeon New Hall Hosp., Salisbury, 1986—; cons. ophthalmic plastic surgeon Moorfields Eye Hosp., London, 1997—99. Vis. cons. ophthalmic plastic surgeon St. John Eye Hosp., Jerusalem, 1995—. Author: (surgical textbook) Colour Atlas of Ophthalmic Plastic Surgery, 3rd edit., 2007; contbr. chapters to books. Vol. vis. cons. ophthalmic plastic surgeon St. John Eye Hosp., Jerusalem, 1995—. Mem.: European Soc. Ophthalmic Plastic and Reconstructive Surgeons (trustee 1990—, pres. 2009—), Brit. Assn. Aesthetic Plastic Surgeons, Brit. Oculo-Plastic Surgery Soc. (pres. 2005—07). Office: New Hall Hosp Salisbury SP54EY England also: Salisbury Health Care Found Trust Odstock Road SP2 8BJ Salisbury England Office Fax: 44-1722-425155. Business E-Mail: anthony.tyers@salisbury.nhs.uk.

TYKHOMYROV, ARTEM ALEXANDROVICH, biochemist; b. Dnieprodzerzhinsk, Dniepropetrovsk, Ukraine, Oct. 5, 1977; PhD in Biochemistry, Dniepropetrovsk Nat. U., 1999. Asst. prof. Dniepropetrovsk Nat. U., 2000—10; sr. rschr. Palladin Inst. Biochemistry NAS Ukraine, 2011—. Mem.: Ukrainian Physiol. Soc., Fedn. European Biochemical Socs. Avocations: travel, music, classical music, football, ping pong/table tennis. Office: Palladin Inst Biochemistry Dept Neurochemistry Leontovicha 9 Kyiv 01601 Ukraine

TYKOCINSKI, MARK L., dean, educator, molecular immunologist, gene therapist; b. Lakewood, NJ, Nov. 26, 1952; married, 1978; 4 children. BA, Yale U., 1974; MD, N.Y. U., 1978. Resident in internal medicine Columbia-Presbyn. Med. Ctr., 1978-79; resident in anatomy pathology NYU Med. Ctr., 1979-81; med. staff fellow immunogenetics Nat. Inst. Allergy & Infectious Diseases/NIH, 1981-83; prof. pathology Sch. Medicine Case Western Reserve U., 1973-98; staff physician U. Hosps., Cleve., 1983-98; Simon Flexner prof., chair dept. pathology and lab. medicine U. Pa., 1998—2008; Anthony and Gertrude DePalma prof., dean Jefferson Med. Coll. Thomas Jefferson U., Phila., 2008—. Recipient Warner-Lambert/Parke-Davis award Am. Soc. for Investigative Pathology, 1995. Mem. Am. Assn. Pathologists, Am. Assn. Cancer Rsch. Achievements include research in genetically engring. proteins for immunotherapy protein factors. Office: Thomas Jefferson University Jefferson Med Coll 1025 Walnut St College Rm 100 Philadelphia PA 19107 Office Phone: 215-955-1628. *

TYLER, DAVID EARL, veterinary medical educator; b. Carlisle, Iowa, July 12, 1928; s. Guy Earl and Beatrice Virginia (Slack) T.; m. Alice LaVon Smith, Sept. 6, 1952; children: John William, Anne Elizabeth. BS, Iowa State U., 1953, D.V.M., 1957, PhD, 1963; MS, Purdue U., 1960. Instr. dept. vet. sci. Purdue U., 1957-60; asst. prof. dept. pathology Coll. Vet. Medicine, Iowa State U., 1960-63, asso. prof., 1963-66; prof., head dept. pathology and parasitology Coll. Vet. Medicine, U. Ga., 1966-71, head dept. pathology, 1971-79, prof., 1971-91, prof. emeritus, 1991—; ret., 1991. Co-founder internat. vet. pathology slide bank, 1984, co-dir., 1984-98; apptd. discussant Charles L. Davis Found. for Advancement Vet. Pathology, 1977-91. Cub Scout master, 1967-69, scout com. chmn., 1970-72; elder Disciples of Christ Ch., 1968—, chmn. ch. bd., 1973-74, 92-94; mem. citizens com. to County Bd. Edn., 1968-70; bd. dirs. Christian Coll., Ga., 1974-77. With AUS, 1946-48. Recipient Borden award Gail Borden Co., 1956, Norden Disting. Teaching award Norden Labs., 1964, 69, 81, 85, 91, Prof. of Yr. award Coll. Vet. Medicine, Iowa State U., 1965, Outstanding Prof. award Coll. Vet. Medicine, U. Ga., 1970, 76, 80-81, 83, 86, 87-88, 90, Joshia Meigs Teaching award, 1985, Stange award Coll. Vet. Med., Iowa State U., 1987, Phi Zeta Teaching award, 1985, N.Am. Outstanding Tchr. award, 1991, Omicron Delta Kappa Outstanding Prof. award U. Ga., 1981, Harold W. Casey award C.L. Davis Found., 1995. Mem. AVMA, Farm House, Am. Coll. Vet. Pathologists (mem. council 1975-77, exam. com. 1982-85), Am. Assn. Vet. Med. Colls. (chmn. com. teaching-learning materials 1975-77), Nat. Program for Instructional Devel. in Vet. Pathology (adv. com. 1976-77), Aghon, Sigma Xi, Phi Eta Sigma, Alpha Zeta, Gamma Sigma Delta, Phi Kappa Phi, Phi Zeta (chpt. sec.-treas. 1982-84), Omega Tau Sigma. Home: 160 Sunny Brook Dr Athens GA 30605-3348

TYLER, DONALD EARL, retired urologist; b. Ontario, Oreg., Oct. 3, 1926; s. Charles Maurice and Iva (Hess) Tyler; 1 child, Paul Donald. MD, U. Oreg., 1950; JD, U. Denver, 1967. Diplomate Am. Bd. Urology, Am. Coll. Legal Medicine. Fellow in gen. surgery, urology Mayo Found., Rochester, Minn., 1952, 55-58; clin. instr. urology U. Utah Med. Sch., Salt Lake City, 1959-64. Author: A New and Simple Theory of Gravity, 1970, Originations of Life from Volcanoes and Petroleum, 1983, Earliest Man of Am. in Oreg., USA: With Photographs of Paleolithic Artifacts, 1986, Crooked Judges, Lawyers and Ins. Companies, 1990, The Other Guy's Sperm: The Cause of Cancer and Other Diseases, 1994, Homo Americanus: An Original American Species, 1998, American Paleolithic: Boat Building Eight Million Years Ago, 1999, Foreign Sperm: The cause of sexually transmitted diseases, cancers, autoimmune diseases, Alzheimer's, Schizophrenia, and Kuru, 2004, Paleolithic Artifacts of American Early Man, 2007. Lt. USNR, 1944—45, lt. USNR, 1952—54, Korea. Mem.: Phi Eta Sigma, Alpha Omega Alpha. Avocations: archaeology, anthropology, geology, skiing, swimming. Home: 1092 SW 2d Ave Ontario OR 97914-2121 Personal E-mail: detyler@cabbone.net.

TYLER, GAIL MADELEINE, nurse; b. Dhahran, Saudi Arabia, Nov. 21, 1953; (parents Am. citizens); d. Louis Rogers and Nona Jean (Henderson) T.; m. Alan J. Moore, Sept. 29, 1990; 1 child, Sean James. AS, Front Range C.C., Westminster, Colo., 1979; BSN, U. Wyo., 1989. RN, Colo. Ward sec. Valley View Hosp., Thornton, Colo., 1975-79; nurse Scott and White Hosp., Temple, Tex., 1979-83, Meml. Hosp. Laramie County, Cheyenne, Who., 1983-89; dir. DePaul Home Health, 1989-91; field staff nurse Poudre Valley Hosp. Home Care/Poudre Care Connection, 1991-98, Rehab. and Vis. Nurses Assn., Fort Collins, Colo., 1999—2003; resource pool nurse Poudre Valley Hosp., Fort Collins, Colo., 2003—; clin. scholar Front Range CC, Larimer Campus, Ft. Collins, Colo., 2011—. Parish nurse Rocky Mountain Parish Health Ministry Orgn., pres., 2004—05, past. pres., 2005—06. Avocations: doll collecting, sewing, reading, travel. Office: Poudre Valley Hosp 1024 S Lemay Ave Fort Collins CO 80524

TYLER, H. RICHARD, physician; b. Bklyn., Oct. 16, 1927; s. Max M. and Beatrice F. T.; m. Joyce Colby, June 17, 1951; children: Kenneth, Karen, Douglas, Lori. AB, Syracuse U., 1947; BS in Medicine, Washington U., 1951, MD, 1951; MA (hon.), Harvard U., 1989. Diplomate Am. Bd. Neurology and Psychiatry. Intern Peter Bent Brigham Hosp., Boston, 1951-52; resident in neurology Boston City Hosp., 1952-54; public health fellow Neurol. Inst., Queen's Sq., London, Salpêtriére, Paris, 1954-55; asst. in pediatrics and neurology Johns Hopkins Hosp., Balt., 1955-56; neurologist Peter Bent Brigham Hosp., Boston, 1956-74; asst. in neurology Harvard Med. Sch., Boston, 1956-59, assoc. in neurology, 1959-61, from instr. to prof., 1961—98, prof. emeritus, 1998—. Sr. physician Brigham and Women's Hosp., Boston, 1974—, dir. neurol. svc., 1979-88. Co-editor: Current Neurology I and II, 1979, 80; mem. editorial bd.: Jour.

Neurology, 1979-84, Classics on Neurology and Neurosurgery Libr., 1983; contbr. articles to profl. jours. Trustee Brookline Pub. Libr., 1970-2001, chmn. bd. trustees, 1985-86, 90-91. Served with U.S. Army, 1946-47. Mem. Am. Neurol. Assn.(hon.), Am. Acad. Neurology (hon.), Mass. Med. Soc. Office: 1 Brookline Pl Ste 503 Brookline MA 02445-7224 Office Phone: 617-735-8720. Personal E-mail: Htyler1798@aol.com.

TYLER, JOHN DUKE, psychologist, educator; b. Nashville, Nov. 30, 1943; s. John Duke and Eleanora (Hammond) Tyler; m. Shirley Kay Montgomery; 1 child, Wade McLeod. BA, Vanderbilt U., 1965; PhD, U. Tex., Austin, 1970. Bd. cert. diplomate Am. Bd. Profl. Psychology. Prof. psychology U. ND, Grand Forks, 1970—2006; dir. Family Inst., Grand Forks, 1980—2006; prof. emeritus psychology, 2006—. Dir., Psychol. Svcs. Ctr. U. ND, Grand Forks, 1979—98. Contbr. articles to profl. jours. Fellow: Acad. Clin. Psychology; mem.: APA, N.D. Psychol. Assn. (pres. 1982—83).

TYLER, ROBERT R., psychologist, consultant; s. Roy E. and Betty J. Tyler; m. Carol J. Albrecht, Mar. 8, 1968; children: Robert R. Tyler, Jr., M. Suzanne McGann. BS in Bus., Chaminade Coll., 1974; MS in Safety, U. So. Calif., 1981; PhD in Psychology, U. Ctrl. Fla., 1997. Cert. comml. pilot FAA, 1970, modeling and simulation profl. Nat. Tng. Systems Assn., Arlington, VA, 2002. Commd. 2d lt. USMC, 1967, advanced through grades to col., 1993; exec. officer, ops. officer Marine Wing Support Group 17, Marine Corps Base Camp Butler, Okinawa, Japan, 1986—87; commdg. officer Marine Aerial Refueling Transport Tng. Squadron 253, Marine Corps Air Station, Cherry Point, NC, 1987—89; dir. aviation safety Hdqs., USMC, Washington, 1990—93; dir. marine corps programs Naval Tng. Systems Ctr., Orlando, 1993—97; ret. USMC, 1997; chief adminstr., nat. aviation & transp. ctr. Dowling Coll., Oakdale, Long Island, NY, 1998—98; human factors advisor to the faa Advancia Corp., Washington, 1998—99; chief scientist Crown Consulting, Inc., 1999—2001; prin. human factors advisor Trios Associates, 2001—02; divsn. dir., simulation tech. svcs. MTS Technologies, Arlington, Va., 2002—05; rsch. scientist Evidence Based Rsch., Inc., Vienna, Va., 2005—07; prin. investigator simulation VisiTech, Ltd., 2007—. Co-chmn. Internat. / Industry Tng. Simulation and Edn. Conf., Orlando, 1993—97; assoc. editor Marine Corps Gazette, Marine Corps Base Quantico, Va., 1990—93; adj. prof. Embry-Riddle Aero. U., Andrews AFB, 1999—, Dept. Psychology Richland CC, Decatur, Ill., 2010—. Co-pres. Potomac H.S. Crew Booster Club, Dumfries, Va., 1984—86; congl. pres. Holy Trinity Luth. Ch., Falls Church, 2000—02, St. Timothy Luth. Ch., Havelock, NC, 1998—99, Emmanuel Luth. Ch., Va., 2006—08. Decorated 32 Strike Flight Air Medals, Meritorious Svc. medal,, Legion of Merit,. Mem.: APA, Marine Corps Aviation Assn., Human Factors and Ergonomic Soc., Aircraft Owners and Pilots Assn., Phi Kappa Phi. Office: VisiTech 500 Montgomery St Ste 400 Alexandria VA 22314 Home: 324 Greenway Ln Decatur IL 62521 Personal E-mail: robttyler@msn.com. Business E-Mail: tyler@visitech.com.

TYVOLD, STIG SVERRE, anesthesiologist; Cand med, U. Oslo, 1998; PhD student, Norwegian U. Sci. and Tech., 2008—. Cert. in anestesiology Den Norske Legeforening, 2007. Head, anesthesia Aleris Hosp. and Med. Ctr., Trondheim, Norway, 2008—. Mem.: Den norske legeforening. Achievements include research in bronchial microdialysis.

TZIMA, NATALIA, physician, director; b. Thessaloniki, Greece, Feb. 11, 1973; MSc, U. Athens, MD, 1996; PhD, Harokopeio U., 2009. Physician NHS Greece, 1996—2004; internist Euroclinic, 2003—04, Med. Unit Hellenic Parliament, 2004—09, asst. dir., 2009—10, dir., 2010—. Tchg. and rsch. staff Harokopeio U., Dept. Dit and Nutrition, Course Pathophysiology, 2003—06; tchr. homeopathy Hellenic Assn. Homeo. Med. Cooperation, 2005—. Recipient Best Paper award, Hellenic Homeo. Assn., 2009. Mem.: European Com. Homeopathy, Hellenic Soc. Atherosclerosis. Avocations: theater, philosophy. Home: Aktaiou 3 Str Athens Attica 11851 Greece Personal E-mail: ntzima@parliament.gr.

TZIMAS, NICHOLAS ACHILLES, orthopedic surgeon, educator; b. Greece, Apr. 18, 1928; arrived in U.S.A., 1955, naturalized, 1960. s. Archilles Nicholas and Evanthia B. (Exarchou) T.; m. Helen J. (Papastylopoulos), Apr. 22, 1958; children: Yvonne and Christina. MD, U. Athens, Greece, 1952. Intern St. Mary's Hosp., Hoboken, NJ, 1955—86; resident in gen. surgery Misericordia Hosp., NYC; resident in orthopedic surgery Bellevue Hosp., NYC, 1957—60; instr. orthopedic surgery N.Y. U. Sch. Medicine, 1961—63, asst. clin. prof., 1963—65, asso. clin. prof., 1965—71, clin. prof., 1971—. Staff Univ. and Bellevue Hosp.; chief children's orthopedics, 1966; orthopedic cons. Inst. Rehab. Medicine, NYU, 1966, St. Agnes Hosp., White Plains, NY, 1972; advisory com. Bur. Handicapped Children, NYC, 1975; spl. invitations for tchg., Osaka, Japan, 1970, Jerusalem, 1974, São Paolo, Brazil, 1976, Taranto, Italy, 1977, Bari, Italy, 1978, Barquisimeto, Venezuela, 1979, Bogotá, Colombia, 1983, Buenos Aires, Argentina, 1983. Author of articles on spina bifida child mgmt. Served with M.C. Greek Army, 1952-55. Named Ofcl. Knight of Italian Republic, 1979 Fellow Am., Internat. Coll. Surgeons; mem. N.Y. Acad. Medicine, N.Y. State, N.Y. County Med. Soc., Am. Acad. Orthopedic Surgeons, Am. Congress Rehab. Medicine, Am. Acad. Cerebral Palsy. Mem. Greek Orthodox Ch.; Archon of the Ecumenical Patriarchate of Constantinople. Home: 33 Edgewood St Tenafly NJ 07670-2909 Office: 530 1st Ave New York NY 10016-6402 Office Phone: 212-263-7278. Personal E-mail: ntzimas@aol.com. Business E-Mail: nicholasotzimas@med.nyu.edu.

TZVETKOV, NIKOLAY TZVETANOV, hematologist, director; b. Rouse, Bulgaria, Apr. 29, 1955; s. Tzvetan Kolev Tzvetkov and Zdravka Kirilova Boianova; m. Diana Ivanova Pavlova, Aug. 22, 1982; children: Anna Nikolaeva Tzvetkova, Alexander Nikolaev. Magister of medicine, Med. U., Pleven Bulgaria, 1981; PhD, Med. U., 2001. Diploma internal diseases Ministry of Health Bulgaria, 1986, diploma clinical hematology Ministry of Health Bulgaria, 1988. Asst. Clinic Hematology U. Hosp., Pleven, 1982—2006, head clinic hematology, 2006—, dir. diagnostic and treatment of out-patients dept., 2006—; head dept. internal diseases Med. U., 2006—, Assoc. prof., 2005. Home: Jk Drujba bl 333 vh B apart 8 Pleven 5806 Bulgaria Office: Univ Hosp Clinic Hematology Georgi Kochev 8A Pleven 5800 Bulgaria Office Fax: +359064886507. Personal E-mail: tzvetkovn@yahoo.com.

UAHWATANASAKUL, YONG, physician; b. Bangkok, June 24, 1937; s. U. Chu Liang and Tan Liang Enah; m. Jeamjit (Peck-Chuau Leow) Sethbhakdi, June 8, 1963; children: Suchart Kenneth, Kesara, Kuntida, Kalaya. BA in Chemistry cum laude, Harvard Coll., 1959; MD, Harvard U., 1963. Diplomate Am. Bd. Internal Medicine, Thai Bd. of Internal Medicine, Thai Bd. Endocrinology. Intern Newton-Wellesley Hosp., Newton Lower Falls, Mass., 1963-64; asst. resident New England Deaconess Hosp., Boston, 1964-66; fellow Josline Clinic, Boston, 1965-66; clin. fellow in endocrinology Mass. Gen. Hosp., Boston, 1966-67; rsch. fellow in medicine Harvard Med. Sch., Boston, 1966-67; lectr. in medicine Chulalongkorn U., Bangkok, Thailand, 1968-97. Chmn., bd. dirs. CMB Packaging, Thailand, 1984-94; vice chmn., bd. dirs. Bangkok Met. Bank, 1974-97; chmn., exec. com. Hwa Chiew Gen. Hosp., Bangkok, 1981-92. Author: (with others) World Book of Diabetes in Practice, 1982, Diabetes Melitus in General Medicine, 1983. Bd. trustees Pok Tek Tung Found., Bangkok, 1981—, U. Chu Liang Found., Bangkok, 1974-99, Chulalongkorn Med. Sch. Found., Bangkok, 1980-84. Fellow Royal Coll. of Physicians (Thailand); mem. Am. Diabetes Assn., The Royal Thai Sports Club (life), Thai Mgmt. Assn. (life), Harvard Club of Thailand (life mem.). Avocation: photography. Office: Medi-Clinic Regent Ho 5 Fl 183 Rajdamri Rd Bangkok 10330 Thailand Home: Soi Srinakorn 204 10120 Bangkok Bangkok Thailand Office Phone: (662) 254-8793, 02-2548792-4. Personal E-mail: yong_uah@yahoo.com.

UBA, ALAN KEITH, pediatrician, educator; b. Oct. 23, 1961; MD, U. Calif., San Francisco, 1988. Cert. in pediat. Am. Bd. Med. Specialties. Intern in pediat. Children's Hosp. at LA, resident in pediat.; assoc. clinical prof. pediat. U. Calif. San Francisco, 1992—. Recipient Chief Residents' Commendation, U. Calif. San Francisco Dept. Pediat., 1992—93, Faculty Tchg. award, 1993; named to Top Docs - the Top 425 Doctors in the Bay Area, San Francisco Mag., 1999, 2005. Office: Dept Pediat U Calif San Francisco Med Sch 505 Parnassus Ave San Francisco CA 94143 Office Phone: 415-353-2790. Office Fax: 415-353-2000, 415-353-2680. Business E-Mail: ubaa@peds.ucsf.edu.

UBBIALI, ALESSANDRO, clinical psychologist, researcher; b. Genoa, Italy, July 30, 1973; Degree in Psychology, Vita-Salute San Raffaele U., Milan, 2001, PhD in Clin. Psychology, 2006. Registered pychotherapist Italian Order Psychologist, 2006. Rschr. Dept. Clin. Neurosciences H San Raffaele Turro, Milan, 2001—08, clin. psychologist, 2006—; lectr. personality assessment methods Vita-Salute San Raffaele U., 2007—08. Rschr. Dept. Clin. Neurosciences - H San Raffaele Turro, Milan, 2001—. Promising Young Profls. scholarship, U. Milan, 2002. Mem.: Psyche-dendron Asn (founder mem. & vice pres.), Soc. Exploration Psychotherapy Integration, Internat. Soc. Study Personality Disorders, Soc. Psychotherapy Rsch. Office Fax: 390229533237. Business E-Mail: ubbiali.alessandro@psyche-dendron.eu.

UCCELLI, RAFFAELLA, biologist, researcher; b. Rome, Aug. 27, 1958; d. Alfredo Josè Uccelli and Maria Antonietta Taurino. Degree in Biol. Scis., U. Rome La Sapienza, 1982; MS. Cert. in multidisciplinary assessment of environmental risk limits Siena U. Summer Sch., 1988, postgrad. in European cmty. course, pollution and human health Kuopio U., 1992, internat. course in epidemiology Cath. U. Sacred Heart, Rome, 2007. Predoctoral fellow ENEA, Rome, 1980—82, project investigator, 1983—87, rschr., 1987—. Supr., instr. flow cytometry Italian Nat. Agy. New Techs., Energy and Environment, Rome, Lerici, 1983—85; mem., del. Italian Air Quality Nat. Group, Ministry Health, Rome, 1988—90; instr. athmospheric and noise pollution Pub. Instrn. Ministry, Rome and Civitavecchia, 1993—96; asst. to vice-dir. dept. evironment Italian Nat. Agy. New Techs., Energy and Environment, 1994—95; del. for definition of priority in epidemiol. and toxicological rsch. activities Italian Nat. Agy. New Techs., Energy and Environment-Italian Nat. Inst. Health, 1994—; asst. to dir., sect. urban environment and mobility Italian Nat. Agy. New Techs., Energy and Environment, 1996—99; instr. 7th issue course on environ. epidemiology Italian Nat. Inst. Health, Rome, 1996; instr. mortality, traffic and cigarette smoking course Italian Assn. Doctors Environment, Pontignano, Siena, Italy, 2001; del. coordination of epidemiol. and toxicological researches and tng. activities Italian Nat. Agy. New Techs., Energy and Environment-Italian Assn. Drs. Environment, Rome, Arezzo, 2001—; tchr. of environ. epidemiology in the course of prevention technics in the environment and in work places Tor Vergata U., Rome, 2007—09. Contbr. articles to profl. jours. Mem.: Chemistry, Biology & Physics Panel Nato Sci. (peace & security com. mem. 2008—), Italian Assn. Epidemiology (assoc.), Italian Group Cytometry (assoc.). Achievements include research in ecological, toxicological and epidemiological fields aimed to protect environment and human health. Avocations: travel, yoga, skiing, sailing. Office: ENEA Via Anguillarese 301 123 Rome RM Italy Office Phone: 0039 06 30486417. Business E-Mail: raffaella.uccelli@enea.it.

UCHI, MASAYUKI, physical therapist, researcher; b. Tokyo, May 10, 1963; s. Uchi Hiroshi and Uchi Ayako. Diploma in Rehab., Goto Coll. Med. Arts & Scis., Tokyo, 1986; BA in Liberal Arts, Hoso U., Tokyo, 1997; PhD in Med., Toho U., Tokyo, 2006. PT Nat. Bd. Cert., 1986, cert. specialist in cardio-respiratory phys. therapy Japanese Phys. Therapy Assn., 2006, specialist in phys. agy. phys. therapy 2006, specialist in fundamental phys. therapy 2006, specialist in bone & joint phys. therapy 2009. Phys. therapist, dept. orthop. surgery Toho U. Omori Hosp., Ota-ku, Tokyo, 1986—97, chief therapist, dept. rehab., 1997—2003, head therapist, dept. rehab., 2006—10, dir. dept. rehab., 2010—. Guest lectr. Saitama Med. Welfare Coll., Japan, 2001—06, Tokyo Met. U. Health Scis., 2002—06. Mem. editl. staff. Jour. Physical Therapy, editl. staff Jour. Japanese Physical Therapy Assn. Recipient Excellent Article award, Japanese Coll. Cardiology, 2006. Mem.: Japanese Acad. Health Scis., Japanese Laser Therapy Assn., Japanese Coll. Cardiology, Japanese Phys. Therapy Assn. Avocations: surfing, dance. Home: 513-1-210 Tsu Kamakura Kanagawa 248-0032 Japan Office: Toho Univ Omori Med Ctr 6-11-1 Omori-Nishi Tokyo Ota-ku Japan Business E-Mail: masayuki@med.toho-u.ac.jp.

UCHIDA, KAZUO, retired technologist, director; b. Kyoto, Kyoto-Fu, Japan, Oct. 31, 1938; s. Toshinosuke and Hana Uchida; m. Akiko Terao, Feb. 22, 1936; 1 child, Akio. Technologist, Kyoto U., Japan, 1961. Chief chemist Kobe Steel. Co Ltd. Hosp., Hyogo-Ken, Japan, 1961—72; head chemist Japan Med. Labs., Ibaraki, Osaka-Fu, 1972—84; dir. Kyoto Med. Sci. Lab., 1984—2008. Leader Kobe City Coop. Soc., 1990—2000. Recipient award, Ogata Tomio Granting Body, 1993, Katoh Katuya award, Nagoya Pub. Health Inst., 1995. Mem.: Japanese Electorophoresis Soc. (assoc.), Japan Soc. Clin. Chemistry (assoc.; coun. Tokyo chpt. 1978, coun. Osaka chpt. 1999), Japanese Soc. Lab. Medicine (assoc.), Japan Soc. Clin. Lab. Automation (assoc.), Japanese Assn. Med. Technologists (assoc.). Citizens. Buddhist. Achievements include patents in field. Avocations: travel, tennis, reading. Home: 102-30-4-3 Morikita-cho Higashinada-ku Hyogo Kobe 658-0001 Japan E-mail: kzuchida@kxa.biglobe.ne.jp.

UCHIDA, KENTARO, medical educator; b. Tokyo, May 9, 1981; PhD, Kitasato U., 2009. Asst. prof. Kitasato U., 2009—. Office: Minamiku Kitasato 1-15-1 Sagamihara Kanagawa 252-0374 Japan Business E-Mail: kuchida@med.kitasato-u.ac.jp.

UCHIN, ROBERT ALLEN, dean, endodontist; b. Phila., Apr. 19, 1933; s. Harry and Doris (Goodman) U.; m. Marlene Florence Neiman; children: Andrew, Richard, Carol. Student, Franklin and Marshall Coll., 1951-53; DDS, Temple U., 1957. Diplomate Am. Bd. Endodontics. Fellow research teaching. dept. endodontics Temple U., Phila., 1959-60, instr. Sch. of Dentistry, 1960-69; co-chmn. endodontic sect. Dade County (Fla.) Dental Research Clinic, 1961-75; founding v.p., chmn. Endodontic sect. Broward County (Fla.) Dental Research Clinic, 1974-79; clin. assoc. Sch. of Dentistry U. Fla., Gainsville, 1970; practice dentistry specializing in endodontics Ft. Lauderdale, Fla., 1960—2000; assoc. dean, dir. extramural programs Coll. Dental Medicine, Nova Southeastern U., Ft. Lauderdale, Fla., 1996—2000, dean, 2000—. Chmn. Endodontic sect. Atlantic Coast Research Clinic, 1971-75; vis. lectr. Emory U., 1965, U.N.C., 1970, 72, U. Wash., 1972, U. Pitts., 1974, U. Pa., 1973-89; cons. VA Hosp., Miami, 1968-86, Cen. Office, 1972-84, dir. endodontic residency, 1972-79; bd. dirs., founding chmn. Gold Coast Savs. and Loan Assn. of Fla., 1984-90, Commonwealth Savs. and Loan of Fla., Ft. Lauderdale, 1979-84; adv. dir. Landmark First Nat. Bank, Ft. Lauderdale, 1974-81; vice chmn. Fla. Dental Assn. Services, Inc. Assoc. editor Jour. Endodontics and Traumatology, 1981-89; contbr. numerous articles to profl. jours. Pres., Temple Emanu-El Reform Congregation, Ft. Lauderdale, 1967-69; trustee, Vanguard Sch., Haverford, Pa., 1971-77; bd. dirs., Vanguard Sch., Ft. Lauderdale, 1970-73, Performing Arts Found., Broward County, Fla., 1986-90. Served to capt. USAF, 1957-59. Fellow: Am. Assn. Endodontists (pres. 1976), Internat. Coll. of Dentists, Am. Coll. of Dentists; mem.: Broward County Dental Assn. (pres. 1982), Fla. Dental Assn. (past pres.), Am. Dental Assn. Holding Co. (past pres.), Fla. Assoc. of Endodontics, So. Endodontic Study Group, Am. Dental Assn., Rotary (pres. Ft. Lauderdale 1969—70). Republican. Jewish. Avocations: fly fishing, stamp collecting/philately, orchids. Office: Coll Dental Medicine Nova Southeastern U 3200 S Univ Dr Fort Lauderdale FL 33328 Office Phone: 954-262-7312. Office Fax: 954-262-1782. Business E-Mail: ruchin@nova.edu.

UCHINO, AKIRA, radiologist, educator; b. Fukuoka, Japan, May 28, 1952; s. Kuniharu and Hatsuyo (Shimizu) U.; m. Machiko Osada, Feb. 26, 1978; children: Akemi, Hiromi, Yoshimi. MD, Kyushu U., 1977, PhD, 1985. Cert. Japanese Bd. Radiology. Resident Kyushu U. Hosp., Fukuoka, Japan, 1977-80, asst. prof., 1983-84, lectr., 1991-92; staff Kyushu Kosei-Nenkin Hosp., Kitakyushu, Japan, 1981-82, chief, 1993-94, Kyushu Rosai Hosp., Kitakyushu, 1985-90; assoc. prof., vice chair dept. radiology Saga (Japan) Med. Sch., 1994—2007; prof. Dept. Diagnostic Radiology Saitama Med. U., 2007—. Mem. Japanese Neuroradiol. Soc. (councilor), Soc. Japanese Interventional Radiology (councilor), Japan Radiol. Soc., Soc. Japanese Magnetic Resonance in Medicine (councilor, editl. bd. mem.), European Soc. Neuroradiology, Am. Soc. Neuroradiology. Office: Saitama Med University International Med Ctr Dept Diagnostic Radiology 1397-1 Yamane Hidaka Saitama 350-1298 Japan Business E-Mail: auchino@saitama-med.ac.jp.

UCHINO, MAKOTO, neurologist, researcher; b. Kumamoto, Japan, Oct. 13, 1945; d. Minoru and Yukiko Uchino; m. Fumiko Matsumoto Uchino, Apr. 16, 1972; children: Katsuhisa, Yohsuke, Yuko. MD, Kumamoto U., 1970, PhD, 1978. Resident Kumamoto U. Hosp., 1970—72; rsch. fellow W.Va. U., Morgantown, 1979—80; asst. prof. Kumamoto U. Sch. Medicine, Japan, 1982—88, assoc. prof., 1993—95, prof. dept. neurology, 1995—. Cons. neurologist Bd. Cert. Minamata Disease, Kumamoto, 1983—. Recipient Meritorious Svc. medal on preservation of the environment, Environment Ministry, 2000. Mem.: Am. Assn. Electrodiagnostic Medicine (overseas mem.), Japanese Soc. Neurol. Therapy (bd. trustees), Japanese Soc. Neurology (bd. trustees). Avocations: Karate, walking, swimming, composing haiku. Office: Kumamoto U Med Sch Dept Neurology Honjo 1-1-1 Kumamoto 860-0811 Japan

UCHIYAMA, NACHIKO, oncologist; b. Mie, Japan, Oct. 28, 1967; MD, Nippon Med. Sch., 1992. Head staff Nat. Cancer Ctr., Tokyo, 2007—. Mem.: JRS, RSNA. Office: 5-1-1 Tsukiji Chuo-Ku Tokyo 1040045 Japan Business E-Mail: nuchiyam@ncc.go.jp.

UDELL, IRA, ophthalmologist, educator; BS, U. Pitts.; MD, Tulane U. Internship Long Island Jewish Med. Ctr., resident; fellow Harvard Med. Sch.; chief divsn. of corneal and external diseases LIJ Med. Ctr., 1981, chmn. ophthalmology; vice chmn. North Shore Univ. Hosp., chmn. ophthalmology, 1997—2004; prof. ophthalmology Albert Einstein Coll. of Medicine, 1996. State counselor NY Am. Acad. of Ophthalmology; dir. Contact Lens Assn. of Ophthalmology; exec. dir. NY State Ophthalmology Soc. Achievements include research in corneal transplantation; DSAEK; ocular infections; ocular surface disorders. Office: Long Island Jewish Medical Center 270-05 76th Ave New Hyde Park NY 11040 Office Phone: 718-470-7000, 516-470-7000.

UDELSON, JAMES ERIC, cardiologist, educator; b. Dec. 16, 1955; MD, NY Med. Coll., 1981. Cert. Internal Medicine, 1984, Cardiovascular Disease, 1989. Resident Newton-Wellesley Hosp., Mass., 1981—84; fellowship cardiology Nat. Heart Lung and Blood Inst., NIH, Bethesda, Md., 1985—87; assoc. chief Tufts-New England Med. Ctr., Boston, 1989, assoc. chief Divsn. Cardiology, dir. nuclear cardiology, co-dir. Heart Failure Ctr. and Hypertrophic Cardiomyopathy Ctr., dir. Cardiac Imaging Core Lab. Assoc. prof. Tufts U. Sch. Medicine, Boston, 1989—. Assoc. editor Circulation, mem. editl. bd., guest editor Jour. Am. Coll. Cardiology. Mem.: Am. Coll. Cardiology, Am. Soc. Nuclear Cardiology (past pres.). Office: Tufts Med Ctr 800 Washington St Boston MA 02111 Office Phone: 617-636-8066.

UDEY, MARK C., dermatologist, researcher; B in chemistry, U. Wis., Madison; MD, PhD, Washington U., St. Louis. Med. intern Barnes Hosp., St. Louis, dermatology resident; faculty mem. in dermatology Wash. U., St. Louis; chief Dermatology Br., sr. investigator Ctr. Cancer Rsch., Nat. Cancer Inst., NIH, Bethesda, Md., dep. dir. Office: Dermatology Br Ctr Cancer Rsch 10 Center Dr Bldg 10 Rm 12N238 Bethesda MD 20892-1908 Office Phone: 301-496-1741. Office Fax: 301-496-5370. E-mail: udey@helix.nih.gov. *

UDOFF, ERIC JOEL, diagnostic radiologist; b. Balt., Oct. 8, 1948; s. Melvin Jerome and Esther (Fisher) U.; m. Ronni Ann Chapin, June 7, 1980; children: Brian Evan, Jonathan Andrew. AB, Washington U., 1969; MD, U. Rochester, 1973. Intern, resident in diagnostic radiology U. Chgo., 1973-77; instr. in cardiovasc. radiology Johns Hopkins U., Balt., 1977-79; radiologist Sinai Hosp., Balt., 1979-86, Mt. Sinai Med. Ctr., Milw., 1986-88, Sinai Hosp., Balt., 1988-90; asst. prof. radiology Johns Hopkins U. Hosp., 1990-91; radiologist North Fulton Regional Hosp., Roswell, Ga., 1991-97; instr. thoracoabdominal imaging U. Va., 1997-98, Radiologist, Diagnostic Imaging Specialists, Atlanta, 1998—. Mem. AMA, Am. Roentgen Ray Soc., Am. Coll. Radiology, Radiol. Soc. N.Am., Ga. Radiol. Soc., Phi Beta Kappa. Avocations: reading, tennis. Office: 6000 Lake Forrest Dr Ste 475 Atlanta GA 30328 Office Phone: 404-459-8440. Personal E-mail: ejurad@yahoo.com.

UDOU, TAKEZO, retired healthcare educator; b. Kumamoto, Japan, June 21, 1945; s. Kiyomatsu Udou; m. Sawako Hisazumi, Oct. 11, 1971; children: Iori, Yoshi, Toyoaki. PhD (hon.), Tottori U. Sch. Medicine, Japan, 1983. Cert. Japanese Coll. Infection Ctrl. Drs., 2000. Asst. assoc. prof. U. Occupl. and Environ. Health, Sch. Medicine, Kitakyushu, Fukuoka, Japan, 1979—93, prof. U. Occupl. and Environ. Health, Sch. Health Scis., Kitakyushu, 1996—2005, Higashi Chikushi Coll. Food and Nutrition, Kokura, Japan, 2006—. Dir.: American Review of Respiratory Disease. Mem.: Royal Soc. Tropical Medicine and Hygene, Am. Soc. Microbiology. Home: 2-2-11 Takasunishi Wakamatsu-Ku Kitakyushu Fukuoka 808-0145 Japan Office: Higashichikushi Coll Food and Nutr 5-1-1 Shimoitozu Kokurakita-Ku Kitakyushu Fukuoka 803-8511 Japan Office Fax: 81 93 561 9728. Business E-Mail: udou@hcc.ac.jp.

UDRISTIOIU, AURELIAN, physician, researcher; b. Valari, India, May 11, 1954; MD, U. din Craiova, 1983; Specialist in Lab. Medicine, U. Medicine, Bucharest, 1991. Specialist, lab. medicine, primary scientist physician Emergency County Hosp. Targu Jiu, 1998—, lab. dir., clin. labs., 1998—2011. Mem.: Biophysics Soc., SRML (Romania), NACB, AACC. Office: Progresului 18 Hosp Targu Jiu Targu Jiu Gorj 210218 Romania Office Fax: 40253210432. Personal E-mail: aurelianu2007@yahoo.com.

UDUPA, NAYANABHIRAMA, pharmaceutical science educator; b. Kinnigoli, Karnataka, India, July 15, 1953; s. Sri K. Anantha Padmanabha and Kamalakshi Udupa; m. Vijayalaxmi K., Feb. 12, 1979; children: Pavithra, Shravan Kumar. B in Pharm, Banaras Hindu U., India, 1974; PharmM, Banaras Hindu U., Varanasi, India, 1976, PhD, 1987. Product devel. scientist Indian Drugs and Pharms. Ltd., Rishikesh and Gurgaon, 1976-81; product devel. exec. Citadel Fine Pharms. Ltd., Madras, India, 1981-84; lectr. pharmaceutics Banaras Hindu U., Varanasi, India, 1984-87; reader in pharmacy Coll. Pharmacy K.M.C., Manipal, India, 1987-89, prof., 1989—, prin., 1997—. Convenor and organizer symposium and workshop on drug delivery, Manipal, 1991, 95, 96, 2000, 2001; prin. investigator rsch. projects on niosome encapsulated anticancer drugs CSIR, New Delhi, 1990, 95, controlled release preparations UGC, New Delhi, U. Saskatchewan (Can.), 1990—, new drug delivery systems, Dr. T.M.A. Pai Found., 1991-99, chief coord., Indian Pharmcological Congress, 2010; lectr. in field; editor Indian J. Comm. Pharm., Indian Jour. Hosp. Pharam. Author: (editor) Drug Discovery and Management, Concepts in Chrunopharmcology, Nanotechnology for Healthcare, Selected Topics in Industrial Pharmacy, 1990, Progress in Drug Delivery-Manipal Experience, 1995, Battle Against Cancer with Pharmaceutical Weapon, 1998, others; editor Pharmag Quarterly Rsch. Jour., 1989—; mem. editl. bd. Indian Jour. Pharm. Sci., Pharm. Today, Pharma Times, Indian Drugs, Indian Jour. Pharm. Edn.; contbr. over 400 rsch. papers, 100 reviews to internat. profl. jours. Joint sec. 42d Indian Pharm. Congress, Manipal, 1990. Recipient Best Paper awards, 1996, Dr. P.C. Dandiya Rsch. award 1996, Prin. of Yr. award Assn. Pharmacy Tchrs. India, 2001; Japanese Drug Delivery Soc. fellow, Kyoto, 1993, FIP fellow, The Netherlands, 1994, AICTE and Dr. T.M.A. Pai Found. fellow, New Delhi, 1995; rsch. grantee Dandiya Endowment Trust, 1997, numerous others, DST, DBT, ICMR, UGC, State Inc., New Delhi, name Pharma. Scientist Yr., IAPST, 2008, IPA Fellowship award, 2008. Mem. Indian Pharm. Assn. (pres. 1995—, sec. Manipal br. 1987-93), Indian Inst. Indsl. Engring., Indian Soc. Nano Sci. (founde, pres.) Office: Coll Pharmacy KMC Manipal Coll Pharm Scis Manipal Karnataka 576104 India also: Manipal Coll Pharm Scis Madhav Nagar Manipal Karnataka 576104 India Home: 4-237A Dasranthanarga Jayanilaya 576 104 Manipal India Home Phone: 91 0820 2572297; Office Phone: 91 0820 2922433, 91 820 2922482. Office Fax: 918202571998, 91 820 2570061. Business E-Mail: n.udupa@manipal.edu.

UEDA, HIROSHI, science educator, researcher; b. Tokyo, May 23, 1963; s. Satoshi and Reiko Ueda. BS, U. Tokyo, 1986, MS, PhD, 1991. Rsch. assoc. U. Tokyo, 1991—97, lectr., 1997—2000, assoc. prof. Kashiwa, Chiba, Japan, 2001—03, assoc. prof., dept. chem. biotech., 2003—; vis. rschr. Ctr. Protein Engring. Med. Rsch. Coun., Cambridge, England, 1998—2000; rschr. Presto, JST, Tokyo, 2004—07. Vis. rschr. Med. Rsch. Coun., Cambridge, Eng., 1998-2000, Presto Inst., 2004—; precursory rschr. for embryonic sci. and tech. Japan Sci. and Tech. Agy. Contbr. articles to profl. jours. Recipient Promotion award Chem. Engring. Soc., 1995, Rsch. award Chem. Egnring. Soc., 2002; Japanese Ramsay fellow Ramsay Meml. Fellowship Trust, 1997. Achievements include invention of open sandwich immunoassay; patents for various immunoassays; research in noncompetitive detection of various biomolecules, basic & applied aspects of bioluminescence. Avocations: bicycling, travel. Office Fax: 81-3-5841-7362.

UEDA, HIROSHI, medical educator; b. Osaka, Japan, Feb. 21, 1954; MSc, Kyoto U., 1976, PhD, 1981. Prof. Nagasaki U., 1996—. Recipient Encouragement prize, Soc. Japanese Pharm. Scis., 1981, Soc. Japanese Pharmacology, 1986. Office: 1-14 Bunkyo-machi Nagasaki 852 8521 Japan Office Fax: 81-95-819-2420. Business E-Mail: ueda@nagasaki-u.ac.jp.

UÉDA, KENJI, neuroscientist; b. Osaka, Japan, Dec. 1, 1952; BSc, U. Osaka, 1976, MSc, 1978; PhD, U. Kyoto, 1988. Rsch. scientist Basic Rsch. Labs, Toray Industry Inc., Kamakura, Kanagawa, Japan, 1981—85; rsch. fellow Nat. Inst. Genetics, Mishima, Shizuoka, Japan, 1985—87; vis. scholar, dept. neuroscis. U. Calif. Sch. Medicine, La Jolla, 1987—91, asst. rsch. neuroscientist, 1991—93; sr. rsch. scientist dept. molecular biology Tokyo Inst. Psychiatry, Setagaya, Tokyo, Japan, 1993—96; vis. rsch. prof. Tokyo Met. U. Sch. Sci., Hachioji, Tokyo, Japan, 1995—96; vis. rsch. scientist Tokyo Met. U., Sch.of Sci., 1996—99; sr. rsch. scientist dept. neurochemistry Tokyo Inst. Psychiatry, Setagaya, Tokyo, Japan, 1996—2001, sr. rsch. scientist dept. neural plasticity, 2001—05, sr. rsch. scientist divsn. psychobiology, 2005—11; vis. prof. Capital Med. U., Beijing, 2001—, co-dir. lab. for neurodegenerative diseases Xuanwu Hosp., 2001—; sci. advisor to dir. gen. Internat. Biog. Ctr., Cambridge, England, 2007—; vis. lectr. Hosei U., Sch. Engring., 2008—10; sr. rsch. scientist, dept. dementia rsch. and higher brain function Tokyo Inst. Med. Sci., Setagaya, 2011—. Recipient Universal award, Am. Biog. Inst. Achievements include discovery of human Alpha-Synuclein/NACP, the mutations of which cause Parkinson's disease and dementia with Lewy bodies. Office: Tokyo Inst Med Sci 2-1-6 Kamikitazawa Setagaya Tokyo 156-8506 Japan Personal E-mail: ueda-kj@igakuken.or.jp, kenueda121@gmail.com.

UEDA, TADASHI, medical research professor; b. Japan, Jan. 28, 1958; PhD, Kyushu U., 1988. Prof. Grad. Sch. Pharm. Scis. Kyushu U., 2003—. Office: 3-1-1 Maidashi Higashi Fukuoka 812-8582 Japan Office Fax: 81-92-642-6667. Business E-Mail: ueda@phar.kyushu-u.ac.jp.

UEDA, WASA, medical educator; b. Osaka, Japan, Oct. 26, 1943; s. Kasaburo and Fumiko (Fukuo) U.; m. Kazuko Akamatu, Mar. 3, 1972; children: Kennichi, Yasuko. Med. degree, Okayama U., Japan, 1969. Intern USAF Hosp., Tachikawa Tokyo, Japan, 1970-71, jr. staff Okayama Univ. Hosp., Japan, 1971-72, asst. prof., 1976-80; resident U. Vt., Burlington, 1972-74, asst. prof., 1974; dept. head Kochi Prefectural Hosp., Kochi, Japan, 1974-76; vis. prof. U. Iowa, Iowa City, 1980-81; assoc. prof. Kochi Med. Sch., 1981-2000, prof., 2000—09, dir. student health svc. unit, 2007—09, emeritus prof., instr. anesthesiology, 2009. Mem. Japan Soc. Anesthesiology, Am. Soc. Anesthesiologists. Avocations: tennis, mechanics, amateur radio. Office: Kochi Med Sch Nankoku Kochi 783-8505 Japan Business E-Mail: uedaw@kochi-u.ac.jp.

UEDA, YUTAKA, medical educator; b. Nara, Japan, July 16, 1970; MD, Osaka U. Med. Sch., 1996, PhD. Asst. prof. Osaka U. Grad. Sch. Medicine, 2002—. Home: 3-3-5-909 Shinsenri-Minamimachi Toyonaka Osaka 560-0084 Japan Personal E-mail: zvf03563@nifty.ne.jp.

UEHARA, TAKASHI, pharmacologist, educator; b. Tokyo, May 11, 1965; s. Masao and Shizuko Uehara; m. Motoko Omori, May 11, 1996; 1 child, Hikari. BA in Pharm. Scis., Hokkaido U., Sapporo, Japan, 1989, MS in Pharm. Scis., 1991, PhD in Pharm. Scis., 1995. Lic. pharm. Japan, 1993. Instr. Hokkaido U., 1994—2000, assoc. prof., 2000—02, 2004—10; rschr. Burnham Inst., La Jolla, Calif., 2002—04; prof. Okayama U., 2010—. Contbr. articles to profl. jours. Recipient award Young Scientists, Pharm. Soc. Japan, 2003, award Young Investigator, Japanese Soc. Neurochemistry, 2005. Mem.: Soc. Neurosci., NO Soc. Japan, Japanese Soc. Neurochemistry, Japanese Biochemical Soc., Japanese Pharmacological Soc., Pharm. Soc. Japan. Achievements include research in mechanism of nitric oxide-induced neuronal death via ER dysfunction. Office: Okayama University Dept Medicinal Pharmacology 1-1-1 Tsushima-Naka Okayama 700-8530 Japan Office Phone: 81-86-251-7939. Personal E-mail: takashi_uehara@mac.com. Business E-Mail: uehara@pharm.okayama-u.ac.jp.

UEHLEKE, HARTMUT, retired pharmacology and toxicology educator; b. Holzminden, Germany, Aug. 17, 1924; s. Rudolf and Paula Uehleke; m. Inge Patzke, Apr. 16, 1955; children: Bernhard, Marianne, Rainer. MD, U. Marburg, Germany, 1953; PhD, U. Munich, Germany, 1958. Rsch. asst. Max-Planck-Inst. Psychiatry, Munich, 1954-56, Max-Planck-Inst. Cellular Chemistry, Munich, 1957-58; sci. asst. Inst. Pharmacology U. Tübingen, 1958-62, lectr., 1962-68, prof., 1969-74; chief dir. toxicology Fed. German Health Office, Berlin, 1975-88. Editor Arch. Toxicol., 1966-75; mem. editl. bd. Toxicology, 1974-98, Xenobiotica, 1972-82, Res. Com. Chem. Path. Pharmacol, 1970-92, Eur.J. Drug Metab. Pharmacokin., 1976; contbr. more than 200 articles to profl. jours. Recipient E. Merck award E. Merck Darmstadt Germany, 1965, Golden Merit award Italian Soc. Toxicology, 1972, Svc. award U. Ghent, 1972; WHO cancer fellow, 1967-68. Mem. N.Y. Acad. Sci. Evangelical-Lutheran. Avocations: tennis, hiking, music, sailing. Home: Karwendelstr 13 12203 Berlin Germany

UEJIMA, TETSU, anesthesiologist, hospital administrator; b. Naha, Japan, Dec. 26, 1955; BS in Chemistry, U. Chgo., 1977; MD, U. Chgo., Pritzker Sch. Medicine, 1981. Dir., cardiac transplant anesthesia Children's Meml. Hosp., 1985—89, dir., anesthesia, Children's Meml. Splty. Ctr. Westchester, 1991—94, dir., liver-intestinal transplant anesthesia, 1997—, staff anesthesiologist, 1985—, med. dir., risk mgmt., 2005—. Instr. in anesthesia, dept. anesthesiology Northwestern U., 1985—89, asst. prof. anesthesiology, 1989—2008, assoc. prof. anesthesiology, Feinberg Sch. Medicine, 1989—; anesthesia patient safety editl. bd. mem. Am. Soc. Anesthesiologists, 2007—; mem., affiliate adv. coun. Smart Tots, 2011—. Mem.: Am. Soc. Healthcare Risk Mgmt., Am. Coll. Physician Execs., Soc. Pediat. Anesthesia, Internat. Anesthesia Rsch. Soc., Am. Soc. Anesthesiologists. Office: 2300 Children's Plz Chicago IL 60614 Office Fax: 773-880-3331. Business E-Mail: tuejima@childrensmemorial.org.

UEMATSU, FUMIYUKI, medical researcher; b. Odawara, Kanagawa, Japan, Oct. 1, 1962; s. Yoshihiro and Suwa Uematsu. MD, Tohoku U., 1988, PhD, 1992. Staff mem., dept. medicine Inst. Tb and Cancer, Tohoku U., Sendai, Miyagi, Japan, 1992—94; med. staff Miyagi Prefectural Semine Hosp., Semine, Japan, 1994—96; postdoctoral rschr., dept. tumor biology M.D. Anderson Cancer Ctr., U. Tex., Houston, 1996; vis. scientist Inst. Molecular Medicine, Irvine, Calif., 1996—97, Inst. Biosciences and Tech., Tex. A&M U., Houston, 1997—2002; rschr. Sasaki Inst., Tokyo, 2002—06; assoc. prof. dept. molecular genetics med. rsch. inst. Tokyo Med. and Dental U., 2006—. Author: Kairyu, 2005, Chihei, 2006; contbr. scientific papers to profl. jours., chapters to books. Internat. Rsch. Communication grant, Ichiro Kanehara Found., 2003. Mem.: Japanese Soc. Toxicology, Japanese Soc. Biochemistry, Japanese Soc. Cancer. Achievements include research in polymorphism in cancer patients; gene expression in cancer patients. Office: Dept Med Genetics Med Rsch Inst Tokyo Med and Dental Univ 1-5-45 Yushima Bunkyo-ku Tokyo 113-8510 Japan Personal E-mail: cqn13552@nifty.com. Business E-Mail: uemgen@tmd.ac.jp.

UEMURA, HIROJI, urologist, oncologist; b. Nakatsu, Oita prefecture, Japan, Aug. 18, 1959; s. Hitoshi and Eiko Uemura; m. Keiko Miyawaki, Nov. 10, 1961; children: Ann, Sho. MD, Yokohama City U. Sch. Medicine, 1985, PhD, 1998. Asst. prof. Yokohama City U., 1998—2003, assoc. prof., 2003—. Recipient Award Yr., Yokohama Med. Congress, 2004, Umehara award, 2007. Mem.: Am. Assn. of Cancer Rsch. (corr.). Achievements include research in Molecular Biology Of Prostate Cancer. Office Fax: +81-45-786-5775. Business E-Mail: hu0428@med.yokohama-cu.ac.jp.

UEMURA, TERUKI, child brain developmentalist; b. Tokyo, Mar. 25, 1944; came to U.S., 1973; s. Kiichi and Teru (Koizumi) U. BA, Keio U., Tokyo, 1967, diploma in bus. adminstr., 1972; M Mgmt., Northwestern U., Evanston, Ill., 1975; postgrad., U. Pa., Phila., 1976-81. Mem. staff Aichi Steel Works, Ltd., Nagoya, Japan, 1967-81; coord. Insts. for Achievement Human Potential, Phila., 1984—; vice dir. intellectual growth at The Children's Ctr. The Children's Ctr., Phila., 1984-91; vice dir. The Children's Ctr. Insts. for Achievement Human Potential, Phila., 2001; vice dir. Insts. Achievement of Intellectual Excellence, Phila., 1994—; mem. Instrem Divsn., Jour. Lawyers Sch., Phila., 2010. Rsch. asst. Harvard U., Cambridge, Mass., 1972-74, U. Pa., Phila., 1979-81; translator U.S. State Dept., Washington, 1980— Program coordinator Coun. Internat. Visitors, Phila., 1978 81. Recipient Brazilian Gold medal of Humanitics, World Orgn. for Human Potential, 1984, 88, Sakura Koro Sho award, 1986, Leonardo da Vinci award, 1993, Founder's award Internat. Acad. Child Brain Devel., 1998. Fellow Internat. Acad. Child Brain Devel.; mem. Friends of Japanese House and Garden (bd. dirs.), Japan Am. Soc. Greater Phila., Barnus Found., Lory World Gardens. Avocations: reading, tennis, travel, history, science.

UENG, STEVE WEN-NENG, orthopedist, surgeon; b. Taipei, Taiwan, Dec. 12, 1950; s. Ueng Chin-Gee and Lin Fon-Zau Ueng; m. Lin Mei-Ling, June 4, 1977; children: Ruey-Shiuan, Lih-Shuoh. MD, Taipei Med. Coll., 1977. From resident in surgery to attending orthopedist Chang Gung Meml. Hosp., Taiwan, 1979—, chief dept. orthopedics, 1994—97, chief Hyperbaric Oxygen Ctr., 1994—97. Assoc. prof. Chang Gung U., 1994—99, prof., supt., 1999—, vice supt., 1997. Grantee, Nat. Sci. Coun., Taiwan, 1993, 1995—2000, 2002—. Mem.: European Soc. Bone and Joint Infection, Undersea and Hyperbaric Med. Soc., Orthopedic Assn. Republic China. Avocations: tennis, golf, painting. Office: Chang Gung Meml Hosp #5 Fu-Hsing St Kweishan Taoyuan Taiwan Business E-Mail: wenneng@cgmh.org.tw.

UENO, EI, surgeon; b. Kumanogawa, Japan, Sept. 29, 1950; s. Tamehaya and Takako (Miyamae) U.; m. Keiko Yokoyama, Apr. 23, 1977; 1 child, Fuyo. MD, Tokyo Med. Coll., 1976; PhD, U. Tsukuba, 1995. Jr. resident Jichi Med. Sch., Minamikawachi, Japan, 1976-78, sr. resident, 1978-81, asst., 1981-82; asst. prof. U. Tsukuba, Japan, 1983—2005, assoc. prof., 2004—06, hosp. prof., 2006—08; dir. Breast Ctr., Tsukuba Med. Ctr., 2009—. Adv. bd. Internat. Breast Ultrasound Sch.; guest assoc. prof. Tokyo Med. U., 1998—2005; pres. Breast Cancer Conf., 1999—; clin. prof. Tsukuba U. Hosp., 2010—. Author, editor: Breast Ultrasound, 1991, Atlas of Breast Surgery, 1993, rev. edit., 1998; author: Mastologia Dinamica, 1995, Ultrasound of Superficial Structures, 1995, Color Atras of Surgery, 2006, Breast Ultrasound, 2007. Fellow Japan Surg. Soc., Japan Soc. of Ultrasound in Medicine (councillor 2000—); mem. Japanese Breast Cancer Soc. (councillor 1992—), Ibaraki Soc. of Breast Disease (pres. 1995—), Internat. Assn. of Breast Ultrasound (organizing com. 1989—, pres. 2001-06), Japanese Assn. Breast amd Thyroid Sonology (pres. 1998-2004), 13th Internat. Congress Ultrasonic Exam. of Breast (chmn. 2003), Breast Cancer Conf., Soc. kumanogenjin (pres., 2008, Wakayama Sightseeing ambassador, 2008). Avocations: swimming, skiing, surfing, spear fishing. Home: 2-2-15 Sengen Tsukuba 305-0047 Japan Office: Breast Ctr Tsukuba Med Ctr 1-3-1 Amakubo Tsukuba 305-8558 Japan Home Phone: 81-29-851-0076; Office Phone: 81-29-851-3511. Business E-Mail: e-ueno@tmch.or.jp.

UENO, SATORU, physics professor; b. Kanagawa, Japan, Sept. 29, 1961; PhD, Grad. Sch. Biosphere Scis., 1992. Prof. Grad. Sch. Biosphere Scis., 2010—. Mem.: Japanese Assn. Crystal Growth (bd.

mem. 2008—), Japanese Soc. Food Sci. & Tech., Am. Oil Chemists' Soc., Japan Oil Chemists' Soc., Phys. Soc. Japan. Avocations: walking, mountain climbing. Office: Grad Sch Biosphere Scis Higashi Hiroshima739-8528 Japan Office Fax: 81 82 424 7910. Business E-Mail: sueno@hiroshima-u.ac.jp.

UEOKA, RYUICHI, biochemistry professor; b. Ozu Town (Kumamoto), Japan, Oct. 10, 1946; s. Seiichi and Teruko (Noguchi) U.; m. Toshiko Hokazono, June 16, 1974; children: Kana, Hidetsugu. BS, Kumamoto U., Japan, 1969, PharmD, 1989; MS, Kyushu U., Fukuoka, Japan, 1975, PhD in Engring., 1982. Assoc. prof. chemistry Sojo U. (formerly Kumamoto Inst. Tech.), 1977-91, prof., 1991—, chmn., 1995—, dept. life sci. head prof., 2000—. Author: Supramolecular Chemistry, 1996, Advances in Biochemical Production Technologies, 2002; contbr. articles to profl. jours.; patentee in field. Recipient Encouragement award Soc. Synthetic Chemistry Japan, 1987, Young Scholar Lecture award The Chem. Soc. Japan, 1986, Best Tchg. award Sojo U., 2004, Outstanding Paper award Jour. Japanese Soc. Pediat. Surgeons, 2006. Avocations: fishing, painting, kendo. Home: Izumi 3-9-1 Kumamoto 862-0941 Japan Office: Sojo Univ Ikeda 4-22-1 Kumamoto 860-0082 Japan Office Phone: 81 96 326 3952. Business E-Mail: ueoka@life.sojo-u.ac.jp.

UGRAS REY, SANDRA, emergency physician; arrived in US, 1979; d. Edip and Susan Sermin Ugras. D of Osteopathy, U. Medicine & Dentistry NJ, Stratford, 2001. Emergency physician Newark Beth Israel Med. Ctr., 2006—. Mem.: Am. Coll. Osteo. Physicians, Am. Coll. Emergency Physicians, Am. Osteo. Assn. Home: 394 Valley View Ave Paramus NJ 07652 Personal E-mail: sandraugras@yahoo.com.

UGURBIL, KAMIL, radiologist, neuroscientist, educator; b. Turkey, July 11, 1949; AB in physics, Columbia Coll., 1971; MA in chem. physics, Columbia U., 1974, MPhil in chem. physics, 1976, PhD in chem. physics, 1977; PhD (hon.), U. Utrecht, 2005. Fellow Bell Labs., 1977—79; asst. prof. biochemistry Columbia U., 1979—82; assoc. prof. biochemistry U. Minn., 1982—85, prof. radiology, neuroscience and medicine, 1985—2007, dir. Ctr. Magnetic Resonance Rsch., 1991—, Margaret and H.O. Peterson chair neuroradiology, 1996—2003, McKnight presdl. endowed chair prof., 2003—. Dir. Hochfeld Magnetresonanz Zentrum Max Planck Inst. fur Biologische Kybernetik, Tubingen, Germany, 2003—08. Recipient Hammett award, 1976, Irma T. Hirschl Career Scientist award, 1980, Rsch. Career Devel. award, NIH, 1983, Gold medal, Internat. Soc. Magnetic Resonance Rsch., 1996. Fellow: Internat. Soc. Magnetic Resonance in Medicine; mem.: Inst. Medicine, Am. Acad. Arts and Sciences, Soc. Neuroscience. Office: Ctr Magnetic Resonance Rsch U Minn Med Sch 2021 6th St SE Minneapolis MN 55416 E-mail: kamil@cmrr.umn.edu.

UHDE, THOMAS WHITLEY, psychopharmacology, psychiatrist; s. George Irwin and Maurine U.; m. Marlene Ann Kraus, Oct. 22, 1977; children: Miles August, Katherine Kraus. BS, Duke U., 1971; MD, U. Louisville, 1975. Diplomate Am. Bd. Psychiatry and Neurology. Postdoctoral fellow Yale U., New Haven, 1975-79, chief resident clin. rsch. unit, 1979; rsch. fellow NIMH, 1979-81; pvt. practice in psychiatry Bethesda, Md., 1979-93; clin. adminstr. sect. psychobiology BPB, NIMH, ADAMHA, Bethesda, Md., 1979-80, chief unit on anxiety and affective disorders, 1982-89, chief 3-West clin. rsch. unit, 1980-90, chief sect. on anxiety and affective disorders, 1989-93; asst. clin. prof. Uniformed Svcs. U. Health Scis., Bethesda, Md., 1982-85, assoc. clin. prof. uniformed svcs., 1985-91; attending staff Clin. Ctr. NIH, Bethesda, Md., 1982-93; chmn. dept. psychiatry Detroit Receiving Hosp. and Harper Hosp., 1994-98; psychiatrist in chief Detroit Med. Ctr., 1993—2001; clin. prof. Uniformed Svcs. U. Health Scis. Sch. Medicine, Bethesda, 1991—; chmn. dept. psychiatry and behavorial neuroscis. Wayne State U. Sch. Medicine, Detroit, 1993—2001; prof. dept. pharmacology Wayne State U. Sch. of Medicine, Detroit, 1993—2003, 1999—2001; prof., chair dept. psychiatry Penn State Coll., Hershey, Pa., 2004—, dir. ctrl. Pa. Psychiatric Inst., 2004—, dir. neurosci. rsch. inst., 2004—06. Prof., psychiatry and behavioral neuroscis. dept., Wayne State U. Sch. Medicine, 1993-2003, assoc. dean rsch. and grad. programs, 1999-2001; asst. dean neuroscis., 2001-03; mem. sci. adv. com. Bethesda, Md., 1990; cons. Rsch. Scientist Devel. Rev. Com., HHS, ADAMHA, 1983, Career Devel. Program Awards Com., VA, Washington, 1986, Primary Care Rsch. Program, ADAMHA, 1988; exec. bd. Anxiety Disorders Assn. Am., 1991-93, 99-, chair sci. adv. bd., Rockville, Md., 1991-93; biomed. instr. review bd. Penn State U., 2004-; mem. sci. adv. bd. VA VISN4 MIREXX, 2005-. Editor-in-chief (jour.) Anxiety 1993-1996; Co-editor-in-chief (jour.) Depression and Anxiety 1996-2002; Editor-in-chief (jour.) Depression and Anxiety 2002--; mem. editl. bd. Actualities Medicales Internationales en Psychiatrie, 1983, Jour. Affective Disorders, 1986, Jour. Anxiety Disorders, 1987-95, Biol. Psychiatry, 1998—2001; contbr. more than 300 sci. articles to profl. jours. Sr. asst. surgeon US Pub. Health Svc., 1979—80, surgeon US Pub. Health Svc., 1980—84, sr. surgeon US Pub. Health Svc., 1984—91, med. dir. US Pub. Health Svc., 1991—93. Recipient Ackerly award, Nat. Rsch. Svc. award, A.E. Bennet Neuropsychiat. Rsch. Found. award, Brain, Body & Mind award Uniformed Svc. Univ. Health Sci., Recognition award ADAA; Am. Coll. Neuropsychopharmacology travel fellow; Commendation medal, US Public Health Svc.; Meritous Svc. medal; named disting. lectr., U. Va., Heninger Lectr., Yale, Highly Cited Scientist in Psychology/Psychiatry, ISI. Fellow Am. Psychiatric Assn. (disting.); mem. Am. Coll. Neuropsychopharmacolgoy, Am. Coll. Psychiatry, Am. Soc. of Clin. Psychopharmacology, Internat. Brain Rsch. Orgn., Sleep Rsch. Soc., Biol. Psych. Soc., Am Psych Assoc., Penn Psych. Soc., Anx. Dis. Assoc. Am., Anx. Assoc. Argentina (hon), Am. Assoc. Chair Dept. Psych., Int. Soc. Psychoneurology. Independent. Unitarian Universalist. Avocations: art, piano, hiking, boating. Office: Penn State Coll Medicine Dept Psychiatry PO Box 850 500 University Dr Hershey PA 17033-0850 Business E-Mail: tuhde@psu.edu.

UHLENHUTH, EBERHARD HENRY, psychiatrist, educator; b. Balt., Sept. 15, 1927; s. Eduard Carl Adolph and Elisabeth (Baier) Uhlenhuth; m. Helen Virginia Lyman, June 20, 1952; children: Kim Lyman, Karen Jane, Eric Rolf. BS in Chemistry, Yale U., 1947; MD, Johns Hopkins U., 1951. Intern Harborview Hosp., Seattle, 1951-52; resident in psychiatry Johns Hopkins Hosp., Balt., 1952-56, asst. psychiatrist in charge outpatient dept., 1956-61, psychiatrist in charge, 1961-62; chief adult psychiatry clinic U. Chgo. Hosps. Clinics, 1968-76; instr. psychiatry Johns Hopkins U., 1956-59, asst. prof., 1959-67, assoc. prof., 1967-68, U. Chgo., 1968-73, prof., 1973-85, acting chmn., 1983-85; prof. psychiatry U. N.Mex., Albuquerque, 1985-97, prof. emeritus, 1997—, Disting. Univ. prof., 2005—, vice chmn. for edn., 1991-94. Cons. in field; mem. clin. psychopharmacology rsch. rev. com. NIMH, 1968-72, mem. treatment devel. and assessment rsch. rev. com., 1987-88; mem. psychopharmacology adv. com. FDA, 1974-78; adv. group to Treatment of Depression Collaborative Rsch. Program, NIMH, 1978-92; study rev. com. Xanax discontinuation program Upjohn Co., 1988-92, Nat. Adv. Coun. on Drug Abuse, NIDA, 1989-92, Coop. Studies Evaluation Com., VA, 1989-92. Mem. editl. bd. Jour. Affective Disorders, 1978—, Psychiatry Rsch., 1979-96, Behavioral Medicine, 1982—, Neuropsychopharmacology, 1992-95, Exptl. and Clin. Psychopharmacology, 1992-99, Depression and Anxiety, 1992—2008; contbr. articles to profl. jours. Recipient Rsch. Career Devel. award USPHS, 1962-68, Rsch. Scientist award, 1976-81. Fellow: Collegium Internat. Neuro-Psychopharmacologicum, Am. Psychopath. Assn., Am. Psychiat. Assn., Am. Coll. Neuropsychopharmacology (pres. 1986); mem.: Psychiat. Rsch. Soc., Balt.-Washington Soc. Psychoanalysis. Office: Univ N Mex Dept Psychiatry Ctr Psychiatric Rsch MSC 11 60351 Univ New Mex Albuquerque NM 87131-0001 Home Phone: 505-265-0663; Office Phone: 505-272-8876. Business E-Mail: uhli@unm.edu.

UIBU, TOOMAS, pulmonologist; MD, Tampere U., Finland, 1998, degree in Pulmonary Medicine and Allergology, 2005. Respiratory cons. Tampere U. Hosp., 2005—; CEO Ihoakatemia, Esthetic Dermatology and Plastic Surgery Clinic, Helsinki, Finland, 2008—. Mem.: Finnish Respiratory Soc. Achievements include research in retroperitoneal fibrosis and asbestos exposure. Office: Ihoakatemia Mannerheimintie 5 C 6 Fl Helsinki 00100 Finland Office Phone: 358-106-168989. Business E-Mail: toomas.uibu@ihoakatemia.fi.

UJI, MASAYO, psychiatrist; d. Susumu and Shizuko Uji. MD, Torroti U., Yonago, 1991; PhD, Kumamoto U., Japan, 2006. Resident physician Kumamoto U. Hosp., 1991—94; psychiatrist, dir. Kanto Ctrl. Hosp., Setagaya, Tokyo, Japan, 1997—2000; psychiatrist Kumamoto U. Hosp., 1994—97, 2000—02, 2006—. Fellow Japan Young Psychiatrist Orgn., Tokyo, 2002—. Contbr. articles various rsch. papers. Mem.: Japanese Soc. for Child and Adolescent Psychiatry, Japan Psycho-Analytical Assn., Japanese Soc. of Psychiatry and Neurology. Office: Kumamoto U Hosp 1-1-1 Honjo Kumamoto 8608556 Japan Office Phone: 81-(0)96-373-5183. Office Fax: 81-(0)96-373-5181. Business E-Mail: ujimasayo@excite.co.jp.

UJULA, TIINA, biochemist; b. Ruukki, Finland, Feb. 3, 1976; PhD, U. Turku, 2011. Rsch. scientist Turku PET Ctr., Finland, 2003—10; project chemist MAP Med. Techs., Helsinki, Finland, 2010—. Mem.: Cancer Rsch. Soc. Turku, Finnish Soc. Nuc. Medicine. Home: Yrttikuja 8 Porvoo FI-06100 Finland Personal E-mail: tiina.ujula@utu.fi.

UKISU, RYUTAROU, radiologist; s. Haruhiko and Reiko Ukisu. MD, Showa U. Sch. Medicine. Lic. Japan, Japanese Coll. Radiology. Chief radiologist Ohta-Atami Gen. Hosp., Fukushima, Japan, 1995—99; chief of neuroradiology, head and neck radiology section, dept. radiology Showa U. Hosp., Tokyo, 1999—2001; chief neuroradiology, head and neck radiology section, dept. radiology Showa U. No. Yokohama Hosp., Japan, 2001—03, asst. prof., chief neuroradiology, head and neck radiology section, dept. radiology, 2003—10, assoc. prof., 2010—. Recipient Cert. Merit award, 89th Radiol. Soc. N.Am., Best Interactive Radiol. Poster Presentation, First Internat. Soc. Radiol. Virtual Congress, Cert. Merit award, 95th Radiol Soc. N. Am. Achievements include research in serial diffusion-weighted MRI of Creutzfeldt-Jakob Disease; diffusion-weighted MR imaging of early-stage Creutzfeldt-Jakob Disease: typical and atypical manifestations; skin injuries caused by fluroscopically guided interventional procedures. Personal E-mail: ryu.ukisu@gmail.com. Business E-Mail: ukisu@med.showa-u.ac.jp.

ULICNY, GARY R., rehabilitation center executive; BA in Special Edn., UNC Chapel Hill; MA in Special Edn., Appalachian U.; PhD in Behavorial Psychology, U. Kansas. Regional v.p. Learning Services Corp., NH, exec. dir.; adminstrv. dir. rehab. services WakeMed Hosp. System, Raleigh, NC; pres., CEO Shepherd Ctr., Atlanta, 1994—. Mem. Ga. Dept. Cmty. Health, 2005—. Mem.: American Coll. Healthcare Executives, American Congress of Rehab. Medicine (v.p.), Ga. Hosp. Assn. (bd. trustees 2009—, chmn. rehab. council). Office: Shepherd Ctr 2020 Peachtree Rd NW Atlanta GA 30309-1402

ULIUKIN, IGOR, epidemiologist; b. Leningrad, Russia, May 2, 1958; s. Mikhail Uliukin and Tatiana (Orlova) Uliukina; m. Olga Arkhipova, July 31, 1981; 1 child, Olga Uliukina. MD, Russian Mil. Med. Acad., Leningrad, 1981; PhD, Russian Mil. Med. Acad., St. Petersburg, 2000. Cert. expert in infectious disease Russian Mil. Med. Acad., 1987. Resident in bacteriology Podolsk Mil. Hosp., 1983; fellow dept. infectious diseases Russian Mil. Med. Acad., Leningrad, 1985—87; physician Russian HIV/AIDS Clin. Ctr./Pediat. HIV/AIDS Clin. Ctr. of Russia, St. Petersburg, 1997—99; head rsch. and info. dept. Pediat. HIV/AIDS Clin. Ctr. of Russia, St. Petersburg, 2000—. Mem. editl. bd. Terra medica nova med. jour., 2003—; contbr. chapters to books, articles to profl. jours. Lt. col. Soviet Army, 1981—95. Office: AIDS Clin Ctr Russia Pediat HIV Shlisselburgskoye Shosse 3 196245 Saint Petersburg Sankt-Pyetyerburg Russia

ULLERYD, PETER, infectious disease specialist; MD, Sahlgrenska U. Hosp., 1986; PhD, U. Göteborg, 2001. Faculty dept. infectious diseases Sahlgrenska Univ. Hosp., Göteborg, Sweden; regional med. officer Dept. Communicable Disease Control. Office: Dept Communicable Disease Control Kaserntorget 11B 411 18 Goteborg Sweden Business E-Mail: peter.ulleryd@vgregion.se.

ULLMAN, SUSANNE, dermatologist, educator; b. Copenhagen, May 15, 1938; d. Gunner Enoch and Ida Zeuthen-Aagaard; m. Niels Ullman (div.). MD, U. Copenhagen, 1965, splty. degree in dermatology, 1976, D of Med. Sci., 1988. Vis. prof. U. Minn., Mpls., 1974—76; prof. dermatology Righospitalet, U. Copenhagen, 1979—, Bispebjerg Hosp. and Righospitalet, U. Copenhagen, 1996—. Coord. for edn. of dermatologists in Denmark, 1983—90; mem. adv. group on AIDS Nat. Bd. Health, Denmark, 1984—89, mem. adv. group on sexually transmitted diseases, 1987—96; mem. com. Robert J. Gorlin Conf. on Dysmorphology, Mpls., 1996—2006; vis. prof. King Faisal U., Dahran, Saudi Arabia, 1981, Hunan Med. U., China, 1989. Contbr. numerous articles to profl. jours. Mem. People to People del., China, 1986. Office: Bispebjerg Hosp Dept Dermatology Bispebjerg Bakke 23 2400 Copenhagen Denmark Office Phone: (0045) 35316494. Business E-Mail: sull0001@bbh.regionh.dk. E-mail: susanne.ullman@dadlnet.dk.

ULLMAN, THOMAS A., gastroenterologist, educator; MD, Cornell U., 1992. Diplomate Am. Bd. Internal Medicine-gastroenterology. Resident internal medicine NY Hosp., 1993—95; fellow gastroenterology Yale-New Haven Hosp., New Haven, 1996—99; assoc. prof. medicine gastroenterology Mt. Sinai Sch. of Medicine, NYC; attending physician Mt. Sinai Med. Ctr., NYC. Office: Mount Sinai Medical Center Department of Medicine 1470 Madison Ave New York NY 10029 Office Phone: 212-241-4299. Office Fax: 212-426-5099.

ULLRICH, AXEL, science association director; b. Lauban, Schlesien, Germany, Oct. 19, 1943; Diploma in bioChemistry, U. Tubingen, Germany, 1971; postgrad., U. Munster, Inst. Biochemistry, 1972; PhD, U. Heidelberg, Germany, 1975. Asst. biochemist U. Munster, Inst. Biochemistry, 1971—72; fellow U. Heidelberg, Inst. Molecular Genetics, Heidelberg, 1972—74; postdoctoral fellow dept. biochemistry and biophysics U. Calif., San Francisco, 1975—77; postdoctoral fellow Deutsche Forschungsgemeinschaft, Bonn, Germany, 1975—77; asst. rsch. biochemist U. Calif., San Francisco, 1977—78; sr. scientist Genetech, Inc., South San Francisco, 1979—84, staff scientist, 1984—88; dir. dept. molecular biology Max Planck Inst., Martinsried, Germany, 1988—. Mem. sci. adv. bd., founder, cons., chief scientist SUGEN, Inc., South San Francisco, 1991—99; hon. prof. 2d Mil. Med. U., Shanghai, 1996; prof. Sorbonne, Acad. de Paris, Paris, 1996—98; founder, vice-chmn. acad. bd. 2d Mil. Med. U., Coop. Lab. for Biol. Signal Transduction Rsch., Shanghai, 1996—; founder, cons., chief sci. advisor Axxima Pharm. AG, Martinsreid, Germany, 1998—; mng. dir. Max Planck Inst. for Biochemistry, Martinsreid, Germany, 1999; bd. dirs. BioImage A/S, Soborg, Sweden; co-chmn. clin. sci. adv. bd. SUGEN, Inc./Pharmacia Upjohn, South San Francisco, Calif., 1999—, sci. advisor, 1999—; hon. prof. U. Tubingen, Tubingen, Germany, 2000—; bd. dirs. ProteoMD GmbH, Tubingen; mem. sci. adv. bd. Neurotech SA, 1998—, Bionomics Ltd., 1996—, Wistar Inst., 1995—, Garching Innovation GmbH, 1992—96, Hagedorn Rsch. Inst., 1991—95; chmn. sci. adv. bd. Garching Innovation GmbH, 1996—; vice chmn. sci. adv. bd. Hans Knoll Inst., 1992—. Mem. editl. bd.: Cancer Rsch., DNA and Cell Biology, Genomics, Growth Factors, Molecular Brain Rsch., Receptors and Channels, Neoplasia. Recipient Paul Langerhans medal, Deutsche-Diabetes-Gesellschaft, 1987, 1st Ann. Ray A. and Robert L. Kroc lectr., The Kroc Found., 1987, John W. Cline Meml. lectr., Am. Cancer Soc. and UCLA, 1987, Berthold medal, German Soc. Endocrinology, 1988, Mildred Scheel Meml. lectr., Modern Trends in Human Leukemia Conf., 1990, 11th Ann. Ray A. and Robert L. Kroc lectr., The Kroc Found., 1996, Prix Antoine Lacassagne, La Ligue Nat. Francaise Contre le Cancer, 1991, Gold medal and XXII Lorenzini Ann. lectr., Fondazione Giovanni Lorenzini, 1997, German Cancer prize, German Cancer Soc., 1998, Ludwig Heilmeyer lectr., Internat. Soc. Gastroenterol. Carcinogenesis, 1999, Bruce F. Cain Meml. award, Am. Assn. for Cancer Rsch., 2000, Wolf Prize in Medicine, Wolf Found., 2010. Mem.: AAAS, European Molecular Biology Orgn. (elected), N.Y. Acad. Scis., Internat. Life Sci. Forum, Deutsche Krebsgesellschaft, Internat. Union Against Cancer, Am. Assn. for Cancer Rsch., Gesellschaft fur Biochemie and Molekularbiologie e.V., Am. Soc. Cell Biology, Academia Europaea. Office: Max Planck Inst for Biochemistry Am Klopferspitz 18A 82152 Martinsried Germany *

ULLRICH, DIETER, physician; b. Bergneustadt, Germany, Apr. 11, 1955; s. Hansjurgen and Friederike (Ertl) U.; m. Holle Bertl Schiefer, Aug., 1982; children: Katja, Franziska. Diploma in medicine, Gesamthochschule Essen, Germany, 1980, D, 1982. Resident biochem. pharmacology U. Göttingen, Germany, 1980—82, resident pediat., 1982—89, resident clin. pharmacology, 1988—89, resident ear, nose, throat clinic, 1989—93; pvt. practice Wedemark, Germany, 1993—. Author: HNO-Erkrankungen im Kindesalter, 1994; contbg. author: Biochemical Basis of Carcinogenesis, 1984, Advances in Glucuronide Formation, 1985, Hepatic Encephalopathy, 1988, Head and Neck Cancer-Advances in Basic Research, 1996; contbr. articles to profl. jours. Avocations: sailing, running, golf. Office: Wedemarkstr 83 30900 Wedemark Germany Office Phone: 0049(0)5130373787. Personal E-mail: ullrich-dieter@t-online.de.

ULMAN, DOUG, foundation administrator; BS in History, Brown U., Providence, 1999. Founder, pres. Ulman Cancer Fund for Young Adults, 1997—, exec. dir., 1997—2001; dir. survivorship, chief mission officer Lance Armstrong Found.: LIVESTRONG, Austin, Tex., 2001—07, pres., CEO, 2007—. Mem. exec. bd. Ulman Cancer Fund for Young Adults; founder LIVESTRONG Young Adults Alliance. Chmn., director's consumer liaison group Nat. Cancer Inst., 2005—09. Recipient Austin Under-40 award, healthcare, 2003, Health Care Hero award, Austin Bus. Jour., 2008. Mem.: Am. Soc. Clin. Oncology. Avocations: soccer, running. Office: Lance Armstrong Found 2201 E Sixth St Austin TX 78702 *

ULMER, CHRISTOPH, general surgeon, visceral surgeon, chief consultant; b. Berlin, July 27, 1970; s. Peter Paul and Traude Ulmer; m. Heike Ulmer; children: Hannah-Marie, Ann-Sophie. MD, Albert Einstein U., Ulm, Baden-Wuerttemberg, Germany, 2006. Cert. approbator Albert Einstein U., 1999. Intern gen. surgery LI Jewish Hosp., Albert-Einstein-U, NYC, 1998—99; resident gen. surgery U. Medicine Charite, Berlin, 1999—2004, Robert-Bosch-Krankenhaus Stuttgart, Baden-Wuerttemberg, 2004—07, cons. gen. surgery, 2007—. Mem.: Rotary Club. Office Phone: 004910171191013439. Business E-Mail: christoph.ulmer@rbk.de.

ULMER, WILLIAM H., SR., retired dentist; b. Wilmington, Del., Sept. 20, 1946; s. Horace Hiate Ulmer and Lillian Palmer Queripel; m. Patricia Ann Kokoszka, July 10, 2004; m. Loreta Harriet Pasquine, June 6, 1970 (div. Oct. 15, 2001); children: Robert John II, William H. Jr., Alison Theresa Kristunas. BS in Biology, Pa. Mil. Coll., 1967; DDS, Fairleigh Dickenson U., Teaneck, NJ, 1971. Cert. forensic dentistry Armed Forces Inst. Pathology, 1990, forensic odontology Northwestern U., 1990. Intern gen. dentistry Del. State Hosp., 1972; dentist Dental Assocs. Del., Hockessin, 1972—2010; pvt. practice Del. Forensic dentist Office of the Med. Examiner, State Del., Wilmington, 1989—; forensic facial recontruction sculptor Office of the Med. Examiner, State of Del., Wilmington, Del., 1992—; forensic dentist Pa. Dental Identification Team, Harrisburg, 1990—, Dept. Health Dimort Team, 1994—2001; cert. police instr. Del. State Police, Wilmington. Dental surgeon Team Health Care, Towaco, NJ, 2002—03, Jamaica. Recipient Gold medal Weight Lifting, Sr. Olympics, 2006. Master: TaeKwonDo Internat. (4th Degree Black Belt 2006); fellow: Acad. Dentistry Internat., Acad. Forensic Sciences, Acad. Gen. Dentistry; mem.: Surfers Med. Assn., Am. Dental Soc., Del. State Dental Soc. (chmn. emergency response team 1990—2007). Avocations: trumpet, guitar. Home Fax: 302-239-3657. Personal E-mail: wulmer@pol.net.

ULSHEN, MARTIN HOWARD, pediatric gastroenterologist, researcher; b. NYC, Mar. 5, 1944; s. Lawrence F. and Dorothy C. Ulshen; divorced; children: Sarah Powell, Daniel; m. Sue Ellen McRae, Dec. 17, 1988. BA, U. Rochester, 1965, MD, 1969. Diplomate Am. Bd. Pediat., sub-bd. pediatric gastroenterology, 1990. Intern in pediatrics Univ. NC, 1969-70; resident in pediatrics Univ. Colo., 1972-74, fellow in pediat. gastroenterology, 1974-75, Childrens Hosp., Boston, 1975-77; prof. Univ. NC, Chapel Hill, 1977—97; fellow in pediat. gastroenterology St. Mary's Hosp. & Good Samaritan Hosp., W. Palm Beach, Fla., 1996—99, Duke Univ. Med. Ctr., Durham, NC, 1999, prof., division chief pediatric gastroenterology, hepatology & nutrition, 1999—. Assoc. editor Jour. Pediat.; med. editor Pediat. Gastroenterology, Am. Bd. Pediat.; contbr. articles to profl. jours. With USPHS, 1970-72. Office: Duke Univ DUMC 3009 Durham NC 27710 Office Phone: 919-684-5068. Office Fax: 919-684-4836. Business E-Mail: martn.ulshen@duke.edu.

ULSTROM, ROBERT A., retired pediatrician; b. Mpls., Feb. 23, 1923; m. Mary Janet McGrath, 1946 (dec. 1981); 3 children; m. Betty Bernard, 1982 (div. 1985). BS, U. Minn., 1944, MD, 1946; postgrad., Strong Meml. Hosp. Lic. physician, Minn., Calif.; diplomate Am. Bd. Pediatrics with subsplty. in endocrinology (bd. dirs. 1980-86, v.p. 1985, chmn. rsch. and devel. com. 1980-86, tech. adv. com. for devel. of computerized exams. 1983-86), Am. Bd. Emergency Medicine (bd. dirs. 1982-86). Intern, resident in pediats. U. Rochester, 1946-48; instr., asst. prof. U. Minn., Mpls., 1950-53, assoc. prof., 1956-61, prof. pediatrics, 1961-64, 66-90, prof. emeritus, 1990—, mem. Ctr. for German and European Studies, Inst. for Global Studies, 2004—, acting head dept. pediats., 1961—62, assoc. dean Coll. Med. Scis., 1967-70; asst. prof. UCLA, 1953-56, prof., 1964-67, chmn. dept. pediatrics, 1964-67; vis. prof. medicine U. So. Calif., 1982-83, ret. Chief pediats. 97th Gen. Hosp., 1949-50; cons. in pediats. Harbor Gen. Hosp., L.A., 1953-56, 64-67, Mpls. Gen. Hosp., 1956-64, Hennepin County Gen. Hosp., 1967-90, hon. staff, 1990—; Well Child Clinic cons. City of L.A., 1953-56; track physician Donneybrooke Racetrack, Brainerd, Minn., 1968-73; dir. Reg. Ctr. for Metabolic Defects, 1975-79; cons. Ellwood & Assocs., 1986-87; med. legal cons. various plantiffs, 1985-95; mem. med. adv. bd. Group Health, Inc., 1967-90, Diabetes Detection and Edn. Ctr., 1969-71; mem. grants review com. Human Growth Inc., 1974-78; mem. tech. adv. com. on human genetics Minn. State Bd. Health, 1976-90; mem. pers. selection com. NIH, 1979, mem. gen. medicine study sect. NIH, 1964-68; mem. divsn. med. scis. NRC, 1961-64; oral examiner Am. Bd. Pediats., 1970-89; expert witness for prosecution U.S. Fed. Dist. Ct., Mpls., 1994-95; instr. computer course for beginners Elder Learning Inst., Coll. Continuing Edn., U. Minn., 1995—, bd. dirs., 1996-2000, webmaster, author, 1997-2002, v.p., 1998-99, mentor undergrad. students Coll. Liberal Arts, 1992—2004. Mem. editl. bd. Jour. Pediats., 1962-65; contbr. articles to profl. jours. Sec.-treas. Minn. Med. Found., 1967-68. With M.C., U.S. Army, 1948-50. Markle scholar in med. scis., 1954-59; Pew Found. fellow, 1985-86; recipient Wyeth award for med. rsch., 1963. Mem. AAAS, Am. Pediat. Soc., Am. Soc. Clin. Investigation, Ctrl. Soc. for Clin. Rsch., Endocrine Soc., Pediat. Endocrine Soc. (founding mem., membership com. 1971-75, chmn. 1975), Midwestern Pediat. rsch. Soc. (coun. 1961-64), Soc. for Pediat. Rsch. (NRC rep. 1961-64), Western Soc. for Clin. rsch., Western Soc. for Pediat. Rsch., Alpha Omega Alpha, Phi Rho Sigma. Home: 4616 Sunset Rdg Minneapolis MN 55416-3335

ULU, K. GÖRKEM, medical researcher; b. Ankara, July 29, 1981; PhD, Ankara U., 1999. Rsch. asst. Sdü Dis Hek, 2005—. Mem.: IADR. Office: Sdü Dis Hek Fak Pedodont 30 Isparta Merkez 32260 Turkey Personal E-mail: gorkemulu@yahoo.com.

ULVUND, MARTHA J., veterinarian, educator; d. Gunleiv and Inger Jakobsen; m. Aasmund Ulvund, Aug. 16, 1970; children: Sindre, Inger Ulvund Svihus. Cand med vet, NVH, Oslo, 1970, Dr Scient, 1973, Dr med vet, 1990. DipECSRHM Ebvs, Eu, 2008. Rsch. asst. NVH, 1970—73, prof. Sandnes, Norway, 1993—, sen res. officer, 1981—93, State Vet. Res. Sta., Sandnes, 1973—79, NORAD, Karatina, Kenya, 1979—81. Bd. mem. NUFU, Bergen, Norway, 2006—, NCE Culinology, Norway, 2006—, Stavanger U. Fund, Norway, 2008—. Recipient Rsch. prize, Rogaland Acad., 1990. Home: Muningate 2C Sandnes 4306 Norway Office: Norwegian Sch Vet Sci Kyrkjevegen 332-334 Sandnes 4325 Norway Office Fax: 4751603509. Business E-Mail: martha.ulvund@veths.no.

UM, KYUNG IL, medical educator; b. Seoul, Dec. 1, 1945; s. Jang Sup Um and Bok Nam Park; m. Keum Soon Choi; children: So Hyun, Jin Hyun. PhD, Seoul Nat. U., 1975—81. Guest rschr. NIH, Bethesda, Md., 1983—84; vis. prof. U. Md., Balt., 1996—97. Author: Molecular Cell Biology. 1st It. Inf., 1968—70, Korea. Mem.: Genetics Soc. Korea (v.p. 1999—2000). Home: 8-2 Dongdaesin-dong 2ka Pusan 602-102 Republic of Korea Office: Dong-A Univ 840 Hadan-dong Saha-Ku Pusan 604-714 Republic of Korea Office Fax: 051-200-7269. Business E-Mail: kium@dau.ac.kr.

UMBAUGH, SCOTT E., engineering educator, design engineer, consultant; b. Columbus, Ohio, Mar. 31, 1957; s. Richard Eugene and Elnora Mae (Wolfe) U.; children: Robin Marie, David Scott; m. Jeanie Marie Tassin, May 31, 2003; children: Angi, Kayla, Michael. BSE with honors, So. Ill. U., 1976-82; MSEE, U. Mo., Rolla, 1983-86, PhD, 1986-90. Intern McDonnell Douglas, St. Louis, 1981; computer engr. ITT North Electric, Columbus, 1982-83, Affinitec Corp., St. Louis, 1983-86; grad. teaching asst., rsch. asst. U. Mo., Rolla, 1986-89; prof. elec. engring. So. Ill. U., Edwardsville, 1989—. Cons. Ctr. for Advanced Mfg. and Prodn., So. Ill. U., 1990, Stoecker and Assocs., Rolla, 1991-92, 94, Camber Corp., St. Louis, 1994—, Sys. Dynamics Internat., St. Louis, 1993-94, Camber Corp., St. Louis, 1994—. Author: Computer Vision and Image Processing, 1998, Computer Imaging: Digital Image Analysis and Processing, 2005, Digital Imaging Processing and Analysis 2nd Edit., 2011; contbr. chpts. to books, articles to profl. jours. Chancellor's fellow U. Mo., Rolla, 1986-89; numerous grants in field. Mem. IEEE (sr.), Am. Soc. Engring. Edn., Pattern Recognition Soc. Office: So Ill U PO Box 1801 Edwardsville IL 62026-1801

UMBDENSTOCK, RICHARD J., medical association administrator; b. 1950; BA in Politics, Fairfield U., Conn., 1972; MSc in Health Svcs. Adminstrn., SUNY, Stony Brook, 1974; LLD (hon.), Gonzaga U., Spokane, Washington, 2003. Diplomate Am. Coll. Healthcare Execs. Ind. cons. for voluntary hosp. governing boards in US and Can.; pres., CEO Providence Svcs., Spokane, Wash., 1993—2006; chmn. Premier, Inc., Charlotte, NC, 2006; exec. v.p. Providence Health & Svcs. (merger of Providence Svcs. & Providence Health Sys.), 2006; spl. asst. to pres. Am. Hosp. Assn., Inc., Chgo., trustee, 2000—04, chmn.-elect, 2005, chmn., COO, pres.-elect, 2006, pres., CEO, 2007—. Mem. nat. bd. advs. Ctr. Healthcare Governance; bd. dirs. Nat. Quality Forum, Nat. Priorities Partnership; chair Hosp. Quality Alliance. Author: several books and articles for hosp. bd. audiences, nat. survey reports for Am. Hosp. Assn., Health Rsch. Ednl. Trust, Am. Coll. Healthcare Execs. Fellow: American Coll. of Healthcare Executives. Office: American Hospital Assn 325 Seventh St NW Washington DC 20004 Office Phone: 202-626-2363. Office Fax: 202-422-2303. *

UMEDA, TOMOHIRO, engineer, educator; b. Japan, Sept. 3, 1974; MS in Engring., Tokyo U. Sci., 1999; MD, Toho U., Sch. Medicine, 2006. Engr. Mitsubishi Materials Co., 1999—2004, Olympus Co., 2004—06; asst. prof. U. Tokyo, 2006—. Asst. prof. Keio U., 2010—; guest assoc. prof. Tokyo U. Sci., 2010—. Fellow: Acad. Human Informatics; mem.: Soc. Inorganic Materials (Japan). Home: 315 1-32-20 Kamiikebukuro Toshima Tokyo 170-0012 Japan Home Fax: 81-3-3940-4500. Personal E-mail: umeda4993tomohiro@yahoo.co.jp.

UMEZULIKE, AUGUSTINE CHIBUZOR, obstetrician, gynecologist, consultant; b. Enugu, Nigeria, Jan. 7, 1960; s. Joy Iwegbunam and Boniface Nweke Umezulike; m. Clara Akaduchieme Diei, Nov. 22, 1989; children: Jennifer Ifeoma, Glory Chukwudumebi, Samuel Chibuzor-Junior. MB, BChir, U. Benin, Nigeria, 1986; Fellowship West African Coll. on Surgeons, U. Nigeria Tchg. Hosp., Enugu State, 1992—98; Mashav-Israeli fgn. ministry postgrad. med. tng. grad. ob-gyn., endoscopic surgery, 2003—04, diploma advanced gynaecological endoscopic surgery, Israeli Tng. Endoscopic Ctr., 2004; JP, Milleneal Jerusalem Pilgrim, 2004. Cons. obstetrician and gynaecologist Nat. Hosp., Abuja, Fct, Nigeria, 1999—; fistula surgeon Mararaba Gurku Med. Centre, Nasarawa, Nigeria, 2003—. Coord., initiator First Internat. Gynecol. Endoscopic Surgery Workshop, 2005. Author: (poems) Cherished (Second World Prize, 1994); dir.: (surgical operations on prisoners) First Surgical Operation In Nigerian Prison (Ministerial Commendation, 1989). Mem. Deeper Life Bible Ch. Ministries, Abuja, Fct, Nigeria, 1998—2003. Fellow: Internat. Coll. Surgeons (life; chmn. conf. sc. sub-com. 2000—00, Nigerian nat. sect.); mem.: Med. And Dental Consultants Nigeria (life; asst. sec. gen. 2002—03), Soc. Gynaecologist and Obstetricians Nigereria (life), Nigerian Med. Assn. (life), Women Health Issues (life; founder, coord. 2002—03). Achievements include founding of Women Health Issues; First Surgeon to operate in a Nigerian Prison; Establishment of Abuja Vesico-Vaginal Fistula Ctr; Counselling in Infertility; Counselling in HIV in developing countries; introduction of gynecological endoscopic surgery into Nigerian practice. Avocations: sports/waching of american wrestling, poetry, writing, reading, nature admiration, ping pong/table tennis. Home: Flt 2 Blk 3 Yedseram St Maitama Fct Abuja 234 Nigeria Office: Nat Hosp PO Box 4509 Garki Ctrl Dist Garki Fct Abuja 234 Nigeria Office Fax: +234-09-2342632. Personal E-mail: acumezulike@yahoo.com.

UMSTAD, MARK PETER, obstetrician, gynecologist; b. Sydney, NSW, Australia, July 16, 1961; s. Peter Denis and Barbara May (Robinson) U.; m. Julie McChristie, Dec. 17, 1983; children: Lauren, Callum, Emily. MB, BChir, U. Melbourne, 1984, MD, 1994. Sr. registrar Royal Women's Hosp., Melbourne, 1991, fellow maternal-fetal medicine, 1993, cons. obstetrician, 1994-96, head obstetric unit, 1997—. Vis. registrar Queen Mother's Hosp., Glasgow, Scotland, 1992. Editor: Royal Women's Hosp. Fetal Monitoring Manual; contbr. articles to profl. jours. Fellow Royal Australian Coll. Ob-gyn., Royal Coll. Ob-gyn., Australian Med. Assn., Australian Perinatal Soc. Avocations: computers, wine, cars. Office: Frances Perry House 20 Flemington Rd Parkville VIC 3052 Australia Business E-Mail: umstad@bigpond.net.au.

UÑA CIDÓN, ESTHER, oncologist, educator; b. Zamora, Spain, Oct. 19, 1975; Degree in Medicine & Surgery, U. Salamanca, 1999; degree in Clin. Oncology, Ctrl. U. Hosp. Oviedo, 2004; M in Palliative Medicine, U. Valladolid, 2006, PhD, 2009; student in Polit. Sci., Nat. U. Distance Edn.; M in Molecular Oncology, Nat. Ctr. Cancer Rsch., Madrid, 2010. Cert. specialist in clinical Oncology; in clin. oncology, & evaluation costs health. Specialist registrar clin. oncology Ctrl. U. Hosp. Oviedo, 2000—04; specialist clin. oncology cons. staff Clin. U. Hosp. Valladolid, 2004—, sec. com. colorectal tumours, 2008—, histology and tumours com. mem., 2010—; prof. medicine & oncology Sch. Medicine, U. Valladolid, 2007—. Spkr. in fields; bd. mem. Health Care Adv., Canada, 2009—; mem. Colorectal Tumours Working Group of Castilla-León, 2010; assoc. editor Global Jour. Surgery Oncology; mem. editl. bd. Jour. US China Med. Sci.; editor-in-chief The Challenge of Colorectal Cancer: A Review Book; sr. editor Jour. Solid Tumors. Contbr. articles to profl. jours.; editor in chief Colorectal Cancer a review book; contbr. chapters to books. Recipient Nat. Profesor Barea awards, Clin. Mgmt. & Health Costs, 2009—10. Mem.: Internat. Soc. Gastrointestinal Tumours, European Assn. Clin. Rsch., Soc. Transl. Oncology (charter mem 2008—10), Am. Assn. Clin. Oncology, Spanish Soc. Med. Oncology, Assn. Oncology Castilla-León. Achievements include studies of biomarkers and tumoral markers in digestive tumours; clinical oncology associated cost reduction. Avocations: reading, bicycling, coin collecting/numismatics, languages, running. Office: Clin University Hosp Oncology Dept C/ Ramon y Cajal s/n 47005 Valladolid Spain Office Phone: 34678938050. Personal E-mail: aunacid@hotmail.com.

UNAKAR, NALIN JAYANTILAL, biological sciences educator; b. Karachi, Sindh, Pakistan, Mar. 26, 1935; came to U.S., 1961; s. Jayantilal Virshankar and Malati Jaswantrai (Buch) U.; m. Nita Shantilal Mankad; children: Rita, Rupa. BS, Gujerat U., Bhavnagar, India, 1955; MSc, Bombay U., 1961; PhD, Brown U., 1965. Research asst. Indian Cancer Research Ctr., Bombay, 1955-61; USPHS trainee in biology Brown U., Providence, 1961-65; research assoc. in pathology U. Toronto, Ont., Canada, 1965-66; asst. prof. biology Oakland U., Rochester, Mich., 1966-69, assoc. prof., 1969-74, prof., chmn. biology dept., 1974-87, prof., 1974-2000, prof. emeritus, 2000—, adj. prof. biomed. scis., 1984—. Mem. coop. cataract research group Nat. Eye Inst., Bethesda, Md., 1977—; mem. visual scis. study sect. NIH, Bethesda, 1982-86, mem. cataract panel, 1980—. Mem. vis. bd. Lehigh U., Bethlehem, Pa., 1986-89. Grantee Nat. Cancer Inst., NIH, 1967-70, Nat. Eye Inst., NIH, 1976-97. Mem. AAAS, Am. Soc. Cell Biology, Assn. Rsch. in Vision and Ophthalmology, Sigma Xi. Home: 2822 Rhineberry Rd Rochester Hills MI 48309-1912

ÜNAL, ABDULLAH MERIÇ, orthopedist; b. Isparta, Turkey, Nov. 26, 1979; MD, Hacettepe U. Sch. Medicine, 2003; MD in Orthopedics and Trauma surgery, Dokuz Eylül U. Sch. Medicine Orthopedics And Traumatology; PhD, Dokuz Eylül U. Sch. Medicine Orthopaedics And Traumatology, 2008. Physician, orthopedics & trauma fellow Henriettenstiftung Hosp., Hannover, Germany, 2007; surgeon dept. orthopedics & trauma Dokuz Eylül U. Hosp., 2008—09; surgeon dept. orthopedics & trauma, dept. chief Dogubayazit Govt. Hosp., Agri, Turkey, 2009—10, Isparta özel Sifa Hosp., Turkey, 2010—. Mem.: Turkish Sssn. Sports Medicine, Arthroscopy and Knee Surgery, Turkish Assn. Orthopedics and Traumatology, Internat. Soc. Arthroscopy, Knee Surgery and Sports Medicine. Avocations: running, history, ping pong/table tennis, football, mountain climbing. Office: Özel Isparta Sifa Hastanesi Yayla Mah Isparta 32100 Turkey Personal E-mail: abdmunal@yahoo.com.

UNAL, SEVIM, oncologist; b. Eskisehir, Jan. 21, 1965; PhD, Hacettepe U., 1990. Mem. childrens hematology oncology rsch. hosp. Republic Turkey Ministry of Health, 2002—. Office: Irfan Bastug Cd Ankara Diskapi 06210 Turkey Business E-Mail: sevimunal@yahoo.com.

UNANUE, EMIL RAPHAEL, immunopathologist; b. Havana, Cuba, Sept. 13, 1934; married, 1965, 3 children. B.Sc., Inst. Secondary Edn., 1952; MD, U. Havana Sch. Medicine, Cuba, 1960; MA, Harvard U., 1974. Assoc. exptl. pathology Scripps Clin. and Research Found., 1960-70; intern in pathology Presbyn. Univ. Hosp., Pitts., 1961-62; research fellow in exptl. pathology Scripps Clin. and Research Found., 1962-65; research fellow immunology Nat. Inst. Med. Research, London, 1966-68; from asst. prof. to assoc. prof. pathology Harvard U. Med. Sch., Boston, 1971-74, Mallinckrodt prof. immunopathology, 1974—85; prof., chmn. dept. pathology Washington U. Sch. Medicine, St. Louis, 1985—2006, Paul and Ellen Lacy prof. pathology. Recipient T. Duckett Jones award, Helen Hay Whitney Found., 1968, Park-Davis award, Am. Soc. Exptl. Pathology, 1973, Albert Lasker award for Basic Med. Rsch., Lasker Found., 1995, Gairdner Found. Internat. award, 2000. Office: Washington U Sch Medicine Dept Pathology and Immunology Box 8118 Saint Louis MO 63110-1093 Office Phone: 314-362-7440. Office Fax: 314-362-4096. E-mail: unanue@pathbox.wustl.edu. *

UNDAR, AKIF, research scientist, biomedical engineer, educator; b. Istanbul, Turkey, Aug. 3, 1963; arrived in U.S., 1987; s. Fikret and H. Neriman Undar; m. F. Pinar Albayrak; children: Damla, Akifcan. BS, Yildiz U., Istanbul, 1986; MS, S.W. Tex. State U., 1992; MSE, U. Tex., 1994, PhD, 1996. Asst. instr., dir. surg. rsch. U. Tex. Health Sci. Ctr., San Antonio, 1996—97; instr. Baylor Coll. Medicine, Houston, 1997—99, asst. prof. surgery, 1999—2002, assoc. prof., 2002—03; assoc. prof. pediat., surgery & bioengring. Pa. State Coll. Medicine, Hershey, 2003—09, prof. pediat., surgery & bioengring., 2009—. Tchg. asst. U. Tex., Austin, 1994—96; dir. perfusion rsch. Tex. Children's Hosp., Houston, 1997—2001, dir. rsch., 2001—03; presenter, lectr. in field. Mem. editl. bd. Artificial Organ, 2003—, ASAIO Jour., 2004—; contbr. articles to profl. jours. Rsch. grantee, AHA Tex. affiliate, 1998-2000, Tanox, Inc., 1999-2001, NIH, 2000, NHLBI, 2005—, Pa. Health Dept., 2004—. Mem.: Children's Miracle Network (grant 2003—), Pa. State Hershey Ctr. Pediat. Cardiovas. Rsch. (founder, dir. 2009—), Internat. Soc. Pediat. Mech. Circulatory Support (founder, pres. 2010—), Internat. Soc. Rotary Blood Pumps, Biomedical Engring. Soc., Internat. Soc. Artificial Organs. Office: Pa State Milton S Hershey Med Ctr Pa State Children's Hosp Dept Pediat 500 University Dr P Box 850 Hershey PA 17033 Office Phone: 717-531-6706. Business E-Mail: aundar@psu.edu.

UNDERBERG, JAMES A., internist, educator; BS, MS, U. Penn., MD, 1982—89. Diplomate Am. Bd. Internal Medicine, cert. clin. lipidology, diplomate Am. Soc. of Hypertension-specialist in clin. hypertension, cert. menopause practitioner North Am. Menopause Soc. Intern Bellevue Hosp. Med. Ctr., resident; asst. clin. prof. dept. medicine NYU Langrone Med. Ctr. Named recognized for execellence in preventive cardiovascular medicine, Am. Heart Assn. Heart-Stroke Recognition Program. Fellow: Soc. of Vascular Medicine and Biology; mem.: Nat. Lipid Assn., NY Preventive Cardiovascular Soc. (founder and pres.). Office: New York University Langone Medical Center 550 First Ave New York NY 10016 Office Phone: 212-263-7300.

UNDERBERG-DAVIS, SHARON J., radiologist; BA, Swarthmore Coll., 1983; MD, Harvard U., 1988. Diplomate Am. Bd. Radiology, 1993, Am. Bd. Radiology-pediatric radiology, 1995. Intern Brigham and Women's Hosp., Boston, 1988—89; resident diagnostic radiology Hosp. of the Univ. of Pa., Phila., 1989—93; fellow pediatric radiology The Children's Hosp. of Phila., 1993—94; with Robert Wood Johnson Univ. Hosp., New Brunswick, NJ. Office: University Radiology Group 579-A Cranbury Rd East Brunswick NJ 08816 Office Phone: 732-390-0040. Office Fax: 732-390-1856.

UNDERWOOD, BRENDA S., information specialist, microbiologist, grants administrator; b. Oak Ridge, Tenn., Mar. 19, 1948; d. William Henry Hensley and Maudell Townsend; m. Thomas L. Janiszewski, Feb. 14, 1984; 1 child, Thomas Zachary Janiszewski. BS, U. Tenn., 1970; MS, Hood Coll., 1980; MBA, Mt. St. Mary's Coll., 1993. Scientist I chem. carcinogenesis Frederick (Md.) Cancer Rsch. Ctr., 1977-84; microbiologist NCI/NIH, Bethesda, Md., 1984-86; sci. tech. writer Engring. and Econs. Rsch., Germantown, Md., 1987-88; spl. asst. to dir., program dir. grants div. Cancer Biology Diagnosis Ctrs., NCI/NIH, Bethesda, 1988-91; indexer, divsn. extramural activities Rsch. Analysis and Evaluation br. NCI/NIH, Bethesda, 1991—, sect. chief for rsch. documentation sect., supr. tech. info. specialist, 1991—2002; br. chief, referral and program analysis br. NICHD/NIH, 2002—. Vol. Riding for the Handicapped, Frederick, 1990-96; mem., recreational sec. Capital Hill Equestrian Soc., Washington, 1988. Mem. AAAS, Am. Soc. for Microbiology, Am. Assn. for Cancer Rsch., Women in Cancer Rsch., Federally Employed Women. Avocations: english riding, hiking, swimming, biking, gardening. Office: NICHD NIH RPAB Divsn Extramural Activ Bethesda MD 20892-0001

UNDERWOOD, CATHERINE H., healthcare association administrator; b. Sept. 02; BS, U. Wis., Stout; MBA, Kellogg Sch. Mgmt., Northwestern U., 1984. Cert. Assn. Exec. Exec. dir. Am. Pain Soc., 1999—; account exec. Assn. Mgmt. Ctr., 2002—; exec. dir. Nat. Assn. Neonatal Nurses. Office: American Pain Soc 4700 W Lake Ave Glenview IL 60025 Office Phone: 847-375-4715. Business E-Mail: cunderwood@ampainsoc.org. *

UNDERWOOD, PAUL BENJAMIN, gynecologist, oncologist, educator; b. Greer, SC, Aug. 8, 1934; s. Paul Benjamin and Gladys (Guest) Underwood; m. Peggy Joyce Outen, July 7, 1957; children: Paul Benjamin III, Mary Barton. MD, Med. U. S.C., 1959. Diplomate Am. Bd. Ob-gyn., Am. Bd. Gynecol. Oncology. Intern Med. U. S.C., Charleston, 1959—60, resident, 1960—64; fellow M.D. Anderson Hosp. and Tumor Inst., Houston, 1966—67; asst. prof. U. S.C., Charleston, 1967—70, assoc. prof., 1970—74, prof., 1974—99, staff, dir. gynecology, assoc. dean admissions Med. Sch., 1999—, dir. divsn. gynecol. oncology, 2002; chmn. dept. ob-gyn. U. Va. Sch. Medicine, Charlottesville, 1979-99. Contbr. articles to profl. jours. With USN, 1964—66. Recipient Alumni of Yr. award, Med. U. S.C., 1989. Mem.: Thegos Soc., S.C. Ob-Gyn. Soc., Charlottesville Med. Soc., So. Med. Soc., Felix Rutledge Soc. (pres. 1977), Am. Assn. Ob-Gyn. (sec. 1992—95, pres. 1999—), Soc. Gynecol. Oncologists (mem. coun. 1972—75, v.p. 1977—78, pres. 1983), Am. Coll. Ob-Gyn., Am. Gynecol. Club (pres. 1996), Alpha Omega Alpha. Office: 171 Ashley Ave Charleston SC 29425-0001 Office Phone: 843-792-4026. Business E-Mail: underwp@musc.edu.

UNDERWOOD, PAUL LESTER, cardiologist; b. Knoxville, Tenn., Mar. 23, 1960; MD, Mayo Med. Sch., 1984. Diplomate Am. Bd. Cardiovascular Disease. Intern Henry Ford Hosp., Detroit, 1984-85; resident internal medicine Mayo Grad. Sch. Medicine, Rochester, Minn., 1985-87; fellow in cardiology Cleve. Clinic, 1990-93; fellow in interventional cardiology Iowa Heart Ctr., Des Moines, 1993; dir. emergency medicine, dir. ICU St. Croix Hosp., U.S. V.I., 1987-90; staff N. Phoenix Heart Ctr., Ariz., 2001—07; dir. rsch. Sonoran Health Specialists-Eclipse Clin. Rsch. Assoc., 2007—. Mem. AMA, Nat. Med. Assn., Assn. Black Cardiologists (former pres.), Am. Coll. Cardiology (councilor), Am. Heart Assn. (bd. dirs. Ariz. affiliate), Soc. for Cardiac Angiography and Interventions. Office: Sonoran Health Specialists Eclipse Clin Rsch Assoc 8414 E Shea Bld Ste 103 Scottsdale AZ 85260 Home: 4727 E Berneil Dr Phoenix AZ 85028-5506 Office Phone: 480-767-3877. Business E-Mail: punderwood@sonoranhealth.com.

UNEMORI, MASAKO, dental educator; b. Japan, June 29, 1951; DDS, Kyushu U., PhD, 1976. Rschr. Kyushu U., 1976, asst. prof., 1980. Office: 3-1-1 Maidashi Higashi-ku Fukuoka 8128582 Japan Office Fax: 81 92 642 6366. Business E-Mail: unemori@dent.kyushu-u.ac.jp.

UNG, LIM ENG, physician; b. Ipoh, Perak, Malaysia, May 16, 1942; s. Cheow Khek Ung and Ean Phaik Khoo; m. Huang Sek Chang, Aug. 29, 1968; children: Casey, Coreen. MBBS, U. Singapore, 1967; MD (hon.), Open Internat. U., Colombo, 1993; diploma in practical dermatology, U. Wales, Cardiff, 1997. Cert. in aviation medicine. House officer Gen. Hosp., Kuala Lumpur, Malaysia, 1967-68; gen. practitioner Ungenglim Health Svcs., Lahad Datu, Malaysia, 1971—. Cons. Felda Sahabat, Lahad Datu, 1985—. Capt. Royal Malaysian AF, 1968-71. Mem. Malaysian Med. Assn., Malaysian Soc. Ultrasound in Medicine, Malaysian Soc. Hypnosis, Lahad Datu Golf and Country Club (pres. 1995-05). Avocations: golf, jogging. Office: Ungenglim Health Svcs PO Box 60291 91112 Lahad Datu Sabah Malaysia Home Phone: 6 089 881481; Office Phone: 6 089 881731. Personal E-mail: elung98@hotmail.com, elung06@gmail.com.

UNGAR, JUDIT, medical association administrator; Pres., exec. dir. Tourette Syndrome Assn., Inc., Bayside, NY. Office: Tourette Syndrome Assn Inc 42-40 Bell Blvd Bayside NY 11361 Office Phone: 718-224-2999. Office Fax: 718-279-9596. Business E-Mail: judit.ungar@tsa-usa.org. *

UNGER, GERE NATHAN, emergency physician, fund raising counsel, lawyer; b. Monticello, NY, May 15, 1949; s. Jessie Aaron and Shirley (Rosenstein) Unger; m. Alice J. McGowan, July 21, 1990; children: Elijah, Breena, Ari, Sasha, Arlen. JD, Bernadean U., 1979; MD, Inst. Polytecnico, Mexico City, 1986; D Phys. Medicine, Met. U., Mexico City, 1987; postgrad., Boston U., 1993, Harvard Law Sch., 1994-96; LLM in Med. Law, U. Glasgow, 2001. Diplomate Am. Bd. Forensic Examiners, Am. Bd. Med. Legal Analysis Medicine and Surgery, Am. Bd. Forensic Medicine, Am. Bd. Risk Mgmt., Am. Bd. Disability Analysts. Med. dir. Vietnam Vets. Post-Traumatic Stress Disorder Program, 1988-90; emergency rm. physician, cons. in medicaid fraud Bronx (N.Y.)-Lebanon Hosp., 1990—; clin. legal medicine Paladin Profl. Group, P.A., Palm Beach, Fla., 1992-98; pres. Albany Law Jour. Co., Inc., 1998—; jurisconsult Office of Gere Unger, M.D., J.D., 1999—; with Inalienable Rights Project Justice Watchdog Group. Mem. surg. critical care com. Am. Soc. Critical Care Medicine, 1992; mem. peer rev. com. Nat. Inst. Disability and Rehab. Rsch., Office Spl. Edn., U.S. Dept. Edn., 1993; mediator, arbitrator, negotiator World Intellectual Property Orgn., 1994; mem. clin. ethics com. Inst. Medecine Legale et de Medecine Sociale, Strasbourg, France, 1994; mediator, arbitrator World Bank, 2000—; chmn. Vet.'s Collaborative; pres., CEO Barista Solutions, civil ct. mediator. Mem. editl. bd. Am. Bd. Forensic Examiners, 1993, Jour. Neurol. and Orthopaedic Medicine and Surgery, 1993. Comdt. Broward County Marine Corps League, 1995—. With USMC, 1968—72. Fellow: The Cognitive Sci. Soc., Exec. Practice Mgmt., Am. Coll. Forensic Examiners, Am. Coll. Legal Medicine, Internat. Coll. Surgeons (mem. ethics com. 1994, mem. emergency response program eastern region 1994), Am. Acad. Neurol. and Orthopedic Surgeons; mem.: FBA (mem. health com., rep. ABA 1994, chmn. med. malpractice/tort com., liaison to AMA), ABA, ATLA (N.Y. state capt. 1992), Internat. Soc. Mil. Law and the Law for War, Mass. Med. Assn., Assn. Corp. Counsel, Internat. Soc. Mil. Law and Law of War, Judge Advs. Assn., Intarnat. Acad. Collaborative Profls., Internat. Assn. Collaborative Profls., N.Y. State Defenders Assn., Nat. Am. Indian Ct. Judges Assn., N.W. Indian Bar Assn., Internat. Assn. Prosecutors, Am. Soc. Investigative Pathology, Internat. Criminal Law Network (The Hague), Internat. Assn. Prosecutors, Internat. Royal Soc. Medicine (London), Nat. Assn. Forensic Econs., Am. Soc. Laser Medicine and Surgery, Kennedy Inst. Ethics, Am. Coll. Physician Execs. (chair forum law and med. mgmt. 1995), Internat. Bar Assn., Nat. Coll. Advocacy. Avocations: flying, boating. Office Phone: 508-759-0009, 202-466-1679, 508-291-7777. Personal E-mail: barristermd@yahoo.com, irproj@yahoo.com. E-mail: barista@lodge-advocate.com.

UNGER, ROBIN, surgeon; b. Toronto, Can., Mar. 31, 1968; BA, McGill U., 1992; MD, Sackler Sch. Medicine, Tel Aviv U., 1999. Physician in hair loss and hair transplant surgery, pres. Unger MDPC, 2001—. Asst. prof. Mt. Sinai Sch. Medicine, 2006—11. Master: Am. Bd. Hair Restoration; mem.: AMA, Ops. Restore, Internat. Soc. Hair Restoration. Avocations: painting, reading. Office: 710 Park Ave New York NY 10021 Office Fax: 212-249-4032. Personal E-mail: drrobinunger@yahoo.com.

UNHJEM, MICHAEL BRUCE, lawyer; b. Fargo, ND, Aug. 22, 1953; s. Kalmer Joseph and Lorelei Mae (Myhra) U.; children: Kaia Mary, David Burges, Kirsten Elizabeth. BA magna cum laude, Jamestown Coll., 1975; JD with distinction, U. N.D., 1978. Bar: N.D. 1978. Pvt. practice, Jamestown, ND, 1978-86; compliance officer Norwest Bank, Jamestown, ND, 1981-84; planned giving officer Jamestown Coll., Anne Carlsen Sch., Jamestown, 1984-86; asst. to pres., gen. counsel Blue Cross Blue Shield of N.D., Fargo, 1986-91, pres., chief exec. officer, 1991—2009, Pioneer Mutual Life Ins. Co., Fargo, 1997—99; atty. at law ND Supreme Ct. Chmn. bd. dirs. Lincoln Mut. Life & Casualty Ins. Co., Fargo, Noridian Adminstr. Svc., LLC, Fargo, Noridian Ins. Svc., Inc., Fargo; chmn. TriWest HC All, Cass Clay United Way; mem. bd. dirs. Prime Ther, Western Conf. Prepaid Health Plans, Jamestown Coll., Blue Cross Blue Shield Assn. State rep. N.D. Legis. Assembly, Bismarck, 1974-86; mem. Nat. Conf. Commrs. on Uniform State Laws, Chgo., 1981—, chmn., Bismarck, 1982-86; co-chmn. Bush for Pres. Com., 1980, 88, 92; presdl. appointee Nat. Coun. on Disability, Washington, 1990.chmn. ND Caring Found., pres. Mental Health Assn., mem. bd. dirs. Jamestown Hosp. Named Outstanding Young North Dakotan, N.D. Jaycees, 1983; recipient Nat. Excellence in Leadership award State of N.D., 1988, Disting. Leadership award N.D. Psychol. Assn., 1988, Spl. Presdl. Commendation award Am. Psychiatric Assn., 1989, Toastmaster Internat. Comm. and Leadership award, 1992, brand excellence awards, BCBS Assn. Mem. ABA, N.D. Bar Assn., Cass County Bar Assn., Kiwanis, Elks, Masons, Shriners. Republican. Lutheran.

UNIS, MARCOS D., veterinarian; b. LA, Calif., Aug. 18, 1978; BS in Biology, Colo. State U., 2002; DVM, St. George's U., Grenada, West Indies, MS in Vet. Anatomy, 2007. Emergency veterinarian Animal Emergency Care Ctr., 2007; intern, small animal medicine & surgery U. Ill. Vet. Med. Tchg. Hosp., 2007—08; resident, small animal surgery Kans. State U. Vet. Med. Tchg. Hosp., 2008—11; vet. surgeon VCA All Care Animal Referral Ctr., 2011. Intern Grad. Edn. Minority Students Program U. Colo. Heath Scis. Ctr., 2002—02; rsch. cons. Toxicology Lab., Colo. State U., 2003—05; rsch. asst. Minority Biomedical Rsch. Support Program Reproductive Physiology Lab., U. Southern Colo., 2000—02. Recipient Excellence award, Ft. Dodge Animal Health, Outstanding Achievement award, Grad. Edn. Minority Students, Reproductive Physiology Lab., U. Southern Colo. Mem.: AVMA, Am. Coll. Vet. Surgeons, Tribeta Biol. Honor Soc. Achievements include research in evaluation of intra- and interobserver variability and repeatability of tibial plateau angle measurements with digital radiography using a novel digital radiographic. Office: 18440 Amistad St Fountain Valley CA 92708 Business E-Mail: munis@vet.ksu.edu.

UNLAP, TINO, biotechnologist, educator; b. Micronesia, June 22, 1965; BS, Western Ky. U., 1981; PhD, Kans. State U., 1990. Asst. prof. Tulane Med. Sch., 2007—08, U. Ala. at Birmingham Med Sch., 2000—07, assoc. prof., 2008—. Dir. Heritage Ctr. Biotech. Program, 2002—07; co-dir. BiotekWorks, 2005—07; adj. prof. OLOL Nurse Anesthesia, 2006—07; mem. editl. bd. Trade Sci. Inc, Biotech., 2010—11, Jour. Biotech. and Biomaterial, 2010—11. Recipient Dean's Award, U. Ala at Birmingham Grad. Sch., Excellence award, Sch. Health Professions, U. Ala at Birmingham. Avocations: martial arts, racquetball, tennis. Office: SHPB476 1705 University Blvd Birmingham AL 35294 Office Fax: 205-975-7302. Business E-Mail: unlap@uab.edu.

UNO, YASUHIRO, research scientist; b. Osaka, Japan, Feb. 19, 1969; DVM, Hokkaido U., 1994, PhD, 2008. Asst. prof. Hokkaido U., Grad. Sch. Pharm. Scis., 2003—06; group leader Shin Nippon Biomed. Labs., Ltd., 2006—. Mem.: Molecular Biology Soc. Japan, Japanese Soc. Study Xenobiotics (Young Scientists award), Japanese Soc. Vet. Sci., ASPET. Office: Shin Nippon Biomed Labs Kainan Wakayama 642-0017 Japan E-mail: uno-yasuhiro@snbl.co.jp.

UNSGÅRD, GEIRMUND, neurosurgeon, educator; b. Trondheim, Norway, Feb. 14, 1948; s. Iver Johan and Alma Unsgård; m. Anne Katrine Momyr; children: Ingrid Alma, Åsne Kristine, Runa Geirmundsdatter, Vigdis Bergitte, Sunniva. MD, U. Oslo, 1974; PhD, U. Trondheim, 1979; specialist in neurosurgery, 1989. Jr. registrar dept. surgery U. Hosp. Trondheim, 1979-81, jr. registrar dept. neurosurgery, 1982-84, sr. registrar dept. neurosurgery, 1984-86, cons. dept. neurosurgery, 1986-96, chief dept. neurosurgery, 1996—, chief neurodivsn. neurosurgery and neurology, 2003. Prof. Norwegian U. Sci. and Tech., Trondheim, 1989—, vice dean med. faculty, 1991-93, dean med. faculty, 1993-98; mem. Nat. Govts. Coun. for Highly Specialized Hosp. Medicine, Norway, 1991-2001. Contbr. over 130 articles to profl. publs. Rep. City Coun. Trondheim, 1987-94; aast. chmn. bd. Trondheim Bus Co., 1987-91, Trondheim Energy Co., 1991-94; mem. bd. Trondheim Cleaning Dep., 1987-91. Recipient prize for excellent rsch. Found. for Indsl. and Tech. Rsch., Trondheim/Oslo, 2000, Knight, St. Olavs Orden, 2010. Mem. Royal Sci. Soc. Norway, Norwegian Acad. Technol. Scis., Norwegian Neurosurg. Assn. (chmn. 1992-94), Scandinavian Neurosurg. Assn. (treas. 1992-94, bd. mem. 1995-98), European Assn. Neurol. Socs. (tng. com. 1988-2004, rsch. com. 1995-2001, v.p. 2003-07). Achievements include 3 patents in field; research interest; immunology and tumor biology; metabolism in brain tissue measured by MRS; ultrasound in brain surgery; ultrasound guided neurosurgery which has led to development of SonoWand an ultrasound based neuronavigation system that is commercialized. Home: Vinge 7510 Skatval Norway Office: St Olav Univ Hosp Neurosurg Dept Trondheim Norway Business E-Mail: geirmund.unsgard@ntnu.no.

UNTEREKER, WILLIAM J., cardiologist, educator; Attended, Columbia U., 1973. Diplomate Am. Bd. Internal Medicine, 1976, Am. Bd. Internal Medicine-cardiovasc. medicine, 1979. Intern internal medicine Mt. Sinai Hosp., 1974—76, resident cardiovasc. diseases, 1976—78, fellow, 1978—79; clin. assoc. prof. of medicine Univ. of Pa.; assoc. dir. cardiology divsn. Penn Presbyn. Med. Ctr. Recipient Top Doctors, Phila. Mag., 2005—06, 2010—11; named one of, 2002, Best Doctors in America, 2003—04, 2005—06, 2009—10. Fellow: Phila. Acad. of Cardiology, ACP, Am. Heart Assn., Am. Coll. of Cardiology; mem.: Soc. of Cardiol. Angiography. Office: Penn Presbyterian Medical Center Philadelphia Heart Institute 4th Fl Ste 400 51 N 39th St Philadelphia PA 19104 Office Phone: 800-789-7366.

UNTERWEGER, MARTIN, diagnostic radiologist; MD, U. Zürich, Switzerland; MBA, U. Zürich, EMM, 1995. Cert. radiologist Europe, 2001. Resident U. Hosp. Zürich, 1994—2000; fellow U. Hosp. Basel, Basel, Switzerland, 2000—02. Contbr. articles to profl. jours. Office: Cantonal Hosp Baden Im Ergel 5404 Baden Switzerland Office Phone: 056 486 3810. Business E-Mail: munterweger@gmx.ch.

UOTILA, LASSE JUHA, physician; b. Leppavirta, Finland, Aug. 1, 1946; s. Arvi and Aili (Taivalaho) U.; m. Marita T. Yli-Tokko, June 15, 1979; children: Martti, Suvi. MD, U. Helsinki, Finland, 1971, PhD in Med. Biochemistry, 1974, docent's competence med. biochemistry, 1979, docent's competence clin. lab. medicine, 1986. Fellow European Bd. Med. Biopathology, 2004; instr., sr. lectr. dept. med. chemistry U. Helsinki, 1972-82; acting specialist clin. chemistry, acting adminstrv. dep. Helsinki U. Ctrl. Hosp., 1982-90, dept. head lab., 1991—. Clin. lab. med. intern Clin. Lab., Helsinki U. Ctrl. Hosp., 1975, 76-78; postdoctoral rsch. fellow dept. biochemistry U. Stockholm, 1975-76, U. Wis., Madison, 1979-81; cons. clin. chemistry Labquality Inc., Helsinki, 1988—. Contbr. articles to profl. jours. Recipient Gustaf Komppa prize Finnish Chem. Soc., 1975. Fellow European Bd. Med. Biopathology; mem. Finnish Soc. Clin. Chemistry (former treas.), Societas Biochemica, Biophysica et Microbiologiae Fenniae, Finnish Med. Assn., Am. Assn. for Clin. Chemistry Avocations: classical music, old steamships, computers, sailing. Office: Helsinki U Ctrl Hosp Clin Lab Haartmaninkatu 4 00290 Helsinki Finland E-mail: lasse.uotila@hus.fi.

UPADHYAY, SANJAY, scientist; b. Varanasi, India, Feb. 14, 1966; MSc, B.H.U., Varanasi, 1989, PhD, 1993. Rschr. Def. Rsch. & Devel. Establishment, 2007, scientist 'E' dep. dir., 2007—. Mem.: Indian Sci. Congress Assn. Avocations: reading, music, movies, cricket, football. Office: Def Rsch & Devel Establishment Gwalior Madhya Pradesh 474002 India Office Fax: 91-751-2341148. Personal E-mail: sanjayupad@rediffmail.com.

UPADHYAY, YOGENDRA NATH, physician, educator; b. Gorakhpur, India, Dec. 21, 1938; arrived in U.S., 1963; s. Murlidhar and Vansraji (Pande) U.; m. Cecile R. Yonish; children: Asha, Sameer, Sanjay. MB, BS, All India Inst. Med. Scis., New Delhi, 1962. Diplomate Am. Bd. Psychiatry and Neurology, Am. Bd. Psychiatry and Child and Adolescent Psychiatry. Instr. in pediatrics Johns Hopkins U. Sch. Medicine, Balt., 1969-71; fellow in child psychiatry Johns Hopkins Hosp./Johns Hopkins U., Balt., 1971-72; resident, then sr. resident in psychiatry Albert Einstein Coll. Medicine/Bronx Mcpl. Hosp. Ctr., 1972-74, fellow in child psychiatry, 1974-75; chief, partial hosp. program for children, dept. psychiatry Brookdale Hosp., Bklyn., 1976-77; med. dir. West Nassau Mental Health Ctr., Franklin Sq., NY, 1977-80; asst. prof. clin. psychiatry SUNY, Stony Brook, 1978-92; dir. child and adolescent psychiatry Nassau County Med. Ctr., East Meadow, NY, 1980-92; sr. psychiatrist South Oaks Hosp., Amityville, NY, 1992—, pres. med. staff, 1995-97, svc. med. dir. child and adolescent psychiatry, 1995-97, med. dir., 1997—; sr. v.p., Medical Affairs South Oak Hosp. and Broadlawn Nursing Home, 2001—. Sr. v.p. med. affairs LI Home, Amityville, NY, 2001—. Fellow Am. Psychiat. Assn. (cons. task force treatments psychiat. disorders 1989—), Am. Acad. Child and Adolescent Psychiatry, Allmsonians of Am. (founding pres. 1982-86), Disting. Life, Am. Psychiat. Assn.,

Am. Acad. Child and Adolescent Psychiatry. Office: S Oaks Hosp 400 Sunrise Hwy Amityville NY 11701-2508 Office Phone: 631-608-5227. Business E-Mail: yupadhyay@south-oaks.org.

UPADYA, ANUPAMA, internist, researcher; b. Kundapur, Karnataka, India, Feb. 11, 1973; m. Shrikanth Upadya; children: Kunal, Nisha. Student, Ramnarain Ruia College, Bombay, India, 1988—90; B Medicine and Surgery, Lokmanya Tilak Mcpl. Coll., Bombay, 1990—96; MD, Yale U., 2001. Diplomate Am. Bd. Internal Medicine, Am. Bd. Pulmonary Medicine, Am. Bd. Sleep Medicine, cert. BLS, ACLS. Intern Lokmanya Tilak Mcpl. Coll., Bombay, 1996—98; resident in internal medicine Yale U., Bridgeport, Conn., 1998—2001, chief resident, 2001, fellow in pulmonary care, 2002—03. Mem. residency rev. com. Yale U., Bridgeport, 1998, mem. interim radiology residency review com., 2000, mem. chief residents com., 2001—. Contbr. articles to profl. jours. Grantee, Bridgeport Hospital, 2001; scholar, Indian Council of Medical Research, 1996. Mem.: ACP, AMA, Am. Acad. Sleep Medicine, Am. Coll. Chest Physicians, Soc. Critical Care Medicine, Am. Thoracic Soc. Office: 753 Hwy 466 Lady Lake FL 32159

UPADYA, SHRIKANTH PY, internist; b. Bangalore, India, May 8, 1967; arrived in U.S., 1993; s. Yogesha P. and Susheela P. Y. Upadya; m. Anupama Upadya, Apr. 7, 1996; children: Kunal, Nisha. MBBS, Mysore Med. Coll., India, 1991; MD, Interfaith Med. Ctr., 1996. Diplomate Am. Bd. Internal Medicine, cert. Bd. Nuc. Cardiology, Echocardiography. Intern Shekar Hosp., Bangalore, India, 1990—91; fellow orthop. Grant Med. Coll., Mumbai, 1991—93; resident Interfaith Med. Ctr., NYC, 1993—96, chief resident, 1996—97; internist Chest Medicine Assocs., Apple Valley, Calif., 1997—99, Health & Hosp. Corp. with St. Barnabas Health & PHS, NYC, 1999—2001; fellow in heart failure, cardiac transplant Yale U. Sch. Medicine, New Haven, 2001—02; fellow in echo, nuc. cardiology St. Luke Roosevelt Hosp., NYC, 2002—03; fellow in cardiology Bridgeport Hosp. Yale U., New Haven, 2003—05; fellow in interventional cardiology Lenox Hill Hosp., NY, 2005—06; pvt. practise, 2006—. Presenter in field. Contbr. articles to profl. jours. Mem.: ACP, AMA, Am. Soc. Echocardiography, Am. Heart Assn., Am Coll. Cardiology, Am. Soc. Internal Medicine (dir. at large, resident physician 1994). Avocations: photography, sports, travel. Office: Bridgeport Hosp Cardiology Dept Bridgeport CT 06825

UPSHAW, HARRY STEPHAN, psychologist, educator; b. Birmingham, Ala., July 10, 1926; s. N.H. and Florence (Arnold) U.; m. Paula Binyon, June 18, 1950; children: Alan Binyon, Phyllis, David Arnold, Stephan Lipner. Student, U. Ala., 1946-47; AB, U. Chgo., 1949; MA, Northwestern U., 1951; PhD, U. N.C., 1956. Asst prof. psychology U. Ala., 1954-57; spl. instr. psychology Simmons Coll., Boston, 1957-58, research asso. Edtl. Research Corp., Cambridge, Mass., 1957-58; asst. prof., then assoc. prof. pub. health U. N.C., 1958-61, lectr., assoc. prof. psychology, 1958-64, rsch. prof. psychology, 1991-97; assoc. prof. Bryn Mawr (Pa.) Coll., 1961-65; assoc. prof., then prof. emeritus psychology U. Ill., Chgo., 1965-91, prof. emeritus, 1991—, dept. head, 1968-72; assoc. dir. Office of Social Sci. Rsch., 1981-87. Guest prof. U. Mannheim, Germany, 1975, Fulbright scholar Technische U., Berlin, 1978-79; vis. scholar Inst. for Rsch. in Social Sci., U. NC, 1991-92; del. to South Africa, People to People Amb. Program, 2004. Editorial cons., Jour. Exptl. Social Psychology, Research in Personality, Jour. Applied Social Psychology, Jour. Personality Social Psychology; Contbr. articles to profl. jours. Served with AUS, 1944-46. Fellow Am. Psychol. Assn., Soc. Exptl. Social Psychol. Office Phone: 312-819-0408.

UPTON, ARTHUR CANFIELD, experimental pathologist, educator; b. Ann Arbor, Mich., Feb. 27, 1923; s. Herbert Hawkes and Ellen (Canfield) Upton; m. Elizabeth Bache Perry, Mar. 1, 1946; children: Rebecca A., Melissa P., Bradley C. Grad., Phillips Acad., Andover, Mass., 1941; BA, U. Mich., 1944, MD, 1946. Intern Univ. Hosp., Ann Arbor, 1947, resident, 1948—49; instr. pathology U. Mich. Med. Sch., 1950—51; pathologist Oak Ridge (Tenn.) Nat. Lab., 1951—54, chief pathology-physiology sect., 1954—69; prof. pathology SUNY Med. Sch. at Stony Brook, 1969—77, chmn. dept. pathology, 1969—70, dean Sch. Basic Health Scis., 1970—75; dir. Nat. Cancer Inst., Bethesda, Md., 1977—79; prof., chmn. dept. environ. medicine NYU Med. Sch., NYC, 1980—92, prof. emeritus, 1993—; clin. prof. radiology U. N.Mex. Sch. Medicine, 1993—95, clin. prof., pathology, 1992—95; clin. prof. environ. and cmty. medicine U. Medicine and Dentistry N.J.-Robert Wood Johnson Med. Sch., 1995—. Attending pathologist Brookhaven Nat. Lab., 1969—77; dir. Inst. Environ. Medicine, Med. Sch., NYU, 1980—92; mem. various coms. nat. and internat. orgns.; lectr. in field; mem. adv. bd. GM Cancer Rsch. Found. Assoc. editor Cancer Rsch., mem. editl. bd. Internat. Union Against Cancer. With US Army, 1943—46. Recipient Ernest Orlando Lawrence award for atomic field, 1965, Claude M. Fuess award, 1980, Sarah L. Poilley award for pub. health, 1983, CHUMS Physician of Yr. award, 1985, Basic Cell Rsch. in Cytology Lectureship award, 1985, Fred W. Stewart award, 1986, Ramazzini award, 1986, Lovelace Med. Found. award, 1993; named nat. lectr., Sigma Xi, 1989—91. Fellow: N.Y. Acad. Sci., Soc. Risk Analysis (Outstanding Achievement award 1997); mem.: AAAS, Ramazzini Inst. (pres. 1992—2003), Assn. Univ. Environ. Health Sci. Ctrs. (pres. 1982—90), Internat. Assn. Radiation Rsch., N.Y. State Health Rsch. Coun. (chmn. 1982—90), Soc. Exptl. Biology and Medicine, Sci. Rsch. Soc. Am., Gerontol. Soc., Peruvian Oncology Soc. (hon.), Japan Cancer Assn. (hon.), Am. Soc. Exptl. Pathology (pres. 1967—68), Am. Assn. Cancer Rsch. (pres. 1963—64), Internat. Assn. Radiation Rsch. (pres. 1983—87), Radiation Rsch. Soc. (councilor 1963—64, pres. 1965—66), Inst. Medicine of NAS (Comfort-Crookshank award 1979), Internat. Acad. Pathology, Am. Assn. Pathologists and Bacteriologists, Sigma Xi, Nu Sigma Nu, Alpha Omega Alpha, Phi Gamma Delta, Phi Beta Kappa. Achievements include research in pathology of radiation injury and endocrine glands, on cancer, on carcinogenesis, on experimental leukemia on aging. Home: 250 E Alameda Apt 636 Santa Fe NM 87501 Office: 303 George St Ste 110 New Brunswick NJ 08901 Office Phone: 732-579-1092. Business E-Mail: acupton@cresp.org.

URAKAMI, KATSUYA, medical educator; b. Okayama, July 3, 1956; D. Tottori U., 1983. Prof. Tottori U., 2000—. Office: Nishimachi 86 Yonago Tottori 683-8503 Japan Office Fax: 81-859-38-6350. Business E-Mail: kurakami@med.tottori-u.ac.jp.

URAKAMI, YUKO, physiatrist, educator; b. Sapporo City, Hokkaido, Japan, Aug. 23, 1959; d. Sho-ji and Yasuko Suzuki; m. Shin-ya Urakami; children: Kentaro, Maiko. MD, Juntendo U., Tokyo, 1985. Chief Nat. Rehab. Ctr. Persons with Disabilities, Tokorozawa City, Saitama, Japan, 1999—; instr. Juntendo U., 2006—. Achievements include research in clinical neurophysiology. Office: Nat Rehab Ctr 4-1 Namiki Tokorozawa Saitama 359-8555 Japan Office Fax: 81-4-2995-0355. Business E-Mail: urakami-yuko@rehab.go.jp.

URBAN, NICOLE D., biostatistician; b. Trenton, NJ, Aug. 16, 1946; d. James Ross Stewart and Patricia Bryant Urban; m. Lee Emery Edlefsen (div.); children: Kerstin Lara Edlefsen, Paul Thatcher Edlefsen. BA in English lit., Simmons Coll., 1970; MS in Biostatistics, Harvard Sch. of Pub. Health, 1973, ScD in Biostatistics and Health Services Adminstrn., 1978. Prin. investigator, Specialized Program of Rsch. Excellence grant in ovarian cancer NIH/Nat. Cancer Inst., Seattle, 1999—; sci. dir. Marsha Rivkin Ctr. for Ovarian Cancer Rsch., Seattle, 1996—2005; mem., cancer prevention rsch. program, divsn. of pub. health sciences Fred Hutchinson Cancer Rsch. Ctr., Seattle, 1998—2005; rsch. prof., dept. of health services, sch. of pub. health and cmty. medicine U. of Wash., Seattle, 2000—; program head, gynecologic cancer rsch. program Fred Hutchinson Cancer Rsch. Ctr., Seattle, 2001—. Mem., p30/p50 working group Nat. Cancer Adv. Bd., 2002—; participant, strategic planning project meeting, applied cancer screening rsch. br. Nat. Cancer Inst., 2001—; mem., external adv. com., specialized program of rsch. excellence in breast cancer Vanderbilt U., 2001—; mem., med. adv. bd. Nat. Ovarian Cancer Coalition, 2001—; chair, external adv. com., specialized program of rsch. excellence in ovarian cancer U. of Tex., 2000—; co-chair, gynecologic cancers progress rev. group Nat. Cancer Inst., 2000—; mem., wash. state cancer registry adv. coun. Wash. State Dept. of Health, 1996—, mem., breast and cervical early detection exec. com., 1994—; mem. molecular diagnostic program, divsn pub. health scis. Fred Huthinson CRC, Seattle, 2006—. Contbr. articles to profl. jours. Grant, Nat. Institutes of Health/Nat. Cancer Inst., 1999—, US Dept. of Def., 2002—, Nat. Institutes of Health/Nat. Cancer Inst., 1997—2002, 1997—2002, US Dept. of Def./United States Army Med. Rsch. and Materiel Command (Ovarian Cancer Rsch. Program), 1998—2001. Mem.: Am. Assn. for Cancer Rsch., South West Oncology Group, Assn. for Health Services Rsch., Am. Soc. of Preventive Oncology, Soc. for Clin. Trials. Office: Fred Hutchinson Cancer Rsch Ctr Box 358080 1100 Fairview Ave N MP900 Seattle WA 98109-1024

URBANETTI, JOHN SUTHERLAND, internist, consultant; b. Mineola, NY, Aug. 14, 1943; s. Anthony Joseph and Mildred S. U.; children: Andrew, Alexis. AB, Johns Hopkins U., 1964, MD, 1967. Diplomate Am. Bd. Internal Medicine and Pulmonary Diseases. Internal medicine intern Johns Hopkins Hosp., Balt., 1967-68, internal medicine resident, 1968-69; fellow in pulmonary cardiology McGill U., Montreal, Can., 1971-74; asst. prof. medicine and dir. pulmonary lab. Tufts New Eng. Med. Ctr. Hosp., Boston, 1974-80; asst. prof. clin. medicine and pulmonary diseases Yale U., New Haven, Conn., 1980—. Cons. toxic inhalation US Surgeon Gen., U.S. Army, USN, USAF, 1974—; cons. biochem. terrorism Dept. of Def., Dept. Justice, 1974—, Dept. State, 1999—. Author: Carbon Monoxide Poisoning, 1980, Pulmonary Management of Surgical Patients, 1982, Battlefield Chemical Inhalation, 1988, Chemical and Biological Warfare, 1997; contbr. articles to profl. jours. Capt. USAF, 1969-71. Recipient Commdr's award for pub. svc. U.S. Army, 1990. Fellow Royal Coll. Physicians and Surgeons (Can.), Am. Coll. Physicians, Am. Coll. Chest Physicians; mem. Am. Thoracic Soc., Aerospace Medicine Soc.; gov. Soc of the Descendants and the Founders of the Hartford 2005-. Avocation: swimming. Office: Southeastern Pulmonary Assocs 155 Montauk Ave New London CT 06320-4842 Office Phone: 860-444-2223. Business E-Mail: jsu@jhu.edu.

URBANI, CARLO ENRICO, dermatologist; b. Milan, June 1, 1961; s. Stellio Urbani and Vittorina Lorini; m. Paola Quinteri, May 7, 1988 (separated). Degree in Medicine & Surgery summa cum laude, U. Milan, 1986, specialization in dermatology, 1989, specialization in chemotherapy, 1993. Resident dept. internal medicine Hosp. Sacco, Milan, 1983-86; fellow resident dept. dermatology Hosp. San Paolo, Milan, 1986-89; cons. dermatologist Sci. Inst. for Hospitalization-Treatment Hosp. San Raffaele-Resnati, Milan, 1989—. Cons. dermatologist Hosp. Ctr. Multimedica, Sesto S. Giovanni, Milan, 1998—, Occupl. and Environ. Dermatologic Svc. of Centro Medico Resnati, Milan, 2000—; designated med. practitioner in immigation med. exams. of Can. health programs, 1990—; spkr. in field. Author: Accessory Mammary Tissue in Clinical Practice, 1996, (with others) Complementary Medicine in Dermatology, 1998; reviewer: (jours.) Dermatology, Dermatologic Therapy, European Jour. Pediats., Breast Disease; contbr. chpt. to book, more than 118 articles to med. jours. Recipient Disting. Leadership award in dermatology and human genetics, 2000. Fellow Am. Acad. Dermatology; mem. Internat. Soc. Dermatology, Internat. Soc. Plastic and Aesthetic Dermatology, Dermoscopy Working Group (task force for melanoma prevention program), Dermatology Found., Italian Soc. Dermatology and Venereology, Italian Soc. Dermatologic Surgery and Oncology, Italian Med. Assn., Italian Soc. Chemotherapy, Italian Assn. for Atopic Eczema, European Acad. Dermatology and Venereology, NY Acad. Scis. Roman Catholic. Avocations: swimming, trekking, jogging, ping pong/table tennis. Home: Via G Frua 11 20146 Milan Italy Office: U Milan Dermatology Svc Via Santa Croce 10/A 20122 Milan MI Italy Office Phone: +39-02-295 295 71. E-mail: ceurbani@tin.it.

URBINA, CHRISTOPHER E., public health service officer, state official; married; 2 children. BS in Biology, Stanford U.; MS in Pub. Health, Johns Hopkins U.; MD, U. Colo., 1980. Cert. family practice and preventive medicine. Assoc. prof. U. Colo. Sch. Medicine; assoc. chair, assoc. prof. Dept. Family and Cmty. Medicine U. N.Mex.; dist. health officer N.Mex. Health and Environment Dept.; joined Denver Pub. Health Dept., 2004, dir.; exec. dir., chief med. officer Colo. Dept. Pub. Health and Environment, 2011—. Co-chair Colo. Pub. Health Improvement Plan-From Act to Action. Recipient Excellence in Public Health Practice, Colo. Sch. of Pub. Health, 2009—10; named one of Best Doctors in Pub. Health and Preventive Medicine, 5280 Mag. Mem.: Colo. Pub. Health Assn. (pres.), Ctr. for Pub. Health Practice Adv. Com., American Acad. of Family Physicians, Assn. of Teachers of Preventive Medicine. Office: Colorado Department of Public Health and Environment 4300 Cherry Creek Dr S Denver CO 80246-1530 Office Phone: 303-692-2000. *

URBSCHAT, STEFFI, biologist; b. Landstuhl, Germany, Jan. 10, 1964; d. Irma and Valentin Lutz; children: Henk Duncan, Marik, Naomi, Lilli Charlotte. Diploma in Biology, U. Kaiserslautern, 1989; PhD, Humangenetics, Homburg, Saar, 1992. Postdoc. Inst. Humangenetics, Hombur-Saar, Germany, 1996—; team leader and pvt. lectr. Neurooncology rsch. group, Homburg-Saar, 2005—. Contbr. articles to rsch. jours. Mem.: Deutsche Gesellschaft Humangenetik, Eano. Achievements include development of a new method:A two-colour technique for chromosome in situ hybridization in tissue sections. Avocations: modern jazz, dance. Home: Obere Himmelsberg str 46 Zweibrucken D 66482 Germany Office Fax: 49-68411626636. Business E-Mail: hgsmur@uks.eu, steffi.urbschat@uks.eu.

URDANETA, FELIPE, anesthesiologist; b. Bogota, Colombia, July 1, 1965; MD, U. del Rosario, 1992. Anesthesiologist U. Fla. NFS-GVHS, 1999—. Recipient Tchg. award, U. Fla.; named Intern of Yr., Outstanding Tchr. of Yr. Mem.: FSA, SAM, ASA. Avocations: tennis, sports, exercise. Office: PO Box 100254 Gainesville FL 32608

URFER, ROMAN, research scientist; b. Winterthur, Switzerland, May 7, 1963; s. Fritz Albert and Berta Urfer; m. Anne Marie Urfer-Buchwalder, Sept. 30, 1995; 1 child, Fabienne. PhD, U. of Basel, 1989—92. Drug discovery program head Novartis Pharma AG, Basel, Switzerland, 1996—2001; sr. v.p. drug discovery & devel. AGY Therapeutics, South San Francisco, Calif., 2001—. First lt. Inf., 1983—87, Switzerland. Mem.: Am. Heart Assn., Am. Soc. for Neuroscience. Achievements include research in structure/function relationship in neurotrophins; pathological pathways in neurodegenerative disorders; chemokine modulation in anti-inflammatory therapy; patents for novel neurotrophic factors; patents pending for novel targets for treatment of stroke; therapeutic antibody directed at chemokine MCP-1.

URICIUC, WILLI ANDREI, dentist, educator; b. Vatra Dornei, Suceava, Romania, Feb. 16, 1980; Cert. specialist dental lab. technician Faculty Dental Medicine Cluj-Napoca, 2007, specialist in materials processing engring. Faculty Materials Sci. Engring., 2009. Assoc. dental specialist rsch. Tech. U. Cluj Napoca, Faculty Materials Sci. and Engring., Dept. Materials Processing Engring., Corrosion and Anticorrosion Protection Lab., 2008—; tchg. dental technician U. Medicine and Pharmacy Cluj-Napoca, Faculty Dental Medicine, 2005—08, assoc. prof. dental lab. technician students dept. dental materials & ergonomy, 2009—. Recipient Best Young Scientist award, Med. Biotechnology Field, 2009. Avocations: painting, skiing, tennis. Home: C Brancoveanu 35/6 Cluj-Napoca Cluj 400467 Romania Personal E-mail: willidenty@yahoo.com.

URICK, JAMES R., dentist; DDS, UCLA Sch. Dentistry, 1996. Resident, chief resident, clin. instr. U. Calif. San Francisco Gen. Dentistry Residency, 1997—98, co-founder Calif. Ctr. Aesthetic Dentistry, DDS & Associates, San Francisco, 2002—. Named Best of the Bay, San Francisco Mag., Top Doc. Mem.: San Francisco Dental Soc., Calif. Dental Assn., Am. Dental Assn., Am. Acad. Cosmetic Dentistry. Office: DDS & Associates 230 California St Ste 200 San Francisco CA 94111

URQUHART, JOHN, medical researcher, educator; b. Pitts., Apr. 24, 1934; s. John and Wilma Nelda (Martin) U.; m. Joan Cooley, Dec. 28, 1957; children: Elizabeth Urquhart Vdovjak, John Christopher (dec. 1965), Robert Malcolm, Thomas Jubal. BA with honors, Rice U., 1955; MD with honors, Harvard U., 1959; D honoris causa, U. Utrecht, 1997. Lic. physician, Calif. Walter B. Cannon fellow in physiology Harvard Med. Sch., Boston, 1956, Josiah Macy, Jr. fellow, 1956-58, 59-61; intern in surgery Mass. Gen. Hosp., 1959-60, asst. resident, 1960-61; investigator Nat. Heart Inst., NIH, Bethesda, Md., 1961-63; asst. prof. physiology U. Pitts. Sch. Medicine, 1963-66, assoc. prof., 1966-68, prof., 1968-70; prof. biomed. engring. U. So. Calif., LA, 1970-71; prin. scientist ALZA Corp., Palo Alto, Calif., 1970-86, dir. biol. scis., 1971-74, pres. rsch. divsn., 1974-78, dir., 1976-78, chief scientist, 1978-82, sr. v.p., 1978-85. Co-founder APREX Corp., Fremont, Calif., pres., 1986-88, dir., 1986-95, chmn., 1988-91, chief scientist, 1988-95; co-founder, chief scientist AARDEX Ltd., Zug, Switzerland, 1995-2009; chmn. & chief scientist AARDEX Group Ltd., Sion, Switzerland, 2009-; vis. prof. pharmacology U. Limburg Sch. Medicine (now Maastricht U.), Maastricht, Netherlands, 1984-85, vis. prof. pharmacoepidemiology, 1986-91, extra ordinary prof. pharmacoepidemiology, 1991-2004, prof. emeritus, 2004-; adj. prof. bioengring. & therapeutic scis. U. Calif., San Francisco, 1984-; dir.'s adv. com. NIH, 1986-88; Boerhaave lectr. U. Leiden, Netherlands, 1991, 94-95, 97; bd. dirs. HBM BioVentures Ltd., Cayman Islands. Co-author: Risk Watch, 1984; contbr. articles to profl. jours.; patentee therapeutic systems for controlled drug delivery and regimen compliance monitoring. Trustee Kettering U. (formerly GMI Engring. and Mgmt. Inst.), Flint, Mich., 1983-2010. Served with USPHS, 1961-63. Recipient Disting. Alumni award, Rice U., 2002; NIH grantee, 1963-70. Fellow AAAS, Royal Coll. Physicians Edinburgh, Royal Soc. Edinburgh (corr.), Am. Assn. Pharm. Scientists, Internat Soc. Pharmacoepidemiology, Biomed. Engring. Soc. (pres. 1976, Disting. Svc. award 2005); mem. Boylston Med. Soc., Am. Soc. Clin. Pharmacology and Therapeutics, Endocrine Soc., Saturday Morning Club Palo Alto, Am. Physiol. Soc. (Bowditch Lectr. award 1969), Calif. Acad. Medicine, Illuminati Edinburgh. Home and Office: 975 Hamilton Ave Palo Alto CA 94301-2213 Office Phone: 650-321-3961. E-mail: urquhart@ix.netcom.com.

URSCHEL, HAROLD CLIFTON, JR., thoracic surgeon, educator; b. Toledo; s. Harold Clifton and Loma Elizabeth Urschel; m. Elizabeth Urschel; children: Harold Clifton III, Bradley VanFleet, Stuling Locke, amanda Elizabeth, Susanna Mckinley Powell. MD, Harvard U., Boston; LLD (hon.), Pikeville Coll.; DS (hon.), Bowling Green State U. Cert. in thoracic surgery Bd. Thoracic Surgery, in vascular surgery Am. Bd. Surgery, in gen. surgery Am. Bd. Surgery. Prof. dept.

cardiovasc. & thoracic surgery U. Tex. Southwestern Med. Sch., Dallas, 1975—; hon. prof. dept. thoracic surgery U. Toronto Med. Sch., Toronto, Ontario, Canada, 1990—, Brigham & Women's Hosp., Harvard Med. Sch., Boston, 1995—; chair dept. cardiovasc. & thoracic surg. rsch., edn. & clin. excellence Baylor U. Med. Ctr., Dallas, 2002—; chief sci. advisor Jon H. DeHaan Found., Naples, Fla.; chair bd. dirs. Mary Crowley Med. Rsch. Ctr., Dallas. Bd. dirs. Electronic Data Sys., Dallas, Med. Tech. Leadership Forum, 1999—, Aastrom Biosci. Inc., Ann Arbor, Mich., 2009—; pres. Am. Coll. Chest Physicians, 1979, Internat. Acad. Chest Physicians, 1979, Southern Thoracic Surg. Assn., 1979, North Tex. Chpt. ACS, 1994, Tex. Surg. Soc., 1994—94; bd. governors ACS, adv. coun. to bd. regents; nat. adv. bd. Humana Hosp., Cardiovasc. Ctr. Excellence; med. adv. bd. Mercy Ship, 2005—; dir., examiner Am. Bd. Thoracic Surgery; clin. adv. bd. Cyberknife, 2006; pres. Soc. Thoracic Surgeons, 1984; chmn.: cardiovasc. surgery com. Am. Coll. Cardiology; chmn. Southern Assn. Vascular Surgery; edn. com. Thoracic Surgery Found. for Rsch. & Edn.; mem. Am. Assn. Thoracic Surgery; dir. Mass. Gen. Hosp. Surg. Soc., Found. Rsch. & Edn. of Thoracic Surgery; chmn. dept. thoracic & cardiovasc. surgery Residency Rev. Com.; vice chmn. Baylor U. Med. Ctr. Rsch. Found., Dallas; internat. adv. panel Hyal Pharm. Corp.; internat. adv. bd. World Heart Found., 2003—; assn. dir. Mass. Gen. Hosp. Surg. Alumni, Boston. Author: (book) The Atlas of Thoracic Surgery; editor: Robotic Radiosurgery Volume II: Tumors That Move With Respiration., Thoracic Surgery, Esophageal Surgery. Recipient Hon. Membership award, Western Thoracic Surg. Soc., Hon. Faculty award, First Internat. Symposium on Thoracoscopy, 1993, Disting. Svc. ward, Soc. Thoracic Surgeons, 1998, Thoracoscopy Course Nat. Faculty award, Am. Assn. Thoracic Surgery & Soc. Thoracic Surgeons, Adv. Coun. Joint Com. Thoracoscopy award; Tchg. Fellowship, Harvard Med. Sch. Achievements include research in cardiovascular & thoracic surgery. Office: Harold C Urschel Jr MD & Assoc 3600 Gaston Ave Dallas TX 75246 Office Phone: 214-824-2503. Business E-Mail: drurschel@me.com.

URSEKAR, TRIVIKRAM NILKANTH, ophthalmologist, consultant; b. Kadus, India, Jan. 11, 1924; s. Nilkanth Gajanan and Girija Nilkanth Ursekar; m. Lata Harihar Rajurkar, June 28, 1959; children: Atul, Mahesh, Rahul. MB, BChir, Govardhandas Sunderdas Med. Coll., Mumbai, India, 1950; MS in Ophthalmology, G.S. Med. Coll., Mumbai, India, 1955; diploma in Ophthalmology, Inst. Ophthalmology, London, 1957. Asst. ophthalmic surgeon Khan Bahadur Haji Bachooali Ophthalmic and E.N.T. Hosp., Mumbai, 1958—64; chief ophthalmic surgeon Khan Bahadur Haji Bachodali Ophthalmic and Ent Hosp., Mumbai, 1964—86; asst. ophthalmic surgeon, assoc. clin. prof. King Edward Meml. Hosp., Seth G.S. Med. Coll., Mumbai, 1959—69; assoc. ophthalmic surgeon, assoc. clin. prof. K.E.M. Hosp., Seth G.S. Med. Coll., Mumbai, 1969—73, ophthalmic surgeon, clin. prof. ophthalmology, 1973—82; prof., head dept. ophthalmology Dr. R.N. Cooper Mcpl. Gen. Hosp., Mumbai, 1982—84; chief retinal surgeon Retina Clinic Taparia Inst. Ophthalmology, Bombay Hosp., Mumbai, 1982—89. Advisor ophthalmology Govt. Maharastra, Mumbai, 1991—99; chmn. ophthalmology postgrad. tchrs. com. U. Mumbai, 1973—82; lectr. in field. Fellow: ACS, Royal Coll. Ophthalmologists; mem.: Maharashtra Ophthal. Soc. (Life Time Achievement award 2004), Ahmed Nagar Ophthal. Acad. (Hon. award 2004), Maharashtra and Bombay Ophthalmology (sr.; pres. 1980—81), All India Ophthalmol. Soc. (sr.; mem. mng. com. 1972—78), Bombay Ophthalmic Assn. (Hon award 2004), Vitreo Retinal Soc. India (founder, pres. 1990). Office: Ursekar Ctr Jnof Karve Rd & RR Roy Rd Mumbai 400004 India

URSO, IDA, psychologist; arrived in U.S., 1954; BA, Kent State U., 1969; MA, UCLA, 1974, PhD, 1983; cert., N.Y. Open Ctr., 1997. Sr. staff assoc. Ctr. for Human Interdependence, Orange, Calif., 1986—90; lectr. Chapman Coll., Orange, 1988—90; dir. World Goodwill, NYC, 1990—96; integrative spiritual psychologist Chaitanya, Hoboken, NJ, 1997—; pres., founder Aquarian Age Cmty., Jersey City, 1998—. Elem. sch. cons. St. Pedro St. Sch., LA, 1976—77; bd. mem. Calif. Coun. for UN U., LA, 1982—84; lectr. Immaculate Heart Coll. Ctr., LA, 1985, LA, 98; organizer, presenter seminars on consciousness and spirituality of UN, 1999—. Writer, editor: newsletter Diamond Light, 1997—; contbr. chapters to books. Bd. mem. Orange County chpt. UN Assn./USA, 1988—90; edn. chairperson UN Assn., Orange County, 1989—90; UN Dept. Publ. Info., Non Govtl. Orgn. World Goodwill, NYC, 1990—96, Children of Earth Lifebridge, NYC, 1998—2000, Aquarian Age Cmty., NYC, 2003—. Mem.: Assn. Humanistic Psychology, Nicholas Roerich Mus., Am. Mus. Natural History. Avocations: community service, reading, music, meditation. Office Phone: 201-659-3060 ext. 45. Business E-Mail: un@aquaac.org.

URSONIU, SORIN, medical educator; b. Timisoara, Romania, June 7, 1963; MD, Victor Babes U. Medicine and Pharmacy Timisoara, Romania, 1988, PhD, 1992. Asst. prof. Victor Babes U. Medicine and Pharmacy Timisoara, 1990—97, sr. lectr., 1998—2007, assoc. prof., 2008—. Mem.: Internat. Epidemiol. Assn. (Bursary award), European Pub. Health Assn. (Bursary award). Avocation: tennis. Office: Pta Eftimie Murgu 2 Timisoara Timis 300041 Romania Office Fax: 40256220479. Business E-Mail: sursoniu@umft.ro.

URSUA, ANITA GOODWIN, reflexologist, massage therapist; b. Norfolk, Va., Feb. 28, 1950; d. Otis Ashby Goodwin and Margaret Fairview (Russell) Cruz; m. Randy K. Ursua, July 29, 1967; children: Donavan, Jessica, Randy Jr. Student, East Side Beauty Coll., San Jose, Calif., 1983, Milpitas Massage Coll., Calif., 1995, Consumnes River Coll., Sacramento, 1997—; studied with, NLP Coaching Inst. Calif., 2008. Cert. massage therapist; cert. herbalogist; cert. reflexologist; cert. natural health profl.; cert. master practitioner neuro-linguistic programming; lic. cosmetologist, life coach & NLP master practitioner CNHP. Reflexologist, Elk Grove, Calif., 1972—; cosmotologist, 1983—; realtor, 2004—. Condr. alternative health edn. classes, 1998—. Author: How to Get Healthy and Stay Healthy in an Unhealthy World, 2001 (Am. Authors Assn. Gold Book award, 2004); paintings and lithoprints. Avocations: art, writing, horses, travel, health. Office: 9116 Elk Grove Blvd 125 Elk Grove CA 95624 also: Perfect Balance NLP Life Coaching 8051 Beachmont Way Sacramento CA 95828 Office Phone: 916-230-3070. E-mail: perfectbalance@elkgrove.net.

US, MELIH, cardiovascular surgeon; b. Ankara, Turkey, Nov. 4, 1964; s. Cengiz Kadir and Senses Us; m. Hulya Us; 1 child, Piril. Diploma, Gulhane Med. Faculty, 1988. Mem. cardiovasc. surgery staff GATA Haydarpasa Tng. Hosp., Istanbul, Turkey, 1996—2001, assoc. prof., 2001—. Cons. GATA Haydarpasa Tng. Hosp., Istanbul, 2001—05. Col. Gulhane Mil. Med. Acad., 1988—2005, Turkey. Mem.: European Soc. Cardiovasc. Surgery Assn., Galatasaray Club. Home: Erenköy Cami Sok Soley Apt No 2 Istanbul 34999 Turkey Office: GATA Military Training Hosp Haydarpasa Istanbul Turkey Office Fax: +90216 302 99 29; Home Fax: +90216 302 99 29. Business E-Mail: usmelih@yahoo.com.

USAI SATTA, PAOLO, gastroenterologist, researcher; b. San Gavino, CA, Italy, Sept. 12, 1964; s. Carlo Usai and Cristina Satta; m. Mariantonia Lai, June 19, 1994; children: Carlo Usai, Francesca Usai. Degree in Medicine and Surgery, U. Cagliari, Italy, 1989, postgrad. in Gastroenterology, 1993. Vis. physician Motility Unit-Gastroneterology, San Giovanni Rotondo, Foggia, Italy, 1992—94; fellow, internal medicine dept. U. Cagliari, 1994—97; med. dirs. gastroenterology Brotzu Hosp., Cagliari, 2000—. Cons. Consensus Conf. Hydrogen Breath Tests, Rome, 2007—08; reviewer Medical Science Monitor. Recipient Neurogastroenterology and Motility Rsch. award, 1998. Mem.: European Soc. Neuro Gastroenterology Motility, Italian Motility Study Group (GISMAD), Index Copernicus Scientists Panel. Achievements include high specialization in alimentary intolerance. Office: Brotzu Hosp Piazzale Alessandro Ricchi 1 9121 Cagliari CA Italy Office Fax: 39070532050. Business E-Mail: paolousai@aob.it.

USAMI, MASAHISA, physician, director; b. Tokyo, Sept. 6, 1931; s. Tomohisa Ishiyama and Terui Usami; m. Kohko Tomihira, Nov. 3, 1968; children: Atsuko, Masaya. B, U. Chiba, Japan, 1956. Med. dr. Chief dr. internal medicine Sumitomo Hosp., Osaka, Japan, 1971-89, vice dir., 1989-96, Sumitomo Life Ins. Co., Osaka, 1997—2004; head med. dir. Higashitemma Clinic, Osaka, 2004—. Mem. Japan Soc. Physical Fitness and Sports Medicine. Mem. Japan Soc. Internal Medicine (specialist), Japan Soc. Circulation (specialist), Japanese Soc. Avocations: fishing, gardening. Home: 5-6 Koyoenhigashiyama-cho Nishinomiyashi Hyogoken 662-0012 Japan Office: Higashitemma Clinic 1-15 Higashitemma 1 Osaka 530-0044 Japan Office Phone: 06-6352-7465. Personal E-mail: usami@e-temma.jp.

USCINSKI, RONALD HENRY, medical educator; b. NYC, Apr. 3, 1943; s. Henry John and Marie Antionette Uscinski; m. Donna Lyn Cutsail, May 25, 1975; children: Benjamin Joseph, David Michael, Daniel Eric, Jessica Lyn. BS, Fordham U., NYC, 1964; MD, Georgetown U., Washington, 1968. Clin. prof. neurol. surgery & pediat. Georgetown U., Washington, 1980—; clin. prof. neurol. surgery George Wash. U., 1995—. Lt. USN, 1969—71. Scholar, Potomac Inst. Policy Studies, Arlington, Va., 2004—. Fellow: ACS (life); mem.: Congress Neurosurgeons (licentiate), Am. Assn. Neurol. Surgeons (licentiate), Polish Acad. Neurosurg. (corr.), Potomac Boat Club. Roman Catholic. Avocations: rowing, music, writing. Business E-Mail: ruscinski@potomacinstitute.org.

USICHENKO, TARAS IVANOVICH, anesthesiologist, educator; b. Krivoy Rog, Ukraine, Nov. 18, 1967; s. Ivan Gnatovich and Lydia Antonovna Usichenko; m. Tamara Leonidovna Tarasova, Oct. 9, 1983; children: Anna Tarasovna, Anastasia Tarasovna. Cert. with first class honor, Med. Inst., Kiev, Ukraine, 1993; D magna cum laude, Justus-Liebig U., Giessen, Germany, 1998. Rsch. fellow dept. pain therapy Justus-Liebig Univ. Hosp., Giessen, Germany, 1993—94, rsch. fellow dept. clin. immunology, 1995—97; intern in anesthesiology City Hosp., Lich, Germany, 1997—98; fellow in anesthesiology Ctr. of Heart Surgery, Dresden, Germany, 1998—99; resident in anesthesiology City Hosp., Dresden, 1999—2001; resident in anesthesiology, rsch. fellow dept. anesthesiology Ernst-Moritz-Arndt Univ. Hosp., Greifswald, Germany, 2002—04, adj. prof. in anesthesiology and pain rsch., 2004—. Contbr. articles to profl. jours.; editor Evidence Based Complementary and Alternative Medicine jour. Served with Soviet Army, 1986—88, Russia. Recipient German prize for pain rsch., 2005, Carl Ludwig Schleich prize, German Soc. Anesthesiology, 2007; fellow German Acad. Exch. Svc., 1993—94. Master: Internat. Coun. Acupuncture and Related Techniques (corr. Ukrainian rep.); fellow: Internat. Coll. Acupuncture and Electro-Therapeutics; mem.: European Soc. Anesthesiology (assoc.). Office: Anesthesiology Dept Friedrich-Loeffler-Str. 23B 17489 Greifswald Germany Office Fax: +493834865802. Business E-Mail: taras@uni-greifswald.de.

USKOVA, ANNA, medical educator; b. St Peterburg, Russia, Jan. 26, 1966; MD, Kazan Med. U., 1989. Asst. prof. UPMC, 2004—. Mem.: ASRA, ASA. Avocations: skiing, tennis, travel. Office: 5230 Ctr Ave Pittsburgh PA 15232 Business E-Mail: uskoaa@anes.upmc.edu.

USMANI, SHARJEEL, physician; b. Karachi, May 17, 1978; MBBS, Dow Med. Coll., 2001, MS, CBNC, Dow Med. Coll.; FEBNM, EBNM, 2007. Registrar nuc. medicine Ministry of Health, Kuwait, 2006. Nuc. physician Hussain Makki Al Jumma Centre Specialized Surgery, Kuwait, 2006. Recipient hon. Officer, Civil Hosp. Karachi. Master: Pakistan Inst. Engring. & Applied Scis.; fellow: Bd. Nuc. Cardiology, European Bd. Nuc. Medicine; mem.: Soc. Nuc. Medicine. Avocations: music, surfing, photography, cricket. Home: Flat 11 Bldg 102 St 11 Block Kuwait 1488 Kuwait Personal E-mail: dr_shajji@yahoo.com.

USTA, MUSTAFA FARUK, urologist, researcher; b. Rize, Turkey, Aug. 30, 1968; s. Memis Ali and Nazmiye Usta; m. Sibel Surmen, Apr. 9, 1999; 1 child, Zeynep. MD, Istanbul U., 1992. Faculty Akdeniz U., Antalya, Turkey, 2000, chief sect. andrology, 2003—; rsch. fellow Tulane U., New Orleans, 2001—03. Recipient Jean Francois Finestie prize, Internat. Soc. Sexual Medicine, 2002, New Investigator award, Am. Soc. Andrology, 2003, Thomas SK Chang Traniee award, 2003, Dean of Sch. Medicine award, Tulane U., 2003; Bayer fellow, 2002. Mem.: Am. Urol. Assn. (assoc.). Achievements include research in diabetes related erectile dysfunction. Avocations: basketball, music. Home: Liman Mahallesi Antalya 07070 Turkey Office: Akdeniz Univ Sch Medicine Dumlupinar Bulvari Kampus 7070 Antalya Antalya Turkey Home Fax: +90-242-227-4482. Personal E-mail: mususta53@hotmail.com. Business E-Mail: musta@akdeniz.edu.tr.

UTSUNOMIYA, DAISUKE, medical educator; b. Fukuoka, Jan. 15, 1971; MD, Kumamoto U. Sch. Medicine, Japan, 1996; PhD, Grad. Sch. Med. Scis., Kumamoto U., 2006. Lectr. to asst. prof. dept. diagnostic image analysis faculty life scis. Kumamoto U., 2010—. Recipient Cert. of Merit, Am. Roentgen Ray Soc. Office: 1-1-1 Honjo Kumamoto 860-8556 Japan Office Fax: 81-96-362-4330. Business E-Mail: utsunomi@kumamoto-u.ac.jp.

UTSUNOMIYA, TAKAFUMI, gynecologist; b. Oita, Japan, Mar. 30, 1949; married. MD, Med. Coll. Kumamoto U., Japan, 1973; PhD, Kyusyu U., Fukuoka, Japan, 1981. Cert. Japan Soc. Ob-Gyn. Bd., 1987, bd. cert. endoscopy technician Japan Soc. Gynecologic and Obstetric Endoscopy, 2003, bd. cert. reproductive med. preceptor Japan Soc. Reproductive Medicine, 2006, bd. cert. endoscopy technician Japan Soc. Endoscopic Surgery, 2008. Pres. St. Luke Clinic, Oita, 1992—; dir. St. Luke Rsch. Inst. Reproductive Medicine, 1998—. Councilor Japan Soc. Reproductive Medicine, Chiyoda-ku, Tokyo, 1993—2006; dir. Japanese Soc. Mammalian Ova Rsch., Fujisawa, Kanagawa, 2003—, Japanese Instn. Standardizing Assisted Reproductive Tech., Nishi-ku, Osaka, Japan, 2003—, Japan Assn. Psychol. Counseling Reproductive Medicine, Yokohama, Kanagawa, 2003—, Oita City Med. Assn., 2004—, Japan Soc. Fertilization and Implantation, Minato-ku, Tokyo, 2005—, NPO Japan Reproductive Health Assn., Ota-ku, Tokyo, 2006—, Japan Soc. Reproductive Regeneration, Yokohama, 2007—; chief Internat. Assn. Pvt. Assisted Reproductive Tech. Clinics and Labs. Japan, Shinjuku-ku, Tokyo, 2005—08; del. Japan Soc. Reproductive Medicine, Chiyoda-ku, Tokyo, 2006—; exec. dir. Japanese Soc. Mammalian Ova Rsch., 2007—. Recipient ISIVF Meml. award, Japan Soc. Fertilization and Implantation, 2003, JSMOR Academic Incentive award, Japanese Soc. Mammalian Ova Rsch., 2004. Office: Saint Luke Clinic 5 Tsumori-Tomioka Oita 8700947 Japan Business E-Mail: st-luke@oct-net.ne.jp.

UTTAL, WILLIAM R(EICHENSTEIN), psychology and engineering educator, research scientist; b. Mineola, NY, Mar. 24, 1931; s. Joseph and Claire (Reichenstein) U.; m. Michiye Nishimura, Dec. 20, 1954; children: Taneil, Lynet, Lisa. Student, Miami U. Oxford, Ohio, 1947-48; BS in Physics, U. Cin., 1951; PhD in Exptl. Psychology and Biophysics, Ohio State U., 1957. Staff Psychologist, mgr. behavioral sci. group IBM Rsch. Ctr., Yorktown Heights, NY, 1957-63; assoc. prof. U. Mich., Ann Arbor, 1963-68, prof. psychology, 1968-86, rsch. scientist, 1963-86, prof. emeritus, 1986—; grad. affiliate faculty dept. psychology U. Hawaii, 1986-88; rsch. scientist Naval Ocean Systems Ctr.-Hawaii Lab., Kailua, 1985-88; prof., chmn. dept. psychology Ariz. State U., Tempe, 1988—90, prof. dept. indsl. engring., 1992—99, affiliated prof., Dept. of Computer Sci. and Engring., 1993-98, prof. emeritus, 1999—. Vis. prof. Kyoto (Japan) Prefectural Med. U., 1965-66, Sensory Sci. Lab., U. Hawaii, 1968, 73, 2003-10, U. Western Australia, 1970-71, U. Hawaii, 1978-79, 80-81, U. Auckland, 1996, U. Freiburg, 1997, U. Sydney, 1999; pres. Nat. Conf. on On-Line Uses Computers in Psychology, 1974. Author: Real Time Computers: Techniques and Applications in the Psychological Sciences, 1968, Generative Computer Assisted Instruction in Analytic Geometry, 1972, The Psychobiology of Sensory Coding, 1973, Cellular Neurophysiology and Integration: An Interpretive Introduction, 1975, An Autocorrelation Theory of Visual Form Detection, 1975, The Psychobiology of Mind, 1978, A Taxonomy of Visual Processes, 1981, Visual Form Detection in Three Dimensional Space, 1983, Principles of Psychobiology, 1983, The Detection of Nonplanar Surfaces in Visual Space, 1985, The Perception of Dotted Forms, 1987, On Seeing Forms, 1988, The Swimmer: A Computational Model of a Perceptual Motor System, 1992, Toward a New Behaviorism: The Case Against Perceptual Reductionism, 1998, A Computational Model of Vision: The Role of Combination, 1999, The War Between Mentalism and Behaviorism, 2000, The New Phrenology: Limits on the Localization of Cognitive Processes in the Brain, 2001, A Behaviorist Looks at Form Recognition, 2002, Psychomythics, 2003, Dualism, 2004, Neural Theories of Mind, 2005, Human Factors in the Courtroom, 2006, The Immeasurable Mind, 2007, Time, Space and Number in Physics and Psychology, 2008; editor: Readings in Sensory Coding, 1972, Neuroscience in the Courtroom, 2008, Distributed Neurol Systems, 2009; assoc. editor Behavioral Rsch. Method and Instrn., 1968—90, Computing: Archives for Electronic Computing, 1963—75, Jour. Exptl. Psychology, Perception and Performance, 1974—79, cons. editor Jour. Exptl. Psychology: Applied, 1994—97; contbr. articles to profl. jours. Served to 2d lt. USAF, 1951-53. USPHS spl. postdoctoral fellow, 1965-66; NIMH research scientist award, 1971-76 Fellow AAAS, APA, Am. Psychol. Soc. (charter), Soc. Exptl. Psychologists (chmn. 1994-95). Achievements include patents in field. Office: Ariz State U Dept Indsl Engring Tempe AZ 85287-1104 Business E-Mail: aowru@asu.edu.

UTUMI, ESTEVAM RUBENS, oral surgeon; b. São Paulo, Brazil, Jan. 8, 1978; Grad. in Dentistry, U. Paulista, 2001; MS in Odontological Sci. and Oral Maxillofacial Surgery, U. São Paulo, 2005. Lt. Brazilian Air Force Hosp. São Paulo, 2009—. Resident Hosp. das Clínicas São Paulo, 2002—05. Avocations: Karate, Ju Jitsu. Home: Rua Pelotas 284 Ap 21 São Paulo 04012-000 Brazil Home Fax: 11 55 55498241. Personal E-mail: estevamutumi@uol.com.br.

UURTUYA, SHUUMARJAV, physiologist; b. Ulaanbaatar, June 25, 1978; MS, Health Scis. U. Mongolia, 2003; PhD, Jichi Med. U., Japan, 2009. Lectr. Health Scis. U. Mongolia, 2003, pathophysiology, 2003—. Fellowship, Japan Ultrasound Soc. Mem.: European Atherosclerosis Soc. Office: Zorig -3 Ulaanbaatar 14210 Mongolia E-mail: sh_uur2004@yahoo.com.

UURUYA, SHUUMARJAV, pathologist; b. Mongolia, June 25, 1978; M, Health Scis. U. Mongolia, 2005; PhD, Jichi Med. U., Japan, 2009. Pathophysiologist Health Scis. U. Mongolia, 2005—. Lectr., pathophysiology, 2005. Mem.: EAS. Office: Zorig-3 Ulaanbaatar Choidog 14210 Mongolia E-mail: sh_uur2004@jichi.ac.jp.

UYEHARA, CATHERINE FAY TAKAKO (YAMAUCHI), physiologist, educator, pharmacologist; b. Honolulu, Dec. 20, 1959; d. Thomas Takashi and Eiko Uyehara; m. Alan Hisao Yamauchi, Feb. 17, 1990. BS, Yale U., 1981; PhD in Physiology, U. Hawaii, Honolulu, 1987. Postdoctoral fellow SmithKline Beecham Pharms., King of Prussia, Pa., 1987-89; rsch. pharmacologist Kapiolani Med. Ctr. for Women and Children, Honolulu, 1990-91; chief, dept. clin. investigation, 2007—. Statis. cons. Tripler Army Med. Ctr., Honolulu, 1984-87, 89—, chief rsch. pharmacology, 1991—, dir. collaborative rsch. program, 1995—, mem. grad. faculty in pharmacology, pediatrics, physiology, U. Hawaii John A. Burns Sch. Medicine, 1991—; grad. faculty Interdisciplinary Biomed. Sci. program, 1991—. Contbr. articles to profl. jours. Decorated Med. Merit Order Mil. Mem. Am. Fedn. for Med. Rsch., Am. Physiol. Soc., Am. Heart Assn., Soc. Uniformed Endocrinologists, Endocrine Soc., We. Soc. Pediatric Rsch., Hawaii Acad. Sci., Sigma Xi. Democrat. Avocations: swimming, diving, crafts, horticulture, music. Office: Dept Clin Investigation 1 Jarrett White Rd Bldg 40 Tamc HI 96859 Office Phone: 808-433-6709.

UZMAN, BETTY BEN GEREN, retired pathologist; b. Ft. Smith, Ark., Nov. 17, 1922; d. Benton Asbury and Myra Estelle (Petty) Geren; m. L. Lahut Uzman, Dec. 17, 1955 (dec.); 1 dau., Betty Tuba. Student, Ft. Smith Jr. Coll., 1939—40; BS, U. Ark., 1942; MD, Washington U., 1945; postgrad., MIT, 1948—50; MA (hon.), Harvard U., 1968. Intern Childrens Hosp., Boston, 1945—46; resident pathology Barnes Hosp., St. Louis, 1946—48; Am. Cancer Soc. rsrch. fellow MIT, Cambridge, 1948—50; chief biol. ultra structure and exptl. pathology Children's Cancer Rsch. Found., Boston, 1950—71; instr. Harvard Med. Sch., Boston, 1949—53, assoc., 1953—56, rsch. assoc., 1956—67, assoc. prof., 1967—71, prof., 1971-72; head rsch. dept. Sparks Regional Med. Ctr., Ft. Smith, 1972—74; prof. pathology La. State U., Shreveport, 1974—77, U. Tenn., Memphis, 1978—89, ret., 1989. Assoc. chief staff rsch. VA, Shreveport, 1974-77; staff pathologist VA, Memphis, 1978-89, chief lab. svc., 1986-87; chief field ops., spl. asst. to dir. VA Ctrl. Office, Washington, 1978-79, dir. med. rsch. svcs., 1979-80; chmn. pathology A Study sect. NIH, 1973-76; cons. to sci. dir. Children's Cancer Rsch. Found., Boston, 1971-73; mem. adv. com. on prevention, diagnosis and treatment Am. Cancer Soc., 1970-73, 77-80; mem. adv. bd. Office Regeneration Rsch., VA, 1985-89; disting. vis. investigator Inst. Venezolano Investigation Cientificas, Caracas, 1972-74 Decorated Order Andres Bello 1st class Venezuela; recipient Weinstein award United Cerebral Palsy, 1964 Mem. AAAS, Am. Soc. Cell Biology (emerita), Microscopy Soc. Am. (emerita, Diatome poster award 1985), Internat. Acad. Pathology (emerita), Am. Assn. Neuropathology (emerita, assoc.), Soc. Neurosci. (emerita), Am. Assn. Cancer Rsch. (emerita). Home and Office: Geren Farm 16048 E State Hwy 197 Scranton AR 72863-0048 Personal E-mail: bettyguzman@centurylink.net

UZODINMA, MINTA LAVERNE SMITH, retired nursing administrator, nurse midwife; b. Des Moines, Mar. 29, 1935; d. Gerald Stanley and Dorothy LaVerne (Miles) Smith; m. John E. Uzodinma, Aug. 8, 1957 (dec. June 1994); children: Chinwe Uzodinma Thomas, Chika Uzodinma Hunter, Eze A., Amechi J. BSN, U. Iowa, 1957; cert nurse-midwifery, U. Miss., Jackson, 1970, MSN, 1975. Staff-head nurse pediatrics unit, supr. insvc. edn. Univ. Hosp., Iowa City, 1957-58, 61-64; clin. instr. med.-surg. nursing Iowa Meth. Sch. Nursing, Des Moines, 1958-59, 60; staff nurse, instr., assoc. dept. ob-gyn-dir. midwifery svc. U. Miss. Med. Ctr., Jackson, 1966-74, instr. nurse-midwifery edn., 1974-77, asst. prof., 1979-85, module coord. nurse-midwifery edn., 1977-81; staff nurse VA Med. Ctr., Jackson, 1985-87; nurse-midwife Coastal Family Health Ctr., Gulfport, Miss., 1987-89; asst. dir. nursing Miss. Dept. Health, Jackson, 1989-95, chief nurse cons., 1995—2001; clin. instr. nursing U. Miss. Med. Ctr., Jackson, 1992—2001, ret., 2001. Acting dir. nursing area Rust Coll., Holly Springs, Miss., 1975; mem. Miss. Bd. Nursing, 1979-84, treas., 1980-82, pres., 1983-84. Asst. editor region 3 Jour. Nurse-Midwifery, 1986-94; contbr. article to nursing jour. Bd. dirs. Hinds County unit Am. Cancer Soc., 1976-83; v.p. Poindexter Elem. Sch. PTA, 1966, pres., 1974-75. Recipient Alton B. Cobb Lifetime Achievement award Miss. Pub. Health Assn., 1996, Thelma Workman award LWV Miss., 1998, Nursing Alumni of Decade award U. Miss., 1998; U. Iowa scholar, 1953-56; named Maternal-Child Health Cmty. Nurse of Yr., Miss. March of Dimes, 1995,98. Fellow Am. Coll. Nurse-Midwives (chpt. sec.-treas. 1985-86, treas. 1978-80, proctor divsn. examiners 1975-85, nat. chmn. nominating com. 1978-79, mem. task force on refresher programs 1984-88, chpt. chair 1991-94, bd. rev. 1987-90, sec. region III chpt. 4 1984-86, bd. govs. regional gov. 1997—, award for excellence 1997); mem. ANA, Miss. Nurses Assn. (chmn. affirmative action com. 1977-78, continuing edn. approval unit 1990-95, nurse practitioner spl. interest group 1984—, dir. edn. 1995-97, Pub./Cmty. Health Nurse of Yr. 1998, named Nurse of Yr. 2001, Hall of Fame 2009), Eliza Pillars RN Assn., AAUW, U. Miss. Alumni Assn. (Nursing Alumni of Decade award 1971-80, 1998), Sigma Theta Tau. Home: 2832 Gretna Green St Jackson MS 39209-6907 Home Phone: 601-354-1908. Personal E-mail: muzocnm@aol.com.

VAAMONDE-MARTIN, DIANA MARIA, biologist, embryologist, researcher, educator; b. Las Palmas, Spain, Oct. 28, 1976; d. Ricardo Vaamonde-Lemos and Maria Inmaculada Martin-Alvarez; m. Marzo Edir Da Silva-Grigoletto, Mar. 18, 2005; children: Daniel Alvaro Oquendo-Vaamonde, Diana Kym Da Silva-Vaamonde. BS cum laude, Wash. and Lee U., Lexington, Va., 1998; MS, Old Dominion U./ The Jones Inst. for Reproductive Medicine, Norfolk, Va., 2004; PhD cum laude, U. Cordoba, Spain, 2006. Cert. Colegio Oficial de Biologos de Andalucia, 2000. Dir. Andrology and Embryology Lab. Ctr. Embriologia and Reproduccion Asistida, Cordoba, 2000—04; asst. prof. Anatomy and Embryology Sch. Medicine U. Cordoba, 2004—; postdoc. rschr. Hosp. Clin. Porto Alegre, Brazil, 2009—. Rschr. Sport Scis. Sch. Medicine U. Cordoba, 2002—; consulting biologist and rschr. Ctr. Iberoamericano Reproduccion Asistida, Punta del Este, Uruguay, 2005—, Insemine Ctr. Reproduçao Humana, Porto Alegre, Brazil, 2007—; invited lectr. in field. Ad hoc referee to numerous sci. jours.:; contbr. chapters to books, articles to profl. jours. Mem.: Spanish Fertility Soc., Spanish Soc. Histology and Tissue Engring. (mem. orgnl. com. XIV Nat. Congress and II Internat. 2007—), Assn. Study Biology Reproduction, Alpha Epsilon Delta. Roman Catholic. Achievements include research in the existing relationship between male infertility and physical activity; the effect of novel training method for muscle and strength improvement; the effect of reactive oxygen species on sperm endometriosis; embryo metabolism, embryo implantation events, confocal microscopy and physiology of pregnancy special media insert in work in her work 2009 ESHRE congress. Avocations: travel, Brazilian capoeira and dance, music, horseback riding, skiing. Office: Sch Medicine Univ Cordoba Avda Menendez Pidal s/n Cordoba 14071 Spain Home: Calle Damasco 6-1 14004 Cordoba Spain Office Phone: 01134957218262. Home Fax: 011-34-957410509. Personal E-mail: fivresearch@yahoo.com.

VACA, CLAUDIA PATRICIA, pharmacist, educator; b. Colombia, June 17, 1968; Degree in Pharmacoepidemiology, U. Autónoma de Barcelona, 2003. Cert. pharmacist U. Nat. de Colombia, 1995. Prof. U. Nat. de Colombia, 2005—. Cons. Ministerio de la Protección Social, 2010—. Recipient Premio Nacional de farmacología, Asociación Colombiana de Farmacología, 2007, Premio Nacional de Atención Farmacéutica, Colegio Nacional de Químicos Farmacéuticos, 2010; fellowship, Panamerican Health Orgn. Mem.: Colegio de Farmacéuticos. Home: Cra 63 22 10 Bogotá Cundinamarca 1111111 Colombia Business E-Mail: cpvacag@unal.edu.co.

VACANTI, JOSEPH PHILIP, pediatric and transplant surgeon; b. Omaha, Oct. 31, 1948; BS summa cum laude, Creighton U., 1970; MD with high distinction, U. Nebr., 1974. Diplomate in gen. surgery and pediatric surgery Am. Bd. Surgery. Clin. fellow in surgery Harvard Med. Sch., Boston, 1979-83; asst. in surgery Children's Hosp., Boston, 1983-90, sr. assoc. in surgery, 1990-98, dir. organ transplant, 1990-98, dir. lab. for transplant and tissue engring., 1990—; asst. prof. surgery Harvard Med. Sch., Boston, 1983-90, assoc. prof., 1990-97, prof., 1997—; John Homans prof. surgery Harvard Med. Sch./Mass. Gen. Hosp., 1998—; dir. Lab. Tissue Engring. and Organ Fabrication Mass. Gen. Hosp., 1998—, dir. Pediat. Transplant, 1998—, chief Dept. Pediat. Surgery, 2003—; surgeon-in-chief Mass. Gen. Hosp. Children, 2003—. Rsch. affiliate MIT, Cambridge, 1988—. Author some 30 book chpts. and more than 150 sci. articles; co-founder, sr. editor Tissue Engring.; mem. editl. bd. Cell Transplantation; mem. editl. adv. bd. Tissue Engring. Intelligence Unit, R.G. Landes. Recipient Sidney Farber award Children's Hosp., 1983, Spl. Recognition award Am. Liver Found., 1987. Fellow ACS; mem. Tissue Engring. Soc. (co-founder, pres.), Am. Soc. Transplant Surgeons, Transplantation Soc., Am. Pediat. Surg. Assn., Soc. Univ. Surgeons, Inst. Medicine. Office: Mass Gen Hosp 55 Fruit St Boston MA 02114-2696 Office Phone: 617-724-1725. Business E-Mail: jvacanti@parthners.org.

VACHIRAMON, AMORNPONG, oral surgeon, orthodontist, consultant; b. Bangkok, July 27, 1974; s. Tharin and Chaweewan Vachiramon. DDS, Chulalongkorn U., Bangkok, 1997; MSc in Oral and Maxillofacial Surgery, U. London, 2001, MSc in Orthodontics, 2003; DBA, So. Calif. U., 2001. Lic. dentist Thailand. Resident Chulalongkorn U., Bangkok, 1997—99; v.p. Centrelite Internat. Ltd., Bangkok, 2003—. Guest faculty Mahidol U., Bangkok, 2002—; moderator Lingual Orthodontists Discussion Group, 2002—. Master: Internat. Congress Oral Implantologists (diplomate) (mem. internat. credentials com.); fellow: Royal Coll. Surgeons Eng.; mem.: Am. Acad. Maxillofacial Prosthetics (mem. internat. rels. com. 2002—), Royal Coll. Surgeons Edinburgh (specialist mem.). Office: Vachiramon Ctr for Face and Dental Care 46 Soi Kasemsan 1 Rama 1 Rd Pathumwan Bangkok 10330 Thailand Home Phone: (662) 2153058; Office Phone: (662) 2153043. Business E-Mail: amornpong@vachiramon.org.

VACULIN, SIMON, medical educator, researcher; b. Prague, Czech Republic, Sept. 8, 1971; MVD, Vet. and Pharm. U. Brno, 1997; PhD in Medicine, Charles U. Prague, 2004. Assoc. prof. Charles U., 3rd Faculty Medicine, 2004—. Editor in chief, chmn. editl. bd. Czech Vet. Sci. Jour., Veterinarni lekar, 2003—07. Mem.: Internat. Assn. Study of Pain, Soc. Neurosci. Avocations: sports, literature. Office: Ke Karlovu 4 Prague 120 00 Czech Republic Business E-Mail: svaculin@lf3.cuni.cz.

VADGAMA, PANKAJ, physician; b. Nairobi, Kenya, Feb. 16, 1948; s. Maganlal V.; m. Dixa; children: Reena, Roosnin, Preeya. MB, BS, Newcastle U., 1971, BS, 1976, PhD, 1984. Demonstrator Newcastle U., U.K., 1972-73, dir. biosensor rsch. group, 1983-88; researcher Royal Victoria Infirmary, U.K., 1973-77; prof. clin. biochemistry Manchester U., U.K., 1988-2000; dir. of IRC in biomaterials Queen Mary and Westfield Coll./U. London, 2000—. Author revs. in field. Mem. Assn. Clin. Biochemists. Avocations: reading, walking. Office: Queen Mary University London Lincoln Mile End London E1 4NS England Office Phone: +44 20 7882 5151. Business E-Mail: p.vadgama@qmul.ac.uk.

VADHERA, RAKESH B., anesthesiologist, educator; b. India, Aug. 15, 1957; MBBS, Maulana Azad Med. Coll., 1978. Prof., dir. OB anesthesiology U. Tex. Med. Br., 2001—. Fellow: RCS Ireland, Royal Coll. Anesthetist (Eng.); mem.: Tex. Soc. Anesthesiology, Soc. Obstetric Anesthesiology and Perinatology, Am. Soc. Anesthesiologist. Office: Dept Anesthesiology 301 University Blvd Galveston TX 77555 Office Fax: 409-772-1224. Business E-Mail: rbvadher@utmb.edu.

VAGAL, ACHALA, radiologist, educator; b. Secunderabad, India, Oct. 1, 1970; MD, LTMGH, 1997. Asst. prof. U. Cin. Med. Ctr., 2007—. Neuroradiology ct dir. Dept. Radiology, 2010. Recipient Cert. of Merit, Am. Roentgen Ray Soc., 2008; fellowship, U. Cin., 2004. Mem.: Am. Soc. Neuroradiology. Office: 234 Goodman St Cincinnati OH 45267 Office Fax: 513-584-9100. Personal E-mail: achalavagal@yahoo.com.

VAGHOLKAR, KETAN RAMESH, surgeon, educator; s. Ramesh Khanderao and Shaila Ramesh Vagholkar; m. Suvarna Ketan Manjrekar, May 12, 1995; 1 child, Parth Ketan. MBBS, T.N. Med. Coll., Mumbai. India, 1989, M in Surgery, 1993. Diplomate Nat. Bd. Examinations, India, 1993, cert. ECFMG. Asst. lectr. Pad. Dr. D.Y. Patil Med. Coll., Nerul, Navi Mumbai, Maharashtra, India, 1996—2000, assoc. prof., 2001—04, prof. surgery, 2005—. Cons. surgeon Rajawadi Mcpl. Gen. Hosp., Mumbai, 1996—, Pad. Dr. D.Y. Patil Hosp. and Rsch. Centre, 2004—, Dr. Vagholkar Hosp., Thane, Maharashtra, 1994—. Contbr. articles to profl. jours. Recipient Rashtriya Rattan award for Med. Excellence, 2006. Fellow: ACS (life fellow 2003); mem.: Royal Coll. Physicians and Surgeons (Glasgow), Assn. Surgeons India (life), Nat. Acad. Med. Sci. (life), European Digestive Soc. (life), Soc. Surgery Alimentary Tract (life). Independent. Hindu. Office Phone: 0091 22 25426205. Personal E-mail: kvagholkar@yahoo.com.

VAGN-HANSEN, CARSTEN PETER MATHIAS, health consultant, physician; b. Copenhagen, Apr. 5, 1938; s. Christian Ebbe Theodor and Annie Margaretha Vagn-Hansen; m. Joan Poula Kruse, June 30, 1962; children: Christian Aksel, Mette Marie, Lotte Marie, Rikke Marie. MD, U. Copenhagen, 1965. Jr. dr. Aabenraa Hosp., Denmark, 1965-67; registrar Naestved County (Denmark) Hosp., 1967-68, sr. registrar, 1968-70; gen. practitioner Aabenraa, Denmark, 1970-88; health cons. Denmark, 1988—. Temp advisor WHO, 1983. Author: Type 2 Diabetes, 1980, 2d edit., 1986, Politike, 1984, 3rd edit., 1996, Health and Well-Being, 1986, Live Your Life, 1993, When It Hurts, 1996, The Good Life, 1999, Ask About Your Health, 1999, Healthy Pages, 2001, On Sorrow and Care, 2003, Type 2 Diabetes and Nature, 2004, The Stomach--Your Best Friend, 2005, Depression, natural treatment, 2006; med. editor HELSE mag., 1988-2000; editor, host Denmark's radio and TV, 1985-2005, TV DK4, 2005—, When it Really Hurts Natural Treatment of Pain, 2009, What Ails You and Why On Natural Health, 2011. Recipient Hippocrates medal Soc. Internat. Med. Gen., Klagenfurt, Austria, 1988, Pharmacia prize Danish Coll Gen. Practice, 1988, Dandy prize, Denmark, 1991, Health for All prize Denmark Com. on Health Info., 1992, Internat. Nature Medicine Honorary prize, 2002. Mem. Danish Med. Assn., Danish Coll. Gen. Practitioners (bd. dirs. 1975-82). Avocation: singing. Office Phone: 01145-75829599. Business E-Mail: cavaha@radiodoktoren.dk.

VAGUNDA, VACLAV, pathologist, researcher; b. Uherske Hradiste, Moravia, Czech Republic, Dec. 16, 1959; s. Josef Vagunda and Hedvika Vagundova; m. Marcela Svedova, Sept. 1, 1984; children: Klara Vagundova, Marek. MD, Masaryk U., 1985, PhD, 2004. Diplomate Czech Republic, 1985. Resident 2d inst. pathology Faculty Children Hosp., Brno, Moravia, Czech Republic, 1985—88; med. rschr. Rsch. Inst. of Clin. & Exptl. Oncology, Brno, 1988—93; cons. pathologist 1st inst. pathology Faculty Hosp., Brno, 1993—95; head pathology dept. Masaryk Meml. Cancer Inst., Brno, 1995—2003, Sanatorium Helios, Brno, Czech Republic, 2004; head pathology lab. Cedelab Ltd., Velke Mezirici, Czech Republic, 2005—. Lectr. faculty of medicine Masaryk U., Brno, 1993—. Contbr. articles to profl. jours. Founding pres., vice-chmn. League Against Cancer, Brno, 1990—2002. Mem.: WHO, Soc. Melanoma Rsch., European Soc. Pathology, Soc. Clin. Cytology, Czech Med. Soc., Soc. of Pathologists, Internat. Acad. of Pathology, Orgn.of European Cancer Inst. Avocations: philosophy, music. Office: Cedelab Ltd Hosp St Zdislava Mostiste 105 594 01 Velke Mezirici Czech Republic Office Fax: 420 566 520 940. Business E-Mail: vagunda@cedelab.cz.

VAHC, YOUNG WOO, medical physics educator; b. Seoul, Republic of Korea, Mar. 12, 1951; s. Sun Bok Vahc and Hee Kyoung Choi; m. Hee Sook Kang; children: Zaiyoun, Zuhyoun. PhD in Med. Physics, Yonsei U., Seoul, 1986. Prof. Wonju (Republic of Korea) Coll. Medicine Yonsei U., Kangwon-Do, 1983—, chmn. basic sci., 1998—. Contbr. articles to profl. jours. Mem.: Internat. Soc. Radiaiton Oncology (mem. adv. com. 1999—), European Soc. Therapeutic Radiology and Ocology, Korean Phys. Soc., Korean Soc. Therapeutic Radiology and Oncology, Korean Soc. Med. Physics. Office: Yonsei U Wonju Coll Medicine Ilsan-Dong 162 220-701 Wonju Gangwon-do Republic of Korea Office Phone: 82-33-741-0361. Office Fax: 82-33-745-0547. Business E-Mail: va23233@wonju.yonsei.ac.kr.

VAIDYA, RAHUL, orthopedist; b. Mandi, Himachal Pradesh, India, Jan. 3, 1966; BSc, Dalhousie U., 1984; MD, McGill U., Montreal, Can., 1991. Orthop. trauma fellow, Locum staff U. BC, Vancouver, Canada, 1997—98; spine fellow McGill U., Montreal, Canada, 1998—99; orthop. trauma, spine surgeon Hotel Dieu Hosp. Met Hosp. Winsor Ont., 1999—2001; chief spine surgery, orthop. trauma surgeon Henry Ford Hosp., 2001—06; specialist chief orthop. surgery Detroit Med. Ctr. Wayne State U., 2006—, clin. assoc. prof. surgery, 2007—11, clin. assoc. prof. surgery/neurosurgery, 2011. Orthop. trauma surgeon Can. Army Res., 2008; clin. assoc. prof. surg. specialities Mich. State U., 2009; orthop. surgeon Winter Olympic Games, Vancouver, 2010. Named one of America's Best Doctors, Americas Best Doctors, America's Top Surgeons, Consumers Rsch. Coun. America. Fellow: Royal Coll. Surgeons Can.; mem.: AO N. Am., Mich. Orthop. Soc., Can. Armed Forces, Orthop. Trauma Assn., Am. Acad. Orthop. Surgeons. Avocations: hockey, golf. Office: Detroit Receiving Hosp 4D4 University Health Ctr 4201 Detroit MI 48201 Office Fax: 313-966-8400. Personal E-mail: rvaidya@dmc.org.

VAIL, THOMAS PARKER, orthopaedic surgeon; m. Lisa Ann Giannetto. MD, Loyola U., 1985. Diplomate Am. Bd. Orthopaedic Surgery. Prof. orthop. surgery Duke U. Med. Ctr., Durham, NC, 1992—2007; prof. and dept. chmn. orthop. surgery U. Calif., San Francisco, 2007—. Office: Univ Calif San Francisco MU 320W 500 Parnassus Ave San Francisco CA 94143-0728 Office Phone: 415-502-5183. *

VAIN, ARVED, research scientist; b. Tartumaa, Estonia, Oct. 29, 1936; s. August and Linda Vain; m. Violetta Tarhanova, Nov. 18, 1982; children: Anneli, Astrid; m. Aino Künnap, Apr. 28, 1964 (div. Nov. 20, 1982). Degree in Mech. Engring., Tallinn Poly. Inst., Estonia, 1961; PhD, U. Tartu, Estonia, 1970—70; D, Latvian Inst. Traumatology and Orthops., Riga, 1993. Sr. rschr., assoc. prof. U. Tartu, 1970—83, 1989—2002, head dept. gymnastics and biomechanics, 1983—89, sr. rschr., 2002—. Chmn. supervisory bd. OÜ Müomeetria, Tartu, 1999—. Contbr. articles to profl. jours.; editor Acta Olympique Academiae Estoniae, 2002. Founder Estonian Olympic Acad., Tartu; mem. sci. coun. on biomechanics Acad. Scis., Moscow, 1983—92. Recipient Innovation award, U. Tartu, 1998, Academic Chellenge award, Tech. U. Munich, 2002. Mem.: Internat. Physiol. Soc. (assoc.), Internat. Biomech. Soc. (assoc.). Achievements include patents for method and device for recording damped natural oscillations of soft biological tissues. Avocations: gardening, music, literature. Office: MÈ-omeetria OÈ£ Soola 8 51013 Tartu Estonia E-mail: arved.vain@ut.ee.

VAISMAN, NACHUM, nutritionist; b. Jerusalem, Sept. 3, 1948; MD, Tel Aviv U., 1978. Head unit clin. nutrition Tel Aviv Sourasky Med. Sch., 1999—. Mem.: Israeli Med. Soc., European Soc. Clin. Nutrition. Avocations: reading, mountain climbing. Office: 6 Wietzmann St Tel Aviv 62342 Israel Office Fax: 97236973191. Business E-Mail: vaisman@tasmc.health.gov.il.

VAJO, ZOLTAN, physician; s. Peter Vajo and Emilia Szollosi; 1 child, Adam Erdman-Vajo. MD in Internal Medicine and Endocrinology, Semmelweis Med. Sch., Budapest, 1991; PhD, Nat. Acad. Scis., Hungary, 1999. Med. resident Maricopa Med. Ctr., Phoenix, 1993—96; fellow NIH, Bethesda, Md., 1996—98, VA Med. Ctr., Phoenix, 1998—2000, rsch. scientist, 2000—02; head dept. medicine Nat. Inst. Psychiatry and Neurology, Budapest, 2003—. Adj. prof. Ariz. State U., Tempe, 2000—03. Contbr. articles to profl. jours., chapters to books. Recipient Young Investigators award, Livial Expert Meeting, 1999. Mem.: AMA, Phoenix Cross Town Endocrinology Soc. Achievements include discovery of novel human gene sequence, timing gene CLK1. Home: Gyongyvirag u 26 Erd 2030 Hungary Personal E-mail: zvajo@hotmail.com.

VAKIL, NIMISH, gastroenterologist, educator; b. India, Nov. 27, 1954; MD, U. Bombay, 1980; degree in Gastroenterology, Northwestern U., 1987. Prof. U. Wis. Sch. Medicine and Pub. Health, 1993—. Gastroenterologist Aurora Health Care, 2011. Recipient prize, European H pylori Rsch. Group, Rsch. award, DAAD. Fellow: ACP, Am. Gastroent. Assn., Am. Coll. Gastroenterology. Avocations: kayaking, bicycling, travel. Office: Aurora Summit Hosp 36500 Aurora Dr Oconomowoc WI 53066 Office Phone: 262-434-5700. Business E-Mail: nvakil@wisc.edu.

VALACHIS, ANTONIS, oncologist; b. Heraklion, Crete, Greece, Mar. 13, 1984; MD, U. Crete, Greece, 2007, PhD. Asst. physician Med. Oncology Pvt. Svc., Lamia, Greece, 2009; oncologist Gen. Hosp. Eskilstuna, Sweden, 2010—. Rsch. assoc. Panhellenic Assn. Continual Med. Rsch., Greece, 2006; rsch. assoc., dept. internal medicine U. Crete, 2007. Rsch. grant, Devel. Cardiac Auscultation Manikin. Mem.: Swedish Assn. Oncology, Panhellenic Assn. Continual Med. Rsch. Avocations: painting, history, sports. Home: Carlavägen 20A Eskilstuna Sörmland 63350 Sweden Personal E-mail: valachis@hotmail.com. Business E-Mail: antonis.valachis@dll.se.

VALACHOVIC, RICHARD WILLIAM, medical association administrator; Former assoc. prof. oral medicine Harvard U., former chief dentistry, Health Svcs.; exec. dir. Am. Dental Edn. Assn. (formerly Am. Assn. Dental Schs.), Washington, 1996—, Internat. Fedn. Dental Edn. Associations; pres. Fedn. Associations Schools of Health Professions. Mem. Washington Higher Edn Secretariat. Fellow: Am. Coll. Dentists, Am. Acad. Pediat. Dentistry. Office: Am Dental Edn Assn Ste 1100 1400 K St NW Washington DC 20005 Office Phone: 202-289-7201. Business E-Mail: ValachovicR@adea.org. *

VALBUENA, AUGUSTIN, psychiatrist; b. Barcelona, June 14, 1940; s. Angel Valbuena and Francisca Briones; m. Lina Vicente Valbuena, Apr. 1, 2001. Licenciado Medicina, U. Barcelona, 1964; DPM, Royal Coll. Physicians, 1970; MD, U. Barcelona, 1971. Prof. psychology Autonoma U., Madrid, 1978; clin. prof. psychiatry Alcala U., Madrid, 1981—90, 1993—96; staff psychiatrist Ramon Cajal Hosp., 1978—90, 1993—2001; head dept. psychiatry Penitentiary Hosp., 1990—93; staff psychiatrist Nino Jesus Hosp., 2001—. Med. dir. Smith Kline & French, Madrid, 1975; psychiat. expert Med. Coun. of Madrid, 2001; mental health advisor Ministry of Health, Madrid, 1987—89. Author: Las Toxico Manias, 1986, 1993, Hamlet and Segismundo, 1993. Mem.: Assn. Writers Psychiatry, Soc. Psiquiatria, Royal Coll. Psychiatrists of London. Avocations: ballroom dancing, sailing, opera. Office: Hosp Nino Jesus Avenida Menendez Pelayo 65 28009 Madrid Spain Office Phone: 915320295. Business E-Mail: agustin.briones@terra.es.

VALCÁRCEL, MARTA IRIS, pediatric educator; b. Santurce, P.R., Mar. 26, 1931; d. Jose and Solveida (Teruel) V. BS, U. P.R., 1951, MD, 1955. Diplomate Am. Bd. Pediatrics. Intern, then resident Kings County Hosp., NYC, 1955-58; fellow in neonatology Columbia Presbyn. Med. Ctr., 1968; chief perinatalneonatal sects. and neonatal ICU U. P.R. Sch. Medicine, San Juan, 1968—2011, pediat. dept. chmn., 1977—96; prof., chmn. dept. pediatrics U. P.R. Sch. Medicine Neonatal Care Unit, San Juan, 1977—2011; assoc. dean for clin. affairs U. P.R. Sch. Medicine, San Juan, 1976-77; exec. dir. Univ. Children's Hosp., San Juan, 1980-86; dir. newborn svcs. U. Dist. Hosp., San Juan, 1967-78, 91, pres. med. staff, 1975-76. Mem. Am. Pediatric Soc., Am. Acad. Pediatrics, P.R. Mked. Assn., So. Soc. Pediatric Rsch., Assn. Med. Sch. Pediatric Dept. Chmn. Roman Catholic.

VALDEMARSSON, STIG, endocrinologist, educator; b. Simrishamn, Aug. 11, 1946; PhD, Lund U., 1983, MD. Asst. prof. Lund U. Hosp., 1978. Mem.: Swedish Thyroid Group, Swedish Endocrine Group. Office: Lund University Hosp Lund Skane S-221 85 Sweden E-mail: stig.valdemarsson@med.lu.se.

VALDERRAMA, ANA MARIA, physician, researcher; b. Bogota, Colombia, Aug. 27, 1959; MD, Pontificia U. Javeriana, 1986; degree in Clin. Pathology, U. Degli Studi di Messina, 1991. Exec. dir.-clin. ops. Pfizer Inc., 2009—. Head, clin. ops. for L.Am., Africa and Mid. East Pfizer, 1987—2011. Recipient Charlie Award, Pfizer Inc. Mem.: Drug Info. Assn. Avocation: piano. Office: 235 E 42nd St New York NY 10017 Business E-Mail: ana.valderrama@pfizer.com.

VALDEZ, ERNESTO VENEGAS, pharmacologist, consultant, educator; b. Dagupan, Philippines, Nov. 18, 1927; s. Juan Gutierrez and Juliana Estrella (Venegas) Valdez; m. Resurreccion Edillor Jamias, Apr. 16, 1958; children: Marylou, Ernesto, Eduardo, Rosalind, Eileen. AA, U. Philippines, 1948, MD, 1953. Instr. pharmacology U. Philippines Coll. Medicine, 1953—60, asst. prof., 1961—65, assoc. prof., 1966—69, prof., 1969—92, prof. emeritus, 1992—, mem. adv. bds., cons., 1953—, asst. coll. sec., 1967—70, coll. sec., 1970—73, chmn. pharmacology, 1973—75, 1988—91. Med. dir. Johnson & Johnson, Manila, 1974—87, med. cons., 1987—95; mem. NRC Philippines; lectr. pharmacology U. Calif. San Francisco, 1959—60, postdoctoral fellow, 1960; postdoctoral fellow cardiovasc. rsch. Ga. Med. Coll., 1960; postdoctoral fellow, vis. assoc. prof. Kans. U. Med. Ctr., 1968. Assoc. editor: Physician's Drug Index, 1965, 1967, Philippine Drug Reference, 1984, Philippine Med. Assn. Compendium, 1988, Philippine Nat. Drug Formulary, 1990. Recipient 1st prize for basic sci. rsch., Manila Med. Soc., 1954, 1957, 1st prize for clin. rsch., 1962, Cultural Heritage award, Govt. of The Philippines, 1963, Meritorious Svc. award, Phi Kappa Phi, 1994; named Outstanding Educator, Med. Alumni Soc., 1999. Fellow: Philippine Soc. Advancement Sci., Philippine Coll. Pharm. Medicine, Philippine Soc. Microbiology and Infectious Diseases, Philippine Soc. Exptl. and Clin. Pharmacology. Roman Catholic. Avocations: tennis, bowling, classical music. Office: U Philippines Coll Medicine 547 Pedro Gil Ermita Manila Philippines Home: Monte Vista Subdivsn Nat Capital Region 9 Guijo St Marikina City 1802 Philippines Office Phone: 632-521-8251. Personal E-mail: ernesto_v_valdez@yahoo.com.

VALDEZ, JOSH, health insurance company executive; A, CC AF; BS, Nat. U. Sacramento; MBA, Golden State U.; D in Bus. Adminstrn., Southern Calif. U., 2006. CFO, exec. dir. West Covina Med. Group, 1994—98; v.p. med. ops and managed care AltaMed Health Svcs., Calif., 1998—2001; CFO, exec. dir. Eastland Med. Group, Combined Mgmt. Svcs.; regional dir., western US and Pacific Territories US Dept. Health and Human Svcs., 2001—03; sr. v.p. Blue Cross Blue Shield, Calif., 2003—07; pres., CEO Josh Valdez, Inc., 2007—, Right Way Healthcare Consulting, 2007—; pres., owner Health Care Strategic Partners, 2008—. Health care adminstr. USAF. Named Man of Yr., Hollenbeck Youth Ctr./Inner-City Games LA, 2005; named one of Top 10 Latinos in Healthcare, LatinoLeaders mag., 2004. Office: Blue Cross and Blue Shield 225 N Michigan Ave Chicago IL 60601 Office Phone: 312-297-6000. Office Fax: 312-297-6609.

VALE, FERNANDO LUIS, medical educator; b. San Juan, San Juan, PR, Dec. 8, 1965; s. Jose Luis Vale and Carmen Dalila Diaz; m. Lynda M. Vale, June 8, 1991; children: Gabriela, Fernando. BS with magna cum laude, U. P.R., 1987, MD, 1991. Cert. bd. cert. neurosurgery. Intern U. Ala. Hosps., Birmingham, 1991—92, resident in neurosurgery, 1992—97; asst. prof. U. South Fla., Tampa, 1997—2004, assoc. prof., 2004—10, prof., 2010—. Residency program dir., neurosurgery U. of South Fla. Contbr. articles to profl. jours. Recipient Thompson Best Tchr. award, Dept Neurosurgery, U. South Fla., 2008—09, Honor's Dean List; named Best Doctors in America; Clin. fellowship, Congress Neurol. Surgeons, 1997. Mem.: AMA, Southern Neurol. Soc., Tampa Bay L.Am. Med. Soc., Am. Epilepsy Soc., Congress Neurol. Surgeons Stereotactic and Functional Neurosurgery, Am. Assn. Neurol. Surgeons, America's Registry Outstanding Profls., Alpha Omega Alpha. Office: USF Health 7th Fl 2 Tampa Gen Cir Tampa FL 33606 Home Phone: 813-920-9277; Office Phone: 813-259-0605. Business E-Mail: fvale@health.usf.edu.

VALE, WYLIE W., biochemist; BS, Rice U., 1964; PhD in Physiology & Biochemistry, Baylor U., 1968. Biochemist The Salk Inst., La Jolla, Calif., 1970-78, Clayton Found. Lab. Peptide Biology br. The Salk Inst., La Jolla, 1978—; Helen McLoraine prof. molecular neurobiology Salk Inst. Biol. Studies, pres. Clayton Found. Labs. for Peptide Biology, chmn. faculty; academic co-founder, chief scientific advisor Neurocrine Biosciences, Inc., San Diego, 1992—. Bd. trustees Salk Inst. Biol. Studies; founding bd. scientific & med. advisors Neurocrine Biosciences, Inc., San Diego, 1992—, bd. dirs, 1992; adj. prof. U. Calif. San Diego; elected mem. Inst. of Medicine, 2000. Recipient Fred Conrad Koch award Endocrine Soc., 1997. Mem.: Internat. Soc. Endocrinology (former pres.), Am. Endocrine Soc. (former pres., Fred Conrad Koch award 1997), Inst. Medicine, AAAS, NAS. Office: Salk Inst Biological Sciences PO Box 85800 San Diego CA 92186-5800 also: Neurocrine Biosciences Inc 12790 El Camino Real San Diego CA 92130 E-mail: vale@salk.edu.

VALENCIA MARTÍN, JOSÉ, interventional cardiologist; b. Teruel, Spain, Jan. 15, 1972; s. José Valencia Fernández and María Jesús Martín Valero; PhD, U. Miguel Hernández, Elche-Alicante, 2005; MD, U. Alicante, 1996. Cert. specialist in cardiology Edn. and Sci. Spanish Dept., 2002. Cardiologist asst. Hosp. Gen. de Alicante, Spain, 2002—. Rschr. (Valenciano Inst. of Heart, Valencia, 1998—; expert cons. health and sci. Iberoamerican Soc. Sci. Info., Buenos Aires, 2003—; grant rschr. Instituto de Cultura Juan Gil-Alber. Contbr. articles to profl. pubs. Recipient First prize for best doctoral thesis, Colegio Ofcl. de Medicos de Alicante, 2005. Mem.: Valenciana Soc. Cardiology, Spanish Soc. Cardiology (assoc.), European Soc. Cardiology (assoc.), Spanish Soc. Cardiology (assoc.; mem. hemodynamic sect.). Office: Hospital General de Alicante Avdapintor Baeza sn 3010 Alicante Spain Home: Avda Goleta 25 Alicarte 03540 Spain Office Phone: 0034-965938561. Office Fax: 0034-965938269; Home Fax: 0034-965938269. Personal E-mail: josevalenciamartin@hotmail.com. Business E-Mail: valencia_jos@gva.es. E-mail: jvalenciam@hotmail.com.

VALENSI, PAUL ELIE, physician, researcher, educator; b. Tunis, Tunisia, Mar. 14, 1953; arrived in France, 1958; s. Guy David Victor and Dora Allegra (Luisada) V.; m. Joelle Suzanne Maquaire, Sept. 19, 1981; children: Marine, Audrey, Alexandre. BA, Lycee Jacques Decourt, Paris, 1969; MA in Physiology, U. Paris, 1979, MA in Immunology, 1983, MA in Biochemistry, 1985. Specialist in nutrition, cardiology, internal medicine, endocrinology and metabolic diseases. Resident various hosps. Pub. Assistance, Paris, 1978-82, sr. resident Bobigny and Bondy, France, 1982—; lectr. U. Paris-Nord, 1982—, rsch. team, 1982—, prof. nutrition, 1993—. Expert in clin. and pharmacol. trials in the fields of diabetology, nutrition, endocrinology, hypertension, microcirculation, coronary heart disease, Bondy, 1982—; expert for internat. reviews of Diabetology and Cardiology; head dept. endocrinology-diabetology-nutrition Jean Verdier Hosp., Bondy, 2005—; dir. lab. for rsch. in nutrition U. Paris Nord, 1995—. Assoc. editor Jour. Diabetes and Metabolism, 2004-; contbr. more than 250 articles on diabetes, obesity, cardiovascular diseases microcirculation and thyroid function to profl. jours. Mem. Council of Adminstrn., U. Paris-Nord, 1986-90, Council of Mgmt, Faculty of Medicine of Bobigny, 1987-90. Officer Air Army, 1977-78, France. Recipient Silver medal Faculty Lariboisiere, Paris, 1982, prize French Assn. for Study Diabetes and Metabolic Diseases, 1989. Mem.: French Group Prevention Type 2 Diabetes (pres. 2009—), European Group for Study of Diabetes and Cardiovasc. Disease (mem. exec. com. 2007—), European Group for Study of Diabetic Neuropathy (pres. 2002—05), French Group of Heart and Diabetes (pres. 2002—05), French Assn. for Study of Obesity (v.p. 2002—05), Diabetes Edn. Study Group (past pres. French sect.), French Soc. Microcirculation, French Soc. Nutrition (adminstrn. coun.), French Soc. Endocrinology, European Assn. for Study of Diabetes, French Assn. for Study of Diabetes and Metabolic Diseases (adminstrn. coun.). Avocation: tennis. Office: Hopital Jean Verdier Avenue du 14 Juillet 93140 Bondy France Office Phone: 33-1-48-02-65-96. Personal E-mail: paul.valensi@noos.fr. Business E-Mail: paul.valensi@jvr.aphp.fr.

VALENTA, JANET ANNE, substance abuse professional; b. Cleve., Sept. 22, 1948; d. Frank A. and Ann (Kogoy) Shenk; m. Mario Valenta, May 22, 1971. BA, Cleve. State U., 1970; postgrad., Rutgers U., 1973, U. Cin., 1976-84. Cert. prevention cons. Ohio, nat. trauma and loss school specialist 2009, nat. trauma loss in children cons. 2009. Purchasing clk./typist Restaurant div. Stouffer Foods Corp., Cleve., 1967-71; cmty. info. specialist Trumbull Warren Office of Econ. Opportunity, Warren, Ohio, 1972; edn. dir. Trumbull County Coun. on Alcoholism, Warren, 1973-78; rehab. counselor Trumbull County Bur. Vocat. Rehab., Niles, Ohio, 1979-80; owner, operator Ironsmith, Niles, 1978-79; cons., trainer Ohio Network Tng. and Assistance to Schs. and Cmty., Youngstown, Ohio, 1987—2002; prevention edn. coord. Cmty. Recovery Resource Ctr., Youngstown, 1979-94; prevention coord. Neil Kennedy Recovery Clinic, Youngstown, 1994—2010. Ohio tng. coord. Babesworld Home, Inc., Detroit, 1986-99; nat. chair pub. health caucus Nat. Assn. Prevention Profls., Chgo., 1976-77. Publicity chair Trumbull Art Guild, Warren, 1974—76; policy coun. Youngstown Cmty. Action, Headstart, 1988—90; active Summer Arts Butler Art Mus., 1997—2002, Ohio Violence Prevention Process, 2002; mem. Tri County Family Violence Prevention Coalition Speaker's Bureau, 2005, MYCAP Headstart Policy Coun., 2009—10; bd. dirs. All Children Learn Differently, 2008; bd. dirs.fiscal officer ACLD-Mollie Kessler Sch., 2009—11; bd. dirs. Ebony Life Support Group, Inc., Youngstown, 1992. Named Woman of Yr., Warren Bus. and Profl. Women's Assn., 1978. Mem. Alcohol and Drug Abuse Prevention Assn. Ohio, Alliance for Substance Abuse Prevention, Am. Inst. Cancer Rsch. Office: Neil Kennedy Recovery Clinic 2151 Rush Blvd Youngstown OH 44507-1535 Office Phone: 330-743-6671 ext 112.

VALENTIN, ANTONIO, medical educator; b. Madrid, Mar. 8, 1969; s. Antonio Valentin and Rosa Huete; m. Eva Pena-Charlon, Aug. 19, 2001; children: Isabel Valentin-Pena, Lucia Valentin-Pena, Antonio Valentin-Pena. Degree in Med., U. Complutense, Madrid, 1993, PhD, 1999; MD, U. London, 2008. Cert. in informatics health U. Complutense, 1994. Clin. rsch. fellow Clin. Neurophysiology, King's Coll. Hosp., London, 1999—2008, hon. practitioner, 2007—; clin. lectr. Dept. Clin. Neuroscis., Inst. Psychiatry, King's Coll., London, 2007—. Co-dir. MSc course epileptology Inst. Psychiatry, London, 2007—. Recipient Intercapital prize, Fund Epilepsy, 2007, Rsch. prize, Epilepsy Action, 2007; Charles Sykes Meml. Fund grant, Fund Epilepsy, 2007. Mem.: Movement Disorder Soc., Gen. Med. Coun. Achievements include development of techniques for diagnosis and identification of brain areas responsible for epilepsy. Office: Kings College London Institute of Psychiatry Dept Clin Neuroscis 16 de Crespigny Park SE5 8AF London England Office Fax: 44 0 207 848 5440. Business E-Mail: antonio.valentin@iop.kcl.ac.uk.

VALENTINE, MARK CONRAD, dermatologist; b. Parkersburg, W.Va., Sept. 26, 1948; s. Sestel and Margaret Elaine (Sabolo) V.; m. Elizabeth Michelle Monezis, Apr. 21, 1975; children: Perry Martin, Owen Mark. BA, W.Va. U., 1970; MD, Johns Hopkins U., 1974. Intern, resident U. Hosps. Cleve., 1974-76, resident, 1976-79; dermatologist pvt. practice, Everett, Wash., 1979—. Clin. prof. U. Wash., Seattle, 1979—; active med. staff Providence Everett Gen. Med. Ctr., 1979—. Editl. bd. Jour. of Am. Acad. Dermatology, 1998—2005. Bd. dirs., sec. City Libr. Bd., Mukilteo, Wash., 1994-99; bd. dirs., v.p. Everett Symphony Bd., 1982-85, 2001—2006; bd. dirs. Book Arts Guild, Seattle, 1988-90. Nat. Merit scholar, 1966. Mem. AMA, Am. Acad. Dermatology (adv. coun. 1983-86), Wash. State Dermatol. Assn. (pres.-elect 1996, pres. 1996-97), Seattle Dermatology Soc. (pres. 1985-86), Snohomish County Med. Soc. (bd. dirs. 2001—, pres. 2006), Rotary (Everett), Phi Beta Kappa. Avocations: book collecting, book binding, guitar, piano. Office: 3327 Colby Ave Everett WA 98201-6403 Home Phone: 425-348-6256; Office Phone: 425-258-6767. Personal E-mail: mark1105@aol.com.

VALENTINE, VINCENT, medical director; b. New Orleans, Aug. 19, 1961; m. Cathy Valentine; children: Kristen L. Oalmann, Olivia C. MD, LSU Sch.Medicine, New Orleans, 1987. Med. dir. lung transplant Ochsner Health Sys., New Orleans, 1994—2007; med. dir. Tex. Transplant Ctr., UTMB, Galveston, 2007—. Contbr. articles to profl. jours. Recipient award, LSU Sch. Medicine, 1987, Arthur Kornberg award, 1987, Timothy F. Beckett, Jr. award, Stanford U. Med. Ctr., 1992, 1994, award, Dupont Pharmaceuticals, 1994, Clin. Tchg. award, UTMB John P. McGovern Acad., 2009; named to Best Spkr. award, ABIM Bd. Rev., 1998. Fellow: ACP, Am. Coll. Chest Physicians; mem.: Phi Beta Kappa, Phi Kappa Phi. Office: UTMB Galveston 301 Univ Galveston TX 77555-0772

VALENTINE, WILLIAM NEWTON, retired physician, educator; b. Kansas City, Mo., Sept. 29, 1917; s. Herbert S. and Mabel W. Valentine; m. Martha Hickman Winfree; children: William, James, Edward. Student, U. Mich., 1934—36, U. Mo., Columbia, 1936—37; MD, Tulane U., 1942. Diplomate Am. Bd. Internal Medicine. Intern Strong Meml. Hosp., Rochester, NY, 1942—43, asst. resident in medicine, 1943, chief resident in medicine, 1943—44; specialist, attending physician in internal medicine Wadsworth Hosp., LA, 1949—88, VA Ctr., LA, 1949—88; specialist, attending physician in internal medicine Ctr. Health Scis. UCLA, 1949—, prof. medicine,

1957—88, chmn. dept., 1963—71, prof. emeritus medicine, 1988—. Contbr. articles to profl. jours. Capt. MC AUS, 1944—47. Recipient Mayo Soley award for excellence in rsch., Western Soc. Clin. Rsch., 1978, 53d Annual UCLA faculty rsch. lectr., 1978. Master: ACP (John Phillips Meml. award for disting. achievements in internal medicine 1979); fellow: Am. Soc. Hematology (Henry Stratton lectr. 1978), Internat. Soc. Hematology (v.p. U.S. 1976—80); mem.: NAS, Am. Acad. Arts and Scis., We. Soc. Clin. Rsch., We. Assn. Physicians (pres. 1969—70), Assn. Am. Physicians, Am. Soc. Clin. Investigation (v.p. 1962), Am. Bd. Internal Medicine. Republican.

VALENTINI, ROBERTO, medical educator; b. Trieste, Italy, Sept. 20, 1958; Degree in Medicine, U. Trieste, 1984, degree in Orthop. and Legal Med., 1989. Adj. prof. U. Trieste, 2006—. Mem.: Italian Orthop. Traumatologic Soc. Office: strada Fiume 417 Trieste 34143 Italy Business E-Mail: roberto.valentini@aots.sanita.fvg.it.

VALENZUELA, JOSE IGNACIO, healthcare educator; b. Neiva, Huila, Colombia, Sept. 1, 1978; MD, Pontificia U. Javeriana, 2002; MSc in Health Infomatics, City U., London, 2006. Rsch. fellow, project coord., connecting health Ealing Hosp. NHS Trust. London, 2006; sub-dir., divsn. edn., coord. ctr. telehealth Found. Santa Fe Bogota, 2007—10, cons., eHealth, 2010—; prof., health info. sys. Pontificia U. Javeriana, 2008—; ind. cons., eHealth, 2010—. Cons., techs. healthcare edn. Ministry Social Protection, 2001—. Recipient Rsch. Excellence award, Found. Santa Fe Bogotá, Innovator award, Healthcare Informatics, Profl. award, Nat. Health Svc. Mem.: Inter-Am. Devel. Bank, Health. European Union, Colombian Assn. eHealth (founding com. mem.), Internat. Med. Informatics Assn. Avocations: writing, music, walking. Home: Cll 129 7D-26 Bogota Colombia Personal E-mail: joseival@gmail.com.

VALERA, EVE MARIE, neuroscientist; d. Ernest and Arlene Valera; m. Kevin Mark Spencer, Nov. 4, 2001. BA Summa Cum Laude, Siena Coll., 1992; AM, U. Ill., 1996, PhD, 1999. Postdoctoral fellow Harvard Med. Sch., Mass Gen. Hosp., Charlestown, Mass., 2000—03; postdoctoral fellow in clin. neuropsychology Mass. Mental Health Ctr. and Beth-Israel Deaconess Ctr., Boston, 2000—02; asst. prof. Harvard Med. Sch., 2007—, Mass Gen. Hosp., Charlestown, Mass., 2007—. Contbr. articles to profl. jours. Recipient Lilly Fellowship award, Eli Lilly and Co., 2003, Herman-Eisen award for Profl. Contbn. to Psychology, U. Ill., 1998, Career Devel. award, NIH, 2005—, ACNP Travel award, 2009; grantee Grad. Coll. Thesis Project Grant, U. Ill., 1996, Nat. Rsch. Svc. award, NIH, 2002-2003, 1998-1999, Women's Studies Funding for Feminist Scholarship, U. Ill., 1996, scholar FMRI Tng. Course Scholarship, APA, 2001; Grad. Coll. fellow, U. Ill., 1993, Excellence grant, Harvard Med. Sch., 2007. Mem.: Internat. Soc. for Traumatic Stress Studies, Internat. Neuropsychol. Soc., Cognitive Neurosci. Soc. Office: Mass Gen Hosp 149 13th St Rm 2651 Charlestown MA 02129 E-mail: eve_valera@hms.harvard.edu.

VALERO, EDELMIRA, chemistry professor; b. Albacete, Spain, Feb. 5, 1961; Degree in Chemistry, U. Murcia, 1985. Rsch. fellow U. Castilla La Mancha, 1986—89, asst. prof., 1989—90, assoc. prof., 1990—, co-dir., phys. chemistry dept., 1996—2002. Mem.: Soc. Biofísica España, Soc. Española Bioquímica, Real Soc. Española Química. Avocations: reading, music, walking. Office: Sch Industrial Engineering Physic Albacete E-02071 Spain Office Fax: 34 967 599224. Business E-Mail: edelmira.valero@uclm.es.

VALFRE, MICHELLE WILLIAMS, nursing educator, administrator, writer; b. Reno, Feb. 12, 1947; d. Robert James and Dolores Jane (Barnard) Williams; m. Adolph A. Valfre, Nov. 7, 1998. BSN, U. Nev., Reno, 1973; M Health Svc., U. Calif., Davis, 1977. RN, Oreg., Ariz. Staff nurse VA Hosp., Reno, 1973—77; family nurse practitioner Tri-County Indian Health Svc., Bishop, Calif., 1977—81; instr. nursing Rogue C.C., Grants Pass, Oreg., 1981—82; psychiat. nurse VA Hosp., Roseburg, Oreg., 1982; dir. edn. Josephine Meml. Hosp., Grants Pass, 1983—84; geriat. nurse practitioner Hearthstone Manor, Medford, Oreg., 1984—86; chmn. nursing dept. Rogue C.C., Grants Pass, 1986—; CEO Health and Ednl. Cons. Inc., Forest Grove, Oreg., 1989—. Instr. social scis. Rogue C.C., 1997-98; DON Highland House Nursing Ctr., Grants Pass, 1990; bd. dirs. Tri-County Indian Health Svc.; cons. for nursing svcs. in long-term care facilities Author: Professional Skills for Leadership, Foundations of Mental Health Care, 5th edit.; contbr.: Fundamental Health Care: Concepts and Skills. Mem. Josephine County Coalition for AIDS, Grants Pass, 1990. With USN, 1965-69 Mem. NAFE, Nat. League Nursing, Oreg. Ednl. Assn., Oreg. State Bd. Nursing (re-entry nursing com. 1992-93) Office: PO Box 807 Forest Grove OR 97116 Home Phone: 503-357-2221; Office Phone: 503-357-2215. E-mail: avalfre@mindspring.com.

VALLANCE-OWEN, ANDREW JOHN, group medical director; b. London, Sept. 5, 1951; s. John and Renee Audrey Jean V.; m. Frances Mary Glover, Apr. 2, 1977; children: Anthony, Simon, Nicola. MB ChB, Birmingham U. Med. Sch., England, 1976; FRCSEd, 1981; MBA, Open U., England, 1993. Surg. registrar Nat. Health Svc., Newcastle-upon-Tyne, England, 1979—83; provincial sec. Brit. Med. Assn., Leeds, England, 1983-85, Scottish sec. Edinburgh, Scotland, 1985-89, under sec. London, 1989-94; med. dir. Brit. United Provident Assn., London, 1994-95, group med. dir., 1995—. Dir. Health Dialog Svcs. Corp., Boston, 1998—2011; dept. chmn. Coun. Royal Med. Found. Epsom Coll., England, 1995—2010, chmn., 2010—; dir. Outcome Technologies Ltd., London, 2002—05; sec. BMA Charitable Trusts, London, 1989—94. Author: The Health Debate Live, 1992; co-author: Medical Audit and Accountability. Found. gov. Latymer Sch. Edmonton, London, 1994—; gov. Queenswood Sch., England, 2001—; pres. Birmingham U. Guild Students, England, 1974—75; dep. chmn. Nat. Hosp. Jr. Staff Coms., BMA, 1982—83; mem. faculty medicine adv. bd. U. Warwick. Leopold Salomons scholar Epsom Coll., England, 1970. Fellow Royal Coll. Surgeons Edinburgh, Royal Soc. Medicine, Royal Soc. Arts; mem. Worshipful Soc. Apothecaries. Avocations: music, jazz, sailing, hill walking, travel. Office: BUPA House 15-19 Bloomsbury Way London WC1A 2BA England Home: 13 Lancaster Avenue EN4 0EP Barnet Herts England Office Phone: 020 7656 2037. E-mail: vallanca@bupa.com.

VALLBONA, CARLOS, physician; b. Granollers, Barcelona, Spain, July 29, 1927; came to U.S., 1953, naturalized, 1967; s. José and Dolores (Calbó) V.; m. Rima Gretel Rothe, Dec. 26, 1956; children: Rima Nuria, Carlos Fernando, María Teresa, Marisa. BA, BS, U. de Barcelona, 1944, MD, 1950. Diplomate Am. Bd. Pediatrics. Child health physician Escuela de Puericultura, Barcelona, 1952, Stagier Etranger Hôpital des Enfants Malades, Paris, 1952-53; intern, resident U. Louisville, 1953-55; resident Baylor Coll. Medicine, Houston, 1955-56, prof. rehab. medicine, 1967—, assoc. prof. physiology and pediatrics, 1962-69, prof., chmn. dept. community medicine, 1969-95, prof. family medicine, 1980-95, Disting. Svc. prof. family and cmty. medicine, 1995—. Adj. prof. U. Tex. Sch. Pub. Health, U. Tex. Health Sci. Ctr., Houston; chief community medicine service Harris County Hosp. Dist.; staff gen. med. service Tex. Children's Hosp.; staff The Inst. Rehab. and Research; staff St. Luke's Episcopal Hosp., con. staff VA Med. Ctr., Houston; Fulbright vis. prof., 1967; cons. WHO, NIH, Nat. Center Health Stats. Pan Am. Health Orgn., Nat. Center Health Service Research; advisor Conseller Sanitat, Catalunya. Author numerous articles in field; editorial bd. several Sci. jours. French Ministry of Edn. fellow, 1952; Children's Internat. Center fellow, 1953; co-recipient Gold medal 6th Internat. Congress Phys. Medicine, 1972; Public Citizen of Yr. San Jacinto chpt. Nat. Assn. Social Workers, 1974; Outstanding Tchr. award Baylor Coll. Medicine Class of 1980, 83, 85, 87, 88; decorated officer Order of Civil Merit (Spain), Medalla Narcis Monturiol (Catalunya). Mem. Am. Acad. Family Physicians, Am. Coll. Med. Informatics (founding mem. 1984), Nat. Acad. Practice (disting. practitioner 1984), Soc. Pediatric Research (emeritus), AMA, Tex. Med. Assn., Am. Coll. Chest Physicians, Am. Pub. Health Assn. (chmn. elect med. care sect. 1989-90), Am. Coll. Preventive Medicine, U.S.-Mex. Border Health Assn., AAAS, Am. Congress Rehab. Medicine, Catalan Soc. Pediatrics (hon.), Argentinian Soc. Internal Medicine (hon. 1986), Argentinian Med. Soc. (hon. 1986), Spanish Acad. Pediatrics (ambulatory pediatrics sect. hon. 1987), Assn. Tchrs. Preventive Medicine, Spanish Profls. Am. (pres. 1988), Soc. Catalana Hipertensio (hon. pres.), Sigma Xi, Alpha Omega Alpha. Roman Catholic. Home: 2001 Holcombe Blvd #2903 Houston TX 77030-4222 Office: Baylor Coll Medicine One Baylor Plz Rm 650E Houston TX 77030-3404

VALLE, RAFAEL F., obstetrician, gynecologist, educator; b. Mendoza, Veracruz, Mex., Sept. 6, 1935; came to US, 1966; MD, Madrid U., 1965. Diplomate Am. Bd. Ob-Gyn. Intern Mt. Sinai Hosp., Mpls., 1966-67, resident in surgery, 1967-69; resident in ob-gyn. U. Minn., Mpls., 1969-72; attending physician Hennepin County Med. Ctr. and U. Minn. Hosps., 1972—75, Northwestern U. Meml. Hosp., Chgo., 1975—; practice in ob-gyn. Northwestern U. Hosp., Chgo., 1975—. Prof. ob-gyn. Northwestern U. Med. Sch., 1994—. Mem. Am. Coll. Obstetricians and Gynecologist, Am. Coll. Surgeons, Am. Soc. for Reproductive Medicine, Assn. Prof. Obs. Gynecol., Am. Assn. Gynecol. Laparoscopists, Chgo. Gynecol. Soc., Internat. Soc. Gynecol. Endoscopy, European Soc. Human Reproduction and Embryology. Office: Northwestern U Med Sch 880 N Lake Shore Dr Ste 20-C Chicago IL 60611 Business E-Mail: r-valle@northwestern.edu. *

VALLEJO, ENRIQUE, cardiologist, researcher; s. Vallejo Edmundo and Venegas Imelda; m. Vallejo Hernandez, Apr. 24, 1993; children: Vallejo Santiago, Vallejo Tania. MD, U. Nat. Autonoma de Mex., 1992. Cert. internal medicine 1995, cardiology 1998, nuclear cardiology Yale U., 1999, cardiac tomography Cleve. Clinic, 2005. Assoc. prof. Inst. Nat. de Cardiologia, Mexico City, 1999—, U. Nat. Autonoma de Mex., Mexico City, 2000—; cons. Hosp. Angeles del Pedregal, Mexico City, 1999—, U. de Radiodiagnostico, Mexico City, 2000—. Contbr. to numerous sci. jours. Postdoc. fellow, Yale U., 1998—99. Fellow: Am. Soc. Nuc. Cardiology. Independent. Avocation: running. Office: Inst Nat de Cardiologia Juan Badiano No1 Sect XVI Mexico City Tlalpan 14080 Mexico Office Fax: 525555730994. E-mail: cpvv2@hotmail.com.

VALLEJO-SOTO, MANUEL, gastroenterologist, bariatric and general surgeon; b. Mex., DF, Oct. 17, 1957; s. Manuel Vallejo-Pérez and Graciela Soto-Centeno; m. Martha Patricia Leal-Pérez; children: Manuel Vallejo, Daniela Vallejo. Bachelor degree, U. La Salle, México City, 1975. Médico cirujano Facultad Medicina, U. La Salle, 1980. Past pres. Gastroenterology Soc. State Queretaro, Mexico, 1990—91; gen. sec. Med. Coll., Queretaro, 1996—98. Home: Escobedo 107 Edif3-301 Col Centro Queretaro Qro 76000 Mexico Office: Clínica Cirugía y Gastroenterología Bernardino Razo No 21-110 Queretaro Qro 76178 Mexico Home Phone: 52-442-224-1253; Office Phone: 52-442-192-3028. Office Fax: 52-442-215-6957. Business E-Mail: mvallejos@prodigy.net.mx.

VALLI, GIORGIO, neurologist, educator; b. Lodi, Sept. 28, 1938; MD, State U. Milan, 1964, specialization in Neurology, 1967. Assoc. prof. neurology State U. Milan, 1983—2008. Cons. Maj. Hosp. Milan, 1971—2005. Recipient Gold medal, Maj. Hosp. Milan. Mem.: Am. Acad. Neurology. Avocations: mountain climbing, skiing, swimming. Home: Via Carlo Osma 2 Milan Lombardia 20151 Italy Home Fax: 39 2 3085663. Personal E-mail: valli.giorgio@fastwebnet.it.

VALONE, KEITH EMERSON, psychologist, psychoanalyst; b. Austin, Tex., Aug. 3, 1953; s. James Floyd and Elizabeth Niles (Emerson) V.; m. Leona Marie Lagace, July 22, 1978; children: Kyle Stephen James, Christienne Marie. BA, U. So. Calif., 1975; MA, U. Ill., 1979, PhD, 1981; PsyD, Inst. Contemporary Psychoanaly, LA, 1995; MS in Clin. Psychopharmacology, Alliant Internat. U., 2010. Lic. psychologist, Calif. Pvt. practice, Pasadena, Calif., 1983—; chief psychology svc. Las Encinas Hosp., Pasadena, 1988; dir. psychology Ingleside Hosp., Rosemead, Calif., 1990-92. Clin. asst. prof. dept. psychology Fuller Theol. Sem., Pasadena, Calif., 1984—85; asst. clin. prof. dept. psychology UCLA, 1984—87; clin. asst. prof. psychiatry and behavioral scis. U. So. Calif. Keck Sch. Medicine, LA, 2006—. Contbr. articles to profl. jours. Mem. APA, Calif. State Psychol. Assn., Phi Beta Kappa. Episcopalian. Office: Ste 321 One W California Blvd Pasadena CA 91105 Office Phone: 626-405-9066. Business E-Mail: valone@thearroyos.org.

VALVERDE, EDUARDO, epidemiologist; b. Lima, Peru, Feb. 12, 1962; MPH, Fla. Internat. U., 1998. Epidemiologist Ctrs. Disease Control and Prevention, 2006—11. Mem.: Internat. AIDS Soc. Avocation: art. Home: 4425 Wieuca Rd NE Atlanta GA 30342 Personal E-mail: eduardovalverde@bellsouth.net.

VALVERDE, PALOMA, biochemist, educator; b. Murcia, Murcia, Spain, Jan. 15, 1968; d. Gregorio Valverde and Paz de los Angeles Hernandez; m. David Irwin Sherris, Nov. 2, 1997; children: Gregory Alexander Sherris children: Michael Gregory Sherris. BSc, U. Murcia, Spain, 1990, MSc, 1991, PhD, 1994. Scientist Human Nutrition Rsch. Ctr. of Aging, Tufts U., Boston, 2002—04; chair dept. scis. Wentworth Inst. Tech. Vis. scientist Boston Biomed. Rsch. Inst., 2007—; biology lectr. Simmons Coll., 2009—; biology instr. Wentworth Inst. Tech., 2008—; dept. chair & asst. prof., 2011—, Wentworth Inst. Tech., Dept. Scis. Contbr. articles to profl. jours. John W. Hein Rsch. fellow, Forsyth Inst., Boston, 1999—2002. Mem.: Am. Physiol. Soc., Internat. Assn. for Biomed. Rsch. (v.p. 2004—). Achievements include discovery of first mutations in human melanocortin receptor 1; gene called WW45 or Salvador; first to use of scorpion venom to treat periodontal disease; development of first antibody to recognize WW45/Salvador gene; discovery of axl receptor tyrosine kinase is ubiquitinated by its ligand Gas6; RANKL and BSP induce bone loss synergistically. Avocations: painting, writing. Home: 37 Neillian Crescent Jamaica Plain MA 02130 Personal E-mail: pvalverde@aol.com. Business E-Mail: valverdep@wit.edu.

VALVO, BARBARA-ANN, lawyer, surgeon; b. Elizabeth, NJ, June 7, 1949; d. Robert Richad and Vera (Kovach) V. BA in Biology, Hofsta U., 1971; MD, Pa. State U., 1975; JD, Loyola Sch. Law, New Orleans, 1993. Bar: La. 1993; diplomate Am. Bd. Surgery. Surg. intern Nassau County Med. Ctr., East Meadow, NY, 1975-76; resident gen. surgery Allentown-Sacred Heart Med. Ctr., Pa., 1976-80; asst. chief surgery USPHS, New Orleans, 1980-81; pvt. practice gen. surgery New Orleans, 1981-89; pvt. practice med. malpractice law, 1995—. Upjohn scholar, 1975. Fellow ACS; mem. ABA, Fed. Bar Assn., La. Bar Assn., La. Trial Lawyers Assn. Republican. Avocations: computers, raising animals. Office: 41 Harley Pl Willow Spring NC 27592 Personal E-mail: bavalvo@nc.rr.com.

VAMVAKAS, ELEFTHERIOS CHRISTOS, pathologist, researcher; b. Drama, Greece, June 26, 1959; s. Christos Eleftherios and Eugenia Vamvakas. MD, Nat. U. Athens, Greece, 1983; MPH, Harvard U., 1986; MPA, NYU, 1989, MPhil, 1991; PhD, 1992. Diplomate Am. Bd. Pathology. Asst. prof. pathology Harvard Med. Sch., Boston, 1994—97; asst. dir. blood transfusion svc. Mass. Gen. Hosp., Boston, 1994—97; assoc. prof. pathology NYU Sch. Medicine, NYC, 1997—2002; chief pathology and lab. medicine svc. NY Dept. Vet. Affairs Med. Ctr., NYC, 1997—99; dir. blood bank and transfusion svc. NYU Med. Ctr., NYC, 1999—2002; exec. v.p., med., scientific, and rsch. affairs Canadian Blood Svcs., Ottawa, 2002—. Author: Evidence-Based Practice of Transfusion Medicine, 2001; editor: Immunomodulatory Effects of Blood Transfusion, 1999; contbr. articles to profl. jours. Office: Canadian Blood Svcs Head Office 1800 Alta Vista Dr Ottawa ON Canada K1G 4J5 Office Phone: 613-739-2190. Business E-Mail: stephen.vamrakas@bloodservices.ca.

VAN AKEN, HUGO KAREL, anesthesiologist, educator; b. Mechelen, Belgium, Mar. 2, 1951; s. Albert and Elisa (Flies) Van A.; m. Grete Maria Gantenbrink; children: Pieter, Caroline, Margareta. MD, Cath. U., Leuven, Belgium, 1976, specialist in Anesthesiology, 1980; promotion, Med. Faculty U. Hosp., Münster, Germany, 1981; habilitation, U. Hosp., Münster, Germany, 1983, transfusion medicine specialist, 1986. Asst. dept. anesthesiology Cath. U., Leuven, 1976-78, asst. clinic anesthesiology and intensive care Westfälische Wilhelms U., Münster, 1979-80, sr. staff physician clinic anesthesiology and intensive care, 1980-83, pvt. tutor, 1983, dir. clinic, poly-clinic for anesthesiology, intensive care, 1985—; ordinary prof. anesthesiology Cath. U., Leuven, Belgium; dir. Klinik und Poliklinik f. Anaesthesiologie/Op. Inten. Universitätsklinikum Münster, 1995—. Editor: Neuro-Anesthetic Practice, 1995, Anesthesia and Analgesia; guest editor: Baillière's Clinical Anesthesiology, 1993, Anesthesia & Analgesia, 2000; editor-in-chief: Current Opinion in Anesthesiology. Fellow Royal Coll. of Anesthetists, European Acad. Anesthesiology (hon. senator, hon. sec., pres. 2000—03), Polish Soc. Anesthesiology and Intensive Therapy (hon.), Assn. Univ. Anesthesiologists, hon., U.S., Am. Soc. Anesthesiology (hon.), European Fed. Anaesthesiology (pres. 2003), Multidisciplinary Joint Com. of Intensive Care Med. (pres. 2003), German Nat. Acad. Scis. (Leopoldine) (hon.), German Soc. Anesthesiology and Intensive Care Medicine (pres. 2007-08); mem. Assn. Anaesthesiologists Ga. (hon.) Avocations: sailing, golf. Office: Universitätsklinikum Münster Dept Anaesth & Intensive Care Medicine 48129 Münster Germany

VAN ARSDALEN, KEITH NORMAN, urologist; b. Plainfield, NJ, Sept. 26, 1951; s. Norman Charles and Thelma Marie Svendsen Van Arsdalen; children: Bryce, Leigh, Jill, Kyle. BS, Muhlenberg Coll., 1973; MMS, CMDNJ, 1975; MD, Med. Coll. Va., 1977. Intern, resident U.Md., Balt., 1977-79; resident Med. Coll. Va., Richmond, 1979-82; asst. prof. surgery, urology U. Pa., Phila., 1983-89, asst. prof. surgery, urology, radiology, 1989-97, prof. surgery, urology, radiology, 1997—. Dir. male fertility sect. U. Pa. Sch. Medicine Divsn. Urology, 1983—, dir. shock wave lithotripsy svcs., 1985—; attending urologist Children's Hosp. Phila., 1989—; chief urology sect. Phila. V.A. Med. Ctr., 1990—2001; expert adv. panel U.S. Pharm. Conv., Rockville, Md., 1990—95; mem. scientific bd. Nat. Kidney Found., NYC, 1992—98. Asst. editor Jour. Endourology, 1987-2003; contbr. articles to profl. jours., chpts. to books. Recipient Paul Rodin Leberman Teaching award Urology Residents, Phila, 1993, 98, Alumni Star award Va. Commonwealth U., 1993, John Morgan Soc. award, 1998; U. Pa. NKF-AUA rsch. fellow, 1982-83. Fellow: ACS (program com. 1992); mem.: AAAS, Urodynamics Soc., Soc. Univ. Urologists, Soc. Study Male Reproduction, Soc. Study Impotence, Soc. Reproductive Surgeons, Soc. Minimally Invasive Therapy, Soc. Laparoendoscopic Surgeons, Soc. Basic Urologic Rsch., Internat. Soc. Urology, Phila. Urol. Soc. (sec.-treas. 1992—98, pres.-elect 1998—99, pres. 1999—2000), Urol. Assn. Pa., Assn. Acad. Surgery, Am. Soc. Reproductive Medicine, Am. Soc. Andrology, Am. Assn. Clin. Urologists, Am. Urol. Assn., Coll. Physicians Phila. (mid-Atlantic sect. edn. com. 1989—90, rsch. com. rep. 1990—94, local arrangements com. 1991—94, chmn. 1992—93, program com. 1996—97, rsch. com. rep. 1999—2002). Avocations: fishing, skiing, swimming, reading, house restoration. Office: Urology 9 Penn Tower 3400 Spruce St Philadelphia PA 19104-4206 Home Phone: 856-428-1273; Office Phone: 215-662-6790.

VANARSDALL, ROBERT LEE, JR., orthodontist, educator; b. Crewe, Va., Feb. 7, 1940; s. Robert Lee Sr. and Margie Mae (Jenkins) V.; m. Sandra E. Hoffman, Aug. 11, 1962; children: Robert Lee III, Lesley, Ashley. BA in Econs., Coll. William and Mary, 1962; DDS, Med. Coll. Va., 1970; cert. Orthodontics and Periodontics, U. Pa., 1973. Diplomate Am. Acad. Periodontology, Am. Bd. Orthodontics. Staff Children's Hosp., Phila., 1973—; prof. orthodontics, chmn. dept. orthodontics U. Pa., Phila., 1981—2011, prof., chmn., 2011; prof. dentistry, chmn. Med. Coll. Pa., Phila., 1989—99; dir. Divsn. Advanced Dental Edn., Advanced Dental Edn., 2009—. K.G. prof. orthodontics U. Sydney, Australia, 2001; bd. dir. Nat. Dental Ins. Co., Denver. Editor: Internat. Jour. Adult Orthodontics and Orthognathic Surgery, 1986-2003, Orthodontics: Current Principles and Techniques, 2d edit., 1994, 4th edit., 2005, 5th edit., 2011, Applications of Orthodontic Mini-Implants, 2007; editl. bd. profl. jours.; contbr. articles to profl. jours. Bd. dirs. Phila. Soc. William and Mary Alumni Assn. Lt. USNR, 1962-65. Fellow Coll. Physicians of Phila. 1978, Am. Coll. Dentistry 1980. Mem. ADA, Am. Assn. Orthodontists, Stomatological Club Phila., Angle Soc. Orthodontists (v.p. ea. component, pres. 2004-2005), Phila. Soc. Orthodontists (pres. 1989, chmn. sci. affairs coun. 1990—), Internat. Coll. of Dentists. Roman Catholic. Avocations: antiques, architecture. Home: 208 Ashwood Rd Villanova PA 19085-1504 Office: 711 W Lancaster Ave Bryn Mawr PA 19010 Office Phone: 610-520-4600. Office Fax: 215-898-0998. Business E-Mail: rlv@pobox.upenn.edu.

VANAUKER, LANA, recreational therapist, educator; b. Youngstown, Ohio, Sept. 19, 1949; d. William Marshall and Joanne Norma (Kimmel) Speece; m. Dwight Edward VanAuker, Mar. 16, 1969 (div. 1976); 1 child, Heidi. BS in Edn. cum laude, Kent State U., Ohio, 1974; MS in Edn., Youngstown U., 1989. Cert. tchr. Ohio, nat. cert. activity cons. Phys. edn. instr. St. Joseph Sch., Campbell, Ohio, 1973—75; program dir. YWCA, Youngstown, 1975—85; exercise technician Youngstown State U., 1985—86; health educator Park Vista Retirement Ctr., Youngstown, 1986—87; tchr. Salem (Ohio) City Sch., 1987—88; recreational therapist Trumbull Meml. Hosp., Warren, Ohio, 1988—. Activity cons. Mahoning/Trumbull Nursing Homes, Warren, 1990-92; adv. bd. rep. Ohio State Bur. Health Promotion Phys. Fitness, 1996—; adv. bd. Ohio State Exec. Phys. Fitness Dept. Health, 1996; tchr. Mohican Youth Ctr., Loudonville, Ohio, 1998-99; dance instr., 2004—; owner, instr. Lanas Dance Studio, 2005—; bd. dirs. USA Dance; presenter in field. Prodr.: Exercise is the Fountain of Youth, 1993; photographer, choreographer; cover photography feature Mahoning County Med. Soc. Bull., 2000, Stars photo in Columbus, Ohio, Secret Window, 2009; exhibited in group show Forum Health, 1999. Vol. Am. Cancer Soc., 1980—, Am. Heart Assn., 1986—, Dance for Heart, 1980-86; mem. State of Ohio Phys. Fitness Adv. Bd., 1996-97. Youngstown State U. scholar, 1986-89; recipient 1st pl. Kodak Internat. Newspaper Snapshot award, 1998-99, 1st Place Internat. Libr. Photography, 2000, Ballroom Dance Gold medal Sr. Olympics, 2006, 1st Pl. award Photo Contest, Youngstown State U., 2007, Excellence award State Activity Personnel Convention, Columbus, Ohio, 2007, Excellence award Resident Activity Assn., Ohio State Conv., 2008. Mem.: AAHPERD, U.S. Amateur Ballroom Dance Assn. (v.p. 2002—03), Pa. Activity Profl. Assn. (pres., spkr. 2001), Resident Activity Profl. Assn. (pres. 1994—96, 2001—03), Youngstown Photography Club (treas. 2006—), Youngstown Camera Club (social chair 1989—90, pres. 1993—95, treas. 2004—), Kappa Delta Pi. Democrat. Presbyterian. Avocations: photography, dance, volleyball, aerobics, travel. Home: 4133 S Turner Rd Canfield OH 44406-8737 Office: 4N Unit Forum Health 1350 E Market St Warren OH 44483-6608 Home Phone: 330-533-5470; Office Phone: 330-219-0008. Business E-Mail: lvanauker@fitnesstoyouth.net.

VAN BOSSE, HAROLD J.P., orthopedic surgeon; MD, U. Ill., 1984—89. Cert. Orthopedic Surgery, 1997. Residence orthopedics U. Ill., Chgo.; fellow Hosp. for Sick Children, Toronto, 1994—95; surgeon Schneider Children's Hosp. Long Island Jewish Med. Ctr.; pediatric orthopedic surgeon NYU Hosp. for Joint Diseases, 1998—; asst. prof. orthopaedic surgery NYU Med. Ctr. Founder A Leg to Stand On, India, 2003; vol. surgeon Silver Service Children's program, Colombia. Named one of Medical Marvels, New York Mag., 2006. Mailing: NYU Hosp for Joint Diseases 301 East 17 St New York NY 10003 Office: 4 Weber Ave Malverne NY 11565 also: 240 E 18th S 1st Fl New York NY 10003 Office Phone: 212-598-2310, 516-596-2514. Office Fax: 212-598-2311.

VAN BREUKELEN, GERARD J.P., statistician, educator; b. Oss, Netherlands, Apr. 12, 1959; married. MD in Math. Psychology (hon.), Radboud U. Nijmegen, Netherlands, 1984, PhD in Math. Psychology, 1989. Asst. prof. math. psychology Radboud U., 1988—90; biostatistician Med. Rsch. Bur. Intnat., Arnhem, Netherlands, 1990—91; asst. prof. stats. Maastricht U., Netherlands, 1991—2005, assoc. prof. stats., 2005—. Contbr. chapters to books, articles to profl. statis. jour. Office: Maastricht Univ Postbus 616 6200 MD Maastricht Netherlands E-mail: gerard.vbreukelen@maastrichtuniversity.nl.

VANCE, RALPH BROOKS, SR., oncologist, educator; b. Jackson, Miss., Dec. 4, 1945; s. Brooks C. and Chrystine G. (Gober) V.; m. Mary Douglas Allen, June 18, 1979; children: Brooks, Barrett. BA in Biology and German, U. Miss., 1968, MD, 1972. Asst. prof. medicine U. Miss., Jackson, 1978—86, assoc. prof. medicine, 1986—93, prof. medicine, 1993—. Chief of staff U. Miss. Hosp. and Clinics, Jackson, 1989-90; pres. faculty senate Univ. Med. Ctr., Jackson, 1986-87, univ. clin. assoc., pres., 1987-89. Author (with others) Development in Molecular Virology: Herpes Virus DNA, 1982; contbr. numerous articles and abstracts to profl. jours. Nat. pres. Am. Cancer Soc., 2003—04, bd. dirs. Atlanta, nat. pres., exec. com.; bd. dirs. ARC, Jackson; bd. Blue Cross/Blue Shield Miss., Jackson, 1989—92. Named to Hall of Fame, U. Miss., 1968. Fellow ACP; mem. Am. Assn. for Cancer Edn., Am. Fedn. for Clin. Rsch., Am. Soc. Clin. Oncology, Am. Assn. for Cancer Rsch., Miss. Acad. Scis., S.W. Oncology Group, U. Miss. Alumni Assn.(bd.dirs. 2009-), Sigma Xi. Office: University Miss Sch Medicine 2500 N State St Jackson MS 39216-4505 Home: 2105 Old Taylor Rd Oxford MS 38655 Office Phone: 601-984-5590. Business E-Mail: rvance@umc.edu.

VAN CITTERS, ROBERT LEE, medical educator, physician; b. Alton, Iowa, Jan. 20, 1926; s. Charles and Wilhemina (Heemstra) Van C.; m. Mary E. Barker, Apr. 9, 1949; children: Robert, Mary, David, Sara. AB, U. Kans., 1949; MD, U. Kans. Med. Ctr., Kansas City, 1953; Sc.D. hon., Northwestern Coll., Orange City, Iowa, 1977. Intern U. Kans. Med. Ctr., Kansas City, 1953-54, resident, 1955-57, fellow, 1957-58; research fellow Sch. Medicine, U. Wash., Seattle, 1958-61, asst. prof. physiology and biophysics, 1962-65, Robert King chair of cardiovascular rsch., 1962—, assoc. prof., 1965-70, prof., 1970—, prof. medicine, 1970—, assoc. dean, 1968-70, dean, 1970-81. Mem. staff Scripps Clinic and Research Found., La Jolla, Calif., 1961-62; exchange scientist joint U.S.-U.S.S.R. Sci. Exchange, 1962; mem. Liason Commn. on Med. Edn., Washington, 1981-85; mem. various coms., nat. adv. research council NIH, Bethesda, Md., 1980-83; mem. Va. Spl. Med. Adv. Commn., 1974-78, chmn., 1976-78; chmn. working group on mech. circulatory support systems Nat. Heart, Lung and Blood Inst. NIH, 1985—, mem. adv. coun. clin. applications and prevention, 1985-89. Contbr. numerous articles to profl. jours. Served to 1st lt. U.S. Army, 1943-46, PTO; to capt. M.C., USAF, 1953-55. Recipient research career devel. USPHS Fellow AAAS; mem. Assn. Am. Med. Colls. (adminstrv. bd. and exec. council 1972-78, Disting. Service mem.), Am. Coll. Cardiology (Cummings medal 1970), Nat. Acad. Sci. Inst. Medicine, Am. Heart Assn., Wash. State Med. Assn. (hon. life) *

VAN DALEN, ELVIRA CAROLINE, epidemiologist, researcher; b. Rotterdam, Netherlands, Aug. 16, 1976; m. Jorrit Willem Van As, Sept. 2, 2005. MD, U. Amsterdam, 2001, PhD, 2007. Rschr. Emma Children's Hosp., Amsterdam, 2002—. Achievements include research in anthracycline-induced cardiotoxicity in childhood cancer patients; pediatric oncology. Office: Emma Children's Hosp / AMC Dept Pediatric Oncology Meibergdreef 9 1105 AZ Amsterdam Netherlands E-mail: e.c.vandalen@amc.uva.nl.

VAN DAM, HEIMAN, psychoanalyst; b. Leiden, Netherlands; s. Machiel and Rika van D.; m. Barbara C. Strona, Oct. 6, 1945; children: Machiel, Claire Ilena, Rika Rosemary. AB, U. So. Calif., 1942, MD, 1945. Fellow in child psychiatry Pasadena (Calif.) Child Guidance Clinic, 1950; gen. practice psychiatry and psychoanalysis LA, 1951—2006; instr. L.A. Psychoanalytic Inst., LA, 1959—2000, co-chmn. com. on child psychoanalysis, 1960-67, tng. and supervising psychoanalyst, 1972—; supr. child and adolescent psychoanalysis So. Calif. Psychoanalytic Inst., 1986—. Cons. Reiss Davis Child Study Center, 1955-76, Neighborhood Youth Assn., LA, 1964-69; assoc. clin. prof. psychiatry and pediats. UCLA Sch. Medicine, 1960-96, clin. prof. psychiatry and pediats., 1996—; vis. supr. child psychoanalysis San Francisco Psychoanalytic Inst., 1969-79, 2002—, Denver Psychoanalytic Inst., 1972-74; adv. bd. Western State U. Coll. Law, Fullerton, Calif., 1965-83. Corr. editor Arbeits Hefte Kinderanalyse, 1985—2005; contbr. articles to profl. jours. Trustee, edn. com. Center for Early Edn., 1964-92, v.p., 1978-79; bd. dirs. Child Devel. and Psychotherapy Tng. Program, LA, 1975-80, pres., 1975-77; bd. dirs. LA Child Devel. Center, 1977-86, treas., 1978-80; mem. cult clinic Jewish Family Service, L.A., 1978-86; bd. dirs. Lake Arrowhead Crest Estates, 1990-99. Capt. M.C. AUS, 1946-48. Mem. Am. Psychoanalytic Assn. (com. on ethics 1977-80), Assn. Child Psychoanalysis (councillor 1966-69, sec. 1972-74, nominating com. 1978-84, membership com. 1988—2005, Marianne Kris lectr. 1995), Internat. Assn. Infant Psychiatry (co-chmn. program com. 1980-83), Internat. Soc. Adolescent Psychiatry (sci. adv. com. 1988-2004), Phi Beta Kappa. Office: 2864 McConnell Dr Los Angeles CA 90064-4658 Office Phone: 310-839-3232. Business E-Mail: opa5x@ucla.edu.

VAN DAM, ROB M., epidemiologist, educator; MSc in Nutrition & Epidemiology, Wageningen U., 1998; PhD, Vrije U. Amsterdam Med. Sch., 2003. Researcher Nat. Inst. for Pub. Health & Environ., 1998—2002; asst. prof. nutrition & health Inst. for Health Sciences, 2002—; rsch. scientist Harvard Sch. Pub. Health, 2005—07; co-dir. epidemiology & genetics core Boston Obesity & Nutrition Rsch. Ctr., 2006—; assoc. epidemiologist Brigham & Women's Hosp., 2006—; asst. prof. Harvard Med. Sch., 2007—. Office: Harvard School Of Public Health 665 Huntington Ave Boston MA 02115 E-mail: rvandam@hsph.harvard.edu.

VAN DE BOGART, DEBRA SCHERWERTS, medical/surgical nurse, researcher; b. Claremont, NH, Aug. 6, 1954; d. William Earl and Barbara Louise (Hadley White) Scherwerts. RN, Sacred Heart Sch. Nursing, Manchester, NH, 1975; student, Cypress Coll., Calif., 1976, U. Calif., Riverside, 1978. RN Calif., 1975, cert. home health nurse, Calif., 1997. Charge nurse, med.-surg. pediat. West Anaheim Cmty. Hosp., Anaheim, Calif., 1975—84; charge nurse, med.-surg. geriat. Humana West Anaheim, Anaheim, Calif., 1984—87; home health nurse, obstet. Physician's Care, Brea, Calif., 1988—90, Am. Home Health, Santa Ana, Calif., 1988—92; staff nurse, rsch. clin. studies ctr. Harbor-UCLA Med. Ctr., Torrance, Calif., 1993—94; nurse rschr. various profit and non-profit orgns., Anaheim, Calif., 1994—, RN coord., cons., 1994—. Contbr. workshop Focus on Health, 1982; mem. citizens adv. com., health Calif. State Assembly, 1982—; cons., home care for MD's Am. Home Health We. Med. Ctr., Santa Ana, 1991—; RN clin. advisor, staff devel. Cmty. Svcs. Projects, Orange and LA Counties, 2000—. Recipient cert. of recognition, Calif. State Legis., 1982. Mem.: ANA, Assn. Am. Acad. Bereavement, Sigma Theta Tau. Democrat. Roman Catholic. Avocations: violin, travel.

VAN DECKER, WILLIAM ARTHUR, cardiologist; b. Passaic, NJ, May 27, 1957; s. William and Louise Adelaide (Meli) Van D.; m. Generosa Grana; children: Stephanie, William, Christopher. BS in Biology summa cum laude, Fairfield U., Conn., 1979; MD, Georgetown U., 1983. Diplomate Am. Bd. Internal Medicine, Cert. Bd. Nuclear Cardiology. Am. Bd. Cardiovascular Diseases; Am. Soc. Echocardiography spl. competency testing, Bd. Cardiovascular CT. Intern Temple U. Hosp., Phila., 1983—84, resident internal medicine, 1984—86, cardiology fellow, 1986—88, non-invasive cardiology imaging tng./rsch. fellow, 1988—89; assoc. dir. Non-Invasive Imaging, dir. Cardiology Clinic Med. Coll. Pa. Hosp.-Drexel U. Coll. Medicine, Phila., 1989—2004, asst. prof. medicine and cardiology, 1989—2004, dir. Heart Sta., 1990—2004; assoc. prof. medicine Temple U., Phila., 2004—. Mem. com. on radiation safety, 1990-2004, chmn. 1993-2004, mem. pharmacy and therapeutics com., 1992-2004, chmn. pharmacy and therapeutics com. 1993-2004, mem. continuing med. edn. com., 1992-96, vice-chmn. quality assurance com., 1993-2004, group leader freshman bioethics, 1992-95, med. student advisor, 1992-2004; presenter in field, bd. dirS. Cert. Bd. Nuclear Cardiology, 2003-08, prof. medicine Temple U., 2010-Manuscript Peer reviewer Annals of Internal Medicine, 1993—; contbr. articles to profl. jours. Fellow Am. Heart Assn., Am. Coll. Cardiology, Am. Coll. Chest Physicians; mem. AMA, ACP, Am. Soc. Echocardiography, Am. Fedn. Med. Rsch.(ea. sect. chair 2001-2002), Pa. Med. Soc., Soc. Nuc. Medicine, Am. Assn. Nuc. Cardiology (founder), Am. Soc. Nuc. Cardiology (founder, bd. dirs., chmn. membership com. 2000—, bd. dirs. cert. bd. 2002—, nat. v.p. 2003-, pres. 2008), Soc. Cardiovasc. Magnetic Resonance (founding mem.), Philadelphia County Med. Soc. (ho. of dels. 1996—, bd. dirs. 2002—), Alpha Epsilon Delta, Alpha Omega Alpha, Phil County Med. Soc.(pres., 2008) Office: Temple Univ Hosp 3401 North Broad St Philadelphia PA 19140 Office Phone: 215-707-3347. Business E-Mail: vandecwa@tuhs.temple.edu.

VANDELLI, CARMEN, gastroenterologist, educator; b. San Cesario sul Panaro, May 11, 1948; MD, Modena U., 1974; degree in gastroenterology, clin. immunology, 1978. Rsch. scientist Modena U., 1975—2004; prof. Dipartimento di Medicine e Specialità Mediche, 2005. Mem.: ASPImF, AISF, EASL. Avocations: gardening, auto restoration. Office: Via del Pozzo 71 Modena Emilia Romagna 41100 Italy Office Fax: 390594223007. E-mail: vandelli@unimore.it.

VANDENBERG, BYRON F., cardiologist; b. Sacramento, Aug. 15, 1953; s. John Byron and Jeannette Vandenberg; m. Anne Carroll. BA, Occidental Coll., 1975; MD, Georgetown U., 1980. Diplomate cert. Bd. of Nuc. Cardology, cert. in internal medicine, in cardiology, in echocardiography, in lipidology. Intern, resident Parkland Hosp., Dallas, 1980-83; fellow Med. Coll. Va., 1983—85, U. Iowa, 1985—86; mem. faculty U. Iowa Coll. Medicine, Iowa City, 1986—97, 2008—; cardiologist Prairie Cardiovascular Cons., Springfield, Ill., 1997—2003, Northern Calif. Cardiology Assoc., Sacramento, 2003—08. Med. dir. adult echocardiography lab. Prairie Heart Inst., Springfield, 1997-2003; mem. editl. bd. Am. Jour. Cardiology, Dallas, 1997-2006. Contbr. articles to profl. jours. Named Best Drs. in Am., Woodward/White, 2001-02, 05-06, 07-08, 09-. Fellow ACP, Am. Coll. Cardiology, Am. Heart Assn., Am. Soc. Echocardiography. Office: Univ Iowa Coll Medicine Divsn Cardiovasc Medicine 200 Hawkins Dr Iowa City IA 52242

VAN DEN HEEVER, PATRICK, lawyer; b. Bloemfontein, South Africa, May 30, 1958; s. Daniel Victor and Georgina Petronella Van Den Heever; m. Luana Jehane Theron. LLB, U. Free State, 1979, LLM, 1981, U. Cape Town, 1997; LLD, U. Pretoria, 2002. Cand. attorney Israel Sackstein, 1979—81; asst. prof. Cape Town, 1984—85; ptnr. Kruger, Du Toit, Kraus and Van den Heever, Cape Town, 1985—94; dir. Erasmus Inc., Cape Town, 1996—98; sr. dir. Millers Inc., Cape Town, 1998—. Judge appeal Cape High Ct., 2004—10; adv. High Ct. South Africa, 2008; external examiner U. Pretoria. Recipient cert. of Commendation, SAAF, 1983, Digma prize for contributions to De Rebus, 1992, cert. for Landmark Contbn. of the Yr., Cape Law Soc., 2003. Office: 401 Advocates Ste 42 Keerom St Chambers Cape Town 4224034 South Africa Home: 31 Highlevel Rd Green Point 8000 Cape Town South Africa Office Phone: 0214216994, 0214224034. Business E-Mail: pvdh@law.co.za.

VANDEPUTTE, DIXIE DIANNE, retired psychologist, educator; b. Little River, Kans., Oct. 16, 1942; d. William Dean and Charlotte Juanita Wright; m. Gregory Charles Vandeputte, Aug. 21, 1959; children: Holly Ann Bell, Gregory Jr., Kerry Lynn Doll. BA summa cum laude in English and Psychology, U. Colo., 1990, MA in Psychology, 1992; PhD in Clin. Psychology, U. Kans., 1997. Lic. clin. psychologist Colo. Program mgr., lead clinician Pikes Peak Mental Health, Colo. Springs, Colo., 1997—2002; dir. Rocky Mountain Brain Injury Rehabilitation Day Clinic, Colo. Springs, 2002—03; dir. Counseling and Testing Ctr. U. Colo., Colo. Springs, 2003—08. Mem. first del. to Vietnam and Cambodia APA, 2006; instr. U. Colo., 2003—08; presenter in field. Contbr. articles to profl. jours. Sec. bd. dirs. Suicide Prevention Partnership, Colo. Springs, 2001—08; sec. bd. Nat. Alliance for the Mentally Ill-CS, Colo. Springs, 2002—08; mem. steering com. KP Women's Endowment, Colo. Springs, 2003—08; bd. dirs. Suicide Prevention Edn. and Advocacy Coalition, Colo. Springs, 2004—08. Recipient Outstanding Undergrad. Social Sci. award, U. Colo., 1990. Republican. Avocations: reading, hunting, crafts.

VANDER, JAMES F., ophthalmologist; grad., MD, U. Mich. Diplomate Am. Bd. Ophthalmology. Intern William Beaumont Hosp.; resident ophthalmology Univ. of Ophthal.; fellow Wills Eye Hosp.; with Mid Atlantic Retina, 1990; med. co-dir. Wills Eye Inst. Ambulatory Surgery Ctr.; pres. faculty ophthalmic edn. Wills Eye Inst.; clin. prof. ophthalmology Thomas Jefferson Univ.; mng. mem. retina svc. Wills Eye Inst. Author of numerous publications on vitreoretinal diseases; reviewer (for numerous ophthalmology jours.); contbr. of over one dozen ophthalmic textbooks; prin. editor (textbook) Ophthalmology Secrets. Named Top Doc, Phila. Mag.; named one of Best Doctors in America. Mem.: Ophthalmic Club of Phila., Am. Soc. of Retinal Specialists, Retina Soc., NJ Med. Soc., Pa. Med. Soc., Pa. Acad. of Ophthalmology, Am. Acad. of Ophthalmology (Honor award). Office: Wills Eye Institute 10th Fl 840 Walnut St Philadelphia PA 19107 Office Phone: 215-928-3300. Office Fax: 215-825-2443.

VANDER AARDE, STANLEY BERNARD, retired otolaryngologist; b. Orange City, Iowa, Sept. 26, 1931; s. Bernard John and Christina (Luchtenberg) Vander A.; m. Agnes Darlene De Beer, June 19, 1956; children: Paul, David, Debra, Mary. BA, Hope Coll., 1953; MD, Northwestern U., 1957. Diplomate Am. Bd. Otolaryngology. Intern Cook County Hosp., Chgo., 1957-59; resident in otolaryngology Northwestern U. Hosp., Chgo., 1966-70; mem. staff Mary Lott Lyles Hosp., Madanapalle, India, 1961-66, 71-87, Affiliated Med.

Clinic, Willmar, Minn., 1987-95; ret., 1995. Served to capt., USAF, 1959-60. Fellow ACS, Am. Bd. Otolaryngology, Am. Acad. Otolaryngology. Republican. Mem. Reformed Church in America. Home: 708 2nd St SE Apt 112 Orange City IA 51041-2165

VAN DER GAAG, ANNA DANIELLE, speech professional, educator; b. Rudgwick, England, Oct. 21, 1959; d. Gerth Frans van der Gaag and Mary Elizabeth (Mudford); m. David James Robertson, Apr. 17, 1993; children: Lauren Vida Robertson, Josh James Robertson. BSc in Speech and Lang. Therapy, U. Coll. London, 1981; MSc in Neurology, U. London, 1986; PhD in Speech and Lang. Therapy, U. Strathclyde, 2000. Rsch. speech therapist Glasgow (Scotland) Health Bd., 1985—88, U. Oxford, England, 1989—92; sr. lectr. U. Strathclyde, Glasgow, 1993—2004; hon. rsch. fellow U. Glasgow, 2004—; pres. Health Profs. Coun., 2006—. Mem. coun. Health Professions Coun., London, 2000—, pres.; advisor Med. Rsch. Coun., Edinburgh, 2001—03. Author: Communication Assessment Profile for Adults with Learning Disabilities, 1988; co-author: Communication and Adults with learning Disabilities, 1993, Audit: an introduction for Speech and language Therapists, 1993, The Early Communication Audit Manual, 1999; editor: Communicating Quality: professional standards for speech and language therapists, 1996, Clinical Guidelines by Consensus for Speech and Language Therapists, 1998; co-editor: Issues in Professional Practice, 2005; contbr. more than 50 articles to profl. jours. Grantee, U.K. Dept. Health, Biomed. Rsch. Coun., Dunhill Med. Trust. Fellow: Royal Soc. Medicine; mem.: Royal Coll. Speech and Lang. Therapists (rsch. com. 1993—97, nat. steering group learning disabilities 2001—05, cons. 2004—, grantee), Ctr. Evidence Based Practice. Achievements include development of first and only U.K.standardised communication assessment for adults with learning disabilities; CPD scheme for U.K. wide speech and language therapy profession; design of innovative study of therapy for people with communication disabilities following stroke; development of first audit manual for speech and language therapists in the U.K; first customised audit software package for speech and language therapists in the U.K. Office Phone: 44 0207 852 0866. Business E-Mail: anna.vandergaag@hpc-uk.org.

VANDERHEYDEN, JEAN-EMILE ERNEST, neurologist; b. Brussels, July 16, 1953; s. Ernest Vanderheyden and Yvette Stampart; children: Nicolas, Melissa, Sebastien. MD, Free U. Brussels, 1978, neurologist, 1983, expert, 1995. Resident neurologist CHU Vesale, Montigny Le Tilleul, Belgium, 1983—95, chief neurology dept., 1996—2005. Head Parkinson Unit CHU Vesale, Montigny Le Tilleul, 1988—2009; mem. adv. bd. Belgian Parkinson Assn., 1998—. Author: Traiter le Parkinson, 2004, 2nd edit., 2010, Approach du Divorce Conflictuel, 2008, Prise en Change de Dimences, 2009. Head pub. interest commn. Rotary, RC Charleroi 7, 1996—. Recipient Hippocrate d' Or, Jour. Medecin, 1997. Avocations: jogging, tennis, golf, marathons. Home and Office: Ave General Jourdan 1 B-6220 Fleurus Belgium Office Phone: 0032497719804.

VAN DER HOEK, SHERRY A., counselor; b. Chgo., July 20, 1956; d. John Albert and Stella Rose (dec.) Troike; m. Herman Vanderhoek (dec.); stepchildren: Michiel, Martin. AAS, Prairie State Coll., 1992; BA, Govs. State U., 1994, MA, 1997. Lic. profl. counselor, Ill.; cert. counselor Nat. Bd. Cert. Counselors. Counselor South Suburban Coun. on Alcoholism, East Hazel Crest, Ill., 1990-93, South Suburban Family Shelter, Hazel Crest, Ill., 1996-97; facilitator Aunt Martha's Youth Svcs. Ctr., Inc., Park Forest, Ill., 1991-92; grad. asst. Govs. State U., University Park, Ill., 1995-97; pvt. practice counselor Matteson, Ill., 1998—. Mem.: ACA, Aunt Martha's Youth Svcs. Ctr. (founding mem. 1972), Ill. Alcoholism and Drug Dependence Assn., Assn. Counselor Edn. and Supervision (Outstanding Grad. Student Scholarship award 1997), Internat. Assn. Addiction and Offender Counselors, Ill. Counselor Educators and Suprs. (Outstanding Grad. Student award 1996), Ill. Alcohol and Other Drug Profl. Cert. Assn., Ill. Counseling Assn. (founder Govs. State Chpt., pres. 1996, regional gov. 1997—2000), Chi Sigma Iota (chpt. sec. 1995), Psi Chi (chpt. founder, pres. 1997). Avocations: cooking, cross stitch. Home and Office: 3761 W 216th Pl Matteson IL 60443

VAN DER LINDEN, PAUL J.Q., gynecologist; b. Heerlen, The Netherlands, Mar. 28, 1960; s. Jan H. Van Der Linden and Elizabeth Van Eyden; m. Mirjam C.A. Papendrecht, Oct. 4, 1991; children: Joep, Daan, Twan. MD, U. Limburg, The Netherlands, 1984; PhD, U. Limburg, 1995. Cert. ob-gyn. The Netherlands. Intern U. Linsurg, Netherlands, 1983—84; reisdent U. Utrecht, 1986—91; gynecologist Univ. Hosp., Maastricht, 1992—96, De Venter Hosp., Deventer, 1996—. Contbr. articles to profl. jours. Recipient Jan Swammerdam Fertility prize, VFS, 1996; fellow, U. Hosp. Maalhicht, Netherlands, 1992—96. Mem.: Dutch Soc. Ob-Gyn., Royal Dutch Med. Soc., European Soc. Human Reproduction and Embryology, Am. Soc. Reproductive Medicine. Avocation: swimming. Office: Deventer Hosp Postbus 5001 7400 GC Deventer Netherlands Home Phone: 31.570.593014; Office Phone: 31.570.646741.

VAN DER MEER, AUDREY LUCIA HENDRIKA, psychologist; b. Velsen, The Netherlands, Oct. 1, 1966; d. Nicolaas Hendrikus Wilhelmus and Lena (Van den Berg) van der M.; m. Frederikus Roelof van der Weel; children: Zoë H.F., Yvo F., Mats N., Rikke H., Leah M. MS, Free U., Amsterdam, 1988; PhD in Psychology, U. Edinburgh, 1992. Rsch. fellow med. rsch. coun. U. Edinburgh, Scotland, 1992, lectr. dept. psychology, 1993-95; sr. lectr. dept. psychology U. Trondheim, Norway, 1995-96; prof. devel. neuropsychology Norwegian U. Sci. and Tech., 1997—. Contbr. articles to profl. jours. Grantee Med. Rsch. Coun. U.K., 1992-95. Mem. Edinburgh Ctr. for Rsch. in Child Devel., Royal Norwegian Soc. Scis. and Letters. Achievements include research in fundamental perceptuo-motor skills in infants and early diagnosis of brain damage in premature babies. Office: Norwegian U Sci & Tech Dept Psychology 7491 Trondheim Norway Office Phone: (47) 73550249. E-mail: audrey.meer@svt.ntnu.no.

VAN DER MEULEN, JOSEPH PIERRE, neurologist; b. Boston, Aug. 22, 1929; s. Edward Lawrence and Sarah Jane (Robertson) Van Der Meulen; m. Ann Irene Yadeno, June 18, 1960; children: Elisabeth, Suzanne, Janet. AB, Boston Coll., 1950; MD, Boston U., 1954. Diplomate Am. Bd. Psychiatry and Neurology. Intern Cornell Med. div. Bellevue Hosp., NYC, 1954-55, resident, 1955-56, Harvard U., Boston City Hosp., 1958-60, instr., fellow, 1962-66; assoc. Case Western Res. U., Cleve., 1966-67, asst. prof., 1967-69, assoc. prof. neurology and biomed. engring., 1969-71; prof. neurology U. So. Calif., LA, 1971—2006, prof. emeritus, 2006—, chmn. dept., 1971—78, v.p. health affairs, 1977—2005, v.p. health affairs emeritus, 2006—, dean Sch. Medicine, 1985—86, 1995—97, vice dean med. affairs, 1995—97; dir. Ind. Health Professions, LA, 1991—2005. Dir. dept. neurology LA County/U. So. Calif. Med. Ctr., 1971—78; vis. prof. Autonomous U., Guadalajara, Mexico, 1974; pres. Norris Cancer Hosp. and Rsch. Inst., 1983—98, chmn., 2004; pres. Scott Newman Ctr., 1987—89. Contbr. articles to profl. jours. Mem. med. adv. bd. Calif. chpt. Myasthenia Gravis Found., 1971—75, chmn., 1974—75, 1977—78; mem. adv. bd. Amyotrophic Lateral Sclerosis Found., Calif., 1973—75, chmn. Calif., 1974—75; mem. Com. to Combat Huntington's Disease, 1973—; bd. dirs. Calif. Hosp. Med. Ctr., Good Hope Med. Found., LA Hosp. Good Samaritan, Barlow Respiratory Hosp., U. So. Calif. Univ. Hosp., chmn., 1991—2004; bd. dirs. Assn. Acad. Health Ctrs., chmn.; bd. dirs. Children's Hosp. LA, Eisenhower Med. Ctr. Served to lt. M.C. USN, 1956—58. Nobel Inst. fellow, Karolinska Inst., Stockholm, 1960—62, NIH grantee, 1968—71. Mem.: AMA, LA Acad. Medicine, Calif. Med. Soc., LA Med. Assn., LA Soc. Neurology and Psychiatry (pres. 1977—78), Am. Acad. Neurology, Am. Neurol. Assn., Phi Kappa Phi, Alpha Omega Alpha (councillor 1992—). Roman Catholic. Home: 39 Club View Ln Palos Verdes Peninsula CA 90274-4208 Personal E-mail: annvander@aol.com.

VANDERPLOEG, JAMES M., preventive medicine physician; b. Upland, Calif., Nov. 22, 1950; BS, Calvin Coll., 1972; MD, U. Iowa Coll. Medicine, 1975; MPH, U. Texas Sch. Public Health, 1980. Cert. Aerospace Medicine and Occupational Medicine. Intern U. Hosp./U. Calif., San Diego, 1975-76; resident in otolaryngoloty U. Iowa Hosps., Iowa City, 1978-79; resident in occupational medicine U. Tex. Sch. Pub. Health, Houston, 1980-82, assoc. prof. occupational health; mem. staff St. John Hosp., Nassau Bay, Tex.; pres., partner Ctr. Aerospace & Occupl. Medicine, Houston; assoc. prof. preventive medicine and community health, divsn. clinical preventive medicine U. Texas Medical Branch, assoc. prof. family medicine. Bd. mem. Am. Bd. Preventive Medicine, Schiller Park, Ill., 1993—98, exec. dir., 1998—. Mem. Am. Coll. Occupational Medicine, ACPrM-AerosMA. Office: U Texas Medical Branch 301 University Blvd Galveston TX 77555-0144

VANDER POORTEN, VINCENT L.M., surgeon, educator; s. Paul Vander Poorten and Agnes Reynaert; m. Mia I.A. Van Oyen, July 16, 1994; children: Cleo, Sandor, Ralph. MD, Cath. U. Leuven, Belgium, 1994; MSc in Epidemology, Free U. Amsterdam, Netherlands, 1996; PhD in Med. Sci., U. Amsterdam, Netherlands, 2002. Cert. otorhinolaryngologist and head and neck surgeon Belgium, 1999. Adjoint clin. head U. Hosp. Leuven, 2001—; assoc. prof. otorhinolaryngology, head and neck surgery Cath. U. Leuven, 2002—. Mem. Ao-CMF Aktionsgescushaft fur Osteosyntase Fragen Ganio Maxillofacial Group. Recipient Rsch. award, Glaxo Smith Kline, 1999; grantee, European Cmty., 1995. Mem.: European Salivary Gland Soc., European Acad. Facial Plastic Surgery, European Head & Neck Soc., Flemish Head and Neck Soc. (pres. 2006—), Royal Belgian Soc. Otorhinolaryngology, Head and Neck Surgery, Netherlands Epidemiol. Soc., Netherlands Soc. Otorhinolaryngology, Head and Neck Surgery, Am. Head and Neck Soc. (corr.). Office: Univ Hosp Leuven Dept ENT and Head and Neck Surgery Herestraat 49 Leuven 3000 Belgium Office Fax: 003216332335; Home Fax: 003216332335. Business E-Mail: vincent.vanderpoorten@uzleuven.be.

VANDERVEEN, JOHN E., nutritionist, federal agency administrator; b. Prospect Park, NJ, May 13, 1934; m. Ernestine Neuhardt, June 3, 1967; children: Keith Bradley, Kimetha Leigh. BS, Rutgers U., 1956; PhD, U. N.H., 1961. Nutritionist USAF, 1961-75; dir. divsn. nutrition FDA, Washington, 1975-92, dir. office plant & dairy foods and beverages, 1992-98, scientist emeritus, 1998—. Served to 1st lt. USAF, 1961-64. Office: FDA Ctr Food Safety and Applied Nutrition 5100 Paint Branch Parkway College Park MD 20740-3335 Office Phone: 301-436-2006. Business E-Mail: jvanderv@cfsan.fda.gov, john.vanderveen@fda.hhs.gov. *

VANDERVEEN, R. PETE (RANDALL L. VANDERVEEN), dean, pharmacist, educator; b. Lafayette, Ind., Nov. 6, 1950; BS in Pharmacy, Purdue U., West Lafayette, Ind., 1974, MS in Clin. Pharmacy, 1976; PhD in Univ. Adminstrn., Mich. State U., 1987; grad. leadership devel. prog., Duke U. Fuqua Sch. Bus., 1998. Cert. psychiatric pharmacist. Instr. Ferris State U., Big Rapids, Mich., 1976-77, asst. prof., 1977-79, assoc. prof., chair clin. pharmacy dept., 1979-88; asst. dean pharmacy practice Oreg. State U., Corvallis, 1988—98; assoc. prof. Oreg. Health & Sci. U., Portland, 1988—98, dir. pharmacy prog., 1994—98; prof. Duquesne U. Grad. Sch. Pharm. Scis., Pits., dean Mylan Sch. Pharmacy, 1998—2005; dean U. So. Calif. Sch. Pharmacy, LA, 2005—, John Stauffer Dean's Chair in pharm. scis., 2005—. Bd. dirs. Nat. Inst. Pharm. Tech. & Edn. (NIPTE); mem. edn. adv. com. Nat. Assn. Chain Drug Stores; former cons. Oreg. Med. Assistance Prog., Mich. Dept. Mental Health, Providence Med. Ctr., Oreg. Health Sci. Hosp., Portland. Contbr. articles to profl. jours. Fellow: Am. Soc. Health-Sys. Pharmacists, Am. Pharmacists Assn.; mem.: Nat. Cmty. Pharmacists Assn., Coll. Psychiat. & Neurologic Pharmacists, Acad. Managed Care Pharmacists, Am. Coll. Clin. Pharmacy, Am. Soc. Cons. Pharmacists, Am. Assn. Pharm. Scientists, Am. Assn. Colleges of Pharmacy (past bd. dirs.).

VANDERWAGEN, W. CRAIG (WILLIAM CRAIG VANDERWAGEN), physician, former federal agency administrator; b. Grand Rapids, Mich., 1949; m. Suzanne M. Vanderwagen; 3 children. BA, Calvin Coll. & Seminary; MD, Mich. State U., 1978. Advanced through ranks to rear adm. upper half US Pub. Health Svc. Corps., 2006; chief pub. health Coalition Provisional Authority, Iraqi Ministry of Health; dir., Office Clin. & Preventative Services, acting chief med. officer, Zuni Indian Hosp. Indian Health Svc., Albuquerque; spl. asst. to the dep. sec. for preparedness US Dept. Health & Human Services (HHS), Washington, asst. sec. for pub. health emergency preparedness, 2006, dep. asst. sec. for preparedness & response, chief preparedness officer, 2006—07, asst. sec. for preparedness & response, 2007—09. Decorated Meritorious Svc. medal; recipient Disting. Svc. award for leading fed. disaster response to Hurricanes Katrina and Rita, AMA, 2006; named Alumni of Yr., Mich. State U. Coll. Human Medicine, 2005.

VAN DEVENTER, VASI, psychology professor; MSc, U. Stellenbosch, South Africa; PhD, U. South Africa, Pretoria. Prof. psychology dept. U. South Africa. Contbr. articles to profl. jours. Mem.: Internat. Soc. Theoretical Psychology (pres. 2009—11). Office: Univ South Africa Dept Psychology PO Box 392 3 Pretoria South Africa Office Phone: 2712 429 8210. Business E-Mail: vdevesh@unisa.ac.za. *

VAN DIJL, JAN MAARTEN, molecular biologist, educator; b. Zwolle, Overijssel, The Netherlands, June 1, 1961; s. Jan and Annemarie Berta Zilla (Eichentopf) van D.; m. Henrica Maria Werink, June 28, 1991; children: Lotte, Mark. MSc cum laude, U. Groningen, Netherlands, 1985, PhD in Math. and Natural Scis., 1990. Rschr. U. Groningen, Netherlands, 1990—94, rschr., lectr., 1996—2004, prof. Medical Micriobiology, 2004—; rschr. Biozentrum, U. Basel, Switzerland, 1994-96. Spkr. in field. Patentee in field; contbr. articles to profl. jours. Dutch Orgn. Fundamental Scientific Rsch. scholar, 1994; European Union fellow, 1994, European Molecular Biology Orgn. fellow, 1994. Avocations: sailing, horseback riding, literature. Office: Dept Med Microbiology Hanzeplein 1 PO Box 30001 Groningen 9700 RB Netherlands

VAN DIXHOORN, JAN, medical educator, researcher; b. Delft, Netherlands, Apr. 2, 1948; s. Jan Van Dixhoorn and Nel Verheem; m. Irmgard Verhoeven. MD, U. Amsterdum, 1977; PhD, Erasmus U., Rotterdam. Head, dept. biofeedback J de Deo Hosp., Haarlem, Netherlands, 1977—83; dir. Ctr. Breathing Therapy, Amersfoort, Netherlands, 1977—; coord. & supr. cardiac rehabiltation Kennmer Hosp., Haarlem, Netherlands, 1986—; pres. Iternat. Stress Mgmt. Found., Netherlands Br., Leersum, Netherlands, 1993—. Home: F van Blankenheymstraat 10 Amersfoort 3817 AG Netherlands

VAN DYCK, CHRISTOPHER HANS, geriatric psychiatrist, educator; BA, Yale U., 1978; MD, Northwestern U., 1984. Diplomate Am. Bd. Psychiatry and Neurology, 1991, Am. Bd. Psychiatry and Neurology-geriatric psychiatry, 2005. Resident in psychiatry Yale-New Haven Hosp., Conn., 1988, fellow geriatric psychiatry, 1990; psychiatrist prof. Yale Med. Group, neurobiology prof., neurology prof., dir. alzheimer's disease rsch. unit; hosp. affiliation includes Yale-New Haven Hosp. Author: (articles) Clinically relevant doses of methylphenidate significantly occupy norepinephrine transporters in humans in vivo, 2010, Discovering genetic associations with high-dimensional neuroimaging phenotypes: A sparse reduced-rank regression approach, 2010, Voxelwise genome-wide association study (vGWAS), 2010, Reduced sample sizes for atrophy outcomes in Alzheimer's disease trials: baseline adjustment, 2010, Effects of BDNF Val66Met polymorphism on brain metabolism in Alzheimer's disease, 2010. Recipient Best Doctors, NY Mag., 2010. Office: Yale-New Haven Hospital Yale Alzheimer's Disease Research Unit 1 Church St 600 Ste New Haven CT 06510 Office Phone: 203-764-8100. Office Fax: 203-764-8111.

VAN DYKE, TERRY ANN, geneticist, researcher; b. Wake Island, Hawaii, May 2, 1955; d. Harold Quinton and Betty Irene (Wolf) Van D.; m. Richard Jude Samulski, Aug. 14, 1982; children: Danielle, Richard. BS, U. Fla., 1977, PhD, 1981. Postdoctoral fellow U. Fla., Gainesville, 1981-82, SUNY, Stonybrook, NY, 1982-84; rsch. assoc. Princeton U., NJ, 1984-86; asst. prof. U. Pitts., Pa., 1986, animal facilities chair, 1989-91, grad. student curriculum, 1990-91; faculty mem. U. NC, Chapel Hill, 1993—, faculty dir. Animal Models Core Faculty, 1998, founder Carolina Mutant Mouse Regional Resource Ctr. (MMRRC), 1999, Sarah Graham Kenan disting. prof. genetics; dir. Mouse Cancer Genetics Program (MCGP) Ctr. Cancer Rsch., Nat. Cancer Inst., NIH, Frederick, Md., 2007—, head cancer pathways and mechanisms. Named Predoctoral trainee Nat. Inst. Health, 1978-81; postdoctoral fellow Am. Cancer Soc., 1982-84. Mem. AAAS, Am. Soc. for Microbiology, N.Y. Acad. Sci., Pitts. Cancer Inst. Avocations: swimming, dance, hiking. Office: Nat Cancer Inst at Frederick Bldg 560 Rm 22-63 PO Box B Bethesda MD 20892 Office Phone: 304-846-1988. Office Fax: 304-846-1290. E-mail: vandyket@mail.nih.gov. *

VANECKOVA, IVANA, physiologist; b. Prague, Czech Republic, Feb. 18, 1964; d. Vaclav Skuhravy and Marcela Skuhrava; m. Michal Vanecek, 1987; children: Lukas Vanecek, Jana. MA, Charles U., 1987; PhD, Inst. Physiology, 2001. Postdoctoral fellow Inst. Physiology, Prague, Czech Republic, 1987—2001, asst. rsch. prof., 2010—, Inst. Clin. and Experimental Medicine, Prague, 2001—10. Mem.: Am. Physiology Soc. (assoc.). Home: Podolská 1486/10 Prague 147 00 Czech Republic Office: Inst Physiology ASCR Videnska 1083 Prague 14200 Czech Republic Business E-Mail: ivanava@biomed.cas.cz.

VAN ETTEN, PETER WALBRIDGE, foundation executive; b. Boston, May 10, 1946; s. Royal Cornelius Van Etten and Peggy June (Walbridge) Hutchins; m. Mary Peters French, Sept. 5, 1968; children: Molly, Clarissa, Ellen. BA, Columbia U., 1968; MBA, Harvard U., 1973. Br. mgr. BayBanks, Brookline, Mass., 1968-71; loan officer Bank of Boston, 1973-76; CFO Univ. Hosp., Boston, 1976-79; exec. v.p., CFO New Eng. Med. Ctr., Boston, 1979-89; pres., CEO Transition Systems, Boston, 1986-89; dep. chancellor U. Mass. Med. Ctr., Worcester, 1989-91; CFO Stanford U., Calif., 1991-94; pres., CEO Stanford Univ. Hosp., 1994-97; CEO UCSF Stanford Health Care, 1997-99; exec. com. U. Healthsystem Consortium, 1997-99, vice chmn., 1998-99; dir. Calif. Healthcare Assn., 1998-99, IDX Sys., Inc., 1999-2001; pres., CEO Juvenile Diabetes Found. Internat., NYC, 2000—06. Dir. Transition Sys., Inc., 1996—98, Duke U. Health Sys., 2003—, vice chmn., 2007—; dir. Rsch. Am., 2005—06. Chair campaign United Way San Francisco, 1998. Business E-Mail: pvanetten1@yahoo.com.

VAN FAASEN, WILLIAM C., health insurance company foundation executive; BA in Psychology, Hope Coll., Michigan; MBA, Michigan State U. Past sr. v.p. operational svcs. Blue Cross/Blue Shield Mich.; exec. v.p., COO Blue Cross/Blue Shield Massachusetts, Boston, 1990-92, pres., CEO, 1992—2005, interim pres., CEO, 2010, chmn., 2002—07, Blue Cross/Blue Shield Massachusetts Found., Boston,

2005—. Bd. dirs. IMS Health, Inc., 1996—, Liberty Mut. Holding Co., Inc., 2002—, NSTAR, 2002—, PolyMedica Corp., 2005—08. Chmn. United Way, Boston. Recipient Lifetime Achievement award in Health Care, Health Care for All, Maimonides award for Anti-Defamation League, Disting. Eagle Scout award, Boy Scouts of America, New Eng. Council's New Englander of the Yr.; named Disting. Bostonian, Greater Boston C. of C. Office: Blue Cross/Blue Shield MA Landmark Ctr 401 Park Dr Boston MA 02215-5000 *

VAN GORDER, CHRIS, medical executive; MS in Health Adminstrn., U. So. Calif., 1984, MS in Pub. Adminstrn., 1986. Chief of health care opers., exec. v.p. Scripps Health System, 1999—; pres., CEO Scripps Health, 2000—. Office: Scripps Health 4275 Campus Point Ct San Diego CA 92121 *

VAN HEERTUM, RONALD LANNY, physician; b. Englewood, NJ, Nov. 23, 1940; s. Arnold and Irene Gladys (Ostheimer) V.; children: Richard Jonathan, Beth Jennifer, Jonathan Jason, Kristin Ashley; m. Elyse Ann Murphy, Apr. 3, 2004. BA, Gettysburg Coll., 1962; MD, N.J. Med. Sch., 1966. Diplomate Nat. Bd. Med. Examiners, 1967, Am. Bd. Radiology, 1971, Am. Bd. Nuclear Medicine, 1973. Intern Hackensack Hosp., NJ, 1966-67; resident in radiology St. Vincent's Hosp. & Med. Ctr. NY, 1967—70, fellow in radiology and nuclear medicine, 1970-71, clin. asst. dept radiology, 1971, asst. chief nuclear medicine sect., asst. attending radiologist, 1975-76, chief nuclear medicine sect., 1977-91, assoc. attending physician depts. radiology and medicine, 1977-78, attending physician depts. radiology and medicine, 1978-91, dir. Nuclear Radiology Residency Tng. Program, 1980-88, 80-91, asst. dir. dept. radiology, 1981-91, med. dir. Sch. Nuclear Medicine Tech., 1982-91; asst. chief nuclear medicine svc. Tripler Army Med. Ctr., Honolulu, 1972, chief nuclear medicine svc., 1972-74; adj. prof. Sch. Pharmacy U. Pacific, Stockton, Calif., 1973-74; fellow in nuclear medicine SUNY, 1974-75; clin. asst. prof. of radiology Sch. Medicine NYU, 1977-83; assoc. prof. clin. radiology NY Med. Coll., Valhalla, 1983-88, prof. clin. radiology, 1988-91; dir. mini-fellowship program St. Vincent's Hosp. Cerebral SPECT Learning Ctr., 1991—2001; prof. clin. radiology Coll. Physicians & Surgeons of Columbia U., NY, 1991—2001; attending physician dept. radiology Columbia-Prsbyn. Med. Ctr., 1991—, dir. nuclear medicine residency tng. program, 1980—88, 1991—; attending physician dept brain imaging NY Psychiatric Inst., 1993—, attending physician Dept. Neurosci., 1996—; vice chmn. dept. radiology Coll. Physicians and Surgeons Columbia U., 1993—, prof. radiology, 2002—; intern chair radiology Coll. Physicians & Surgeons, 2008—09; exec. vice-chair CAO radiology, 2009—. Cons. nuclear medicine Catholic Med. Ctr. of Bklyn. and Queens, 1979-88, The Long Island Coll. Hosp., 1980-88, dept. radiology St. Vincent's Hosp. and Med. Ctr. of NY, 1991-92, biol. studies unit NY Psychiat. Inst., 1993—, The Oxford Project to Investigate Memory and Aging, The John Radcliffe Infirmary and Dept. of Clin. Pharmacology Oxford U., 1993—; alt. del. Am. Coll. Nuclear Physics, 1980-82; core mem. DOE Sponsored Consensus Panel Brain SPECT Perfusion Imaging: Optimizing Image Aquisition and Processing, 1991; vis. prof. Brooke Army Med. Ctr., San Antonio, 1978, Howard U. Med. Coll., Washington, 1980, South Hills Health Systems, Pitts., 1981, St. Barnabas Med. Ctr., Livingston, NJ, 1989, Eastern Va. Med. Sch. Norfolk Gen. Hosp., 1990, U. PR Med. Ctr., VA Med. Ctr., 1993, U. Wash. Med. Ctr., Seattle, 1994, Washington U., St. Louis, 1998, Robert Wood Johnson Med. Sch., 1999, Stonybrook Health Sci. Ctr., 2005, U. Puerto Rico, 2005; mem. Am. Bd. Nuc. Medicine, 1995-, vice chair, 1999-2000, chair, 2000-02; dir. Columbia Kreitchman PET Ctr., 1993-2010. Contbr. articles to profl. jours. Major USAR, 1971-74. Recipient Physician Recognition award AMA, 1974-93; numerous rsch. grants in field. Fellow Am. Coll. Radiology (commn. on nuc. medicine 1994-2000, chmn. nuc. medicine accreditation com. 2000-06, chair accreditation program chiefs com., 2002-06, vice chmn., 2002-06), NY Acad. Medicine (sec. nuclear medicine sect. 1993—); mem. Am. Roentgen Ray Soc., Radiological Soc. N. Am., NY Roentgen Soc., Soc. Nuclear Medicine (mem. bd. govs. greater NY chpt. 1982-84, 86-89, mem. acad. coun. 1988, mem. brain imaging coun. 1988—, sub-chmn. gastroenterology sci. program com. 1989-90, pres. elect brain imaging coun. 1990-92, pres. 1992-94, sub.-chmn. psychiatry-clin. sci. program com. 1993-94), Soc. Thoracic Radiology (sr. mem.). Presbyterian. Business E-Mail: rvh5@columbia.edu.

VAN HEMELRYCK, FRANÇOISE, pharmaceutical executive; b. Brussels, May 2, 1966; Degree in Social Comm., U. Catholique Louvain, 1989. Sr. project mgr. Fleishman Hillard, 1995—98; head health & pharm. practice area Adamson BSMG Worldwide, 1998—2001; project mgr. European Cancer Orgn., 2001—. Office: 83 Ave E Mounier Brussels 1200 Belgium Business E-Mail: francoise@ecco-org.eu.

VAN HORN, FRANK OAKS, retired counselor, consultant; b. Grand Junction, Colo., Apr. 16, 1926; s. Oertel F. and Alta Maude (Lynch) Van H.; m. Dixie Jeanne MacGregor, Feb. 1, 1947 (dec. Nov. 1994); m. Evelyn Anne Carroll, Mar. 22,1998; children: Evelyn (dec.), Oertel (dec.), Jeanne AA, Mesa Coll., 1961; BA, Western State Colo., 1963; MEd, Oreg. State U., 1969. Counselor, mgr. State of Oreg.-Employment, Portland and St. Helens, 1964-88; pvt. practice counselor and cons. St. Helens, 1988-96. Chair Task Force on Aging, Columbia County, 1977-79; advisor Western Interstate Commn. on Higher Edn., Portland, 1971, Concentrated Employment and Tng., St. Helens, 1977, County Planning Bd., Columbia County, Oreg., 1977-80, City Planning Bd., St. Helens, 1978, Youth Employment Coun., St. Helens, 1978, Task Force on Disadvantaged Youth, St. Helens, 1980; counselor Career Mgmt. Specialists Internat.; instr. Portland C.C. Mem. ACA, Oreg. Counseling Assn., Internat. Assn. Pers. in Employment Svc. (Outstanding Achievement award 1975), Nat. Employment Counselors Assn. Democrat. Avocation: singing. Home: 464 Leelo Ct Florence OR 97439

VAN HOYWEGHEN, MAGDA JOZEF HENDRIK MARIA, retired surgeon; d. Maria Amelberga Servotte and Hendrik Van Hoyweghen. Gymnasium, Onze Lieve Vrouw Presentatie, Sint Niklaas, Belgium, 1953. Cert. MD Utrecht State U., Netherlands, 1966. Surg. resident, NYC, 1967—71; gen. surgeon Local Govt., Mwanza, Tanzania, 1973—77, Caritas, Juba, Sudan, 1977—78, Med. Mission Sisters, Attat, Ethiopia, 1978, Terre Des Hommes, Serabu, Sierra

Leone, 1978; sr. surgeon Local Govt., Lilongwe, Malawi, 1981—92; mem. gen. govt. Med. Mission Sisters, Nairobi, Kenya, 1992—98. Recipient European Masters Bioethics, U. Louvain, 2004; fellow, ACS, 1975—, East African Coll. Surgeons, 1987; fellowship, John L. Madden Surg. Soc., 1972, Internat. Coll. Surgeons, 1980. Mem.: Internat. Soc. Med. Mission Sisters.

VANIER, ALAIN, psychiatrist, psychoanalyst; b. Boulogne, France, June 20, 1948; s. André Vanier and Nadia Grynszpan; m. Catherine Mathelin; m. Nadia El Hefnaoui, Dec. 19, 1977 (div. Sept. 2001); children: David, Judith, Noémie. Licence ès Lettres, U. Paris 7, 1972, MA in Clin. Psychology, 1978, MD, 1985, PhD in Clin. Psychology, 1995, habilitation a diriger les recherches, 2000. Psychoanalyst Bonneuil Exptl. Psychiat. Home for Disturbed Children, France, 1975—99; pvt. practice psychoanalysis Paris, 1977—; pvt. practice in psychiatry, 1987—; psychiat. resident in psychiatry and child psychiatry U. Paris 6, 1981—86. Psychiatre des hôpitaux, Paris, 1986—97; assoc. prof. U. Paris 7, 1996—2001, prof., 2001—, dir. grad. studies 2001—, chmn. sci. rsch. dept. clin. scis., 2001—; editl. dir. Espace Analytique Collection edit. Denoel, Paris, 1998—. Author: Lacan, 2000, English translation, 2000; contbr. articles to profl. jours. Mem.: Ctr. for Tng. and Rsch. in Psychoanalysts (v.p 1982—95), Assn. de Formation Psychanalytique et de Recherches Freudiennes Espace Analytique (pres. 1998—2001). Office: 14B Rue Raynouard 75016 Paris France Office Phone: 33 1 45 04 55 06. E-mail: alainvanier@noos.fr.

VANITALLIE, THEODORE B., physician; b. Hackensack, NJ, Nov. 8, 1919; s. Dorus Christian and Lucy M. (Pohle) VanI.; m. Barbara Cox, Sept. 25, 1948 (div. Mar. 1992); children: Lucy M., Theodore B., Christina M., Elizabeth B., Katharine R.; m. Sallie Newton Calhoun, Mar. 11, 1992. BS, Harvard U., 1941; MD, Columbia U., 1945. Diplomate: Am. Bd. Internal Medicine. Intern in medicine St. Luke's Hosp., NYC, 1945-46, asst. resident in internal medicine, 1948-49, resident, 1949-50, dir. nutrition and metabolism rsch. lab., 1952-55; assoc. Peter Bent Brigham Hosp., Boston, 1955-57; dir. medicine St. Luke's Hosp. Center, NYC, 1957-75. Dir. Obesity Rsch. Ctr., 1974-85, co-dir., 1986-88; asst. prof. Sch. Pub. Health, Harvard U., 1955-57; assoc. clin. prof. medicine Columbia, N.Y.C., 1957-65, clin. prof., 1965-71, prof., 1971-88, prof. emeritus, 1988—; vis. prof. internal medicine Am. U. Beirut, 1968-69, trustee, 1976-93; spl. advisor on human nutrition Surgeon Gen., 1980-81; mem. sci. adv. bd. Nutrition Found., 1967-71; pres. Am. Bd. Nutrition, 1968-71; mem. food and nutrition bd. NRC, 1970-76; med. adv. com. on cyclamates HEW, 1969-70; mem. gastrointestinal and nutrition tng. com. NIH, 1969-73, mem. adv. coun. Nat. Arthritis, Diabetes, Digestive and Kidney Diseases, NIH, 1978-81; mem. joint nutrition monitoring evaluation com. USDA and HHS, 1982-86; dir. Miles Labs., 1976-84; vis. physician Rockefeller U. Hosp., 1986-89; adj. prof. Rockefeller U., 1986-89; vis. prof. medicine in psychiatry, U. Pa., 1990-94, trustee, St. Luke's-Roosevelt Hosp. Ctr., 1988-94. Mem.* editorial bd.: Diabetes, 1960-71; editor-in-chief: Am. Jour. Clin. Nutrition, 1979-81. Mem. Englewood (N.J.) Bd. Edn., 1960-65, v.p., 1964-65; Lt. (j.g.) USNR, 1946-48. Recipient citation FDA, 1983. Fellow ACP (disting. physicians award 1987), AAAS, Am. Inst. Nutrition; mem. AMA (mem. coun. on foods and nutrition 1967-74, vice chmn. 1974, Joseph B. Goldberger award 1985), Am. Soc. Clin. Investigation, Soc. Exptl. Biology and Medicine, Am. Clin. and Climatol. Assn., Am. Soc. Clin. Nutrition (coun. 1970-73, pres. 1976-77, Elmer V. McCollum award 1985), Soc. Study of Ingestive Behavior (disting. sci. award 1994), Order of Malta (knight comdr. Quebec priory 1990—), Century Assn., Fla. Hist. Soc. (bd. dirs. 1995—2004, pres. 2002-04). Research and contbr. numerous publs. on obesity, body composition, pancreatic hormone, glucagon, mechanism of energy balance regulation, treatment of pruritus and hypercholesteremia in biliary cirrhosis, physiology and clin. use of medium chain triglyceride, induced hyperketonemia in treatment of Parkinson Disease. Mailing: 16 Coult Ln Old Lyme CT 06371 Personal E-mail: drvanitallie@comcast.net.

VAN KIRK, JOHN ELLSWORTH, retired cardiologist; b. Dayton, Ohio, Jan. 13, 1942; s. Herman Corwin and Dorothy Louise (Shafer) Van K.; m. Patricia L. Davis, June 19, 1966 (div. Dec. 1982); 1 child, Linnea Gray. BA cum laude, DePauw U., Greencastle, Ind., 1963; BS, Northwestern U., Chgo., 1964, MD with distinction, 1967. Diplomate Am. Bd. Internal Medicine, Am. Bd. Internal Medicine subspecialty in cardiovasc. disease; cert. Nat. Bd. Med. Examiners. Intern Evanston (Ill.) Hosp., 1967-68; staff assoc. Nat. Inst. of Allergy & Infectious Diseases., Bethesda, Md., 1968-70; resident internal medicine U. Mich. Med. Ctr., Ann Arbor, 1970-72, fellow in cardiology, 1972-74, instr. internal medicine, 1973-74; staff cardiologist Mills Meml. Hosp., San Mateo, Calif., 1974—2001, vice-chief medicine, 1977-78, dir. critical care, 1978-96, critical care utilizaton rev., 1988-99, dir. pacemaker clinic, 1976-99; staff cardiologist Mills-Peninsula Hosp., Burlingame, Calif., 1996-99; ret., 1999. Dir. transitional care, 1996—99; mem. courtesy staff Sequoia Hosp., 1984—2001, ret., 1999. Contbr. rsch. articles to profl. jours. Recipient 1st prize in landscaping Residential Estates, State of Calif., 1977. Fellow Am. Coll. Cardiology; mem. AMA (Physician's Recognition award 1968, 72, 75, 77, 80, 82, 85, 87, 89, 93, 97, 2000), Calif. Med. Assn., San Mateo County Med. Soc., Am. Heart Assn., San Mateo County Heart Assn. (bd. dirs. 1975-78, mem. Bay area rsch. com. 1975-76, mem. edn. com. 1975-77, pres.-elect 1976-77, pres. 1977-79), Alpha Omega Alpha, Republican. Mem. United Brethren Ch. Avocations: gardening, tennis, woodworking, amateur radio. Home: 235 Amherst Ave San Mateo CA 94402-2201 Personal E-mail: John_VanKirk@msn.com.

VAN KUIJK, FREDERICUS J. (ERIK VAN KUIJK), medical association administrator, researcher; b. Boxmeer, Netherlands, Aug. 3, 1959; MD, U. Nijmegen, PhD cum laude, 1988. Vice chair, med. dir. ophthalmology U. Tex. Med. Br., 2001—. Fellow: European Bd. Ophthalmology; mem.: Assn. Rsch. Vision and Ophthalmology, Am. Acad. Ophthalmology. Avocation: hiking. Office: 700 University Blvd Galveston TX 77555-1106 Business E-Mail: fjvankui@utmb.edu.

VANLARE, JORDAN M., medical student; b. NY; m. Jane Lynch. AB in Biomed. Sciences, magna cum laude, Harvard U., Cambridge, Mass., 2004; med. student, Columbia U. Coll. Physicians and Surgeons, NY. Engagement mgr. McKinsey & Co.; program analyst US

Dept. Health and Human Services, Washington. Contbr. articles to profl. jours. Mem.: AMA (bd. trustees 2011—, regional chmn. med. student sect., vice chmn. med. student sect. com. on economics in medicine, former mem. AMA Found. bd. dirs.). Office: c/o AMA Bd Trustees 515 N State St Chicago IL 60654 *

VAN MIDDLESWORTH, LESTER, physiology, biophysics and medicine educator, internist; b. Washington, Jan. 13, 1919; s. Lester and Hazel Lucile (Brandt) VanM.; m. Nellie Rue Franklin, June 29, 1948; children: Linda V. Anderson, Jane V. Norman, Frank L., Paul E. BS in Chemistry, U. Va., 1940, MS in Chemistry, 1942, MS in Physiology, 1944; PhD in Physiology, U. Calif., Berkeley, 1946; MD, U. Tenn., 1951, DSc (hon.), 2008. Teaching asst. dept. physiology U. Va., 1944, U. Calif., Berkeley, 1944—45; instr. U. Tenn. Med. Units, Memphis, 1946—52, instr. in medicine, 1953—57, asst. prof. physiology, 1952—54, assoc. prof., 1954—59, prof., 1959—89, prof. emeritus physiology and biophysics, 1989—, asst. prof. medicine, 1957—61, assoc. prof., 1961—72, prof. medicine, 1972—89, prof. medicine emeritus, 1989, Disting. prof. physiology and medicine, 1986—; U. disting. prof., 2007. Rotating intern City of Memphis Hosps., 1951-52; cons. chief chemist Piedmont Apple Products Corp., Charlottesville, Va., 1940-46, Crocker Radiation Lab., U. Calif., Berkeley, 1946-47, Oak Ridge Inst. Nuclear Studies, 1950-54; guest co-investigator Endocrine Labs. Tufts Med. Coll., Boston, summers 1954, 55, 56, 59, 61, 64, 66, 69, Scripps Clinic and Rsch. Found., La Jolla, Calif., 1957; guest investigator in endocrinology Harbor Gen. Hosp., UCLA, 1971, Frederick Joliot Hosp., Orsay, France, 1972, Lawrence Livermore Radiation Lab. U. Calif., 1970; staff mem. clinic for med. thyroid disease patients, City of Memphis and U., Tenn., 1951—; mem. internat. com., 1990-2002. Author 153 publs. in profl. jours., 192 abstracts and oral presentations; work on permanent display Smithsonian Nat. Mus. Am. History, Washington, D.C. Recipient Disting. Svc. award, 1985, Disting. Alumnus award, U. Tenn. Coll. Medicine, 1989, USPHS career rsch. grantee, 1962-89; nominee Prince Mahidol award, U. Tenn. Health Sci. Com., 2007. Mem. Am. Chem. Soc., Am. Physiol. Soc., AAAS, Soc. Exptl. Biology and Medicine, Am. Soc. Clin. Investigation, So. Soc. Clin. Investigation, Health Physics Soc., Endocrine Soc., Am. Thyroid Assn. (Disting. Svc. award 1988), Sigma Xi (rsch. award 1944, 86, nat. lectr. 1989-91), Alpha Chi Sigma. Achievements include research in audiogenic siezures and worldwide radioiodine fallout, and radium in normal human thyroid glands; first to observe and report worldwide spread of radioiodine fallout in animal thyroid glands. Office: U Tenn Health Sci Ctr 894 Union Ave Memphis TN 38163-3514 Home: 648 Des Moines Dr Hermitage TN 37076-1557 Office Phone: 901-448-5837. Personal E-mail: vanruehonve@gmail.com. *

VAN NAGELL, JOHN RENSSELAER, oncologist, gynecologist; b. NYC, Sept. 16, 1939; s. John Rensselaer and Rosamond Musgrave Van Nagell; m. Elizabeth Gay, June 10, 1977; children: John R Van Nagell III, Elizabeth Knox Pfister, Lucy Tepper. MD, U. Pa., 1967. Diplomate Am. Bd. Ob/Gyn. Prof., dir. divsn. gynecol. oncology U. Ky. Med. Ctr., Lexington, 1973—, Am. Cancer Soc prof. clin. oncology. Cons. NCI - PLCO Trial, Bethesda, Md., 1992—. Author: Modern Concepts of Gynecologic Oncology. Lt. USN, 1971—77. Named one of Top Doctors for Women, Ladies Home Jour., 2001—08, Ams. Top Doctors, Castle Connolly, 2002—10. Mem.: Masters of Foxhounds Assn. (bd.dirs. 2005, v.p. 2008), Soc. Gynecol. Oncologists (pres. 1994—95). Avocations: horseback riding, fox hunting. Business E-Mail: jrvann2@email.uky.edu.

VANNELA, RAVEENDER, biotechnologist, environmental scientist; s. Lalitha and Hanmandlu Vannela; m. Archana Puliroju, Aug. 14, 2002; children: Aditi, Amogha. BS, Osmania U., Hyderabad, India, 1995; MS, Kakatiya U., Warangal, Andhra Pradesh, India, 1997; MPhil, Pondicherry U., India, 1999; PhD, Birla Inst. Tech. and Sci., Pilani, India, 2003. Cert. biotech. techniques Birla Inst. Tech. Sci., 2002. Rsch. assoc. Iowa State U., Ames, 2003—04; rsch. fellow scientist U. Mich., Ann Arbor, Mich., 2004—. Contbr. articles to profl. jours., chapters to books. Pres. Nat. Student Union India, Nizamabad, Andhra Pradesh, 1995—98; active Swadyaya, Nizamabad, 1987—91. Recipient Young Scientist Travel award, Fedn. European Microbiological Soc., 2002. Mem.: Assn. Environ. Engrs. and Sci. Profs., Am. Soc. for Microbiology, Am. Chem. Soc. (Best Paper Excellence award 2005), Indian Nuc. Chem. and Allied Scientists (life). Achievements include patents for photobioreactor SCALE-Up and DNAzyme-based nanosensor for Hg2+ and As5+; development of SpiSORB for Hg (II) removal; discovery of SpiSORB materials; development of Sun Greens nutraceuticals. Office: Ariz State U Biodesign Inst 1001 S McAllister Ave Tempe AZ 85287 Home: 1118 E Euclid Ave Gilbert AZ 85297 Office Fax: 480-727-0889. Personal E-mail: rvannela@gmail.edu. Business E-Mail: rvannela@asu.edu.

VANNELLI, ALBERTO, surgeon; b. Milan, Feb. 29, 1972; D, Scundary Sch. Focusing Humanities, Milan, 1991. Bd. cert. diplomate 1997, bd. cert. diplomate in gen. surgery specialist tng. 2003. Physician Inst. Exptl. Surgery and Liver Transplantation, Milan, 1995—98, Gen. Surgery Divsn., Ospedale San Paolo, Milan, 1998—2000, Plastic and Reconstructive Surgery Divsn., Ospedale Fatebenefratelli, Milan, 2000—01; physician and cons. Divsn. Senology Nat. Cancer Inst., 2001; vice dir. and physician Divsn. Colon-Proctology Nat. Cancer Inst., 2001—. Author: (book) Evoluzione Della Chirurgia Rettale; exhibitions include XXV Congresso Nazionale Associazione Italiana Studio Pancreas (Best Oral Comunication award, 2001), XXVI Congresso Nazionale Associazione Italiana Studio Pancreas (Best Oral Comunication award, 2002); contbr. articles to profl. jours. Achievements include invention of pelvic lymphedema theory. Home: Corso di Porta Nuova 46 Milan 20121 Italy Office: Nat Inst Tumor Milan Via Giacomo Venezian 1 20133 Milan MI Italy Home Phone: 390223902616; Office Phone: 393392335772. Office Fax: 390223902338. Business E-Mail: a.vannelli@tiscali.it.

VAN NOSTRAND, DOUGLAS, nuclear medicine physician, director; b. NYC, Apr. 10, 1947; BS, Duke U., 1969; MD, Emory U. Sch. Medicine, 1973. Dir., divsn. nuc. medicine Malcolm Grow Med. Ctr., 1978—80, Walter Reed Army Med. Ctr., 1980—87, Good Samaritan Hosp., 1988—99, Wash. Hosp. Ctr., 1999—. Prof. medicine Georgetown U. Med. Ctr., 2004—11. Grant, Multiple Founds. and Cos.

Fellow: ACP, Am. Coll. Nuc. Medicine; mem.: Am. Thyroid Assn., Soc. Nuc. Medicine. Office: 110 Irving St NW Ste GA60B Washington DC 20010 Office Fax: 202-877-6606. Business E-Mail: douglas.van.nostrand@medstar.net.

VAN NOY, TERRY WILLARD, health care executive; b. Alhambra, Calif., Aug. 31, 1947; s. Barney Willard and Cora Ellen (Simms) V.; m. Betsy Helen Pothen, Dec. 27, 1968; children: Bryan, Mark. BS in Bus. Mgmt., Calif. State Poly. U., 1970; MBA, Pepperdine U., 1991. CLU. Group sales rep. Mutual of Omaha, Atlanta, 1970-74, dist. mgr., 1974-77, regional mgr. Dallas, 1977-82, nat. sales mgr. Omaha, Neb., 1982-83, v.p. group mktg., 1983-87, div. dir. Orange, Calif., 1987-95; pres., CEO, Amil Internat., Las Vegas, 1995-98; prin. Van Noy Consulting Group, Henderson, Nev., 1998—. Vice-chmn. State Nev. Reinsurance Bd., mem. divsn. ins. health adv. com.; presenter in field. Vice-chmn. Morning Star Luth. Ch., Omaha, 1987; adv. bd. Chapman U. Sch. Bus.; exc. com. ABL Orgn.; chmn. bd. trustees Desert Rsch. Inst. Found. Mem. Am. Soc. CLU, Orange County Employee Benefit Coun., We. Pension and Benefits Conf., Las Vegas Valley Soaring Assn. (v.p.), Great Basin Soaring Inc. (pres.), Internat. Found. Employee Benefit Plans. Republican. Avocations: skiing, scuba diving, soaring. Home and Office: 2312 Prometheus Ct Henderson NV 89074-5324 Office Phone: 702-433-9677. Personal E-mail: tvannoy@earthlink.net.

VAN OST, LYNN, physical therapist, Olympic team official; b. Englewood, NJ, Sept. 7, 1960; d. William Carlisle and Marijane Dorward Van Ost. BSN, West Chester State Coll., Pa., 1982; MEd, Temple U., Phila., 1987; BS Phys. Therapy, Temple U., 1988. RN Pa, 1982; cert. athletic trainer Nat. Athletic Trainer's Assn., 1984. Staff nurse Abington Meml. Hosp., Pa., 1982—84; nurse/ athletic trainer U.S. Sports Acad., Mobile, Ala., 1984—85; coord. sports medicine Providence Hosp., Mobile, 1985—86, Del. County Meml. Hosp., Drexel Hill, Pa., 1988—90; staff phys. therapist Hunterdon Phys. and Sports Therapy, Flemington, NJ, 1990—91, Sports Phys. Therapy, Somerset, NJ, 1991—92; clin. specialist sports medicine Thomas Jefferson U. Hosp., Phila., 1992—98; asst. dir. Sports Phys. Therapy Inst., Princeton, NJ, 1998—2000, dir. Flemington, 2000—02; clin. specialist, sports phys. therapy Hunterdon Med. Ctr., Flemington, 2002—. Vol. athletic trainer U.S. Olympic Com., Colorado Springs, 1989—96, U.S. Field Hockey, Colorado Springs, 1993—96, U.S. Short Track Speed Skating, Lake Placid, NY, 1994—99. Author: (study guide) Athletic Training Student Guide to Success, 2003, 4th edit., 2009, (cd rom) Goniometry, 1999, Cram Session in Goniometry, 2010. Scholar Athletic Tng., Temple U., 1982—84. Mem.: Nat. Athletic Trainer's Assn., Abbes' Soc., Panhellenic (pres. 1981—82), Alpha Phi (panhellenic rep. 1980—81). Achievements include patents for Athletic Tng. Jacket. Avocations: golf, travel. Home: 2 Riverview Drive West Trenton NJ 08628 Office: Hunterdon Med Ctr 2100 Wescott Drive Flemington NJ 08822-4604 Office Phone: 908-237-7096. Personal E-mail: kmanfrc@verizon.net.

VAN PRAAG, HERMAN MEIR, psychiatrist, educator, researcher; b. Schiedam, The Netherlands, Oct. 17, 1929; s. Marinus Maurits and Charlotte Frederique (Leverpoll) V.P.; m. Cornelia Eikens; children: Marinus, Gido, Charlotte, Bart. MD, Leiden U., The Netherlands, 1956; PhD in Neurobiology, U. Utrecht, The Netherlands, 1962. Chief of staff dept. psychiatry Dijkzigt Hosp., Rotterdam, The Netherlands, 1963-66; founder, prof., head dept. biol. psychiatry Psychiat. Univ. Clinic State U., Groningen, Netherlands, 1966-77; prof., head dept. psychiatry Acad. Hosp. State U., Utrecht, 1977-82, prof. head dept. psychiatry; prof., head dept. psychiatry Albert Einstein Coll. Medicine, Bronx, NY, 1982—92; prof., head dept. psychiatry and neuropsychology Acad. Hosp. U. Maastricht, Netherlands, 1992—99, sci. advisor dept. psychiarty and neuropsychology, 1999—. Emeritus prof. Albert Einstein Coll. Medicine, 1992—; psychiatrist-in-chief Montefiore Med. Ctr., Bronx, 1982—92; Lady Davis vis. prof. Hebrew U. Hadassah U. Hosp., Jerusalem, 1976—77; head WHO Nat. Ref. Ctr. for Study of Psychotropic Drugs, 1969, WHO Collaborating Ctr. for Rsch. and Tng. in Biol. Psychiatry, 1974; founder Interdisciplinary Soc. Biol. Psychiatry, 1966, Found. for Psychiatry and Religion, 1998; guest lectr. numerous univs. around the world. Editor: Psychiatria Neurologia Neurochirurgia, 1968-70, Advances in Biological Psychiatry, 1978—; editor-in-chief Psychiatria Neurologia Neurochirurgia, 1971-74, Biology of Behavior, 1975-82, Handbook of Biological Psychiatry, 1975-81, Einstein Monograph Series in Experimental and Clinical Psychiatry, 1988—; European chief-editor Progress in Neuro-Psychopharmacology, 1993—; mem. editl. bd. numerous publs. in field; reviewer Am. Jour. Psychiatry, Archives of Gen. Psychiatry, Jour. Nervous and Mental Disease; mem. internat. scientific commn. Jour. Brazilian Psychiat. Assn. Decorated knight Order of the Dutch Lion, Queen Beatrix of The Netherlands; recipient numerous awards and honors. Fellow Am. Coll. Neuropsychopharmacology, Am. Psychiat. Assn.; mem. Royal Acad. Scis. of The Netherlands, Soc. Biol. Psychiatry, Collegium Internationale Neuro-Psychopharmacologicum, Assn. for Advancement of Psychotherapy, Internat. Group for Study of Affective Disorders, Internat. Soc. Psychoneuroendocrinology, European Brain and Behavior Soc., Internat. Assn. for Suicide Prevention, Brit. Pharmacol. Soc., European Soc. for Clin. Investigation, Bataafsch Genootschap der Proefondervindelijke Wijsbegeerte, Am. Coll. Neuropharmacology, Deutsche Gesellschaft fur Psychiatrie und Nervenheilkunde, Israel Med. Assn., Psychiat. Rsch. Soc., NY Acad. Medicine, Am. Psychopathol. Assn., Internat. Coll. Neurobiology, Biol. Psychiatry and Psychopharmacology, Serotonin Club, Internat. Soc. for Rsch. on Emotion, Internat. Soc. Psychoneuroendocrinology, Arbeitsgemeinschaft fur Neuropsychpharmakologie und Pharmakopsychiatrie, World Psychiat. Assn. (chmn. religion, spirituality and psychiatry sect.). Office: Acad Hosp Maastricht Postbus 5800 6202 AZ Maastricht Netherlands Office Phone: 31-55-5760795. Personal E-mail: h.m.van.praag@vanpraag.com.

VANREEK, JAN, epidemiologist; b. Oostvoorne, The Netherlands, July 10, 1945; MD, Leyden U., The Netherlands, 1969. Epidemiologist Maastricht (The Netherlands) U., 1975—92, 1993—. Author: The ultra modern endgame study, 1989, Grand strategy, 2000; contbr. articles to profl. jours. Achievements include formulated present Dutch anti-smoking policy in 1985. Home: De Erk 8 6269 BJ Margraten Netherlands Home Phone: 0434582004. Home Fax: 0434583144.

VAN ROOD, JON (JOHANNES) JOSEPH, immunologist; b. Hague, Netherlands, 1926; MD, PhD. Prof. U. Leiden, Netherlands, ret., 1991. Founder Eurotransplant, Lieden, Netherlands, 1967, BMDW (Bone Marrow Donors Worldwide), Lieden, 1988; chmn. editl. bd. Europdonor Found. Editor: Immunobiology of Hla Class-I and Class-II Molecules (Progress in Allergy), 1984; co-author: The Role of Micro-Organisms in Non-Infectious Diseases, 1990; contbr. articles to numerous profl jour. Recipient Robert Koch prize for excellence in biomed. scis., 1977, Wolf Found. prize in medicine, Israel, 1978, Arbois Brillot prize, 1985, E. Zung prize, 1989, Heineker prize, 1990, Erica Scierzapos la Pace prize, 1995, Medawar prize, 1996. Mem.: World Marrow Donor Assn. (pres. 1994, pres. emeritus), European Soc. Organ Transplants. Achievements include research in understanding of the complexity of the HL-A system in man and its implications in transplantation and in disease. Office: Europdonor Found Plesmanlaan 1B 2333 BZ Leiden Netherlands Office Fax: 31 653244415. *

VAN ROSTENBERGHE, HANS LUC ASTER, neonatologist, consultant, researcher; b. Oudenaarde, East Flanders, Belgium, Oct. 18, 1964; s. Romain Achiel Van Rostenberghe and Mariette Coleta Heyse; m. Maraina Che Hussin, May 4, 1991; children: Johan Suhardi Hans, Joshua Aiman Hans. B of Med. Scis., U. Ghent, Belgium, 1985, MD, 1989. Cert. pediats. U. Ghent, 1994; lead auditor Internat. Register Cert. Auditors, UK, 2005. Trainee for specialist in pediats. U. Ghent, 1989—94; lectr. U. Sains Malaysia, Kubang Kerian, Kelantan, Malaysia, 1994—2000, assoc. prof., 2000—. Head neonatal ICU U. Sains Malaysia, Kubang Kerian, 1997—, chmn. med. based master of medicine program, 2000—. Contbr. articles to profl. jours. Chmn., vol. ogrn. Sahabat Yokuk, Kota Bharu, Kelantan, 2004—. Recipient Boddaert award, U. Ghent, 1988; Rsch. grants, U. Sains Malaysia, 1995—. Mem.: Nat. Perinatal Com., Perinatal Soc. Malaysia, Parenteral and Enteral Nutrition Soc. Malaysia (life), Malaysian Pediat. Assn. (life). Achievements include development of High Frequency Oscillating Ventilation and other modern applications services in Neonatal Intensive Care Unit, Hospital Universiti Sains Malaysia. Home: 764 Kampung Nipah Kelantan Bachok 16300 Malaysia Office: Univ Sains Malaysia Jalan Raja Perempuan Zainab II Kelantan Kubang Kerian 16150 Malaysia Office Fax: 60 9 7653370; Home Fax: 60 9 7782716. Personal E-mail: hansvro@yahoo.co.uk. Business E-Mail: hansvr@kb.usm.my.

VAN SAENE, HENDRIK KAREL, pathologist, researcher; b. Aalst, Belgium, May 19, 1946; s. Maurits Van Saene and Madeleine Beeckman. MD, U. Leuven, Belgium, 1973; PhD, U. Groningen, The Netherlands, 1982. Trainee U. Groningen, Netherlands, 1974—77, cons., 1977—87; sr. lectr. U. Liverpool, England, 1987—97, reader, 1997—. Editor: Infection Control in ICU by SDD, 1989, Infection and Anaesthetist, 1991, Infection Control in ICU, 1998, 3rd edit., 2011, Management of Infection, 2001. Fellow: Royal Coll. Pathologists. Avocations: art, early Renaissance. Office: Sch Clin Scis Duncan Bldg. Daulby St Liverpool L69 3GA England Office Phone: 44 151 7064923. Business E-Mail: nia.taylor@liv.ac.uk.

VAN SCHIL, PAUL EMILE, surgeon, researcher; b. Antwerp, Belgium, July 7, 1957; s. Willy Karel and Martha Sidonia (De Maeyer) Van S.; m. Renelde Esther Ruelle, July 27, 1984; 1 child, Kristof. MD, U. Antwerp, 1982; PhD, U. Nijmegen, The Netherlands, 1992. Resident in gen. surgery Imelda Hosp.-Univ. Hosp. of Antwerp, Bonheiden and Edegem, Belgium, 1982—88; fellow in thoracic-vascular surgery Antonius Hosp., Nieuwegein, The Netherlands, 1989—90; rsch. fellow U. Antwerp, 1990—96; mem. staff dept. surgery divsn. thoracic & vascular surgery Univ. Hosp. Antwerp, 1990—, prof. thoracic and vascular surgery, 1996—, chief dept. thoracic and vascular surgery, 2000—. Contbr. numerous articles to sci. jours. Lt. Belgian Med. Svc., 1988-89. Fellow Am. Soc. Angiology, NY Acad. Scis.; mem. Belgian Soc. Surgery (Duprez award 1989, Fund Prof. Dr. A. Lacquet 1998), Internat. Soc. Surgery, European Soc. for Surg. Rsch., Soc. Thoracic Surgery Office: U Hosp Antwerp Dept Thoracic and Vascular Surgery Wilrijkstraat 10 B-2650 Edegem Antwerp Belgium Home Phone: 32-3-8870147; Office Phone: 32-3-8214360. Business E-Mail: paul.van.schil@uza.be.

VANSELOW, NEAL ARTHUR, retired academic administrator, internist; b. Milw., Mar. 18, 1932; s. Arthur Frederick and Mildred (Hoffmann) Vanselow; m. Mary Ellen McKenzie, June 20, 1958; children: Julie Ann, Richard Arthur. AB, U. Mich., 1954, MD, 1958, MS, 1963. Diplomate Am. Bd. Internal Medicine, Am. Bd. Allergy and Immunology. Intern Mpls. Gen. Hosp., 1958—59; resident Univ. Hosp., Ann Arbor, Mich., 1959—63; instr. medicine U. Mich., 1963—64, asst. prof., 1964—68, assoc. prof., 1968—72, prof., chmn. dept. postgrad. medicine and health professions edn., 1972—74; dean Coll. Medicine U. Ariz., Tucson, 1974—77; chancellor med. ctr. U. Nebr., Omaha, 1977—82, v.p., 1977—82; v.p. health scis. U. Minn., 1982—89, prof. internal medicine, 1982—89; chancellor Tulane U. Med. Ctr., New Orleans, 1989—94, chancellor emeritus, 1997—; prof. internal medicine Tulane U., New Orleans, 1989—97, prof. internal medicine emeritus, 1997—. Adj. prof. health sys. mgmt. Tulane U., New Orleans, 1993—99, prof. emeritus, 1999—; chmn. Joint Bd. Osteo. and Med. Examiners Ariz., 1974—77; chmn. coun. on Grad. Med. Edn. Dept. Health and Human Svcs., 1986—91; mem. com. on educating dentists for future Inst. Medicine NAS, 1993—95, chairperson com. on future of primary care, 1994—96, co-chairperson com. on U.S. physician supply, 1995—96, scholar in residence, 1994—95, mem. com. to assess occupl. health and safety tng. needs, 1999—2000, chmn. com. on introducing social and behavioral sci. into med. sch. curriculum, 2002—04; chairperson continuing eval. panel Am. Internat. Health Alliance, 2000—01; mem. adv. com. Medschool.com, 2000—01; adj. prof. Sch. Health Adminstrn. and Policy Ariz. State U., 2000—05; mem. spl. emphasis panel NIH, 2005; mem. Health Sci. Adv. Com. U. Ariz., 2009—, Rio Verde Bd. Fire Commrs., Ariz., 2009—; bd. dirs. U. Ariz. Healthcare Corp., 2010—. Panel on interdisciplinary health profl. edn. Nat. League Nursing, 1996—97; exec. com. United Way Midlands, 1980—82, vice-chmn. 1981 campaign; mem. Commn. on Health Professions Pew Charitable Trusts, 1990—92, 1997—99, Commn. on the Future of Med. Edn. U. Calif, 1996—97; mktg. mgmt. governing coun. U. Hosp. Consortium, 1993—95; trustee Meharry Med. Coll., 1996—, chair presdl. search com., 2006; pres., chmn. bd. Am. Friends London Sch. Hygiene and Tropical Medicine, 1998—2002; com. on relationships between medicine and nursing Josiah Macy Jr. Found., 1999—2000; mem. Gov.'s Pan Am. Commn., La., 1991—92; bd. dirs. Devel. Authority for Tucson's Economy, 1975—77, Minn. High Tech. Coun., 1983—86, Minn. Coalition for Health Care Costs, 1983—87, La. Health Care Authority, 1989—90, United Way Greater New Orleans Area, 1992—97; bd. dirs., exec. com. Health Planning Coun. Midlands, Omaha, 1978—82, v.p., 1981—82. Recipient Disting. Alumnus award, U. Mich. Med. Ctr. Alumni Soc., 2007. Fellow: ACP (workgroup on physician workforce and financing med. edn. 1996), Ariz. Acad. Arts, Sci. and Tech. (bd. govs. 2005—07, founding mem.), Am. Coll. Physician Execs., Am. Acad. Allergy; mem.: Inst. Med. NAS, Soc. Med. Adminstrs., Assn. Acad. Health Ctrs. (bd. dirs. 1983—89, chmn. bd. dirs. 1988), Rio Verde (Ariz.) Cmty. Assn. (bd. dirs. 2000—04), Phi Beta Kappa, Nu Sigma Nu, Beta Theta Pi, Alpha Omega Alpha, Sigma Xi. Home: 18942 E Mountainaire Dr Rio Verde AZ 85263-7093 Personal E-mail: nvanselow@gmail.com.

VAN SLOOTEN, RONALD HENRY JOSEPH, dentist; b. Paterson, NJ, July 12, 1937; s. Henry and Edythe (De Marco) Van S.; m. Joyce Elenor Mandel, 1962 (div. 1969); children: Ronald Henry Jr., Timothy Jay, Lauren; m. Barbara Rose Durante, July 1, 1979; children: Jonathan Henry, Brian Joseph. DDS, Fairleigh Dickinson U., Teaneck, NJ, 1962. Dentist pvt. practice, Paterson, 1965-76, Ridgewood, NJ, 1969-78, Ho Ho Kus, NJ, 1978—; staff mem. Bainert Meml. Hosp., Paterson, 1966-75, Ridgewood Valley Hosp., 1975—2004; assoc. prof. Fairleigh Dickinson Dental Sch., Hackensack, NJ, 1973-90; pres. Van Slooten Harbour Marina Inc., Port Henry, NY, 1989—. Cons. NJ Mfrs. Ins. Co., Trenton, 1966-2003. Pres. Fairleigh Dickinson Sch. Dentistry Alumni Assn., 1976-77. Lt. comdr. USN, 1962-65. Fellow Acad. Gen. Dentistry, Acad. Dentistry Internat.; mem. ADA, Internat. Dental Health Found., NJ Dental Soc., Bergen County Dental Soc. (chmn. Nat. Dental Health Week citation 1970), Moriah C. of C., Ho-Ho-Kus C. of C. Republican. Roman Catholic. Avocations: racquetball, fishing, boating. Office: Ho Ho Kus Profl Bldg 110 Warren Ave Ste 1 Ho Ho Kus NJ 07423-1561 Office Phone: 201-447-1116.

VAN STEENWYK, JOHN JOSEPH, healthcare plan consultant; b. Mpls., July 25, 1931; s. Elmer Arnold and Marion Ione (Thompson) van S.; m. Janice Kevin Sharp, July 11, 1959; children: Jennifer Lee, Edward Arnold, Julie Anne AB, Oberlin Coll., 1953; MBA, U. Pa., 1955. V.p., cons. The Segal Co., NYC, 1957—81; pres. Health Econs., Inc., Spring House, Pa., 1982—. Clin. asst. prof. cmty. and preventive medicine N.Y. Med. Coll., Valhalla, NY, 1980—2002; population health assoc. Sch. Population Health, Jefferson U., 2009—. With USN, 1955-57. Sr. scholar, Dept. Health Policy, Jefferson U., 2005—09. Mem.: APHA, Am. Health Ins. Plans, Acad. Health. Episcopalian. Avocation: gardening. Home: 921 Tennis Ave Ambler PA 19002-2312 Office: Health Economics Inc 768 N Bethlehem Pike PO Box 710 Spring House PA 19477 Office Phone: 215-628-3838.

VAN STONE, WILLIAM WEBB, retired psychiatrist; b. Denver, Mar. 14, 1929; s. Wilfred Douglas and Cora Coleman (Kampf) Van S.; m. Joan Kay Kinnear, Nov. 27, 1958 (dec. Dec. 2004); children: Lisa Kay, Kathryn Louise, David William; m. JoAnn Tuttle Seover, July 30, 2010. BA, Swarthmore Coll., 1951; MD, Cornell U., 1955. Cert. in psychiatry. Intern Mary Hitchcock Meml. Hosp., Hanover, N.H., 1955-56; resident Menninger Sch. Psychiatry, Topeka, 1958 61; unit chief Topeka VA Hosp., 1963-67; asst. chief of staff Palo Alto (Calif.) VA Med. Ctr., 1967-89, chief treatment svcs., 1989-2000; assoc. chief for psychiatry VA Central Office, Washington, 2001—09. Clin. assoc. prof. psychiatry emeritus Stanford (Calif.) U. Med. Sch., 1968—; mem. faculty Menninger Sch. Psychiatry, 1963-67, mem. & com. chair Group Advancement Psychiatry, 1975-2000. Contbr. 35 articles to profl. jours., chpts. to books. Chmn. bd. Miramonte Mental Health Assn., Palo Alto, 1976; pres. No. Calif. Psychiat. Soc., San Francisco, 1986-87, bd. dirs. Cmty. Sch. Music and Arts, Mountain View, Calif., 1969-75, bd. dirs. DC Chptr., Parents Family and Friends of Lesbians and Gays, 1996-2003. Capt/ Res. USN, 1956—77. Postdoctoral fellow C.F. Menninger Meml. Hosp., 1961-63. Fellow Am. Psychiat. Assn. (disting. life); mem. Phila. Psychiat. Assn. Avocation: singing. E-mail: wvsdc@aol.com.

VAN TILBURG, MIRANDA A.L., medical educator; b. Turnhout, Belgium, Mar. 29, 1971; MA, Tilburg U., 1994, PhD, 1998. Asst. prof. medicine U. NC, 2002—. Office: 130 Mason Farm Rd CB 7080 Chapel Hill NC 27516 Business E-Mail: tilburg@med.unc.edu.

VAN UMMERSEN, CLAIRE A., academic administrator, biologist, educator; b. Chelsea, Mass., July 28, 1935; d. George and Catherine (Courtovich); m. Frank Van Ummersen, June 7, 1958; children: Lynn, Scott. BS, Tufts U., 1957, MS, 1960, PhD, 1963; DSc (hon.), U. Mass., 1988, U. Maine, 1991; LHD (hon.), U. New Eng., 2005. Rsch. asst. Tufts U., 1957-60, 60-67, grad. asst. in embryology, 1962, postdoctoral tchg. asst., 1963-66, lectr. in biology, 1967-68; asst. prof. biology U. Mass., Boston, 1968-74, assoc. prof., 1974—86, assoc. dean acad. affairs, 1975-76, assoc. vice chancellor acad. affairs, 1976-78, chancellor, 1978-79, dir. Environ. Sci. Ctr., 1980-82; assoc. vice chancellor acad. affairs Mass. Bd. Regents for Higher Edn., 1982-85, vice chancellor for mgmt. systems and telecom., 1985-86; chancellor Univ. System NH, Durham, 1986-92; sr. fellow New Eng. Bd. Higher Edn., 1992-93; sr. fellow New Eng. Resource Ctr. Higher Edn. U. Mass., 1992-93; pres. Cleve. State U., 1993—2001, pres. emerita, 2001—; v.p., dir. Office of Women Am. Coun. Edn., Wash., DC, 2001—05, v.p. Ctr. for Effective Leadership, 2005—. Cons. Mass. Bd. Regents, 1981-82, AGB, 1992—, Kuwait U., 1992-93; asst. Lancaster Course in Ophthalmology, Mass. Eye. and Ear Infirmary, 1962-69, lectr., 1970-93, also coord.; reviewer HEW; mem. rsch. team which established safety stds. for exposure to microwave radiation, 1958-65; participant Leadership Am. program, 1992-93; bd. dirs. Nat. Coun. Sci. Environment, 1998—, mem. subcom. for future and fin. Active NH Ct. Systems Rev. Task Force, 1989-90, Leadership Cleve. Class '95, Ohio Gov.'s Coun. on Sci. and Tech., 1996-98, Strategy

Coun. Cleve. Pub. Schs., 1996-98, Cleve. Sports Commn., 1999-2001, Cleve. Mcpl. Sch. Dist. Bd., 1999-2001; New Eng. Bd. Higher Edn., 1986-92, exec. com., 1989-92, NH adv. coun., 1990-92; chair Rhodes Scholarship Selection Com., 1986-91; bd. dirs. NH Bus. and Industry Assn., 1987-93; governing bd. NH Math. Coalition, 1991-92; exec. com. 21st Century Learning Cmty., 1992-93; state panelist NH Women in Higher Edn., 1986-93; bd. dirs. Urban League Greater Cleve., 1993-2001, strategic planning com., chair edn. com., 1996-99, sec., exec. com., 1997-99; bd. dirs. Great Lakes Sci. and Tech. Ctr., 1993-2001, edn. com., 1995-2001; bd. dirs. Greater Cleve. Growth Assn., 1994-2001, Civic Vision 2000 and Beyond, Cleve., 1997-98; bd. dirs., exec. com. Sci. and Tech. Coun. Cleve. Tomorrow, 1998-99; rep. NE Ohio Tech. Coalition, 1999-2001; trustee Ohio Aerospace Inst., 1993-2001, exec. com., 1996-2001; strategic planning com. United Way, 1996-2000, chair environ. scan subcom. 1996-2001; leadership devel. com. ACE, 1995-98, women's commn., 1999-2001; bd. dirs. United Way, 1995-2001; co-chair Pub. Sector Campaign, 1997-98; bd. dirs. NCAA, divsn. 1, exec. com., 1999-2001; mem. AGB Ctr. for Pub. Higher Edn. Trusteeship and Goverance, 2001-03, Assn. Liaison Officers Adv. Com., 1998-2001. Recipient Disting. Svc. medal U. Mass., 1979, Woman of the Yr. Achievement award YWCA, 1998; Am. Cancer Soc. grantee Tufts U., 1960. Mem. Am. Coun. on Edn. (com. on self-regulation 1987-91), Nat. Conf. Cmty. and Justice (program com. 1996-2001), Nat. Coun. for Sci. and the Environment (bd. dirs. 1999-, fin. and futures coms.), State Higher Edn. Exec. Officers (fed. rels. com., 1986-92, cost accountability task force, exec. com. 1990-92), ACE (com. leadership devel.), Nat. Assn. Sys. Heads (exec. com. 1990-92), Nat. Ctr. for Edn. Stats. (network adv. com. 1989-92), New Eng. Assn. Schs. and Colls. (commn. on higher edn. 1990-93), North Ctrl. Assn. Schs. and Colls. (evaluator 1993-2001, chair accreditation teams 1986-90), Greater Cleve. Round Table (bd. dirs. 1993-2001, exec. com. 1995-2001), Cleve. Playhouse (trustee 1994-2001), Nat. Assn. State Univs. and Land Grant Colls. (exec. com. on urban agenda, mem. commn. tech. transfer), Am. Assn. State Colls. and Univs. (state rep. 1994-96, commn. on urban agenda 1996-2001, bd. dirs. 1996-99, mem. emerging issues task force 1996-98), Phi Beta Kappa, Sigma Xi. Office: American Coun on Edn One DuPont Cir NW Washington DC 20036-1193 Home Phone: 202-965-3072; Office Phone: 202-939-9376. Business E-Mail: claire_van_ummersen@ace.nche.edu.

VAN VELDHUIZEN, PETER JAY, oncologist, hematologist; b. Bellflower, Calif., Oct. 18, 1959; s. Peter and Grace (Van Surksum) Van V. BS in Chemistry, U. S.D., 1982, MD, 1986. Resident U. Kans. Med. Ctr., Kansas City, 1986-89, fellow, 1989-92; staff physician VA Med. Ctr., Kansas City, Mo., 1992—. Mem. AMA, ACP, Phi Beta Kappa, Alpha Omega Alpha. Home: 1229 W 69th St Kansas City MO 64113-1909

VAN VLIET, IRENE M., psychiatrist; Diploma in pharmacy, Utrecht U., The Netherlands, 1981, MD, 1987, PhD, 1996. Mem. dept. neurology Utrecht U. Med. Ctr., 1987—89, mem. dept. psychiatry, 1989—2001, Leiden U. Med. Ctr., Netherlands, 2001—. Mem. Dutch Multidisciplinary Guidelines Anxiety Disorders, 2003—09, Dutch Multidisciplinary Guidelines ECT. Author, editor: ECT, 2005, 2009, Anxiety Disorders, 1995, 1999, 2003, SEKR Specific Items in Psychiatry, Gender Issues in Psychiatry, 2002, 2006. Recipient Marina de Wolf award, Dutch Patient Assn. Anxiety and Phobic Disorders. Mem.: Dutch Psychiat. Assn. (Quality of Care award 2006), Am. Psychiat. Assn., European Coll. Neurophysiopharmacology. Office: Leiden U Med Ctr Dept Psychiatry B1-P Postbus 9600 2300 RC Leiden Netherlands

VAN WIMERSMA GREIDANUS, TJEERD BUWE, pharmacology educator; b. Utrecht, The Netherlands, July 17, 1936; s. Herman Theodorus and Catharina Esther (Jaeger) van W.; m. Jenny Koekkoek, Mar. 23, 1962 (div.) children: Buwe, Hajo Tjeerd (dec.), Ydke Hendrike; m. Anja Francisca Van Dam, July 22, 1983; 1 child, Daniel Cornelis. Degree Biology, Utrecht U., 1966; PhD, 1970, experimental pharmacologist, 1977. Asst. prof. dept. med. pharmacology U. Utrecht, 1972-76, assoc. prof., 1976-80, prof., 1980-2001, chmn. dept. med. pharmacology, 1985-99; ret., 2001. Chmn. Netherlands Soc. Olympic Participants, 1986-99; bd. dirs. Med. Faculty U. Utrecht, 1984-87, chmn. preclin. sect., 1975-78; chmn. Netherlands Ctr. Doping Affairs, Arnhem, 1989-2001; mem. coun. Utrecht U., 1995-99; chmn. adv. bd. U. Ctr. Sportsmedicine Ultrecht U., 2003—. Author and editor of over 250 scientific papers and chapters in neuroendocrinology, sports and doping. Mem. bd. Dutch Rowing Assn., Amsterdam, 1967-71; chef d'equipe Dutch Rowing Team European Champions, Olympic Games Mex., 1967-68; chef de Mission Netherlands Olympic Team, Sarajevo, L.A., 1984; bd. mem. Netherlands Olympic Com., The Hague, 1985-89, Netherlands Inst. Sportsjurisdiction, Amsterdam, 2004-06. Sgt. Royal Air Force, 1956-58. Recipient medal of Honor, Netherlands Olympic Com., 1985, Faculty Medicine Utrecht U., 1997, medal of honor, Utrecht U., 2001, regal decoration Queen's Birthday Honour, 2001; named Hon. mem. Utrecht Students Rowing Club Triton, 1965. Mem. Netherlands Soc. Olympic Participants (hon.). Home: Rembrandthage 272 Nieuwegein 3438 JT Netherlands E-mail: t.greidanus@planet.nl.

VAN ZEE, KIMBERLY J., surgeon, educator; Grad. summa cum laude, Pomona Coll.; MD, Harvard Med. Sch., 1987. Diplomate Am. Bd. Surgery. Resident in surgery NY Hosp.- Cornell, 1988—90, 1993—94; fellow in rsch. Cornell Univ. Med. Coll., 1990—93, prof. surgery. Named one of Top Doctors, NY Metro Area, Castle Connolly, Best Doctors in NY, NY mag., 2009. Fellow: ACS. Office: Memorial Sloan- Kettering Cancer Center 1275 York Ave New York NY 10065 Office Phone: 212-639-2000. Office Fax: 212-639-3576.

VAN ZWIETEN, PETER A., clinical pharmacologist, educator, consultant; b. Heemstede, The Netherlands, May 20, 1937; s. Frans C. Van Zwieten and Dora Van Son. PhD, U. Amsterdam, The Netherlands, 1961; MD, U. Kiel, Germany, 1968; degree (hon.), Med. U., Beijing, 1995, Tongji Med. U., Wuhan, China, 1997. Bd. cert. clin. pharmacologist. Postdoctor U. Vienna, Austria, 1963-65; lectr. U. Kiel, Germany, 1965-68, assoc. prof., 1968-71; prof. faculty pharmacy Acad. Hosp., U. Amsterdam, 1971-85, prof. faculty medicine, 1985—; cons. clin. pharmacology, 1985—. Dean faculty pharmacy U. Amsterdam, 1972-85. Author: (with others) Drug Therapy in Cardio-Thoracic Surgery, 1997, Antihypertensive Drugs, 1997; contbr. articles to profl. jours. With Royal Netherlands Army, 1961-63, reserve officer, 1963-99. Mem. German Acad. Scis., Academia Europea, Order of Netherlands' Lion (knight). Avocations: art, languages. Office: U Amsterdam Acad Med Ctr Meibergdreef 15 1105 AZ Amsterdam Netherlands Office Fax: 31-20-676-0511.

VAN ZYL, ANDRE WILLEM, periodontist, educator; b. Cape Town, South Africa, Apr. 4, 1959; BChD, U. Stellenbosch, 1983, MChD, 1989. Asst. prof. U. Stellenbosch, 1998—2003, U. Pretoria, 2006—. Fellow: Internat. Team Implantology; mem.: South African Soc. Periodontology, Deutsche Gesellschaft fur Orale Implantologie. Avocation: photography. Office: Oral and Dental Hosp Bophelo Rd Pretoria Gauteng 0001 South Africa Office Fax: 27 12 326 3375. Business E-Mail: andrevanzyl@up.ac.za.

VAN ZYL, PAULINA MARIA, pharmacologist; b. Calvinia, Sept. 8, 1961; MBChB, U. Stellenbosch, 1985; PhD in Clin. Pharmacology, U. Free State, 2010. Physician U. Free State, U. Hosp., 2001—. Avocation: history. Office: University Free State Nelson Mandela Bloemfontein Free State 9300 South Africa Office Fax: 0514441523. E-mail: vzylpm@ufs.ac.za.

VAN ZYL, ROBYN LYNNE, pharmacologist, educator; b. South Africa, Apr. 7, 1968; BSc with honors in Pharmacology, U. Witwatersrand, 1989, PhD in Pharmacology, 1997. Assoc. prof., acting head pharmacology divsn. U. Witwatersrand, 1992—. Large Rsch. grant, Carnegie, Thuthuka: Women Rsch. grant, South African Nat. Rsch. Found. Mem.: Parasitology Soc. South Africa, Toxicology Soc. South Africa, South African Soc. Basic and Clin. Pharmacology (bd. dirs. 2006—11, treas.). Achievements include research in malaria and novel antimalarial agent discovery and metal homeostasis in malaria and mammalian cells. Avocations: sports, reading, painting. Office: 7 York Rd Parktown Johannesburg Gauteng 2193 South Africa Office Fax: 27-11-643-5415. Business E-Mail: robyn.vanzyl@wits.ac.za.

VAPNEK, JONATHAN, urologist; BA in Molecular Biophysics and Biochemistry summa cum laude with honors, Yale U., 1978—82; MD, U. of Calif. San Diego Sch. of Medicine, 1982—86. Diplomate Am. Bd. Urology, 1995. Resident surgery Univ. of Calif. San Diego Med. Ctr., 1987—88, resident urology, 1988—92; fellow neurourology Univ. of Calif. Davis Med. Ctr., 1992—93; asst. attending urologist Mt. Sinai Hosp., 1993—2001, 2001—; attending staff physician Bronx Veterans Affairs Med. Ctr., 1993—2002. Asst. prof. urology Mt. Sinai Sch. of Medicine, 1993—2001; clin. assoc. prof. urology, 2001—. Author-co author (more than 35 papers, and having made over 50 academic presentations). Fellow: ACS; mem.: NY Acad. of Medicine, Soc. for Urodynamics and Female Urology, Am. Spinal Injury Assn., Am. Paraplegia Soc. (bd. dirs., program com., edn. com.), NT Sect. Am. Urol. Assn., Am. Urol. Assn. Office: 229 E 79th St Suite 1A New York NY 10075 Office Phone: 212-717-9500.

VARANI, KATIA, pharmacologist, educator; b. Sassoferrato, Nov. 15, 1959; Degrees in Biol. Scis., U. Ferrara, 1988, PhD, 1995. Tech. asst. U. Ferrara, 1998—2003, rschr., 2004—06, assoc. prof., 2006—. Mem.: Italian Soc. Pharmacology, Purine Club. Office: via Fossato di Mortara 17-19 Ferrara 44121 Italy Office Phone: 0390532455217. Office Fax: 0390532455205. Business E-Mail: vrk@unife.it.

VARGAS, PILAR, physician, consultant; b. Rio Pedras, PR, June 5, 1944; d. Pedro Vargas and Pilar Bodas de Vargas; m. Sten H. Vermund, Apr. 8, 1978; children: Julian, Gabriel. BS in Chemistry, U. P.R., Rio Piedras, 1966; PhD in Biology, CUNY, 1975; MD, Albert Einstein Coll. Medicine, 1977. Diplomate Am. Bd. Neurology and Psychiatry. Intern medicine N.Y. Med. Coll., NYC, 1977-78; resident psychiatry Bronx (N.Y.)-Mcpl. Hosp. Ctr., 1978-80, fellow child psychiatry, 1981-83; instr. psychiatry Albert Einstein Coll Medicine Yeshiva U., NYC, 1983-89; cons. State of Ala. Dept. Edn., Birmingham, 1995—2006; cons. Dept. Human Svcs., State Tenn., 2007—. Contbr. articles to profl. jours. Fellow NIMH, Bronx, 1981-82. Mem. Am. Psychiat. Assn., Am. Acad. Child and Adolescent Psychiatry. Office: State Tenn Dept Human Svcs Metro Ctr 200 Athens Way Nashville TN 37202 Office Phone: 615-782-6038. Personal E-mail: pilarvv@aol.com.

VARGHESE, CHACKO, pharmacist; b. Mathra, India, Oct. 7, 1956; arrived in U.S., 1984; d. Chacko Varghese and Chacko Thankamma; m. Lizyamma George Varghese, July 22, 1987; children: Joshua, Janeen, Jensine. BS in Pharmacy, Northeastern U., Boston, 1990; D of Pharmacy, Nova Southea. U., 1999. Registered pharmacist Mass., Fla., Tenn., cons. pharmacist Fla. Pharmacist Whidden Meml. Hosp., Everett, Mass., 1990, Eckerd Drug Co. Inc., Ft. Lauderdale, Fla., 1990—98, Pharmerica, Pompano Beach, Fla., 1998—99; clin. pharmacist Broward Gen. Med. Ctr., Ft. Lauderdale, 1999—2000, Meml. Hosp. West, Pembroke Pines, Fla., 2000—01; clin. pharmacist, coord. McKennson Medication Mgmt., Plantation, Fla., 2001—02; pharmacist Walgreens Pharmacy, Ft. Lauderdale, 2002—04, dist. diabetic rep., 2004—. Preceptor Bd. Pharmacy, Fla., 1995—96, 2001. Mem.: Am. Pharmacists Assn., Am. Soc. Healthsys. Pharmacists. Mem. Ch. Of God. Avocations: travel, bicycling, reading. Home: 5444 NW 52d Ave Coconut Creek FL 33073 Office: Walgreens Pharmacy 4351 W Sample Rd Coconut Creek FL 33073 Office Phone: 954-978-4979. E-mail: chackliz5444@aol.com.

VARGO, JOHN, gastroenterologist; b. Elmira, NY, May 17, 1959; BA, U. Rochester, 1981, MD, 1985. Interim chair, dept. gastroenterology Cleve. Clinic, 1994—. Fellow: ACP, Am. Gastroent. Assn., Am. Coll. Gastroenterology, Am. Soc. Gastrointestinal Endoscopy; mem.: Bockus Alumni Internat. Soc. Gastroenterology. Office: Cleve Clinic 9500 Euclid Ave Cleveland OH 44195 Business E-Mail: vargoj@ccf.org.

VARGO, ROBYN, orthopedist, surgeon; DO, Ohio Univ. Coll. Osteopathic Medicine, Athens. Cert. Bd. Orthopaedic Surgery Examiners. Intern, resident Brentwood Hosp., Cleve.; fellow in adult reconstructive foot and ankle surgery Centennial Med. Ctr., Nashville; staff physician Hinsdale Hosp., Ill., Good Samaritan Hosp., Hinsdale Surg. Ctr., Ill., Salt Creek Surgery Ctr.; ptnr. Hinsdale Orthopaedic Assoc., Ill., 1995—. Contbr. articles to numerous profl. jours. Mem.: DuPage County Med. Soc., Am. Osteopathic Assn., Am. Osteopathic Acad. Orthopaedics, Am. Orthopaedic Foot and Ankle Soc. Office: Hinsdale Orthopaedic Assoc 550 W Ogden Ave Hinsdale IL 60521

VARIK, KARIN, surgeon; b. Estonia, Aug. 30, 1950; PhD, Tartu U., 1976. Sr. tchg. physician Tartu U. Hosp., 1977—, sr. asst., 1980. Master: Estonian Assn. Paedit. Surgeons; mem.: World Assn. Paedit. Surgeons, European Assn. Paedit. Surgeons, Baltic Assn. Paedit. Surgeons. Office: Puusepa 8 Tartu 51014 Estonia Business E-Mail: karin.varik@kliinikum.ee.

VARJU, DEZSOE, biologist, educator; b. Gasztony, Hungary, May 22, 1932; arrived in Germany, 1956; s. Johann and Anna (Hirschmann) V.; m. Heide Agner. Diploma Physics, U. Budapest, Hungary, 1956; PhD, U. Goettingen, Germany, 1958; univ. tchr., U. Tuebingen, Germany, 1967. Rsch. asst., rsch. assoc. Max Planck Inst., Tuebingen, 1958-59, 60-68; postdoctoral fellow Calif. Tech., Pasadena, 1959-60; prof. U. Tuebingen, 1968-97, prof. emeritus, 1997—. Author: Systems Theory, 1977, Mit den Ohren Sehen und den Beinen Hören, 1998; co-author: Polarized Light in Animal Vision, Polarization Patterns in Nature, 2004; editor: Localisation and Orientation in Biology and Engineering, 1984; co-editor: Biological Cybernetics Jour., 1993-2000; mem. adv. bd. Jour. Comp. Physiology. Avocations: gardening, skiing, tennis. Office: U Tuebingen Auf der Morgenstelle 28 72076 Tübingen Germany Business E-Mail: dezsoe.varju@unituebingen.de.

VARLOTTA, LAURIE, pediatrician, pulmonologist; b. Oct. 27, 1959; MD, SUNY Downstate Med., Brooklyn, 1985; BA in chemistry, Emory U., Atlanta, 1981. Fellow pediat. pulmonology Children's Hosp. Phila., 1989-92; attending pulmonologist St. Christopher's Hosp. Children, Phila., 1992—, acting chief pulmonology, 1999-2000, chief sect. pulmonology and allergy, 2000—01, dir. Cystic Fibrosis Ctr., 1999—, med. dir. respiratory therapy, 1998—2002, med. dir. pulmonary function lab., 1998—, clin. dir. sect. pulmonology, 2004—07. Lectr. in field. Contbr. articles to profl. jours. Co-chair mid-atlantic consortium Cystic Fibrosis Found., 2000—, ctr. com., 2006—, bd. dirs. Del. Valley chpt., 2005—. Mem.: Cystic Fibrosis Found. Ctr. Com.

VARMA, DATLA G.K., radiologist, researcher; b. Bobbili, Andhra, India, June 2, 1951; came to U.S., 1976; now naturalized; s. Datla V. Raju and Datla Satyavathi; m. Siva Kumari, Dec. 20, 1980; children: Datla Kirti, Datla Vivek. MBBS, Andhra Med. Coll., 1975. Diplomate Am. Bd. Radiology, Am. Bd. Nuclear Medicine. Intern King George Hosp., Visakha Patnam, India, 1974-75; resident in anat. pathology Good Samaritan Hosp., Cin., 1977-78; resident in nuclear medicine Univ. Hosp., Cin., 1978-80, resident in radiology, 1980-83; asst. prof. radiology Tulane U., New Orleans, 1983-88, med. dir. diagnostic svcs./radiology dept., 1987-89, assoc. prof. radiology, 1988-89, sect. chief body CT, 1983-89, sect. chief body MRI, 1988-89; assoc. prof. radiology U. Tex./M.D. Anderson Cancer Ctr., Houston, 1989-99, acting sect. chief MRI, 1991-99, prof. radiology, 1999—. Contbr. articles to profl. jours., chpts. to books. Avocations: sports, travel, reading. Home: 3915 Marlowe St Houston TX 77005-2045 Office: Md Anderson Cancer Ctr PO Box 57 Houston TX 77001-0057 Business E-Mail: dvarma@mdanderson.org.

VARMA, SANDEEP, nephrologist, educator; b. Ernakulam, Kerala, India, Feb. 27, 1973; MBBS, Govt. Med. Coll., Thrissur, 1999; DM in Nephrology, Govt. Med. Coll., Thiruvananthapuram, 2007. Asst. prof., internal medicine, head, divsn. nephrology, cons. nephrologist Sree Gokulam Med. Coll., Thiruvananthapuram, 2008—. Asst. prof. Govt. Med. Coll., 2007—08; cons. nephrologist Jubilee Hosps., Thiruvananthapuram, 2010—, S. K. Hosp., Thiruvananthapuram, 2010—. Mem.: Nephrology Assn. Kerala, Indian Med. Assn. Home: Parakkode Ln Kariyam Thiruvananthapuram Kerala 689017 India Personal E-mail: drsandeepvarma@yahoo.com.

VARMA, SURENDRA K., pediatrician, educator; b. Lucknow, India, Dec. 10, 1939; arrived in U.S., 1968; s. Raghubir P. and Leela Varma; m. Kamlesh Varma, Feb. 25, 1967; children: Rishi Anand, Ritu. MB, BChir, King George Med. Sch., Lucknow, 1962, MD, 1968. Diplomate in pediatrics and in pediat. endocrinology Am. Bd. Pediat. Rsch. assoc. MIT, Cambridge, Mass., 1972—74; asst. prof. Tex. Tech. U. Health Sci. Ctr., Lubbock, 1974—78, assoc. prof., 1978—83, prof., 1983—98, univ. dist. prof., 1998—. Instr. Harvard Med. Sch., Boston, 1973—74; vice chair resident rev. com. pediat. Accreditation Coun. Grad. Med. Edn., Chgo., 1997—; presenter in field; Ted Hartman Endowed chair, 2007—; assoc. dean Grad. Med. Edn., 2008—. Contbr. articles to profl. jours. Lt. col. US Army, 1990—91. Fellow: Am. Coll. Clin. Endocrinology, Am. Acad. Pediat.; mem.: Alpha Omega Alpha. Home: 4617 5th St Lubbock TX 79416 Office: Tex Tech Univ Health Scis Ctr 3601 4th St Lubbock TX 79430 Office Phone: 806-743-2312. Business E-Mail: surendra.varma@ttuhsc.edu.

VARMA, hematologist; b. Patyani, Feb. 6, 1956; MBBS, HPMC, Simla, 1980; MD, PGIMER, Chandigarh, 1986. Prof., head dept. hematology PGIMER, 2006—. Fellowship, WHO. Mem.: Cytometry Soc. India, European Hematology Assn., Indian Soc. Human Genetics Nat. Acad. Med. Scis., Indian Assn. Pathologists & Microbiologists, Indian Assn. Cancer Rsch., Indian Soc. Hematology and Blood Transfusion. Avocations: music, cricket, reading. Office: 1036 Sector 24 B Chandigarh 160023 India Office Fax: 911722747124. E-mail: varmaneelam@yahoo.com.

VARMUS, HAROLD ELIOT, federal agency administrator, cell biologist, educator, former hospital administrator; b. Oceanside, NY, Dec. 18, 1939; s. Frank and Beatrice (Barasch) Varmus; m. Constance Louise Casey, Oct. 25, 1969; children: Jacob Carey, Christopher Isaac. BA in English, Amherst Coll., Mass., 1961; MA in English Lit., Harvard U., 1962; MD, Columbia U. Coll. Physicians & Surgeons, NYC, 1966. Intern, resident Columbia-Presbyn. Hosp., 1966-68; clin. assoc. Nat. Inst. Arthritis & Metabolic Disease, Bethesda, Md., 1968-70; lectr. dept. microbiology U. Calif., San Francisco, 1970-72, asst. prof., 1972-74, assoc. prof., 1974-79, prof. dept. microbiology & immunology, 1979—93, prof. dept. biochemistry & biophysics, 1982—93, American Cancer Soc. prof. molecular virology, 1984—93; dir. NIH, Bethesda, 1993—99; pres., CEO Meml. Sloan-Kettering Cancer Ctr., NYC, 2000—10; dir. Nat. Cancer Inst.,

Bethesda, Md., 2010—. Chmn. bd. on biology NRC, 1991—93; mem. WHO Commn. Macroeconomics & Health, 2000—02; co-founder, chmn. bd. Pub. Libr. of Sci. (PLoS), 2003—; mem., co-chair Pres.'s Coun. Advisors on Sci. & Tech. (PCAST), 2009—10. Author: The Art and Politics of Science, 2009; contbr. articles to profl. jours. Chair sci. bd. Grand Challenges in Global Health initiative, Bill & Melinda Gates Found., 2003—08; bd. dirs. Campaign to Defend the Constn., Scientists & Engineers for America. Surgeon USPHS, 1968—70. Recipient Albert Lasker award for Basic Med. Rsch., 1982, Passano Found. award, 1983, Shubitz Cancer prize, 1984, Gardner Found. Internat. award, 1984, Alfred P. Sloan award, GM Cancer Rsch. Found., 1984, Vannevar Bush award, NSF, 2001, Nat. Medal Sci., The White House, 2002; co-recipient Scientist of Yr. award, Calif. Acad. Sci., 1982, Nobel prize in Physiology/Medicine, The Nobel Found., 1989; named one of America's Best Leaders, US News & World Report, 2007. Mem.: NAS, Am. Soc. Biochemistry & Molecular Biology, Am. Acad. Arts & Scis., Am. Soc. Cell Biology, Am. Soc. Microbiology, Am. Soc. Virology, Inst. Medicine. Democrat. Office: National Cancer Institute HIH 6116 Executive Blvd Bethesda MD 20892 Mailing: PLoS Hdqs 185 Berry St St 3100 San Francisco CA 94107 *

VARNER, CHARLEEN LAVERNE MCCLANAHAN, nutritionist, educator, administrator, dietitian; b. Alba, Mo., Aug. 28, 1931; d. Roy Calvin and Lela Ruhama (Smith) McClanahan; m. Robert Bernard Varner, July 4, 1953. Student, Joplin (Mo.) Jr. Coll., 1949—51; BS in Edn., Kans. State Coll. Pittsburg, 1953; MS, U. Ark., 1958; PhD, Tex. Woman's U., 1966; postgrad., Mich. State U., 1955, U. Mo., 1962. Registered lic. dietitian. Apprentice county home agt. U. Mo., 1952; tchr. Ferry Pass Sch., Escambia County, Fla., 1953—54; tchr. biology, home econs. Joplin Sr. HS, 1954—59; instr. home econs. Kans. State Coll., Pittsburg, 1959—63; lectr. foods, nutrition Coll. Household Arts and Scis., Tex. Woman's U., 1963—64; rsch. asst. NASA Grant, 1964—66; assoc. prof. home econs. Ctrl. Mo. State U., Warrensburg, 1966—70, adviser to Colhecon, 1966—70; adviser Alpha Sigma Alpha, 1967—70, 1972; bd. adv. Honors Group, 1967—70; prof., head dept. home econs. Kans. State Tchrs. Coll., Emporia, 1970—73; prof., chairperson dept. home econs. Benedictine Coll., Atchison, Kans., 1973—74; prof., head, dept. home econs. Baker U., Baldwin City, Kans., 1974—75; owner, operator Diet-Con Dietary Cons. Enterprises, cons. dietitian, 1973—, Home-Con Cons. Enterprises, 1975—; adj. prof. Highland (Kans.) CC, 2003—. Active mem. Joplin Little Theater, 1956—60. Mem.: AAUP, AAUW, NEA, Assn. Edn. Young Children, Am. Vocat. Assn., Alumni Assn. Kans. State Coll. Pittsburg, U. Ark. Alumni Assn., Mo. Acad. Scis., Kans. Home Econs. Assn., Mo. Home Econs. Assn., Am. Home Econs. Assn., Kans. Dietetic Assn., Mo. Dietetic Assn., Am. Dietetic Assn., Kans. State Tchr. Assn., Mo. State Tchr. Assn., Kappa Phi (organist), Theta Alpha Pi, Phi Upsilon Omicron, Kappa Kappa Iota, Delta Kappa Gamma, Alpha Sigma Alpha, Beta Beta Beta, Beta Sigma Phi, Sigma Xi. Methodist. Home: Main PO Box 1009 Topeka KS 66601-1009 Home Phone: 785-640-7002.

VARNER, DALE EDWARD, surgeon, thoracic surgeon; b. Dec. 5, 1961; MD, UCLA Sch. Medicine, 1988. Flight surgeon Colo. Air Nat. Guard, 1996—2006; worked electronic med. record implementation team Kaiser Permanente; gen. surgeon, thoracic surgeon Colo. Permanente Med. Group, 2000—, assoc. med. dir. resource stewardship. Former bd. dir. Colo. Permanente Med. Group; former chmn. surgery Exempla Good Samaritan Med. Ctr.; former asst. clin. prof. U. Colo. Sch. Medicine. Office: Colorado Permanente Medical Group 280 Exempla Cir Lafayette CO 80026 *

VARNEY, RICHARD ALAN, health facility administrator; b. Concord, NH, July 8, 1950; s. John Berry and Hattie Elizabeth (Harrington) V.; m. Suzanne Glaab, Dec. 31, 1983; stepchildren: Alysen Suzanne Bidle, Craig Judson Bidle. BS in Phys. Edn., U. N.H., 1972; MHA in Healthcare Adminstrn., Baylor U., 1984; diploma, Command and Gen. Staff Coll., 1986. Commd. 2d lt. U.S. Army, 1973, advanced through grades to lt. col., 1991; dep. asst. CEO Cutler Army Hosp., Ft. Devens, Mass., 1973—76; field med. asst. 38th ADA Bde., Osan Air Base, Republic of Korea, 1977—78; dep. asst. CEO 15th Med. Battalion, Ft. Hood, Tex., 1979—81; adminstrv. resident Ireland Army Hosp., Ft. Knox, Ky., 1982—83; COO, exec. officer U.S. Army Dental Activity, Ft. Knox, 1983—86; grad. instr. Army-Baylor Healthcare Program, San Antonio, 1986—90; project mgr. Office of the Army Surgeon Gen., Washington, 1990—93; ret. U.S. Army, 1993; office mgr. Aebi, Ginty, Romaker & Sprouse MD's, Inc., Lancaster, Ohio, 1993—2000; dir. gen. internal medicine program The Ohio State U. Med. Ctr., Columbus, 2000—04; dir. ops. Fairfield Dept. Health, Lancaster, 2005—09; dir. organizational devel. Fairfield Cmty. Health Ctr., Lancaster, Ohio, 2010. Mem. Source Selection Evaluation Bd.-Champus Reform, Arlington, Va., 1987; mem. adv. com. for assoc. degree program in med. assisting Ohio U., Lancaster, 1998-2000. Adult leader Boy Scouts Am., Tex., Va. and Ohio, 1988-97, 2003—; mem. Lancaster City Bd. of Health, 1996-2001, pres. pro tem, 1999-2001; mem. Fairfield County Combined Gen. Health Dist. Bd., 2002-04. Officer US Army Med. Svc. Corps, 1973—93. Decorated Legion of Merit, Order of Mil. Med. Merit award, Expert Field Med. badge; named to Hon. Order Ky. Cols., 1989, Outstanding Young Man of Am., 1982. Fellow Am. Coll. Healthcare Execs.; mem. Ctrl. Ohio Health Adminstrs. Assn., Ohio Med. Group Mgmt. Assn., Mid-Ohio Med. Mgmt. Assn., Profl. Assn. Med. Mgrs., Am. Assn. Procedural Coders, Lancaster Area Soc. for Human Resource Mrmt. (legis. rep. 1998-99, membership chair 1999—2008, sec. 2009-), Am. Hosp. Assn., Nat. Eagle Scout Assn., The Ret. Officers Assn., Am. Legion, Fraternal Order of Eagles, Alpha Phi Omega. Avocations: home improvement, music. Home: 1025 E 5th Ave Lancaster OH 43130-3276 Home Phone: 740-681-5665; Office Phone: 740-277-6043. Personal E-mail: richvarneyosu@yahoo.com. Business E-Mail: rvarney@fairfieldchc.org.

VARRAY, ALAIN L., scientist, specialized in human exercise physiology and rehabilitation; b. Montpellier, Hérault, France, Mar. 6, 1960; s. Robert and Rose-Lise Varray; m. Marie-Pierre Remy, July 15, 1982; children: François, Sylvie, Christophe. Master's in Adapted Phys. Activity, U. Montpellier, 1983, PhD in Human Movement Scis., 1990. Rsch. fellow faculty sports scis. U. Montpellier, 1986—89, asst. prof. faculty sports scis., 1990—97, prof. faculty sports scis., 1990—97, classe exceptionnelle prof., 2010. Dir. lab. sport, performance and health U. Montpellier, 1999—2003, rsch. vice-dean faculty sport scis., 2005—; pres. rsch. coun., rehab. group clinics FontalVie, Toulouges, Pyrénées Orientales, 1992—; mem. coun. Human Movement Scis. Doctoral Sch. Contbr. articles to profl. jours. Recipient Lawrence Rarick award, Internat. Fedn. Adapted Phys. Activity, 2005. Mem.: Nat. Coun. Universities, Nat. Council Univs., Rsch. and Devel. Sport and Health (pres. 1998). Office: Univ of Montpellier 1 700 avenue du Pic Saint Loup 34090 Montpellier F-34090 France Office Phone: 33 411 75 90 70. Business E-Mail: alain.varray@univ-montp1.fr.

VARRE, SREEDEVI, geneticist; b. Nalgonda, Jan. 1, 1972; PhD, 1993; MSc, Osmania U., Hyderabad Andhra Pradesh, India, PhD, 2002. Scientist Rsch. Orgn., tchr. Inst. Genetics and Hosp. Genetic Diseases, Osmania U., 2004—. Fellowship, BC Welfare. Mem.: Third World Orgn. Women Sci., Indian Soc. Human Genetics. Avocation: singing. Office: Osmania University Inst Genetics and Hosp Genetic Diseases Begumpet Hyderabad Andhra Pradesh 500016 India Personal E-mail: sreedevi_vreey@yahoo.co.in.

VARSHAVSKY, ALEXANDER JACOB, molecular biologist, educator; b. Moscow, Nov. 8, 1946; arrived in US, 1977; s. Jacob M. and Mary B. (Zeitlin) Varshavsky; m. Vera Bingham, Aug. 30, 1990; children: Roman, Anna, Victoria. BS in Chemistry, Moscow State U., 1970; PhD in Biochemistry, Moscow Inst. Molecular Biology, 1973. Rsch. fellow Moscow Inst. Molecular Biology, 1973—76; asst. prof. dept. biology MIT, Cambridge, 1977-80, assoc. prof., 1980-86, prof., 1986-92; Howard & Gwen Laurie Smits prof. cell biology Calif. Inst. Tech., Pasadena, 1992—. Mem. molecular cytology study sect. NIH, 1983—87; vis. fellow Internat. Inst. for Advanced Studies, Kyoto, 2001; bd. dirs. Encyclopedia Molecular Cell Biology & Molecular Medicine, 2002—05; mem. med. adv. bd. Gairdner Found., Canada, 2002—06. Contbr. articles to profl. jours. Recipient Novartis-Drew award in biomed. sci., Novartis, Inc./Drew U., 1998, Merit award, NIH, 1998, Gairdner Found. Internat. award, 1999, Alfred P. Sloan Jr. prize, GM Cancer Rsch. Found., 2000, Lasker award for basic med. rsch., 2000, Hoppe-Seyler award, German Soc. Biochemistry & Molecular Biology, 2000, Merck award, Am. Soc. Biochemistry & Molecular Biology, 2001, Pasarow award in cancer rsch., Pasarow Found., 2001, Wolf Found. prize in medicine, Israel, 2001, Massry Found. prize, 2001, Max Planck Rsch. prize, Germany, 2001, Louisa Gross Horwitz prize, Columbia U., 2001, Wilson medal, Am. Soc. Cell Biology, 2002, Stein & Moore award, Protein Soc., 2005, March of Dimes prize in devel. biology, 2006, Gagna & Van Heck prize, Belgium, 2006, Griffuel Cancer Rsch. prize, France, 2006, Schleiden medal, Germany, 2007, Gotham prize for cancer rsch., 2008, Vilcek prize, 2010. Fellow: AAAS, Am. Acad. Arts & Scis., Am. Acad. Microbiology; mem.: NAS, Acad. Europaea, European Molecular Biology Orgn., Am. Philos. Soc. Achievements include patents in field. Office: CalTech Divsn Biology 147 75 1200 East California Blvd Pasadena CA 91125-0001 Office Phone: 626-395-3785. Office Fax: 626-440-9821. Business E-Mail: avarsh@caltech.edu. *

VARSOS, VASSILIOS, neurosurgeon, department chairman; b. Lamia, Greece, July 5, 1948; s. George and Ariadni Varsos; 1 child. MD, Aristotles U., Thessaloniki, Greece, 1973; PhD, U. Athens, Greece, 1984. Resident in neurosurgery Polyclinic Athens, 1974—80; rsch. fellow in neurosurgery Mass. Gen. Hosp., Harvard U., Boston, 1980—82, fellow in neurosurgery, 1983; registrar in neurosurgery Radcliffe U., Oxford, England, 1983—85; vis. prof. Harvard U., Boston; chief neurosurgeon Red Cross Hosp., Athens. Mem.: several neurol. soc.s. Office: Red Cross Hosp Dept Neurosurgery Athens Greece Address: Paleo Psychiko Karkavitsa 4 154 52 Athens Greece Business E-Mail: varsosdr@hol.gr.

VARUGHESE, SANTOSH, nephrologist, educator; b. Nilambur, India, Oct. 8, 1972; MBBS, Christian Med. Coll. Vellore, MD, 1995, DM in Nephrology, 2007. Assoc. prof. Christian Med. Coll. Vellore, 2007—, cons. nephrologist, 2007—. Recipient Achievement award, Indian Med. Assn., Young Clinician award, Asian Am. Internat. Med. Soc., Wayne State U., award, B. Braun Med. Trust Found., 2005. Mem.: Indian Soc. Peritoneal Dialysis, Indian Soc. Nephrology (Southern Chpt.) (Gold medal), Internat. Soc. Nephrology. Avocations: reading, writing. Office: Dept Nephrology Christian Med Coll Vellore Tamil Nadu 632004 India Office Fax: 914162232035. E-mail: santosh.vellore@gmail.com.

VARVAROVSKÁ, JANA, pediatrician, educator; b. Klatovy, Czech Republic, Jan. 24, 1951; d. Jan Karnolt and Libuse Karnoltová; m. Václav Varvarovský, July 20, 1975; children: Jan Varvarovský, Václav Varvarovský. MD, Charles U., 1975, PhD, 2005. Cert. Pediat., 2nd Degree Inst. for Further Med. Edn., 1987, Pediatr., 1st Degree Inst. for Further Med. Edn., 1978, lic. Pediatrician Czech Med. Soc., 1992, Immunologist Czech Med. Soc., 1992. Jr. physician Charles U. Hosp., Plzen, Czech Republic, 1975—82; jr. lectr. Charles U., 1982—90; chief outpatient clinic pediat. dept. Charles U. Hosp., Plzen, 1990—94, chief in-patient dept. pediat. dept., 1995—2002; sr. lectr., cons. Charles U., Plzen, 2003—. Author articles in med. jours. Grantee Barrande 2000, French Fgn. Office and Czech Ministry Edn., 2000, Iga Mz Cr, Ministry of Health, Prague, 2003—, Barrande 2000, French Fgn. Office and Czech Ministry Edn., 2001; scholar, Schwarzenberger Fund, 1992, French Fgn. Office, 1996. Mem.: Internat. Diabetes Fedn. (licentiate), Czech Soc. Diabetology (licentiate), Czech Soc. Clin. Immunology and Allergology (licentiate), Czech Pediat. Soc. (licentiate). Avocations: travel, history, music, movies. Office: Charles Univ Hosp Alej Svobody 80 323 00 Plzen Czech Republic Office Fax: +420377104694. E-mail: varvarovska@fnplzen.cz.

VAS, ADAM, clinical pharmacologist; b. Budapest, Hungary, Apr. 1952; s. Károly Vas and Berta Scheitz; m. Gabriella Zsámboki, July 1, 1975; children: Michaela, Fruzsina. MD, Semmelweis U.Medicine, Budapest, 1977. Cert. internal medicine 1982, clin. pharmacology 1985, hypertension care 1999. Jr. rsch. fellow St. John's Hosp., Budapest, 1977—82; sr. rsch. fellow Postgrad. Med. U., Budapest, 1982—93; rsch. dir. Gedeon Richter Ltd., Budapest, 1993—2000, sr. rsch. advisor, 2000—; prof. medicine Szeged Univ. Sci., Hungary, 2002—. Hypertension Clinic Head Semmelweis U., Budapest; curator Zoltan Bay Found. for Applied Rsch., 2002—05. Introduction to Clinical Pharmacology (in Hungarian), 1992. Mem.: European Fedn. Pharm. Scis., Hungarian Pharm. Mfrs. Assn. Scientific and Tech. Com. (pres. 1997), Hungarian Thrombosis Soc., Hungarian Hypertension Soc. (mem. bd. 1993—98), Hungarian Stroke Soc., Hungarian Soc. Internal Medicine, German Soc. Clin. Pharmacology, European Assn. Clin. Pharmacology and Therapy (bd. dirs. 2003—), Hungarian Soc. Exptl. and Clin. Pharmacology (treas. 1995), Rotary Club Budapest-Sasad (pres. 2001—02, Paul Harris Award 2001). Roman Catholic. Avocations: swimming, music, literature, history, nature. Home Phone: (+36-1)-355-9762; Office Phone: (+36-1)-431-4200. Office Fax: (+36-1)-262-8301. Business E-Mail: a.vas@richter.hu.

VASANTHARAJU, S. G., pharmacist, educator; b. Chitradurga, June 16, 1965; PharmM, Birla Inst. Tech., 1995. Educator Bapuji Pharmacy Coll. Pharmacy, 1995—2006, Manipal Coll. Pharm. Scis., 2006—. Contbr. articles to numerous profl. jours. Recipient Sri Shamanur Shivashankarappa Parvathamma Gold medel, Kuvempu U., Karnataka, IPC Cash award, Mysore U., Karnataka. Mem.: Assn. Pharm. Tchrs. India. Avocation: music. Office: Dept Pharm Quality Assurance Manipal Karnataka 576104 India E-mail: sgvasanth65@gmail.com.

VASELLA, DANIEL LUCIUS, pharmaceutical company executive; b. Fribourg, Switzerland, Aug. 15, 1953; came to U.S., 1988; s. Oskar Emil and Ursulina Isabella (Vieli) V.; m. Anne-Laurence Moret, May 12, 1978; children: Emilia Anna, Mauro Giovanni, Flavio Bernardo Placi. Fed. physician diploma, U. Berne, Switzerland, 1979, MD, 1980; postgrad., Harvard U., 1989; PhD (hon.), U. Basel, 2002. Resident in pathology U. Berne, Berne, 1980-81; resident in internal medicine Inselspital, Berne, 1982-83, Waid-Spital, Zurich, Switzerland, 1983-84; psychoanalyst U. Berne, Berne, 1983-88; attending physician Inselspital, Berne, 1984-88; mgr. spl. projects Sandoz Pharmaceuticals Corp., East Hanover, NJ, 1988-90, product mgr., 1990-91; dir. mktg. Sandoz PharmaceuticalsCorp., East Hanover, NJ, 1991-92; CEO Sandoz Pharmaceuticals AG, Basel, Switzerland, 1992-96, Novartis AG, Basel, Switzerland, 1996—99, chmn., CEO, 1999—2010, chmn., 2010—. Bd. dirs. Novartis AG, 1996-, PepsiCo, Inc., 2002-, Alcon, Inc., 2008-; lectr. U. Fribourg, Berne and Fribourg, 1985-88 Author: (with others) Psychosomatische Medizin, 1986; contbr. articles to profl. jours. Speaker various orgns., U.S.A. and Switzerland, 1985-92. Recipient Patron award U. Mich., 1992, AJ Congress Humanitarian award, 1998, Appeal of Conscience award, 2000, Ordem Nacional do Cruzeiro do Sul, Brazil; named Chevalier, Ordre National de la Légion d'Honneur, France. Mem. Am. Mgmt. Assn., Swiss Med. Assn. (bd. cert. for internal medicine 1985), Swiss Soc. for Geriatrics, Swiss Psychosomatic Assn., Swiss Psychoanalytical Assn. (candidate), Deutsches Kollegium fuer Psychosomatik; pres. Internat. Fdn. of Pharma. Manufacturers Assn., Am. Acad. Arts & Scis.(hon.fgn.) Avocation: art. Office: Novartis Ag 4002 Basel Switzerland *

VASENIUS, JARKKO, physician, director; b. Helsinki, Feb. 9, 1961; MD, Helsinki U., PhD, 1988. Assoc. prof. Helsinki U. Ctrl. Hosp., 1998—2007; med. dir. Dextra Hand Clinic, 2007—. Mem.: European Soc. Surgery Hand, Finnish Soc. Surgery Hand. Office: Raumantie 1 A Helsinki Finland Business E-Mail: jarkko@vasenius.fi.

VASHISTHA, ASHUTOSH, cardiologist, consultant; s. Ram Kishore and Urmila Vashistha; m. Meenu Sharma, June 21, 1990; children: Ashlesha, Anshuman. MBBS, G.S.V.M. Med. Coll., 1983—88. Chief of cardiology, med. dir. Lifeline Hosp. & Heart Ctr., Lucknow, India, 1993—; registrar Jaslok Hosp., Mumbai, India, 1992—92. Med. dir. Lifeline Hosp. & Heart Ctr., Lucknow, 1993—; cons. cardiologist, 1997—. Chmn. sci. com. Assn. of Clin. Cardiology, Lucknow, India, 2000. Fellow: Royal Coll. Physicians, Am. Coll. Chest Physicians, Am. Coll. Of Cardiology (life); mem.: Royal Soc. Medicine, Genesis Club (life). Office: Lifeline Hospital & Heart Centre B-49 Mandir Marg Mahanagar Lucknow 226006 India Home: B-49 Mandir Marg 226 006 Lucknow India Office Fax: 91 522 2364673; Home Fax: 91 522 2364673. E-mail: ashutosh_lifelinehospital@hotmail.com, av@lifelineheart.com.

VASILEIADIS, GEORGE T., pediatrician, researcher; s. Theodore and Afrodite Vasileiadis; m. Fenia Konstantinidou, Dec. 26, 1999; children: Theodore, Aristeidis. Med. Degree, U. Ioannina, Med. Sch., Greece, 1989; MS in Med. Biophysics, U. Western Ont., London, Can., 2004. Specialist pediatrician Health Directorate, Aristotle U., Greece, 1999, specialist neonatologist-perinatologist U. Western Ont., Royal Coll. Physicians Can., 2003. Jr. and sr. resident pediat. AHEPA U. Hosp., Thessaloniki, Greece, 1993—98; jr. and sr. resident neonatology Sunderland Royal Hosp., England, 1998—99; fellow neonatal-perinatal medicine U. Western Ont., 2000—03; clin. academic staff Med. Sch., U. Nottingham, England, 2005—10; cons. neonatologist BHR U. Hosps. NHS Trust, 2010—. Affiliated scientist Lawson Health Rsch. Inst., London, 2003—05. Contbr. scientific papers to profl. jours. With RIBI, Nottingham, 2009. Med. officer Health Svcs. - Land Forces, 1990—92, Greece. Recipient Rsch. award, Lawson Health Rsch. Inst., 2003; grantee Rsch. Imaging, U. Nottingham, 2006. Mem.: European Soc. Pediatric Rsch., Rotary Internat. (club adminstrn.). Achievements include first to impact of IVH on cortical development, Sex model of early brain development & white matter development model following prematurity; development of multisequencial brain imaging research. Personal E-mail: gtvasileiadis@gmail.com.

VASILENKO, TATYANA, physiologist, researcher; b. Atamanovo, Russia, July 18, 1952; d. Fedor and Vera Vasilenko; m. Victor Muravyev, Nov. 12, 1978; children: Antonina Ivanova, Irena Muravyeva. DSc in Biology, State U., St. Petersburg, 1980, State Acad. Vet. Medicine and Biotech., Moscow, 2008. Jr. rschr. Inst. of Biology Komi Dept. Acad. of Scis. of URSS, Syktyvkar, Russia, 1981—86; rschr. Inst. of Physiology, Komi Sci. Centre, Ural Divsn., Russian Acad. of Sci., Syktyvkar, Russia, 1986—91, sr. rschr., 1991—2004; head lab. physiology of ruminant animal Inst. of Physiology, Komi Sci. Ctr., Ural Divsn., Russian Acad. of Sci., Syktyvkar, Russia, 2004—. Author: Integrative Zoology, 2006, Doklady Biol. Sci., 2008. Mem.: Physiol. Soc. Achievements include patents for Stimulation of female animal estrus activity by the application of food additives from

Asteraseae plants; Methods of determination of functional state of female ovary; Application of additives from cow placenta tissue for the stimulation of female animal reproduction. Avocations: travel, gardening, crocheting. Office: Inst Physiology ul. Pyervomayskaya 50 167000 Syktyvkar Komi Ryesp. Russia Office Fax: (8212) 44 78 90; Home Fax: (8212) 21 66 47. Business E-Mail: vasilenko@physiol.komisc.ru.

VASILIADIS, HARIS S., orthopedist, educator; b. Thessaloniki, Feb. 6, 1974; MD, Aristotle U. Thessaloniki, 1998. Assoc. rschr. Molecular Cell Biology and Regenerative Medicine, Sahlgrenska Acad., U. Gothenburg, Sweden, 2008; lectr., orthops. U. Ioannina, Greece, 2011—. Avocations: mountain climbing, diving, travel. Home: Neokaisareia PO Box 363 Ioannina 45500 Greece Personal E-mail: vasiliadismd@gmail.com.

VASINA, LUBOMIR, psychotherapist, educator; b. Brno, Czech Republic, Aug. 22, 1948; s. Antonin Vasina and Marie Vasinova; m. Radka Ponizilova, Apr. 29, 2005; 1 child, David. PhD, Faculty Arts, Brno, 1975; PhD in Clin. Psychology, Masaryk's U., Brno, 1983. Cert. assoc. prof. clin. psychology Masaryk's U., 1997, assoc. prof. gen. psychology 1987. Asst. prof. U. Komensky Dept. Psychology, Bratislava, Slovakia, 1975—79; vocat. asst. prof. Masaryk's U. Faculty Arts, Dept. Psychology, 1979—87, assoc. prof., 1987—. Mem.: Internat. Brain Rsch. Orgn., Czech Med. Soc. J. E. Purkyne. Office: Inst Psychology MU Brno A Novaka 1 Brno 66088 Czech Republic Home Phone: 0042 072 3120233; Office Phone: 0042 0549 497941. Office Fax: 00420549491523. Business E-Mail: vasina@phil.muni.cz.

VASLEF, STEVEN NICHOLAS, surgeon; b. Colorado Springs, Colo., Aug. 16, 1958; s. Nicholas P. and Irene I. (Koncz) V.; m. Maria E. Vaslef, July 11, 1988. BS, MIT, 1980; MD, U. Va., 1984; PhD, Northwestern U., 1990. Diplomate Am. Bd. Surgery with subspecialty in surg. critical care. Intern U. Ill., Chgo., 1984-85, resident in gen. surgery, 1985-92; mem. staff Evanston/Glenbrook Hosps., 1992-94; asst. prof. surgery, asst. pro. bio-med. engring. Northwestern U. Med. Sch., Chgo., 1992-94; asst. prof. surgery Duke U. Med. Ctr., Durham, N.C., 1994-2000, assoc. prof., 2000—, asst. prof. bio-med. engring., 1994—97, asst. prof. anesthesiology, 1996—. Mem. ACS; mem. Soc. Critical Care Medicine, Am. Soc. Artificial Internal Organs, Soc. for Surgery of Alimentary Tract, Am. Assn. Surgery of Trauma, Ea. Assn. for Surgery of Trauma. Office: Duke Univ Med Ctr Dept Surgery Box 2837 Durham NC 27715-2601 Home Phone: 919-382-8208. E-mail: vasle001@mc.duke.edu. *

VASSILOPOULOU-SELLIN, RENA, researcher; b. Dec. 29, 1949; MD, Albert Einstein Coll. Medicine, 1974. Resident Montefiore Hosp., Bronx, 1974-77; fellow Northwestern U., Chgo., 1977-80; prof. Univ. Tex., Houston, 1980—. Fellow ACP, Am. Assn. Clin. Endocrinol.; mem. AAAS, AMA, Am. Soc. Bone and Mineral Rsch., Am. Diabetes Assn., Am. Soc. Clin. Oncology, Endo Soc. Office: Anderson Cancer Ctr 1515 Holcombe Blvd # 15 Houston TX 77030-4009

VASSILYADI, MICHAEL, pediatric neurosurgeon; b. Istanbul, Turkey, Nov. 25, 1961; s. Irakli and Cristal Vassilyadi; m. Anastasia Lyras, Aug. 23, 1986; children: Frank Photios, Christal, Anthony Irakli. BSc, McGill U., 1980—83, MSc, 1984—86, MD, CM, 1986—90. Diplomate Am. Bd. Pedait. Neurol. Surgery, Am. Bd. Neurol. Surgery. Med. staff Children's Hosp. of Ea. Ont., Ottawa, Canada, 1996—. Asst. prof. surgery U. of Ottawa, 1996—2003; assoc. prof. surgery and pediat. U. Ottawa, 2003—; investigator Children's Hosp. Ea. Ont. Rsch. Inst., Canada; mentor faculty medicine U. Ottawa, Spina Bifida & Hydrocephalus Assn. Ontario Med. Adv. Contbr. articles to profl. jours.; mem. editl. bd. Pediat. Neurosurgery. Ottawa chpt. dir. Think First Can. Recipient Matching Travel award, Children's Hosp. of Ea. Ont. Rsch. Inst., 1998, 2003—05, Best sci. posters, Neurol. Sciences of Que., 1995, Tchg. Skills Attainment award, Faculty of Medicine, U. Ottawa, 2007; Farquharson Rsch. scholarship, Med. Rsch. of Can., 1987, Dr. James Douglas Rsch. fellowship in Pathology, McGill U., 1985. Fellow: ACS, Am. Acad. Pediat., Royal Coll. Physicians and Surgeons Can.; mem.: Can. Neurol. Scis. Fedn., Can. Pediat. Neurosurgery Group, Am. Bd. Neurol. Surgery, Am. Bd. of Pediat. Neurol. Surgery, Can. Neurosurg. Soc., Am. Soc. Pediatric Neurosurgeons, Coll. Physicians and Surgeons Ont., Coll. des Medecins du Que., Can. Med. Assn., Am. Epilepsy Soc., Am. Assn. Neurol. Surgeons (pediat. neurol. surgery sect.), Ont. Med. Assn., Internat. Soc. Pediatric Neurosurgery, Congress Neurol. Surgeons (pediat. neurol. surgery sect.). Greek Orthodox. Achievements include research in pediatric neurosurgery. Office: Children's Hosp of Eastern Ontario 401 Smyth Rd Ottawa ON Canada K1H 8L1 Business E-Mail: vassilyadi@cheo.on.ca.

VASU, SULOCHANA PALLICKADAVIL, research scientist; b. Kollam, Apr. 25, 1953; BSc, Med. Coll., Trivandrum, 1978, MBBS; PGCBT&IH, Inst Immunohematology, Kerala U., Mumbai, 1995; PGCCC, Inst Immunohematology, Kerala U. Blood transfusion officer Sree Chitra Tirunal Inst. Med. Scis. & Tech., 1986—91, scientist d, 1991—96, scientist e, 1996—2001, scientist f, 2001—08, scientist g, 2008—. Mem.: Indian Soc. Blood Transfusion & Immunohematology. Avocations: reading, movies. Office: Med Coll Trivandrum Kerala 695011 India E-mail: pvs@sctimst.ac.in.

VATAKAS, LEANDROS CONSTANTINOS, ophthalmologist; b. Thessaloniki, Macedonia, Greece, June 29, 1942; s. Constantinos Leandros and Eve Nikolaos (Asimopoulou) V.; m. Victoria George Samaras, Dec. 14, 1968; children: Constantinos, Helen; m. Andriana Pipiliago Poulou, Dec. 15, 1999. MD, Aristotels U., Thessaloniki, Greece, 1968, diploma in ophthalmology, 1972. Asst. ophthalmology Hippokration Hosp., Thessaloniki, 1969-72, sr. registrar Eye Clinic, 1974-77; hon. registrar Moorfields Eye Hosp., London, 1972-73; rsch. fellow Inst. Ophthalmology, London, 1973-74; pvt. practice Thessaloniki, 1974—. Cons. eye dept. Sarafianos Gen. Clinic, Thessaloniki, 1977-90, eye dept. Galinos Gen. Clinic, Thessaloniki, 1990—; responsible for doctors Amnesty Internat., Thessaloniki, 1984-87; gen. sec. Pvt. Practice Doctors, Thessaloniki, 1985-87, Soc. Practising Ophthalmologists, Thessaloniki, 1980-83; responsible for Thessaloniki Experiment in Internat. Living, 1962-63; co-founder, joint-owner Irmos Art Galery, Thessaloniki, 1984—; founder, owner Protipo Ophthal. Thessaloniki's, Greece, 2002-. Translator, editor: T.S. Eliot - Collected Poems, 1994, Theatrical Works, 1998; producer 16 sci. films, 1970-77; contbr. numerous articles to profl. jours. Elected mem. City Coun., Thessaloniki, 1982-86; pres. 1st Sch. Com. Thessaloniki, 1987-92; gen. sec. Assn. Thessalonikean Students Aristotel's U., 1960-63; bd. dirs. Mcpl. Theatre Orgn. Thessaloniki, 1985-88. Recipient Hon. Diploma, Mayor and City Coun. Thessaloniki, 1988, Hon. Diploma and Medal, Mayor and City Coun., 1992. Fellow Royal Coll. Ophthalmologists (U.K.); mem. Greek Ophthal. Soc., Greek Soc. Cataract and Refractive Surgeons, Ophthal. Soc. No. Greece, N.Y. Acad. Scis., European Soc. Cataract and Refractive Surgeons, Panhellenic Ophthal. Soc., Bridge Club Thessaloniki, Mensa Internat. (spkr.). Liberal Democrat. Mem. Christian Orthodox Ch. Avocations: art, poetry, bridge, classical music, reading. Home: Lida-Maria Danai 2 57001 Thermi Thessaloniki Greece Office: Hermou Str 55 546 23 Thessaloniki Greece Office Phone: 0003 2310 265132, 302310265132. Personal E-mail: vatakas@perfectuision.gr.

VATER, YOURI L., medical educator; b. Riga, Latvia, Apr. 14, 1954; m. Hanna Vater; 1 child, Maxim; 1 child, Roman. MD, Riga Univ. Sch. of Medicine, Riga Latvia, 1977; PhD, U. Tartu, Estonia, 1988. Cert. sr. bd. anesthesia Israel, 1997. Rsch. fellow Riga Med. Sch., 1980—87, sr. rsch. fellow, 1987—90; dir. cardioanesthesiology dept. Heart Surgery Ctr. Sch. of Medicine Republic of Latvia, Riga, Latvia, 1980—90; residency anesthesia U. Tel Aviv Sackler Med. Ctr., Ichilov, 1990—97; assoc. prof., attending anesthesiologist U. Wash. Sch. of Medicine, Seattle, 1999—. Contbr. articles various profl. jours. Active participant Doctors for Democracy, Tel Aviv, Israel, 1995. Lt. Israeli Mil. Forces., 1995—2004, Israel. Mem.: Am. Soc. Transplantaion Anesthesiologists, Latvian Soc. Anesthesiologists, Am. Soc. Anesthesiologists, Israeli Soc. Anesthesiologists. Achievements include Art Show Promotions. Avocation: travel. Home: 11323- 24 th Ave NE Seattle WA 98125 Office: U Wash 1959 Pacific St POB 356540 Seattle WA 98105-6540 Home Phone: 206-367-3356; Office Phone: 206-598-4260. Personal E-mail: yvater@yahoo.com.

VATNER, STEPHEN F., physiologist, department chairman; m. Dorothy E. Vatner; children: Jonathan, Daniel, Ralph. BA, Grinnell Coll., Iowa, 1961; MD, NYU, NYC, 1965; MD (hon.), Kagawa U., Japan, 1992. Lic. cardiologist. Internship, residency U. Va., Charlottesville, 1966—67; postdoctoral fellow U. Wash., Seattle, 1969; asst. rsch. physiologist U. Calif., San Diego, 1969—70, asst. prof. medicine, 1971—72, Harvard Med. Sch., Boston, 1972—74; assoc. prof. medicine Peter Bent Brigham Hosp., Harvard Med. Sch., Boston, 1974—90; prof. medicine Harvard Med. Sch., 1990—97; prof., dir. cardiovasc. and pulmonary rsch. inst. Allegheny U. Health Scis., Pitts., 1997—99; dir. Weis Ctr. Rsch., Henry Hood Rsch. Program, Charles B. Degenstein Prof., Penn State Coll. Medicine, Danville, Pa., 1999—2000; prof. medicine, dir. Cardiovasc. Rsch. Inst., U. Medicine and Dentistry, New Jersey Med. Sch., Newark, 2000—01; chair, dept. cell biology and molecular medicine UMDNJ, New Jersey Med. Sch., Newark, 2001—. Vis. prof. U. Nebr., 1993. Editl. bd. mem.: Am. Jour. Physiology, 1979—81, 1985—90, bd. med. editors:, 1998; editor: (editor-in-chief) Circulation Rsch.; cons. editor: Jour. Molecular and Cellular Cardiology, 2000, mem. editl. bd.: Am. Jour. Physiology; contbr. manuscript publs. and articles to peer-reviewed jours. Recipient Hawthorne Lecture award, Howard U., 1990, Wiggers award, Am. Physiology Soc., 1995, Thomas L. O'Donohue Meml. Lecture in Neuropharmacology award, DC, 1997, Merit award, NIH; named Konrad Witzig Meml. Lectr., Cardiovasc. Sys. Dynamics Soc., 1996, Foaud A. Bashour Disting. Physiologist Lectr., U. Tex., 1996, J.R. Neely Lectr., Geisinger Clinic, 1997, Hon. Prof., Fourth Mil. Med. U., Xian, China, 1998; grantee Rsch. grants, NIH, 1997—2002, 2001—06. Fellow: Internat. Soc. Heart Rsch.; mem.: Am. Heart Assn. (exec., credentials, program and nominating coms. 1968, chmn. council on circulation, program com. 1982—85, co-dir., sci. sessions of councils on sci. and circ. 1986, vice-chmn., coun. on circulation 1988—90, chmn., coun. on circulation 1990—92, v.p. 1990—92, bd. dirs. 1997, chmn., nominating com., coun. on circulation 1997—99, co-dir. sci. sessions of councils on sci. and circ., Established Investigatorship award 1974—79, George E. Brown Lecture award 1986, Rsch. Achievement award, Disting. Achievement award), Circulation (editl. bd. mem. 1999), Circulation Rsch. (editor-in-chief 1991—99, consulting editor 1999), Hypertension (editl. bd. mem. 1983—89), Coun. on Circulation, AHA (assoc.), Am. Soc. Clin. Investigation (assoc.), Am. Fedn. Clin. Rsch. (assoc.), Am. Assn. Accreditation of Lab. Animal Care (assoc.; bd. trustees), Biophysical Soc. (assoc.), Am. Physiol. Soc. (assoc.), Am. Soc. Pharmacology and Exptl. Therapeutics (assoc.), Am. Assn. Physicians (assoc.), Soc. Exptl. Biology and Medicine (editl. bd. mem. 1981—87), Circulation Rsch. (editl. bd. mem. 1981—87). Office: UMDNJ PO Box 1709 185 So Orange Ave Ste G609 Newark NJ 07101-1709 Business E-Mail: vatnersf@umdnj.edu.

VAUGHAN, EDWIN DARRACOTT, JR., urologist, surgeon; b. Richmond, Va., May 13, 1939; s. Edwin Darracott and Blanche V. (Bashaw) V.; m. Virginia Anne Lloyd, June 30, 1962; children: Edwin Darracott III, Barbara Anderson. BS, Washington and Lee U., 1961, DSc, 1982; MD, U. Va., 1965, MS, 1969. Diplomate Am. Bd. Urology (trustee, v.p. 1988, pres. 1989). Intern Vanderbilt U., 1965—66, asst. resident, 1966—67; chief resident in urology U. Va., 1970—71, asst. prof. urology, 1973—75, assoc. prof., 1975—78, prof., 1978; clin. rsch. fellow Columbia U., 1971—72, rsch. assoc. dept. medicine, 1972—73; James J. Colt prof. urology, chmn. dept. urology Cornell U. Med. Coll., NYC; attending urologist-in-chief NY Hosp., NYC, 1978—2001; sr. assoc. dean clin. affairs Cornell U. Med. Coll., NYC, 1993—2001, chmn. dept. urology, 1993—2001, exec. vice dean sr. assoc. dean clin affairs, 2005—10, prof. emeritus urology, 2010. Chief med. officer Cornell Physician Orgn., 1997-2005; sci. adv. bd. Nat. Kidney Found., 1977-81; sec.-treas. Urology Coun., 1977-80, chmn., 1980-81; med. adv. bd. Coun. High Blood Pressure, 1977; acting co-chief exec. officer Columbia-Cornell Care, L.L.C., 1997; adv. coun. Nat. Diabetes and Digestive and Kidney Diseases, 2002-06; bd. Med. Ctr. Operating U. Va., 2002-. Editor: Seminars in Urology, 1983-95, Timely Topics in Urology, 2007; assoc. editor Investigative Urology, 1977-78, mem. editl. bd., 1978-94, assoc. editor, 2004; mem. editl. bd. Brit. Jour. Urology, 2004; editor Campbell's Urology; assoc. editor Brit. Jour. Urology, 2004, asst. editor, 2004—; editor-in-chief Timely Topics in Urology, 2007; contbr. articles to profl. jours. Mem. adv. coun. Nat. Diabetes and Digestive and Kidney Diseases, 2002—06; bd. visitors, chair med. ctr. oper. bd. U. Va., 2002—10. Recipient Rsch. Career Devel. award NIH, 1976-78, Russell and Mary Hugh Scott award Am. Found. Urol. Disease, 1998, J.K. Latimer award NY-NJ Kidney Found., 1999, Valentine medal NY Acad. Medicine, 2000, Maurice R. Greenberg Disting. Svc. award, 2002, Good Scout award, BSA, 2002, Presdl. award Soc. Basic Sci. Rsch., 2004, Walter Reed award U. Va. Med. Sch., John Latimer award, NY nat. Found., 2005, John C. Coleman Tchg. award, Dept. Urology, Weill-Cornell Med. Sch., 2008, Austrian Cross, Australian Govt., 2008, Raymon Guiteras award Am. Urol. Assn., 2011, Disting. Alumni award Washington & Lee U., 2011; NIH tng. grantee, 1967-68; USPHS grantee, 1971-77; Am. Heart Assn. grantee, 1976-79, Mem. ACS, AAAS, Internat. Soc. Urology, NY Acad. Scis., Soc. Univ. Urologists, Am. Urol. Assn. (hon., chmn. rsch. com. 1980-91, treas. NY sect. 1985, v.p. NY sect. 1986, pres. NY sect. 1987, bd. dirs. 1992-97, pres.-elect 2000, pres. 2001, immediate past pres. 2002, Golden Cystoscope award 1981, Disting. Contbn. award 1992, Hugh Hampton Young award 2000, Russell Lavengood award, NY sect., 2008), Urol. Soc. Australasia (hon.), Soc. Exptl. Biology and Medicine, Soc. Univ. Surgeons, Soc. Internat. Urology (chmn. bd. 1997—), Am. Found. Urol. Disease (pres. 1987-92, Presdl. Founder award 2004), NY Med. Surgical Soc. (pres. 2005), Soc. Basic Urol. Rsch. (Pres. award 2004), Nat. Kidney and Urol. Disease Adv. Bd. (dep. chmn.), Intersoc. for Kidney and Urol. Disease Rsch. (chmn. 1987), Am. Assn. Genito-Urinary Surgeons Coun.(pres. elect 2009, pres. 2011; Barringer medal 1993), Am. Surg. Assn., Brit. Assn. Urol. Surgeons (hon., St. Paul's medal), Japanese Urol. Soc. (hon.), Clin. Soc. Genitourinary Surgeons (pres. 2006), Sigma Chi (Significant Sig award 2000), Alpha Omega Alpha (award 1976), Omicron Delta Kappa (award 1981). Address: Anne & Darracott Vaughan Eaglestone 89 Hollow Creek Rd Sheridan WY 82801 Business E-Mail: evaughan@med.cornell.edu.

VAUGHAN, THERESE MICHELE, insurance educator; b. Blair, Nebr., June 12, 1956; d. Emmett John and Lonne Kay (Smith) V.; m. Robert Allen Carber, Aug. 15, 1993; children: Kevin Leo Vaughan-Carber, Thomas S. Vaughan-Carber. BBA, U. Iowa, 1979; PhD, U. Pa., 1985. CPCU. Asst. prof. Baruch Coll., CUNY, 1986-87; cons. Tillinghast, NYC, 1987-88; dir. ins. ctr. Drake U., Des Moines, 1988-94; ins. commr. State of Iowa, Des Moines, 1994—2004; Robb B. Kelley Disting. prof. ins. and actuarial sci. Drake U., 2005—. Bd. dirs. Endurance Splty. Holdings, Prin. Fin. Group, Nat. Coun Comp. Ins. Editor Jour. Ins. Regulation, 2005—; co-author: Fundamentals of Risk and Insurance, 1996, 99, 2003, 08, Essentials of Insurance: A Risk Management Approach, 1995, 2001; contbr. articles to profl. jours. S.S. Huebner fellow U. Pa., 1979-82; recipient Outstanding Young Alumnus award U. Iowa, 1996; named to Iowa Ins. Hall of Fame, 2003. Mem. Nat. Assn. Ins. Commrs. (pres. 2002, CEO), Ins. Marketplace Stds. Assn. (bd. dirs. 2004—), Am. Risk and Ins. Assn. (pres. 2008), Beta Gamma Sigma, Omicron Delta Epsilon. Avocations: hiking, biking, reading. Home: 4632 Elm St West Des Moines IA 50265-2993 Office: Drake Univ 2507 University Ave Des Moines IA 50311 Office Phone: 515-271-2830. Business E-Mail: terri.vaughan@drake.edu. *

VAUGHAN, WINSTON C., otolaryngologist, surgeon; b. Kingston, Jamaica, Sept. 2, 1964; BA in Biology with Honors, John Hopkins U., 1987; MD, Stanford Sch. Medicine, 1992. Cert. Calif., Ga. Composite State Bd. Med. Examiners, Otolaryngology. Intern, gen. surgery Stanford U. Med. Ctr. and Affiliates, 1992—93; resident, otolaryngology-head and neck surgery Stanford U. Med. Ctr., 1993—97, chief resident, dept. otolaryngology, 1997; fellow, rhinology and advanced sinus surgery Ga. Rhinology and Sinus Ctr., Savannah, Ga., 1997—98; fellow, staff surgeon Meml. Med. Ctr., St. Joseph's and Candler Hosp., Ga., 1997—98; dir., faculty. dept. otolaryngology-head and neck surgery Stanford Sinus Ctr., Stanford U. Sch. Medicine, 1998—2005; dir. Stanford Rhinology & Sinus Surgery Fellowship; dir., founder California Sinus Inst., E. Palo Alto and San Ramon, 2005—; mem., founder California Sinus Found., 2005—; otolaryngologist surgeon Stanford Hosp., Palo Alto Veterans Hosp., Lucille Packard Children's Hosp., Santa Clara Valley Med. Ctr. (Calif). Dir. Caribbean Endoscopic Sinus Surgery Course, 2000—; mem. otolaryngology resident edn. com. Stanford U. Sch. Medicine, 1998—2002, coord., resident cadaver dissections, 1999—2001, co-ord., annual otolaryngology symposium, 1999—2004, coord., endoscopic sinus surgery courses, 1999—2005; dir., scientific adv. bd., cons. Sinus Pharmacy, Santa Barbara, Calif., 2000—; cons. Bayer, Ortho-McNeil, Wallace, 1998—, GE Surgical Navigation (VTI, Boston, Mass.), 2000—, Sinus Pharma, Carpentaria, Calif., 2002—, BrainLab Surgical Navigation, 2002—04, Exploramed, 2004—; presenter in field. Reviewer Am. Jour. Rhinology, 2001—, Otolaryngology Head and Neck Surgery, 2002—; contbr. articles to profl. jours., chapters to books. Bd. trustee John Hopkins U., 1987—91; vol. physician Free Clinic, Meml. Med. Ctr., 1997—98; vol. doctor Calif. AIDS ride, San Francisco to LA, 2000, 2004. Fellow: Am. Bd. Otolaryngology-Head and Neck Surgery, Am. Rhinology Soc. (cons. 1999—2003, bd. dir. 2004—, chmn. edn. com. 2002—04); mem.: AMA, Am. Rhinologic Assn., Am. Laryngological, Rhinological and Otological Soc., Am. Acad. Otolaryngology-Head and Neck Surgery, Caribbean Assn. Otolaryngologists, Nat. Med. Assn., Calif. Med. Assn. Achievements include pioneering the development, use and research into nebulized medications for the management of difficult chronic sinus cases since 2000. *

VAUGHN, LISA DAWN, physician, educator; b. Ashland, Ky., May 10, 1961; d. Charles Clinton and Mildred Darlene (Cantrell) V. AS in Biology, U. Ky., 1981, BS in Zoology, 1983; DO, W.Va. Sch. Osteo. Medicine, 1988. Diplomate Nat. Osteo. Med. Bd., cert. Am. Assn. Med. Rev. officer, 1996. Gen. intern Doctors Hosp. Inc., Massillon, Ohio, 1988-89, family practice resident, 1989-91; emergency room physician Coastal Emergency Svcs., Snowpark, Ohio, 1989-90; urgent care physician Acute Care Specialists, Akron, Ohio, 1991; physician Portage Family Practice Clinic, North Canton, Ohio, 1991-95, First Care Family Health & Immediate Care Ctr., Canton, Ohio, 1995-95; dir. occupl. medicine First Care, Canton, 1996, med. dir. urgent care sys., 1996-97; physician Mercy Health Ctr. Jackson, Ohio, 1997—. Clin. asst. faculty Ohio U. Coll. Medicine, Athens, 1990-91, adj. clin. faculty, 1992—; asst. dir. family practice residency Ohio U. Coll.

Medicine-Doctors Hosp. Inc., Massillon, 1992-95; urgent CARE physician First Care, Canton, Ohio, 1995—; med. dir. family home health svc. Doctors Hosp., 1992-94, chmn. dept. family medicine, 1994-95; med. dir. Riczo and Co. Managed Care Orgn., 1997-2010; med. adv. to Canton City Schools, Med. Assisting Program; med. advisor Boy Scouts Med. Explorers, Massillon, 1989-90; med. career advisor Girl Scouts Career Day, Canton, 1990; affiliate physician Cleve. Clinic, 1991—; med. advisor Canton City Sch. Med. Assisting Program, 1997-2010. Contbr. poems. Col. Ky. Cols. Assn., Ashland, 1989—; vol. United Way of Stark County, 1990-91. Mem. Cleve. Clinic Found. (affiliate physician), AMA, Am. Coll. Osteo. Family Physicians, Am. Osteo. Assn. (cert.), Ohio State Med. Assn., W.Va. Soc. Osteo. Medicine, Sigma Sigma Phi (sec. 1985-86). Democrat. Avocations: writing, reading, history. Office: Statcare Jackson 7452 Fulton Dr NW Massillon OH 44646-9393

VAVALA, DOMENIC ANTHONY, medical research scientist, educator, retired military officer; b. Providence, Feb. 1, 1925; s. Salvatore and Maria (Grenci) V BA, Brown U., Providence, 1947; MS, U. RI, Kingston, 1950; MA, Trinity U., San Antonio, 1954; PhD Physiology, Accademia di Studi Superiori "Minerva", Italy, 1957; MEd, U. Houston, 1958; LittD, Univ. Internazionale Sveva "Frederick II", Bergamo, Italy, 1979; DSc (hon.), Nobile Accademia di Santa Teodora Imperatrice, Rome, 1966, DMS (hon.), 1970; DPH (hon.), Nobile Accademia di Santa Teodora Imperatrice, 1983; D Pedagogy (hon.), Studiorum Universitas Constantiniana of Sovrano Ordine Constantiniano di San Giorgio, Rome, 1966; EdD (hon.), Imperiale Accademia di San Cirillo, Pomezia, Italy, 1977; D Health Scis. (hon.), Johnson & Wales U., 1993; LLD (hon.), Fridericus II U., Capua, Italy, 1997; MD (hon.), Frederick II U., Providence, 1999. Cert. Yale U. Army Specialized Tng. Program, 1944. Asst. tumor rsch. U. R.I., also asst. entomol. rsch., 1950; rsch. asst. pharmacology Boston U. Sch. Medicine, 1950—51; commd. 2d lt. med. svc. USAF, 1951, advanced through grades to lt. col., 1968; rsch. team physiologist cold injury Army Med. Rsch. Lab., Osaka Army Hosp., Osaka, Japan, 1951—52; rschr. aviation physiologist USAF Sch. Aviation Medicine, Randolph AFB, Tex., 1952—54, 3605th USAF Hosp., Ellington AFB, Tex., 1955—57, chief physiol. tng., 1957; cons. aviation physiology, film prodn. dept. U. Houston, 1956; rschr. aviation physiologist, head acad. sect. dept. physiol. tng. Wilford Hall USAF Hosp., Lackland AFB, Tex., 1957—58; vis. prof. physiology Incarnate Word Coll., San Antonio, 1958; rschr. aviation physiologist, chief physiol. tng. comdr. 832d Physiol. Tng. Flight, 832d Tactical Hosp., Cannon AFB, N.Mex., 1958—64; adjunct prof. Ea. N.Mex. U., Portales, 1959—64; instr. adult edn. divsn. Clovis Mcpl. Schs., N.Mex., 1960; rschr. aviation physiologist, comdr. 15th Physiol. Tng. Flight, 824th USAF Dispensary, Kadena Air Base, Okinawa, 1965—66; rsch. scientist, directorate fgn. tech., aerospace med. divsn. Brooks AFB, Tex., 1966—68; chief R & D support and interface divsn., dep. dir. for fgn. tech., 1969—70; adj. instr. Johnson & Wales U., Providence, 1973—74; instr. humanities Johnson and Wales U., Providence, 1974—75, asst. prof. humanities, 1975—77, prof. health scis. and nutrition, 1977—93, prof. emeritus, 1993—, coord. biomed. and behavioral scis. Day Coll. divsn., 1973—75, psychology coord. vets. divsn. Coll. Continuing Edn., 1974—76, assoc. dean adj. faculty, 1975, dean faculty, 1975—77, coord. acad. devel., 1977—78, dir. mus. series, 1990—, curator Chapel Empress St. Theodora, 1992—; with Vet. Adminstrn. Med. Ctr., Providence. Pres. corp., chmn. bd. dir. Sovereign Constantinian Order of St. George, Inc., R.I., 1986—; pres. corp., chmn. bd. dir. The Noble Acad. of Empress St. Theodora of R.I., Inc., 1988—2008; instr. anatomy, physiology and med. terminology R.I. Hosp., Providence, 1987-90, rector & emeritus pres. The Constantinian U., 2010- Writer, prodr.: (TV Series) Your Body in Flight, Sta. KUHT, Houston, 1956; (TV series) Highway to Health, Okinawa, 1965; compiled and edited: Fifty Years of Progress of Soviet Medicine, 1917-67; abstractor, translator in medicine Chem. Abstracts Svc., Am. Chem. Soc., Ohio State U., 1963-74; editor: (Cath. parish newspaper) The Logos, Kadena Air Base, Okinawa, 1965-66 (1st pl. 5th Air Force chapel printed news contest); contbr. articles to profl. jours Pres. Holy Name Soc., Kadena Air Base, Okinawa, 1965-66; trustee, Gov. Ctr. Sch., Providence, 1979-85; mem. scholarship com. St. Sahag and, St. Mesrob Armenian Apostolic Ch., Providence; choir master, music dir. Cannon AFB, Cath. Parish, 1958-65; received in pvt. audience Pope John Paul II, 1997. Served with AUS, 1943-44 Recipient Disting. Svc. award Clovis Jaycees, 1959, Acad. Palms Gold medal Accademia Studi Superiori "Minerva", 1960, citation, chief chaplains USAF, 1970, commendation medal USAF, 1970, chief biomed. scientist insignia, biomed. scis. corps USAF Med. Svc., 1970, spl. faculty citation Johnson and Wales U., 1981, contbn. awd. doctoral program ednl. leadership Alan Feinstein Grad. Sch., Johnson and Wales U., Providence, 1999, academician divsn. scis. Accademia di Studi Superiori "Minerva", 1960; Min. Plenipotentiary for U.S. of Nobile Accademia di Santa Teodora Imperatrice, Rome, 1967, rector pro tempore, France, 1980, Achievement cert. Dept. Army Headquarters, US Army Ryukyu Islands, APO San Francisco, 1966; decorated knight grand officer Merit Class, Sovereign Constantinian Order St. George, Rome, 1969, Knight of Grand Cross with Constantinian neckchain, Justice Class, Sovereign Constantinian Order St. George, 1969, Knight of Grand Cross Justice Class, Order St. John of Jerusalem, Knights of Malta, Bari, Italy, 1984, Knight of Grand Cross Justice Class, Order St. John of Jerusalem, Knights of Cyprus, Rhodes and Malta, Bari, 1984, Knight of Grand Cordon Justice Class, Order Teutonic Knights, Sao Paulo, 1986, Knight of Grand Cross Justice Class, Mil. Order St. Gereon, Sao Paulo, 1986, Knight of Grand Cross Justice Class, Mil. and Hospitalier Order St Jean d'Acre and St. Thomas, Capua, Italy, 1987, Knight of Grand Cross Justice Class, Mil. and Hospitalier Order St. Mary of Bethlehem, Capua, 1987, Knight of Grand Cross Disting. Assoc. of Am. Soc., Italian Legions of Merit, Class of 2007; recipient Ednl. Professionalism award Domei Toastmasters Internat., 1965; named Magnificent Rector, The Constantinian U. (Studiorum Universitas Constantiniana), Italy, 1970, named Magnificent Rector and Pres. Emeritus, 2010 Marquis of Royal Throne of Swabia of Hohenstaufen Dynasty, Prince Jean von Schwaben, Bergamo, Italy, 1984, Duke of the New Rome, Constantinople, of Imperial Dynasty of Amorium by His Imperial Highness Prince Don Francesco Amoroso d'Aragona, Capua, 2000, Citizens Citation, Hon. Vincent A. Cianci Jr., Mayor City Providence, 1995, Spl. Citation, Johnson & Wales U., Alan Shawn Feinstein Grad. Sch., Sch. Edn., 2007; Nominee Nations Ten Outstanding Young Men awards, US Jr. CC, 1959 Fellow AAAS (emeritus, life), RSPH (emeritus), Tex. Acad. Sci.(life), Royal Soc. Health (London; emeritus), Royal Soc. Pub. Health (UK) (emeritus, 2009), Am. Inst. Chemists (emeritus); mem. Assn. Mil. Surgeons US (life), Nat. Assn. Doctors US (founder 1958, sec.-treas. 1958-85, editor-in-chief The NADUS Jour. 1963-68), Accademia di San Cirillo Italy (hon.), NY Acad. Scis., Phi Sigma, Kappa Delta Pi, Phi Kappa Phi, Alpha Beta Kappa (charter, pres. RI Alpha chpt. Johnson and Wales U. 1984-92, Vavala Nutrition award, Noble Acad. of Empress Saint Theodora award, Outstanding Culinary Fellow award), Acad. Europea for Econ. Cultural Rels. (acad. senate, medallion 2004), 1916 Soc. RI Found., Providence; Dir., Singing Chapel Prog., The Bridge at Cherry Hill Assisted Living Cmty. (dir. chapel svcs.), One Cherry Hill Rd., Johnston Rhode Island, Am. Legion, Disabled Am. Vets., Mil. Officers Assn. America. Personal E-mail: davavala@cox.net.

VAZIRI, NOSRATOLA DABIR, internist, nephrologist, educator; came to U.S., 1969, naturalized, 1977; s. Abbas and Tahera Vaziri. MD, Tehran U., Iran, 1966. Diplomate Am. Bd. Internal Medicine, Am. Bd. Nephrology; cert. hypertension specialist Am. Soc. Hypertension. Intern Cook County Hosp., Chgo., 1969-70; resident Berkshire Med. Ctr., Pittsfield, Mass., 1970-71, Wadsworth VA Med. Ctr., LA, 1971-72, UCLA Med. Ctr., 1972-74; prof. medicine U. Calif.-Irvine, 1979—, prof. physiology and biophysics, 2001—, prof. biol. scis., 2006—, chief nephrology and hypertension divsn., 1977—2011, dir. hemodialysis unit, 1977-94, vice chmn. dept. medicine, 1982-94, chmn. dept. medicine, 1994-98, chair faculty Coll. Medicine, 2000—02. Sr. assoc. editor: Jour. Spinal Cord Medicine, 1991-2005; mem. editl. bd. Kidney Internat., 2003—, Am. Jour. Nephrology, 1999-02, Nephron, 1999-02, Advancements in Renal Replacement Therapies, 1999-04, Internat. Jour. Artificial Organs, 1990—, Spinal Cord Medicine, 1991-2005, Jour. Renal Nutrition, 2006—11, Jour. Clin. Exptl. Hypertension, 2010-; contbr. articles to profl. jours. Mem. sci. adv. coun. Nat. Kidney Found., 1977—. Recipient Golden Apple award, U. Calif. Irvine Coll. Medicine, 1977, Lauds and Laurels award, U. Calif. Irvine Alumni Assn., 1999, Spirit Nephrology award, Nat. Kidney Found., 2002, Athalie Clarke's Outstanding Health Sci. Rschr. award, 2003, Presdl. Lectureship award, Can. Hypertension Soc., Disting. Svc. award, Western Assn. Physicians, 2007. Master: ACP (Laureate award 2010); fellow: Am. Heart Assn. (fellow coun. high blood pressure rsch.); mem.: Internat. Soc. Uremia Rsch. and Toxicity (councilor 2009—), Am. Soc. Hypertension, Internat. Soc. Nephrology, Assn. Profs. Medicine, Western Assn. Physicians (councilor 2003—05, pres. 2006—07), Am. Paraplegia Soc. (pres. 1992—94, Donald Munro award 2002), Am. Physiol. Soc., Am. Soc. Nephrology, Alpha Omega Alpha. Avocation: gardening. Home: 66 Balboa Cv Newport Beach CA 92663-3226 Office: U Calif Irvine Med Ctr Div Nephrology Dept Medicine 101 The City Dr Orange CA 92868-3201 Business E-Mail: ndvaziri@uci.edu.

VAZZANA, THOMAS, cardiologist, educator; Attended, St. Georges U., Grenada, 1985. Diplomate Am. Bd. Cardiology, Am. Bd. Cardiology-interventional cardiology, Am. Bd. Internal Medicine. Resident in internal medicine St. Joseph's Hosp. & Med. Ctr., Paterson, NJ, 1987—89; fellow in cardiovascular disease St. Vincent's Hosp. & Med. Ctr., SI, NY, 1989—91; asst. prof. medicine NY Med. Coll.; with Richmond Univ. Med. Ctr.; cardiologist SI Univ. Hosp. Office: Staten Island University Hospital 501 Seaview Ave Ste 200 Staten Island NY 10305 Office Phone: 718-663-6400. Office Fax: 718-663-6490.

VEARRIER, DAVID JAMES, toxicologist, educator; b. Mission Viejo, Calif., July 3, 1978; BA, U. Calif., Berkeley, 2000; MD, U. Calif., San Diego, 2005. Attending physician Abington Meml. Hosp., 2008—10; core faculty Albert Einstein Healthcare Network, 2010—11; asst. prof. Drexel U. Coll. Medicine, 2011—. Mem.: Am. Acad. Emergency Medicine, Am. Coll. Emergency Physicians, Am. Coll. Occupl. and Environ. Medicine, Am. Coll. Med. Toxicology, Am. Acad. Clin. Toxicology. Home: 530 S 2nd St Unit 824 Philadelphia PA 19147 Home Fax: 610-639-3191. Business E-Mail: david.vearrier@drexelmed.edu.

VEAZIE, PETER J., preventive medicine physician, educator; b. Seattle, July 18, 1963; PhD, U. Minn., 2003. Assoc. prof. U. Rochester, 2004—. Mem.: Soc. Med. Decision Making, Academy-Health. Office: University Rochester Dept Community and Preventive Medicine Rochester NY 14642-0644 Business E-Mail: peter_veazie@urmc.rochester.edu.

VEDDER, NICHOLAS BLAIR, plastic surgeon, educator; b. Chgo., Mar. 27, 1955; s. Beverly Blair and Geraldine (Bovbjerg) V.; m. susan Russell Heckbert, June 26, 1978; children: Katherine Anne, Nicholas Russell. BS with distinction in Biology, Stanford U., 1977; MD, Case Western Res. U., 1981. Diplomate Am. Bd. Surgery with added qualification in hand surgery, Am. Bd. Plastic Surgery, Nat. Bd. Med. Examiners; lic. physician, Wash., Mass. Resident in surgery U. Wash., Seattle, 1981-86, NIH rsch. fellow, 1986-88, hand surgery fellow, 1990-91, asst. prof. plastic surgery and orthop., 1991-95, assoc. prof. plastic surgery and orthop., 1995—, head divsn. plastic surgery Harborview Med. Ctr.; resident in plastic surgery Mass. Gen. Hosp., Boston, 1988-90. Attending surgeon U. Wash. Hosps., 1990—, Children's Hosp. and Med. Ctr., VA Med. Ctr.; lectr. in field; vis. prof. Johns Hopkins U., Balt., 1991, Nat. Heart and Lung Inst., London, 1991, So. Ill. U., 1991 Contbr. numerous articles to profl. jours., chpts. to books; referee Jour. Clin. Investigation, Am. rev. of Respiratory Diseases, Jour. Surg. Rsch., Jour. Pharmacology and Exptl. Therapeutics, Jour. of trauma, Plastic and Reconstructive Surgery, Annals of Plastic Surgery. Recipient Peter Gingrass award Plastic Surgery Rsch. Coun., 1995; ACS First Prize Nat. scholar, 1987; grantee NIH, 1988-89, 89-94, 91-92, 95—, Genentech, Inc., 1991-93, Biomembrante Inst., 1993-94, Cell Therapeutics, Inc., 1995-96, CDC, G.D. Searle, Inc., 1995-96. Fellow ACS; mem. AAAS, Henry N. Harkins Surg. Soc., N.W. Soc. Plastic Surgeons, Wash. Soc. Plastic Surgeons, seattle Surg. Soc., King County Med. Soc., Wash. Med. Soc., Assn. Acad. Chmn. Plastic Surgery, Am. assn. Hand Surgery, Assn. Acad. Surgery, Am. Soc. Plastic and Reconstructive Surgeons (Robert H. Ivy award 1994), Am. Soc. Surgery or the Hand, Plastic Surgery Ednl. Found., Sigma Xi. Office: Divsn Plastic Surgery Harborview Med Ctr Univ Wash Box 359796 325 Ninth Ave Seattle WA 98104-2499 Office Fax: 206-731-3656.

VEDHA HARI, B. N., medical educator; b. Thiruvallur, Tamil Nadu, India, July 5, 1981; B in Pharmacy, Dr. M. G. R. Med. U., Tamil Nadu, 2004; PharmM, Bharathidasn U., 2008. Asst. prof. SASTRA U., 2008—. Contbr. articles to profl. jours. Recipient Kavi Kurisil award, Thiruvaiyaru Tamil U., India, Painthamil Thilagam award, Kavi Thenii award, Tamil Nadu Naadaga Ilakkiaya Mandram Chennai, India, Swami Vivekananda award, Bharathi Vidhyalaya, Madurai, India. Mem.: India Pharmacist Assn. (life), Assn. Cmty. Pharmacist India (life), Assn. Pharm. Tchrs. India (life). Avocations: writing, reading, cricket, poetry. Office: SASTRA University Thirumalasamudram Thanjavur Tamil Nadu 613 401 India Business E-Mail: vedhahari@scbt.sastra.edu.

VEERASAMY, RAVICHANDRAN, pharmacist, educator; b. Pattukkottai, May 19, 1975; BS, K. M. Coll. Pharmacy, 1996; MPharm, Dr. Harisingh Gokr U. Sagar, Madhya Pradesh India, 1998; PhD in Pharm. Scis., Dr. Harisingh Gour U., Sagar, Madhya Pradesh, India, 2009. Asst. prof. Fathima Coll. Pharmacy, Kadayanallur, India, 1999—2001, KMCH Coll. Pharmacy, Coimbatore, India, 2001—05; rsch. scholar Dr. Harisingh Gour U., 2005—08; prof. Alshifa Coll. Pharmacy, Kerala, India, 2008—09; assoc. prof. Aimst U., Malaysia, 2009—. Contbr. articles to numerous sci. profl. jours. Jr. Rsch. fellowship, U. Grant Commn., New Delhi, Rsch. fellowship, All India Coun. Tech. Edn. Mem.: Indian Pharm. Assn. Office: Faculty Pharmacy Aimst University Semeling Kedah 08100 Malaysia E-mail: phravi75@rediffmail.com.

VEGA, WILLIAM A., psychiatrist, educator; b. LA; BA in sociology, U. Calif., Berkeley, MA, PhD in criminology, 1971. Prof. U. Calif. Berkeley Sch. Pub. Health, 1990—99; prof. psychiatry, Robert Wood Johnson Med. Sch. U. Medicine and Dentistry of NJ, rsch. dir. behavioral healthcare; prof. family medicine, David Geffen Med. Sch. UCLA, 2007—, co-founder, dir. Multicultural Rsch. Network on Health and Healthcare, founding dir., assoc. vice provost Luskin Ctr. Innovation, 2008—. Founding mem. WHO Internat. Consortium Psychiat. Epidemiology. Mem.: Inst. Medicine. Office: Luskin Ctr Innovation 2333 Murphy Hall Box 951405 Los Angeles CA 90095-1405

VEGA-BRICENO, LUIS ENRIQUE, pediatrician; b. Lima, Peru, Feb. 20, 1972; s. Luis E. Vega and Carmen L. Briceno. MD, Universidad Peruana Cayetano Heredia, Lima, Peru, 1998. Pediatric rschr. Pontificia Univ. Catolica De Chile, Santiago De Chile, 2003—. Editor: Chilean Pediatric Respiratory Jour. European Travel And Accomodation, European Respiratory Soc., 2003. Mem.: Chilean Pediatric Soc. (assoc.). Office: Pontificia Univ Catolica De Chile Lira 85 5th Fl 114-D Santiago Chile E-mail: levega@puc.cl.

VEGSO, GYULA, surgeon, oncologist; b. Budapest, Hungary, July 1, 1963; s. Gyula Vegso and Emilia Domotor; m. Maria Toth, July 25, 1998; children: Gergely, Balazs. MD, Semmelweis U. Budapest; PhD, Med. U., Budapest, 1988. Transplant surgeon Semmelweis U., 1993—. Mem.: Hungarian Transplantation Soc., Hungarian Oncological Soc., Hungarian Surg. Soc., European Assn. Cancer Rsch. Office: Semmelweis Univ Dept Transplant & Surg Baross St 23 Budapest 1082 Hungary Business E-Mail: vegso@trans.sote.hu, vegso.gyula@med.semmelweis-univ.hu.

VEIT, CLAIRICE GENE TIPTON, retired measurement psychologist; b. Monterey Park, Calif., Feb. 20, 1939; d. Albert Vern and Gene (Bunning) Tipton; children: Steven, Barbara, Laurette, Catherine. BA, UCLA, 1969, MA, 1970, PhD, 1974. Asst. prof. psychology Calif. State U., LA, 1975—77, assoc. prof. psychology, 1977—80; rsch. psychologist Rand Corp., Santa Monica, Calif., 1977—2004; ret., 2004. Rsch. cons. NATO Tech. Ctr., The Hague, The Netherlands, 1980-81; faculty Rand Grad Sch., Santa Monica, 1993—97. Mem. NOW, L.A. Opera League, Sierra Club. Achievements include development of subjective transfer function method to complex sys. analysis and the mental health inventory. Avocations: mountain climbing, playing piano, travel, music, theater. Personal E-mail: ctvest1@gmail.com.

VEIT, KENNETH, dean, educator; DO, Phila. Coll. Osteo. Medicine, 1976. Med. dir. So. Huntington Co. Med. Ctr., 1977—79; med. coord. Nat. Health Svc. Corp., Region III (USPHS), 1980—81; chief clin. consultation br. U.S. Pub. Health Svc., 1980—81; interim dean, asst. dean. gad. med. edn., dir. med. edn., chmn. divsn. cmty. medicine, dir. health care ctrs. Phila. Coll. Osteo. Medicine, provost, dean, sr. v.p. acad. affairs, 2002—. Lectr. in field; served numerous cmty. and govt. appts.; mem. several rev. bds. Recipient Humanitarian medal, USPHS, 1981. Office: Office of Dean Phila College Osteopathic Medicine 4170 City Ave Philadelphia PA 19131 *

VEIT, LINDA J., research scientist; b. Syracuse, NY, May 7, 1962; BS, LeMoyne Coll., 1984. Rsch. support specialist Upstate Med. U., 1985—93, clin. rsch. assoc., 1993—2010, project staff assoc. cancer ctr., 2010—. Clin. rsch. assoc. com. CALGB, 1998—2011. Mem.: Assn. on Clin. Rsch. Profls., Soc. Clin. Rsch. Profls. Office: 750 E Adams St Syracuse NY 13210 Business E-Mail: veitl@upstate.edu.

VEITH, FRANK J., vascular surgeon, researcher, educator; Cert. in gen. sugery 1961, in thoracic surgery 1968, in vascular surgery 1983. William J. von Liebig chmn. for vascular surgery Montefiore Med. Ctr., Bronx, NY, vice-chmn., prof. surgery, Albert Einstein Coll. Medicine, Bronx, NY. Ann. host VEITHsymposium. Contbr. more than 1,000 articles and chapters in profl. med. jours. and books.; serves on editl. bds. for four major vascular jours., editor-in-chief Vascular. Recipient Julius H. Jacobson, II, MD award for Physician Excellence, Vascular Disease Found., 2004. Mem.: Internat. Soc. for Vascular Surgery (founding sec.), Eastern Vascular Soc. (past pres.), Soc. for Vascular Surgery (past pres.). Considered role model in the field of vascular surgery; heading effort to have vascular surgery as a specialty board under the umbrella of the American Board of Specialties. Office: Cleveland Clinic 4455 Douglas Ave Ste 11E Bronx NY 10471 Business E-Mail: fjvmd@msn.com.

VEJAPHURTI, KHACHORN, obstetrician, gynecologist, nursing educator; s. Lamchuan and Sup Vejaphurti; m. Amata Ninsananda, Nov. 16, 1980; children: Chatchakarn, Acharee. MD, Mahidol U., Bangkok, 1967. Registered Mich. Ob-gyn. Hua Chiew Hosp., Bangkok, 1968—69, 1974—2004, chmn. ob-gyn. dept., 2000—02; trainee, 1969—74. Spl. lectr. faculty nursing Hua Chiew Chalerm Prakiat U., Bangkok, 1978—. Author: (travel and healthcare column) Thai Globe Trotter Mag., 1983—88, (health knowledge column) Hua Chiew Bull., 2002—05. Active Poh Tek Tung Found., Bangkok, 1974—2005; attendant World Fellowship Buddhist, World Buddhist U., Bangkok, 2000—, participant, 2000—; mem. Thai Med. Coun. Mem.: Thai Med. Coun., Siriraj Med. Sch. Alumni, Royal Thai Coll. Ob-gyn., Med. Assn. Thailand. Avocations: stamp collecting/philately, photography. Home: 18/1 Soi Charoenchai Ekamai Rd Bangkok 10110 Thailand Home Phone: 66023919039.

VELAZQUEZ MEDINA, LAURA EUGENIA, biomedical researcher; b. Mex. City, Mar. 9, 1965; d. Salvador Velazquez Arellano and Emma Flavia Medina Urbizu. BS in Biomed. (hon.), U. Nat. Autonoma Mex., Mex. City, 1990; M in Human Genetics, U. Paris 7, 1991, PhD in Human Genetics, 1994. Postdoc. rschr. Samuel Lunenfeld Rsch. Inst., Mt. Sinai Hosp., Toronto, Ont., Canada, 1995—2002, Inst. Cochin, Hosp. Cochin, Paris, 2002—03; sr. rschr. class I Ctr. Nat. Rsch. Sci., Paris, 2003—. Contbr. articles to profl. jours. Primary sch. tchg. vol. Missionaries Charity, Toronto, 1997—99. Fellowship, Med. Rsch. Coun., Can., 1995, Found. pour la Rsch. Med., France, 2002, Academic grant, Institut Nat. Sante Rsch. Med., 2003. Mem.: European Mast Cell and Basophil Rsch. Network, Internat. Cytokine Soc. Achievements include research in identification of the tyrosine kinase protein Tyk2 in the Interferon alpha signaling pathway in immune cells; role of the adaptor protein LNK in early hematopoiesis through analysis of an animal model; identification of the important function of the adaptor LNK in the migration of primary hematopoietic cells; functional role of the adaptor LNK in human myeloproliferative disorders. Avocations: swimming, tennis, travel, dance. Office: UMR U978 Inserm/ University Paris 13 74 rue Marcel Cachin Bobigny Ile-de-France 93017 France Business E-Mail: laura.velazquez@inserm.fr.

VELCEK, FRANCISCA, pediatric surgery, educator; Grad., U. Philippines, 1966. Diplomate Am. Bd. Surgery, Am. Bd. Surgery-pediatric surgery. Intern Saint Clare's Hosp. Ctr., 1967, resident, 1971; fellow Kings County Hosp.; prof. surgery State Univ. of NY Health Sci. Ctr.; with Lenox Hill Hosp., Univ. Hosp. of Bklyn. Office: Lenox Hill Hospital 965 Fifth Ave New York NY 10075 Office Phone: 212-744-9396. Office Fax: 212-879-1910.

VELCULESCU, VICTOR E., oncologist, educator; MD in Medicine, Johns Hopkins U., Balt., PhD in Human Genetics and Molecular Biology. Postdoctoral fellow Sidney Kimmel Comprehensive Cancer Ctr. at Johns Hopkins, Balt.; assoc. prof. oncology, dir. cancer genetics Ludwig Cancer Ctr. at Johns Hopkins, Balt. Contbr. articles to profl. jours. Named one of Brilliant 10, Popular Sci. mag., 2003. Office: 1650 Orleans St Rm 5M05 Baltimore MD 21231 Office Phone: 410-955-8878. E-mail: velculescu@jhmi.edu.

VELEZ, INES, oral pathologist, educator; b. Bogota, Colombia, Apr. 15, 1946; arrived in US, 1999; d. Jose and Emilia (Marulanda) Velez; m. Eduardo Tamara (div.); children: Luis Tamara, Clara Lucia Tamara; m. Guillermo Torres, Mar. 30, 1992. DDS, Colombian Coll. Odontology, 1979; postgrad., U. Fla., 1982—84; MEd, U. Los Andes, 1989; M in Laser Dentistry, Acad. Laser Dentistry, 1997. Cert. tchr. Fla. Chair., prof. pathology Colombian Coll. Odontology, 1984—92, pres. asst., 1989—92, dir. biopsy svc., 1984—95; chair, prof., dir. biopsy svc. Columbian Sch. Medicine, 1991—98, dir. bioclinical area, 1997—98; asst. prof. to assoc. prof., dir. oral and maxillofacial pathology, dir. biopsy svc. Nova Southeastern U., Ft. Lauderdale, Fla., 2000—. Lectr. in field. Contbr. articles to profl. jours. Recipient Best Student award, Coll. Sans Facon, 1963, Colombian Coll. Odontology, 1979, Educator award, Fla. Dental Assn., 2003, Golden Apple award, Nova Southeastern U., 2003, Ctr. of Excellence award, 2004. Mem.: ADA, Broward County Dental Assn., Fla. Dental Assn., Pierre Fouchard Acad., Acad. Laser Dentistry, Columbian Acad. Oral Pathology (founder), Am. Acad. Oral and Maxillofacial Pathology, Omicron Kappa Upsilon. Home: 3524 Parkside Dr Davie FL 33328 Office: Nova Southeastern U 3200 S University Dr Fort Lauderdale FL 33328 Home Phone: 954-262-7382; Office Phone: 954-472-7810. Business E-Mail: ivelez@nova.edu.

VELISSARIOU, IOANNA MICHAEL, pediatrician, researcher; b. Athens, Greece, Oct. 21, 1974; d. Michael George Velissarios and Evangelia-Ypakoi John Velissariou; m. Vasilios George Kosmas, June 20, 2003; 1 child, Francesca Vasilis Kosmas. MD with honors, U. Athens, PhD in Pediats. with honors, 2006. Diplomate U. Thessaly, 1998. House officer internal medicine, gen. surgery, obstetrics and gen. pediats. Gen. Hosp. Larissa, Greece, 1997—98; sr. house office in gen. medicine Gen. Hosp. Karystos, Greece, 1998—2000; sr. house officer in gen. pediats. Fairfield Gen. Hosp., Bury, Manchester, England, 2000—01; sr. house officer in neonatology New Cross Hosp., Wolverhampton, England, 2001—02; sr. house officer in pediat. accident and emergency Birmingham Children's Hosp., England, 2002—03; sr. house office pediat. hematology/oncology, 2003—04; academic assoc. P and A Kyriakou Children's Hosp., U. Athens, 2003—; specialist registrar in paediatric intensive care unit Athens Med. Ctr., 2003—, Mitera Maternity Hosp., Athens, 2006—. Mem.: Royal Coll. Paediatrics and Child Care. Achievements include research in pediatric chronic cough and asthma. Home: Amfitritis 3 175 61 Palio Faliro Athens Greece Home Phone: 00306944863635; Office Phone: 00306944863635. Personal E-mail: jane_vel@hotmail.com.

VELLA, VENANZIO, epidemiologist, health economist and planner; b. Tripoli, Libya, Sept. 17, 1954; s. Natale Vella and Italia Buia; m. Alessandra Pirozzi, Sept. 10, 1996. MD, U. La Sapienza, Rome, 1978, degree in Pediat., 1981; MS in Epidemiology, London Sch. Hygiene, 1982, PhD, 1990; MS in Health Econs., U. York, England, 2000. Cert. Italian Med. Assn., 1978. Assoc. expert WHO, Geneva, 1984—86; primary health care officer UNICEF, Kampala, Uganda, 1986—89; pub. health specialist The World Bank, Washington,

1992—99; epidemiologist, health economist Italian Cooperation, Pietermaritzburg, KwaZulu-Natal, South Africa, 2001—08, health info. sys. cons. Fed. Ministry Health Addis Ababa, Ethiopia, 2009—. Knight fellow, U. London, 1981—83. Mem.: Italian Med. Assn. Personal E-mail: thevellas@yahoo.it.

VELLAICHAMY, GANESAN, chemist; b. Eriyodu, Tamil Nadu, India, Feb. 23, 1972; PhD in Chemistry, 2001. Rschr. Banaras Hindu U., 2004—. Office: Dept Chemistry Sci Faculty Varanasi Uttar Pradesh 221005 India Personal E-mail: velganesh@yahoo.com.

VELT, PAUL MARK, radiologist; s. Irwin and Beulah Velt; m. Lynn Pugan, Feb. 4, 1979; children: Jennifer, Eric. MD, U. of Brussels, 1971—79. Cert. Radiologist Am. Bd. Radiology, 1985, Cert. of Added Qualification Am. Bd. Radiology, 1999. Assoc. radiologist Braff Associates, Clifton Springs, NY, 1985—97, Monroe Radiology, Rochester, NY, 1997—99, The Ide Group, Rochester, 1999—2001; chief of radiology Suncoast Imaging Ptnrs., Spring Hill, Fla., 2002—. Mem.: AMA, Soc. Breast Imaging, Soc. Invasive Radiology, Am. Coll. Radiology. Office: SunCoast Imaging Ptnrs 3959 Van Dyke Rd#188 Lutz FL 33558

VELUPILLAI, YOGA NATHAN, medical educator; s. Parimalam Ponnampalam; 3 children. MBBS, Karnatak U., India, 1973; MPH, Glasgow U., Scotland, 1997, PhD, 2001. House officer Dist. Civil Hosp., Belgaum, India, 1974—75, Gen. Hosp., Johore Bahru, Malaysia, 1976, sr. house officer Malacca, Malaysia, 1977—81; gen. practitioner Pvt. Practice, Malacca, 1982—83, Klang, Malaysia, 1984—89; gp trainer Med. Aid Palestinians, Beirut, 1990—95, Tyre, Lebanon, 1990—95; rschr. Pub. Health Dept., Glasgow, 1997—2000; pub. facilitator Glasgow Med. Sch., 1998—2007; r & d mgr. Argyll & Clyde Health Bd., Paisley, Scotland, 2000—04; pub. health programme mgr. Glasgow Ctr. Population Health, 2005—08; hon. clin. tchr., divsn. cmty. based scis. U. Glasgow, 2006—; lectr. Epidemiology & Pub. Health Dept., Cork, Ireland, 2008—; tutor Limerick Med. Sch., Ireland, 2008—. Contbr. articles to profl. jours. Mem.: Soc. Social Medicine (UK), Faculty Pub. Health (hon.).

VEMULPAD, SUBRAMANYAM RAMACHANDRA, microbiologist, educator; b. Anantapur, India, Feb. 11, 1956; arrived in Australia, 1994; s. Ramachandra and Sitalakshmi (Devarakonda) V.; m. Chandrika Narsapura, Aug. 15, 1986; 1 child, Anirudh. BSc, Nat. Coll., Bangalore, India, 1973; MSc, Jawaharlal Inst. Med. Edn., Pondicherry, India, 1976; PhD, Maulana Azad Med. Coll., Delhi, India, 1982. Demonstrator MA Med. Coll., Delhi, 1977-82; R&D scientist Anil Starch Products Ltd., Ahmedabad, India, 1983-84; sr. rsch. officer Indian Coun. Med. Rsch., Bhubaneswar, India, 1984-90, asst. dir., 1990-94; sr. lectr. Coll. Medicine, Blantyre, Malawi, 1994-95, assoc. prof., 1995-96; pub. health officer Western Sydney Pub. Health Unit, 1996-99; project officer South Western Sydney Pub. Health Unit, 1999—2000; assoc. prof. faculty sci. Macquarie U., Sydney, 2000—. Head divsn. microbiology Indian Coun. Med. Rsch., Bhubaneswar, 1984-94; mem. HIV/AIDS Tech. Adv. Com., Govt. Orissa, India, 1992-94; head dept. microbiology Coll. Medicine, Blantyre, 1994-96. Mem. Australian Soc. Microbiology, Assn. Microbiologists India (life), Indian Assn. Med. Microbiologists (life). Hindu. Avocations: indian classical music, travel, homeopathy. Home: 105 Ballandella Rd Toongabbie NSW 2146 Australia Office: Macquarie University Faculty Sci Bldg E7a Rm 226 Herring Rd 2109 Sydney NSW Australia Office Phone: 612-9850 9385. Business E-Mail: subramanyam.vemulpad@mq.edu.au.

VENEMAN, ANN MARGARET, former international organization official, former United States Secretary of Agriculture; b. Modesto, Calif., June 29, 1949; d. John G. and Nita D. (Bomberger) Veneman. BA in Polit. Sci., U. Calif., Davis, 1970; MA in Pub. Policy, U. Calif., Berkeley, 1971; JD, U. Calif. Hastings Coll. Law, San Francisco, 1976; D (hon.), Calif. Poly. State U., San Luis Obispo, 2001, Lincoln U., Mo., 2003, Del. Dtate U., 2004, Middlebury Coll., Vt., 2006. Bar: Calif. 1976, US Supreme Ct. 1981. Staff atty. gen. counsel's office Bay Area Rapid Transit Dist., Oakland, Calif., 1976-78; dep. pub. defender Stanislaus County, Modesto, 1978-80; assoc., then ptnr. Damrell, Damrell & Nelson, Modesto, 1980-86; assoc. adminstr. Fgn. Agrl. Svc., USDA, Washington, 1986—89, dep. under sec. for internat. affairs & commodity programs, 1989-91, dep. sec., 1991-93, sec., 2001—05; atty. Patton, Boggs & Blow LLP, Washington, 1993—95; sec. Calif. Dept. Food & Agr., 1995—99; atty. Nossaman LLP, Sacramento, 1999—2001; exec. dir. UNICEF, 2005—10. Bd. dirs. Close Up Found., Malaria No More, NYC, 2006—, Alexion Pharmaceuticals, Inc., 2010—. Recipient Cal Aggie Alumni Citation for Excellence, 1995, Nat. Farm-City Week award, Kiwanis Club Greater Modesto, 1995, Outstanding Woman in Internat. Trade award, 2001, Outstanding Alumna of Yr. award, U. Calif. Davis, 2001, Food Rsch. & Action Ctr. award, 2001, Nat. 4-H Alumni Recognition award, 2002, Dutch Am. Heritage award, 2002, Statesman of Yr. award, Jr. Statesman Found., 2002, United Fresh Fruit & Vegetable Disting. Svc. award, 2002, Golden State award, Calif. Coun. Internat. Trade, 2002, John Chafee award for Disting. Pub. Svc., Rep. Main St. Partnership, 2004; named Calif. Agriculturalist of Yr., 2003; named one of The 100 Most Powerful Women, Forbes mag., 2009. Mem.: US Afghan Women's Coun. (hon.), Sigma Alpha (hon.).

VENIER, ANTONIO, medical educator; b. Siena, Italy, Dec. 4, 1942; Degree, U. Sacred Heart Rome, 1970. Prof. U. Sacred Heart Rome, 1980—. Office: Largo Gemelli 8 Rome 00168 Italy Business E-Mail: antonio.venier@rm.unicatt.it.

VENKATACHALAM, SANKAR, anatomist, educator; b. Thiruthuraipoondi, Tamil Nadu, India, May 2, 1971; MSc in Anatomy, U. Madras, 1994, PhD, 2000. Asst. prof., anatomy U. Madras, 2000—. Postdoc. rsch. assoc. Rutgers U. Mem.: Assn. Anatomists (Tamil Nadu), Anat. Soc. India, Internat. Placenta Stem Cell Soc. Office: Dept Anatomy University Madras Chennai Tamil Nadu 600113 India Personal E-mail: venkatsankar@yahoo.com.

VENKATARAMAN, ANANTHARAMAN, emergency physician, educator; b. Singapore, Oct. 2, 1951; MBBS, U. Singapore, 1975. Sr. cons. Singapore Gen. Hosp., 1994—; clin. prof. Nat. U. Singapore, 2004—. Chmn. Splty. Tng. Com. Emergency Medicine, 1990—2009, Emergency Medicine Svcs. Com., Ministry of Health, Singapore,

1994—2008, Med. Adv. Com., Ministry of Home Affairs, Singapore, 1997—2010, Nat. Resuscitation Coun., Singapore, 2007—11; founder pres. Asian Soc. Emergency Medicine, 1998—2001. Recipient Pub. Svc. medal, Nat. Day Honors award, Singapore, 2009, Best Tutor award, Nat. U. Singapore Med. Soc., 2010. Fellow: RCP (Edinburgh), RCS (Edinburgh), Internat. Fedn. Emergency Medicine; mem.: Singapore Med. Assn., Soc. Emergency Medicine Singapore. Avocations: reading, walking. Office: Dept Emergency Medicine Singapore Outram Rd Singapore 169608 Singapore Office Fax: 6562260294. Business E-Mail: ananthararaman@sgh.com.sg.

VENKATARAMAN, RAMASWAMY, chemist, educator; b. Tirunelveli, Tamil Nadu, India, May 31, 1962; s. Ramaswamy Iyer Nettur Venkataraman and Ruckmani Rajagopala Iyer. BSc, Sri Paramakalyani Coll., Alwarkurichi, India, 1982; MSc, Ayya Nadar Janaki Ammal Coll., Sivakasi, India, 1984; PhD, Manonmaniam Sundaranar U., Tirunelveli, 2000; postgrad in Herbal Medicine, Manonmaniam Sundaranar U. R&D chemist Kothari Phytochems., Nagari, Madurai, India, 1985; lectr. Sri Paramakalyani Coll., Alwarkurichi, 1985—2000, reader, 2000—. Prin. investigator UGC Minor Rsch. Project, Alwarkurichi, 1997—99; co-investigator DST; reviwer RASAYAN, Jour. Pharmacy Rsch. Contbr. articles to profl. jours. Treas. Sri Paramakalyani Coll. Alumni Assn.; sec. Sri Paramakalyani Coll. Staff & Student's Coop. Stores. Mem.: Madurai Kamaraj-Manonmaniam Sundaranar U. Tcrhs. Assn. (zonal exec. 1988—). Achievements include research in isolation and characterization of new organic compound, furofuran type, from medicinal plant, ecbolium linneanum kurz, traditionally used for jaundice. Avocation: music. Office: Sri Paramakalyani Coll Alwarkurichi Sivasailam Rd Tirunelveli 627412 India Personal E-mail: rvraman3@rediffmail.com.

VENKATA RAMANA MURTHY, KUSUMA, urologist; b. Rajahmundry, India, May 5, 1976; MS, Post Grad. Inst. Med. Edn. and Rsch., 2003; MCh, Osmania Med. Coll., 2009. Sr. resident Post Grad. Inst. Med. Scis., 2003—04, Nizams Inst. Med. Scis., 2005—06; higher splty. trainee Osmania Med. Coll., 2006—09; jr. cons. Hyderabad Inst. Med. Scis., 2009—10; cons. urologist Kamineni Inst. Med. Scis., 2010—. Contbr. articles to profl. jours. Named Best Citizen of India, Indian Internat. Friendship Soc. Fellow: RCS (Edinburgh); mem.: Assn. Surgeons India, Urol. Soc. India. Avocation: guitar. Home: D/N: 2-23-39 Sector 6 MVP Colony Visakhapatnam Andhra Pradesh 530017 India Personal E-mail: murthy.kusuma@rediffmail.com.

VENKATESH, PRADEEP, ophthalmologist, educator; s. Venkatesh Suryanarayana Rao and Leelavathi Venkatesh; m. Geetha Srinivasan, Feb. 19, 1999; 1 child, Raghavi P. Rao Chinnu. MBBS, Bangalore Med. Coll., 1991; MD in Ophthalmology, All India Inst. Med. Sci., New Delhi, 1994. Diplomate in ophthalmology Nat. Bd. Examinations, New Delhi, 1997. Sr. resident vitreo-retina AIIMS, New Delhi, 1998; asst. prof. Dr. RP Centre, AIIMS, New Delhi, 2000—. Co-investigator numerous clin. studies. Author: (textbook) Fluorescein Angiography- A User's Manual, Step by Step Optical Coherence Tomography, Step by Step Fluorescein and Indocyanine Green Angiography. Recipient Prof. Narsing A. Rao prize, Uveitis Soc. India, 2004. Mem.: European Vitreo-Retinal Soc., Uveitis Soc. India, Vitreoretinal Soc. India, All India Ophthal. Soc. (life). Hindu. Achievements include development of new technique of giving subtenon injection. Avocations: music, ping pong/table tennis, hockey, walking. Office: All India Inst Med Scis Dr RP Centre Ansari Nagar New Delhi 110029 India Home: E-8 Khel Gaon Marg 110 049 New Delhi India Office Fax: 91-11-26862663. Personal E-mail: venkyprao@yahoo.com.

VENKATESH, YELDUR PADMANABHA, biochemist, immunologist; b. Kalale, Karnataka, India, Dec. 2, 1953; arrived in U.S., 1981; s. Padmanabha and Anasuya (Bai) Rao; m. Poornima Venkatesh, June 26, 1981; 1 child, Madhava. BS in Chemistry, Bangalore U., India, 1970; MS in Biochemistry, U. Mysore, 1974; PhD in Biochemistry, Indian Inst. Sci., Bangalore, 1981. Lectr. biochemistry Kasturaba Med. Coll., Manipal, India, 1974-75; postdoctoral fellow Washington U. Sch. Medicine, St. Louis, 1981-83, NIH trainee in immunology, 1984-85; rsch. assoc. Smith Kline & French Labs., King of Prussia, Pa., 1985-87; rsch. scientist ImmunoGen, Inc., Cambridge, Mass., 1987-92, sr. rsch. scientist, 1992-95; scientist fellow Ctrl. Food Technol. Rsch. Inst., Mysore, India, 1996-97, scientist, 1997—2002, sr. scientist, 2002—06, prin. scientist, 2006—11, sr. prin. scientist, 2011—. Overseas assoc. Govt. of India Dept. of Biotechnology Fla. State U., Tallahassee, 2002—03; editl. bd. mem. TANG & Case Reports Allergy. Contbr. articles to profl. jours. in biochemistry, immunology and allergology. Recipient CFTRI Found. Day award, 2005; Rsch. fellow, Univ. Grants Commn., 1975—79, Nat. Rsch. Svc. fellow, NIH, 1984—85. Fellow: Indian Acad. Allergy, Indian Coll. Allergy, Asthma and Applied Immunology; mem.: Bd. Studies Biosci., U. Mysore, Indian Immunology Soc., Assn. Food Scientists and Technologists (India), Soc. Biol. Chemists (India) (Prof. P. B. Rama Rao Meml. award 2009), Indian Inst. Sci. Alumni Assn. Hindu. Achievements include research in protein structure-function relationships in bovine pancreatic ribonuclease A, human complement protein C3, ricin, blocked ricin, and monoclonal antibodies; development of affinity chromatography media for separation of biologicals; novel cross-linkers for the preparation of antibody heteroconjugates, protocols for removal of toxic contaminants and minimizing aggregation in the proprietary toxin (blocked ricin) and immunotoxins; influence of chemical deglycosylation on the biological properties of blocked ricin; first demonstration that a single amino acid substitution affects the kinetics of protein folding in ribonuclease A; evidence for third galactose binding site in ricin B-chain, chemistry and biology of food allergens; mannitol in pomegranate and mushroom; 21 kD allergen (thaumatin-like protein) in sapodilla; horsegram lectin (Dol b Agglutinin); 60-71 kD allergens (polyphenol oxidase) in eggplant; almond profilin (Pru du 4), identification of polyphenol oxidase as a multigene family in eggplant; generation of antibodies to haptens (mannitol, erythritol, xylitol, and ribitol) for devel. immunoassays for specific sugar alcohols; role of lectins (potato, banana, garlic and horsegram) in non-allergic food hypersensitivity; non-specific activation of basophils/mast cells by dietary lectins; protein and polysaccharide; immunomodulators from plant sources (garlic, onion, guduchi, herbs and spices). Office: CFTRI Dept Biochem & Nutrition Mysore 570

020 India Home: 95 1st B Cross New Kantharaja Urs Rd Nivedithanagar Mysore 570022 India Home Phone: 91-821-2546991; Office Phone: 91-821-2514876. Personal E-mail: venkatyp@yahoo.com. Business E-Mail: ypv@cftri.res.in.

VENKATESWARAN, GOVINDARAJALU, biotechnologist; b. Chennai, Mar. 13, 1959; PhD, Mysore U., 1999; MPhil, Bharathiyar U., 1984. Asst. prof., head dept. Erode Arts & Sci. Coll., Erode, 1982—84; rsch. assoc. Sugarcane Breeding Inst., Coimbatore, 1984—86; sr. scientist Ctrl. Food Technol. Rsch. Inst., Mysore, Karnataka, India, 1986—, rsch. supr., 1986—2011. Named one of Best Biotechnologists, ABI, US. Mem.: Indian Yeast Group, Soc. Biol. Chemists (India), Assn. Microbiologists India, AFST (Mysore). Avocations: music, photography. Office: Ctrl Food Technological Rsch Inst Mysore Karnataka 570 020 India Office Fax: 91 821 2517233. Personal E-mail: venkatcftri@gmail.com.

VENKATIAH, JAYANTHI, medical educator; b. Bangalore, India, Mar. 13, 1969; MBBS, KIMS, Bangalore, 1991; MS, KIMS, Hubli, 1997. Assoc. prof., asst. prof., lectr. M. S. Ramaiah Med. Coll., 1997—2009; prof., head Vydehi Inst. Med. Scis., 2009—11, Saptagiri Inst. Med. Scis. and Rsch. Ctr., 2010—. Editor in chief Anatomica Karnataka Jour., 2009—11. FAIMER fellowship, Advanced Internat. Med. Edn. Mem.: Saptagiri Inst. Med. Edn. Avocations: singing, flower arranging. Office: 16 Chikkasandra Hessargatta Main Rd Bangalore Karnataka 560090 India Personal E-mail: drjayanthi_anatomy@yahoo.com.

VENTENILLA, AURORA CURAMEN, psychiatrist; b. San Jose, The Philippines, Nov. 7, 1939; came to U.S., 1968; d. Tereso and Petra (Patricio) Curamen; m. Doroteo Olba Ventenilla, Oct. 22, 1966; children: Anna, Enrique. MD, Manila Ctrl. U., 1963. Diplomate Am. Bd. Psychiatry and Neurology. Staff psychiatrist Cleve. VA Med. Ctr., 1974—96; contract psychiatrist COMPHEALTH, Salt Lake City, 1996—; staff psychiatrist Windsor Hosp., Chagrin Falls, Ohio, 1999—2001, Fremont (Ohio) Meml. Hosp., 2000—, Ctr. for Families and Children, Parma, Ohio, 1999—. Chief of psychiatry 256 Gen. Hosp. U.S. Army Res., Parma, Ohio, 1986-92. Lt. col. U.S. Army Res., 1982-92. Decorated Army Commendation medal Operation Desert Storm, 1991. Mem. Am. Profl. Practice Assn., Assn. Philippine Physicians in Am., Assn. Philippine Physicians in Ohio. Home: 9826 Tamarack Trl Brecksville OH 44141-4109

VENTER, J. CRAIG (JOHN CRAIG VENTER, CRAIG VENTER), science foundation director, geneticist; b. Salt Lake City, Oct. 14, 1946; m. Claire Fraser, 1981 (div. 2005). BS in Biochemistry, U. Calif., San Diego, 1972, PhD in Physiology and Pharmacology, 1975; D (hon.), Ariz. State U., 2007. Prof. SUNY, Buffalo; with Roswell Pk. Meml. Inst.; sect. and lab chief Nat. Inst. Neurol. Disorders and Stroke NIH, Bethesda, Md., 1984—92; co-founder, chair, chief scientist The Inst. for Genomic Rsch., 1992—98; co-founder, CEO, pres., chief sci. officer Celera Genomics Corp., Rockville, Md., 1998—2002; chmn. sci. adv. bd. Applera Corp., Norwalk, Conn.; chmn., co-founder, pres. The J. Craig Venter Sci. Found. Joint Tech. Ctr., 2003—, J. Craig Vetner Inst.; co-founder, pres. Ctr. for the Advancement Genomics, 2003—, Inst. for Biol. Energy Alternatives, 2003—. Bd. dirs. High Tech. Coun. Md.; mem. sci. adv. bd. ValiGene; chmn., bd. trustees The Inst. for Genomic Rsch. Contbr. several articles to profl. jours.; author: A Life Decoded, My Genome: My Life, 2007. Served in USN, 1967—68, South Vietnam. Recipient Beckman award, 1999, Chiron Corp. Biotech. Rsch. award, 1999, King Faisal Internat. award for sci., 2000, Taylor Internat. prize in medicine, Robarts Rsch. Inst., 2001, Gairdner Found. Internat. award, 2002, Indsl. Application of Sci. award, NAS, 2002, Eni award for rsch. & environment, 2008, Nat. Medal Sci., NSF, 2009; named one of The 100 Most Influential People in the World, TIME mag., 2007, 2008, 10 People Who Mattered, Newsweek, 2008, The 100 Agents of Change, Rolling Stone mag., 2009. Fellow: Am. Soc. Microbiology, Am. Acad. Arts & Sciences; mem.: NAS. Achievements include research in functional and comparative analysis of genome and gene products in viruses, eubacteria, pathogenic bacteria, archea and eukaryotes, both in plants and animals including humans; first to use automated gene sequencers; development of expressed sequence tags (ESTs); discovery of more than half of all human genes. Office: J Craig Venter Inst 9712 Medical Ctr Dr Rockville MD 20850 also: J Craig Venter Sci Found 5 Research Pl Rockville MD 20850 *

VENTIMIGLIA, VINCENT J., JR., consulting firm executive, former federal agency administrator; b. 1962; married; 5 children. BA magna cum laude, Yale U., 1984; JD, Georgetown U., 1990. Legis. asst. to Senator Gordon Humphrey US Senate Com. on Health Issues, Washington, 1985—88; dir. Capitol Hill Housing Improvement Partnership, 1988—90; staff atty. US Sentencing Commn., 1990—94; counsel to Senator Dan Coats US Senate Labor & Human Resources Com., 1995—98; dir. Govt. Affairs Office Medtronic, Inc., 1998—2001; health policy dir. Health Policy Team US Senate Health Edn. Labor & Pensions Com., 2001—05; policy dir. US Senate Budget Com., 2005; asst. sec. for legis. US Dept. Health & Human Services (HHS), 2005—09; sr. v.p. health & life sciences practice B&D Consulting, Washington, 2009—. Mem.: Md. State Bar Assn. Office: B&D Consulting 1050 K St NW Ste 400 Washington DC 20001 Office Phone: 202-312-7463. Office Fax: 202-312-7460. E-mail: vincent.ventimiglia@bakerd.com.

VENTOLINI, GARY, obstetrician, researcher, gynecologist, educator; b. Peru, Sept. 26, 1953; MD, Padova U., Italy, 1977. Bd. cert. in ob-gyn., family practice. Assoc. prof., divsn. dir. Wright State U., Boonshoft Sch. Medicine, 2002—06, prof., chair ob-gyn. dept., 2006—. Contbr. articles to profl. jours., chapters to books. Fellow: Am. Acad. Family Practice, Am. Congress Obstetricians and Gynecologists. Office: 128 E Apple St Ste 3800 CHE Dayton OH 45409 Business E-Mail: gary.ventolini@wright.edu.

VENTOR, DEON J., pathologist; Assoc. prof. Cancer Functional Genomics Lab., Murdoch Children's Rsch. Inst., Melbourne, Australia, chief pathologist, cancer genomics; head, cancer epidemiology program, dept. pathology U. Melbourne; dir. Genetic Technologies Ltd., Melbourne, exec. dir.; co-dir. pathology Mater Hosp., Brisbane, Australia. Bd. advisors Gendia Found.; cons. WHO, pharm. cos. biotech. startups. Contbr. articles to profl. jours. Fellow: Royal Coll. Pathologists, Australasia. Achievements include research in cancer genetics and genetic-based diagnostics. Avocation: triathalons. Office: Genetic Technologies Ltd PO Box 115 Fitzroy Vic 3065 Australia Office Phone: 61 3 9415 7688. Office Fax: 61 3 9416 4076.

VENTURA, HECTOR OSVALDO, cardiologist; b. Buenos Aires, Mar. 21, 1951; came to U.S., 1981; s. Osvaldo Domingo and Nelida (Scocozza) V.; m. Laurie Anne Zeringue, Apr. 21, 1990; children: Austin Alejandro, Leighton Leandro, Kendra Mariel. BS, Nat. No. 10 Coll., Buenos Aires, 1968; MD, U. Buenos Aires, 1974. Diplomate Am. Bd. Internal Medicine with subspecialty in cardiovascular diseases. Resident in internal medicine Mil. Hosp., Argentina, 1975-78; rsch. fellow hypertension Ochsner Found., New Orleans, 1981-84; internal medicine resident Oschsner Found. Hosp., New Orleans, 1984-86, cardiology fellow, 1986-88; heart failure/heart transplant fellow Loyola U., Chgo., 1989; co-dir. heart failure heart transplant Oshsner Med. Inst., New Orleans, 1989-97, transplant adv. bd., 1992-97, ethics com., 1995-97; assoc. prof. medicine La. State U. Sch. Medicine, New Orleans; co-dir. advanced heart failure/cardiac transplant Tulane U. Med. Ctr., New Orleans, 1998-2000; prof. medicine Tulane U. Sch. Medicine, New Orleans, 2000—. Dir. cardiovasc. disease tng. program and edn. Ochsner Clinic Found., New Orleans, 2000—09; chmn. Grad. Med. End. Com., Ochsner Clin. Found., 2004-; jour. manuscript reviewer. Mem. editl. bd. Jour. Heart & Lung Transplantation, 1994; contbr. articles to profl. jours. 1st lt. Argentine Army, 1974-80. Ochsner Found. fellow, 1985-86. Fellow Am. Coll. Cardiology; mem. Am. Soc. Transplant (organ thoracic com. 1993—), Am. Heart Assn. Roman Catholic. Avocations: tennis, aerobic exercise. Home: 3746 Rue Chardonnay Metairie LA 70002-1500 Office: Ochsner Clinic Found 1514 Jefferson Hwy New Orleans LA 70121 Office Phone: 504-842-5638. Business E-Mail: hventura@ochsner.org.

VENTURINI, MASSIMO, radiologist; b. Ancona, Italy, Oct. 9, 1961; s. Claudio Venturini and Gianna Leonardi; m. Laura Valle, Feb. 12, 2002; 1 child, Carolina Micol. Diploma, Classic HS Rinaldini, Italy, 1980; MD, U. Milan, Italy, 1988. Cert. Bd. Cert. Radiology U. Of Milan, Italy, 1992. Staff radiologist San Raffaele Sci. Inst., Milan, Milan, Italy, 1992—. Contbr. articles various profl. jours. Achievements include research in aascular and interventional radiology. E-mail: venturini.massimo@hsr.it.

VERDIER, DAVID D'OOGE, ophthalmologist, educator; b. Grand Rapids, Mich., Jan. 22, 1949; s. Leonard D'Ooge and Anita Beatrice (Carvalho) V.; m. Beverly Deane Johnson; children: Renée Leigh, Travis D'Ooge, Eric Leonard, Nora Claire. BA in Polit. Sci., U. Mich., 1971; MD, U. Mich. Med. Sch., 1977. Resident in family practice Med. U. S.C., Charleston, 1977-80; resident in ophthalmology Pitts. Eye and Ear, U. Pitts., 1980-83; corneal and external eye fellowship U. Iowa, Iowa City, 1983-84; pvt. practice med. and surg. ophthalmology Verdier Eye Ctr. P.L.C., Grand Rapids, Mich., 1984—; clin. prof. Mich. State U. Coll. Medicine, East Lansing, 1986—. Med. dir. Mich. Tissue Bank, Lansing, Mich., 1995-98; mem. med. adv. bd. Eye Bank Assn. Am. 2003-, Cape Elethra Found., 2004—. Contbr. articles to profl. jours. and textbook chpts. Bd. dirs. East Grand Rapids (Mich.) Sch. Found., 1992-2000, Macatawa Bay Yacht Club, Holland, Mich., 1988-90, 94-95, Grand Rapids Art Mus., 1995-2001; bd. dirs. Macatawa Park Cottagers Assn., Holland, 1993-99, pres., 1993-98. Named to Galens Hon. Med. Soc., 1975-77. Mem. Mich. Ophthalmologic Soc. (bd. dirs. 1994-2000), Mich. State Med. Soc. (del. 1993-2000, Eye Bank Assn. Am. (med adv bd. 2003—). Home: 3043 Mary St SE Grand Rapids MI 49506-3150 Office: Verdier Eye Center PLC 1000 E Paris Ave SE Ste 130 Grand Rapids MI 49546-3680

VERDILE, VINCENT PAUL, dean, emergency physician; b. Troy, NY, Aug. 13, 1955; s. Raphael Mario and Frances (Marinucci) V.; m. Louise Ann Wickware, Aug. 30, 1985. BS, Union U., 1977, MS, 1980; MD, Albany Med. Coll., 1984. Cert. American Bd. Emergency Medicine, 1990. Intern U. Pitts., 1984-85, resident in emergency medicine, 1985-87; assoc. med. dir. dept. pub. safety City of Pitts., 1985—93; flight physician Ctr. for Emergency Medicine, Pitts., 1988—93; chair. dept. of emergency med. Albany Med. Coll., 1993—2000, interim dean, 2000, exec. v.p. health affairs, exec. med. dir., dean, 2001—. Mem. adj. staff dept. emergency medicine Mercy Hosp., Pitts, 1987—93; med. dir., emergency med. technician Community Coll. Allegheny Coll., 1987—93; attending physician emergency dept. Presbyn.-Univ. Hosp., 1987—93; assoc. program dir. residency in emergency medicine Univ. of Pitts., 1987—93, asst. prof. medicine, 1987—93. Contbr. numerous articles to profl. jours. Mem. Soc. Acad. Emergency Medicine, Nat. Assn. Emergency Med. Svcs. Physicians (chmn. membership com. 1988—), Am. Coll. Emergency Physicians, Pa. chpt. Am. Coll. Emergency Physicians, Pa. State Med. Soc., Allegheny County Med. Soc., Am. Assn. Poison Control Ctrs. Roman Catholic. Office: Albany Med Coll Emergency Medicine Group 47 New Scotland Ave MC 139 Albany NY 12208 Office Phone: 518-262-3773. Office Fax: 518-262-3236. *

VERDUGO, GEORGINA C., federal agency administrator; BA, UCLA; JD, U. San Francisco; LLM, London Sch. Economics; MPA, Harvard U. Kennedy Sch. Govt. Chief of staff rep. Lucille Roybal-Allard US House of Reps., Washington; head Washington office Mexican American Legal Def. & Ednl. Fund (MALDEF); dep. asst. atty. gen. Office Legis. Affairs, US Dept. Justice; exec. dir. Americans for a Fair Chance, Washington, 2000—02; asst. US atty. (so. dist.) Calif. US Dept. Justice, San Diego, 2002—03; assoc. counsel LA Unified Sch. Dist., 2004—08; pvt. practice atty. LA, 2008—09; dir. Office Civil Rights, US Dept. Health & Human Services, Washington, 2009—. Named one of 100 Most Influential People in Bus. Ethics, Ethisphere Mag., 2009. Office: Office Civil Rights HHS 200 Independence Ave SW Washington DC 20201 Office Phone: 202-619-0403. E-mail: OCRMail@hhs.gov. *

VEREB, TERESA B., psychiatrist; b. Poland; d. Joseph and Henryka Biskup; m. Bartholomew Vereb, Aug. 3, 1968; children: Bartholomew Jr., Teresa Tilden. MD, Acad. Medicine, Warsaw, 1966. Cert. stress mgmt. Am. Acad. Experts in Traumatic Stress, 2005. Resident psychiatry Hosp. Wolsky, Warsaw, 1966—68, Med. Sch. Safarik U., Kosice, Czech Republic, 1968—70, staff psychiatry, 1971—72; resident psychiatry SUNY, Buffalo, 1977—78; clin. instr. psychiatry Meyer Meml. Hosp., Buffalo, 1977—78; resident psychiatry U. Fla., Gainesville, 1978—80; pvt. practice gen. psychiatry Bradenton, Fla., 1980—; staff psychiatrist Blake Hosp., Bradenton, 1980—, Manatee Meml. Hosp., Bradenton, 1980—, chief psychiatry, sectional chief psychiatry, 1981—85, 1987—91, chairperson psychiat. sect., 2000. Active Sacred Heart Cath. Ch., Bradenton, 1980—. Recipient Disting. Physician award, Fla. Med. Assn., 2005; named Profl. of Yr., 2008; named to Am. Top Psychiatrists, Consumer's Rsch. Coun. Am., 2006, 2007. Mem.: AMA (Physician Recognition award 1995—2002, 2005—06), Am. Acad. Experts in Traumatic Stress, Manatee County Med. Soc., Fla. Psychiat. Assn., Fla. Med. Assn. (Physician Recognition award 1995—2005, Rogeriem Pfizer Re-Commn. 1999, Am. Top Rate Physician 1999, Top Psychiatrist 2004—08, Boar Cert. for stress mgmt. 2005, Am. Top Rate Physician 2008), Am. Psychiat. Assn. Achievements include successfully climbed Mount Kilimanjaro, 1997. Avocations: water-skiing, skiing, swimming, hiking, mountain climbing. Office: Vereb and Vereb MDs PA 5015 Manatee Ave West Bradenton FL 34209

VEREBEY, KARL GEZA, toxicologist, pharmacologist, educator; b. Budapest, Hungary, Mar. 12, 1938; came to U.S., 1956; s. Karoly and Etelka (Szabo) V.; m. Debra Adler, Feb. 22, 1962; children: Rita, Todd, Marc. AA, Eotvos J. Gimnazium, Budapest, Hungary, 1956; BA, Hunter Coll., 1965; MA, CUNY, 1968; PhD, Cornell U. Med. Coll., 1972. Diplomate Am. Bd. Forensic Toxicology; cert. in high complexity., clin. lab. dir. Am. Bd. Bioanalysis; lic. clin. lab. dir., N.Y., N.J., Vt. Dir. clin. pharmacology State of N.Y., NYC, 1973-88; dir. clin. lab. Psychiat. Diagnostic Lab. Am., South Plainfield, N.J., 1982-89; chief toxicologist City of N.Y., 1989-92; dir. toxicology N.Y. State Inst. Basic Rsch., SI, 1992-95; pres., dir. Leadtech Corp., North Bergen, NJ, 1992—2001; dir. Ammon Analytical Lab., 1999—. Assoc. prof. SUNY Health Sci. Ctr., 1978-2000; mem. exec. com. Drug Abuse Adv. Bd., N.Y. State Dept. Health, 1985; advisor subcom. on trace metals analysis to Nat. Com. Clin. Lab. Stds., 1992; insp. Nat. Lab. Cert. Program dept. Health and Human Svcs., 1989. Mem. editl. bd. Jour. Addictive Diseases, 1981; contbr. over 100 articles to sci. jours., chpts. to books. With U.S. Army, 1961-63. Rsch. fellow USPHS, 1968-73; grantee Cornell U. Med. Coll., 1974-77, Narcotic and Drug Rsch., Inc., 1974-76, 79-81, DuPont Pharm., 1985; inductee Hunter Coll. Hall of Fame, 1989; named Water Polo Nat. Champion, NY Athletic Club, 1959, 60, 61. Fellow Am. Acad. Forensic Sci.; mem. Am. Soc. Pharmacology and Exptl. Therapeutics, Soc. Forensic Toxicologists. Internat. Assoc. Forensic Toxicologists. Avocations: water polo, kayaking, tennis, photography. Home: 638 Debehar Ct River Vale NJ 07675-6409 Office Phone: 908-862-4404. Personal E-mail: k.verebey@att.net.

VERECZKEY, LASZLO FERENC, physician, researcher; b. Budapest, Hungary, June 16, 1942; s. Laszlo and Ilona (Sulkovszky) V.; m. Erzsebet Kalocsai, Dec. 30, 1968; children: Ildiko, Katalin. MD, Semmelweiss U., Budapest, Hungary, 1967; PhD, Hungarian Acad. Scis., 1983. Asst. prof. Semmelweis U., Budapest, 1967-71; head dept. Chem. Works of Gedeon Richter, Budapest, 1971-90; dep. dir. Inst. for Drug Rsch., Budapest, 1990-92; sci. dir. Biorex Ltd., Budapest, 1993; head dept. Chem. Rsch. Ctr. Hungarian Acad. Scis., Budapest, 1991—. Author: (with O. Gaal and G. Medgyesi) Electrophoresis in the Separation of Biological Micromolecules, 1980; contbr. articles to profl. jours. Mem. Internat. Soc. Study Xenobiotics (councillor 1991-94, 96-99, 2008-11). Avocations: swimming, latin language. Office: Hung Acad Scis/Chem Rsch Ctr Pusztaszeri ut 59-67 Budapest H-1025 Hungary Home Phone: (36) 1-325-7029. E-mail: vela@chemres.hu.

VERED, MARILENA, dentist, educator; b. Iasi, Romania, Aug. 23, 1966; DMD, Hebrew U., Jerusalem, 1992. Sr. lectr. oral pathology Tel Aviv U., 2007—. Office: 4 Klatchkin Tel Aviv 69978 Israel Office Fax: 972-3-6409250. Business E-Mail: lmy@netvision.net.il.

VERGHESE, ABRAHAM CHEERAN, medical educator, writer; b. Addis Ababa, Ethiopia, May 30, 1955; arrived in US, 1980; MD, Madras U., India, 1979; MFA, U. Iowa, 1991; DSc (hon.), Swarthmore Coll., 2001; LHD (hon.), U. Northern Ill., 2007. Diplomate Am. Bd. Internal Medicine, cert. in pulmonary disease. Intern Govt. Gen. Hosp., Madrass Med. Coll., 1979-80; resident, chief resident East Tenn. State U., Johnson City, 1980-83, instr. in medicine, 1982-83, asst. prof. medicine, 1985-88, assoc. prof. medicine, 1988-90; fellow in infectious diseases Boston U. Sch. Medicine, 1983-85; chief infectious diseases VA Med. Ctr., Johnson City, 1986-90, asst. chief medicine, 1988-90; vis. assoc. U. Iowa, Iowa City, 1990-91; prof. medicine Tex. Tech. U., El Paso, 1991—2002, chief infectious diseases, Regional Acad. Health Ctr., 1991-97; prof. medicine, founding dir. Ctr. Med. Humanities & Ethics, U. Tex. Health Sci. Ctr., San Antonio, 2002—07; prof. theory & practice of medicine, sr. assoc. chair dept. internal medicine Stanford U. Med. Sch., Calif., 2007—, residency program dir., dept. medicine, 2009—. Author: (nonfiction) My Own Country: A Doctor's Story of a Town and Its People in the Age of AIDS, 1994 (one of 5 Best Books of Yr., TIME mag., NY Times Notable Book), The Tennis Partner: A Doctor's Story of Friendship and Loss, 1998, (novels) Cutting for Stone, 2010; contbr. numerous articles to profl. jours. Recipient John P. McGovern Medal, Osler Soc., Montreal, 2007. Master: ACP; fellow: Coll. Chest Physicians, Infectious Diseases Soc. America, Royal Coll. Physicians Can.; mem.: Soc. Exptl. Biology & Medicine, Am. Soc. Microbiology, Am. Fedn. Clin. Rsch., Am. Geriat. Soc. Office: Stanford U Dept Medicine 300 Pasteur Dr S102C MC 5109 Stanford CA 94305 Office Phone: 650-721-6966. Office Fax: 650-725-8381. *

VERHEY, LYNN JAMES, retired medical educator; b. Holland, Mich., Apr. 13, 1940; BA, Kalamazoo Coll., 1962; PhD, U. Ill., 1968. Chief physics divsn. dept. radiation oncology U. Calif., San Francisco, 1991—2008, assoc. prof., 1991—95, prof., 1995—2008, prof. emeritus, 2008—. Chief of physics divsn. in dept. of radiation oncology U. of Calif., San Francisco, 1991—2008. Fellow: Am. Assn. Med. Physics, Am. Soc. Therapeutic Radiation Oncology. Avocations: tennis, golf. Home: 49 Oak Hill Ln Stonington ME 04681 Business E-Mail: lverhey@radonc.ucsf.edu.

VERMA, ANOOP KUMAR, pediatrician; b. Raipur, Chhattisgarh, India, Oct. 20, 1959; MBBS, Mediacal Coll. Raipur, 1984; MD in Pediat., Med. Coll. Raipur, 1988. Nat. v.p. Indain Acad. Pediat., 2005—06, nat. chairperson neurology chpt., 2009—. Ctrl. working com. mem. Indian Med. Assn., 1990. Fellow: Fellow Coll. Gen. Practitioner, IMA Acad. Med. Scis. Avocations: writing, photography. Home: Swapnil Nursing Home Civil Lines Raipur Chhattisgarh India Personal E-mail: anoopve@yahoo.com.

VERMA, BALAK R., surgeon, department chairman; MBBS, U. Delhi, New Delhi, 1964; MD, Wayne State U., Detroit, 1973. Diplomate Am. Bd. Surgery, Am. Bd. Thoracic Surgery. Clin. assoc. prof. surgery WSU Sch. Medicine, Detroit; chmn. Indus Hosp., Shimla, India, 1993—. Named Himachal Ratan, Intellectual Soc. India, New Delhi, 2001. Fellow: RCS (Can.), Am. Coll. Surgeons. Office: Indus Hosp Shimla India Office Phone: 91-177-2841401. Business E-Mail: chairman@indushospital.org.

VERMA, INDER M., biochemist; b. Sangrur, Punjab, India, Nov. 28, 1947; MSc in Biochemistry, Lucknow U., India, 1966; PhD in Biochemistry, Weizmann Inst. Sci., Rehovot, Israel, 1971. Postdoc. fellow biology MIT, 1971—74; asst. prof. Salk Inst. Biol. Studies, La Jolla, Calif., 1974—79, assoc. prof., 1979—83, sr. mem., Molecular Biology & Virology Lab., 1983-85, prof. molecular biology, 1985-95, Am. Cancer Soc. prof. molecular biology, 1990—, prof., Irwin & Joan Jacobs chair exemplary life sci., Lab. Genetics, 1995—. Adj. assoc. prof. U. Calif., San Diego, 1979—83, adj. prof. biology, 1983—; Franklin D. Roosevelt investigator March of Dimes Birth Defects Found., 1997. Recipient Medal for outstanding scientist, Assn. Scientists Indian Origin in America, 1985, Merit award, NIH, 1987, Outstanding Investigator award, 1988, Thrombosis Rsch. Inst. award, London, 1993, Charaka award, Assn. Indians in America, 1995; fellow Jane Coffin Childs Meml. Fund, 1970—73; Reverend Solomon B. Caulker Meml. fellowship, 1967—70. Fellow: Am. Acad. Microbiology, Nat. Acad. Scis. India (fgn.); mem.: NAS (coun. mem. 2006—09), Am. Soc. Gene Therapy (pres. 2000—01), European Molecular Biology Orgn. (assoc.), Third World Acad. Scis., Inst. Medicine. Office: Salk Inst Biol Studies PO Box 85800 10010 N Torrey Pines Rd San Diego CA 92186-5800 Office Phone: 619-453-4100. Business E-Mail: verma@salk.edu.

VERMA, NIKHIL, orthopedist; b. Feb. 8, 1973; BS with highest distinction in Cellular and Microbiology, Univ. Mich., 1994; MD, Univ. Penn. Sch. Med., 1998. Cert. orthopaedic surgery ABOS, 2003. Orthopaedic resident Rush-Presbyterian St. Luke's Med. Ctr., Chgo., 1998—; fell., sports med. Hosp. Spl. Surgery, 2003—04. Recipient James B. Angell Scholar, Univ. Mich., 1994, Gallo award Young Rschrs., The Cancer Inst. NJ, 1995, Jorge O. Galante MD Excellence in Rsch. award, Rush-Presbyterian St. Lukes Med. Ctr., 2001—02. Mem.: Asian Pacific Am. Med. Students Assn. Home: 1611 W Harrison St # 300 Chicago IL 60612-4861 Office Fax: 312-243-8925. Business E-Mail: nverma@rushortho.com.

VERMA, NITIN, pharmacist, educator; b. Meerut, India., Aug. 14, 1982; PhD, UPTU, 2004; PharmM, BU, Bhopal, 2006. Asst. prof., rsch. fellow MIET, Meerut, Uttar Pradesh, India, 2006—08; assoc. prof., rsch. assoc. BIT, Meerut, 2008—; assoc. prof., sr. rsch. assoc. IPES, Baddi U., Himachal Pradesh, India, 2011—. Contbr. scientific papers to profl. publs. Fellow: Soc. Free Radical Rsch.; mem.: Internat. Soc. Ethanopharmacology (London), Indian Soc. Pharmacognosy (India), Assn. Pharm. Tchrs. India. Avocation: writing. Office: Inst Pharmacy & Emerging Sci Baddi Himachal Pradesh 173 205 India Office Fax: 01795-247352. E-mail: nitinmiet14@rediffmail.com.

VERMA, RAJESH KUMAR, special education educator; b. Varanasi, Uttar Pradesh, India, Aug. 19, 1973; BA in Mental Retardation, 2000, MEd in Spl. Edn., 2008. Lectr. in vocat. tng. Nat. Inst. Mentally Handicapped, 2003—08; asst. academic dir. Rehab. Coun. India, New Delhi, 2009—. Avocations: cricket, ping pong/table tennis. Office: B-22 Qutub Institutional Area New Delhi Delhi 110016 India Personal E-mail: rajeshrk_verma@rediffmail.com.

VERMA, RISHENDRA, veterinarian, researcher; b. Tilhar, Uttar Pradesh, India, Jan. 9, 1953; s. Lakshmi Narain and Shivkumari Verma; m. Chitra Verma, Dec. 11, 1979; children: Harshit, Mohit. BSc, Bareilly Coll., 1973; B of Vet. Sci. and Animal Husbandry, Vet. Coll., Mathura, 1977, M of Vet. Sci., 1979; diploma in journalism, Mysore U., 1989; MSc, The Med. Sch., Birmingham, Eng., 1990; PhD, Indian Vet. Rsch. Inst., Izatnagar, 1995. Cert. in ednl. techs. Continuing Edn. Ctr., Asian Inst. Tech., Bangkok. Dist. sheep and wool ext. officer, artificial insemination ext. officer, gov. Govt. Rajasthan, Izatnagar, Rajasthan, India, 1979—80; vet. officer, gen. mgr. Sabarkantha Milk Prodrs. Union Ltd., Himmatnagar, Gujrat, India, 1980; devel. officer, dir. Animal Husbandry, Lucknow, Uttar Pradesh, 1980; asst. disease investigation officer (poultry), vice chancellor Haryana Agrl. U., Hisar, India, 1980—81; scientist S-1, pres. Indian Coun. Agrl. Rsch., New Delhi, 1981—87, scientist sr. scale, 1989—95, sr. scientist, 1995—2001, prin. scientist, 2000—01; scientist C, dir. Ctr. Drug Rsch. Inst., Lucknow, Uttar Pradesh, 1987—89, scientist S-1, 1989; head govt. analyst divsn. biol. standardization Indian Vet. Rsch. Inst., Izatnagar, Uttar Pradesh, 2001—; joint dir. Ctr. Animal Diseases Rsch. Diagnosis. Cons. in field. Editor: Indian Jour. Vet. Rsch. Fellowship, FIAAVR, FISVIB, FPHVA, FIAVPHS, FIYAVSC, FNAASC, FNASC. Home: 1219/6E Block Rajendranagar Uttar Pradesh Bareilly 243122 India Office: Indian Vet Rsch Inst Izatnagar 243 122 Bareilly 243122 India Office Fax: 0581-2303284; Home Fax: 0581-2302188. Personal E-mail: rishendra_verma@yahoo.com.

VERMA, SACHIT, medical researcher; b. India, Oct. 11, 1977; MBBS, Govt. Med. Coll., Amritsar, India, 2000. Rschr. Thomas Jefferson U., Phila., 2006. Recipient Exec. Coun. award, Am. Roentgen Ray Soc., 2008, Rsch. award, Radiol. Soc. N.Am., 2008; fellowship, Soc. Radiologists Ultrasound, 2008. Office: 132 S 10th St Philadelphia PA 19107 Personal E-mail: medskv@yahoo.com.

VERMETTE, RAYMOND EDWARD, retired health facility administrator; b. Lewiston, Maine, June 30, 1942; m. Ernestine Pero, Dec. 29, 1963; children: Tamara, Gregory. BS in Bacteriology, U. Maine, 1964; MS in Biochemistry, U. Wis., 1966; MBA, Temple U., 1973; master tchr.'s cert., Cath. Diocese Boston, 1981. Cert. in pers. mgmt., Va. Supr. animal toxicology Hazleton Labs., Vienna, Va., 1967-71; pers. mgr. Damon Clin. Lab., Phila., 1971-73, ops. mgr., 1973-75, gen. mgr. Needham Heights, Mass., 1975-90; v.p. ops. Damon Corp., Needham Heights, 1983-87, corp. v.p., 1987-89, sr. v.p., 1990—93; sr. v.p., gen. mgr. Corning/MetPath, Westwood, Mass., 1994-95; ret., 1995. Vis. lectr. fin. mgmt. and bus. adminstrn. Framingham State Coll., 1978—84; instr. mgmt. Newbury Jr. Coll., Boston, 1976—79; health care mgmt. cons., 2001—. Author: (with B. Kliman and E. Kolowrat) What You Should Know About Medical Lab Tests, 1979. V.p. fin. com., Framingham, Mass., 1982—84; mem. capital budget com. Town of Framingham, 1987; mem-elect Framingham Town Meeting, 1987—90, Govt. Study Com., 1995—97, mem. fin. com., 1997—2001; chmn. bd. religious edn. Cath. Ch., Framingham, 1981—84, co-chmn. pre-marriage preparation coun., 1981—99, organist, 1979—. Republican. Home: 2 Old Town Hwy Unit 16 East Haven CT 06512-4530 *

VERMUND, STEN HALVOR, epidemiologist, educator; b. Mpls., Jan. 31, 1954; s. Halvor and Karen (Bergfjord) V.; m. Pilar Vargas, Apr. 8, 1978; children: Julian, Gabriel. BA, Stanford U., 1974; MD, Albert Einstein Coll. Medicine, 1977; MSc, London Sch. Hygiene and Tropical Medicine, 1981; PhD, Columbia U., 1990. Diplomate Am. Bd. Pediatrics, Am. Bd. Preventive Medicine. Intern Presbyn. Hosp., NYC, 1977-78, resident in pediat., 1978-80; asst. prof. Columbia U., NYC, 1982-85, Albert Einstein Coll. Medicine, Bronx, NY, 1985-88; chief epidemiology br. divsn. AIDS Nat. Inst. Allergy and Infectious Diseases, Bethesda, Md., 1988-92, chief vaccine trials and epidemiology br. divsn. AIDS, 1992-94; prof. epidemiology, internat. health, medicine & pediat. U. Ala., Birmingham, 1994—2005, chmn. dept. epidemiology, 1994-98, dir. divsn. geog. medicine, 1994—2005, sr. scientist Comprehensive Cancer Ctr., 1994—2005, assoc. dir. Ctr. for AIDS Rsch., 1994—2003, pres. Gorgas Meml. Inst., 1995—2005, dir. John J. Sparkman Ctr. for Internat. Pub. Health Edn., 1999—2005; prof. pediat., medicine, preventive medicine and ob/gyn Vanderbilt U., Nashville, 2005—, dir., inst. for global health, 2005—, Amos Christie chair in global health, 2005—. Cons. NYC Dept. Environ. Protection, 1986-88, Med. Bd. Nat. Coun. Chs., NYC, 1984-85, CDC, Atlanta, 1989—, FDA, Rockville, Md., 1991-94, NIH, 1994—; mem. Inst. Medicine Panel on Perinatal Transmission of HIV, 1997-98, mem. Inst. Medicine Panel on HIV Prevention, 1999-2000. Contbg. author: AIDS Epidemiology, 1993, Until the Cure: Caregiving for Women with HIV, 1993, Parasitic Protozoa, 2d edit., vol. 6, 1993, HIV in Women, 1995, AIDS, 4th edit., 1997; co-editor, contbg. author: Preventing HIV Infection in Developing Countries, 1999; contbr. articles to profl. jours. Mem. adv. bd. health rsch. tng. program N.Y.C. Dept. Health, 1986—88; mem. sci. adv. bd. World AIDS Found., 1994—95; mem. adv. com. Office AIDS Rsch., NIH, 2000—. Recipient Curnan award Babies Hosp., NYC, 1980, Lalcaca medal U. London, 1981, Commrs. Spl. Svc. award NYC Dept. Health, 1988, Merit award USPHS, Bethesda, 1989, Cert. of Appreciation, U.S. Surgeon Gen., 1993, Superior Svc. award USPHS, 1994; med. rsch. grantee Ctrs. for Disease Control, Nat. Cancer Inst., Nat. Inst. Allergy Infectious Diseases, Nat. Inst. Child Health and Devel., others, 1986-88, 94—. Fellow Am. Acad. Pediatrics (sec., founding mem. regional com. on homeless children 1986-88), Am. Coll. Epidemiology, Soc. Adolescent Medicine, Royal Soc. Tropical Medicine and Hygiene, Infectious Disease Soc. Am.; mem. APHA, Internat. AIDS Soc., Internat. Epidemiologic Assn., Am. Soc. Tropical Medicine and Hygiene. Avocations: hiking, tennis, violin, ping pong/table tennis. Office: Vanderbilt U Inst Global Health Light Hall 319 0242 Nashville TN 37232 E-mail: sten.vermund@vanderbilt.edu.

VERNET, GUY JEAN JACQUES, medical researcher, director; b. France, July 21, 1959; PhD, U. Lyon, 1984. Postdoc. rsch. assoc. CIRAD, 1984—86; assoc. prof. U. Basel, Switzerland, 1986—90; rsch. dir. Biomerieux, 1990—2007; sci. dir. Found. Merieux, 2008—. Office: 17 Rue Bourgelat Lyon 69002 France Business E-Mail: guy.vernet@fondation-merieux.org.

VERNILLET, LAURENT, pharmacologist, researcher; b. La Garenne-Colombes, Hauts de Seine, France, Oct. 27, 1959; s. Serge Raymond and Raymonde Marguerite Vernillet; m. Maryse Renee Muller, Sept. 7, 1985; children: Cathelyne Sylvie, Emeline Josiane, Johann Remi, Chloe Valerie. BTech in Biochemistry, Nat. Sch. Chemistry, Biology and Physics, Paris, 1977; Diploma in Applied Biology, U. Tech. Inst., Caen, France, 1979; PharmD, Rene Descartes U., Paris, 1983; Diploma in Pharmacokinetics and Drug Metabolism, U. Paris-South, Chatenay-Malabry, France, 1984; PhD in Exptl. and Clin. Pharmacology, Rene Descartes U., Paris, 1992. Asst. chemist Thibault's Pharmacy, Saint-Mande, Val de Marne, France, 1983—86; sr. rsch. scientist Novartis (formely Sandoz), Rueil-Malmaison, Hauts de Seine, France, 1987—95; rsch. fellow, drug metabolism and pharmacokinetics dept. Sanofi-Aventis (formely Rhone-Poulenc Rorer), Antony, Hauts de Seine, France, 1995—2000; sr. pharmacokineticist, pharmacokinetics, pharmacodynamics and trial simulations dept. Eli Lilly and Co Ltd., Windlesham, England, 2000—02; asst. dir. drug metabolism and pharmacokinetics dept. TAP Pharm. Products Inc., Lake Forest, Ill., 2002—06; sr. scientist and group leader, pharmocokinetics, pharmacodymamics and bioanalytical sci. Genentech Inc., South San Francisco, Calif., 2006—08; dir. Clin. Pharmacology, Vertex Pharm. Inc., Cambridge, Mass., 2008—. Presenter at profl. meetings and confs.; peer reviewer clin. pharmacology chptrs. in scientific books. Contbr. scientific papers, articles to profl. jours. Recipient Laroze Found. prize, 1992. Fellow: Am. Soc. Clin. Pharmacology and Therapeutics; mem.: Am. Coll. Clin. Pharmacology. Achievements include significant involvement in the development of some key drugs such as ciclosporin (immunosuppresant), docetaxel and irinotecan (oncology) and febuxostat (metabolic disorder). Avocations: skiing, volleyball, tennis, genealogy, stamp collecting/philately. Office: 130 Waverly St Cambridge MA 02139 Personal E-mail: golden2003@verizon.net.

VERNON, BRENT LEON, biomedical engineer, educator; b. San Antonio, July 17, 1968; BSE, Ariz. State U., 1993; PhD, U. Utah, 1999. Asst. prof. Ariz. State U., 2000—06, assoc. prof., grad. program chair, 2006—. Faculty Banner Good Samaritan Orthop. Residency Program, 2005. Grant, NIH, Am. Heart Assn. Mem.: Biomed. Engring. Soc. Avocations: camping, travel, reading. Office: ECG334 Tempe AZ 85287-9709 Office Fax: 480-727-7624. Business E-Mail: brent.vernon@asu.edu.

VERNON, WESLEY, forensic practitioner researcher; b. Stockport, Eng., Jan. 23, 1958; s. Denis and Irene Vernon; m. Val Vernon, Nov. 13, 1982; children: Rachel, Wesley. Diploma in podiatric medicine, U. Salford, Eng., 1980; further edn. tchrs. cert., Stockport Coll. Tech., 1981; cert. in health svcs. mgmt., Sheffield Hallam U., 1987, PhD in Podiatry/Forensic Podiatry, 2000; BSc in Podiatry with honors, U. Brighton, Eng., 1990. Registered podiatrist Health Professions Coun., Eng. Sr. podiatrist Derbyshire (Eng.) Area Health Authority, 1980—81; sector chief podiatrist North Derbyshire Dist. Health Authority, 1981—85; divisional chief podiatrist Sheffield Cmty. Svc. Unit, 1985—93; head podiatry svc. Sheffield Primary Care Trust, 2003—07. Podiatry advisor South Yorkshire Workforce Devel. Confedn., Sheffield, 2002—07; rsch. lead Sheffield Cmty. Svcs., 2003—; past peer reviewer for Physiotherapy Jour. Chartered Soc. Physiotherapists, London, 1996; peer reviewer Scottish Health Bd., Edinburgh, 2003; peer reviewer for rsch. tng. fellowship award scheme The Health Found., London, 2002—05; forensic podiatry cons., High Peak, England, 1995—; vis. prof. Staffordshree U., 2004—, Huddersfield U., 2010—; hon. rsch. fellow Sheffeld Hallam U., 2004—06; peer reviewer Jour. Foot & Ankle Rsch., Brit. Med. Jour., Medinian Swiss Law British Radical Jous. Contbr. articles to profl. jours. Mem. emeritus, bd. dirs. Am. Soc. Forensic Podiatrists, 2004—11. Recipient travel award, Cmty. Health Sheffield NHS Trust, 1997, Royal Soc., Hong Kong, 2005, Queen's Golden Jubilee medal, Officer of the Order, The Brit. Empire; grantee, Trent Focus, 2002, Sheffield Health and Social Rsch. Consortium, 2003, 2005. Fellow: Faculty Podiatric Medicine, Forensic Sci. Soc.; mem.: Coll. Podiatric Mgmt., RfPB (grant 2009), Ctr. Internat. Forensic Assistance, Can. Identification Soc., Internat. Assn. for Identification (life; chair. sub-com., Disting. Membership award 1998), Brit. Assn. Human Identification (editor forensic podiatry sect. 2002—08), Podiatric Rsch. Forum (chair 1998—2007, travel award 1998, 2002), Forensic Sci. Soc., Soc. Chiropodists and Podiatrists (seat of faculty of podiatric medicine 1980—, faculty mem. of podiatric medicine 1998—2007, fellow, faculty mgmt.). Methodist. Avocations: martial arts, Asian cooking, music, cave exploration. Home: Jordanthorpe Health Ctr Dyche Close Sheffield S88DJ England Office Fax: 114-2371185.

VERNOUX, JEAN-PAUL, engineering educator; b. Burie, Chte. Mme., France, Mar. 23, 1948; s. Edmond and Yvonne V.; m. Anita Greaux, Dec. 22, 1970; children: Teva, Nicolas, Guillaume. Engr., Inst. Nat. Scis. Appliqués, Lyon, France, 1969; Master, U. Montreal, Montreal, Canada, 1972; PhD, U. Bordeaux, France, 1981, PhD, 1986. Prof. Ministry of Edn. and Rsch., 2003. Engr. for rsch. Inst. Recherche Meds. Louis Malarde, Papeete, Tahiti, French Polynesia, 1972—76; head biochemistry dept. Universite Hassan II, Casablanca, Morocco, 1978—87; asst. prof. U. Caen (France), 1987—2002, prof., 2003—; head food dept. IUP. Expert cons. Agence Française Securite Sanitaire Aliments, Paris, 2003—; ciguatera cons. Ciguatera Ctr., Woods Hole, Mass., 2003—. Author: Coral Fishes of the West Indies, 1988. Roman Catholic. Office: IUP Agro_alimentaire Rue Sainte Paix 14000 Caen 14000 Cedex France Office Fax: 02 31 56 61 79. Business E-Mail: jean-paul.vernoux@unicaen.fr.

VERONESI, UMBERTO, surgeon; b. Milan, Nov. 28, 1925; m. Susy Razon, Apr. 13, 1961; children: Paolo, Marco, Alberto, Pietro, Giulia, Silvia, Francesco. Grad., Milan U., 1951, MD (hon.), 2005, U. Cordoba, Argentina, 1988, U. Porte Alegre, Brazil, 1989, U. Athens, Greece, 1993, U. Antwerp, Belgium, 1995. Dir. gen. Nat. Cancer Inst., Milan, 1975—94; prof. pathology Perugia U., Italy, 1957—; prof. surgery Milan U., 1961—; chmn. Melanoma Group, WHO, Milan, 1967—. Chmn. Melanoma Group, WHO, Milan, 1967—; sci. dir. European Inst. Oncology, 1994—2000, 2000—; min. health Italian Govt., 2000—01; mem. adv. com. GM Cancer Rsch. Found. Author: Surgical Anatomy, 1961, Clinical Oncology, 1973, Europe Textbook on Surgical Oncology, 1989; dir.: Jour. Clin. and Exptl. Oncology. Founder Umberto Veronesi Found. for Sci. Progress. Recipient Nat. award, Am. Cancer Soc., 1977, Gold medal, Italian Ministry Health, 1978, Lucy Wortham James Clin. Rsch. award, Soc. Surg. Oncology, 1982, King Faisal Internat. prize, Saudi Arabia, 2003, Disting. Svc. award for Sci. Achievement, Am. Soc. Clin. Oncology, 2003, Pathfinder award, Am. Soc. Breast Disease, 2006, others. Mem.: Internat. Soc. Chemoprevention, Fedn. of European Cancer Socs., European Soc. Mastology, European Soc. Surg. Oncology (founder, chmn. 1982—), European Orgn. for Rsch. in Cancer Treatment (pres. 1985), Internat. Union Against Cancer (pres. 1978—82). Office: European Inst Oncology Via Giuseppe Ripamonti 435 20141 Milan MI Italy E-mail: direziane.scientifica@ico.it.

VÉRONNEAU-TROUTMAN, SUZANNE, retired ophthalmologist; b. Coaticook, Que., Can., Oct. 30, 1928; d. Sarto Veronneau and Victorine Marcoux; m. Richard C. Troutman, July 12, 1967; stepchildren: David Troutman, Anne Troutman, Richard Troutman. BA, Coll. St. Maurice, St. Hyacinthe, Que., 1951; BSc II, U. Montreal, Que., 1952, MD, 1957; postgrad. in ophthalmology/pathology, Inst. Ophthalmology, London, 1960—61. Diplomate ophthalmology Royal Coll. Physicians of London, Royal Coll. Surgeons of Eng., lic. Med. Coun. Can., physician N.Y. State, diplomate ophthalmology Coll. of Physicians and Surgeons Province of Que., Royal Coll. of Physicians and Surgeons of Can., Am. Bd. of Ophthalmology. Sr. plastic surgery, neurosurgery resident Notre Dame Hosp., Montreal, 1957—58; resident in ophthalmology Hosp. Maisonneuve, Montreal, 1958—59; asst. in ophthalmology Hosp. Edouard Herriot, Lyon, France, 1959—60; clin. asst., OPD officer Royal Eye and Moorfields Eye Hosps., London, 1961; ophthalmic surgeon Gandhi Eye Hosp., Aligarh, India, 1962; instr. basic scis., asst. opthalmologist Maisoneuve Hosp., Montreal, 1963—67; clin. assoc. prof. ophthalmology SUNY Downstate Med. Ctr., Bklyn., 1971—82; clin. instr. dept. ophthalmology Cornell U. Med. Coll., NYC, 1971—74, clin. asst. prof. ophthalmology, 1974—77, clin. assoc. prof. ophthalmology, 1977—98, clin. prof. ophthalmology, 1998—2000; clin. prof. emeritus Weill Med. Coll. of Cornell U., NYC, 2000—. Dir. strabismus clinic and orthoptics Maisoneuve Hosp., Que., 1963—67; chief ocular motility clinic Manhattan Eye Ear and Throat Hosp., NYC,

1970—2000; asst. attending physician dept. surgery, divsn. ophthalmology Hosp. of the Holy Family, 1973—77, assoc. attending physician, 1977—80; asst. dir. dept. motor anomalies N.Y. Eye and Ear Infirmary, 1970—74, assoc. attending surgeon, 1971—82, assoc. dir., 1974—82; adj. attending ophthalmologist Bronx Lebanon Hosp. Ctr., 1975—77, assoc. attending ophthalmologist, 1977—79; cons. dept. ophthalmology Beth Israel Med. Ctr., 1979—87; lectr. in field. Editor, transl.: Hugonniers' textbook Strabismus, heterophoria, ocularmotor paralysis, 1st edit., 1969; author: (textbook translated in French, Japanese and Portuguese) Prisms in the Medical and Surgical Management of Strabismus; contbr. 32 chpts. to books, articles more than 35 articles to sci. jours. Established endowment of biennial internat. prize Pan Am. Assn. Ophthalmology, 1991; established ann. prize Women in Ophthalmology, San Francisco, 1997; established perpetual endowment ann. scholarships and prize dept. edn. U. Que., Montreal, 1999; established perpetual endowment ann. scholarships dept. ophthalmology U. Montreal, 2006. Recipient Residents award for outstanding tchg., N.Y. Eye and Ear Infirmary, 1970, Spl. Achievement medal, U. Montreal, 1993. Fellow: ACS (life), Royal Coll. Surgeons Can.; mem.: AMA (life), Am. Ophthalmol. Soc., Am. Acad. Ophthalmology (life Honor award 1981), Pan Am. Assn. Ophthalmology (life; bd. dirs. 1993—2003), Med. Soc. of the State of N.Y. (life), Am. Assn. Pediat. Ophthalmology and Strabismus (life; charter mem.). Home: 10175 Collins Ave Apt 1506 Bal Harbour FL 33154 Personal E-mail: sveronneautroutman@me.com.

VEROUX, MASSIMILIANO, physician, researcher; b. Catania, Italy, Sept. 28, 1971; s. Gastone Veroux and Giovanna Santisi. Diploma in sci., U. Catania, Italy, 1989; D in Traumatology, 2003. Fellow Dept Surg. Transplant and Adv. Technology, Catania, Italy, 1995—98, Dept. Surg. and Gastroenterol. Scis., Padova, Italy, 1998—2000, Dept. Surg. and Transplantation, Catania, Italy, 2000—01; rschr. Dept. Surg., Transplantation, and Advanced Technologies, Catania, Italy, 2001—, assoc. prof. surgery, 2002. Cons. Dept. Surg., Transplantation, and Advanced Technologies, Catania, Italy, 2003—. Author: (book) Chirurgia (Premio Ruggeri award, 2001), (journal) Neurotoxicity In Tacrolimus-treated Renal Transplant Recipients (Premio Consorzio Interuniversitario Trapianti d'Organo award, 2002). Mem.: Italian Soc. Surgery (assoc. premio ruggeri 2001). Avocations: waterpolo, travel, swiming, computer. Office: Dept Surg Transplant and Adv Tech Via Santa Sofia 78 Catania 95128 Italy Home: Viale Raffaello Sanzio 60 95128 Catania CT Italy Office Fax: 39-095-3782206; Home Fax: 39-095-3782207. Personal E-mail: mveroux@yahoo.it. Business E-Mail: veroux@unict.it.

VERRICO, MARGARET MARY, pharmacist; d. Michael P. and Corinne E. Lynam, James R. Lynam (Stepfather); m. Anthony J. Verrico, June 5, 1976; children: Teresa M.(dec.), Anthony J., Maria E. BS summa cum laude in Pharmacy, U. Pitts., 1993. Registered pharmacist Pa., 1993. Drug info. pharmacist Thrift Drug, Pitts., 1993—94, U. Pitts., 1994—. Faculty mem. Sch. Pharmacy U. Pitts., 1994—; co-chmn. allergy task force U. Pitts. Med. Ctr., 2003—09, co-chmn. adverse drug event subcom., 1994—2009. Contbg. author: Pharmacotherapy: A Patient-Focused Approach. First Edition, 1997, Pharmacotherapy: A Patient-Focused Approach. Instructor's Guide, 1997; contbr. articles to profl. jours., chapters to books. Mem. U. Pitts. Senate Libr. Com., 2010—, United Way Women's Leadership Initiative, 2003—. Recipient Dean's award, McNeil Pharms., 1992, Excellence in Pharmacy award, Mylan Pharms., 1993, Clin. Practice Poster award, Am. Soc. Pain Mgmt. Nurses, 2000, Quality and Innovation Fair for UPMC Presbyn.-Patient Safety award, 2010; Semple Meml. scholar, U. Pitts., 1989—93, U. Pitts. scholar, 1991—93. Mem.: Am. Soc. Health Sys. Pharmacists, Rho Chi (assoc.), Nat. Golden Key Soc. (assoc.). Roman Catholic. Office: University Pitts PFG 01-01-01 200 Lothrop St Pittsburgh PA 15213 Office Fax: 412-647-4362. Business E-Mail: verricomm@upmc.edu.

VERSFELT, MARY G., pediatrician, educator; Attended, Columbia U. Coll. Physicians and Surgeons, 1978. Diplomate Am. Bd. Pediatrics. Intern Columbia-Presbyn. Med. Ctr., NYC, resident in pediat., 1979—81; assoc. clin. prof. pediat. Columbia-Presbyn.; with Westchester Med. Ctr.; pediatrician Greenwich Hosp. Office: Greenwich Hospital Pediatrics Associates - NE Medical Group 26 Rye Ridge Plz Rye Brook NY 10573 Office Phone: 914-251-1100. Office Fax: 914-251-1109.

VERSIANI, MARCO AURÉLIO, dentist; b. Belo Horizonte, May 23, 1971; Degree in Dentistry, U. Fed. Minas Gerais, 1992; PhD, U. Sao Paulo, 2011. Dept. head Polícia Militar Minas Gerais, 2002—. Adj. prof. U. São Paulo, 2009—. Decorated Brazilian Mil. Decoration Bronze medal Polícia Militar Minas Gerais. Mem.: Internat. Assn. Dental Rsch. Avocations: guitar, running. Office: FORP/USP Av do Café Ribeirão Preto São Paulo 14040-904 Brazil E-mail: marcoversiani@yahoo.com.

VERST, CYNTHIA L., pharmaceutical executive; BS in Biology and Chemistry, No. Ky. U.; MS in Structural and Cellular Biology, U. Ill.; BS in Pharmacy, U. Cin., PharmD. Sect. head N.Am. med. & tech. affairs P&G Pharmaceuticals, Cin., 1994—2002; v.p. late phase Kendle Internat. Inc., Cin., 2002—07; sr. v.p. late phase rsch. i3 Innovus Inc., Medford, Mass., 2007—11; global head late phase ops. Quintiles, Durham, NC, 2011—. Office: Quintiles 4820 Emperor Blvd Durham NC 27703 Office Phone: 919-998-2000. Office Fax: 919-998-2003.

VER STEEG, DONNA LORRAINE FRANK, nurse, sociologist, educator; b. Minot, ND, Sept. 23, 1929; d. John Jonas and Pearl H. (Denlinger) Frank; m. Richard W. Ver Steeg, Nov. 22, 1950; children: Juliana, Anne, Richard B. BSN, Stanford, 1951; MSN, U. Calif., San Francisco, 1967; MA in Sociology, UCLA, 1969, PhD in Sociology, 1973. Clin. instr. U. ND Sch. Nursing, 1962-63; USPHS nurse rsch. fellow UCLA, 1969-72, asst. prof. Sch. Nursing, 1973-79, assoc. prof. Sch. Nursing, 1979-94, asst. dean Sch. Nursing, 1979-81, chmn. primary ambulatory care Sch. Nursing, 1976-87, assoc. dean Sch. Nursing, 1983-86, prof. emeritus chair primary care Sch. Nursing, 1994-96, prof. emeritus Sch. Nursing, 1996—; spl. cons., mem. adv. com. on physicians' assts. and nurse practitioner progs. Calif. State Bd. Med. Examiners, 1972-73. Co-prin. investigator PRIMEX Project Family Nurse Practitioners, UCLA Ext., 1974—76; assoc. cons. Calif. Postsecondary Edn. Commn., 1975—76; spl. cons. Calif. Dept. Consumer Affairs, 1978; chair nurse practioner/physician's asst. statewide program planning com. Calif. Area Health Edn. Ctr., 1978—89; mem. Calif. State Legis. Health Policy Forum, 1980—81; accredited visitor Western Assn. Sch. and Coll., 1985; mem. nurse practitioner adv. com. Calif. Bd. RN, 1995—97; mem. Edn. Industry Interface, Info. Devel. Mktg. Sub Com., 1995—99, recruitment, 1999—2001; archivist Calif. Strategic Planning Com. Nursing/Colleagues in Caring Project, 1995—. Contbr. chpts. to profl. books, articles to profl. jours. Recipient Leadership award Calif. Area Health Edn. Ctr. Sys., 1989, Commendation award Calif. State Assembly, 1994; named Outstanding Faculty Mem., UCLA Sch. Nursing, 1982. Fellow Am. Acad. Nursing; mem. AAAS, AAUW, ANA (Calif.) (pres. 1979-81, interim chair 1995-96), Nat. League Nursing, Calif. League Nursing, N.Am. Nursing Diagnosis Assn., Am. Assn. History Nursing, Stanford Nurses Club, Sigma Theta Tau (Alpha Eta chpt. Leadership award Gamma Tau chpt. 1994), Sigma Xi. Office: UCLA Sch Nursing Box 956917 Los Angeles CA 90095-6917 Home: Behmont Village 425 10775 Wilshire Blvd Los Angeles CA 90024 Personal E-mail: dversteeg@aol.com. Business E-Mail: dverstee@sonnet.ucla.edu.

VERTREES, AMY E., surgeon; b. Feb. 21, 1974; BS, Ga. Tech, 1995; MD, Uniformed Svcs. U. Health Scis., 2004. Gen. surgery resident Walter Reed Army Med. Ctr., 2004—10, attending surgeon, maj. AUS, 2010—; deployed gen. surgeon 745th Forward Surg. Team, Afghanistan, 2011. Decorated Army Achievement medal US Army; recipient Outstanding Med. Student award, Assn. Mil. Surgeons US, 2004, Outstanding Resident award, Assn. Women Surgeons, 2009, D'Avis award, Dept. Surgery, Walter Reed Army Med. Ctr., 2010. Mem.: AMA, ACS, Soc. Am. Gastrointestinal and Endoscopic Surgeons, Assn. Mil. Surgeons US, Assn. Women Surgeons. Avocations: reading, running. Home: 11506 Alma St Silver Spring MD 20902 Personal E-mail: vertrees57@yahoo.com.

VESELL, ELLIOT SAUL, pharmacologist, educator; b. NYC, Dec. 24, 1933; s. Harry and Evelyn (Jaffe) Vesell; m. Kristen Paige Peery, Mar. 24, 1968; children: Liane Clark, Hilary Peery. AB magna cum laude, Harvard U., 1955, MD magna cum laude, 1959; DSc (hon.), Phila. Coll. Pharmacy & Sci., 1988; PhD (hon.), Philipps U., Marburg, Germany, 1991. Intern, children's med. svc. Mass. Gen. Hosp., Boston, 1959-60; rsch. assoc. Rockefeller U., NYC, 1960-62; asst. resident medicine Peter Bent Brigham Hosp., Boston, 1962-63, clin. assoc. Nat. Inst. Arthritis Metabolic Diseases, NIH, Bethesda, Md., 1963-65; head sect. pharmacogenetics Nat. Heart Inst., NIH, Bethesda, 1965-68; Evan Pugh prof. pharmacology Pa. State U., Hershey, 1968—, asst. dean grad. edn., 1973-96, chmn. dept. pharmacology Coll. Medicine, 1968—2000, Bernard B. Brodie prof., 1991—. Pfizer vis. prof.; Burroughs Wellcome vis. prof. Editor: The Life and Works of Thomas Cole, 1964, Progress in Basic and Clin. Pharmacology, 1990, others; contbr. articles to profl. jours. Recipient Von Humboldt award, 1988. Fellow: AAAS, Royal Soc. Medicine (Frohlich vis. prof. 1985); mem.: Am. Soc. Clin. Pharmacology Therapeutics (Oscar B. Hunter Meml. award 1991), Am. Coll. Clin. Pharmacology (pres. 1980—82, Disting. Investigator award 1999), Am. Soc. Pharmacology Exptl. Therapeutics (sec.-treas. 1995—98, Exptl. Therapeutics award 1971, Harry Gold award clin. pharmacology 1985), Am. Soc. Clin. Investigation, Assn. Am. Physicians, Phi Beta Kappa, Alpha Omega Alpha. Office: Pa State U Coll Medicine Dept Pharmacology PO Box 850 Hershey PA 17033-0850 Office Phone: 717-531-8285. Business E-Mail: esv1@psu.edu.

VEST, GAYLE SOUTHWORTH, obstetrician, gynecologist; b. Duluth, Minn., Apr. 7, 1948; d. Russell Eugene and Brandon (Young) Southworth; m. Steven Lee Vest, Nov. 27, 1971; 1 child, Matthew Steven. BS, U. Mich., 1970. Diplomate Am. Bd. Ob-Gyn. Intern in ob-gyn. Milw. County Gen. Hosp., 1974-75, So. Ill. U. Sch. Medicine, 1975-78; pvt. practice Chapel Hill (N.C.) Ob-Gyn., 1978-80; asst. attending physician dept. ob-gyn. U. N.C. Sch. Medicine, Chapel Hill, 1978-80; clin. assoc. dept. ob-gyn. Duke U. Med. Ctr., Durham, NC, 1978-80; pvt. practice Big Stone Gap (Va.) Clinic, 1980-88, Norwise Ob-Gyn. Assocs., Norton, Va., 1988—. Fellow: ACOG; mem.: Med. Soc. Va., Christian Med. and Dental Assn. Avocations: skiing, kayaking, travel.

VEST, STEVEN LEE, gastroenterologist, hepatologist, internist; b. Mpls., July 30, 1948; s. Lee Herbert and Marian Mize (Rains) V.; m. Gayle Maureen Southworth, Nov. 27, 1971; 1 child, Matthew Steven. BA, U. Minn., 1970, MD, 1974. Diplomate Am. Bd. Internal Medicine, Am. Bd Gastroenterology. Intern internal medicine Milw. County Hosp., 1974—75; resident internal medicine So. Ill. U., Springfield, 1975—77; fellow gastroenterology and hepatology Duke U. Med. Ctr., Durham, NC, 1978—80; cons. gastroenterology-hepatology and internal medicine Lonesome Pine Hosp., Big Stone Gap, Va., 1980—; cons. gastroenterology and internal medicine Norton Cmty. Hosp., Norton, 1985—. Chmn. med. care evaluation, Lonesome Pine Hosp., Big Stone Gap, 1984-88, chmn. pharmacy, therapeutics and transfusion com., 1992-94; chief of medicine Norton Cmty. Hosp., 1991-93, 97-99, exec. com., bd. dirs., 1993-2002, 05—, mem. credentials com., 1995-97, bylaws com., 1996-97 Fellow ACP-Am. Soc. Internal Medicine, Am. Coll. Gastroenterology, Am. Gastroent. Assn.; mem. Am. Soc. Internal Medicine, Va. Med. Soc. (state del. 1992), Wise County Med. Soc. (treas. 1984-86, v.p. 1991-92, pres. 1992-93), Am. Assn. Christian Counselors, Wise County C. of C. Methodist. Avocations: kayaking, jogging, skiing, photography, Karate. Home: Powell Valley 1800 Egan Rd Big Stone Gap VA 24219-4224 Office: NCH Med Arts Bldg 2 98 15th St NW Ste 202 Norton VA 24273-1600 Office Phone: 276-679-0244. Business E-Mail: slvest9815nch1@verizon.net.

VETROVEC, GEORGE WAYNE, cardiologist, medical researcher, educator; b. Akron, Ohio, Aug. 12, 1943; MD, U. Va., 1970. Diplomate Am. Bd. Internal Medicine, Am. Bd. Cardiovascular Medicine. Intern, medicine Med. Coll. Va., Richmond, 1970-71, resident, cardiology, 1971-74, fellow in cardiology, 1974-76; faculty mem. Va. Commonwealth U., Richmond, 1976—, chmn., prof. med. cardiology, 1986—, chmn. divsn. cardiology, Pauley Heart Ctr., dir. Adult Cardiac Catheterization Lab., assoc. chmn. of medicine for clin. affairs, Dept. Internal Medicine, Martha M. and Harold W. Kimmerling, M.D. chair cardiology. Mem. staff Med. Coll. Va.; mem. VCUHS Authority Bd. Dirs. Contbr. several articles to journals, chapters to books; mem. of several editl. bds. Recipient W. Robert Irby Philanthropic Leadership Award, MCV Found.; named Clinician of Yr., 1997; named one of Best Doctors in Am., Best Doctors Inc.; named to AOA Med. Honor Soc. Fellow: ACP, European Soc. Cardiology, Royal Coll. Physicians of Thailand, Soc. Cardiac Angiography and Interventions (past pres.), Am. Coll. Cardiology, Am. Coll. Chest Physicians; mem.: Irish Cardiac Soc., Assn. Univ. Cardiologists (past pres.), Assn. Profs. Cardiology (past pres.), Physician Workforce Adv. Com. (former chmn. bd. trustees), Am. Heart Assn. (former pres. Richmond Coun. and Va. Affiliate, chmn. Mid Atlantic Regi, chmn. Catheterization Com, Coun. Clin. Cardiology, Nat. Award of Merit 1991, Richmond Golden Heart Award 1997). Office: Divsn Cardiology Virginia Commonwealth U Health Sys PO Box 980036 Richmond VA 23298-0036 Office Phone: 804-828-8885. Business E-Mail: gvetrovec@mcvh-vcu.edu.

VETTER, LOUISE, medical association administrator; CEO Am. Lung Assn., NYC, 2000—09, Huntington's Disease Soc. America, NYC, 2009—. Office: Huntington's Disease Soc America 505 Eighth Ave Ste 902 New York NY 10018 Office Phone: 212-242-1968 ext. 220. Office Fax: 212-239-3430. Business E-Mail: lvetter@hdsa.org. *

VETTER, VICTORIA L., pediatric cardiologist, educator; b. Louisville, Aug. 15, 1946; d. Albert Elmo and Mildred Irene Vetter; m. Anthony S. Jennings, June 8, 1974; children: Jennifer, Jonathan, Jason. BA in Chemistry, U. Ky., 1968, MD, 1972; MPH, U. Pa., 2009, MS in Health Policy, 2010. Bd. cert. Am. Bd. Pediat. in Pediat. and Pediat. Cardiology. Intern pediat. Johns Hopkins Hosp., Balt., 1972—73, resident pediat., 1973—74; sr. resident pediat. Vanderbilt U. Hosp., Nashville, 1974—75; fellow pediat. cardiology The Children's Hosp. Phila., 1975—78, asst. cardiologist, 1978—82, assoc. cardiologist, 1982—89, sr. cardiologist, 1989—, dir. pediat. electrophysiology lab., 1978—95, dir. pediat. electrocardiography lab., 1978—, chief divsn. cardiology, 1993—; sr. physician dept. pediat. U. Pa. Sch. Medicine, 1989—. Instr. pediat. U. Pa. Sch. Medicine, 1978, asst. prof. pediat., 1978—81, prof. pediat., 1999—; asst. prof. pediat. The Children's Hosp. Phila., U. Pa. Sch. Medicine, 1981—87, assoc. prof. pediat., 1987—99, Evelyn R. Tabas chair in pediatric cardiology, 2005—; lectr. in field. Sci. reviewer: jours. Circulation, Am. Jour. Cardiology, Jour. Am. Coll. Cardiology, Pediat. Cardiology, Pacing and Clin. Electrophysiology, Pediat. Rsch., Clin. Pediat., Annals of Internal Medicine, New Eng. Jour. Medicine, Jour. Cardiovasc. Electrophysiology, Jour. Pediat., Am. Jour. Diseases of Children, Pediat. Emergency Care; contbr. chapters to books, articles and abstracts to jours. Grantee in field. Fellow: Am. Coll. Cardiology (mem. emergency cardiac care com. 1992—98, mem. pediat. cardiology com. 1994—96, mem. 1996 annual sci. session program com. 1995—96, mem. credentials com. 1997—2000), Am. Acad. Pediat. (mem. exec. com. pediat. cardiology subsect. 1989—92, Young Investigator award sect. on cardiology 1978); mem.: AMA, Nat. Heart, Lung & Blood Inst. (prin. investigator 2001—), John Morgan Soc., Phila. Arrhythmia Group, Pediat. Arrhythmia Group (mem. steering com.), Phila. County Med. Soc., Internat. Registry for Drug-Induced Arrhythmias (mem. sci. adv. com.), Sudden Arrhythmia Death Syndromes Found. (mem. sci. adv. bd.), Cardiac Arrhythmias Rsch. and Edn. Found., Inc. (mem. sci. adv. bd., Heart of the Child award 1996), N.Am. Soc. Pacing and Electrophysiology (mem. annual sci. sessions program com. 1998—2001, mem. pediat. com. 1998—2001), Pediat. Electrophysiology Soc., Am. Heart Assn. Coun. on Cardiovasc. Disease in the Young (mem. exec. com. 1993—98, mem. com. on tng. in pediat. cardiology 1994—96, mem. com. on electrocardiography and arrhythmias 1995—97, mem. membership com. 1996—97, chair Rashkind lecture selection com.), Am. Heart Assn. (med. spokesperson), Am. Heart Assn. Southeastern Pa. Affiliate (mem. rsch. peer rev. com. 1987—92, program chairperson 1988—90, mem. exec. com. 1988—93, v.p. 1989—90, pres.-elect 1990—91, pres. 1991—92, past-pres. 1992—93, mem. bd. dirs. 1993—96, mem. bd. govs. 1994—96, mem. pediat. sub-com. cardiac support coalition 1997—, post-doctoral fellow 1976—77, 1978—79), Alpha Omega Alpha, Phi Beta Kappa. Home: 110 Willow Way Cherry Hill NJ 08034-3049 Office: The Childrens Hosp Phila 34th St & Civic Center Blvd Philadelphia PA 19104 Home Phone: 856-429-5745; Office Phone: 215-590-3529.

VEYRAT, COLETTE F., cardiologist research, consultant; d. André J. Tardy and Marguerite E. Deshayes; m. Jean-Gérald M. Veyrat, June 27, 1957; children: Stéphane M., Elisabeth E. MD, U. Paris Faculté Médecine, 1963. Cert. cardiologist Ctr. Nat. Rsch. Sci., 1967. Sr. rschr. Ctr. Nat. Rsch. Sci., Paris, 1967—97; pres. Internat. Cardiac Doppler Soc., Seattle, 1990—94; rschr. dir. echolaboratory Ins. Nat. Rsch. Sci., Paris, 1994—2001. Dir. echo-laboratory and non-invasive techniques rschr. Asst. Publique-Hôpitaux Paris, 1967—2001, ednl. cons., 1967—2001. Contbr. articles to profl. med. jours. Recipient Silver medal Faculty Medicine, 1963; grant, INSERM, 1982—88. Achievements include first woman cardiologist to launch the cardiac Doppler technique using the first directional Doppler Flowmeter, first computerized continuous analysis of myocardial velocities. Business E-Mail: colette.veyrat.resedal@noos.fr.

VEZERIDIS, MICHAEL PANAGIOTIS, surgeon, educator; b. Thessaloniki, Greece, Dec. 16, 1943; came to U.S., 1974; s. Panagiotis and Sofia (Avramidis) V.; m. Therese Mary Statz; children: Peter Statz, Alexander Michael. MD, U. Athens, 1967; MA ad eundem (hon.), Brown U., 1989. Diplomate Am. Bd. Surgery. Fellow surg. rsch. Harvard Med. Sch./Mass. Gen. Hosp., Boston, 1974-77; resident U. Mass., Worcester, 1977-80; fellow in surg. oncology Roswell Park Meml. Inst., Buffalo, 1980-81, attending surgeon, 1981-82; staff surgeon VA Med. Ctr., Providence, 1982-84; asst. prof. surgery Brown U., Providence, 1982-88; chief surg. oncology VA Med. Ctr., Providence, 1984—, assoc. chief surgery, 1986-98, chief surgery, 1998—; cons. in surgery R.I. Hosp., Providence, 1987—, co-dir. multidisciplinary Melanoma program, 2000—; surg. oncologist Roger Williams Med. Ctr., Providence, 1989—; assoc. dir. divsn. surg. oncology Brown U., Providence, 1989—98, assoc. prof. surgery, 1988-94, prof., 1994—; prof. surgery Boston U. Sch. Medicine, 1999—. Chmn. profl. edn. com. R.I. divsn. Am. Cancer Soc., Providence, 1987-89, pres.-elect 1989-91, pres. 1991-93, del. dir. to nat. bd. dirs., 1993-96, mem.

Nat. Assembly of the Am. Cancer Soc., 1997-2003, mem. internat. activities adv. com., 2003-07, bd. dirs. New Eng. divsn., 1997-2005, chief med. officer New. Eng. divsn., 1999-2001; chmn. R.I. State Cancer Liaison Program Am. Coll. Surgeons, 1999-2008, mem. commn. on cancer, 2003-09, bd. dirs. Rhode Island Cancer Coun., 2004-; vis. prof. U. Patras (Greece) Med. Sch., 1988; mem. sci. adv. com. Clin. Rsch. Ctr., Brown U., Providence, 1989-91. Co-dir. Multidisciplinary Melanoma Program, 2000-; contbr. articles to profl. jours. and chpts. in med. books. Mem. parish coun. Ch. of Annunciation, Cranston, R.I., 1985-91; v.p. Hellenic Cultural Soc. Southeastern New Eng., Providence, 1987-89. Decorated Navy Commendation medal; named Profl. Fed. Employee of Yr., R.I. Fed. Exec. Coun., 1987; recipient St. George medal Am. Cancer Soc.; Merit Rev. Cancer Rsch. grantee VA, 1983-89. Fellow ACS (treas. R.I. chpt. 1996-2000, pres.-elect 2000-2002, pres. 2002-2004, gov.-at-large, 2009-); mem. Soc. Surg. Oncology, Assn. for Acad. Surgery, Am. Soc. Clin. Oncology, N.Y. Acad. Scis. (life), Soc. for Surgery Alimentary Tract, Am. Assn. for Cancer Rsch., Collegium Internat. Chirurgiae Digestivae, Assn. Mil. Surgeons U.S., Soc. for Metastasis Rsch., New Eng. Cancer Soc., New Eng. Surg. Soc., Quidnessett Country Club. Greek Orthodox. Avocations: classical music, reading, fencing, tennis, squash, cross country skiing. Home: 50 Limerock Dr East Greenwich RI 02818-1643 Office: Univ Surg Assocs Ste 470 Two Dudley St Providence RI 02905 Office Phone: 401-331-1036. Business E-Mail: michael_vezeridis@brown.edu.

VEZNIK, ZDENEK, medical researcher, educator; b. Brno, Czech Republic, June 30, 1928; s. Frantisek Veznik and Marie Veznikova; m. Dagmar Horálkova, Dec. 21, 1955; children: Dagmar Velehradska, Zdena Sabelova. DVM, U. Vet. Scis., Brno, 1953; PhD, U. Vet. and Pharm. Scis., Brno, 1961, DSc, 1994. Rschr. Tchg. Hosp., Brno, 1953—55; scientist Vet. Rsch. Inst., Brno, 1956—2005, head dept. reproduction, 1961—2001, head nat. reference lab. for spermatology, 2002—. Lectr., post-grad. tchr. State Vet. Adminstrn., Prague, Czech Republic, 1976—; lectr. Mendel U. Agr. and Forestry, Brno, 1992—, U. Pardubice, Czech Republic, 1996—. Author: (book) Chlamydia Infections, Continuing Professional Education In Spermatology and Andrology; mem. editl. bd.: Vet. Med.-Czech, 1995—2005; contbr. articles to profl. jours. Head Horse Riding Sect., Brno, 1980—2005. Recipient medal for cooperation with human medicine, Masaryk U., Brno, 1998. Master: Vet. Med. Coun. (pres. 1990—92), Czech Acad. Agrl. Scis. (sect. vet. medicine 1995—2004, presidium mem. 1995—2004); mem.: Czechoslovak Soc. Biology. Achievements include patents for Automatic Curette For Endometrial Sample Collection From Animals. Avocations: music, gardening, painting, horseback riding. Home: Veveri 52 602 00 Brno Czech Republic Office: Veterinary Research Institute Hudcova 70 621 00 Brno Czech Republic Office Fax: 00 4205 4121 1229. Business E-Mail: veznik@vri.cz.

VIALLE, LUIZ, orthopedist, educator; b. Curitiba, Brazil, Apr. 15, 1947; MD, 1970, PhD. Prof. orthopaedics Cath. U. Parana, 1980—. Internat. chmn. AOSpine Internat. - AO Found., 2009—. Office: Brigadeiro Franco 979 Curitiba Parana 80.430-210 Brazil E-mail: vialle@uol.com.br.

VIANNA, CAIO BRITO, cardiologist, educator; b. Sao Paulo, Brazil, Oct. 18, 1954; MD, U. Sao Paulo, 1979, PhD, 1999. Asst. physician heart inst., adj. prof. U. Sao Paulo, Med. Sch., 1999—. Mem.: Brazilian Soc. Cardiology. Avocation: fishing. Home: Consolação St 2984 Apt 71 Sao Paulo 01416000 Brazil Home Phone: 30695387. Home Fax: 30695348. Personal E-mail: caio.vianna@incor.usp.br.

VIANNA, ROSSANA CRISTINA X. F., physician; b. Maringá, Paraná, Brazil, Nov. 30, 1960; Degree, Faculdade Evangélica Medicina do Paraná, 1984; MS, Pontificia U. Cath. do Paraná, 2007. Physician, médica Prefeitura Mcpl. Saúde Colombo, 1992, Secretaria do Estado da Saúde do Paraná, 1983—, cons., 2003. Mem.: Com. Estadual Ética em Pesquisa do Estado do Paraná, Com. Prevenção da Mortalidade Infantil do Estado do Paraná. Avocations: dance, music. Home: Rua João Waldir Teixeira de Faria 11 Curitiba Paraná 82700-560 Brazil Home Fax: 55 41 35853665. Personal E-mail: rossanacxfv@yahoo.com.br.

VICARIO, PASQUALE P., retired biochemist; b. East Stroudsburg, Pa., Feb. 12, 1950; BS, Moravian Coll., 1972; PhD, Rutgers U., 1988. Sr. rsch. assoc. Merck & Co., 1979—2005; group leader for R & D Hydromer, Inc., 2006—10. Home: 197 Harding Ave North Plainfield NJ 07063 Personal E-mail: ppv50@aol.com.

VICAS, LAURA GRATIELA, pharmacist, educator; b. Oradea, Jan. 17, 1967; Degree in pharmacy, U. Medicine & Pharmacy 'Iuliu Hatieganu', Cluj Napoca, 1991. Prof. U. Oradea, 2008—. Master: Coll. Pharmacists; mem.: Romanian Soc. Pharm. Scis. Avocations: piano, bicycling. Office: Leaganului Oradea Bihor 410003 Romania Office Fax: 0040359410944. Personal E-mail: laura.vicas@gmail.com.

VICENCIO, ALFIN GEMIL, pediatrician; s. Alfin S. and Miguela Vicencio; life ptnr. Rose Anne Mallon. MD, Med. Coll. Ohio, Toledo, 1996. Cert. in medicine NY. Pediatric resident, babies and childrens hosp. Columbia U., NYC, 1996—99; fellow, pediatric pulmonology Yale U., New Haven, 1999—2002; attending physician Children's Hosp. Montefiore, Bronx, NY, 2002—.

VICK, DANA JAMES, physician; b. Rochester, Minn., June 21, 1962; s. Alan George and Patricia Ann (Korum) V.; m. Anne Marie Troisi, Oct. 30, 1993. BA, U. Va., 1984; postgrad., Piedmont Va. C.C., Charlottesville, 1985-89; MD, Va. Commonwealth U., 1994; MBA in Healthcare Mgmt., Regis U., 2008. Cert. grad. with honors Inducted to Alpha Sigma Nu, 2008. Summer rsch. student The Mayo Clinic, Rochester, Minn., 1982, 83; telemktg. rep. Comdial Corp., Charlottesville, Va., 1984-86; lab. specialist U. Va. Sch. of Medicine, Charlottesville, 1986-89, summer rsch. student, 1990; commd. 2d lt. USAR, 1989, advanced through grades to maj., 2000, honorable discharge, 2003; transitional intern Walter Reed Army Med. Ctr., Washington, 1994-95, Nat. Capital Consortium pathology resident, 1995-99; chief anat. pathology DeWitt Army Cmty. Hosp., Ft. Belvoir, Va., 1999—2002; chief anat. pathology, med. dir. microbiology Eisenhower Army Med. Ctr., Ft. Gordon, Ga., 2002—03; assoc. pathologist St. Josph's Pathology, P.C., Syracuse, NY, 2003—10; med. advisor microbiology Lab. Alliance Ctrl. N.Y., 2003—10; v.p. med. affairs, chief med. officer Oneida Healthcare, NY, 2011—. Adj. asst. prof. dept. pathology USUHS, Bethesda, Md., 1996-2003; lectr. specialist in blood banking program Walter Reed Army Med. Ctr., Washington, 1996-99; guest lectr. specialist in blood banking NIH, Bethesda, 1997-99; guest lectr. immunohematology rev. course, 1996—99. Contbr. articles to profl. jours. Chair U.S. Army delegation AMA-RFS, 1996-99, reference com., 1997, Md. state coord. Smoking is Not for Me Nat. Essay Contest, 1998. Decorated Meritorious Svc. medal (2), Army Commendation medal; recipient Excellence in Medicine Leadership award, AMA Found., 2006, NY State Conspicuous Svc. Cross. award, 2006. Fellow Coll. Am. Pathologists (chmn. NY delegation, 2005-11), Royal Soc. Medicine, Am. Soc. Clin. Pathology; mem. AMA (mem.-at-large AMA-RFS governing coun. 1998-99, US Army del. young physicians sect. 1999-2001, mem.-at-large AMA-YPS governing coun. 2001—03, NY state alternate del. AMA-HOD, 2009-), Wash. Soc. Pathologists (exec. coun.), Am. Soc. Cytopathology, Assn. Mil. Surgeons of US, Nat. Med. Vets. Soc.(bd. dirs., 2004-05), US and Can. Acad. of Pathology, Med. Soc. State NY, NY State Soc. Pathologists (chmn. profl. affairs com. 2004-06, sec. & treas. 2007-11), Onondaga County Med. Soc., Soc. Med. Cons. to the Armed Forces, Syracuse Symphony Orch. (bd. dirs. 2008-11), Alpha Sigma Nu, Med. Soc. State NY (vice chair com. emergency preparedne & bioterrorism response 2008-, mem. budget fin. com. 2008-, vice chair benefits com. 2006-, mem. forensic medicine com. 2011-), Health Care Adv. Com. NY's 25th Congl. Dist. Avocations: instrumental and choral music, photography, golf. Home: 4443 Treetops Cir Manlius NY 13104 E-mail: djvick615@pol.net.

VICK, NICHOLAS A., neurologist; b. Chgo., Oct. 3, 1939; MD, U. Chgo., 1965. Diplomate Am. Bd. Neurology. Intern U. Chgo. Hosps., 1965, resident in neurology, 1966-68; fellow in neurology NIH, Bethesda, Md., 1968-70; staff Evanston (Ill.) Hosp., 1975—; prof. neurology Northwestern U. Med. Sch., Evanston, Ill., 1978—. Mem.: Am. Bd. Psychiatry and Neurology (past exec. dir.). Office: North Shore Univ Health Sys Dept Neurology 2650 Ridge Ave Evanston IL 60201-1781 Office Phone: 847-570-2570. Business E-Mail: nvick@enh.org, nvick@northshore.org.

VICKREY, HERTA M., microbiologist; b. San Gregorio, Calif. m. William David Vickrey; children: Ellean H., Carlene L. Smith, Corrine A. Pochop, Arlene A.; m. Robert James Fitzgibbon, Dec. 28, 1979. BA, San Jose State U., 1957; MA, U. Calif., Berkeley, 1963, PhD in Bacteriology and Immunology, 1970. Cert. immunologist, pub. health microbiologist, clin. lab. scientist. Pub. health microbiologist Viral & Rickettsial Diseases Lab., Calif. State Dept. Pub. Health, Berkeley, 1958-60, 61-62, 1964; postgrad. rsch. bacteriologist dept. bacteriology U. Calif., Berkeley, 1963-64; bacteriologist Children's Hosp. Med. Ctr. No. Calif., Oakland, 1958-70; asst. prof. U. Victoria, B.C., Can., 1970-72; rsch. assoc. rsch. dept. Wayne County Gen. Hosp., Wayne, Mich., 1972-83; lab. supr. med. rsch. and edn. U. Mich., Ann Arbor, 1977-83; pub. health lab. dir. Shasta County Pub. Health Svcs., Redding, Calif., 1983-84; sr. pub. health microbiologist Tulare County Pub. Health Lab., Tulare, Calif., 1984—2007, tech. supr. Visalia, Calif., 1992-93; med. technologist Hillman Health Clin. Lab., Tulare, Calif., 1994-96, clin. lab. scientist, 1996—2007. Vis. scientist MIT, Cambridge, 1982; organizer, lectr. mycology workshop Tulare County Health Dept. Lab., Visalia, 1988; USPHS trainee U. Calif., Berkeley, 1965, 66. Author: Isolation and Identification of Mycotic Agents, 1987-88; contbr. articles to profl. jours. Fundraiser Battered Women's Shelter, Redding, 1983, Real Opportunities for Youth, Visalia, 1985, 86, Open Gate Ministries, Dinuba, Visalia, 1987-94, 97-99, 2003, Leukemia and Lymphoma Soc., 2003, 04, 05, 06-11. Fellow NIH, 1966-69, Dr. E.E. Dowdle rsch. fellow, U. Calif., 1969-70; grantee U. Victoria, 1970-72, Med. Rsch. and Edn. and Med. Adminstrn., U. Mich., 1973-83. Mem. No. Calif. Assn. Pub. Health Microbiologists, Calif. Scholarship Soc., Am. Soc. Clin. Pathologists (assoc.), Phi Beta Kappa, Delta Omega, Phi Kappa Phi, Beta Beta Beta. Avocations: biking, swimming. Home: 3505 W Campus Dr Apt 5 Visalia CA 93277-1869

VICKY, LESTER HULTS, small business owner; b. Charleston, SC, Nov. 25, 1953; EdD, PhD, U. N.Mex, 2000. Owner Eternal Youth Med. Spa, 2009, mgr., 2009. Recipient Leadership award, Milken. Mem.: Albuquerque C. of C. Home: 4019 Silvery Minnow Pl Albuquerque NM 87120 Home Fax: 505-344-1352. Personal E-mail: lesterv433@aol.com.

VICO, LAURENCE, research scientist; b. St. Germain en Laye, France, June 6, 1958; PhD, U. Lyon, 1984, PhD, 1990. Dir. rsch. INSERM, 2000—. Lab. dir. INSERM and U., 2003. Recipient Les Scis. Du Vivant Dans L'espace award, Philip Morris. Mem.: Am. Soc. Bone and Mineral Rsch. Avocation: travel. Office: LBTO Inserm U1059 Medicine Faculty 15 R Saint-Etienne Loire 42023 French Guinea Office Fax: 33-477-55-57-72. Business E-Mail: vico@univ-st-etienne.fr.

VICTOR, LUI WC, psychiatrist; b. Hong Kong, Nov. 2, 1970; MB, U. Hong Kong, BChir, 1994; MS in Health and Hosp. Mgmt., U. Birmingham, 2003. Assoc. cons. Tai Po Hosp., 2006—. Hon. clin. asst. prof., dept. psychiatry Chinese U. Hong Kong, 2006—; mem. Guardianship Bd., Govt. Hong Kong Spl. Adminstrv. Region, 2008—. Hon. treas. Chinese Dementia Rsch. Assn., 2009—. Recipient Pfizer Rsch. award, Hong Kong Psychogeriatric Assn. Fellow: Hong Kong Acad. Medicine, Hong Kong Coll. Psychiatrists; mem.: Royal Coll. Psychiatrists. Avocation: photography. Office: Dept Psychiatry Tai Po Hosp Hong Kong Hong Kong

VIDAILLET, HUMBERTO J., JR., physician, administrator, researcher; b. Santiago, Cuba, Sept. 24, 1954; arrived in U.S., 1968; s. Humberto J. and Caridad Vidaillet; m. Debbie Vidaillet, June 6, 1981; children: Kelsey, Daniel, Corbin. MD, U. Okla., 1981. Resident in internal medicine Mayo Clinic, Rochester, Minn., 1981-84; tng. in cardiology/electrophysiology Duke U. Med. Ctr., Durham, NC, 1984-87; dir. cardiac electrophysiology Marshfield Clinic, Wis., 1987—2006, bd. dirs., 1989—, prin. investigator, Wis. Genomics Initiative, 2008—, exec. com. mem., 2009—, mem. bd. dirs., 2009—; assoc. clin. prof. medicine U. Wis. Sch. Medicine, Madison, 1994-2000, clin. prof. medicine, 2000—; assoc. dir. U. Wis. Inst. Clin. and Translational Rsch., 2007—; bd. dirs. Security Health Plan, 2009—. Prof. medicine U. Chile Sch. Medicine, 1994; cons. prof. medicine Inst. Med. Sci., Sch. Medicine, Medellin, Colombia, 1999; med. dir. arrhythmia svcs. St. Joseph Hosp., Marshfield, 1992-2006; mem. hosps. and clinics bd. and authority U. Wis., 2005—; rsch, and publs. com. Nat. Implantable Cardioverter Defibrillator Registry the Am. Coll. Cardiology, Bethesda, Md., 2006-08; bd. mem., Nat. Assn. Cuban Am. Educators, 2008-; adv. bd., Cuban Heritage Jour. Culture, 2008-; cons. in field. Contbr. articles to profl. jours. Parish coun. Our Lady of Peace Cath. Ch., Marshfield, 1996-2001; bd. dir. U. Wis. Found.; exec. com. Marshfield; vice chmn. bd. trustees Marshfield Clinic Rsch. Found., 1990-93, 2000-03, elected clin. physician rep. to bd. trustees, 2000—, vice-chair, 2003—05; coord., local prin. investigator clin. trials med. rsch., dir., Marshfield Clin. Rsch. Found., 2005-, dir. med. rsch., Marshfield Clin. Rsch. Found., 2005-; bd. dirs. New Visions Gallery, 1992-98; mem. found. bd. U. Wis. Marshfield/Wood County Campus, 1992-98. Am. Heart Assn. sr. investigator award, 1997, 15th Annual Gwen D. Sebold Rsch. Fellow ACP (chair internat. com. 1989-92, winner clin. paper competition 1984, 86, 87, faculty ann. sci. sessions, rsch. and publ. subcom.), Am. Coll. Cardiology (mem. edn. com., faculty sci. ann. sessions sr. investigator award 2000), Am. Coll. Chest Physicians, Heart Rhythm Soc. (faculty ann. sessions); mem. N.Am. Soc. Electrophysiology and Pacing (faculty ann. sci. sessions), Internat. Soc. Internal Medicine (sci. program commn.), Inter Am. Congress Cardiology (sci. program com. 2003), Intern Am. Coll. Cardiology (US rep. to sci. com., faculty ann. sci. session), Human Rights Worker Internat, Heart Rhythm Soc. Office: Marshfield Clinic 1000 N Oak Ave Marshfield WI 54449-5702 Business E-Mail: vidaillet.humberto@mcrf.mfldclin.edu.

VIDAL, MICHEL, medical educator; b. Castres, France, Nov. 27, 1966; s. René Vidal and Georgette Cros. Asst. prof. Faculté de Pharmacie, Paris, 1998—2005, prof., 2005—. Recipient, Chancellerie des U. de Paris, 1996. Achievements include patents for in field. Avocations: cooking, botany, travel. Office: Faculté de Pharmacie PAris Descartes Univ 4 avenue de l'Observatoire Paris 75006 France Personal E-mail: vidal.michel1@free.fr. Business E-Mail: michel.vidal@parisdescartes.fr.

VIDAVER, ANNE MARIE, plant pathology educator; b. Vienna, Mar. 29, 1938; came to U.S., 1941; d. Franz and Klara (Winter) Kopecky; children: Gordon W.F., Regina M. BA, Russell Sage Coll., 1960; MA, Ind. U., 1962, PhD, 1965. Lectr. U. Nebr., Lincoln, 1965-66, rsch. assoc., 1966-72, asst. prof., 1972-74, assoc. prof., 1974-79, prof. plant pathology, 1979—, interim dir. Ctr. Biotech., 1988-89, head dept. plant pathology, 1984-2000, 2003—06; chief scientist USDA's NRICGP, 2000—02. Contbr. articles to profl. jours. and books; patentee in field. Recipient Pub. Svc. award Nebr. Agri-Bus., 1977, Sci. award for excellence NAMA, New Orleans, 1991. Fellow AAAS, Am. Phytopath. Soc., Am. Soc. Microbiology; mem. Intersoc. Consortium for Plant Protection, Internat. Soc. Plant Pathology, Alliance for Prudent Use of Antibiotics. Avocations: indoor gardening, reading. Office: U Nebr Dept Plant Pathology Lincoln NE 68583-0722 Office Phone: 402-472-2858. E-mail: avidaver1@unl.edu.

VIDAVER, ROBERT MAXWELL, medical educator; b. Mpls., June 17, 1932; s. Robert William and Helen Mary (Ford) Vidaver; m. Virginia Moore Sewell, May 27, 1960. AB, Columbia U., 1953; MD, SUNY, 1956; MA (hon.), Dartmouth Coll., 1993. Diplomate Am. Bd. Psychiatry and Neurology, 1963. Intern in medicine U. Md., Balt., 1956—57; resident in psychiatry Yale U. Sch. Medicine, New Haven, 1957—60; asst. prof., coord. undergrad. edn. U. Md., Balt., 1962—65; state dir. psychiat. edn. Md. Dept. Health & Mental Hygiene, Balt., 1965—71; instr., asst. prof. Johns Hopkins Sch. Medicine, Balt., 1965—72; pres. First Md. Health Care Corp., Balt., 1971—72; assoc. prof. medicine and psychiatry N.J. Med. Sch., Newark, 1973—81, assoc. dean for hosp. affairs, 1979; med. dir. Martland Hosp., N.J. Med. Sch., Newark, 1974—78; prof., chmn. dept. psychiatry and behavioral sci. Ea. Va. Med. Sch., Norfolk, 1981—88; med. dir. N.H. Hosp., Concord, 1988—2008; prof., vice chmn. dept. psychiatry Dartmouth Med. Sch., Hanover, NH, 1988—2008, prof. emeritus, 2008—. Bd. dirs. NH Hosp., Concord, 1988—2004. Author: Developments in Human Services' Education and Manpower, 1973; contbr. articles to profl. jours. Capt. US Army, 1960—62. NY State Regents scholar, NY State Dept. Edn., Columbia U., 1949—53, NY State Profl. scholar, SUNY Coll. Medicine, 1952—56. Fellow: Am. Psychiat. Assn. (life; Disting.); mem.: NH Psychiat. Assn. (councillor), Alpha Omega Alpha (Leonard Tow Humanism in Medicine award, NH bd. medicine 2008). Episcopalian. Office: NH Hosp 36 Clinton St Concord NH 03301-2359 Personal E-mail: vvidaver@hotmail.com.

VIDELA, SEBASTIAN, medical researcher; b. Barcelona, Mar. 20, 1963; s. Eugenio Videla and Angeles Cés; m. Anna Maria Ristol; children: Laia, Alba. MD, Autonomous U. Barcelona, 1987, PhD, 1991. Cert. profl. pharmacologist U. Barcelona, 1993, clin. pharmacolgy specialist Spanish Health Ministry, 2001. Jr. rschr., pharmacology dept. Clin. Trial Unit, Clin., Hosp. Sant Pau, Barcelona, 1986—89; rschr. Digestive Sys. Unit, Vall Hebron Hosp., Barcelona, 1989—2008; clin. rsch. mgr. ESTEVE, Barcelona, 1997—; advisor, rschr. Lluita Contra la SIDA Found., Badalona, 2001—. Achievements include research in human papilloma virus co-infections in patients infected by the human immunodeficiency virus; clinical painkilers; gastrointestinal bleeding; intestinal microflora in chronic inflammation and ulceration of the rat colon; antifungals. Office: Esteve Avinguda Mare de Deu de Montserrat 221 8041 Barcelona Spain Office Fax: 34 93 456 87 74. Business E-Mail: svidela@esteve.es.

VIDELL, JARED STEVEN, cardiologist; b. Phila., Apr. 9, 1947; s. Harry and Rose (Malken) V.; m. Cyla Trocki, Dec. 27, 1969; children: Haviv Elana, Mikhael Alon, Samara Pilar. BEd, U. Miami, 1969; DO, Phila. Coll. Osteo. Medicine, 1976. Resident and chief resident in internal medicine Atlantic City (N.J.) Med. Ctr., 1976-79; fellow in cardiovascular diseases Albert Einstein Med. Ctr., Phila., 1979-81; rsch. fellow in nuclear cardiology Deborah Heart and Lung Ctr., Browns Mills, NJ, 1981-82, dir. employee health svcs., 1982-84; asst.

dir. cardiology Pritikin Longevity Ctr., Downington, Pa., 1984-87; cardiologist, dir. clin. lab. Physician Care, P.C., Towanda, Pa., 1987-90; from co-chmn. intensive care to dir. cardiac stress lab. Meml. Hosp., Towanda, 1987-90; dir. house staff, intensive/cardiac care Lower Bucks Hosp., Bristol, Pa., 1992-94; dir. house staff ICU-CCU North Phila. Health Systems, 1994-97; med. dir. North Phila. Health Sys. Girard Med. Ctr., 1997—, chmn. clin. medicine, 1997—. Med. dir. Am. Cancer Soc. chpt., 1989-90; state peer rev. KEPRO, 1989-90. LTC MC USAR. Fellow: Am. Soc. Angiology; mem.: POMA, AOA, Alumni Assn. Phila. Coll. Osteo. Medicine, Internat. Soc. Endovascular Surgery, Internat. Soc. Internal Medicine, Am. Soc. Internal Medicine, Am. Coll. Chest Physicians. Avocations: travel, fishing. Office Phone: 609-823-1989. Office Fax: 609-823-1989.

VIDJAK, NEDA, psychotherapist; b. Split, Croatia, Jan. 29, 1966; d. Nediljko Sucur and Irma Vidjak. Mathematician-informatician, Math.-Informatics Sch., Split, 1984; MD, Med. U., Zagreb, Croatia, 1989; theologian, Theol. U., Split, 1993; M of Med. Scis., Med. U., Zagreb, 2001. Dr. trainee Health's Home, Split, 1989—90; prof. Nursing Sch., Split, 1991—92; psychotherapist Meeting Comty., Split, 1992—. Vol. psychotherapist Tele-Apel Ctr., Split, 1990—92, Meeting Comty., Split, 1990—92, Refugees Ctr., Split, 1991, Prison, Split, 1992—93; leader Counseling Ctr. Meeting Cmty., Split, 1992—; rev. Croatian Med. Jour., 2003—. Mem. Adv. Coun. Archbishop, Split, 1992—2004. Mem.: Mensa. Roman Catholic. Avocations: fine arts, antiques, horticulture, travel. Home: R.Boskovica 12 21-000 Split Croatia Office Phone: 385 21 361 200, 385 21 345 288. Business E-Mail: nedavidjak@lnt.lr. E-mail: neda.vidjak@st.htnet.hr.

VIDUETSKY, ALEXANDER, sonologist, medical researcher; b. Vinnitsa, Ukraine, June 14, 1967; s. Vladimir and Galina Viduetsky; m. Lucy Veshchikova, Apr. 9, 1995. MD, Vinnitsa Med. Inst., Ukraine, 1994; PhD, Ternopil Med. Acad., Ukraine, 1998. Registered Am. Registry Diagnostic Med. Sonographers, 2000. Rschr. Vinnitsa State Med. U., 1994—98, sr. rschr., 1998—99; chief sonographer Advanced Radiology Beverly Hills, Calif., 1999—. Mem.: Am. Inst. Ultrasound in Medicine, Am. Soc. Echocardiography. Achievements include research in Ultrasound characteristics of Thyroid in children of Ukraine. Office: Advanced Radiology Beverly Hills 8641 Wilshire Blvd # 105 Beverly Hills CA 90211

VIEHBACHER, CHRISTOPHER J., pharmaceutical company executive; b. Canada, Mar. 26, 1960; m. Alison Viehbacher; 3 children. Chief. fin. acct. Wellcome GmbH, Germany, 1988—89, fin. dir., 1989—93; pres., CEO Burroughs Wellcome Inc., Canada, 1993—95; v.p. strategy/integration Glaxo Wellcome France, 1995—96, gen. mgr., 1996—97, chmn., mng. dir., 1997; pres. Europe Pharmaceuticals GlaxoSmithKline PLC, 2001—03, pres. US Pharmaceuticals, 2003—08, pres. N. Am. Pharmaceuticals, 2008; CEO Sanofi-Aventis, 2008—; pres., CEO Genzyme Corp., 2011—. Bd. dirs. Pharm. Rsch. Manufacturers of America (PhRMA), CEO Roundtable on Cancer, Research!America, NC GlaxoSmithKline Found., Sanofi-Aventis, 2008—. Bd. mem. Triangle United Way, Cardinal Club. Recipient Légion d'Honneur award, France, 2003. Office: Sanofi-Aventis 174 avenue de France 75013 Paris France also: Gynzyme Corp 500 Kendall St Cambridge MA 02142 *

VIEL, JEAN-FRANCOIS DENIS CLAUDE, medical educator, researcher; b. Le Havre, Upper Normandy, France, Oct. 23, 1956; s. André Viel and Renée Martin; m. Christine Marlène, Ghislaine Thibaut, July 31, 1982, children: Clément, Martin, Brieuc, Bérengère. MD, U. Caen Lower-Normandy, France, 1981; MPH, U. Rennes, France, 1984; PhD in Biostats. and Epidemiology, Paris South U., 1992. Pub. health physician Regional Hosp., Metz, Lorraine, France, 1988—90; rsch. asst. Biostats. and Epidemiology, U. Hosp., Caen, Lower Normandy, 1984—88, lectr. Besancon, France, 1990—93, prof., 1993—. Author: (book) Public Health Atomized; contbr. articles to profl. rsch. publs. Recipient Environment, Health, Quality Life award, French Acad. Medicine, 1992. Office: Faculty Medicine 2 Ave Du Prof Leon Bernard Rennes Brittany 5043 France Office Fax: 33 381 218 735. Business E-Mail: jean-francois.viel@univ-rennes1.fr.

VIERCK, CHARLES JOHN, JR., retired neuroscience educator; b. Columbus, Ohio, July 6, 1936; s. Charles John and Esther (Amadon) V.; m. Cheryl Stogner; children: Kenneth Christopher, Karl Frederick. BSc, U. Fla., Gainesville, 1959, MSc, 1961, PhD, 1963. Postdoctoral fellow U. Pa., Phila., 1963-65; asst. prof. U. Fla., Gainesville, 1965-71, assoc. prof., 1971-77, prof., 1977—2004, prof. emeritus, 2004. Adj. prof. U. NC, Chapel Hill, 1977—2007; dir. Ctr. Neurobiol. Scis. U. Fla., 1975-2005. Mem. editorial bd. Somatosensory Motor Research, Am. Pain Soc. Jour., Jour. Neurosci.; contbr. articles to profl. jours., chpts. to books Grantee NIH, NIMH, NSF, VA, 1966—. Mem. Soc. Neurosci., Internat. Assn. Study Pain Democrat. Avocations: jazz, golf. Home: 6519 SW 37th Way Gainesville FL 32608-5146 Personal E-mail: vierck@mbi.ufl.edu.

VIERLING, ELIZABETH, botanist, educator; b. Hackensack, NJ, Jan. 15, 1953; BS, U. Mich., Ann Arbor, 1975; PhD, U. Chgo., 1982. Regents prof. U. Ariz., 1985—; prof. U. Mass., 2011—. Fellowship, Guggenheim Found., Sr. Rsch. fellowship, Alexander von Humboldt Found., Germany. Fellow: AAAS; mem.: ASBMB, Am. Soc. Plant Biology. Avocations: ceramics, gardening. Office: 710 N Pleasant St Amherst MA 01003 Business E-Mail: vierling@biochem.umass.edu.

VIERLING, JOHN MOORE, physician; b. Bellflower, Calif., Nov. 20, 1945; s. Lester Howard and Ruth Ann (Moore) V.; m. Gayle Aileen Vandermast, June 30, 1968 (div. 1984); children: Jeffrey M., Janet A; m. Donna Marie Sheps, May 4, 1985; children: Matthew R., Mark L. (dec.). BA in Biology with great distinction, Stanford U., 1967, MD, 1972. Intern then resident Strong Meml. Hosp. U. Rochester, N.Y., 1972-74; clin. assoc. liver unit NIH, Bethesda, Md., 1974-77; gastroenterology fellow U. Calif., San Francisco, 1977-78, instr. medicine, 1978-79; from asst. to assoc. U. Colo. Sch. Medicine, Denver, 1979-90; dir. hepatology, med dir. liver transplantation Cedars-Sinai Med. Ctr., LA, 1990—. Assoc. prof. medicine UCLA, 1990-96, prof. medicine & surgery, 1996—2005; chief hepatology, Baylor Coll. Med., Houston, 2005-. Assoc. editor: Prinicples and Practice of Gastroenterology and Hepatology, 1992; editorial bd. Hepatology, 1985-90, Gastroenterology, 1993-98, Liver Transplantation, 2004-; co-editor Liver Immunology, 2002, 2007; co-patentee in hybridization assay for hepatitis virus, 1992; mouse model for hepatitis C, 1997. Fellow ACP; mem. Am. Assn. Study Liver Diseases (pres. 2006), Am. Clin. and Climatol. Assn., Am. Gastroenterolog. Assn., Internat. Assn. for Study Liver, European Assn. for Study Liver, Am. Liver Found. (chmn. bd. dirs. 1994—2000, sec. treas., Digestive Disease Week 2008-). Avocations: photography, tennis, hiking. Office: 1709 Dryden Ste 1500 Houston TX 77030

VIETA, ANA, pharmacist, director; b. Barcelona, Oct. 10, 1976; MSc in Health Policy Planning and Financing, LSE-LSHTM, 2005. Pharmacist Barcelona U., 2000. Strategic and applied market access assoc. dir. IMS Health, 2008—. Prof. ESAME, 2008—. Home: Freixa 46 Barcelona Cataluña 08021 Spain Personal E-mail: avieta@es.imshealth.com.

VIETA, EDUARD, psychiatrist, educator; b. Barcelona, Jan. 16, 1963; s. Eduardo and Maria Dolores (Pascual) V.; m. Gloria Fernandez-Esparrach, June 26, 1994. MD, Autonomous U., Barcelona, 1987; PhD, U. Barcelona, Spain, 1994. Cert. psychiatrist. Resident Hosp. Clinic, Barcelona, 1988-91, rsch. fellow, 1992, staff psychiatrist, 1993-94, staff psychiatrist, liaison psychiatry unit, cons., 1994—, dir. bipolar disorders program, 1998; rsch. dir. clin. inst. psychiatry and psychology U. Barcelona, 2000; staff psychiatrist, liaison psychiatry unit, cons. Hosp. Clinic Barcelona, 1994—. Sci. cons. Investigacion Medica Permanente, Barcelona, 1991-92; congress organizer European Assn. Psychiatry, Barcelona, 1992; prof. psychiaty, U. Barcelona, 2005. Contbr. articles to profl. jours. in the field. Founder pres. Nat. Bipolar Assn., Barcelona, 1994. Grantee Clinic Found., Barcelona, 1992; named Best Young Investigator Soc. Española de Medicina Psicosomática, 1993, Doctor of Year, 2005; recipient award Best Original Pub., 2004, 2005. Mem. AAAS, Catalan Psychiat. Soc. (sec. 1997-99), Spanish Biol. Psychiatr. Soc. (Best Doctoral Theses Second award). Avocations: literature, music, soccer, chess, anthropology. Office: U Barcelona Hosp Clinic Villarroel 170 08036 Barcelona Spain Office Phone: +34932386535. Business E-Mail: evieta@clinic.ub.es.

VIGANÒ, CATERINA, medical association administrator, researcher; b. Milan, Oct. 7, 1963; Grad. in Medicine, U. Milan, 1992, PhD in Psychiatry and Rels., 1996. Dir., simple unit residential high intensity psychiat. rehab. ctr. psychiat. unit ii mental health dept. L. Sacco U. Hosp., U. Degli Studi di Milano, 2007—. Prof., faculty medicine U. Milan, 2004. Master: Italian Psychiat. Rehab. Soc.; mem.: Centro Italiano Psicologia Analitica, Italian Med. Psychotherapy Soc., Italian Psychatric Rehab. Soc. Office: GB Grassi 74 Lombardia Milan 20157 Italy Business E-Mail: caterina.vigano@unimi.it.

VIGÁRIO, PATRÍCIA, physical education educator; b. Rio de Janeiro, Sept. 26, 1981; Degree in Phys. Edn., Fed. U. Rio de Janeiro, 2004. Prof. Jose Bonifácio Found., 2004. Home: Avenida Rainha Elizabeth 637/701 Rio de Janeiro 22081030 Brazil Personal E-mail: patriciavigario@yahoo.com.br.

VIGMO, JOSEF, retired geriatrician; b. Reykjavík, Iceland, Nov. 12, 1922; arrived in Sweden, 1956; s. Olaf Johan Olsen-Vigmostad and Aline Josefine (Zachariassen) Hervík; m. Soffía Axelsdóttir, Jan. 24, 1953; children: Terje, Sylvi Aline. MD, U. Iceland, 1953; postgrad., U. Gothenburg, Sweden, 1960. Lic. in internal medicine, cardiology, geriatrics, Sweden. Asst. med. officer Sandträsks Tuberculosis Sanatorium, Sweden, 1953-54, resident in pulmonary diseases, 1956-57; rotating intern White Meml. Hosp. and Clinic, Loma Linda U., LA, 1954-55; resident in internal medicine Piteå County Hosp., Sweden, 1958-59, Kalix and Skene County Hosps., Norrköping Gen. Hosp., Sweden, 1961-65; sub-chief med. officer Hultafors Health Ctr., Sweden, 1960; sub-chief med. officer geriatric dept. Borås Gen. County Hosp., Sweden, 1966-77, chief med. officer geriatric dept., 1977-87; ret., 1987. Consulting cardiologist, Borås Gen. County Hosp., 1978—, lectr. Sch. Nursing, 1967—. Recipient Gold medal Älvsborg County Council, 1987. Mem. Swedish Med. Assn., Swedish Geriatrics Assn., Swedish Assn. Chief Med. Officers, South-Älvsborg County Assn. Chief Med. Officers. Lutheran. Avocations: linguistics, genealogy. Home: Båleröd Sjövägen 1 S-452 97 Strömstad Sweden

VIGNESWARAN, WICKII THAMBIAH, cardiothoracic surgeon, educator; b. Jaffna, Sri Lanka, Jan. 25, 1955; arrived in USA, 1991, naturalized, 1994; s. Murugesu and Rajapoopathy (Nagalingam) Thambiah; m. Jnanarupy Thillainayagam, Dec. 3, 1984; children: Yalini, Hari, Janani. MB BChir, U. Sri Lanka, Peradeniya, 1978. Cert. in cardiothoracic surgery. Advanced cardiothoracic surg. fellow Mayo Clinic, Rochester, Minn., 1991-93; dir. gen. thoracic surgery U. Ill.-Chgo. Med. Ctr., 1994-98; dir. thoracic organ, dir. cardiothoracic transplant U. Ill.-Chgo., 1994-98; chief cardiothoracic surgery Westside VA Med. Ctr., Chgo., 1994-98; staff mem. Hines VA Med. Ctr., Chgo., 1998—2005; chief thoracic surgery Loyola U. Med. Ctr., Maywood, Ill., 1998—2005, dir. lung transplantation, 1998—2005; prof. surgery U. Chgo., 2006—; assoc. chief cardiac and thoracic surgery, dir. lung and heart-lung transplant U. Chgo. Hosps., 2006—. Contbr. numerous articles to med. jours. including Thorax, Jour. Cardiovasc. Surgery, Jour. Clin. Transplantation. Sen. U. Ill.-Chgo., Champaign and Rockford, Ill., 1996-98; chmn. cardiothoracic subcom. Regional Organ Bank of Ill., Chgo., 1996-97. Recipient Trainee Investigator award Midwestern Award Cen. Soc. for Clin. Investigation and Am. Fedn. for Clin. Rsch., 1993, Young Investigator award DuPont Pharm./ACP, 1993; named to Top Surgeons List Consumer Rsch. Coun. Am. Fellow: ACS, Royal Coll. Physicians and Surgeons Can., Royal Coll. Surgeons Edinburgh; mem.: AMA, AAAS, European Soc. Cardiothoracic Surgery, Internat. Coll. Surgeons (v.p. 2003—06, pres. 2009, chair coun. surg. spltys., chair bd. 2010), Am. Coll. Chest Physicians (bd. regents 2005—09, trustee Chest Found. 2009—), Chgo. Surg. Soc., Gen. Thoracic Surgery Club, Ill. Thoracic Surg. Soc. (pres. 2001, 2003), Soc. Thoracic Surgeons, Royal Coll. Surgeons Eng., Internat. Soc. Heart and Lung Transplantation. Hindu. Avocations: travel, nature, medical missions. Office: U Chgo 5841 S Maryland Ave MC5040 Chicago IL 60637-1470 Office Phone: 773-795-1267, 773-834-7812. Business E-Mail: wvignesw@surgery.bsd.uchicago.edu.

VIGUERA, ADELE CASALS, psychiatrist, researcher; MD, Dartmouth Med. Sch.; MPH, Harvard Sch. Pub. Health. Intern & resident Mass. Gen. Hosp., assoc. dir. Perinatal & Reproductive Psychiatry Program, 1996—, Cleveland Clinic; asst. prof. psychiatry Harvard Med. Sch., 1996—. Mem.: North Am. Menopause Soc., Am. Teratology Soc., Am. Psychiatric Assn. Office: Womens Health Center Simches Research Bldg 185 Cambridge St Ste 2200 Boston MA 02114

VIIKKI, MERJA, physician; b. Oulu, Finland, May 13, 1971; d. Jussi and Elli Klaavu; m. Olli Viikki, Aug. 13, 1994; children: Ville, Atte. MD, U. Tampere Med. Sch., Finland, 1997, PhD, 1999. Sr. lectr. U. Tampere Med. Sch., 2007—. Recipient Found. Psychiatric prize, 2011. Mem.: Finnish Med. Assn. Office: University Tampere Med Sch Arvo Tampere 33014 Finland Personal E-mail: merja.viikki@gmail.com.

VIJAYAKUMAR, MADHAVAN, pharmacist; b. Rajapalayam, Tamilnadu, India, July 27, 1978; MPharm, Birla Inst. Tech., Ranchi, India, 2002; PhD, Manipal U., 2008. Sr. rsch. asst. Nat. Bot. Rsch. Inst., 2002—05, scientist, 2005—. Sr. Rsch. fellowship, Coun. Sci. & Indsl. Rsch., India. Mem.: Indian Pharmacy Grad. Assn., Indian Pharm. Assn. Avocations: reading, cricket. Home: SA/D 11 NBRI Colony 21 Gokhale Marg Lucknow Uttar Pradesh 226001 India Personal E-mail: herbalvijay@gmail.com.

VIJAYAN, V. K., cardiologist, pulmonologist, consultant; s. V. K. Govindan Vydiar and P. P. Lakshmi; m. A. M. Reetha, Apr. 29, 1981. MB, BChir, Calicut Med. Coll., Kerala, 1971; MD, Delhi U., 1977; PhD, Madras U., Tamil Nadu, 1990; DSc, Tamil Nadu Med. U., 1996. Sr. house surgeon Willington Hosp., New Delhi, 1972—73; asst. rsch. officer cardiology GB Pant Hosp., New Delhi, 1973—74; resident V.P. Chest Inst., Delhi, 1974—75; resident in medicine, sr. rsch. fellow Lady Hardinge Med. Coll. and Willington Hosp., New Delhi, 1975—77; clinical rsch. officer Indian Coun. Med. Rsch., Madras, 1977—81, sr. clinical rsch. officer, head cardio-pulmonary medicine unit, 1981—87, asst. dir., head cardio-pulmonary medicine unit, 1987—91, dep. dir., head cardio-pulmonary medicine unit, 1991—96, sr. dep. dir., head cardio-pulmonary medicine unit, 1996—98; dir. V.P. Chest Inst. U. Delhi, 1998—. Spkr. in field. Editor: Indian Jour. Chest Diseases and Allied Scis., 1999—, Lung India, 1996—99; mem. editl. bd.: Indian Jour. Chest Diseases and Allied Scis., 1992—98, Indian Jour. Cardiology, 1998—, Thorax (South Asian edit.), 2001, Internal Medicine Jour. Thailand, 2001—, Jour. Environ. Medicine, 2001—, Lung India, 2001—, Indian Jour. Tuberculosis, 2003—, Chest, 2006—, others; contbr. articles to profl. jours., chapters to books. V.p. World Lung Found., South Asia, 2005—. Recipient Saroj-Jyothi award, Indian Chest Soc., 1987, Shrimati Yashodhara Meml. award, 1997, Dr. O.A. Sarma Endowment Lectr. award, Tuberculosis Assn. Andhra Pradesh, 1989, Prof. B.K. Aikat Oration award, Indian Coun. Med. Rsch., 1991, Amrit-Modi Unichem award, 1994, Oration award, Calicut Med. Coll., 1994, Silver medal, Internat. Labour Office/Japan Indsl. Safety and Health Assn., Japan, 1997, Medicine Endowment Lectr. award, U. Madras, 1998, Sir Ronald Ross Meml. Oration award, post-grad. med. edn. and rsch., 2005, Dr. M. Santosham Meml. Oration award, Indian Assn. Bronchology, 2005, Dr. Prem-Sobti-ABC Found. Excellence award for Best Chest Specialist of India, 2005; Merit scholar, State Govt., 1956—62, Nat. Merit scholar, Govt. India, 1962—70, Sr. Rsch. fellow, All India Heart Found., 1977, British Coun. fellow, Brompton Hosp., London, 1983. Fellow: Indian Coll. Cardiology, Am. Coll. Chest Physicians (treas. South India chpt. 1990—93, gov. 1993—2000, nominating com. 1995—97, founder pres. Indian chpt. 1999—2000, internat. regent India 2000—06), Nat. Acad. Med. Scis., Indian Soc. Cardiology (life), Nat. Coll. Chest Physicians (life Cipla Oration award 2004); mem.: Nat. Inst. Occupl. Health (Ahmedabad) (sci. adv. com. mem. 2007—), Am. Thoracic Soc., Indian Soc. for Sleep Rsch. (life), Indian Pharmacol. Soc. (life), Geriat. Soc. India (life), Indian Sleep Disorders Assn. (life), Indian Coll. Allergy, Asthma and Applied Immunology (life; pres. 2007—08, DN Shivpuri Meml. Oration award 2000), Cardiological Soc. India (life), Assn. Physicians India (life), Indian Soc. Electrocardiology (life), Indian Chest Soc. (life), Indian Immunology Soc. (life), Indian Soc. Clinical Pharmacology and Therapeutics (life), Assn. Physiologists and Pharmacologists India (life), Hypertension Soc. India (life), Nat. Acad. Med. Scis. (life), Indian Assn. for Biomed. Scientists (life), Indian Med. Assn. (life), Indian Soc. for Study Lung Cancer (life), Asian Pacific Soc. Respirology (chmn. clin. respiratory medicine assembly 2006—07, ctrl. planning com. 2007—08, exec. com. 2007—08), Indian Assn. Med. Jour. Editors, Tuberculosis Assn. India (spl. invitee exec. com. 2005—, Prof. K.C. Mohanty award 1994, Ranbaxy-Robert Koch Oration award 1999), Indian Soc. for Bronchology (governing coun. mem. 1997—2001, v.p. 2002—04, pres.-elect 2004—05, pres. 2005—06). Achievements include research in effects of methyl isocyanate exposure on respiratory sys., flexible fibreoptic bronchoscopy, prevalence of asthma, sleep related breathing disorders. Avocation: travel. Office: VP Chest Inst Univ Delhi New Delhi 110007 India Home: VP Chest Inst Directors Bunglow 110 007 New Delhi India Personal E-mail: vijayanvk@hotmail.com.

VIJAYAPPA, MADHU BUKKASAGARA, neurologist; MD, Bangalore Med. Coll., 1999. House staff radiation oncology All India Inst. Med. Scis., New Delhi, 2000—01; clin. rsch. fellow Harvard Med. Sch., Boston, 2003—05; house staff medicine OSF St. Francis Hosp., Peoria, Ill., 2005—08, chief resident neurology, 2008—, fellow endovascular surg. neuroradiology, 2010—. V.p. Vivekananda Youth Assn., Tumkur, Karnataka, India, 1995—96. Recipient Best Resident poster, OSF St. Francis Hosp., 2007, Best Resident Poster, 2008; fellow Clin. Rsch. Fellow, Harvard Med. Sch., 2003—05; Travel grant, Internat. Stroke Conference, 2005, Am. Acad Neurological Surgery meeting, 2005. Mem.: AMA, Soc. Vascular and Interventional Neurology, Am. Heart Assn. Stroke Coun., Am. Acad. Neurology. Achievements include research in the rate of stroke associated with the use of thoratec ventricular assist device in older patients. Office: OSF St Francis Hosp 530 NE Glen Oak ave Peoria IL 61637 Personal E-mail: mbvijay1@yahoo.com.

VIJEYARASA, RAMONA, lawyer, researcher; b. Sydney, Aug. 9, 1981; LLB, U. NSW, 2005, PhD candidate, 2009—; LLM in Internat. Legal Studies, NYU, 2007. NYU internat. law and human rights fellow Internat. Ctr. Transitional Justice, 2007; internat. legal fellow Ctr. Reproductive Rights, 2007—08; corr. Reproductive Health Reality Health Check, 2008—10; cons. Internat. Orgn. Migration, 2008—09; rschr., sch. social scis. and internat. studies U. NSW, 2009—. Adv. com. mem. Women Won't Wait: End HIV & Violence Against Women Now Campaign, 2011. Recipient Australian Postgrad. award, Govt. of Australia, prize, United Assn. Women, U. NSW. Avocations: running, cooking. Home: Calle Mejico 33 1 C Madrid 28028 Spain Personal E-mail: rvijeyarasa@gmail.com.

VIKEN, RICK J., psychology professor; BA, St. Olaf Coll., 1976; MA, U. Iowa, 1981, PhD, 1984. Prof. psychology Ind. U., Bloomington, dir. clin. tng. program. Office: Dept Psychol and Brain Sciences Ind Univ 1101 East 10th St Bloomington IN 47405 Office Phone: 812-855-1697. Office Fax: 812-855-4691. E-mail: viken@indiana.edu.

VILA, BRYAN, research scientist, educator; b. Salt Lake City, Jan. 1947; MPA, Pepperdine U., 1990; PhD, U. Calif., Davis, 1990. Chief, br. emergency preparedness US Dept. Interior, 1984—86; assoc. prof. U. Calif., Irvine, 1990—97, U. Wyo., 1997—2002; dir., crime control & prevention rsch. divsn. Nat. Inst. Justice, US Dept. Justice, 2002—05; prof. Wash. State U., 2005—. Dir., trust ter. bur. investigation US Trust Ter. Pacific Islands, 1978—84. Decorated Purple Heart medal USMC, Vietnam Campaign medal, Vietnam Svc. medal, Nat. Def. Svc. medal. Mem.: AAAS, Am. Soc. Criminology, Sleep Rsch. Soc. Avocation: reading. Office: Sleep and Performance Rsch Ctr Spokane WA 99210-1495 Business E-Mail: vila@wsu.edu.

VILABOA, NURIA ELDA, medical researcher; b. Lugo, Spain, Aug. 11, 1965; BS, U. Complutense de Madrid, 1989, PhD, 1995. Rsch. fellow Ctr. de Investigaciones Biológicas CIB-CSIC, Madrid, 1991—95, postdoc. assoc., 1998—2000, U. Miami Sch. Medicine, 1995—98; postdoc. rsch. fellow Inst. de Investigaciones Biomédicas Alberto Sols UAM-CSIC, Madrid, 2000—02; prin. investigator Hosp. U. La Paz, 2001. Grant, Ministry of Sci. and Innovation CYCIT, Spain, Fundación Mutua Madrileña, Cell Mechanics grant, Networking Rsch. Ctr. Bio-engring., Biomaterials and Nanomedicine CIBER-BBN, Spain. Office: Paseo de La Castellana 261 Madrid 28011 Spain Business E-Mail: nvilaboa.hulp@salud.madrid.org.

VILARDELL, FRANCISCO, gastroenterologist, educator; b. Barcelona, Apr. 1, 1926; s. Jacinto Vilardell and Mercedes Viñas; m. Leonor March; children: Mercedes, Carmen, Xavier. MD, U. Barcelona, 1949, DSc, 1961; DSc in Medicine, U. Pa., Phila., 1962; PhD (hon.), U. Toulouse, France, 1974, U. Zaragoza, Spain, 1990. Resident medicine Hosp. del Mar, Barcelona, 1949-52; fellow gastroenterology Hosp. de la Santa Cruz & San Pablo, 1952-55, chief gastroenterology svc., 1963—; fellow gastroenterology Grad. Hosp., Phila., 1959-62; prof., dir. Postgrad. Sch. Gastroenterology U. Barcelona, 1970—; hon. prof. U. Valparaiso, Chile, 1996. Pres. European Assn. Study Liver, 1975-76, Coun. Internat. Orgns. Med. Scis. coms., 1987-91; sec.-gen. World Orgn. Gastroenterology, 1974-82, pres., 1982-90. Editor: Enfermedades Difusas del Estomago, 1962, others; assoc. editor Bockus Gastroenterology, 3rd edit., 1972, editl. cons., 4th edit., 1986; contbr. articles to profl. jours. Asst. dir. gen. med. edn. Spanish Ministry Health, 1978-80, dir. gen. health planning, 1980-82, mem. med. rsch. coun., 1982-91. Fellow ACP, Royal Coll. Physicians, Royal Coll. Physicians Edinburgh, Am. Coll. Gastroenterology; mem. Catalan Soc. Bioethics (pres. 1994-96); hon. mem. French Gastroenterology Soc., Brit. Gastroenterology Soc., German Gastroenterology Soc., Japanese Gastroenterology Soc., Spanish Gastroenterology Soc., Polish Gastroenterology Soc., Hungarian Gastroenterology Soc., Portuguese Gastroenterology Soc., Argentinian Gastroenterology Soc., Colombian Gastroenterology Soc., Nat. Health Coun. Avocations: music, philology, medical history. Home: Reina Victoria 26 08021 Barcelona Spain Office: Hosp Santa Cruz & San Pablo 08025 Barcelona Spain

VILCEK, JAN TOMAS, immunologist, medical educator; b. Bratislava, Czechoslovakia, June 17, 1933; came to U.S., 1965, naturalized, 1970. s. Julius and Friderika (Fischer) V.; m. Marica F. Gerhath, July 28, 1962 MD, Comenius U., Bratislava, 1957; CSc (PhD), Czechoslovak Acad. Sci., Bratislava, 1962. Fellow Inst. Virology, Bratislava, 1957-62, head of lab., 1962-64; asst. prof. microbiology NYU Med. Ctr., NYC, 1965-68, assoc. prof., 1968-73, prof., 1973—. Chmn. nomenclature com. WHO, 1981—86; mem. adv. com. Am. Cancer Soc., 1981—87, chmn., 1983; mem. sci. adv. bd. Max Planck Inst., Munich, 1987—95; pres. Vilcek Found., 2003—. Author: Interferon, 1969; editor in chief Archives of Virology, 1975-86, Cytokine and Growth Factor Revs., 1995-2005; editor: Interferons and the Immune System, 1984, Tumor Necrosis Factor: Structure, Function and Mechanism of Action, 1991, Cytokine Reference, 2000; mem. editl. bd. Virology, 1979-81, Archives of Virology, 1986-92, Infection and Immunity, 1983-85, Antiviral Rsch., 1984-88, Jour. Interferon and Cytokine Rsch., 1988—, Jour. Immunological Methods, 1986—, Natural Immunity and Cell Growth Regulation, 1986-92, Jour. Immunology, 1987-89, Lymphokine Rsch., 1987-94, Jour. Biol. Chemistry, 1988-90, ISI Atlas Sci., Immunology, 1988-89, Jour. Cellular Physiology, 1988-2008, Cytokine, 1989—, Biologicals, 1989-95, Acta Virologica, 1991—, Internat. Archives of Allergy and Immunology, 1992-98, Folia Biologica, 1993-96, Cellular Immunology, 1993-96, Jour. of Inflammation, 1994-97, Cytokines, Cellular & Molecular Therapy, 1998-2005; contbr. articles to profl. jours.; co-inventor of anti-inflammatory drug infliximab used in rheumatoid arthritis and Crohn's disease, other inflammatory disorders. Mem. rev. panel Israel Cancer Rsch. Fund, 1993-96; mem. fellowship rev. com. Am. Heart Assn., 1992-94. Recipient Rsch. Career Devel. award, USPHS, 1968—73, Recognition award, Japanese Inflammation Soc., 1989, Outstanding Investigator award, Nat. Cancer Inst., NIH, 1991—98, Elliott Osserman Disting. Svc. Cancer Rsch. award, Israel Cancer Rsch. Fund, 1996, Disting. Alumnus award and medal, Comenius U., Bratislava, 2001, Albert Gallatin medal, NYU, 2005, Jan E. Purkyne medal, Czech Acad. Scis., 2008; grantee, USPHS, others. Fellow AAAS; mem. Am. Soc. Microbiology, Am. Assn. Immunologists, Internat. Soc. Interferon and Cytokine Rsch. (hon. life), Czech Immunology Soc., Internat. Cytokine Soc. (hon. life, pres. 1997-98), Czechoslovak Soc. Microbiology. Business E-Mail: jan.vilcek@nyumc.org.

VILJOEN, DEON ANDRE, sports medicine physician, consultant; b. Dunnottar, South Africa, Feb. 1, 1952; MBChB, U. Pretoria, 1980; MPhil in Sports Medicine, U. Cape Town, 1997. Occupl. medicine cons. Hunter Indsl. Medicine, 2005—. Mem.: Australasian Faculty Occupl. and Environ. Medicine. Avocations: bicycling, golf, surfing. Home: 39A Pell St Merewether NSW 2291 Australia Home Fax: 61249636842. Personal E-mail: deonviljoen@bigpond.com.

VILLA, ROBERTO FEDERICO, physician, biologist, educator; b. Spessa Po, Pavia, Italy, Feb. 13, 1948; s. Pietro Mario and Mariuccia Marina (Bacci) V.; m. Roberta Ida Clemente, Sept. 1, 1979; children: Eleonora, Elisa. MD, U. Pavia, 1990, DSc, 1972. Doctor U. of Pavia, 1972, U. of Pavia, 1990. Prof. sch. medicine and surgery U. Pavia, Italy, 1977-93, prof. Sch. Biol. Sci., 1993—, prof. pharmacology, 2002—. Rschr. U. Pavia, 1973-97, prof. Sch. Chemistry, 1991-. Author: Principi di Farmacologia, 1993, 2008; about 320 papers in Pharmacology of Central Nervous System; contbr. articles to profl. jours. With Rome Mil. Engring., 1973-74. Seargent Mil. Engring., 1973—74, Rome. Mem.: Am. Coll. Clin. Pharmacology, N.Y. Acad. Sci., Clin. Neuropharmacology, Internat. Brain Rsch. Orgn., Soc. Neurosci. Home: Via Alcuino 5 20149 Milan MI Italy Office: University Pavia Via Ferrata 9 Pavia 27100 Italy Office Phone: 39-0382-986391. E-mail: robertofederiw.villa@unipv.it.

VILLA, THAIS RODRIGUES, child neurologist; b. Marilia, Sao Paulo, Brazil, May 26, 1979; MD, PUCCAMP, 2002; PhD, UNIFESP, 2011. Rsch. scientist, divsn. investigation and treatment headaches UNIFESP, 2006—. Mem.: Brazilian Headache Soc. (Best Rsch. award 2009), Internat. Headache Soc. (Best Rsch. award 2008). Avocation: travel. Home: Potenji 60 Ap 93 Sao Paulo 04139020 Brazil Office Phone: 551150846339.

VILLABLANCA, JAIME ROLANDO, neuroscientist, medical educator; b. Chillàn, Chile, Feb. 1929; arrived in U.S., 1971, naturalized, 1985; s. Ernesto and Teresa (Hernàndez) V.; m. Guillermina Nieto, Dec. 3, 1955; children: Amparo C., Jaime G., Pablo J., Francis X., Claudio I. Bachelor in Biology, Nat. Inst. Chile, 1946; licentiate medicine, U. Chile, 1953, MD, 1954. Cert. neurophysiologist. Rockefeller Found. postdoctoral fellow in physiology John Hopkins and Harvard Med. Schs., 1959-61; Fogarty internat. rsch. fellow in anatomy UCLA, 1966-68, assoc. research anatomist and psychiatrist, 1971-72; assoc. prof. psychiatry and biobehavioral scis. UCLA Sch. Medicine, 1972-76; prof. psychiatry and biobehavioral scis. UCLA, 1976—2004, prof. neurobiology, 1977—2004, disting. prof. psychiatry and biobehavioral scis., neurobiology, 2004—07, disting. emeritus prof., 2007—. Mem. faculty U. Chile Sch. Medicine, 1954-71, prof. exptl. medicine, 1970-71; vis. prof. neurobiology Cath. U. Chile Sch. Medicine, 1974; cons. in field. Author numerous rsch. papers, book chpts., abstracts; chief regional editor Developmental Brain Dysfunction, 1988-99; editor Intermaliomal Journal of Developments Neuroscience, 2007-. Decorated Order Francisco de Miranda (Venezuela), 1987; recipient Premio Reina Sofia, Madrid, Caracas (Spain), 1990, Lifetime Achievement award UCLA Sch. Medicine, 2001, Emeritus award Colegio Medico de Chile, 2004; fellow Rockefeller Found., 1959-61, Fogarty Internat. Rsch. fellow NIH, 1966-68; grantee USAF Office Sci. Rsch., 1962-65, Found. Fund Rsch. Psychiatry, 1969-72, USPHS-Nat. Inst. Child Human Devel., 1972-96, USPHS-Nat. Inst. Drug Abuse, 1981-85, USPHS-Nat. Inst. Neurol. Disorders and Stroke, 1988-92, Fgn. Scientist Traveling grant Tokyo Met. Govt., 1995. Mem. AAAS, AAUP, Sleep Rsch. Soc. (Significant Early Contbr. award 2003), Intellectual & Developmental Disabilities Rsch. Ctr., Brain Rsch. Inst., Internat. Brain Rsch. Orgn., Am. Physiol. Soc., Soc. for Neurosci., Assn. Venezolana Padres de Niños Excepcionales, Soc. Child and Adolescent Psychiatry and Neurology (Chile, hon.), Johns Hopkins Med. and Surg. Assn., Sigma Xi. Home: 200 Surfview Dr Pacific Palisades CA 90272-2911 Office: UCLA Dept Psychiatry & Biobehavioral Scis Los Angeles CA 90024-1759 Business E-Mail: jvillablanca@mednet.ucla.edu.

VILLADSEN, JAN ALEXANDER, rheumatologist; b. Copenhagen, Oct. 17, 1956; MD, Aarhus U., 1993; MD in Clin. Immunology, Trondheim U., 2003. Staff specialist 1, medical specialist Danis Soc. Reumatology, King Christian X Hosp. Rheumatology, 2010—. CEO, founder owner ViVoX Ltd., 1997; bd. mem. Earth Fertilizer Ltd.; ptnr. Metoxia, EU 7th Framework Programme, Large Integrated Network, 2009—. Fellow: Royal Danish Yacht Club; mem.: Danish Med. Assn., Norveigian Soc. Clin. Immunology, Danish Soc. Reumatology. Avocations: yachting, gardening. Office: King Christian X Rheumatology Hosp Graasten DK-6300 Denmark Business E-Mail: jan.villadsen@dadlnet.dk.

VILLAFLOR, VIVENCIO V., JR., surgeon, director; b. Manila, Philippines, Oct. 26, 1936; s. Vivencio V. Villaflor, Sr. and Pilar N. (Villaseñor) Villaflor; m. Gregoria Ferrer Poblete, June 26, 1966; children: Vivencio Jose III, Ma Pilarcita, Vicente Jose, Aurora Ysabel, Francisco Jose. BSc, U. Philippines, 1958, MD, 1962, student, 1962—67. Lic. physician Philippine Med. Bd. Exam., 1962. Resident in surgery Dept. Surgery Philippine Gen. Hosp., 1962—67; assoc. prof. Dr. F.Q. Duque Med. Found. Lyceum N.W. U., Dagupan, Philippines. Chmn. Pangasinan Cardiovasc. Diagnostic Ctr., Dagupan, 1988—, Dagupan Breast Imaging Ctr., 2000, Dagupan Endoscopic Laparoscopic Ctr., Inc., 2001—; pvt. practice, Dagupan, 2001. Accredited physician US Peace Corps., Philippines, 1983—; pres. Pangasinan Med. Soc., 1975; chmn. Dagupan City Fiesta and Rizal Day Celebration, Philippines, 1979—; pres. Pangasinan Anti-Drug Abuse Found., 1988—91; mem. organizing com. Pistay Dayat and Bangus Festival, 2002; mem. exec. com. Dagupan City Fiesta, 2002; chmn. Nat. Movement Free Elections, Dagupan, 1984, 1986, 1988, 1992; commr. restoration project Lingayen-Dagupan Archdiocese Cathedral, 1991—2003; mem. planning and devel. coun. Dagupan City, 1992; vice chmn., dir. Dagupan City C. of C. and Industry, 1999—2002; vice chmn. Darapal City chpt. Philippine Nat. Red Cross, Pangasinan, 2004—06; life mem. YMCA. Recipient Outstanding Project Chmn. award, Operation Barrio Clinic, 1973; named Most Outstanding Citizen in pub. svc., City of Dagupan, 1982, Civic Leader of Yr., Weekly Vibrations, 1989. Fellow: ACS, Philippine Soc. Gen. Surgeons, Internat. Coll. Surgeons, Philippine Coll. Surgeons (life); mem.: Philippine Med. Assn. (dist. gov. 1980—81, 1991—92, Most Outstanding Physician in Pangasinan 1979, Dr. Jose P. Rizal award 2000), UP Med. Alumni Assn. (life Cmty. Svc. award Luzon 2000), Rotary (trustee Dagupan Found. 1982—, pres. Dagupan sect. 1988—89, pres. Rotary Club Found. 1990—91, Rotary Internat. Svc. award profl. excellence 2005, Paul Harris fellow). Roman Catholic. Avocation: stamp collecting/philately. Office: Dagupan Drs Villaflor Meml Hosp Mc Arthur Hwy 2400 Dagudan Ilicos Region Philippines Office Phone: (6375) 522-7629.

VILLAGOMEZ, JOSEPH K., state agency administrator, public health service officer; MA. Addiction services mgr. Cmty. Guidance Ctr., Saipan, Northern Mariana Islands; dir. mental health & social services Dept. Pub. Health, Saipan, sec. health, 2006—. Sec. Pacific Islands Health Officers Assn., bd. dirs., pres. Mem.: APA. Office: Dept Pub Health PO Box 500409 CK Saipan MP 96950 Office Phone: 670-236-8201. Office Fax: 670-234-8930. Business E-Mail: jkvsaipan@saipan.com.

VILLA-KOMAROFF, LYDIA, molecular biologist, educator, health product executive, academic administrator; b. Las Vegas, N.Mex., Aug. 7, 1947; d. John Dias and Drucilla (Jaramillo) V.; m. Anthony Leader Komaroff, June 18, 1970. BA, Goucher Coll., 1970; PhD, MIT, 1975; DSc (hon.), St. Thomas U., 1996, Pine Manor Coll., 1997; PhD (hon.), Goucher Coll., 1997; DSc (hon.), Regis Coll., 2010. Rsch. fellow Harvard U., Cambridge, 1975-78; asst. prof. dept. microbiology U. Mass. Med. Ctr., Worcester, 1978-81, assoc. prof. dept. molecular genetics micro, 1982-85; assoc. prof. dept. neurology Harvard Med. Sch., Boston, 1986-95; sr. rsch. assoc. neurology Children's Hosp., Boston, 1985-95, assoc. dir. mental retardation rsch. ctr., 1987-94; prof. dept. neurology Northwestern U., Evanston, Ill., 1995—2002, assoc. v.p. rsch., 1995-97, v.p. rsch., 1998—2002; v.p. for rsch., COO, Whitehead Inst. for Biomed. Rsch., Cambridge, Mass., 2003—05; chief sci. officer Cytonome, Inc., 2005—; CEO Ctyonome Inc., 2006—09; chief sci. officer Cytonome ST LLC, 2009—. Mem. mammalian genetics study sect. NIH, 1982-84, mem. reviewers rsch., 1989, mem. neurol. disorders program project rev. com., 1989-94; mem. adv. bd. Biol. Sci. Directorate, NSF, 1994-99; bd. dirs. Nat. Ctr. Genome Rsch., 1995-00, TransKaryotic Therapies, 2003-05, chair 2005, bd. dirs. Mass. Life Sci. Ctr., 2008-; mem. adv. coun. Nat. Inst. Neurol. Disorders and Stroke, NIH, 2000-04; bd. trustees Pine Manor Coll., 2004—, chair, 2007-2011; sr. lectr. Sloan Sch. Mgmt. MIT, 2003--05. Contbr. articles and abstracts to profl. jour.; patentee in field. Recipient Hispanic Engr. Nat. Achievement award, 1992, Nat. Achievement award Hispanic Mag., 1996, Lifetime Achievement award, Hispanic Bus. Mag., 2008; inducted Hispanic Engr. Nat. Achievement Hall of Fame, 1999; selected 50 most important Hispanics by "business & Tech., Hispanic Engr. & Info. Tech." mag. 2003; named Hispanic Scientist of Yr. Mus. Sci. and Industry, Tampa, 2008; Helen Hay Whitney Found. fellow, 1975-78; NIH grantee, 1978-85, 89-96. Mem. AAAS (bd. dirs. 2000-05), Am. Soc. Microbiology, Assn. for Women in Sci., Soc. for Neurosci., Am. Soc. Cell Biology, Soc. for Advancement Chicanos and Native Ams. in Sci. (founding, bd. dir. 1987-93, v.p. 1990-93), Internat. Soc. for Cellular Therapy, Am. Soc. for Blood and Marrow Transplantation. Office Phone: 617-330-5030 ext. 354. Business E-Mail: lvk@cytonomest.com.

VILLAR, JOSE, physician, educator; b. Sevillla, Nov. 14, 1947; MD, Facultad Medicina Sevilla, 1970, PhD, 1973. Jefe clinico Andalouse Health Svc., 1973; catedrático U. Sevilla, 1984—. Avocation: music. Home: Trajano Sevilla 41002 Spain Personal E-mail: jvillar@us.es.

VILLARUEL, ANTONIA M., nursing educator; BSN, Nazareth Coll., Kalamazoo, Mich., 1978; MSN, U. Pa., Phila., 1982; PhD, Wayne State U., Detroit, 1993. RN. Fellow U. Mich., Ann Arbor, 1995; prof. risk reduction and health promotion U. Mich. Sch. Nursing, Ann Arbor, dir. Ctr. Health Promotion. Named to Mich. Nurses Hall of Fame, 2004. Fellow: Am. Acad. Nursing; mem.: Inst. Medicine, Nat. Assn. Hispanic Nurses, Nat. Coalition Ethnic Minority Nursing Associations (founding mem., v.p.). Office: U Mich Sch Nursing Rm 4320 400 N Ingalls Bldg Ann Arbor MI 48109-0482 Office Phone: 734-615-9696. Office Fax: 734-647-0351. E-mail: avillarr@umich.edu.

VILLAVECES, JAMES WALTER, allergist, immunologist, consultant; b. San Luis Obispo, Calif., Nov. 4, 1933; s. Robert and Solita (Combariza) V. BA, UCLA, 1955; MD (hon.), U. Calif. Med. Sch., 1960. Diplomate Am. Bd. Allergy and Immunology. Intern Sawtelle VA Hosp., LA, 1960-61; preceptorship in adult allergy LA County Hosp., 1964-66; tchg. fellow in allergy White Meml. CCM, LA, 1966-67; co-chief allergy divsn. Ventura Med. Ctr., Calif., 1969—87; spkr. Earth Day in Ventura County, 1974; practice medicine specializing in allergy-immunology Ventura, 1984—; lectr. Wellpoint Calif. RAST, IVIG; co-dir. Allergy Clinic Ventura Co Hosp.; ptnr. Earth Day Vastnra Country Air Pollution Containment. Founder botanical weed allergy walks, 1970; cons. Enviracaire HEPA Filter Co., 1970; cons. in allergy/immunology, Blue Cross, 1991-96; medical invention cons., Inventor's Internat. Co., Inc., 1970-73, screener for med. inventions, 1968; inventor, cons. Sprixx: Alcohol-gel Clip on Dispensers, 2001, cons. Western RAST Panel Forum; mem. Pharmacy and Therapeutics Com., Wellpoint (Blue Cross Calif.) Inc., 1991-96; prodr. Ventura County cities street-tree guide for asthma patients; peer reviewer Blue Cross So. Calif. Wellpoint, 1980, 1984-95; co-dir. allergy Clinic Ventura Hosp., lectr. allergy-immunology pediat., internal medicine for family practice residency program, Ventura, Calif., 1968-83; rschr. Dartmouth U. Hosp., 2008; cons., lectr., peer reviewer in field. Writer, prodr., editor films; contbr. articles on biology of pollens and molds of Ventura County to profl. jours.; patentee in field. Bd. dir. Am. Lung Assn., Ventura, 1969-85, pres., 1974, advisor air pollution control com., 1971-74, Ventura County APD & Liason & Ventura Med. Soc.; judge Ventura Sci. Fair, 1970-85; lectr. in field. Recipient commendation County Bd. Suprs., Ventura, 1974; named one of Am.'s Top Physicians Consumers Rsch. Coun. Am., 2003-05. Fellow Am. Acad. Allergy (emeritus mem.), Am. Coll. Allergy, Asthma, Immunology; mem. Calif. Soc. Allergy-Immunology, Calif. Med. Assn., Ventura County Med. Assn., Gold Coast Tri-County Allergy Soc. (pres. 1987), CAL Club (hon.), Ventura County Sports Hall of Fame (mem. founding bd.), Mensa. Republican. Achievements include development of infection protection device for hospital; research in sprixx invention has cut infection rate; set standard for RAST use for Wellpoint to Calif. Blue Cross governing standard for and use of IVIG. Avocations: writing, photography, lecturing, pistol target shooting, fishing. Home: 928 High Point Dr Ventura CA 93003-1415 Office: Dudley Profl Ctr 4080 Loma Vista Rd Ste M Ventura CA 93003-1811 Office Phone: 805-656-0433. Personal E-mail: allergycare2006@yahoo.com.

VILLEGAS GALVEZ, VICTORIA EUGENIA, biology professor; b. Cali, Colombia, Aug. 22, 1968; Degree in Biology, U. Valle, 1996; M, Pontificia U. Javeriana, 2005. Asst. prof. U. Rosario, 2005—. Avocation: movies. Office: Calle 64 con carrera 24 Bogota 11001 Colombia Business E-Mail: victoria.villegas@urosario.edu.co.

VILLELA, MARCOS MARREIRO, biologist, educator; b. Pelotas, Rio Grande do Sul, Brazil, Mar. 19, 1981; Grad in Biology, U. Fed. de Pelotas, Brazil, 2001; PhD, Fundação Oswaldo Cruz, 2008. Adj. prof. human parasitology U. Fed. de Pelotas, 2008—. Writer Editora Atheneu., 2007—11. Avocations: reading, writing, Karate. Home: Gal Osório 1213 Pelotas Rio Grande do Sul 96020-000 Brazil Personal E-mail: marcosmvillela@bol.com.br.

VILLET, MARTIN H., entomologist, educator; b. Ndola, Zambia, Dec. 27, 1961; MSc, Wits, 1986, PhD, 1989. Prof. Rhodes U., 1993—. Dir. Southern African Forensic Entomology Rsch. Lab., 1998; editor African Entomology, 2006—09. Author: Forensic Entomology. Mem.: South African Soc. Systematic Biology, Royal Soc. South Africa, Entomol. Soc. South Africa. Office: Sommerset St Box 94 Grahamstown Eastern Cape 6140 South Africa Office Fax: 27 46 622 8959. Business E-Mail: m.villet@ru.ac.za.

VILLORIA, JESUS FRANCISCO, writer; b. Madrid, Dec. 6, 1967; married. MD, Complutense U., Madrid, 1992; DStat, Autonomous U., Barcelona, 2007. Cert. in English proficiency Trinity Coll., London, 1985. Clin. rsch. assoc. Item Pharma, Madrid, 1994—96; project mgr. Phoenix Internat., Madrid, 1996—99; med. writer Staticon Internat., Madrid, 1999—2001, sr. med. writer, 2001—02; head med. writing PRA Internat., Madrid, 2002—04; head med. writing dir. Medicxact S.L., Alpedrete, Madrid, 2004—. Singer: (classical choral works) Bass. 1st lt. San. Corps, 1991—93, Madrid. Honor grant, Escuelas Pías de San Fernando, 1996. Mem.: European Med. Writers Assoc., Coll. Physicians Madrid. Office: Medicxact SL Plz Ermita 4 Alpedrfete 28430 Madrid Spain Office Fax: 34911031979. Business E-Mail: villoriajesus@medicxact.es.

VILLUMSEN, STEEN, physician, b. Denmark, Apr. 20, 1973; MD, U. Copenhagen, 2002, PhD, 2011. Physician Statens Serum Inst., 2005—, cons., 2011; rschr., dept. infectious diseases Hvidovre Hosp., 2011—. Cons. Statens Serum Institut, 2011. Office: Statens Serum Inst Artillerivej 5 Copenhagen 2300 Denmark E-mail: stv@ssi.dk.

VIÑAS, LUIS A., plastic surgeon; Attended, U. Puerto Rico, 1977—78, U. Mass., 1978—79; MD, Universidad Central del Caribe, 1980—83. Diplomate Am. Bd. of Plastic Surgery, 1993, lic. Puerto Rico, Fla., 1990, Nev. State Bd. of Med. Examiners, 2004. Resident in gen. surgery Nassau County Med. Ctr., East Meadow, NY, 1984—87, fellow in burn care, 1987—88, resident in plastic surgery, 1988—90; surg. asst. Hosp. Gen. San Carlos, 1984—84; med. spa dir. Alesandra Salon and Spa, Boynton Beach, Fla., 2009—; hosp. affiliations include St. Mary's Med. Ctr., JFK Med. Ctr., Good Samaritan Med. Ctr. Cons. & faculty ethicon endo-surgery Johnson & Johnson, Cincinnati, Ohio, 2008—; cons. TEI Biosciences, Boston, 2008—. Recipient Susan G. Komen Breast Cancer Found. Appreciation award, Messenger of Peace & Hope award, 2004, Physician Hero award, Heroes in Medicine award, 2005. Mem.: AMA, Fla. Med. Assn., Palm Beach Med. Soc., Fla. Soc. of Plastic and Reconstructive Surgeons, Am. Bd. of Plastic Surgery, Am. Soc. of Plastic Surgeons, Am. Soc. for Aesthetic Plastic Surgery. Office: LA Viñas Plastic Surgery & Med Spa 550 South Quadrille Blvd West Palm Beach FL 33401 Office Phone: 561-655-3305. Office Fax: 561-655-3951.

VINCENT, FREDERICK MICHAEL, SR., neurologist, educator; b. Detroit, Nov. 19, 1948; s. George S. and Alyce M. (Borkowski) Vincent; m. Patricia Lucille Cordes, Oct. 7, 1972; children: Frederick Michael Jr., Joshua Peter, Melissa Anne. BS in Biology, Aquinas Coll., 1970; MD, Mich. State U., 1973. Cert. in neurology Am. Bd. Psychiatry and Neurology, 1979, Am. Bd. Electrodiagnostic Medicine, 1992, Am. Bd. Forensic Examiners, 1996, Am. Bd. Forensic Medicine, 1996, in neurology with subspecialty of clin. neurophysiology Am. Bd. Psychiatry and Neurology, 1996. Intern St. Luke's Hosp., Duluth, Minn., 1974; resident in neurology Dartmouth Med. Sch., Hanover, NH, 1975—77, instr. dept. medicine, chief resident neurology, 1977—78; chief neurology sect. Munson Med. Ctr., Traverse City, Mich., 1978—84; asst. clin. prof. medicine and pathology Mich. State U., East Lansing, 1978—84, chief sect. neurology Coll. Human Medicine, 1984—87, clin. prof. psychiatry and internal medicine, 1989—2004, clin. prof. medicine, 1990—, clin. prof. neurology and ophthalmology, 2001—; pvt. practice Lansing, Mich., 1987—. Clin. and rsch. fellow neuro-oncology Mass. Gen. Hosp., Boston, 1985; clin. fellow in neurology Harvard Med. Sch., Boston, 1985; cons. med. asst. program Northwestern Mich. Coll., Traverse City, 1983—84; neurology cons. radio call-in show Sta. WKAR, East Lansing, 1984—2000, Sta. WCMU-TV, 1987, 1993—. Author: (book) Neurology: Problems in Primary Care, 1987, 2d edit., 1993; contbr. articles to profl. jours. Fellow, NSF, 1969, Nat. Multiple Sclerosis Soc., 1971. Fellow: ACP, Am. Bd. Legal Medicine, Am. Assn. Neuromuscular and Electrodiagnostic Medicine (computer electronics com. 1995—98, profl. practice com. 1999—2000, practice rev. panel 2000—03), Am. Acad. Neurology (program accreditation devel. subcom. 1993—2001), Am. Bd. Forensic Examiners; mem.: Am. Coll. Legal Medicine, Inuit Art Soc., Alpha Omega Alpha. Independent. Roman Catholic. Avocations: art, fishing. Home: 825 Pebblebrook Ln East Lansing MI 48823-2163 Personal E-mail: vincen11@msu.edu. Business E-Mail: vincent11@ousu.edu.

VINCENT, JOAN EVELINE, anthropologist, educator; b. Surrey, Eng., Nov. 17, 1928; BSc in Economics, London Sch. Economics, 1957; MA in Polit. Sci., Chgo. U., 1964; PhD, Columbia U., 1968. Prof., 1945—; prof., rsch. head, grad. dept. Bernard Coll. Columbia U., 1968—2011. Chair, rsch. com. Harvard Testimonial; mem. Nat. Humanities Ctr., Princeton, 1989—90. Co-author: Aids Research in Uganda. Recipient Wheeler Voegelin prize, Am. Soc. Ethnohistory; Rsch. fellowship, Inst. Soc. & Econ. Rsch., Mekerere, Uganda, 1966—67, Burcaess fellow, Columbia U., 1967—68, John Simon Guggenheim Meml. Found. fellowship, 1973—74. Mem.: Rsch. Inst. Study of Man, Inst. Devel. Studies, Social Hist. Soc. Ireland, Am. Anthrop. Assn. Avocations: tennis, stamp collecting/philately, writing. Home: C/O Rosemary Cottage Pyecombe St Pyecombe West Sussex England Office: 3 Fordham Hill Oval Apt 9H Bronx NY 10468

VINCENT, ROBERT, otolaryngologist, surgeon; b. Chateaubriant, France, Oct. 28, 1960; s. Julien and Henriette Vincent; m. Martine Augeix, July 23, 1988; children: Julie, Marion, Romain. MD, Nancy U., 1990. Interne des hopitaux Nancy U. Hosp., France, 1985—91; otologist surgeon Jean Causse Ear Clinic, Colombiers, France, 1991—. Mem. Otosclerosis study group. Author (co-authors): (cd-rom) OTO-ROM 2, Intercative trip in Otology-Neurotology (First Prize at the FILMED (Internat. festival of med. films), 1998); author: OTO-ROM 1, Interactive trip in Otology, (book) 3D Atlas of the ear, (scientific publication) Stapedotomy for tympanosclerotic stapes fixation: is it safe and efficient? A review of 68 cases (Accepted for publ. in Otology-Neurotology Jour., 2002), Malleus ankylosis: a clinical, audiometric, histologic and surgical study of 123 cases. (Accepted for publ. in the Otology-Neurotology Jour., 1999). Dir. Internat. music festival, Mazaugues. Recipient Gordon Smyth Lectr., Royal Soc. Medicine and Brit. Assn. Head and Neck Surgeons, 2002. Fellow: Royal Coll. Surgeons Edinburgh (hon.); mem.: French ENT Soc. (Otosclerosis study group), European Acad. Otology-Neurotology, Am. Acad. Otolaryngology Head and Neck Surgery (corr.), Prosper Meniere Soc. Achievements include design of Middle Ear Prostheses. Avocations: music, literature, skiing, tennis. Home: 7 allée du Chablis 34500 Béziers France Office: Jean Causse Ear Clinic Traverse de Béziers 34440 Colombiers France Office Fax: 00 33 4 67 35 62 00. Personal E-mail: robvinc@aol.com.

VINDIGNI, VINCENZO, medical educator, researcher; b. Udine, Italy, Feb. 14, 1971; m. Chiara Pavan, Dec. 20, 2003. MD, U. Padova, Italy, 1997. Diploma in plastic and reconstructive surgery U. Padova, 2002, diploma in philosophy tissue engring. 2006. Rschr. dept. histology U. Padova, 2005, asst. prof. plastic surgery, 2007—. Author various manuscripts; contbr. articles to profl. jours. Mem.: Italian Soc. Microsurgery, Italian Soc. Plastic and Reconstructive Surgery. Home: Via Roma n° 74 Padova 35100 Italy Office: Univ Padova Via Giustiniani 2 Padua 35100 Italy Office Phone: +39 049 8212701. Office Fax: +39 049 8213687. Business E-Mail: vincenzo.vindigni@unipd.it.

VINGOE, FRANCIS JAMES, clinical and forensic psychologist, consultant; b. San Diego, Oct. 20, 1931; arrived in U.K., 1934, arrived in UK, 1975; s. Alfred and Mary Ellen (James) V.; m. Dolores Marguerite Chevillard, Apr. 1957 (div. 1965); 1 child, Sylvie Lamorna; m. Grace Roberta Cameron, Apr. 15, 1966; children: Lisa Michelle, Wendy Sue, Michael Jan. BA with honors, Calif. State U., San Diego, 1956; MA, Calif. State U., San Francisco, 1960; PhD, U. Oreg., 1965. Diplomate in hypnosis Am. Bd. Psychol. Examiners; chartered clin. psychologist, forensic psychologist, expert witness. Teaching asst. U. Nebr., Lincoln, 1956-57; instr. math. Cogswell Poly. Coll., San Francisco, 1959-61; ednl. psychologist Bremerton (Wash.) Pub. Schs., 1961-63; instr. psychology Olympic Coll., Bremerton, 1961-63; clin. psychology intern Napa State Hosp., 1963-64; lectr. Napa Coll., 1963-64, counselor, psychometrist, instr. U. Oreg., Eugene, 1964-65; rsch. assoc. State of Oreg., 1965; asst. prof. psychology Colo. State U., Ft. Collins, 1965-68; assoc. prof. psychology SUNY, Cortland, 1968-71; sr. lectr. clin. psychology U. Groningen, The Netherlands, 1971-75; prin. clin. psychologist Univ. Hosp. Wales, Cardiff, 1975-85; lectr. U. Wales Coll. Medicine, Cardiff, 1975-92; pvt. practice cons. clin. and forensic psychologist, 1994—; coastal watch officer Gwennap Head, Cornwall, 2004—. Cons. clin. psychologist Univ. Hosp. Wales, Cardiff, 1985-94; cons. Poudre R-1 Schs., Ft. Collins, 1966-68, Tri County Head Start Programme, Torrington, Wyo., 1967-68; vis. lectr. Wells Coll., Aurora, N.Y., 1968-70; single joint expert witness, 1999—. Author: Clinical Psychology and Medicine, 1981; cons. editor Internat. Jour. Clin. and Exptl. Hypnosis; assoc. editor Brit. Jour. Exptl. and Clin. Hypnosis, 1982, Jour. Contemporary Hypnosis, 1991; clin. editor Brit. Jour. Exptl. and Clin. Hypnosis, 1982; contbr. articles to profl. jours. With USN, 1949-53. Faculty Rsch. fellow SUNY, Cortland, 1970; Faculty Rsch. grantee Colo. State U., 1968. Fellow Brit. Psychol. Soc. (divsn. clin., forensic, and neuropsychology); mem. Brit. Soc. Exptl. and Clin. Hypnosis (chmn. Wales and West of Eng. br. 1982-85), Brit. Soc. Clin. and Exptl. Hypnosis (chmn. 1985-2000) Internat. Soc. Hypnosis (coun. reps. 1991-2001). Avocations: swimming, boating, fishing, travel, reading. Home and Office: 1 the Parade TR19 6PR Mousehole Penzance England Office Phone: 01736 732 597. E-mail: vincam76@globalnet.co.uk.

VINH, THOSON, medical educator; b. June 28, 1944; MD, Medicine Sch., 1972, PhD, 1980. Prof. Cochin Rene Descartes Med. Sch., 1982—. Recipient Neer award, Am. Shoulder & Elbow Surgeons. Mem.: Soc. Française Chirurgie Orthopédique et Traumatologique, Soc. Chirurgie de la Main, Soc. Internat. Chirurgie Orthopedique Traumatologique. Conservative. Buddhist. Home: 20 Rue du Moulin Vert 75014 Paris France Home Phone: 0140445588. Business E-Mail: thoson.vinh@cch.aphp.fr.

VINH-HUNG, VINCENT, oncologist, researcher; s. Buu and Aubriet; life ptnr. Bee Keyzer. Baccalaureat, Lycee J.J. Rousseau, Saigon, Vietnam, 1969. Cert. in radiation oncology Belgium, 1984. Head breast radiation unit Oncologisch Centrum, UZ Brussel, Jette, 2006—. Achievements include research in data modeling in breast cancer. Office: Oncologisch Centrum UZ Brussel Laarbeeklaan 101 Jette Brussels 1090 Belgium Office Phone: 32 2 477 6041. Office Fax: 32 2 477 6212. Personal E-mail: anhxang@gmail.com. E-mail: conrvhgv@uzbrussel.be.

VINOGRADSKY, BORIS V., surgeon; Grad., Stanley Kaplan Ednl. Ctr., Winooski Vt., 1992—93; MD with summa cum laude, Yaroslavl Med. Acad., Russia, 1980—86. Lic. USMLE Steps I, II and III 1995, 1996, BLS, ACLS and ATLS 1996, US Drug Enforcement Adminstrn. Lic. 1999, cert. ECFMG 1995, Gen. Surgery State Ohio Med. Lic., 1999. Postdoc. rsch. fellow biochemistry and medicine Univ. Vermont, Burlington, 1993—95; resident gen. surgery Univ. Ky., Lexington, 1996—98, Med. Coll., Toledo, 1998—2002; fellow CT surgery Case Western Res., Cleve., 2002—03; tng. treatment rectal prolapse and hemorrhoids Columbus, Ohio, 2003; pvt. practice gen. surgery Cleve., 2003—; with lake hosp. system lake West and Lake East Hosps., 2003—; with cleve. clinic system Hillcrest Hosp., 2005—09; tng. laparoscopic colon workshop Norwalk, 2006, Cleve., 2006; tng. Hernias workshop Akron, Ohio, 2006; tng. modified kugel mesh hernia repair workshop Pismo Beach, Calif., 2006; with univ. hosp. system Geauga Hosp., 2006—; tng. SILS course Cleve., 2009; with univ. hosp. system Richmond Hosp., 2009—; pres. and owner Boris V. Vinogradsky MD Inc., pvt. practice gen. surgery, trauma and surg. critical care. Instr. physiology Yaroslavl Med. Acad., 1986—87, instr. otolaryngology, 1990—91. Co-author various abstacts including "Treatment of throat cancer in the Emergency Hospital, 1991" and "Genetically engineered endothelial cells: Increased surface fibrinolysis and potential adaptation to endovascular stenting, 1995"; contbr. articles Surgical approach to the treatment of disorders of the lymphatic system of the extremities, 1985, Treatment of obliterative atherosclerosis, 1986, chapters to books Disorders of the Stomach, Prostaglandins, Thromboxane, and Leukotrienes, numerous publs. in the RAMA jour., 2004-2009. Recipient Resident of the Year, Surgery, MCO Toledo Ohio, 2002; scholar Russian Nat. Merit, Yaroslavl Med. Acad., 1983. Fellow: Am. Coll. Surgeons; mem.: Russian Am. Med. Assn. (USA) (chmn. of the bd.), Lake County Med. Soc., Ohio State Med. Assn., Am. Med. Assn., Acad. Medcine Northeast Ohio, Am. Soc. Laparoscopic Surgeons, Am. Soc. Breast Surgeons, SAGES. Avocations: photography, travel, reading, cooking. Office: Boris V Vinogradsky MD Incorporated 36100 Euclid Ave Ste 330-B Willoughby Ohio 44094 United States Office Phone: 4409538055. Office Fax: 4409530242. *

VIOLET, WOODROW WILSON, JR., retired chiropractor; b. Sept. 19, 1937; s. Woodrow Wilson and Alice Katherine (Woods) V.; m. Judith Jane Thatcher, June 15, 1963; children: Woodina Lonize, Leslie Alice. Grad. with honors, U.S. Army Med. Svc. Sch., 1955, student, Ventura Coll., 1961-62; grad., L.A. Coll. Chiropractic, 1966. Pvt. practice chiropractic medicine, Santa Barbara, Calif., 1966-73, London, 1973-74, Carpinteria, Calif., 1974-84. Past mem. coun. roentgenology Am. Chiropractic Assn. Former mem. Parker Chiropractic Rsch. Found., Ft. Worth. With USAF, 1955-63. Recipient award merit Calif. Chiropractic Colls., Inc., 1975, cert. of appreciation Nat. Chiropractic Antitrust Com., 1977. Mem.: Nat. Geog. Soc., Delta Sigma. Patentee surg. instrument.

VIRGO, KATHERINE SUE, medical researcher; b. East Alton, Ill., Feb. 14, 1959; d. John William and Doris Ann (Spencer) Ulmrich; m. John Michael Virgo, Sept. 6, 1980. BSBA, So. Ill. U., 1981, MBA, 1983; PhD in Health Svcs. Rsch., St. Louis U., 1991. From asst. coord. to exec. adminstr. Atlantic Econ. Soc., Edwardsville, Ill., 1976—86; co-founder, exec. adminstr. Internat. Health Econs. and Mgmt. Inst., Edwardsville, 1983—87; health sci. specialist VA Med. Ctr., St. Louis, 1986—93, clin. rsch. coord., 1993—2008; asst. prof. St. Louis U., 1991—96, assoc. prof., 1996—2001, prof., 2001—08, dir. health svcs. rsch. Am. Cancer Soc., 2008—10; adj. prof. Emory U., 2008—; mng. dir. health svcs. rsch. Am. Cancer Soc., 2010—. Bd. dir. Internat. Health Econs. and Mgmt. Inst., Edwardsville, 1983-87. Assoc. editor: Atlantic Econ. Jour., 1994—, dep. editor: Internat. Advances in Econ. Rsch., 1995—; co-editor: Cancer Patient Follow-Up, 1997, The Bionic Patient, 2005; ad hoc reviewer: JAMA, 1995—96, Med. Care, 1995—, Women's Health Issues, 2000—01, Jour. Spinal Cord Medicine, 2002—, Jour. Behavioral Health Svc. Rsch., 2000—, Jour. Gen. Internal Medicine, 2005, mem. editl. bd.: Surg. Oncology, 2007—, ad hoc reviewer: Internat. Jour. Oncology, 2005—; ad hoc reviewer Am. Journal Pub Health, 2008—; contbr. articles to profl. jours. Mem. St. Louis Cathedral Basilica Choir, 2000—08, Sacred Heart Basilica Choir, 2009—, Sacred Heart Basilica Schola, 2010—. VA grantee. Mem.: APHA (sect. councilor 2003—06, program chair 2005—08, health svc. rsch. com. chair 2008—, chair-elect 2010—11, chair 2011—), Soc. Internat. Geriatric Oncology, Am. Paraplegia Soc., Health Econs. Rsch. Orgn., Acad. of Health, Am. Soc. Clin. Oncology (health svcs. rsch. com. 2002—05, sci. program com. mem. 2008—09, methods subcom., dissemination and implementation subcom.), Internat. Health Econs. Assn. Democrat. Roman Catholic. Avocations: singing, piano, travel, reading, swimming. Office: Am Cancer Soc Health Svc Rsch Intramural Res Dept 250 Williams St NW Atlanta GA 30303-1002 Home: 1360 Stephens Dr NE Atlanta GA 30329-3714 Business E-Mail: kvirgo@emory.edu.

VISCO, FRANCES M., foundation administrator; married; 1 child. BS with honors, St. Joseph's U.; JD, Villanova U., 1983. Ptnr. Cohen, Shapiro, Polisher, Shiekman and Cohen, Phila.; first pres. Nat. Breast Cancer Coalition, Washington, 1992—. Mem. breast cancer rsch. program integration panel Dept. Def.; bd. dirs. Linda Creed Breast Cancer Found., Nat. Breast Cancer Coalition, mem. exec. com.; consumer adv. bd. Temple U. Comprehensive Breast Ctr.; apptd. mem. Pres. Clinton's Cancer Panel, 1993. Editor The Villanova Law Rev. Named Person of Week ABC World News Tonight with Peter Jennings, 1993; recipient Judge Learned Hand award Phila. chpt. of Am. Jewish Com. 1994, Powerhouse award Mirabella mag., 1995. Mem. Am. Cancer Soc. (Phila. divsn., legis. affairs com.), Greater Phila. C. of C., Women's Ctr. for Health Promotion (adv. com.), Thomas Jefferson Univ. Hosp. (adv. coun.). Office: Nat Breast Cancer Coalition/Fund 1101 17th St NW Ste 1300 Washington DC 20036 Office Phone: 202-296-7477. Office Fax: 202-265-6854. *

VISCONTI, ERNEST, pediatrician; Attended, SUNY Upstate Med. U., Syracuse NY, 1971. Diplomate Am. Bd. Pediatrics, Am. Bd. Pediatrics-pediatric infectious disease. Tng. RI Hosp.; tng. infectious disease NY Presbyn. Hosp.; tng. pediat. cornell campus Presbyn. Hosp.; resident in pediat. NY Hosp., 1972—74; fellow in infectious disease RI Hosp., Providence, 1976—78; with Richmond Univ. Med. Ctr.; pediatrician Lutheran Med. Ctr., Brooklyn. Office: Lutheran Medical Center Seaview Medical 314 Seaview Ave Staten Island NY 10305 Office Phone: 718-668-3417. Office Fax: 718-668-3420.

VISHNU, PRAKASH, physician, scientist, hematologist, oncologist; b. Bangalore, Karnataka, India, Nov. 3, 1976; s. Vishnu and Sudhamani; m. Madhavi Chivukula, Apr. 30, 2001; children: Sai Pranati Prakash, Sai Pragna Prakash. MD, Bangalore Med. Coll., 2000; postgraduate diploma in Molecular Medicine and Pathology, U. Auckland, New Zealand, 2005. Diplomate Med. Coun. India, 2001, Am. Bd. Internal Medicine, 2008. Rsch. assoc. U. Auckland, 2003—05, U. Mich., Ann Arbor, 2005—06; ho. officer Detroit Med. Ctr., 2005—08, Mayo Clinic, 2008—11, Hematology-Oncology, Mayo Clinic, 2008—11. Recipient Internat. Scholar in Tng., Am. Assn. Cancer Rsch., 2007, Am. Soc. Hematology Travel award, 2010. Mem.: AMA, ACP, Am. Soc. Hematology, Am. Assn. Cancer Rsch. (assoc.), Am. Soc. Clin. Oncology (assoc.). Achievements include research in breast, ovary and lung cancers; hematopoietic stem cells; radiation pneumontis; Crohn's disease. Avocations: photography, travel. Office: Va Mason Med Ctr 1100 9th Ave # C2-Hem Seattle WA 98101 Office Phone: 206-223-6193. Business E-Mail: prakash.vishnu@vmmc.org.

VISKONTAS, INDRE, neuroscientist; b. Etobicoke, Ont., Can., Oct. 7, 1976; BSc, U. Toronto, 1999; PhD, UCLA, 2006. Cognitive neuroscientist Memory & Aging Ctr., UCSF, 2006—. TV host Oprah Winfrey Network, 2011; assoc. editor Neurocase, 2007—11. Avocation: singing. Office: Memory and Aging Ctr 350 Parnasses A San Francisco CA 94143-1207 Business E-Mail: iviskontas@memory.ucsf.edu.

VISO-GUROVICH, FELA, pharmacist, educator; b. Mexico City, Mex., Sept. 2, 1946; d. Alfredo Viso and Perla Gurovich. PhD, Centro Investigacion Estudios Avanzados del Instituto Politécnico Nacional, Mexico City, 1970—73; Postdoctoral, U. Cambridge, Eng., 1973—75; BS in Chemistry, Pharmacy, and Biology, Sch. Chemistry Nat. Automous U., Mex., 1970. Coord., pharmacy curriculum Universidad Autónoma Metropolitana Xochimilco, Mexico City, 1975—78, Universidad Nacional Autónoma de México, Mexico City, 1982—84; subdir., Mexican Pharmacopeia Secretaria de Salud, Mexico City, 1987—93; dean, sch. of pharmacy Universidad Autónoma Estado de Hidalgo, Pachuca, 1993—2005; coord., msc degree Universidad Autónoma del Estado de Hidalgo, Pachuca, 2005—. Cons. Secretaria de Salud, 1985—2005; pres. Colegio Nacional de Químicos Farmacéuticos Biologos México AC, Mexico City, 1995—97; coord., rsch. & postgrad. studies Universidad Autónoma del Estado de Hidalgo, 1996—98; pres. Mexican Assn. Hosp. Pharmacists, Pachuca, 2004—. Pharmacist Design of Clinical Pharmacy Curriculum (Nat. award on Pharm. Scis., 1999); contbr. articles to profl. jours. and pubs. Active Servicios de Salud de Hidalgo, Pachuca, 1993—93. Grantee Support for Postdoctoral Studies, Brit. Coun., 1973—75, Scholar in Residence, Am. Soc. Health-Sys. Pharmacists, 2004. Mem.: Can. Soc. Hosp. Pharmacists (hon.), Asociación Mexicana de Farmacéuticos de Hosp., AC (assoc.), Colegio Nacional de Químicos Biologos, México.AC (assoc.), Internat. Pharm. Fedn. (assoc.), Am. Soc. Health Sys.-Pharmacist (assoc.), Academia Nacional de Ciencias Farmacéuticas (assoc.). Achievements include research in pharmacoepidemiology in Mexico. Home: Hacienda de Tecajete 120 Hidalgo Pachuca 42083 Mexico Office: Secretaria de Salud del Estado Blvd Neuvo #102 Pachuca Hidalgo Mexico also: Health Ministry of the State Hidalgo Blvd Nuevo Pachuca Hidalgo 42083 Mexico Office Fax: 52 (771) 7105421; Home Fax: 52 (771) 7105421. Personal E-mail: visoguro@yahoo.com.mx.

VISONÀ, ENRICO, orthopedist; b. Montebelluna, May 27, 1980; MD, U. degli Studi Padova, 2005. Orthopedist, traumatologist Clinica Orthop., Padua, 2011; orthop. surgeon ULSS 17, 2011—. Mem.: SIGASCOT, SICSeG, SIOT. Avocations: rugby, motorcycling. Home: Via Marchesi 5 Padua Veneto 35126 Italy Personal E-mail: e.visona@libero.it.

VISU-PETRA, LAURA ALEXANDRA, researcher, psychologist educator; b. Bistrita, Bistrita-Nasaud, Romania, Feb. 5, 1981; d. Vasile and Elena Petra; m. George Visu, May 27, 2006. MA in Clin. Psychology, Babes-Bolyai U., Cluj-Napoca, 2004, PhD Summa cum laudae, 2008. Cert. psychotherapist Albert Ellis Inst., NY, 2004. Asst. prof. Dept. Psychology, Babes-Bolyai U., 2006—. Mem. editl. bd. Romanian Assn. Cognitive Scis., Cluj-Napoca, 2005—08. Contbr. articles to profl. jours. Active mem. Devel. Psychology Lab., Cluj-Napoca, 2006—08. Scholar SOCRATES, Erasmus, Ministry of Edn., 2005; Young Doctoral Rsch. grant, NRC, 2006—08. Mem.: Internat. Brain Rsch. Orgn., Soc. Rsch. in Child Devel. Office: Dept Psychology Babes-Bolyai Univ Republicii str no 37 Cluj-Napoca Cluj 40015 Romania Office Fax: 0040264590967. Business E-Mail: laurapetra@psychology.ro.

VISWANATHAN, GOPALAKRISHNAN, neurosurgeon, educator; b. New Delhi, Nov. 15, 1976; MBBS, Trivandrum Med. Coll., 2000; MS in Gen. Surgery, Trivandrum Med. Coll., Trivandrum, Kerala, 2004; MCh in Neurosurgery, Sree Chitra Tirunal Inst. Med. Scis. and Tech., Trivandrum, 2007. Postdoc. fellow Sree Chitra Tirunal Inst. Med. Scis. and Tech., 2008, asst. prof., 2008—. Recipient Best Paper award, 49th Ann. Conf. Internat. Coll. Surgeons, Indian chpt., 2003, Gold medal, Trivandrum Med. Coll., Jr. Sci. Talent Search award, Govt. of Delhi. Mem.: Congress of Neurol. Surgeons, Neurol. Soc. India. Achievements include research in surgical treatment of brain tumors, pediatric cerebrovascular disorder. Avocations: music, reading, sports. Office: Sree Chitra Tirunal Inst Med Scis and Tech. 7th Fl Surg Block Trivandrum Kerala 695011 India Office Phone: 91 471 2524492. Office Fax: 91-471-2550728. Personal E-mail: doc_gopal@yahoo.com.

VITHOULKAS, GEORGE, homeopath; b. Athens, Greece, July 25, 1932; m. Zissoula Antoniadou (Zissoula) V. Diploma in Homeopathy, Indian Inst. Homeopathy, India, 1966. Prof. classical homeopathic medicine, Athens, 1967—; founder and dir. Ctr. Homeopathic Medicine, Athens, 1970—; dean Internat. Acad. Classical Homeopathy, Alonissos, Greece, 1995—. V.p. Greece LIGA Medicorum Internat. Homeopatica; founder (with others) Internat. Found. Homeopathy, United States, 1978—; cons. Vithoulkas Expert Sys. U. Namur, Belgium, 1987—91; collaborating prof. med. faculty Basque U., Bilbao, Spain, 1999; collaborating prof. Aegean U., Greece, 2004. Author: Homeopathy-Medicine of the New Man, 1975, 2d edit., 1992, The Science of Homeopathy, 1980, Materia Medica Viva, A New Model for Health and Disease, Talks on Classical Homeopathy, Essence of Materia Medica Le Essenze Rubate, 1988, Essenzen Homoopathischer, 1990, Homeopatttisia Laakeainekuvia, 1992, Homeopathic Conference Esalen The Bern Seminar, 1980; creator Greek Homeopathic Jour., 1972—2003; creator, editor European Jour. Classical Homeopathy, 1995—98. Recipient honors, Internat. Hemeopathic Med. Soc., 1974, Gold medal, Internat. Congress LIGA, 1989, Alternative Nobel Prize, Sweden, 1996, Hungarian Democracy Gold medal, Pres. Republic of Hungary, 2000; named Homeopath of Millenium, Min. Health Ctrl. Govt. of India, 2000, Prof. honoris causa, Kiev Med. Acad., 2000. Mem. AAAS, Internat. Found. Homeopathy (pres.), Hellenic Homeopathic Med. Soc. (hon. pres.), Greek Soc. Homeopathic Medicine (founder), N.Y. Acad. Scis., Hahnemann Soc. Eng. (hon. v.p.), Sci. and Med. Network, Soc. Authors. Avocations: ecology, gardening, politics. Office: Inter Acad Clas Homeopathy 37005 Alonissos Greece Office Phone: 0030-24240-65142. Business E-Mail: academy@vithoulkas.com.

VITT, DAVID AARON, health products executive; b. Phila., Aug. 3, 1938; s. Nathan and Flora B.; m. Renee Lee Salkever, Oct. 20, 1963; children: Nadine Lori Einiger, Jeffrey Richard. BS, Temple U., 1961. Sales engr. X-Ray Corp., Phila., 1961-65, Midwest Am., Chgo., 1965-67, product mgr., 1967-68, product mgr. regional sales, 1968-70; dir. mktg. Valtronic & Living Wills, Bronx, NY, 1970-74; v.p., gen. mgr. dental divsn. Siemens Med. Sys. Inc., Iselin, NJ, 1974—86, past corp. v.p., gen. mgr. dental divsn.; CEO, pres. Pelton & Crane, Charlotte, NC, 1986-89; v.p. govt. sales, ret. Siemens Med. Sys., 1994; founder, pres., CEO D.A.V., Inc., 1995—; founder, co-owner RealDental.com. Pres. Denx Am. Inc., 1998; industry rep. to Am. Nat. Stds. Inst.; co. rep. U.S.-USSR Trade and Econ. Coun.; co-founder Enter Am. Group Exec. Consultants, vice chmn. Gnonnds & Beautification Com. Greenbmer, Whittingham, Safety & Infrustructural Group Greenbnauat Whittingham. Bd. dirs. Am. Fund for Dental Health; apptd. mem. Charlotte Mecklenburg Cmty. Rels. Com.; mem. bd. visitors U. N.C., Charlotte; officer, mem. exec. com. Jr. Achievement. Served in USAR, 1961-68. Mem. Am. Mgmt. Assn. (bd. dirs. N.J. chpt.), Am. Mktg. Assn., Am. Dental Trade Assn. (bd. dirs.), Dental Mfrs. Am. (past pres.), Am. Acad. Dental Radiology, Charlotte C. of C. (bd. advisors), Acad. Gen. Dentists (bd. mem. found.), Masons (32d deg.), Shriners. Republican.

VITTETOE, MARIE CLARE, retired clinical laboratory science educator; b. Keota, Iowa, May 19, 1927; d. Edward Daniel and Marcella Matilda Vittetoe. BS, Marycrest Coll., 1950; MS, W.Va. U., 1971, EdD, 1973. Staff technologist St. Joseph Hosp., Ottumwa, Iowa, 1950-70; instr. Ottumwa Hosp. Sch. Med. Tech., 1957-70, St. Joseph Hosp. Sch. Nursing, Ottumwa, 1950-70; asst. prof. U. Ill., Champaign-Urbana, 1973-78; prof. clin. lab. scis. U. Ky., Lexington, 1978-94; cons. Nat. Pub. Health Lab Port au Prince, Haiti, 2005—10, Hosp. U. Paix Port au Prince, Haiti, 2009, Project Hope Haiti, 1985—87; cons. labs. Barbados, Guyana, Jamaica, 1992. Mem. Sisters of Humility of Mary, 1946—; chair Congregation of Humility of Mary; clin. lab. cons. 6 clinics in Haiti, 2000—10; cons. Nat. Pub. Health Lab., Port au Prince, Haiti, 2007—10. Author: Vittetoe Family Tree and Scrapbook, 2000, Peiffer-Berg Family Tree and Scrapbook, 2000, Lutz/Peiffer Family Tree Update, 2002, Vittetoe Family Tree Update, 2002; contbr. articles to profl. jours. Vol. hosp. labs., Haiti, 1999—2011; apptd. to advisory bd. CRUDEM Found., 2005—. Recipient Kingston award for Creative Tchg., Recognition award for svc. to edn., Commonwealth of Ky. Coun. on Higher Edn., disting. grad. award, Nat. Cath. Ednl. Assn., 1995, devel. of youth award, Iowa 4-H Found., 1996, award for devel. Best Little Lab. in Haiti, 2002, award, CRUDEM Found., 2009; named Ky. Col., Marie Vittetoe award for excellence in svc. named for her, U. Ky., 1999. Mem. Am. Soc. for Med. Tech. (chmn. 1986-89, Profl. Achievement award 1991, Ky. Mem. of Yr. award 1994), Am. Soc. Clin. Lab. Scis., Am. Soc. Clin. Pathologists (assoc.), Alpha Mu Tau. Avocations: walking, genealogy.

VITTONE, BERNARD JOHN, psychiatrist, researcher; b. Latrobe, Pa., Oct. 5, 1951; s. Felix Edward and Jessie (Mosso) V.; children: Matthew, Victoria. BS in Psychology, Georgetown U., 1973, DMS, 1977. Diplomate Am. Bd. Psychiatry Neurology. Intern flexible medicine, resident psychiatry St. Vincent's Hosp and Med. Ctr., NYC, 1977-82; resident ophthalmology Wills Eye Hosp., Phila., 1978-79; staff psychiatrist Phila. State Hosp., Phila., 1979; med. staff fellow NIMH, Bethesda, Md., 1982-84; dir. Nat. Ctr. Treatment Phobias, Anxiety, Depression, Washington, 1985—. Cons. Roundhouse Sq. Psychiat. Ctr., Alexandria, Va., 1984-85; guest rschr. NIMH, 1984-93; tng. com. St. Vincent's Hosp. Med. Ctr., NYC, 1980-81; attending staff Dominion Hosp., 1991-92; faculty Washington Sch. Psychiatry, 1997—; featured expert CNN, Nightline, Washington Post, Newsweek, others. Contbg. author to profl. jours. and books. Mem. instnl. rev. bd. Inst. Behavior Health, Rockville, Md., 1988-91; dir. adv. bd. Am. Against Drugs, 1990-94. Recipient Outstanding achievement award microbiology, Georgetown Univ., 1976; named Top Washington Psychotherapist, Washingtonian mag., 1998, 2009, Top Washington Doctor, 2010. Fellow Am. Psychiat. Assn.; mem. AMA, Washington Psychiat. Soc., Anxiety Disorders Assn. Am., Alpha Omega Alpha. Avocations: tennis, ping pong/table tennis, billiards, swimming, darts. Office: NCTPAD 2423 Pennsylvania Ave NW Washington DC 20037-1718 Office Phone: 202-363-7792, 202-363-3900.

VITZ, PAUL CLAYTON, psychologist, educator; b. Toledo, Aug. 27, 1935; m. Evelyn Birge; 6 children. BA high honors in Psychology, U. Mich., 1953; PhD, Stanford U., 1962. Instr. psychology Pomona (Calif.) Coll., 1962-64; asst. prof. NYU, 1965-70, assoc. prof., 1970-85, dir. psychology dept. undergrad. program, 1973-79, prof., 1985—2004, prof. emeritus, 2004—. Adj. prof. John Paul II Inst. on Marriage and Family, Washington, 1990-2003, Internat. Acad. Philosophy, 1994-98; prof./sr. scholar Inst. for Psychol. Scis., 2000—; lectr. in field. Author: Psychology as Religion: The Cult of Self-Worship, 1977, 2d edit., 1994, (with A.B. Glimcher) Modern Art and Modern Science: The Parallel Analysis of Vision, 1984, Censorship: Evidence of Bias in Our Children's Textbooks, 1986, Sigmund Freud's Christian Unconscious, 1988, Faith of the Fatherless: The Psychology of Atheism, 1999; editor: (with S. Krason) Defending the Family: A Sourcebook, 1998, (with S. Felch) The Self: Beyond the Postmodern Crisis, 2006; contbr. articles to profl. jours., chpts. to books. Grantee Nat. Inst. Mental Health, 1963-64, 64-66, 66-67, Nat. Inst. Neurol. Diseases and Blindness grantee, 1970-73, 73-74, Nat. Inst. Edn., 1983, 84-85, Dept. Edn., 1986-87. Office: Inst for the Psychol Scis Ste 511 2001 Jefferson Davis Hwy Arlington VA 22202

VIVEK, AHYA N., pulmonologist, educator; MD, Boston U. Resident Barnes-Jewish Hosp. Wash. Univ.; fellow Hosp. of the Univ. of Pa.; asst. prof. medicine Sch. of Medicine Univ. of Pa.; med. dir. Lung Transplantation Program Univ. of Pa. Med. Ctr., Phila. Contbr. various med. compilations. Office: University of Pennsylvania Medical Center 832 West Gates Bldg 3400 Spruce St Philadelphia PA 19104 Office Phone: 215-349-5824. Office Fax: 215-662-3226. Business E-Mail: ahyav@uphs.upenn.edu.

VIVERO-ESCOTO, JUAN LUIS, chemist; b. Mex., Jan. 19, 1977; BSc, Nat. Poly. Inst. Mex., 2000; PhD, Iowa State U., 2009. Rsch. asst. Nat. Poly. Inst. Mex., 2000—04, Iowa State U., 2005—09, tchg. asst., 2004—05; postdoc. rsch. assoc. U. NC, Chapel Hill, 2010—. Application chemist Hercules Inc., 2000—03. Recipient Alpha Sigma Chi Rsch. award, Iowa State U., Travel award, Procter & Gamble, award, Telmex Found.; Faculty Diversity fellowship, Office Vice Chancellor Rsch., U. NC. Mem.: Am. Chem. Soc., Materials Rsch. Soc., Chemistry Dept. Postdoc. Assn. UNC-CH, Sigma Xi Sci. Rsch. Soc. Avocation: reading. Home: 6 Lanark Rd Chapel Hill NC 27517 Personal E-mail: viej770119@yahoo.com.

VIVIANI, GIORGIO LUCIANO, physician, educator; b. Rodos, Greece, Oct. 8, 1948; MD, U. Genova, 1974, degree in Geriat., 1977. Assoc. prof. medicine U. Genova, 1992—. Mem.: ADA, EASD. Office: viale benedetto XV 6 Genova 16132 Italy Office Fax: 3903537541. Business E-Mail: vivianig@unige.it.

VIVIANO, PAUL STEVEN, medical center administrator; b. LA, Mar. 23, 1953; s. Al and Edythe (Buck) V.; m. Carole Viviano, Aug. 5, 1979; children: Allison, Megan. BA in Polit. Sci., U. Calif., Santa Barbara, 1975; MPA, UCLA, 1976. Pres., CEO Norris Comprehensive Cancer Ctr., U. SC Hosp.; with The St. Joseph Health System; adminstrv. asst. Orange County Pub. Health Dept., Orange, Calif., 1976, dir. adminstrn., 1976-78; asst. adminstr. Dominguez Valley Hosp., Compton, Calif., 1978-80; adminstr. Lakewood Gen. Hosp., Calif., 1980-81; exec. dir. Los Alamitos Med. Ctr., Calif., 1981-85; CEO Long Beach Community Hosp., Calif., 1985—87; pres., CEO St. Jude Med. Ctr., Fullerton, Calif., 1987; COO Alliance HealthCare Services, Inc., 2003—04, chmn., pres., 2003—, CEO, 2004—. Bd. dirs., treas. Preferred Health Network; mem. liaison com. Blue Cross; bd. dirs. COHR Connection. Bd. dirs. Huntington Harbour br. Am. Cancer Soc., Calif. Spl. Olympics. Mem. Young President's Orgn. Roman Catholic. Avocations: sailing, tenniss, volleyball. Office: Alliance HealthCare Services 100 Bayview Cir Ste 400 Newport Beach CA 92660 Office Phone: 949-242-5300. Personal E-mail: pviviano@alliancehealthcareservices-us.com. *

VIVINO, FREDERICK B., rheumatologist, educator; Am. Bd. Internal Medicine-internal medicine, rheumatology, lic. to practice Pa., 1985. Intern, resident Med. Coll. Pa., fellow rheumatology, 1989; intern internal medicine Hahnemann Univ. Hosp., 1984, resident internal medicine, 1986; chief rheumatology Penn Presbyn. Med. Ctr.; dir. Penn Sjogren's Syndrome Ctr.; clin. assoc. prof. medicine. Named Top Doc, Phila. Mag., 2008—11; named one of America's Top Doctors, 2008, 2010. Office: Penn Presbyterian Medical Center 51 N 39th St Philadelphia PA 19104 Office Phone: 215-662-8000.

VIXNER, LINDA, medical researcher; b. Orsa, Mar. 21, 1972; BS in Physiotherapy, Linköping U., 1997; PhD, Karolinska Inst. Lectr., med. sci. Dalarna U., 2007; rschr. Karolinska Inst., 2010—. Recipient Gyllene Pekpinnen award, Lärarnas Riksförbund. Office: Högskolan Dalarna Falun Dalarna 791 80 Sweden Business E-Mail: lvi@du.se.

VLACHOJANNIS CHRUBASIK, JULIA ELODIE, orthodontist; b. Offenbach am Main, Germany, Oct. 7, 1980; MSc, Columbia U. NYC, PhD in Med. Dentistry, 2009. Recipient Postgrad. Birnberg Rsch. award, William Jarvie Soc. Home: Lofou 4A EKALI 14578 Athens Greece Personal E-mail: jvlachojannis@gmail.com.

VLADECK, BRUCE CHARNEY, healthcare consultant, former academic administrator; b. NYC, Sept. 13, 1949; s. Stephen Charney and Judith (Pomarlen) V.; m. Fredda Wellin, Aug. 5, 1973; children—Elizabeth Charney, Stephen Isaiah, Abigail Sarah. BA, Harvard U., Cambridge, Mass., 1970; MA, U. Mich, 1972, PhD in Polit. Sci., 1973. Assoc. social scientist NYC-Rand Inst., 1973-74; asst. prof. Columbia U., NYC, 1974-78, assoc. prof., 1978-79; asst. commr. health planning and resources devel. NJ Dept. Health, Trenton, 1979-82; asst. v.p. Robert Wood Johnson Found., Princeton, NJ, 1982-83; pres. United Hosp. Fund, NYC, 1983-93; adminstr. HCFA, Washington, 1993-97; prof. health policy and geriatrics Mt. Sinai Med. Ctr., NYC, 1997—2004; prin. Health Scis. Adv. Svcs. Ernst & Young LLP, 2004—06, 2007—09; interim pres. U. Medicine and Dentistry NJ, Newark, 2006—07; sr. advisor Neycera Inc., 2009—. Mem. NY State Coun. on Health Care Financing, Albany, 1978-92; mem. com. on nursing home regulation Inst. Medicine, Washington, 1983-85, chmn. com. on health care for homeless people, 1986-88, mem. prospective payment assessment com., 1986-93; mem. Nat. Bipartisan Commn. on Future of Medicare, 1997-98. Author: Unloving Care: The Nursing Home Tragedy, 1981. Contbr. numerous articles to profl. publs. Fellow N.Y. Acad. Medicine; mem. Inst. Medicine, Nat. Acad. Scis., Phi Beta Kappa. Office Phone: 212-773-0111, 212-506-5453. Personal E-mail: bvladeck@earthlink.net. Business E-Mail: bruce.vladeck@ey.com, bvladeck@nexevaconsultancy.com.

VLADIMÍR, MUSIL, information scientist; b. Prague, May 30, 1976; PhD, Charles U. Prague, 2006. Dep. head Ctr. Sci. Info., 1994—. Mem.: Czech Info. Soc. Avocation: singing. Office: Ruska 87 Prague 10000 Czech Republic Business E-Mail: vladimir.musil@lf3.cuni.cz.

VLADUTIU, ADRIAN O., physician, educator; b. Bucharest, Romania, Aug. 5, 1940; came to U.S., 1969, naturalized 1974; s. Octavian and Veturia (Chirescu) Vladutiu; m. Georgirene V. Dietrich;

children: Christina Lynn, Catherine Joy. MD, Sch. Medicine, Bucharest, 1962; PhD in Immunopathology, Sch. Medicine, Jassy, Romania, 1968. Diplomate Am. Bd. Pathology. Asst. prof. physiopathology Sch. Medicine, Bucharest, 1968-71; assoc. prof. pathology SUNY Sch. Medicine, Buffalo, 1978-81, prof. pathology, 1981—, pathologist, 1974—2006; dir. clin. labs. Buffalo Gen. Hosp., 1982—2001, prof. microbiology, 1982—, prof. medicine, 1985—. Cons. Niagara Falls (N.Y.) Meml. Hosp., 1976—82, Tri-County Hosp., Gowanda, NY, 1991—93; acting head dept. pathology Buffalo Gen. Hosp, 1985—86; dir. lab. Deaconess Hosp. Buffalo, 1982—91, Columbus Meml., Buffalo, 1996—98. Author: Pleural Effusion, 1986; contbr. chapters to books, articles to profl. jours. Med. Rsch. Coun. Can. fellow, 1968, Buswell fellow, 1969; recipient rsch. prize Ministry Edn. Romania, 1965, rsch. award NIH, 1985. Fellow: ACP, Nat. Acad. Clin. Biochemistry, Coll. Am. Pathologists; mem.: Am. Soc. Investigative Pathology, Am. Assn. Immunologists. Achievements include first demonstration of the association of autoimmunity with major histocompability antigens; discovery of Buffalo thyroxine binding globulin gene. Home: 80 Oakview Dr Buffalo NY 14221-1420 Business E-Mail: vladutiu@buffalo.edu. E-mail: guthormones@yahoo.com.

VLAHOV, DAVID, epidemiologist; b. Washington, Aug. 31, 1952; s. William John and Helga Rose Vlahov; m. Robyn Randice Mione; children: Alexander, Alexandra Gershon. BA, Earlham Coll., 1974; BSN, MS, U. Md., 1980; PhD, Johns Hopkins U., 1988. RN 1977. Prof. epidemiology Sch. Pub. Health Johns Hopkins U., Balt., 1988—2001; dir. Ctr. for Urban Epidemiologic Studies, v.p. for rsch. NY Acad. Medicine, NYC, 1999—; prof. clin. epidemiology Sch. Pub. Health Columbia U., NYC, 1999—. Mem. nat. adv. coun. on drug abuse Dept. HHS. Contbr. more than 550 sci. papers to profl. jours.; editor: Jour. Urban Health, 2000—. Recipient Merit award, NIH, 1995—2005; grantee, 1990—, CDC, 1990—, Robert Wood Johnson Found., 1990—, NY Cmty. Trust, 1990—. Fellow: NY Acad. Medicine, Infectious Disease Soc. of Am.; mem.: Am. Pub. Health Assn., Am. Epidemiol. Soc., Soc. for Epidemiol. Rsch. Home: 401 E 86th St Apt 12 E New York NY 10028 Office: NY Acad Medicine 1216 Fifth Ave New York NY 10029 Office Phone: 212-822-7382. Business E-Mail: dvlahov@nyam.org.

VLASIN, MICHAL, medical educator, researcher; b. Brno, Czech Republic, Sept. 1, 1967; s. Jaromir Vlasin and Olga Vlasinova; m. Vera Marcinkova, Oct. 11, 1997; children: Michal, Christina Vlasinova. DVM, Vet. U., Brno, Czech Republic, 1992; PhD, U. of Vet. and Pharm. Scis. Brno, 2000. Rsch. fellow Henderson Rsch. Centre, Hamilton, Ontario, Canada, 1998—2002; assoc. prof. U. of Vet. and Pharm. Scis. Brno, Czech Republic, 2004—. Cons. Czech Vet. Coll., Brno, 2003—. Second lt. Ctrl. Army Vet. Hosp., 1993—94, Czech Republic. Grantee Rsch. grant, Czech Grant Agy., 1996, 2005. Master: Czech Soc. for Thrombosis and Haemostasis (assoc.; chmn. 2003); mem.: Czech Small Animal vet. Assn. (assoc.). Office: Univ of Vet and Pharml Palackeho 1 3 Brno 612 42 Czech Republic Business E-Mail: vlasinm@vfu.cz.

VLASOV, YAN VLADIMIROVICH, neurosurgeon; b. Kuybyshev, Russia, Nov. 16, 1967; MA, Samara State Med. U., 1992, PhD, 1995. Neurology and neurosurgery physician Samara State Med. U., 1995—. Pres. All-Russian Pub. Orgn. Disabled People with Multiple Sclerosis, 2007—11. Mem.: European Multiple Sclerosis Platform, Multiple Sclerosis Internat. Fedn. Avocations: tennis, travel. Office: Yuria Pavlova pereulok 8 office 4 Samara 443009 Russia Office Fax: 7 846 995 86 45. Business E Mail: sams99@inbox.ru.

VLASTARAKOS, PETROS V., medical doctor; b. Athens, Attica, Greece, June 3, 1974; s. Vassilios P. Vlastarakos and Christina Psaropoulou Vlastarakou; m. Evangelia Filothei Tavoulari, Mar. 8, 2008. U. Diploma, Athens U. Sch Medicine, 1999; MS in Healthcare Adminstrn., Athens U. Dept. Nursing, 2005; PhD in Otolaryngology, Athens U. Sch. Medicine, 2009. Diplomate in otolaryngology Ministry Health, Greece, 2008. Sr. ho. officer internal medicine therapeutics Provincial Hosp. Sparta, Laconia, Greece, 1999, P.&A. Kyriakou Children's Hosp. surgery, Athens, 2001; gen. practitioner Provincial Health Ctr. Gytheion, Sparta, 1999—2000; ENT registrar Hippokrateion Gen. Hosp., Athens, 2004—09; staff grade otolaryngologist Lister Hosp., East & North Hertfordshire, NHS Trust, Stevenage, England, 2009—. Reviewer African Jour. Microbiology rsch., 2003—; rschr. Athens U., 2005—; commd. reviewer Nat. Med. Rsch. Coun., Singapore, 2007; reviewer Indian Jour. Dental Rsch., 2007—, Expert Rev. Vaccines Jour., London, 2008—, Internat Jour. Pediat. Otolaryngology, 2009, Jour. Bacteriology Rsch., 2009—, Laryngoscope, 2009—, Jour. Pediat. Biochemistry, 2010, Swiss Med. Weekly, 2010, Clin. Reviews & Opinions, 2010, Annuals Indian Acad. Neurology, 2003—, Internat. Jour. Medicine & Med. Scis., 2009—, Neurology India, 2009—. Contbr. articles to profl. sci. jours. Vis. E.N.T. dr. Doctors of World (Athens br.), 2005—; attending physician Gytheion Charity Instn. Elderly People, Sparta, 2000. Sgt. (md) Greek Airforce, 2002—03. Decorated Letter Recognition Greek Airforce-Training Adminstrn.; Scholarship Healthcare Adminstrn., Alexandros S. Onassis Found., 2004—05, Excellence Healthcare Adminstrn., Greek State Scholarship's Found., 2005, 2006. Office: Lister Hosp ENT Dept Coreys Mill Ln Stevenage Herts SG1 4AB England Home: Dhardhanellion 29 113 63 Athens Greece Office Phone: 00447774567429. Personal E-mail: pevlast@hotmail.com. Business E-Mail: pevlast@yahoo.gr.

VLODAVER, ZEEV A., cardiologist; b. Lomas de Zamora, Argentina; arrived in U.S., 1970; s. Marcos Vlodaver and Dora Weledniger; m. Dalia Puterman, July 3, 1962; children: Aner, Sagit, Royee. MD, Buenos Aires U., 1956. Fellow in cardiology Tel Aviv U., 1969; sr. rsch. assoc. cardiolovasc. pathology rsch. United Hosp., St. Paul, 1970-80; med. dir. non invasive cardiology Unity Hosp., Fridley, Minn., 1977—; clin. assoc. prof. U. Minn., Mpls., 1982—. Author: Coronary Art in Congenital Heart, 1975, Coronary Heart Disease, 1976; contbr. over 60 articles to profl. jours., 3 chpts. to books; chief editor: Med. Jour. of Allina, 1992—99 (Clarion award, 92). Fellow Am. Coll. Cardiology, Am. Heart Assn. Avocations: jogging, travel, archaeology, classical music. Home: 6 Edgcumbe Pl Saint Paul MN 55116-2308 Office: Unity Hosp-Allina 650 Osborne Rd NE Fridley MN 55432-2762 Personal E-mail: zeev.vlodaver@gmail.com. Business E-Mail: zeevvoldave@allina.com.

VODICKA, PAVEL ERIK, physician; b. Uherské Hradišti, Feb. 21, 1956; MD, Charles U., Prague, 1981; PhD, Nat. Inst. Pub. Health, 1986. Head dept. Inst. Exptl. Medicine, Acad. Sci. Czech Republic, 1998—. Grant, Ministry of Health Czech Republic. Mem.: Czech Med. Soc. Avocation: history. Office: Videnska 1083 Prague Central Bohemia 14200 Czech Republic Business E-Mail: pvodicka@biomed.cas.cz.

VODOLAZHSKAYA, MARGARITA GENNADIEVNA, physiologist, educator; b. Stavropol, Russia, Apr. 3, 1963; d. Gennadiy Grigorievich Vodolazhsky and Valeriya Alexandrovna Vodolazhskaya; m. Igor Michailovich Rosly; 1 child. Candidate in Biology, MSPU, Russia, 1993; D of Biology, KSMA, Russia, 2000. Postgrad. Stavropol State U., Russia, 1988—91, asst., 1991—93, assoc. prof., 1998—2000, prof., 2000—02, chief rsch. work dept., 2000—11, chief biomedicine lab., 2004—. Mem. dissertation bd. Stavropol State U., Russia, 2002, SSAU, Russia, 2002. Grantee, Russian Acad. Sci., Moscow, 2002—03. Mem.: Internat. Psychoneuroendocrinol. Soc., Russian Pharmacol. Soc., Russian Physiol. Soc. Avocations: travel, music. Office: Stavropol State Univ ul. Pushkina 1 355017 Stavropol Stavropol'Skiy Kray Russia Business E-Mail: biomed@stavsu.ru.

VOETSCH, BARBARA, neurologist, researcher; b. Nürtingen, Germany, July 4, 1969; d. Karl Paul and Doris Voetsch; m. Marc A. Forgione. MD, State U. Campinas, São Paulo, 1992, PhD in Med. Scis. and Neurology, 2002. Cert. Brazilian Fed. Neurology, lic. Brazil. Intern State U. Campinas, São Paulo, Brazil, 1993—94, resident in neurology, 1994—97, stroke fellow, 1997—98; stroke rsch. fellow Harvard Med. Sch., Boston, 1999—2000; coord. Stroke in the Young Clinic, State U. Campinas, São Paulo, 1997—99; rsch. assoc. Whitaker Cardiovasc. Inst. Boston U., 2000—04, postdoctoral fellow, 2002—04, asst. prof. medicine, 2004—; intern Boston Med. Ctr., 2005—06; resident in neurology Mass. Gen. Hosp., Brigham and Women's Hosp. Harvard Med. Sch., Boston, 2006—. Author: Thrombosis and Hemorrhage, 2002, Recent Advances in Hematology, 2004; reviewer Circulation Rsch., Stroke, Lancet, New England Jour. of Medicine; reviewer: Jour. Neurol. Scis., Circulation, Clin. Genetics, Blood Coagulation and Fibrinolysis; contbr. articles to profl. jours. Recipient Neurology award for best rsch., Brazilian Acad. Neurology, 1998, Fellow's Clin Rsch. award, Astra Zeneca Young Investigator Forum, 2000; grantee Found. for Higher Edn. and Grad. Tng., 1999—2000. Mem.: Brazilian Soc. Cerebrovascular Diseases, Brazilian Acad. Neurology, Med. Assn. São Paulo, Am. Heart Assn. (mem. stroke coun.). Avocations: tennis, volleyball.

VOGEL, CARL-WILHELM ERNST, biomedical scientist, clinical pathologist; b. Hamburg, Germany, Mar. 9, 1951; came to U.S., 1979; s. Erich Hermann Walter and Lisbeth Klara (Barbulla) V.; m. Candice G. McMullan, 1989. MD, U. Hamburg, Germany, 1976; diploma in biology, 1980, PhD in Biochemistry, 1986. Diplomate Am. Bd. Pathology; cert. Bd. Lab. Medicine and Bd. Med. Biochemistry (Germany). Predoctoral rsch. fellow Tropical Inst., Hamburg, 1973-75; intern Univ. Hosps., Hamburg and Kiel, Germany, 1976-78; postdoct. rsch. fellow Rsch. Inst. Scripps Clinic, La Jolla, Calif., 1979-82; asst. prof. biochemistry and medicine Georgetown U., Washington, 1982-87, assoc. prof., 1987-91, adj. prof., 1991-99, resident in medicine, pathology, allergy/immunology, 1984-86, 88-89; prof., chmn. dept. biochemistry and molecular biology U. Hamburg, Germany, 1990-99; prof. pathology U. Hawaii John A. Burns Sch. Medicine, Honolulu, 1999—, dir., Cancer Rsch. Ctr., 1999—2008, prof., Cancer Rsch. Ctr., 1999—. Mem. Vincent T. Lombardi Cancer Rsch. Ctr., Washington, 1982-92; mem. Internat. Ctr. for Interdisciplinary Studies of Immunology, Washington, 1982-94, sci. dir., 1987-91; vis. prof. pathology and lab. medicine Ind. U.-Purdue, Indpls., 1996-97; mem. examiner Bd. Lab. Medicine (Germany), 1991-99, Bd. Med. Biochem. (Germany), 1998-99; adj. prof. U. Guam, 2001—; cons. to biomed. corps Mem. editl. bd. Jour. Devel. and Comparative Immunology, 1984-96. Recipient Nat. Cancer Inst./NIH Rsch. Career Devel. award; overseas rsch. fellow Studienstiftung des Deutschen Volkes, 1978-79, U.S.A. rsch. fellow Deutsche Forschungsgemeinschaft, 1980-82; NIH rsch. grantee, 1983-94, 99—. Fellow Am. Soc. Clin. Pathology, Coll. Am. Pathologists; mem. AMA, AAAS, Am. Chem. Soc., German Soc. Biochemistry and Molecular Biology, Am. Soc. Microbiology, Am. Assn., Immunologists, Am. Soc. Biochemistry and Molecular Biology, Am. Assn. Cancer Rsch., Am. Soc. Clin. Oncology, European Soc. Med. Oncology, Am. Soc. Tropical Medicine and Hygiene, Internat. Soc. Devel. and Comparative Immunology, Am. Fedn. Med. Rsch., Gesellschaft Immunologie, Gesellschaft Deutscher Chemiker, Am. Soc. Clin. Investigation, Am. Soc. Investigative Pathology, German Soc. Cell Biology, German Soc. Lab. Medicine, Japanese Biochem. Soc., Australasian Soc. Immunology, Japanese Cancer Assn., German Cancer Soc., European Assn. Cancer Rsch., Hawaii Med. Assn., Sigma Xi. Office: Cancer Rsch Ctr Hawaii 1236 Lauhala St Honolulu HI 96813-2424 Office Phone: 808-586-3013. Fax: 808-586-3052. E-mail: cvogel@crch.hawaii.edu.

VOGEL, GERHARD HANS, pharmacologist, toxicologist; b. Bucarest, Roumania, Sept. 9, 1927; s. Eugen Georg and Emilie Katharina (Sturm) V.; m. Anna Theresia Zoller, Dec. 23, 1988. Pharmacist degree, U. Erlangen, 1951; physician degree, U. Tubingen, 1955; assoc. prof. degree, U. Marburg, 1967; assoc. prof. degree (hon.), U. Frankfurt, 1979. Resident City Hosp., Heidenheim, Germany, 1956-57; sr. scientist endocrinology lab. Dept. of Pharmacology, Hoechst AG, Frankfurt, Germany, 1958—69, dir., 1967—78, Pharma Rsch. Exptl. Medicine, Hoechst AG, Frankfurt, Germany, 1977—79, Pharma Preclinical Evaluation and Devel., Hoechst AG, Frankfurt, Germany, 1980—88, Decision Bd. on Pharm. Devel., Hoechst AG, Frankfurt, Germany, 1989—90; cons. Pharm. and Med. Rsch. Devel., Aalen, Germany, 1990—. Mem. several scientific assns., Germany/USA, 1970—; cons. in drug evaluation and devel. Editor: Drug Discovery and Evaluation: Pharmacological Assays, 1997, 2d edit., 2002, 3rd edit., 2007, Drug Discovery and Evaluation: Safety and Pharmacokinetic Assays, 2006; contbr. over 100 articles on biomechanics to profl. jours. Home: Bohlstr 28 D 73430 Aalen Germany Home Phone: 0049-7361-980806. E-mail: profgerhardvogel@aol.com.

VOGEL, H. VICTORIA, psychotherapist, educator, research social writer, stress disorder and addiction recovery counselor; BA, U. Md., 1968; MA, NYU, 1970, MA, 1975; MEd, postgrad., Columbia U., 1982—; cert., Am. Projective Drawing Inst., 1983; CASAC, New Sch. U. for Social Rsch., 2000. Diplomate Am. Acad. Experts in Traumatic Stress; cert. addiction recovery counselor, expert in traumatic stress, alcohol and substance abuse counselor, addictions treatment, addiction counseling alcohol and substance abuse. Art therapist Childville, Bklyn., 1962-64; tchr. Montgomery County (Md.) Jr. H.S., 1968-69; with H.S. divsn. N.Y.C. Bd. Edn., 1970—; guidance counselor, instr., psychotherapist in pvt. practice; edn. administr. Tchrs. Coll. Columbia U., NYC, 1982. Med. guidance counselor, instr., psychotherapist in pvt. practice; clin. counseling cons. psychodiagnosis and devel. studies, art/play therapy The Modern Sch., 1984—; art/play therapist Hosp. Ctr. for Neuromuscular Disease and Devel. Disorders, 1986—; employment counselor-adminstr. N.Y. State Dept. Labor Concentrated Employment Program, 1971-72; intern psychotherapy and psychoanalysis psychiat. divsn. Ctrl. Islip Hosp., 1973-75, Calif. Grad. Inst., L.A.; intern psychol. counseling and rehab. N.J. Coll. Medicine, Newark, 1979. Author: The Never Ending Story of Alcohol, Drugs and Other Substance Abuse, 1992, Variant Sexual Behavior and the Aesthetic Modern Nudes, 1992, Psychological Science of School Behavior Intervention, 1993, Joycean Conceptual Modernism: Relationships and Deviant Sexuality, 1995, Electronic Evil Eyes, 1995 (U.S. Cert. of Recognition, 1996), Psychological Paradigms of Alcohol Violence Suicide Trauma Addiction Variant Pathologies PTSD and Schizophrenia, 1999. Mem. com. for spl. events NYU, 1989; participant clin. and artistic perspectives Am. Acad. Psychoanalysis Conf., 1990, participant clin. postmodernism and psychoanalysis, 1996; aux. police officer N.Y. Police Dept., 1994—; chair bylaws com. Columbia U., 1995—. Mem.: ACA, AAAS, APA, NY Acad. Sci., Tchrs. Coll. Adminstrv. Women in Edn., Assn. Humanistic Psychology (exec. sec. 1981), Art/Play Therapy, N.Y. Art Tchrs. Assn., Am. Acad. Experts Traumatic Stress (diplomate in expert traumatic stress), Am. Soc. Group Psychotherapy and Psychodrama (publs. com. 1984—), Am. Orthopsychiat. Assn., Am. Psychol. Soc., Phi Delta Kappa (editor chpt. newsletter 1981—84, exec. sec. Columbia U. chpt. 1984—, chmn. nominating com. for chpt. officers 1986—, rsch. rep. 1986—, pub. rels. exec. bd. dirs. 1991, NYU chpt. v.p. programs 1994—).

VOGEL, HANS-PETER ERICH, neurologist; b. Neuruppin, Germany, Feb. 27, 1945; s. Erich and Liselotte (Becker) V.; m. Heide Marie Vatter, July 1, 1973; children: Katja, Sabine. MD, Free U. Berlin, 1970. Bd. cert. diplomate neurology and psychiatry. Intern pediat., Berlin, 1970; intern medicine and surgery, 1972-73; rsch. fellow U. Birmingham, Eng., 1970-71; lectr. U. Riyadh, Saudi Arabia, 1971-72; rsch. fellow with specialist tng. in neurology & psychiatry U. Berlin, 1973-81, cons., 1980-93; head dept. Klinikum Buch, Berlin, 1994—; lectr. Free U. Berlin, 1990; prof. Humboldt U., Berlin, 1997—2010; ret., 2010. Author: Nebenwirkungen der Antiparkinson-Medikamente und Myotonolytika, 1983, Profile der Parkinson-Medikamente, 1984, Palliativmedizinische Aspekte Neurologischer Erkrankungen, 1997, author, co-editor: Anamneseerhebung und Untersuchung des Nervensystems, 1996. Fellow German Neurol. Soc.; mem. Neurol. and Psychiat. Soc. Berlin (sec. 1993, pres. 2001, head. dept. 2010). Office: Klinikum Buch Schwanebecher Chaussee 50 D-13125 Berlin Germany Office Phone: 4930-940154200. E-mail: hans-peter.vogel@berlin.helios-kliniken.de.

VOGEL, JAMES M., hematologist, oncologist; b. NYC; s. Peter Vogel and Helen M. Mandlebaum; m. Judith Anne Resnick, 1 child, Jennifer. BA, Wesleyan U., 1958, MA, 1959; MD, Columbia U., 1962. Diplomate Am. Bd. Internal Medicine, Am. Bd. Hematology, Am. Bd. Med. Oncology. Intern Mt. Sinai Hosp., NYC, attending physician - medicine, 1968—, resident in hematology and internal medicine; chief hematology/med. oncology medicine divsn. Beth Israel Hosp., NYC, 1968; assoc. prof. medicine Mt. Sinai Sch. Medicine, NYC, 1986—; fellow in med. oncology Nat. Cancer Inst., Bethesda, Md. Author: How to Live with Hemophilia, 1972. Lt. comdr. USPHS, USCG, 1964—66. Named Best Doctor in N.Y., Met. Area Connally Rehab., 1995—, N.Y. Mag., 1998—. Avocations: skiing, stamps, military history. Office: 1125 Park Ave New York NY 10128 Office Phone: 212-369-4250. Personal E-mail: drjvogel@aol.com.

VOGEL, THOMAS TIMOTHY, surgeon, educator, lay worker; b. Columbus, Ohio, Feb. 1, 1934; s. Thomas A. and Charlotte A. (Hogan) V.; m. M.M. Darina Kelleher, May 29, 1965; children: Thomas T., Catherine D., Mark P., Nicola M. AB, Coll. of Holy Cross, 1955; MS, Ohio State U., 1960, PhD, 1962; MD, Georgetown U., 1965. Pvt. practice surgery, Columbus, 1971-2001; chmn. liturgy com., pres. parish coun. St. Catharine Parish, Columbus, 1971-73; chmn. diocesan adminstrn. com. Diocesan Pastoral Coun., Columbus, 1972-73, chmn., 1973-75; vice prefect Sodality of Holy Cross, 1953-55; mem. Ohio Bishop's Adv. Coun., Columbus, 1976-79. Clin. asst. prof. surgery Ohio State U., Columbus, 1974—; past trustee Peer Rev. Sys., Inc.; assoc. med. dir. United Health Care, Columbus, 1997-2000; cons. Rehabilitation Svcs.; commr., surveillance utilization rev. mem. Medicaid, State of Ohio, 1998-2000; assoc. med. dir. Palmetto GBA, 1999—2011. Contbr. articles to profl. jours. Chmn. coun. grad. students Ohio State U., 1961; bd. dirs. St. Vincent's Children's Ctr., 1975-83, chmn., 1981-82; past chmn. bd. trustees St. Joseph Montessori Sch. Recipient Layman's award, Columbus Ea. Kiwanis, 1972; named Knight of the Holy Sepulchre, Equestrian Order of the Holy Sepulchre of Jerusalem, 2001. Mem. ACS, Am. Physiol. Soc., Assn. for Acad. Surgery, Ohio State Med. Assn. (del. 1993—), Sigma Xi, Delta Epsilon Sigma. Roman Catholic. Home: 247 S Ardmore Rd Columbus OH 43209-1701 Office: 621 S Cassingham Rd Columbus OH 43209-2403

VOGEL, VICTOR GERALD, medical educator, researcher; b. Bethlehem, Pa., Mar. 14, 1952; s. Victor Gerald Jr. and Margaret Moser (Smith) V.; m. Saralyn Sue Schaffner, June 25, 1977; children: Heather Marie, Christiaan Keith. Diplomate Am. Bd. Internal Medicine, Am. Bd. Preventive Medicine, Nat. Bd. Med. Examiners. Resident in internal medicine Balt. City Hosps., 1978-81; fellow in med. oncology Johns Hopkins Oncology Ctr., Balt., 1983-86; Andrew W. Mellon fellow Johns Hopkins Sch. Hygiene Pub. Health, Balt., 1984-86; asst. prof. medicine and epidemiology U. Tex./M.D. Anderson Cancer Ctr., Houston, 1986-93, assoc. prof. clin. cancer prevention, 1993-95; asst. prof. epidemiology U. Tex. Sch. Pub. Health, Houston, 1987-95; prof. medicine and epidemiology U. Pitts. Cancer Inst./Magee-Womens Hosp., 1996—2008, dir. MAGEE/UPCI breast cancer program, 1996—2002, dir. MAGEE/UPCI breast cancer prevention program, 2003—08; v.p. Rsch. Am. Cancer Soc., Atlanta, 2009—10; dir. Cancer Inst., Geisinger Health Sys., 2010—. Epidemiologist Tex. breast screening project Am. Cancer Soc., 1986-93; mem. data and safety monitoring bd. Women's Health Initiative, NIH, 1994—2004; bd. dirs. Nat. Surg. Adjuvant Breast and Bowel Project Found., Inc., 1997-2011, AMC Cancer Ctr., Denver, 1996-99; protocol chmn. Nat. Cancer Inst. Study of Tamoxifen and Raloxifene. Contbr. articles to profl. jours. Mem. Nat. Surg. adjuvant Breast and Bowel Project Found., Inc.; founding pres. Internat. Soc. Cancer Risk Assessment and Mgmt., 2003. Served with USPHS, 1981-83. Recipient award, Am. Cancer Soc., 1987, career devel. award, 1990—93, Impact award, Nat. Constorium Breast Ctrs., 2008; named Med. Vol. of Yr., Am. Cancer Soc., 1983; fellow, Susan G. Komen Breast Cancer Found., 1990—93. Fellow Am. Coll. Preventive Medicine, ACP; mem. Am. Soc. Clin. Oncology, Am. Soc. Preventive Oncology, Christian Med. and Dental Assn., Am. Assn. Cancer Rsch. Republican. Presbyterian. Avocation: flying. Office: Geisinger Health Sys 100 N Academy Ave Danville PA 17822 Home: 82 Red Fox Ln Lewisburg PA 17837 Office Phone: 570-271-8228. Business E-Mail: vgvogel@geisinger.edu.

VOGELSTEIN, BERT, oncology educator; b. Balt., June 2, 1949; BS in Math., U. Pa., 1970; MD, Johns Hopkins U. Sch. Medicine, 1974. Rsch. assoc. Nat. Cancer Inst., 1976—78; pediatric intern and resident Johns Hopkins U. Sch. Medicine, Balt., 1974—76, asst. prof., 1978—83, assoc. prof., 1983—89, Clayton prof. oncology and pathology, 1989—, Howard Hughes Med. Inst. investigator, 1995—. Advisor NIH Sci. Rev. Groups, Nat. Cancer Inst.; bd. reviewing editors Science; assoc. editor Molecular Cell and Cancer Cell; sci. adv. bd. U, Calif., San Francisco, Cancer Ctr., GMP Genetics, Morphotek; sci. review bd. Pediatric Brain Tumor Found., US. Assoc. editor: Genes, Chromosomes and Cancer, mem. bd. reviewing editors: Sci. mag.; contbr. articles to profl. jours., 99 US patents in the field. Recipient Alfred G. Knudson award, Nat. Cancer Inst., Anne & Jason Farber Lecture award, Am. Acad. Neurology, 1991, Internat. award, Gairdner Found., 1992, Medal of Honor, Am. Cancer Soc., 1992, Richard Lounsbery award, NAS, 1993, Baxter Rsch. award, Assn. Am. Med. Coll., 1994, laureates Passano Found., 1994, G.H.A. Clowes Meml. award, Am. Assn. Cancer Rsch., 1995, Paul Erlich and Ludwig Darmstaedter prize, Paul Erlich Found., 1997, William Beaumont prize, Am. Gastroenterological Assn., 1997, Sartstedt Rsch. prize, Inst. Clin. Chemistry, 1997, Louisa Gross Horwitz prize, Columbia U. Med. Ctr., 1998, William Allan award, Am. Soc. Human Genetics, 1998, Charles S. Mott prize, GM Cancer Rsch. Found., 2000, Prince of Asturias award in Sci., 2004. Mem.: NAS, European Molecular Biology Orgn., Am. Philosophical Soc., Inst. Medicine, Am. Acad. Arts and Scis. Achievements include revolutionizing our understanding of complex genetic mutations that occur when an normal bowel epithelial cell is transformed into a malignant cell. Office: Johns Hopkins Sch Medicine 589 Cancer Rsch Bldg 1650 Orleans St Baltimore MD 21231

VOGIATZIDIS, KONSTANTINOS, cardiologist; b. Athens, Aug. 30, 1971; MD, U. Thessaly, Greece, 1999, PhD, 2010. Resident internal medicine Agia Olga Gen. Hosp., Ionia, Attica, 2003—05; resident cardiology Tzaneio Gen. Hosp., Piraeus, Attica, 2005—09. Contbr. articles to profl. jours. Recipient Best Oral Presentation award, Hellenic Thoracic Soc., 2004, Best Basic Rsch. award, Athens Med. Soc., 2006, BLS/AED, ACLS Spl. awards, 2000, 2005, 2009. Avocations: travel, movies, martial arts. Home: 23 Charilaou Trikoupi Piraeus Attica 18536 Greece Personal E-mail: consvog@yahoo.gr.

VOGT, STEPHAN, orthopedist, researcher; b. Kirchhellen, Nordrhein-Westfalen, Germany, Aug. 17, 1970; s. Wilfried and Monika Vogt; m. Britta Kuckuck; 1 child, Lisa. Degree, Nordrhein-Westfalen, 1997; MD, U. Essen, Germany, 1999. Sci. fellow U. Heidelberg, Berlin, 1998—2000; postdoc. rschr. Molecular Pharmacology, Free U. Berlin, 2000—03; group leader tissue engr. gene therapy TU Munich, Dept. Orthop. Traumatology, 2003, physician, 2003, orthop. surgeon, 2008, assoc. prof., 2009. Contbr. articles to profl. jours. Recipient award, DFG, 2003—, KKF, 2003—, AO, 2003—, German Arthritis Found., 2003—, Don Joy award, AGA, 2006. Mem.: DGOOC (award 2003—). Achievements include research in regular gene transfer methods. Home: Am Lilienberg 1 München Bavarian 81669 Germany Office: TU Munich Klinikum Rechts Der Isar Ismaninger Str 22 München Bavarian 81675 Germany

VOGT-LOWELL, ROBERT W., pediatric cardiologist; b. Havana, Cuba, Aug. 28, 1959; B, Univ. Miami; MD, Univ. Puerto Rico, 1986. Diplomate Am. Bd. Pediatrics, 1989, in pediatric cardiology Am. Bd. Pediatrics, 1996. Intern in pediatrics, resident in pediatric cardiology Miami Children's Hosp., 1986—89; fellow in pediatric cardiology LI Jewish Med. Ctr., Albert Einstein Med. Ctr., NY, 1989—92, asst. prof., 1992—94; pediatric cardiologist Single Source Pediatric Heart Ctr., Miami, Fla., 1994, Miami Children's Hosp., 1998—. Office: Miami Children's Hosp Ste 110 7765 SW 87th Ave Miami FL 33173 Office Phone: 305-595-1833, 866-756-9355. Office Fax: 305-595-2024.

VOHS, JAMES ARTHUR, health plan administrator; b. Idaho Falls, Idaho, Sept. 26, 1928; s. John Dale and Cliff Lucille (Packer) Vohs; m. Janice Hughes, Sept. 19, 1953 (dec. Oct. 1999); children: Lorraine, Carol, Nancy, Sharla; m. Eileen Galloway, Oct. 8, 2005. BA, U. Calif., Berkeley, 1952; postgrad., Harvard Sch. Bus., 1966. Employed by various Kaiser affiliated orgns., 1952—92; chmn., pres., CEO Kaiser Found. Hosps. and Kaiser Found. Health Plan, INc., Oakland, Calif., 1975—92, chmn. emeritus; chmn. bd. dirs. Holy Names Coll., 1981—92; chmn. Marcus Foster Inst., 1981—. Chmn. Fed. Res. Bank San Francisco, 1991—94. Mem. Oakland Bd. Port Commrs., 1993—96; bd. dirs. Oakland-Alameda County Coliseum Complex, 1986—96, Bay Area Coun., 1985—94, chmn., 1991—92. With US Army, 1946—48. Mem.: Inst. Medicine NAS. Personal E-mail: javohs1@comcast.net.

VOIGT, MICHAEL D., medical researcher; b. Pretoria, South Africa, Feb. 16, 1955; MBCLB, Pretoria U., South Africa, 1978; FCP, Coll. Medicine, South Africa, 1985; MMed., U. Cape Town, 1988. Diplomate Am. Bd. Internal Medicine, 2000; cert. ECFMG 1978, lic. South Africa. Intern Baragwanath Hosp., Dept. Ob-Gyn. Dept. Medicine South African Defense Force, 1979; med. officer South African Def. Force, 1980—81; sr. house officer dept. neurology & emergency medicine U. Cape Town, 1982, resident Dept. Medicine, 1983—85, fellow divsn. gastroenterology & hepatology, 1986—87; register Dept. Medicine, 1983—86; sr. registrar GI Heapatology, 1987; sr. cons. Dept. Medicine, Groote Schuur Hosp., South Africa, 1991—94; asst. prof. clin. medicine Divsn. Gastroenterology Hepatology, Dept. Internal Medicine, U. Iowa, 1996—98, asst. prof., 1998—2003, prof. clin. medicine, 2004—; specialist physician Liver Clinic, Dept. Medicine, 1988—91; dep. head med. firm Groote Schuur Hosp. South Africa, 1991—94; chief liver svc. Liver Clinic & Hepatology Svc., Groote Schuur Hosp., 1994—95; med. dir. liver failure and transplant U. Iowa, 1997—. Tchr. GI-Hepatology Jour. Club, 1999—; co-dir. Iowa City Transplant Forum, 2003—; mem. Update Hepatology Iron Metabolism, Grand Rounds Iron Benches & Beds, 2005, Emergency Medicine Acute Liver Failure Lecture, 2007; grad. tchr. Adv. Group, 1995, DDC Com. Tchg., 1996, ICD Com. M2 Curriculum, 2000—; co-dir. FCPIV, 1997; adv. com. mem. Office Consultation & Rsch. Med. Edn., 2003—04; resident adv. Usman Secldiqui Nat. Edn. Related Presentations, 2001—03; tchr. in fields; peer reviewer South African Med. Jour., 1986, South African Jour. Conf. Med. Edn., 1990, South African Jour. Critical Care, 1992; vis. prof. Trinity Hosp. Phoenix Ariz., U. Pretoria, South Africa, 2003; reviewer Am. Assn. Study Liver Diseases Health Svcs. Rsch., 2008—; mem. European Assn. Study Liver Disease, 2006—, UNOS Regional Review Bd., 1997—, Am. Assn. Transplant Physicians, 1997—, UNOS Region Liver Review Com., 1997—, Ctrl. Soc. Clin. Rsch., 1999—, European Assn. Study Liver Disease, 2006—, UNOS Bd. Dirs. Councilor, 2009—11, UNOS Region 8 Councilor, 2009—11. Contbr. chapters to books. Recipient Hoechst prize, 1975, Protea award, 1978, Med. Rsch. Coun. Career Devel. award, 1988—89, South African Gastroenterological Soc. Investigator award, 1989, Jr. Investigator award, South African Pulmonology Soc., 1990, award, Critical Care Soc., 1993, Patients' Choice award, 2008—10, Recognition award, Dept Nursing & Patient Care Svcs., 1998, award, Am. Assn. Study Liver Diseases Surgery & Liver Transplant Com., 1998—2000, Iowa Dept Pub. Health Recognition & Hepatitis Task Force, 2004, Above & Beyond award, 2002—05, MRC award, 1988—89, MRC Liver Rsch. Ctr. award, 1990—95, Joint award, South African Gastroenterological Soc., 1993—94, award, Hoechst & Glaxo Drug Trials, 1993—95; named America's Top Gastroenterologists, 2008, America's Top Physicians, 2009—10, Best Doctors in America, 2009—. Achievements include research in liver transplantation, acute liver failure, ascites and hepatorenal failure, hepatitis C in liver transplantation, transplantation in liver cancer; multivariate analysis of factors in progression of hepatitis C post transplant, interferon ribavirin therapy for HCV infection post liver transplantation; predictive value of percent necrosis in Acute Liver Failure; albumin octreotide and midodrine in hepatorenal syndrome. Office: University Iowa Iowa City IA 52242 Office Phone: 319-356-1461. Office Fax: 319-356-7918. E-mail: michael-voigt@uiowa.edu.

VOISIN, GUY-ANDRÉ, immunologist, researcher; b. Paris, Dec. 11, 1920; s. Maurice Roger and Marguerite Jeanne (Nommés) V.; m. Janine Edmée Terrassier, July 16, 1959; children: Jacques-André, Jean-Michel, Véronique. MS, U. Paris, Sorbonne, 1943; MD, U. Paris, 1945, DSc, 1958. Intern, resident Hosps. of Paris, 1947-51; fellow Johns Hopkins U., Balt., 1951-52; chief clinics Faculty Medicine Paris, 1953-54; dir. rsch. team CNRS, Paris, 1968-87; dir. rsch. Claude Bernard Assn. of Hosps. of Paris, 1964-90; sci. dir. INSERM Rsch. unit on immunopathology and exptl. immunology, 1970-88; dir. Ctr. Immunopathology Claude Bernard Assn. of Hosps. of Paris, 1971-90, dir. rsch. emeritus, 1991—. Sci. advisor in immunology Clin-Midy/Sanofi, Montpellier, France, 1974-87; organizer med. scis.; mem. several nat. sci. coms.; lectr. in field. Author, editor: Immunologie de la Reproduction, 1990; patentee in field; contbr. numerous sci. articles to internat. jours. and books. Med. lt. French Army, 1944-46. Decorated Chevalier Légion d'Honneur, France, 1975; recipient Prix Prince Albert 1st de Monaco, Nat. Acad. Medicine, 1971. Mem. French Soc. Immunology (pres. 1974-78), Internat. Soc. Immunology Reprodn. (pres. 1986-89, pres. of honor), French League Against Multiple Sclerosis (pres. med. and sci. com. 1988-96, pres. of honor), Assn. Scientists Forever (pres. 1998-2001), European Soc. Reproductive and Devel. Immunology (founding pres. 1996-99). Avocations: history of arts and sciences, swimming, skiing. Home: 40 rue Condorcet 75009 Paris France Office: Hosp Paul Brousse bâtiment Fred Siguier 94800 Villejuif France Office Phone: 33 145593495. Personal E-mail: guyandre.voisin@dbmail.com.

VOITL, PETER K., pediatrician; b. Vienna, July 10, 1962; MD, Med. U. Vienna, 1987, PhD, 2008, MBA. Cert. sonography lectr. Pediat. cardiologist Ambulatorium Kinderkardiologie, 2004—. Reviewer in fields. Recipient Gesundheitspreis Stadt Wien, Vienna. Office: Donaucitystrasse 1 Vienna 1220 Austria Office Phone: 4312637979. Office Fax: 431263797979. Business E-Mail: office@kinderarzt.at.

VOJACEK, JAN, cardiologist, educator; b. Prague, Apr. 27, 1947; s. Jan and Jana (Zavadilova) V.; m. Ivana Zelena, Aug. 16, 1973; 1 child, Lenka. MD, Charles U., Prague, 1971, DSc, 1997; PhD, 1981. Rsch. fellow Inst. Clin. and Exptl. Medicine, Prague, 1976-79, rschr., 1980-86; rsch. fellow Royal Infirmary, Edinburgh, 1979-80; head cardiologist Cen. Bohemia, Prague, 1987-90; assoc. prof. medicine Charles U., Prague, 1991-99, prof. cardiology, 1999—; head divsn. cardiology U. Hosp. Motol, Prague, 1999—2003; head dept. medicine I Charles Univ., Univ. Hosp., Hradec Kralove, 2004—. Vis. prof. Tex. Heart Inst., Houston, 1993. Author: (books) Silent Myocardial Ischemia, 1994, Coronary Stenting, 1997, Acute Coronary Syndromes, 1998, Arterial and Venous Thrombosis in Clinical Practice, 2003, Clinical Cardiology, 2008; contbr. sci. papers. Grantee Min. of Health, Czech Republic, 1986, 92, 95, 99, 2003, 07, 09. Fellow European Soc. Cardiology, Am. Coll. Cardiology; mem. Czech Soc. of Cardiology (pres. working group interventional cardiology 1994-2004, pres. working group acute cardiac care 2005-10), European Assn. Percutaneous Cardiovasc. Interventions, ESC, Internat. Soc. Holter Monitoring. Avocations: classical music, opera, sports, literature. Office: Univ Hosp Dept Medicine Hradec Králové Czech Republic

VOKURKA, MARTIN, medical educator, writer; b. Prague, Czech Republic, Oct. 17, 1962; s. Frantisek Vokurka and Marta Vokurkova; m. Alexandra Hakaufova; children: Frantiska Sylva Vokurkova, Filipa Klara Vokurkova. MD, PhD, Charles U., Prague, 1987. Assoc. prof., vice dean First Faculty Medicine, Charles U., Prague, 1987—; sr. rschr. Ctr. Exptl. Hematology, Prague, 2006—. Cons. Maxdorf Pub., Prague, 1998—. Author: (stories) Rozpady; contbr. articles to profl. med. jours., to med. dictionaries. Mcpl. dep., Brandys n.L-St. Boleslav, Czech Republic, 2006—. Recipient Rector prize, Charles U., 2003. Office: Charles Univ First Med Faculty U Nemocnice 5 Prague 12853 Czech Republic Office Fax: +420 224912834. Business E-Mail: mvoku@lf1.cuni.cz.

VOLANAKIS, JOHN EMMANUEL, immunologist, rheumatologist; b. Thessaloniki, Greece, Mar. 17, 1938; arrived in US, 1968, naturalized, 1978; s. Emmanuel (Manolis) John and Cleo (Agathonos) Volanakis; children: Emmanuel (Manolis) John, Marina Cleo. MD, Aristotle U., Thessaloniki, 1962; DMed, Nat. U. Athens, Greece, 1968, PhD (hon.), 2003. Cert. Bd. Internal Medicine Ministry Health, Greece, 1967. Fellow rheumatology Cleve. Met. Gen. Hosp., 1968—71; instr. dept. medicine U. Ala., Birmingham, 1971—73, asst. prof. dept. medicine, 1973—77, assoc. prof. dept. medicine, 1977—83, prof. dept. medicine, 1983—2003; pres., sci. dir. Biomedical Sciences Rsch. Ctr. Alexander Fleming, Vari, Greece, 1997—2003. Dir., rsch. component Multipurpose Arthritis Ctr., Birmingham, Ala., 1984—97. Editor: The Human Complement System in Health and Disease; contbr. articles to profl. jours. Cadet Mil. Med. Sch., 1956—61, Thessaloniki, Greece. Recipient Alexander von Humbolt, Rsch. award for Sr. U.S. Scientists, Alexander von Humbolt Stiftung, 1996—97; named Anna Lois Waters Chair of Medicine in Rheumatology, U. Ala., 1989—97; Robert M. Stecher fellow, Arthritis Found. Ohio, 1969—71, Fogarty Sr. Internat. Rsch. fellow, NIH, 1978—79. Mem.: Assn. Am. Physicians. Achievements include patents for crystals of human factor D. Avocation: literature. Home: 2900 Redmont Park C 302W Birmingham AL 35205 Office: University Alabama 1530 3rd Ave S Shel 411 Birmingham AL 35294-0012 Business E-Mail: volanaki@uab.edu.

VOLBERDING, PAUL ARTHUR, academic physician; b. Rochester, Minn., Sept. 26, 1949; s. Walter A. and Eldora M. (Prescher) V.; m. Juline Christofferson, June 15, 1971 (div. June 1976); m. Mary M. Cooke, June 6, 1980; children: Alexander, Benjamin, Emily. AB, U. Chgo., 1971; MD, U. Minn., 1975. Resident in internal medicine U. Utah, Salt Lake City, 1975-78; fellow in oncology U. Calif., San Francisco, 1978-81; dir. med. oncology San Francisco Gen. Hosp., 1981—, dir. AIDS program, 1983—; dir. Ctr. for AIDS Rsch. U. Calif., San Francisco, 1988—, prof. medicine, 1990—. Bd. dirs. Dignity Ptnrs. Inc., 1996—; elected mem., Inst. of Medicine, 1999. Editor: Medical Management in AIDS, 1986; editor Jour. of AIDS, 1990—. Fellow ACP, AAAS; mem. Internat. AIDS Soc. (founder, chmn. bd.). Office: San Francisco VA Med Ctr 4150 Clement St San Francisco CA 94121 Office Fax: 415-750-2182. Business E-Mail: paul.volberding@va.gov.

VOLGIN, DENYS V., medical researcher; b. Melitopol, Ukraine, Apr. 19, 1973; s. Victor E. Volgin and Ludmila I. Volgina; m. Valeria Dovbik, June 12, 2003; children: Anastasia, Darya D. MS biology, chemistry (hon.), Melitopol State Pedagogical U., Ukraine, 1990—95; PhD physiology of human and animals, Bogomolets Inst. Physiology, Kiev, Ukraine, 1996—99. Asst. tchr. physiology Melitopol State Pedagogical U., Ukraine, 1995—96; postgraduate rschr. Bogomolets Inst. Physiology, Kiev, 1996—99; postdoctoral rschr. U. Pa., Phila., 1999—2002, rsch. assoc., 2002—06, rsch. asst. prof. physiology, 2006—. Recipient Faculty Career Advancement award, Am. Acad. Sleep Medicine, 2004; fellow Soros Fellowships, Internat. Renaissance Found., 1994, 1996. Mem.: Internat. Soc. Neurochemistry, Am. Acad. Sleep Medicine. Achievements include research in pharmacological correction of hypoxic states; study of the role of nitric oxide in central control of breathing in neonatal animals; single-cell gene expression profiling of upper airway motoneurons; study of GABAergic mechanisms in hypothalamic neurons involved in sleep/wake control study of GABAergic regulation of gene expression. Avocations: poetry, the arts. Office: Univ Pa 3800 Spruce St 209 E/Vet Philadelphia PA 19104 Home: 4528 Spruce St Philadelphia PA 19139 Business E-Mail: dvolgin@vet.upenn.edu.

VOLGMAN, ANNABELLE SANTOS, cardiologist, educator; b. Quezon City, The Philippines, Oct. 30, 1957; arrived in U.S., 1970; d. Raymundo Jocson and Purificacion Villatuya Santos; m. Keith Allen Volgman, Apr. 23, 1988; children: Robert Keith, Caroline Annabelle. BA, Barnard Coll., 1980; MD, Columbia U., 1984. Internal medicine resident U. Chgo. Hosps. and Clinics, 1984—87; cardiology fellow Northwestern Meml. Hosp., Chgo., 1987—90; asst. prof. Rush U., Chgo., 1990—2000, assoc. prof., 2001—, med. dir. Heart Ctr. Women. Cons. and spkr. in field. Contbr. articles to profl. jours. Bd. dirs. Lookingglass Theatre, 2006—. Named one of America's Top Dr.'s, Castle Connolly Med. Ltd., 2008, Top Dr.'s, Chgo. Mag., 2008. Fellow: Am. Coll. Cardiology; mem.: Am. Heart Assn. (med. chair women's legacy luncheon 2000—02, bd. dirs. 2002—, pres.-elect midwest affiliate metro bd. 2008, Spl. Merit award 2001—02, Women with Heart award 2005), Menomonee Club (bd. dirs. 2002—04). Avocations: running, bicycling, triathlons, reading, swimming. Office: Rush Heart Inst Ste 1159 1725 W Harrison St Chicago IL 60612 Office Phone: 312-942-6569. Business E-Mail: annabelle_volgman@rush.edu.

VOLICER, LADISLAV, physician, educator; b. Prague, Czechoslovakia, May 21, 1935; came to U.S., 1969, naturalized, 1977; s. Ladislav and Vilma (Molnarova) V.; m. Olga Holeckova, July 14, 1959 (div. 1970); children: Irena, Katerina; m. Beverly J. Beers, May 20, 1972 (div. 1998); children: Zuzka, Marika, Nadine, m. Joyce Simard, Jan. 1, 2009. MD, Charles U., 1959; PhD of Pharmacology, Czechoslovak Acad. Scis., 1964. Rsch. assoc. Czechoslovak Acad. Sci., Prague, 1966—68; rsch. asst. prof. U. Munich, 1968—69; from asst. prof. to assoc. prof. pharmacology Boston U. Sch. Medicine,

1969—77, asst. prof. medicine, 1975—2004, prof. pharmacology, 1977—2004, prof. psychiatry, 1985—2004, mem. inst. rev. bd., 1975—78; courtesy prof. Sch. Aging Studies U. South Fla., Tampa, 2004—; external prof., head 3d med. faculty Charles U., Prague, Czech Republic, 1995—. Clin. pharmacologist E.N. Rogers Meml. Vets. Hosp., Bedford, Mass., 1980-87, dep. dir. Geriatric Research Edn. Clin. Ctr., 1987-92, clin. dir., 1992-2004; mem. drug formulary com. State Mass., Boston, 1977-83; mem. inst. rev. bd. McLean Hosp., Belmont, Mass., 1980-2000, rsch. psychiatrist, 1997-2004 Editor: Clinical Aspects of Cyclic Nucleotides, 1977, Clinical Management of Alzheimer's Disease, 1988, Hospice Care for Patients with Advanced Progressive Dementia, 1998; Enhancing Quality of Life in Advanced Dementia, 1999, Management of Challenging Behaviors in Dementia, 2000; contbr. papers to profl. publs. Grantee Nat. Inst. Aging, 1986-2004, Nat. Inst. Alcoholism and Alcohol Abuse, 1972-79, Nat. Inst. Drug Abuse, 1973-78, Merck, Sharp & Dohme, 1971; recipient Alcoholism Research award VA, 1979-85. Fellow Gerontol. Soc. Am., Am. Acad. Nursing Democrat. Unitarian Universalist. Office: U South Fla Sch Aging Studies 4202 E Fowler Ave MHC 1342 Tampa FL 33620 Home: 2337 Dekan Ln Land O Lakes FL 34639 Office Phone: 813-909-0539. E-mail: lvolicer@cas.usf.edu. *

VOLK, STEPHAN ALBERT, neurologist, psychotherapy educator; b. Frankfurt Am Main, Germany, July 20, 1955; s. Hans Joachim and Gertrud Amalie (Ahlborn) V.; m. Sigrid Anne Meyer, Aug. 26, 1983; children: Jan-Eric, Robin John, Tom Hendrik. MD Psychiatry, Neurology, Psychotherapy, Heidelberg U., 1981. Postgrad. Max Planck Inst., Munich, 1981—83; jr. physician Univ. clinics, Frankfurt, 1983—88, sr. physician, 1988—; asst. prof. psychiatry Heidelburg U., 1991—2001, prof. psychiatry and psychotherapy, 2001—. Head sleep disorders dept. Univ. Clinics, Frankfurt, 1988, head outpatient dept., 1990; instr. psychiatry Frankfurt U., 1990, assoc. prof., 1996—; gen. mgr., dir. Psychosomatic Hosp., Hofheim, 1998—. Author: Obsessive-Compulsive Disorders, 1994; contbr. more than 100 articles to profl. jours. Max Planck Soc. rsch. fellow, 1981. Mem. Internat. Soc. of Brain Imaging in Psychiatry, World/European/German Sleep Rsch. Socs. (spkr. edn. in sleep medicine sect. 1988-90). Avocations: classical music, historical cars, german history. Address: Psychosomatic Hosp Hofheim GmbH/Kurhausstr 33 Hofheim 65719 Germany Office Phone: 0049 6192 291 1401. Business E-Mail: stvolk@kliniken-mtk.de. E-mail: jrtvvv@web.de.

VOLKMAN, ALVIN, retired physician, research scientist, educator; b. Bklyn., June 10, 1926; s. Henry Phillip and Sarah Lucille (Silverstein) V.; m. Winifred Joan Grinnell, June 12, 1947 (div. Aug. 1967); children: Karl Frederick, Nicholas James, Rebecca Jane Evans, Margaret Rose Werrell, Deborah Ann Falls; m. Carol Ann Fishel, Jan 26, 1973 (dec. Sept. 1992); 1 child, Natalie Fishel; 1 stepchild, Jeffrey C. Moore, m. A. Suzanne Hiss, Oct. 6, 1997. BS, Union Coll., 1947; MD, U. Buffalo, 1951; D in Philosophy, U. Oxford, Eng., 1963. Diplomate Nat. Bd. Med. Examiners, Am. Bd. Pathology. Intern Mt. Sinai Hosp., Cleve., 1951-52; rsch. fellow dept. anatomy Western Res. U. Sch. Medicine, 1952-54; resident, then sr. resident, then asst. in pathology Peter Bent Brigham Hosp., Boston, 1956-60; asst. prof. pathology Columbia U. Coll. Physicians and Surgeons, 1960-66; asst. mem., then assoc. mem. Trudeau Inst., Saranac Lake, NY, 1966-67; prof. dept. pathology East Carolina U. Sch. Medicine, Greenville, NC, 1977—, acting chmn. dept. pathology, 1989-90, assoc. dean for rsch. and grad. studies, 1989-95, prof. emeritus, 1995—, ret., 1999. Mem. NIH study sect. immunological scis., 1975-79, chmn., 1977-79 Contbr. articles to sci. jours. Served to lt. USNR, 1954-56. Am. Cancer Soc. scholar, 1961-63, Arth and Rheumat Found. fellow, 1952-54. Mem. AAAS, Am. Soc. Investigative Pathology, Am. Assn. Immunologists, Am. Soc. Hematology, Reticuloendothelial Soc., Am. Soc. Microbiologists, N.Y. Acad. Scis., Soc., Leukocyte Biology (hon. life). Personal E-mail: alvolk390@gmail.com

VOLKMAR, FRED ROBERT, psychiatrist, educator, director; b. Highland, Ill., Mar. 26, 1950; s. Fred Harwood and Ella Josephine (Smith) Volkmar; m. Elizabeth Anne Wiesner, Sept. 2, 1984; children: Lucy Amelia, Emily Louisa. BS, U. Ill., Urbana-Champaign, 1972; MA, MD, Stanford U., Calif., 1976. Diplomate Am. Bd. Psychiatry and Neurology. Resident psychiatry Stanford U., Calif., 1976—80; fellow child psychiatry Yale U., New Haven, 1980—82; asst. prof. Child Study Ctr., 1982—88, assoc. prof., 1988—98, prof., 1998—, Irving B. Harris chair, 2003—, chmn., dir., chief child psychiatry Yale New Haven Hosp., 2006—. Cons. psychiatrist Benhaven Sch., New Haven, 1984—, med. dir., 1982—85; mem. sci. com. Nat. Ctr. for Clin. Infant Programs, Washington, 1985. Recipient Sandoz award, 1980, Ittelson award, Am. Psychiat. Assn., Faculty Scholar award, William T. Grant Found., 1982, Rsch. Career award, NIMH, 1983, Tarjan award, Am. Acad. Child Adolescent Psychiatry, 2007; James scholar, Laughlin fellow, 1982. Mem.: Am. Acad. Child Psychiatry, Soc. for Rsch. in Child Devel., Phi Beta Kappa. Democrat. Avocations: astronomy, photography, sailing. Office: Yale U Child Study Ctr 230 S Frontage Rd PO Box 207900 New Haven CT 06519-1124 Home Phone: 203-481-0743; Office Phone: 203-785-5759. Business E-Mail: fred.volkmar@yale.edu.

VOLKOV, ILIA, physician; b. Kiev, Ukraine, Oct. 17, 1955; arrived in Israel, 1991; s. Daniel and Pesya Volkov; m. Tatyana Dil, Jan. 23, 1981; 1 child, Ruslan Ilan. MD, Novosibirsk Med. Inst., Russia, 1986; degree, Clalit Health Svcs., 1996. Cardiologist Local Hosp., Novosibirsk, 1986—88, head internal medicine dept., 1988—89; physician Diagnostic Ctr., Kiev, 1989—91; resident Clalit Health Svcs., Beer sheva, Israel, 1992—96, family physician, 1996—; student clerkship coord. Ben Gurion U., Beer-sheva, 1996—, lectr., 2008. Mem.: Israel Med. Assn. (assoc.). Achievements include research in Vitamin B12; recurrent aphthous stomatitis. Office: Lehavim Med Clinic Lehavim Ctr 10 Lehavim Israel Office Fax: 972-8-6510290. Personal E-mail: r0019@zahav.net.il.

VOLKOW, NORA DOLORES, federal agency administrator, medical researcher; b. Mexico City, Mar. 27, 1956; m. Steven Adler. BA, Modern Am. Sch., Mexico City, 1974; MD, Nat. U. Mex., 1980. Diplomate Am. Bd. Psychiatry & Neurology. Rsch. asst. Registro Nacional de Anatomia Patologica, Mexico City, 1975-76, Miles Lab. Exptl. Therapeutics, Mexico City, 1977-78; intern St. Anne Psychiat. Hosp., Paris, 1979-80; resident dept. psychiatry NYU, 1981—84; asst. prof. U. Tex. Med. Sch., Houston, 1984-87; attending physician psychiat. unit Herman Hosp., Houston, 1985-87; assoc. scientist dept. medicine Brookhaven Nat. Lab., Upton, NY, 1987-89, assoc. chief of staff, Clin. Rsch. Ctr., 1990, dir. nuclear medicine divsn., 1994—2003, dir, NIDA/DOE Imaging Ctr., 1997—2003, assoc. dir. life scis., 1999—2003; assoc. prof. dept. psychiatry SUNY, Stony Brook, 1991—2003, assoc. dean, Sch. Med., 1997—2003; dir. Nat. Inst. Drug Abuse (NIDA) NIH, Washington, 2003—. Elected mem. Inst. Medicine, 2000; mem. adv. com. minority tng. in psychiatry, Washington, 1991—; mem. study sect. clin. neuroscis. NIH, Washington, 1992—. Co-editor: Positron Emission Tomography in Schizophrenia Research, 1991. Recipient Premio Robins award, U. Mex., 1978, Premio Gabino Barrera award, 1981, Laughlin fellowship, Am. Coll. Psychiatry, 1984, Scanditronix scholarship, 1985, Paul C. Aebersold award, Soc. Nuclear Medicine, 2003; named Innovator of Yr., US News & World Report, 2000; named one of The World's Most Influential People, TIME mag., 2007, The 100 Most Powerful Women in DC, Washingtonian mag., 2009; named to Who's Next in 2007, Newsweek. Office: NIDA Neuro Sci Ctr Rm 5213 6001 Exec Blvd MS 9581 Bethesda MD 20892-9581 Office Phone: 301-443-6480. Office Fax: 301-443-9127. Business E-Mail: nora.volkow@nih.gov. *

VOLPE, ALESSANDRO, urologist, educator; b. Torino, Italy, May 26, 1972; MD, U. Torino, Italy, 1998, Splty. in Urology, 2003. Assoc., urologic oncology, urooncology fellow U. Health Network Toronto Gen. Hosp. and Princess Margaret Hosp., Toronto, Ont., Canada, 2004—05; staff urologist, divsn. urology S. Giovanni Battista Hosp., Torino, 2006; staff urologist, dept. urology S. Luigi Gonzaga Hosp. U. Torino, Italy, 2006—08; asst. prof., urology U. Eastern Piedmont Maggiore Della Carità Hosp., Novara, Italy, 2008—. Reviewer, European urology, urologic oncology Brit. Jour. Urology & Endourology, 2008; mem. Post Publ. Peer Rev. Faculty 1000 New Tech. Sect., 2009, Guidelines Com. Italian Soc. Urology, 2010, EAU Young Academic Urologists Renal Cancer Group, 2011; mem., editl. bd. Jour. Archivos Españoles de Urologia, 2011. Contbr. articles to profl. jours. Recipient Recognition award, Indsl. Union Torino. Fellow: Am. Soc. Urologic Oncology; mem.: Italian Endourological Assn., Italian Soc. Urologic Oncology, Italian Soc. Urology, European Assn. Urology. Avocations: reading, basketball, travel. Home: Via Villar Focchiardo 14 Torino 10139 Italy Business E-Mail: alessandro.volpe@med.unipmn.it.

VOLPE, EUGENE ARNOLD, oncologist, immunologist, researcher; b. Moscow, Oct. 31, 1947; arrived in Latvia, 1966, came to U.S., 2000; naturalized, 2010. s. Arnold Maxim and Olga Pavel (Nikitina) V; m. Mary Lenore Gruver-Volpe, Mar. 10, 2005. MS in Medicine, Faculty General Medcine, Riga (Latvia) Med. Inst., 1972; postgrad. Tumor Immunology, Inst. Exptl. & Clin. Oncology, USSR Acad. Med. Scis., Moscow, 1972-75, PhD in Medicine, 1976, MD, Inst. Exptl. and Clin. Medicine, Riga, 1992, Dr. habil. medicine, 1997. Postdoctoral rsch. fellow in natural anti-tumor resistance Inst. Carcinogenesis, N.N. Blokhin Ctr. for Cancer Rsch., Moscow, 1989-95; jr. rschr. scientist Inst. Exptl. and Clin. Medicine, Riga, 1975-80, sr. rsch. scientist, 1981-94, leading rsch. scientist, 1994—2000; vis. scientist, assoc. investigator Dept. Exptl. Hematology-Oncology, tumor immunologist St. Jude's Children's Rsch. Hosp., Memphis, 2000; rsch. assoc. Rsch. Inst. for Genetic and Human Therapy, Washington, 2001—02; rsch. assoc. dept. pharmacology Georgetown U. Med. Ctr., Washington, 2002, rsch. assoc. dept. oncology Vincent T. Lombardi Comprehensive Cancer Ctr., 2002—04, rsch. assoc. dept. surgery, 2004—08, sr. rsch. asst. dept. neurosurgery, Mischer Neuro sci. Inst. Vivian L. Smith Ctr. for Neurologic Rsch., U. Tex., Houston, 2008—09; rsch. assoc. Dept. Opthalmology, Ocular Surface Ctr., The Roy and Lillie Cullen Eye Inst., Baylor Coll. Medicine, Houston, 2009—. Mem. sci. group leaderships Lab. Host Biostimulators, Dept. Oncology, Inst. Exptl. and Clin. Medicine, Riga, 1981-2000; vis. scientist Mario Negri Inst. for Pharmacol. Rsch., Milan, 1996, St. Jude's Children's Rsch. Hosp., Memphis, 2000; mem. coun. for Theses Habilitation and Promotion, Univ. Latvia, Riga (specialty theoretical medicine), rsch. bd. advisors The Am. Biog. Inst., Inc., Raleigh, N.C. Contbr. articles to sci. jours. Named Sr. Rsch. Worker, USSR Highest Attestation Com., 1983; recipient diploma Red Cross Soc., 1975, Award for Profl. Excellence, 1975, Badge of Honor for Profl. Achievements, 1977, travel award Ares-Serono Found., Switzerland, 1991, Travel award Belgian Cancer Assn., 1993, Mr. George Soros' Internat. Sci. Found., Single award for profl. achievements, 1993, Travel Fund award 4th Internat. TNF Congress, The Netherlands, 1994, Travel award Novartis Internat. AG, Switzerland, 1997, Travel award Soros Found.-Latvia, 1997, Silver medal award 2000 Outstanding Achievements, U.K., 1997, Travel award Immuno-Designed Molecules S.A., France, 1998, Recognition and Appreciation award, Georgetown U., Washington, 2007, Travel award, Nat. Eye Inst., Bethesda, 2011; Long-term Rsch. grant Latvian Coun. Sci., 1994-96, 97-2000, Mr. George Soros' Internat. Sci. Found., 1994-95; Paolo Baffi Study grantee European Sch. Oncology, Milan, Italy, 1996. Mem. Internat. Soc. for Preventive Oncology (travel award 1994), Baltic Immunol. Soc., European Assn. for Cancer Rsch. (travel awards 1991, 93, 94, 98), European Macrophage Soc., Soc. Exptl. Biology and Medicine, Soc. Leukocyte Biology (travel award 1997, 99), N.Y. Acad. Sci., Pancreas Club, Inc., Assn. Rsch. in Vision & Opthalmology, Team Film & Ocular Surface Soc., Internat. Ocular Surface Soc. Avocations: bookbinding, literature, photography, travel. Personal E-mail: eugenevolpe@yahoo.com.

VOLPICELLI, GIOVANNI, physician; b. Catania, Italy, Feb. 27, 1962; s. Domenico Volpicelli and Gemma Zeno; m. Anita Trisoglio, Oct. 13, 1999; children: Gemma, Vittorio. MD, U. Catania, Italy, 1987. Cert. specialization metabolism U. Catania, Italy, 1990, lic. emergency medicine U. Catania, 1997. Internal medicine intern Garibaldi Hosp., Catania, 1986—90, internal medicine resident, 1990—96; trainee sch. of diabetes and metabolism U. Catania, 1987—90, granted rsch. fellow, chair on metabolism, 1990—92, trainee sch. emergency medicine, 1992—97; rsch. fellow dept. internal medicine Radcliffe Infirmary, Oxford, England, 1988; rsch. fellow Salgrenska Hosp., Goteborg, Sweden, 1996—96; mng. emergency medicine physician, attending emergency room physician Asti Civil Hosp., Italy, 1998—2000; crit. care physician Gradenigo Hosp., Torino, Italy, 2000—02; mng. emergency physician San Luigi Gonzaga Hosp., Orbassano, Torino, 2002—. Tng. in non-invasive ventilation in emergency care U. Torino, 2001, tng. in emergency ultrasound, 03; expert emergency ultrasound, 2003—. Contbr. articles to profl. jours., chapters to books. Fellow: Am. Coll. Emergency Physicians, Am. Coll. Chest Physicians, European Soc. Emergency Medicine, Italian Soc. Emergency Medicine; mem.: World Interactive Network Focused on Critical Ultrasound. Achievements include being one of the main experts in the development of new diagnostic applications of lung ultrasound in the emergency medicine and critical care setting; co-inventor of new methods for the assessment of insulin resistance. Avocations: spear fishing, sailing. Home: Strada di Fenestrelle 238 10132 Turin TO Italy Home Phone: 39 011 8997530; Office Phone: 39 330 368347, 390119026603. Personal E-mail: gio.volpicelli@tin.it.

VON ALLMEN, DANIEL, pediatric surgeon; b. Boston, June 4, 1958; BA, Williams Coll., Mass., 1980; MD, U. Vt. Coll. Medicine, 1986. Diplomate Am. Bd. Surgery, cert. in pediatric surgery. Intern U. Cin., 1986—87, resident, 1987—93; fellow Children's Hosp. Med. Ctr., Cin., 1993—95; asst. prof. surgery & pediat. U. NC Sch. Med., Chapel Hill, 1995—96, assoc. prof. then prof. surgery, divsn. chief pediatric surgery, 2003—; surgeon in chief NC Children's Hosp.; asst. prof. surgery U. Pa. Sch. Med., Phila., 1996—2003. Contbr. articles to profl. jours. Named a Top Doc. for Kids, Phila. Mag., 2001. Office: UNC Dept Surgery Divsn Pediatric Surgery 170 Manning Dr CB 7223 Chapel Hill NC 27599 Office Phone: 919-966-4643. Office Fax: 919-843-2497.

VONBERG, RALF-PETER, medical educator; MD, Med. Sch. Hannover, 2001. Cert. infection control specialist Ärztekammer Niedersachsen, 2006; microbiologist Ärztekammer Niedersachsen, 2009. Physician Med. Sch. Hannover, Germany, 2001—. Office: Med Sch Hannover Carl-Neuberg-Str. 1 30625 Hannover Germany Office Phone: 0049-511-532-4431. Office Fax: 0049-511-532-4366. Business E-Mail: vonberg.ralf@mh-hannover.de.

VON BOSE, MICHAEL JOERG, physician, consultant, educator; b. Munich, Feb. 13, 1948; s. Hans-Juergen Karl and Margit (Niedermeier) Boettner; m. Janet Patricia Powell, Apr. 9, 1980 (div. Jan. 1985); m. Dorothee Marianne Scheid (div. Apr. 2001); children: Julia Teresa, Fiona Olga Louisa; m. Eva-Maria Bermbach, May 11, 2001. Dr.med, Ludwig-Maximlian U., 1978; MD (FLEX-examm), Boston, 1982. Bd. cert. Neurology and Psychiatry, 1994 (Germany). Resident Dept. Surgery, U. Hosps., Munich, 1977-78; resident dept. anesthesiology Krecke Hosp., Munich, 1978-79, resident Dept. Surgery, Bklyn.-Cumberland Med. Ctr., NYC, 1979-82, Dept. Surgery, Jersey City Med. Ctr., NJ, 1982-86, Dept. Neurology Stådt Krankenhaus Bogenhausen, Munich, 1987-90, 90-94, attending physician ICU, 1994—. Am. Heart Assn., ACLS instr., course dir. UMDNJ, Newark 1993—; adj. asst. prof. dept. emergency medicine George Washington U., Washington, 1999. Co-author: manual on personality disorder examination, 1996; contbr. articles to profl. jours. Lt. German Navy, 1969-72. Recipient grant from The Laerdal Found., Norway, 1994, scholarship Max-Planck Soc., Munich, 1987-90. Fellow Assn. Resus citation Tng. (chmn. 1994—), Am. Coll. Emergency Medicine. Avocations: cruise ship medicine, critical care medicine, sailing, diving. Home: Aschafeldstr 10 83250 Marquartstein Germany Office: Hohenesterstr. 12 81245 Munich Germany Fax: 01149-8641-591181. E-mail: vonbose@mac.de.

VONDERHAAR, BARBARA K., retired medical researcher; Grad., Clarke Coll., Dubuque, Iowa, 1965; PhD, U. Wis., Madison. Postdoctoral training in mammary gland biology NIH; chief Mammary Biology and Tumorigenesis Lab. Ctr. Cancer Rsch., Nat. Cancer Inst., head Molecular and Cellular Endocrinology Sect., Mammary Biology and Tumorigenesis Lab., chair Breast and Gynecologic Malignancies Faculty, co-chair Intramural Program for Rsch. on Women's Health, scientist emeritus, 2010—. Recipient Award for Excellence in Mentoring, Bethesda Assn. for Women in Sci., 2000, Helen F. Cserr Award for outstanding woman scientist, Mt. Desert Island Biol. Laboratories, 2004. Office: Mammary Biology and Tumorigenesis Lab Ctr Cancer Rsch 37 Convent Dr Bldg 37 Rm 1106A1 Bethesda MD 20892-4254 Office Phone: 301-435-7587. Office Fax: 301-480-4727. E-mail: vonderhb@mail.nih.gov. *

VONDRACEK, PETR, neurologist, researcher, consultant, professor; b. Brno, Czech Republic, Apr. 25, 1971; s. Vaclav Vondracek and Helena Vondrackova; 1 child, Veronika Vondrackova. MD, Masaryk U., 1995, PhD, 2005. Diplomate Inst. Postgrad. Med. Edn., Czech Republic. Resident in neurology Masaryk U. Hosp., Brno, 1995—2001, cons. pediat. neurology, 2001—. Profl. guarantor Parent Project Czech Republic, Brno, 2003—. Author: (book) Focus on Birth Defects Research, 2006; contbr. articles to profl. jours.; author: (book) White Matter Involvement in Neuromascular Disorders, 2009, New Perspective and Innovative Ideas in The Treatment of Inherited Neurovascular Disorders, 2011. Grantee, Internal Grant Agy., Ministry Health Czech Republic, 2000—05. Mem.: Treat NMD Global Database Oversight Com. Newcastle, Tyne, Czech Soc. Clin. Neurophysiology, Czech Neurol. Soc., World Muscle Soc. Achievements include development of treatment of pediatric patients with spinal muscular atrophy; on-line database of patients with Duchenne muscular dystrophy; research in new mutations in Connexin 32 And Calpain 3 genes; discovery of new forms of congenital muscular dystrophies. Home: U Sokolovny 14 Brno 635 00 Czech Republic Office: Dept Pediatric Neurology Cernopolni 9 Brno 625 00 Czech Republic Home Phone: 420723216022; Office Phone: 420532234934. Personal E-mail: neurovon@volny.cz. Business E-Mail: pvondracek@fnbrno.cz.

VONDRASOVA, PETRA, physical therapist; b. Klatovy, Jan. 14, 1979; MS, Charles U., Prague, 2001, PhD, 2007. Owner physiotherapist Pvt. Physiotherapy Clinic, 2009—. Mem.: Czech Biomechanics Soc., Czech Podology Soc., Czech Physiotherapy Assn. Avocations: sports, dance. Office: Voriskova 49 Manesova 871 Klatovy 33901 Czech Republic Business E-Mail: info@fyziop.cz.

VON ESCHENBACH, ANDREW C., oncologist, former federal agency administrator; b. Phila., Oct. 30, 1941; BS, St. Joseph's U., Phila., 1963; MD, Georgetown U., 1967. Diplomate Am. Bd. Urology. Intern U. Pa./Phila. Gen. Hosp., 1967—68; resident gen. surgery Pa. Hosp., Phila., 1971—72, resident urology, 1972—75; instructor, urology U. Pa. Sch. Medicine; fellow urol. oncology U. Tex. MD Anderson Cancer Ctr., Houston, 1976—77, prof. urology, 1980—2002, chmn. dept. urology, 1983—96, cons. prof., cell biology, prof. urology, exec. v.p., chief acad. officer, dir. program ctr. Genitourinary Cancer Ctr. Houston, 1997—2002, founding dir., Prostate Cancer Research Prog., 1996, v.p. for academic affairs, Roy M. and Phyllis Gough Huffington Clin. Rsch. Disting. Chair in Urologic Oncology; dir. Nat. Cancer Inst., NIH, Bethesda, Md., 2002—06; acting commr. FDA, Rockville, Md., 2005—06, commr., 2006—09; sr. adv. to sec. US Dept. Health & Human Services, Washington, 2006—09. Founding mem. C-Change. Contbr. articles to profl. jours., chapters to books. Lt. comdr. US Navy Med. Corps, 1968—71. Recipient Carpe Diem award, Lance Armstrong Found., 2007, Julie Rogers "Spirit of Love" award; named one of 100 Most Influential People in the World, TIME Mag., 2006, Best Doctors in Am., Am. Radium Soc., 2007. Mem.: AMA, Am. Med. Writers Assn., Soc. Surg. Oncology, Am. Urological Assn., Am. Cancer Soc. (pres.-elect 2002), Uniformed Svcs. Univ. of Health Sciences (Cert. Meritorious Svc. for outstanding contbn. to prostate disease rsch.).

VON FRIEDERICHS-FITZWATER, MARLENE MARIE, researcher; b. Beatrice, Nebr., July 14, 1939; d. Paul M. and Velma B. (von Friederichs) Fitzwater; children: Richard Nielson, Kevin T. Young, James L. Nielson, Paul M. Nielson. BS, Westminster Coll., 1981; MA, U. Nebr., Omaha, 1981; PhD, U. Utah, 1987; cert. in death edn., Temple U., 1982; MPH, Waden U., 2008. Various pub. rels., writing and editing positions, 1957-78; teaching fellow in comm. U. Nebr., Omaha, 1978-83, U. Utah, Salt Lake City, 1978-83; asst. prof. mass comm. U. So. Colo., Pueblo, 1983-85; prof. comm. studies Calif. State U., Sacramento, 1985—, chair comm. studies, 1996-2000; assoc. clin. prof. family practice Sch. Medicine U. Calif., Davis, 1987—, asst. adj. prof. internal medicine, 2003—, adj. asst. prof. hematology and oncology, 2005—; dir., outreach rsch. and edn. US Davis Cancer Ctr., 2005—. Condr. workshops on communication skills for health care profls. Bergan Mercy Hosp., Omaha, 1980-81, Mercy Care Ctr., Omaha, 1980-81, Am. Cancer Soc., 1981-82, Hospice of Salt Lake, Utah, 1981-82; condr. seminars, workshops and courses on health communication, death and dying, patient edn. and compliance, other related topics, 1983—; presenter in health communication various profl. orgn. meetings and confs., 1981—; dir., co-founder The Health Communication Rsch. Inst., Sacramento, 1988—. Contbr. articles to profl. jours. Trainer United Way, Sacramento, project mgr., 1986—; pres. bd. dirs. Hospice Care Sacramento, Inc., 1986-87; instr. vol. tng. program Hospice Consortium Sacramento; hospice vol. 1980—. Recipient Lifetime Achievement award Sacramento Pub. Rels. Assn., also numerous state, regional and nat. awards for writing, editing, publ. design and photography. Fellow Am. Acad. on Physician & Patient; mem. Internat. Communication Assn. (health communication div., newsletter editor 1987-89, sec. 1989-91), AAUP, Assn. Behavioral Scis. and Med. Edn., Assn. Women in Sci., Pub. Rels. Soc. Am. (bd. dirs. Calif. Capital chpt. 1987-91), Soc. Tchrs. Family Medicine, Soc. Health Care Pub. Rels. and Mktg. No. Calif. Office: Calif State U Communication Studies Dept 6000 J St Sacramento CA 95819-2605 Office Phone: 916-734-8810. E-mail: marlene.vonfriederichs-fitzwater@ucdmc.ucdavis.edu.

VON HOFF, DANIEL DOUGLAS, oncologist, researcher; b. Oshkosh, Wis., Apr. 29, 1947; BS, Carroll Coll., 1969; MD, Columbia U. Coll. Physicians & Surgeons, 1973. Diplomate Am. Bd. Internal Medicine, Am. Bd. Oncology. Intern internal medicine U. Calif., San Francisco, 1973-74, resident internal medicine, 1974-75; med. oncology fellow Nat. Cancer Inst.; faculty, prof. dept. medicine, dept. cellular & structural biology U. Tex. Health Sci. Ctr., San Antonio, 1975—99; founding dir. Inst. Drug Devel., Cancer Therapy & Rsch. Ctr., San Antonio, 1989; prof. medicine, dir. Cancer Ctr. U. Ariz., 1999—; exec. v.p., dir. translational drug devel. divsn., head pancreatic cancer rsch. program Translational Genomics Rsch. Inst. (TGen), Phoenix, 2003—. Mem. Nat. Cancer Adv. Bd., 2004—, acting chair, 2005—06. Recipient Block Award, Ohio State U., 2003, Frances E. Bull Award, U. Mich. Comprehensive Cancer Ctr., 2003, Weinberg Award, Harvard Med. Sch. Dana Farber Cancer Ctr.; grantee Frederick S. Philips Lectureship, Meml. Sloan-Kettering Cancer Ctr., Michel Clavel Lectureship, European Orgn. Rsch. & Treatment of Cancer, Bagshawe Lectureship, Brit. Assn. Cancer Rsch. Fellow: Am. Coll. Physicians; mem.: AMA, Am. Soc. Clin. Oncology, Am. Assn. Cancer Rsch. (pres. 1999—2000, Richard and Hinda Rosenthal Found. award 1997). Office: Translational Genomics Rsch Inst Ste 660 445 N 5th St Phoenix AZ 85004

VON HOFSTEN, CLAES, psychology professor; PhD in Psychology, Uppsala U., Sweden, 1973, docent, 1976; D honoris causa (hon.), U. de Normandie, 1996. Lectr. Uppsala U., 1973—79, reader, 1979—82, prof. psychology, 1998—; vis. prof. U. Minn. Inst. Child Devel., 1982—83; sr. lectr. Umea U., Sweden, 1984—85, prof. psychology, 1985—97, chmn. psychology dept., 1994—97; vis. prof. U. Va., 1997—99. Mem. adv. coun. Internat. Assn. the Study Attention and Performance, 1992—. Editor: Scandinavian Jour. Psychology, 1985—88; assoc. editor: Ecological Psychology, 1988—97, mem. editl. bd.: Jour. Motor Behavior, 1982—97, Human Movement Sci., 1983—97, Cahiers de Psychologie Cognitive, 1986—92, Infant and Child Devel., 1990—, assoc. editor: Human Devel., 1997—2002, Devel. Psychology, 2006—; contbr. articles to profl. jours. Named XVth Gibson Lectr., Cornell U., NY, 2001; fellow, MIT Ctr. Cognitive Sci., 1983—84, Stanford U. Ctr. Advanced Study in the Behavioral Sciences, 1988—89; Northern scholar, Edinburgh U., 1984, 2003. Mem.: Am. Acad. Arts & Sciences. Office: Uppsala Univ Dept Psychology Tradgardsgatan 20 Box 1225 SE 751 42 Uppsala Sweden Office Phone: 018-471 21 33. Office Fax: 018-471 21 23. Business E-Mail: Claes.von_Hofsten@psyk.uu.se.

VON HOLDEN, MARTIN HARVEY, psychologist; b. Bronx, NY, May 29, 1942; s. Leon and Gertrude (Fishbein) Von H.; m. Virginia T. Brown, Dec. 17, 1971; 1 child, Mark Walter; children by previous marriage: Sandi Gwen Bitton, David Lawrence; 1 stepchild, Theresa Ann Brilli-Rogers. BA, NYU, 1964; MA, U. Toledo, 1965; D Pub. Adminstrn., NYU, 1981. Sr. psychologist N.Y. State Dept. Mental Hygiene, Rockland State Hosp., Orangeberg, 1966-67, team leader, 1970-71, dir. interdisciplinary tng. team, 1971-73; chief of service Metro Unit Harlem Valley Psychiat. Ctr., Wingdale, NY, 1973-74, dep. dir. programs, 1974-75; dep. dir. treatment svcs. Pilgrim Psychiat. Ctr., West Brentwood, NY, 1975-76; dir. Matteawan State Hosp., Beacon, NY, 1977, Ctrl. N.Y. Psychiat. Ctr., Marcy, NY, 1977-82; exec. dir. Rochester (N.Y.) Psychiat. Ctr., 1982-97; privatization project mgr. Fla. Dept. Children & Families, Tallahassee, 1997-98; from svc. team coord. to adminstr. G. Pierce Wood Meml. Hosp., Arcadia, Fla., 1998-2000; adminstr. G. Pierce Wood Meml., Arcadia, Fla., 2000—02; ops. mgmt. cons. mgr. DeSoto Juvenile Correctional Facility, 2002—06; cons. mental health Fla. Dept. Juvenile Justice, 2006—, sr. psychologist, Detention North Region, 2008—10; dir., Dr. Martin H. Von Holden assoc. cons. Mental Health & Forensic Mental Health. Assoc. dir. Inst. Motivation Rsch., Croton-on-Hudson, N.Y., 1965-73; dir. Martin H. Von Holden Assocs., motivation rsch., Fairlawn, N.J., 1970-74; cons. psychologist, group therapist Green Haven Correctional Facility, Stormville, N.Y., 1970-77; cons. psychologist, group therapist Auburn (N.Y.) Correctional Facility, 1977-94, Butler Correctional Facility, 1994-96, Willard Drug Treatment Ctr., 1997; clin. assoc. prof. dept. psychiatry Sch. Medicine, U. Rochester, 1983-97; cons. in field; spkr. in field. Contbr. articles to profl. jours. Mem. adv. coun. N.Y. State Commn. Quality Care to Mentally Disabled, 1989-97. Capt. MSC, U.S. Army, 1967-70. Recipient James Gordon Bennett prize NYU, 1964, Outstanding Achievement award United Way of N.Y. State, 1994. Fellow Am. Assn. Mental Health Adminstrs. (cert. mental health adminstr.); mem. Am. Psychol. Assn., Am. Correctional Assn., Am. Assn. Correctional Psychologists, Assn. Facility Dirs. N.Y. State Office Mental Health (pres. 1984-85), Order of Arrow, Psi Chi, Fla. Suicide Prevention Coun. Jewish. Home: 1250 Peppertree Ln Port Charlotte FL 33952-1357 Personal E-mail: vonholden@comcast.net.

VON JAKO, RONALD ANDREW, physician executive; s. Geza Julius and Maria Magdolna von Jako; m. Ava Cecilia Novak, Aug. 17, 2003; 1 child, Christian Andrew. MD, PhD, U. Pecs, Hungary, 1984—90, attending, 2006—. Med. and surgical externships Melrose Wakefield Hosp. & Harvard Affiliated Hosps., Boston, 1990—93; surg. rsch. fellow Lahey Clinic Med. Ctr., Burlington, Mass., 1993—94; v.p. clin. affairs & devel. Atlantis Surg., Ryebrook, NJ, 1995—2000; clin. leader Visualization Tech. Inc., Wilmington, Mass., 2000—02; chief med. officer & surg. devel. leader GE Healthcare Surgery & Interventional, Salt Lake City, 2002—; v.p. clin. R & D Internat. Surg. Tech., Boston; vis. prof. surgery hon Semmelweis Med. U. Surg. tech. cons Edward Weck Surg. Instruments a Baxter Co., Research Triangle Pk., NC, 1990—92, US Surg. Corp., Norwalk, Conn., 1992—93; surg. devel. cons. Spine Tech. Inc., Mpls., 1993—94; surg. rschr. & devel. cons. Kaieser Aerospace, Carlsbad, Calif., 1994—95; med. tech. cons. Medtronic, Mpls., 1995—96. Contbr. articles to profl. jours. Exec., Internat. Surg. Tech., Melrose, Mass., 1989—; res. dep. sheriff Essex County Sheriffs Dept., Salem, Mass., 1986—94; fund raiser GE Healthcare Surgery, Lawrence, Mass., 2007—; dist. ward chmn. Melrose, 1990—91; vice chmn. Rep. Party, Melrose, 1991—92; bd. dirs. Cardian Mountain Sch., NH. Decorated Hungarian Order of Knights Vitezi Rend; recipient awards, Amer. Coll. Surgeons, 1993, 1994, Keynote Spkr. award, Mass. Inst. Tech., 2007—08, Internat. Brain Mapping Soc. & U. Calif. LA, 2008, Tech. award, GE Healthcare, 2004—, Pres. award, 2009; Surg. Rsch. grant, 2006, Minimally Invasive Surgery fellowship, Lahey Clinic Med. Ctr., 1993—94. Mem.: AMA (corr.), Congress Neurol. Surgeons, Am. Acad. Otolaryngology Head & Neck Surgery, Am. Spine Radiology Assn., Spine Arthroplasty Soc., N.Am Spine Soc., Mass. Med. Soc. (corr.). Achievements include invention of surgical instruments for minimally invasive surgery; development of less invasive surgical techniques for general and vascular surgery; design of novel endoscopic and fiberoptic instruments for surgery; patents for surgical instruments for spine, orthopedics and general cardio-vascular surgeries; pioneer in special fiberoptic retractor scopes for minimally invasive spine, orthopedics and cardiovascular surgeries and use of surgical navigation in cochlear implantation; first to use of 3D fluoroscopic navigation in sinus surgery and first in electromagnetic stereotactic navigation in minimally invasive spine and trauma surgery. Avocations: mountain climbing, hiking, lacrosse, travel. Personal E-mail: drvonjako@comcast.net. Business E-Mail: ron.vonjako@med.ge.com.

VON KROGH, GEO, retired dermatologist, venereologist; b. Bergen, Norway, Jan. 25, 1943; arrived in Sweden, 1970; s. Morten and Aslaug (Hegland) von K. MD, U. Bergen, 1967; PhD, Karolinska Inst., Stockholm, 1981. Intern Hosp. Drammen, Norway, 1967-68; resident in diving medicine Naval Hosp. Bergen, 1969-70; resident in dermatology and venereology So. Hosp., 1970-78; resident in psychiatry Hosp. Beckomberga, Stockholm, 1970; rsch. dermatologist U. Calif., San Francisco, 1979-82, asst. prof., 1983; assoc. prof., staff dermatologist Karolinska Hosp., Stockholm, 1988—2006; assoc. prof. dermatology Karolinska Inst., Dept. Medicine, Dermatology and Venerology Unit, Karolinska U., Stockholm, 2006; ret., 2006. Cons. in field. Author: (chpts.) Safety and Efficacy of Topical Drugs and Cosmetics, 1982, Dermatotoxicology, 2d edit., 1983, Occupational Skin Disease, 1983, Dermatology, 2d edit., Vol. 1, 1984, Infections in Reproductive Health, Vol. II, 1985, Dermatologic Immunology and Allergy, 1985, Treatment of Sexually Transmitted Diseases, 1986, Papillomaviruses, 1987, Genitoanal Papilloma Virus Infection: A Survey for the Clinician, 1989, Genital Papillomavirus Infections: Advances in Modern Diagnosis and Therapy, 1990, Papillomavirus in Human Pathology, 1990, Clinics in Dermatology, Vol. 3, 1991, Orticaria Angioedema, 1991, Dermatology & Perspectives, 1993, Papillomavirus in Human Pathology, 1995, Current Problems in Dermatology, Vol. 24, 1996; contbr., editor Human Papillomavirus Infections in Dermatovenereology, 1997; editor: Sexually Transmitted Diseases, 1990; co-editor: Genitoanal Papilloma Virus Infection, 1989, Diagnostic and Therapy in Primary Care, 1990, Papilloma Viruses, Part Two, 1997, Human Papilloma Virus Infection. A Clinical Atlas, 1997; contbr. 80 articles to profl. jours. and 2 textbooks. With Norwegian Navy, 1969-70. Mem. Swedish Acad. Dermatology, Scandinavian Soc. Genito-urinary Medicine, Internat. Soc. Study Vulvar Disease, Internat. Papillomavirus Workshop Group, Swedish Physicians Against AIDS, European Acad. Dermatology Venereology, Internat. AIDS Soc., Internat. Soc. STD Rsch., Med. Soc. Study Venereal Diseases, Am. Venereal Disease Assn., Swedish Soc. Dermatologic Surgery, European Human Papilloma Virus Associated Pathology (pres. 1993-96), Internat. Union Against Sexually Transmitted Infections (bd. sci. mem. 1996, European br., mem. editl. bd. Genital Infectious and Neoplasia Update 1998, hon. treas.), Internat. Union Against Venereal Diseases and Treponematoses (hon. treas. European br.), Internat. Union against Sexually Transmitted Infections. Home: Sjokvarnsbacken 12 13171 Nacka Sweden Office Phone: 46 70 768 2755. Personal E-mail: geo.von.krogh@ownit.net.

VON MITZLAFF, HANS-CHRISTOPH, neurologist; b. Ludwigshafen, Germany, Sept. 3, 1960; arrived in Switzerland, 1989; s. Conrad and Ruth von Mitzlaff; m. Astrid von Hirschheydt, 1987; children: Christian, Konstantin, Benjamin. MD, U. Göttingen, Germany, 1990; specialist in neurology, Ärztekammer, Reutlingen, Germany, 1997. Collaborator Max-Planck Inst., Göttingen, 1988; asst. physician Valbella Hosp., Davos, Switzerland, 1989-90, U. Hosp., Bern, Switzerland, 1990-94, Elisabethen Hosp., Ravensburg, Germany, 1994-95, Swiss Epilepsy Ctr., Zürich, 1995-97; med. dir. Neurorehab. Ctr., Wald, Switzerland, 1998—2000; pvt. practice Pfäffikon, SZ, 2001—. Active humanitarian activites, Johanniter, Poland, 1982. Grantee, Studienstiftung des Deutschen Volkes, 1984. Mem.: German Soc. Clin. Neurophysiology, Swiss Soc. Clin. Neurophysiology, Swiss Neurol. Soc., German Med. Assn., Swiss Med. Assn. Office: Oberdorfstrasse 11 8808 Pfäffikon Switzerland

VON NETTELHORST, HERWIG, medical products executive, biomedical engineer; b. Wittenberg, Germany, Mar. 30, 1945; s. Peter von and Brigitta von Nettelhorst; m. Brigitte Schoo, Mar. 3, 1971; children: Gesa von Nettelhorst, Gerald von Nettelhorst. MSc in Engring., U. Trier Kaiserslautern, 1974; DSc in Engring., Tech. U. Berlin, 1978. Head R&D Biotronik GmbH, Berlin, 1978—84; CEO Getemed AG, Teltow, Germany, 1984—. Mem. supervisory bd. Nexus Ag, Villingen-Schwenningen, Germany, 2003—06. Recipient Innovation award, Berlin, 1987. Achievements include patents for various pacemaker related instruments; design of BabyGuard apnea monitor; VitaGuard.

VON OEFELE, KONRAD ANDREAS, psychiatrist; b. Munich, May 2, 1954; s. Walter Konrad and Elisabeth Ada von Oefele; m. Anne Lisa Wings; children: Alexandra, Ulrike, Julia, Regina. MD, U. Munich, 1980. Cert. psychiatrist, psychotherapist, forensic psychiatrist. Asst. physician, Mainkofen, Germany, 1980—81; rsch. fellow U. Munich, 1981—91; dir. Landgerichtsarzt, Munich, 1991—. Author: Das Betreuungsrecht, 1992, 8th edit., 2009, Forensische Psychiatrie, 1998, 2nd edit., 2011; contbr. articles to profl. jours. and books. Mem.: Cusanuswerk. Roman Catholic. Office: Landgerichtsarzt Nymphenburger str 16 80097 Munich Germany

VON WERDER, KLAUS, medical educator; b. Darmstadt, Germany, Dec. 15, 1940; s. Fritz and Gerda (von Esmarch) von W.; children: Julia, Konstantin, Alexander. MD, U. Munich, 1968. Endocrine fellowship U. Calif., San Francisco, 1968—70; asst., chief neuroendocrinology unit U. Munich, 1970—88; chief dept. medicine Schloßpark-Klinik, Humboldt U., Berlin, 1988—2005; endocrinologist pvt. practice, 2005—. Guest physician Hop. Pitié, Paris, 1978, IAEA cons. U. Chiang-Mai, Thailand, 1980; Royal Soc. vis. prof., 1993. Contbr. articles to profl. jours. Recipient Marius Tausk award, German Endocrine Soc., 1974, Endocrinology Trust medal European Soc. Endocrinology, Copenhagen, 1987. Fellow Royal Coll. Physicians (London); mem. German Endocrine Soc., Am. Endocrine Soc., Polish Endocrine Soc. (hon.), European Neuroendocrine Assn. (pres. 1995-99), Bulgarian Endocrine Soc. (hon.), Rotary (pres. 2002-03). Home: Birkensteinstr 81 83730 Fischbachau Germany Office: Endokrinologikum Promenadeplatz 12 80333 Munich Germany Home Phone: 0049 08028 661; Office Phone: 0049 089 2429670. Personal E-mail: klaus@vonwerder.de.

VON ZUR MÜHLEN, ALEXANDER MEINHARD, internist, educator; b. Riga, Latvia, May 13, 1936; arrived in Germany, 1939. s. Alexander and Kira (Velitschkowski) von zur M.; m. Karen Berg, 1958 (div. 1977); children: Insa, Friederike, Patrick; m. Ulrike Warnecke, 1977; children: Constantin, Nicolas. Grad., Med. Sch. Freiburg, Fed. Republic Germany, 1963. Asst. Med. Sch. Göttingen, Fed. Republic Germany, 1965-74, sr. asst., 1974; prof. Internal Medicine Med. Sch. Hannover, Fed. Republic Germany, 1974—. Contbr. articles to profl. jours. Mem. German Soc. Endocrinology, German Soc. Internal Medicine. Office: Med Hochschule Hannover Konstanty-Gutschow Str 8 D-30625 Hannover Germany Home Phone: 0049-511-513332. Business E-Mail: a.muehlen@endokrinologikum.com. E-mail: dr.alexander@muehlen.net.

VON ZUR MÜHLEN, CONSTANTIN, cardiologist, researcher; b. Hannover, Germany, June 9, 1977; s. Alexander and Ulrike von zur Mühlen; m. Daria Kaps. MD, U. Würzburg, Würzburg, 2003. Med. diploma U. Würzburg, Germany, 2003. Fellow cardiology U. Hosp. Freiburg, Germany, 2003—, head rsch. lab.; cardiology rsch. fellow U. Oxford, 2005—06. Contbr. articles to profl. jours. Recipient W.P Harvey prize, U. Freiburg, 2007; grantee Acute Coronary Syndrome 2004, Merck Sharp&Dohme, 2004. Mem.: German Soc. Internal Medicine, German Cardiac Soc., European Heart Assn. Achievements include invention of a contrast agent targeting activated platelets; patents pending for targeted contrast agents. Office: Univ Hosp Freiburg Hugstetter St 55 Freiburg Baden-Württemberg 79106 Germany

VOORHESS, MARY LOUISE, pediatric endocrinologist; b. Livingston Manor, NY, June 2, 1926; d. Harry William and Helen Grace (Schwartz) V. RN, City Hosp. Sch. Nursing, Binghamton, NY, 1946; BA in Zoology, U. Tex., 1952; MD, Baylor Coll., Houston, 1956. Diplomate Am. Bd. Pediatrics and Pediatric Endocrinology. Rotating intern Albany (N.Y.) Med. Ctr., 1956-57, asst. resident pediatrics, 1957-58, chief resident pediatrics, 1958-59; rsch. fellow pediatric endocrinology and genetics SUNY Health Sci. Ctr., Syracuse, 1959-61, asst. prof. pediatrics, 1961-65, assoc. prof. pediatrics, 1965-70, prof. pediatrics, 1970-76, acting chmn. dept. pediat., 1970—72, SUNY Sch. Medicine and Biomed. Scis., Buffalo, prof. pediatrics, 1976-91, prof. pediatrics emeritus, 1991—; co-chief div. endocrinology Children's Hosp. Buffalo, 1976-91; retired, 1997; acting chmn. SUNY Sch. Medicines & Biomed. Scis., Buffalo, 1988—89. Mem. nat. adv. environ. health scis. coun. NIH, 1980-83. Ad hoc reviewer Jour. Pediat., Pediat., Am. Jour. Diseases Children, others, 1960-97;

contbr. sci. articles to profl. jours., chpts. to books. Mem. adv. bd. Interim Healthcare inc., 1991-97; mem. devel. coun. Children's Hosp. Buffalo Found., 1991-97; med. dir. Children's Growth Found., Buffalo, 1976-97; cmty. advisor Assn. for Rsch. Childhood Cancer, Buffalo, 1990-97. Recipient rsch. career devel. award Nat. Cancer Inst., 1961-71, Dean's award SUNY Sch. Medicine and Biomed. Scis., 1991. Fellow Am. Acad. Pediatrics, AAAS; mem. Soc. Pediatric Rsch. (emeritus), Am. Pediatric Soc. (emeritus), Endocrine Soc. (emeritus), Pediatric Endocrine Soc. (emeritus), Phi Beta Kappa, Alpha Omega Alpha. Presbyterian. Home: Apt 33 5707 Williamsburg Landing Dr Williamsburg VA 23185-8008 E-mail: mvoorhess@cox.net.

VORKO-JOVIC, ARIANA, epidemiologist, educator, scientist; b. Zagreb, Croatia, June 26, 1946; d. Egon and Draga Vorko; m. Franjo Jovic, Oct. 10, 1981; children: Alan Jovic, Ozren Jovic. PhD, MD, Med. Sch., Zagreb, 1971. Asst. in epidemiology Sch. of Pub. Health Med. Sch., Zagreb, 1972—93, asst. prof. Sch. Pub. Health, 1994—99, assoc. prof., 2000—, prof., 2009—. Contbr. articles to profl. jours. Mem.: Croatian Acad. Med. Sci. (life).

VORMANN, JUERGEN, nutritionist, researcher; b. Herford, Germany, Apr. 25, 1953; s. Heinz and Gerda Vormann; 1 child, Helen. Abitur, Nordseegymnasium, Langeoog, 1972; Dr. rer. nat., U. Hohenheim, Stuttgart, Germany, 1981; Habilitation in Biochemistry, Free U. Berlinl, Germany, 1991. Cert. nutritionist U. Hohenheim, 1978, registered prof. Free U. Berlin, Germany, 1997. Rschr. Inst. Molecular Biology and Biochemistry, Free U., Berlin, 1980—96; med. dir. Protina Pharm., Ismaning, Germany, 1996—99; dir. Inst. Prevention and Nutrition, IPEV, Ismaning, 2000—. Recipient Hermes Mineral award, 1994. Office: Inst Prevention & Nutrition Adalperostr 37 Ismaning Munich 85737 Germany Business E-Mail: vormann@ipev.de.

VOROBYEVA, NATALYA MIKHAYLOVNA, cardiologist; b. Russia, Aug. 2, 1976; MD, Tyumen State Med. Acad., 1999, PhD, 2004. With Cardiology Rsch. and Prdn. Ctr., 2006—. Recipient Young Investigator award, XXII Congress ISTH, Boston, 2009. Office: ul 3-ya Cherepkovskaya 15a Moskva 121552 Russia Business E-Mail: natalyavorobjeva@mail.ru.

VOSA, CARLO, cardiologist; b. Torre del Greco, Feb. 5, 1946; Degree in Medicine and Surgery, U. Naples, 1971; degree in Cardiac Surgery, U. Padua, 1980. Chief pediat. cardiac surgery dept. Second U. Naples, Monaldi Hosp., 1997—2007; chief adult and pediat. cardiac surgery dept. AOU Federico II U. Hosp., 2007—. Prof. cardiac surgery U. Naples, 2000—11. Recipient Gold medal, Pres. Italian Republic. Mem.: Ministry of Health (mem. nat. com. sci. rsch.), Italian Soc. Cardiac Surgery. Home: Via Tasso 480 Villa Gloria Naples 80127 Italy Business E-Mail: carlo.vosa@unina.it.

VOSS, EDWARD WILLIAM, JR., immunologist, educator; b. Chgo., Dec. 2, 1933; s. Edward William and Lois Wilma (Graham) V.; m. Virginia Hellman, June 15, 1974; children: Cathleen, Valerie. AB, Cornell Coll., Iowa, 1955; MS, Ind. U., 1964, PhD, 1966. Asst. prof. microbiology U. Ill., Urbana, 1967-71, assoc. prof., 1971-74, prof., 1974-98, prof. emeritus, 1999—, adj. prof. dept. vet. pathobiology, 2001—, dir. cell sci. ctr. Urbana, 1988-94, Coll. Liberal Arts and Scis. Jubilee prof., 1990. Rev. panel on molecular biology gene structure USDA, Washington, 1985-86, U.S. Dept. Energy Rsch., 1994; panel mem. in biol. scis. NSF Minority Grad. Fellowships, Washington, 1986-88, sci. adv. bd. Biotech. Rsch. and Devel. Corp., 1989-1992, mem. Peer Review Com. AHA, 1993-96; study sect. innovation grant program for approaches in HIV vaccine rsch. NIH, 1997; adj. prof. U. Hawaii, Manoa, 1999-2001, Coll. Vet. Medicine, 2001—. Author, editor Fluorescein Hapten: An Immunological Probe, 1984, Anti-DNA Antibodies in SLE, 1988, adv. editor Immunochemistry, 1975—78, Molecular Immunology, 1980—2002, mem. editl. bd. Applied and Environ. Microbiology, 1979—99; contbr. articles to profl. jours. Apptd. to pres.'s coun. U. Ill. Found., 1995. Served with U.S. Army, 1956-58. NIH fellow, 1966-67, NSF fellow, 1975-77; NIH grantee, 1967—, NSF grantee, 1967—; recipient Disting. Lectr. award U. Ill., 1983; named 1st James R. Martin Univ. scholar, 1994; recipient Exemplary Contbn. award Lupus Found. Am., 1994. Ednl. Aid award E.I. DuPont, 1994, 95. Fellow Am. Inst. Chemists; mem. AAAS, Fedn. Am. Scientists, Am. Assn. Immunologists, Am. Assn. Biol. Chemists, Reticuloendothelial Soc., Am. Lupus Soc. (hon. bd. dirs. Cen. Ill. chpt. 1986—, named to Nat. Lupus Hall of Fame 1988, Cmty. Svc. award 1996), N.Y. Acad. Scis., U.S. Pharmacopeial Conv., Inc., Nat. Geog. Soc., Am. Chem. Soc. (tour speaker 1984-87), Protein Soc., Sigma Xi. Home: 555 Hahaione St 8H Honolulu HI 96825-1460 E-mail: edwardv307@aol.com.

VOSS, JULIE E., plastic surgeon, educator; married; 2 children. MD summa cum laude, U. Calif. Diplomate Am. Bd. Dermatology. Resident in dermatology Univ. Calif., Irvine; asst. prof. Sch. of Medicine Univ. Wash.; founder Cascade Dermatology and Surgicenter; dir. dept. of dermatology Northwest Face med. and aesthetic svcs. Fellow: Am. Acad. for Cosmetic Surgery, Am. Soc. Dermatologic Surgery. Avocations: gardening, swimming, hiking, skiing. Office: Northwest Face Medical and Aesthetic Services 3100 Carillon Point Kirkland WA 98033 Office Phone: 425-576-1700.

VOSS, MIRANDA, surgeon; b. London, Apr. 4, 1963; MBChB, Aberdeen U., 1987. Sr. specialist Worcester Hosp., 1996—. Lectr. U. Stellenbosch, 2009; exec. com. mem. Surg. Rsch. Soc. South Africa, 2010. Fellow: RCS (Eng), Coll. Surgeon South Africa. Office: Worcester Hosp Murray St Worcester Western Cape 6850 South Africa Business E-Mail: mvoss@worcestersurgery.co.za.

VOS SAVANT, MARILYN, columnist, medical products executive; b. St. Louis, Aug. 11, 1946; d. Joseph Mach and Marina vos Savant; m. Robert Koffler Jarvik, 1987; children: Mary, Dennis. Attended, Washington U., St. Louis; LittD (hon.), Coll. NJ, 2003. 'Ask Marilyn' columnist Parade mag., 1986—; v.p., CFO Jarvik Heart, Inc., NYC, 1988—. Author: Omni I.Q. Quiz Contest, 1985, Ask Marilyn: Answers to America's Most Frequently Asked Questions, 1992, The World's Most Famous Math Problem: The Proof of Fermat's Last Theorem and Other Mathematical Mysteries, 1993, More Marilyn: Some Like It Bright!, 1994, "I've Forgotten Everything I Learned in School!": A Refresher Course to Help You Reclaim Your Education, 1994, Of Course I'm for Monogamy: I'm Also for Everlasting Peace and an End to Taxes, 1996, The Power of Logical Thinking: Easy Lessons in the Art of Reasoning and Hard Facts about Its Absence in Our Lives, 1996, The Art of Spelling: The Madness and the Method, 2000, Growing Up: A Classic American Childhood, 2002; co-author: Brain Building: Exercising Yourself Smarter, 1990. Mem. adv. bd. Nat. Assn. Gifted Children, Nat. Women's History Mus.; bd. dirs. Nat. Coun. Econ. Edn. Recipient Women Making History award, Nat. Women's History Mus.; named one of Five Outstanding Speakers, Toastmasters Internat., 1999, Women of the New Millennium, White House Vital Voices: Women in Democracy Campaign; named to Guinness Book of World Records Hall of Fame, 1988. Achievements include listed under "Highest IQ" in the Guinness Book of World Records, 1985-1989. Avocations: skiing, travel. Office: Jarvik Heart Inc 333 W 52nd St New York NY 10019-7451 Mailing: c/o Parade Publs 711 3rd Ave New York NY 10017 *

VOTH, DOUGLAS W., physician, health facility administrator; MD, U. Kans., 1959. Diplomate Am. Bd. Internal Medicine, 1966. Intern U. Kans. Sch. Medicine, Kansas City, 1959—60, resident in internal medicine, 1960—61, 1964—65, assoc. prof. medicine, 1971—73, prof. medicine, chair dept. and dir. residency program, 1974—84, pres. corp., 1978—84; fellow in infectious diseases Upstate Med. Ctr., Syracuse, NY, 1961—64; mem. sect. infectious diseases Kans. U. Med. Ctr., 1965—73; prof. medicine U. Okla. Sch. Medicine, 1973—74; med. dir., chief med. svc. King Fahad Hosp, Al Baha, Saudi Arabia, 1985—86; overseas advisor Royal Coll. Physicians, England, 1987—; prof. medicine U. Okla. Coll. Medicine, Oklahoma City, 1987—, acting chair dept. neurology, 1990—92, exec. dean, 1992—96; dean Faculty of Medicine and Health Scis., United Arab Emirates, 1996—2000; dir. med. edn. Sheikh Zayed Hosp., Abu Dhabi, 2000—01; dir. alumni and devel. U. Okla. Health Scis. Ctr., 2001—02, 2007—10; dean U. Okla. Coll. Pharmacy, Oklahoma City, 2002—07. Trustee U. Presbyn. Neurol. Inst., Oklahoma City, 1994—96. Recipient Delp award, 2006; named Regents' Prof., 2010. Fellow: ACP, Infectious Diseases Soc. Am. Office: Univ Okla Health Sci Ctr 1000 Stanton L Young Blvd Ste 162 Oklahoma City OK 73190 Home Phone: 405-340-6267; Office Phone: 405-271-2300. Business E-Mail: douglas-voth@ouhsc.edu. *

VOUDOURIS, COSTAS PANAGIOTIS, rheumatologist, consultant; b. Thessaloniki, Macedonia, Greece, Jan. 4, 1938; s. Panagiotis and Joan (Homatas) V.; m. Caterina Kioussis, Jan. 3, 1965; children: Panagiotis, Eleana. Grad., Am. Coll., Thessaloniki, 1956; MD, U. Thessaloniki, 1972. Med. asst. Ctrl. Hosp., Thessaloniki, 1964-66; sr. house officer Gen. Hosp., Wakefield, Eng., 1967-68; registrar Regional Rheumatology Centre, Liverpool, 1968-70, A IKA Hosp., Thessaloniki, 1971-75, dir. dept. medicine, 1976-85; dir. dept. rheumatology First Gen. Hosp., Thessaloniki, 1986—2004; lectr., prof. Open U., Thessaloniki, 1989. Rschr., mem. coun. Hellenic Found. for Rheumatol. Rsch., Athens, 1992—. Author: Diagnostic Rheumatology, 1987, Rheumatological Encyclopedic Dictionary, 1998; co-author: Advances in Medicine, 1991; co-editor: Primer in Rheumatology, 1993, 2d edit., 2004; editor Med. Clinics N.Am. (Greek edit.), 1972-76. Lt. Med. Svcs. Greek Mil., 1963-64. Recipient hon. medal Municipality of Thessaloniki, 1990, hon. diploma Hellenic Soc. Continued Edn., 1992. Mem. Hellenic Soc. Rheumatology (pres. 1989-90), Med. Soc. Thessaloniki (v.p.) 1988-92), N.Y. Acad. Scis. Mem. Conservative Party. Greek Orthodox. Avocations: sailing, gardening, political philosophy. Office Phone: 003 2310 277866. E-mail: kb@hol.gr.

VOUKELATOU, KONSTANTINA, biomedical engineer, researcher; b. Patras, Greece, June 10, 1967; d. Christos Voukelatos and Denise Voukelatou. BSc in Bioelectronics Engring, 1990; MSc in Bioelectronics Engring, U. St. Petersburg, Russia, 1992. Registered profl. engr., Greece, 1994. Engring. rschr., cons. Italian Nat. Agy. New Techs., Energy & Sustainable Econ. Devel. Rsch. Ctr., Bologna, Italy, 2000—; applied engr. Inst. Biomed. Tech., Greece, 1992—95, U. Patras, Netherlands, 1992—95, Hellas Med. Svc., Greece, 1992—95; Quality Auditor CRITO, Italy, 1996—98; mgr. to coord. Monrif Group SpA, Italy, 1998—99; rschr. to project coord. Italian Nat. Agy. New Techs., Energy & Sustainable Econ. Devel., Italy, 1999—. Mem.: Engrs. Register. Achievements include research in calculation methods. Avocations: travel, swimming, reading, music. Home: Pietro Miliani 7/3 Bologna 40132 Italy Office: ENEA Rsch Ctr Via Martiri di Monte Sole 4 40129 Bologna BO Italy Office Phone: 0039-051-6098293. Home Fax: 0039-051-6098738. Personal E-mail: nadia.voukelatou@enea.it.

VREDENBURGH, JAMES JOSEPH, medical educator; b. Mt. Kisco, NY, Feb. 17, 1957; BA in Psychology, U. Va., Charlottesville, 1979; MD, U. Vt., 1983. Lic. Conn., NH, Vt., NC, cert. Med. Oncology, Hematology. Resident St. Francis Hosp. and Med. Ctr., Hartford, Conn., 1983—86; fellow Dartmouth-Hitchcock Med. Ctr., Hanover, NH, 1986—90; instr., medicine Dartmouth Med. Sch., Hanover, NH, 1986—90, assoc. medicine, 1990; asst. prof. Duke U. Med. Ctr., Durham, NC, 1990—96, assoc. prof. medicine, dept. medicine, dept. surgery, divsn. neurosurgery, 1996—2003, prof. medicine, 2003—, med. dir., adult clin. services. Med. dir. stem cell cryopreservation lab., 1990—2002; med. dir. Hillandale Clin. Lab., 1992—2002; interim dir. bone marrow transplant program, 1995; mem. cancer protocol review com., 1991—2001, 2004—; med. dir., pharmacology lab., 1995—; mem. clin. microbiology users com., 1998—; mem. cancer ctr. users exec. com., 2000—; med. dir. clin. ops., 2005—. Contbr. several articles to profl. jours.; refereed journals. Mem.: Soc. Neuro-Oncology, Internat. Soc. for Hematotherapy and Graft Engring., Am. Soc. Blood & Marrow Transplantation, Am. Soc. Hematology, Am. Soc. Clin. Oncology, Phi Beta Kappa, Sigma Xi, Alpha Omega Alpha. Office: Duke U Med Ctr DUMC Box 3624 Durham NC 27710 Office Phone: 919-668-2993. Office Fax: 919-684-6674. Business E-Mail: vrede001@mc.duke.edu.

VREDEVOE, DONNA LOU, academic administrator, microbiologist, educator, biomedical researcher; BA in Bacteriology, UCLA, 1959, PhD in Microbiology, 1963. USPHS postdoctoral fellow Stanford (Calif.) U., 1963—64; instr. bacteriology UCLA, 1963, postgrad. rsch. immunologist dept. surgery Ctr. Health Scis., 1964-65, asst. rsch. immunologist dept. surgery Ctr. Health Scis., 1964-67, asst. prof. Sch. Nursing, Ctr. Health Scis., 1967-70, assoc. prof., 1970-76; prof. Sch. Nursing, Ctr. Health Scis., 1976—, assoc. dean Sch. Nursing, 1976-78, acting assoc. dean Sch. Nursing, 1985-86, asst. dir. space planning Cancer Ctr., 1976-78, dir. space planning, 1978-90, cons. to lab. nuc. medicine and radiation biology, 1967-80, acting dean Sch. Nursing, 1995-96. Chair acad. senate UCLA, 1999—2000, vice chancellor acad. pers., 2001—06, spl. asst. to chancellor, 2006—07, prof., vice chancellor emerita, 2006—; pres. UCLA Emerita Assn., 2010—11, past pres., 2011—. Contbr. articles to profl. publs. Postdoctoral fellow USPHS, 1963-64; Mabel Wilson Richards scholar UCLA, 1960-61; rsch. grantee Am. Cancer Soc., Calif. Inst. Cancer Rsch., Calif. divsn. Am. Cancer Soc., NIH, USPHS, Am. Nurses Found., Cancer Rsch. Coordinating Com. U. Calif., Dept. Energy, UCLA. Mem Am. Soc. Microbiology, Am. Assn. Immunologists, Am. Assn. Cancer Rsch., Nat. League Nursing (2d v.p. 1979-81), Sigma Xi, Alpha Gamma Sigma, Sigma Theta Tau (nat. hon. mem.). Office: UCLA Sch Nursing 700 Tiverton Ave 3-232 Factor Bldg Box 951702 Los Angeles CA 90095-1702 Office Phone: 310-206-6619.

VRIEND, WILLEM HENDRIK, retired rural surgeon; b. Haarlem, The Netherlands, Sept. 24, 1928; arrived in Australia, 1990; s. Cornelis and Engelina Maria Adriana (Van Kampen) V.; m. Engeltje Gijsbertha de Jong, Sept. 27, 1955; children: Evertje Engeline, Cornelis, Ingeborg Johanna, Adriaan, Simonjan. MD, U. Leiden, The Netherlands, 1955, postgrad., 1956; PhD, Vrije Universiteit Amsterdam, 2003. Cert. health inspector for Indonesian govt.; med. expert Dutch Fgn. Office, pioneer/cmty. worker Highlands of Irian Jaya. Intern Deaconess Hosp., Leiden, 1955-56, resident in gen. surgery, ob-gyn. and urology, 1959-60, 64-65, resident in orthopedics and neurosurgery Utrecht, The Netherlands, 1975-76, intern in orthopedics and neurosurgery Leiden, 1975-76; resident in tubal surgery U. Leiden, 1981-82, intern in tubal surgery, 1981-82; mission doctor, tropical surgeon, health inspector Gereja Masehi Injili Timor Min. Health, Kupang, Indonesia, 1956-59; mission physician, tropical surgeon Gereja Kristen Injili, Angguruk, Irian Jaya, Indonesia, 1960-75; bilateral med. expert, tropical surgeon Gereja Kristen Injili Secretariat Cabinet Republic Indonesia, Wamena, Irian Jaya, 1976-86; mission doctor, tropical surgeon Gereja Kristen Injili-World Mission Australia, Wamena, 1987-93; ret., 1993. Pioneer Gereja Keristen Injili-Opening of the Yalimo area, 1961-65; cmty. developer Gereja Keristen Injili, Angguruk, 1965-75, rural surgeon, Angguruk and Wamena, 1961-93. Author: (film) SPT 100, 1970, (book trilogy) Smoky Fires, The Merits of Development Cooperation for Inculturation of Health Improvements, 2000. Grantee SIMAVI, The Netherlands, 1956-93, VEM, Barmen-Wuppertahl, 1965, Prof. Dr. P.H. van Thiel, The Netherlands, 1956-94. Mem. Uniting Ch. of Australia. Home: 13 Cronin Dr 4160 Brisbane QLD Australia Personal E-mail: wimvr@ozemail.com.au.

VROCHIDES, DIONISIOS, surgeon, director; b. Thessaloniki, Greece, July 25, 1969; MD, Aristotle U. Thessaloniki, 1994, PhD, 2000. Resident, chief resident, dept. surgery Brown U., 2000—05, asst. instr. in surgery, 2004—05; fellow in HPB and transplant surgery, multi-organ transplant dept. McGill U., 2005—07, adj. prof. in surgery, 2009; dir. Ctr. HPB Surgery, Euromedica Geniki Kliniki Gen. Hosp., 2008—. Bd. dirs. Zoe Hosp. Oncology, 2010. Recipient Humanism & Excellence in Tchg. award, Brown U., Dean's Tchg. Excellence award, Dept. Surgery Resident Tchg. award, Haffenreffer House Staff Excellence award, RI Hosp.; Ernest and Merilyn Avrith fellowship, McGill U. Fellow: ACS; mem.: Can. Assn. Gen. Surgeons, Am. Soc. Transplant Surgeons, Internat. Liver Transplantation Soc., Internat. Hepato-Pancreato-Biliary Assn., AHPBA. Avocations: sailing, basketball, skydiving. Office: 2 Gravias Thessaloniki MKD 54645 Greece Personal E-mail: vrochides@yahoo.com.

VUISSOZ, PIERRE-ANDRÉ, engineer; b. Aigle, Vaud, Switzerland, Jan. 20, 1969; Diploma in Physics, ETHZ, 1993; PhD, EPFL, 1999. Rsch. engr. Imagerie Adaptative Diagnostique et Interventionnelle, UHP - INSERM U947, 2004—. Mem.: ISMRM. Office: Imagerie Adaptative Diagnostique et Interventionnelle UHP - INSERM U947 Tour Drouet 4 Vandoeuvre les Nancy Lorraine 54511 France Office Fax: 33-3-83-15-40-62. Business E-Mail: pa.vuissoz@chu-nancy.fr.

VUKASINOVIC, ZORAN STANISA, orthopedic surgeon, educator; b. Valjevo, Serbia, July 12, 1959; s. Stanisa Milijan and Vukosava Sava (Urosevic) V.; m. Zorica Momcilo Zivkovic, Dec. 22, 1984; children: Ivan, Teodora. MD, H.S. Medicine, Belgrade, Serbia, 1982, MSc, 1991, PhD, 1993. Resident Inst. Orthop. Surgery Banjica, Belgrade, 1982—89, chief ultrasound diagnostics, 1990—94, head paediat. orthop. dept., 1995—; asst. prof. Univ. H.S., Belgrade, 1989—96, prof., 1996—. Author: Sport Traumatology, 1993, Paediatric Hip, 1994, Paediatric Orthopaedics, 1999, General Orthopaedics, 2002, Special Orthopaedics, 2004; editor: Acta Orthopaedica Iugoslavica. Mem.: European Fedn. Orthop. Surgeons and Traumatologists (nat. del. 1997—), Internat. Fedn. Pediat. Orthop. Socs. (founder, nat. del.), European Paediat. Orthop. Soc. (nat. del. 1997—), World Orthop. Assn., Serb Orthop. and Traumatology Assn. (v.p. 2007—). Home: 9 Kneginje Zorke 11000 Belgrade Serbia Office: Inst Orth Surg Banjica 28 Mihajla Avramovica 11041 Belgrade Serbia Office Phone: 38111 6666447. Business E-Mail: zvukasin@beotel.net.

VUKSTA, MICHAEL JOSEPH, surgeon; b. Pitts., Apr. 25, 1926; s. Michael and Mary Sarah (Hanulya) V.; m. Dorothy Ann Bosak, Sept. 12, 1953; children: Patricia, Michael, Carol, Janet. BA, Youngstown State U., 1949; MD, Ohio State U., 1957. Diplomate Am. Bd. Surgery. Enlisted USN, advanced through grades to capt., 1974; intern St. Elizabeth Hosp., Youngstown, Ohio, resident in gen. surgery, 1958-62; pvt. practice gen. surgery Youngstown, 1962-89; head blue team surgery Oak Knoll U.S. Naval Hosp., Oakland, Calif., 1989-93; assoc. prof. surgery NEOUCOM. Capt. USN retired. Fellow ACS, Am. Coll. Sports Medicine, Southwestern Surg. Congress; mem. Nat. Athletic Trainers Assn. (advisor). Byzantine Catholic. Home: 131 Lovett Pl Pensacola FL 32506-5265 E-mail: mvukie@aol.com.

VULIC, DUSKO, cardiologist, medical researcher; b. Banja Luka, Bosnia-Herzegovina, Apr. 21, 1960; s. Bosko and Stoja Vulic; m. Branka Kragulj, Jan. 20, 1990; children: Sonja, Sasa. MD, Med. Faculty, 1978; specialist in Internal Medicine, Mil. Med. Acad., 1989—93; student in Cardiology, Med. faculty, 1995—97; PhD, Sch. Medicine Belgrade, Serbia, 2005. Cardiologist Assn. of Med. Drs., 2001. Head of ctr. for med. rsch. Ctr. for med. rsch., Med. electronics, Banja Luka, Serbia and Montenegro, 1987—90; coord. of sci. work Ctr. for Med. Rsch., Med. Electronics, Banja Luka, Bosnia-Herzegovina, 1990—95; head of the cardiology unit Ctr. of Med. Rsch., Banja Luka, Bosnia-Herzegovina, 1995—; nat. coord. for prevention cardiovasc. disease Ministry of Health Care Republic of Srpska, Banja Luka, Bosnia-Herzegovina, 1999—. Dir. Found. of Health and Heart, Banja Luka, Bosnia-Herzegovina, 1999—. Mem. Healthcare Found., Banja Luka, Bosnia-Herzegovina, 1998—2000. Fellow: European Soc. of Cardiology (licentiate; nat. coord. European guidelines 2003—06); mem.: Serbian Acad. Scis. and Arts (coun. cardiovascular pathology), Acad. Scis. and Arts Rep. Srpska (coun. cardiovascular pathology), Working Group Epidemiology and Prevention European Soc. of Cardiology (assoc.), European Arteriosclerosis Soc. (assoc.), European Assn. Cardiovascular Prevention and Rehab., Working Group of Epidemiology and Prevention World Hear Fedn. Home: Kralja Alfonsa XIII 43 Republika Srpska Banja Luka 78000 Bosnia-Herzegovina Office: Center for Med Rsch Medelectron Vuka Karadzica 6 Republika Srpska Banja Luka 78000 Bosnia-Herzegovina Office Phone: 38751241239. Office Fax: 38751215075; Home Fax: 38751217979. Business E-Mail: dule@blic.net.

VULPOI, CARMEN, physician, educator; b. Iasi, Romania, Nov. 22, 1956; MD, U. Medicine Iasi, 1983. Prof. U. Medicine and Pharmacy Gr.T.Popa, 2007—. Fellow: Soc. Romana de Endocrinologie; mem.: European Thyroid Assn., Soc. Francaise d'Endocrinologie, Endocrine Soc. Avocations: literature, music. Office: Blvd Independentei nr 1 Iasi 700111 Romania Office Phone: +40723204603. Office Fax: +40232229940. E-mail: c.vulpoi@yahoo.fr.

VUORI, TERO, psychologist, vision specialist, researcher; s. Urho and Raila Vuori; m. Anna Peltola, Dec. 5, 1998; children: Tiitus, Taavi, Toivo. BA, U. Helsinki, Finland, 2003, MS, 2002. Cert. legalized psychologist Health Care Supervision Ctr., Finland, 2002. Asst. psychologist Helsinki U. Ctrl. Hosp., 2000—01; cons. adult edn. Adulta Inc., Helsinki, 1999—2001; imaging specialist Nokia Tech. Platforms, Helsinki, 2001—. Cpl. coastal arty., 1995—96, Hanko, Finland. Mem.: Sigchi Finland, Finnish Psychol. Assn., ACM, Internat. Soc. Optical Engring., IS&T, SID. Lutheran. Achievements include patents pending for image adjustment with tone rendering curve. Avocations: travel, gardening, trivia. Office: Nokia Itämerenkatu 11 Helsinki 00180 Finland Office Fax: 358718037135.

VUORISTO, MERI-SISKO KRISTIINA, oncologist, consultant; b. Isojoki, Finland, Apr. 2, 1958; d. Pentti and Aira Haavisto; m. Esko Vuoristo, Aug. 27, 1988. Lic. in medicine, U. Turku, Finland, 1984; splty. degree in oncology and radiotherapy, U. Tampere, Finland, 1992, PhD, 1996. Cons. oncologist Tampere U. Hosp., 1992—. Contbr. articles to profl. jours. Mem.: EORTC Melanoma Group, Finnish Melanoma Study Group (chair 1997—2004), Finnish Soc. Oncology. Avocations: literature, ballet, cats. Office: Tampere U Hosp Dept Oncology PL 2000 33521 Tampere Finland

VUPPALAPATI, GUNASEKAR, plastic surgeon, registrar; b. Kodivalasa, India, June 25, 1972; s. Varadarajulu Naidu and Dorasaniamma Vuppalapati; m. Rajani Chirumamilla, Dec. 4, 1998; 1 child, Nirmitha. MB BS, MR Med. Coll., Gulbarga, 1994; MS in Gen. Surgery, Coimbatore Med. Coll., India, 1999; MChir in Plastic Surgery, Stanley Med. Coll., Chennai, India, 2002. Ho. surgeon Krishna Rajendra Hosp., Mysore, India, 1994—95; sr. ho. surgeon Coimbatore Med. Coll. Hosp., 1996—99; registrar Inst. for Rsch. and Rehab. Hand, Dept. Plastic Surgery Stanley Hosp., Chennai, India, 2000—02; cleft fellow Sri Ramachandra Cleft and Craniofacial Ctr., Chennai, 2002—02; sr. ho. officer Royal Preston (Eng.) Hosp., 2002—03; registrar St. Andrews Centre for Plastic Surgery and Burns, Chelmsford, England, 2003—05; sr. clin. fellow Queen Victoria Hosp., East Grinstead, England, 2005—. Contbr. articles to profl. jours. Fellow: Royal Coll. Surgeons Edinburgh (licentiate). Hindu. Achievements include discovery of Commissural Artery of Digital Webspace; design of Islanded Tripier flap; patents pending for In Vivo Tissue Engineering. Office: Queen Victoria Hospital Holtye Road East Grinstead RH19 3DZ England Office Fax: 0044 1342 414122. Personal E-mail: guna@doctor.com. Business E-Mail: gunasekar.vuppalapati@qvh.nhs.uk.

VUYLSTEKE, ALAIN, anesthesiologist, researcher; b. Zweibrucken, Germany, Sept. 29, 1966; arrived in Eng., 1995; BSc, U. Notre Dame Paix, Namur, Belgium, 1987; MD, U. Cath. Louvain, Brussels, 1991, anesthesiology tng., 1998. Cons. Papworth Hosp. Nat. Health Svc. Trust, Cambridge, England, 1998—, dir. anesthesia rsch. unit, 1999—, dir. critical care unit, 2002—. Fellow: Royal Coll. Anesthetists; mem.: Faculty Intensive Care Medicine. Office: Papworth Hosp NHS Trust Papworth Everard CB23 3RG Cambridge England Office Phone: 44(0) 1480 830541. Fax: 44(0) 1480 364936. E-mail: alain@vuylsteke.net.

VYDELINGUM, NADARAJEN AMEERDANADEN, cell biologist, educator, researcher, health administrator; b. Curepipe, Mauritius, June 1, 1945; came to U.S., 1977, U.S. citizen, 1985; s. Vythilingum Francis Vydelingum and Mareeaya Paratian; m. Rosemary Dowland, Nov. 6, 1971 (div.); children: Natalie, Eric; m. Nancy Yurman, 2005. BS in Cell Biology with honors, Birkbeck London U., Eng., 1972, MS in Biochemistry, 1974; PhD in Clin. Biochemistry, St. Mary's Med. Sch., London, 1979; postgrad., Inst. Biology London U., 1990. Adj. asst. prof. cell biology U. Wis., Milw., 1979; asst. prof. medicine and pharmacology Med. Coll. Wis., Milw., 1979-86; dir. rsch. and surg. metabolism lab. Sloan-Kettering Cancer Ctr., NYC, 1986-91; health sci. adminstr. bioengring. and physiology NIH, Bethesda, Md., 1991—; core lab. dir. Gen. Clin. Rsch. Ctr. Med. Coll. Milw.; dep. dir. Nat. Cancer Inst., 2001—08, Ctr. to Reduce Cancer Health Disparities; biologist, health scientist admin. Nat. Cancer Inst., 2008—. Reviewer Health Sci. Consortium Peer Rev. Bd., Carrboro, NC, 1984—, for Sci. Book, Boston U.; peer reviewer Am. Diabetic Assn., 1989-96; faculty mem. Found. for the Advancement of Edn. in the Scis., NIH, 1993—; lectr. cell biology Johns Hopkins U., Balt., 1994-98. Contbr. articles to profl. jours. Am. heart Assn. fellow, 1979-81; NIH grantee, 1985—. Fellow: Soc. of Biology (UK) (charter mem.), Nat. Acad. Clin. Biochemistry, Royal Soc. Pub. Health; mem. Am. Assn. Cancer Rsch. (mem. sci. adv. bd.), Am. Diabetes Assn. (grantee 1982-84), NY Acad. Scis., Soc. Biology UK MSB, European Profl. Biologists, Math. Biology, Union Concerned Scientists, Am. Assoc. Advancement Sci., Am. Assn. Clin. Biochemistry, European Countries Biol. Assn. Democrat. Unitarian Universalist. Avocation: drums. Home: 17629 Prince Edward Dr Olney MD 20832-2140 Office: NIH 6130 Executive Blvd MSC 7315 Bethesda MD 20892-7315 Office Phone: 301-402-6837. Personal E-mail: drums12@verizon.net. Business E-Mail: vydelinn@mail.nih.gov.

VYUNOVA, TATIANA VLADIMIROVNA, neurochemist, chemist, biologist, researcher; b. Moscow, Mar. 20, 1980; d. Elena Pavlovna V'unova. MS in Chem. Tech. and Biotech., D. Mendeleyev U. Chem. Tech. Russia, 2003; PhD in Biotech., Moscow State Acad. Fine Chem. Tech., 2009. Jr. rsch. asst. Inst. Molecular Genetics, Russian Acad. Scis., Moscow, 2003—08, scientist, 2009—. Contbr. scientific papers to profl. jours. Achievements include research in regulatory peptides (neuropeptides) molecular mechanism and drug design. Avocations: yachting, travel, sports. Office: IMG RAS Kurchatova Sq 2 Moscow 123182 Russia Office Fax: 74991960216. Business E-Mail: vunova2@mail.ru.

WABBY, JAMES PATRICK, quality assurance professional, educator; b. Pitts., Apr. 20, 1976; s. James and Patricia Wabby. BSc in Biol. Scis., Duquesne U., 2000, MSc in Health Mgmt. Systems, 2002. HIPAA cons. C.C. Allegheny County, Pitts., 2002—03, adj. prof., 2003—04; clin. regulatory affairs and quality assurance Abbott Labs., Chgo., 2004—, sr. global compliance, 2008; auditor Abbott Vascular. Mem. bioethics oversight com. Abbott Labs., Chgo., 2004—, mem. human factors coun., 2004—; adj. prof. Robert Morris Coll. Ill., Chgo., 2005—. Mem. philanthropy team Abbott Labs., Pitts., 2004—; polit. campaign mgr. Dist. Justice, Pitts., 1998. Recipient Health Sci. award, Duquesne U., 2000. Mem.: Regulatory Affairs Profl. Soc., Am. Soc. Law, Medicine, and Ethics, Am. Health Lawyers Assn. Avocations: fishing, running, exercise, reading, travel. Home: 4783 Willow Dr Pittsburgh PA 15236

WACHTEL, MITCHELL STEVEN, pathologist; b. NYC, May 22, 1959; s. Herbert Leonard and Lenore Esther Wachtel; m. June Grace Wagner, July 20, 1984. BA in Chemistry, Columbia Coll., 1981; MD, U. Miami, 1985. Cert. anatomic and clin. pathology Am. Bd. Pathology, 1991. Resident New England Deaconess Hosp., 1985—89; fellowship Meml. Sloan Kettering Cancer Ctr., 1989—92; assoc. prof. Tex. Tech. health Scis. Ctr., Lubbock, 2004—, dir. cytology, 2004—05; asst. prof. Oregon Health Svcs. Ctr., UAML, 1992—94; pathologist Associated Pathologists Chartered, Las Vegas, 1994—97, Fair Fox Pathology Assocs., 1997—2000, Austin Pathology Assocs., 2000—04. Contbr. articles to profl. jours. Alt. del. Coll. Am. Pathologists, Chgo., 2003—05. Mem.: Alpha Omega Alpha. Achievements include research that proved Bayes' thoerem does not apply in certain situations; proof that grades on tabular and ductal carcinoma of the breast do not mean the game thing; the first statistically validity histologic model of mouse asthma. Office: TTUHSC-School of Medicine Dept Pathology STOP 8115 Lubbock TX 79430-8115 Office Fax: 806-743-2117. Personal E-mail: mitchellwachtel@msn.com. E-mail: mitchell.wachtel@ttuhsc.edu.

WÄCHTLER, MARTIN, internist, epidemiologist; D., U. Frankfurt, 1984. Diplomate U. of Frankfurt Main, 1983, specialist for internal medicine Bavarian Med. Assn., 1993, specialist for infectious diseases German Soc. for Infectious Diseases, 2003, Bavarian Assn. Physicians, 2006, cert. in hepatology Deutsche Gesellschaft Verdauungs und Stoffwechsel-Krankheiten, 2008. Resident German Heart Ctr., Munic, 1985—87, Munic Schwabing Hosp., Academic Tchg. Hosp. of U. of Munic, 1988—. Mem.: German Soc. of Infectious Diseases. Office: Munic Schwabing City Hosp Kölner Platz 1 Munic 80804 Germany Office Fax: 00498930683844. Personal E-mail: waechtler@extern.lrz-muenchen.de. Business E-Mail: martin.waechtler@kliniukm-muenchen.de.

WACHUKU, KAY VICTOR, mental health services professional, researcher; arrived in U.S., 1979, naturalized; s. S. A.J. Wachuku and Vidah Odor; m. Stephanie Lou Robison; children: Ejikay, Sonnia, Kyle, Klyde. BA, Hampton U., 1983; MA, So. U., 1985; PhD, Breining Inst., 2001. Prof. Bethune-Cookman Coll., Daytona Beach, Fla., 1985—90; dir. Oakwood Drug Tx Ctr., San Bernardino, Calif., 1990—96; substance abuse specialist Inland Empire Job Corps, San Bernardino, 1996—2002; assoc. dean ITT Tech. Inst., San Bernardino, 2003—. Cons. Inland Redevel. Found., San Bernardino, 1998—. Author: Relapse Prevention Workbook, 1999 (Dept. of Labor award, 2001), Anthology of Monographs on Addiction Studies, 2001, Marijuana Impaired Youths, 2003. Mem.: Calif. Assn. Alcohol and Drug Abuse Counselors (cert.). Achievements include design of youth drug treatment protocol for substance abuse. Avocations: swimming, martial arts, yoga, bodybuilding. Home: PO Box 87 San Bernardino CA 92402-0087 E-mail: orosi@verizon.net.

WACKER, WARREN ERNEST CLYDE, retired internist; b. Bklyn., Feb. 29, 1924; s. John Frederick and Kitty Dora (Morrissey) W.; m. Ann Romeyn MacMillan, May 22, 1948; children: Margaret Morrissey, John Frederick. Student, Georgetown U., 1946—47; MD, George Washington U., 1951; MA (hon.), Harvard U., 1968. Intern George Washington U. Hosp., 1951-52, resident in internal medicine, 1952-53; resident Peter Bent Brigham Hosp., Boston, 1953-55; Nat. Found. Infantile Paralysis fellow, 1955-57; investigator Howard Hughes Med. Inst., Boston, 1957-68; from faculty to prof. hygiene Harvard U., Cambridge, Mass., 1955-71, assoc. prof. medicine, 1968—71, acting master Mather House, 1974-75, acting master Kirkland House, 1975-76, master Cabot House, 1978—82; sr. med. cons. Risk Mgmt. Found., Cambridge, 1992—2011; Henry K. Oliver prof. hygiene emeritus Harvard U., Cambridge, 1995—. Dir. health svcs. Harvard U., Cambridge, 1971-89; vis. scholar St. Mary's Hosp. Med. Sch., 1964; vis. prof. U. Tel Aviv, 1987; chmn. bd. Applied Mgmt. Sys., Burlington, Mass., 1982-97, Millipore Corp., Bedford, Mass., 1971-94. Author: Magnesium and Man, 1981; sec., editl. adv. bd. Biochemistry, 1962-76; assoc. editor Magnesium; mem. editl. bd. Toxiogical and Environ. Chemistry, 1989-2006; contbr. articles to profl. jours. Vestryman St. Paul's Episc. Ch., Brookline, Mass., 1965-68, 76-79, 91-94; bd. dirs. Harvard Cmty. Health Plan, Boston, 1973-84, mem. fin. com., 1984-86, mem. corp., 1986-96; bd. dirs. Bishop Rhinelander Found., Cambridge, 1973-76, 78-84, Controlled Risk Ins. Co., 1976-78; pres. bd. overseers Peter Bent Brigham Hosp., Boston, 1979-80; trustee Brigham and Women's Hosp., Boston, 1980-89, Risk Mgmt. Found., 1979-92; mem. mgmt. bd. MIT, 1985-95; mem. corp. Mt. Auburn Hosp., Cambridge, 1986—2006; mem. adv. bd. hospitality program Episc. Diocese Mass., 1989-95. 1st lt. USAAF, 1942-45. Decorated Air medal, D.F.C., Liberation medal, Greece; named Disting. Alumnus, George Washington U., 1963; recipient Cert. of Merit, Soc. Magnesium Rsch., 1985. Mem. AMA, Am. Chem. Soc., Am. Soc. Biol. Chemistry, Am. Soc. Clin. Investigation, Mass. Med. Soc., ACP, Am. Coll. Health Assn. (pres. 1981, Boynton award 1986), Biochemistry Soc. (London), Am. Coll. Nutrition, Harvard Club (Boston), Sigma Xi, Alpha Omega Alpha. Home: 77 Pond Ave Apt 401 Brookline MA 02445

WACKYM, P. ASHLEY, otolaryngologist, educator; b. Balt., Dec. 25, 1957; BA in Chemistry, Calif. State U., 1980; MD, Vanderbilt U. Sch. Medicine, 1985. Asst. prof. UCLA Sch. Medicine, 1991—94; assoc. prof., chief ear svc. Mt. Sinai Sch. Medicine, 1994—98; John C. Koss prof., chmn., dept. otolaryngology and communication scis. Med. Coll. Wis., 1998—2009; v.p. rsch. Legacy Health, 2009—. Pres. Ear and Skull Base Inst., 2009. Recipient Edmund Prince Fowler award, Am. Laryngol., Rhinol. and Otol. Soc., Nicholas Torok Vestibular award, Am. Neurotology Soc. Fellow: ACS, Am. Acad. Pediat.; mem.: Am. Otol. Soc., Am. Acad. Otolaryngology-Head and Neck Surgery (Disting. Svc. award), Collegium Oto-Rhino-Laryngologicum Amicitae Sacrum. Avocations: kayaking, reading. Office: Ear and Skull Base Inst 1225 NE 2nd Ave Portland OR 97232 Office Fax: 503-233-8558. Business E-Mail: wackym@neurotology.org.

WADA, HIROSHI, engineering educator; b. Sendai, Japan, Jan. 18, 1949; s. Toyoji and Keiko Wada; m. Mieko Sato, May 2, 1977; children: Madoka, Ei. BA, Tohoku U., 1972, MA, 1974, PhD, 1977. With Tohoku U., Sendai, Japan. Dept. head Tohoku U., Sandai, Japan, 1994—95, 1997—98, 2006—07, 2008—; hon. prof. U. Queensland, 2004—. Recipient Disting. Scholarly Achievements award, Japan Soc. Mech. Engrs., 2003; grantee British Coun. Scholarship, UK, 1983—84, Human Frontier Sci. Program Orgn., 2003—06. Fellow: Japanese Soc. Mech. Engrs.; mem.: Assn. Rsch. Otolaryngology, Acoustical Soc. Am., Internat. Inst. Acoustics and Vibrations (dir. 2001—05), Internat. Soc. Audiology (com. mem. 1998, editor 2005—). Achievements include patents for US Patent No. 5,063,946. Avocations: tennis, skiing, cars. Home: 4109 Hachiman Aoba-ku Sendai 980-0871 Japan Office: Dept Bioengring and Robotics Tohoku U 6-6-01 Aoba-Yama Sendai 980-8579 Japan Home Phone: 81 22 272 1452; Office Phone: 81 22 795 6938. E-mail: wada@cc.mech.tohoku.ac.jp.

WADA, KEITA, medical educator; b. Yamagata, Japan, Mar. 30, 1971; MD, Teikyo U., 1996, PhD, 2002. Asst. prof. Teikyo U. Hosp., 2007—. Recipient Young Investigator's award, 5th Internat. Hepato-Pancreato-Biliary Surgery. Mem.: Pancreas Club. Avocation: golf. Office: 2-11-1 Kaga Itabashi Tokyo 1738605 Japan Office Fax: 81-3-5375-6097. Business E-Mail: wada@med.teikyo-u.ac.jp.

WADA, NORIHITO, surgeon; MD, Keio U., Tokyo, 1992, PhD, 2004. Lic. physician Japan, 1992. Intern Keio U. Hosp., 1995—97; resident dept. surgery, Sch. Medicine Keio U., 1997—2001; instr. surgery Keio U., 2005—. Fellow: ACS. Office: Keio Univ Dept Surg 35 Shinanomachi Tokyo Shinjuku-ku 160-8582 Japan Office Phone: 81-3-3353-1211.

WADA, TAKURO, medical educator; b. Ebetsu, Hokkaido, Japan, Jan. 29, 1960; married. MD, PhD, Sapporo Med. U., Hokkaido. Cert. med. dr. Japan, 1984. Asst. prof. Sapporo Med. U., 2000—. Office: Sapporo Med Univ S 1 West 16 Chuo-ku Sapporo Hokkaido 060-8543 Japan Office Fax: 011-641-6026. Business E-Mail: twada@sapmed.ac.jp.

WADDELL, WILLIAM JOSEPH, pharmacologist, toxicologist; b. Commerce, Ga., Mar. 16, 1929; s. Daniel and Lillian Marie (Vollrath) Waddell; m. Grace Carolyn Marlowe, Oct. 19, 1974; children: William Joseph, James Glenn, Martin Christie, Amy Allison. AB in Chemistry, U. N.C., 1951, MD, 1955. Postdoctoral rsch. fellow U. N.C. Sch. Medicine, 1955-58, asst. prof. pharmacology, 1958-62, asso. prof., 1962-72, assoc. prof. oral biology Dental Rsch. Ctr., 1967-69, prof., 1969-72, assoc. dir., 1968-72; prof. pharmacology U. Ky. Coll. Medicine, Lexington, 1972-77; prof., chmn. dept. pharmacology and toxicology U. Louisville, 1977-97, emeritus chmn., 1997—, prof. emeritus, 1998—. Centennial Alumni Disting. vis. prof. U. N.C. Sch. Medicine, 1979. Contbr. articles to profl. jours. Fellow: Acad. Toxicological Scis.; mem.: Soc. Toxicology, Soc. Exptl. Biology and Medicine, Internat. Soc. Study Xenobiotics, Am. Teratology Soc., Am. Physiol. Soc., Am. Soc. Pharmacology and Exptl. Therapeutics, Sigma Xi. Home: 14300 Rose Wycombe Rd Prospect KY 40059-9024 Office: U Louisville Dept Pharmacology Louisville KY 40292-0001 Office Phone: 502-228-4220. Business E-Mail: bwaddell@louisville.edu.

WADDEN, THOMAS ANTONY, psychologist, educator; b. Richmond, Va., Sept. 3, 1952; s. Thomas Antony Jr. and Mary Lloyd (Cradock) W.; m. Jan Robin Linowitz, Nov. 11, 1984; children: David Joseph, Michael James, Steven Zachary. AB magna cum laude, Brown U., 1975; PhD, U. NC, 1981; MA (hon.), U. Pa., 1994. Psychology intern Boston VA Med. Ctr., 1980-81; instr. in psychology U. Pa. Sch. Medicine, Phila., 1981-82, asst. prof. psychology, 1982-87, assoc. prof. psychology, 1987-91, prof. psychology, 1994—; prof. psychology, dir. clin. tng. Syracuse U., NY, 1992-93. Clin. dir. Obesity Rsch. Group, U. Pa., Phila., 1983-91, dir. Ctr. for Weight and Eating Disorders, 1994—; dir. Ctr. for Health and Behavior, Syracuse U., 1992-93. Author (with K.D. Brownell): LEARN Program for Weight Control Behaviour Therapy, 1998; assoc. editor: Annals of Behavioral Medicine, 1990—93, Obesity, 2007—, mem. editl. bd.: Internat. Jour.

Eating Disorders Health Psychology, Internat. Jour. Obesity, Jour. Cons. and Clin. Psychology, Obesity Rsch.; editor (with T.B. Vanltallie): Treatment of the Seriously Obese Patient, 1992; editor: (with A.J. Stunkard) Obesity: Theory and Therapy, 1993, Handbook of Obesity Treatment, 2002; editor: (with A.J. Stunkard & R.I. Berkowitz) Obesity: A Guide for Mental Health Professionals, 2005; contbr. chapters to books; writer: numerous sci. papers; editor: Surgery of obesity and related disorder. Recipient Nat. Rsch. Svc. award NIMH, 1983-85, Rsch. Scientist Devel. award, 1987-91, 94-2000, Midcareer Investigator award in patient oriented rsch., 2003—. Mem. APA, Soc. Behavioral Medicine (bd. dir. 1987-90), Assn. for Advancement of Behavior Therapy (New Rschr. award 1986), Acad. Behavioral Medicine, Obesity Soc. (v.p. 2003-04, pres. 2005-06), Germantown Cricket Club, Cosmos Club, Phi Beta Kappa, Sigma Xi. Democrat. Avocations: squash, music. Office Phone: 215-746-5046. Business E-Mail: wadden@mail.med.upenn.edu.

WADE, ESTELLE B., psychologist, psychoanalyst; b. Bklyn., July 20, 1938; d. David and Selma Jobyna Schwartz; m. Donald E. Wade (div.); m. Alan L. Cantor. BA magna cum laude, Clark U., 1959; MA, Brandeis U., 1961; PhD, Columbia U., 1971. Lic. psychologist NY, 1972, cert. profl. qualification psychology Assn. State Provincial Bds., 2001; bd. cert. found. fellow Am. Coll. Advanced Practice Psychologists, 1999. Postdoctoral fellowship in psychoanalysis Post-grad. Ctr. Mental Health, NYC, 1980—83; counselor Inst. Crippled & Disabled, NYC, 1961—62, N.Y.C. Dept. Hosps., Bklyn., Queens, 1962—65; psychology intern VA, NYC, 1966—68; tchg. asst. Columbia U., NYC, 1968—69; lectr. psychology CUNY, 1969—70; staff psychologist Queens County Neuropsychiatric Inst., Jackson Heights, 1969—71, chief psychologist, 1971—81; supervising psychologist Fifth Ave. Ctr. Psychotherapy, NYC, 1981—84; pvt. practice psychoanalysis & psychotherapy NYC, 1977—. Host several radio programs, 1971—75. Singer: Amato Opera Chorus, 1976—77. Mem. Pinewoods Folk Music Soc., 1966—75, program chair, 1971—75; mem. Queens Ind. Democrats, Jackson Heights, 1967—69, Sloop Clearwater-NYC Chapter, 1969—75, program chair, 1973—75. Mem.: APA (life; program chair divsn. independent practice 1980—81, psychologist psychoanalyst practitioner, divsn. psychoanalysis 1984—), NY State Psychological Assn. (emeritus), Nat. Register Health Svc. Providers Psychology (platinum registrant 1994), Phi Beta Kappa (hon. Honor Roll 2010). Democrat. Jewish. Avocations: classical music, opera, reading, walking. Office: 141 E 55th St Ste 9B New York NY 10022 Office Phone: 212-935-1213.

WADE, NATHANIEL G., psychology professor; b. Pa., Feb. 9, 1972; BA, Wheaton Coll., 1994; PhD, Va. Commonwealth U., 2003. Assoc. prof. Iowa State U., 2003—. Recipient Margaret Gorman Early Career Rsch. award, Divsn. 36 of APA; grant, Fetzer Inst. Mem.: APA. Avocation: soccer. Office: W112 Lagomarcino Hall Ames IA 50011 Business E-Mail: nwade@iastate.edu.

WADLINGTON, WALTER JAMES, law educator; b. Biloxi, Miss., Jan. 17, 1931; s. Walter and Bernice (Taylor) Wadlington; m. Ruth Miller Hardie, Aug. 20, 1955; children: Claire, Charlotte, Ian(dec.), Susan, Derek Alan. AB, Duke U., 1951; LLB, Tulane U., 1954. Bar. La. 1954, Va. 1965. Pvt. practice, New Orleans, 1954—55, 1958—59; asst. prof. Tulane U., 1960—62; mem. faculty U. Va., 1962—, prof law, 1964—, James Madison prof., 1970—2002, James Madison prof. emeritus, 2002—, prof. legal medicine Med. Sch., 1979—2002, Harrison Found. rsch. prof., 1990—92. Tutor civil law U. Edinburgh, Scotland, 1959—60; vis. Tazewell Taylor prof. law Coll. William and Mary, 1986; dir. med. malpractice program Robert Wood Johnson, 1985—91, mem. adv. com. clin. scholars program, 1989—97; chmn. nat. adv. bd. Improving Malpractice Prevention and Compensation Sys., 1994—98; disting. health law tchr. Am. Soc. Law, Medicine and Ethics, 1988; trustee-at-large Edn. Commn. Fgn. Med. Grads., 1995—2003. Author (with O. Brien): Cases and Materials on Domestic Relations, 1970, 6th edit., 2007, Family Law in Perspective, 2001; author: 2d edit., 2007; author: (with Waltz and Dworkin) Cases and Materials on Law and Medicine, 1980; editor-in-chief: Tulane U. Law Rev., 1953—54; author (with Davis, Scott, and Whitebread): Children in the Legal System, 3rd edit., 2004; author: 4th edit., 2009. Fulbright scholar, U. Edinburgh, 1959—60. Home: 1620 Keith Valley Rd Charlottesville VA 22901-3018 Office: U Va Sch Law 580 Massie Rd Charlottesville VA 22903-1738 Office Phone: 434-293-5261. Personal E-mail: wjwadlington@gmail.com. Business E-Mail: wjw@virginia.edu.

WAGA, JANINA JADWIGA, ophthalmologist; b. Warsaw, Oct. 16, 1952; MD, U. Lund, 1977, PhD, 1999. Cert. profl. musician clarinete & saxophone. Sr. physician, sr. staff mem. dept. ophthalmology U. Hosp. Skåne, 1980—. Avocation: violin. Home: Hövadsvägen 19 Veberöd Skåne 247 60 Sweden Business E-Mail: janina.waga@med.lu.se.

WAGATSUMA, KENJI, physician, director; b. Miyagi, Mar. 23, 1963; MD, Jikei U., PhD, 1988. Dir., divsn. interventional cardiology Toho U. Omori Med. Ctr., 2003—. Fellow: Soc. Cardiovasc. Angiography and Interventions. Office: 6-11-1 Omori-nishi Ota-ku Tokyo 143-8541 Japan Office Fax: 81-3-3761-5405. Business E-Mail: kwaga@med.toho-u.ac.jp.

WAGHMARE, LALITBHUSHAN SHRIKRISHNA, medical association administrator; b. Kharagpur, India, July 1, 1977; MBBS, NKP SIMS Nagpur U., 1999; MD, Govt. Med. Coll., Nagpur, 2004. Assoc. prof., physiology Datta Meghe Inst. Med. Scis., 2008, dir., inovations, 2009—. Recipient B. C. Roy award, Med. Coun. India. Mem.: Am. Physiology Soc. Office: Datta Meghe Inst Med Sci Nagpur Maharashtra 440022 India Office Fax: 91-712-2245318. Personal E-mail: drlalitwaghmare@rediffmail.com.

WAGNER, ANNETTE M., dermatologist, surgeon; b. Halifax, Nova Scotia, Can., Sept. 14, 1960; d. Ronald Clarence and Thelma May Dillman; children: Hadley Ann, Kirstin Laurel, Michela Jean, Charles Norman, Madison Leah, Gavin Lewis. BSc, U. Calgary, Alberta, Can., 1984; MDCM, McGill U., Montreal, Quebec, Can., 1988. Cert. in pediat. Tucson, 1997, in dermatology 1995, in pedait. dermatology 2006. Dir. pediats. dermatol. surgery Children's Meml. Hosp., Chgo., 1994—, attending physician, 1994—; intern. pediat. U. Ariz., 1988—89, resident pedait., 1989—91, resident dermatalogy, 1991—94. Clin. practice dir. Childrens Meml. Hosp., Chgo., 1996—98. Office: Childrens Meml Hosp 2300 Children's Plz Box 107 Chicago IL 60524 Office Fax: 708-836-4805; Home Fax: 773-327-3448. *

WAGNER, AUREEN PINTO, psychologist, educator; d. Baptist and Winifred Pinto; m. Scott C. Wagner, June 25, 1994; 2 children. BA, St. Agnes Coll., Mangalore, India, 1981; MA, Mysore U., India, 1983; PhD, U. Iowa, 1989. Lic. psychologist NY. Clin. intern Yale U. Child Study Ctr., New Haven, 1988—89; postdoctoral fellow Brown U., Providence, 1989—91; asst. prof. psychiatry/psychology U. Rochester (NY) Sch. Medicine and Dentistry, 1991—98; founder, dir. Lighthouse Press, Inc., Rochester, 1998—2006, The Anxiety Wellness Ctr., Rochester, 2006—; clin. assoc. prof. neurology U. Rochester (NY) Sch. Medicine and Dentistry, 2003—. Mem. profl. adv. bd. Tourette Syndrome Assn. Rochester, 1997—; dir. The Anxiety Wellness Ctr., Rochester, 2006—; mem. sci. adv. bd. Obsessive Compulsive Found., Boston, 2005—; internat. spkr. in field. Author: Up and Down the Worry Hill: A Children's Book about Obsessive-Compulsive Disorder and its Treatment, 2000 (Reader's Preference Editors' Choice Award, 2003), What to Do When Your Child Has Obsessive-Compulsive Disorder: Strategies and Solutions, 2002, (manual) Treatment of OCD in Children and Adolescents, 2003, Worried No More: Help and Hope for Anxious Children, 2002, 2d edit., 2005. Grantee J.N. Tata scholar, Tata Found., Bombay, India, 1984—88; Lady Meherbai Tata scholar, Lady Meherbai Tata Edn. Trust, Bombay, India, 1984—88, Robert J. Haggerty Rsch. scholar, U. Rochester Sch. of Medicine, 1995, Nat. Merit scholar, Govt. of the State of Karnataka, India, 1981—83. Mem.: APA, Genesee Valley Psychol. Assn. (chmn. newsletter com. 2005—), Anxiety Disorders Assn. Am., Obsessive Compulsive Found. Roman Catholic. Achievements include development of conceptual framework to explain treatment of OCD to children. Avocations: travel, gardening, choral music, walking. Office: 2000 Regency Pky # 204 Cary NC 27518 Office Phone: 919-371-8230. Office Fax: 919-469-8639. Personal E-mail: awagner@anxietywellness.com.

WAGNER, DONALD BERT, health facility administrator; b. York, Pa., July 27, 1930; s. Bert Daniel and Mary Elizabeth (Roelke) W.; m. Janet Louise Bankert, July 12, 1952; children: Kimberly, Susan, David, John. Student, Franklin & Marshall, 1948-50; BS in Phys. Therapy, Columbia U., 1952; MHA, Baylor U., 1960. Commd. 2d lt. USAF, 1952, advanced through grades to brig. gen., 1982; physical therapist Randolph AFB, San Antonio, 1952-55; asst. adminstr. USAF/RAF S. Ruislip, London, adminstr. USAF/RAF Bentwaters, Ipswich, England, 1955-58; various adminstrv. roles USAF Hosps. and Commands, Europe and U.S., 1958-73; dep. comdr. USAF Sch. Health Care Sci., Wichita Falls, Tex., 1973-75; adminstr. Wilford Hall Med. Ctr., San Antonio, 1975 79; chief med. svc. corps Office Surgeon Gen. USAF, San Antonio, 1979-82; dep. surgeon gen. USAF Med. Svc. Ctr., San Antonio, 1981-82, ret., 1982; adminstr., assoc. v.p. M. D. Anderson/U. Tex. Cancer Ctr., Houston, 1982-85; chief exec. officer Meml. Southwest Hosp., Houston, 1985-91; v.p. Meml. Hosp. System, Houston, 1985 91, internal cons., interim hosp. CEO, 1991—2005; mem. adv. bd. Grad. Program in Healthcare Adminstrn. Texas Women's U., Houston. Adj. prof. Baylor and Trinity U., San Antonio, 1975-82, assoc. prof. U. Houston, St. Louis U., 1982 88, CEO Woodlands Hosp., Angleton-Danbury Hosp., Prevention and Recovery Ctr., Bellville Hosp., MHHS Long Term Acute Care Hosp., MH S.E. Hosp.; chief operating officer St. Joseph Med. Ctr.; cons., El Salvador, Nicaragua, China, Saudi Arabia, Japan, Korea, 1991-02. Bd. dirs. Hospice at the Med. Ctr., 1982-2001, Child Advocates, Houston, 1985-89, Kidney Found., Houston, 1985-88, Westland YMCA, Houston, 1985-88, 90-94, Ft. Bend County YMCA, 1998-03, Greater Houston Hosp. Coun., 1983-87, Sam Houston area Alzheimer's Assn. 1990-94; mem.n. external adv. bd. Sch. Allied Health, U. Tex. Med. Br.; mem. adv. bd. gradrogram healthcare adminstrn. Tex. Women's U., Houston. Named Disting. Alumnus Baylor U. Program in Healthcare Adminstrn., 1993. Fellow Am. Coll. Healthcare Execs. (life fellow, edn. com., ethics com., comm. com.), Royal Soc. Health; mem. Am. Hosp. Assn. (bd. dirs. hosp. rsch. and edn. found. 1990—), Tex. Hosp. Assn., Assn. Mil. Surgeons U.S. (Am. coll. healthcare exec. Ray E. Brown award 1982, Lifetime Achievement award, 2009, Outstanding Sr. Level Healthcare Exec. Regents award 1991, Regents Lifetime Achievement award 2004), Am. Mgmt. Soc. Republican. Methodist. Avocation: music. Home and Office: 1746 Carriage Way Sugar Land TX 77478-4201 Home Phone: 281-980-5613.

WAGNER, EDWARD HARRIS, epidemiologist, educator; b. Buffalo, 1940; AB, Princeton U., 1961; MD, SUNY: Buffalo, 1965; MPH, U. NC, Chapel Hill, 1972. Cert. Internal Medicine, 1972. Intern Buffalo Gen. Hosp., 1965—66; asst. dir. VA outpatient dept. McDonald Army Hosp., Ft. Eustis, Va., 1967—68; resident SUNY Buffalo, 1968—70, chief tchg. fellow, 1970—71; instr. medicine and family medicine U. NC, Chapel Hill, 1971—72, asst. prof. epidemiology and medicine, 1972—78, assoc. prof. epidemiology and medicine, 1978—83, dep. dir. health services rsch. ctr., 1980—83, prof. epidemiology and medicine, 1983, clin. prof. epidemiology, 1984—, assoc. Cecil G. Sheps Ctr. Health Services Rsch., 1995—, adj. prof. epidemiology, 2000—; dir. Ctr. Health Studies Group Health Coop. of Puget Sound, Seattle, 1983—98, dir. W.A. MacColl Inst. Healthcare Innovation, 1992—; prof. health services U. Wash. Sch. Pub. Health and Cmty. Medicine, Seattle, 1984—. Bn. surgeon US Army, 1966—76, Vietnam. Recipient Gilbert S. Beck award, 1965, Cecil G. Sheps Disting. Investigator award, U. NC, 1988, John Atkinson Ferrell prize, 1999, Disting. Alumnus award, 1999, Tyroler Alumni award, 2008, Edward Henderson award, Am. Geriatrics Soc., 2004, Pres.'s award, NY Health and Hospitals Corp., 2006, Health Care Quality award, Nat. Com. Quality Assurance, 2007, Picker award, Picker Inst., 2007. Fellow: ACP, Soc. Behavioral Medicine; mem.: Inst. Medicine, Am. Heart Assn., Assn. Teachers of Preventive Medicine, Internat. Epidemiologic Assn., Soc. Gen. Internal Medicine, Assn. Health Services Rsch., HMO Rsch. Network, Delta Omega, Alpha Omega Alpha. Office: 1730 Minor Ave Ste 1290 Seattle WA 98101 Office Phone: 206-287-2877. E-mail: wagner.e@ghc.org.

WAGNER, GERALDINE MARIE, nursing educator, consultant; b. Renton, Wash., Apr. 12, 1948; d. Ernest F. and Vera P. (Temiraeff) W. AA, Pasadena City Coll., 1970; BA cum laude, Calif. State U., Northridge, 1977; BSN, Calif. State U., LA, 1982; MEd summa cum laude, Azusa Pacific U., 1993. Cert. pub. health nurse, Calif. Dept. Health Svcs. In utilization mgmt. Blue Cross, Woodland Hills, Calif., 1987-88, Healthmarc, Pasadena, Calif., 1988-90; nursing educator, asst. dir. vocat. nursing program Casa Loma Coll., LA, 1991-92, dir. program planning and devel., and coord. continuing edn. Lake View Terrace, 1992-93; dir. vocal. nursing program Glendale (Calif.) Career Coll., 1994-95; with patient care rev. svcs. U. So. Calif. U. Hosp., LA, 1996—; med.-legal nurse cons., 2000—. Docent Mission La Purisima Concepcion. Capt. Nurse Corp, U.S. Army, 1979-84. Mem.: ASPCA, VFW, G.K. Chesterton Soc., Calif. Mission Studies Assn., Assn. for Women in Math., Fellowship Cath. Scholars, Computer Using Educators, Nat. Coun. Tchrs. Math., Am. Math. Soc., Blue Army Our Lady Fatima, Soc. Cath. Social Scientists, Mil. Officer Assn. Am., Assn. Hebrew Catholics, Order of Preachers, Inst. Religious Life, AMVETS, Res. Officers Assn. U.S., Army Nurse Corps. Assn., Cath. War Vets, History Channel Club, Disabled Am. Vets., Am. Legion, Sigma Theta Tau, Pi Lambda Theta. Roman Catholic. Home: 924 Rock Rose Ln Lompoc CA 93436 Office Phone: 805-735-3575. Personal E-mail: sistergeraldinemarie@comcast.net.

WAGNER, LORI A., medical educator; b. Jamestown, NY, Aug. 31, 1961; BS, U. Utah, 1984, PhD, 1993. Scientist Idaho Tech., 1999—2001; asst. prof. U. Utah, 2002—. Grant, NIH. Mem.: AAAS, Internat. Eosinophil Soc. Avocation: skiing. Office: 30 North 1900 East Salt Lake City UT 84132 Business E-Mail: lori.wagner@hsc.utah.edu.

WAGNER, MURIEL GINSBERG, nutrition therapist; d. Irving A. and Anna Ginsberg; 1 child, Emily Lucinda Faith. BA, MS, Wayne State U.; PhD, U. Mich. Registered dietitian. Nutritionist Merrill-Palmer Inst., Detroit; pvt. practice, nutritional therapist Southfield, Mich. Cons. select com. on nutrition U.S. Senate, Ford Motor Co., Dearborn, Mich., Detroit Dept. Consumer Affairs; adj. faculty mem. Wayne State U., Detroit, U. Mich., Dearborn. Author: (cookbook) Tun...ahhh; contbr. articles to profl. publs.; writer, publisher (newsletter) Eating Younger. Vol. Am. Heart Assn. of Mich.; also various local and nat. govtl. groups Recipient Outstanding Cmty. Svc. award Am. Heart Assn.; named Outstanding Profl., Mich. Dietetic Assn. Fellow Am. Dietetic Assn. (organizer Dial-A-Dietitian); mem. Am. Diabetes Assn. Avocations: cooking, recipe development, gardening. Office: 4000 Town Ctr Ste 8 Southfield MI 48075-1401 Home Phone: 248-548-3215; Office Phone: 248-350-1190.

WAGNER, PETER KARL, surgeon; b. Schankweiler, Germany, Mar. 8, 1949; s. Karl and Maria Wagner; m. Dr. Ingrid Steinbach; children: Eva-Maria, Tilmann. MD, Univ. Mainz, Germany, 1976; prof. of surgery (hon.), Univ. Marburg, Germany, 1989, Univ. Munich, 1994. Head physician Univ. Marburg, Dept. Surgery, 1987—93; chief surgeon Klinikum Rosenheim, Dept. Surgery, 1993—. Capt. Bd. of Health, Munich. Mem.: Berufsverband Chirurgie, Deutsche Gesellschaft Chirurgie. Roman Catholic. Avocations: music, gardening. Office: Klinikum Pettenkoferstr 10 D-83022 Rosenheim Germany Office Phone: 04908031-363201. E-mail: peter.wagner@kliro.de.

WAGNER, WOLFGANG, pharmaceutical industry executive; b. Hohenpeissenberg, Germany, June 29, 1950; s. Josef and Irmgard (König) W.; m. Karin Schuett, Dec. 23, 1997. MD & PhD, U. Munich, 1975; DiplPharmMed, FAPI, 1997. Med. dir. Duphar Pharma (Solvay Group), Hannover, Germany, 1984-91; internat. clin. dir. Solvay Pharms., Marietta, Ga., 1991-93; corp. med. dir. Solvay Human Health Divsn., Hannover, 1993-94; v.p. global drug safety and surveillance worldwide Solvay Pharmaceuticals, Hannover, 1995—; hon. prof. Albert-Schweitzer Internat. U., Geneva, 2001; prof. European Acad., Brussels, 2001—. Lectr. in med. ethics and clin. pharmacology. Contbr. to books and articles to profl. jours. Decorated Internat. Order of Merit. Fellow Faculty of Pharm. Medicine, Royal Colls. Physicians of U.K.; mem. Acad. Ethics in Medicine, Kennedy Inst. Ethics Georgetown U., World Order Sci., Culture, Edn. (cavalier), Internat. Diplomatic Acad. Avocation: music. Home: Schneewittchen Weg 23 D 30179 Hannover Germany Office: Solvay Pharmaceuticals Hans-Böckler-Allee 20 D-30173 Hannover Germany

WAH, ROBERT M., reproductive endocrinologist, obstetrician, gynecologist; b. Oreg., July 10, 1957; m. Debra Ann Wah; 1 child, Renee Megan. BA in Chemistry, U. Oreg.; MD, Oreg. Health Scis. U. Diplomate American Bd. Ob-gyn., cert. in reproductive endocrinology/infertility. Resident ob-gyn. Nat. Navel Med. Ctr., Bethesda, Md.; reproductive endocrinology fellowship Harvard Med. Sch./Brigham & Womens Med. Ctr., Boston; physician, instr. Nat. Naval Med. Ctr. in Md., Bethesda, Walter Reed Army Med. Ctr., Washington; assoc. chief info. officer Military Health Sys., US Dept. Def.; dep. nat. coord. for health info. tech. US Dept. Health & Human Svcs., Washington, 2005—06; v.p. pub. sector, chief med. officer Computer Scis. Corp. (CSC), Falls Church, Va., 2007—. Faculty Uniformed Svcs. U.Health Scis., Harvard Med. Sch., U. Calif., San Diego. Capt, USN Med. Corps. Named one of 50 Most Powerful Physician Execs. in US, Modern Physician/Modern Healthcare mags., 2008, 2009. Mem.: AMA (bd. trustees 2005—, chair bd. trustees 2011—), American Congress Ob-gyn., American Soc. Reproductive Medicine, Assn. Mil. Surgeons US (exec. adv. coun.), Oreg. Med. Assn., Med. Soc. Va. Office: CSC 3170 Fairview Park Dr Falls Church VA 22042 *

WAHABI, HAYFAA ABDELMAGEED, obstetrician, consultant; b. Khartoum, Sudan, Jan. 18, 1963; d. Abdelmageed Ahmed Wahabi and Suad Salih Abdelazim; m. Abdelmonim Ali Abdelrahman, Oct. 25, 1991; children: Lena Tasneem Abdelrahman, Alla Abdelrahman, Mohamed Abdelrahman. MS in Reproduction Tech., U. Nottingham, Eng., 1998; MS in Med. Edn., U. Maastricht, Netherlands, 2007. Tng. registrar Rochford Hosp., Southend On Sea, England, 1990—2000; cons. Nat. Gaurd Hosp., Riyadh, Saudi Arabia, 2000—, dir. women cmty. health project, 2005—, chairperson rsch. com., 2005—. Pres. sudan evidence-based medicine assn. Sudan Evidence-Based Medicine Assn., Khartoum, 2005—. Author: (cochrane systematic rev.) Cochrane Library (First Cochrane Rev. from Saudi Arabia, 2008); contbr. scientific papers. Fellow: Royal Coll. Obstetrican and Gynecologists (Eng.), Royal Coll. Obstetrican and Gynecologists (Edinburgh); mem.: Royal Coll. Obstetrican and Gynecologists (Eng.).

Achievements include development of women health community project with the establishment of secondery health care system in the national gaurd hospitals providing unique services of preconception and genetic counselling. Office: King Abdulaziz Med City Sheikh Jabir St Riyadh 11426 Saudi Arabia

WAHDAN, TAREK MOHAMED, director; b. Cairo, Sept. 3, 1961; Ph.D, Poitiers U., France, 1994. Assoc. prof. chemistry Suez Canal U., Egypt, 2005, vice dean student affairs, 2006—07; cultural and ednl. chancellor Egyptian Embassy, United Arab Emirates, 2007—11; dir. Am. U., Cairo, 2011—. Contbr. articles to profl. publs. Mem.: Sci. Syndicate (Cairo). Avocations: reading, swimming, football. Home: 30 Mahmoud Hasanen off Adelsalam Aref Mansoura Dakahlia 32654 Egypt Personal E-mail: tarekwahdan@yahoo.com.

WAHJOEPRAMONO, EKA JULIANTA, neurosurgeon, educator; MD, U. Med. Sch., Semarang, Indonesia, 1983; PhD in Neurosci, Hasanuddin U., Makassar, Indonesia; attending, Pelita Harapan U, Jakarta, Indonesia, 2006—. Cert. neurosurgery specialist Padjadjaran U., Med. Sch. Bandung, Indonesia, Indonesian Nat. Bd. Neurosurgery, 1994. Exec. com. mem. Asian Conf. Neurol. Surgeon, 1996—98; prof., chmn. dept. surgery, medical faculty Pelita Harapan U., dean med. faculty; founder Indonesian Brain Found.; founder, mem. World Acad. Neurol. Surgeons; chmn. Neurosci. Ctr. Siloam Hosps.; with com. & tng. edn. World Fedn. Neurosurg. Socs., skull-base com. mem.; treas. Asian Congress Neurol. Surgery; pres. Indonesia Soc. Neurorehab. and Neuroreconstrn. Editl. bd. mem. Jour. Neurosurgery, Asian Jour. Neurosurgery, Jour. Clin. Neurosci., Jour. Experimental And Clin. Medicine, Australasia Clin. Neurosci.; sr. adv. panel mem. World Neurosurgery; vis. prof. in fields. Contbr. scientific papers to profl. publs. Recipient Ksatria Bakti Husada Arutala, Ministry Health Republic of Indonesia. Mem.: Am. Assn. Neurosurgeons, Collegium Internat. Gero (sci. com. mem.), Indonesische Gesellschaft fur Medizine, Indonesia Soc. Gerontology, Indonesia Neurosurg. Soc., Internat. Skull Base Congress (sci. adv. com. mem. 2004), Asian Oceanian Skull-base Soc. (coun. mem., exec. mem.), Asian Congress Neurosurgery (del.), World Congress Neurol. Surgery, Indonesia Soc. Neurosurgeon, Indonesia Med. Assn., Japan Neurosurg. Soc. (hon.). Office: University Pelita Harapan Sch Medicine Siloam Hosps Dept Neurosurgery Jakarta 15811 Indonesia Office Fax: 62215460921. Business E-Mail: eka@siloamhospitals.com. E-mail: ekabrain@gmail.com.

WAHL, HANS GUENTHER, medical educator, director; b. Reutlingen, Baden-Wuerttemberg, Germany, Feb. 18, 1956; Diploma in Chemistry, U. Tübingen, 1990; PhD, U. Tuebingen, 1994, MD, 1998. Oberarzt Klinikum Fulda, Germany, 2000—02; asst. prof. Klinikum der Universitaet Marburg, Germany, 2002—. Grantee, Deutsche Forschungsgemeinschaft, 1998—2000; fellow Grad. Study U. of Kans., Gerhard Roesch Stiftung, 1979—80, In vivo studies, U. of Tex., Deutsche Gesellschaft fuer Klinische Chemie, 1994—95; scholar Studienfoerderung, Robert Bosch Stiftung, 1977—84, Studienstiftung des Deutschen Volkes, 1981—84.

WAHL, ROSEMARIE, biologist, educator; d. Arnold Spencer and Rosemary Doyle Wahl; m. Michael Leroy Tumlinson, May 31, 1992; m. Miroslav Synek (div.); children: Mary Rose Synek, Thomas Robert Synek. BS, MIT, 1956; MS, U. Chgo., 1961, PhD, 1967. Instr. U. Ill., Chgo., 1965—66; asst. prof. Tex. Christian U., Ft. Worth, 1967—72; assoc. prof. St. Mary's U., San Antonio, 1976—83, prof., 1983—, chair dept. biol. scis., 1979—2004. Vis. asst. prof. U. Tex., Austin, 1972—75; chief advisor health professions St. Mary's U., 1979—2004, chair premed./predental adv. com., 1979—2004. Mentor, advisor on biotechnology, mayor, city ofcl. City of San Antonio, 1984—95. Recipient Disting. Faculty award, St. Mary's U. Sch. Sci., Engring and Tech., 1986. Mem.: MIT Class 1956 (v.p. 2001—), Tex. Genetics Soc., Tex. Assn. Advisors for Health Professions (exec. com.), Am. Soc. Microbiology, Sigma Xi. Avocation: travel. Office: St Marys U Dept Biol Scis 1 Camino Santa Maria San Antonio TX 78228 Office Phone: 210-431-8064. Business E-Mail: rwahl@stmarytx.edu.

WAHL, SINDI, psychology professor; b. South Africa, Jan. 2, 1982; MEd in Psychology, Stellenbosch U., 2007. Project founder and coord. Macias Restis Support Programme Aids Orphans Kayamandi, 2007—08; ednl. psychologist Stellenbosch U., 2007—. Recipient Innovation prize, Ctr. Student Counselling and Devel. Office: Victoria St Stellenbosch 7600 South Africa Business E-Mail: swahl@sun.ac.za.

WAIBEL, JILL STEWART, dermatologist; b. Indpls., Apr. 28, 1970; BS, Ind. U., 2001; MD, Wright State U., 2001. Owner, physician Miami Dermatology and Laser Inst., 2010—. Faculty, voluntary U. Miami, 2008—11. Recipient Enhancement Pub. and Cmty. Edn. HIV Infection award, Surgeon Gen. Fellow: ASDS, ASLMS, AAD; mem.: WDS, AMA. Office: 7800 SW 87th Ave Miami FL 33173 Personal E-mail: jwaibelmd@aol.com.

WAID, THOMAS HENRY, physician, researcher, educator; b. Ashtabula, Ohio, May 21, 1949; s. Carl Thomas and Ruth Agusta Waid; m. Nancee Ann Bartlett; children: Ashley Nicole, Andrew McClellan. BS in Pharm., U. Cin.; MS; MD, U. Ky., Lexington. Cert. internal medicine, nephrology Am. Bd. Internal Medicine, 1985. Med. dir. kidney transplantation U. Ky. Med. Ctr., 1985—; prof. medicine U. Ky., 2000—. Med. dir. heart transplantation U. Ky. Med. Ctr., 1992—, med. dir. lung transplantation, 1992—, med. dir. pancreas transplantation, 1994—, med. dir. dialysis, 1996—2007. Recipient Lifetime Achievement award, Harbor HS, Chief Residents Faculty award, 1991, 1994—95. Mem.: Rho Chi Soc., Lexington Med. Soc. (svc. coun. chair. elect 2005—). Republican. Methodist. Achievements include research in immunosuppression. Avocations: golf, fishing, travel, ballroom dancing, water-skiing, antiques. Office: Univ Ky Med Ctr 800 Rose St C-347 Lexington KY 40536

WAILOO, KEITH ANDREW, historian, educator; BA in chem. engring., Yale U., 1984; MA, U. Pa., 1989, PhD in history and sociology of sci., 1992. From asst. prof. to prof. U. NC, Chapel Hill, 1992—2001; prof. history Rutgers U., New Brunswick, 2001—, prof. Inst. for Health, Health Care Policy, and Aging Rsch., 2001—, founding dir. Ctr. Race and Ethnicity, 2006—, Martin Luther King, Jr. prof. history, 2006—. Vis. prof. Harvard U., 1998—99. Author: Drawing Blood, 1997 (Arthur Viseltear award, Am. Pub. Health Assn., 1997), Dying in the City of the Blues, 2001 (Lillian Smith book award, Southern Regional Coun., 2002, NJ Coun. Humanities Honor book, 2002, Am. Polit Sci. Assn. award, 2002, Susanne Glasscock Humanities book award, 2003, William H. Welch medal, Am. Assn. History of Medicine, 2005); co-author (with Stephen Pemberton): The Troubled Dream of Genetic Medicine, 2006; co-editor: A Death Retold, 2006. Fellow Ctr. Advanced Study Behavioral Sciences, Stanford U., 2006—07; Investigator award, Robert Wood Johnson Found., 2002—05, Centennial fellow in the history of sci., James S. McDonnell Found., 1999—2008. Mem.: Inst. Medicine, Assn. for the History of Medicine, Am. Hist. Assn., Orgn. Am. Historians. Office: Inst Health Health Care Policy and Aging Rsch Rutgers U 30 Coll Ave New Brunswick NJ 08901 also: Dept History Rutgers U 16 Seminary Pl New Brunswick NJ 08901 Office Phone: 732-932-8419. Office Fax: 732-932-1358. E-mail: kwailoo@rci.rutgers.edu, kwailoo@ifh.rutgers.edu, kwailoo@history.rutgers.edu.

WAINBERG, MARK ARNOLD, medical educator, director; b. Montreal, Quebec, Canada, Apr. 21, 1945; s. Abe Wainberg and Fay Haffner; children: Zev, Jonathan. PhD, Columbia U., NY, 1972. Cert. med. rschr. McGill U., 1972. Assoc. prof. McGill U. AIDS Ctr., Montreal, 1974—89, prof. & dir., 1989—. Pres. Internat. AIDS Soc., Geneva, 1998—2000. Contbr. scientific papers. Recipient honor, Officer Order of Canada, Govt. of Can., 2001, Officer Order of Que., Govt. of Que., 2005, Legion of honor, Govt. of France, 2008, Lifetime Achievement award, AIDS Soc. India, 2009. Fellow: Royal Soc. Can., Coll. Physicians & Surgeons Can. (hon.). Home: 6506 Fern Rd Montreal PQ Canada H4V 1E4 Office: McGill University AIDS Ctr Jewish Gen Hosp 3755 Cote Ste Catherine Montreal PQ Canada H3T 1E2 Office Phone: 514-340-8307. Business E-Mail: mark.wainberg@mcgill.ca.

WAINBLATT, MARK EFRAIM, pediatrician, hematologist, oncologist; Studied, Yeshiva U., 1976. Cert. pediatric hematology-oncology, diplomate Am. Bd. of Pediatrics. Resident Bronx Mcpl. Hosp. Ctr., 1977—79; fellow Children's Hosp. of LA, 1979—81; with Nassau Univ. Med. Ctr.; prin. investigator children's oncology group Winthrop Univ. Hosp., chief pediatric hematology-oncology divsn. Mem.: Am. Soc. for Pediatric Hematology, Am. Soc. of Clin. Oncologists, Am. Soc. for Hematology. Office: Winthrop University Hospital Ste 460 120 Mineola Blvd Mineola NY 11501 Office Phone: 516-663-9400. Office Fax: 516-663-9482.

WAINSCOTT, CYNTHIA, medical association administrator; BA, Met. State Coll., Denver. Edn. dir. Mental Health Assn. Minn., 1987—90; exec. dir. Nat. Mental Health Assn. Ga., 1990—2003; mem. bd. dirs. Mental Health America (formerly Nat. Mental Health Assn.), Alexandria, former bd. chair, acting pres., CEO, 2006. Mem., nat. mental health adv. coun. Ctr. for Mental Health Svcs., 2000—04; adv. coun. Ga. Gov. Mental Health, Mental Retardation and Substance Abuse Adv. Coun.; drug utilization rev. bd. Ga. Medicaid Agy.; bd. dir. Ga. Parent Support Network; adv. com. Fuqua Ctr. for Late Life Depression, Emory Univ., Ga. Cmty. Trust. Mem.: Ga. Prevention Credentialing Consortium (founding mem.).

WAINWRIGHT, MARK STEPHEN, pediatric neurologist, educator; s. William Wainwright and Kathleen MacCormack; m. Natalie Eve Silberman, Jan. 13, 1982; children: Callista, Sinead. MD, PhD, U. Chgo., 1995. Diplomate Am. Bd. Psychiatry and Neurology, Inc., cert. in child neurology. Assoc. prof. Northwestern U. Feinberg Sch. Medicine, Chgo., 2000—; dir., ctr. interdisciplinary rsch. pediatric critical illness Children's Meml. Hosp., Chgo., 2007—; dir. Pediatric Neurocritical Care Program, 2007—. Achievements include research in role of inflammation in the mechanisms of acute brain injury in children and research and clinical practice in pediatric critical care neurology. Office: Children's Memorial Hosp no 51 2300 Children's Plaza Chicago IL 60614 Office Phone: 773-880-4921. Business E-Mail: m-wainwright@northwestern.edu.

WAISMAN, WARNER, pharmacist; b. NYC, Apr. 22, 1931; s. Abraham Herbert and Pearl (Brand) W. BS in biochemistry, BS in sociology, Queens Coll., 1955; BS in pharmacy, Bklyn. Coll. Pharmacy, 1958. Registered pharmacist, N.Y., La. Pharmacist Schreir Pharmacy, NYC, 1962-63; pharmacist Dew Drug, NYC, 1963-66, Raysol Pharmacy, NYC, 1966-70, 72-75, Bellevue Hosp., NYC, 1970-72, Bronx State Hosp., NYC, 1975-78, Coler Hosp., NYC, 1978-95, Hamtini Pharmacy & Surg. Supplies, 2008—. Recipient Outstanding Contbr. award, Remington Registry Healthcare & Pharm. Coms., 2011. Democrat. Jewish. Home: 132-15 Rico Pl Ozone Park NY 11417-2017 Office: Hamtini Pharmacy & Surg Supplies 615 Seneca Ave Ridgewood NY 11385 Office Phone: 718-326-3673. Office Fax: 718-326-3675.

WAISWA, PETER, healthcare educator; b. Iganga, Uganda, Aug. 29, 1971; Degree in medicine, Mbarara U. Sci. and Tech., 1989; PhD in medicine, Karolinska Inst., Sweden, Makerere U., Uganda, 2010. Intern physician Rubaga Hosp., Uganda, 1997—98; nat. health officer Uganda Red Cross Soc., 1998—2000; med. officer Ministry of Health, Iganga Dist. Health Svcs., 2000—08; lectr. Makerere U. Sch. Public Health and Karolinska Inst., 2008—; health sys. expert, maternal and child health. Bd. vice chair Uganda Devel. and Health Assocs., 2008—. Mem.: Reproductive Health Uganda (bd. chairperson, Busoga region 2007—10), Uganda Red Cross Soc. (bd. chmn., Iganga Br. 2007—10), Uganda Med. Assn. Office: Karolinska Inst Nobels Väg Stockholm Sweden Business E-Mail: pwaiswa@musph.ac.ug.

WAIT, SCOTT D., neurosurgeon; MD, East Carolina U. Resident in neurosurgery St. Joseph's Hosp. & Med. Ctr. Office: 350 West Thomas Rd Phoenix AZ 85013 Office Phone: 602-406-3000.

WAITE, LAWRENCE WESLEY, osteopathic physician, educator; b. Chgo., June 27, 1951; s. Paul J. and Margaret E. (Cresson) W.; m. Courtnay M. Snyder, Nov. 1, 1974; children: Colleen Alexis, Rebecca Maureen, Alexander Quin. BA, Drake U., 1972; DO, Coll. Osteo Medicine and Surgery, 1975; MPH, U. Mich., 1981. Diplomate Nat. Bd. Osteo. Med. Examiners; bd. cert. family practice, holistic medicine, neuromusculoskeletal medicine, Osteopathic Manipulative Medicine. Intern Garden City Osteo. Hosp., Mich., 1975—76; practice gen. osteo. medicine Garden City, 1979—82, Battle Creek, 1982—96, La Crosse, Wis., 1996—2004; emergency rm. physician, 2004—; sect. head Onalaska Family Practice, 1999—2002, coord. rsch., chmn. dept., 1996—99, chmn. integrative medicine edn./rsch. com., 2002—04, vice chair, dept. integrative medicine, 2004. Cons. Nat. Bd. Examiners Osteo. Physicians and Surgeons, 1981—88, 1998—; chief med. examiner Calhoun County, 1991—93; preceptor U. Wis. Med. Sch., 1997—2000, assoc. clin. prof., 2000—, Mich. State U. Coll. Osteo. Medicine, East Lansing, 1979—97, Lakeview Gen. Osteo. Hosp., Battle Creek, Mich., 1983—87; mem. profl. adv. coun. Good Samaritan Hosp., Battle Creek, 1982—83; exec. bd. Primary Care Network, 1994—96; assoc. clin. prof. Des Moines U. Coll. Osteo. Medicine, 2002—05; mem. evaluations registry Commn. on Osteo. Coll. Accreditation, 2006—; vol. radio announcer Wis. Pub. Radio, 2006—. Writer TV program Cross Currents Ecology, 1971; editor radio series Friendship Hour, 1971-72 Bd. dirs. La Crosse YMCA, 2000-03, Internat. Log Rolling Assn., 2000-04; cert. judge U.S. Log Rolling Assn., 2006—; bd. dirs., instr. Hospice Support Services, Inc., Westland, Mich., 1981-86; exec. bd. officer Battle Creek Area Urban League, 1987-91; bd. dirs., mem. exec. com. Clearwater Farm Found., Inc., 1999-04; vestryman St. Thomas Episcopal Ch., 1990-93; bd. mem. Eagle Bluff Environ. Learning Ctr., Lanesboro, 2003-; leader Boy Scouts Am.; bd. sec. Internal Soc. Complementary Medicine Rsch., 2004-05. Served to lt. comdr. USN, 1976-79. U. Wis. fellow, Madison, 2003-04; State of Iowa scholar, 1969. Mem.: Wis. Assn. Osteopathic Physicians (bd. officer 2011—), US Log Rolling Charitable Found. (officer 2009—), Am. Coll. Osteo. Emergency Physicians (govtl. affairs com. 2007—), Am. Acad. Osteopathy, South Ctrl. Osteo. Assn. (officer, state del. 1983—96), Am. Osteo. Assn., Internat. Soc. Complementary Medicine Rsch. (sec. 2004—05), Population Inst. (population action coun. 1984—99), Upper Miss. River Osteopathic Study Group (sec. 2008—), Brotherhood St. Andrews (life), Bermuda Hist. Soc. (life), Nat. Eagle Scouts Assn. (life). Avocations: geography, medieval history, genealogy. Home and Office: 2110 Evenson Dr Onalaska WI 54650-8772 Office Phone: 608-397-6678. Business E-Mail: lwwaite@wisc.edu.

WAITZKIN, HOWARD BRUCE, internist, sociologist, educator; b. Akron, Ohio, Sept. 6, 1945; s. Edward and Dorothy (Lederman) W.; m. Jean Ellis-Sankari, Nov. 12, 2005; 1 stepchild, Daren; 1 child, Sofia. BA summa cum laude, Harvard U., 1966, MA, 1969, MD, PhD, 1972. Diplomate in internal & geriat. medicine Am. Bd. Internal Medicine. Resident in medicine Stanford U. Med. Ctr., Calif., 1972-75, Robert Wood Johnson clin. scholar depts. sociology-medicine, 1973-75; sr. resident in medicine Mass. Gen. Hosp., Boston, 1977-78; assoc. prof. sociology, clin. asst. prof. medicine U. Vt., Burlington, Vt., 1975-77; vis. assoc. prof. health and med. scis. U. Calif., Berkeley, 1978-82, clin. asst. prof. medicine San Francisco, 1978-82; internist La Clínica de la Raza, Oakland, Calif., 1978-82; prof. medicine and social scis. U. Calif., Irvine, 1982-96, chief div. gen. internal medicine and primary care, 1982-90; med. dir. U. Calif.-Irvine-North Orange County Community Clinic, Anaheim, 1982-90; disting. prof. U. N.Mex., 2005—, prof. sociology, family and cmty. medicine, internal medicine and Latin Am. studies, 1997—, sr. fellow, Robert Wood Johnson Found. Ctr. Health Policy, 2008—; internist El Centro Family Health, N.Mex., 2007—09, Taos Med. Group, N.Mex., 2009—. Regional rep., nat. sec. bd. dir. Physicians for Nat. Health Program, Cambridge, Mass., 1989-91; cons. documentary Health Care Across the Border, Nat. Pub. TV, NYC, 1989-90, documentary on US health care system Nat. TV Austria, 1991; cons. BBC, 1992, Pew Health Professions Commn., 1992-94, Assn. Am. Med. Colls., 1992-93, Robert Wood Johnson Found., 1992, Rsch. and Tng. Group in Social Medicine, Santiago, Chile, 1990—, Eisenhower Rural Health Ctr., Idyllwild, Calif., 1995-96, office of pres. breast cancer rsch. initiative U. Calif, 2001, John D. & Catherine T. MacArthur Found., 2004, 09, Korean Med. Assn., 2011; nat. coord. Civilian Med. Resources Network, 2005-; lectr. med. sociology U. Amsterdam, The Netherlands, 1977; vis. prof. Northwestern U., 1994, U. Ill., Chgo., 1994, U. Wash., 1996, U. N.Mex., 1996, U. Ky., 1996, U. Guadalajara, 1997, 2002, 03, Simon Fraser U., 1997, U. Campinas, Brazil, 1999, Cornell Med. Coll., 1999, U. Utah, 2002, Nat. Inst. Pub. Health, Cuernavaca, Mex., 2003, 06, Robert Wood Johnson Sch. Medicine and Dentistry, NJ, 2003-04, State U. Rio de Janerio, Brazil, 2008, Patan Acad. Health Scis. Kathmandu, Nepal, 2011; expert panel on comm. with elderly patients Nat. Inst. Aging, 1997; prin. investigator US Agy. for Healthcare Rsch. and Quality, NIMH, 1991-, Robert Wood Johnson Found., 2003-05, 08-09. Co-author: The Exploitation of Illness in Capitalist Society, 1974; author: The Second Sickness: Contradictions of Capitalist Health Care, 1983, paperback edit., 1986, revised edit., 2000, The Politics of Medical Encounters: How Patients and Doctors Deal with Social Problems, 1991, paperback edit., 1993, At the Front Lines of Medicine: How the Health Care System Alienates Doctors and Mistreats Patients...and What We Can Do About It, 2001, paperback edit., 2004, Medicine and Public Health at the End of Empire, 2011; mem. editl. bd. Internat. Jour. Health Svc., Social Problems, Western Jour. Medicine, Cambio y Salud (Chile), Investigacion en Salud (Mex.), Internat. Jour. Cuban Health and Medicine, Cuadernos Medico Sociales, Chile. Cons. on health policy Jesse Jackson Presdl. Campaign, 1988; bd. dirs., mem. com. on litigation Orange County Pub. Law Ctr., 1990-96. Fellow in ind. study and rsch. NEH, 1984-85, Fulbright fellow, 1983, 88-90, 93-94, sr. fellow NIA, 1989-91, Fogarty Internat. Ctr., NIH, 1994-98, Fulbright New Century Scholar, 2001-02, Guide to Am. Top Physicians, 2002-, John Simon Guggenheim Meml. Found. fellow, 2002-03, Jonathan Mann Award for Lifetime Commitment to Pub. Health and Social Justice Issues, N.Mex. Pub. Health Assn., 2003. Fellow ACP, Am. Acad. Physician and Patient, Soc. for Applied Anthropology; mem. APHA, Am. Sociol. Assn. (nat. coun.-at-large med. sociology sect. 1989-92, coord. resolution process concerning nat. health program 1990-91, Leo G. Reeder award for disting. career in medicine and social sci., 1997, sect. chair 2009-10), Soc. Gen. Internal Medicine, Phi Beta Kappa, Salvador Allende Program Social Medicine (pres. 2006-). Avocations: music, athletics, gardening, mountain hiking. Office: U NMex Sociology MSC05 3080 Rm 1103 1915 Roma NE Albuquerque NM 87131 Office Phone: 505-277-0860. Business E-Mail: waitzkin@unm.edu.

WAKABAYASHI, TOSHIHIKO, neurosurgeon; b. Koganei City, Tokyo, Aug. 22, 1954; s. Hiroshi and Misako Wakabayashi; m. Midori Maehara; 1 child, Nobuhiko. MD, Nagoya U. Sch. Medicine, Aichi, Japan, 1981, PhD, 1985. Prof. and chmn. Nagoya U. Sch. Medicine, 2008—. Assoc. prof. Nagoya U. Hosp., 2004—08. Dir.: (neurosurgery medicine) (Ann. award, Japan Gene Therapy Assn., 2007). Office: Dept Neurosurg Nagoya Univ 65 Tsurumai Showa Nagoya Aichi 466-8550 Japan Home: 3-10-16 Chiyoda Naka-ku Nagoya Aichi 460 0012 Japan Office Phone: 81-52-744-2355. Office Fax: 81-52-744-2361; Home Fax: 81-52-323-1213. Personal E-mail: waka0822@aol.com. Business E-Mail: wakabat@med.nagoya-u.ac.jp.

WAKAI, TOSHIFUMI, surgeon, educator; b. Ojiya, Niigata, Japan, Jan. 29, 1966; s. Sadao and Kiyo Wakai; m. Mikiko Aikawa, May 30, 1995; children: Chika, Rika. MD, Yamanashi U., Sch. Medicine, Japan, 1992; PhD in Surg. Oncology, Niigata U., 1999. Lic. Japanese Ministry Health, 1992. Surg. resident Niigata U., Med. & Dental Hosp., 1992—94; surg. fellow Niigata U., Med. & Dental Hosp., Divsn. Digestive & Gen. Surgery, 1999—2003, asst. prof. Japan, 2003—09, assoc. prof., 2010—. Fellow: Japanese Hepato-Pancreato-Biliary Assn. (assoc.), Japanese Soc. Gastroenterology (assoc.), Japan Surg. Soc. (assoc.), Japanese Soc. Gastroent. Surgery (assoc.); mem.: Internat. Soc. Digestive Surgery (assoc.), Internat. Assn. Surgeons and Gastroenterologists (assoc.), Internat. Hepato-Pancreato-Biliary Assn. (assoc.), Internat. Surg. Soc. (assoc.). Office: Niigata U 1-757 Asahimachi-dori Niigata 951-8510 Japan Office Phone: 81-(0)25-227-2228. Office Fax: +81-(0)25-227-0779. Business E-Mail: wakait@med.niigata-u.ac.jp.

WAKAMATSU, YUKO, retired biologist; b. Kyoto, Oct. 13, 1945; d. Saburo and Shigeko Wakamatsu; life ptnr. Kenjiro Ozato. BS, Konan U., Kobe, 1968; PhD, Kyoto U., 1981. Tech. staff Kyoto U., 1968—73, asst. prof., 1973—88, assoc. prof., 1988—94, Nagoya U., Japan, 1994—2002, prof., 2002—09; guest rschr. U. Wuerzburg, Germany, 2009—. Achievements include first to the establishment of a novel method for the fish nuclear transfer of adult somatic cells using diploidized eggs as recipients in medaka fish; invention of fish model that is transparent throughout life. The main organ systems are visible from the outside of the body of living adult fish to the naked eye. Office: University Wuerzburg Physiological Chemistry I Bioctr Am Hubland 97074 Wuerzburg Germany

WAKE, DAVID BURTON, biology professor; b. Webster, SD, June 8, 1936; s. Thomas B. and Ina H. (Solem) W.; m. Marvalee Hendricks, June 23, 1962; 1 child, Thomas Andrew BA, Pacific Luth. U., 1958; MS, U. So. Calif., 1960, PhD, 1964. Instr. anatomy and biology U. Chgo., 1964-66, asst. prof. anatomy and biology, 1966-69; assoc. prof. zoology U. Calif., Berkeley, 1969-72, prof., 1972-89, John and Margaret Gompertz prof., 1991-97, prof. integrative biology, 1989—2003, prof. emeritus integrative biology, 2003—, faculty rsch. lectr., 2004, prof. grad. sch., 2005—. Dir. Mus. Vertebrate Zoology U. Calif., Berkeley, 1971-98; curator Herpetology Mus. Vertebrate Zoology, U. Calif., 1969-; vis. Alexander Agassiz prof. Mus. Comparative Zoology, Harvard U., 2002. Author: Biology, 1979; co-editor: Functional Vertebrate Morphology, 1985, Complex Organismal Functions: Integration and Evolution in the Vertebrates, 1989. Recipient Quantrell Tchg. award U. Chgo., 1967, Outstanding Alumnus award Pacific Luth. U., 1979, Joseph Grinnell medal Mus. Vertebrate Zoology, 1998, Henry S. Fitch award Am. Soc. Ichthyologists and Herpetologists, 1999, Joseph Leidy medal Acad. Nat. Sci. Phila., 2006, Berkeley Citation award U. Calif., 2006; grantee NSF, 1965—; Guggenheim fellow, 1982. Fellow AAAS, Am. Acad. Arts and Scis.; mem. NAS, NRC (bd. biology 1986-92), Am. Philos. Soc., Internat. Union for Conservation of Nature and Natural Resources (chair task force on declining amphibian populations 1990-92), Am. Soc. Zoologists (pres. 1992), Am. Soc. Naturalists (pres. 1989), Am. Soc. Ichthyologists and Herpetologists (bd. govs.), Soc. Study Evolution (pres. 1983, editor 1979-81), Soc. Systematic Biology (coun. 1980-84), Herpetologist's League (Disting. Herpetologist 1984), Save the Redwoods League(Coun., 2005-) Home: 999 Middlefield Rd Berkeley CA 94708-1509 Home Phone: 510-845-1627. Business E-Mail: wakelab@uclink.berkeley.edu.

WAKE, MADELINE MUSANTE, academic administrator, nursing educator; Diploma, St. Francis Hosp. Sch. Nursing, 1963; BS in Nursing, Marquette U., 1968, MS in Nursing, 1971; PhD, U. Wis., Milw., 1986. Clin. nurse specialist St. Mary's Hosp., Milw., 1971-74, asst. dir. nursing, 1974-77; from dir. continuing nursing edn. dean nursing to provost Marquette U., Milw., 1977—2007, provost, 2002—07, prof., 2008—. Mem. devel. team Internat. Classification for Nursing Practice, Geneva, 1991-99. Chmn. bd. dirs. Trinity Meml. Hosp., Cudahy, Wis., 1991-96; bd. dirs. Blood Ctr. Wis., 2003-. Recipient Profl. Svc. award Am. Diabetes Assn.-Wis. affiliate, 1978, Excellence in Nursing Edn. award Wis. Nurses Assn., 1989; named Disting. Lectr. Sigma Theta Tau Internat., 1991. Fellow: Am. Acad. Nursing; mem.: ANA, Am. Assn. Colls. and Univs., Vis. Nurs Assn. Wis. (bd. dirs.), Am. Assn. Coll. Nursing (bd. dirs. 1999—2002). Office: Marquette Univ Clark Hall Milwaukee WI 53201-1881 Office Phone: 414-288-7511, 414-288-7878.

WAKEFIELD, MARK RICHARD, urologist, educator; b. Sacramento, Calif., Jan. 18, 1968; s. James L. and Mary K. Wakefield; m. Lara Lynn Creech; children: Maria, James. BS in Zoology, U. Tex., Austin, 1990; MD, U. Mo., Columbia, 1994. Med. specialty bd. cert. Am. Bd. Urology, 2002. Asst. prof. surgery, urology U. Mo. Sch. Medicine, Columbia, 2004—10, assoc. prof. surgery, urology, 2010—, interim chief divsn. urology, 2011. Dir. and primary surgeon, renal transplantation U. Mo. Health Care, 2004—. Bd. mem. Midwest Transplant Network, Kans. City, Kans., 2007—08. Maj. staff urologist USAF, 2000—04, Wright-Patterson AFB, Ohio. Recipient Tow Humanism in Medicine awards, Gold Found., 2008. Fellow: ACS (state chpt. v.p. 2008—). Office: Univ Mo Sch Medicine M562 One Hospital Dr Columbia MO 65212 Office Phone: 573-882-1151. Office Fax: 573-884-7453.

WAKEFIELD, MARY KATHERINE, federal agency administrator, former medical educator; b. Aug. 12, 1954; BSN, Mary Coll., Bismarck, ND, 1976; MSN, U. Tex., Austin, 1978, PhD, 1985; grad. program for sr. mgrs. in govt., Harvard U., 1991. RN. Staff nurse intensive care unit St. Alexius Hosp., Bismarck, 1975-76; nurse United Hosp., Grand Forks, ND, 1976-77, part-time staff nurse, 1979—86; acad. asst. Univ. Tex. Sch. Nursing, Austin, 1977-78; instr. Brackenridge Sch. Nursing, Austin Cmty. Coll., 1978-79; legis. asst. then chief of staff to Senator Quentin Burdick US Senate, Washington, 1987-89, chief of staff to Senator Kent Conrad, 1993—96; prof., dir. Ctr. Health Policy, Rsch. & Ethics George Mason Univ., Fairfax, Va., 1996—2001; prof., dir. Ctr. Rural Health, assoc. dean Univ. ND Sch. Medicine & Health Sciences, Grand Forks, 2001—09; adminstr. Health Resources & Services Adminstrn. (HRSA), US Dept. Health & Human Services, Rockville, Md., 2009—. Mem. President's Adv. Commn. Consumer Protection & Quality in Health Care Industry, 1997—98, Medicare Payment Adv. Commn.; past chair nat. adv. coun. Agy. Healthcare Rsch. & Quality; chair inst. of medicine (IOM) com. Health Care Quality for Rural America; bd. trustees Cath. Health Initiatives. Mem. editl. bd. Journal Rural Health, Annals Family Medicine, Nursing Economics; contbr. articles to profl. journals. Recipient Nurse Rsch. award, American Orgn. Nurse Execs., 2006, Margaret D. Sovie Writer's award, Nursing Economics, 2008; named one of The Top 25 Women in Healthcare, Modern Health mag., 2011. Fellow: American Acad. Nursing; mem.: AAUW, ANA, Nat. League Nursing, ND Acad. Sci., Philippine Nurses Assn. Met. Washington (hon.), Inst. Medicine (mem. Com. Quality of Health Care in America, chair Com. Future of Rural Health Care), Sigma Xi, Sigma Theta Tau. Office: US Department of Health and Human Services 200 Independence Ave SW Washington DC 20201 also: Health Resources & Services Administration 5600 Fishers Ln Rockville MD 20857 Office Phone: 877-696-6775. E-mail: Administrator@hrsa.gov. *

WAKISAKA, MASAMI, urologist; b. Nakasuge, Tottori, Japan, June 6, 1947; parents Urao and Kikue (Shinohara) W. MD, Chiba U., Japan, 1981. Lectr. Chiba (Japan) U., 1976-81, asst. prof., 1981-88; dir. sect. Funabashi (Japan) Chu-oh Hosp., 1988—. Contbr. articles to profl. jours. Mem. Japanese Urol. Assn., Japanese Cancer Assn., Japan Soc. Cancer Therapy, N.Y. Acad. Scis. Avocations: tennis, swimming, going to the theater. Office: Social Ins Funabashi Chu-oh Hosp 6 13 10 Kaijin Funabashi 273 8556 Japan Business E Mail: m-waki@iris.ocn.ne.jp.

WAKSMAN, BYRON HALSTED, immunologist, educator, medical association administrator; b. NYC, Sept. 15, 1919; s. Selman A. and Bertha (Mitnik) W.; m. Joyce Ann Robertroy, Aug. 11, 1944; children: Nan, Peter. BS, Swarthmore Coll., 1940; MD, U. Pa., 1943. Intern Michael Reese Hosp., Chgo., 1944; fellow Mayo Found., 1946-48; NIH fellow Columbia U. Med. Sch., 1948-49; assoc., then asst. prof. bacteriology and immunology Harvard Med. Sch., 1949-63; rsch. fellow, then assoc. bacteriologist (neurology) Mass. Gen. Hosp., 1949-63, prof. microbiology Yale U., 1963-74, prof. pathology, 1974-78, chmn. dept., 1964-70, 72-74, prof. pathology and biology, 1979-89; v.p. rsch. programs Nat. Multiple Sclerosis Soc., NYC, 1979—87, v.p. rsch. and med. programs, 1987-89; adj. prof. pathology NYU, 1979—2001, rsch. prof. biomedicine and sci. edn., 2002—, dir. (ad interim) programs for prep. edn. sci. and medicine, 2002—03, sr. advisor collaborative edn. programs, 2003—; vis. scientist in neurology Harvard U., 1990—. Mem. expert panel immunology WHO, 1963—83, microbiology fellowships panel and study sect. mem. NIH, 1961—69; bd. trustees Found. for Microbiology, 1968—, pres., 1970—2000, chmn. bd. trustees, 2001—09; bd. trustees Biosis, 1988—91; dir. sci. writing fellowships program Marine Biol. Lab., Woods Hole, Mass., 1990—95; Humboldt prof. Max Planck Inst., Martinsried, 1991—92; dir. European Initiative for Communicators Sci., 1992—95; chmn. bd. Sci. Counsellors Nat. Inst. Aging, 1977—79. Contbr. articles to profl. jours.; editor: Progress in Allergy/Chemical Immunology, 1962—; mem. editl. adv. bd.: Cellular Immunology, 1970—95, Immunol. Comms., 1970—95, Inflammation, 1975—90, assoc. editor: Bacteriol. Revs., 1963—67, Jour. Immunology, 1962—66, Internat. Archives Allergy and Applied Immunology, 1962—95. Served as psychiatrist AUS, 1944-46. Fellow Am. Acad Arts and Scis.; mem. Am. Assn. Immunologists (councillor 1965-70, pres. 1970-71), Brit. Soc. Immunology, Am. Soc. Microbiology (councillor 1967-71), Am. Acad. Microbiology, Am. Acad. Neurology, Am. Neurol. Assn. Home: Brookhaven at Lexington 1010 Waltham St Apt 462 Lexington MA 02421-8069 Office Phone: 781-862-3839. Business E-Mail: bwaksman@partners.org.

WALACH, HARALD, psychologist, researcher; b. Augsburg, Germany, Feb. 6, 1957; s. Ulrich and Frieda (Eichinger) W.; m. Johanna Riepl, Apr. 11, 1986; children: Gregor Riepl, Ulrich, Maria-Theresia, Raphael. Diploma in Psychology, U. Freiburg, Germany, 1984; PhD, U. Basle, Switzerland, 1991; also PhD, U. Vienna, 1995. Rschr. U. Freiburg, 1991—93, lectr. in psychology, 1994—2005; rsch. prof. psychology U. Northampton Sch. Social Sci., England, 2005—09. Dir. European office Samueli Inst., 2001—. Author: Homeopathy as Basic Therapy, 1986, Homeopathic Remedy Prufung, 1992, Experiential Knowledge of God, 1996, Clinical Research in Complementary Therapies, 2002, Psychology: Philosophical Foundations, Theory of Science History, 2005-09; editor Jour. Research in Complementary Medicine, 2000—, Spirituality & Health Internat., 2007—09, Experiential Knowledge of God Vol 2, 2010, Spirituality, 2011, Get Rid of the Pills, 2011, Neuroscience Consciousness Spirituality; contbr. articles to profl. jours. Cusanuswerk scholar, Bonn, Germany, 1979-84, 1988-90. Mem. AAAS, GIRI (bd. dirs. 1993-96, v.p. 1996), German Assn. Transp. Psychology (founding mem. 2000), Internat. Soc. Complementary Medicine Rsch. (pres. 2007-), Soc. for Sci. Exploration, German Soc. Epidemiology. Roman Catholic. Avocations: hiking, singing, mountain climbing. Office: Viadrina European University Inst Transcultural Health Studies PO Box 1786 Frankfurt D-15207 Germany Office Phone: 004933555342380. Business E-Mail: harald.walach@northampton.ac.uk, walach@europa-uni.de.

WALADKHANI, ALI-REZA, nutritionist; b. Theran, Iran, Sept. 3, 1963; arrived in Germany1, 1983; s. Ahmad Waladkhani and Fatemeh Rastdju. Degree in Sci. of Nutrition, U. Hohenheim, 1992, PhD in Exptl. Sci., 1996. Nutrition adviser Krankenanstalt Mutterhaus, Trier, Germany, 1997—, study coord., 1999—. Dir. Med. and Nutrition Cons., Trier, 1999—. Mem.: Am. Soc. Quality. Home: Olewiger 154A Rheinland-Pfalz Trier 54295 Germany Office: Klinikum Mutterhaus Feldstr 16 Rheinland-Pfalz Trier 54290 Germany Office Fax: 0049 651 9472344; Home Fax: 0049 651 9472344. Personal E-mail: waladkhani@mutterhaus.de. Business E-Mail: waladkha@uni-trier.de.

WALBERG, HERBERT JOHN, psychologist, educator, consultant; b. Chgo., Dec. 27, 1937; s. Herbert J. and Helen (Bauer) W.; m. Madoka Bessho, Aug. 20, 1965; 1 child, Herbert J. III. BE in Edn. and Psychology, Chgo. State U., 1959; ME in Counseling, U. Ill., 1960; PhD in Ednl. Psychology, U. Chgo., 1964. Instr. psychology Chgo. State U., 1962—63, asst. prof., 1964—65; lectr. edn. Rutgers U., New Brunswick, NJ, 1965—66; asst. prof. edn. Harvard U., Cambridge, Mass., 1966—69; assoc. prof. edn. U. Ill., Chgo., 1970—71, prof., 1971—84, rsch. prof., 1984—, external examiner, 1981. External examiner, 1981; ednl. cons. numerous orgns.; external examiner Monash U., 1974, 76, Australian Nat. U., 1977; speaker in field; former coord. worldwide radio broadcasts on Am. Edn. Voice of Am., USIA, Office Pres. U.S., cons. Ctr. for Disease Control U.S. Pub. Health Svcs., 1985-90. Author, editor: 49 books, chmn. editl. bd.: Internat. Jour. Ednl. Rsch., 1985—; contbr. over 350 articles to profl. jours., chapters to books. Mem. Chgo. United Edn. Com., also other civic groups, 1971-86; bd. dirs. Family Study Inst., 1987; chmn. bd. dirs. Heartland Inst., 1995. Nat. Inst. Edn. rsch. grantee, 1973, NSF rsch. grantee, 1974, March of Dimes rsch. grantee, 1976, numerous others. Fellow AAAS, Am. Psychol. Assn., Royal Statis. Soc.; mem. Internat. Acad. Edn. (founding), Am. Ednl. Rsch. Assn., Assn. for Supervision and Curriculum Devel., Brit. Ednl. Rsch. Assn., Nat. Soc. for Study Edn., Evaluation Rsch. Soc., Internat. Acad. Scis., Phi Delta Kappa (Disting. Rsch. award U. Chgo. chpt. 1971, cert. of recognition 1985), Phi Kappa Phi (hon.). Lutheran. Avocation: travel. Office: U Ill 1040 W Harrison St Chicago IL 60607-7129 Office Phone: 312-505-0528.

WALCOTT, CHARLES, neurobiology and behavior educator; b. Boston, July 19, 1934; s. Charles Folsom and Susan (Cabot) W.; m. Jane Clayton Taylor, Aug. 14, 1976; children: Thomas Stewart, Samuel Cabot. AB, Harvard U., 1956; PhD, Cornell U., 1959. Asst. prof. div. engring. and applied physics Harvard U., Cambridge, Mass., 1961-65; asst. prof. biology Tufts U., Medford, Mass., 1965-67; assoc. prof. dept. biology SUNY, Stony Brook, 1967-74, prof. dept. biology, 1974-81; prof., exec. dir. Cornell Lab. of Ornithology, Ithaca, NY, 1981-93, Louis Agassiz Fuertes dir., 1992-95; prof. neurobiology and behavior Cornell U., 1981—2008, prof. emeritus, grad sch. prof., 2008—, dir. divsn. biol. scis., 1998-99, assoc. dean of the univ. faculty, 2000—03, dean, univ. faculty, 2003—08, U. Ombudsman, 2011—. Cons., dir. Elem. Sci. Study, Watertown, Mass., 1961-67; dir. 3-2-1- Contact, Children's TV Workshop, N.Y.C., 1978—80; dir. L.A. Fuertes. Contbr. many rsch. papers to sci. jours. Dir. sci. TV, Mass. Audubon, Lincoln, 1959—61. Avocations: gardening, sailing, photography. Home: 84 Besemer Hill Rd Ithaca NY 14850-9656 Office: Cornell U Dept Neurobiology Behavior W255 Seeley Mudd Hall Ithaca NY 14853 Office Phone: 607-254-4382. Business E-Mail: cw38@cornell.edu.

WALD, ARNOLD, gastroenterologist; b. NYC, June 10, 1942; s. Jack and Ruth (Fox) W.; m. Ellen Faith Rashkow, June 26, 1966; children: Elissa Karen, Eric Lawrence. BA, Colgate U., 1964; MD, SUNY, NYC, 1968. Diplomate Am. Bd. Internal Medicine, Am. Bd. Gastroenterology. Intern Kings County Hosp., Bklyn., 1968-69, resident, chief resident, 1969-71; fellow in medicine Johns Hopkins Hosp., Balt., 1973-75; asst. prof. medicine U. Pitts. Sch. Medicine, 1978-83, assoc. prof., 1983-91, prof., 1991—2006; chief gastroenterology divsn. Montefiore U. Hosp., Pitts., 1991-95; assoc. chief divsn. gastroenterology and hepatology U. Pitts. Med. Ctr., 1993—2000, dir. fellowship tng. and edn. divsn. gastroenterology, hepatology and nutrition, 1999—2006, prof. medicine, obstetrics, gynecology and reproductive scis., 2005—06; prof. medicine U. Wis. Sch. Medicine and Pub. Health, Madison, 2006—. Head gastroenterology unit Montefiore Hosp., Pitts., 1985-91; mem. adv. bd. Internat. Found. Bowel Dysfunction, 1992—; bd. dirs. Pitts. chpt. Nat. Found. Ileitis and Colitis, Inc., 1980-84. Contbr. articles to profl. jours and books. Maj. U.S. Army, 1971-73. Master Am. Coll. Gastroenterology (bd. trustees 1991-98, gov. western Pa. 1988-90, chmn. internat. rels. com. 1993); fellow Am. Gastroent. Assn., Ctrl. Soc. Clin. Rsch. (councillor 1985-90, chmn. gastroent. sect. 1989-90), Am. Motility Soc., Internat. Found. Functional Gastrointestinal Disorders, Gastroenterology Rsch. Group. Democrat. Jewish. Avocations: tennis, reading, hiking. Office: Divsn GI and Hepatology UWMF Centennial Bldg 1685 Highland Ave Madison WI 53705 Home: 2510 Marshall Pkwy Madison WI 53713 Office Phone: 608-263-4033. Business E-Mail: axw@medicine.wisc.edu.

WALD, NIEL, public health educator; b. NYC, Oct. 1, 1925; s. Albert and Rose (Fischel) W.; m. Lucienne Hill, May 24, 1953; children: David, Phillip. AB, Columbia U., NYC, 1945; MD, NYU, 1948. Sr. hematologist Atomic Bomb Casualty Commn., Hiroshima, Japan, 1954-57; head biologist health physics divsn. Oak Ridge Nat. Lab., 1957-58; med. rsch. and tchg. specializing in radiation medicine and cytogenetics Pitts., 1958—; mem. faculty U. Pitts. Grad. Sch. Pub. Health and Med. Sch., 1958—2004, prof. radiation health, 1962-91, prof. environ. and occupl. health, 1991—2004, prof. radiology, 1965—2004; prof. human genetics U. Pitts., 1991—2004, prof. emeritus, 2004—; chmn. dept. radiation health U. Pitts. Grad. Sch. Pub. Health and Med. Sch., 1969-76, 77-89, chmn. dept. occupl. health, 1975-76, chmn. dept. indsl. environ. health scis., 1976-77. Dir. radiation medicine dept. Presbyn.-Univ. Hosp., 1966-2004; med. dir. Clin. Cytogenetics Lab., U. Pitts., 1982-99, chmn. Radiation Safety Com. 1960-2005, radiation cytogenetics cons., 1999-2004; dir. U.S. Dept. Energy postdoctoral fellowship program in radiation scis., 1997-2004; cons. U.S. NRC Office of Nuc. Materials Safety and Safeguards, mem. adv. panel for decontamination of Three Mile Island Nuc. Power Sta. Unit 2, 1981-93, cons. adv. com. on reactor safeguards, 1989-94; mem. U.S. working group on health effects, U.S.-USSR Joint Coordinating Com. for Civilian Nuc. Reactor Safety, 1989-92; cons. USN, nuc. industries and utilities; chmn. radiol. health study sect. USPHS, 1967-71; mem. Nat. Coun. Radiation Protection and Measurements, 1969-81, consociate mem., 1981—; mem. Gov. Pa. Adv. Com. Atomic Energy Devel. and Radiation Control, 1966-84, chmn., 1974-76; mem. Pa. Dept. Environ. Protection adv. com. on low level radioactive waste disposal, 1985-2009; mem. U.S. nuc. tech. adv. group Internat. Stds. Orgn., 2003-. Contbr. numerous articles to sci. and med. publs. Vol. U.S. Citizens Def. Corps Air Warden Svc., 1943—45, capt. USAF, 1952—54. Recipient Health Physics Faculty Rsch. award U.S. Dept. Energy, 1992-95. Mem. Health Physics Soc. (pres. 1973-74), Am. Pub. Health Assn. (governing coun. 1971-73, program devel. bd. 1973-74), Radiation Rsch. Soc. (assoc. editor jour. 1965-68), Soc. Nuc. Medicine (assoc. editor jour. 1959-69), Am. Soc. Human Genetics, Am. Coll. Occupl. & Environ. Medicine, AAAS, AMA, Internat. Soc. Hematology. Achievements include research in the diagnosis and treatment of accidental human radiation injury, in human radiation dosimetry by automatic image analysis of radiation-induced chromosome aberrations, in the cytogenetics of murine radiation-induced leukemia and in health studies of irradiated human populations in U.S., Japan and Russia. Office: University Pitts Grad Sch Pub Health A713 Crabtree 130 Desoto St Pittsburgh PA 15261 Office Phone: 412-624-2735. Business E-Mail: wald@pitt.edu.

WALDEN, ROTRAUT, architectural psychologist, researcher; d. Arno and Maria Walden. Diploma in Psychology, U. Giessen, Germany, 1983; PhD, U. Paderborn, Germany, 1992; PD Dr. Phil., U. Coblence. Sr. lectr. U. Coblence, Koblence, Germany, 1992—. Author: Lively Living: Developing Psychological Guidelines for Quality of Living, Assessing the Performance of Offices of the Future, Happiness and Unhappiness: Experiences of Happiness and Unhappiness from the Interactionistic Perspective, Architectural Psychology: Elementary School, High School, University and Office of the Future; co-author: Psychology and the Built Environment - Concepts, Methods and Examples of Applications, Places for Children - Kindergarten From the Point of View of Architectural Psychology, Schools for the Future, 6th. edit.; editor: Schools for the Future: Design Proposals from Architectural Psychology for Kindergartens; contbr. articles to profl. jours. Mem.: Environ. Design Rsch. Assn., German Assn. Psychology (divsn. environ. psychology). Roman Catholic. Achievements include 23 projects in 11 countries & in 5 continents. Office: University of Coblence Universitaetsstr 1 D-56070 Koblenz Germany Office Phone: 49-261-287-1930. Office Fax: 0049/261/287-1921. Business E-Mail: walden@uni-koblenz.de.

WALDHAUSEN, JOHN ANTON, retired surgeon, editor; b. NYC, May 22, 1929; s. Max. H. and Agnes H. (Stettner) W.; m. Marian Trescher, June 4, 1957; children: John H., Robert Rodney, Anthony Gordon Scarlett. BS magna cum laude, Coll. Great Falls, 1950; MD, St. Louis U., 1954. Diplomate Am. Bd. Surgery, Am. Bd. Thoracic Surgery. Intern Johns Hopkins Hosp., 1954-55, resident, 1955-57; clin. asst. Nat. Heart and Lung Inst., NIH, 1957-59; resident Hosp. U. Pa., 1959, Ind. U. Med. Ctr., 1960-62; practice medicine specializing in cardiothoracic surgery Indpls., 1962-66, Phila., 1966-70; mem. staff Milton S. Hershey Med. Ctr., Hershey, Pa., 1969-96. From instr. to asst. prof. Ind. U. Med. Ctr., 1962—66; assoc. prof. surgery U. Pa., Phila., 1966—70; prof. surgery Pa. State U. Coll. Medicine/Milton S. Hershey Med. Ctr, 1966—83, chmn. dept. surgery, 1969—94, sr. mem. grad. faculty, 1970—94, interim provost, dean, 1972—73, assoc. dean health care, 1973—75, assoc. dean and dir. Univ. Physicians, 1993—96, J.W. Oswald prof., 1983—99, J.W. Oswald prof. emeritus, 1999—; trustee U. Great Falls, Mont., 2001—04. Mem. editl. bd. Jour. Cardiovasc. Surgery, 1985-93, Jour. Pediatric Surgery, 1972-78, Jour. Thoracic and Cardiovasc. Surgery, 1982, editor, 1994-2000; cons. editor Archives of Surgery, 1972-74; contbr. chpts. to books and articles to med. jours. Recipient Career Devel. award USPHS, 1964. Fellow AAAS; mem. AMA, ACS (chpt. pres. 1974-75, gov. 1979-85, chmn. adv. coun. cardiothoracic surgery 1992-97), Am. Acad. Pediat., Am. Assn. Surgery of Trauma, Am. Coll. Cardiology (sec. 1981-82, trustee 1984-89, mem. editl. bd. jour. 1983, assoc. editor 1986-89), Am. Fedn. Clin. Rsch., Am. Heart Assn., Am. Physiol. Soc., Am. Soc. Artificial Internal Organs, Am. Assn. Thoracic Surgery (1st v.p. 1990-91, pres., 1991-92), Am. Surg. Assn. (1st v.p. 1984-85), Ctrl. Surg. Assn., Internat. Cardiovasc. Soc. (chpt. recorder 1969-74), Pa. Assn. Thoracic Surgery (pres. 1977-78), Thoracic Surgery Dirs. Assn. (pres. 1977-79), Societe International de Chirurgie (membership chmn. 1987-92, treas. 1992-94), Soc. Clin. Surgery (treas. 1971-80, v.p. 1981-82, Pres. 1982-83), Soc. Surg. Chairmen, Soc. Thoracic Surgeons, Soc. Univ. Surgeons, Soc. Vascular Surgery, So. Surg. Assn., Sigma Xi, Alpha Omega Alpha. Home: 515 Bridgeview Dr Lemoyne PA 17043 Office: Pa State U Coll Med MS Hershey Med Ctr PO Box 850 Hershey PA 17033-0850 Office Phone: 717-531-8329. Personal E-mail: jwaldhausen@aol.com.

WALDINGER, ROBERT JON, psychiatrist; b. Omaha, Mar. 1, 1951; s. David and Miriam (Passman) W.; m. Jennifer Abby Stone, May 26, 1986; children: Daniel Cane, David Stone. AB, Harvard U., 1973, MD, 1978. Diplomate Am. Bd. Psychiatry and Neurology. Fellow in psychol. rsch. McLean Hosp., Belmont, Mass., 1982-85, asst. dir. residency tng., 1985-90; dir. tng. Mass. Mental Health Ctr., Boston, 1990-96; rsch. assoc. Judge Baker Children's Ctr., Boston, 1997—2003; assoc. prof. psychiatry Harvard Med. Sch., 2003—04; dir., study adult devel. Mass. Gen. Hosp., 2004—. Mem. faculty Boston Psychoanalytic Inst., 1987-. Author: Psychiatry for Medical Students, 1984, Effective Psychotherapy with Borderline Patients, 1987. Knox fellow Harvard U., 1973. Fellow Am. Psychiat. Assn. (Falk fellow 1980-82). Democrat. Jewish. Office: Mass General Hosp 15 Parkman St Wang 812 Boston MA 02114 Office Phone: 617-525-6133, 617-643-4339. Business E-Mail: rwaldinger@partners.org.

WALDMANN, ANNIKA, epidemiologist, researcher; b. Aurich, Germany, July 13, 1974; d. Klaus Waldmann and Dagmar Anna Irmgard Blecken-Kirschner. Diploma in U. entrance, Gymnasium Ulricianum, Aurich, 1994; diploma in Food Sci., Leibniz U. Hannover, Germany, 2000, diploma in German Lang., 2000, PhD, 2004. Cert. in intro. biostatistcs for epidemiologists U. Muenster, Germany, 2001, in clin. epidemiology U. Halle, Germany, 2006; in epidemiology DGEP, 2010. Sci. rschr. Inst. Food Sci., Hannover, 2001—04, Inst. Social Medicine, Luebeck, Germany, 2004—06, Inst. Cancer Epidemiology, Luebeck, 2004—08, Cancer Registry Schleswig-Holstein, 2009—10, Inst. Clin. Epidemiology, Luebeck, 2011—. Author: (book) Ernährungsphysiologische Aspekte von Brot; contbr. chapters to books, articles to sci. jours. Recipient award, German Soc. of Prevention Rehab., 2008. Fellow: Inst. Clin. Epidemiology; mem.: German Soc. Epidmiology, German Nutrition Soc. Lutheran. Office: Inst Clin Epidemiology Ratzeburger Allee 160 Luebeck 23538 Germany Office Phone: 00494515005447. Office Fax: 00494515005455. Business E-Mail: annika.waldmann@uk-sh.de.

WALDMANN, THOMAS ALEXANDER, medical researcher, physician; b. NYC, Sept. 21, 1930; s. Charles Elizabeth (Sipos) Waldmann; m. Katharine Emory Spreng, Mar. 29, 1958; children: Richard Allen, Robert James, Carol Ann. AB, U. Chgo., 1951; MD, Harvard U., 1955; PhD (hon.), U. Med. Sch., Debrecin, Hungary, 1991. Diplomate Am. Bd. Allergy and Immunology. Intern Mass. Gen. Hosp., Boston, 1955—56; clin. assoc. Nat. Cancer Inst., NIH, Bethesda, Md., 1956—58, sr. investigator, 1958—68, head Immunophysiology Sect., 1968—73, chief Metabolism Br., 1971—. Cons. WHO, 1975, 78; bd. dirs., v.p. Found. Advanced Edn. in Scis., Bethesda, 1980—2002, treas., 1988—90, v.p., 1990—92; William Dameshek vis. prof. U. Calif., Irvine, 1984; mem. med. adv. bd. Howard Hughes Med. Inst., 1987—93; vis. com. mem. Harvard Med. Sch., Boston, 1988—94; mem. sci. adv. com., chmn. Mass. Gen. Hosp., 1992—96; chmn. sci. adv. bd. HealthCare Investment Corp., Princeton, NJ, 1986—2003. Author: Plasma Protein Metabolism, 1970; contbr. articles to profl. jours. With USPHS, 1956—58, 1959—63, 1975—94. Recipient Henry M. Stratton medal, Am. Hematology Soc., 1977, G. Burroughs Mider award, NIH, 1980, DSM, Dept. Health and Human Svcs., 1983, Abbott Lab. award in Clin. and Diagnostic Immunology, Am. Soc. Microbiology, 2002, Debrecen prize, Debrecen Med. Sch., Hungary, 2005, Dana Found. prize, Am. Assn. Immunologists, 2007; named Man of Yr., Am. Leukemia Soc., 1980. Fellow: Am. Acad. Allergy (Bela Schick award 1974, John M. Shelton award 1984, Lila Gruber prize 1986, Simon Shubitz prize 1987, CIBA-GEIGY Drew award 1987, Milken Family Med. Found. Disting. Basic Scientist prize 1991, Artois Latour Internat. Rsch. prize 1991, Bristol-Myers Cancer prize 1992, Paul Ehrlich medal 1997), Acad. Med. Scis. (hon.); mem.: NAS (chmn. 1985—89), UK Acad. Med. Scis., Clin. Immunology Soc. (pres. 1988), Am. Soc. Clin. Investigation (mem. editl. bd. 1978—80, 1983—88), Hungarian Acad. Scis. (hon.), Assn. Am. Physicians, Inst. Medicine, Am. Acad. Arts and Scis. Achievements include research in defining structure multisubunit IL-2 receptor; identifying novel cytokine IL-15; forms of IL-2R-directed therapy using alpha and beta-emitting radionuclide chelate versions of humanized monoclonal antibodies (Zenapax daclizumab) for treatment cancer and Multiple Sclerosis; analysis immunoglobulin gene rearrangements define clonality and classifying human lymphoid neoplasia; discovery of intestinal lymphangeictasia and allergic gastroenteropathy. Office: Nat Inst Health Bldg 10, Rm 4N115 10 Center Dr Bethesda MD 20892-1374 Office Phone: 301-496-6656. Business E-Mail: tawald@helix.nih.gov. *

WALDO, ALBERT LEON, cardiologist, educator; b. NYC, Nov. 25, 1936; MD, SUNY Coll. Medicine, Bklyn., 1962. Cert. in internal medicine, specialty in clin. cardiac electrophysiology, specialty in cardiovasc. Intern Kings County Hosp., Bklyn., 1962-63, resident in medicine, Balt. City Hosps., 1963-65, chief resident medicine SUNY downstate med. ctr., 1965—66; fellow Coll. Physicians and Surgeons Columbia U., 1966—68, from assoc. to asst. prof. dept. pharmacology, Coll. Physicians and Surgeons, 1969—72; fellow cardiology Columbia-Presbyn. Med. Ctr., NYC, 1968-69; from assoc. prof. to prof. medicine U. Ala., 1972—86; with U. Hosps. Case Med. Ctr., Cleve., 1986—, dir., clin. cardiac electrophysiology program; prof. medicine Case Western Res. U., Cleve., 1986—, Walter H. Pritchard Prof. Cardiology, prof. medicine, and prof. Biomedical Engineering. Cons., Circulatory Sys. Devices Panel of the Medical Devices Advisory Com., FDA. Serves or has served on the editl. bds. of peer reviewed journals in the field, including Circulation, Journal American College Cardiology, American Journal Cardiology, Pacing and Clinical Electrophysiology, Journal Cardiovascular Electrophysiology, Journal Electrocardiology, Heart Rhythm, (audio journals) American College of Cardiology (ACCEL), North American Society of Pacing and Electrophysiology (NASPETapes) (also editor-in-chief); contbr. articles to profl. jours. Recipient award for Achievements in Clin. and Exptl. Cardiology, Found. Hartsvrienden RESCAR of The Netherlands, Master Tchr. award, SUNY-Downstate Coll. Medicine, 2002. Fellow Am. Coll. Cardiology (past pres. Ohio Chpt., Disting. Scientist award, 2009), ACP, Am. Coll. Chest Physicians, Am. Heart Assn., Heart Rhythm Soc. (founding mem., past pres. formally called N.Am. Soc. Pacing and Electrophysiology, Disting. Scientist award, 1997, Founders award, 2007, Michel Mirowski Award of Excellence, 2007) mem. Am. Physiol. Soc., Am. Soc. Clin. Investigation, Assn. Am. Physicians, Assn. Univ. Cardiologists, Cardiac Electrophysiology Soc. (past pres.), Am. Coll. Cardiology (Disting. Scientist award, 2009). Office: U Hosps Case Med Ctr 11100 Euclid Ave Cleveland OH 44106-1736 Office Phone: 216-844-7690.

WALDUM, HELGE LYDER, gastroenterologist; b. Norway, May 11, 1946; MD, U. Oslo, 1971; PhD, U. Tromso, 1980; Docteur d' Etat, U. Paris, 1987, Docteur d' Etat, 1993. Prof., head dept. Norwegian U. Sci. and Tech., Hosp. St. Olav, 1981—. Mem.: AGA. Avocation: cross country skiing. Home: Jakobstien 4 Trondheim N-7021 Norway Business E-Mail: helge.waldum@ntnu.no.

WALENTIK, CORINNE ANNE, pediatrician; b. Rockville Centre, NY, Nov. 24, 1949; d. Edward Robert and Evelyn Mary (Brinskele) Finno; m. David Stephen Walentik, June 24, 1972; children: Anne, Stephen, Kristine. AB honors, St. Louis U., 1970, MD, 1974, MPH, 1992. Diplomate Am. Bd. Pediat., Am. Bd. Neonatal and Perinatal Medicine, cert. physician exec. Certifying Commn. on Med. Mgmt., Am. Coll. Physician Execs. Resident pediat. St. Louis U. Group Hosps., 1974—76, fellow neonatology, 1976—78; neonatalogist St. Mary's Health Ctr., St. Louis, 1978—79; from co-dir. to dir. neonatal unit St. Louis City Hosps., 1979—85; dir. neonatology St. Louis Regional Med. Ctr., 1985—96; asst. prof. pediat. St. Louis U., 1990—94, assoc. clin. prof., 1994—98, assoc. prof. pediat., 1998—2001, prof. pediat., 2001—. Supr. nursery follow-up program Cardinal Glennon Children's Hosp., St. Louis, 1979—, neonatologist, physician exec. for managed care and pub. policy, 1997—; dir. nurseries St. Mary's Health Ctr., Richmond Heights, Mo., 2004—07; chair provider svcs. adv. bd. St. Louis Regional Health Commn. Contbr. articles to profl. jours. Mem. adv. com. Mo. Perinatal Program., 1983-86; chair cmty. adv. bd. Mo. Found. Health., bd. mem., 2009-. Fellow: Am. Acad. Pediat. (pres. Mo. chpt., com. on child healthcare financing); mem.: APHA, St. Louis Met. Med. Soc., Mo. State Med. Assn., Nat. Perinatal Assn. (coun. 1984—87), Mo. Perinatal Assn. (pres. 1983), Mo. Pub. Health Assn. (pres. St. Louis chpt. 1995—96). Roman Catholic. Avocations: bridge, baseball, sports. Home: 7234 Princeton Ave Saint Louis MO 63130-3027 Office: Cardinal Glennon Children's Hosp 1465 S Grand Blvd Saint Louis MO 63104-1003 Office Phone: 314-577-5642. Business E-Mail: walentca@slu.edu. *

WALI, ANJILNA, research scientist; b. Kashmir, Jammu and Kashmir, India, Aug. 1, 1977; PhD, Postgrad. Inst. Med. Edn. & Rsch., 2006. Rsch. scientist Nat. AIDS Rsch. Inst., 2007, Chembiotek, 2008; postdoc. rsch. fellow, dept. biotech. U. Pune, 2009—, scientist, 2009—11. Recipient Nat. Eligibility Test award, Coun. Sci. & Industry Rsch., Gold medal, U. Kurukshetra; DS Kothari fellowship, U. Grants Commn. Avocations: sports, travel, gardening. Home: 102 Bldg I Da Vinci Maestros W Pune Maharashtra 411040 India Personal E-mail: anjlinawali@gmail.com.

WALID, MOHAMMAD SAMI, medical researcher; MD, Tishreen U., Syria, 1996; PhD, Kuban State Med. U., Russia, 2006. Med. rschr. Med. Ctr. Ctrl. Ga., 2006—. Contbr. articles to profl. jours. Recipient Top Ten Socioeconomic Paper award, World Congress Neurol. Surgeons Annual Meeting, New Orleans, LA, 2009, First Pl., Am. Asson. Nerol. Surgeons, Denver, Colo., 2011. Mem.: AMA, Nat. Med. Assn. Achievements include research in IUGR, gynecologic laparoscopy, pain, and opioid dependence. Office: Med Ctr Ctrl Georgia 840 Pine St Ste 880 Macon GA 31201 Office Phone: 720-533-8746. Office Fax: 586-628-5932. E-mail: mswalid@yahoo.com.

WALINSKY, PAUL, cardiology educator; b. Phila., June 21, 1940; s. Aaron and Bess (Kleiman) W.; m. Stephanie Sosenko, Nov. 27, 1971; children: Shira, Daniel. BA, Temple U., 1961; MD, U. Pa., 1965. Cert. Nat. Bd. Med. Examiners, Am. Bd. Internal Medicine Cardiovascular. Instr. medicine Thomas Jefferson U., Phila., 1973-75, asst. prof. medicine, 1975-79, assoc. prof. medicine, 1979-82, prof. medicine, 1982—. Cons. EP Technologies, Mountain View, Calif., 1991-93, Baxter Edwards, Irvine, Calif., 1988-91, C.R. Bard, Billerica, Mass., 1994, ESP Pharma, 2002. Contbr. articles to profl. jours.; reviewer profl. jours.; inventor method for high frequency ablation, percutaneous microwave catheter angioplasty. Capt. USAF, 1967—69. Fellow Am. Coll. Cardiology, ACP; mem. AMA, Pa. Med. Soc., Phila. County Med. Assn. Achievements include 14 U.S. patents in field of perfusion balloon catheter, microwave aided balloon angioplasty with lumen measurement, intravascular ultrasonic imaging catheter and method for making same, and acoustic catheter with rotary drive. Office: Thomas Jefferson U 925 Chestnut St Philadelphia PA 19107-5084 Personal E-mail: paulwalinsky@comcast.net. Business E-Mail: paul.walinsky@jefferson.edu.

WALKER, AUDREY THAYER, clinical social worker, psychotherapist; b. Quincy, Mass., June 29, 1935; d. Paul Clifton and Dorothy Ritchie Thayer; m. David A. Walker, Aug. 21, 1982; children: Elizabeth Penniman Billett Bilhartz, Matthew Thayer Billett. AB, Wheaton Coll., Ill., 1957; MSS/MSW, Smith Coll., Northampton, Mass., 1959. Acad. Cert. Social Workers, 1963, LICSW DC, 1985, bd. cert. diplomate in clin. social work 1990. Caseworker Ch. Home Soc., Boston, 1959—61; caseworker, family therapist Family Svc. Agy. of Sacramento, 1961—63; chief psychiat. social worker, supr. dept. psychiatry George Washington U., 1969—90, adj. assoc. prof., 1971—, dir. social work tng., 1975—90; adj. assoc. prof. Smith Coll. Sch. for Social Work, Northampton, Mass., 1971—2003; pvt. practice clin. social worker, psychotherapist, 1990—; adj. faculty Counseling and Psychiat. Svcs., Georgetown U., 1993—2006; field faculty advisor Smith Coll. Sch. for Social Work, Northampton, Mass., 1996—2003, adj. assoc. prof., 2006—07. Co-chair Smith Coll Sch. Social Work/Washington Psychoanalytic Inst. Jour. Club, 1975—76; co-leader theoretical integrative seminar Smith Coll. Sch. for Social Work, 2003—07, Clin. Social Work Inst., Washington, clin. cons. advisor, founding task force adj. faculty, 1999—2009; lectr., presenter m-svc. tng. faculty Am. U., lectr. student counseling & psychiat. svc., 1990—2000. Author: Psychoanalysis and Society: Can Psychoanalysis Help to Understand Modern Conflicts?, Freud at 150: Twenty-First Century Essays on a Man of Genius, 2008; contbr. articles to profl. jours. Administrv. collaboration Life Cycle Courses George Washington U. Dept. Psychiatry, Washington Psychoanalytic Inst., 1975—85; co-chair benefit ann. lectures Smith Coll. Sch. for Social Work Alumni Assn., Washington, 1978—88. Recipient Day-Garrett award for significant and maj. contbns. to social work, Smith Coll. Sch. Social Work, 2005, Disting. Practitioner award, Nat. Acads. of Practice, 2005—; Grad. Study scholar, Episcopal Ch. of Am., Youth Svcs. Divsn., 1957-1959, Sr. Class Grad. Study awardee and scholar, Wheaton Coll. Sr. Class, 1957, Freudian Scholar presenter, Austrian Embassy Symposium, 2006. Mem.: Inst. Contemporary Psychology & Psychoanalysis, Washington Ctr. Psychoanalytic (elected full mem. 2009—10), Am. Psychoanalytic Assn. (psychotherapy assoc.), Psychoanalysis and Brain Study Group, Am. Assn. Psychoanalysis in Clin. Social Work (diversity com. 2008—11, presenter nat. conf. psychoanalysis & cultural competency 2009—11), Am. Group Psychotherapy Assn. (clin. mem. 1982—2004), Smith Coll. Sch. for Social Work Alumni Assn. (Greater Washington chpt. steering com. 1974—93, bd., 1918 fellowship 1982—88, 2002—), Greater Washington Soc. for Clin. Social Work (v.p. profl. affairs 1990—94, bd. mem.-at-large, advisor 1994—2005, continuing edn. com. 1995—2008, founding chair consultation svcs. com. 1997—98, ethics conf. com. 2004, 2006, ad hoc ethics com. 2006—07, ethics conf. com. 2008, 2010, Cert. of Appreciation 1991—97, 2002—06, 2008, 2010, 2011), Nat. Membership Com. Psychoanalysis Social Work (Washington-Balt. area chair 1997—2003, area chair 1997—2007), Smith Coll. Club (Washington) (bd. dirs. 1983—87), Social Sci. Honor Soc. Avocation: art. Office: 3 Washington Cir NW Ste 406 Washington DC 20037 Office Phone: 202-331-1547. Business E-Mail: audreythayerwalker@gmail.com.

WALKER, DAVID H., medical educator; b. Nashville, May 31, 1943; s. William and Sarah Huddleston Walker; m. Marjorie B. Walker, May 31, 1968. BA, Davidson Coll., 1965; MD, Vanderbilt U. Sch. Medicine, 1969; Docteur Honoris Causae (hon.), U. Mediterranee, Marseille, France, 1999. Asst. surgeon USPHS, 1973—75; rsch. med. officer CDC, Atlanta, 1973—75; clin. asst. prof. Emory U., 1974—75; asst. prof. U. NC, Chapel Hill, 1975—80, assoc. prof., 1980—86, prof., 1986—87; prof., chmn. U. Tex. Med. Br., Galveston, 1987—; com. mem. Def. Health Bd., 2006—11; with, nat. rsch. coun. standing com. US Dept. Def., 2007—10. Com. mem. Nat. Biodefense Network, 2003—; mem. sci. adv. bd. Armed Forces Inst. Pathology, 1996—2004. Editor: (book) Tropical Infectious Diseases: Principles, Pathogens, and Practice, 8 books; contbr. articles to profl. jours., chapters to books. Grantee, NIH, 1980—2011. Mem.: Am. Soc. Rickettsiology, Am. Soc. Tropical Medicine and Hygiene, US-Can. Acad. Pathology. Achievements include patents for ehrlichia Disulfide Bond Formatiopn (DSB) proteins and uses thereof; an immunoreactive ferric binding protein of ehrlichia canis and uses thereof; p153 and p156 antigens for the immunodiagnosis of canine and human ehrlichioses; immunoreactive 38-kda ferric binding protein of ehrlichia canis and uses thereof; rickettsia felis outer membrane protein; 28-kda immunoreactive protein gene of ehrlichia canis and uses thereof; p43 antigen for the immunodiagnosis of canine ehrlichiosis and uses thereof; ehrlichia canis 120-kda immunodominant antigenic protein and gene; immunodominant 120 kda surface-exposed adhesion protein genes of ehrlichia chaffeensis. Office Phone: 409-772-3989.

WALKER, DUARD LEE, medical educator; b. Bishop, Calif., June 2, 1921; s. Fred H. and Anna Lee (Shumate) Walker; m. Dorothea Virginia McHenry, Aug. 11, 1945; children: Douglas Keith, Donna Judith, David Cameron, Diane Susan. AB, U. Calif., Berkeley, 1943, MA, 1947; MD, U. Calif., San Francisco, 1945. Diplomate Am. Bd. Microbiology. Intern, U.S. Naval Hosp., Shoemaker, Calif., 1945—46; asst. resident internal medicine Stanford U. Service San Francisco Hosp., 1950—52; asso. prof. med. microbiology and preventive medicine U. Wis., Madison, 1952—59, prof. med. microbiology, 1959—88, prof., chmn. med. microbiology, 1970—76, Paul F. Clark prof. med. microbiology, 1977—88, prof. emeritus, 1988—, prof., chmn. med. microbiology, 1981—88. Cons. Naval Med. Rsch. Unit, Gt. Lakes, Ill., 1958—74; mem. microbiology tng. com. Nat. Inst. Gen. Med. Scis., 1966—70; mem. nat. adv. Allergy and Infectious Diseases Coun., 1970—74; mem. adv. com. on blood program rsch. ARC, 1978—79; mem. study group on papovaviridae Internat. Com. on Taxonomy of Viruses, 1976—90; mem. vaccines and related biol. products adv. com. FDA, 1985—89; mem. rev. panel postdoct. rsch. fellowships for physicians Howard Hughes Med Inst., 1990—93. Mem. editl. bd. Infection and Immunity, 1975—83, Archives of Virology, 1981—83, Microbial Pathogenesis, 1985—90. Served to lt. (j.g.) USNR, 1943—46, served to capt. USNR, 1953—55. Fellow NRC postdoctoral virology, Rockefeller Inst. Med. Rsch., N.Y.C., 1947—49, USPHS immunology, George Williams Hooper Found., U. Calif., San Francisco, 1949—50. Fellow: Infectious Diseases Soc. Am., Am. Acad. Microbiology, Am. Pub. Health Assn.; mem.: Arts and Letters, Wis. Acad. Sics., Am. Soc. Virology, AAUP, Reticulendothelial Soc., Soc. Exptl. Biology and Medicine, AAAS, Am. Soc. Microbiology, Am. Assn. Immunologists, NAS. Home: 618 Odell St Madison WI 53711-1435 Office: U Wis Med Sch 600 Highland Ave Madison WI 53792-1510 Office Phone: 608-233-9279. Personal E-mail: dlwalke1@facstaff.wisc.edu.

WALKER, HENRY GILBERT, health care executive, consultant; b. Gowanda, NY, Feb. 16, 1947; s. Henry George and Grace Dayton (Moore) W.; m. Elaine Ruth Darbee, July 18, 1970 (div. Dec. 1979); 1 child, Matthew Case; m. Patricia Ann Andrade, May 14, 1983; children: Michael David, Christopher John. BS in Indsl. Engring., Cornell U., 1969; MBA, U. Chgo., 1975. Evening adminstr. Rush-Presbyn. St.-Luke's Med. Ctr., Chgo., 1973-75; mgmt. cons. Booz, Allen & Hamilton, Chgo., 1975-79; regional adminstr., v.p. S.W. Community Health Service, Albuquerque, 1979-83, adminstr., v.p., 1983-86; exec. v.p. Presbyn. Healthcare Services, Albuquerque, 1986-92; pres., CEO Tucson Med. Ctr., 1992—95, Health Ptnrs. of Ariz., 1995—97, Providence Health System, Seattle, 1997—2004; ptnr. Andrade Walker Consulting, LLC, Bellevue, Wash., 2004—. Bd. dirs. Park Dist., Elmhurst, Ill., 1978, 1979, Rural.Metro Corp., 1997—; mem. Dist. III Cmty. Action Com., Albuquerque, 1985; divsn. chmn. United Way of Albuqueque, 1985, 1988; bd. trustees St. Joseph Health Sys., 1999—; adv. bd. mem. U. Ariz. Coll. Pub. Health, 2005—. Recipient Hosp. Survey award U. Chgo., 1975, Bachmeyer award U. Chgo., 1975, Outstanding Midshipman award Cornell U., 1969; named one of Emerging Healthcare Leaders, Healthcare Forum, 1985, 86, Healthcares Up and Comers, Modern Healthcare Mag., 1987. Mem.: Healthcare Forum (bd. dirs., chmn.), N.Mex. Hosp. Assn. (chmn. bd. dirs. 1983—85, treas.). Independent. Presbyterian. Avocations: reading, hiking, bicycling.

WALKER, JASON A., gynecologist; b. Aberdeen, Md., Feb. 18, 1972; BA, Wake Forest U., 1993; MD, Wake Forest U. Sch. Medicine, 1997. Physician Catawba Women's Ctr., 2001—. Fellow: Am. Coll. Obstetrics & Gynecology; mem.: AMA, Internat. Soc. Clin. Densitometry, NC Obstetrics & Gynecology Soc., Phi Beta Kappa. Office: 1501 Tate Blvd SE Ste 201 Hickory NC 28601 E-mail: jwalker@catawbawomenscenter.com.

WALKER, JOAE BROOKS, retired psychiatrist; b. Boston, June 14, 1926; d. Collins and Hannah Slade (Benton) Graham; m. Bernard Charles Brooks, Jan. 11, 1976, m. Samuel Elwood Walker, Nov. 29, 2008; children by previous marriage: Anne Benton Millman, Jane Graham Selzer. Nursing degree, Mass. Gen. Hosp. Sch. Nursing, 1947; AB with distinction, U. Rochester, 1950, MD, 1954. Diplomate Am. Bd. Psychiatry and Neurology. Intern in medicine Duke Hosp., Durham, N.C., 1954-55; resident in psychiatry Mass. Mental Health Ctr., Boston, 1955-57; resident in child psychiatry Beth Israel Hosp., Boston, 1957-59, mem. staff, 1959-97; pvt. practice Brookline, Mass., 1959-97. Cons. New Eng. Home for Little Wanderers, Boston, 1959-75, Kimberly Clark Corp., 1983-97; asst. clin. prof. psychiatry Harvard U. Med. Sch., Boston, 1978-97; vol. psychiatrist Sr. Friendship Ctr. Health Clinic, Naples, Fla., 1998-2007; mem. bd. Registration in Medicine of Mass., 1991-95. Author: No More Diapers! A Guide to Toilet Training, 1971, 2d edit., 1991, When Children Ask About Sex-A Guide for Parents, 1975, I'm A Big Kid Now! A Guide to Toilet Training for Children and Parents, 1989, Let Go Of Me! You're Not My Daddy!, 2006. Distinguished fellow APA (life), Acad. Child and Adolescent Psychiatry (life); mem. Mass. Psychiat. Soc., New Eng. Coun. Child Psychiatry (bd. dirs. 1979-82, pres. 1987-89). Personal E-mail: s5019w2009@hotmail.com.

WALKER, JOHN ERNEST, molecular biologist, researcher; b. Halifax, Yorkshire, Eng., Jan. 7, 1941; s. Thomas Ernest and Elsie (Lawton) Walker; m. Christina Jane Westcott, 1963; children: Esther, Miriam. BA in Chemistry, St. Catherine's Coll., U. Oxford, 1964, MA, PhD, 1969; DSc (hon.), U. Buenos Aires, 1998, U. Huddersfield, 1998, U. Oxford, 1999, U. Manchester Inst. Sci. & Tech., 1999, Groningen U., 1999, U. Leeds, 1999, U. London, 2002, U. Sussex, 2003, U. Liverpool, 2004, U. East Anglia, Norwich, 2006, Moscow State U., 2007. Postdoc. fellow U. Wis., Madison, 1969—71; NATO rsch. fellow French Nat. Ctr. Sci. Rsch. (CNRS), Gif-sur-Yvette, France, 1971—72; European Molecular Biology Orgn. rsch. fellow Pasteur Inst., Paris, 1972—74; sci. staff mem., Molecular Biology Lab. Med. Rsch. Coun., Cambridge, England, 1974—82, sr. scientist lab. molecular biology, 1982—98, dir. Mitochondrial Biology Unit (formerly Dunn Human Nutrition Unit), 1998—. Hon. prof. Peking Union Med. Coll., Beijing, 2001—. Contbr. articles to profl. jours. Recipient Johnson Found. prize, U. Pa. Med. Sch., 1994, CIBA medal, Biochem. Soc., 1995, Peter Mitchell medal, European Bioenergetics Congress, 1996, Gaetano Quagliariello prize, U. Bari, Italy, 1997, Nobel prize in chemistry, 1997, Messel medal, Soc. Chemistry & Industry, 2000, Lifetime Achievement award, GeneExpression Systems Inc., Mass., 2008. Fellow: Royal Soc., Acad. Med. Scis. London (founding fellow), Soc. Biology London (hon.); mem.: NAS (fgn. assoc.), Academia Europaea, European Molecular Biology Orgn., Royal Netherlands Acad. Arts & Scis. (fgn.). Avocations: cricket, opera music, walking. Office: Mitochondrial Biology Unit Wellcome Trust MRC Bldg Hills Rd Cambridge CB2 0XY England Business E-Mail: walker@mrc-dunn.cam.ac.uk.

WALKER, KIM NORMAN, nursing educator, researcher; b. Auckland, New Zealand, July 30, 1954; BSc, Lincoln Inst. Health Scis., 1987; PhD, La Trobe U., 1994. Prof., rschr. Nursing Rsch. Inst., 2008—. Adj. prof. U. Tasmania, U. Tech. Sydney, 1997. Grant, St Vincent's Clinic Found. Fellow: Australasian Coll. Health Svc. Mgmt.; mem.: Health Svcs. Rsch. Assn. Australia and New Zealand. Office: 406 Victoria Sydney NSW 2010 Australia Business E-Mail: kim.walker@acu.edu.au.

WALKER, MICHAEL CHARLES, SR., retired services executive; b. Rochester, NY, Mar. 4, 1940; s. Charles Boyle and Evelyn Esther (Young) W.; m. Patricia Ann Camelio, Feb. 2, 1963; children: Michael Charles Jr., Lyn, Lea, Matthew. BA, U. Colo., 1962; MBA, Columbia Pacific U., 1982, DBA, 1984. Adminstrv. trainee Lincoln Rochester (N.Y.) Trust Co., 1962-64, mktg. officer, 1964-68; asst. v.p. Lincoln First Bank of Rochester, 1968-72, v.p., 1972-77; pres. M.C. Walker Co., Inc., Spencerport, NY, 1977-80; CEO, PRCC, Rochester, 1980—89; pres., CEO Presbyn. Homes and Svcs. Genesee Valley, Inc., Rochester, 1999—2002. Lectr. SUNY, Brockport, 1982—89; v.p., dir. Kilian and Caroline Schmitt Found., Rochester, 1985—; mem. adv. bd. Chase Manhattan Bank, Rochester, 1989—92; trustee Rochester Hearing and Speech Ctr., 1989—95, chmn., 1993—94; bd. dirs. Genesee Region Home Care Assn., Rochester, 1990—2000; trustee Greater Rochester C. of C., 1981—89. Author: Introduction to Bank Marketing Research, 1969, rev. edit., 1972, Practical Handbook of Marketing Definitions, 1970, 2d edit., 2004, Marketing to Seniors, 2004; contbr. articles to profl. jours. Leader task force Spencerport Ctrl. Schs. Bd. Edn., 1977, 80-81, 85; chmn. Monroe County Svs. Bond Com., Rochester, 1972-97; mem. United Way Evaluation Team, 1990-94; bus. adv. bd. SUNY, Brockport, 1993—2004; mem. N.Y. State Bd. Profl. Med. Conduct, 1993-2006; profl. adv. com. Self Help for Hard of Hearing, 1994-96; trustee Nazareth Coll., 2005—. Recipient Pres.'s Geneseekers award, Rochester Area C. of C., 1979, Innovation of Yr. award, NYAHSA, 1989, Cmty. Svc. award, Self Help for Hard of Hearing, 1997, Patriotic Svc. award, U.S. Treasury, 1997. Mem. Am. Mktg. Assn. (pres. Rochester chpt. 1969-70), N.Y. State Bankers Assn. (pres. residential mortgage com. 1975-76), N.Y. Assn. Homes and Svcs. for Aging (various coms.), Rochester Rotary, Am. Legion. Episcopalian. Avocations: golf, reading, travel, physical fitness.

WALKER, PAUL, otolaryngologist; b. NYC; s. Kenneth Edward and Philomena Catherine Walker; m. Krysia Ulaszyn, Feb. 28, 1982; children: Tom, Ally. Advanced tng. registrar Australian Soc. Otolaryngology Head And Neck Surgery, Sydney, 1988—91; fellow paediat. otolaryngology Hosp. Sick Children, Toronto, Ont., Canada, 1991—92; paediat. otolaryngologist John Hunter Children's Hosp., Newcastle, NSW, Australia, 1992—. Conjoint assoc. prof. surgery and paediat. U. Newcastle, 2001—. Fellow: ACS, Royal Australasian Coll. Surgeons; mem.: Australian Med. Assn., Am. Soc. Pediat. Otolaryngology, Australian Soc. Paediat. Otolaryngology, Australian Soc. Otolaryngology Head and Neck Surgery. Office: Paediat Otolaryngology Croudace St 2305 New Lambton NSW Australia Office Fax: 61 2 49572960.

WALKER, PHILIP CHAMBERLAIN, II, retired health facility administrator; b. Big Spring, Tex., July 7, 1944; s. Philip Chamberlain and Mary Catherine (St. John) W.; m. Linda Jane Holsclaw, Jan. 21, 1978; children: Shannon M., Meghan M. BA, Cen. Wash. State Coll., 1970; MS, U. Idaho, 1971. Exec. dir. Multnomah Found. for Med. Care, Portland, Oreg., 1972-81; chief exec. officer Peer Rev. Orgn. for Wash. State, Seattle, 1981-84; dir. Preferred Provider Orgn. devel. Provident Life and Accident, Chattanooga, 1984-88; v.p. Maxicare Health Plans, LA, 1988-91; v.p., gen. mgr. Maxicare Health Plans Midwest, Chgo., 1991-92; pres. Health Plus, Peoria, Ill., 1992—2007; CEO, chmn. bd. HCH Adminstrn., Peoria, Ill., 1992-98; sr. v.p. Health Care Horizons, Albuquerque, 1992-98; exec. v.p. Proctor Health Sys., 1998—2007. Bd. dirs. RMR Group, HCH Adminstrn., Health Care Horizons; cons. in field. Contbr. articles to profl. jours. Bd. dirs. Boys and Girls Club of Greater Peoria, 2003—06; v.p. Boys and Girls Club Peoria, 2004—06; Ctrl. Ill. regional adv. bd. Multiple Sclerosis Assn., 2002—04; chmn. Hult Health Edn. Ctr., 1999—2003; bd. dirs. Boys & Girls Clubs Olympic Peninsula, 2008—10, Olympic Med. Ctr. Found., 2008—; mem. Olympic Area Agy. Aged Coun., 2008—; bd. dirs. Hult Health Edn. Ctr., Cancer Ctr. for Health Living, 2001—03, Heart of Ill. United Way, 2004—07. With USAF, 1961—66, Vietnam. Mem.: Rear Commadore, Sequim Bay Yacht Club, Creve Coeur Club (bd. govs., pres.). Business E-Mail: pcwalkerii@yahoo.com.

WALKER, R. DALE, psychiatrist, educator; BS in Microbiology, U. Okla., 1968, MD, 1972. Diplomate Am. Bd. Psychiatry and Neurology-psychiatry, 1982, Am. Bd. Psychiatry and Neurology-addiction psychiatry, 1993. Resident psychiatry Univ. Okla. Med. Ctr., 1972—73, Univ. Calif. San Diego Med. Ctr., 1975—77; prof. psychiatry Oreg. Health & Sci. Univ., prof. pub. health and preventive medicine; dir. One Sky Nat. Resource Ctr. for Am. Indian/Alaska Native Substance Abuse Svcs., Ctr. for Am. Indian Health Edn. and Rsch. Recipient Award of Outstanding Svc., Seattle Indian Health Bd., 1985, VA Svc. Award, 1995, Outstanding Svc. to Am. Indian People, Indian Health Svc., 1995, Mental Health Excellence Award, 1996, Outstanding Svc., Oreg. Indian Coun., 1999; named Physician of the Yr., 1989, 2009; named one of Best Doctors in America, Woodward White Publs., 1992—96, Best Doctors in the Pacific NW, 1996—, Best Mental Workers, Good Housekeeping, 1994, The Best Med. Specialists in North America, 1995; scholar Lew Wentz Scholarship, 1964—66. Fellow: Internat. Assn. of Social Psychiatry, Am. Psychiat. Assn.; mem.: Am. Acad. of Addiction Psychiatry, Am. Assn. for Affirmative Action, Am. Assn. of Cmty. Psychiatrists, Am. Assn. of Chairs of Dept. of Psychiatry, Am. Hosp. Assn., Wash. State Psychiat. Assn., Rsch. Soc. on Alcoholism, Assn. of Transcultural Psychiatry, Soc. for the Study of Culture and Psychiatry, Assn. of Am. Indian Physicians (pres.), Am. Coll. of Psychiatry. Office: Oregon Health & Science University 3181 SW Sam Jackson Park Rd Portland OR 97239-3098 Office Phone: 503-494-3703. E-mail: walkerrd@ohsu.edu.

WALKER, RICHARD HAROLD, pathologist, educator; b. Cleve., Dec. 2, 1928; s. Harold Deford and Bernice Margaret (Wright) W.; m. Carolyn Franklin, Sept. 28, 1954; children: Bruce, Lynn, Cara, Leah. BS, Emory U., 1950, MD, 1953. Intern City of Memphis Hosps., 1953-54; resident in pathology Coll. Medicine U. Tenn., Memphis, 1954-55, 57-59, prof. pathology, 1966-70; Am. Cancer Soc. clin. fellow U. Tenn. Coll. Medicine, 1957-59; med. dir. blood bank and transfusion svc. City of Memphis Hosps., Memphis, 1961-70; chief of blood bank and transfusion service William Beaumont Hosp., Royal Oak, Mich., 1970-95, med. dir. Sch. Med. Tech., 1970-91. Clin. prof. pathology Sch. Medicine Wayne State U., Detroit, 1982-95. Contbr. articles on blood transfusion, blood group genetics and transfusion medicine to med. jours. Capt. USNR ret. Recipient Murray Thelin Humanitarian award Memphis chpt. Nat. Hemophilia Found., 1968. Mem. AMA, Coll. Am. Pathologists, Am. Soc. Clin. Pathologists (Disting. Svc. award 1977, Ward Burdick award 1992), Am. Assn. Blood Banks (pres. 1976-77, John Elliott Meml. award 1986), Tenn. Assn. Blood Banks (L.W. Diggs award 1986), Internat. Soc. Blood Transfusion, Am. Soc. for Histocompatibility and Immunogenetics. Republican. Presbyterian. Home: 4204 Fleet Landing Blvd Atlantic Beach FL 32233-4590

WALKER, RICHARD HUGH, orthopaedic surgeon; b. Elgin, Ill., Jan. 29, 1951; m. Wendy Allen; children: Ashley Elizabeth, Blake Allen, Emily Paige. AB cum laude, Occidental Coll., 1973; MD, U. Chgo., 1977. Diplomate Nat. Bd. Med. Examiners, Am. Bd. Orthopaedic Surgery. Jr. resident in surgery UCLA, 1977-79; jr. resident in orthopaedic surgery Stanford (Calif.) U., 1979-81, sr. resident, 1981-82, chief resident, 1982-83; clin. mem. divsn. orthop. surgery, sect. lower extremity reconstructive surgery Scripps Clinic, La Jolla, Calif., 1983—, co-dir. lower extremity reconstructive surgery fellowship, divsn. orthopaedic surgery, 1989—, assoc. head. divsn. orthopaedic surgery, 1990-97, chmn. dept. surgery, 1998—; v.p. surg. radiol. svcs. Golden Gate U., 2001—. Staff physician dept. surgery Scripps Green Hosp., La Jolla, 1983—; mem. exec. com. Green Hosp. of Scripps Clinic, La Jolla, 1994—2001, chief of staff, 1995—97; Team physician San Diego Padres, 1983—86, team physician, 1995—99; Clin. instr. dept. orthopaedics and rehab. U. Calif., San Diego, 1983—92, asst. clin. prof., 1992—; Mem. bd. dir. Scripps Clinic Med. Group, La Jolla, 1992—, mem. exec. com., 1998—, med. dir. surg. specialties, 1998—2001, mem. joint exec. bd., 1992—93. Cons. reviewer Clin. Orthopaedics and Related Rsch., 1989—, Jour. Bone and Joint Surgery, 1994—; contbr. articles to profl. jours. Mem. AMA, ACS, Am. Acad. Orthopaedic Surgeons, We. Orthopaedic Assn. (program chmn. San Diego chpt. 1994-95, treas. 1995-96, v.p. 1996-97, pres. 1997-98, Resident Paper award 1983), Calif. Orthopaedic Assn., Assn. Arthritic Hip and Knee Surgery (charter mem. 1991), Am. Assn. Hip and Knee Surgeons, Assn. Bone and Joint Surgeons (Nicholas Andry Rsch. award 1997). Office: Scripps Clinic Divsn Orthop Surgery 10666 N Torrey Pines Rd La Jolla CA 92037-1092 Office Phone: 858-554-9882. Business E-Mail: rwalker@scrippsclinic.com.

WALKER, RONALD EDWARD, psychologist, educator; b. East St. Louis, Ill., Jan. 23, 1935; s. George Edward and Marnella (Altmeyer) W.; m. Aldona M. Mogenis, Oct. 4, 1958; children: Regina, Mark, Paula, Alexis. BS, St. Louis U., 1957; MS, Northwestern U., 1959, PhD, 1961. Lectr. psychology Northwestern U., 1959-61; faculty dept. psychology Loyola U., Chgo., 1961—, asst., then asso. prof., 1961-68, prof., chmn. dept., 1965—73, prof. emeritus, 1999—, acting dean Coll. Arts and Scis., 1973-74; dean Loyola U. (Coll. Arts and Scis.), 1974-80, academic v.p., 1980-81, sr. v.p., dean faculties, 1981-89, exec. v.p., 1989-99. Cons. VA, Chgo., 1965-74; Am. Psychol. Assn.-NIMH; vis. cons., 1969; vis. scientist Am. Psychol. Assn. NSF, 1968; Cook County (Ill.) rep. from Ill. Psychol. Assn., 1969-72; cons.-evaluator North Cen. Assn., 1986-99. Contbr. articles to profl. jours. Bd. trustees St. Francis Hosp., Evanston, Ill., 1986—92, Chgo. Archdiocesan Sems., 1985—97, Loyola Acad., Wilmette, Ill., 1987—93, St. Louis U., 1988—97; bd. dirs. Holy Family Villa Nursing Home, Lemont, Ill., 2002—05. Recipient Disting. Psychologist of Yr. award Ill. Psychol. Assn., 1986. Business E-Mail: rwalker@luc.edu.

WALKER, STEPHEN R., urologist; Grad. magna cum laude, Muhlenberg Coll.; MD, Jefferson Med. Coll., 1983. Diplomate Am. Bd. Urology, lic. Pa. Resident gen. surgery Lehigh Valley Hosp. Ctr., Allenton, 1983—85; resident urology Thomas Jefferson Univ. Hosp., 1985—89, assocs. urology, 1989; clin. asst. prof. Temple Univ.; urologist Taylor Hosp., Springfield Hosp., Acad. Urology of Pa.,

Crozer-Chester Med. Ctr., Ridley Park. Named Top Dr. in Urol. Surgery, Main Line Today, Recognized Dr., HealthGrades; named one of the Top Doctors, Phila. Mag. Fellow: ACS; mem.: Del. County Med. Soc., Pa. Med. Soc., Urol. Assn. Pa., Am. Assns. of Clin. Urologists, Am. Urologic Assn. Office: Crozer Chester Medical Center One Medical Center Blvd Upland Chester PA 19013 Office Phone: 610-447-2000. Office Fax: 610-447-2969.

WALKER, WALDO SYLVESTER, retired biologist, retired academic administrator; b. Fayette, Iowa, June 12, 1931; s. Waldo S. and Mildred (Littelle) W.; m. Marie J. Olsen, July 27, 1952 (div.); children: Martha Lynn, Gayle Ann; m. Rita K. White, June 16, 1984. BS cum laude, Upper Iowa U., Fayette, 1953; MS, U. Iowa, 1957, PhD, 1959; D of Sci. (hon.), Upper Iowa U., 2004. Mem. faculty Grinnell (Iowa) Coll., 1958, assoc. dean coll., 1963-65, chmn. div. Natural Scis., 1968-69, dean of adminstrn., 1969-73, exec. v.p., 1973-77, dean coll., 1973-80, provost, 1977-80, exec. v.p., 1980-90, exec. v.p. and treas., 1988-90, v.p. for coll. svcs., 1990-95, prof. biology, 1968-2001, prof. emeritus, 2001—. Research assoc. U. B.C. Dept. of Botany, 1966-67. Author articles on plant physiology, ultrastructural cytology. Served with U.S. Army, 1953-55. Fellow NSF Sci. Faculty, 1966-67; recipient NSF research grants, 1960-63, 68. Mem. Am. Assn. Colls., Am. Conf. Acad. Deans (nat. chmn. 1977-78), Am. Assn. Higher Edn., Sigma Xi. Home: 1920 Country Club Dr Grinnell IA 50112-1130 Address: 1920 Country Club Dr Grinnell IA 50112 E-mail: walkerws@iowatelecom.net.

WALKER, WILLIAM EASTON, surgeon, educator, lawyer; b. Glasgow, Scotland, Aug. 7, 1945; came to U.S., 1969; s. William Telfer and Josephine Blair (Easton) W.; m. Mary Fraley Cooley, June 23, 1973; children— Sarah Cooley, Blair Easton, Denton Arthur Cooley, William Easton, II MD, Glasgow U., Scotland, 1968; PhD, Johns Hopkins U., 1975; JD, South Tex. Coll Law, 1993. Diplomate Am. Bd. Surgery, Am. Bd. Thoracic Surgery, Am. Bd. Vascular Surgery. Intern, resident Johns Hopkins U., Balt., 1969-75; resident Vanderbilt U., Nashville, 1975-79; assoc. prof., dir. div. thoracic and cardiovascular surgery U. Tex. Med. Sch., Houston, 1979-94. Cons. M.D. Anderson Hosp., Houston, 1979—. Recipient Harwell Wilson award Vanderbilt U., Nashville, 1979 Fellow ACS, So. Surg. Assn., Royal Coll. Surgeons, Am. Coll. Cardiology; mem. Am. Assn. Thoracic Surgery, Coun. Fgn. Rels., Houston Country Club, Belle Meade Country Club, Cosmos Club (Washington), Krewe of Endymion (New Orleans), Phi Beta Kappa, Sigma Xi. Republican. Presbyterian. Avocations: law, bridge, Wagner, World War I history, cooking. Home and Office: 2831 Sackett St Houston TX 77098-1125 Home Phone: 713-204-4267; Office Phone: 713-520-0021. E-mail: ww19@comcast.net.

WALKLEY, EDWARD I. (TED WALKLEY), pediatric emergency medicine physician; MD, Harvard U., 1970. Diplomate Am. Bd. Pediatrics, 1976, cert. pediatric emergency medicine 2007. Intern Children's Hosp. Med. Ctr., Boston, resident, 1971—73; physician emergency dept. Mary Bridge Children's Hosp., Tacoma. Fellow: Am. Coll. of Emergency Physicians (FACEP), Am. Acad. of Pediat. (FAAP). Office: Mary Bridge Childrens Hospital 317 Martin Luther King Jr Way Tacoma WA 98405 Office Phone: 253-403-1408. Office Fax: 253-403-1406.

WALKUP, JOHN TIMOTHY, psychiatrist, educator; b. St. Paul, Oct. 11, 1951; s. John William and Lydia Sadie Ester (Natzke) W.; m. Jennifer Ann Haythorenthwaite. BA in Humanities, U. Minn., 1975, MD, 1982. Diplomate Am. Bd. Psychiatry and Neurology. Resident in adult psychiatry Yale U. Med. Sch., New Haven, 1982-85; resident in child psychiatry Yale Child Study Ctr., New Haven, 1985-88; asst. prof. psychiatry Johns Hopkins U., Balt., 1988, assoc. prof. psychiatry, dep. dir. child and adolescent psychiatry. Co-editor: Treating Tourette Syndrome and Tic Disorders, A Guide for Practitioners, 2007; co-author: Managing Tourette Syndrome, 2008. Laughlin fellow Am. Coll. Psychiatrists, 1987. Mem. AMA, Am. Psychiat. Assn., Am. Acad. Child and Adolescent Psychiatry (presdl. scholar 1987), Nat. Tourette Syndrome Assn. (chmn. med. adv. bd., sci. adv. bd.) Office: Johns Hopkins Hosp CMSC 314 600 N Wolfe St Baltimore MD 21287-5371 Office Phone: 410-955-5823. Office Fax: 410-955-8691. E-mail: jwalkup@jhmi.edu.

WALL, CONRAD, III, lab administrator, researcher; b. Boston, June 13, 1939; s. Conrad and Nell Kennedy Wall; m. Susan Ann Vieth; children: Conrad Carter, Richard Alison. BS in Physics, Tulane U., New Orleans, 1961, MS in Physics, 1968; PhD in Bioengineering, Carnegie Mellon U., Pitts., 1975; MS in Biomedical Sci., Harvard Med. U., 2010. Engring. tech. staff Boeing Co., New Orleans, 1965—70; postdoc. fellow (NIH) U. Pitts. Med. Sch., 1975—76, rsch. asst. prof. otolaryngology, 1976—82; dir., Raymond Jordan human vestibular lab. Eye and Ear Hosp., Pitts., 1982—87; assoc. prof. otology and laryngology Harvard Med. Sch., Boston, 1987—; founding dir., jenks vestibular diagnostic lab. Mass. Eye and Ear Infirmary, Boston, 1987—; assoc. prof., affiliated faculty, HMS-MIT health scis. and tech. MIT, Cambridge, 1987—, rsch. affiliate, man-vehicle lab., dept. aero. engring., 1989—; affiliated rsch. assoc. prof., neuromuscular rsch. ctr. Boston U., 2003—; otology and laryngology prof. Harvard Med. Sch., Boston, 2010. Mem., human studies com. Schepens Eye Rsch. Inst., Boston, 1991—; chair, working group on basic vestibular function test battery Am. Nat. Standards Inst., Washington, 1992—; assoc. team lead, nat. space biomedical rsch. inst. NASA, Houston, 2000—06. Mem. corp. Old North Ch., Boston, 2005—10. 1st lt. US Army, 1963, Fort Eustis, Va. Fellow: Am. Inst. Medicine and Biol. Engring. (elect 2008). Episcopalian. Achievements include first to electric stimulation of the human posterior ampullary nerve which demonstrate robust nystagmus eye movements -a crucial step in showing feasibility of balance prosthesis implants. Avocations: skeet shooting, fly fishing. Office: Massachusetts Eye & Ear Infirmary 243 Charles St Boston MA 02114 Office Fax: 617-573-4154. Business E-Mail: cwall@mit.edu. *

WALL, SONJA ELOISE, nursing administrator; b. Santa Cruz, Calif., Mar. 28, 1938; d. Ray Theothornton and Reva Mattie (Wingo) W.; m. Edward Gleason Holmes, Aug. 1959 (div. Jan. 1968); children: Deborah Lynn, Lance Edward; m. John Aspesi, Sept. 1969 (div. 1977); children: Sabrina Jean, Daniel John; m. Kenneth Talbot LaBoube, Nov. 1, 1978 (div. 1989); 1 child, Tiffany Amber; m. Charles Borsic, July 2002. BA, San Jose Jr. Coll., 1959; BS, Madonna Coll., 1967; postgrad., Wayne State U., 1967—68; student, U. Mich., 1968—70. RN, Calif., Mich., Colo. Staff nurse Santa Clara Valley Med. Ctr., San Jose, Calif., 1959-67, U. Mich. Hosp., Ann Arbor, 1967-73, Porter and Swedish Med. Hosp., Denver, 1973-77, Laurel Grove Hosp., Castro Valley, Calif., 1977-79, Advent Hosp., Ukiah, Calif., 1984-86; motel owner LaBoube Enterprises, Fairfield, Point Arena, Willits, Calif., 1979—; staff nurse Northridge Hosp., LA, 1986-87, Folsom State Prison, Calif., 1987; co-owner, mgr. nursing registry Around the Clock Nursing Svc., Ukiah, 1985—; critical care staff nurse Kaiser Permanente Hosp., Sacramento, 1986-89; nurse Snowline Hospice, Placerville, Calif., 1989-92; carepoint home care and travel nurse Hosp. Staffing Svcs. Inc., Placerville, 1992-94, interim home health nurse, 1994-95; nurse Finders Home Health Care, 1996; owner Sunshine Manor Residential Care Home, Placerville, 1995—, Rainbow Manor Residential Care Home, 2000—02; psychol. and trauma RN Folsom State Prison, 2002—04, Calif. Dept. Mental Health, Placerville, Calif., 2004—. Owner Royal Plantation Petites Miniature Horse Farm. Contbr. articles to profl. jours. Leader Coloma 4-H, 1987-91; mem. mounted divsn. El Dorado County Search and Rescue, 1991-93; docent Calif. Marshall Gold Discovery State Hist. Park, Coloma, Calif. Mem. AACN, NAFE, Oncology Nurses Assn., Soc. Critical Care Medicine, Am. Heart Assn. (CPR trainer, recipient awards), Calif. Bd. RNs, Calif. Nursing Rev., Calif. Critical Care Nurses, Soc. Critical Care Nurses, Alzheimers Aid Soc. No. Calif., Am. Motel Assn. (beautification and remodeling award 1985), Nat. Hospice Nurses Assn., Cmty. Residential Care Assn. Calif., Soroptimist Internat. Calif., Am. Miniature Horse Assn. (winner nat. grand championship 1981-83, 85, 89), DAR (Jobs Daus. hon. mem.), C. of C. of El Dorado County, Kiwanis, Cameron Park Country Club. Republican. Episcopalian. Avocations: pinto, paint and miniature horses, real estate development, swimming. E-mail: sunshinemanor@directcon.net.

WALLACE, BEVERLY B., hospital administrator; b. Jan. 14, 1951; B in Acctg. with honors, U. West Fla. Various positions, includingCFO, hosp., market & divsn. Humana, Inc., Fla., 1983—93; various positions Galen (merged with HCA Inc.); joined HCA, Inc., 1993, CFO, Mid-America Divsn., 1994—96, CFO, 1996—97, pres., Homecare Divsn., 1997—98, v.p., Managed Care, 1998—99, sr. v.p., Revenue Cycle Ops. Mgmt., 1999—2003, pres., Fin. Svcs. Group, 2003—06, pres., Shared Svcs. Group, 2006—. Former bd. dirs., mem., Governance Com. Healthcare Fin. Mgmt. Assn. (HFMA); bd. dirs. Fedn. of Am. Hosps. Office: HCA Inc 1 Park Plz Nashville TN 37203 Office Phone: 615-344-9551. Office Fax: 615-344-2266. Business E-Mail: beverly.wallace@hcahealthcare.com. *

WALLACE, CHARLES ALAN, plastic surgeon; b. Ft. Worth, Tex., Feb. 13, 1957; MD, U. Tex. Southwestern Med. Sch., 1982. Cert. Am. Bd. Plastic Surgery. Intern, gen. surgery U. Hawaii, Honolulu, 1982—83; resident Baylor U. Med. Ctr., Dallas, 1984—87, resident, plastic surgery, 1986—87; resident St. Joseph-MD Anderson, Houston, 1987—89; private practice Dallas, 1989—. Fellow: ACS; mem.: Tex. Soc. Plastic and Reconstructive Surgeons, Dallas Soc. Plastic Surgeons, Cronin and Brauer Soc., AMA, Tex. Med. Assn., Dallas County Med. Assn., Am. Soc. Plastic Surgeons, Soc. Baylor Surgeons. Avocations: riding motorcycles, fixing cars, boats & airplanes. Office: 17110 Dallas Pky Ste 100 Dallas TX 75248 Office Phone: 972-380-7090. Office Fax: 972-380-7016.

WALLACE, DESIREE, investigational drug pharmacist, pharmacy educator; d. Divinia and Russell Wilkinson; m. Craig Wallace; children: Joshua children: Isabella. PharmD, U. So. Calif., 1996. Investigational drug pharmacist Loma Linda U. Med. Ctr., Calif., 1999—; asst. prof. pharmacy practice Loma Linda U. Sch. Pharmacy, Calif., 2002—. Mem. bd. instl. rev. Loma Linda U., 1999. Contbr. articles to profl. jours. Mem. Ch. Calif. Stewat C4th, O-Lee TJ; bd. dirs. Am. Cancer Soc., Upland, Calif., 1997—99. Achievements include research in ginko biloba and acetazolamide prophylaxis for acute mountain success. Business E-Mail: dwallace@ahs.llumc.edu, dwallace@llu.edu.

WALLACE, MARK ALLEN, hospital administrator; b. Oklahoma City, Apr. 24, 1953; s. William Howell and Mollie Marie (Godsy) W.; children: Emily, Benjamin. BS, Okla. Bapt. U., 1975; MS, Washington U., St. Louis, 1978. Adminstrv. asst. Bapt. Med. Ctr., Oklahoma City, 1975-77; administrv. resident Meth. Hosp., Houston, 1977-78; asst. v.p. Tex. Meth. Hosp., Houston, 1978-80, v.p., 1980-83, sr. v.p., 1983-89; pres., CEO Tex. Children's Hosp., Houston, 1989—. Adj. instr. Washington U., 1984—; adj. asst. prof. Tex. Womans U., Houston, 1983—; bd. dirs., chmn. fin. com., treas. Greater Houston Hosp. Svc. Corp., 1986-90; bd. trustees, Nat. Assn of Children's Hospitals and Related Institutions Contbr. articles to profl. jours. Chmn. campaign drives United Way, Houston, 1984, 86, corporate walk for Juvenile Diabetes Found. Walk to Cure Diabetes, 2000; class chmn. alumni vision for excellence and growth for future campaigns Okla. Bapt. U., 1982; bd. dirs. Tex. Gulf Coast chpt. March of Dimes Birth Defects Found., 1985-91, Zoological Society of Houston, Sam Houston Area Coun. of the Boy Scouts, World Health & Golf Assn., Greater Houston Partnership (vice-chair Flood Control Task Force), Greater Houston Community Found.; bd. governors, Houston Forum; active mem. Second Baptist Ch., Houston, Young Presidents' Orgn., and Houston Country Club Recipient Emerging Leaders in Health Care award Healthcare Forum Mag. and Korn/Ferry Internat., 1987. Fellow Am. Coll. Healthcare Execs. (com. on membership, subcom. on recruitment 1990—, Robert S. Hudgens Meml. award, 1992, Young Healthcare Exec. of Yr., 1992); mem. Am. Heart Assn. (med. adv. com. 1990-91), Healthcare Forum (pres. emerging leaders alumni group 1988-91), Am. Hosp. Assn., Tex. Hosp. Assn. (bd. dirs., bd. dirs. polit. action com. 1988—, chmn. bd. trustees, 1998-1999), Greater Houston Hosp. Coun. (bd. dirs. 1991—, chmn. 1993-1994), Houston Area Health Care Coalition, Childrens Hosp. Assn. Tex. (pres. 1992—, chmn. 2002-2003), Tex. Gulf Coast Arthritis Found. (bd. dirs. 1990-91). Republican. Baptist. Office: Tex Children's Hosp 6621 Fannin St Houston TX 77030 also: PO Box 300630 Houston TX 77230-0630

WALLACE, ROBERT BRUCE, retired surgeon; b. Washington, Apr. 12, 1931; s. William B. and Anne E. W.; m. Betty Jean Newel, Aug. 28, 1955; children: Robert B., Anne E., Barbara N. BA, Columbia U., 1953, MD, 1957. Diplomate Am. Bd. Surgery, Am. Bd. Thoracic Surgery. Chmn., prof. dept. surgery Mayo Clinic and Mayo Med. Sch., Rochester, Minn.; bd. govs. Mayo Clinic, 1968-79; prof. dept. surgery Georgetown U. Sch. Medicine, 1980—96, chmn. dept. surgery, 1980-95, surgeon and chief univ. hosp., 1980-95; retired, 1996. Trustee Mayo Found., 1970—78; chmn. sci. adv. com. LeDucq Found., 2000—05. Recipient Disting. Alumni award, Mayo Clinic, 2008. Mem. ACS (bd. govs. 1975-79), Am. Surg. Assn., Soc. Clin. Surgery, Am. Assn. Thoracic Surgery (pres. 1994-95), Internat. Cardiovascular Soc., Soc. Vascular Surgery, Thoracic Surgery Found. Rsch. & Edn. (bd. dirs. 1993-2001, pres. 1998-2001). Home: 1322 Darnall Dr Mc Lean VA 22101-3009 E-mail: rbwallace@cox.net.

WALLACE, WILLIAM EDWARD, thoracic surgeon; BS, Stephen F. Austin State U., 1972; MS, Tex. Tech. U., Lubbock, 1974; MD, U. North Tex. Health Sci. Ctr., Forth Worth, 1980. Diplomate Nat. Bd. Med. Examiners, in surgery and surg. critical care Am. Bd. Surgery, Am. Bd. Thoracic Surgery. Intern Tulsa Regional Med. Ctr., 1980—81; resident in gen. surgery Dallas-Fort Worth Med. Ctr., Grand Priarie, Tex., 1981—85; fellow in cardiothoracic-vascular surgery Tex. Heart Inst., Houston, 1985—86, 1989—90; pvt. practice Forth Worth, 1986—. Physician, bd. dirs. Osteo. Med. Ctr. Tex., Fort Worth, 2000—03, chief of staff, 1993—2000; clin. asst. prof. U. North Tex. Health Sci. Ctr., Fort Worth, 1987—, adj. prof. Cardiovasc. Rsch. Inst., 2001—. Contbr. articles to sci. jours. Fellow: Am. Osteo. Assn., Am. Coll. Health Sci., Am. Coll. Chest Physicians; mem.: Soc. Critical Care Medicine, Tex. Med. Found., Tex. Med. Assn. Office: 4315 Booth Callaway Rd Ste 311 North Richland Hills TX 76180 Home Phone: 817-929-1503. Business E-Mail: wwallace@mededge.com. E-mail: william.wallace@heartplace.com.

WALLACH, EDWARD ELIOT, obstetrician, gynecologist, educator; b. NYC, Oct. 8, 1933; s. David Abraham and Madeleine (Spiro) W.; m. Joanne Levey, June 24, 1956; children: Paul, Julie. BA, Swarthmore Coll., 1954; MD, Cornell U., 1958; MA (hon.), U. Pa., 1970. Diplomate Am. Bd. Ob-Gyn. (bd. dirs. 1989-97, dir. divsn. reproductive endocrinology 1989-96), Am. Bd. Reproductive Endocrinology. Intern 2d med. div. Bellevue Hosp., NYC, 1958-59; resident obstetrics and gynecology Kings County Hosp., Bklyn., 1959-63; asst. instr. State U. N.Y. Downstate Med. Center, Bklyn., 1962-63; mem. faculty U. Pa. Sch. Medicine, 1965-84, prof. obstetrics and gynecology, 1971-84, chief endocrinology sect., div. human reprodn., dept. obstetrics and gynecology, 1968-71, mem. admissions com., 1970-73, mem. community health com., 1966-71, mem. student adv. com., 1966-84, mem. com. for appointments and promotions, 1972-77, chmn., 1974-77; dir. dept. obstetrics and gynecology Pa. Hosp., 1971-84, sec., treas. profl. staff, 1972-75; prof., chmn. dept. ob-gyn. Johns Hopkins U. Sch. Medicine, 1984-94, chmn. med. staff, 1991-94, prof., 1984-94. Vis. prof. ob-gyn. U. Kyoto Sch. Medicine, 1981; vis. prof. Keio U. Sch. Medicine, 1987; mem. fertility and maternal health drugs adv. com. FDA, 1992-2006; bd. dirs. Am. Bd. Emergency Medicine, 1998—. Assoc. editor: Fertility and Sterility, 1974—; co-editor: Modern Trends in Infertility and Conception Control; editor-in-chief Postgrad. Ob-Gyn., 1980—; mem. editl. bd. Fertility and Sterility, 1970—, Ob-Gyn., 1976-79, Contemporary Ob-Gyn., 1976-99, Biology of Reprodn., 1978-84; editor-in-chief Current Opinion in Ob-Gyn., 1989-93; contbr. to med. jours. Trustee Marriage Council Phila., 1970-78; chmn. finance com. Phila. Coordinating Council for Family Planning, 1972-73, chmn. med. adv. com., 1973-76; trustee Balt. Chamber Orch., 1989-97. Served as surgeon USPHS, 1963-65. Trainee NIH, 1961-62; recipient Lindback Found. Disting. Teaching award U. Pa., 1971 Fellow Am. Coll. Ob-Gyn., Am. Fertility Soc. (dir. 1977-81, pres. 1985-86); mem. Am. Gynecol. and Obstet. Soc. (v.p. 1983-84), Soc. Gynecol. Investigation (pres. 1986-87), Am. Bd. Ob-Gyn. (bd. dirs. 1989-97, dir. divsn. reproductive endocrinology 1989-96), Phila. Endocrine Soc., Obstet. Soc. Phila. (program chmn. 1969-70, 70-71, 71-72, mem. coun. 1972-83, v.p. 1976-77, pres. 1979-80), Soc. Study Reprodn., Inst. Medicine/NAS, Am. Fertility Soc. (pres. 1985-86), Soc. Gynecol. Investigation (pres. 1986-87), Am. Gynecol. and Obstet. Soc. (v.p. 1984), Phila. Obstet. Soc. (pres. 1980), Inst. of Medicine, Alpha Omega Alpha. Office: Johns Hopkins Med Instn 600 N Wolfe St Baltimore MD 21287-0005 Office Phone: 410-583-2751.

WALLACH, HELENE SUZANNE, clinical psychologist, lecturer, researcher; b. NYC, June 3, 1954; d. Anita and David Simke; m. Ben Wallach, Oct. 9, 1975; children: Shai Dror, Orlee Inbal, Limor Shiri. BA in Psychology and Stats., Tel-Aviv U., Ramat-Aviv, Israel, 1977; MA in Clin. Psychology, Lakehead U., Thunder-Bay, Ont., 1982; PhD in Clin. Psychology, U. Western Ont., London, Ont., 1988. Hypnotherapist Israel, 1997, Family and Couple Therapist Israel, 1996, Registered Clinical Psychologist Israel, 1990. Psychometrist Ont. Correctional Instn., Brampton, Ontario, 1981—83; psychologist London Psychiat. Hosp., Outpatient Unit, London, Ontario, Canada, 1987—88; psychologist, mgr. Tal Inst. Psychotherapy, Karmiel, Israel, 1989—; lectr. Western Galilee Coll., Acco, Israel, 1994—2004; psychologist Rivka Sieff Hosp., Psychiat. Unit, Israel, 1989—97; chairperson criminology, dept. behavioral studies Emek Yezreel Coll., Afula, Israel, 2000—07; lectr. U. Haifa, 2004—. Workshop dir. Ednl. Psychol. Units, Various cities in Northern Isreal, Israel, 2002—04; workshop presenter Family and Marital Therapy Conf., Zichron Yaakov, Israel, 2000—00; conf. organizer and moderator Emek Yezreel Coll., Afula, Israel, 2004—04; reviewer for rsch. proposals Chief Scientist, Ministry of Health, Karmiel, Israel, 2003—03. Contbr. articles to profl. jours. Chairperson of pta High-School, Karmiel, Israel, 1990—92; mem. of nat. coun. Shinui Party, National, Israel, 1992—99; head of local party Shinui, Karmiel, Israel, 1992—98; mem. of local city coun. (mem.: governing body, dir. in econ. body; mem. committees: contracts, edn., allocation, city planning City Coun., Karmiel, Israel, 1993—98; chairperson of the com. synagogue, Karmiel, Israel, 1998—2000. Pvt. NACHAL, 1972—74, Jericho, Golan, Coast. Recipient Spl. Achievements In Stats., Tel-Aviv U., 1975, Spl. Achievements In Psychology, 1977, Spl. Achievements In Stats., 1976, Spl. Achievements In Psychology, 1976, 1975, MRC Scholarship, Can., 1985-1988, Ont. Govtl. Assistance, 1984-1985, Grad. First In Class In Stats., Tel-Aviv U., 1977; grantee, Chief

Scientist, Ministry of Health, 2000-2002, Collaboration 2000, 1999-2002, Chief Scientist, Ministry of Health, 1996-1998; scholar, U. of Western Ont., 1985, U. Western Ont., 1984, 1984. Mem.: Israeli Bridge Assn. (Bronze Master), Israeli Equastrian Fedn. Achievements include design of Guidelines for students: I writing a term paper; II writing a theroretical seminar; III writing a research seminar; Guidelines for local municipalities for funding voluntary organizations; development of BA program in criminology within behavioral sciences in Emek Yezreel College. Avocations: horseback riding, bridge, photography. Office: Tal Inst Psychotherapy 49 Morad Hagay Karmiel 20100 Israel Home: 21, Zamir St 20100 Karmiel Israel Personal E-mail: helenwa@yahoo.com.

WALLACH, STANLEY, medical educator, consultant, administrator; b. Bklyn., Dec. 10, 1928; s. Abraham and Ida Helen Wallach; m. Pearl Small, 1973; children: Sara Lynn, Rhonda, Peter, Francine, Shellie, Allen, Corinne, Mara. AB, Cornell U., 1948; MA in Phys. Chemistry, Columbia U., 1949; MD, SUNY Downstate Med. Ctr., 1953. Diplomate Am. Bd. Internal Medicine, Am. Bd. Endocrinology and Metabolism. Intern Kings County Hosp., Bklyn., 1953-54; resident in internal medicine VA Hosp./Salt Lake Gen. Hosp., Salt Lake City, 1954-56; fellow in endocrinology and metabolism Mass. Gen. Hosp., Boston, 1956-57; attending physician Kings County Hosp., Bklyn., 1957-73, SUNY Hosp., Bklyn., 1966-73, Albany (N.Y.) Med. Ctr., 1973-83; chief of med. svc. VA Med. Ctr., Albany, 1973-83, Bay Pines, Fla., 1983-90, cons. Tampa, Fla., 1991-92; attending physician Tampa Gen. Hosp., 1991—92, Moffitt Cancer Ctr., 1991-92; dir. med. edn. Cath. Med. Ctr., Jamaica, N.Y., 1992-93; dir. endocrinology and co-dir. osteoporosis ctr. Hosp. for Joint Diseases, NYC, 1993—2001; instr. in medicine SUNY Downstate Med. Ctr., 1957-58, from asst. prof. to assoc. prof., 1960-71, prof., 1971-73; prof., asst. chmn. dept. medicine Albany Med. Coll., 1973-77, prof., assoc. chmn. dept. medicine, 1977-83; prof. internal medicine Coll. Medicine U. South Fla., 1983-92, assoc. chmn. dept. internal medicine, 1988-92; exec. dir. Am. Coll. Nutrition, 1993—2003; clin. prof. medicine NYU Sch. Medicine, NYC, 1995—. Pres. Certification Bd. for Nutrition Specialists, 1992-96; career scientist Health Rsch. Coun., City of N.Y., 1967-71; program dir. USPHS Clin. Rsch. Ctr., SUNY Downstate Med. Ctr., 1966-73; rsch. collaborator Brookhaven Nat. Lab., Upton, N.Y., 1970-82; vice-chmn. Gordon Rsch. Conf. on Magnesium in Biochem. Processes and Medicine, 1987, chmn., 1990; cons. NIH, NSF, USDA, Nat. Osteoporosis Found., Nat. Arthritis Found., U.S. Pharmacopeial Conf. Mem. editl. bd. Jour. Am. Coll. of Nutrition, 1981—, Magnesium and Trace Elements, 1982—90, Jour. Trace Elements in Exptl. Medicine, 1987—90; reviewer Am. Jour. Medicine, Annals of Internal Medicine, Archives of Internal Medicine, Jour. Clin. Endocrinology and Metabolism, Endocrinology, Metabolism, Calcified Tissue Internat., Jour. Bone and Mineral Rsch., Osteoporosis Internat., Procs. of Soc. Exptl. Biology and Medicine, Jour. Nutritional Biochemistry; contbr. numerous articles to profl. jours. Capt. med. corps. USNR, 1968—99. Co-recipient Hektoen Silver award AMA Conv., 1959, John D. Johnson award Paget's Disease Found., 1989, honoree of 20th ann. gala, 1998. Fellow ACP (emeritus), Am. Coll. Clin. Pharmacology, Am. Coll. Endocrinology, Am. Coll. Nutrition (bd. dirs. 1982-93, v.p. 1983-85, pres.-elect 1985-87, pres. 1987-89, sec., treas. 1991-93, exec. dir. 1993-2003), Am. Soc. Nutrition (emeritus).; mem. Assn. Am. Physicians, Am. Soc. for Clin. Investigation (emeritus), Am. Fedn. Clin. Rsch. (emeritus), Am. Soc. Bone and Mineral Rsch. (emeritus), Am. Assn. Clin. Endocrinology (emeritus), Endocrine Soc. (emeritus), Paget's Disease Found. (pres., bd. dirs. med. adv. panel), Internat. Bone and Mineral Soc., Internat. Soc. Trace Element Rsch. in Humans. Office: 1200 80th St S Saint Petersburg FL 33707 Personal E-mail: stanthemensch@gmail.com. *

WALLER, JOHN LOUIS, anesthesiologist, educator; b. Loma Linda, Calif., Dec. 1, 1944; s. Louis Clinton and Sue (Bruce) W.; m. Jo Lynn Marie Haas, Aug. 4, 1968; children: Kristina, Karla, David. BA, So. Coll., Collegedale, Tenn., 1967; MD, Loma Linda U., 1971. Diplomate Am. Bd. Anesthesiology. Intern Hartford (Conn.) Hosp., 1971—72; resident in anesthesiology Harvard U. Med. Sch.-Mass. Gen. Hosp., Boston, 1972—74, fellow, 1974—75; asst. prof. anesthesiology Emory U. Sch. Medicine, Atlanta, 1977—80, assoc. prof., 1980—86, chmn. dept. anesthesiology, 1986—2000, prof., 1986—2001, prof. emeritus, 2001—; chief anesthesiology Emory U. Hosp., Atlanta, 1986-94, med. dir., 1993-95; assoc. v.p. info. svcs. Woodruff Health Scis. Ctr., 1995-97; chief info. officer Emory U. System Healthcare, Atlanta, 1995-97; prof. anesthesiology Med. U. S.C., Charleston, 2002—, chmn. dept. anesthesia and perioperative medicine, 2002—05, dir. med. informatics, 2005—. Cons. Arrow Internat., Inc., Reading, Pa., 1988—; mem. adv. com. on anesthetic and life support drugs FDA, Washington, 1986—92; numerous vis. professorships and lectures. Contbr. articles to med. jours. Bd. dir. Picis Inc., 2006—. Maj. MC USAF, 1975—77. Recipient cert. of appreciation Office Sec. Def., 1983. Fellow: Am. Coll. Chest Physicians, Am. Coll. Anesthesiologists; mem.: Assn. Cardiac Anesthesiologists, Soc. Acad. Anesthesia Chmn. (councillor 1989—), Assn. Univ. Anesthesiologists, Internat. Anesthesia Rsch. Soc. (trustee 1984—2002, sec. 1996—98, chair 1998—2000), Soc. Cardiovascular Anesthesiologists (pres. 1991—93), Am. Soc. Anesthesiologists. Avocations: fishing, sailing, swimming. Office: Med Univ SC Dept Anes and Perioperative Medicine 167 Ashley Ave Ste 301 Charleston SC 29425 Business E-Mail: wallerj@musc.edu.

WALLER-NIEWOLD, MARILYN J., podiatric surgeon; m. John W. Niewold; 5 children. Student, Bethel Coll., 1969-71; BS, U. Minn., 1975; postgrad., Calif. Poly., 1983-86; DPM, Calif. Coll Podiatric Medicine, 1990. Cert. foot and ankle surgeon Calif. Bd. Podiatric Medicine, Oreg. Bd. Med. Examiners; cert. physician in wound care, CMET. Resident in podiatric surgery VA Med. Ctr., San Francisco, 1990—93; rsch. fellow in HBO and wound healing VA Med. Ctr./Travis AFB, San Francisco, 1992-93; pvt. practice Hayward, Calif., 1993—2003; chief podiatry svcs., dir., amputation prevention Warm Springs Health and Wellness Ctr., Oreg., 2003—. Fellow Am. Profl. Wound Care Assn., 2008. Mem. Am. Podiatric Med. Soc., Am. Diabetes Assn., Am. Assn. Women Podiatrists, Fed. Podiatric Med. Soc., Am. Assn. for Advancement of Wound Care, Am. Coll. Foot & Ankle Orthops. & Medicine, Omicron Nu. Avocations: gardening, needlecrafts, photoscrapbooking. Business E-Mail: marilyn.waller@ihs.gov.

WALLERSTEIN, JUDITH SARETSKY, psychologist, researcher; b. NYC, Dec. 27, 1921; d. Samuel Saretsky and Augusta (Tucker) Weinberger; m. Robert S. Wallerstein, Jan. 26, 1947; children: Michael, Nina, Amy. BA, CUNY, 1943; MS, Columbia U., 1946; PhD in Psychology, Lund U., Sweden, 1978. Sr. lectr. U. Calif., Berkeley, 1966—91, sr. lectr. emeritus, 1991—; dir. Calif. Children of Divorce Project, Marin County, 1971—. Founder, former exec. dir. Judith Wallerstein Ctr. Family in Transition, Corte Madera, Calif., 1980—93. Author: (book) Surviving the Breakup, 1980, Second Chances, 1989, The Good Marriage, 1995, The Unexpected Legacy of Divorce, 2000, What About the Kids, 2003; contbr. articles to profl. jours. Mem. adv. com. family law Calif. Senate Subcom. Adminstrn. Justice, 1977—79; mem. task force family equity Calif. State Senate, 1986. Recipient Koshland award in social welfare, San Francisco Found., 1975, Renè Spitz award, Denver Psychoanalytic Soc., 1991, Geri Taylor Meml. award, No. Calif. Psychiat. Soc., 1993, Presdl. citation, APA Divsn. Family Psychology, 1995, Dale Richmond award, Am. Acad. Pediat., 1996, award, ABA Section on Family Law, 2001, Presdl. citation, APA, 2001; fellow, Ctr. Advanced Study in the Behavioral Scis., Stanford, Calif., 1979—80, Rockefeller Found. Study Ctr., Bellagio, Italy, 1992. Mem.: NASW, Internat. Psychoanalytical Assn., Assn. Family Conciliation Cts., Assn. Child Psychoanalysis (mem. exec. coun. 1977—80), Am. Orthopsychiat. Assn., San Francisco Psychoanalytic Soc. (interdisciplinary mem.), N.Y. Freudian Soc. (hon.), Am. Psychoanalytic Assn. (hon.), Phi Beta Kappa. Achievements include principal investigator follow-up study effects of divorce on children and their parents; principal investigator study of good marriages. Office Phone: 415-435-3417. Personal E-mail: judywall@comcast.net.

WALLERSTEIN, ROBERT SOLOMON, retired psychiatrist; b. Berlin, Jan. 28, 1921; s. Lazar and Sarah (Guensberg) Wallerstein; m. Judith Hannah Saretsky, Jan. 26, 1947; children: Michael Jonathan, Nina Beth, Amy Lisa. BA, Columbia U., 1941, MD, 1944; postgrad., Topeka Inst. Psychoanalysis, 1951-58. Assoc. dir., then dir. rsch. Menninger Found., Topeka, 1954-66; chief psychiatry Mt. Zion Hosp., San Francisco, 1966-78; tng. and supervising analyst San Francisco Psychoanalytic Inst., 1966—; clin. prof. U. Calif. Sch. Medicine, Langley-Porter Neuropsychiat. Inst., 1967-75, prof., chmn. dept. psychiatry, also dir. inst., 1975-85, prof. dept. psychiatry, 1985-91, prof. emeritus, 1991—, ret. Vis. prof. psychiatry La. State U. Sch. Medicine, New Orleans Psychoanalytic Inst., Pahlavi U., Shiraz, Iran, 1977, Fed. U. Rio Grande do Sul, Portol Alegre, Brazil, 1980; mem., chmn. rsch. scientist career devel. com. NIMH, 1966—70, fellow Ctr. Advanced Study Behavioral Scis., Stanford, Calif., 1964—65, 1981—82, Rockefeller Found. Study Ctr., Bellagio, Italy, 1992. Author: 21 books; mem. editl. bd.: numerous profl. jours.; contbr. 385 articles to profl. jours. With US Army, 1946—48. Recipient Heinz Hartmann award, N.Y. Psychoanalytic Inst., 1968, Disting. Alumnus award, Menninger Sch. Psychiatry, 1972, J. Elliott Royer award, U. Calif., San Francisco, 1973, Outstanding Achievement award, No. Calif. Psychiat. Soc., 1987, Mt. Airy gold medal, 1990, Mary Singleton Sigourney award, 1991, Outstanding Contbn. to Psychoanalytic Edn. award, Internat. Fedn. Psychoanalytic Edn., 1999. Fellow: ACP, Am. Orthopsychiat. Assn., Am. Psychiat. Assn., Am. Coll. Psychoanalysts; mem.: Group Advancement Psychiatry, Brit. Psycho-Analytic Soc. (hon.), Mex. Psychoanalytic Assn. (hon.), Mex. Assn. Psychoanaltyic Practice, Tng. Rsch. (hon.), Internat. Psychoanalytic Assn. (v.p. 1977—85, pres. 1985—89, hon. v.p. 1999—), Am. Psychoanalytic Assn. (pres. 1971—72), Phi Beta Kappa, Alpha Omega Alpha. Office Phone: 415-435-3417.

WALLNER, MARTIN, pharmacologist, educator; b. Vorau, Austria, Apr. 9, 1962; Diploma in Engring., Graz Inst. Tech., 1988, PhD, 1995. Asst. prof., dept. molecular and med. pharmacology UCLA, 2007—. Mem.: Soc. Neurosci. Avocation: sports. Office: 650 Charles E Young Dr S Rm 23 338 CHS Los Angeles CA 90095-1735 Business E-Mail: mwallner@mednet.ucla.edu.

WALSEMANN, KATRINA M., healthcare educator; b. Calif., Dec. 28, 1975; BA, U. Calif., Davis, 1997; PhD, U. Mich., Ann Arbor, 2005. Postdoc. rsch. fellow U. Mich., Ann Arbor, 2005—07; asst. prof. U. SC, 2007—. Recipient Anna Olcott Smith award, U. Mich., Ann Arbor. Mem.: Population Assn. Am. Office: 800 Sumter St Rm 216 Columbia SC 29204 Business E-Mail: kwalsema@sc.edu.

WALSH, CHRISTINE ANN, cardiologist; b. Bklyn., Dec. 31, 1947; d. Martin and Loretta (Lesniewski) Kull; m. Sean Michael Walsh, June 10, 1978; children: Kathleen, Sean, Stephen. BS, Fordham U., 1969; MD, Yale U., 1973. Diplomate Am. Bd. Pediatrics, Am. Bd. Critical Care Medicine, Am. Bd. Pediatric Cardiology. Intern, then resident Babies Hosp., N.Y., Columbia-Presbyn. Med. Ctr., N.Y.; fellow in pediatric cardiology Columbia U., N.Y., asst. prof. Coll. Physicians and Surgeons NYC, 1980-84; asst. prof. Albert Einstein Coll. of Medicine, NYC, 1984-91; asst. attending physician N.C. Bronx Hosp., 1984—; asst. attending pediatrician Jacobi Med. Ctr., Bronx, 1984—; dir. Pediat. Dysrhythmia Ctr. Montefiore Med. Ctr., Bronx, 1984—, from asst. to assoc. attending pediatrician, 1984-98, attending pediatrician, 1998—, chief sect. pediat. cardiology, 2002—07, co-dir., cardiogenetics, 2008—; assoc. prof. pediat. Albert Einstein Coll. of Medicine, Bronx, 1991-98, prof., 1998—, co-chair admissions com., 1998—. Cons. Adult Arrhythmia Svc., Montefiore Med. Ctr., Pacemaker Ctr., epilepsy unit, Cranio-facial Ctr.; postdoctorate in cardiac electrophysiology and phramcology Columbia U. Coll. Physicians and Surgeons, NYC, 1978—80. Editor: Adolescent Medicine, State of Art Revs., Adolescent Cardiology; contbr. articles to profl. jours. Bd. dirs. Velo-Cardio-Facial Syndrome Ednl. Found., NYC, 1995—. Grantee, Albert Einstein Interdivisional, 1995, 1999. Fellow: Am. Acad. Pediat., Am. Coll. Cardiology; mem.: N.Y. Soc. Pediatric Critical Care Assn., Am. Heart Assn., Pediat. Electrophysiology Soc., Pediatric Cardiology Soc. (treas. 1987—88, sec. 1988—89, v.p. 1989—90, pres. 1990—91), Heart Rhythm Soc., Assn. Yale Alumni Medicine (sec.), Phi Beta Kappa. Avocations: gardening, skiing, scuba diving, piano, camping. Home: PO Box 258 Flushing NY 11363-0238 Office Phone: 718-741-2310, 718-741-2343. *

WALSH, DANIEL P., retired hospital administrator; BA in Economics, Rutgers U.; M in Bus. Adminstrn., Mich. State U.; M in Health Adminstrn., U. Minn. Diplomate Am. Coll. of Healthcare Execs., lic. Nursing Home Adminstr. Dir. Health Care Facility Planning and Rev., 1974; CEO Nassau-Suffolk Hosp. Coun., 1978; dep. exec. dir. Nassau-Suffolk Health Sys. Agy., chmn.; joined Good Samaritan Hosp. Med. Ctr., 1981, pres. and CEO; chmn. NY State Cath. Health Conf.; pres. and CEO Winthrop-Univ. Hosp., 1999—2009. With Fireman's Mus., Ursuline Sisters. Recipient David award, Networking Mag., 2007. Fellow: Am. Coll. of Health Care Execs. (Execs. award); mem.: Soc. of the Friendly Sons of St. Patrick (Friendly Son 2007), Am. Hosp. Association's Regional Policy Bd., Greater NY Hosp. Assn. (bd. dir.), Healthcare Assn. of New York State (bd. dir.), Hosp. Fin. Mgmt. Assn. Office: c/o Winthrop-University Hospital 259 First St Mineola NY 11501 Office Phone: 516-663-0333.

WALSH, DAVID JOSEPH, pediatric neurologist, educator; b. St. Louis, Oct. 5, 1946; s. Joseph Lloyd and Dorothy Ann Walsh. BS, Georgetown U., Washington, DC, 1968; MD, Med. U. SC, 1973. Diplomate Am. Bd. Psychiatry and Neurology, Am. Bd. Pediat. Asst. prof. neurology and pediat. Jacksonville Health Edn. Program, U. Fla., Jacksonville, 1981—82; asst. prof. pediat. and neurology U. Kans., Kansas City, 1982—88; pvt. practice Allegheny Neurol. Assoc., Pitts., 1988—90; asst. prof. neurology Med. Coll. Wis., Milw., 1990—2004; assoc. prof. neurology St. Louis U., St. Louis, 2004—11, prof. neurology psychiatry, 2011—. Program dir. pediat. residency U. Kans., Kansas City, 1982—87; program dir. pediat. neurology residency program Med. Coll. Wis., Milw., 2001—03; chief med. staff, divsn. neurology Children's Hosp. Wis., Milw., 2001—04; chief sect. child neurology St. Louis U., St. Louis, 2004—11. Author: (short story) Upping the Ritalin. Chair profl. adv. bd. Epilepsy Found. S.E. Wis., Milw., 1992—2004, pres., 1994—2004; sec. profl. adv. bd. Epilepsy Found., 2006—; pres. profl. adv. bd. Epilepsy Found. Greater St. Louis area, 2008—11. Lt. USNR, 1974—76. Fellow: Am. Acad. Neurology; mem.: Assn. U. Profs. Neurology, Harvard Med. Alumni Assn., Med. U. SC Alumni Assn., Child Neurology Soc. Independent. Roman Catholic. Avocations: Aikido, opera, travel. Office: Cardinal Glennon Children's Hosp 1465 S Grand Blvd Glennon Hall Rm 7514 Saint Louis MO 63104 Business E-Mail: walshdj@slu.edu.

WALSH, EUGENIA LAURA, psychologist; b. Cortland, NY, Apr. 30, 1927; d. Melvin James Wilkin and Laura Eda Wills; m. Maurice Edwin Becker (div.); children: Sylvia Pow, Stanley Becker, Sheryl Savas, Gary Becker; m. Robert R. Walsh, 1978. AA in Psychology, Lansing CC, Mich., 1969, BA in Social Sci. summa cum laude, Mich. State U., East Lansing, 1971; MA in Clin. Psychology, Ctrl. Mich. U., Mt. Pleasant, 1973. Ltd. lic. psychologist Mich., cert. social worker Mich. Comml. artist Photographic Sci. Lab. Cornell U., Ithaca, NY, 1944—47; asst. dir. Common Ground Crisis Ctr., St. Johns, Mich., 1974; rsch. analyst Mich. Dept. Social Svcs., Lansing, 1974—75; clin. psychologist Mich. Dept. Corrections, Jackson, 1975—78, 1981, Robert R. Walsh, PhD & Assocs., Jackson, 1979—83, Psychol. Svcs. Cons., Brooklyn, Mich., 2001—. Bus. owner antiques store, Jackson, 1979—80. Author: The Kids' Pages, 1998. Mem. Concerned Ams. of Mich., Lansing, 1969—71, Jackson County Vols. Against Pound Seizure, Jackson, 2004—; vol. psychologist Clinton County Cmty. Mental Health, St. Johns, Mich., 1974. Fellow, Ctrl. Mich. U., 1971; scholar, Mich. State U., 1969. Mem.: NAACP (exec. bd. 1999—2000), Jackson Civic Art Assn., Jacksonburgh Branch - The Questers, Coalition for Corrections Reform, Bklyn. Artists Assn., Mich. Assn. Profl. Psychologists, Mensa, Jackson Camera Club (photographer, Best of Yr. 1989), Phi Theta Kappa. Avocations: photography, art, writing. Home: PO Box 429 Brooklyn MI 49230 Office: Psychol Svcs Cons PO Box 429 Brooklyn MI 49230

WALSH, JOSEPH BRENNAN, ophthalmologist; b. Troy, NY, Mar. 6, 1941; s. Joseph Edward and Edna Margaret (Molloy) W. BS in Biology, Georgetown U., 1962, MD, 1966. Diplomate Am. Bd. Ophthalmology. Intern SUNY Upstate Med. Ctr., Syracuse, 1966-67; resident in medicine Univ. Hosp., Boston, 1968—69; resident in ophthalmology The N.Y. Eye and Ear Infirmary, NYC, 1970-73; retina fellow Montefiore Hosp. and Med. Ctr./Albert Einstein Coll. Medicine, Bronx, 1973-74; from instr. to assoc. prof. dept. ophthalmology Montefiore Med. Ctr./Albert Einstein Coll. of Medicine, Bronx, N.Y., 1973-88; chmn., prof. dept. ophthalmology NY. Eye and Ear Infirmary, NY. Med. Coll., 1988—, pres., 2008—, Belingba Bingam & Gerald G. Pierce disting. chair; chapter mem. Hosp. St. John Jerusalem, 1988—, hospitaller, 1994—2001, gov., 1995—2008, chancellor, 2001—05. Lectr. in field. Capt. M.C. USAF, 1968—70. Decorated Knight Hospitaller Am. Priory of the Most Venerable Order Hosp. St. John Jerusalem; recipient Belinda Bingham Pierce and Gerald G. Pierce, MD Disting. Chair Ophthalmology, 2007. Fellow N.Y. Acad. Medicine (Charles H. May Meml. lectr. 1998—), N.Y. Acad. Scis., Royal Coll. Ophthalmologists, Am. Acad. Ophthalmology; mem. Assn. for Rsch. in Vision and Ophthalmology, Ophthalmic Laser Surg. Soc. (pres. 1992-94), Macula Soc., Retina Soc., N.Y. Soc. for Clin. Ophthalmology (pres. 1984-85, Schoenberg lectr. 1993—), N.Y. Ophthalmol. Soc. (sec. 2002, pres. 2008). Office: NY Eye and Ear Infirmary 310 E 14th St New York NY 10003-4201 Office Phone: 212-979-4447. Office Fax: 212-979-4268. Business E-Mail: jwalsh@mee.edu, jwalsh@nyee.com, jwalsh@nyee.edu. E-mail: rlewis212@aol.com.

WALSH, NICOLAS EUGENE, rehabilitation services professional, educator; b. Mpls., July 1, 1947; s. Leonard Cyril and June Alice Walsh; m. Wendy Sarah Allnutt, June 1, 1973; children: Meghan, Rorey, Katlin, Alaine. BS, USAF Acad., 1969; MS, Marquette U., 1974; MD, U. Colo., 1979. Asst. prof. naval sci. Marquette U., Milw., 1972—74; from asst. prof. to assoc. prof. rehab. medicine U. Tex. Health Sci. Ctr., San Antonio, 1982—89, prof., chmn. rehab. medicine, 1989—, exec. assoc. dean Sch. Medicine, 1999—2000, disting. prof., 2001—. Dir. Am. Bd. Phys. Medicine and Rehab., Rochester, Minn., 1994—2006, sec., 1996—98, chmn., 1998—2005; pres., CEO Univ. Physician Group, 1998—2001. Author book chpts.; editor:

Rehabilitation of Chronic Pain, 1991; editor-in-chief Archives of Phys. Medicine and Rehab., Chgo., 1994—2000; mng. editor: Rehabilitation Medicine: Principles and Practices, 2005. Recipient Excellence in Rsch. award, Am. Jour. Phys. Medicine and Rehab., 1991; named Health Care Profl. of Yr., Gov.'s Com. for Disabled Persons, 1989. Fellow: Am. Acad. Phys. Medicine and Rehab. (Richard and Hinda Rosenthal Found. award 1991, Zieter lectr. 2003), Am. Bd. Pain Medicine (v.p. 1993—94, sec. 1994—96); mem.: Phys. Medicine and Rehab. Edn. and Rsch. Found. (pres. 1993—2000, Excellence in Rsch. award 1991), Assn. Acad. Physiatrists (v.p. 1993—95, pres. 1996—98). Office: U Tex Health Sci Ctr Mail Code 7872 7703 Floyd Curl Dr San Antonio TX 78229-3900 Home Phone: 210-493-1174; Office Phone: 210-567-5350. Business E-Mail: walshn@uthscsa.edu.

WALSH, PATRICK CRAIG, urologist; b. Akron, Ohio, Feb. 13, 1938; s. Raymond Michael and Catherine N. (Rodden) W.; m. Margaret Campbell, May 23, 1964; children— Christopher, Jonathan, Alexander. AB, Case Western Res. U., 1960, MD, 1964. Intern in surgery Peter Bent Brigham Hosp., Boston, 1964-65, asst. resident in surgery, 1965-66; asst. resident in pediatric surgery Children's Hosp. Med. Center, Boston, 1966-67; resident in urology UCLA Med. Ctr., 1967-71; dir., chmn. James Buchanan Brady Urol. Inst., urologist-in-chief Johns Hopkins Hosp., Balt., 1974—2004; prof., dir. dept. urology Johns Hopkins U. Sch. Medicine, 1974—2004, prof. urology, 2004—. Contbr. articles to med. jours. Served to comdr. M.C. USN, 1971-73. Recipient Charles F. Kettering medal GM Cancer Rsch. Found., 1996, King Faisal Internat. prize, 2007. Mem. Am. Assn. Genitourinary Surgeons, Clin. Soc. Genitourinary Surgeons, Am. Urol. Assn., Am. Surg. Assn. Inst. Medicine of NAS, Alpha Omega Alpha. Roman Catholic. Office: Johns Hopkins Med Inst 600 N Wolfe St Baltimore MD 21287-0005 Office Phone: 410-955-6100.

WALSH, R. MATTHEW, surgeon, gastroenterologist; Grad., Creighton U.; MD, Med. Coll. Wis. Intern & resident Loyola U. Med. Ctr. Foster G. McGaw Hosp.; fellow Mass. Gen. Hosp., Cleveland Clinic, hepato-pancreato-biliary & transplant surgeon. Office: Cleveland Clinic 9500 Euclid Ave MC-A80 Cleveland OH 44195 Office Phone: 216-445-7576.

WALSH, SCOTT WESLEY, reproductive physiologist, researcher; b. Wauwatosa, Wis., July 23, 1947; s. Virgil C. and Harriet E. (Jacobson) W.; m. Cynthia Lee Sorenson, Oct. 10, 1981 (div. Mar. 1987); m. Margaret Ann Dahmus, Apr. 16, 1994. BS with honors, U. Wis., 1970, MS, 1972, PhD, 1975. Asst. prof. U. N.D. Sch. Medicine, Grand Forks, 1975-76; asst. to assoc. scientist Oreg. Primate Ctr., Beaverton, 1976-80; asst. prof. Oreg. Health Scis. U., Portland, 1978-80, Mich. State U., E. Lansing, 1980-85; assoc. prof. U. Tex. Health Sci. Ctr., Houston, 1985-90; prof. Va. Commonwealth U. Med. Ctr., Richmond, 1990. Grant reviewer Nat. Inst. Child Health and Human Devel., Washington, 1988—, editl. bd. mem. Hypertension Pregnancy. Mem. editl. bd. Reproductive Scis. Named to Dean's Tchg. Excellence List, U. Tex. Health Sci. Ctr., 1989; recipient Shannon award Nat. Inst. Child Health and Human Devel., NIH, grantee 1983—, Grant-in-aid Am. Heart Assn., 1999-2002. Mem. Soc. for Gynecologic Investigation, Am. Physiol. Soc., Endocrine Soc., Soc. for Study Reprodn., Soc. for Free Radical Biology and Medicine, Internat. Soc. for Study Hypertension in Pregnancy. Achievements include discovery of imbalance of increased thromboxane, decreased protacyclin and increased lipid peroxides, decreased antioxidants in placentas obtained from women with pregnancy-induced hypertension. Office: Va Commonwealth U Med Ctr Dept Ob-Gyn PO Box 980034 Richmond VA 23298-0034

WALSH, THOMAS DECLAN, pharmacologist, educator; b. Cork, Ireland, July 24, 1947; came to U.S., 1983; s. Thomas and Ann (Cahill) W.; married; children: Richard, Conor, Rory. MB BChir, BA of Obstetrics, Univ. Coll., Dublin, 1971; MS in Clin. Biochemistry, U. Newcastle-upon-Tyne, Tyne-on-Wear, Eng., 1976. Bd. cert. in internal medicine and med. oncology. Intern St. Vincent's Hosp., Dublin, 1971; rsch. fellow in clin. pharmacology St. Christopher's Hospice, London, 1979-84; JM Found. oncology/pharmacology fellow devel. chemotherapy Meml. Sloan Kettering Cancer Ctr., NYC, 1984-87; dir. palliative care program Cleve. Clinic Taussig Cancer Ctr., 1987—, endowed chair palliative medicine, 1996; prof. internal medicine Ohio State U. Coll. Medicine, 1999; med. dir. CCF Healthcare Ventures, Inc., 1998, exec. dir., 1999; interim dir. Rehab. Inst. Cleve. Clinic. Med. dir. Cleve. Clinic Home Care Svcs., 1999—. Editor: (book) Symptom Control, 1988. Fellow ACP, Royal Coll. Physicians; mem. European Assn. Palliative Care (founding mem.), Am. Acad. Hospice and Palliative Medicine (founding mem.). Avocations: music, military history. Office: Cleve Clinic Found M76 9500 Euclid Ave # M76 Cleveland OH 44195-0001 Fax: 216-445-5090. E-mail: walsht@ccf.org.

WALSH, THOMAS JOHN, infectious disease physician, oncologist, researcher, educator; BA in Biology/Chemistry, Assumption Coll., Worcester, Mass., 1974; MD, The Johns Hopkins U., 1978. Diplomate in internal medicine, infectious diseases, med. oncology Am. Bd. Internal Medicine. Resident in medicine Michael Reese Hosp., U. Chgo., 1978-82; fellow pathology Johns Hopkins Hosp. and Univ., Balt., 1979-80; fellow infectious diseases U. Md., Balt., 1982-85, fellow med. oncology, 1985-86, Nat. Cancer Inst., Bethesda, Md., 1986-87, sr. staff fellow, 1987-88, med. officer, 1988—91, sr. investigator, 1991—, head mycology unit, 1991—, chief immunocompromised host sect., 1996—; prof. U. Md. Sch. Medicine, Balt., 1999—. Prof. The Johns Hopkins U. Sch. Medicine, Balt., 1985—, Edward J. Hook vis. prof., U. va., 2008, Temple W. Williams Jr., vis. prof., Methodist Hosp., Cornell U., 2008. Contbr. chpts. to Management of Infections in Patients with Cancer, 1985, Critical Problems in Trauma Care, Vol. II Medical Management, Current Therapy in Hematology/Oncology, 1987, Diagnosis and Therapy of Systemic Mycoses, 1989, Respiratory Diseases in the Immunosuppressed Host, 1990, Hematology: Basic Principles and Practice, 3d edit., 1999, Medical Microbiology, 3d edit., 1991, Pediatric AIDS, 1990, Current Therapy in Critical Care Medicine, 1990, Emerging Targets in Antibacterial and Antifungal Chemotherapy, 1991, The Principles and Practice of Medical Intensive Care, 1993, Aspergillus: The Biology and Industrial Applications, 1991, New Strategies in Fungal Disease, 1992, Oral Fungal Infections in Immunocompromised Patients, 1991, Current Therapy in Pediatric Infectious Diseases, 3d edit., 1993, Hematopoietic Growth Factors and Mononuclear Phagocytes, 1993, Fungal Diseases of the Lung, 2d edit., 1993, Manual of Clinical Microbiology, 7th edit., 1994, Infectious Diseases, 1994, Infectious Complications of Cancer, 1995, Principles and Practice of Pediatric Oncology, 5th edit., 2006, Current Therapy in Adult Medicine, 4th edit., 1997, Cutaneous Infection and Therapy, 1997, Manual of Bone Marrow Transplantation, 1997, Adrenomedullin, 1998, Transplant Infections, 1998, Hunter's Tropical Medicine, 1999, Cancer: Principles and Practice of Oncology, 2001, 05, 08, others; editor: Medical Mycology. Infectious Diseases Clinics of North America, Vols. I an II, 2002-03, Antimicrobial Resistance, 2008, Aspegillus Fumigatus and Aspergillosis, 2008; contbr. more than 700 publs. and 500 rsch. abstracts. Recipient Med. Mycology Fellow award Nat. Found. for Infectious Diseases, 1984, Young Investigator award ICAAC and Am. Soc. Microbiology, USPHS Commendation medal, 1993, 01, Outstanding Svc. medal, USPHS, 1996, Meritorious Svc. medal, 2003, Disting. Clin. Tchr. award NIH, 2002, Nat. Emergency Preparedness award, 2004, Rhoda Benham award 2008, Med. Myrological Soc. Am., 2008, Lucille Georg medal Internat. Soc. Human & Animal Mycology, 2009. Fellow ACP, Am. Acad. Microbiology, Infectious Diseases Soc. Am., Am. Coll. Chest Physicians). Achievements include development of experimental and clinical found. for new approaches to diagnosis, treatment and prevention of life-threatening infections in immunocompromised children and adults; development of new understanding of pathogenesis, diagnosis, and treatment of emerging mycoses; devel. new approaches to augmentation of host defenses in immunocomprised children and adults with cancer; development of direct clinical care leading to life saving interventions in children and adults with severe infections; mentoring a new generation of experts in the study and care of patients with serious infections.

WALSH, THOMAS JOSEPH, ophthalmologist; b. NYC, Sept. 18, 1931; s. Thomas Joseph and Virginia (Hughes) W.; m. Sally Ann Maust, June 21, 1958; children: Thomas Raymond, Sara Ann, Mary Kelly, Kathleen Meghan. BA, Coll. Fordham, 1954; MD, Bowman Gray Med. Sch., 1958; degree in Mgmt., Yale U., 1998. Intern St. Vincent's Hosp., NYC, 1958-59; resident ophthalmology Bowman Gray Med. Sch., Winston-Salem, NC, 1961-64; fellow neuro-ophthalmology Bascom Palmer Eye Inst., Miami, Fla., 1964-65; practice medicine specializing in neuro-ophthalmology Stamford, Conn., 1965—; dir. neuro-ophthalmology service, asst. prof. ophthalmology and neurology Yale Sch. Medicine, New Haven, 1965-74, assoc. prof., 1974-79, prof., 1979—, also bd. permanent officers; dir. ophthalmology Stamford Hosp., 1978-83; mem. staff St. Joseph Hosp., Yale New Haven Hosp. Cons. to surgeon gen. army in neuro-ophthalmology Walter Reed Hosp., Washington, 1966—, VA Hosp., West Haven, 1965—, Silver Hill Found., New Canaan, Conn., 1974—; adj. prof. Dartmouth Med. Sch.; telemedicine bd. ORBIS Internat.; cons. mem. of bd. Orbis Internat.; lectr. in field. Contbr. articles to various publs. Adv. bd. Stamford Salvation Army, 1972-92; med. bd. Darien Nurses Assn., Conn., 1972—; surgeon Darien Fire Dept., 1969—. With AUS, 1959-61. Decorated Knight of Malta; Centennial fellow Johns Hopkins, 1976; named one of Top Opthalmologists, Best Doctors.com, 2004 Mem. AMA, Conn., Fairfield County med. socs., Acad. Ophthalmology, Oxford Ophthal. Congress, Acad. Neurology, Am. Assn. Neurol. Surgeons, Internat. Neuro-Ophthalmology Soc., Soc. Med. Cons. to Armed Forces, Cosmos Club (Washington), Darien County Club, Yale Club (N.Y.C), Lions, Army-Navy Club, Orbis Internat. (cybermedicine bd. mem.). Office: Yale Dept Ophthalmology PO Box 208061 330 Cedar St Stamford CT 06520-8061 Home Phone: 203-866-0220; Office Phone: 203-785-6444. Personal E-mail: twalsh13@optonline.net. Business E-Mail: thomas.walsh@yale.edu.

WALSH, WILLIAM P., health facility administrator; Sr. v.p. North Bronx Healthcare Network; exec. dir. Jacobi Med. Ctr. of NYC Health and Hosps. Corp. Office: Jacobi Medical Center 125 Worth St New York NY 10013 Office Phone: 212-788-3321. Office Fax: 212-788-0040.

WALSKI, MICHAEL, pathophysiologist, molecular biologist; b. Osielec, Cracow, Poland, Mar. 15, 1941; s. Stefan and Anna (Heisig) W.; m. Renata Celary, Dec. 19, 1984; children: Anna, Łukasz. MS, Poznań U., 1965; PhD, Med. Acad., Warsaw, 1969, MScD, 1986. Asst. Med. Acad., Warsaw, 1965-74, adj., 1974-90; assoc. prof. Med. Rsch. Centre, Warsaw, 1990—. Contbr. articles to profl. jours. Grantee Japan Soc for Promotion of Sci., Kyoto, 1972, Bristol (Eng.) U., 1981, Harvard Sch. Pub. Health, Boston, 1985. Mem. Polish Soc. Pathologists, Polish Soc. Parasitologists, N.Y. Acad. Scis., Polish Soc. Neuropathologists, Inst. Soc. Neuropathologists, European Respiratory Soc. Roman Catholic. Avocations: opera, history, architecture. Office: Polish Acad Scis Pawińskiego 5 02-106 Warsaw Poland Home: Ul. Filtrowa 59/43 02-056 Warsaw Poland Business E-Mail: walski@cmdik.pan.pl.

WALTER, JOHN, medical association administrator; With Bristol Meyers Squibb, Donald, Lufkin & Jenrette, March of Dimes, 1984—95; sr. v.p. fin. and IT Leukemia & Lymphoma Soc., CFO, exec. v.p. strategic alliances and new bus. devel., COO, pres., CEO, 2008—. Office: Leukemia & Lymphoma Soc 1311 Mamaroneck Ave White Plains NY 10605 *

WALTER, PETER, biochemist; b. Berlin; Diploma in Chemistry, Free U. Berlin, 1976; MSc in Organic Chemistry, Vanderbilt U., 1977; PhD in Cell Biology, Rockefeller U., 1981. Prof., chmn. dept. biochemistry & biophysics U. Calif., San Francisco; investigator Howard Hughes Medical Inst. Harvey lectr. Rockefeller U., 1996; Feodor-Lynen lectr. Mosbach Kolloquium, 1998. Co-author: Molecular Biology of the Cell, 2002, Essential Cell Biology, 2003. Recipient Searle Scholar award, 1983, Passano award, 1988, Eli Lilly award, 1988, Alfred P. Sloan award, 1989, Merit award, Nat. Insts. Health, 1990, Wiley Prize biomedical sciences, 2005, Gairdner Found. Internat. award, 2009. Fellow: Am. Acad. Microbiology, Am. Acad. Arts and Scis.; mem.: NAS, European Molecular Biology Orgn. (assoc.). Office: U Calif San Fransisco Dept Biochemistry & Biophysics Genentech Hall N312 600 16th St San Francisco CA 94143-2200 Office Phone: 415-476-5017. Office Fax: 415-476-5233. Business E-Mail: walter@cgl.ucsf.edu. *

WALTER, VIRGINIA LEE, psychologist, educator; b. Temple, Tex., Oct. 30, 1937; d. Luther Patterson and Virginia Lafayette (Wilkins) W.; m. Glen Ellis, 1958 (div.); children: Glen Edward, David Walter; m. Robert Reinehr, 1963 (div.); 1 son, Charles Allen; m. Robert Bruininks, 1975 (div.). BS, U. Tex., Austin, 1959, MEd, 1967; postgrad. internship program in spl. Edn. Adminstrn., 1970; EdD, U. Houston, 1973. Prof. ednl. psychology dept. ednl. psychology U. Minn., Mpls., 1973-85; pres. Sch. Resource Ctr., Austin, Tex., 1985-90; tchr. Llano Pub. Schs., 1988-97; dir. Walter Resources, 1998—. Chmn. State Adv. Coun. for Inservice Tng. Regular Classroom Tchrs., 1977-79; cons. spl. ednl. various sch. dists., state depts. and agys. Editl. cons.: Jour. Ednl. Psychology, 1979, Reading Rsch. Quar., 1982; assoc. editor: Exceptional Children, 1979-84; assoc. editor Teaching Exceptional Children, 1985-89; contbr. articles to profl. jours., papers to profl. confs. Named Minn. Spl. Educator of Yr., 1978; recipient Svc. award Internat. Coun. Exceptional Children, 1978; HEW Office of Human Devel. Svcs. grantee, 1976-80; Dept. Edn. contractee, 1980-83 Mem. Coun. for Exceptional Children, Nat. Assn. Children with Learning Disabilities (dir. Minn. chpt. 1978-80), Nat. Assn. Retarded Citizens, AAUP, Assn. Supervision and Curriculum Devel. Home and Office: 7108 Running Rope Austin TX 78731-2128

WALTERHOUSE, DAVID OTTO, physician; b. Ann Arbor, Mich., June 23, 1956; BS, U. Mich., 1978, MD, 1983. Physician Children's Meml. Hosp., 1989—. Mem. Intergroup Rhabdomyosarcoma Study Group, 1998—2000; pediat. hematology-oncology fellowship program dir. Northwestern U. Feinberg Sch. Medicine, 1999—2008, Mem.: Fedn. Am. Socs. Exptl. Biology, Am. Assn. Cancer Rsch., Am. Soc. Pediat. Hematology/Oncology, Am. Soc. Cell Biology, Children's Oncology Group (mem. soft tissue sarcoma com. 2000—11). Office: Children's Memorial Hosp 2300 Children's Plz Chicago IL 60614 Office Phone: 773-880-3223. Business E-Mail: d-walterhouse@northwestern.edu.

WALTERS, ARTHUR SCOTT, neurologist, educator, clinical research scientist; b. Balt., Feb. 20, 1943; s. Charles Henry and Jean Vivian (Scott) W.; m. Bokyun Kim, May 18, 1985 (div. Oct. 1992); m. Lesley J. Gill, Dec. 19, 1992. BA, Kalamazoo Coll., 1965; MS, Northwestern U., 1967; MD, Wayne State U., 1972. Diplomate Am. Bd. Psychiatry and Neurology; diplomate Am. Bd. Sleep Medicine; lic. med. faculty, Tenn.,2008. Intern Oakwood Hosp., Dearborn, Mich., 1972-73; resident in neurology SUNY Downstate Med. Ctr., Bklyn., 1976-79; movement disorder fellow Neurol. Inst., NYC, 1982-84; asst. prof. neurology Robert Wood Johnson Med. Sch., U. Medicine & Dentistry NJ, New Brunswick, 1984-91, assoc. prof. neurology, 1991-99, clin. prof. neurology, 1999—2008; asst. chief divsn. neurology Lyons VA Med. Ctr., NJ, 1985-89, neurology cons., 1984-99; prof. neurosci. Seton Hall U. Sch. Grad. Med. Edn., South Orange, NJ, 1999—2008, NJ Neurosci. Inst., Edison, 1999—2008; prof. neurology Vanderbilt U. Sch. Medicine, Nashville, 2008—. Nat. chmn. med. adv. bd. Restless Legs Syndrome Found., 1992-98; chair Internat. Restless Legs Study Group, 1992-2007; head Restless Legs Syndrome and Periodic Limb Movement Coun. for the Nat. Sleep Found., 1994-96; neurology cons. Coney Island Hosp., Bklyn., Bklyn. Jewish Hosp., 1980-81; presenter in field. Contbr. articles to profl. publs., chpts. to books; organizer symposia. Named Rschr. of Yr. in medicine Seton Hall U. Sch. Grad. Med. Edn., 2003-04, Michael S. Aldrich hon. lectr. in sleep medicine for outstanding contbns. to patient care, rsch. and edn. U. Mich., 2006, Best Vol. neurology faculty member UMDNJ-Robert Wood Johnson Med. Sch., 2007; recipient Disting. Svc. award Internat. Restless Legs Syndrome Study Group, 2007, Tchg. award, Sleep Fellows and Cmty. Sleep Physicians NJ Neurosci. Inst. JFK Med. Ctr., 2008; grantee UMDNJ, 1984-86, VA RAG, 1985-86, Sandoz Corp., 1985-88, VA Merit Rev., 1989-98, Clemente Found., 1994-95, Purdue Pharma, 2000—, NIH, 2002-07, EKBOM award, Disting. Svc. award Restless Legs Syndrome Found., 1998, Bronze Oak LEAF Disting. Svc. award, Lyons Va. Med. Ctr, 1998, Disting. Faculty Medical License, Tenn., 2008, Excellence in Sleep Resch., Am. Acad. Neurology Sleep Sci. award, 2010, Vice Chairperson Speciality Com. Sleep Medicine, World Pediat. Chinese Medicine Socs., 2011-. Fellow Am. Acad. Neurology, Am. Acad. Sleep Medicine; editl. bd., (journal) Sleep, Sleep Medicine; mem. AAAS, Am. Neurol. Assn., Sleep Rsch. Soc., Movement Disorder Soc., NY Acad. Scis., NJ Sleep Soc. (sec. 1995-96, treas. 1996-97, v.p. 1998-99). Achievements include Formed the first med. advisory bd. of the Restless Legs Syndrome Found; formed the Int. RLS study group compriseed of 130 physicians & scientists from 17 countries dedicated to resch on RLS & Periodic Lim Movements in sleep. Office: Dept Neurology Vanderbilt Univ Sch Medicine MCN A-0118 1161 21st Ave S Nashville TN 37232-2551 Office Phone: 615-322-0283. Personal E-mail: artumdnj@aol.com. Business E-Mail: arthur.walters@vanderbilt.edu.

WALTERS, CLAYTON WILLIAM, health facility administrator, rehabilitation services professional, consultant; b. Jellico, Tenn., June 7, 1951; s. Phillip Gordon and Sarah Eileen Walters; m. Susan Louise Brandau; children: David Clayton, Christopher, Matthew, Cassandra. AA in Humanities, Dutchess C.C., Poughkeepsie, NY, 1979. Exec. dir. Baldwin Rsch. Inst., Amsterdam, NY, 2003—04, v.p. cons., 2004—06; v.p. ops. St. Jude Thaddeus Inc., Des Moines, 2006—08, St. Gregory Retreat Ctr., 2008—. Republican. Episcopalian. Avocations: reading, book collecting, sailing. Home: PO Box 310 Bayard IA 50029 Office: Saint Gregory Retreat Ctr 5875 Fleur Dr Des Moines IA 50321 Office Phone: 515-419-8788. Business E-Mail: clayton@stgregoryctr.com.

WALTERS, FARAH M., health services company administrator, former hospital administrator; b. Feb. 10, 1945; BS, Ohio State U., 1968; MS, Case Western Res. U., 1975, MBA, 1984. Sr. v.p., gen. mgr. Univs. Hosps., Cleve., 1987-89, exec. v.p., 1989-91, exec. dir., 1991-92, pres., CEO, 1992—2002, QualHealth, LLC, 2005—. Mem.

Ohio Commn. to Study the Ohio Econ. & Tax Structure; bd. dirs. PolyOne Corp., Celanese, 2007—. Recipient Ellis Medal of Honor; named to Bus. Hall of Fame, Bus. mag., 2000, Ohio Women's Hall of Fame, 2001.

WALTERS, MARIAN R., research administrator; b. Washington, 1948; PhD, U. Houston, 1975. Prof. physiology Tulane U. Sch. Medicine, New Orleans, 1980—2004, dir. tuxcoe leadership core, 1999—2004, dir. of grad. studies in physiology, 1983—2004; assoc. dean rsch. and grad. studies Penn State U., Harrisburg, 2004—. Author: (book chapter) Encyclopedia of Hormones: Calcium Regulating Hormones. Mem.: Grants Resource Ctr. (adv. bd. mem. 2008—10), Soc. Exptl. Biology and Medicine (coun. mem. 2001—08, treas. 2006—08). Office: Penn State Harrisburg 777 W Harrisburg Pike Middletown PA 17057 Office Phone: 717-948-6303.

WALTERS, MARK DOUGLAS, obstetrician, gynecologist, director; b. Toledo, July 21, 1954; s. Donald Walters; m. Virginia Walters; children: Samantha, Maxwell, Zoe. BS in biology, U. Cincinnati, 1976; MD, Ohio State U., 1980. Cert. Am. Bd. Ob-Gyn. Intern Tufts U. Sch. Medicine, Boston, 1980—81, resident in ob-gyn., 1981—84; asst. prof. dept. ob-gyn. U. Tex. Health Sci. Ctr., San Antonio, 1984—90; assoc. prof. dept. reproductive biology and ob-gyn. Case Western Reserve U. Sch. Medicine, Cleve., 1990—93; med. dir. Women's Health Ctr. U. Hospitals of Cleve., 1990—93; head sect. gen. gynecology, dir. urogynecology The Cleve. Clinic, 1993—, dir. fellowship program in urogynecology/reconstructive pelvic surgery, 1997—, vice-chair gynecology, 2006—; prof. surgery Cleve. Clinic Lerner Coll. Medicine, 2006—. Vice chair gynecology Cleve. Clinic, 2006—. Author: (book) Clinical Urogynecology, 1993, Urogynecology and Reconstructive Pelvic Surgery, 3d edit., 2006. Recipient Ann. Resident Tchg. award, MetroHealth Med. Ctr., 1996, 1999, 2000, 2002. Fellow: Am. Coll. of Obstetricians and Gynecologists; mem.: Cleve. Soc. of Ob-gyn., Soc. of Gynecologic Surgeons, Am. Urogynecology Soc., Jour. of Gynecologic Surgery (editl. bd.), Internat. Urogynecology Jour. (editl. bd.). Office: The Cleve Clinic Dept Ob-gyn 9500 Euclid Ave Desk A81 Cleveland OH 44195 E-mail: walterm@ccf.org.

WALTON, G. CLIFFORD, physician; b. Richmond, Va., Jan. 5, 1968; s. Eugene Marion and Mary Ann (McNabb) W.; m. Tami Marie Daniel, June 26, 1998. BS summa cum laude, Hampden-Sydney Coll., 1990; MD, Med. Coll. Va., 1994. Intern Med. Coll. Va., Richmond, 1994-95; resident Blackstone (Va.) Family Practice, 1995-97; pvt. practice, Kenbridge, Va., 1997-99, Richmond, 1996—. Med. examiner Va. Dept. Health, Powhatan, 1996—; mem. housestaff coun. Med. Coll. Va., 1995-97. Sci. fair judge Southside Va. H.S., Farmville, 1988-97. Mem. AMA, Am. Acad. Family Physicians, Med. Soc. Va., Phi Beta Kappa, Sigma Xi, Omicron Delta Kappa. Avocations: baseball card collecting, gardening, photography. Home: 1640 Jeter Rd Powhatan VA 23139-6907 Office: Patient First 12101 South Chalkley Rd Chester VA 23831 Office Phone: 804-796-3636.

WALTON, ROBERT LEE, plastic surgeon; b. Lawrence, Kans., May 30, 1946; s. Robert L. and Thelma B. (Morgan) W.; m. Elisabeth K. Beahm, Oct. 7, 2000; children: Marc, Morgan, Lindsey. BA, U. Kans., 1968; MD, U. Kans., Kansas City, 1972. Diplomate Am. Bd. Surgery, Am. Bd. Plastic Surgery. Resident in surgery Johns Hopkins Hosp., Balt., 1972-74, Yale-New Haven (Conn.) Hosp., 1974-78; chief of plastic surgery San Francisco Gen. Hosp., 1979-83; prof. and chmn. dept. plastic surgery U. Mass. Med. Ctr., Worcester, 1983-94; prof., chmn dept. plastic surgery U. Chgo., 1994—2004, prof. dept. plastic surgery, 2004—. Contbr. articles to profl. jours. Founder Projecto Mira Found. for Handicapped Children, Santurce, P.R., 1990. Mem. ACS, Am. Assn. Plastic Surgeons, Am. Soc. Plastic and Reconstructive Surgery, Am. Soc. Reconstructive Microsurgery, Alpha Omega Alpha. Office: Plastic Surgery Chgo 60 East Delaware Pl Ste 1430 Chicago IL 60611 Home Phone: 312-944-0972; Office Phone: 312-337-7795. Personal E-mail: notlaw72@sbcglobal.net. Business E-Mail: drrwalton@sbcglobal.net.

WALTON, SHELLEY FAYE, immunologist, educator; b. New Zealand, Dec. 2, 1959; BSc in Biology, Ctrl. Queensland U., 1989; PhD, U. Sydney, 1998. Prin. rsch. scientist Menzies Sch. Health Rsch., 1998—2010, hon. assoc. prof., 2010; assoc. prof. immunology U. Sunshine Coast, 2010—. Recipient Chief Min.'s Rsch. and Innovation award, Northern Ter. Rsch. and Innovation Awards. Mem.: Australian Soc. Parasitology, Australian Soc. Immunology. Office: University Sunshine Coast Locked Bag 4 Maroochydore Queensland 4558 Australia Business E-Mail: swalton1@usc.edu.au.

WALTON, SHIRLEY DAWN, retired medical technician; b. Jamestown, NY, Dec. 12, 1935; d. Kenneth Everett and Wilma Alene Lewis; m. Okley Homa Walton, May 3, 1963 (dec.); 1 child, William W. Cert. respiratory care practioner Fla., 1993. Trainee Women's Christian Hosp., Jamestown, 1956—61; nurse's aid St. Joseph's Hosp., Tampa, Fla., 1963—64, cardiology technician, 1964—74; cardiology tech. U. Hosp., Tampa, 1975—82, respiratory therapist, 1982—88; cardiology tech. East Pasco Med. Ctr., Zephyrhills, Fla., 1988—98; ret., 1998. Methodist. Home: 6801 Woodsman Dr Zephyrhills FL 33544 Home Phone: 813-929-3544.

WALTRIP, ROBERT L., orthopedist; MD, John Hopkins Sch. Medicine, Balt., 1996. Cert. Orthopaedic Surgery, sports medicine Orthopaedic Surgery. Intern Univ. Pitts., resident orthopaedic surgery; fellow sports medicine Am. Sports Medicine Inst., Birmingham, Ala.; hosp. affiliations include Univ. Pitts. Med. Ctr., Butler Meml. Hosp. Office: Tri Rivers Surgical Associates Incoporated 9104 Babcock Blvd Number 2120 Pittsburgh PA 15237 Office Phone: 412-367-0600.

WALTZ, CAROLYN ANN, healthcare educator; d. Alexander J. and Reda P. Feher; m. Carroll G. Waltz, May 16, 1964; children: Laura Ann Hudson, Jennifer Lynne Hodges. BSN, U. Md., Sch. Nursing, Balt., 1963, MS, 1968; PhD, U. Del. Coll. Edn., Newark, Delaware, 1976. Cert. RN, State Bd. Nursing, Md., 1963. Instr. U. Md., Balt., 1968—72, asst. prof. grad. cmty. health nursing, prof.; assoc. prof. U. Md. Sch. Nursing, Balt., Md., 1976—90, asst. prof., 1972—75, dir. measurement clin. and ednl. outcomes project, 1983—88, coord. evaluation, prof., 1990—95, 1995—97, acting asst. dean continuing edn. and internat. programs, 1997—97, prof., 1997—2003, prof. internat. activities and evaluation, 2004, dir. planning and accountability, dir. doctoral program and evaluation, assoc. dean academic affairs, dir. internat. activities and evaluation, course coord., 2010—. Project dir. accreditation outcomes project Nat. League Nursing, New York City, 1986—88; vis. prof. U. Alta., Coll. Nursing, Edmonton, Canada, 1993, Nat. Taipei, Coll. Nursing, Taiwan, 1994; mem. editl. rev. bd. Jour. Cardiovasc. Nursing; mem. nursing edn. Innovative Ctr. Column. Contbr. articles to profl. jours. (Am. Jour. Nursing Book Yr. awards, manuscript reviewer, 2008, editl. bd. mem., 2008, award, 2010); author (Waltz, CF Strickland, OL, Lenz, ER): Measurement in Nursing and Health Research, 2010. Vol. evaluator Mid. States Accrediting Commn. on Higher Edn. Recipient Citation Contributions award, Taiwan Nurses Assn., Republic of China, 2000, Adj. Mem. award, GRISM, 2007—; grant, Fed. and Pvt. Funding Agencies, 1981—2003, Elected fellowship, Am. Acad. Nursing, 1981—. Mem.: APA, ANCC (mem. commn. 1993—96, visitor mem. exec. comm), Phi Kappa Phi (hon.), Royal Coll. Nursing (mem. internat. sci. adv. panel), Sigma Theta Tau Internat. (reviewer), Nat. League Nursing Accrediting Commn., Internat. Network Doctoral Edn. (exec. com. mem. 1999—2008, program planning com., publ. co.), Commn. Grads. Fgn. Nursing Schs. (mem. rsch. 1992—97, evaluation com.), Nat. League Nursing (accreditation site visitor 1981—2008, mem. bd. rev.), ANA (com. 1968—2008). Office: Univ Maryland Sch Nursin 655 W Lombard St Baltimore MD 21201

WALTZ, JAMES RICHARD, physician; b. Massillon, Ohio, June 30, 1935; AB, Ohio U., 1957; MD, Ohio State U., 1962. Intern Milw. County Hosp., 1962-63; resident U. Ill. Rsch. Edn. Hosps., 1963-67; gen. surgeon Liberty Hosp. Mem. ACS. Office: 15724 Oakmont Dr Kearney MO 64060-9251 Office Phone: 816-628-6699. *

WALTZ, JOSEPH MCKENDREE, neurosurgeon, educator; b. Detroit, July 23, 1931; s. Ralph McKinley and Bertha (Seelye) W.; m. Janet Maureen Journey, June 26, 1954; children: Jeffrey McKinley, Mary Elaine, David Seelye, Stephen McKendree; m. Marilyn Liska, June 5, 1967; 1 child, Tristana McKendree. Student, U. Mich., 1950; BS, U. Oreg., 1954, MD, 1956. Diplomate Am. Bd. Neurol. Surgery, Am. Bd. Forensic Medicine, Am. Bd. Forensic Examiners, lic. NY, 1963, Calif., 1960, NJ, 1969, Mich., 1958; cert. DABNS Bd.; bd. cert. neurosurgeon. Surg. intern U. Mich. Hosp., 1956-57, gen. surg. resident, 1957-58, clin. instr. neurosurgery, 1960-63; neurosurg. assoc. St. Barnabas Hosp., NYC, 1963—; assoc. dir. Inst. Neurosci., 1974—, dir. dept. neurol. surgery, 1977—2002; attending Neurosci. Inst. Our Lady of Mercy, 1998—2009; with AANS CNS Joint Sections, 1993—, U. Mich. Med. Ctr., Ann Arbor, 2001—; attending neurosurgeon Neurosci. Inst., 1998—2008, St. Barnabas Hosp., dir., 1976—98, chief neurosurgery dept., 1998—2002, bd. trustees, 1976—2001, chmn. operating review bd., 1963—95, chmn. institutional review bd., 1975—90; asst. prof. NY Coll. Osteopathic Medicine, Old Westbury, NY, 1989—2002; bd. dirs. U. Mich. Med. ctr., Ann Arbor, 1995—2001, exec. bd., 1995—2001; bd. dir. alumni assn. U. Mich., 1996—99, presdl. club mem., 1977; clin. prof. dept. neurosurgery NYU Med. Ctr., 1974—79; student asst. dept. anatomy U. Oregon Dental Sch., Portland, Oreg., 1952—56; asst. resident dept. gen. surgery U. Mich. Med. Ctr., Ann Arbor, 1957—58, jr., sr. clin. instr., 1960—63. Assoc. cons. in neurosurgery Englewood (N.J.) Hosp., 1964—; assoc. prof. neurosurgery NYU Med. Str., 1974—; asst. prof. dept. surgery (neurosurgery) N.Y. Coll. Osteo. Medicine, 1989—; mem. alumni bd. U. Mich. Med. Ctr., 1995; dir. Med. Ct. Graphics; gen. surgery internship U. Mich. Med. Ctr., Ann Arbor, 1956—57. Author: (chpt.) Cryogenic Surgery, Neurology, 1982, Advances in Neurology, 1983, Textbook of Stereotactic and Functional Neurosurgery, 1997; contbr. 60 articles to profl. jours. Mem. sci. adv. bd. Dystonia Med. Research Found., 1980—2006; trustee St. Barnabas Hosp., 1980—. Served to capt. M.C. AUS, 1958-60. Capt. med. corps US Army, 1958—60, with US Army, 1960—62. Recipient Bronze award Am. Congress Rehab. Medicine, 1967, World Cmty. Svc. award Rotary, Disting. Trustee award United Hosp. Fund, 1995, Outstanding Contribution award, Neurostimulation Found., Appreciation NY State Supreme Ct., Med. Malpractice Mediation Panel, award, Electronics & Info. Scis., 1984, award, Inrternat. Biographical Ctr., Cambridge, fellow. Rsch. grant, Rockefeller Found., named. Yr. Book Sci. & Future, 1984, Notable Americans, Am. Biographical Inst., 1981, Best Doctors America, 1978, 2008, Top Doctors NY Metro Area, Americas Top Surgens, 2002-03. Mem. AMA, Am. Paralysis Assn., World Soc. Stereotactic and Functional Neurosurgery, Congress Neurol. Surgeons, Math. Assn. Am., Internat. Neural Network Soc., Soc. for Cryobiology, N.Y. State Med. Soc., Bronx County Med. Soc., N.Y. State Neurosurg Soc., Congress Neurological Surgeons, Joint Sect. Neurotrauma & Critical Care, Joint Sect. Stereotactic & Functional Neurosurgery, Joint Sect. Spine & Peripheral Nerves, Am. Acad. Pain Mgmt., Am. Acad. Spine Physicians, NY Med. Soc., Bronx County Med. Soc., Internat. Neural Network Soc., Math. Assn. America, NY Acad. Sci., Am. Assn. Advancement Sci., Nat. Ski Patrol, Phi Beta Pi. Achievements include spl. rsch. on neurophysiology and treatment of epilepsy, basal ganglia disorders, abnormal movement disorders, cerebral palsy, also neurosurg. application stereotactic thalamic surgery and spinal cord stimulation, patent for multi electrode catheter assembly for spinal cord stimulation. Office: 150 Purchase St Ste 7 Rye NY 10580 Office Phone: 914-967-6577. Personal E-mail: joemwaltz@aol.com.

WAMALA, SARAH PROSSIE, public health service officer; b. Nkozi, Uganda, Jan. 16, 1967; MS in Biostats., Stockholm U., 1994; PhD in Medicine, Pub. Health, Karolinska Inst., 1999. Rsch. scientist-epidemiology, biostats. Karolinska Inst., 1995—2000, assoc. prof., 2001; unit head, rsch. mgr.- social environment and health Swedish Nat. Inst. Pub. Health, 2000—06; head dept.-health promotion and disease control Stockholm County Coun., 2006—08; dir. gen. Swedish Nat. Inst. Pub. Health, 2008—. Recipient Excellent Contbn. award, Internat. Soc. Behavioral Medicine; Promising Young Scientist fellowship, Knut-Alice Wallenbergs Stiftelse. Office: Swedish Nat Inst Pub Health Ostersund 83140 Sweden Office Fax: 46863 19 96 02. Business E-Mail: sarah.wamala@fhi.se.

WAN, JUN, orthopedist; b. Nanchang, Jiangxi, Jan. 11, 1981; MD, Ctrl. South U., 2011, PhD. Attending physician, dept. orthopaedics Xiangya Hosp., 2005—, Xiangya 2nd Hosp. Med. translator Yimaitong, 2006—. Mem.: Chinese Med. Doctor Assn. Avocations: reading, cooking. Office: Renmin Mid Rd 139 Xiangya Rd 1 Changsha Hunan 410013 China Personal E-mail: spinewanjun@gmail.com.

WAN, LEI, medical educator, researcher; b. Nantou, Taiwan, June 11, 1973; s. Liang-Jun Wan and Jing-Zhi Chen; m. Jane Liu, Oct. 26, 2002; children: Alan, Sunny. PhD, Nat. Tsing-Hua U., Hsinchu, 2003. Diplomate medical technologist Ministry Edn., Taiwan, 1995. Assoc. rschr. China Med. U. Hosp., Taichung, Taiwan, 2004—; prof. China Med. U., Taichung, 2010—. Translator: (textbook) Molecular Biology Understanding the Genetic Revolution, Arthur M. Lesk: Introduction to Bioinformatics; author: Medical Microbiology and Immunology. Recipient Outstanding Student award, Taiwan Soc. Lab. Medicine, 1995. Mem.: Chinese Soc. Cell & Molecular Biology. Home: 11 Renti 2nd St Dali City Taichung County 412 Taiwan Office: Sch Chinese Medicine 91 Hsueh-Shih Rd Taichung 404 Taiwan Personal E-mail: lei.joseph@gmail.com.

WAN, SONG, cardiac surgeon, educator; b. Shanghai, Dec. 4, 1963; s. Ling-Ying Wan; m. Yu Gu, Aug. 1, 1968; 1 child, Joyce. MD, Beijing Med. U., 1987; PhD, U. Libre Brussels, 1997. Resident Beijing Med. U., 1987-94; clin. fellow U. Hosp. Erasme, Brussels, 1994-98; cardiac surgeon Chinese U. Hong Kong, 1998—. Contbr. chapters to books, more than 130 articles to profl. jours. Recipient Young Investigators award Am. Coll. Chest Physicians, 1996, Study Visit award Royal Soc., U.K., 1999, Travel award Asian Soc. Cardiovascular Surgery, 2000. Fellow: Coll. Surgeons Hong Kong, Royal Coll. Surgeons Eng.; mem.: Am. Assn. Thoracic Surgery, Internat. Soc. for Minimally Invasive Cardiac Surgery, Chinese Med. Assn., Internat. Soc. Cardiovascular Surgery, Soc. Thoracic Surgeons. Office: Chinese U Hong Kong Prince of Wales Hosp Hong Kong China Office Phone: (852) 2632 2629. Fax: 2637 7974. E-mail: swan@cuhk.edu.hk.

WAN, THOMAS SHEK KONG, clinical scientist; s. Koon Keung Wan and Mui Cheung; m. Mary Mei Yee Lo, Jan. 20, 1991; children: Conan Pok Hin, Eden Pok Yeung. BS, Nat. Taiwan U., 1984; MPhil, U. Hong Kong, 1992, PhD, 1997. Cert. Chartered biologist Inst. Biology, 1992, mem. Assn. Genetic Technologists, US, 1991, chartered scientist Sci. Coun., 2005. Technician U. Hong Kong, 1984—90, hon. asst. prof., dept. pathology, 1999—2005, hon. assoc. prof., dept. pathology, 2005—; med. technologist Queen Mary Hosp., U. Hong Kong, 1990—2004, sci. officer & cytogeneticist in-charge, 2004—; hon. prof. First Clin. Coll., Harbin Med. U., China, 2005—. Mem. rev. bd. Jour. Assn. Genetic Technologists, Lenexa, Kans., 2004—, mem. editl. bd. Atlas Genetics & Cytogenetics Oncology & Haematology, France, 2006—, Assoc. Genetic Technologists Cytogenetics Lab Manual, Lenexa, 2006—, Jour. Cancer Sci. & Therapy, 2010—; mem. editl. acad. Internat. Jour. Oncology, Greece, 2007—; vis. prof. Fujian Med. U., China, 2010—. Contbr. articles to profl. jours. Pres. Hong Kong Soc. Cytogenetics, 2009—, hon. sec., 2007—09; coun. mem. Hong Kong Soc. Molecular Diagnostic Scis., 2008; mem. Rotaract Club Hong Kong Island East, 1987—91. Fellowship, Inst. Biomed. Sci., 1993. Fellow: Royal Coll. Pathologists Australia, Royal Coll. Pathologists (Eng.); mem.: Am. Assn. Cancer Rsch. Office: Queen Mary Hosp Univ Hong Kong Dept Pathology-Haematology Pokfulam Rd Hong Kong Hong Kong Business E-Mail: wantsk@hku.hk.

WANDERLEY, TEREZA CONRADO, physician, educator; b. Serra Talhada, Oct. 5, 1064; MD, 1988; MS, U. Pernambuco, 2008. Physician Hosp. Agamenom Magalhaes, 1988—, tutor, 2002—. Master: U. Pernambuco. Avocations: exercise, travel, reading. Home: Frei Leandro Recife Pernambuco 510111600 Brazil Home Fax: 8133267051. Personal E-mail: terezaconrado@hotmail.com.

WANEBO, HAROLD J., surgeon, educator; b. Denver, Feb. 12, 1935; s. Clifford P. and JoAnn (Curtin) W.; m. Claire Anne Wanebo, Oct. 27, 1964; children: John Eric, Michael David, Jacqueline Elise. BS, Regis Coll., 1957; MD, U. Colo., 1961. Intern Cornell Med. divsn. Bellevue Hosp., N.Y., 1961-62, resident N.Y., 1962-63; surg. resident U. Calif. Med. Ctr., San Francisco, 1963-65, 67-69; fellow in tumor immunology Meml. Sloan-Kettering Cancer Ctr., N.Y., 1965-67, sr. surg. fellow N.Y., 1971-73, clin. asst. attending surgeon N.Y., 1973-74, assoc. N.Y., 1973-77, asst. attending surgeon N.Y., 1974-77, assoc. scientist N.Y., 1977-83, cons. clin. immunology svc. N.Y., 1977-90; instr. surgery Cornell U.-N.Y. Hosp. Med. Ctr., 1973-75, asst. prof. surgery, 1975-77; chief divsn. surg. oncology Med. Ctr., prof. surgery U. Va., Charlottesville, 1977-87; prof. surgery, dir. surg. oncology Brown U., Providence, R.I., 1987—; prof. surgery Boston U. Med. Sch., 2006—; editor (pelvic surgery) Clinics North Surgical, 2005. Editor: Hepatic and Biliary Cancer, 1987, Common Problems in Cancer Surgery, 1990, Colorectal Cancer, 1993, Surgery for Gastrointestinal Cancer, 1996, Surgical Clinic North America, Surgical Management Pelvic Malignancy, 2005, Surgical Clinic of North America Regional Therapy of Malignancy, 2008; numerous presentation papers to books and articles to profl. jours. Maj. U.S. Army, 1969-71, Vietnam. Decorated Bronze star; recipient Commendation medal with device. Mem. ACS, Am. Assn. Cancer Edn., Am. Assn. Cancer Rsch., Am. Assn. Immunologists, Am. Cancer Soc. (Jr. Faculty Clin. Fellowship award 1974-77), Am. Surg. Assn., Am. Soc. Clin. Oncology, Assn. Am. Vol. Physicians, Med. Soc. State of N.Y., Med. Soc. R.I., Med. Soc. Va., Nafzigger Surg. Soc., New Eng. Surg. Soc., N.Y. Acad. Scis., N.Y. Surg. Soc., Soc. Surgery of Alimentary Tract, Soc. Surg. Oncology, Soc. Univ. Surgeons, Southeastern Surg. Congress, So. Surg. Assn., Soc. Head and Neck Surgery. Office: Landmark Med Ctr Divsn Surg Oncology 206 Cass Ave Woonsocket RI 02895 Office Phone: 401-767-1595. Business E-Mail: hwanebo@rwmc.org.

WANER, MILTON, otolaryngologist, pediatric facial plastic surgeon; MD, U. Witwatersrand Med. Sch., Johannesburg, South Africa, 1977. Cert. Otolaryngology, South African Med. and Dental Coun., 1986. Resident, surgery U. Witwatersrand, Johannesburg, 1980, resident, otolaryngology, 1981—84; lectr. U. Sydney, Australia; resident, otolaryngology U. Ark. for Med. Sciences, Little Rock, 1984—85, prof. otolaryngology, 2001, dir., Laser Inst.; Benjamin and Milton Waner Endowed chair in pediat. facial plastic and reconstructive surgery Ark. Children's Hosp., Little Rock; dir. Vascular Anomalies Ctr., Ark. Children's Hosp.; fellow, otolaryngology and maxillofacial surgery U. Cin. Med. Ctr., Ohio, 1984—85; co-dir. Vascular

Birthmarks Inst. NY, Beth Israel Med. Ctr. and St. Luke's-Roosevelt Hosp. Ctr. Author and co-author of several textbooks; contbr. chapters to books, med. papers. Recipient Power of One award, Vascular Birthmarks Found., Children's Miracle award, Children's Miracle Network, 2004; named one of Best Doctors, NY Mag., 2008, Top Doctors: New York Metro Area, Castle Connolly, 2008. Mem.: Am. Acad. Otolaryngology Head and Neck Surgery (award), Am. Acad. Facial Plastic and Reconstructive Surgery, Am. Soc. for Laser Medicine and Surgery (surgical rep. on bd. dirs.), British Acad. Aesthetic Plastic Surgeons (hon.). Achievements include being an internationally recognized authority on hemangiomas and vascular malformations; patents in field. Office: Vascular Birthmark Inst 126 W 60th St New York NY 10023 Office Phone: 212-636-3977. Office Fax: 212-636-3979. Business E-Mail: waner@NYHNI.org.

WANG, BEVERLY Y., pathologist, educator; Attended, Jiangxi Med. Coll., 1982. Diplomate Am. Bd. Pathology, 1998, Am. Bd. Pathology-cytopathology, 1999. Resident in pathology Mt. Sinai Med. Ctr., 1995—98; clin. fellow in cytopathology Mt. Sinai Sch. Medicine, 1998—99; adjunct prof. NYU Sch. Medicine; dir. surg. pathology and otolaryngology depts. Tisch Hosp. Co-author: (jour. articles) The appearance and significance of neuron-specific enolase in the development of the nervous system of rats, 1986, Parotid polycystic sclerosing adenosis , 2000, Metastatic balloon cell malignant melanoma: a case report and literature review, 2011, numerous other jour. articles. Achievements include research in Histologic risk assessment of oral squamous carcinoma; Mucosal melanoma in head and neck. Office: New York University Langone Medical Center Tisch Hospital 560 1st Ave Fl 4th Rm 461 New York NY 10016 Office Phone: 212-263-6032. Office Fax: 212-263-7916.

WANG, BINGHE, medical educator, department chairman; b. Beijing, May 25, 1962; PhD, U. Kans., 1991. Prof., chair Ga. State U., 2003—. Scholar drug discovery Ga. Rsch. Alliance, 2003; disting. cancer scientist Ga. Cancer Coalition, 2003; editor-in-chief Medicinal Rsch. Revs.; book series editor Wiley Series Drug Discovery & Devel.; mem. editl. adv. bd. Chem. Biology and Drug Design. Recipient Disting. Alumni Prof. award, Ga. State U., Outstanding Faculty award, U. Ga. Office: Petit Sci Ctr 100 Piedmont Ave SE 313 Atlanta GA 30303 Business E-Mail: chemrr@langate.gsu.edu.

WANG, CHEN, hospital administrator; Pres. Beijing Chao Yang Hosp.; dep. dir. Beijing Inst. of Respiratory Medicine. Sr. mem. Fedn. of Chinese Can. Professionals (FCCP); chief WHO. Recipient Nat. Sci. and Tech. Achievement Award, Chinese Med. Sci. and Tech. Award, Outstanding Contrbn. for Tobacco Control Award, WHO. Achievements include research in Respiratory Critical Care Medicine; Diagnosis and Treatment of Pulmonary Embolism; Respiratory Tract Infection; Severe Acute Respiratory Syndrome (SARS); Avian Flu; Influenza. Office: Beijing Chao Yang Hospital 8 Gongren Tiyuchang Nanlu Chaoyang District Beijing 100020 China Office Phone: 01085231000. *

WANG, CHIN KUN, academic administrator, medical educator; b. Changhwa, Taiwan, Feb. 4, 1966; s. Dar-Shyong Wang and Shiang-Guey Lin; m. Hui-Fang Chiu, Oct. 25, 1993; children: Pei-Wen, Bo-Yuan. BA in Food Sci., Nat. Chung Hsiung U., Taichung, Taiwan, 1989; PhD in Food Sci. and Tech., Nat. Taiwan U., 1993. Asst. rsch. fellow dept. food sci. Nat. Chung Hsiung U., 1988—89; asst. prof. Sch. Nutrition Chung Shan Med. U., Taichung City, 1993—96, prof., 1996—, chair Sch. Nutrition, 1998—2001, dean student affairs, 2001—02, dean Coll. Healthcare & Mgmt., 2002—08, v.p., 2006—10, pres., 2010—. Profl. com. mem. Consumers' Found. Chinese Taipei, 1997—; coun. mem. Healthy City Constrn. Ctr., Taichung, 1999—. Recipient Rsch. award, Nat. Sci. Coun., Taiwan, 1994, 1996—98, 2000, Excellent Prof. award, Chung Shan Med. U., 1996, 2003. Mem.: Chinese Dietetic Soc., Internat. Soc. Nutraceuticals & Functional Foods (bd. dirs. 2008—, founding mem.), Taiwan Assn. Med. Edn., Taiwan Assn. Food Sci. Tech. (bd. dirs. 2007—), Nutrition Soc. Taiwan (pres. 2009—), Health Food Soc. Taiwan (bd. dirs. 1999—). Buddhist. Avocations: travel, running, music. Office: Chung Shan Med Univ 110 Sec1 Chien-Kuo North Rd Taichung 40201 Taiwan Home: 55 Fuxin St Taichung Taiwan Office Phone: 886-4-24730022 ext. 1101. Office Fax: 886-424759950; Home Fax: 886-424825975. Personal E-mail: wangchinkun1@yahoo.com.tw. Business E-Mail: wck@csmu.edu.tw.

WANG, CHUN-HSIANG, physician; b. Tainan, Taiwan, Sept. 19, 1958; s. Hsiu-Tao Wang Huang; m. Tsui-Chen Chang, May 4, 1965; children: Michael, Ruby, Vivian. MD, Chung Shan Med. U., 1986; MSc, Oxford U., 1991. Diplomate Gastro-enterol. Soc. Taiwan, 1995. Instr. Chung Jung U., Tainan, Taiwan, 1998; cons. hepatologist, chair, med. rsch. com. Tainan Mcpl. Hosp., 1991—. Vis. clinician Mayo Clinic, Rochester, Minn., 1990—91; vis. fellow Endoscopy Unit Hamburg U., Germany, 1995; vis. scholar Liver Ctr. U. So. Calif., LA, 2004—05. Translator: (translation) The Interpretation of Laboratory Data, Life, love and learning; editor: (collections of essays) The story of Chung Shan; contbr. articles to profl. jours.; co-author (with Lein Ray Mo, Kuo Kwan Chang, Ruey Chang Lin): A Cohort Study to Investigate Hepatocellular Carcinoma Risk In Hepatitis C Patients Hepato Gastroenterology, 2011. Mem.: AAAS, NY Acad. Sci., Inst. Ultrasound in Medicine, Am. Gastro-enterol. Assn., Formal Med. Assn. (corr.). Achievements include research in Hepatitis, Liver Disease; Video-endoscopic ultrasonography in staging gastric carcinoma; Villous adenoma of common bile duct; A Survival Model in Patients Undergoing Radical Resection of Ampullary Adenocarcinoma; Rapid diagnosis of choledocholithiasis using biochemical tests in patients undergoing laparoscopic cholecyetctomy; Multiple anomalies of pancreaticobiliary ductal system: report of a case; Helicobacter pylori infection and the risk of peptic ulcer among cirrhotic patients; Whipple disease in a Taiwanese woman: report a case; Preoperative assessment of choledocholithiasis in laparoscopic cholecystectomy; Statistic model for predicting variceal hemorrhage in patients with liver cirrhosis using endoscopy, clinical parameters, and Doppler flowmetry; Statistic model for predicting variceal hemorrhage in patients with liver cirrhosis using endoscopy, clinical parameters, and Doppler flowmetry; Hemodynamic study of hepatocellular carcinoma: correlation between power Doppler ultrasonography and histologic grading; Helicobacter pylori infection and the risk of peptic ulcer among cirrhotic patients; Hepatitis C virus impairs DNA damage-repair to induce chromosomal instability; Does Type and Duration of Antiretroviral Therapy Attenuate Liver Fibrosis in HIV/HCV Coinfected Patients?; Preoperative endoscopic sphincterotomy in the treatment of patients with cholecystocholedocholithiasis; Ballon sheath miniprobe compared to conventional EUS in the staging of colorectal cancer; artificial neural network model is superior to logistic regression model in predicting treatment outcomes of interferon based combination therapy in patients with chronic hepatitis C intervirology; pharcogenomics of chronic hepatitis C therapy with genome-wide association studies; hepatitis C virus inhibits DNA damage repair through reactive oxygen and nitrogen species and by interfering with ATM-NBS1/Mre11/Rad50 DNA repair pathway in monocytes and hepatocytes; a cohort study to investigate hepatocellular carcinoma risk in hepatitis C patients. Office: Tainan Municipal Hospital 670 Chongde Road Tainan 701 Taiwan Personal E-mail: chunhsiang@gmail.com.

WANG, CLIFFORD, medical association administrator; b. Calif., Oct. 19, 1961; MPH, U. Calif., 1987; MD, U. Calif., Irvine, 1992. Clin. assoc. prof. medicine Stanford U., 2008—11; pres., med. staff Santa Clara Valley Med. Ctr., 2007—10, chief, inpatient medicine, 2005—. Bd. dirs. Nat. Pub. Health and Hosp. Inst., 2001—09. Fellow: ACP. Office: 751 South Bascom Ave San Jose CA 95128 Office Fax: 408-885-3625. Business E-Mail: clifford.wang@hhs.sccgov.org.

WANG, FEI, pharmacist, educator; d. Ke-Chiang and Iok Meng Lee Wang; m. Cunegundo Manuel Vergara; children: Leander Vergara, Chiu Yen Vergara. BS in Pharmacy, St. John's U., Jamaica, NY, 1983, MS in Pharmacy, 1994, PharmD, 1996. Cert. pharmacotherapy specialist Am. Pharm. Assn., DC, 1998, smoking cessation specialist Nat. Smoking Cessation Program, U. Pitts., 1998. Cmty. pharmacist Genovese Drug Stores, Inc., Fort Lee, NJ, 1983—84, supervising pharmacist Astoria, NY, 1985—90; hosp. pharmacist Cornell Med. Ctr., NY Hosp., NYC, 1990—93, target drug clin. coord., 1993—95; specialty residency in adult internal medicine Med. U. SC, Charleston, 1996—97, clin. pharmacist in surgery & trauma, 1996—97; clin. specialist in ambulatory care Hartford Hosp., Conn., 1997—. Adj. preceptor St. John's U., NYH-CMC, 1993—94; adj. instr. Med. U. SC, 1996—97; clin. preceptor U. Conn., 1997—2005, asst. clin. prof. Sch. Pharmacy, 1997—, dir. ambulatory care residency and fellowship program, 2001—; presenter in field; lectr. in field. Contbr. articles to profl. jours. Grant, Hartford Hosp. & Boehringer Ingelheim, 2002—05. Mem.: Conn. Soc. Health Sys. Pharmacists, Am. Soc. Health Sys. Pharmacists, Am. Coll. Clin. Pharmacy. Office: U Conn Dept Pharmacy Practice 69 North Eagleville Rd Unit 3092 Storrs Mansfield CT 06269-3092 Business E-Mail: fwang@harthosp.org.

WANG, FENG, engineering educator; b. Shandong, China, Aug. 15, 1962; PhD, Tohoku U., 2000. Assoc. prof. Maebashi Inst. Tech., 2006—; rsch. assoc. Tohoku U., 2000—06. Recipient award, Japan Soc. Applied Electromagnetic Mechanics, Silver prize, Jt. Internat. Conf. JFSIM & SMABA, 2005. Mem.: IEEE. Avocations: photography, reading. Office: 460-1 Kamisadori-Machi Maebashi Gunma 371-0816 Japan E-mail: f.wang@maebashi-it.ac.jp.

WANG, FREDERICK MARK, pediatrician, ophthalmologist, educator; b. NYC, Feb. 17, 1948; Student, Northwestern U., 1968; MD, Yeshiva U., 1972. Diplomate Am. Bd. Ophthalmology, Am. Bd. Pediats., Nat. Bd. Med. Examiners. Intern in pediats. H.C. Moffitt-U. Calif. San Francisco Hosps., 1972-73; resident in pediats. Bronx Mcpl. Hosp. Ctr.-Albert Einstein Coll. Medicine, 1973-74, resident in ophthalmology, 1976-79; Heed fellow in ophthalmology and strabismus Children's Hosp. Nat. Med. Ctr., Washington, 1979-80; asst. prof. ophthalmology Albert Einstein Coll. Medicine, Bronx, 1980-82, asst. clin. prof., 1982-85, assoc. clin. prof., 1985-95, clin. prof., 1995—, asst. prof. pediats., 1980-82, asst. clin. prof. pediats., 1982-92; dir. pediat. ophthalmology and strabismus svc. Montefiore Med. Ctr., Bronx, 1980-90. Cons. ophthalmologist Children's Evaluation & Rehab. Ctr., Rose Kennedy Ctr. for Rsch. in Mental Retardation and Human Devel., Bronx, 1980—, Craniofacial Ctr., Montefiore Med. Ctr., Bronx, 1980—; attending physician in ophthalmology Bronx Mcpl. Hosp./Montefiore Med. Ctr., 1980—; asst. attending physician in ophthalmology North Ctrl. Bronx Hosp., 1980-98; attending physician Strabismus Svc., N.Y. Eye & Ear Infirmary, N.Y.C., 1982-99, attending surgeon, 1999—; mem. dept. ophthalmology Lenox Hill Hosp., N.Y.C., 1988—; sci. reviewer Jour. Am. Acad. Ophthalmology, 1980-86; mem. profl. adv. bd. Found. for Children with Learning Disabilities, N.Y.C., 1983-89; mem. sci. adv. bd. The Glaucoma Found., N.Y.C., 1986-92; mem. profl. adv. bd. Nat. Assn. for Visually Handicapped, N.Y.C., 1988—; coord. pediat. sect. Greater N.Y. Ophthalmology Clin. Lectr. Series, 1990-93; mem. Velo-Cardio-Facial Syndrome Ednl. Found., 1994—, nominating com., 1995—. Mem. editl. bd. Jour. Pediat. Ophthalmology and Strabismus, 1998—; contbr. articles to profl. jours., chpts. to books. Referee, U.S. Soccer Fedn. Maj. med. officer USAF, 1974-76. Mem. Am. Acad. Pediats., Am. Acad. Ophthalmology, Am. Assn. for Pediat. Ophthalmology and Strabismus, N.Y. Soc. for Pediat. Ophthalmology and Strabismus (program chmn. 1987-89, pres. 1990-92), N.Y. Soc. for Clin. Ophthalmology (corr. sec. 1988-90, membership chmn. 1990-91, program chmn. 1991-92, pres. 1992-93), N.Y. Acad. Medicine (sec. sect. on ophthalmology 1993-94, sect. chmn. 1995-96), Alpha Omega Alpha. Avocations: fishing, chess, swimming, soccer refereeing. Office: Pediat Ophthalmology NY 30 E 40th St New York NY 10016-1201 Home Phone: 914-723-7122; Office Phone: 212-684-3980.

WANG, FU-WEI, physician; b. Tainan, Taiwan, Dec. 10, 1966; MS, Kaohsiung Med. U., 2006. Vis. staff dept. family medicine Kaohsiung Vets. Gen. Hosp., 1998—. Vis. scholar geriatric medicine and gerontology Emory U. Sch. Medicine, 2003. Fellow: Gerontol. Soc. Taiwan, Taiwan Assn. Hospice Palliative, Taiwan Assn. Family Medicine (Merck Found. Rsch. award 2010). Avocations: baseball, hiking, movies. Office: 386 Ta-Chung 1st Rd Kaohsiung 80424 Taiwan Business E-Mail: wfwvghks@yahoo.com.tw.

WANG, GWO JAW, orthopedic surgery educator; Lillian T. Pratt prof. and chmn. orthopedic surgery U. Va. Sch. Medicine, Charlottesville, 1992—2000; pres. Kaohsiung Med. U., Taiwan, 2000—06; prof. emeritus Nat. Cheng-Kung U., 2008—, U. Va., 2009—. Vis. prof. orthop. surgery Kaohsiung Med. U., Taiwan, 2006—. Recipient U. Va. Pres.'s Report award, 1992, Otto Aufranc award, Hip Soc. and Am. Acad. Orthop. Surgeons, 1992, 1997, Stinchfield award, 1986, Nicholas Andry award, 1998, Va. career award, Va. Orthop. Soc., 2007. Office: Kaohsiung Med Univ 100 Shih Chuan 1st Rd Kaohsiung Taiwan Home Phone: 886-7-537-1179; Office Phone: 886-7-3121101 ext.5390. Business E-Mail: gwojaw@cc.kmu.edu.tw.

WANG, HONGBO, gynecologist; b. Tongcheng, Anhui, China, Apr. 24, 1969; MD, Tongji Med. Coll., Huazhong U. Sci. & Tech., 1993; PhD, Tongji Med. Coll., 2002. Prof. ob-gyn. Union Hosp. Tongji Med. Coll., 1993, dir. HR, 2011. Recipient Paper award, Pacific Coast Reproduction Soc. Avocation: travel. Office: 1277 Jiefang Ave Union Hosp Wuhan Hubei 430022 China Office Fax: 0086-2785776343. Business E-Mail: whbdf@yahoo.com.

WANG, HUIRU, biotechnologist, researcher; b. Beijing, Feb. 25, 1957; MD, PhD, U. Tokyo, Med. Sch., 1997. Postdoc Med. Coll. Wis., 1997—2000; scientist Blood Ctr. Wis., 2000—01; asst. prof. U. Ill. at Chgo., 2001—05; rsch. asst. prof. Northwestern U., 2005—08; pres. B&H Biotechs. LLC, 2007—. Adj. investigator Nat. Influenza Ctr., China CDC, 2007—11; cons. Coll. Pharmacy, U. Ill. at Chgo., 2010, China Nat. Biotec Group Inst., Sinopharma, 2011; mm. editl. bd. World Jour. Virology, 2011—. Grant, NIH, Am. Liver Found., HHS/IRS. Mem.: Ill. Biotech. Indsl. Orgn. (grant), Am. Assn. Study Liver Diseases, Am. Assn. Immunologists. Avocations: cooking, travel, swimming. Office: 2201 W Campbell Park Dr Lab 322 Chicago IL 60612 Business E-Mail: jhwang@bh-biotech.com.

WANG, HWA-CHAIN ROBERT, biomedical researcher, educator; PhD, U. Va., 1990. Postdoctoral rsch. assoc. Harvard U., 1990—94; rsch. scientist Ohio State U. Comprehensive Cancer Ctr., Columbus, 1994—97; assoc. prof. molecular oncology U. Tenn., Knoxville, 1997—2010, prof., 2010—. Office: Univ Tenn Coll Vet Medicine 2407 River Dr Knoxville TN 37996 Business E-Mail: hcrwang@utk.edu.

WANG, JEFFREY C., surgeon; b. Mitchell, SD, July 30, 1965; s. YuSan and Linda Wang; m. Christina Jennet Lee, June 28, 1992; children: Christopher Jeffrey, Benjamin Jeffrey. BS, Stanford U., Calif., 1987; MD, U. Pitts., 1991. Chief spine surgery UCLA Comprehensive Spine Ctr., 1997—. Office: UCLA Comprehensive Spine Center 1250 16th Street Suite 745 Santa Monica CA 90404 Office Phone: 310-319-3334. Office Fax: 310-319-5055. *

WANG, JIAXI, molecular biologist, educator; b. Gaizhou City, China, Jan. 19, 1940; s. Yun Chang Wang and Ji Hua Yang; m. Hongming Fu, Sept. 1, 1967; children: Di, Tie. MD, Dalian Med. U., China, 1963. Diplomate. From rsch. asst. to prof. Beijing Inst. Basic Med. Sci., 1965—92, prof., 1992—. Vis. scholar dept. molecular genetics U. Brussels, 1979—81; vis. scholar dept. animal biology U. Pa., Phila., 1986—87. Editor: Chinese Jour. Biochem. & Molecular Biology, 1998—; co-editor-in-chief: Jour. Exptl. Hematology. Achievements include patents in field. Avocations: poetry, reading, walking, writing, mountain climbing. Office: Beijing Inst Basic Med Sci 27 Taiping Rd Beijing 100850 China Home Phone: 010-68151628; Office Phone: 010-66931322. Business E-Mail: wangjx@nic.bmi.ac.cn.

WANG, JONG HWAN, otolaryngologist; b. Seoul, Republic of Korea, Oct. 8, 1971; s. Chi Hong Wang and Hong Soon Kim; m. Won Hee Lee, Sept. 5, 2004; children: Min Ji, Yu Bin. MD, Hallym U., 2001; PhD in Otolaryngology, U. Ulsan, 2009. Cert. Korean Bd. Otolaryngology, 2006, residency in otolaryngology Asan Med. Ctr., 2006. Clin. instr. Asan Med. Ctr., Seoul, 2008—09; chief otolaryngology dept. Gimpo Woori Hosp., Gimpo-si, Gyeonggi-do, 2010. With Korean Army, 1994—95. Cert. fellow, Asan Med. Ctr., 2007. Mem.: Korean Rhinologic Soc., Korean Otolaryngologic Soc., Korean Med. Assn. Democrat. Buddhist. Achievements include discovery of mechanism accounting for rhinovirus-induced bacterial infection in nasal epithelial cells; drugs inhibiting rhinovirus-induced inflammation and bacterial infection; human parainfluenza virus 3 as one of the causative virus of postviral olfactory dysfunction; long-term natural course of retention cyst of the maxillary sinus; correlation between subjective palatine tonsil size and objective palatine tonsil size in patients with sleep-disordered breathing; palatine tonsil size difference between normal-weight and obese children with sleep-disordered breathing; the effect of Staphylococcus aureus infection on the pathogenesis of nasal polyp by inflammation and tissue remodelling in patients with chronic rhinosinusitis. Avocations: swimming, badminton, bicycling, golf. Office: Gimpo Woori Hosp Dept Otolaryngology Geolpo-Dong 389-15 Gyeonggi-do 415-020 Gimpo-si Gyeonggi-do Republic of Korea Home Phone: 82 2 817 6638; Office Phone: 82 31 999 1773. Personal E-mail: entwang@naver.com.

WANG, JONG-SHYAN, physical therapist, physiologist, researcher; b. Kaoshuing, Taiwan, Sept. 2, 1965; s. Sia-Zong Wang and Shian-Lam Hong; m. Gai-Ping Lam; children: Yu-Ann, Yu-Wien. PhD, Nat. Cheng -Kung U., 1996. Physical Therapist Min. of Exam., R.O, C., 1996. Prof. Grad. Inst. of Rehab. Sci., Chang Gung U., Tao-Yuan, Taiwan, 1997—. Editor, cons. Phys. Therapy Assn. of Taiwan, 1998—. Recipient Wu Ta-You award, Nat. Sci. Coun., R.O.C., 2002. Fellow: Phys. Therapy Assn. of Taiwan; mem.: Internat. Soc. on Thrombosis and Haemostasis, Am. Physiologic Soc. Office Phone: 886-3-2118800. Office Fax: 886-3-2118700. Business E-Mail: s5492@mail.cgu.edu.tw.

WANG, JOON HO, surgeon, orthopedist, educator; b. Seoul, Republic of Korea, Mar. 10, 1969; s. Young Gu Wang and Soon Sik Oh; m. Myung Ju Shin, June 4, 1970; children: Sang Rok, Seo Yeon. BA, Korea U., 1990, MS in Med. Sci.; PhD in Med. Sci., Korea U., Seoul, 2004. Diplomate Korea Med. Assn., 1994. Residency orthopedic surgery Korea U. Med. Ctr., Seoul, 1998—2002; fellow orthopedic surgery and sports medicine Samsung Med. Ctr., Seoul, 2002—03; fellow orthopedic surgery and arthroscopy Korea U. Guro Hosp., Seoul, 2003—04; clin. asst. prof. Korea U. Ansan Hosp., 2004—05, asst. prof., 2005—08, assoc. prof., 2008—10, Sungkyunkwan U., Samsung Med. Ctr., 2010—. 1st lt. South Korean Mil., 1995—98. Home: Woosung Apt 1-801 Seocho-Dong Se Seoul 137-773 Republic of Korea Office: Dept Orthop Samsung Med Ctr Irwon-dong Gangnan-gu Seoul 135-710 Republic of Korea Office Fax: 082-2-3410-0061; Home Fax: 082-31-405-9006. Personal E-mail: mdwang88@gmail.com.

WANG, JOSEPHINE L. FEN, physician; b. Taiwan, China, Jan. 2, 1948; arrived in US, 1974; d. Pao-San and Ann-Nam (Chen) Chao; m. Chang-Yang Wang, Dec. 20, 1973; children: Edward, Eileen. MD, Nat. Taiwan U., Taipei, 1974. Diplomate Am. Bd. Pediat., Am. Bd. Allergy and Immunology. Intern Nat. Taiwan U. Hosp., 1973—74; resident U. Ill. Hosp., Chgo., 1974—76; fellow Northwestern U. Med. Ctr., Chgo., 1976—78, instr. pediat., 1978—; cons. Holy Cross Hosp., Chgo., 1978—, Meth. Hosp. Ind., 1979—, St. Anthony Hosp., 1985—, Christ Hosp., 1995—. Fellow: Am. Coll. Allergy; mem.: AMA, Am. Acad. Allergy. Office: 9012 Connecticut Dr Merrillville IN 46410-7170 also: 4901 W 79th St Burbank IL 60459-1554 Office Phone: 708-425-1320, 219-769-6177.

WANG, JULIE, pediatric allergist, educator; b. Calif., July 13, 1974; MD, Cornell U., 2000. Asst. prof., pediat. Mt. Sinai Sch. Medicine, 2006. Office: Mt Sinai Sch Medicine One Gust L Levy Pl Box 1198 New York NY 10029

WANG, KUNGSUN, health facility administrator; MD, Shanghai Jiao Tong U. Med. dir. New Vision Eye Clinic. Vis. scholar Sinai Hosp., United States. Mem.: Internat. Soc. of Refractive Surgery, Am. Academy of Opthalmology. Office: New Vision Eye Clinic International Patient Services 12th Fl 197 Rui Jin Er Rd Shanghai 200025 China Office Phone: 8602164377445. *

WANG, LI-JEN, radiologist, educator; m. Yon-Cheong Wong. MD, Sch. Medicine, Kaohsiung Med. Coll., Taiwan, 1988. Cert. radiologist Radiol. Soc., Republic of China., 1992. Attending staff Chang Gung Meml. Hosp., 1994—, asst. prof., 1996—2004, assoc. prof., 2004—11, prof., 2011—. Contbr. articles to profl. jour. Recipient award, Jour. Computed Assisted Tomography, 1997. Mem.: European Soc. Radiology, Radiol. Soc. N. Am., Radiol. Soc., Repubic of China (award 2007). Achievements include research in imaging diagnosis of urinary tuberculosis, angiomyolipoma, urinary stones and transitional cell carcinoma. Office: Chang Gung Meml Hosp 5 Fu-Hsing St Gueishan Taoyuan 333 Taiwan Office Fax: 886-3-3970074. Business E-Mail: ljw33db@adm.cgmh.org.tw.

WANG, MARILENE, medical educator; b. NYC, July 5, 1963; MD, Loma Linda U., 1986. Prof. UCLA Sch. Medicine, 1992—. Chief, otolaryngology VA Greater LA Healthcare Sys., 1994. Grant, NIH. Fellow: ACS, Am. Head and Neck Soc., Triological Soc., Am. Rhinologic Soc., Am. Acad. Otolaryngology. Office: 200 UCLA Med Plz Ste 550 Los Angeles CA 90095 Business E-Mail: mbwang@ucla.edu.

WANG, MATTHEW NAI-HWEI, surgeon, educator; s. Shih-Ling Wang and Huan Wang-Lin; life ptnr. Sylvia Shun-Hui Kuo, Dec. 12, 1975; 1 child, Raymond Jen-Chih. MD, Kaohsiung Med. U., Taiwan, 1974. Diplomate Dept. of Health, Exec. Yuan, China, 1974. Chief divsn. pediat. orthop. Vet.'s Gen. Hosp., Taipei, Taiwan, 1985—96; supt. Tachia br. Kuang Tien Gen. Hosp., Taichung, 1996—. Prof. Hung Kuang U., Taichung, 2004—. Mem.: Taiwan Orthop. Assn. (com. mem. 1998—, editl. bd.), Pediat. Orthop. Soc. N.Am. (corr.). Avocation: golf. Office: Kuang Tien Gen Hosp 321 Chiu Kuo Rd Tachia Taichung 437 Taiwan Office Phone: 04-26888989. Business E-Mail: admin_tachia@ktgh.com.tw.

WANG, MICHAEL, psychologist, educator; b. Sheffield, England, Jan. 15, 1956; s. Man Gee and Patricia Mavis Wang; m. Madeleine Valerie Taylor, Aug. 26, 1978; children: Naomi, James, Miriam, Benjamin. BSc in Psychology with hons., Manchester U., Eng., 1978, MSc in Clin. Psychology, 1980, PhD in Psychiatry, 1991. Clin. psychologist U. Hosp. South Manchester, 1980—83, sr. clin. psychologist, 1983—88; clin. dir. psychology U. Hull, Kingston upon Hull, England, 1988—97, head dept. clin. psychology, 1997—2005; prof. U. Leicester, England, 2005—, head Dept. Clin. Psychology, 2005—. Cons. in field; lectr. in field. Contbr. articles to profl. jours. Grantee, N.E. Yorks Workforce Devel. Confedn., 2000, Cancer Rsch. Campaign, 2002, European Commn., 2002. Fellow: Royal Soc. Medicine, Brit. Psychol. Soc. (chmn. divsn. clin. psychology, chmn. symposium organizing com.); mem.: Brit. Assn. Behavioral and Cognitive Psychotherapy, Brit. Assn. Christians in Psychology. Avocations: piano, skiing, tennis, films. Office: Univ Leicester 104 Regent Rd Leicester LE1 7LT England Business E-Mail: mw125@le.ac.uk.

WANG, NANCY, pathologist, educator; b. An-Wei, China, Sept. 2, 1944; m. Tingchung Wang; children: Jessie, Melissa. BS, Nat. Taiwan U., 1966; MS, U. Minn., 1968, PhD, 1978. Diplomate Am. Bd. Med. Genetics. Instr. Dept. Pathology & Lab. Med. U. Minn., Mpls., 1978-79, asst. prof., 1980-82, Dept. Pathology, Tulane Med. Sch., 1982-83, assoc. prof., 1984-86, U. Rochester, NY, 1986-93, prof. NY, 1993—. Mem.: Am. Assn. Human Gennetics. Office Phone: 585-275-6597. Business E-Mail: nancy_wang@urmc.rochester.edu.

WANG, PAIR DONG, physician, internist, researcher; s. Wan-Fu Wang and Sha-En Wang-Lee; m. Yuh-Yeh Pan, Dec. 25, 1972. PhD in pub. health, Nat. Taiwan U., 1991—95. Internal Medicine Specialist Dept. Health, Taiwan, 1992, Family Medicine Specialist Dept. Health, Taiwan, 1989. Dep. supt. Taipei Mcpl. Chronic Disease Hosp., Taiwan, 1995—2000, cons. physician, 2000—. Reviewer Am. Jour. of Infection Control, NYC, 2000—. Contbr. articles to profl. jours. Recipient Health medal, Dept. of Health, The Exec. Yuan / Taiwan, 1997, Pub. Svc. Outstanding award, The Exec. Yuan / Taiwan, 1989, 1991, Shin-Lin award, Taipei Med. Assn., 1993. Fellow: Taiwan Soc. of Internal Medicine (licentiate), Family Medicine Assn. (licentiate), Taiwan Med. Assn. (licentiate), Med. Ultrasonic Assn. (licentiate). Buddhist. Achievements include research in menopause problems, osteoporosis as well as research on the causes & prevention of different chronic diseases. Avocations: reading, jogging, hiking, travel, music. Office: Taipei Mcpl Chronic Disease Hosp # 530 Lin-Shan North Rd Taipei 104 Taiwan Fax: 886-2-2367-6222. E-mail: pdw@ms34.hinet.net.

WANG, QINHONG, research scientist; b. Zhejiang, China, May 14, 1968; PhD, FuDan U., China, 2004. Sci. rsch. fellow Duke U. Med. Ctr., 2008—. Recipient Rsch. award, Nat. Natural Sci. Rsch. Found., Shanghai, 2000—01. Mem.: Am. Soc. Hematology, Am. Assn. Cancer Rsch. Home: 2752 Campus Walk Ave Apt 29H Durham NC 27705 Personal E-mail: qinhong_wang@yahoo.com.cn.

WANG, RONALD CHI CHIU, medical researcher, educator; s. Chun Fai Wang and Chen Yuk Lee; m. Sally Wu, Mar. 31, 1996; 1 child, Nicole. MBBS, Jinan U., 1994; PhD in Surg. Sci., Chinese U. Hongkong, 1998; PhD in Genetics, Nat. Inst. Genetics, Japan, 2011. Cert. in Acupuncture Guangzhou U. Traditional Chinese Medicine, China, 1990, Inst. Traditional Chinese Medicine, 1989, in Traditional Chinese Medicine Inst. Traditional Chinese Medicine, 1990. Ho. officer and surgeon Overseas Chinese Hosp., Guangzhou, China, 1993—94; rsch. assoc. Chinese U. Hong Kong, Shatin, 1998—2001, asst. prof., 2002—06, assoc. prof., 2006—, in charge Analytical Biochemistry Lab. Dept. Ophthalmology and Visual Sci., 2002—; postdoctoral fellow Inst. Biochemistry Humboldt U., Berlin, 1999; postdoctoral fellow Nat. Inst. Genetics, Mishima, Japan, 2001—02; hon. sci. officer Prince Wales Hosp., 2006; dep. dir. Prenatal Genetic Diagnosis Ctr. Prince Wales Hosp., 2006. Rsch. fellow Nat. Inst. Genetics, 2002—. Recipient Regional Svc. award, Australasian Assn. Clin. Biochemists, Asian and Pacific Fedn. Clin. Biochemistry, and Internat. Fedn. of Clin. Chemistry, 2004, Travel award, Human Genome Orgn., 2006, Bursary award, Internat. Fedn. Clin. Chemistry and Lab. Medicine, 2007, Young. Investigator award, Asia Assn. Rsch. Vision and Ophthalmology, 2007, Loke award, Internat. Fedn. Placental Assn., 2007, Organising Com. award, Soc. Gynecologic Investigation, 2009, 2009; fellow, Japan Soc. Promotion Scis., 2000, 2009—11, German Academic Exch. Svc., 1999; scholar, Asian-Pacific Fedn. Clin. Chemistry, 2006, Keystone Symposium, 2007, scholarship, Internat. Soc. Immunology and Reprodn., 2007; Internat. Travel grant, Am. Assn. Clin. Chemistry, 2005, Norvatis Travel fellow, Asia Assn. Rsch. Vision and Ophthalmology, Jr. fellowship, Internat. Union Toxicology. Mem.: Royal Soc. Chemistry UK, Hong Kong Soc. Mass Spectrometry (corr.), Hong Kong Soc. Clin. Chemistry (corr. Roche award 2003), Hong Kong Soc. Devel. Biology (corr.), Internat. Soc. Stem Cell Rsch. (corr. award), Obstetrics and Gynecol. Soc. Hong Kong (assoc. Trust Fund award 2005, 2008, 2010), Asia Pacific Soc. Eye Genetics (life). Office: Chinese Univ Hong Kong Dept Ob Gyn Prince of Wales Hosp Shatin Hong Kong Office Phone: 852-2632-2810. Office Fax: 852-2636-0008. Business E-Mail: ccwang@cuhk.edu.hk.

WANG, RUEY-HSIA, nursing educator, director; b. Tainan, Taiwan, Nov. 6, 1959; d. Jian-Zhang Wang and Jin-Que Chen; m. Jin-Ze Chen, Apr. 8, 1986; children: Yu-Tsung Chen, Yu-Wen Chen. BSN, Kaohsiung Med. U., Taiwan, 1982; MS in Pub. Health, Kaohsiung Med. U., 1985, PhD in Nursing, 2005. RN Dept. Health, 1983. Tchg. asst., Inst. and Dept. Pub. Health Kaohsiung Med. U., 1983—85, lectr. coll. nursing, 1985—93, nurse practitioner, Chung-Ho Meml. Hosp., 1991—92, assoc. prof., coll. nursing, 1993—2006, adminstrn. tchr., coll. nursing, 1995—2001, adminstrn. leader, dept. rschr. and devel., 2005—06, supr., Chung-Ho Meml. Hosp., 2005—06, prof., dir. coll. nursing, 2006—. Trustee Sin-Sim Nursing Found., Bd. of Trustees, Taiwan, Kaohsiung, Taiwan, 2001—, com. mem. Sch. Health Com. Kaohsiung City, 2004—05, Cmty. Health Devel. Ctr. San-min Dist., Kaohsiung Med. U., 2005—06; com. mem., dept. health Health Edn. and Promotion Com., Taipei, 2006—. Author: (book) Health Promotion and Theory: Theory and Practice; contbr. articles to profl. journ. Recipient Rsch. award, NSC, Taipei, 1990, 1992, Excellent Nurse award, Internat. Lions Club, Kaohsiung, 1995, Kaohsiung Nurses Assn., Taiwan, 1997, Svc. Decoration award, Ministry Edn., Taipei, Taiwan, 1995, 2005, Excellent Tutor award, Kaohsiung Med. U., Taiwan, 1995, Excellent Postgrad. Student award, 2005. Mem.: Assn. Chinese Sch. and Coll. Health Nursing (dir. 2000—03), Taiwan Health Promotion and Edn. Assn., Taiwan Nurses Assn. (cmty. health nursing com. mem. 2006—), Kaohsiung Nurses Assn. (exec. dir. 2007—), Sigma Theta Tau. Office: Kaohsiung Med Univ 100 Shih-Chuan 1st Rd Kaohsiung 807 Taiwan Office Fax: 886 7 3218364. Business E-Mail: wrhsia@kmu.edu.tw.

WANG, SHAN, hospital administrator; B in Mgmt. Studies, Beijing Med. Coll., 1983; MD, Beijing Med. U., 1992. Rsch. fellow Beijing Med. Univ., China, 1986—92; resident dept. surgery Beijing Med. Univ. People's Hosp., China, 1983, chief resident dept. surgery, 1986, attending surgeon dept. surgery, 1988—93, assoc. prof. dept. gen. surgery, 1993—98, asst. to pres., 1998—99; dir. lab. surg. oncology Peking Univ. People's Hosp., China, 1999, dep. dir. divsn. gastrointestinal surgery, 2001, v.p., 2003, pres. Edit. bd. mem. various publs. Recipient 1st prize Peking Univ. Tchg. Achievement, 2005, 1st prize Nat. Tchg. Achievement, 2nd prize Beijing Tchg. Achievement. Office: Peking University Peoples Hospital S St Xicheng Dist Beijing 100044 China Office Phone: 8688326666. *

WANG, SHIH-TIEN, surgeon, educator; b. Taipei, Taiwan, July 3, 1962; s. Ya-Song and Wei Wang; m. Su-Jane You; children: Yun-Shiuan, Yun-Ling. B, Nat. Defence Med. Ctr., Taipei, 1987. Lic. physician Taiwan, 1987, diplomate Taiwan Bd. Exam. Surgery, 1991, Taiwan Bd. Exam. Orthop. Surgery, 1991. Surgeon, divsn. spine surgery, dept. orthopedics and traumatology Taipei Veterans Gen. Hosp., 1997—; assoc. prof., dept. orthopedics Sch. Medicine, Nat. Yang Ming U., Taipei, 2008—. Sec. gen. Taiwan Spine Soc., Taipei, 2008—; sec. Jour. Orthop. Surgery, Taiwan, Taipei, 2006—. Contbr. articles to numerous med. jours. Mem.: Taiwan Spinal Soc., Taiwan Orthop. Assn., Taiwan Surg. Assn. Achievements include patents for anterior spinal instrumentation. Home: 2nd Fl 201 Sec 2 Shih-Pai Rd Taipei 112 Taiwan Office: Taipei Veterans Gen Hosp 201 Sec 2 Shih-Pai Rd Taipei 112 Taiwan Office Fax: 886-2-28745839. Personal E-mail: s_twang@yahoo.com. Business E-Mail: stwang@vghtpe.gov.tw.

WANG, SHU-LI, epidemiologist, educator, researcher; b. Changhua, Taiwan, Sept. 15, 1967; d. Ming-Jing and Gua lee Wang; m. Shih-Ming Wang, Sept. 21, 1993; children: Yu-Ning, Yu-Tzu. BS, Nat. Taiwan U., Taipei, 1990; PhD, U. Coll. London, 1995. Fellow in gerontology U. Cambridge, England, 1995—96; fellow Acad. Sinica, Taipi, 1996—97; asst. prof. Chung-Shan Med. U., Taichung, Taiwan, 1997—2000; asst. prin. investigator Nat. Health Rsch. Inst., Kaohsiung, Taiwan, 2000—04, assoc. prin. investigator, 2004—. Adj. assoc. prof. Kaohsiung Med. U., 2004—; data coord. WHO project U. London, 1991—94; mem. adv. bd. Nat. Sci. Coun., Taipei, 2005—, Kaohsiung County Dept. Health, 2005—. Contbr. articles to profl. jours. Recipient, Internat. Diabetes Fedn., 1995, 1996, Spl. Rsch. award, Nat. Sci. Coun., 1999, Young Scientist award, Asian Conf. on Occupl. Health, Taipei, 2002. Mem.: European Assn. for Study of Diabetes, Soc. Toxicology, Internat. Soc. Environ. Epidemiology. Avocations: mountaineering, painting. Office: Nat Health Rsch Inst No 35 Keyan Rd Zhanan 350 Taiwan Home Phone: 886-(3)-5586955; Office Phone: 886-(37)-246166 ext. 36509. Personal E-mail: slwang.tw@gmail.com. Business E-Mail: slwang@nhri.org.tw.

WANG, WEILIN, surgeon; s. Xian Wang; m. Yanxin Gao; 1 child, Zheng. PhD, China Med. U., 1995. Cert. pediat. surgeon Chinese Med. Assoc., 1982. Dep. chmn. Chinese Assn. Pediat. Surgeons, Beijing, 2002—; chmn. Br. Assn. Pediat. Surgeons, Shenyang, Liaoning, China, 2004—. Dir., dept. pediat. surgery Shenjing Hosp. China Med. U., Shenyang, 1998—. Recipient Nat. award, Chinese Assn. Pediat. Surgeons, 2007; grant, Nat. Ministry Sci. and Tech., 2008. Achievements include research in basic and clinical research of congenital anorectal malformations. Avocations: swimming, travel, photography, painting. Home and Office: China Med Univ Shengjing Hosp 36 Sanhaojie 110004 Shenyang Lißonngsheng China Office Fax: 86-24-23892617. Personal E-mail: wweilin@hotmail.com.

WANG, WILLIAM WEIQI, physician; b. Shanghai, June 3, 1962; arrived in U.S., 1989; s. Junmin Wang and Shanlai Gan; m. Lini Son-Will Wang; children: Will, Louis. MD, Shanghai Med. U., 1985; PhD, U. Medicine and Dentistry N.J., Newark, 1995. Fellow NIMH, Bethesda, Md., 1995—96; rsch. assoc. Baylor Coll. Medicine, Houston, 1997—98; resident psychiatry Washington U., St. Louis, 1998—2002; attending psychiatrist SSM Healthcare, St. Louis, 2002—; clin. instr. St. Louis U. Med. Sch., 2003—. Dir. med. rsch. Advent Rsch. Inst., 2006—10; bd. dir. Impact Group, LLC; med. dir. geriatric transitional program SSM St. Joseph Health Ctr., 2007—; med. dir. Olimedics Inst., 2008—. Author: Psychiatry Pearls of Wisdom, 1999, Psychiatry for the Boards, 2002, 2007, Comprehensive Psychiatry Review, 2009; contbr. articles to profl. jours. Recipient Clin. Rec. award, Shanghai Mpcl. Health Bur., 1988. Mem.: Am. Psychiat. Assn. Avocations: fine arts, history. Office: 255 Spencer Rd Saint Peters MO 63376 Office Phone: 636-939-2550. Personal E-mail: wwwang@rocketmail.com.

WANG, XIAOLONG, biology professor; b. Ningguo, Anhui, China, June 3, 1972; PhD, Ocean U. China, 2006. Assoc. prof. Ocean U. China, 1999—. Grant, Nat. Natural Sci. Found. Mem.: AAAS. Avocations: music, mountain climbing. Office: 5 Yushan Rd Qingdao Shandong 266003 China Business E-Mail: xiaolong@ouc.edu.cn.

WANG, YONG, mathematics professor; b. Mongolia, Aug. 1, 1976; PhD, Acad. Math. and Sys. Sci., Chinese Acad. Scis., 2005. Assoc. prof. Acad. Math. and Sys. Sci., Chinese Acad. Scis., 2007—. Mem.: Ops. Rsch. Soc. China. Avocations: swimming, tennis, reading. Office: 55 Zhongguancun East Rd Haidian Beijing 100190 China Business E-Mail: ywang@amss.ac.cn.

WANG, YOUQING, engineering educator; b. Laiwu City, Shandong, June 7, 1981; PhD, Tsinghua U., 2008. Sr. investigator U. Calif., Santa Barbara, 2008—10; prof. Beijing U. Chem. Tech., 2010—. Adj. sr. investigator Sansum Diabetes Rsch. Inst., 2008—11. NSFC grant, Nat. Nature Sci. Found. China. Mem.: IEEE, Am. Diabetes Assn., Sigma Xi. Avocation: badminton. Office: 15 BeiSanHuan East Rd Mail Box 4 Beijing 100029 China Personal E-mail: kewangyq@gmail.com.

WANG, YUH-FENG, nuclear medicine physician; b. Fengyuan, Taichung, Taiwan, Aug. 28, 1966; s. Chin-Ping Wang and Me-Lee Huang; m. Mei-Hua Chuang; children: Alex Daniel, Ilya Joyce, Austin Wesley, Avery Landon. MD, Nat. Defence Med. Ctr., Taipei, Taiwan, 1991, MS in Microbiology and Immunology, 1995. Diplomate Taiwan, 1991, cert. Assn. Occupl. Medicine, Taiwan, 1997, Soc. Nuc. Medicine, Taiwan, 1998. Chief residency Dept. Nuc. Medicine, Tri-Service Gen. Hosp., Taipei, 1995—99, attending staff, 1999—2000; consulting staff Dept. Nuc. Medicine, Armed Forced Taichung Gen. Hosp., 1999—2004; dir. Dept. Nuc. Medicine, Buddhist Dalin Tzu Chi Gen. Hosp., Chiayi, Taiwan, 2000—. Instr. Dept. Radiology, Nat. Defence Med. Ctr., 1997—2000; instr. dept. internal medicine Tzu Chi U., Hualien, Taiwan, 2001—07, asst. prof., 2007—. Recipient Young Investigator's award, Tri-Service Gen. Hosp., 1999, 22nd World Congress Pathology and Lab. Medicine, 2003, Best Poster award, 9th Congress World Fedn. Nuc. Medicine and Biology, 2006. Mem.: Soc. Nuc. Medicine, Taiwanese Com. Clin. Lab. Std., Assn. Occupl. Medicine. Office: Buddhist Dalin Tzu Chi Gen Hosp No2 Min-Sheng Rd Dalin Chiayi 622 Taiwan Office Fax: 886-5-2648508. Personal E-mail: yuhfeng@gmail.com. E-mail: nment@ms7.hinet.net.

WANG, YUQI, hospital administrator; b. Beijing, 1947; Grad., China Union Med. U.; MS, Shanghai Med. U., 1982. Clin. tng. vascular surgery Austin Hosp. Univ. Melbourne, Australia; sr. vascular surgeon Zhongshan Hosp. Fudan Univ., Shanghai, dir. inst. vascular surgery, med. dir. Edtl. bd. mem. Chinese Jour. Surgery, Chinese Jour. Expptl. Surgery. Mem.: Internat. Soc. Cardiovascular Surgery, Internat. Coll. Angiology, Asian Vascular Soc., Chinese Soc. Vascular Surgery (vice chmn.). Office: Zhongshan Hospital Fudan University 180 Fenglin Rd Shanghai China Office Phone: 862164041990. Business E-Mail: yqwang@shmu.edu.cn. *

WANG, ZHI, biomedical researcher; b. Lanchou City, Ganshu, China, June 2, 1950; m. Xia Zhang, June 24, 1953; 1 child, Ruibing. MD, Xi'an Sch. Medicine, 1981. Action dir., asst. prof. Tufts U. Sch. Medicine, Boston, 1999—2000; dir., prof. Boston U. Sch. Medicine, 2001—. Recipient Assn. Rsch. award, Am. Laryngol. Assn., 1994; grantee, NIH, 2001. Fellow: Am. Acad. Otolaryngology Head and Neck Surgery. Achievements include research in less side-effects in cancer treatment/surgery. Office: Boston Univ Sch Medicine 88 E Newton St D616 Boston MA 02118 Home: 9 Hialeah Lane Framingham MA 01701-3585 Personal E-mail: zhiw@hotmail.com. Business E-Mail: zwang@bu.edu.

WANG, ZHIWEI, medical educator, researcher; b. China, June 18, 1970; PhD, Wayne State U., 2006. Rsch. assoc. Wayne State U., 2007—11; instr. Harvard Med. Sch., 2011—. Recipient Postdoc. fellowship, Dept. Def. Mem.: Am. Assn. Cancer Rsch. Avocations: soccer, travel, reading. Office: 330 Brookline Ave CLS-637 BIDMC Boston MA 02115 Personal E-mail: wangzw2001@yahoo.com.

WÄNGBERG, BO INGEMAR, surgeon, educator; b. Mariestad, Skaraborg, Sweden, Apr. 15, 1953; s. Ingemar Mattias and Kjersti Fredrika (Boorg) W.; m. IngaMai Elisabeth Pettersson, June 5, 1982; children: Julia, Victoria, Axel. MD, U. Göteborg, Sweden, 1978, PhD, 1992. Authorized specialist of gen. surgery, Sweden. Resident County Hosp., Bohuslän, Sweden, 1978-86, cons., 1986-87, Sahlgrenska Univ. Hosp., Göteborg, 1987-94, assoc. prof. surgery, 1994—. Expdn. surgeon Swedish Antarctic Rsch. Project, Royal Swedish Acad. Scis., 1988-89; rschr. Med. Rsch. Coun., 1995—, chmn. MRC planning group on abdominal tumors, 2005—. Contbr. more than 100 articles to profl. jours. Recipient numerous rsch. grants from local/nat. instns. Fellow Swedish Surg. Soc.; mem. N.Y. Acad. Scis., Internat. Soc. Surgery, Internat. Assn. Endocrine Surgeons (mem. coun. 2004—), Swedish Assn. Endocrine Surgeons (pres. 2000—). Avocations: skiing, tennis, mountain climbing, literature. Home: Högadalsg 16 S-431 69 Mölndal Sweden Office: Sahlgrenska Univ Hospital Dept of Surgery S-413 45 Goteborg Sweden Office Phone: 46-31-3428092. E-mail: bo.wangberg@surgery.gu.se.

WANGYANG, YU, pharmacologist; b. Hefei, Anhui, China, Feb. 17, 1980; PhD, Shandong U., 2007. Rschr. Shandong Provincial Key Lab. Microparticles Drug Delivery Tech., 2010—. Home: 1# XinYu Rd Ji'nan Shandong 250000 China Personal E-mail: younger_cpu@yahoo.com.cn.

WANI, MANSUKHLAL CHHAGANLAL, chemist; b. Nandurbar, Maharastra, India, Feb. 20, 1925; came to U.S., 1958, naturalized, 1977; s. Chhagnalal Kikabhai and Maniben Chhanganlal (Shah) W.; m. Ramila Mansukhlal Dalal, Dec. 4, 1954; 1 child, Bankim M. BS with honors, St. Xavier's Coll., Bombay U., 1947, MS, 1950; PhD, Ind. U., 1962. Lectr. chemistry Bhavan's Coll., Bombay, 1951-58; rsch. asst. Ind. U., Bloomington, 1958-61; rsch. assoc. U. Wis., Madison, 1961-62; prin. scientist Rsch. Triangle Inst., Rsch. Triangle Park, NC, 1962—. Inventor anticancer drugs. Recipient B.F. Cain Meml. award Am. Assn. Cancer Rsch., 1994, City of Medicine award Durham, N.C., 1994, Award of Recognition Nat. Cancer Inst., 1996, Charles E. Kettering prize GM Cancer Rsch. Found., 2000, Ranbaxy Rsch. award. Mem. AAAS, Am. Chem. Soc., Am. Soc. Pharmacognosy, N.Y. Acad. Scis., India Assn. (pres. 1970-72), Hindu Soc. (dir. 1976-81), Assn. Indians in Am., Indo-Am. Forum, Sigma Xi, Phi Lambda Upsilon. Democrat. Avocations: reading, travel, sports. Home: 2801 Legion Ave Durham NC 27707-1921 Office: Rsch Triangle Inst 3040 W Cornwallis Rd Research Triangle Park NC 27709-2194 Home Phone: 919-489-2573; Office Phone: 919-541-6685. Business E-Mail: mcw@rti.org.

WANI, NISAR AHMAD, veterinarian, researcher; s. Abdul Aziz Wani and Hajra Begum; m. Shabeena Mustafa, June 27, 1994; children: Sadan, Shahzan. B of Vet. Sciences and Animal Husbandry, SK U. Agrl. Sciences and Tech., 1992; M of Vet. Sci., SK U. Agrl. Sci. and Tech., Srinagar, Kashmir, India, 1996; PhD in Vet. Reproduction, Gynecology and Obstetrics, G.B.Pant U. Agr. and Tech., Pantnagar, India, 2002. From sr. rsch. asst. to asst. prof., jr. scientist SK U. Agrl. Sci., Srinagar, 1992—2003; sr. scientist Ctrl. Vet. Rsch. Lab., Dubai, United Arab Emirates, 2003—. Recipient Best Young Scientist award, J&K State Coun. for Sci. and Tech., 1996. Mem.: Indian Soc. Agribusiness Profls., Internat. Embryo Transfer Soc., Indian Soc. for Study of Animal Reproduction (life Dr. S.N. Luktukae award 1999, Dr. G.B. award 2000, Outstanding Young Scientist award 1996). Office: Central Veterinary Rsch Lab Zabeel Dubai United Arab Emirates Office Fax: +971 4 3368638; Home Fax: +971 4 3368638. Personal E-mail: drnawani@hotmail.com.

WANK, GERALD SIDNEY, periodontist, educator; b. Bklyn., Jan. 20, 1925; s. Joseph and Sadie (Ikowitz) W.; m. Gloria Baum, June 4, 1949; children: David, Stephen, Daniel. BA, NYU, 1945, DDS, 1949; cert. in orthodontia, Columbia U., 1951, cert. in periodontia, 1956. Intern Bellevue Hosp., 1949-50; pvt. practice NYC, Great Neck, N.Y., 1949—; instr. dept. periodontia, oral medicine NYU Dental Sch., 1956-63, asst. clin. prof. dept. periodontia, 1963-67, asst. prof. periodontia, oral medicine, former postgrad. dir. periodontal-prosthesis dept. fixed partial prosthesis, 1970—, clin. assoc. prof. periodontia and oral medicine, 1970-77, clin. prof. dept. periodontia and implantology, 1977—, postgrad. dir. periodontia, 1968-71, Disting. prof. periodontics, 2002; lectr. periodontology Harvard U. Sch. Dental Medicine, 1971—74; vis. lectr. N.Y.C. C.C. Sch. Dental Hygiene, 1960-65, Albert Einstein Coll. Medicine, 1967-96; sr. asst. attending staff North Shore U. Hosp., 1974-77, sr. asst. attending divsn. surgery, 1977—. Cons. orthodontic panel N.Y. State, N.Y.C. depts. health, 1953-80; cons. periodontal prosthesis, Goldwater Meml. Hosp., N.Y.C.; former postgrad. instr. 1st Dist. Dental Soc. Postgrad. Sch., dist. claims com.; lectr. in field; mem. com. admissions N.Y. U. Coll. Dentistry, 1975-86, chmn. fund raising, 1976-77; cons. N.Y. VA Hosp., 1996—. Contbr. to: Practice of Periodontia, 1960, Dental Clinics of North America, 1972, 81, Manual of Clinical Periodontics, 1973; contbr. articles to profl. jours. Capt. USAF, 1953-55. Recipient Alumni Meritorious Service award NYU, 1981, Coll. Dentistry Alumni Achievement award NYU, 1983, Disting. Prof. Periodontics award NYU Coll. Dentistry, 2002, named to Leaders in Am. Sci., 1963-64. Fellow APHA, Am. Acad. Oral Medicine, Acad. Gen. Dentistry, N.Y. Acad. Dentistry (life), Internat. Coll. Dentists (life), Am. Coll. Dentistry (life), Am. Acad. Oral Medicine (pres. N.Y. sect. 1971-72); mem. N.Y. Coll. Dentists (dir.), ADA, Dental Soc. N.Y.C. (dir. 1st dist., chmn. ethics com. 1985-86, peer rev. com.), Fedn. Dentaire Internat., Am. Assn. Dental Schs., N.Y. State Pub. Health Assn., AAUP, Pan Am. Med. Assn. (life), AAAS, ADA, Am. Acad. Periodontology, Sci. Rsch. Soc. Am., Northeastern Soc. Periodontia (life), Am. Acad. Dental Medicine, Acad. Gen. Dentistry, Internat. Acad. Orthodontia, Am. Assn. Endodontists (life), Am. Acad. Periodontia (life), Am. Acad. Oral Medicine (life), NYU Coll. Dentistry Alumni Assn. (dir., sec. 1973-74, v.p. 1974-75, pres. 1976-77), Am. Assn. Endodontists, NYU Coll. Dentistry Dental Assocs. (charter), Acad. Oral Rehab. (hon.), First Dist. Dental Soc. (program chmn. 1984, chmn. continuing edn. 1983, sec., 1985, v.p. Eastern Dental Soc. br. 1986, pres.-elect 1987, pres. br. 1988, bd. dirs. 1989—, Meritorious Svc. award 1997), NY County Dental Soc. (peer rev. com.), Am. Acad. Osseointegration (life), NYU Gallatin Assocs., Alumni Fedn. NYU (dir. 1976-81), N.Y. County Dental Soc. (Dist. Claims Com.), Soc. of the Torch, Masons, Century Club, NYU Club, Fresh Meadow Country Club, Omicron Kappa Upsilon (life), Alpha Omega. Jewish. Home and Office: 40 Bayview Ave Great Neck NY 11021-2819 Office: 30 E 40th St New York NY 10016-1201 Office Phone: 516-487-7877. Personal E-mail: gwank@aol.com.

WAN PUTEH, SHARIFA EZAT BINTI, medical educator; b. Malaysia, Oct. 2, 1970; MD, Nat. U. Malaysia, 1996; MPH, U. Kebangsaan Malaysia, 2004. Assoc. prof. Nat. U. Malaysia, 2000—. Cons., assoc. prof. Nat. U. Malaysia Med. Ctr., 2004—11. Recipient Rsch. award, 4th Internat. Ispor Conf. Phuket Thailand, Clin. Rsch. award, UKM Med. Ctr. Malaysia. Mem.: Ispor Outcome Rsch. Malaysia, Nat. Pub. Health Assn. Avocations: reading, travel, horseback riding. Home: 35 Jalan Pulau Angsa U10/43A Sunway Alam Shah Alam Selangor 40170 Malaysia Home Fax: 60391456670. Personal E-mail: sh_ezat@yahoo.com.

WAPNER, KEITH LESLIE, orthopedic surgeon, educator; b. Phila., Sept. 27, 1953; s. Paul Mordecai and Evelyn (Locke) W.; m. June Carosia, Jan. 16, 1982; children: Peter, Charles. BA, U. Pa., 1976; MD, Temple U., 1980. Diplomate Am. Bd. Orthopedic Surgery. Intern in surgery Hosp. of U. Pa., 1980-81, fellowship in orthop., 1981-82, resident in orthop. surgery, 1982-85, clin. prof. orthop. surgery, dir. orthop. foot and ankle surgery Phila., 2000—; asst. prof. Thomas Jefferson U., Phila., 1986-93, assoc. prof., 1993-95; prof. Allegheny U., Phila., 1996—2000. Adj. prof. orthop. Preyol Coll. Medicine, 2000-, clin. prof. U. Pa., 2000-. Mem. editl. bd. Seminars in Arthroplasty, 1990, Operative Techniques in Orthopaedics, 1990, Foot and Ankle, The Official Jour. of Am. Orthop. Foot and Ankle Soc., 1992, Clin. Orthops. and Related Rsch., 1993; reviewer Am. Jour. Sports Medicine, 1993; contbr. numerous articles to profl. jours. Bd. dirs. Ohev Shalom Hebrew Sch., Wallingford, Pa., 1995. Named one of Top Doctors, Phila. Mag., 2002, 2004-08. Fellow Am. Coll. Surgeons, Am. Acad. Orthop. Surgery, Am. Orthop. Foot and Ankle Soc.; mem. Am. Diabetes Soc., Pa. Med. Soc., Phila. Med. Soc., Phila. Orthop. Soc., Phila. Rheumatism Soc. Office: PennCare Farm Journal Bldg 5th Fl 230 W Washington Sq Philadelphia PA 19106

WARBURTON, DAVID, pediatrician, researcher; s. William Henry and Margaret Warburton; m. Leslie J. Nangle, June 13, 1971; children: Nicole Marie, Andrew David, Christopher Douglas. BSc, MBBS, U. London, 1973, DSc, 2006; MBA in Med. Mgmt., Marshall Sch. Bus., U. Southern Calif., 2009. Lic. Calif., 1979. Faculty U. Southern Calif., 1979—; prof. pediats., surgery and craniofacial biology dir. devel. biology and regenerative Medicine Program, Saban Rsch. Inst.; dir. Calif. Inst. for Regenerative Medicine Tng. Program and Stem Cell Core Facilites, Calif.-Mongolia Med. Project. Officer Most Excellent Order of Brit. Empire for Svcs. to USA-UK. Contbr. over 300 sci. papers in field. Venture crew advisor Boy Scouts Am., La Canada, Calif. Recipient Order of the Silver Falcon of Mongolia. Fellow: Royal Coll. Surgeons Eng., Royal Coll. Phys. Edinburgh. Achievements include research in molecular basis of organogenesis, tissue injury repair and regeneration with special focus on the lung. Avocations: opera, literature, languages, gardening. Office: Childrens Hosp 4650 Sunset Blvd Los Angeles CA 90027 Business E-Mail: dwarburton@chla.usc.edu. *

WARCHOL, STANISLAW, pediatrician, surgeon; b. Warsaw, Mazowsze, Poland, May 8, 1956; s. Stanislaw and Maria Warchol; m. Teresa Barbara Dudek, Oct. 3, 1982; 1 child, Ewa Maria. MD, Med. U. Warsaw, 1980, PhD, 1995. Jr. asst. dept. pediat. surgery Med. U. Warsaw, 1980—82, asst. dept. pediat. surgery, 1983—86, asst. lectr. dept. pediat. surgery, 1987—94; lectr. dept. pediat. surgery Med. U. of Warsaw, 1995—. Cons. dept. pediat. and nephrology Med. U. Warsaw, 1992—; cons. Dept. of Pediatric Nephrology and Cardiology, Bialystok, Podlaskie, Poland, 1999—. Mem.: Polish Assn. Pediat. Nephrology (assoc.), Baltic Assn. Pediat. Surgeons (assoc.), Polish Assn. Pediat. Surgeons (assoc.). Roman Catholic. Achievements include development of Introduction Of Presternal Peritoneal Dialysis Catheter In Children; Introduction Of Silver-Coated Peritoneal Dialysis Catheters In Children; Introduction Of New Techniques Of Peritoneal Dialysis Catheter Implantation In Children; Introduction Of Uniform Strategy In Arteriovenous Fistula Construction For Haemodialysis Purposes In Children; Introduction Of Surgical Implantation Of Permanent Haemodialysis Catheter In Children. Avocations: skiing, swimming, travel, reading. Office: Dept Genl Pediat Surgery Marszalkowska 24 Mazowsze Warsaw 00 576 Poland Office Fax: (+4822)6214631; Home Fax: (+4822)6214631. Personal E-mail: swarchol@poczta.onet.pl.

WARD, CHESTER LAWRENCE, physician, consultant; b. Woodland, Calif., June 8, 1932; s. Benjamin Briggs and Nora Elizabeth Ward; m. Sally Diane Ward, Dec. 10, 1960; children: Katharine, Lynda. BA, U. Calif., Santa Barbara, 1955; MPH, U. Calif., Berkeley, 1966; MD, U. So. Calif., 1962; grad., Indsl. Coll. Armed Forces, 1978. Commd. 2d lt., inf. U.S. Army, 1954, advanced through grades to brig. gen., 1980; surgeon 5th Spl. Forces, Ft. Bragg, NC, Vietnam, 1963-64; chief aviation medicine, preventive medicine and aeromed. consultation service Ft. Rucker, Ala., 1967-68; surgeon Aviation Brigade and USA Vietnam Aviation Medicine Cons., 1968-69; flight surgeon Office of U.S. Army Surgeon Gen., 1970-71; physician The White House, Washington, 1971-75, 76; dir. environ. quality rsch. U.S. Army Med. Rsch. and Devel. Commd., 1975-76; comdr. Womack Cmty. Hosp., 1978—80; surgeon XVIII Airborne Corps, Ft. Bragg, 1978-80; comdr. William Beaumont Army Med. Ctr., El Paso, Tex., 1980-82; med. dir. Union Oil Co., Schaumburg, Ill., 1982-83, dir. domestic medicine LA, 1983-84; exec. dir. continuing med. edn. and clin. prof. emergency medicine U. So. Calif. Sch. Medicine, LA, 1984-85; dir., health officer Dept. Pub. Health, Butte County, Calif., 1985-95; cons., contractor, pvt. practice medicine, 1996—; med. dir. NorCal EMS, 2001—05. Trustee, pres. Oroville Union HS Dist., 1998—2002; chmn. Citizen's Bond Oversight Com., 2003—05; dir. The Estuary Owners' Assn., 2006—08, pres., 2007—08; mem. state bd. pilot commr. Pilot Fitness Cmty., 2009—; chmn.Health & Safety Cmty. Cardinal Pt. Res. Assn., 2010—; apptd. by Gov. Wilson Calif. Commn. Emergency Med. Svcs., past commr. Decorated DSM, Legion of Merit (2), Bronze Star, Air medal (5). Fellow: Aerospace Med. Assn., Am. Coll. Preventive Medicine (past regent); mem.: No. Calif. Emergency Med. Svcs. Inc. (governing bd. 1987—2006, dir.), Calif. Med. Assn. (past del.), Butte-Glenn County Med. Soc. (past pres.), Mil. Officers Assn. (past chpt. pres.).

WARD, DANIEL HOWARD, dentist; b. Columbus, Ohio, Dec. 14, 1953; AB, Ohio U., BS, 1976; DDS, Ohio State U., 1979. Diplomate Am. Bd. Aesthetic Dentistry. Pvt. practice, 1979—. Asst. clin. prof., instr. Ohio State U. Coll. Dentistry, 1996—2009. Fellow: Am. Coll. Dentists, Am. Soc. Dental Aesthetics, Acad. Gen. Dentistry; mem.: ADA, CDS, ODA, Am. Acad. Cosmetic Dentists. Avocations: guitar, music. Office: 1080 Polaris Pky Ste 130 Columbus OH 43240 Office Fax: 614-430-8995. E-mail: dward@columbus.rr.com.

WARD, DEBORA ELLIOTT, psychologist; b. Malone, NY, Mar. 24, 1954; d. Donald Joseph and Marion Pearl (Briggs) Elliott; m. Bernard Daniel Ward, Sept. 26, 1987; 1 child, Daniel Elliott. BA in Psychology with honors, Binghamton U., NY, 1976; MS in Clin. Psychology, Syracuse U., NY, 1978, PhD in Clin. Psychology, 1983. Lic. in psychology, Maine. Psychol. asst. Neuropsychology Lab., Hutchings Psychiatric Ctr., Syracuse, N.Y., 1978-79, Syracuse U. Counseling Ctr., 1979-80; psychology assoc. West Haven (Conn.) VA Med. Ctr., 1980-81; rsch. asst. Syracuse U., 1981-82; psychology trainee Syracuse VA Med. Ctr., 1982; staff psychologist Bangor (Maine) Mental Health Inst., 1983-91; psychiat. clinician Acadia Hosp., Bangor, Maine, 1992-98, staff psychologist, 1998—. Cons. psychologist Greater Bangor Area Crisis Stabilization Svcs., 1995-98. Contbr. articles to profl. jours. Trustee Simpson Meml. Libr., Carmel, Maine, 2004—, pres., 2009—. USPHS fellow, 1976-78. Mem. APA, Maine Psychol. Assn., Phi Beta Kappa, Phi Beta Kappa Assn. Maine (v.p. 2004-). Avocations: seashell collecting, flower gardening, painting. Home: 313 Cook Rd Carmel ME 04419-9622 Office: Acadia Hosp 268 Stillwater Ave Bangor ME 04401-3980 Office Phone: 207-973-6349.

WARD, JACQUELINE ANN BEAS, nurse, healthcare administrator, legal nurse consultant; b. Somerset, Pa., Oct. 23, 1945; d. Donald C. and Thelma R. (Wable) Beas; divorced; children: Charles L. Jr., Shawn M. BSN, U. Pitts., 1966; MA in Counseling and Guidance, W.Va. Coll. Grad. Studies, 1976; MBA, Columbus Coll., 1983; AS in Health Svcs. Mgmt./Nursing Home Adminstrn., St. Petersburg Jr. Coll., 1997. Cert. advanced nursing adminstrn., legal nurse cons., 2007; adult living facility adminstr., nursing home adminstr. preceptor. Staff nurse W.Va. U. Hosp., Morgantown, 1966—67; staff nurse, head nurse Meml. Hosp, Charleston, W.Va., 1967—69; staff nurse Santa Rosa Hosp., San Antonio, 1969; staff nurse, supr. Bexar County Hosp., San Antonio, 1970; charge and staff nurse Rocky Mountain Osteo. Hosp., Denver, 1971; from staff nurse to asst. DON Charleston Area Med. Ctr., 1971—82; DON H.D. Cobb Meml. Hosp., Phenix City, Ala., 1982—84; v.p. nursing Venice Hosp., Fla., 1984—90, v.p. ops., 1990—94; exec. dir., v.p. Life Counseling Ctr., Osprey, Fla., 1994—95; dir. skilled unit and spl. projects Bon Secours/Venice Hosp., 1995—97; adj. clin. nursing faculty Manatee CC, Bradenton, 1998—99; interim adminstr. DON Contracting, Sarasota, 1999—2000; adminstr. Ctrs. for Long Term Care Venice Beach, 2000—01, Lake Towers-Sun Terrace Health Care Ctr., Sun City Center, Fla., 2002—05, Tandem Health Care Sarasota, 2005—07; exec. dir. Beneva Park Club, Sarasota, 2005. Clin. instr. Chattahoochie Valley C.C., Phenix City, 1982—84; support svcs. cons. Bon Secours Healthcare, Venice, 1996—97; support svcs. cons., interim adminstrn. Long Term Care, 1997—98; legal nurse cons., 2007—. Office Phone: 941-377-7535.

WARD, JEANNETTE POOLE, retired psychologist, educator; b. Honolulu, June 19, 1932; d. Russell Masterton and Bessie Naomi (Hammett) Poole; children: John Russell Ward, Lisa Joy Ward. BA, Birmingham So. Coll., Ala., 1963; PhD in Psychology, Vanderbilt U., 1969. NSF summer rsch. asst. U. Iowa, Iowa City, 1962, Vanderbilt U., Nashville, 1963, NASA fellow, 1963-66, NIH postdoctoral fellow, 1966-67; spl. rsch. fellow Duke U., Durham, NC, 1970-71; asst. prof. psychology U. Memphis, 1967—72, assoc. prof., 1972—77, prof., 1977—2000; ret., 2001. Editor: Current Research in Primate Laterality, 1990, Primate Laterality, 1992; mem. editl. bd. Jour. Comparative Psychology, 1988-95, Internat. Jour. of Comparative Psychology, 1995—; contbr. chpts. to books and articles to profl. jours. Fellow APA; mem. Psychonomic Soc., Animal Behavior Soc., Am. Primatology Soc., Southeastern Psychol. Assn., Soc. for Neurosci., Internat. Soc. for Comparative Psychology (treas. 1989-90, pres.-elect 1996-98, pres. 1998-2000), Sigma Xi (pres. Memphis State U. chpt. 1989-90, rsch. award 1985). Democrat. Avocations: reading, art, music.

WARD, JEWELL C., clinical geneticist, educator; MD, Indiana U., 1971. Cert. Am. Bd. Clin. Genetics-Med. Genetics, 1982, Am. Bd. Clin. Biochemical Genetics-Med. Genetics, 1982. Intern Children's Hosp., Ohio, 1973, resident pediat. Ohio, 1972—74; fellow Indiana Univ. Hosp., 1972, fellow med. genetics, 1974—75, Johns Hopkins Univ. Hosp., 1975—79; prof. pediat. Univ. Tenn.; physician Methodist Hosp. Office: Methodist Hospital 777 Washington Ave Ste 400 Memphis TN 38103 Office Phone: 901-866-8818.

WARD, JOHN F., medical educator; b. Pitts., Dec. 10, 1964; MD, Georgetown U., 1991. Asst. prof. UT MD Anderson Cancer Ctr., 2006—. Office: 1515 Holcombe - Unit 1373 Houston TX 77030 Business E-Mail: jfward@mdanderson.org.

WARD, LOUIS EMMERSON, retired physician; b. Mt. Vernon, Ill., Jan. 19, 1918; s. Henry Ben (Pope) and Aline (Emmerson) Ward; m. Nan Talbot, June 5, 1942; children: Nancy, Louis, Robert, Mark; m. Marian Mansfield, Jan. 27, 1979. AB, U. Ill., 1939; MD, Harvard, 1943; MS in Medicine, U. Minn., 1949. Intern Ill. Research and Ednl.

Hosp., Chgo., 1943; fellow medicine Mayo Found., 1946—49; cons. medicine, rheumatology Mayo Clinic, 1950—83, chmn. bd. govs., 1964—75. Contbr. articles to profl. jours. Vice chmn. bd. trustees Mayo Found., 1964—76; past bd. dirs. Fund for Republic, Ctr. for Study Dem. Instns., Arthritis Found., Northwestern Bell Telephone Prin. Fin. Group; mem. Nat. Coun. Health Planning and Resource Devel., 1976—83. With M.C. US Army, 1944—46. Recipient Achievement award, U. Ill., 1968, Disting. Alumnus award, Mayo Found., 1983. Master: Am. Coll. Rheumatology; mem.: Inst. Medicine, So. Minn. Med. Assn., Zumbro Valley Med. Soc., Minn. Med. Soc., Ctrl. Soc. Clin. Rsch., Nat. Soc. Clin. Rheumatologists, AAAS, AMA, Phi Delta Theta, Alpha Omega Alpha, Sigma Xi, Phi Beta Kappa. Home: Apt 916 211 2nd St NW Rochester MN 55901-2820

WARD, PATRICIA ANN, pharmaceutical executive; b. Vincennes, Ind., Aug. 12, 1956; d. Harold Edgar and Thelma Lucille (Mason) Hudson; m. Steven Joe Ward, Aug. 31, 1974; children: Jennifer Jo, Jade Steven. Student, Vincennes U., 1984; diploma in radiologic tech., Good Samaritan Sch. Radiologic Tech., Vincennes, 1986; BS in Mgmt., Oakland City U., 1992, MS, 2003. Nat. cert. radiologic technician; cert. radiologic technologist, Ind. Sales exec. Takeda Pharm. N.Am. Vol. United Cerebral Palsy Ind., Vincennes, 1983, VFW, Newburgh, 1995, Colonnade Club, Delta Zeta, Evansville, 1994—; cons. Girl Scouts U.S.A., Bicknell, Ind., 1984; parent vol. Castle H.S., Newburgh, Ind., 1992—; mem. Comdr.'s Club, DAV, Newburgh, 1995—. Mem. Am. Soc. Radiologic Technologists, Ind. Soc. Radiologic Technologists (mem. dist. 8 radiologic technologists). Avocations: golf, floral arranging, swimming, travel. Home: 3177 Graceland Ct Newburgh IN 47630-2689

WARD, ROBERT F., pediatric otolaryngologist; b. Bklyn., June 8, 1950; MD, Cornell Univ., 1981. Cert. Am. Bd. Otolaryngology, 1986. Intern NY Hosp., NYC, 1981—82, resident surgery, 1982—83, resident otolaryngology, 1983—86; fellow in pediatric otolaryngology Children's Hosp., Harvard Med. Coll., Boston, 1986; prof. otolaryngology Weill Med. Coll., Cornell Univ., NYC. Recipient Achievement award, Am. Acad. Otolaryngology-Head & Neck Surgery, 1996, Seymour Cohen award, Am. Bronchoesophagologic Assn., 1981; named one of Best Doctors, NY Mag., 2008—09. Office: Weill Cornell Med Coll 5th Fl 1305 York Ave New York NY 10021 Office Phone: 646-962-2224. Office Fax: 646-962-0100.

WARD, VERNON GRAVES, retired internist; b. Palisade, Nebr., Mar. 5, 1928; s. Charles Bennett and Mildred Belle (Graves) W.; m. Eleanore Mae Farstveet, Aug. 28, 1952; children: Scott (dec.), Margo, Alison, Barry. BA, Nebr. Wesleyan U., 1948; MD cum laude, U. Nebr., Omaha, 1954. Diplomate Am. Bd. Internal Medicine. Instr. and rsch. fellow, anatomy Columbia U. Coll. Physicians and Surgeons, NYC, 1948—50; intern U. Wis., Madison, 1954—55, resident internal medicine, 1955—58, chief resident, physician, 1957—58; fellow in neurophysiology and psychosomatic medicine U. Okla., Oklahoma City, 1960—61; asst. clin. prof. medicine U. Wis., Madison, 1961—62; pvt. practice internal medicine Kearney, Nebr., 1962—67, asst. prof. U. Nebr. Coll. Medicine, Omaha, 1967—69; assoc. clin. prof. medicine U. Nebr., Omaha, 1969—; pvt. practice internal medicine Omaha, 1969—2005; ret. Chmn. dept. internal medicine Clarkson Hosp., Omaha, 1976-78, 96-98. Contbr. articles to profl. jours. including JAMA, Nebr. State Med. Jour., Wis. State Med. Jour., Am. Heart Jour., Postgrad. Medicine. Pres. Nebr. chpt. Arthritis Found., 1969-71. Lt. comdr. USNR, 1958-60. Recipient Cmty. Based Tchg. award ACP-ASIM, 2000; named Hutton Traveling Scholar Coll. of Physicians, 1965. Fellow ACP, Am. Coll. Rheumatology; mem. AMA, Nebr. State Med. Soc., Omaha Med. Soc., Am. Soc. Internal Medicine (Cmty.-Based Tchg. award 2000), Am. Psychosomatic Soc., Nebr. Soc. Internal Medicine (pres. 1980-82, Disting. Internist award 1990), Phi Kappa Phi, Alpha Omega Alpha (pres. Nebr. chpt. 1984-85), Phi Chi (grand sec.-treas. 1986—2006, co-chmn. nat. conv. Omaha 1953, emeritus trustee 2006—), Phi Kappa Tau. Republican. Lutheran. Home: 302 N 54th St Omaha NE 68132-2813 Home Phone: 402-558-7641.

WARDELL, TAMARA LYNN, critical care nurse; b. Terre Haute, Ind., Feb. 19, 1952; d. Donald Meredith Wardell, Jr. and Patricia Ernestine Cooksey Wardell. BSN, Duke U., Durham, NC, 1974; MSN in Nursing Edn., U. Pitts., 1986; postgrad., Duquesne U., Pitts., 1995—. Instr. St. Francis Med. Ctr., Sch. Nursing, Pitts., 1986—87; critical care instr. We. Pa. Hosp., Pitts., 1987—88; staff nurse, surg. intensive care unit, med., IV team St. Francis Med. Ctr., Pitts., 1988—92; nurse mgr., patient care coord., supr. VA Med. Ctr., Pitts., 1992—94; grad. rsch., tchg. asst. Duquesne U., Sch. Nursing, Pitts., 1996—2001. Clin. instr. Carlow U., Sch. Nursing, Pitts., 1994—95; exec. com. past pres. Exec. Commn., Nat. PRP Commn., 2004—06; news letter editor, 1998—2000. Editor: (newsletter) Western Pennsylvania Mensa Phoenix, 1987—; contbr. monthly column. Leader Girl Scouts America, 1989—2008, mem., Daisy leader Trillium Coun., 1984—94, mem. svc. unit mgr., 1992—94; sec. Pleasant Ridge Resident's Coun., McKees Rocks, Pa., 2007—09; chair Food Pantry Com., 2007—09; interviewer Duke U. Alumni Admissions Adv. Com., Pitts., 1991—2009. Kuhnel scholar, Mensa Edn. and Rsch. Found., 2005. Mem.: Oncology Nursing Soc. (chair awards and oncology nursing found. com. 2002—03), Therapeutic Touch Assoc. Internat., Inc (nursing initiative on aging task force 2006—07, regional membership coord. 2008—11), Am. Assn. Critical Care Nurses (nat. scholar rev. com. 2006, nat. rev. panel mem. 2011), Am. Mensa (proctor 1992—, scholar chair 1997—2004, 2006—08, publicity chair 2006—07), Coll. Club Carnegie (bridge & recreation chair 2005—09), Golden Key Internat. Honor Soc., Sigma Theta Tau (media guide health care experts 1997—2009, pres.-elect 2006—07, Creative Arts Competition winner 2003). R-Conservative. Lutheran. Avocations: gardening, reading, needlecrafts, bridge. Home: 341 Potomac Ave Terre Haute IN 47803-1663 Home Phone: 812-235-4514. Personal E-mail: tamwardell@frontier.com.

WARDLE, JON, physician; b. Darwin, Northern Ter., Australia, Sept. 22, 1979; ND, Australian Coll. Natural Medicine, 2004; PhD, U. Queensland, 2011. Lectr., clin. supr. Australian Coll. Natural Medicine, 2005—08; nat. health and med. rsch. coun. pub. health scholar U. Queensland, 2007—11. Dir., rsch. capacity bldg. Network of Rschrs. Pub. Health Complementary and Alternative Medicine, 2008—11; assoc. editor Founds. Naturopathic Medicine Project, 2010—11; editor-in-chief Internat. Jour. Naturopathic Medicine, 2011. Trans-Pacific fellowship, U. Wash. Mem.: Nat. Herbalists Assn. Australia, Pub. Health Assn. Australia. Office: University Queensland Sch Population Health Herston Qld 4006 Australia Business E-Mail: j.wardle@sph.uq.edu.au.

WARE, J(OE) ANTHONY, cardiologist; b. Topeka, Dec. 12, 1952; s. Joe F. and Jane C. (Casper) Ware; children: Gabriel, Rachel, Emily. BS summa cum laude, Washburn U., 1974; MD, Kans. U., 1977. Diplomate Am. Bd. Internal Medicine, Am. Bd. Cardiovasc. Disease. Intern, resident Baylor Coll. Medicine, Houston, 1977-81, chief resident, 1981, clin. fellow in cardiovasc. disease, 1981-84; rsch. fellow Beth Israel Hosp., Med. Sch. Harvard U., Boston, 1984-86, assoc. prof. medicine, 1986-97; Sidney L. & Miriam K. Olson prof. cardiology Albert Einstein Coll. Medicine and Montefiore Med. Ctr., NYC, 1997-2001, chief cardiovasc. divsn., 1997-2001; v.p. cardiovasc. rsch. and clin. investigation Eli Lilly and Co., Indpls., 2001—. Dir. CCU Beth Israel Hosp., Med. Sch. Harvard U., 1992—93, dir. vascular biol. unit, 1992—97. Author, editor: book Angiogenesis in Cardiovascular Disease, 1999; contbr. articles to profl. jours. Fellow: Am. Coll. Cardiology; mem.: Molecular Medicine Soc., Assn. Profs. Cariology, Assn. Univ. Cardiologists, Am. Soc. Clin. Investigation, Am. Heart Assn., Am. Soc. Cell Biology, Am. Soc. Hematology, Assn. Am. Physicians, Interurban Clin. Club. Office: VP Lilly Rsch Labs Eli Lilly and Co DC 6072 Indianapolis IN 46285 Office Phone: 317-651-1034. Business E-Mail: jaware@lilly.com.

WARGO, ANDREA ANN, retired public health service officer; b. Pottsville, Pa., Dec. 27, 1941; d. John Andrew and Anna Mary (Blischok) W.; m. Roger Fredrick Sies, Mar. 31, 1981. BS in Biology, Chestnut Hill Coll., 1972; PhD in Biology, Georgetown U., 1978. Educator, adminstr. Cath. Archdiocese Phila., 1961-74; tchg. asst. Georgetown U., Washington, 1974-78, postdoctoral fellow, 1978-80; acting br. chief FDA, Silver Spring, Md., 1980-86, acting chief gen. hosp. and personal use devices, 1986-88; assoc. adminstr. Agy. for Toxic Substances and Disease Registry, Washington, 1988-2001; ret., 2001. Mem. Surgeon Gen.'s Policy Adv. Coun., 1996-2001. Contbr. articles to sci. publs. Grantee NSF, 1972, 73, Kidney Found., 19790-80. Mem. Assn. Women in Sci. (treas. Washington-Balt. chpt. 1979-80), Commd. Officers Assn., Georgetown U. Alumni Assn., Toastmistress Club (pres. Bethesda chpt. 1978-79), Pub. Health Svc. (scientist profl. adv. com., exec. sec. 1984-86, vice chmn. 1986-87), Sigma Xi. Avocations: languages, computers, financial planning, handwriting analysis, crossword puzzles. Home: 17604 N Stone Haven Dr Surprise AZ 85374 Home Phone: 623-546-5625. Personal E-mail: aw12rf8@cox.net.

WARING, GEORGE ORAL, III, ophthalmologist, surgeon; b. Buffalo, Feb. 21, 1941; s. George Oral Waring and Mary Jane Fitzpatrick-Waring; children from previous marriage: George Oral IV, John Timothy, Joy Waring-Harty, Matthew. BS cum laude, Wheaton Coll., Ill., 1963; MD, Baylor Med. Coll., Houston, 1967. Diplomate Am. Bd. Ophthalmology (assoc. examiner, 1980, 89). Rotating intern Ben Taub Gen. Hosp., Houston, 1967—68; resident Wills Eye Hosp. and Rsch. Inst., Phila., 1970—73, Heed fellow in corneal and external disease, 1973—74; staff physician Hosp. Ship Hope, Natal, Brazil, 1973; asst. prof. U. Calif., Davis, 1974—79, assoc. prof., 1979; surg. dir. Sacramento Valley Eye Bank, 1976—79; staff physician Emory Clinic, Inc., Atlanta, 1979—82, clinic ptnr., 1982—2002, with, 2002—04; mng. dir. Emory Vision Correction Ctr., 1994—2001; founding surgeon InView Vision (formerly Emory Vision), 2001—; pvt. practice Atlanta, 2004—. Affiliate scientist Yerkes Regional Primate Rsch. Ctr. Emory U. Sch. Medicine, Atlanta, 1982—92, assoc. prof., 1979—83, prof., dir. refractive surgery, 1983—2004, clin. prof., 2006—; rsch. assoc. French Ministry Rsch. & Tech., 1992; Fogarty sr. internat. fellow US NIH, 1992; vis. prof. Ain Shams U., Cairo, 1992—93; chmn. dept. ophthalmology, dir. rsch. dept. El-Magrabi Eye Hosp. and Med. Ctr., Jeddah, Saudi Arabia, 1992—95; cons. Summit Tech., 1990—95, Chiron Corp., 1993—2000, Nidek, Inc., 2001—, Bausch and Lomb, 2001—05, Advanced Med. Optics, 2005—, Schwind Corp., 2006—08; mem. sci. adv. bd. Calhoun Vision, 2002—; mem. sci. adv. bd., clin. investigator AcuFocus, 2005—; lectr. in field. Author 2 textbooks; mem. editl. bd.: Am. Jour. Ophthalmology, 1981—87, mem. consultative bd.:, 1987—97; mem. editl. bd. Jour. Refractive Surgery, 1985—87; assoc. editor: Jour. Refractive Surgery, 1987—88, editor-in-chief:, 1989—, mem. editl. bd.: numerous jours.; contbr. more than 50 chpts. to books, more than 500 articles to profl. jours. Lt. USPHS, 1968—70. Recipient Hon. medal, Ain Shams U., Ceiro, 1989, Barraquer prize, Internat. Soc. Refractive Keratoplasty, 1992, Gold medal, Pan Arab Coun. Ophthalmology, 1993, 1997, Gregg medal, Royal Assn. Coll. Ophthalmology, 1996, Buasch and Lomb Visionary award, 2004, Kritzinger medal, South Africa Cataract Refraction Surgery; co-recipient Emmy award, NATAS, 1977; grantee, NIH, 1978—81, 1980—, 1980—91, others, U. Calif., Davis, 1973—76, 1982—83, 1987—88, others, various industries; Pew Found. scholar, 1971—72, Training grantee, NIH, 1971. Fellow: ACS (mem. com. applicants 1991), Eye Bank Assn. Am. (mem. constitution and by-laws com. 1984—86, mem. program com. 1985, mem. adv. bd.), Royal Coll. Ophthalmologists, Am. Acad. Ophthalmology (mem. interprofessional edn. com. 1978—81, mem. instrn. adv. com. 1978—81, cons. 1983—, Honor, Sr. Honor and Life Achievement awards 2004), Explorer's Club; mem.: AMA (mem. ophthalmology program com. 1975—79, Physician's Recognition award 1989—95), Wills Eye Hosp. Ex-Resident's Soc., Soc. Heed Fellows (mem. Heed award nomination com. 1983—84, 2000—04, chmn. 2004, Outstanding Ophthalmologist 1978), Saudi Ophthal. Soc., Paton Corneal Transplant Soc., Internat. Soc. Refractive Surgery of Am. Acad. Ophthalmology (trustee 1981—89, editor Jour. Refractive Surgery 1989—, Lans award 1986, Berraguer award 1992, Lifetime Achievement award in Refractive Surgery 1997, Kvitzinger award 2003), Egyptian Soc. Ocular Implants and Refractive Surgery (hon.), Internat. Ophthalmic Microsurgery Study Group, Ga. Soc. Ophthalmology (mem. pub. edn. com. 1981—84, mem. govtl. com. 1988—89, mem. laser com. 1991—92), Dekalb Med. Soc., Coun. Refractive Surgery Quality Assurance, Castroviejo Cornea Soc. (mem. exec. com. 1981—85, program chmn. 1983—85, Castroviejo medal 2004), Assn. Rsch. Vision and Ophtalmology (mem. cornea sect. com. 1985—88, chmn. cornea sect. com. 1987—88, Weisenfeld award 2008), Am. Ophthal. Soc., Commd. Officers Assn. USPHS, Am. Eye Study Club (emeritus mem. 1988—). Avocations: art, kayaking, mountain climbing, scuba diving, sailing. Home: 36 Willow Glen Atlanta GA 30342 Office: INView 4780 Ashford Dunwoody Rd Atlanta GA 30338-5564 Office Phone: 678-222-5102. Office Fax: 404-250-9006.

WARITZ, RICHARD STEFAN, toxicologist, researcher; b. Portland, Oreg., Apr. 1, 1929; s. Anton John and Theresa (Stegelmaier) W.; m. Ruth Evelyn White, June 7, 1950; children: Joyce E., Gary S., Sharon J., Carol L. BA, Reed Coll., 1951; PhD, Stanford U., 1957. Diplomate Am. Bd. Toxicology. Sr. rsch. scientist E.I. DuPont de Nemours & Co., Wilmington, Del., 1957-64, mgr. inhalation toxicology, 1964-72, mgr. bio-scis., 1972-75; sr. toxicologist Hercules Inc., Wilmington, 1975-80, mgr. toxicology, 1980-92; pres. BioSante Internat., Inc., 1992—2009; fellow Acad. Toxicological Scis. Grad. toxicology edn. adv. bd. Rutgers U., Piscataway, N.J., 1980-2005, vis. prof. toxicology, 1993-2005; life scis. adv. bd. U.S. Army, Aberdeen, Md., 1982-92; toxicology peer rev. bd. U.S. Army Ctr. for Health Promotion and Preventive Medicine, 1992—2008. Contbr. articles to profl. jours. Fellow: Acad. Toxicological Scis.; mem.: Am. Chem. Soc., Am. Conf. Govtl. Indsl. Hygienists, Am. Indsl. Hygiene Assn., Internat. Union Toxicol. Socs. (councillor 1983—88), Soc. Toxicology (treas. 1981-85, pres. Mid-Atlantic chpt. 1989). Roman Catholic. Avocations: golf, fishing, bowling. Home: 2613 Turnstone Dr Wilmington DE 19808-1638 Personal E-mail: waritztox@verizon.net.

WARNATH, MAXINE AMMER, psychologist, arbitrator; b. NYC, Dec. 3, 1928; d. Philip and Jeanette Ammer; m. Charles Frederick Warnath, Aug. 20, 1952; children: Stephen Charles, Cindy Ruth. BA, Bklyn. Coll., 1949; MA, Columbia U., 1951, EdD, 1982. Lic. psychologist Oreg. Various profl. positions Hunter Coll., U. Minn., U. Nebr., U. Oreg., 1951-62; asst. prof. psychology Oreg. Coll. Edn., Monmouth, 1962-77; assoc. prof. psychology, chmn. dept. psychology & spl. edn. Western Oreg. U., Monmouth, 1978-83, prof., 1983—96, prof. emeritus, 1996—. Dir. organizational psychology program, 1983—96; pres. Profl. Perspective Internat., Salem, Oreg., 1987—; cons., dir. Orgn. R&D, Salem, Oreg., 1983—87; seminar leader Endeavors for Excellence program. Author: Power Dynamism, 1987. Mem.: APA (com. pre-coll. psychology 1970—74), Western Psychol. Assn., Oreg. Psychol. Assn. (pres. 1980—81, pres.-elect 1979—80, legis. liaison 1977—78), Oreg. Acad. Sci., N.Y. Acad. Scis., Am. Psychol. Soc. Home and Office: 658 Village Dr Pompano Beach FL 33060-7767 Office Phone: 954-786-3108, 954-707-0199. Business E-Mail: warnathm@wou.edu.

WARNER, CHRISTOPHER HUGH, psychiatrist; b. Steubenville, Ohio, Apr. 2, 1974; s. William Norman and Diana Lynn Warner; m. Carolynn Marie Stocum, Mar. 3, 1997; children: Timothy Jordan children: Jacob Thomas, Aaron Christopher, Matthew Dylan. BS, U.S. Mil. Acad., West Point, NY., 1996; MD, Uniformed Svcs. U. of Health Sci., Bethesda, Md., 2000. Lic. physician Ind., 2000, diplomate Am. Bd. of Family Practice, 2005, Am. Bd. Psychiatry & Neurology, 2009. Resident in family practice and psychiatry Walter Reed Army Hosp., Washington, 2000—05; chief resident NCC Family Practice Psychiatry, Washington, 2003—05; divsn. psychiatry 3rd Inf. Divsn., Fort Stewart, Ga., 2005—08; chief dept. bd. medicine Winn Army Hosp., Fort Stewart, Ga., 2008—10; comdr., gen. staff Coll. Ft. Leavenworth, Kans., 2010—11; dep. comdr. clin. svcs. US Army Med. Activity Ala., 2011—. Maj. US Army, 1992—, Fort Stewart, GA. Decorated Bronze Star US Army; recipient Award for Outstanding Leadership in Psychiatry, Assn. of Acad. Psychiatry, 2004, George Ginsberg Award for Accomplishment in Edn. and Tng. in Psychiatry, Am. Assn. of Dirs. of Psychiat. Residency Tng., 2004, Gen. Graves B. Erskine Award for Most Outstanding Resident, Walter Reed Army Med. Ctr., 2005, Al Glass Award for Outstanding Leadership in Mil. Psychiatry, 2005, Physician Recognition award, US Army Surgeon Gen., 2006; named Martin Fenton Nat. Resident of the Yr., Assn. of Medicine and Psychiatry, 2005, Resident Tchr. of the Yr., Soc. of Tchrs. of Family Medicine, 2005. Mem.: Assn. for Acad. Psychiatry (assoc.), Am. Psychiat. Assn. (assoc.; regional chpt. jr. devel. officer 2005), Am. Acad. of Family Physicians (assoc.). Christian. Achievements include research in examining the ethics training of psychiatric residents; on eating disorders in military recruits; on depression in military recruits; on the characteristics and practices of FP/Psych trained individuals; on leadership development in medical residency training; psychological effects of combat exposure on soldiers. Office: Student Detached Command Gen Staff Coll Fort Leavenworth KS 66027 Home: 1312 Bastogne Ct Fort Wainwright AK 99703 Personal E-mail: christopher.h.warner@us.army.mil.

WARNER, DENNIS ALLAN, psychology professor; b. Idaho Falls, Idaho, Apr. 27, 1940; s. Perry and Marcia E. (Finlayson) W.; m. Charyl Ann DeHart, Dec. 12, 1962; children: Lisa Rae, Sara Michelle, David Perry, Matthew Arie. BS, Brigham Young U., 1964; MS with honors, U. Oreg., 1966, PhD, 1968. Asst. prof. edn. Wash. State U., Pullman, 1968-72, assoc. prof. edn., 1972-78, prof. edn., 1978-85, dir. tchr. edn., 1983-85, prof., chmn. ednl. counseling psychology, 1985-93, interim dir. Partnership Ctr., 1993—94, 2004—06, prof. edn. leadership and counseling psychology, 1994—, assoc. dean Coll. Edn., 1999—2005, exec. assoc. dean Coll. Edn., 2006—07, dir. H.S. equivalency program, 2004—. Vis. asst. prof. psychology U. Idaho, Moscow, 1971. Author: Interpreting and Improving Student Test Performance, 1982; contbr. articles to profl. jours. Postdoctoral research assoc. U. Kans., 1976-77. Fellow: APA. Mem. Lds Ch. Home: 645 SW Mies St Pullman WA 99163-2057 Office: Wash State Univ Coll Edn Cleveland Hl Rm 160B Pullman WA 99164-2114 Office Phone: 509-335-5652. Business E-Mail: dawarner@wsu.edu.

WARNER, KENNETH E(DGAR), dean, public health educator, consultant; b. Washington, Jan. 25, 1947; s. Edgar W. Jr. and Betty (Strasburger) W.; m. Patricia A. Hilty, Oct. 1, 1977; children— Peter, Andrew AB, Dartmouth Coll., 1968; MPhil, Yale U., 1970, PhD, 1974. Lectr. dept. health mgmt. and policy Sch. Pub. Health, U. Mich., Ann Arbor, Mich., 1972—74, asst. prof., 1974—77, assoc. prof., 1977—83, prof., 1983—, chmn., 1982—88, 1992—95, Richard D. Remington Collegiate prof. pub. health, 1995—2001, dir. Tobacco Rsch. Network, Avedis Donabedian Disting. Univ. prof. pub. health, 2001—, dean, 2005—. Cons., Washington, 1976—95, Office on

Smoking and Health, USPHS, Rockville, Md., 1978—, Inst. Medicine, Nat. Acad. Scis., Washington, 1984—, numerous additional pub. and pvt. orgns.; mem. bd. sci. counselors divsn. cancer prevention and control Nat. Cancer Inst., Bethesda, Md., 1985—89. Author: (with Bryan Luce) Cost-Benefit & Cost Effectiveness Analysis in Health Care, 1982; contbr. articles to profl. jours. Trustee Am. Lung Assn., Mich., Lansing, 1982; mem. subcom. on smoking Am. Heart Assn., Dallas, 1983-87; mem. com. on tobacco and cancer Am. Cancer Soc., N.Y.C., 1984-92; bd. dirs. Am. Legacy Found., 1999-2003. Hon. Woodrow Wilson fellow, 1968; W.K. Kellog Found. fellow, 1980-83; vis. scholar Nat. Bur. Econ. Research, Stanford, Calif., 1975-76; recipient Surgeon Gen.'s medallion Dr. C. Everett Koop, 1989. Fellow Assn. Health Svcs. Rsch.; mem. APHA (leadership award 1990), Inst. Medicine, Phi Beta Kappa. Office: U Mich Dept Health Sch Pub Health 109 Observatory St Ann Arbor MI 48109-2029 Office Phone: 734-763-5454. Business E-Mail: kwarner@umich.edu.

WARNER, LESLEY RAE, biology educator; b. Milton, New Zealand, July 21, 1940; arrived in Australia, 1970; d. Raymond John and Fay Catherine (Sanders) Wilson; m. Roger Joseph Smales (div. 1981); children: Alastair Grantly, Fiona Ruth; m. George Oliver Warner (div. 2005). BHSc, Otago U., Dunedin, New Zealand, 1961, BSc, 1963, MSc with honors, 1965; PhD, Adelaide U., Australia, 1975; diploma in edn., Adelaide Coll. Arts/Edn., 1981. Sr. lectr. Gippsland Inst., Churchill, Victoria, Australia, 1982—85; head dept. biology Capricornia Inst., Rockhampton, Australia, 1986—89; dean Sch. Sci. Univ. Coll. Ctrl. Queensland, Rockhampton, 1989—90, head dept. biology, 1991—94; assoc. prof. biology dept. Ctrl. Queensland U., 1995—2001, head Sch. Biol. and Environ. Scis, 2001—04, prof. biology dept., 2002—05, prof. emeritus, 2006—. Hon. rsch. assoc. South Australian Mus., Australia, 2006—. Author: Gippsland Flavours, 1988. Fellow: Australian Soc. Parasitology (coun. mem. 1994—95, pres.-elect 1996, pres. 1997, v.p. 1998, coun. mem. 2010—), Royal Soc. South Australia; mem.: Helminthological Soc. Wash. Mem. Uniting Ch. of Australia.

WARNER, MARK A., anesthesiologist; b. Greenville, Ohio, Oct. 7, 1953; s. Paul C. Jr. and Mildred G. Warner; m. Mary Ellen Bunch, Oct. 14, 1978; children: Paul, Mark, Matthew, Daniel. AB in Chemistry, Miami U., Oxford, Ohio, 1976; MD, Med. Coll. Ohio, 1979. Diplomate Am. Bd. Anesthesiology. Intern, resident Mayo Clinic, Rochester, 1979-82, prof. and chmn. dept. anes., 1999—2005, dir. hosp. ops., 1995-99, exec. bd., 2005—. Bd. dirs. Anesthesia Patient Safety Found., Boston, 1996—. Bd. dirs. Rochester Family YMCA, Rochester, 1998—, Rochester Airport Co., 1992—, Mayo Med. Transp. Sys., Rochester, 1995-2002, Gold Cross Ambulance, Rochester, 1995-2002. Mem. American Bd. Anesthesiology, Raleigh, N.C., (bd. dirs. 1999-, pres. 2009), American Soc. Anesthesiologists (bd. dirs. 1996-2008, 1st v.p. 2008-09, pres. elect 2009-10, pres. 2010-11). Office: Mayo Clinic 200 1st St SW Rochester MN 55905-0001 E-mail: warner.mark@mayo.edu. *

WARNER, ROBERTA ARLENE, retired accountant, financial services executive; b. Binghamton, NY, Dec. 31, 1938; d. Murrilan Earl and Ethel Margaret (Bell) W. BA, SUNY, Binghamton, 1960; MBA, Ind. U., 1962, MHA with highest distinction, 1973. CPA, N.Y.; lic. nursing home adminstr., N.Y. Sr. acct. Arthur Young & Co., CPA, Buffalo, 1962—66; acctg. supr. Children's Hosp., Buffalo, 1966—68; contr. King Manor Nursing Homes-Ave. Bldg. Corp., Buffalo, 1968—71; asst. dir. health fin. Hosp. Assn. N.Y. State, Albany, 1973—80, dir. health fin., 1980—93, Healthcare Assn. N.Y. State, Albany, 1994—97, dir. data analysis and stds., 1997—98; pres. Roberta A. Warner Co., 1999—2003, ret., 2003. Author articles in field. Trustee Ednl. Found. of Am. Women's Soc. CPA, Am. Soc. Women Accts., 1985-87; pres. hist. preservation com. Windsor Ctrl. Sch. Dist., 2006-; mem. Historic Windsor Adv. Com., 2010. Fellow Healthcare Fin. Mgmt. Assn.; mem. AICPA, Am. Acctg. Assn., Am. Soc. Women Accts. (pres. Buffalo chpt. 1967-68), Am. Women's Soc. CPA, N.Y. State Soc. CPA, Ind. U. Alumni Assn. (life), Binghamton U. Alumni Assn. (life), Grange. Methodist. Home: 569 NY Rte 79 Windsor NY 13865-2714

WARNKE, PATRICK H. H., maxillofacial surgeon, plastic surgeon, researcher; b. Germany, Apr. 20, 1969; s. Hans Dieter and Inge Warnke; m. Frauke Peters Warnke; 2 children. DDS, U. Kiel, Germany, 1995, MD, 2001; degree in maxillofacial surgery, 2005, PhD, 2006, degree in plastic surgery, 2007. Assoc. prof. faculty health scis. and medicine Bond U., Gold Coast, Australia; head European Rsch. Consortium Myjoint, 2004—. Contbr. articles to profl. jours. With German Air Force, 1988—89. Recipient Outstanding Rsch. award, Faculty of Medicine U. Kiel, 2004. Mem.: German Assn. Maxillofacial Surgeons. Office: Dept Oral and Maxillofacial Surgery Univ Kiel Arnold Heller Str 16 24105 Kiel Germany E-mail: pwarnke@hotmail.com.

WARNKE, ROGER ALLEN, pathology educator; b. Peoria, Ill., Feb. 22, 1945; s. Delmar Carl and Ruth Armanelle (Peard) W.; m. Joan Marie Gebhart, Nov. 18, 1972; children: Kirsten Marie Warnke Woolf, Lisa Marie. BS, U. Ill., 1967; MD, Washington U., St. Louis, 1971. Diplomate Am. Bd. Pathology. Intern in pathology Stanford (Calif.) U. Med. Sch., 1971-72, resident in pathology, 1972-73, postdoctoral fellow in pathology, 1973-75, postdoctoral fellow in immunology, 1975-76, asst. prof. pathology, 1976-82, assoc. prof., 1983-90; prof., 1991—; Ronald F. Dorfman prof. hematopathology Stanford (Calif.) U., 2003. Cons. Becton Dickinson Monoclonal Ctr., Mountain View, Calif., 1982-88, IDEC, Mountain View, 1985-90, Coulter Pharm., Inc., 1997-98; sci. advisor Ventana Med. Systems, Inc., Tucson, 1986-94. Contbr. over 300 articles to profl. jours., chpts. to books. Recipient Benjamin Castleman award Mass. Gen. Hosp., 1981; Agnes Axtel Moule faculty scholar Stanford U., 1979-82; Rsch. grantee Nat. Cancer Inst. and NIH, 1978-2005 Mem. So. Bay Pathology Soc., Calif. Soc. Pathologists, U.S. Can. Acad. Path., Am. Soc. Investigative Pathology, Soc. for Hematopathology, European Assn. for Haematopathology, Coll. Am. Pathologists, Internat. Lymphoma Study Group. Home: Stanford University Sch Medicine 845 Tolman Dr Stanford CA 94305-1025 Office: Stanford U Dept Pathology Stanford CA 94305

WARPEHA, RAYMOND LEONARD, surgeon, educator; b. Mpls., Dec. 5, 1934; s. Frank Joseph and Sophie Helen (Fryzlewicz) Warpeha; m. Ivy Lee Kloth; children: Katherine, John, Joseph, Frank. BS, U. Minn., 1956, DDS, 1958; MD, Northwestern U., 1965, PhD in Anatomy, 1966. Cert. Am. Bd. Surgery, 1971, plastic surgery Am. Bd. Surgery, 1973. Instr. anatomy Northwestern U. Med. Sch., Chgo., 1963—65, instr. surgery, 1969—72; asst. prof. surgery and anatomy Loyola U. Stritch Sch. Medicine, Maywood, Fla., 1973—75, assoc. prof. surgery and anatomy, 1975—80, prof. surgery and anatomy, 1981—2000, prof. emeritus, 2000—. Cons. surgery Cook County Hosp., Chgo., 1970—72; founder, dir. Burn Ctr. Loyola U. Hosp., 1972—91; dir. surg. anatomy dept. surgery Loyola Med. Sch., 1972—2000. Author: 59 articles and 9 book chpts., Clinics of Plastic Surgery North America, 1981; mem. editl. bd.: Chgo. Medicine. Chmn. Ill. Burn Surgeons adv. group Ill. Dept. Med. Svcs., Springfield, 1973—80; chmn. burn surgeons adv. group Divsnl. Med. Svcs., Washington, 1975; mem. bd. trustees Ill. Trauma Soc.; trustee Am. Soc. Maxillofacial Surgery. Recipient award for Lifetime Med. Contbns. and Pub. Svc. to Burn and Fire Victims and Survivors, Knapp Burn Found., Chgo., 1999, Disting. Svcs. award, 2007, lectureship award, 2008; postdoctoral Am. Heart Assn. fellow, Northwestern Med. Sch., 1962—63. Fellow: Am. Coll. Surgeons (chmn. membership com. Dist. 3 1995—99); mem.: Am. Soc. Plastic and Reconstructive Surgeons, Soc. Head and Neck Surgeons, Am. Assn. Plastic Surgeons, Am. Soc. Maxillofacial Surgeons, Am. Burn Assn., Chgo. Soc. Plastic Surgery (pres. 1983—84, treas. 1981—82, v.p. 1982—83). Roman Catholic. Avocations: fishing, botany. Office: Loyola Med Ctr Dept Surgery 2160 S First Ave Maywood IL 60153

WARREN, BRYAN FREDERICK, pathologist, consultant; b. Tiverton, Eng., Apr. 15, 1958; s. William Frederick and Edith (Dimeloe) Warren. MBChB, Liverpool U., Eng., 1981. Sr. house officer in medicine, Liverpool, 1982—85; registrar in pathology, 1985—87; lectr. in pathology Bristol, 1987—96; cons. gastrointestinal pathologist Oxford Hosps., 1994—; hon. sr. lectr. U. Oxford, 1997—; hon. prof. Queen Mary, U. London, 2009—. Meetings sec. Brit. Divsn. of Internat. Acad. Pathology, England, 2005—; chair pathology sect. Brit. Soc. Gastroenterology, England, 2002, Basil Morson lectr., 09; mem. coun., hon. mem. Assn. Coloproctology, Ireland, 2010. Author: Morson and Dawson's Gastrointestinal Pathology, 2003, Challenges in Inflammatory Bowel Disease, 2006. Fellow: Royal Coll. Physicians, Royal Coll. Pathologists, Linacre Coll. Oxford; mem.: Athenaeum Club. Anglican. Avocations: driving, restoring automobiles. Office: John Radcliffe Hosp Cellular Pathology Dept Headley Way OX3 9DU Oxford England

WARREN, DANIEL CHURCHMAN, health facility administrator; b. Washington, Sept. 23, 1939; s. Walter Thomas and Laura Katherine W.; m. C. Frederica Lescure, June 5, 1958(dec. Mar. 7, 2007), Elaina Gianatasio, Apr. 5, 2008; 1 child, Christopher C. BS, Roanoke Coll., 1960; MD, Med. Coll. Va., 1964; MPH, U. N.C., 1971; MMAS, U.S. Army Command & Gen. Coll., 1974. Diplomate Nat. Bd. Med. Examiners, Am. Bd. Preventive Medicine, lic. physician VA; ordained Anglican Cath. priest 2002. Intern Georgetown U. Hosp., 1964-65; resident in surgery Med. Coll. Va., 1967-68, William Beaumont Gen. Hosp., 1968-69; resident in preventive medicine Walter Reed Army Inst. Rsch., 1971-73; commd. 2d lt. U.S. Army, 1965, advanced through grades to col., 1986; asst. med. dir. HealthAm. Va., 1986; pvt. practice travel, 1987-89; dir. Peninsula Health Dist., Newport News, Va., 1990—2001; warden Holyrood Sem., 2001—03; rector St. Matthews Anglican Cath. Ch., 2002—09; priest-in-charge All Saints ACC, 2007—; warden Scott Sch. Theology, 2003—. Clin. asst. prof. family and cmty. medicine Ea. Va. Med. Sch., Norfolk; cons. Riverside Regional Med Ctr., Newport News. Active Gloucester County Rep. Com., 1987-96, chmn. 1992-95, Gloucester County Redistricting Adv. Com., 1991, 2001; hon. chmn. Combined Va. Campaign United Way the Va. Peninsula, 1992. Fellow: Am. Coll. Preventive Medicine; mem.: Knight of the Order St. Lazarus Jerusalem, Order Founders Patriots America, Jamestowne Soc., Med. Soc. Va. Republican. Anglican. Avocation: English and Virginia history. Business E-Mail: dwarrenmd@cox.net.

WARREN, DONALD WILLIAM, medical and dental educator; b. Bklyn., Mar. 22, 1935; s. Sol B. and Frances W.; m. Priscilla Girardi, June 10, 1956; children: Donald W. Jr., Michael C. BS, U. N.C., 1956, DDS, 1959; MS, U. Pa., 1961, PhD, 1963; D in Odontology (hon.), U. Kuopio, Finland, 1991. Asst. prof. dentistry U. N.C., Chapel Hill, 1963-65, dir. Craniofacial Ctr., 1963-2000, assoc. prof., 1965-69, prof., 1969-80, chmn. dept. dental ecology, 1970-85, Kenan prof., 1980—2004, Kenan prof. emeritus, 2004—, rsch. prof. otolaryngology, 1985—2004; ret. Cons. NIH, Bethesda, Md., 1967-2000, R. J. Reynolds-Nabisco, Winston-Salem, N.C., 1986-99; owner Cabin Banch Tack Shop, 1995-. Contbr. articles to profl. jours. Recipient Honor award Am. Cleft Palate Assn./Craniofacial Assn., 1992, O. Max Garner award U. N.C. Bd. Govs., 1993, honors award Angle Orthodontic Soc., 1998. Fellow AAAS, Internat. Coll. Dentists, Am. Speech and Hearing Lang. Assn. (Editors award 1998, Honors award 2003), Internat. Assn. Dental Rsch., Acoustical Soc. Am., Am. Cleft Palate Assn. (pres. 1981-82, Disting. Svc. award 1984), Am. Cleft Palate Edn. Found. (pres. 1976-77), Am. Equest Trade Assn. (treas. 2008-, pres. 2010). Avocations: horse related activities, running, farming. Home: PO Box 1356 Southern Pines NC 28388-1356

WARREN, DWIGHT WILLIAM, III, physiology educator; b. LA, Dec. 21, 1942; s. Dwight William Jr. and Edna (Rainen) W.; m. Grace Anita Sturm, Nov. 24, 1965; 1 child, Jennifer Anne. AB, U. Calif., Berkeley, 1964; PhD, U. So. Calif., LA, 1972, MSEd, 2000. Asst. prof. U. So. Calif., LA, 1972-78, assoc. prof., 1978-88, prof. dept. physiology and biophysics, 1988—2006, prof. and acting chmn., dept. Pharmacology and Nutrition, 1992-94; prof. dept. cell and neurobiology U. Southern Calif., LA, 1994—2010, emeritus prof., 2011—, prof. dept. ophthalmology LA, 1993—99, assoc. dean for curriculum, 1994—99, emeritus prof., 2011—; vice dean, chair dept. biomed. sci. Charles E. Schmitt Coll. Sci. Fla. Atlantic U., 1999—2006, emeritus prof. biomed. sci., 2006—. Mem. editl. bd. Reproductive Scis., 1989-93, Biology of Reproduction, 1989-95; contbr. articles to profl. jours. Nat. rsch. svc. sr. fellow USPHS, 1980-81; Fulbright scholar USIA, Finland, 1990. Mem. AAAS, Endocrine Soc., Soc. Study Reproduction, Am. Soc. Andrology, N.Y. Acad. Scis., Assn. Rsch. in Vision and Ophthalmology. Business E-Mail: dwarren@usc.edu.

WARREN, JOHN ROBIN, retired physician, pathologist; b. Adelaide, Australia, June 11, 1937; s. John Roger Hogarth and Helen Josephine (Verco) Warren; m. Winifred Teresa Williams, May 5, 1962 (dec.); children: John Campbell, David Daniel, Patrick Stephen, Andrew Timothy, Rebecca Ruth, Eliza. Grad., St. Peters Coll., Adelaide, 1954; MB, BChir, U. Adelaide, 1961; MD (hon.), U. Western Australia, 1997; D (hon.), U. Adelaide, 2006, U. Toyama, Japan, 2007, Otto-von-Guericke U., Germany, 2007. Jr. resident med. officer Queen Elizabeth Hosp., Woodville, South Australia, 1961; registrar haematology and clin. pathology Inst. Med. & Vet. Sci., Adelaide, 1962—63; lectr. pathology U. Adelaide, 1963—64; registrar clin. pathology Royal Melbourne Hosp., Victoria, Australia, 1964—68; pathologist Royal Perth Hosp., Western Australia, 1968—99, emeritus cons. pathology, 1998—; emeritus prof. U. Western Australia; ret. Contbr. articles to profl. jours. Recipient Warren Alpert prize, Harvard U., 1994, Howard Florey Centenary medal, 1998, Nobel prize in physiology/medicine, 2005, Premier's Sci. award, Govt. Western Australia, 2007, Disting. Pathologist medal, Internat. Acad. Pathology, 2008; named Western Australian of Yr., 2007. Fellow: Australian Acad. Sci., Royal Coll. Pathologists Australasia (Paul Ehrlich award 1997), Royal Australian Coll. Physicians (hon.); mem.: Am. Soc. Clin. Pathology (Spl. Rocognition award 2007), German Soc. Pathology, Polish Soc. Gastroenterology, Australian Soc. Cytology, Internat. Acad. Pathology, Australian Med. Assn. Achievements include development of a convenient diagnostic test for detecting Helicobacter pylori, bacterium linked to the development of duodenal and gastric ulcers, in patients. Avocations: photography, stamp collecting/philately. Office: Ste 10 3 Centro Ave Subiaco WA 6008 Australia Office Fax: 61 89382 2313. *

WARREN, KENNETH R., federal agency administrator; Grad., City Coll. NY; D in Biochemistry, Mich. State U., 1970. Postdoc. fellow UCLA, U. Mich. Mental Health Rsch. Inst.; rschr. Walter Reed Army Inst. Rsch., Rockville, Md., 1974; staff mem. rsch. divsn. Nat. Inst. Alcohol Abuse & Alcoholism (NIAAA), NIH, Bethesda, Md., 1976, chief biomed. rsch. br., dep. dir. Divsn. Extramural Rsch., dir. Office Sci. Affairs, 1984—2005, assoc. dir. Office Basic Rsch., 2002—07, acting dir. Office Sci. Policy & Comm., 2007—08, dep. dir., 2008, acting dir., 2008—. Contbr. articles to profl. jours. Recipient Superior Svc. award, USPHS, 1982, Seixas award, Rsch. Soc. Alcoholism, 1994, Henry Rosett award, 2002; named to Tom & Linda Daschle Hall of Fame, Nat. Orgn. Fetal Alcohol Syndrome, 2007. Achievements include research in the effects of alcohol use during pregnancy including fetal alcohol syndrome and fetal alcohol spectrum disorders. Office: Nat Inst on Alcohol Abuse and Alcoholism 5635 Fishers Ln MSC 9304 Rockville MD 20852 Office Phone: 301-443-5494. Office Fax: 301-443-6077. Business E-Mail: kenneth.warren@nih.gov. *

WARREN, MICHELLE PALMIERI, internist, endocrinologist; b. NYC, 1939; MD, Cornell U. Med. Coll., 1965. Cert. Internal Medicine with subspecialty in endocrinology and reproductive endocrinology. Intern, medicine Bellevue Hosp. Ctr., NYC, 1965—66, resident, 1966—68; resident, endocrinology Meml. Hosp. Cancer, NYC, 1966—68; fellow Columbia U., Coll. Physicians & Surgeons, 1968—71, asst. prof., 1971—75, assoc. prof. clin. ob/gyn & clin. medicine, 1975—96, prof. ob/gyn & medicine, 1996—; attending St. Luke's Roosevelt Hosp., NYC, 1975; founder, med. dir., Ctr. for Menopause, Hormonal Disorders and Women's Health Columbia U. Med. Ctr., NYC, 1997—, prof. medicine and obstetrics and gynecology, Wyeth Ayerst prof. women. Cons. Wyeth Pharm.; lectr. in field. Contbr. articles to profl. jours., chapters to books; publ;ished a book on sports and hormones. Named Best Doctors in NYC, NY Mag.; named one of Best Doctors In America, 2004—05. Achievements include first to identify skeletal problems, including scoliosis and stress fractures that occur in young women because of menstrual irregularities. Address: Ctr for Menopause Hormonal Disorders and Women's Health Dept Ob/Gyn Columbia U Med Ctr 622 W 168th St PH 16 New York NY 10032 Office: 16 E 60th St Ste 490 New York NY 10022 Office Fax: 212-737-4664, 212-744-9353.

WARREN, RICHARD M., experimental psychologist, educator; b. NYC, Apr. 8, 1925; s. Morris and Rae (Greenberg) W.; m. Roslyn Pauker, Mar. 31, 1950. BS in Chemistry, CCNY, 1946; PhD in Organic Chemistry, NYU, 1951. Flavor chemist Gen. Foods Co., Hoboken, N.J., 1951-53; rsch. assoc. psychology Brown U., Providence, 1954-56; Carnegie sr. rsch. fellow NYU Coll. Medicine, 1956-57, Cambridge (Eng.) U., 1957-58, rsch. psychologist applied psychology rsch. unit, 1958-59; rsch. psychologist NIMH, Bethesda, Md., 1959-61; chmn. psychology Shimer Coll., Mt. Carroll, Ill., 1961-64; assoc. prof. psychology U. Wis., Milw., 1964-66, prof., 1966-73, rsch. prof., 1973-75, disting. prof., 1975-95, rsch. prof., disting. prof. emeritus, 1995—. Vis. scientist Inst. Exptl. Psychology, Oxford (Eng.) U., 1969-70, 77-78. Author: (with Roslyn Warren) Helmholtz on Perception: Its Physiology and Development, 1968, Auditory Perception: An Analysis and Synthesis, 3rd edit., 2008; contbr. articles to profl. jours. Fellow APA, Am. Psychol. Soc., Acoustical Soc. Am.; mem. AAAS, Am. Chem. Soc., Am. Speech and Hearing Assn., Sigma Xi. Office: Univ of Wisconsin-Milwaukee Dept Psychology PO Box 413 Milwaukee WI 53201 Office Phone: 414-229-5328. Business E-Mail: rmwarren@uwm.edu. *

WARREN, RICHARD WAYNE, obstetrician, gynecologist; b. Puxico, Mo., Nov. 26, 1935; s. Martin R. and Sarah E. (Crump) W.; m. Rosalie J. Franzoia, Aug. 16, 1959; children: Lani Marie, Richard W., Paul D. BA, U. Calif., Berkeley, 1957; MD, Stanford U., Calif., 1961. Diplomate Am. Bd. Ob-Gyn. Intern Oakland Naval Hosp., Calif., 1961-62; resident on ob-gyn. Stanford Med. Ctr., 1964-67; pvt. practice specializing in ob-gyn. Mountain View, Calif., 1967—. Mem. staff Stanford Hosp., El Camino Hosp.; pres. Warren Medical Corp.; assoc. clin. prof. ob-gyn. Stanford Sch. Medicine. Contbr. articles to profl. jours. With USN, 1961-64. Fellow Am. Coll. Ob-Gyn.; mem. AMA, Am. Fertility Soc., Am. Assn. Gynecologic Laparoscopists, Calif. Med. Assn., San Francisco Gynecol. Soc., Peninsula Gynecol. Soc., Assn. Profs. Gynecology and Obstetrics, Royal Soc. Medicine,

Shufelt Gynecol. Soc. Santa Clara Valley. Home: 102 Atherton Ave Menlo Park CA 94027-4021 Office: 2500 Hospital Dr Mountain View CA 94040-4106 Office Phone: 650-961-8111. Personal E-mail: warren423@sbcglobal.net.

WARREN, RUSSELL FREDERICK, orthopedist; b. Burlington, Vt., June 18, 1939; MD, SUNY, Syracuse, 1966. Bd. cert. orthopedic surgery. Intern St. Lukes Hosp. Ctr., NYC, 1966—68; resident orthopedic surgery Hosp. for Spl. Surgery, NYC, 1970—73, surgeon in chief, 1993—2003, surgeon-in-chief emertius, 2003; fellow in shoulder surgery Columbia Presbyn. Med. Ctr., NYC, 1977; prof. surgery, chmn. divsn. orthopaedic surgery Weill Med. Coll., Cornell U.; physician New York Giants. Editor-in-chief Techniques in Shoulder and Elbow Surgery. Recipient Neer award for shoulder rsch., 1989, 1995, 2005, 2006, O'Donohue award for sports medicine rsch., 1982, 1991, 1994, Humana award for sports medicine, 1992, Mr. Sports Medicine award, Am. Orthopaedic Soc. Sports Medicine, 2003. Mem.: Am. Orthop. Soc. Sports Medicine (pres. 1994—95), Am. Shoulder and Elbow Soc. (pres. 1994—95). Achievements include research in shoulder and knee instability; ligament reconstruction and arthroscopy; joint replacement-knee and shoulder; rotator cuff disease and sports injuries. Mailing: Hosp for Spl Surgery 535 E 70th St New York NY 10021 Office: Belaire Bldg 1st Fl 525 E 71st St New York NY Office Phone: 212-606-1178, 212-606-1075. Business E-Mail: warrenr@hss.edu.

WARREN, SETH C.R., hospital administrator; B, U. Richmond; MBA, Syracuse U. Compensation coord. CentraState Med. Ctr., Freehold, NJ; benefits and compensation coord. St. Agnes Med. Ctr., Fresno, Calif.; asst. v.p. The Hunter Group, Raleigh, NJ; dir. ops. St. Francis Hosp. and Health Centers, exec. dir. Mooresville, Ind.; exec. v.p. and COO St. Anthony Meml. Health Centers, Mich. City, Ind.; pres. St. Anthony Med. Ctr., St. Louis; regional CEO and pres. St. James Hosp. and Health Centers, 2008—. Office: St. James Hospital and Health Centers 1423 Chgo Rd Chicago Heights IL 60411 Office Phone: 708-756-1000.

WARREN, STEPHEN THEODORE, geneticist, educator; b. Grosse Point, Mich., Nov. 30, 1953; s. Theodore Stephen and Frances (Fedo) W.; m. Karen Lee Pierce, Aug. 27, 1978; 1 child, Thomas. BS, Mich. State U., 1976, PhD, 1981. Diplomate American Bd. Med. Genetics. Grad. asst. Mich. State U., East Lansing, 1976 81; rsch. assoc. U. Ill., Chgo., 1981-83, instr., 1983-85; asst. prof. Emory U. Sch. Medicine, Atlanta, 1985 91, assoc. prof., 1991 93, William Patterson Timmie prof. human genetics, 1993—, chmn. dept. human genetics, 2001—; investigator Howard Hughes Med. Inst., 1992—2002. Vis. scientist European Molecular Biol. Lab., Heidelberg, Germany, 1984.; cons. Ctrs. for Disease Control, Atlanta, 1988-89, NIH, Bethesda, Md., 1989—; collaborator Ctr. D'Etude du Polymorphysme Humain, Paris, 1989—. Editor-in-chief Am. Jour. Human Genetics, 2000-2005; mem. editl. bd. Human Molecular Genetics, Am. Jour. Human Genetics, Cytogenetics, Cell Genetics, Mammalian Genome, others; contbr. chpts. to books and more than 200 articles to profl. jorus. Recipient Sigma Xi prize Mich. State Sigma Xi, East Lansing, 1981, NIH fellowship NIH, Bethesda, 1982, Basil O'Connor award March of Dimes, N.Y.C., 1986, Albert E. Levy award Emory U., Atlanta, 1987, William Rosen Rsch. award Nat. Fragile X Found., 1996, Mich. State U. Outstandinf Alumni award, 2007, Brandwein award in Genetic Rsch., "Champion for Babies" award March of Dimes, 2008, Jacob's Ladder Internat. Rsch. prize, 2009, American Acad. Neurology "Frontiers in Clinical Neuroscience" award, 2009; inductee Nat. Inst. Child Health & Human Devel. Hall of Fame Honor, 2003. Fellow American Coll. Med. Genetics; mem. American Soc. Human Genetics (nominating com. 1991, awards con. 1992—, bd. dirs. 1997—, William Allan award 1999), American Soc. Biochemistry and Molecular Biology, American Soc. Microbiology, Genetics Soc. America, American Soc. Human Genetics (pres., 2005), Human Genome Orgn., Inst. Medicine., NAS Achievements include research on molecular genetic studies of the fragile X syndrome and other human genetic diseases. Office: Emory University School Medicine 301 Whitehead Bldg 615 Michael St Atlanta GA 30322-4218 Office Phone: 404-727-5979. E-mail: swarren@emory.edu. *

WARREN, WILLIAM MICHAEL, JR., hospital administrator, lawyer; b. Bryan, Tex., June 8, 1947; s. William Michael and Rebecca Carolyn (Glass) W.; m. Anne Candler McLeod, June 5, 1968; children: William Powers, Laura Anne, Amy Lynn. BA, Auburn U., 1968; JD, Duke U., 1971. Bar: Ala. 1971. Assoc. Bradley, Arant, Rose & White, Birmingham, Ala., 1971-77, ptnr., 1977-83; v.p., gen. counsel Ala. Gas Corp., Birmingham, 1983-84, pres., COO, 1984; pres, COO Energen Corp., Birmingham, 1987-91; pres., CEO Children's Health System, bd. trustees, 1988—. Bd. dirs. AmSouth Bank Birmingham N.A., Energen Corp., Ala. Gas Corp., So. Gas Assn., Inst. Gas Tech., Protective Life Corp., 2001-. Contbr. articles to periodicals. Bd. dirs. Ala. Symphony Assn., 1988-90, pres., 1990—, chmn., 1991-92; chmn. Met. Devel. Bd., 1989-90; trustee Ala. Inst. for Deaf and Blind, 1988—, 1st lt. USAF, 1971-72. Mem. Ala. State Bar, ABA, Am. Gas Assn. (edn. 2000 com. 1991—), So. Gas Assn. (bd. dirs. 1989—), Inst. Gas Tech. (bd. trustees 1989—), Birmingham Area C. of C. (bd. dirs. 1986—, v.p 1989), Summit Club (bd. dirs. 1989). Lodges: Rotary. Democrat. Methodist. Home: 3533 Mill Springs Rd Birmingham AL 35223-1637 Office: Childrens Health System 1600 7th Ave S Birmingham AL 35233 Office Phone: 205-939-9100. Business E-Mail: mike.warren@chsys.org. *

WARRICK, PAUL DAVID, otolaryngologist; b. May 15, 1972; MD, McMaster U., Hamilton, Ont., 1995—99. Diplomate Am. Bd. Otolaryngology, 2005. Intern dept. surgery U. Toronto, 1999—2000, resident dept. otolaryngology, 2000—04; otolaryngologist Affinity Med. Group, Appleton, Wis., 2004—08. Fellow: ACS, Royal Coll. Surgeons Can., Am. Acad. Otolaryngology-Head and Neck Surgery; mem.: Am. Acad. Otolaryngic Allergy. Achievements include research in vocal tremor. Avocations: golf, baseball, volleyball, stamp collecting/philately. Office: Piedmont Vista ENT Allergy & Sleep Assocs PLLC 1733 Connelly Spring Rd Lenoir NC 28645 Office Fax: 828-728-2215. Business E-Mail: pwarrick@piedmontvista.com.

WARSHAL, DAVID P., gynecologic oncologist, educator; MD, Pa. State U. Diplomate Am. Bd. Ob-Gyn, Am. Bd. Ob-Gyn-gynecologic oncology. Intern Nassau County Med. Ctr.; resident Strong Meml. Hosp., NY, fellow, Pa. Hosp.; assoc. prof. ob-gyn Cooper Univ. Hosp., dir. gynecologic cancer ctr., head divsn. of gynecologic oncology. Office: Cooper University Hospital 1 Cooper Plz Camden NJ 08103 Office Phone: 856-342-2000.

WARTH, JAMES ARTHUR, physician, researcher; b. NYC, Apr. 30, 1942; s. Peter and Anne Warth; m. Maria Archer Russell, May 3, 1969; children: David M., Andrew A. BS, Tufts U., 1963, MD, 1967. Diplomate Am. Bd. Internal Medicine, Am. Bd. Hematology, Am. Bd. Oncology. Hematologist Harvard Health Svc. Harvard U., Cambridge, Mass., 1976—77, officer, 1976—77; attending hematologist Harper Grace Hosp., Detroit, 1977—84; asst. prof. medicine Wayne State U., Detroit, 1977—84; rsch. scientist New Eng. Med. Ctr., Boston, 1984—86; attending hematologist, oncologist Faulkner Hosp., Boston, 1986—; asst. prof. medicine Tufts U. Sch. Medicine, Boston, 1986—, course dir. phys. diagnosis Faulkner Hosp., 1992—, assoc. course dir. phys. diagnosis, 1996—; dir. dept. medicine, physician asst. program Faulkner Hosp., Boston, 1996—97; lectr. medicine Harvard Med. Sch., Boston, 2000—, patient Dr. II, 2001—06, sect. leader, tutor hematologic pathophysiology, 2004—. Guest appearance NBC affiliate NBC News, Detroit, 1980; cons. in hematology NIH, Bethesda, Md., 1980—83, 1987, rsch. lectr., NY, 86; invited lectr. Columbia U., 1982, Harvard U., 1984, SUNY, Syracuse, 1991, New Eng. Med. Ctr., Tufts Univ., 1992, Northwestern U., 2004, Brigham and Women's Hosp., 2004; vis. prof. Yale Univ., New Haven, 1986; faculty advisor Tufts U. Sch. Medicine, 1991—98; cons. in hematology Mass. Profl. Rev. Orgn., Waltham, 1991—93, 2004—; Medfield State Hosp., Mass., 1993—99; Max Millman meml. lectr. in medicine Bay State Med. Ctr., Tufts U., Springfield, Mass., 2000; bd. dirs. Faulkner Physicians Assn., Inc., Boston, 1994—; mem. melanoma adv. bd. N.E. region Schering Plough Co., Kenilworth, NJ, 1995. Contbg. author: textbook Hematologic Disorders in Maternal-Fetal Medicine, 1990, reviewer: Am. Jour. Hematology, 1986, Jour. Andrology, 1990—92; contbr. articles to profl. jours. Preceptor Nat. Youth Forum, 1996—98. Maj. US Army, 1969—71. Recipient Mark Aisner M.D. Award for Excellence in Tchg. Physical Diagnosis, Tufts U. Sch. Medicine, 2001, 25 Yrs. Tchg. award, 2010; named to Guide to America's Top Physicians, Consumer Rsch. Council of America, 2003, 2005; Spl. Fellow, NIH, 1974—76, rsch. grantee, 1980—83, 1983 86. Fellow: ACP; mem.: Bio Membranes Sickle Cell Rsch. Group, Am. Fedn. Med. Rsch., Am. Soc. Hematology. Achievements include discovery of new human red blood cell, sequestrocyte accepted into Am. Soc. Hematology slide bank, 1995 and referenced in Textbooks of Hematology. Avocations: art, music, architecture, tennis. Office: Faulkner Hosp 1153 Centre St Rm 5950 Boston MA 02130-3446 Office Phone: 617-739-7776. Business E-Mail: james_warth@hms.harvard.edu.

WARTMAN, STEVEN A., medical association administrator; Grad., Cornell U., 1966, MD, Johns Hopkins U., 1970, PhD Sociology, 1979. Diplomate Am. Bd. Internal Medicine. Dir. med. svs., chmn. medicine Mount Sinai Med. Ctr., Miami Beach; prof. medicine U. Miami; sr. residency in internal medicine Baltimore City Hosp.; intern in internal medicine Stanford U. Med. Ctr.; resident in internal medicine Yale-New Haven Hosp.; prof. medicine Albert Einstein Coll. Medicine; physician-in-chief L.I. Jewish Med. Ctr.; with Edward Meilman Disting. Chair Medicine; dir. Ctr. Quality Rsch. North Shore-L.I. Jewish Health Sys.; dean U. Tex. Med. Sch. San Antonio, 2000—05; pres. Assn. Acad. Health Centers, Washington, 2005—. Contbr. more than 120 peer-reviewed jour. articles, abstracts, chapters to books. Recipient Leadership and Achievement award, Soc. Gen. Internal Medicine, 1997, Excellence award, U.S. Health Resources and Svcs. Adminstrn., 1999; fellow Internat. in Health Care, Yugoslavia, 1969, Primary Care Policy, USPHS, 1991; scholar Henry Luce, Indonesia, 1975—76, Robert Wood Johnson Clin., Johns Hopkins U., 1976—78. Fellow: ACP; mem.: Alpha Omega Alpha, Phi Beta Kappa. Office: Assn Academic Health Centers Ste 720 1400 Sixteenth St NW Washington DC 20036

WARYE, KATHY L., healthcare organization executive; BA, U. Md. Mgr. continuing edn. Am. Acad. Otolaryngology-Head & Neck Surgery; dir. profl. devel. Spl. Libraries Assn., 1985—88, asst. exec. dir. profl. growth, 1988—93; cons. Wilson Learning Corp.; sr. v.p. edn. & govt. rels. Assn. Advancement Med. Instrumentation; pres. Nat. Sci. Tech. Edn. Partnership; exec. dir. Assn. Professionals in Infection Control & Epidemiology (APIC), 2004—06, CEO, 2006—. Contbr. articles to profl. jours. Bd. dirs. Nat. 4-H Coun., Northern Va. Tech. Coun. Mem.: Greater Washington Soc. Assn. Execs., Am. Soc. Assn. Execs. (Excellence in Edn. award 1989, Associations Advance America award 2002). Office: APIC 1275 K St NW Ste 1000 Washington DC 20005 Office Phone: 202-789-1890. Office Fax: 202-789-1899. E-mail: kwarye@apic.org. *

WASFIE, TARIK JAWAD, surgeon, educator; b. Baghdad, Iraq, July 1, 1946; m. Barina Y. Wasfie, Mar. 11, 1975; children: Giselle, Nissan. BS, Central U., Iraq, 1964; MD, Baghdad Med. Sch., 1970. Cert. gen. surgeon. Surg. rsch. assoc. Sinai Hosp. of Detroit/Wayne State U., 1981-85; clin. fellow Coll. Phys. & Surg., Columbia U., NYC, 1985-91, postdoctoral rsch. scientist, 1987-91; attending surgeon Mich. State U./McLaren Hosp., Flint, 1991—. Contbr. articles to profl. jours. NIH grantee, 1984. Fellow ACS, Internat. Coll. Surgeons; mem. AMA, Mich. State Med. Soc., Flint Acad. Surgeons, Am. Soc. Artificial Internal Organs, Internat. Soc. Artificial Organs, Soc. Am. Gast. Endoscopic Surgeons. Achievements include production of antiidiotypic antibodies and their role in transplant immunology; development of percutenous access device. Home: 1125 Kings Carriage Rd Grand Blanc MI 48439-8715

WASHINGTON, A. EUGENE, dean, medical educator; b. Houston, 1950; BS in Zoology, Howard U., 1972; MD, U. Calif., San Francisco, 1976; MPH in Epidemiology, U. Calif., Berkeley, 1975; MSc in Health Policy, Harvard U., 1978. Diplomate Am. Bd. Ob-Gyn., Am. Bd. Gen. Preventive Medicine. Intern USPHS, Staten Island, N.Y., 1976-77; resident Preventive Medicine Harvard U., 1977-79; resident Ob-Gyn. Stanford U., 1986-89; fellow Health Policy Inst. Health PS/U. Calif., San Francisco, 1983-86; prof. Ob-Gyn., Preventive Medicine, Epidemiology & Biostatistics U. Calif., San Francisco, prof. chair., obstetrics, gynecology, 1989—2010, exec. vice chancellor & provost, 2004—10; vice chancellor UCLA Health Sciences, 2010—; dean UCLA David Geffen Sch. Medicine, 2010—. Mem. AAAS, APHA, Soc. for Epidemiol. Rsch., Inst. Medicine (coun. mem.) Office: UCLA Geffen Sch Medicine Office of Dean BOX 951722 12-138 CHS Los Angeles CA 90095-1722 Office Phone: 310-825-5687. Office Fax: 310-825-4955. Business E-Mail: ewashington@mednet.ucla.edu. *

WASHINGTON, REGINALD LOUIS, pediatric cardiologist; b. Colorado Springs, Colo., Dec. 31, 1949; s. Lucius Louis and Brenette Y. (Wheeler) W.; m. Billye Faye Ned, Aug. 18, 1973; children: Danielle Larae, Reginald Quinn. BS in Zoology, Colo. State U., 1971; MD, U. Colo., 1975. Diplomate Nat. Bd. Med. Examiners, Am. Bd. Pediat., Pediatric Cardiology. Intern U. Colo. Med. Ctr., Denver, 1975—76, resident in pediat., 1976-78, chief resident, instr., 1978-79, fellow in pediatric cardiology, 1979-81, from asst. prof. pedit. to assoc. clin. prof. pediat., 1982—2005, clin. prof. pediat., 2005—; staff cardiologist Children's Hosp., Denver, 1981-90; v.p. We. Cardiology Assocs., Divsn. for Fetal, Pediatric and Adult Congential Heart Disease, Denver, 1990—2004; med. dir. Rocky Mountain Pediatrix Cardiology, Denver, 2004—08; chief med. officer Rocky Mountain Hosp. For Children, Denver, Colo., 2008—; chief of staff Presbyn./St. Lukes Med. Ctr., 1999-2001. Admissions com. U. Colo. Sch. Medicine, Denver, 1985-89; chmn., bd. dirs. Coop. Health Care Agreements, 1994-98; chmn. dept. pediatrics Presbyn./St. Lukes Med. Ctr, Denver, 1996-99, 2003-05, pres.-elect med. staff, 1997-99, chmn. ethics com., 2003-07; adv. coun. Nat. Heart Lung Blood Inst., NIH, 1996-986 Cons. editor Your Patient and Fitness, 1989-92; mem. editl. bd. Jour. Pediats., 2004—, Congenital Heart Disease, 2006-. Chmn. Coop. Health Care Agreements Bd., State of Colo., 1994-98; adv. bd. dirs. Equitable Bank of Littleton, Colo., 1984-86; bd. dirs. Rocky Mountain Heart Fund for Children, 1984-89, Rainbo Ironkids, 1989-95, Ctrl. City Opera, 1989-95, Cleo Parker Robinson Dance Co., 1992-94, Nat. Coun. Patient Info. and Edn., 1992-98, Children's Heart Alliance, 1993-94, Colo. State U. Devel. Coun., 1994-2003, Caring for Colo. Found., 1999-2001; nat. bd. dirs. Am. Heart Assn., 1992-96; trustee Denver Ctr. Performing Arts, 1994—, Regis U., 1994-99; mem. Gov.'s Coun. Phys. Fitness, 1990-91; bd. govs. Colo. State U., 1996-2004, pres., 2001-03; trustee Colo. Trust, 2002-; trustee Helen Bonfils Found., 2003—, Temple Hoyne Buell Found., 2007-. Recipient William E. Morgan Alumnus Achievement award Colo. State U., 2004, Cardiologist of Yr., HCA, 2004, named Salute Vol. of Yr. Big Sisters of Colo., 1990; honoree NCCJ, 1994, Physician of Yr., Nat. Am. Heart Assn., 1995, Civis Princeps award Regis U., 2007, Gold heart award Nat. Am. Heart Assn., 2008. Fellow Am. Acad. Pediat. (cardiology subsect., chmn. sports medicine and fitness com. 2000-2004, chmn. task force on obesity 2003—08, Thomas Shaffer award 2007), Am. Coll. Cardiology, Am. Heart Assn. (coun. on cardiovasc. disease in the young, exec. com. 1988-91, nat. devel. program com. 1990-94, vol. of yr. 1989, pres. Colo. chpt. 1989-90, Torch of Hope 1987, Gold Heart award Colo. chpt. 1990, bd. dirs. Colo. chpt., exec. com. Colo. chpt. 1987-2000, grantee Colo. chpt. 1983-84, mem. editl. bd. Pediat. Exercise Scis. 1988-2002), Soc. Critical Care Medicine; mem. Am. Acad. Pediat. Perinatology, Am. Acad. Pediat./Pediat. Cardiology (exec. com. 1996-2004), N.Am. Soc. Pediat. Exercise Medicine (pres. 1986-87), Colo. Med. Soc. (chmn. sports medicine coun. 1993-94), Leadership Denver 1990, Glenmoor Golf Club. Democrat. Roman Catholic. Avocations: golf, fishing. Office: Rocky Mountain Hosp Children 1719 East 19th Ave Denver CO 80218 Office Phone: 303-839-6100. Business E-Mail: rlwash@aol.com.

WASIK, BARBARA HANNA, psychologist, educator; b. Douglas, Ga., May 29, 1942; d. Frank Joseph and Josephine (Nahoom) Hanna; m. John L. Wasik, June 24, 1966; children— John Gregory, Mark Timothy, Jeffrey Joseph AB, U. Ga., 1963; MA, Fla. State U., 1965, PhD, 1967. Lic. psychologist, N.C. Postdoctoral research fellow Duke U., Durham, NC, 1967-68; dir. research Ford Found. grant, Durham, NC, 1968-69; from asst. prof. to assoc. prof. U. N.C., Chapel Hill, 1969-77, prof., 1977—, William R. Kenan Jr. disting. prof., 2003—, assoc. dean Grad. Sch., 1972-75, chmn. div. human devel. and psychol. services, 1975-77, assoc. dean Sch. Edn., 1977-83, 1988—92, sr. investigator Child Devel. Ctr., 1972—. Mem. commn. NAS, 1998—2000; co-facilitator Nat. Forum Home Visiting, 1999—2006. Assoc. editor Jour. Applied Behavior Analysis, 1972; mem. editorial bd. Behavioral Assessment, 1984-85; contbr. chpts. to books and articles to profl. jours. Mem. N.C. Psychological Assn. (sec. 1982-85, pres. 1988-89), Am. Psychol. Assn. (divsn. 25 sec-treas. 1983-86, coun. rep. 1994-99, bd. edn. affairs 1999-2001, chair bd edn. affairs 2001), Soc. Research in Child Development, Southeastern Psychol. Assn., Assn. Advancement Behavior Therapy. Democrat. Roman Catholic. Home: 609 Brookview Dr Chapel Hill NC 27514-1402

WASILUK, ALICJA, medical educator; b. Bialystok, Poland, Apr. 21, 1960; MD, Med. U. Bialystok, 1985, PhD, 2010. Prof., dept. neonatology Med. U. Bialystok, 2011—. Recipient Sci. award, Polish Ministry Health, Rector Med. U. Bialystok. Mem.: Polish Soc. Neonatology, European Assn. Perinatal Medicine, Am. Soc. Hematology. Avocation: diving. Office: Sklodowskiej-Curie 24a Bialystok 15-276 Poland Office Fax: 48 85 7468663. Business E-Mail: awasiluk@umwb.edu.pl.

WASSENBERG, EVELYN M., retired medical/surgical nurse, educator; b. Oct. 8, 1933; d. Patrick A. and Mary A. (Kieffer) L'Ecuyer; m. Maurice P. Wassenberg, Oct. 29, 1955; children: Sherry Ann Gaines, Laura Marie O'Neil. Diploma in nursing, Marymount Sch. Nursing, Salina, Kans., 1955; BS in Nursing, Marymount Coll., Salina, 1982; MN, Wichita State U., Kans., 1987. Cert. nurse specialist. Dir. nursing svc. Community Meml. Hosp. Inc., Marysville, Kans., 1962-79; house supr. Luth. Hosp., Beatrice, Nebr., 1980-82; primary nurse Beatrice Cmty. Hosp., 1983; instr. Ft. Scott C.C., Kans., 1983-2001; nurse Girard Hosp., Kans., 2001; ICU nurse Nevada Regional Health Ctr., Mo., 2001—03, clin. instr., 2003—06, Ft. Scott CC Kans; ret., 2006. Mem. Mary Queen of Angels Cath. Ch. Named Nurse of Yr. Bourbon County Kans., 1992. Mem. Am. Nursing Assn., Kans. State Nursing Assn., Sigma Theta Tau. Address: 216 S Crawford St Fort Scott KS 66701-3231

WASSENICH, LINDA PILCHER, retired health policy analyst, social worker; b. Washington, Aug. 27, 1943; d. Mason Johnson and Vera Bell (Stephenson) Pilcher; m. Mark Wassenich, May 14, 1965; children: Paul Mason, David Mark. BA magna cum laude with honors, Tex. Christian U., Fort Worth, 1965; MSW, U. N.C., Chapel Hill, 1970. Licensed advanced practitioner, cert. social worker, Tex. Counselor family ct. Dallas County Juvenile Dept., 1970-73, 75-76; dir. govt. rels. Vis. Nurse Assn., Dallas, 1980-84, exec. officer of hospice, 1984-85; exec. dir. Incest Recovery Assn., Dallas, 1985-86; assoc. exec. dir. Lone Star Coun. Camp Fire, Dallas, 1986-89; exec. v.p. Vis. Nurse Assn. Found., Dallas, 1989-91; dir. policy and resource devel. Vis. Nurse Assn. Tex., 1992-99; ret. Field instr. U. Tex. Arlington Sch. Social Work, 1993-99. Contbr. articles to profl. publs. Mem. Leadership Dallas, 1988—89; bd. dirs. Women's Coun. Dallas County, 1986—95, 1999—2001, pres., 1992—93; mem. adv. bd. Maternal Health and Family Planning Dallas, 1990—94; chmn. Dallas County Welfare Adv. Bd., 1991—95; bd. dirs. United Way of Met. Dallas, 1992—94, Youth Impact Ctrs., Dallas, 1993—94; trustee Simmons Family Found., Dallas, 2000—; mem. bd. dirs. Cmty. Coun. Greater Dallas, 2004—, sec., 2007, v.p., 2008; chair governance com. Human Rights Initiative North Tex., Dallas, 2004—10; chair adv. coun. Dallas Area Agy. on Aging, 2005—; bd. mem. Tex. Christian U., Harris Coll. Nursing & Health Scis., 2008—, exec. com. mem., 2006—. Recipient Heart award Lone Star Coun. Camp Fire USA, 1990, Laurel award AAUW, Dallas, 1995, Valuable Alumna award Tex. Christian U. Alumni Assn., 2003, Women of Spirit award Am. Jewish Congress, Dallas, 2005; named Field Inst. of Yr., U. Tex. Arlington Sch. Social Work, 1999, Golden Rule award finalist JC Penney, 2000, Exceptional Tex. Woman Vet. Feminists America. Mem.: LWV (bd. dirs. Dallas 1974—80, pres. 1995—99, bd. dirs. Tex. 1999—, Tex. v.p. pub. rels. 2001—10, Myrtle Bales Bulkley award 2000, Pres. award 2005), NASW (co-chmn. Dallas unit 1981—82, chair Tex. nominating com. 1990—92, Tex. bd. dirs., Social Worker of Yr. award 1988, Lifetime Achievement in Social Work award 2002), Assn. Fundraising Profls. (bd. dirs. Dallas chpt. 1994—97, v.p. governance 1995—96, cert., Outstanding Fund Raising Exec. of Yr. 1999), Acad. Cert. Social Workers. Home: 5221 Pebblebrook Dallas TX 75229-5504

WASSERHEIT, JUDITH N., social services administrator; b. NYC, 1954; m. Jeffrey Harris, 1981; one child. BA cum laude, Princeton U., 1974; MD, Harvard U., 1978; MPH, Johns Hopkins U., 1989. Co-dir., co-developer Harborview Med. Ctr., U. Wash., 1982-84; infectious disease physician Internat. Ctr. for Diarrheal Disease Rsch., 1984-86; asst. chief Sexually Transmitted Disease Clin. Svcs. Balt. City Health Dept., 1986-89; chief Sexually Transmitted Disease Br. Nat. Inst. Allergy and Infectious Diseases, NIH, 1989-92; dir. Sexually Transmitted Disease Prevention Disease Ctr. for Disease Control & Prevention, HHS, 1992—2001; dir. HIV Vaccine Trials Network, Seattle, 2001; prof. allergy and infectious disease U. Wash. Sch. Pub. Health, Seattle, vice chair, prof. global health. Affiliate investigator Fred Hutchinson Cancer Rsch. Ctr., Seattle; amb. Paul G. Rogers Soc. Global Health Rsch., 2007—. Editor: Reproductive Tract Infections: Global Impact and Priorities for Women's Health, 1992; contbr. articles to profl. jours. Recipient Spl. Recognition award Pub. Health Svc., 1990, 91, Young Profl. award Maternal-Child Health, APHA, 1991, Presdl. Meritorious Rank award, 1996; Pub. Health Leadership Inst. Scholar, 1993. Mem. Phi Beta Kappa, Sigma Xi. Office: U Washington Box 355065 1705 NE Pacific St Seattle WA 98195 also: Harborview Med Ctr 325 9th Ave Seattle WA 98109 Office Phone: 206-685-1894. Office Fax: 206-685-8519. E-mail: jwasserh@u.washington.edu.

WASSERMAN, DANUTA ELISABETH, medical educator; b. Warsaw, Mar. 19, 1945; arrived in Sweden, 1968; d. Nikolai Stefan and Stefania Maria (Smolarek) Wolk; children: Janek, Susanne, Camilla; m. Jerzy Wasserman, June 16, 1979 MD, Med. Faculty, Uppsala, Sweden, 1972; PhD, Karolinska Inst., Stockholm, 1986. Cert. psychoanalyst. Med. and psychiat. resident, Uppsala and Stockholm, 1972—93; sr. psychology cons. Karolinska Hosp., 1994—; rschr. Med. Rsch. Coun., Stockholm, 1989—92; assoc. prof. Karolinska Inst., Stockholm, 1990—95, prof. psychiatry & suicidology, NASP, 1995—, head Nat. Swedish Ctr. Suicide Rsch. & Prevention Mental Ill Health, 1995—, chmn. dept. pub. health scis., 2002—07, dir. WHO collaborating ctr. suicide rsch. and prevent Geneva, Copenhagen, 1997—. Hon. pres. Estonian-Swedish Suicidological Inst, Tallinn, Estonia, 1993—; mem. Club 13 Karolinska Inst., 1993—, Internat. Assn. Suicide Prevention and Crisis Intervention, 1995—. Author and co-author of several books; editor: Suicide an unnecessary death, 2001, Martin Dunitz, 2001 (translated to Chinese, Russian and Japanese 2003), Depression-The Facts, 2006, The Oxford Textbook of Suicidology and Suicide Prevention: A Global Perspective, 2009; mem. editl. bd. Crisis, Archives Suicide Rsch.; dir. editl. bd. Epidemiol. Surveillance of Suicidal Behaviours; contbr. 300 articles to profl. jours. Task force for suicide prevention Swedish Med. and Swedish Psychiat. Assn., 1994. Mem. Internat. Assn. Suicide Prevention and Crisis Intervention (v.p. 1995-97, dir. task force for identification of rsch. priorities in suicidology 1993—, Erwin Stengel Rsch. award 1993), Internat. Assn. Suicide Rsch. (pres. 2005-07, past pres., 2007-09), Swedish Med. Assn. (rsch. award 1993), Am. Found. Suicide Prevention (Rsch. award, 2005, German Hans-Rost Suicidology prize, 2005, Nordic Mins. Coun. award for significant achievement to improve mental health and prevent suicide, 2008), NY Acad. Scis., European Psychiatric Assn. (chair, sect. suicidology & suicide prevention, 2005-, bd. mem., 2008-, pres. elect), World Psychiat. Assn. (co-chair, suicidology sect., 2005-08, chair, suicidology sect., 2008-). Avocations: reading, history, travel, piano, gardening. Office: Nat Ctr Suicide Rsch/Prevention Mental Health NASP Karolinska Inst Box 230 171 77 Stockholm Sweden

WASSERMAN, GARY, urologist; MD, Tulane U., 1985. Diplomate Am. Bd. Urology. Resident surgery George Washington Univ. Med. Ctr., 1986—87; resident urology Tulane Univ. Med. Ctr., 1987—91. Office: 180 N Dean St Englewood NJ 07631 Office Phone: 201-503-9100. Office Fax: 201-816-1777.

WASSERMAN, HAL STUART, interventional cardiologist, educator; s. Jules Wasserman; m. Lisa Ann Haas, Feb. 7, 1987. MD, Columbia U., 1982. Diplomate Am. Bd. Internal Medicine-cardiovascular disease, Am. Bd. Internal Medicine-interventional cardiology. Resident in internal medicine Columbia-Presbyn. Med. Ctr., NY, 1982—85, fellow in cardiovascular disease, 1985—88; assoc. clin. prof. medicine Columbia Univ.; cardiologist NY- Presbyn. Hosp.; prin. investigator Danbury Hosp. Office: Danbury Hospital 24 Hospital Ave 7 Tower Danbury CT 06810 Office Phone: 203-739-7600.

WASSERMAN, ROBERT HAROLD, biology professor; b. Schenectady, Feb. 11, 1926; s. Joseph and Sylvia (Rosenberg) W.; m. Marilyn Mintz, June 11, 1950; children: Diane Jean, Arlene Lee, Judith Rose. BS, Cornell U., 1949, PhD, 1953; MS, Mich. State U., 1951. Research assoc. AEC project U. Tenn., Oak Ridge, 1953-55; sr. scientist med. div. Oak Ridge Inst. Nuclear Studies, 1955-57; assoc. prof. dept. phys. biology N.Y. State Vet. Coll., Cornell U., 1957-63, prof., 1963—, James Law prof. physiology, 1989-97, James Law prof. emeritus, 1998—, acting head phys. biology dept., 1963-64, 71, 75-76, chmn. dept. /sect. physiology, 1983-87, mem. exec. com. div. biol. sci., 1983-87. Vis. fellow Inst. Biol. Chemistry, Copenhagen, 1964-65; chmn. Conf. on Calcium Transport, 1962; co-chmn. Conf. on Cell Mechanisms for Calcium Transfer and Homeostasis, 1970; mem. adv. bd. Vitamin D Symposia, 1976—; adv. bd. Symposia Calcium-Binding Proteins, 1977-2001, chmn., 1977; food and nutrition bd. NRC; cons. NIH, Oak Ridge Inst. Nuclear Studies; pub. affairs com. Fedn. Am. Socs. Exptl. Biology, 1974-77; chmn. com. MPI, NRC; pre-doctoral fellowship panel Howard Hughes, 1999-2000, 03. Bd. editors: Calcified Tissue Research, 1977-80, Procs. Soc. Exptl. Biol. Medicine, 1970-76, Cornell Veterinarian, Jour. Nutrition; contbr.: articles to profl. jours. Served with U.S. Army, 1944-45. Recipient Mead Johnson award, 1969, Andre Lichtwitz prize INSERM, 1982, W.F. Neuman award Am. Soc. Bone and Mineral Rsch., 1990, Merit award NIH, 1993-96, Brown U. Rsch. award, 2004; Guggenheim fellow, 1964-65, 72, fellow NSF-OECD, 1964-65. Fellow Am. Inst. Nutrition, mem. Am. Physiol. Soc., Soc. Exptl. Biology and Medicine, AAAS, Nat. Acad. Scis., Sigma Xi, Phi Kappa Phi, Phi Zeta Home: 358 Savage Farm Dr Ithaca NY 14850-1758 Business E-Mail: rhw2@cornell.edu.

WASSERMAN, STEPHEN IRA, medical association administrator, allergist, immunologist, educator; b. LA, Dec. 17, 1942; m. Linda Morgan; children: Matthew, Zachary. BA, Stanford U., 1964; MD, UCLA, 1968. Diplomate Am. Bd. Internal Medicine, Am. Bd. Allergy and Immunology. Intern, resident Peter B. Brigham Hosp., Boston, 1968-70; fellow in allergy, immunology Robert B. Brigham Hosp., Boston, 1972-75; asst. prof. medicine Harvard U., Boston, 1975-79, assoc. prof., 1979, U. Calif.-San Diego, La Jolla, 1979-85, prof. medicine, 1985—, chief allergy tng. program Sch. Medicine, 1979-85, chief allergy div. Sch. Medicine, 1985-93, acting chmn. dept. medicine, 1986-88, chmn. dept. medicine, 1988-2000, Helen M. Ranney prof., 1992—2001, chief allergy tng.program Sch. Medicine, 2001—05. Co-dir. allergy sect. Robert B. and Peter B. Brigham Hosps., 1977-79; dir. Am. Bd. Allergy and Immunology, pres. 2010-; dir. Am. Bd. Internal Medicine., chair, 1999-2000. Contbr. articles to profl. jours. Served to lt. comdr. USPHS, 1970-72, San Francisco. Fellow Am. Acad. Allergy and Immunology (pres. 1997-98); mem. Am. Soc. Clin. Investigation, Assn. Am. Physicians, Am. Assn. Immunologists, Collegium Internationale Allergologicum, Phi Beta Kappa, Alpha Omega Alpha. Office: American Bd Allergy and Immunology 111 S Independence Mall E Ste 701 Philadelphia PA 19106-2515 also: University Calif San Diego Stein Clin Rsch Bldg Rm 244 9500 Gilman Dr MC 0637 San Diego CA 92093-0637 Office Phone: 858-822-4261. Office Fax: 858-534-7517. Business E-Mail: swasserman@ucsd.edu. *

WASSON, GREGORY D., retail executive; b. 1958; BS in Pharmacy, Purdue U., 1981. Various positions Walgreen Co., Deerfield, Ill., 1980—86, dist. mgr., 1986—99, regional v.p. store ops., 1999—2001; exec. v.p. Walgreens Health Initiatives Inc. (WHI), 2001—02, pres., 2002; v.p. Walgreen Co., Deerfield, Ill., 2001—04, sr. v.p., 2004—05, exec. v.p., 2006—07, pres., COO, 2007—09, pres., CEO, 2009—. Bd. dirs. Walgreen Co., 2009—. Office: Walgreen Co 200 Wilmot Rd Deerfield IL 60015 *

WASTERLAIN, CLAUDE GUY, neurologist; s. Desire and Simone (De Taeye) W.; m. Anne Marguerite Thomsin, Feb. 28, 1967; 1 child, Jean Michel. Cand. Sci., U. Liege, 1957, MD, 1961; degree in Libr. Sci., Molecular Biology summa cum laude, Free U. Brussels, 1969. Resident Cornell U. Med. Coll., NYC, 1964-67, instr. neurology, 1969-70, asst. prof., 1970-75, assoc. prof., 1975-76, UCLA Sch. Medicine, 1976-79, prof., 1979—2005, vice-chair dept. neurology, 1976—, disting. prof., 2005—; chief neurology svc. VA Med. Ctr., Sepulveda, Calif., 1976—98; chair neurology Greater LA VA Health Care Sys., 1998—. Attending neurologist UCLA Ctr. Health Scis., 1976—. Author, editor: Status Epilepticus, 1984, Neonatal Seizures, 1990, Molecular Neurobiology and Epilepsy, 1992, Progressive Nature of Epileptogenesis, 1996, Status Epilepticus: Mechanism Management, 2006; contbr. articles to med. jours. Recipient N.Y. Neurol. Soc. Young Investigator award, 1965; Rsch. Career Devel. award NIH, 1973-76; William Evans fellow, U. Auckland, New Zealand, 1984; Worldwide AES award for rsch. in epilepsy, 1992; Golden Hammer Tchg. award, 1996; Amb. for Epilepsy, Internat. League Against Epilepsy, 2003; Pierre Gloor award Am. Clin. Neurophysiology Soc., 2006. Fellow Am. Acad. Neurology; mem. Am. Neurol. Assn., Am. Soc. Neurochemistry (coun. mem. 1991-97), Internat. Soc. Neurochemistry, Am. Epilepsy Soc., Royal Soc. Medicine. Avocations: tennis, skiing, jazz, theater. Office: West LA Va Med Ctr 127 11301 Wilshire Blvd Los Angeles CA 90073

WATABE, KENJI, gastroenterologist, educator; b. Hino, Tokyo, Japan, Feb. 21, 1969; s. Tadashi and Junko Watabe; m. Miyuki Watabe, Nov. 23, 1995; children: Hana, Megumi. PhD, Osaka U., Japan, 2001. Cert. bd. mem. Japanese Soc. Internal Medicine, 2003, in gastroenterologist Japanese Soc. Gastroenterology, 2005, in supervisory dr. Japanese Soc. Internal Medicine, 2007. Rsch. fellow (CEO program) Osaka U., Suita, 2002—04, asst. prof., 2004—. Cancer Rsch. grant, Osaka Cancer Found., Japan, 2001, Rsch. grant, Ministry Edn., Culture, and Sports Japan, 2005, 2007.

WATABE, NORIMITSU, marine biologist, educator; b. Kure, Hiroshima, Japan, Nov. 29, 1922; came to U.S., 1957; s. Isamu and Matsuko (Takamatsu) W.; m. Sakuko Kobayashi, Dec. 12, 1952; children: Shoichi, Sachiko. BS, 1st Nat. High Sch., Tokyo, 1945; MS, Tohoku U., Sendai, Japan, 1948, DSc, 1960. Rsch. investigator Fuji Pearl Co., Mie-ken, Japan, 1948-52; instr. Prefect U. Mie, Tsu, Mie-ken, 1952-55, asst. prof., 1955-59; rsch. assoc. Duke U., Durham, N.C., 1957-70; assoc. prof. U. S.C., Columbia, 1970-72, prof. biology and marine sci., 1972-93, disting. prof., 1993-94, disting. prof. emeritus, 1994—. Cons. Ford Found., 1968; vis. prof. U. Bonn, Germany, 1976-77; dir. Electron Microscopy Ctr., 19770-95; cons. in field. Author: Studies on Pearls, 1959; editor: Mechanisms of Mineralization, 1976, Mechanisms of Biomineralization, 1980, Hard Tissue Mineralization and Demineralization, 1991; assoc. editor, Jour. Morphology, 1999—; contbr. articles to profl. jours. Recipient Pearl Rsch. award Elmer W. Ellsworth, 1952, Alexander Von Humboldt award Govt. of Germany, Russel award U. SC, 1981; grantee NIH, 1971-76, NSF, 1973-95. Fellow AAAS; mem. Am. Micros. Soc. (life). Avocation: music.

WATANABE, AKINARI, ophthalmologist; b. Japan, June 20, 1973; MD, Fukushima Med. Coll., 1999. Dir. Watanabe Eye Clinic, 2009—. Office: 1-3-1 Shioe Amagasaki Hyogo 661-0976 Japan Office Fax: 81-6-6423-9720. Business E-Mail: akinari@watanabe-eye.net.

WATANABE, HIROKO, medical researcher; b. Japan, Oct. 4, 1961; PhD, U. Tokyo, 2007. Registered midwife. Rsch. scientist, women's health Shiga U. Med. Sci., 2009—. Office: Seta Tsukinowa-cho Otsu 520-2192 Japan Office Fax: 81-77-548-2433.

WATANABE, HIROSHI, doctor of internal medicine, educator; b. Kitakyushu, Fukuoka, Japan, Feb. 18, 1961; s. Shinsaku JItouzono and Aiko Jitouzono; m. Yoko Watanabe; children: Yusaku, Shunsaku. MD, Nagasaki U., Japan, 1988, PhD, 2001. Cert. Japanese Soc. Internal Medicine, 1995, Japanese Assn. Infectious Diseases, 1996, infection control doctor 2000, physician Japanese Respiratory Soc., 1997. Asst. prof., dept. internal medicine, inst. tropical medicine Nagasaki U., 1988—2006; prof., divsn. infectious diseases dept. infectious medicine Kurume U., Fukuoka, 2006—. Short-term cons. World Health Orgn., Geneva, 2003. Recipient award, Japanese Soc. Chemotherapy, 2005. Office: Kurume Univ Sch Medicine 67 Asahimachi Kurume Fukuoka 830-0011 Japan Office Fax: 81-942-31-7697. Business E-Mail: hwata@med.kurume-u.ac.jp.

WATANABE, KYOICHI A(LOYSIUS), pharmacology educator, chemist; b. Amagasaki, Hyogo, Japan, Feb. 28, 1935; s. Yujiro and Yoshiko Francisca (Hashimoto) W.; m. Krystyna Lesiak; children: Kanna, Kay, Kenneth, Kim, Kelly, Katherine. BA, Hokkaido U., 1958, PhD, 1963. Lectr. Sophia U., Tokyo, 1963; rsch. assoc. Sloan-Kettering Inst., NYC, 1963—66, assoc., 1968—72, assoc. mem., 1972—81, mem., 1981—95; rsch. fellow U. Alta., Edmonton, Canada, 1966—68; assoc. prof. Cornell U. Med. Coll., NYC, 1972—81, prof. pharmacology, 1981—98; dir. organic chemistry Codon Pharm., Inc., Gaithersburg, Md., 1996—98; v.p. R&D Pharmasset Inc., Tucker, Ga., 1998—2003; vis. prof. U. Minn., 2003—. Study sect. NIH, Washington, 1981-84. Recipient Szalecki medal, Wojzkowa Akademia Medyczna, 1989, Marie Sklodowska Curie medal, Polish Chem. Soc., 1993, František Šorm Meml. award, Czech Acad. Scis., 2002. Mem. Polish Chem. Soc. (hon.), Russian Acad. Sci. (bd. sci. cons. Engelhardt Inst. Molecular Biology 1994-97). Achievements include rsch. in total synthesis of nucleoside antibiotics, novel heterocycle ring transformation, C-nucleoside chemistry, antiviral and anticancer nucleosides, intercalating agents, modified oligonucleotides, triplex DNA for gene repair.

WATANABE, MAKOTO, medical educator; b. Mabi-cho, Japan, Feb. 7, 1951; s. Kazuo and Takako Watanabe; m. Reiko Higashi, Apr. 3, 1974; children: Eiko, Shoko, Utako. MD, Okayama U., Japan, 1975, DMS (hon.), 1979. Asst. prof. Shimane Med. U., Izumo, Japan, 1981—94, assoc. prof., 1994—2001; dep. dir. Mihara (Japan) Red Cross Hosp., 2001—05; dir. Tsuyama The First Hosp., 2005—08; prof. Fukuyama U., 2008—. Contbr. articles to profl. jours. Fellow: Am. Coll. Gastroenterology Internat.; mem.: Am. Soc. Gastrointestinal Endoscopy, Japanese Soc. Gastroenterology, Japan Soc. Hepatology. Avocations: travel, photography, golf. Home: 534-7 Ide Soja 719-1125 Japan Office: Fukuyama Univ 1 Gakuen-cho Fukuyama 729-0292 Japan Office Phone: 81-84-936-2111. Office Fax: 81-84-936-2213. Business E-Mail: watanabe@fubac.fukuyama-u.ac.jp.

WATANABE, MARK DAVID, pharmacist, educator; b. Santa Monica, Calif., Dec. 7, 1955; s. Jack Shigeru and Rose Nobuko (Iida) W. BA in Chemistry, U. Calif., Irvine, 1977, BS in Biol. Sci., 1978; PharmD, U. Calif., San Francisco, 1982, PhD in Pharm. Chemistry, 1990. Lic. pharmacist Calif., Oreg., Ill., Mass. Pharmacy intern various locations, San Francisco, 1979-82; pharmacist Kaiser Permanente, San Francisco, 1981-87; clin. scis. rsch. fellow in psychiat. pharmacy U. Tex., Austin, 1987-89; clin. asst. prof. pharmacy practice U. Ill., Chgo., 1989-98. Rsch. asst. U. Calif., San Francisco, 1980-87; clin. pharmacy cons. Ill. Dept. Mental Health & Devel. Disabilities, 1994-98; med. sci. mgr. Bristol-Myers Squibb, 1998-99; clin. pharmacy specialist, Alameda Co., Calif., 1999-2003; asst. cli. prof. clin. pharmacy, U. Calif., San Francisco, 1999-2003; asst. clin. specialist Northeastern U., 2003-07, asst. clin. prof., 2007-08, clin pharm. cons. U. Mass. Med. Sch., 2008-10, asst. clin. prof. Northeastern U., 2010-Regents scholar U. Calif., San Francisco, 1979-82; recipient Excellence in Teaching award Long Found., San Francisco, 1984. Mem.: Coll. Psychiatric Neurologic Pharmacists, Am. Pharm. Assn., Am. Soc. Health-Sys. Pharmacists, Am. Coll. Clin. Pharmacy, Mensa, Phi Lambda Sigma, Rho Chi. Unitarian Universalist. Avocations: individual and fitness sports, reading, travel, music. Office: Northeastern Sch Pharm 360 Huntington Ave Boston MA 02115

WATANABE, NORIHITO, gastroenterologist, educator; b. Japan, May 27, 1953; MD, Keio U. Sch. Medicine, PhD, 1979. Prof. Tokai U. Sch. Medicine, 2007—. Asst. dir. Tokai U. Hachioji Hosp., 2010—11. Mem.: Japanese Soc. Gastroenterology, Japan Soc. Hepatology. Avocation: gardening. Office: 1838 Ishikawamachi Hachioji Tokyo 192-0032 Japan Office Fax: 42-639-1144. Business E-Mail: norihito@is.icc.u_tokai.ac.jp.

WATANABE, SATORU, public health service officer; b. Yokohama, Japan, June 25, 1968; PhD, Grad. Sch. Tokyo Met. U., 2010. Chief clk. Kitasato U. Kitasato Inst. Med. Ctr. Hosp., 1998—. Mem.: World Confederation Phys. Therapy. Achievements include generalization of prism adaptation for wheelchair driving task in patients with unilateral spatial neglect. Office: 6-100 Arai Kitamoto Saitama 3648501 Japan Office Fax: 81-48-593-1239. Business E-Mail: s-watan@insti.kitasato-u.ac.jp.

WATANABE, SHUN-ICHI, thoracic surgeon, educator; b. Mishima, Shizuoka, Japan, June 26, 1953; s. Shigeru and Shigeyo Watanabe; m. Rieko Nagano, June 2, 1984; children: Yu, Satoko, Akiko, Tomoko. MD, Nat. Defence Med. Coll., Tokorozawa, 1974—80; DMS (hon.), Kagoshima U., 1994. Diplomate Japan Bd. Surgery, 1999, Japan Bd. Thoracic Surgery, 1996, Japan Bd. Chest Surgery, 1997. Staff, cardiovasc. surgeon Nat. Minamikyusyu Ctrl. Hosp., Kagoshima, Japan, 1991—92, Miyazaki Prefecture Hosp., Miyazaki, Japan, 1992—94; instr. 2nd Dept. Surgery, Kagoshima U., Faculty Medicine, Kagoshima, Japan, 1994—2000, asst. prof., 2000—. Avocations: travel, walking, golf, writing, reading. Home: 2-3-3 Murasakibaru Kagoshima 890-0082 Japan Office Fax: +81-99-265-8177; Home Fax: +81-99-251-2961. Personal E-mail: marble@m5.dion.ne.jp. E-mail: shun@khosp2.kufm.kagoshima-u.ac.jp.

WATANABE, TAKAHIRO, medical educator; b. Kawaguchi-ko, Yamanashi, Japan, Mar. 24, 1967; s. Takao and Masuko Watanabe; m. Mariko Watanabe, May 11, 2003. MD, PhD, U. Tokyo, 1991. Lic. dermatologist Tokyo, 1996. Resident dept. dermotology Tokyo U., 1991—93, rsch. assoc. dept. dermatology, 1995—99, lectr. dept. dermatology, 2002—07; rsch. assoc. dept. dermatology Internat. Med. Ctr. Japan, 1993—95; rsch. fellow Nat. Cancer Inst., Bethesda, Md., 1999—2002. Fellow: Am. Acad. Dermatology. Office: Futaba Dermatology Clinic 3-7-2 Horikiri Katsushika Tokyo 124-0006 Japan Business E-Mail: takahiro-tky@umin.ac.jp.

WATANABE, TAKUYA, medical educator; b. Fukushima, Japan, Mar. 2, 1970; MD, Niigata U., PhD, 1994. Assoc. prof., dept. internal medicine & gastroenterology Nippon Dental U. Niigata, 2009—. Editl. bd. mem. World Jour. Gastroenterology, China, World Jour. Gastrointestinal Oncology, China, Gastroenterology Rsch. & Practice, India, Chemotherapy Rsch. & Practice, India, Clin. & Experimantal Gastroenterology, United States, Rare Tumors, Italy; editl. bd. mem., regional editor Gastroenterology Insights, Italy. Editor: Recent Patents on Anti Cancer Drugs Discovery; assoc. editor Gastroenterology & Hepatology From Bed to Bench, Iran. Recipient ICHIDA's award, Niigata U. 3rd Dept. Internal Medicine, 2010. Office: 1-8 Hamauracho Chuo-ku Niigata 951-8580 Japan Office Phone: 81-025-267-1500. Office Fax: 81-025-267-1582.

WATANABE, TORU, pediatrician; b. Niigata, Japan, May 2, 1960; s. Isuke and Sachiko Watanabe; m. Chieko Hoshi, Apr. 29, 1985; children: Sayo, Shyu, Shizuka, Ryo. MD, Niigata U., 1985, PhD, 2003. Lic. physician The Japanese Ministry of Welfare, 1985. Resident Niigata City Gen. Hosp., 1985—90, staff, 1991—. Guest rschr. dept. cell biology, faculty medicine, Inst. Nephrology, Niigata U., 1997—2001. Mem. editl. bd.: Jour. Pediatric Nephrology, 2008—, Jour. Pediat. Biochemistry, 2009—; contbr. articles to profl. jours. Recipient The Plenary Presentation award, Japanese Soc. of Pediat. Nephrology, 1994, The best clin. rsch. award, 1999. Mem.: Japanese Soc. of Pediat., Japanese Soc. of Pediat. Nephrology, Internat. Pediat. Nephrology Assn. (editl. bd. pediat. nephrology 2008—). Avocations: reading, walking. Office: Niigata City Gen Hosp 463-7 Shumoku Chuoku Niigata 950-1197 Japan Office Fax: 8125 2815169. Personal E-mail: ruruchankiiro@ecatv.home.ne.jp. Business E-Mail: twata@hosp.niigata.niigata.jp.

WATANABE, YASUHIRO, pharmacologist educator; b. Osaka, Japan, Mar. 15, 1950; s. Kohei and Chieko W.; m. Noriko Iwamoto, Aug. 21, 1981; children: Mirei, Haruka. MD, Osaka U., Japan, 1974, PhD, 1981. Physician Mcpl. Hosp., Ikeda, Osaka, Japan, 1975-76, The Ctr. for Adult Diseases, Osaka, Japan, 1976-78; asst. Osaka U. Sch. Medicine, Japan, 1979-87, asst. prof., 1987-92; prof. Nat. Def. Med. Coll., Tokorozawa, Saitama, Japan, 1992—. Recipient Award for Encouragement of Young Investigators, Japanese Pharmacology Soc., 1989. Avocation: travel. Office: Nat Def Med Coll Dept Pharmacology Namiki 3-2 Tokorozawa 359-8513 Japan

WATANABE, YASUYUKI, medical educator; b. Okayama, Japan, Sept. 30, 1954; s. Toru and Mitsuko Watanabe; m. Hiroko Ota; children: Wakako, Hirofumi, Atsuhiro. Grad. cum laude, Hiroshima U. Sch. of Medicine, Japan, 1973—79; PhD, Hiroshima U. Grad. Sch. of Medicine, 1985—88. Diplomate 1979. Resident in internal medicine Hiroshima U. Hosp., Hiroshima, Japan, 1979—81; med. staff in internal medicine Onomichi Gen. Hosp., Onomichi, Hiroshima, Japan, 1981—83; rsch. student First Dept. of Internal Medicine, Hiroshima U. Sch. of Medicine, Hiroshima, Japan, 1983—84, med. staff, 1984—85, instr., 1988—91, 1993—94, asst. prof., 1994—96; dir. Watanabe Clinic, Kasaoka, Okayama, Japan, 1996—. Dir. Kasaoka Med. Assn., Kasaoka, Okayama, Japan, 1999—2002; part time lectr. First Dept. of Internal Medicine, Hiroshima U. Sch. of Medicine, Hiroshima, Japan, 1997—2002; vis. scholar div. clin. immunology U. Calif. Davis Sch. Medicine, Calif., 1991—93; part time lectr. dept. medicine and molecular sci. divsn. frontier med. sci. Hiroshima U. Sch. Medicine, 2003—. Author: New Trends in Hepatology, 1986, Cytoprotection & Biology, 1987, Cells of the Hepatic Sinusoid, 1991, Frontier in Hepatology ' 94, 1994; contbr. articles to profl. jours. and publs., 2000. Mem. Nat. Geographic Soc., Washington, 1999—2002. Recipient Kajiyama, First Dept. of Internal Medicine, Hiroshima U. Sch. of Medicine, 1987. Mem.: AAAS (Washington DC), AMA (assoc.), N.Y. Acad. of Scis. (New York 1817), Japanese Soc. of Allergology (Tokyo), Japan Soc. of Ultrasonics in Medicine (Tokyo), Japan Gastroenterol. Endoscopy Soc. (Tokyo), Japanese Soc. of Hepatology (Tokyo), Japanese Soc. of Gastroenterology (Tokyo 1898), Japanese Soc. of Internal Medicine (Tokyo 1903), Japan Med. Assn. (Tokyo). Avocations: running, golf, travel. Business E-Mail: wata-cl@pluto.dti.ne.jp.

WATANABE, YOSHIO, cardiologist; b. Tokyo, Nov. 8, 1925; s. Yoshisada and Setsuko (Shiga) W.; m. Keiko Ohta, Nov. 18, 1958; children: Mari, Yuri. MD, Keio Gijuku U., 1951, DMS, 1960. Asst. instr. medicine Keio U. Hosp., Tokyo, 1952-60; assoc. prof. medicine, physiology and biophysics Hahnemann Med. Coll., Phila., 1961-72; prof. medicine, dir. cardiovascular inst. Fujita Health U., Toyoake, Japan, 1972-95; hosp. dir. Toyota Regional Med. Ctr., Japan, 1995—99; cons. cardiologist Chiba Tokushukai Hosp., Funabashi, Japan, 1999-2000, Shonan Kamakura Gen. Hosp., Kamakura, Japan, 2001—03, Nagoya Tokushukai Gen. Hosp., Kasugai, Japan, 2004—. Scientific chmn. 5th Internat. Symposium Cardiac Pacing, Tokyo, 1976. Author: Cardiac Arrhythmias, Electrophysiologic Basis for Clinical Interpretation, 1977, Beyond Brain Death, 2000; co-author: International Textbook of Cardiology, 1986, Cardiac Electrophysiology, From Cell to Bedside, 1990; editor: Cardiac Pacing, 1977, Heart and Vessels, 1985-99. Recipient Kato Meml. prize Physiology and Medicine Kato Meml. Found., Tokyo, 1981. Fellow Am. Coll. Cardiology (co-dir. annual program on cardiac arrhythmias 1965-99), Heart Rhythm Soc. (mem. health policy com. 1997-2000); mem. Japanese Soc. Electrocardiology (hon., pres. 1989-90), Brit. Cardiovasc. Soc., Portuguese Soc. Cardiology (hon. mem.), Japanese Circulation Soc. (extraordinary mem.), Japanese Cardiac Arrhythmia Soc. (hon. mem.), Coun. Clin. Cardiology, Am. Heart Assn. (internat. fellow). Buddhist. Avocations: cello, astronomy, hiking. Home: 2-6-3 Kugenuma-Fujigaya Fujisawa 251 Japan Office: Nagoya Tokushukai Gen Hosp 2 28 1 Kozoji-cho Kasugai 487 0013 Japan Office Phone: 81-568-51-8711.

WATARI, JIRO, medical educator; b. Hokkaido, Japan, Nov. 17, 1960; s. Hiroshi and Umeko Watari; m. Hiroyo Asakawa, July 3, 1994; 1 child, Sayako. MD, Asahikawa Med. Coll., Japan, PhD, 1986. Lectr. Asahikawa Med. Coll., 2005—07; assoc. prof. Hyogo Coll. Medicine, 2009—. Recipient Shirakabe award; named Eminent Scientist of Yr., Internat. Rsch. Promotion Coun., 2011. Business E-Mail: watarij@hyo-med.ac.jp.

WATAYA-KANEDA, MARI, dermatologist, educator; b. Japan, Apr. 22, 1955; MD, Ehime U., 1980; PhD, Osaka U., 1985. Med. staff dermatology Mino-City Hosp., 1987—88; vis. asst. rsch. dermatologist dept. dermatology U. Calif., San Francisco, 1988—90; sr. resident dermatology Osaka U. Hosp., 1991—2006; vis. assoc. prof., rsch. fellow Dept. Dermatology, Grad. Sch. Medicine, Osaka U., 1991—2006, assoc. prof., 2007—. Bd. mem. Japanese Soc. von Recklinghausen Disease, 2009. Grants, Ministry of Edn., Culture, Sports, Sci. and Tech. Japan, Ministry of Health, Labor and Welfare Japan. Mem.: Japanese Soc. Japanese Soc. Human Genetics (specialist clin. genetics 2010), Japanese Soc. Investigative Dermatology (bd. mem. 2008), Japanese Soc. Dermatology (specialist dermatology 1988). Office: 2-2 Yamadaoka Suita Osaka 565-0871 Japan Office Fax: 81-6-6879-3039. Business E-Mail: mkaneda@derma.med.osaka-u.ac.jp.

WATCHKO, JON F., pediatrician, educator; MD, U. Pitts., 1980. Diplomate Am. Bd. Pediatrics, Am. Bd. Pediatrics-neonatal perinatal medicine, lic. Nat. Bd. of Med. Examiners. Resident Upstate Med. Ctr., Syracuse, NY, 1983; fellow Univ. of Wash., Seattle, 1986, hosp. affliation include/s Magee Womens Hosp. of UPMC, Children's Hosp. of Pitts. of UPMC, UPMC Mercy, prof. pediatrics and obstetrics gynecology reproductive sci. Univ. of Pitts., sr. scientist Magee-Womens rsch. inst. Co-author of numerous publications. Mem.: Am. Physiol. Soc., Soc. for Pediatric Rsch., Soc. for Pediatric Rsch., Midwest Soc. for Pediatric Rsch., Perinatal Rsch. Soc., Am. Pediatric Soc. Office: Magee-Womens Hospital of UPMC 300 Halket St Pittsburgh PA 15213 Office Phone: 412-641-1834. Office Fax: 412-641-5313. E-mail: jwatchko@mail.magee.edu.

WATERMAN, MICHAEL SPENCER, mathematics and biology professor; b. Coquille, Oreg., 1942; s. Ray S. and Bessie E. Waterman, m. Vicki Lynn Buss, 1962 (div. 1977); 1 child, Tracey Lynn BS, Oreg. State U., 1964, MS, 1966; MA, Mich. State U., 1968, PhD, 1969. Assoc. prof. Idaho State U., Pocatello, 1969-75; mem. staff Los Alamos Nat. Lab., 1975-82, cons., 1982—; prof. math. and biology U. So. Calif., LA, 1982—, U. So. Calif. Assocs. Endowed Chair, 1991—. Vis. prof. math. U. Hawaii, Honolulu, 1979-80; vis. prof. structural biology U. Calif., San Francisco, 1982; vis. prof. Mt. Sinai Med. Sch., NYC, 1988; 150th anniversary vis. prof. Chalmers U., 2000; Aisenstadt chair U. Montreal, 2001 Author: Introduction to Computational Biology, 1995; editor: Mathematical Methods for DNA Sequences, Calculating the Secrets of Life, 1995, Genetic Mapping and DNA Sequencing, 1996, Mathematical Support for Molecular Biology, 1999; Annals of Combinatories, Methodology and Computing in Applied Probability, Genomics, Computational Methods in Science and Technology, Acta Biochimica et Biophysica Sinca; editor-in-chief: Jour. Computational Biology; contbr. articles to profl. jours. Recipient Gardner Found. Internat. award, 2002; grantee, NSF, 1971, 1972, 1975, 1988—, Los Alamos Nat. Lab., 1976, 1981, Sys. Devel. Found., 1982—87, NIH, 1986—99, Sloan Found., 1990—91; fellow, Guggenheim Found., 1995. Fellow AAAS, Am. Acad. Arts and Scis., Inst. Math. Stats.; mem. NAS, French Acad. Sci., Am. Statis. Assn., Soc. Math. Biology, Soc. Indsl. and Applied Math. Office: U So Calif Dept Biol Sci Los Angeles CA 90089-1340 *

WATERS, PAUL F., thoracic surgeon; MD, U. Toronto, 1974. Diplomate Am. Bd. Surgery, 2004, Am. Bd. Surgery-gen. surgery, Am. Bd. Thoracic Surgery. Resident gen. surgery Univ. of Toronto Med. Ctr., Canada, 1975—79, resident thoracic surgery, 1979—80; fellow esophageal surgery Univ. of Chgo. Med. Ctr., Chgo., 1980—81; med. staff Greenwich Hosp., Conn. Office: Greenwich Hospital 77 Lafayette Pl Ste 302 Greenwich CT 06830 Office Phone: 203-863-4341. Office Fax: 203-863-4249.

WATERSTON, ROBERT HUGH, medical educator, researcher, medical geneticist, department chairman; b. Detroit, Sept. 17, 1943; BSE, Princeton U., NJ, 1965; PhD, MD, U.Chgo., 1972. Postdoctoral fellow divsn. cell biology MRC Lab Molecular Biology, Cambridge, England, 1972—74; intern in pediatric medicine Children's Hosp. Med. Ctr., Boston, 1974—75; postdoctoral fellow divsn. cell biology MRC Lab Molecular Biology, Cambridge, England, 1975—76; asst. prof. dept. anatomy and neurobiology Washington U., St. Louis, 1976—89; asst. prof. genetics Washington U. Sch. Medicine, St. Louis, 1980—81, assoc. prof. genetics, 1981—87, prof. genetics, 1987—91, prof. and acting head dept. genetics, 1991—93, James S. McDonnell prof. and chmn. dept. genetics, 1993—2003, head, dept. genetics Seattle, dir., Genome Sequencing Ctr., chmn. dept. genome sci., 2002—, William B. Gates III endowed chair biomed. scis., 2003—. Founder Genome Sequencing Ctr., St. Louis; ad hoc mem. Molecular Cytology Study Sect., 1977, 83; regular mem. Molecular Cytology Study Sect., NIH, 1987—88, chmn., 1989—91; mem. NIH, 1985—86, mem. adv. coun., chmn. Molecular Cytology Study Sect., mem. nat. adv. coun. for human genome rsch., 1998—2002; mem. fellowship rev. subcom. Molecular Dystrophy Assn., 1982—87, mem task force on genetics, 1983; mem. organizing com. Fourth Internat. C. elegans Meeting, Cold Spring Habor, NY, 1985. Contbr. over 80 articles to profl. jours.; mem. editl. bd. Jour. Cell Biology, 1988—91. Recipient Beadle award, Gen. Soc. Am., Dan David Prize, Peter H. Raven Lifetime award, 2000, Gairdner Found. Internat. award, 2002, Alfred P. Sloan, Jr. prize, GM Cancer Rsch. Found., 2003, Genetics prize, Peter Gruber Found., 2005; named NIH predoctoral trainee, 1968—71, Am. Heart Assn. Established Investigator, 1980—85; grantee, NIH, 1997—99, 1998—2001, Merck & Co., 1994—99; fellow Am. Cancer Soc. (postdoctoral), 1972—74, Muscular Dystrophy Assn. (postdoctoral), 1975—76, John Simon Guggenheim, 1985—86. Fellow: Am. Acad. Arts & Sciences; mem.: NAS (coun. mem. Inst. Medicine 2006—), Am. Soc. Cell Biology: STS, Genetics Soc., Alpha Omega Alpha, Sigma Xi. Office: U Wash 1705 NE Pacific St HSB-K357 Seattle WA 98195-7730 Office Phone: 206-685-7347. Business E-Mail: waterston@gs.washington.edu. *

WATHEN, CHRISTOPHER G., physician; b. Bebington, Cheshire, Eng., Aug. 11, 1955; s. John R. and Cicely W. BSc with honors, Edinburgh U., Scotland, 1976, MBChB with honors, 1979, MD, 1980. Intern Hammersmith Hosp., London, 1981-82; lectr. in medicine Royal Infirmary, Edinburgh, 1982-89; sr. registrar City Hosp., No. Gen. Hosp., Royal Infirmary, Edinburgh, 1989-91; lectr. in medicine Royal Infirmary, Edinburgh, 1990-91; cons. physician Wycombe Hosp., High Wycombe, England, 1991—, Stoke Mandeville Hosp., England, 2000—. Mem. edn. com. Nat. Asthma Campaign, London, 1992—; sr. lectr. U. Oxford. Contbr. numerous articles to profl. jours. Fellow Royal Coll. Physicians Edinburgh, Royal Coll. Physicians London; mem. Brit. Thoracic Soc., Am. Thoracic Soc., Am. Heart Assn. Office: Buckinghamshire Healthcare NHS Trust Queen Alexandra Rd High Wycombe HP11 2TT England

WATKINS, CAROLE S., human resources specialist, medical products executive; b. 1960; BS in Bus., Franklin U., Columbus, Ohio, 1983. With O.M. Scott & Sons, Lazarus, Huntington Banks, Ltd. Brands, Columbus, Ohio, 1989—96; v.p. human resources pharm. distbn. Cardinal Health, Inc., 1996—2000, sr. v.p. pharm. distbn. and provider svcs., 1999, exec. v.p. human resources, 2000, chief human resources officer, 2000— . Bd. pres. Action for Children, Ohio. Office: Cardinal Health 7000 Cardinal Pl Dublin OH 43017 *

WATKINS, CHARLES REYNOLDS, medical equipment company executive; b. San Diego, Oct. 28, 1951; s. Charles R. and Edith A. (Muff) W.; children: Charles Devin, Gregory Michael, Joshua Thomas. BS, Lewis and Clark Coll., 1974; postgrad., U. Portland, 1976. Internat. salesman Hyster Co., Portland, Oreg., 1975-80, Hinds Internat. Corp., Portland, 1980-83; mgr. internat. sales Wade Mfg. Co., Tualatin, Oreg., 1983-84; regional sales mgr. U.S. Surg., Inc., Norwalk, Conn., 1984-86; nat. sales mgr. NeuroCom Internat., Inc., Clackamas, Oreg., 1986-87; pres. Wave Form Systems, Inc., Portland, 1987-98; pres., dir. Wave Form Mfg., Inc., Portland, 1998—2007; prin. Wave Form Lithotripsy LLC, Portland, 1998—, Cryo Ptnrs., LLC, Portland, 2003—; pres., CEO Wave Form Guild, Inc., Columbus, Ohio, 2011—. Bd. dirs. Portland World Affairs Coun., 1980. Mem. Am. Soc. Laser Medicine and Surgery, Am. Assn. Gynecol. Laparoscopists, Ind. Med. Distbrs. Assn., Portland City Club. Republican. Avocations: flying, photography, travel. Office: Wave Form Sys Inc PO Box 3195 Portland OR 97208-3195 Office Phone: 503-626-2100. Business E-Mail: chuckw@waveformsys.com.

WATKINS, DEBORAH KAREN, epidemiology investigator, educator; b. Mt. Pleasant, Pa., Sept. 10, 1950; d. Thomas Earl and Berniece Helen (Kapelewski) W. AB, George Washington U., 1972; MS, Georgetown U., 1990. Production editor Am. Pub. Health Assn., Washington, 1972-79; exec. dir. Soc. for Occupational and Eviron. Health, Washington, 1979-81; dir. legis. affairs Pa. Environ. Coun., Phila., 1982-83; rsch. asst. prof. dept. family medicine Georgetown U., Washington, 1983—2002, dep. dir. divsn. occupl. health studies, 1990—2002; mng. scientist Exponent, Inc., Washington, 2004—06; owner Watkins Consulting, Arlington, Va., 2007—. Adj. asst. prof. Georgetown U., Washington, 2002—. Mem. Soc. Occupl. and Eviron. Health (gov. coun. 1987-93), Soc. Epidemiologic Rsch., Soc. Profl. Journalists. Avocations: British history, needlepoint. Office: Watkins Consulting 4831 N 9th St Arlington VA 22203 Business E-Mail: dwatkins@ginevan.com.

WATKINS, JEFFREY CLIFTON, neuroscientist; b. Perth, Australia, Dec. 20, 1929; s. Colin Hereward and Amelia Miriam (Smith) W.; m. Beatrice Joan Thacher, Apr. 5, 1973; children: Timothy Douglas, Katherine Helen. BS, U. Western Australia, Perth, 1949, BS with honors, 1950, MS, 1954; PhD, U. Cambridge, Eng., 1954. Rsch. fellow chemistry U. Cambridge, 1954-55, Yale U., New Haven, 1955-57; rsch. fellow in physiology Australian Nat. U., Canberra, 1958-61, fellow, 1961-65; vis. rsch. scientist Agrl. Rsch. Coun., Inst. Animal Physiology, Babraham, England, 1963—64, sci. officer, 1965-67; sci. staff mem. neuropsychiatry unit Med. Rsch. Coun., Carshalton, Surrey, England, 1968-73; sr. rsch. fellow in physiology/pharmacology U. Bristol, England, 1973-83, hon. sr. rsch. fellow in pharmacology, 1983-89, hon. prof. pharmacology, 1989-99, prof. emeritus, 1999—. Cons. Sandoz Pharma, Berne, Switzerland, 1983-94, Tocris Neuramin Ltd., Bristol, 1985-94, dir., 1992-94; cons. and dir. Tocris-Cookson Ltd., Bristol, 1994—2006. Co-editor: The NMDA Receptor, 1989, 2d edit. 1994; contbr. articles to profl. jours.; patentee in field. Recipient Wakeman Found. award, 1992, Charles A. Dana Found. award, 1994, Bristol-Myers Squibb award, 1995, Thudichum medal Brit. Biochem. Soc., 2000. Fellow Royal Soc. London, Inst. Biology London, Acad. Med. Sci. London, Brit. Pharm. Soc. (hon., Wellcome Gold medal 2001); mem. Brit. Physiol. Soc., Academia Europaea. E-mail: jeffwatkins@onetel.com.

WATKINS, JOAN MARIE, osteopath, physician; b. Anderson, Ind., Mar. 9, 1943; d. Curtis David and Dorothy Ruth (Beckett) W.; m. Stanley G. Nodvik, Dec. 25, 1969 (div. Apr. 1974). BS, West Liberty State Coll., 1965; Cert. of Grad. Phys. Therapy, Ohio State U., 1966; DO, Phila. Coll. Osteo., 1972; M of Health Professions Edn., U. Ill., Chgo., 1986; MPH, U. Ill., 1989. Diplomate Osteo. Nat. Bds., Am. Bd. Preventive Medicine, Am. Bd. Occupl. and Environ. Medicine, Am. Bd. Emergency Medicine. Resident in phys. medicine and rehab. U. Pa., 1973—74; emergency osteo. physician Cooper Med. Ctr., Camden, 1974-79, Shore Meml. Hosp., Somers Point, NJ, 1979-81, St. Francis Hosp., Blue Island, Ill., 1981-82, Mercy Hosp. and Med. Ctr., Chgo., 1982-90, dir. emergency ctr., 1984-88; resident in occupl. and preventive medicine U. Ill., 1988-90; corp. med. dir. occupl. health svc. Univ. Cmty. Hosp., Tampa, 1992—2006; assoc. prof. environ. & occupl. health Coll. Pub. Health, USF; cons. in field, 2006—; with Tampa Occupl. Health Svcs. Fellow Am. Coll. Occupl. and Environ. Medicine, Am. Soc. Preventive Medicine, Fla. Assn. Occupl. and Environ. Medicine (pres. 1999-2001). Avocations: sailing, needlecrafts, swimming. Home: 4306 Harbor House Dr Tampa FL 33615-5408 Office: 2919 Swann Ave 102 Tampa FL 33609 Office Phone: 813-414-9400. Business E-Mail: ywatkin9@tampabay.rr.com, jwatkins@health.usf.edu.

WATKINS, PAUL B., academic administrator, medical educator; b. Schenectady, NY, Feb. 17, 1953; s. George Daniels and Carolyn Lenore (Nevin) W.; m. Joanne Carol Spalty, July 4, 1981; children: Andrew James, Melanie Ann. BA, Cornell U., 1975; MD, Cornell Med. Sch., 1979. Intern NY Hosp.-Cornell Med. Ctr., 1979-80, resident, 1980-82; fellow Med. Coll. Va., 1982-84, from instr. to asst. prof., 1984-86; physician admission ward Khao-I-Dang Cambodian Refuge Camp, Thailand, 1982; asst. prof. U. Mich., Ann Arbor, 1986-91, assoc. prof. medicine, 1991-97, prof. medicine, 1997-99, prof. pharmacology, 1997—99, assoc. dir., Gen. Clin. Rsch. Ctr., 1991, dir., Gen. Clin. Rsch. Ctr., 1992—99; Verne S. Caviness Disting. prof. medicine U. NC, Chapel Hill, 1999—, prof. pharmacotherapy, 1999—, prof. toxicology, prof. exptl. therapeutics; dir., Gen. Clin. Rsch. Ctr. U. NC Hospitals, 1999—; dir., Inst. for Drug Safety Sciences Hamner Inst. and U. NC, Rsch. Triangle Park, 2009—. Advisor toxic waste orgn. Inst. Medicine, Washington, 1993-96; mem. toxicology study sect. NIH, Bethesda, Md., 1992-96; mem. steering com. for the Pharmacogenetics Network, Nat. Inst. Gen. Med. Sciences; steering com. chair, Drug Induced Liver Injury Network; sci. cons. Parke-Davis Pharm., Organon Internat., Wyeth-Ayerst, Proctor and Gamble, Abbott Labs., Bristol-Meyers Squibb, Severe Adverse Events Consortium, Preclinical Safety Testing Consortium; FDA cons., 1997—. Contbr. articles to profl. jours. Mem. St. Andrews Ch., Ann Arbor, 1990—. Recipient VA Career Devel. Associate Investigator award, 1984-86, Rsch. Assoc. award, 1987-91, Annual Therapeutic Frontiers' award Am. Coll. Clin. Pharmacy, 1998, NIH Merit award, 1998. Fellow ACP; mem. AAAS, Am. Soc. Clin. Investigation (elected), Am. Assn. Study Liver Disease, Am. Gastroent. Assn., Am. Fedn. Clin. Rsch., Midwest Gut Club, Ctrl. Soc. Clin. Rsch., Internat. Assn. Study Liver, Internat. Soc. Study Xenobiotics. Avocations: jogging, skiing, wind surfing, tennis, scuba diving. Home: 116 Carolina Ave Chapel Hill NC 27514-3200 Office: U NC 3312 Kerr Hall CB#7360 Chapel Hill NC 27599-7360 Address: Hamner Inst for Health Sciences 6 Davis Dr PO Box 12137 Research Triangle Park NC 27709-2137 Office Phone: 919-966-1435. Business E-Mail: pbwatkins@med.unc.edu.

WATNICK, TERRY J., medical educator; b. Newark, Jan. 8, 1959; BSc, Brown U., 1981; MD, Yale Sch. Medicine, 1987. Assoc. prof. Johns Hopkins Sch. Medicine, 1996—. Med. adv. bd. Md. Kidney Found., 2002—11; sci. adv. bd. Polycystic Kidney Disease Found., 2006—11. Mem.: Am. Assn. Nephrology. Home: 855 N Wolfe St Rangos Bldg Baltimore MD 21205 Home Fax: 443-287-7679. Business E-Mail: twatnick@jhmi.edu.

WATSCHINGER, KATRIN, research scientist; b. San Candido, Italy, Mar. 17, 1979; Mag. rer. nat., Innsbruck U., 2004; PhD, Innsbruck Med. U., 2007. Postdoc. fellow Innsbruck U., 2004—07, Innsbruck Med. U., 2007—. Recipient prize, Sanofi-Aventis Austria, 2010. Mem.: Internat. Soc. Pteridinology (Blair-Curtius-Pfleiderer-Wachter award). Avocations: reading, travel, dance. Office: Fritz-Preglstr 3 Innsbruck 6020 Austria Business E-Mail: katrin.watschinger@i-med.ac.at.

WATSON, ANTHONY L. (TONY), health facility executive; b. Okla., 1942; m. Desiree Boiling Boiling; children: Alayja Boiling, Sheridan Boiling. Attended, U. Okla., 1959, Columbia U.; advance cert., U. Pa., Cornell U.; BA in Polit. Sci., Ctrl. State Coll., Okla., 1966; LHD (hon.), NY Coll. of Podiatric Medicine. Supervising pub. health advisor dept. health edn. and welfare Ctr. for Disease Control, Pub. Health Svc., 1966-70; dep. dir. Comprehensive Health Planning Agy., NYC, 1970-76; exec. dir. Health Planning, NYC, 1976—85; exec. v.p., COO HIP Health Plan of NY, NYC, 1985—91, chmn., CEO, 1991—, Emblem Health, Inc. (parent co. of HIP Health Plan (HIP) and Group Health, Inc. (GHI)), 2006—. Instr. health planning Herbert J. Lehman Coll. of the City of New York, 1972—74; mem. Nat. Bipartisan Commn. on the Future of Medicare, 1999; chmn. bd. dirs. centralized lab. svcs. HIP Health Plan; chmn. bd. dirs. HIP Health Plan of NJ, 1995—99, HIP Health Plan of Fla., HIP Health Plan Pa.; bd. dirs. HIP Health Plan of NY; dir. Sierra Health Services, Inc., 2000—, America's Health Ins. Plans; bd. dirs. Emblem Health. Co-author of several academic publications. Pres., chmn. HIP Found.; mem. Cmty. Coun. Greater NY; dir. Alliance For Downtown NY, NYC 2012, Inc.; mem. NY Hosp. NY Review and Planning Coun., Gov.'s Health Care Adv. Bd., Econ. Panel of NY Governor's Coun. on Fiscal and Econ. Priorities, Borough Pres.'s Health Adv. Coun., Nat. Conf. of Christians and Jews, YMCA of NY, NYC Partnership; dir. Money Store, Inc., 1991. Recipient Schlesinger award for outstanding contributions to Cmty. Health Planning, John Lawe Meml. award, Leadership award of the One Hundred Black Men, Inc., Award of the Jewish Nat. Fund, Congl. Recognition award of the US House of Representatives, NY Urban League award, Norman Vincent Peale award for Positive Thinking, Blanton-Peale Inst. Fellow NY Acad. of Medicine; mem. American Health Planning Assn., American Hosp. Assn., American Assn. of Health Plans (chmn. 2000-01) Office: HIP Health Plan of NY 55 Water St New York NY 10041 *

WATSON, DONALD CHARLES, JR., cardiothoracic surgeon, educator; b. Fairfield, Ohio, Mar. 15, 1945; s. Donald Charles and Pricilla H. Watson; m. Susan Robertson Prince, June 23, 1973; children: Kea Huntington, Katherine Anne, Kirsten Prince. BA in Applied Sci., Lehigh U., 1968, BSME, 1969; MSME, Stanford U., 1969; MD, Duke U., 1972; MBA, Vanderbilt U., 1992. Diplomate Am. Bd. Thoracic Surgery, Am. Bd. Surgery. Intern Stanford U. Med. Ctr., Calif., 1972-73, resident in cardiovasc. surgery Calif., 1973-74, resident in surgery Calif., 1976-78, chief resident in heart transplant Calif., 1978-79, chief resident in cardiovasc. and gen. surgery Calif., 1978-80; clin. assoc. surgery br. Nat. Heart and Lung Inst., 1974-76, acting sr. surgeon, 1976; assoc. cardiovasc. surgeon dept. child health and devel. George Washington U., Washington, 1980-84, asst. prof. surgery, asst. prof. child health and devel., 1980-84, attending cardiovasc. surgeon dept. child health and devel., 1984-89, assoc. prof. surgery, 1984-89; assoc. prof. pediats. U. Tenn.-Memphis, 1984-90, prof. surgery, 1990—2006, prof. pediats., 1990—2006, chmn. cardiothoracic surgery, 1984-99, assoc. chief med. officer, 1999—2001. Mem. staff Le Bonheur Children's Med. Ctr., Memphis, 1984—2006, chmn. cardiothoracic surgery, 1984-99; cons. in field; instr. advanced trauma life support; profl. cons., program reviewer HHS. Contbr. chpts., numerous articles, revs. to profl. publs. Bd. dirs. Airlift Hope Am., Internat. Children's Heart Found., Child Health Alliance Mid-South. Served to lt. comdr. USPHS, 1974-76. Smith Kline & French fellow Lehigh U., 1967; NSF fellow Lehigh U., 1968; univ. interdepartmental scholar and univ. scholar Lehigh U., 1968. Fellow Am. Coll. Cardiology, ACS; mem. Am. Assn. Thoracic Surgery, Soc. Thoracic Surgeons, So. Thoracic Surg. Assn., Andrew G. Morrow Soc., Norman E. Shumway Soc. (multiple bd. dirs.), NIH Alumni Assn., Stanford U. Med. Alumni Assn., Stanford U. Alumni Assn., Lehigh U. Alumni Assn., Smithsonian Assocs., U. Tenn. Pres.'s Club, LeBonheur Pres's Club, Pilots Internat. Assn., Nat. Assn. Flight Instrs., Aircraft Owners and Pilots Assn., Biltmore Forest Country Club, Phi Beta Kappa, Tau Beta Pi, Pi Tau Sigma, Phi Gamma Delta. Republican. Presbyterian. Achievements include established a regional referral center for the treatment of congenital heart disease. Avocations: golf, sailing, mountain climbing, flying.

WATSON, JAMES DEWEY, retired molecular biologist; b. Chgo., Apr. 6, 1928; s. James Dewey and Jean (Mitchell) W.; m. Elizabeth Lewis, 1968; children: Rufus Robert, Duncan James. BS in Zoology, U. Chgo., 1947; PhD in Zoology, Ind. U., 1950; DSc (hon.), U. Chgo., 1961, Ind. U., 1963; LLD (hon.), U. Notre Dame, 1965; DSc (hon.), L.I. U., 1970, Adelphi U., 1972, Brandeis U., 1973, Albert Einstein Coll. Medicine, 1979, Hofstra U., 1976, Harvard U., 1978, Rockefeller U., 1980, Clarkson Coll., 1981, SUNY, 1983, Rutgers U., 1988, Bard Coll., 1991, U. Cambridge, 1993, Fairfield U., 1993, U. Stellenbosch, 1993, U. Oxford, Washington Coll., 1999, U. Judaism, 1999, U. Coll. London, 2000, Ill. Wesleyan U., 2000, Widener U., 2001, Dartmouth, 2001, Trinity Coll., Dublin, 2001; MD (hon.), U. Buenos Aires, Argentina, 1986, Charles Univ., Prague, 1998. Rsch. fellow NRC, U. Copenhagen, 1950-51; Nat. Found. Infantile Paralysis fellow Cavendish Lab., Cambridge U., 1951-52, 55-56; sr. rsch. fellow biology Calif. Inst. Tech., 1953-55; asst. prof. biology Harvard U., 1955-58, assoc. prof., 1958-61, prof., 1961-76; dir. Cold Spring Harbor Lab., Watson Sch. Biol. Sci., NY, 1968—94, pres. NY, 1994—2004, chancellor NY, 2004—07; assoc. dir. Nat. Ctr. for Human Genome Rsch., NIH, 1988-89, dir. Nat. Ctr. for Human Genome Rsch., 1989-92. Newton-Abraham vis. prof. Oxford U., 1994; inst. advisor Allen Inst. for Brain Sci., Seattle, Washington. Author: Molecular Biology of the Gene, 1965, 4th edit., 1986, The Double Helix, 1968, (with John Tooze) The DNA Story, 1981, (with others) The Molecular Biology of the Cell, 1983, 2nd edit., 1989, 3rd edit. 1994, (with John Tooze and David Kurtz) Recombinant DNA, A Short Course, 1983, 2nd edit., 1992, A Passion for DNA, 2000, Genes, Girls and Gamow, 2001, DNA: The Secret of Life, 2003, Avoid Boring People: Lessons From a Life in Science, 2007 Named Hon. fellow Clare Coll., Cambridge U., Hon. Knight of Brit. Empire, 2002; recipient (with F.H.C. Crick) John Collins Warren prize Mass. Gen. Hosp., 1959, Eli Lilly award in biochemistry American Chem. Soc., 1959, Albert Lasker prize American Pub. Health Assn., 1960, (with F.H.C. Crick) Rsch. Corp. prize, 1962, (with F.H.C. Crick and M.H.F. Wilkins), Nobel Prize in Medicine, 1962, Presdl. Medal of Freedom, 1977, Kaul Found. award for Excellence, 1993, Nat. Biotech. Venture award, 1993, Copley Medal, 1993, Charles A. Dana award, 1994, Lomonosov medal Russian Acad. Sci., 1995, Nat. Medal of Sci., 1997, Liberty medal City of Phila., 2000, Benjamin Franklin medal for Disting. Achievement in Sciences American Philos. Soc., 2001, Gairdner Found. award for Merit, 2002, Lotos Club Medal of Merit, 2004. Mem. NAS (Carty medal 1971), Am. Philos. Soc., Am. Assn. Cancer Rsch., Am. Acad. Arts and Scis., Am. Soc. Biol. Chemistry, Royal Soc. (London), Acad. Scis. Russia, Danish Acad. Arts and Scis. Achievements include co-discovery of Double-Helix DNA; has become the first person to receive his own personal genome map in 2007. *

WATSON, KAROL ELIZABETH, internist, educator; b. Gary, Ind., Dec. 15, 1963; MD, Harvard Med. Sch., 1989. Cert. Am. Bd. Internal Medicine, 1993, Am. Bd. Internal Medicine, Cardiovascular Disease, 2004. Intern, internal medicine UCLA Sch. Medicine, 1990—91, resident, internal medicine, 1991—92, fellow, cardiology, 1992—97, assoc. prof. medicine; dir., Cholesterol and Lipid Mgmt. Ctr. UCLA CHAMP (Cholesterol, Hypertension, and Atherosclerosis Mgmt. Program); physician, medicine, endocrinology, diabetes and hypertension Gonda Diabetes Ctr. Office: UCLA Med-Cardio Mail Code 167917 Dept Code 1553 Box 951679 BH-307 CHS Los Angeles CA 90095-1679 Office Phone: 310-794-7121. Office Fax: 310-206-9133. Business E-Mail: kwatson@med.net.ucla.edu.

WATSON, LISA A., minister; b. Murfreesboro, Tenn., Sept. 25, 1963; BA, U. Dubuque, 1996; MDiv, U. Dubuque Theol. Sem., 1998. Staff chaplain Regions Hosp., 2001—. Mem.: Assn. Profl. Chaplains. Presbyterian. Office: 640 Jackson St MS 11102J Saint Paul MN 55101 Business E-Mail: lisa.a.watson@healthpartners.com.

WATSON, MICHAEL S., medical geneticist, educator; BS, Am. U., Washington DC; MS in Med. Genetics, U. Ala., PhD in Physiology & Biophysics. Cert. Am. Bd. Med. Genetics. Exec. dir. Am. Coll. Med. Genetics; dir. clinical & molecular cytogenetics Wash. U., 1986—2000, adj. prof. pediatrics St. Louis. Office: 9650 Rockville Pike Bethesda MD 20814-3998 E-mail: mwatson@acmg.net.

WATSON, PETER GORDON, ophthalmologist, surgeon; b. Newport, Eng., Apr. 30, 1930; s. Ralph and Renée Watson; m. Ann Wollaston Macintosh, Aug. 6, 1953; children: Andrew, James, Louisa, Hamish, Elizabeth. MA, Queens Coll., 1956; MB, BChir, U. Cambridge, Eng., 1956. Cons. opthalmic surgeon Addenbrookes Hosp., Cambridge, 1965—95, Moorfields Eye Hosp., London, 1970—95; boerheave prof. U. Leiden, Netherlands, 2000—05. Chmn. examinations com. Internat. Coun. Ophthalmology, 1994—2008. Author: Metabolic Integrations, 1956, 2d edit., 1959, Sclera and Systemic Disease, 1977, 2d edit., 2004, Atlas Sclera & Disease, 1992. 2d lt. Royal Arty., 1948—50. Fellow: Royal Coll. Surgeons, Royal Coll. Ophthalmology (hon.; sr. v.p. 1994—95); mem.: Academia Ophthalmologica Internationalis (pres.), Soc. Apothacaries (liveryman). Avocations: sailing, painting. Home and Office: 11 Perry Ct Clerk Maxwell Rd CB3 0RS Cambridge England Office Phone: 44 1223 353789.

WATSON, RALPH EDWARD, internist, educator; b. Cin., Apr. 4, 1948; s. John Sherman and Evelyn (Moore) W.; m. Demetria Rencher, Sept. 9, 1972; children: Ralph Edward, Monifa. BS, Xavier U., 1970; MD, Mich. State U., East Lansing, 1976. Diplomate Am. Bd. Internal Medicine; cert. clin. hypertension specialist. Intern U. Cin. Med. Ctr., 1976-77, resident in internal medicine, 1977-79, asst. clin. prof. internal medicine, 1980-88; asst. prof. internal medicine Mich. State U., East Lansing, 1988-94, assoc. prof., 1994—. Attending physician in hypertension clinic Mich. State U., 1988-91, assoc. dir. hypertension clinic, 1991-94, dir. hypertension clinic, 1995—, program dir. transitional yr. residency, 1990-96, assoc. program dir. internal medicine residency, 1996-2003; mem. U.S. HHS Office Minority Health Resource Person Network. Fellow ACP, Internat. Soc. Hypertension in Blacks, Am Assn. Black Cardiologists; mem. Nat. Med. Assn., Am. Soc. Internal Medicine, Lansing Area Am. Heart Assn., Am. Black Cardiologists (chair rsch. com.), Am. Soc. Hypertension, Xavier U. Alumni Assn., Alpha Omega Alpha. Office: Mich State U 338B Clinical Ctr East Lansing MI 48824-1313 Office Phone: 517-353-4811.

WATSON, RICHARD A., surgeon, director; b. Yonkers, NY, Feb. 17, 1942; BA, NYU, 1964; MD, Georgetown Sch. Medicine, 1968. Prof. surgery UMDNJ NJ Sch. Medicine, 1995; dir., residency edn. urology Hackensack U. Med. Ctr., 2002—. Col. US Army, 1966—93. Decorated Superior Svc. award Dept. of Def., Legion of merit US Army. Fellow: ACS; mem.: Assn. Mil. Surgeons, Cath. Med. Assn., Alpha Omega Alpha Soc. Home: 360 Essex St Ste 403 Hackensack NJ 07601 Home Fax: 201-336-8221. Personal E-mail: rwatson@aol.com.

WATSON, RITA MARIE, cardiologist; b. Omaha, Nebr., Dec. 11, 1945; BA, U. Nebr.; MD, Harvard U., 1976. Diplomate Am. Bd. Internal Medicine, Nat. Bd. Medical Examiners, Am. Bd. Cardiovascular Disease, Cert. Bd. Nuclear Cardiology. Intern U. Pa. Hosp., Phila., 1976-77, resident, 1977-79; fellow in cardiovascular diseases NIH, Bethesda, Md., 1979-81; prof. medicine Grad. Sch. Medicine Seton Hall U., South Orange, NJ, 1993—; ptnr. Monmouth Cardiology Associates, LLC, Long Branch. Pvt. practice Cardiovascular Diseases, Elizabeth, N.J., 1988—; hosp. appt. St. Elizabeth Hosp., Elizabeth. Fellow Internat. Andrea Gruentzig Soc., Soc. Cardiac Angiography and Interventions (exec. officer), Am. Coll. Cardiology. Office: Monmouth Cardiology Associates LLC 215 Brighton Ave Long Branch NJ 07740 Office Phone: 732-222-5143. Office Fax: 732-222-4862.

WATSON, ROBERT JOE, retired health facility administrator, retired career officer; b. Wellington, Kans., Nov. 12, 1934; s. Charles Bruce and Marguerite B. (Scholes) W.; m. Ursula Eschenroeder, Dec. 26, 1983; children: Stephanie Watson-Zollinger, Stacy Watson Bruce, Susannah Watson Gold; stepchildren: Jurgen Wanke, Claudia Beeck. MS in Edn., Kans. State Tchrs. Coll., 1963; MBA, U. Hawaii, 1969; MHA, George Washington U., 1973, EdD, 1976; student, Command-Gen. Staff Coll., 1973, U.S. Army War Coll., 1986. Commd. 2nd lt. U.S. Army, 1963, advanced through grades to col., 1989; stationed at Tripler Army Med. Ctr., Honolulu, 1967-69, USARV Surgeons Office, Long Binh, Vietnam, 1969-70, Surgeon Gen.'s Office, Washington, 1970-74, Walter Reed Med. Ctr., Washington, 1974-76, Acad. Health Svcs., Ft. Sam Houston, Tex., 1976—80, 68th Med. Group, Ziegenberg, Germany, 1980-82, U.S. Army Hosp., Ft. Riley, Kans., 1982-84, 34th Gen. Hosp., Augsburg, Germany, 1984-87; assoc. dean USA Med. Field Svc. Sch., Ft. Sam Houston, Tex., 1987—89; assoc. dir. Student Health Ctr. U. Fla., Gainesville, 1989—2005; ret., 2005. Fellow Am. Coll. Healthcare Execs. (adv., regent 1982-84). Episcopalian. Avocations: tennis, golf, gardening.

WATSON, S. MICHELE, nursing educator; b. Selma, Ala., Apr. 21, 1965; d. Kenneth and Linda (Bishop) Wilds; m. H. Alan Watson, May 30, 1987. AAS, Cleveland State Community Coll, Tenn., 1987, AS, 1985. RN, Tenn. ICU staff Meml. Hosp., 1987-88; emergency rm. staff Cleveland (Tenn.) Cmty. Hosp., 1988; team leader Bradley Meml. Home Health, Cleveland, 1988-2001; sch. nurse Cleveland City Schs., 2001—06; nurse St. Mary's Hosp., 2006—; health sci. tcr. Spring Hill HS, 2010—. Home: PO Box 7416 Columbia TN 38401 also: PO Box 746 Columbia TN 38402-0746 Office Phone: 423-907-1200. Personal E-mail: watson.michele@yahoo.com.

WATSON, SHARON GITIN, psychologist; b. NYC, Oct. 21, 1943; d. Louis Leonard and Miriam (Myers) Gitin; m. Eric Watson, Oct. 31, 1969; 1 child, Carrie Dunbar. BA cum laude, Cornell U., 1965; MA, U. Ill., 1968, PhD, 1971. Cert. psychologist Calif. Psychologist City NY Prison Mental Health, Riker's Island, 1973-74, Youth Svcs. Ctr., LA County Dept. Pub. Social Svcs., 1975-77, dir. clin. svcs., 1978, dir., 1978-80; exec. dir. Crittenton Ctr. for Young Women and Infants, LA, 1980-89, Assn. Children's Svcs. Agys. So. Calif., LA, 1989—92, LA County Children's Planning Coun., 1992—99; cons. LA County Chief Exec. Office, 2001—04, Edn. Coordinating Coun., 2004—; mem. LA City Commn. for Children, Youth and Their Families, 2000—06, LA County Children's Planning Coun., 2001—08. Mem. LA delegation Pres.'s Summit for Am.'s Future, 1997. Mem. Commn. for Children's Svcs. Family Preservation and Family Support Policy

Com., 1989—99, Interagy. Coun. Child Abuse and Neglect Policy Com., 1993—99, Mayor's Com. on Children, Youth and Families, 1993—95; bd. dirs. Adolescent Pregnancy Childwatch, 1985—89, LA Ednl. Partnership, 1999—2003, LISC Health Sector, 1996—99, LA Roundtable for Children, 1988—94; trustee LA Ednl. Alliance for Restructuring Now, 1992—99. Recipient award honoree, LA County Children's Planning Coun. 'Improving Children's Lives', 2001, LA County Bd. of Supervisors, Foster Care Hero, 2010. Mem.: Assn. Children's Svcs. Agys. So. Calif. (sec. 1981—83, pres. elect 1983—84, pres. 1984—85), Calif. Assn. Svcs. for Children (sec.-treas. 1983—84, pres. elect 1985—86, pres. 1986—87), US Figure Skating (bd. dirs. 1992—2006, chmn. sanctions and eligibility 1993—96, membership com. 1996—99, strategic planning com. 2000—02, regional vice chmn. competitions com. 2000—02, sec. 2002—06, mem. exec. com. 2002—06, nat. competition judge: singles, pairs, and synchronized skating, nat. data/video operator, regional technical controller, regional referee), US Olympics Com. (Jr. Olympics com. 1998—2000), Pasadena Figure Skating Club (pres. 1985—87, 1989—90, bd. dirs. 1983—), So. Calif. Inter-Club Assn. of Figure Skating Clubs (vice chair 1989—91, chair 1991—93). Home and Office: 4056 Camino Real Los Angeles CA 90065-3928 Personal E-mail: sharonla12@aol.com.

WATSON, STANLEY ELLIS, clergyman, small business owner; b. New Orleans, July 25, 1957; s. Joseph and Dorothy (Jones) W. EdB, Jarvis Christian Coll., Hawkins, Tex., 1977; MRE, Tex. Christian U., Ft. Worth, 1979; spl. edn., So. U. A&M, Baton Rouge, 1986; grad., U.S. Acad. Pvt. Investigation, 1991; DD (hon.), Charter Ecumenical Ministries, 1994; student in Christian Counseling, Christian Bible Coll. and Sem., 2005—. Cert. tchr.; registered notary Mich.; lic. pvt. investigator, La. Asst. min. Jarvis Christian Coll., Hawkins, Tex., 1974-77; tchr. pub. sch., Daingerfield, Tex., 1977-78; sr. pastor Truevine Christian Ch., 1977—79; asst. min. Park Manor Christian Ch., Chgo., 1980-81; asst. mgr. K- Mart, Shreveport, La., 1981-82; min. United Christian Ch., Jackson, Miss., 1982-83; tchr. pub. sch., Napoleonville, La., 1986-87, Zachary, La., 1987-88; min. Vt. Christian Ch., Flint, Mich., 1988—92, sr. pastor, 1990; assoc. min. Buena Vista Bapt. Ch., St. James, La. Owner, mgr. Watson Diversified Fin. Co., 1989—, Watson Detective Agy., Donaldsonville, La., 1992—; v.p. DVY Sys., Inc., 1997—; CEO Watson and Julien Cmty. Mission, Inc., Donaldsonville, La.; clin. pastoral counseling, christian counseling, 2001.e Mem. NAACP, NEA. Recipient Presdl. citation Nat. Assn. for Equal Opportunity in Higher Edn.; Christian Women's fellow, 1975-77, St. Louis Bd. Edn. fellow, 1977-79, Tex. Christian U. Brite Div. Sch. scholar, 1977; Jarvis Christian Coll. cert. of Honor and Merit, 1974-77; named Rev. Stanley Watson Day City of Flint, Mich., 1989, Disting. Alumnus, Jarvis Christian Coll., 1995. Mem. Nat. Assn. Investigative Specialists, Am. Inst. Profl. Bookeepers, Am. Fin. Coord. Assn. (fin. coord.), Christian Counselors Assn., Nat. Assn. Investigative Specialist, Nat. Assn. Federated Tax Preparers, Am. Soc. Notaries, Aircraft Owners and Pilots Assn. Coun. for Exceptional Children, Forgotten Man Ministries, Jarvis Christian Coll. Alumni Assn. (v.p.), NAACP, Urban League of Flint, Urban Coalition of Greater Flint, Flint C. of C., Internat. Reading Assn., NEA, Am. Sailing Assn., Phi Beta Sigma, Kappa Delta Pi. Mem. Tex. Christian U. Alumni Assn. Democrat. Avocations: beekeeping, stamp collecting/philately. Home and Office: PO Box 668 Donaldsonville LA 70346-0668 Home Phone: 225-473-3364; Office Phone: 225-323-3025. Personal E-mail: jarvis19771@gmail.com, jarvis19771@yahoo.com, tcu1980@gmail.com.

WATTANAKRAI, KAMOL, plastic surgeon; b. Suphanburi, Thailand, Aug. 30, 1954; s. Heng Khiam and Payoong Lim; m. Penpun Wattanakrai, Mar. 25, 1993; 1 child, Pisacha. MD, Mahidol U., Bangkok, 1979. Dir. Bangkok Plastic Surgery Ctr., 1990—; head divsn. plastic surgery Bhumiboladulyadej Hosp., Royal Thai Air Force, Bangkok, 1997—2005, chmn. dept. surgery, 2005—. Organizing sec. 9th Internat. Congress Oriental Soc. Aesthetic Plastic Surgery, 2004. Group capt. Royal Thai Air Force, 1980—. Fellow: ACS; mem.: Soc. Plastic and Reconstructive Surgeons of Thailand (sec. 2005—), Soc. Aesthetic Plastic Surgeons of Thailand (sec. 2002—). Avocations: swimming, reading, travel, golf, dining. Office: Bangkok Plastic Surgery Ctr 1/16 Paholyothin Rd 10220 Bangkhen Bangkok Thailand Office Phone: (661) 8120565. Fax: (662) 5212236. Personal E-mail: kamolw@gmail.com. Business E-Mail: kamol@plasticsurgery.or.th.

WATTERS, ANN OLIVA, psychologist, educator; d. George Verdelli II and Dorothy Austin Oliva; m. Thomas A. Watters, Aug. 30, 1975; children: Andrew George, Michael Thomas. BA in English, U. Calif., Berkeley, 1974; MA in English Lit., Washington U., St. Louis, 1976; MA in Health Psychology, Calif. Sch. Profl. Psychology, 1997, PhD in Psychology, 1999. Emeritus lectr. rhetoric and English Stanford U., Calif., 1987—; pvt. practice clin. psychology San Mateo, Calif., 1999—; asst. clin. prof. psychiatry U. Calif., San Francisco, 2005—. Author, editor: Global Exchange: Reading/Writing in a World Context, 2005; co-author: Creating America: Reading & Writing Arguments, 4th edit., 2005, Writing for Change: A Community Reader. Former chair bd. dirs. San Mateo Med. Ctr. Found. Mem.: AAUP, APA, Calif. Psychol. Assn. Office Fax: 650-375-8398. Business E-Mail: watters@stanford.edu. *

WATTLEWORTH, ROBERTA ANN, physician; b. Sioux City, Iowa, Dec. 26, 1955; d. Roland Joseph and Elizabeth Ann (Ahart) Eickholt; m. John Wade Wattleworth, Nov. 7, 1984; children: Adam, Ashley. BS, Morningside Coll., Sioux City, 1978; D of Osteopathy, Coll. Osteo. Medicine/Surgery, Des Moines, 1981; M.Healthcare Administrn., U. Osteo. Med. and Health Scis., Des Moines, 1999; MPH, Des Moines U., 2004. Intern Richmond Heights (Ohio) Gen. Hosp., 1981-82, resident in anesthesiology, 1982-84; anesthesiologist Doctor's Gen. Hosp., Plantation, Fla., 1984-85; resident in family practice J.F. Kennedy Hosp., Stratford, NJ, 1985-87; educator family practice U. Osteo. Medicine and Health Scis., Des Moines, 1987-89; family practitioner McFarland Clinic, P.C., Jewell, Iowa, 1989-94; lectr. family practice Osteopath. Med. Ctr., Des Moines U., 1999—, prof., chair dept. family medicine, 2003—. Med. dir. nursing home Bethany Manor, Story City, Iowa, 1990-99, Jewell Vol. Fire and Rescue Squad, 1990-99. Bd. dirs. Heartland Sr. Svcs., 1995—99, Iowa Rural Health Assn. Named Nat. Outstanding Osteo. Educator of Yr., Nat. Student Osteo. Med. Assn., 2001—02, Inaugural fellow, Nat. Acad. Osteopathic Med. Educators, 2009. Fellow Am. Coll. Osteo. Family Physicians; mem. Am. Osteo. Assn., Am. Med. Dirs. Assn. (sec.-treas. Iowa chpt. 1997-99), Am. Coll. Osteo. Family Physicians (pres. Iowa chpt. 1995-96), Iowa Osteo. Med. Assn. (trustee 1995-99, v.p. 1999—, pres.-elect 2000-01, pres. 2001-02, Physician of Yr. 2004-05), Soc. Tchrs. Family Medicine. Lutheran. Avocations: gardening, cooking, painting. Office: 3200 Grand Ave Des Moines IA 50312-4104 Office Phone: 515-271-7816. Business E-Mail: Roberta.Wattleworth@dmu.edu.

WATTS, RAY L., dean, neurologist, educator; b. Birmingham, Ala. BS in Engring., U. Ala., Birmingham, 1976; MD, Wash. U., St. Louis, 1980. Internship, residency in neurology Mass. Gen. Hosp., Boston; clin. fellowship Harvard U. Med. Sch., Mass.; fellowship in motor control and movement disorders NIH, 1984—86; mem. neurology faculty Emory U., Atlanta, 1986—2003, prof., vice chmn. neurology dept., 1998—2003; John N. Whitaker prof. and chmn. neurology U. Ala., Birmingham, 2003—10, sr. v.p. medicine, dean sch. medicine, 2010—, James C. Lee endowed chmn., prof. neurology, 2010—; pres. U. Ala. Health Services Found., 2005—; interim CEO U. Ala. Birmingham Health Sys., 2008; chief neurology U. Ala. Hosp. Co-editor: Movement Disorders: Neurologic Principles and Practice, 1997—. Office: University Ala Birmingham Office of Sr VP and Dean of Sch Medicine 1530 3d Ave S FOT 1203 Birmingham AL 35294-3412 Office Phone: 205-934-1111. Office Fax: 205-996-4039. Business E-Mail: rlwatts@uab.edu. *

WAUBANT, EMMANUELLE, medical educator, director; b. France, Feb. 16, 1964; MD, Lille, France, 1987; PhD, Paris, 2003. Assoc. prof., neurology UCSF, 2001—, dir., clin. rsch. MS, 2005—, dir., pediatric MS, 2006—. Office: 350 Parnassus Ave Ste 908 San Francisco CA 94117 Office Fax: 415-514-2470. Business E-Mail: emmanuelle.waubant@ucsf.edu.

WAUGH, THEODORE ROGERS, orthopedic surgeon; b. Montreal, Sept. 21, 1926; s. Theodore Rogers and Anne Maude (Lawlor) W.; children: Susanne Rogers, Margaret Stewart, Theodore Rogers. BA, Yale U., 1949; MD, CM, McGill U., 1953; DMS, U. Goteborg, Sweden, 1968. Diplomate Am. Bd. Orthop. Surgery. Intern Royal Victoria Hosp., Montreal, 1953-54; asst. resident in pathology McGill U., 1954-55; asst. resident in surgery NYU Bellevue Med. Ctr., 1955-56; capt., M.C. USAF, 1956—58, lt. col., res., CMDR 695th MSCSU, 1959—66; asst. resident, resident, fellow N.Y. Orthop. Hosp., Columbia U., 1958-62, instr., clin. asst. prof. orthop. surgery, 1962-68; asst. attending Presbyn. Hosp., NYC, 1962-68; prof., chief divsn. orthop. surgery U. Calif., Irvine, 1968-78; prof., chmn. dept. orthop. surgery NYU Med. Ctr., 1978—97, emeritus prof., 1997—. Adj. prof. surgery Dartmouth U. Sch. Medicine, 1998-2003, adj. prof. orthopaedics, 2003—11. Contbr. numerous articles to profl. jours. Fellow ACS, Royal Coll. Surgeons (Can.), Am. Acad. Orthop. Surgeons, Scoliosis Rsch. Soc., Assn. Bone and Joint Surgeons, Am. Orthop. Assn., Am. Orthop. Soc. Sports Medicine; mem. 20th Century Orthopedic Club, Alpha Omega Alpha. Presbyterian. Achievements include developing designer surgical devices used in orthopaedic surgery, in-vivo measurement of forces in correction of spinal deformity (scoliosis). E-mail: trwmd3@comcast.net.

WAUGH, WILLIAM HOWARD, physician, research scientist; b. NYC, May 13, 1925; s. Richey Laughlin and Lyda Pearl (Leamer) W.; m. Eileen Loretta Garrigan, Oct. 4, 1952; children: Mark Howard, Kathleen Cary, William Peter. Student, Boston U., 1943, W.Va. U., 1944; MD, Tufts U., 1948, postgrad., 1949—50. Cardiovascular rsch. trainee Med. Coll. Ga., Augusta, 1954-55, asst. rsch. prof. physiology, 1955-60, assoc. medicine, 1957-60; assoc. prof. medicine U. Ky., Lexington, 1960-69; Ky. Heart Assn. Chair in cardiovascular rsch. Ky. Heart Assn., Lexington, 1963-71; prof. medicine U. Ky., Lexington, 1969-71; prof. medicine and physiology East Carolina U., Greenville, 1971—2001, rsch. prof. physiology, 2001—04, prof. emeritus, 2001—. Head renal sect. U. Ky. Coll., Lexington, 1960-68; chmn. dept. clin. scis. East Carolina U., Greenville, 1971-75, chmn. policy and rev. com. on human rsch., 1972-90. Contbr. articles to profl. jours. With AUS, 1943-46; capt. USAF, 1952-54. Recipient NC Med. Soc. award, 1998. Fellow: ACP; mem.: AAAS, Microcirculatory Soc. (50-Yr. club), Am. Physiology Soc., NC Med. Soc. (life). Achievements include basic advances in excitation contraction coupling in vasc. smooth muscle; basic advances in autoregulation of renal blood flow and urine flow; adj. therapy in acute lung edema; noncovalent antisickling agents and amino acid nutrient in sickle cell hemoglobinopathy; oral citrulline as dietary supplement in man; daily intermittent peritoneal dialysis; R-Lipoate salt & vitamin C for late cognitive health. Home: 119 Oxford Rd Greenville NC 27858-4954 Personal E-mail: ewwaugh@suddenlink.net.

WAXMAN, HARVEY L., cardiologist; Attended, Mt. Sinai Sch. of Medicine. Diplomate Am. Bd. Internal Medicine, 1977, Am. Bd. Internal Medicine-cardiovasc. medicine, 1979, Am. Bd. Phys. Therapy Specialties-clin. electrophysiology, 1992. Intern NY Univ., resident; fellow Hosp. of the Univ. of Pa., Univ. of Miami; chief cardiology divsn. Penn Presbyn. Med. Ctr. Named one of Best Doctors in America, 2003—04, 2005—06, 2009—10, Top Doctors, Del. Valley Consumers Checkbook, 2003, Phila. Mag., 2005—11, America's Top Doctors, 2007—08, 2010. Mem.: Am. Coll. of Cardiology, ACP, AMA. Office: Penn Presbyterian Medical Center Philadelphia Heart Institute 4th Fl Ste 400 51 N 39th St Philadelphia PA 19104 Office Phone: 800-789-7366.

WAXMAN, SAMUEL, oncologist, hematologist, medical educator; b. NYC, July 26, 1936; s. Leo and Sally Berkwitz Waxman. BS, Cornell U., Ithaca, NY, 1957; MD summa cum laude, SUNY Downstate Med. Ctr., Bklyn., 1963. Diplomate American Bd. Internal Medicine, cert. in hematology. Intern Mount Sinai Hospital, NYC, 1963—64, med. resident, 1964—66, rsch. fellow hematology, 1966—68, asst. attending physician, 1970—74, head Rochelle Belfer Chemotherapy Found. Lab., 1972—, assoc. attending physician, 1974—83, attending in medicine, 1983—; asst. clin. prof. dept. medicine Mount Sinai School Medicine, 1970—74, assoc. clin. prof. medicine, 1974—83, clin. prof. medicine, 1983—94, Zena & Michael A. Wiener prof. medicine, divsn. hematology/oncology, 1994—2004, Albert A. & Vera G. List prof. medicine, 2004—07, disting. svc. prof. medicine, hematology and med. oncology, 2007—. Founder, sci. dir. Samuel Waxman Cancer Rsch. Found., NYC, 1976—; cons. prof. Shanghai Second Med. U., China, 1992—; bd. dirs. Brookdale Sr. Living, Inc., 2005—. Contbr. articles to profl. jours. Trustee, mem. med. adv. bd. Leukemia Soc. America, 1975—. Recipient Magnolia award, Shanghai Mcpl. Govt., 1997; named to Hall of fame of NY Physicians, NY Mag., 1998. Fellow: ACP; mem.: Internat. Soc. Preventive Oncology, American Soc. Clin. Investigation, American Assn. Cancer Rsch., American Soc. Hematology, American Soc. Clin. Nutrition, American Fedn. Clin. Rsch., Harvey Soc., Alpha Omega Alpha. Avocations: outdoors, golf, music, art, travel. Office: Samuel Waxman Research Foundation 420 Lexington Ave Ste 825 New York NY 10170 also: Mt Sinai Med Ctr One Gustave Levy Pl New York NY 10029 Office Phone: 212-289-2828. Business E-Mail: samuel.waxman@mssm.edu. E-mail: samuel.waxman@brookdaleliving.com. *

WAY, BARBARA HAIGHT, retired dermatologist; b. Franklin, NJ, Dec. 27, 1941; d. Charles Padley and Alice Barbara (Haight) Shoemaker; m. Anthony Biden Way; children: Matthew Shoemaker Way, Sarah Shoemaker Way. AB in Music cum laude, Bryn Mawr Coll., 1962, postgrad., 1963-64; MD, U. Pa., 1968. Diplomate Am. Bd. Dermatology. Systems engr. IBM, Balt., 1962—63; mem. dean's staff Bryn Mawr (Pa.) Coll., 1963—64; med. intern U. Wis. Hosps., Madison, 1968—69, resident in dermatology, 1969—72; physician emergency rm. St. Francis Hosp., La Crosse, Wis., 1969—72, founder dept. dermatology, 1972; asst. prof. dept. dermatology Tex. Tech U. Sch. Medicine, Lubbock, 1972—73, from asst. clin. to assoc. clin. prof., 1973—74, asst. prof., assoc. chair, 1974—76, assoc. prof., chair, 1976—81, assoc. clin. prof., 1981—92; clin. prof. Tex. Tech. U. Health Scis. Ctr., Lubbock, 1995—2005, founder, dir. dermatology residency tng. program, 1978—81, pvt. practice, 1973—74, 1981—2006; acting dir. Lubbock City Health Dept., 1982—83; ret., 2006. Mem. credentials com. Covenant Hosp., Lubbock, 1990, 92, 94, 95, founding dir. phototherapy unit, 1990-91, 93, exec. com., 1991, 93, 98, chief dermatology sect., 1991, 93, 98, subsect. chief, 1992, 94. Alumna admissions rep. Bryn Mawr Coll., 1972-75, 87-96; mem. selection com. outstanding physician Lubbock chpt. Am. Cancer Soc., 1991-94, chmn., 1991; bd. dirs. Tex. Tech. U. Med. Found., 1987-89, Double T. Connection, 1988-90. Fellow Am. Acad. Dermatology (reviewer jour.); mem. Tex. Dermatol. Soc. (chmn. roster com. 1980), Tex. Med. Assn. (mem. sexually transmitted diseases com. 1986-90, mem. coun. pub. health 1990-92, vice councillor dist. III 1992-98, councillor dist. III 1998-2000, chmn. reference com. fin. and orgnl. affairs ann. session 1992), Lubbock County-Garza County Med. Soc. (mem. various coms. 1980-2000, chmn. sch. and pub. health com. 1983, mem. bd. censors 1983-85, chair 1985, sec. 1986, v.p. 1987, liaison with Tex. Tech. U. Health Scis. Ctr. com. 1988-91, co-chmn. pub. rels. com. 1988-89, alt. Tex. Med. Assn. del. 1988-89, del. 1990-95, 98-2000, pres.-elect 1989, pres. 1990, chmn. ad hoc bylaws com. 1991-94, chmn. Hippocratic award 1991), Women's Dermatologic Soc. (founding sec.), Dallas County Medical Res. Corp. Personal E-mail: anthony.way@ttuhsc.edu.

WAY, E(DWARD) LEONG, pharmacologist, toxicologist, educator; b. Watsonville, Calif., July 10, 1916; s. Leong Man and Lai Har (Shew) Way; m. Madeline Li, Aug. 11, 1944; children: Eric, Linette. BS, U. Calif., Berkeley, 1938, MS, 1940; PhD, U. Calif., San Francisco, 1942. Pharm. chemist Merck & Co., Rahway, NJ, 1942; instr. pharmacology George Washington U., 1943-46, asst. prof., 1946-48; asst. prof. pharmacology U. Calif., San Francisco, 1949-52, assoc. prof., 1952-57, prof., 1957-87, prof. emeritus, 1987—, chmn. dept. pharmacology, 1973-78. USPHS spl. rsch. fellow U. Berne, Switzerland, 1955-56, China Med. Bd.; rsch. fellow, vis. prof. U. Hong Kong, 1962-63; Sterling Sullivan disting. vis. prof. Martin Luther King U., 1982; hon. prof. pharmacology and neurosci. Guangzhou Med. Coll., 1987; adv. com. Pharm. Rsch. Mfrs. Assn. Found., 1968-98; mem. coun. Am. Bur. for Med. Advancement in China, 1982; bd. dirs. Li Found., 1970—, pres., 1985-98, bd. dirs. Haight Ashbury Free Clinics, 1986-93; Tsumura prof. neuropsychopharmacology med. sch. Gunma U., Maebashi, Japan, 1989-90; sr. staff fellow Nat. Inst. on Drug Abuse, 1990-91; rschr. on drug biodisposition, analgetics, devel. pharmacology, drug tolerance, drug dependence and Chinese materia medica. Editor: New Concepts in Pain, 1967, (with others) Fundamentals of Drug Metabolism and Drug Disposition, 1971, Endogenous and Exogenous Opiate Agonists and Antagonists, 1979; mem. editl. bd. Clin. Pharmacology, Therapeutics, 1975-87, Drug, Alcohol Dependence, 1976-87, Progress in Neuro-Psychopharmacology, 1977-91, Research Communications in Chem. Pathology and Pharmacology, 1978-91, Alcohol and Drug Dependence, 1986-91, Asian Pacific Jour. Pharm., 1985—, Jour. Chinese Medicine, 1993—; contbr. numerous articles and revs. to profl. publs. Recipient Faculty Rsch. Lectr. award, U. Calif., San Francisco, 1974, San Francisco Chinese Hosp. award, 1976, Cultural citation and Gold medal, Ministry of Edn., Republic of China, 1978, Nathan B. Eddy award, Coll. on Problems in Drug Dependence, 1979, Mentorship award, Coll. on Problems in Drug Dependence, San Juan, 2004, Chancellor's award, U. Calif., 1986, Disting. Alumnus award, U. Calif., San Francisco, 1990, Asian Pacific Am. Systemwide Alliance award, 1993, Lifetime Achievement award, Chinese Hist. Soc., 2001, Outstanding Overseas Chinese award, Chinese Cons. Benevolent Assn., Chinese Womens Assn., 2005, Cert. of Honor, Mayor Gavin Newsome, San Francisco, 2005. Fellow Am. Coll. Neuropsychopharmacology (life, emeritus), Am. Coll. Clin. Pharmacology (hon.), Coll. on Problems of Drug Dependence (exec. com. 1978-92, chmn. bd. dirs. 1978-82, Nathan B. Eddy award 1979, Mentorship award 2004); mem. AAAS (life), Am. Soc. Pharmacology, Exptl. Therapeutics (bd. editors 1957-65, pres. 1976-77, Torald Sollman award 1992), Fedn. Am. Socs. Exptl. Biology (exec. bd. 1975-79, pres. 1977-78), Am. Pharm. Assn. (life, Rsch. Achievement award 1962), AMA, Soc. Aid and Rehab. Drug Addicts (Hong Kong, life), Western Pharmacology Soc. (pres. 1963-64), Japanese Pharm. Soc. (hon.), Coun. Sci. Soc. Pres.' (exec. com. 1979-84, treas. 1980-84), Chinese Pharmacology Soc. (hon.), Academia Sinica (academician), Leong Man Way Found. (founder & pres. 1976-78). Office: University Calif Dept Clin Pharmacy C152 PBX 0622 San Francisco CA 94143-0001 Office Phone: 415-476-2722.

WAYNE, VICTOR SAMUEL, cardiologist; b. Melbourne, Australia, Jan. 7, 1953; s. Mark Isaac and Anita (Selzer) W.; m. Karen Susan Eisinger; children: Fairlie, Stephanie. MB, BS with honors, Monash U., 1976. Diplomate Australian Soc. Ultrasound in Medicine. Intern, resident med. officer, registrar Alfred Hosp., Melbourne, 1976-79, cardiology registrar, 1980-81; advanced cardiology fellow St. Vincent Hosp., Worcester, Mass., 1982-83; instr. medicine U. Mass., Worcester, 1982-83; sr. cardiologist, chmn. Divsn. Cardiology Cabrini Health, Melbourne, 1983. Vis. physician, cardiologist Alfred Hosp., Monash U., Melbourne, 1983—; lecturer in field. Contbr. articles to profl. jours; co-author books. Mem. governing body Cabrini Health, Melbourne, Australia, 2004—, chmn., sr. med. staff, 2004—. Grantee Nat. Heart Found., Alfred Hosp., 1982. Fellow Royal Australasian Coll. Physicians, Am. Coll. Chest Physicians, Internat. Acad. Chest Physicians and Surgeons, N.Y. Acad. Scis., Am. Coll. Cardiology, Internat. Coll. Angiology, European Soc. Cardiology; mem. Cardiac Soc. Australia and New Zealand, Australian Soc. Echocardiography, Internat. Soc. and Fedn. Cardiology, Australian Friends Tel Aviv U. (pres.), Internat. Bd. Gov.'s Tel Aviv U., Spiritgrow Ctr., Melbourne (pres.), Melbourne Hebrew Congregation (exec. mem.); Clubs: Nat. Golf Australia, Mensa Australia. Jewish. Avocations: reading, travel, theater, property investment, piano. Home: 8 Carmyle Ave Toorak Victoria 3142 Australia Office: Cabrini Med Ctr 183 Wattletree Rd Melbourne Victoria 3144 Australia

W. D. JI, medical association administrator; b. Henan, Oct. 1, 1966; D, West China Med. U., 2002. Vice dir. Shanghai Changning Mental Health Ctr., 2008—. Office: 299 Xiehe Rd Shanghai Changning 200335 China Personal E-mail: breeze1999@126.com.

WEATHERALL, DAVID JOHN, medical scientist, academic administrator; b. Liverpool, Eng., Mar. 9, 1933; s. Harry and Gwendoline Charlotte Miriam (Tharme) Weatherall; m. Stella Isabel Mayorga-Nestler, June 20, 1962; 1 child, Mark William. MB, BChir, U. Liverpool, 1956, LLD (hon.), 1992, U. Bristol, 1994; DSc (hon.), U. Manchester, 1988, U. Edinburgh, 1989, U. Aberdeen, 1991, U. Leicester, 1991, U. London, 1993, U. Keele, 1993, Oxford Brookes U., 1995, South Bank U., 1995, Mahidol U., 1997, U. Exeter, 1999, McGill U., 1999, Cambridge, 2004; MD (hon.), U. Leeds, 1988, U. Sheffield, 1989, U. Nottingham, 1993. Rsch. fellow Johns Hopkins Hosp., Balt., 1961-65; lectr. medicine U. Liverpool, 1965-66, sr. lectr. medicine/hematology, 1966-69, reader hematology, 1969-71, prof. hematology, 1971-74; Nuffield prof. clin. medicine U. Oxford, 1974-92, Regius prof. medicine, 1992—2000, hon. dir. Inst. Molecular Medicine, 1989—2000; chancellor Keele U., Staffordshire, England, 2002—. Author: New Genetics and Clinical Practice, 1991, Science and the Quiet Art, 1995, Oxford Textbook of Medicine (numerous edits.); contbr. articles to profl. jours. Recipient Feldberg Found. award for biosci., 1984, Helmut Horten Rsch. award, 1995, Prince Mahidol prize in medicine, 2002, Allen award, Am. Soc. Human Genetics, 2003, Mendel Medal, Genetics Soc., 2006, Lasker-Koshland Spl. Achievement award in med. sci., 2010. Fellow: Royal Soc. (Royal Medal 1989), Royal Coll. Physicians; mem.: NAS (fgn. assoc.), Am. Philos. Soc., Brit. Assn. Advancement Sci., Assn. Am. Physicians, Am. Soc. Hematology (hon.), Am. Acad. Arts & Scis., Assn. Physicians Gt. Britain & Ireland, Brit. Soc. Hematology. Office: John Radcliffe Hosp Weatherall Inst Molecular Medicine Headley Way OX3 9DU Oxford England

WEAVER, ARTHUR LAWRENCE, rheumatologist, consultant; b. Lincoln, Nebr., Sept. 3, 1936; s. Arthur J. and Harriet Elizabeth (Walt) Weaver; m. JoAnn Versemann, July 6, 1980; children: Arthur Jensen, Anne Christine. BS (Regents scholar) with distinction, U. Nebr., 1958; MD, Northwestern U., 1962; MS in Medicine, U. Minn., 1966. Diplomate Am. Bd. Internal Medicine, Am. Bd. Rheumatology. Intern U. Mich. Hosps., Ann Arbor, 1962-63; resident Mayo Grad. Sch. Medicine, Rochester, Minn., 1963-66; practice medicine specializing in rheumatology and internal Lincoln, 1968—2002; med. dir. Arthritis Ctr. Nebr., 1968—2002; ret., 2002. Staff mem., chmn. rheumatology dept. Bryan Meml. Hosp., 1976—78, 1982—85, 1989—91, vice-chief staff, 1984—87; chmn. fin. com. Bryancare, 1995—96; courtesy staff St. Elizabeths Hosp., Lincoln Gen. Hosp.; cons. staff VA Hosp.; chmn. Juvenile Rheumatoid Arthritis Clinic, 1970—88; asst. prof. Internal Medicine Dept. U. Nebr., Omaha, 1976—88, assoc. prof., 1988—95, clin. prof. Rheumatology divsn., 1995—2008, clin. prof. medicine emeritus, 2008—; med. dir. Lincoln Benefit Life Co., 1972—90, Assurity Life Ins. Co., 1995—2003, bd. dirs., 1992—2007; adv. com. Coop. Systematic Studies in Rheumatic Diseases III; bd. dirs. M.G.I. Pharma Inc., 1998—2008, Internat. Rheumatology Network, 2003—06, AZANO, 2007—08, CORRONA; cons. in field. Editl. bd. mem. Nebr. Med. Jour., 1982—96; contbr. articles to profl. jours. Mem. tech. cons. panel for rheumatology Harvard Resource Based Relative Value Study; trustee U. Nebr. Found., 1974—. Capt. med. corps US Army, 1966—68. Recipient Outstanding Nebraskan award, U. Nebr., 1958, C.W. Boucher award, 1958, Philip S. Hench Rheumatology award, Mayo Grad. Sch. Medicine, 1966, Founders award Nebr. chpt., Arthritis Found., 1997. Fellow: ACP (Nebr. coun. 1983—85, Laureate award Nebr. chpt. 1996), Am. Coll. Rheumatology (bd. dirs. 1985—96, planning com. 1987—96, sec. 1991—93, pres. rsch. and edn. found. 1991—93, exec. com. 1991—96, 2d v.p. 1993—94, 1st v.p., pres.-elect 1994—95, pres. 1995—96, chmn. nominating com. 1996—97, master 2001, 1st Paulding Phelps award 1989), Am. Rheumatism Assn. (pres.-elect Ctrl. region 1983—84, com. on rheumatologic practice 1983—87, pres. Ctrl. region 1984—85); mem.: AMA (life), Minn. Med. Assn., Midwest Coop. Rheumatic Disease Study Group (chmn. exec. com. 1986—92), Nat. Soc. Clin. Rheumatology (program chairperson 1986—87, exec. com. 1987—92, program chairperson 1988), Arthritis Found. (life; profl. del.-at-large 1987—88, 1989, 1990, 1995—96, blue ribbon rsch. com. 1995—96, bd. dirs. Nebr. chpt., Nat. Vol. Svc. citation 1988, Founder award 1997), Arthritis Health Professions Assn. (com. on practice 1984—87), Nebr. Soc. Internal Medicine (Internist of Yr. 1988), Am. Soc. Internal Medicine (coord. com. phys. payment svcs. 1988—93), U. Minn. Med. Sch. Alumni Assn., U. Mich Med. Sch. Alumni Assn., Mayo Grad. Sch. Medicine Alumni Assn., Phi Rho Sigma, Pi Kappa Epsilon, Alpha Omega Alpha, Sigma Xi, Phi Beta Kappa. Republican. Presbyterian. Home and Office: 9914 Weavers Point Rd Pequot Lakes MN 56472-6472 Office Phone: 218-562-5351. Personal E-mail: weaver2aj@tds.net.

WEAVER, CONNIE MARIE, foods and nutrition educator; b. LaGrande, Oreg., Oct. 29, 1950; d. Robert Chesley and Averil Jean (Harris) Shelton; m. Lloyd Rollin Weaver, Dec. 22, 1971; children: Douglas, Mark, Richard. BS in Nutrition, Oreg. State U., 1972, MS in Nutrition, 1974; PhD in Nutrition, Fla. State U., 1978. Tchg. asst. dept. foods & nutrition Oreg. State U., Corvallis, 1973-74; instr. dept. foods & nutrition Grossmont Coll., El Cajon, Calif., 1974-75; rsch. assoc. dept. food & resource chemistry U. RI, Kingston, 1975; tchg. asst. Fla. State U., Tallahassee, 1975-78; asst. prof. foods & nutrition Purdue U., West Lafayette, Ind., 1978-84, assoc. prof., 1984-88, prof., 1988—2000, head dept. foods & nutrition, 1991—, disting. prof. dept. foods & nutrition, 2000—, dir. Botanicals Ctr. Age-Related Diseases, 2000—, dep. dir. Clin. Translational Sci. Inst., 2008—. Rsch. fellow Kraft, Inc., Glenview, Ill., 1988; W. O. Atwater lecturership Agrl. Rsch. Svc., USDA/American Soc. Nutritional Scis., 2003. Mem. editl. bd. Jour. Nutritional Biochemistry, 1990—2001, Advances in Food & Nutrition Rsch., 1997—, Nutrition Rsch. Reviews, 1998—, American Jour. Clin. Nutrition, 2001—07, Jour. Bone & Mineral Rsch., 2004—; contbr. articles to profl. jours. Sci. advisor food, nutrition & safety com., North American br. Internat. Life Scis. Inst., 1993—97, bd. trustees, 1998—; bd. sci. counselors Nat. Space Biomedical Rsch. Inst., Houston, 1998—2001; mem. women's adv. bd. Mead Johnson & Co., 1998—; adv. coun. Joint Inst. Food Safety & Applied Nutrition, College Park, Md., 2000—04. Recipient Centennial Laureate award, Fla. State U., 0005, Harrison award, Ohio State U., 2008; named to Purdue U. Foods & Nutrition Hall of Fame, 2006. Fellow: American Coll. Nutrition (Career award 2005), Inst. Food Technologists (chair nutrition divsn. 1990, mem. exec. com. 1991—93, Outstanding Rsch. award 1991, Babcock Heart award 1997); mem.: Inst. Medicine, Internat. Bone & Mineral Soc., American Soc. Bone & Mineral Rsch., Soc. Exptl. Biology & Medicine, American Soc. Nutrition (treas., coun. mem. 1992—96, pres. 1998—99, Robert H Herman award 2009), Gamma Sigma Delta (pres. Hoosier chpt. 1989—90), Kappa Omicron Nu, Phi Tau Sigma (pres. Hoosier chpt. 1986—87), Sigma Xi (pres. Purdue chpt. 2003—04). Achievements include research in building peak bone mass during adolescence and bone loss in postmenopausal women. Office: Purdue U Foods & Nutrition 700 W State St West Lafayette IN 47907-1186 Office Phone: 765-494-8228. Office Fax: 765-494-0674. E-mail: fandn@purdue.edu. *

WEAVER, KENNETH, gynecologist, researcher; b. Whitetop, Va., Dec. 4, 1933; s. Grover Cleveland and Violet Elaine (Baldwin) W.; children: Teresa Marie, Janice Eileen, Beverly Lynn, Pamela Jean, Cynthia Ann; m. Shelby Jean Davis, June 15, 1966. BA, U. N.C., 1957, MD, 1960. Diplomate Am. Bd. Ob-Gyn. Intern U.S. Pub. Health Svc., Boston, 1960-61; med. officer Cherokee (N.C.) Indian Hosp., 1961-64; gen. physician Haywood County Hosp., Waynesville, N.C., 1964-70, obstetrician, gynecologist, 1974-77; resident U. Ark. Med. Ctr., Little Rock, 1970-74; asst. prof. U. Ark., Little Rock, 1977-78, acting chmn., dept. ob-gyn., 1978; pvt. practice Johnson City, Tenn., 1978—. Mem. Gov. Com. on Cancer, Raleigh, N.C., 1970-71; dir. Maternity and Infant Care, Little Rock, 1977-78; assoc. prof. James H. Quillen Coll. Medicine, Johnson City, 1978-83. Contbr. articles to sci. jours. Honoree Wisdom Hall of Fame, 1998. Fellow Am. Coll. Ob-Gyn., Am. Coll. Nutrition, Am. Assn. Gynecol. Laparoscopists, N.Y. Acad. Scis. Achievements include six patent devices having to do with laser surgery and other gynecol. and urol. uses; rsch. in magnesium and preeclampsia, in magnesium and migraine, in relationship between magnesium and blood platelet function. Office: 1103 Jackson Blvd Jonesborough TN 37659 Office Phone: 423-753-4177.

WEAVER, LOIS JEAN, physician, educator; b. Wheeling, W.Va., May 23, 1944; d. Lewis Everett and Ann Weaver. BA, Oberlin Coll., 1966; MD, U. Chgo., 1970. Pulmonary fellow Northwestern U., Evanston, Ill., 1975-77; trauma fellow U. Wash. Harborview Hosp., Seattle, 1977-79, research assoc., instr. medicine, 1979-81, clin. asst. prof. medicine, 1983—; clin. research fellow Virginia Mason Med. Research Ctr., Seattle, 1981-82; mem. med. staff Swedish Hosp., Seattle, 1984-92. Pulmonary cons. Fred Hutchinson Cancer Research Inst., Seattle, 1984-86, regional med. advisor and med. cons., disability quality br. Social Security, Seattle, 1985—. Contbr. sci. articles to profl. jours. La Verne Noyes scholar U. Chgo., 1966; Parker B. Francis fellow Northwestern U., 1975. Mem. Sigma Xi. Avocations: gardening, music. Home: PO Box 2098 Kirkland WA 98083-2098 Office: 701 5th Ave Ste 2900 MIS 105 Seattle WA 98104-7075

WEAVER, MICHAEL GLEN, pharmacist; b. Tuscola, Ill., Sept. 11, 1955; S. Glen and Margaret (Long) W.; m. Catherine (Paynic), 1978; children: Jennifer, Michelle, Gregory. BS in Pharmacy, St. Louis Coll. of Pharmacy, 1978; MBA, So. Ill. U., 1989. Registered pharmacist Ill. Clin. coordinator, staff pharmacist St. Elizabeth Med. Ctr., Granite City, Ill., 1975-87; dir. pharmacy Freeport Meml. Hosp. (now Freeport Health Network), Ill., 1987-92, dir. pharmacy and info. systems, 1992-97, dir. info. and telecom. svcs., 1997—2002; dir. pharmacy Freeport Health Network, 2002—. Dir. Ill. Bd. Pharmacy, 1995—99. Allocations com. United Way of NW Ill., 2000-, bd. dirs. 2006-11; Girl Scouts, Green Hills, 2005-09, bd. dirs., 2005-09, exec. com., 2006-09, Girl Scouts Northern Ill. Audit Ctr., 2009-. Mem.: Am. Coll. Healthcare Execs., Ill. Coun. Hosp. Pharmacists (dir. ednl. affairs 1991—94, dir. orgnl. affairs 2004—05, pres.-elect 2005—06, pres. 2006—07, treas. elect. 2008—09, treas 2009—), Am. Soc. Hosp. Pharmacists, Kiwanis (bd. dirs. Lincoln-Douglas chpt. 1998—2009, v.p. 2003—04, pres. elect 2004—05, pres. 2005—06), Delta Sigma Theta, Beta Gamma Sigma, Phi Kappa Phi. Republican. Avocations: music, computers. Home: 1346 Carriage Hill Ln Freeport IL 61032-6168 Office: Freeport Health Network 1045 W Stephenson St Freeport IL 61032-4899 Office Phone: 815-599-6113.

WEAVER, VALERIE M., medical educator; b. Can., Aug. 28, 1957; PhD, U. Ottawa, 1992. Postdoc. fellow U. Ottawa, 1994; prof. depts. surgery & anatomy UCSF, 2006—. Dir. Ctr. Bioengring. & Tissue Regeneration, 2006; co-dir. Bay Area Ctr. Phys. Scis. & Oncology, 2009. Recipient Outstanding Achievement award Lawrence Berkeley Nat. Lab., Lawrence Berkeley Nat. Lab., U. Calif., Berkeley; Postdoc. grant, U. Calif. Breast Cancer Rsch. Program. Mem.: Internat. Soc.Stem Cell Rsch., Am. Assn. Cancer Rsch., Am. Soc. Cell Biology, Biophys. Soc. Office: 513 Parnassus Ave Rm HSE 560 San Francisco CA 94143 Business E-Mail: valerie.weaver@ucsfmedctr.org.

WEAVER, W(AYNE) DOUGLAS, cardiologist, researcher, medical educator; b. Ft. Fairfield, Maine, Mar. 14, 1945; 1 child, John. BA, U. Maine, 1967; MD, Tufts U., 1971. Diplomate Am. Bd. Internal Medicine, Am. Bd. Cardiovasc. Disease. Intern, then resident U. Wash., Seattle, 1971-74, fellow in cardiology, 1974-76, prof. medicine/cardiology, 1979-96; head divsn. cardiology, dir. Henry Ford Cardiovascular Inst. Henry Ford Health Sys., Detroit, 1996—, also Darin chair cardiology; prof. medicine Wayne State U. Contbr. over 350 articles to profl. jours. (articles), assoc, editor numerous jours. Named one of Am.'s Best Cardiologists; named to Top Doctors List, Hour Mag. Fellow: Am. Coll. Cardiology (pres. 2008—09, former v.p.), Am. Heart Assn. (bd. trustee-Metro Detroit). Avocations: skiing, boating, golf. Office: Henry Ford Hosp 2799 W Grand Blvd Detroit MI 48202-2689 Office Phone: 313-916-4420. Business E-Mail: wweaver1@hfhs.org.

WEBB, CHRISTIAN A., research scientist; b. Toronto, Ont., Can., Sept. 6, 1981; BA, McGill U., 2005; MA, U. Pa., 2008, PhD student in Clin. Psychology, 2007—. Rsch. fellow, intern U. Pa. Harvard Med. Sch. McLean Hosp., 2007—. Fellowship, Social Scis. and Humanities Rsch. Coun. Can., Benjamin Franklin fellowship, U. Pa. Mem.: APA, Assn. Behavioral and Cognitive Therapies, Sigma Xi. Avocations: golf, travel. Office: University Pa Dept Psychology 3720 Walnut St Philadelphia PA 19104 Business E-Mail: webb@sas.upenn.edu.

WEBB, DAVID JOHN, pharmacology educator, medical researcher, consultant; b. Greenwich, London, Sept. 1, 1953; s. Alfred William Owen and Edna May (Parish) W.; m. Margaret Jane Cullen, June 23, 1984 (dissolved); m. Louise Eleanor Bath, Mar 14, 2009 children: David Matthew, Matthew Owen Cullen, Mark Ewen. MB, BS, U. London, 1977, MD, 1990; DSc, U. Edinburgh, 2000. Clin. rsch. fellow Med. Rsch. Coun. Blood Pressure Unit, Glasgow, Scotland, 1982-85; lectr. in pharmacology St. George's Hosp. and Med. Sch. U. London, 1985-89; sr. lectr. dept. medicine U. Edinburgh, Scotland, 1990-95, Christison prof. therapeutics and clin. pharmacology, 1995—, head Ctr. Cardiovascular Sci., 1998—2004; deputy dir. Scottish Clinical Pharm. & Pathology Prog., 2010—. Hon. cons. physician Lothian U. Hosps., NHS Trust, Edinburgh, 1990—, head dept. medicine, 1997-2001; dir. clin rsch. ctr. U. Edinburgh, 1990-95; mem. physiol. medicine grants com. Med. Rsch. Coun., 1996; leader Wellcome Trust Cardiovasc. Rsch. Initiative, 1997-2001; mem. MRC Adv. Bd., 1997, Wellcome Trust Physiology and Pharmacology Panel, 1997-2000 chmn. Lothian Area Drug and Therapeutics Com., 1998-2005; head Ctr. for Cardiovascular Sci., 2000-04; chmn. Scottish Medicine Consortium, 2005—08; chmn. project grant com. Brit. Heart Found., 2004—09, v.p. Royal Coll. Physicians Edinburgh, 2007-09; head Wellcome Trust Scottish Translational Medicine and Therapeutics Initiative, 2009-. Author: (with others) The Endothelium in Hypertension, 1997; contbr. articles to profl. jours. Hon. trustee, rsch. dir. High Blood Pressure Found., Edinburgh, 1991—. Recipient SmithKline Beecham prize and Silver medal, 1994, Lilly Biennial prize and Gold medal for clin. rsch., Brit. Pharmacol. Soc., 2003; fellow, Am. Heart Assn. Fellow Royal Coll. Physicians Edinburgh (v.p. 2006-09), Royal Coll. Physicians (UK), Royal Coll. Physicians London, Brit. Pharmacology Soc., Am. Heart Assn., Faculty of Pharm. Med., Acad. Med. Sci. (U.K.), Royal Soc. Edinburgh, European Soc. Cardiology; mem. Med. Rsch. Soc., Scottish Soc. for Exptl. Medicine (coun. 1994), Brit. Hypertension Soc. (exec. com. 1991-94), European Soc. Hypertension, Internat. Soc. Hypertension, Brit. Pharmacological Soc. (exec. com. clin sect. 1994-99, sec. 1995, Hon. sec., dir., trustee 1996-99), Scottish Cardiac Soc., Rsch. Defence Soc., Am. Heart Assn. (Hypertension and Cardiology), European Network of Therapeutics Tchrs., Assn. Physicians of Great Brit. and Ireland, Scottish Soc. Physicians (pres. 2010), Assn. Clin. Profs. Medicine, Soc. for Medicines Rsch., U.K. Heads and Profs. Clin. Pharmacology (chmn. 2004—), Internat. Union Basic and Clin. Pharmacology (exec. com. 2005), European Assn. Clin. Pharmacology & Therapeutics (pres., 2009), Scottish Mountaineering Club. Avocations: mountain climbing, opera, bridge, chess. Office: Queens Med Rsch Inst 47 Little France Crescent Rm E322 Edinburgh EH16 4TJ Scotland Home: 75 Great King St Edinburgh EH3 6RN England Home Phone: 0131 556 7145.

WEBB, GARY DOUGLAS, cardiologist; s. John Douglas Webb and Jeannie Hardy Penman; m. Anne Michelle Phillips, Dec. 22, 1984; children: Laura Madeline, Natalie Anne, Geoffrey Cameron, Lindsay Anne. BS, McGill U., Montréal, 1965, MD, 1967. Chief cardiology Wellesley Hosp., Toronto, Ont, 1972—80; cardiologist Toronto Gen. Hosp., 1980—2004; dir., congenital cardiac ctr. adults U. Toronto, 1986—2004; dir., adult congenital heart ctr. U. Pa., Phila., 2004—09; dir. adolescent and adult congenital heart ctr. Cin. Children's Hosp., Phila., 2009—. Pres. Can. Adult Congenital Heart Network, Toronto, 1992—2004, Internat. Soc. Adult Congenital Cardiac Disease, Raleigh, NC, 1993—94; cochair, 32nd Bethesda conf. Am. Coll. Cardiology, Wash., 2000—01, chair, adult congenital working group, 2005—; chmn., chmn., med. adv. bd. Adult Congenital Heart Assn., Phila., 2007—. Editor: (textbook) Diagnosis and Management of Adult Congenital Heart Disease, Cases in Adult Congenital Heart Disease. Recipient 700th Anniversary medal, Charles U., Prague, Czech Republic, 1998; named one of America's Top Doctors, Castle Connolly Med. Ltd., 2008; fellowship, RCPS, 1972, Am. Coll. Cardiology, 1976. Fellow: Am. Heart Assn. Office: Adolescent and Adult Congenital Heart Ctr Cin Children's Hosp 3333 Burnet Ave Cincinnati OH 45223 Office Fax: 513-803-1778. Business E-Mail: gary.webb@cchmc.org.

WEBB, KATHARINE, counselor; b. Bklyn., Sept. 13, 1931; d. Joseph Norris and Thelma (Black) Norris Sharpton; m. John James Webb, May 25, 1956 (div. Aug. 1971); children: John, Tyra, Lori. BS in Home Econs., Hunter Coll., 1954, MS in Home Econs., 1957; MS in Guidance and Counseling, Western Mich. U., 1969; PhD in Guidance and Psychol. Svcs., Ind. State U., 1972. Tchr. home econs. N.Y.C. Bd. Edn., Bklyn., 1954-65, counselor, 1965-68, Ind. State U., Terre Haute, 1970-72; assoc. prof. counselor edn. SUNY-Brockport, 1972-79; commr. N.Y. State Commn. of Correction, Albany, 1979-85; dir. guidance and counseling N.Y. State Dept. Correctional Svcs.,

1985-98. Mediator, arbitrator Cmty. Dispute Ctr., Rochester, N.Y., 1973-79; mediator, fact-finder N.Y. State Pub. Employees Rels. Bd., Albany, 1975-79; adj. prof. Maria Coll., Albany, N.Y., 1987-2004. Pres. bd. dirs. Brockport Childcare Ctr., N.Y., 1973-74, Nat. Migrant Found., Inc., Albany, 1983-84; bd. dirs. YWCA of Rochester, N.Y., 1975-77, YWCA of Albany, 1985-92, Albany Cath. Family and Cmty. Svcs., 1991-94, St. Casimir's Regional Sch., 1991-96; elected mem. Albany Sch. Bd., 1998-2002; mem. N.Y.S. Regent's Adv. Coun. Accreditation, 2000—09. Recipient cert. recognition YWCA of Rochester, 1975, cert. disting. svc. Urban League Rochester, 1976, award for disting. spl. programs SUNY Office Spl. Programs, Albany, 1978, award for support and contbns. Rochester Ednl. Opportunity Ctr., 1978, award for svc. Mental Health Assn. Rochester, 1979, Disting. Alumni award Ind. State U., 1986, Albany Humanitarian award, 1988. Mem. Delta Kappa Gamma Soc. (past chpt. pres.), Delta Sigma Theta. Democrat. Roman Catholic. *

WEBB, ORVILLE LYNN, retired physician, pharmacologist, educator; b. Tulsa, Okla., Aug. 29, 1931; s. Rufus Aclen and Berla Ophelia (Caudle) W.; m. Joan (Liebenheim), June 1, 1954 (div. Jan. 1980); children: Kathryn, Gilbert, Benjamin; m. Jeanne P. (Heath), Aug. 24, 1991. BS, Okla. State U., 1953; MS, U. Okla., 1961; PhD in Pharmacology, U. Mo., 1966, MD, 1968. Diplomate Nat. Bd. Med. Examiners, Am. Bd. Family Practice, Okla Bd. Basic med. Scis.; cert. med. examiner, 1999. Rsch. assoc. in pharmacology U. Okla., 1959—61; rsch. fellow NIH, 1962—66; instr. pharmacology U. Mo., Columbia, 1966—68, asst. prof., 1968—69; intern U. Mo. Med. Ctr., 1968—69; family practice New Castle, Ind., 1969—89; med. dir. VA Clinic, Lawton, Okla., 1989—94, Comanche County Hosp., Lawton, Okla., 1994—98; pvt. practice medicine Lawton, Okla., 1998—2002; owner Comanche County Med. Clinic, Lawton, Okla., 1998—2002, Okla. Med. Clinic, Lawton, 1999—2003; ret., 2003. Clin. assoc. prof. family medicine U. Okla. Coll. Medicine, 1989—; adj. assoc. prof. pharmacology U. Okla. Coll. Medicine, 1989—; mem. U. Okla. Medicine Admissions Bd., 1995-98; mem. staff Henry County Meml. Hosp., New Castle, Ind. 1969-89; guest prof. pharmacy and pharmacology Butler U. Coll. Pharmacy, Indpls., 1970-75; owner, dir. Carthage Clinic, 1975-89; clin. assoc. prof. family medicine Ind. U. Coll. Medicine, 1986-89; county physician, jail med. dir. Henry County, Ind., 1976-89. Author: (with Blissitt, Stanaszek, Lea, and Febiger) Clinical Pharmacy Practice, 1972, Bd. Wichita Mtn Homeowners Assn.(pres., 2003-); contbr. numerous articles to profl. journals. Bd. dir. Lawton Philharm., 1990-95. Recipient Cert. of Merit in Pharmacol. and Clin. Med. Rsch., 1970, Med. Student Rsch. Essay Award Am. Acad. Neurology, 1968, Fellow Am. Bd. Family Practice, 1973 Fellow Am. Acad. Family Physicians, Am. Coll. Physician Exec.; mem. AMA (ann. award recognition 1975-2001), AAAS, Ind. State Med. Assn., Am. Coll. Sports Medicine, Am. Coll. Occupl. and Environ. Medicine, N.Y. Acad. Sci., Am. Soc. Contemporary Medicine and Surgery, Okla. State Med. Assn., Festival Chamber Music Soc. (bd. dirs. Indpls. 1981-87), Nat. Fraternity Eagle Scouts, Mensa, Columbia Club, Skyline Club, Country Club, Kiwanis, Elks, Sigma Xi, Phi Sigma. Achievements include research in harmful effects of anabolic steroids on athletes; cholesterol and other lipids. Home: 85 Quail Creek Dr NW Lawton OK 73507-9026

WEBB, PAUL, physiologist, educator, researcher, consultant; b. Cleve., Dec. 2, 1923; s. Monte F. and Barbara (Webb) Bourjaily; m. Eileen Whalen, Mar. 13, 1948; children: Shaun P., Paula S. Womacks. BA, U. Va., 1943, MD, 1946; MS in Physiol., U. Wash., 1951. Asst. prof. physiology U. Okla. Sch. Medicine, Oklahoma City, 1952—54; chief environ. sect. Aeromed. Lab., Wright-Patterson AFB, Ohio, 1954-58; prin. assoc. Webb Assocs., Yellow Springs, Ohio, 1959-82; vis. scientist INSERM, Paris, 1983; vis. prof. U. Limburg, Maastricht, The Netherlands, 1986, U. Uppsala, Sweden, 1988-89; clin. prof. cmty. health Wright State U. Sch. Medicine, Dayton, Ohio, 1980—; rsch. prof. bioengring. Wright State U., Dayton, 2005—. Cons. aerospace and undersea medicine, energy balance and thermal physiology, Yellow Springs, 1980—. Author: Human Calorimeters, 1985; contbr. articles to profl. jours. Village councilman Village of Yellow Springs, Ohio, 1969-75; mem. Air Force Scientific Adv. Bd., Washington, 1984-88. Recipient Ely award Human Factors Soc., 1972. Fellow Aerospace Med. Assn. (Aerospace Indsl. Life Scis. Assn. award 1969), Am. Inst. Med. and Biol. Engring.; mem. Am. Physiol. Soc., Undersea & Hyperbaric Med. Soc. (oceaneering internat. award 1979, pres. 1980-81). Home and Office: 14 Cedar Ct Yellow Springs OH 45387-1958

WEBB, WATTS RANKIN, surgeon; b. Columbia, Ky., Sept. 8, 1922; s. Frank Elbert and Susie Josephine (Rankin) W.; m. Frances Luella Cooke, Aug. 19, 1944; children: Michael Andrew, Paul Alan, Harvey Elbert, Gordon Lewis. BA, U. Miss., 1942; MD, Johns Hopkins U., 1945. Diplomate Am. Bd. Surgery, Am. Bd. Thoracic Surgery, Am. Bd. Surg. Critical Care. Intern Barnes Hosp., St. Louis, 1945-46; resident in surgery VA Hosp., Biloxi, Miss., 1946-48; resident in gen. and thoracic surgery Barnes Hosp., 1948-52; chief surgeon Miss. State Sanatorium, 1952-63; instr. surgery U. Miss., 1955-56, asst. prof. surgery, 1956-58, prof., 1958-63; prof., chmn. div. thoracic and cardiovascular surgery U. Tex. Southwestern Med. Sch., Dallas, 1964-70; prof., chmn. dept. surgery SUNY Upstate Med. Center, Syracuse, 1970-77; chmn. dept. Tulane U., New Orleans, 1977-89, prof. surgery, 1977-93, La. State U., New Orleans, 1993—, Streveport, 2007—, Huey P. Long Hosp., Alexandria, 2007—. Author: Pulmonary Problems in Surgery, 1974, Surgery in Acute Coronary Problems, 1974, Aneurysms, 1983, Cardiovascular Emergencies, 1986, Atlas of Pulmonary Resections, 1988, (with others) Surgical Management for Chest Injuries, Vol. VII, 1990; mem. editl. bd.: Annals of Thoracic Surgery, 1968-79, Surg. Rounds, 1978-82, Surgery Clinics, 1980-82, Microcirculation, 1983-84, Brit. Jour. Surgery, 1981-89; contbr. articles to profl. jours. Recipient award Hadassah, 1965, Knockers Soc. Outstanding Tchr. award SUNY Upstate Med. Ctr., 1972, Owl Club Clin. Tchr. of Yr. award Tulane U. Med. Sch., 1978, 86, 88-93, Gloria P. Walsh award for best tchr. in Med. Sch., 1992, Aesculapian Tchr. of Yr. award La. State U., 1995, 96. Fellow ACS, Am. Coll. Chest Physicians; mem. AMA, Am. Assn. Thoracic Surgery, Am. Coll. Cardiology, Am. Fedn. Clin. Research, Am. Heart Assn. (Silver medal 1963), Am. Physiol. Soc., Am. Surg. Assn., Am. Thoracic Soc., Halsted Soc., La. Med. Soc., Orleans Parish Med. Soc., New Orleans Surg. Soc., Societe International de Chirurgie, Soc. Cryobiology, Soc. Thoracic Surgeons, Soc. Univ. Surgeons, Southeastern Surg. Congress, So. Med. Assn., So. Soc. Clin. Research, So. Surg. Assn. (Shipley medal 1961), So. Thoracic Soc., So. Thoracic Surg. Assn., Surg. Assn. La., Surg. Biology Club II, Internat. Soc. Heart Transplantation, Gulf Coast Vascular Soc., Sigma Xi, Alpha Omega Alpha, Pi Kappa Pi, Beta Beta Beta, Alpha Epsilon Delta. Methodist. Office: La State U Huey P Long Hosp PO Box 5352 Pineville LA 71361-5352 Office Phone: 318-448-0811. Personal E-mail: webbwatts@yahoo.com. *

WEBBER, CAROLYN ANN (MRS. GERALD E. THOMSON), pathologist, educator; b. Aiken, SC, Mar. 28, 1936; d. Paul Rainey and Clemmie Vivian (Embly) Webber; m. Gerald Edmund Thomson Webber, July 26, 1958; children: Gregory Alan, Karen Blair. BS, SC State Coll., 1956; MD, Howard U., 1960. Diplomate Am. Bd. Pathology. Rotating intern Kings County Hosp., Bklyn., 1960—61, resident in pathology, 1961—63, 1964—66; clin. fellow pathology Am. Cancer Soc., 1962—63, 1964—65, attending physician, 1969—; instr. pathology SUNY Downstate Med. Ctr., Bklyn., 1966—69, asst. prof., 1969—73, clin. asst. prof., 1973—, attending physician, 1970—. Contbr. articles to profl. jours. Fellow: ACP; mem.: NY Pathol. Soc., Am. Med. Women's Assn. (pres. 2005—06), Assn. Women Sci., Am. Soc. Cytology. Office: SUNY Downstate Med Ctr Pathology Box 25 450 Clarkson Ave Brooklyn NY 11203-2056 Office Phone: 718-245-5401. Business E-Mail: cwebber@netmail.hscbklyn.edu.

WEBBER, JOHN BENTLEY, orthopedic surgeon; b. Morristown, NJ, Jan. 27, 1941; s. George Bentley and Gladys (Moody) W.; m. Mary Christina Thometz, Feb. 25, 1978; children: John Bentley, Edward Alan BA, Lehigh U., 1962; MD, Temple U., 1966. Intern Rochester Gen. Hosp., NY, 1966-67; resident Temple U. Med. Ctr., Phila., 1967-70; Stelrling Bunnell fellow in hand surgery Pacific Med. Ctr., San Francisco, 1971; assoc. prof. orthopedic surgery and rehab. Hahnemann Med. Coll. and Hosp., Phila., 1973—2001, chief sect. on hand surgery, 1973—2005; attending surgeon St. Christopher's Hosp. for Children, Phila., 1996—. Cons. in hand surgery Mcpl. Med. Svcs., Phila., 1973-87, USPHS, Phila., 1973-76, burn ctr. St. Agnes Med. Ctr., Phila., 1973—, Phila. unit Shriners' Hosp. for Crippled Children, 1979-95. Served to maj. USAF, 1971-73. Fellow ACS (Pa. com. on trauma), Am. Acad. Orthopedic Surgeons; mem. AMA, Am. Soc. for Surgery of Hand, Bunnell Hand Club (pres. 1978-80), Assn. for Acad. Surgery, Eastern Orthopedic Soc., Pa. Med. Soc., Phila. Orthopedic Soc., Phila. Hand Soc. (pres. 1987-89), Phila. County Med. Soc., Phila. Coll. Physicians, Meigs Med. Assn., Rotary, Union Leauge, Riverside Yacht Club (fleet surgeon), Phila. Country Club, Delaware Valley Ducks Unltd. (chmn. 1983-88), U.S. Coast Guard (cert. master). Republican. Congregationalist. Home: 138 Montrose Ave Town House 51 Bryn Mawr PA 19010 Personal E-mail: handweb@aol.com.

WEBEL, CHARLES PETER, human science and psychology educator; b. LA, Dec. 23, 1948; s. James Webel and Jeanne (Herbert). BA, U. Calif., Berkeley, 1969, PhD, 1976; postgrad. in pub. health/social medicine, Harvard U., 1989-91. Chair Ctr. Ednl. Change, Berkeley, 1968-70; filmmaker Nat. Ednl. TV, NYC, 1969-70; lectr. social scis. U. Calif., Berkeley, 1976-78, dir. grad. programs Western Inst. Social Rsch., Berkeley, 1977-78; asst. prof. sociology New Coll., Sarasota, Fla., 1978-79; exec. editor social scis. Columbia U. Press, NYC, 1980-83; asst. prof. philosophy Calif. State U., Chico, 1984-89, teaching fellow gen. edn. Harvard U., Cambridge, Mass., 1990-91; gen. editor scholarly book series Peter Lang Pub., NYC, 1990—. Rsch. assoc. dept. anthropology U. Calif., Berkeley, 1990—94, lectr. Sch. Social Welfare, 2000-01; prof. human sci. and psychology Saybrook Inst., San Francisco, 1990—2001; Fulbright prof. U. Heidelberg, Germany, 2002-03, dir. Ctr. for Peace Studies, prof. social scis. U. Tromso, Norway, 2004-05; UNESCO chair for the philosophy of people U. Castellon, Spain, 2005-06; Fulbright sr. specialist and prof. U. Rome; prof., dir., peace & conflict studies U. NY, Prague, Czech Republic. Author: Terror, Terrorism and the Human Condition, 2006-07; author, editor: Marcuse Critical Theory and The Promise of Utopia, 1988; co-author: Peace and Conflict Studies, 2008; co-editor: Handbook of Peace and Conflict Studies, 2007; filmmaker: Lifestyle, 1969. Organizer Congress Racial Equality, N.Y.C., 1965-66; West Coast sec. Internat. Philosophers for Prevention Nuclear Omnicide, 1985-89. Fulbright scholar Fulbright Commn., Germany, 1971-72; regents fellow U. Calif., Berkeley, 1972-73, dissertation fellow Social Sci. Rsch. Coun., N.Y.C., 1974-76, grad. fellow Harvard U., 1989-91, NEH summer fellow Harvard U., 1986, NEH fellow Cornell U., 1998. Mem. Am. Philos. Assn., Am. Sociol. Assn., Internat. Soc. Polit. Psychology, World Affairs Coun. Avocations: classical music, film, global travel, sports, humor. Mailing: Za Poricskou Brßnou 16 ZA 186 00 Prague Czech Republic *

WEBER, ADELHEID LISA, retired nurse, chemist; b. Cottbus, Germany, June 1, 1934; came to the U.S., 1958; d. Johannes Gustav Paul and Johanna Katinka (Askevold) Haertwig; m. Joseph Cotrell Weber (dec. 1986), Oct. 25, 1957; children: Robert Andreas, Miriam Lisa. RN, Stadtisches Hosp., Dortmund, Germany, 1956; BS in Distributive Sci., Am. U., 1983; MBA, U. Md., 1991; postgrad., New Eng. Acupuncture Sch., 2000. RN. Nurse Krankenhaus, Wuppertal, Germany, 1956—57; pvt. nurse Wellesley, Mass., 1969—74; lab. tech. Microbiol. Assoc., Bethesda, Md., 1979—84; switchboard operator Best Products Co., Bethesda, 1983—87; lab. tech. Uniformed Svcs. U. Health Scis., Bethesda, 1984—90; info. rsch. tech. Info. Rsch. Internat. Inc., Bethesda, 1987; chemist USDA, Beltsville, Md., 1990—93, ret., 1993; distbr. Morinda Health Product-Noni Juice, 1999—; nurse Comfort Keepers In Home, Cape Cod, Mass., 2005—08; selfemployed, 2008—. Vol. Sibley Meml. Hosp., Washington, 1991. Recipient Cert. award County of Montgomery, Md., 1988, Whitman Walker Clinic, 1987. Mem. NAFE, Soc. for Rsch. Adminstrs., Am. Chem. Soc., Nat. Assn. for Amputees, Soc. for Applied Spectroscopy, Nat. Trust for Historic Preservation, Hemlock Soc. Nat. Capital Area, Nat. Mus. for Women in Arts, Wash. Performing Arts Soc. Avocations: stained glass, pottery, gardening, needlecrafts, reading. Home: 23 Sunset Ln Osterville MA 02655-2036 E-mail: heidiweb_2003@comcast.com.

WEBER, CHARLES WALTER, nutrition educator; b. Harold, SD, Nov. 30, 1931; s. Walter Earl and Vera Jean (Scott) W.; m. Marylou Merkel Adam, Feb. 3, 1961; children: Matthew, Scott. BS, Colo. State U., 1956, MS, 1958; PhD, U. Ariz., 1966. Research asst. U. Ariz., Tucson, 1963-66, asst. prof., 1966-68, assoc. prof., 1969-72, prof. nutrition, 1973-97, prof. emeritus, 1997—. Cons. Hermosillo, Mex., 1970-74, Inst. of Health, Cairo, 1981-82, U. Fortaleza, Rio de Janiero, 1986. Contbr. articles to sci. jours. Served as cpl. U.S. Army, 1952-54. Mem. Am. Assn. Cereal Chemists, Am. Inst. Nutrition, Inst. Food Technologists, N.Y. Acad. Scis., Am. Soc. Clin. Nutrition, Poultry Sci. Assn., Ariz. Referees Assn., Sigma Xi. Clubs: Randolph Soccer (Tucson) (pres. 1976-79). Avocation: stamp collection. Home: 4031 E Calle De Jardin Tucson AZ 85711-3410

WEBER, CHRISTOPH KURT, gastroenterologist, consultant; m. Wibke Weber. MD, Justus-Liebig-U., Giessen, 1990; Habilitation, U. Ulm, Germany, 2002. Cert. internal medicine U. Ulm, 1999, gastroenterology 2001. Gastroenterology cons. Spital Sonnenhof, Bern, Switzerland, 2004—. Sci. advisor Signalomics, Vienna, 2006—. Fellow: European Socitey Gastroenterology; mem.: Am. Pancreatic Assn., Deutsche Gesellschaft für Verdauungs und Stoffwechselkrankheiten. Office: Spital Sonnenhof Buchserstrasse 30 Berne 3006 Switzerland Office Phone: 0041-31-358-1547. Business E-Mail: christophweber@sonnenhof.ch.

WEBER, DONALD FRANK, obstetrician, gynecologist; b. Minot, ND, May 15, 1956; s. Sebastian and Loretta Mae Weber; m. Kathleen Ann Weeks, Apr. 21, 1979; children: Christine Marie, Brian Joseph, Eric James. BS, U. ND, 1978, MD, 1982. Diplomate Am. Bd. Ob-Gyn. Resident Mt. Sinai Med. Ctr., U. Wis. Sch. Medicine, 1982—86; obstetrician-gynecologist LutherMidelfort, Eau Claire, Wis., 1986—; chair, credentials com. Luther Hosp., Eau Claire, 1996—. Clin. asst. prof. U. Wis. Sch. Medicine, 1987—; chief of staff Luther Hosp., Eau Claire, 1994—96. Bd. dirs. Big Bros. Big Sisters of the Chippewa Valley, Eau Claire, Wis., 1994—2002, Perinatal Found., Madison, Wis., 2001—10, Barron Meml. Med. Ctr., Wis., 1999—2002. Recipient Meritorius Svc., State Med. Soc. Wis., 2001, WAPC Appreciation award, Wis. Assn. for Perinatal Care, 1992, 2003, Callon-Leonard award, WAPC, 2007. Fellow: Am. Coll. Ob-Gyn. (vice chair Wis. sect. 2001—05, chair Wis. sect. 2005—08, Nomination Com. award 2009, Com. Healthcare Underserved Wolien award 2011—); mem.: AMA, Ctrl. Assn. Ob-gyn., Wis. Assn. for Perinatal Care (treas., pres. 1996—98), Am. Inst. Ultrasound in Medicine. Avocations: golf, ice hockey, history, travel. Office: LutherMidelfort 1400 Bellinger St Eau Claire WI 54702-1510 Office Phone: 715-838-6100. E-mail: weber.donald@mayo.edu.

WEBER, FRANK, neurologist, research scientist; b. Hassfurt, Bavaria, Germany, Oct. 2, 1963; s. Bernhard and Christel Weber; m. Gertraud von Gise, Apr. 30, 1990; children: Michael, Katharina. MD, Julius-Maximilians U., Würzburg, Germany, 1990; habilitation, Georg-August U., Göttingen, 1999. Cert. specialist in neurology, electromyography, specialist in neurol. intensive care. Scholar dept. neuroimmunology Max-Planck-Inst. Psychiatry, Martinsried, Germany, 1990—92, cons. sect. neurology Munich, 2000—; resident Georg-August U., Göttingen, 1992—98, cons., 1998—2000. Head rsch. group Chronic Inflammatory Ctrl. Nervous Sys. Diseases. Contbr. articles to profl. jours. Grantee, Hertie Stiftung, Göttingen, 1994, German Rsch. Coun., Göttingen, 1997; scholar, German Rsch. Coun., Martinsried, 1990—92. Mem.: European Neurol. Soc., German Neurol. Soc., German MS Soc. (med. adv. bd.). Home Phone: 49-0-89-66000514. Business E-Mail: fweber@mpipsykl.mpg.de.

WEBER, GEORG FRANZ, cancer researcher; b. Erlangen, Germany, July 7, 1962; came to U.S., 1989; s. Otto and Margret (Hartung) W.; m. Chitra Edwin, Sept. 21, 1991; 1 child, Ramona Sara. BS, Ohm-Gymnasium, Erlangen, Germany, 1981; MD, PhD, Julius Maximilians U., Wuerzburg, Germany, 1988. Rsch. assoc. U. S. Ala., Mobile, 1989; rsch. fellow dept. biochemistry and Dana-Farber Cancer Inst. Harvard U., Boston, 1990-91, rsch. assoc. dept. pathology and Dana-Farber Cancer Inst., 1991-93, instr., 1993-2000; asst. prof. in radiation oncology New Eng. Med. Ctr. and Tufts U., Boston, 1999—2004; assoc. prof. pharmacy U. Cin., 2004—. Founder, CEO, Biotech. Co. MetaMol Theranostics, 2007. Deutsche Forschungsgemeinschaft fellow, 1989-91, award, Purdue U. Business Plan Competetion, 2008, Intellectual Property award, Cin. Innovates award, 2010, Emerging Entrepreneurial Achievement award, U. Cin., 2010. Mem. AAAS, AMA, Deutscher Aerzteverband, Am. Assn. Cancer Rsch., Metastasis Rsch. Soc. Achievements include research into reactive oxygen species in medicine, immunology, cancer research, theory of chess, biomechanics. Office: U Cin Med Ctr Coll Pharmacy 3225 Eden Ave Cincinnati OH 45267-0004

WEBER, GEORGE, oncology and pharmacology educator, researcher; b. Budapest, Hungary, Mar. 29; came to U.S., 1959; s. Salamon and Hajnalka (Arvai) W.; m. Catherine Elizabeth Forrest, June 30, 1958; children: Elizabeth Dolly Arvai, Julie Vibert Wallace, Jefferson James. BA, Queen's U., 1950, MD, 1952; MD (hon.), U. Chieti, Italy, 1979, Med. Faculty, Budapest, 1982, U. Leipzig, Fed. Republic of Germany, 1987, Tokushima U., Japan, 1988; degree, Kagawa U., Japan, 1992. Rsch. assoc. Montreal Cancer Inst., 1953-59; prof. pharmacology Ind. U. Sch. Medicine, Indpls., 1959—; dir. Lab for Exptl. Oncology Sch. Medicine, Ind. U., Indpls., 1974—; Milan Panič prof. oncology Ind. U., Indpls., 1994—, Wellcome prof., 1995—; prof. Lab. for Exptl. Oncology Sch. Medicine, Ind. U., Indpls., 1974-90, disting. prof. Lab. for Exptl. Oncology, 1990—. Chmn. study sect. USPHS, Washington, 1976-78; sci. adv. com. Am. Cancer Soc., N.Y.C., 1972-76, 94-98, Damon Runyon Fund, N.Y.C., 1971-76; mem. U.S. Nat. Com., Internat. Union Against Cancer, Washington, 1974-80, 90-94, NAS, Washington, 1974-80, 90-94, U.S. Army Med. Rsch. and Breast Cancer Rsch. Program, 1996-97; prof. Brit. cancer campaign U. Oxford, Oxford, Eng., 2001; vis. prof. U. Bologna, Italy, 2001—. Editor: Advances in Enzyme Regulation, Vols. 1-49, 1962—; assoc. editor Jour. Cancer Rsch., 1969—80, 1982—89. Recipient Alecce Prize for cancer rsch. Tiberine Acad., Rome, 1971, Best Prof. award Student AMA, Indpls., 1966, 68, G.F. Gallanti prize for enzymology Internat. Soc. Clin. Chemists, 1984, Outstanding Investigator award Nat. Cancer Inst., NIH, 1986-94, Semmelweis medal & diploma Budapest, Hungary, 2001, medal

Gastroenterological Soc., Aliga, Hungary, 2001, Prestigious External Award Recognition Ind. U., Indpls., Ind., 2002. Mem. Am. Soc. for Pharmacology and Exptl. Therapeutics, Am. Assn. Cancer Rsch. (G.H.A. Clowes award 1982), Russian Acad. Sci. (hon.), Hungarian Cancer Soc. (hon.), Hungarian Acad. Scis. (hon.), Acad. Scis. Bologna (Italy) (hon.). Home: 7307 Lakeside Dr Indianapolis IN 46278-1618

WEBER, JEROME CHARLES, human relations educator, retired academic administrator; b. Bklyn., Sept. 1, 1938; s. Meyer and Ethel (Shier) W.; m. Elizabeth Lynn Wiley, July 18, 1975; children: Amy Elizabeth, Jeffrey Glenn. BS, Bklyn. Coll., 1960; MA, Mich. State U., 1961, PhD, 1966. Mem. faculty U. Okla., Norman, 1964—, prof. edn., phys. edn., human rels. and social work, 1973—, Regents' prof. edn. and human rels., 1991—, asst. and acting dean, 1969-72, dean Univ. Coll., 1973-91, vice provost instructional svcs., 1979-91; chmn. ednl. leadership and policy studies, 1991-93. Author: (with D.R. Lamb) Statistics and Research in Physical Education, 1970, (with G. Henderson) College Survival for Student-Athletes, 1985, (with R. Cintron) Enduring Enigmas: Issues in Adult and Higher Education, 1997; contbr. chpts. to books; contbr. articles to profl. jours. Bd. dirs. Univ. div. United Way, 1970; pres. Norman Kindergarten Assn., 1968; commr. Norman Bd. Parks, 1971-79. Recipient Outstanding Faculty award, Okla. U., 2007; named to Higher Edn. Hall Fame, Okla., 2005. Fellow Am. Coun. Sports Medicine; mem. Am. Assn. Higher Edn., Coun. Sports Psychology, Am. Coun. on Edn. Democrat. Jewish. Home: 5 Pebble Creek Rd Norman OK 73072-2822 Office: 630 Parrington Oval Norman OK 73069-8813 Office Phone: 405-325-3629. E-mail: jcweber@ou.edu.

WEBER, KATHLEEN M., sports medicine physician, orthopedist; BS in Nursing, Coll. Mt. Joseph, Cin., Oh.; MS in Exercise Physiology, George Williams Coll., Downers Grove, Ill.; Post-Baccalaureate in Health Sci., Loyola Univ., Chgo.; MD, Rush Med. Coll., Chgo., 1996. Cert. in sports medicine, in internal medicine, lic. Ill., Calif. Intern in health promotion Hinsdale Hosp. Cardiology Dept., Ill.; intern in corp. health promotion CF Industries, Inc., Long Grove, Ill., Amoco Corp. Hdqs., Chgo.; intern in cmty. health progrms Naperville YMCA, Naperville, Ill.; resident, internal medicine Rush Univ. Med. Ctr., Chgo., 1996—99, chief resident, internal medicine, 1999—2000; fellow in sports medicine U. Calif. San Diego Med. Ctr., 2000—01; health dir., cons. The LaSalle Club, Chgo.; cons., owner Leisure and Fitness Svcs., Evanston, Ill.; attending physician, dir. primary care/sports medicine and women's sports medicine Midwest Orthopaedics at Rush Univ. Med. Ctr. Team physician for various HS athletic departments; mem. med. staff for various sports competitions; team physician U. Calif. San Diego Athletic Dept., 2000—01, San Diego Spirits, 2001, Chgo. Blaze, WNBL, US Soccer, Chgo. White Sox, DePaul U. Athletic Dept. Contbr. articles to profl. jours., chapters to books. Recipient Outstanding Work as an Intern, Rush Univ. Med. Ctr. Dept. Medicine, 1997, Aesculapius award, Rush Med. Coll., 1998, Dept. Medicine award Resident Yr., Rush Univ. Med. Ctr., 1999, Dept. Medicine award Outstanding Tchr., 2000; named to Top Doctor's, Chgo. Mag., 2009. Mem.: Am. Soc. Internal Med., Am. Coll. Physicians, Am. Med. Soc. Sports Med., Am. Coll. Sports Med. Office: Midwest Orthopaedics at Rush Ste 1063 1725 W Harrison St Chicago IL 60612 Office Fax: 312-431-3400.

WEBER, MICHAEL A., physician, researcher; m. Sandra Du Bro, Sept. 12, 1971; children: Mark S., David S. BS, Sydney U., Australia, 1967; MD, Sydney U. Sch. of Medicine, Australia, 1967. Cert. Medicine Royal Australasian Coll. of Physicians, 1977, ACP, 1977. Resident in medicine NYU Med. Ctr., 1968—71; rsch. fellow Sydney Hosp., U. Sydney, 1971—75; asst. prof. medicine Cardiovasc. Ctr., Cornell U. Med. Ctr., NYC, 1975—77; chief, sect. clin. pharmacology and hypertension, Irvine Coll. Medicine U. Calif., 1977—95, assoc. prof. medicine, 1977—82, prof. medicine, 1982—85; chmn., dept. medicine Brookdale U. Med. Ctr., Bklyn., 1995—2000; prof. medicine SUNY Downstate Coll. Medicine, Bklyn., 1995—, assoc. dean clin. rsch., 2000—04. Served on Cardiovascular and Renal Drugs Adv. Bd. FDA; cons. FDA; serves on steering committees of several nat. and internat. clin. outcomes trials; retained cons. and mem. speakers bur. Novartis, Merck, Boehringer Ingelheim, Bristol-Myers Squibb and Sanofi. Author: (jour. articles) Lancet; editor: (med. ref. book) Hypertension Medicine, Ambulatory Blood Pressure Monitorins; editor in chief (Jour. Clin. Hypertention); co-editor (mem. editl. bd.): Med Reviews; contbr. several articles to profl. jours. Pres. Am. Soc. of Hypertension, NYC, 1998—2000; chmn. ASH Specialists Program in Hypertension, NYC; cons., ctr. for drug evaluation and rsch. FDA, Washington, 1993—2009. Fellow: Am. Coll. Clin. Pharmacology, Am. Coll. Physicians, Am. Heart Assn. (fellow, coun. for high blood pressure rsch.), Am. Coll. of Cardiology; mem.: Am. Soc. Hypertension (founder, past pres., chair, hypertension specialists program). Office: SUNY Downstate Coll Medicine 450 Clarkson Ave Box 97 Brooklyn NY 11203 Office Fax: 212-584-9192. Personal E-mail: michaelwebermd@cs.com.

WEBER, STEFAN, anesthesiologist, researcher; b. Germany; MD, J. W. Goethe U., 1995. Cert. LÄK Hessen, Germany, 1997, diploma European Soc. Anesthesiology, 2007. Resident Max-Planck Inst., Bad Nauheim, Germany, 1996—97; post-doctoral rschr. U. Calif., Berkeley, 1997—2000; resident U. Bonn Med. Ctr., Germany, 2000—05, staff anesthesiologist, leader flow cytometry lab., 2005—. Author: (sci. handbook) Methods in Enzymology, 2000, Handbook of Cosmetic Science and Technology, 2002, Handbook of Exercise and Oxygen Toxicity, 2006, (sci. ref. book) Current Problems in Dermatology 29, 2006, Clinical Critical Care Medicine, 2006; contbr. (to book chpts.). Recipient Optolind award for skin rsch., Hermes Co., 2000, Poster award, German Soc. Intensive Care Medicine, 2006, Award, Capitol Conf. on Anesthesiolgy and Intensive Care Medicine, 2007; Rsch. grantee, U. Bonn, 2002. Mem.: European Soc. Intensive Care Medicine, German Soc. Anesthesiology and Intensive Care Medicine, European Soc. Critical Care Medicine, Soc. Critical Care Medicine. Office: Univ Bonn Med Ctr Sigmund-Freud-Str 25 D-53105 Bonn Germany Personal E-mail: drsweber@yahoo.de.

WEBER, WALTER PAUL, surgeon, researcher; b. NYC, Dec. 1, 1973; s. Walter Weber and Elisabeth Weber-Stadelmann. MD, U. Basel, Switzerland, 2000. Cert. gen. surgeon FMH, 2007. Resident surgeon Basel U. Hosp., 2001—07; postdoc. rsch. fellow Johns Hopkins Med. Insts., Balt., 2008—. Contbr. scientific papers. With Spl. forces, 1993—, Switzerland. Grant, FAG, 2006, 2007, Swiss Nat. Found., 2007, Novartis-Stiftung, 2007, Huggenberger Krebsstiftung, 2008. Home: Schützenmattstrasse 1 Basel 4051 Switzerland Office: Basel Univ Hosp Spitalstrasse 21 Basel 4031 Switzerland Office Phone: 011-41-61-3286149. Personal E-mail: weberwa@gmx.ch. Business E-Mail: waweber@uhbs.ch.

WEBER, WENDELL WILLIAM, pharmacologist; b. Maplewood, Mo., Sept. 2, 1925; s. Theodore William and Flora Ann (Holt) W.; m. La Donna Tavis, Sept. 29, 1952; children— Jane Holt, Theodore Wendell. AB, Central Coll., 1945; PhD in Phys. Chemistry, Northwestern U., 1950; MD, U. Chgo., 1959. Diplomate Am. Bd. Pediatrics; lic. Mich., N.Y., Calif. Asst. prof. chemistry U. Tenn., Knoxville, 1949-51; mem. ops. research staff U.S. Army Chem. Center, Edgewood, Md., 1951-55; successively instr., asst. prof., asso. prof., prof. pharmacology N.Y. U. Sch. Medicine, NYC, 1963-74; prof. U. Mich., Ann Arbor, 1974-98, Disting. lectureship in Biomedical Rsch., 1993, emeritus prof., 1998—; Disting. lectureship Ctr. for Environ. Genetics U. Cin., 1997. Mem. pharmacology-toxicology com. NIH, 1969-73, rev. coms., 1968— Mem. editl. bd. Bioessays, 1984-91, Pharmacogenetics, 1990—2005, Am. J. Pharmacogenetics, 2000-2005, Personalized Medicine, 2004—09, Molecular Diagnosis and Therapy; author: Pharmacogenetics, 1997, 2nd edits., 2008, The Acetylator Genes and Drug Response, 1987 NIH spl. fellow, 1962-65; research grantee, 1967—98; recipient Career Scientist awards N.Y.C. Health Research Council, 1965-70, 70-74 Fellow N.Y. Acad. Scis.; mem. Am. Soc. Pharmacology and Therapeutics, Am. Chem. Soc., Am. Soc. Human Genetics, Soc. Toxicology (hon.), AAAS, Sigma Xi, Phi Lambda Upsilon. Achievements include research specialty in pharmacogenetics. Home: 14 Geddes Hts Ann Arbor MI 48104-1724 Office: Dept Pharmacology U Mich Ann Arbor MI 48109-0632 Office Phone: 734-764-1316. Business E-Mail: wwweber@umich.edu.

WEBSTER, FLEUR BELINDA, public health service officer, consultant; b. Cowra, NSW, Australia, Mar. 19, 1970; d. Mervyn John and Shirley Maude Webster; m. David Louis Hobson, Oct. 23, 1999; children: Zoe Anastasia Hobson, William Louis Hobson, Mia Eloise Hobson, Samuel Jack Hobson. BSc with honors, U. Sydney, 1991, MScVSc, MPH, U. Sydney, 1996. Coord. hereditary bowel cancer program NSW Cancer Coun., Sydney, 1995—96; project officer best practice Nat. Breast and Ovarian Cancer Ctr., Sydney, 1996—97, mgr. early detection, 1998—2002, cons. project mgr., 2002—. Address: 18 Ironstone Ave Bathurst NSW 2795 Australia Business E-Mail: fleur.webster@nbocc.org.au.

WEBSTER, HENRY DE FOREST, neuroscientist; b. NYC, Apr. 22, 1927; s. Leslie Tillotson and Emily (deForest) W.; m. Marion Havas, June 12, 1951; children: Christopher, Henry, Sally, David, Steven. AB cum laude, Amherst Coll., 1948; MD, Harvard U., 1952. Diplomate in Neurology Am. Bd. Psychiatry Neurology, 1959. Intern Boston City Hosp., 1952-53, resident, 1953-54; resident in neurology Mass. Gen. Hosp., 1954-56, rsch. fellow in neuropathology, 1956-59, prin. investigator NIH rsch. grants, electron micros. studies peripheral neuropathy, 1959-69, mem. staffs; instr. neurology Harvard Med. Sch., Boston, 1959-63, assoc. in neurology, 1963-66, asst. prof. neuropathology, 1966; assoc. prof. neurology U. Miami Sch. Medicine, Fla., 1966-69, prof., 1969; chief sect. cellular neuropathology Nat. Inst. Neurol. Diseases and Stroke, Bethesda, Md., 1969-97; chief Lab. Exptl. Neuropathology, 1984-97; scientist emeritus NIH, 1997—2009. Disting. scientist, lectr. dept. anatomy Tulane U. Sch. Medicine, 1973; Royal Coll. lectr. Can. Assn. Neuropathologists, 1982; Saul Korey lectr. Am. Assn. Neuropathologists, 1992; chmn. Winter Conf. on Brain Rsch., 1985-86; head neuropathology del. to visit China in 1990, Citizen Amb. Program, People to People Internat.; exec. com. rsch. group on neuromuscular disease World Fedn. Neurology, 1986-93. Author: (with A. Peters and S.L. Palay) The Fine Structure of the Nervous System, 1970, 3rd edit., 1991, Cellular Neuroscience: Projects and Images, 2006, (with K.E. Aström) Gliogenesis: Historical Perspectives, 1839-1985, 2009; contbr. sci. articles, revs. to profl. jours. and books. With USNR, 1945—46. Recipient Superior Svc. award USPHS, 1977, A. von Humboldt award Germany, 1985, Sci. award Peripheral Neuropathy Assn., 1994; named hon. prof. Norman Bethune U. of Med. Scis., Chanchun, China, 1991. Mem. Am. Assn. Neuropathologists (v.p. 1976-77, pres. 1978-79, Weil award 1960, Meritorious Contbns. to Neuropathology award 2001), Internat. Soc. Neuropathology (hon., councillor 1976-80, v.p. 1980-84, exec. com. 1980-84, 86-94, pres. 1986-90), Internat. Congress Neuropathology (sec. gen. VIII 1978), Peripheral Nerve Study Group (exec. com. 1975-93, chmn. 1977 meeting), Japanese Soc. Neuropathology (hon.), Am. Neurol. Assn., Am. Acad. Neurology, Royal Soc. Medicine, Am. Soc. Cell Biology, Soc. Neurosci., Rotary Internat., Ausable Club (exec. com.). E-mail: mhwebster@verizon.net.

WEBSTER, JAMES RANDOLPH, JR., physician; b. Chgo., Aug. 25, 1931; s. James Randolph and Ruth Marian (Burtis) W.; m. Joan Burchfield, Dec. 28, 1954; children: Susan, Donovan, John. BS, U. Chgo.-Northwestern U., 1953; MD, MS, Northwestern U., 1956. Diplomate: Am. Bd. Internal Medicine (sub bd. pulmonary disease and geriatrics). Intern Phila. Gen. Hosp., 1956-57; resident in medicine Northwestern U., 1957-60, NIH fellow in pulmonary disease, 1962-64; chief medicine Northwestern Meml. Hosp., Chgo., 1976—88; prof. medicine Northwestern U. Med. Sch., 1977—, chief gen. med. sect. dept. medicine, 1987-88; chief exec. officer Northwestern Med. Group Practice, 1978-88; dir. Buehler Ctr. on Aging Northwestern U. Med. Ctr., 1988-2000. Chief staff Northwestern Meml. Hosp., 1988-90; pres. Chgo. Bd. Health, 2002—, Inst. Medicine, Chgo., Ill., 2002-04, exec. dir., 2004—; chair Ill. Ad Hoc Com. to Defend Health Care. Contbr. chpts. to books, articles to med. jours. Capt. U.S. Army, 1960-62. Recipient Outstanding Clin. tchr. award Northwestern U. Med. Sch., 1974, 77, 84, 86, Alumni Merit award Northwestern U., 1979, Henry P. Russe-Inst. of Medicine award for exemplary compassion in health care, 1997, Aeschulapian award as Physician of Yr., Anti Defamation League, 1998, Lifetime Achivement award,2009, Luminary Sr. award, Chgo., 2006 Master: ACP (gov. for Ill. 1988—92, chair sub-com. on aging 1993, Clayppole award 1994); mem.: Ill. Geriatrics Soc. (pres. 1992—94), Am. Geriatrics Soc., Alpha Omega Alpha. Office: Inst Medicine Chgo Ste 525 332 S Michigan Ave Chicago IL 60604 Home: PO Box 274 Lakeside MI 49116 Office Phone: 312-663-0040. Business E-Mail: j-webster@northwestern.edu.

WEBSTER, JOHN GOODWIN, biomedical engineering educator, researcher; b. Plainfield, NJ, May 27, 1932; s. Franklin Folger and Emily Sykes (Boody) W.; m. Nancy Egan, Dec. 27, 1954; children: Paul, Robin, Mark, Lark BEE, Cornell U., 1953; MSEE, U. Rochester, 1965, PhD, 1967. Engr. North American Aviation, Downey, Calif., 1954-55; engr. Boeing Airplane Co., Seattle, 1955-59, Radiation Inc., Melbourne, Fla., 1959-61; staff engr. Mitre Corp., Bedford, Mass., 1961-62, IBM Corp., Kingston, NY, 1962-63; asst. prof. elec. engring. U. Wis., Madison, 1967-70, assoc. prof. elec. engring., 1970-73, prof. elec. and computer engring., 1973-99, prof. biomed. engring., 1999—2001, prof. emeritus biomed. engring., 2001—. Author: (with others) Medicine and Clinical Engineering, 1977, Sensors and Signal Conditioning, 1991, 2d edit., 2001, Analog Signal Processing, 1999; editor: Medical Instrumentation: Application and Design, 4th edit., 2009, Clinical Engineering: Principles and Practices, 1979, Design of Microcomputer-Based Medical Instrumentation, 1981, Therapeutic Medical Devices: Application and Design, 1982; Electronic Devices for Rehabilitation, 1985; Interfacing Sensors to the IBM-PC, 1988, Encyclopedia of Medical Devices and Instrumentation, 2d edit., 2006, Tactile Sensors for Robotics and Medicine, 1988, Electrical Impedance Tomography, 1990, Teaching Design in Electrical Engineering, 1990, Prevention of Pressure Sores, 1991, Design of Cardiac Pacemakers, 1995, Design of Pulse Oximeters, 1997, The Measurement Instrumentation, and Sensors Handbook, 1999, Encyclopedia of Electrical and Electronics Engineering, 1999, Mechanical Variables Measurement, 2000, Minimally Invasive Medical Technology, 2001, Electrical Measurement, Signal Processing and Displays, 2004, Bioinstrumentation, 2004. Recipient Rsch. Career Devel. award NIH, 1971-76; NIH fellow, 1963-67; recipient Western Electric Fund award Am. Soc. Engring. Edn., 1978, Best Reference Work award, 1999, Theo C. Pilkington Outstanding Educator award, 1994. Fellow IEEE (3d Millennium medal 2000, IEEE-EMBS Career achievement award 2001), Am. Inst. Med. and Biol. Engring., Inst. Physics, Instrument Soc. Am. (Donald P. Eckman Edn. award 1974), Assn. for Advancement Med. Instrumentation (Found. Laufman-Greatbatch prize 1996), Biomed. Engring. Soc. Democrat. Unitarian Universalist. Office: Univ Wis Dept Biomed Engring 1550 Engineering Dr Madison WI 53706-1609 Home Phone: 608-233-8410; Office Phone: 608-263-1574. Business E-Mail: webster@engr.wisc.edu.

WEBSTER, JOHN KINGSLEY OHL, II, health administrator, rehabilitation manager; b. LA, July 27, 1950; s. John Kingsley Ohl and Inez (Gilbert) Webster; children: David Lilly, Jason Kingsley McKnight. AA, Pasadena City Coll., Calif., 1973; BS, San Jose State U., Calif., 1975; MS, Calif. State U., LA, 1989. Registered occupl. therapist Calif. Supervising occupational therapy cons. San Gabriel Valley Regional Ctr., 1976-79; supr. II occupational therapy cons. San Diego Regional Ctr., 1979-83; sr. occupational therapist Mesa Vista Hosp., 1983-84; pvt. practice Vista, Calif., 1983-85; occupational therapy cons. Calif. Children Svcs., State Dept. Health Svcs., LA, 1985-86, regional adminstrv. cons., 1986-90; dir. occupational therapy Eureka Gen. Hosp., 1990; dir. ops. and mktg. Life Dimensions Inc., Newport Beach, Calif., 1990; occupational therapy cons., licensing and cert. Calif. Dept. Health Svcs., 1990-93; program dir. rehab. svcs. Scripps Meml. Hosp., Encinitas, Calif., 1993-94; dir. rehab. Vista Knoll, 1994; clin. dir. occupational therapy Sundance Rehab., San Diego, 1994-95; regional dir. ops. Quest Rehab, LA, 1995-96; area mgr. Am. Therapy Svc., 1996; western divsn. dir. of ops. Accelerated Care Plus, LA, 1996-97; clin. svcs. mgr. Tustin Rehab. Hosp., 1998-99; supr. therapist Calif. Childrens Svcs., 1999; regional dir. ops. Healthpoint, Vista, Calif., 1999-2000; chief restorative svcs. Calif. Vets. Home, Barstow, 2000—03; correctional health svcs. adminstr. Calif. Instn. Women, Corona, Calif., 2003—06; adminstr. correctional health svcs. R.J. Donovan, San Diego, 2006—09, therapy specialists, 2009—10, Interpro Rehab, 2010—. Cons. Hopi and Navajo Tribes, Winslow, 1978; dir. Imperial County SPRANS grant, El Centro, Calif., 1986—88; pres., owner Ergonomix & Regs., San Diego, 1988—. Recipient Esquire title Lady Elliot of STOBS, Edinburough, Scotland, 1973, spl. dept. recognition, Calif. State U., 1989. Mem.: Am. Occupl. Therapy Assn. Avocations: painting, sculpting, producing films, woodworking, tennis. Personal E-mail: ergonomixjw@netzero.net.

WEBSTER, LESLIE TILLOTSON, JR., pharmacologist, educator; b. NYC, Mar. 31, 1926; s. Leslie Tillotson and Emily (de Forest) W.; m. Alice Katharine Holland, June 24, 1955; children: Katharine White, Susan Holland Webster Van Drie, Leslie Tillotson III, Romi Anne. BA, Amherst Coll., 1947, Sc.D. (hon.), 1982; student, Union Coll., 1944; MD, Harvard U., 1948. Diplomate: Am. Bd. Internal Medicine. Rotating intern Cleve. City Hosp., 1948-49, jr. asst. resident in medicine, 1949-50; asst. resident medicine Bellevue Hosp., NYC, 1952-53; research fellow medicine Harvard and Boston City Hosp. Thorndike Meml. Lab., 1953-55; from demonstrator to instr. medicine Sch. of Medicine Western Res. U., 1955-60; research assoc. to sr. instr. biochemistry Case Western Res. U. Sch. Medicine, 1957—60, asst. prof. medicine, 1960-70, asst. prof. biochemistry, 1960-65, asst. prof. pharmacology, 1965-67, assoc. prof., 1967—70, prof. pharmacology, 1976-92, chmn. pharmacology dept., 1976-91, prof. medicine, 1980-86, prof. emeritus pharmacology dept., 1992—; rsch. prof., divsn. pediat. pharmacology and critical care Rainbow Babies and Children's Hosp., Case Western Res. U. Sch. Medicine, 1992—2006, cons. dept. pharmacology, 2007—. Prof., chmn. pharmacology dept. Northwestern U. Med. and Dental Sch., 1970—76; dir. med. scientist tng. program Case Western Res. U. Sch. Medicine, 1979—92; mem. gastroenterology nutritional tng. grants com. NIAMD, NIH, 1965—69; mem. sci. working group on schistosomiasis WHO, 1977—83, chmn. subsect. on chemotherapy biochemistry, 1977—83; mem. exec. com. Gt. Neglected Diseases Network, Rockefeller Found., 1978—86; mem. cellular and molecular basis of disease rev. com. NIGMS, NIH, 1984—88; cons. World Bank, Laos, 2003. Served to lt. med. corps. USNR, 1950-52. Russell M. Wilder fellow Nat. Vitamin Found., 1956-59; Sr. USPHS Research fellow, 1959-61; USPHS Rsch. Career Devel. awardee, 1961-69; Macy faculty scholar, 1980-81. Mem. ACP (life), Central Soc. Clin. Rsch. Coalition (emeritus), Am. Soc. Clin. Investigation (emeritus), Am. Soc. Biochemistry and Molecular Biology (emeritus), Assn. Med. Sch. Pharmacology (emeritus), Am. Soc. Pharmacology and Exptl. Therapeutics (emeritus), Alpha Omega Alpha (hon.). Home: 12546 Cedar Rd No 4 Cleveland Heights OH 44106-3294 Office: Dept Pharmacology Case Western Res Univ 10900 Euclid Ave Cleveland OH 44106-4965 Office Phone: 216-368-0850. Business E-Mail: ltw2@case.edu.

WEBSTER, STEPHEN BURTIS, dermatologist, educator; b. Chgo., Dec. 3, 1935; s. James Randolph Webster and Ruth Marion (Burtis) Holmes; m. Katherine Griffith Webster, Apr. 4, 1959; children: David Randolph, Margaret Elizabeth, James Lucian. BS, Northwestern U., 1957, MD, 1960. Diplomate Am. Bd. Dermatology (bd. dirs. 1992—, v.p. 1997-98, pres.). Intern Colo. Gen. Hosp., Denver, 1960-61; resident Walter Reed Gen. Hosp., Washington, 1962-65; staff physician Henry Ford Hosp., Detroit, 1969-71, Gundersen Lutheran Med. Ctr., La Crosse, 1971—; assoc. clin. prof. U. Wis., Madison, 1976—; clin. prof. U. Minn., Mpls., 1978—. Lt. col. U.S. Army, 1962-69. Fellow Am. Acad. Dermatology (sec.-treas. 1985-88, pres. 1991); mem. AMA, Am. Dermatol. Assn. (pres. 1996-97), Am. Bd. Dermatology (v.p. 1997-98, pres. 1999-2000, assoc. exec. dir. 2001—08, asst. exec. dir., 2009-), Wis. Med. Soc., La Crosse County Med. Soc., Soc. Investigative Dermatology, Alpha Omega Alpha. Independent. Congregationalist. Avocations: bagpipes, model trains. Home: N2062 Wedgewood Dr E La Crosse WI 54601-7175 Office: Gundersen Clinic Ltd 3111 Gundersen Dr MS NC3-006 Onalaska WI 54650 Business E-Mail: sbwebste@gundluth.org.

WECHSLER, DANIEL STEVEN, medical educator; s. Morris Herschel and Ann Wechsler; m. Stephanie Burns, Aug. 21, 1994; children: Caroline Susannah, Julie Rebecca. AB, Harvard U., Cambridge, Mass., 1982; MD, McGill U., Montreal, 1987; PhD, McGill U., 1987. Diplomate Am. Bd. Pediat. Assoc. prof. U. Mich. Med. Sch., Ann Arbor, 1994—. Dir. pediat. hematology-oncology fellowship tng. program U. Mich., 2000—. Mem.: Am. Soc. Pediatric Hematoloy-Oncology (tng. com. 2003—06). Achievements include research in chromosomal translocations in infant leukemia. Office: U Mich 1500 E Medical Ctr Dr CCGC 4312 Ann Arbor MI 48109-0936 Home: 4110 Champaign Dr Durham NC 27707-3077 Office Fax: 734-647-9654. E-mail: dwechsl@umich.edu.

WECHSLER, JILL, editor, writer; b. NYC, July 5, 1946; BA, Vassar Coll., 1968; MA, Hunter Coll., 1974. Editor Managed Healthcare Exec., 1990—, Pharm. Exec. Mag., 1990—. Mem.: Am. Soc Journalists & Authors, Nat. Assn. Sci. Writers, Assn. Healthcare Journalists. Office: 7715 Rocton Ave Chevy Chase MD 20815 Business E-Mail: jillw2@olg.com.

WECHSLER, TONI, healthcare educator, writer; MPH, U. Calif., Los Angeles, 1985. Founder Fertility Awareness Counseling & Training Seminars (FACTS), 1986—. Author: Taking Charge of your Fertility, Cycle Savvy: The Smart Teen's Guide to the Mysteries of Her Body. Office: Ovusoft LLC 120 W Queens Way Ste 202 Hampton VA 23669 Office Phone: 757-722-0991, 757-722-7998. E-mail: info@ovusoft.com.

WEDNER, H. JAMES, physician, researcher; b. Pitts., May 12, 1941; s. Benjamin Mayer and Lucille Ruth (Jacobs) W.; m. Maureen Patricia Martin, June 18, 1978 (div.); children: Bryna Kimberly, Jason Oliver. BS, Cornell U., 1963; MD, Cornell Med. Coll., 1967. Intern Barnes Hosp., St. Louis, 1967—68; resident internal medicine Washington U. Med. Sch., St. Louis, 1970—71, fellow allergy and immunology, 1971—73; lt. comdr. USPHS, Govenor's Island, NY, 1968—70; prof. medicine Washington U. Med. Sch., St. Louis, 1990—, dir. tng. program allergy and immunology, 1986—95, 2001—, chief clin. allergy and immunology, 1988—, med. dir. The Asthma and Allergy Ctr., 2000—, acting chief Divsn. Allergy and Clin. Immunology, 2001—02, chief, 2002—. Vis. prof. Am. Coll. of Allergy and Immunology, Little Rock, 1991, U. Buffalo Med. Sch., 1999; William Pierson vis. prof. Ea. Va. Med. Sch., 2003; prin. investigator psychosocial aspects of asthma, St. Louis Asthma Study Unit; chmn. steering com. Nat. Coop. Inner City Asthma Study; prin. investigator Fungal Alleries Innercity Homes. Editor: Allergy: Theory and Practice, 1984, 2d rev. edit., 1991; mem. editl. bd. Jour. Immunology, 1980-82, Jour. Allergy and Clin. Immunology, 1991-96; assoc. editor Anaphylaxis and Drug Allergy Current Allergy Reports, 2000—; sect. editor Anaplylaxis and Drug Allergy, Current Allergy and Asthma Reports; mem. exec. com., bd. dirs. Asthma and Allergy Found. America, St. Louis. Fellow Am. Acad. Allergy Asthma Immunology, Am. Coll. Physicians; mem. Internat. Soc. Immunopharmacology, Am. Coll. Allergy Asthma Immunology, Am. Assn. Immunology, Clin. Immunology Soc., European Acad. Allergology and Clin. Immunology. Achievements include initial description of Parthenium hysterophruis allergy; research on asthma and the psychosocial aspects of asthma, molecular characterization of plant and fungal allergens and the role of fungi in asthma. Office: Washington U Med Sch Campus Box 8122 660 S Euclid Ave Saint Louis MO 63110-1010 Office Phone: 314-454-7376. Personal E-mail: wednerj@att.net. Business E-Mail: jwedner@im.wustl.edu, jwedner@dom.wustl.edu.

WEEDIN, JOHN WILLIAM, urologist; b. LA, May 20, 1980; BA in History, Molecular and Cell Biology, U. Calif., Berkeley, 2002; MD, U. Calif., San Diego, 2006. Physician Baylor Coll. Medicine, Scott Dept. Urology, 2007—. Mem.: Am. Urol. Assn. Avocations: golf, reading, baseball, softball. Home: 4518 Holt St Bellaire TX 77401 Home Fax: 713-798-5553. Personal E-mail: jweedin@hotmail.com.

WEEKER, ELLIS, emergency physician; b. New Orleans, June 7, 1944; s. Harry and Marion W.; m. Gail Otis, July 3, 1982; children: Michael, Lisa, Elizabeth, Matthew. BS, Tulane U., 1966; MD, La. State U., 1970. Diplomate Am. Bd. Emergency Medicine. Intern Kaiser Found. Hosp., Oakland, 1970-71, resident in internal medicine, 1972-73, Highland Gen. Hosp., Oakland, 1972-73, assoc. chief emergency svcs., 1973-75; staff physician Calif. Emergency Physicians Med. Group, Oakland, 1975—, mem. bd. dirs., 1975—2009, divsn. v.p., 2008—. Med. dir. Calif. Emergency Physicians Med. Group, Oakland, 1976-95, regional med. dir., 1978-2008, chmn. bd. dirs., 1979-87, divsn. v.p., 2008-; mem. staff Good Samaritan Hosp., San Jose, Calif., 1975—, chmn. emergency dept., 1977-82. Commnr. Emergency Med. Care Commn., Santa Clara County, Calif., 1990-92. Mem. Am. Heart Assn. (chmn. bd. Santa Clara chpt. 1991-92, pres. 1988-89, nat. affiliate faculty ACLS 1982-91). Republican. Roman Catholic. Avocations: music, skiing, sailing. Home: 2105 S Bascom Ave Ste 360 Campbell CA 95008-3270 Office Phone: 510-350-2860.

WEEKS, GERALD, psychologist, educator; b. Morehead City, NC, Nov. 20, 1948; s. Marion G. and Ada (Willis) W. BA in Philosophy and Psychology, East Carolina U., 1971, MA in Gen. Psychology, 1973; PhD in Clin. Psychology, Ga. State U., 1979. Diplomate Am. Bd. Profl. Psychology (pres. 1987-88, bd. dirs. 1982-87), Am. Bd. Family Psychology, Am. Bd. Sexology; cert. marital and family therapist; lic. practicing psychologist, Nev., Pa.; bd. cert. sexologist. Intern in family therapy Harlem Valley Psychiat. Ctr., Wingdale, NY, 1978-79; assoc. prof. psychology U. N.C., Wilmington, 1979-85; dir. tng. Penn Coun. for Relationships, 1985—; clin. asst. prof. psychology Sch. Medicine U. Pa., Phila., 1985-87, clin. assoc. prof., 1988-98; chair, prof. dept. counseling U. Nev.-Las Vegas, 1999—. Pvt. practice Carolina Ob-gyn. Ctr., Wilmington, 1980-85. Author: Paradoxical Therapy, 1982, Treating Couples: The Intersystem Model of the Marriage Council of Philadelphia, 1989, Promoting Change through Paradoxical Therapy, 1991, Paradoxical Psychotherapy: Theory and Practice with Individuals, Couples, and Families, 1982; co-author: (with L. L'Abate) Family Therapy: Basic Concepts and Terms, 1985, (with L. L'Abate) Integrating Sex and Marital Therapy: A Clinicians Guide, 1987, Erectile Dysfunction, 2000, (with N. Gambescia) Couples in Treatment, 1992, rev. edit., 2001, Integrative Solutions: Treating Common Problems in Couple's Therapy, 1995, (with Hof and TREAT) Focused Genograms: Intergenerational Assessment of Individuals, Couples and Families, 1999, (with DeMaria & Hof) Hypoactive Sexual Desire, 2002, Treating Infidelity, (with Gambescia and Jenkins) Handbook of Family Therapy, 2003, (with Odell and Muthuen) If Only I Had Known: Common Mistakes in Couples Therapy, 2004, (with K. Hertlein & Mambescia) Muida to Systemic Sex Therapy, 2008, Systemic Sex Therapy, A Clinician's Guide to Systemic Sex Therapy; contbr. articles to profl. jours. Recipient Outstanding Family & Marriage Therapy award, AAMNFT, 2009. Fellow Am. Assn. Marital and Family Therapy (clin. mem., nat. adv. bd., approved supr.); mem. APA, Acad. Family Psychology, Interpersonal and Social Skills Assn. (founding mem.), Acad. Psychologists in Marital, Sex, and Family Therapy, Am. Assn. of Sex Educators (clin. mem.), Counselors of Therapists. Office: Dept Marriage and Family Therapy PO Box 453045 4505 S Maryland Pky Las Vegas NV 89154-3045 Office Phone: 702-895-1392. Business E-Mail: gerald.weeks@unlv.edu.

WEEKS, SANDY CLAIRE, medical researcher; b. Adelaide, Australia, Sept. 18, 1950; d. Henry Vernon and Valda Dorothy (Wahlqvist) W. Student in med. sci., U. So. Australia, Adelaide, 1977-82. Justice of the Peace. Surgical rsch. asst. Adelaide U., 1968-76, Flinders U. Med. Ctr., Adelaide, 1976-81, med. rsch. scientist, 1982-88, sr. med. rsch. scientist, 1989- . Lectr. in biol. scis. So. Australian Colls. for Advanced Edn., Adelaide, 1973-78; dir. Flinders Credit Union, 1985-99; devel. cons. Diagnostic Rsch. Labs., Australia, 1987-90; spkr. Asian & Pacific Fedn. Cancer Rsch. and Control, Bangkok, 1993, others; keynote spkr. World Conf. for Breast Cancer, Can., 1997, 2002, keynote spkr., internat. adv. bd., 2002. Author: The Anti Cancer Cookbook, 1990, 2d edit., 1993, How Not To Take Medicine, 1995, 3d edit., 2000, Hot to Trot, 1998, Hormone Replacement Therapy-Friend or Foe?, 1998, Prostate Puzzles-More Than a Mind Teaser!, 1999, Quackbusters Chronicles, 2003, The Cancer Pack-Taking the Fear Out of Cancer, 2003, Apocalypse Or A Golden Age?, 2011; contbr. articles to profl. jours. Cmty. preceptor in preventive cancer edn. Mem. N.Y. Acad. Scis., Australian Inst. Med. Scientists (spkr.), Internat. Soc. Preventive Oncology (spkr.), Australian and New Zealand Soc. Cell Biology. Avocations: writing travel documentaris, fiction, music, classi cal piano. Office: Flinders U Dept Anatomical Pathology Flinders Med Ctr Bedford Park 5042 Australia Office Phone: 618 8204 4685. Business E-Mail: sandy.weeks@flinders.edu.au.

WEEMS, KERRY N., former federal agency administrator; b. Portales, N.Mex., 1956; BA in Philosophy, N.Mex. State U., 1978, BBA in Mgmt., 1978; MBA, U. N.Mex., 1981. Staff mem. Appropriations Com. US Senate, 1981—83; program & budget analyst US Dept. Health & Human Services, Washington, 1983—88, program analyst Office of Budget, 1988—91, chief budget planning br., 1991—96, dir. divsn. budget policy, execution & mgmt., 1996—2002, acting dep. asst. sec. budget, 2001—02, acting asst. sec. for budget, tech. & fin., 2003—05, dep. chief staff, 2005—07, adminstr. Centers for Medicare & Medicaid Services, 2007—09.

WEERAKIET, SAWAEK, gynecologist; b. Chumporn, Feb. 15, 1956; Diplomate Thai Bd Ob-Gyn., Thai Med. Coun., Bangkok, 1994, in reproductive medicine Thai Sub-Bd., 2000. Head, dept. ob-gyn. Faculty Medicine Ramathibodi Hosp., Mahidol U., 2008—. Office: Praram 6 Bangkok Ratchathevi 10400 Thailand Office Fax: 6622011416. Business E-Mail: raswt@mahidol.ac.th.

WEFERS, KLAUS PETER, dentist; b. Bottrop, Germany, Oct. 10, 1955; s. Heinrich Johann and Maria Theodora (Hilgert) W.; m. Sabine Kovermann, Aug. 22, 1986. DDS, Giessen U., 1986; DMD; attending in Health Bus. Adminstrn., Nuremberg U., 2010—. From dental asst. to head subdept. gerodontology Giessen U., Germany, 1983-97; head Blend-a-med Rsch., Germany, 1997—2001; asst. med. dir. Jena U., Germany, 2002—11; specialist gerodontology, 2008. Cons. Cen-Tec, Brussels, 1986-87, Stiftung Warentest, Berlin, 1996—, Deutsches Inst. für Normung, Berlin, 1998—; legal expert in prosthodontics, 1988—. Mem. Nat. Soc. Gerodontology(pres. 1990-97), European Coll. Gerodontology (councillor 1993-98). Avocations: model railways, architecture. Office: Friedrich-Schiller U, ZZMK D-07743 Jena Germany Business E-Mail: kp.wefers@med.uni-jena.de.

WEG, JOHN GERARD, physician; b. NYC, Feb. 16, 1934; s. Leonard and Pauline M. (Kanzleiter) W.; m. Mary Loretta Flynn, June 2, 1956; children: Diane Marie, Kathryn Mary, Carol Ann, Loretta Louise, Veronica Susanne, Michelle Celeste. BA cum laude, Coll. Holy Cross, Worcester, Mass., 1955; MD, N.Y. Med. Coll., 1959. Diplomate: Am. Bd. Internal Medicine. Commd. 2nd lt. USAF, 1958, advanced through grades to capt., 1967; intern Walter Reed Gen. Hosp., Washington, 1959-60; resident, then chief resident in internal medicine Wilford Hall USAF Hosp., Lackland AFB, Tex., 1960-64, chief pulmonary sect., 1964-66, chief inhalation sect., 1964-66, chief pulmonary and infectious disease service, 1966-67; resigned, 1967; clin. dir. pulmonary disease div. Jefferson Davis Hosp., Houston, 1967-71; from asst. prof. to assoc. prof. medicine Baylor U. Coll. Medicine, Houston, 1967-71; assoc. prof. medicine U. Mich. Med. Sch. Univ. Hosp., Ann Arbor, 1971-74, prof., 1974—2001, prof. emeritus, 2001—. Physician-in-charge pulmonary divsn., 1971-81, physician-in-charge pulmonary and critical care med. divsn., 1981-85, instnl. rev. bd. mem., 1996-2003, co-chair INSTL rev. bd., 2004-11; cons. Ann Arbor VA, 1971—2001, Wayne County Gen. Hosps., 1971-84; mem. adv. bd. Washtenaw County Health Dept., 1973—85; mem. respiratory and nervous sys. panel, anesthesiology sect. Nat. Ctr. Devices and Radiol. Health, FDA, 1983-88, chmn., 1985-88. Contbr. med. jours., reviewer, mem. editorial bds. Decorated Air Force Commendation medal; travelling fellow Nat. Tb and Respiratory Disease Assn., 1971; recipient Aesculpaius award Tex. Med. Assn., 1971 Master ACP (chmn. Mich. program com. 1974); fellow Am. Coll. Chest Physicians (chmn. bd. govs. 1976-79, gov. Mich. 1975-79, chmn. membership com. 1976-79, prof.-in-residence 1972—74, chmn. critical care coun. 1982-85, chmn. ethics com. 1998, master FCCP, 2002-), Am. Coll. Chest Physicians and Internat. Acad. Chest Physicians (master, exec. council 1976-82, pres. 1980-81); mem. AAAS, Am. Fedn. Clin. Rsch., AMA, Am. Thoracic Soc. (sec.-treas. 1974-76), Am. Assn. Inhalation Therapy, Air Force Soc. Internists and Allied Specialists, Soc. Med. Consultants to Armed Forces, Internat. Union Against Tb, Mich. Thoracic Soc. (pres. 1976-78), Mich. Lung Assn. (dir., Bruce Douglas award 1981), Am. Lung Assn., Rsch. Club U. Mich., Assn. Advancement Med. Instrumentation, Central Soc. Clin. Rsch., Am. Bd. Internal Medicine (subsplty. com. on pulmonary disease 1980-86, critical care medicine test com. 1985-87, critical care medicine policy com. 1986-87), N.Y. Med. Coll. Alumni Assn. (medal of honor 1990), Alpha Omega Alpha. Home: 3060 Exmoor Rd Ann Arbor MI 48104-4132 Home Phone: 734-971-6156; Office Phone: 734-763-2540. E-mail: jweg@umich.edu.

WEGELIUS, OTTO CARL, retired medical educator; b. Oct. 21, 1920; MD, Helsinki U., 1947, PhD, 1952. Asst. tchr. Dept. Medicine, Helsinki, 1956—59, prof. IV, 1959—64, assoc. prof., 1964—71; full prof., 1971—83, prof. emeritus, 1983—. Contbr. articles to profl. jours.; author: Slumpens Vagar, 1998, Slumpens Skordar, 2008, Vemod Poems, 2008. Mem.: Endocrine Soc., Am. Coll. Rheumatology. Home: Mynt Gaard Myntbolevagen 2 Espoo 02780SF Finland

WEGNER, KARL HEINRICH, retired pathologist, educator, farmer; b. Pierre, SD, Jan. 5, 1930; s. Lester and Nell (Norbeck) W.; m. Mary Josephine Waddell, June 15, 1957 (dec. 2003); children: Madeleine Jean, Peter Norbeck, Mary Nell; m. Margaret Ann Cash, Apr. 28, 2004. BA, Yale U., 1952; MD, Harvard U., 1959. Intern, resident Mass. Gen. Hosp./Harvard U., 1959-62; pathologist Sioux Valley Hosp., Sioux Falls, S.D., 1962-90; pathologist, dir. Lab. Clin. Medicine, Sioux Falls, 1962-90; prof., chmn. dept. pathology U. SD, 1968-73, v.p. health affairs, founding dean Sch. Medicine, 1973-79, Regents Disting. prof. emeritus, 1992—; owner Meadowlark Farms, Montrose, S.D.; ret. Mem. Bd. of Regents for Higher Edn., State of S.D., pres. bd. regents, 1996-97. Bd. dirs. U. S.D. Found.; pres. bd. dirs. Sioux Valley Hosp. Found., Sioux Falls Area Cmty. Found.; pres., Friend of Yr., 2006, SD Symphony. With USMC, 1952—54, capt. Reserves USMC, 1954—58. Karl H. Wegner Endowed Professorship; recipient Disting. Svc. award S.D. State Med. Assn., 1984, Community Svc. award, 1975, Philanthropist of Yr. award, S.D., 2002; inducted to S.D. Hall of Fame, 1987; Karl and Mary Jo Wegner Health Scis. Info. Ctr. named in their honor, 1998. Fellow Coll. Am. Pathologists, Internat. Acad. Pathologists, Am. Soc. Pathologists; mem. Am. Pathology Found. (pres. 1984-85, Am. Pathologist of Yr. award, 1989), Alpha Omega Alpha. Home: 5010 S Sunnymede Cir Sioux Falls SD 57108-2823 E-mail: khwegner@sio.midco.net.

WEGNER, ROLF-DIETER, geneticist; b. Berlin, Aug. 14, 1949; PhD, Humboldt U. Berlin (formerly Free U. Berlin), 1979. Cert. Prof. Charite Humboldt U. Berlin, 1997. Head lab. postnatal diagnosis, genetic counseling unit Free U. Berlin, 1978—91; head cytogenetic dept., genetic counseling unit berlin Humboldt U. Berlin, 1991—95; head Zentrum Praenataldiagnostik Kudamm199, Berlin, 1999—. Contbr. articles to profl. jours. Leading team ch. cmty. Protestantic Ch. Berlin Brandenburg, Berlin, 1971—. Office: Zentrum Praenataldiagnostik Kurfuerstendamm 199 Berlin 10719 Germany Office Phone: 49 30 8804 3151. Office Fax: 49 30 8804 3176. Business E-Mail: wegner@kudamm-199.de.

WEHBE, MARWAN A., orthopaedic surgeon, educator; Attended, Inter Am. U., Beirut. Diplomate Am. Bd. Orthopaedic Surgery, 1983, Am. Bd. Orthopaedic Surgery-hand surgery, 1989. Clin. prof. Thomas Jefferson Univ.; staff Bryn Mawr Hosp., 1985—, attending physician; staff Paoli Hosp., 2002—. With mktg. com. Am. Assn. Hand Surgery, 1994—97; with numerous coms. Am. Soc. Surgery of the Hand, 1994—; cons. reviewer Jour. of the Hand Surgery, 2000—. Author: (clin. studies) "Anatomy of the Extensor Mechanism of the Hand and Wrist", Hand Clinics, 1995, "Extensor Physiology in the Hand and Wrist", Hand Clinics, 1995, "Ulnar Shortening using the AO Small Distractor", J. Hand Surgery, 1995, "Early Motion after Hand and Wrist Reconstruction", Hand Clinics, 1996, "Early Motion Protocols in Hand and Wrist Reconstruction", Hand Clinics, 1996, numerous other clin. studies. Named one of the Top Doctors, Phila. Mag., 2011. Mem.: AMA, ACS, Am. Acad. Orthop. Surgeons, Am. Assn. Hand Surgeons, Am. Soc. Surgery of the Hand. Office: Bryn Mawr Hospital Susquehanna Bank Bld 101 Bryn Mawr Ave Ste 300 Bryn Mawr PA 19010 Office Phone: 610-525-1000. Office Fax: 610-525-1001.

WEHBY, MONICA C., pediatric neurosurgeon; b. Nashville; 4 children. BS in Microbiology, U. Notre Dame, Ind., 1984, BA in Psychology, 1984; MD, Baylor Coll. Medicine, Houston, 1988. Cert. American Assn. Neurol. Surgeons, American Bd. Pediat. Neurosurgeons. Resident in neurosurgery UCLA Med. Ctr., 1988—95; fellow in pediat. neurosurgery U. Utah Children's Med. Ctr., 1996—97;

neurosurgeon, ptnr. Microneurosurgical Consultants PC, 1997—2008; med. dir. pediat. neurosurgery The Children's Hosp. at Legacy Emanuel, Portland, Oreg.; pediat. neurosurgeon Legacy Med. Group - Pediat. Neurosurgery, Portland. Bd. trustees Oreg. Assn. Hospitals and Health Services, Legacy Health Systems Found. Mem.: AMA (mem. House Dels. 1986—, bd. trustees 2011—), American Assn. Neurol. Surgeons (mem. bd. dirs., mem. Congress Neurol. Surgeons' Wash. com.), Oreg. Med. Soc. (past pres.), Med. Soc. Met. Portland (past pres., Presdl. citation). Office: Legacy Med Group Pediat Neurosurgery Med Office Bldg Ste 330B 501 N Graham St Portland OR 97227 Office Phone: 503-413-3690. Office Fax: 503-287-0705. *

WEHNERT, MANFRED SIEGFRIED, human molecular geneticist, educator; b. Stralsund, Germany, Feb. 7, 1951; s. Siegfried and Erika (Stripp) W.; m. Susanne Christine Kittner, Oct. 6, 1989; children: Hendrikje, Sabine Susanne. Diploma in Biology, U. Greifswald, Germany, 1973, PhD, 1980, Habilitation, 1991. Cert. human geneticist. Faculty U. Greifswald, 1978—91, sr. faculty, 1994—, prof. human molecular genetics, 1999—; postdoctoral Baylor Coll., Houston, 1991—94. Recipient award Johann-Lukas-Schoenlein Soc., Germany, 1990, award Fed. Min. Sci. and Tech., Germany, 1991. Fellow AAAS, Am. Soc. Human Genetics, European Soc. Human Genetics, World Muscle Soc. Achievements include research in post-and prenatal biochemical diagnosis of inborn; errors of metabolism; introduction of molecular genetics diagnosis of clotting disorders and muscle diseases; identification and characterization of human genes; codiscovery of the gene for Miller-Diecker-Lisencephaly. Office: Inst Human Genetics Fleischmannstr. 42/44 17489 Greifswald Germany Office Phone: 49-3834-865374. Business E-Mail: mwehnert@uni-greifswald.de.

WEI, BO, thoracic surgeon; b. Shanxi, China, July 10, 1973; MD, Capital Med. U., PhD, 2004. Thoracic surgeon Beijing Shijitan Hosp., Capital Med. U., 2006—. Office: 10 Tieyi Rd Haidian Dist Beijing 100038 China Personal E-mail: greatweibo@yahoo.com.cn.

WEI, I. HUA, medical educator; b. Taichung, Feb. 10, 1974; PhD, Nat. Taiwan U. Coll. Medicine, 2004. Asst. prof. Sch. Medicine, China Med. U., Taiwan, 2005—. Office: 91 Hsueh-Shih Rd Taichung 404 Taiwan

WEI, JOHN THOMAS, urologist, educator; b. Hong Kong, Jan. 3, 1967; came to U.S., 1972; s. John K.C. and Lina Ko Wei; m. Mary Lee Wei, Sept. 25, 1993; children: Nicholas John, Katherine Britney. BS, Northwestern U., Chgo., 1989; MD, Northwestern U. Med. Sch., Chgo., 1991; MS, U. Mich. Sch. Pub. Health, 1999. Resident in surgery North Shore Univ. Hosp., Manhasset, NY, 1991-93; resident in urology Cornell-N.Y. Hosp., NYC, 1993-97; Robert Wood Johnson clin. scholar U. Mich., Ann Arbor, 1997-99, lectr. medicine and surgery, 1997-99, asst. prof. surgery, 1999—, assoc. prof., dept. urology, asst. prof. urology, dir., clin. rsch. and quality assurance, assoc. dir., Clin. Rsch. Tng. Program in Urology; staff urologist Ann Arbor VA Med. Ctr., 1997—. Voting mem. R&D com. Ann Arbor VA, 2000—. Chmn. prostate cancer com. Mich. Cancer Consortium, 1999. Am. Found. for Urologic Disease scholar, 1997. Mem. Am. Assn. Clin. Urologists, Am. Urol. Assn., Chinese Am. Med. Soc. Avocations: gardening, wood craft, aquariums. Office: Univ of Mich Taubman Ctr 3875 1500 E Medical Center Dr Ann Arbor MI 48109-0330 Mailing: Livonia Ctr for Specialty Care 19900 Haggerty Rd Fl 1 Ste 111 Livonia MI 48152-1052 Office Phone: 734-615-3040, 734-936-7030. E-mail: jtwei@umich.edu.

WEI, KEVIN S., cardiologist, educator; b. Hong Kong, China, Nov. 24, 1963; BS, U. Toronto, 1986, MD, 1989. Asst. prof. medicine U. Va., 1997—2003, assoc. prof. medicine, 2003—05; prof. medicine Oreg. Health & Sci. U., 2005—. Recipient Young Investigator award, Am. Coll. Cardiology, 1997, Am. Soc. Echocardiography, 2000, Feigenbaum Lectr. award, 2005. Fellow: Am. Coll. Cardiology, Am. Soc. Echocardiography; mem.: Am. Heart Assn. Avocations: bicycling, piano. Office: 3181 SW Sam Jackson Park Rd UHN62 Portland OR 97239 Office Fax: 503-494-8550. Business E-Mail: weik@ohsu.edu.

WEI, SHI, medical educator; b. China, Feb. 24, 1964; MD, China Med. U., 1989. Asst. prof. U. Ala., Birmingham, 2009. Office: West Pavilion P220 619 19th St S Birmingham AL 35249 Business E-Mail: swei@uab.edu.

WEI, WILLIAM I., surgeon; MBBS, 1974, MS, 1991. Chief of svc. ear, nose and throat dept. Queen Mary Hosp., Hong Kong; fellow Am. Coll. of Surgeon, 1984; fellow ear, nose and throat Royal Coll. of Surgeons, England, 1986, fellow gen. surgeon, 1979, fellow, 2000; fellow otorhinolaryngology Hong Kong Acad. of Medicine, 1993, fellow surgeon, 1997; hon. fellowship Royal Australasian Coll. of Surgeons, 2004. Prof. surgery dept. Univ. of Hong Kong, chmn. surg. sciences group, faculty medicine. Author 203 refereed jours., 70 non refereed jours., 20 book chpts., 2 books. Mem.: Hong Kong Head & Neck Soc. (pres. 2004—05), Hong Kong Coll. of Otorhinolaryngologists (pres. 1996—2002). Office: Queen Mary Hospital Professorial Block Rm 206 Pokfulam Rd Hong Kong Office Phone: 85228554237. Office Fax: 85228184407. Business E-Mail: hrmswwi@hkucc.hku.hk. *

WEI-CHIEN, HUANG, medical educator, researcher; b. Tainan, Taiwan, Mar. 4, 1974; PhD, Nat. Taiwan U., 2003. Asst. prof. Grad. Inst. Cancer Biology, China Med. U., 2007—. Mem.: Taiwan Pharmacology Soc., Am. Assn. Cancer Rsch. Office: 9F 6 Hsueh-Shih Rd Taichung 404 Taiwan Business E-Mail: whuang@mail.cmu.edu.tw.

WEIDANZ, WILLIAM P., microbiologist, immunologist, educator; b. Jackson Heights, NY, Jan. 30, 1935; BS in Pharmacy, Rutgers Coll. Pharmacy, 1956; MS in Bacteriology, U. RI; PhD in Microbiology, Tulane U., 1961. Asst. prof. microbiology La. State U., 1964—66; prof. microbiology & immunology Hahnemann Coll. Medicine, 1966—90, assoc. dean academic affairs, 1983—85; prof., chair, med. microbiology & immunology, Sch. Medicine U. Wis., 1990—2000, prof. med. microbiology and immunology, Sch. Medicine and Pub. Health, 2000—. Editl. bd. mem. Infection and Immunity, 1983—87, Vaccine Rsch., 1995—2005, Exptl. Parasitology, 1995—2005; sect. editor Immunoparasitology, Jour. Immunology, 1990; study sect. mem., tropical medicine and parasitology NIH, 1985—89; mem. sci. cons. group Malaria Vaccine R & D Program US AID, 1988—2007; adj. prof. medicine U. Ala., Birmingham, 1990; adj. prof. microbiology Drexel U. Coll. Medicine, 2002; adj. prof. pharm. scis. Tex. Tech U., 2005. Recipient Excellence in Tchg. award, Lindback Found.; Eleanor Roosevelt Internat. Cancer fellowship, Am. Cancer Soc., U. Rsch. Coun. Faculty fellowship, La. State U. Mem.: Am. Soc. Tropical Medicine and Hygiene, Am. Soc. Microbiology. Avocations: gardening, fishing, reading. Office: 1550 Linden Dr Madison WI 53706-1521 Office Fax: 608-262-8418. Business E-Mail: wweidanz@facstaff.wisc.edu.

WEIDINGER, MARIELUISE, biologist; b. Düsseldorf, Germany, Jan. 20, 1953; d. Franz and Helga Weidinger. Baccalaureat, Luxemburg, 1971; PhD, U. Salzburg, Austria, 1978. Sci. employee U. Bielefeld, Germany, 1978—83; sci. officer U. Vienna, 1984—. Contbr. scientific papers to profl. publs. Adminstr. Internat. Bahai Cmty., Vienna, 1972—2009. Mem.: Internat. Socs. Electron Microscopy. Office: Univ Vienna Biology Ctr Althanstrasse 14 Vienna A-1090 Austria Business E-Mail: marieluise.weidinger@univie.ac.at.

WEIDNER, STANISLAW MARIAN, biochemistry, enzymology and proteomics educator; b. Wrzesnia, Poznan, Poland, Mar. 22, 1947; s. Jozef and Ludwika (Rominska) Weidner; m. Maria Magdalena Minakowska, Aug. 12, 1976; children: Magdalena, Janusz. Master, Olsztyn U., Poland, 1971, Doctor, 1980. Asst. Olsztyn U. Agr. and Tech., 1971-80, adj., 1980-89, asst. prof., 1989-92, assoc. prof., 1992—2001; prof. biology U. Warmia and Mazury, Olsztyn, 2001—, head dept. biochemistry, 2005—. Vis. prof. Okayama U., 1998—99. Editor (with Waclaw Minakowski): (books) Biochemistry of Vertebrates, 1998 (Antoni Dmochowski award, 2008), 2nd edit., 2005 (Minister's prize, 1999, 2006), 2007, 2010; mem. editl. bd. Acta Physiologiae Plantarum, 2000—; contbr. over 80 refereed articles to profl. jours.; presenter numerous conf. papers. Recipient Silver and Gold Cross for achievements in sci. and ednl. fields, Pres. of Poland, 1994, 2003, medal, Nat. Edn. Commn., 2009; fellow Internat. Rsch. and Exch. Bd., 1990, Kosciuszko Found., 1997; State Com. for Sci. Rsch. grantee, 1993—2001, 2004—10, COST Project European Coop. grant, 1996—2001, 2003—. Mem.: Soc. for Seed Sci., Polish Soc. for Exptl. Biology, Polish Bot. Soc., Fedn. European Socs. Plant Biology, Fedn. European Biochem. Socs. Roman Catholic. Office: Univ Warmia and Mazury Oczapowskiego St 1A 10-957 Olsztyn Poland Home: Ul, Jaroslawa Iwaszkiewicza 41/3 10-089 Olsztyn Poland Office Phone: (4889) 5234883. Business E-Mail: weidner@uwm.edu.pl.

WEIGEL, OLLIE J, dentist, former mayor; b. Guthrie County, Iowa, Sept. 29, 1922; s. Verne Noble and Ethel Rebecca (Johnson) W.; m. Mary Kathryn Finnegan, June 3, 1944 (dec. Sept. 1999); children: John, Marilyn, Larry, Susan. DDS, U. Iowa, 1951. Practice dentistry, Ankeny, 1951-94; mayor City of Ankeny, 1974-93. Mem. Metro Planning Orgn., 1995-2000; bd. dirs. Neveln Resource Ctr., 1995-2000. Mem. Ankeny Bd. Adjustment, 1953-58, Ankeny Planning and Zoning Commn., 1953-65, Ankeny City Coun., 1966-73, Des Moines Area C.C. Found. Bd., 1993—, mem. emeritus; mem. Des Moines Area Metro Forum, 1985-93, found. bd. On With Life, 1994-2000; life mem. Ankeny Indsl. Devel. Corp.; mem. adv. bd. dirs. Brenton Bank of Ankeny, 1994-2000; mem. Polk County Aviation Authority, 2001-2003. 1st lt. USAAF, 1943-45, ETO. Recipient Person of Vision award, Ankeny Indsl. Devel. Corp. (1st recipient), 2001; named to Mayors Hall of Fame, 1993—96. Mem. ADA (life), Iowa Dental Assn. (life), Des Moines Dist. Dental Assn., Ankeny C. of C. (charter mem., life, pres. 1953, 70, Outstanding Citizen 1976, 93), Mid Iowa Assn. Local Govts. (chmn. 1983), League of Iowa Municipalities (pres. 1976-77), Ctrl. Iowa Regional Govts. (pres. 1978), Am. Legion (life), Ankeny Cmty. Dist. Sch. Found. (bd. dirs.)(named Hall of Fame 2007) Republican. Methodist. Avocation: fishing. Home and Office: 2506 NW 4th St Ankeny IA 50023-1002

WEIGER, WENDY ANNE, physician, researcher; b. Baltimore, Dec. 10, 1961; d. Robert William and Nadine Luxmore Weiger. BA, Harvard Coll., Cambridge, MA, 1983; PhD, Harvard U., Cambridge, 1995; MD, Harvard Med. Sch., Boston, 1997. Rsch. fellow Beth Israel Deaconess Med. Ctr., Boston, 1999—2002; rsch. assoc. Harvard Med. Sch. Osher Inst., 2002—. Author: (review) Complementary Cancer Therapies Annals Internal Med., Seratonin and Behavior Biological Reviews; contbr. articles to profl. jours. Bd. dirs. Only A Child, Guatemala City, Guatemala, 2000—03, Arlington St. Ch., Boston, 2002—03. Recipient Elizabeth Cary Agassiz Scholar, Radcliffe Coll., 1979-1984; fellow Albert J. Ryan Fellow, Albert J. Ryan Found., 1988-1995. Mem.: Earthjustice Legal Def. Fund, Nature Conservancy. Democrat. Unitarian Universalist. Achievements include research in integrative medicine with a focus on therapies commonly used in cancer. Avocation: nature writing. Office: Harvard Med Sch Osher Inst The Landmark Ctr 401 Park Dr Boston MA 02215 E-mail: wendy_weiger@hms.harvard.edu.

WEIGHTMAN, ESTHER LYNN, emergency trauma nurse; b. Tawas City, Mich., June 13, 1966; d. Garrie Lee and Naomi Ruth (Atwood) Schneller; m. Robert Thomas Weightman, Dec. 31, 1996; children: Erin Elizabeth, Kaili Marie. BS in Christian Secondary Edn., Ozark Bible Inst. & Coll., Neosho, Mo., 1988; BSN, Ind. Wesleyan U., Marion, 1991; MS in Cmty. Health Nursing, U. Colo. Health Scis. Ctr., Denver, 1995. RN, Colo.; cert. ACLS, pediatric advanced life support, trauma nurse core course; Profl. Spl. Svcs. licensee Colo. Dept. Edn. Staff nurse emergency dept. Marion Gen. Hosp., 1991-92, Penrose-St. Francis Healthcare Sys., Colorado Springs, Colo., 1992-95; staff nurse registry QS Nurses Corp., Colorado Springs, 1992-2001; staff devel. nurse 302d ASTS-USAFR, Peterson AFB, Colo., 1994-2001; staff nurse emergency dept. Med. Ctr. of Aurora, Colo., 1997-2001; staff nurse ICU St. Peter's Hosp., Helena, Mont., 2001—02, VA Mont. Healthcare Sys., Ft. Harrison, Mont., 2002—04; staff devel. nurse Mont. Air N.G., Great Falls, 2003—05; nurse surg. intensive care unit VA, Omaha, 2004—05, Omaha nurse urgent care, 2005—08, charge nurse urgent care Sioux Falls, SD, 2008—09; clin. nurse 710th Med. Squadron, USAFR, Offutt AFB, Nebr., 2005—09; case mgr., Home Based Primer Ops. Enduring Freedom-Ops. Iraq Freedom, Sioux Falls, SD, 2009; clin. nurse 302d ASTS-USAFR, Peterson AFB, Colo., 2009—, chief nurse, 2011—; case mgr. DEF OIF, Sioux Falls, 2009—10, home health nurse case mgr., 2010. Mentor various healthcare instrnl. facilities, 1991—; vol. tchr. health classes Knowledge is Power, Red Cross Shelter, Colorado Springs, 1995-96; health fair vol. Mem.: Emergency Nurses Assn., Res. Officers Assn., Sigma Theta Tau. Avocations: cooking, orchestra (trumpet).

WEIHRAUCH, THOMAS ROBERT, internist, consultant, gastroenterologist, educator; b. Munich, Nov. 23, 1942; s. Hans Robert and Elna Sophie (Birch) W.; m. Birgit Eggers, Mar. 7, 1969; children: Martin Robert, Julia Christine. MD, PhD, U. Munich, 1970; Habilitation in Internal Medicine, U. Mainz, Germany, 1979. Diplomate German Bd. Internal Medicine, German Bd. Gastroenterology. Intern U. Kiel (Germany) Clinics, 1969—70, Maricopa County Hosp., Phoenix, 1970—71; resident in internal medicine Univ. Clinic Medicine I, Mainz, 1971—79, chief resident, 1979—82; assoc. in exptl. pharmacology U. Mainz, 1971—75, lectr. clin. medicine, pathophysiology and clin. pharmacology, 1971—89; life prof. internal medicine and gastroenterology Free U. Berlin Klinikum Steglitz, 1981; head dept. clin. rsch. I Bayer AG Pharm. Rsch. Ctr., Wuppertal, Germany, 1982—85, head dept. medicine and devel., 1985—95, sr. v.p. global med. strategy and rels., 2000—02; prof., lectr. clin. medicine and pathophysiology U. Düsseldorf, Germany, 1989—, head med. affairs internat., 1995—2000; cons. Bayer Healthcare, 2002—. Med. examiner for clin. pharmacology; bd. bus. group for self-medication Bayer AG, Leverkusen, Germany, 1984-87, bd. bus. group pharma, 1991-93; bd. spokesman Paul-Martini-Found., Bonn, Germany, 1992-95; vice chmn. Ctr. Medicine Rsch. Internat., Carshalton, Eng., 1993-95, chmn. R&D bd., 1996—2000; mem. bd. Faculty Pharm. Medicine, UK; adv. chemotherapy WHO, 2005—. Editor: Therapy in Internal Medicine, 1975, 18th edit., 2010; reviewer: German and internat. jours., pub. houses, sci. founds. and award coms.; contbr. articles to profl. jours. With German Army, 1962-63. Fellow Royal Soc. Medicine (London), Royal Coll. Physicians Faculty Pharm. Medicine UK (with distinction); mem. German Soc. Internal Medicine (spokesman for corp. mems. 1993-2005). Avocations: jogging, skiing, archaeology. Business E-Mail: weihrauch@uni-duesseldorf.de.

WEIJERMAN, PHILIP CARL, urologist, educator; b. Penang, Malaysia, July 24, 1962; s. Robert Arthur Weijerman and Edda Perini; m. Mari-José Kerremans, Apr. 27, 1991; children: Sebastian, Mark, Francesca. MD, Leiden U., Netherlands, 1988; PhD, Erasmus U. Rotterdam, The Netherlands, 1997. Urology intern Westeinde Hosp., The Hague, The Netherlands, 1988-89; resident in surgery St. Francis Hosp., Rotterdam, 1990-91, Erasmus U. Rotterdam, 1993-96, Sophia Children's Hosp., 1993-96, St. Francis Hosp., 1993-96; mem. urology staff Rynstate Hosp. Arnhem, The Netherlands, 1996—, head Dept. Urology, 2002—, head Residency Program, 2006—. Contbr. articles to profl. jours. Fulbright grantee, 1992; Felix Guyon fellow European Bd. Urology, 1992, Stanford (Calif.) U., 1992-93. Fellow European Bd. Urology; Royal Dutch Med. Soc., Internat. Med. Assn. Lourdes, Dutch Urology Assn., European Assn. Urology, Am. Urol. Assn., Internat. Round Table, Rotary. Roman Catholic. Avocations: golf, guitar. Home: Poggenbeekstr 31 Arnhem 6813 KD Netherlands Office: Rynstate Hosp Wagner Ln PO Box 9555 6800 Arnhem Netherlands

WEIJUN, PENG, radiologist; s. Yao Xiangrong and Peng Yumei; married; 1 child, Peng Lei. MD, Fudan U., Shanghai, 1994. Diplomate Fudan U. Bd., 1994. Chmn. Dept. Radiology, Shanghai, 2003—, Tumor Imaging Com. CACA, Shanghai, 2005—08. Achievements include patents in field. Personal E-mail: weijunpeng@yahoo.com.

WEIKEL, MALCOLM KEITH, healthcare company executive; b. Shamokin, Pa., Mar. 9, 1938; s. Malcolm J. and Marian Eleanor (Faust) Weikel; m. Barbara Joan Davis, Dec. 17, 1960; children: Richard, Kristin. BSc in Pharmacy, Phila. Coll., 1960; MSc in Pharmacy, U. Wis., 1962, PhD in Mktg. and Economics, 1966. Chmn. Alliance for Quality Nursing Home Care. Inc.; brand mgr., mgr., Health Economics Roche Labs., 1966—70; commr., Med. Svcs. Adminstrn. HEW, Washington, 1970—77; group v.p. Am. Med. Internat., 1978—82, pres., CEO, 1982—84; exec. v.p., COO Manor Healthcare Corp., Silver Spring, Md., 1984—86; exec. v.p., gen. mgr., Midwest Divsn. Health Care & Retirement Corp., Toledo, 1986—88, sr. exec. v.p., dir., Ops., 1988—91; sr. exec. v.p., COO Manor Care, Inc., 1991—2006, bd. dirs., 1992—2006, dir., Emeritus, 2006—. Bd. dirs. Lab. Corp. of America Holdings, 2003—, Direct Supply, Inc., 2007—. Chmn. Fedn. of Am. Hospitals, Found. for the Future of Aging. Recipient Sec.'s Spl. citation, HEW, 1975, 1977, Disting. Bus. Alumnus award, Wis. Sch. Bus., 2008. Mem.: Am. Health Care Assn. (v.p. 1990—, chmn. multifacility group 1990—93). Office: Laboratory Corp of America Holdings Bd Directors 531 S Spring St Burlington NC 27215 Office Phone: 336-436-5274. Office Fax: 336-436-1569. E-mail: weikelm@labcorp.com. *

WEIL, ANDREW THOMAS, physician, educator; b. Phila., June 8, 1942; s. Daniel Pythias and Jenny (Silverstein) Weil. AB in Biology, Harvard U., 1964; MD, Harvard Med Sch., 1968. Intern Mt. Zion Hosp. Med. Ctr., San Francisco, 1968-69; fellow Inst. Current World Affairs, NYC, 1971-75; rsch. assoc. Harvard Bot. Mus., Cambridge, Mass., 1971-84; lectr. U. Ariz., Tucson, 1983—96, founder, program dir. Ariz. Ctr. Integrative Medicine (formerly Program in Integrative Medicine), 1994—, clin. prof. medicine, 1996—, Lovell-Jones endowed chair integrative rheumatology, 2005—; founder, chmn. Weil Found., Vail, Ariz., 2005—, Weil Lifestyle, LLC, Phoenix, 2005—. Dir. integrative health & healing Miraval Life in Balance Resort, Catalina, Ariz. Author: The Natural Mind: An Investigation of Drugs and the Higher Consciousness, 1972, Marriage of Sun and Moon: Dispatches from the Frontiers of Consciousness, 1980, Health and Healing, 1984, Natural Health, Natural Medicine, 1995, Spontaneous Healing, 1995, 8 Weeks to Optimum Health, 1997, Eating Well for Optimum Health, 2000, Healthy Aging, 2005, Why Our Health Matters, 2009, Spontaneous Happiness, 2011; co-author: (with Winifred Rosen) From Chocolate to Morphine: Everything You Need to Know About Mind-Altering Drugs, 1983, (with Rosie Daley) The Healthy Kitchen, 2002; author: (monthly newsletter promoting general health and healthy aging) Dr. Andrew Weil's Self Healing; monthly columnist Prevention mag., maintains website and daily blog Dr. Weil.com. Recipient Inaugural award, American Acad. Osteopathy, 2001, John P. McGovern award in behavioral scis., Smithsonian Associates, 2005; named a Pioneer in Integrative Medicine, Inst. Health & Healing, San Francisco, 2006; named one of The 25 Most Influential Americans, TIME mag., 1997, The 100 Most Influential People in the World, 2005; named to American Acad. Achievement, 1998. Democrat. Buddhist. Achievements include honored by mycologists Dr. Gustan Guzman, Fidel Tapia and Paul Stamets in 1995 by naming a newly discovered mushroom, Psilocybe weilii after him. Avocation: gardening. Office: Arizona Center Integrative Medicine PO Box 245153 Tucson AZ 85724-5153 also: Weil Found PO Box 13006 Tucson AZ 85732 *

WEIL, RICHARD, III, surgeon, medical educator; b. NYC, Feb. 22, 1936; s. Richard Jr. and Allene (Hall) W.; m. Polly Edgar, Aug. 22, 1959; children: Wendy, Richard. AB, Princeton U., 1957; MD, Columbia U. Coll. Physicians and Surgeons, 1961. Diplomate Am. Bd. Surgery, Nat. Bd. Med. Examiners. Intern in surgery Presbyn. Hosp., 1961-62, asst. resident in surgery, 1962-63, 65-67, chief resident in gen. surgery, 1968; chief resident in pediat. surgery Babies Hosp., 1969, chief resident in vasc. surgery, 1969, asst. attending surgeon, chmn. surg. house staff com., 1970-74, dir. kidney transplantation, 1973-74; asst. in surgery Columbia U. Coll. Physicians and Surgeons, 1967-68, instr. surgery, 1969, asst. prof. surgery, 1970-74; fellow in transplantation surgery U. Minn., 1970; assoc. prof. surgery U. Colo., 1974-79, prof. surgery, 1979-87, dir. transplantation, 1980-87; prof. surgery, dir. transplantation NYU, 1987-93; assoc. dean medicine, prof. surgery Brown U., Providence, 1993-98. Cons. surgeon Manhattan VA Hosp., 1989-92, Denver VA Hosp., 1980-87, Denver Gen. Hosp., 1980-87, St. Anthony-Ctrl. Hosp. Denver, 1980-87; attending surgeon Bellevue Hosp. Ctr., 1989-93 Contbr. more than 130 articles to profl. jours. including Surg. Forum, Am. Jour. Surgery, Transplantation, Surgery, Jour. Pediat. Surgery, Surgery, Gynecology & Obstets., among others. Capt. U.S. Army Med. Corps, 1963-65, Germany. Mem. Am. Assn. Tissue Banks, ACS, Am. Fedn. Clin. Rsch., Am. Soc. Transplant Surgeons, Am. Soc. for Artificial Internal Organs, Am. Surg. Assn., Assn. for Acad. Surgery, Allen O. Whipple Surg. Soc. (recorder 1976-78), Ctrl. Surg. Assn., Clin. Immunology Soc., Denver Acad. Surgery, Harvey Soc., Intermountain End-Stage Renal Disease Network (exec. com. 1975-79), Internat. Cardiovasc. Soc., N.Y. Ctr. for Liver Transplantation, N.Y. Clin. Soc., N.Y. Regional Transplant Program (pres. 1991-92), N.Y. Surg. Soc., Rocky Mountain Vasc. Surg. Soc., Soc. Internat. de Chirurgie, Soc. Vascular Surgery, Soc. U. Surgeons, Transplantation Soc., Western Assn. Transplant Surgeons, United Network for Organ Sharing (councilor for Colo., Wyo., Nebr., Kans., Iowa, Mo. 1986-87). Personal E-mail: rweiliii@msn.com. *

WEIL, RICHARD MARK, exercise physiologist; Private practice; with Cardio-Fitness Ctr., NYC, 1983—84, Payne Whitney Clinic, NY Hosp./Cornell Med. Ctr., 1987—88, Comprehensive Weight Control Ctr., NY Hosp./Cornell Med. Ctr., 1987—96, Life Extension Inst., NYC, 1989—91, Diabetes Treatment Program, Cabrini Med. Ctr., NYC, 1993—96, Joslin Diabetes Ctr., St. Luke's-Roosevelt Med. Ctr., NYC, 1994—99, VanItallie Ctr. for Nutrition and Weight Mgmt., St. Luke's-Roosevelt Hosp., 1994—2002, Behavioral Health Program, NYU Med. Ctr., 1995—99, Naomie Berrie Diabetes Ctr., Columbia Presbyn. Med. Ctr., NYC, Centers for Obesity Rsch. and Edn. (C.O.R.E), 1999—2003; exercise physiologist, dir. NY Obesity Rsch. Ctr. Weight Loss Program, St. Luke's-Roosevelt Hosp. Ctr., 2003—. Athletic coach experience U. NC, Chapel Hill, 1979—81, U. Pa., 1981—82, tchg. experience, 1981—82, Temple U., Pa., 1982—83, New Sch. for Social Rsch., NY, 1987—90; mem. adv. bd. Mt. Sinai Hosp., Adult Diabetes Treatment Ctr., 1994—97; wrote questions for the cert. exam for diabetes educators given by Nat. Cert. Bd. of Diabetes Educators, 1999; cons. Nat. PTA Com. to address problems of childhood obesity, 2001; invited presenter in field. Mem. adv. bd. D-Life TV, editl. bd. Diabetes Self-Management Mag., writes articles and answers fitness questions on www.medicinenet.com, WebMD-.com, writer of weekly fitness column Slim-Fast.com, 2002—03; contbr. several articles to profl. jours., chapters to books; media appearances include New York Post, Women's Day, O-Oprah Winfrey Mag., Cosmopolitan, CBS News Radio, Conn. Pub. TV, Phil Donahue TV Show, PBS TV, Knoll Pharm. Edn. Video, NY Daily News, CBS This Morning, WRIL Rhode Island Radio, WMCA Radio, Channel 54, D-Life TV, 20/20. Mem.: Diabetes Exercise and Sports Assn. (bd. dirs.), N.Am. Assn. for the Study of Obesity, Nat. Strength and Conditioning Assn., Am. Diabetes Assn., Am. Coll. Sports Medicine, Am. Assn. Diabetes Educators. Office: St Luke's Hosp 1111 Amsterdam Ave WH1020 New York NY 10025 Business E-Mail: rweil@chpnet.org.

WEIL, THOMAS P., retired health services consultant; b. Mount Vernon, NY, Oct. 2, 1932; s. H.M. and Alice (Franc) W.; m. Janet Whalen, Feb. 13, 1965. BA, Union Coll., 1954; MPH, Yale U., 1958; PhD, U. Mich., 1964. S.S. Goldwater fellow Mount Sinai Med. Ctr., NYC, 1957-58; assoc. cons. J.G. Steinle Assocs., Garden City, NY, 1958-61; asst. prof. UCLA, 1962-65; assoc. dir. Touro Infirmary, New Orleans, 1964-66; prof., dir. U. Mo., 1966—71; v.p. E.D. Rosenfeld Assocs., NYC, 1971-75; pres. Bedford Health Assocs. Inc., NY, NC, 1975-2000; ret. Chmn. Health Edn. & Applied Rsch. Found., Washington, 1981-83; bd. dirs. Albany Med. Ctr., Inc., NY, 1974-77; cons. to numerous hosps., med. schs., health related orgs., 1958-2000. Contbr. articles profl. jours. Named vis. prof. W.K. Kellogg Found., Sydney, Australia, 1969; recipient svc. award Am. Assn. Healthcare Cons., 1982; Weil Disting. Prof. in Health Svcs. Mgmt., U. Mo., 1991-2001. Fellow APHA (emeritus), Am. Assn. Healthcare Cons. (emeritus), Am. Coll. Healthcare Execs. (emeritus). Jewish. Office Phone: 828-252-1616. Personal E-mail: tpweil@aol.com.

WEILL, HANS, medical educator; b. Berlin, Aug. 31, 1933; came to U.S., 1939; s. Kurt and Gerda (Philipp) W.; m. Kathleen Burton, Apr. 3, 1958; children: Judith, Leslie, David. BS, Tulane U., 1955, MD, 1958. Diplomate: Am. Bd. Internal Medicine. Intern Mt. Sinai Hosp., NYC, 1958-59; resident Tulane Med. Unit, Charity Hosp. La., New Orleans, 1959-60, chief resident, 1961-62, sr. vis. physician, 1972—; NIH research fellow dept. medicine and pulmonary lab. Sch. Medicine Tulane U., New Orleans, 1960-61, instr. medicine, 1962-64, asst. prof. medicine, 1964-67, assoc. prof., 1967-71, prof. medicine, 1971—, Schlieder Found. prof. pulmonary medicine, 1985-97; chief Environ. Medicine sect. Tulane Med. Center, 1980-96; dir. univ. Ctr. for Bioenviron. Rsch., 1989-93; dir. interdisciplinary research group in occupational lung diseases Nat. Heart, Lung and Blood Inst., 1972-92, mem. nat. adv. council, 1986-90, chmn. pulmonary disease adv. com., 1982-84; active staff Tulane Med. Center Hosp., 1976—; program dir. Nat. Inst. for Environ. Health Sci., 1992-96. Cons. pulmonary diseases Touro Infirmary, New Orleans, 1962—; cons. NIH, Nat. Inst. Occupational Safety and Health, Occupational Safety and Health Adminstrn., USN, NAS, EPA; lectr., participant workshops and confs. profl. groups in U.S., France, Can., U.K.; dir. Nat. Inst. Environ. Health Scis Superfund. Basic Rsch. Program, 1992-96. Mem. editorial bd. Am. Rev. of Respiratory Disease, 1980-85, CHEST, 1987-91; editor Respiratory Diseases Digest, 1981; guest editor Byssinosis conf. supplement, CHEST, 1981. Fellow Am. Acad. Allergy, Royal Soc. Medicine, ACP; mem. Am. Thoracic Soc. (pres. 1976), Am. Lung Assn. (bd. dirs. 1975-78), New Orleans Acad. Internal Medicine (sec., treas. 1973-75), Am. Coll. Chest Physicians (gov. for La. 1970-75), Am. Fedn. Clin. Research, So. Soc. Clin. Investigation, N.Y. Acad. Scis., Brit. Thoracic Assn., Internat. Epidemiol. Assn., Am. Heart Assn. (task force on environment and cardiovascular system 1978), Brit. Thoracic Soc., Phi Beta Kappa, Alpha Omega Alpha. Home and Office: 110 Bellshire Dr Flat Rock NC 28731 Personal E-mail: hweill@bellsouth.net. *

WEIMER, ROBERT JAY, geology educator, energy consultant, civic leader; b. Glendo, Wyo., Sept. 4, 1926; s. John L. and Helen (Mowrey) Weimer; m. Ruth Carol Adams, Sept. 12, 1948; children: Robert Thomas, Loren Edward(dec.), Paul Christner, Carl Scott. BA, U. Wyo., Laramie, 1948, MA, 1949; PhD, Stanford U., Calif., 1953; DEng (hon.), CSM, 2008. Registered profl. engr., Colo. Geologist Union Oil Co. Calif., 1949-54; cons. geologist U.S. and fgn. petroleum exploration, 1954—; prof. geology Colo. Sch. Mines, 1957-83, prof. emeritus, 1983—, Getty prof. geology, 1978-83; vis. prof. U. Colo., 1961, U. Calgary, Can., 1970, Inst. Tech., Bandung, Indonesia, 1975; dir. dept. head Geol. Mus., 1965—70. Fulbright lectr. U. Adelaide, South Australia, 1967; disting. lectr. and continuing edn. lectr. Am. Assn. Petroleum Geologists, Soc. Expl. Geophysicists; ednl. cons. to petroleum cos., 1964—; mem. energy rsch. adv. bd. Dept. Energy, 1985-90, Bd. on Mineral and Energy Resources, Nat. Rsch. Coun., 1988. Editor: Guide to Geology of Colorado, 1960, Symposium on Cretaceous Rocks of Colorado and Adjacent Area, 1959, Denver Earthquakes, 1968, Fossil Fuel Exploration, 1974, Studies in Colorado Field Geology, 1976, Petroleum System, Denver Basin, 1996. Trustee Colo. Sch. Mines Research Found., 1967-70; pres. Rockland Found., 1982-83; bd. dirs. Foothills Art Ctr., 1997-2002. With USNR, 1944-46. Recipient Disting. Alumnus award U. Wyo., 1982, Mines medal Colo. Sch. Mines, 1984, Brown medal, 1990, Parker medal Am. Inst. Profl. Geologists, 1986, Exemplary Alumni award U. Wyo., 1994, ISEM Hedberg award, 2001, Carla Coleman Conservation award, 2005, Hall of Fame award IPAMS, 2006. Fellow Geol. Soc. Am. (chmn. Rocky Mountain sect. 1966-67, Sloss award 2003), AAAS; mem. Am. Assn. Petroleum Geologists (hon. pres. 1992, Sidney Powers medal 1983, Dist. Educator award 1996), Soc. for Sedimentary Geology (hon., sec.-treas. 1966-67, v.p. 1971, pres. 1972, Twenhofel medal 1995), Colo. Sci. Soc. (hon., pres. 1981), Rocky Mountain Assn. Geologists (hon., pres. 1969, found. bd. 1976-86, Scientist of Yr. 1982, Legend award 2003), Nigerian Mining and Geoscis. Soc. (hon.), Can. Soc. Petroleum Geologists (hon.), Wyo. Geol. Assn. (hon.), Colo. Sch. Mines Alumni Assn. (hon., Coolbaugh award 1996), Am. Geol. Inst. Found. (sec., treas. 1984-88, Legendary Geosci. award 2006-), Geol. Soc. Am. Found. (bd. dirs. 1999-04), Nat. Acad. Engring. (ch. sec. 11 1999), Northwoodside Inc. Land Conservancy Found. (v.p. 1995-96, pres. 1997—, Carla Coleman Conservation award 2005, Arthur Lakes Public Svc. award, 2008), Mt. Vernon Country Club (Golden, bd. dirs. 1956-59, 81-84, pres. 1983-84). Home: RR 3, 25853 Mt Vernon Rd Golden CO 80401-9699 Office Phone: 303-526-0247. Business E-Mail: rweimer@mines.edu.

WEIMER, TANIA DE AZEVEDO, retired pharmacist, educator; b. Salvador, Bahia, Brazil, July 30, 1945; d. Antonio Soares and Eunice Soares Azevedo; m. Günter Weimer, July 6, 1974; children: Ricardo de Azevedo, Rodrigo de Azevedo. PhD, U. Fed. do Rio Grande do Sul, Porto Alegre, RS, Brazil, 1980. Diplomate pharmacist U. Fed. da Bahia, 1970. Prof. U. Fed. do Rio Grande do Sul, 1976—2000; full prof. U. Luterana do Brazil, Canoas, Rio Grande do Sul, 2001—08; ret., 2008. Cons. CNPq, Brasilia, Distrito Federal, Brazil, 1980—. Achievements include research in genetic investigation of human andnimal variability, animal health, animal conservation, microevolution.

WEINAND, CHRISTIAN, plastic surgeon, hand surgeon; b. Luebeck, Germany, July 6, 1969; MD, U. Saarland, 1998, PhD, 2000. Resident U. Hosp. Leipzig, Germany, 2001—02; prin. investigator Harvard Med. Sch., Mass. Gen. Hosp., Lab. Tissue Engring. and Organ Fabrication, 2002—05; resident, dir. lab. Burn & Tissue Regeneration Wash. Hosp. Ctr., 2005—08; resident plastic & hand surgery, mgr. lab. hand surgery U. Hosp. Bern, Switzerland, 2009; attending physician, co-dir. burn dept., mgr. lab. regenerative medicine U. Hosp. Cologne, Germany, 2009—. Bd. mem. German Soc. Hand Surgery, 2002, Jour. Tissue Engring., 2004, Jour. Biomed. Material Rsch., 2009—. Contbr. articles to profl. publs. Recipient Lit. Highlight award, Internat. Soc. Stem Cell Rsch., 2005, Young Rschr. award, Radiol. Soc. N.Am., 2005, Resident award, Ea. Vascular Soc., 2006; Rsch. grant, AO/ASIF, Am. Soc. Surgery Hand. Master: Rsch. Gate (sci. advisor 2008—); fellow: German Soc. Plastic, Reconstructive and Aesthetic Surgery, Am. Burn Assn. (cons., provider 2007—), German Soc. Hand Surgery. Avocations: Judo, trumpet. Office: Ostmerheimer Strasse 200 Cologne Northrhine Westfalia 51109 Germany

WEINBERG, CARL, psychoanalyst; b. Rockaway Beach, Queens, NY; BA in Govt., St. John's U., Jamaica, NY, BS in Psychology; M in Psychology, The New Sch. Social Rsch., NYC; advanced tng., Nat. Psychol. Assn. for Psychoanalysis, NYC. Pvt. practice modern psychoanalyst, NYC. Bd. trustees The Tng. Inst., supervising and tng. analyst. Trauma counselor American Red Cross; developer clin. services practice Gay Men's Health Crisis; developer AIDS outreach program and HIV telephone hotline NYC Dept. Health; trauma & grief counselor NYC Fire Dept. Mem.: Nat. Psychol. Assn. Psychoanalysis (nat. pres.). Office: 350 W 50th St Ste 2kk New York NY 10019 Office Phone: 212-581-4070. Business E-Mail: cw@carlweinberg.com. *

WEINBERG, DAVID SETH, gastroenterologist, department chairman; Undergrad. magna cum laude, Yale U.; MS, U. Pa., 1995; MD, Cornell U., 1989. Diplomate Am. Bd. Internal Medicine, Am. Bd. Internal Medicine-gastroenterology, lic. Pa., 1992. Intern Beth Israel Deaconess Med. Ctr., 1990, resident, 1992; fellow gastroenterology and clin. epidemiology Pa. Hosp., 1995; dir. gastroenterology Fox Chase Cancer Ctr., 2001, chmn. medicine dept., Audrey Weg Schaus and geoffrey Alan Weg chair med. sci., 2008—. Author: In The Clinic: Colorectal Cancer Screening, 2008; co-author: Gene Environmental Risk Assessment For Colorectal Cancer Risk In Primary Care Practice Settings: A Pilot Study, 2007, Knowledge And Attitudes About Microsatellite Instability Testing Among Individuals Diagnosed With Colorectal Cancer, 2007, Reasons Patients With A Positive Fecal Occult Blood Test Result Do Not Undergo Complete Diagnostic Evaluation, 2008, Association of GUCY2C Expression In Lymph Nodes With Time To Recurrence And Disease Free Survival In PN0 Colorectal Cancer, 2009. Recipient Rsch. Thesis award, Cornell Univ.; named one of the Top Doctors, Phila Mag., 2011; fellow Nat. Rsch. Svc. award. Mem.: NIH (clin. oncology emphasis panel mem.), Am. Coll. Gastroenterology, Am. Gastroent. Assn., Am. Assn. for Cancer Rsch., Alpha Omega Alpha. Office: Fox Chase Cancer Center 333 Cottman Ave Philadelphia PA 19111-2497 Office Phone: 215-728-6900.

WEINBERG, EUGENE DAVID, microbiologist, educator; b. Chgo., Mar. 4, 1922; s. Philip and Lenore (Bergman) W.; m. Frances Murl Izen, Sept. 5, 1949; children— Barbara Ann, Marjorie Jean, Geoffrey Alan, Michael Benjamin. BS, U. Chgo., 1942, MA, 1948, PhD, 1950. Instr. dept. microbiology Ind. U., Bloomington, 1950-53, asst. prof., 1953-57, asso. prof., 1957-61, prof., 1961—, head microbiology sect., med. sci. program, 1978—92. Mem. sci. adv. bd., chair publs. Iron Disorders Inst., 1998—. Served with AUS, 1942-45. Mem.: Am. Soc. Microbiology. Office: Ind U Biology Dept Jordan Hall Bloomington IN 47405 Office Phone: 812-336-5556. Fax: 812-855-6705. Business E-Mail: eweinber@indiana.edu.

WEINBERG, GERALD C., medical association administrator; Joined staff Muscular Dystrophy Assn., NYC, 1957, campaign dir., dir. field ops., sr. v.p., COO, dir., pres., CEO Tucson, 2006—. Bd. dirs. Muscular Dystrophy Assn. Venture Philanthropy. Office: Muscular Dystrophy Assn USA Nat Hdqs 3300 E Sunrise Dr Tucson AZ 85718 Office Phone: 520-529-2000. *

WEINBERG, GERARD, pediatrics surgery, educator; MD, Albert Einstein Coll. of Medicine, 1973. Diplomate Am. Bd. Surgery, Am. Bd. Surgery-pediatric surgery. Resident surgery Albert Einstein Coll. of Medicine, 1974—76, prof. surgery; resident pediatric surgery Childrens Hosp., 1976—77; fellow pediatric surgery Univ of Miami Hosp., 1978—79; with Montefiore Med. Ctr. Office: Montefiore Medical Center 3355 Bainbridge Ave Bronx NY 10467 Office Phone: 718-920-7200.

WEINBERG, HUBERT, plastic surgeon; b. Clermont-Ferrant, France, Feb. 2, 1950; came to U.S., 1955; s. Paul and Esther Weinberg; m. Rita Weinberg, June 24, 1974; children: Deborah, Nevin, Michael, Jennifer, Lauren, Aimee. BA, Yeshiva U., 1971; MD, Cornell U., 1975. Diplomate Am. Bd. Plastic Surgery. Intern, resident Mt. Sinai Hosp.; instr. Mt. Sinai Med. Ctr., NYC, 1982-84, assoc. prof., 1984-97, prof., 1998-2000; clin. prof., 2000—; assoc. attending physician Mt. Sinai Med. Ctr., NYC, 1984-97, dir. microsurgery rsch. dept., 1982-2000, attending physician, 1998—, Westchester Med. Ctr., Valhalla, N.Y., 2000—. Adj. prof. N.Y. Med. Coll., 2000—. Author: (with others) Musculoskeletal Oncology, 1992; contbr. articles to profl. jours. including Current Surgery, Plastic Reconstr. Surgery, and Jour. Reconstructive Microsurgery. Recipient 2d pl. award Plastic Surgery Ednl. Found., 1983. Fellow ACS, N.Y. Acad. Scis. (1st prize awards 1987, 93); mem. Am. Soc. Plastic and Reconstructive Surgeons, Am. Assn. Plastic Surgeons. Avocations: computer graphics, gardening, landscaping. Business E-Mail: hubert.weinberg@mssm.edu. *

WEINBERG, JEFFREY B., physiatrist, educator; MD, NYU, Valhalla, 1980. Diplomate Am. Bd. Physical Medicine and Rehab., 1985. Resident physical medicine & rehab. NYU Langone Med. Ctr., NYC, 1981—83, fellow geriatric medicine Bellevue Hosp., 1984—86; asst. clin. prof. physical medicine & rehab. SUNY Downstate Med. Ctr.; attending physician SI Univ. Hosp., NY. Office: Staten Island University Hospital Rehabilitation Medicine 475 Seaview Ave Staten Island NY 10305 Office Phone: 718-226-9463. Office Fax: 718-226-9955.

WEINBERG, LAURENCE, anesthesiologist; b. Johannesburg, Apr. 14, 1968; s. Jack and Elaine Weinberg; m. Jacqueline Lyndsay Bowman, Dec. 8, 1996; children: Rachel Beth, Hannah Rose, Aaron Brian. BSc, University of Cape Town Med. Sch., South Africa, 1991; MBBCh, U. Witwatersrand Med. Sch., South Africa, 1997. Anesthesiologist Austin Hosp., Heidelberg, Victoria, Australia, 2007—. Presenter to professional confs. Contbr. scientific papers, articles to profl. jours. Fellow: Australian and New Zealand Coll. Anaesthetics; mem.: Royal Coll. Physicians (London). Jewish. Avocations: sports, travel. Office: Austin Hosp Jtudley Rd Heidelberg Victoria 3163 Australia Office Phone: 0061-3-94965000. Business E-Mail: laurence.weinberg@austin.org.au.

WEINBERG, MILTON, JR., retired cardiovascular and thoracic surgeon; b. Sumter, SC, Aug. 8, 1924; s. Milton and Ethel (Harper) W.; m. Joan Ehrenstrom, Nov. 24, 1956; children: Caryl, Susan, Amy. Student, Duke U., 1941-43, MD, 1947. Diplomate Am. Bd. Surgery, Am. Bd. Thoracic Surgery. Attending surgeon Rush Presbyn.-St. Luke's Med. Ctr., Chgo., 1957-90, emeritus attending, 1990—; attending surgeon Cook County Hosp., Chgo., 1956-80, Luth. Gen. Hosp., Park Ridge, Ill., 1986—2003, mem. governing coun., 1996—2001; assoc. prof. Rush Med. Coll., Chgo., 1969-78, prof. surgery, 1978-90, emeritus prof., 1990—; clin. prof. U. Chgo., 1990-99; ret., 2003. Chmn. dept. surgery Luth. Gen. Hosp., Park Ridge, 1988-94, vice-chmn. dept. surgery, 1994-2003; pres. med. staff

Rush Med. Ctr., Chgo., 1977-79; presenter movies at mtgs. ACS. Mem. editorial bd. Annals of Thoracic Surgery, 1968-79; contbr. articles to profl. jours., chpts. to surg. textbooks. Trustee The Presbyn. Home, Evanston, Ill., 1984—2010; life dir. 2010-; bd. dirs. Chgo. Symphony Orch., 1985-95; advocate Charitable Found. Bd., 1996-2002. Maj. U.S. Army, 1951-53. Decorated Bronze Star. Fellow: ACS, Am. Coll. Cardiology, Am. Coll. Chest Physicians; mem.: Ctrl. Surg. Soc., Soc. Vascular Surgery, Soc. Thoracic Surgeons, Am. Assn. Thoracic Surgery. Avocations: fly fishing, fly rod building, photography. Home: 983 Kirkhill Ln Lake Forest IL 60045-4209 E-mail: mw983@yahoo.com.

WEINBERG, PAUL M., pediatric cardiologist, educator; BS, Pa. State U., 1967; MD, Thomas Jefferson U., Phila., 1969. Diplomate Am. Bd. Pediatrics, Am. Bd. Pediatrics-pediatric cardiology, lic. Pa., 1970, NJ, 1983. Intern The Children's Hosp. Phila., 1970, resident, 1971, fellow, 1973, hosp. affiliations includes; resident Children's Hosp. Med. Ctr., Boston, 1977; dir. Resident Edn. in Cardiology, Cardiology Fellowship Tng. Program; prof. pediat. sch. medicine Univ. Pa. Co-author: (publs.) Usefulness of Magnetic Resonance Imaging for the Diagnosis of Right Ventricular Dysplasia in Children, 2006, Heterotaxy Syndrome with Functional Single Ventricle: Does Prenatal Diagnosis Improve Survival?, 2006, Delayed-enhancement Cardiovascular Magnetic Resonance Identifies Fibrous Tissue in Children after Surgery for Congenital Heart Disease, 2007, Membranous Remnant of Left Venous Valve of Inferior Vena Cava: Implications for Device Closure of Atrial Septal Defects, 2007, Neurological Complications Associated with the Treatment of Patients with Congenital Cardiac Disease: Consensus Definitions from the Multi-Societal Database Committee for Pediatric and Congenital Heart Disease, 2008, and numerous others. Named one of Top Doctors, Phila. Mag., 2011. Office: The Children's Hospital of Philadelphia 34th St and Civic Center Blvd Philadelphia PA 19104 Office Phone: 215-590-3274. E-mail: weinberg@email.chop.edu.

WEINBERG, RICHARD M., internist, pulmonary and critical care physician, consultant; b. NYC, July 13, 1946; s. Abraham and Grace F. Weinberg; m. Ellen L. Oberman, June 7, 1947; children: Joshua D., Aaron M., Jeremy O. BS, Rensselaer Poly. Inst., Troy, NY, 1966; MD, Albany Med. Coll., Union U., 1970. Diplomate Am. Bd. Internal Medicine, 1974, pulmonary disease Am. Bd. Internal Medicine, 1976, critical care medicine Am. Bd. Internal Medicine, 1987; cert. physician exec. Certifying Commn. in Med. Mgmt., 2003. Attending physician Overlook Hosp., Summit, NJ, 1975—2003, Morristown Meml. Hosp., NJ, 1975—2003, med. dir. dept. of respiratory therapy, 1978—95, sect. head, pulmonary and critical care medicine dept. medicine, 1978—95; med. dir. Morristown Meml. Physician-Hosp. Orgn., NJ, 1993—94, pres., CEO, 1995—97; sr. v.p. Morristown Meml. Hosp., NJ, 1995—97; v.p. physician network devel. Atlantic Health Sys., Florham Park, NJ, 1997—98; v.p. med. affairs Bayonne Hosp., NJ, 1999—2000; chief med. officer St. Francis Health Sys., Pitts., 2001—02; med. dir. quality improvement Univ. Hosp., Univ. Medicine and Dentistry of NJ, 2004—06; chief quality officer Stamford, Conn., 2006—. Mem. bd. Bayonne Behavioral Health Sys., NJ, 1999—2000; med. advisor N.J. Assn. for Respiratory Therapy; health care cons., Short Hills, NJ, 1999—2000, Short Hills, 2002—; mem. steering com. joint project in DVT prevention and treatment. Joint Commn. Accreditation Healthcare Orgns. and Nat. Quality Forum; mem. quality improvement adv. com. NJ Dept. Health and Sr. Svcs. Bd. mem. Congregation B'Nai Jeshurun, Short Hills, NJ, 1988—92. Fellow Pulmonary Medicine, Am. Lung Assn., 1974-1975. Mem.: Am. Coll. Physician Execs. Achievements include first to negotiate, secure and manage first two physician organization global risk managed care contracts in N.J; development and implementation of process to measure the cost-effectiveness of one of the most widely used new technology medications. Office Phone: 203-276-4156, 973-610-7814. E-mail: rmw@evisitmd.com.

WEINBERG, ROBERT ALLAN, biochemist, educator; b. Pitts., Nov. 11, 1942; s. Fritz E. and Lore (Reichhardt) Weinberg; m. Amy Schulman Weinberg, Nov. 19, 1976; children: Aron, Leah Rosa. BS, MIT, 1964, PhD, 1969; PhD (hon.), Northwestern U., Ill., 1984, Uppsala U., Sweden, 2007; DSc (hon.), Tufts U., 2009. Instr. Stillman Coll., Tuscaloosa, Ala., 1965—66; rsch. fellow Weizmann Inst., Rehovoth, Israel, 1969—70, Salk Inst., LaJolla, Calif., 1970—72; asst. prof. to assoc. prof. biology & ctr. cancer rsch. MIT, Cambridge, 1973—82, prof. biology, 1982—, Daniel K. Ludwig prof. cancer rsch., 1997—. Founding mem. Whitehead Inst., Cambridge, Mass., 1982—; rsch. prof. Am. Cancer Soc., 1985; mem. adv. bd. GM Cancer Rsch. Found. Author: (books) Racing to the Beginning of the Road: The Search for the Origin of Cancer, 1996, One Renegade Cell: How Cancer Begins, 1998, One Renegade Cell: The Quest for the Origin of Cancer, 1999, The Biology of Cancer, 2006; contbr. articles articles to profl. jours. Recipient Bristol Myers award for Disting. Achievement in Cancer Rsch., 1984, Brown-Hazen award, NY Dept. Health, 1984, Sloan prize, GM Cancer Rsch. Found., 1987, Rsch. Recognition award, Samuel Roberts Noble Found., 1990, Gairdner Found. Internat. award, 1992, Harvey Prize, Technion, 1994, G.H.A. Clowes Meml. award, 1996, Nat. Medal of Sci., 1997, Wolf Found. prize in medicine, 2004, Landon-AACR prize for Cancer Rsch., 2006, Otto Warburg medal, 2007; named Scientist of Yr., Discover mag., 1982. Fellow: Am. Acad. Arts & Scis.; mem.: NAS, Inst. Medicine, Royal Swedish Acad. Scis. Achievements include identified and characterized both the first oncogene and the first tumor suppressor gene; demonstrated how certain gene regulators, or transcription factor, contribute to cancer metastasis. Avocations: genealogy, house building. Office: Whitehead Inst Biomed Rsch 9 Cambridge Ctr Cambridge MA 02142-1479 Office Phone: 617-258-5159. Fax: 617-258-5213. E-mail: weinberg@wi.mit.edu. *

WEINBERGER, MICHAEL, pain medicine physician, anesthesiologist, educator; MD, Columbia U., 1983. Diplomate Am. Bd. Internal Medicine, Am. Bd. Anesthesiology, cert. pain medicine. Resident internal medicine St. Vincent's Hosp. and Med. Ctr., 1984—86; resident anesthesiology Columbia Presbyn. Med. Ctr., 1986—89; fellow pain mgmt. Meml. Sloan Kettering Cancer Ctr., 1990; assoc. clin. prof. anesthesiology Columbia U. Office: New York Presbyterian Hospital 622 West 168th St PH 5 East Room 500 New York NY 10032-3784 Office Phone: 212-305-2500.

WEINBERGER, STEVEN ELLIOTT, medical association administrator, internist, educator; b. Phila., Jan. 28, 1949; s. Leon and Ruth (Shoemaker) W.; m. Janet Harrison Brauer, June 14, 1970; children: Eric, Mark. AB, Princeton U., 1969; MD, Harvard U., 1973. Diplomate Am. Bd. Internal Medicine, Am. Bd. Pulmonary Disease, Am. Bd. Critical Care Medicine. Intern, then resident U. Calif. Med. Ctr., San Francisco, 1973-75, intern, 1973-74, resident, 1974-75; fellow Nat. Heart Lung and Blood Inst., NIH, 1975-78; attending physician Beth Israel Hosp., Boston, 1978—2004, clin. dir. pulmonary and critical care div., 1986-94, exec. vice chmn. dept. medicine, 1992—2004, chief pulmonary and critical care divsn. Boston, 1994—2004; sr. v.p. med. edn. and pub. American Coll. Physicians, Phila., 2004—10, dep. exec. v.p., 2009—10, exec. v.p., CEO, 2010—. Instr. Harvard Med. Sch., Boston, 1978-80, asst. prof., 1980-89, assoc. prof., 1989-95, prof. medicine 1995-2004; former exec. dir. Carl J. Shapiro Instn. Edn. and Rsch.; adj. prof. medicine U. Pa. Sch. Medicine. Author: Principles of Pulmonary Medicine, 1986, 2d edit., 1992, 3d edit., 1998; mem. editl. bd. New Eng. Jour. Medicine, 1992-2000; contbr. articles to profl. jours., chapters to books. Fellow ACP, Am. Coll. Chest Physicians. Avocations: piano, tennis. Office: American Coll Physicians 190 N Indenedence Mall W Philadelphia PA 19106-1572 *

WEINEL, PAMELA JEAN, general health scientist; b. Olney, Md., Dec. 14, 1956; d. Clarence Dawson and Jean Elizabeth (Woodward) Weinel; m. Nathan Richards, May 6, 1995. AA in Elem. Edn., Montgomery Coll., Rockville, Md., 1976; BSN, U. Md., Balt., 1986, M in Sci. Adminstrn., 1998; MBA, U. Balt., 2001. Oncology staff nurse George Washington U. Med. Ctr., Washington, 1986—88, Bone Marrow Transplant coord., 1988—90; adminstrv. coord. Walter Reed Army Med Ctr., Washington, 1990—98; advice nurse Kaiser Permanente, Kensington, Md., 1991—98; rsch. program mgr. Clin. Rsch. and Protocol Mgmt. Office U. Md. Greenebaum Cancer Ctr., Balt., 1999—2002; IVF nurse Shady Grove Fertility Ctr., Rockville, Md., 2003—04; project mgr. Social and Sci. Sys., Inc. CODA Divsn. FDA MedSun Project, Silver Spring, Md., 2004—06; asst. dir. program ops. FDA, CDRH, ODE, Rockville, Divsn. Reproductive, Abdominal and Radiological Devices, 2006—10; faculty assoc., grad. nursing prog. U. Md., Balt., 2006—11; regulatory health project mgr. FDA, Office of Commr., Office of Spl. Med. Programs, Office of Pediat. Therapeutics, 2010—. Cons., mem. People to People Internat., Russia, 1992, Vietnam, 93; roundtable facilitator Internat. BMT Symposium, Omaha, 1992; lectr. Contemporary Forums, San Francisco, 1994. Contbr., 1993—94. Sponsor for adults Resurrection Roman Cath. Ch., Burtonsville, Md., 1997—2000, CCD instr. 7th grade, 2001—02. Named an Outstanding Young Woman in Am., 1997. Mem.: Sigma Iota Epsilon, Phi Kappa Phi, Phi Theta Kappa, Sigma Theta Tau (scholar 1996). Avocations: travel, photography, writing. Office: FDA 10903 New Hampshire Ave Bldg 32 Rm 5147 Silver Spring MD 20993-0002 Business E-Mail: pam.weinel@fda.hhs.gov.

WEINER, ANNE LEE, social worker; b. Chelsea-Malden, Mass., Nov. 2, 1932; d. Nathan and Edith E. (Sigel) Varnick; m. Paul J. Weiner, Jan. 25, 1959; children: Berdine R., Ronald M. Diploma in med. sec., Chandler Sch. for Women, 1952; AA in Social Work, Middelsex CC, 1974; BSW, Salem Coll., 1987. Med. sec. New Eng. Med.-Boston U. Hosp., Boston, 1952—60; social worker Lynn-Union Hosp., Lynn, Mass., 1968-1982; home care social worker Mass. Elder Care, Peabody, 1982-1987; dir. Dept. Social Work Logan Homes, Wingate Homes, Hill Haven Homes, Mass., 1987-99. Mem. region bd. Hadassah steering com. social work, Hadassah Boston and Fla. Atlantic region; pres. Chessed, 2003—09; active Hist. Soc. Peabody; organizer social work support groups North Shore, Mass., 1987—99. Personal E-mail: lighthousealw@bellsouth.net.

WEINER, BEN-ZION, pharmaceutical executive; BSc, MSc, Hebrew U., PhD in Chemistry, 1975. Post doctoral rsch. Schering-Plough Corp.; with Teva Pharm., Israel, 1975, v.p., R&D, 1996—2002, group v.p., global producst, 2002—06, Office of CEO as chief R&D officer, 2006—. Mem. core mgmt. com. Teva Pharm., Israel; current non-exec. dir. XTL Biopharmaceuticals Ltd., 2005—. Achievements include being granted twice the Rothschild Prize for Innovation/Export, in 1989 for the development of alpha D3 for Dialysis and Osteoporosis & in 1999 for the development of Copaxone for Multiple Sclerosis. Office: Teva Pharmaceutical Industries Ltd 5, Basel St 49100 Petah Tiqwa Israel Office Phone: 01197239267267. Office Fax: 01197239234050.

WEINER, HOWARD MARC, physician; b. Feb. 25, 1946; BSc, Marietta Coll., 1967; MD, U. Cin., 1971; MPH, Med. Coll. Wis., 1994. Diplomate Am.Bd. Allergy, Asthma and Immunology, Am. Bd. Preventive Medicine/Occupl. Medicine. Intern medicine Temple U. Hosp., Phila., 1971—72, resident internal medicine, 1972—74; fellow allergy and clin. immunology Hosp. U. Pa., Phila., 1974—76; pres., physician Allergy & Asthma Assocs. West Boca, Boca Raton, Fla., 1988—; pres., med. dir. Med. Assessment Inst. Inc., Boca Raton, Fla., 1997—. Chmn. ethics com. Palm Beach County Med. Soc., West Palm Beach, Fla., 1994-97; bd. dirs. Primus Physicians Svcs., Inc., So. Fla. Mem. Omicron Delta Kappa Soc., Pi Kappa Epsilon. Office: Med Assessment Inst Inc 2385 NW Executive Ctr Dr Ste 100 Boca Raton FL 33431 Office Phone: 561-451-0200.

WEINER, IRVING BERNARD, psychologist; b. Grand Rapids, Mich., Aug. 16, 1933; s. Jacob H. and Mollie Jean (Laevin) W.; m. Frances Shair, June 9, 1963; children: Jeremy Harris, Seth Howard. BA, U. Mich., Ann Arbor, 1955, MA, 1957, PhD, 1959. Diplomate Am. Bd. Profl. Psychology. From instr. to prof. psychiatry and pediat. U. Rochester, NY, 1959-72; head divsn. psychology U. Rochester Med. Center, 1968-72; prof. psychology, chmn. dept. Case Western Res. U., 1972-77, dean grad. studies, 1976-79; vice chancellor for acad. affairs U. Denver, 1979-83, prof. psychology, 1979-85; v.p. for acad. affairs Fairleigh Dickinson U., Teaneck, NJ, 1985-89, prof. psychology, 1985-89; prof. psychiatry U. South Fla., Tampa, 1989—. Adv. editor John Wiley & Sons, 1967-93, 99—, Lawrence Erlbaum Assocs., 1993-99; psychology edn. rev. com. NIMH, 1977-81. Author: Psychodiagnosis in Schizophrenia, 1966, Psychological Disturbance in Adolescence, 1970, rev. edit., 1992, Rorschach Handbook, 1971, Child Development, 1972, Principles of Psychotherapy, 1975, rev. edit., 1998, 2009, Development of the Child, 1978, Child and Adolescent Psychopathology, 1982, Rorschach Assessment of Children and Adolescents, 1982, rev. edit., 1995, Adolescence, 1985, rev. edit., 1995, Handbook of Forensic Psychology, 1987, rev. edit., 1999, 2006, Principles of Rorschach Interpretation, 1998, rev. edit., 2003, Handbook of Psychology, 2003, Handbook of Personality Assessment, 2008; editor: Readings in Child Development, 1972, Clinical Methods in Psychology, 1976, 83, Adult Psychopathology Case Studies, 2004, Jour. Personality Assessment, 1985-93, Rorschachiana, 1989-96; mem. editl. bd. Profl. Psychology, 1971-76, Jour. Adolescent Health Care, 1979-87, Children and Youth Svcs. Rev., 1979-91, Jour. Pediat. Psychology, 1981-87, Devel. and Behavioral Pediat., 1985-96, Studi Rorschachiani, 1985-1996, European Jour. Psychol. Assessment, 1985—, Jour. Adolescent Rsch., 1986-91, Jour. Personality Disorders, 1986-92, Psychol. Assessment, 1994—2003, Jour. Personality Assessment, 2003—, Assessment, 2004—, Jour. Child Custody, 2005—. Recipient Disting. Profl. Achievement award Genesee Psychol. Assn., 1974, Disting. Profl. Contbr. award, Soc. Clin. Psychology, 2010 Fellow APA, Acad. Clin. Psychology, Acad. Forensic Psychology, Acad. of Assessment Psychology (Lifetime Achievement awrd 2001); mem. Assn. Advancement Psychology, Soc. Personality Assessment (pres. 1976-78, 2005-07, Disting. Contbn. award 1983), Assn. Internship Ctrs. (exec. com. 1971-76), Soc. Rsch. in Adolescence, Soc. for Rsch. in Child and Adolescent Psychopathology, Soc. for Exploration Psychotherapy Integration, Soc. Pediat. Psychology, Am. Psychol. Law Soc., Internat. Rorschach Soc. (pres. 1999-2005), Assn. Psychol. Sci., Soc. Clin. Psychology (pres. 2008), Phi Beta Kappa, Sigma Xi, Phi Kappa Phi. Home and Office: 13716 Halliford Dr Tampa FL 33624-6903 Office Phone: 813-961-8032. Business E-Mail: iweiner@health.usf.edu.

WEINER, KAREN COLBY (KAREN LYNN COLBY), psychologist, lawyer; b. Oak Park, Ill., Oct. 28, 1943; d. Leonard L. and Mildred Irene (Berman) Colby; m. J. Laevin Weiner, July 26, 1964; children: Joel Laevin, Doren Robin, Anthony Justin. BA, Mich. State U., East Lansing, 1964; JD, U. Detroit, 1977, MA, 1986, PhD, 1988. Bar: Mich. 1977, D.C. 1978. Speech therapist Oak Park Sch. Dist., 1965-68; law clk. justice G. Mennen Williams Mich. Supreme Ct., Lansing, 1977-79; assoc. Dickinson, Wright, Moon, Van Dusen & Freeman, Detroit, 1979-83; intern in psychology Detroit Psychiat. Inst., 1986-88; psychologist Northland Clinic, Southfield, Mich., 1987-88; postdoctoral intern Wyandotte (Mich.) Hosp. and Health Ctr., 1988-90; psychologist Counseling Assocs., Southfield, 1988—2004, dir. psychol. svcs., quality assurance coord., 1991-99; bd. dirs. Mich. Psychoanalytic Inst. Found., 2004—. Hearing panelist Atty. Discipline Bd., Detroit, 1982-95; hearing referee Mich. Civil Rights Commn., Detroit, 1983-91; mem. Mich. Bd. Psychology, 1999—2007, vice chair, 2004-07; adj. prof. U. Detroit Mercy, 2001-03; Grad. Inst. Life Coach Tng. adj. prof. Inst. Life Coach Tng., 2008. Author: The Little Book of Ethics for Coaches, rev. edit., 2007; contbr. articles to profl. jours. Mem. adv. bd. Mich. chpt. Anti-Defamation League, 1981-90. Fellow Mich. Psychol. Assn. (mem. ethics com. 1992-2000, chmn. legis. com. 1993, chmn. ethics com. 1997-99, pres. 2008); mem. APA, Internat. Coach Fedn. (ethics and stds. com.), Mich. Soc. for Psychoanalytic Psychology (pres. 1995-97, sec. 1991-92, treas. 1992-94), Women Lawyers Assn. Mich. (pres. 1981-82, pres. Found. 1982-83), Mich. Bar Assn. Jewish. Home: 2501 Long Lake Rd West Bloomfield MI 48323 Office: 29260 Franklin Rd Ste 115 Southfield MI 48034-1144 Office Phone: 248-353-1020. Personal E-mail: drkcw@comcast.net.

WEINER, LESLIE PHILIP, neurology educator, researcher; b. Bklyn., Mar. 17, 1936; s. Paul Larry and Sarah (Paris) W.; m. Judith Marilyn Hoffman, Dec. 26, 1959; children: Patrice, Allison, Matthew, Jonathan. BA, Wilkes Coll., 1957; MD, U. Cin., 1961. Diplomate Am. Bd. Psychiatry and Neurology. Intern in medicine SUNY, Syracuse, 1961-62; resident in neurology Johns Hopkins Hosp., Balt., 1962-65, fellow, 1967-69; resident Balt. City Hosp., 1962-63; fellow in virology Slow Virus Lab., Nat. Inst. Neurol and Communicative Disorders-Stroke, NIH, Balt., 1969; asst. prof. neurology Johns Hopkins U., 1969-72, assoc. prof., 1972-75; prof. neurology and microbiology U. So. Calif. Sch. Medicine, LA, 1975—, chmn. dept. neurology, 1979—2003, Richard Angus Grant Sr. chair in neurology, 1987—. Chief neurologist U. So. Calif. Univ. Hosp., 1991-96, mem. bd. govs.; chief neurologist L.A. county-U. So. Calif. Med. Ctr., 1979-94,; chmn. U. So. Calif. Gen. Clin. Res. Ctr., 1994-95; mem. neurosci. tng. study sect. NIH, 1990-93; mem. sci. adv. bd. Hereditary Disease Found., 1992—, chmn., 1994-96; mem. programs rsch. adv. com. Nat. Multiple Sclerosis Soc., 2000-07; mem. com. review adverse effects vaccines Inst. Medicine Nat. Acads, Washington, 2009-; cons. in field. Editor: Neural Stem Cells Methods and Protocols, 2007; assoc. editor: Neurobase, 1994-95, Neuronet; mem. editl. bd. Infectious and Geographic Neurol., 1994—; contbr. chpts. to books; contbr. over 150 articles to profl. jours. Chmn. Conn. Stem Cell Peer Review Com., 2007—; bd. dirs. Starbright Found., LA, 1991—99. Capt. M.C. US Army, 1965—67. Grantee, Conrad Hilton Found., 1995—97, Kenneth Norris Found., 1995—, NIH, 1999—, Race to Erase MS Nancy Davis Ctrs. Without Walls, 2000—, McDonald Found., Oxnard Found., Gogian Found., Heron Found.; grant, Teva Neurosci., 2009—. Fellow: Am. Acad. Neurology; mem.: AAAS, Nat. MS Soc. (mem. adv. com. rsch. program 2000—07, grant 2000—), Coalition Advancement Med. Rsch., Assn. Univ. Profs. Neurology, L.A. Acad. Medicine, Johns Hopkins U. Soc. Scholars, Soc. Neurosci., Am. Neurology Assn., Am. Health Assistance Found., Alpha Omega Alpha. Democrat. Jewish. Avocation: theater. Office: RMR 506 2025 Zonal Ave Los Angeles CA 90089 Home Phone: 323-934-0633; Office Phone: 323-442-3020. Office Fax: 323-442-5500. Business E-Mail: lweiner@usc.edu.

WEINER, LOUIS MARC, oncologist; b. Phila., May 21, 1951; married. BA in Biology with honors, U. Pa., 1973; MD, Mt. Sinai Sch. Medicine, NYU, NYC, 1977. Diplomate Am. Bd. Internal Medicine, cert. Am. Bd. Internal Medicine, Med. Oncology. Intern U. Vt. Med. Ctr. Hosp., resident, chief resident; from assoc. mem. divsn. med. sci. to chmn. Fox Chase Cancer Ctr., Phila., 1985—94, chmn. med. oncology, 1994—, G. Morris Dorrance, Jr. endowed chair in med. sci., 2002—, v.p. translational rsch., 2002—; dir. Lombardi Comprehensive Med. Ctr. Georgetown U. Hosp., Washington, 2007—. Asst. prof. Temple U., Phila., 1987—95, prof., 1995—; sci. adv. bd. Merrimack Pharms., Cambridge, Mass., 2007—. Contbr. articles to profl. jours.;

mem. editl. bd.: Cancer Rsch., Clin. Cancer Rsch. Steering com. translational rsch. working group Nat. Cancer Inst.; mem. cancer immunopathology and immunotherapy study sect. NIH. Recipient Clin. Investigtor award, Nat. Cancer Inst., 1986, Targeted Therapy award, Janssen Pharm. Found., 1998, Research award, American Cancer Soc.; grantee, NIH, 1986, 1989, 1990, 1993, 1996, 1999, 2000, Dept. of Defense, 1996, 1998—99, clin. and rsch. fellowships, Tufts U., Boston. Mem.: Am. Assn. Cancer Rsch. (chair immunology task force), Am. Soc. Clin. Oncology.

WEINER, MICHAEL A., pediatrician, educator, hematologist, oncologist; Studied, SUNY, 1972. Diplomate Am. Bd. of Pediatrics, cert. pediatric hematology-oncology. Intern Montefiore Med. Ctr.; resident Thomas Jefferson Univ. Hosp.; fellow NYU Med. Ctr., 1974—76, Johns Hopkins Hosp., 1977; prof. pediat. coll. of physicians and surgeons Columbia Univ. Office: Morgan Stanley Children's Hospital Irving Pavilion FL 7 161 Fort Washington Ave New York NY 10032-3710

WEINER, RICHARD DAVID, psychiatrist, researcher; b. NYC, Nov. 25, 1945; BS, MIT, 1967; M of Systems Engring., U. Pa., 1969; MD, PhD, Duke U., 1973. Diplomate Am. Bd. Psychiatry and Neurology. Prof. psychiatry Duke U. Med. Ctr., Durham, NC, 1997—, dir. electroconvulsive therapy program, 1991—; chief, mental health svc. line VA Med. Ctr., Durham, 1993—. Office: Duke U Med Ctr PO Box 3309 Durham NC 27710-3309 Home: Box 3309 DUMC Durham NC 27710

WEINER, STEVEN H., plastic surgeon; BA in Biosciences magna cum laude, Lehigh U., 1982; MD, U. Pa., 1986. Diplomate Am. Bd. Plastic Surgery, 2000, Am. Bd. Medical Specialties, 2000, lic. NY, Calif., Md. Resident gen. surgery John Hopkins Med. Instn.; resident plastic surgery Albany Med. Coll.; former med. dir. comprehensive wound healing ctr. Paradise Valley Hosp., Phoenix; academic affiliations include Univ. of Ariz., Midwestern Univ., Tourno Univ. Contbr. publs. Vol. Interplast Internat., Operation Smile. Mem.: Am. Soc. for Aesthetic Plastic Surgery, Am. Soc. of Plastic Surgeons. Office: New Image Plastic Surgery 7425 E Shea Blvd Ste 105 Scottsdale AZ 85260 Office Phone: 480-596-6886.

WEINER, STUART, obstetrician, gynecologist, educator; b. Phila., Sept. 26, 1946; BA, Princeton U., 1968; MD, U. Pa., 1972. Prof. ob gyn. Thomas Jefferson U., 1982—. Dir., divsn. reproductive imaging & genetics, maternal fetal medicine, 2002. Fellow: Am. Coll. Obstetricians & Gynecologists; mem.: Internat. Soc. Ultrasound ob-gyn., Am. Inst. Ultrasound Medicine, Soc. Maternal Fetal Medicine. Avocations: scuba diving, backpacking, bicycling, reading. Office: 834 Chestnut St Ste 400 Philadelphia PA 19107 Business E-Mail: sweinermd@comcast.net.

WEINER, SYLVIA, surgeon, researcher; b. Zschopau, Sachsen, Germany, Mar. 30, 1979; d. Rudolf Alfred and Carla Else Weiner; m. Detlef Weiß; children: Sophia Dora Weines, Rafael Alfed. MD, U. Würzburg, 2005. Surgeon KH Sachsenhausen, Frankfurt, Germany, 2005—. Organizer Frankfurter Meeting Laparoscopic Surgery Obesity & Metabolic Disorders, 1999—. Recipient Poster award, IFSO, 2005. Office: Krankenhaus Sachsenhausen Schulstr31 Frankfurt Hessen 60594 Germany

WEINER, TIMOTHY M., pediatric surgeon; b. Bethesda, Md., Jan. 9, 1961; BA in biology, Oberlin Coll., 1983; MD, Georgetown Univ., 1989. Cert. Am. Bd. Surgery, 1997, in Pediatric Surgery Am. Bd. Surgery, 2000. Intern in pediatric surgery Univ. NC Sch. Med., Chapel Hill, 1989—90, resident in pediatric surgery, 1990—93; rsch. fellow Lineberger Comprehensive Cancer Ctr., Univ NC, Chapel Hill, 1991—93; sr. resident pediatric surgery Univ. NC Sch. Med., Chapel Hill, 1993—95; fellow in pediatric surgery Children's Hosp. Pitts., Pa., 1995—97; asst. prof. pediatric surgery Univ. NC Sch. Med., Chapel Hill, 1997—2004, assoc. prof. pediatric surgery, 2004—. Contbr. articles to profl. jours. Recipient Nat. Rsch. Svc. award, 1992—93, James Ewing Travel award, Soc. Surgical Oncology, 1993. Office: UNC Sch Med Dept Surgery CB#7210 3010 Old Clinic Bldg Chapel Hill NC 27599-7210 Office Phone: 919-966-4220. Office Fax: 919-966-8806.

WEINGAST, MARVIN, laboratory executive; b. Bklyn., Jan. 1, 1943; s. Abe and Rose (Altein) W. BS, L.I. U., 1967, MS, 1971; postgrad., Poly. Inst., 1967-68. Analytic and pollution chemist Amerada Hess Corp., Pt. Reading, N.J., 1969-73; asst. lab. dir. Chem. Constrn., North Brunswick, N.J., 1973-74; dir. Indsl. Hygiene Lab. Nat. Starch and Chemical, Bridgewater, N.J., 1974—. Grant com. mem. Ctr. for Hazardous and Toxic Substance Mgmt., Newark, 1988—; mem. Sourland Regional Citizens Planning Coun., Neshanic, N.J., 1989—. Contbr. to book: Small Business Programs, 1980; contbr. articles to profl. jours. Recipient Chemistry Dept. award L.I. U., 1967, Teaching fellowship Poly. Inst., 1967, L.I. U., 1968. Mem. MENSA, Am. Chem. Soc., Am. Conf. Chem. Labeling, Soc. Toxicology. Achievements include development of improved system for identification of hazardous chemicals; organization of first global monitoring of indsl. workers to hazardous workplace chemicals. Office: Nat Starch & Chem Co 10 Finderne Ave Bridgewater NJ 08807-3355 Personal E-mail: weingast@weingast.com.

WEINHOLD, LINDA LILLIAN, psychologist, researcher; b. Reading, Pa., Nov. 9, 1948; d. Aaron Zerbe Weinhold and Nancy Louise (Spotts) Weikel; m. Jack Wayne Prisk, Jan. 21, 1967 (div. 1969). Lic. practical nurse, AVTS, 1970; BS, Penn State U., 1975; MS, C.W. Post Ctr., 1982; PhD, Fordham U., 1986. LPN; cert. profl. counselor. Instr., asst. prof. Gettysburg Coll., Pa., 1985-86; post doc. fellow John Hopkins U., Balt., 1986-88; staff fellow NIH NIDA Addiction Rsch. Ctr., Balt., 1988-93; cons. NIH NIDA Medications Devel., Rockville, Md., 1993-94; soc. sci. program coord. Med. Ctr. NIDA Rsch., Washington, 1994-95; cons. The Clin. Cons. Group Antech, Inc., Balt., 1995; substance abuse counselor Hope Village, Inc., Washington, 1996—. Various presentations. Mem. Am. Psychol. Assn., Am. Counseling Assn., Bah'a'i', Phi Kappa Phi, Sigma Xi. Avocations: singing, dance, painting, photography, reading. Home: 2611 Bowen Rd SE Apt 203 Washington DC 20020-6623 Office: Hope Village Inc 2840 Langston Pl SE Washington DC 20020-3241 Office Phone: 202-678-1077.

WEININGER, MARKUS, radiologist; b. Wuerzburg, Germany; s. Erich and Gerlinde Weininger; m. Heidi Weininger. MD, U. Wuerzburg, Germany, 2000. Cons. KPMG Consulting, Frankfurt, Germany, 2001—02; mktg. mgr. Siemens Med. Solutions, Malvern, Pa., 2003—04, Erlangen, Germany, 2002—04; med. dir. Calyx Partners, LLC, Orlando, Fla., 2004; radiologist U. Hosp. Wuerzburg, 2004—10; radiologist dept. radiology Med. U. SC, Charleston, 2010—. Med. dir. Caly Ptnrs., 2004—09; ptnrs. Pease Weininger & Co, LLC, Orlando, 2009—, Evelus LLC, Orlando, Fla., 2009—. Home: 1650 William Hapton Way Mount Pleasant SC 29466 Personal E-mail: mweininger1@yahoo.com. Business E-Mail: markus@peaseweininger.com, markus@weininger.us.

WEINMAN, STEVEN ALAN, emergency nurse practitioner, educator, writer, health facility administrator; b. St. Louis, July 17, 1962; s. Stanley I. Weinman and Diana Raye (Kessler) Schrader; m. Carol Angela Daiber, July 27, 1986; children: Erin Elizabeth, Sarah Katherine. Diploma in Nursing, Jewish Hosp. of St. Louis, 1986; BSN, Webster U., Kansas City, 1996. RN, Mo., NY, NJ; cert. emergency nurse. Emergency nurse Jewish Hosp. of St. Louis, 1986-87, Truman Med. Ctr.-West, Kansas City, Mo., 1987-93, clin. nurse mgr., 1987-93, clin. educator, 1993-95, St. Luke's Northland Hosp., Kans. City, Mo., 1996-97; prin. ptnr. Emergency Care Cons. Greater NY, Somerville, NJ, 1996—; instr. dept. emergency medicine NY Hosp.-Cornell Med. Ctr., NYC, 1997-2001; sr. dir. Med. Ed. and Custom Publ., Excepta Med. Elsevier, Hillsborough, NJ, 2001—02; dir. Office of Continuing Med. Edn. Elsevier Health Scis. Divsn., 2004; sr. dir. Ctr. for Accredited Healthcare Edn., Princeton, NJ, 2004—, Inst. Med. and Nursing Edn., Princeton, 2004—. Nurse rschr. Clin. Multiphase Rsch., 1991—2000; rsch. coord. dept. emergency medicine Truman Med. Ctr., Kansas City, 1991—96; mem. editl. adv. bd. Roadrunner Press/ENA, 1999—2001; per diem instr. in emergency and trauma care N.Y. Presbyn. Hosp.-Cornell Med. Ctr., NYC, 2001—; dept. health and human svcs. NNRT Region II, 2003—; deputy chief EMS & spl. operations Somerville Rescue Squad, NJ. Editor textbooks and monographs; mem. editl. bd. Clin. CORNERSTONE, 2001-03, Excerpta Medica, Inc.; contbg. author books and book chpt, contbr. articles to profl. jour. Adv. bd. Kansas City chpt. ARC, 1991-94; chief nurse EMS, Kansas City Spiritfest, 1989-95; emergency med. technician Somerville Rescue Squad, State of NJ, 2002, edn. and tng. officer, 2003—, crew chief, 2003—, EMS capt., 2006—, mem. exec. bd., 2004—. Recipient Spl. Recognition award Emergency Nursing Found., Spl. Recognition award Somerville Rescue Squad, Extrication Save award, 2004, Lifesaving awards, 2004-07, Rescue award, 2006-07. Mem.: Am. Orgn. Nurse Execs., NJ State Nurses Assn., Nat. Assn. EMS Educators, Global Alliance for Med. Edn., Alliance for Continuing Med. Edn., Soc. Trauma Nurses, Am. Trauma Soc., Emergency Nurses Assn. (treas. Greater Kansas City chpt. 1989—91, pres. 1994, state coun. exec. com. 1993—95, sec. 1991, state del. 1991—95, Recognition award 1991, 1993, Edn. award 1993, Recognition award 1994, Educator of Yr. 1994, 1996, Recognition award 2000—01, Disting. Svc. award 2000, 2003—04). Avocations: photography, writing, computers, travel. Home: 29 W Spring St Somerville NJ 08876-1627 Office: 201 Carnegie Ctr Ste 104 Princeton NJ 08540 Personal E-mail: rescsteve@aol.com.

WEINMANN, JUDY P. MUNGER, retired nurse, educator; b. Georgetown, Tenn., June 1, 1943; d. Paul and Martha Edith (Smith) Powell; m. David Finley Munger, Dec. 6, 1963 (div. June 1985); children: David Finley Jr., Robert Powell (dec.). Grad., Erlanger Hosp., Chattanooga, 1964; AS, Cleve. State CC, Tenn., 1982; BS, U. Tenn., 1984. RN Tenn., cert. occupl. health nurse specialist (COHN-S), Tenn. Med. staff nurse Bradley Meml. Hosp., Cleveland, 1964; office nurse William I. Proffitt, M.D., Cleveland, 1964-65; occupl. health nurse Singer-Cobble Co., Chattanooga, 1966-67, Burlington Woolens Co., Cleveland, 1967-68, Am. Uniform Co., Cleveland, 1972-73, M&M/Mars, Cleveland, 1979-91; sch. nurse Cleveland State Coll., 1968-72, Bradley High Sch., Cleveland, 1973-79; dir. nursing Open Arms Care Corp., Ooltewah, Tenn., 1992-93, Tenn. Home Health, Hixson, Tenn., 1993; dir. cmty. edn./case mgmt. Med. Shares Home Care, Chattanooga, 1994—2000; adminstr. occupl. health svcs. Parkridge Med. Ctr., 2000—02; account exec. Med Shares Home Care, 2002—03; patient care rep. Home Health Care of East Tenn., 2003—; account mgr. M.E.D. of Tenn., 2003—04; nurse educator Hospice of Chattanooga, 2005—09. Presenter in field. Nurse ARC, Cleveland, 1979-; chmn. Bradley County Substance Abuse Com., Cleveland, 1980-87; com. mem. Am. Cancer Soc., Chattanooga, 1984—; acct. mgr. Med. Equipment Distrs., 2003. Recipient Schering award as Tenn. outstanding occupational health nurse Schering-Plough Co., 1989, Lifetime Achievement award, Elizabeth Newbert, 2003. Mem.: Case Mgrs. Soc. Am., Cleve. Area Safety Coun. (Safety award 1988), Chattanooga Occupational Health Nurses Assn. (v.p., bd. dirs., Pres.'s award 1989), Chattanooga Nurses Assn., Tenn. Occupational Health Nurses Assn. (bd. dirs. 1986—), Tenn. Nurses Assn., Sigma Theta Tau. Democrat. Baptist. Avocations: dance, reading, music, gardening, crafts. Home: 1200 King Arthur Rd Chattanooga TN 37421-4020 Personal E-mail: judyweinmann@comcast.net.

WEINMANN, ROBERT LEWIS, neurologist; b. Newark, Aug. 21, 1935; s. Isadore and Etta (Silverman) Weinmann; m. Diana Weinmann, Dec. 13, 1980 (dec. Dec. 1989); children: Paul, Chris, Dana, Paige. BA, Yale U., 1957; MD, Stanford U., 1962. Diplomate Am. Bd. EEG and Neurophysiology (v.p.), Am. Acad. Pain Mgmt., Am. Bd. Forensic Medicine, cert. med. evaluator Calif. Intern Pacific Presbyn. Med. Ctr., San Francisco, 1962-63; resident in neurology Stanford (Calif.) U. Hosp., 1963-66, chief resident, 1965-66; pvt. practice San Jose, Calif., 1969—. Former clin. instr. neurology Stanford U. Chmn. editl. bd. Clin. EEG Jour., mem. editl. bd. Clin. Evoked Potentials Jour.; contbr. articles to various publs. Capt. M.C. US Army, 1966—68. Recipient award, State of R.I., Santa Clara County Med. Soc., Calif. State Assembly, U.S. Congress, other orgns.; fellow, U. Paris, 1957—58. Fellow: Am. Coll. Forensic Medicine; mem.: Ind. Practice Assn., Union Am. Physicians and Dentists (bd. dirs. 1972—, pres. Calif. fedn. 1989—2006, pres. 1993—, pres. Ind. Practice Assn. 2007—). Avocations: softball, tennis, music, theater, martial arts. Mailing: 2040 Forest Ave San Jose CA 95128-4810 Office Phone: 408-292-0802.

WEINREB, JEFFREY C., radiologist, educator; MD, Mt. Sinai Sch. Medicine, NY, 1978. Diplomate Am. Bd. Radiology, Am. Bd. Radiology-diagnostic radiology, 1983. Intern internal medicine LI Jewish Med. Ctr., NYC, 1978—79, resident diagnostic radiology, 1979—81, chief resident diagnostic radiology, 1981—82; fellow ultrasound/computed tomography Hosp. of the Univ. of Pa., Phila., 1982—83; prof. diagnostic radiology Yale Univ., New Haven; dir. med. imaging Yale-New Haven Hosp., chief body imaging and MRI. Office: Yale-New Haven Hospital 2nd Fl S Pavilion 20 York St New Haven CT 06510 Office Phone: 203-785-5913. Office Fax: 203-785-3061.

WEINRYB, JOAN, physician, internist; MD, Yeshiva U. Diplomate Am. Bd. Internal Medicine, 1986, Am. Bd. Internal Medicine-geriatric medicine, 1992. Intern Grad. Hosp., Phila.; resident Albert Einstein Med. Ctr. Yeshiva Univ.; corp. clin. med. dir. Presbyn. homes and svcs. Penn Presbyn. Med. Ctr. Named one of the Top Doctors, Phila. Mag., 2008—11. Mem.: Pa. Med. Dirs. Assn., Gerontologic Soc. of America, Del. Valley Geriatric Soc., Am. Geriatric Soc., Am. Med. Dirs. Assn., ACP. Office: Penn Presbyterian Medical Center Ralston Penn Center 3615 Chestnut St Philadelphia PA 19104 Office Phone: 215-662-2746.

WEINSHENKER, NAOMI JOYCE, clinical psychiatrist, educator, researcher; b. Ridgewood, NJ, Mar. 28, 1961; d. Theodore and Anne Betty (Jaffe) W. BA summa cum laude, Yale U., 1983; MD, U. Pa., 1989. Diplomate Am. Bd. Psychiatry and Neurology. Rotating intern Overlook Hosp., Summit, NJ, 1989-90; resident in adult psychiatry Mass. Mental Health Ctr., Harvard U. Med. Sch., Boston, 1990-92, fellow in child and adolescent psychiatry, 1992-93, Boston Childrens Hosp., Harvard Med. Sch., 1993—94; staff psychiatrist Choate Health Systems, Woburn, Mass., 1994-96; asst. prof. clin. psychiatry U. Medicine and Dentistry of N.J., Newark, 1996-2000; asst. prof. clin. psychiatry Sch. Medicine NYU, 2000—10; pvt. practice psychiatry, 2006—; freelance medical reporting News12, Norwalk, Conn., 2006—07; med. corr. Med. Missions Children, 2007—08; cons. expert witness Dechert LLP, 2009; adv. bd. mem. NJ Life Health & Beauty Mag., 2010—; med. reporter Ebru TV, Somerset, NJ, 2010—. Staff psychiatrist U. Behavioral HealthCare, Newark, 1996—97; asst. dir. U. Hosp. Psychiat. Outpatient Ctr., 1998—2000; mem. faculty NYU Child Study Ctr., 2000—06; cons. child outpatient svcs. Tri-City Mental Health and Retardation Ctr., Inc., Medford, Mass., 1996; dir., young adult inpatient program Tisch Hosp., 2000—04. Contbr. articles to profl. jours.; editl. asst. Emergency Medicine mag., 1983-84. Vol. psychiatry unit, coord. psychiatry vols., Yale-New Haven Hosp., 1979-83; vol. recruitment coord. Phila. Adult Spl. Olympics, 1985. Mem. Am. Psychiat. Assn., Am. Acad. Child-Adolescent Psychiatry, NJ Psychiat. Assn. (Essex County rep. Tri-County chpt. 1997-98, treas. 1998-99, sec. 1999-00, v.p. 2000-2001, pres.-elect 2001-02, co-chair, com. on women 2010-), NJ Coun. Child/Adolescent Psychiatry, Phi Beta Kappa, Sigma Xi. Democrat. Jewish. Avocations: theater, nutrition, vegetarianism, weightlifting, aerobics. Office Phone: 973-471-4440. Personal E-mail: naomi_weinshenker@yahoo.com.

WEINSTEIN, CAROL, psychiatrist; b. NYC; BS, Cornell U., 1980; MD, SUNY, Buffalo, 1984. Cert. psychiatry. Psychiatrist, co-med. dir., med. dir. inpatients units Four Winds Hosp., Katonah, NY, 1988—92; asst. dir. psychiat. emergency svc. Montefiore Hosp. Ctr., Bronx, 1993—96, assoc. dir. psychiat. emergency svcs., 1996—97, assoc. dir. inpatient psychiatry, 1997—99; staff psychiatrist St. Vincents Westchester, Harrison, 1999—. Recipient Alumni award Contbn. Residency program, Cornell-N.Y. Hosp. Mem.: Am. Soc. Clin. Psychopharmacology, Am. Psychiat. Assn. Office: St Vincents Hosp 275 North St Harrison NY 10528

WEINSTEIN, GREGORY S., otolaryngologist, educator; MD, NYU. Diplomate Am. Bd. Otolaryngology. Resident Univ. of Iowa; fellow Univ. of Calif.; prof. otolaryngology: head and neck surgery Univ. of Pa.; vice chmn. otolaryngology: head and neck surgery dept. Penn Medicine, co-dir. ctr. for head and neck cancer, dir. head and neck surgery divisn. and head and neck surgery clinic, dir. head and neck oncology fellowship. Named one of the Top Docs, Phila. Mag., 2004—11, Best Doctors in America, 2003—04, 2005—06, 2007—08, 2009—10, America's Top Doctors, 2007, 2008, 2010. Office: Hospital of the University of Pennsylvania 5 Silverstein 3400 Spruce St Philadelphia PA 19104 Office Phone: 215-662-2777.

WEINSTEIN, JAY, internist; MD, Hahnemann U. Diplomate Am. Bd. Internal Medicine. Resident internal medicine St. Vincent Hosp.; hospital affiliation includes Beth Israel Med. Ctr.; internist specializing in mgmt. of chronic area. Bd. dirs. PHO. Named one of Top Doctors of NY Metro Area, Castle Conolly, Top Family Doctors, Town and Country Mag., 2001. Mem.: ACP, Clin. Competency Com., Faculty Practice Steering Com. Office: Saint Vincent Hospital 170 W 12th St New York NY 10011

WEINSTEIN, MELVIN PHILLIP, physician educator; b. Long Branch, NJ, Apr. 27, 1944; s. Joseph and Selma Joyce (Nathanson) W.; m. Dustra Lee Anderson, July 13, 1969; children: Joanna Lee, Michael Jacob. BA in Zoology with distinction, Rutgers U., 1966; MD, George Washington U., 1970. Diplomate Nat. Bd. Med. Examiners, Am. Bd. Internal Medicine, Am. Bd. Infectious Diseases, Am. Bd. Pathology (Med. Microbiology). Intern Hartford (Conn.) Hosp., 1970-71, resident, 1973-75; fellow in infectious diseases U. Colo. Health Sci. Ctr., Denver, 1975-77, fellow in clin. microbiology, 1983; asst. prof. medicine U. Medicine and Dentistry N.J., New Brunswick, 1977-83, assoc. prof. medicine and pathology, 1983-91, prof. medicine and pathology, 1991—; staff Robert Wood Johnson U. Hosp., New Brunswick, 1977—. Cons. staff St. Peter's U. Hosp., 1998-2005; cons. Roosevelt Hosp., Edison, N.J., 1986-89; vis. assoc. prof. Rutgers U., New Brunswick, 1986-98; vis. prof. Rutgers U. Coll. Pharmacy, 1998—; trustee Am. Bd. Med. Microbiology, Washington, 1991-97; mem. area com. on microbiology, 1997-2003, mem. subcom. antimicrobial susceptibility testing Clin. and Lab. Stds. Inst., Wayne, Pa., 1993—, vice chair area com. on microbiology, 1998-2002; dir. Microbiology Lab., Robert Wood Johnson U. Hosp., New Brunswick, 1983—, HIV-Antibody Counselling and Testing Svc., 1985-87, 91—; chief divsn. of allergy, immunology and infectious diseases Robert Wood Johnson Med. Sch., 2001—; lectr. in field. Mem. editl. bd. Jour. Clin. Microbiology, 1984-99, Am. Jour. Infection Control, 1987-2000, Diagnostic Microbiology and Infectious Disease, 1989—, Clin. Microbiol. Rev., 2002-; sect. editor Clin. Infectious Diseases, Manual Clin. Microbiology, 8th, 9th and 10th edit.; contbr. chpts. to books, articles to profl. jours. Comdr. USPHS, 1971-73. Henry Rutgers Rsch. fellow, 1965-66. Fellow ACP, Infectious Diseases Soc. Am., Am. Acad. Microbiology; mem. Am. Soc. Microbiology (BD award for rsch. in Clin. Microbiology 2004), Soc. Hosp. Epidemiologists Am., N.J. Infectious Disease Soc. (founding mem.), Alpha Omega Alpha. Avocation: golf. Office: Robert Wood Johnson Med Sch 1 Robert Wood Johnson Pl New Brunswick NJ 08901-1928 Office Phone: 732-235-7713. *

WEINSTEIN, MILTON CHARLES, decision scientist, educator; b. Brookline, Mass., July 14, 1949; s. William and Ethel (Rosenbloom) W.; m. Rhonda Kruger, June 14, 1970; children: Jeffrey William, Daniel Jay. AB, AM, Harvard U., 1970, MPP, 1972, PhD, 1973. Asst. prof. John F. Kennedy Sch. Govt., Harvard U., Cambridge, Mass., 1973-76, assoc. prof., 1976-80; prof. policy and decision scis. Harvard Sch. Pub. Health, Boston, 1980-86, Henry J. Kaiser prof. health policy and mgmt., 1986—; prof. medicine Harvard Med. Sch., Boston, 1992—2005; v.p. Innovus Rsch. Inc., Medford, Mass., 1998—; prin. cons. i3 Innovus, Medford, 2005—. Adj. prof. cmty. and family medicine Dartmouth Med. Sch., Hanover, N.H., 1981-87; vis. lectr. Intermountain Health Care, Salt Lake City, 1997—; cons. U.S. Office Tech. Assessment, 1979-87, HHS, 1979—, VA, 1984-86, EPA, 1983—, New Eng. Med. Ctr., 1986-87, Intermountain Health Care, 1987—; mem. adult treatment panel Nat. Cholesterol Edn. Program, NIH; co-chair Panel on Cost-Effectiveness in Health and Medicine, USPHS, 1993-96. Author: Clinical Decision Analysis, 1980, Hypertension: A Policy Perspective, 1976, Cost-Effectiveness in Health and Medicine, 1996, Decision Making in Health and Medicine, 2001; mem. editl. bd. Med. Decision Making, 1981-94, Jour. Environ. Econs. and Mgmt., 1986-88, Jour. Clin. Oncology, 1996-99; assoc. editor Med. Decision Making, 1994-2001. NSF fellow, 1972. Mem. Inst. Medicine of NAS (com. on priorities new vaccine devel., com. to evaluate the NIH artificial heart program), Soc. Med. Decision Making (trustee 1980-82, pres. 1984-85), Internat. Health Econs. Assn., Internat. Soc. Pharmacoens. and Outcomes Rsch., Am. Med. Joggers Assn., US Speedskating (bd. dirs. 1996-00), Phi Beta Kappa.

WEINSTEIN, RONALD S., pathologist, educator; b. Schenectady, NY, Nov. 20, 1938; s. H. Edward and Shirley (Diamond) W.; m. Mary Dominica Corabi, July 12, 1964; children: Katherine Eiliesh, John Benjamin. BS, Union Coll., Schenectady, 1960; MD, Tufts U., 1965. Diplomate: Am. Bd. Pathology; 1972. Chemist Marine Biol. Lab., Woods Hole, Mass., 1960-62; intern Mass. Gen. Hosp., Boston, 1965-66, clin. and research fellow, 1965-70, resident in pathology, 1966-70; dir. Mixter Lab., 1966-70; vice chmn. pathology Aerospace Med. Research Labs., Dayton, Ohio, 1970-72; asso. prof. pathology Tufts U., 1972-75; Harriet Blair Borland prof., chmn. dept. pathology Rush Med. Coll. and Rush-Presbyn.-St. Luke's Med. Center, Chgo., 1975-90; prof., head dept. pathology U. Ariz. and U. Med. Ctr., Tucson, 1990—; dir. Ariz. Telemedicine Program, Tucson, 1996—. Teaching fellow Harvard Med. Sch., 1966-70; dir. Central Pathology Lab., Nat. Bladder Cancer Group, 1983-89, mem. editorial bd. Pathology, 1991—, J. Urologic Pathology, 1992—. Mem. editorial bd. Ultrastructural Pathology, 1979—, Human Pathology, 1980—, assoc. editor, 1983-92, mem. editorial bd. Lab. Investigation, 1983—; assoc. editor Advances in Pathology, 1985-91, editor, 1991—; contbr.: articles profl. jours. Served as maj. USAF, 1970-72. Ford Found. fellow, 1959; Congressional intern, 1959; USPHS fellow, 1965-68 Mem.: AMA, Am. Telemed. Assn. (v.p. 2001—), Internat. Coun. Soc. Pathology (v.p. 1992—98, pres. 1998—), Internat. Soc. Urologic Pathology (pres.-elect 1992—94, pres. 1995—96), Chgo. Pathol. Soc. (pres. 1979—80), Assn. Pathology (chmn., sec. treas. 1989—90, v.p. 1998—), U.S. and Can. Acad. Pathology (pres. 1988—89), Internat. Acad. Pathology (councilor 1980—82, internat.councilor 1982—84), Am. Soc. Cell Biology. Office: U Ariz Dept Pathology 1501 N Campbell Ave Tucson AZ 85724-0001

WEINSTEIN, WILFRED M., medical educator; b. Melville, Can., Mar. 14, 1940; MD, Queen's U., Kingston, Can., 1964. Rsch. and clin. fellow, gastroenterology U. Wash. Sch. Medicine Gastroenterology, 1967—70; prof., medicine David Geffen Sch. Medicine UCLA, 1979—, dir., gastroenterology fellowship program, 2001—08. Faculty, gastroenterology, advisor to prof., medicine U. Alta. Edmonton AB Can., 1970—79; pres. Can. Assn. Gastroenterology, 1978—79; dir., med. procedures unit and endoscopy, gastroenterology biopsy lab. Dept. Medicine Digestive Diseases David Geffen Sch. Medcine UCLA, 1979—2001; guest lectr. Ann. Meeting Queensland Gastroenterology Soc. Colum Australia, 1997. Recipient Schindler Career Achievment award, Am. Soc. Gastrointestinal Endoscopy, 2003. Mem.: Am. Gastroent. Assn. (governing bd., Am. Soc. Gastrointestinal award). Avocation: reading. Office: UCLA 16010 Valley Wood Rd Sherman Oaks CA 91403 Office Fax: 310-825-3133. Personal E-mail: zevzmw@gmail.com.

WEINSTOCK, MARTIN ARTHUR, dermatologist, epidemiologist, educator; b. NYC, Oct. 31, 1956; s. Irvin and Mae Weinstock; m. Gail Gilkey, June, 1981; children: Hannah, Clara. BA in Math. summa cum laude, Williams Coll., 1977; MPhil in Epidemiology, Columbia U., 1981, PhD in Epidemiology, 1982, MD, 1983; MA (hon.), Brown U., 1995. Diplomate Am. Bd. Dermatology; lic. Mass., R.I. Resident in internal medicine U. Pitts. Hosps., 1983-84; resident in dermatology Harvard U. Hosps., Boston, 1984-87; Andrew W. Mellon Found. fellow in clin. epidemiology Harvard Med. Sch., Boston, 1987-88; chief of dermatology, staff physician Dept. Vets. Affairs Med. Ctr., Providence, 1988—; asst. prof. medicine (dermatology) Brown U., 1988—94, assoc. prof. medicine (dermatology), 1994—96, dir. rsch., divsn. dermatology, 1995—96, assoc. prof. dermatology, 1996—98, dir. rsch., dept. dermatology, 1996—, prof. dermatology, 1998—2003, prof. dermatology and cmty. health, 2003—. Staff physician Mass. Gen. Hosp. Chelsea Health Ctr., Boston, 1985-86, South Boston Community Health Ctr., 1986-88, Dept. Medicine Children's Hosp., Boston, 1987-88, Miriam Hosp., Providence, 1994-2002, RI Hosp., 1994-; dir. RI pigmented lesion unit, dir., photomedicine, Roger Williams Med. Ctr., Providence, 1988-97, 1997-, staff physician, 1988-98; vis. prof., Skin Diseases Rsch. Ctr., Case Western Reserve U., 2000; mem. med. faculty exec. com., Brown U., 2001-04, vice-chair, 2001-02, chair 2002-03, past chair, 2003-04; mem. exec. com., Brown U. 2002-03, and others. Mem. editl. bd. Jour. Am. Acad. Dermatology, 1993-98, asst. editor 1998-, Jour. Cutaneous Medicine and Surgery (also editor), 1995-97, Dermatology Lexicon Project, 2003-04, others; guest editl. bd. Health Edn. and Behavior, 1998; contbg. editor, Year Book of Dermatology, 1985-; assoc. editor Jour. Investigative Dermatology, 2002-, Jour. Am. Acad. Dermatology, 2004-; asst. sect. editor, Archives of Dermatology, 2004-; cons. editor, Sun and Skin News, 1991, 1994; contbr. articles to profl. jours.; reviewer for grants; reviewer for sci. jours. Grantee NIH, VA; recipient Benedict award-First prize in Math., 1974, Dept. Vet. Affairs Spl. Contbn. award, 1990, Diabled Am. Veterans Dept. RI Outstanding Physician award, 1993, Fed. Employee of Yr., Profl. Category (for RI), 1993. Mem. APHA, Am. Dermatological Assn., Assn. Professors of Dermatology, Am. DermatoEpidemiology Assn., Internat. DermatoEpidemiology Assn. (founder, pres. 2002-2003, bd. dirs. 2003-04, steering com., 2006-), Internat. Soc. Cutaneous Lymphomas, Med. Dermatology Soc.(bd. dirs. 2004-06, mentorship program com. 2004-05, pres.-elect, 2006-2008), Nat. Assn. VA Dermatologists (v.p. 1991-92, pres. 1992-93, nominating com. 1993-97, chair nominating com., 1996-97), Am. Acad. Dermatology(mem. epidemiology com., 1996-2000, environment coun., 1995-98, computer tech./computer and informatics com., 1996-2000, database develop. task force/task force on computers in edn. and rsch., 1996-2000), Soc. Epidemiologic Rsch., Soc. Investigative Dermatology (com. on sci. programs, abstract reviewer, 1993—), New Eng. Dermatol. Soc., Am. Cancer Soc. (Chair skin cancer adv. group, 1997-, bd. dirs. RI divsn. 1992-97, mem. exec. com. RI divsn. 1994-97), RI Dermatol. Soc., R.I. Med. Soc., Phi Beta Kappa, Sigma Xi. Office: VA Med Ctr 111D 830 Chalkstone Ave Providence RI 02908-4734 also: Warren Alpert Med Sc of Brown U Dept Dermatology Box G-A Providence RI 02912 Business E-Mail: MAW@brown.edu, Martin_Weinstock_MD@brown.edu.

WEINTRAUB, JOSHUA L., vascular and interventional radiologist; MD, Wayne State U., 1991. Diplomate Am. Bd. Radiology-diagnostic radiology, cert. vascular and interventional radiology. Resident transitional William Beaumont Hosp., Mich.; resident radiology Beth Israel Deaconess Med. Ctr., Boston, 1992—96; fellow radiology U. Pa., 1996—97; assoc. prof. radiology Mount Sinai Sch. of Medicine, assoc. prof. surgery; chief, vascular and interventional radiology Mt. Sinai Med. Ctr. Named one of Top Doctors, Castle Connolly, 2007, 2008, 2009. Office: Mount Sinai Medical Center 1176 Fifth Ave New York NY 10029 Office Phone: 212-241-8333. Office Fax: 212-348-7403. E-mail: joshua.weintraub@mountsinai.org.

WEIR, BRYCE KEITH ALEXANDER, neurosurgeon, neurologist, educator; b. Edinburgh, Apr. 29, 1936; arrived in U.S., 1992, arrived in Can., 2002; s. Ernest John and Marion Weir; m. Mary Lou Lauber, Feb. 25, 1976; children: Leanora, Glyncora, Brocke. BSc, McGill U., Montreal, Que., Can., 1958, MD, CM, 1960, MSc, 1963. Diplomate Am. Bd. Neurol. Surgery, Nat. Bd. Med. Examiners. Intern Montreal Gen. Hosp., 1960-61; resident in neurosurgery Neurological Inst., Montreal, 1962-64, 65-66, NY Neurol. Inst., NYC, 1964—65; neurosurgeon U. Alta., Edmonton, Can., 1967-92, dir. div. neurosurgery, 1982-86, Walter Anderson prof., chmn. dept. surgery, 1986-92; surgeon-in-chief U. Alta. Hosps., 1986-92; Maurice Goldblatt prof. surgery and neurology U. Chgo., 1992—2002, dir. Brain Rsch. Inst., 1993—2001, interim dean biol. scis. divsn. and Pritzker Sch. Medicine, v.p. med. affairs, 2001—02. Past pres. V Internat. Symposium on Cerebral Vasospasm; mem. neurology A study sect. NIH, 1991—93; invited speaker at over 135 profl. meetings; vis. prof. over 68 univs., including Yale U., Cornell U., Columbia U., Duke U., U. Toronto, U. Calif., San Francisco; lectr. in field. Author: Aneurysms Affecting the Nervous System, 1987, Subarachnoid Hemorrhage-Causes and Cures, 1998, Cerebral Vasospasm, 2001; co-editor: Primer on Cerebrovascular Diseases, 1997, Stroke: Pathophysiology, Diagnosis and Management, 4th edit., 2004; mem. editl. bd. Jour. Neurosurgery, chmn. bd, 1993—94, mem. editl. bd. Neurosurgery Quar., Jour. Cerebrovascular Disease, Neurosurgery; contbr. over 275 articles to profl. jours. Named Officer of the Order of Can., 1995. Fellow: ACS, Royal Coll. Surgeons Can., Royal Coll. Surgeons Edinburgh (hon.); mem.: Can. Neurosurg. Soc. (Inaugural Lifetime Achievement award 2006), Interurban Neurosurg. Soc. (chmn.), Nat. Acad. Scis., Inst. Medicine, Japan Neurosurg. Soc. (hon.), Soc. Neurol. Surgeons (Grass gold medal 1992), Am. Acad. Neurol. Surgeons, James. IV Assn. Surgeons, Am. Surg. Assn. Achievements include rsch. in cerebral vasospasm and the surgical management of intracranial aneurysms. Home: 1262 Saturna Dr Parksville BC V9P 2X6 Canada

WEIR, NEIL FRANCIS, otolaryngologist, consultant; b. Guildford, Surrey, Eng., Aug. 7, 1942; s. James MacDonald and Elizabeth Mary (Motton) W.; m. Susan White, May 7, 1966; children: Justin Neil MacDonald, Robert Thomas MacDonald. MB, BS, Westminster Med. Sch., London, 1965; MA in Bioethics, U. Surrey, 2005; MD, U. London. Fellow Royal Coll. Surgeons Eng. Registrar ENT St. Thomas' Hosp., London, 1969-72; sr. register ENT Royal Free Hosp., London, 1972-78; cons. otolaryngologist Royal Surrey County Hosp., Guildford, England, 1987—2002, hon. cons., 2002—. Hon. con. otologist Atkinson Morley's Hosp., St. George's Healthcare Trust, Wimbledon, London, 1987-97; founder Britain Nepal Otology Svc., 1988; med. trustee Order St. John Care Trust, 2004-. Author: Otolaryngology, An Illustrated History, 1990 (George Davey Howells Meml. prize U. London 1990); editor, bd. dirs. Jour. Laryngology and Otology, 1992-2004, chmn. 2005—10; contbr. chpts. to books and articles to profl. jours. Decorated knight Magistral Grace, Sovereign Mil. Order of Malta; Order of Gorkha Dakshin Bahu (Nepal). Fellow: Royal Soc. Medicine (hon. editor 1996-2000, mem. coun., v.p. 2002-04); mem. Brit. Voice Assn. (coun. mem. 1990-98, chmn. 1990-91), Worshipful Soc. Apothecaries London (liveryman 1984—, chmn. livery com. 1998-2000). Roman Catholic. Avocations: sculpture, opera, sailing. Office Phone: 440 1252783265. Personal E-mail: neilweir@btinternet.com.

WEISBERGER, JAMES DAVID, hematopathologist; b. Wilkes-Barre, Pa., Aug. 25, 1955; s. Seymour and Sally Weisberger; m. Linda Ellen Cohen, May 20, 1984; children: Nicholas, Laura. BS, Stanford U., 1977, MS, 1978; MD U. Pa., 1983. Intern, resident internal medicine Calif. Pacific Med. Ctr., San Francisco, 1983—86; internist Fairmount Med. Group, El Cerrito, Calif., 1986—89, Cmty. Health Care Plan, New Haven, 1988—89; resident pathology NY Med. Coll., Valhalla, NY, 1990—94; fellow hematopathology NY Hosp. Cornell Med. Ctr., NYC, 1994—95; asst. prof. pathology and medicine NY Med. Coll., Valhalla, 1995—99, clin. asst. prof. pathology, 1999—; dir. hematopathology IMPATH, Inc., NYC, 1999—2003; v.p. chief med. officer Bio-Reference Labs., Elmwood Park, NJ, 2003—. Contbr. articles various profl. jours. Office: Bio-Reference Labs 481 Edward Ross Dr Elmwood Park NJ 07407

WEISBURGER, JOHN HANS, retired medical researcher; b. Stuttgart, Germany, Sept. 15, 1921; came to U.S., 1943, naturalized, 1944; s. William and Selma (Barth) W.; children: William, Diane, Andrew. AB, U. Cin., 1947, MS, 1948, PhD, 1949; MD (hon.), U. Umeå, Sweden, 1980. Officer USPHS, 1950—; mem. staff Nat. Cancer Inst., NIH, Bethesda, Md., 1950-61, head carcinogen screening sect., 1961-72; dir. bioassay segment, Carcinogenesis Programs Nat. Cancer Inst., Bethesda, Md., 1971-72; v.p. rsch. Am. Health Found., Valhalla, NY, 1972-87; dir. Naylor Dana Inst. for Disease Prevention, Valhalla, 1972—87; rsch. prof. pathology N.Y. Med. Coll., Valhalla, 1974—; pres. Weisburger Assocs., North White Plains, NY, 1987—. Mem. biochemistry and nutrition study sect. NIH, 1957—58; mem. interdepartmental panel on carcinogens FDA, USDA, USPHS, 1962—71; chmn. carcinogenesis subcom. Nat. Large Bowel Cancer Project, 1972—75; mem. expert panel on nitrites and nitrosamines USDA, 1973—77; mem. Nat. Cancer Inst. Clearinghouse on Environ. Carcinogens, 1976—78; co-chmn. organizing com. US-Japan Coop. Workshop on GI Tract Cancer, 1979; chmn. sci. rev. panel NJ State Commn. Cancer Rsch., 1988—90; co-chmn. internat. symposium on health effects of tea, NY, 1991; chmn. nutrition and cancer sect. 3d Anticarcinogenesis & antimutagenesis conf., Italy, 1991; chmn. study sect. NIH-Nat. Cancer Inst., Bethesda, Md., 1991; rsch. fellow Japanese Found. for Promotion of Cancer Rsch. Nat. Cancer Ctr. Rsch. Inst., Tokyo, 1992; adv. com. rev. RDA Food & Nutrition Bd. NAS, 1993; lectr. numerous lectures in field; chmn. numerous confs. national & internat.; editl. bd. Internat. Jour. Tea Sci., 2006—. Assoc. editor Jour. Nat. Cancer Inst., 1960-62, Xenobiotica, 1971—2004, Archives of Toxicology, 1977-87, Internat. Jour. Toxicology, 1982-2002, Preventive Medicine, 1988-2004; mem. internat. editl. adv. bd. Food and Chem. Toxicology, 1967—2004; assoc. editor Cancer Rsch., 1969-80, mem. cover editl. bd., 1987-99; mem. editl. bd. Chemico-Biol. Interactions, 1969-88, Carcinogenesis, 1979-87, Inst. Sci. Info. Atlas of Sci., 1987-89, Cancer Epidemiology Biomarkers Prevention, 1991-98, Cancer Detection Prevention, 1994-2004; mem. guest editl. bd. Japanese Jour. Cancer Rsch., 1987—; hon. editor Protective Effects of Tea on Human Health, 2006; contbr. articles to profl. jours. With US Army, 1944—46, Italy, Austria, ret. col. USPHS. Decorated D.S.M.; recipient Meritorious Svc. medal USPHS HEW, 1970, Outstanding Service award Westchester div. Am. Cancer Soc., 1984, Meyer and Anna Prentis award Mich. Cancer Ctr., 1987; named one of 1000 most cited scientists, ISI List, 1981. Leadership plaque N.J. State Commn. Cancer Rsch., 1990. Fellow N.Y. Acad. Scis., Am. Coll. Nutrition; mem. Am. Assn. Cancer Rsch. (hon. mem., rep. to European Assn. Cancer Rsch. 1985-89), Am. Chem. Soc. (hon., com. environ. improvement 1992-94, chmn. lectr. chemistry and health 31st Middle Atlantic regional meeting 1997, chmn. symposium tea and health, N.Y., 2003), Am. Gastroent. Assn., Am. Soc. Biochem. Molecular Biologists, Am. Soc. Preventive Oncology (founding mem., bd. dirs. 1983-90, Disting. Svc. award 1990), Biochem. Soc. (London, emeritus), Environ. Mutagen Soc., European Assn. Cancer Rsch. (coun. 1985-90), Japan Cancer Assn. (hon. life), Soc. Exptl. Biol. Medicine, Soc. Toxicology (chmn. bd. publs. 1968-71, councilor 1972-74, amb. toxicology Mid-Atlantic divsn. 1990, hon. mem. 1995, emeritus mem. 2010-, Award of Merit 1981), Westchester Chem. Soc. (Disting. Scientist 1996), Sigma Xi, Alpha Chi Sigma (pres. Washington profl. chpt. 1967-68), Phi Lambda Upsilon. Achievements include rsch. in lifestyle and chronic disease prevention, relevant mechanisms, and medical care cost reduction. Home: 4 Whitewood Rd White Plains NY 10603-1137 Personal E-mail: johnweisburger@aol.com.

WEISFELDT, MYRON LEE, cardiologist, educator; b. Milw., Apr. 25, 1940; s. Simon Charles and Sophia (Price) W.; m. Linda Nan Zaremski, Dec. 29, 1963; children— Ellyn Joy, Lisa Janel, Sara Michelle Student, Northwester U., 1958-60; BA, Johns Hopkins U., 1962, MD, 1965. Intern and resident Columbia-Presbyn. Med. Ctr., NYC, 1965-67; fellow in cardiology Mass. Gen. Hosp., Boston, 1970-72; asst. prof. medicine Johns Hopkins U., Balt., 1972-78, prof. medicine, 1978-91, Robert L. Levy prof. cardiology, 1979-91; Samuel Bard prof. medicine, chair dept. Columbia-Presbyn. Med. Ctr., NYC, 1991—2001; William Osler prof. medicine, dir. dept. medicine Johns Hopkins Med. Sch., 2001—; physician in chief Johns Hopkins Hosp., 2001. Dir. cardiology Johns Hopkins Med. Inst., Balt., 1975-91, Peter Belfer Lab. for Johns Hopkins, Ischemic Heart Disease Spl. Ctr. Rsch., 1977-91; nat. pres. Am. Heart Assn., 1989-90; cardiology adv. com. Nat. Heart, Lung and Blood Inst., 1986-90, chmn., 1988-90; mem. adv. coun. Nat. Inst. on Aging, 1999-2002; study chair resuscitation outcomes consortium Nat. Heart Lung and Blood Inst., 2004—; study chair Resuscitation Outcomes Consortium, NIH, DOD, 2006-. Editor: The Aging Heart, 1980; editorial bd. Jour. Clin. Investigation, 1984-88, Circulation, 1980-86, 88—2004, Jour. Am. Coll. Cardiology, 1987-93, Jour. Molecular and Cellular Cardiology, 1975-80, 86-89, Circulation Rsch., 1988-94. With USPHS, 1967—69. NIH grantee, 1977-91; recipient Golden Heart award Am. Heart Assn., 1998, Harrick award, 2004. Fellow AAAS, ACP (Phillips award in clin. medicine 2006), Am. Coll. Cardiology; mem. Assn. Univ. Cardiologists, Am. Soc. Clin. Investigation, Assn. Am. Physicians, Assn. Prof. Medicine (Diversity award, 2008), Inst. of Medicine, Phi Beta Kappa, Alpha Omega Alpha, Interurban Clin. Club. Jewish. Office: Johns Hopkins Medicine 1830 E Monument St Ste 9026 Baltimore MD 21287 Office Phone: 410-955-6642. Business E-Mail: mlw5@jhmi.edu.

WEISFUSE, ISAAC BRAM, city health department administrator; b. New Hyde Park, NY, Apr. 27, 1955; m. Evelyn Horn; children: Ari, Lois. MD, SUNY Downstate Med. Ctr., Bklyn., 1982; MPH in Health Policy and Mgmt., Columbia U., NYC, 1991. Diplomate Am. Bd.

Internal Medicine. Intern/resident internal medicine LI Jewish Med. Ctr., 1982—85; fellow epidemiology & pub. health Epidemic Intelligence Svc., Ctr.'s for Disease Control & Prevention, 1985—87; with NYC Dept. Health & Mental Hygiene, 1987—, various positions including dir. Office AIDS Rsch., asst. commr. Bur. Sexually Transmitted Diseases, dir. emergency preparedness activities, 1999—, agy. incident comdr. for World Trade Ctr. disaster, dep. commr. disease control, 2002—. Assoc. prof. clin. pub. health of epidemiology Columbia U. Mailman Sch. Pub. Health; faculty Johns Hopkins Sch. Pub. Health, Balt. Contbr. articles to profl. jours. Office: NYC Dept Health & Mental Hygiene 125 Worth St Rm 326 CN#22 New York NY 10013 Business E-Mail: iweisfus@health.nyc.gov.

WEISMAN, GARY ANDREW, biochemist; b. Bklyn., June 18, 1951; s. Joseph Herman and Elaine (Melman) W.; m. Sandra Kay Hille, Aug. 4, 1979; children: Laura Joanne, Pamela Michelle, Veronica Evelyn. BS, Polytechnic U., 1972; postgrad., U. Bordeaux, France, 1972-74; PhD, U. Nebr., 1980. Postdoc. rsch. assoc. Cornell U., Ithaca, NY, 1980-85; asst. prof. U. Mo., Columbia, 1985-92, assoc. prof., 1992-98, prof., 1998—. Spl. reviewer NIH, mem. ODCS Study Section; reviewer NSF, Am. Jour. Physiology, Jour. Biol. Chemistry, Molec. Pharmacology, Euro. Jour. Pharmacol. GLIA; editl. bd. Purinergic Signalling. Contbr. articles to profl. jours. Grantee USDA, 1987—, NIH, 1988—, CF Found., 1994-2000, Am. Diabetes, 1995-2002, Am. Heart Assn. 1994-. Mem. AAAS, Am. Chem. Soc., Am. Soc. Biochem. and Molecular Biology, Am. Diabetes Assn., Am. Heart Assn., NY Acad. Scis., Soc. for Neurosci., Am. Soc. Nutr. Scis., Am. Soc. Pharmacol. and Exptl. Therapeut. Home: 1804 University Ave Columbia MO 65201-6004 Office: U Mo Dept Biochemistry 540E Life Scis Ctr Columbia MO 65211-7310 Business E-Mail: weismang@missouri.edu.

WEISS, CAROL JULIET, psychiatrist; b. NYC, Mar. 5, 1957; d. Eugene and Rose (Schwartz) Weiss. BA, Wesleyan U., 1977; MD, Johns Hopkins U., 1983. Diplomate Am. Bd. Psychiatry and Neurology. Intern N.Y. Hosp., NYC, 1983—84; resident Payne Whitney Clinic, N.Y. Hosp., NYC, 1984—87; asst. psychiatrist Payne Whitney Clinic - N.Y. Hosp., NYC, 1983—87; clin. fellow Cornell U., NYC, 1987—89, instr. and clin. affiliate in psychiatry and pub. health, 1989—, clin. asst. prof. in psychiatry and pub. health NYC, 1992—; pvt. practice NYC, 1987—. Cons. in field. Contbr. articles to profl. jours., chpts. to books. Mem. Am. Psychiat. Assn., Am. Soc. Addiction Medicine, Phi Beta Kappa. Office: 1044 Madison Ave New York NY 10075 Office Phone: 212-988-1209.

WEISS, EARLE BURTON, physician; b. Waltham, Mass., Nov. 23, 1932; s. Murray E. and Ruth R. (Pill) W.; m. Ruth Lithwick, Dec. 1, 1963; children: Ilana, Joshua. BS with honors, Northeastern U., Boston, 1955; MS, MIT, Cambridge, 1957; MD, Albert Einstein Coll. Medicine, NYC, 1961. Intern King's County Hosp., Bklyn., 1961—62; resident Boston City Hosp., 1962—64, Nat. Heart Inst. fellow, 1964—66; sr. rsch. assoc. Tufts Lung Sta., 1964—71; founder/first dir. respiratory ICU, sr. attending physician pulmonary & med. svc. Boston City Hosp., 1964—71, dir. Pulmonary Physiology Lab., 1966—71; assoc. chief of medicine Tufts Med. Svc./Boston City Hosp., 1969—71; dir. divsn. respiratory diseases St. Vincent Hosp., Worcester, Mass., 1971—89, also acting med. dir., 1985—87; prof. medicine U. Mass. Med. Sch., 1977—; sr. pulmonary rsch. scientist, dept. anesthesia Rsch. Labs. Brigham and Womens Hosp., Boston, 1989—. Cons. medical devices adv. panel FDA, 1975-77; cons. in physiology Norfolk County Sanitorium, 1966-69; lectr. medicine Tufts Med. Sch., 1978-; assoc. prof. life scis. Worcester Poly. Inst., Mass., 1976—; vis. prof. Faculty of Medicine, dept. of anesthesia Harvard Med. Sch., 1990-2002, vis. prof. U. Guadalajara, Mexico, 1973, 77, prof. extraordinario faculty medicine, 1977, 82; med. dir. Found. Rsch. in Bronchial Asthma and Related Diseases, 1980—; Tb cons. Commonwealth of Mass., 1972-89; dir. regional inpatient Tb and outpatient Tb clinic, Worcester County, 1972-89, spl. asst. to dir., Astronomy Dept. & Whitin Obs. Wellesley Coll., 2011. Author: Bronchial Asthma, 1976, 2d edit., 1985, 3d edit., 1993, Status Asthmaticus, 1978; contbr. (with artist Frank H. Netter) Ciba Collection: The Respiratory System Anatomy of Lung and Asthma Sections and Clinical Symposia Bronchial Asthma, Acute Respiratory Failure in COPD, 1969; contbr. over 90 articles to profl. jours., abstracts, audio tapes and book chpts. Capt. USAFR, 1965-70. Recipient 1st Dr. J. McKeever Meml. award for outstanding med. educator, 1970, The Acad. Honor Soc., Tchg. and Patient Care award, Boston City Hosp. (I-III), 1971; named Extraordinary Prof, U. Guapalajara Faculty Medicine, 1977; named one of Am.'s Top Physicians, 2003—. Fellow ACP, Am. Coll. Chest Physicians, Royal Coll. Physicians; mem. AAAS, AMA, Mass. Thoracic Soc. (pres. 1976-78, Chadwick medal for meritorious contbn. in Respiratory Diseases 1990), Am. Thoracic Soc. (co-founder clin. assembly, rep. councilor 1979-82, founder, chmn. med. devices com. 1972-79, rep. ANSI med. tech. adv. bd. 1973-75, med. edn. com. 1972-74), Am. Assn. Clin. Scientists, Am. Soc. Internal Medicine, Soc. Free Radical Rsch., NY Acad. Scis., Am. Acad. Med. Dirs., Interasthma, Astron. Soc. of the Pacific, Soc. for Astron. Scis., Royal Astron. Soc. Can., Planetary Soc., British Astron. Assn., Sigma Xi, (MIT chpt.). Achievements include introduction and pioneering use of controlled mechanical ventilation in acute respiratory failure of chronic lung disease and asthma, arterial blood gas profiles in status asthma, "cross-over" point in status-severe asthma, recording of breath sounds, the theory of the role of calcium and oxygen toxic products in causing asthma and airways reactivity 1979, percutaneous lung biopsy for diagnosis of respiratory infections, effect thyroid hormones upon cerebral cortex maturation and first isolation of alpha-hydroxy acid oxidase; establishment student research fellowship at Albert Einstein College of Medicine. Home: 57 South St Natick MA 01760-5526 Office: Brigham and Womens Hosp Dept Anesthesia Rsch L Boston MA 02115 Personal E-mail: drwe@comcast.net. Business E-Mail: eweiss@bics.bwh.harvard.edu, eweiss@wellesley.edu.

WEISS, GERSON, endocrinologist, educator; b. NYC, Aug. 1, 1939; s. Samuel and Lillian (Wolpe) Weiss; m. Linda Gordon, Dec. 24, 1959; children: Jonathan, David, Michele, Andrew. BA, NYU, 1960, MD, 1964. Diplomate Am. Bd. Ob-Gyn. Intern, fellow dept. medicine Johns Hopkins Sch. Medicine, 1964-65; resident ob-gyn NYU Med. Ctr., 1964-69; rsch. fellow physiology U. Pitts. Sch. Medicine, 1971-73; asst. prof. ob-gyn NYU Med. Ctr., 1971-76, assoc. prof., 1976-80, prof., 1980-85; dir. div. reproductive endocrinology NYU Med. Center, 1975-85; prof. ob-gyn U. Med. and Dentistry NJ-NJ Med. Sch., 1986—, chmn. dept., 1986—; dir. divsn. reproductive endocrinology Hackensack U. Med. Ctr., NJ, 1996—2002. Rep. Am. Bd. Med. Spltys., bd. dirs., 2004—. Mem. editl. bd.: Fertility and Sterility Jour., 1986—93, Gyn.-Ob. Investigation; contbr. scientific papers to profl. jours. Served to maj. MC US Army, 1969—71. Rsch. grantee, NIH, 1975—, United Cerebral Palsy Found., 1977—83, Mellon Found., 1982—85, Rsch. fellow, John Polachek Found. Mem.: ACOG, Liason Com. Ob-Gyn. (chair 2009—), Soc. Study Reprodn., NY Gynecol. Soc. (pres. 1989—90), NY Obstet. Soc. (pres. 1990—91), Soc. Gynecol. Investigation (pres. 2005—06), Endocrine Soc., Am. Bd. Ob-Gyn. (mem. divsn. reproductive endocrinology 1985—90, mem. ob-gyn. residency rev. com. 1995—2000, bd. dirs., treas. 1997—98, pres. 1998—2002, chmn. 2002—06), Am. Gyn.-Ob. Soc., Alpha Omega Alpha, Sigma Xi, Phi Beta Kappa. Home: 185 West End Ave Apt 7MN New York NY 10023 Office: UMDNJ NJ Med Sch Dept Ob-Gyn 185 S Orange Ave Newark NJ 07103-2757 Business E-Mail: weissge@umdnj.edu.

WEISS, JAMES LLOYD, cardiology educator; b. Chgo., Jan. 15, 1941; s. Edward Huhner and Ruth (Wingerhoff) W.; m. Susan Forscher Weiss. July 23, 1967; children: Ethan James, Lisa Fleur. BA, Harvard Coll., 1963; MD, Yale U., 1968. Intern, resident U. Mich. Hosp., Ann Arbor, 1968-70; staff fellow NIH, Bethesda, Md., 1970-72; resident medicine Johns Hopkins Hosp., Balt., 1972-73, fellow cardiology, 1973-75, dir. Heart Station, 1976—, asst. prof. Medicine, 1975-81, assoc. prof. Medicine, 1981-90, prof. Medicine, Cariology, 1990—, Michael J. Cudahy prof. of cardiology, 1992—, assoc. dean admissions and acad. affairs, 1999—, dir. cardiology fellowship and tng. program, 1999—. Mem. editl. bd.: Johns Hopkins Med. Letter, 1991—, Jour. Am. Coll. Cardiology, 1995—; contbr. 120 articles to profl. jours. Recipient Harvard Book prize, 1959. Fellow Am. Coll. Cardiology, AHA Coun. on Circulation; mem. Harvard Club N.Y.C., Ctr. Club. Office: Cardiology Divsn Johns Hopkins Hosp 600 N Wolfe St Baltimore MD 21287-0005 Home Phone: 410-321-1145; Office Phone: 410-955-6834. E-mail: jlweiss@jhmi.edu. *

WEISS, KEVIN BARTON, medical association administrator, epidemiologist; b. Nov. 20, 1956; BA, Washington U., Mo., 1977; MS, MD, U. Chgo., 1981; MPH, Harvard U., 1985, MS, 1987. Bd. cert. internat medicine 1984. Intern internal medicine Cook County Hosp., Chgo., 1981—82, resident internal medicine, 1982—84, resident, 1984—85; tng. epidemiology US Nat. Inst. Allergy and Infectious Diseases, NIH, US Nat. Ctr. for Health Statistics, Ctrs. for Disease Control and Prevention; with Med. Ctr. George Wash. U., DC, asst. prof. healthcare scis.; assoc. prof. internal medicine Rush Med. Coll.; dir. Ctr. Health Services Rsch. Rush Primary Care Inst. Rush-Presbyn.-St. Luke's Med. Ctr., Chgo.; prof. divsn. gen. medicine, dir. Inst. for Healthcare Studies, co-dir. Inst. Health Svcs. & Policy Northwestern U.; dir. Ctr. for Mgmt. Complex Chronic Care Hines and Chgo. Veterans Affairs Med. Ctr.; pres., CEO Am. Bd. Med. Specialties, 2008—. Bd. regents ACP; initiator Nat. Cooperative Inner-City Asthma Study; prin. investigator Pediat. Asthma Care Patient Outcomes Rsch. Team Agy. for Healthcare Rsch. and Quality; prin. investigator Chgo. Initiative to Raise Asthma Health Equity Nat. Heart, Lung and Blood Inst.; mem. expert panel Asthmas Guidelines Nat. Heart, Lung and Blood Inst./Nat. Asthma Edn. and Prevention Program; chair Guideline Implementation panel Nat. Asthma Edn. and Prevention Program; chair asthma measure adv. panel NAt. Com. on Quality Assurance; chair various federally sponsored national asthma workshops. Contbr. articles to profl. pubs., chapters to books. Achievements include research in the epidemiology of asthma and asthma-related problems. Office: American Board Medical Specialties 222 N La Salle St Ste 1500 Chicago IL 60601-1117 Office Phone: 312-436-2600. *

WEISS, LYN DENISE, physician; b. Bethpage, NY, Apr. 13, 1959; d. Eugene and Lois Zanger; m. Jay M. Weiss, Apr. 7, 1984; children: Ari, Helene, Stefan, Richard. BA, U. Va., 1981; MD, SUNY, Bklyn., 1985. Diplomate Am. Bd. Electrodiagnostic Medicine, Nat. Bd. Med. Examiners, Am. Bd. Phys. Medicine and Rehab. Resident Dept. Phys. Medicine & Rehab. Nassau U. Med. Ctr., East Meadow, NY, 1985—89; attending physician Dept. Phys. Medicine & Rehab. Nassau U. Med. Ctr., 1989—94, dir. Electrodiagnostic Medicine Dept. Phys. Medicine Rehab., 1991—; dir. residency tng. Dept. Phys. Medicine & Rehab. Nassau U. Med. Ctr., 1993—; acting chmn. Dept. Phys. Medicine & Rehab. Nassau U. Med. Ctr., 1994—96; chmn. Dept. Phys. Medicine & Rehab. Nassau U. Med. Ctr., 1996—. Author: Cumulative Trauma Disorders, 1997, Skin Care Triad, 2000, Easy EMG, 2004, Easy Injections, 2007, Oxford Handbook of PM&R, 2010.

WEISS, MARGARET, dermatologist, educator; Grad., Princeton U.; MD, Johns Hopkins U. Diplomate Am. Bd. Dermatology. Resident dermatology Johns Hopkins U., asst. prof., dermatology; physician Maryland Laser, Skin, and Vein Inst. Appeared in (TV shows) Good Morning, America, Health Week, PBS; co-author: (textbook) Vein Diagnosis & Treatment: A Comprehensive Approach, 2001. Fellow: Am. Soc. of Dermatologic Surgery, Am. Acad. of Dermatology; mem.: Md. Dermatologic Soc., Am. Coll. of Phlebology. Office: Maryland Laser, Skin, & Vein Institute, LLC 54 Scott Adam Rd Ste 301 Aspen Mill Profl Bldg Hunt Valley MD 21030 Office Phone: 410-666-3960. Office Fax: 410-666-3981.

WEISS, MARISA C., breast cancer oncologist, non-profit breast cancer organization executive; married; 3 children. Attended, U. Pa., MD, 1984. Intern radiological oncology Crozer-Chester Med. Ctr., Pa., 1984—85; resident radiological biology U. Pa. Hosp., 1985—88, fellow radiological oncology, 1988—90; practicing breast cancer oncologist Lankenau Hosp., part of Main Line Health Hospitals of the Thomas Jefferson U. Health System, 1992—; dir. breast radiation oncology, dir. breast health outreach Lankenau Hosp.; asst. prof. dept. radiation oncology U. Pa.; founder, past pres. Living Beyond Breast Cancer (LBBC), 1990—2007; pres., founder, spokesperson Breastcancer.org. Mem. director's consumer liaison group Nat. Cancer Inst., 2000—07; mem. profl. adv. bd. Mommy's Light Lives On, Phila. Wellness Cmty.; keynote spkr. on internat. women's health conference circuit, including Speaking of Women's Health, Europa Donna, Irish Cancer Soc., and John Hopkins; mem. Marine Biol. Lab., Woods Hole, Mass.; hosp. appointment Paoli Meml. Hosp., Pa., 1992—94, Chester Co. Hosp., Pa., 1992—94, Brandywine Hosp., Pa. Co-author (with mother Ellen Weiss): Living Beyond Breast Cancer, 1997, 1998; co-author: (with daughter Isabel Friedman) Taking Care of Your Girls: A Breast Health Guide for Girls, Teens and In-Betweens, 2008; author: 7 Minutes!: How to Get the Most from Your Doctor Visit, 2007; frequently consults by TV, print and radio media; performer: (ednl. video) Doctor, Doctor, Lend Me Your Ear: An Up-Close Look at Patient-Doctor Relationship; multiple guest appearances on Today Show, 1998—2007, Good Morning America and ABC News.com, 2007—08, guest appearances CNN House Call during Breast Cancer Awareness Month, 2003—06, (NPR) Fresh Air with Terry Gross, Radio Times with Mary Moss-Coane, CNN Radio, ABC Radio, CBS Radio, Washington Post Radio and the radio partner of Cosmopolitan Mag., med. editor (TV films) Why I Wore Lipstick to My Mastectomy, Lifetime TV, In Matters of Life and Dating, guest spkr. WebMD's spl. breast cancer feature, 2001—04, interviewed and regularly quoted in New York Times, USA Today, Wall Street Journal, Washington Post, Philadelphia Inquirer and articles for the AP newswire, People, Cosmopolitan, Ladies' Home Journal, Redbook, More, Shape, Self, Allure and O., serves on advisory bd. Women's Health mag. Recipient of several honors from Am. Cancer Soc., 2003 Professor of Survivorship award, Susan G. Komen Found. (now Susan G. Komen for the Cure); named Top Doc (cover story), Philadelphia Mag., 2005. Mem.: Am. Soc. Therapeutic Radiation Oncology, Am. Soc. Clin. Oncology. Office: Breastcancer.org 7 E Lancaster Ave 3rd Fl Ardmore PA 19003

WEISS, MARTIN HARVEY, neurosurgeon, educator; b. Newark, Feb. 2, 1939; s. Max and Rae W.; m. R. Debora Rosenthal, Aug. 20, 1961; children: Brad, Jessica, Elisabeth. AB magna cum laude, Dartmouth Coll., 1960, BMS, 1961; MD, Cornell U., 1963. Diplomate Am. Bd. Neurol. Surgery (bd. dirs. 1983-89, vice chmn. 1987-88, chmn. 1988-89). Intern Univ. Hosps., Cleve., 1963-64, resident in neurosurgery, 1966-70; sr. instr. to asst. prof. neurosurgery Case Western Res. U., 1970-73; asso. prof. neurosurgery U. So. Calif., 1973-76, prof., 1976-78, prof., chmn. dept., 1978—2004, Martin H. Weiss chair in neurol. surgery, 1997—. Chmn. neurology B study sect. NIH; mem. residency rev. com. for neurosurg. Accreditation Commn. for Grad. Med. Edn., 1989—, vice chmn., 1991—93, chmn., 1993—95, mem. appeals coun. in neurosurg., 1995—; vis. prof. U. Mich. 1987; vis. prof. Med. Sch. Harvard U., 1988; vis. prof. U. Wash., 1988, U. Calif., San Francisco, 1994, U. Oreg., 1995, Tufts U., 1996, U. Melbourne, 1996, U. Sydney, 1996, U. Erlangen/Nurnberg, 1999, U. Geneva, 1999, U. Tex., 2004, U. Oreg., 2004, Stanford U., 2005; vis. prof., Bronson Ray lectr. Cornell U., 2005—06; Afrox traveling prof. South African Congress Neurol. Surgeons, 1989; hon. guest Royal Coll. Physicians Endocrine Sect., London, 2001; lectr. in field. Author: Pituitary Diseases, 1980, assoc. editor Bull. L.A. Neurol. Socs., 1976-81, Jour. Clin. Neurosci., 1981—; mem. editl. bd. Neurosurgery, 1979-84, Neurol. Rsch., 1980—, Jour. Neurosurgery, 1987—, chmn., 1995—, assoc. editor, 1996—; editor-in-chief Clin. Neurosurgery, 1980-83, Neuro Sociological Focus, 1996-. Served to capt. USAR, 1964—66, assoc. in gen. surgery USAH, USMA, 1964—66, West Point, NY. Spl. fellow in neurosurgery NIH, 1969-70; recipient Jamieson medal Australasian Neurosurg. Soc., 1996, Pevehouse medal Calif. Assn. Neurol. Surgeons, 2008. Mem. ACS (adv. coun. neurosurgery 1985-88), Soc. Neurol. Surgeons (v.p. 1999, pres.-elect 2000—, pres. 2001-02, Disting. Svcs. award, 2011), Neurosurg. Soc. Am., Am. Acad. Neurol. Surgery (exec. com. 1988-89, v.p. 1992-93), Rsch. Soc. Neurol. Surgeons, Am. Assn. Neurol. Surgeons (bd. dirs. 1988-91, sec. 1994-97, pres.-elect 1998-99, pres. 1999-00, past pres. 2000-01, Kurze Lectr. 2005, Cushing Medalist, 2005), Congress Neurol. Surgeons (v.p. 1982-83), Western Neurosurg. Soc. (Cloward medal 2006), Neurosurg. Forum, So. Calif. Neurosurg. Soc. (pres. 1983-84), Neurosurgeon Rsch. & Edn. Found. (chmn., exec. com. 2004-), Phi Beta Kappa, Alpha Omega Alpha. Home: 357 Georgian Rd La Canada Flintridge CA 91011-3520 Office: 1200 N State St Los Angeles CA 90033-1029 Home Phone: 818-790-7467; Office Phone: 323-226-7421. Business E-Mail: weiss@usc.edu.

WEISS, PAUL RICHARD, plastic surgeon; b. Bklyn., July 4, 1942; s. Murray and Belle (Edelman) W.; m. Linda Wayne, Aug. 23, 1964; children: Fredda Susan, Jonathan Michael. BS, Tufts U., Medford, Mass., 1964; MD, Tulane U., New Orleans, 1969. Diplomate Am. Bd. Plastic Surgery, 1977, Am. Bd. Surgery, 1975. Intern Bronx Muni Hosp Ctr., NY, 1969—70, resident surgery, 1970—72, Montefiore Hosp. Med. Ctr., NY, 1972—74, resident plastic surgery, 1974—76; attending plastic surgeon Montefiore Med. Ctr., NY, 1976—, Albert Einstein Coll. Med. Hosp., NY, 1976—, Beth Abraham Hosp., NY, 1976—, Jewish Home & Hosp., NY, 1976—, Beth Israel Med. Ctr., NY, 1986—2005; clin. prof. plastic surgery Albert Einstein Coll. Medicine, Bronx, NY, 1994—; clin. prof. surgery Albert Einstine Coll., 2007—. Adv. bd. FOJP Medical Malpractice, N.Y.C., 1988—. Named one of Top Doctor, NY Mag. Fellow ACS (Bronx chpt., pres. 1995-96); Am. Soc. Plastic Surgeons, Am. Assn. Plastic Surgeons, Am. Soc. Aesthetic Plastic Surgery, NY Regional Soc. Plastic Surgeons (pres. 1992-93), Montefiore Med. Ctr. Staff Alumni Assn. (pres. 1994-97), Am. Assn. Hand Surgery, Northeastern Soc. Plastic Surgeons, World Profl. Assn. Transgender Health. Jewish. Avocations: landscape gardening, vintage automobiles, stamp collecting/philately, collecting and restoring antique furniture. Office: 1049 5th Ave Ste 2D New York NY 10028-0115 Office Phone: 212-861-8000. Office Fax: 212-861-8376. Personal E-mail: pweissmd@verizon.net.

WEISS, ROBERT, pediatric nephrologist, educator; MD, Georgetown U., 1971. Diplomate Am. Bd. Pediatrics, Am. Soc. Pediatric Nephrology-pediatric nephrology. Resident pediat. Bellevue Hosp. Ctr., NY, 1972—74; fellow pediatric nephrology Montefiore Med. Ctr., Bronx, NY, 1976—78; chief pediatric nephrology Children's and Women's Physicians of Westchester, LLP; affiliated White Plains Hosp. Ctr., Westchester Med. Ctr. Prof. pediat. NY Med. Coll. Office: Children's and Women's Physicians of Westchester LLP Munger Pavilion Rm 123 Valhalla NY 10595 Office Phone: 914-594-4280.

WEISS, ROBERT A., dermatologist, educator; Grad., Columbia U.; MD, Johns Hopkins U., 1978. Diplomate Am. Bd. Dermatology. Resident dermatology John Hopkins Univ.; fellow dermatologic rsch.

Nat. Inst. of Health; assoc. prof. dermatology Johns Hopkins Univ.; physician Md. Laser, Skin, & Vein Inst. Author: (textbooks) Vein Diagnosis & Treatment: A Comprehensive Approach, Cosmetic Dermatology; appeared in (TV shows) 20/20, The Today Show, contbg. editor Jour. Dermatologic Surgery, 2003—, editorial bd. Lasers in Surgery and Medicine. Mem.: Internat. Soc. for Dermatologic Surgery (bd. dirs.), Am. Soc. for Laser Medicine and Surgery (bd. dirs.), Am. Coll. of Phlebology (pres.), Am. Soc. of Dermatologic Surgery (treas.). Office: Maryland Laser, Skin, and Vein Institute, LLC 54 Scott Adam Rd Ste 301 Aspen Mill Profl Bldg Hunt Valley MD 21030 Office Phone: 410-666-3960. Office Fax: 410-666-3981.

WEISS, ROBERT ARNOLD, medical association administrator; b. NYC, Jan. 31, 1953; BA, Columbia U., 1974; MD, Johns Hopkins U Sch. Medicine, 1978. Dir. Md. Laser Skin and Vein Inst., 1985—. Fellow: Am. Acad. Dermatology. Office: 54 Scott Adam Rd Hunt Valley MD 21030 Office Fax: 410-666-0203. Business E-Mail: rweiss@mdlsv.com.

WEISS, ROBERT M., urologist, educator; b. NYC, Jan. 13, 1936; s. David and Laura W.; m. Ilana Shemer, May 20, 1973; children: Erik Daniel, Dana Alexandra. BS magna cum laude, Franklin and Marshall Coll., Lancaster, Pa., 1957; MD, SUNY, Bklyn., 1960; MA (hon.), Yale U., New Haven, Conn., 1976. Diplomate: Am. Bd. Urology, Nat. Bd. Med. Examiners. Intern Cornell Med. Divsn., Bellevue Hosp., NYC, 1960-61; resident in gen. surgery Beth Israel Hosp., NYC, 1961-62; resident in urology Squier Urol. Clinic, Presbyn. Hosp., NYC, 1963-64, 65-67; vis. fellow Columbia U. Coll. Physicians and Surgeons, NYC, 1964-65, adj. assoc. prof. pharmacology, 1975-77, adj. prof. pharmacology, 1977—; mem. faculty Yale U. Med. Sch., New Haven, 1967—, prof. urology, 1976-88, prof., chief sect. of urology, 1988—, Donald Gutherie prof. surgery, 2001—, interim chmn. dept. surgery, 1999-2001; attending urology Yale-New Haven Hosp., New Haven, 1967-88, head sect. of urology, 1988—, interim chief dept. surgery, 1999—2001, pres. med. staff, 2004—06. Cons. West Haven VA Hosp. Contbr. articles to profl. jours. Trustee Am. Bd. Urology, 1998-2004. With USAR, 1962-63. Fellow ACS, Am. Acad. Pediat.; mem. AAAS, Am. Assn. Genito-Urinary Surgeons, Am. Surg. Assn., Am. Physiol. Soc., Soc. Gen. Physiologists, Assn. Univ. Urologists, Soc. Pediatric Urology, Am. Urol. Assn., Clin. Soc. Genito-Urinary Surgeons, New Eng. Surg. Soc., New Eng. Urol. Assn., Phi Beta Kappa, Sigma Xi. Office: Yale U Sch Medicine Dept Urology PO Box 208041 New Haven CT 06520-8041 Office Phone: 203-785-2815. Business E-Mail: robert.weiss@yale.edu.

WEISS, ROBERT STEPHEN, medical manufacturing company operating executive; b. Oct. 25, 1946; s. Stephen John and Anna Blanche (Lescinski) W.; m. Marilyn Annette Chesick, Oct. 29, 1970; children: Christopher Robert, Kim Marie, Douglas Paul. BS in Acctg. cum laude, U. Scranton, 1968. CPA, N.Y. Supr. KPMG (formerly Peat, Marwick, Mitchell & Co.), NYC, 1971-76; asst. corp. contr. Cooper Labs., Inc., Parsippany, N.J., 1977-78; group contr. Cooper Vision, Inc., 1980; v.p., corp. contr. Cooper Labs., Palo Alto, Calif., 1981-83, The Cooper Cos., Inc. (formerly CooperVision, Inc.), Palo Alto, Calif., 1984-89; v.p., treas., CFO The Cooper Cos., Inc., Pleasanton, Calif., 1989—2005, sr. v.p., 1992-95, exec. v.p. fin., 1995—2005, COO, 2005—07, CEO, 2007—, pres., 2007—. Bd. dirs. The Cooper Cos., Inc., Pleasanton, Calif, 1996-, Accuray Inc., Sunnyvale, Calif., 2007-. With U.S. Army, 1969-70. Decorated Bronze Star with oak leaf cluster, Army Commendation medal. Mem. AICPA, N.Y. State Soc. CPAs. Office: The Cooper Companies Inc Ste 590 6140 Stoneridge Mall Rd Pleasanton CA 94588 Office Phone: 925-460-3610. Business E-Mail: rweiss@cooperco.com.

WEISS, SAMUEL, neurobiologist, educator; BSc in Biochemistry, McGill U., Montreal; PhD in Neurobiology, U. Calgary. Postdoctoral fellow Alberta Heritage Found. for Med. Rsch. and Med. Rsch. Coun. Can., 1983—88; asst prof. to prof., Alberta Heritage Found. for med. rsch. scientist, dept. cell biology & anatomy & pharmacology & therapeutics, faculty medicine U. Calgary, 1988—, co-founder, inaugural chair, genes and develop. rsch. group; dir. Hotchkiss Brain Inst. Recipient Alberta Innovation-Growing Brain Cells, Heritage Cmty. Found., 2002, Gairdner Found. Internat. award, 2008; named a Researcher of the Month, Canadians for Health Rsch., 2005. Achievements include discovery of with Fritz Stadeczek discovered the metabotropic glutamate receptor in 1985; adult neural stem cells in mammalian brain and its importance in nerve cell regeneration in 1992; patents in field. Office: U Calgary Hotchkiss Brain Inst 2263-3330 Hospital Dr NW Calgary AB Canada T2N 4N1 Business E-Mail: weiss@ucalgary.ca. *

WEISS, SAMUEL ABRAHAM, psychologist, psychoanalyst; b. NYC; m. Alice Langer, May 20, 1958; children: Benjamin Z., Naomi E., Susan J. BA, Yeshiva U., 1944; MA, NYU, 1948, PhD, 1957. Diplomate in clin. psychology, Am. Bd. Profl. Psychology. Intern Bellevue Psychiat. Hosp., NYC, 1955—56; assoc. rsch. scientist NYU Med. Ctr., NYC, 1956—59, rsch. scientist, 1959—68, assoc. dir. amputee psychology rsch., 1958—66; assoc. prof. psychology Yeshiva U., NYC, 1961—71, psychol. cons. Stern. Coll. for Women, 1960—71; psychologist, psychotherapist, psychoanalyst in pvt. practice NYC, 1972. Cons. N.Y. State Div. Vocat. Rehab., 1958-73. Contbr. articles to profl. jours. Fellow AAAS (Rosette award 1991), APA (editl. cons. rehab. psychology 1972-80), Assn. Psychological Sci. Jewish. Achievements include new research on medical factors in phantom limb pain and rehabilitation. Home: 80-40 Lefferts Blvd Kew Gardens NY 11415-1723 Office Phone: 212-686-8324.

WEISS, SUSAN ELLEN, adult nurse practitioner, educator; b. Youngstown, Ohio, Oct. 25, 1951; d. Robert Cochran and Clara Olive (Cyphert) Stetson; m. Paul Wm. Weiss, Dec. 27, 1975; children: David, Rebecca, Noah, Simon, Solomon. AAS, Youngstown State U., 1971, BSN, 1975; cert. adult nurse practitioner, SUNY, 1981. Cert. adult nurse practitioner, legal nurse cons., 1998. Nurse practitioner St. Joseph Riverside Hosp., Warren, Ohio; emergency room nurse St. Elizabeth Hosp., Youngstown; ICU-CCU nurse Youngstown Osteo. Hosp.; dir. advanced nursing edn. NP Sch. Based Clinic, 1994. Pro-bono adult nurse practitioner Drs. James and Chris Ventresco, Family Practice, 2004—05. Mem.: AACN, Am. Acad. Nurse Practitioners, Cardiovascular Nursing Assn., Oncology Nursing Soc., Nat. League Nursing, Am. Coll. Cert. Legal Nurse Cons., Am. Coll. Nurse Practitioners. Home: 1275 Sageberry Dr North Lima OH 44452-8575 Personal E-mail: weissan@aol.com.

WEISSBLUTH, MARC, pediatrician, educator; b. 1943; MD, U. Wash., Seattle, 1970; grad., Stanford U. Cert. in pediat. Am. Bd. Med. Specialties, 1975. Intern St. Louis Children's Hosp., resident; prof. clinical pediat. Feinberg Sch. Medicine, Northwestern U.; pediatrician Children's Meml. Hosp., Chgo., Northwestern Children's Practice, Chgo. Author: Crybabies, Sweet Baby: How to Soothe Your Newborn, Your Fussy Baby, Healthy Sleep Habits, Happy Child. Mem.: Children's Cmty. Physicians Assn. Avocations: fishing, boating, golf, skiing, tennis. Office: Northwestern Childrens Practice 680 N Lake Shore Dr Ste 123 Chicago IL 60611 also: Childrens Meml Hosp Box 86 2300 Childrens Plz Chicago IL 60614 Office Phone: 312-642-5515, 773-880-4549. Office Fax: 312-642-0753.

WEISSENBACH, JEAN, science foundation director, researcher; b. Strasbourg, Feb. 13, 1946; B in Math., U. Strasbourg, 1964, grad. in Chemistry, 1969, DSc in Molecular Biology, 1977. With U. Strasbourg, Pasteur Inst., Genethon; dir. CNRS (French Ctr. for Scientific Rsch.); CEO Genescope, French Nat. Sequencing Ctr., Envy, France, 1997—. Advisor, com. on mapping and sequencing of the human genome US Acad. Sci., 1987; mem. genome com. French Ministry for Rsch., 1989, 91; mem. adv. group Sanger Ctr. Scientific, 1994—; mem. scientific bd. GREG, 1994—95; mem. coll. scientific advisors Pasteur Inst., 1994—96; mem. scientific be. GIS Infobiogen, 1994—99; mem. scientific com. for rsch. into the human genome German Ministry for Edn., Sci., Rsch. and Tech., 1995—96; chmn. scientific com. Max-Planck Inst. Molecular Genetics, Berlin, 1997; mem. scientific com. Lillie Biology Inst., 1998, Genomics Pathogins Lab., Pasteur Inst., 1998; mem. scientific bd. Genomics Program of French Ministry responsible for rsch., 1999. Mem. editl. com. Cytogenetics and Cell Genetics, 1992—97, Human Molecular Genetics, 1994—98, Annals Human Genetics, 1994—, Genome Research, 1995—. Recipient Maurice Nicloux prize, French Biol. Chemistry Soc., 1979, Mergier-Bourdeix prize, French Acad. Sci., 1992, Mauro Baschirotto prize, European Soc. Human Genetics, 1995, Athena Found. prize, 1996, Platinum Tech. 21st Century Pioneer Partnership award, Smithsonian Inst., 1999, Gairdner Found. award, 2002. Mem.: Acad. Sci., Molecular Medicine Soc., French Soc. Human Genetics, French Soc. Genetics, Human Genome Orgn., European Molecular Biology Orgn., French Soc. Biochemistry and Molecular Biology, HUGO. Office: Genoscope Nat Ctr of Sequencing 2 rue Gaston Crémieux CP 5706 91057 Evry France Office Phone: 33 0 1 60 87 25 00. Office Fax: 33 0 1 60 87 25 14. *

WEISSENBORN, SÖNKE J., virologist, chemist; b. Bad Segeberg, Germany, May 23, 1966; s. Johannes and Frauke Weissenborn; m. Inke Diana Schaper, Mar. 11, 2006; children: Mira Nandy, Julias. PhD in Genetics, U. Cologne, Germany, 2003. Chemist Rheinisch-Westfälische Technische Hochschule Aachen, Germany, 1998. Rsch. assoc. Inst. Virology U. Cologne, 2003—05, asst. prof. and rsch. group leader, 2005—. Lectr. for chemistry Tech. Coll. for Lab. Assistants in Medicine U. Cologne, 2001—. Contbr. articles to profl. pubs. Mem.: Internat. Papillomavirus Soc. (assoc.), German Soc. Virology (assoc.).

WEISSERT, ROBERT, neurologist, educator, neuroimmunologist; b. Stuttgart, Germany, Apr. 18, 1964; s. Nikolaus and Ingeborg Weissert; m. Katrien L. de Graaf, June 9, 2000; children: Emma Laura, Helena Sophie. MD, U. Tuebingen, Germany, 1994; PhD, Karolinska Inst., Sweden, 1999. Cert. specialization in neurology Germany, 2002. Internship, neurology U. Tuebingen, 1993—95, resident, neurology, 1998—2000, resident, psychiatry, 2000—01, cons., multiple sclerosis outpatient clinic, 2002—07, adj. prof., neurology, 2006—; postdoc. fellowship, neuroimmunology Karolinska Inst. & Hosp., Stockholm, 1995—98; Heisenberg fellowship, German rsch. found. Hertie Inst. Clin. Brain Rsch., Tuebingen, 2002—07; leader, rsch. in pharm. industry Merck Serono SA, Geneva, 2007—10; invited prof., neurology U. Geneva, 2007—10, U. Regensburg, 2011—. Cons. Faster Cures, Washington, 2008—; expert Innovative Medicines Initiative, Brussels, 2011—. Contbr. articles. Recipient Multiple Sclerosis prize; Rsch. fellowship, German Rsch. Found., 1995—97, grants, 1999—2007, Ministry Edn. & Health, 1999—, Rsch. fellowship, European Cmty., 1997—98. Achievements include patents in field. Mailing: Am Invslenhole 4 Nittendorf D-93152 Germany Office Phone: 49-941-941-0. Business E-Mail: robert.weissert@googlemail.com.

WEISSMAN, ALLAN M., medical researcher; BS in biochemistry, SUNY, Stony Brook, 1977; MD, Albert Einstein Coll. Medicine, 1981. Resident in internal medicine Washington U.; postdoctoral fellow Cell Biology and Metabolism Br. Nat. Inst. Child Health & Human Devel., NIH, 1984; ind. investigator Nat. Cancer Inst., NIH, 1989, chief Regulation of Protein Functions Lab. Ctr. Cancer Rsch., 2001—03, acting chief Regulation of Cell Growth Lab., chief Lab. Protein Dynamics and Signaling, 2003—. Mem.: Assn. Am. Physicians, Am. Soc. Clin. Investigation, Alpha Omega Alpha. Office: Lab Protein Dynamics and Signaling Nat Cancer Inst Frederick 1050 Boyles St, Bldg 560, Rm 22-103 Frederick MD 21702-1201 Office Phone: 301-846-1222. Office Fax: 301-846-1666. E-mail: amw@nih.gov. *

WEISSMAN, IRVING L., medical researcher; b. Great Falls, Mont., Oct. 21, 1939; married, 1961; 4 children. BSc, Mont. State Coll., 1961, DSc (hon.), 1992; MD, Stanford U., 1965; Doctorate (hon.), Columbia U., 2006, Mt. Sinai Sch. Medicine, NYC, 2007. NIH fellow dept. radiology Stanford U., 1965—67, rsch. assoc., 1967—68, asst. prof. dept. pathology, 1969—74, assoc. prof. dept. pathology, 1974—81, prof. dept. pathology, 1981—, chmn. immunology program, 1986—2001; Karel & Avice Beekhuis Prof. Cancer Biology Stanford U. Sch. Medicine, 1987—, prof. devel. biology, 1989—, dir., Inst. of Stem Cell Biology and Regenerative Medicine, 2003—, prof. by courtesy, biology and neurosurgery, 1990—. Sr. Dernham fellow Calif. divsn. Am. Cancer Soc., 1969—73; mem. immunobiology study sect. NIH, 1976—80; mem. founding scientific adv. bd. Amgen, 1981—89, DNAX, 1981—92; James McGinnis Meml. lectr. Duke U., 1982; mem. sci. rev. bd. Howard Hughes Med. Inst., 1986; George Feigen Meml. lectr. Stanford U., 1987; Albert Coons Meml. lectr. Harvard U., 1987; Jame Stahlman lectr. Vanderbilt U., 1987; mem. sci. adv. com. Irvington House Inst., 1987; 5th Ann. vis. prof. cancer biology U. Tex. Health Sci. Ctr., 1987; R. E. Smith lectr. U. Tex. Sys. Cancer Ctr., 1988; co-founder SyStemix, Inc., 1988, bd. dirs., 1988—97; mem. founding scientific adv. bd. T-Cell Scis. (now Avant, Inc.), 1988—92; Chauncey D. Leake lectr. U. Calif., 1989; Harvey lectr. Rockefeller U., 1989; Rose Litman lectr., 90; disting. lectr. Western Soc. Clin. Investment, 1990; investigator Howard Hughes Med. Inst., 1990—92; chmn. U.S.-Japan Immunology Bd., 1992—94; chmn. sci. adv. com. McLaughlin Rsch. Inst., 1992—, trustee, 1992—; bd. govs. Project Inform, 1995—; co-founder StemCells, 1996—, mem. bd. dirs.; co-founder Celtrans (now Cellerant), 2001—; chair scientific adv. bd. Cellerant; spkr. in field. Contbr. articles to profl. publications. Recipient Faculty Rsch. award, Nat. Am. Cancer Soc., 1974—78, Basic Cell Rsch. award, Am. Soc. Cytopathology, Pasarow Award for cancer rsch., 1989, Kaiser Award for Excellence in Preclinical Teaching, Outstanding Investigator Award, NIH, E. Donnall Thomas Award, Am. Soc. Hematology, 1999, deVillers Award for Outstanding Achievements in Leukemia Rsch., Leukemia Soc. Am., 1999, J. Allyn Taylor Internat. Prize in Medicine, 2003, Bass Award, Soc. Neurological Surgeons, 2003, Elliott Proctor Joslin medal, Am. Diabetes Assn., 2003, Van Bekkum Stem Cell Award, 2003, Disting. Scientist Award, Am. Assn. Cancer Inst., 2003, Alan Cranston Awardee, Alliance for Aging Rsch., 2004, Rabbi Shai Shacknai Mem. Prize in Immunology and Cancer Rsch., Lautenberg Ctr. for Gen. and Tumor Immunology, 2004, medal for Disting. Contributions to Biomedical Rsch., NY Acad. Medicine, 2004, Jeffrey Modell Dare to Dream award, 2005, Commonwealth Cub of Calif. 18th Ann. Disting. Citizen award, 2006, American-Italian Cancer Found. prize for Scientific Excellence in Medicine, NYC, 2006, John Scott award, City of Phila., 2006, I. & H. Wachter Found. award, 2007, Robert Koch Found. award, Berlin, Germany, 2008, Rosentiel award, Brandeis U., 2009, Passano Found. award, 2009; named One of Top 100 Alumni, Mont. State U., 1993, Mont. Conservationist of Yr., Mont. Land Reliance, 1994, Calif. Scientist of Yr., 2002; scholar, Josiah Macy Found., 1974—75. Fellow: AAAS, Am. Acad. Arts and Scis.; mem.: Inst. of Medicine (IOM), NAS (steering com. NIOM AIDS panel 1985—86, chair, Panel on Sci. & Med. Aspects of Human Reproductive Cloning, Jessie Stevenson Kovalenko Medal 2004), Internat. Soc. for Stem Cell Rsch. (pres.-elect), Inst. Immunology, Am. Assn. Cancer Rsch., Am. Soc. Microbiology, Am. Assn. Pathologists, Am. Assn. Univ. Pathologists, Am. Assn. Immunologists (pres. 1994—95). Achievements include research in phylogeny and developmental biology of cells that make up blood-forming and immune systems; first to isolate, in mice and in man, the blood-forming stem cell; knowledge expected to lead to improved treatment of people with myeloma, lymphoma and breast cancer. Avocations: football, ballet, fly fishing. Office: Stanford U Sch Medicine Dept Pathology B257 Beckman Ctr Stanford CA 94305-5323 E-mail: irv@stanford.edu.

WEISSMANN, GERALD, internist, researcher, educator, editor, writer; b. Vienna, Aug. 7, 1930; came to U.S., 1938; s. Adolf and Greta (Lustbader) W.; m. Ann Raphael, Apr. 1, 1953; children: Lisa, Andrew. BA with honors, Columbia U., NYC, 1950; MD, NYU, 1954. Diplomate Am. Bd. Internal Medicine. Intern Mt. Sinai Hosp., NYC, 1954-55, asst. resident medicine, 1957-58; chief resident medicine Bellevue Hosp., NYC, 1959-60; fellow depts. biochemistry and medicine Arthritis and Rheumatism Fedn., NYU, 1958-59; rsch. asst. dept. medicine NYU Sch. Medicine, 1959-60, instr. medicine, 1959-62, asst. prof., 1962-65, assoc. prof., 1966-70, prof., 1970—, dir. div. cell biology, 1969-73, dir. div. rheumatology of dept. medicine, 1973-2000; dir. Ctr. Biotech. Studies, 2000—. USPHS spl. rsch. fellow dept. biophysics Strangeways Lab., Cambridge, Eng., 1960-61; sr. investigator Arthritis and Rheumatism Found., N.Y.C., 1961-65; career rsch. scientist Health Rsch. Coun. N.Y.C., 1966-71; instr. physiology Marine Biol. Lab., Woods Hole, Mass., 1973-77, investigator, 1970—, trustee, 1993—; vis. investigator ARC Inst. Animal Physiology, Babraham, Eng., 1964-69, Centre de Physiologie et d'Immunologie Cellulaires, Hosp. St. Antoine, Paris, 1973-74, William Harvey Rsch. Inst., London, 1987; mem. postdoctoral fellowships rev. com. Pfizer Internat., N.Y.C., 1983-89; mem. scholarship selection com. Pew Scholars in Biomed. Scis., New Haven, 1984-94; lectr. Johns Hopkins U., 1976, 89, Med. Coll. Ga., Augusta, 1980, Med. Coll. Pa., 1988, William Harvey Rsch. Inst., London, 1987, others; nat. adv. bd. Ellison Med. Found, 1997—; chair Prix Galien USA award com. Author: The Woods Hole Cantata, 1995, They All Laughed at Christopher Columbus, 1987, The Doctor With Two Heads, 1990, The Doctor Dilemma, 1992, Democracy and DNA, 1996, Darwin's Audubon, 1998, The Year of the Genome, 2001, Galileo's Gout, 2007; editor-in-chief Inflammation, 1975-01, Advances in Inflammation Rsch., 1979—, MD Mag., 1989-94, The FASEB Jour., 2005-; mem. editl. bd. Clin. Immunology and Immunopathology, 1972-88, Advances in Prostaglandin, Thromboxane and Leukotriene Rsch., 1975—, Am. Jour. Medicine, 1976-88, Tissue Reactions, 1979, Immunopharmacology, 1982; contbr. over 300 articles to profl. jours. Capt. M.C., U.S. Army, 1955-57. Recipient Allesandro Robecchi prize Internat. League Against Rheumatism, 1972, Marine Biol. Lab. award, 1974, 1979, U. Bologna medal, Italy, 1978, Lila Gruber Cancer Rsch. award Am. Acad. Dermatology, 1979, Solomon A. Berson Med. Alumni Achievement award NYU, 1980, Merit award NIH, 1987, Centennial award Marine Biol. Lab., 1988, others; Guggenheim Found. fellow, N.Y.C., 1973-74. Fellow AAAS; mem. Am. Coll. Rheumatology (pres. 1982-83, Disting. Investigator award 1992, Presdl. Gold medal 2005, master 1996), Am. Fedn. Clin. Rsch., Soc. Exptl. Biology and Medicine, Am. Soc. Pharmacology and Exptl. Therapeutics, Am. Soc. Exptl. Pathology, Assn. Am. Immunologists, Am. Soc. Cell Biology, Am. Soc. Clin. Investigation, Am. Soc. Biol. Chemistry and Molecular Biology, Assn. Am. Physicians, Harvey Soc. of N.Y. (pres. 1981-82), Interurban Clin. Club, PEN Am. Ctr., Cosmos Club, Phi Beta Kappa, Alpha Omega Alpha, fgn. mem. Accademia Nazionale dei Lincei (Rome) Avocation: tennis. Office: NYU Med Ctr Dept Medicine BCD686 550 1st Ave New York NY 10016-6402

WEISZ, JOHN R., psychology professor, child psychologist; b. Newton, Miss. m. Jenny Graves; 4 children. BA in Psychology, Miss. Coll., Clinton; MS, PhD in Clin. and Devel. Psychology, Yale U., New Haven. Diplomate Am. Bd. Profl. Psychology, cert. in clin. child &

adolescent psychology, lic. Calif., Mass. Asst. prof. Cornell U., NYC, 1975—78; from asst. to assoc. prof., then prof. U. NC, Chapel Hill, 1978—90; prof. dept. psychology UCLA, 1990—2004, dir. grad. program clin. psychology, 1991—94, prof. dept. psychiatry & biobehavioral scis., 2000—04; prof. psychology Harvard U., Cambridge, Mass., 2004—, affiliated faculty, Ctr. on Developing Child, 2008—; pres., CEO Judge Baker Children's Ctr. Harvard Med. Sch., Boston, 2004—. Prof. Med. Coll. Va., Richmond, 1987—88; dir. rsch. & psychol. svcs. Va. Treatment Ctr. Children, 1987—88; dir. clin. training UCLA Psychology Clinic, 1991—94; dir. rsch. network on youth mental health John D. & Catherine T. MacArthur Found., 2001—; chair sci. adv. group Nat. Acad. Parenting Profls., Inst.Psychiatry, Univ. Coll. London, 2008—. Prin. editor clin. psychology TheScientificWorld, 2000—, assoc. editor Jour. Consulting & Clin. Psychology, 2000—01, Perspectives on Psychol. Sci., 2007—09, mem. editl. bd. Devel. Psychology, 1978—79, Child Devel., 1980—81, Jour. Clin. Child Psychology, 1992—0996, Jour. Clin. Psychology, 1996—2000, Mental Health Svcs. Rsch., 1997—, Report Emotional & Behavioral Disorders in Youth, 2000—08, Child & Adolescent Mental Health, 2001—, Clin. Psychology: Sci. & Practice, 2002—05; contbr. articles to profl. jours. Peace Corps vol. Kenyatta Nat. Hosp., Nairobi, Kenya, 1968—71. Recipient Disting. Tchg. award, UCLA, 2001, Disting. Sci. Achievement in Psychology award, Calif. Psychol. Assn., 2004. Fellow: Am. Acad. Clin. Child & Adolescent Psychology, Am. Psychol. Assn. (Nicholas Hobbs award 2004); mem.: Soc. Clin. Child & Adolescent Psychology (pres. 2000, chair com. on evidence 2001—, Disting. Sci. Contbn. award 2005), Soc. Clin. Psychology (chair com. on sci. & practice 2000—02), Internat. Soc. Rsch. Child & Adolescent Psychopathology (pres. 2001—03). Office: Judge Baker Childrens Ctr Harvard Med Sch 53 Parker Hill Ave Boston MA 02120 also: Harvard U Dept Psychology William James Hall 33 Kirkland St Cambridge MA 02138 Office Phone: 617-278-4299. Office Fax: 617-730-5440. Business E-Mail: jweisz@jbcc.harvard.edu. *

WEITBERG, ALAN BARRY, physician, researcher, dean; b. Phila., Mar. 2, 1950; s. Sidney and Esther Weitberg; m. Katherine Raphaela Bick, Sept. 6, 1975 (div. Apr. 1993); children: Allison Ross, Seth Raphael. AB, Cornell U., Ithaca, NY, 1972; MD, Univ. Medicine and Dentistry NJ, Newark, 1976; MEd (hon.), Brown U., Providence, 1992. Lic. MD RI, 1978, Mass., 1982, cert. Nat. Bd. Med. Examiners, 1977, Internal Medicine, 1980, Med. Oncology, 1987, Hematology, 1988. Resident and chief resident in medicine Roger Williams Med. Ctr. and Brown Med. Sch., Providence, 1976—80; hematology fellow Mass. Gen. Hosp. and Harvard U., Boston, 1980—82; instr. med. sch. Harvard Med. Sch., Boston, 1982—85; chief divsn. hematology, oncology Brown Med. Sch. and Roger Williams Med. Ctr., Providence, 1985—91; prof. and chmn., dept. medicine Roger Williams Med. Ctr. and Boston U. Sch. Medicine, Providence, 1991—; asst. dean acad. affairs Boston U. Sch. Medicine, 2007—. Dir. divsn. med. oncology Brown U., 1988—; prof. medicine Boston U. Sch. Medicine. 1988—, asst. dean acad. affairs, 2007; bd. trustees Roger Williams Med. Ctr., 2002—04. Author: Cancer of the Lung, 2002; contbr. more than 75 sci. papers to profl. jours., chapters to books, articles to over 60 profl. jours. Critical care, med. appraisal, med. audit, med. rec. Roger Williams Hosp., 1979—80, infection control, nutritional support, patient care/greivence, 1979—80, intern selection, clin. competence com., 1985—, chmn. cancer com., 1986—99, chmn. credentials com., 1987—91, transfusion com., 1988—92, physician's adv. com., 1989—, exec. com., 1991—, strategic planning com., 1992—, joint conf. com., 1992—, quality improvement steering coun., 1992—, oncology task force, 1995—, pres., med. assoc., 1996—, bd. trustees, 2002—, Univ. Med. Group, 1999—, exec. com. bd., 2001—; chmn. admissions com. for an integrated med. residency program Brown U., 1990—; com. sectional chiefs Boston U., 1997—. Recipient Dean Charles L. Brown award, Univ. Medicine and Dentistry NJ, 1976, Tchr. of Yr. award, Brown U. Sch. Medicine, 1992, Eminent Scientist award, Internat. Rsch. Promotion Coun., Physician's Recognition award with commendation, AMA, 2005; named to Top Dr. Am., 2009; named to Mu Eplison Delta Hon. Soc., Cornell U., 1971, Watts Scholarship Soc., Cornell Univ., 1971; nominee Ernesta Nuti Internat. prize for Cancer Rsch., Rome, 1992; Arts and Sci. Dean's scholar, Cornell U., 1969, over 30 rsch. grants from various colls. and univs. Fellow: ACP (exec. coun. RI chpt. 1992—, Lifetime Achievement award RI chpt. 2010); mem.: AMA (Physicians Recognition award 2005—), AAAS, Cancer Trials Support Unit, Assn. Acad. Med. Ctr., Clin. Oncology Group, Am. Soc. Hematology, Assn. Am. Med. Coll., Leukemia Soc. Am. (bd. dirs. 1989—), Am. Bd. Internal Medicine (recertification com. 1993—), Am. Soc. Cancer Rsch. (chmn. carcinogeneses sect. 1987—, state legis. com. 1992—), Am. Soc. Clin. Oncology (chmn. lung cancer sect. 1987—), Am. Cancer Soc. (chmn. nominating com. 1992, instl. rsch. grant rev. study sect. 1992—), Am. Fedn. for Clin. Rsch. (chmn. hematology sect. 1993—), Internat. Soc. Free Radical Rsch., Sigma Xi. Avocations: painting, opera, running, reading. Office: Roger Williams Med Ctr Dept Medicine 825 Chalkstone Ave Providence RI 02908 Business E-Mail: awietherg@rwmc.org.

WEITZ, HOWARD HY, cardiologist, educator; b. Phila., July 6, 1952; s. Thelma and Arnold Weitz; m. Barbara Malett, May 3, 1987; children: Aaron Richard, Benjamin Isaac, Hannah Sarah. BS, Muhlenberg Coll., Pa., 1974, DS (hon.), 2003; MD, Jefferson Med. Coll., Phila., 1978. Diplomate Am. Bd. Internal Medicine, 1981, cert. Cardiovascular Diseases Am. Bd. Internal Medicine, 1985. Dir. divsn. cardiology Jefferson Med. Coll., Phila., 1995—98, prof. medicine, 2005—, sr. vice-chmn., dept. of medicine, 2005—, dir. dept. cardiology, 2008; co-dir. Jefferson Heart Inst., Phila., 1998—, dir., 2008; commr. Fed. Medicaid Commn., Washington, 2005—06. Author: Medical Management of the Surgical Patient, 1992 (NBI Healthcare Found. Humanism in Medicine Faculty award, 1998), 2d edit., 1998, 3rd Edit., 2008, Peripheral Vascular Disorders, 2004. Fellow: Am. Coll. of Cardiology, ACP. Office: Jefferson Heart Inst 925 Chestnut St Philadelphia PA 19027 Business E-Mail: howard.weitz@jefferson.edu.

WEIZHONG, LI, engineering educator; b. Dalian, China, Feb. 17, 1956; PhD, Nottingham Trent U., 2002. Prof. Dalian U. Tech., 2002—. Avocations: sports, music. Office: Linggong Rd Dalian Liaoning 116024 China Business E-Mail: wzhongli@dlut.edu.cn.

WELCH, HENRY GILBERT, internist; b. Alexandria, Va., Apr. 21, 1955; BA in Economics, Harvard Coll., Cambridge, Mass., 1976; MD, U. Cin. Med. Ctr., 1982; MPH, U. Wash., Seattle, 1990. Diplomate Am. Bd. Internal Medicine. Intern internal medicine Conemaugh Valley Meml. Hosp., Johnstown, Pa., 1982—83; commd. lt. comdr. USPHS; resident U. Utah, Salt Lake City, 1985—87; VA/Robert Wood Johnson clin. scholar U. Wash., 1988—90; prof. medicine and cmty. & family medicine Dartmouth Med. Sch., Hanover, NH, dir. Ctr. Medicine & the Media. Co-dir. VA outcomes group VA Med. Ctr., White River Junction, Oreg. Author: Should I Be Tested for Cancer? Maybe Not and Here's Why, 2004; contbr. articles to pofl. jours. Recipient Visiting Scientist award, Internat. Agy. Rsch. on Cancer, 2001—02. Fellow: ACP, Am. Soc. Clin. Investigation. Office: VA Outcomes Group 111B VA Med Ctr 215 N Main St White River Junction VT 05009 Office Phone: 802-296-5178. E-mail: H.Gilbert.Welch@dartmouth.edu. *

WELCH, ROBERT ALAN, obstetrician-gynecologist, perinatologist maternal-fetal medicine; b. Perrysburg, Ohio, Aug. 1, 1951; s. Robert Chester and Dorothy Jean (Hamilton) W.; m. Sally Elizabeth Straits, June 24, 1972; children: Olivia, Robert Jr., Kathryn. BS, U. Toledo, 1973; MD, La. State U., 1980; MSA, Ctrl. Mich. U., 2000. Diplomate Am. Bd. Maternal Fetal Medicine. Resident in ob-gyn. Wayne State U., Detroit, 1980-84, fellow in perinatal dept., clin. instr., 1984-86; exec. chief resident Detroit Med Ctr., 1983-84; assoc. prof. ob-gyn. Wayne State U., Detroit, 1986-91; dir. maternal and fetal medicine Providence Hosp., Southfield, Mich., 1991-95, chmn., program dir. dept. ob-gyn., 1995—, med. dir. women's svcs., 1998—. Dir. high risk pregnancy unit Hutzel Hosp., Detroit, 1986; lectr. in field. Patentee modified surgical gloves, self-capping needle, digital device for dispensing medicine, cervical ring; contbr. articles to profl. jours., chpts. to books. Recipient Morris Bachman award, Stephenson Prize award Detroit Med. Ctr., 1983-84. Fellow: Am. Coll. Ob-Gyn. (Mich. sect. adv. com., Searle Donald F. Richardson Meml. prize 1986, Ephraigm McDowell award 1985); mem.: AAAS, AMA, Soc. Maternal Fetal Medicine, Oakland County Med. Soc., Am. Coll. Physician Execs., Am. Fedn. Clin. Rsch., Am. Assn. Med. Edn. and Rsch. in Substance Abuse, Assn. Profs. in Gynecology and Obs., N.Y. Acad. Sci., Am. Fertility Soc., Am. Inst. Ultrasound in Medicine, Am. Soc. Gynecologic Laparoscopists, Wayne County Med. Soc., Mich. State Med. Soc. Avocation: microcomputing. Office: Providence Hosp Dept Ob Gyn Southfield MI 48075 also: PO Box 2043 16001 W 9 Mile Rd Southfield MI 48075-4818

WELCH, ROBERT BOND, ophthalmologist, educator; b. Balt., May 24, 1927; s. Robert S.G. and Sally (Bond) W.; m. Elizabeth Truslow, May 30, 1953. AB, Princeton U., NJ, 1949; MD, Johns Hopkins U., Balt., 1953. Diplomate: Am. Bd. Ophthalmology. Intern in internal medicine Duke U. Hosp., 1953-54; resident in ophthalmology Wilmer Inst., Johns Hopkins U., 1954-57, chief resident in ophthalmology, 1959, co-dir. retina service, 1959-84, dir. retina service, 1984-85; retinal cons. in ophthalmology Walter Reed Army Hosp., 1961—2003, Bethesda Naval Hosp, 1976-99; assoc. prof. ophthalmology Johns Hopkins U.; chmn. dept. ophthalmology Greater Balt. Med. Ctr., 1985-91. Author: (with others) The Wilmer Institute 1925-1975, 1976; author: The Wilmer Opthalmological Institute 1925-2000, 2000; editor Transactions Am. Ophthal. Soc., 1984-91; mem. editorial staff Retina mag., 1980-86. Served with USNR, 1945-47. Recipient Disting. Alumnus award, Johns Hopkins U., 2001, Superior Civilian Svc. award, U.S. Army, 2004, Robert Bond Welch professorship in opthalmology, Johns Hopkins Medicine and Wilmer Eye Inst., 2006. Mem. Am. Ophthal. Soc. (v.p. 1992-93, pres. 1993-94, editor 1984-90), Retina Soc. (pres. 1981-83), Pan. Pacific Surg. Assn. (v.p. 1972-80), Md. Soc. Eye Physicians and Surgeons (pres. 1963-64), Md. Club., Elkridge Club, South River Club. Democrat. Episcopalian. Home: 4409 Atwick Rd Baltimore MD 21210-2811 Office: 86 State Cir Annapolis MD 21401-1906 Office Phone: 410-263-3492.

WELCKER, KATRIN, thoracic surgeon, director; b. Hamburg, Germany, Oct. 26, 1965; 2 children. MD, PhD. Asst. surgeon U. Munich, Bavaria, 1992—2000; jr. registrar, dept. thoracic surgery Asklepios Fachkliniken Munich-Gauting, 2000—03, Krankenhaus Großhansdorf, Hamburg, Germany, 2003—05; asst. med. dir., dept. thoracic surgery Klinikum Bremen-Ost gGmbH, 2005—08, sr. asst. med. dir., dept. thoracic surgery, 2008—. Mem. coun. woman Deutsche Gesellschaft für Thoraxchirurgie, Berlin, 2003; mem. coun. German Soc. Surgeons, Deutsche Gesellschaft für Chirurgie, Berlin, 2008—. Grantee German study found., U. Study, 1985—92, Münchner Medizinische Wochenschrift, Reseach, 1998, German Soc. of Surgeons, For Visit internat. centers for thoracic surgery, 2005. Fellow: European Bd. Thoracic & Cardiovasc. Surgeons; mem.: Soc. Bavarian Surgeons, Deutscher Ärztinnenbund, Deutsche Gesellschaft Pneumologie, European Soc. Thoracic Surgeons, Deutsche Gesellschaft Thoraxchirurgie, Deutsche Gesellschaft Chirurgie, European Respiratory Soc. Evangelical. Avocation: tennis. Office: Klinikum Bremen-Ost gGmbH Züricher Str 40 Bremen D 28325 Germany Business E-Mail: katrin.welcker@klinikum-bremen-ost.de.

WELDON, DAVID JOSEPH, JR., former United States Representative from Florida; b. Amityville, NY, Aug. 31, 1953; s. David Joseph and Anna Weldon; m. Nancy Sourbeck, Aug. 18, 1979; children: Kathryn, David. BS, SUNY, Stony Brook, 1978; MD, SUNY, Buffalo, 1981. Intern Letterman Army Med. Ctr., 1981-82, resident in internal medicine, 1982-84; pvt. practice, Melbourne Internal Medical Assoc, 1987—94; mem. US Congress from 15th Fla. dist., Washington, 1995—2009; mem. appropriations com. Served in US Army, 1981—97 USAR, 1987—92. Fellow: ACP; mem.: AMA, Fla. Med. Assn. Republican. Protestant.

WELDON, VIRGINIA V., retired food products executive, pediatrician; b. Toronto, Sept. 8, 1935; arrived in US, 1937; d. John Edward and Carolyn Edith (Swift) Vernal; children: Ann Weldon Doyle, Susan Weldon Erlinger. AB cum laude, Smith Coll., 1957; MD, SUNY-Buffalo, 1962; LHD (hon.), Rush U., 1985. Diplomate Am. Bd. Pediat., Am. Bd. Pediatric Endocrinology and Metabolism, Nat. Bd. Med. Examiners (bd. dirs. 1987-89). Intern Johns Hopkins Hosp., Balt., 1962-63, resident in pediat., 1963-64; fellow pediatric endocrinology Johns Hopkins U., Balt., 1964-67, instr. pediat., 1967-68; from instr. to assoc. prof. Wash. U., St. Louis, 1968—79, prof., 1979-89, v.p. Med. Ctr., 1980-89, dep. vice chancellor med. affairs, 1983-89, dir. Ctr. Study Am. Bus., 1998-99; v.p. sci. affairs Monsanto Co., St. Louis, 1989, v.p. pub. policy, 1989-93, sr. v.p. pub. policy, 1993-98. Mem. gen. clin. rsch. ctrs. adv. com. NIH, Bethesda, Md., 1976—80, mem. rsch. resources adv. coun., 1980—84; adv., dir. Monsanto Co., 1989—98. Contbr. articles to sci. jours. Mem. risk assessment mgmt. commn. EPA, 1992—97; commr. St. Louis Zool. Pk., 1983—92; mem. Pres.'s Com. Advs. Sci. and Tech., 1994—2000; trustee Calif. Inst. Tech., 1996—, Whitaker Found., 1997—99, St. Louis Sci. Ctr.; bd. dirs., vice chmn., chmn. St. Louis Symphony Orch., 1993—2005, hon. trustee, 2005—; bd. dirs. United Way Greater St. Louis, 1978—90, St. Louis Regional Health Care Corp., 1985—91; mem. adv. com. on agrl. biotech. USDA, 2000—01. Fellow: AAAS, Am. Acad. Pediat.; mem.: PT @ CC, St. Louis Med. Soc., Soc. Pediat. Rsch., Endocrine Soc., Am. Pediat. Soc., Assn. Am. Med. Colls. (disting. svc. mem., del., chmn. coun. acad. socs. 1984—85, chmn. assembly 1985—86), Nat. Acads. (nat. assoc.), Inst. Medicine, Alpha Omega Alpha, Sigma Xi. Roman Catholic. Home: 242 Carlyle Lake Dr Saint Louis MO 63141-7544

WELDON, WILLIAM CONRAD (BILL WELDON), pharmaceutical executive; b. Bklyn., Nov. 26, 1948; m. Barbara Weldon; 2 children. BS in Biology, Quinnipiac U., 1971. With sales and mktg. McNeil Pharm. Johnson & Johnson, 1971—82; mgr. ICOM Regional Develop. Ctr., 1982—84; v.p. mng. dir. Korea Mcneal Ltd., 1984—86; mng. dir. Orthro-Cilag Pharm., 1986—89; v.p. sales mktg. Janssen Pharm., 1989—92; pres. Ethicon Endo-Surgery, 1992, group chmn., 1995, chmn., pharm. group, 1998; vice-chmn. Johnson & Johnson, New Brunswick, NJ, 2001—02, chmn., CEO, 2002—. Bd. dirs. Johnson & Johnson, 2001—, J.P. Morgan Chase & Co., 2005—; chmn. Pharm. Rsch. & Manufacturers, 2005—. Serves Liberty Sci. Center Chmn.'s Adv. Coun.; mem. Sullivan Commn. on Diversity in the Healthcare Workforce; trustee Quinnipiac Univ. Avocation: basketball. Office: Johnson & Johnson 1 Johnson & Johnson Plaza New Brunswick NJ 08933 *

WELKER, KRISTINA DIANE, psychologist, b. July 9, 1960; BA, U. Ctrl. Okla., Edmond, 1989; MA, Ottawa U., Phoenix, 2000; PhD in Psychology, U. Southern Calif., 2006. Lic. profl. counselor 2006. Pharm. sales rep. Mead Johnson Labs., Phoenix, 1992—94; profl. counselor, 2001—06; psychotherapist Well Within, LLC, 2006—. Contbr. articles to Ahwatukee foothills news. Mem.: Am. Assn. Christian Counselors, Am. Counselling Assn. Office: 12020 S Warner Elliot Loop Ste 104 Phoenix AZ 85044 Personal E-mail: drkristina@drkristinawelker.com.

WELKOWITZ, WALTER, biomedical engineer, educator; b. Bklyn., Aug. 3, 1926; s. Samuel and Shirley (Rosenblum) W.; m. Joan Horowitz, June 17, 1951; children: David, Lawrence, Julie. BS, The Cooper Union, NYC, 1948; MS, U. Ill., 1949, PhD, 1954. Profl. engr., N.J. Rsch. assoc. U. Ill., Urbana, 1948-54, Columbia U., NYC, 1954-55; asst. to pres., gen. mgr. Gulton Industries, Inc., Metuchen, NJ, 1955-64; prof., chmn. elec. engring. Rutgers U., Piscataway, NJ, 1964-86, prof. biomed. engring., 1986—, chmn. biomedical engring., 1986-90. Cons. Gulton Industries, Metuchen, N.J., 1964-74. Author: Engineering Hemodynamics: Application to Cardiac Assist Devices, 1977, 2d edit., 1987; co-author: Biomedical Instruments: Theory and Design, 1976, 2d edit., 1992, author numerous chpts. in books; contbr. more than 100 articles to profl. jours. With U.S. Navy, 1944-46. Rutgers U. Rsch. Coun. fellow, 1974-75; recipient Centennial medal IEEE, 1984, Excellence in Rsch. award Rutgers Bd. Trustees, 1985, IEEE Career Achievement award Soc. Engring. Med. Biology, 1991; Llewellyn Thomas vis. prof. U. Toronto, Can., 1989. Fellow IEEE (engring. in medicine and biol. soc. career achievement award 1991), N.Y. Acad. Medicine, Am. Inst. of Medicine and Biol. Engring. Achievements include 26 patents for Electron Tube, Ultrasonic Flowmeter, Ultrasonic Transducer, Piezoelectric Heart Assist Apparatus, Method and Apparatus for Non-Invasive Monitoring Dynamic Cardiac Performance, and others. Home: 197 Water St Apt 400 Keene NH 03431-4260 Home Phone: 603-903-7875; Office Phone: 813-626-8776. Personal E-mail: wwelkowitz@aol.com.

WELLEMS, THOMAS E., federal agency administrator; b. Anaconda, Mont., Aug. 2, 1951; BS in Physics and Chemistry, N.Mex. Inst. Mining & Tech.; PhD in Biophysics, U. Chgo., 1980; MD, U. Chgo. Pritzker Sch. Medicine, 1981. Diplomate Am. Bd. Internal Medicine. Intern internal medicine U. Pa. Hosp., Phila., 1981—82, resident tropical medicine, 1982—84; fellow NIH, Bethesda, Md., 1984—86, sr. staff fellow Nat. Inst. Allergy & Infectious Diseases (NIAID), 1987—91, head malaria genetics sect., 1991—, chief Lab. Malaria & Vector Rsch., 2002—. Recipient Sanofi-Aventis US award, Am. Soc. Microbiology, 2007. Mem.: NAS, Inst. Medicine. Address: NIAID 6610 Rockledge Dr MSC 6612 Bethesda MD 20892-6612 Office: Malaria & Vector Rsch Lab Twinbrook II 12441 Parklawn D 3E10A Bethesda MD 20892-0001 Office Phone: 301-496-2487. Business E-Mail: twellems@niais.nih.gov. *

WELLER, ELIZABETH BOGHOSSIAN, child and adolescent psychiatrist; b. Aug. 7, 1949; m. Ronald A. Weller, Feb. 18, 1978; children: Andrew, Christine. BS, Am. U., Beirut, Lebanon, 1971, MD, 1975. Lic. psychiatrist, Lebanon, Mo., Ohio, Pa. Intern Am. U. of Beirut, 1974-75; resident Renard Hosp./Washington U., St. Louis, 1975-78; fellow U. Kans. Med. Ctr., Kansas City, 1978-79; asst. prof. psychiatry U. Kans. Med. Sch., Kansas City, 1979-85; chief child/adolescent psychiatry Ohio State U., Columbus, 1985-94, assoc. chair dept. psychiatry, 1994-96; prof. psychiatry and pediat. U. Pa., 1996—, chmn. dept. psychiatry child and adolescent psychiatry, 1996-99, vice chmn. dept. psychiatry, prof. psychiatry/pediatrics, 1996—. Fred Allen chair dept. psychiatry Children's Hosp. of Phila., med. dir. Child Guidance Ctr., 1996-99; pres. Am. Bd. Psychiatry and Neurology, 2004. Co-author: Psychiatric Disorders in Child/Adolescent, 1990, Current Perspectives on Major Depressive Disorders in Children, 1984, Children's Interview for Psychiatric Syndromes, 1999. Fellow APA, Am. Acad. Child/Adolescent Psychiatry; mem. ACP, World Fedn. for Mental Health, Soc. Biol. Psychiatry,

Am. Bd. Psychiatry and Neurology (pres. 2004). Office: 3440 Market St Philadelphia PA 19104-4399 Office Phone: 215-590-7573, 215-590-7574. Office Fax: 315-590-7537. Business E-Mail: weller@email.chop.edu.

WELLER, ROY OLIVER, retired neuropathologist; b. London, May 27, 1938; s. Leonard Arthur and Myrtle Weller; m. Francine Michelle Cranley, Dec. 22, 1960; children: Adrienne, Timothy. BSc in Anatomy with honors, Guy's Hosp., 1959, MB BS, 1962, PhD in Pathology, 1967, MD, 1971. House officer, intern Guy's Hosp., London, 1961-62, lectr. in pathology, 1963-67, sr. lectr., cons., 1968-72; postdoctoral fellow NIH, NYC, 1967-68; sr. lectr. U. Southampton, 1973-78, prof. neuropathology England, 1978—2003, emeritus prof. Dep. dean of medicine U. Southampton, 1980-84, curator U. Libr., 1984-88, dir. pathology, 1989-93; editor Neuropathology and Applied Neurobiology, 1989-98. Author: Pathology of Peripheral Nerves, 1977, Atlas of Neuropathology, 1984; editor: Clinical Neuropathology, 1983, Systemicpathology-Neuropathology, 1991, Diagnostic Pathology of Nervous System Tumours, 2002; contbr. over 170 articles to profl. jours. Rsch. grant, Multiple Sclerosis Soc., 1990—99. Fellow Royal Coll. Pathology; mem. British Neuropathol. Soc. (pres. 2001-02), Internat. Soc. Neuropathology (v.p. 2000-02, series editor neurodegeneration, muscles books 2011-). Achievements include research in neuropathology including Multiple Sclerosis and Alzheimer's disease. Home: 22 Abbey Hill Road SO23 7AT Winchester England E-mail: row@soton.ac.uk.

WELLS, ADRIAN, professor, clinical psychologist, researcher, consultant, originator of metacognitive therapy; b. Doncaster, England, Feb. 2, 1962; s. Kenneth Arthur and Marian (Johnson) W. BS with honors, Aston U., Birmingham, 1984, PhD, 1987; MS, Leeds U., 1989; Diploma, U. Pa., Phila., 1990. Chartered clin. psychologist. Rsch. fellow U. Pa., Phila., 1989-90; sr. rsch. clin. psychologist U. Oxford, 1990-95; reader, cons. U. Manchester, 1995—2003, prof., 2004—; prof. II U. Trondheim, 2003—. BABCP rep. U.K. Coun. Psychotherapy, London, 1992-93; mem. steering group cognitive behavior therapy,CBT-Tng. Program U. Oxford, 1992-95; assoc. editor Behav. Cognitive Psychotherapy, 1994—, dir. Metacognitive Therapy Inst.; cons. NHS. Author: (books) Attention & Emotion: A Clinical Perspective, 1994, (with G. Matthews) Cognitive Therapy of Anxiety Disorders, 1997, Emotional Disorders and Metacognition: Innovative Cognitive Therapy, 2000, Bulimia Nervosa: A Self-Help Cognitive Therapy Programme, 2000, Metacognitive Therapy for Anxiety and Depression, 2009, Metacognitive Therapy: Distinctive Features, 2009; contbr. numerous articles to profl. jours. Mem. British Psychological Soc. (assoc. fellow), British Assn. Behav. & Cognitive Psychotherapy, Fellow: Acad. Cognitive Therapy. Avocations: watercolour painting, music, classic cars. Office: U Manchester/Manchester Royal Infirmary Dept Clin Psychology Rawnsley Bldg Oxford Rd M13 9WL Manchester England E-mail: adrian.wells@manchester.ac.uk.

WELLS, GERTRUDE BEVERLY, psychologist; b. Haverhill, Mass., July 14, 1940; d. True Franklyn Wells and Priscilla Eleanor (Browne) Duerstling. BS, SUNY, Fredonia, 1962; MA, Coll. St. Rose, Albany, NY, 1969; PhD, U. Mo., Columbia, 1976; PhD in Clin. Psychology, Fielding Grad. U., Santa Barbara, Calif., 1999. Tchr. speech pathology N.Y. Pub. Schs., Albany and Clifton Park, 1962-70; lectr. SUNY, Albany, 1970-73; asst. prof. Coll. St. Rose, Albany, 1975-77; assoc. prof. U. No. Iowa, Cedar Falls, 1977-78; prof. U. of La., Lafayette, 1978-85; prof., program dir. Calif. State U. Stanislaus, Turlock, 1985-87; prof. comm. Calif. State U., San Francisco, 1987—92; chief exec. officer West Coast Inst., 1992—2000; clin. psychologist, pvt. practice, 2001—. Author: Stuttering Treatment, 1987; contbr. articles to profl. jours. Health svc. provider Nat. Register of Health Svc. in Psychology. Mem.: APA, Am. Acad. Health Care Providers in Addictive Disorders. Avocations: writing, bicycling, gardening. Office: 16 Joost Ave San Francisco CA 94131 Office Phone: 415-585-5212.

WELLS, JOHN TIMOTHY, pediatric neurologist; MD, Sch. Med. SUNY, Stony Brook, 1988. Cert. Am. Bd. Pediatrics, 1991, in Child Neurology Am. Bd. Pediatrics, 1996. Resident in pediatrics Long Island Jewish Med. Ctr., 1988—91; fellow in neurology NYU Med. Ctr., 1991—94; fellow in pediatric neurology Yale Univ., 1994—95; clinical assoc. prof., Dept. Neurology NYU Med. Ctr., NYC. Contbr. articles to profl. jours. Office: NYU Dept Neurology 109 E 67th St New York NY 10021 Office Phone: 212-772-6683. Office Fax: 212-452-3131.

WELLS, KAREN KAY, medical library manager; b. Petaluma, Calif., Jan. 9, 1956; d. Albert Lee and Miyoko (Kay) W.; m. John Edward Guth, Aug. 4, l979 (div. l986). BS with honors, U. Colo., 1977; MEd with honors, U. Ill., 1980, MS with honors, 1982. Cert. tchr., Colo., Ill. Grad. asst. grad. libr. U. Ill., Urbana, 1981—82; asst. prof. med. libr. svcs. sch. medicine Mercer U., Macon, Ga., 1982—88; libr., head dept. Presbyn. Denver and St. Luke's Med. Ctr., 1983; instr., cons. dialog pharm. database AMI-St. Luke's Hosp. Health Scis. Libr., Denver, 1985—87; head libr. Manville Health, Safety and Environ. Libr., Denver, 1988—91; info. cons. Wells Info. Svc., Denver, 1989—91, sr. admistrv. assessor, 1996—98; libr. mgr. Exemple Luth. Med. Ctr., Wheat Ridge, Colo., 2000—. Mem. ALA, Med. Libr. Assn., Colo. Coun. Med. Librs. (cons. med.-sci. databases l984—), U. Colo. Alumni Assn., U. Ill. Alumni Assn., Beta Phi Mu, Kappa Delta Pi. Democrat. Roman Catholic. Avocations: racquetball, diving. Office: Exempla Luth Med Ctr 8300 W 38th Ave Wheat Ridge CO 80033

WELLS, MICHAEL J., medical educator; b. Cardston, Alberta, Can., Nov. 10, 1969; BS, U. Ctrl. Ark., 1992; MD, U. Ark., Miss., 1997. Assoc. prof. Tex. Tech U. HSC, 2001—. Fellow: Am. Acad. Dermatology; mem.: AMA, Am. Coll. Mohs Surgery. Office: 3601 4th St TTUHSC Dept Dermatology Lubbock TX 79430 Business E-Mail: mjwells@pol.net.

WELLS, SAMUEL ALONZO, JR., surgeon, educator; b. Cuthbert, Ga., Mar. 16, 1936; s. Samuel Alonzo and Martha Steele W.; m. Barbara Anne Atwood, Feb. 13, 1964; children: Sarah, Susan. Student, Emory U., 1954—57, MD, 1961. Intern Johns Hopkins Hosp., Balt., 1961—62, resident in internal medicine, 1962—63; asst. resident in surgery Barnes Hosp., St. Louis, 1963—64; resident in surgery Duke U., Durham, NC, 1966—70; guest investigator dept. tumor biology Karolinska Inst., Stockholm, 1967—68; asst. prof. surgery Duke U., Durham, NC, 1970—72, assoc. prof., 1972—76, prof., 1976—81; clin. assoc. surgery br. Nat. Cancer Inst., NIH, Bethesda, Md., 1964—66, sr. investigator surgery br., 1970—72, cons. surgery br., 1975—; prof., chmn. dept. surgery Washington U., St. Louis, 1981—98; dir. ACS, Chgo., 1998—99, group chair, prin. investigator, oncology group, 1998—2005, exec. dir. internat. thyroid cancer study group, 2005—09; sr. clin. surgery br. Nat. Cancer Inst. Dir. Duke U. Clin. Rsch. Ctr., 1978—81; mem. Residency Rev. Com. Surgery, 1987—93, chmn., 1991—93; mem. bd. regents ACS, 1989—98, vice chmn. bd. regents, 1998—; prof. surgery Duke U. Sch. Medicine, 2001—07. Mem. editl. bd.: Annals of Surgery, 1975—93, Surgery, 1975—93, Jour. Surg. Rsch., 1981—93, editor in chief: World Jour. Surgery, 1983—92, Current Problems in Surgery, 1989—. Pres. GM Cancer Rsch. Found., 1996—2006. Lt. comdr. USPHS, 1964—66. Fellow: AAAS; mem.: ACS, Soc. Internationale de Chirurgie (pres. 2001), Soc. Surg. Oncology (pres. 1993—94), Halsted Soc. (pres. 1987), Nat. Cancer Adv. Bd., Inst. Medicine of NAS, Am. Soc. Clin. Investigation, Soc. Clin. Surgery (treas. 1980—86, v.p. 1986—88, pres. 1988—90), Soc. Univ. Surgeons (exec. coun. 1976—78), Am. Surg. Assn. (mem. coun. 1986—91, pres. 1995—96, recorder, Sci. Achievement medallion 2004), Am. Bd. Surgery (exec. com. 1986—89, vice chmn. 1987—88, chmn. 1988—89), Alpha Omega Alpha. Office: Nat Cancer Inst NIH Bldg 10 Room 3-2571 MSC 1206 9000 Rockville Pike Bethesda MD 20892 Office Phone: 301-435-7854. Business E-Mail: wellss@mail.nih.gov.

WELSH, GEORGE FRANKLIN, plastic surgeon, educator; b. Charles City, Iowa, Oct. 13, 1940; s. George S. Welsh and Aldeen (Paris) Welsh Taylor; m. Rosemary Dahlen, June 23, 1973; children: Christopher Franklin, Penelope Cosette, Bradford Alexander. BA, Carleton Coll., 1962; BS, U. N.D., 1964; MD, Harvard U., 1966; M in Hosp. Adminstrn., Xavier U., 1994; cert. in Horticulture, U. Cin., 2002. Diplomate Am. Bd. Surgery, Am. Bd. Plastic Surgery; cert. physician exec; Health Care Garden Design, Chgo., 2004. Commd. officer USAF, 1966, advanced through grades to lt. col., 1974, intern Hosp. San Antonio, 1966—67, flight surgeon Takhli RTAFB Thailand, 1967—69, plastic surgeon Dayton, Ohio, 1975—78; flight surgeon, dir. base med. svcs. United Arab Emirates, 1991, Air War Coll., 1988; resident in surgery Mayo Clinic, Rochester, Minn., 1969—73; resident in plastic surgery U. Okla. Health Sci. Ctr., Oklahoma City, 1973—75; Maytag Fellow in plastic surgery U. Miami, Fla., 1976; ret. col. USAFR, 1996; pvt. practice Cin., 1978—. Cons. on healthcare adminstrn., Cin., 1994—; asst. clin. prof. surgery Wright State U. Sch. Medicine, Dayton, 1975-78; vol. asst. prof. surgery U. Cin. Sch. Medicine, 1978-. Contbr. chpt. to book; contbr. articles to profl. jours. including Surg. Clinics N.Am., Jour. Thoracic and Cardiovasc. Surgery, So. Med. Jour., Plastic and Reconstructive Surgery, Aesthetic Plastic Surgery, Brit. Jour. Plastic Surgery. Mem. Leadership Cin., 1981; citizen amb. People to People Internat., Albania, Russia, 1994, Cuba, 2000, Egypt, 2003, China, 2008. Fellow ACS, Am. Coll. Physician Execs.; mem. Am. Soc. Plastic Surgeons, Millard Plastic Surg. Soc. (programs.), English Spkg. Union (past pres. Cin. br.), Gen. Soc. Colonial Wars (sec. gen.), Ohio Soc., (programs), Cin. Hort. Soc. (chmn. bd.), Harvard Alumni Assn. Avocations: medical missions, gardening, fishing. Office: Aesthetic Plastic Surgery Ctr 6200 Pfeiffer Rd Ste 320 Cincinnati OH 45242-5861 Office Phone: 513-793-0302. Personal E-mail: fwelsh@aol.com.

WELSH, JACK DARYL, retired medical educator, writer; b. Grand Island, Nebr., Nov. 29, 1928; s. Robert Edward and Avis L. Welsh; children: Deborah Ann Frazier, Jack R., James J. BS, U. Nebr., Lincoln, 1951; MD, U. Nebr., Omaha, 1954. Diplomate Am. Bd. Internal Medicine, Am. Bd. Gastroenterology. From instr. to prof. Okla. Med. Sch., Oklahoma City, 1959—90, David Ross Boyd prof. medicine emeritus, 1990. Author: Medical Histories of Confederate Generals, 1995, Medical Histories of Union Generals, 1996, Two Confederate Hospitals and Their Patients, 2005. Sgt. US Army, 1946—47. Home: 610 Greenlea Chase West Oklahoma City OK 73170

WELSH, WILLIAM DANIEL, geriatric medicine family practice physician; b. Balt., May 18, 1950; s. Joseph Leo and Bessie Mary (Tangires) W.; m. Loraine Lynn Barkhaus, July 11, 1985; children: Sean William Welsh, Ryan Daniel. Student, Johns Hopkins U., 1971; BS in Biology cum laude, Fairleigh Dickinson U., 1972; DO, Coll. Osteo. Medicine-Surgery, Des Moines, 1975. Diplomate Nat. Bd. Osteo. Physicians; cert. ATLS; approved supr. physician assts. Osteophatic Med. Bd. Calif.; radiography and fluoroscopy x-ray supr., operator Calif. Intern Martin Place Hosp., Madison Heights, Mich., 1975-76, resident in internal medicine, 1976-77; pvt. practice Detroit, 1977-79; pvt. practice, Whittier, Calif., 1979—. Instr. ACLS, L.A., 1980-92; bd. dirs. Whittier Hosp. Med. Ctr., 1981, vice chief staff, 1982-84, med. dir. family asthma forum, 1979-88, med. dir. Summit Place alcohol treatment program, 1983-88; med. dir. Mirada Hills Rehab. Hosp., La Mirada, Calif., 1980-88; former clin. preceptor Coll. Osteo. Med. Pacific, Pomona, Calif., clin. assoc. prof. internal medicine, clin. assoc. prof. family practice; mem. dept. family practice, physician rev. com. Friendly Hills Regional Med. Ctr., La Habra, Calif., 1994-97; mem. staff Presbyn. Intercmty. Hosp., Whittier, Whittier Hosp. Med. Ctr., chmn. by laws com. 1999-2001, mem. exec. com. 1999-2001; med. dir. Royal Ct. Convalescent Hosp.; med. dir. First Choice Home Health Agy.; assoc. prof. family medicine Western U. Health Scis.; spkr. in field. Participant Calif. Beach Clean Up Day, 1996, med. dir. Hospice Care of West, 2007-09, Hosp. Touch Lpng Beach, Med. Mission, Mex, med. dir. First Choice Home Health, med. dir., Socal Post Acute Care. Recipient Physician Recognition award AMA, 1991, 95, 96, Commn. of Merit Rep. Nat. Com., 1995, Physician of Yr. award, Rep. Nat. Com., 2006, named on of Top Doctors Recognition award, 2009-11. Mem. Am. Osteo. Assn., Am. Coll. Osteo. Family Physicians, Osteo. Physicians and Surgeons Calif., Am. Coll. Osteopathic Family Practitioners (bd. cert. family practice 1991, geriatrics 2000), Cancer Prevention award, Am. Cancer Soc. Republican. Roman Catholic. Avocations: boating, skiing, reading, tennis. Home: 16871 Marina Bay Dr Huntington Beach CA 92649-2913 Office Phone: 562-945-9333. Personal E-mail: wdwelsh@socal.rr.com, drwdwelsh@yahoo.com.

WELTERS, ANTHONY, healthcare service executive, lawyer; BA in Economics, Manhattanville Coll.; JD, NYU. Atty. SEC; exec. asst. to Senator Jacob Javits; sr. level positions Amtrak, US Dept. Transp.; chmn., pres., CEO, founder AmeriChoice Corp., 1989—2006; exec. v.p. UnitedHealth Group, Inc., 2006—, pres., pub. and sr. markets group, 2007—. Bd. dirs. West Pharm. Svcs., Inc., 1997—, C.R. Bard, Inc., 1999—, Qwest Commun. Internat. Inc., 2006—. Bd. trustees Healthcare Leadership Coun.; vice chmn. bd. Morehouse Sch. Medicine; mem. bd. NYU Law Sch., Wolf Trap Found. Recipient Horatio Alger award, 1998. Office: UnitedHealth Group Inc 9900 Bren Rd E Minnetonka MN 55343 Office Phone: 952-936-1300. Office Fax: 952-936-1819. Business E-Mail: anthony.welters@qwest.com. *

WELTMAN, JOEL KENNETH, immunologist; b. NYC, May 22, 1933; s. Charles and Frances (Seasonwein) W.; m. K. Reulla Avatichi, June 28, 1956; children: Alica C., Orlee R. BA, NYU, 1954; MD, SUNY, Bklyn., 1958; PhD, U. Colo., 1963; MA, Brown U., Providence, 1972. Diplomate Am. Bd. Allergy and Immunology. Clin. emeritus prof. medicine Brown U., Providence, 2005—. Fellow Am. Soc. Biol. Chemists; mem. Am. Soc. Biol. Chemistry, Molecular Biology, New Eng. Soc. Allergy (treas. 1995—98, pres. 1999-2000). Achievements include patent for screening antibodies.

WELTMAN, NATHAN Y., medical researcher; b. Peoria, Ill., Jan. 23, 1985; BSED in Exercise Physiology, U. Va., 2007, MEd in Exercise Physiology, 2008; attending, U. SD, 2008—. Rsch. fellow Sanford Sch. Medicine U. SD, 2008—. Recipient Margaret Dullea Simko award, Am. Dietetic Assn. Ann. Meeting. Mem.: AMA, Am. Diabetes Assn. (Clin. Scientist Tng. award), Am. Physician Scientist Assn., Am. Med. Student Assn. Home: 4309 S Bedford Ave Sioux Falls SD 57103 Business E-Mail: nathan.weltman@usd.edu.

WELTZ, MARTIN DAVID, hematologist; b. Phila., Jan. 18, 1948; children: Michael, Adam. BS in Biology, Bklyn. Coll., 1969; DO, Kans. City U. Medicine Biosci., 1973; MBA, Johns Hopkins U., 2002, MPH, 2003. Diplomate Nat. Bd. Med. Examiners for Osteo. Physicians and Surgeons, Am. Bd. Internal Medicine, (subspecialty of med. oncology, subspecialty of hematology, subspecialty hospice and palliative medicine). Commd. 2d lt. USMC, 1973, advanced through grades to lt. col., 1981; intern Walter Reed Army Med. Ctr., Washington, 1973-74, resident, 1974-76, fellow hematology and med. oncology sect., 1976-79, attending physician dept. internal medicine, 1979-81, staff hematologist, med. oncologist, dir. med. edn., 1979-80, chief divsn. head Clin. Cancer Chemo-Pharmacology Rsch. Lab., 1979-80, asst. chief, dir. clin. pharmacy hematology-med. oncology, 1980-81; resigned USMC, 1981; pvt. practice, sr. v.p., founder Hematology-Oncology Cons., Greenbelt, Md., 1983—2011, v.p., treas., 1986—2011; pres. med.-dental staff Laurel Regional Hosp., 1993-99; chmn. dept. internal medicine Washington Adventist Hosp., 1997-2001; bd. dir. Md. Oncology-Hematology, 2011—. V.p., sec., 1986—; attending med. staff AMI Drs. Hosp., Prince George's County, Lanham, Md., 1983, Washington Adventist Hosp., Takoma Park, Md., 1983—, sec.-treas. dept. internal medicine, 1991-94, asst. chmn., 1994-97; asst. chief hematology/med. oncology Prince Georges Hosp. Ctr., 1986—; staff Laurel Regional Hosp., 1983—, chmn. hematology-med. oncology, 1989-1998, med. dir. Hospice in Prince George's County, 1989—, chmn. dept. internal medicine, 1989-92, chmn. tumor bd., 1989—, chmn. employees ann. benefit med.-dental staff, 1990-2000, chmn. med. exec. com., 1993-2000, pres. med. and dental staff, 1993-99, trustee, 1993-99; bd. dirs. Dimensions Corp., Landover, Md., sec.-treas. bd. dirs., 1990-99; pres. Med. Dental Staff laurel Regional Hosp., 1993-99; vice chmn. Dept. Internal Medicine, Washington Adventist Hosp., 1994-96; chmn. Dimensions Health Care Network PHO, 1994-99; med. dir. Hospice in Prince Georges County, 1990-98, Hospice of the Chesapeake, 1999-; bd. dirs. Universal Health Care Network, Medi-Cen of Md.; bd. dirs., found. chmn. med. exec. com., pres. med.-dental staff Laurel Region Hosp., 1993—; bd. dirs. Dimensions Healthcare Network, Dimensions Health Care Corp. Medi-Cen of Md. and Universal Healthcare Corp., Cancer Care, Inc.; chmn., founder tumor bd. Laurel Regional Hosp. and Washington Adventist Hosp., 1988—; chmn. transfusion com. Washington Adventist Hosp., 1990—; sec. Laurel Hosp. Found., 2000-05. Contbr. articles to profl. jours. Bd. dirs. Am. Cancer Soc., Prince George's County, 1981—; med. advisor cansurmount program Am. Cancer Soc., Montgomery County, Md., 1982-90; ring dir. Ea. Regional Karate Tournament, Montgomery Coll., Rockville, Md., 1987—; mem. advisor Md. Blood Ctr., 1987-88; mem. med. adv. bd. Hospice Prince George's County, Largo, Md., 1991-99, active archtl. and design com., capital campaign com., bldg. com., 1992—; mem. com. Parent Fund and Centurion Campaign; bd. dirs. Found. Laurel Regional Hosp., 1993—, others. Named one of America's Top Oncologists, 2009—. Fellow ACP, Acad. Medicine N.J.; mem. AMA, Am. Soc. Internal Medicine, Am. Soc. Clin. Oncology, Am. Soc. Hematology, Acad. Hospice and Polliative Medicine, Am. Coll. Clin. Pharmacology, Am. Coll. Osteo. Internists, Am. Soc. Clin. Oncologists, Am. Coll. Physician Execs., Am. Soc. Clin. Pharmacology and Therapeutics, Am. Soc. Contemporary Medicine and Surgery, Am. Fedn. for Clin. Rsch., Royal Soc. Medicine (London), Md. Osteo. Assn., Oncology Soc. N.J., N.J. Soc. Internal Medicine, N.Y. Acad. Scis., N.Y. Oncology Soc., Md. Soc. Clin. Oncology, George Washington U. Parent Assn., Luther Rice Soc., Johns Hopkins Alumni Assn. (life). Office: Greenway Center Dr Greenbelt MD 20770 Personal E-mail: martinweitz@aol.com. Business E-Mail: martinweitz@jhsph.com.

WEN, CHUN-YANG, gastroenterologist, pathologist; b. Jilin, China, May 18, 1962; m. Ai-Ping Wang, Sept. 17, 1962; children: Wen, Xin. MD, Nagasaki U., Japan, 2002. Lic. China, 2000. Lectr. Jilin Med. Coll., 1983—2002; asst. prof. Nagasaki U., 2002—. Mem. editl. bd.: World Jour. Gastroenterology, 2002—03. Home: Kawaguchi 5-1 Kawaguchi Apt #513 Nagasaki 852-8108 Japan Office Fax: +81-95-849-7108; Home Fax: +81-95-846-6352. Personal E-mail: chunyangwen103@yahoo.com.cn. E-mail: cywen518@net.nagasaki-u.ac.jp.

WEN, ZHI-HONG, science educator; m. Yc Chang. PhD, Nat. Def. Med. Ctr., Taipei, 2003. Asst. prof. Nat. Sun Yat-sen U., Kaohsiung, Taiwan, 2004—. Achievements include discovery of marine-derived drugs. Home and Office: Nat Sun Yat-sen Univ 70 Lien-Hai Rd Kaohsiung 804 Taiwan Office Fax: 886-7-5252021. Business E-Mail: wzh@mail.nsyus.edu.tw.

WENDA, SKIP THOMAS, occupational health nurse; b. St. Paul, Aug. 24, 1952; BA, NDSU, 1978; PhD, U. Minn., 1996. With occupl. health Gerdau Ameristeel, 2007—. Bd. dirs. Bnai Emet Synagogue, 2007—08. Recipient Concours D'honneur award, Am. Assn. Tchrs. French. Mem.: APA, Sigma Theta Tau Nat. Honor Soc. Nursing. Avocations: travel, languages. Office: 1678 Red Rock Rd Saint Paul MN 55119 Office Fax: 651-731-6552. Business E-Mail: skipind@umn.edu.

WENDER, RICHARD C., medical educator, department chairman; b. Pitts., Sept. 25, 1953; BS, Princeton U., 1975; MD, U. Pa., 1979. Chair, dept. family and cmty. medicine Thomas Jefferson U., 2002—. Pres., CEO JeffCare Jefferson's Physician Hosp. Orgn., 2005—11; nat. pres. Am. Cancer Soc., 2006—07. Office: 1015 Walnut Philadelphia PA 19107 Office Fax: 215-955-0640. Business E-Mail: richard.wender@jefferson.edu.

WENDT, VERNON EARL, internist, cardiologist; b. Cleve., Mar. 26, 1931; s. Raymond C. and Esther L. (Naujoks) Wendt; m. Hildegarde Caroline Moeller, Aug. 14, 1953; children: David, Frederick, Kathryn, Elizabeth, Doralyn, James, Vernon Earl Jr. BS in Zoology and Chemistry cum laude, Baldwin-Wallace Coll., 1952; MD, Columbia U., 1956. Diplomate Am. Bd. Internal Medicine. Intern Detroit Receiving Hosp., 1956—57, resident, 1959—62; USPHS postdoctoral fellow in cardiology Wayne State U. Sch. of Medicine, Detroit, 1962—65, from instr. to asst. prof. medicine, 1961—65; dir. rsch. Blodgett Meml. Med. Ctr., Grand Rapids, Mich., 1965—67; pvt. practice Grand Rapids, 1967—2000. Chief elder Game Letter Ch. W. Young, Mich., head elder. Capt. M.C. USAF, 1957—59. Head Elder grant, Lauren Ch., Wyoming, Mich., 2008—. Fellow: ACP, Coun. Geriatric Cardiology, Am. Coll. Angiology, Am. Coll. Cardiology; mem.: AMA, Mich. State Med. Soc., Mich. Health Coun. (trustee 1998—), Am. Acad. Anti-Aging Medicine, Kent County Med. Soc., Mich. Soc. Internal Medicine (pres. 1991—92), Am. Lung Assn. Mich. (pres. 1978—80), Am. Heart Assn. Mich. (trustee 1973—93, pres. 1987—88). Lutheran. Avocations: golf, gardening, walking. Home and Office: 1620 Andover Rd SE Grand Rapids MI 49506 Office Phone: 616-949-9292. Personal E-mail: v.h.wendt@comcast.net.

WENER, BRIAN D., psychologist; s. Martin M. and Rachel Wener; 1 child, Sara. BA in Psychology with honors, Carleton U., 1971; MA in Psychology, SUNY, Plattsburgh, 1975; D of Psychology, Ctrl. Mich. U., 1982. Lic. psychologist NH, 1983, Mass., 1995, cert. sch. psychologist NH, 1981. Clin. psychologist Riverbend Counseling, Concord, NH, 1983—87; psychologist II Philbrook Ctr., 1975—78; clin. psychologist pvt. practice, Portsmouth, 1987—, sch. psychologist Hampton Schs., 2000—06. Cons., evaluator NH Medicaid Disability Unit, Concord, 1990—. Fellow, NH Psychol. Assn. (bd. dirs. 1992—94); mem.: APA, Nat. Assn. Sch. Psychologists. Avocations: photography, guitar. Office: 404 The Hill Portsmouth NH 03801-3736 Office Phone: 603-431-1294. Personal E-mail: shaman426@gmail.com. *

WENER, MARK HOWARD, rheumatologist, medical educator; b. Chgo., Mar. 14, 1949; s. Leon E. and Sadie (Freedland) W.; m. Corinne L. Fligner, Aug. 8, 1982; children: Leah, Zachary. AB in Chemistry, U. Chgo., 1970; MD, Washington U., St. Louis, 1974. Diplomate Am. Bd. Internal Medicine, Am. Bd. Rheumatology, Am. Bd. Diagnostic Lab. Immunology. Resident in medicine U. Iowa Hosp., Iowa City, 1974-78, fellow in rheumatology, 1978-79, assoc. in rheumatology and internal medicine, 1979-80; fellow in rheumatology and immunology U. Wash., Seattle, 1980-82, dir. immunology divsn. dept. lab. medicine, 1983—, asst. prof., 1983-89, assoc. prof. depts. lab. medicine and medicine, 1989—2005, prof. dept. lab. medicine, 2005—; dir. clin. lab., adj. rheumatology divsn., dept. medicine U. Wash. Med. Ctr., Seattle, 2005—. Contbr. articles to profl. jours., chpts. to book, profl. ednl. software. Bd. dirs. Wash. State Arthritis Found., 1989-92, med. and sci. com. chair. Fellow Am. Coll. Rheumatology; mem. ACP (bd. dirs. 2011-), Acad. Clin. Lab. Physicians and Scientists, Am. Assn. Clin. Chemists, Assn. Med. Lab. Immunologists. Office: U Wash Dept Lab Medicine Dept Lab Medicine Box 357110 Seattle WA 98195-0001 Office Phone: 206-598-4615.

WENG, RHAY-HUNG, medical educator; b. Taichung, Taiwan, May 31, 1977; s. Chiou Dung Wu; m. Long Liu Huang. PhD in Health Care Mgmt, Bus. Adminstrn., Nat. Chung Cheng U., Taiwan, 2006. Asst. prof. Chia Nan U. Pharmacy & Sci., 2003—. Office: 60 Erh-Jen RD Sect 1 Jen-Te Tainan 717 Taiwan Office Phone: 886-9-12182673. E-mail: wonhon@mail2000.com.tw.

WENGER, NANETTE KASS, cardiologist, medical researcher, educator; b. NYC, Sept. 3, 1930; d. Aaron Zelig and Edith (Malkin) Kass; m. Julius Wenger; children: Deborah, Judith, Beth. BA summa cum laude, Hunter Coll., 1951; MD, Harvard U., 1954. Intern Mt. Sinai Hosp., NYC, 1954—55, chief resident in cardiology, 1956—57; sr. resident in medicine Grady Meml. Hosp., Atlanta, 1958; fellow in cardiology Emory U. Sch. Medicine, Atlanta, 1958—59, instr. medicine, 1959—62, assoc. in medicine, 1962—64, asst. prof. cardiology, 1964—68, assoc. prof., 1968—71, prof. medicine Divsn. Cardiology, 1971—; cons. Emory Heart and Vascular Ctr., Atlanta; mem. med. staff Crawford W. Long Hosp., Atlanta, 1977—; chief cardiology Grady Meml. Hosp., Atlanta. Dir. cardiac clinics Grady Meml. Hosp., 1960—, chief cardiology, 1998—; cons. cardiology VA Med. Ctr., Atlanta, 1988—; participant numerous profl. symposiums and confs.; mem. cardiovas. and renal drugs adv. com. U.S. FDA, 1978-82; co-chair nat. plan for cardiac rehab. com. Div. Vocat. Rehab., Social and Rehab. Svcs., HEW, 1973-90; mem. Internat. Task Force for Prevention of Coronary Heart Disease, 1989—; founding fellow Soc. Geriatric Cardiology, 1986, bd. dirs., 1987—, pres., 1994-95; former chair, US Nat. Heart, Lung, and Blood Inst. Conf. on Cardiovascular Health and Disease in Women; cons. Emory Heart Ctr.; heads the Emory U. component of the Heart and Estrogen-Progestin Replacement Study (HERS). Mem. editl. bd. various profl. publs. including Cardiac Rehab. Quar., 1974-79, Primary Care, 1975-79, Internat. Jour. Sports Cardiology, 1983—, Med. Month, 1983-84, Jour. Cardiovasc. and Pulmonary Medicine, 1983—, Geriatric Cardiology, 1986—, Nutrition, Metabolism and Cardiovasc. Disease, 1989—; reviewer publs. including Am. Jour. Medicine, 1972—, Am. Jour. Cardiology, 1979—, Am. Heart Jour., 1975—, European Heart Jour., 1983—; editor Am. Jour. Geriatric Cardiology, editor-in-chief; assoc. editor The Heart; co-editor (with Peter Collins) Women and Heart Disease, 2005; contbr. articles to profl. jours.; contbr. book chpts. Chair Heart Sunday program, 1968-69, program chair Fulton County Heart Unit, 1969-71, bd. dirs., 1969-79, 80-82, pres., 1977-78; fellow coun. clin. cardiology, Am. Heart Assn., 1970, chair rehab. com., 1972-75, chair artherosclerosis task force, 1973-74, program v.p., 1975-76, pres., 1977-78, bd. dirs., 1975-79, mem./past mem. numerous other coms.; mem. med. adv. and cardiovasc. health coms. Butler St. YMCA, 1980-82; chair, WHO Expert Com. on Rehabilitation after Cardiovascular Disease; co-chair, Guideline Panel on Cardiac Rehabilitation, US Agy. for Healthcare Policy and Rsch. Recipient Myrtle Wreath award Atlanta Hadassah, 1967, award of Achievement, Nat. Ctr. for Vol. Action, 1978, Outstanding Profl. Achievement award, Hunter Coll., 1993, President's Women in Sci. award, Am. Med. Women's Assn., 1993, Citation, Am. Coll. Sports Medicine, 1994, Jan J. Kellermann Meml. award for Cardiovascular Prevention and Rehabilitation, Internat. Soc. Heart Failure, 1995, Juha P. Kokko award for Excellence in Cardiovascular Lecturing and Edu., Dept. Med. Housestaff, Emory Univ. Sch. Med., 1999-2000, Emory Williams Disting. Tchg. award, 2004, Evangeline Papageorge Alumni Tchg. award, 2004, Shining Star award Atlanta Women in Law and Medicine, 2000, Atlanta Bus. Chronicle Health-Care Heroes Lifetime Achievement award, 2005; Disting. Fellow Soc. Geriatric Cardiology, 2002; honoree Women of Yr. issue Time Mag., 1976; named Joseph B. Wolff Meml. Lectr., Am. Coll. Sports Medicine, 2001; named one of the 10 Most Important Women in Medicine, Ladies Home Jour., 1994; named to Best Doctors in Am.; recognized by McCall's Mag. for rsch. into causes and treatments for heart disease in women. Fellow Am. Heart Assn.(active Ga. affiliate 1960-, first woman president Ga. affiliate, fellow coun. clin. cardiology, 1970, chair rehab. com., 1972-75, chair artherosclerosis task force, 1973-74, program v.p., 1975-76, pres., 1977-78, bd. dirs., 1975-79, mem./past mem. numerous other coms., Bronze Disting. Svc. medallion Ga. affiliate Am. Heart Assn., 1970-71, Silver Disting. Svc. medallion, 1978, Gold Disting. Svc. medallion, 1979, named Physician of Yr., 1998, Disting. Achievement award, Sci. Coun., Women in Cardiol. Mentoring award, 1999, R. Bruce Logue award for Excellence in Medicine, 2001, Gold Heart award, 2004), Am. Coll. Cardiology (gov. for Ga. 1983-86, trustee 1987-89, various coms.), Am. Coll. Chest Physicians; master ACP (James D. Bruce Meml. award 2000); mem. AMA, WHO (expert adv. panel on cardiovasc. disease 1989—), Am. Assn. Cardiovasc. and Pulmonary Rehab. (trustee 1985-88, chairperson ethics com. 1985—, 2nd Ann. Lecture award 1987), Nat. Heart, Lung and Blood Inst., Internat. Soc. and Fedn. Cardiology (pres. sci. coun. on rehab. of cardiac patients 1984-88), Soc. Geriatric Cardiologists (officer, pres. 1994-95), Med. Assn. Ga., Med. Assn. Atlanta, Atlanta Clin. Soc.(emeritus), Soc. for Prevention of Heart Disease and Rehab. (hon.), Soc. Women's Health (bd. dirs. 2000—, vice chair 2002—), Philippine Heart Assn. (hon.), Philippine Coll. Cardiology (hon.), Omicron Delta Kappa. Office: Emory Univ Sch Medicine Grady Meml Hosp Glenn Bldg E278 49 Jesse Hill Jr Dr SE Atlanta GA 30303 Home Phone: 404-237-4802, Office Phone: 404-616-4420. Business E-Mail: nwenger@emory.edu.

WENGER, RONALD DAVID, surgeon; b. Phila., May 1, 1944; s. Christian Showalter and Helen Grace (Heisey) W.; m. Judith Kay Anderson, Jan. 24, 1970; children: Clayton, Lera. BA, Ohio Wesleyan U., 1966; MD, Case Western Res. U., 1970. Diplomate Am. Bd. Surgery. Intern U. Oreg. Med. Sch., Portland, 1970-71; fellow Mayo Clinic Surgery Dept., Rochester, Minn., 1973-77; clin. prof. surgery U. Wis. Med. Sch., Madison, 1977—; pvt. practice, Madison, 1977—; asst. chief surgery St. Mary's Hosp., Madison, 1980-00; chief surgery Dean Med. Ctr., Madison, 1988-93. Recipient Best Drs. in Dane County, Madison Mag., 2008—10; named one of, 2006. Mem. ACS (also Wis. chpt.), AMA, SAGES, Am. Assn. Endocrine Surgeons, Wis. State Med. Soc., Madison Surg. Soc., Wis. Surg. Soc. (pres. 2005—), Soc. for Surgery of Alimentary Tract. Avocations: skiing, bicycling, sailing, travel, reading. Home: 726 Farwell Dr Madison WI 53704-6032 Office: 1821 S Stoughton Rd Madison WI 53716-2257 Home Phone: 608-241-4216.

WENGER, SHARON LOUISE, cytogeneticist, researcher, educator; b. Washington, Sept. 25, 1949; d. William Fred and Lois Helen (Compton) W.; m. George E. Fromlak Jr., Jan. 10, 1976; children: Nicholas Edward, Holly Louise, Andrea Lee. BA in Biology, Thiel Coll., 1971; MS in Human Genetics, U. Pitts., 1973, PhD in Human Genetics, 1976. Cert. in clin. cytogenetics Am. Bd. Med. Genetics. Asst. prof. U. Pitts. Sch. Med., 1980-89, assoc. prof., 1989—97; prof. pathology W. Va. U., 1997—. Contbr. articles to profl. jours. Mem. Am. Soc. Human Genetics, Am. Coll. Med. Genetics, Assn. Genetic Technologists, Assn. Molecular Pathology. Achievements include research of sister chromatid exchange and fragile sites, chromosome syndromes and mechanism of tissue limited mosaicism. Home: 50 Crescent Heights Morgantown WV 26505 Office: W Va U Dept Pathology PO Box 9203 Morgantown WV 26506-9203 Office Phone: 304-293-3212.

WEN-LONG, SHI, hospital administrator; b. Tainan City, Taiwan, Feb. 25, 1928; married; 3 children. Co-founder Chi Mei Plastics Corp., 1953—59; chmn. Chi Mei Corp., 1959—2004, Chi Mei Mus., 1977—, Tainan Opera Orch., 1986—88, Chi Med. Ctr., 1987—; nat. policy advisor Rep. of China, 1996—2000, presdl. sr. advisor, 2000—06. Office: Chi Mei Medical Center No 901 Zhonghau Rd Yongkang Dist Tainan Taiwan Office Phone: 88662812811. *

WENNBERG, JOHN E., epidemiologist; b. June 2, 1934; BA, Stanford U., 1956; MD, McGill Med. Sch., 1961; MPH, Johns Hopkins Sch. Hygiene and Pub. Health, 1966. Intern DC Gen. Hosp., Washington, 1961-62; assoc. med. resident Johns Hopkins Hosp., Balt., 1962-63, fellow in renal disease & pharmacology, 1963-65; resident in chronic disease Balt. City Hosp., 1966-67; dir. No. New England Regional Med. Program, Burlington, Vt., 1967-71; interim dir. Coop. Healthcare Info. Ctr., Burlington, 1972-73; sr. assoc. Harvard Ctr. Cmty. Health & Med. Care, Boston, 1973-75; asst. prof. Dartmouth Med. Sch., NH, 1975, prof. cmty. and family medicine (epidemiology) NH, 1980—, prof. of medicine NH, 1989—, Peggy Y. Thomson Prof. (Chair) for the Evaluative Clin. Sciences NH. Founder, dir. to dir. emeritus Dartmouth Inst. for Health Policy and Clin. Practice, Lebanon, NH.; bd. dirs. Am. Med. Rev. Rsch. Ctr.; physicians adv. group NY Health & Hosps. Corp.; co-founder Ctr. for Shared Decision Making, Dartmouth-Hitchcock Med. Ctr. Contbr. several articles to profl. jours.; founder and first editor Dartmouth Atlas of Health Care. Co-founder Found. for Informed Med. Decision Making. Recipient Assn. for Health Svcs. Research;s Disting. Investigator award, Richard and Hinda Rosenthal Found. award in Clin. Medicine, Baxter Found. Health Svcs. Rsch. prize, Joint Commn. Ernest Amory Codman award, 2007; co-recipient Picker Inst. award for the Advancement of Patient Centered Care. Mem. Am. Hosp. Assn. (coun. rsch. & devel. 1973-75), Inst. Medicine (Gustav O. Lienhard award, 2008), Johns Hopkins Soc. Scholars. Office: Dartmouth Med Sch HB 7251 35 Centerra Pkwy Ste 300 Rm 3018 Lebanon NH 03766 Office Phone: 603-653-0876. Office Fax: 603-653-0896. Business E-Mail: John.Wennberg@dartmouth.edu.

WENNERBERG, JOHAN PHILIP, head and neck surgeon; b. Borås, Elfsborg, Sweden, May 22, 1951; s. Bengt and Ellen (Bengtsson) W.; m. Gunilla Månsson; children: Henrik, Erik. MD, Lund U., Sweden, 1976, PhD, 1984. Intern U. Hosp. Lund S.W., 1976-78, resident dept. otorhinolaryngology, head and neck surgery, 1979-83, specialist in otorhinolaryngology, head and neck surgery, 1983—; sr. surgeon dept. otorhinolaryngology, head and neck surgery U. Hosp. Lund S.E., prof. otorhinolaryngology, head and neck surgery, 1998—, head clin. dept., 1999—2006. Chmn. Scandinavian Soc. Head and Neck Oncology, 2008. Recipient A-G Crafoord's prize, Lund, 1985, Carl-Axel Hamberger prize Swedish Med. Soc., Stockholm, 1991. Office: U Hosp Lund Dept ORL Head and Neck Surgery S-221 85 Lund Sweden Office Phone: 46 46 172810. Business E-Mail: johan.wennerberg@med.lu.se.

WENTS, DORIS ROBERTA, psychologist; b. LA, Aug. 26, 1944; d. John Henry and Julia (Cole) W. BA, UCLA, 1966; MA, San Francisco State U., 1968; postgrad., Calif. State U., LA, 1989—90, Claremont Grad. U., Calif., 1990—. Lic. ednl. psychologist, credentialed sch. psychologist, Calif. Sch. psychologist Diagnostic Sch. for Neurologically Handicapped Children, LA, 1969—86; pvt. practice Monterey Park, Calif., 1986—89; cons. rsch. psychologist orgnl. behavior, 1993—. Instr. Calif. State U., L.A., 1977. Co-author: Southern California Ordinal Scales of Development, 1977. Mem.: Western Psychol. Assn., Acad. Mgmt., L.A. Conservancy, Sigma Xi, Zeta Tau Alpha (officer Santa Monica alumnae chpt. 1970—, Cert. of Merit 1979). Avocations: travel, watersports, theater, bridge, photography. Personal E-mail: wentsd@uclalumni.net.

WENTZEL, KLAUS, orthopedist, radiologist, oncologist; b. Creuzburg, Germany, Nov. 2, 1947; s. Robert and Hanna (Ludewig) Wentzel; m. Renate Ullmann; children: Lieselotte, Anne, Klaus-Robert. Student, Friedrich-Schiller U., 1968—73; MD, U. Jena, 1975. Ward doctor Radiol. Clinic U., Jena, Germany, 1973—80, Orthop. Clinic U., Jena, 1980—84, asst. med. dir., 1984—88, vice chmn., 1986—95; med. dir. Hosp. Eisenberg, Germany, 1986—91; exec. med. supt. Orthop. Clinic U., Bad Schmiedeberg, Germany, 1995—. Counselor Ctr. Rheumatism, Jena, 1985—93, founder, vice chmn., 1988—91; vice chmn. Ctr. Oncology, Jena, 1982—94; lectr. U. Jena, 1992. Contbr. articles to profl. jours. Mem. com. German Coun. Road Safety, Berlin, 2001—; chmn. Union Orthop., Sachsen-Anhalt, Germany, 1998—. Recipient Gottfried-Herder medal, 1963. Avocations: hunting, sailing, oldtimer rally. Office: Orthopedic Clinic Kur-Promenade 1 6905 Bad Schmiedeberg Germany Office Phone: 034925 63070.

WERBINSKI, JANICE LOUISE, medical association administrator; b. Pontiac, Mich., Oct. 29, 1947; BS, Western Mich. U., 1969; MD, Med. Coll. Wis., 1975. Assoc. clin. prof. Kalamazoo Ctr. Med. Studies, Mich. State U., 1979—2011; fellow Am. Congress Ob-Gyn., 1985—2011; divsn. chief ob-gyn. Borgess Health, 2002—04; med. dir. Bronson Women's Ctr., 1988—96, Borgess Women's Health, 2007—. Founding pres., bd. dirs. Am. Coll. Women's Health Physicians, 1996—2010; bd. dirs. Am. Med. Women's Assn., 2006—11; editl. bd. SW Mich. Med. Jour., 2003—08; med. dir. YWCA Sexual Assault Nurse Examiner Program, 2003—11; state liaison AMA Women Physicians Congress, 1998—2011. Recipient Clin. Tchg. award, Mich. State U. Coll. Human Medicine, Clin. Excellence award, Nat. Assn. Profl. Women's Health, Glass Ceiling award, Kalamazoo Women's Network, Pres.'s award, Am. Med. Women's Assn., Mich. State Med. Soc. Fellow: Am. Congress Ob-Gyn.; mem.: Mich. State Med. Soc., N.Am. Menopause Soc., Am. Med. Women's Assn., Am. Coll. Women's Health Physicians. Avocations: oil painting, boating. Office: 9875 Currier Dr Portage MI 49002 Office Fax: 269-321-7011. Personal E-mail: drwerb@aol.com.

WERBITT, WARREN, gastroenterologist, educator; b. Phila., Jan. 29, 1939; s. Saull Boris and Pearl (Weiner) W,; m. Drue Natalie Engman Werbitt, Aug. 30, 1964; children: Julie Michele, Jeffrey Brian. BS in Pharmacy, Temple U., 1960; D in Osteopathy, Des Moines U., Coll. Osteopathic Medicine, 1966; MD, Drexel U. Coll. Med., 1973. Diplomate Am. Osteo. Bd. Internal Medicine, also sub-splty. bd. Gastroenterology; diplomate Am. Bd. Internal Medicine, also sub-splty. bd. Gastroenterology. Intern Doctor's Hosp., Columbus, Ohio, 1966-67, resident in internal medicine, 1967-68, Kennedy Meml. Hosps., Cherry Hill, NJ, 1968-69, Mercy Cath. Med. Ctr., Phila., 1969-70, Drexel U. Coll. Medicine, Phila., 1971—72, fellow in gastroenterology, 1970-71, 72-74, instr., 1973—, attending physician and cons. in gastroenterology, 1977-94; instr. Phila. Coll. Osteo. Medicine, Phila., 1973-75, chmn. divsn. gastroenterology, 1975-77; clin. assoc. prof. medicine U. Medicine and Dentistry, NJ, 1977—; attending physician and cons. in gastroenterology Vet. Adminstrn. Hosp., Phila., 1972-75; chmn. Div. Gastroenterology, Dept. Medicine Phila. Coll. Osteopathic Medicine, 1975-77; chmn. Dept. Medicine Kennedy Meml. Hosp. U. Med. Ctr., Cherry Hill,

1979-81, chmn. subsect. Gastroenterology, 1979-87; assoc. fellow AGAF Am. Gastroentology. Contbg. editor NJ Jour. for Osteo. Physicians and Surgeons, 1980—; mem. scientific adv. com. Phila. chpt. Nat. Found. Ileitis and Colitis, Inc., 1982—; contbr. articles to profl. jours. Recipient Profl. Svc. award Med. Soc. N.J., 1991., Named Top Dr. South Jersey Mag., 2007-08 Fellow Am. Coll. Physicians, Am. Coll. Gastroenterology, Am. Gastroenterol. Assn., Acad. Med. N.J.; mem. AMA, Am. Soc. Gastrointestinal Endoscopy, Am. Soc. Parenteral and Enteric Nutrition, Am. Inst. Ultrasound in Medicine, Am. Assn. Gynecologic Laparoscopists, Phila. Gastrointestinal Rsch. Forum, State Med. Soc. N.J., Camden County Med. Soc., N.J. Endoscopic Soc., Del. Valley Soc. for Gastrointestinal Endoscopy, South Jersey Gastroenterol. Soc., Am. Osteo. Assn., N.J. Soc. Osteo. Physicians and Surgeons, Am. Coll. Osteopathic Internists, Camden County Osteo. Assn., Am. Cancer Soc. (bd. dirs. N.J. chpt.), Crohn's and Colitis Found. Am. Inc. (Phila. and Del.), Pres.'s Circle Am. U., N.Y. Acad. Scis., John Sherman Myers Soc., Med. Club Phila., Lambda Omicron Gamma. Avocations: golf, running, music, reading. Office: Profl Gastroenterology Assn 1939 Route 70 E Ste 250 Cherry Hill NJ 08003-4507 Office Phone: 856-429-4433. Business E-Mail: progastro@comcast.net.

WERCHNIAK, ANDREW EUGENE, dermatologist; s. Wolodymyr and Anna Werchniak; m. Jeanine Courchesne Courchesne, Jan. 7, 1994; children: Andrew Morris, Anne, Alexander, Ethan, Elias, Kiernan. BSEE, U. Md., 1993; MD, U. Va., 2000. Cert. Am. Bd. Dermatology, 2004. Intern Dartmouth Med. Sch., 2000—01, resident, 2001—04; dermatologist Brigham & Women's Hosp., Boston, 2004—, Dana Farber Cancer Inst., Boston, 2004—. Fellow: Am. Acad. Dermatology; mem.: AMA. Office: Brigham & Women's Dana Farber 221 Longwood Ave Boston MA 02115 Office Phone: 617-732-4918.

WERDENSCHLAG, LORI B., psychologist, educator; b. Livingston, NJ, Apr. 20, 1965; d. Stephen Robert and Sandra Joyce Werdenschlag; m. William Alden Barbour, Aug. 5, 2000; 1 child, Jordan Sara Barbour. BA in Psychology and Anthropology, Emory U., Atlanta, 1987; MS in Developmental Psychology, Tulane U., New Orleans, 1990; PhD in Developmental Psychology, Tulane U., 1992; postgrad., Lyndon State Coll. Prof. dept. psychology Lyndon State Coll., Lyndonville, Vt., 1992—; devel. home provider Washington County Mental Health, Vt., 1999—2006. Creator organizer Lyndon State Coll. Ann. Cultural Festival, 1996—; resource provider Coalition: Success by Six, Headstart, Vt. Dept. Health, 2003—, St. Johnsbury Daycare Provider Network, 2003—; condr. tng. workshops in field. Contbr. articles to profl. jours. Big sister Big Bro./Big Sisters, New Orleans, 1990—; sch. bd. mem. Barnet Sch., Vt., 2008; exec. bd. dirs. AIDS Cmty. Awareness Project/Vt. Cares Orgn., 1996—2000. Fellow, PEW Found., 1991—92; Advanced Study grantee, Lyndon State Coll., 1995, 1999, 2000, 2007, Learning Cmtys. Fund grantee, Vt. State Colls., 1996—97, 2007—, Faculty fellow, 2002—04. Avocations: reading, travel, skiing. Office: Lyndon State Coll 1001 College Rd Lyndonville VT 05851 Office Phone: 802-626-6435. E-mail: lori.werdenschlag@lyndonstate.edu. *

WERHAGEN, LARS, neurologist; b. Stockholm, Apr. 20, 1952; MD, Karolinska Inst., 1985, PhD, 2008. Staff neurologist Stockholms Läns Landsting, 1995—. Cons. AFA Assurance Co., 1997. Mem.: ISCOS. Avocation: antiques. Home: Banergatan 50 Stockholm S-115 26 Sweden Personal E-mail: lars.werhagen@ki.se.

WERLIN, LAWRENCE B., obstetrician, gynecologist, reproductive endocrinologist; b. Albany, NY, 1948; s. Esther (Caplan) W.; m. Sally Rosso, Dec. 24, 1970; children: Rachel, Evan, Emma. BA, Boston U.; MD, Mt. Sinai Sch. Medicine, NYC, 1976. Diplomate Am. Bd. Ob-Gyn. Intern Harbor Gen. Hosp., Torrance, Calif., 1976-77, resident in ob-gyn., 1977-80; nat. fellow in reproductive endocrinology NIH, Bethesda, Md., 1980-82; mem. staff Hoag Meml. Hosp., Newport Beach, Calif. Mem. AAAS, Am. Soc. Reproductive Medicine, Soc. for Assisted Reproductive Tech., Pacific Coast Fertility Soc. Office: Coastal Fertility Med Ctr 4900 Barranca Pky Ste 103 Irvine CA 92604-8603 Business E-Mail: werlmd@coastalfertility.com.

WERMAN, DAVID SANFORD, psychiatrist, psychoanalyst; b. NYC, Jan. 1, 1922; s. Morris and Blanche (Heftel) W.; m. Marjolijn R. de Jager, Oct. 25, 1958 (div. 1975); children: Marco W., Claudia J. BA, Queens Coll., 1942; postgrad., Columbia U., 1946-47; MD, Cert. d'Etudes Medicales, U. Lausanne, Switzerland, 1952. Diplomate Am. Bd. Obstetrics and Gynecology, Am. Bd. Psychiatry and Neurology. Intern Beth Israel Hosp., NYC, 1953-54, resident, 1954-57, Montefiore Hosp., Bronx, NY, 1964-67; pvt. practice specializing in ob-gyn. NYC, 1957-64; faculty acad. psychiatry U. NC, Chapel Hill, 1967-76, assoc. prof., instr. psychoanalytic tng. program, 1974—; prof. psychiatry Duke U. Med. Ctr., Durham, NC, 1976—, supervising and tng. analyst psychoanalytic tng. program, 1981-97, Honored prof. psychiatry, 1990—, prof. emeritus, 1992—, supervising and tng. analyst emeritus, 1997—. Cons. Durham VA Hosp. Author: The Practice of Supportive Psychotherapy, 1984. Contbr. chpts. to books, articles to profl. jours. With AUS, 1943-45 Named Outstanding Tchr. psychiatry U. N.C., 1975, honored tchr. psychiatry Duke U., 1978, hon. prof., 1990. Fellow ACS, Am. Psychiat. Assn., Am. Coll. Psychoanalysts, others Home and Office: 111 E 85th St 23G New York NY 10028 Home Fax: 212-722-0744. Personal E-mail: davidwerman@aol.com.

WERNEKE, URSULA, psychiatrist, consultant, educator, researcher; Grad., Heinrich Heine U., Duesseldorf, Germany, 1989, MD, 1990; MSc, London Sch. Hygiene and Tropical Medicine, 1994. Lic. medicine State of Northrhine-Westphalia, Germany, 1991, registered specialist psychiatry Specialist Tng. Authority, Med. Royal Colls., UK, 2002, med. and specialist registration psychiatry Nat. Bd. Health and Welfare, Sweden, 2007. Ho. officer Heinrich-Heine U., Duesseldorf, 1990—91; rsch. fellow U. La Plata, Argentina, 1991—93, London Sch. Hygiene and Tropical Medicine, 1994—96; coord. German breast cancer screening program Ctrl. Rsch. Inst. for Ambulatory Care, Cologne, Germany, 1996—97; resident in psychiatry Maudsley Hosp., London, 1997—2002; cons. psychiatrist Homerton U. Hosp., London, 2002—07, Vrinnevi Hosp., Norrkoeping, Sweden, 2007—, Sunderby Hosp., Lulea, 2008—; assoc. prof. in psychiatry Umea U., Sweden, 2011—. Mem. Kew-Kings-Square Network on Pharmacognosy; peer reviewer for several med. jours. and granting bodies; adv. bd. Quantum Paradigms Psychopathology. Contbr. chapters to books, articles to profl. jours. Rsch. project grantee, German Academic Exch. Svc., 1991—93, Cancer Rsch. UK, 1999—2002. Mem.: European Assn. Consultation Liason Psychiatry & Psychosomatics, Swedish Acupuncture Assn., European Assn. Consultation-Liaison Psychiatry and Psychosomatics (Sweden) (co-ord.), Swedish Assn. Liaison Psychiatry, Swedish Psychiatric Assn., Swedish Med. Assn., Royal Coll. Psychiatrists UK. Achievements include research in complementary and alternative medicine. Office: Sunderby Hosp Dept Psychiatry 971 80 Luleå Sweden Personal E-mail: uwerneke@gmail.com.

WERNER-JACOBSEN, EMMY ELISABETH, developmental psychologist; b. Eltville, Germany, May 26, 1929; came to U.S., 1952, naturalized, 1962; d. Peter Josef and Liesel (Kunz) W. BS, Johannes Gutenberg U., Germany, 1950; MA, U. Nebr., 1952, PhD, 1955; postgrad., U. Calif., Berkeley, 1953-54. Research asso. Inst. Child Welfare, U. Minn., 1956-59; vis. scientist NIH, 1959-62; asst. prof. to prof. human devel., rsch. child psychologist U. Calif., Davis, 1962-94, rsch. prof., 1995—; mem. dept. psychiatry Sub-Saharan Orphans and Vulnerable Children Working Group, Stanford U., 2009—. Sr. author: The Children of Kauai, 1971, Kauai's Children Come of Age, 1977; author: Cross-Cultural Child Development: A View from the Planet Earth, 1979, Vulnerable, but Invincible, 1982, 3d edit., 1998, Child Care: Kith, Kin and Hired Hands, 1984, Overcoming the Odds, 1992, Pioneer Children on the Journey West, 1995, Reluctant Witnesses: Children's Voices From the Civil War, 1998, Through the Eyes of Innocents: Children Witness World War II, 2000, Unschuldige Zeugen, 2001, Journeys From Childhood to Mid Life: Risk, Resilience and Recovery, 2001, A Conspiracy of Decency: The Rescue of the Danish Jews in World War II, 2002, In Pursuit of Liberty, 2006, Passages to America, 2009, Yudayajin o Sokue!, 2010; contbr. articles to profl. jours. Recipient Disting. Sci. Contbn. to Child Devel. award, Soc. Rsch. Child Devel., 1999, Dolly Madison Presdl. award for outstanding lifelong contbns. to devel. and wellbeing of children and families, Zero to Three, 1999, Arnold Gesell award, German Soc. Pediat., 2001, award for disting. career contbns. to sci. study of lifespan devel., Soc. for Study of Human Devel., 2005. Fellow: Assn. Psychol. Scis., Soc. Rsch. Child Devel., German Acad. Social Pediats. (hon.). Business E-Mail: eewerner@ucdavis.edu.

WERRBACH, JOHN, hospital administrator; m. Nancy Werrbach. B, Northeastern Ill. U., Chgo.; MBA, Northern Ill. U. Sch. of Bus., DeKalb, Ill. Clin. lab. supr. Alexian Brothers Med. Ctr., exec. v.p. hosp. ops., interim CEO, 2007, pres., CEO Elk Grove Village, Ill., 2008—; corp. v.p. ops. Alexian Brothers Health System; COO, chief adminstrv. officer Lincoln Pk. Hosp. (formerly Grant Hosp.), Chgo.; adminstrv. dir., v.p. Merit Health Sys., St. James Hosps. and Health Centers, Chgo. Heights. Office: Alexian Brothers Medical Center 800 Biesterfield Rd Elk Grove Village IL 60007 Office Phone: 847-437-5500.

WERTHAMMER, JOSEPH WILLIAM, pediatrician; b. Huntington, W.Va., July 28, 1947; s. Siegfried and Elsa Werthammer; m. Toby Sims, May 26, 1973; children: Matthew, Jeffrey, Nicholas. BS, Marshall U., Huntington, WV, 1969; MD, W.Va. Sch. Medicine, Morgantown, 1973. Diplomate Am. Bd. Pediat., 1978, 1981. Resident pediat. U. California, San Diego, 1973—76; fellow neonatology Harvard Med. Sch. Boston Childrens Hosp., Boston, 1979—81; prof. and chmn. dept. pediat. Joan C. Edwards Sch. Medicine-Marshall U., Huntington, 1988—. Recipient Outstanding Svc. award, Am. Acad. Pediat., 1991, Children award, TEAM W.Va. Children, 2007; named Pediatrician of Yr., W.Va. Chpt. Am. Acad. Pediat., 2001. Mem.: Alpha Omega Alpha. Office: Dept Pediat Ste 3500 1600 Med Ctr Dr Huntington WV 25701 Office Fax: 304-691-1375. Business E-Mail: werthammer@marshall.edu.

WERYNSKI, PIOTR, cardiologist; b. Mielec, Mar. 7, 1973; PhD, Jagiellonian U., 1998. Pediat. cardiologist, 2001—. Office: Wielicka 265 Cracow Malopolska 30-663 Poland Business E-Mail: werpiotr@interia.pl.

WESBURY, STUART ARNOLD, JR., health science association administrator, educator; b. Phila., Dec. 13, 1933; s. Stuart Arnold and Jennie (Glazewska) W.; m. June Carol Davis, Feb. 23, 1957; children: Brian, Brent, Bruce, Bradford. BS, Temple U., 1955; MHA, U. Mich., 1960; PhD, U. Fla., 1972. Capt. USPHS, 1955, served as adminstrv. officer, hosp. and clinic pharmacist, resigned, 1958; adminstrv. asst. Del. Hosp., 1960-61; asst. adminstr. Bronson Meth. Hosp., 1961-66; assoc. dir., asst. prof. U. Fla. Tchg. Hosp., 1966-67, dir., assoc. prof., 1967-69; v.p. Computer Mgmt. Corp., Gainesville, Fla., 1969-72; dir., prof. grad. studies in health svcs. mgmt. U. Mo., Columbia, 1972-78; pres. Am. Coll. Healthcare Execs., Chgo., 1979-91; sr. v.p. TriBrook Group, Inc., Westmont, Ill., 1992-94; prof. Sch. of Health Adminstrn. and Policy Ariz. State U., Tempe, 1994-2000, dir., exec. edn. programs Coll. Bus., 1996-2000, prof. emeritus, 2000—. Chmn. bd. trustees, trustee emeritus Blood Sys., Inc., Scottsdale, Ariz. Co-author: Why We Spend Too Much on Health Care; contbr. articles to profl. jours. Bd. dirs. Health Task, Inc., Atlanta, Boys Clubs, Gainesville, Heartland Inst.; chmn. bd. dirs. Mid-Am. chpt. ARC, 1988-91, DuPage County Dist., 1984-87; active Boy Scouts Am.; chmn. adminstrv. bd. Meth. Ch.; trustee Nat. Blood Found.; Rep. Congl. candidate Dist. 13, Ill. Recipient Award of Honor, Temple U.; named to Health Care Hall of Fame, 2005, Gallery of Success, Temple U. Fellow Am. Coll. Health Care Adminstrs. (hon.), Am. Coll. Healthcare Execs. (Silver Medal award 1991); mem. APHA, Am. Hosp. Assn., Hosp. Mgmt. Sys. Soc., Assn. Univ. Programs in Health Adminstrn. (chmn. 1977-78), Am. Assn. Healthcare Cons. (hon.), Rotary (past pres.). Home and Office: 950 Willow Valley Lakes Dr H-312 Willow Street PA 17584 Home Phone: 717-464-4560. Business E-Mail: stu.wesbury@asu.edu.

WESCOTT, WILLIAM BURNHAM, oral maxillofacial pathologist, educator; b. Pendleton, Oreg., Nov. 10, 1922; s. Merton Girard and Josephine (Creasey) W.; m. Barbara L., Dec. 31, 1944 (dec. June 12, 1969); children: William Douglas, Diane Elizabeth; m. Gloria Greer-Collins, Aug. 28, 1989. DMD, U. Oreg., Portland, 1951, MS, 1962. Asst. prof. to assoc. dean admin. U. Oreg. Dental Sch., Portland, 1953-72; co-dir. oral disease rsch. VA, Houston, 1972-75, dir. dental edn. ctr. LA, 1980-85; acting dir. Reg. Med. Edn. Ctr., Birmingham, Ala., 1978-80; chief dental svc. Dept. of Veteran's Affairs, San Francisco, 1985-94; clin. prof. U. Calif., San Francisco, 1994—2006; cons. Northern System of Clinics Dept. Vets. Affairs, 1994—. Dental surgeon, Oreg. Air N.G., Portland, 1954-68; cons. Madigan Army Med. Ctr., Ft. Lewis, W. Va., 1971-74, VA Med. Ctrs., No. Calif., 1985—, prof. pathology Duke U. Med. Sch., 1977-79; cons. U. Med. Ctr., Fresno, 1998—2006; mem. Enloe Hosp. Head and Neck Malignancy Tumor Bd.; featured spkr. Meml. Day, Gridley-Biggs Cemetery, 2010; spkr. in field. Contbr. 80 articles to profl. jours. and several chpts. to profl. books; 4 chtps. to books. Dist. chmn. Boys Scouts Am., Portland, 1965-67; bd. dirs. Am. Cancer Soc., Portland, 1964-67; comdr. Veterans Foreign Wars Post 5731, Gridley, Calif., 1994-95, comdr., 1996-98; chmn. Mil. Vets Ct. of Honor Meml., No. Calif., 1997—. With Oreg. N.G., 1938-40; with U.S. Army, 1940-42; lt. col. USAF, 1942-68. Decorated DFC with oak leaf cluster USAF, Oreg. N.G. Merit Svc. Medal, Portland, Fedn. des Anciens Combattants Français medal; named Man of Yr., Gridley C. of C., 2009. Fellow Am. Acad. Oral and Maxillofacial Pathology, Am. Coll. Dentists, Mil. Officers Assn. Am. (sec. 2000—05), Omicron Kappa Upsilon, Sigma Xi. Avocations: woodworking, fishing. Home: 437 Justeson Ave Gridley CA 95948-9434 Office: U Calif Sch Dentistry S 512 San Francisco 3rd & Parnassus San Francisco CA 94143-0424 Business E-Mail: wesco83@sbcglobal.net.

WESSEL, MORRIS ARTHUR, retired pediatrician; b. Providence, Nov. 1, 1917; s. Morris Jacob and Bessie (Bloom) Wessel; m. Irmgard Rosenzweig, June 1, 1952; children: David, Bruce, Paul, Lois. BA, Johns Hopkins U., 1939; MD, Yale U., 1943. Diplomate Am. Bd. Pediat. Intern Babies Hosp., NYC, 1943-44; fellow in pediat. Mayo Found., Rochester, Minn., 1947-48; rooming-in fellow in pediat. Yale U. Sch. Medicine, 1948-51; asst. dir. pediatric outpatient clinic Yale-New Haven Hosp., 1951-52, dir. pediatric outpatient clinic, 1952-57; staff pediatrician, collaboration project Yale U. Sch. Medicine, 1957-62, instr. pediat., 1950-53, clin. asst. prof., 1963—71, clin. assoc. prof., 1961-75, clin. prof., 1975-97; ret., 2005. Bd. dirs. Clifford Beers Child Guidance Clinic, New Haven, 1950—55, cons. pediatrician, 1967—2005; bd. dirs. Women's Health Svc., New Haven, 1992—97, Child Welfare League, NYC, 1979—91. Author: Parents Book on Raising a Healthy Child, 1987. Maj. US Army, 1944—47, ETO. Mem.: New Haven County Med. Soc., Conn. Med. Soc., Soc. Adolescent Medicine, Am. Acad. Pediatrics (Practitioner Rsch. award 1994, C. Anderson Aldrich award 1997). E-mail: morriswessel@comcast.net.

WESSELINGH, STEVEN LODEWYK, medical educator; b. Adelaide, Australia, Jan. 12, 1959; s. Bernard Johannes and Elizabeth Wesselingh; married. PhD, Flinders U., S. Australia, 1988. Registered South Australian Registration, 1982, Victorian Registration, 1999, cons. physician 1989, ECFMG, 1990. Lectr. dept. microbiology Flinders U., Australia, 1988—91, sr. lectr. dept microbiology & infectious diseases, 1994—98; prof. microbiology & medicine Monash U., Melbourne, Victoria, Australia, 2003, dean faculty medicine, nursing & health scis., 2007—, dir., 1999—2002, MacFaqlane Burnet Inst. Med. Rsch. and Pub. Health, Melbourne, 2003—07; asst. prof., dept neurology John Hopkins Sch. Medicine, Balt., 1992—93; prof. Alfred Hosp., Melbourne, 1999—2002; exec. dir. South Australian Health & Med. Rsch. Inst., 2011. Professorial fellow U. Melbourne Dept. Microbiology, 2003. Contbr. articles to profl. jours. and publs. Recipient Glaxo award, 1996, Postdoc. award, AMRAD, 1994; fellow, NHMRC, 1991—95; Rsch. grant, various orgns. Fellow: RACP; mem.: Victorian Inst. Forensic Medicine Coun. (coun. mem. 2007), Baker Heart Rsch. Inst. Bd., Baker Heart Rsch. Inst., Sci. Adv. Com., Mental Health Rsch. Inst. (mem. bd. dir. 2007), Australian Ctr. HIV and Hepatitis Rsch. (dep. dir. 2002). Avocations: soccer, windsurfing. Office: Monash Univ Faculty Medicine, Nursing & Health Scis Bldg 64 Wellington Rd 3800 Clayton VIC Australia also: S Australian Health & Med Rsch Inst 121 King William St Adelaide 5001 Australia Office Fax: 623 99055566.

WESSELLS, HUNTER, urologist, researcher; b. Bryn Mawr, Pa., May 24, 1963; s. Henry Walton Wessells III and Nancy Hunter Wessells; m. Bokgi Choi, Sept. 16, 1995; 1 child, Callista Lee. BS in Psychology, Georgetown U., 1984, MD, 1988. Diplomate Am. Bd. Urology, Nat. Bd. Med. Examiners. Surgical resident U. Pa., Phila., 1988—90, urology resident, 1990—94; fellow, reconstructive urology and trauma U. Calif., San Francisco, 1994—95; instr., dept. surgery U. Pa. Sch. Medicine, 1993—94; clin. instr. U. Calif., San Francisco, 1994—95; asst. prof., clin. surgery/urology U. Ariz. Coll. Medicine, Tucson, 1995—2000, assoc. prof., surgery, 2000—01; assoc. prof., urology U. Wash. Sch. Medicine, Seattle, 2001—03, prof., chief of urology, 2005—. Faculty mem. Biomedical Engring. Interdisciplinary Program Grad. Coll., U. Ariz., 1998—2001; com. mem. 1st and 2nd Internat. Consultation on Erectile and Sexual Dysfunction WHO, Paris, 1999, Paris, 2003; mem. panel NIH/Nat. Inst. Diabetes and Digestive and Kidney Diseases, Bethesda, Md., 2001—; affiliate Diabetes Endocrinology Rsch. Ctr., U. Wash. Sch. Medicine, Seattle, 2001—, Harborview Injury Prevention Rsch. Ctr., 2002—; hosp. appointments Harborview Med. Ctr., Seattle, 2001—, chief urology, 2002—, mem. med. exec. bd., 2002—, mem. trauma coun., 2002—, mem. ambulatory care adv. coun., 2002—, mem. surgical coun., 2004—; hosp. appointments U. Calif., San Francisco, 1994—95, San Francisco Gen. Hosp., 1994—95, U. Med. Ctr., Tucson, 1995—2000, So. Ariz. VA Health Care Sys., Tucson, 1995—2000, U. Wash. Med. Ctr., Seattle, 2001—, Puget Sound VA Health Care Sys., Seattle, 2001—; dir., urodynamics and sexual dysfunction unit U. Ariz. Health Sciences Ctr., 1996—99; several vis. professorships; invited lectr. in field. Contbr. chapters to books, articles to profl. jours.; Ad Hoc reviewer for several peer-related jours. Rsch. grantee, NIH/NIDDK, 2000, 2003. Fellow: ACS (mem. urology adv. com. 2002), Seattle Surgical Soc. (assoc.); mem.: Western Urologic Forum, Northwest Urol. Soc., Soc. Univ. Urologists, Sexual Medicine Soc. N. Am., Am. Assn. for the Surgery of Trauma, Am. Urol. Assn. (chair young urologists com. 2002), European Assn. Urology (assoc.), U. Barge Club (Founder's Cup 1991). Avocations: bicycling, swimming. Office:

Harborview Med Ctr Dept Urology Box 359868 325 Ninth Ave Seattle WA 98104 Office Phone: 206-731-3205. Office Fax: 206-731-4709. E-mail: wessells@u.washington.edu.

WESSELMANN, GLENN ALLEN, retired health facility administrator; b. Cleve., Mar. 21, 1932; s. Roy Arthur and Dorothy (Oakes) W.; m. Genevieve De Witt, Sept. 6, 1958; children: Debbie, Scott, Janet. AB, Dartmouth, 1954; MBA with distinction, Cornell U., 1959. Research aide Cornell U., Ithaca, NY, 1958-59; adminstrv. resident Meml. Hosp., NYC, 1957-58, adminstrv. asst., 1959-61, asst. adminstr., 1961-65, asst. v.p., 1965-68; v.p. for adminstrn. Meml. Hosp. for Cancer and Allied Diseases, NYC, 1968-79; exec. v.p., chief operating officer St. John Hosp., Detroit, 1979-84; pres., CEO St. John Health System, 1984-95, vice chmn., 1995-97; chmn., pres., CEO St. John Hosp. & Med. Ctr., 1984-94, ret., 1995. Mem. bus. adv. bd. City of Detroit, 1991-95, chmn., 1993-94; mem. exec. com. Greater Detroit Area Health Coun.; bd. dirs. Caymich Ins. Co. Ltd., Mich. Health Care Alliance, SelectCare, Detroit Econ. Growth Corp. Trustee Sisters of St. Joseph Health System 1981-94, Sisters of St. Joseph Health Svc., 1983-95, St. John Hosp. and Med. Ctr., 1979-95, St. John Health System, 1984-95, The Oxford Inst., 1984-95, Eastwood Clinics, 1992-95; pres. Providence Ch. Corp., Hilton Head Island, S.C., chmn. ch. fin. ocm., corp. pres. session; mem. bus. adv. bd.! City of Detroit, 1991-95, chmn. 1993-94. Served with MC AUS, 1955-57. Fellow ACHE; mem. Am. Hosp. Assn., Internat. Hosp. Fedn., Mich. Hosp. Assn. (trustee, chmn. 1994-95, mem. exec. com.), Assn. Am. Med. Colls. (Coth rep.), Am. Cancer Soc. (regional adv. bd. 1994-95), Med. Group Mgmt. Assn., Soc. Health Service Adminstrs., Sigma Phi Epsilon. Home: 63 Big Woods Dr Hilton Head Island SC 29926-2604 Personal E-mail: glengen@hargray.com.

WESSON, DAVID, surgeon, educator; b. July 12, 1948; MD, U. Toronto, Ont., 1976. Asst. prof. surgery U. Toronto, 1981—94; prof. surgery Cornell U. Med. Coll., NYC, 1994—97, Baylor Coll. Medicine, Houston, 1997—. Mem.: ACS. Office: Baylor Coll Medicine 6701 Fannin Houston TX 77030 Office Fax: 832-825-3141.

WEST, BOB, pharmaceutical executive; b. Ellenville, NY, Mar. 7, 1931; s. Harry and Elsie May Wicentowsky; m. Betty Parker, May 9, 1957 (div.); children: Debra Ellen, Elizabeth Ann, Sharon Lynn; m. Jacqueline Cutler, Jan. 3, 1982. BS, Union U., 1952; MS, Purdue U., 1954, PhD, 1956; postgrad. mgmt. seminar, U. Chgo., 1972. Pres., dir. research Food, Drug, Chem. Svcs., Stamford, Conn., 1975—; pres., dir. research Bob West Assocs., Inc., Stamford, 1975—. Pres Drug Info. Assn., Phila., 1974-75; sci. adv. bd. Fountain Pharms., Inc., Largo, Fla., 1993—, Dovetail Techs., Inc., College Park, Md., 1996—, Phytopede, Inc., Sarasota, Fla., 1999—. Mem. editl. bd. Drug Info. Assn. Jour., Phila., 1977-85; contbr. articles to profl. jours. Mem. ASPET, Soc. Toxicology, Acad. Pharm. Scis., Assn. Rsch. Dirs., Drug Info. Assn., Assn. Univ. Tech. Mgrs. Home and Office: Food Drug Chem Svcs 7925 Meadow Rush Loop Sarasota FL 34238-4319 Home Phone: 941-925-8325; Office Phone: 941-925-8958. Personal E-mail: bjwest22@verizon.net.

WEST, CLARK DARWIN, pediatric nephrologist, educator; b. Jamestown, NY, July 4, 1918; s. Clark Darwin and Frances Isabel (Blanchard) W.; m. Ruthann Asbury, Apr. 12, 1944 (div.); children: Charles Michael, John Clark, Lucy Frances; m. Dolores Lachenman, Mar. 1, 1986. AB, Coll. of Wooster, 1940; MD, U. Mich., 1943. Intern Univ. Hosp., Ann Arbor, Mich., 1943-44, resident in pediatrics, 1944-46; fellow in pediatrics Children's Hosp. Research Found., Cin., 1948-49, research asso., 1951-89, asso. dir., 1963-89, dir. div. immunology and nephrology, 1958-89, with cardiopulmonary lab. chest service Bellevue Hosp., NYC, 1949-51; attending pediatrician Children's Hosp., 1951-89; asst. prof. pediatrics U. Cin., 1951-55, asso. prof., 1955-62, prof., 1962-89. Mem. coms. NIH, 1965-69, 1972-73 Mem. editorial bd.: Jour. Pediatrics, 1960-79, Kidney Internat., 1977-89, Clin. Nephrology, 1989-96; contbr. articles to profl. jours. Served to capt. M.C., AUS, 1946-47. Decorated Army commendation medal; recipient recognition award Cin. Pediat. Soc., 1980, Mitchell Rubin award, 1986, Henry L. Barnett award, 1995, Daniel Drake medal, 1996, John P. Peters award, 1996; Founders award, 2008. Mem. Soc. Pediatric Research (sec.-treas. 1958-62, pres. 1963-64), Am. Pediatric Soc., Am. Soc. Pediatric Nephrologists (pres. 1973-74, Founders award 2008), Am. Physiol. Soc., Am. Assn. Immunologists, Am. Soc. Nephrology, Internat. Pediatric Nephrology Assn., Sigma Xi, Alpha Omega Alpha. Achievements include research on immunopathogenesis and treatment of glomerulonephritides and in the complement system. Home: 11688 Aristocrat Dr Harrison OH 45030-9753 Personal E-mail: CWest_2865@fuse.net.

WEST, DANIEL CHARLES, dentist; b. Trenton, NJ, July 23, 1955; s. Harry E. and Alma R. (Washburn) W.; m. Deborah L. Scott, May 28, 1977; children: Lauren Elizabeth, Colin Jeffrey, Aaron Samuel. BS, Ea. Nazarene Coll., 1977; DMD, U. Pitts., 1982; M, Acad. Gen. Dentistry, 2003. Min. youth music South Hills Ch. of the Nazarene, Bethel Park, Pa., 1977-82; pvt. practice Terre Hill, Pa., 1982-95; prin., owner New Holland (Pa.) Dental Care, 1995—. Mem. Internat. Gen. Bd. Ch. of Nazarene, Kansas City, Mo., 1989—2002, lay mem. dist. adv. bd. Phila. dist., Frazer, Pa., 1985—2007, coord. work and witness program, 1988—90, dir. compassionate ministries, 1990—; bd. dirs. Mission Am.; dir. Phila. Dist. IMPACT, 1982—89, 2001—05; trustee Ea. Nazarene Coll., Wollaston, Mass., 1984—, mem. exec. com., chmn. dept. fin., chmn. bd. dirs., 2002—06; mem. clin. faculty U. Pa. Sch. Dental Medicine, Med. U. Ukraine, Kiev, Pediat. Med. U., Moscow; mem. Mission Am. Bd., 1997—; mng. ptnr. Ctrl Am. Partnership, 2007—; regional v.p. ACCRU Wealth Inc., 2009—. Contbr. articles to jours. Bd. dirs. Garden Spot Village Retirement Cmty., 1996—97; interim min. music Fairview Village Ch. of Nazarene, 2001—02; mng. ptnr. CIS Partnership for Ministry, 1998—2002; chmn. bd. trustees Eastern Nazarene Coll., 2002—06, mem. found. bd., 2004—06. Lt. USPHS, 1982—85. Recipient Alumni Achievement award, Eastern Nazarene Coll., 1996, Citation for Exceptional Achievement, Pa. Ho. Reps., 2004; named Bus. Man of Yr., Pa., 2007. Fellow: Internat. Coll. Oral Implantologists, Master Am. Acad. Gen. Dentistry; mem. ADA (Cert. Recognition for Internat. Svc. in a Fgn. County 1996), Am. Acad. Cosmetic Dentistry, Pa. Dental Assn., Lancaster County Dental Soc. Republican. Office: 650 E Main St New Holland PA 17557-1410 Office Phone: 717-354-3200. Personal E-mail: dcwdmd@comcast.net.

WEST, JOHN BURNARD, physiologist, educator; b. Adelaide, Australia, Dec. 27, 1928; came to U.S., 1969; s. Esmond Frank and Meta Pauline (Spehr) W.; m. Penelope Hall Banks, Oct. 28, 1967; children: Robert Burnard, Joanna Ruth. MB, BChir, Adelaide U., 1951, MD, 1958, DSc, 1980; PhD, London U., 1960; DSc (hon.), U. Barcelona, Spain, 1987, U. Ferrara, Italy, 2004, U. Athens, 2006. Resident Royal Adelaide Hosp., 1952, Hammersmith Hosp., London, 1953-55; physiologist Sir Edmund Hillary's Himalayan Expdn., 1960-61; dir. respiratory rsch. group Postgrad. Med. Sch., London, 1962-67, reader medicine, 1968; disting. prof. medicine and physiology U. Calif., San Diego, 1969—. Leader Am. Med. Rsch. Expdn. to Mt. Everest, 1981; U.S. organizer China-U.S. Conf. on respiratory failure, Nanjing, 1986; mem. life scis. adv. com. NASA, 1985-88, task force sci. uses of space sta., 1984-87, aerospace med. adv. com., 1988-89, chmn. sci. verification com. Spacelab SLS-1, 1983-92, commn. on respiratory physiol. Internat. Union Physiol. Scis., 1985—, commn. on clin. physiol., 1991—, commn. gravitation physiol., 1986—, study sect. NIH, chmn., 1973-75; prin. investigator Spacelabs SLS 1, 2, LMS, Neurolab, 1983—; co-investigator European Spacelabs, D2, Euromir, 1987—; external examiner Nat. U. Singpore, 1995; Wiltshire lectr., London, 1971, Schwidetzky lectr., 1975, Fleischner lectr., 1977, Robertson lectr. Adelaide U., 1978, I.J. Flance lectr. Washington U., 1978, W.A. Smith lectr. Med. Coll. SC, 1982, S. Kronheim lectr. Undersea Med. Soc., 1984, McClement lectr. NYU, 1996, Harry Fritts Jr. Lectr., Stony Brook U., 2007, Moran Campbell Lectr., Brit. Thoraic Soc., 2007, Allan J. Ersler Meml. lectr. Jefferson Med. Coll., 2010, McDwell lectr. Kings Coll., London, 2010; Julian Johnson lectr. U. Pa., 2011, William Paton lectr., Physiol. Soc., Eng., 2011. Author: Ventilation/Blood Flow and Gas Exchange, 1965, Respiratory Physiology-The Essentials, 1974, Translations in Respiratory Physiology, 1975, Pulmonary Pathophysiology-The Essentials, 1977, Translations in Respiratory Physiology, 1977, Bioengineering Aspects of the Lung, 1977, Regional Differences in the Lung, 1977, Pulmonary Gas Exchange (2 vols.), 1980, High Altitude Physiology, 1981, High Altitude and Man, 1984, Everest-The Testing Place, 1985, Best and Taylor's Physiological Basis of Medical Practice, 1985, 91, Study Guide for Best and Taylor, 1985, High Altitude Medicine and Physiology, 1989, The Lung: Scientific Foundations, 1991, 2d edit., 1997, Lung Injury, 1992, Respiratory Physiology: People and Ideas, 1996, High Life: A History of High Altitude Physiology and Medicine, 1998; Pulmonary Physiology and Pathology: An Integrated, case-based approach, 2001, Gravity and the Lung, 2001; founder, editor-in-chief High Altitude Medicine and Biology, 2000-. Recipient Ernest Jung prize for medicine, Hamburg, 1977, Presdl. citation Am. Coll. Chest Physicians, 1977, Kaiser Tchg. award 1980; scholar Macy Found., 1974; Jeffries Med. Rsch. award AIAA, 1992. Fellow Royal Coll. Physicians (London), Royal Australasian Coll. Physicians, Royal Geog. Soc. (London), AAAS (med. sci. nominating com. 1987-93, coun. del. sect. med. scis.), Am. Inst. for Med. and Biol. Engring. (founding fellow 1992), Am. Heart Assn. (G.C. Griffith lectr. 1978, D.W. Richards lectr. 1980), Internat. Soc. for Mountain Medicine (pres. 1991-94), Am. Acad. Arts and Scis.; mem. NAS (com. space biology and medicine 1986-90, subcom. on space biology 1984-85, com. advanced space tech. 1992-94, panel on small spacecraft tech. 1994), Am. Assn. Thoracic Surgery (hon.), Nat. Bd. Med. Examiners (physiology test com. 1973-76), Am. Physiol. Soc. (pres. 1984-85, coun. 1981-86, chmn. sect. on history of physiology 1984-92, hist. pubs. adv. com., Reynolds prize for history 1987, Ray Daggs award 1998, Guyton Tchg. award 2002, Julius H. Comroe lectr. 2003), Inst. of Medicine of NAS, Am. Soc. Clin. Investigation, Physiol. Soc. Gt. Britain, Am. Thoracic Soc. (Edward Livingston Trudeau medal 2002), Royal Soc. of Medicine (Hickman medal, 2007), Assn. Am. Physicians, Western Assn. Physicians, Russian Acad. Sci. (elected fgn. mem.), Explorers Club, Fleischner Soc. (pres. 1985), Harveian Soc. (London), Royal Instn. Gt. Britain, Royal Soc. Medicine (London), Hurlingham Club (London), La Jolla Beach & Tennis Club. Home: 9626 Blackgold Rd La Jolla CA 92037-1110 Office: U Calif San Diego Sch Medicine 0623 Dept Medicine La Jolla CA 92093 Office Phone: 858-534-4192. Business E-Mail: jwest@ucsd.edu.

WEST, JOHN THOMAS, retired surgeon; b. Live Oak, Fla., June 23, 1924; s. James Whitaker and Lelah Eulalia (Moore) W.; m. Ruth Marita Blakely, June 18, 1948; children: Phyllis Ann, Rebecca Ruth, James Carl, Jeffrey Moore, Paul Blakely. BS, U. Mich., 1946; MD, Vanderbilt U., 1951. Diplomate Am. Bd. Surgery. Commd. officer USPHS, 1951, advanced through grades to capt., 1963; rotating intern USPHS Hosp., Seattle, 1951—52; chief surgery USPHS Alaska Native Hosp., Anchorage, 1957—60, resident gen. surgery, 1954—57; chief surgery USPHS Hosp., Seattle, 1963—69, USPHS Indian Hosp., Phoenix, 1969—71; sr. investigator surg. br. Nat. Cancer Inst. USPHS, Bethesda, Md., 1960—63, ret. Nat. Cancer Inst., 1971; clin. asst. prof. U. Wash., Seattle, 1964—68; clin. assoc. prof. Tex. Tech U., Lubbock, 1974—77; pvt. practice La Grange, Ga., 1971—74, 1977—94; ret., 1994. Mem. active staff West Ga. Med. Ctr., La Grange, 1971-74, 77-94. Bd. dirs. Ga. divsn. Am. Cancer Soc., 1972-77, 77-92. Recipient Meritorious Svc. medal USPHS, 1968. Fellow ACS (sr.), Soc. Surg. Oncology (sr.). Presbyterian. Achievements include report of facilitation of major hepatic resection by an innovation in the surgical exposure of the liver. Home: 134 Hickory Ln Lagrange GA 30240-8622 Home Phone: 706-884-1654. Personal E-mail: rutom.west@gmail.com.

WEST, KEITH PARKER, JR., nutritionist; b. Darby, Pa., Dec. 1949; BS, Drexel U., 1971; DPH, Johns Hopkins Sch. Hygiene and Pub. Health, 1987. George G Graham prof. infant and child nutrition Johns Hopkins Bloomberg Sch. Pub. Health, 1982—. Mem.: Am. Dietetic Assn. (registered dietitian 1971—), Am. Soc. Nutrition (Internat. Nutrition prize). Avocation: music. Office: Johns Hopkins Bloomberg Sch Pub Health Dept Internat Health Baltimore MD 21205 Office Fax: 410-955-0196. Business E-Mail: kwest@jhsph.edu.

WEST, MICHAEL ALAN, retired hospital administrator; b. Waseca, Minn., Aug. 4, 1938; s. Ralph Leland and Elizabeth Mary (Brann) W.; m. Mary Thissen, Jan. 21, 1961; children— Anne, Nancy, Douglas. BA, U. Minn., 1961, MHA, 1963. Sales corr. Physicians and Hosps. Supply Co., Mpls., 1959-60; adminstrv. resident R.I. Hosp., Providence, 1962-63, adminstrv. asst., 1963-65, asst. dir., 1965-68; exec. asst. dir. Med. Center U. Mo., Columbia, 1968-70, assoc. dir., 1970-74, asst. prof. community health and med. practice, 1968-74; v.p. for adminstrn. Luth. Gen. Hosp., Park Ridge, Ill., 1974-80, exec. v.p., 1980-84; pres., CEO Akron Gen. Med. Ctr., Ohio, 1984-97, Akron Gen. Health Sys., 1997—2002. Bd. dirs. Vol. Hosps. Am. Inc.; chair VHA-Ctrl., Inc. Bd. dirs. Great Trails Coun. Boy Scouts Am. Mem. Am. Coll. Healthcare Execs., Akron Regional Hosp. Assn. (chmn.), Portage Country Club, Akron City Club, Catawba Island Club, Noreaster Club. Home: 495 Woodbury Dr Akron OH 44333-2780

WEST, ROBERT MACLELLAN, science educator, consultant; b. Appleton, Wis., Sept. 1, 1942; s. Clarence John and Elizabeth Ophelia (Moore) West; m. Jean Sydow, June 19, 1965; 1 child, Christopher. BA, Lawrence Coll., 1963; SM, U. Chgo., 1964, PhD, 1968. Rsch. assoc. Princeton (N.J.) U., 1968-69; asst. prof. Adelphi U., Garden City, NY, 1969-74; curator geology Milw. Pub. Mus., 1974-83; dir. Carnegie Mus. Natural History, Pitts., 1983-87, Cranbrook Inst. Sci., Bloomfield Hills, Mich., 1987-91; prin. RMW Sci. Action, Washington, 1992-95; pres. Informal Sci., Inc., Washington, 1993-98, Informal Learning Experiences, Inc., Washington, 1999—. Adj. prof. U. Wis., Milw., 1974—83. Contbr. articles to profl. jours. Bd. dirs. Friends New Zoo, Pitts., 1984—87; treas. E. Mich. Environ. Action Coun., Birmingham, 1987—92. Recipient Arnold Guyot prize, Nat. Geographic Soc., 1982; named Man of the Yr. in Sci., Vectors Pitts., 1988; NSF fellow, 1965—68, NSF Rsch. grantee, 1970—82, Nat. Geographic Soc. Rsch. grantee, 1973, 1976, 1977, 1979, 1980, 1982. Mem.: Visitor Study Assn. (bd. dirs. 2005—11), Am. Assn. Mus., Mus. Group, Soc. Vertebrate Paleontology, Nat. Ctr. Sci. Edn. (bd. dirs. 1984—88, 1992—), Explorers Club, Rotary. Avocations: nature, history, sports. Office: Informal Learning Experiences Inc PO Box 42328 Washington DC 20015-0928 Home Phone: 202-686-1696; Office Phone: 202-362-5823. Personal E-mail: rmacwest@gmail.com. Business E-Mail: ileinc@informallearning.com.

WEST, SYNTHA JANE TRAUGHBER, mental health services professional; b. Gladewater, Tex., Oct. 22, 1938; d. Jimmy J. and Virginia Lavon (Wood) Traughber; m. Royce Glen West; children: Rock David, Royal Jim. BA, Baylor U., 1961; MEd, Tex. A&M U. Commerce, 1965, PhD, 1971. Lic. profl. counselor, marriage and family therapist, cert. counselor, expert in traumatic stress and bereavement trauma. Adj. asst. prof. East Tex. State U., Commerce, 1975—76; lead H.S. counselor Longview (Tex.) Ind. Sch. Dist., 1975—77; head H.S. counselor Marshall (Tex.) Ind. Sch. Dist., 1977—80; counselor Tyler Jr. Coll., Tex., 1992; Mid. and H.S. counselor Winona (Tex.) Ind. Sch. Dist., 1980—97; mental health therapist Walker & Assocs., Tyler, 1997—98, Andrews Ctr., Tyler, 1998—99. Dir. guidance Brewer H.S., White Settlement, Tex., 1971—75, Kerens (Tex.) Ind. Sch. Dist., Kerens, 1966—69, Rains Ind. Schs. Dist., Emory, Tex., 1966; spkr. in field. Author: Today's Dreams, Tomorrow's Realities, 2001, (poetry) Poetry Gems 2000, 2001, America at the Millennium, 2000. Pianist, asst. First Bapt. Ch., Owentown, Tex., 2000—; pres. Gladewater (Tex.) Former Students, 1997—. Recipient Ms. Congeniality, 2006, Ms. Tex. Sr., America, Winner, 2008; named Ms. Congeniality, Ms. Tex. Sr. Pageant, 2000, Ms. Tex. Sr., 2001; nominee Tex. Women's Hall of Fame, 1999, 2000. Mem.: Tex. Ret. Sch. Pers., Piney Woods Counseling Assn., Tex. Counseling Assn., Sheriff's Assn. Tex. Avocations: dancing (clog and jazz), twirling batons, patriotic flag routine, piano. Home: 12446 Chapman Rd Tyler TX 75708-3210 Office Phone: 903-877-3013, 903-530-9941. Personal E-mail: drsynthawest@yahoo.com.

WESTBROOK, GARY L., neurologist; BA in Zoology, Miami U., Oxford, Ohio, 1970; MSE in Biomed. Engring., Case Western Res. U., Cleve., 1974, MD, 1976. Diplomate Am. Bd. Internal Medicine, 1979. Intern, resident in internal medicine Mt. Auburn Hosp., Harvard U., Cambridge, Mass., 1976—78; resident in neurology Barnes Hosp., Wash. U., St. Louis, 1978—81; PRAT fellow, pharmacology sci. program NIH Nat. Inst. Gen. Med. Sciences, Bethesda, Md., 1981—83; staff & sr. staff fellow, lab. devel. neurobiology NIH, Bethesda, 1983—87; asst. prof. neurology Oreg. Health Sci. U., Portland, 1987—88, assoc. prof. neurology, 1988—92, prof. neurology & physiology, pharmacology, 1992—; asst. scientist Vollum Inst., Portland, 1987—90, sr. scientist, 1990—, co-dir., 2005—; attending neurologist Univ. Hosp., Portland, 1988—, physician, epilepsy program, 1989—2003. Assoc. editor: Jour. Neurosci. Cellular Neurosci. Sect., 1988—93, editor:, 1995—97, sr. editor: Jour. Neurosci. Cellular and Molecular Neurosci., 1997—2002, editor-in-chief: Jour. Neurosci., 2003—07, mem. editl. bd.: Molecular Pharmacology, 1995—98; contbr. articles to profl. jours. Mem. Dana Alliance, 2005—; sci. adv. bd. Myelin Repair Found., 2004—, chmn., 2007—; chmn. ad hoc Max Planck Inst. Exptl. Medicine, 2006—; adv. coun. NINDS, NIH, 2006—. Recipient Devel. award, McKnight Endowment Fund Neurosci., 1988, Javits Neurosci. Investigator award, NINDS, NIH, 1993, MERIT award, 1997, Max Planck Rsch. award for internat. cooperation, 2003. Mem.: Inst. Medicine, Am. Acad. Arts & Sciences, Phi Beta Kappa, Omicron Delta Kappa. Office: Vollum Inst Oreg Health & Sci Univ 3181 SW Sam Jackson Park Rd Portland OR 97239-3098 Office Phone: 503-494-8311.

WESTEN, DREW, psychology professor; b. 1959; married; 2 children. BA, Harvard U.; MA in Social & Polit. Thought, U. Sussex, Eng.; PhD in Clin. Psychology, U. Mich. Tchr. U. Mich.; chief psychologist Cambridge Hosp., Mass.; assoc. prof. psychiatry Harvard Med. Sch.; rsch. assoc. prof. Boston U., psychologist, Ctr. Anxiety and Related Disorders; prof. Emory U., 2002—, dir. Lab. Personality and Psychopathology, prof. Dept. Psychology, prof. Dept. Psychiatry and Behavioral Sciences. Founder Westen Strategies, LLC; advised a range of candidates & organizations, from presdl. & congl. campaigns to major progressive organizations, to Fortune 500 companies. Performer: (albums) I'm a Professor: Songs for Mediocre Guitar and Inadequate Vocals, (songs) Oy, to be a Goy on Christmas; author: Self and Society: Narcissism, Collectivism, and the Development of Morals, The Political Brain: The Role of Emotion in Deciding the Fate of the Nation, 2007; co-author: Psychology, Study Guide, 2004; occassional commentator All Things Considered, Nat. Pub.

Radio, 1998—; contbr. several articles to profl. jours.;, author of several scholarly articles. Recipient Theodore Millon award, Am. Psychol. Found., 2004. Office: Emory U 308 Psychology Bldg 532 Kilgo Cir Atlanta GA 30322 Office Phone: 404-727-7407. Office Fax: 404-727-0372. E-mail: dwesten@emory.edu.

WESTERBERG, SIV ÖMAN, lawyer, physician; b. Borås, Sweden, June 11, 1932; d. Bror and Magda (Karlsson) Öman; m. Per G. S. Westerberg, June 19, 1964; children: Eva, Carl, Gösta. Medicine Kandidat, U. Uppsala, Sweden, 1954, Medicine Licentiat, 1960; Juris Kandidat, U. Lund, Sweden, 1982. Bar: Sweden 1982, European Commn. Human Rights 1983, European Ct. Human Rights 1987. Physician U. Clinics, Gothenburg, Sweden, 1960—64; physician, rschr. Clin. Labs., U. Hosp. Sahlgrenska Sjukhuset, Gothenburg, 1961—63; pvt. practice gen. medicine Gothenburg, 1964—79; pvt. practice law, 1982—. Author (with H. A. Hansen): A Handbook of Laboratory Work, 1962; author: Vaccination of Persons Travelling Abroad, 1964, To Be a Physician, 1978, Punishment Without a Crime, 2004; contbr. articles on renal physiology to med. jours., on child welfare to Swedish and fgn. newspapers. Lutheran. Home and Office: Skårsgatan 45 SE-412 69 Gothenburg Sweden Office Phone: 46 31 402988.

WESTERDAHL, JOHN BRIAN, nutritionist, health educator; b. Tucson, Dec. 3, 1954; s. Jay E. and Margaret (Meyer) W.; m. Doris Mui Lian Tan, Nov. 18, 1989; 1 child, Jasmine Leilani. AA, Orange Coast Coll., 1977; BS, Pacific Union Coll., 1979; MPH, Loma Linda U., 1981; PhD, Pacific Western U., 2001; MA, Calif. Grad. Sch. Theology, 2008. Registered dietitian, master herbalist; cert. nutrition specialist; bd. cert. anti-aging health practitioner. From nutritionist, health educator to dir. Castle Med. Ctr., Kailua, Hawaii, 1981—89, dir. wellness and lifestyle medicine and nutritional svc., 1998—2006; dir. nutrition and health rsch. Health Sci., Santa Barbara, Calif., 1989-90; sr. nutritionist, project mgr. Shaklee Corp., San Francisco, 1990-96; dir. nutrition Dr. McDougall's Right Foods, Inc., South San Francisco, 1996—98; mem. faculty staff, dir. continuing edn. Am. Acad. Nutrition, 1996—2006; staff nutritionist Millennium Restaurant, San Francisco, 1995—; dir. Murad Inclusive Health Ctr., Murad Med. Group, El Segundo, 2006—07, Bragg Health Found., 2007—; dir. health scis. Bragg Live Food Products Inc., Santa Barbara, Calif., 2007—. Radio talk show host Nutrition and You KGU Radio, Honolulu, 1983—89, KWAI Radio, Honolulu, 1999—; nutrition com. mem. Hawaii div. Am. Heart Assn., Honolulu, 1984—87; mem. nutrition study group Gov.s Conf. Health Promotion and Disease Prevention, Hawaii, 1985. Author: Medicinal Herbs: A Vital Reference Guide, 1998, The Millennium Cookbook: Extraordinary Vegetarian Cuisine, 1998; editor: Nourish Mag., 1995-96; nutrition editor: Veggie Life Mag., 1995—2003. Recipient Bausch & Lomb Hon. Sci. award, 1972, award, Letterman Orange Coast Coll. Swim Team, 1976—77, Disting. Achievement award, Men Achievement Cambridge, 1988, Outstanding State Coord. award, Vegetarian Nutrition Diatetic Practice Group Am. Dietetic Assn., 2006, Outstanding Svc. award, Nutrition Complementary Care Dietetic Group Am. Dietetic Assn., 2006, IBC Gold medal; named Internat. Health Profl. of Yr., 2008; named one of 10 Outstanding Young Persons, Hawaii Jr. C. of C., 1988. Mem.: Calif. Dietetic Assn., Am. Coll. of Lifestyle Medicine (bd. dirs. 2006—09), Seventh-day Adventist Dietetic Assn., Hawaii Dietetic Assn., Hawaii Nutrition Coun. (v.p. 1983-86, pres.-elect 1988-89, pres. 1989), Inst. Food Technologists, Am. Soc. Pharmacognosy, Am. Coll. Nutrition, Am. Dietetic Assn. (Hawaii coord. vegetarian nutrition dietetic practice group 1998—2006), Am. Acad. Anti-Aging Medicine, Am. Coll. Sports Medicine, AAAS. Republican. Seventh-Day Adventist. Avocations: swimming, scuba diving. Office: Bragg Health Found 199 Winchester Canyon Rd Santa Barbara CA 93117 Office Phone: 800-446-1990, 800-968-1020. Business E-Mail: drwesterdahl@bragg.com.

WESTERMAN, LIANE MARIE, research scientist executive; b. Long Branch, NJ, June 20, 1949; d. Charles Wilson and Edith Doris (Johnson) Case; m. S. Thomas Westerman; children: David Aaron, Charles Paul. BA in Psychology, Monmouth U., West Long Branch, NJ, 1972; MA in Teaching, Coll. of N.J., 1979. Cert. tchr. of handicapped, N.J. Tchr. spl. edn., dir. afternoon program S.E.A.R.C.H., Ocean, NJ, 1972-74; tchr. spl. edn. Jackson (N.J.) Twp. Sch. System, 1974-79; exec. dir. Otologic Edn., Inc., Shrewsbury, NJ, 1980-88; dir. clin. rsch. Nat. Patent Analytical Systems, Inc., Roslyn Heights, NY, 1983-86, v.p. rsch., 1986-88; pres. Westerman Rsch. Assocs., Inc., Shrewsbury, NJ, 1988—2007. Participant numerous convs., profl. organs. and spl. interest groups, U.S.A., Israel and The Netherlands, 1974—; software devel. expert to knowledge engr. for Visual Perceptual System, 1984—; v.p. Otologic Edn., Inc., Shrewsbury, 1988-2007. Co-contbr. articles and chpts. to profl. publs.; U.S. and Can. patentee computer-aided drug-abuse detection. Fundraiser Am. Heart Assn., 1991; bd. dirs. Women's Coun. for Leon Hess Cancer Ctr. at Monmouth Med. Ctr., 2003—; active MADD; activist Nat. Audubon Soc. Mem. Am. Acad. Otolaryngology, Head and Neck Surgery (assoc.), Psi Chi, Sigma Xi. Avocations: travel, classical music, creative writing. Office: Liane Westerman 170 Ave at the Common Ste 6 Shrewsbury NJ 07702-4003

WESTERMANN, JUERGEN, biomedical engineer, researcher; b. Uelzen, Niedersachsen, Germany, Feb. 1, 1959; s. Richard and Charlotte Westermann; m. Claudia Westermann-Behnke, Nov. 12, 2005; children: Kim-Jennifer, Lennart. Dipl. Ing. in Bioengring., U. Applied Sci., Hamburg, Germany, 1984. Engr. Immuno Biological Lab., Hamburg, Germany, 1985—2000, head product devel., 2000—08; head radio immunoassay devel Euroimmun Ag, 2008—. Contbr. articles to profl. jours. Mem.: Gesellschaft Deutscher Chemiker. Achievements include patents for Cis-Diol affinity plate. Office: EUROIMMUN AG Seekamp 31 D-23560 Luebeck Germany Business E-Mail: j.westermann@euroimmun.de.

WESTHEIMER, GERALD, optometrist, educator; b. Berlin, May 13, 1924; naturalized, 1944, came to U.S., 1951; s. Isaak and Ilse (Cohn) W. Optometry diploma, Sydney Tech. Coll., Australia, 1943, fellowship diploma, 1950; BSc, U. Sydney, 1947; PhD, Ohio State U., 1953; DSc (hon.), U. NSW, Australia, 1988; ScD (hon.), SUNY, 1990; MD (hon.), U. Tubingen, 2005. Practice optometry, Sydney, 1945-51; research fellow Ohio State U., 1951-53; prof. physiol. optics U. Houston, 1953-54; asst. prof., then assoc. prof. physiol. optics Ohio State U., 1954-60; postdoctoral fellow neurophysiology Marine Biol. Lab., Woods Hole, Mass., 1957; vis. researcher Physiol. Lab., U. Cambridge, Eng., 1958-59; mem. faculty U. Calif. at Berkeley, 1960—, prof. physiol. optics, 1963-68, chmn. group physiol. optics, 1964-67, prof. physiology, 1968-89, prof. neurobiology, 1989—, head div. neurobiology, 1987-92; adj. prof. Rockefeller U., N.Y., 1992—; hon. prof. U. Electronic Sci. & Tech. China, Chengdu, 2010—. Sackler lectr. Tel Aviv U. Med. Sch., 1988, D.O. Hebb lectr. McGill U., 1991, Grass Found. lectr. U. Ill., 1991, Wertheimer lectr. U. Frankfort on the Main, 1998; mem. com. vision NRC, 1957-72; mem. visual scis. study sect. NIH, 1966-70, chmn. visual scis. B study sect., 1977-79; mem. vision, research and tng. com. Nat. Eye Inst., NIH, 1970-74, chmn. bd. sci. counselors, 1981-83; mem. exec. council com. vision NAS-NRC, 1969-72; mem. communicative scis. cluster Pres.'s Biomed. Rsch. Panel, 1975, Enoch Lectr., Wash. U. Med. Sch., 2009. Author rsch. papers; editor: Vision Rsch., 1972-79; editl. bd. Investigative Ophthalmology, 1973-77, Exptl. Brain Rsch., 1973-89, Optics Letters, 1977-78, Spatial Vision, 1985—2009, Ophthalmic and Physiological Optics, 1985—, Vision Rsch., 1985-92, Jour. of Physiology, 1987-94. Recipient Von Sallman prize Columbia U., 1986; Prentice medal Am. Acad. Optometry, 1986, Bicentennial medal Australian Optometric Assn., 1988, B. Collin Rsch. medal Optometrists Assn. Australia, 2010; Named Order of Australia, 2009 Fellow AAAS, Royal Soc. London (Ferrier lectr. 1992, editl. bd. procs. 1990-96, 2000-06), Am. Acad. Arts and Scis., Optical Soc. Am. (Tillyer medal 1978, assoc. editor jour. 1980-83), Am. Acad. Optometry; mem. Royal Soc. New So. Wales (hon.), Soc. Neurosci., Assn. Rsch. in Vision and Ophthalmology (Proctor medal 1979), Internat. Brain Rsch. Orgn., Physiol. Soc. Gt. Britain, Sigma Xi, Gen. Divsn. AM (order of Australia 2009), Royal Soc. NSW (hon.). Home: 582 Santa Barbara Rd Berkeley CA 94707-1746 Business E-Mail: gwestheimer@berkeley.edu.

WESTHEIMER, RUTH SIEGEL (DR. RUTH, KAROLA WESTHEIMER), psychologist, television personality; b. Frankfurt, Fed. Republic Germany, June 4, 1928; came to U.S., 1956; m. Manfred Westheimer (dec. 1997); children: Miriam, Joel. Grad. psychology, U. Paris Sorbonne; Master's degree, New Sch. for Social Research, NYC, 1959; EdD, Columbia U., 1970; Science Degree (hon.), Bronx HS; PhD (hon.), Westfield State Coll., 2008. Research asst. Columbia U. Sch. Pub. Health, NYC, 1967-70; assoc. prof. Lehman Coll., Bronx, N.Y., 1970-77; with Bklyn. Coll., West Point Milit. Acad.; counsellor, radio talk show hostess Sexually Speaking Sta. WYNY-FM, NYC, 1980-90; hostess TV series Good Sex, Dr. Ruth Show, Ask Dr. Ruth, 1987-92; pvt. practice NYC, 1976—. Adj. assoc. prof. to full prof. NYU; leader seminars for residents and interns in pediats. on adolescent sexuality Brookdale Hosp.; hon. pres., Coun. on Sexuality and Aging, Nat. Sexuality Resource Ctr. Author: Dr. Ruth's Guide to Good Sex, 1983, First Love: A Young People's Guide to Sexual Information, 1985, Dr. Ruth's Guide for Married Lovers, 1986, (autobiography) All In a Lifetime, 1987, Sex and Morality: Who is Teaching Out Sex Standards?, 1988, Dr. Ruth's Guide to Erotic and Sensuous Pleasures, 1991, Dr. Ruth's Guide to Safer Sex, 1992, Dr. Ruth Talks to Kids, 1993, The Art of Arousal, 1993, Dr. Ruth's Encyclopedia of Sex, 1994, Heavenly Sex, 1995, Sex for Dummies, 1995, The Value of Family, 1996; co-author: (with Steven Kaplan) Surviving Salvation; contbr. articles to mags.; appeared in film A Woman or Two, 1986; appeared on TV show Quantum Leap, 1993, Play Boy Making Love Series (video), 1996, All New Dr. Ruth Show (nominated 5 times by Ace awards, Ace award for excellence in cable TV, 1988), What's Up, Dr. Ruth (gold medal Internat. Film and TV Festival for excellence in ednl. TV), You're on the Air with Dr. Ruth, Never Too Late, 1992—, Dr. Ruth's House, (calendar) Dr. Ruth's Good Sex Night-to-Night Calendar, 1993, 94, (boardgame) Dr. Ruth's Game of Good Sex; exec. prodr. documentary on Ethiopian Jews Surviving Salvation, 1991; columnist Ask Dr. Ruth. Pres. YMHA, Washington Heights. Recipient Mother of Yr. award Nat. Mother's Day Com., Liberty medal City of N.Y.; named to Women in Technology Internat. Hall of Fame, 2010. Fellow N.Y. Acad. Medicine.

WESTHOF, ERIC, cell biologist, medical researcher, educator; b. Uccle, Belgium, July 25, 1948; M in Physics, Liege U., PhD. Prof. structural biochemistry U. Louis Pasteur, Strasbourg, France, 1988—, v.p. rsch. and doctoral studies, 2007—08; dir. Inst. Molecular and Cellular Biology Nat. Ctr. Sci. Rsch. (CNRS), Strasbourg, France, 2006—, dir. architecture and reactivity of RNA, 2005—; prof. biophysics and structural biochemistry U. Strasbourg, France, v.p. rsch. and doctoral studies, 2009—. Burroughs Wellcome Fund vis. prof. Rutgers U., 2001—02. Exec. editor RNA, Nucleic Acids Rsch. Fellow: AAAS, Inst. Physics, London; mem.: French Acad. Scis. (Charles-Leopold Mayer Prize 2007). Office: Inst for Molecular & Cellular Biology 15 Rue Rene Descartes 67084 Strasbourg France Office Phone: (+33) 3 88 41 70 37. Office Fax: (+33) 3 88 60 22 18. *

WESTHOFF, CAROLYN LOUISE, obstetrician, gynecologist, epidemiologist, educator; b. Nov. 17, 1951; MD, U. Mich., 1977. Cert. Ob-Gyn., 1986. Intern in ob-gyn. Henry Ford Hosp., Detroit, 1977—78; resident in epidemiology SUNY Downstate, Bklyn., 1978—82; fellow London Sch. Hygiene and Tropical Medicine, 1982—83; prof. ob-gyn. Columbia U., NYC, prof. epidemiology and population and family, dir. family planning and preventive medicine. Mem.: Inst. Medicine. Office: Presbyn Hosp Rm 1669 630 W 168th St New York NY 10032 Office Phone: 212-305-9368. E-mail: clw3@columbia.edu.

WESTIN, STEINAR, physician, educator; b. Oslo, June 21, 1944; s. Sverre and Karen (Skjeseth) W.; m. Rigmor Austgulen, Dec. 28, 1970 (div. 1985); Kamilla, Johanna, Andreas; m. Lise Skjaak Braek, May 25, 1991. Student, Brandeis U., Mass., 1966-67, U. Bergen, Norway, 1970; MD, U. Trondheim, Norway, 1990. Specialist gen. practice and family medicine. Jr. registrar Neevengaarden Psychiat. Hosp., 1971; rsch. fellow dept. psychiatry U. Bergen, 1972; intern Haraldsplass Hosp., Bergen, 1972-73; gen. practice Asköy Dist., Norway, 1973-78; asst. prof. cmty. medicine and gen. practice U. Trondheim, 1979-83, assoc. prof., 1983-90, prof., dept. chmn., 1990—. Vis. prof. Royal Australian Coll. Gen. Practitioners, 1995; mem. organizing com. for postgrad. tng. in gen. practice Norwegian Med. Assn., 1986-96. Author: Research in General Practice, 1983, The Educational Handbook for General Practitioners, 1985, 2d edition, 1996, Problem Solving in General Practice, 1987, Unemployment and Health: Medical and Social Consequences of a Factory Closure in a Ten-Year Controlled Follow-up Study, 1990, Becoming Disabled: A Sociomedical Analysis of Individual Adaptations to Life After Long-Term Unemployment, 1990; chmn. editl. bd. Jour. Norwegian Med. Assn., 1996-2004; mem. editl. bd. British Med. Jour., 1995-2002, European Jour. Gen. Practice, 1994—; editor: Textbook of Social Medicine, 2004, Textbook of Social Epidemiology, 2009 Wien/Fulbright scholar Brandeis U., Mass., 1966-67. Avocations: skiing, windsurfing. Home: Övre Allé 9 N-7030 Trondheim Norway Office: Norwegian U Sci & Tech Dept Pub Health and Gen Practice N-7489 Trondheim Norway Office Phone: 47-73598887. Business E-Mail: steinar.westin@ntnu.no.

WESTMAN, JACK CONRAD, child psychiatrist, educator; b. Cadillac, Mich., Oct. 28, 1927; s. Conrad A. and Alice (Pedersen) W.; m. Nancy K. Baehre, July 17, 1953; children— Daniel P., John C., Eric C. MD, U. Mich., 1952. Diplomate Am. Bd. Psychiatry and Neurology. Intern Duke Hosp., Durham, NC, 1952-53; resident U. Mich. Med. Ctr., 1955-59; dir. outpatient svcs. Children's Psychiat. Hosp., Ann Arbor, Mich., 1961-65; assoc. prof. U. Mich. Med. Sch., 1964-65; coord. diagnostic and treatment unit Waisman Ctr., U. Wis., Madison, 1966-74, prof. psychiatry, 1965-96, prof. emeritus, 1997—. Cons. Joint Commn. on Mental Health of Children, 1967-69, Madison Pub. Schs., 1965-74, Children's Treatment Ctr., Mendota Mental Health Inst., 1965-69 Author: Individual Differences in Children, 1973, Child Advocacy, 1979, Handbook of Learning Disabilities, 1990, Who Speaks for the Children?, 1991, Licensing Parents, 1994, Born to Belong, 1997, Parenthood in America, 2001, Breaking the Adolescent Parent Cycle, 2009, The Complete Idiot's Guide to Child and Adolescent Psychiatry, 2011; editor Child Psychiatry and Human Devel., 1984-99; contbr. articles to profl. jours. Vice-pres. Big Bros. of Dane County, 1970-73; v.p. Wis. Assn. Mental Health, 1968-72; co-chmn. Project Understanding, 1968-75; pres. Wis. Cares, 1998—. With USNR, 1953-55. Fellow Am. Psychiat. Assn., Am. Coll. Psychiatrists, Am. Acad. Child and Adolescent Psychiatry, Am. Orthopsychiat. Assn. (bd. dirs. 1973-76); mem. Am. Assn. Psychiat. Svcs. for Children (pres. 1978-80), Multidisciplinary Acad. Clin. Edn. (pres. 1992-98), Canyon Scholars (treas. 2000-). Home: 1234 Dartmouth Rd Madison WI 53705-2214 E-mail: jwestman@wisc.edu.

WESTNEY, OUIDA LENAINE, urologist, educator; b. Balt., May 4, 1967; BS, Howard U., 1988; MD, Johns Hopkins U., 1992. Assoc. prof. MD Anderson Cancer Ctr., 2005—. Mem.: Soc. Urodynamics and Female Urology, Am. Urol. Assn. Avocations: cooking, travel. Office: 1515 Holcombe Blvd Unit 1373 Houston TX 77006 Business E-Mail: owestney@mdanderson.org.

WESTOFF, CHARLES FRANCIS, demographer, educator; b. NYC, July 23, 1927; s. Frank Barnett and Evelyn (Bales) Westoff; m. Joan P. Uszynski, Sept. 11, 1948 (div. Jan. 1969); children: David, Carol; m. Leslie Aldridge, Aug. 1969 (div. Feb. 1993); m. Jane DeLung, May 1997. AB, Syracuse U., NY, 1949, MA, 1950; PhD, U. Pa., Phila., 1953. Instr. sociology U. Pa., 1950—52; rsch. assoc. Milbank Meml. Fund, NYC, 1952—55; rsch. assoc. Office Population Rsch. Princeton U., NJ, 1955—62, Maurice P. During '22 prof. demographic studies and sociology, 1962—99, prof. emeritus, 1999—, sr. rsch. demographer, 1999—, chmn. dept. sociology, 1965—70, assoc. dir. Office Population Rsch., 1962—75, dir., 1975—92; assoc. prof. sociology NYU, also chmn. dept. sociology Washington Sq. Coll., 1959—62; vis. sr. fellow East-West Population Inst., Honolulu, 1979—81; Disting. vis. prof. Am. U., Cairo, 1979; mem. vis. com. Harvard-MIT Joint Ctr. for Urban Studies, 1980—83. Exec. dir. Commn. Population Growth and Am. Future, 1970—72; mem. adv. com. on population stats. US Bur. Census, 1973—79; chmn. Nat. Com. for Rsch. on 1980 Census, 1981—88; bd. dirs. Alan Guttmacher Inst., 1977—88, 1989—; sr. tech. advisor Demographic Health Surveys, 1984—; bd. dirs. Population Resource Ctr., 1985—, Population Ref. Bur., 1988—94, Population Commns. Internat., 1992—98; com. on population NAS, 1983—88. Co-author: Family Growth in Metropolitan America, 1961, The Third Child, 1963, College Women and Fertility Values, 1967, The Later Years of Childbearing, 1970, From Now to Zero, 1971, Reproduction in the United States, 1965, 1971, Toward the End of Growth: Population in America, 1973, The Contraceptive Revolution, 1976, Demographic Dynamics in America, 1977, Mass Media and Reproductive Behavior in Africa, 1997, New Estimate of Unmet Need and the Demand for Family Planning, 2006, Unmet Need at the End of the Century, 2002, Reproductive Preferences in Developing Countries at the Turn of the Century, 2002, Trends in Marriage and Early Childbearing in Developing Countries, 2006, Recent Trends in Contraception and Abortion in Twelve Countries, 2005, The Stall in the Fertility Transition in Kenya, 2006, Religion, Religiousness and Fertility in the US and in Europe, 2007, Religiousness and Fertility in the among European Muslims, 2007; contbr. articles on demography and sociology to profl. jours.; co-author: A New Approach to Estimating Abortion Rats, 2009. Recipient Irene Taueber award for Outstanding Rsch. Contbns., 1995. Fellow: Am. Acad. Arts and Scis.; mem.: Internat. Union Sci. Study Population (Laureate award 2007), Population Assn. Am. (bd. dirs. 1960—62, 1968—70, 1st v.p. 1972—73, pres. 1974—75), Planned Parenthood Fedn. Am. (dir. 1978—81), Inst. Medicine-NAS. Home: 1 Highland Rd Princeton NJ 08540 Office: Princeton U Wallace Hall Princeton NJ 08544 Business E-Mail: westoff@princeton.edu.

WESTON, GEORGE W., plastic surgeon; b. Aug. 14, 1953; married. Attended, U. Ala., 1971—75, Samford U., 1975—77, U.South Ala., 1977—81. Diplomate Am. Bd. Plastic Surgery, 1990. Resident gen. surgery and plastic surgery Wake Forest Univ. Med. Ctr., 1981—86; fellow plastic surgery Charlotte Plastic Surgery Ctr., 1986, Univ. of Ala. Med. Ctr., 1986; hosp. appointment Fairfax Hosp.; joined Austin-Weston Ctr. for Cosmetic Surgery, 1987, pres. Invited panelist Aesthetic Surgery Jour., 1999; invited faculty perspectives and advances in plastic surgery, Vail, Colo., 2000, 04; invited faculty Perioral Plastic Surgery Symposium, 2003, Australian Sci. and Math. Sch. Mid-Face Symposium, 2004; invited spkr. NC Soc. of Plastic Surgeons, 2006; invited panelist Am. Soc. of Aesthetic Plastic Surgery,

2006. Author: (publs.) Rejuvenating the Aging Mouth, 1993—2007. Named one of Top Plastic Surgeons, Washingtonian Mag., 1989, Am. Rsch. Coun., 2007—10, Northern Va. Mag., 2010. Mem.: Nat. Capital Soc. of Plastic Surgeons, Va. Soc. of Plastic Surgery, AMA, Am. Soc. of Plastic Surgeons. Office: Austin-Weston Center for Cosmetic Surgery 1825 Samuel Morse Dr Reston VA 20190 Office Phone: 703-893-6168.

WESTON, LOUANNE C., marriage and family therapist; Grad., Coll. William & Mary, Western Inst. for Social Rsch., Berkeley, Inst. Advanced Study Human Sexuality, San Francisco. Lic. Marriage & Family Therapist, diplomate Am. Coll. Sexologists, 1983, Am. Bd. Sexology, 1989. Marriage, family & child counselor pvt. practice. Fellow: Am. Acad. Clinical Sexologists; mem.: Am. Bd. Sexology (clinical supr.), Am. Assn. Marriage & Family Therapists, Calif. Assn. Marriage & Family Therapists, Soc. for the Scientific Study of Sexuality. Office: 5006 Sunrise Blvd Ste 106 Fair Oaks CA 95628 Office Phone: 916-961-2490. Office Fax: 916-965-1960. E-mail: louannecoleweston@sexmatters.com.

WESTON, WILLIAM LEE, retired dermatologist; b. Grand Rapids, Minn., Aug. 13, 1938; s. Eugene and Edith Kathryn (Lee) W.; m. Janet J. Atkinson, June 9, 1964; children: Elizabeth Carol, William Kemp. AB, Whitman Coll., 1960; B in Med. Sci., U. S.D., 1963; MD, U. Colo., 1965. Resident in pediatrics U. Calif., San Francisco, 1967-68; intern, then resident in pediatrics U. Colo., Denver, 1965-67, resident in dermatology, 1970-72, asst. prof. dermatology & pediatrics, 1976, prof., 1976—2006, chmn. dept. dermatology, 1976—2001, emeritus prof. dermatology, 2006—. Author: Practical Pediatric Dermatology, 1979, rev. edit., 1985, Color Textbook of Pediatric Dermatology, 1991, rev. edits., 1996-2001, 07; editor-in-chief Current Problems in Dermatology, 1988-93. With AUS, 1968-70. Mem. Soc. Pediatric Dermatology (founder, sec.-treas. 1975-80, pres. 1984-85), Colo. Dermatol. Soc. (hon., pres.), Soc. Investigative Dermatology (bd. dirs.), Am. Acad. Dermatology (bd. dirs.). Methodist. Home: 8550 E Ponderosa Dr Parker CO 80138-8233

WESTRICK, HEIDI LYNN, medical/surgical nurse; b. Johnstown, Pa., Dec. 15, 1966; d. Thomas and Karol Anne (Kirchner) Zwiener; m. Daniel D. Westrick, Sept. 4, 1999. Diploma, Conemaugh Valley Meml. Hosp., Johnstown, 1987; BSN, U. Pitts., Johnstown, 1993. Bd. cert. RNC-BSN Med. Surg. Nursing. 2000, cert. trauma and acute rehabilitation nursing, head injuries; peritoneal dialysis, cardiac monitoring, Am. nursing credential, registered med. surg. nursing, 1990; cert. CPR, BDLS, CDLS. Nurse Conemaugh Valley Meml. Hosp., Johnstown, Pa., 1987—; admissions coord. Conemaugh Hosp., Crichton Ctr. Advanced Rehab., Johnstown, Pa., 1996—. Vol. Red Cross Blood Dr., St. Nicholas Ch., eucharistic min. Sheetz Family Christmas. Mem. Conemaugh Valley Alumni (sec., peer rev. com., bd. mem. rehab. creation ctr.), Alumni of U. Pitts. at Johnstown, PENNA, FEMA, Fed. Disaster Reserve Assn. (Pa. med. reserve mem., Pa. serve vol. RN). Office Fax: 814-940-4090. Personal E-mail: daniel440@verizon.net, donielyy@clgon.net

WESTROPE, MARTHA RANDOLPH, psychologist, consultant; b. Gaffney, SC, May 19, 1922; d. Gordon Robert and Hannah (Brown) Westrope; 1 adopted child, Ashley Randolph. BS, Winthrop Coll., Rock Hill, SC, 1942; MA, U. NC, Chapel Hill, 1944; PhD, U. Iowa, Iowa City, 1952. Lic. psychologist SC. Pvt. practice, Greenville, S.C., 1960—; part-time pvt. practice, 1987-96; part-time staff mem. Spartanburg Mental Health Clinic, SC, 1971-73, Greenville Mental Health Ctr., 1974-85, Patrick B. Harris Psychiat. Hosp., Anderson, S.C., 1985-87; med. cons. SC Vocat. Rehab. Dept., Greenville, 1987-91, part-time med. cons., 1993-99. Cons. SC Parole Bd. Psychol. Evaluation SC Dept. Corrections, 1983—87. Mem.: Coun. Nat. Register Health Svc. Providers Psychology, Am. Group Psychotherapy Assn., Greenville County Mental Health Assn., Am. Assn. Advancement Psychology, SC Psychol. Assn., Southeastern Psychol. Assn., Am. Psychol. Assn. Democrat. Presbyterian. Avocations: wildlife preservation, fine arts. Home: 11 Darien Way Greenville SC 29615-3236

WETHERBE, HERBERT JOHN, pharmacist; b. Montague, Mass., Sept. 18, 1943; s. John Bond Wetherbe, Dorothy Mildred Wetherbe; m. Linda Ann Stines. MDiv, Trinity Evang. Div. Sch., 1979; PharmD, U. Ill., 1992. Registered pharmacist Ill., N.Y. Chemist Inmont Corp., Detroit, 1969—71; chief pharmacist Walgreens Drug Co., Deerfield, Ill., 1979—83; staff pharmacist VA Hosp., Danville, 1983—87, King Khaled Eye Specialist Hosp., Riyadh, Saudi Arabia, 1987—89; clin. pharmacist Northwestern Meml. Hosp., Chgo., 1992—93, Security Forces Hosp., Riyadh, 1993—96; pharmacist Kinney Drugs, Gouverneur, NY, 1996; clin. cons. hosp. info. sys. Nat. Consulting Bur. Huff Barrington Owens Alan Cooper, Inc., Safat, Kuwait, 1996—97, Integrated Solutions for Bus., Riyadh, 1998—2002, Nat. Consulting Bur. Huff Barrington Owens Alan Cooper, Inc., Safat, 2002—03, Kinney Drugs, Gouveneur, 2003—, supervising pharmacist/floating pharmacist, 2003—. Mem.: Northern NY Pharmacists Soc., Intravenous Nurses Soc., Pharmacists Soc. State N.Y., Am. Soc. Health Sys. Pharmacists, Am. Pharm. Assn., Am Inst. Chemists, Am. Chem. Soc., Gen. Soc. Mayflower Descs., N.Y. State Coun. Health Sys. Pharmacists. Republican. Avocation: travel. Personal E-mail: hjwetherbe@yahoo.com.

WEWALKA, FRIEDRICH, physician; b. Vienna, July 2, 1957; MD, Vienna U., 1982. Oberarzt Krankenhaus der Elisabethinen Linz, 2010—. Mem.: Austrian Soc. Gastroenterology and Hepatology, ESGE. Office: Fadingerstraße 1 Linz 4010 Austria Business E-Mail: friedrich.wewalka@elisabethinen.or.at.

WEXLER, ANDREW MARK, plastic surgeon; b. Leominster, Mass., Aug. 25, 1952; AB, Dartmouth Coll., 1974; MA, Boston U., MD, 1980. Chief plastic surgery, regional dir. craniofacial svcs. Southern Calif. Kaiser Permanente, 1990—. Clin. prof. plastic surgery U. Southern Calif., 2003—; med. adv. bd. Operation Smile Internat., 2000—. Fellow: ACS; mem.: Am. Cleft Lip and Palate Soc., Am. Soc. Maxillofacial Surgeons (pres. 2007—08), Am. Assn. Plastic Surgeon, Am. Soc. Plastic Surgeons (bd. dirs. 2009—). Office: 6041 Cadillac Ave Los Angeles CA 90034 E-mail: surgiwex@gmail.com.

WEXLER, DEBORAH LEE, physician; b. Minn., Mar. 16, 1950; MD, U. Minn., 1982. Exec. dir. & founder Immunization Action Coalition. Editor Needle Tips, Vaccinate Adults, Vaccinate Women, IAC Express, Hep Express. Office: Immunization Action Coalition 1573 Selby Ave Ste 234 Saint Paul MN 55104 Office Phone: 651-647-9009. Office Fax: 651-647-9131. E-mail: admin@immunize.org.

WEXLER, LAURA F., cardiologist, academic administrator; b. Washington, Jan. 26, 1947; d. Michael and Helen (Fooner) Wexler; m. David N. Glass, Nov. 9, 1980; children: Stephanie, Eleanor, Benjamin. BA, Barnard Coll., NYC, 1967; MD, Washington U. Sch. Medicine, St. Louis, 1971. Diplomate Am. Bd. Internal Medicine, cert. in Cardiology. Intern, resident Boston City Hosp./Harvard Med. Sch.; fellow internal medicine/cardiology Mass. Gen. Hosp., Boston; asst. prof. medicine Boston U. Sch. Medicine, 1976-87; assoc. prof. medicine U. Cin. Coll. Medicine, 1987—91, prof. medicine, 1991—99, interim dir. divsn. cardiology, 1999—2001, assoc. dean student affairs/admissions, 2001—. Chief cardiology Cin. Vets. Affairs Med. Ctr., 1987—98; chair clin. biennium curriculum com., reappointment, promotions and tenure com. U. Cin. Coll. Medicine. Editor: Cardiology Alert, 1978—87; contbr. articles to profl. jours. Fellow: Am. Heart Assn., Coun. Clin. Cardiology, Am. Coll. Cardiology. Achievements include research in heart disease in women; sleep apnea in patients with heart failure. Office: U Cin Coll Medicine Divsn Cardiovasc Diseases 231 Albert Sabin Way Cincinnati OH 45267-0001 Office Phone: 513-558-4721. Office Fax: 513-558-3116. Business E-Mail: wexlerl@ucmail.uc.edu.

WEXLER, LEONARD HOWARD, pediatric oncologist; b. Bklyn., Nov. 21, 1961; s. Theodore and Florence Wexler; m. Beth Sue Brown, Sept. 1999. BA, Boston U.; MD, Boston U. Sch. Medicine, 1985. Cert. Pediatrics, Pediatric Hematology-Oncology. Intern, pediatrics Albert Einstein/Montefiore, Bronx, NY, 1985—88, resident, pediatrics, 1985—88; fellow, pediatric hematology and oncology NIH-Nat. Cancer Inst., Bethesda, Md., 1988—92, sr. clin. investigator, pediatric branch, 1992—96; dir. clin. services Babies & Children's Hosp., NYC, 1996—99, assoc. mem. dept. pediatrics Meml. Sloan-Kettering Cancer Ctr., NY, 1999—; asst. prof. pediatrics Uniformed Services Univ. of the Health Sciences; assoc. prof. pediatrics, divsn. pediatric oncology Columbia U., NY, 1996—99; assoc. prof. pediatrics Weill Med. Coll.-Cornell U., NY, 1999. Co-chair of internat. study to evaluate the effectiveness of chemotherapy for the treatment of children with osteosarcoma, co-investigator clin. trial that evaluates a novel combination of chemotherapy agents & radiotherapy techniques for the treatment of children with rhabdomyosarcoma, Meml. Sloan-Kettering. Med. editl. adv. bd. Libby Shriver Sarcoma Initiative. Named one of Medical Marvels, New York Mag., 2006. Office: Dept Pediatrics #210 Meml Sloan Kettering Cancer Ctr 1275 York Ave New York NY 10021 Office Phone: 212-639-7990. Business E-Mail: wexlerl@mskcc.org.

WEXLER, NANCY SABIN, clinical neuropsychology educator; b. Washington, July 19, 1945; d. Milton and Leonore Wexler. AB cum laude, Radcliffe Coll., 1967; PhD in Clin. Psychology, U. Mich., 1974; DHL (hon.), NY Med. Coll., 1991; DSc (hon.), U. Mich., 1991. Lic. psychologist, N.Y. Psychol. intern, teaching fellow U. Mich., 1968-74; asst. prof. psychology grad. faculty New Sch. Social Rsch., NYC, 1974-76; pvt. practice psychology NYC, 1974-76; health sci. adminstr. Nat. Inst. Neurol., Comm. Disorders and Stroke, NIH, 1978-83; pres. Hereditary Disease Found., Santa Monica, Calif., 1983—; prof. neurology & psychology Coll. Phys. and Surgeons, Columbia U., NYC, 1985-92, Higgins prof. clin. neuropsychology, 1992—. Mem. Ctr. for Brain and Behavior Coll. Phys. and Surgeons of Columbia U., 1985; mem. adv. com. Human Genome Ctr., Lawrence Berkeley Labs. and U. Calif., 1988—; mem. external adv. com. Ctr. for Human Genome Studies, Los Alamos Nat. Labs., 1990-; co-chairperson ethical, legal and social issues com. Human Genome Orgn., 1991—, mem. dir. search Nat. Ctr. for Human Genome Rsch., NIH, 1992; chairperson Joint NIH/Dept. of Energy Ethical, Legal, Social Issues Working Group on Human Genome, 1989-; chair, Ethics Working Group, Human Genome Project. Contbr. articles to profl. jours. Trustee Nat. Huntington's Disease Assn., 1983-85, Marine Biol. Lab., 1984-86, Eleanor Roosevelt Inst. Cancer Rsch., 1985-91, Found. for Care and Cure of Huntington's Disease, 1988-. Fulbright scholar U. West Indies, Jamaica, 1967-68; fellow The Hastings Ctr., 1990—; recipient award Robert J. and Claire Pasarow Found., 1987, Living Legacy award Women's Internat. Soc., 1988, Alumnae Athena award Alumnae Coun. U. Mich., 1989, award Gov.'s Office, Zulia, Venezuela, 1989, Venezuelan Presdl. award, 1990, Legis. Commendation N.Y. State, 1990, Disting. Svc. award Nat. Assn. Biology Tchrs., 1993, Foster Elting Bennett award, 1993, Nat. Med. Rsch. award Nat. Health Coun., 1993, Albert Lasker Pub. Svc. award, 1993, Benjamin Franklin medal in Life Sciences, Franklin Inst., 2007. Mem. AAAS (bd. dirs. 1993—), APA, Am. Soc. Law and Medicine, Soc. Neurosci. (chairperson social issues com. 1988-90, organizing com. Neurobiology of Human Diesease Workshop 1980—), Am. Psychol. Soc., Am. Soc. Human Genetics, World Fedn. Nuerology, Rsch. Group on Huntington's Disease, Am. Neurol. Assn., Inst. Medicine (coun. mem.). Achievements include discovery of the gene responsible for Huntington's Disease. Office: Columbia U Coll Phys & Surg NY State Psychiat Inst 1051 Riverside Dr Rm 371 Unit 6 New York NY 10032-1013 also: Hereditary Disease Found 6th fl 3960 Broadway New York NY 10032 Office Phone: 212-543-5667. Office Fax: 212-543-6002. Business E-Mail: nancywexler@hdfoundation.org. E-mail: wexlern@pi.cpmc.columbia.edu. *

WEXLER, PATRICIA SUSAN, dermatologist, surgeon; b. Bronx, NY, Oct. 26, 1951; m. Eugene Wexler; children: Perri, Jane. MD, U. Libre de Bruxelles, Belgium, 1979. Diplomate Am. Bd. Internal Medicine 1983, Am. Bd. Dermatology 1986. Intern Beth Israel Med. Ctr., N.Y.C., 1979—80, resident in internal medicine, 1980—82, fellow in infectious disease, 1982—83, attending physician, Mt. Sinai Hosp., N.Y.C.; private practice Wexler Dermatology, N.Y.C. Assoc. clin. prof. dept. dermatology Mt. Sinai Med. Ctr., N.Y.C.; cons. in devel. of several skin care and make-up lines. Author medical rsch. publs. Recipient Am. Acad. Cosmetic Surgery award for Excellence in Cosmetic Surgery. Fellow: Am. Soc. Dermatologic Surgery. Office: 145 E 32nd St 7th Fl New York NY 10016-6055 Office Phone: 212-684-2626. E-mail: crespi666@aol.com.

WEYLANDT, KARSTEN HENRICH, internist; b. Hamburg, Germany, July 26, 1973; s. Joachim Heinrich and Brigitte Weylandt. MD, U. Heidelberg, Germany, 1997; DPhil, Oxford U., 2000. Rschr. Mass. Gen. Hosp. and Harvard Med. Sch., Boston, 1995—96, Hammersmith Hosp., London, 1999—2000; physician Kantonsspital, Basel, Switzerland, 2001, Charité U. Hosp., Berlin, 2002—; instr. medicine Harvard Med. Sch., 2008; rsch. fellow Mass. Gen. Hosp., 2008; MSD Oncology scholar, 2008; Wesner-Creutzfeldt scholar, 2008. Author: (internal medicine handbook) DDInnere. With German Mil., 1992—93. Scholar, German Nat. Scholarship Found., 1994-1999, German Academic Exch. Svc., 1997-1998; Marie-Curie Rsch. Fellow, European Union, 1998-2000. Mem.: German-Israelis Soc., German Soc. for Digestive and Metabolic Diseases, Endocrine Soc., European Affairs Soc. Lutheran. Avocations: reading, tennis. Office: Charité U Hosp Augustenburger Platz 1 Berlin D-13353 Germany Business E-Mail: karsten.weylandt@charite.de.

WHANG, KWANGYOUN, nutritionist, educator; MSc, Ohio State U., Columbus, 1988; PhD, U. Ill., Urbana-Champaign, 1995. Mgr. Am. Soybean Assn., Seoul, Republic of Korea, 1988—91; Swine rsch. mgr. Mark II Plan, Indpls., 1995—98; prof. Korea U., Seoul, 1998—. Mem.: Am. Soc. Animal Sci. Office: Korea Univ Anam-dong Seongbuk-Gu Seoul 136-713 Republic of Korea Office Fax: 82-2-3290-3499. Business E-Mail: kwhang@korea.ac.kr.

WHANG, MATTHEW IHN SEONG, urologist; b. Seoul, Republic of Korea, June 28, 1960; s. Mike Dae Yun and Ok Joo Whang; m. Margaret K. Nam, June 18, 1988; children: Dana Youngha, Nicole Yoonha, Michael Joonha. BA in Biochemistry, Duke U., 1983; MD, Columbia U., NYC, 1987. Diplomate Am. Bd. Urology, 1995. Surgery resident Columbia Presbyn. Med. Ctr., 1987—89, urology resident, 1989—93; physician Physicians in Urology, Livingston, NJ, 1993—99; pres. Modern Urology, West Orange, NJ, 2000—. Dir. transplant urology St. Barnabas Med. Ctr., Livingston, NJ, 1999—. Contbr. articles to profl. jours., chapters to books. Fellow: ACS; mem.: Assn. Korean Am. Med. Graduates (v.p. 1997—99, pres. 1999—2001), Korean AMA (chmn. membership com. 1998—99, chmn. sci. and edn. com. 1999—2000, sec. gen. 2000—02, exec. v.p. 2002—04). Roman Catholic. Avocation: golf. Office: Modern Urology 1001 Pleasant Valley Way West Orange NJ 07052 Personal E-mail: matthewmd@msn.com.

WHANG, SUKOO JACK, pathologist, microbiologist; b. Seoul, South Korea, Feb. 3, 1934; arrived in U.S., 1963, naturalized; m. Chung A. Park, Nov. 30, 1963; children: Selena, Stephanie, John. BS, Oreg. State U., 1957; MS, UCLA, 1960, PhD, 1963; MD, Korea U., Seoul, 1972. Diplomate Am. Bd. Tropical Medicine, Am. Bd. Forensic Medicine, Am. Bd. Pathology, Am. Bd. Med. Microbiology. Intern Good Samaritan Hosp., Dayton, Ohio, 1973—74; resident White Meml. Med. Ctr., L.A., 1974—77, clin. pathologist, 1977—90, chmn. infection control com., 1977—87, dir. Sch. Med. Tech., 1977—87; dep. med. examiner L.A. County Coroner's Dept., LA, 1991—2000. Recipient Physician's Recognition award, AMA, 1980—. Fellow: ACP, Coll. Am. Pathologists (Pathology Continuing Med. Edn. award 1984—), Am. Coll. Forensic Medicine, Am. Coll. Tropical Medicine, Am. Soc. Clin. Pathologists. Republican. Seventh Day Adventist. Avocations: swimming, reading. Home: 1325 Via Del Rey South Pasadena CA 91030

WHANG, WILLIAM, cardiologist; MD, Columbia U. Coll. Physicians & Surgeons. Cert. cardiovascular disease, clinical cardiac electrophysiology. Intern & resident Columbia U. Med. Ctr.; fellow Mass. Gen. Hosp.; cardiologist NY-Presbyterian Hosp. Office: 622 W 168th St New York NY 10032 Office Phone: 212-305-8559. Office Fax: 212-305-3137.

WHARTON, RALPH NATHANIEL, psychiatrist, educator; b. Boston, June 15, 1932; s. Nathaniel Philip and Deeda (Levine) W.; children: Naida, Philip, Laura. AB cum laude, Harvard U., 1953; MD, Columbia U., 1957, degree in psychoanalysis, 1970. Cert. Neurology and Psychiatry 1969. Intern Cornell divsn. Bellevue Hosp., NYC, 1957—58; resident Columbia-Presbyn. Med. Ctr., 1961—64; pvt. practice psychiatry/pharm., 1964—; assoc. psychiatry Coll. Physicians and Surgeons, 1964—69, asst. prof. clin. psychiatry, 1969—72, assoc. prof., 1972—83, prof., 1984—; sr. rsch. psychiatrist NY State Psychiat. Inst., 1964—70; assoc. attending psychiatry Columbia-Presbyn. Hosp., 1970—80, attending psychiatrist, 1980—; sr. cons. supr. psychiatric svc. NY Presbyteriuan Hosp. Ex-officio mem. bd. trustees Columbia-Presbyn. Med. Ctr., pres. soc. practitioners, 1980—82, attending, 1984—; exec. dir. Wharton Fund for Brain Rsch.; med. dir. Black Sea project Macalester Coll., 1994—98; co-dir. Reiner for Behaviour and Psychosomatic Rsch. and Tchg. Columbia U. Med. Ctr., 2004—; exec. dir. Wharton Fund Brain Rsch., 1993—; co dir. Reiner Ctr. Psychosomatic Medicine, Columbia Med. Ctr. Author: Landmark Papers, Lithium Carbonate for Affective Disorders, 1966; contbr. Mood and Anxiety chapters, Merritt's Textbook of Neurology, 2005, 08, AARP chapter, Art of Aging, 2006, numerous papers, publs. in profl. jours. and chpts. to books. Mem. alumni campaign com. Coll. Physicians and Surgeons, Columbia U., 2001—. Served to Capt. M.C., US Army, 1958-60, US Army Hosp. Orleans, France, 1960-61 Capt. med. corp US Army, 1958—60. Recipient NIH Obama Basin Rsch. award, 2008—11; named Disting. Practitioner of Yr., Columbia U. Med. Ctr., Soc. Practitioners, 2010; named one of Best Drs., NY Mag. Fellow: Am. Coll. Psychoanalysts (pres. 1996, bd. dirs. 1996—), NY Acad. Medicine, Am. Psychiat. Assn. (life Hon. Life fellow 2002); mem.: AMA, Group for Advancement Psychiatry, Internat. Assn. Study of Pain (founding mem.), Royal Soc. Medicine, Soc. Practitioners (exec. com. 1990—), Harmonie Club, Harvard Club (class agent 1953—), Salon de Virtuosi (founding bd. mem. 1991—, treas. 1991—), Lotos Club. Achievements include sponsor of Wharton Professorship in Psychiatry at Columbia U. Health Ctr., 2008. Avocations: skiing, sailing, literature. Office: Columbia-Presbyn Med Ctr Atchley Pavilion Ste 209 161 Ft Washington Ave New York NY 10032-3713 Office Phone: 212-860-2666. Business E-Mail: rnw1@columbia.edu.

WHAYNE, THOMAS FRENCH, JR., cardiologist, educator; b. Ft. Leavenworth, Kans., Aug. 25, 1937; s. Thomas French and Mary Lutenia (Porter) W.; m. Eugenia McDonald Ingram, June 22, 1963; children: Thomas French III, James Givens, Katherine Ingram. AB in Chemistry, U. Pa., 1959, MD, 1963; PhD in Biochemistry, U. Calif., San Francisco, 1970. Cert. Am. Bd. Internal Medicine, 1972, in cardiovasc. disease Am. Bd. Internal Medicine, 1974. Intern in medicine The N.Y. Hosp., 1963-64, resident in medicine, 1964-66; fellow in cardiovascular disease Cardiovascular Rsch. Inst., San Francisco, 1966-69, U. Toronto, Ontario, Can., 1969-70; asst. prof. medicine Ohio State U., Columbus, 1970-72; assoc. prof. medicine U. Okla., Oklahoma City, 1972-77; clin. prof. medicine U. Ky., Lexington, 1977-98, prof. medicine cardiovascular medicine, 1998—. Assoc. mem. Okla. Med. Rsch. Found., 1972-77; staff cardiologist Lexington Clinic, 1977-98; lectr., presenter in field, Spanish presentations in Spanish speaking countries. Contbr. abstracts, chapters to books, articles to profl. jours., multiple articles in Spanish. Supporter U. Ky. Dept. Hispanic Studies, Gill Heart Inst., U. Pa. Undergrad. Sch., U. Pa. Sch. Medicine, U. Pa. Rowing, Vesper Boat Club Phila. With med. corps. USAR, 1963—72. Named Man of Yr., Okla. Heart Assn., 1975—76. Fellow: ACP, Internat. Coll. Angiology, Coll. Physicians of Phila., Am. Heart Assn., Am. Coll. Cardiology; mem.: Vesper Boat Club, Rotary. Presbyterian. Avocations: Spanish language, golf, scuba diving, photography. Office: Divsn Cardiovascular Medicine 326 Wethington Bldg 900 S Limestone Lexington KY 40536-0200 Office Phone: 859-323-3705.

WHEAT, MYRON WILLIAM, JR., cardiothoracic surgeon; b. Sapulpa, Okla., Mar. 24, 1924; s. Myron William and Mary Lee (Hudiburg) W.; m. Erlene Adele Plank, June 12, 1949 (div. June 1970); children: Penelope Louise, Myron William III, Pamela Lynn, Douglas Plank; m. Carol Ann Karmgard, June 18, 1970 (div. Apr. 1996); 1 child, Christopher West. AB, Washington U., St. Louis, 1949; MD cum laude, Washington U., 1951. Diplomate Am. Bd. Surgery, Am. Bd. Thoracic Surgery. Instr., clin. fellow Washington U., St. Louis, 1956—58; asst. prof. surgery U. Fla., Gainesville, 1958—65, prof. surgery, 1965—72; dir. profl. svcs., chief clin. physician U. Fla. Shands Tchg. Hosp., Gainesville, 1968—72; prof. surgery, dir. thoracic and cardiothoracic surgery U. Louisville Sch. Medicine, 1972—75, clin. prof. surgery, 1975—; cardiothoracic surgeon Cardiac Surg. Assocs., P.A., St. Petersburg, Fla., 1975—91; cons., thoracic surgery Bay Pine VA Hosp., St. Petersburg, 1994—; clin. prof. surgery U. So. Fla. Sch. Medicine, Tampa, 1995—; cardiothoracic surgeon Cardiac Surg. Assocs., P.A., Clearwater, Fla., 1991—. Clin. prof. surgery U. South Fla., 1995—; cons. Bay Pines VA Hosp., St. Petersburg, 1991—; mem. Am. Bd. Thoracic Surgery, 1969-75 Author (with others) 18 books; mem. editl. bd. Am. Heart Jour., 1971; contbr. over 100 articles to profl. jours.; developed drug therapy for acute dissecting aneurysms of the aorta 1st lt. USAF, 1943-46, ETO Decorated DFC Air medal (4), Presdl. Citation; named First Howard W. Lillenthal Meml. lectr. Mt. Sinai Hosp., 1963. Fellow ACS (gov.), Am. Coll. Cardiology (chmn. bd. govs. 1968-69); mem. Am. Surg. Assn., Am. Assn. Thoracic Surgery (sec. 1972-78), So. Surg. Assn., So. Thoracic Surg. Assn., Soc. Thoracic Surgeons, Soc. Thoracic Surgeons Gr. Britain and Ireland, Alpha Omega Alpha Republican. Home and Office: 8413 SW 55th Pk Gainesville FL 32608 Personal E-mail: myronwheat@msn.com.

WHEATLEY, CHARLES HENRY, III, information technology executive; b. Balt., Aug. 11, 1932; s. Charles Henry Jr. and Rebecca W. (Cloud) Wheatley; m. Charlotte Beryl Davis, June 11, 1955; children: Charles H. IV, Craig A., Cheryl L.W. Wilhelm. BA in Polit. Sci. (hon.), Western Md. Coll., 1954; JD (hon.), U. Md., 1959. Bar: Md. 1960, DC 1981, US Supreme Ct. 1964. Tchr. Carroll County Pub. Sch., Westminster, Md., 1955-56; officer, missiles, judge adv. U.S. Army, 1957-62; law clk. assoc. judge William R. Horney Md. Ct. Appeals, Annapolis, 1959-60; pvt. practice Md. and Washington, 1960—; mem. Md. Ho. of Del., Annapolis, Md., 1962-66; pres., COO, advisor corp. rels., dir. Cell Works, Inc., Balt., 1997—2002; cons. mktg. govt. CCC Diagnostics LLC, 2004—. SOI Assoc., real estate, ins. exec. AID Realty & Ins. Co., Balt., 1960—; adj. coll. instr. Western Md. Coll., Westminster, 1963-65, Villa Julie Coll., 1980-86, Balt. C.C., 1966-72, Caroll C.C., 2002—; chmn. bd., CEO Regional Mfg. Inst., Balt., 1993-96; nat. del. White House Conf. on Small Bus., Washington, 1985; pres. Fish Am., Inc., 1990—, Replex, Inc., 1986—, Life, Inc., 1994—; spkr. in field. Contbr., editor: (weekly newspaper) Maryland Teacher, 1974-77; guest News Makers program WJZ-TV, 1985; contbr. articles to profl. jours. Md. del. Md. State Constitutional Conv., Annapolis, 1967-68; councilman Balt. City Coun., 1971-74; trustee Balt. County Gen. Howp., 1963-65; chmn. Carroll County Com. Aging, Md., 2005-, Carroll County Bd. Zoning Appeals, 2006-. 1st lt. Missile Brigade, JAG US Army, 1957—62. Received Cell Works Co. Computerworld-Smithsonian Science Innovation laureate award, 1999. Mem.: Carroll County Bar Assn., Md. State Tchrs. Assn. (exec. sec. 1974—77), Supreme Ct. Bar, Dist. Columbia Bar Assn., Md. State Bar Assn., Md. Commn. Mfg. Competitiveness, Phi Beta Kappa, Order of Coif, Pi Gamma Mu. Methodist. Avocations: education, music, writing, photography, health. Office: 707 Wheatley Dr Westminster MD 21157 Office Phone: 410-871-1112. Personal E-mail: lifeinc@earthlink.net.

WHEELER, BEVERLY B., cardiology and cardiothoracic clinical nurse specialist; b. St. Stephens, NB, Can., Nov. 9, 1946; parents Am. citizens; d. Robert George and Elizabeth B. (Rideout) Barnes; m. Wylie Thompson; children: Jeffrey, Tami. AA, Mohegan C.C., Norwich, Conn., 1981; BSN in Gerontology, George Mason U., Fairfax, Va., 1989, MSN, 1991; postgrad., Mich. State U., 1999. RN, Tex.; cert. and registered clin. nurse specialist, Va.; cert. ACLS. Various civilian adminstrv. positions U.S. Navy, Groton, Conn., Arlington, Va., 1974-87; vis. nurse Comprehensive Health Agy., Springfield, Va., 1984-86; nursing agy. pers. SRT Med.-Staff Internat., Springfield, 1982-88; legal asst. Office of Asst. Sec. of Navy for Rsch., Engring. and Sys., Washington, 1987-89; staff nurse Arlington Hosp., 1986-90, Fairfax Hosp., Falls Church, Va., 1991—2006; cardiology/cardiothoracic surgery clin. nurse specialist Nat. Naval Med. Ctr., Bethesda, Md., 1989—2006; clin. inst. U. Tex. Health Sci. Ctr., Sch. Nursing, San Antonio, 2008—. Mem. test devel. com. Am. Nurses Credetialing Ctr., 1996-99; textbook cons., 1994-2004; legal cons. and expert witness; rschr. in field; adj. clin. nursing instr. Marymount U., Arlington, Va., 2000-06. Contbr. articles to profl. nursing jours. Vol. Am. Heart Assn., 1994—2002. Mem. ANA, NAFE, ANCC, Tex. Nurses Assn., Am. Heart Assn. Episcopalian. Avocations: aerobics, reading, gardening, crocheting. Personal E-mail: beverly.wylie@sbcglobal.net. Business E-Mail: wheelerb3@uthscsa.edu.

WHEELER, CASS (M. CASS. WHEELER), healthcare consultant, former health science association administrator; b. Tex. BA in Bus., U. Texas, Austin, 1963. Stockbroker NY Stock Exch. firm, Dallas, 1969—73; with Am. Heart Assn., Austin, Tex., 1973—82, COO Dallas, 1982—96, sr. v.p., field ops., 1996—97, CEO, 1997—2008, ret., 2008. Guest lectr. Harvard U. Sch. Bus. & Pub. Health, U. Texas Sch. Mgmt., Dallas, U. Texas Lyndon B. Johnson Sch. Pub. Affairs, Austin; former bd. chmn. Nat. Health Coun.; bd. mem. Partnership for Prevention, Research! America, Nat. Ctr. Tobacco-Free Kids, Nat. Assembly Health & Human Svc. Organizations; advisory bd. mem. Discovery Health Media, Inc.; former mem. President's Commn. Improving Econ. Opportunity in Communities Dependent on Tobacco Production While Protecting Pub. Health; bd. dirs. Am. Legacy Found. Avocations: running, skiing, bicycling.

WHEELER, HEWITT BROWNELL, surgeon, educator; b. Louisville, July 21, 1929; s. Arville and Lois (Vance) W.; m. Elizabeth Jane Maxwell, July 21, 1956; children: Stephen, Elizabeth, Jane, Mary. Student, Vanderbilt U., 1945-48; MD, Harvard U., 1952. Diplomate Am. Bd. Surgery (bd. dirs. 1984-90). Cushing fellow Harvard Med. Sch., Boston, 1953, Peters fellow, 1956, research fellow, 1959-60, instr. surgery, 1961-64, clin. assoc. surgery, 1964-67, asst. clin. prof. surgery, 1967-70, assoc. prof. surgery, 1970-71; asst. in surgery Peter Bent Brigham Hosp., Boston, 1959-60, jr. assoc. surgery, 1961-64, assoc. surgery, 1964-69, sr. assoc. surgery, 1969-71; asst. chief surgery Roxbury VA Hosp., Boston, 1961-62, chief surgery, 1962-71, chief of staff, 1968-71; cons. surgery U. Mass. Med. Sch., Worcester, 1966-71; prof., chmn. dept. surgery U. Mass. Med. Sch. at Worcester, 1971-96, Harry M. Haidak disting. prof. surgery, 1985-98, prof. emeritus, 1998—; chief staff U. Mass. Hosp., 1974-76, surgeon-in-chief, 1976-96; exec. dir. Ctr. for Advanced Clin. Tech., 1995—; affiliate prof. biomed. engring. Worcester Poly. Inst., 1974—; lectr. surgery Harvard Med. Sch., 1974-96; chief surgery St. Vincent Hosp., Worcester, 1971-75. Cons. Meml. Hosp., Worcester City Hosp., 1970-96, Worcester Hahnemann Hosp., 1974-94, Peter Bent Brigham Hosp., 1973-96; chmn. surg. research program com. VA, Washington, 1965-67, nat. participant surg. cons., 1965-69, chmn. ad hoc adv. com. surgery, 1969-71. Pres. Mass. Compassionate Care Coalition, 2000—04; trustee Ctrl. Mass. Health Care Found., 1975—77, Worcester Found. for Biomed. Rsch., 1996—2004, Hospice Ctrl. Mass. Inc., 1997—2000, U. Mass. Meml. Found., 1998—2005, Boston Med. Libr., 1996—2002. 1st lt. M.C. AUS, 1953—55. Mem. ACS (bd. govs. 1984-90, coun. Mass. chpt. 1973-76, pres. 1980), AAAS, AMA, Am. Surg. Assn., Soc. Univ. Surgeons, Internat. Cardiovascular Soc., New Eng. Surg. Soc. (treas. 1977-84, v.p. 1986-87, pres. 1989-91), Boston Surg. Soc. (pres. 1995-96), Worcester Surg. Soc. (pres. 1973-75), Transplantation Soc., Mass. Med. Soc. (100th Shattuck lectr. 1990; lifetime achievement award 2005), Worcester Dist. Med. Soc. (sec. 1996-99, v.p. 1999-00, pres. 2000-01), New Eng. Vascular Soc. (v.p. 1985-86, pres. 1988-89). Achievements include rsch. in exptl. transplantation, blood vessel surgery, method to detect blood clots, improving end-of-life care. Home: 52 Cloyster Rd South Portland ME 04106-5110 E-mail: bwheele1@maine.rr.com.

WHEELER, JOHN S., JR., urologist; s. John S. Wheeler Sr. and Virginia S. Wheeler; m. Michele A. Marganski, June 4, 1977; children: Nicholas, Anne. BA, Dartmouth Coll., 1972; MD, Georgetown U., 1977. Lic. physician Ill., cert. Mass. Resident gen. surgery Boston Med. Ctr., 1977—79, resident urology, 1979—82, urodynamics fellowship, 1983; faculty Loyola U. Med. Ctr., Maywood, Ill., 1983—; staff urologist Hines VA Hosp., 1983—, RML Hosp., Hinsdale, 2003—. Cons. in field. Contbr. articles to profl. jours., chapters to books. Fellow, Boston U. Med. Ctr., 1982—83. Mem.: Am. Paraplegia Soc. (rsch. com. 1984—), Am. Coll. Surgeons, Am. Urological Assn., Alpha Omega Alpha. Roman Catholic. Avocations: golf, skiing. Office: Loyola U Med Ctr Dept Urology 2160 S First Ave Maywood IL 60153 Office Phone: 708-216-4076. Business E-Mail: jwheeler@lumc.edu. *

WHEELER, ROBERT CHANNING, JR., health maintenance organization executive; b. Evanston, Ill., Mar. 4, 1952; s. Robert Channing Wheeler and Mary M. (Whitmire) Brown; m. Elizabeth Joan Mellor, (div. 2001); children: Joy Carolyn, Anne Miriam; m. Leslle Quint Eisen 10,2001. BA, BS, Stanford U., 1977, MA, 1978; MBA, UCLA, 1983. Program assoc. Community Cancer Control L.A., 1979-80; dir. prevention UCLA Cancer Ctr., Westood, 1980-83; sr. staff mgr. FHP Inc., Fountain Valley, Calif., 1983-84; dir. provider rels. Maxicare Health Plans, LA, 1984-85, v.p., exec. dir., 1985-86, regional v.p., 1987—89; various executive positions CIGNA Healthcare, 1989—94; CEO UnitedHealth Group (Northeast Region), 1995—98, Uniprise (sub. UnitedHealth group), 1998—2004; exec. v.p. United Health Group, 2004—05; commercial dir. gen. health Whitehall, London, 2007—08; commercial dir. gen. dept. health Nat. Health Svc., England, 2007—08. Avocations: scuba diving, sailing. Home: 11 Surf Rd Westport CT 06880 Office Phone: 203-247-2893. Personal E-mail: cwheel9999@aol.com, chanwheeler@aol.com.

WHELAN, ALISON JEAN, clinical geneticist, educator; MD, Wash. U., St. Louis, Mo., 1986. Diplomate Am. Bd. Internal Medicine, 1989, cert. Am. Bd. Clin. Genetics-Med. Genetics, 2010. Intern Barnes Jewish Hosp., 1988, resident internal medicine, 1987—89; fellow rsch. Wash. Univ., 1989—91, resident pediat., 1992—94, fellow clin. genetics, 1993—94, prof. medicine; fellow St. Louis Children's Hosp.; hosp. affiliation includes Siteman Cancer Ctr., Barnes Jewish Hosp., St. Louis Children's Hosp. Office: Saint Louis Children's Hospital Center for Advance Medicine 4921 Parkview Pl Ste 5C Saint Louis MO 63110 Office Phone: 314-454-6093.

WHELAN, RICHARD L., colon and rectal surgeon, educator; MD, Columbia U., NY, 1982. Diplomate Am. Bd. Colon and Rectal Surgery, 1989. Resident in gen. surgery NY Presbyn. Med. Ctr., 1983—87; fellow in colon and rectal surgery Univ. Minn., 1987—88; prof. surgery College of Physicians and Surgeons Columbia Univ.; chief colon and rectal surgery NY Presbyn. Hosp./Columbia Univ. Med. Ctr., assoc. dir. surgical oncology, 2007—09; chief colon and rectal surgery svc. St. Luke's Roosevelt Hosp., NY, dir. basics sci. and clin. rsch. lab., 1996—, chief surgical oncology, 2009—. Author: various publs. Named Patients Choice; named one of Best Doctors in NY, America's Top Doctor, Top Doctor for Cancer. Mem.: Soc. for Surgery of the Alimentary Tract, Soc. Am. Gastrointestinal Endoscopic Surgeons (bd. govs.), NY Soc. Colon and Rectal Surgeons (pres. 2004—06), Am. Soc. Colon and Rectal Surgeons. Office: St Lukes Roosevelt Hospital 425 W 59th St Ste 7B New York NY 10019 Office Phone: 212-523-8172.

WHERRY, DAVID COLWELL, surgeon, educator; b. Pawnee City, Nebr., Dec. 18, 1926; MD, George Washington U., 1952. Diplomate Am. Bd. Surgery. Intern George Washington U. Hosp., Washington, 1952-53; surg. resident Mount Alto VA Hosp., Washington, 1953-54, 56-59. Prof. surgery Uniformed Svcs. U. Health Scis., 1991—; clin. prof. surgery George Washington U., 1991—, clin. prof. surgery Georgetown U., 2002. Fellow ACS, Royal Coll. Surgeons (Eng.); mem. Royal Soc. Medicine. Office Phone: 301-295-3155. Personal E-mail: cenya.wherry@aol.com. *

WHIDDEN, ROBERT LEE, JR., healthcare consultant; b. Beverly, Mass., Oct. 10, 1943; s. Robert Lee and Phyllis Alma (Patch) W.; m. Lois Ann Lapeza, Mar. 4, 1972. AB in English, Harvard U., 1965. Div. dir. Lowell (Mass.) Gen. Hosp., 1970-75; asst. adminstr. Union Hosp., Lynn, Mass., 1975-85; pres. Surgi/1 div., 1984-86, R.L. Whidden and Co., Andover, Mass., 1986—, Query, Andover, Mass., 1986—. Prin. cons. Charlton Meml. Hosp., Fall River, Mass., 1987—, Boston Regional Med. Ctr., Stoneham, Mass., 1988—; hosp. rep. delegated rev. com. Eastern Mass. Profl. Standards Rev. Orgn., bd. dirs., 1984—; ex-officio mem. Integrated Data Demonstration Grant Com. Blue Cross Mass., 1982—; health care advisor Govt. of Anguilla, Brit. West Indies, 1989-91; cons. health affairs Brit. Dept. Territories, 1990-93; bd. dirs. Lowell Area Continuing Edn. Ctr., Nat. Found. Environ. Control, 1971, Hospice of North Shore, Inc.; bd. dirs., chmn. Northshore Manpower Coalition; corp. edn. adv. bd. North Shore C.C., 1981—; mem. North Shore Econ. Coun., 1981—; mem. Mass. Health Data Adv. Coun. Nat. Merit scholar, 1960-61; named to Hon. Order Ky. Cols. Fellow Am. Coll. Health Care Execs. (life); mem. Mass. Hosp. Assn. (life; program rev. com. 1982—, chmn. mgmt. com. 1984—, facilities and svc. com. class of 1987), New Eng. Hosp. Assembly, Am. Soc. Law and Medicine, Health Care Mgmt. Assn., Am. Mgmt. Assn., Order Paul Revere Patriots, Phi Beta Kappa, Myopia Polo Club (patron), Hasty Pudding Club, Andover Tennis Club. Episcopalian. Home and Office: 3 Spruce Cir Andover MA 01810-4020 Home Phone: 978-470-1230. Personal E-mail: rwhidden@aol.com.

WHIFFEN, JAMES DOUGLASS, surgeon, educator; b. NYC, Jan. 16, 1931; s. John Phillips and Lorna Elizabeth (Douglass) W.; child from a previous marriage, Gregory James; m. Sally Vilas Runge, Aug. 21, 1993. BS, U. Wis., 1952, MD, 1955. Diplomate: Am. Bd. Surgery. Intern Ohio State U. Hosp., 1955-56; resident U. Wis. Hosp., 1956-57, 59-61; instr. dept. surgery U. Wis. Med. Sch., 1962-64, asst. prof., 1964-67, asso. prof., 1967-71, prof., 1971-96, vice chmn. dept., 1970-72, acting chmn., 1972-74; asst. dean Med. Sch., 1975-96; prof. emeritus U. Wis. Med. Sch., 1996—; mem. exam. council State of Wis. Emergency Med. Services, 1974-77. Bd. dirs. Wis. Heart Assn. Served to lt. comdr. USNR, 1957-59. John and Mary R. Markle scholar in acad. medicine, also; Research Career Devel. award NIH, 1965-75 Fellow A.C.S., Am. Soc. Artificial Internal Organs. Clubs: Maple Bluff Country, Achievements include research publs. on biomaterials, thrombo-resistant surfaces and the physiology of heart-lung bypass procedures. Home: 17 Cambridge Ct Madison WI 53704-5906 Office: 600 Highland Ave Madison WI 53792-0001 E-mail: jwhiffen@wisc.edu.

WHINERY, MICHAEL ALBERT, physician; b. Herts Watsford, Eng., June 30, 1951; s. Leo Howard and Doris Eileene Whinery and Alma Piper; m. Tatijana Dunnebier, 1976 (dec. Jan. 1981); m. Judy Renee Wright, Apr. 30, 1982; children: Rhiannon Daire Eileene, Terron Rae Lee. BS, Okla. U., 1976; D of Osteopathy, Okla. State U., 1980. Diplomate Am. Bd. Family Practice. Intern Hillcrest Health Ctr., Oklahoma City, 1980-81; with McLoud Clinic, McLoud, Okla., 1981-98; staff physician Okla. Vets. Ctr., Claremore, 2000—. House physician McLoud Nursing Ctr., 1988—; med. examiner Pottawatomie County Health, McLoud, 1983--. Author: Poetic Voices of America, 1991; composer lyrics and music at Stella Gospel Rec. Studio, 2000, A Soldier Last Prayer. Mem. Presdl. Order Merit Nat. Repub. Senatorial Com., Washington, 1991, Presdl. Task Force, 1983—, Senatorial Commn. Repub. Senatorial Inner Circle, Washington, 1991; mem. U.S. Congrl. Adv. Bd., 1993. Served with USMC, Vietnam era. Recipient Acknowledgement of Outstanding Contbn. in Clin. Rsch. award SANDOZ Labs., 1992, Rep. Presdl. Legion of Merit, 1994, Rep. Majority medal, U.S. Senate, 1997, Rep. Task Force medal of merit, 1997. Mem. Am. Legion, C. of C., Jr. C. of C., U.S. Senatorial Club (preferred mem.), U.S. Congressional Act Bd. (state advisor 1990-91). Baptist. Avocations: fishing, music, composing songs, poetry and writing lyrics. Office: PO Box 2745 3001 W Bluestarr Claremore OK 74018-2745 Office Phone: 918-342-5432 ext. 217. Business E-Mail: mwhinery@odva.state.ok.us.

WHISNANT, JACK PAGE, neurologist; b. Little Rock, Oct. 26, 1924; s. John Clifton and Zula I. (Page) W.; m. Patricia Anne Rimmey, May 12, 1944; children: Elizabeth Anne, John David, James Michael. BS, U. Ark., 1948, MD, 1951; MS, U. Minn., 1955; MD (hon.), U. Edinburgh, Scotland, 1996. Intern Balt. City Hosp., 1951-52; resident in medicine and neurology Mayo Grad. Sch. Medicine, Rochester, Minn., 1952-55, instr. neurology, 1956-60, asst. prof., 1960-64, asso. prof., 1964-69, prof., 1969—; Meyer prof. neurosci. Mayo Med. Sch.; chmn. dept. neurology Mayo Clinic, Mayo Med. Sch., Mayo Grad. Sch. Medicine, 1971-81; chmn. dept. health scis. research Mayo Clinic and Mayo Med. Sch., 1987-93. Cons. neurology Mayo Clinic, 1955-96, head sect. neurology, 1963-71; dir. Mayo Cerebrovascular Clin. Rsch. Ctr., 1975-96. Contbr. articles on neurology and cerebrovascular disease to med. jours. Trustee YMCA, Rochester, pres.,

1977. With USAAF, 1942-45. Decorated Air medal. NIH grantee, 1959-96. Fellow Am. Heart Assn., Am. Acad. Neurology (pres. 1993-95); mem. AMA, Am. Neurol. Assn. (pres. 1981-82), Am. Bd. Psychiatry and Neurology (bd. dirs. 1983-90, pres. 1989), Zumbro Valley Med. Soc., Minn. Med. Assn., Minn. Soc. Neurol. Scis., Ctrl. Soc. Neurol. Rsch. (pres. 1964), Alumni Assn. Mayo Found. (Disting. Alumnus award 2003). Presbyterian. Office: Mayo Clinic Dept Health Scis Rsch 200 1st St SW Rochester MN 55905-0001 Home: 211 2nd St NW Apt 716 Rochester MN 55901-2813 Personal E-mail: whisnant24@charter.net. Business E-Mail: whisnant@mayo.edu.

WHITAKER, CHERYL RUCKER, healthcare company executive; b. July 18, 1967; BS in Biology, Emory U., 1989; MD, Washington U. Sch. Med., 1993; MPH, Harvard U. Sch. Pub. Health, 1995. Intern Stanford Univ. Hosp., 1994—95; resident U. Calif., San Francisco, 1995—97; dir. internal medicine Friend Family Health Ctr., Chgo., 1997—99; physician U. Chgo. Medical Ctr., 1997—99; staff physician Provident Hosp. Cook County, 1999—2001; asst. prof. preventive & internal medicine Rush Univ. Medical Ctr., 2001—09; sr. program officer Chgo. Cmty. Trust, 2009—11; chief med. officer Merge Healthcare Inc., Chgo., 2011—. Chmn. Ill. Health Info. Exch. Authority. Recipient Chapter Laureate award, Illinois Chpt. of the American Coll. Physicians, 2009. Office: Merge Healthcare 200 E Randolph St Suite 2435 Chicago IL 60601 Office Phone: 312-565-6868. Office Fax: 312-565-6870. *

WHITAKER, ERIC E., academic administrator, former state agency administrator; b. Chgo. m. Cheryl Whitaker; children: Caleb, Caitlin. BS, Grinnell Coll., 1987; MPH, Harvard Univ., 1991; MD, Univ. Chgo., 1993. Attending physician internal med. John H. Stroger Jr. Hosp. (Cook County Hosp.), Chgo.; asst. prof. Rush Med. Coll., Chgo.; dir. Ill. Dept. Public Health, Springfield, 2003—07; exec. v.p. strategic affiliations U. Chgo. Med. Ctr., 2007—, assoc. dean cmty. based rsch., 2007—. Co-founder Project Brotherhood Black Men's Clinic, Chgo., 1998; past pres. Am. Med. Student Assn. Office: Univ Chgo Med Ctr 5841 S Maryland Ave Chicago IL 60637

WHITAKER, IAIN STUART, registrar, plastic surgeon; b. Manchester, Cheshire, Eng., Jan. 21, 1976; s. Stuart Geoffrey and Geraldine Margaret Whitaker. BA, U. Cambridge, Eng., 1997, MB, BChir, 2000, MA, 2001. Demonstrator anatomy dept. anatomy U. Cambridge, 2003—04; specialist registrar dept. plastic surgery Morriston Hosp., Swansea, Wales, 2005—. Contbr. to over 50 manuscripts in peer reviewed surg. jours. Mem.: Royal Coll. Surgeons. Achievements include research in microsurgery. Home: 8 Avonlea Rd Sale M334HZ England Personal E-mail: iainwhitaker@fastmail.fm.

WHITAKER, LINTON ANDIN, plastic surgeon; b. Navasota, Tex., Nov. 16, 1936; s. Ira Andin and Lena Rivers (Stedman) W.; m. Renata Grasmanis, Dec. 20, 1963; children: Derek Andin (dec.), Ingrid Marlena, Brandon Andrew. BA, U. Tex., 1958; MD, Tulane U., 1962. Diplomate Am. Bd. Surgery, Am. Bd. Plastic Surgery. Founder, dir. ctr human appearance U. Pa. Med. Ctr. Phila. 1988—; resident in gen. surgery Dartmouth Affiliated Hosps., Hanover, NH, 1965-69; resident in plastic surgery U. Pa. Hosp., Phila., 1969-71; chief plastic surgery Grad. Hosp., 1971-77, U. Pa. Hosp., Phila., 1987—2005, attending surgeon, 1971—; chief plastic surgery Children's Hosp. Phila., 1981—2001, attending surgeon, 1971—; v.p. med. staff Children's Hosp., Phila., 1992-94, pres. med. staff, 1994-96; attending physician VA Hosp., 1971—, Phila. Gen. Hosp., 1971-77; assoc. in plastic surgery Sch. Medicine, U. Pa., Phila., 1971-73, asst. prof. in plastic surgery, 1973-76, assoc. prof., 1976-81, prof., 1981—; founder, dir. ctr. human appearance U. Pa. Med. Ctr., Phila., 1988—. Vis. prof. South Australia Craniofacial Unit, Adelaide, Australia and New Zealand, 1981, U. Hawaii, 1983, Brown U., Providence, 1983, Mass. Gen. Hosp., Boston, 1984, U. Utah, Salt Lake City, 1984, U. B.C., Vancouver, 1986, U. Pitts., 1988, U. Calif., San Diego, 1992, Ohio Valley Soc. for Plastic and Reconstructive Surgery, 1992, N.Y. U., 1994; Curts vis. prof. Dartmouth U. Med. Ctr., Hanover, N.H., 1990, Kazanjian vis. prof. Mass. Gen. Hosp., Boston, 1990; First Seiichi Ohmori Meml. lectr. All Asiatic Congress on Aesthetic Surgery, Tokyo, 1988; vis. speaker Inst. Cosmotology and Inst. Stomatology, Moskow, Russia, 1985, vis. prof. Seoul Nat. U. and vis. speaker Korean Soc. for Plastic Surgeons, 1994; hon. vis. spkr. Chinese Plastic Surgery Soc., Beijing, 1996; lectr., speaker at univs., assns. in field. Co-author: Atlas of Cranio-maxillofacial Surgery, 1982, Aesthetic Surgery of the Facial Skelton, 1992; editor (with P. Randall): Symposium on the Reconstruction of Jaw Deformity, Clinics in Plastic Surgery, 1987, 1991; co-editor: Yearbook of Plastic and Reconstructive Surgery, 1980—97; assoc. editor: Seminars in Complementary Medicine, 2001—, mem. editl. bd.: Jour. Cutaneous Aging and Cosmetic Dermatology, 1988—; contbr. articles to profl. jours. Capt. M.C., U.S. Army, 1963-65. Foederer fellow Foederer Fund for Excellence, 1985-88; NIH grantee, 1976-79, 81-87, 82-85, 89, Plastic Surgery Edn. Found. Rsch. grantee, 1980-82; recipient James IV Surg. Traveller award, 1979. Fellow ACS, Am. Soc. Ophthalmic Plastic and Reconstructive Surgery (hon.); mem. AMA, Am. Assn. Plastic Surgeons (mem. program com. 1988, chmn. 1989, Rsch. grantee 1984-85), Am. Surg. Assn., Am. Alpine Workshop in Plastic Surgery (founding mem.), Am. Cleft Palate Assn. (chmn. com. classification craniofacial anomalies 1976-80, mem. program com. for 1978 mtg. 1977, mem. long-range planning com. 1980, mem. coun. 1981-84, chmn. internat. rels. com. 1981-83), Am. Cleft Palate Ednl. Found. (bd. dirs. 1975-84, chmn. rsch. com. 1975-78, chmn. instrl. courses 1980-81), Am. Soc. Aesthetic Plastic Surgery, Am. Soc. Craniofacial Surgery (mem. coun. 1992—), Am. Soc. Maxillofacial Surgeons (Spl. Honors 2003, bd. dirs. 2003—), Am. Soc. Plastic and Reconstructive Surgeons, mem. plastic surgery speakers bur. 1977—), Am. Soc. Plastic and Reconstructive Surgeons Ednl. Found. (chmn. ednl. assessment com., maxillofacial truama and craniofacial anomalies 1975-78, mem. clin. symposia com. 1978-82, chmn. clin. symposia com. 1981-82), Internat. Cleft Palate and Related Craniofacial Anomalies Soc., Internat. Soc. Aesthetic Surgery, Internat. Soc. Craniofacial Surgeons (founding mem., organizer, mem. exec. com. 1987—, sec and treas. 1993-95, pres. 1995-97), Phila. Med. Soc., Phila. Acad. Surgery, Coll. Physicians Phila., Assn. Acad. Surgery, Northeastern Soc. Plastic Surgeons N.Y. (chmn. program com. 1987, mem. programcom. 1988), Plastic Surgery Rsch. Coun., John Morgan Soc., Robert H. Ivy Soc., The Columbian Soc. Plastic, Maxillofacial and Hand Surgery (hon.), Academia Medica Lombarda (Italy, hon.), Sociedad Jamie Planas de Cirugia Plastica (Spain, hon.), Mt. Kenya Safari Club (hon.), Japan Soc. Craniomaxillofacial Surgeons (hon.), Asian Pacific Cranofacial Assn., Japan Soc. Plastic and Reconstructive Surgery (hon.), Phila. Club, Merion Cricket Club, Confrerie des chevaliers du Tastevin, Grand Senechat. Avocations: mountain climbing, skiing, wines. Office: U Pa Med Ctr 10 Penn Tower 3400 Spruce St Philadelphia PA 19104-4206 Office Phone: 215-662-2048. Business E-Mail: linton.whitaker@uphs.upenn.edu.

WHITAKER, SUSANNE KANIS, veterinary medical librarian; b. Clinton, Mass., Sept. 10, 1947; AB in Biology, Clark U., 1969; MS in Library Sci., Case Western Res. U., 1970. Regional reference libr. Yale Med. Libr., New Haven, 1970-72; med. libr. Hartford Hosp., Conn., 1972-77; asst. libr. Cornell U., Ithaca, NY, 1977-78; vet. med. libr. Coll. Vet. Medicine, Cornell U., 1978-98, vet. pub. svcs. libr., 1998—. Mem. Med. Libr. Assn. (vet. med. librs. sect. 1983-84, chmn. 1984-85, chmn. pub. rels. com. 2000—), Med. Libr. Assn. (Upstate NY and Ont. chpt.), Acad. Health Info. Profls. (disting. mem.), Am. Vet. Med. History Soc. (sec.-treas. 2004—), Phi Beta Mu, Phi Zeta. Home: 23 Wedgewood Dr Ithaca NY 14850-1064 Office: Cornell U Coll Vet Medicine Flower-Sprecher Libr Ithaca NY 14853-6401 Home Phone: 607-257-9248; Office Phone: 607-253-3499. Business E-Mail: skw2@cornell.edu.

WHITE, AUGUSTUS AARON, III, orthopaedic surgeon; b. Memphis, June 4, 1936; s. Augustus Aaron and Vivian (Dandridge) White; m. Anita Ottemo; children: Alissa Alexandra, Atina Andrea, Annica Akila. BA cum laude in Psychology, Brown U., Providence, 1957, DMS (hon.), 1997; MD, Stanford U., Calif., 1961; PhD, Karolinska Inst., Sweden, 1969; degree in Mgmt., Harvard U., Cambridge, Mass., 1984; DHL (hon.), U. New Haven, Conn., 1987; DS (hon.), So. Conn. State U., New Haven, 2000; DMS (hon.), Meharry Med. Sch., 2011. Diplomate Nat. Bd. Examiners, Am. Bd. Orthopaedic Surgery. Intern U. Mich. Hosp., Ann Arbor, 1961-62; asst. resident in gen. surgery Presbyn. Med. Center, San Francisco, 1962-63; asst. resident in orthopaedic surgery Yale Med. Center, New Haven, 1963-65, sr. instr., resident orthopaedic surgery, 1965-66; asst. prof. orthopaedic surgery Yale Med. Sch., 1969-72, assoc. prof., 1972-76, prof., 1977-78, dir. biomech. rsch. dept. orthopaedics, 1970-78; prof. orthopaedic surgery Harvard Medical School, 1978—; orthopaedic surgeon-in-chief Beth Israel Deaconess Med. Ctr., Boston, 1978-92, orthopaedic surgeon-in-chief emeritus, 1996—; sr. assoc. orthopaedic surgery Children's Hosp. Med. Ctr., Boston, 1979-89; assoc. in orthopaedic surgery Brigham & Women's Hosp., Boston, 1980-89; cons. div. surgery Sidney Farber Cancer Inst., Boston, 1980—; Ellen and Melvin Gordon disting. prof. med. edn., prof. orthopaedic surgery Harvard Med. Sch., 2002—, dir. culturally component care edn. program. Rschr. biomechanics lab. Beth Israel Deaconess Med. Ctr.; chair sci. adv. bd., dir. OrthoLogic, Inc., Phoenix; sci. adv. bd. Am. Shared Hosp. Svcs., San Francisco; chair sci. adv. bd., bd. dirs. Zimmer Holding, Inc., 2001—10; cons. orthop. surgery West Haven VA Hosp., Conn., 1970—78, Hill Health Ctr., New Haven, 1970—78; chief orthop. surgery Conn. Health Care Plan, 1976—78; adv. coun. Nat. Inst. Arthritis, Metabolism and Digestive Disease, NIH, 1979—82; mem. admissions com. Yale Med. Sch., 1970—72; presenter, moderator Symposium on Cervical Myelopathy, San Francisco, 1987; chmn. grant rev. com. NIH, 1985; founding mem., bd. overseers Brown U. Sch. Medicine, 1996—99; bd. overseers WGBH Radio/TV, Boston, 1996—98, trustee, 1998—2007, mem. adv. bd., bd. overseers, 2007—; Alfred R. Shands Jr. lectr. Am. Orthop. Assn., 2001; W. Montague Cobb lectr. W. Montague Cobb/ Nat. Med. Assn. Health Inst., 2008; pres. guest lectr. Scoliosis Rsch. Soc., 2001; chair com. culturally competence care Harvard Med. Sch., 2002—06; hon. staff orthopaedics Beth Israel Deaconess Med. Ctr., 2005—09; mem. adv. coun. biology and medicine Brown U., 2005; mem. adv. coun. Nat. Ctr. for Minority Health and Health Disparities, NIH, 2001—06. Author: Clinical Biomechanics of the Spine, 1978, 2d edit., 1990, (with M. Panjabi) Biomechanics in the Musculoskeletal System, 2001, Symposium on Idiopathic Low Back Pain, 1982, Your Aching Back-A Doctor's Guide to Relief, 1983, rev. edit., 1990, translated in German, 1992, (with P. Philips) 3rd revised edit., 2010, (with D. Chanoff) Seeing Patients. Unconscious Bias in Health Care, 2011; guest editor Clin. Orthop. and Related Rsch., 1999; contbr. articles to profl. jours., chpts. to books. Trustee Brown U., Providence, 1971-76, bd. fellows, 1981-92, fellow emeritus, 1992—, chmn. corp. com. on minority affairs, 1981-86, chmn. corp. com. on med. edn., 1989-96, chmn. vis. com. on diversity; trustee Northfield Mt. Hermon Sch., Northfield, Mass., 1976-81; bd. dirs. The Partnership, Boston, 1984—. Capt. AUS, 1966-68. Decorated Bronze Star medal; named one of 10 Outstanding Young Men US Jr. C. of C., 1969, Selected for Exceptional Black Scientist poster series CIBA-GEIGY Corp., 1982; recipient Martin Luther King, Jr. Med. Achievement award, 1972, Kappa Delta award, nat. prize for outstanding rsch. in orthopaedics field, 1975; nat. award for spinal rsch. Eastern Orthopaedic Assn., 1980, Disting. Svc. award Northfield Mt. Hermon Sch. Alumni Assn., 1983; William Rogers award Associated Alumni Brown U., 1984, Outstanding Achievement award Delta Upsilon, 1986, Brown Bear award Brown Alumni Assn., Lifetime Achievement award Beth Israel Deaconess Med. Ctr., 2005, Candle in the Dark in Medicine award Morehouse Coll., 2006, J.E. Wallace Sterling Lifetime Achievement award Stanford Med. Sch., 2006, Smith and Nephew Disting. Clin. Educator award Am. Orthop. Assn., 2006; Am.-Brit.-Canadian Travelling fellow Am. Orthopedic Assn., 1975, Disting. Clin. Educator award, 2006; Ann. Spine Symposium named in his honor Beth Israel Deaconess Med. Ctr., 2004, William W. Tipton Jr. Leadership award, Am. Acad. Orthop. Surgeons, Orthop. Rsch. Soc., 2010, Ivy Football Assn. award, Brown Football Assn. Hon., 2011, Outstanding Svc. award Mass. Orthop. Assn., 2011, Living Legend award Mus. African Am. History, 2011. Fellow Am. Acad. Orthopaedic Surgeons (chmn. diversity com. 1997-2001, Diversity award 2006), Scoliosis Rsch. Soc.; mem. The Acad. Harvard Med. Sch., Orthopaedic Rsch. Soc., Cervical Spine Rsch. Soc., Internat. Soc. for Study Lumbar Spine, Internat. Soc. Orthopaedic Surgery and Traumatology, Nat. Med. Assn. (Orthopaedic Scholar award 1994), Cervical Spine Rsch. Soc. (pres. 1988), N.Am. Spine Soc., Acad. Orthopaedic Soc. (co-chmn. com. on diversity), Clin. Orthopedic Soc. (Nix Ethics award 2002), J. Robert Gladden Orthopaedic Soc. (founding pres. 2000-03), Fedn. of Spine Assns. (pres. 1998), Sigma Xi, Sigma Pi Phi, Delta Upsilon (pres. Brown U. chpt. 1956, Charles Evan Hughes award for advancement of justice 2006, Augustus White III award for excellence in medicine established 2006, 09). Office: HMS Landmark East 401 Park Dr Boston MA 02215 Office Phone: 617-998-8802. Business E-Mail: augustus_white@hms.harvard.edu.

WHITE, BEVERLY JANE, retired cytogeneticist; b. Seattle, Oct. 9, 1938; Grad., U. Wash., 1959, MD, 1963. Diplomate Nat. Bd. Med. Examiners, Am. Bd. Pediatrics, Am. Bd. Med. Genetics; lic physician and surgeon, Wash., Calif. Rsch. trainee dept. anatomy Sch. Medicine U. Wash., Seattle, 1960-62, pediatric resident dept. pediatrics, 1967-69; rotating intern Phila. Gen. Hosp., 1963-64; rsch. fellow med. ob-gyn. unit Cardiovascular Rsch. Inst. U. Calif. Med. Ctr., San Francisco, 1964-65; staff fellow lab. biomed. scis. Nat. Inst. Child Health and Human Devel. NIH, Bethesda, Md., 1965-67, sr. staff fellow, attending physician lab. exptl. pathology Nat. Inst. Arthritis, Metabolism and Digestive Diseases, 1969-74, acting chief sect. cytogenetics, 1975-76, rsch. med. officer, attending physician sect. cytogenetics lab. cellular biology and genetics, 1974-86, dir. cytogenetics unit, interinstitute med. genetics program clin. ctr., 1987-95; dir. cytogenetics Corning Clin. Labs., Teterboro, NJ, 1995-96; assoc. med. dir. cytogenetics Nichols Inst.-Quest Diagnostics, San Juan Capistrano, Calif., 1996-97, med. dir. cytogenetics, 1998—2008, med. dir. genetics divsn., 2000—02. Vis. scientist dept. pediat. divsn. genetics U. Wash. Sch. Medicine, 1983-84; intramural cons. NIH, 1975-95; cons. to assoc. editor Jour. Nat. Cancer Inst., 1976; cons. dept. ob-gyn. Naval Hosp., Bethesda, 1988-89; lectr., presenter in field. Recipient Mosby Book award, 1963, Women of Excellence award U. Wash. and Seattle Profl. chpt. Women in Comm., 1959, Reuben award Am. Soc. for Study Sterility, 1963. Fellow Am. Coll. Med. Genetics (founding), Am. Acad. Pediatrics; mem. AMA. Am. Soc. Human Genetics, Assn. Genetic Technologists (program com. 1989). Personal E-mail: bjwsur@comcast.net.

WHITE, BURTON LEONARD, retired educational psychologist, writer, consultant; b. Boston, June 27, 1929; s. Jack J. and Evelyn S. W.; m. Janet Hodgson-White; children— Laura, Emily, David, Daniel. BSM.E., Tufts Coll., 1949; BA, Boston U., 1956, MA, 1957; PhD, Brandeis U., 1960. Research assoc. Brandeis U., 1960-62, M.I.T., 1962-65; sr. research assoc. Harvard Grad. Sch. Edn., 1965-78; head Center Parent Edn., Newton, Mass., 1978-99, ret., 1999. Author: books including Human Infants, 1971, Experience and Environment, Vol. I, 1973, Vol. II, 1978, The First Three Years of Life, 1975, latest edit. 1995, The Origins of Competence, 1979, Educating the Infant and Toddler, 1988, Raising A Happy, Unspoiled Child, 1994, The New First Three Years of Life, 1995; contbr. articles to profl. jours. Served with AUS, 1951-53. Home: 115 Pine Ridge Rd Newton MA 02468-1616 Personal E-mail: todours1@aol.com.

WHITE, CHARLES IRWIN, geneticist; b. Adelaide, Australia, Apr. 28, 1959; BSc with honors, U. Adelaide, 1980; PhD, MRC Nat. Inst. Med. Rsch., London, 1985. Postdoc. fellow Brandeis U., 1985—89, Inst. Curie, 1992—93, Ctr. Nat. de la Rsch. Sci., U. Paris XI, 1990—91, chargé de recherche, 1993—2001; conseil de l'unité de recherche CNRS UMR6547, commn. de spécialistes sects. 64 et 65 U. Blaise Pascal, 1998—2007, dir. rsch. Ctr. Nat. de la Recherche Sci., 2001—. Conseil de l'unité de recherche ISV, CNRS Gif sur Yvette and IBP, U. Paris Sud, Orsay, 1990—98; commn. des scis. biologiques et médicales Inst. Recherche pour la Dévélop., 2008—11. Grant, European Union, Agence Nat. Recherche. Mem.: Soc. Française de Génétique. Avocations: walking, travel, bicycling. Office: Université Blaise Pascal CNRS UMR6247 Clermont Ferrand Auvergne 63171 France Business E-Mail: charles.white@univ-bpclermont.fr.

WHITE, CHRISTINE A., internist, oncologist, pharmaceutical executive; BA in Biology, U. Chgo., MD. Cert. Internal Medicine, Med. Oncology. Mem. clin. staff Scripps Meml. Hospitals, San Diego, 1984—94, med. dir. oncology rsch., 1990—94, chair dept. medicine, 1994; dir. clin. oncology rsch. Sidney Kimmel Cancer Ctr., San Diego, 1994—96; various sr. positions including sr. v.p. global med. affairs Biogen Idec, Cambridge, Mass., 1996—2005. Bd. dirs. Pharmacyclics, Inc., Sunnyvale, Calif., 2006—, Arena Pharm., Inc., San Diego, 2006—, Monogram Biosciences, Inc., 2008—09, Genoptix, Inc., Carlsbad, Calif., 2009—. Mem. editl. bd. Cancer Biotherapy and Radiopharmaceutical, Expert Rev. of Anti-Cancer Therapy, Jour. Immunotherapy, several others; contbr. articles to profl. jours. Office: c/o Pharmacyclics Inc 995 E Argues Ave Sunnyvale CA 94085 Business E-Mail: cwhite@arenapharm.com. *

WHITE, CLIFTON R., JR., dermatologist; MD, U. Calf., LA; MD dermatology, Oreg. Health & Sci. U.; MD dermatopathology, NY U. School of Med. Editor in chief Am. Journal of Dermatopathology; chief of dermatology Portland Veterans Administration Med. Ctr., dir. dermatopathology; prof. Oreg. Health & Sci. Univ. Mem.: Am. Bd. Dermatology (pres. 2006). Office: c/o Oregeon Health & Science University 3181 SW Sam Jackson Park Rd Portland OR 97239

WHITE, GILBERT CASE, II, internist, hematologist; b. Durham, NC, Nov. 19, 1944; s. Finley Tomlinson and Jane Dinsmoor White; m. Judy Camp Atkins White; children: Ingle Tomlinson, Mason Carpenter, Andrew Eliot. BA, U. NC, 1966, MD, 1971. Diplomate Am. Bd. Internal Medicine. Intern then resident Georgetown U., Washington, 1971—73; from resident to prof. U. NC, Chapel Hill, 1973—2004; dir. Blood Rsch. Inst. Blood Ctr. Wis., Milw., 2004—; assoc. dean Med. Coll. Wis., Milw., 2004—. John C. Pk.er prof. U. NC, 1999—2004. Bd. dir. Great Lakes Hemophilia Found., 2005—, GTI Inc., 2005—08; Chair Gordon Rsch. Conf. Cell Biology Megakaryocytes and Platelets, 2009. Recipient NIH Clinical Assoc. Physician award, 1979—81, Basil O'Connor Award, 1979—81, Armand J. Quick Lectr. award, Med. Coll. Wis., 1988, Arthur L. Bloom Lectr. award, Brit. Soc. Hematology, 2000. Fellow: RCP; mem.: Am. Clin. and Climatological Assn., Assn. Am. Physicians, Soc. Expt. Biology and Medicine, Am. Soc. Biochemistry and Molecular Biology, Southern Soc. Clin. Investigation, Internat. Soc. Thrombosis and Hemostasis (exec. dir. 1999—2009, Investigator Recognition award 1997), Am. Heart Assn. (exec. com. mem 1994—97, Med. and Sci. Advisory

Com. mem. 1995—99, leadership com. 2001—09, Spl. Recognition award), Nat. Hemophilia Found. (bd. dir. 2010—, 2010, Murray N. Thelin Award 1996, Kenneth M. Brinkhous Award 2007). Business E-Mail: gcwhite@bcw.edu.

WHITE, HAROLD JACK, pathologist; b. Bklyn., Jan. 4, 1920; s. Abraham and Jennie (Warshawsky) W.; m. Lucette Darby, July 19, 1962; children: Elizabeth, Darby, Matthew, Esther. BS, Harvard U., 1941; MD, U. Geneva, 1952. Diplomate Am. Bd. Pathology. Intern, resident in pathology Yale U. Sch. Medicine, New Haven, 1953-58, fellow, 1957-58; assoc. pathologist Brigham and Women's Hosp., Boston, 1962-66; chief lab. svc. VA Hosp., West Roxbury, Mass., 1962-66, Little Rock, 1966-80; sr. scientist, acting head biomed. sci. dept. GM Rsch. Labs., Warren, Mich., 1980-85, cons., 1985—. Prof. pathology, microbiology U. Ark. Med. Sch., Little Rock, 1966—; vis. scientist dept. comparative medicine, MIT, Cambridge, 1988—. Contbr. over 100 articles, abstracts in pathology, microbiology, immunology, toxicology, biomedicine to profl. jours. 1st lt. USAAF, 1942-46. Fellow Coll. Am. Pathologists, Internat. Coll. Pathology. Home: 24 Bass Rocks Rd Gloucester MA 01930-3276 Office: 35 Main St Gloucester MA 01930-5730 Office Phone: 978-281-3531. Personal E-mail: hjwriverrun@aol.com.

WHITE, JEFFREY D., oncologist, federal agency administrator; BS in Applied and Engring. Physics, Cornell U., Ithaca, NY, 1979; MD, Howard U. Coll. Medicine, Washington, 1984. Diplomate Am. Bd. Internal Medicine, cert. in med. oncology. Internal medicine resident Washington Hosp. Ctr., 1984—87, oncology & hematology fellow, 1987—90; med. staff fellow metabolism br. Nat. Cancer Inst., 1990—97; dir. Clin. Trials and Clin. Care Program, Metabolism Br. Nat. Cancer Inst., NIH, Bethesda, Md., dir. clin. trials & clin. care program, 1997—98, dir. Office Cancer Complementary & Alternative Medicine, 1998—. Oncology cons., Office Alternative Medicine NIH, 1995—98; vis. prof. Inst. Biomedical Scis., Academia Sinica, Taipei, Taiwan. Mem.: Ernest E. Just Biomedical Soc. Office: Office Cancer Complementary & Alternative Medicine Nat Cancer Inst 6116 Executive Blvd Ste 609 MSC 8339 Bethesda MD 20892 Office Phone: 301-435-7980. Office Fax: 301-480-0075. Business E-Mail: jeffrey.white@nih.gov. *

WHITE, JEFFREY GEORGE, healthcare consultant; b. Lawrence, Mass., Apr. 16, 1944; s. Alfred James and Ruth Virginia (Maylum) W.; children: Jennifer L., Tracy E. AB in Econs., Bowdoin Coll., 1966; MBA, U. N.H., 1985. Asst. pers. dir., then asst. adminstr. Maine Med. Ctr., Portland, 1967-71; asst. adminstr. Regional Meml. Hosp., Brunswick, Maine, 1971, adminstr., 1971-74; assoc. dir. Elizabeth Ann Seton Hosp., Waterville, 1974-75; assoc. adminstr. Mid-Maine Med. Ctr., 1975-79, v.p. ops., 1979-83; asst. dir. Wentworth-Douglass Hosp., Dover, NH, 1983-85; exec. v.p. Frisbie Meml. Hosp., Rochester, NH, 1985-89, pres., 1989-92; sr. cons., prin. Helms & Co., Inc., Concord, NH, 1992—. Interim pres. New London (NH) Hosp., 2002-03, Copley Hosp., Morrisville, Vt., 2006-07; preceptor dept. health mgmt. and policy U. NH, Durham, 1985-92, adj. asst. prof., 1991-93, asst. prof., 1993-97, dean's leadership coun. sch. health human svcs., 1998-2007; bd. dirs. Riverwoods at Exeter, 2000-2003. Vol. pub. TV sta.; bd. dirs. Greater Seacoast United Way, 1991-94, chmn. comty. campaign, 1993; pres. Greater Rochester C. of C., 1990. Fellow Am. Coll. Healthcare Execs. (past regent for N.H.); mem. N.H. Hosp. Assn. (trustee emeritus). Independent. Avocations: walking, skiing, reading, travel. Office: Helms & Co Inc 1 Pillsbury St Concord NH 03301-3556 Home: 10th North Rd Alexandria NH 03222 Home Phone: 603-744-5579; Office Phone: 603-225-6633. E-mail: jwhite@helmsco.com.

WHITE, JOHN VINCENT, surgeon, consultant; b. Chgo., May 7, 1952; s. Ralph and Angela White. BS, Northwestern U., 1974; MD, Columbia U., 1978. Diplomate Am. Bd. Surgery. Instr. surgery Columbia U., NYC, 1982-83; asst. prof. surgery Temple U., Phila., 1984-88, assoc. prof. surgery, 1988-94, prof. surgery, 1994-99; clin. prof. surgery U. Ill. Sch. Medicine; chmn. dept. surgery Luth. Gen. Hosp., Park Ridge, Ill., 1999—. Adj. sr. fellow Sch. Health Econs. U. Pa., Phila., 1994—; tech. cons. Boston Scientific Corp., Natick, Mass., 1995—; surg. cons. Dept. of Health N.Y. State, 1993; surg. tech. cons. Congl. Office of Tech. Assessment, Washington, 1995; laser tech. cons. Office of Naval Rsch., Washington, 1993-97, cons. NSF Biomed. Engring. Program, 2007-09. Editor: Hemodilution in Patient Care, 1989, Alternatives to Open Vascular Surgery, 1995, Surgical Clinics of North America, 1998; founding editor: Jour. Laparoendoscopic Surgery, 1990. Recipient Samuel D. Gross award Phila. Acad. Surgery, 1992; grant NSF, 2007-10. Mem. Am. Soc. Laser Medicine and Surgery, Soc. Univ. Surgeons (mem. found. bd. dirs. 1994-98), Del. Valley Vascular Soc. (pres. 1995—), Soc. Vascular Surgery (mem. com. outcomes analysis 1994—), Midwestern Vascular Soc., Alpha Omega Alpha. Office: Lutheran Gen Hosp 1775 Dempster St Park Ridge IL 60068-1173 Office Phone: 847-723-7200. Office Fax: 847-696-3394. Business E-Mail: john.white-md@advocatehealth.com.

WHITE, JULIAN, physician; b. May 23, 1952; MBBS, U. Adelaide, 1976, MD, 1988. Cranio-facial registrar Women's & Children's Hosp., 1979—84, haematology registrar, 1984—90, head, toxinology, 1990—. Assoc. prof., dept. pediat. U. Adelaide, 2001. Sec. IST, 2009—. Recipient Excellence award, Women's & Children's Hosp. Fellow: Australasian Coll. Tropical Medicine; mem.: Internat. Soc. Toxinology. Office: Women's & Children's Hosp 72 King William Rd North Adelaide 5006 Australia Office Fax: 08-81618024. Business E-Mail: julian.white@adelaide.edu.au.

WHITE, KENNETH SPENCER, SR., lawyer; b. Lynchburg, Va., Oct. 31, 1939; s. Kenneth L. and Bertha (Spencer) W.; m. Jane Stafford Baber, June 23, 1962; children: Virginia White O'Keefe, Kenneth Spencer Jr., Charles B. BS, U. Va., 1962, JD, 1965. Bar: Va. 1965. Ptnr. Edmunds & Williams, P.C., Lynchburg, 1966—2000, of counsel, 2000—08. Chmn. bd. dirs. Bank of James Fin. Group, Inc., 2000—09, Centra Health, Inc., 2009—. Mem. bd. dirs. Sweet Briar Coll., 1980-90; pres. Va. Bd. of Edn., 1983-86, Greater Lynchburg Cmty. Trust, 2001-04; mem. Govs. Commn. Excellence Edn., 1986-87; chmn. Va. Pub. Sch. Authority, 1990-94; mem. Commonwealth Transp. Bd., 2002—10. Fellow Am. Bar Found., Va. Law Found. (trustee 1981-86); mem. ABA (chmn. standing com. on profl. utilization and career devel. 1978-80), Va. Bar Assn. (exec. com. 1977-80), Lynchburg Bar Assn. (pres. 1977). Episcopalian. Home: 1616 Langhorne Rd Lynchburg VA 24503-3118 Office Phone: 434-384-3546.

WHITE, KERR LACHLAN, retired physician, foundation administrator; b. Winnipeg, Man., Can., Jan. 23, 1917; s. John Alexander and Ruth Cecelia (Preston) Stevenson; m. Isabel Anne Pennefather, Nov. 26, 1943; children: Susan Isabel, Margot Edith. BA with honors (Oliver Gold medal), McGill U., 1940, MD, CM, 1949; DM (hon.), U. Leuven, 1978; postgrad., London Sch. Hygiene and Tropical Medicine, 1960; DSc (hon.), McMaster U., 1983. Intern, resident in medicine Mary Hitchcock Meml. Hosp., Hanover, NH, 1949—52; Hosmer fellow McGill U. and Royal Victoria Hosp., Montreal, Que., Canada, 1952—53; asst. prof. medicine U. N.C. Sch. Medicine, Chapel Hill, 1953—57, assoc. prof. medicine and preventive medicine, 1957—62; Commonwealth advanced fellow Med. Rsch. Coun., Social Medicine Rsch. unit London Hosp., 1959—60; chmn., prof. epidemiology and community medicine U. Vt., Burlington, 1962—64; prof. Sch. Hygiene and Pub. Health Johns Hopkins U., Balt., 1965—76, chmn. dept. health care orgn., 1965—72; dir. Inst. Health Care Studies United Hosp. Fund N.Y., 1977—78; dep. dir. health scis. Rockefeller Found., NYC, 1978—97, ret., 1997. Chmn. U.S. Nat. Com. Vital and Health Stats., 1975—79; mem. health adv. panel Office of Tech. Assessment, U.S. Congress, 1975—82; cons. Nat. Ctr. Health Stats., 1967—83, WHO, 1967—. Editor: Manual for Examination of Patients, 1960, Medical Care Research, 1965, Health Care: An International Study, 1976, Epidemiology as a Fundamental Science, 1976, Task of Medicine, 1988, Healing the Schism, 1991; mem. editl. bd.: Med. Care, 1962—73, Inquiry, 1967—79, Internat. Jour. Epidemiology, 1971—81, Internat. Jour. Health Svcs., 1971—; contbr. chapters to books, articles to profl. jours. Trustee Case-Western Res. U., 1974—79; bd. dirs. Found. for Child Devel., 1969—80. With Can. Army, 1942—45. Recipient Pew Primary Care Achievement award, 1995, Baxter Found. award, 1996, Wood award for lifetime contbns. to primary care rsch., 1999. Fellow: APHA (gov. coun. 1964—68, 1971—73, coun. med. care sect. 1962—65), NAS (Inst. Medicine coun. 1974—76, chmn. membership com. 1975—77), ACP, AAAS, Am. Heart Assn., Am. Acad. Preventive Medicine, Royal Soc. Medicine (hon.); mem.: AMA, Kerr L. White Inst. Health Svcs. Rsch. (hon. dir. 1995—), Internat. Epidemiol. Assn. (hon.; life, pres. 1974—77, treas., exec. com. 1964—71, 1974—77, coun. 1971—81), Am. Hosp. Assn. (adv. coun. ednl. and rsch. trust 1965—68), Assn. Tchrs. Preventive Medicine (coun. 1963—68), Century Club (N.Y.C.), Cosmos Club (Washington), Alpha Omega Alpha, Sigma Xi. Office Phone: 434-972-2499. Business E-Mail: klw2j@virginia.edu.

WHITE, LISA JANE, mathematician; b. Eng., Sept. 29, 1971; Degree in Applied Math., U. Warwick, 1993, PhD in Biol. Scis., 2001. Head, math. modelling MahoMahidol Oxford Tropical Medicine Rsch. Unit, 2007—. Avocation: Kung Fu. Office: Faculty Tropical Medicine Mahidol University Bangkok 10400 Thailand Business E-Mail: lisa@tropmedres.ac.

WHITE, LOWELL ELMOND, JR., retired medical educator; b. Tacoma, Wash., Jan. 16, 1928; s. Lowell E. and Hazel (Conley) W.; m. Margie Mae Lamb, June 21, 1947; children: Henry, Leanna White Maynes, Inger-Britt White Peterson. BS in Pharm., U. Wash., 1951, MD, 1953. Diplomate Am. Bd. Neurol. Surgery. Intern N.C. Meml. Hosp., Chapel Hill, 1953-54; resident neurosurgery, asst. to instr. U. Wash., 1954-60, asst. prof., 1960-64, assoc. prof., 1964—68; asso. dean U. Wash. Sch. Medicine, 1965-68; prof. surgery & neurosic., chief divsn. neurol. surgery U. Fla., 1968—72; prof. neurosci. U. South Ala., 1972—94, chmn. divsn. neurosci., 1972-77, ret., 1994. Adj. prof. speech pathology audiology Ala. Sch. Math. and Sci., 1993-94; chmn. nat. adv. com. Animal Resources NIH, 1966-70; cons. rsch. facilities and resources NIH; cons. divsn. hosp. and med. facilities USPHS; cons. grants adminstrn. policy U.S. Dept. HEW. Contbr. articles profl. jours. Bd. dirs. Mobile County Emergency Med. Svcs. Com., 1973-82, Epilepsy chpt. Mobile, 1973-89, Mobile cpt. Myasthenia Gravis Found. Am., 1974-90, Mobile, Ala. Mental Health Assn., 1979-89, Spl. Edn. Action Com., 1985-97, pres. 1996; vol. Homeland Security Med. Res. Corps and ARC, 2005-. With USN, 1946—47, with USNR, 1948—66. Guggenheim fellow, 1958-59 Mem. AMA, Am. Assn. Neurol. Surgeons, Am. Assn. Neuropathologists, Am. Acad. Neurol. Surgeons, Soc. for Neurosci., Assn. Am. Med. Colls., Am. Assn. Anatomists, Rsch. Soc. Neurol. Surgeons, Neurosurg. Soc. Ala. (pres. 1975), Am. Physicians Poetry Assn., Odyssey U. South Ala., Soc. for Arts in Healthcare, Snohomish County Med. Soc., Sigma Xi. Home: 100 Timber Ridge Way NW Unit 1103 Issaquah WA 98027

WHITE, MARTHA VETTER, allergist, immunologist; b. Richmond, Va., Oct. 23, 1951; d. Robert Joseph and Miriam Ernestine (Thomas) Vetter; m. Frederick Joseph Kozub, Oct. 11, 1975 (div. June 1982); m. John Irving White, Feb. 18, 1984; children: Josh, Christie. Student, Vanderbilt U., Nashville, 1969-71; BA, U. Richmond, 1973; MD, Va. Commonwealth U., Richmond, 1978. Cert. m. Bd. Pediatrics, Am. Bd. Allergy and Immunology. Pediatric intern and resident Va. Commonwealth U., Richmond, 1978-81; locum tenans Pub. Health, Richmond, Va., 1981-82; fellow Allergy and Immunology U. Southern Calif., LA, 1983-84, Georgetown U., 1983-84; sr. staff fellow Food and Drug Adminstrn., Bethesda, Md., 1984-85; NSRA fellow Nat. Inst. Allergy and Infectious Diseases, Bethesda, Md., 1985-88; sr. staff fellow, 1988-93; rsch. dir. Inst. for Asthma and Allergy, Wheaton, Md., 1993—. Cons. Sandoz Pharms., Marion Merrell Dow, Glaxo, Boehringer Ingleheim, Ciba-Geigy, Miles Genentech; rschr. Glaxo, Abbott, Pfizer, Marion Merrell Dow, Miles, Rhône Poulenc Rhoen, Sanofi, Adams, Astra, Merck, Neurbiol. Techs., 3M, Zeneca, Wyeth, Smith-Kline Beecham; bd. dirs. Allery & Asthma Network/Mothers of Asthmatics, 1987—; med. editor MA Report, 1986—; assoc. editor Allergy, Asthma and Immunology Guide, 1989-90. Contbr. numerous scientific papers, abstracts, chpts. and reviews in field. Recipient Norwich Eaton Rsch. award, 1987; Merrell Dow scholar in allergy, 1989; Geigy fellow, 1984. Mem.: Soc. Prin. Investigators (pres. 2002—03), Am. Thoracic Soc., Am. Coll. Allergy and Immunology, Adm. Acad. Allergy and Immunology, Am. Acad. Pediat., Am. Assn. Immunologists, Gamma Sigma Epsilon, Psi Chi, Beta Beta Beta. Office: Inst Asthma and Allergy 11002 Veirs Mill Rd # 414 Wheaton MD 20902 Home Phone: 301-962-1600; Office Phone: 301-962-5800.

WHITE, MILES D., pharmaceutical executive; b. Mpls., Mar. 10, 1955; m. Kim White. BS in Mech. Engring., Stanford U., 1978, MBA, 1980. Mgmt. cons. McKinsey & Co.; joined Abbott Laboratory, Inc., 1984, v.p. diagnostic sys. and ops., 1993-94, sr. v.p. diagnostic ops., 1994-98, exec. v.p., 1998-99; CEO Abbot Labs., 1998—99; chmn., CEO Abbott Laboratory, Inc., 1999—. Bd. dirs. Abbott Labs., 1998—, Motorola Inc., 2005—09, The Tribune Co., 2005—06, McDonalds Corp., 2009—, Fed. Res. Bank, Chgo., 2002—, chmn., 2002—04, 2005—07. Bd. trustee Field Mus., Chicago, Northwestern U., Joffrey Ballet, Chicago, Culver Ednl. Found.; mem. Stanford Grad. Sch. of Bus. Adv. Coun., Stanford Adv. Coun. on Interdisciplinary Biosciences. Mem.: American Acad. Arts & Sciences, Econ. Club of Chgo., Executives' Club of Chgo. (chmn.). Office: Abbott Labs 100 Abbott Park Rd Abbott Park IL 60064-6400 *

WHITE, PERRY MERRILL, JR., orthopedic surgeon; b. Texarkana, Ark., Oct. 11, 1925; s. Perry Merrill and Mary Gladys (Shelton) W.; m. Lucy Katherine Freeman, Dec. 23, 1947; children: Perry Merrill III, MD., Georgia Lynette, Katherine Landis White Long, John David. BS, Baylor U., 1948, MD, 1953; postgrad., Vanderbilt U., 1948-49. Diplomate Am. Bd. Orthopedic Surgery. Intern VA Hosp., Houston, 1953-54; gen. practice medicine Spearman, Tex., 1955-57; resident orthopedic surgery Eugene Talmadge Meml. Hosp., Augusta, Ga., 1957-61; pvt. practice orthopedic surgery Atlanta, 1961-83; chief Ga. Adult Amputee Clinic, 1965-79; active staff Scottish Rite Hosp. for Crippled Children, Decatur, Ga., 1965-73; instr. orthopedic surgery residency program Ga. Bapt. Hosp., 1965-83; orthopedic panelist Ga. Dept. Vocat. Rehab. Cons. Ga. Crippled Children's Service, 1965-76 Former mem. bd. dirs. Haggai Inst., Atlanta, London, Singapore. Served with USNR, 1944-46. Fellow ACS, Am. Acad. Orthopedic Surgeons; mem. So., Ga., Atlanta med. assns., Eastern Orthopedic Assn., Ga., Atlanta orthopedic socs., Alpha Kappa Kappa. Republican. Baptist (deacon). Home: 1547 Cave Rd NW Atlanta GA 30327-3119 E-mail: kaper1947@bellsouth.net. *

WHITE, PETER, radiographer, educator; b. Haverfordwest, Pembrokeshire, Wales, June 3, 1961; s. Edward William and Mary White; m. Imelda Cabalza, Mar. 6, 1998; children: Morgan Ellis, Joshua William, Dylan Lloyd. LLM, U. Wales, 1996; PhD, Hong Kong Poly. U., 2004. DCR Coll. Radiographers, 1983, TDCR Coll. Radiographers, 1993, HDCR Coll. Radiographers, 1992. Therapy radiographer Velindre Hosp., Cardiff, South Glamorgan, Wales, 1983—89, clin. instr., 1991—92; lectr. U. Wales Coll. Medicine, Cardiff, 1995—96; asst. prof. Hong Kong Poly. U., Kowloon, 1997—. Reviewer The Radiographer Jour., Australia, 2004—06. Mem. editl. bd.: Jour. Radiotherapy in Practice, 1998; contbr. articles to profl. jours. Mem. human subjects ethics subcom. Hong Kong Poly. U., 2000—. Ctrl. Earmarked Rsch. grant, U. Grants Com., Hong Kong, 2001, Devel. grant, Hong Kong Poly. U., 2002. Mem.: Soc. Radiographers (licentiate State Registered 1983), Internat. Soc. Radiographers and Radiologic Technologists (assoc. Assoc. membership 2001). Episcopalian. Achievements include research in legal aspects of telemedicine/teleradiology; health care law and ethics. Avocations: travel, squash, soccer. Home: Flat 18B Tower 8 Laguna Verde Hung Hom Hong Kong Kowloon Hong Kong Office: Hong Kong Poly University Dept Health Tech Info Hung Kwong St Hong Kong Kowloon Hong Kong Office Fax: 852 2362 4365.

WHITE, RAYMOND LESLIE, geneticist; b. Orlando, Fla., Oct. 23, 1943; s. Lawrence and Marjorie White; m. Joan Palmer Distin, June 1, 1968; children: Juliette, Jeremy. BS in Microbiology, U. Oreg., 1965; PhD in Microbiology, MIT, 1971; postdoctoral studies, Stanford. Rsch. assoc., instr. MIT, Cambridge, 1971-72; postdoctoral fellow Sch. Medicine Stanford U., Calif., 1972-75; asst. prof. Dept. Microbiology U. Mass. Sch. Medicine, Worcester, 1975-78, assoc. prof. Dept. Microbiology, 1978-80; investigator Howard Hughes Med. Inst. U. Utah Med. Ctr., 1980-94; assoc. prof. Dept. Cellular, Viral and Molecular Biology U. Utah Sch. Medicine, 1980-84, co-chmn. Dept. Human Genetics, 1984-94, prof. Dept. Oncological Scis., 1985—; prof. Dept. of Human Genetics U. Utah Sch. of Medicine, 1985—; chmn. Dept. Oncological Scis. U. Utah Sch. Medicine, 1994—, dir. Huntsman Cancer Inst., 1994—2000; chief sci. officer DNA Scis., Inc., Fremont, Calif., 2000—02; dir. Ernest Gallo Clinic & Rsch. Ctr. U. Calif. San Francisco, Emeryville, Calif., 2002—, vice chair, prof. neurology, 2002—. Ad hoc mem. NIH Gen. Med. Sci. Inst. Coun., 1984, mem. NIH study sect., 1979-83. Consulting editor Jour. Clin. Investigation; subject area editor Genomics, 1987-90; contbr. articles to profl. jours. Woodrow Wilson fellow, 1965-66, NIH grad. fellow, 1966-71, Jane Coffins Childs Found. fellow, 1971-75; Nat. Cancer Inst. Cancer Ctr. Support grantee, 1995—; recipient Sword Hope award Am. Cancer Soc., 1995, Lewis S. Rosenstiel award Disting. Work Basic Med. Scis., Brandeis U., 1992, Rosenblatt award for excellence, 1993, Nat. Med. Rsch. award Nat. Health Coun., 1991, Friedrich von Recklinghausen award Nat. Neurofibromatosis Found., 1990, Charles S. Mott prize Gen. Motors Cancer Rsch. Found., 1990, Raymond Bourfine award, Paris, 2002. Mem. NAS, Am. Soc. Human Genetics (Allen Cancer Rsch. award 1989, assoc. editor Cancer Rsch.), Utah Acad. Scis., Inst. Medicine. Achievements include the development of a new technology for mapping and ultimately identifying human genes causing disease and the discovery of fundamental genes and genetic mechanisms important in the inherited and cellular pathways to cancer. Office: Ernest Gallo Clinic & Rsch Ctr Ste 200 5858 Horton St Emeryville CA 94608 Office Phone: 510-985-3102. Office Fax: 510-985-3101. E-mail: rayw@egcrc.net.

WHITE, RAYMOND PETRIE, JR., dentist, educator, dean; b. NYC, Feb. 13, 1937; s. Raymond Petrie and Mabel Sarah (Shutze) White; m. Betty Pritchett, Dec. 27, 1961; children: Karen Elizabeth, Michael Wood. Student, Washington and Lee U., 1955—58; DDS, Med. Coll. Va., 1962, PhD, 1967. Diplomate Am. Bd. Oral and Maxillofacial Surgery. Postdoctoral fellow anatomy Med. Coll. Va., Richmond, 1962—67, resident in oral surgery, 1964—67; asst. prof. U. Ky., Lexington, 1967—70, assoc. prof., 1970—71, chmn. dept.

oral surgery, 1969—71; prof., asst. dean adminstrn. Va. Commonwealth U., Richmond, 1971—74; prof. Sch. Dentistry U. N.C., Chapel Hill, 1974—, Dalton L. McMichael disting. prof., 1993—, dean Sch. Dentistry, 1974—81, assoc. dean Sch. Medicine, Sch. Dentistry, 1981—92. Mem. staff U. N.C. Hosps., mem. exec. com., 1974—98, sec., 1977—78, assoc. chief staff, 1981—92; mem. adv. panel on dentistry U.S. Pharmacopial Conv., 1985—; sr. program cons. The Robert Wood Johnson Found., 1982—90. Author (with E.R. Costich): Fundamentals of Oral Surgery, 1971; author: (with Bell and Proffit) Surgical Correction of Dentofacial Deformities, 1980; author: (with W.R. Proffit) Surgical Orthodontic Treatment, 1990; author: (with M.R. Tucker, B.C. Terry, J.E. Van Sickels) Rigid Fixations for Maxillofacial Surgery, 1991; co-editor: Internat. Jour. Adult Orthodontics and Orthodontic Surgery, 1985—2002; asst. editor: Jour. Oral and Maxillofacial Surgery, 1993—; author (with W.R. Profit, R.P. Jr., and D. Sarver): Contemporary Treatment of Dentofacial Deformity, 2002; contbr. sci. articles to profl. jours. Bd. dirs. Am. Fund for Dental Health, 1978—86, v.p., 1982—85. Recipient Disting. Svc. award, Am. Fund Dental Health, 1987, Dental Found. N.C., 1981, John C. Brauer award for acad. distinction, U. N.C. Alumni Assn., 2000, Daniel M. Laskin award, 2002, Rsch. Excellence award, Oral and Maxillofacial Surgery Found., 2003. Mem.: AAAS, ADA, N.C. Assn. Oral and Maxillofacial Surgeons, Am. Assn. Oral and Maxillofacial Surgeons (gen. chmn. sci. sessions com. 1974—76, chmn. strategic planning com. 1990—96, Outstanding Svc. award as committeeman 1976, William Gies award 2000, Disting. Svc. award 2003), Chalmers J. Lyons Acad. Oral Surgery, Inst. Medicine of NAS, Internat. Assn. Dental Rsch. (pres. Ky. sect. 1970), N.C. Dental Soc., Sigma Xi, Omicron Kappa Upsilon, Sigma Zeta, Alpha Sigma Chi, Delta Tau Delta, Psi Omega. Roman Catholic. Home: 1506 Velma Rd Chapel Hill NC 27514-7601 Office: U NC Sch Dentistry Dept Oral/Maxillofacial Surgery Chapel Hill NC 27599-7450 Office Phone: 919-966-1126. Business E-Mail: ray_white@dentistry.unc.edu.

WHITE, ROBERT DENNIS, pediatrician, director; b. South Bend, Ind., Dec. 29, 1949; s. Alfred Butler and Mary Ruth (Gibbens) White; m. Kathy Lynn Samuels, Aug. 15, 1970; children: Luke Alfred, James Samuels, Kieran Claire, Benjamin Robert. Student, U. Notre Dame, 1967-69; BA, John Hopkins U., 1969-70, MD, 1970-74. Diplomate Am. Bd. Pediatrics. Resident in pediatrics Johns Hopkins Hosp., Balt., 1974-76, fellow in neonatology, 1976—77; sr. rsch. scientist Wellcome Rsch. Labs., London, 1980; dir. regional newborn program Meml. Hosp., South Bend, 1981—. Clin. asst. prof. pediat. Ind. U. Sch. Medicine, 1983—; adj. prof. psychology U. Notre Dame, 1989—; chmn. Recommended Stds. Newborn ICU Design, 2006. Co-editor: (book) Lifespan Perspectives on Health and Illness, 1999. Fellow: Am. Acad. Pediat. Office: Meml Hosp 615 N Michigan St South Bend IN 46601-1087 *

WHITE, RONALD A., colon and rectal surgeon; Attended, Boston U., BA in Med. Sci./Sociology summa cum laude, MD, 1981; LLB with honors, Rutgers Sch. Law, 2007. Diplomate Am. Bd. Colon and Rectal Surgery, 1988. Resident surgery Montefiore Hosp., Bronx, NY, 1981—86; fellow colon & rectal surgery Univ. Medicine and Dentistry NJ Robert Wood Johnson Med. Sch., Piscataway, NJ, 1986—87; chief surgery Bergen Regional Med. Ctr.; colon and rectal surgeon Valley Hosp., Englewood Hosp. and Med. Ctr. Named one of Best Doctors, NY Mag., 1999, 2002—07, NJ Monthly, 2003. Fellow: NY Soc. Colon and Rectal Surgeons, Am. Soc. Colon and Rectal Surgeons, Am. Coll. Surgeons. Office: Englewood Hospital & Medical Center 350 Engle St Englewood NJ 07631 Office Phone: 201-894-3000.

WHITE, RONALD JOSEPH, biomedical researcher, physiologist, educator; b. Opelousas, La., Dec. 4, 1940; s. John Wesley and Alma Louise (LaSalle) White; m. Margaret Helen Launey, June 8, 1963; children: Joseph LaSalle, Angela Alma, Margaret Leslie. BS in Chemistry, U. S.W. La., 1963; PhD in Phys. Chemistry, U. Wis., 1968. NSF postdoctoral fellow in theoretical chemistry U. Oxford, England, 1967-68; rsch. assoc. Bell Tel. Labs., Murray Hill, NJ, 1968-70; from asst. prof. to assoc. prof. math. U. S.W. La., Lafayette, 1970—76, prof. math., dir. Univ. Honors Program, 1976—80; rsch. assoc. dept. physiology and biophysics U. Miss. Med. Ctr., Jackson, 1973-75; sr. scientist GE Co./Mgmt. and Tech. Svcs. Co., Washington and Houston, 1980-85; chief scientist Life/Biomed. Scis. and Applications Divsn. NASA, Washington, 1985—96; rsch. prof. physiology Uniformed Svcs. U. Health Scis., Bethesda, Md., 1985—96; prof. dept. otorhinolaryngology Baylor Coll. Medicine, Houston, 1996—2003; assoc. dir. Nat. Space Biomed. Rsch. Inst., 1997—2003; sr. fellow Univs. Space Rsch. Assn., Houston, 2003—09; v.p. rsch. SD Sch. Mines & Tech., Rapid City, 2009—. V.p. Assn. Gifted and Talented Students, La., 1977—80; pres. La. Collegiate Honors Coun., 1978—79. Editor (assoc. life scis.): Simulation, 1974—75; editor: (spl.) Medicine and Sci. in Sports and Exercise, 1996; contbr. numerous chpts. to books, papers to profl. jours. Recipient NASA traineeship, 1963—66, Am. Inst. Chemists award, 1963, Disting. Prof. award, 1978, Med. Info. Processing Best Paper award, 15th ann. Hawaii Internat. Conf. on Systems Sci., 1982, Hon. Mem. award, Soc. NASA Flight Surgeons, 1992, Exceptional Achievement medal, NASA, 1992; fellow, Woodrow Wilson Found., 1963. Fellow: Aerospace Med. Assn. (assoc.); mem.: Internat. Soc. Computational Biology, Internat. Acad. Astronautics (bd. trustees 1997—2009, commr. space life scis. 2001—03, chair life scis. 2001—09, commr. space life scis. 2009—, Luigi Napolitano Lit. award 1996), Am. Soc. Gravitational and Space Biology (charter mem.), Am. Phys. Soc., Sigma Xi (rsch. award 1976), Phi Kappa Phi. Office: SD Sch Mines & Tech 501 E Saint Joseph St Rapid City SD 57701 Home: 3010 Calle Baja Rapid City SD 57702 Office Phone: 605-394-2493. Personal E-mail: ronwhite@earthlink.net. Business E-Mail: ronald.white@sdsmt.edu.

WHITE, RUSSELL DENNY, surgeon, educator; b. Maryville, Mo., Sept. 28, 1947; BA, U. Mo., 1969, MD, 1974. Prof. medicine, orthopaedic surgery U. Mo., Kansas City Sch. Medicine, 2005—, dir. sports medicine fellowship program, 2006—, head team physician, 2009—. Med. dir. event medicine Tropicana Field, St. Petersburg, 1997—2005; clin. assoc. prof. medicine U. South Fla., Tampa, 1997—2005; med. dir. sports medicine ctr. Truman Med. Ctr. Lakewood, 2007—11. Recipient 'Giant of Medicine' award, U. Mo. Med. Ctr.; named one of Kans. City 'Super Drs.' in Sports Medicine, Colleagues and Super Doctors Orgn. Fellow: Am. Coll. Sports Medicine, Am. Acad. Family Physicians, Am. Bd. Family Physicians; mem.: Am. Assn. Clin. Endocrinologists, Am. Diabetes Assn., Alpha Omega Alpha Honor Med. Soc. Avocations: jazz, woodworking, motorcycling. Office: Truman Medical Ct Lakewood 7790 Lee Kansas City MO 64139 Office Fax: 816-404-7142. Personal E-mail: jockdoc2000@hotmail.com.

WHITE, SHELLEY D., medical association administrator; b. Syracuse, NY, Oct. 10, 1965; BSc, St. Lawrence U., 1987; MSc, New Sch. Social Rsch., 1993. Assoc. adminstr. Upstate Med. U., 1993—. Named one of Best Leader, Upstate Med. U. Fellow: Am. Coll. Healthcare Execs.; mem.: Healthcare Fin. Mgmt. Assn., Nat. Assn. Healthcare Access Mgrs. Office: 750 E Adams St 250 HS Syracuse NY 13210 Office Fax: 315-464-5062. Business E-Mail: whites@upstate.edu.

WHITE, SUSIE MAE, school psychologist; b. Madison, Fla., Mar. 5, 1914; d. John Anderson and Lucy (Crawford) Williams; m. Daniel Elijah White, Oct. 20, 1958 (dec. Sept. 29, 1968) BS, Fla. Meml. Coll., St. Augustine, 1948; MEd, U. Md., 1953; postgrad., Mich. State U., 1955, Santa Fe C.C., 1988; Cert. Child Care Supervision, W.T. Loften Edn. Ctr., Gainesville, Fla., 1994. Tchr. elem. Grove Park Elem. Sch., Fla., 1943; tchr. Douglas H.S., High Springs, Fla., 1944—55; sch. psychologist Alachua County Sch. Bd., Gainesville, Fla., 1956—69, coord. social svcs., 1970; owner, dir. Mother Dear's Child Care Ctr., Gainesville, 1988—. Author: Determined--in spite of...Autobiography of Susie Mae Williams White, 1998, Lord, Fix Me Inspirational Poems, 2000 Del. Bapt. World Alliance, Bapt. Conv. Fla., Tokyo, 1970; state dir. leadership Fla. Bapt. Gen. Conv., 1971-85 Recipient trophy, Lincoln HS Alumni Assn. Inc., 1923—70, Golden Anniversary award, A.L. Membane HS Class, Cert. of Appreciation, 1958, Fla. State Dept. Edn., 1971, Reonition Disting. Achievement Golden Dem., Appreciation for Disting. Svc. award, Fla. Gen. Bapt. Conv., 1979, Hall of Fame award, Martin Luther King Jr. Hall of Fame, 1994, Cert. Appreciation for Outstanding Svc. & Leadership, Mt. Sinai Woman's Conv., 1997, The Susie Mae White scholarship fund established, Mt. Sinai Congress Christian Edn., 1995, Cert. Appreciation, Friendship Bapt. Ch., 2000, Deloris Keith Meml. Good Neighbor award, East Gainesville Devel. Task Force, Inc., 1999, Trophy for Being Inspiration to Young Women, Alachua Practical Acad. Cultural Edn. Ctr. for Girls, Inc., 2001, Plaque for Appreciation of 60 Yrs. of Svc., Friendship Baptist Ch., 2001, Plaque for Appreciation of Leadership & Dedication to Cmty., Faith Tabernacle of Praise Mins., Inc., 2001, Moderator's Appreciation Legacy award, Reconition Valuable Contbr's Mt. Sinai Missionary Baptist Assn., 2007—08, Cmty Svc. award, Ebony Appreciation awards, Com. Inc., Silver Anneversary award, Pleasant St. Historic Soc., 2009, Lifetime Achievement award, Cmty. Svc. Religion; named to Hall of Fame, Susie Mae White Cmty. Svc., 2010. Mem. AAUW, Nat. Ret. Tchrs. Assn., Alachua County Tchrs. Assn., Fla. Meml. Coll. Nat. Alumni Assn., Heroines of Jericho, Masons Democrat. Avocations: gardening, speaking, working with police on crime prevention. Office: Child Care Ctr 811 NW 4th Pl Gainesville FL 32601-5049

WHITEHEAD, ROBERT P., oncologist; b. Mpls., Sept. 13, 1945; BA, Johns Hopkins U., 1967; MD, U. Md., 1971. Sr. mem., med. oncology Nev. Cancer Inst., 2010—. Prof. U. Nev. Sch. Medicine, 2010. Mem.: Ea. Coop. Oncology Group, Am. Assn. Cancer Rsch., Am. Soc. Clin. Oncology. Office: One Breakthough Way Las Vegas NV 89135 Business E-Mail: rwhitehead@nvcancer.org.

WHITEHEAD, TANYA DIANNE GRUBBS, psychologist, educator, researcher; b. Scottsbuff, Nebr., June 23, 1953; d. William Elliott Grubbs and Esther Mary Cooper Grubbs; m. William Downing Whitehead, Aug. 12, 1971; children: Shana Alexandra, Thomas William, Bethany Rose. B in Psychology summa cum laude, Ottawa U., 1990; M in Clin. Psychology, Avila U., 1992; D in Psychology, U. Mo., 2001. Cert. specialist, developmental and handicapping conditions U. Kans. Sch. Medicine, 1993. Clin. instr. U. Kans. Sch. Medicine, Kansas City, 1987—96; rsch. prof. U. Mo., Kansas City, 1996—. Psychol. consulting burn unit, craniofacial team, spina bifida clinic, pediatric gastroenterology Sch. Medicine, U. Kans., Kansas City, 1987—96; state, regional and nat. advisor People First Self Advocacy Tng. Adults With Devel. Disabilities, 1997—2001; peer grant rev. facilitator and chair US Depts Health and Human Svcs., Corp. for Nat. Svc., Washington, 1999—; program evaluator, impact of asset bldg. on youth from disadvantaged circumstances Office of Cmty. Svc., US Dept. Health and Human Svs.; program evaluation: promoting higher edn. partnerships for global devel. US AID, Assn. Liaison Office for U. Cooperation in Devel., Cape Town, South Africa; dir. AmeriCorps VISTA Project in Self Advocacy, Statewide, Mo., 1998—2000; cons.: cmty. movement for urban progress cmty. devel. corp. Urban Core Cmty. Devel. Project, Kansas City, 2002—04; sr. program evaluator; assets for independence demonstration project, us hhs, office cmty. svcs. PeopleWorks, Inc., Washington, 2000—01. Author: (Self Determination Workshops) New Media Workshops for Adults with DD, (book) Exploring Self Advocacy from a Social Power Perspective, Disability Accommodations from a Person Centered Perspective, (film) Enslaved Minds: Final Barrier to Freedom and Justice; contbr. new media toolkit (Crystal Communicator Award, 2001); author: (disability accommodation guide) Exchange City Accommodation Guide. Recipient Sr. Specialist Fulbright, Sr. Devel. Specialist, USAID; fellow Ctr. for the City, U. Mo., 2004-2005; fellow, Studies in Cmty. Change, 2000. Mem.: ANA (mem. commn. accreditation 2006—08), AAUP, AAUW, APA, LWV, Am. Nurses Credentialing Ctr. (bd. Commn. on Accreditation). Home: 1850 N Clark St Apt 1908 Chicago IL 60614-5339 Business E-Mail: whiteheadt@umkc.edu.

WHITEHOUSE, FRED WAITE, endocrinologist, researcher; b. Chgo., May 6, 1926; s. Fred Trafton Waite and Grace Caroline (Peters) W.; m. Iris Jean Dawson, June 6, 1953; children: Martha, Amy, Sarah. Student, Northwestern U., 1943-45; BS, U. Ill., Chgo., 1947, MD, 1949. Diplomate Am. Bd. Internal Medicine; cert. endocrinology and metabolism. Intern, then resident Henry Ford Hosp., Detroit, 1949-53, staff physician, 1955—, chief divsn. metabolism, 1962-88, chief divsn. endocrinology and metabolism, 1988-95; divsn. head emeritus, 1995—; fellow Joslin Clinic, Boston, 1954-55. Cons. FDA, Washington, 1980-2008; mem. Coalition Diabetes Edn. and Minority Health, 1989-91. Contbr. articles to profl. jours. Bd. dirs. Wheat Ridge Found., 1984-93. Lt. USNR, 1951-53. Master ACP; mem. NIH (nat. diabetes adv. bd. 1984-88), Am. Diabetes Assn. (pres. 1978-79, Banting medal 1979, Outstanding Clinician award 1989, Outstanding Physician Educators award 1994, Best award 1994), Detroit Med. Club (pres. 1976), Detroit Acad. Medicine (pres. 1991-92). Lutheran. Avocations: bicycling, gardening. Home: 1265 Blairmoor Ct Grosse Pointe Woods MI 48236-1230 Office: Henry Ford Med Group 3031 W Grand Blvd Ste 800 Detroit MI 48202 Home Phone: 313-884-1324; Office Phone: 313-916-5812. Office Fax: 313-916-8343. Business E-Mail: fwhiteh1@hfhs.org.

WHITEHURST, WILLIAM OSCAR, lawyer; b. Ardmore, Okla., Oct. 23, 1945; s. William Oscar and Freddie Elizabeth (Ormsby) W.; m. Stephanie Anne Evans, June 22, 1968; children: Emilee Dawn, Rebecca Danielle. BS in Pharmacy, U. Okla., 1968; JD, U. Tex., 1970. Bar: Tex. 1971, U.S. Dist. Ct. (we. dist.) Tex. 1971, U.S. Ct. Mil. Appeals 1971, U.S. Ct. Appeals (5th cir.) 1971, U.S. Supreme Ct. 1971; bd. cert. in personal injury trial law, Tex.; bd. cert. civil trial adv. Assoc. Fulbright & Jaworski, Houston, 1971; counsel, staff dir. jud. affairs com. Tex. Ho. Reps., Austin, 1975; sr. shareholder Whitehurst, Harkness & Brees Cheng & Imhotf, P.C., Austin, 1975—. Mem. Senate-House Select Com. on the Judiciary, 1983-84, subcom. on Svc. Delivery, subcom. on Jurisdicition; faculty law U. Tex., 1979-86, 88, Tex. Coll. Trial Adv., 1984—. Served to capt. JAGC, USAF, 1971-75. Fellow Am. Bar Found., Tex. Bar Found. (chmn. bd. trustees 1992-93), Am. Coll Trial Lawyers, Internat. Acad. Trial Lawyers (pres. 2008-09); mem. ABA (chmn. standing com. legal aid and indigent defendants 2003-06), Nat. Conf. Bar Pres. (exec. coun. 1992-95), Tex. Bar Assn. (pres. 1986-87, exec. com. 1981-84, 85-88, bd. dirs. 1981-84, active various coms.), Travis County Bar Assn. (sec. 1980-81, bd. dirs. 1979-81), Am. Bd. Trial Advs., Tex. Young Lawyers Assn. (pres. 1982-83, bd. dirs. 1979-84), Austin Young Lawyers Assn. (pres. 1978-79), Tex. Trial Lawyers Assn. (pres. 1995), Am. Soc. Pharmacy Law, Am. Soc. Law and Medicine, Order of Barristers, Univ. Club, Austin Country Club. Democrat. Presbyterian. Avocations: flying, skiing, travel. Home: 2703 Westlake Dr Austin TX 78746-1909 Office: Whitehurst Harkness et al 5113 Southwest Pky Ste 150 Austin TX 78735 Office Phone: 512-476-4346. Business E-Mail: bwhitehurst@austintriallaw.com.

WHITELAW, BRUCE, biotechnologist, educator; b. Malaya, Aug. 19, 1959; BSc, U. Edinburgh, 1982; PhD, U. Glasgow, 1986. Divsn. head BBSRC Roslin Inst., 2005—07; prof. animal biotech. U. Edinburgh, 2007—. Sci. adv. bd. mem. Immunogenes AG, 2007, Recombinetics Inc., 2010; frontiers sci. jury mem. BBVA Found., 2008; v.p. animal biotech. NewVectys SAS, 2011. Mem. Internat. Soc. Transgenic Techs. Office: Roslin Inst Easter Bush Campus Edinburgh Midlothian EH25 9RG Scotland Business E-Mail: bruce.whitelaw@roslin.ed.ac.uk.

WHITE LOVETT, ANNESHA, pharmacist, researcher; b. LA, Calif., Jan. 14, 1977; d. Henry C. and Brenda V. White; m. John C. Lovett III, Oct. 27, 2007. PharmD, Fla. A&M U., Tallahassee, 2001, MS, 2003; PhD, U. Fla., Gainesville, 2010. Cert. geriatric care mgmt. U. Fla., 2007. Health policy analyst Govt. Accountability Office, Washington, 2002—02; tchg. asst. Fla. A&M U., Tallahassee, 2001—03; intern Agy. Health Care Adminstrn., Tallahassee, 2001—01, Wyeth Pharmaceuticals, Collegeville, Pa., 2005—05; tchg. asst. U. Fla., Gainesville, 2003—05, rsch. asst., 2005—10; asst. prof. Mercer U., Atlanta, 2010—. Pharmacy intern Walgreens, Tallahassee, 1999—2001, Jackson Meml. Hosp., Fla., 2000—01; peer reviewer Jour. Managed Care Pharmacy, 2003—. Author jour. articles Vol. Miracle Hill Nursing Home, Tallahassee, 1999—2003; dir. Health & Spiritual Wellness Six Ministeries Hopewell Missionary Bapt. Ch., 2011—; chair health ministry Hopewell Missionary Bapt. Ch., Norcross, Ga., 2008—10. Recipient Grad. Student Tchg. award, Fla. A&M U., 2003, Grad. Student Rsch. award, 2003, Nat. Minority Leadership award, 2000, ISPOR Disting. Svc. award, Internat. Soc. Pharmacoeconomics Outcomes Rsch., 2006, 2007, Student Achievement award, South Fla. Soc. of Health-System Pharmacists, 2000, Assn. of Black Health Sys. Pharmacists, 2000, award, Inst. Learning Retirement, 2008; Alumni Fellowship, U. Fla., 2003-2006, Pre Doctoral fellowship, 2009, fellowship, Pharm. Rsch. and Mfrs. America, 2009. Mem.: Am. Assoc. Colls. Pharmacy, Acad. Managed Care Pharmacy, Acad. Health, Am. Pharmacists Assn., Am. Soc. Health-System Pharmacists, Internat. Soc. Pharmacoeconomics Outcomes Rsch. (student network chair 2006—07). Home Phone: 404-771-6546; Office Phone: 678-547-6134. Personal E-mail: anneshalovett@gmail.com. Business E-Mail: lovett_aw@mercer.edu.

WHITEN, (DAVID) ANDREW, psychologist, researcher; b. Apr. 20, 1948; BSc in Zoology with 1st class honors, Sheffield U., England, 1969; PhD, Bristol U., England, 1972. Conversion fellow Queen's Coll., Oxford, England, 1972—75; lectr. in psychology St. Andrew's U., Fife, Scotland, 1975—90, reader, 1990—97, Leverhulme rsch. fellow Fife, Scotland, 2003—06; SSRC postdoc. rsch. fellow Dept. Experimental Psychology U. Oxford, 1972—75, prof. evolutionary & devel. psychology, 1997, wardlaw prof. psychology, 2000—; vis. prof. U. Zurich, 1992, Emory U., 1996. Vis. prof. Zurich U., Switzerland, 1992; F.M. Bird prof. Emory U., Atlanta, 1995—96; rsch. reader Brit. Acad., 1999—2001. Co-editor (with R. Byrne): Machiavellian Intelligence: Social Expertise and the Evolution of Intellect, 1988; co-editor: (with E. Widdowson) Natural Diet and Foraging Strategy of Monkeys, Apes and Humans, 1992; co-editor: Machiavellian Intelligence II: Extensions and Evaluations, 1997, 2000; author: Natural Theories of Mind: Evolution, Development and Simulation of Everyday Mindreading, 1991; contbr. articles to profl. publs. Recipient Rivers medal, Royal Anthrop. Inst. Gt. Britain and Ireland, 2007, Osman-Hill medal, Primate Soc. Gt. Britain, 2010; sr. rsch. fellow, Royal Soc. Leverhulme Trust, 2006—07. Fellow: FRSE, FBA, FBPsS. Avocations: art, painting, films, music, gardening. Office: U St Andrews Sch Psychology Fife KY16 9JU Scotland Business E-Mail: a.whiten@st-and.ac.uk.

WHITESCARVER, JACK EDWARD, federal agency administrator; b. Palestine, Tex., May 16, 1937; s. A.B. and Elizabeth Lorraine (Kimball) Whitescarver. BS, Sam Houston State U., Huntsville, Tex., 1959, MS, 1965; PhD, U. Medicine Dentistry NJ, 1974. Rsch. assoc. Harvard U. Sch. Pub. Health, Boston, 1976-77; grants assoc. NIH, Bethesda, Md., 1977, spl. asst. to dir., Nat. Inst. Allergy & Infectious Diseases (NIAID), 1978-84, dep. dir., Office AIDS Rsch. (OAR), 1988—2000, acting dir. OAR, 2000—02, dir. OAR, assoc. dir. AIDS rsch., 2002—; asst. dean rsch. & devel. Emory U. Sch. Medicine, Atlanta, 1984-86, assoc. dean, 1986-88, asst. prof. pathology, 1985-88. Contbr. numerous articles to profl. jours., chapters to books. Recipient Disting. Svc. award, HHS; named Alumnus of Yr., UMDNJ Grad. Sch. Biomed. Scis., 1991; fellow Albert Soiland Cancer Found., 1967—70. Mem.: Internat. AIDS Soc., Infectious Diseases Soc. America, Am. Acad. Allergy & Immunology. Office: NIH Office AIDS Rsch MSC 9308 5635 Fishers Ln Rockville MD 20852 Office Phone: 301-496-0357. Office Fax: 301-496-2119. Business E-Mail: jack.whitescarver@nih.gov. *

WHITFIELD, GRAHAM FRANK, orthopedic surgeon; b. Eng., 1942; arrived in U.S., 1969, naturalized, 1975; BSc, King's Coll., U. London, 1963; PhD, Queen Mary Coll., U. London, 1969; MD, NY Med. Coll., 1976. Rsch. scientist Unilever Rsch. Lab., England, 1963-66; postdoctoral fellow dept. chemistry Temple U., 1969-71, instr., 1971-72, asst. prof., 1972-73; resident in surgery NY Med. Coll. Affiliated Hosps., NYC, 1976-78, resident in orthopedics, 1978-79, sr. resident in orthop. surgery, 1979-80, chief resident, 1980-81; attending orthop. surgeon Good Samaritan Hosp., West Palm Beach, Fla., 1981-87, St. Mary's Hosp., West Palm Beach, 1981—82, JFK Med. Ctr., Lake Worth, Fla., 1981—, Palms Wellington Surg. Ctr., West Palm Beach, 1994-96, Wellington Regional Med. Ctr., West Palm Beach, 1996—, Bethesda Health City, Boynton Beach, Fla., 1996—2009, Palms West Hosp., Loxahatchee, Fla., 1997—2004, Columbia Hosp., West Palm Beach, 1997—2002. Instr. health professions divsn. Nova Southeastern U., North Miami, Fla., 1994-95, clin. asst. prof. dept. surgery, Coll. Osteo. Medicine, Nova Southeastern U., Ft. Lauderdale, Fla., 1995—, expert med. advisor, Divsn. Managed Care & Health Quality, Bureau Managed Health Care Workers Compensation Unit Agy. Health Care Administrn. & Judges Compensation Claims, 1996-2008 Author: (with Joseph Cohn and Louis Del Guercio) Critical Care Readings, 1981; editl. bd., contbg. editor Hosp. Physician, 1978-82; cons. editor Physician Asst. and Health Practitioner, 1979-82; orthop. cons. Conv. Reporter, 1980-82; assoc. editor-in-chief Critical Care Monitor, 1980-82; editl. bd. Complications in Orthopedics, 1986-96; practice panel cons. in orthop. surgery Complications in Surgery, 1982-96. Vol. with med. mission Orthop. Splty. Med. Care to the indigenous population, Andes Mountains Ecuador, 2007—08. Recipient N.Y. Med. Coll. Surg. Soc. award, 1976. Fellow: Internat. Coll. Surgeons; mem.: AMA, Fla. Orthop. Soc., So. Orthop. Assn., Royal Inst. Chemistry (Eng.), Palm Beach County Med. Soc., Fla. Med. Assn., Soc. the Four Arts, Rotary, Explorer's Club (N.Y.C.), Brit. Schs. and Univs. Club, Soc. Sons of St. George (N.Y.C.), Sigma Xi. Avocation: travel. Office: 2150 S Congress Ave West Palm Beach FL 33406-7604 Office Phone: 561-965-5200. Business E-Mail: doctorwhitfield@aol.com.

WHITFIELD, JONATHAN MARTIN, pediatrician; b. Edinburgh, Sept. 26, 1946; s. Robert Percy and Miriam (Rosenberg) W.; m. Clare Anne Larabie; children: Mark, Andrew, Nicola. MB BChir cum laude, Glasgow U., Scotland, 1970. Fellow in neonatology U. Toronto, Ont., Can., 1977-78, U. Colo., 1976-77, from asst. prof. to assoc. prof. pediats., 1978-91; dir. neonatology and pediat. critical care Baylor U. Med. Ctr., Dallas, 1991-94, chmn. pediats., 1994—. Comdr. M.C. USN, 1986—. Fellow Am. Coll. Chest Physicians, Am. Acad. Pediats., Royal Coll. Physicians Can. Avocations: music, skiing, sailing, diving. Office: Baylor U Med Ctr 3500 Gaston Ave Dallas TX 75246-2096

WHITING, DONALD M., neurologist, educator; MD, Thomas Jefferson U. Diplomate Am. Bd. Neurol. Surgery. Intern Geisinger Med. Ctr.; resident Cleveland Clinic, fellow; clin. assoc. prof. neurosurgery Drexel Univ.; fellow Allegheny Gen. Hosp., practice in neurosurgery, surgical dir. Named one of Top Doctors, Pitts. mag. Office: Allegheny General Hospital 320 E N Ave Pittsburgh PA 15212 Office Phone: 412-359-3131. Office Fax: 412-359-4108.

WHITING-SORRELL, ANNA, state agency administrator; b. Hot Springs, Mont., July 1, 1957; m. Gene Whiting-Sorrell; 1 child, Katy. BA in Polit. Sci. with honors, U. Mont., Missoula, 1980, MPA, 1993. Instr. Two Eagle River Sch., Mont., 1980—82, academic supr., curriculum devel. specialist, 1982—83; adminstr., Alcohol and Substance Abuse Program Confederated Salish and Kootenai Tribes Tribal Adminstrn., 1984—92, social services adminstr., Alcohol and Substance Abuse Program, 1991—93, health systems planner, 1993—94, program analyst, 1994—2002, dir. office support services, 2002—05; dir. Native Am. Outreach Senator John Kerry's Presdl. Campaign, 2004; dep. policy dir. Gov. Elect. Schweitzer and Lt. Gov. Elect Bohlinger Transition Team, 2004; policy advisor on families to Gov. Brian Schweitzer Office of the Gov., Mont., 2005—08; dir. Mont. Dept. Pub. Health and Human Services, Helena, 2008—. Mem. Ronan Sch. Dist. Indian Parent Com., chairwoman, 1995—97; co-chair, cmty. partnership com. Ronan Sch. Office civil Rights, 2003; mem. Kellogg Leadership Cmty. Change Program, 2004; enrolled mem. Confederated Salish and Kootenai Tribes; mem. Salish Kootenai Devel. Bd. Dirs. Recipient Cert. Disting. Svc., Tribal Coun., Confederated Salish and Kootenai Tribes, 1987, Outstanding Performance award, 1992, 1998, Group Citation award, US Dept. Health and Human Services Indian Health Service, 1988, Outstanding Svc. award, Ctr. Substance Abuse Prevention, 1997, 25 Yrs. Honoring 25 Individuals award, Nat. Assn. Children of Alcoholics, 2008. Democrat. Office: Mont Dept Pub Health and Human Services 111 N Sanders Rm 301 Helena MT 59620 Office Phone: 406-444-5622. Office Fax: 406-444-1970.

WHITLEY, RICHARD, state agency administrator; BA, Willamette U., Oreg.; MS in Counseling Psychology, Oreg. State U., Corvallis. Sr. psychologist Nev. Women's Correctional Facility; chief, bur. cmty. health Nev. Dept. Health and Human Services, Carson City, dep. adminstr., health divsn., 2004—08, adminstr., health divsn., 2008—. Office: Nev Dept Health and Human Services Health Divsn 4150 Technology Way Ste 300 Carson City NV 89706 Office Phone: 775-684-4200. Office Fax: 775-684-4211.

WHITLEY, RICHARD JAMES, pediatrician, educator; b. Nutley, NJ, Sept. 15, 1945; s. Robert Jackson and Helen (Sigemund) W.; m. Sally Bendroth, Apr. 11, 1973; children: Kevin, Christopher, Catherine, Jennifer BA, Duke U., 1967; MD, George Washington U., 1971. Diplomate Am. Bd. Pediatrics. Intern in pediatrics U. Ala., Birmingham, 1971-72, resident in pediatrics, 1972-73, fellow dept. pediatrics, 1973-76, asst. prof. pediatrics, 1976-77, asst. prof. pediatrics and microbiology, assoc. scientist Cancer Research and Tng. Ctr., 1977-78, assoc. prof. pediatrics, asst. prof. microbiology, 1978-80, scientist Cancer Research and Tng. Ctr., dir. clin. research unit Univ. Hosp., 1978-80, assoc. prof., vice chmn. dept. pediatrics, asst. prof. microbiology, 1980-81, scientist Cancer Research and Tng. Ctr., dir. clin. research unit Univ. Hosp., 1980-81, prof., vice chmn. dept., assoc. prof. microbiology, 1981-83, scientist Cancer Research and Tng. Ctr., dir. clin. research unit, Univ. Hosp., 1981-83, prof., acting chmn. dept. pediatrics, assoc. prof. microbiology, 1983-84, scientist Cancer Rsch. and Tng. Ctr., dir. clin. rsch. unit, Univ. Hosp., 1983-84, prof. pediatrics and microbiology, 1985-87, prof. medicine, 1988—, vice chmn. dept. pediatrics, 1989—, acting dir. div. perinatal medicine, 1989-91, scientist Cancer Rsch. and Tng. Ctr., dir. clin. rsch. unit, Univ. Hosp., 1984-88, Loeb eminent scholar chair in pediatrics, 1992; staff physician U. Ala. in Birmingham Hosps. and Clinics, Children's Hosp., Birmingham. Cons. in field; mem. virology sect. NIH, 1985-89, chmn. Nat. Inst. Allergies and Infectious Diseases Data Safety and Monitoring Bd., 1986—, reviewer, site visitor; pres. IDSA, 2009-10. Sect. editor Intervirology, 1986—; editor Antiviral Rsch., 1987—; mem. editorial bd. Jour. Infectious Diseases, 1988—, Sexually Transmitted Diseases, 1989—; contbr. numerous articles to profl. jours. Bd. dirs. Ala. Sch. of Fine Arts, Birmingham, 1982-90 Recipient award of Commendation U. Ala. in Birmingham, 1977, Pres.'s medal, 2007, named Disting. Prof., 2009. Mem. Am. Soc. Virology (bd. dirs. 1988—), Internat. Soc. Antiviral Rsch. (pres. 1988-90), Soc. for Health and Human Values, Transplantation Soc., Infectious Diseases Soc. (past pres. 2010-11), Soc. for Pediatric Rsch., Alpha Omega Alpha Home: 216 Shades Crest Cir Birmingham AL 35216-1316 Office: U Ala Dept Pediatrics 1600 7th Ave S Birmingham AL 35233-1711 *

WHITLOCK, ANDY, medical association administrator; b. San Francisco, Oct. 14, 1975; BS, The Citadel, 1997; PhD, Med. U. SC, 2003. Assoc. dir., preclin. ocular pharmacology Lexicon Pharms., 2004—. Mem.: ARVO. Office: 8800 Tech Forest Pl The Woodlands TX 77381 Business E-Mail: awhitlock@lexpharma.com.

WHITMAN, BURKE WILLIAM, health services executive; b. Newport, RI, Feb. 26, 1956; s. Homer William and Anne (Sarran) W. BA cum laude, Dartmouth Coll., 1978; MBA, Harvard U., 1984. Project mgr. HCB Contractors/Barker Interests Ltd., Atlanta, Houston, 1979-85; investment banker Morgan Stanley & Co. Inc., NYC, 1988-92; v.p. fin./devel. Almost Family Inc., Balt., 1992-94; pres., CFO Deerfield Healthcare Corp., Balt., 1994-99; CFO Triad Hosps., Inc., Plano, Tex., 1999—2005; pres., COO Health Mgmt. Assocs., Inc., Naples, Fla., 2005—07, pres., CEO, 2007—08. Bd. dirs. Fedn. Am. Hosps., chmn. audit com., 2005—06. Former bd. dirs. Outward Bound, Police Athletic League; bd. advisors Marine Corps U.; mem. Founders Group, Nat. Mus. Marine Corps. With USMC, 1985—2005, lt. col. USMCR, 1988—. Mem.: Fedn. Am. Hosps. (bd. dirs.), Piedmont Driving Club. Episcopalian. Avocations: hiking, bicycling, outdoor sports.

WHITMER, W. CARL, hospital administrator; BS, Western Ky. U. Sr. mgr. KPMG LLP, 1986—94; v.p., fin., treas. & CFO PhyCor Inc., 1994—2000; v.p., treas. IASIS Healthcare LLC, 2000—01, CFO, 2001—10, pres., CEO, 2010—. Bd. dirs. Fenwall Inc. Office: IASIS Healthcare LLC 117 Seaboard Ln Bldg E Franklin TN 37067 Office Phone: 615-844-2747. Office Fax: 615-846-3006. Business E-Mail: wwhitmer@iasishealthcare.com. *

WHITMORE, DOUGLAS MICHAEL, physician; b. Cambridge, Mass., Oct. 30, 1947; s. Donald Herbert and Marcela (Klein) W.; m. Ana Maria Lopez. BS, MS in Physics, U. Ill., Champaign-Urbana, 1969; MS in Physics, Stanford U., 1970, PhD in Physics, 1975; MD, U. Miami, 1978. Diplomate Am. Bd. Internal Medicine, Am. Bd. Pulmonary Disease, Am. Bd. Critical Care Medicine, Am. Bd. Geriatric Medicine. Physician Holy Cross Hosp., Ft. Lauderdale, Fla., 1983—. Pres. med. staff Holy Cross Hosp., 1996-97, chief of medicine, 1995-98. Trustee Holy Cross Hosp., 1995-98. Fellow ACP, Am. Coll. Chest Physicians; mem. Caducean Med. Soc. (pres. 1996-97), Am. Thoracic Soc. Office: Med Complex West 1930 NE 47th St Ste 205 Fort Lauderdale FL 33308-7728 *

WHITMORE, KRISTENE E., medical educator, director; MD, Hahnemann U. Diplomate Am. Bd. Urology. Resident gen. surgery Hahnemann Univ. Hosp., resident urology; fellow Female Pelvic Medicine and Reconstructive Surgery; founder Pelvic and Sexual Health Inst., various positions, med. dir. Phila.; prof. urology and ob-gyn. dept. Drexel Univ., chair urology, female pelvic medicine and reconstructive surgery; program dir. Univ. Medicine and Dentistry of NJ. Author: Overcoming Bladder Disorders: Compassionate, Authoritative Medical and Self-Help Solutions for Incontinence, Cystitis, Interstitial Cystitis; contbr. Jour. of Urology, Urology, Am. Jour. of Obstetrics and Gynecology, Clin. Obstetrics and Gynecology, Internat. Jour. of Urogynecology, Prevention Mag., Cosmo, Ladies Home Jour., US News and World Report. Adv. bd. mem. Women's Health Found., Simon Found.; bd. dirs. Am. Urogynecologic Soc. Found. Mem.: Interstitial Cystitis Assn. (adv. bd. mem.), Nat. Assn. for Continence (adv. bd. mem.). Office: Pelvic and Sexual Health Institute 4th Fl 207 N Broad St Philadelphia PA 19102 Office Phone: 215-863-8100. Office Fax: 215-587-6252.

WHITSELL, JOHN CRAWFORD, II, general surgeon; b. St. Joseph, Mo., Dec. 21, 1929; s. Ora Earl and Lorena (Spratt) W. AB, Grinnell Coll., Iowa, 1950; MD, Washington U., St. Louis, 1954. Diplomate Am. Bd. Surgery, Am. Bd. Thoracic Surgery. From instr. to clin. prof. surgery Cornell U. Med. Ctr., NYC, 1963—70; from asst. attending to attending in surgery NY Hosp., NYC, 1964—70; surg. dir. Rogosin Kidney Ctr. NY Hosp.-Cornell Med. Ctr., NYC, 1973—75; attending in surgery NY Hosp., 1970—98, hon. attending surgeon, 2001—; clin. prof. surgery Cornell Med. Coll., 1970—98, clin. prof. surgery emeritus, 1998—. Surg. cons. Rogosin Kidney Ctr., 1975—, Sharon Hosp., Conn., 1976-2001. Contbr. articles to profl. jours. Capt. USAF, 1961-63, Eng. Fellow ACS; mem. Transplantation Soc., NY Surg. Soc., Am. Soc. Transplant Surgeons, NY Soc. for Thoracic Surgery, Soc. Thoracic Surgeons, NY Acad. Medicine, Union Club of NY, Phi Beta Kappa. Avocations: golf, fishing, auto racing. Personal E-mail: rmwhitsell@aol.com.

WHITTEMORE, ANTHONY DUNSTER, vascular surgeon, chief medical officer; b. Boston, Nov. 5, 1944; s. Anthony Rogers Whittemore and Kathrine Gansevoort Binnian Howe; m. Rhoda Belknap Stetson, June 18, 1966; children: Anthony Rogers, Joshua Stetson, Sarah Belknap. BS, Trinity Coll., 1966; MD, Columbia U., 1970. Resident surgery Columbia Presbyn. Med. Ctr., 1970—76; rsch. assoc. Columbia U., NYC, 1972—73; trainee NIH, 1975—76; vascular fellow Peter Bent Brigham Hosp., Boston, 1976—77; chief vascular surgery Naval Regional Med. Ctr., Portsmouth, Va., 1977—79; instr. surgery Harvard Med. Sch./Peter Bent Brigham Hosp., Boston, 1979—80; asst. prof. surgery Harvard U., 1981—87, assoc. prof. surgery, 1987—93, prof. surgery Med. Sch., 1993—. Dir. surg. tng. program Harvard Med. Sch./Brigham and Women's Hosp., 1979; mem. med. staff. Brigham and Women's Hosp., 1979—, chief divsn. vascular surgery, 1990—99, apptd. dir. Vascular Ctr., 1991, chief med. officer, 1999—; grant investigator NIH, 1979, 83; cons. Bard CardioSurgery, Billerica, Mass., 1982—, Meadox Meds., Oakland, NJ, 1983—, Instrumentation Labs., North Andover, Mass., 1980—. Contbr. articles to profl. pubs. Served to lt. comdr. USN, 1977—79. Decorated Commendation award USN. Fellow: ACS; mem.: Soc. Internat. de Chirurgie, New Eng. Soc. Vascular Surgery, New Eng. Surg. Soc., Soc. Vascular Surgey, Internat. Cardiovascular Soc., Boston Surg. Soc., Soc. U. Surgeons, Am. Surg. Soc., Am. Soc. for Artificial Internal Organs (program com. 1982—), Am. Surg. Assn., Assn. Acad. Surgery, Country Club. Achievements include patents in field. Home: 148 Farm Rd Sherborn MA 01770-1622 Office: Brigham & Women's Hosp 75 Francis St Boston MA 02115-6106 Office Phone: 617-732-8515.

WHITTEMORE, PAUL BAXTER, psychologist; s. Harry Ballou and Margaret B. Whittemore; m. Jane Moore, Apr. 22, 1995. BA in Religion, Ea. Nazarene Coll., 1970; MDiv., Nazarene Theol. Sem., 1973; MA in Theology, Vanderbilt U., 1975, PhD in Theology, 1978; PhD in Clin. Psychology, U. Tenn., 1987. Cert. in clin. psychology Am. Bd. Profl. Psychology, lic. psychologist Calif. Asst. prof. philosophy Trevecca Nazarene Coll., Nashville, 1973—76; asst. prof. philosophy and religion Point Loma Coll., San Diego, 1976—80; asst. prof. philosophy Mid. Tenn. State U., Murfreesboro, 1980—83; clin. psychology intern LA County/U. So. Calif. Med. Ctr., LA, 1986—87; coord. behavior health ctr. Calif. Med. Ctr., LA, 1987—88; clin. asst. prof. family medicine U. So. Calif. Sch. Medicine, LA, 1988—; pvt. practice Newport Beach, Calif., 1991—. Mem. behavioral sci. faculty Glendale Adventist Family Practice Residency Program, Glendale, Calif., 1989—90; inpatient group therapist Ingleside Hosp., Rosemead, Calif., 1990—92; founder, pres. Date Coach, 1992—2000. Contbr. articles to profl. jours. Recipient Andrew W. Mellon Postdoctoral Faculty Devel. award, Vanderbilt U., 1981. Mem.: AAUP (chpt. v.p. 1982—83), APA, Orange County Psychol. Assn. (bd. dirs. 1996—2001), Calif. Psychol. Assn. (media divsn. sec.-treas. 1997—98), Am. Philos. Assn., Am. Acad. Religion. Achievements include discovery of link between phenylthiocarbamide tasting and depression. Office: 1001 Dove St Ste 145 Newport Beach CA 92660-2123

WHYBROW, PETER CHARLES, psychiatrist, educator, director, author; b. Hertfordshire, Eng., June 13, 1939; U.S. citizenship, 1975; s. Charles Ernest and Doris Beatrice (Abbott) W.; children: Katherine, Helen Student, U. Coll., London, 1956—59; MB BS, U. Coll., 1962; diploma psychol. medicine, Conjoint Bd., London, 1968; MA (hon.), Dartmouth Coll., 1974, U. Pa., 1994. House officer endocrinology U. Coll. Hosp., 1962, sr. house physician psychiatry, 1963—64; house surgeon St. Helier Hosp., Surrey, England, 1963; house officer pediat. Prince of Wales Hosp., London, 1964; resident psychiatry U. N.C. Hosp., 1965—67, instr., rsch. fellow, 1967—68; mem. sci. staff neuropsychiat. rsch. unit Charshalton, Surrey, 1968—69; dir. residency tng. psychiatry Dartmouth Med. Sch., Hanover, NH, 1969—71, prof. psychiatry, 1970—84, chmn. dept., 1970—78, exec. dean, 1980—83; prof., chmn. dept. psychiatry U. Pa., Phila., 1984—96, Ruth Meltzer prof. psychiatry, 1992; chief psychiatrist Hosp. U. Pa., 1984—96; prof. psychiatry and biobehavioral scis., chmn. dept. psychiatry Sch. Medicine UCLA, 1996—, dir. Semel Inst. for Neurosci. and Human Behavior, 1996—, physician-in-chief CEO Rsch. Neuropsychiat. Hosp., 1996—, Judson Braun disting. prof. psychiatry, 1999—. Dir. psychiatry Dartmouth Hitchcock Affiliated Hosp., 1970-78; vis. scientist NIMH, 1978-79; cons. VA, 1970—, NIMH, 1972—; chmn. test com. Nat. Bd. Med. Examiners, 1977-84; rschr. psychoendrocrinology; vis. prof. Queen's Coll., Oxford U., 2009-. Author: Mood Disorders: Toward a New Psychobiology, 1984, The Hibernation Response, 1988, A Mood Apart, 1997, American Mania: When More Is Not Enough, 2005 (Gradiva Book award, Nat. Assn. Advancement Psychoanalysis, 2006); editor: Psychosomatic Medicine, 1977 (Ann. Book award NAMI 2005); mem. editl. bd. Cmty. Psychiatry, Psychiat. Times, Directions in Psychiatry, Neuropsychopharmacology, Depression; contbr. articles to profl. jours Recipient Anclote Manor award psychiat. rsch. U. N.C., 1967, Sr. Investigator award Nat. Alliance for Rsch. into Schizophrenia and Depression, 1989; scholar Josiah Macy Jr. Found., 1978-79, vis. scholar Oxford U., 2009-; fellow Ctr. Advanced Studies in Behavioral Sci., Stanford, 1993-94; recipient Lifetime Investigator award NDMDA, 1996; decorated Knight of Merit, Sovereign Order of St. John of Jerusalem, 1993; Disting. Prof. U. Calif., 2004, Silver Ribbon award for Sci. Leadership NARSAD, 2008. Fellow AAAS, Am. Psychiat. Assn., Royal Coll. Psychiatrists (founder), Am. Coll. Psychiatrists, Ctr. Advanced Study of Behavioral Scis. (hon.), Soc. Psychosomatic Rsch. London (hon.); mem. Am. Assn. Chmn. Depts. Psychiatry (pres. 1977-78), Royal Soc. Medicine, Am. Psychopath Assn., Am. Coll. Neuropsychopharmacology, Soc. Biol. Psychiatry, N.Y. Acad. Scis., Soc. Neurosci., Sigma Xi, Alpha Omega Alpha Office: UCLA Semel

Inst Neuroscience & Human Behavior 760 Westwood Plz Los Angeles CA 90095-8353 Office Phone: 310-206-1233. Fax: 310-825-3942. Business E-Mail: pwhybrow@mednet.ucla.edu.

WHYTE, MICHAEL P., genetics educator, researcher, director; b. NYC, Dec. 19, 1946; s. Michael Paul and Sophie (Dziuk) W.; m. Gloria Frances Golenda, Oct. 26, 1974; 1 child, Catherine Alexandra. BA in Chemistry, NYU, 1968; MD, SUNY, Bklyn., 1972. Diplomate Am. Bd. Internal Medicine, Nat. Bd. Med. Examiners. Intern, 1st yr. resident dept. medicine NYU Sch. Medicine Bellevue Hosp., NYC, 1972-74; clin. assoc. devel. and metabolic neurology br. Nat. Inst. Neurol. and Communicative Disorders and Stroke NIH, Bethesda, Md., 1974-76; fellow divsn. bone and mineral metabolism dept. medicine Washington U. Sch. Medicine, 1976-79, instr. dept. medicine, 1979-80, asst. sci. dir. Clin. Rsch. Ctr., 1979—; asst. physician Barnes Hosp., 1979—; staff physician St. Louis Children's Hosp., 1979—; NIH clin. assoc. physician Clin. Rsch. Ctr. Washington U. Sch. Medicine, 1980-82, asst. prof. medicine dept. medicine, 1980-86, assoc. prof. medicine dept. medicine, 1986-91, asst. prof. pediat. Edward Mallinckrodt dept. pediat., 1982-89, assoc. prof. pediat. Edward Mallinckrodt dept. pediat., 1989-92, prof. medicine dept. medicine, 1991—, prof. pediat. Edward Mallinckrodt dept. pediat., 1992—, prof. genetics James S. McDonell dept. genetics, 1997—; med. dir. Metabolic Rsch. Unit Shriners Hosp. for Children, St. Louis, 1982-2000, mem. staff, 1983—; assoc. attending physician Jewish Hosp., 1983—. Mem. editl. bd. Calcified Tissue Internat., 1995-2000, Jour. Bone and Mineral Rsch., 1994—; med. adv. bd. Osteogenesis Imperfecta Found., 1986—, med. adv. panel Paget's Disease Found., 1986—; chmn. med. adv. com., bd. dirs. Osteogenesis Found., 1995—; med.-sci. dir. Ctr. for Metabolic Bone Disease and Molecular Rsch. Shriners Hosp. for Children, St. Louis, 2000—. Assoc. editor: Primer on Metabolic Bone Diseases and Disorders of Mineral Metabolism, 1990, 93, 96, 99, 2003, 06; assoc. editor Calcified Tissue Internat., 1989-2000; contbr. chpts. to books, articles to profl. jours. Lt. comdr. USPHS, 1974-76. Fellow Am. Coll. Endocrinology; mem. ACP (assoc.), Assn. Am. Physicians, Am. Soc. Cell Biology, Am. Soc. Clin. Investigation, Am. Fedn. Clin. Rsch., Am. Soc. Advancement Sci., Am. Soc. Bone and Mineral Rsch. (ednl. com. 1987—, Fuller Albright award 1987, Young Investigator award 1983, Dr. Boy Frame award 1997, Frederic C. Bartter award, 2007, Charles Slemenda award 2009, Henning Andensen prize 2010), Am. Soc. Human Genetics, Endocrine Soc., Soc. Exptl. Biology and Medicine, Japanese Soc. Inherited Metabolic Disease (hon.), NY Acad. Scis. Office: Shrinens Hosp Children 2001 S Lindbergh Blvd Saint Louis MO 63131 Business E-Mail: mwhyte@shrinenet.org.

WIACEK-ZUBRZYCKA, MAGDALENA, physical therapist; b. Klodzko, Nov. 23, 1976; d. Maria Wiacek; m. Igor Z. Zubrzycki; 1 child, Igor Klaudiusz Zubrzycki. PhD, Nicoluas Copernicus U., Bydgoszcz, Poland, Rostock U., Germany, 2003. Asst. Rzeszow U., Poland, 2005—08. Contbr. articles to profl. publs. Home: Ul. Gen. Kazimierza Sosnkowskiego 11 52-207 Wroclaw Poland Personal E-mail: magdalenawiacek@yahoo.de.

WIATR, CHRISTOPHER LOUIS, microbiologist; b. Chgo., Jan. 5, 1948; s. Joseph Thomas and Beatrice Harriet (Kaminski) Wiatr; m. Jeanne Lynn Malecki, Oct. 20, 1978; children: Kelli Jean, Christopher Joseph, Kaycee Lynn, Kirby Ann, Nicholas Aloysius. BS, Ill. Benedictine Coll., 1969; MS, IIT, 1974; PhD, U. Ill., Chgo., 1985. Cert. tchr. grades 9-12 Ill. Tchr., coach St. Rita High Sch., Chgo., 1969-74; rsch. microbiologist Swift & Co./Esmark/Beatrice Foods, Chgo., 1974-75, lab. mgr., 1975-76, tech. dir. rsch. and quality assurance, 1976-79; sr. microbiologist water and wastewater treatment R&D Nalco Chem. Co., Naperville, Ill., 1985-87; sr. rsch. microbiologist Nalco Chem. Co. Water and Waste Treatment R & D, Naperville, Ill., 1988, group leader water microbiology, 1989-91; group leader Pulp & Paper Chems. R & D, Naperville, Ill., 1991-94; mgr. biocides R&D Calgon-ECCI, Pitts., 1994—95, dir. microbiology and biochemistry, 1995—2000; tech. dir. formulator chem. divsn. Buckman Labs., Memphis, 2000—04, tech. dir. performance chem. divsn., 2005—; assoc. Water Techs. Tech. Com., 2000—, assoc. water com., 2001—, assoc. tech. presentations presentations subcom., 2001—02. Reviewer Nat. Assn. Corrosion Engrs; chmn. biocide and biofilms session Internat. Water Conf., 1996-98; conducted workshops Mont. State U., Bozeman, 1990, Ill. Inst. Tech., Chgo., 1993, U. Ga., Athens, 1995, SUNY, Farmington, 1999. Contbr. chapters to books, articles to profl. jours. Eagle scout, merit badge counselor Boy Scouts Am., 1963—; com. Maplebrook I Swim Club, Naperville, 1990-94; football coach St. Raphael, Naperville, 1993-94. Named Researcher of Yr., Nalco Chem. Co., 1987. Mem. TAPPI (microbiology and microbiol tech. and water quality com. 1993-98), Am. Chem. Soc., Nat. Assn. Corrosion Engrs., Soc. Indsl. Microbiology, Am. Soc. for Microbiology, Assn. Water Technologies (cooling water com., tech. com., biocide com., featured spkr. ann. meeting 2001, 03, 05), Cooling Tower Inst. (featured spkr., 2005), Soc. Tribologists and Lubricant Engrs. (spkr.), Sigma Xi (pres. Nalco chpt. 1991-92). Roman Catholic. Achievements include 20 patents; enzyme applications for controlling bacterial adhesion on equipment and surfaces; nontoxic biocontrol; recognition as expert on biofilms, biocides, microbiologically influenced corrosion and antimicrobial resistance. Business E-Mail: clwiatr@buckman.com.

WICHA, MAX S., oncologist, educator; b. NYC, Mar. 24, 1949; m. Sheila Crowley; children: Jason, Allyson. BS in Biology summa cum laude with honors, SUNY, Stony Brook, 1970; MD, Stanford U., 1974. Diplomate Am. Bd. Internal Medicine; lic. physician, Mich., Ill. Intern in internal medicine U. Chgo. Hosps. and Clinics, 1974-75, jr., sr. resident in internal medicine, 1975-77; rsch. assoc. lab. pathophysiology Nat. Cancer Inst./NIH, Bethesda, Md., 1977-79, fellow in clin. oncology, 1978-80, investigator lab. pathophysiology, 1979-80; asst. prof. internal medicine divsn. hematology and oncology U. Mich., Ann Arbor, 1980-83, assoc. prof., 1983-88, prof. internal medicine, disting. prof. oncology, 1988—, mem. tumor metastasis, extracellular matrix, reproductive endocrinology programs, 1982—, chief, divsn. hematology and oncology, dept. internal medcine, dir. Simpson Meml. Rsch. Inst., 1984-93, mem. program in cellular and molecular biology, 1984—, founding dir. Comprehensive Cancer Ctr., 1987—. Mem. cancer rsch. com. U. Mich., 1981—, sci. adv. bd. dental rsch. inst., 1983—, dean's adv., 1988—, reproductive endocrinology selection com., breast care ctr. exec. com., 1988—, exec. dir.'s adv. coun., 1992—, chair instl. rev. com. gene therapy program project., 1992—, dean's adv. com. Howard Hughes Med. Inst., 1992—, strategic planning policy and organizational com. health scis. info. tech. and networking, 1992—; vis. prof. Mich. State U., 1985, Harvard U., Boston, 1986, Wash. State U., 1986, Boston U., 1986, Wayne State U./Harper Grace Hosps., 1987, U. Ill., 1987, Med. Coll. Wis., 1987., U. Chgo., 1987, Eppley Inst. for Rsch. in Cancer and Allied Diseases, Omaha, 1988, U. Nebr., Omaha, 1988, U. Minn./Minn. VA Hosp., 1988, MD Anderson Cancer Ctr., Houston., Mt. Sinai Med. Ctr., N.Y.C., Am. Cancer Soc., Kalamazoo, 1989, Gainesville, Fla., 1990, Orlando, Fla., 1990, Pezcoller Symposium, Rovereto, Italy, 1990, Prince Henry's Hosp., Melbourne, Australia, 1990, Northwestern U. Med. Ctr., Chgo., 1990, Meml. Sloan-Kettering Cancer Ctr., N.Y.C., 1990, Tex. S.W. U., Dallas, 1990, Mich. State U., 1991; lectr. U. Mich., 1990; mem. NIH Site Visit team U. Calif. Cancer Rsch. Lab., Berkeley, 1985; ad hoc mem. cell biology and physiology study sect. NIH, 1985, 86, study sect., Bethesda, 1991; mem. NCI Site Visit team Norris Cotton Dartmouth Cancer Ctr, 1989, Howard U., Wash., 1989, Howard U. Parent Com., 1989, MD Anderson Cancer Ctr., Houston, 1992; sci. advisor U. Colo. Cancer Ctr., Denver, 1990, Samuel Waxman Cancer Rsch. Found., Mt. Sinai Med. Ctr., N.Y.C., 1988-93; mem. NCI Adv. Panel, Bethesda, 1991; mem. sci. adv. com. U. Tex. San Antonio Cancer Ctr., U. Miami Sylvester Cancer Ctr., Mich. State U., East Lansing, Norris-Cotton Cancer Ctr., Dartmouth-Hitchcock Med. Ctr., Hanover, N.H., Mich. Cancer Found., Detroit, V. T. Lombardi Cancer Rsch. Ctr., Georgetown U., Washington, 1992—, MD Anderson Cancer Ctr., Houston, 1992—; mem. extramural sci. adv. bd. UCI Clin. Cancer Ctr., U. Calif. Irvine, Orange, 1992—; mem. NCI SPORE in Prostate Cancer Study Sect., 1992; chair NCI Cancer Ctr. Support Rev. Com., 1993; NCI Site Visit chair Jefferson Cancer Ctr., Phila., 1992, Worcester (Mass.) Cancer Found., 1993, Duke U. Cancer Ctr., Durham, N.C., 1993, Lineberger Comprehensive Ctr., Chapel Hill, N.C., 1993; mem. NCI Comprehensive Cancer Ctrs. Review, 1993, chmn. parent com. Cancer Ctr. Support Rev. Com., 1992—; cons. Warner Lambert Co., 1980—. Assoc. editor: Molecular and Cellular Differentation, 1993; co-editor: The Hematopoietic Microenvironment, 1993, mem. editorial bd. Blood, Molecular and Cellular Differentiation, Jour. Lab. and Clin. Medicine, Cancer Rsch., 1993—, Oncology, Cancer Prevention Internat.; reviewer Nature, Science, Proceedings of NAS, Jour. Clin. Investigation, Jour. Cell Biology, Exptl. Cell Rsch., Exptl. Hematology, Cancer., Clin. and Exptl. Metastasis, Jour. Nat. Cancer Inst., Tissue & Cell, Am. Inst. Biol. Scis., Am. Jour. Pathology, Jour Immunology, Jour. Med. Scis., NSF, Oncology Rsch., Lab. Investigation, Breast Cancer Rsch. and Treatment; contbr. over 110 articles and to profl. jours., chpts. to books.; invited lectr. in field. With USPHS, 1977-80. Recipient NSF RSch. award SUNY, 1969, Eli Luke and David Jacob Rsch. award Stanford U. Sch. Medicine, 1974, Upjohn Achievement Excellence in Medicine award, Outstanding Med. Resident award U. Chgo. Hosps., 1977, Jerome Conn Excellence in Rsch. award, 1983; grantee NIH, 1991—, 93—, Am. Cancer Soc., 1992—, Suntory Rsch. Inst., 1992-93. Mem. AAASN, Am. Assn. for Cancer Rsch. (state legis. com. 1992—, finance com. 1992—), Am. Fedn. for Clin. Rsch. (selections com. midwest sect. 1986—, comm. com., 1986—, awards com., 1986—), Am. Soc. for Cell Biology, Am. Soc. Hematology (com. on publs. 1991-93), Assn. Am. Cancer Insts. (bd. dirs. 1993—), Am. Soc. for Clin. Investigation, Am. Soc. Clin. Oncology (award selection com. 1992—), Ctrl. Soc. for Clin. Rsch., Mich. Soc. Hematology and Oncology, Southwest Oncology Group, Assn. Community Cancer Ctrs. Achievements include patents for antibodies to human mammary cell growth inhibitor and methods of production and use, human mammary cell growth inhibitor and methods of production and use; research in regulation of cell growth and differentiation, molecular mechanisms of tumor metastasis. Mailing: U Mich Cancer Ctr Rm 6302 1500 E Medical Ctr Dr Ann Arbor MI 48109-0942 Office Phone: 734-936-1831. Office Fax: 734-615-3947. Business E-Mail: mwicha@umich.edu.

WICHMANN, DAVID S., insurance company executive; Ptnr. Arthur Andersen; sr. v.p. corp. develop. UnitedHealth Group, Inc., Minnetonka, Minn., 1998—2004, pres., COO specialized care services, 2001—03, CEO specialized care services (Now OptumHealth), 2003—04, pres., COO UnitedHealthcare, 2004—06, exec. v.p., pres. comml. group, 2006—08, exec. v.p., 2006—, pres. group ops., 2008—, CFO, 2011—. Office: UnitedHealth Group Inc PO Box 1459 Minneapolis MN 55440-1459 also: UnitedHealth Group Inc 9900 Bren Rd E Minnetonka MN 55343 *

WICK, MITCHELL A., physician; b. NYC, July 15, 1954; s. Edwin and Doris Wick. BA in Chemistry, U. South Fla., 1976; postgrad., U. Miami, Coral Gables, Fla., 1972—73; D.O., Kirksville Coll. Osteo. Medicine, Mo., 1980. Diplomate Am. Osteo. Bd. Family Physicians, Am. Acad. Pain Mgmt., Am. Assn. Integrative Medicine. Intern Southeastern Med. Ctr., N. Miami, Fla., 1980—81; resident Parkview Hosp., Toledo, 1981—83; staff physician Walk-in Family Medicine Ctr., Boynton Beach, Fla., 1983—86; physician Davie-Dania Med. Ctr., Fla., 1986—96; staff physician Meml. Pembroke Hosp., Pembroke Pines, Fla., 1991—. Author: Megaphysics, A New Look at the Universe, 2003. Named Internat. Scientist of Yr., 2006. Mem.: Internat. Biog. Ctr. Cambridge Eng., Fla. Osteo. Med. Assn., Am. Osteo. Assn. Achievements include research and copywrite on physics theory regarding the fractal nature of spacetime manifolds and how matter and energy interact with thereof utilizing string theory. Avocations: physics, tensor calculus. Home: 11715 Louise Ave Granada Hills CA 91344-2432 Personal E-mail: mitchell598@comcast.net, wickmitchell@gmail.com.

WICKER, SABINE, occupational health physician; b. Alsfeld, Germany, Nov. 4, 1965; d. Alfons and Gertraud Wicker. Cert. MD Med. Sch., U. Giessen, 1998, occupational health specialist Landesarztekammer Hessen, 2003, emergency medicine 1997. Head occupl. health svc. U. Hosp. Frankfurt, Germany, 2003—. Recipient award, Theodor Stern Stiftung, 2006, Robert Koch-Inst., 2009. Mem.: DGAUM (standing com. vaccination mem.). Office: Univ Hosp Frankfurt Theodor-Stern-Kai 7 Frankfurt 60590 Germany Business E-Mail: sabine.wicker@kgu.de.

WICKLIFFE, CHARLES WALTON, cardiologist; b. Gaffney, SC, Mar. 17, 1943; s. Charles Walton and Maude W. Badgett; m. Melody Anne Craig, Mar. 25, 1965; children: Charles, Andrew. MD cum laude, Emory U., 1967. Cert. Am. Bd. Internal Med., 1973, Am. Bd. Cardiovascular Diseases, 1975. Fellow cardiology Emory U. Sch. of Medicine, Atlanta, 1973-75, asst. prof. medicine, cardiology faculty, 1975-76; co-dir. cardiac cath lab. Grady Meml., Atlanta, 1975—76; clin. asst. prof. of medicine, cardiology Emory U. Sch. of Medicine, Atlanta, 1976-87, clin. assoc. prof., 1987—; pvt. practice internal med., cardiovascular diseases Cardiology of Ga., P.C., Atlanta, 1976—. Chmn., bd. trustees West Paces Ferry Hosp., Atlanta, 1984, bd. trustees, 1981—84; chmn. credentials Piedmont Hosp., Atlanta, 1995, pres. elect-med. staff, 1996—97, pres. med. staff, 1998—2000, trustee, bd. dirs., 1996—; chmn. Specialty Physician Orgn. Piedmont Clin.; chmn. bd. dirs. Piedmont Healthcare, 2002—. Editor: (of profl. jours.) Med. Assn., 1985—89. Venue med. officer ACOG; com. Olympic games, 1995—96. Flight surgeon USN, 1969, lt. comdr., flight surgeon USN, 1969—72. Fellow: Am. Coll. Clinical Cardiology, Am. Heart Assn., Atlanta Diabetes Assn., Am. Coll. Cardiology; mem.: Med. Assn. Atlanta, Med. Assn. Ga., Am. Med. Assn., Atlanta Clinical Soc., Atlanta Cardiology Forum. Democrat. Methodist. Avocations: reading, horseback riding, golf, fishing. Office: 275 Collier Rd NW Ste 500 Atlanta GA 30309-1749 Office Phone: 404-605-2800. Personal E-mail: docwickliffe@aol.com.

WICKWIRE, PATRICIA JOANNE NELLOR, psychologist, educator; d. William McKinley and Clara Rose (Pautsch) Nellor; m. Robert James Wickwire, Sept. 7, 1957; 1 child, William James. BA cum laude, U. No. Iowa, Cedar Falls, 1951; MA, U. Iowa, Iowa City, 1959; PhD, U. Tex., Austin, 1971; postgrad., U. So. Calif., LA, UCLA, Calif. State U., Long Beach. Lic. ednl. psychologist, marriage and family therapist, Calif.; nat. cert. counselor. Tchr. Ricketts Ind. Schs., Iowa, 1946-48; tchr., counselor Waverly-Shell Rock Ind. Schs., Iowa, 1951-55; reading cons., head dormitory counselor U. Iowa, Iowa City, 1955-57; tchr., sch. psychologist, adminstr. S. Bay Union H.S. Dist., Redondo Beach, Calif., 1962-82, dir. student svcs. and spl. edn. Cons. mgmt. and edn.; pres. Nellor Wickwire Group, 1981—; mem. exec. bd. Calif. Interagy. Mental Health Coun., 1968-72, Beach Cities Symphony Assn., 1970-82; chmn. Friends of Dominguez Hills, Calif., 1981-85. Contbr. articles in field to profl. jours. Pres. Calif. Women's Caucus, 1993-95, 2003-06. Mem. APA, AAUW (exec. bd., chpt. pres. 1962-72), Nat. Career Devel. Assn. (media chair 1992-98), Am. Assn. Career Edn. (pres. 1991—), LA County Dirs. Pupil Svcs. (chmn. 1974-79), LA County Pers. and Guidance Assn. (pres. 1977-78), Assn. Calif. Sch. Adminstrs. (dir. 1977-81), LA County SW Bd. Dist. Adminstrs. for Spl. Edn. (chmn. 1976-81), Calif. Assn. Sch. Psychologists (bd. dirs. 1981-83), Am. Assn. Sch. Adminstrs., Calif. Assn. for Measurement and Evaluation in Guidance (dir. 1981, pres. 1984-85, 98-2000, 04-05), ACA (chmn. Coun. Newsletter Editors 1989-91, mem. com. on women 1989-92, mem. com. on rsch. and knowledge 1994-97, chmn. 1995-97, mem. and chmn. bylaws com. 1998-2001, rep. to joint com. on testing practices 2001-07), Assn. Measurement and Eval. in Guidance (Western regional editor 1985-87, conv. chair 1986, editor 1987-90, exec. bd. dirs. 1987-91, chair position statements and stds. 2001—10), Calif. Assn. Counseling and Devel. (exec. bd. 1984—2006, pres. 1988-89, jour. editor 1990-2002), Nat. Assn. for Ind.-Edn. Coop. (bd. dirs. 2002-05), Internat. Career Assn. Network (chair 1985-2011), Internat. Women's Rev. Bd. (Women's Inner Cir. of Achievement 2008-), Calif. Edn. Found. (bd. dirs. 1987—), World Future Soc., Pi Lambda Theta, Alpha Phi Gamma, Psi Chi, Kappa Delta Pi, Sigma Alpha Iota, Phi Delta Kappa, AACE (editor, 1991-) Office: The Nellor Wickwire Group 2900 Amby Pl Hermosa Beach CA 90254-2216 Office Phone: 310-376-7378.

WIDDIG, WALTER LAURENTIUS, neuroscientist, speech pathology/audiology services professional; b. Bergisch Gladbach, North Rhine-Westfalia, Germany, Aug. 7, 1949; s. Johann Widdig and Elisabeth Widdig-Bierganns; m. Ploni van der Stoep, July 22, 1953; children: Esther Christine, Anne-Martine, Jan-David. PhD, U. Cologne, Paris, 1981. Cert. speech pathologist North Rhine-Westfalia, 1981; grammar school tchr. North Rhine-Westfalia, 1978. Grammar sch. tchr. Bergisch Gladbach H.S., Cologne, 1981—85; sci. asst. U. Cologne, 1984—89; head lab. neuropsychology and linguistics Ruhr U. Hosp. Bergmannsheil, Bochum, Germany, 1989—. Contbr. articles to profl. jours. Achievements include invention of online therapy of cortical blindness. Office: Ruhr-Univ Hosp Bergmannsheil Bürkle de la Camp-Platz 1 North-Rhine Westfalia Bochum 44789 Germany Office Fax: +49 234 330734. E-mail: walter.widdig@rub.de.

WIDGREN, BENGT, physician; b. Gothenburg, June 12, 1950; MD, Med. Sch., 1985; PhD, 1991. Head Dept. Rsch., Edn. and Devel., 2010—. Assoc. prof. Sahlgrenska Acad., 1993. Master: METTS/RETTS (mem. Nordic steering group). Home: Maleviksbacken 5 Kullavik Halland S-429 35 Sweden Personal E-mail: bengt.widgren@gu.se.

WIDIMSKY, JIRI, cardiologist, educator; b. Pilsen, Czechoslovakia, Mar. 31, 1925; s. Bohus and Marie (Breiska) Widimsky; m. Dagmar Petrovicka; children: Petr Widimsky, Jiri Widimsky Jr. MD, Charles U., Prague, Czechoslovakia, 1950, PhD, 1956, cert. prof., 1976, DSC, 1971. Intern Karlovy Vary, 1950-51; resident Inst. Cardiovascular Diseases, Prague, 1951-56; cardiologist Inst. Cardiovascular Disease, Prague, 1951-61, chief cardiopulmonary lab., 1962-70; head dept. cardiology Inst. Clin. and Exptl. Medicine, Prague, 1970-83, Postgrad. Med. Sch., Prague, 1983-93, prof. cardiology, 1993—. Cons. WHO, Geneva, 1975—85, Novartis, Prague, 1989—2006. Contbr. articles to profl. jours. Fellow: European Soc. Cardiology (hon.); mem.: Internat. Soc. Hypertension, European Soc. Hypertension (hon.), Czech Soc. Internal Medicine (hon.), Czech Cardiol. Soc. (hon.), Czech. Med. Soc. (hon.). Roman Catholic. Office: IKEM Dept Cardiology 1958/9 Videnska 14 21 Prague Czech Republic Home: Lukesova 7 142 00 Prague 4 Czech Republic Home Phone: 420241713439; Office Phone: 420261365420. Home Fax: 420241713439. Personal E-mail: widimsky@seznam.cz.

WIDMANN, ROGER FRANKLIN, pediatric orthopaedic surgeon; m. Miriam A. Leventhal, Mar. 1988. B summa cum laude, Yale Univ., 1985, MD, 1989. Cert. Am. Bd. Orthopaedic Surgery, 1997. Resident in pediatric orthopaedic surgery Mass. Gen. Hosp., Harvard Univ.,

1989—94; fellowship in pediatric orthopaedic surgery Children's Hosp., Boston, 1994—95; assoc. attending orthopaedic surgeon, Pediatric Orthopaedic Surgery Svc. Hosp. for Spl. Surgery, NYC, 1995—, chief, Pediatric Orthopaedic Surgery Svc., 2004—, co-chief, Limb-Lengthening Svc. & mem. Scoliosis Svc.; dir. pediatric orthopaedic trauma NY Hosp.; assoc. prof., clinical orthopaedic surgery Weill Cornell Med. Coll., NYC. Contbr. articles to profl. jours. Recipient Donjoy Prize for MD Thesis, Yale Sch. Med., 1989. Mem.: AMA, Am. Bd. Orthopaedic Surgery, Am. Acad. Pediatrics, Am. Acad. Orthopaedic Surgeons, Am. Acad. Cerebral Palsy & Develop. Med., Phi Beta Kappa, Sigma Xi. Office: Hosp for Spl Surgery 535 E 70th St New York NY 10021 also: Burke Rehabilitation Office 785 Mamaroneck Ave White Plains NY 10605 Office Phone: 212-606-1325. Office Fax: 212-717-0673.

WIDMER, CHARLES GLENN, dentist, researcher; b. Daytona Beach, Fla., Jan. 8, 1955; s. Ernest Clyde and Martha Elizabeth (Hunter) Widmer; m. Alyson Lynn Byrd, July 11, 1981; children: Kathryn Michelle, Elizabeth Ann. BS, Emory U., 1977, DDS, 1981; MS, SUNY, 1983. Asst. prof. Emory U. Sch. Dentistry, Atlanta, 1983-91; assoc. prof. Coll. Dentistry U. Fla., Gainesville, 1991—, acting assoc. dean rsch., 1996-97, dir. clin. rsch. Facial Pain Ctr., 2004—06, coord., orthodontic grad. rsch., 2007—. Mem. spl. grants rev. com. NIH/NIDCR, 2002—08, head, divsn. facial pain, 2008—; mem. dental scis. rev. com. Can. Inst. Health Rsch., 2002—05. Mem. editl. bd. Cells Tissues Organs, 1999—, Jour. Dental Rsch., 2005—08, Open Dentistry Jour., 2007—, Jour. Stomatological Investigation, 2007—; contbr. articles to profl. jours. Active Atlanta Zoo, 1985—91. Recipient Rsch. Career Devel. award, NIH, 1991—96; grantee, 1986—. Mem.: ADA, N.Y. Acad. Scis., Am. Assn. Dental Rsch. (bd. dirs. 1998—2000), Internat. Brain Rsch. Orgn., Soc. Neuroscience, Assn. Univ. Temporomandibular Disorders and Orofacial Pain Programs (sec., treas., v.p., pres. 1990—95), Internat. Assn. Dental Rsch. (sec., treas., v.p., pres., councilor neuroscience group 1989—95). Office: U Fla Dept Orthodontics PO Box 100444 Gainesville FL 32610-0444 Business E-Mail: widmer@dental.ufl.edu.

WIDMER, HANS RUDOLF, neuroscientist, director; b. Aarau, Switzerland, 1957; PhD, U. Zurich, Switzerland, 1989. Rsch. assoc. U. Southern Calif., LA, 1991—93; dir. rsch. dept. neurosurgery U. Bern, Switzerland, 1996—, assoc. prof., 2008. Bd. mem. Network European Cns Transplantation and Restoration, 2003—05. Contbr. articles to med. jour. Fellow: Am. Soc. Neural Therapy and Repair; mem.: Swiss Soc. Pharmacology and Toxicology, European Tissue Culture Soc., Swiss Soc. Neurosci., Soc. Neurosci., Cell Transplant Soc. Office: Univ Hosp Dept Neurosurgery 3010 Bern Switzerland Office Fax: 41 (0)31 382 2414. Business E-Mail: hanswi@insel.ch.

WIDMER, NICOLAS ANTOINE, pharmacist; b. Lausanne, Switzerland, Jan. 27, 1976; s. François and Chantal Favre Widmer; m. Cindy Inès Haller, July 28, 2007. MS in Pharmacy, U. Lausanne, 2000; MAS in Hosp. Pharmacy, U. Geneva, 2005; PhD in Life Scis., U. Lausanne, 2006; diploma in Clin. Pharmacology, SGKPT, Swiss Soc. Clin. Pharmacology and Toxicology, 2009. Cert. hosp. pharmacist FPH, Swiss Soc. Pharmacists, 2005, clin. pharmacy FPH, Swiss Soc. Pharmacists, 2011. Asst. Pharmacy Svs., Hosp. Ctrs., Lausanne, Sion, 2002—05, Divsn. Clin. Pharmacology and Toxicology, U. Hosp. Ctr., Lausanne, 2005—06, pharmacist in charge, TDM, 2006—. Pharmacist Pharmacie 24, Lausanne, 2001—09. Recipient Scis. Faculty award, U. Lausanne, 2001, Claude V. Perrier award, Found. Promotion Tchg. and Rsch. Pharmacotherapy, 2006, Biology & Medicine Faculty award, U. Lausanne, 2007. Office: Univ Hosp Ctr avenue de Beaumont 29 1011 Lausanne Switzerland

WIE, MYUNG-BOK, neuroscientist, educator; b. Yecheon, Republic of Korea, Oct. 9, 1958; s. Seong-Won Wie and Jung-Hee Kim; m. Kyung-Ae Kang (div.); 1 child, Seok-Hyun; m. Chun Hee Park. BS, Kyungpook Nat. U., Taegu, 1981, MSc, 1986, PhD, 1990. Lic. vet. Ministry Agr. and Forestry, 1981. Food insp. officer Ministry Nat. Def., Chunchoen and Sokcho, Republic of Korea, 1981—84; rsch. asst. sch. medicine Hallym U., Chuncheon, Republic of Korea, 1985—90, rsch. instr. sch. medicine, 1990—92; postdoctoral rschr. dept. neurology Wash. U., St. Louis, 1992—94; prin. rsch. scientist ctrl. rsch. inst. Samchondang Pharm. Co., Seoul, Republic of Korea, 1994—97; instr. Cheju Nat. U., Jeju, Republic of Korea, 1997—99, asst. prof., 1999—2001; vis. prof. divsn. neurology Alta. U., Edmonton, Canada, 2001—02; assoc. prof. sch. vet. medicine Kangwon Nat. U., Republic of Korea, 2002—, dir. inst. vet. sci., 2006—. 1st lt. Korean Army, 1981—84. Named to Leading Health Professionals of World, Internat. Biog. Ctr., 2006. Mem.: Soc. Neuroscience. Roman Catholic. Achievements include invention of neuroprotective agents; patents in field. Avocations: travel, tennis. Office: Kangwon Nat Univ 192-1 Hyoja 2-Dong 200-701 Chuncheon Gangwon-do Republic of Korea Office Fax: 82-33-244-2367. Business E-Mail: mbwie@kangwon.ac.kr.

WIEBE, ROBERT, internist, insurance company executive; m. Joni Rubin; 1 child, Claire. BA in Math. summa cum laude, U. Mo., Columbia, MD; MPA, U. Calif., Berkeley; MBA, Stanford U. Diplomate American Bd. of Internal Medicine, lic. Calif., Nevada. Several positions with Veterans Health Adminstrn., dir., Veterans Integrated Svc. Network 21, US Dept. Veterans Affairs; exec. v.p., chief med. officer Catholic Healthcare West, 2008—.

WIEBKING, GUY R., health facility administrator; MBA, U. Md., College Park. Divisional v.p. Major Health Care Systems, Hosp. Products Divsn. Abbott Labs., Abbott Park, Ill.; charter mem. bd. dirs. Provena Health, Mokena, Ill., 1997—, chmn. bd., 2002—06, interim pres., CEO, 2006—07, pres., CEO, 2008—. Bd. mem. Clara Abbott Found., Abbott Park, Ill., San Miguel Schools, Chgo. Office: Provena Health Suite 300 19065 Hickory Creek Dr Mokena IL 60448 *

WIEDEMANN, CHARLES LOUIS, dentist; b. Belvidere, NJ, May 6, 1936; s. Charles and Clothilde Paulina (Fischer) W.; m. Jacqueline Burdzy, June 11, 1960 (dec. Jan. 31, 2009); children: Lorraine Carol, Julie Patricia. BA in Biol. Sci., Rutgers U., 1957; DDS with honors, Fairleigh Dickinson U., 1962; grad., U.S. Army Med. Field Svc. Sch., 1962; postgrad. student, Inst. for Grad. Dentists, 1968-69, St. Clare's Hosp. Continuing Edn., NJ, 1972—, U. Pa., 1974-75, Boston U. Sch. Grad. Dentistry, 1991. Pvt. practice dentistry, Hackettstown, N.J., 1966—; internship residency US Army Field Hosp. Munich, Germany. Founder dental sect. staff dept. surgery Hackettstown Regional Med. Ctr., chief dentistry, 1973-75, 77-78, chief of staff dental sect. dept. surgery, 1974, 80, 85; dental health dir. Clarence W. Sickles Med. Ctr., Hackettstown, 1970-90; co-dir. Stargazer, Bd. of Ed, Online Mag. telecomm. sys., 1985-86; pres. Rexxcom Sys. Electronic Pub. and Computer Software, Co., 1990—; lectr. in field. Author: The Now Philosophy for Dentistry, 1972, Fantastic Facts About Dental Health, 1975, (computer software) The Format Machine, 1987, Autofont, 1990, The Magic Font Machine (Magifont, Magivue, Magishow), 1990, News 1, 1991, Digipad, 1993, The Autofont Titler, 1994; co-author: Autodoc, 1990, rev. edit., 1993, Font Mania, 1991;; rev. edit., 1996, XL1000, 1993, XL2000, 1993, XL2001, 1994, rev. edit., 1995, E-Z Book, 1995, Autofont Titler, 1995; editl. adv. panel: Dental Econs. Jour., 1979—80; editor: DPA News, 1993—95; contbr. articles to profl. jours. and mags.; columnist: Hackettstown Gazette, 1983—85; author: The Gospel of John in Modern English, 2010. Chmn. Bd. of Health, Washington Twp., Morris County, N.J., 1975-78; co-dir. telecomm. sys. Hunterdon Ctrl. Regional H.S., 1989-98; presentations to Morris, Warren, and Sussex Counties, N.J. elem. schs. ann., 1966-93. Capt. Dental Corps., U.S. Army, 1962-65. Recipient cert. Stuart L. Isler Found. for Preventive Dentistry, 1986. Emeritus Fellow Acad. Gen. Dentistry, Am. Endodontic Soc. (Harold Katz Meml. award 1983); mem. ADA (life mem., panel on quar. survey of pvt. practitioners 1990-93), Digital Pub. Assn. (founder, bd. dirs.), Am. Analgesia Soc., Internat. Analgesia Soc., N.J. Dental Assn., Warren-Sussex Dental Soc., Tri-County Dental Soc. (tchr. dental practice adminstrn. 1970-71), Hackettstown Dental Study Group (co-founder 1974-2006), Found. for Motivation in Dentistry (founder, chmn., bd. dirs.), Hosp. Assn. Neighborhood Dentists. Republican. Achievements include design of computer fonts, modules, graphics simulations; development of painless dental injections; improved nerve-block anesthesia technique; first to develop electronic publishing software; invention of Rexxcom character set; Gentle Numb injection syringe for dental anesthesia. Office: 110 Mill St Hackettstown NJ 07840-2343 Office Phone: 908-852-0880.

WIEDMANN, MARCUS WOLF, internal medicine physician, gastroenterologist, diabetologist, medical oncologist; b. Wuerzburg, Germany, Apr. 26, 1969; s. Roland Wolf and Heidemarie Wiedmann; m. Tong Wu, Nov. 15, 2001; children: Jeanette Weiqiang children: Patrick Weilei. MD, Wuerzburg Med. Sch., 1996. Jr. resident medicine U. Leipzig, Germany, 1996—99, sr. resident medicine, 2001—04, fellow gastroenterology, 2004—05, asst. prof., 2005—08, attending, 2005—08; chief Medicine Dept., St. Mary Hosp., Berlin, 2008—; rsch. fellow MGH Cancer Ctr., Harvard U., Boston, 1999, Sch. Medicine, Brown U., Providence, 1999—2001. Contbr. articles to profl. jours. Obergefreiter Inf., 1988—89, Veitshoechheim and Hammelburg. Mem.: Am. Soc. Clin. Oncology, German Assn. Gastroenterology, German Internal Medicine Assn., European Soc. of Med. Oncology, German Assn. for Study of Liver Disease, Am. Assn. for the Study of Liver Diseases. Roman Catholic. Avocation: dining. Office Fax: 011-49-30-76783425. Business E-Mail: wiedmann@marienkrankenhaus-berlin.de.

WIEGERINK, ROBIN L., medical association administrator; CAE. Exec. dir, CEO Am. Soc. Echocardiography, 2001—. Office: Am Soc Echocardiogrphy 2100 Gateway Centre Blvd Ste 310 Morrisville NC 27560 Office Phone: 919-297-7164. Office Fax: 919-882-9900. Business E-Mail: rwiegerink@asecho.org. *

WIEHLER, STEPHAN ROBERT GEORG, neurologist; b. Hannover, Germany, Nov. 16, 1953; s. Gerhard Georg Bernhard and Sabine Elisabeth (Lesse) W.; m. Gudrun Ingrid Below, May 30, 1981; children: Antonius, Flavia, Claudia. MD, MHH U., Hannover, 1979. Resident in internal ZVBKH Regional Hosp., Bad Oeynhausen, Germany, 1979-80; intern in neurology MHH Univ. Hosp., Hannover, 1980-86; sr. physician, dep. chief dept. neurology Gilead Hosp./VBA Bethel, Bielefeld, Germany, 1986-94; pvt. practice Bielefeld, 1995—. Cons. neurologist Hosp. City of Bielefeld, 1987—; lectr. in field. Capt. German Med. Svc., 1982-83. Mem. German Ultrasound Soc., German Soc. Electrophysiol. Diagnostic Avocations: music, violin (string quartet), literature, modern and medieval painting. Home: Kerkebrink 4 33619 Bielefeld Germany Office: Oberustr 5 33602 Bielefeld Germany Office Phone: 0049-521-177400. Personal E-mail: swiehler@t-online.de.

WIELAND, EBERHARD H., physician, educator; b. Mainz, Germany, July 9, 1956; s. Theodor and Irmgard Wieland; m. Maria T. Shipkova; children: Johannes, Victoria. MD, Ruprecht-Karls-U., Heidelberg, 1982; Habilitation, Georg-Aug.-U., Goettingen, 1997. Cert. Facharzt für Laboratoriumsmedizin Aerztekammer Niedersachsen, 1993, EurClinChem European Register Clin. Chemists, 2005, Klinischer Chemiker Deutsche Gesellschaft fuer Klinische Chemie, 1993. Intern U. Hosp., Heidelberg, Germany, 1983—85; postdoc. fellow U. Calif. San Diego, 1985—87; jr. physician U. Hosp., Goettingen, Germany, 1987—96, sr. physician, 1996—2000; c3 prof. Georg-August-U., Goettingen, 2000—03; apl. prof. Eberhard-Karls-U., Tuebingen, Germany, 2007—, Ctrl. Inst. Clin. Chemistry & Lab. Medicine, Stuttgart, Germany, 2003—, head physician, 2003. Mem.: European Atherosclerosis Soc., Transplantation Soc., Am. Heart Assn., Soc. Free Radical Rsch., Internat. Assn. Therapeutic Drug Monitoring & Clin. Toxicology, Am. Assn. Clin. Chemistry. Achievements include research in oxidative stress, atherosclerosis, immunosuppression. Office: Klinikum Stuttgart Kriegsbergstrasse 60 Stuttgart D-70174 Germany Office Phone: +49-711-27834800. Office Fax: +49-711-2784809.

WIELAND, GILBERT DARRYL, medical researcher, anthropologist, gerontologist; b. Hagerstown, Md., Oct. 31, 1951; s. Gilbert Hugh and Joan Kanaga Wieland; m. Manhal A. Wieland, Apr. 26, 1980; 1 child, Christopher. BA cum laude in Anthropology, Am. U., Washington, DC, 1972; PhD in Anthropology, U. Rochester, NY, 1982; MPH in Health Svcs., UCLA, 1983. Sr. rsch. scientist VA Geriatric Rsch., Edn. and Clin. Ctr., Sepulveda, Calif., 1982—96; rsch. dir. Beverly Found., Pasadena, Calif., 1987—90; assoc. rsch. prof. divsn. geriat. UCLA, 1991—96; prof. USC Sch. Medicine, Columbia, 1996—; rsch. dir. geriat. Palmetto Health Richland, Columbia, 1998—. Prof., divsn. geriat., dept. medicine USC Sch. Medicine, 1996; dep. editor Jour. Gerontology A Med. Scis., 2005—11. Dep. editor Journal of Gerontology: Medical Sciences, 2005—, assoc. editor Aging: Clinical and Experimental Research, 2005—, mem. editl. bd., reviewer 30 med. and sci. jours., —; editor: Geriatric Assessment Technology, 1995, Cultural Diversity & Geriatric Care, 1994, Case-Based Geriatrics, 2011. Recipient Spl. Recognition award, Am. Geriat. Soc., 2011. Fellow: Soc. Applied Anthropology, Gerontol. Soc. Am. (chair pub. policy com. 2000—02, chair rsch. task force), Am. Geriatrics Soc. (mem. rsch. com. 2000—05, mem. publ. ed. com. 2008—). Office Fax: 803-434-4331. Business E-Mail: darryl.wieland@palmettohealth.org.

WIEMEYER, ANDREW S., prosthodontist; married; 3 children. Grad., Milton Acad., Middlebury Coll., U. Conn., 1998, postgrad. Cert. specialty prosthodontics. Resident Univ. Conn.; owner Wiemeyer Dentistry, Mass., prosthodontist. Coach Duxbury Minisoccer Program, Mass. Mem.: Am. Coll. of Prosthodontists, Am. Dental Assn., Shamrock Dental Study Club. Avocations: tennis, bass guitar. Office: Wiemeyer Dentistry 104 Tremont St Duxbury MA 02332 Office Phone: 781-934-5292.

WIENS, ARTHUR NICHOLAI, psychology professor; b. McPherson, Kans., Sept. 7, 1926; s. Jacob T. and Helen E. (Kroeker) W.; m. Ruth Helen Avery, June 11, 1949; children: Barbara, Bradley, Donald. BA, U. Kans., 1948, MA, 1952; PhD, U. Portland, 1956. Diplomate: Am. Bd. Examiners Profl. Psychology. Clin. psychologist Topeka State Hosp., 1949-53; sr. psychologist outpatient dept. Oreg. State Hosp., Salem, 1954-58, chief psychologist, 1958-61, dir. clin. psychology internship program, 1958-61; clin. instr. U. Oreg. Med. Sch., Portland, 1958-61, asst. prof., 1961-65, assoc. prof., 1965-66; prof. med. psychology, 1966—96; prof. emeritus med. psychology, 1997—. Field assessment officer Peace Corps, 1965; cons. psychologist Portland Ctr. for Hearing and Speech, 1964—67, Dammasch State Hosp., 1967—69, Raleigh Hills Hosp., 1968—84, Oreg. Vocat. Rehab. Divsn., 1973—2001, mem. state adv. com., 1976—93; cons. William Temple Rehab. House, Episcopal Laymen's Mission Soc., 1968—88; chmn. State Oreg. Bd. Social Protection, 1971—84, State of Oreg. Bd. Psychologist Examiners, 1963—66, 1974—77; v.p. bd. dirs. Raleigh Hills Rsch. Found., 1974—80. Contbr. articles to profl. jour. Fellow AAAS, APA (chmn. com. on vis. psychologist program 1972-76, chmn. accreditation com. 1978, mem. task force edn. and credentialing 1979-84); mem. Am. Assn. State Psychology Bd. (pres. 1978-79), Nat. Register Health Svc. Providers in Psychology (bd. dirs. 1985-92, chmn. 1989-92), Profl. Exam. Svc. (bd. dirs. 1982-88, 90-96, chmn. 1986-88), Sigma Xi. Home: 74 Condolea Way Lake Oswego OR 97035-1010 Office: Oreg Health Scis U Portland OR 97201

WIERNIK, PETER HARRIS, oncologist, educator; b. Crocket, Tex., June 16, 1939; s. Harris and Molly (Emmerman) W.; m. Roberta Joan Fuller, Sept. 6, 1961; children: Julie Anne, Lisa Britt, Peter Harrison. BA with distinction, U. Va., 1961, MD, 1965; Dr. honoris causa, U. Republic, Montevideo, Uruguay, 1982. Diplomate Am. Bd. Internal Medicine, Am. Bd. Med. Oncology (mem. writing com. 1981-87). Intern Cleve. Met. Gen. Hosp., 1965—66, resident, 1969—70; resident Osler Svc. Johns Hopkins Hosp., Balt., 1970—71; sr. asst. surgeon USPHS, 1966, advanced through grades to med. dir., 1976; sr. staff assoc. Balt. Cancer Rsch. Ctr., 1966—71, chief med. oncology sect., 1971—76, chief clin. oncology br., 1976—82, dir., 1976—82; assoc. dir. cancer treatment divsn. Nat. Cancer Inst., 1976—82; assoc. dir. Albert Einstein Cancer Ctr., Bronx, 1982—98, prof. medicine, 1983—98, prof. radiation oncology, 1996—98, head med. oncology divsn.; pres. Cancer Rsch. Fdn., 1998—; dir, leukemia program St. Lukes Roosevelt Med. Ctr., 2010—. Asst. prof. medicine U. Md. Sch. Medicine, Balt., 1971-74, assoc. prof., 1974-76, prof., 1976-82; prof. medicine and radiation oncology NY Med. Coll., 1998—; cons. hematology med. oncology Union Meml. Hosp., Greater Balt. Med. Ctr., Franklin Sq. Hosp.; bd. dirs. Balt. City unit Am. Cancer Soc., 1971-78; chmn. patient care com., 1972-75, profl. edn. grants com., NYC divsn., 1983-90, nat. clin. fellowship com., 1984-96; med. adv. com. Nat. Leukemia Assn., 1976-88, chmn. med. adv. com., 1989—; chmn. adult leukemia com. Cancer Leukemia Group B, 1976-83; prin. investigator Ea. Coop. Oncology Group, 1982-94, 96—; chmn. gynecol. oncology com., 1986-88, chmn. leukemia com., 1988-94; sci. cons. Vt. Regional Cancer Ctr., 1987—2008; dir. OLM Comprehensive Cancer Ctr., NY Med. Coll., 1998—2008, dir. Cancer Ctr. Montefiore Med. Ctr., North Divsn., 2008-10, cons. editor, Diagnosis Oncology Jours., Clin. Oncology, 2010-, coun. eastern divsn. Am. Fed. Med. Rsch., 2010-, councillor at large Nat. Coun., 2011-. Editor: Controversies in Oncology, 1982, Supportive Care of the Cancer Patient, 1983, Neoplastic Diseases of the Blood, 1985, 4th edit., 2003, Adult Leukemias, 2001; editor: (assoc.) Medical Oncology and Tumor Pharmacotherapy, 1987—91; editor: (sr.), 1991—; editor: (assoc.) Am. Jour. Therapeutics, 1994—; co-editor: Year Book of Hematology, 1986—98, Handbook of Hematologic and Oncologic Emergencies, 1988—98, Bone Marrow Transplantation (textbook), 1995, Am. Jour. Medical Scis., 1976—81; editor: Jour. of Cancer Rsch. and Clin/ Oncology, 1986—89, Jour. Clin. Pharmacology, 1985—; mem. editl. bd. Cancer Treatment Reports, 1972—76, Leukemia Rsch., 1977—86, 1991—2005, Leukemia, 1986—2003, Cancer Clin. Trials, 1977—, Jour. of Therapeutic Rsch., 1994—, Hospital Practice, 1979—, Jour. of Clin. Oncology, 1989—91, consulting edit., 2010—, Leukemia and Lymphoma, 1989—2007, PDQ National Cancer Inst., 1987—94, Cancer Investigation, 1998—2007, Serbian Archives Medicine, 2005—; contbr. articles to profl. jours., chapters to books. Recipient Z Soc. award U. Va., 1961, Byrd S. Leavell Hematology award U. Va. Sch. Medicine, 1965, Gold medal 1st Polish Congress Oncology, 2002, Statesman award Am. Soc. Clin. Oncology, 2008. Fellow AAAS, ACP, Am. Coll. Clin. Pharmacology (awards com. 1999—), Internat. Soc. Hematology, Royal Soc. Medicine (London), NY Acad. Medicine; mem. Am. Soc. Clin. Investigation (instl. rep. 1997—2001), Am. Soc. Clin. Oncology (chmn. edn. tng. com. 1976-79, 84, subcom. clin. investigation 1980-82, program com. 1990, pub. issues com., 1990-95, com. rsch. awards 1996-2000, com. health svcs. rsch. 2000-2003), Am. Assn. Cancer Rsch. (clin. cancer rsch. com. 2002—), Am. Soc. Hematology, Am. Fedn. Clin. Rsch., Am. Acad. Clin. Toxicology, Internat. Soc. Exptl. Hematology, NY Acad. Sci., Am. Soc. Hosp. Pharmacy, Am. Soc. Clin. Pharmacology Therapeutics, Am. Radium Soc. (program com. 1987-93, exec. com. 1988-95, publ. com. 1988-

92, sec. 1990-91, pres.-elect, 1992-93; pres. 1993-94, Janeway medalist, 1996), Polish Oncology Soc. (hon., Gold medal), Harvey Soc., Uruguayan Hematology Soc. (hon.), Acad. Medicine Uruguay (corr.), European Assn. Cancer Rsch., European Soc. Hematology, Phi Beta Kappa (assoc.), Sigma Xi, Alpha Omega Alpha, Phi Sigma (award 1961), FDA Grant Application Review Panel, Faculty 1000 Biology (faculty mem. 2007-, Celgene Career Achievement award 2009), Assn. Patient Oriented Rsch. (founding mem., 1999-, bd. dir. 2010-). Office Phone: 212-636-3338. Personal E-mail: pwiernik@aol.com. Business E-Mail: pwiernik@chpnet.org.

WIERSBITZKY, SIEGFRIED KARL WILHELM, retired pediatrician; b. Neuruppin, Germany, Jan. 2, 1940; s. Siegfried W. and Sofia M. (Kuhnert) W.; m. Helga Kurzbein, Dec. 31, 1959; children: Mark Siegfried Kurt, Claudia Sofia Helga. MD, U. Greifswald, 1963, MS, 1973. Pediatrician, Germany, 1968—; pediatric bronchopneumologist, 1983—; pediatric infectiologist, 1983—; neonatologist, 1993—; dir. Children's Hosp. U., Greifswald, 1991—2005, ret., 2005. Cons. allergologist Ärztekammer Prov. Med. Assn., Mecklenburg-Vorpommern, 1991-2008; leader Gesellschaft für Allergologie M/V, Germany, 1993-95; sci. bd. Paul Ehrlich-Inst., 1992-2005, v.p. sci. bd., 1998-2001. Author, editor 32 books; contbr. over 390 articles to profl. jours. Mem.: Gesellschaft für Paediat. Pneumologie, Deutsche Gesellschaft für Paediat. Infekt., Arbeitsgemeinschaft für Paediatrische Pneumologie und Allergologie, Ärzteverband Deutscher Allergologen, Deutsche Gesellschaft für Kinder-und Jugendmedizin. Home Phone: 49 3834-823867. Personal E-mail: siegfried.wiersbitzky@arcor.de.

WIERSMA, SUSAN RENEE, pediatrician; b. Milw., Wis., May 5, 1958; MD, Case Western Reserve Univ., 1984. Cert. Am. Bd. Pediatrics, 1989, in Pediatric Hematology-Oncology Am. Bd. Pediatrics, 1992. Intern in pediatrics Univ. Minn., Mpls., 1985, resident in pediatrics, 1986—87; fellowship in pediatric hematology-oncology Children's Hosp., LA, 1987—90; assoc. prof. Case Western Reserve Univ., Cleve.; dir., pediatric stem cell transplant program Univ. Hospitals, Cleve. Contbr. articles to profl. jours.

WIERZBIETA, WOJCIECH, anesthesiologist, researcher, health facility administrator; b. Warsaw, Dec. 20, 1948; s. Wincenty Maciej and Janina (Wolkanowska) Wierzbieta. MD, Med. Acad., Warsaw, 1974, 1st degree specialization, 1977, 2d degree specialization, 1979. Head anesthesia and intensive care dept. Ctrl. Children Traumatology Hosp., Warsaw, 1978-82; cons. in anesthesia and intensive care M.O.H., Benghazi, Libya, 1982-87, Ctrl. Railway Hosp., Warsaw, 1987-88; scientific coord. Upjohn, Warsaw, 1988-93, med. dir., 1993-96, Pharmacia & Upjohn, Warsaw, 1996; gen. mgr. Innovex/Quintiles, Warsaw, 1997; mgr. clin. ops. ctrl. ea. Europe Paroxel, Warsaw, 1998-2000; med. advisor Astellas Pharma, Warsaw, 2000—06, clin. ops. mgr., 2006—. Lectr. 3d Internat. Congress of Anesthesiologists, Poland, 1979. Contbr. articles to med. jours. Mem. Polish Soc. Anaesthesiology and Intensive Care, Drug Info. Assn., Nat. Geographic Soc., Profl. Assn. Diving Instrs. (instr.), Divers Alert Network (instr.). Roman Catholic. Avocations: diving, skiing, archaeology. E-mail: wojciech.wierzbieta@pl.astellas.com.

WIESCHAUS, ERIC F., molecular biologist, educator; b. South Bend, Ind., June 8, 1947; m. Gertrud Schüpbach; children: Ingrid, Eleanor, Laura. BS in Biology, U. Notre Dame, South Bend, 1969; PhD in Biology, Yale U., New Haven, 1974. Rsch. fellow Zool. Inst., U. Zurich, Switzerland, 1975-78; group leader European Molecular Biol. Lab., Heidelberg, Germany, 1978-81; asst. prof.biology Princeton U., NJ, 1981—83, assoc. prof., 1984—87, prof., 1987—, Squibb prof. molecular biology. Fellow Molecular Genetics Lab., Nat. Ctr. Sci. Rsch (CNRS), France, 1976; vis. rschr. Ctr. Pathobiology, U. Calif., Irvine, 1977; mem. sci. adv. coun. Damon Runyon-Walter Winchell Cancer Fund, 1987—92; mem. adv. coun., dept. biology Rice U., Houston, 1988—; adj. prof. biochemistry Univ. Medicine & Dentistry NJ (UMDNJ)-Robert Wood Johnson Med. Sch. Contbr. articles to profl. jours. Recipient Nobel prize in physiology/medicine, 1995. Fellow: Am. Acad. Arts & Scis.; mem.: NAS, Fedn. Am. Scientists, Am. Philos. Soc. Office: Princeton U Dept Molecular Biology Moffett Lab 435 Washington Rd Princeton NJ 08544-0001 Office Phone: 609-258-5383. Business E-Mail: efw@princeton.edu. *

WIESE, NEVA, retired critical care nurse; b. Hunter, Kans., July 23, 1940; d. Amil H. and Minnie (Zemke) W. Diploma, Grace Hosp. Sch. Nursing, Hutchinson, Kans., 1962; BA in Social Sci., U. Denver, 1971; BSN, Met. State Coll., 1975; MS in Nursing, U. Colo., Denvr, 1978; postgrad., U. N.Mex., 1986; PhD, Kennedy Western U., 1999. RN, N.Mex. Cardiac ICU nurse U. N.Mex. Hosp., Albuquerque; coord. critical care edn. St. Vincent Hosp., Santa Fe, charge nurse CCU, clin. nurse III intensive and cardiac care. Recipient Mary Atherton Meml. award for clin. excellence St. Vincent Hosp., 1986. Mem.: AACN, ANA. Home: 849 Rio Vista St Santa Fe NM 87501-1549

WIESEL, TORSTEN NILS, neurobiologist, educator; b. Upsala, Sweden, June 3, 1924; arrived in US, 1955; s. Fritz Samuel and Anna-Lisa Elisabet (Bentzer) Wiesel; 1 child, Sara Elisabet. MD, Karolinska Inst., Stockholm, 1954; MD (hon.), Karolinska Inst, Stockholm, 1989, Harvard U., 1967, Linköping U., 1982; DSc (hon.), NYU, 1987, U. Bergen, 1987. Asst. dept. child psychiatry Karolinska Hosp., 1954—55; fellow in ophthalmology Johns Hopkins U., Balt., 1955—58, asst. prof. ophthalmic physiology, 1958—59; assoc. in neurophysiology and neuropharmacology Harvard Med. Sch., Boston, 1959—60, asst. prof. neurophysiology and neuropharmacology, 1960—64, asst. prof. neurophysiology, 1964—67, prof. physiology, 1967—68, prof. neurobiology, 1968—74, chmn. dept. neurobiology, 1973—82, Robert Winthrop prof. neurobiology, 1974—82; Vincent & Brooke Astor prof. neurobiology Rockefeller U., NYC, 1982—98, pres., 1991—98, Vincent & Brooke Astor prof. emeritus, pres. emeritus, 1998—, dir. Shelby White and Leon Levy Ctr. Mind, Brain & Behavior. Lectr. Coll. de France, 1977; Hitchcock prof. U. Calif., Berkeley, 1980; sec.-gen. Human Frontier Sci. Program, Strasbourg, France, 2000; chair sci. adv. bd. Nat. Inst. Biol. Sci., Beijing; co-chair bd. governors Okinawa Inst. Sci. & Tech. Contbr. numerous articles to profl. jours. Pres. Internat. Brain Rsch. Orgn., 1998—2004; bd. governors NY Acad. Scis., 2001—06, chmn., interim dir., 2001—02; adv. bd. mem. European Brain Rsch. Inst.; chmn. bd. dirs. Aaron Diamond AIDS Rsch. Ctr., NYC, 1995—2001; bd. dirs. Hosp. Spl. Surgery, NYC, Pew Ctr. Global Climate Change. Recipient Jules Stein award, Trustees Prevention of Blindness, 1971, Lewis S. Rosenstiel prize, Brandeis U., 1972, Friedenwald award, Assn. Rsch. Vision & Ophthalmology, 1975, Louisa Gross Horwitz prize, Columbia U., 1978, Dickson prize, U. Pitts., 1979, Nobel prize in physiology/medicine, 1981, W.H. Helmerich III award, 1989, Nat. Medal Sci., 2005, Ramon Y Cajal Gold medal, Spanish Nat. Rsch. Coun., 2006, Marshall M. Parks, MD medal, Children's Eye Found., 2007. Mem.: NAS (chmn. com. on human rights 1994—2004, David Rall medal 2005), AAAS, Serbian Acad. Scis. & Arts, Royal Swedish Acad. Scis. (fgn.), Royal Soc. (fgn.), Soc. Neurosci. (pres. 1978—79), Swedish Physiol. Soc., Nat. Acad. Arts & Scis., Am. Acad. Arts & Scis., Am. Philos. Soc. (Karl Spencer Lashley prize 1977), Am. Physiol. Soc. Office: Rockefeller U 1230 York Ave New York NY 10021-6399 E-mail: Torsten.Wiesel@rockefeller.edu.

WIESEN, KAREN, dietician; BS in Nutrition, Pa. State U., 1977; MS in Clinical Dietetics, St. Louis U., 1987. Renal dietitian Wash. U. Sch. Medicine-Barnes Jewish Dialysis Ctr., 1999—. Chair Nat. Kidney Foundation-Coun. Renal Nutrition, 2009—11; adj. clin. instr., clin. preceptor, dept nutrition St. Louis U., 2007—. Recipient NRF Recognized Renal Dietitian award, Am. Assn. Diabetes Educators. Office: Washington University Sch Medicine 4205 Forest Park Ave Saint Louis MO 63108 Office Fax: 314-286-0855. Business E-Mail: kwiesen@dom.wustl.edu.

WIESENFELD, HAROLD C., obstetrician, gynecologist, epidemiologist; MD, McGill U. Sch. of Medicine, Montreal, Can., 1987. Diplomate Am. Bd. Ob-Gyn., lic. to practice Pa., 1992. Resident McGill U. Sch. of Medicine, Montreal, Canada; hosp. affiliations include Magee-Womens Hosp. of Univ. of Pitts. Med. Ctr. (UPMC), UPMC Mercy, UPMC Presbyn. Co-author: (articles) Antimicrobial Prophylaxis for Cesarean Delivery Before Skin Incision, 2009, 2010. Fellow: Am. Congress Obstetricians and Gynecologists. Office: University of Pittsburgh Physicians Womens Health Gynecology Specialties 300 Halket St Ste 0610 Pittsburgh PA 15213 Office Phone: 412-641-6412.

WIESENTHAL, ANDREW MICHAEL, physician; b. NYC, Mar. 5, 1950; s. Jerome Mitchell and Gladys Hortense (Heilig) W.; m. Dillie Sue Gunkel Wiesenthal, July 1, 1978. BA, Yale U., 1971; MD, SUNY, 1975; MS, Harvard U., 2004. Cert. Pediatrics and Pediatric Infectious Disease Am. Bd. Pediatrics. Internship, residency pediatrics U. Colo. Health Scis. Ctr., Denver, 1975-78; epidemic intelligence svc. officer Ctrs. for Disease Control, Atlanta, 1978-80; fellowship pediatric infectious diseases U. Colo. Health Scis. Ctr., Denver, 1980-83, pediatrician Colo. Permanente Med. Group, PC, Denver, 1983-2000, chief pediat. arapahoe med. office, 1986-89, physician dir. quality assurance, 1988-93, assoc. med. dir., 1994-2000; assoc. exec. dir. for clin. info. systems Fedn. Permanente Med. Groups, Oakland, Calif., 2000—10, dir. Deloitte Consulting, 2010—. Bd. dirs. Colo. Permanente Med. Group, PC, Denver, 1988—93, chair, 1991—93; govs. hemophilia adv. coun. State of Colo., 1990—2000; bd. dirs. Nat. Com. for Quality Assurance, Washington, 1996—2001, Care Mgmt. Inst. Fedn. Permanente Med. Groups, Oakland, Calif., clin. assoc. prof. U. Colo. Health Scis. Ctr., Denver, 1996—2000; commr. Cert. Commn. Health Info. Tech., 2006—10; US mgmt. bd. rep. Internat. Health Terminology Standards Devel. Orgn., 2007—, trustee, 2011—. Contbr. numerous articles to profl. jours. Vol. pediatric clinic Samaritan House Homeless Shelter, 1990—2000, Warren Village Single Parent Housing, 1995—2000; mem., bd. dirs. AIDS Project, East Bay, 2008—. Fellow Am. Acad. Pediat.; mem. Pediat. Infectious Disease Soc, Epidemic Intelligence Svc. Alumni Assn., No. Calif. Yale Assn., Infectious Disease Soc. Am., Healthcare Info. Mgmt. Svcs. Soc. Jewish. Avocations: running, biking, hiking, camping, crossword puzzles. Office: Deloitte Consulting 555 Mission St San Francisco CA 94105 Office Phone: 415-783-5849. Business E-Mail: awiesenthal@deloitte.com.

WIESMÜLLER, GERHARD ANDREAS, physician, educator; b. Wesseling, Nordrhein-Westfalen, Germany, Sept. 30, 1962; s. Adolf and Ursula Wiesmüller; m. Vera Schumacher; 1 child, Christina Alexandra. MD, Sch. Medicine, Cologne U., 1992. Pre-registration house officer Med. Inst. Environ. Hygiene, Heinrich-Heine-U., Düsseldorf, Nordrhein-Westfalen, 1991—92, sci. employee, 1992—97, Inst. Hygiene and Environ. Medicine, U. Hosp., RWTH Aachen U., Nordrhein-Westfalen, 1997—99, sci. asst. c1, 1999—2002, sr. asst. c2, 2002—06; intern Med. Clinic III, U. Hosp. RWTH Aachen U., 1998—99, asst. prof., 2002, assoc. prof., 2006; head dept. environ specimen bank human tissues Med. Faculty Westphalian Wilhelms-U. Münster, Nordrhein-Westfalen, 2006—10; head dept. infectious and environ. hygiene Pub. Health Dept. Cologne, 2010—. Mem.: Rotary Internat. (Koln Halanentor). Home: Am Obersten Bruch 98 Kerpen Nordrhein-Westfalen 50170 Germany Office: Public Health dept Dept Infectious & Environme Hygiene A Teachener Str 220 Colognr Nordrhein-Westfalen 50931 Germany Office Phone: 49 251 8356066, 99 221 221 25993. Office Fax: 49 251 8355524, 99 221 221 23553; Home Fax: 49 2275 918952. Personal E-mail: ga.wiesmueller@t-online.de. Business E-Mail: ga.wiesmueller@uni-muenster.de, gerhard.wiesmuller@stadt.koeln.de.

WIESNER, DALLAS CHARLES, immunologist, researcher; b. Brookings, SD, Mar. 19, 1959; s. Charles Howard Wiesner and Coleen Marie (Hendrickson) Bailey; m. Priscilla Anne Semon, 1992. BS in Microbiology with high honors, S.D. State U., 1982. HIV product devel. tech. Abbott Labs., Diagnostic Div., Abbott Park, Ill., 1985-87, HIV retrocell product mgr. North Chicago, Ill., 1987-88, sect. mgr. infectious disease and immunology Abbott Park, Ill., 1988-90; mgr. sexually transmitted diseases tech. product devel. Diagnostic div. Abbott Labs., Abbott Park, Ill., 1990-91, sect. mgr. retrovirus tech. product devel., 1991-96; with hepatitis r&d diagnostic divsn. Abbott Labs, Abbott Park, 1996—. Mem. Am. Assn. Clin. Chemistry, Am. Soc. for Microbiology, Phi Kappa Phi. Lutheran. Avocations: fishing, camping, scuba diving, photography, amateur radio. Home: 8710 Lakeshore Dr Pleasant Prairie WI 53158-4721 Office: Abbott Labs 200 Abbott Pk Rd North Chicago IL 60064-3500 Office Phone: 847-937-1873.

WIESNER, RUSSELL H., internist, gastroenterologist, educator; b. Milwaukee, Wis., Jan. 22, 1947; BS in Pharmacy, U. Wis., Madison, 1970; MD, Med. Coll. Wis., 1975. Cert. Internal Medicine, 1978, Gastroenterology, 1981. Internship, pharmacy U. Wis., Milwaukee; intern, internal medicine Mayo Grad. Sch. Medicine, Rochester, Minn., 1975—76, resident, internal medicine, 1976—78, fellowship, gastroenterology, 1978—81, prof. medicine, med. dir. Former pres. United Network for Organ Sharing; spkr. in field. Editor: Liver Transplantation; reviewer (med. jours.); contbr. articles to profl. jours., abstracts. Recipient Am. Soc. Transplantation/Astellas Clin. Sci. Established Investigator award, 2005. Office: Mayo Clinic Transport Ctr 200 First St SW Rochester MN 55905 Office Phone: 507-266-1586.

WIFFLER, THOMAS P., healthcare company executive; BBA, Iona Coll., New Rochelle, NY. Joined as dir. fin. Ill. health plan UnitedHealthCare Svcs., Inc., 1999, various positions including CFO, nat. CFO large accounts, COO UnitedHealthcare Ill., COO ctrl. region, then pres., CEO UnitedHealthcare Ill., 2007—. Bd. dirs. Ill. C. of C. Maj. US Marine Corps Res. Named one of 40 Under 40, Crain's Chgo. Bus., 2009. Office: UnitedHealthcare 233 N Michigan Ave Chicago IL 60601 Office Phone: 312-424-4460. Business E-Mail: thomas_p_wiffler@uhc.com. *

WIG, JYOTSNA, anesthesiologist; b. Ludhiana, Panjab, India, Apr. 23, 1949; d. Chhabil Das and Sita Devi Ahuja; m. Jai Dev Wig, Sept. 17, 1972; children: Surabhi, Swati. MBBS, Christian Med. Coll. Ludhiana, India, 1971; MD, Postgraduate Inst. Med. Edn. and Rsch., India, 1975. cons. in anesthesiology Post Grad. Inst. of Med. Ed. & Rsch.(PGIMER), 1978—. Sr. resident, anesthesia Post Graduat Inst. of Med. Ed. & Rsch. (PGIMER), Chandigarh, India, 1973-78, lectr., 1978-83, asst. prof., 1983-86, assoc. prof., 1986-90, additional prof., 1990-95, prof., 1995—. Author: (with others) Surgical Gastroenterology, 1986, 90, Head Injury, 1998; contbr. articles to profl. jour. Warden Lady Doctor's Hostel, 1993-95. British Commonwealth fellowship, 1986-87; recipient Award FAMS, 1999. Mem. Indian Med. Assn. (life), Neurol. Soc. of India (life), Indian Soc. for the Study of Pain. Avocations: site seeing, watching movies, writing letters. Office: Postgrad Inst Med Edn and Rsch Dept Anesthesia Sector 12 PGI Campus Chandigarh 160012 India Home: 8-H/5 SEC 12 PGI Campus 160 012 Chandigarh India Home Phone: 0172-2745234; Office Phone: 0172-2756501. Personal E-mail: jdwsjni@hotmail.com.

WIGLEY, CAROLINE, neuroscientist, educator; married. Staff scientist Imperial Cancer Rsch. Fund, London, 1979—85; lectr., sr. lectr. Kings Coll. London, 1985—2002; sr. hon. tchg. fellow Peninsula Coll. Medicine and Dentistry, Exeter, Devon, England, 2003—. Dep. editor, cancer surveys OUP, Oxford, 1980—86; sect. editor Gray's Anatomy Elsevier, London, 2000—, microstructure editor, 2000—. Mem.: Inst. Learning and Tchg., European Tissue Culture Soc. (pres. 1994—97)

WIGLEY, DIANA GAIL, respiratory therapist; d. Roland Eugene and Jewel Maxine Box; children: Trent Matthew, Kyle Brandon. Diploma, Ind. Voc. Tech Sch., 1984. Registered respiratory therapist Ind., 1997, EEG Tech & Evoked Potenial Tech Ind., 2003. Staff therapist Bedford Med. Ctr., Ind., 1980—90; staff therapist, lead therapist James W. Riley Children's Hosp., Indpls., 1990—92; area supr. Golden Care, 1993—96; staff therapist, EEG tech Wash. County Hosp., Washington, 1996—97; registered respiratory therapist Bloomington Hosp., 1997—, registered EEG tech, IOM tech, 2000—. Office: Bloomington Hosp 402 West 2nd St Bloomington IN 47402 Office Fax: 812-353-5220. Personal E-mail: blmgtneeg@verizon.net.

WIGTON, ROBERT SWIFT, medical educator; b. Phila., Jan. 22, 1942; s. Robert Spencer and Marcia Catherine (Swift) W.; m. Deborah Ann Adkins, Jan. 9, 1976. BA, Harvard Coll., 1965; BS, U. Nebr., 1967, MD, 1969, MS, 1973. Diplomate Am. Bd. Internal Medicine. Cert. Nebr. State Bd. Med. Examiners, 1969. Instr. Dept. Physiology U. Nebr. Coll. Medicine, Omaha, 1969-71, residency med., 1971—74, asst. prof. Dept. Internal Medicine, 1974-81, dir. House Officer Program, 1976-79, asst. dean for grad. med. edn., 1976-87, assoc. prof. Dept. Internal Medicine, 1981-89, assoc. dean for acad. affairs and grad. med. edn., 1986-93, prof. Dept. Internal Medicine, 1989—, chief Sect. Gen. Internal Medicine, 1993—2002, assoc. dean for grad. med. edn., 1993—. Vis. scholar Dept. Medicine U. Pa. Sch. Medicine, Phila., 1982-83; editl. bds. Med. Decision Making, MD Computing, Jour. Gen. Internal Medicine. Editor: (CD-ROM multimedia text) Procedures in Internal Medicine, 1996; contbr. articles to profl. jours. Recipient Disting. Alumnus award, U. Nebr. Coll. Med., 2010; named Hall of Fame, Omaha Ctrl. HS, 2009. Fellow ACP (Tchg. and Rsch. scholar 1973-76, Nebr. Laureate award 2006), Am. Coll. Med. Informatics; mem. Soc. for Med. Decision Making (v.p. 1988-89, trustee 1985-88, Eugene Saenger award 1996), Soc. Gen. Internal Medicine (coun. 1985-88, Elnora Rhodes award, 2005), Assn. Am. Med. Colls. (regional chair group on ednl. affairs 1994-95), Alpha Omega Alpha (pres. Alpha chpt. 1996-97, counselor 1997—2010), Phi Rho Sigma (Irving Cutter medal, 2007). Avocations: music, photography, hiking, drawing, computers. Office: University Nebr Med Ctr 985524 Nebraska Med Ctr Omaha NE 68198-5524 E-mail: wigton@unmc.edu.

WIKLUND, K. LARS C., anesthesiologist, researcher, educator; b. Uppsala, Sweden, Oct. 10, 1943; s. Knut and Elisabeth (Rabenius) W.; m. Ulla B. Anderson; children: Per K.E., Clara M.E. MD, Uppsala U., 1969, PhD, 1975. Clin. researcher dept. anesthesiology Univ. Hosp. Uppsala, 1969-75, asst. prof., then assoc. prof. neuroanesthesia, 1975-86, prof., chmn. dept. anesthesiology and intensive care, 1986—99, chair dept surg. Sci., 2002—10. Contbr. articles to med. jours. Bd. mem. The Laerdal Found. for Acute Medicine, 1993—. Recipient Hon. prize in acute medicine Oslo U., 1991. Fellow: Royal Coll. Anesthetists; mem.: Swedish Resuscitation Coun. (bd. mem. 2009—), Swedish Med. Soc. (bd. mem. 2005—10), Scandinavian Soc. Anaesthesiology and Intensive Care (bd. dirs. 2002—11), European Soc. Anaesthesiology, European Resuscitation Coun., Critical Care Soc., Am. Soc. Anesthesiologists. Home: Sveavägen 2 S 75236 Uppsala Sweden E-mail: lars.wiklund@surgsci.uu.se.

WIKNER, JOHAN NILS PONTUS, physician, researcher; b. Stockholm, June 18, 1956; s. Nils and Essie (Henden) W.; m. Birgitta Norstedt, June 22, 1985; children: Cecilia, Axel, Gustav. MD, Karolinska Inst., Stockholm, 1982, PhD, 1998. Resident in internal medicine and cardiology Karolinska Hosp., Stockholm, 1985-91, Södersjukhuset Hosp., Stockholm, 1985—91, cons. dept. internal medicine and endocrinology, 1991—. Contbr. articles to profl. jours. Named Tutor of the Yr., Student Union, Sch. medicine, Karolinska Inst., 1997, Med. Tchr. of Yr., 2007, Karolinska Inst. Mem. Swedish Soc. Cardiology, Swedish Soc. Endocrinology, Swedish Soc. Diabetology. Office: Södersjukhuset Hosp Dept Internal Medicine 11883 Stockholm Sweden Business E-Mail: johan.wikner@sodersjukhuset.se.

WILBANKS, DONNIE JO, healthcare educator; b. Oklahoma City, Okla., Feb. 21, 1950; s. James Henry and Laura Aneice (Henderson) Wilbanks; m. Sandra Kay Smith, Aug. 6, 1977; children: Kimberly Lynn, Eric Leslie. BA, Mo. Bapt. Coll., St. Louis, 1976; MA in Tchg., Webster U., St. Louis, 1991. Vocat. instr. State of Mo. and State of Ill. Assoc. pastor Fourth Bapt. Ch., St. Louis, 1972—76; alcoholism counselor Project Promised Land, St. Louis, 1972—75; bus. agt. Svc. Employees Internat. Union, St. Louis, 1985—86; children's svc. worker Mo. Family Svcs., 1986—93; in-home family therapist Mo., 1993—98; instr. psychology, anatomy, physiology St. Louis Coll. Health Careers, 1998—. Author: (textbook) Applied Psychology in Health Care, 2008. Vol. fund raising ARC, St. Louis, 2006. Cpl. USMC, 1968—71. Recipient Outstanding Svc. award, St. Louis Coll. of Health Careers, 2004; named Instr. of the Quarter, 2004, Instr. of the Yr., 2005. Mem.: MENSA, Am. Assn. of Profl. Hypnotherapists. Office: St Louis Coll of Health Careers 909 S Taylor Saint Louis MO 63110 Personal E-mail: donnie.wilbanks@yahoo.com.

WILBUR, RICHARD SLOAN, medical association administrator, physician; s. Blake Colburn and Mary Caldwell (Sloan) Wilbur; m. Betty Lou Fannin, Jan. 20, 1951; children: Andrew, Peter, Thomas. BA, Stanford U., 1943, MD, 1946; JD, John Marshall, 1990. Cert. ABIM (Gastroenterology Am. Bd. Internal Medicine, 1954. Intern San Francisco County Hosp., 1946—47; resident Stanford Hosp., 1949—51, U. Pa. Hosp., 1951—52; postgrad. tng. U. Mich. Hosp., 1957, Karolinska Sjukhuset, Stockholm, 1960; staff Palo Alto (Calif.) Med. Clinic, 1952—69; dep. exec. v.p. AMA, Chgo., 1969—71, 1973—74; asst. sec. for health and environment dept. def., 1971—73; sr. v.p. Baxter Labs., Inc., Deerfield, Ill., 1974—76; exec. v.p. Council Med. Splty. Socs., 1976—91, sec. accreditation coun. for continuing med. edn., 1979—91; assoc. prof. medicine Georgetown U. Med. Sch., 1971—77, Stanford Med. Sch., 1952—69; pres. Nat. Resident Matching Plan, 1991—92. Chmn. bd., CEO Inst. Clin. Info., 1994—99; sr. v.p. healthcare Buckeye Corp. Pte, Ltd., Singapore, 1997—2000; CEO Medic Alert, 1992—94; pres. Am. Bd. Med. Mgmt., 1992; mem. Am. Bd. Electrodiagnostic Medicine, 1993—98; chmn. med. adv. bd. Med. City, Bangalore, India, 1997—2000; bd. visitors Drew U. Postgrad. Med. Sch. Contbr. articles to profl. jours. Bd. govs. ARC; chmn. Mid-Am. Blood Svcs. Bd., Lifesource Blood Bank, 1996—98; vice-chmn. Rep. Cen. Com. Santa Clara County, Calif., 1966—89; bd. dir. Nat. Adv. Cancer Coun., Nat. Health Coun., 1993—95; chmn. bd. dir. Medic Alert Found.; chmn. bd. Calif. Med. Assn., 1968—69, Calif. Blue Shield, 1966—68, Am. Med. Found., 1987—; pres. Royal Soc. Medicine Found., 1998—2004. With USNR, 1942—58. Recipient Disting. Svc. medal, Dept. Def., 1973, Scroll of merit, Nat. Med. Assn., 1971. Fellow: ACP, Am. Coll. Physician Execs. (bd. regents 1985—89, pres. 1988—89), Am. Coll. Legal Medicine (pres. 2006—07), Internat. Coll. Dentistry (hon.); mem.: World Assn. Med. Law (editor 2010—), Am. Soc. Internal Medicine, Am. Gastroent. Assn., Santa Clara County Med. Soc. (hon.), Lake County Med. Soc., Ill. Med. Assn., Inst. Medicine, Cedars Club, Pacific Interurban Clin. Club, Alpha Omega Alpha, Phi Beta Kappa. Home: 985 Hawthorne Pl Lake Forest IL 60045-2217 Office: APT Management Inc 736 N Western Ave #222 Lake Forest IL 60045 E-mail: aptmgmnt@aol.com.

WILCHEK, MEIR, biochemist, educator; b. Warsaw, Oct. 17, 1935; arrived in Israel, 1949; s. Eliezer Nechemia and Rachel (Zaidenberg) Wilchek; m. Esther Edlis, Mar. 14, 1960; children: Eliezer Yizhak, Yael Zvia, Hagit Zipora. BS, Bar-Ilan U., Ramat Gan, Israel, 1960, PhD (hon.), 1995; PhD in Biochemistry, Weizmann Inst. Sci., Rehovot, Israel, 1965; DSc (hon.), U. Waterloo, Can., 1989; PhD (hon.), U. Jyvaskyla, Finland, 2000, Ben-Gurion U., Beer-Sheva, Israel, 2000. Chief chemist Yeda Co., Rehovot, 1960-62; rsch. assoc. dept. biophysics Weizmann Inst. Sci., 1965-66, sr. scientist, 1968-71, assoc. prof., 1971-74, prof., 1974—, head dept. biophysics, 1977-78, 83-87; vis. fellow NIH, Bethesda, Md., 1966-67, rsch. assoc., 1967-68. Vis. scientist NIH, 1972, 1974—75. Contbr. articles to profl. jours., chapters to books;, editor various med. texts. Recipient Rothschild prize in chemistry, Israel, 1984, Pierce prize for biorecognition tech., Ill., 1987, Israel prize in life scis., 1990, Sarstedt prize, Germany, 1990, Disting. Clin. Chemist award, Internat. Fedn. Clin. Chemistry, 1996, Christian B. Anfinsen award, Protein Soc., 2004, Wilhelm-Exner medal, Austria, 2004, Emet prize, Israel, 2005; co-recipient Wolf Found. prize in medicine, 1987; named an Hon. Citizen, City of Rehovot, 2004; Fogarty Internat. Scholar, 1981—82. Mem.: Israeli Acad. Scis. & Humanities, Israel Immunological Soc., Israel Chem. Soc., Israel Biochem. Soc., European Acad. Sci. & Art, European Molecular Biology Orgn., Inst. Medicine, Am. Chem. Soc., Am. Soc. Biol. Chemistry (hon.). Office Phone: 893 438 08. E-mail: meir.wilchek@weizmann.ac.il. *

WILCOX, CHRISTOPHER, nephrologist; b. Sept. 15, 1942; PhD, London U., 1974. Divsn. chief, nephrology and hypertension Georgetown U. Med. Ctr., 1994—. Office: 3800 Reservoir Rd 6PHC Washington DC 20057 Business E-Mail: wilcoxch@georgetown.edu.

WILCOX, GISELA, endocrinologist, researcher; b. Newcastle-upon-Tyne, Northumberland, Eng., Mar. 19, 1966; d. Max Wilcox and Patricia Loraine Wilcox (nee Young); m. Boyd Josef Gimnicher Strauss, Aug. 21, 1996. BSc with hons. in Medicine, Monash U., Victoria, Australia, 1990, MBBS with hons., 1990. Lic. physician Australia. Intern Monash Med. Ctr., Clayton, Victoria, Australia, 1991—92, clin. biochemistry registrar, 1994—95, cons. physician Clin. Nutrition and Metabolism Unit, 2001—; mem. staff Austin and Repatriation Hosp., Heidelberg, Victoria, Australia, 1992—94; metabolic registrar St Vincent's Hosp., Fitzroy, Victoria, Australia, 1995—96; diabetes registrar Internat. Diabetes Inst., Caulfield, Victoria, Australia, 1996—97; endocrinology registrar Alfred Hosp., Prahran, Victoria, Australia, 1997—98, clin. biochemistry registrar, 1998—2000; fellow in metabolic medicine Murdoch Children's Rsch. Inst., Melbourne, Victoria, Australia, 1999—2001; project officer food and nutrition monitoring & surveillance program Monash U., 2001—02; chem. pathologist Melbourne Pathology, 2004—. Chem. pathologist Mayne Health Dorevitch Pathology, Heidelberg, Australia, 2002—04; cons. Baker Med. Rsch. Inst., Prahran, Australia, 1997—2003; steering com. Nat. Iodine Nutrition Survey, 2002—03; hon. sr. lectr. dept. medicine Monash U., 2004—; dir. clin. tng. Monash Med. Ctr. Com. mem. Temple Beth Israel, Melbourne, 2000—03. Grantee, Sanitarium Health Food Co., 1999, Perpetual Trustees, 2000. Fellow: Royal Coll. Pathologists Australisia, Royal Australasian Coll. Physicians; mem.: Australasian Clin. Nutrition Soc. (newsletter editor 2003—), Australasian Soc. Study Obesity, Soc. Study Inborn Errors of Metabolism, Nutrition Soc. of Australia, The Endocrine Soc., Endocrine Soc. of Australia, Australasian Assn. Clin. Biochemists (Exam. prize 1998), N.Y. Acad. Scis. Achievements include research in early clinical research in phytoestrogens. Avocations: music, bicycling, natural history. Office: Monash Med Ctr 246 Clayton Rd Clayton VIC 3168 Australia Office Fax: +61 3 9594 6370. Business E-Mail: gisela.wilcox@southernhealth.org.au.

WILCOX, RYAN ALAN, medical educator; b. Allegan, Mich., Oct. 17, 1973; BS, Hope Coll., BA, 1996; MD, Mayo Med. Sch., PhD, 2004. Asst. prof., medicine Mayo Clinic, 2009—. Recipient Patterson Meml. prize, Hope Coll.; Gen. Mills Found. Clinician-Investigator grant, Mayo Clinic. Mem.: Am. Assn. Cancer Rsch., Am. Soc. Clin. Oncology, Am. Soc. Hematology, Phi Beta Kappa. Avocations: cooking, hiking, scuba diving. Business E-Mail: rywilcox@med.umich.edu.

WILCZOK, TADEUSZ MARIAN, biochemist, educator; b. Katowice, Poland, June 22, 1934; s. Pawel and Roza Rozanska W.; m. Gizela Brezezina, Mar. 17, 1956; 1 child, Adam. BS in Chemistry, U, 1952; MS in Chemistry, Higher Pedag Sch., 1955; PhD in Biochemistry, U, 1960, DS in Biochemistry, 1962. Asst. Higher Pedagog Sch., Katowice, Poland, 1955; researcher Acad. Sci., Moscow, 1956-58; dozent Inst. Oncology, Gliwice, Poland, 1958; from asst. prof. to prof. Med. U. Silesia, Katowice, 1966—. Vis. prof. Gutenberg U., Mainz, 1959, Sloan Kettering Inst., N.Y.C., 1964, EPA Gulf Breeze, Fla., 1978; mem. Com. Biochemistry, Biophysics Polish Acad. Sci., Warsaw, 1968; chmn. Com. Med. Physics, Warsaw; pres. Polish Biophysics Soc., 1985; dean Pharm. faculty, 1984-96; v.p. Silesian Med. Acad., 1996—; rector U. Med. of Silesia, 1999—. Editor Atlas of Metabolic Pathways, 1993; contbr. over 200 scientific articles to profl. jours. Mem. Acad. Sci. Pharm. (France). Avocation: hunting. E-mail: rektor@infomed.slam.katowice.pl.

WILD, JAMES ROBERT, biochemistry and genetics professor; b. Sedalia, Mo., Nov. 24, 1945; s. Robert Lee and Frances Elleta (Wheeler) W.; m. Ann Lynn Brenner, Aug. 1, 1973; 1 child, Kalli Ann. BA in Zoology, U. Calif., Davis, 1967; PhD in Cell Biology, U. Calif., Riverside, 1971, post doctoral fellow, 1972. From asst. to assoc. prof. genetics and biochemistry Tex. A&M U., Coll. Sta., Tex., 1975-84, prof., chair genetics faculty, 1984—, prof. biochemistry & genetics, 1984—2000, head biochemistry and biophysics dept., 1986-90, exec. assoc. dean Coll. Agr. and Life Scis., 1987—92, prof., head dept. biochemistry and biophysics Coll. Agr. and Life Scis., 1994—2000, chmn. faculty genetics. Fellow faculty Tex. Agrl. Experiment Sta., 1999. With USN, 1972-75. Recipient So. Regional award for excellence in coll. anduniv. tchg. in food and agrl. scis., Higher Edn. program USDA, 1992. Fellow AAAS. Methodist. Office: Tex A&M U 2128 Biochemistry Bldg Rm 332 College Station TX 77843-2128 Office Phone: 979-845-6539. Business E-Mail: j-wild@tamu.edu.

WILDENTHAL, CLAUD KERN, physician, educator; b. San Marcos, Tex., July 1, 1941; s. Bryan and Doris (Kellam) W.; m. Margaret Dehlinger, Oct. 15, 1964; children: Pamela, Catharine. BA, Sul Ross Coll., 1960; MD, U. Tex. Southwestern Med. Ctr., Dallas, 1964; PhD, U. Cambridge, Eng., 1970. Intern Bellevue Hosp., NYC, 1964-65; resident in medicine, fellow cardiology Parkland Hosp., Dallas, 1965-67; rsch. fellow Nat. Heart Inst., Bethesda, Md., 1967-68; vis. rsch. fellow Strangeways Rsch. Lab., Cambridge, 1968-70; asst. prof. to prof. internal medicine and physiology U. Tex. Southwestern Med. Ctr., Dallas, 1970-76, prof., dean grad. sch., 1976-80, prof., dean Southwestern Med. Sch., 1980-86, prof., pres., 1986—2008, prof., 2008—; pres. Southwestern Med. Found., 2008—. Hon. fellow Hughes Hall, U. Cambridge, 1994—. Author: Regulation of Cardiac Metabolism, 1976, Degradative Processes in Heart and Skeletal Muscle, 1980; contbr. articles to profl. jours. Bd. dirs. Lasker Found., Dallas Ctr. Performing Arts, Dallas Symphony, Dallas Opera, Dallas Mus. Art, Dallas Citizen's Coun., Dallas Regional C. of C., Cambridge in Am., Hoblitzelle Found., Reves Found. Recipient rsch. career devel. award NIH, 1972; spl. rsch. fellow USPHS, 1968-70; Guggenheim fellow, 1975-76. Mem. AMA, Inst. Medicine/NAS, Am. Soc. Clin. Investigation, Royal Soc. Medicine Gt. Britain, Am. Physiol. Soc., Internat. Soc. Heart Rsch. (past pres. Am. sect.), Am. Fedn. Clin. Rsch., Assn. Am. Physicians, Am. Heart Assn. (past chmn. sci. policy com.), Assn. Acad. Health Ctrs. (past chmn. sci. policy com.). Home: 4001 Hanover Ave Dallas TX 75225-7010 Office: 3963 Maple Ave Ste 100 Dallas TX 75219

WILDER, ROBERT THEODORE, anesthesiologist; b. Pomona, Calif., July 14, 1955; BS, Stanford U., 1977; MD, Vanderbilt U., PhD, 1984. Assoc., anesthesiology Children's Hosp., Boston, 1990—2000; cons., anesthesiology Mayo Clinic, 2000—. Office: Mayo Clinic Dept Anesthesiology Rochester MN 55905 Office Fax: 507-255-6463. Business E-Mail: wilder.robert@mayo.edu.

WILDING, JOHN PAUL HOWARD, medical educator, consultant; DM, Southampton U., 1985, 1994. Sr. lectr. U. Liverpool, 1996—2001, reader medicine, 2001—05, prof. medicine England, 2005—08, head dept. obesity, endocrinology, 2010—. Cons. U. Hosp. Aintree, Liverpool, 1996—. Fellow: Royal Coll. Physicians; mem.: Soc. Endocrinology, Assn. for Study of Obesity (chmn. 2006—09). Achievements include research in obesity and diabetes. Office: Univ Liverpool Aintree Hosp Longmoor Ln L9 7AL Liverpool England

WILDING, PETER, retired biochemist; b. Chester, Eng., Dec. 16, 1934; BSc with honors, U. Birmingham, Eng., 1961, PhD, 1965. Dir. pathology BUPA Med. Ctr., London, 1969—72; dep. dir. Wolfson Rsch. Labs., U. Birmingham, 1972—77; v.p. diagnostics Technicon Instruments Corp., 1977—82; v.p. r & d SmithKline Beckman/Geometric Data, 1982—86; prof. U. Pa., 1986—2004, emeritus prof., 2004—. Pres. & CEO, bd. dirs. Aviva Bioscis., San Diego, 2001—03; sec., bd. dirs. PhenoTech Inc., Phila., 2006—08. Recipient Clin. Innovator award, U. Pa. Sch. Medicine, Kone award, Assn. Clin. Biochemists, UK, Hon. Prof., West China U. Med. Scis., Chengdu, China. Fellow: Internat. Union Pure & Applied Chemistry, Nat. Acad. Clin. Biochemistry, Royal Soc. Chemistry (UK), Royal Coll. Pathologists (UK); mem.: Am. Assn. Clin. Chemistry (Outstanding Contbn. award). Avocations: golf, theater, singing. Home: 14 Callery Way Malvern PA 19355 Home Fax: 610-240-0234. Business E-Mail: pwilding@mail.med.upenn.edu.

WILENSKY, GAIL ROGGIN, economist; b. Detroit, June 14, 1943; d. Albert Alan and Sophia (Blitz) Roggin; m. Robert Joel Wilensky, Aug. 4, 1963; children: Peter Benjamin, Sara Elizabeth. AB (hon.), U. Mich., 1964, MA in Economics, 1965, PhD in Economics, 1968; degree (hon.), Hahnemann U., 1993, Rush U., 1997, U. Sciences, Phila., 2002. Trustee, Nat. Opinion Rsch. Ctr. University of Chicago; trustee, combined benefits fund United Mineworkers of America; mem. Inst. of Medicine & its Governing Coun.; pres. Def. Health Bd.; economist President's Commn. on Income Maintenance Programs; exec. dir. Md. Coun. of Econ. Advs., 1969-71; sr. rschr. Urban Inst., Washington, 1971-73; assoc. rsch. scientist, pub. policy and pub. health University of Michigan, Ann Arbor, 1973-75, vis. asst. prof. econs., 1973-75; sr. rsch. mgr. Nat Ctr. for Health Svcs. Rsch., Hyattsville, Md., 1975-83; assoc. profl. lectr. George Washington U., 1976-78; v.p. div. health affairs Project HOPE, Millwood, Va., 1983-90; adminstr. Health Care Fin. Adminstrn., Washington, 1990-92; dep. asst. to the Pres. for policy devel. The White House, 1992-93; sr. fellow Project HOPE, Bethesda, Md., 1993—, chair phys. payment rev. com., 1995-97; chmn. Medicare Payment Adv. Commn. (MedPAC), 1997—2001; co-chair Pres.'s Task Force to Improve Healthcare Delivery for Vets., 2001—03, Dept. Def. Task Force on Future of Mil. Health Care, 2006. Vice chmn. Md. Health Care Commn.; bd. dirs. Gentiva Health Svcs., Quest Diagnostics, Inc., SRA Internat., Inc., UnitedHealth Group, Cephalon, Inc., The BrainScope Co., Inc., 2009—. Contbr. 100 articles in field to profl. jours. Dir. Am. Heart Assn., 1980-85, bd. dirs., 2002—; mem. health adv. com. Compt. Gen. U.S., 1987-90; bd. dirs. United Healthcare Corp., Cephalon, Quest Diagnostics; mem. vis. com. med. sch. U. Mich., 1993-97; trustee United Mine Workers Am. Retirement Fund, 1993—; commr. WHO Commn. on the Social Determinants of Health, 2005-08. Flinn Found. disting. scholar, 1985; recipient Dean Conley award Am. Coll. Healthcare Execs., 1989. Mem. NAS Inst. Medicine (coun. mem. 2006-), Am. Econ. Assn. (women's com. 1982-84), Fedn. Orgn. of Profl. Women (chmn. econ. task force 1981-83), Am. Statis. Assn., Nat. Tax Assn., Washington Women Economists, Assn. Health Svc. Rsch. (dir. 1984-87), Found. Health Svc. Rsch. (bd. dir. 1987-90), Acad. Health (chair bd. dir. 2000—, Cosmos Club (Washington). Office: Cephalon Inc Bd. Directors 41 Moores Rd Frazer PA 19355 Office Phone: 610-344-0200. Business E-Mail: gwilensky@projecthope.org, gwilensky@cephalon.com. *

WILENSKY, JACOB T., ophthalmologist, educator; b. New Orleans, Aug. 16, 1942; BA, Tulane U., 1964, MD, 1968. Prof. ophthalmology U. Ill. Coillege Medicine, Chgo., 1990—2010, Wilensky prof. ophthalmology, 2010—. Cons. JBWSVA Hosp., 1976—2011. Fellow: Am. Acad. Ophthalmology; mem.: Am. Ophthal. Soc., Am. Glaucoma Soc. Office: 1855 W Taylor Chicago IL 60612 Business E-Mail: jacowile@uic.edu.

WILEY, JOHN EDWIN, cytogeneticist; b. Roanoke, Va., Mar. 2, 1951; s. James Edwin and Marie Rita (Cassell) W. BA, U. N.C., Greensboro, 1973, MA, 1976; PhD, N.C. State U., 1981. Diplomate Am. Bd. Med. Genetics-Clin. Cytogenetics. Biomed. rschr. St. Paul's Coll., Lawrenceville, Va., 1981-82; postdoctoral trainee U. Wis., Madison, 1982-84; mem. faculty East Carolina U. Sch. Medicine, Greenville, NC, 1984—. Contbr. articles to profl. jours. Biomed. rsch. support grantee United Way, Greenville, 1986-87, USPHS, Washington, 1987-90. Mem. AAAS, Am. Soc. Human Genetics, Am. Soc. Zoologists, Am. Soc. Ichthyologists and Herpetologists. Democrat. Achievements include observation that certain genes on frog chromosomes seem to move frequently around, that chromosome constitution in many breast cancer tumors seems normal, that in some patients with ring X chromosomes the ring may not be turned off, that the addition of tumor promoting agents helps white blood cells in many vertebrates to divide, and that DNA sequences on ends of frog chromosomes are the same as those on the ends of human chromosomes. Office: East Carolina U Brody Sch Medicine 600 Moye Blvd Greenville NC 27834-4300 Home: 206 Ravenwood Dr Greenville NC 27834-6737 Home Phone: 252-758-0621; Office Phone: 252-744-2525. E-mail: wileyj@ecu.edu.

WILEY, JOSEPH MICHAEL, pediatrician, department chairman; b. Balt., Oct. 13, 1956; married; 1 child. BA, Loyola Coll. Balt., 1978; MD, U. Md. Sch. Medicine, 1982. Asst. prof. pediat. and oncology Johns Hopkins Sch. Medicine, 1988—93; chief pediat. hematology, oncology and pediat. bone marrow transplantation U. NC, Chapel Hill, 1993—2000; physician exec., dept. chmn. Lifebridgehealth, 2000—11, chmn., dept. pediat., Sinai Hosp. Balt., 2000—. Pediat. Cancer Rsch. grant, Hyundai Found. Pediat. Cancer Rsch., Fungal Infection Rsch. grant, Children's Cancer Found. Md. Fellow: Am. Acad. Pediat. Avocations: cooking, travel, golf. Office: 2401 W Belvedere Ave Baltimore MD 21215 Office Fax: 410-601-8766. Business E-Mail: jwiley@lifebridgehealth.org.

WILEY CENE, CRYSTAL, medical educator; b. Burlington, NC, June 28, 1973; MD, Brody Sch. Medicine, East Carolina U., 2002; MPH, Bloomberg Sch. Pub. Health, Johns Hopkins U., 2006. Asst. prof. U. NC, Chapel Hill, 2008—. Recipient Mentored Patient-

Oriented Rsch. Career Devel. award, NIH, Nat. Heart Lung and Blood Inst. Mem.: Am. Heart Assn., Soc. Gen. Internal Medicine. Avocations: tennis, travel. Office: 5034 Old Clinic Bldg #7110 Chapel Hill NC 27599 Office Fax: 919-966-2274. Business E-Mail: crystal_cene@med.unc.edu.

WILFERT-KATZ, CATHERINE M., medical association administrator, pediatrician, epidemiologist, educator; b. LA, July 26, 1936; m. Samuel L. Katz; children: Rachel, Catherine stepchildren: John, David, William, Deborah, Susan, Penelope. BA with distinction, Stanford Coll., 1958; MD cum laude, Harvard U., 1962. Med. intern Boston City Hosp., 1962—63; resident in pediat. Children's Hosp., Boston, 1964—66, fellow in infectious diseases, 1966—68; asst. prof. pediat. and virology Duke U., 1969—73, assoc. prof. pediat., 1974—79, prof. pediat. and microbiology, chief pediatric infectious diseases, 1980—96, prof. emeritus; sci. dir. Elizabeth Glaser Pediat. AIDS Found., Santa Monica, Calif., 1997—2009. Chair Adv. Com. on Immunization Practices, 1980, Perinatal Working Group of Prevention Trials Network, NIH; mem. adv. com. Office of AIDS Rsch., 1999—2005. Recipient Christopher award, Am. Acad. Pediat., 2007. Mem.: NIH AIDS Coms., Inst. Medicine, Infectious Diseases Soc. Am. (pres. 2000). Home Fax: 919-968-0447. Personal E-mail: wilfert@mindspring.com.

WILGIS, E F SHAW, surgeon; b. Balt., Dec. 17, 1936; MD, U. Md., 1962. Chief hand surgery Curtis Nat. Hand Ctr., Union Meml. Hosp., 1983—2000, dir. rsch., 2000—. Chmn., bd. dirs. Medstar Health Rsch. Inst., 2006—10. Mem.: Am. Soc. Surgery Hand. Avocations: golf, bicycling. Office: Curtis Nat Hand Ctr 3333 N Calv Baltimore MD 21218 Office Fax: 410-261-8175. Business E-Mail: shaw.wilgis@medstar.net.

WILHELM, GARY BRETZ, physician; s. Norman E. and Madeleine Bretz Wilhelm; 1 child. BA in Biology, Capital U., Columbus, Ohio, 1974; PhD in Human Anatomy and Neuroscis., U. Tex., Galveston, 1980; MD, U. Tex., San Antonio, 1986. Postdoctoral fellow dept. pathology U. Tex. Health Sci. Ctr., San Antonio, 1980—81, instr. in human anatomy, 1980—82; intern Brooke Army Med. Ctr., Fort Sam Houston, Tex., 1987; resident in orthop. William Beaumont Army Med. Ctr., Fort Bliss, Tex., 1991—96; commd. 2d lt. US Army, 1986, advanced through grades to col.; physician extender staff US Army Acad. Health Scis., San Antonio, 1990—91, resident physician Fort Bliss, 1991—96; chief, phys. exams clinics and aerospace medicine Munson Army Health Ctr., Ft. Leavenworth, Kans., 1996—; flight surgeon Mo. Army Nat. Guard, Jefferson City, 1996—; chif med. officer Cmty. Based Health Care Orgn., Ala., 2006—08; med. dir. Gentry Family Practice Clinic, 2007—. Orthopedic tech. course dir. Acad. Scis., Fort Sam Houston, 1990—91. Contbr. articles to profl. publs. Co-dir. Nat. Student Rsch. Forum, Galveston, 1978—79. Col. med. corps, flight surgeon Mo. Army NG. Decorated Meritorious Svc. medal US Army, Civilian Achievement award, Army Commendation Medal Cmty. Based Health Care Orgn., Nat. Def. Svc. medal, Global War Terrorism Medal; named Flight Surgeon of Yr., Soc. Army Flight Surgeons, 1988. Episcopalian. Avocations: flying, fox hunting, reading.

WILHELM, KLAUS PETER, dermatologist, educator, consultant; b. Bremen, Germany, Mar. 3, 1960; s. Alfred and Annette (Geissler) W.; m. Dorothea Schmidt, Mar. 7, 1986; children: Jan-Sebastian, Florian-Alexander, Antonia-Sophie. MD, Med. U. Lubeck, Germany, 1986, PhD, 1995. Cert. dermatologist, allergologist. Resident in dermatology Med. U. Lübeck, 1990-93, sr. dermatologist, 1993-94; pres., med. dir. proDERM, Schenefeld, Germany, 1994—, prof., 2002. Vis. postdoctoral fellow U. Calif. Med. Sch., San Francisco, 1988-90. Co-editor: (handbooks) Bioengineering of the Skin-Methods and Instrumentation, 1996, Bioengineering of the Skin-Surface Imaging and Analysis, 1997, Dermatotoxicology, 2008. Capt. M.C. German Army, 1986-88. Rsch. grantee Deutsche Forschungsgemeinschaft, 1990-92, 92-94, postdoctoral stipend, 1988-90. Mem. Internat. Soc. Bioengring. and the Skin (mem. bd. 1994—, sec. 2003-10, pres. 2010-), Am. Acad. Dermatology. Home: Fruteweg 3 22559 Hamburg Germany Office: proDERM Kiebitzweg 2 22869 Schenefeld Germany Business E-Mail: kpw@proDERM.de.

WILHELM, MORTON, retired surgeon; b. Roanoke, Va., June 22, 1923; s. Walter LeRoy and Della Mae (Turner) W.; m. Jean Osborne, June 3, 1949; children: Melissa, Christina. BS, Va. Mil. Inst., 1944; MD, U. Va., 1947. Diplomate Am. Bd. Surgery. Intern, resident in surgery VA Mason Hosp., Seattle, 1947-51, 52-53; fellow, instr. surgery Med. Ctr. U. Va., Charlottesville, 53-54, 56-66, assoc. prof. surgery Med. Ctr., 1966-80, prof. surgery Med. Ctr., 1980-93, chief dept. surg. oncology Med. Ctr., 1990-93, Joseph Farrow prof. surg. oncology Med. Ctr., 1990-93. Pres. Va. div., mem. nat. bd. dirs. Am. Cancer Soc., Meritorious Svc. award, Horsley award, Nat. Teresa Lasser award. Lt. U.S. Army, 1951-53. Fellow ACS (vice chmn. commn. on cancer 1989-90, pres. Va. chpt., mem. bd. govs.); mem. So. Surg. Assn., So. Soc. Clin. Surgeons, Soc. Surg. Oncology. Avocations: tennis, golf, woodworking.

WILHELM, SCOTT M., physician, educator; b. Toledo, Ohio, Oct. 11, 1969; MD, U. Cin., Coll. Medicine, 1995. Assoc. prof. surgery U. Hosps., Case Med. Ctr., 2003—. Office: University Hospitals Case Med Ctr Cleveland OH 44106 Office Fax: 216-983-7230. Business E-Mail: scott.wilhelm@uhhospitals.org.

WILHIDE, STEPHEN D., medical association administrator; BA in Social Scis., Frostburg State U., Md., 1965; MSW, U. Md., 1972; MPH, U. Pitts., 1976. Exec. dir. So. Ohio Health Svcs. Network, 1976—2002, Nat. Rural Health Assn., Alexandria, Va., 2002—. Vol. VISTA, NC. With US Army, Vietnam. Named one of Most Powerful People in Healthcare, Modern Healthcare mag., 2003. Office: National Rural Health Association 1108 K St NW Fl 2 Washington DC 20005-4094 Office Phone: 703-519-7910. Business E-Mail: wilhide@nrharural.com.

WILKENS, PHILIP IVERSEN, chiropractor; b. Oslo, Apr. 28, 1978; MS, Anglo European Coll. Chiropractic, 2005. Rsch. fellow Oslo U. Hosp., 2006—. Rsch. fellow U. Oslo, 2006. Avocations: exercise, running. Home: Ivan Bjørndalsgate 10 Oslo 0472 Norway Personal E-mail: phililip.wilkens@medisin.uio.no.

WILKES, DAVID STEPHEN, immunologist, educator; b. Phila., Sept. 5, 1956; m. Toni Eldridge-Wilkes; children: Kristen, David Jr. BS, Villanova U., Pa., 1978; MD, Temple U. Sch. Medicine, Phila., 1982. Diplomate Nat. Bd. Med. Examiners, Am. Bd. Internal Medicine, cert. in critical care medicine, in pulmonary disease. Internal medicine residency Temple U. Hosp., 1982—85; pulmonary & critical care fellow U. Tex. Southwestern Med. Ctr., Dallas, 1989—92; asst. prof. dept. medicine Ind. U. Sch. Medicine, Indpls., 1992—97, assoc. prof., 1997—2004, dir. Ctr. Immunobiology, 2004—, Dr. Calvin H. English prof. medicine, 2004—09, August M. Watanabe prof. med. rsch., assoc. dean rsch. affairs, 2009—. Clin. instr. dept. medicine U. Tex. Southwestern Med. Ctr./Parkland Meml. Hosp., 1986—89; staff physician Ind. U. Med. Ctr./Wishard Meml. Hosp., 1992—; v.p. med. staff Vencor Hosp., Indpls., 1993—95, pres. med. staff, 1996—98; mem. nat. adv. coun. Nat. Inst. Allergy & Infectious Diseases, NIH, 2006—; founder, chief sci. oficer ImmuneWorks, Indpls., 2009—. Contbr. articles to profl. jours. Maj. med. corp USAF, 1985—88. Fellow: ACP, Am. Coll. Chest Physicians; mem.: AAAS, Am. Soc. Transplantation, Internat. Sco. Heart & Lung Transplantation, Am. Assn. Immunologists, Assn. Am. Physicians (hon.), Am. Lng Assn. Ind., Am. Fedn. Med. Rsch., Am. Thoracic Soc. (bd. dirs. 2005—07). Office: Ind U Sch Medicine Fairbanks Hall Rm 6200 340 W 10th St Indianapolis IN 46202 also: ImmuneWorks 351 W 10th St Indianapolis IN 46202 Office Phone: 317-278-7020. E-mail: dwilkes@iupui.edu. *

WILKIE, DONALD WALTER, retired biologist, aquarium administrator; b. Vancouver, BC, Can., June 20, 1931; s. Otway James Henry and Jessie Margaret (McLeod) W.; m. Patricia Ann Archer, May 18, 1980; children: Linda, Douglas, Susanne. BA, U. B.C., 1960, M.Sc., 1966. Curator Vancouver Pub. Aquarium, 1961-63, Phila. Aquarama, 1963-65; exec. dir. aquarium-mus. Scripps Instn. Oceanography, La Jolla, Calif., 1965-93, exec. dir. emeritus, 1993—; founding dir. Birch Aquarium of Scripps, 1992. Cons. aquarium design, rschg. exhibit content; sci. writer and editor naturalist-marine edn. programs. head coach, Scholastic Clay Targets Prog., 2003-08. Author books on aquaria and marine ednl. materials; contbr. numerous articles to profl. jours. Bd. mem. San Diego Shotgun Sports Assn., 2008; pres. UCSD Retirement Assn. 1999-02. Mem. San Diego (Calif.) Zool. Soc., Writingentstory Aquariums Scripps Instn. San Diego. Home: 4548 Cather Ave San Diego CA 92122-2632 Office: U Calif San Diego Scripps Instn Oceanography Libr 9500 Gilman Dr La Jolla CA 92093-0219 E-mail: dwilkie@ucsd.edu, donwilkie1@mac.com.

WILKINS, ROBERT HENRY, neurosurgeon, editor, educator; b. Pitts., Aug. 18, 1934; s. George H. and Mary M. (Lemon) W.; m. Gloria A. Kohl, Dec. 28, 1957; children: Michael I., Jeffrey K., Elizabeth A. BS, U. Pitts., 1955, MD, 1959. Diplomate Am. Bd. Neurol. Surgery. Intern, resident gen. surgery Duke U. Med. Ctr., Durham, NC, 1959-61, resident in neurosurgery, 1963-68, asst. prof. neurosurgery, 1968-72, prof. neurosurgery, 1976—2004, chief divsn. neurosurgery, 1976-96, emeritus prof. neurosurgery, 2005—; clin. assoc. surgery br. Nat. Cancer Inst., Bethesda, Md., 1961-63; chmn. dept. neurosurgery Scott and White Clinic, Temple, Tex., 1972-75; assoc. prof. neurosurgery U. Pitts., 1975-76. Lectr. Cook County Grad. Sch. Medicine, Chgo., 1976-96; attending neurosurgeon Durham VA Hosp., 1968-72, 78-98; mem. Nat. Adv. Coun. Nat. Inst. Neurol. Disorders and Stroke, 1989-92. Co-editor: Neurosurgery, 2d edit., 3 vols., 1996, Neurosurgery Updates I and II, 1990, 91, Neurosurgical Operative Atlas, 1991-2000, Principles of Neurosurgery, 1994; editor Clin. Neurosurgery, 1972-75; assoc. editor Surg. Neurology, 1975-76; founding editor Neurosurgery, 1977-82, mem. editl. rev. bd., 1997-2001; mem. editl. bd. Jour. Neurosurgery, 1987-96, chmn., 1996-97, mem. adv. bd., 1997—; neurosurgery editor Key Neurology and Neurosurgery, 1993-96, Yr. Book of Neurology and Neurosurgery, 1994-97. Recipient Travel award Copenhagen, Nat. Inst. Neurol. Diseases and Blindness, 1965, Royal Australasian Coll. Surgeons, Found. lectr. Adelaide 1986. Fellow ACS (gov. 1996); mem. Congress Neurol. Surgeons (pres. 1979-80), Am. Assn. Neurol. Surgeons (treas. 1989-92), So. Neurosurg. Soc. (sec. 1988-91, pres. 1992-93), Soc. Neurol. Surgeons (v.p. 1995-96), Am. Bd. Neurol. Surgery (dir. 1991-97, chmn. 1996-97), Phi Beta Kappa, Alpha Omega Alpha. Democrat. Avocation: medical writing and editing. Office: Duke U Med Ctr PO Box 3807 Durham NC 27710-0001 Personal E-mail: rhwilkins@aol.com.

WILKINSON, BARBARA J., pediatrician, educator; b. Mitcham, Surrey, Eng., June 5, 1946; came to U.S., 1954, naturalized, 1963. d. Arthur Frederick and Elizabeth (Law) Wilkinson. BA in Zoology with highest distinction, U. Maine, 1969; MD, Boston U., 1973. Diplomate Am. Bd. Pediatrics, 1981. Pediatric intern Boston City Hosp., 1973-74; fellow in neonatology U. Rochester/Strong Meml. Hosp., Rochester Gen. Hosp., Rochester, N.Y., 1976-78; resident in pediatrics Maine Med. Ctr., Portland, 1974-76, assoc. neonatologist, outreach educator, 1979-83, attending staff, courtesy staff, 1979—, lectr. for pediatric med. students, 1983—2003; clin. instr. pediatrics part time faculty U. Vt. Coll. Medicine/Maine Med. Ctr., Portland, 1980-83, clin. asst. prof. pediatrics part time faculty, 1983—2004. Participant at emergency and family practice grand rounds on bereavement Maine Med. Ctr., early 1990s, co-facilitator Sudden Infant Death Support Group, 1980-2004; adj. faculty in allied health scis. So. Maine Vocat. Tech. Inst., South Portland, 1984-86; adj. faculty pathophysiology courses So. Maine Tech. Coll., South Portland, 1998-2000. Mem., contact person Maine Children's Meml. Libr. Bereaved Parents; precinct ward clk. Elections, Portland, 1990s-01. Fellow Am. Acad. Pediatrics; mem. AAUW (life), Am. Acad. Pediat., Altrusa Internat., Nat. Honor Soc., Phi Beta Kappa, Phi Kappa Phi (life). Avocations: watercolor painting, silk screening, photography, reading. Home: 4435 Summerwood Dr Cumming GA 30041-9445

WILKINSON, DAVID STANLEY, pathologist, consultant, researcher, educator; b. Richmond, Va., Feb. 2, 1945; s. Herbert Carroll and Hattie Mae (Vaughan) Wilkinson; m. Judith Farish Pace, June 16, 1967; children: Jill Marie, Julie Lynne, Virginia Ann. BS in Chemistry, Va. Mil. Inst., Lexington, 1967; PhD in Exptl. Oncology and Pathology, U. Wis.-Madison, 1971; MD, U. Miami, 1978. Diplomate Am. Bd. Pathology. Fellow McArdie Lab. Cancer Rsch. U. Wis., 1967—71; asst. prof. biochemistry U. South Fla., Tampa, 1972—76; resident in pathology Walter Reed Army Med. Ctr., Washington, 1978—82; instr. pathology Uniformed Svc. U. Health Sci., Bethesda, 1979—82; chief clin. pathology Eisenhower Army Med. Ctr., Ft. Gordon, Ga., 1982—84; instr. pathology Med. Coll. Ga., Augusta, 1982—84; assoc. prof. pathology George Washington U. Med. Ctr., 1984—89, dir. clin. pathology div., 1984—92, prof. pathology, 1989—93; med. dir. George Washington U. Hosp., 1992—93; prof. pathology, chmn. dept. pathology Va. Commonwealth U., 1993—. Lectr. in field. Editor: (other) Clinical Laboratory Management Review, 1989—2004; contbr. articles to profl. jours. Commd. 2nd lt. US Army, 1967, advanced through grades to maj. US Army, 1982. Fellow: Coll. Am. Pathologists, Am. Soc. Clin. Pathology; mem.: AMA, Assn. Pathology Chairs (pres. 2004—06), Med. Soc. Va. (del.), Richmond Acad. Medicine (trustee), U.S. and Canadian Acad. Pathology, Am. Soc. Investigative Pathology, Am. Assn. Blood Banks, Am. Assn. Clin. Chemistry, Soc. Exptl. Biology and Medicine, Am. Assn. Cancer Rsch., VMI Keydet (Lexington, Va.). Republican. Office: Va Commonwealth Univ Dept Pathology PO Box 980662 Richmond VA 23298-0662

WILKINSON, LOUISE CHERRY, psychology professor, dean; b. Phila., May 15, 1948; BA magna cum laude, Oberlin Coll., 1970; EdM, EdD, Harvard U., 1974. Prof., chmn. dept. ednl. psychology U. Wis., Madison, 1976-85; prof., exec. officer Grad. Sch. PhD Program CUNY, NYC, 1984-86; disting. prof., dean Grad. Sch. Edn. Rutgers U., 1986—2003; dean Sch. Edn. Syracuse (NY) U., 2003—05, disting. prof. edn., psychology and comm. scis., 2003—. Chair ednl. strategic planning Rutgers U.; mem. nat. rev. bd. Nat. Inst. Edn., 1977, 85, 87; cons. Nat. Ctr. for Bilingual Rsch., 1982, 84, US Dept. Edn., 1995—96; adv. bd. Nat. Reading Rsch. Ctr., 1992—98; co-chair commn. on literacy leadership Internat. Reading Assn.; vis. prof. U. London, 2006—, East China Normal U., 2006—, Igroun U., 2007—10; hon. guest prof. Beijing Normal U., 2001—05. Co-author: Communicating for Learning, 1991; editor: Communicating in Classroom, 1982, Social Context of Instruction, 1984, Gender Influences in the Classroom, 2002; co-editor: Literacy and Language Learning, 2004, Improving Literacy Achievement in Urban Schs., 2008; contbr. articles to profl. jours.; mem. editl. bds. various publs.:; co-editor: The Education of English Language Learners, 2010. Fellow: APA, Am. Assn. for Applied and Preventive Psychology, Am. Psychol. Soc.; mem.: NJ Coun. Acad. Policy Advisors, Am. Ednl. Rsch. Assn. (v.p. 1990—92, program chair 1997). Home: 315 Riverside Dr #15A New York NY 10025

WILKINSON, RALPH RUSSELL, retired biochemistry educator, toxicologist; b. Portland, Oreg., Feb. 20, 1930; s. Tracy Chandler and Lavern (Russell) W.; m. Evelyn Marie Wickman, Aug. 5, 1956. BA, Reed Coll., 1953; PhD, U. Oreg., 1962; MBA, U. Mo., Kansas City, 1974. Rsch. chemist VA Hosp., Kansas City, Mo., 1973-74, sr. rsch. chemist Midwest Rsch. Inst., Kansas City, 1975-84, prof. Rockhurst Coll., Kansas City, 1985-86, Cleve. Chiropractic Coll., Kansas City, 1987-99, prof. emeritus, 1999—2011. Cons. in biochemistry, toxicology, environ. impact, tech. assessment, Kansas City, 1981—. Author: (book) Neurotoxins and Neurobiological Function, 1987; contbr. articles to profl. jours. Mem. Southtown Coun., Kansas City, Mo., 1989—, Spina Bifida Assn. Am., Kansas City, 1989—. NSF fellow, 1959-60. Mem. Am. Chem. Soc., Sigma Xi. Avocations: travel, history, music, antiques. Home: 7911 Charlotte St Kansas City MO 64131-2175

WILKINSON, SUSAN MARY, nursing educator, researcher; b. Norwich, Eng., Jan. 3, 1945; MSc in Nursing, U. Manchester, 1986, PhD, 1991. Hon. sr. lectr. palliative care ret. head palliative care rsch. marie curie cancer care Dept. Mental Health Scis. Royalfree Hosp. Med. Sch. U. Coll. London, 1998—. Recipient Sci. of Yr. award, Internat. Rsch. Promotion Coun., 2009. Fellow: Royal Soc. MedicineLife; mem.: EONS, Palliative Care Forum, Royal Coll. Nursing, Palliative Care Rsch. Soc. Home: Bakery Cottage Chases Ln Friston Suffolk IP171PJ England Home Phone: 447974561213. Home Fax: 441728688419. Personal E-mail: susie.wilkinson@medsch.ucl.ac.uk, drsusie@btinternet.com.

WILKOW, BRIAN RICHARD, hospital administrator and clinician; b. Bklyn., June 3, 1964; s. Elliot and Marcia W. BS, Touro Coll., 1987. Lic. physician asst. Nat. Commn. on Cert. Physician Assts. Coord. physician assts. Luth. Med. Ctr., Bklyn., 1989—96; dir. physician asst. svcs. N.Y. Meth. Hosp., Bklyn., 1996—. Adj. lectr. Coll. Staten Is., N.Y., 1993—; EMT instr. coord. Staten Is. Emergency Med. Tng., 1993—; preceptor SUNY, Bklyn., 1996—. Pres. Shorefront Vol. Ambulance Corps, Bklyn., 1990-2000, Bklyn. Critical Incident Stress Mgmt. Team, 1999—; v.p. Temple Beth Ahavath Sholom, Bklyn., 1997-2001, pres. 2001—. Fellow Am. Acad. Physician Assts., Am. Assn. Surg. and Physician Assts., N.Y. State Soc. Physician Assts. Office: NY Meth Hosp 506 6th St Brooklyn NY 11215-3645 E-mail: brwpac@aol.com.

WILLARDSEN, JOSEPH G, cosmetic dentist; Grad., Loma Linda U.; completed Comprehensive Aesthetic Reconstruction Program, Las Vegas Inst., completed Laser Certification, completed K6/K7 Neuromuscular tng.; tng. with Dr. Dick Barnes Group, Arrowhead Internat., completed Anterior Aesthetics tng., completed Total Team Tng., completed Aesthetic Symposium; grad., Occlusion Connections. Official dentist Miss Nev. U.S.A. pageant; official dental adv. LPG/Technoderm USA; bd. mem. Occlusion Connections; founder Esthetic Alliance, TrueVT.com, True Aesthetics. Editl. mem. adv. bd. Aesthetic Dentistry. Contbr. article; featured in popular magazines including Cosmopolitan, Harpers Bazaar, Town & Country, Marie Claire, Redbook, Vegas, Aesthetic Dentistry, Dental. Mem.: ADA, Occlusion Connections study group, Am. Acad. of Cosmetic Dentistry, Nev. Dental Assn., Southern Nev. Dental Soc. Office: True Dentistry 9061 W Post Rd Las Vegas NV 89148 Office Phone: 702-434-4800. Office Fax: 702-433-4806.

WILLDEN, MICHAEL J., public health service officer, state official; BBA, Southern Utah U., 1973. Various positions including eligibility worker, internal auditor, program specialist, program chief, dep. adminstr. & adminstrv. svcs. officer Nev. Dept. Health & Human Services (DHHS), Carson City, 1976—2000, state welfare adminstr., 2000—01, dir., 2001—. Mem. Governor's Working Group Methamphetamine Use Members, Nev. Named Cmty. Advocate of Yr., Nev. chpt. Nat. Assn. Social Workers, 2005; named a Citizen of Distinction, Foundation for Ind. Tomorrow, 2005. Office: Nevada Department of Health & Human Services 4126 Technology Way Rm 100 Carson City NV 89706 *

WILLERSON, JAMES THORNTON, cardiologist, researcher, medical educator; b. Lampasas, Tex., Nov. 16, 1939; m. Nancy Beamer; 2 children. BS, U. Tex., Austin, 1961; MD, Baylor Coll. Medicine, 1965. Diplomate Internal Medicine 1972, Cardiovascular Disease 1974. Intern, internal medicine Mass. Gen Hosp., Boston, 1965—66, resident, cardiology, 1966—67, fellow, 1969—72; clin. assoc. NIH, Bethesda, Md.; former chief, cardiology St. Luke's Episcopal Hosp.; former chief, med. svcs. Meml. Hermann Hosp.; joined faculty, held positions including prof. medicine and dir., cardiovascular divsn. U. Tex. Southwestern Med. Sch., Dallas, 1972—89; chair, dept. medicine U. Tex. Med. Sch., Houston, 1989—2001, Edward Randall II Chair, dept. internal medicine, 1989—; prof. medicine U. Tex. Health Sci. Ctr., Houston, 1976—, Alkek/Williams Disting. Prof., 1989—, interim pres., 2000—01, pres., 2001—08; med. dir., chief cardiology rsch., co-dir. Cullen Cardiovascular Rsch. Lab. Tex. Heart Inst., St. Luke's Episcopal Hosp., 1993—, pres.-elect, 2004—07, pres., 2007—. Adj. prof. medicine Baylor Coll. Medicine, U. Tex. MD Anderson Cancer Ctr.; invited lectr. in field. Editor-in-chief Circulation, 1993—2004; contbr. several articles to profl. jours.; editl. bd. mem. of several peer-reviewed jours., author and co-author of several textbooks; co-editor: Cardiovascular Medicine, 3rd edit., 2007. Recipient James B. Herrick award, Am. Heart Assn., 1993, Disting. Svc. award, Coun. Clin. Cardiology, Am. Heart Assn., 2002, Merit medal, Internat. Acad. Cardiovascular Scis., 2004, Career Achievement award, Transcatheter Cardiovascular Therapeutics Mtg., 2005, Ignacio Chavez Medallion, Nat. Autonomous U. Mex., 2008; named Disting. Alumnus, U. Tex. Austin, 1999, Disting. Scientist, Am. Coll. Cardiology, 2000, Outstanding Cardiologist, Shanghai Internat. Symposium Cardiology, 2006, Lewis Katz Vis. Prof. in Cardiovascular Rsch. and Katz prize in Cardiovascular Rsch., Columbia U. Med. Ctr., 2007. Fellow: Royal Soc. Medicine; mem.: Nat. Am. Heart Assn. (former chmn. rsch. com. & NIH Cardiovascular & Renal Study Sect., bd. dirs. and steering com.), Inst. Med., Alpha Omega Alpha, Phi Beta Kappa. Achievements include creation of the Brown Foundation Institute of Molecular Medicine for the Prevention of Human Diseases; being honored as an international honorary member of the Japanese Circulation Soc. Among the first 7 physicians outside of Japan to be inducted & one of only 2 Americans to receive this honor in 2006. Home: 6601 Westchester Ave Houston TX 77005 Office: Texas Heart Inst 6770 Bertner MC 3-116 Houston TX 77030

WILLETT, KEITH M., professor of orthopaedic trauma surgery; b. Eng., 1957; BS, Charing Cross Med. Sch., London, 1981, MB. Cert. LRCP Royal Coll. Surgeons Eng., 1985, MRCS, FRCS. Cons. trauma surgeon Oxford Radcliffe Hosp. s NHS Trust, England, 1992—2004; prof., orthop. trauma surgery U. Oxford, 2004; nat. clin. dir. Trauma Care, Dept. Health, England, 2009—. Chmn. Injury Minimisation Programme Schs., Oxford, 1994—. Fellow: Brit. Orthopaedic Association. Achievements include research in trauma outcomes. Office: John Radcliffe Hosp Kadoorie Rsch and Edn Ctr Headley Way OX3 9DU Oxford England Office Fax: 441865857611.

WILLETT, WALTER CHURCHILL, epidemiologist, educator; b. Hart, Mich., June 20, 1945; s. Elwin Lintin and Lawain (Churchill) W.; m. Gail Valerae Pettiford, June 11, 1973; children: Amani, Kamali. Studied food sci., Mich. State U., 1963-66; MD, U. Mich., 1970; MPH, Harvard U., 1973, DPH, 1980. Diplomate Am. Bd. Internal Medicine. Lectr. in medicine U. Dar es Salaam, Tanzania, 1974-75, head community health dept., 1975-77; fellow clin. epidemiology Channing Lab. Med. Sch., Harvard U., Boston, 1977-80; asst. prof. epidemiology Sch. Pub. Health, Harvard U., Boston, 1980-84, assoc. prof. epidemiology, 1984-88, Fredrick John Stare prof. epidemiology and nutrition, 1987—, chmn. dept. nutrition, 1991—; prof. epidemiology and nutrition Harvard Med. Sch., 1992—. Statis. cons. New Eng. Jour. Medicine, Boston, 1987—; spkr. in field. Author: Nutritional Epidemiology, 1989, Eat, Drink and Be Healthy: The Harvard Medical School Guide to Healthy Eating, 2001, Nutritional Epidemiology, 2nd Edit.; contbr. over 900 articles to sci. publs. Recipient Charles S. Mott prize, GM Cancer Rsch. Found., 2001, Brinker award, Komen Found., 2003, Linus Pauling Inst. Prize Health Rsch., 2003, Rogers award, AAMC, 2003, Discovery Health Channel Med. Honors, 2004. Mem. Am. Epidemiol. Soc., Soc. for Epidemiol. Rsch., Am. Inst. Nutrition, Alpha Omega Alpha. Avocations: gardening, woodworking, skiing, bicycling, kayaking. Office: Harvard Sch Pub Health Dept Nutrition Bldg II Rm 311 651 Huntington Ave Boston MA 02115 Office Phone: 617-432-4680.

WILLEY, CHRISTOPHER, medical association administrator; b. Berlin, Vt., July 31, 1972; BS with honors, Charter Oak State Coll., 2007. Exec. dir. Cardiology Assoc. Fairfield County PC, 2008—. Mem.: Am. Coll. Cardiology Practice Adminstr., Am. Soc. Nuc. Cardiology, Am. Registry Radiol. Technologists. Avocations: bicycling, yoga. Home: 126 Meadow Park Dr Milford CT 06461 Personal E-mail: cwilley@cafconline.com.

WILLHAM, RICHARD LEWIS, zoology educator; b. Hutchinson, Kans., May 4, 1932; s. Oliver S. and Susan E. (Hurt) W.; m. Esther B. Burkhart, June 1, 1954; children: Karen Nell, Oliver Lee. BS, Okla. State U., 1954; MS, Iowa State U., 1955, PhD, 1960. Asst. prof. Iowa State U., Ames, 1959-63, assoc. prof., 1966-71, prof. dept. animal sci., 1971-78, Disting. prof., 1978—; assoc. prof. Okla. State U., Stillwater, 1963-66. Cons. in field; tchr. livestock history; guest curator exhbn. Art About Livestock, 1990. Author: A Heritage of Leadership - The First 100 Years of Animal Science at Iowa State University, 1996;Portrait Hangs in S & S Club Gallery of Livestock Industry Leaders. Recipient Svc. award Beef Improvement Fedn., 1974, Edn. and Rsch. award Am. Polled Herefore Assn., 1979, Rsch. award Nat. Cattlemen's Assn., 1986, 91, Disting. Alumnus award Okla. State U., 1978, Regents Faculty Excellence award Iowa State U., 1993; named to Hall of Fame Am. Hereford Assn., 1982, Am. Angus Assn., 1988. Fellow Am. Soc. Animal Sci. (animal breeding and genetics award 1978, industry service award 1986). Home: 2316 Hamilton Dr Ames IA 50014-8201 Office: Iowa State U Dept Animal Sci Ames IA 50011-0001 Home Phone: 515-268-5216; Office Phone: 515-294-3533. E-mail: rwillham@iastate.edu.

WILLHITE, CALVIN CAMPBELL, toxicologist; b. Salt Lake City, Apr. 27, 1952; s. Jed Butler and Carol (Campbell) W. BS, Utah State U., 1974, MS, 1977; PhD, Dartmouth Coll., 1980. Toxicologist USDA, Berkeley, Calif., 1980—85, State of Calif., Berkeley, 1985—2010, NSF Internat., 2011—. Adj. assoc. prof. toxicology Utah State U., 1984—94; mem. data safety rev. bds. Johns Hopkins Sch. Medicine, 1996; mem. Calif./OSHA Gen. Industry Safety Order PEL Adv. Bd., 1994, 96; mem. sci. adv. com. Nat. Toxicology Program, 2002—05; rev. bd. Nat. Inst. Environ. Health Sci. Ctr. Evaluation Risk Human Reprodn., 2001; mem. com. toxicology NAS, 2001—04; devel. toxicity/structure-activity task group Internat. Life Sci. Inst., 2003—05; sci. rev. panel Burnham Inst., 2002, Am. Enterprise Inst., 2010; mem. US EPA Nat. Adv. Com., 2005—09. Mem. editl. bd.: Toxicology and Applied Pharmacology, 1989—; editor: NY Acad. Sci., 1993, Toxicology, 1996—, Jour. Toxicol. Environ. Health (B), 1997—, Toxicology Letters, 1998—2002, Reproductive Toxicol., 2001—05; contbr. articles on birth defects to profl. jours. Mem. WHO IARC Cancer Prevention Work Group, 1999, European Union/OECD validation regulatory methods ENV/EHS, 2002; commr. City of Novato, Calif., 2000—2010. Nat. Inst. Child Health and Human Devel. grantee, 1985-92, March of Dimes Birth Defects Found. grantee, 1987-91, Hoffmann LaRoche grantee, 1992-94. Mem. NIH (Health Promotion/Disease Prevention Study sect. 1998), NSF (mem. health effects adv. bd. 1986—2010), Am. Conf. Govt. Indsl. Hygienists (mem. threshold limit values com. 1989-99), Soc. Toxicology (program com. 1995-99, Frank R. Blood award 1986). Home: 99 Newport Landing Novato CA 94949 Office: NSF Internat 99 Newport Landing Novato CA 94949 Office Phone: 510-540-3766. Personal E-mail: calvinwillhite@hotmail.com.

WILLI, STEVEN MATTHEW, physician, educator, researcher; s. John Edward and Doris Mae (Smith) Willi; m. Maria Szpiech, July 27, 2002. BA cum laude, Johns Hopkins U., 1981, MD, 1985. Diplomate in pediatrics and pediatric endocrinology Am. Bd. Pediatrics. Resident in pediat. Children's Hosp. of Phila., 1985—88; fellow in pediatric endocrinology Children's Hosp. Phila., 1988—91; instr. pediat. U. Pa., Phila., 1991—92, assoc. prof. pediat., 2004—; asst. prof. pediat. Med. U. S.C., Charleston, 1992—98, assoc. prof., 1998—2004. Contbr. chpts. to books, articles to profl. jours. Med. dir. Camp Adam Fisher for Children with Diabetes, Summerton, S.C., 1995-2003; bd. dirs. Juvenile Diabetes Found., 1995-99; dir. Diabetes Ctr. for Children, Children's Hosp. of Phila., 2004—. Recipient Nat. Rsch. Svc. award NIH, 1990, Clin. Assoc. Physician award NIH, 1996; Healfman scholar, 1985. Fellow Am. Acad. Pediatrics; mem. Endocrine Soc., Lawson Wilkins Pediatric Endocrine Soc., Am. Diabetes Assn. Avocations: bicycling, photography. Office: Childrens Hosp of Phila Divsn Endocrinology/Diabetes 34th St Civic Ctr Blvd Philadelphia PA 19104-0001 Office Phone: 215-590-3174.

WILLIAM, HARRIS T., medical educator; b. Jan. 13, 1972; BS in Materials Engring., 1994; MD, Southwestern U., 1999. Asst. prof. UAB, 2008—. Office: 1600 7th Ave S Ste ACC 620 Birmingham AL 35233 Office Fax: 205-975-5983. Personal E-mail: wthmd@yahoo.com.

WILLIAMS, ANDRE, medical association administrator; b. Fairfax, Va., Aug. 31, 1961; BS, Lincoln U., 1983. Ceo Assn. Black Cardiologists, Inc., 2008—. Mem.: ASAE. Office: 2400 N St NW Ste 604 Washington DC 22003 Business E-Mail: awilliams@abcardio.org.

WILLIAMS, CECILIA LEE PURSEL, optometrist; b. Lewisburg, Pa., Nov. 15, 1948; d. Lee LaVerne and Geraldine May (Steininger) Pursel; m. Richard Lee Williams, May 17, 1975; 1 son, Kent Lee. Student, Lycoming Coll., 1966—68; BS, Pa. Coll. Optometry, 1970, OD, 1972. Lic. and/or cert. optometrist, D.C., Pa., N.Y., N.J., Va. Rsch. optometrist in soft lens materials Gumpelmayer Optik, Vienna, Austria, 1973; optometrist Sterling Optical Co. Contact Lens Ctr., Washington, 1974-79; pvt. practice optometry Springfield, Va., 1980—. Recipient Clin. Efficiency award Pa. Coll. Optometry, 1972; Women's Aux. of Pa. Optometrists scholar, 1968-70, 70-72; Pa. State grantee, 1968-70, 70-72. Mem. Optometric Ctr. of Nation's Capital (dir. 1977-80), Am. Optometric Assn., Va. Optometric Assn., No. Va. Optometric Soc., Nat. Honor Soc. for Optometry, Omega Delta. Home: 3600 Wilton Hall Ct Alexandria VA 22310-2176 Office: 7241 Commerce St Springfield VA 22150-3411 Office Phone: 703-866-9364.

WILLIAMS, CHARLES LAVAL, JR., retired preventive medicine physician; b. New Orleans, Jan. 19, 1916; s. Charles Laval and Lewise (McLaurine) W.; m. Ellen Clendenin Ustick, Dec. 14, 1946; children: Ellen Clendenin, Katherine McLaurine. Student, U. Va., 1933-35; MD, Tulane U., 1940; M.P.H., U. Mich., 1945. Diplomate: Am. Bd. Preventive Medicine and Pub. Health. Intern U.S. Marine Hosp., New Orleans, 1941; with USPHS, 1941-67; assigned N.C. State Health Dept., 1941-44, USPHS States Relations div., 1944, U. Mich., 1944-45, Am. Acad. Pediatrics Nat. Study Child Health Services, 1945-47; chief planning unit, asst. chief div. commd. officers, 1947-51; with US/AID Div. Pub. Health, 1951-62; chief pub. health adviser AID Mission to Peru, 1959-62; asso. dir. internat. relations Office Internat. Health, 1962-64; chief Office Internat. Research, NIH, Bethesda, Md., 1965-66; dep. dir., then dir. Office Internat. Health, Office Surgeon General, USPHS, Washington, 1966-67; dep. dir. Pan Am. Health Orgn., 1967-79; ret.; exec. v.p. Am. Assn. World Health, 1980-84. U.S. del./alt. or advisor to eight world health assemblies between 1955 and 1967, and to ten sessions of the Directing Coun. of the Pan Am. Health Orgn. between 1953 and 1966. Fellow Am. Pub. Health Assn.; mem. U.S.-Mexico Border Pub. Health Assn., Phi Kappa Phi, Delta Omega. Home: 5600 Wisconsin Ave Apt 1009 Chevy Chase MD 20815-4411

WILLIAMS, CHRISTOPHER A., ophthalmologist; MD, U. Iowa, 1988. Diplomate Am. Bd. Ophthalmology. Resident Wills Eye Hosp., Phila, Pa.; divsn. chief ophthalmology Crozer Chester Med. Ctr., Upland, Pa.; asst. physician Wills Eye Physician. Mem.: Am. Acad. of Ophthalmology. Office: Ophthalmic Surgical Associates 30 Medical Center Blvd CCMC POB1 Ste 104 Chester PA 19013 Office Phone: 610-874-5261. Office Fax: 610-874-0318.

WILLIAMS, CONRAD JAMES, emergency physician; b. Cambridge, Eng., Aug. 27, 1970; MBBS, U. Adelaide, 1994. Physician Lyell McEwin Hosp. Emergency Dept., 2008—. Sr. instr. Royal Australasian Coll. Surgery, Emergency Mgmt. Severe Trauma, 2001; staff specialist emergency physician Lyell McEwin Hosp., 2008; instr. Resuscitation Coun., Advanced Life Support, 2009; clin. lectr. U. Adelaide Med. Sch., 2010. Fellow: Australasian Coll. Emergency Medicine; mem.: South Australian Salaried Med. Officers Assn., South Australian Br. Australian Med. Assn. Avocations: camping, cooking. Office: Lyell McEwin Hosp Haydown Rd Elizabeth Vale 5112 Australia Office Fax: 08 8182 9179. Business E-Mail: conrad.williams@health.sa.gov.au.

WILLIAMS, DAVID OWEN, cardiologist; b. Phila., May 18, 1943; Graduate, Trinity Coll., Hartford, Conn., 1965; MD, Hahnemann Med. Coll., 1969. Cert. Nat. Bd. Med. Examiners, 1970, Am. Bd. Internal Medicine, 1972, Subspecialty Bd. Cardiovascular Disease, 1975, Interventional Cardiology 1999, lic. RI, 1976, Mass., 1996. Intern, resident, internal medicine Hahnemann Hosp., Phila., 1969—70, fellow in tchg., 1971—72; fellow in cardiology U. Calif. Sch. Medicine, Davis, 1972-74, asst. prof. med., 1974—76; asst. prof. medicine, divsn. biol., med. sci. Brown U., 1976—80, assoc. prof. medicine, divsn. biol., med. sci., 1980—85, prof., medicine, 1985—; asst. chief, dept. medicine Martinez Vet. Affairs Med. Ctr., Calif., chief, cardiology sect. Calif., 1974—76; cardiologist, divsn. cardiology RI Hosp., Providence, 1976—, physician in medicine, 1976—, assoc. physician in medicine, 1976—, physician-in-charge, 1989—91, dir., cardiac catheterization lab., 1976—, dir., interventional cardiology, 1992—. Adj. asst. prof. biomed. engring. U. RI, 1977—; consulting staff, dept. medicine Miriam Hosp., Providence, 1981—, Women and Infants Hosp. RI, 1982—, Roger Williams Gen. Hosp., Providence, 1987—; bd. mem. Interventional Cardiology Test Com. Am. Bd. Internal Med., 1997—. Serves on editl. bds. of several profl. jours. in medicine, serves as an editl. reviewer for several profl. jours.; contbr. articles to profl. jours.; editl. cons. Jour. Am. Coll. Cardiology, 1990—92, 2002—06, Med. Letter, 1990—. Cardiac care advisory com. RI Dept. Health, 1987—. Recipient Sci. & Tech. award, Gov. RI, 1991, Andreas R. Gruentzig award, Gruentzig Soc., 2006; named Alumnus of Year, Hahnemann U., 1990; named an Outstanding Med. Specialist Cardiology US, Town & Country mag., 1989; named one of Best Dr.'s America, 1992—93, 1993—94, Country's Best Heart Dr.'s, Good Housekeeping mag., 1996, Best Dr.'s America, American Health mag., 1996, Top Docs in RI, RI Monthly mag., 1994, 2002. Fellow: Soc. Cardiac Angiography (com. on interventional cardiology 1986), Am. Coll. Cardiology; mem.: Assn. U. Cardiologists, Am. Heart Assn., ACP, RI Med. Soc., Am. Fedn. Clinical Rsch., Am. Heart Assn. (exec. com., coun. cardiovascular radiology 1984—87, program com., scientific sessions 1989—91, clin. coun., com. on cardiac catheterization 1989—97, page award com., coun. on atherosclerosis 1993—95, coun. rep., coun. on clin. cardiology 1993—96, mem. cardiac catheterization and interventional cardiology com. 1995—97, coun. rep., coun. on clin. cardiology 1997—2000, fellow, coun. on arteriosclerosis, thrombosis and vascular biology 1997—, exec. com., coun. on clin. cardiology 1998, fellow, coun. on clin. cardiology 1998—, fellow, coun. cardiovascular radiology 2004—, bd. dirs., RI affiliate 1976—85). Office: RI Hosp Div Cardiology 593 Eddy St APC 814 Providence RI 02903-4971 Office Phone: 401-444-4581. E-mail: David_Williams@Brown.EDU.

WILLIAMS, DAVID R., healthcare educator; b. Anaheim, Calif., Dec. 23, 1961; PhD, UAB, 2003. Assoc. prof. Appalachian State U., 2003—. Fellow: Am. Coll. Healthcare Execs.; mem.: Assn. U. Programs Health Adminstrn. Office: Appalachian State University LS Dougherty Hall Boone NC 28608 Business E-Mail: willimsdr@appstate.edu.

WILLIAMS, DREW DAVIS, surgeon; b. San Augustine, Tex., Jan. 18, 1935; s. Floyd Everett and Villamae (Morehead) W.; m. Marilyn Raus, June 27, 1958; children: Leslie, Cynthia, Matthew, Jennifer, Amelia. BS, Tex. A&M Coll., 1957; MD, U. Tex., 1960; grad., naval flight surgeon, U.S. Naval Sch. Aviation Medicine, 1963. Diplomate Am. Bd. Surgery, Am. Bd. Quality Assurance and Utilization Rev. Physicians. Intern USPHS Hosp., Seattle, 1960-61; resident in gen. surgery U. Tex. Med. Br., Galveston, 1961-62, 64-68; resident in pulmonary svc. M.D. Anderson Hosp., Houston, 1968; pvt. practice Baytown, Tex., 1968—. Active staff San Jacinto (Tex.) Meth. Hosp., 1968-95, chief of surgery, 1972, 73, pres. med. staff, 1976; mem. courtesy staff Bay Coast Hosp., Baytown, 1968-95; cons. staff Baytown Med. Ctr. Hosp., 1972-95; 1st chmn. dept. surgery in devel. of family practice residency program affiliated with Tex. Med. Sch., Houston, 1977; mem. Tex. State Bd. Med. Examiners, 1983-89, sec.-treas., 1984-88, pres., 1988-89; unit med. dir., clin. instr. dept. preventive medicine and cmty. health U. Tex. Med. Br., Galveston, 1995-99. Contbr. chpt. to book and articles to profl. jours. Mem. Baytown Area Citizen's Adv. Panel. Flight surgeon USN, 1962—64, lt. comdr. USNR, ret., 1967. Clin. fellow, Am. Cancer Soc., 1966—67. Mem.: SAR (past pres. local chpt.), AMA (Physicians Recognition award), ACS, Ret. Physicians Orgn. (med. reserve com.), Houston Surg. Soc. (past pres.), Baytown Surg. Soc., East Harris County Med. Soc. (pres. 1982), Harris County Med. Soc. (exec. bd. 1994, chmn. coun. med. splty., co-chmn. disaster response com. of ret. physician orgn.), Singleton Surg. Soc. (past pres.), Tex. Surg. Soc., Tex. Med. Assn., Sovereign Colonial Soc.-Am. of Royal Descent, Colonial Order of the Crown, Soc. Descendents of Colonial Clergy, Sir William Osler Soc., Sons of Republic of Tex. (at large life), Magna Carta Barons, Am. Cancer Soc. (pres. Baytown chpt. 1970—71), Knights Templar, Shriners, Masons (32 degree). Democrat. Mem. Ch. of Christ. Avocations: hunting, fishing, genealogy, painting, gardening. Home and Office: 1217 Kilgore Rd Baytown TX 77520-3912 Office Phone: 281-422-7969. Business E-Mail: ddw@hal-pc.org.

WILLIAMS, EMILY C., healthcare educator, researcher; b. Moscow, Idaho, Aug. 31, 1976; BA, Lewis & Clark Coll., 1998; MPH, Boston U., 2003; PhD, U. Wash., 2009. Tobacco prevention educator Multnomah County Health Dept. and Portland Pub. Schs., 2000—01;

rsch. assoc. Boston U. & Med. Ctr., 2001—03; rsch. project dir. Dept. Vets. Affairs Health Svcs. Rsch. & Devel., 2003—10; traveling faculty Internat. Honors Program Health and Cmty. Track, 2009—10; core investigator, asst. prof. Dept. Vets. Affairs Health Svcs. Rsch. & Devel. U. Wash., 2010—. Reviewer Jour. Addiction Medicine, Jour. Studies on Alcohol and Drugs, Addictive Behaviors, Drug and Alcohol Dependence, Jour. Behavioral Health, 2006; assoc. editor Addiction Sci. & Clin. Practice Jour., 2011. Recipient Pres.'s award, Lewis & Clark Coll., Troy Ridenour Meml. award, New Investigator Travel award, Nat. Insts. Alcohol Abuse and Alcoholism, 2008, 2010. Mem.: Substance Use Disorders Quality Enhancement Rsch. Initiative Alcohol Misuse Workgroup, Rsch. Soc. Alcoholism. Avocations: yoga, travel, reading. Office: 1100 Olive Way Ste 1400 Seattle WA 98101 Business E-Mail: emily.williams3@va.gov.

WILLIAMS, ERIC S., cardiologist, educator; b. Louisville, 1946; MD, Ind. U., 1971. Diplomate Internal Medicine 1974, Cardiovascular Disease 1977. Intern, internal medicine Ind. U. Hosps., Indpls., 1971—72, resident, cardiology, 1972—73, fellow, 1973—75, resident, cardiology, 1975—76; prof. medicine, assoc. dir. Ind. U. Sch. Medicine, Dept. Medicine, Krannert Inst. Cardiology, Methodist Hosp., Indpls. Co-prog. dir., Clarian Cardiovascular Ctr. Ind. U. Sch. Medicine, Dept. Medicine, Krannert Inst. Cardiology, assoc. dean for Clarian Affairs. Mem.: Am. Coll. Cardiology (pres. Ind. chpt., chmn ECG com.), Am. Heart Assn., Nat. Bd. Governers. Office: Methodist Hosp Rm KI E480 1701 Senate Blvd Indianapolis IN 46202-1239 Office Phone: 317-962-0551. Business E-Mail: ewillia@iupui.edu.

WILLIAMS, GARY MURRAY, pathologist, educator; b. Regina, Sask., Can., May 7, 1940; s. Murray Austin and Selma Ruby (Domstad) W.; m. Julia Christine Lundberg; children: Walter, Jeffrey, Ingrid. BA, Washington and Jefferson Coll., 1963; MD, U. Pitts, 1967. Diplomate Am. Bd. Pathology, Am. Bd. Toxicology. Assoc. prof. pathology Temple U., Phila., 1971-75; mem. Fels Rsch. Inst., Phila., 1971-75; rsch. prof. N.Y. Med. Coll., Valhalla, 1975-98, prof. pathology, environ. pathology and toxicology, dir., 1999—. Mem. working group Internat. Agy. Rsch. on Cancer, Lyon, France, 1976, 80, 1982—83, 1985—87, 1989, 91, 1996—99; mem. subcom. on upper reference levels of nutrients NRC, 1999—2003, com. health effects dioxin, 2004—06; advisor joint expert com. on food additives WHO, 2001—10. Mem. editl. bd. Archives of Toxicology, 1988—, assoc. editor Food and Chem. Toxicology, 2005—; contbr. more than 510 articles to profl. jours.; editor or co-editor 8 books, —. Lt. comdr. USPHS, 1969-71. Recipient Sheard-Sanford award Am. Soc. Clin. Pathologists U. Pitts., 1967, Dean's Disting. Rsch. award NY Med. Coll., 2006, 50th Anniversary 5 Yr. Svc. medal WHO, 2006; named Disting. Scientist Am. Chem. Soc., 2005. Fellow Internat. Acad. Toxicol. Pathology (accreditation com. 2000), Royal Coll. Pathologists; mem. Soc. Toxicology (Arthur J. Lehman award 1982, Lectr. award 1996, Advancement Animal Welfare award 2002, Merit award, 2009), Soc. Toxicol. Pathology, Phi Beta Kappa, Alpha Omega Alpha. Home: 8 Elm Rd Scarsdale NY 10583-1410 Office: Dept Pathology NY Med Coll Valhalla NY 10595-1549 Home Phone: 914-723-8739; Office Phone: 914-594-4146. Business E-Mail: gary_williams@nymc.edu.

WILLIAMS, GERALD FRANCIS, nursing administrator; b. Melbourne, Victoria, Australia, Jan. 11, 1964; s. Francis Bert and Maureen Anne Williams; m. Tracey Anne Lee; children: Katherine, Brendan, Rachel, Matthew. Nursing degree, Lincoln Inst., Victoria, 1984; MS in Health Adminstrn., U. NSW, Australia, 1998; MS in Law, Queensland U. of Tech., Australia, 2003; grad., Australian Inst. Co. Dirs. Cert. critical care nursing, Alfred Hosp., Victoria, midwifery, Lincoln Inst.; pub. sector mgmt. Griffith U. Chief nurse N. T. Health, Darwin, Northern Territory, Australia, 2000—03; DON Alice Springs Hosp., Northern Territory, Australia, 1996—2003; dir. World Fedn. Socs. of Intensive and Critical Care Medicine, London, 2001—; founding chair World Fedn. Critical Care Nurses, Philippines, 2001—. Fellow: Am. Acad. Nursing, Australian Coll. Health Svc. Execs.; mem.: Gold Coast Health Svc. Dist. (exec. dir., nursing and Midwifery svcs. 2007—), Australian Coll. Critical Care Nurses (life; pres., treas. 1997—2001). Office: 108 Nerang St Southport 4215 Queensland Australia Business E-Mail: ged_williams@health.qld.gov.au.

WILLIAMS, GRAEME P., physician, director; b. Australia, Oct. 12, 1951; BAppSc in Pathology, Melbourne U., 1975; BSc in Medicine, Monash U., 1977, MBBS, 1981. Med. dir. Dr. Graeme Williams Specialist Med. Practice, 2000—. Dir., prin. investigator Internat. Rsch. Inst. Disease Prevention, 2005—10. Office: PO Box 1574 Noosa Heads Queensland 4567 Australia Office Fax: 61754556577. Business E-Mail: graemewilliams8@bigpond.com.

WILLIAMS, HENRY NEAL, microbiologist, educator; b. Rocky Mount, NC, Sept. 18, 1943; BS, N.C. A&T State U., 1965; MS, U. Md., Balt., 1972, PhD, 1979. Asst. prof. U. Md., Balt., 1981—87, assoc. prof., 1987—97, asst. v.p. rsch., 1993—95, prof. microbiology, 1998—2002, 2003—; asst. v.p. Morgan State U., Balt., 1998—2002. Cons. U. of D.C., Washington, 2002, Savannah State U., Ga., 2000, Novaflux, Inc., Princeton, NJ, 1998—2000, Nat. Assn. for Equal Opportunity in Edn., 2003. Contbr. articles to profl. jours., chpts. to books. Founding mem. Sci. and Tech. Polit. Action Com.; pres. Md. Classified Employees Assn., Balt., 1977—79, 1997—99. With US Army, 1965—67. Recipient Martin Luther King Jr. Drum Maj. award, Martin Luther King Jr. Awards Com., 2003; grantee Congl. Sci. fellow, Am. Soc. for Microbiology, 1980. Mem.: Am. Soc. Microbiology (co-chair minority task force 1997, pres. Md. br. 1988—89, William A. Hinton award 2003). Avocation: physical training.

WILLIAMS, J. KELL, medical educator; b. Detroit, Aug. 14, 1946; BS, U. Mich., 1968; MD, Wayne State U., 1972. Prof. U. South Fla. Coll. Medicine, 1982—. Cons. Fla. Dept. Profl. Regulation, 1985—91; bd. dirs. Fla. Birth-Related Neurologic Injury Compensation Assn., 1988—89; chmn. Maternal Mortality Com., Fla., 1990—95; exec. bd. Fla. Obstetric & Gynecologic Soc., 1992—; adv. coun. Am. Coll. Obstetricians & Gynecologists, 1998—. Recipient Diamond award, Wayne State U., 1st Pl. Sci. Presentation, So. Perinatal Assn., Cert. Appreciation, Fla. Acad. Family Physicians. Fellow: Am. Coll. Obstetricians & Gynecologists (Outstanding Residency Program Dir. award); mem.: Fla. Obstetric & Gynecologic Soc., Assn. Profs. Gynecology & Obstetrics. Avocations: travel, hockey. Office: 2 Tampa Gen Cir Rm 6028 Tampa FL 33606 Business E-Mail: jkwillia@health.usf.edu.

WILLIAMS, JOHN N., dean, dental educator; BA with honors, Transylvania U., Lexington, KY, 1974; DMD, U. Louisville, 1980, MBA, 1987. Asst. u. provost U. Louisville, 1988—91; dean U. Louisville Sch. Dentistry, 1999—2005; assoc. dean for ednl. programs U. of Louisville Sch. of Dentistry, 1991—98; prof. dept. periodontics, endontics and dental hygiene U. Louisville Sch. Dentistry; dean U. N.C. Sch. Dentistry, Chapel Hill, NC, 2005—. Mem. editl. bd. Jour. Contemporary Dental Practice. Mem.: Am. Acad. Devel. Medicine and Dentistry. Avocations: boating, classical & choral singing. Office: Sch Dentistry NC Univ CB #7450 1090 Old Dental Bldg Chapel Hill NC 27599-7450 Office Phone: 919-966-2731. Business E-Mail: john_williams@dentistry.unc.edu.

WILLIAMS, JOHN R., professor; BA, Sem. Christ the King, Mission, Can., 1963, U. Windsor, Can., 1965; MA, U. Toronto, 1966; PhD, U. St. Michael's Coll., Toronto, 1970; D, Université des Sciences Humaines de Strasbourg, France, 1975. Prof. religious studies Meml. U. Nfld., St. John's, Canada, 1971—86; prin. rsch. assoc. Ctr. Bioethics Clin. Rsch. Inst. Can., Montreal, 1986—91; dir. ethics Can. Med. Assn., Ottawa, 1991—2003, World Med. Assn., Ferney-Voltaire, France, 2003—06; ethics cons. Ottawa, 2007—. Adj. prof. U. Ottawa, Carleton U., Ottawa. Author: (books) WMA Medical Ethics Manual, Christian Perspectives on Bioethics, Bioéthique Régionale: Une Introduction, Biomedical Ethics in Canada, Martin Heidegger's Philosophy of Religion, FDI World Dental Federation Dental Ethics Manual; co-author: (book) Bioethics in Canada, Canadian Physicians and Euthanasia; editor: Canadian Churches and Social Justice. Mem. Oxfam-Canada, 1972—80. Grantee Profl. Leadership award, Can. Internat. Devel. Agy., 1999; fellow, Can. Coun., 1967—70; Rsch. grant, 1974—75, 1977, 1978, Aid to Publ. grant, Humanities Rsch. Coun. Can., 1979, Rsch. grant, Social Sci. and Humanities Rsch. Coun. Can., 1980, 1982, 1985, 1988—90. Office Fax: 613-829-3089.

WILLIAMS, JOSEPH DALTON, pharmaceutical executive; b. Washington, Pa., Aug. 15, 1926; s. Joseph Dalton and Jane (Day) W.; m. Mildred E. Bellaire, June 28, 1973; children: Terri, Daniel. BS in Pharmacy, U. Nebr., 1950; DSc (hon.), Union U., 1991, U. Nebr., 1989; LHD (hon.), Albany Coll. Pharmacy, Union U., 1980, Rutgers U., 1987, Long Island U., 1988; DSc (hon.), Phila. Coll. Pharmacy and Sci., 1988, Long Island U., 1988, Albany Coll. Pharmacy of Union U., 1991; D Human Svcs. (hon.), Caldwell Coll., 1989; LLD (hon.), Bethune-Cookman Coll., 1990, Coll. St. Elizabeth, 1990, Seton Hall U., 1990, U. Md., 1991, St. Augustine Coll., 1992. Pres. Parke-Davis Co., Detroit, 1973-76; pres. pharm. group Warner-Lambert Co., Morris Plains, NJ, 1976-77; pres. Internat. Group, 1977-79; pres., dir. Warner-Lambert Corp., 1979-80, pres., chief operating officer, 1980-84, chmn., CEO, 1985-91, chmn. exec. com., 1991-97; retired, 1997. Bd. dirs. AT&T, 1984-1997, J.C. Penny & Co., 1985-1998, Exxon Corp., 1985-1997, Rockefeller Fin. Svcs. Inc., Rockefeller and Co., Inc., 1992-1999, Eckerd Corp., 1997-2000. Trustee emeritus Columbia U. With USNR, 1943—46. Mem. Am. Pharm. Assn., Links Club, Pine Valley Golf Club, Baltusrol Golf Club, Mid Ocean Club. Office: Warner-Lambert Co 55 Madison Ave Morristown NJ 07960-7397 Office Phone: 973-285-3277.

WILLIAMS, KIM ALLAN, cardiologist, educator; b. Chgo., Ill., Nov. 10, 1954; Attended, Coll. U. Chgo., 1971—75; MD, U. Chgo. Pritzker Sch. Med., 1979. Cert. Cardiology, Internal Medicine, 1982, Nuclear Medicine, 1986, Nuclear Cardiology. Intern, internal medicine Emory U., Atlanta, 1979—80, resident, cardiology, 1980—82; fellow, cardiology U. Chgo., 1982—85, fellow, clin. pharmacology Ill., 1984—85, fellow, nuclear medicine Ill., 1984—86; practicing, 1986—; assoc. prof. medicine U. Chgo. Pritzker Sch. Medicine, prof. medicine, radiology, dir., nuclear cardiology. Contbr. articles to profl. jours. Named one of Top Doctors, Chgo. Mag., 1996, 2000, 2004. Fellow: Assn. Black Cardiologists, Am. Heart Assn., Am. Soc. Nuclear Cardiology (chair, coalistion of cardiovascular organizations 2006—07, past pres.), Am. Coll. Cardiology (bd. trustee); mem.: AMA (chair, nuclear medicine sect. coun., AMA specialty svc. soc. 2006—07), Soc. Nuclear Medicine, Nat. Med. Assn., Assn. U. Radiologists, Am. Soc. Echocardiography. Office Phone: 312-702-6258. Office Fax: 773-702-4386, 773-702-3512. Business E-Mail: kwilliam@medicine.bsd.uchicago.edu.

WILLIAMS, LEWIS T. (RUSTY WILLIAMS), chemicals executive; MD, PhD, Duke U. Faculty mem. Harvard Medical School; co-founder, bd. dirs. COR Therapeutics, Inc.; adj. prof., medicine University of California, San Francisco, investigator, Howard Hughes Med. Inst.; founder, exec. chmn. FivePrime Therapeutics; chief scientific officer, bd. dirs. Chiron Corp.; pres. Chiron Technologies, Chiron R&D, 1994, chief scientific officer, 1999. Bd. dirs. Beckman Coulter Inc.; bd. trustees Duke U.; bd. dirs. Juvaris BioTherapeutics. Mem. Nat. Acad. of Sciences; fellow Am. Acad. of Arts and Sciences. Office: Five Prime Therapeutics Inc 1650 Owens St 200 San Francisco CA 94158-2261 Office Phone: 415-365-5600. Business E-Mail: lewis.williams@fiveprime.com. *

WILLIAMS, LUTHER STEWARD, research scientist; b. Sawyerville, Ala., Aug. 19, 1940; s. Roosevelt and Mattie B. (Wallace) W.; m. Constance Marie Marion, Aug. 23, 1963; children: Mark Steward, Monique Marie. BA magna cum laude, Miles Coll., 1961; MS, Atlanta U., 1963; PhD, Purdue U., 1968, DSc (hon.), 1987, U. Louisville, 1992, Capitol Coll., 1996, Bowie State U., 1996, Tuskegee U., 1997, U. DC, 1999. NSF lab. asst. Spelman Coll., 1961-62, Atlanta U., 1962-63, instr. biology, faculty rsch. grantee, 1963-64, asst. prof. biology, 1969-70, prof. biology, 1984-87, pres., 1984-87; grad. tchg. asst. Purdue U., West Lafayette, Ind., 1964-65, grad. rsch. asst., 1965-66, asst. prof. biology, 1970-73, assoc. prof., 1973-79, prof., 1979-80, NIH Career Devel. awardee, 1971-75, asst. provost, 1976-80; dean Grad. Sch., prof. biology Washington U., St. Louis, 1980-83; v.p. acad. affairs, dean Grad. Sch. U. Colo., Boulder, 1983-84; Am. Cancer Soc. postdoctoral fellow SUNY-Stony Brook, 1968-69; assoc. prof. biology MIT, 1973-74; spl. asst. to dir. Nat. Inst. Gen. Med. Scis., NIH, Bethesda, Md., 1987-88; dep. dir. Nat. Inst. Gen. Med. Scis. NIH, Bethesda, 1988-89; sr. sci. advisor to dir. NSF, Washington, 1989-90, asst. dir. for edn. and human resources, 1990-99; visiting scholar Payson Ctr. Internat. Devel./Tech., Arlington, Va., 1999-2000, edn. cons., 2000—; provost, v.p. for acad. affairs Tuskegee U., Ala., 2006—10; mem. Nat. Adv. Coun. Nat. Ctr. Minurity Health Disabilities NIH, 2007—10, Coun. NIH, 2009—. Educator, cons., 2000—; dir. edn., sr. advisor to dir. Mo. Bot. Garden, St. Louis, 2001-05; chmn. rev. com. MARC Program, Nat. Inst. Gen. Med. Scis., NIH, 1972-76; grant reviewer NIH, 1971-73, 76, NSF, 1973, 76-80, Med. Rsch. Coun. of N.Z., 1976; mem. life scis. sreening com. recombinant DNA adv. com. HEW, 1979-81; mem. nat. adv. gen. med. sci. council NIH, 1980-85; mem. adv. com. Office Tech. Assessment, Washington, 1984-87; chmn. fellowship adv. com. NRC Ford Found., 1984-85; mem.-at-large Grad. Record Exam. Bd., 1981-85, chmn. minority grad. edn. com., 1983-85; mem. health, safety and environ. affairs. com. Nat. Labs., U. Calif., 1981-87; mem. adv. panel Office Tech. Assessment, US Congress, 1985-86; mem. fed. task force on women, minorities and the handicapped in sci. and tech., 1987-91; mem. adv. panel to dir. sci. and tech. ctrs. devel. NSF, 1987-88; mem. nat. adv. com. White House Initiative on Historically Black Colls. and Univs. on Sci. and Tech., 1986-89; numerous other adv. bds. and coms. Contbr. sci. articles to profl. jours. Vice-chmn. bd. advisors Atlanta Neighborhood Justice Ctr., 1984-87; bd. dirs. Met. Atlanta United Way, 1986-87, Butler St. YMCA, Atlanta, 1985-87; trustee Atlanta Zool. Assn., 1985-87, Miles Coll., 1984-87, Atlanta U., 1984-87, 90-96; mem. nominating com. Dana Found; mem. St. Louis CC Found. Bd., 2004-06. NIH predoctoral fellow Purdue U., 1966-68; recipient William A. Hinton Rsch. Trng. award, Am. Soc. Microbiology, 1998, trustee award Acad. Scis. St. Louis, 2004; named to Black Coll. Hall of Fame, 2002. Fellow Am. Acad. Microbiology, Acad. Sci. St. Louis; mem. Am. Soc. Microbiology, Am. Chem. Soc., Am. Soc. Biol. Chemists (mem. ednl. affairs com. 1979-82, com. on equal opportunities for minorities 1972-84). Home and Office: 15286 Brightfield Manor Dr Chesterfield MO 63017 Business E-Mail: lswilliams1968@sbcglobal.net. E-mail: luther.williams@tuskegee.edu.

WILLIAMS, MARTHA JANE SHIPE, psychologist, retired educator; b. Houston, June 28, 1935; d. Charles Edward and Florence Mae (Coons) Shipe; m. John Gregor Williams, June 4, 1958; children— John, David, Susan, Thomas. BA, U. Tex., Austin, 1957, MA, 1962, PhD, 1963. Sec. U. Tex., Austin, 1954-57; sec. pers. and sales div. Tenneco, 1957-58, teaching and rsch. asst. U. Tex., Austin, 1958-61, rsch. assoc., 1961-66, asst. prof., 1966-69, assoc. prof., 1969-75, prof., 1975-91, prof. emeritus, 1991—; asst. dir. Inst. Higher Edn. Mgmt., U. Tex. System Adminstrn., Austin, 1979-81; dean, centennial prof. Sch. Social Work, U. Tex., Austin, 1981-91; dean health scis. U. Wyo., Laramie, 1991—98, prof., 1998—2006, prof. emerita, 2006—. Author books, book chpts.; contbr. articles to profl. jours. Chairperson Tex. Gov.'s Commn. for Women, 1983-85. Univ. fellow, 1959, NSF fellow, 1960-61 Mem. APA, Coun. Social Work Edn., Am. Ednl. Rsch. Assn., Phi Delta Kappa, Sigma Xi. Home: 1312 E Park Ave Laramie WY 82070-4146 Home Phone: 307-742-9179. Business E-Mail: mswllms@uwyo.edu. *

WILLIAMS, MARTHA SPRING, psychologist; b. Dallas, Oct. 5, 1951; d. Thomas Ayers and Emma Martha (Felmet) Spring; m. James Walter Williams, June 30, 1979; children: Dane Ayers, Jake Austin BA, Tex. A&M Commerce, 1972, MEd, 1974, EdD, 1978. Cert. and lic. psychologist, Tex.; lic. profl. counselor, marriage and family therapist. Tchr. Dallas Ind. Sch.; grad. asst. to dean Coll. Edn. East Tex. State U., 1975—77; intern Terrell State Hosp. Outreach Clinic and Hunt County Clinic, Greenville, Tex., 1975—76; intern Counseling Ctr. East Tex. State U., 1976—77; learning dir. Man and His Environ. Program, 1978—85; pvt. practice psychology Dallas, 1981—. Adolescent group therapist in-patient psychiat. facility, 1986-91; mem. staff Baylor/Richardson (Tex.) Med. Ctr., clin. dir. allied mental health profls., 1992-94; v.p. for provider rels. Advanced Behavioral Health Care Sys., Inc., 1995—2000; mem. staff Lake Pointe Hosp., St. Paul Author: (with others) The Role Innovative Woman and Her Positive Impact on Family Functioning, 1981, Women and Intimacy, 1982, Premenstral Syndrome: A Family Affair, 1984, The Expanding Horizons of Traditional Private Practice: High Tech High/Touch, 1986, Adolescent Suicide: Consequences of an Anti-Child Society, 1986, Therapist as a Partner, 1987 Nat. del. Dem. Conv., San Francisco, 1984, LA, 2000, Boston, 04; Dem. county chair Kaufman County, 1990-95; mem. state Dem. Exec. Com. 1993—, Boston LA, 2000-. Mem.: Tex. State Soc. Lutheran. Avocations: skiing, travel, politics, tap dancing. Home: PO Box 1119 Terrell TX 75160-7144 Office: 12840 Hillcrest Rd Ste E-101 Dallas TX 75230-1599 Office Fax: 972-386-6558.

WILLIAMS, MATHEW R., cardiologist, surgeon; BA in Philosophy, Columbia U., 1992, MD, 1996. Resident gen. surgery UCLA Med. Sch., 1996—98; rsch. fellowship cardiothoracic surgery Columbia U. Coll. Physicians and Surgeons, NYC, 1998—2001, asst. prof. surgery, 2007—; resident gen. surgery NY Presbyn. Hosp. / Columbia U. Med. Ctr., 2001—03, fellowship cardiothoracic surgery, 2004—05, fellowship interventional cardiology, 2006, attending surgeon, interventional cardiologist, 2007—, surgical dir. cardiovascular transcatheter therapies, 2007—. Contbr. articles to med. jours. Named one of 40 Under 40, Crain's NY Bus., 2010. Office: NY-Presbyterian Hosp/Columbia Milstein Hosp Bldg, Rm 7-435 177 Fort Washington Ave New York NY 10032 Office Phone: 212-305-9320. Office Fax: 212-342-3520. *

WILLIAMS, MICHAEL LLEWELYN, pediatrician, director; b. Melbourne, Apr. 14, 1949; MBBS with honors, Monash U., 1972; M in Med Sci., Newcastle U., 1995. Dir. child and adolescent health Queensland Health, 1990—, sr. staff specialist tele-health Children's Health Svc., 2010—. Outstanding Rural fellow, RACP. Fellow: Royal Australasian Coll. Physicians; mem.: Mackay Conservation Group. Office: PO Box 8245 Mt Pleasant Mackay Queensland 4740 Australia Office Fax: 0748856067. Business E-Mail: michael_williams@health.qld.gov.au.

WILLIAMS, NOEL BROWN, hospital administrator; b. Pasadena, Tex., Mar. 15, 1955; 2 children. B Engring. in Computer Sci. & Math., Vanderbilt U., 1977; MS in Healthcare Fin. Mgmt., U. SC, 1987. Chief info. officer Am. Svc. Group, Brentwood, Tenn., Prison Health Svcs., Inc., 1996—97; various positions HCA, Inc., 1979—93, various info. svcs. dept. positions, including v.p., info. svcs., 1994—95; pres. HCA Info. Tech. & Svcs., Inc. (subs. HCA, Inc.); sr. v.p., chief info. officer HCA, Inc., 1997—. Office: HCA Inc One Park Plz Nashville TN 37203 Office Phone: 615-344-9551. Office Fax: 615-320-2266. Business E-Mail: noel.williams@hcahealthcare.com. *

WILLIAMS, PAUL E., immunologist, consultant; b. Caerfyrddin, Wales, Nov. 11, 1954; s. Tom Williams and Mary Hannah Thomas; m. Sian Eleanor Fowden, Jan. 16, 1988; children: Fiona Catrin, Sarah Angharad. BA, Oxford U., 1976, MB, BCh, 1979. Sr. ho. officer in medicine East Birmingham Hosp., England, 1980—82; registrar in gen. medicine Univ. Hosp. of Wales, 1982—84; registrar in thoracic medicine Llandough Hosp., Wales, 1984—86; rsch. fellow Royal Infirmary, Edinburgh, Scotland, 1986—90, Walter Reed Army Inst. Rsch., Washington, 1990—91; sr. registrar in immunology Birmingham Heartlands Hosp., England, 1991—95; cons. clin. immunologist Cardiff Hosps., Wales, 1995—. Fellow: Royal Coll. Pathologists (U.K.), Royal Coll. Physicians (U.K.). Achievements include patent for cellbeads, a novel way of using fixed fluorescence-labelled cells as a bead for the purposes of accurately counting cells in a cell-suspension. Avocations: music, inventing, computers, gardening, skiing. Office: Univ Hosp Wales Dept Med Biochemistry & Immunology CF14 4XW Cardiff Wales Office Phone: +44/0 29 2074 8358. Business E-Mail: williamspe@cardiff.ac.uk.

WILLIAMS, PHILIP COPELAIN, obstetrician, gynecologist; b. Vicksburg, Miss., Dec. 9, 1917; s. John Oliver and Eva (Copelain) Williams; m. Constance Shielda Rhetta Williams, May 29, 1943; children: Philip, Susan Carol, Paul Rhetta. BS magna cum laude, Morehouse Coll., 1937; MD, U. Ill., 1941. Diplomate Am. Bd. Ob-Gyn. Intern Cook County Hosp., Chgo., 1942—43, resident ob-gyn., 1946—48; resident gynecology U. Ill., 1948—49; practice medicine specializing ob-gyn. Chgo., 1949—; mem. staff St. Joseph Hosp., Ill. Masonic Hosp., Cook County Hosp., McGaw Hosp.; clin. prof. Med. Sch. Northwestern U., Chgo. Bd. dirs. Am. Cancer Soc. Chgo. Unit & Ill. Divsn. Contbr. articles to profl. jours. Served with US Army, 1943—45. Recipient Civic award, Loyola U., 1970, Edwin S. Hamilton Interstate Teaching award, 1984. Fellow: ACS, Internat. Coll. Surgeons; mem.: AAAS, AMA, NY Acad. Scis., Inst. Medicine, Am. Fertility Soc., Chgo. Gynecol. Soc. (treas. 1975—78, pres. 1980—81), Chgo., Ill. Med. Socs., Plaza, Carlton, Barclay. Presbyterian.

WILLIAMS, RALPH CHESTER, JR., physician, educator; b. Washington, Feb. 17, 1928; s. Ralph Chester and Annie (Perry) W.; m. Mary Elizabeth Adams, June 23, 1951 (dec.); children: Cathy, Frederick (dec.), John (dec.), Michael, Ann AB with distinction, Cornell U., 1950, MD, 1954; MD (hon.), U. Lund, Sweden, 1991. Diplomate Am. Bd. Internal Medicine. Intern Mass. Gen. Hosp., Boston, 1954-55, asst. resident in internal medicine, 1955-56; resident in internal medicine N.Y. Hosp., 1956-57; chief resident Mass. Gen. Hosp., Boston, 1959-60; guest investigator Rockefeller Inst., NYC, 1961-63; physician in internal medicine and rheumatology, 1963—; assoc. prof. U. Minn., Mpls., 1963-68, prof., 1968-69; prof., chmn. dept. medicine U. N.Mex., Albuquerque, 1969-88; Schott prof. rheumatology and medicine U. Fla., Gainesville, 1988-98; with rheumatology dept. U. N.Mex. Sch. Medicine, Albuquerque, 1998, emeritus prof. medicine, 1998—. Assoc. editor: Jour. Lab. and Clin. Medicine, 1966-69; mem. editl. bd.: Arthritis and Rheumatism, 1968—; contbr. articles to profl. jours. Capt. USAF, 1957—59. Recipient Regents' Meritorious Svc. award, U. N.Mex., 2003. Master Am. Coll. Rheumatology (Gold medal 2004); fellow ACP; mem. Am. Assn. Immunology, Assn. Am. Physicians, Am. Fedn. Clin. Rsch., Am. Soc. Clin. Investigation, Ctrl. Soc. Clin. Rsch., Western Soc. Clin. Investigation, Phi Beta Kappa, Alpha Omega Alpha. Achievements include research in immunologic processes and connective tissue diseases. Home: 624 E Alameda St Apt 13 Santa Fe NM 87501-2293 Personal E-mail: coolypatch22@cybermesa.com.

WILLIAMS, REDFORD BROWN, medical educator; b. Raleigh, NC, Dec. 14, 1940; s. Redford Brown Sr. and Annie Virginia (Betts) W.; m. Virginia Carter Parrott, August 9, 1940; children: Jennifer Betts, Lloyd Carter. AB, Harvard U., 1963; MD, Yale U., 1967. Diplomate Am. Bd. Internal Medicine. Intern, then resident Yale-New Haven Med. Ctr., 1967-70; sr. surgeon USPHS, Bethesda, Md., 1970-72; asst. prof. Duke U. Med. Ctr., Durham, NC, 1972, prof. psychiatry, 1977—, prof. psychology, 1990—, dir. behavioral medicine rsch. ctr., 1985—; CEO Williams LifeSkills, Inc., 1997—. Cons. NIH rev. coms., Bethesda, 1977—. Author: The Trusting Heart, 1989, Anger Kills, 1993, Lifeskills, 1998, In Control, 2006; contbr. articles to profl. jours. Dir. NC Heart Assn., Chapel Hill, 1980-83. Recipient Rsch. Scientist award NIMH, 1974—; NIH grantee, 1976—. Fellow Soc. Behavioral Medicine (pres. 1984-85, Upjohn Disting. Scientist award 1992), Acad. Behavioral Medicine Rsch. (pres. 1995—); mem. Am. Psychosomatic Soc. (bd. dirs. 1978-81, pres. 1992), Internat. Soc. Behavioral Medicine (pres.-elect 2004-06, pres. 2006-08). Unitarian Universalist. Avocation: tennis. Office: Duke U Med Ctr PO Box 3926 Durham NC 27710-0001 Office Phone: 919-684-3863. Business E-Mail: redfordw@duke.edu.

WILLIAMS, RICHARD DWAYNE, physician, educator, urologist; b. Wichita, Kans., Oct. 7, 1944; s. Errol Wayne and Roseanna Jane (Page) W.; m. Beverly Sue Ferguson, Aug. 29, 1964; 1 child, Wendy Elizabeth. BS, Abilene Christian U., 1966; MD, Kans. U., 1970. Diplomate Am. Bd. Urology, Nat. Bd. Med. Examiners. Intern, then resident in gen. surgery U. Minn., Mpls., 1970-72, resident in urology, 1972-76, asst. prof., 1976-79, U. Calif., San Francisco, 1979-84, assoc. prof., 1984; prof., chmn. dept. urology U. Iowa, Iowa City, 1984—. Chief urology VA Med. Ctr., San Francisco, 1979-84, VA Med. Ctr., Iowa City, 1984-88; mem. task force on bd. exams Am. Bd. Urology, 1981-85, guest examiner Oral exams, 1984-, trustee, 1994-2000; Rubin H. Flocks chair in urology U. Iowa, 1994, program com. chair Soc. Internat. Urology (SIU), 2007-09; mem. nat. adv. coun. NIDDK, NIH. Author: (with others) Advances in Urologic Oncology, 1987, Genitourinary Cancer: Basic and Clinical Aspects, 1987, Adult and Pediatric Urology, 1987, General Urology, 1988, Textbook of Medicine, 1988, also others; editor: Advances in Urologic Oncology, 1987; guest editor Seminars in Urology, 1985, Problems in Urology: Prostate Cancer, 1989; bd. editors Jour. Urology, 1980-88; mem. editorial bd. Urology, Jour. Urology; also articles. Bd. dirs. Iowa chpt. Nat. Kidney Found., bd. sci. advisors 1989-92; pres. Am. Found. Urologic Diseases, 2003-05. Maj. USAR, 1971-77. Bordeau scholar Kans. U. Med. Ctr., 1968-69; NIH, VA, Am. Cancer Soc. grantee. Fellow ACS (chmn. urology sect. No. Calif. chpt. 1980-82, chmn. ann. meeting programs 1988, mem. residency rev. com. urology 1993-99, vice chair 1995, chair 1997); mem. AAAS, Iowa Med. Soc., Iowa Urologic Soc., Am. Urologic Assn. (dir. seminar on residency evaluation 1987, bd. editors alt. 1988-, rep. North Ctrl. sect., prodr. slide presentations 1988, recipient prizes 1982, 87, com. mem. 1987-, bd. dirs. 1994, pres.-elect 1997, Hugh Hampion Young award, 2009), Am. Assn. for Cancer Rsch., Am. Soc. Clin. Oncology, Am. Assn. GU Surgeons, Clin. Soc. Genitourinary Surgeons (sec.-treas. 1997-2000), Soc. Internat. D'Urologie (pres. US sect. 2003-, program chair, 2007-), Soc. Univ. Urologists (chmn. com. on residency evaluation 1986-88, councillor 1987-, pres. 1993), Soc. Surg. Oncology, Soc. Urologic Oncology (chmn. membership com. 1987-90, sec. 1990-94, pres.-elect 1995, pres. 1996), Johnson County Med. Soc., Flock's Soc., Western Urologic Forum, Alpha Omega Alpha. Republican. Office: U Iowa Dept Urology 200 Hawkins Dr Iowa City IA 52242-1009 Office Phone: 319-356-0760.

WILLIAMS, ROBERT SANDERS (SANDY WILLIAMS), health facility administrator; b. Athens, Ga. m. Jennifer Williams; children: Molly, Nicholas, Owen. Degree, Princeton U., 1970; MD, Duke U., 1974. Internship, residency, Internal Medicine Mass. Gen. Hosp., 1974—76; fellowship, Cardiology Duke U. Med. Ctr., 1977—80; vis. prof., Biochemistry Dept. Oxford U., 1984—85; chief, Cardiology, prof., Internal Medicine, Biochemistry, & Molecular Biology, dir., Ryburn Ctr. for Molecular Cardiology U. Tex. Southwestern Med. Ctr., 1990—2001; vis. scientist Cold Spring Harbor Lab., NY, 1995—96; asst. prof., Medicine, Physiology & Cell Biology Duke U. Sch. medicine, 1980—84; assoc. prof., Medicine & Microbiology Duke University School Medicine, 1986—90, dean, vice chancellor, Acad. Affairs, 2001—07, sr. vice chancellor, Acad. Affairs, 2007—. Bd. advisor Nat. Heart, Lung and Blood Inst.; bd. dirs. NIH, Laboratory Corp. of America Holdings, 2007—. Contbr. more than 150 scholarly articles to biomed. jours., Proceedings of the Nat. Acad. Scis. Mem. Inst. of Medicine of the Nat. Acad. of Sciences; fellow Am. Assn. for the Advancement of Science; pres. Assn. of U. Cardiologists; chmn., Rsch. Com. Am. Heart Assn. Recipient Disting. Alumnus Award, Duke U. Sch. Medicine, 2000. Fellow: AAAS; mem.: NAS, Inst. of Medicine, Assn. Univ. Cardiologists, Am. Heart Assn. Achievements include being the leader of the Dallas Heart Disease Prevention Project, an innovative program of research in the genetic epidemiology of cardiovascular disease. Office: Laboratory Corp of America Holdings Bd Directors 531 S Spring St Burlington NC 27215 Office Phone: 336-436-5274. Office Fax: 336-436-1569. E-mail: williamsr@labcorp.com. *

WILLIAMS, SANKEY VAUGHAN, health services researcher, internist; b. San Antonio, Apr. 15, 1944; s. James Sankey and Helen (Long) W.; m. Constance Hess, June 27, 1972; children: Elizabeth Helen, Jennifer Lee. AB, Princeton U., 1966; MD, Harvard U., 1970. Diplomate Am. Bd. Internal Medicine. Intern Hosp. of U. Pa., 1970-71, jr. resident, 1971-72, chief med. resident, 1974-75; assoc. dir. clin. rsch. Ctr. for Study of Aging, U. Pa., 1982-86; assoc. dir. for med. affairs Leonard Davis Inst. for Health Econs., U. Pa., 1978-90; dir. clin. scholars program U. Pa., Phila., 1988-96; prof. health care systems Wharton Sch., U. Pa., Phila., 1989—; prof. medicine U. Pa., Phila., 1989—, chief div. gen. internal medicine, 1992—, Sol Katz prof. medicine, 1992—. Commr. Prospective Payment Assessment Commn., U.S. Congress, Washington, 1988-91; chairman health svcs. rsch. devel. grants study sect. Agy. for Health Care Policy and Rsch., 1991-94; counselor for med. affiars to the pres. U. Pa., 1990-92. Co-editor: The Physician's Practice, 1980; author 35 revs, chpt. or editorials; contbr. 62 articles to various sci. jour., assoc. editor, annals of Internal Medicine, 2003-. Lt. comdr. USPHS, 1972-74. Recipient Career Devel. award Henry S. Kaiser Family Found., 1981-86. Mem. ACP (master, chmn. clin. privileges com. 1989-93, Soc. for Med. Decision Making (pres. 1985-86), Soc. for Gen. Internal Medicine (coun. 1979-84, editor Jour. Gen. Internal Medicine 1994-99, pres. 2000-01). Office: Hosp Univ of Pa Divsn Gen Internal Medicine 1220 Blockley Hall 423 Guardian Dr Philadelphia PA 19104-6021

WILLIAMS, SHAUNA T., colon and rectal surgeon; MD, U. Hawaii, 1984. Diplomate Am. Bd. Surgery, 2009, Am. Bd. Colon and Rectal Surgery, 2010. Intern Oreg. Health Sciences Univ. Hosp., resident, 1985—90; fellow in colon and rectal surgery Mayo Clinic, Rochester, Minn., 1990—91; hosp. affiliations include St. Luke's Regional Med. Ctr., St. Alphonsus Regional Med. Ctr., Idaho. Fellow: Am. Soc. of Colon and Rectal Surgeons, ACS, Am. Cancer Soc. Oncology; mem.: Ada County Med. Soc., Idaho Med. Soc., Priestly Soc. (mayo clinic), Northwest Soc. Colon and Rectal Surgeons. Office: St Alphonsus Regional Medical Center 1072 N Liberty St Ste 201 Boise ID 83704 Office Phone: 208-367-3059. Office Fax: 208-377-2273.

WILLIAMS, SID, psychiatrist; b. Australia, Oct. 12, 1942; MBBS, U. Sydney, 1966. Staff specialist to clin. dir. psychiatry Bankstown-Lidcombe Hosp., Sydney, 1974—97; clin. dir. aged care psychiatry svc. Braeside Hosp., Sydney, 1996—98; conjoint sr. lectr. U. NSW, 1996—98; assoc. prof. psychiatry, faculty medicine U. Sydney, 1989—91; vis. med. officer NSW Health, 1996—. Chair, adv. com. psychiatry old age NSW Inst. Psychiatry, 1985—90; convenor, psychogeriatric working party Ministerial Implementation Com. Mental Health & Devel. Disability, Health NSW, 1988; mem., standing com. tng. psychiatrists NSW Inst. Psychiatry, 1993—96; mem., com. care older people Australian Med. Assn., 1995—2003. Fellow: Royal Australian & New Zealand Coll. Psychiatrists (bd. practice standards 1990—94, mem., Faculty Psychiatry Old Age), Australasian Assn. Gerontology, Australian Med. Assn.; mem.: Internat. Psychogeriatric Assn., Australian & New Zealand Soc. Geriatric Medicine. Office: PO Box 4035 Homebush NSW 2140 Australia Office Phone: 0297646395.

WILLIAMS, STEPHEN G., urologist, educator; b. Bryn Mawr, Pa., July 12, 1965; BA, Princeton U., 1987; MD, Loyola U. Stritch Sch. Medicine, 1993. Dir., urologic oncology Kaiser Permanente, 2002—, academic faculty mem., ctr. med. edn., dept. urology, 2003—, residency program dir., urology, 2007—10, chmn., nat. urology symposium, 2007—10. Clin. instr., dept. urology U. So. Calif. Sch. Medicine, 1999—2001; asst. clin. prof. surgery, divsn. urology U. Calif., San Diego, 2002—03. Fellowship, U. So. Calif., LA County Hosp., Norris Comprehensive Cancer Ctr., LA, Calif. Mem.: Calif. Med. Assn., Western Sect., Am. Urologic Assn., Soc. Urologic Oncology, Am. Urologic Assn. Office: 10800 Magnolia Ave Riverside CA 92505 Business E-Mail: stephen.g.williams@kp.org.

WILLIAMS, STEPHEN L., city health department administrator; M Ed, Auburn U., 1980; MPA, Baruch Coll., NYC, 1986. Exec. mgr. health, human services and veteran services Travis County, Tex.; exec. mgr. combined health dept. Austin and Travis County; dir. public health City of Houston, 2004—. Office: Houston Dept Health 8000 N Stadium Dr Houston TX 77054-1823 Office Phone: 713-794-9320.

WILLIAMS, STEPHEN MEREDITH, psychologist, writer; b. London, Feb. 2, 1950; s. Peter Meredith and Bettina Primrose (Hyams) Williams; m. Brigitte Johanna Strater, July 4, 1980; children: Conrad Meredith, Stella Gael. BA with honours in Psychology-Philosophy, Cambridge U., Eng., 1972; DPhil in Exptl. Psychology, U. Sussex, Eng., 1980. Chartered psychologist. Rschr. Open U., Milton Keynes, England, 1978-79; lectr. psychology U. Ulster, Coleraine, Eng., 1979-90, N.E. Essex Health Authority, Colchester, Eng., 1990-94; pvt. practice psychology, Colchester, 1994—. Author: Psychology on the Couch, 1988, Environment and Mental Health, 1994, Psychology: The Study of Mind, 1996, Key Articles in Psychology, 1997, Social Psychology-Intro, 2002, Further, 2005, Advanced, 2008; contbr. over 50 articles to sci. jours. Mem. coun. Social Dem. Party, 1989; gov. Myland Sch., Colchester, 1992-96. Scholar Trinity Coll., Cambridge U., 1968, sr. scholar, 1970. Fellow Brit. Psychol. Soc. (assoc.); mem. Brit. Fedn. for Correspondence Chess (sec. 1996-2000, mag. editor 2008-), English Chess Fedn. (minutes sec. 1995-97, 2002, 10), U. Sussex Alumni Soc., European Soc. for Study of Cognitive Sys., Internat. Assn. for Religious Freedom (Brit. chpt.), Soc. Authors. Avocations: chess, computers, reading. Home and Office: Taylor View 18a Fingringhoe Rd Old Heath Colchester C02 8DZ England Business E-Mail: steve.williams7@ntlworld.com.

WILLIAMS, STEVEN D., plastic surgeon; b. Mpls., Minn. m. Yvonne Christian William, June 1, 1991. BA, U. Chgo., 1979; MD, Loyola U., Maywood, Ill., 1985. Former cert. State Med. Bd. OH, Mich. Bd. Medicine, former lic. State Med. Bd. OH, Mich. Bd. Medicine, cert. State Ill. Med. Bd., Fed. Drug Enforcement Adminstrn., lic. State Ill. Med. Bd., Fed. Drug Enforcement Adminstrn., bd. cert. Nat. Bd. Med. Examiners, Am. Bd. Plastic Surgery, splty. bd. cert. Am. Bd. Plastic Surgery, 1998. Resident, intern, gen. surgery U. Ill., 1985—89, chief resident, gen. surgery, 1989—90; fellow, staff attending-burn fellowship, dir. ICU Cook County Hosp., 1990—91; resident, plastic and reconstructive surgery Med. Coll. OH, Toledo, 1991—92, adminstrv. chief resident, plastic and reconstructive surgery, 1992—93; attending physician, plastic surgeon, pvt. practice Ctr. Reconstructive Surgery, 1993—95, Cmty. Health Ctr. Bourbonnais, 1995—. Chmn., chief surgery Riverside Med. Ctr. & St. Mary's Hosp., 2005—, chmn. operating room coms.; mem. Med. Ctr. Trauma Com., Kankakee, Ill., Riverside Med. Ctr. Dept. Profl. Edn., Kankakee, Riverside Med. Ctr. Oper. Rm. Com., Kankakee, Riverside Med. Ctr. Physicians Adv. Bd., Kankakee, Provena St. Mary's Hosp. Oper. Rm. Com., Ill.; presenter, spkr. in field; med. dir. Riverside Ambulatory Surgery Ctr. Contbr. articles to profl. jours. Mem. Am. Breast Cancer Found., Am. Cancer Soc., Am. Diabetes Assn., Am. Found. for Blind, Am. Fedn. Police, Am. Heart Assn., Am. Inst. Cancer Rsch., Alzheimers Assn., Amnesty Internat., Arthritis Found., Cath. Charities, Covenant House, Cystic Fibrosis Found., Feed the Children, Hospice Edn. Inst., Internat. Humane Soc., Habitat for Humanity, Macular Degeneration Rsch. Found., Mercy Home Boys & Girls, Multiple Sclerosis Assn. Am., NAACP, Nat. Found. Cancer Rsch., Nat. Geog. Soc., Nat. Hort. Soc., Nat. Humane Soc., Nat. Osteoporosis Found., Nat. Parkinsons Found., Nat. Pub. & Chgo. Pub. Radio, Oblate Missions, Pub. TV, United Negro Coll. Found., USO, Sacred Heart League, World Conf. Religion & Peace; ptnr. Spl. Olympics; vol., vision and blood pressure screening test; mem. Big Bros./Big Sisters Met. Chgo., Chgo. Anti-Cruelty Soc., Harbor House Kankakee, Maryknoll Fathers and Bros., So. Poverty Law Ctr., St. Jude's Childrens Hosp. Assn., St. Labre Am. Indian Sch., LWV; ch. lector. Fellow: Am. Coll. Surgeons, ACS; mem.: AMA, Kankakee County Med. Soc., Phenylketonuria Action Group, Karl A. Meyer Surg. Soc. of Cook County Hosp., Kanakakee County Med. Soc. (v.p. 2005—, pres. 2006—), Chgo. Med. Soc., Ill. State Med. Soc., Am. Burn Assn., Chgo. Soc. Plastic Surgeons, Midwest Assn. Plastic Surgeons (v.p.), Am. Soc. Plastic Surgeons, VFW, Am. Vets. Assn., Paralyzed Vets. Found., Consumers Union, U. Chgo. Varsity Athletic Letterman's Club, Phi Gamma Delta. Avocations: bicycling, hiking, guitar, photography, travel.

WILLIAMS, TANISHA YARWEH, microbiologist; b. Griffin, Ga., Feb. 2, 1971; BS in Biology, Ga. State U., 1994, MS in Biology, 2002. Microbiologist FDA, 2009—. Mem.: Am. Soc. Clin. Pathology. Home: 6380 The Trail Stone Mountain GA 30087 Personal E-mail: tayar123@yahoo.com.

WILLIAMS, THOMAS EUGENE, pediatric hematologist and oncologist, pharmaceutical executive; b. Texarkana, Ark., May 13, 1936; s. Thomas Earle and Frankie Jo (Garner) W.; m. Peggy Jane O'Neill, May 31, 1958; children: Thomas Eugene, Elizabeth Anne, James David. BA, Yale U., 1958; MD, U. Tex. Southwestern Med. Sch., 1962. Rotating intern Hermann Hosp., Houston, 1962-63; pediat. resident Children's Med. Ctr., Dallas, 1963-65; fellow pediat. hematology-oncology U. Va. Hosp., Charlottesville, 1967-68; rsch.

assoc. Cancer Rsch. Lab., U. Va., Charlottesville, 1968-69; asst. prof. pediat. and pathology U. Tex. Health Sci. Ctr., San Antonio, 1969-72, assoc. prof. pediat., asst. prof. pathology, 1972-73, assoc. prof. pediat. and pathology, 1973-79, assoc. prof. pediat., 1985-94; assoc. dir. med. Cetero, San Antonio, 2008; med. dir. ONYX Pharm. Inc., 2009—10. Med. dir. Santa Rosa Children's Hosp. Cancer Rsch. and Treatment Ctr., 1974—79, South Tex. Comprehensive Hemophilia Ctr., 1977—79, dir. pediat. bone marrow transplantation program, 1986—93; sr. clin. rsch. scientist Burroughs Wellcome Co., 1979—85; dir. new drug devel. Orphan Med., Inc., 1994—96; dir. med. affairs Ilex Oncology Svcs., Inc., 1997—98, ILEX Oncology Products, Inc., 1998—2002; clin. assoc. prof. pediat. U. N.C. Sch. Medicine, 1979—85; clin. fellow bone marrow transplantation program Johns Hopkins U. Sch. Medicine, Balt., 1985; sr. dir. Divsn. Oncology ICON Clin. Rsch., Inc., 2002—07; pres., CEO Thistle Advisors Internat. Inc., 2007—; chief med. officer Amplimed Corp., 2008. Contbr. articles to profl. jours. Exec. dir. Episcopal Med. Missions Found., 1997—. Lt. comdr. USNR, 1965—67. Recipient travel award Am. Soc. Pharmacology and Exptl. Therapeutics, 1968; Am. Cancer Soc. advanced clin. fellow, 1968-69, 70-72. Mem. Am. Soc. Clin. Oncology, Am. Soc. Hematology, Am. Assn. for Cancer Rsch. Episcopalian. Office Phone: 210-979-8400. Business E-Mail: twilliams@thistleoncology.com.

WILLIAMS, THOMAS FRANKLIN, physician, educator; b. Belmont, NC, Nov. 26, 1921; s. T. F. and Mary L. (Deaton) Williams; m. Catharine Carter Catlett, Dec. 15, 1951; children: Mary Wright, Thomas Nelson. BS, U. N.C., 1942; MA, Columbia U., 1943; MD, Harvard U., 1950; DSc (hon.), Med. Coll. Ohio, 1987, U. N.C., 1992; DMS, Thomas Jefferson U., 2003. Intern Johns Hopkins, Balt., 1950—51, asst. resident physician, 1951—53; resident physician Boston VA Hosp., 1953—54; research fellow U. N.C., Chapel Hill, 1954—56, instr. dept. medicine and preventive medicine, 1956—57, asst. prof., 1957—61, assoc. prof., 1961—68, prof., 1968; attending physician Strong Meml. Hosp., Rochester, NY, 1968—; cons. physician Genesee Hosp., Rochester, NY, 1973—; prof. medicine, preventive medicine and cmty. health U. Rochester, 1968—92, prof. radiation biology and biophysics, 1968—91, on leave, 1983—91, prof. emeritus, 1992—; clin. prof. medicine U. Va., 1983—89; lectr. medicine Johns Hopkins U., 1983—89; clin. prof. depts. family medicine and medicine Georgetown U., 1983—89; dir. Nat. Inst. on Aging NIH, 1983—91; asst. surgeon gen. USPHS, 1983—91, ret., 1991; attending physician Monroe Cmty. Hosp., Rochester, 1991—, vice-chmn. cmty. coalition for long term care, 1991—; disting. physician VA Med. Ctr., Canandigua, NY, 1995—98. Adv. bd. U. Rochester Sch. Medicine and Dentistry, 1968—83; med. dir. Monroe Cmty. Hosp., Rochester, 1968—83; mem. rev. coms. Nat. Ctr. for Health Svcs. Rsch.; adv. bd. St. Ann's Home; mem. gov. bd. NRC, 1981—83; sci. dir. Am. Fedn. Aging Rsch., 1992—; cons. in field. Contbr. articles to profl. publs. With USNR, 1943—46. Recipient Civic award for health care, Rochester N.Y. C. of C., 1998; fellow, USPHS, 1966—67; scholar Markle scholar, 1957—61. Fellow: ACP, APHA; mem.: NAS (coun. 1980—83, governing bd. 1981—83, Gustav O. Lienhard award Inst. Medicine 1969), AAAS, Am. Clin. Climatol. Assn., N.C. Coun. for Human Rels. (chmn. 1963—66), Rochester Regional Diabetes Assn. (pres. 1977—79), Am. Gerontol. Soc., Am. Geriatrics Soc., Soc. Exptl. Biology and Medicine, Am. Fedn. Clin. Rsch., Am. Diabetes Assn. (bd. dirs. 1974—80), Monroe County Med. Soc., N.Y. State Med. Soc., Assn. Am. Physicians, Inst. Medicine. Episcopalian. Home: 287 Dartmouth St Rochester NY 14607-3202 Office: Monroe Cmty Hosp Office Med Dir Rochester NY 14620

WILLIAMS, UNA JOYCE, retired psychiatric social worker; b. Youngstown, Ohio, June 24, 1934; d. Samuel Wilfred and Frances Josephine (Woods) Ellis; children: Wendy Louise, Christopher Ellis, Sharon Elizabeth. BA, U. Ala., 1957; MSW, Adelphi U., 1963. Diplomate in profl. counseling Internat. Acad. Behavioral Medicine, Counseling and Psychotherapy. Dir. Huntington Program Sr. Citizens, 1963—67; psychiat. social worker-supr. N.Y. State Dept. Mental Hygiene, Suffolk Psychiat. Hosp., Central Islip, 1969—72; info.-referral counselor Mental Health Assn. Nassau County, Hempstead, NY, 1993—; therapist Madonna Heights Family Clinic, Dix Hills, NY, 1994—99; med. and psychiat. social worker Northport VA Med. Ctr., NY, 1994—2005, psychiat. social worker acute psychiat. treatment svcs., 2005—08, med. social worker dialysis svcs., 2007—08. Cons. on programs for aging Luth. Social Svcs. Met. N.Y., 1959, sr. citizens programs, Bd. Edn. Port Jefferson, N.Y., 1961-63. Chmn. Huntington Twp. Com. Human Rels., 1970; sec. bd. trustess Unitarian Universalist Fellowship Huntington, 1984. Mem. NASW (diplomate in social work), Am. Assn. Family Counselors and Mediators,Germany Philatelic Soc. (pres. chpt. 30, 1990, Mem. of Yr. 1987). Avocations: painting, stamp collecting/philately, music (voice & piano), genealogy. Home: 316 Lenox Rd Huntington Station NY 11746-2640

WILLIAMS, WILLIAM JOSEPH, retired hematologist, educator; b. Bridgeton, NJ, Dec. 8, 1926; s. Edward Carlaw and Mary Hood (English) W.; m. Margaret Myrick Lyman, Aug. 12, 1950 (dec. Aug., 1985); children: Susan Lyman, William Prescott, Sarah Robb; m. Karen A. Hughes, Feb. 18, 1989. Student, Bucknell U., 1943-45; MD, U. Pa., 1949. Diplomate: Am. Bd. Internal Medicine. (hematology com. 1976-80). From intern to assoc. prof. U. Pa., Phila., 1949—61, assoc. prof. to prof. medicine, chief hematology, 1961—69; sr. instr. microbiology Case We. Res. U., 1952; asst. prof. medicine Washington U., St. Louis, 1959—60; rsch. fellow Oxford U., England, 1960—61; mem. hematology tng. com. Nat. Inst. Arthritis and Metabolic Disease, 1964—68, mem. rsch. career program com., 1968—72; chmn. dept. medicine SUNY Health Sci. Ctr., Syracuse, 1969—92, prof. medicine, 1969—2006, interim dean Coll. Medicine, 1991—92, dean coll. medicine and v.p. biomed. scis., 2002—04, disting. svc. prof., 2002—06, disting. svc. prof.emeritus, 2006—, dean emeritus Coll. Medicine, 2004—. Vis. scientist Walter and Eliza Hall Inst., Melbourne, Australia, 1980; vis. prof. Monash U., Melbourne, 1980; mem. thrombosis adv. com. Nat. Heart and Lung Inst., 1969-73, chmn., 1971-73; adv. coun. Nat. Arthritis, Metabolism and Digestive Diseases, 1975-79; mem. residency rev. com. internal medicine Accreditation Coun. Grad. Med. Edn., 1983-89, mem. bd. appeals panel for internal medicine, 1989-2000; mem. NY State Coun. Grad. Med. Edn., 1987-89. Editor-in-chief: Hematology, 1972, 4th edit., 1989, Williams Hematology Companion Handbook, 1996; co-editor: Williams Manual of Hematology, 2003; contbr. articles to med. lit. Trustee Everson Mus. Art, 1975-81, 83-89. With USNR, 1944-46, 52-54. Recipient Research Career Devel. award Nat. Heart Inst., 1963-68; Daland fellow Am. Philos. Soc., 1955-57; Markle scholar, 1957-62 Mem. ACP (gov. Upstate N.Y. 1976-81), Am. Soc. Biochemistry and Molecular Biologists, Am. Soc. Clin. Investigation, Assn. Am. Physicians, Am. Clin. and Climatol. Assn., Am. Soc. Hematology, Interurban Clin. Club (sec. 1964-70), Alpha Omega Alpha. Mem. Soc. Friends. Home: 5160 Peck Hill Rd Jamesville NY 13078-9724 Office: 750 E Adams St Syracuse NY 13210-2306 Home Phone: 315-446-0546; Office Phone: 315-464-9788. Business E-Mail: williamw@upstate.edu.

WILLIAMS, WINFRED W., molecular biologist; MD, NYU. Resident Brigham & Women's Hosp.; program scientist dept. molecular biology Mass. Gen. Hosp. Co-chmn. Multicultural Affairs Office Adv. Bd. Mass. Gen. Hosp., adv. bd. Ctr. for Faculty Devel. Office: Massachusetts General Hospital 55 Fruit St BUL 123 Boston MA 02114-2696 Office Phone: 617-726-5050. Office Fax: 617-724-1122.

WILLIAMS-LATNIE, VERONICA MYRES, psychotherapist, social worker; b. Shreveport, La., May 11, 1947; d. McEura and Margie Virgina (Reagan) Myres; divorced; children: Nicole Leann, Jennifer Lyn, Erica Maria; m. Melvin Latnie Nov. 17, 2007 BA, La. Tech. U., Ruston, 1969; MSW, U. Mich., Ann Arbor, 1977; PhD, So. Calif. U., 2001. Diplomate Am. Bd. Clin. Social Workers, Am. Psychotherapy Assn.; cert. social worker, Mich. Probation counselor Citizens Probation Authority, Flint, Mich., 1970-72; unit dir., therapist Svcs. to Overcome Drug Abuse Among Teenagers, Flint, 1972-74; psychiat. therapist Psycho-Therapeutic Treatment Clin., P.C., Flint, 1974-77; psychiat. social worker Hurley Med. Ctr., Flint, 1977-79; field instr. Sch. Social Work U. Mich., Ann Arbor, 1978-79, 86—; psychiat. social worker Inst. Mental Health, Flint, 1979-81, Psychotherapeutic Treatment Clinic, 1981-83; clin. social worker Flint Bd. Edn., 1979-83; pupil appraisal spl. edn. Caddo Parish Sch. Bd., Shreveport, La., 1983—85; psychiat. therapist Mott Children's Health Ctr., 1986—92, Oakland Psychol. Clinic, P.C., 1991—92; owner and dir. V. Williams, PhD, MSW, ACSW, BCD, PC, Flint, Mich., 1992—2009; dir. behavior health svcs. Hamilton Cmty. Health Network, Flint, Mich., 2009—. Developer dropout prevention program Flint Bd. Edn., 1986-98; Beecher Sch. Dist., 1998-2006. Bd. dirs. Boys & Girls Club. Mem. NASW, ACSW, NEA, Mich. Edn. Assn. Democrat. Office: Ste 3001 225 E 5th St Flint MI 48502 Home Phone: 810-695-5610; Office Phone: 810-232-0018. E-mail: drvmwilliams@comcast.net.

WILLIAMSON, DONALD ELLIS, state agency administrator, public health service officer; b. Louisville, Miss., June 17, 1955; m. Anita Hudspeth; 1 child, Jonathan Stuart. Student, East Miss. Jr. Coll., 1972-73, Miss. State U., 1973-75; MD cum laude, U. Miss., 1979. Diplomate Am. Bd. Internal Medicine. Intern, resident in internal medicine U. Va. Hosp., Charlottesville, 1979-82; with East Miss. State Hosp., Meridian, 1979; state TB control officer Miss. State Dept. Health, 1982-86; dir. divsn. disease control Ala. Dept. Pub. Health, 1986-88, dir. bur. preventive health svcs., 1988-92, state health officer, 1992—. Faculty mem. Injury Control Rsch. Ctr. U. Ala., Birmingham; clin. assoc. prof. dept. internal medicine U. South Ala.; presenter in field. Contbr. articles to profl. jours. Chmn. Ala. Pub. Health Care Authority, Ala. Radiation Adv. Bd. Health; mem. Ala. Commn. Aging, State Bldg. Commn., Statewide Health Coordinating Coun., Ala. Youth Svcs. Bd., Ala. Child Abuse & Neglect Prevention Bd., Ala. Resource Devel. Com., Ala. Anat. Bd., Planning and Adv. Coun. Devel. Disabilities, Ala. Bd. Med. Scholarship Awards, Pesticides Adv. Com., Gov.'s Interagy. Coordinating Coun., Ala. Juvenile Justice Coordinating Coun., Emergency Med. Svcs. Adv. Coun., 1986 92, Legis. Adv. Com. AIDS, 1988-90, Atty. Gen.'s Task Force Med-.Waste, 1989, Water Resources Adv. Coun., exec. coun. Ala. Children's Svcs. Facilitation Team, 1993—; mem. med. adv. com. ARC. Recipient Mosby Book award, 1979, Dr. Robert Ramsey award, 1993; Pub. Health Leadership Inst. scholar, 1996. Mem. APHA, Assn. State and Territorial Health Ofcls. (exec. com. 1995-2000, pres. 1997-98), Am. Acad. of Pediatrics (Child Health Advocate of the Yr. award 1999), Pub. Health Found. (Theodore R. Ervin award 1999), Med. Assn. State Ala., Ala. Pub. Health Assn. (bd. dirs. 1991—, chmn. disease control and epidemiology sect. 1991-92, D.G. Gill award 1997), Pub. Health Found. (bd. dirs. 1995-99, treas. 1997—), Phi Theta Kappa, Phi Kappa Phi, Alpha Omega Alpha. Home: 8113 Lichfield Ct Montgomery AL 36117-5124 Office: Ala Dept Pub Health PO Box 303017 201 Monroe St Montgomery AL 36104-3735

WILLIAMSON, MARVEL, dean, nursing administrator, sexologist, educator; b. Holton, Kans., Nov. 4, 1953; d. Thomas Arthur and Lois M. (Ihrig) Ansley; m. Paul Williamson, May 12, 1973; children: Marcus W., Sean W. BS in Nursing, Wichita State U., 1976; MS in Nursing, U. Ky., 1978; PhD, U. Iowa, 1987. Cert. sex educator, nurse educator. Fellow Acad. Nursing Edn. Prof. U. Iowa, Iowa City, 1980-89; dir. patient svcs. Ransom Meml. Hosp., Ottawa, Kans., 1989-91; dir. schs. nursing at Rolla, Sikeston and Kansas City Park Coll., Parkville, Mo., 1991-97; prof. Albany (Ga.) State U., 1997-99; sexologist Silver Spring, Md., 1999—2001; dean Kramer Sch. Nursing, Oklahoma City U., 2001—. Contbr. articles to profl. jours. Mem. ANA, Am. Assn. Sex Educators, Counselors and Therapists, Sigma Theta Tau. Home and Office: 3141 NW 18th St Oklahoma City OK 73107 Office: Oklahoma City U 2501 N Blackwelder Oklahoma City OK 73106 Office Phone: 405-208-5900.

WILLINGER, RHONDA ZWERN, optometrist; b. Bklyn., Apr. 26, 1962; d. Jerome Max and Jeanette (Zwern) Willinger; m. Wayne Ken Chan, Aug. 26, 1990; children: Jamie S. Chan, Jared Max. BS, U. Miami, 1983; OD with honors, New Eng. Coll. Optometry, 1987. Resident in optometry VA Med. Ctr., Bedford, Mass., 1987-88; pvt. practice, Burlington, Mass., 1988-89; pvt. practice specializing in contact lenses Framingham, Mass., 1989—; exec. bd. dirs. Mass Soc., 2009—. Clin. investigator for contact lens companies. Vol. Metrowest Free Clinic. Scholar New Coll., U. South Fla., 1979-81; honors scholarship U. Miami, 1981-83. Mem. Am. Optometric Assn. (contact lens sect.), Mass. Soc. Optometrists. Avocation: violin. Home: 228 Lowell Ave Newton MA 02460-1830 Office: 659 Worcester Rd Framingham MA 01701-5204 Office Phone: 508-872-2722. Personal E-mail: studio.optics1@verizon.net.

WILLIS, ARNOLD JAY, urologic surgeon, educator; b. Phila., Feb. 12, 1949; s. Alexander and Rosaline May (Dortort) W.; m. Lilian Marie Mortensen, Aug. 29, 1981; children: Adam Mark, Simon Matt, Andreas Morton. BA, Franklin & Marshall U., 1970; MD, Thomas Jefferson Med. Ctr., 1974. Intern George Washington U. Hosp., Washington, 1974-75, resident in surgery, 1975-77, resident in urology, 1977-80; instr. in urology George Washington U. Med. Ctr., Washington, 1980-82, asst. clin. prof., 1982-88, assoc. clin. prof., 1988—; founder, pres. NY Cryotherapy, LLC, CEO, founding mem.; assoc. dean, clin. scis. Aureus U. Sch. Medicine, Aruba. Mem. Del Marva Found. Med. Care, Washington, 1985-90; profl. adv. bd. Nat. Kidney Found., Washington, 1988-92; med. dir., founder Met. Ambulatory Urologic Inst., Mid Atlantic Prostate Inst., Mid Atlantic Cryotherapies, LLC; med. dir., founder Continence Treatment Ctr. of Md.; expert on transgluteal brachytherapy for prostate cancer; med. dir., founder Met. Brachytherapy Assocs.; keynote spkr. 12th Copenhagen Urologic Symposium on Brachytherapy; CEO NY Cryotherapy LLC, Greenbelt Urologic Inst., founder; cons. 21st Century Oncology, organizer First Focal Minimally Invasive Therapy Prostate, Renal Cancer Ebeltoft, Denmark; cons. in field. Mem. editl. bd. Health Educator, 1995-96; contbr. articles to sci. jours.; inventor ultrasound guide. Founder profl. sports league/major league roller hockey; owner Washington Power profl. hockey team. Clin. Oncology Tng. grantee NIH, 1974; named Tchr. of Yr., Georgetown Family Practice Residency, 1991. Fellow Internat. Coll. Surgeons (v.p. U.S. sect. 1986—, Washington regent); mem. Am. Urologic Assn., Am. Assn. Clin. Urologists, Washington Urol. Assn. (Resident's prize 1980). Jewish. Avocations: tennis, squash, skiing, fishing, sailing. Home: 2011 Whiteoaks Dr Alexandria VA 22306-2432 Office: 650 Pennsylvania Ave SE Ste 480 Washington DC 20003-4373 Home Phone: 301-474-3636; Office Phone: 202-546-1107. Personal E-mail: powerajw@aol.com.

WILLIS, GLADDEN WILLIAMS, retired pathologist, scientific photographer, tree farmer; b. Minden, La., Mar. 26, 1939; s. John Stillmon and Virgie Williams Willis; m. Lydia Hall, May 14, 1966; children: Charles Austin, Loye Stillmon. BS, Centenary Coll., 1960; MD, Tulane U., 1964. Intern La. State U. Med. Ctr., Shreveport, 1964-65, resident, 1965-69; fellow Meml. Sloan-Kettering Med. Ctr., NYC, 1969-71; pathologist St. Luke's Hosp., Houston, 1971-72, St. Mary's Hosp., Roswell, N.Mex., 1972-73, Ochsner Clinic Found., New Orleans, 1973—2005, dir. anat. pathology, 1976—2003, vice chmn. lab. medicine, 1996—2003. Contbr. articles to profl. jours., 2622 sci. photographs to encys. and books. Past pres. Jefferson Performing Arts Soc., Metarie, La. Capt. USAF, 1966—72. Recipient George Washington Honor medal, Valley Forge Found., 1996. Fellow Arthur Purdy Stout Soc., Royal Microscopical Soc.; mem. Assn. Dirs. of Anatomic Pathology, Internat. Acad. Pathology, Am. Soc. Media Photographers, NY Acad. Scis. Republican. Methodist. Avocation: photography. Home and Office: PO Box 719 Doyline LA 71023 Office Phone: 318-745-2251. Personal E-mail: gladdenandlydia@gmail.com.

WILLIS, ROBERT ADDISON, dentist; b. Wichita, Kans., Apr. 27, 1949; s. Everett Clayton and Mary Ann (Rohlin) W.; m. Janet Sue Jones, Jan. 21, 1968 (div. Dec. 1986); children: Gregory, Jeffrey; m. Sherryl Ann Galloway, Apr. 26, 1991; children: Wes Misak, Wendy Misak. Student, Okaloosa Walton Jr. Coll., Niceville, Fla., 1970-71, Wichita State U., 1972-74; DDS, U. Mo., 1978. Dentist, Wellington, Kans., 1978—. Cons. Sumner County Regional Hosp., 1980—, Lakeside Lodge Nursing Home, Wellington, 1980—. Bd. dirs. Kans. Babe Ruth Leagues, Inc., dist. commr., 1990—2009, state commr., 2009-, mgr. Classic West team, 1990, 2005; website devel., webmaster Kansasbaberuthleagues.com, 1995—; bd. of elders Calvary Luth. Ch., 1989-94, treas., 2003—, mem. fin. com., 2003—. With USAF, 1968-71. Named to Kans. Babe Ruth Leagues Hall of Fame., 2005. Mem. ADA, Acad. Gen. Dentistry, So. Dist. Dental Soc. (pres. 1980), Kans. Dental Assn. (coun. on peer rev. 1988-89), Wellington Dental Soc. (treas. 1981—), Optimist CLub, Wellington Area C. of C. (com. on indsl. devel. 1992), Am. Legion, Xi Psi Psi. Republican. Avocations: golf, photography, jogging, collecting music records, woodworking. Home: 620 Circle Dr Wellington KS 67152-3206 Office: 204 E Lincoln Ave Wellington KS 67152-3061 Home Phone: 320-326-2711. Business E-Mail: rwillis@sutv.com.

WILLIS, WILLIAM DARRELL, JR., neuroscientist, educator; b. Dallas, July 19, 1934; s. William Darrell and Dorcas (Chamberlain) W.; m. Jean Colette Schini, May 28, 1960 (dec. Jan. 1, 2006); 1 child, Thomas Darrell. BS, BA, Tex. A&M U., 1956; MD, U. Tex. Southwestern Med. Sch., 1960; PhD, Australian Nat. U., 1963. Postdoctoral research fellow Nat. Inst. Neurol. Diseases and Blindness, Australian Nat. U., 1960-62, Istituto di Fisiologia, U. Pisa, Italy, 1962-63; from asst. prof. to prof. anatomy, chmn. dept. U. Tex. Southwestern Med. Sch., Dallas, 1963-70; chief lab. comparative neurobiology Marine Biomed. Inst., prof. anatomy and physiology U. Tex. Med. Br., Galveston, 1970—, dir. Marine Biomed. Inst., 1978—2004, chmn. dept. anatomy and neurosci., 1986—2004, Ashbel Smith prof., 1986-95, Cecil and Ida Green prof., 1995—. Mem. neurology B study sect. NIH, 1968 72, chmn., 1970 72, mem. neurol. disorders Program Project rev. com., 1972-76, Nat. Adv. Neurol. and Communicative Disorders and Stroke Coun., 1987-90; tng. grant com. Nat. Inst. of Neurol. Disorders and Stroke, 1994-98. Mem. editl. bd. Neurosci., Exptl. Neurology, 1970-90, Archives Italienne Biologie, Neurosci. Letters, 1976-92; chief editor Jour. Neurophysiology, 1978-83, Pain, 1986-89; assoc. editor Jour. Neurosci., 1986-89, editor-in-chief, 1993-94; sect. editor Exptl. Brain Rsch., 1990-92, 1995-2004. Mem. AAAS, Am. Assn. Anatomists (exec. com. 1980-86), Am. Pain Soc. (pres. 1982-83), Internat. Assn. Study Pain (coun. 1984-90), Am. Physiol. Soc., Soc. Exptl. Biol. Medicine, Soc. Neurosci. (pres. 1984-85), Internat. Brain Rsch. Orgn., Cajal Club, Sigma Xi, Alpha Omega Alpha. Office: U Tex Med Br 301 University Blvd Galveston TX 77555-1069 Home: 7312 Seawall Blvd Apt 109 Galveston TX 77551-1994 Business E-Mail: wdwillis@utmb.edu.

WILLMAN, JOSEPH HOWARD, pathologist; b. Indpls., Oct. 14, 1966; s. Joe Irvin and Barbara Ellen Willman; m. Ran Yoon Willman, June 19, 1994; 1 child, Josephine Yoon-Yung. BA, U. Chgo., 1989; diploma of pub. health, U. Otago, 1996; MD, Ind. U., 1997. Resident in pathology U. Utah, Salt Lake City, 1997—2001; dermatopathology fellow U. Colo., Denver, 2001—03; pathologist Clin. Pathology Assocs., Austin, Tex., 2003—. Office: Clin Pathology Assoc 9200 Wall St Austin TX 78754

WILLOCK, MARCELLE MONICA, retired medical educator; b. Georgetown, Guyana, Mar. 30, 1938; came to U.S. 1954; d. George and Renee W. BA, Coll. New Rochelle, 1958; MD, Howard U., 1962; MA, Columbia U., 1982; MBA, Boston U., 1989. Diplomate Am. Bd. Anesthesiology. Asst. clin. prof. med. ctr. NYU, 1968-72, assoc. clin. prof. med. ctr., 1972-74; asst. prof. clin. anesthesiology Columbia U., NYC, 1978-82; prof. Boston U., 1982, chmn. dept. anesthesiology, 1982—98, asst. provost cmty. affairs, 1998—2002; dean Coll. Medicine Charles R. Drew U., LA, 2002—05; ret., 2005. Sec. The Med. Found., Boston, 1991-94. Contbr. articles to profl. jours. Pres. Louis and Marthe Deveaux Found., Panama, 1965—; trustee Coll. New Rochelle, NY, 1976-82, 2006—. Mem. Am. Soc. Anesthesiologists (del. 1986—, alt. dir. 1990-94, bd. dirs. 1994—, asst. sec. 1999-2001), Mass. Soc. Anesthesiologists (pres. 1988-89), Soc. Acad. Anesthesia Chairs (sec.-treas. 1989-91, pres.-elect 1993-94, pres. 1994—), Wood Libr. Mus. (bd. developers 2010-), Alpha Omega Alpha. Roman Catholic. Personal E-mail: mwillock@bu.edu. *

WILLOUGHBY, WILLIAM FRANKLIN, II, retired physician, scientist, military officer; b. Washington, Feb. 4, 1936; s. William Westel and Patricia (De Zychlinska) W.; m. Mary Scott Fishburne, 1963 (div. 1974); children: Westel Woodbury, William Franklin III, Laura Fishburne, Mary Scott; m. Judith Eleanor Barbaras, Oct. 25, 1975; 1 child, Robert Alexander Willoughby. AB, Johns Hopkins U., 1957, MD, 1965, PhD in Microbiology, 1965; grad. with distinction, USAF War Coll., 1985. Diplomate Am. Bd. Pathology. Intern then resident in pathology Johns Hopkins Hosp., 1965—67; asst. prof. depts. pathology and microbiology Case Western Res. U., Cleve.; dir. Virginia Mason Rsch. Ctr., Seattle, 1972—75; assoc. prof. dept. pathology Sch. Medicine, Johns Hopkins U., Balt., 1975—87; prof., chmn. dept. pathology Sch. Medicine, U. S.C., Columbia, 1987-92; dir. labs. Cook County Hosp., Chgo., 1992-98, interim med. dir., 1994-96; ret., 1998. Cons. NIH, Bethesda, Md., 1979-98, mem. pathology A study sect., 1982-86; cons. NRC, Washington, 1981-84; mem. res. component med. coun., Dept. Def., Pentagon, 1991-93; maj. USAFR, 1975, advanced through ranks to maj. gen., 1993; dep. surgeon gen. for res. affairs, USAF, Bolling AFB, D.C., 1993-95; asst. surg. gen., Operation Desert Storm/Desert Shield, 1990-91, ret. 1995. Author: The Zychlinski Family: Their Polish Ancestors and American Descendants, 2007; mem. editorial bd. Am. Rev. Respiratory Disease, 1978-84; contbr. articles to profl. jours., reviewer numerous sci. manuscripts. Vestryman Trinity Episcopal Ch., Long Green, Md., 1984-87; bd. dirs. Ctrl. S.C. chpt. ARC, Columbia, 1989-92; bd. fellow Norwich U., 1992-95. Decorated D.S.M., Legion of Merit; recipient Edwin E. Osgood prize Va. Mason Rsch. Ctr., 1973; Arthritis Found. fellow Scripps Clinic and Rsch. Found., 1967-69; Poncine scholar Poncine Found., 1972-74; NIH rsch. grantee, 1976-91. Fellow Coll. Am. Pathologists; mem. AAAS, Am. Lung Assn. (nat. rsch. grant rev. com. 1978-82, chmn., 1981-82), Am. Soc. Investigative Pathology, Am. Assn. Immunologists, Am. Soc. Cell Biologists, Chgo. Coun. Fgn. Rels., Internat. Acad. Pathology, Assn. Pathology Chmns., Aerospace Med. Assn., Soc. USAF Flight Surgeons (bd. govs. 1993-96), Am. Thoracic Soc., Assn. Mil. Surgeons U.S., Soc. Med. Cons. to Armed Forces, Army Navy Club, Air Force Assn., Univ. Club Chgo., Silver Wings Assn., Johns Hopkins Club, City Club Chgo. Avocations: music, genealogy, antique automobiles, Chinese art. Home: 1416A S Federal St Chicago IL 60605-3057 Personal E-mail: wwilloughby@sbcglobal.net.

WILLS, MICHAEL STEPHEN, nutritionist, quality assurance professional, photographer; b. Roslyn, NY, Mar. 10, 1953; s. Thomas Francis and Catherine Ann Wills; m. Svetlana Victorivna Shiryaeva, Jan. 26, 1994 (div. Aug. 2005); m. Barbara Ann Keegan, Jan. 15, 1979 (div. June 20, 1985); m. Pamela Jayne Sprinkle, Mar. 20, 2009; stepchildren: Laleh Archin, Dara Lee Archin, Denna Archin(dec.), Charles Clancy, Kseniya Andreevna Shiryaeva; 1 child, Sean Michael. BS with high honors, U. Ariz., 1975. Registered dietitian Am. Dietetics Assn., Ill., 1976. Newspaper carrier LI Newsday, Albertson, NY, 1966—69; dietetic technician Ariz. Med. Ctr., Tucson, 1972—73; dietetic practicum US Army, San Francisco, 1973—73; dietetic technician Tucson Med. Ctr., 1973—75; dietetic internship U. Ariz., Tucson, 1975—76; dir. of food svc. Catskill Meml. Hosp. and Nursing Home, NY, 1976—77; food svc. dir. New Rochelle Nursing Home, NY, 1977—79; dir. of food svc. Grace Plz., Inc., Great Neck, NY, 1979—82; corp. dietitian Data Control Info., Inc., Hornell, NY, 1982—84, dir. software devel., 1984—86; quality assurance and customer support rep. The CBORD Group, Inc., Ithaca, NY, 1986—87, mgr. support and quality assurance, 1987—88, mgr. quality assurance, 1988—98, dir. quality assurance, 1998—2007, sr. adv. Analyst, 2007—; owner www.MichaelStephenWills.com. Cons. ServiceMaster, Downers Grove, Ill., 1986—94, Abbot Labs., Chgo., 1987—88, Brown U., Providence, 1987—92, Hallmark Cards, Kansas City, Kans., 1987—94, 1988 Winter Olympics, Calgary, Alberta, Canada, 1987—88, Disneyland, Paris, 1993, The Walt Disney World Co., Orlando, Fla., 1993—2003, Cornell U., Ithaca, NY, 1995, Kaiser Permanente, LA, 2001—03, NSW Dept. Health, Sydney, 2002—04, Children's Hosp. Eastern Ontario, 2002—, Disneyland, Anaheim, Calif., 2003, H.E.B. Markets, San Antonio, 2004, Calif. Inst. of Tech., Pasadena, Calif., 2004, Gordon's Food Svc., Aramark, 2006—, The Ottawa Hosp., 2009—, Children's Hosp. of Eastern Ontario; presenter in field. Contbr. articles to profl. jours. Alumni bd. dirs. U. Ariz. Coll. Agrl. & Life Scis., 2005—; mem. Unitarian Universalist Assn., Ithaca, 1992—2004. Recipient Photography awards, Photographic Soc. Am., 2005—09; scholar Promising Student, Herricks HS PTA, 1971, U. Ariz., 1973—74; NY State Regents scholar, NY State Dept. Edn., 1971, Syntex Dietetic Internship scholar, Syntex Corp., 1975. Mem.: Am. Dietetic Assn. (licentiate), Amercian Soc. for Quality (assoc.; paper reviewer 2002—04), Photographic Soc. Am. (assoc.), Kappa Omicron Nu. Democrat. Roman Catholic. Achievements include development of functional reliability approach for software development; creation of an algorithm for calculating probability of concurrence for multi-user software applications; creation of a system of equations with algorithm to quantity software performance; creation of Olvera Valenzuela Memorial Scholarship for University of Arizona. Avocations: astronomy, writing, backpacking. Home: 20 West Malloryville Rd PO 258 Freeville NY 13068 Office: The CBORD Group Inc 61 Brown Rd Ithaca NY 14850 Personal E-mail: mwills@twcny.rr.com. Business E-Mail: msw@cbord.com.

WILLSON, TONI MARIE, medical/surgical nurse, educator; b. Adelaide, South Australia, Australia, Sept. 16, 1962; d. Jeffery Cleveland and Patricia Mary Willson; m. Neil David Smark, Apr. 18, 1987 (div. Oct. 5, 1992). BNg, Flinders U. of South Australia, Adelaide, 1999, BNg with honors, 2000, grad. in Health, 2001. Credentialled Diabetes Educator, Australian Diabetes Educators Assn., 2002. Adminstrn./co-ordinator Fire Fighting Enterprises (SA) Pty Ltd, Adelaide, South Australia, Australia, 1981—96; rsch. asst. The Royal Adelaide Hosp., Adelaide, South Australia, Australia, 1997—98; RN Women's and Children's Hosp., Adelaide, South Australia, Australia, 1999; diabetes nurse educator The Queen Elizabeth Hosp. and Health Svcs., Adelaide, South Australia, Australia. Grant assessor Diabetes Australia Rsch. Trust, Sydney, 2001—. Contbr. articles to profl. publs. Chairperson Women With Diabetes, Inc., Adelaide, South Australia, Australia, 1994—99; consumer rep./advocacy Ministerial Diabetes Adv. Com., Adelaide, South Australia, Australia, 1997—2001. Grantee Consumer and Provider Partnership in Health Project - Consumer Focus Strategy, Commonwealth Dept. of Health and Aged Care (Australia), 2000; Diabetes Nurse Educator grantee, Eli Lilly Australia, Pty. Ltd., 2002, Diabetes Australia Rsch. Trust grantee, 2002, Rsch. grantee, Novo Nordisk Pharms., 1995. Mem.: Endocrine Nurses Soc. of Australia Inc., Australian Diabetes Educators Assn., Golden Key (life Outstanding scholastic achievement and excellence 1998). Avocations: painting, piano. Office: Queen Elizabeth Hosp Diabetes Centre 8 Woodville Rd 5011 Woodville SA Australia Office Fax: (08) 8222 6044. E-mail: toni.willson@nwahs.sa.gov.au.

WILMOT, IRVIN GORSAGE, former hospital administrator, educator, consultant; b. Nanking, China, June 30, 1922; s. Frank Alonzo and Ethel (Ranney) W.; m. Dorothy Agnes Mohlfeld, Feb. 6, 1943; children: Marcia Beth, David Michael. BS, Northwestern U., 1955; MBA, U. Chgo., 1957. With Internat. Register Co., Chgo., 1946-47; buyer U. Chgo., 1947-49; adminstrv. asst., then asst. supt. U. Chgo. Clinics, 1949-61; adminstr. NYU Med. Ctr.-Univ. Hosp., 1961-68, exec. v.p., 1968-81, Blue Cross-Blue Shield Greater N.Y., 1981-83, dir., 1977-81; exec. v.p., COO Montefiore Hosp. and Med. Ctr., NYC, 1984-85; healthcare cons., 1985—. Instr. then asst. prof. U. Chgo., 1957-61; assoc. prof. NYU, 1961-68; prof., 1968—; assoc. dir. U. Chgo. Grad. Program Hosp. Adminstrn., 1959-61; mem. hosp. rev. and planning coun. State of N.Y., 1979-87. Bd. dirs. N.Y. Blood Ctr., 1978-81. With USN, 1940-46. Fellow Am. Coll. Hosp. Adminstrs. (life, chmn. ctrl. com. insts. 1959-65, regent N.Y. State and P.R. 1974—); mem. Assn. U. Programs Hosp. Adminstrs. (exec. sec. 1959-61), Am. Hosp. Assn. (mem. coun. rsch. and planning 1965-68, coun. on mgmt. 1979-80, coun. on fin. 1981-84, trustee 1979-81), Assn. Am. Med. Colls. (chmn. coun. tchg. hosps. 1970-71), Greater N.Y. Hosp. Assn. (bd. govs., pres. 1973-74), Hosp. Assn. N.Y. State (trustee, chmn. 1976-77). Home: 300 E Overlook #337 Port Washington NY 11050

WILMUT, IAN, biologist; b. Hampton Lucey, Eng., July 7, 1944; s. Jack and Eileen Mary (Dalgleish) W.; m. Vivienne Mary Craven, Sept. 9, 1967; children: Helen, Naomi, Dean. BSc in Agrl. Sci., Nottingham U., Eng., 1967, DS, 1998; PhD in Animal Genetic Engring., Cambridge U., Eng., 1971. Sr. scientist ABRO (Animal Rsch. Breeding Station, which is now known as the Roslin Inst.), Edinburgh, 1973-93; prin. investigator Roslin Inst., Midlothian, Scotland, 1993—, mem. sr. mgmt., joint head dept. gene expression and develop. Scientific advisor Geron Bio-Med, a wholly owned subsidiary of the Geron Corp., Menlo Park, Calif.; lectr. in field. Editor Jour. Reproduction Fertility, 1993—; co-author (with Colin Tudge and Keith Campbell) The Second Creation: Dolly and the Age of Biological Control, 2000, (with Roger Highfield) After Dolly: The Uses and Misuses of Cloning, 2006; contbr. articles to profl. jours. Hon. fellow U. Edinburgh, 1993; recipient Lord Lloyd of Kilgerran prize, Sir John Hammond Meml prize Soc. Study Fertility, Rsch. medal Royal Agrl. Soc. Eng., Sir William Young award Royal Highland & Agrl. Soc. Scotland; co-recipient Shaw prize in life sci. and medicine, 2008. Mem. Internat. Embryo Transfer Soc. (pres. 1994), NAS (fgn. assoc.), Order of the British Empire; fellow Royal Soc. Edinburgh, Acad. Med. Scis. Achievements include creating the first calf ever produced from a frozen embryo, named Frosty in 1973; with Keith Campbell, the birth of Megan and Morag, two Welsh mountain sheep cloned from differentiated embryo cells in 1995; with Keith Campbell, the production of a mammal cloned from adult cells, the lamb named Dolly in 1996; with Keith Campbell, creating Polly, a sheep cloned from fetal skin cells that had been genetically altered to contain a human gene in 1997; granted a license to clone human embryos for medical research in 2005. Avocations: hill walking, photography, curling, gardening. E-mail: ian.wilmut@bbsrc.ac.uk.

WILNER, ERIC MARK, radiologist; b. Tulsa, Okla., Dec. 5, 1949; s. Sol and Selma Wilner; m. Patricia. Harrison Wise, Aug. 10, 1997; children: Emily K., Allison A.; m. S. Scott, May 31, 1976 (div. July 17, 1996). BA, Northwestern U., Evanston, Ill., 1972; MD, Med. Coll. Wis., Milw., 1976. Diplomate Nat. Bd. Med. Examiners, 1977, in diagnostic radiology Am. Bd. Radiology, 1980, cert. fellowship in computed tomography & ultrasound Boston Va Med. Ctr., Mass., 1981, resident in diagnostic radiology New Eng. Med. Ctr. & Affiliated Hosps., 1980, flexible intern Cambridge Hosp., 1977. Ptnr. NE Radiology Associates, Mass., 1981—; staff radiologist Amesbury Health Ctr., Mass., 1981—, Health Diagnostics, Hallmark Health, Stoneham, Mass., 1999—2010, Metronorth MRI, Medford, Mass., 2002—, Inmed Diagnostic Svcs. Ma, Stoneham, Mass., 2004—, Anna Jaques Hosp., Newburyport, Mass., 1981—, chief radiologist, 1985, 1988, 1991—92. Contbr. articles to profl. jours. Mem. radiology delegation to South Africa People to People Citizen Amb. Programs, 2009. Recipient Champion, Med. Am. Solutions, 2010, Champion award, Medicine-Am. Solution, 2010; named one of America's Top Radiologists, Consumers Rsch. Coun. America, 2009—10, Leading Physician World, 2010, The Leading Physucians of the World, 2010. Mem.: Radiol. Soc. N. Am., Am. Coll. Radiology. Office: 25 Highland Ave Newburyport MA 01950 Personal E-mail: emw125@comcast.net.

WILSON, ADEL MICHEL, plastic surgeon; b. Cairo, Dec. 2, 1965; s. Michel and Soad Jimmy (Tadros) W. MD, Cairo U., 1988, M in Surgery, 1992, PhD, 1997. Registrar in surgery Cairo U., 1990-93, prof. in plastic surgery, 1996—; registrar in plastic surgery U. Coll., London, 1994-95; cons. plastic surgery Ministry of Health, Cairo, 1997—, Al-Salam Hosp., Cairo, 1996—. Dir. Infection Control com., Cairo, 1997-98, Microsurgery Unit, Cairo, 1996-98; mem. Environ. Care com., 1998—. Author: Case Presentations for MRCS, 1997; contbr. articles to profl. jours. Mem. bd. Gezira Sporting Club, Cairo, 1996. Fellow Royal Coll. Surgeons; mem. Royal Soc. of Medicine (hon.), British Assn. of Plastic Surgeons. Avocations: reading, ping pong/table tennis, chess. Home: 37 Batal Ahmed Abdel-Aziz Giza 12411 Egypt Office: 42 Dokki St Flat 132 Dokki 12311 Egypt Office Phone: 20122144209. Business E-Mail: adelwilson@esprs.com.

WILSON, CECIL BRUCE, internist; b. Columbus, Ga., 1935; m. Betty Jane Wilson; 3 children. BA in History, Emory U., Atlanta; MD, Emory U. Sch. Medicine, 1961. Diplomate American Bd. Internal Medicine. Intern US Naval Hosp., Portsmouth, Va., 1961—62; resident internal medicine US Naval Hosp., San Diego, 1966—69; internal medicine pvt. practice Winter Park, Fla. Past pres. med. staff Winter Park Meml. Hosp., Fla. Hosp. Med. Ctr., Orlando. Nat. fellow, advisor Ctr. Global Health & Med. Diplomacy, U. North Fla.; past pres. Fla. Statewide Health Coun.; past chair Local Health Coun. East Ctrl. Fla. Flight surgeon, comdr. USN. Master: ACP (past chair bd. regents); mem.: World Med. Assn. (coun. mem.), American Soc. Internal Medicine, AMA (House of Delegates 1992—, bd. trustees 2002—, chair bd. trustees 2006—07, pres. 2010—11, immediate past pres. 2011—), Orange County Med. Soc. (past pres.), Fla. Med. Assn. (past pres., Cert. of Merit 2003). Office: Cecil B Wilson MD 1341 Orange Ave Winter Park FL 32789-4911 Office Phone: 407-647-2122. Office Fax: 407-647-6701. *

WILSON, CHARLES STEPHEN, cardiologist, educator; b. Geneva, Nebr., June 14, 1938; s. Robert Butler and Naoma Luella (Norgren) Wilson; m. Linda Stern Walt, Aug. 21, 1960; children: Michael Scott, Amy Lynn, Cynthia Lee. BA cum laude, U. Nebr., 1960; MD, Northwestern U., 1964. Diplomate Am. Bd. Internal Medicine subsplty. bd. cardiovascular disease, Nat. Bd. Med. Examiners. Intern Fitzsimons Gen. Hosp., Denver, 1964-65; fellow in internal medicine and cardiology Mayo Grad. Sch. Medicine, Rochester, Minn., 1968-72; practice medicine specializing in cardiology Lincoln, Nebr., 1972—; attending staff Bryan Meml. Hosp., 1972—, chmn. cardiology, 1976-79; clin. prof. medicine and cardiology U. Nebr. Med. Ctr., Omaha; med. dir. Bryan LGH Med. Ctr. Ultrafast CT Scanner, Lincoln, 2001—, Sch. Health Profl, Bryan LGH Coll. of Health Scis., 2002—. Mem. Mayor's Coun. on Emergency Med. Svcs., Lincoln, 1974-78; founder, chmn. Nebr. State Hypertension Screening Program; med. dir. Lincoln Mobile Heart Team, 1977-80, Lincoln Cardiac Rehab. Program, 1978-79; co-founder, pres. Nebr. Heart Inst., 1987; co-founder Lincoln Cardiac Transplant Program, 1987. Contbr. articles to profl. jours.; editorl. cons. Chest, 1975-76; assoc. editor Nebr. Med. Jour., 1981-88. Trustee U. Nebr. Found., 1983—, chmn. Nebr. Coordinating Commn. for Postsecondary Edn., 1984-88; mem. bd. regents U. Nebr., 1991—2009, chmn. 1994, 2001, 07. Served as maj. M.C., USAR, 1963-68. Gen. Motors Nat. scholar, 1956—60, Nat. Found. med. scholar, 1960—64, Mead Johnson scholar, ACP, 1968—71. Fellow ACP, Am. Coll. Cardiology (bd. govs. 1990-93, pres. Nebr. affiliate 1992-93), Am. Coll. Chest Physicans, Am. Heart Assn. (dir. Nebr. affilate 1973-80, pres. 1976-77); mem. Mayo Cardiovascular Soc., Nebr. Cardiovascular Soc. (pres. 1989-90), Nebr. Coun. on Pub. Higher Edn. (steering com. 1991—2002), Lincoln Heart Assn. (dir. 1972-75, pres. 1974-75), AMA, Nebr. Med. Assn. Lancaster County Med. Soc., Am. Soc. Internal Medicine, Lincoln Found., U. Nebr. Chancellor's Club, Lincoln U. Club (dir. 1981-84), U. Nebr. Pres. Club, Phi Beta Kappa, Sigma Xi, Alpha Omega Alpha, Phi Delta Theta (pres. Nebr. Alpha chpt. 1959-60). Home: 7430 N Hampton Rd Lincoln NE 68506-1624 Office: Bryan LGH Ultrafast CT Scanner 1500 S 48th St Lincoln NE 68506

WILSON, CHRISTINE JESSICA, physical therapist; b. Queensland, Australia, Aug. 21, 1957; B in Physiotherapy, U. Queensland, 1978. Cons. physiotherapist, paediatric med. conditions Royal Children's Hosp., Children's Health Svcs., Qld Health, 1990—. Vis. lectr., sch. health & rehab. scis. U. Queensland, St Lucia, Brisbane, Queensland, Australia, 1994—2006; vis. lectr., sch. exercise sci. & physiotherapy Griffith U., Gold Coast, 2003; asst. prof., health scis. & medicine Bond U., Gold Coast, 2009. Recipient Advanced Clinician award, Queensland Health, 2003; Rsch. grant, Roche Products, 2002—04. Fellow: Australian Coll. Physiotherapists; mem.: Nat. Paediatric Group, APA, Cardiorespiratory Physiotherapy Australia, APA, Internat. Physiotherapy Group Cystic Fibrosis, Australian Physiotherapy Assn. Office: Physiotherapy Royal Children's Hosp Brisbane Queensland 4029 Australia Office Fax: 61 7 3636 5181. Business E-Mail: christine_wilson@health.qld.gov.au.

WILSON, DANIEL JAMES, physical education educator; b. Lonpoc, Calif., Apr. 13, 1964; s. James Leonard and Shirley Irene (Gerjets) Wilson; m. Jennie Lynn Gorham, Feb. 14, 1997; children: Tawnie Lucille, Danielle Lynn. BS, Saginaw Valley Coll., 1986; MA, Mich. State U., 1989, PhD, 1993. Asst. prof. U. Mo., Columbia, 1993—96, NIH fellow, 1995—99, clin. asst. prof., 1998—99, dir. Gait Lab., 1998—99; asst. prof. S.W. Mo. State U., Springfield, 1999—2003, assoc. prof., 2003—, lab. dir., 2003—. Author: Botulinum Toxin Type A in Pain Management, 1999, Botulinum Toxin Type A in Pain Management, 2d edit., 2002. Mem.: Mo. Acad. Scis., Am. Alliance for Health, Phys, Edn., Recreation & Dance, Internat. Soc. Biochemist in Sports. Avocations: fishing, running. Office: Southwest Mo State Univ 901 S National Ave Springfield MO 65804

WILSON, DONALD EDWARD, internist, educator, former dean; b. Worcester, Mass., Aug. 28, 1936; s. Rivers Rivo and Licine (Bradshaw) Wilson; m. Patricia C. Littell, Aug. 27, 1977; children: Jeffrey D.E., Sean D., Monique, Sheila L. AB, Harvard U., 1958; MD, Tufts U., 1962. Diplomate Am. Bd. Internal Medicine. Intern St. Elizabeth Hosp., Boston, 1962—63; resident in medicine, research fellow in gastroenterology VA Hosp. and Lemuel Shattuck Hosp., Boston, 1963—66; assoc. chief gastroenterology Bklyn. Hosp., 1968—71; instr. medicine SUNY Downstate Med. Center, Bklyn., 1968—71; asst. prof. medicine U. Ill., Chgo., 1971—73, asso. prof., 1973—75, prof., 1975—80, acting head dept. medicine, 1976—77; dir. divsn. gastroenterology U. Ill. Hosp., Chgo., 1971—78, chief of gastroenterology, 1973—80, physician-in-chief, 1976—77; prof., chmn. dept. medicine SUNY Downstate Med. Center, Bklyn., 1980—91; physician-in-chief State U. and Kings County Hosp., 1980—91; dean U. Md. Sch. Medicine, Balt., 1991—2006, v.p. of med. affairs, 1999—2006, dir. Program in Minority Health and Health Disparities Edn. and Rsch. Vis. prof. medicine U. London, Kings Coll. Med. Sch., 1977—78; mem. gastrointestingal drugs adv. bd. FDA, 1985—87, chmn., 1986—87; mem. Part II test com. Nat. Bd. Med. Examiners, 1985—88; mem. nat. digestive adv. bd. NIH, 1985—87, chmn., 1986—87, mem. gen. clin. rsch. ctrs. com., 1987—; mem. nat. adv. com. Agy. for Health Care Policy and Rsch., Dept. HHS, 1991—94, chmn., 1992—94; mem. residency rev. com. for internal medicine Acque, 1993—; mem. nat. com. fgn. med. edn. and accreditation U.S. Dept. Edn., 1994—; mem. nat. adv. rsch. resources com. NIH, 1997—2000; bd. dirs. Provident Bank Corp., 2002—. Contbr. articles to med. jours.; mem. editl. bd. Tufts Med. Alumni Bulletin, 1993—2002. Bd. vis. Harvard Sch. Pub. Health, 1992—94; bd. overseers Tufts U. Med. Sch., 2002—; bd. dirs. Balt. Symphony Orch., 1997—2004, Kernan Hosp., Balt., 1991—98, bd. dirs., Endowment Fund, 1996—; bd. dirs. Alliance to End Childhood Poisoning, 1992—95, The Baer Sch., Balt., 1992—, Mercy Med. Ctr., Balt., 1991—, U. Md. Med. Sys., 1991—. Capt. M.C. USAF, 1966—68. Recipient Rsch. award, HEW, 1971, 1974, John A. Hartford Found., Inc., 1972—79, Distilled Spirits Coun. U.S., 1972—74, VA, 1974. Master: ACP; mem.: AAAS, NAS, Inst. of Medicine, Assn. Profs. Medicine (sec. treas. 1990 91), Am. Clin. and Climatol. Assn., Nat. Med. Assn., Assn. for Acad. Minority Physicians (sec./treas. 1986—), Assn. Am. Physicians, Chgo. Soc. Gastrointestinal Endoscopy (pres. 1979—80), N.Y. Soc. Gastroenterology, N.Y. Acad. Medicine, N.Y. Acad. Scis., Soc. Exptl. Biology and Medicine, Midwest Gut Club, Digestive Disease Found., Chgo. Soc. Gastroenterology (pres. 1978—79), Ctrl. Rsch. Club, Ctrl. Soc. Clin. Rsch., Accreditation Coun. Grad. Med. Edn. (rev. com. internal medicine), Am. Assn. Study Liver Disease, Am. Fedn. Clin. Rsch., Am. Gastroent. Assn., Md. Med Comprehensive Ins. Trust (mem. 1998—, chmn. 1998—2000, 2002—04), The Ctr. Club (Balt.), Med. Club Bklyn., 14 West Hamilton St. Club (Balt.), Harvard Club (Chgo., N.Y.C.), Sigma Pi Phi (grand boule). Office: U Md Sch Medicine 655 W Baltimore St Rm HSFII S441 Baltimore MD 21201-1509 Office Phone: 410-706-7410. Office Fax: 410-706-0235. E-mail: drwilson@som.umaryland.edu.

WILSON, DONALD HURST, III, biopharmaceutical industry executive; b. Balt., Mar. 1, 1946; s. Donald H. and Winifred W.; m. Catharine A. MacKinnon, June 21, 1968 (div. 1972); m. Beverly Lee Wright, Oct. 3, 1975 (div. 1998); m. Constance Fisher Neely, Sept. 23, 2000; children: Beverly Callaway, Sarah Elizabeth. AB, Yale U., 1968; MBA, JD, Harvard U., 1976. Bar: Mass. 1977, N.C. 2003; cert. Superior Ct. mediator NC Dispute Resolution Commn., 2007. Cons. Boston Cons. Group, 1976-78; dir. mktg. I/C divsn. Black & Decker, Hampstead, Md., 1978-83; pres. MWI Tng. Svcs., Inc., Hunt Valley, 1983—96; v.p. Innoversity Edn. Ctrs., Global Knowledge Network, Inc., Md., 1996—97; pres. and COO Endacea, Inc. (formerly Link Tech., Inc.), Raleigh, 1997—98, pres. and CEO, 1998—2000, v.p. and COO, 2001—02, v.p., gen. counsel, 2003, pres., CEO and gen. counsel, 2004—. Bd. dirs. Endacea, Inc. (formerly Link Tech., Inc.), Raleigh, 1997—. Mem. vestry St. John's Episcopal Ch., 1993-96, lay eucharistic min., 1995-97; dir. The Bishop Claggett Ctr., 1995-97. Mem.: Info. Tech. Tng. Assn. (founder and dir. 1992—95), Assn. Microcomputer Distbrs. (founder and dir. 1988—90), Archaeol. Soc. Md. (trustee 1994—98). Republican. Avocations: archaeology, golf. Home: 1112 Baslow Brook Ct Raleigh NC 27614-8866

WILSON, EDWARD OSBORNE, biologist, educator, writer; b. Birmingham, Ala., June 10, 1929; s. Edward Osborne and Inez (Freeman) W.; m. Irene Kelley, Oct. 30, 1955; 1 child, Catherine Irene. BS, U. Ala., 1949, MS, 1950, LHD (hon.), 1980; PhD, Harvard U., 1955; DPhil, Uppsala U., Sweden; DSc (hon.), Duke U., 1978, Grinnell Coll., 1978, U. West Fla., 1979, Lawrence U., 1979, Fitchburg State Coll., 1989, Macalester Coll., 1990, U. Mass., 1990, Oxford U., 1993, Ripon Coll., 1994, U. Conn., 1995, Ohio U., 1996, Bates Coll., 1996, Coll. Wooster, 1997, U. Guelph, 1997, U. Portland, 1997, Kenyon Coll., 2002, U. of the South, 2002, Harvard U., 2004, Clark U., 2005; LHD (hon.), Hofstra U., 1986, Muhlenburg Coll., 1998, Yale U., 1998, Pa. State U., Bradford Coll., 1997, Conn. Coll., 2000, U. South Ala., 2003, Albion Coll., 2005, U. Puget Sound, 2006, Rockefeller U., 2007, Williams Coll., 2007; LLD, Simon Fraser U., Emory U., 2008, Grad. Theol. Found., 2008, U. Miss. Lavelle, 2008; DHC, U. Madrid Complutense, 1995, U. Montreal, 2004; DrRerNat, U. Würzburg, 2000. Jr. fellow Soc. Fellows, Harvard U., 1953—56, faculty, 1956—, Baird prof. sci., 1976—94, Pellegrino U. prof., 1994—97, rsch. prof., 1997—2002, curator entomology, 1971—97, hon. curator entomology, 1997—. Selection com. Guggenheim Found., 1982—89; bd. dirs. World Wildlife Fund, 1983—94, Orgn. Tropical Studies, 1984—91, N.Y. Bot. Garden, 1991—95, Am. Mus. Natural History, 1992—2002, Am. Acad. Liberal Edn., 1993—2004, Nature Conservancy, 1994—2002, Conservation Internat., 1997—. Author: The Insect Societies, 1971, Sociobiology: The New Synthesis, 1975, On Human Nature, 1978 (Pulitzer prize for non-fiction, 1979), Promethean Fire, 1983, Biophilia, 1984, Success and Dominance in Ecosystems, 1990, The Diversity of Life, 1992 (Nat. Wildlife Assn. award, Deutsche Umweltstiftung Book award, Sir Peter Kent Conservation prize), Naturalist, 1994 (L.A. Times Book prize sci., 1995), In Search of Nature, 1996, Consilience: The Unity of Knowledge, 1998 (Forkosch award Internat. Acad. Humanism, 2000), Biological Diversity: The Oldest Human Heritage, 1999, The Future of Life, 2002 (Natural World Book prize, U.K., 2002), Pheidole in the New World: A Dominant, Hyperdiverse Ant Genus, 2003 (Julia Ward Howe prize, 2003), From So Simple A Beginning, 2005, Nature Revealed, 2006, The Creation: An Appeal to Save Life on Earth, 2006; author: (with R.H. MacArthur) The Theory of Island Biogeography, 1967; author: (with C.J. Lumsden) Genes, Mind and Culture, 1981; author: (with Bert Holldobler) The Ants, 1990 (Pulitzer prize for non-fiction, 1991), Journey to the Ants, 1994 (Phi Beta Kappa prize sci., 1995), The Creation, 2006 (Green Book award, Stevens Inst. Tech. Ctr. Sci. Writings, 2007), The Superorganism, 2008; others. Recipient Cleve.-AAAS Rsch. prize, 1967, Mercer award, Ecol. Soc. Am., 1971, Nat. Medal Sci., 1976, Disting. Svc. award, Am. Inst. Biol. Scis., 1976, Archie Carr medal, U. Fla., 1978, Leidy medal, Acad. Natural Sci., Phila., 1979, Tyler Ecology prize, 1984, Silver medal, Nat. Zool. Park, 1987, German Ecol. Inst. prize, 1987, Weaver award scholarly letters, Ingersoll Found., 1989, Crafoord prize in Biosciences, Royal Swedish Acad. Sciences, 1990, Prix di'Inst. de la Vie, Paris, 1990, Revelle medal, 1990, Gold medal, Worldwide Fund for Nature, 1990, Achievement award, Nat. Wildlife Fedn., 1992, Shaw medal, Mo. Bot. Garden, 1993, Internat. prize biology, Govt. of Japan, 1993, Eminent Ecologist award, 1994, Ecol. Soc. Am. Audubon medal, Audubon Soc., 1995, Pub. Understanding Sci. award, AAAS, 1995, John Hay award, Orion Soc., 1995, Schubert prize, Germany, 1996, Washburn medal, Mus. Sci., 1996, Hutchinson medal, Garden Club Am., 1997, Stone award, New Eng. Aquarium, 1999, Nonino prize, Letters and Sci., Italy, 2000, King Faisal Internat. prize for sci., 2000, Kistler prize, Found. for the Future, 2000, Phillips Meml. medal, World Conservation Union, 2000, Lewis Thomas prize, Rockefeller U., 2001, Nierenberg prize, Scripps Oceanographic Inst., 2001, Thoreau medal, Thoreau Soc., 2001, Lifetime Achievement award, Time, 2001, Global Environment Citizens award, Harvard U., 2001, Busk medal, Royal Geog. Soc., 2002, Presdl. medal, Republic of Italy, 2002, Silver Cross of Christopher Columbus, Dominican Republic, 2003, Lowell Thomas award, Explorers Club, 2004, Frances Hutchinson medal, Chgo. Bot. Garden, 2004, Gov.'s award, Island Alliance, Mass., 2004, Rachel Carson award, Internat. Soc. Ecotoxicology and Chemistry, 2004, Rungius medal, Am. Mus. Wildlife Art, 2005, Prince William of Orange medal, Leiden U., 2006, TED prize, Sampling Found., 2006, George B. Stibbitz Comms. Pioneer award, Am. Computer Mus., 2006, TED Biotech. Prize, 2007, Catalonia prize, Spain, 2007, Terceuteram Silver medal, Linnear Soc., 2007, Pirk award, Nat. PKC Assn., 2008; Guggenheim Found. fellow, 1978. Fellow: Deutsche Akad. Naturforsch, Am. Philos. Soc. (Franklin medal 1998), Am. Acad. Arts and Scis.; mem.: NAS, Royal Soc. Sci. Uppsala (Sweden), Russian Acad. Sci., Royal Entomol. Soc. (hon. life), Finnish Acad. Sci. and Letters, Royal Soc. London, Netherlands Entomol. Soc. (hon. life), Royal Soc. Edinburgh (life), Assn. Tropical Biology (hon. life), Acad. Humanism (hon. life), Am. Humanist Assn. (Disting. Svc. award 1982, hon. life, Humanist of Yr.), Zool. Soc. London (hon. life), Entomol. Soc. Am. (Founders Meml. award 1972, L.O. Howard award 1985, hon. life), Brit. Ecol. Soc. (hon. life), Am. Genetics Assn. (hon. life), Explorers Club (life, hon. life, medal). Home: Apt A-208 1010 Waltham St Lexington MA 02421 Office: Harvard U Mus Comparative Zoology Cambridge MA 02138 Office Phone: 617-495-2315. Business E-Mail: ewilson@oeb.harvard.edu.

WILSON, ELIZABETH M., medical association administrator; BS, So. Ill. U.; grad. mgmt. cert., Loyola U. Grad. Sch. Bus., Chgo. Positions of increasing responsibility Edelman Pub. Rels., Am. Hosp. Assn., Loyola U.; nat. dir. pub. rels. Alzheimer's Assn.; exec. dir., comm. and pub. affairs Nat. Safety Coun.; exec. dir. Am. Brain Tumor Assn., Des Plaines, Ill., 2008—. Office: Am Brain Tumor Assn 2720 River Rd Des Plaines IL 60018 Office Phone: 847-827-9910. Office Fax: 847-827-9918. *

WILSON, FRANCES HELEN, retired occupational therapist; b. Pitts., Oct. 17, 1929; d. J. Vernon and Margaret Hassler (Prugh) Wilson. BA, Conn. Coll., 1951; advanced standing cert., Columbia Sch. Occupl. Therapy, 1953. Therapist Washington (Pa.) County Soc. Crippled Children and Adults, 1953-54; staff therapist Oakland VA Hosp., U. Pitts., 1955-66; supr. Occupl. Therapy Clinic, Aspinwall VA Hosp., Pitts., 1966-74, 81-85, Occupl. Therapy Clinic, Oakland VA Hosp., Pitts., 1974—85, ret., 1985. Active Jr. League Pitts., Inc.; vol. Pitts. (Pa.) Children's Mus. Mem. Western Pa. (treas. 1967-69), Am. Occupl. Therapy Assns., Presbyn. Univ. Hosp. Pitts. Vol. Assn., Pitts. (Pa.) Symphony Assn., Acad. Lifelong Learning, Conn. Coll. Club (treas. 1971-94), Twentieth Century Club (Pitts.). Republican. Presbyterian. Home: Washington Plz 1116 1420 Centre Ave Pittsburgh PA 15219

WILSON, FRED M., II, ophthalmologist, educator; b. Indpls., Dec. 10, 1940; s. Fred Madison and Elizabeth (Fredrick) W.; m. Karen Joy Lyman, Sept. 10, 1959 (div. June 1962); 1 child, Teresa Wilson Kulick; m. Claytonia Leigh Pemberton, Aug. 28, 1964; children: Yvonne Wilson Hacker, Jennifer Wilson DeLong, Benjamin James. AB in Med. Scis., Ind. U., 1962, MD, 1965. Diplomate Am. Bd. Ophthalmology. Intern Sacred Heart Hosp., Spokane, Wash., 1965-66; resident in ophthalmology Ind. U., Indpls., 1968-71, fellow in ophthalmology, 1971-72, F.I. Proctor Found., San Francisco, 1972-73; from asst. prof. to assoc. prof. ophthalmology Ind. U., Indpls., 1972-76, prof. ophthalmology, 1981—2005, prof. emeritus, 2005—; cons. vets. Administrn. Mede. Ctr., Indpls., 1976—. Med. dir. Ind. Lions Eye Bank, Inc., Indpls., 1973-99; cons. surgeon Ind. U., Indpls., 1973-2005. Contbr. articles to profl. jours., chapters to books. Lt. comdr. USNR, 1966-68, PTO. Mem. Am. Acad. Ophthalmology (assoc. sec. 1988-93, Sr. Teaching award 1989), Assn. Proctor Fellows, Soc. Heed Fellows, Am. Ophthalmol. Soc., Am. Bd. Ophthalmology (bd. dirs. 1993-2000), Ill. Soc. Ophthalmology (hon.), Mont. Acad. Ophthalmology (hon.), Pacific-Coast Ophthalmol. Soc. (hon.). Republican. Avocations: photography, guitar, history, language, natural history. Home: 12262 Crestwood Dr Carmel IN 46033-4323

WILSON, GEORGE SPENCER, retired chemistry professor; b. Bronxville, NY, May 23, 1939; AB, Princeton U., 1961; PhD, U. Ill., 1965. Asst. prof. to assoc. prof., chemistry U. Ariz., 1967—79, prof., chemistry, 1979—87; disting. prof., chemistry and pharm. chemistry, emeritus U. Kans., 1987—2010, assoc. vice provost, rsch. and grad. studies, 2004—10. Vis. prof. U. Paris VII, 1981; mem., metallobiochemistry study sect. NIH, 1982—86; editl. bd. mem. Biosensors and Bioelectronics, 1986; pres., phys. and biophys. chemistry divsn. Internat. Union Pure and Applied Chemistry, 2000—01. Recipient C.N. Reilley award, Soc. Electroanalytical Chemistry. Fellow: AAAS, Internat. Soc. Electrochemistry; mem.: Electrochem. Soc., Am. Chem. Soc., Sigma Xi. Avocations: travel, fishing.

WILSON, H. DAVID, dean; b. West Frankfort, Ill., Sept. 13, 1939; m. Jeannette Wilson; children: Jennifer, Jacqueline, Mary Jeanne. AB in Zoology, Wabash Coll., 1961; MD, St. Louis Sch. Medicine, 1966. Diplomate Nat. Bd. Med. Examiners, Am. Bd. Pediatrics. Intern pediatrics Cardinal Glennon Meml. Hosp. for Children, St. Louis U., 1966—67; resident dept. pediatrics U. Ky. Med. Ctr., Lexington, 1967—68, chief resident, 1968—69; NIH rsch. fellow U. Tex. Health Scis. Ctr., Dallas, 1971—73; fellowship Am. Coun. on Edn., 1988—89; dir. admissions Coll. of Medicine, U. Ky., 1986—88; assoc. dean for acad. affairs, prof. Coll. Medicine, U. Ky., 1989—95; dean, prof. U. N.D. Sch. of Medicine, Grand Forks, 1995—2009, v.p. for health affairs, 2001—09; dean U. Kans. Sch. Medicine, Wichita, 2009—. Author: (TV series) For Kids Sake, 1987-88; dir. pediatric infectious diseases U. Ky. Med. Ctr., Lexington, 1973-95, dir. cystic fibrosis care and tchg. ctr., 1975-80, med. dir., clin. virology lab., 1982-95; staff United Hosp., Grand Forks, 1995—; elected univ. senate U. Ky., 1993-96, bd. trustees Gluck Equine Rsch. Found., 1991-95, rules and elections univ. senate standing com., 1991-92, steering com. for U.K. self-study, 1990-95, co-chmn. steering com., 1990-95, chmn. review and search com. for chmn. dept. obstetrics and gynecology, 1990, chmn. curriculum com. Coll. of Medicine, 1989-95; elected acad. coun. of med. ctr. U. Ky. Med. Ctr., 1989-92; lectr. in field. Contbr. numerous articles to profl. jours. Fellow Pediatric Infectious Dieseases Soc.; mem. AMA (past mem. Coun. on Med. Edn.), Am. Soc. of Microbiology, Am. Thoracic Soc., Am. Acad. Pediatrics, Pan Am. Group for Rapid Viral Diagnosis. Office: University Kans Sch Medicine Office of Dean 1010 N Kansas Wichita KS 67214-3199 Office Phone: 316-293-2602. Business E-Mail: hdwilson@kumc.edu. *

WILSON, IAN ANDREW, molecular biology educator; b. Perth, Scotland, Mar. 22, 1949; BS in Biochemistry, U. Edinburgh, Scotland, 1971; DPhil in Molecular Biology, Oxford U., Eng., 1976; DSc, Oxford U., 2000. Tutor and tchg. asst. in biochemistry Harvard U., 1978-82, rsch. assoc. biochemistry and molecular biology, 1980-82; asst. mem. dept. immunology Scripps Rsch. Inst., La Jolla, Calif., 1982—83, asst. mem. dept. molecular biology, 1983—84, assoc. mem. dept. molecular biology, 1984—90, chmn. structure and chem. affinity group, 1987—, prof., lectr. structural biology and biophysical chem., 1988—, prof. molecular biology, 1991—, prof. Skaggs Inst. Chem. Biology, 1996—. Adj. prof. U. Calif., San Diego, 1998—. Contbr. articles to profl. jours. Recipient Newcomb-Cleve. prize, 1996-97. Fellow: Royal Soc. London; mem.: Acad. Arts and Sci., Am. Chem. Soc., Protein Soc., Brit. Soc. Immunologists, Am. Crystallographic Assn., Am. Assn. Pathologists, Am. Soc. Virologists, Brit. Biophys. Soc. Office: Scripps Rsch Inst BCC206 Dept Molecular Biol 10550 N Torrey Pines Rd La Jolla CA 92037-1000 *

WILSON, INYANG, physician assistant; b. Nigeria, Aug. 3, 1959; BA, Charles R Drew U., 1992. CEO PA Fresno-Arcola Family Med. Clinic, 2003—. Recipient Leading Physicians of World. Avocations: running, reading, camping, hiking. Office: 12125 Hwy 6 Ste B Fresno TX 77545 Office Fax: 281-431-9474. E-mail: fresnoclinic@yahoo.com.

WILSON, JAMES MILLER, IV, cardiovascular surgeon, educator; b. Atlanta, Mar. 11, 1946; s. James Miller Wilson III and Sara Sharp; m. Lisa VanLandingham; children: James Miller V, Robert Paul, Michael Simpson, Sara Ann. Student, Emory U.; MD, Duke U., 1971. Diplomate Am. Bd. Surgery, Am. Bd. Thoracic Surgery. Intern N.Y. Hosp., 1971-72; resident N.Y. Hosp.-Cornell Med. Ctr., 1972-73, U. Calif., San Francisco, 1975-80; attending staff Christ Hosp., Cin., 1980—, Bethesda Hosp., Cin., 1980—, Jewish Hosp., Cin., 1980—, Univ. Hosp., Cin., 1982—, Deaconess Hosp, Cin., 1982—, VA Med Ctr., Cin., 1983—, Children's Hosp., Cin., 1984—, Good Samaritan Hosp., Cin., 1994—; assoc. prof. clin. surgery U. Cin. Coll. Med., 1985—; chmn. dept. cardiovasc. surgery Deaconess Hosp., 1985—2001; dir. cardiac surgery Mercy Hosp., 2001—. Mem. open heart surgery adv. com., Ohio, 1995—; tech. adv. panel on cardiac surgery Nat. Quality Forum, chmn. Contbr. articles to profl. jours. Lt. Comdr. submarine svc. USN, 1973-75. Fellow ACS, Am. Coll. Cardiology, Am. Heart Assn. (cardiovasc. coun.), Am. Coll. Chest Physicians; mem. AMA, U.S. Naval Submarine League, UDT/SEAL Assn., U.S. Submarine Vets., Inc., Am. Assn. Thoracic Surgery, Thoracic Surgery Found., Assn. Acad. Surgery, Soc. Thoracic Surgeons, Ohio State Med. Assn., Cin. Acad. Medicine, Howard C. Nafziger Soc. Avocations: music, diving, hiking, skiing, horses. Home Phone: 513-271-9060; Office Phone: 513-603-8600. E-mail: jmwilson@alumni.duke.edu.

WILSON, JEAN DONALD, endocrinologist, educator; b. Wellington, Tex., Aug. 26, 1932; s. J. D. and Maggie E. (Hill) Wilson. BA in Chemistry, U. Tex., 1951, MD, 1955. Diplomate Am. Bd. Internal Medicine. Intern, then resident in internal medicine Parkland Meml. Hosp., Dallas, 1955—58; clin. assoc. Nat. Heart Inst., Bethesda, Md., 1958—60; instr. internal medicine U. Tex. Southwestern Med. Sch., Dallas, 1960—61, prof., 1968—. Editor: Jour. Clin. Investigation, 1972—77. Sr. asst. surgeon USPHS, 1958—60. Recipient Fuller prize, Am. Urol. Assn., 1983, Lita Annenberg Hazen award, 1986, Dale medal, Soc. for Endocrinology, 1991, Pincus medal, Worchester Found., 1992. Fellow: Royal Coll. Physicians; mem.: NAS, Endocrine Soc. (Oppenheimer award 1972, Koch award 1993), Am. Soc. Biochemistry and Molecular Biology, Soc. Exptl. Biology and Medicine, Am. Philos. Soc., Assn. Am. Physicians (Kober medal 1999), Am. Soc. Clin. Investigation, Inst. Medicine, Am. Acad. Arts and Scis. (Amory prize 1977). Office: U Tex Southwestern Med Ctr Dept Internal Medicine 5323 Harry Hines Blvd Dallas TX 75390-8857 Home Phone: 214-351-1837; Office Phone: 214-648-3469. Office Fax: 214-648-8917. Business E-Mail: jwils1@mednet.swmed.edu.

WILSON, JOANNE A.P., gastroenterologist, educator; b. Raleigh, NC, July 22, 1947; d. John H. and Conorah L. (Watson) Peebles; m. Kenneth H. Wilson, Aug. 15, 1969; children: Nora, Court, Sarah. BS in Chemistry, with highest honors, U. NC, Chapel Hill, 1969; MD, Duke U. Sch. Medicine, Durham, NC, 1973. Diplomate Am. Bd. Internal Medicine, cert. in Pediatric Gastroenterology. Intern, resident internal medicine Peter Bent Brigham Hosp., Harvard Med. Ctr., Boston, 1973-75; resident gastroenterology Georgetown Hosp., Washington, 1975—76; fellowship gastroenterology Vets. Affairs Med. Ctr., Washington, 1976-78; asst. prof. medicine U. Mich., Ann Arbor, 1978-86; assoc. prof., assoc. chief gastroenterology for outpatient svcs. Duke U. Med. Ctr., 1986-95, prof. gastroenterology, 1995—. Med. dir. Crohn's & Colitis Found., 1988—90; apptd. mem. Nat. Comm. on Digestive Diseases NIH, 2006. Contbr. articles to profl. jours. Bd. trustees Durham Acad. Recipient Trailblazer award, Duke Student Nat. Med. Assn., 2007. Fellow: ACP; mem.: Am. Soc. Gastrointestinal Endoscopy, Am. Gastroenterological Assn. (sec. 1997—2003, named one of Outstanding Women in Sci. 2008), Alpha Omega Alpha, Phi Beta Kappa. Achievements include being the first African American female to matriculate at Duke School of Medicine; first female secretary of the American Gastroenterological Association. Office: DUMC Dept Medicine PO Box 3858 Durham NC 27710-0001 Office Phone: 919-684-1817. Office Fax: 919-681-8147. Business E-Mail: joanne.wilson@duke.edu.

WILSON, LINDA SMITH, retired academic administrator; b. Washington, Nov. 10, 1936; d. Fred M. and Virginia D. Smith; m. Malcolm C. Whatley, June 29, 1957 (div. 1969); 1 child, Helen K. Whatley; m. Paul A. Wilson, Jan. 22, 1970; 1 stepchild, Beth A. BA, Tulane U., 1957, HLD (hon.), 1993; PhD, U. Wis., 1962; DLitt (hon.), U. Md., 1993. Rsch. assoc. U. Md., College Park, 1962—64, rsch. asst. prof., 1964—67; vis. asst. prof. U. Mo., St. Louis, 1967—68; asst. to vice chancellor for rsch., asst. vice chancellor for rsch., assoc. vice chancellor for rsch. Washington U., St. Louis, 1968—75; assoc. vice chancellor for rsch. U. Ill., Urbana, 1975—85; assoc. dean U. Ill. Grad. Coll., Urbana, 1978—85; v.p. for rsch. U. Mich., Ann Arbor, 1985—89; pres. Radcliffe Coll., Cambridge, Mass., 1989—99, pres. emeritus, 1999; sr. lectr. Harvard Grad. Sch. Edn., 1989—2003; bd. dirs. Myriad Genetics, Tulane U., Tulane Murphy Found. Rsch. resources adv. coun. NIH, Bethesda, Md., 1978—82; mem. Nat. Commn. on Rsch., Washington, 1978—80; dir.'s adv. coun. NSF, Washington, 1980—89; com. on govt.-univ. relationships NAS, 1981—83, govt.-univ.-industry rsch. roundtable, 1984—89, coord. coun. for edn., 1991—93; energy rsch. adv. bd. Dept. of Energy, 1987—90; chmn. adv. com. office sci. and engring. pers. NRC, 1990—96; adv. com. edn. and human resources NSF, Washington, 1990—95; sci., tech. and states task force Carnegie Commn. on Sci., Tech. and Govt., 1991—92; overser Mus. Sci., Boston, 1992—2001; trustee Mass. Gen. Hosp., 1992—99, hon. trustee, 1999—2002; trustee Com. on Econ. Devel., 1995—; bd. dirs. Inacom, Inc., 1997—2003, Citizens Fin. Group, Inc., 1997—2000, Value Line, Inc., 1998—2000; bd. vis. Coll. Letters and Sci. U. Wis., 1999—2005; dean's adv. coun. Newcomb Coll., 1999—2006. Contbr. articles to profl. jours. and book chpts. Adv. bd. Nat. Coalition for Sci. and Tech., Washington, 1983—87; bd. govs. YMCA, Champaign, Ill., 1980—83. Recipient Centennial award, Newcomb Coll., 1986, Disting. Alumni award, U. Wis., 1997, Radcliffe medal, 1999; named One of 100 Emerging Leaders, Am. Coun. Edn. and Change Mag., 1978, Outstanding Alumna, Class of 1957, Tulane U., 2007. Fellow: AAAS (bd. dirs. 1984—88); mem.: Am. Coun. Edn. (commn. on women in higher edn. 1991—93, chair 1993), Inst. Medicine (coun. mem. 1986—89, com. on setting NIH priorities, com. on govt.-industry collaboration in biomed. edn. and rsch.), Assn. for Biomed. Rsch. (bd. dirs. 1983—86), Nat. Coun. Univ. Rsch. Adminstrs., Soc. Rsch. Adminstrs. (Disting. Contbn. to Rsch. Adminstrn. award 1984), Am. Chem. Soc. (bd. coun. com. on chemistry and pub. affairs 1978—80), Phi Kappa Phi, Phi Delta Kappa, Alpha Lambda Delta, Sigma Xi, Phi Beta Kappa. Home: 26 Honey Locust Dr Topsham ME 04086 Home Phone: 207-729-9129.

WILSON, M. ROY, academic administrator, medical educator; b. Yokohama, Japan, Nov. 28, 1953; BS, Allegheny Coll., 1976; MD, Harvard Med. Sch., 1980; MS in Epidemiology, UCLA, 1990. Diplomate Nat. Bd. Medicine, Am. Bd. Ophthalmology. Intern Harlem Hosp. Ctr., NYC, 1980-81; resident in ophthalmology Mass. Eye & Ear Infirmary/Harvard Med. Sch., Boston, 1981-84, glaucoma, 1984-85; clin. fellow in ophthalmology Harvard Med. Sch., 1980-85, clin. asst. ophthalmology, 1985-86; clin. instr. dept. surgery, Divsn. Ophthalmology Howard U. Sch. Medicine, Washington, 1985-86; asst. prof. ophthalmology UCLA, 1986-91; asst. prof., chief Divsn. Ophthalmology Charles R. Drew U. of Medicine and Sci., LA, 1986-90, assoc. prof., chief Divsn. Ophthalmology, 1991-94, acad. dean, 1993-95, dean, 1995-98, prof., 1994-98, UCLA, 1994-98; dean sch. medicine Creihton U., Omaha, 1998—, interim v.p., 1999-2000, vice pres. health scis., 2001—; pres. Tex. Tech. U. Health Sci. Ctr., Lubbock, 2003—06; chancellor U. Colo at Denver Health Scis. Ctr., 2006—. Asst. in ophthalmology Mass. Eye and Ear Infirmary, 1985-86; cons. ophthalmologist, Victoria Hosp., Castries, St. Lucia, 1985-86; hosp. appointment, UCLA; chief physician Martin Luther King, Jr. Hosp., L.A., 1986—; project dir. Internat. Eye Found., Ministry of Health, 1985-86; biology lab instr., Allegheny coll., 1975; instr. in biochemistry Harvard U. Summer Sch., 1977-78; instr. Harvard Med. Sch., 1980-85, others; cons. and presenter in field; participant coms. in field. Mem. AMA, APHA, Assn. Rsch. in Vision and Ophthalmology, Chandler-Grant Glaucoma Soc., Nat. Med. Assn., Am. Acad. Ophthalmology, Inst. Medicine (elected 2003), Soc. Eye Surgeons Internat. Eye Found., Mass. Eye and Ear Infirmary Alumni Assn., So. Calif. Glaucoma Soc., West Coast Glaucoma Study Club, Assn. Univ. Profs. in Ophthalmology, L.A. Eye Soc., Calif. Med. Assn., Am. Glaucoma Soc., Soc. Epidemiol. Rsch. Office: U Colo at Denver Health Scis Ctr 35 SYS Boulder CO 80309-0035

WILSON, MARY ELIZABETH, physician, educator; b. Indpls., Nov. 19, 1942; d. Ralph Richard and Catheryn Rebecca (Kurtz) Lausch; m. Harvey Vernon Fineberg, May 16, 1975. AB, Ind. U., 1963; MD, U. Wis., 1971. Diplomate Am. Bd. Internal Medicine, Am. Bd. Infectious Diseases. Tchr. of French and English Marquette Sch. Madison, Wis., 1963-66; intern in medicine Beth Israel Hosp., Boston, 1971-72, resident in medicine, 1972-73, fellow in infectious diseases, 1973-75; physician Albert Schweitzer Hosp., Deschapelles, Haiti, 1974-75, Harvard Health Svcs., Cambridge, Mass., 1974-75; asst. physician Cambridge Hosp., 1975-78; hosp. epidemiologist Mt. Auburn Hosp., Cambridge, 1975-79, chief of infectious diseases, 1978—2002, dir. Travel Resource Ctr., 1996—2002, mem. consulting staff, 2003—05. Mem. adv. com. immunization practices CDC, Atlanta, 1988—92; mem. acad. adv. com. Nat. Inst. Pub. Health, Mexico, 1989—91; cons. Ford Found., 1988; site dir. GeoSentinel Network, 1999—2002, spl. cons., 2002—; instr. medicine Harvard Med. Sch., Boston, 1975—93, asst. clin. prof., 1994—99, assoc. prof. medicine, 1999—2004, assoc. clin. prof., 2004—; assoc. Ctr. Health and Global Environment, 1996—2000; asst. prof. depts. epidemiology and population and internat. health Harvard Sch. Pub. Health, 1994—99, assoc. prof. population and internat. health, 1999—2008, assoc. prof. global health & population, 2008—; lectr. Sultan Qaboos U., Oman, 1991; chair Woods Hole Workshop, Emerging Infectious Diseases, 1993. Author: A World Guide to Infections: Diseases, Distribution, Diagnosis, 1991; co-editor (with Richard Levins and Andrew Spielman): Disease in Evolution: Global Changes and Emergence of Infectious Diseases, 1994; mem. editl. bd. Current Issues Pub. Health, 1999—2003, Global Change and Human Health, 1999—2003; sect. editor travel medicine and tropical diseases: Infectious Diseases Clin. Practices; mem. editl. bd. Infectious Diseases Clin. Practices, 2006—; assoc. editor: Jour. Watch Infectious Diseases, 1997—; mem. editl. adv. bd. Clin. Infectious Diseases, 1999—2004, spl. sect. editor Emerging Infections, Clinical Infectious Diseases, 2006—. Mem. Cambridge Task Force AIDS, 1987—90; bd. dirs. Horizon Comm., West Cornwall, Conn., 1990—97; mem. Nat. Commn. on Indsl. Farm Animal Prodn., 2006—08; bd. mem. FXB USA, 2007—; bd. sci. counselors Ctr. Disease Ctrl. & Prevention, 2008—; bd. trustees Internat. Ctr. Diarrhea Disease Rsch., Bangladesh, 2009—; bd. dirs. Alliance Prudent Use of Antibiotics, 2010—. Recipient Lewis E. and Edith Phillips award, U. Wis. Med. Sch., 1969, Cora M. and Edward Van Liere award, 1971, Mosby Scholarship Book award, 1971, Leo Blacklow Tchg. award, 1999, Emanuel Wolinsky award, 2008; named to Northwestern Sch. Corp. Disting. Alumni Hall of Fame, 2007; fellow, Ctr. Advanced Study Behavioral Scis., Stanford, Calif., 2002; scholar-in-residence, Bellagio (Italy) Study Ctr., Rockefeller Found., 1996. Fellow: ACP, Royal Soc. Tropical Medicine and Hygiene, Infectious Diseases Soc. Am.; mem.: Am. Soc. Tropical Medicine Hygiene (councilor 2006—10), Soc. for Vector Ecology, Internat. Soc. Travel Medicine, Peabody Soc., Am. Soc. Microbiology, Aesculapian Club, Alpha Omega Alpha, Phi Sigma Iota, Sigma Sigma. Avocations: flute, hiking, reading, travel.

WILSON, MIRIAM GEISENDORFER, retired physician, educator; b. Yakima, Wash., Dec. 3, 1922; d. Emil and Frances Geisendorfer; m. Howard G. Wilson, June 21, 1947; children— Claire, Paula, Geoffrey, Nicola, Marla. BS, U. Wash., Seattle, 1944, MS, 1945; MD, U. Calif., San Francisco, 1950. Mem. faculty U. So. Calif. Sch. Medicine, LA, 1965—, prof. pediatrics, 1969—2004, emeritus prof. pediatrics, 2004—. Office: U So Calif Med Ctr 1129 N State St Rm 1g24 Los Angeles CA 90033-1044 Personal E-mail: mfgwil@verizon.net.

WILSON, MYRON ROBERT, JR., retired psychiatrist; b. Helena, Mont., Sept. 21, 1932; s. Myron Robert, Sr. and Constance Ernestine (Bultman) Wilson. BA, Stanford U., 1954, MD, 1957. Diplomate Am. Bd. Psychiatry and Neurology. Dir. adolescent psychiatry Mayo Clinic, Rochester, Minn., 1965—71; pres., psychiatrist in chief Wilson Ctr., Faribault, Minn., 1971—86, chmn., 1986—90; ret., 1990. Assoc. clin. prof. UCLA, 1985—99. Contbr. articles to profl. jours. Chmn., CEO C. B. Wilson Found., LA, 1972—2006; bd. dirs. Pasadena (Calif.) Symphony Orch. Assn., 1987; vestryman, treas. St. Thomas' Parish, LA, 1993—96. Lt. comdr. USN, 1958—60. Fellow, Mayo Grad. Sch. Medicine, Rochester, 1960—65. Fellow: Internat. Soc. Adolescent Psychiatry (founder, treas. 1985—88, sec. 1985—88, treas. 1988—92), Am. Soc. Adolescent Psychiatry, Am. Psychiat. Assn.; mem.: Order St. John of Jerusalem, Sigma Xi (Mayo Found. chpt.). Episcopalian. Office Phone: 760-325-4956. Personal E-mail: wilsonchababl@aol.com.

WILSON, NANCY JEANNE, laboratory consultant, medical technologist; b. Neptune, NJ, Apr. 17, 1951; d. Harry E. Sr. and Kathryn E. (O'Shea) W. BS, Monmouth Coll., 1975; MPA, Fairleigh Dickinson U., 1988. Cert. assisted living adminstr. NJ Dept. Health, State of NJ. Clin. intern med. tech., staff med. technologist Riverview Med. Ctr., 1975; staff med. technologist Rush Clin. Labs., Red Bank, NJ, 1976, Kimball Med. Ctr., Lakewood, NJ, 1977—78, clin. lab. supr., 1978—86; infection control practice Jersey Shore Med. Ctr., Neptune, N.J., 1990; dir. lab. and diagnostic svcs. Carrier Clinic, Belle Mead, NJ, 1990—2002, lab. and infection control cons., 2002—04, clin. lab. adminstr., infectious control coord., 2004—. Mem. Am. Soc. Clin. Pathologists (diplomate lab. mgmt.), Am. Assn. Clin. Chemistry, Am. Soc. Microbiology, Clin. Lab. Mgmt. Assn., Am. Soc. Clinics Lab. Sci., Assn. for Profls. in Infection Control, Pi Alpha Alpha. Avocations: golf, walking, relaxing. Home: 42 Monument St Freehold NJ 07728-1721 Office Phone: 908-281-1340. Personal E-mail: nwilson@carrierclinic.com.

WILSON, RALPH SLOAN, retinal surgeon; b. El Dorado, Ark., Nov. 12, 1937; s. George Evander and Lauree Eta (Doss) Wilson; m. Sarah Mignon Ross, Dec. 27, 1958; m. Ann Jameson, 1987; children: Ralph Sloan, William Gregory, Steven Robert 1 stepchild, John Matsek. AB, Davidson Coll., 1959; BS, MD, U. Ark., 1963. Diplomate Am. Bd. Ophthalmology. Postgrad. ophthalmology Harvard Med. Sch., Boston, 1964—65; intern U. Ark. Hosps., Little Rock, 1963—64, resident ophthalmology, 1965, U. Tex. Med. Br., Galveston, 1965—67; Heed fellow retinal pathology and surgery Mass. Eye and Ear Infirmary, Harvard Med. Sch., Boston, 1969; asst. prof. and dir. retina svc. dept. ophthalmology U. Ark. Med. Ctr., Little Rock, 1970—75, assoc. prof., 1975—81, prof., 1981—95, prof. emeritus, 1995—, acting chmn. ophthalmology dept., 1974—75; pvt. practice Little Rock, 1975—99; mem. Ark. State Bd. Dispensing Opticians; dir. Retina Svc., US VA Hosp., Little Rock; trustee Lyon Coll., 1982—, student life com. chmn., 1988—97, edn. com. chmn., 2001—. Pres. & bd. dirs. Retinal Rsch. Fund; bd. dirs. Ark. Eye & Kidney Bank, Ark. Soc. Prevention Blindness, 1971—73. Contbr. articles to profl. jours. Served to lt. comdr. USNR, 1967—69. Recipient Physicians Recognition award, AMA, 1969—99; Hoffmann La Roche grant, 1966—67. Mem.: AAUP, AMA, Assn. Mil. Surgeons, Ark. Ophthalmology Sect. Ark. Med. Soc. (pres. 1977—78), Assn. VA Ophthalmologists, Ark. Found. Med. Care, Ark. Acad. Ophthalmology (pres. 1975—76), Retina Soc., Little Rock Acad. Surgery, Soc. Heed Fellows, U. Med. Group, U. Tex. Med. Br. Ophthalmology Alumni Assn. (pres. 1970—72), Internat. Eye Found., Soc. Eye Surgeons, New Orleans Acad. Ophthalmology, Soc. Boliviana Oftalmologia, Soc. Française d'Ophthalmologie, Pan Am. Soc. Ophthalmology, Southern Med. Assn., Rsch. Prevent Blindness, Am. Ophthal. Soc. (athletic chmn.), Ark. Assns. Ophthalmology, Pulaski County Med. Socs., Assn. Rsch. and Vision Ophthalmology, Am. Acad. Retinal Surgeons (charter mem.), Am. Acad. Ophthalmology (spkrs. bur., pub. info. com. mem. 1986—96, chmn., com. on drugs 1990—96, Hon. award, Sr. Hon. award), Sigma Xi, Alpha Tau Omega, Alpha Omega Alpha. Achievements include research in ocular melanomas, ocular fireworks injuries, mechanism of human accomodation and multiple ocular surgical techniques; patents in field. Home: 140 Washington Rd Rye NH 03870 Personal E-mail: cottagers@comcast.net. E-mail: cottagers@aol.com.

WILSON, RAYMOND ERNEST, surgeon; s. Victor Mills and Sarah Wilson; m. Doreen Alice Bunting, July 10, 1968; children: Andrew William, Caroline Sarah Walker, Stephen Raymond, Philip Boyd. MBBS with hons., U. Sydney, 1966. Lic. physician NSW Med. Bd., 1966, Queensland Med. Bd., 2005. Resident med. officer Royal Prince Alfred Hosp., Sydney, Nsw, 1966—67; surg. registrar South Shields Gen. Hosp., 1968—69; sr. surg. registrar Royal Victoria Hosp., Belfast, Northern Ireland, 1969—70; gen. practitioner Blakehurst Med. Practice, Sydney, 1971—2004; specialist skin surgeon Australian Skin Cancer Group, Sydney, 2004—05, Solarderm, Brisbane, Australia, 2005—. Vis. surgeon Hurstville (Australia) Cmty. Hosp., 1971—2004, mem. surg. com., 1980—94; tutor clin. surgery U. NSW, Sydney, 1976—86. Author: Jenner of George Street, 2000; contbr. Spotlight on Israel; contbr. scientific papers to Med. Jour. Australia, articles to profl. publs. Elder Bexley Christian Assembly, Sydney, 1978—2005, Bethany Christian Assembly, Brisbane. Fellow: Royal Coll. Surgeons Edinburgh, Royal Australasian Coll. Surgeons; mem.: Australian Med. Assn. Home: 10 Jabiru Drive Queensland Mango Hill 4509 Australia

WILSON, RICHARD K., microbiologist, researcher; AB in Microbiology, Miami U., 1981; PhD in Biochemistry, U. Okla., 1986. Rsch. fellow Calif. Inst. Technol., 1986—90; prof. genetics & molecular microbiology Washington U. Sch. Medicine, 1990—, dir. Genome Sequencing Ctr., 1990—; founder & mng. dir. Orion Genomics, 1998—; researcher Siteman Cancer Ctr. Contbr. of several articles to profl. journals. Office: The Genome Center Washington University School of Medicine 4444 Forest Park Ave Campus Box 8501 Saint Louis MO 63108 Office Phone: 314-286-1804. Office Fax: 314-286-1810. Business E-Mail: rwilson@wustl.edu.

WILSON, ROBERTA BUSH, retired psychotherapist, accountant; b. Watertown, NY, Dec. 23, 1937; d. Robert King and Barbara P. (Wiggins) Banks; m. Marvin D. Bush, Feb. 28, 1959 (div. 1977); m. Asa A. Wilson, July 29, 2004. BA, Glenville State Coll., 1977; MS, W.Va. U., Morgantown, 1985. Lic. profl. therapist W.Va. Acct. GE Plastics, Parkensburg, W.Va., 1959—77; lit. vol. Parkensburg, 1977—89; outpatient site head Abraxas, Parkensburg, 1989—95; psychotherapist Westbrook Health Svc., Parkensburg, 1996—97; ret., 1997. Pres., bd. dirs. Lit. Vol. Program of Wood County, Parkersburg. Mem.: Profl. Women's Assn. (pres., bd. dirs., Hall of Fame 1995). Episcoplian. Avocations: gardening, travel, photography. Home: 915 Lenore St Parkersburg WV 26101-6160

WILSON, SAMUEL MAYHEW, surgeon; b. Phila., June 26, 1950; m. Dorothy Hay Barrus, June 9, 1990; children: Elisabeth, Mary. BA, Swarthmore Coll., Pa., 1972; MS, Drexel U., Phila., 1975; MD, Temple U., Phila., 1979. Diplomate Am. Bd. Surgery. Resident in surgery Temple U. Hosp., Phila., 1979-84; fellow in vascular surgery Presbyn.-U. Pa. Med. Ctr., 1984-86; attending surgeon Evang. Cmty. Hosp., Lewisburg, 1986-88, Albert Einstein Med. Ctr., Phila., 1988-95. Attending surgeon Elkins Park Hosp., Pa., 1988-95, Frankford Hosp., Phila., 1988-95, JFK Meml. Hosp., Phila., 1988-95; staff surgeon Bayhealth Med. Ctr.-Kent Gen. Hosp., Dover, 1996-2010, staff surgeon, laurens Country Health Care Sys. Clinton, SC, 2011-, chair dept. surgery, 2006-07, med. exec. com., 2005-07, sec./treas., 2005-06; asst. clin. instr. surgery U. Pa. Med. Sch., Phila., 1984-85, assoc. clin. instr., 1985-86; clin. instr. surgery Temple U. Sch. Medicine, Phila., 1988-95; sec.-treas. med. exec. com. Kent Gen. Hosp., 2005-06. Contbr. articles to profl. jours. Active Christ Episcopal Ch., Dover, 1996—2010, vestry, 2005-07, Corp. USMCR, 1972-78. Fellow ACS, Southeastern Surg. Congress; mem. AMA (Physician Recognition award), Delaware Valley Vascular Soc., Ea. Vascular Soc. Avocations: sailing, skiing, hiking, photography, reading. Office: 1012 Med Ridge Rd Clinton SC 29325 Office Phone: 864-833-3852.

WILSON, SHANDRA SHEPPARD, urologist; b. Wheatrige, Colo., Mar. 9, 1972; d. Sharon Marie and William David Sheppard; m. David Alliott Wilson; children: Amanda Nicole, Andrew Gabriel. BA, Denver U., 1993; BS; MD, Washington U., St. Louis, 1997. Resident U. Southern Calif., LA, 2000—03; fellow, urology, oncology U. Colo., 2003—04, asst. prof. Aurora, 2004—. Presenter in field. Contbr. articles to profl. jours. Local Bladder Cancer grant, U. Colo., 2006. Mem.: Am. Urologic Assn. Avocations: hiking, camping. Home: 16 Mountain Willow Dr Littleton CO 80127 Office: Univ Colorado HSC 12631 E 17th Ave MS 319 Aurora CO 80045 Office Fax: 720-848-0170; Home Fax: 720-848-0180. Business E-Mail: shandra.wilson@ucdenver.edu.

WILSON, THOMAS JOSEPH, insurance company executive; b. 1957; m. Jill Garling; 3 children. BSBA, U. Mich., 1979; M of Mgmt., Northwestern U., 1980. Various fin. positions Amoco Corp., Chgo., 1980-86; mng. dir. mergers and acquisitions Dean Witter Reynolds, Chgo., 1986-93; v.p. strategy and analysis Sears, Roebuck and Co., Chgo., 1993-95; sr. v.p., CFO Allstate Corp., Northbrook, Ill., 1995-98; chmn., pres. Allstate Fin., 1999—2002; pres. Allstate Protection, 2003—05; pres., COO Allstate Corp., Northbrook, Ill., 2005—06, pres., CEO, 2007—08, chmn., pres., CEO, 2008—. Bd.

dirs. The Allstate Corp., 2006—. Bd. dirs. Rush-Presbyn.-St. Luke's Med. Ctr. and Fed. Res. Bank Chgo. Office: The Allstate Corp 2775 Sanders Rd Northbrook IL 60062-6110 *

WILSON, TIMOTHY D., psychology professor; BA in Psychology, Hampshire Coll., Amherst, Mass., 1973; MA in Psychology, U. Mich., Ann Arbor, 1975, PhD in Psychology, 1977. Rsch. asst., Hwy. Safety Rsch. Inst. U. Mich., 1974, rsch. asst., Inst. Social Rsch., 1974—77, tchg. asst., 1975—76; asst. prof. Duke U., Durham, 1977—79, U. Va., Charlottesville, 1979—84, assoc. prof., 1984—93, assoc. chair dept. psychology, 1987—88, prof., 1993—2001, dir. grad. studies, 1995—97, 1998—99, chair dept. psychology, 2001—04, Sherrell J. Aston prof. psychology, 2001—. Co-author (with E. Aronson, R. Akert): Social Psychology: The Heart and the Mind, 1994, 2d edit., 1997, 3d edit., 1998, Can. edit., 2001, 4th edit., 2002, 5th edit., 2005, Can. 3d edit., 2007, 6th edit., 2007; author: Strangers to Ourselves: Discovering the Adaptive Unconscious, 2002; assoc. editor: Jour. Personality and Social Psychology: Attitudes and Social Cognition, 1999—2001; contbr. articles to profl. jours., ad hoc reviews to profl. jours. Grantee, NSF, 1986—, Nat. Inst. Mental Health, 1986—2007, Russell Sage Found., 2005—08; vis. scholar, U. Wash., 1986, Stanford U., 1992; vis. faculty mem., U. BC, 2008. Fellow: Am. Psychol. Soc., Soc. Personality and Social Psychology; mem.: APA, Am. Acad. Arts & Sciences, Soc. Exptl. Social Psychology, Internat. Soc. Self and Identity, Assn. the Scientific Study Consciousness, Phi Beta Kappa. Office: U Va Dept Psychology 102 Gilmer Hall PO Box 400400 Charlottesville VA 22904-4400 Office Phone: 434-924-0674. Office Fax: 434-982-4766. Business E-Mail: twilson@virginia.edu.

WILSON, VALERIE PETIT, health science association director; b. New Orleans, Jan. 24, 1950; d. Alvin Joseph and Lorraine Catherine (Kelly) Petit; children: Daniel Lawrence, Craig Anthony. BS, Xavier U. La., 1970; PhD, Johns Hopkins U., 1976. Dir. policy USPHS, Washington, 1990—92, dept. dir., 1992, asst. dir. nat. AIDS policy office, 1992—93; dir. health scis. policy Inst. Medicine Nat. Acad. Scis., Washington, 1993—98; dep. dir. Tulane/Xavier Ctr. Bio-Environ. Rsch., New Orleans, 1998—2003; exec. dir. leadership alliance, clin. prof. cmty. health Brown U., Providence, 2004—. Cons. NIH, Fairfax County Schs. Contbr. articles to profl. jours. Mem. AAAS, Am. Soc. Biochemists and Molecular Biologists. Avocations: quilting, gardening. Office: Brown U Leadership Alliance Cranston RI 02920-2699 Home Phone: 401-228-8642; Office Phone: 401-863-1474. Business E-Mail: valerie_wilson@brown.edu.

WILSON, VICTORIA JANE SIMPSON, medical/surgical nurse; b. Floresville, Tex., Nov. 30, 1952; d. Joseph Eugene and Eva Gertrude (Ferguson) Simpson; m. Richard Royce Wilson, May 15, 1976; children: Sarah Beth, Nathan Lawrence. BSN, U. Cen. Ark., 1977; MS in Nursing, Northwestern State U., 1981; attending, U. Ark., Little Rock. Charge nurse surg. St. Vincent Infirmary, Little Rock; staff nurse ICU La. State U. Med. Ctr., Shreveport, La.; patient edn. coord. White River Med. Ctr., Batesville, Ark.; co-owner, CEO Health Plus, Stuttgart, Ark.; co-owner Wilson Enterprises, Humphrey, Ark., 1992—99; prin. nurse St. Vincent Health Sys., 2000—01; mem. faculty Southeast Ark. Coll., 2000; Level I coord. faculty Jefferson Sch. Nursing, Pine Bluff, Ark., 2001—06; instr. U. Ark., Pine Bluff, 2006—07; staff nurse U. Ark. Med. Scis., 2007—. Mem.: ANA, Nat. League Nursing, Ark. Nurses Assn., Sigma Theta Tau. Home: 51 Wilson Ln Humphrey AR 72073-9097 Office Phone: 870-830-5442.

WILSON, WAYNE JAMES, science educator, researcher; b. Brisbane, Australia, Dec. 4, 1970; s. James McKendrick and Vicki Hazel Wilson. BSc with honors, U. Queensland, 1991, PGDipAud, 1993; PhD, U. Witwatersrand, Johannesburg, 2001. Diploma in co. directorship Australian Inst. Co. Dirs., Brisbane, 2008; cert. in clin. practice Audiol. Soc. Australia, 1996. Clin. audiologist Queensland Neurootology Clinic, 1993—96, Starship Childrens' Hosp., Auckland, New Zealand, 2001—02; lectr. in audiology U. Witwatersrand, Johannesburg, 1996—2001, U. Auckland, 2001—02, U. Queensland, 2002—. Co-chair ctrl. auditory processing task force Health Professions Coun. South Africa, Johannesburg, 1999—2002; reviewer various sci. jours., 2000—; presenter in field. Contbr. more than 50 articles to profl. jours. Grantee, U. Witwatersrand, 1998, 1998-2001, 1999, U. Queensland, 2003-2004, 2004, 2004-2005, 2007—09, U. Hong Kong, 2007—09, The John and Mark Kibble Trust, 2004-2005, Australian Rsch. Coun. First-link Fund, 2005-2006, Symbiosis Group Ltd., 2007—, Australian Gov.'s Comet, 2007, Australian Gov.'s Comready, 2007—08, Queensland and NHMRC Equip, Queensland Med. DEvel. Incentive, 2008; numerous grants. Mem.: Pacific Soc. for Study of Speech, Language and Hearing, Audiol. Soc. Australia. Office: University Queensland Divsn Audiology St Lucia 4072 Queensland Brisbane Australia Office Fax: +61 7 3365 1877. Business E-Mail: w.wilson@uq.edu.au.

WILSON, WILLIAM HARWELL, psychiatrist, educator; b. Memphis, Feb. 6, 1951; s. Joseph Harwell Wilson and Helen Wilson (Cobb) Carruthers; m. Paula Rea, Oct. 18, 1986; children: Rea Xan, Sanford Shepherd. BA, Brown U., 1973; MD, U. Pa., 1981. Diplomate Am. Bd. Psychiatry and Neurology, Nat. Bd. Med. Examiners. Resident in psychiatry U. Wis., Madison, 1981-85; asst. prof. psychiatry U. Pitts. Sch. Medicine, 1985-86, Med. Coll. Pa., Phila., 1986-89, Oreg. Health Scis. U., Portland, 1989—93, asst. dir. pub. psychiatry tng. program, 1989—94, assoc. prof. psychiatry, 1993—2003, prof. psychiatry, 2003—. Dir. prof. edn. unit Dammasch State Hosp., Wilsonville, Oreg., 1989-94; attending psychiatrist Oreg. Health Scis. U. Hosp., 1994—; dir. Inpatient Psychiatric Svc., 2002-11; supr. Outpatient Clin. Svcs., 2011-. Contbr. numerous articles on treatment of schizophrenia to sci. jours. Grantee NIMH, 1989-93; Recipient of Mental Health award of Excellence, State Oreg. Disting. fellow Am. Psychiat. Assn.; mem. Soc. for Biol. Psychiatry, Psychiatry, World Fedn. Mental Health, Nat. Alliance for Mentally Ill (Exemplary Psychiatrist award 1992, 98), Am. Soc. Clin. Psychopharmacology. Office: Oreg Health Scis U Mail Code UHN-80 3181 SW Sam Jackson Park Rd Portland OR 97239-3011 Office Phone: 503-494-7353. Business E-Mail: wilsonw@ohsu.edu.

WILSON, WILLIAM JULIUS, sociology educator; b. Derry Twp., Pa., Dec. 20, 1935; s. Esco and Pauline (Bracy) W.; m. Mildred Marie Hood, Aug. 31, 1957; children: Colleen, Lisa; m. Beverly Ann Huebner, Aug. 30, 1970; children: Carter, Paula. BA, Wilberforce U., 1958; MA, Bowling Green State U., 1961; PhD, Wash. State U., 1966; LHD (hon.), U. Mass., 1982, L.I. U., 1982, Columbia Coll., Santa Clara U., Loyola Coll., 1988, De Paul U., 1989; LLD (hon.), Marquette U., Mt. Holyoke Coll., 1989; LHD (hon.), New Sch. for Social Rsch., 1991, Bard Coll., 1992, John Jay Sch. Criminal Justice, 1992, U. Pa., 1993, So. Ill. U., 1993, Northwestern U., 1993, Bowling Green State U., 1994, SUNY, Binghamton, 1994, Princeton U., 1995, Columbia U., Rutgers U., Haverford Coll., 1996, Johns Hopkins U., Morehouse Coll., Niagara U., 1997, Dartmouth Coll., 1997, U. Amsterdam, 1998, Clarion U., 1999, Colgate U., 1999, Clark U., 1999, Bates Coll., 1999; D (hon.), Northeastern U., 1999, Macalester Coll. Ohio State U., 2001; DHL (hon.), Occidental Coll., 2001, Rensselaer Poly. Inst., 2001, Lawrence U., 2001, U Miami, 2002, others. Asst. prof. U. Mass., Amherst, 1965-69, assoc. prof., 1969-71; vis. asso. prof. U. Chgo., 1971-72, assoc. prof. dept. sociology, 1972-75, prof., 1975—, chmn. dept. sociology, 1978—, Lucy Flower prof. urban sociology, 1980-84, Lucy Flower disting. service prof., 1984—; Lucy Flower univ. prof., 1990-96; Malcolm Wiener Prof. of social policy Harvard U., 1996-98, Lewis P. and Linda L. Geyser Univ. Prof., 1998—. Mem. bd. univ. publs. U. Chgo. Press, 1975-79; bd. dirs. Ctr. for Nat. Policy, 1987-92, Ctr. Budget and Policy Priorities, 1987—, Ctr. for Advanced Study of Behavioral Scis., 1988-2002, Twentieth Century Fund (now called Century Found., 1992—, Jerome Levy Inst., 1992-2002, Manpower Demonstration Rsch. Corp., 1993—; bd. dirs. Pub./Pvt. Ventures, Phila., 1994-2002, 02-. Author: Power, Racism and Privilege, 1973, Through Different Eyes, 1973, The Declining Significance of Race, 1978, The Truly Disadvantaged, 1987, The Ghetto Underclass, 1993, Sociology and the Public Agenda, 1993, When Work Disappears, 1996 (award Sidney Hillman Found. 1997), The Bridge Over the Racial Divide, 1999. Bd. dirs. Social Sci. Rsch. Coun., 1979-84, Chgo. Urban League, 1983-97, Spencer Found., 1987-97, George M. Pullman Found., 1986-93, Russell Sage Found., 1989-98, Nat. Humanities Ctr., 1990-95, PolicyLink, 2000-; mem. Com. on Sci., Engring. and Pub. Policy, NAS, 1995-2001; nat. bd. dirs. A. Philip Randolph Inst., 1981-, Inst. Rsch. on Poverty, 1983-87; trustee Spelman Coll., 1989-98, Bard Coll., 2001-;bd. govs. Levy Econs. Inst., 2001-; mem. Pres. Commn. on White House Fellowships, 1994-2001; mem. Pres. Com. Nat. Medal Sci., 1994-98; trustee Wilberforce U.; bd. advisors Frederick D. Patterson Rsch. Inst., 1995-, United Negro Coll. Fund, 1996—; mem. scholars' coun. Libr. of Congress, 2002-, coun. academic advisors Congl. Black Caucus Found., 2003-. With U.S. Army, 1958-60. Recipient Disting. Tchr. of Year award U. Mass., Amherst, 1970, Regents Disting. Alumnus award Wash. State U., 1988, Burton Gordon Feldman award Brandeis U., 1991, Frank E. Seidman Disting. award in polit. econ., 1994, Martin Luther King Jr. Nat. award, 1998, Nat. Medal of Sci. 1998, A. Philip Randolph/Bayard Rustin Humanitarian award, 2003; MacArthur Prize fellow, 1987. Fellow AAAS, Am. Acad. Polit. and Social Sci., Am. Acad. Arts and Scis. (Talcott Parsons Social Scis. prize, 2003); mem. NAS, Nat. Acad. Edn., Am. Philos. Soc., Inst. of Medicine, Brit. Acad., Am. Sociol. Assn. (pres. 1989-90, com. for pub. understanding of sociology award 1998, Sydney M. Spivack award 1977, DuBois, Johnson, Frazier award 1990, Lester F. Ward Disting. Contbns. to Applied Sociology award 1998), Soc. for Study Social Problems (C. Wright Mills award 1988), Sociol. Rsch. Assn. (pres. 1987-88), Consortium of Social Sci. Assn. (pres. 1993-94), Internat. Sociol. Assn., Chgo. Urban League (Beautiful People award 1979). Democrat. Home: 75 Cambridge Pkwy Unit E406 Cambridge MA 02142-1229 Office: John F Kennedy Sch Govt Harvard Univ 79 John F Kennedy St Cambridge MA 02138-5801

WILSON, WILLIAM PRESTON, retired psychiatrist; b. Fayetteville, NC, Nov. 6, 1922; s. Preston Puckett and Rosa Mae (VanHook) W.; m. Dorothy Elizabeth Taylor, Aug. 21, 1950; children: William Preston, Benjamin V., Karen E., Tammy E., Robert E. BS, Duke U., 1943, MD, 1947. Diplomate Am. Bd. Psychiatry and Neurology (examiner). Intern Gorgas Hosp., Ancon, Panama; from resident psychiatry to prof. emeritus Duke U. Med. Ctr., Durham, NC, emeritus prof. psychiatry, 1985—; assoc. prof. psychiatry, dir. psychiat. rsch. U. Tex. Med. Br., Galveston, 1958-60; dir. Inst. Christian Growth, Durham, NC, 1985—; dist. prof. counseling Carolina Grad. Divinity Sch., Greenshore, NC, 1996—2007; ret., 2007. Chief neurophysiol. labs. VA Hosp., Durham, N.C., 1961-76; sec. Am. Bd. Qualification in Electroencephalography, 1971-77; mem. N.C. Gov.'s Task force on Diagnosis and Treatment; mem. med. adv. com. N.C. Found. Mental Health Rsch.; bd. dirs. nat. divsn. Contact Teleminstry USA, also mem. internat. commn. healing; cons. numerous area hosps.; Finch lectr. Fuller Theol. Sem., Pasadena, Calif., 1974; vis. prof. psychiatry Marshall U. Sch. Medicine, Huntington, W.Va., 1985-89. Co-author: The Grace to Grow; editor: Applications of Electroencephalography in Psychiatry; co-editor: EEG and Evoked Potentials in Psychiatry and Behavioral Neurology; contbr. articles to med. jours.; Author: The Nuts and Bolts of discipleship. Mem. ofcl. bd. Asbury United Meth. Ch., Durham; mem. program and curriculum com. United Meth. Ch., 1973-81; trustee Meth. Retirement Home, Durham; pres. United Meth. Renewal Svcs., Inc., 1978-82. Served with AUS, 1943-46. Recipient Ephraim McDowell award Christian Med. Found., 1982, Pioneer in Christian Psychiatry award Congress on Christian Counseling, 1988; named Educator of Yr., Christian Med. and Dental Assn., 1996, Pres. Heritage award, 2011; EEG Montreal Neurol. Inst. fellow, 1954-55, postdoctoral fellow NIMH. Mem. Am. Psychiat. Assn., So. Psychiat. Assn. (pres. 1977-78), AMA, So. Med. Assn. (chmn. sect. neurology and psychiatry 1970), Med. Soc. N.C., Durham-Orange County Med. Soc. (chmn. student recruitment com. 1965), Soc. Biol. Psychiatry, Am. EEG Soc. (councillor), So. EEG Soc. (pres. 1964), Assn. Rsch. Nervous and Mental Diseases, Am. Epilepsy Soc., AAAS, Am. Acad. Neurology, Sigma Xi, Alpha Omega Alpha, U.S. Power Squadron Club (comdr. Durham 1971), AACC Republican. Home and Office: 1209 Virginia Ave Durham NC 27705-3263 Personal E-mail: williamwilson622@gmail.com.

WILSON-COSTELLO, DEANNE E., pediatrician, educator; b. Warren, Ohio, June 18, 1964; BS, Grove City Coll., Pa., 1991; MD, Wright State U., 1991. Prof., pediat. Rainbow Babies and Children's Hosp., 1991—, dir., high risk follow-up, 1997. Named one of Top Dr., Top Drs. Inc. Fellow: Am. Acad. Pediat. Avocations: violin, piano, baseball. Home: 16771 Staffordshire Ct Chagrin Falls OH 44023 Home Fax: 216-844-3380. Personal E-mail: drfjcmd@aol.com.

WILT, JEFFREY LYNN, pulmonary and critical care physician, educator; b. Fairmont, W.Va., Nov. 15, 1963; s. Paul Lynn and Linda (Amos) W. BA, U. Mich., 1986, MD, 1988. Diplomate Am. Bd. Internal Medicine, Am. Bd. Pulmonary Diseases, Am. Bd. Critical Care Medicine, Am. Bd. Med. Examiners, Am. Bd. Nutrition Support; cert. ACLS instr. Fellow sect. pulmonary and critical care medicine W.Va. U., Morgantown, 1992-95; resident in internal medicine Blodgett-St. Mary's Hosp., Grand Rapids, Mich., 1988-91, chief med. resident in internal medicine, 1990-91; asst. dir. internal medicine residency St. Mary's Hosp., Grand Rapids, 1991-92; pvt. practice, Grand Rapids, 1995—. Asst. dir. med. ICU, Blodgett Meml. Med. Ctr., co-dir. transitional residency, 1997-98, COO internal medicine residency, 1998, program dir., 1998-99; assoc. program dir. internal medicine residency Mich. State U., Grand Rapids, 1999—, asst. prof. medicine, 1999-2003, assoc. prof., 2003—. Fellow ACP (Nat. Clin. Vignette winner 1991), Am. Coll. Chest Physicians (Young Investigators award 1993); mem. AMA, Am. Thoracic Soc., Soc. Crit. Care Medicine. Republican. Avocations: bicycling, Tae Kwon Do, magic, reading, chess. Home: 4995 Sequoia Dr SE Grand Rapids MI 49512-9622 Office: 1900 Wealthy St SE Ste 150 Grand Rapids MI 49506-2969

WILTROUT, ROBERT H., federal agency administrator, medical researcher; b. Kutztown, Pa., Sept. 13, 1950; BA, Kutztown U., 1972; MS in microbiology, Pa. State U., U. Park, 1975; PhD in immunology, Wayne State U., Detroit, 1979; studied, Queens U., Kingston, Ontario, Can., 1981. Postdoctoral studies Lab. Immunodiagnosis NIH, Bethesda, Md.; staff fellow Biol. Response Modifiers Program Nat. Cancer Inst., NIH, Bethesda, Md., head exptl. therapeutics sect. of Lab. Expt. Immunology, 1986—, prin. dep. dir. Ctr. for Cancer Rsch., 2002—05, dir. Ctr. for Cancer Rsch., 2005—, sci. dir. basic rsch. Ctr. for Cancer Rsch. Fellow USPHS, 1979. Mem.: Soc. Biol. Therapy, Soc. Leukocyte Biology, Am. Assn. Cancer Rsch., Am. Assn. Immunology. Office: Ctr for Cancer Rsch Nat Cancer Inst 31 Center Dr, Bldg 31, Rm 3A11 Bethesda MD 20892 Office Phone: 301-496-4345. E-mail: wiltrour@mail.nih.gov. *

WIMALASENA, JAY, medical researcher, educator; b. Sri Lanka, June 7, 1946; MB, U. Southampton, 1970; PhD, U. Colo. Med. Ctr., 1978. Asst. prof. U. Nebr. Med. Sch., 1986—92; prof. U. Tex. Med. Ctr., 1992—. Sci. editor Endocrine Related Cancer Jour., 2005. Numerous grants, NIH, Am. Cancer Soc. Mem.: AAAS, Endocrine Soc., Am. Soc. Biochemistry and Molecular Biology, Am. Assn. Cancer Rsch. Avocation: travel. Office: University Tex Med Ctr 1924 Alcoa Hwy Knoxville TN 37920 Office Fax: 865-305-6863. Business E-Mail: jwimalas@utmck.edu.

WIMMER, MARKUS ANTON, biomedical engineer, educator; PhD, Tech. U. Hamburg, Germany, 1999. Rsch. Arbeitsgemeinschaft Osteosynthesefragen Rsch. Inst., Davos, Switzerland, 1997—2001; assoc. prof., sect. dir. Rush Med. Ctr., Chgo, 2001—. Office: Rush Med Ctr 1653 W Congress Pkwy Ste 1417 Chicago IL 60612 Business E-Mail: markus_a_wimmer@rush.edu.

WINAWER, SIDNEY J., physician, educator; b. NYC; s. Nathan and Sally Winawer; children: Daniel, Jonathan, Joanna. BA, NYU, 1952; MD, SUNY, 1956; DSc (hon.), SUNY Downstate Med. Ctr., 2005. Asst. in medicine Harvard Med. Sch., Boston, 1962—66; asst. physician Harvard Med. Svc. Boston City Hosp., 1964—66; with Meml. Sloan-Kettering Cancer Ctr., NYC, 1968—, chief gastroent. and nutrition svc., 1978—98, mem. with tenure of title, 1988—, Paul Sherlock chair, 1991—; prof. medicine Cornell U. Coll. Medicine, NYC, 1980—, dir. integrative oncology program, 1997—98. Head Ctr Prevention Cancer WHO, Geneva, 1985—2000; liaison rep Nat Cancer Adv Bd, Washington, 1984—89; mem adv comt cancer prevention Am Cancer Soc, 1988—90; mem sci adv bd ICRF; consult varios rev comts Nat Cancer Inst, Washington. Editor: (book) Prevention Colorectal Cancer, 1980, Basic and Clinical Perspectives of Colorectal Polyps and Cancer, 1988, Lar Bowel Cancers: Policy, Prevention, Research and Treatment, 1991, Management of Gastrointestinal Disease, 1992, Gastrointestinal Cancer, 1992, Cancer of the Colon, Rectum and Anus, 1994, Cancer Free, 1995, Healing Lessons, 1998; contbr. chapters to books, articles to profl jours. Capt USAF, 1959—61. Recipient Clin. Achievement award, Meml. Sloan Kettering Cancer Ctr., 1997, Alumni award, 1998, SUNY Downstate Med. Ctr., 2000, Disting. Gastroenterology award, SUNY, 2003, Constantine Medal, Italian Govt., 2002, Internat. Laurel award, Cancer Rsch. and Prevention Found., 2004, others, Disting. Achievement award, 2010; grantee Nat. Cancer Inst., 1974, 1977, 1980, 1985, 1988, 1990, 1993, 1999, 2003. Master: Am. Coll. Gastroenterology (pres. 1979—80, Baker Presdl. lectr. 1992, Disting. Sci. Achievement award 1982, Clin. Achievement award 1997); fellow: ACP; mem.: Internat. Digestive Cancer Alliance (co-chair), NY Soc Gastrointestinal Endoscopy (founder, pres. 1978—79, ann. lectr. 1985, Florence Lefcourt disting. svc. award 2006, Florence Lefcourt State of the Art award 2006), Am. Assn. Cancer Rsch., Am. Soc. Clin. Oncology (Am. Cancer Soc. award 2001), Am. Gastroentrol. Assn. (nat. chmn. cancer sect. 1989—91, U.S. multisoc. colorectal cancer task force, Joseph B. Kirsner award 1999, Disting. Achievement award 2011), Am. Soc. Gastrointestinal Endoscopy (bd. dirs. 1974—78, disting. lectr. 1985, co-chair guidelines com. 1997—, Schindler award 1994). Jewish. Avocations: music, cross country skiing, dance, swimming, bicycling. Office: Meml Sloan-Kettering Cancer Ctr 1275 York Ave New York NY 10021-6094 Home: 1275 York Ave New York NY 10021 Office Phone: 212-639-7678. Business E-Mail: winawers@mskcc.org.

WINCHESTER-DIDSBURY, ETHEL A., chaplain, counselor, educator, theologian; b. Tucson, Ariz., Oct. 7, 1939; d. Russell Crayden and Ethel M. (Birmingham) Winchester; children: Crayden E. Didsbury, Lawrence J. Didsbury, Catherine M. Bean, Teresa M. Anspach. BS, U. Houston, 1975; M in Theol. Studies, St. Mary's Sem., Houston, 1977, MA in Theology, 1980; DMin, Grad. Theol. Found., 1993. Lic. chem. dependence counselor Tex.; bd. cert. chaplain Assn. Profl. Chaplains. Educator, theology dept. head, campus ministry St. Agnes Acad., Houston, 1970—77; educator religious studies, bioethics, psychology Duchesne Acad., Houston, 1978—91; fellow Oxford U., England, 1991; educator scripture and ministry Diocese of Galveston-Houston, 1991—92; chaplain, educator, counselor Valley Bapt. Med. Ctr., Harlingen, Tex., 1993—94, Diocese of Brownsville, Tex., 1994—, Brownsville Med. Ctr., 1994—98, Valley Regional Med. Ctr., Brownsville, 1994—2003; dir., developer, educator, pastoral care provider, counselor L'Peregrine, Brownsville, 2003—. Mem. ethics com. Valley Regional Med. Ctr., Brownsville, 1995—, mem. Inst. Rsch. Bd. com./rsch., 2000—; presenter in field. Author: My Left Hand: An Anthology of Stories, 1993; co-author (with Ann Umscheid): (cdp) Mother St. Andrew Feltin: From the Past into the Future within the Present, 1992; contbr. articles to profl. jours., papers to confs. and seminars. Mem.: Assn. Clin. Pastoral Edn. (clin. mem.), S. Tex. Cath. Chaplains Network (co-founder, facilitator), Soc. Biblical Studies, Brownsville Healthy Cmtys. Initiative (health com. 1995—), Cameron County Task Force on Family Violence (com. mem. 1998—), Nat. Assn. Cath. Chaplains, Assn. Profl. Chaplains (state cert. com. 2002, 2003), Nat. Assn. Addiction Profls., Tex. Assn. Addiction Profls., Valley Assn. Addiction Profls. (treas., v.p.), Am. Acad. Religion. Roman Catholic. Avocations: nature, environment, hiking, gardening, writing. Office: L Peregrine PO Box 5107 Brownsville TX 78523

WINCOR, MICHAEL Z., psychopharmacology educator, clinician, researcher, director; b. Chgo., Feb. 9, 1946; s. Emanuel and Rose (Kershner) Wincor; m. Emily E.M. Smythe; children: Meghan Heather, Katherine Rose. SB in Zoology, U. Chgo., 1966; PharmD, U. So. Calif., 1978. Rsch. project specialist U. Chgo. Sleep Lab., 1968-75; psychiat. pharmacist Brotman Med. Ctr., Culver City, Calif., 1979-83; asst. prof. U. So. Calif., LA, 1983-97, assoc. prof., 1997—, interim chair dept. pharmacy, 2001—02, assoc. dean external programs, 2003—06, dir. continuing pharmacy edn. and internat. programs, 2006—09; assoc. dean Globalization & Continuing Profl. Devel., 2009—. Cons. Fed. Bur. Prisons Drug Abuse Program, Terminal Island, Calif., 1978—81, Nat. Inst. Drug Abuse, Bethesda, Md., 1981, The Upjohn Co., Kalamazoo, 1982—87, 1991—92, Area XXIV Profl. Stds. Rev. Orgn., LA, 1983, Brotman Med. Ctr., Culver City, Calif., 1983—88, SmithKline Beecham Pharms., Phila., 1990—93, Tokyo Coll. Pharmacy, 1991, 2008—10, G.D. Searle & Co., Chgo., 1992—97, 1999—2001, Pfizer, NY, 1998—2004, Wyeth-Ayerst, Phila., 1999—2001, Novartis, East Hanover, NJ, 2002—04, AstraZeneca, Wilmington, Del., 2003—04, Nat. Assn. Bd. Pharmacy Continuing Profl. Devel. Com., 2003—04, Sanofi-Aventis, 2004—08, Takeda Pharms. N.Am., Inc., 2005—08, Meijo U., 2006, Showa Pharm U., 2007—08, U. Kebangsaan Malaysia, 2007, Cyberjaya U., Coll. Med. Scis., 2009, Nat. Taiwan U., 2010, China Med. U., 2010, Kaoshing Med. U., 2010. Contbr. more than 75 articles to profl. jours., chpts. to books, papers presented at nat. and internat. meetings and reviewer. Mem. adv. coun. Franklin Avenue Sch., 1986-89; bd. dirs. K.I. Children's Ctr., 1988-89; trustee Sequoyah Sch., 1992-93; mem. tech. com. Ivanhoe Sch., 1993-96; U. So. Calif. Amb., 2000—. Faculty scholar U. So. Calif. Sch. Pharmacy, 1978; recipient Cert. Appreciation Mayor of LA, 1981, Bristol Labs award, 1978, DuPont Pharma Innovative Pharmacy Practice award, 1995, Pharmacy Coun. Mental Health award, 1996, Outstanding Chpt. Advisor award Am. Pharm. Assn.-Acad. Students of Pharmacy, 2003. Mem. Am. Coll. Clin. Pharmacy (chmn. constn. and bylaws com. 1983-84, mem. credentials com. 1991-93, 95-97, edtl. affairs com. 1994, constn. and bylaws com. 1999-00), Am. Assn. Colls. Pharmacy (focus group on liberalization profl. curriculum 1990-92, mem. pharmacy practice planning commn. 1996-97, chmn. pharmacy practice awards com. 1998-00, mem. bylaws and policy devel. com. 2001-03, mem. computer tech. in edn. task force 2001-02, chmn. coun. of faculties strategic planning and resolutions com. 2001-03, mem. continuing pharmacy edn. ACPE liaison com., 2004-06, chair elect global pharmacy edn., 2008-09, chair global pharmacy edn., 2009-2010, mem., grad. & rsch. affairs com., 2009-10), Am. Soc. Health-Sys. Pharmacists (chmn. edn. and tng. adv. working group 1985-88, chmn. com. on academia 1996-97), Am. Pharm. Assn. (del. ann. meeting ho. of dels. 1989, 1998), Sleep Rsch. Soc., Nat. Sleep Found., Am. Acad. Sleep Medicine, Calif. Pharmacists Assn. (trustee 1997-01, chmn. editl. rev. com. 1998-03), Hollywood-Wilshire Pharmacists Assn. (pres. 2006—07), U. So. Calif. Sch. Pharmacy Alumni Assn. (bd. dirs. 1979—, pres. 1998—2008), Coll. Psychiat. Neurol. Pharmacists (chmn. recertification com. 2003-06, chmn. program com. 2006-07, Judith J. Saklad Meml. Lecture award 2007), Rho Chi (regional councilor & mem. nat. exec. coun., 2008-, Alumni award 2007), Phi Lambda Sigma. Avocation: photography. Office: 1985 Zonal Ave Los Angeles CA 90089-9121

WINDER, ALVIN ELIOT, public health educator, clinical psychologist; b. NYC, Feb. 17, 1923; s. Martin Winder and Frances (Erdrick) Isaacson; m. Barbara Dietz, July 19, 1949; children: Mark, Joshua, Sarah, Susan; m. Doris M. Raphael, Aug. 18, 2001. BA, CUNY, 1947; MS, U. Ill., 1948; PhD, U. Chgo., 1952; MPH, U. Calif., Berkeley, 1980. Lic. clin. psychologist, Mass. Chief psychologist VA Hosp., Downey, Ill., 1953-56; rsch. asst., asst. prof. Clark U., Worcester, Mass., 1956-58; chief psychologist VA Clinic, Springfield, Mass., 1958-61; assoc. prof. psychology Springfield Coll., 1961-63; chmn. psychology dept. Westfield (Mass.) State Coll., 1963-65; assoc. prof. counseling edn. Sch. Edn., U. Mass., Amherst, 1965-69, prof., dir. grad. program div. nursing, 1969-78, prof. Sch. Pub. Health, 1978-93; dir. planning, cons. Springfield (Mass.) Pub. Health Dept., 1993-95; prof. B U. Med. Sch., 2004—05. Adj. prof. Sch. Pub. Health, Boston U., 1995—; assoc. to exec. sec. Asian Pacific Assn. for Control of Tobacco, 1988—; cons. Mass. Dept. Pub. Health, 1998—. Author: Introduction to Health Education, 1984, Solid Waste Education Recycling Directory, 1989; editor: Adolescence Contemporary Studies, 1974; guest editor Jour. Applied Behavior, 1970; co-editor: Internat. Quar. of Cmty. Health Edn., 1992-96. Sr. selectman Town of Leverett, Mass., 1988-90; Lilly Found. mentor U. Mass., 1989. Grantee U.S. Childrens Bur., 1966, 67, Dexter Found., 1969, NIMH, 1974, Mass. Cancer Soc., 1997, Nat. Cancer Inst., 1986-91. Mem. APHA, APA, Mass. Assn. Older Ams. (v.p. 2002). Avocation: tennis. Home and Office: 70 Seminary Ave Newton MA 02466 Personal E-mail: march1931@aol.com.

WINDER, CLARENCE LELAND, psychologist, educator; b. Osborne County, Kans., June 16, 1921; s. Clarence McKinley and Edna (Ikenberry) W.; m. Elizabeth Jane Jacobs, Aug. 14, 1943; children: David William, Christina Louise. Student, Santa Barbara State Coll., 1941; AB with honors, U. Calif. at Los Angeles, 1943; MA, Stanford U., 1946, PhD, 1949. From instr. to assoc. prof. Stanford U., 1949-61; dir. Psychol. Clinic, 1953-61; prof., dir. Psychol. Clinic, Mich. State U., 1961-62, prof. psychology, 1961-91, prof. emeritus, 1991—, chmn. dept., 1963-67; dean Coll. Social Sci. Mich. State U., 1967-74, assoc. provost, 1974-77, provost, 1977-86, provost emeritus, 1991—; prof., dir. Psychol. Svcs. Ctr., U. So. Calif., 1962-63. 1st lt. USAAF, 1943-45. Decorated Air medal with 7 clusters, D.F.C. Fellow APA, AAAS; mem. Sigma Xi. Achievements include research in psychol. aspects schizophrenia, parent-child rels., personality devel., and higher edn. adminstrn. Home: 2700 Burcham Dr Rm 542 East Lansing MI 48823-3895

WINDHAGER, ERICH ERNST, physiologist, educator; b. Vienna, Nov. 4, 1928; came to U.S., 1954; s. Maximilian and Bertha (Feitzinger) W.; m. Helga A. Rapant, June 18, 1956; children: Evelyn Ann, Karen Alice. MD, U. Vienna, 1954. Rsch. fellow in biophysics Harvard Med. Sch., Boston, 1956—58; instr. in physiology Cornell U. Med. Coll., NYC, 1958—61; vis. scientist U. Copenhagen, 1961—63; asst. to prof. physiology Cornell U. Med. Coll., NYC, 1963—, Maxwell M. Upson prof. physiology and biophysics, 1978—2002, chmn. dept. physiology, 1973—2002, acting chmn. dept. cell biology, 1998—2002. Recipient Homer W. Smith award N.Y. Heart Assn., 1978, Berliner-Abbott award Am. Physiol. Soc., 1999. Office: Weill Med Coll Cornell U Dept Physiology 1300 York Ave New York NY 10021-4805 Home Phone: 201-567-8688; Office Phone: 212-746-6386. E-mail: ewindhag@med.cornell.edu.

WINDSOR, LESTER JACK, science educator; b. Apr. 20, 1959; s. William R. and Carrie A. Windsor; m. Elizabeth Walker, Dec. 13, 1989 (div. Apr. 23, 1999); children: Ashley, Garrett, Amanda. BS in Biology, Samford U., 1981; PhD in Biochemistry, U. Ala., 1993. Grad. tchg. asst. Samford U., Birmingham, Ala., 1981—83; rsch. asst. U. Ala., Birmingham, 1983—87, rsch. lab. supr., 1993—94, rsch. instr., 1994—95, rsch. asst. prof., 1995—98, assoc. scientist cell adhesion and matrix rsch. ctr., 1995—98, assoc. scientist comprehensive cancer ctr., 1997—98, grad. faculty, 1997—98; asst. prof. dept. oral biology Ind. U. Sch. Dentistry, Indpls., 1999—2005, grad. faculty, 2000—, assoc. prof. dept. oral biolgy, 2005—; grad. faculty Ind. U., Indpls., 2000—, adj. asst. prof. dept. anatomy and cell biolgy, 2000—05, adj. assoc. prof. dept. anatomy and cell biology, 2005—. Contbr. articles to profl. jours. Grantee, NIH, 1992—98, 1992—98, 1994—97, 1994—99, 1996—2001, Nat. Cancer Inst., 1995—96, 1997—99, 1997—2002, Ind. U. Sch. Dentistry, 2002—04, Ind. U. Cancer Ctr., 2002—03. Mem.: AAAS (assoc.), N.Y. Acad. Scis. (assoc.). Office: Indiana University School of Dentistry 1121 W Michigan St Indianapolis IN 46202-5186 Office Phone: 317-274-1448. Office Fax: 317-278-1411. Business E-Mail: ljwindso@iupui.edu.

WINEGAR, BRADFORD CHARLES, otolaryngologist, surgeon, researcher; b. Killeen, Tex., Apr. 27, 1955; s. Albert Lee and Phyllis Marie Winegar; m. Stacy J. Jones, Oct. 28, 1979; children: Bradford Reed, Ross Alan, Chad Evan. MD, Southwestern Med. Sch., Dallas, 1980. Attending physician, ptnr. Austin Ear, Nose & Throat Clinic, Tex., 1985—. Cons. Roxane Labs., Inc., Columbus, Ohio, 2006—; investigator Cedra Clin. Rsch., LLC, Austin, 2006—; mem. adv. bd. Aeriflux, Inc., Austin, 2005—. Morgan Goode fellow, Southwestern Med. Sch., 1977. Fellow: Am. Acad. Otolaryngology, Head and Neck Surgery, Inc.; mem.: AMA (life), Tex. Assn. Otolaryngology, Head and Neck Surgery, Travis County Med. Assn., Tex. Med. Assn., Austin Coun. Fgn. Affairs, Rotary Club. Office: Austin Ear Nose & Throat Clinic 3705 Medical Pky Ste 320 Austin TX 78705-1023 Office Phone: 512-925-5207.

WINEMILLER, MARK, medical educator; b. 1968; BA, U. Minn., 1992; MD, Mayo Med. Sch., 1996. Asst. prof. Mayo Clinic, 2000—. Mem.: AAP, AAPM&R. Avocation: music. Office: 200 First St SW Rochester MN 55905 E-mail: markw1420@gmail.com.

WINER, ERIC P., hematologist, oncologist, educator; b. Boston, Dec. 8, 1956; s. Richard Shepherd and Rhoda Ruth (Woogmaster) W.; m. Nancy M. Borstelman, June 23, 1984; children: Jeffrey, Joel, Emily. BA magna cum laude, Yale U., 1978, MD, 1983. Diplomate Nat. Bd. Med. Examiners, Am. Bd. Internal Medicine, Med. Oncology; lic. N.C. Intern internal medicine Yale-New Haven Hosp., Conn., 1983-84, resident internal medicine, 1984-86, chief resident, internal medicine, 1986-87; instr. dept. medicine Yale U. Sch. of Medicine, New Haven, 1986-87; staff physician Yale New-Haven Hosp., 1986-87; fellow hematology/oncoolgy Duke U. Med. Ctr., Durham, N.C., 1987-89, assoc. in medicine, 1989-90, physician, 1989, asst. prof. medicine divsn. hematology-oncology, 1990-96, assoc. prof., 1996—97; dir. breast oncology ctr. Dana-Farber Cancer Inst., Boston, 1997—, chief divsn. women, 2007—; active staff mem., dept. medicine Brigham and Women's Hosp., 1997—; assoc. prof. Harvard Med. Sch., 1997—2008, prof. medicine, 2008—. Cadre mem. psycho-oncology com. Cancer and Leukemia Group B, 1989—, breast com., 1990—, co-chair, 2009-, GU working com., 1991-94, clin. econ. working group, 1995—; co-dir. multi-disciplinary breast oncology program, 1993—, mem. hematology-oncology fellowship com.; PI for Duke U. Nat. Surgical Adjuvant Breast Program, 1992—; reviewer Jour. Clin. Oncology, Jour. AMA, Archives of Internal Medicine, Cancer Chemotherapy and Pharmacology, Transplantation, New Eng. Jour. Medicine, Breast Diseases; assoc. prof. Harvard Med. Sch.; chief scientific adviser, Susan G. Komen for the Cure, 2007-. Contbr. numerous articles, abstracts to profl. jours., chpts. to books. Recipient Kushlan award for outstanding intern, jr. resident Yale U. Sch. Medicine, 1984, 85; Am. Cancer Soc. Career Devel. award, 1991-94, Wendell Rosse award, 1994, Claire W. and Richard P. Morse Rsch. award, 2002; grantee: A.W. Mellon Found., 1990-91, Glaxo, Inc. pharmacoecon. divsn., 1991-92, NIH, 1991—. Mem. Am. Soc. Clin. Oncology, Acad. Hospice Physicians, Alpha Omega Alpha. Office: Dana-Farber Cancer Inst Mayer 228 44 Binney St Boston MA 02115 Office Phone: 617-632-6876. Office Fax: 617-632-1930. Business E-Mail: ewiner@partners.org.

WINET, HOWARD, research scientist, medical educator; b. Chgo., Sept. 13, 1937; s. Maurice Winet and Lillian Silver; m. Carol Katherine Kasper; children: Evan Darwin, Wendy Lynn. BS in Zoology, U. Ill., 1959; MA in Zoology, UCLA, 1962, PhD in Zoology, 1969. Cert. tchr. secondary edn., Calif. Tchr. secondary sch. sci. L.A. City Schs., 1962—66; postdoctoral fellow engring. sci. Calif. Inst. Tech., Pasadena, 1970—74, rsch. engr., 1974—77; assoc. prof. physiology So. Ill. U., Carbondale, 1977—80; assoc. prof. rsch. orthopaedics U. So. Calif., LA, 1980—98, assoc. prof. rsch. biomed. engring., 1996—98; lectr. biomed. engring. UCLA, 1998—, adj. prof. orthop., 1998—. Cons. Commonwealth Sci. & Indsl. Rsch. Orgn., Canberra, Australia, 1979; vis. assoc. prof. math. U. Wis., Madison, 1982; Fogarty internat. fellow orthopaedics Gothenburg U., Sweden, 1984; sr. assoc. U.S. Army M.C., Walter Reed Hosp., Washington, 1990—92. Contbr. (book chpts.) Engineering Science, Fluid Dynamics, 1990, Encyclopaedic Handbook of Biomaterials and Bioengineering, 1995, Clinically Applied Microcirculation Research, 1995, Bone Mechanics Handbook, 2001; mem. sci. editl. bd.: European Cells and Materials Jour. Grantee Rsch. grant, NIH, 1978—81, 1986—89, 1994—97. Mem.: Assn. Rsch. Circulation Osseous (v.p.), Soc. Biomaterials (vice chair spl. interest groups 2002). Avocation: fly fishing. Office: Orthopaedic Hosp UCLA 2400 Flower St Los Angeles CA 90007 Home Phone: 626-792-3500; Office Phone: 213-742-1007. Business E-Mail: hwinet@ucla.edu.

WINFIELD, JOHN BUCKNER, rheumatologist, educator; b. Kentfield, Calif., Mar. 19, 1942; s. R. Buckner and Margaret G. (Katterfelt) Winfield; m. Patricia Nichols (div. 1968); 1 child, Ann Gibson; m. Teresa Lee McGrath, 1969 (div. 2000); children: John Buckner III, Virginia Lee; m. Leigh Fleming Callahan, 2001. BA, Williams Coll., 1964; MD, Cornell U., 1968. Diplomate Am. Bd. Internal Medicine. Intern in medicine N.Y. Hosp., NYC, 1968-69; staff assoc. LI/Nat. Inst. Allergy and Infectious Diseases NIH, Bethesda, Md., 1969-71; resident in medicine, fellow in rheumatology U. Va. Sch. Medicine, Charlottesville, 1971-73; fellow in immunology Rockefeller U., NYC, 1973-75; asst. prof. medicine U. Va. Sch. Medicine, Charlottesville, 1975-76, assoc. prof. medicine, 1976-78, U. N.C., Chapel Hill, 1978-81, prof. medicine, 1981—2006, chief div. rheumatology and immunology, 1978-99; dir. Thurston Arthritis Rsch. Ctr., U. N.C. Sch. Medicine, Chapel Hill, 1982—2001; dir Daughtridge Arthritis Ctr., Lenoir, NC, 2002—07; consulting rheumatologist Appalachian Regional Rheumatology, 2007—; Smith prof. medicine U. NC Sch. Med., Chapel Hill, 1987—2006, emeritus, 2006—, adj. prof. exercise sports physiology, 2003—; adj. prof. endodontics Neurosensory Disorders Ctr., UNC Sch. Dentistry, sr. mem.; owner Winfield Medical, L.L.C., 2004—. Adv. coun. Nat. Inst. Arthritis and Musculoskeletal and Skin Diseases, NIH, 1988-92; chmn. edn. com. Am. Rheumatism Assn., Atlanta, 1980-84; immunol. scis. study sect. NIH, 1979-83, Arthritis Musculoskeletal and Skin study sect., 1992-96; vice-chair fellowship com. Arthritis Found., 1982; med. coun. Lupus Found. Am., 1987-96. Author more than 130 med. and sci. articles in peer reviewed rheumatology and immunology jours.; mem. editl. bd. Arthritis and Rheumatism, Bull. Rheumatic Diseases, Rheumatology Internat., Clin. Exptl. Rheumatology, Am. Jour. Medicine, Clin. Immunology, Current Rev. Rheumatology. Sr. asst. surgeon with USPHS, NIH, Bethesda, Md., 1968-71. Recipient Borden prize Cornell U. Med. Coll., 1964, numerous rsch. grants NIH and Arthritis Found., 1975—, Sr. Investigator award Arthritis Found., 1976-79, Kenan award U. NC, 1985, NIH merit award, 1992. Fellow ACP; mem. Am. Assn. Immunologists, Am. Fedn. Clin. Rsch., Am. Soc. Clin. Investigation, Assn. Am. Physicians, Am. Clin. Climatol. Assn., Nat. Soc. Clin. Rheumatologists (treas. 1997-02), Henry Kunkel Soc. (councilor 2000-02), Chapel Hill Country Club; master, Am. Coll. Rheumatology. Republican. Episcopalian. Avocations: golf, on and off-road motorcycling, scuba diving instructor, skiing. Home: 102 Greenwood Ln Chapel Hill NC 27514-5957 Office Phone: 828-263-8370. Business E-Mail: john_winfield@med.unc.edu.

WING, EDWARD JOSEPH, biomedical researcher, educator, dean; b. Mineola, NY, June 19, 1945; s. Maurice John and Frances Elliott Wing; m. Rena Rimsky, Aug. 19, 1967; children: Jonathan Frederick, Kenneth Elliott. BA magna cum laude, Williams Coll., 1967; MD cum laude, Harvard U., 1971. Resident in medicine Peter Bent Brigham Hosp., Boston, 1971-73; asst. surgeon USPHS, Pitts., 1973-75; fellow infectious diseases Stanford U., Palo Alto, Calif., 1975-77; asst. prof. medicine U. Pitts., 1977-82, assoc. prof. medicine, 1982-88, prof. medicine, 1989—; physician-in-chief, dept. medicine Montefiore Univ. Hosp., Pitts., 1990, vice chmn. dept. medicine, 1991; physician-in-chief RI Hosp., Miriam Hosp.; exec. physician-in-chief Meml. Hosp. of RI, Vet. Affairs Med. Ctr., Women & Infants Hosp.; chair Dept. Medicine Brown U., Joukowsky Family prof. medicine; dean medicine and biological scis. Alpert Med. Sch., Brown U., 2008—. Jour. referee numerous med. and sci. jours.; grant reviewer NIH and VA. Contbr. numerous articles to profl. jours. NIH grantee, 1983, 84, 87, 91, 94, 2003, 2006. Fellow Infectious Disease Soc. Am.; mem. Am. Clin. and Climatological Assn., Assn. of Professors of Medicine (mem. 2001, bd. dirs. 2006), Council of Deans. Avocations: tennis, skiing, photography, sailing. Office: Brown U Med Sch Divsn of Biology and Medicine Box G-A Providence RI 02912 Office Phone: 401-863-3330. E-mail: Edward_Wing_MD@Brown.EDU. *

WINGARD, JOHN REID, medical educator; b. Charleston, SC, Jan. 30, 1947; m. Frances Diane Phillips, 1974; children: Ellen, Emily, Sally, Benjamin. BA in English, Yale U., 1969; MD, The Johns Hopkins U., 1973. Diplomate Am. Bd. Internal Medicine, subspecialty of Med. Oncology. Intern City of Memphis Hosp./U. Tenn. Ctr. for Health Scis., 1973-74, resident, 1974-76; chief resident V.A. Hosp., Memphis, 1976-77; instr. in medicine U. Tenn. Ctr. for Health Scis., Memphis, 1976-77; fellow in oncology and internal medicine The Johns Hopkins U. Sch. Medicine, Balt., 1977-79, various to asst. prof. oncology, 1977-87, assoc. prof. oncology, 1987-91, assoc. prof. medicine, 1990-91; prof. medicine Emory U. Sch. Medicine, Atlanta, 1991-96, prof. Winship Cancer Ctr., 1992-96; dir. bone marrow transplant program, prof. medicine U. Fla., Gainesville, 1996—; dep. dir. U. Fla. Shands Cancer Ctr., 2011—. Dir. bone marrow transplant program Emory U. Sch. Medicine, 1991-96; dir. Bone Marrow Transplant Outpatient Clinic, Johns Hopkins Oncology Ctr., 1984-91; cons. Office of Disability Programs, Social Security Adminstrn., Balt., 1981-91; study group Nat. Inst. Allergy and Infectious Diseases,

1988—; adv. com. Internat. Bone Marrow Transplant Registry, 1989-91, 95—, sec.-treas., 1998—; chair, steering com. Blood and Marrow Transplant Clin. Trials Network, 2001—; bd. dirs. Found. Cellular Therapies, Nat. Marrow Donor Program. Contbr. articles to profl. jours.; contbr. chpts. to books; assoc. editor: Biology of Blood and Marrow Transplantation. Mem. Am. Soc. Microbiology, Am. Soc. Clin. Oncology, Am. Soc. Hematology, Internat. Soc. Exptl. Hematology, Am. Soc. Blood and Marrow Transplantation (pres. 2002-2003). Office: U Fla Coll Medicine PO Box 100277 Gainesville FL 32610-0277 Home: 9297 SW 31st Pl Gainesville FL 32608-7936 Office Phone: 352-273-7760, 352-273-8010. Business E-Mail: wingajr@medicine.ufl.edu, wingajr@ufl.edu.

WINGATE, DAVID, physician, researcher; b. London, Apr. 17, 1935; s. Harold and Minnie Wingate; m. Pauline Griffith, Dec. 24, 1958; children: William, Richard, Guy. BA with honors, U. Oxford, England, 1956, MSc, 1958, BMBCh, MA, MD, U. Oxford, England, 1960. Various postgrad. tng. posts Middlesex Hosp., London, 1960—70; rsch. fellow Mayo Clinic, Rochester, 1970—71; sr. lectr. London Hosp. Med. Coll., 1971—87, prof. gastrointestinal sci., 1987—2000; hon cons. gastroenterologist Royal London Hosp., 1975—2000; mem., rsch. ethics com. Nat. Rsch. Ethics Svc., London, 1994—; emeritus prof. gastrointestinal sci. Queen Mary U. London, 2000—, hon. fellow, 2005. Contbr. scientific papers. Trustee HH Wingate Charitable Found., London, 2000. Recipient Gotch Meml. medal, U. Oxford, 1959. Fellow: RCP.

WINGO, CHARLES, medical educator; b. Jan. 1, 1950; MD, LSU New Orleans Sch. Med., 1975. Prof. medicine, physiology, functional genomics U. Fla., 1990—. Mem. Am. Physiol. Soc., 1983, Am. Soc. Clin. Invest, 1990. Fellow: ACP. Office: University Fla Div Nephrology PO Box 100224 Gainesville FL 32610 Business E-Mail: cswingo@ufl.edu.

WINHUSEN, THERESA, medical researcher, educator; b. Cin., Mar. 17, 1968; BA, U. Cin., 1990; PhD, Ind. U., 1996. Rsch. assoc. prof. U. Cin. Coll. Medicine, 2006—. Assoc. dir. Cin. Addiction Rsch. Ctr., 2000. Recipient Outstanding Contbns. award, Nat. Inst. Drug Abuse Clin. Trials Network, 2010. Mem.: Coll. Problems Drug Dependence. Office: 3210 Jefferson Ave Cincinnati OH 45220 Business E-Mail: winhusen@carc.uc.edu.

WINICK, MARTIN, pediatric surgeon; b. NYC, Feb. 20, 1935; s. David Winick and Sadie Zubress Winicj; m. Marianne Winick; children: Stephen, Suzanne, Vanessa, Jonathon. BS magna cum laude, CCNY, 1956; MD, SUNY, Bklyn., 1960. Rotating intern Jewish Hosp. Bklyn., 1960—61, gen. surgery resident, 1961—65; pediat. surgery resident St. Christopher's Hosp. for Children., Phila.; pediatric surgeon pvt. practice, Suffolk, NY, 1968. Lt. comdr. USPHS, 1966—68. Fellow: Am. Coll. Surgeons; mem.: Am. Pediatric Surg. Assn. Republican. Jewish. Home: 5 Pine Point Huntington NY 11743 Office: 158 E Main St Huntington NY 11743-2988 Office Phone: 631-427-1300.

WINICK, MYRON, nutrition professor, physician; b. NYC, May 4, 1929; s. Charles B. and Ruth E. (Gesser) W.; m. Elaine L. Lasky, Sept. 19, 1964; children: Jonathan, Stephen. AB, Columbia U., 1951; MS, U. Ill., 1952; MD, SUNY, 1956. Intern U. Pa., Phila., 1956-57; asst. resident pediatrics Cornell U. Med. Coll., NYC, 1957-59, chief resident, 1959-60, attending pediatrician Stanford U. Hosp., 1963-64; asst. prof. pediatrics Cornell U. Med. Coll., NYC, 1964-68, assoc. prof. pediatrics and nutrition, 1968-70, prof., 1970-71; dir. Inst. Human Nutrition Columbia U. Inst. Human Nutrition, 1972-87, prof. pediatrics, 1972-89, R.R. Williams prof. nutrition, 1973-89, R.R. Williams prof. emeritus, 1990—; pres. U. Health Scis./Chgo. Med. Sch., North Chgo., Ill., 1990-93; dir. Ctr. for Nutrition, Genetics and Human Devel., 1975-87. Vis. prof. pediatrics U. Chile, Santiago, 1967; asst. attending pediatrician NY Hosp., NYC, 1964-68, assoc. attending pediatrician, 1968-70, attending pediatrician, 1970-71; attending pediatrician Presbyn. Hosp., NYC, 1972-89; cons. Pan Am. Health Orgn., 1966—; med. dir. Weight Watchers Internat., 1997—; sr. scientist Am. Health Found., 1999—. Author: Malnutrition and Brain Development, 1976; textbook Nutrition in Health and Disease, 1980; Growing Up Healthy; A Parent's Guide to Good Nutrition, 1982; For Mothers and Daughters: A Guide to Good Nutrition for Women, 1983; Your Personalized Health Profile: Choosing the Diet That's Right for You, 1985; Nutrition, Pregnancy and Early Infancy, 1989; The Fiber Prescription, 1992; editor: textbook Current Concepts in Nutrition, 1972—, Nutrition: Pre- and Postnatal Development, Vol. I, Human Nutrition: A Comprehensive Treatise, 1979, Columbia Ency. of Nutrition, 1988, (with Joan Lunden) Growing Up Healthy, 2004, Final Stamp: The Jewish Doctors in the Warsaw Ghetto, 2007; contbg. editor Nutrition Revs., 1969-76; mem. editl. bd. Jour. Nutrition, 1972-76, 82-86, The Year in Metabolism (now Contemporary Metabolism), 1975—; assoc. editor Growth, 1984—; nutrition editor Cancer Prevention, 1994—. Trustee Found. for Internat. Child Health; mem. nutrition interdisciplinary cluster Pres.' Biomed. Research Panel, 1975; mem. panel on infants and children Pres.' Commn. on Mental Health, 1977; cons. Office of Tech. Assessment, U.S. Congress, 1976-78; mem. Food and Nutrition Bd. NRC, 1982-88. With USNR, 1960-62. Bank of Am.-Gianini Found. fellow Stanford, 1962; NIH Spl. fellow, 1963; recipient NIH Career Devel. award, 1968-71; E. Mead Johnson award pediatric research, 1970; Osborne and Mendel award Am. Inst. Nutrition, 1976; Agnes Higgins award March of Dimes Found., 1983 Fellow Royal Soc. Health, Am. Soc. Nutritional Scis., Am. Acad. Pediatrics; mem. AAAS, Am. Soc. Cell Biology, Soc. Developmental Biology, Harvey Soc., Soc. Pediatric Rsch., Royal Soc. Medicine, Brit. Nutrition Soc., Am. Soc. Clin. Nutrition, NY Acad. Scis., NY Acad. Medicine, Soc. for Exptl. Biology and Medicine, Soc. for Neurosci., Internat. Soc. for Devel. Neurosci., Cosmos Club. Home: 165 West End Ave Apt 10K New York NY 10023 Business E-Mail: mw29@columbia.edu. *

WININGER, MARTIN, dermatologist; b. NYC, Mar. 22, 1939; s. Samuel Wininger and Mary Wirshborn; m. Jean Gallancy-Wininger, Sept. 8, 2005; m. Carol Manberg (dec.); children: Aaron, Eric, Danielle. AB, NYU, 1959, MD, 1963. Intern Jewish Hosp. Bklyn., 1963—64; fellow NYU, NYC, 1966—67; resident Kings County Hosp.-Bklyn. VA Hosp., 1967—69; pvt. practice dermatology Elmhurst, Merrick, NY, 1969—. Capt. US Army, 1964—66, Korea. Mem.: AMA, L.I. Dermatology Soc., N.Y. Dermatology Soc., Am. Acad. Dermatology. Home: 65 Wensley Dr Great Neck NY 11020 Office: Lashinsky & Wininger 80-37 Broadway Elmhurst NY 11373 also: 1955 Merrick Rd Merrick NY 11566 Office Phone: 718-898-8600, 516-223-1223.

WINK, MICHAEL, biologist, educator; b. Esch Bad Münstereifel, Fed. Republic Germany, Apr. 10, 1951; s. Alfred and Johanna (Remmen) W.; m. Coralie Oberhoffer, Mar. 11, 1978; children: Leonie, Charlotte, Lucie, Adrian. Diploma in Biology, U. Bonn., Fed. Republic Germany, 1977; Dr. rer. nat., U. Braunschweig, Fed. Republic Germany, 1980, Habilitation, 1985. Scientist U. Braunschweig, 1980-85; Heisenberg fellow U. Munich, 1986-88; assoc. prof. U. Mainz, Fed. Republic Germany, 1988-89; prof. faculty pharmacy and faculty biology U. Heidelberg, Fed. Republic Germany, 1989—. Dir. Inst. Pharm. Biology, Heidelberg, 1989-2001, vice dean, 1990-91, 93-97, dean faculty pharmacy, 1991-93, 97-2001, student dean, 2001-05, vice dean faculty of life sci., 2006—, Inst. Pharmacy and Molecular Biotech., Heidelberg, Germany, 2002—; vis. prof. U. Nanjing, China, 1998, U. Cordoba, Argentina, 1996, Harbing, 2004, 05, adj. prof. Southern cross U., Australia, 2011 Author four books on ornithology and Lupinen, 1991, Lupius, 1991 Research, Cultivation and Utilization, 1992, PCR in Medical and Biological Laboratories, 1994, Progress in Lupin Research and Cultivation, 1995, Therapy of Rheumatism With Plant Drugs, 1998, Alkaloids: Biochemistry, Ecology and Medicinal Applications, 1998, Lupins in Research and Application, 1998, Phytomedicines to Treat Disorders of the Nervous System, 1998, Biochemistry of Plant Secondary Metabolism, 1999, Function of Plant Secondary Metabolites and their Exploitation in Biotechnology, 1999, Evolutionary Biology, 2001, Vererbung und Milieu, 2001, Medicinal Plants of the World, 2004, Handbook of Medicinal Plants, 2004, Molekulare Biotechnologie, 2004, Birds of the Rhineland, 2005, Introduction to molecular biotechnology, 2007, Evolutionsbiologie, 2008, Mind-altering and Poisonous Plants of the World, 2008, Handbuch der Giftigen und Psychoaktiven Pflanzen, 2008; contbr. over 500 articles on natural products, chem. ecology, molecular evolution, ornithology, medicinal plants and plant physiology to profl. jours. Recipient Rheinlandtaler award Cultural Achievements Landschaftsverband Rheinland, Köln, 1988, G. Niethammer award for ornithology. Mem. AAAS, N.Y. Acad. Scis., Brit. Ornithologist's Union, Deutsche Ornithologen Gesellschaft, Gesellschaft fur Biologische Chemie, Internat. Soc. Molecular Evolution, Internat. Soc. Chem. Ecology, Phytochemical Soc. Europe, other sci. socs., Rotary. Office: University Heidelberg Inst Pharmacy and Molecular Biotech Im Neuenheimer Feld 364 69120 Heidelberg Germany E-mail: wink@uni-hd.de.

WINKELMANN, ANNE, counselor; b. Bayonne, NJ, Oct. 21, 1941; d. Francis Xavier and Marguerite Mary Agnes (Finnerty) Winkelmann; BS in Edn., Chestnut Hill Coll., 1972; MA in psychology, 2002. Cert. criminal justice specialist, chem. dependency supr., addictions counselor, alcohol and drug counselor; tchr. Pa., N.J., lic. clin. alcohol and drug counselor N.J., 2004. Tchr. Sisters of St. Joseph, N.J. and Pa., 1960—85; counselor Seabrook House, NJ, 1985—93, Maryville Inc., Williamstown, NJ, 1995—2004; chief clin. officer SODAT Inc. of NJ, 2004—. Spkr. in field; specialist MICA (Mentally Ill Chemically Addiction). Mem. spkrs. bur. Maryville; former mem. Mayor's Com. on Drug and Alcohol Prevention, Vineland, NJ, cons. Sacred Heart Regional Grammar Sch; vol. alcoholism counselor Trenton Detox; childcare worker Paradise Sch. for Delinquent Adolescent Males, 1980—85. Mem.: NAATP (Nat. Alcohol Addictions Treatment Prevention), NAADAC, N.J. Assn. Alcoholism and Drug Abuse Counselors.

WINKELSTEIN, JERRY ALLEN, retired pediatrician; b. Syracuse, NY, Sept. 5, 1940; s. Warren W. and Lillian (Sirkin) Winkelstein; m. Marilyn Link, June 21, 1969; children: Beth, Amy. BA, Syracuse U., 1961; MD, Einstein Med. Sch., 1965. Diplomate Am. Bd. Pediatrics, 1972. Intern in pediatrics Johns Hopkins Hosp., Balt., 1965—66, resident in pediatrics, 1966—68, fellow in pediatrics, 1970—73, resident in immunology, 1971—72; asst. prof. pediat. Johns Hopkins U., Balt., 1973-76, assoc. prof., 1976-82, Eudowood prof. pediat., 1982—2005, prof. medicine, 1990—2005, prof. pathology, 1998—2005; dir. divsn. immunology dept. pediat. Johns Hopkins Hosp., Balt., 1980—2004. Contbr. articles to sci. jours. Trustee Eudowood Bd., 2008—. Lt. comdr. USPHS, 1968—70. Recipient Mead-Johnson award, Am. Acad. Pediat., 1982, Lifetime Achievement award, Modell Found., 1996, Scientific Achievement award, Immune Deficiency Found., 2004. Mem.: Infectious Disease Soc., Am. Soc. Clin. Investigation, Soc. Pediatric Rsch., Am. Pediatric Soc. Home: 609 Stoney Spring Dr Baltimore MD 21210 Home Phone: 410-243-2766. *

WINKELSTEIN, WARREN, JR., physician, educator; b. Syracuse, NY, July 1, 1922; s. Warren and Evelyn (Neiman) W.; children: Rebecca Winkelstein Yamin, Joshua, Shoshana; m. Veva Kerrigan, Feb. 14, 1976. BA, U. N.C., 1942; MD cum laude, Syracuse U., 1947; MPH, Columbia U., 1950. Diplomate Am. Bd. Preventive Medicine. Intern Charity Hosp., New Orleans, 1947-48; with ICA (Vietnam), 1951-53; from dir. div. communicable disease control to 1st dep. comdr. local, environ. health svcs. Erie County Health Dept., 1953-62; from assoc. prof. to prof. SUNY, Buffalo, 1962-68; prof. epidemiology, dean pub. health U. Calif., Berkeley, 1972-96, prof. emeritus, 1996. Dir. Internat. Environ. Epidemiology Inst., 1997. Author: Basic Readings in Epidemiology, 1972; contbr. articles profl. jours. With AUS, 1944-46. Mem. APHA, AAAS, Internat. Am. Epidemiol. Socs., Am. Heart Assn. Address: Dept Epidemiol Univ Calif Sch Pub Health Berkeley CA 94720-7360

WINKENWERDER, WILLIAM, JR., consulting firm executive, former federal agency administrator; b. Ashville, NC, Apr. 27, 1954; BS, Davidson Coll., 1976; MD, U. N.C., 1981; MBA, U. Pa., 1986; postgrad., Stanford U., 1991. Resident internal medicine N.C. Meml. Hosp. U. N.C., 1981-84; instr. dept. medicine Sch. Medicine U. Pa., 1984-87; spl. asst. to adminstr. Health Care Financing Adminstrn. US Dept. Health & Human Services, 1987-88; dir. quality assurance and utilization mgmt. Southeast Permanente Med. Group, Kaiser Permanente, Atlanta, 1988-90, assoc. med. dir., 1990-92; v.p. CMO so. ops. Prudential Health Care, Atlanta, 1992-95; v.p. primary care svcs. Emory Health Care, Atlanta, 1996-98; assoc. v.p. health affairs Robert Woodruff Health Scis. Ctr. Emory U., 1996-98; exec. v.p. health care svcs., vice chmn. Blue Cross Blue Shield Mass., Boston, 1998—2001; asst. sec. for health affairs US Dept. Def., Washington, 2001—07; founder, chmn. The Winkenwerder Co., LLC, Alexandria, Va., 2007—. Mem. exec. com. Emory Healthcare, Emory Clinic, 1996-98; chmn. CMO com. Prudential Healthcare, 1992-95; bd. dirs. Care Sci. Corp., Wharton Sch. Bus. Health Care Alumni, Fed. Employees Program-Blue Cross Blue Shield Assn., The Reed and Barton Co.; founder HCFA Effectiveness Initiative, U.S. Dept. Health and Human Svcs., participant Task Forces on Health and Human Svcs. AIDS and Minority Health, 1987-88, U.S. Pub. Health Risk Assessment and Quality Assurance, Sec.'s Minority Health, Sec.'s Catastophic Illness; rep. Prudential on Med. Dirs. Com. on Group Health Assn. Am.; spkr. in field. Contbr. articles to profl. jours. Kaiser Family Found. fellow, 1984-86, 87-88, Kellogg Pub. Health Policy fellow U. Pa., 1986, Wharton Washington fellow U. Pa., 1986. Mem.: AMA, Am. Soc. Internal Medicine, Health Care Forum's Physician Leader Network, Am. Assn. Health Plans (bd. dirs.), Am. Coll. Physician Execs., Am. Coll. Physicians, Davidson Coll. Alumni Assn. Office: The Winkenwerder Co LLC 330 John Carlyle St Ste 220 Alexandria VA 22314 Office Phone: 703-836-1035. Office Fax: 703-836-1743.

WINKLER, DOLORES EUGENIA, retired health facility administrator; b. Milw., Aug. 10, 1929; d. Charles Peter and Eugenia Anne (Zamka) Kowalski; m. Donald James Winkler, Aug. 18, 1951; 1 child, David John. Grad., Milw. Bus. Inst., 1949. Acct. Curative Rehab. Ctr., Milw., 1949-60; staff acct. West Allis (Wis.) Meml. Hosp., 1968-70, chief acct., 1970-78, reimbursement analyst, 1978-85, dir. budgets and reimbursement, 1985-95; ret., 1995. Mem. adv. coun., fin. com. Tau Home Health Care Agy., Milw., 1981—83. Mem.: Inst. Mgmt. Accts. (pres. 1983—84, nat. dir. 1986—88, pres. Mid Am. Regional Coun. 1988—89, award of excellence 1989), Healthcare Fin. Mgmt. Assn. (pres. 1989—90, Follmer Bronze award 1980, Reeves Silver award 1986, Muncie Gold award 1989, medal of honor 1993), Beta Chi Rho (pres. 1948). Avocations: travel, photography, golf. Home: 12805 W Honey Ln New Berlin WI 53151-2652

WINKLER, KARL, clinical pathologist, consultant; b. Worms/Rhein, Rheinland-Pfalz, Germany, Nov. 16, 1963; s. Hans Paul and Irene Winkler. Student, Freiburg U. Med. Sch., 1985—87; BS with first class honors in Biol. Scis., Brock U., St. Catharines, Ont., Can., 1988; MD, U. Freiburg Med. Sch., Germany, 1992. Bd. lic. clin. pathologist Ärztekammer Baden-Württemberg, 2000, cert. clin. chemist Deutsche Vereinte Gesellschaft für Klinische Chemie und Laboratoriums, 2001. Intern U. Freiburg, 1993—94, residency dept. clin. chemistry, 1994—2000, dep. head dept. clin. chemistry, 2004—. Head outpatients ward for lipid disorders U. Freiburg, 2005—. Recipient Gödecke Forschungspreis, U. Freiburg, 1991, Förderpreis der Dr. Walter Freundlich und Luise Freundlich Stiftung, U. Frankfurt, 1997. Mem.: Deutsche Vereinte Gesellschaft für Klinische Chemie und Laboratoriumsmedizin, European Atherosclerosis Soc., Deutsche Gesellschaft für Atheroskleroseforschung. Office: Dept Clinical Chemistry Univ Hugstetter Str 55 D-79106 Freiburg Germany Office Fax: 49 761 270 3444. Business E-Mail: kwinkler@ukl.uni-freiburg.de.

WINKLER, SHELDON, dentist, educator; b. NYC, Jan. 25, 1932; s. Ben and Lillian (Barsh) W.; m. Sandra M. Cohen, Aug. 13, 1961; children: Mitchell, Lori. BA, Washington Sq. Coll., 1953; DDS, NYU, 1956. Asst. prof. denture prosthesis NYU Coll. Dentistry, NYC, 1958-61, 66-68, rsch. asst. prof., 1962-63; dir. materials rsch. Consol. Metal Products Industries Inc., Albany, NY, 1963-65, cons. materials rsch., 1966-68; asst. prof. removable prosthodontics sch. dentistry SUNY, Buffalo, 1968-70, assoc. prof., 1970-79; prof., chmn. dept. prosthodontics Temple U. Sch. Dentistry, Phila., 1979-86, 94-96, asst. dean for advanced studies, continuing edn./rsch., 1987-89, acting asst. dean, 1993-95, prof. restorative dentistry, 1996—2006; prof. dentistry Ariz. Sch. Dentistry and Oral Health, Mesa, 2006—07, Midwestern U. Coll. Dental Medicine, Glendale, Ariz., 2007—, Sch. Oral Health Scis., U. Tech., Jamaica, 2011—. Asst. dir. dental dept. NYU Med. Ctr. Goldwater Meml. Hosp., NYC, 1966—68, vis. dentist dental dept., 1966—68; attending in prosthodontics E.J. Meyer Meml. Hosp., Buffalo, 1975—79; postgrad instr. First Dist. Dental Soc. NY, NYC, 1963—2005; cons. Coe Labs., Chgo., 1967—87, Harkness Ctr., Buffalo, Rosa Coplon Home & Infirmary, Buffalo, 1970—79, Erie C.C., Buffalo, 1979—, Lever Bros. Co., NYC, 1981—2005, VA Hosp., Phila., 1989—2005, Ivoclar N. Am., Amherst, NY, 2000—; lectr. dept. dental hygiene NYC C.C., 1967—68; hon. prof. Pierre Fauchard Sch. Dentistry, Asuncion, Paraguay, 1999—. Author: (with A. Davidoff and M.H.M. Lee) Dentistry for the Special Patient: The Aged, Chronically Ill and Handicapped, 1972, Essentials of Complete Denture Prosthodontics, 1979, 2d edit., 1988, 3rd edit., 2010; editor: Resins in Dentistry, 1975, Complete Dentures, 1977, Removable Prosthodontics, 1984, (with B.R. Lang, F.R. Lauciello and G.P. McGivney) Contemporary Complete Denture Occlusion, 2001; editor Jour. Implant Dentistry, 1990-97; sr. editor Jour. Oral Implantology, 2000—; contbr. articles to profl. lit.; co-designer McGowan-Winkler complete denture trays. Served as capt. AUS, 1956-58, 61-62. Recipient Outstanding Layman award Vocat. Tech. Alumni and Student Assn., SUNY, Buffalo, 1974, Internat. Edn. award Internat. Congress Oral Implantologists, 1992, journalism award Internat. Coll. Dentists, 1993, Academic Devotion award Chulalongkorn U., Bangkok, 1995. Fellow Am. Coll. Dentists, Greater N.Y. Acad. Prosthodontics; mem. ADA, Internat. Assn. Dental Rsch., Am. Assn. Dental Schs., Am. Acad. Implant Prosthodontics (exec. dir., 1998-, Outstanding Personality Implant Prosthodontics award, 2002), Sci. Rsch. Soc. Am., Acad. Plastics Rsch., Am. Prosthodontic Soc., Am. Soc. Geriatric Dentistry, Internat. Congress of Oral Implantologists, Sigma Xi, Sigma Epsilon Delta, Omicron Kappa Upsilon. Home: 8672 E Eagle Claw Dr Scottsdale AZ 85266-1058 Office Phone: 480-588-8062. E-mail: swinkdent@cox.net.

WINN, H. RICHARD, surgeon; b. Chester, Pa., 1942; BA, Princeton U., 1964; MD, U. Pa., 1968. Diplomate Am Bd. Neurol. Surgeons. Intern U. Hosp., Cleve., 1968-69, resident surgery, 1969-70; resident neurolog. surgery U. Hosp. Va., Charlottesville, 1970-74; neurol. surgeon U. Wash. Hosp., Seattle, 1983—2002; prof., chmn. neurol.

surgery U. Wash., Seattle, 1983—2002; prof. neurosurgery and neurosci. Mt. Sinai Med. Sch., NYC, 2003—. Bd. dirs. Am. Bd. Neurol. Surgery, 1995-2001, vice chmn., 2000-01. Founding editor Neurosurgical Clinics of North America; mem. editl. bd. Jour. Neurosurgery, 1995-2001, chair, 2001-2002; mem. editl. bd. Am. Physiology, 1995-2000, Am. Jour. Surgery. Recipient Disting. Alumnus, Haverford Sch., 2000. Fellow AAAS, Soc. Brit. Neurol. Surgeons (hon.); mem. AMA, Am. Assn. Neurol. Surgeons, Soc. Neurol. Surgeons (Grass prize 1999, Disting. Svc. award 2005), Congress Neurol. Surgeons. Office: Dept Neurosurgery Mount Sinai Sch Medicine One Gustave L Levy PO Box 1136 New York NY 10029 Office Phone: 212-241-9128. Business E-Mail: richard.winn@mountsinai.org.

WINNEM, BJØRN MAGNE, anesthesiologist; b. Evenes, Norway, Sept. 21, 1947; s. Erling and Mary Irene (Burchard) W.; m. Dina Navjord, June 25, 1976; children: Marcus, Andreas. Student, U. Vienna, Austria, U. Bergen, Norway, 1967, MD, 1976. Cert. anesthesiologist. Resident in surgery SIA, Oslo, 1976; resident in medicine Torsby Hosp., Sweden, 1977, Narvik Hosp., Norway, 1977; physician Narvik Health Authority, 1977-78; clin. resident in anesthesiology U. Trondheim, Norway, 1978-79; resident in anesthesiology U. Tex. Health Sci. Ctr., San Antonio, 1979; resident anesthesiology and cardiology cardiovascular physiology U. Clin. Trondheim, 1980-83; rsch. fellow Inst. for Biomed. Tech., U. Trondheim, 1984-86; cons. Innherred Hosp., Levanger, Norway, 1986-87, Lillehammer Hosp., Norway, 1987-97; head anesthesia, intensive care Unprofor Normedcoy, Tuzla, 1994; mem. crictical care staff Ulleval Univ. Clinic, 1998-99; staff anesthesiologist Ullevål Univ. Clinic, 1999—; trauma anesthesiology expert Med. Readiness br. Hdqrs. Def. Command of Norway, 2002—. Contbr. articles to profl. jours. With UN Protection Force, Bosnia-Herzegovina, 1994, Internat. Security Assistance Force, Kabul, Afghanistan, 2003, Meymaneh, Afghanistan, 2006. Maj. M.C. Norwegian Mil., 1994. Recipient Golden Ball, Norwegian Football Assn., 1963; Nat. Rsch. Coun. grantee, 1984-86. Mem. Norwegian Med. Assn. (trustee 1996-98), Norwegian Anesthesiology Assn., Scandinavian Anesthesiology Assn., European Soc. Intensive Care Medicine, Internat. Trauma Anesthesiology and Critical Care Soc., Soc. of Critical Care Medicine. Avocations: soccer, scuba diving, skiing, mountain climbing, sailing. Office: Ulleval Univ Clin Dept Anesthesiology Military Med Ops Ctr N 0407 Oslo Norway Home: Sigrid Undsets Veg 8 2615 Lillehammer Norway Business E-Mail: bmwinnem@mil.no. E-mail: bmw@winnem.com.

WINOCOUR, PETER HOWARD, endocrinologist, consultant; b. Glasgow, Scotland, Feb. 12, 1956; s. Bertram and Sandra Winocour; m. Janice Eve Winocour, Mar. 25, 1990; children: David, Leanne. MB ChB, U. Glasgow, 1979, MD, 1989. Rsch. fellow, 1982—89; lectr., 1989—93; cons. physician dept diabetes and endocrinology Queen Elizabeth II Hosp., 1993—. Mem.: Assn. Brit. Clin. Diabeteologists (sec. 2002—08, chmn. 2008—11), Royal Coll. Physicians. Office: Queen Elizabeth II Hospital Dept Diabetes and Endocrinology Howlands AL7 4HQ Welwyn Garden City AL7 4HQ England

WINOKUR, THOMAS, pathologist; b. Eglin AFB, Fla., Jan. 30, 1953; BS, Stanford U., 1975; MD, Wash. U., 1979. Pathologist Fox Chase Cancer Ctr., 1984—88; sr. staff fellow NIH, 1988—93; assoc. prof. pathology U. Ala., Birmingham, 1993—. Master: US-Canadian Acad. Pathology; fellow: Coll. Am. Pathology (surg. pathology com.); mem.: AAAS, Am. Soc. Investigative Pathology, Soc. Cardiovasc. Pathology. Office: University Ala Dept Pathology NP3541 Birmingham AL 35233 Business E-Mail: tinokur@uab.edu.

WINSTEAD, DANIEL KEITH, psychiatrist; b. Cin., Dec. 30, 1944; s. Daniel Sebastian and Betty Jane (Kirsch) W.; m. Jennifer Reiner, June 15, 1968; children: Laura Suzanne, Nathaniel Scott. BA, U. Cin., 1966; MD, Vanderbilt U., 1970. Diplomate Am. Bd. Psychiatry and Neurology. Resident U. Cin., 1970-72, fellow, 1972-73; chief VA Med. Ctr. psychiat. svc. Tulane U., New Orleans, 1976-79, dir., consultation/liaison psychiat. tng., 1979-83, dir. psychiatric edn. and residency tng., 1983-87, assoc. prof., 1979-84, prof., 1984—, chmn. dept. psychiatry and neurology, 1987—; chief psychiat. svc. VA Med. Ctr., New Orleans, 1976-80; assoc. chief staff for edn. VA Med Ctr., New Orleans, 1979-87; staff psychiatrist VA Med. Ctr., New Orleans, 1987—. Med. dir. Jefferson Parish Substance Abuse Clinic, 1980-81; cons. E.R. Squibb and Sons, 1985-86; vis. physician psychiatry Charity Hosp., New Orleans, 1979-90. Contbr. articles to profl. jours. Maj. U.S. Army, 1973-76. Mem. AMA, Am. Bd. Psychiat. and Neurology (pres. bd. dirs. 2006), Am. Coll. Psychiatrists, Am. Acad. Psychiatry and Law, Am. Psychiat. Assn., La. State Med. Soc., So. Assn. for Rsch. in Psychiatry, Acad. Psychosomatic Medicine (pres.), Am. Assn. Chairmen Depts. Psychiatry (pres.-elect), Am. Assn. Dirs. Psychiat. Residency Tng., Assn. Acad. Psychiatry, La. Psychiat. Assn. (pres. 1991-92, 2009-2010), Soc. Biol. Psychiatry, New Orleans Area Psychiat. Assn., New Orleans Neurol. Soc., Orleans Parish Med. Soc. Republican. Presbyterian. Avocations: oenology, travel. Office: Tulane Med Sch 1440 Canal St Ste 1000 New Orleans LA 70112-2703 Home: 5348 Bellaire Dr New Orleans LA 70124-1033 E-mail: winstead@tulane.edu.

WINSTON, ARNOLD, psychiatrist, educator; b. NYC, May 1, 1935; s. Irving and Eva (Barban) W.; m. Beverly M. Winston, Oct. 21, 1938; children: Roy, Eric, Michael. AB, U. Chgo., 1956; MD, SUNY Med. Ctr., Bklyn., 1960. Med. intern Downstate Med. Ctr-Kings County Hosp., Bklyn., 1960-61, psychiatry resident, 1961-62, 63-65, chief psychiatry treatment unit, 1966-72; chief of svc. South Beach Psychiat. Ctr., SI, N.Y., 1972-74, dep. dir., 1974-75, dir., 1975-78; chmn. dept. psychiatry Beth Israel Med. Ctr., NYC, 1978—. Asst. prof. psychiatry SUNY, Bklyn., 1971-75, clin. assoc. prof. psychiatry, 1975-78; prof. psychiatry Mt. Sinai Coll. Medicine, N.Y.C., 1978-94; prof. psychiatry Albert Einstein Coll. Medicine, Bronx, N.Y., 1994—, vice chmn. dept., 1996; Ostmarka lectr. U. Trondheim, 1989; vis. prof. U. Vt., 1983. Author: Short-Term Psychotherapy, 2002, Learning Supportive Psychotherapy: An Illustrated Guide, 2011; contbr. numerous chpts. to books, articles to profl. jours. Psychotherapy rsch. grantee NIMH, 1993-95. Fellow Am. Psychiat. Assn. (disting. life fellow), Am. Coll. Psychiatrists, Am. Bd. Psychiatry and Neurology (diplomate). Avocations: tennis, skiing, gardening, golf. Office: Beth Israel Med Ctr 1st Ave & 16th St New York NY 10003 Home Phone: 212-593-0076; Office Phone: 212-420-2555. Business E-Mail: awinston@bethisraelny.org.

WINSTON, LISA GAIL, medical educator; b. LA, Nov. 29, 1969; AB, Harvard U., 1990; MD, Johns Hopkins U., 1994. Assoc. clin. prof. U. Calif., San Francisco, 2001—. Office: 1001 Potrero Ave San Francisco CA 94110 Business E-Mail: lisa.winston@ucsf.edu.

WINTER, CHESTER CALDWELL, surgeon, educator, historian, writer; b. Cazenovia, NY, June 2, 1922; s. Chester Caldwell and Cora Evelyn (Martin) W.; m. Mary Antonia Merullo, Oct. 22, 1983; children by previous marriage: Paul, Ann, Jane. BA, U. Iowa, 1943, MD, 1946. Diplomate: Am. Bd. Urology. Intern Meth. Hosp., Indpls., 1946-47; med. resident St. Luke's Hosp., Cedar Rapids, Iowa, 1947; physician Calif., 1950-51; resident gen. surgery VA Hosp., Los Angeles, 1952-53; resident urology VA Hosp.-UCLA Med. Ctr., 1953-57; clin. asst. surgery UCLA, 1954-57, instr. surgery and urology, 1957-58, asst. prof. surgery and urology, 1958-59, asst. prof. Step II, 1959-60; prof. surgery and urology Ohio State U., 1960-88, prof. emeritus surgery and urology, 1988—, Louis Levy prof. urology, 1980-88. Dir. urology Ohio State U. Hosp., Columbus, 1960-78; cons. urology VA, Air Force hosps., Dayton, 1960-80. Author: Radioisotope Renography, 1963, Correctable Renal Hypertension, 1964, Nursing Care of Patients with Urologic Diseases, 4th edit, 1977, Practical Urology, 1969, Vesicoureteral Reflux, 1969, A Concise History of the U.S. and the State of Ohio, 2002, A Bicentennial History of the State of Ohio, 2003, Ohio Cities: Historical Descriptions, 2004, Concise Biographies of Notable Ohioans, 2005, A Concise History of Columbus Ohio and Franklin County, 2009; editl. cons. Exerpta Medica: Nuclear Medicine, Jour. AMA; mem. editl. bd. Andrology, Jour. Urology; contbr. articles to profl. jours. Served to capt. M.C. U.S. Army, 1943-46, 48-49. Fellow Am. Acad. Pediatricians, Am. Coll. Surgeons; mem. Am. Assn. Genitourinary Surgeons, Am. Urol. Assn., Soc. Univ. Surgeons, Soc. Pediatric Urology, Soc. Univ. Urologists, Internat. Soc. Urology, Urol. Investigators Forum, Ohio State Med. Assn., Columbus Surg. Soc., Central Ohio Urology Soc., Columbus Acad. Medicine, Ohio State U. Med. Soc. Home: 6425 Evening St Worthington OH 43085-3054 E-mail: cwinter3@ameritech.net. *

WINTER, DUNCAN FORBES, ophthalmologist; b. Garden City, NY, Oct. 23, 1952; s. Clark Burritt and Margery Forbes Winter; m. Delphine Stillger, Aug. 1, 1981; children: Cornelia, Lauren. BA, Washington & Lee U., 1975; MS, MBA, Adelphia U., 1978; MD, Albany Med. Sch., 1984. Bond trader Shields Mode, NYC, 1975—76; commodity trader Gill & Duffus, NYC, 1976—78; intern in surgery Albany Med. Ctr., 1985, resident in ophthalmology, 1986—90, fellow in ocular pathology, 1987; ophthalmologist Adirondack Eye Ctr., Saranac Lake, NY, 1990—, dir. surg. eye care, 1990—. Bd. dirs. Lake Placid (NY) Film Festival, 2000—03. Fellow: ACS, Am. Assn. Ophthalmology; mem.: Franklin County Med. Soc. (pres.-elect). Achievements include invention of surgical instruments for ophthalmologic surgery. Avocations: skiing, tennis, flying, polo. Home: Peninsula Rd Lake Placid NY 12986 Office: Adirondack Eye Ctr 86 Main St Saranac Lake NY 12983 Office Phone: 518-891-5189. Personal E-mail: dwinter007@adelphia.net.

WINTER, HANS, veterinary pathologist; b. Vienna, Dec. 1, 1922; arrived in Australia, 1954; s. Rudolf and Rosina (Kozler) W.; m. Jean Isobel McRae, Dec. 18, 1962; children: Christopher, Alexander, Richard, Harold. Degree in vet., Vet. U., Vienna, 1950, DVM, 1951; D Vet Sci, U. Queensland, Brisbane, Australia, 1966. Diplomate Am. Coll. Vet. Pathologists. Asst. dept. vet. pathology Vet. U., Vienna, 1950-54; pathologist Vet. Sch., U. Queensland, Brisbane, 1954-87, head dept. vet. pathology, 1980-85, rsch. cons., 1986—. Cons. FAO/UN, Rangoon, Burma, 1966-67; prof. 1968; sr. cons. in vet. pathology FAO/UN, Iran, Iraq, India, Bhutan, 1970-85; sr. cons. Asian Developing Bank, Bhutan, 1988-91; sr. fgn. scientist U.S. Nat. Sci. Found., Mich. State U., East Lansing, 1968; hon. vet. Brookfield Show Soc., Brisbane, 1970—; founding pres. Australian Assn. Vet. Pathologists, 1974-82, pres. World Assn. Vet. Pathologists, 1979-87. Author: Postmortem Examinations of Ruminants, 1966, Spanish edit., 1968, Burmese edit., 1968, Farsi edit., 1970, Arabic edit., 1980; contbr. articles to profl. jours. Fulbright fellow Cornell U., Ithaca, N.Y., 1951-52; sr. scientist fellow Deutscher-Akademischer Austausch Dienst, Munich, 1973, 78; recipient Austrian Cross of Honor for Sci. and Arts First Class, Pres. Austria, 2004. Mem. Australian Coll. Vet. Scientists, Royal Coll. Vet. Surgeons, Australian Vet. Assn. (coun. mem. 1974-83), European Soc. Vet. Pathology, Royal Queensland Yacht Squadron, Phi Zeta (hon.), Sigma Xi. Avocations: equestrian, sailing. Home: 175 Boscombe Rd Brookfield Brisbane QLD 4069 Australia Personal E-mail: hanswinter@gmail.com.

WINTER, HOWARD J., surgeon; MD, Yeshiva U., NYC, 1974. Diplomate Am. Bd. Surgery, lic. NJ, 1978, Pa., 1986. Intern Albert Einstein Med. Ctr., resident; hosp. affiliations include Centennial Surg. Ctr., Summit Surg. Ctr., Virtua Hosp. Berlin, Virtua Hosp. Marlton, Virtua Hosp. Voorhees. Named one of Top Doctors, Phila. Mag., 2011. Fellow: ACS; mem.: Soc. of Am. Gastrointestinal and Endoscopic Surgeons, Am. Soc. of Colon and Rectal Surgeons. Office: Virtua Hospital Voorhees 100 Bowman Dr Voorhees NJ 08043 Office Phone: 856-247-3000.

WINTER, JANE, medical educator; b. NYC, 1952; MD, U. Pa., 1977; intern, U. Chgo., 1977-78, resident int. medicine, 1978-80. Fellow in hematology and oncology Columbia P&S, NYC, 1980-81, Northwestern U., 1981-83, prof., 1983—. Mem.: Ea. Coop. Oncology Group, Am. Soc. for Blood and Marrow Transplantation, Am. Assn. Cancer Rsch., Am. Soc. Clin. Oncology, Am. Soc. Hematology. Office: Divsn Hematology/Oncology 676 N St Clair St Ste 850 Chicago IL 60611-2978 Office Phone: 312-695-0990. E-mail: j-winter@northwestern.edu.

WINTER, JONATHAN, dermatologist; Attended, Albert Einstein Coll. of Medicine. Diplomate Am. Bd. Dermatology. Intern Montefiore Med. Ctr.; resident Albert Einstein Med. Ctr.; dermatologist Cooper Univ. Hosp. Office: Cooper University Hospital Ste A1 00 Kingsway E Sewell NJ 08080 Office Phone: 856-589-3331. Office Fax: 856-589-3416.

WINTER, PETER MICHAEL, anesthesiologist, educator; b. Sverdlovsk, Russia, Aug. 5, 1934; arrived in U.S., 1938, naturalized, 1944; s. George and Anne Winter; m. Michelle Yakopec, Dec. 28, 1991; children: Karin Anne, Christopher George, Lia Lynn, Tori Anne. BA, Cornell U., 1958; MD, U. Rochester, 1962. Diplomate Am. Bd. Anesthesiology. Intern U. Utah, Salt Lake City, 1962-63; resident in anesthesiology, pharmacology and respiratory physiology Mass. Gen. Hosp., Boston, 1963-65; USPHS fellow Harvard U. Med. Sch., Mass., 1964-66; Buswell fellow dept. physiology, asst. prof. SUNY, Buffalo, 1966-69; assoc. prof. dept. anesthesiology Sch. Medicine, U. Wash., Seattle, 1969-74, prof., 1974-79; prof., chmn. dept. anesthesiology and critical care medicine U. Pitts. Sch. Medicine, 1979-96, Peter and Eva Safar prof. anesthesiology/critical care med., 1987—96, prof. emeritus, dir. faculty devel., 1996—. Anesthesiologist in chief Univ. Health Ctr. Hosps., Pitts., 1979—96. Editl. cons.: Anesthesiology CCMJ; contbr. chapters to books, papers and abstracts to publs. With US Army, 1953—56. Recipient Career Devel. award, NIH, 1971. Mem.: AMA, Assn. univ. Anesthetists, Internat. Anesthesia Rsch. Soc., Undersea Med. Soc., Soc. Critical Care Medicine, N.Y. Acad. Scis., Royal Soc. Medicine, Am. Soc. Anesthesiologists, Am. Coll. Chest Physicians, Morton Soc., Am. Alpine Club. Office: 3471 5th Ave Ste 910 Pittsburgh PA 15213-3221

WINTER, ROBIN OKNER, health facility administrator; b. Newark, Mar. 10, 1953; BA, Haverford Coll., Haverford, Pa., 1974; MD, Albert Einstein Coll. Medicine, 1978; M in Med. Mgmt., Carnegie Mellon U., 1999. Diplomate Am. Bd. Family Medicine (cert. in geriatric medicine). Dir. family medicine residency program JFK Med. Ctr., Edison, NJ, 1989—. Mem.: Assn. Family Medicine Residency Dirs. (pres. 2003—04). Office: JFK Med Ctr 65 James St Edison NJ 08818 Office Fax: 732-906-4986. *

WINTER, STEVEN, internist, cardiologist; b. Bklyn., July 25, 1950; s. Nathan Harold and Magda (Markowitz) W.; m. Florence Stein, Aug. 20, 1972; children: Amy R., Daniel. BA, Yeshiva U., 1972; MD, U. Med./Dentistry of N.J., 1976. Diplomate Am. Bd. Internal Medicine with subspecialty in cardiovascular disease. Intern North Shore Univ. Hosp., Manhasset, N.Y., 1976-77; resident in medicine North Shore Univ. Hosp, Manhasset, N.Y., 1976-79, Meml. Sloan Kettering Cancer Ctr., Cornell Cooper Tng. Hosp., 1977-79; fellow in cardiology R.I. Hosp.-Brown U., Providence, 1979-81; pvt. practice SI, N.Y.; attending in medicine and cardiology S.I. U. Hosp., 1981—, St. Vincent's Med. Ctr., Richmond, 1985—; asst. clin. prof. SUNY, Bklyn., 1985—. Fellow ACP, Am. Coll. Cardiology; mem. AMA, Am. Heart Assn- .(Named Top Drs. NY Castle Connolly, 2000-10) Office: 2627B Hylan Blvd Staten Island NY 10306-4353

WINTERHOLLER, BERT WELCH, oral and maxillofacial surgeon; b. Lovell, Wyo., Mar. 20, 1947; s. Bert William and Alys Winterholler; m. Laurel Ann Warner, Aug. 4, 1970; children: Sheridan Ringhiser, Melissa Hodges, William B., Erika Sadler, Cody. Student, U. Wyo., 1965—66; BA, Brigham Young U., 1972; DDS cum laude, Creighton U., 1977; degree in oral and maxillofacial surgery, U.S. Naval Hosp., Portsmouth, Va., 1983. Diplomate Am. Bd. Oral and Maxillofacial Surgery. Dental officer USN, 1973—86; resident in oral and maxillofacial surgery U.S. Naval Hosp., Portsmouth, 1980—83; mem. staff oral and maxillofacial surgery Fargo (N.D.) Clinic, 1986—88; ptnr. OMS, P.C., Fargo, 1988—89, Oral and Maxillofacial Surgery, P.C., Gt. Falls, Mont., 1989—93, Billings, Mont., 1993—. Cons. St. Paul Fire & Marine, Mpls., 1987—, MRI of Am., Salt Lake City, 2001—; clin. instr. U. P.R., San Juan, 1983—86. Mem. fireworks prevention com. City of Billings, 2001—02; mem. Tobacco Prevention Adv. Bd. State of Mont., Helena, 2003—; missionary LDS Ch., Germany, 1966—68. Comdr. USN, 1973—83. Fellow: Am. Assn. Oral and Maxillofacial Surgeons; mem.: ADA, Am. Coll. Oral and Maxillofacial Surgeons. Mem. Lds Ch. Avocations: gemology, wooden boat building, music, sport aviation. Home: 2522 Riveroaks Dr Billings MT 59105 Office: Oral and Maxillofacial Surgery PC 2520 17th St W Billings MT 59102 E-mail: bgrdrm@aol.com.

WINTERKORN, JACQUELINE MARJORIE SCHUKER, neuro-ophthalmologist; b. NY, Jan. 2, 1947; m. Thomas H. Meikle (dec.); m. David V.C. Lincicome; children: Elisabeth B., Margaret K. AB, Barnard Coll., Columbia U., NYC, 1967; PhD, Cornell Med. Coll., Ithaca, NY, 1973, MD, 1983. Instr. dept. anatomy Cornell U. Med. Coll., NYC, 1975-76, asst. prof. dept. anatomy, 1976-81, lectr. dept. cell biology and anatomy, 1981-86, asst. prof. ophthalmology, 1989-93, assoc. prof. ophthalmology, 1993-96, assoc. prof. neurology and neurosci., 1994-96, clin. prof. ophthalmology, neurology and neurosci., 1997—. Heed fellow in ophthalmology, 1987-88; recipient William Warner Hoppin award N.Y. Acad. Medicine, 1985, Am. Acad. Ophthalmology Achievement award, 1999. Fellow: N.Am. Neuro-ophthalmology Soc., Am. Acad. Ophthalmology; mem.: AMA, Nassau County Med. Soc., N.Y. State Med. Soc., Internat. Neuro-ophthalmology Soc., Am. Assn. for Study Headache, Alpha Omega Alpha, Sigma Xi. Office: 26 North St PO Box 222 Roxbury CT 06783-0222

WINTERS, JILL MARY, nursing educator, director; b. Milw., June 30, 1955; d. John Paul Gabor and Ann Lorraine (Ladish) Gordy; m. Jack Mark Winters; children: David, Michael. BSN, U. Wis., Milw., 1978; MS in Nursing, Marquette U., 1991; PhD, U. Wis., 1996. Cert. CCRN. Nurse various hosps., Milw., 1978—85, Peck Foods Corp., Milw., 1985-88; asst. prof. U. Wis.-Milw., 1996—2001; assoc. prof., dir. rsch. Marquette U., Milw., 2001—. Contbr. numerous book chpts. and articles to profl. jours. Grantee, Nat. Inst. Nursing Rsch., Wis. Women's Health Found., Nat. Inst. Disability and Rehab. Rsch., Nat. Inst. Child Health and Human Devel., Children's Hosp. Wis. Mem. AACCN (grantee 1997), ANA, Midwest Nursing Rsch. Soc., Am. Nurses Found., Sigma Theta Tau (v.p. local chpt. 1997-99). Roman Catholic. Achievements include research in use of music to improve cardiac function and reduce anxiety after myocardial infarction, heart rate variability in infants with serious congenital heart defects and prematurity; heart rate variability with myocardial infarction and heart failure, accessibility of medical equipment for persons with disabilities, exercise and heart failure, and telehealth applications. Avocations: golf, running, cross country skiing. Home: 10320 N Provence

Ct Mequon WI 53092-5228 Office: Marquette U Coll Nursing PO Box 1881 Milwaukee WI 53201-1881 Home Phone: 262-242-3922. Business E-Mail: jill.winters@marquette.edu.

WINTERSTEIN, JAMES FREDRICK, academic administrator; b. Copperas Cove, Tex., Apr. 8, 1943; s. Arno Fredrick Herman and Ada Amanda Johanna (Wagnr) W.; m. Diane Marie Bochmann, July 13, 1963 (dec. August, 2002); children: Russell, Lisa, Steven, Amy; m. Cynthin Sportelli Mar. 16, 2010. Student, U. N.M., 1962; D of Chiropractic cum laude, Nat. Coll. Chiropractic, 1968; cert., Harvard Inst. for Ednl. Mgmt., 1988. Diplomate Am. Chiropractic Bd. Radiology; lic. chiropractic, Ill., Fla., S.D., Md. Night supr. x-ray dept. DuPage Meml. Hosp., Elmhurst, Ill., 1964-66; x-ray technologist Lombard (Ill.) Chiropractic Clinic, 1966-68, asst. dir., 1968-71; chmn. dept. diagnostic imaging Nat. Coll. Chiropractic, Lombard, Ill., 1971-73, chief of staff, 1985-86; pres. Nat. U. Health Scis., Lombard, Ill., 1986—; pvt. practice West Chicago, Ill., 1968-73, Fla., 1973-85. Faculty Nat. Lincoln Coll. Post-Profl., Grad. and Continuing Edn., 1967—; chmn. x-ray test com. Nat. Bd. Chiropractic Examiners, 1971-73; govs. adv. panel on coal worker's pneumoconiosis and chiropractic State of Pa., 1979; v.p. Am. Chiropractic Coll. Radiology, 1981-83; mem. adv. coun. on radiation protection Dept. Health and Rehabilitative Svcs. State of Fla., 1984-85; cons. to bd. examiners State of S.C., 1983-84, State of Fla., 1980-85; cons. to peer review bd. State of Fla., 1980-84; trustee Chiropractic Centennial Found., 1989-90; mem. adv. com. Aids Alternative Health Ptnrs., 1996-2000, Consortial Ctr. for Chiropractic Rsch., 1998—; bd. dirs. Fedn. Ill. Ind. Colls. and Univs., 1995—; bd. dirs. Alternative Medicine, Inc., 1999—; spkr. in field. Pub. Outreach (Nat. Univ. Health Scis. monthly); author numerous monographs on chiropractic edn. and practice; co-inventor composite shielding and mounting means for x-ray machines; contbr. articles to profl. jours. Chmn., bd. dirs. Trinity Luth. Ch., West Chgo., 1970-72, Luth. High Sch., Pinellas County, Fla., 1979-82, St. John Luth. Ch., Lombard, 1988; chmn. bd. edn. First Luth. Sch., 1975-79; chmn. First Luth. Congregation, Clearwater, Fla., 1979-82; chmn. bldg. planning com. Grace Luth. Ch. and Sch., St. Petersburg, Fla., 1984-85; bldg. planning com. ch. expansion, new elem. sch., First Luth. Sch., 1975-79; stewardship adv. coun. Fla./Ga. dist. Luth. Ch. Mo. Synod, 1983-85; trustee West Suburban Regional Acad. Consortium, 1993-99. With U.S. Army, 1961-64. Recipient Cert. Meritorious Svc. Am. Chiropractic Registry of Radiologic Technologists, Cert. Recognition for Inspiration, Guidance, and Support Delta Tau Alpha, 1989, Cert. Appreciation Chiropractic Assn. South Africa, 1988, 1st pl. Fund Raiser Ride for Kids award Pediat. Brain Tumor Found. U.S., 1997, Cert. Appreciation Ill. Chiropractic Soc., 1997, Hope and Support award Alternative Health Ptnrs., 1998, Chiropractor of Yr., Ill. Chiropractic Soc., 2000, Person of the Yr., Alternative Medicine, Inc., 2001, NUHS Bd. Trustees Disting. Svc. award, 2002, President's citation award Maryland Chiropractic Assn., 2003. Mem. APHA, Am. Chiropractic Assn., Am. Chiropractic Coll. Radiology (pres. 1983-85, exec. com. 1985-86), Am. Chiropractic Coun. on Diagnostic Imaging, Am. Chiropractic Coun. on Diagnosis and Internal Disorders, Am. Chiropractic Coun. on Nutrition, Nat. Univ. Alumni Assn., Am. Acad. Chiropractic Physicians (sec.), Assn. Chiropractic Colls. (sec.-treas. 1986-91), Coun. Chiropractic Edn. (sec.-treas. 1988-90, v.p. 1990-92, pres. 1992-94, immediate past pres. 1994-96), Fla. Chiropractic Assn. (chmn. radiol. health com. 1977-85, Disting. Svc. award 1999). Republican. Lutheran. Avocations: reading, automobile rehabilitation, harley-davidson motorcycles, fishing.

WINZOR, DONALD JOHN, retired chemistry professor; b. Gawler, Australia, May 16, 1935; BSc in Chemistry, U. Adelaide, 1956, PhD, 1961, DSc, 1976. Rsch. scientist, sr. rsch. scientist Commonwealth Sci. and Indsl. Rsch. Orgn., 1960—68; sr. lectr., biochemistry U. Queensland, 1968—72, reader, biochemistry, 1973—93, prof., biochemistry, 1993—2000, prof. emeritus, 2000—. Mem.: Australian Soc. Biochemistry and Molecular Biology. Home: 20/12 Bellevue Parade Brisbane Queensland 4068 Australia Office Fax: 61-7-2265-4699. Business E-Mail: d.winzor@uq.edu.au.

WIOT, JEROME FRANCIS, radiologist; b. Cin., Aug. 24, 1927; s. Daniel and Elvera (Weisgerber) W.; m. Andrea Kockritz, July 29, 1972; children— J. Geoffrey, Jason. MD, U. Cin., 1953. Diplomate: Am. Bd. Radiology (trustee, pres.). Intern Cin. Gen. Hosp., 1953-54, resident, 1954-55, 58-59; gen. practice medicine Wyoming, Ohio, 1955-57; mem. faculty U. Cin., 1959-67, 68—, prof., chmn. radiology, 1973-93, acting sr. v.p., provost for med. affairs, 1985-86, prof. emeritus, 1998—; practice medicine specializing in radiology Tampa, Fla., 1967-68. Contbr. articles to med. jours. Bd. dirs. Ruth Lyons Fund, U. Cin. Found., 1997—2003, U. Cin. Hosp., 2005—. Served with USN, 1945-46. Fellow Am. Coll. Radiology (pres. 1983-84, chmn. commn. on diagnostic radiology); mem. Radiol. Soc. N.Am., Am. Roentgen Ray Soc. (pres. 1986-87), Am. Bd. Radiology (pres. 1982-84), Ohio Med. Assn., Cin. Acad. Medicine, Radiol. Soc. Greater Cin., Ohio Radiol. Soc. Office: U Cin Med Ctr Dept Radiology 234 Goodman St Cincinnati OH 45267-1000 Office Phone: 513-475-8755. E-mail: jfwiot@hotmail.com.

WIRRELL, ELAINE C., neurologist, educator; b. Vancouver, BC, Jan. 12, 1963; BSc, Simon Fraser U., 1985; MD, U. BC, 1989. Pediat. neurologist U. Sask., 1996—2000, Alta. Children's Hosp., 2000—07; prof. neurology, dir. pediat. epilepsy Mayo Clinic, 2007—. Recipient Tchg. award, PA Residents and Interns, Alta., CR 20 award, Mayo Found., Dean Sci. award, Simon Fraser U., Dr. Whitelaw award, U. BC, CIBA Geigy prize. Mem.: Am. Neurol. Assn., Am. Acad. Neurology, Am. Epilepsy Soc. Avocations: hiking, gardening. Office: Mayo Clinic 200 First St SW Rochester MN 55905 Office Fax: 507-284-0727. Business E-Mail: wirrell.elaine@mayo.edu.

WIRTH, FREMONT PHILIP, JR., neurosurgeon, educator; b. Nashville, July 23, 1940; s. Fremont P. and Willa (Dean) W.; children: Fremont Philip III, Andrew Simpson, Carolyn Howe. BA with honors in History, Williams Coll., 1962; MD, Vanderbilt U., 1966. Diplomate Am. Bd. Neurol. Surgery (guest examiner 1989, bd. dirs. 1992-98, vice chmn. 1997-98), Nat. Bd. Med. Examiners; cert. advanced trauma life support ACS. Surg. intern Johns Hopkins Hosp., Balt., 1966-67, resident and fellow in surgery, 1967-68; asst. resident in neurosurgery Barnes Hosp., Washington U., St. Louis, 1970-72, fellow in neurosurgery, 1972-74; pvt. practice, Savannah, Ga., 1974—. Asst. clin. prof. neurosurgery Med. Coll. Ga., Augusta, 1991—, vis. prof., 1978, 79, 86, 87; mem. staff, neurosurg. ICU, St. Joseph's Hosp., 1974—, dir. neurosurg. ICU, 1978—; mem. staff Meml. Med. Ctr., 1974-75, dir. rehab., 1983; mem. staff Candler Gen. Hosp., 1974—; med. dir. Head and Spinal Cord Injury Prevention Project for Ga., 1984-96; presenter in field, 1970—; vis. prof. U. Md., Balt., 1981, Tufts New Eng. Med. Ctr., Boston, 1982. Series editor (with R.A. Ratcheson) Concepts in Neurosurgery, 1986-93; editor: (with Ratcheson) Neurosurgical Critical Care, Concepts in Neurological Surgery, Vol. 1, 1987, Ruptured Cerebral Aneurysms, Concepts in Neurological Surgery, Vol. 6, 1994; contbr. articles and book revs. to med. jours., chpts. to books. Elder Skidaway Island Presbyn. Ch., 1981-83; mem. pack 57 com. Cub Scouts Am., Savannah, 1979-84; mem. troop 57 com. Boy Scouts Am., Savannah, 1980-85, mem. fin. com. Coastal Empire coun., 1987-90, mem. adv. bd., 1990-96; chmn. physicians' solicitation United Way Coastal Empire, 1987; bd. dirs. Think First Found., 1990-95. With USPHS, 1968-70. Fellow ACS (bd. govs. 1984-90, sr. mem. trauma com. 1991-93); mem. AMA (physician's recognition award 1973-76, 77-79, 80-82, 83-85, 88-91, 91-94, 95-98, 98—), Congress Neurol. Surgeons (profl. conduct com. 1989-93, v.p. 1985-86, Disting. Svc. award 1989), Am. Acad. Neurol. Surgeons, Neurosurg. Soc. Am., Am. Assn. Neurologic Surgeons (nominating com. 1994-96, bd. dirs. 1998-2001, v.p. 2002-03, pres. 2005-06), Brain Surgery Soc., Ga. Med. Soc. (pres. 1995, bd. trustees 1996-2001, chmn. 2000-01), Med. Assn. Ga. (editl. bd. 1987-93), Ga. Neurosurg. Soc. (exec. com. 1981-88, pres. 1988-89), So. Neurosurg. Soc. (exec. com. 1982-91, pres. 1988-89, Semmes lectr. 1997), N.Am. Skull Base Soc., Am. Heart Assn. (fellow stroke coun.). Avocations: golf, fly fishing, hunting. Office: Neurol Inst Savannah 4 E Jackson Blvd Savannah GA 31405-5810

WIRTH, GARRETT ANDREW, plastic surgeon; s. Carl and Caroline Wirth; m. Christine Wirth; children: Kerilee, Ryan, Christopher, Quinn, Hannah, Garrett. BS, Muhlenberg Coll., Allentown, Pa., 1992; MS, Albany Med. Coll., NY, 1995, MD, 1998. Diplomate Am. Bd. Plastic Surgery, 2006. Assoc. clin. prof. plastic surgery U. Calif., Irvine Med. Ctr., Orange, 2005—. Fellow: ACS. Office: Aesthetic and Plastic Surgery Inst 200 S Manchester Ste 650 Orange CA 92868 Office Fax: 714-456-7718.

WIRTHLIN, MILTON ROBERT, JR., periodontist; b. Little Rock, July 13, 1932; s. Milton Robert and Margaret Frances (Clark) W.; m. Joan Krieger, Aug. 1, 1954; children: Michael, Steven, Laurie, David, Aina. DDS, U. Calif., San Francisco, 1956, MS, 1968. Diplomate Am. Bd. Periodontology. Commd. ensign USN, 1955, advanced through grades to capt., 1976, retired, 1985; assoc. prof. U. Pacific, San Francisco, 1985-86; assoc. clin. prof. U. Calif., San Francisco, 1986-96, clin. prof., 1996—, dir. postgrad. periodontology, 1996-99, clin. prof. emeritus, 2000—. Contbr. articles to profl. jours. Asst. scoutmaster Boy Scouts Am., San Bruno, Calif., 1968, com. chmn. Explorer Post, San Francisco, 1981-83; bd. dirs. ARC, Chgo., 1976-81, chair social svc. com., San Francisco, 1981-83. Decorated Meritorious Svc. medal with 2 gold stars; recipient Gabbs prize U. Calif., 1956. Fellow Internat. Coll. Dentists; mem. Am. Dental Assn., Am. Acad. Perdiodontology, Western Soc. Periodontology, Med-Dental Study Guild San Francisco (pres. 1993), Internat. Assn. Dental Rsch., Omicron Kappa Upsilon. Avocations: ho scale model railroading, fly tying, trout fishing, genealogy. Office: U Calif Med Ctr Sch Dentistry San Francisco CA 94143 0762 *

WISDOM, PEGGY JEAN, neurologist; b. OKeene, Okla., Nov. 4, 1947; d. Clarence W. and Grace V. Wisdom. BS in Biology/Chemistry, Northwestern State Coll., DWA, Oreg., 1968; MD, U. Okla., Norman, 1972. Diplomate Am. Bd. Psychiatry and Neurology. Resident in neurology U. Fla., 1972-76; asst. prof. neurology U. Okla., Oklahoma City, 1976-90, assoc. prof. neurology, 1990—2002, prof. neurology, 2002—, vice chair dept. neurology, 1981—; med. dir. neurologic rehab. O'Donoghue Rehab. Inst., Oklahoma City, 1981-89, chief of staff, 1986-90; chief neurology VA Med. Ctr., Oklahoma City, 1994-97, chief neurology/rehab., 1997—. Cons. Commn. on Accreditation of Rehab. Facilities, Tuscon, 1990-2006, Okla. Dept. Rehab. Svcs., Oklahoma City, 1993-96. Sci. adv. bd. Omniplex Mus., Oklahoma City, 1994. Mem. Am. Acad. Neurology, Am. Acad. Neurology (chmn. women issues in neurology sect. 1999-2001), Am. Epilepsy Soc. Republican. Presbyterian. Office: U Okla Health Scis Ctr # 215 711 Stanton L Young Blvd Oklahoma City OK 73104-5021 Office Phone: 405-271-4113. Business E-Mail: peggy-wisdom@ouhsc.edu.

WISE, ALLEN F., healthcare company executive; b. Wichita, Kans., Aug. 20, 1942; BS, Wichita State U. Exec. v.p. of operations Health Care Systems Inc., 1985—90; pres., CEO Keystone Health Plan, 1991-94; COO Independence Blue Cross, Phila., 1991—94; exec. v.p. Metra Health Co., 1994—95; pres., CEO Wise Health System, 1994; exec. v.p. United HealthCare Corp., 1995—96; pres., CEO Coventry Health Care, Inc., Bethesda, Md., 1996—2004, non-exec. chmn., 2004—08, exec. chmn., 2008—09, exec. chmn., CEO, 2009—. Bd. dir., chmn. HealthMarkets Inc.; bd. dir. Magellan Health Services Inc., NCP Group Inc. Office: 6705 Rockledge Dr Ste 900 Bethesda MD 20817-1814 *

WISE, BRET W., health products executive; m. June Wise; 3 children. BS, Ind. U. CPA. Ptnr. KPMG; v.p., CFO WCI Steel, Inc., Warren, Ohio; sr. v.p., CFO Ferro Corp., Cleve., 1999—2002; CFO, sr. v.p. DENTSPLY Internat. Inc., York, Pa., 2002—05, exec. v.p., 2005—06, pres., COO, 2006, chmn., pres., CEO, 2006—09; chmn., CEO DENTSPLY International, Inc., York, Pa., 2009—. Bd. dir. Dental Trade Alliance. Mem. AICPA, Fin. Execs. Inst. Office: DENTSPLY Internat Inc Susquehanna Commerce Ctr 221 W Philadelphia St York PA 17405 *

WISE, EDMUND JOSEPH, retired physician assistant, industrial hygienist; b. Pitts., June 18, 1947; s. Edmund Joseph and Marian Elizabeth (Burdelski) W. BA in Biology, Washington and Jefferson Coll., 1969; B of Health Scis., Duke U., 1974, cert. occupl. and environ. medicine, 2000; MPH, U. Tenn., 1990. Clin. care tech. II Duke U. Med. Ctr., Durham, N.C., 1971-72; physician asst. Oak Ridge Nat. Lab., Tenn., 1974—; ret., 2003; chief adj. faculty South Coll., 2008—. Mem. hazardous waste com. Oak Ridge Nat. Lab., 1993-2003, ergonomics com., 1994-2003, hearing conservation com., 1984-2003; mem. toxic substance control act task team Lockheed Martin Energy Sys., Oak Ridge, 1995-97; adj. prof. physician asst. program South College, Knoxville, Tenn., 2007-, mem. physician asst. adv. com., 2007-, mem. physician asst. selection com., 2007, chmn. Hall of Fame Com. Tenn., Acad. Physicians Asst., 2007-. Author: History Medical Activities 1/12 Infantry, 1970; co-author: AAPA Guidelines Continuing Medical Education, 1977, ORNL Hazwoper Program Manual, 1993; contbr. articles to profl. jours., chpt. to book. Mem. malpractice review bd. Tenn. Dept. Pub. Health, Nashville, 1981—, chief adj. faculty South Coll., student faculty advisor, South Coll., Hist. Tenn. Acad. Physicians Assts. Decorated Bronze Star, Combat Med. badge, Army commendation medal; recipient Gold cert. of Appreciation, Am. Heart Assn., 1983, Mem. awards, Com. Tenn. Acad. Physician Asst., 2008-. Fellow Am. Acad. Physician Assts. (house del. 1979, 86, profl. and continuing med. edn. com. 1975-80), Tenn. Acad. Physician Assts. (co-founder, v.p. 1975, pres. 1977, mem. awards com. 2008, named Hall of Fame, 2002, 08); Tenn. Heart Assn. (cert. BCLS, affiliate faculty 1978-2000), East Tenn. Region Heart Assn. (CPR-Emergency Cardiac Care com. 1980-99), N.C. Acad. Physician Assts. (affiliate), Soc. for Preservation of Physician Asst. History, Duke U. Alumni Assn., Nat. 4th Infantry Divsn. Assn., Washington and Jefferson Alumni Assn. Roman Catholic. Avocations: model railroading, stamp collecting/philately, gardening, tennis. Home: 1238 Venido Dr Knoxville TN 37932-2598 Personal E-mail: wiseeddiej@gmail.com.

WISE, MICHAEL, insurance company executive; m. Cynthia Wise; 3 children. BA in Economics, U. Rochester; MBA with distinction, U. Mich. Sr. mgmt. Deloitte & Touche Mgmt. Consulting; CFO Kaiser Permanente, Physicians Quality Care; served in a variety of sr.-level roles Cigna Healthcare, 1999—2005, sr. v.p. fin. and med. analysis, v.p. fin. tri-state region, sr. v.p. network mgmt.; exec. v.p., CFO ConnectiCare, 2005—10, pres., 2010—. Bd. dirs. CBIA; bd. Ins. and Fin. Svc. Cluster. Office: ConnectiCare PO Box 4050 175 Scott Swamp Rd Farmington CT 06034-4050 Office Phone: 860-674-5757.

WISE, PHYLLIS M., academic administrator, physiologist, educator; BA, Swarthmore Coll., 1967; MA, U. Mich., 1969, PhD, 1972; DSc (hon.), Swarthmore Coll., 2008. Postdoctoral fellow U. Mich., 1972—74; rsch. assoc. physiology U. N.Mex., 1974—75, adj. asst. prof. physiology, lectr. biology, 1975—76; asst. prof. physiology U. Md., Balt., 1976—82, assoc. prof. physiology, 1982—87, prof. physiology, 1987—93; prof. and chair physiology U. Ky., Lexington, 1993—2001; disting. prof. neurobiology, physiology, behavior and membrane biology U. Calif., Davis, 2002—05, dean divsn. biol. sciences, 2002—05; prof. physiology, biophysics, ob-gyn. and biology U. Wash., Seattle, 2005—, v.p. academic affairs, 2005—07, provost, 2005—, exec. v.p., 2007—, interim pres., 2010—11. Vis. sci. ob-gyn. U. Goettingen, Germany, 1985—86; bd. dirs. NIKE, Inc., 2009—. Recipient Rsch. Career Devel. award, NIH, 1982—87, Merit award, 1986—96, 2001—10, Nathan W. Shock award, 1991, Burroughs-Wellcome professorship, 1997, Robert W. Kellemeier award, Gerontol. Soc. Am., 1999, Albert D. and Elizabeth H. Kirwan Meml. prize, 2000, Excellence in Sci. award, Fedn. Am. Societies for Exptl. Biology, 2002, Women in Endocrinology Mentor award, 2003, Roy O. Greep award, 2004, Women of Influence award, Puget Sound Bus. Jour., 2008; fellow Ford Found., 1972—74. Fellow: AAAS; mem.: Inst. Medicine, Am. Physiol. Soc. (Solomon Berson award 1998), Endocrine Soc., Soc. for Neuroscience (Presdl. Speaker 1997), Soc. for the Study of Reproduction. Office: University of Washington 301 Geberding Hall Box 351237 Seattle WA 98195-1230 Office Phone: 206-543-7632. E-mail: pmwise@u.washington.edu. *

WISH, JAY BARRY, nephrologist, specialist; b. Hartford, Mar. 30, 1950; s. Martin and Evelyn Lillian (Lassman) W.; m. Linda Kristina Hansen, June 29, 1971; (div. 1980); children: Allen Jeremy, Robin Lindsey; m. Diane Elizabeth Perkins, June 5, 1983 (div. 2006); children: Jeffrey Bryan, David Phillip. BA, Wesleyan U., 1970; MD, Tufts U., 1974. Diplomate Am. Bd. Internal Medicine, Am. Bd. Nephrology. Resident in medicine New England Med. Ctr., Boston, 1974-79; instr. in medicine Tufts U., Boston, 1978-79; lectr. in health sci. Northeastern U., Boston, 1978-79; asst. prof. of medicine Case Western Res. U., Cleve., 1979-85, assoc. prof. of medicine, 1985-96, prof. medicine, 1996—; dir. hemodialysis U. Hosps. of Cleve., 1980—, dir. continuing edn., 1987-95. Chmn. Med. Adv. Bd. Kidney Found. of Ohio, Cleve., 1985-88. Author: Renal Disease and Hypertension, 1982, Disorders of Potassium, 1984, Metabolic Diseases, 1986, Rheumatic Diseases of the Kidney, 1993, Acid-Base and Electrolyte Disorders in the Critically Ill Patient, 1993, Assuring Quality of Care in Dialysis Patients, 1994, Algorithms and Care Paths for Quality Improvement, 2000, Adequacy of Hemodialysis, 2008, Quality, Safety and Accountability in Dialysis, 2008; contbr. articles to med. jours. Chmn. med. rev. bd. End-Stage Renal Disease Network #22, Pitts., 1982-87, End-State Renal Disease Network #9, Indpls., 1992-2000, pres., 2001-06; mem. exec. com. Forum of End-Stage Renal Disease Networks, 1992-2006, v.p., 1996-98, pres., 1998-2001; bd. dirs. Renal Phys. Assn., 1993-99, sec. 1996-97, treas., 1997-98; mem. Nat. Kidney Found. Fellow Am. Coll. of Physicians; mem. Am. Soc. of Nephrology, Internat. Soc. of Nephrology, Alpha Omega Alpha. Democrat. Jewish. Avocation: performing arts. Office: U Hosps Cleve 11100 Euclid Ave Cleveland OH 44106-1736 Home Phone: 216-849-3950; Office Phone: 216-844-3163. Personal E-mail: jaywish@earthlink.net.

WISH, LESLIEBETH BERGER, psychotherapist, writer, management consultant; d. Irving L. and Miriam Solomon Berger; m. Peter A. Wish, Nov. 16, 1984; 1 stepchild, Carly Sidra. AB in History & English, Carnegie Mellon U., 1970; MA in English, Ohio U., 1971; MA in Social Svc. Mgmt., Byrn Mawr Coll., 1976; EdD in Human Devel., U. Mass., 1996. Lic. clin. social worker Md., 1980, Mass., 1982, Fla., 2003, diplomate clin. social work Bd. Examiners, 1988; cert. aquatics fitness instr. 2005. Post doctoral tng. in marriage & family therapy sys. Georgetown U. Med. Sch., DC, 1979—82; dir. social work & families The Linwood Sch., Ellicott City, Md., 1980—81; dir. human resource devel. & clin. svcs. The New England Inst. Family Rels., Framingham, Mass., 1982—94; faculty coord., admissions acad. advisor Grad. Ctr. Bus. & Counseling Webster U., Sarasota, 2001—04; v.p. Gulfcoast Healthstyle, Sarasota, Fla.,

1994—. Girls' career workshop developer Girls, Inc., Sarasota, Fla., 2006—07; lectr., cons. in field; founder lovevictory.com; adv. bd. mem. & feature writer, expert Qualityhealth.com; mem. med. adv. bd., columnist Relationship Realities, 2009—. Author: Incest, Women & Work, 1998; author, contbg. editor: Trafalgar Publs., 2001—06; contbr. articles to popular mags., websites;, author numerous poems; contbr. columns in newspapers. Chair Sarasota Women's Advisory Commn., 1994—2001; pres. coun. Easter Seals, 2002—; co-coord. counseling network, spl. ops. Warrior Found., 2006—; co-coord. counselor network Spl. Ops. Warrior Found.; co-coord. Child Abuse Task Force, Sarasota, 2006—07; program and workshop devel. The Women's Resource Ctr., Sarasota, 2007—, bd. mem., 2009—; active bd. mem. Womens Resource, Sarasota, Fla., 2009, U. South Fla., Acad. Lifelong Learning Faculty, 2008—; adv. bd. mem. & writer qualityhealth.com, 2009—; columnist Rels. Realities, www.qualityhealth.com, Rels. & Sexual Health Newsletter Online. Recipient Md.'s Best Small Press award, Md. Arts Commn., 1981. Mem.: Am. Biog. Inst. (Woman Yr. 2006), Women's Leadership & Acad. Honor Society (mortar bd. 1970), Phi Kappa Phi. Achievements include first to expand sex education and awareness of sexual issues at work and home for The New England Institute of Family Relations; research in the connection between childhood sexual abuse and its impact on work and career in women; on career-family history inventory. Avocations: travel, opera, writing, painting.

WISHNICK, MARCIA MARGOLIS, pediatrician, geneticist, educator; b. NYC, Oct. 10, 1938; d. Hyman and Tillie (Stoller) Margolis; m. Stanley Wishnick, June 12, 1960; 1 child, Elizabeth Anne. BA, Barnard Coll., 1960; PhD, NYU, 1970, MD, 1974. Diplomate Am. Bd. Pediatrics, Nat. Bd. Med. Examiners. Rsch. technician Lederle Labs./Am. Cyanamid, Pearl River, NY, 1960-66; postdoctoral fellow N.Y. Pub. Health Lab., NYC, 1970-71; resident in pediatrics NYU-Bellevue Med. Ctr., NYC, 1974-77, asst. prof. pediatrics, 1977-82; clin. assoc. prof. pediatrics Bellevue Med. Ctr. NYU Med. Ctr., NYC, 1982-87; clin. prof. pediatrics NYU-Bellevue Med. Ctr., NYC, 1987—2003; pvt. practice, NYC, 1977—2003. Contbr. articles to profl. jours. Fellow Am. Acad. Pediatrics; mem. AMA, N.Y. Pediatric Soc., N.Y. Med. Soc.

WISLOWSKA, MARGARET, rheumatologist; b. Warsaw, Mar. 10, 1949; d. Stanislaw and Anna (Wawrzyniewicz) Gawdzinski; m. Janusz Wislowski, July 4, 1971; children: Aleksandra, Andrzej. MD, Med. U., Warsaw, 1972; PhD in Rheumatology, Med. Acad., Warsaw, 1986; postdoc., Med. Acad. Warsaw, Med. Acad. Lublin, 2009. Gen. practitioner Policlinic Indsl., Warsaw, 1973—75, Hosp. Warsaw, 1974—75; rheumatologist Policlinic, Warsaw, 1974—79; gen. practitioner Ctr. Hosp. Warsaw, 1979—81, rheumatologist, cons., 1981—, head of rheumatology dept., 2003—; asst. prof. Med. Acad., Warsaw and Lublin, prof., 2009. Cons., presenter, rschr. in field. Author: Rheumatoid Arthritis and Changes in Heart in Noninvasive Examinations, 1998; contbr. chapters to books, articles to profl. jours. Mem. Rheumatological Soc., N.Y. Acad. Scis., Osteoarthritis Rsch. Soc. Roman Catholic. Avocations: gardening, travel, skiing. Home and Office: Ctrl Hosp Warsaw Ul. Woloska 137 02-507 Warsaw Poland Office Phone: 048-22-508-1524.

WISNICKI, JEFFREY LEONARD, plastic surgeon; b. NYC, May 15, 1957; s. Joseph and Lorraine (Justman) Wisnicki; m. Rebecca Lynn O'Shields, Feb. 2, 1997; children: Justin Robert, Brandon Lawrence. BS summa cum laude, Rensselaer Poly. Inst., 1976; MD cum laude with honors, Union U., 1980. Diplomate Am. Bd. Plastic Surgery. Intern in surgery Stanford (Calif.) U. Med. Ctr., 1980-81, resident in gen., plastic and reconstructive surgery, 1981-84, chief resident in plastic and reconstructive surgery, 1985-86; fellow in plastic and reconstructive surgery Dartmouth-Hitchcock Med. Ctr., Hanover, NH, 1984; active staff Good Samaritan Hosp., West Palm Beach, Fla., 1986—, Wellington Regional Hosp., West Palm Beach, 1986—; chief divsn. plastic surgery John F. Kennedy Meml. Hosp., West Palm Beach, 1990-93; chmn. dept. surgery Palms West Hosp., West Palm Beach, 1991-93, chief med. staff, 1994-97, chmn. bd. trustees, 1997—2002, trustee, 2002—03; chief divsn. plastic surgery Good Samaritan and St. Mary's Hosp., West Palm Beach, 1997—2001, Good Samaritan Hosp., 2001—04. Clin. instr. surgery U. Calif., San Francisco, 1985; bd. dirs. Interplast, 1985-86, clin. faculty, 1986—90; presenter in field. Contbr. chpts. to books and articles to profl. jours. Named Best Plastic Surgeon, Palm Beach Mag., 1998. Fellow ACS; mem. Am. Soc. Plastic & Reconstructive Surgeons, Alpha Omega Alpha. Office: 13005 Southern Blvd Ste 133 Loxahatchee FL 33470 Office Phone: 561-798-1400. Business E-Mail: info@drwisnicki.com.

WISNIEWSKI, P. MICHELLE, retired obstetrician, gynecologist; b. Oneida, NY, June 26, 1945; d. Henry Francis Wisniewski and Kathryn Starr Holloway; m. Anna Cebula Costello, Sept. 20, 1998 (div. Apr. 14, 2010); m. Louise Marie Benyovszky, Sept. 22, 1984 (div.); children: Ladislaus Michael, Alexander Paul. BS, Georgetown U., 1967; MD, Universidad Autonoma de Guadalajara, Mexico, 1975. Bd. Cert. Am. Bd. of Ob/Gyn, 1983, lic. Physican and Surgeon NJ, Pa., 1977, Residency in Ob/Gyn Hahnemann U., 1980. Chairperson, dept of ob/gyn Health Care Plan of NJ., Cherry Hill, NJ, 1980—82; attending physician ob/gyn NE Hosp., Phila., 1882—1987, Nazareth Hosp., Phila., 1984—90, Pa. Hosp., Phila., 1987—91; chairperson, dept. of ob/gyn Mercy Hosp., Wilkes-Barre, Pa., 1991—92. Author: (medical research) Journal of Reproductive Medicine (Fellowship, Internat. Soc. for the Study of Vulvovaginal Disease, 1987), (photographic exibit) The Natural and Scenic Beauty of the Florida Keys, 2003, Butterflies & Warblers in the Florida Keys, 2008—, Key West Bottanical Garden & Tropical Forest; exhibitions include Butterflies of Biscayne, Nat. Pk., 2010, Butterflies of Big Cypress, Nat. Pk., 2011; author: Butterflies of the Everglades, 2009. Chmn. Fla. Keys Coun. People with Disabilities, Key West, Fla., 2002—08; sr. dir. Disability and Disaster: Surviving the Fla. Keys, Serving People Who are Deaf or Hard of Hearing, 2007; lobbyist Key West City Coun., Monroe County Commn., Key West, Fla., 2001—07; active plaintiff Assn. for Disabled Am., Miami, Fla., 2001—, pres., 2006—. 1st lt. US Army, 1967—70, Rep. Vietnam. Decorated Bronze Star Medal, Air Medal for Valor, Mil. Medal of Honor & Gallantry Cross Rep. Vietnam; recipient Hon. Conch Cert., Monroe Fla. County Mayor, 2002. Fellow: Am. Coll. Ob-Gyn. (life). Achievements include led the struggle to make the Florida Keys accessible for people with disabilities; aided passage of transgender civil rights legislation. Personal E-mail: kwimages@bellsouth.net.

WISOFF, JEFFREY HOWARD, neurosurgeon, medical educator; b. Jan. 24, 1953; MD, George Washington U. Sch. Medicine & Health Scis., 1978. Diplomate Am. Bd. Neurol. Surgery 1990. Intern surgery Mt. Sinai Med. Ctr., NYC, 1978—79; resident neurosurgery NYU Med. Ctr.-Bellvue Hosp., 1979—84; fellow pediatric neurosurgery NYU Med. Ctr., 1984—85, dir. divsn. pediatric neurosurgery, 1985—; assoc. prof. dept. neurosurgery and pediat. NYU Sch. Med., 1985—. Mem. med. adv. bd. Hydrocephalus Assn.; mem. profl. adv. bd. Children's Brain Tumor Found. Named one of Top Doctors for NY Metro Area, Castle Connolly Med. Ltd., 1999—2009, America's Top Doctors for Cancer, 2005—07, America's Top Doctors, 2006—09. Mem.: Am. Soc. Pediatric Neurosurgeons, Am. Assn. Neurol. Surgeons, Congress Neurol. Surgeons. Office: NYU Lagone Med Ctr 550 First Ave New York NY 10016 also: WHT 10 1002 317 E 34 St New York NY 10016 also: 185 Canal St 6th Fl New York NY 10013 Office Phone: 212-263-6419. Business E-Mail: Jeffrey.Wisoff@nyumc.org. *

WITHERS, HUBERT RODNEY, radiotherapist, radiobiologist, educator; b. Queensland, Australia, Sept. 21, 1932; arrived in U.S., 1966; s. Hubert and Gertrude Ethel (Tremayne) W.; m. Janet Macfie, Oct. 9, 1959; 1 child, Genevieve. MB BS, U. Queensland, Brisbane, Australia, 1956; PhD, U. London, 1965, DSc, 1982. Bd. cert. Ednl. Coun. Fgn. Med. Grads. Intern Royal Brisbane and Associated Hosps., 1957; resident in radiotherapy and pathology Queensland Radium Inst. and Royal Brisbane Hosp., 1958-63; U. Queensland Gaggin fellow Gray Lab., Mt. Vernon Hosp., Northwood, Middlesex, England, 1963—65, Royal Brisbane Hosp., 1966; radiotherapist Prince of Wales Hosp., Randwick, Sydney, Australia, 1966; vis. rsch. scientist lab. physiology Nat. Cancer Inst., Bethesda, Md., 1966-68; assoc. prof. radiotherapy sect. exptl. radiotherapy U. Tex. Sys. Cancer Ctr. M.D. Anderson Hosp. & Tumor Inst., Houston, 1968-71, prof. radiotherapy, chief sect. sect. exptl. radiotherapy, 1971-80; prof. dir. exptl. radiation oncology dept. radiation oncology UCLA, 1980-89, 1991—94, prof. vice chair, dir. exptl. radiation oncology dept. radiation oncology, 1991—94, Am. Cancer Soc. Clin. Rsch. prof. dept. radiation oncology, 1992—94, interim dir. Jonsson Comprehensive Cancer Ctr., 1994—95, chmn. radiation oncology, 1994—2005. Assoc. grad. faculty U. Tex., Grad. Sch. Biomed. Scis, Houston, 1969-73, mem. grad. faculty, 1973-80; prof. dept. radiotherapy Med. Sch., U. Tex. Health Sci. Ctr., Houston, U. Tex. Med. Sch., Houston, 1975-80; prof., dir. Inst. Oncology, The Prince of Wales Hosp., U. NSW, Sydney, Australia, 1989-91; mem. com. mortality mil. pers. present-at-atmosphere tests of nuc. weapons Inst. Medicine, 1993-94; mem. radiation effects rsch. bd. NRC, 1993-99; mem. com. neutron dose reporting Internat. Commn. Radiation Units and Measurements, 1982-93, mem. report com. clin. dosimetry for neutrons, 1993-98; mem. task force non-stochastic effects radiation Internat. Com. Radiation Protection, 1980-84, mem. com. 1, 1992-00; mem. radiobiology com. Radiation Therapy Oncology Group, 1979-89, mem. dose-time com., 1980-89, mem. gastroenterology com., 1982-89; fellow Royal Australian Coll. Radiologists Edn. Bd., 1989-91; trustee Am. Bd. Radiology, 1995-04; mem. cancer rsch. coord. com. U. Calif., 1991-97, mem. standing curriculum com. UCLA biomed. physics grad. program, 1993-2007; cons. exptl. radiotherapy U. Tex. Sys. Cancer Ctr., 1980—. Mem. Am. editl. bd.: Internat. Jour. Radiat. Oncol. Biol. Phys., 1982-89, 1991-2007, internat. editl. bd., 1989-91; cons. editor: The European Jour. Cancer, 1990-95; editl. bd. dirs.: Endocurietherapy/Hyperthermia Oncology, 1991—2001, Radiation Oncology Investigations, 1992-2002; assoc. editor: Cancer Rsch., 1993-94, editl. bd. 1995-97. Mem. Kettering selection com. Gen. Motors Cancer Rsch. Found., 1988-89, chmn., 1984, 1989, 1990-94, 2002-04, awards assembly, 1990-94, 2002-04, adv. coun., 1994-2006. Decorated officer Order of Australia, 1998; Named Gilbert H. Fletcher lectr. U. Tex. Sys. Cancer Ctr., 1989, Clifford Ash lectr. Ont. Cancer Inst., Princess Margaret Hosp., 1987, Erskine lectr. Radiol. Soc. N.Am., 1988, Ruvelson lectr. U. Minn., 1988, Milford Schultz lectr. Mass. Gen. Hosp., 1989, Del Regato Found. lectr. Hahnemann U., 1990, Bruce Cain Meml. lectr. New Zealand Soc. Oncology, 1990; recipient Medicine prize Polish Acad. Sci., 1989, Second HS Kaplan Disting. Scientist award Internat. Assn. Radiation Rsch., 1991, Gray medal Internat. Commn. Radiation Units, 1995, U.S. Dept. Energy Fermi award 1997, Radiation Rsch. Soc. Failla award, 1988, Gold medal Royal Australian and N.Z. Coll. Radiologists, 1997, Charles F. Kettering prize GM Cancer Rsch. Found., 1998; Emmanuel van der Schueren medal Belgian Rad One Soc., 2004, Gold medal Gilbert H. Fletcher Soc., 2005, Gold medal Radiol. Soc. N.Am., 2005. Fellow Am. Coll. Radiology, ACS Oncology Group (ethics com. oncology 2002—), Royal Australasian Coll. Radiologists (bd. cert., Gold medal 1997), Am. Bd. Radiology (bd. cert. therapeutic radiology 1977, Am. Coll. Radiology adv. com. patterns of care study 1988-93, radiation oncology adv. group 1993-98, others, Gold medal 2004), Am. Radium Soc. (credential com. 1986-89, 93-94, treas. 1993-94, pres. 1996-97, others, Janeway medal 1994), Am. Soc. Therapeutic Radiology and Oncology (Gold Medal awards com. 1982, 93, 00, publs. com. 1993-97, vice-chair publs. com., 1996-97, keynote address 1990, Gold medal 1991, Fellow 2006), Nat. Cancer Inst. (ad-hoc rev. coms. 1970—, radiation sudy sect. 1971-75, cons. U.S.-Japan Coop. Study high LET Radiotherapy 1975-77, cancer rsch. emphasis grant rev. com. 1976, clin. cancer ctr. rev. com. 1976-79, toxicology working group 1977-78, reviewer outstanding investigator grants 1984-93, bd. sci. counselors, 1986-88), Nat. Cancer Inst. Can. (adv. com. rsch. 1992-95), Pacific N.W. Radiol. Soc. (hon.), Tex. Radiol. Soc. (hon.), So. Calif. Radiation Oncology Soc. (sec., treas., 1992-94, pres. 1997-98), European Soc. Therapeutic Radiology and Oncology (hon.; Regaud lectr. 2000), Polish Oncology Soc. (hon., Gold medal 2002), Austrian Radiation Oncology Soc. (hon.), Phila. Roentgen Ray Soc. (hon.), Radiation Rsch. Soc. (pres. 1982-83, honors and awards com. 1984-88, ad hoc com. funds utilization 1987-89, adv. com. Radiation Rsch. Jour. 1988-96, Failla awardm 1988). Office: David Geffen Sch Medicine UCLA 10833 Le Conte Ave Los Angeles CA 90095-1714 Office Phone: 310-825-8278. Business E-Mail: hwithers@mednet.ucla.edu.

WITHERSPOON, LYNN RALPH, physician, information technology executive; b. Mt. Pleasant, Mich., Nov. 11, 1942; m. Glory Ann Smith, Jan. 27, 1980; children: Eric W., Kevin B., Heather A. BA, Fla. State U., 1964; MD, U. Wis., 1968. Diplomate Am. Bd. Nuclear Medicine, Am. Bd. Internal Medicine. With Ochsner Clinic/Alton Ochsner Med. Found., New Orleans, 1974—, dir. radioimmunology lab., 1975-95, chmn., dir. med. informatics, 1994-96; chief info. officer Ochsner Clinic, 1997—2001; chief info. officer, v.p. Ochsner Clinic Found., 2001—06; intern, then resident in internal medicine Ochsner, New Orleans, 1968-70; fellow in nuclear medicine Duke U., Durham, N.C., 1972-74, chief resident in nuclear medicine, 1973-74; chief info. officer, system v.p. Ochsner Health System, 2006—09; chief med. info. officer, system v.p. Ochsner Health Sys., 2009—. Contbr. numerous articles to profl. jours. Elder Jefferson (La.) Presbyn. Ch., 1982—; mem. adv. bd. Sta. WWNO, New Orleans, 1985—2005. Lt. comdr. USNR, 1970-72. Fellow ACP; mem. Soc. Nuclear Medicine, Southwestern Soc. Nuclear Medicine (v.p. 1980-81, sec. 1983-86, pres. 1988-89), Soc. Nuclear Medicine (trustee 1988-89), La. Healthcare Quality Farm Health Info. Tech. Com., 2008-. Presbyterian. Avocations: violin, swimming. Office: Ochsner Clinic 1514 Jefferson Hwy New Orleans LA 70121-2483 Office Phone: 504-842-4033. E-mail: lwitherspoon@ochsner.org. *

WITHERSPOON, WALTER PENNINGTON, JR., orthodontist; b. Sept. 3, 1938; s. Walter P. and Florence Evelyn (Jones) W.; m. Joyce Ann Smith, Sept. 6, 1970; 1 child, Annie Melissa. BS, U. S.C., 1960; DDS, U. N.C., 1964, MSO, 1969. Pvt. practice, Columbia, 1969—. Med. staff Bapt. Med. Ctr., Columbia, 1970—, Lexington County Hosp., West Columbia, 1974—. Host Nite Line Broadcasting Co. Adv. bd. 1st Palmetto Bank and Trust, West Columbia, 1982; mem. adv. bd. 1st Citizens Bank; candidate S.C. Ho. of Reps., 1994; del. S.C. Rep. Com., 1989—; mem. platform com. S.C. Rep. Party Conv., poll com., 1992; del. Rep. Nat. Conv., Houston, 1992, rules com., task force on edn.; Rep. nat. committeeman, 1996-2008, rules com., rep. nat. com.; pres. Rep. Electoral Coll., 1996, 2000-04; bd. dirs. Southeastern Coll. Assemblies of God, Lakeland, Fla., 1984, Brookland Plantation Home for Boys, Orangeburg, S.C.; pres. Friends of Irmo Libr.; chmn. Lexington County Rep. Party; commr. Richland/Lexington Counties Commn. for Tech. Edn., S.C. Commn. on Alcohol and Drug Abuse; bd. dirs. Centerplace for Homeless; mem. Presdl. Visit-Ticket Com.; amb. Irmo C. of C.; vol. lockup telethon Muscular Dystrophy Assn. Lt. USN, 1964-66; candidate US Senate, 2008; treas. Fin. Devel. Champions For Life, Columbia, SC. Recipient Century Mem. award Boy Scouts Am., 1984. Mem. ADA, Greater Columbia Dental Assn. (pres. 1975-76), U NC Dental Alumni Assn. (bd. dirs.), SC Dental Assn. (ho. of dels. 1971-73, 91-96, legis. com. 1993), SC Orthodontic Assn. (ctrl. dist. dir., state rep.), Am. Assn. Orthodontists, (polit. action com.), Sertoma (pres. 1975-76), Am. Legion (mem. baseball com.), So. Assn. Orthodontists (SC rep. Am. Assn. Orthodontists polit. action com.), Cen. Dist. Dental Soc., 1st Founds. Inc. (bd. dirs.). Home: 250 Lancer Dr Columbia SC 29212-1216

WITHROW, LUCILLE MONNOT, nursing home administrator; b. Alliance, Ohio, July 28, 1923; d. Charles Edward Monnot and Freda Aldine (Guy) Monnot Cameron; m. Alvin Robert Withrow, June 6, l945 (dec. 1984); children: Cindi Withrow Johnson, Nancy Withrow Townley, Sharon Withrow Hodgkins (dec.), Wendel Alvin. AA in Health Adminstrn., Eastfield Coll., Mesquite, Tex., 1976. Lic. nursing home adminstr., Tex.; cert. nursing home ombudsman. Held various clerical positions, Dallas, 1950-72; office mgr., asst. adminstr. Christian Care Ctr. Nursing Home, Mesquite, Tex., 1972-76; head adminstr. Christian Care Ctr. Nursing Home and Retirement Complex, Mesquite, 1976-91; nursing home ombudsman Tex. Dept. Aging and Tex. Dept. Health, Dallas, 1991-93; legal asst. Law Offices of Wendel A. Withrow, Carrollton, Tex., 1993—. Com. on geriatric curriculum devel. Eastfield Coll., Mesquite, 1979, 87; ombudsman adv. com. Sr. Citizens Greater Dallas; cons. in field. Vol. Dallas Arboretum and Bot. Soc.; mem. Ombudsman adv. com. Sr. Citizens of Greater Dallas; charter mem. Stage Show Prodns. Recipient Volunteerism award, Tex. Atty. Gen., 1987, Tex. Gov., 1992. Mem. Tex. Assn. Homes for Aging, Am. Assn. Homes for Aging, Health Svcs. Speakers Bur., White Rock Kiwanis. Mem. Ch. Of Christ. Avocations: reading, travel, theater. Home: 11344 Lippitt Ave Dallas TX 75218-1922 Office: Law Office of W A Withrow 1120 Metrocrest Dr Ste 200 Carrollton TX 75006-5872

WITKIN, EVELYN MAISEL, retired geneticist; b. NYC, Mar. 9, 1921; d. Joseph and Mary (Levin) Maisel; m. Herman A. Witkin, July 9, 1943 (dec. July 1979); children— Joseph, Andrew. AB, NYU, 1941; MA, Columbia U., 1943, PhD, 1947; DSc honoris causa, N.Y. Med. Coll., 1978, Rutgers U., 1995. Mem. staff genetics dept. Carnegie Inst., Washington, 1950-55; mem. faculty State U. N.Y. Downstate Med. Center, Bklyn., 1955-71, prof. medicine, 1968-71; prof. biol. scis. Douglass Coll., Rutgers U., 1971-79, Barbara McClintock prof. genetics, 1979-83, Waksman Inst. Microbiology, 1983-91; Barbara McClintock prof. emerita Waksman Inst. Microbiology, Rutgers U., 1991—. Author articles; mem. editorial bds. profl. jours. Postdoctoral fellow Am. Cancer Soc., 1947-49; fellow Carnegie Instn., 1957; Selman A. Waksman lectr., 1960; Phi Beta Kappa vis. scholar, 1980-81; grantee NIH, 1956-89; recipient Prix Charles Leopold Mayer French Acad. Scis., 1977, Lindback award, 1979, Nat. Medal of Science award, 2002. Fellow AAAS, Am. Acad. Microbiology; mem. NAS, Am. Acad. Arts and Scis., Environ. Mutagen Soc., Am. Genetics Soc. (Thomas Hunt Morgan medal, 2000), Am. Soc. Microbiology. Home: 1 Firestone Ct Princeton NJ 08540-5220 E-mail: ewitkin@aol.com.

WITTE, ARNOLD STEWART, neurologist; b. NYC, Dec. 14, 1952; s. Henry Dennis Witte and Shirley Block; m. Debra J. DeLuca, Apr. 29, 1984; children: Samantha, Russell, Daniel, Larissa. BS, SUNY, Stony Brook, 1973; MD, Tufts U., 1977. Diplomate Am. Bd. Internal Medicine, Am. Bd. Neurology & Psychiatry, Am. Bd. Electrodiagnostic Medicine, lic. NJ, Pa. Intern U. Hosps. Cleve., Cleve., 1977—78, resident, 1978—79; resident in neurology Hosp. of U. Pa., Phila., 1980—81, fellow, 1982—83; asst. prof. neurology Thomas Jefferson U. Hosp., 1983—86; mem. staff Capital Health Sys. at Mercer, 1986—, chief dept. neurology, 1989—96, 1999, vice chief dept. neurology, 2000—. Cons. Trenton Psychiat. Hosp., 1987—, Forensic Psychiat. Hosp., 1987—; courtesy staff St. Francis Med. Ctr.,

1993—. Contbr. articles to profl. jours. Mem.: AMA, Mercer County Med. Soc., Am. Acad. Neurology, Alpha Omega Alpha. Office: 2 Princess Rd Lawrenceville NJ 08648 Office Phone: 609-895-9000.

WITTE, KRISTEN LEE, molecular biologist; b. Madison, Wis., Mar. 16, 1987; BS, U. Wis., Madison, 2009. Assoc. rsch. specialist, dept. biomolecular chemistry U. Wis., 2009—. Home: 308 Forest St 6 Madison WI 53726 Business E-Mail: kwitte@wisc.edu.

WITTENBERG, HENRY TAYLOR, JR., physician, surgeon; b. Kansas City, July 5, 1933; s. Henry Taylor and Ruby Lena (Pratt) Wittenberg; m. Helen Marie Marlar, Sept. 7, 1963; children: Heather Melanee, Henry Taylor III. BS in Pharmacy, U. Kans., Lawrence, 1956; DO, Kansas City U. Medicine and Bioscis., 1960. Lic. Mo., 1960, Okla., 1962, cert. Am. med. dir. 1998. Intern Lakeside Hosp., Kansas City, 1960—61; preceptor Claremore Health Ctr., Okla., 1962—64; physician pvt. practice, Independence, Mo., 1961—62, Blue Star Clinic, Claremore, 1962—, Claremore Regional Hosp., 1962—; interim home health med. dir., 2004—. Chief staff Claremore Regional Hosp., 1962—; founder, bd. mem. First Bank of Okla., 1977, v.p. bd., 1977—87; founding mem. Okla. chpt. Am. Med. Dirs., 1991, v.p. bd., 1991—95; med. dir. Wood Manor Nursing Home, 1987—, Claremore Nursing Home, 1989—, Trinity Hospice, 2000—, Colonial Care Nursing Home, 2002—; mem. gov.'s com. Emergency Med. Svc., 1995—2000; mem. adv. bd. Unicare Welfare HMO, 2002—04. Editor-in-chief: U. Kans. Jayhawker U. Kans. Yearbook, 1956. Founding mem., pres. Claremore Jaycees; chmn. Rogers County March of Dimes, 1965—67; Jaycee founder group, original cast mem. Claremore Gridiron, 1966—; lay reader St. Paul's Episcopal Ch., jr. warden, 1998, sr. warden, 1999. Recipient Omicron Delta Kappa Scholastic award, Kans. U., Otto Schnellbacjer award Outstanding Contbr. Campus L:ife, Nat. Leadership award, Nat. Rep. Congressional Com., cert. for contbns. to ambulatory care and pub. health, CDC; named Physician of Yr., Claremore, Okla., 1996, Rep. of Yr., Nat. Rep. Congressional Com. and Bus. Adv. Coun., 2001; named one of Am.'s Top Family Doctors, Consumer Rsch. Coun. Am., 2004, 2007. Mem.: Rogers County Med. Soc. (v.p. 1986, program dir. 1986—97), Okla. Osteo. Assn. (life), U. Kans. Gold Medal Club, Shrine (Potentate's Honor award 2003), Scottish Rite, Masons, Rho Sigma Chi, Sigma Sigma Phi, Psi Sigma Alpha, Kappa Psi (pres.), Delta Chi. Episcopalian. Achievements include delivery over 3000 babies. Office: Blue Star Clinic 206 E Blue Star Dr Claremore OK 74017 Home Phone: 918-341-4278; Office Phone: 918-341-4040.

WITTICH, CHRISTOPHER MARTIN, physician; b. Mount Pleasant, Iowa, Dec. 30, 1974; PharmD, U. Iowa, 1999; MD, Mayo Med. Sch., 2003. Physician Mayo Clinic, 1999—2011. Fellow: ACP; mem.: AMA, Assn. Med. Edn. Europe, Assn. Program Dirs. Internal Medicine, Soc. Academic Continuing Med. Edn. Avocations: cooking, travel. Office: 200 First St SW Rochester MN 55905 Business E-Mail: wittich.christopher@mayo.edu.

WITTMER, JAMES FREDERICK, preventive medicine physician, educator; b. Carlinville, Ill., Dec. 30, 1932; s. Franklin Benjamin and Eva Caroline (Zihlman) W.; m. Juanita Lou Wilkey, June 29, 1962; children: Ellen, Carol, Nancy. MD, Washington U., St. Louis, 1957; MPH, Harvard U., 1961. Diplomate Am. Bd. Preventive Medicine. Intern U. Va. Hosp., Charlottesville, 1857-58; commd. capt. USAF, 1958, advanced through grades to col., 1971; ret., 1979; dean allied health U. Tex. Health Sci. Ctr., San Antonio, 1979-80, asst. med. dir. Conoco Oil Co., Ponca City, Okla., 1980-81; assoc. med. dir. Mobil Oil Corp., NYC, 1981-83; dir. health, environ. and safety ITT, NYC, 1983-95, corp. v.p., 1990-95. Clin. prof. medicine Cornell U. Med. Coll., NYC, 1984—; lectr. environ. medicine NYU, NYC, 1984—; adj. prof. U. Tex. Sch. Pub. Health, Houston, 1987—, prof. occupl. health, 1996—97, nat. coord. com. on clin. preventive svcs. USPHS, 1994—97; cons. office hearings and appeals U.S. Social Security Adminstrn., 1997—2003; cons. Met. Health Dist., San Antonio, 2002—08. Mem. Pres.'s Com. on Employment People with Disabilities, Washington, 1986-2000, chmn. med. and ins. com., 1986-90. Fellow ACP, Am. Coll. Occupational and Environ. Medicine (bd. dirs. 1990-97, sec. 1992-94), Am. Coll. Preventive Medicine, Aerospace Med. Assn., N.Y. Acad. Medicine; mem. AMA. Home and Office: 159 Sabine Rd Boerne TX 78006-6217 Home Phone: 830-537-4782; Office Phone: 830-537-4782. Business E-Mail: wittmer@gvtc.com.

WITTY, ANDREW, pharmaceutical executive; BA in Economics, Nottingham U., 1985. Joined Glaxo UK, 1985; dir. pharmacy & distribution Glaxo Pharms. UK; dir. bus. devel. Biocompatibles Ltd.; internat. product mgr. Glaxo Holdings plc; mng. dir. Glaxo South Africa, area dir. South & East Africa; v.p., gen. mgr. mktg. Glaxo Wellcome Inc.; sr. v.p. Asia Pacific, Pharms. Internat. GlaxoSmithKline plc, Singapore, 2001—03, pres. Europe pharmaceuticals Brentford, England, 2003—08, CEO, 2008—. Mem. working group Pharma Futures; econ. adviser Gov. of Guangzhou, China, 2000—02; bd. mem. Singapore Econ. Devel. Bd., Singapore Land Authority Bd., Min. of Law, 2002—03; bd. dirs. GlaxoSmithKline plc, 2008—; non-exec. dir. Office Strategic Coordination Health Rsch. Mem. Imperial Coll. Commercialization Adv. Bd., Health Innovation Coun., INSEAD UK Coun. Recipient Pub. Svc. medal, Govt. of Singapore, 2003; named a Power Player, Advt. Age, 2009. Office: GlaxoSmithKline plc One Franklin Plaza PO Box 7929 Philadelphia PA 19101 also: 980 Great W Rd Brentford TW8 9GS England *

WITTY, THOMAS EZEKIEL, III, psychologist, researcher; b. Greensboro, NC, Oct. 11, 1955; s. Thomas Ezekiel, Jr. and Peggy (Coggins) Witty; m. Ginger Lynell Kissee, June 28, 1997; children: Ezekiel Thomas, Zoe Anne. BA in English, U. N.C., Greensboro, 1980; MS, Va. Commonwealth U., 1989; PhD, U. Mo., 1995. Lic. psychologist Miss., cert. in rehab. Am. Bd. Profl. Psychology, 2008. Tchr. secondary English, debate and cross-country coach Henry County Pub. Schs., Collinsville, Va., 1981-87; fin. aid. counselor asst. Va. Commonwealth U., Richmond, 1987-89; substance abuse counselor Dist. 19 Alcoholism Svcs., Petersburg, Va., 1990; grad. rsch. asst. U. Mo., Columbia, 1990-94, grad. instr., 1992-94; postdoctoral fellow Rusk Rehab. Ctr., Columbia, 1995-98; chief psychology Mo. Rehab. Ctr., Mt. Vernon, 1998-2001; psychologist North Miss. Med. Ctr., Tupelo, 2001—. Rsch. cons. Coun. on Rehab. Edn., Inc., Champaign, Ill., 1991; ad hoc reviewer Jour. Rehab. Psychology, 1995—98; internship selection com. U. Mo. Health Svcs. Consortium, Columbia, 1996—98; faculty Family Medicine Residency Ctr., Tupelo, Miss., 2001—; alt. mem. instl. rev. bd. N. Miss. Med. Ctr., 2002—. Contbr. articles to profl. jours. Walter Scott Monroe Rsch. fellow, U. Mo., 1992—95, Postdoctoral fellow, NIH, 1995—98, Rsch. grantee, U. Mo. Rsch. Bd., 1997. Mem.: APA (divsn. 17, 22, 38, 50), Miss. Psychol. Assn., Sierra Club, KC, Kappa Delta Pi. Democrat. Roman Catholic. Avocations: running, swimming, bicycling, hiking, camping. Office: North Miss Med Ctr Dept Behavioral Health 830 S Gloster St Tupelo MS 38801 Business E-Mail: twitty@nmhs.net.

WITZ, GISELA, research scientist, educator; b. Breslau, Federal Republic of Germany, Mar. 16, 1939; came to U.S., 1955. d. Gerhardt Witz and Hildegard (Sufeida) Minzak. BA, NYU, 1962, MS, 1965, PhD, 1969. Assoc. rsch. scientist NYU Med. Ctr., NYC, 1970-73, rsch. scientist, 1973-77, asst. prof., 1977-80, U. Medicine and Dentistry of N.J.-Robert Wood Johnson Med. Sch., Piscataway, NJ, 1980-86, 1986—93, prof., 1993—2000, prof. emeritus, 2001—. Dep. dir. Joint Grad. Program in Toxicology, Rutgers U./Univ. Medicine and Dentistry of N.J.-Robert Wood Johnson Med. Sch., 1988, assoc. dir. 1992-2000; cons. Nat. Rsch. Coun., Washington, 1982-83, 85-86. Recipient Dupont Teaching award, NYU, 1966, Univ. Scholar, Founders Day award, N.Y. U., 1969, Student Appreciation award Rutgers Assn. Toxicology Grad. Students, 1996, Faculty Vol. award UMDNJ-Robert Wood Johnson Med. Sch., 2004, 06; honoree 3d Ann. Women in Sci. Symposium, 2000. Fellow Oxygen Soc.; mem. Am. Assn. Cancer Rsch., Am. Chem. Soc., Soc. Toxicology, N.Y. Acad. Sci., Sigma Xi. Avocations: gardening, painting. Office: U Medicine and Dentistry NJ Robert Wood Johnson Med Sch Piscataway NJ 08854 E-mail: witz@eohsi.rutgers.edu.

WITZEL, LOTHAR GUSTAV, physician, gastroenterologist; b. Mannheim, Fed. Republic Germany, July 27, 1939; s. Gustav and Martha (Pilger) Witzel; m. Heidemarie Stiffel; children: Lothar Gustav, Angelika, Stefan, Eva-Maria. MD, U. Freiburg, Fed. Republic of Germany, 1965; PhD, U. Berlin, 1983. Substitute medicine supt. U. Bern (Switzerland) Med. Sch., 1973-77; dir., med. supt. German Red Cross Hosp., Berlin, 1978-93. Contbr. articles to profl. jours.; patentee in field. Mem. Indian Soc. Gastroenterology (hon.), European Congress Endoscopy (sec. gen. 1981), Swiss Soc. Gastroenterology (corr. mem. 1989, Award of Gastroenterology 1981). Avocation: jazz music. Office: Ansbacher Str 13 Berlin 10787 Germany Office Phone: 00493021005720. Business E-Mail: lothar@prof.-dr.-witzel.de.

WIVEL, NELSON AUBURN, physician, medical researcher, educator, biotechnology consultant; b. Denver, Sept. 4, 1935; s. Claude Burns and Aubrey (Angus) W.; m. Carol Henderson, June 16, 1963 (dec. 1999); children: Mark Auburn, Ashley Elizabeth. BS, Ea. N.Mex. U., 1957; MD, Stanford U., 1961. Diplomate Am. Bd. Pathology. Intern Cornell U., NYC, 1961-62, asst. resident in medicine, 1962-63; asst. resident in pathology Stanford U., Calif., 1963-65; rsch. trainee in pathology Washington U., St. Louis, 1965-66; head ultrastructural studies sect. Nat. Cancer Inst., Bethesda, Md., 1966-70, head ultrastructural biology sect., 1970-86; med. officer for AIDS rsch. Gen. Clin. Rsch. Ctrs., NIH, Bethesda, 1986-89, dir. Office of Recombinant DNA Activities, 1989-96; dep. dir. Inst. Human Gene Therapy Sch. Medicine U. Pa., Phila., 1996—2007. Adj. prof. molecular and cellular engring., program chair ethics and pub. policy rsch. program U. Pa. Med. Ctr., Phila., 1996-2007, exec. dir. recombinant DNA adv. com. NIH; biotech. cons., 2007—. Assoc. editor Jour. Nat. Cancer Inst., 1968-70, Human Gene Therapy, 1993-2009, Jour. Biolaw and Bus., 1996—, Transplant Video Jour., 2002-04, Pre Clinica, 2003-05; contbr. more than 100 articles to profl. jours. including Sci., Nature, Jour. of Virology, Virology. Recipient Commendation medal USPHS, 1990. Mem. Am. Soc. Cell Biology, Am. Soc. Virology, Am. Soc. Gene Therapy. Achievements include research on murine retroviruses that can function as moveable genetic elements (transposons). Office Phone: 215-836-1519.

WLODAWER, ALEXANDER, medical researcher; b. Poland; PhD, UCLA, 1974; Doctor Honoris Causa, Tech. U., Lodz, Poland, 2004. Postdoctoral training Stanford U.; joined Nat. Bur. Standards, 1976; joined ABL Basic Rsch. Program, Ctr. Cancer Rsch., Nat. Cancer Inst., NIH, Frederick, Md., 1987, chief Macromolecular Crystallography Lab., 1999—, head protein structure sect. Vis. fellow Sidney Sussex Coll., U. Cambridge, 1998—99; adj. prof. biochemistry and molecular biology George Washington U., assoc. mem. Inst. Biomedical Sciences; editor FEBS Jour.; mem. editl. bd. Protein Sci., Acta Biochimica Polonica. Mem.: Polish Acad. Sciences (fgn. mem.), Protein Soc., Am. Crystallographic Assn. Office: Macromolecular Crystallography Lab NCI Frederick Bldg 536 Rm 5 PO Box B Frederick MD 21702-1201 Office Phone: 301-846-5036. Office Fax: 301-846-6322. E-mail: wlodawer@nih.gov. *

WOEBER, KENNETH ALOIS, physician; b. Feb. 2, 1935; MB, BChir, MD, U. Witwatersrand, Johannesburg, South Africa, 1957. Intern Johannesburg Hosp., 1958-59; rsch. fellow Harvard Med. Sch., 1962-64, instr. medicine, 1965-68, asst. prof. medicine, 1968-70, assoc. prof. medicine, 1970-72; prof. clin. medicine U. Calif., San Francisco, 1975—, vice-chmn. medicine, 1981-2000, chief clin. endocrinology, 2000—. Chmn. subsplty. bd. endocrinology and metabolism Am. Bd. Internal Medicine, 1985-87. Contbr. articles to profl. jours. Recipient Van Meter prize Am. Thyroid Assn. Fellow Royal Coll. Physicians of Edinburgh. Home: 6 Bartel Ct Belvedere Tiburon CA 94920-1656 Office: U Calif San Francisco at Mt Zion PO Box 1640 San Francisco CA 94143-1640 Office Phone: 415-885-7574. Business E-Mail: ken.woeber@ucsf.edu. *

WOEHRLEN, ARTHUR EDWARD, JR., dentist; b. Detroit, Dec. 9, 1947; s. Arthur Edward and Olga (Hewka) W.; m. Sara Elizabeth Heikoff, Aug. 13, 1972; 1 child, Tess Helena. DDS, U. Mich., 1973. Resident in gen. dentistry USAF, 1973-74; gen. practice dentistry Redwood Dental Group, Warren, Mich., 1976—. Instr. Sinai Hosp., Detroit, 1977—; chief of dentistry St. John's Hosp., Macomb Ctr., Mt. Clemens, Mich., 1982—; mem. dentistry staff Hutzel Hosp., Warren; reviewer Chubb Ins. Co. (malpractice claims), 1978-89; bd. mem. Mich. Acad. Gen. Dentistry (chmn. State of Mich. Continuing Dental Edn. Accreditation). Contbr. articles on dentistry to profl. jours. Served to capt. USAF, 1973-76. Fellow Internat. Coll. of Oral Implantologists; mem. ADA, Acad. Gen. Dentistry (Master), Mich. Dental Assn., Acad. Gen. Dentistry, Am. Acad. Oral Medicine, Fedn. Dentaire Internationale, Acad. Dentistry for the Handicapped, Am. Acad. Oral Implantologists, Internat. Coll. Oral Implantologists, Macomb Dist. Dental Soc.; panel mem. Am. Arbitration Assn. Independent. Home: 25460 Dundee Rd Royal Oak MI 48067-3018 Office: 13403 E 13 Mile Rd Warren MI 48088-3188

WOJCIECHOWSKI, KRZYSZTOF JAN, virologist, consultant, writer, researcher, editor; s. Zdzislaw Jacek Wojciechowski and Irena Zygfryda Wojciechowska; m. Barbara Carmel Ivory, Apr. 1, 1981; m. Marcjanna Grazyna Mackiewicz, Jan. 21, 1961 (div. June 21, 1978); children: Piotr Kazimierz, Paulina Ewa. Vet. surgeon, Warsaw Agrl. U., 1961, D of Vet. Sci.-Microbiology, 1967; DSc, Nat. Vet. Rsch. Inst., Pulawy, Poland, 1974. Microbiologist, mycologist, master production-fermentation of antibiotics Polfa Farmaceuticals, Warsaw-Tarchomin, 1961—62; rsch. fellow vet. faculty Warsaw Agrl. U., 1963—66; head virology sect. Lab. of Vet. Hygiene, Warsaw, 1967—77, docent-assoc. prof. virology sect., 1974—84; advisor Labs. Vet. Hygiene, Virology Diagnosis to Ministry Agr., Poland, 1974—77; project mgr., animal health officer-virology FAO-UN, Kabul, Afghanistan, 1977—81, animal health officer-virology hdqrs. Rome, 1982—99, global cons., regional tech. coop. program project (epidemiology) for Balkans, 2001—03; freelance internat. cons. on viral disease control and animal health Warsaw, Dublin, 2000—. Advisor Vet. Dept.-Ministry of Agr., Warsaw, 1973—77; univ. lectr. vet. propedeutics vet. faculty Warsaw Agrl. U., 1967—77, part-time univ. lectr. virology, epizootiology vet. faculty, 1974—77, co-initiator vet. biotech. devel. in Poland, 1991—98, co-initiator Dept. Viral Rsch. and Preparation of Anti-viral Biol. State Vet. Inst., 1975—77, advisor to dean faculty vet. medicine, 2000—04; asst. custodian Ctr. History of Vet. Medicine, Warsaw, 1959—77, voluntary custodian, 2004—; founder, co-coord. CENTAUR - FAO Established Network of Vet. Biotech./Epidemiology/Food Safety, 1996—; adv. bd. mem. Centaur News Flash Info and the Centaur webpage, Vet. Rsch. Inst., Brno, Czech Republic, 1998—; FAO/UN fellow dept. virology Cen. Vet. Lab., Weybridge, Surrey, England, 1971—72; mem. Biomed. Tech. Epidemiology & Food Soc. Centaur Global Network. Contbr. reports, articles, and papers to profl. jours.; editor: Memoirs of K.M. Millak 1886-1920, 2003; author: Mikolaj Rej Lycee in Warsaw in the Peak of Stalinism, 2006, Preparation of History of Polish Society of Veterinary Sciences, 2010. Recipient Letter of Appreciation, Govt. of Afghanistan, 1981, Mark of Distinction, Min. of Agr. and Food Economy, Poland, 1998, Cert. of Appreciation, Pan African Veterinary Vaccine Ctr., 2006; named George C. Poppensiek Vis. Prof. in Internat. Vet. Medicine, Cornell U., 2001. Mem.: AAAS, Am. Soc. for Microbiology, Polish Soc. Vet. Sci. (chmn. Warsaw br. 1975—77, head sect. history of vet. medicine 2007—10, Fad mfg. GREP & Celebration mem. 2011, golden diploma vol. surgeon u. lifescis. 2011, Mark of Distinction 1992), Polish Soc. Vet. Sci. (hon.), Former UN Staff Mems. Assn. (life). Roman Catholic. Achievements include participation in the development of PanAfrican Rinderpest Eradication Campaign; scientific supervision of 10 FAO associate professional officers and the FAO André Mayor Research fellowship holder; invited speaker to 15 international expert consultations, congresses, meetings or seminars, representing FAO during 7 meetings of the International Office of Epizootics-OIE; establishing Virology Section (including the National Veterinary Reference Laboratory on Rabies Diagnosis), Laboratory of Veterinary Hygiene, Warsaw; participation in the development of The Concept South Asia Rinderpest Eradication Campaign SAREC; initiating the establishement of Veterinary Vaccine Quality Control in Central, Eastern and Southern Africa, Ethiopia, and co-initiating the PanAfrican Veterinary Vaccine Centre PANVAC; co-initiating Global Rinderpest Eradication Campaign (GREP); attempts to initiate and design PAN MEAL TU pan africa center for American Health co-initiation and contribution to the development of the FAO Biotechnology Programmes on Animal Health; development of control and eradication of Newcastle Disease with special emphasis on use of the ND4 vaccine for rural poultry; co-initiation and co-management of CANAPS-Computer Assisted Network on Nucleid Acids and Protein Sequencing in Latin America and Carribean; managing the establishment and upgrading of Veterinary Laboratories (Diagnostic or Vaccines) in 17 Countries of Africa, Asia and Middle East; contribution to coordination of the FAO Reference Laboratories (21) and Collaborating Centres; backstopping implementation of 130 national and 20 regional FAO projects; West Asia Rinderpest Eradication Campaign Coordination; organization and implemenation of regional training workshops; African Swine Fever Control in Latin Americas, Carribean: 1982-84, Carribean: 1996-98, Africa: 1985-99; Participating in the work of EMPRES-FAO Emergency Prevention System for Transboundary Animal and Plant Pests and Diseases-Livestock Component; control and eradication of rabies in cooperation with the World Health Organization (WHO); control and eradication of exotic and transboundary diseases of livestock and poultry; initiation and coordination of applied research related to infectious diseases control-in cooperation with international centres of excellence; design of contribution to the team work on designing of 95 national and regional FAO projects; presentation of CENTAUR to international philosophical meetings Dialogue and Universalism in Warsaw and the veterinary conference by Ukrainian Academy of Sciences in Feodosia, Crimea 2003, Odessa,2010; Food and Agriculture Organization of UN/International Atomic Energy Agency 2004; co introduction of rabies laboratory diagnostic (fluorescent antibody test) at worthy level including verifications. Avocations: philosophy, history, literature, jazz, skiing. E-mail: krisjwojciechowski@gmail.com.

WOJTCZAK, ANDRZEJ MACIEJ, physician, educator; b. Bielsko, Poland, Dec. 11, 1933; s. Jozef Antoni and Maria Wanda (Wolska) Wojtczak; m. Krystyna Teresa Cichonczyk, Apr. 12, 1961; children: Krzysztof, Hanna. BS magna cum laude, Med. Sch. Poznan, Poland, 1955, MD, 1962, PhD, DMSc, Med. Sch. Poznan, Poland, 1966. Cert. specialty in internal medicine 1961, sub-specialty in nephrology Poznan, Poland, 1968. Assoc. prof., head, dept. nephrology Med. Sch. Poznan, Poland, 1968—71; prof. medicine, head, dept. medicine Nat. Rsch. Inst. Lung Disease and Tuberculosis, Warsaw, 1972—86; prof. medicine, head, dept. internat. health faculty of social medicine Sch. Postgrad. Med. Edn., Warsaw, 1991—96, dean, faculty of social medicine, 1996—2001, prof. emeritus, 2001—. Vis. scientist Hosp. U. Pa., Phila., 1965—66, Hammersmith Hosp., London, 1965—66; dir., nat. health policies & sys., rsch. & human resources WHO, Copenhagen, 1979—86, coord., program of cooperation with european mem. states, 1984—86; exec. dir. WHO Rsch. Ctr. for Health Devel., Kobe, Japan, 1996—99; dir. Inst. for Internat. Med. Edn., White Plains, NY, 1999—; vis. prof., sch. social policy Kwansei Gakuin U., Hyogo, Japan, 1999—2002. Contbr. articles to numerous profl. med. jours.; editor: Textbook of Internal Medicine, 1981—83, Textbook of Internal Medicine 2d edit., 1995. Dir., dept. med. edn. & sci. Ministry of Health and Social Welfare, Warsaw, 1971—78, undr-sec. of state for health, 1989—91, vice-chmn, nat. coun. of med. cons., 1994—96; mem., adv. coun. on social policy to Pres. of Rep. of Poland, 1992—96; mem., adv. group on health issues to Spkr. of Sen. of Rep. of Poland, 1993—96; mem., bur. european health com. Coun. of Europe, Strasbourg, France, 1994—96. Fellow, Rockefeller Found., 1958—59. Mem.: Internat. Assn. of Med. Sci. Educators, Warsaw Scientific Soc., Polish Acad. Sci. (mem. com. of social aspects in medicine 1992—), Polish Soc. Social Medicine and Pub. Health (v.p. 1991—96), Assn. for Med. Edn. for Europe (mem. exec. com. 1982—99, pres. 1992—96), European Health Care Mgmt. Assn. (hon.), Polish Med. Alliance (hon.). Home: Ul. Inflancka 163 00-189 Warsaw Poland Office Phone: 914-253-6682. E-mail: wojtczak@iime.org.

WOLAHAN, CARYLE GOLDSACK, nursing educator, consultant; b. Somerville, NJ, July 27, 1942; d. Wilbur Wood and Jane (Hadley) Goldsack; m. Thomas Warren Hussey, June 26, 1965 (dec. Oct. 1970); 1 child, Timothy Stephen; m. William Kevin Wolahan, Sept. 30, 1983 (dec. Jan. 2001). BS, Wagner Coll., 1964; MEd, Columbia U., 1973, EdD, 1979. Sch. nurse, tchr. Malverne Pub. Schs., NY, 1966—67, Dover-Wingdale Pub. Schs., Dover Plains, NY, 1967—68; head nurse Harlem Valley State Hosp., Wingdale, NY, 1968—69; asst. prof., acting dir. div. nursing Trenton State Coll., NJ, 1973—77; assoc. prof., acting dir. Felician Coll., Lodi, NJ, 1979—80, dir. divsn. nursing, 1982—87; dir. nursing program Stern Coll., Yeshiva U., NYC, 1980—82; assoc. dean Coll. Nursing SUNY Health Sci. Ctr., Bklyn., 1987—91, acting dean Coll. Nursing, 1991—92; dean sch. nursing Adelphi U., 1992—2000; prof. nursing Adelphi U. Sch. Nursing, 2000—05; ret., 2005; nursing edn. cons., 2005—. Contbr. articles to profl. jours., chpts. to books; editor Topics in Clin. Nursing, 1983. Trustee Cath. Med. Ctrs. Bklyn. and Queens, 1989-2000, chair continuous quality improvement com., 1998-2000; regional bd. St. Vincent's Cath. Med. Ctrs. Recipient NEAA award, Disting. Trustee award United Hosp. Fund, 2000; named Woman of Achievement Alpha Omicron Pi; named to Nursing Hall of Fame Tchrs. Coll. Columbia U., 1999. Mem. ANA (del. 1978-87), NJ State Nurses Assn. (coun. on edn. 1976-82, chmn. com. on ednl. preparation 1984-88), NY State Nurses Assn. (chair pub. rels. com. 1990-92, spkrs. bur., recruitment com. Dist. 14, 1990, chair coun. on edn.), Nat. League for Nursing (accreditation com. 1985-90, site visitor 1984-98), Am. Acad. Nursing, Nursing Edn. Alumni Assn. Tchrs. Coll. (pres. 1990-94. v.p. 2003-04, pres. 2004-06), Lake Hopatcong Yacht Club (fleet surgeon 2004—), Sigma Theta Tau. Episcopalian. Avocations: boating, reading, theater, hand crafts. Home: 1143 Crim Rd Bridgewater NJ 08807-2344 Home Phone: 973-398-8308. Personal E-mail: dublin@optonline.net. Business E-Mail: wolahan@adelphi.edu.

WOLANSKYJ, ALEXANDRA, hematologist; d. Bohdan Markian Wolanskyj and Urania Wolanskyj nee Vassalakis; m. Robert Jay Spinner, Dec. 3, 2000; children: Maxwell Alexander Spinner, Noah Daniel Spinner. BSc with honors, Concordia U., Montreal, Que., 1987; MD, U. Montreal, 1992; MS in Internal Medicine, Mayo Grad. Sch. Medicine, Rochester, Minn., 1995, MS in Hematology-Oncology, 1998. Registered Am. Bd. Internal Medicine, 1995, in hematology Am. Bd. Internal Medicine, 1998, in oncology Am. Bd. Internal Medicine, 1998. Asst. prof. medicine Mayo Clinic, Rochester, 2004—, chair edn., divsn. hematology, 2006—. Chair, hematology course Mayo Clinic Coll. Medicine, Med. Sch., 2006—. Prodr.: (musical album) Lesya (Winner Best Original Song, 1987, Album of Yr., 1987); contbr. articles to profl. med. jours. Named Tchr. of Yr., Med. Coll. Ohio, 2001, Mayo Grad. Sch. Medicine, 2006; grantee Edn. Innovation, Mayo Coll. Medicine, 2004. Fellow: Royal Coll. Surgeons and Physicians Can.; mem.: ACP, Am. Soc. Clin. Oncology, Am. Soc. Hematology.

WOLCOTT, HUGH DIXON, obstetrics and gynecology educator; b. NYC, Jan. 12, 1946; s. Charles Edmund and Joan Degrau (Loveland) W.; m. Jane Jarrell Smith; children: Allison, James. BS, U.S. Naval Acad., 1967; MSE, Princeton U., 1969; MD, Northwestern U., 1979. Diplomate Am. Bd. Ob-Gyn, Am. Bd. Med. Examiners. Commd. ensign USN, 1967, advanced through grades to capt., 1990; aviator, Fighter Squadron 14 Naval Air Station, Oceana, Va., 1971-74; test pilot Naval Air Test Ctr., Patuxent River, Md., 1974-76; staff physician Naval Hosp., Portsmouth, Va., 1984, Jacksonville, Fla., 1984-86, dir. colposcopy and laser clins. Portsmouth, Va., 1986-89, dir. ob-gyn. residency program, 1989-91, acting chmn. dept. ob-gyn., 1990-91; ret., 1991; asst. prof. Med. Coll. Hampton Roads, Norfolk, Va., 1991—. Chmn. dept. ob-gyn. Sentara Hosps, Norfolk, 1996—2001; ob-gyn. splty. advisor Sentara Health Mgmt. Corp., 2000—09; chmn. bd. mgrs. Mid-Atlantic Women's Care, LLC, 2005—08; mem. Congl. Adv. Com. Healthcare, 2006—09; program chmn. MAWC Patient Safety Conf., 2010. Contbr. articles profl. jours. Mem. steering com. Sentara ObRight Patient Safety Initiative, 2005—. Awarded 1st prize scientific paper by resident physician Am. Coll. Obstetricans and Gynecologists; recipient Guggenheim fellowship Princeton U., 1967-68, MVP award Am. Coll. Ob-gyn. PAC, 2010; Trident scholar U.S. Naval Acad., 1966-67, named one of Most Valuable Player, Am. Coll. Ob-Gyn., 2010, named Super Drs., Hampton Rds., Va., 2011. Fellow Am. Coll. Ob.-Gyns. (chmn. Navy sect. armed forces dist. 1989-91), Assn. Profs. Ob.-Gyns. (assoc.); mem. Am. Assn. Gynecol. Laparoscopists. Episcopalian. Home: 835 Botetourt Gdns Norfolk VA 23507-1814 Office: Woman Care Ctrs 100 Kingsley Ln Ste 400 Norfolk VA 23505 Home Phone: 757-627-1290.

WOLDMAN, SHERMAN, pediatrician; b. Buffalo, Apr. 1, 1932; s. Joseph Harry and Sadie (Weinstein) W. m. Fern Marlene Weinstein, Dec. 28, 1952; children: Deborah Janine Case, Scott Alan, Sabina Heide Muller. BS in Pharmacy magna cum laude, U. Buffalo, 1953, MD with high honors, 1957. Diplomate Am. Bd. Pediat. Intern Millard Fillmore Hosp., Buffalo, 1957-58; resident in pediat. Womens & Children's Hosp., Buffalo, 1958—60, active staff, 1961—2004, emeritus, 2005; pvt. practice Buffalo, 1961-66, Cheektowaga, NY, 1962—2004; mem. active staff Millard Fillmore Hosp., Buffalo, 1961—2004, chmn. dept. pediat., 1985-91, emeritus, 2005; pediatrician pvt. practice, 2005, Clermont, NJ, 2006. Clin. asst. pediat. SUNY Sch. Medicine, Buffalo, 1962, clin. assoc. 1970, clin. asst. prof., 1973, clin. assoc. prof., 2001, preceptor Sch. Nursing, 1976-82; attending pediatrician Booth Meml. Hosp., Buffalo, 1969-72; sch. physician Williamsville Ctrl. Schs., NY, 1962-94, chmn. of physicians, 1970-94, courtesy staff St. Joseph Intercmty. Hosp., Cheektowaga, 1963-80, Kenmore Mercy Hosp., NY, 1963-70, 1974-82, Sisters of Charity Hosp., Buffalo, 1991-2003, Erie County Med. Ctr., Buffalo, 1979-83, Buffalo Gen. Hosp., 1987-95; provisional staff Mercy Hosp., Buffalo, 1982-83, courtesy staff, 2000-03; sch. physician LTES, Cape May, NJ, 2005-07, fed. advisor, 2007-. Vol. Leukemia and Lymphoma Soc., 1975, bd. trustees Western & Ctrl. NY chpt. 1975-2005, pres. 1977-79, v.p. 1979-81, profl. edn. com. 1975-2005, Vol. So. NJ/Shorechapter 2005-, nat. bd. trustees 1978-87, vice chmn. patient aid com., 1980-87; task force on sch. health Erie County Health Dept., NY; trustee Temple Beth David Ner-Israel, Buffalo, 1964-65; vol. staff pediatrician, vol. in medicine clinic Cape May Courthouse, NJ, 2006—07. Co-recipient recognition cert. Cheektowaga NY C. of C., 1982; Myron L. Woldman Vol. of Yr. award Western NY chpt. Leukemia Soc. Lymphoma, 1987, nat. chmn.'s citation 1999; Disting. Physician award Millard Fillmore Health Sys., 1995. Mem.: Maimonides Med. Soc. (pres. Buffalo chpt. 1982—83), Med. Soc. County of Erie, N.Y. (chmn. pub. health com. 1978—79), Buffalo Pediat. Soc. (pres. 1969—70), Med. Soc. State of N.Y., Am. Acad. Pediat. (PREP fellow 1979—85, 1992—94, 1994—96, 1997—99, 2000—02), Gibson Anat. Soc. (hon.), Phi Lambda Kappa (alumni pres. 1965, v.p. alumni 1980—81), Rho Chi, Alpha Omega Alpha. Avocations: gardening, computers. Personal E-mail: swoldman@comcast.net.

WOLEVER, RUTH Q., psychologist, researcher; BA in Spanish, U. Va.; PhD in Clinical Psychology, U. Miami, 1994. Lic. clinical psychologist, cert. health svcs. provider. Intern U. NC Chapel Hill Sch. Medicine, 1994; rsch. dir. Duke Integrative Medicine; asst. clinical prof. dept. psychiatry & behavioral sciences Duke U. Sch. Medicine. Former instr. Dade County Pub. High Sch.; former dir. South Fla. Youth Program. Office: Duke Center for Living Campus 3475 Erwin Rd Durham NC 27705 Office Phone: 919-660-6610.

WOLF, ARON S., healthcare consultant, psychiatrist; b. Newark, Aug. 25, 1937; married; children: Jon, Lisa, Laurie. BA, Dartmouth Coll., 1959; MD, U. Md., 1963; cert. in med. mgmt., Tulane U., 1998, Master's in Med. Mgmt., 2000. Diplomate Am. Bd. Psychiatry and Neurology, Am. Bd. Forensic Psychiatry; cert. med. mgmt. Tulane U., 1999. Intern U. Md. Hosp., Balt., 1963-64; resident in psychiatry Psychiat. Inst. U. Md. Hosp., Balt., 1964-67, chief resident, 1966-67; pvt. practice specializing in adminstrv. medicine and psychiatry Anchorage, 1967—. Dir. Springfield Hosp. Alcholic Clinic, Balt., 1966-67; psychiat. cons. Levindale Hebrew Home and Infirmary, Balt., 1966-67, McLaughlin Youth Ctr., Anchorage, 1969-72; mem. staff Providence Hosp., chief psychiatry sect., 1977-81, 94; mem. staff Humana Hosp., Alaska, Kodiak Island Hosp., Palmer Valley Hosp., Valdez Cmty. Hosp., Bethel Cmty. Hosp., Cordova Alaska Hosp.; mem. staff Charter North Hosp., exec. com., 1984-86; staff psychiatrist Landon Psychiat. Clinic, 1970-71; ptnr. Langdon Clinic, Anchorage, 1971-97, clinic pres., 1981-95; clin. prof. U. N.Mex., 1991—; med. dir. Cordova Cmty. Mental Health Ctr., 1976-80, 84—, ptnr., dir. comprehensive substance dependence program Breakthrough, 1989; assoc. adminstr. Med. Affairs Providence Hosp., Anchorage, 1995-2000; rural adminstr. Providence Health Sys. Alaska, 2000-03; pres. Wolf Healthcare Cons., 2003—; cons. Alaska Native Med. Ctr., 1975-77, Woman's Resource Ctr., Anchorage, 1977-81; instr. dept. psychology U. Alaska, Anchorage, 1968-75; assoc. clin. prof. psychiatry U. Alaska, Fairbanks, 1974-85, clin. prof., 1985—; assoc. clin. prof. U. Wash., 1974-85, clin. prof., 1985—, clin. prof. psychiatry Sch. Medicine U. N.Mex.; participant weekly mental health TV talk show, Anchorage, 1970—; guest lectr. to various profl. and civic groups, 1967—. Contbr. articles to psychiatry to profl. jours. Vice pres. Greater Anchorage Area Borough Sch. Bd., 1971-72, pres. 1973-74; pres. Chugach Optional Sch. Parent Adv. Bd., 1976-77; mem. med. adv. com. Alaska Kidney Found., 1977-82; mem. Alaska Gov.'s Mental Health Adv. Bd., 1976-84, chmn., 1983; mem. Gov.'s Task Force on Criminally Committed Patients, 1980—; bd. dirs. Greater Anchorage Drug Mgmt. Group, 1972-73. With M.C., USAF, 1967-70. Recipient Wendell-Muncie award Md. Med. Soc. 1967. Fellow Am. Psychiat. Assn. (pres. Alaska dist. br. 1975, sec. Alaska br. 1984-85, del. assembly 1975-81, 86, 89-93, area III chmn. assembly procedures com. 1982—, nat. planning com. 1981, nat. membership com. 1981-86, 89—, chmn. confidentiality com., 1986—, recorder of assembly 1984-85, chmn. 1988, Alaska del., 1986—, chair nat. membership com. 1992—, disting. life fellow), Am. Acad. Psychiatry and Law (mem. ethics com., 1987), Am. Coll. Physician Execs.; mem. Am. Soc. Law and Medicine, Soc. Air Force Psychiatrists, ACLU, AMA (chmn. mental health com. 1971-75, medicine and law com. 1980-81), Alaska Med. Assn., N.Y. Acad. Scis., Am. Assn. of Med. Adminstrn. Home: 8133 Sundi Dr Anchorage AK 99502-4198 Office: 4120 Laurel St Anchorage AK 99508 E-mail: aronwolf@aol.com.

WOLF, BARRY, geneticist, pediatric educator; b. Chgo., June 19, 1947; s. Bert D. and Toby E. W.; children: Michael Loren, Bryan Phillip. BS, U. Ill., 1969; MD, U. Ill. Coll. Medicine, 1974; PhD, U. Ill., 1974. Diplomate Am. Bd. Pediatrics, Med. and Biochem. Genetics. Intern, resident in pediatrics Childrens Meml. Hosp., Northwestern U., Chgo., 1974-76; fellow Yale U. Sch. Medicine, New Haven, 1976-78; prof. human genetics Med. Coll. Va., Richmond, 1978-2001, vice chair for rsch. dept. pediatrics, 1996-2000; dir. rsch. Conn. Children's Med. Ctr., 2001—05; assoc. chmn., dir. rsch. Dept. Pediats. Sch. Medicine U. Conn., 2001—01; chmn. Dept. Med. Genetics Henry Ford Hosp., Detroit, 2005—. Author over 200 jour. articles and book chpts. dealing with inherited disorders of metabolism and biochem. genetics, specifically disorders of biotin metabolism. Recipient E. Mead Johnson award for pediatric rsch. Am. Acad. Pediatrics, 1988, Borden award in nutrition Am. Inst. Nutrition, 1987, Outstanding Scientist of Va. award Va. Sci. Mus., 1986, Ounce of Prevention award Action for Prevention of Va., 1985. Mem. Am. Soc. Clin. Investigation, Am. Pediat. Soc., Soc. Pediatric Rsch., Soc. Inherited Metabolic Diseases, Soc. Study Inborn Errors of Metabolism, Am. Soc. Human Genetics. Avocation: japanese cloisonne. Office: Henry Ford Hosp Dept Med Genetics 3031 W Grand Blvd Suite 700 Detroit MI 48202 Home Phone: 248-433-9003; Office Phone: 313-916-3116. Business E-Mail: bwolf1@hfhs.org.

WOLF, DALE B., health facility administrator; BA, U. Colo.; MBA, U. Denver. V.p., Splty. Ops. The Travelers, 1988—94; sr. v.p., Bus. Devel. MetraHealth Cos., Inc., 1995; exec. v.p. SpectraScan Health Svcs., Inc., 1995—96; sr. v.p Coventry Health Care Inc., Bethesda, Md., 1996—98, CFO, treas., 1996—2004, exec. v.p., 1998—2004, CEO, 2004—09, pres., 2008—09. Bd. dir. HealthExtras Inc.; bd. dirs. Catalyst Health Solutions, Inc. Mem.: Soc. of Actuaries. Office: Catalyst Health Solutions Inc 800 King Farm Blvd Rockville MD 20850 Office Phone: 301-548-2900. Office Fax: 301-548-2991. E-mail: dwolf@healthextras.com. *

WOLF, GERALD, biological and medical scientist; b. Limbach, Germany, Feb. 22, 1943; s. Herbert and Hedwig (Müller) W.; m. Hella Körner, Dec. 22, 1967; children: Ronald, Antje. MS, U. Leipzig, Germany, 1970, PhD, 1979. Scientist asst. U. Leipzig, 1967-79; univ. lectr. Med. Acad. Magdeburg, Germany, 1979-81, univ. prof., 1991-92, U. Magdeburg, 1992—, v.p., 2000—02. Dir. Inst. Biology Med. Acad. Magdeburg, 1979-92, Inst. Med. Neurobiology, 1992—2008. Author: Wissenschaftliches Taschenbuch Neurobiologie, 1974, 76, Seele oder Program?, 1982, 85, Das Gehirn. Substanz, die sich selbst begreift, 1996; author, editor: Fachlexikon der Neurobiologie, 1989, Methoden der Hirnforschung, 1997, (novel) The Brain God, 2005, Der Hirngott, 2005, Glaube Mir Mich Gibt es Nicht, 2009; contbr. articles to profl. jours. Recipient Johannes Müller Preis Gesellschaft für Experimentelle Medizin, 1981. Mem. Internat. Brain Rsch. Orgn., Soc. for Neurosci., Gesellschaft für Neurowissenschaften. Achievements include research in glutamate transmitter metabolism and neurodegeneration, electron microscopic localization of the enzyme family of nitric oxide synthases as well as neurobiology in general and neurophilosophy. Home: Schrotebogen 12/153 D-39126 Magdeburg Germany Office: Univ Magdeburg Haus 39 Leipziger Str 44 D-39120 Magdeburg Germany Office Phone: 49-391-6714278. Business E-Mail: gerald.wolf@medizin.uni-magdeburg.de.

WOLF, GREGORY H., insurance company executive; b. Erie, Pa. married; 2 children. BS, Penn State U.; MS in Hosp. and Health Svcs. Adminstrn., Ctrl. Mich. U.; postgrad., Cornell U., U. Pa. V.p. mktg. and sales, then sr. v.p., exec. v.p., pres. Employers Health, Green Bay, Wis., 1988-95; sr. v.p. sales and mktg. Humana Inc., Louisville, 1995-96, COO, pres., 1996—97, CEO, pres., 1997—99; pres., Small Bus. Initiative Cigna Inc., 2001—02; pres. Cigna Group Ins., 2002—. Chmn., CEO nextHR.com, 2000—01. Bd. dir. Boys and Girls Club of Green Bay, Cystic Fibrosis Found., Green Bay. Office: Cigna Corp 1 Liberty Place Philadelphia PA 19192-1550

WOLF, IRNA LYNN, psychologist; b. Dunottar, South Africa, Aug. 30, 1949; came to U.S., 1977; d. John and Tolsa W.; m. Raymond Frank Shamos, Feb. 22, 1976; children: Lorin Iver, Richard Lance, Ilan Hiram, Troy Joseph. MFA cum laude, U. Witwatersrand, 1976; MA, U. Rochester, 1983; PhD, Ariz. State U., 1991, postgrad., 1997. Lic. psychologist, Ariz., diplomate Am. Bd. Psychology; cert. sch. psychologist. Rsch., tchg. asst. Ariz. State U., Tempe, 1984-89; ind. rsch., 1989-97; pvt. practice Phoenix, 1997—. Lectr. in field; cons. Human Info. Processing, 1997—. Contbr. articles to profl. jours. Recipient Certificate of Appreciation Paradise Valley Police Dept., 1992. Mem. APA, Am. Psychol. Soc., Nat. Assn. Sch. Psychologists, We. Psychol. Assn., Ariz. Psychol. Assn., Phi Kappa Phi. Republican. Avocations: painting, drawing, hiking, swimming. Home: 4516 E Onyx Ave Phoenix AZ 85028-4200

WOLF, JEFFREY STEPHEN, physician; b. Hartford, Conn., July 30, 1946; s. Abraham and Norma Wolf; m. Nina Loving Lockridge; children: Sarah Loving, Lawren Hiley. BS, McGill U., 1968; MD, Med. Coll. Va., 1972, MS, 1973. Diplomate Am. Bd. Colon and Rectal Surgery. Intern in surgery Mt. Sinai Hosp., NYC, 1972-73, resident, 1973-75, N.Y. Med. Coll.-Met. Hosp., NYC, 1975-77; chief resident in surgery Met. Hosp., NYC, 1977-78; fellow colon-rectal surgery Grtr. Balt. Med. Ctr., 1978-79; colon-rectal surgeon Portsmouth, Va., 1979—. Fellow ACS, Am. Soc. Colon and Rectal Surgery; mem. AMA, Portsmouth Acad. Medicine, Med. Soc. Va., Am. Soc. Colon and Rectal Surgeons, So. Med. Assn., Chesapeake Colon-Rectal Soc., S.E. Va. Soc. Colon-Rectal Surgeons. Office: 3235 Academy Ave Ste 200 Portsmouth VA 23703-3200 Office Phone: 757-484-9653.

WOLF, ROBERT EDWARD, physician, educator; b. Houston, Jan. 20, 1942; s. John Eaton and Ruby Lucile (Bukowski) W.; m. Ann Elizabeth Killebrew, Dec. 23, 1967 (dec. Sep. 29, 2009); 1 child, Robert Edward, Jr. BA, Baylor U., 1964; MA, U. Tex. Med. Br., 1968, MD, 1969, PhD, 1973. Diplomate Am. Bd. Internal Medicine. Intern in internal medicine U. Tex. Med. Br., Galveston, 1969-70, resident in internal medicine, 1970-71; fellowship in rheumatology U. Tex. Health Scis. Ctr., Dallas, 1973-75; rsch. assoc. VAMC, Dallas, 1975-77; asst. prof. of medicine U. Tex. Health Scis. Ctr., Dallas, 1975-77; staff physician, chief rheumatology VA Med. Ctr., Shreveport, La., 1977—; chief rheumatology La. State U. Health Scis. Ctr., 1997—2003, assoc. prof. medicine, 1977-89, prof. medicine, 1989—2003, dir. Arthritis Ctr., 1990—2003, prof. emeritus, 2004—. Mem. faculty promotions com. La. State U. Health Scis. Ctr., 1994—98, rsch. adv. coun., 1992—2003, adminstrv. coun., 1994—2003, utilization rev. com., 1983—95. Contbg. author: Selected Topics in Clinical Chemistry, 1972, Serum Protein Abnormalities, 1975; contbr. articles to profl. jours. Undergrad. edn. com. Arthritis Found., Atlanta, 1979-82, pres., 1983-85, exec. com.; Shreveport. Lt. comdr. USPHS, 1971-73. Recipient Grand (Student) award Nat. Rsch. Forum, Galveston, 1968, 3rd (Resident) award, 1970, Multipurpose Arthritis Ctr. award NIH, Bethesda, Md., 1977, Ctr. of Excellence-Arthritis award State of La., Baton Rouge, 1990-2003. Fellow: Am. Coll. Rheumatology. Office: VA Med Ctr 510 E Stoner Ave Shreveport LA 71101 Business E-Mail: robert.wolf@va.gov.

WOLF, SHARON ANN, psychotherapist; b. Dallas, May 13, 1951; d. Frank Allan and Ursula (Mohnblatt) W.; 1 child, Allan. BA in Psychology, New Eng. Coll., 1973; MA in Counseling Psychology, Antioch Grad. Sch., 1976; PhD in Clin. Psychology, Union Grad. Sch., 1989. Cert. Mental Health Counselor, 1997. Behavioral spl. ednl. planner Philbrook Children's Learning Ctr., Concord, N.H., 1972; asst. to spl. edn. cons. N.H. Hosp., Concord, 1972-73; spl. edn. planner Rochester (N.H.) Child Devel. Ctr., 1973; counseling practicum Morrill Sch., Concord, N.H., 1973, Contoocook Valley Mental Health Ctr., Henniker, N.H., 1973-74, counseling psychology intern, 1974-76; lab. instr. New Eng. Coll., Henniker, 1973; ednl. and guidance counselor asst. Hillsboro (N.H.)-Deering Sch. Dist., 1973-74; pediatric psychology intern parent-infant devel. program Ctrl. N.H. C.M.H. Ctr., Concord, 1986-87; assoc. psychologist Easter Seal Rehab. Ctr., Manchester, N.H., 1976-80, Ctrl. N.H. Community Mental Health Svcs., Concord, 1980-88; intern forensic psychology Concord Dist. Ct., 1987-88; pvt. practice Northfield, N.H., 1988—. Psychol. cons. children and youth program Twin Rivers Counseling Ctr., Franklin, N.H. 1980-83, therapist, 1984-86; therapist Ctrl. N.H. Comm. Mental Health Ctr., 1980-83, Parent-Infant Devel. Program, Concord, N.H., 1983-88. Fellow Am. Orthopsychiat. Assn.; mem. Am. Assn. Suicidology, Am. Assn. Counseling and Devel., New England Coun. on Crime and Delinquency, N.H. Assn. of the Deaf, N.H. Registry of Interpreters for the Deaf. Avocations: rug hooking, music. Office: PO Box 253 Tilton NH 03276-0253

WOLF, STEVEN E., surgeon, educator; b. Balt., Oct. 16, 1964; s. Gerald Wayne and Margaret Louise (Melcher) W.; m. Kristin Steele, Dec. 2, 1989; children: Travis O., Hailey E. BS in Zoology cum laude, U. Tex., 1986; MD, U. Tex. Med. Br., Galveston, 1990. Diplomate Am. Bd. Surgery, Tex. State Bd. Med. Examiners, Mo. State Bd. Healing Arts. Resident in surgery U. Mo., Kansas City, 1990-95; rsch. fellow in trauma and burns Shriners Hosp. for Children, Galveston, 1995-96, staff surgeon, 1996, clin. fellow in critical care and burns, 1996—97; asst. prof. surgery U. Tex., Galveston, 1996; vice-chair for rsch., dept. surgery U. Tex. Health Sci. Ctr., San Antonio, Betty and Bob Kelso Disting. Chair in Burn and Trauma Surgery, 2007—; dir., US Army Inst. Surgical Rsch. Burn Ctr. Brooke Army Med. Ctr., Fort Sam Houston, Tex. Chmn. info. sys. steering Shriners Burns Inst., 1996-97; mem. pharmacy and therapeutics com. U. Tex., 1997; mem. burn adv. bd. Beiersdorf-Jobst Internat., 1997. Co-author (chpt.) Baillere's Clinical Endocrinology, 1996; contbr. several articles to profl. jours. Mem. ACS (assoc.), Soc. Parenteral & Enteral Nutrition, Am. Burn Assn., Assn. Acad. Surgery, AMA, Am. Soc. for Parenteral and Enteral Nutrition, Assn.for Academic Surgery, AAAS, J. Bradley Aust Surgical Soc., Shock Soc., Singleton Surgical Soc., Soc. for Critical Care Medicine; elected to Am. Assn. for the Surgery of Trauma, Eastern Assn. for the Surgery of Trauma, Soc. U. Surgeons, So. Surgical Assn., Surgical Infection Soc., Tex. Surgical Soc. Republican. Methodist. Achievements include work with mortality determinants in massive pediatric burns, team member that developed an adaptable arm sling for military burn patients. Office: U Tex Health Sci Ctr Dept Surgery 7703 Floyd Curl Dr San Antonio TX 78229-3900 Business E-Mail: wolfs@uthscsa.edu.

WOLFBERG, MELVIN DONALD, optometrist, educational association administrator, consultant; b. Altoona, Pa., June 24, 1926; s. Max Alex and Claire (Schiffman) Wolfberg; m. Audrey Iris Koch, Apr. 26, 1952; children: Debra Lynn, Michael Alex, Daniel Ben; m. Linda Diane Machesic, Dec. 4, 1979. OD, Pa. Coll. Optometry, Phila., 1951; D of Ocular Sci. (hon.), New England Coll. Optometry, 1989, Ill. Coll. Optometry, 1990; LHD (hon.), Pa. Coll. Optometry, 1998. Lic. optometrist, Pa. Pvt. practice and ptnr. optometric practice, Selinsgrove, Pa., 1951-79; pres. Pa. Coll. Optometry, Phila., 1979-89, chmn. bd., 1976-79; v.p. profl. rels. Bausch and Lomb, Rochester, NY, 1991-95; pres. In Vision Inst., Boston, 1991-95, ptnr., dir. Sylvan Learning Ctr., Vero Beach, Fla., 1996—2009. Cons. to sec. HEW, Washington, 1970-77; dir. Better Vision Inst., N.Y.C., 1960-80. Mem. Selinsgrove City Coun., 1961-62; pres. Selinsgrove Community Chest, 1957; chmn. Optometrists Rep. Nat. Com., 1972, 76; chmn. Nat. Inter-Profl. Health Coun., Washington, 1972-77; dir. Univ. City Sci. Ctr., Phila., 1980-87; adv. com. Coun. Higher Edn., Commonwealth Pa., 1980-89. Served with U.S. Army, 1944-46, ETO. Decorated Purple Heart, Bronze Star, Silver Star; named Man of Yr. Central Pa. Optometric Soc., 1964, Alumnus of Yr. Pa. Coll. Optometry, 1970; recipient Carel C. Koch Meml. medal, 1989. Fellow Am. Acad. Optometry (pres. 1985-86, Eminent Svc. award, 2005); mem. Pa. Assn. Colls. and Univs. (exec. com. 1982-89, sec.-treas. 1985-88, vice chmn. 1988-89), Pa. Optometric Assn. (pres. 1959-61, Optometrist of Yr., Ewalt Meritorious Svc. award 2003), Am. Optometric Assn. (pres. 1969-70, Disting. Svc. award 1994, named to Nat. Optometry Hall Fame 2004), Pa. Coll. Optometry Alumni Assn. (pres. 1957), Beta Sigma Kappa. Personal E-mail: machesic@msn.com.

WOLFE, GIL I., neurologist; b. NYC, Apr. 26, 1963; s. Asher Wolfe and Haia Goldenberg; m. Amy Bolk, Dec. 10, 1989. MD, U. Tex., Dallas, 1989. Diplomate in neurology, neuromuscular medicine and clin. neurophysiology Am. Bd. Psychiatry and Neurology. Neuromuscular medicine prof. U. Tex. Southwestern Med. Sch., Dallas, 1994—. Contbr. chapters to books, articles to profl. jours. Disting. chair in neuromuscular disease rsch. Dr. Bob and Jean Smith Found. Fellow: Am. Acad. Neurology; mem.: Am. Neurol. Assn. Office: University Tex Southwestern Med Sch 5323 Harry Hines Blvd Dallas TX 75390-8897

WOLFE, NATHAN, epidemiologist, educator; BA in Human Biology, with honors, Stanford U., Calif., 1993; MA in Biol. Anthropology, Harvard U., 1995, DSc in Immunology & Infectious Disease, 1998. Postdoc. fellow dept. internat. health Johns Hopkins U., Balt., 1999—2003, asst. prof. dept. epidemiology, dept. molecular microbiology & immunology, 2003—06; prof. dept. epidemiology UCLA, 2006—. Cons. Ctrs. Disease Control, Nat. Ctr. Infectious Diseases, 1996—2000, US Mil. HIV rsch. program, Walter Reed Army Inst. Rsch., Silver Spring, Md., 2001—04, Internat. AIDS Vaccine Initiative, 2002—03, Ind. U. Sch. Medicine, 2008—, Bloodsystems Rsch. Inst., San Francisco, 2008—. Contbr. articles to profl. jours. Recipient Internat. Rsch. Scientist Devel. award, NIH Fogarty Internat. Ctr., 1999, Dir.'s Pioneer award, NIH, 2005—; named one of Brilliant 10, Popular Sci. mag., 2006, The 100 Agents of Change, Rolling Stone mag., 2009; Fulbright fellow, 1997—98. Mem.: AAAS, Internat. Soc. Ecosystem Health, Internat. Primatological Soc., Ecol. Soc. America, Am. Soc. Virology, Am. Soc. Tropical Medicine & Hygiene (Travel award 1998), Am. Soc. Microbiology. Achievements include patents in field.

WOLFERSTEIG, JEAN LOIS, retired medical association administrator; b. Kingston, NY, July 13, 1950; d. Evelyn Anna Schupp and John Raymond Wolfersteig; m. William Edward Miller. AS in Liberal Arts, Ulster County CC, 1970; BA in Secondary Edn., State U. Coll., 1972; MS in Pub. Svc. Adminstrn., Russell Sage Coll., Albany, New York, 1983. Unit mgr. Wassaic Devel. Ctr., Wingdale, NY, 1972—75, staff devel. specialist, 1976—79; dir. of staff devel. and tng. Westchester Devel. Disabilities Svcs. Office, Tarrytown, NY, 1979—84, Hudson River Psychiat. Ctr., Poughkeepsie, NY, 1984—92, quality mgmt. dir., 1992—98, dir. for facility admin. svcs., 1998—2002, CEO, 2002—07. Bd. mem. Cmty. Adv. Bd. for Marist Coll., Poughkeepsie, 1985—90; adj. faculty Westchester CC, Valhalla, 1981—84; bd. mem. Adv. Bd. for Orange County CC. Forensic Mental Health Program, Middletown, NY, 1985—85. Co-author: (international presentations) Balanced Scorecard and Performance Improvement. Chairperson of selection com. Herman B. Snow Scholarship Fund, Poughkeepsie, 1991—2001. Recipient Salute to Women in Industry, Dutchess County YWCA, 1992, Leadership and Svc. award, Nat. Alliance for Mentally Ill (Mid-Hudson), 2006, NY State Legis. Resolution, Hudson River Pyschiat. Ctr., 2007, Disting. Svc. award, Eliot Spitzer, Gov. NY State, 2007, Mental Health Cert. of Appreciation, 2007. Mem.: Nat. Alliance Mentally Ill (Leadership award 2006), Nat. Assn. of State Mental Health Dirs., Phi Kappa Phi. Avocations: writing, sailing, travel, gardening.

WOLFF, EDWARD, physician; b. NYC, Apr. 15, 1941; s. Julius and Molly W.; m. Marilyn Alice Pels; children: Shana, Loryn, Kimberly. BS, Muhlenberg Coll., 1962; MD, Georgetown U., 1966. Intern U. Ala. Hosp., Brimingham, 1966-67; resident N.Y. Med. Coll., NYC, 1967-71; physician pvt. practice, Great Neck, NY, 1976—. Attending physician North Shore U. Hosp., Manhasset, NY, St. Francis Hosp. Heart Ctr., Roslyn, NY. Fellow Am. Coll. Physicians; mem. AMA, N.Y. State Med. Soc., Nassau County Med. Soc. Office: Ste 404 107 Northern Blvd Great Neck NY 11021 Office Phone: 516-498-1818.

WOLFF, KLAUS, dermatologist, educator, researcher; b. Hermannstadt, Romania, Dec. 4, 1935; arrived in Austria, 1947; s. Helmut Konrad and Hedwig (Orendi) W.; m. Marilies von Artens, June 12, 1962 (div. Dec. 12, 1970); m. Elisabeth Christine Schreiner, July 7, 1971 (div. Dec. 1998); children: Philippa, Eva, Bernhard; m. Gabriele Robitschek, Jan. 8, 1999. MD, U. Vienna, 1962; MD (hon.), U. Kiel, 1997, U. Budapest, 1999, U. Sibiu, 2003. Med. diplomate; diplomate dermatology. Prof. U. Vienna, 1974-76, head divsn. exptl. dermatology, 1974-76; prof., chmn. dept. dermatology U. Innsbruck, Austria, 1976-81; chmn. dept. dermatology U. Vienna Gen. Hosp., 1981—2004. Editor: Dermatology in General Medicine, 1979, 87, 93, 99, 2003, 08, Vasculitis, 1979, Color Atlas and Synopsis of Clinical Dermatology, 1993, 97, 2000, 01, 05; contbr. 450 articles to profl. jours. Fellow: Royal Coll. Physicians; mem.: German Acad. Natural Scis., Austrian Acad. Scis., 16 internat. sci. socs. (hon.), European Soc. Dermatol. Rsch. (pres. 1975—76), Internat. League of Dermatol. Socs. (mem. internat. com. of dermatology, pres. 1987—92). Avocations: literature, opera, tennis, skiing. Office: Vienna Gen Hosp Dept Dermat 18-20 Währinger Gürtel A-1090 Vienna Austria Office Phone: 431404007707. Business E-Mail: klaus.wolff@meduniwien.ac.at.

WOLFINGER, GLENN J., dentist, educator; BS in Biology, Villanova U., Pa., 1986; DMD, Tufts U., 1990. Diplomate Am. Bd. Prosthodontics, 1998. Resident gen. practice Albert Einstein Med. Ctr., Phila., 1990—91; resident combined prosthodontics Veterans Adminstrn. Outpatient Clinic, Boston, 1991—93; clin. fellow dept. prosthodontics sch. dental medicine Harvard Univ., Boston, 1991—93; asst. clin. prof. dept. prosthodontics sch. dentistry Temple Univ., Phila., 1993—95; dir. prosthodontics and implant dentistry Dept. Veterans Affairs Med. Ctr., Phila., 1993—; bd. cert. prosthodontist Prosthodontics Intermedia Dental Ctr., Fort Washington, Pa., 1993—; courtesy staff dept. surgery divsn. dentistry Suburban Gen. Hosp., Norristown, Pa., 1994—; prosthodontic instr. pediatric dental residency program Episcopal Hosp., Phila., 1996—; lectr. dept. prosthodontics sch. dental and oral surgery Columbia Univ., NYC, 2001—. Mem. Acad. of Gen. Dentistry, 1990—95, Am. Assn. of Hosp. Dentists, 1994—96, Am. Soc. for Geriatric Dentistry, 1994—96, Am. Acad. of Implants Prothodontics, 1999—2004; invited spkr. - implant course gen. practice residency program Albert Einstein Med. Ctr., Phila., 1997—. Co-author: (publs.) Patient Attitudes Before and After Dental Implant Rehabilitation, 1994, Management of an Abscess Around the Apex of a Mandibular Root Form Implant: Clinical Report, 1994, Fabrication of a Gingival Mask: A Removable Gingival Replacement Unit, 1995, Conversion Prosthesis: A Transitional Fixed Implant Prosthesis, 1996, Prosthodontic Management of a Combination Transosteal/Endosteal Implant, 1996, Restoring Lost Vertical Dimension of Occlusion Using Dental Implants: A Clinical Report, 1996, Two Implant Supported Single Molar Replacement: Interdental Space Requirements and Comparison to Alternative Options, 1997, and numerous others. Recipient Second Place, Second Ann. Steven R. Gordon Postgrad. Prosthodontic Essay Contest, 1993, Award of Appreciation, Temple Univ. Sch. Dentistry, 1995, First Place Alumni Day Table Clinic, 1995, Aeard of Appreciation for Outstanding Dedication to Students and Excellence in Tchg. Fixed Prosthodontics, Stomatognathic Honor Soc., Temple Univ. Sch. Dentistry, 1995; fellow, Acad. of Osseointegration, 2004. Mem.: Columbia Univ., Sch. of Dental & Oral Surgery The Alfred Owre Soc. (faculty group leader 2003—), Internat. Coll. of Prosthodontists, Del. Valley Acad. of Osseointegration, ADA, Pa. Prosthodontic Assn., Pa. Dental Assn., Montgomery-Bucks Dental Assn., Joseph E. Ewing Dental Study Group, Acad. for Sports Dentistry, Am. Assn. for Dental Rsch., Phila. Sect., Albert Einstein Med. Ctr. Resident Alumni Soc., Tufts Univ. Sch. of Dental Medicine Alumni Assn., Villanova Univ. Alumni Assn., La Salle Coll. High Sch. Alumni Assn., Alpha Phi Delta Frat., Gamma Zeta Chpt. Achievements include research in effects of diabetes on osseointegration; mandibular flexure clinical evaluation; immediate loading of branemark implants; osseointegration in older patients; and numerous others. Office: Prosthodontics Intermedia 467 Pennsylvania Ave Ste 201 Fort Washington PA 19034 Office Phone: 215-646-6334. Office Fax: 215-643-1149.

WOLFMAN, EARL FRANK, JR., surgeon, educator; b. Buffalo, Sept. 14, 1926; s. Earl Frank and Alfreda (Peterson) W.; m. Lois Jeannette Walker, Dec. 28, 1946; children— Nancy Jeannette, David Earl, Carol Anne. BS cum laude, Harvard U., Cambridge, Mass., 1946; MD cum laude, U. Mich., 1950. Diplomate Am. Bd. Surgery. Intern U. Mich., Ann Arbor, 1950-51, asst. resident in surgery, 1951-52, resident in surgery, 1954-55, from jr. clin. instr. surgery to assoc. prof., 1955-66, asst. to dean, 1960-61, asst. dean, 1961-64; practice medicine specializing in surgery, 1957—, Sacramento, 1966—; prof. surgery Sch. Medicine, U. Calif., Davis, 1966—, founding chmn. dept. surgery, 1966-78, founding assoc. dean, 1966-76, mem. staff, chief surg. svcs. Med. Ctr., 1966-78, founding chmn. div. surg. scis., 1966-78. Contbr. articles to profl. jours. Served to lt. M.C. USNR, 1952-54. Fellow ACS; mem. AMA (del. 1987-99), Ctrl. Surg. Soc., Western Surg. Soc., Sacramento Surg. Soc., Pacific Coast Surg. Soc., Frederick A. Coller Surg. Soc., Soc. Surgery Alimentary Tract, Am. Assn. Endocrine Surgeons, Sierra Sacramento Valley Med. Soc., Calif. Med. Assn. (trustee 1991-2000), Am. Soc. Gen. Surgeons. Office Phone: 916-734-7886. Business E-Mail: efwolfman@ucdavis.edu.

WOLFORD, LARRY M., surgeon; s. Donald Ralph and Wilma Irene Wolford; m. Denise Hazel LeBlanc, June 11, 1983; children: Dax Patrick, Dallas Danielle, Demi Denise, Dylan Dion, Dash Larry. BS, U. Pitts., 1965; DMD, Temple U., Phila., 1969; cert. in Oral Surgery, U.Tex. Southwestern Med. Sch., Dallas, 1973; diploma of Hon. Merit (hon.), U. São Paulo, Brazil, 1995. Diplomate Am. Bd. Oral and Maxillofacial Surgery. Asst. dir. dept oral and maxillofacial surgery and ctr. for correction dentofacial deformities John Peter Smith Hosp., Fort Worth, 1973—83, coord. Ft. Worth cleft palate program, 1973—83; prof. oral and maxillofacial surgery Baylor Coll. Dentistry, Dallas, 1983—87, dir. of oral and maxillofacial surgery grad. program, 1984—86, clin. prof. of oral and maxillofacial surgery, 1987—; dir. oral and maxillofacial surgery fellowship program Baylor Coll. Dentistry Tex. A&M U. Sys. and Baylor U. Med. Ctr., Dallas, 1985—. Mem. adv. com. Am. Bd. Oral and Maxillofacial Surgery, 1985—91. Co-author (Epker, WolFord): Dentofacial Deformities: Surgical Orthodontic Correction, 1980; co-author: (WolFord, Hilliard, Dugan) Surgical Treatment Objective: A Systematic Approach to the Prediction Tracing, 1985; co-editor (Fonseca, Baker, WolFord): Cleft / Craniofacial / Cosmetic Surgery, 2000; contbr. 22 chapters to books;, author 170 manuscripts. Recipient 1st William F. Harrigan award, William F. Harrigan Soc., 1982, Diplomat Am. Coll. Dentists award, Am. Coll. Dentistry, 1987, William J. Gies Found. Oral and Maxillofacial award for major contributions, 1990. Mem.: ADA, Am. Soc. Tempormandibular Joint Surgeons, Am. Assn. Oral and Maxillofacial Surgeons (mem. com. ann. sci. sessions 1977—83, chmn. planning com. combined meeting AAO/AAOMS 1980, chmn. com. annual sci. sessions 1980—82, spl. cons. com. annual sci. sessions 1982—83, mem. planning com. combined meeting AAO/AAOMS 1983). Achievements include development of many surgical procedures and instruments; research in over 100 clin. and lab. studies; porous block hydroxyapatite (Interpore 200) for bone grafting in the craniofacial area; tempormandibular joint concepts for total joint prostheses for reconstruction, mitek mini anchors for disc repositioning in tempormandibular joint surgery. Avocation: sports cars. Office: 3409 Worth St Ste 400 Dallas TX 75246 Office Phone: 214-828-9115.

WOLFSON, AARON HOWARD, radiation oncologist, educator; b. Nashville, May 13, 1955; s. Sorrell Louis and Jacqueline Adele (Falis) W.; m. Adrienne Sue Mates, Dec. 16, 1979; children: Alexis Ellyn, Andrew Lane. BA, U. Fla., 1978, MD, 1982. Diplomate Am. Bd. Radiology. Intern internal medicine Jackson Meml. Hosp., Miami, Fla., 1982—83; staff physician Pub. Health Svc., Miami, 1983—85; pvt. practice Palm Beach Gardens, Fla., 1985—86; resident in radiation oncology Med. Coll. Va., Richmond, 1986—89; from instr. to assoc. prof. radiation oncology U. Miami, Miller Sch. Medicine, 1989—2003, prof., 2003—, vice chair dept. radiation oncology, 2005—. Co-dir. Gynecology Site dis. group Sylvester Cancer Ctr., 2001—. Contbr. articles to profl. jours. Bd. dirs. Children's Home Soc., Ft. Lauderdale, Fla., 1993—, Temple Beth Israel, Sunrise, Fla., 1994—; mem. spkrs. bur. U. Miami, 1993—; vol. spkr. Broward County Schs., 1990—; exec. v.p. Temple Beth Israel, 1996-98, pres., 1998-99. Sylvester Cancer Ctr. grantee, 1992. Mem. Gynecologic Oncology Group (bd. dir. 2007-), Radiation Therapy Oncology Group, Am. Soc. Therapeutic Radiology and Oncology. Jewish. Achievements include research on malignant tumors of the female genital tract; patent for radiation implant for gynecologic cancer. Office: Univ Miami 1475 NW 12th Ave # D-31 Miami FL 33136-1002 Home Phone: 954-370-8038; Office Phone: 305-243-4210. Business E-Mail: awolfson@med.miami.edu.

WOLFSON, DAVID H., pediatrician; MD, U. Pitts. Diplomate Am. Bd. Pediatrics, Am. Bd. Pediatrics-adolescent medicine. Resident Children's Memorial Hosp.; fellow Harvard Univ.; clin. prof. pediatrics U. Pitts.; with Children's Hosp. of Pitts., Magee-Womens Hosp. Office: Children's Hospital of Pittsburgh of UPMC Cranberry Business Park 3104 Unionville Rd Ste120 Cranberry Township PA 16066 Office Phone: 724-776-4433.

WOLINSKY, EMANUEL, internist, educator; b. NYC, Sept. 23, 1917; s. Jacob and Bertha (Siegel) W.; m. Marjorie Claster, Nov. 15, 1946; children: Douglas, Peter. BA, Cornell U., 1938, MD, 1941. Diplomate Am. Bd. Med. Microbiology. Intern, resident medicine N.Y. Hosp., 1943-45; bacteriologist Trudeau Lab., Saranac Lake, NY, 1947-56; mem. faculty Case Western Res. U. Sch. Medicine, 1956-98, prof. medicine, 1968-88, prof. pathology, 1981-88, prof. emeritus, 1988-98, ret., 1998. Dir. microbiology Cleve. Met. Gen. Hosp., 1959-91, acting dir. dept. pathology, 1980-86, chief div. infectious diseases, 1961-83. Co-editor Textbook of Pulmonary Diseases, 5th edit., 1993; Asso. editor: Am. Rev. Respiratory Diseases, 1973-79; Contbr. articles to profl. jours., textbooks. Mem. Tb panel U.S.-Japan Co-op. Med. Sci. Program, 1969-75. Recipient Crystal Cross award Ohio Thoracic Soc., 1995, Louis Weinstein award Clin. Infectious

Diseases, 1995, Maurice Saltzman award Mt. Sinai Healthcare Found., 1999; named to Med. Hall of Fame, Cleve. Mag., 1998. Mem. Am. Soc. Microbiology (Gardner Middlebrook award 1998), Am. Thoracic Soc. (Trudeau medal 1986), Infectious Diseases Soc. Am. (Soc. Citation award, 2004), Phi Beta Kappa, Alpha Omega Alpha. Home: 24761 S Woodland Rd Cleveland OH 44122-3327

WOLINTZ, ARTHUR HARRY, neurologist, ophthalmologist; b. Bklyn., May 30, 1937; s. Louis and Celia (Ragofsky) W.; m. Carol Sue Bergstein, Nov. 28, 1963; children: Robyn Joy, Ellen Sharon. Student, NYU, 1955-58; MD summa cum laude, SUNY, Bklyn., 1962; postgrad., Columbia U., 1967-68. Diplomate Am. Bd. Psychiatry and Neurology, Am. Bd. Ophthalmology; licensee Nat. Bd. Med. Examiners, U. State of N.Y. Intern Maimonides Hosp., Bklyn., 1962-63, jr. resident in medicine, 1963-64; resident Nat. Inst. Neurol. Diseases and Blindness, Bethesda, Md., 1964-66; chief resident Mt. Sinai Hosp., NYC, 1966-67; clin. asst. prof. neurology Downstate Med. Ctr. SUNY, Bklyn., 1968-69, resident in ophthalmology, 1969-71, from asst. prof. to prof., 1971—, prof. clin. ophthalmology and clin. neurology, 1977—, interim chief ophthalmology, 1983, acting regional chmn. dept. ophthalmology, 1984, prof. ophthalmology, 1987—, chmn. dept. ophthalmology, 1987-96; Disting. tchg. prof., chair emeritus dept. ophthalmology SUNY-Health Sci. Ctr. Bklyn., 1995, 96—; asst. neurologist Presbyn. Hosp., NYC, 1967-68; instr. neuropathology Coll. Physicians and Surgeons Columbia U., NYC, 1967-68; instr. neurology Mt. Sinai Sch. Medicine, NYC, 1967-68; assoc. dir. neurology Maimonides Med. Ctr., Bklyn., 1968-69; asst. neurologist Coney Island Hosp., Bklyn., 1968-69. Vis. neurologist Kings County Hosp. Ctr., Bklyn, 1968-69; chief divsn. ophthalmology and neuro-ophthalmology Kingsbrook Jewish Med. Ctr., Bklyn., 1971, sec. med. and dental staff 1976-77, v.p. 1978-79, pres. 1980-81, dir. ophthalmology 1981; attending physician State Univ. Hosp., Bklyn., 1971, Kings County Hosp. Ctr., Bklyn., 1971; cons. Luth. Med. Ctr., Beth Israel Med. Ctr., Brookdale Hosp. Med. Ctr., Bklyn., L.I. Coll. Hosp., Bklyn., Maimonides Med. Ctr., Cath. Med. Ctr. Bklyn. and Queens, Bklyn. VA Hosp. Author: Essentials of Clinical Neuro-Ophthalmology, 1976; contbr. chpts. to sci. textbooks and handbooks, articles to profl. jours. Pres. Flatbush Jewish Ctr., Bklyn. With USPHS 1964-66. Recipient J. Eugene Chalfin Meml. Lectr. award Alumni Assn. State Univ.-Kings County, 1981, Tchr. of Yr. award dept. ophthalmology Interfaith Med. Ctr., 1988, Greats in Ophthalmology in Bklyn. award SUNY Downstate Med. Ctr. Dept. Ophthalmology, 2004, Alumni Svc. award SUNY Downstate Med. Ctr. Coll. Medicine, 2007. Fellow ACP, ACS, Am. Acad. Ophthalmology and Otolaryngology, Am. Acad. Neurology; mem. AMA, AAAS, Med. Soc. County Kings, Med. Soc. State N.Y., Bklyn. Ophthal. Soc., N.Y. Acad. Medicine, Am. Acad. Neurology, Alumni Assn. SUNY (pres.-elect 1989, pres. 1990-91, Richard C. Troutman M.D. Master Tchr. award in ophthalmology 1987, Disting. Alumni Achievement award 1997, Frank L. Babbott M.D. Meml. award 2002, Clarence and Mary Dennis Dedicated Svc. award 2004, Kingbrook Pres.'s award 2004), Oddfellows, Alpha Omega Alpha. Home and Office: 100 Ocean Pky Apt 4H Brooklyn NY 11218-1755 Office Phone: 718-854-7360. Personal E-mail: ahwolintz@aol.com.

WOLK, MICHAEL JAY, cardiologist, educator; b. NYC, Nov. 21, 1938; BA, Colgate U., Hamilton, NY, 1960; MD, Columbia U. Coll. Physicians & Surgeons, 1964. Diplomate Am. Bd. Internal Medicine, 1971, Am. Bd. Cardiovascular Disease, 1973. Intern, internal medicine SUNY Downstate Med. Ctr., Bklyn., 1964-65, resident, internal medicine, 1965-67, chief resident, 1966—67; resident cardiology New Eng. Med. Ctr., Boston, 1967-69; fellow cardiology Cornell U. Med. Ctr., NYC, 1969-70; mem. staff NY Hosp., 1969—; assoc. clin. prof. Weill Med. Coll., Cornell U., 1969—98, clin. prof. medicine, 1998—; pvt. practice NYC, 1969—. Contbr. several articles to profl. jours. Named a Med. Honoree, 12th Ann. Heart of the Hamptons Gala, 2008. Fellow: ACP, Am. Coll. Cardiology (past pres., exec. com., chair, budget, fin. and investment com.). Office: 425 E 61st St New York NY 10065 also: Michael Wolk Md 425 E 61st St Fl 6 New York NY 10065-8795 Office Phone: 212-752-2000.

WOLKOV, HARVEY BRIAN, oncologist, researcher; b. Cleve., Feb. 8, 1953; s. Sidney and Norma Wolkov; m. Lauren Cronin, Jan. 9, 1993; 1 child, Nicole. BSc, Purdue U., West Lafayette, Ind., 1975, MSc, 1977; MD, Med. Coll. Ohio, Toledo, 1979. Diplomate Am. Bd. Radiology. Intern U. Calif., San Francisco, 1979-80; resident Stanford Med. Ctr., Calif., 1980-83, chief resident, 1982; rsch. asst. Stanford U., 1982; from asst. clin. prof. to assoc. clin. prof. U. Calif., Davis, 1983-97, assoc. clin. prof., 1997—; med. dir. Mercy Hosps., Sacramento, 1987-90, Sutter Cancer Ctr. Dept. Radiation Oncology, Sacramento, 1990—. Mem. adv. bd. Nat. Graves Disease Found., Jacksonville, Fla., 1993—; dir. Sutter Gamma Knife Ctr., 1997—; co-prin. investigator radiation oncology Children's Oncology Group, 2001—. Author (with others): (book) Intraoperative Radiation, 1989, Frontiers in Radiation, 1991, Textbook Radiation Oncology, 2004; contbr. articles to profl. jours. Bd. dirs. Sutter Hosps. Found., Sacramento. Mem.: Am. Coll. Radiation Oncology (chancellor 2010—, economics com. mem. 2010—), Calif. Radiol. Soc. (exec. com. 2001—), Sutter Inst. Med. Rsch. (chair rsch. com. 1996—, hosp. chair oncology com. 2003—, neuroscience inst. leadership com. 2003—), Calif. Radiation Oncology Soc. (pres.-elect 1999, pres. 2000—01), Am. Soc. Therapeutic Radiology and Oncology (bd. dirs. 2000—03, vice chair outcome rsch., fin. com., corp. rels., workforce, comm., mem. ethics comm. coronary artery radiation therapy coms., Internat. Travel award 1987, inaugural fellow 2006), Radiation Therapy Oncology Group (com. chair 1986—90, publ. com. 1990—, mem. com. 1990—, lung and brain com. 1990—), No. Calif. Radiation Oncology Soc. (pres. 1999—2001), Coun. Affiliated Radiation Oncology Soc. (pres. 1999—2000), Assn. Residents Radiation Oncology (exec. com. 1997—2000, faculty advisor 1997—2000, advisor emeritus 2000—), Am. Cancer Soc. (reviewer 1990—, fellow 1978, 1983), Am. Coll. Radiology (chmn. stds. accreditation com. 1997—2003, councilor at large 1999, alt. councilor 2000—03, councillor 2003—, mem. expert panels, credentials com., fellow 1997). Avocations: painting, sculpture, travel, cello. Office: Sutter Cancer Ctr 2800 L St Ste 10 Sacramento CA 95816-5616 Personal E-mail: hbwolkov@comcast.net. Business E-Mail: wolkovh@radiological.com.

WOLL, BENCIE, neuroscientist, linguist; b. NYC, Feb. 22, 1950; d. Lazar B. Woll and Fannie Woll Avrin. BA, U. Pa., 1970; MA, U. Essex, Colchester, Eng., 1971; PhD, U. Bristol, Eng., 1991. From. rsch. asst. to sr. lectr. U. Bristol, 1973-95; prof., chair sign lang. & deaf studies City U., London, 1995—2005, Univ. Coll. London, 2005—. Dir. Deafness, Cognition and Lang. Rsch. Ctr., 2006—. Author: Sign Language, 1985, The Linguistics of BSL, 1999 (Deaf Nation prize, 1999, BAAL Book prize, 2000), BSL Receptive Skills Test, 1999. Trustee Deaf Studies Trust, Bristol, 1995—2005. Wyndham Deedes fellow Anglo-Israel Assn., 1982, Royal Netherlands Sci. Inst. fellow, 2005. Mem.: Coun. Advancement of Communication With Deaf People, Sign Lang. Adv. Com., Royal Assn. Deaf People (vice chair 2002—, trustee 2008), Penn Club (NY). Avocations: music, travel, cats, Yiddish. Home: Flat 4 24 Inverness Ter London W2 3HU England Office: Deafness Cognition and Language Rsch Ctr 49 Gordon Sq London WC1H 0PD England Office Fax: 44-20-7679 8691. Business E-Mail: b.woll@ucl.ac.uk.

WOLLACK, JAN B., pediatrician, neurologist, educator; Attended, Columbia U., 1981. Diplomate Am. Bd. of Psychiatry and Neurology, 1987, Am. Bd. of Pediatrics, 1988, Am. Bd. of Psychiatry and Neurology, 2001. Intern pediat. Columbia Presbyterian Med. Ctr., NY, NY, 1981—83, resident pediat. & neurology, 1983—86; with Bristol Myers Squibb Children's Hosp., Robert Wood Johnson Univ. Hosp.; assoc. prof. pediat. Robert Wood Johnson Med. Sch., chief divsn. of child neurology and neurodevelopmental, dir. neurodevelopmental disabilities, dir. child neurology program, dir. pediat. epilepsy program. Office: UMDNJ-RWJ Medical School 89 French St 2nd Fl New Brunswick NJ 08901 Office Phone: 732-235-7875. Office Fax: 732-235-6620.

WOLLEMANN, MARIA, neuroscientist, consultant; b. Budapest, Hungary, July 6, 1923; d. Victor and Ilona (Barta) Wollemann. MD, U. of Sci., Szeged and Budapest, 1947. Sr. rsch. assoc. Inst. of Neurosurgery, Budapest, Hungary, 1954—70; dir. BRC Inst. Biochemistry Hungarian Acad. Scis., Szeged, Hungary, 1978—83. Sci. cons. Biol. Rsch. Ctr. Inst. Biochemistry Hungarian Acad. Scis., Szeged, Hungary, 1985—98. Author: (book) Biochemistry of Brain Tumors, 1974 (Academic award, 1977). Mem. Nature Protection Assn., Szeged, Hungary, 1973—2002. Recipient Academic award, Hungarian Acad.of Sci.Biol.Section, 1977. Mem.: Hungarian Soc Biochemistry. (Straub F.Bruno prize 1984). Achievements include research in Isozymes Of Brain Tumors, Free Radicals Of Chlorpromazine, Subtypes Of Opioid Kappa Receptors. Avocations: swimming, birdwatching, farming. Office: Biol Rsch Ctr Institute of Biochemistry HAS Temesvari korut 62 Hungary Szeged 6701 Hungary Office Phone: 36-62-599600. Office Fax: 36-62-433-506. E-mail: wollemann@brc.hu.

WOLLENHAUPT, JURGEN H., rheumatologist; b. Neuss, Germany, June 4, 1957; s. Karl-Heinz and Elfriede (Abstoss) W.; m. Katharina B. Krauch, 1987; children: Hannah Sophie, Charlotte Marie, Carl Christian. MD, U. Dusseldorf, Germany, 1983; PhD, Hannover Med. Sch., Germany, 1998. Diplomate German Bd. Internal Medicine, German Bd. Rheumatology, German Bd. Phys. and Rehab. Medicine. Rsch. fellow divsn. immunology U. Heidelberg, Germany, 1985-86; rsch. assoc. U. Dusseldorf, 1986-89; staff mem. Hannover Med. Sch., 1989-92, sr. lectr., 1992-98, assoc. prof., 1998—2002, prof. rheumatology, 2002—, head dept. rheumatology, 1999—. Assoc. editor Aktuelle Rheumatologie. Maj. German Air Force, 1984-85. Office: Klinikum Eilbek Dehnhaide 120 D-22081 Hamburg Germany Office Phone: 49-40-20921351. Business E-Mail: wollenhaupt@rheumatologikum.de.

WOLLENSAK, GREGOR JOSEF, ophthalmologist; b. Erlangen, Germany; s. Josef Wollensak and Roswitha Sauer. Abitur, Canisius Coll., Berlin, 1979. Cert. in facharzt augenheilkunde Aerztekammer Baden Württemberg, 1996. Ophthalmologist U. Freiburg Br., Germany, 1991—96, pathologist, 1991—96; rsch. fellow Wilmer Eye Inst., Balt., 1997—98; oberarzt Dept. Ophthalmology, Klinikum Carl Gustav Carus, Dresden, Germany, 1998—2006, Dept. Ophthalmology, Martin Luther U., Halle, Germany, 2007—, Saale, Germany, 2007—. Contbr. articles to profl. jours. Recipient Rsch. award, German Ophthal. Soc., 2003. Home: Wildentensteig 4 Berlin D-14195 Germany

WOLLESEN, FLEMMING, endocrinologist; b. Mar. 30, 1935; MD, Copenhagen U. Med. Sch., 1963; post grad. studies, UCLA Med. Sch., 1971—73. Lic. in medicine and surgery Albany, NY, 1974, cert. in internal medicine Copenhagen, 1980, in endocrinology Copenhagen, 1984, Am. Bd. Eligible In Internal Medicine, 1989, in internal medicine & endocrinology Stockholm, 1983. Intern and resident, internal medicine U. Hosp., Copenhagen, 1963—68; rsch. fellow, endocrinology Copenhagen County Hosp., Copenhagen, 1969—70; sr. rschr. Danish Govt. Med. Rsch. Coun., Copenhagen, 1969—70; chief resident endocrinology UCLA Med. Sch., 1971—73; asst. prof. endocrinology Coll. Physicians & Surgeons, Columbia U., NY, 1973—75, Copenhagen U. Hosp., 1976—86; assoc. prof. endocrinology Kalmar County Hosp., Sweden, 1986—91; asst. prof. endocrinology Uppsala U. Hosp., Sweden, 1992—99; personal physician, endocrinology to the pres. United Arab Emirates, 2000—04; specialist endocrinology Stockholm, 2004—. Contbr. articles to profl. jours. Rsch. grant, Danish Govt. Med. Rsch. Coun., 1970. Fellow: Am. Coll. Physicians, Philadelphia; mem.: Am. Diabetes Assn., The Endocrine Soc. America, Swedish Soc. Diabetology, Swedish Endocrine Soc., Swedish Med. Assn., Danish Soc. Internal Medicine, Danish Endocrine Soc., Danish Med. Assn. Home: Sysslomansgatan 41 B Uppsala 75227 Sweden Office: Engelbrekts Clinic Östermalmsgatan 47 114 27 Stockholm Sweden Office Phone: 0046 8 101500. Home Fax: 0046 18121215. Business E-Mail: flemming.wollesen@medicin.uu.se.

WOLLMAN, GLENN DAVID, physician, medical guide; b. Brooklyn, Ny, June 24, 1946; s. Leonard and June. MD, U. Miami, Coral Gables, 1972. Med. dir. integrative medicine program St. Francis Med. Ctr., Santa Barbara, Calif., 1998—2002; chief med. officer EmCare, Santa Barbara, Calif., 1999—2003; prof. Santa Barbara Coll. of Oriental Medicine, Santa Barbara, Calif., 2003—. Cmty. lectr. Santa Barbara City Coll., Santa Barbara, Calif., 1998. Fellow: Am. Coll. Emergency Physicians (life); mem.: St Ynez Valley Cottage Hosp. (hon.), Lompoc Healthcare Dist. (hon.), Cottage Hosp. Med. Staff (hon.). Achievements include Medical Guide (a new field in medicine), hospital based integrative medicine program. Avocations: meditation, music, painting, martial arts. Home and Office: Living Suite 1543 Portesuello Ave Santa Barbara CA 93105

WOLMAN, ERIC, health care consultant; b. NYC, Sept. 25, 1931; s. Leo and Cecil (Clark) W.; m. Sandra Rosman, July 27, 1963; children: Karin, Alastair. AB in Math., Harvard Coll., 1953; PhD in Applied Math., Harvard U., 1957. Mem. tech. staff AT&T Bell Labs., Murray Hill, Holmdel, NJ, 1957—66, dept. head traffic rsch. and network engrng. Holmdel, NJ, 1966—77, dept. head ops. rsch. and computing sys. West Long Branch, NJ, 1977—82, dept. head human performance engrng. Piscataway, Summit, NJ, 1983—87; v.p. cmty. programs and rsch. Mich. Cancer Found., Detroit, 1988—91; asst. leader cancer prevention and control program Prentis Comprehensive Cancer Ctr. Met. Detroit, 1990—94; mem. faculty grad. program in cancer biology Wayne State U. Sch. of Medicine, Detroit, 1992—96; vis. rsch. prof. dept. sys. engrng and ops. rsch. George Mason U., Fairfax, Va., 1996—. Mem. evaluation panel for fire programs Nat. Bur. of Standards, Gaithersburg, Md., 1966-74, evaluation panel for nat. engrng. lab., 1974-80, working group on info. tech. NSF, Arlington, Va., 1980-81. Contbr. articles to profl. jours. Trustee Rumson (N.J.) Country Day Sch., 1973-81, Sea Edn. Assn., Woods Hole, Mass., 1981-2004, Overseer, 2004-. Fellow AAAS, Inst. Ops. Rsch. and Mgmt. Scis. (coun. 1979-82), INFORMS; mem. Seabright Beach Club, Harvard Club (NYC). Avocation: cruising. Home: 7806 Hidden Meadow Ter Potomac MD 20854-1792 Office Phone: 301-983-0698. Personal E-mail: eric.wolman@erols.com.

WOLRAICH, MARK LEE, pediatrician, educator; BA, SUNY, Binghamton, 1966; MD, SUNY, Syracuse, 1970. Diplomate Am. Bd. Pediat. Pediatric intern SUNY, Syracuse, 1970-71; pediatric resident U. Okla. Health Scis. Ctr., Oklahoma City, 1973-74; pediatric fellowship U. Oreg. Health Scis. Ctr., 1974-76; asst. prof. U. Iowa, 1976-81, assoc. prof., 1981-86, prof., 1986-90, Vanderbilt U., 1990-2001, dir. divsn. child devel., dir. child devel. ctr., 1990-99, dir. ctr. for chronic illnesses and disabilities in children, 1990-2000; investigator J.F. Kennedy Ctr. for Rsch. on Edn. and Human Devel., 1990-2001; prof. pediat., dir. Child Study Ctr. Okla. U. Health Scis. Ctr., 2001—, Edith Kinney Gaylord presdl. prof., 2010. Med. supr. U. Iowa Divsn. of Devel. Disabilities, 1980-90; vis. prof. Great Ormond St. Hosp. for Sick Children, London, 1983, U. Cape Town, Rondebosch Cape, South Africa, 1986, Columbus Children's Hosp., Ohio State U., Dept. Pediat., 1988; mem. Iowa State Foster Care Rev. Bd. Co-editor Advances in Developmental and Behavioral Pediatrics, 1981-92; cons. editor Am. Jour. on Mental Deficiency; editl. adv. bd. A Guide to Parent Counseling; editor The Classification of Child and Adolescent Mental Disorders in Primary Care-Diagnostic and Statistical Manual for Mental Disorders in Primary Care Child and Adolescent Version, 1996; cons. reviewer Developmental Medicine and Child Neurology, Pediatrics, Nutrition and Behavior, Jour. Pediatrics, Jour. of Social and Personal Relationships, Applied Rsch. in Mental Retardation, Jour. of Clin. Psychology, Jour. Developmental and Behavioral Pediatrics, Clin. Pediatrics, others; contbr. numerous articles to profl. publs. Mem. Children and Adults with Attention Deficit, 2003—. Recipient Disting. and Dedicated Svc. award Spina Bifida Assn. Iowa, 1979, Lou Holloway award Health Scis. Edn., Presdl. Professorship award U. Okla. Health Scis. ctr., 2010; grantee NIMH, 1987-90, 98-2001, Nat. Inst. on Disability and Rehab. Rsch., 1987-89, NIH, 1988-91, Iowa Dept. Human Svcs., 1986-89, U. Iowa, 1979-87, United Cerebral Palsy Rsch. and Endl. Found., Inc., 1978-87, Iowa March of Dimes, 1980, Sugar Assn., Inc., 1983, Internat. Life Scis. Inst., 1988-91, W.T. Grant Found., 1989; MCH Lend grant, 1999—, CDC grant, 2002; named to Children and Adults with Attention-Deficit/Hyperactivity Disorder Hall of Fame, 2003. Fellow Am. Acad. Pediat. (com. 1992-2000, chair com. on psychosocial aspects child and family health 1997-2000, chair child and adolescent health action group 2000-04, chair-elect mgmt. com., 2004-, chmn. mgmt. com. 2006—, Aldrich award, Sect. Devel. and Behavioral Pediats. 2011), Am. Acad. Cerebral Palsy and Devel. Medicine; mem. Soc. for Devel. and Behavioral Pediat. (pres. 1994-95, program dir. 1990-93), Soc. Pediatric Psychology Assn. (assoc., Lee Salk award for disting. svc.), Soc. for Pediatric Rsch. (sr.), Am. Acad. on Comm. in Healthcare (charter), Am. Pediatric Soc., Ctr. Diseases Control & Prevention (mem. bd. sci. counsellors). Office: Okla U Health Scis Ctr 1100 NE 13th St Oklahoma City OK 73117

WOLSTEIN, ARTHUR, podiatrist; b. NYC, Nov. 22, 1914; s. Hyman Wolstein and Rose Kornbluth; m. Diane Teichberg, May 29, 1947; children: Deborah, Lewis, Peter, Marianne. D in Podiatric Medicine, N.Y. Coll. Podiatric Medicine, 1937. Past chmn. Visions summer camp for the blind, 1997; chmn. bd. R.A.I.N., 1998—; vol. Chaplains Programs Bronx Vets. Med. Ctr.; vol. spkr. Srs. Outspeaking NY Medicare Rights Ctr. Staff sgt. US Army, 1942—46. Named to Westchester Hall of Fame, 2009. Mem.: DAV (elected comdr. Bronx chpt. #23 1999—2001), APHA, Am. Assn. Hosp. Podiatrists (past pres.), Bronx County Podiatry Soc. (pres. 1955), Am. Acad. Ambulatory Foot Surgery, Am. Podiatric Med. Assn. (del. 1955—65), Nat. Order Trench Rats, Bronx Hist. Soc., Disabled Am. Vets, B'nai B'rith, Bronx Coun. on Arts, AARP, Rotary (treas. 1997, pres. 2003—05), Comdrs. Club. Jewish. Avocation: N.Y. Yankees. Home: 11 Morrison Dr New Rochelle NY 10804-1710 Office Phone: 718-863-3338.

WOLTER, NICHOLAS, health facility administrator; b. Minn., Oct. 31, 1947; BA in English, Carleton Coll.; MA in American Culture, U. Mich., MD, 1977. Cert. Internal Medicine, Pulmonary Medicine. Intern internal medicine Mary Imogene Bassett Hosp., Cooperstown, NY, 1977—78, resident critical care medicine, 1978—80; fellow in pulmonary and critical care medicine U. Mich., 1980—82; CEO Billings Clinic, Mont. Bd. dirs. Billings Clinic Found., LifeCenter Northwest, VHA Health Found., 2003—06; past chmn. MHA (Assn. of Mont. Health Care Providers); bd. chmn. VHA Mountain States; commissioner on Medicare Payment Adv. Commission (MedPAC). Named Physician Exec. of Yr., Med. Group Mgmt. Assn. Mem.:

American Hosp. Assn. (bd. dirs.), American Coll. Physician Executives, American Med. Group Assn. (bd. dirs.). Office: Billings Clinic 801 North 29th St PO Box 35100 Billings MT 59107-7000 Office Phone: 406-238-2500.

WOLYNN, TODD H., lactation consultant; MD, U. Pitts. Diplomate Am. Bd. Pediatrics, cert. lactation cons. Resident UPMC Mercy, hosp. affiliation include/s, Magee-Womens Hosp. of UPMC, Children's Hosp. of Pitts. of UPMC; clin. instr. Univ. of Pitts. Named one of Top Doctors, Pitts. Mag., 2010. Office: Kids Plus Pediatrics 4070 Beechwood Blvd Pittsburgh PA 15217 Office Phone: 412-521-6511.

WON, CHONG HYUN, medical educator, dermatologist; b. Seoul, Republic of Korea, Sept. 28, 1972; s. Chul Hee Won and Oh Sook Kwon; m. Jee Soo An, Feb. 24, 2007. MD, Seoul Nat. U. Sch. Medicine, PhD, 2007. Lic. Korean Med. Lic. Exam., 1997. Clin. fellow Seoul Nat. U. Boramae Hosp., 2005—06, asst. prof., 2006—. Office: Boramae Hosp 39 Boramaegil Shindaebangdong Dongjakgu Seoul 156-707 Republic of Korea Business E-Mail: chwon98@chol.com.

WON, CHULHO, biomedical engineer, educator; b. Geo-Je, Kyung-Nam, Republic of Korea, Feb. 3, 1968; s. Seok-Joon Won and Kui-Ja Kim; m. Jean-Sook Park, Jan. 9, 1999; children: Eric S., Seung-min. PhD, Kyunpook Nat. U., Daegu, Republic of Korea, 1998. Assoc. prof. Kyungil U., Kyungsan, Republic of Korea. Recipient Herbert M. Stauffer Award: Outstanding basic sci. paper, Academic radiology, Assn. of Univ. Radiologist, 2003; fellow, Coll. Medicine, Keimyung U., Deagu, 1998—99, U. Iowa Hosps. and Clinics, 1999—2002. Home: Hyo-mok 2 Dong Daegu 701-776 Republic of Korea Office: Kyungil U Hayang-Up 33 712-701 Kyung Republic of Korea Office Fax: +82-53-850-7612. Business E-Mail: wonchulho@msn.com.

WON, DONG IL, medical educator; b. Wonju, Republic of Korea, Oct. 28, 1966; s. Ki Yun Won and Jung Ja Sung; m. Myeong Sin Chae, Aug. 21, 1995; children: Ye Jin, Jung Ha. MB, Yonsei U., Seoul, 1991, MM, 1997, PhD, 2004. Doctor Ministry Health and Welfare Republic of Korea, 1991, cert. bd.lab. medicine Korean Soc. for Lab. Medicine, 1996. Assoc. prof. Sch. Medicine Kyungpook Nat. U., Daegu, Republic of Korea, 2002—. Mem. editl. bd.: Korea Jour. Lab. Medicine, 2006—; contbr. articles to profl. jours. Recipient Oral Presentation award, Korean Soc. Lab. Medicine, 2006, 2008, 2009. Mem.: Clin. Cytometry Soc. Home: Beomeo-Dong 2025 Suseong-Gu Daegu 706-947 Republic of Korea Office: Kyungpook Nat Univ Hosp Dept Laboratory Medicine Samduk-Dong 2 Ga Jung Gu 50 700 721 Daegu Daegu Republic of Korea Office Fax: 82-53-426-3367. Personal E-mail: wondi@hanmail.net. Business E-Mail: wondi@knu.ac.kr.

WON, JONG-HO, medical educator; b. Incheon, Republic of Korea, Dec. 7, 1959; s. Joong-Hee Won and Jeung-Hee Kim; m. Young-Hyun Ahn, Sept. 29, 1991; children: Sang-Yon, Joo-Hee. MD, Soonchunhyang U. Coll. Medicine, Asan, South Korea, 1984; PhD, Ulsan U., South Korea, 1996. Cert. in dr. medicine Ministry Health & Welfare, Korea, 1984, internal medicine Ministry Health & Welfare, Korea, 1991, med. hematology oncology Ministry Health & Welfare, Korea, 1996. Chief divsn. hematology oncology Soonchunhyang U. Hosp., Seoul, 2001—, dir. stem cell Therapy Ctr., 2004—, chair, gen. mgr. out & in-patient, 2008—. Contbr. articles to profl. jours. First lt. flight surgeon, 1984—87, Seosan, South Korea. Recipient award for Best Scientist, Korean Soc. BRM, 2001, award for Best Article, Korean Soc. Cancer, 2004. Mem.: Korean Soc. Blood & Marrow Transplantation (chmn. clin. trial com. 2007—), Korean Soc. Cancer, Korean Soc. Hematology (chmn., sci. com. 2009), Internat. Soc. Exptl. Hematology, European Hematology Assn., Am. Soc. Hematology. Office: Soonchunhyang University Hosp 22 Daesagwan-gil Yongdan-Ku Seoul 140-743 Republic of Korea Office Fax: 82-2-709-9200. Business E-Mail: jhwon@hosp.sch.ac.kr.

WON, KYOUNG SOOK, nuclear medicine physician; b. Jinangun, Chonbuk, Republic Of Korea, Aug. 15, 1967; d. Yong Sung and Mak Rae (Shin) Won; m. Keun Uk Park, Mar. 14, 1993; children: Sang Hyuk Park, Min Hyuk Park, Jun Hyuk Park. MD, Chonbuk Nat. U., Jeonju, 1991; PhD, U. Ulsan, Seoul, 2001. Cert. physician Min. of Health and Welfare, Republic of Korea, 1991, specialist of nuc. medicine Min. of Health and Welfare, Republic of Korea, 1998, specialist of internal medicine Min. of Health and Welfare, Republic of Korea, 1996. Intern Nat. Med. Ctr., Seoul, Republic of Korea, 1991—92, resident in internal medicine, 1992—96; clin. fellow nuc. medicine Asan Med. Ctr., Seoul, Republic of Korea, 1996—97; dir. nuc. medicine Asan Gangnung Hosp., Gangwon, Republic of Korea, 1997—2002; instr. nuc. medicine Keimyung U., Daegu, Republic of Korea, 2002—04, asst. prof., 2004—08, assoc. prof., 2008—. Postdoctoral fellow M.D. Anderson Cancer Ctr., Houston, 2006—07. Contbr. articles to profl. jours. Mem.: Korean Soc. Nuc. Medicine (assoc.). Office: Keimyung Univ Dongsan Med Ctr Dongsandong 194 700-712 Daegu Daegu Republic of Korea Office Fax: 82-53-250-8128. Personal E-mail: wildrose1@hanmail.net. Business E-Mail: won@dsmc.or.kr.

WON, SUN JAE, medical educator; b. Seoul, Republic of Korea, June 24, 1976; MD, Cath. U., 2001. Clin. asst. prof., dept. rehab. medicine Korea U. Guro Hosp., 2009—. Asst. adminstr. info. com. Korean Acad. Rehab. Medicine, 2011. Mem.: Korean Soc. Prosthetics and Orthotics, Korean Acad. Neuromusculoskeletal Sonography, Korean Acad. Electrodiagnostic Medicine, Korean Assn. Pain Medicine, Korean Acad. Rehab. Medicine. Avocations: meditation, reading, travel. Home: Bongcheon-dong 1596-11 303 Gwanak-gu Seoul 151-050 Republic of Korea Personal E-mail: gstinfog@naver.com.

WONG, BRIAN, medical educator; b. Santa Monica, Calif., July 20, 1948; AB, Harvard U., 1970; MD, SUNY Downstate, 1974. Prof. medicine, molecular microbiology & immunology, dir., divsn. infectious diseases Oreg. Health & Sci. U., 2006—. Office: OHSU Infectious Diseases Divisn 3181 Portland OR 97239 Office Fax: 503-494-4264. Business E-Mail: wongbri@ohsu.edu.

WONG, BRIAN JET-FEI, surgeon; b. LA, Sept. 23, 1963; s. Richard Toy and Hazel F. (Lue) W. BS, U. So. Calif., 1985; postgrad., Oxford U., 1985-86; MD, Johns Hopkins U., 1990; PhD, U. Amsterdam, 2001. Resident U. Calif., Irvine, 1990-96, clin. instr., 1997-98, asst. prof., 1998—2001, assoc. prof., 2001—06, prof., 2006—07, vice chmn. Rsch. assoc. Beckman Laser Inst., Irvine, 1994—. Recipient Physician Excellence, Orange County Med. Assn.; named one of Best Dr. in USA. Mem. ACS, Biomed. Optical Soc., SPIE, Am. Acad. Facial Plastic Surgery. Avocation: surfing. Office: Univ Calif Irvine Beckman Laser Inst 1002 Health Scis Rd Irvine CA 92612 Office Phone: 714-456-5753.

WONG, CARLOS, biochemist, educator, researcher; b. Magdalena, Sonora, Mexico, Aug. 9, 1932; s. Carlos Wong-Sun and Juana Ramirez; m. María Isabel Baeza; children: María Isabel Wong-Baeza, Carlos Wong-Baeza. B in Pharmacy, Nat. Poly. Inst., Mex., 1959, PhD in Biochemistry, 1968; postgrad., U. Calif., LA, 1969. Pharmacy dept. chair Nat. Poly. Inst., 1965—75, biochemistry dept. chair, 1980—83, biochemistry grad. studies chair, 1984—91, enzymology lab head, 1980—, prof. biochemistry, 1980—. Adv. Sci. & Tech. Bd., Distrito Fed., Mexico, 2001—02. Recipient Acad. Merit medal, Ednl. Bd., 1992, von Behring award, Acad. Medicine, 1999; grantee Investigation 2000, Nat. Inst. Poly., 2001. Fellow: Nat. Sys. Rsch. Roman Catholic. Achievements include design of N-propyl and N-isopropyl oxamates as a selective inhibitors of alpha-hydroxyacid dehydrogenase, an enzyme that participates in the energetic metabolism of T. cruzi; research in ethyl esters of N-isopropyl and N-propyl oxamates exhibited trypanocidal activity on T. cruzi strains including those that were resistant to Nifurtimox and Benznidazol; patents in field. Avocations: football, baseball. Office: Instituto Politécnico Nacional ENCB Apartado postal 4-129 Distrito Federal Mexico City 11340 Mexico Home: Amado Nervo 172 6400 Mexico City Distrito Federal Mexico Office Fax: 5255926614. Business E-Mail: cwong@encb.ipn.mx.

WONG, DENNIS CHUNG TAK, surgeon; MBBS. Specialist upper GI and bariatric surgeon Pamela Youde Nethersole Ea. Hosp., Dept. Surgery, Chai Wan, Hong Kong, 2001—. Contbr. articles to profl. jours. Mem.: FHKAM, FCSHK, FRACS, MRCS. Office: Pamela Youde Nethersole Eastern Hosp 3 Lok Man Rd Chai Wan Hong Kong Personal E-mail: dctwong@gmail.com.

WONG, FAYE LING, public health service officer; BS in Dietetics, U. Wash., 1972; MPH, U. Calif.-Berkeley, 1973. Registered dietitian, lic. Ga. Relief dietary supr. Va. Mason Hosp., Seattle, 1968—72; chief Bur. of Nutrition Coconino County Dept. Pub. Health, Flagstaff, Ariz., 1974—76; nutrition cons. Office of Cmty. Health Svcs., Oreg. State Health Divsn., Portland, 1976—81; dir. Sentinel Site project Detroit Health Dept., 1981—83; pub. health nutritionist field svcs. br. Ctr. for Health Promotion and Edn. CDC, Atlanta, 1983—89, program analyst Ctr. for Chronic Disease Prevention and Health Promotion, 1988—89, chief field svcs. br. divsn. nutrition, 1989—92, chief program ops., program svcs. br., 1992—94, asst. chief divsn. cancer prevention and control, 1994 95, asst. chief policy and devel., 1995—96, assoc. dir. diabetes edn., dir. nat. diabetes edn. program, 1996—2000, dir. Youth Media Campaign, 2001—. Contbr. numerous articles, abstracts to profl. jours., to resource manuals. Recipient Award for Disting. Svc., Dept. Health and Human Svcs., 2000, Questar Internat. award, 2000, Thoth award., Pub. Rels. Assn. Am., 2000, Aesculapius Awards for Excellence, Nat. Diabetes Edn. Program, 1999, 1998, Award for Excellence in recognition of outstanding leadership and dedicated svc., Assn. of State and Territorial Pub. Health Nutrition Dirs., 1991. Mem.: Am. Diabetes Assn. (mem. health profls. sect. 1996—), Am. Assn. Diabetes Educators (mem. pub. health specialty practice group 1996—), Am. Dietetic Assn. (mem. diabetes care and edn. practice group 1996—, mem. nominating com. 1999—), APHA (mem. food and nutrition sect. 1975—, mem. exec. bd. pub. policy rev. and devel. com. 1995—97, chair editl. bd. Am. Jour. Pub. Health 1997—2000, pres. 2001—02, co-chair task force on aging 2001—03, chair, exec. dir. search com. 2001—, Apple award 1991). Office: 4770 Buford Hwy NE lc 94 Atlanta GA 30341 Business E-Mail: fwong@cdc.gov.

WONG, FRANKLIN C., medical educator; b. Hong Kong, Oct. 14, 1955; MD, Chgo. Med. Sch., PhD, 1986; JD, U. Houston, MBA, 1998. Prof., nuc. medicine and neuro-oncology M.D. Anderson Cancer Ctr., 1992—. Prof. U. Tex. M.D. Anderson Cancer Ctr. Radiation Dosimetry grant, US NIH, 2001—08, US DOD CDMRP Breast Cancer Rsch. Programs, 2003—08. Fellow: Am. Acad. Neurology, Am. Coll. Nuc. Medicine, Am. Coll. Legal Medicine; mem.: State Bar Tex. Avocations: flying, hunting. Office: 1400 Pressler Bellaire TX 77401 Office Fax: 713-563-3694. Business E-Mail: fwong@mdanderson.org.

WONG, JOHNSON TAI, allergist, immunologist, educator; MD, U. Calif., 1980. Diplomate Am. Bd. Internal Medicine, 1983, Am. Bd. Allergy and Immunology, 1985, lic. Mass., 1984. Intern internal medicine Wadsworth Gen. Hosp., 1981, resident internal medicine, 1981—83; fellow allergy and immunology Mass. Gen. Hosp., 1983—86; asst. prof. medicine Harvard Med. Sch.; hosp. affiliations include Mass. Eye & Ear Infirmary, Newton-Wellesley Hosp., Mass. Gen. Hosp. Co-author: (publs.) Simultaneous assessment of cytotoxic T lymphocyte responses against multiple viral infections by combined usage of optimal epitope matrices, anti- CD3 mAb T-cell expansion and "RecycleSpot, 2005, Transience of vaccine-induced HIV-1-specific CTL and definition of vaccine response, 2006, Ten-year study of causes of moderate to severe angioedema seen by an inpatient allergy/immunology consult service, 2008, and other numerous publications. Named one of Top Doctors, Boston Mag., 2009. Office: Massachusetts General Hospital 55 Fruit St Boston MA 02114-2696 Office Phone: 617-726-2000.

WONG, KENNETH, pharmacist; b. Hong Kong, China, Jan. 28, 1961; arrived in U.S., 1961; s. Wing Lee and Lotus Ling Wong; m. Sandra Kwok-Ling Lau, May 30, 1992; children: Julianne Mei-Yun, Kristen Mei-Kei. B, U. So. Calif., 1980; PharmD, U. So. Calif., LA, 1984. Registered pharmacist Bd. Pharmacy, Calif., 1984. Clin. pharmacist Kaiser Permanent, LA, 1985—. Mem.: Calif. Soc. Health-System Pharmacists, Calif. Pharmacists Assn., Am. Soc. Health-System Pharmacists. Achievements include defining the pharmacist's role in ambulatory chronic disease management within a new promary care medical system delivery model; development of web-based Computerized Medication List Program. Office: Kaiser Permanente 4950 Sunset Blvd Los Angeles CA 90027

WONG, KIU FUNG KELVIN, physician; b. Hong Kong, Mar. 21, 1985; MB, Jinan U., 2010. House officer Shenzhen People's Hosp. China, 2009—10; team leader rsch. team first atypical case Silver-Russell Syndrome, China. Team leader rsch. team first atypical case Silver-Russell Syndrome, China; with dept. pediat., First Affiliated Hosp. Jinan U., 2009—10; vice-chief rsch. dir., joint-inventor BIOLAB Svc. Clin. Lab., 2010—. Recipient prize, Sir Edward Youde Meml. Fund Coun., 2003—04; Nat. scholarship, Ministry Edn. People's Republic of China, 2007—08. Mem.: Nat. Med. Pediat. Residents' Assn., Hong Kong New Generation Cultural Assn. (com. mem.), Tsinghua Alumni Assn. Hong Kong Future Leaders, Hong Kong Ergonomics Soc. Home: Flat 407 Block 24 Heng Fa Chuen Hong Kong HKSAR Hong Kong Personal E-mail: wkfkelvin2002@hotmail.com.

WONG, KUTT-SING, surgeon; b. Singapore, Sept. 23, 1967; MBBS, Nat. U. Singapore, 1991. Cons. Nat. U. Hosp., 2004—09, Raffles Hosp., 2009—. Founding mem. Soc. Colorectal Surgeons, Singapore, 2003—11. Decorated Top Cadet Singapore Armed Forces; recipient Gold Reviewer award, Annals, Acad. Medicine, Singapore. Fellow: RCS, AMS. Avocations: chess, running, badminton, tennis, squash. Office: Raffles Hosp 585 N Bridge Rd #01-00 Singapore 188770 Singapore Business E-Mail: wong_kuttsing@rafflesmedical.com.

WONG, NATHAN DONALD, medicine and epidemiology researcher, educator; b. Downey, Calif., Apr. 18, 1961; s. Donald Wah and Mew Lun (Hee) W.; m. Mia K. Park, July 21, 1996; 1 child, David. BA, Pomona Coll., Claremont, Calif., 1983; MPH, Yale U., New Haven, Conn., 1985, PhD, 1987. Lectr. medicine Yale U., New Haven, 1987; asst. prof. U. Calif., Irvine, 1988—94, assoc. prof., 1994—2002, dir. heart disease prevention program, dept. medicine, 1991—, prof., 2003—, prof. dept. epidemiology LA, 2003—, Irvine, 2010—, prof., dept. radiology, 2011—. Prin. investigator Antihypertensive Lipid-Lowering to Prevent Heart Attack Trial and other lipid and cardiovasc. prevention trials, 1994—; co-prin. investigator Women's Health Initiative, 1995—; investigator NIH Multiethnic Study of Atherosclerosis (MESA), Coronary Artery Risk Development in Young Adults, Cardiovascular Health Study, and Epidemiology of Diabetes Interventions and Complications Studies; interviewed for various publs. and programs, including ABC Eyewitness News, L.A. Times, Orange County Register, CBS News, USA Today, N.Y. Times, others; profl. cons. Cedars-Sinai Med. Ctr., 2002—; editor-in-chief textbook Preventive Cardiology, Mcgraw-Hill, 2000, 2d edit, 2005; co-editor (textbook) Metabolic Syndrome and Cardiovascular Disease, 2007. Co-editor: (textbook) Preventive Cardiology: Companion to Braunwald's Heart Disease, 2011; mem. editl. bd.: Preventive Cardiology, Jour. Cardiovascular Drugs, Jour. Cardiometabolic Risk; contbr. chapters to books, approx 200 articles to profl. jours. Mem. Calif. Senate Hearing Panel on Youth Phys. Edn. and Fitness, 1991; chair Calif. Cardiovasc. Disease Prevention Coalition, 1998-99; spkr. numerous internat., nat. and local confs., hosps., and med. spkrs. burs. Rsch. grantee, Bristol Myers-Squibb, Pfizer, Merck, Novartis, Forest. Fellow Am. Coll. Cardiology (membership and credentialing com. 2003—09, prevention of cardiovasc. disease com. 2003-04, taskforce 4, 34th Bethesda Conf. 2003), Am. Heart Assn. Coun. on Epidemiology and Prevention, Am. Soc. Preventive Cardiology (pres. 2010-). Achievements include research in computed tomography, metabolic syndrome, diabetes, lipids, hypertension, preventive cardiology, coronary and aortic calcium. Avocations: running, hiking, skiing, photography. Office: Heart Disease Prevention Program Sprague Hall 112 Univ Calif Irvine CA 92697-4101 Home Phone: 949-240-2840. Business E-Mail: ndwong@uci.edu.

WONG, PO-KEUNG, environmental microbiologist, toxicologist; b. Hong Kong, Aug. 17, 1954; s. Cheung-Sung and Ngau (Mok) Wong; m. Lai-Hor Lee, 1977; children: Carmine, Carol, Carson. BSc in Biology, Chinese U. Hong Kong, 1977, MPhil in Microbiology, 1979; PhD in Microbiology, U. Calif., Davis, 1983. Lectr. Chinese U. Hong Kong, 1986-94, sr. lectr., 1994-96, assoc. prof., 1996-97, prof., 1997—. Vis. rsch. scientist, U. Calif., Davis, 1993; mem. ISO14000 Tech. Com., Hong Kong, 1997—. Editor-in-chief Jour. Environ. Scis. (Chinese Acad. Scis.), 1995—. Mem. Am. Soc. Microbiology, Soc. Toxicology, Soc. Environ. Toxicology and Chemistry, Chartered Instn. Water and Environ. Mgmt., N.Y. Acad. Sci., Am. Chem. Soc., Internat. Soc. Environ. Biotech. Office: The Chinese University Hong Kong Sch Life Scis Shatin NT Hong Kong SAR China Business E-Mail: pkwong@cuhk.edu.hk.

WONG, RAYMOND SHIU-LOONG, radiologist; b. Hong Kong, Jan. 25, 1942; came to U.S., 1958; s. Jason Y. and Nancy L. (Tamm) W.; m. Jo-Lien Hsieh; 1 child, Florence W. BS in Chemistry, UCLA, 1962; MD, U. Chgo., 1966. Diplomate Am. Bd. Radiology with subspecialty in nuclear radiology, Am. Bd. Pediats. Diagnostic radiologist Hollywood Presbyn. Med. Ctr., LA, 1981-94, Huntington Meml. Hosp., Pasadena, Calif., 1994—. Contbr. articles to profl. jours. Mem. Am. Coll. Radiology, Soc. Nuclear Medicine, Calif. Radiol. Soc., L.A. Radiol. Soc., Radiol. Soc. N.Am. Office: Huntington Meml Hosp 100 W California Blvd Pasadena CA 91105-3097

WONG, SAI-SIONG, dermatologist, consultant; b. Malaysia, Jan. 22, 1961; s. Ling-Choon Wong and Guat-Eng Tan; m. Kit-Yue Chan; children: Rebecca, Wing-Yee, Grace, Wing-Eng. MBBCh, University of Wales, Cardiff, 1986. Cert. Specialist in Dermatology Hong Kong, 1998. Sr. house officer in medicine Univ. Hosp. Wales, Cardiff, 1987—88; registrar in medicine Royal Gwent Hosp., Newport, Wales, 1988—89, Llandough Hosp., Cardiff, 1989—90; sr. ho. officer in dermatology Univ. Hosp. Wales, Cardiff, 1990—91; sr. med. officer Evangel Hosp., Hong Kong, 1992—94, Our Lady of Maryknoll Hosp., Hong Kong, 1994—96; registrar in dermatology Nat. Skin Ctr., Singapore, 1996—98, assoc. cons. in dermatology, 1996—98; cons. dermatologist Evangel Hosp., Kowloon,, Hong Kong, 1998—2004; dir., cons. dermatologist Skin and Laser Ctr., Hong Kong Bapt. Hosp., Kowloon, Hong Kong, 2004—06; hon. clin. asst. prof. faculty medicine Chinese U., Hong Kong, 2005—07. Contbr. articles to profl.

jours. Fellow: Royal Coll. Physicians (London), Hong Kong Coll. Physicians, Am. Acad. Dermatology, Acad. Singapore, Hong Kong Acad. Medicine; mem.: Royal Coll. Physicians (London), Dermatol. Soc. Singapore, Hong Kong Soc. Dermatology and Venereology. Avocations: reading, swimming, jogging, tennis, travel. Office: Skin and Laser Ctr Hong Kong Bapt Hosp 222 Waterloo Rd Kowloon Hong Kong Hong Kong Home Phone: 852-23377082; Office Phone: 852-27115221. Personal E-mail: kysswong@yahoo.com.

WONG, SIMON KAM KEE, pediatrician; b. Hong Kong, Oct. 31, 1935; s. Kam Tong and Yu (Wu) W.; m. Doreen Yee Chong Poon, May 5, 1962; children: Carol, Rita, Josephine, Elaine, Judy. MBBS, Hong Kong U., 1960. Pediatric med. officer Queen Mary Hosp., Hong Kong, 1961-68, Queen Elizabeth Hosp., Hong Kong, 1968; cons. pediatrician Caritas Med. Centre, Hong Kong, 1968-79; pvt. practice Hong Kong, 1979—. Hon. cons. John F. Kennedy Centre for Spastics, Hong Kong, 1964-68. Justice of peace Hong Kong Govt., 1984—; chmn. King's Coll. Old Boys Assn., 1963; hon. sec. Hong Kong Spastic Assn., 1966-67; chmn. Fu Hong Soc. Hong Kong, 1981-83, 91-93, pres., 1999-2008; mem. Subvention and Lottery Fund Adv. Com., Hong Kong Govt., 1992-98. Fellow Royal Coll. Physicians Edinburgh, Hong Kong Coll. Pediatrician, Hong Kong Acad. Medicine, Royal Coll. Physicians and Surgeons Glasgow; mem. Hong Kong Pediatric Soc. (chmn. 1976-77), Hong Kong Jockey Club. Roman Catholic. Avocations: tai chi, swimming, antique, ceramic, painting. Office: Rm 402 Prince Comml Bldg 150-152 Prince Edward Rd W Kowloon Hong Kong China

WONG, SIMON S., environmental health scientist, educator; arrived in U.S., 1992; MD, China Med. U., Shenyang, 1982, MPH, 1988. Cons. U. Ariz., Tucson, 1992—93, rsch. assoc., 1994—96, asst. rsch. scientist, 1997—2002, asst. prof., 2003—07, assoc. prof., 2008—. Contbr. articles to profl. jours. Grantee, USAF, 2000—, Am. Lung Assn., 2001—03, Health Effects Inst., 2005—. Mem.: Am. Thoracic Soc., Soc. Toxicology. Office: Univ Ariz 1501 N Campbell Ave Tucson AZ 85724-5073 Office Phone: 520-626-6572. Business E-Mail: shengjun@email.arizona.edu.

WONG, TOM, cardiologist, consultant; s. Kelly and Regia; married; 1 child. MB, ChB, U. Aberdeen, Scotland, 1993; MD, U. Aberdeen, 2007. Specialist registrar North-West Thames London Hosp., 1997—2006; cardiologist cons. Royal Brompton and Harefield Hosp., 2006—. Hon. sr. lectr. Nat. Heart and Lung Inst., Imperial Coll., London, 2006—. Editor: Current Medical Literature, 2001—05. Recipient People of Yr. award, Assn. for Disability and Rehab., 1995, Master's Letter of Commendation, Guild of Air Pilots and Air Navigators, 1996, Gold medal, Young Investigator award, Heart Rhythm UK, 2006; rsch. grantee, Wellcome Trust, 2003. Fellow: European Soc. Cardiology; mem.: Brit. Cardiac Soc., Royal Coll. Physicians (Edinburgh). Avocations: swimming, running. Office: Royal Brompton and Harefield Hosp Sydney St London SW3 6NP England Office Phone: 442073518619. Business E-Mail: tom.wong@imperial.ac.uk. E-mail: tomwong@ic.ac.uk.

WONG, WING KEUNG, trading and electronics company executive, physician; b. Hong Kong, Jan. 5, 1933; s. Lai Cho Wong and Sut Mui Chung; m. Ban Cho, May 28, 1957; children: Hoi Ling, Hoi Yin. MB, BChir, Beijing Med. Coll., 1955. Lic. Med. Coun. Hong Kong. Physician lst Hosp. of Beijing Med. Coll., 1955—2016; with Hosp., Ganshu, China, 1970—73; pvt. practice Hong Kong, 1979—94; dir. Cheung Tai Hong Ltd., Hong Kong, 1974—86; chmn. bd. dirs. Computime Ltd., Hong Kong, 1979—83; dir. Computime Internat. Ltd., British Virgin Islands, 1993—95; dep. chmn. Cheung Tai Hong Holdings Ltd., Bermuda, 1994—95; exec. dir. Cheung Tai Hong Ltd., Hong Kong, 1987—96. Author: Simplicity--A Photograph Album, 2001, Daydream-A Book of Poems and Photos, 2003. Mem. Hong Kong Med. Assn., Dynasty Club. Avocations: travel, music, diving, photography.

WONG KEE SONG, LOUIS MICHEL, gastroenterologist, educator; b. Mauritius, July 4, 1969; MD, U. Montreal, 1992. Cons., gastroenterology and hepatology Mayo Clinic, 2000—, assoc. prof., 2000—. Mem.: Am. Coll. Gastroenterology, Am. Gastroent. Assn., Am. Soc. Gastrointestinal Endoscopy. Office: 200 1st St SW Rochester MN 55905 Office Fax: 507-255-7612. Business E-Mail: wong.louis@mayo.edu.

WONGSTITWILAIROONG, BOONCHAI, medical researcher; b. Bangkok, Nov. 12, 1964; BSc in Med. Tech., Chulalongkorn U., 1986. Med. rsch. technician Lab. QA, USAMC-Armed Forces Rsch. Inst. Med. Scis., 2005—. Mem.: Assn. Clin. Rsch. Profls. Office: Armed Forces Research Inst Med Scis 315/6 Rajvithi Rd Rajathevee Bangkok 10400 Thailand Business E-Mail: boonchaiw@afrims.org.

WONSON, ANGELA CALMAN, health care public relations executive; Attended, U. Calif., San Diego, Harvard U. Kennedy Sch Govt. Asst. dir. editl. NBC 7/39, San Diego; mgr. media rels. MSNBC/CNBC; chief comm. officer Cleve. Clinic; pres. Calman Media; sr. v.p. nat. health media rels. Edelman Pub. Rels.; dir. healthcare media Weber Shandwick, exec. v.p. Tv news prodr.; publicist; media strategist. Office: Weber Shandwick 919 3rd Ave New York NY 10022 Office Phone: 212-445-8000.

WON-TAK, CHO, orthodontist; b. Republic of Korea, May 8, 1968; MSD in Orthodontistry, WonKwang U., 1992. Chief physician Ye Dental Clinic, 1998. Recipient Pierre Fauchard award, Am. Biog. Inst., 2010. Fellow: World Fedn. Orrhodontists; mem.: Korean Assn. Orthodontics. Office: 1291 Dunsan-dong Seogu Gounson B/D 3F Daejeon 302-830 Republic of Korea Office Fax: 82424882834. E-mail: yedentist@gmail.com.

WOO, JEONG-TAEK, endocrinologist, educator; b. Seoul, Republic of Korea, Feb. 2, 1959; s. Soon-myung Woo and Sang-kyu Lim; m. Yong-nan Keum, Oct. 24, 1987; children: Jae-yeon, Jae-sun, Young-jae. MD, Kyung Hee U., 1983, PhD, 1993. Lic. endocrinologist Korean Assn. Internal Medicine, 1994. Intern Kyung Hee U. Hosp., Seoul, Republic of Korea, 1983—84, resident, 1984—87, rsch. and clin. fellow, Dept. Endocrinology, 1991—95, asst. prof. Dept. Endocrinology, 1995—2002; physician Diabetes Ctr. Euliji Hosp., Seoul, Republic of Korea, 1990—91; rsch. assoc. Sch. Medicine Vanderbilt U., Nashville, 1998—2001; assoc. prof. Sch. Medicine Kyung Hee U., Seoul, 2002—. Contbr. articles to profl. jours. Capt. Korean Army, 1987—90. Mem.: Korea Soc. Study of Obesity (chmn. rsch. coun. 2005—), Korea Diabetes Assn. (chmn. nutritional coun. 2004—, Med. Rsch. award 1995, Med. rsch. award 2003). Conservative. Roman Catholic. Avocations: dog training, golf. Office: Dept Endo and Metab Kyung Hee U Coll Med 1 Hoekidong Dongdaemoonku Seoul 130-702 Republic of Korea Office Fax: 822-968-1848. Business E-Mail: jtwoomd@khmc.or.kr.

WOO, JONG-MIN, psychiatrist, educator; b. Seoul, Republic of Korea, Jan. 15, 1968; MD, Seoul Nat. U., PhD, 1992; MPH, Johns Hopkins Bloomberg Sch. Pub. Health, 2009. Asst. prof. Inje U., 2003—10, assoc. prof., 2010—. Dir. dept. psychiatry Inje U. Seoul Paik Hosp., 2010. Recipient Hana Med. award, Korean Neuropsychiatric Assn., Hana Pub. Co. Office: Seoul Paik Hosp Dept Psychiatry Seoul 100-032 Republic of Korea Personal E-mail: jongmin.woo@gmail.com.

WOO, KENNETH ROGER, urologist; b. LA, July 27, 1969; s. Roger and Julie Woo; m. Christine H. Sohn, May 16, 1998. BS in Molecular Biology magna cum laude, UCLA, 1992; MD with distinction, Mt. Sinai Sch. Medicine, NYC, 1996. Resident urology NYU Med. Ctr., 1996—2002. Contbr. articles to profl. jours. Grantee Yamanouchi USA Rsch., 1999. Fellow: Am. Coll. Surgeons; mem.: AMA, Endourol. Soc., Am. Assn. Clin. Urologists, Am. Urol. Assn., Golden Key, Phi Beta Kappa. Avocations: tennis, hiking. Office Phone: 410-879-4879. Personal E-mail: kennethwoo@comcast.net.

WOO, PATRICIA, pediatric rheumatologist; b. Hong Kong, Feb. 12, 1948; arrived in UK, 1961; d. Hing Tak and Chiu Wah (Lam) W. BSc, U. London, 1969, M.B.BS, 1972; PhD, U. Cambridge, UK, 1979. Tng. fellow U. Cambridge, 1976-79; registrar Northwick Park Hosp., London, 1979-81; sr. registrar Guy's Hosp., London, 1981-83; rsch. fellow Boston Children's Hosp., 1983-85; MRC cons. rheumatologist, hon. cons. physician Northwick Park and Great Ormond St. Hosps., London, 1985-94; prof. pediatric rheumatology U. Coll. London, 1994—, Royal Postgrad. Med. Sch., 1994-95; cons. physician Great Ormond St., UCLH, 1994—. House officer Charing Cross Hosp., London, 1973-74, sr. house officer Brompton Hosp., London, 1974-75, Northwick Park Hosp., 1975-76; mem. ILAR and WHO task force on paediatric rheumatology, 1993—. Editor: Oxford Textbook of Rheumatology, 1993, 98, 2004, Paediatric Rheumatology Update, 1989; assoc. editor Rheumatology, 1992—2004; contbr. articles to profl. jours. Named Commander of the British Empire, Queen Elizabeth, 2005. Fellow Royal Coll. Physicians UK, Royal Coll. Pediat. and Child Health, Acad. Med. Scis.; mem. Assn. Physicians UK (coun. mem.), Brit. Paediatric Rheumatology Group (convenor 1993-96), European Pediat. Rheumatology Soc. (pres. 1999-2005). Achievements include research on acute phase gene regulation by cytokines, cytokine network genetic predisposition paediatric rheumatology and clinical research in juvenile arthritis. Office: University Coll London Medical School Rayne Building 5 University St London WCIE 6JF England Business E-Mail: patricia.woo@ucl.ac.uk.

WOO, SEUNG KYOON, medical educator; b. Seoul, Republic of Korea, Aug. 28, 1965; PhD, Seoul Nat. U., 1996. Asst. prof., neurosurgery U. Md., 2006—. Office: 685 W Baltimore St Baltimore MD 21201 Business E-Mail: skwoo@smail.umaryland.edu.

WOO, SUNG-SICK, geneticist; b. Seoul, Republic of Korea, Dec. 22, 1963; BS, Seoul Nat. U., 1986, MS, 1988; PhD, Tex. A&M U., 1996. Postdoc. rschr. U. Calif., Davis, 1996—98; rsch. asst. prof., DNA sequencing ctr. group leader Clemson U. Genomics Inst., 1998—99; asst. prof. Konkuk U., 1999—2000; chief sci. officer Unigen, Inc., 2000—08; chief agrl. officer ECONET Holdings, 2008—. Expert dir. Korean Soc. Health Promotion and Disease Prevention, 2009—; mem. com. Certification Com. OK-EFAPA Program, Control Union Certification Korea, 2009; mem. bd. dirs. Aloecorp China, 2009; mem. commn. Spl. Commn. Agr., Fisheries and Rural Policies, Republic of Korea, 2009; expert advisor in bio-resources and bio-engineering Korea Inst. Planning & Evaluation Tech. Food, Agr., Forestry & Fisheries, 2007—08. Recipient Top Fifty Rsch. Achievement award, Ministry Edn., Sci. and Tech. and Korea Sci. and Engring. Found., 2006. Mem.: AAAS, Korean Soc. Health Promotion & Disease Prevention, Korean Soc. Breeding Sci., Korean Soc. Food Sci. and Tech., Gamma Sigma Delta, Phi Kappa Phi. Avocations: sailing, golf. Home: Sangji Ritzville 3-501 843-15 Bangbae4-dong Seocho-gu Seoul 137-836 Republic of Korea Home Fax: 82-2-467-9988. Personal E-mail: sswoo@unigen.net.

WOO, Y. JOSEPH, thoracic surgeon, educator; MD, U. Pa. Diplomate Am. Bd. Surgery, 2000, Am. Bd. Thoracic Surgery-cardiothoracic surgery, 2002. Intern Hosp. Univ. Pa., resident, fellow; asst. prof. surgery; dir. minimally invasive and robotic cardiac surgery program Pa. Hosp., dir. cardiac transplantation and mech. circulatory support program. Named one of Top Doctors, Phila. Mag., 2009—, America's Top Doctors, 2010. Mem.: Am. Heart Assn. Office: Pennsylvania Hospital Garfield Duncan Bldg Ste 305 700 Spruce St Philadelphia PA 19106 Office Phone: 800-789-7366. E-mail: wooy@uphs.upenn.edu.

WOOD, DOUGLAS LYNN, medical educator; b. Columbia, Mo., June 24, 1951; s. Cecil Vernon and Wilda Fay (Palmer) W.; m. Julia Ann Sandbothe, May 28, 1977; children: Ethan, Amanda, Paul, Benjamin, Ivan. BA cum laude with distinction in Biology, Carleton Coll., 1973; MD magna cum laude, U. Mo., 1977. Diplomate Am. Bd. Internal Medicine, Am. Bd. Cardiovasc. Diseases. Asst. prof. medicine Mayo Grad. Sch. Medicine, Rochester, Minn., 1983—91, assoc. prof. medicine, 1991—2003, vice chmn. dept. medicine, 1993—2007, prof. medicine, 2003—. Cons. cardiovasc. diseases Mayo Clinic, Rochester, 1983-2008, vice-chair dept. medicine, 1993—2009, chair divsn. health care policy and rsch., 2007—; pres., CEO, chmn. bd. dirs. Immanuel-St. Joseph's Mayo Health Sys., Mankato, Minn.; chair Sec.'s Adv. Com. on Regulatory Reform, Dept. HHS, 2001-02, mem. practicing physicians adv. com., 2000-04. Contbr. articles to profl. jours. Mem. coun. on performance measurement Joint Commn. on Accreditation of Healthcare Orgns., Oakbrook Terrace, Ill., 1995-2007; mem. CPT editl. panel AMA, Chgo., 1994-97; chair fin. coun. St. Pius X Ch., Rochester, 1993-97; mem. Minn. Citizens Forum on Health Care Costs, 2003-04; mem. Gov.'s Quality Control Coun., 2006—; trustee Minn. Med. Assn., 2008-. Recipient Disting. Svc. award, Minn. Med. Assn., Merit award, U. Mo. Sch. Medicine. Fellow ACP, Am. Coll. Cardiology (Disting. Svc. award); mem. Am. Coll. Physician Execs., Alpha Omega Alpha, Sigma Xi. Office: Mayo Clinic 200 1st St SW Rochester MN 55905-0002 Home Phone: 507-285-1624; Office Phone: 507-284-1446, 504-284-2511. Business E-Mail: wood.douglas@mayo.edu.

WOOD, FRANCES DIANE, medical secretary, artist; b. Caddo, Okla., Mar. 7, 1950; d. Clovis Lynn and Hilda Dee (Guthrie) Wood; m. Samuel Dante Wolfe, Aug. 20, 1990 (div. Mar. 1992). BA, Southea. Okla. State U., 1972; postgrad., Grayson County Coll., 1987, Rose State Coll., 2002, U. Ctrl. Okla., 2004. Cert. master gardener Okla., 2006. Ins. clk. Sherman Cmty. Hosp., Tex., 1973—74; med. sec. Essin Clinic, Sherman, 1980—83; med. transcriptionist Texoma Med. Ctr., Denison, Tex., 1983—88, Wilson N. Jones Meml. Hosp., Sherman, 1989—95; CEO Designs by Diane, Caddo, 1995—. Conv. del. Blue Cross-Blue Shield Tex., Dallas, 1980—83; v.p. Jett Transcription, Denison, 1988. Exhibitions include paintings in cmty. art shows, Represented in permanent collections Shamrock Bank, Caddo, Indian Terr. Mus., Caddo. Charter mem. Caddo Edn. Found., Okla., 1993-95; sponsor Save the Children, Philippines, 1995. Named Okla. Master Gardener, 2006—. Mem. ASPCA, Friends Internat. Fellowship of Christians and Jews, Physicians Com. for Responsible Medicine, Nat. Trust Hist. Preservation, Okla. Sheriffs Assn. (hon.), Arts Coun. Co-op (life), Nat. Arbor Day Found., Sierra Club, Sacred Heart Auto League, People for Ethical Treatment Animals, Urban League Greater Oklahoma City Democrat. Avocations: pet care and pet psychology, interior decorating, astronomy, holistic and naturopathic medicine, gardening.

WOOD, JACKIE DALE, physiologist, educator, researcher; b. Picher, Okla., Feb. 16, 1937; s. Aubrey T. Wood and Wilma J. (Coleman) Wood Patterson. BS, Kans. State U., 1964, MS, 1966; PhD, U. Ill., 1969. Asst. prof. physiology Williams Coll., Williamstown, Mass., 1969-71; asst. prof. U. Kans. Med. Ctr., Kansas City, 1971-74, assoc. prof., 1974-78, prof., 1978-79; prof., chmn. dept. physiology Sch. Medicine, U. Nev., Reno, 1979-85; chmn. dept. physiology coll. medicine Ohio State U., Columbus, 1985-97, prof. physiology and internal medicine, 1997—. Cons. NIH, Bethesda, Md., 1982-88. Editor: (book) Physiology of the Digestive Tract. Adv. bd. Internat. Found. Functional Gastrointestinal Disorders, Milw., 1997—2008. Recipient Rsch. Career Devel. award NIH, 1974; named Hon. Citizen City of Atzugi Japan, 1987; Alexander von Humboldt fellow, W.Ger., 1976, grantee NIH, 1971—. Fellow Am. Gastroent. Assn.; mem. AAAS, Am. Physiol. Soc. (assoc. editor 1984-96, rsch. award 1986), Soc. Neuroscience. Office: Ohio State U Dept Physiology and Cell Biology 304 Hamilton Hall 1645 Neil Ave Columbus OH 43210-1218 Home Phone: 614-457-2820. Business E-Mail: wood.13@osu.edu.

WOOD, JAMES ANDERSON, cardiac surgeon; b. Newton, Mo., Nov. 5, 1926; s. Frank and Lula Wood; m. Joann Wood, 1950; children: Diane, James, Jeff, Carol. BA, Reed Coll., 1953; MD, U. Oreg., 1957. Diplomate Am. Bd. Thoracic Surgey, Am. Bd. Surgery. Prof. cardiac surgery, 1974—94. Co-founder St. Vincent Hosp. Cardiac Surg. Program, Portland, VA Hosp. Cardiac Surg. Program, Portland; founder Bend OR Cardiac Surg. Program, Portland, Corvallis OR Cardiac Surg. Contbr. articles to profl. jours. With Marine Corps. Recipient Young Rschr. award Am. Heart Assn., Meritorious award AMA, 1965. Mem. AMA, Portland Surg. Soc., U.S. Polo Assn., Robert Wise Surg. Soc., El Dorado Polo Club, William Conklin Surg. Soc., Albert Starr Club, Am. Soc. of Thoracic Surgeons, Portland Acad. of Medicine, Dant Found., Wesley Eager Cardiac Surg. Found. (pres.), Pan Pacific Assn., Pacific Coast Surg., North Pacific Surg., Internat. Cardiovascular. Home: PO Box 5 North Plains OR 97133-0005

WOOD, JOHN, physician; b. Dec. 8, 1977; MD, Temple U. Sch. Medicine, 2004. Assoc. dir. family & cmty. medicine Lancaster Gen. Health, 2007—. Mem.: AAFP. Office: 555 N Duke St Lancaster PA 17604 Business E-Mail: jcwood@lghealth.org.

WOOD, JOHN ALVIN, allergist, immunologist, educator; MD, U. Okla., 1968. Diplomate Am. Bd. Internal Medicine, 1972, Am. Bd. Internal Medicine-pulmonary disease, 1978, Am. Bd. Allergy and Immunology, 1979. Resident internal medicine Univ. Hosp., 1969—70, Barnes Hosp.-Wash. Univ. Sch. Med., 1970—71; fellow pulmonary disease Wash. Univ. Sch. Med., 1975—77, fellow allergy and immunology, 1976—77; asst. prof. medicine Wash. Univ.; hosp. affiliations includes St. Luke's Hosp. Office: Saint Luke's Hospital 232 S Woods Mill Rd Chesterfield MO 63017-3417 Office Phone: 314-434-1500.

WOOD, JOHN M., gastroenterologist; MD, U. Hosp. Cleve. Diplomate Am. Bd. Internal Medicine, Am. Bd. Internal Medicine-gastroenterology. Intern Cleve. Met. Gen. Hosp.; resident Metrohealth Med. Ctr., Cleve.; fellow Cleve. Clinic Hosp. Found.; hosp. affiliation Univ. Pitts. Med. Ctr. St. Margaret; pvt. practice Kelly and Wood Ltd. Office: Kelly & Wood Limited Burrel Medical Center 1600 Wildlife Lodge Rd Ste 300 Lower Burrell PA 15068 Office Phone: 142-784-1110.

WOOD, JOSEPH GEORGE, neuroscientist, educator; b. Victoria, Tex., Dec. 8, 1928; s. Harold Robert and Frances Josephine (Marcak) W.; m. Jane L. Andrews; 1 dau., Marian. BS, U. Houston, 1954, MS, 1958; PhD, U. Tex., Galveston, 1962. Teaching asst. biology, U. Houston, 1956-58; instr. anatomy U. Tex. Dental Br., Houston, 1961, Yale U., 1962-63; asst. prof. U. Ark. Med. Sch., Little Rock, 1963-66; assoc. prof. U. Tex., San Antonio, 1966-70, asst. dean acad. devel., 1967-69, prof. and chmn. dept. neurobiology and anatomy Houston, 1970—84, prof. neurobiology and anatomy, 1984—88; prof., chmn. dept. anat. sci. U. Okla. Coll. Medicine, 1988-93; dir. Okla. Ctr. Neurosci., 1990-95. Guest prof. dept. pathobiology, cell biology and neuroanatomy U. Minn., 1993—96; sr. lectr. molecular and cell biology U. Tex., Dallas, 1997—2007, asst. dean pre-health professions, 1998—2002, assoc. dean pre-health edn., 2002—07, clin. prof. human devel., 2002—07; vis. prof. Philips U., Marburg, Germany, 1984. Served with AUS, 1954-56. Recipient Basic Sci. Tchg. award U.

Ark. Med. Ctr., 1963, U. Tex. Houston, 1972, 75, 86, Disting. Alumnus award U. Tex. Med. Br., 1976 Mem.: Tex. Assn. Advisors for the Health Professions (chair), Tex. Soc. Electron Microscopy (pres. 1970—71, exec. coun. 1971—79), Assn. Anatomy Chmn., Histochem. Soc., Assn. Am. Med. Colls., Soc. Neurosci. (exec. com. Houston chpt. 1971—77, pres. 1973—77, rsch. award 1962), Am. Assn. Anatomists (exec. com. 1974—78), Cajal Club, Alpha Omega Alpha, Sigma Xi, Golden Key, Phi Kappa Phi.

WOOD, MALISSA J., cardiologist, educator; b. Maryville, Mo., Apr. 9, 1963; d. Robert and Malissa (James) Wood; m. David F. Lawlor, June 18, 1997; children: Seamus, Caitlin. MD, U. Mo. Sch. Med., Kansas City, 1987. Diplomate Am. Bd. Internal Medicine, cert. in Cardiovascular Disease. Intern, resident internal medicine Beth Israel Hosp., Boston, 1987-90, chief resident internal medicine, 1990-91, cardiovasc. fellow, 1991-94; fellow interventional medicine U. Tex. Health Scis. Ctr., San Antonio, 1994-95; pvt. practice South Tex. Cardiovasc. Consultants, San Antonio, 1995; now clin. cardiologist, staff physician Cardiac Ultrasound Lab. Mass. Gen. Hosp., Boston. Asst. prof. medicine Harvard Med. Sch., Boston; co-dir. women's health prog. Mass. Gen. Hosp. Heart Ctr. Contbr. articles to profl. jours., chapters to books; spkr. in field. Recipient Vice Chancellors award, U. Mo., 1987. Fellow: Am. Coll. Cariology; mem.: Am. Soc. Echocardiography (bd. dirs. 2006—), Am. Heart Assn. (chair Women in Heart Disease prog. 1997—98), Back Bay Echo Soc. Boston (pres.). Achievements include research in using echocardiography to better understand cardiac adaptations to changing loading conditions, particularly the cardiac response to conditions such as pregnancy, strenuous exercise and exposure to altitude. Avocations: running, bicycling, swimming, kayaking, piano. Office: Mass Gen Hosp Dept Cardiac Ultrasound 55 Fruit St YAW 5 Boston MA 02114 Office Phone: 617-724-1986.

WOOD, MAURICE, medical educator; b. Pelton, Eng., June 28, 1922; came to U.S., 1971; s. Joseph and Eugenie (Lumley) W.; m. Erica Joan Noble, May 1, 1948; children: Roger Lumley, Ashley Michael, Frances Jane. MB BS, U. Durham, Eng., 1945. Diplomate Am. Bd. Family Practice. Sr. ptnr. med. practice South Shields County, Durham, 1950-71; gen. practice teaching group U. Newcastle, Newcastle-on-Tyne, Eng., 1969-71; gen. clin. asst. dept. psychology-medicine South Shields Gen. Hosp., 1966-71; assoc. prof., dir. rsch. in family practice Med. Coll. Va.-Va. Commonwealth U., Richmond, 1971-73, prof., dir. rsch. in family practice, 1973-87, prof. emeritus, 1987—. Cons. advisor WHO, Geneva, 1979-90, chmn. working party to develop a classification for primary care, 1979-90; founding mem. exec. dir. N.Am. Primary Care Rsch. Group, Richmond, 1972-92, past pres., pres. emeritus, 1993—; chmn. com. on cmty. oriented primary care Insts. of Medicine, 1982-84. Assoc. editor Jour. Family Practice, 1970-83. Recipient award for meritorious svc. Va. Acad. Family Physicians, 1976; Maurice Wood award for career achievement in primary care rsch. founded in his honor, 1995. Fellow Royal Coll. Gen. Practitioners, Am. Acad. Family Physicians, World Orgn. Famaly Drs. (WONCA); mem. Inst. Medicine-Nat. Acad. Sci., Soc. Tchrs. Family Medicine (Curtis Hames Career Research award 1984), Ambulatory Sentinel Practice Network, Internat. Primary Care Network (treas., bd. dirs.), N.Am. Primary Care Rsch. Group (treas., bd. dirs., exec. dir., 1982-92), Rotary. Episcopalian. Personal E-mail: wood150w@verizon.net.

WOOD, NANCY ELIZABETH, psychologist, educator; d. Donald Sterret and Orne Louise (Erwin) W. BS, Ohio U., 1943, MA, 1947; PhD, Northwestern U., 1952. Prof. Case We. Res. U., Cleve., 1952—60; specialist, expert HEW, Washington, 1960—62; chief rschr. USPHS, Washington, 1962—64; prof. U. So. Calif., LA, 1965—. Learning disabilities cons., 1960-70; assoc. dir. Cleve. Hearing and Speech Ctr., 1952-60; dir. licensing program Brit. Nat. Trust, London. Author: Language Disorders, 1964, Language Development, 1970, Verbal Learning, 1975 (monograph) Auditory Disorders, 1978, Levity, 1980, Stoneskipping, 1989, Bird Cage, 1994, Out of Control, 1999. Pres. faculty senate U. So. Calif., 1987—88. Recipient Outstanding Faculty award, Trojan Fourth Estate, 1982, Pres.' Svc. award, U. So. Calif., 1992. Fellow APA (cert.), AAAS, Am. Speech and Hearing Assn. (legis. coun. 1965-68); mem. Internat. Assn. Scientists. Republican. Methodist. Office: U So Calif University Park Los Angeles CA 90089-0001 Personal E-mail: woodn@roadrunner.com.

WOOD, ROBERT A., pediatrician, allergist, educator; b. Clifton Springs, NY, Jan. 17, 1956; s. I. Robert and Carol Ann W.; m. Renee M. Wood, May 29, 1982. BA with honors, SUNY, Buffalo, 1978; MD, U. Rochester, 1982. Diplomate Am. Bd. Pediatrics, Am. Bd. Allergy and Immunology. Intern pediat. Johns Hopkins Children's Ctr., Balt., 1982—83, resident allergy and immunology, 1983—85, fellowship, 1986—88; assoc. prof. to prof. pediatrics Johns Hopkins U. Sch. Medicine, Balt., 1988—, dir. Pediat. Allergy Clinics and Pediat. Allergy Consultation Svc., dir. Divsn. Pediatric Allergy and Immunology, 2005—. Dep. editor Pediatric Asthma and Allergy and Immunology, assoc. editor Annals of Allergy and Asthma, editor Pediatric Allergy; contbr. articles to med. jours.; author: Food Allergies for Dummies, 2007. Fellow: Am. Coll. Allergy and Immunology, Am. Acad. Allergy and Immunology, Am. Acad. Pediat. Office: Johns Hopkins Hosp CMSC 1102 600 N Wolfe St Baltimore MD 21287 Office Phone: 410-955-5883. Office Fax: 410-955-0229. E-mail: rwood@jhmi.edu.

WOOD, SHELTON EUGENE, JR., education educator, minister, consultant; b. Douglas, Ga., May 20, 1943; s. Shelton and Mae Lillie (Pheil) Wood; m. Louise Wood, Aug. 25, 1961; children: Shelton John, Deirdre Louise. AA, St. John's U., 1958; BA, U. Nebr., 1959; MEd, Coll. William and Mary, Williamsburg, Va., 1971; PhD, Sussex U., 1973; EdD, Southeastern U., Washington, DC, 1975; MBA, Ctrl. Mich. U., Mount Pleasant, 1977; MA, U. Okla., Norman, 1980; D in Ministry, Wesleyan Bible Coll., 1999; Cert. in Internt. Rels., Fgn. Svc. Inst., 1971; Cert. in Mgmt., Indsl. Coll. Armed Forces, 1970. Area mgr. Marshall Fields Corp., Fla., 1957-58; transp. supr. Greyhound Corp., Jacksonville, Fla., 1959-62; officer US Army, 1963, advanced through grades to inf. col., 1996; with Redstone Readiness Group, 1977-80; chief studies and analysis divsn. Korean Inst. for Def. Analysis, 1981-83; faculty St. John River C.C., 1984-90; nat. and internat. bus. and mgmt. cons., 1995—; sr. pastor Fellowship Wesleyan Ch., Spring Hill, Fla., 1998—2005, asst. dist. supt. Fla., 2005—. Faculty Wesleyan Bible U., 1997—; pres. Georgetown Wesleyan U. of the Americas, 2005-. Author: Strategic for Implementing A Family Life Ministry Ctr., 1997; contbr. articles to profl. jours. Active Boy Scouts Am., 1977—90; lay leader United Meth. Ch., Falls Ch., Va., 1977—79, St. James United Meth. Ch., 1986—90; mem. dist. bd. ministerial develop. Fla. Dist. of Wesleyan Ch., 1999, chair evangelism and ch. growth com., 1999—; bd. dirs. Baby Love. Decorated Bronze Star with 2 oak leaf clusters, Air medal with 3 oak leaf clusters, Purple Heart with 2 oak leaf clusters; Sussex Coll. fellow, 1969-70. Mem. NEA, Am. Soc. Trainers and Developers (pres. S.E. chpt. 1974-75), Am. Def. Preparedness Assn., Putnam County C. of C. (pres. 1990-91), Toastmasters Internat. (Disting. Toastmaster 1989), Kiwanis (pres. 1989-90), Rotary (pres. 2009-), Phi Kappa Delta, Phi Delta Kappa. Address: 8485 Chatsworth St Spring Hill FL 34608 Personal E-mail: ewood11@tampabay.rr.com.

WOOD, THOMAS WILLARD, retired health industry executive, retired military officer; b. Logan, Utah, Jan. 21, 1939; s. Elmer Raymond and Leola (Pitkin) W.; m. Blanche Loila Dowdle, Sept. 11, 1959 (div.); children: Dianna Wood Perry, Jeffery Thomas (dec.); m. Charlene Taulbee, Oct. 5, 1974; children: Douglas Winston Remington, Angela Christine Wood, Thomas Willard II, Michael Joseph, Matthew David. BA, Utah State U., 1962; MS, Cen. Mich. U., 1975; postgrad., Indsl. Coll. Armed Forces, 1975, Armed Forces Staff Coll., 1976. Commd. 2d lt. USAF, 1962, advanced through grades to col., 1983; chief protocol Hdqrs. Air Force Logistics Command, Wright-Patterson AFB, Ohio, 1972-75; chief spl. project div. Hdqrs. 21st Air Force, McGuire AFB, N.J., 1977-78; chief inquiries br. Legis. Liaison, Office of Sec. Air Force, The Pentagon, Washington, 1978-82; dep. dir. Directorate Competition Advocacy Ogden Air Logistics Ctr., Hill AFB, Utah, 1982-85; air attache U.S. Def. Attache Office, Am. Embassy, Wellington, New Zealand, 1985-88; dean New Zealand Mil. Attache Corps, 1986—88; chief protocol, dep. dir. pub. and govtl. affairs Hdqrs. U.S. Comdr.-in-Chief Pacific, Camp Smith, Hawaii, 1988-89; ret., 1989; adminstrv. asst. to v.p. mktg. Hawaii Med. Svc. Assn., Honolulu, 1989-91; sr. account exec. client rels. Baxter Internat. Inc., San Antonio, 1991-92; sr. account exec. prescription svc. divsn. Caremark Inc., San Antonio, 1992-95; with corp. accts. prescription svc. divsn. Caremark Inc., San Antonio, 1996-97; sr. account exec. field ops. Caremark Pharm. Svcs., Medpartners Inc., San Antonio, 1997-99; sr. acct. mgr. field ops. CaremarkRx Inc., San Antonio, 1999-2000. Sr. nat. acct. mgr. Caremark Inc., San Antonio, 2000-02, assoc. nat. acct. exec., 2003-04, strategic acct. exec., 2007-09, ret. High priest LDS Ch., also ch. organist, pianist, tchr.; music chmn., high coun. San Antonio North Stake, 2006-11; mem. groundbreaking and dedication com. San Antonio Tex. Temple, 2002-05. Decorated DFC, Air medal with nine oak leaf clusters; Gallantry Cross with palm (Vietnam); named hon. Royal New Zealand Air Force Navigator, 1988. Mem. Disting. Flying Cross Soc. (pres. Alamo chpt. 2003-08). Avocations: walking, piano, reading. Home: 1351 Grey Oak Dr San Antonio TX 78213-1602

WOOD, WILLIAM CHADWICK, cardiologist; b. Memphis, 1946; BA, U. Miss., 1966; MD, U. Tenn., Sch. Medicine, 1969. Cardiologist, clin. assoc. prof. East Carolina Heart Inst. Fellow: ACP, ACC. Office: East Carolina Heart Inst 115 Heart Dr Greenville NC 27834-4354 Business E-Mail: woodw@ecu.edu.

WOODCOCK, JANET, federal agency administrator; b. Washington, Pa., Aug. 29, 1948; d. John and Frances (Crocker) W.; m. Roger Henry Miller, Nov. 16, 1981; children: Kathleen Miller, Susanne Miller. BS cum laude, Bucknell U., 1970; MD, Northwestern U., Chgo., 1977. Diplomate Am. Bd. Internal Medicine. Intern Hershey Med. Ctr./Pa. State U., 1977-78, resident in internal medicine, 1978-80, chief resident in medicine, 1980-81; fellow in rheumatology U. Calif./VA Med. Ctr., San Francisco, 1982-84; instr. medicine divsn. rheumatology and immunology VA Med. Ctr., San Francisco, 1984-85; med. officer divsn. biol. investigational new drugs Ctr. for Biologics Evaluation and Rsch./FDA, Rockville, Md., 1986-87, group leader divsn. biol. investigational new drugs, 1987-88, dep. dir. divsn. biol. investigational new drugs, 1988, dir. divsn. biol. investigational new drugs, 1988-90; dir. office of therapeutics rsch. and rev. Ctr. for Biologics Evaluation and Rsch., FDA, Rockville, Md., 1992-94, acting dep. dir., 1990-92; dir. Ctr. for Drug Evaluation and Rsch., FDA, Rockville, Md., 1994—2005, 2008—, acting dir., 2007—08; dep. commr. ops., chief med. officer FDA, Rockville, Md., 2005—08. Instr. medicine, asst. prof. divsn. gen. internal medicine Hershey Med. Ctr./Pa. State U., 1981; analytical chemist rsch. divsn. A.B. Dick Co., Niles, Ill., 1971-73. Nat. Merit scholar Bucknell U., 1966, Pa. State scholar, 1966; Rsch. fellow Am. Rheumatism Assn.; VA Investigator grantee, 1985; recipient Presdl. Rank Meritorious Exac. award, Nathan Davis award, AMA, Pub. Svc. award, Am. Assn. Cancer Rsch., Pub. Health Leadership award, Nat. Org. Rare Disorders, VIDA award, Nat. Alliance Hispanic Health, Award for Leadership in Personalized Medicine, Personalized Medicine Coalition, 2005 Mem. Alpha Omega Alpha, Alpha Lambda Delta. Office: Ctr Drug Evaluation & Rsch US Food & Drug Admin 5600 Fishers Lane Rockville MD 20857

WOODHOUSE, CHRISTOPHER RICHARD JAMES, urologist, educator; b. Knebworth, Eng., Sept. 20, 1946; s. Christopher M. and Davina (Lytton) W.; m. Anna M. Philipps, Feb. 27, 1975; children: Jack, Constance. MBBS, Guy's Hosp. Med. Sch., 1970. Sr. registrar St. Peter's Hosp., London, 1978-81, Inst. of Urology, London, 1981—; cons. Royal Marsden Hosp., London, 1981—; prof. adolescent urology Univ. Coll., London, 2005—11, prof. emeritus, 2011—. Hon. cons. urologist Hosp. Children, Great Ormond St., London, 1981—. Author: Long Term Paediactric Urology, 1991, Physiological Basis of Medicine-Disorders of the Kidney and Urinary Tract, 1987, (with others) Management of Urological Emergencies, 2006; chmn. BJU Internat., 2000—10. Fellow Royal Coll. Surgeons; mem. Brit. Assn. Urol. Surgeons (coun. 1991-94), Genito-Uninary Reconstructive Surg. Soc. (coun. 1996—2000), Am. Assn. Genito-Urinary Surgeons. Avocation: gardening. Office: 31 Eustace Bldg 372 Queenstown Rd SW8 4NT London England Office Phone: 44 207 498 9402. Business E-Mail: christopher@crjwoodhouse.fsnet.co.uk.

WOODLE, ERWIN STEVE, transplant surgeon; b. Texarkana, Ark., Jan. 7, 1954; three children. BS summa cum laude, Tex. A&M U., 1976; MD magna cum laude, U. Tex. Med. Br., Galveston, 1980. Diplomate Am. Bd. Surgery, ACS. Intern, gen. surgery U. Tex. Health Sci. Ctr., Houston; resident, gen. surgery U. Calif., Davis, NIH surgical rsch. fellow; fellow, renal and pancreatic transplantation U. Chgo., fellow, hepatic transplantation and hepatobiliary surgery, NIH surgical rsch. fellow; asst. prof. surgery Washington U. Sch. Medicine, St. Louis, 1990—92; asst. prof. surgery & immunology U. Chgo., 1992—98, assoc. prof. surgery & immunology, 1998—99; prof. surgery U. Cin., 1999—, chief, divsn. transplantation, 1999—. Chmn. bd. dirs. Israel Penn Internat. Transplant Tumor Registry; com. mem. Ctr. for Biol. Evaluation and Rsch FDA, Washington, 1994—97; bd. dirs. Ohio State Consortium on Solid Organ Transplantation, 2001—, mem. liver transplantation com., 2001—, mem. pancreas/islet transplantation com., 2001—, mem. kidney transplantation com., 2001—, chmn., program review com., 2002—, vice-chmn., exec. com., 2003, chmn., exec. com., 04; pancreas/islet patient selection subcommittee Ohio Solid Organ Transplantation Consortium, 2000, mem. patient selection com., 2000—, mem. cushion fund com., 2003—; mem. scientific adv. bd. SangStat Med. Corp., Wyeth/Ayerst, Fujisawa, Medimmune, Biogen, Roche, Fujisawa Can., Immu Med, Genzyme, Novartis; several visiting professorship. Contbr. several articles to med. and sci. jours., chapters to books; abstract reviewer World Transplant Congress, 2006, Am. Transplant Congress Scientific Session, 2007, mem. editl. review bds. Clinical Nephrology, Graft, Investigative Drugs, Transplantation and Lancet Oncology, ad hoc, editl. reviewer Am. Jour. Kidney Diseases, Am. Jour. Transplantation, Hepatology, Human Immunology, Internat. Immunology, Jour. Clin. Investigation, Jour. Immunology, Jour. Surgical Rsch., Jour. Vascular and Interventional Radiology, Jour. Vascular Surgery, Lancet, Liver Transplantation, Nature Biotechnology, New England Jour. Medicine, Surgery, Transplantation, Transplant Proceedings and World Jour. Surgery. Mem. med. adv. bd. Kidney Found. (Cin. Chpt.), 2001—02. Recipient Am. Heart Assn. Clinician Scientist award, 1992—96; named one of America's Top Surgeons, 2004, 2006, America's Best Doctors, 2004, Health Care Heroes award, 2006; named to Paul Peters Lectureship, Tex. Transplant Soc., 2003. Mem. AAAS, Am. Assn. for the Study of Liver Diseases, Am. Assn. Immunologists, Acad. Medicine Cin., Am. Soc. Transplant Physicians (mem. scientific studies com., 1995, chairperson, 1996-99, Kidney Pancrease Transplantation com., 1995, co-chairperson, 1996-97, program and publications com., 1996-98, 1997-2000, co-chairperson-liver/intraabdominal sect., 1996-97, chairperson 1997-99, continuing med. edn. com., 1997-2000, chairperson liver/intraabdominal subcommittee, program com., 1997-98, coun. bd. dirs., 1998, pub. policy com. 1999-2003, membership com. 2002-04), Am. Surgical Assn., Assn. for Academic Surgery, Cell Transplant Soc., Ctrl. Surgical Assn. Chgo. Assn. Immunologists, Chgo. Surgical Soc., Cin. Surgical Soc., Clin. Immunology Soc., Erlanger Soc., Ill. Surgical Soc., Internat. Coll. Surgeons, Am. Soc. Transplant Surgeons (bd. dirs., co-chmn. membership com., 2004-05), Am. Soc. Transplantation (mem. kidney pancreas com., 2006-), Internat. Liver, Transplantation Soc., Internat Xenotransplantation Assn. Transplantation Soc., Internal Soc. for Organ Donation and Procurement, Nat. Kidney Found. (mem. med. adv. bd.), Soc. Nuclear Medicine, Soc. for Organ Sharing, St. Louis Surgical Soc., Stanley J. Dudrick Surgical Soc., Transplantation Soc., Earl. F. Wolfman Surgical Soc., Xenotransplantation Soc., Soc. Univ. Surgeons, Western Surg. Assn., Am. Diabetes Assn. (bd. pres., Cin. Cpt., 2001-2002), Mensa, Alpha Omega Alpha. Office: U Cin Dept Surgery 231 Albert Sabin Way PO Box 670558 Cincinnati OH 45267-0559 Office Phone: 513-558-6001. Business E-Mail: WOODLEES@UCMAIL.UC.EDU.

WOODLEY, DAVID TIMOTHY, dermatology educator; b. Aug. 11, 1948; s. Raoul Ramos-Mimoso and Marian (Schlueter) W.; m. Christina Paschall Prentice, May 4, 1974; children; David Thatcher, Thomas Colgate, Peter Paschall. AB, Washington U., St. Louis, 1968; MD, U. Mo., 1973. Diplomate Am. Bd. Internal Medicine, Am. Bd. Dermatology, Nat. Bd. Internal Medicine. Intern Beth Israel Med. Ctr., Mt. Sinai Sch. Medicine, N.Y. Hosp., Cornell U. Sch. Medicine, NYC, 1973-74; resident in internal medicine U. Nebr., Omaha, 1974-76; resident in dermatology U. N.C., Chapel Hill, 1976-78, asst. prof. dermatology, 1983-85, assoc. prof. dermatology, 1985-88; prof. medicine, co-chief divsn. dermatology Cornell U. Med. Ctr., NYC, 1988-89; prof., vice chair dept. dermatology Stanford (Calif.) U., 1989-93; prof., chair dept. dermatology Northwestern U., Chgo., 1993-99. Research fellow U. Paris, 1978-80; expert NIH, Bethesda, Md., 1983-89; prof., assoc. chmn. dermatology Stanford U Sch. Medicine, 1989-93; chmn. dermatology Sch. Medicine Northwestern U., 1993-99; prof., chmn. dermatology U. So. Calif., 1999—; mem. study sect. NIH. Contbr. chpts. to books and articles in field to profl. jours. Mem. Potomac Albicore Fleet, Washington, 1982-83, Chapel Hill, 1983—, Jungian Soc. Triangle Area, Chapel Hill, 1983—. Fellow Am. Acad. Dermatology; mem. ACS (assoc.), Dermatology Found., Am. Soc. for Clin. Rsch., Soc. Investigative Dermatology, Assn. Physician Poets, Am. Soc. for Clin. Investigation., Assn. Am. Physician Office: U So Calif Keck Sch Medicine Dept Dermatology UC Norris Cancer Ctr Topping Tower 3905 1441 Eastlake Ave Los Angeles CA 90033 Office Phone: 323-865-0983.

WOODRING, JOHN HOWELL, radiologist; b. Louisville, Sept. 10, 1951; s. Franklyn Howell and Dorothy Moore Woodring; m. Catherine Anne Martin, Aug. 27, 1977; children: Paul Martin, Mark Reynolds. BS, U. of Louisville, 1972; MD, U. of Ky., 1976. Lic. diagnostic radiology Am. Bd. of Radiology. Intern Louisville Gen. Hosp., 1976—77; resident physician U. of Ky. Med. Ctr., Lexington, 1977—80; asst. prof. of diagnostic radiology U. of Ky., Lexington, 1980—84, assoc. prof. of diagnostic radiology, 1984—92, prof. of diagnostic radiology, 1992—98; staff radiologist Lexington VA Med. Ctr., Lexington, 1999—. Chief of radiology svc. Lexington VA Med. Ctr., 2000—02. Contbr. articles to sci. jours. (Cert. of Merit Am. Roentgen Ray Soc., 1994). Asst. scoutmaster Boy Scouts of Am., Louisville, 1968—77; senior-high counselor 1st United Meth. Ch., Lexington, 1984—87, Sunday sch. tchr., 1992—2000. Fellow: Am. Coll. of Chest Physicians (hon.), Am. Coll. of Radiology (hon.); mem.: Soc. of Thoracic Radiology, Radiol. Soc. of N.Am. (life), So. Med. Assn. Liberal. Presbyterian. Achievements include first to demonstrate role of computed tomography in evaluation of coronary artery disease, and evaluation of cervical spine fractures; propose the use of endobronchial stents in the treatment of right pneumonectomy syndrome; role of computed tomography in the evaluation of congenital lobar emphysema; identify risk factors for the development of salicylate-induced pulmonary edema; demonstrate that there is no statistically significant difference in the distribution of pleural effusion between the right and left hemithorax in congestive heart failure; development of pulmonary artery-bronchus ratio as a means of diagnosing congestive heart failure. Avocations: model trains, antique cars, music, literature. Home: 336 Arcadia Park Lexington KY 40503 Office: Radiology Svc Lexington VA Med Ctr CDD-114 1101 Veterans Dr Lexington KY 40502

WOODRUFF, PETER WALLER ROLPH, academic clinical psychiatry professor; s. Alan Waller Woodruff and Mercia Helen Arnold; m. Catriona Hall; children: Flora, Amelia. MBBS., Med. Sch., Newcastle Upon Tyne, 1981; PhD, U. London, 1997. Vis. lectr. medicine Khartoum Med. Sch., Sudan, 1989, vis. lectr. psychiatry, 1991—92; vis. lectr. medicine Juba Med. Sch., Equatoria, Sudan, 1986, vis. lectr. psychiatry, 1991—92; house surgeon Bishop Auckland Gen. Hosp., County Durham, England, 1981—82; house physician Newcastle Gen. Tchg. Hosp., Tyne and Wear, England, 1982; sr. house physician Sunderland Health Authority, Wearside, England, 1982—84; clin. lectr. medicine King's Coll. Hosp. Med. Sch., London, 1985—86; asst. prof. medicine Internat. Health Program, U. Md., Balt., 1987—88; psychiat. registrar Bethlem, Maudsley Hospitals, London, 1988—91; exch. clin. rsch. psychiatrist Johns Hopkins Med. sch., Balt., 1990—91; clin. lectr. Royal Bethlem Maudsley Hosp., London, 1991—95; hon. sr. registrar Royal Bethlem Maudsley Hosp, 1991—95; fulbright fellow Harvard Med. Sch., Mass. Gen. Hosp., Boston, 1994—95; rsch. fellow Inst. Psychiatry, London, 1995—97; sr. lectr. Inst. Psychiatry Maudsley Hosp., London, 1995—97, cons., 1995—97; sr. lectr. U. Manchester, Salford Mental Health Svc., England, 1997—99, hon. cons. psychiatrist, 1997—99; prof. & head academic clin. psychiatry U. Sheffield, Sheffield Care Trust, 1999—, dir. scanlab., 1999—, hon. cons. psychiatrist, 1999—. Vis. prof. Nanjing Brain Hosp., China, Royal Jordanian Psychiatry Svc., Amman, Jordan, U. Khartoum; mem. Wellcome Trust Clin. Interview Com., London, 2005—09, Acad. Scis., Finland, 2009—. Editor: (book) Empathy in Mental Illness; contbr. articles to numerous sci. papers. Vice-chair Acad. Faculty, Royal Coll. Psychiat., 2009—11, chair, 2011—. Recipient Silver medal, Amateur Rowing Assn., 1974, Home Internat. Regatta rep. Eng., 1974; fellow Fellowship, Fulbright Commn., 1994—95. Fellow: Royal Coll. Psych., Worshipful Soc. Royal Coll. Apothecaries (liveryman), Med. Soc. London (fellow); mem.: RCP (life), Royal Coll. Psych., Athenaeum. Avocations: gardening, history, travel. Office: Univ Sheffield Longley Ctr Norwood Grange Dr Sheffield S5 7JT England Office Phone: 0114 2261501.

WOODS, JAMES ROBERT, JR., obstetrician, gynecologist; b. El Paso, Tex., Dec. 11, 1943; MD, Bowman Gray U., 1970. Cert. in ob-gyn., recert., subspecialty in maternal fetal medicine, recert. Intern Tripler Army Med. Ctr., Honolulu, 1970-71, resident in ob-gyn., 1971-74; fellow in fetal medicine UCLA Med. Ctr., 1974-76; chair, dept. ob-gyn. U. Rochester Med. Ctr. Mem. Soc. for Gynecologic Investigation, Am. Gynecol. and Obstet. Soc., Perinatal Rsch. Soc., Soc. Maternal-Fetal Medicine. Office: Univ Rochester Med Ctr Dept Ob-Gyn 601 Elmwood Ave Rochester NY 14642-0001 Office Phone: 585-275-5201.

WOODS, JAMES STERRETT, retired toxicologist; b. Lewistown, Pa., Feb. 26, 1940; s. James Sterrett and Jane Smith (Parker) W.; m. Nancy Fugate, Dec. 20, 1969; 1 dau., Erin Elizabeth. AB, Princeton U., 1962; MS, U. Wash., 1968, PhD, 1970; MPH, U. N.C., 1978. Diplomate Am. Bd. Toxicology. Rsch. assoc. dept. pharmacology Yale U. Sch. Medicine, New Haven, 1970-72; staff fellow environ. toxicology. Nat. Inst. Environ. Health Scis. br. NIH, Research Triangle Park, NC, 1972-75, head biochem. toxicology sect., 1975-77; sr. rsch. leader environ. occupl. health risk evaluation Battelle Ctrs. for Pub. Health Rsch. and Evaluation, Seattle, 1978—2006; prof. U. Wash., Seattle, 1979—. Pres. Am. Bd. Toxicology, 1997-98. Contbr. articles to profl. jours. With USN, 1962-66. Scholar USPHS, 1966-70; Fellow Am. Cancer Soc., 1970-72. Mem. AAAS, Am. Assn. Cancer Rsch., Am. Soc. Pharmacology and Exptl. Therapeutics, Pacific NW Assn. Toxicologists (founding pres.), Soc. Epidemiology Rsch., Soc. Toxicology, Am. Coll. of Epidemiology, Am. Bd. Toxicology (pres. 1997-98). Home: 4525 E Laurel Dr NE Seattle WA 98105-3838 Office: Univ Wash Ste 100 4225 Roosevelt Way NE Seattle WA 98105 Office Phone: 206-685-3443. Business E-Mail: jwoods@u.washington.edu.

WOODS, JOHN ELMER, plastic surgeon; b. Battle Creek, Mich., July 5, 1929; m. Janet Ruth; children: Sheryl, Mark, Jeffrey, Jennifer, Judson. BA, Asbury Coll., 1949, DHL, 1999; MD, Western Res. U., 1955; PhD, U. Minn., 1966. Intern Gorgas Hosp., Panama Canal Zone, 1955-56, resident in gen. surgery, 1956-57, Mayo Grad. Sch., Rochester, Minn., 1960-65, resident in plastic surgery, 1966-67, Brigham Hosp., Boston, Mass., 1968; fellow, transplant cons. Harvard Med. Sch., Cambridge, Mass., 1969; cons. in gen. and plastic surgery Mayo Clinic, Rochester, 1969-93, vice chmn. Dept. Surgery; asst. prof. Mayo Med. Sch., Rochester, 1973-76, assoc. prof., 1976-80, prof. plastic surgery, 1980-93, Stuart W. Harrington prof. surgery. Vis. prof. Yale Sch. Medicine, New Haven, 1984, Harvard Sch. Medicine, Cambridge, 1984. Contbr. over 200 articles to profl. jours.; also 26 book chpts. and 1 film. Recipient Disting. Mayo Clinician award, 1991, Disting. Mayo Alumnus award, 1999. Mem. AMA (coun. on sci. affairs 1985-87), ACS (grad edn. com. 1985-87), Am. Bd. Med. Specialties, Am. Bd. Plastic Surgery (sec.-treas. 1985-88, chmn. 1988-89), Am. Soc. Plastic Surgeons Ednl. Fedn. (pres. 1984-85). Avocations: skiing, sailing, reading, the arts. Office: Mayo Clinic Plummer N-10 Rochester MN 55905-0001 Business E-Mail: woods.john@mayo.edu.

WOODS, NANCY FUGATE, nursing educator; BS, Wis. State U., 1968; MSN, U. Wash., 1969; PhD, U. NC, 1978; D (hon.), U. Pa., Phila., U. Haifa, Israel, Chiang Mai U., Thailand. Staff nurse Sacred Heart Hosp., Wis., 1968, Univ. Hosp., Wis., 1969-70, St. Francis Cabrini Hosp., 1970; nurse clinician Yale-New Haven Hosp., 1970-71; instr. nursing Duke U., Durham, N.C., 1971-72, from instr. to assoc. prof., 1972-78; assoc. prof. physiology U. Wash., Seattle, 1978-82, prof. physiology, 1982-84, chairperson, dept. parent and child nursing, 1984-90, dir., ctr. women's health rsch., 1989—, prof., dept. family and child nursing, 1990—, dean, sch. nursing, 1998—2008. Pres. scholar U. Calif., San Francisco, 1985-86. Contbr. articles to profl. jours. Named Reid Endowed Dean in Nursing, 2007. Fellow ANA, Am. Acad. Nursing, Inst. Medicare, N.A.S.; mem. AAUP, APHA, Am. Coll. Epidemiology, Soc. Menstrual Cycle Rsch. (v.p. 1981-82, pres. 1983-85), Soc. Advancement Women's Health Rsch. Office: U Wash Sch Nursing PO Box 357260 Seattle WA 98195-7260

WOODS, WALTER EARL, biomedical research and development executive; b. Phila., Sept. 26, 1944; s. Walter Earl and Janet I. (Ferguson) W.; m. Anna Maria Gianfreda, Dec. 4, 1975; children: Jeffrey, Elaine, Roberto, Carlo. BS in Biology, Delaware Valley Coll. Sci. and Agr., 1966. Pilot plant operator Shell Chem., Woodbury, N.J., 1966-67; virologist, tissue culturist 1st U.S. Med. Lab., NYC and Ft. Meade, Md., 1967-69; virologist Merck, Sharpe & Dohme, West Point, Pa., 1969-70; quality control and assurance supr. Richardson-Merrell Inc., Swiftwater, Pa., 1970-74, cons., dir. influenza vaccine mfg. Naples, Italy, 1974-75, mgr. biol. prodn. Swiftwater, 1976-78, Connaught Labs., Inc., Swiftwater, 1978-81, dir. vaccine mfg., 1982-84, dir. mfg. resource planning, class A rating, 1984-88, dir. product devel. and mgmt., 1989-91; chmn. HIB and Pertussis bus. group, 1989—93; project co-dir. SAP software installation Connaught Labs., Inc., Swiftwater, 1997-98; exec. dir. project mgmt. Aventis Pasteur, 1990—98; project leader acellular combination vaccines, 1998—2008; project leader Lic. DAPTACEL in U.S., 2002—; assoc. v.p. R & D Program & Project Leadership, 2009—; bd. mem. C-D Joint Venture @ Daichi Seiyau, Japan. Project dir. licensing Japanese Acellular Pertussis and Japanese Encephalitis Vaccines, 1992, HIB vaccine, 1993, licensed acP vaccine, Germany, 1994, Proj Lead, Dapatacel Lacel Pertussis Vaccine, 5th Dose, global project lead Janefi Pastur R + D Transfution. lic. Pentacel, 2008; mem. joint devel. com. Merck-Connaught Partnership; corp. sponsor for licensing of DTacP vaccine for infant use, 1996. Mem. visitors bd. East Stroudsburg U., bd. dirs. computer sci., 2000; bd. dirs. Northeastern Pa. Indsl. Resource Ctr., Wilkes-Barre, Pa., 1988—91. Recipient Banting-Best award, 1989. Mem. ASM, Pharm. Mfrs., Project Mgmt. Inst., Internat. Assn. Biol. Standardization. Avocations: soccer, music, gardening, reading. Home: 53 Deerfield Way Scotrun PA 18355-9637 Office: Sanofi Pasteur Discovery Dr Swiftwater PA 18370-0187 Office Phone: 570-839-4243. Business E-Mail: wwoods@ptd.net.

WOOD-SMITH, DONALD, plastic surgeon; b. Sydney, June 30, 1937; s. William Frederick and Vera Mary; children: Christina Margaret, Donald William, Phillip Raynor. MB, BChir, Sydney U., 1954. Diplomate Am. Bd. Plastic Surgery. Surg. resident Lewisham Hosp., Sydney, 1954—57, Royal Marsden Hosp., 1957-58; resident plastic surgery NYU Hosp. Med. Ctr., 1960-64, asst., assoc. and attending surgeon, 1964-92; prof. plastic surgery Columbia Presbyn. Med. Ctr., 1991—. Vis. surgeon Bellevue Hosp., 1964-92, London Ind. Hosp., 1999-2005; chmn. plastic surgery Manhattan Eye Ear and Throat Hosp., 1975-77; assoc. prof. plastic surgery NYU, 1977-84, prof., 1984-92; surgeon, dir. plastic surgery Manhattan Eye Ear and Throat Hosp., 1977-84; cons. plastic surgeon NY Eye and Ear Infirmary, chmn. dept. plastic and reconstructive surgery, 1984— Author: Nursing Care of the Plastic Surgery Patient, 1967, Cosmetic Facial Surgery, 1973; contbr. articles to med. jours. Fellow ACS, Royal Coll. Surgeons of Edinburgh; mem. Am. Assn. Plastic Surgeons, Am. Soc. Plastic Surgeons, Am. Soc. Maxillofacial Surgeons, NY Acad. Medicine, Brit. Assn. Plastic, Reconstructive & Aesthetic Surgeons. Office: 830 Park Ave New York NY 10021-2757 Address: 56 Hanley St London WIG 9QA England Home Phone: 212-744-2225; Office Phone: 212-744-2224. Personal E-mail: dw830@aol.com.

WOODSON, GAYLE ELLEN, otolaryngologist; b. Galveston, Tex., June 9, 1950; d. Clinton Eldon and Nancy Jean (Stephens) W.; m. Kevin Thomas Robbins; children: Nicholas, Gregory, Sarah. BA, Rice U., 1972; MD, Baylor Coll. Medicine, 1975. Diplomate Am. Bd. Otolaryngology (bd. dirs., residency rev. com. for otolaryngology, exam. chair). Fellow Baylor Coll. Medicine, Houston, 1976, Inst. Laryngology & Otology, London, 1981-82; asst. prof. Baylor Coll. Medicine, 1982-87; asst. attending Harris County Hosp. Dist., Houston, 1982-86; with courtesy staff Saint Luke's Episcopal Hosp., Houston, 1982-87; assoc. attending The Methodist Hosp., Houston, 1982-87; asst. prof. U. Calif. Med. Sch., San Diego, 1987-89; chief otolaryngology VA Med. Ctr., San Diego, 1987-92; assoc. prof. U. Calif. Sch. Med., San Diego, 1989-92; prof. otolaryngology U. Tenn., Memphis, 1993—2000, So. Ill. U., 2003—. Numerous presentations and lectures in field. Contbr. numerous articles and abstracts to med. jours., also videotapes. Recipient deRoldes award, Am. Layrngol. Assn., 2003. Fellow ACS (bd. govs.), Royal Coll. Surgeons, Soc. Univ. Otolaryngologists (past pres.), Am. Soc. Head and Neck Surgery, Am. Laryngol. Assn. (pres.-elect de Roaldes award, 2003), Triological Soc.; mem. AMA, Am. Acad. Otolaryngology-Head and Neck Surgery (bd. dirs. 1993-96), Am. Med. Women's Assn. (past pres. Memphis br.), Soc. Head and Neck Oncologists Eng., Am. Physiol. Soc., Assn. Women Surgeons, Am. Soc. Head and Neck Surgeons, Johns Hopkins Soc. Scholars, Collegium OtoRhinolaryngolicum Amicus Sacrum. Office: Southern Illinois Univ PO Box 19662 Springfield IL 62794-9662 Home Phone: 217-726-0026. Business E-Mail: gwoodson@siumed.edu.

WOODSON, JONATHAN, federal agency administrator; b. Great Barrington, Mass., July 27, 1956; Grad. magna cum laude, CCNY; MA in Strategic Studies, US Army War Coll., Carlisle, Pa.; MD, NYU Sch. Medicine, 1979. Diplomate American Bd. Internal Medicine, American Bd. Surgery, cert. in vascular surgery and surg. critical care. Resident internal medicine Mass. Gen. Hosp., 1979—82, resident gen. surgery, 1982—86, resident vascular surgery, 1987—88; career officer, positions to brig. gen. US Army Res. Med. Commd.; mil. assignments include surgeon 373rd Gen. Hosp.; surgeon 351st Gen. Hosp., 86th Evacuation Hosp., Operation Desert Storm, Saudi Arabia, 1991; observer/trainer, Hospitals Integrated Lanes Training Program, 87th Maneuver Area Commd. US Army Res. Med. Commd., 1992—94; surgeon 399th Combat Support Hosp., chief profl svc./dep. comdr., acting comdr., 1999—2000; profl. liaison officer 804th Med. Brigade; sr. med. officer, Internat. Surg. and Med. Response Team US Army Res. Med. Commd.; chief profl. svcs./dep. comdr. 865th Combat Support Hosp.; comdr. 399th Combat Support Hosp., Taunton, Mass., 2003—06, 330th Med. Brigade and cons. to Surgeon Gen., Ft. Sheridan, Ill., 2006—09; dep. comdr. US Army Res. Med. Commd., Ft. Sheridan, Ill., 1999—2010; asst. sec. for health affairs US Dept Def., Washington, 2011—, asst. surgeon gen. reserve affairs, force structure & mobilization, Dept. Army, 2009—10. State faculty ACS Mass. Com. on Trauma Advanced Life Support Course, 1990—92; assoc. prof. surgery, assoc. dean students, diversity and multicultural affairs Boston U. Sch. Medicine; sr. attending vascular surgeon Boston Med. Ctr.; adj. asst. prof. surgery Uniformed Svcs. Univ. Health Sciences. Decorated Legion of Merit, Bronze Star Medal, Meritorious Svc. Medal with oak leaf cluster, Army Commendation Medal with 2 oak leaf clusters, Army Res. Components Achievement Medal with 4 oak leaf clusters, Nat. Def. Svc. Medal, Southwest Asia Campaign Medal (2 Bronze Svc. Stars), Armed Forces Res. Medal, Army Svc. Ribbon, Army Res. Component Overseas Training Ribbon, Kosovo Campaign Medal, NATO Medal, Kuwait Liberation Medal, Global War on Terrorism Expeditionary Medal, Order of Mil. Med. Merit; recipient Gold Humanism in Medicine award, Assn. American Med. Colleges, 2009. Fellow: ACS (gov.); mem.: Assn. Mil. Surgeons US, Soc. US Army Flight Surgeons, Mass. Med. Soc., Soc. Clin. Vascular Surgery, New Eng. Surg. Soc., New Eng. Soc. Vascular Surgery, Boston Surg. Soc., Uniform Svcs. Univ. Surg. Associates, Assn. Mil. Surgeons, Assn. Health Services Rsch., Soc. Vascular Surgery, Assn. Academic Surgery. Office: US Dept Defense 1400 Defense Pentagon Washington DC 20301 *

WOODSON, RILEY DONALD, thoracic and cardiovascular surgeon, lawyer; b. Winfield, Kans., Dec. 24, 1931; s. Riley Delma and Virginia Marie Woodson (Stepmother), Ruth Benedict Woodson; married; children: Riley David, Wade Clinton. BA, U. Kans., 1953, MD, 1956; JD, U. Toledo, 1984. Bar: Ohio 1984, US Dist. Ct. (no. dist. Ohio) 1985; Med. Licensure Kans., 1956, Calif., 1961, Ariz., 1962, Ohio, 1968, diplomate Am. Bd. Surgery, 1964, Am. Bd. Thoracic Surgery, 1968, Am. Bd. Cardiothoracic Surgery, 1978. Intern Parkland Meml. Hosp., Southwestern Med. Sch., Dallas, 1956—57; resident in gen. surgery U. Minn. Hosps., Mpls., 1957—63; resident in thoracic and cardiovasc. surgery U. Oreg. Med. Sch., Portland, 1965—67; asst. prof. surgery, asst. chief, thoracic and cardiovasc. surgery U. Ill. Sch. Medicine, Chgo., 1967—69; assoc. prof. surgery, chief, thoracic and cardiovasc. surgery Med. U. Ohio, Toledo, 1969—78, clin. assoc. prof. surgery, 1979—; pvt. practice Toledo, 1978—92, Palm Springs, Calif., 1993—96; contract med. malpractice case analyst Jacobson, Maynard, Tuschman & Kalur, LLC, Toledo, 1997—98; ptnr. Sodeman, Kirkhope & Woodson, LLP, Toledo, 2001—. Pres. Ohio Coll. Chest Physicians, Columbus, 1971—72; medicolegal case cons., Toledo, Port Clinton, Ohio, 1975—2006; mem. jud. and profl. rels. Ohio State Med. Assn., Columbus, 1986—90; bd. dirs. Palm Springs Acad. Medicine, 1994—96. Author 29 works in nat. and internat. med. and legal publs. Nat. basic and advanced CPR faculty Am. Heart Assn., 1976—83; exec. com. mem., bd. trustees sec., med. dir. Regional Emergency Med. Svcs. NW Ohio, Toledo, 1975—79; trustee NW Ohio Heart Assn., Toledo, 1976—80. Capt. USNR, 1963—88. Recipient Owl Soc., U. Kans., 1952, Sachem Cir., Omicron Delta Kappa (Pres.), 1953, Russell Hayden Outstanding Med. Student Rsch. medal, 1956, Outstanding Resident Rsch. award, Portland Surg. Soc., 1967, Am. Outstanding Med. Writing award, NW Medicine, 1967, Golden Apple for Tchg. Excellence, Med. U. Ohio, 1972, Outstanding Physician Vol., NW Ohio Heart Assn., 1980; Summerfield scholar, U. Kans., 1949, Nat. Honor Soc. scholar, 1949, Athletic scholarship Basketball and Track, 1949. Fellow: ACS (sr.), Soc. Vascular Surgery (disting. fellow), Am. Coll. Legal Medicine (sr.), Am. Coll. Angiology (sr.), Am. Coll. Chest Physicians (sr.; gov. 1972—78), Am. Coll. Cardiology (sr.); mem.: AMA, AAUP (sr.), ABA, Am. Soc. Law and Medicine, Soc. Internat. Surgery, Undersea Med. Soc., Assn. Academic Surgery, Assn. Mil. Surgeons of US, Toledo Surg. Soc. (founding mem.), Am. Thoracic Soc. (sr.), Soc. Thoracic Surgeons (sr.), Am. Assn. Surgery of Trauma (sr.), Am. Assn. Vascular Surgery (sr.), Toledo Acad. Med., Ohio Med. Assn., Ottawa County Bar Assn., Toledo Bar Assn. (mem. JD/MD and continuing legal edn. commns. 1985—), Ohio Bar Assn., U. Kans. Varsity K Club, Shrine, Scottish Rite, Knights Templar, Phi Kappa Phi, MENSA, Beta Theta Pi (U. Kans. chpt. pres. 1953). Office: 4445-E Marin Pines Port Clinton OH 43452 Office Phone: 419-797-7311. Office Fax: 419-797-7311. Personal E-mail: rd_woodson2@hotmail.com.

WOODWARD, WENDY ANN, radiation oncologist; BA in Chemistry, Mt. Holyoke Coll., S. Hadley, Mass., 1993; MD, PhD in Molecular Biology, Thomas Jefferson U., Phila., Pa., 2000. Cert. Am. Bd. Radiology, 2006. Med. intern Albert Einstein Med. Ctr., Phila., 2000—01; resident, radiation oncology U. Tex., MD Anderson Cancer Ctr., Houston, 2001—05; rsch. fellow Baylor Coll. Medicine, Houston, 2003—04; asst. prof., breast radiation oncology U. Tex. MD Anderson Cancer Ctr., Houston, 2005—. Contbr. several articles to profl. jours. Recipient Eleanor Montague prize, Resident Manuscript Contest, 2003, Roentgen Rsch. award, Radiological Soc. N.Am., 2004, Fletcher award, 1st pl. Resident Rsch. award, U. Tex. MD Anderson Cancer Ctr., 2005; named Intern of Yr., Albert Einstein Med. Ctr., 2001; Gibbon Scholar, Thomas Jefferson U., 1993—2000, Foerderer Fellowship, 1993, Fellowship, Clin. Epidemiology Workshop, Cancer Edn. Consortium, 2002, ASTRO travel grant, Gordon Conf. on Radiation, 2004, ASTRO Travel grant, Translational Rsch. Symposium, 2006, K12 grant, Ctr. for Clin. and Translational Scis., U. Tex. Health Scis. Ctr., 2006—09. Mem.: Am. Assn. Women in Radiology (mem. exec. com. 2004, mem.-in-tng.-at-large 2004—05), Am. Soc. Therapeutic Radiology and Oncology (mem. rsch. evaluation com. 2005—), Am. Radium Soc. (Young Oncologist Essay award 2003, Travel award, Barcelona, Spain 2005), Am. Soc. Clin. Oncology (Merit award 2003), Gilbert H. Fletcher Soc., Alpha Omega Alpha, Sigma Xi. Office: Univ Tex MD Anderson Cancer Ctr MDA ACB p1-2855 Unit 1202 1515 Holcombe Blvd MDA ACB P1-2855 Unit Houston TX 77030 Office Phone: 713-563-8481. Business E-Mail: wwoodward@mdanderson.org.

WOOLF, ALAN D., pediatrician, educator; MD, U. Chgo., 1976; MPH, U. NC, Chapel Hill. Diplomate Bd. Med. Examiners, 1977. Pediatrician Children's Hosp., Boston, 1983—2008, dir. pediatric environ. health ctr., co-dir. fellowship tng. program in pediatric environ. health; assoc. prof. pediat. Harvard Med. Sch. Contbr. articles to profl. jours. Mem.: American Acad. Clin. Toxicology (mem. bd. trustees, pres. 2010—). Achievements include research in toxicology and poisoning prevention. Office: Children's Hosp Boston 1295 Boylston St Ste 100 Boston MA 02118 Office Phone: 617-355-5187. Office Fax: 617-730-0049. Business E-Mail: alan.woolf@tch.harvard.edu. *

WOOLFENDEN, JAMES MANNING, nuclear medicine physician, educator; b. LA, Nov. 8, 1942; BA with distinction, Stanford U., 1964; MD, U. Wash., 1968. Diplomate Am. Bd. Nuclear Medicine (chmn. credentials com. 1993-94, vice chmn. exams. com. 1993-95, chmn. exam. com. 1995-96, sec. 1994-96, chmn. 1996-97, life mem.), Nat. Bd. Med. Examiners. Med. intern L.A. County-U. So. Calif. Med. Ctr., 1968-69; med. resident West L.A. VA Med. Ctr., 1969-70; nuclear medicine resident L.A. County-U. So. Calif. Med. Ctr., 1972-74; from asst. prof. radiology to assoc. prof. radiology U. Ariz., Tucson, 1974-84, prof. radiology, 1984—2007, prof. emeritus. Med. staff Univ. Med. Ctr., Tucson, 1974-2007; cons. VA Med. Ctr., 1974-2007; cons. med. staff Tucson Med. Ctr., 1975-2004, Carondelet St. Joseph's Hosp., 1974-98, St. Mary's Hosp., Tucson, 1976-90; mem. Nat. Cancer Inst. site visit team NIH, 1976, mem. NHLB Inst. site visit team NIH, 1976, mem. diagnostic radiology study sect., 1989-97, chmn., 1995-97; med. liaison officer network EPA, 1983-85; cons.-tchg. med. staff Kino Cmty. Hosp., 1984-94; med. officer Clin. Ctr., NIH, Bethesda, 1984-85; mem. Ariz. Cancer Ctr., U. Ariz., 1988—, sr. clin. scientist Univ. Heart Ctr., 1990—; Ariz. bd. regents U. Ariz. Presdl. Search Com., 1990-91; chmn. Ariz. Atomic Energy Commn., 1979-80, Ariz. Radiation Regulatory Hearing Bd., 1981—; bd. dirs. Calif. Radioactive Materials Mgmt. Forum, chmn., 1994-95, Western Forum Edn. in Safe Disposal of Low-Level Radioactive Waste, 1990-2000, vice chmn., 1991-92, chmn., 1992-94. Manuscript reviewer: Noninvasive Med. Imaging, 1983-84, Jour. Nuclear Medicine, 1985—, Investigative Radiology, 1989-94, Archives of Internal Medicine, 1990—; contbr. book chpts.: Diagnostic Nuclear Medicine, 2d edit., 1988, Adjuvant Therapy of Cancer, 1977, Fundamentals of Nuclear Medicine, 1988, others; contbr. articles to profl. jours. Mem. Am. Heart Assn. Coun. on Cardiovasc. Radiology. Maj. U.S. Army, 1970-72, Vietnam. Fellow Am. Coll. Nuc. Physicians (long range planning com. 1981-83, govt. affairs com. 1984-94, exec. com. 1987-91, sec. 1989-91, parliamentarian 1991-95, treas. 1996-98, publs. com. 1993-98, chmn. publs. com. 1993-94, pres.-elect 1998-99, pres. 1999-2000, others); mem. AMA (diagnostic and therapeutic tech. assessment reference panel 1982-98), Am. Nuc. Soc., Soc. Nuc. Medicine (com. on audit 1992-99, trustee 1992-96, ho. dels. 1996-2003, fin. com. 1996-99, bd. dirs. 1997-99, bronze medal for sci. exhibit 1984, bd. dirs., sec.-treas. So. Calif. chpt. 1993-95, pres.-elect 1995-96, pres. 1996-99), Assn. Univ. Radiologists, Ariz. Med. Assn., European Assn. Nuc. Medicine, Pima County Med. Soc., Radiol. Soc. N.Am., Soc. for Molecular Imaging. Office: Ariz Health Scis Ctr Radiology Rsch 1501 N Campbell Ave Tucson AZ 85724-5067

WOOLHANDLER, STEFFIE, healthcare educator; b. Oct. 12, 1951; BA, Stanford U., 1975; MD, LSU-NO; MPH, UC, Berkeley, 1979. Prof., medicine Harvard Med. Sch., 2009 —, vis. prof., medicine, 2011; prof., pub. health CUNY, 2010—. Recipient Barker award, Harvard Med. Sch., Barksy award, Physicians Forum; named Humanist of Yr., Ethical Culture Soc. Fellow: ACP; mem.: Physicians Nat. Health Program. Office: Dept Medicine 1493 Cambridge St Cambridge MA 02139 Office Fax: 617-665-1671. Business E-Mail: swoolhandler@challiance.org.

WOOLLEY, MARY ELIZABETH, science administrator, advocate; b. Chgo., Mar. 16, 1947; John Joseph and Ellen Louise (Bakke) McEnerney; m. John Stuart Woolley, Dec. 6, 1969 (div. 1985); children: George Newsom, Nora Ellen; m. Michael Howland Campbell, Jan. 1, 1989 (div. 2004). BS, Stanford U., 1969; MA, San Francisco State U., 1972; postgrad., U. Calif., San Francisco and Berkeley, 1974-75. Assoc. dir. Inst. Epidemiology and Behavioral Medicine, San Francisco, 1979-81; adminstr. Med. Rsch. Inst. of San Francisco, 1981-82, v.p., adminstr., 1982-86, v.p., exec. dir., 1986-90; pres. Research! Am., Alexandria, Va., 1990—. Cons. in fin. and mgmt. NIH, Bethesda, Md., 1984—92; adj. faculty U. Calif. Sch. Pub. Health, Berkeley, 1983—92, mem. Dean's adv. coun., 1995—2002; founding mem. Whitehead Inst. Bd. Assocs., 1995—; bd. dirs. Lovelace Inst., Respiratory Rsch. Inst., vice chmn., 1999—2004; bd. dirs. Children's Rsch. Inst., Washington, 2003—07; lectr. to profl. assns.; mem. bd. visitors Harvard U. Sch. Pub. Health, Cambridge, 2002—; mem. dean's coun. Johns Hopkins Sch. of Nursing, 2002—; mem. bd. advisors IBM Life Scis., 2003—. Editor Jour. of Soc. Rsch. Adminstrs., 1986-89, mem. editl. rev. bd., 1989-95; mem. editl. bd. Jour. Women's Health, 1992-2003, Sci. Comm., 1994—; contbr. articles and editls. to profl. jours. Bd. dirs. Kensington (Calif.) Edn. Found., 1986-89, Enterprise for H.S. Students, 1990-92; mem. capital campaign com. Calif. Shakespeare Festival, 1989-91, v.p. Med. Rsch. Assns. Am., 1993-95; bd. advisors Friends of Cancer Rsch., 1996—; bd. dirs. Nat. Patient Safety Found., 1998-2000, Friends of Nat. Inst. of Nursing Rsch., 2001-07. Recipient Silver Touchstone award Am. Hosp. Assn., 1994, Disting. Svc. award Columbia Coll. Physicians and Surgeons, 1994, Advocacy award Fedn. Am. Socs. Exptl. Biology, 1998, Advocacy award Friends Nat. Inst. Nursing Rsch., 1999, Leadership award Coun. Scientific Soc. Pres.'s, 1999, Advocacy award Friends of Dental Rsch., 2002; honored Women of Vision Am. Com. Weizmann Inst. Sci., 2004, 05, 06, Advocacy award Am. Soc. Biochemistry and Molecular Biology, 2007. Fellow AAAS; mem. Assn. Ind. Rsch. Insts. (pres.-elect 1987-89, pres. 1989-90), Inst. Medicine (coun. mem.), Soc. Rsch. Adminstrs. (bd. dirs. 1986-90, bd. advisors 1990-93, Hartford-Nicholson Svc. award 1990, Disting. Contbn. to Rsch. Adminstrn. award, 1993), Calif. Biomed. Rsch. Assn. (bd. govs. 1986-90), Nat. Press Club. Democrat. Office: Research! Am 1101 King St Ste 520 Alexandria VA 22314-3067 Office Phone: 703-739-2577. Office Fax: 703-739-2372. Business E-Mail: mwoolley@researchamerica.org.

WOOLLING, KENNETH RAU, cardiovascular disease internist; b. Indpls., Mar. 6, 1918; m. Catherine Margaret McColl, Mar. 20, 1948; 2 children. BA magna cum laude, Butler U., 1939; postgrad., Harvard U., 1939-40; MD, Ind. U., 1943; MS in Medicine, U. Minn., 1951; MS, Mayo Found. Grad. Sch. Edn. Diplomate Nat. Bd. Med. Examiners, Am. Bd. Internal Medicine, Am. Bd. Cardiovascular Disease. Intern Indpls. City Hosp. (now Wishard Meml.), Indpls., 1943-44; resident in internal medicine Marion County Gen. Hosp., Indpls., 1947; fellow, first asst. internal medicine Mayo Found., Rochester, Minn., 1948-52; mem. med. staff, mem. tchg. staff postgrad. med. edn. Marion County Gen. Hosp. (name now Wishard Meml. Hosp.), Indpls., 1952—; founder, dir., peripheral vascular diseases clinic Indpls City & Marion County Gen. Hosp. (now Wishard Meml.), Indpls., 1952-68; pvt. practice internal medicine and cardiovascular diseases Indpls, 1952—; founder, dir. peripheral vascular diseases clinic Meth. Hosp., Indpls., 1967-72, founder, dir. vascular lab., 1970-73, mem. med. staff, tchr. staff postgrad. med. edn., 1952—. Mem. med. staff St. Vincent Hosp., St. Francis Hosp. and Winona Meml. Hosp., Indpls., 1952—; charter mem. med. staff Cmty. Hosp., Indpls., 1952—; charter mem. med. adv. com. Butler U., Indpls, 1956—. Contbr. articles to profl. jours., 1950—; author. Recollections of A Mayo Clinic Fellowship at Mid Twentieth Century: 1948-1952, 2010. Capt. Med. Corps U.S. Army, 1944-46. Fellow ACP, Am. Coll. Chest Physicians, Coun. on Cardiology Am. Heart Assn., Am. Coll. Angiology (gov. state of Ind. 1979-80); mem. AMA (50 Yr. award 1993), SAR, Internat. Union Angiology, Am. Soc. Internal Medicine, Am. Diabetes Assn., Ind. State Med. Soc., Ind. Diabetes Assn., Am. Fedn. for Clin. Rsch., N.Y. Acad. Med. Scis., North Ctrl. Clin. Soc., Mayo Cardiovascular Soc., Ind. Hist. Soc., Res. Officers Assn., Indpls. Med. Soc., Am. Legion, Shriners, Masons (Scottish Rite and Mystic Tie Lodge, 50 yr. award 1989), Contemporary Club of Indpls., Indpls. Athletic Club, Columbia Club, Highland Golf and Country Club, Phi Delta Theta (50 yr. award 1985), Phi Kappa Phi, Phi Chi. Presbyterian. Office: PO Box 80192 Indianapolis IN 46280-0192

WOOLLISCROFT, JAMES O., dean, medical educator; BS summa cum laude, U. Minn., 1972, MD, 1976. Resident internal medicine U. Mich., Ann Arbor, faculty Dept. Internal Medicine, 1980, prof. internal medicine, 1993—, prof. Dept. Med. Edn., Josiah Macy, Jr. prof. med. edn., 1996, Lyle C. Roll prof. medicine, 2001, assoc. chair Dept. Internal Medicine; chief of staff U. Mich. Hosps. and Health Ctrs., Ann Arbor, assoc. dean, dir. grad. med. edn. U. Mich. Med. Sch., Ann Arbor, exec. assoc. dean, 1999—2006, interim dean, 2006—07, dean, 2007—. Recipient Career Achievement in Med. Edn. Award, Soc. Gen. Med. Edn., 2004. Office: U Mich Med Sch Office of Dean 1301 Catherine Rd Ann Arbor MI 48109 Office Phone: 734-763-9600. *

WOOLSTON-CATLIN, MARIAN, retired psychiatrist; b. Seattle, Jan. 20, 1931; d. Howard Brown and Katharine Nichols (Dally) Woolston; m. Randolph Catlin Jr., July 5, 1959; children: Laura Louise, Jennifer Woolston, Randolph III. BA cum laude, Vassar Coll., 1951; MD, Harvard U., 1955. Diplomate Nat. Bd. Med. Examiners. Intern in pediatric medicine Children's Hosp., Boston, 1956, asst. resident in pediatric medicine, 1957; resident in psychiatry Mass. Mental Health Ctr., Boston, 1957-59; fellow in child psychiatry Tavistock Clin., London, 1960, spkr. Rhodes House, U. Oxford, 1961; Commonwealth fellow in child psychiatry Harvard U. at Gaebler Children's Unit, Waltham, Mass., 1975-78, clin. instr. psychiatry, 1978-79; pvt. practice Wellesley Hills, Mass., 1978-91, Medfield, Mass., 1991—2006. Clin. instr. psychiatry Harvard U. at Mass. Mental Health Ctr., Boston, 1957-59, 78-82, Tufts U. at Mass. Mental Health Ctr., 1957-59; mem. exec. bd. Parents' and Children's Svcs., Boston, 1983-86. Designer H.H. Hunnewell Meml. Garden for New Eng. Flower Show Mass. Hort. Soc., 1975 (Ames Cup award). Exec. bd. Ext. Divsn. New Eng. Conservatory Music, 1972-75; charter mem. reuse com. Medfield State Hosp., 1992—; charter mem. Nat. Women's History Mus., 2004; corporator Schepens Eye Rsch. Inst., 2005—, adv. bd., rsch. com. 2006—; adv. bd. Women's Eye Health Task Force, 2005—. Fellow Am. Acad. Child and Adolescent Psychiatry; mem. AMA, Am. Psychiat. Assn. (life), Mass. Psychiat. Assn., Mass. Med. Soc., New Eng. Coun. Child and Adolescent Psychiatry (hon.), Boston Vassar Club (exec. bd. 1963-75), Hills Garden Club Wellesley (exec. bd. and design chief 1973-75; Designer Hosp. Gardens Ames Cup award, 1975). Episcopalian. Avocations: landscape design, sculpting. Office Phone: 508-359-8046.

WOO SHIN, KO, Oriental medicine physician, educator; b. Busan, Republic of Korea, Jan. 2, 1963; s. Ko Jin Hong and Oh Chu Ja; m. Jung Soo Jung, Dec. 27, 1992; children: Ko Yeo Kyoung, Ko Kwang Yoon. MD in Oriental Medicine, WonKwang U., Iksan, 1995; PhD, Pusna Nat. U., Busan, 2004. Lic. Oriental medicine physician Ministry of Health of Wellfare, 1988. Dir. Ulsan Dongeui Oriental Medicine Hosp., Republic of Korea, 2006—. Chief Clin. Rsch. Ctr. Oriental Medicine, Dongeui U., Busan, 2005—06. Author: Text of Traditional Korean Dermatology & Surgery. Com. mem. Pub. Welfare of Srs., Ulsan, 2006—07. With, 1988—90, Korean Army. Grantee, Ministry of Health & Welfare, 2005, KOSEF, 2005. Mem.: Korean Oriental Med. Opthalmology & Otolaryngology & Dermatology (pres. 2003—06). Home: Daerim River E Apt 203-2401 Mangmi 2 Dong Suyeong Gu Busan 613-774 Republic of Korea Office: Ulsan Dongeui Oriental Medicine Hosp 479-7 Singung-Dong Nam-Gu 680-824 Ulsan Republic of Korea Office Phone: 82-052-226-8101. Office Fax: 82-052-256-0665. Personal E-mail: wsko@deu.ac.kr.

WORA-URAI, NOPADOL, physician, surgeon; b. Bangkok, Dec. 23, 1946; s. Lert and Saipin Wora-Urai; m. Dusadee Ummaralikit, July 28, 1946; 1 child, Regina Sawadronnapak. BS, Mahidol U., Bangkok, 1966, MD, 1970. Diplomate Am. Bd. of Surgery, 1979, Thai Bd. Surgery Thai Med. Coun., 1980. Resident in surgery Columbus Hosp., Chgo., 1972—77; fellow in hand surgery Cook County Hosp., Chgo., 1977—78; mem. surg. staff Phramongkutklao Hosp. and Coll. of Medicine, Bangkok, 1980—95, chmn. dept. surgery, 1995—98, prof. surgery, 1996—2006; dep. dir. Phramongkutklao Hosp., 1998—2003, advisor, 2003—06, chmn. Trauma Ctr., 2004—06; Thailand nat. del. Internat. Soc. Surgery, Basel, Switzerland, 2003—; chmn. Transplant Ctr. Phramongkutklao Hosp., 2004—06. Editor-in-chief Thai Jour. of Surgery, mem. editl. bd. Jour. Med. Assn. Thailand, 2004—05. Pres. Assn. Gen. Surgeons Thailand, Bangkok, 2004—05. Lt. gen M.C., 2006, Bangkok. Named Disting. Alumnus, Assn. Siriraj Hosp. Physician Alumni, 2002. Fellow: ACS (corr.), Internat. Coll. Surgeons (corr.; pres. 2006—07, co-editor Internat. Surgery 2005—06, pacific fedn. sec. 2005—, pres. Thailand sect. 2006—), Royal Coll. Surgeons Thailand (life; chmn. advanced trauma life support subcom. 2003—05, chmn. definitive surgery trauma care 2003—05, v.p. 2005—); mem.: Asian Surg. Assn. (v.p. 2004—06), Royal Coll. Surgeons Edinburgh. Buddhist. Avocations: travel, reading, gardening, sports, golf. Office: Phramongkutklao Hosp Rajvithee Rd Rajthevee Bangkok 10400 Thailand Home: 88/71 Soi Aree Phaholyothin Rd 10400 Bangkok Bangkok Thailand Office Fax: (66-2) 354-9089; Home Fax: (66-2) 271-1374. Personal E-mail: wnpdol@netscape.net.

WORCESTER, HOWARD LESTER, internist; b. Kansas City, Mo., Jan. 3, 1945; s. Howard Elmer and Alma Jane (Evans) W. div.; m. Tammy Worcester; children: Tiffany, Chase. BS, U. Oregon, 1967, MD, 1971. Diplomate Am. Bd. Internal Medicine, Am. Bd. Forensic Pathology. Intern Harbor Gen. Hosp. UCLA, 1971-72; med. officer U.S. Army, West Germany, 1972-75; resident U. Calif., Irvine, 1975-77, chief med. resident, 1977-78; pvt. practice internal medicine Meml. Hosp., Long Beach, Calif., 1978—. Dir. utilization rev. Long Beach Meml. Hosp., 1983—, trustee, 1983—, also bd. dirs.; cons. Sultanate of Oman, Muscat, Oman, 1984—. Patron L.A. County Mus. Major U.S. Army, 1972-75. Recipient Merck scholarship U. Oreg. Med. Sch., 1969 Mem. Long Beach Meml. Hosp. Med. Group (pres. 1983—), Long Beach Meml. Med. Svc. Orgn. (pres. 1993-96), Phi Beta Kappa, Alpha Omega Alpha. Episcopalian. Avocations: cooking, wine collecting, travel, sports. Home: 11042 Skyline Dr Santa Ana CA 92705-2473 Office: Meml Med Group 2650 Elm Ave Ste 309 Long Beach CA 90806-1600 Office Phone: 562-595-8549. Personal E-mail: lesworcester@hotmail.com.

WORELL, JUDITH P., psychologist, educator; b. NYC; d. Moses and Dorothy Goldfarb; m. Leonard Worell, Aug. 11, 1947 (div.); children: Amy, Beth, Wendy; m. H.A. Smith, Mar. 23, 1985 BS magna cum laude, Queens Coll., 1950; MA, Ohio State U., 1952, PhD in Clin. Psychology, 1954; DHL (hon.), Colby-Sawyer Coll., 1993. Research assoc. Iowa Psychopathic Hosp., Iowa City, 1957-59; research assoc. Okla. State U., 1960-66; asst. prof. U. Ky., Lexington, 1969-71, assoc. prof., 1971-75, prof. ednl. and counseling psychology, 1976—, dir. counseling psychology tng. program, 1980-93, chairperson dept. ednl. and counseling psychology, 1993-97, prof. emerita, 1999—. Author: (with C.M. Nelson) Managing Instructional Problems, 1974; (with W.E. Stilwell) Psychology for Teachers and Students, 1981; Psychological Development in the Elementary Years, 1982; (with Fred Danner) The Adolescent as Decision-maker: Applications to Development and Education, 1989; (with Pam Remer) Feminist Perspectives in Therapy: An Empowerment Model for Women, 1992; (with N. Johnson) Shaping the Future of Feminist Psychology: Education, Research, and Practice, 1997, (with Norine Johnson & Michael Roberts) Beyond Appearance: A New Look at Adolescent Girls, 1999, Encyclopedia of Women and Gender: Sex Similarities and Differences and the Impact of Society on Gender, 2001, (with Pam Remer) Feminist Perspectives in Therapy: Empowering Diverse Women, 2003, (with Carol Goodheart) Oxford Handbook of Girls' and Women's Psychological Health, 2006; assoc. editor Jour. Cons. and Clin. Psychology, 1976-79, mem. editl. bd., 1984-89; assoc. editor Psychol. Women Quar., 1984-89, editor, 1989-95, mem. editorial bd. Sex Roles, 1984-2000, Psychol. Assessment, 1991-97, Clin. Psychology Rev., 1991-97, Women and Therapy, 1992-2000; cons., reviewer 10 jours.; contbr. articles to profl. jours. Named U. Ky. Campus Woman of Yr., 1976, Outstanding Univ. Grad. prof., 1991, Disting. Ky. psychologist, 1990; USPHS fellow, 1953; NIMH rsch. grantee, 1962-69; recipient: APF Gold Medal, 2010 Fellow APA (pres. Clin. Psychology of Women 1986-88, chmn. com. state assn. rels. 1982-83, fellow selection divsn. 35 com. 1983-84, policy and planning bd. 1989-92, publs. and comm. bd. 1992-99, chair 1996-98, chair jours. com., pres. divsn. psychology of women 1997-98, Disting. Leader for Women in Psychology 1990, Carolyn Wood Sherif award, 2001, Psychology of Women Heritage award 2004, coun. rep. 2000-02, chair women's caucus 2002) Soc. Psychol. Study of Social Issues (chmn. fellow com. 2005-), Ky. Psychol. Assn. (pres. 1981-82, rep. at large 1995-97), Southeastern Psychol. Assn. (exec. coun. mem.-at-large, pres.-elect 1993-94 pres. 1994-95), Am. Women in Psychology, Phi Beta Kappa. Home: 3892 Gloucester Dr Lexington KY 40510-9729 Office: U Ky Dept Ednl and Counseling Psychology 245 Dickey Hl Lexington KY 40506-0017 E-mail: jworell@insightbb.com. *

WORMAN, HOWARD JAY, internist, educator; b. Paterson, NJ, May 21, 1959; s. Louis and Dora W. BA, Cornell U., 1981; MD, U. Chgo., 1985. Diplomate Am. Bd. Internal Medicine. Intern NY Hosp., NYC, 1985—86, resident, 1986—87; guest investigator Rockefeller U., NYC, 1987—90; asst. prof. Mt. Sinai Sch. Medicine, NYC, 1990—94; asst. attending physician Mt. Sinai Hosp., NYC, 1990—94; asst. prof. Columbia U. Coll. Physicians and Surgeons, NYC, 1995—98, assoc. prof., 1998—2007, prof., 2007—; asst. attending physician NY Presbyn. Hosp., Columbia-U. Med. Ctr., NYC, 1995—98, assoc. attending physician, 1998—2007, attending physician, 2007—; dir. divsn. digestive and liver diseases NY Presbyn. Hosp., NYC, 1999—2002. Mem. med. adv. com. Muscular Dystrophy Assn., 2000—05. Mem. editl. bd. Hepatology, 1993-2008, Frontiers in Biosci., World Jour. Gastroenterology; assoc. editor Biomed. Ctrl. Cell Biology Nucleus, The Open Jour. Gastroenterology; mem. bd. reviewing editors Molecular Biology of the Cell; contbr. articles to profl. jours. Recipient Physician-Scientist award NIH, 1987-92; Charles E. Culpeper scholar in Med. Scis., 1994-95, Irma T. Hirschl scholar, 1997-2002. Mem. AAAS, ACP, Am. Chem. Soc., Am. Fedn. Med. Rsch. (Trainee award in clin. rsch. 1989, Henry Christian award 1990), Am. Soc. Cell Biology, Am. Assn. Study of Liver Diseases, Am. Gastroent. Assn., Am. Soc. Clin. Investigation, N.Y. Acad. Scis. (vice chmn. biol. scis. sect. 1992-93, chmn. 1993-94), Am. Diabetes Assn., Hon. Order Ky. Cols., Phi Beta Kappa, Assn. Am. Physicians. Democrat. Jewish. Avocations: music, reading. Office: Columbia U Coll Physicians-Surgeons 630 W 168th St New York NY 10032-3795 Office Phone: 212-305-1306. Business E-Mail: hjwl4@columbia.edu.

WORNING, ANNE MARIE, international organization administrator; b. Denmark; MD, U. Copenhagen, 1979. European coord. clin. trials in the pharm. industry; clin. experience in surgery; positions in adminstrn., fin., mgmt., and strategic planning, European and Eastern Mediterranean regional offices WHO, rural hospital worker Burundi, dir. planning, resource coordination and performance monitoring Geneva, exec. dir., office of the dir. gen., 2009—. Former counsellor to the bd. Internat. Soc. Quality Assurance. Mem.: Danish Soc. Quality Assurance in Health Care. Office: WHO avenue Appia 20 1202 Geneva Switzerland *

WORRELL, AUDREY MARTINY, retired geriatric psychiatrist; b. Phila, Aug. 12, 1935; d. Francis Aloysius and Dorothy (Rawley) Martiny; m. Richard Vernon Worrell, June 14, 1958; children: Philip Vernon, Amy Elizabeth. MD, Meharry Med. Coll., 1960. Diplomate Am. Bd. Psychiatry and Neurology. Intern Misericordia Hosp., Phila., 1960-61; resident SUNY-Buffalo Affiliated Hosp., NY, 1961-63, Buffaflo Psychiat. Ctr., NY, 1963-64; dir. capitol region Mental Health Ctr., Hartford, Conn., 1974-77; acting regional dir. Region IV State Dept. Mental Health, 1976-77; asst. chief psychiatry VA Med. Ctr., Newington, Conn., 1977-78, acting chief psychiatry, 1978-79, chief psychiatry, 1978-80; dir. Capitol Regional Mental Health Facilities, Hartford, Conn., 1980-87; clin. prof. psychiatry U. Conn., 1981-87; commr. State Dept. Mental Health, Hartford, 1981-86; CEO, med. dir. Vista Sandia Hosp., Albuquerque, 1986-88; dir. consultation liason Lovelace Med. Ctr., Albuquerque, 1988-89, geriatric psychiatry, 1989-93; dir. geriatric psychiatry Charter Hosp., Albuquerque, 1993-96, St. Joseph Med. Sys., Albuquerque, 1994—; pvt. practice, 1996—2003; part-time cons. Albuquerque VA Hosp., 2003—08. Contbr. articles to profl. jour. Bd. dir. Transitional Svc., Buffalo, 1973-74, ARC, Buffalo, 1973-74, Child and Family Svc., Hartford, 1972-73; co-chmn. United Way/Combined Health Appeal, State of Conn., 1983, 84; active Child Welfare Inst. Adv. Bd., Hartford, 1983—, Conn. Prison Bd., Hartford, 1984-85; chmn. Gov. Task Force on Mental Health Policy, 1982-85; mem. Gov.Task Force on Homeless, 1983-85. Recipient Leadership award Conn. Coun. Mental Health Ctr., 1983, Outstanding Contbn. award to Health Svc., YWCA, Hartford, 1983. Mem. AMA, APHA, NASMHPD (sec., bd. dir. 1982-86), New Eng. Mental Health Commr. Assn., Am. Med. Women's Assn., Conn. Assn. Mental Health and Aging, Conn. Coalition for Homeless Inc., Conn. Rehab. Assn., Am. Assn. Psychiat. Adminstr., Am. Hosp. Assn., Am. Orthopsychiat. Assn., Assn. Mental Health Adminstr., Hosp. and Cmty. Psychiatry Svc., Corporators of Inst. of Living of Hartford, Am. Psychiat. Assn., Conn. Psychiat. Soc., Am. Coll. Psychiatrists, Am. Coll. Mental Health Adminstr.

WORRELL, RICHARD VERNON, orthopedic surgeon, dean; b. Bklyn., June 4, 1931; s. John Elmer and Elaine (Callender) Worrell; m. Audrey Frances Martiny, June 14, 1958; children: Philip Vernon, Amy Elizabeth. BA, NYU, 1952; MD, Meharry Med. Coll., 1958. Diplomate Am. Bd. Orthop. Surgery, Nat. Bd. Med. Examiners. Intern Meharry Med. Coll., Nashville, 1958—59; resident in gen. surgery Mercy-Douglass Hosp., Phila., 1960—61; resident in orthop. surgery State U. N.Y. Buffalo Sch. Medicine Affiliated Hosps., 1961—64; resident in orthop. pathology Temple U. Med. Ctr., Phila., 1966—67; pvt. practice orthop. surgery Phila., 1967—68; asst. prof. acting head divsn. orthop. surgery U. Conn. Sch. Medicine, 1968—70; attending orthop. surgeon E.J. Meyer Meml. Hosp., Buffalo, Millard Fillmore Hosp., Buffalo, VA Hosp., Buffalo, Buffalo State Hosp.; clin. instr. orthop. surgery SUNY, Buffalo, 1970—74; chief orthop. surgery VA Hosp., Newington, Conn., 1974—80; asst. prof. surgery (orthop.) U. Conn. Sch. Medicine, 1974—77, assoc. prof., 1977—83, asst. dean student affairs, 1980—83; prof. clin. surgery SUNY Downstate Med. Ctr., Bklyn., 1983—86; dir. orthop. surgery Brookdale Hosp. Med. Ctr., Bklyn., 1983—86; prof. orthop. U. N.Mex. Sch. Medicine, 1986—97, prof., vice chmn. dept. orthop., 1997—99, prof. emeritus, 1999—; dir. orthop. oncology U. N.Mex. Health Scis. Ctr., 1987—99; mem. med. staff U. N.Mex. Cancer Ctr., 1987—99; chief orthop. surgery VA Med. Ctr., Albuquerque, 1987—97. Cons. in orthop. surgery Newington (Conn.) Children's Hosp., 1968—70; mem. sickle cell disease adv. com. NIH, 1982—86. Bd. dirs. Big Bros. Greater Hartford. Served to capt. M.C. USAR, 1962—69. Fellow: ACS, Royal Soc. Medicine, London, Am. Acad. Orthop. Surgeons; mem.: AMA, N.Mex. Soc. Clin. Oncology, Internat. Soc. Orthop. Surgery and Traumatology, Orthop. Rsch. Soc., Internat. Fedn. Surg. Colls. (assoc.), Am. Soc. Clin. Oncology, Am. Soc. Clin. Pathologists, Am. Orthop. Assn., Alpha Omega Alpha. Personal E-mail: rworrellmd@aol.com. Business E-Mail: rworrell@salud.unm.edu.

WORTH, DAVID ALLEN, rheumatologist, educator; MD, U. Rochester, 1971. Diplomate Am. Bd. Internal Medicine-rheumatology. Resident internal medicine Montefiore Med. Ctr., Bronx, 1972—74, fellow rheumatology, 1974—75, 1977—78; rheumatologist Union Hosp., Overlook Med. Ctr. Asst. clin. prof. medicine Univ. Medicine and Dentistry of NJ. Office: Overlook Medical Center 2376 Morris Ave Union NJ 07083-5707 Office Phone: 908-686-6616. Office Fax: 908-686-5806.

WORTH, MELVIN H., surgeon, educator; b. Norwich, Conn., July 14, 1930; s. Melvin H. and Stella E. (Cline) W.; m. Alice Tenzer, May 17, 1953; children: Nancy, David. AB, Clark U., 1950; MD, NYU, 1954. Diplomate Am. Bd. Surgery. Intern Bellevue Hosp., NYC, 1954-55, resident, 1957-61, dir. trauma svc., 1966-79; dir. surgery S.I. U. Hosp., NYC, 1979-96; assoc. prof. NYU, NYC, 1968-69; prof. clin. surgery SUNY, Bklyn., 1979—96, Uniformed Svc. U. Health Sci. Ctr., 1996—. Chmn. trauma designation com. N.Y.C. Emergency Med. Svc., 1990; mem. Office of Profl. Med. Conduct of N.Y. State, 1983-98. Vice chmn. N.Y. State Health Rev. and Planning Coun., 1988-94, chair, 1995. Capt. USMC, 1955-57. Scholar-in-residence Inst. Medicine, 1996—. Fellow ACS, Am. Coll. Gastroenterology; mem. Internat. Soc. Surgery, Soc. Am. Gastrointestinal Endoscopic Surgeons, Am. Assn. for Surgery of Trauma, Assn. Acad. Surgery, Soc. Critical Care Medicine, Assn. Surg. Edn., N.Y. Surg. Soc. (pres. 1989), Alpha Omega Alpha. Home: 817 Freedom Plaza Cir Apt 104 Sun City Center FL 33573-7210 Personal E-mail: alicemelworth@msn.com.

WORTH, RANDALL GLENN, biology professor; b. Detroit, Sept. 27, 1970; BS, U. Charleston, 1992; PhD, Wayne State U., 1999. Asst. prof. U. Toledo Coll. Medicine, 2005—. Office: University Toledo Coll Medicine Toledo OH 43614 Business E-Mail: randall.worth@utoledo.edu.

WORTH, SHERRI, cosmetic dentist; married; 3 children. BS, DDS, UCLA. Pvt. practice. Mem.: ADA, Esthetic Professionals, European Acad. Esthetic Dentistry, American Acad. Esthetic Dentistry, Acad. of Osseointegration, Acad. of Gen. Dentistry, Assn. of Women Dentists, Newport Harbor Acad. Dentistry, Orange County Dental Soc., Calif. Dental Assn. Avocations: golf, skiing, photography. Office: 1401 Avocado Ave Newport Beach CA 92660 Office Phone: 949-644-6988.

WORTHLEY, DANIEL LINDSAY, gastroenterologist; b. Adelaide, Australia, Sept. 24, 1976; MBBS with Honors, U. Adelaide, 1999; PhD candidate, QIMR, Australia, 2007—. Registered MD Med. Bd. of South Australia, 2000. Med. intern Royal Adelaide Hosp., Australia, 2000, med. resident, 2001—03; gastroenterology registrar Flinders Med. Ctr. and Repatriation Gen. Hosp., Adelaide, Australia, 2004—06. Fellow, RACP.

WORTSMAN, XIMENA, radiologist; b. Tome, Concepcion, Chile, Dec. 4, 1965; d. Isaias Wortsman and Gloria Canovas; m. Rodrigo Ferreira, June 24, 1995; children: Benjamin Ferreira Wortsman, Camila Ferreira Wortsman. MD, Sch. Medicine U. Chile, Santiago, 1990. Cert. radiologist U. Chile and Soc. Chilena Radiologia, 1993. Faculty Hosp. San Juan Dios, Radiology Dept., Santiago, Chile, 1993—96; chief radiology dept. Hosp. del Prof., Santiago, 1993—2006; ultrasound dept. chief Clinica Servet, Radiology dept., Santiago, 2001—. Musculoskeletal ultrasound fellowship Diagnostic Imaging Dept. Henry Ford Hosp., Detroit. Contbr. articles to profl. jours. (Best Presentation Radiology Congress of Chilean Soc. Radiology, 2003, Best Rev. Article Dermatology Chilean Jour., 2006). Mem.: Soc. Chilena Dermatologia, AIUM, Am. Roentgen Ray Soc., RSNA, Soc. Chilena Radiologia. Office: Clinica Servet Radiology Dept Almirante Pastene 150 Providencia Santiago RM Chile Business E-Mail: xwo@tie.cl.

WOTEKI, CATHERINE ELLEN, federal agency administrator; b. Ft. Leavenworth, Kans., Oct. 7, 1947; d. Joseph Jeremiah and Catherine (Costello) O'Connor; m. Thomas Henry Woteki, June 7, 1969. BS, Mary Washington Coll., 1969; MS, Va. Poly. Inst. and State U., 1971, PhD, 1973. Registered dietitian. Asst. prof. Drexel U., Phila., 1975-77; project dir. Congl. Office of Tech. Assessment, Washington, 1977-80; group leader Human Nutrition Info. Services USDA, Washington, 1980-83; dep. dir. Nat. Ctr. for Health Statistics US Dept. Health & Human Services, Washington, 1983-90; dir. Food & Nutrition Bd. Inst. Medicine, Washington, 1990-93; dep. assoc. dir. for sci. Office Sci. & Tech. Policy, Exec. Office of the Pres., Washington, 1994-95; dep. under sec. for rsch., edn. & economics USDA, Washington, 1996, under sec. for food safety, 1997—2001; dean agrl., prof. human nutrition Iowa State U., Iowa City, 2002—05; global dir. sci. affairs Mars, Inc., McLean, Va., 2005—10; under sec. for rsch., edn. & economics USDA, Washington, 2010—. Contbr. articles to profl. jours. Named Outstanding alumna Va. Poly. Inst. and State U., 1987; recipient Elijah White award Nat. Ctr. for Health Statis., 1987, Spl. Recognition award USPHS, 1987, Staff Achievement award Inst. of Medicine, 1991. Mem. American Inst. Nutrition, American Dietetic Assn. Coun. on Rsch., Inst. Food Technologists, Am. Pub. Health Assn., Inst. Medicine (chair food & nutrition bd., 2003-05) Office: USDA 1400 Independence Ave SW Washington DC 20250-0002

WOYSKI, MARGARET SKILLMAN, retired geology educator; b. West Chester, Pa., July 26, 1921; d. Willis Rowland and Clara Louise (Howson) Skillman; m. Mark M. Woyski, June 19, 1948; children: Nancy Elizabeth, William Bruno, Ronald David, Wendelin Jane. BA in Chemistry, Wellesley Coll., Mass., 1943; MS in Geology, U. Minn., Mpls., 1945, PhD in Geology, 1946. Geologist Mo. Geol. Survey and Water Resources, Rolla, 1946-48; instr. U. Wis., Madison, 1948-52; lectr. Calif. State U., Long Beach, 1963-67, lectr. to prof. Fullerton, 1966-91, assoc. dean Sch. Natural Sci. and Math., 1981-91, emeritus prof., 1991—. Contbr. articles to profl. jours.; author lab. manuals; editor guidebooks. Fellow Geol. Soc. Am. (program chmn. 1982); mem. South Coast Geol. Soc. (hon. pres. 1974), Mineral Soc. Am. Home: 2525 Brea Blvd # 119 Fullerton CA 92835-2787

WOY-WOJCIECHOWSKI, JERZY MARIAN, nuclear medicine physician, composer; b. Inowroclaw, Poland, Aug. 9, 1933; s. Henryk and Irena (Przygodzka) Woy-W.; m. Elzbieta Rusiecka, Apr. 19, 1958 (div. 1970); 1 child, Ewelina; m. Alicja Malgorzata Koztowska, Sept. 25, 1971; children: Patrycja, Dominika. MD, U. Warsaw, Poland, 1957, PhD, 1967. Dir. Med. Theatre Eskulap, Poland, 1951-81, Nuclear Med. Dept., Poland, 1968—; pres. Curtis Healthcare, Poland, 1990—, Polish Com. for UNICEF, 1994-99, Polish Med. Assn., 1987—. Prof. U. Warsaw, 1990 Author: Ktoredy do Medycyny, 1967, Poczytanki Zdrowotne, 1998, Opowiesci Lekarza, 2000; chief editor: Med. Problems, 1983—, mem. editl. bd.: Polish Radiol. Rev., 1976—, Nuc. Med. Problems, 1987—, Polish Med. Weekly, 1997—; contbr. articles to profl. jours.; author: Spiewajacy Konsyliarze, 2003. Mem. Health Promotion Com., Office of Pres. Walesa, 1993-96. Recipient Sci. award Ministry of Health, 1974, 77, Gloria Medicinae medal, 1991, A. Jurzykowski award, 1996. Mem. Warsaw Med. Soc. (pres. 1976-87), Polish Med. Acad., European Soc. Nuclear Medicine, Lions Club. Mem. Solidarity. Roman Catholic. Avocations: music, composition. Home: Skrzetuskiego 02-726 Warsaw Poland Office: Polish Med Assn Al Ujazdowskie 24 02-478 Warsaw Poland E-mail: Jerzy.Woy-Wojciechowski@curtisgroup.pl.

WRAY, BETTY BEASLEY, allergist, immunologist, pediatrician; b. Ga., 1935; MD, Med Coll. Ga., 1960. Diplomate Am. Bd. Allergy and Immunology, Am. Bd. Clin. Lab. Immunology. Intern Talmadge Meml. Hosp., Augusta, Ga., 1960-61, resident in pediatrics, 1962, 64-65, fellow in pediatric allergy, 1966-68; staff mem. Med. Coll. Ga., Augusta, 1979—, prof. pediat. medicine, interim dean Sch. Medicine, v.p. clin. activities, 2000—02, prof. emeritus, 2002—; vol. physician David Pk. Comm. Health Ctr., 2007—. Mem.: Am. Coll. Allergy, Asthma and Immunology, Am. Acad. Pediat., Am. Acad. Allergy and Immunology, Am. Pediatric Soc. Office: Med Coll Georgia BG 1009 Augusta GA 30912

WREN, BARRY GEORGE, gynecological endocrinologist, educator, researcher, consultant; b. Canowindra, NSW, Australia, Apr. 8, 1932; s. George Brien and Violel Ada (Bird) W.; m. Loloma Anne Cochrane, Jan. 2, 1957; children: Grahame, David, Michael. MB, BS, Sydney U., Australia, 1956; MD, U. NSW, 1972, M in Health Pers. Edn., 1978. Registrar KEMH, Perth, W. Australia, 1957-61, Hammersmith Hosp., London, 1961-62; dir. Maternity Svcs., We. Nigeria, 1963-64; assoc. prof. ob-gyn U. NSW, Australia, 1964-87; dir. Sydney Menopause Ctr. Royal Hosp. Women, Sydney, 1978-97, 1980—99. Pres. Australian Amarant Found., 1990—92; inaugural pres. Austrlian Menopause Soc., 1988—90. Author: Handbook of Obstetrics and Gynecology, 1978, 83, 87, 95, Your Choice, 1995; author, editor: Clinical Management of Menopause, 1996; editor: Proceedings 8th International Congress on Menopause, 1997. Decorated Order of Australia, 1999; recipient Inaugural Distinction award Australian Menopause Soc., 1995; Fotheringham fellow Royal Australian Coll. Ob-gyn, 1959. Fellow Royal Australian Coll. Ob-gyn., Royal Coll. Ob-gyn., Internat. Gynecol. Endocrinology Soc., Internat. Menopause Soc. (mem. sci. com. 1993-96, mem. exec. com. 1993-99), Australian Med. Assn., Australasian Menopause Soc. (1st pres. 1988-89). Avocations: golf, exploration. Home: 78 John St Woollahra NSW 2025 Australia Office: 506/180 Ocean St Edgecliff NSW 2027 Australia Business E-Mail: barrygwren@bigpond.com.

WRENN, CHRISTOPHER JAY, physician; b. Margarita, Panama Canal Zone, July 16, 1947; s. Earl Walton and Maxine Elizabeth (Luther) Wrenn; m. Nancy Margaret Bowie, June 27, 1970; children: Kristina Elizabeth, Courtney Bowie. BS, Baylor U., 1969; MD, U. Nebr., 1973. Diplomate Am. Bd. Pediatrics, Am. Bd. Allergy and Immunology. Intern pediatrics Children's Med. Ctr., Dallas, 1973-74, resident pediatrics, 1974-76, chief resident pediatrics, 1976-77; staff pediatrician Los Barrios Unidos Community Clinic, Dallas, 1977-78; fellow allergy and immunology Med. Br. U. Tex., Galveston, Tex., 1978-80; practice medicine specializing in allergy Graves-Gilbert Clinic, Bowling Green, Ky., 1980-83, Wichita Clinic, 1983-84, Allergy Clinic, Tyler, Tex., 1984—. Staff pediatrician Dallas County Juvenile Detention Ctr., 1975—78, Buckner Bapt. Children's Home, 1977—78. Co-author: Pediatrics by Self Instruction, 1982. Fellow: Am. Coll. Allergists, Am. Acad. Pediat.; mem.: Am. Acad. Allergy and Immunology. Presbyterian. Avocation: writing fiction and poetry. Office: Allergy Clinic PA 1128 Medical Dr Tyler TX 75701

WRIGHT, ALEXI A., physician; b. Athens, Ohio, Dec. 27, 1972; BA with honors, Stanford U., 1996; degree in Medicine, U. Pa., 2003. Resident Brigham and Women's Hosp., 2003—06; med. oncology fellow Dana-Farber Cancer Inst., 2006—09, attending physician, 2009—. Exec. com. mem. Nat. Comprehensive Cancer Network's Ovarian Cancer Outcomes Database, 2011. Recipient Dunne award, Brigham and Women's Hosp., Mentor award, Wellness Cmty. award. Mem.: Nat. Palliative Care Rsch. Ctr. (Career Devel. award), Am. Soc. Clin. Oncology (Merit award, Young Investigator award, Career Devel. award), Phi Beta Kappa. Avocation: writing. Office: Dana-Farber Cancer Inst 450 Bklyn Ave Boston MA 02215 Office Fax: 617-632-3479. Business E-Mail: alexi_wright@dfci.harvard.edu.

WRIGHT, CREIGHTON BOLTER, SR., cardiovascular surgeon, educator; b. Washington, Jan. 29, 1939; s. Benjamin Washington and Catherine Adele (Bolter) W.; m. Carolyn Eleanor Craver, Jan. 29, 1966; children: Creighton Bolter, Benson, Kathryn, Elizabeth. BA, Duke U., 1961, MD, 1965; MBA, Xavier U., Cin., 1995. Diplomate Am. Bd. Surgery, Am. Bd. Thoracic Surgery, Am. Bd. Gen. Vascular Surgery. Intern Duke U., Durham, NC, 1965—66; resident in surgery U. Va., Charlottesville, 1966—71; asst. prof., then assoc. prof. George Washington U., Washington, 1974—76; assoc. prof., then prof. surgery U. Iowa, Iowa City, 1976—81; prof. clin. surgery, assoc. dean U. Cin., 1982—; prof. clin. surgery Uniformed Svcs. U., 1982—; dir. dept. surgery Jewish Hosp., Cin., 1989—2003; med. dir. cardiovasc. svcs. Health Alliance Cin., 1999—2003; chief of staff VA Med. Ctr., Cin., 2003—07; pres. Cardiac, Vascular & Thoracic Surgeons Inc. Councilor Acad. Medicine, 2003—09; v.p., pres. Acad. Found., 2008—11. Editor: Vascular Grafting, 1983, (with others) Venous Trauma, 1983; contbr. articles to med. jours., chpts. to books. Col. USAR, 1966-93; Jewish Hospital Bd.; Sigma Chi, Cincinnati; UG Health, ZLC Health Bd. Colonel Medical Corps. Decorated Bronze Star; recipient Kindred Resident Tchr. award, 1967, Golden Apple Tchg. award, 1975, Tchg. award Jewish Hosp., 2001; Top Surgeons in Am.; Award of Excellence, Am. Heart Assn. SW Ohio Affiliate, 2003; Distinguished Achievement Award, AHA, Great Rivers Affiliate, 2008-2009; Francis Award, The Friar's Club for Volunteer Serv., Cincinnati, 2009; Dir's Community Leadership Award, Fed. Bureau of Investigation, 2010; Finalist Cin. Healthcare Hero 2011. Mem.: Greater Cin. Vascular Soc. (pres. 1997—98), Cin. Surgery Soc. (pres. 1996), Midwestern Vascular Surgery Soc., So. Thoracic Surgery Assn., Muller Surg. Soc. (pres. 1985—87), Am. Heart Assn. S.W. Ohio (v.p. 1998—, pres. 2000, Kaplan award 1999, award of excellence 2003, Disting. Svc. award 2009), Internat. Soc. Cardiovasc. Surgery, Ctrl. Surg. Assn., Soc. Thoracic Surgery, Am. Assn. Thoracic Surgery, Soc. Vascular Surgery, Soc. Univ. Surgeons, Assn. Acad. Surgery (pres. 1980), Optimists (v.p. 2009, pres. 2010), Comml. Club, Sigma Chi (Significant Sig award 1993, Hall of Fame 2005), Alpha Omega Alpha. Conservative. Episcopalian. Home: 312 E 2d St Covington KY 41011-1704 Office: Cardiac Vascular & Thoracic Surgeons 4030 Smith Rd Ste 300 Norwood OH 45209 Office Phone: 513-421-3494. Personal E-mail: cbw@one.net.

WRIGHT, DANA JACE, retired emergency nurse practitioner; b. Cleve., Apr. 20, 1952; d. William James and Murl Jean (White) Ewing; m. David Alan Samball, June 22, 1968 (div. Apr. 1971); 1 child, David; m. David M. Wright, July 11, 1981; children: William James, Karen Marie. A in Nursing, Valencia C.C., 1973, AA, 1973; BS in Respiratory Therapy, U. Cen. Fla., 1975; MEd, Auburn U., 1979; D in Nursing, Case Western Res. U., 1982. RN, Fla., Ohio, N.Y., Ga.; cert. emergency med. technician; cert. and registered respiratory therapist; cert. med.-surg. nurse; lic. real estate agt., N.Y. Nursing asst.

Holiday Hosp., Orlando, Fla., 1970-71, staff nurse critical care unit, intensive care unit, 1973; pvt. duty nurse Med. Personnel Pool, Orlando, 1973-74; nurse critical care burn team Upjohn, Inc., Augusta, Ga., 1976-77; ednl. dir. dept. respiratory therapy U. Hosp., Augusta, 1975-76; mem. staff respiratory therapy VA Hosp., Augusta, 1976-77; clin. instr. respiratory therapy Med. Coll. Ga., Augusta, 1976-77, Columbus Coll., 1977-78; ednl. dir. respiratory therapy Med. Ctr. Hosp., Columbus, 1977-79; staff nurse, relief supr. Kelly Health Care, Beachwood, Ohio, 1979-81; staff nurse Med. Staff, Inc., Cleve., 1981-83; dir. nursing S.R.T. Med. Staff Inc., Cleve., 1983; pres. Wright Properties, Buffalo, 1987-94, Med. Ctr. Vending, 1994-97; ret. nurse, 1994. Part-time nurse Millard Fillmore Suburban Hosp., 1990-91. Treas. Ch. Women's Assn., Snyder, N.Y., 1985-86, Clerk Ch. Coun., 2008-; mem. nursing resources panel North Ohio Lung Assn., 1981-82, mem. Women Grads.-USA.org, 2007-; mem. Profl. Parent Network, Buffalo, 1987—, Erie Co. Commn. on the Status of Women, 2000-08, vol. Food Shuttle, 1996-; rep. of McLain found. to grantmakers, 2000-; com. reviewer Internat. Charity Project Grants, 2004-09; bd. dirs. Virginia Guildersleeve Internat. Fund., 2008-09, v.p. Mem. ANA (alt. del. 1993-94), AAUW (mem. at large 2003-08), Am. Assn. Nurses Practicing Independently (assoc.), Nat. Nurses Bus., N.Y. State Nurses Assn. (nurse rsch. cons. 1991-92, 94, chair nurse entrepreneurs 1992-94, WNY regional review team 1992-94), Women's Dental Guild, Internat. Fedn. Univ. Women, Internat. Fedn. U. Women. Republican. Home and Office: 49 Colony Ct Buffalo NY 14226-3507 Personal E-mail: dwright394@aol.com.

WRIGHT, DELL, residential care and treatment facility executive; b. Greenville, SC, Aug. 29, 1944; s. Thomas C. and Marie (Tate) W.; m. Ines R. Teran, Oct 22, 1977; children: Anthony, Andre, Fionna, Al-Jonn. Diploma in computer tech., Control Data Inst., 1969. Electronic tester RCA, Marlboro, Mass., 1970-71; customer svc. rep. Honeywell Info. Systems, Inc., Waltham, Mass., 1971-75; computer technician Bendix Field Engring., Columbia, Md., 1975-78; sr. field engr. Ford Aerospace and Comm. Corp., Palo Alto, Calif., 1978-79; systems integration engr. Kentron Internat./NASA/JPL, Pasadena, Calif., 1979-83; sr. fabrication technician Rockwell Internat., Anaheim, Calif., 1983-84; computer engr. Al-Johi Internat., Dhahran, Saudi Arabia, 1984-85; sr. test engr. Gen. Dynamics, San Diego, 1985-88; owner Wrights Food Vending Svc., 1988—90; pres., founder Residential Care and Treatment Facility for Youth, 1991—. Author: Inspirational, 1995, My Life's Journey, 2005; inventor mechanical multiple picture frame. Chair, utilities commr. City of Colton, Calif., 1996—. With U.S. Army, 1962-65. Democrat. Avocations: rv camping, fishing, motorcycling.

WRIGHT, HARRY HERCULES, psychiatrist; b. Charleston, SC, Jan. 4, 1948; s. Harry Vernon and Agnes Lucile (Simmons) W. BS, U. S.C., 1970, MD, MBA, U. Pa., 1976. Resident in psychiatry Wm. S. Hall Psychiat. Inst., Columbia, SC, 1977—79; adminstrv. fellow in psychiatry NIMH, Rockville, Md., 1979; fellow in child psychiatry William S. Hall Psychiat. Inst., 1979—81, instr. child psychiatrist, 1981—; instr. dept. neuropsychiatry and behavioral sci. U. S.C. Sch. Medicine, 1981—82, asst. prof., 1982—86, assoc. prof., 1986—90, prof., 1990—. Contbr. articles to profl. jours. Bd. dirs. Carolina Children's Home, 1992—, Zero to Three, 1997—; bd. trustees, First Steps to Sch. Readiness, 1999-2003; mem. landmarks commn. City of Columbia, 1986-98. Recipient Freed award, Hall Psychiat. Inst., 1978, Outstanding Svc. award, Sickle Cell Found., Clin. Sci. Rsch. award, 1998, Am.'s Top Doctors award, 2001—, Rsch. Advancement award, U. SC, 2002, 2004, 2006, 2008; grantee Falk fellow, 1977—79, Laughlin fellow, 1979. Mem.: Am. Coll. Psychiatrists, Am. Soc. Human Genetics, Soc. Study Psychiatry and Culture, Acad. Orgnl. and Occupl. Psychiatry, So. Med. Assn., Am. Soc. Adolescent Psychiatry, World Assn. Infant Mental Health, World Psychiat. Assn., Am. Acad. Child Psychiatry, Am. Physiatry Assn., Autism Soc. Am., Riverbank Zool. Soc., Sigma Xi, Omicron Delta Kappa. Methodist. Home: PO Box 12474 Columbia SC 29211-2474 Office: 3555 Harden St Ext Ste 301 Columbia SC 29203-6894 Office Phone: 803-434-4250, 803-261-9316. Business E-Mail: harry.wright@uscmed.sc.edu.

WRIGHT, JANE COOKE, oncologist, educator, consultant; b. NYC, Nov. 30, 1919; d. Louis T. and Corinne (Cooke) W.; m. David D. Jones. AB, Smith Coll., 1942; MD with honors, N.Y. Med. Coll., 1945; D in Med. Scis., Women's Med. Coll. Pa., 1965; ScD, Denison U., 1971. Intern Bellevue Hosp., NYC, 1945-46, resident, 1946, mem. staff, 1955-67; resident Harlem Hosp., 1947, chief resident, 1948; clin. Cancer Rsch. Found., Harlem Hosp., 1949-52; dir., 1952-55; mem. staff Harlem Hosp., 1949-55; practice medicine specializing in clin. cancer chemotherapy NYC; mem. faculty dept. surgery Med. Ctr., N.Y. U., NYC, 1955-67, adj. assoc. prof., 1961-67, also dir. cancer chemotherapy services research, 1955-67; prof. surgery N.Y. Med. Coll., NYC, 1967-87, prof. surgery emeritus, 1987—, assoc. dean, 1967-75; mem. staff Manhattan VA Hosp., 1955-67, Midtown, Met., Bird S. Color, Flower-Fifth Ave. Hosps., all NYC, 1967-79, Westchester County Med. Center, Valhalla, NY, 1971-87, Lincoln Hosp., Bronx, NY, 1979-87. Cons. Health Ins. Plan of Greater N.Y., 1962—94, Blvd. Hosp., 1963—, St. Luke's Hosp., Newburgh, NY, 1964—; pelvic malignancy rev. com. N.Y. Gynecol. Soc., 1965—66, St. Vincent's Hosp., NYC, 1966—, Dept. Health, Edn. and Welfare, 1968—70, Wyckoff Heights Hosp., NYC, 1969—, NIH, 1971—, others; adv. bd. Skin Cancer Found. Contbr. articles to profl. jours. Mem. Manhattan coun. State Commn. Human Rights, 1949—, Pres.'s Commn. Heart Disease, Cancer and Stroke, 1964-65, Nat. Adv. Cancer Coun. NIH, 1966-70, N.Y. State Women's Coun., 1970-72; bd. dirs. Medico-CARE, Health Svcs. Improvement Fund Inc.; trustee Smith Coll., Northampton, Mass., 1970-80. Recipient numerous awards, including; Mademoiselle mag. award, 1952; Lady Year award Harriet Beecher Stowe Jr. High Sch., 1958; Spirit Achievement award Albert Einstein Sch. Medicine, 1965; certificate Honor award George Gershwin Jr. High Sch., 1967; Myrtle Wreath award Hadassah, 1967; Smith medal Smith Coll., 1968; Outstanding Am. Women award Am. Mothers Com. Inc., 1970; honored as one of 150 Am. Women Physicians at exhbn. Changing the Face of Medicine at the Nat. Libr. Medicine, NIH, 2003; Golden Plate award Am. Acad. Achievement, 1971; Exceptional Black Scientists Poster Ciba Geigy, 1980. Fellow N.Y. Acad. Medicine; mem. Nat. Med. Assn. (edit. bd. jours.), Manhattan Ctrl. Med. Soc., N.Y. County Med. Soc. (nominating com.), AMA, AAAS, Am. Assn. Cancer Rsch. (dir. Rsch. Salute 1971-74, Appreciation award for 50 Yr.of service, 2004, established Jane Cooke Wright lectureship 2006), N.Y. Acad. Scis., N.Y. Cancer Soc., Internat. Med. and Rsch. Found. (v.p.), Am. Cancer Soc. (dir. div.), N.Y. Cancer Soc. (pres. 1970-71), Am. Soc. Clin. Oncology (sec. treas. 1964-67, Spl. Appreciation award as a founding mem. 2004), Contin Soc., Sigma Xi, Lambda Kappa Mu, Alpha Omega Alpha. Clubs: The 400 (N.Y. Med. Coll.). Achievements include AACR and AACR minorities in Cancer Research (MICR) council has selected to name a lectureship in my honour. Address: 7002 Kennedy Blvd East Apt 9C Guttenberg NJ 07093 Home Phone: 201-662-8922. *

WRIGHT, JEREMY JOHN, cardiologist; b. Lae, Papua New Gunea, May 14, 1973; MBBS (hon.), U. Western Australia, 1997. Cardiologist Hearts First Greenslopes Pvt. Hosp., 2005—. Rsch. grant, Gallipoli Rsch. Found. Fellow: Cardiac Soc. Australia & New Zealand, Royal Australasian Coll. Physicians; mem.: Soc. Cardiovasc. Computed Tomography. Avocation: surfing. Personal E-mail: jeremy@hearts1st.com.

WRIGHT, JESSE HARTZELL, psychiatrist, educator; b. Altoona, Pa., Sept. 21, 1943; s. Jesse H. and Marion (Stone) W.; m. Susanne Judy Wright, July 9, 1967; children: Andrew, Laura. BS, Juniata Coll., 1965; MD, Jefferson Med. Coll., 1969; PhD, U. Louisville, 1976. Diplomate Am. Bd. Psychiatry and Neurology, Am. Bd. Med. Examiners; lic. psychiatrist, Ky. Asst. prof. U. Louisville, 1975-79, assoc. prof., 1979-87, prof., 1987—; clin. dir. Norton Psychiat. Clinic, Louisville, 1975-83, med. dir., 1983—2009; chief adult psychiatry U. Louisville, 2000—09, vice-chmn academic affairs, dir. depression ctr., dept. psychiat., 2009—; resident in psychiatry U. Mich., Ann Arbor, 1970-73. Author: first multimedia computer program for psychotherapy, Good Days Ahead, author: (self help book for depression) Getting Your Life Back, (textbooks with DVD) Learning Cognitive-Behavior Therapy, Cognitive-Behavior Therapy for Severe Mental Illness, High-Yield Cognitive-Behavior Therapy for Brief Sessions (Health Book of Yr. Brit. Med. Soc., 2009), Breaking Free From Defness: Pathways to Wellness, others; chpts. to books; contbr. articles to prof. jours. Fellow Am.Psychiat. Assn., Am. Coll. Psychiatrists; mem. Ky. Psychiat. Assn. (sec. 1979-80, v.p. 1980-81, pres. 1982-83), Acad. Cognitive Therapy (founding pres.), Alpha Omega Alpha. Avocations: gardening, running, theater, skiing. Home: 15 Indian Hills Trl Louisville KY 40207-1532 Office: Univ Psychiatric Group 401 E Chestnut St Louisville KY 40202

WRIGHT, JOHN BARRY DEBENHAM, child psychiatrist, consultant, educator; MB, BS, St Bartholomew's Hosp., London, 1985; M in Med Sci., Leeds U., Eng., 1994; MD, London U., 2000. DCH Royal Coll. Physicians. Sr. registrar in child psychiatry Leeds Rotational Tng. Scheme, 1992—95; cons. child and adolescent psychiatry York, 1995—. Mental health curriculum convenor Hull York Med. Sch., hon. sr. lectr., Clin. Lead Nat. Deaf Child & Adolescent Mental Health Svcs., 2009—, U. Cat Test Devel. Group, 2010—. Author: How to Live with Autism and Asperger Syndrome. A Practical Guide for Parents and Professionals, 2004, (children's book) Slates Pulls it Off, 2003, editor 100 cases in psychiatry textbook; contbr. articles to profl. jours. NIHR Rsch. grants. Fellow: Royal Coll. Psychiatrists. Achievements include leading Child Mental Health Research Programme in Yorkshire. Office: Lime Trees Child and Family Unit 31 Shipton Rd York YO30 5RE England Office Fax: 01904 632893.

WRIGHT, JOHN CHARLES YOUNG, JR., obstetrician, gynecologist; MD, West Va. U. Diplomate Am. Bd. Ob-Gyn, lic. Ohio, 1979, Pa., 1985. Resident Wright-Patterson Med. Ctr., 1982, Miami Valley Hosp., 1982; hosp. affiliations include East Liverpool City Hosp., Ellwood City Hosp., Heritage Valley Beaver, Pa. Fellow: Am. Congress of Obstetricians and Gynecologists. Office: Heritage Valley Beaver 1000 Dutch Ridge Rd Beaver PA 15009 Office Phone: 724-775-6636.

WRIGHT, JOHN ROBERT, retired pathologist, educator; b. Winnipeg, Man., Can., Aug. 18, 1935; came to U.S., 1961, naturalized, 1968; s. Ross Grant and Anna Marie (Crispin) W.; m. Deanna Pauline Johnson, June 25, 1960 (dec. May 24, 2004), Janet Elizabeth, Aug. 21, 2006; children— Carolyn Deanna, David John. MD with honors, U. Man., 1959. Diplomate: Am. Bd. Pathology. Intern Winnipeg Gen. Hosp., 1959-60, resident, 1960-61, Balt. City Hosp., 1961-63, Buffalo Gen. Hosp., 1963-64; teaching fellow in medicine U. Man., 1960-61; instr. in pathology, Buswell fellow SUNY-Buffalo, 1965-67, prof. pathology, chmn. dept. pathology, 1974-96, interim dean medicine, v.p. clin. affairs, 1997-98, dean medicine, 1998—2001; asst. chief pathology Balt. City Hosps. and; asst. prof. Johns Hopkins U., 1967-74; cons. Roswell Park Meml. Inst., 1975—2005, bd. visitors, 1981-97, interim dir., 1985-86, chmn. bd. visitors, 1987-97; ret., 2005. Recipient Louis A. and Ruth Siegel Disting. Teaching award SUNY-Buffalo, 1977, 78, 88, Deans award SUNY, 1987. Fellow Assn. Pathology Chairs (sr., pres. 1994-96); mem. AMA, AAAS, Coll. Am. Pathologists, Am. Soc. Investigative Pathologists, Am. Soc. Clin. Pathologists, U.S. and Can. Acad. Pathology, Alpha Omega Alpha. Achievements include research in amyloidosis and aging. Home: 46 Wynngate Ln Williamsville NY 14221-1840 Office: 206 Farber Hall SUNY Buffalo NY 14214 Personal E-mail: jrwright@buffalo.edu.

WRIGHT, LARRY JAN, epidemiologist; s. J. Evan and Mary Bluemel Wright; m. LaVonda Eddington, June 17, 1960; children: Deborah Hamilton, Karl Larry, Tana Lynn. BS, U. Utah, Salt Lake City, 1960, MD, 1964. Diplomate Am. Bd. Internal Medicine, 1972. Intern, resident on ward medicine Barnes Hosp. Wash. U., St. Louis, 1964—66; clin. assoc. Nat. Inst. Allergy and Infectious Diseases, Bethesda, Md., 1966—68; sr. med. resident U. Wash. Hosps., Seattle, 1968—69; clin. infectious disease fellow U. Wash., Seattle, 1969—71; pvt. practice Inter-Mountain Clinic, Salt Lake City, 1971—89; clin. dir. microbiology, virology, and molecular laboratories LDS Hosp. and Urban Ctrl. Region, Salt Lake City, 1989—2000, infectious disease cons., epidemiology rschr., 1989—2007. Pres. InterMountain Clinic, Inc, Salt Lake City, 1981—86; vice chmn. dept. medicine LDS Hosp., Salt Lake City, 1988—89, pres. med. staff, 1989—90; bd. govs. IHC Corp., Salt Lake City, 1989—91. Contbr. articles to profl. jours. Governing bd. Work Activity Ctr. for Adults with Disabilities, Salt Lake City, 1992—98. Lt. comdr. USPHS, 1966—68. Nat. Found. scholar, March of Dimes, 1960—64. Fellow: ACP, Infectious Disease Soc. Am.; mem.: Am. Soc. for Internal Medicine, Am. Soc. for Microbiology, Alpha Omega Alpha, Phi Beta Kappa. Achievements include research in infectious diseases. Avocations: sailing, skiing, golf, hiking, travel.

WRIGHT, MATTHEW JUSTIN, psychologist, researcher; b. Fresno, Calif., Sept. 26, 1973; s. Tim G. Wright and Helene K. (Burrell) Kipp. BA, Calif. State U., Fresno, 1997, MA, 2001; PhD, Wash. State U., Pullman, 2006. Lic. psychologist Calif., 2009. Postdoc. fellow U. Calif., LA, 2006—08; dir. neuropsychology svcs. & tng. Harbor-UCLA Med. Ctr., Torrance, 2008—. Contbr. chapters to books, articles to profl. jours. Neuropsychology HIV-AIDS fellowship, NIMH, 2006—08. Mem.: APA, Cognitive Neurosci. Soc., Internat. Neuropsychol. Soc. Achievements include development of Item-Specific Deficit Approach (ISDA) to evaluating verbal memory dysfunction. Office: Harbor-UCLA Med Ctr 1124 W Carson St B-4 South PO Box 490 Torrance CA 90502 Business E-Mail: mwright@labiomed.org.

WRIGHT, THEODORE ROBERT FAIRBANK, biologist, educator; b. Kodaikanal, Tamil Nadu, India, Apr. 10, 1928; s. Horace Kepler and Adelaide Caskey (Fairbank) Wright; m. Eileen Marie Yongen, Jan. 6, 1951 (dec. Jan. 2002). AB in Biology, Princeton U., 1949; MA in Biology, Wesleyan U., 1954; PhD in Zoology, Yale U., 1959. Asst. professor biology Johns Hopkins U., Balt., 1959-65; assoc. prof. biology U. Va., Charlottesville, 1965-75, prof. biology, 1975-95; prof. emeritus, 1995—. Vis. scientist Max Planck Inst. for Biology, Tubingen, 1975-76, Devel. Biology Ctr., U. Calif., Irvine, 1982. Editor: The Genetics and Biology of Drosophila, vol. 2a-c, 1978, vol. 2d, 1980, Genetic Regulatory Hierarchies in Development, 1990; co-editor: Advances in Genetics, 1988-92. With U.S. Army, 1950-52. NIH postdoctoral fellow Max Planck Inst. for Biology, Tubingen, Fed. Republic Germany, 1958-59; NSF grantee, 1967-72, 90-93; NIH grantee, 1972-93; Am. Cancer Soc. grantee, 1988-90. Fellow AAAS; mem. AAUP, Genetics Soc. Am., Soc. for Devel. Biology, Va. Acad. Sci., Sigma Xi.

WRIGHT, WILLIAM EVAN, physician, consultant; b. NYC, Aug. 1, 1946; s. Samuel and Frances Elnora (Perpente) W.; m. Diana Claire Dryer, Aug. 15, 1970; children: Jason William, Elizabeth Garland, Edwin Samuel. BA in Music, U. Rochester, 1968; MD, U. Pa., 1972; MSPH, U. Utah, 1979, MS in Physiology, Harvard U., 1980. Diplomate Am. Bd Internal Medicine, Am. Bd. Preventive Medicine, Occupl. Medicine, Am. Bd. Ind. Med. Examiners; ACOEM cert. med. rev. officer; cert. FAA med. examiner, Am. Bd. Disability Analysis. Intern LDS Hosp., Salt Lake City, 1972-73, resident, 1973-75, U. Utah Med. Ctr., Salt Lake City, 1978-79, Harvard Sch. Pub. Health, Boston, 1979-80; asst. prof. U. So. Calif., LA, 1980-86; med. dir. U.S. DEA, Arlington, Va., 1986-96; program mgr., site med. dir. DynCorp, Reston, Va., 1991-96; med. dir. Md. Office, CORE, Inc., Irvine, Calif., 1996—2003; cons. Office of Worker Advocacy, U.S. Dept. Energy, Washington, 2003—05; pres. Work Wright, Inc., 2003—. Cons. Westwood Group, 2003—05; dist. med. cons. U.S. Dept. Labor, 2006—; med. dir. Reliable Review Svcs., Boca Raton, Fla., 2007—. Author, editor: (med. textbook) Couturier's Occupational and Environmental Infectious Diseases, 2009; Contbr. articles to profl. jours. Maj. M.C., U.S. Army, 1975-77. Fellow ACP, Am. Coll. Occupl. and Environ. Medicine, mem. Cosmos Club (Washington), Alpha Omega Alpha. Avocation: music. Home: 6801 Womberly Way Mc Lean VA 22101-1532 Office Phone: 703-356-0092. E-mail: 1we_wright@post.harvard.edu.

WRIGHTMAN, CAROLINE ANNE MCGHEE, nursing educator; b. Mar. 14, 1942; d. William Hanen and Lola Jeanette (Oberg) McGhee; m. Larry Keith Wrightman, Mar. 24, 1974. BSN, Loma Linda U., 1965; MNursing in Psychiatry, UCLA, 1975. Clin. instr. pediat. Pacific Union Coll., Glendale, Calif., 1970—72; clin. instr. psychiat. nursing LA County Sch. Nursing, 1972—73; crisis unit dir., mental health counselor LA County Mental Health, Arcadia, 1976—79; adminstrv. dir. psychiatry Fla. Hosp., Orlando, 1979—84; dir. inpatient svcs. Battle Creek (Mich.) Adventist Hosp., 1984—86; asst. prof. Walla Walla Coll., Portland, Oreg., 1988—91, 1999—2006; case mgr. Pacificare Behavioral Health, 1996—98; county designated mental health profl. Columbia River Mental Health, Vancouver, Wash., 1991—96, nurse care coord., 2006—07; dir. nursing edn. Concorde Career Coll., Portland, Oreg., 2008—11; program dir. Carrington Coll., 2011—. Adventist. Home: 11528 SE Tyler Rd Portland OR 97086-6844 Office: Office Carrington Coll 2010 Lloyd Ctr Portland OR 97232 Office Phone: 503-575-1040. Personal E-mail: wrightmanc@juno.com.

WRÓBEL, ANDRZEJ, neurophysiologist; s. Jerzy and Hanna Wróbel; m. Liliana Wróbel; children: Jacek, Olga. MSc, U. Warsaw, 1969; PhD, DSc, Nencki Inst. Exptl. Biology. Cert. neurosci. prof. 1996. Dir. dept. neurophysiology Nencki Inst. Exptl. Biology, Warsaw, 2002—; chair neurocognition processes Warsaw Sch. Social Psychology, 2005—10. Presidial mem. Internat. Brain Rsch. Orgn., 1996—98. Editor: Acta Neurobiologiae Experimentals; contbr. chapters to books, articles to profl. jours. Recipient Rsch. Excellence award, Polish Acad. Sci., 1975, 1983, 1993, 2001, 2009, Warsaw Sch. Social Psychology, 2006. Mem.: Soc. Neuroscience, Fedn. European Neuroscience Assns., Polish Neuroscience Soc. (pres. 1995—97), European Brain and Behavior Soc. (presidial com. mem. 2004—07). Achievements include research in beta EEG activity as an attentional carrier in the brain. Office: Nencki Inst Exptl Biology L Pasteur 3 Warsaw 02-093 Poland Business E-Mail: wrobel@nencki.gov.pl.

WRONG, OLIVER MURRAY, retired medicine educator, consultant physician; b. Oxford, Eng., Feb. 7, 1925; s. Edward Murray and Rosalind Grace (Smith) W.; m. Marilda Musacchio, June 8, 1956; children: Jessica, Michela. BA, Oxford U., 1945, BM, 1947, DM, 1964. Jr. physician United Oxford Hosps., 1947-51; sr. intern in medicine Toronto (Ont., Can.) Gen. Hosp., 1951-52; clin. rsch. fellow Mass. Gen. Hosp., Boston, 1952-53; tutor in medicine Manchester (Eng.) U., 1954-58; med. asst. Univ. Coll. Hosp. Med. Sch., London, 1959-61; lectr. medicine Royal Postgrad. Med. Sch., London, 1961-69; prof. medicine Dundee (Scotland) U., 1969-72, Univ. Coll., London, 1972-90, dir. dept., 1972-82, prof. emeritus, 1990—. Chmn.

Nat. Kidney Rsch. Fund, U.K., 1976-80; vis. prof. medicine Harvard U., Boston, 1974, Sherbrooke (Que., Can.) U., 1974, U. Toronto, 1976, McGill U., 1976. Co-author: (monograph) The Large Intestine: Its Role in Mammalian Nutrition and Homeostasis, 1981; contbr. articles on renal and intestinal function and disease to med. jours. Capt. M.C., Royal Army, 1948-50. Fellow Royal Coll. Physicians (London), Royal Coll. Physicians (Edinburgh); mem. Royal Soc. Medicine, Assn. Physicians Gt. Britain and Ireland. Avocations: baroque music, country, gardens, travel. Home: Flat 8 96-100 New Cavendish St London W1W 6XN England Office Phone: 020 7637 4740. Personal E-mail: oliverwrong@aol.com.

WRONSKI, IAN, physician, educator; b. Tel-Aviv, Apr. 10, 1951; arrived in Australia, 1951; s. Chaskel and Genia (Borek) W.; m. Maggie Al Grant, Nov. 25, 1983; children: Daniel, Miriam. MB, BS, Monash U., Melbourne, Australia, 1976; diploma, Liverpool U., Eng., 1984; MPH, Harvard U., 1989, SM in Epidemiology, 1990. Resident med. officer Victorian Hosp., Melbourne, 1977—79; fellow Victorian Acad. Gen. Practice, Melbourne, 1980; med. dir. Broome Regional Aboriginal Med. Svc., Australia, 1981—86; dir. health svcs. Kimberley Aboriginal Med. Svcs. Coun., Broome, 1986—92; dir. Anton Breine Ctr. for Tropical Medicine, Townsville, Australia, 1992—99; found. prof., head dept. pub. health and tropical medicine James Cook U., Townsville, 1994—98, exec. dean faculty health and molecular scis., 1997—2000, exec. dean faculty medicine, health and molecular scis., 2000—, pro-vice chancellor medicine, health and molecular scis., 2005—. Assoc. health svcs. adv. com. Healthpartner, 2003—; communicable diseases adv. com. Aboriginal and Torres Strait Islander Commn., 1987—91; mem. health svcs. adv. com. Australian Consumer & Competition Coun., 2003—. Design author: (software) Healthplanner, 1987; contbr. articles to profl. jours. Recipient Surgeon Gen. John White medal, 2008; Life Fellow, Australian Coll. Rural and Remote Medicine, 2007. Fellow Australasian Coll. Tropical Medicine (coun. mem. 1994-96), Australasian Faculty of Pub. Health Medicine, Royal Australian Coll. Gen. Practitioners, Australian Coll. Rural and Remote Medicine (life, pres. 2000-2003); mem. Royal Australasian Coll. Physicians (Aboriginal health com. 1991—), Rural Drs. Assn. Queensland (aboriginal and Torres Strait Island health com. 1993). Avocations: piano, stamp collecting/philately. Office: James Cook Univ Fac Medicine Health & Molecular Scis Townsville 4811 QLD Australia Home Phone: 61-7-47212325; Office Phone: 61-7-47815330. Business E-Mail: ian.wronski@jcu.edu.au.

WROTEN, DAVID, medical association administrator; BA in Fin., Ark. State U., MBA, 1983. Bus. cons. officer Small Bus. Devel. Ctr., Ark. State U., Jonesboro; profl. rels. coord. Ark. Med. Soc., Little Rock, 1983—86, asst. exec. v.p., 1986—2005, exec. v.p., 2005—. Pres., CEO AMS Benefits Inc.; mem. Gov.'s Medicaid Adv. Com. Named to The Power List, ArkansasBusiness.com, 2009. Mem.: Ark Soc. Assn. Executives (pres. 2002—03), Am. Assn. Med. Soc. Executives, Am. Soc. Assn. Executives. Office: Ark Med Soc PO Box 55088 #10 Corporate Hill Dr Ste 300 Little Rock AR 72215 Office Phone: 501-224-8967. Office Fax: 501-224-6489. Business E-Mail: dwroten@arkmed.org. *

WRYE, SCOTT W., plastic surgeon, educator; Grad. with honors, SUNY. Diplomate Am. Bd. Surgery, Am. Bd. Plastic Surgery. Resident in gen. surgery Univ. Colo.; plastic surgery tng. Pa. State Univ.; pvt. practice Hall and Wrye Plastic Surgeons, Nev. Author: various publs. Recipient Intern of the Yr., Outstanding Tchr. Mem.: Alpha Omega Alpha. Office: Hall and Wrye Plastic Surgeons 635 Sierra Rose Dr Ste A Reno NV 89511 Office Phone: 775-284-8296. Office Fax: 775-332-6583.

WU, CARL, medical researcher; m. Gisela Storz; children: Ella, Toby, Felix. Grad., Saint Mary's Coll., Calif., 1974; PhD in Biology, Harvard U., 1979. Postdoc. fellow Harvard U., 1979—82; staff mem. Nat. Cancer Inst., NIH, 1982—, chief Lab. Biochemistry & Molecular Biology, Ctr. Cancer Rsch., 1996—, head Chromosome Structure & Gene Regulation Sect. Contbr. articles to sci. jours. Recipient Outstanding Young Scientist award, Md. Acad. Scis., 1987, Young Investigator award, American Soc. Biochemistry & Molecular Biology, 1992. Mem.: NAS, Inst. Medicine, American Acad. Arts & Scis. Office: Lab Molecular Cell Biology Nat Cancer Inst Ctr Cancer Rsch 37 Convent Dr Bldg 37 Rm 6068 Bethesda MD 20892-4255 Office Phone: 301-496-3029. Office Fax: 301-435-3697. E-mail: carlwu@helix.nih.gov. *

WU, CHING-YI, occupational therapist, educator; d. Chi-pin Wu and Yu-yun Yu. BS, Nat. Taiwan U., Taipei, 1990; MS, Boston U., 1993, DSc, 1997. Registered occupl. therapist Nat. Bd. for Cert. Occupl. Therapy, Inc, 1992, cert. Taiwan Occupl. Therapy Assn., 1998. Occupl. therapist Ya-Tung Meml. Hosp., Paochou, Taiwan, 1990—91; asst. prof. Chang Gung U., Kwei-shan, Taoyuan, Taiwan, 1997—2001, vice chair, dept. occupl. therapy, 1998—2008, assoc. prof., dept. occupl. therapy, 2001—08, prof., dept. occupl. therapy, 2008—; chair Dept. Occupl. Therapy & Grad. Inst. Behavioral Sci., 2008—. Recipient awards for excellence in rsch., Nat. Sci. Coun., Taipei, 1997—99, 2000 Outstanding Intellectuals 21st Century award, 2008—10, 21st Century award, 2008—09; named Leading Educators of World, 2008, Internat. Health Professor of Yr., 2008, Internat. Profl. of Yr., 2008; named to Dictionary of Internat. Biography, 2009; Ann Henderson scholar, Boston U., 1996, Rsch. grant, Nat. Sci. Coun., Taipei, 1998—2003, 2004—, Nat. Health Rsch. Insts., Taipei, 2001—05, 2008—. Mem.: World Fedn. Occupl. Therapists (rev. bd. mem. 1993—95), Taiwan Occupl. Therapists Union (cons. rsch. devel. com. 1993—95, rsch. devel. com. mem. 2004—10, exec. editor 2005—09, dir., academic devel. com. 2010—), Taiwan Occupl. Therapy Assn. (jour. cons. 1998—2000, academic devel. com. mem. 2000—02, internat. affairs com. mem 2006—10, standing dir. 2009—10, dir. acad. devel. com. mem. 2009—10, rsch. devel. com. mem. 2009—, academic devel. com. mem. 2011—, 2011—). Achievements include dictionary of international biography. Office: Chang Gung Univ Dept Occupl Therapy 259 Wen-hwa 1 Rd Taoyuan 333 Taiwan Home: 9 Alley 42 Ln 392 Rude 1 Rd Sijhih City Taipei 221 Taiwan Office Fax: 886 3 2118700.

WU, CHUNG-JUNG, endocrinologist, researcher; b. Taichung, Taiwan, Dec. 28, 1967; MD, Taipei Med. Coll., Taiwan, 1993; MA, Nanhua U., 2005. Intern, resident, 1994—99; internal dr. Taichung Vets. Gen. Hosp., 1994—99; chief attending dr. in endocrinology and metabolism Chia-Yi Vets. Hosp., Taiwan, 1999—. Office: Chia-Yi Vets Hosp 600 Ssu-Hsien Rd Sect 2 Chiayi 60093 Taiwan Office Phone: 886 5 2359630 ext. 2507. Office Fax: 886 5 2369676; Home Fax: 886 4 22428423. Personal E-mail: cjwu_doctor@yahoo.com.tw. Business E-Mail: cjwu@vghtc.gov.tw.

WU, FANG, research scientist; b. China, Apr. 23, 1972; PhD, Sichuan U., 2003. Assoc. prof. SW Jiaotong U., 2006; postdoc. fellow Lab Molecular Biology and Cell Differentiation, Inst. Nat. Santé et de la Recherche Médicale, 2005—06; postdoc. fellow dept. pharm. scis. SUNY, Buffalo, 2009—; postdoc assoc. Ctr. Vaccine Biology and Immunology, U. Rochester Med. Ctr., 2007—09. Office: University Buffalo 544 Hochstetter Hall Buffalo NY 14260 E-mail: wufang3@gmail.com.

WU, HONG, pathologist; arrived in U.S., 1988; d. Xin-Yu Wu and Xu-Zhi Xu; m. Lance Mark Wiseman, Nov. 24, 1999. MD, Peking Union Med. Coll., Beijing, 1986; PhD, U. Va., 1992. Diplomate in surg. and clin. pathology and in dermatopathology Am. Bd. Pathology. Rsch. asst. dept. med. genetics Inst. Basic Med. Scis., Chinese Acad. Med. Scis., Beijing, 1987—88; rsch. assoc. dept. microbiology U. Va. Sch. Medicine, Charlottesville, 1993—94; resident dept. pathology and lab. medicne U. Pa., 1994—99, fellow dept. dermatology, 1999—2000; mem., staff pathologist dept. pathology Fox Chase Cancer Ctr., Phila., 2000—. Contbr. articles to profl. jours. Mem.: Am. Soc. Clin. Pathologists, Internat. Soc. Dermatopathology, Am. Soc. Dermatopathology. Office: Fox Chase Cancer Ctr 333 Cottman Ave Philadelphia PA 19111 Office Phone: 215-728-6900. E-mail: hong.wu@fccc.edu.

WU, HSIN-LUNG, pharmacist, educator, consultant; s. Wan-Der and Pan (Chen) W.; m. Pi-O Chuang, Nov. 12, 1968; children: Yii-Der, Yie-Wen. PhD, Osaka U., Japan, 1985. Cert. pharmacist Dept. Health, 1964. Dir. Hosp. pharmacy Kaohsiung Med. U. Hosp.; dir. libr. Kaohsiung Med. U., Taiwan, 1978—80, dean bus. affairs, 1981—88, dir. natural product rsch. ctr., 1988—91, dir. sch. pharmacy, 1988—94, dir. grad. inst. pharm. sci., founding dir. coll. pharmacy, cons., 2006—, emeritus prof., 2010—. Sr. editor Chinese Pharm. Jour., 1995—; editor Kaohsiung Jour. Med. Scis., 1992-96; cons. Nat. Sci. Coun., 1992-93, Min. Examinations, 1989-94, 2000-10, adv. Taiwan EPA. Contbr. scientific papers (Top Referee, 2007, Outstanding alumni sci., 2006, Excellence in tchg. award, 1998, 2001, 2006). Vol. KMU Pharmacy Alumni Assn., 1988—2009. Recipient Prestige Sr. Educator Award, Ministry of Edn, Sr. Educator award, MInistry of Edn., 2007. Mem. Pharm. Soc. Taiwan, Chinese Chem. Soc., Formosa Assn. Advancement Sci., Chinese Environ. Analytical Soc., Taiwan Mass Spectrometry Soc., Am. Chem. Soc. (Outstanding Alumni in sci. 2006). Office: Kaohsiung Med Univ #100 Shih-Chuan 1st Rd Kaohsiung 807 Taiwan Office Fax: 886-7-3159597. Business E-Mail: hlwu@kmu.edu.tw.

WU, HUAI-NING, engineering educator; b. Anhui, China, Nov. 15, 1972; PhD, Xi'an Jiaotong U., 1997. Postdoc. rschr. dept. electronic engring. Beijing Inst. Tech., 1997—99; assoc. prof. Sch. Automation Sci. and Elec. Engring., Beihang U., 1999—2008, prof., 2008—; rsch. fellow Dept. Mfg. Engring. & Engring. Mgmt., City U. Hong Kong, 2008, 2010. Blue Sky Scholar disting. prof. Beihang U. Recipient First Class Natural Sci. award, Ministry Edn., China, New Century Excellent Talents award, Blue Sky New Star, Beihang U. Mem.: Chinese Assn. Automation, Com. Tech. Process Failure Diagnosis and Safety. Avocations: ping pong/table tennis, hiking. Office: 37 Xue Yuan Rd Haidian Dist Beijing 100191 China Business E-Mail: huainingwu@163.com.

WU, JI, biologist; b. Chenzhou, Hunan, China, Mar. 17, 1963; d. Zhangrong Wu and Heai He; m. Qi Tian; 1 child, Geng Tian. MD, Hengyang Med. Coll., China, 1983; MS, Nanjing Ry. Coll., China, 1994; PhD, Beijing Med. U., 1997. Gynecologist Chenzhou Women's and Children's Hosp., 1983—91; postdoctoral fellow U. Gottingen and German Primate Ctr., 1997—99; postdoctoral rsch. assoc. U. Utah, Salt Lake City, 1999—2001; assoc. scientist Temple U., Phila., 2001—. External assessor Rsch. Grants Coun., Hong Kong, 2004—. Contbr. articles to profl. jours.; mem. editl. bd. (jour.) Reproductive Biology and Endocrinology, 2002—. Recipient Excellent Paper award, China Jour. Ob-Gyn., 1999, Japanese Medicine award, 1st Pharm. Co. of Japan and Internat. Health Exch. Ctr., 1996, award of Extraordinary Abilities Honor in Chenzhou, Pub. Hosue of Flowery City, 1996, Contemporary Famous Dr. Honor in China, Pub. House of Chinese Population, 1998, award of Sci. and Tech., Ministry of Edn., China, 2002, Beijing, 2003; named Disting. Scientist, Pub. House of Chinese Pers. Adminstrn., 1999. Mem.: Internat. Soc. for Embryo, Am. Soc. Cell Biology, Soc. for Study of Reprodn. Office: Temple Univ Dept Anatomy and Cell Biology 3400 N Broad St Philadelphia PA 19140

WU, JING, physician; b. Fanchang, Anhui, China, Apr. 16, 1968; MD, Nanjing U. Chinese Medicine, 2002. Dir. Jiangsu Provincial Hosp. TCM, 2005. Chief dir. English of Clin. Medicine, 2002. Avocations: music, gardening. Office: 155 Hanzhong Rd Nanjing Jiangsu 210029 China Personal E-mail: zhwujing@yahoo.com.cn.

WU, JOHNNY, internist; b. Kaoshiung, Taiwan, Jan. 24, 1972; s. Ching-Yuan and Tsuey-Ling Wu. BA, Johns Hopkins U., 1994; MD, St. George's U., Grenada, 1998. Resident Seton Hall U., Trinitas Hosp., Elizabeth, NJ, 1998—2001; house officer Physician's Practice Enhancement, LLC, Newark, 2001—; ptnr. Ching-Yuan Wu, East Hanover, 2001—04; pres., CEO PrimeCare Med. Cons. LLC, East Hanover, 2002—; med. dir. EMCFW, Clinton, NJ, 2003—06, WCC, Shelton, Wash., 2006—08; regional med. dir. UMDNJ-UCHC, 2008—. Clin. asst. prof. UMDNJ Robert Wood Johnson Med. Sch., 2003—. Mem.: ACP, AMA, Johns Hopkins Alumni Assn., Pi Kappa Alpha. Avocations: golf, tennis.

WU, JULIAN K., neurosurgeon; b. China, Mar. 9, 1956; ScB, Brown U., Providence, 1977; MD, U. Conn., Farmington, 1981. Diplomate Am. Bd. Neurol. Sugery, 1990. Intern Boston City Hosp., 1981—82; resident Tufts New Eng. Med. Ctr., Boston, 1982—87; chief neurosurgery Beth Israel Deconess Med. Ctr., Boston, 1997—2005; assoc. prof. neurosurgery Harvard U. Med. Sch., Boston, 2000—05; assoc. chmn. neurosurgery Tufts Med. Ctr., 2005—, prof. neurosurgery, 2007—. Bd. mem. Brain Tumor Soc., 1994—. Contbg. author (books) The Practice of Neurosurgery, 1996, Cancer Of The Nervous System, 2004. Recipient Charlton Fund award, Tufts U. Med. Sch., Boston, 1991. Master: Sigma Xi; fellow: Am. Coll. Surgeons; mem.: Neursurgeons Soc. Am., Am. Assn. Neurol. Surgeons. Office: Tufts Med Ctr 800 Washington St Boston MA 02111

WU, LINGLING, ophthalmologist, educator; BS, MS, PhD, Zhejiang U., Hangzhou. Assoc. prof., resident 2nd Affiliated Hosp. Zhejiang U., Mangzhou, 1983—2001, prof., 2001—03, Peking U. Third Hosp., Beijing, 2003—. Contbr. scientific papers. Recipient Third prize, Zhejiang Province, 1998. Mem.: Executive Com. Chinese Gloucoma Soc. Office: Peking Univ Third Hosp Peking Univ Eye Ctr Beijing 100083 China Home: 49 North Garden Rd Haidian Dist 100191 Beijing China

WU, LI-TZY, alcohol and drug abuse services professional, researcher; d. Yu-Tsai and Yu-Chi Wu; m. Hsin-Hsong Tseng, Apr. 20, 1992; children: Jonathan Tseng, Harrison Tseng. DSc, Johns Hopkins U., 1998. RN N.J., 1993. Psychiat. epidemiologist RTI Internat., Research Triangle Park, NC, 1999—2005; assoc. prof. Sch. Medicine Duke U., Durham, NC, 2005—. Resident Nat. Inst. on Drug Abuse Women and Gender Jr. Investigator Travel award, 2001; grantee, Nat. Inst. Drug Abuse, 2000—, Nat. Inst. Alcohol Abuse and Alcoholism, 2001—03; fellow, NIH, 1997—99. Mem.: Coll. on Problems of Drug Dependence, Delta Omega (Alpha chpt.).

WU, PAN, dean; b. Guizhou, China, May 22, 1973; PhD, Grad. U. Chinese Acad. Scis., 2002. Vice dean Coll. Resources & Environ. Engring., Guizhou U., 2004—. Master: Ctr. Mining Environ. Engring. & Tech. Avocations: reading, travel, mountain climbing. Office: Guizhou University Guiyang Guizhou 550003 China E-mail: wupan522@sohu.com.

WU, QINGBO, physician; b. Linyi, China, Apr. 7, 1975; MS, Shandong Acad. Med. Scis., 2009. Dir., acupuncturist Jinan Ctr. Hosp. affiliated to Shandong U., 2009—. Commr. Chinese Soc. TCM Pain Br., 2010—. Recipient Sci. and Technol. 2nd prize, Shandong Province. Mem.: China Assn. Chinese Medicine Pain Assn. Avocation: reading. Office: 105 Jiefang Rd Lixia Dist Jinan Shandong 250013 China Business E-Mail: wuqingbo@mail.com.

WU, RUDOLF SHIU-SUN, biology educator; b. Hong Kong, Nov. 29, 1949; s. Kon Choy and Shiu Kee (Yuen) W.; m. Oi-Lee Chong, July 15, 1974; children: Karen Kar-Yan, Cassandra Kar-Chit. BS with honors., Chinese U. Hong Kong, 1971, BS with spl. honors, 1972; MPhil, U. Hong Kong, 1974; PhD, U. B.C., Vancouver, Can., 1978. Rsch. scientist Agr. and Fisheries Dept., Hong Kong, 1978-83, head marine pollution sect., 1983-85, acting head Fisheries Rsch. Sta., 1985-88; prin. lectr. City Polytechnic of Hong Kong, 1988-90; prof., head Victoria U. Technology, Melbourne, Australia, 1990-93; dir. Ctr. for Coastal Pollution and Conservation City U. of Hong Kong, 1993—. Adv. bd. Marine and Freshwater Rsch., 1997—; mem. coastal ocean observations panel Intergovtl. Oceanographic Commn., 2002—04; mem. sci. adv. panel Environ. Agy., U.K. Govt., 2003—; chair biology panel rsch. assessment exercise, univ. grants com. Hong Kong Govt., 2005—, mem. rsch. grants coun., 2006—; mem. Group of Experts Sci. Aspects Marine Environ. Mgmt., 2007—. Contbr. articles to profl. jours.; mem. editl. bd. Australasian Jour Ecotoxicology. Recipient ann. award Can. Soc. Zoologists, 1976, award for excellence AAAS, 1977, Commonwealth scholar Commonwealth Assn., 1974-77. Mem. Marine Biol. Assn. of Hong Kong (vice chmn. 1982-90), Soc. of Environ. Toxicology and Chemistry (Asia Pacific bd. dirs. 2004-06). Office: Sch Biol Scis University Hong Kong Hong Kong Hong Kong E-mail: rudolfwu@hku.hk.

WU, SHINN-CHIH, agriculturist, educator; b. Yunlin, Taiwan, Aug. 30, 1961; BS, Nat. ChungHsing U., 1988; PhD, Nat. Taiwan U., 1999. Rsch. asst. Pig Rsch. Inst. Taiwan, 1990—94; asst. rsch. fellow Animal Tech. Inst. Taiwan, 1994—99, assoc. rsch. fellow, 1999—2004; asst. prof. Nat. Taiwan U., 2004—10, assoc. prof., 2010—. Recipient Outstanding Agriculturist Kiwanis award, Achievement Individual award, 2002, Coun. Agr., 2002, Superior Agriculturist COA award. Avocations: exercise, badminton, reading, cooking. Office: 50 Ln 155 Sect 3 Keelong Rd Taipei 10672 Taiwan Office Fax: 886-2-27324070. Business E-Mail: scw01@ntu.edu.tw.

WU, SHYI-KUEN, physical therapist; b. Taiwan, Oct. 26, 1969; s. Wu and Hsieh; m. Ya-Ju Becky Yu, Dec. 8, 2001; 1 child, Chieh-Ruey Jerry. BS, Kaohsiung Med. U., Taiwan, 1993; MS, U. NC, Chapel Hill, 1998; PhD, Nat. Cheng Kung U., Taiwan, 2007. Cert. phys. therapist Dept. Health, Exec. Yuan, Taiwan, 1996, in spinal manual therapy Manual Concepts, Australia, 2003; personal tng. instr. YMCA, 2008. Sr. phys. therapist Taichung Veterans Gen. Hosp., Taiwan, 1999—2003; assoc. prof. Dept. Phys. Therapy, HungKuang U., Taichung County, Taiwan, 2003—07, dir., 2008—, cons. Phys. Edn. and Rsch. Ctr., 2008; dir. Ednl. Resource Ctr., 2010—. Contbr. articles to profl. jour. Recipient Best Intelligent award, Kaohsiung Med. U., 1993, Rsch. Paper award, HungKuang U., 2008; named Sr. Outstanding Tchr., Pvt. Edn. Assn., 2006. Fellow: Phys. Therapist Assn. Taiwan; mem.: Phys. Therapy Assn. ROC. Achievements include development of a neck motion model to differentiate the movements and posture between upper and lower cervical spines. Home and Office: HungKuang Univ 34 Chung-Chie Rd Shalu Taichung County 433 Taiwan Office Fax: 886-4-26324105. Business E-Mail: skwu@sunrise.hk.edu.tw.

WU, SING-YUNG, physician, researcher; b. China, 1939; MB, Nat. Taiwan U., 1963; PhD, U. Wash., 1969; MD, Johns Hopkins U., 1971. Staff physician VA Med. Ctr., Long Beach, Calif., 1977—; asst. prof. U. Calif., Irvine, 1977—84, assoc. prof., 1985—90, prof. dept. radiol. scis. and medicine, 1990—. Editor: Thyroid Hormone Metabolism, 1991, 1994; author: Gold File-The Transfer of Nationalist China's Gold Reserve from Shanghai to Taiwan in 1949, 2007. Office: Thyroid Rsch Lab 5901 E 7th St Long Beach CA 90822 Office Phone: 562-826-5808. Business E-Mail: sing.wu@va.gov.

WU, SUH-CHIN, science educator; b. Ping-tung, Taiwan, Jan. 15, 1962; s. M.-J. Wu and K.-S. Wang; m. Yu-Min Cheng; children: Jesse, Angela BS, Nat. Cheng-Kung U., Tainan, Taiwan, 1985; MS, Nat. Tsing Hua U., 1987; PhD, Tex. A&M U., 1993. Vis. fellow NIH NCBI, Bethesda, Md., 1994-95; assoc. investigator Nat. Inst. Preventive Medicine, Taipei, Taiwan, 1995-97; asst. prof. dept. life sci. Nat. Tsing-Hua U., Hsinchu, Taiwan, 1997—2000, assoc. prof., 2000—04, prof. Inst. Biotechnology, 2004—; assoc. investigator vaccine R&D ctr. Nat. Health Rsch. Inst., 2004—08; t. investigator vaccin R&D Ctr., Nat Health Rsch. Inst., 2009—. Contbr. articles to sci. jours.; mem. editl. bd.: Enzyme and Microbial Tech., 2005—, The Open Vet. Sci. Jour., 2007—, Internat. Jour. Med. Engring. and Informatics, 2007—. Recipient Sci. Vis. Prog. award, Oak Ridge Nat. Lab., 1993, Rsch. award, Nat. Sci. Coun., Taiwan, 1997—98, Nakajima Found. award, 2001; vis. scholar, NCI Frederick, Md., 2008. Mem.: Am. Soc. Microbiol., Internat. Soc. Vaccines, Am. Chemistry Soc., Am. Inst. Chem. Engrs. Office: Dept Life Sci Nat Tsing Hua U Hsinchu 30013 Taiwan Home Phone: 886 3 5635701. Business E-Mail: scwu@life.nthu.edu.tw.

WU, TAI TE, biological sciences and engineering educator; b. Shanghai, Aug. 2, 1935; m. Anna Fang, Apr. 16, 1966; 1 child, Richard. MB, BS, U. Hong Kong, 1956; BSMechE, U. Ill., Urbana, 1958; SM in Applied Physics, Harvard U., Cambridge, Mass., 1959; PhD in Engring. (Gordon McKay fellow), Harvard U., 1961. Rsch. fellow in structural mechanics Harvard U., 1961-63; rsch. fellow in biol. chemistry Harvard U. (Med. Sch.), 1964, rsch. assoc., 1965-66; rsch. scientist Hydronautics, Inc., Rockville, Md., 1962; asst. prof. engring. Brown U., Providence, 1963-65; asst. prof. biomath. Grad. Sch. Med. Scis., Cornell U. Med. Coll., NYC, 1967-68, assoc. prof., 1968-70; assoc. prof. physics and engring. scis. Northwestern U., Evanston, Ill., 1970-73, prof., 1973-74, prof. biochemistry and molecular biology and engring. scis., 1973-85, acting chmn. dept. engring. scis., 1974, prof. biochem., molecular biology, cell biology and biomed. engring., engring. scis., applied math., 1985-94, prof. biochemistry, molecular biology, cell biology, biomed. engring., 1994—2010, prof. biomed. engring., molecular bioscis., 2010—. Author (with E.A. Kabat and others): Variable Regions of Immunoglobulin Chains, 1976, Sequences of Immunoglobulin Chains, 1979, Sequences of Proteins of Immunological Importance, 1983, Sequences of Proteins of Immunological Interest, 1987, 5th edit., 1991; editor: New Methodologies in Studies of Protein Configuration, 1985, Analytical Molecular Biology, 2001, Best Scientific Discovery or Worst Scientific Fraud of the 20th Century, 2006; contbr. articles to profl. jours. Recipient Progress award Chinese Engrs. and Scientists Assn. So. Calif., LA, 1971, Rsch. Career Devel. award NIH, 1974-79; C.T. Loo scholar, 1959-60. Mem. Am. Soc. Biochem. and Molecular Biology, Sigma Xi, Tau Beta Pi, Pi Mu Epsilon Office: Northwestern University Dept Molecular Bioscis Evanston IL 60208-3500 Office Phone: 847-491-7849. Business E-Mail: t-wu@northwestern.edu.

WU, WEI, pharmacist, educator; b. Xuzhou, Xuzhou, Jan. 26, 1971; BS, Second Mil. Med. U., 1992; PhD, West China U. Med. Scis., 1999. Pharmacist 208 Hosp. PLA, 1992—93; lectr. Sch. Pharmacy, Fudan U., 2000—01, assoc. prof., 2001—06, prof., vice dean, 2007—. Recipient Young Scientist award, Chinese Pharm. Assn., Advances S & T award, People's Liberation Army; named one of Excellent Young Tchrs., Shanghai Commn. Edn. Fellow: Chinese Medicinal Edn. Assn., Chinese Traditional Chinese Medicine Assn., World Traditional Chinese Medicine Union, Shanghai Pharm. Assn. (Pharm. S & T award). Avocations: jogging, badminton. Office: 826 Zhangheng Rd Shanghai 201203 China Business E-Mail: wuwei@shmu.edu.cn.

WU, WEN-YI, surgeon; b. Hong Kong, Mar. 24, 1957; MD, U. Santo Tomas, Philippines, 1984. Hair transplant surgeon Taiwan Hair Transplant, Taipei, 2004—. Achievements include first to perform follicular unit hair transplantation in Taiwan. Home: 8F # 21 Sect 3 Nanjing East Rd Taipei Taiwan Office: Taiwan Hair Transplant 8F #21 Sect 3 Nanjing East Rd Taipei 104 Taiwan Home Fax: 886-225012476. Business E-Mail: wu@hair7838.com.

WU, XIU-XIAN, medical educator; b. China, July 6, 1962; MD, Kyoto U., PhD, 2002. Asst. prof. Kagawa U., 2002. Office: 1750-1 Ikenobe Kitagun Kagawa 761-0793 Japan Business E-Mail: wuxian@kagawa-u.ac.jp.

WU, YU-CHI, electrical engineering educator, consultant, researcher; b. Fengshan, Taiwan, July 19, 1964; s. Shih-Dar and Shang-Feng (Wang) W.; m. Suhua Ho; 1 child, Yi-Hong. PhD in Elec. Engring., MS in Elec. Engring., Ga. Inst. Tech., Atlanta, 1993. Rsch. asst. Ga. Tech., Atlanta, 1989-92; cons. PG&E, San Francisco, 1990; assoc. analyst EDS/EMA, Atlanta, 1992-93, analyst, 1993-94; assoc. prof. dept. elec. engring. United U., Miao-Li, Taiwan, 1994—2002, dir. libr., 2000—01, prof. dept. elec. engring., 2002—, dean student affairs, 2003—06; chmn. Lien Ho Coll. Tech. and Commerce, Miao-Li, Taiwan, 1995—98. Cons. EDS/CMS, Taipei, Taiwan, 1994-95; project prin. investigator, NSC, Taiwan, 1995—. Inventor: IPM-OPF Software, 1993, PHS Software, 1992; contbr. articles to profl. jours. Mem. Youth Goodwill Mission Group, Taiwan, 1983. 2nd Lt. Army, 1984-86, Taiwan. Recipient Acad. award Nat. Kaohsiung Inst. Tech., 1984, Straight A's in MS work, Ga. Tech., 1990. Mem.: IEEE (sr.). Avocations: reading, movies, golf, sports. Home Phone: 886-3-5753392; Office Phone: 886-37-350846, 88637381362. Business E-Mail: ycwu@nuu.edu.tw.

WU-CHE, WEN, medical association administrator; b. Taipei, Taiwan, June 20, 1967; PhD, Nat. Taiwan Normal U., 2000. V.p. Goldenbiotech. Corp., 1996—. Office: Sect 1 Zhong Zheng East Rd 10 F New Taipei Danshui 251 Taiwan Office Fax: 886-2-26261812. Business E-Mail: wwc@goldenbiotech.com.tw.

WUHL, CHARLES MICHAEL, psychiatrist; b. NYC, Sept. 24, 1943; s. Isadore and Sali (Ackner) Wuhl; m. Gail Wuhl; children: Elise, Amy. MD, U. Bologna, 1973. Diplomate Am. Bd. Psychiatry and Neurology. Intern NY Med. Coll., 1975—76, resident in psychiatry, 1976—77; fellow in child psychiatry Columbia Presbyn. Med. Ctr., 1977—78; practice medicine specializing in psychiatry and child psychiatry Englewood, NJ, 1978—; attending staff, mem. faculty NY Med. Coll.; psychiatrist NYU, also asst. clin. prof. psychiatry NYU Sch. Medicine; with Psychosocial Aspects of Pediatric Care, 1978, World Book Ency., 1980—. Fellow: Am. Psychiatric Assn. (life); mem.: AMA, Am. Acad. Child Psychiatry, Am. Psychiat Assn. Office: 163 Engle St Englewood NJ 07631-2530 Office Phone: 201-569-2228. Business E-Mail: cw3@nyu.edu.

WULC, ALLAN E., ophthalmologist; BA, Amherst Coll., 1972—76; MD, U. Pa., 1974—75. Diplomate Am. Bd. Ophthalmology, cert. ophthalmic plastic and reconstructive surgery, cosmetic Surgery, facial, diplomate Am. Bd. of Physician Specialists-plastic surgery. Resident ophthalmology scheie eye inst. Univ. of Pa., 1981—84; fellow eye plastic and reconstructive surgery Univ. of Ariz., 1984—85; fellow orbital and lacrimal surgery Moorefields Eye Hosp., 1985—86; fellow gen. cosmetic surgery Advanced Cosmetic Surgery Ctr., 2000—02; clin. fellow scheie eye inst. Univ. of Pa., 1984—86, asst. prof. dept. of ophthalmology scheie inst., 1986—89, chief oculoplastic svc. scheie eye inst., chief orbital svc. scheie eye inst., assoc. prof. ophthalmology, 1995—96, clin. assoc. prof. ophthalmology, 1996; clin. assoc. prof. ophthalmology & otolaryngology Drexel Univ., 1996; assoc. preceptor Albany Med. Coll., 2007. Asst. instr. dept ophthalmology scheie eye inst. Univ. of Ariz., 1984—85. Recipient William G. Shields 3rd Memorial prize, S. Weir Lewis Memorial prize, Phi Beta Kappa Association prize, Thomas Oliver Memorial prize, Marvin Quickert prize, Golden Apple Resident Teaching award, Uncinate award. Mem.: AMA, ACS, Am. Assn. of Physician Specialist, Phila. Coll. of Physician, Ophthalmic Club of Phila., Pa. Acad. of Ophthalmology and Otolaryngology, Montgomery County Med. Soc., Am. Acad. of Ophthalmology (Junior Honor award, Senior Honor award), European Soc. of Ophthalmic Plastic and Reconstructive Surgery, Aesthetic Soc., Am. Acad. of Liposuction Surgery, Am. Acad. of Cosmetic Surgery, Am. Acad. of Facial Plastic and Reconstructive Surgery, Am. Soc. of Ophthalmic Plastic and Reconstructive Surgery. Office: Abington Memorial Hospital Ste 161 610 W Germantown Pk Plymouth Meeting PA 19462 Office Phone: 610-828-8880. Office Fax: 610-828-8883.

WUNDER, CHARLES COOPER, retired physiologist, biophysicist, educator; b. Pitts., Oct. 2, 1928; s. Edgar Douglas and Annabel (Cooper) W.; m. Marcia Lynn Barnes, Apr. 4, 1962; children: E(dgar) Douglas, David Barnes, Donald Charles. AB in Biology, Washington and Jefferson Coll., 1949; MS in Biophysics, U. Pitts., 1952, PhD in Biophysics, 1954. Assoc. U. Iowa, Iowa City, 1954-56, asst. prof. physiology and biophysics, 1956-63, assoc. prof. physiology and biophysics, 1963-71, prof. physiology and biophysics, 1971-98, prof. emeritus, 1998—. Cons. for biol. simulation of weightlessness U.S. Air Force, 1964; vis. scientist Mayo Found., Rochester, Minn., 1966-67. Author: Life into Space: An Introduction to Space Biology, 1966; also chpts., numerous articles, abstracts Recipient Research Career Devel. award NIH, 1961-66; AEC predoctoral fellow U. Pitts., 1951-53; NIH spl. fellow, 1966-67; grantee NIH, NASA Mem. Am. Physiol. Soc., The Biophys. Soc. (charter), Aerospace Med. Assn., Iowa Acad. Sci. (chmn. physiology sect. 1971-72, 83-84, 96-97), Am. Soc. Biomechanics (founding), Aerospace Physiologist Soc., Iowa Physiol. Soc. (pres. 1996-97), Am. Soc. for Gravitational and Space Biology (Founders award 2000). Presbyterian. Achievements include the establishment of chronic centrifugation as an approach for investigating gravity's role as a biological determinant. Home: 702 W Park Rd Iowa City IA 52246-2425 Office: U Iowa BSB Iowa City IA 52242 Business E-Mail: charles-wunder@uiowa.edu.

WUNGSEOK, CHA, medical educator; s. Bonghwan Cha and Anja Jung; m. Seongbo Kim; children: Jeongmin Cha, Jeonghun Cha. Dr., Kyunghee U., Seoul, Korea., 2001. Cert. oriental med. dr. Ministry of Health & Welfare, Korea, 1994. Part time instr. Kyunghee U., 2001—02, rsch. full time instr., 2002—04, full time instr., 2004—06, asst. prof., 2006—. Rsch. advisor Korea Inst. of Oriental Med., Taejeon, 2002—. Author: (book) Su-Sae-Hyun-Seo; contbr. articles to med. jours. Grantee, Korea Inst. of Sci. and Tech. Evaluation and Planning, 2002, Kyunghee U., 2004, 2006, 2007, 2008, Korea Rsch. Found., 2006. Mem.: Korean Soc. of Med. History, The Assn. of Korean Oriental Med. Achievements include research in construction of modernization base for traditional medicine knowledge data and traditional medical science. Avocations: reading, mountain climbing. Home and Office: KyungHee Univ 130-701 1 Hoegi-Dong Dongdaemoon-Gu Seoul 130-701 Republic of Korea Office Fax: 82 2 965 5969.

WURTH, MARYJANE A., medical association administrator; m. Chris Wurth. BS, SUNY, Cortland; MS in Human Svc. Studies, Cornell U. V.p., continuing care, cmty. health HANYS Solutions, Inc., 1990, pres., CEO, 2001; pres. Ill. Hosp. Assn. (IHA), 1998—. COO Healthcare Assn. of NY State (HANYS); mem. Am. Soc. of Assn. Exec.; bd. dirs. Rensselaer County C. of C.; founding mem., Helen Ptochia Found. African Fistula Hosp. Office: Illinois Hospital Association 1151 E Warrenville Rd Naperville IL 60566 Office Phone: 630-276-5400. *

WURTH, RAINER, physician, researcher; b. Wipperfürth, Germany, Apr. 3, 1971; s. Gerd and Anita Wurth. Cert.: Würzburg Law Sch. 1998; Leipzig Med. Sch., 2008. Doc. rsch. fellow Max Bürger Rsch. Ctr., Leipzig, Saxony, Germany, 2005—; exec. asst. to chmn. Bd. Leipzig U. Hosp., 2010—. Contbr. chapters to books, articles to profl. jours. Recipient Best Poster award, German Soc. Cytometry, 2005. Home: Inselstraße 19 Leipzig Saxony 04103 Germany Office: Liebigstr 18 Leipzig Saxomy 0410 Germany Office Phone: 0049-341-9715913. Business E-Mail: rainer.wurth@medizin.uni-leipzig.de.

WURTMAN, RICHARD JAY, neuroscientist, educator, inventor; b. Phila., Mar. 9, 1936; s. Samuel Richard and Hilda (Schreiber) W.; m. Judith Joy Hirschhorn, Nov. 15, 1959; children: Rachael Elisabeth, David Franklin. AB, U. Pa., 1956; MD, Harvard U., 1960. Intern Mass. Gen. Hosp., 1960-61, resident, 1961-62, fellow medicine, 1965-66, clin. assoc. in medicine, 1985—; research assoc., med. research officer NIMH, 1962-67; mem. faculty MIT, Cambridge, 1967—, prof. endocrinology and metabolism, 1970-80, prof. neuroendocrine regulation, 1980-94, Cecil H. Green disting. prof., 1994—2010; dir. Clin. Rsch. Ctr., MIT, Cambridge, 1985—2005, green prof. emeritus, 2011—. Lectr. medicine Harvard Med. Sch., 1969—; prof. Harvard-MIT Divsn. Health Scis. and Tech., 1978—; Smithies lectr. Oxford U., 2002; sci. dir. Ctr. for Brain Scis. and Metabolism Charitable Trust, 1981—; invited prof. U. Geneva, 1981; Sterling vis. prof. Boston U., 1981; vis. fellow Balliol Coll., Oxford U., 1997; chmn. life scis. adv. com. NASA, 1979-82; chmn. adv. bd. Alzheimer's Disease Assn., 1981-84; assoc. neuroscis. rsch. program MIT, 1974-82; chmn. life scis. adv. bd. USAF, 1985—94; founder, chmn. sci. adv. bd. Interneuron Pharms., Inc., 1989-99; co-founder Wurtco, 1999, Back Bay Sci., 1999. Author: Catecholamines, 1966; (with others) The Pineal, 1968; editor: (with Judith Wurtman) Nutrition and the Brain, Vols. I and II, 1977, Vols. III, IV, V., 1979, Vol. VI, 1983, Vol. VII, 1986, Vol. VIII, 1990, contbr. articles to profl. jours.; chpts. to books. Mem. bd. overseers Boston Symphony Orch., 1997—; trustee New World, Symphony, 2007—; bd. dirs. Fenway Cmty. Health Ctr., Boston, 1998—2003, Provincetown Art Assn. and Mus., 2000—, pres., 2005—09. Recipient various awards and lectureships. Mem. Endocrine Soc. (Ernst Oppenheim award 1972), Am. Physiol. Soc., Am. Soc. Biol. Chemists, Am. Soc. Pharmacology and Exptl. Therapeutics (John Jacob Abel award 1968), Am. Soc. Neurochemistry, Soc. Neurosci., Am. Soc. Clin. Nutrition, Am. Inst. Nutrition (Osborne & Mendel award 1982), Porcellati Lecture ESN, Lands Lecture U. Mich. Achievements include some 1,000 rsch. publications,and 200 US patents on new treatments for diseases and conditions; invention of melatonin for promoting sleep, of dexfenfluramine for treating obesity, of citicoline for treating stroke and of Sarafem for the treatment of premenstrual syndrome, and of phosphatide precursors mixtures for enhancing brain synapse formation in neurodegenerative diseases. Home: 300 Boylston St Boston MA 02116-3923 Office: Mass Inst Tech 77 Massachusetts Ave 46-5009 Cambridge MA 02139-1323 Office Phone: 617-253-6731. Business E-Mail: dick@mit.edu.

WURTZ, ROBERT HENRY, neuroscientist; b. St. Louis, Mar. 28, 1936; s. Robert Henry and Alice Edith (Popplwell) Wurtz; m. Sally Smith, Dec. 20, 1958 (div.); children: William, Erica; m. Emily Otis, Apr. 23, 1983. AB, Oberlin Coll., 1958; PhD, U. Mich., 1962; DSc (hon.), Oberlin Coll., 2009. Rsch. assoc. Com. for Nuclear Info., St. Louis, 1962-63; fellow Sch. Medicine, Washington U., 1962-65; rsch. psychologist NIH, Bethesda, Md., 1965-66, physiologist, 1966-78, sr. scientist Lab. Sensorimotor Rsch., 1978—2002; founding chief Lab. Sensorimotor Rsch., 1978—2002, disting. prof., 2008—. Vis. scientist Cambridge U., England, 1975—76. Editor: Neurobiology of Saccadic Eye Movement, 1989. Recipient Karl Spencer Lashley award, Am. Philos. Soc., 1995. Fellow: AAAS; mem.: NAS, APA (Disting. Sci. Contbn. award 1997), Gruber Found. (Neurosci. prize 2010), Soc. Exptl. Psychologists, Assn. for Rsch. in Vision and Opthalmology, Am. Physiol. Soc., Soc. Neurosci. (pres. 1991, Ralph W. Gerard prize 2006), Am. Acad. Arts and Scis., Inst. Medicine (Dan David Found. prize 2004). Office: NIH Nat Eye Inst Bldg 49 Rm 2A50 Bethesda MD 20892-4435

WUSI, QIU, neurosurgeon, educator; b. Shaoxing, Zhejiang, China, Aug. 6, 1973; s. Qiu Yuechun; married; 1 child, Qiu Mingqi. PhD, Zhejiang U., China, MD, 2007. Diplomate bd. cert. Ministry Pub. Health, China. Asst. tchr. Hangzhou Br., Med. Coll., Zhejiang U., China, 1994—2000; resident physician 2nd Affliated Hosp., Zhejiang U., Hangzhou, China, 2002—. Assoc. prof. Med. Coll., Hangzhou Normal U., Zhejiang, 2000—. Home: 6-3-301 Shuijing Yuan Xiacheng Hangzhou Zhejiang 310015 China Office: Hangzhou 2nd Hosp 126 Wenzhou Rd Hangzhou Zhejiang 310015 China Business E-Mail: shihai954@163.com.

WÜTHRICH, KURT, molecular biologist, biophysicist, educator; b. Aarberg, Switzerland, Oct. 4, 1938; m. Marianne Briner, 1963; children: Bernhard Andrew, Karin Lynn. MS, U. Bern, Switzerland, 1962; PhD in Chemistry, U. Basel, Switzerland, 1964; ChD (hon.), U. Siena, Italy, 1997; PhD (hon.), U. Zurich, Switzerland, 1997, Swiss Fed. Inst. Tech., Lausanne, 2001, U. Sheffield, Eng., 2004, U. Valencia, Spain, 2004, King George's Med. U., India, 2005, U. Pecs, Hungary, 2005, Lomonosov State U., Russia, 2006, U. Verona, Italy, 2007, U. Rene Descartes, Paris, 2007; PhD, U. Del. Norte Asuncion Paraguay, 2007, U. Verona Italy, 2007, U. Rene Descartes, Paris France, 2007. Lectr. in chemistry, physics and math. U. Bern, 1957—62; postdoc. tng. U. Basel, 1964—65, U. Calif., Berkeley, 1965—67; mem. tech. staff Bell Tel. Labs., Murray Hill, NJ, 1967—69; lectr. Swiss Fed. Inst. Tech. (ETH) Zurich, Zürich, 1969—72, asst. prof., 1972—76, assoc. prof., 1976—80, prof. biophysics, 1980—, chmn. dept. biology, 1995-2000; Cecil H. & Ida M. Green vis. prof. structural biology Scripps Rsch Inst., La Jolla, 2001—. Editor: Quar. Rev. Biophysics, 1984—91, 1996—2001, Macromolecular Structures, 1990—2000; mem. editl bd. numerous sci. publs.; contbr. articles to profl. jours. Recipient Friedrich Miescher prize, Swiss Biochem. Soc., 1974, Stein & Moore award, Protein Soc., 1990, Louisa Gross Horwitz prize, Columbia U., 1991, Gilbert Newton Lewis medal, U. Calif., Berkeley, 1991, Marcel Benoist prize, Swiss Confederation, 1992, Louis-Jeantet Found. award, Geneva, 1993, Kaj Linderstrøm-Lang prize, Carlsberg Found., Copenhagen, 1996, Kyoto prize in advanced tech., Inamori Found., Japan, 1998, Otto-Warburg medal, Soc. Biochemistry & Molecular Biology, Germany, 1999, Nobel prize in chemistry, 2002, Ralph & Helen Oesper award, U. Cin., 2010, Bijvoet medal, Utreclet U., 2008, Paul Walden Medal, Riga Tech. U., 2008, Jabir Ibn Hyyan medal, Saudi Chem. Soc., 2009. Fellow: AAAS, Royal Soc. London (fgn. mem.), Indian Nat. Sci. Acad. (fgn. mem.); mem.: NAS (fgn. assoc.), Royal Soc., Swiss Acad. Engring. Scis., German Acad. Scis. Leopoldina, ISMAR (hon.), Korean Magnetic Resonance Soc. (hon.), Nuc. Magnetic Resonance Soc. Japan (hon.), European Acad. Arts & Humanities (hon.), Japanese Biochem. Soc. (hon.), Nat. Magnetic Resonance Soc. India (hon.), Swiss Chem. Soc. (hon.), Royal Soc. Chemistry (hon.), Royal Soc. Edinburgh (hon.), Internat. Soc. Magnetic Resonance in Medicine (hon.), Hungarian Acad. Sci. (hon.), Latvian Acad. Sci. (hon.), Indian Biophys. Soc. (hon.), Latvian Inst. Org. Synthesis (hon.), Korean Acad. Sci. Technol. (hon.), Am. Acad. Arts & Sciences (hon. fgn. mem.), Academia Europea, European Molecular Biology Orgn. Office: ETH Zurich Inst Molecular Biology Biophysics 8093 Zurich Switzerland also: Scripps Rsch Inst Dept Molecular Biology 10550 N Torrey Pines Rd La Jolla CA 92037 Office Phone: 858-459-1768. Business E-Mail: wuthrich@scripps.edu.

WYATT, HAROLD VIVIAN, retired medical researcher; b. Devonport, Eng., June 11, 1926; s. Fred and Emily (Phillips) W.; m. Joan Wilkinson Jones, Feb. 23, 1956; children: Tristram Dick, Ben Timothy. BSc, U. London, 1951, BSc with honors, 1952, PhD, 1957. Chartered biologist. Rsch. asst. St. Bartholomew's Hosp., London, 1954-57; postdoctoral fellow Johns Hopkins Hosp., Balt., 1957-59; ICI fellow U. Leeds, 1959—62, hon. rsch. fellow, 1986—, hon. lectr., philosophy, 2004—09; reader in microbiology U. Bradford, 1962-82; vis. scientist Nat. Cancer Inst., Bethesda, 1969-71; hon. rsch. assoc. U. Manchester, 1980-81; dir. sch. of sci. Coll. of Med. Scis., West Bank, 1982-83; guest rsch. worker Indian Inst. Chem. Biology, Calcutta, India, 1985. Cons. for legal actions for compensation for vaccine damaged children, vis. lectr. philosophy, U. Leeds. Author: AIDS Information, 1988; editor: Information Sources in the Life Sciences, 4th edit., 1997, Poliomyelitis in India, 1998; contbr. over 300 articles to profl. publs. Sgt. Army, 1944-48, U.K. Grantee Royal Soc., 1987, British Libr., Wellcome Trust, 1993, 94. Fellow Soc. Biologist. Achievements include discovery of aggravation of paralytic poliomyelitis by injections and susceptibility of hypo-gamma-globulinemics to oral polio vaccine, incidence and case-fatality of neonatal poliomyelitis, history of brucellosis. Home: 1 Hollyshaw Terr Leeds LS15 7BG England Business E-Mail: nurhvw@leeds.ac.uk.

WYATT, JAMES, medical educator, director; b. Ill., Aug. 16, 1967; AB, Brown U., 1989; PhD, U. Ariz., 1995. Lab. dir. Sleep Disorders Svc. and Rsch. Rush U. Med. Ctr., 2003—06, dir., 2006—; asst. prof., behavioral scis. Rush Med. Coll., 1999—2007, assoc. prof., behavioral scis., 2007—. Grant, NIH, Rsch. grant, Industry & Various Cos. Fellow: Am. Acad. Sleep Medicine; mem.: APA, Soc. Rsch. Biol. Rhythms, Sleep Rsch. Soc. Office: Rush University Med Ctr 1653 West Congress Pky Chicago IL 60612 Business E-Mail: jwyatt@rush.edu.

WYCOFF, CHARLES COLEMAN, writer, retired anesthesiologist; b. Glazier, Tex., Sept. 2, 1918; s. James Garfield and Ada Sharpe (Braden) W.; m. Gene Marie Henry, May 16, 1942 (dec.); children: Michelle, Geoffrey, Brian, Roger, Daniel, Norman, Irene, Teresa. AB, U. Calif., Berkeley, 1941; MD, U. Calif., San Francisco, 1943; postgrad., U. London, 1954-55. Diplomate Am. Bd. Anesthesiology. Intern San Francisco County Hosp., 1943-44; resident in anesthesiology U. Calif. Hosp., San Francisco, 1944-45; tng. in anesthesiology Walter Reed Gen. Hosp., 1945; founder The Wycoff Group of Anesthesiology, San Francisco, 1947-53; chief of anesthesia St. Joseph's Hosp., San Francisco, 1947-52, organizer residency tng. program in anesthesiology, 1950, San Francisco County Hosp., 1954, chief anesthesia, 1953-54; tchr. practice anesthesiology Presbyn. Med. Ctr., NYC, 1955-63; asst. prof. anesthesiology Columbia U., NYC, 1955-63; clin. practice anesthesiology St. Francis Meml. Hosp., San Francisco, 1963-84. Prodr., dir. films on regional anesthesia; contbr. articles to sci. jours. Scoutmaster Boy Scouts Am., San Francisco, 1953-55. Capt. MC, US Army, 1945-47. Mem. Alumni Faculty Assn. Sch. Medicine U. Calif.-San Francisco (councilor-at-large 1979-80). Democrat. Avocations: researching origins of human behavior, writing, gardening, languages. Home: 3875 Castro Valley Blvd Spc 55 Castro Valley CA 94546-4584 Personal E-mail: ccwycoff918@yahoo.com.

WYDERSKI, RICHARD JOSEPH, internist; b. Dayton, Ohio, Apr. 1, 1960; s. Josef and Gertrude Vera Wyderski; m. Karen Louise Wyderski, May 2, 2002 (div. Sept. 2004); m. Mary Teresa Wyderski, June 12, 1982 (div. Sept. 1995); m. Karen Bollie Wyderski, Dec. 1, 2009. BS, U. Dayton, 1982; MD, U. Cin., 1986; M in Med. Mgmt., U. So. Calif., 2002. Diplomate Am. Bd. Internal Medicine, Nat. Bd. Med. Examiners. Resident U. Cin. Dept. Medicine, 1986—89, gen. medicine fellow, 1989—90, chief med. resident, 1990—91; pvt. practice Assoc. Specialists of Internal Medicine, Dayton, 1991—97; med. dir., Bethany Luth. Village Luth. Social Svcs., Centerville, Ohio, 1991—96; med. dir., Ambulatory clinics Miami Valley Hosp., Dayton, 1996—2008; assoc. residency program dir. Wright State U. Dept. Medicine, Dayton, 1997—2009; hosp. physician St. Joseph's Mercy Health Ctr., 2009—11, chief medicine, 2010—11, med. dir. hospitalist program, 2010—11; dir., perioperative medicine Wake Forest U. Bapt. Med. Ctr., 2011—; exec. com. mem. Dayton Internat. Peace Mus., hon. trustee, 2009—. Mem. ethics com. Luth. Social Svcs. of the Miami Valley, Dayton, 1997—2008; mem. quality improvement/utilization mgmt. com. United HealthCare of Ohio, Inc., Dayton/Cin., 1996—2002. Vol.; bd. trustees Alzheimer's Assn. of the Miami Valley, Dayton, 1991—95; treas., mem. bd. trustees Med. Vols. of Cin., 1990—91; founder, chair adv. com. Domestic Abuse and Violence Inst. of Dayton, 1999—2004; trustee Epilepsy Found. We. Ohio, 2002—07, v.p., 2004, pres., 2005. Recipient Leadership award, AMA, Chgo., 1989. Fellow: ACP (assocs. com., Ohio chpt. 2001—02, program com. 2002—03, awards com. 2002—04); mem.: AMA, NAACP (life; asst. treas. and exec. com. mem. Dayton Unit 2009), BMW Car Club of America, Ark. Med. Soc., Dayton Internat. Peace Mus., Am. Geriat. Soc. (Geriat. Recognition award 1998, 2002). Democrat. Roman Catholic. Avocations: automobiles, tennis. Home: 2216 Meadow Hill Rd Winston Salem NC 27106 Office: Medical Center Blvd Winston Salem NC 27157 Office Phone: 336-713-5215. Business E-Mail: rwydersk@wfubnc.edu, rwydersk@wakehealth.edu.

WYKLE, MAY L., dean, educator, researcher; BSN, Case Western Res. U., 1956, MSN Psychiat. Nursing, PhD Edn. Dean and Florence Cellar prof. gerontol. nursing, Frances Payne Bolton Sch. Nursing Case Western Res. U., Cleve., 1988—, faculty assoc., Univ. Ctr. Aging and Health. Established ednl. programs, Europe, Africa, Asia; vis. prof. U. Mich., U. Tex.-Houston, U. Zimbabwe-Africa; del., served on planning com. White House Conf. on Aging, 1993. Contbr. articles, chapters to books; author: Decision Making in Long-Term Care, Practicing Rehabilitation with Geriatric Clients, Stress and Health Among the Elderly, Family Caregiving Across the Lifespan, Service Minority Elders in the 21st Century (AJN Book of Yr. award, 2000). Dir. Robert Wood Johnson Tchg. Nursing Home Project; project dir. several tng. grants; cons. nursing homes, psychiat. hosps.; mem. bd. dirs. numerous cmty. orgns., nursing homes, profl. assns. Recipient Humanitarian award, Outstanding Contbns. to Nursing Profession, 1999, Acad. award, NIMH Geriatric Mental Health, Merit award, Cleve. Coun. Black Nurses, Belle Sherwin award, Cleve. Vis. Nurse Assn., Leadership award excellence in geriatric care, Midwest Alliance in Nursing, Disting. nurse-scholar lectr. award, Nat. Coun. Nursing Rsch., Nursing Educator award, New Cleve. Woman mag.; named first Pope Eminent scholar, Rosalynn Carter Inst. Human Devel. Southwestern State U., Americus, Ga., Outstanding Rschr. in State of Ohio, Ohio Rsch. Coun. on Aging, Ohio Network Edn. Cons. in field of Aging, 1992. Fellow: Gerontol. Soc. Am. (Gerontol. Doris Schwartz Nursing Rsch. award), Am. Acad. Nursing; mem.: NIA, NIMH, NINR, Vets Adminstrn. (geriatric/gerontology adv. com.), Sigma Theta Tau Internat. (pres.-elect 1999). Office: Frances Payne Bolton Sch Nursing 10900 Euclid Ave Cleveland OH 44106

WYLIE-ROSETT, JUDITH, dietician, educator; BS, U. Ark., Fayetteville, 1966; MEd, Teacher's Coll., Columbia U., NYC, 1971, EdD, 1980. Registered Dietitian. Dietetic internship NY Hosp.-Cornell Med. Ctr., NYC, 1967, dietitian, metabolic rsch. unit, 1967—69; assoc. in medicine, dept. medicine Albert Einstein Coll. Medicine, Bronx, NY, 1971—79, head, divsn. nutrition, dept. cmty. health, 1980—84, asst. prof., dept. cmty. health, 1980—84, asst. prof., dept. epidemiology and social medicine, 1984—88, assoc. prof., dept. epidemiology and social medicine, 1988—95, prof., dept. epidemiology and population health, 1995—, head, divsn. health, behavior and nutrition, 1998—. Cons. for NIH clin. trials and studies. Ad Hoc Reviewer Demonstration and Edn. grants Nat. Heart, Lung and Blood Inst., 1985—, mem. of several editl. bds., reviewer for several profl. jours. Coord., nutrition svcs. Door Multi-Svc. Youth Ctr., 1973—78. Fellow: NY Acad. Medicine; mem.: Am. Assn. Diabetes Educators, Am. Dietetic Assn. (award for excellence in the practice of clin. nutrition 1990, Mary P. Huddleson award 1995), Am. Heart Assn., Am. Diabetes Assn. (bd. dirs. 1981—84, award for outstanding profl. educator in the field of diabetes 1991, Woman of Valor award by Bronx Diabetes Coalition 1996), Phi Upsilon Omicron. Office: 1308 Belfer Bldg Albert Einstein Coll Medicine 1300 Morris Park Ave Bronx NY 10461 Office Phone: 718-430-3345. Office Fax: 718-430-8634. E-mail: jwrosett@aecom.yu.edu.

WYLLIE, ANDREW, pathologist, educator; BSc, MB, ChB, PhD, U. Aberdeen. Prof., head dept. pathology U. Cambridge. Hon. cons. Addenbrooke Hosp., Cambridge. Editl. bd. Journal of Pathology. Recipient Bertner award, MD Anderson Cancer Ctr., U. Tex., 1994, Hans Bloemendel award, U. Nijmegen, 1998, Gairdner Found. Internat. award, 1999. Fellow: Royal Soc. Edinburgh, Royal Soc.; mem.: Pathological Soc. (GB & Ireland) (pres. 2009—), British Acad. Med. Sciences (founding mem.). Office: Dept Pathology U Cambridge Tennis Court Rd Cambridge CB2 1QP England Business E-Mail: ahw21@cam.ac.uk. *

WYMYSLO, THEODORE EDWARD (TED WYMYSLO), public health service officer; b. Toledo, July 17, 1952; MD, Ohio State U., 1979. Physician East Dayton Health Ctr., 1983; dir. Miami Valley Hosp. Family Practice Residency Program, Dayton, Ohio, 1986—2008; assoc. clin. prof. Wright State U. Sch. Medicine; co-founder (with Syed Ahmed) Reach Out of Montgomery County; dir. Family Medicine Dayton, Ohio Dept. Health (ODH), 2011—. Recipient Family Physician of Yr. award, Miami Valley Acad. Family Physicians, 2001, Philanthropist of Yr. award, Ohio Acad. Family Physicians, 2002, American Acad. Family Physicians, 2003, Pride in the Profession award, AMA Found., 2006, Disting. Svc. award, Montgomery County Medical Soc., 2006, Ohio Acad. Family Physicians, 2006, Torchlight Leadership Achievement award, 2009. Office: Ohio Department Health (ODH) 246 N High St Columbus OH 43215 E-mail: director@odh.ohio.gov. *

WYNGAARDEN, JAMES BARNES, retired physician; b. East Grand Rapids, Mich., Oct. 19, 1924; s. Martin Jacob and Johanna (Kempers) W.; m. Ethel Vredevoogd, June 20, 1946 (div. 1977); children: Patricia Wyngaarden Fitzpatrick, Joanna Wyngaarden Gandy, Martha Wyngaarden Krauss, Lisa Wyngaarden, James Barnes Jr. Student, Calvin Coll., 1942—43, Western Mich. U., 1943—44; MD, U. Mich., 1948; DSc (hon.), U. Mich., Med. Coll. of Ohio, 1984, U. Ill., 1985, George Washington U., 1986, U. SC, West Mich. U., 1989, Duke U., 2006; PhD (hon.), Tel Aviv U., 1987. Diplomate Am. Bd. Internal Medicine. Intern Mass. Gen. Hosp., Boston, 1948-49, resident, 1949-51; vis. investigator Pub. Health Rsch. Inst., NYC, 1952-53; investigator NIH, USPHS, Bethesda, Md., 1953-56; asso. prof. medicine and biochemistry Duke U. Med. Sch., 1956-61, prof., 1961-65; vis. scientist Inst. Biologie-Physiochemique, Paris, 1963-64; prof., chmn. U. Pa. Med. Sch., 1965-67; physician-in-chief Med. Svc. Hosp. U. PA., Phila., 1965-67; Frederic M. Hanes prof., chmn. dept. medicine Duke U. Sch. of Medicine, Durham, NC, 1967-82; physician-in-chief Med. Svc. Duke U. Hosp., Durham, 1967-82; chief of staff Duke U. Hosp., Durham, 1981-82; dir. NIH, Bethesda, MD, 1982-89; assoc. dir. life scis. Office of Sci. and Tech. Policy, Exec. Office of Pres., The White House, 1989-90; dir. Human Genome Orgn., 1990-91; fgn. sec. NAS, 1990-94; prof. medicine, assoc. vice chancellor for health affairs Duke U., Durham, NC, 1990-94, ret., 1994; mem. staff VA, Durham County Hosps.; sr. assoc. dean internat. med. programs U. Pa., Phila., 1995-97. Cons. Office Sci. and Tech. Exec. Office of Pres., 1966-72; Mem. Pres.'s Sci. Adv. Com., 1972-73; mem. Pres.'s Com. for Nat. Medal of Sci., 1977-80; mem. adv. com. biology and medicine AEC, 1966-68; mem. bd. sci. counselors NIH, 1971-74; mem. adv. bd. Howard Hughes Med. Inst., 1969-82; mem. adv. council Life Ins. Med. Research Fund, 1967-70; adv. bd. Sci. Yr., 1977-81; vice-chmn. Com. on Study Nat. Needs for Biomed. and Behavioral Rsch. Personnel, NRC, 1977-81; bd. dirs. Idera Pharm., prin. Wash. Adv. Group, 1995-02. Author: (with W.N. Kelley) Gout and Hyperuricemia, 1976; mem. editorial bd. Jour. Biol. Chemistry, 1971-74, Arthritis and Rheumatism, 1959-66, Jour. Clin. Investigation, 1962-66, Ann. Internal Medicine, 1964-74, Medicine, 1963-90; editor: (with J.B. Stanbury, D.S. Fredrickson) The Metabolic Basis of Inherited Disease, 1960, 66, 72, 78, 83, (with O. Sperling and A. DeVries) Purine Metabolism in Man, 1974, (with L.H. Smith, Jr.) Cecil Textbook of Medicine, 16th edit., 1982, 19th edit., 1992. Bd. dirs. Royal Soc. Medicine Found., 1971-76, The Robert Wood Johnson Found. Clin. Scholar Program, 1973-78. Ensign USNR, 1943-46; sr. surgeon USPHS, 1951-56, rear adm. USPHS, 1982-90. Recipient Borden Undergrad. Research award, U. Mich., 1948, NC Gov.'s award for sci., 1974, Disting. Alumnus award We. Mich. U., 1984, Robert Williams award Assn. Profs. Medicine, 1985, Dalton scholar in medicine, Mass. Gen. Hosp., 1950, Richard Schweiker Excellence in Govt. award, 1985, Fedn. of Am. Socs. of Exptl. Biology Pub. Svc. award, 1989, Humanitarian award Nat. Orgn. for Rare Diseases, 1990; Royal Coll. Physicians fellow, 1984. Mem. Am. Rheumatism Assn., Am. Fedn. Clin. Rsch., So. Soc. Clin. Investigation (pres. 1974, founder's medal 1978), ACP (John Phillips Meml. award 1980), Am. Soc. Clin. Investigation, AAAS, Am. Soc. Biol. Chemists, Assn. Am. Physicians (councillor 1973-77, pres. 1978, Kober medal 1991), Endocrine Soc., Nat. Acad. Scis., Royal Acad. Scis. Sweden, Am. Acad. Arts and Sci., Inst. Medicine, Sigma Xi. Clubs: Interurban Clinical (Balt.). Democrat. Presbyterian. Avocations: tennis, skiing, painting. *

WYNN, MARTHA MARIE, anesthesiologist, educator; b. Pitts., Sept. 28, 1944; BA, Marquette U., 1966; MD, U. Wis., 1977. Assoc. prof. anesthesiology U. Wis. Sch. Medicine & Pub. Health, 1983—. Fellow: Am. Soc. Anesthesiology; mem.: Soc. Cardiovasc. Anesthesiologists. Office: B6/305 Clin Sci Ctr 600 Highland Ave Madison WI 53705 Business E-Mail: mmwynn@facstaff.wisc.edu.

WYNNE, JAMES J., research scientist; b. Bklyn., Mar. 19, 1943; AB in Physics, Harvard U., 1964, MA in Physics, 1965, PhD in Physics, 1969. Mgr. Laser Physics and Chemistry Group IBM T.J. Watson Rsch. Ctr.; rsch. scientist IBM Watson Rsch. Ctr., 1971—. Contbr. articles, scientific papers. Co-recipient R.W. Wood prize, Optical Soc. Am., 2004; named one of Inventors of the Yr., Ea. NY Intellectual Property Law Assn., 2001; named to National Inventors Hall of Fame, 2002. Achievements include patents in field; development of Lasik eye surgery. Office: Watson Rsch Ctr 1101 Kithawan Rd Ste 134 Yorktown Heights NY 10598

WYNNE, JOSHUA, dean, cardiologist, educator; AB, Boston U., 1971, MD magna cum laude, 1971; MBA with honors, U. Chgo., 2000; MPH, U. Mich., Ann Arbor, 2002. Cert. in internal medicine and cardiovascular diseases. Residency in internal medicine Harvard Med. Sch. Peter Bent Brigham Hosp., 1971—73, fellowship in cardiology, 1975—78; chief cardiology divsn. Wayne State U., Detroit, 1984—87, v.p. affiliated internists, 1993—97, v.p. faculty senate, 1997—99, pres. faculty senate, 1999—2001; sr. analyst Detroit Med. Ctr. Inst. Strategic Analysis and Innovation, 2001—04; exec. assoc. dean, assoc. dean academic affairs U. ND Sch. Medicine and Health Sciences, Grand Forks, 2004—08, assoc. v.p. health affairs, vice dean, 2008—09, interim v.p. health affairs, interim dean, 2009—10, v.p. health affairs, dean, 2010—. Contbr. articles to profl. jours., chapters to books. Councillor Assn. Univ. Cardiologists; bd. mem. Wayne State U. Fund Med. Rsch. and Edn., Wayne State U. Univ. Internists and Affiliated Internists. Recipient Phi Delta Epsilon Women's Club award, Boston U., Disting. Alumnus award, Boston U. Sch. Medicine, Rev. Elmer and Min. West Meml. award, 2008; named a Top Doc in Cardiology, Detroit Monthly; named one of Best Doctors in America, 1996, 1997, 1999, 2001, 2002—10. Fellow: American Heart Assn. (bd. mem. Mich. and Midwest affiliates, various leadership positions within the Mich. affiliate, Dodrill award 2002), American Coll. Cardiology; mem.: Alpha Omega Alpha. Office: University ND Sch Medicine & Health Sciences Office of Dean 501 N Columbia Rd Stop 9037 Grand Forks ND 58202-9037 Office Phone: 701-777-2516. Business E-Mail: jwynne@medicine.nodak.edu. *

WYPKEMA, WYPKE, surgeon, consultant; b. Pretoria, South Africa, Nov. 20, 1927; s. Albertus and Agatha (Beezhold) W.; m. Garda Mimie Krause, Nov. 22, 1952 (dec.); children: Emma Mary, Agatha Jane, Otto, Wypke Jr. MBChB, U. Pretoria, 1950; ChM, U. Witwatersrand, Johannesburg, South Africa, 1964. House doctor Univ. Hosp., Pretoria, 1951; gen. practice Sterkspruit Bronkhorst Spruit, South Africa, 1952; anatomical & surg. prosector Royal Coll. Surgeons, London, 1953; sr. house doctor Guys Hosp. Orpington Hosp., London, 1954, Hammersmith Hosp., London, 1955; registrar, tutor in gen. surgery Bristol (Eng.) Royal Infirmary, U. Bristol, 1956; registrar Cheltenham (Eng.) Gen. Hosp., 1957, Bristol Royal Infirmary/Univ. Bristol, 1958-59; surg. chief, sr. tutor Baragwanath Hosp./Univ. Witwatersrand, Johannesburg, 1960-63; pvt. practice, cons. professorial unit U. WITS, Johannesburg, 1963—. Chmn. Mayo Clinic, Flora Clinic, Arwyp Clinic; lectr. in field. Contbr. articles to profl. jours. Fellow Royal Coll. Surgeons (London). Avocations: sports, tennis. Home: 132 Bellairs Dr Johannesburg 2125 South Africa Office: Mayo Clinic William Nicol Dr PO Box 5137 Weltevreden Roodepoort 1715 South Africa Business E-Mail: mayoww@iafrica.com.

WYRTZEN, JAMES CHARLES, pastoral psychotherapist, marriage, family, group therapist, academic administrator; b. NYC, Aug. 27, 1942; s. James and Malvina Wyrtzen; m. Marcia Metz, Aug. 17, 1975; children: Christy, Andrew Mark, David Christopher. BA, Moravian Coll. and Theol. Sem., 1964, MDiv, 1967; DMin, NY Theol. Sem., 1981; DD (hon.), Moravian Theol. Sem., 1991. Cert. mental health counselor NY, diplomate emeritus Am. Assn. Pastoral Counselors, 2008; cert. in pastoral care Blanton Peale Grad Inst., 1970, in pastoral counseling 1973, lic. marriage and family counselor NY, NJ, Calif. Pastor United Meth. Ch., Westhampton Beach, NY, 1967—70, Whitestone United Meth. Ch., NY, 1970—73; dir. Whitestone Counseling Ctr., 1973—76; staff therapist Yorkville Counseling Ctr., NY, South Nassau Family Counseling Inst., NY; pvt. practice psychotherapy NYC, 1973—2008; exec. dir. Creative Living Counseling Ctr., Allendale, NJ, 1976—88, sr. staff therapist, 1988—; dir. Blanton, Peale Grad. Inst. Inst., 1988—99. Ministry mem. United Meth. Ch., 1966—2008; pres. Hampton Coun. Chs., 1969—70; mem. Nat. Mental Health Leadership Forum, 1988—92; trustee Found. Mental Health, 1988—2000; sec.-treas. Am. Assn. Pastoral Counselors, 1983—87, mem. exec. com., 1983—92, bd. govs., 1983—92, v.p., 1988—90, pres., 1990—92, chmn. advocacy com., 1992—2002; v.p. Alumni Assn. Insts. Religion and Health, 1985—87, pres., 1987—88; mem. Am. Group Psychotherapy Assn., Am. Assn. Marriage and Family Counselors; sec. Nat. Coalition Spiritual Healthcare and Counseling, 1997—98, v.p., 1998—2000, Osher Lifelong Learning Inst., 2011—. Recipient Cora Dosta Moses Homeltics prize, Moravian Theol. Sem., 1967, Disting. Contbn. award, Eastern Region Am. Assn. Pastoral Counselors, 1991, Disting. Alumnus award, Blanton Peale Inst., 1995, award, Metro Chpt. NY Assn. Marriage and

Family Therapy, 1998. Democrat. Methodist. Home: 2086 Avenue Of The Trees Carlsbad CA 92008-1104 Home Phone: 760-720-1759. Personal E-mail: jcw43210@aol.com.

XAVIER, ANDRÉ JUNQUEIRA, medical educator; b. Rio de Janeiro, Sept. 24, 1963; M, U. Fed. de Santa Catarina, 2004; PhD, U. Fed. de São Paulo, 2007. Prof. U. do Sul de Santa Catarina, 2002—. Bd. dirs. Soc. Brasileira de Geriatria e Gerontologia, 2010—. Avocation: sailing. Home: Nicolau Antônio Deschamps 103/ A 201 Florianópolis Santa Catarina 88034404 Brazil Home Fax: 55214832698932. Personal E-mail: andre.xavier@unisul.br.

XAVIER, ARUN, dentist, educator; b. Kerala, Mar. 29, 1983; B in Dental Surgery, AB Shetty Meml. Inst. Dental Scis., Mangalore, India, 2006, M in Dental Surgery, 2010. Clin. asst. prof. Amrita Sch. Dentistry, Amrita Inst. Med. Scis. and Rsch. Ctr., Kochi, Kerala, 2010—. Office: Amrita Inst Med Scis and Rsch Ctr Amrita Dental Sch Ponekkara Ernakulam 41 Kochi Kerala 682041 India

XAVIER, FAUSTO JORGE CANOVA, internist, consultant; b. Lisbon, Portugal, July 26, 1944; s. Fausto Tavares and Paulina Canova Xavier; m. Julia Maria Xavier; children: Fausto Nuno, Jorge Canova. Gen. practitioner, Lisbon U., 1973; ENT specialist, Hosp. Civis, Lisbon, 1980. Gen. practitioner Hosp. Civis, Lisbon, 1973—76, hospitaler ENT asst., 1976—93, Hosp. Pulido Valente, Lisbon, 1994—95; ENT grad. asst. Hosp. Dr. José Antunes, Torres Vedras, Portugal, 1995—2002; ENT dir. Centro Hospitalar, Torres Vedras, 2002—. ENT specialist Brit. Hosp., Lisbon, 1985—; clin. dir. Liga Amigos Hosp., 1980—87. Contbr. articles to profl. jours. Mem. Banda União Sanjoanense, Albergaria-a-Velha, 1995, Banda União Pinheirense, Albergaria-a-Velha, 1995—. Mem.: Médicos da Carreira Hospitalar. Avocation: skiing. Office: R Forno Tijolo 19-2 Lisbon Portugal Home: Rua Professor Carlos Teixeira 1600-608 Lisbon Portugal

XAVIER, RUI, facial plastic surgeon; b. Viseu, Portugal, July 22, 1965; MD, Faculdade Medicina Porto, 1989. Physician Hosp. Arrabida-Porto, 1998. Mem.: European Acad. Facial Plastic Surgery. Avocations: scuba diving, tennis, history. Home: Rua Aristides Sousa Mendes 210 Porto 4150-088 Portugal Personal E-mail: rjxavier@iol.pt.

XIA, GUOHUA, scientist, psychiatrist, psychologist; married; 1 child, M-Y. MB in Clin. Medicine, Beijing Med. U., 1986, MA in Marriage and Family Therapy, U. Nebr., Lincoln, 1998, PhD in Psychology, 2002. Lic. Calif., Ohio, 2007. Physician The 2nd Hosp. of Hebei Med. U., Shijiazhuang, China, 1986—93; counselor Counseling and Psychotherapy Ctr. Peking U., Beijing, 1993—95; tchr. ZhongGuanCun Software Coll., Beijing, 1993—95; database analyst, info. specialist and grad. asst. U. Nebr., Lincoln, 1995—2001; physician U. Texas, Houston, 2001—02, U. Tex. Southwestern Med. Ctr., Dallas, 2002—05; asst. prof. Case Western Reserve U., 2005—07, head, Transcranial Magnetic Stimulation program, 2005—07; asst. clin. prof. U. Calif., Davis, 2007—; prin. investigator TMS, 2007—. Sec. Hebei Mental Health Orgn., Shijiazhuang, 1990—93; assoc. editor Frontiers in Impulsivity, Compulsivity and Behavioral Dyscontrol, 2009—. Contbr. articles to profl. jours., chapters to books. Recipient Young Investigator award, Nat. Alliance for Rsch. on Schizophrenia and Depression, 2005, NCDEU New Investigator award, NIMH, 2006. Mem.: APA, Internat. Soc. Electroconvulsive Therapy and Neurostimulation, Am. Psychiatric Assn., Psychol. Assn. China, Chinese Med. Assn. (Excellent Acad. Paper award 1993), Chinese Mental Health Assn., Am. Psychiatry Assn., Kappa Omicron Nu.

XIA, TONGLI, pathologist, educator; b. Langfang, Hebei, China, Apr. 30, 1938; s. Enpu Xia and Xia Li; m. Lin Zhao, Apr. 10, 1962; children: Jun, Ying. MD, Beijing Med. U., 1961. Asst. Beijing Med. Coll., 1961—63, physician, 1964—78; physician-in-charge Beijing Med. U., 1979—86, assoc. prof., 1987—89, prof., chmn. dept., 1990—. Vis. scientist Emory U.; vis. prof. U. South Ala., 1986—88, U. Tex. MD Anderson Cancer Ctr., U. Va., 1995—96. Chief editor: Prostate Cancer, the Basic and Clinical Aspects, 2000, Contemporary Urologic Pathology, 2002, Oncology, The Specific Diagnosis, 2002, Practical Diagnosis and Treatment for Low Urinary Tract Obstruction, 2003, Laboratory Diagnostics for Cancer, 2005. Recipient Sci. and Tech. Progress award, State Ednl. Com., 1995, Ministry Pub. Health China, 1996, State Sci. and Tech. Com., 1997. Fellow: Coll. Am. Pathologists; mem.: Internat. Soc. Urol. Pathology, Chinese Med. Assn. Office: Peking U Inst Urology 8 Xishiku St Beijing 100034 China Office Phone: 8610-66551122-2579. Business E-Mail: tlxia@163bj.com.

XIA, ZEYANG, research scientist; b. Hubei, China, Oct. 14, 1980; PhD, Tsinghua U., 2008. Vis. scholar Tech. U. Munich, 2005—06; rsch. fellow Nanyang Technol. U., 2008—09; rsch. scientist Ind. U.-Purdue U. Indpls., 2009—. Tech. cons. Ningbo Mecai Automobile Inner Decoration Co. Ltd, China, 2007. Vis. Scholarship, Chinese Scholarship Coun., Chinese Govt. Mem.: IEEE, IEEE/RAS Tech. Com. Robot Learning, IEEE/RAS Tech. Com. Mobile Manipulation, IEEE/RAS Tech. Com. Algorithms Planning and Control Robot Motion, IADR/AADR. Office: 723 W Michigan St SL260 Indianapolis IN 46202 Personal E-mail: zeyangxia@gmail.com.

XIAN, LI JIAN, pharmacologist, educator; B, Sun Yat-Sen U., 1966; MS in Pharmacology, Sun Yat-sen U., Guangzhou, China, 1982. From clin. staff to prof. Sun Yat-sen U. of Med. Sci., 1968—97; prof. Sun Yat-sen U. Med. Sci., 1997—. Dir. dept. antitumor drugs rsch. Sun Yat-Sen U., Guangzhou, China, 1994—, assoc. chief biotherapy ctr., 2000—06, doctoral supr., 2000—; mem. expert group Nat. Natural Scis. Found., China, 1995, Supr. Drugs Agy. of China, 1995. Mem. editl. com.: Chinese Jour. Cancer, 2000. Recipient 2d Class prize advanced scis. and technique, Nat. Edn. Ministry, China, 1997; grantee, Nat. Natural Scis. Found., China, 1990, 1994, 2003, Priority Discipline Found., Nat. Health Ministry, China, 2000. Avocations: music, photography, travel, literature. Office: Cancer Center Sun Yat-sen University 651 Dongfengdongl 510060 Guangzhou Yandongsheng China Office Phone: 86-20-87343186. Business E-Mail: lj_xian@yahoo.com.

XIANFANG, YUE, engineering educator; b. Shanxi, Aug. 31, 1974; D, U. Sci. & Tech. Beijing, 2007. Assoc. prof. U. Sci. & Tech. Beijing, 2010—. Gen. mgr.'s asst. Commonage Constrn. & Devel. Co., Ltd., Tianjin, 1996—99. Recipient Provincial Sci. & Tech. Progress prize. Fellow: Biomed. Engring. and Clin. Medicine. Avocations: travel, mountain climbing, swimming, tai chi. Office: 30 Xueyuan Rd Haidian Dist Beijing 100083 China Office Fax: 86-10-62329145. Business E-Mail: yuexf@me.ustb.edu.cn.

XIANGEN, SHI, neurosurgeon, educator; b. Shaoxing, Zhejiang, Oct. 8, 1956; M, Jilin U., 1986; PhD, Capital Med. U., 1992. Prof., chmn. dept. neurosurgery Beijing Sanbo Brain Hosp., Capital Med. U., 2004—. Mem.: China Dr. Assn. (named Best Neurosurgeon 2010). Avocation: swimming. Office: Xiang Shan Rd Yi Ke Song 50# Haidian Beijing 100093 China Office Fax: 86-1062856902. Business E-Mail: shixen@sina.com.

XIAN-WEN, YANG, biologist, educator; b. Jiangxi, China, Sept. 30, 1976; PhD, Kunming Inst. Botany, Chinese Acad. Scis., 2006. Assoc. prof. South China Sea Inst. Oceanology, Chinese Acad. Scis., 2008—. Office: 164 W Xingang Rd Guangzhou Guangdong 510301 China Business E-Mail: yangxw76@126.com.

XIAO, JIANBO, research scientist; b. Yancheng, Jiangsu, China, Feb. 19, 1979; PhD, Okayama Prefectural U., 2009, Ctrl. South U., 2009. Rsch. scientist Coll. Life & Environment Sci., Shanghai Normal U., 2009—. Editor Jour. Functional Foods Health and Disease; assoc. editor African Jour. Food Sci., Jour. Medicinal Plant Rsch.; editor-in-chief Jour. Toxicology and Environ. Health Sci. Office: Guilin 100 Rd Shanghai 200234 China E-mail: jianboxiao@yahoo.com.

XIAO, YIN, dental educator, educator; b. Wuhan, Hubei, Australia; married. BDSc, Hubei Med. U., Wuhan, China, 1986, MDSc, 1991; PhD, U. Queensland, Brisbane, Australia, 2000. Lectr. and periodontist Wuhan U., Hubei, China, 1991—95; rsch. officer Queensland U. Tech., 2000—02, rsch. fellow, 2002—05, assoc. prof., 2005—. Fellow, NHMRC, 2002. Mem.: ASBTE, ANZORS. Office: Queensland Univ Tech 60 Musk Ave Kelvin Grove Brisbane Queensland 4059 Australia Business E-Mail: yin.xiao@qut.edu.au.

XIAO, ZHIQIANG, medical educator; b. Liling, Hunan, China, Dec. 5, 1963; s. Bangxiong and Zhilan Xiao; m. Jianling Li; 1 child, Ta. BS, Hunan Med. U., Changsha, 1985, MS, 1988, PhD, 1996. Cert. prof. oncology Ministry of Health China, 2001. Asst. prof. Cancer Rsch. Inst., Hunan Med. U., 1988—93, assoc. prof., 1994—97; rsch. assoc. Sch. Medicine, Wayne State U., Detroit, 1997—2001; prof. Xiangya Hosp. Ctrl. South U., Changsha, 2001—, assoc. dir. key lab. cancer proteomics Chinese Ministry of Health, 2003—. Contbr. articles to profl. med. jour. Recipient First prize, Hunan Province Govt. China, 1999, 2005; scholarship, Ministry of Edn. China, 2003, grant, Nat. Natural Sci. Found. China, 2003—04, Ministry of Sci. and Tech. China, 2004. Mem.: Chinese Cancer Assn., Chinese Human Proteomic Orgn. Home and Office: Xiangya Hosp 87 Xiangyal Rd 410008 Changsha H"nBnsheng China Office Phone: 86-731-4327239. Office Fax: 86-731-4327321. Business E-Mail: zqxiao2001@yahoo.com.cn.

XIAODONG, ZHU, surgeon; b. Henan, 1932; Grad., Harbin Med. U., 1956; postgrad. in Cardiovascular Surgery, Peking Union Med. Coll., 1970. Tng. to the UK and Australian heart surgery, 1988, academic exchanges Phillippines, 1980, Iran, Azerbaijan, Australia; cons. Weisheng Bu Health tech. Appraisal; cons. med. sciences degree com. Chinese Acad.; tech. cons. PLA's Navy and Air Force Gen. Hosp.; pres. Fu Wai Hosp., Beijing, 1963—65. Recipient Hon. Title and awards, Inst. Med. Sci., Won the World Surg. Soc., 1988; grantee Outstanding Contributions of Young Med. Experts, State and Tech., 1993. Mem.: Chinese Med. Assn. Soc. of Thoracic and Cardiovascular Surgery (chmn.), Chinese Assn. (cons.). Office: Fu Wai Hospital 167 Beilishi Rd Xicheng Dist Beijing 100037 China Office Phone: 861068313013. Office Fax: 861068313012. *

XIAO-PING, CHEN, medical educator; b. Liuyang, Hunan, China, July 28, 1974; PhD, Ctrl. South U., 2002. Prof. Ctrl. South U., 2005—. Office: Dept Pharmacology 110 Xiangya Rd Changsha Hunan 410078 China Personal E-mail: chenxp74@hotmail.com.

XIE, BIN, medical association administrator; b. Luzhon, Sichuan, China, Nov. 8, 1964; MD, Shanghai Jiao Tong U., 1992. V.p. Shanghai Mental Health Ctr. Shanghai Jiao Tong U., 2003—. Recipient Shanghai Sci. and Tech. Progress award, Shanghai Municipality Govt., 2006, 2009; Young fellow, World Psychiatry Assn., 1999, Harvard Med. Sch. Freeman fellow, 2002—03. Master: Soc. Mental Health, Chinese Assn. Preventive Medicine, Chinese Psychiatrist Assn.; mem.: Chinese Soc. Psychiatry. Office: 600 Wan Ping Nan Rd Shanghai 200030 China Office Fax: 8621-64387986. Personal E-mail: binxie64@gmail.com.

XIE, H. BILL, pathologist, medical educator; s. Zhihe Xie and Peifang Chen; m. Ru Tian, Feb. 25, 1987; children: Tina J., Maria T. MD, Hunan Med. U., Changsha, China, 1982; MS, U. Wis., Madison, 1989, PhD, 1994. Cert. Ednl. Commn. For Fgn. Med. Grads., 1995, diplomate Am. Bd. Pathology, 2000. Instr. Hunan Med. U., Changsha, China, 1983—87; rsch. fellow U. Wis., Madison, 1995—96; resident physician U. Wis. Hosp. and Clinics, Madison, 1996—2000; cytopathology fellow Loyola U. Med. Ctr., Maywood, Ill., 2000—01; asst. prof. Duke U. Med. Ctr., Durham, NC, 2001—. Tchg. asst. U. Wis., Madison, 1991—93; dir. Laser Capture Microdissection Core Lab. Fellowship, Armed Forces Inst. Pathology, 2000. Fellow: Am. Soc. Cytopathology, Am. Soc. Clin. Pathology, Coll. Am. Pathologists; mem.: Can. Acad. Pathology, US Acad. Pathology. Achievements include research in ion transport across the cellular membrane has significant impact on understanding the pathogenesis and guiding the treatment of some of medical diseases, such as renal difficiency, edema, etc; Motoneuron Differentiation has provided significant insights on the mechanisms regulating neuron maturation during development; development of Organotypic Culture on porous membrane modification has been proved to be a versatile and powerful model for research; the results of the Wang Needle Biopsy Review serves as useful guidelines for patient care. E-mail: h.billxie@duke.edu.

XIN, HUA, cell biologist; b. Shanghai, May 20, 1950; d. Wei Xin and Mingnian Zhuang; m. Liming Chen, Mar. 1978; 1 child, Xinzheng Chen. MD, Shandong Med. Coll., Jinan, China, 1976. Hematologist No. 2 Provincial Hosp., Jinan, 1977—78; asst. prof. Shandong Med. Coll., Jinan, 1978—84; vis. scholar Peking U., Beijing, 1984—86; lectr. Shandong Med. U., Jinan, 1985—96; vis. scholar U. Ill., Urbana-Champaign, 1990—91; assoc. prof. cell biology Shandong U. Med. Sch., Jinan, Shandong, 1996—2000; prof., dir. Shandong U. Med. Sch., Inst. Cell Biology, Jinan, 2001—. Author: (book) Medical Cell Biology, in Overview of New Subjects of Medicine, Cell Biological basis of GeneticDiseases, People's Health; editor: Medical Cell Biology, 2004—08; contbr. articles to profl. jours.; editor: (book) Genetic Diseases, 2000, Overeview of New Subjects od Medicine, 2001, Transplant in Brain, 1993; editor: (chief) Medical Cell Biology Experiment, 2001, Advanced Technologies in Cell Biology, 2008; editor: (assoc.) Essential Ultrastructuer in Medcine, 2003, Experiment of Medical Cell and Molecular Biology, 2007. Fellow: Chinese Soc. Cell Biology (assoc.; br. pres. tchg. & popularization sect. 2003—); mem.: Chinese Med. Soc. (pres. med. cell biology sect. 1996—), Shandong Soc. Cell Biology (v.p. 1998—), Chinese Med. Assn. (bd. mem. cell biology section 1998—). Achievements include discovery of gypenosides may protect primary cultures of rat cortical cells against oxidative neurotoxicity. Office: Inst Cell Biology Shandong Univ Med Sch 44 West Wen Hua Rd Shandong Jinan 250012 China

XIONG, GE, surgeon, educator; b. Wuhan, Hubei, China, Mar. 19, 1970; MD, Tongji Med. U., PhD, 1998. Cons., prof., dept. hand surgery Beijing Jishuitan Hosp., 1998—. Mem.: AASH, ASSH. Office: 31 Xinjiekou E St Beijing Xichen 100035 China Personal E-mail: dr_xiongge@hotmail.com.

XIONG, LI, surgeon; b. Changsha, June 28, 1980; D, Ctrl. South U., 2007. Surgeon Second Xiangya Hosp., 2007—11. Office: Renmin Rd 139 Changsha Hunan 410011 China Business E-Mail: lixionghn@163.com.

XIONG, LU, engineering educator; b. Hubei, May 9, 1977; PhD, Hong Kong U. Sci. and Tech., 2004. Assoc. prof. SW Jiaotong U., Chengdu, China, 2006—. Home: SW Jiaotong University Chengdu 610031 China Personal E-mail: luxiong_2004@163.com.

XIONG, TOUSU SAYDANGNMVANG, minister, theology studies educator; b. Hmong Long Cheng, June 23, 1966; arrived in U.S., 1976, naturalized, 1996; s. Nhialue Saydang and May (Vang) X.; m. Zoua Pahoua Moua, Sept. 14, 1993; children: Chivkeeb Genesis Toupa, Naamonunas Ruth, Nujsimloob Hebrews, Nkaujzuapaaj Esther, Naomi Mayvang, Psalm Ntawvnkauj, Johnny Tshwmsim, Eve Nkaujab. BA in Bibl. Studies, Simpson Coll., San Francisco, 1989; MA in Theology, Mennonite Brethren Bibl. Sem., Fresno, Calif., 1991; AS in Computerized Acctg., Phillips Jr. Coll., Fresno, Calif., 1993. Ordained to ministry Christian and Missionary Alliance, 1991. Assoc. min. Hmong San Raphael (Calif.) Bapt. Ch., 1986-88; youth min. Hmong Alliance Ch. of Santa Barbara, Goleta, Calif., 1984-85, Hmong Alliance Ch. of Fresno, 1989—; med. record acct. Dr. Suchat Jariangprasert Med. Clinic, Fresno, Calif., 1993—96; assoc., shareholder Wal-Mart Stores, Inc., Bentonville, Ark., 1998—; attendance com. bd. mem. Mother May Vang Xiong Meml. Found. Inc.; agrl. educator Hmong Lang. Pa Dao Arts, 1946—86, Xieng Khouang Laos, 1986; exec. com. chmn. capt. Nhialue Saydang Xiong Heritage Found. Inc.; lay minister elder chaplain CIA SGU Royal Lao Unit, 1960—75, Long Tieng, Laos, 1996; gen. mgr. Pahoua Moua Xiong Heritage Found. Inc., Walmart Stores Inc.; store mgr. dist. grocery market pers. mgr. Calif. State U. Fresno, Ban Vinai, Thailand, 1976. Mem. Nat. Eagle Scout Assn. Mission Coun. Troop 127, Goleta, Calif.; assoc., com. bd. mem. Phagna Norapamok Gen. Vang Pao Meml. Found., Inc., CIA SGU Royal Lao Unit, 1960—75, Long Tieng Laos, 2011; attendance com. mem. Lao Family Cmty. Fresno, Inc., 1986, Hmong Internat. New Yr. found., Inc., Fresno, 2006—; edn. com. mem. Hmong 18 Clan Coun., Inc., Fresno, Calif., 1991; CEO, owner Hmoob Xiong Ts Hummer H2 Adventure Outdoor Offroad Acad., Fresno, 2009—. Mission coun. Unit Scoutmaster Larry Miller, Santa Barbara, Calif.; scoutmaster Boy Scouts America, 1984—85, life mem., eagle scout, 1983—; life mem. Nat. Eagle Scout Assn., Mission Coun., Troop 127, Goleta, Calif. Recipient Eagle Scout Lifetime Membership award, Boy Scouts America, 1983. Avocation: computers. Office: Hmong Alliance Ch Fresno 8234 E Belmont Ave Fresno CA 93727-9725 Mailing: PO Box 1528 Clovis CA 93613 Personal E-mail: xteagle76@yahoo.com.

XIROUCHAKIS, ELIAS, gastroenterologist; b. Thessaloniki, Jan. 1, 1972; MD, U. Rome La Sapienza, 1996. Registrar NIMTS Vets. Hosp., 2000—02, 1st IKA Hosp., 2002—06; clin. and rsch. fellow Royal Free Hosp., 2007—08; cons. gastroenterologist, hepatologist Athens Med. P. Faliron Hosp., 2008—. Hon. rsch. fellow U. Coll. London, 2007—08; bd. editors Annals Gastroenterology, 2008—10, World Jour. Gastrointestinal Endoscopy, 2010. Fellowship, Hellenic Soc. Gastroenterology and Nutrition, Rsch. grant, Hellenic Soc. Study Liver. Fellow: European Bd. Gastroenterology and Hepatology; mem.: Cochrane Database Systematic Revs., European Assn. Study Liver. Avocations: music, sports. Office: 36 Areos St Palaio Faliro Attiki 17562 Greece E-mail: elmoxir@yahoo.gr.

XU, DONGBING, pediatrician; b. Beijing, July 6, 1965; s. Guoliang Xu and Peihua Zhao; m. Yifu Yang, Sept. 18, 1996; 1 child, Hans Louyang. MD, Capital Inst. Medicine, Beijing, 1988; MS in Clin. Epidemiology, Erasmus U., Rotterdam, Netherlands, 1998; BS in Med. Tech., Bemidji State U., 2000; MS in Med. Tech., U. N.D., Grand Forks, 2002. Lic. pediatrician China, 1988, cert. med. technologist ASCP, 2000. Pediatrician Beijing Children's Hosp., 1988—; clin. lab. scientist Jay County Hosp., Portland, Ind., 2000; med. technologist First Care Med. Svcs., Fosston, Minn., 2000—. Mem.: Chinese Med. Assn. Office: First Care Med Svcs 900 Hilligoss Blvd SE Fosston MN 56542 Home: 402 31st St NE Apt 311 Rochester MN 55906-2851

XU, FENG, research scientist, educator; b. Xiaoshan, Zhejiang, China, Feb. 20, 1964; s. Rupeng Xu and Aiqing Chai; m. Ling Ying, Oct. 6, 1963; 1 child, Duo. PhD, Dalian Inst. Chem. Physics, China, 1999. Assoc. prof. Dalian Inst. of Chem. Physics, Dalian, Liaoning, China, 1999—2001; postdoctoral rschr. analytical instruments divsn.

Shimadzu Corp, Kyoto, 2001—03; postdoctoral rschr. U. Tokushima Dept Medicinal Chemistry, Tokushima, Japan, 2003—05; rsch. assoc. La. State U. Chemistry Dept., Baton Rouge, 2005—. Mem. internat. adv. bd. analytical abstracts Royal Soc. of Chemistry, London, 2004—. Author: Electrophoresis, Analytical Chemistry; contbr. articles to profl. jours. Office: La State U 8000 GSRI Rd Bldg 3100 Baton Rouge LA 70820 Office Phone: 225-578-5248. E-mail: fengxu22@gmail.com.

XU, GUORONG, medical researcher; b. Shanghai, Dec. 3, 1943; s. Wei Geng Xu and Feng Zhu Zhang; m. Lifen Qian; 1 child, Cheng Kai. MD, Shanghai Med. Coll., 1970; PhD, U. London, 1984. Resident in surgery Shuicheng (China) Steel Works Hosp., 1970—73, chief surg. resident in surgery, 1975—78; postdoctoral fellow dept. gen. surgery Zhong Shan Hosp., Shanghai Med. Coll., 1973—75, attending, 1984—88, assoc. dir., cons. surgeon, 1988—89; rsch. assoc. NJ Med. Sch., Newark, 1989—94, asst. prof., 1994—99, assoc. prof. dept. medicine, 1999—2003, prof. dept. medicine, 2003—. Contbr. articles. Grantee Grany-in Aid award, Am. Heart Assn., 1998-1999, Veterans Health Adminstrn., 2001—. Mem.: Am. Soc. Biochemistry and Molecular Biology, Am. Gastroent. Assn. Achievements include research in Created a rabbit model and found dietary cholesterol causes hypercholesterolemia in rabbits but not in rats because it only expands bile acid pool in rabbits that inhibits bile acid synthesis; Found feeding cholesterol increases ASBT expression in the ileum in rabbits but not in rats such that the bile acid pool only expands in rabbits; design of A rabbit model constructed with bile fistula such that the bile acid pool size can be measured & physiological effect of individual bile acid be tested; research in Found the different response to dietary cholesterol in rabbits and rats is due to the nuclear receptor FXR is activated in rabbits but not in rats. Office: GI Research Lab (15A) VA Med Ctr 385 Tremont Ave East Orange NJ 07018-1095 Personal E-mail: xugu@umdnj.edu.

XU, HONG, herbalist, acupuncturist, educator, researcher; arrived in Australia, 1995; d. Houen Xu and Jidi Chen; m. Yan Xu, July 21, 1996; 1 child, Ao-Chen (Julia). MB, Beijing Traditional Chinese Medicine Coll., 1990; PhD, Victoria U., 2002. Registered acupuncturist and Chinese herbalist Chinese Medicine Registration Bd. Victoria, 2002, cert. in osteoporosis Osteoporosis Com. of China Gerontol. Soc., Internat. Chinese Hard Tissue Soc., 1998, in med. radiation safety Dept. Human Svcs., Australia, 1999. Lectr., physician, clin. practice supr. Beijing (China) U. Phys. Edn., 1990—95, dietician Affiliated Olympic Sports Del., 1991—93; lectr. Sch. Health Scis. Victoria U., Melbourne, 1997—2005, coord. Chinese herbal medicine Sch. Health Scis., 2001—03, coord. Chinese medicine discipline Sch. Health Scis., 2003—06, sr. lectr. Sch. Health Scis., 2005—08, assoc. prof., Sch. Biomed. & Health Scis., 2008—. Vis. scholar Prince of Wales Hosp. Med. Sch. Chinese U. Hong Kong, 1993; vis. scholar Faculty Human Devel. Victoria U., 1995—96; practitioner Chinese medicine, mgr. Chinese Medicine Clinic, Melbourne, 1996—; vis. prof. Beijing U. Chinese Medicine, 2005—. Author (editor): The Progress of Resources, Environment and Health in China. SCOPE China III - International Council of Scientific Unions (ICSU), 2004. Recipient Accomplishment award, Beijing U. Phys. Edn., 1993, Sci. Rschr. award, 1995, Disting. Academic Achievement award, Victoria U., 2003, Faculty Health, Engring. & Sci. Tchg. Excellence award, 2008, Vice-Chancello's Citation for Excellence Tchg. & Learning award, 2008. Mem.: Coun. Splty. Com. Gynaecology World Fedn. Chinese Medicine, World Fedn. Acupuncture-Moxibustion Socs. (mem. local academic and sci. adv. com. 2004—), Australian Acupuncture and Chinese Medicine Assn. Ltd., Inaugural Australian Coun. Chinese Medicine Edn. (hon.). Achievements include patents in field. Avocations: tai chi, calligraphy, ping pong/table tennis, reading. Office Phone: 61-3-93261868. Business E-Mail: hong.xu@vu.edu.au.

XU, HONGGUANG, orthopedist, educator; b. Chaoxian, Dec. 20, 1964; MD, Peking Union Med. Coll., 2005. Prof Dept. Orthop., 1985. Office: 2 Zhenshanxilu Yijishan Hosp Wuhu Anhui 241001 China Office Fax: 86-553-5739037. Business E-Mail: xuhg@medmail.com.cn.

XU, HONGLIN, medical researcher; b. Hang Zhou, China, Oct. 16, 1972; PhD, Chinese Acad. Preventive Medicine, 2001. Dept. chief Nat. Vaccine and Serum Inst., 2006—. Office: 4 San Jian Fang Nan Li Chao Yang Dist Beijing 100024 China Personal E-mail: xhyct@yahoo.com.

XU, HUA-ZI, medical educator, department chairman; b. Yueqing, Zhejiang, China, Feb. 22, 1963; MD, Zhejiang Med. U., 1983. Prof. Dept. Orthop. Surgery, Second Affiliated Hosp. Wenzhou Med. Coll., 2000—, chmn., 2006. Recipient Sci. and Technol. awards, Chinese Med. Assn., Dept. Health Zhejiang Province, Med. Tech. award. Fellow: Chinese Assn. Spine and Spinal Cord Injury, Chinese Orthop. Assn.; mem.: North Am. Spine Soc., Internat. Med. Soc. Paraplegia. Avocations: running, mountain climbing. Office: 109 Xue Yuan Xi Rd Wenzhou Zhejiang 325000 China Office Fax: 086-577-88832693. Personal E-mail: spine-xu@163.com.

XU, JIANGUANG, hospital administrator; MD, PhD. Pres. Huashan Hosp., China. Co-author: (publs.) Application of fetal neural stem cells transplantation in delaying denervated muscle atrophy in rats with peripheral nerve injury, 2010. Address: Huashan Hospital Office of the President 19 Fl 12 Wulumuqi Zhong Lu Jing An Shanghai China Office Phone: 62489999 Ext. 1900. *

XU, KAITIAN, chemistry professor; b. China, July 20, 1963; PhD, Hong Kong U. Sci. & Tech., 2000. Prof. Multidisciplinary Rsch. Ctr., Shantou U., 2005. Office: DaXueLu 243 Shantou Guangdong 515063 China Office Fax: 86-754-82901179. Business E-Mail: ktxu@stu.edu.cn.

XU, SHUQIANG, hospital administrator; MB, Beijing U. of Chinese Medicine, M in Medicine; LLD, North-East Normal U. Postdoctoral rsch. fellow in economics Beijing Normal U.; dir. dept. of human resources China-Japan Friendship Hospital, China, 1993—95, asst. pres., 1995—98, v.p., 1998—2004, pres., 2004—. Mem. 11th Chinese People's Polit. Consultative Conf.; standing com. mem. All China Youth Fedn.; vice chmn. Chinese Assn. of Rehab. Medicine, Chinese Assn. of Integrative Medicine, chmn. of mng. com.; vice chmn. Chinese Assn. of Med. Equipment, Chinese Assn. of Med. Rescue, China Japan Med. Sci. and Tech. Exch. Assn., Chinese Assn. of Geriatrics Rsch.; mng. dir. Chinese Hosps. Assn., chmn. hosp. economy mgmt. com.; mng dir. China Doctors Assn., vice chmn. integrative medicine doctor br.; exec. dep. mng. dir. China Assn. of Chinese Medicine, vice chmn of mng. com.; dir. Chinese Med. Assn. Office: China Japan Friendship Hospital 2 East Yinghuayuan St Hepingli Beijing 100029 China Office Phone: 00861064282297. *

XUDONG, LIU, gastroenterologist; b. Lvliang, China, Mar. 5, 1976; MD, Sun Yat-sen U., 2009. Vice dir., dept. liver disease Ruikang Hosp. Guangxi Traditional Chinese Medicine U., 2009—. Office: 10 Huadong Rd Nanning Guangxi 530011 China Personal E-mail: lxdlhx@163.com.

XUE, CHARLIE CHANGLI, medical educator; b. Chaoyang, Guangdong, China, Sept. 14, 1965; s. Song Yuan Xue and Shi Mei Zhuang; m. Bailey K.F. Lim, Dec. 10, 2000. MB, Guangzhou U. Chinese Medicine, China, 1987; PhD, Royal Melbourne Inst. Tech. U., Australia, 2000. Registered Chinese Medicine Registration Bd. of Victoria, 2001. Assoc. lectr. and physician Guangzhou U. of Chinese Medicine, 1987—93; part-time lectr. Royal Melbourne Inst. Tech. U., Bundoora, Victoria, Australia, 1994—95, full time lectr., 1996—98, sr. lectr., head of chinese medicine, 1999—2002, assoc. prof., head Chinese medicine unit, 2003—. Mem. Chinese Medicine Registration Bd. of Victoria, Melbourne, Australia, 2000—; short term cons. WHO, Manila, 2002—; hon. acad. advisor Chinese U. of Hong Kong, Hong Kong, 2001—; co-editor Annals of Chinese Medicine, Singapore, 2003—; chair, program accreditation com. Sydney (Australia) Inst. of Traditional Chinese Medicine, 2002—. Author: more than 40 conf. procs.; contbr. articles to profl. publs. Pres. The First World Congress on Chinese Medicine, Melbourne, 2002—03; mem. Australian Coun. of Chinese Medicine Edn., Brisbane, Queensland, 2003. Fellow: Australian Acupuncture and Chinese Medicine Assn. Achievements include patents pending for Chinese herbal medicine for hay fever; development of five Chinese medicine degree programs. Office: RMIT Univ Plenty Rd 3083 Bundoora VIC Australia Office Fax: 613 99257178; Home Fax: 613 94401218. Personal E-mail: charlie.xue@optusnet.com.au. E-mail: charlie.xue@rmit.edu.au.

XUE, KAIXIAN, biomedical researcher; s. Renjie and Shuzhen (Xia) Xue; m. Dingyi Tang; children: Zhong, Hua. BS, Fudan U., Shanghai, China, 1962; MS, Wuhan U., China, 1965. Rschr. asst. Wuhan U., 1962—67; dir. of asst. Rugao Hosp., China, 1968—78; dir. lab of genetics, prof. Jiangsu Inst. for Cancer Rsch., Nanjing, Jiangsu Province, China, 1979—. Editor-in-chief Cancer Genetics (Nat. Sci. Fund prize, 2000); author: Micronucleus Test, Essential of Human Genetics, National Environmental Protection Agency: Guide for Chemical Test; mem. editl. bd.: Internat. Jour. Med. Genetics; contbr. articles to profl. jours.; editor-in-chief Cancer Epigenetics. Recipient Nat. Sci. Conv. prize, Nat. Govt., 1978, Jiangsu Sci. and Tech. Advancement award, 1987, Chinese Govt., 1997, Nat. Sci. and Tech. Advancement award, 1998. Master: Chinese Environ. Mutagen Soc. (mutagenesis com., editl. bd. Carcinogenesis, Teratogenesis, Mutagenesis), Jiangsu Environ. Mutagen Soc. Achievements include discovery of in vivo micronucleus test in human capillary blood lymphocytes; genotoxicity of tabacco-smoking enhanced by excessive alcohol-drinking and inhibited by tea-drinking habits; synthetic beta-carotene has genotoxicity and natural beta-carotene has antigenotoxicity, in which 9-cis stereoisomers might play a critical role. Office: Jiangsu Inst for Cancer Rsch Bai Zi Ting 42 Jiangsu Province Nanjing 210009 China Personal E-mail: xuekx@yahoo.com.cn.

XUE, YONG QUAN, medical educator, director; b. Shanghai, Jiangsu, China, Nov. 1940; s. Dai Pei Xue and Shen De Zhen; children: Lan, Feng. BS in Medicine, Yan Cheng Med. Sch., 1961; MS in Hematology and Internal Medicine, Suzhou Med. Coll., 1981. Lic. Ministry oHealth, 1980. Resident physician Yan Cheng People's Hosp., Yan Cheng, Jangsu, China, 1961—66; prin. leader med. practitioners She Yang Linhai Hosp., Sheyang, Jiangsu, 1966—73; lectr. Yan Cheng Health Sch., 1973—78; prof., dir. Clin. Hematological Diagnosis Lab., Suzhou, Jiangsu, 1981—; lectr. Suzhou Med. Coll., China, 1983, assoc. prof., 1990—92, prof., 1996. Vis. scholar C.H.U de Poitiers, France, 1983—84; grad. student supr. Suzhou Med. Coll., 1994, postgrad. student supr., 98. Author: (book) Cytogenetics and It's Atlas in Leukemia, 2003; contbr. articles to profl. jours. Recipient Third degree award, Jiangsu Province Admnstrn., 1995, Second degree award, 1998, First degree award, 2009. Office: Jiangsu Inst Hematology 188 Shizi St Suzhou 215006 China Office Fax: 86 512 65113556. Business E-Mail: chromosome8471@yahoo.com.cn.

YADA, HIROTAKA, physician; married. MD, U. Occupl. and Environ. Health, Fukuoka, Japan, 1999; PhD, Keio U., 2008. Physician Keio U., Sch. Medicine, Tokyo, 2003—08. Contbr. articles circulation research; author: (images) Circulation.

YADA, TOYOTAKA, physiologist, researcher; b. Beppu, Japan, Dec. 30, 1955; s. Sunao and Yoshiko Yada; m. Kazuko Iio, Nov. 9, 1956. MD, PhD, Kawasaki Med. Sch., Japan. Diplomate of Cardiology Japanese Circulation Soc. Asst. prof. Kawasaki Med. Sch., Kurashiki, Japan, 1997—. Recipient Rsch. Encouragement award, Japanese Heart Found., 1994, Tanabe award, Am. Heart Found., 2005. Office: Kawasaki Med Sch 577 Matsushima Kurashiki 701-0192 Japan Office Fax: 81-86-463-2975. E-mail: yada@me.kawasaki-m.ac.jp.

YADAV, RAM JANAK, statistician, educator; b. Utter Pradesh, India, Jan. 1, 1954; PhD, Meerut U., 1992. Scientist F, prof. Nat. Inst. Med. Stats., New Delhi, 2004—. Fellow: Indian Soc. Med. Stats. Office: Nat Inst Med Stats New Delhi 110029 India Office Fax: 91-11-26589635. Personal E-mail: rjyadav@hotmail.com.

YAFFE, BRUCE, internist; MD, George Wash. U., 1976. Diplomate Am. Bd. Internal Medicine. Intern Mt. Sinai Hosp., 1977, resident, 1979, fellow, 1980, 1982; med. staff Lenox Hill Hosp. Named one of Top Doctors, Castle Conolly. Mem.: ACP, AMA, Am. Soc. of Gastroenterology, Am. Gastroenterology Assn. Office: Lenox Hill Hospital 100 E 77th St New York NY 10075 Office Phone: 212-434-2000.

YAFFE, STUART ALLEN, physician; b. Springfield, Ill., July 6, 1927; m. Natalie, 1952; children: Scott, Kim Yaffe Schoenburg. BS cum laude, U. Alaska, 1951; MD, St. Louis U., 1956. Diplomate Am. Bd. Family Practice. Intern St. Louis CIty Hosp., 1956-57, resident, 1957-58; physician pvt. practice, 1958—; clin. assoc. prof. So. Ill. U. Sch. Medicine., Springfield, 1971—; ptnr. Springfield Clinic, 1989—. With U.S. Army, 1945-47. Mem. AMA, Am. Acad. Family Physicians, Ill. Acad. Family Physicians, Ill. State Med. Soc., Sangamon County Med. Soc. Office: 1100 Centre West Dr Springfield IL 62704-2100 Home Phone: 217-546-3604, 217-528-9651; Office Phone: 217-528-7541.

YAGATA, HIROSHI, oncologist; b. Japan, Mar. 22, 1964; MD, Kanazawa U., 1990; PhD, Chiba U., 1998. Asst. head physician St. Luke's Internat. Hosp., 2004. Avocation: running. Office: 9-1 Akashi-cho Chuo Tokyo 104-8560 Japan Office Fax: 81-3-3544-0649. Business E-Mail: yagata@mvh.biglobe.ne.jp.

YAGHJYAN, GEVORG V., plastic surgeon; MD with honors, Yerevan State Med. U., Armenia, 1986—92; diploma Microsurgery and Plastic Surgery, Mikaelian Surg. Inst., Armenia, 1992—94. Cert. Republic of Armenia, 1997. Vis. surg. tng. hand surgery dept. Clinic du Parc, Lyon, France, 1994; vis. surg. tng. microsurgery dept. Surgery Ctr., Moscow, 1995; fellowship reconstructive microsurgery and plastic surgery Yerevan State Med. Univ., Armenia, 1994—97. Asst. prof. microsurgery Yerevan State Med. Univ., Armenia. Author: (articles) Microcirculatory systems during acute cholecistitis, 1988 (2nd place, 1988), Substitution of small wrist defects by vascular island flaps, 1995, Use of posterior interosseous flap in treatment of wrist tissue defects, 1996, various articles. Pres. Armenian Br. of Land and Culture Org. Mem.: Armenian Assn. of Plasticand Reconstructive Surgery (sec. gen.). Avocations: tennis, swimming, reading, music, Armenian architecture of the mid. ages. Mailing: Yerevan State Medical University 2 Koryun St 0025 Yerevan Armenia Office Phone: 37410582532. *

YAGI, AKIHIRO, psychologist, educator; b. Osaka, Japan, June 19, 1942; BA, Kwansei Gakuin U., Nishinomiya, Japan, 1966, MA, 1968, PhD, 1981. Rschr. Indsl. Products Rsch. Inst., Tokyo, 1969-76, sr. rschr., 1976-83; assoc. prof. dept. psychol. sci. Kwansei Gakuin U., 1983—86, prof., 1986—2011, vis. prof., 2011—. Dir. Internat. Group for Psychophysiology in Ergonomics, Wuppertal, Germany, 1994-98. Author: Perception and Cognition, 1996, Engineering Psychophysiology, 1999; editor: Brain Images and Cognitive Functions, 1999; guest editor Internat. Jour. Psychophysiology, 2000. Mem. Coun. Indsl. Sci. and Tech., Tokyo. Rsch. grantee New Energy Devel. Orgn., Tokyo, 1996, Ministry of Sci., Edn. and Culture, Tokyo, 1999. Mem.: Japanese Soc. Psychophysiol. Psychology (pres. 2007—10), Japanese Soc. Psychophysiol. Rsch. (bd. dirs. 1980—, Disting. Paper prize 1999), Japanese Psychol. Assn. (bd. dirs. 1995—2001). Avocation: classical music. Office: Kwansei Gakuin U niv Dept Psychol Sci 1-1-155 Uegahara Nishinomiya Hyogo 662 8501 Japan Fax: 81 798 34 6069. Business E-Mail: yagi@kwansei.ac.jp.

YAHIKOZAWA, HIROYUKI, physician; b. Shiojiri, Nagano, Japan, Dec. 15, 1962; s. Yoshiyuki and Fumiko Yahikozawa; m. Kumiko Yahikozawa, Nov. 3, 2000; children: Manae, Yuki. MD, Shinsyu U. Med. Sch., Matsumoto, Nagano, 1988, PhD, 2000. Resident internal medicine Jichi Med. U. Hosp., Minamikouchigun, Tochigi, Japan, 1988—90; resident critical care med. ctr. Met. Bokutou Hosp., Sumida, Tokyo, 1990; physician internal medicine Shinsyu U. Hosp., Matsumoto, 1991—97; chief internal medicine Komoro Kousei Gen. Hosp., Nagano, 1998—2001; chief neurology Nagano Red Cross Hosp., 2001—. Rsch. assoc. microbiology-immunology Northwestern U. Med. Sch., Chgo., 1995—97. Home: Inaba Nagano 380-0917 Japan Office: Nagano Red Cross Hosp Wakasato Nagano 380-8582 Japan

YAHUACA-MENDOZA, PATRICIA, medical educator; b. Mex. City, May 10, 1955; d. Jorge E. Yahuaca Mendoza and Rosalva Mendoza Ortega; m. Jose Luis Alvarado Acosta, Aug. 29, 1981; children: Jose Luis Alvarado Yahuaca, Laura Patricia Alvarado Yahuaca. MS in Pharmacology with honors, Ctr. Rsch. and Advanced Studies, Méx. City, 1983, DSc in Pharmacology, 1989; PhD, SUNY, Syracuse, 1998; diploma in Tutorials, Autonomous U. Zacatecas, Mex., 2004; postdoc, SUNY, 1998; B in in Chemistry Science, Chemist-Pharmacist-Biologist, U. Guadalajara, 1977. Prof. chemistry, Sci. Sch. U. Guadalajara, 1975—81; rsch. prof. Sch. Human Medicine, Autónoma U. Zacatecas, Mexico, 1984—, rsch. prof., pharmacology, 2000—, head, pharmacology, 2004—08. Nat. sys. rschr., Mexico, 1985; invited prof., pharmacology U. Colima, Mexico, 1994—, U. Guadalajara, 2000—; invited prof. in molecular biomedicine Ctr. Rsch. and Advanced Studies, 1995—2001; prof. PROMEP Profile, 1997—; rschr., leader PROMEP-SEP, 2002—; human resource trainer, prof. pharmacology. Contbr. articles to profl. jours. V.p. Zacatecas Acad. Scis., 1994—. Grant, PIFOP, 2002—10, FOMIX-CONACYT, Mex., 2007—09, 2010—, CONACYT Basic Sci., Mex., 2010—, PIFI, 2010—. Mem.: Mex. Assn. Pharmacology. Roman Catholic. Achievements include research in pharmacology, finding some treatments to improve health condition in patients with liver cirrhosis; antioxidant properties of natural products as rosmarinus officinalis, crataegus oxyacantha and uncaria tomentosa applied in diseases such as acute myocardial infarction; diabetes mellitus and liver cirrhosis; pharmacokinetics of drugs in patients with cancer or drug intoxication. Avocations: guitar, singing, history, travel. Office: Doctoral Program in Pharmacology Medicine Sch UAZ Campus UAZ Siglo XXI Labs Bldg 3rd lev Zacatecas-Guadalajara Rd Km 6 Zacatecas 98160 Mexico Office Phone: 52-492-9256690 Ext. 6033. Business E-Mail: yahuacap@uaz.edu.mx.

YAKIMOVA, KRASSIMIRA SIMEONOVA, pharmacologist, researcher; b. Montana, Bulgaria, Mar. 24, 1949; d. Simeon Alexandrov Velkov and Liuba Petrova Velkova; m. Alexander Yakimov Ivanov; 1 child, Alexander Yakimov. MD, Med. U., Sofia, Bulgaria, 1973, PhD, 1987, DMS, 2000. Cert. diploma of speciality in pharmacology. Physician Regional Hosp., Montana, 1974—78; asst. prof. Med. U., Sofia, 1978—98, assoc. prof., 1999—2002, prof., 2002—. Head lab. neuropharmacology Med. U., Sofia, 1991—94, head lab. pharmacology of thermoregulation and pain, 1998—. Contbr. articles to profl.

jours., chapters to books. Mem. Union for protection of animals, Sofia, 1991—2001. Grantee, Max-Planck- Soc., Germany, 1994, 1995, 1996, 1998, DAAD, 2001, 2004, 2009, DFG, 2005; fellow, Fulbright Found., 2004. Mem.: EUROTOX, IBRO, Bulgarian Med. Assn., Soc. Pharmacology, Union of Scientists. Orthodoxal Christian. Avocation: reading. Home: Mladost-2,bl 207,vh 2,ap 67 Sofia 1799 Bulgaria Office: Dept Pharmacology, Med Univ 2 Zdrave Sofia 1431 Bulgaria Office Phone: 00359-2-951-5652. Business E-Mail: kyakim@medfac.acad.bg.

YAKOUN, MAURICE, surgeon, researcher; b. Algiers, Algeria, Dec. 30, 1948; s. Gaston and Renee (Moatti) Y.; m. Muriel Attali, Oct. 13, 1984. MD, U. Montpellier, France, 1975, surg. and oncology specialization, 1989. Intern in surgery U. Hosp. Montpelier; resident in surgery Montpelier Anti-Cancer Ctr.; chief dept. surgery Clinic St.-Jean, Montpellier, 1983—; asst. prof. Anticancer Ctr., Montpellier, 1979-83. Author: Digestive Failure, 1975 (award French Acad. Surgery 1976); editor Nutrition-Metabolism, 1981. With M.C., Tunis Anti-Cancer Ctr., 1975-76. Fellow Am. Soc. for Parenteral and Enteral Nutrition (young rsch. award 1981), N.Y. Acad. Scis. Office: Clinique St-Jean 36 avenue Bouisson Bertrand 34090 Montpellier France Home Phone: 00-33-621058526; Office Phone: 0033 467414148. E-mail: maurice.yakoun@laposte.net.

YAKUBU, ABDULKADIR, surgeon, director; b. Andaza, Nigeria, Apr. 24, 1971; MD, St. Petersburg State Med. U., 1997; PhD, Rostov State Med. U., 2009. Sec. St. Petrsburg Nigerian Students' Union, 1996—97; chief med. dir. Ringim Gen. Hosp., 2001—04; chmn., Jigawa state chpt. Nigeian Med. Assn., 2002—04; chief med. dir. Jahun Gen. Hosp., 2005—07; chief med. dir., cons. surgeon, rschr. Kazaure Gen. Hosp., 2009—. Mem.: Russian Endoscopic Surgeons' Assn., Am. Assn. Gasteroenterologists And Endoscopic Surgeons. Office: Daura Rd Kazaure Jigawa 5550 Nigeria Personal E-mail: drakyakubu@yahoo.com.

YALAM, ARNOLD ROBERT, allergist, immunologist, consultant; b. NYC, Apr. 11, 1940; s. Herman and Sylvia (Taber) Y.; m. Carol Ann Strocker, June 16, 1964; children: John, Matthew. AB, Johns Hopkins U., 1960; MD, U. Md., Balt., 1964. Diplomate Am. Bd. Internal Medicine, Am. Bd. Allergy and Immunology. Intern Jackson Meml. Hosp., Miami, Fla., 1964-65; resident in internal medicine SUNY Downstate Med. Ctr., Bklyn., 1965-67; fellow Scripps Clinic and Rsch. Found., La Jolla, Calif., 1967-68; cons. allergist and immunologist San Diego, 1970—. Maj. US Army, 1968—70. Fellow Am. Acad. Allergy and Immunloy; mem. Am. Soc. Addiction Medicine (cert.), San Diego Allergy Soc.

YALAVARTHI, RAMARAJA, physician; MD, Guntur Med. Coll., India, 1975. Diplomate Am. Bd. Internal Medicine, Am. Bd. Gerontology. Intern Govt. Gen. Hosp., 1974—75, India Ellis Hosp., 1975—76; resident psychiatry SUNY, Stony Brook, 1976—78; resident internal medicine Weiss Meml. Hosp., Chgo., 1978—80; chmn. dept. medicine, pres. med. staff St. James Hosp. and Health Ctrs., Chgo. Heights and Olympia Fields, 2004—05, pres. med. staff, 2004—05; chmn. quality improvement com. South Suburban Hosp.; physician WellGroup Health Partners, Chgo. Heights. Recipient Leadership award (Internat. Med. Grad. Physician), AMA Assn., 2005. Mem.: AMA, Indian Am. Med. Assn., Am. Assn. Physicians from India. Office: WellGroup Health Partners 333 Dixie Hwy Chicago Heights IL 60411 Business E-Mail: rajayalavarthi@aol.net. *

YALÇINDAG, F. NILÜFER, ophthalmologist, educator; b. Turkey, July 25, 1968; MD, Ankara U., 1990. Clin. rsch. fellow U. Aberdeen Sch. Medicine Dept. Ophthalmology, 2005—06; resident Ankara U. Faculty Medicine Dept. Ophthalmology, Turkey, 1997—2001, cons., 2001—, assoc. prof., 2008—. Mem.: Uveitis and Behcet Disease Unit and Cornea Unit, Turkish Ophthal. Soc., Internat. Ocular Inflammation Soc. Avocations: reading, dance, travel. Office: Ankara University Faculty Medicine Ankara 06100 Turkey Office Fax: 90 312 3638082. Business E-Mail: yalcinda@medicine.ankara.edu.tr.

YALIN, ZHANG, medical educator; b. Zhangjiajie, China, July 1, 1951; MD, Hunan Med. U., 1985; PhD, Ctrl. South U., 1998. Prof. Mental Health Inst. Second Xiangya Hosp. Ctrl. South U., 1998—, vice dir., 1998—2011. Recipient Outstanding Tchr. Nat. Top prize, Ministry Edn. of People's Republic of China; grant, China Med. Bd. NY Inc., Nat. Natural Sci. Found. China, Nat. Social Sci. Found. China, Nat. Key Tech. R&D Program. Master: Chinese Med. Assn. (profl. com., social psychiatry, profl. com., psychiatry), China Assn. Mental Health (profl. com., psychol. counseling and psychotherapy, profl. com., suicide and crisis intervention); mem.: WHO Cooperated Rsch. Ctr. Psychosocial Factors and Health. Office: 139 Renmin Rd Changsha Hunan 410011 China E-mail: zhangyl69@vip.sina.com.

YALMAN, DENIZ, medical educator; b. Izmir, Turkey, June 22, 1964; MD, Ege U., 1988. Prof., faculty medicine dept. radiation oncology Ege U., 1990—. Bd. dirs. Turkish Soc. Lung Cancer, 2009—11; regent turkey Internat. Assn. Study Lung Cancer, 2010—. Mem.: Balkan Union Oncology, European Soc. Therapeutic Radiology and Oncology, Am. Soc. Therapeutic Radiology and Oncology. Avocations: music, movies. Office: Ege Universitesi Tip Fakultesi Radyasy Izmir Ege 35100 Turkey Office Fax: 00902323884294. Business E-Mail: deniz.yalman@ege.edu.tr.

YAMADA, HARUKI, professor; b. Tokyo, Oct. 21, 1947; B, Tokyo Coll. Pharmacy, 1970, PhD, 1975. Dir. Basic Rsch. Divsn., Oriental Medicine Rsch. Ctr., Kitasato Inst., 1996—, Ctr. Basic Rsch., Kitasato Inst., 1999—2009; prof. Kitasato Inst. Life Scis. & Grad. Sch. Infection Control Scis., Kitasato U., 2001; dean Grad. Sch. Infection Control Scis., Kitasato U., 2002—10; dir. gen. Kitasato Inst. Life Scis., Kitasato U., 2003—10. Mem. sci. adv. com. DNDi, Japan, 2003—11, chmn. bd. dirs., 2008—09; coop mem. Sci. Coun. Japan, 2006; adv. bd. Consortium Globalization Chinese Medicine, 2007; bd. mem. Med. & Pharm. Soc. WAKAN-YAKU, 2010. Recipient Sibasaburo Kitasato Meml. award, Kitasato Inst., Academic Promoting award, Japanese Soc. Oriental Medicine, Fu-Shi Rsch. award, Chinese Soc. Traditional Vet. Sci., award, Lifu Academic Award Found., Academic award, Med. & Pharm. Soc. WAKAN-YAKU. Mem.: Japanese Soc. Carbohydrate Rsch., Med. & Pharm. Soc. Japan, Pharm. Soc. Wakan-Yaku, Am. Chem. Soc. Avocations: painting, travel. Office: 5-9-1 Shirokane Minato-ku Tokyo 108-8641 Japan Office Fax: 81-3445-1351. E-mail: yamada@lisci.kitasato-u.ac.jp.

YAMADA, HIROSHI, neurologist; married. MD, PhD, Jichi Med. Sch., Tochigi, Japan. Resident Shizuoka Prefecture Gen. Hosp., 1981—83; fellow Yaizu City Gen. Hosp., 1983—86; chief, dept. gen. internal medicine Seirei Hamamatsu Gen. Hosp., 1997—2001; assoc. prof. Gen. Clin. Rsch. Ctr. Hamamatsu U. Sch. Medicine, Japan, 2001—; prof. divsn. drug evaluation and info. U. Shizuoka, Japan, 2005—. Asst. prof. neurology Jichi Med. Sch., Minami-Kawachi, Tochigi prefecture, 1994—97. Fellow: ACP, Japanese Soc. Internal Medicine (licentiate). Home: U Shizuoka Suruga Yada 52-1 Shizuoka Prefecture Shizuoka 422-8526 Japan Office Fax: +81 54 264 5762. E-mail: hyamada@u-shizuoka-ken.ac.jp.

YAMADA, HIROSHI, biomedical engineer, educator; B of Engring., Nagoya U., 1984, M of Engring., 1986, DEng, 1990. Post doctoral fellow Johns Hopkins U., Balt., 1992—93; rsch. asst. Nagoya U., Aichi, Japan, 1989—94, asst. prof., 1994—2001; assoc. prof. Kyushu Inst. Tech., Kitakyushu, Fukuoka, Japan, 2001—08, prof., 2008—. Co-editor (with dr kajzer and dr. tanaka) Human Biomechanics and Injury Prevention, editl. com. mem. Jour. Soc. Biomechanisms, 2001—05. Recipient Young Engrs. award, Japan Soc. Mech. Engrs., 1991, Outstanding Paper medal, 1992, Seguchi award, Divsn. Bioengring. Japan Soc. Mech. Engrs., 1995. Achievements include research in Mechanical evaluation of living tissues and cells at macro- and microscale levels; Theoretical modeling and numerical analysis on living tissues and cells on the basis of continuum mechanics. Office: Kyushu Inst Tech 2-4 Hibikino Wakamatsu-ku Kitakyushu Fukuoka 808-0196 Japan Business E-Mail: yamada@life.kyutech.ac.jp.

YAMADA, KENNETH MANAO, cell biologist; s. Paul Manao and Masaye Yamada; m. Susan Jane Sleeper, July 1, 1973. BA in Biol. Scis., Stanford U., 1966, PhD in Biol. Scis., 1971, MD, 1972. Intern Seton Med. Ctr., Daly City, Calif., 1972-73; commd. lt. USPHS, 1974, advanced through grades to capt., 1982—2003, ret., 2003; sect. chief Nat. Cancer Inst., Bethesda, Md., 1980-90; lab. chief Nat. Inst. Dental and Craniofacial Rsch., NIH, Bethesda, 1990—. Mem. Cell Biology Study sect. NIH, 1979—83; mem. external adv. com. Cancer Rsch. Ctr. Howard U., 1979—88; co-chmn. Gordon Conf. on Fibronectin, 1982; Stadtler lectr. U. Tex. Sys. Cancer Ctr. M.D. Anderson Hosp., 1988; Swerling lectr. Dana-Farber Cancer Inst. Harvard Med. Sch., 1988; Retzius lectr. Karolinska Inst., 2005; Leonardo lectr. San Raffaele Rsch. Inst., Milan. Editor: Jour. Cell Biology, 1999—; contbr. more than 350 publs. to biomed. lit. Recipient Eli Luke and Jacob David Rsch. award, 1972, Sr. Investigator award, Am. Soc. Matrix Bio., 2004, Disting. Scientist award, AADR, 2008. Fellow: AAAS; mem.: Soc. Devel. Biology, Southeastern Cancer Rsch. Assn. (bd. dirs. 1980—83), Am. Soc. Matrix Biology (coun. 2003—), Internat. Soc. Matrix Biology (coun. 1994—2006), Am. Soc. Biochemistry and Molecular Biology, Am. Soc. Cell Biology (coun. 1992—95), Sigma Xi, Phi Beta Kappa. Office: NIDCR Nat Inst Health 30 Convent Dr Bldg 30 Rm 426 Bethesda MD 20892-4370 Office Phone: 301-496-9124. Business E-Mail: kenneth.yamada@nih.gov.

YAMADA, MIKIKO, research scientist; b. Japan; MS in Pharm. Sci., Nagasaki U., Japan, 2000; PharmD, U. Southern Nevada, 2009. Postdoc. rschr. U. Kansas, 2009—. Recipient award, Epilepsy Found. Office: 3901 Rainbow Blvd Mail Stop 4047 Kansas City KS 66160

YAMADA, SEIKO DIANE, gynecologic oncologist; b. Apr. 16, 1964; MD, UCLA. Diplomate Am. Bd. Ob-Gyn. Intern, resident Harbor-UCLA Med. Ctr., Torrance, Calif.; fellowship U. Calif., Irvine; prof. ob.-gyn., chief sect. gynecologic oncology U. Chgo. Med. Ctr. Contbr. articles to profl. jours., chapters to books. Mem.: Soc. Gynecologic Oncologists, Assn. Chgo. Gynecologic Oncologists, Am. Coll. Obstetricians & Gynecologists, Am. Assn. Cancer Rsch. Office: U Chgo Med Ctr 5841 S Maryland Ave MC 2050 Chicago IL 60637 E-mail: sdyamada@babies.bsd.uchicago.edu.

YAMADA, SHIN-ICHI, neurologist, medical researcher; s. Yoneo and Hisako Yamada. MD, Nagoya U. Sch. Medicine, Japan, 1999, PhD in Medicine, 2006. Cert. Nat. Med. Bd., Japan, 1999, Japanese Bd. Neurology, 2005. Resident Nagoya U. Hosp., Japan, 1999—2000; neurologist Gifu Prefectural Tajimi Hosp., Japan, 2000—03; rsch. assoc. dept. neurology Nagoya U. Grad. Sch. Medicine, 2003—. Office: Dept Neurology Nagoya Univ 65 tsurumai Showa Nagoya Aichi 466-8550 Japan Office Fax: 81-52-744-2394. Personal E-mail: y.shinichi@nifty.com.

YAMADA, TADATAKA (TACHI), foundation administrator, gastroenterologist; b. Tokyo, June 5, 1945; BA in History, Stanford U., Calif.; MD, NYU Sch. Medicine, 1971; D (hon.), U. East Anglia, 2007; DSc (hon.), U. Warwick, 2008. Diplomate Am. Bd. Internal Medicine, cert. in pediatric gastroenterology. Intern internal medicine Med. Coll. Va. Hospitals, Richmond, 1971-72, resident gastroenterology, 1972-74; gastrointestinal fellow UCLA, 1977-79; chmn. dept. internal medicine U. Mich. Med. Sch., Ann Arbor; physician-in-chief U. Mich. Med. Ctr.; bd. dirs. SmithKline Beecham Pharm., 1994, pres. healthcare svcs. divsn., 1996—99, chmn. rsch. & devel., 1999—2001, GlaxoSmithKline, 2001—06; exec. dir. Global Health program Bill & Melinda Gates Found., 2006—. Contbr. articles to profl. jours. Recipient Disting. Med. Scientist award, Med. Coll. Va., Disting. Faculty Achievement award, U. Mich., Disting. Achievement award in Gastrointestinal Physiology, Am. Physiol. Soc. Master: ACP; fellow: Imperial Coll. Medicine; mem.: NAS, Acad. Med. Scis., Inst. Medicine, Am. Gastroenterological Assn. (past pres., Friedenwald Medal), Assn. Am. Physicians (past pres.). Office: Bill & Melinda Gates Found PO Box 23350 Seattle WA 98102 *

YAMADA, TOHRU, biologist, educator, researcher, director; b. Hadano, Kanagawa, Japan, June 30, 1975; s. Yoshio and Tamiko Yamada; m. Kaori Horiguchi, Sept. 13, 2005; 1 child, Haruki K. Bachelor's degree, Tokyo Inst. Tech., 1999, Master's degree, 2001, PhD, 2003. Post-doctoral fellow dept. microbiology/immunology U. Ill. Coll. Medicine, Chgo., 2003—04, rsch. asst. prof. dept. surg. oncology, 2004—; dir drug devel. CDG Therapeutics Inc., 2006—; cons. Reuters Insight, 2008—. Editl. bd. mem. Jour. Chinese Clin. Medicine, 2010—; reviewer Internat. Jour. Biomed. Sci., 2010—. Contbr. articles to profl. jours., chapters to books. First Class scholar, Japan Student Svcs. Orgn., 1999. Mem.: Am. Soc. Gene Therapy, Am. Assn. Cancer Rsch., Am. Soc. Microbiology. Office: U Ill Coll Medicine Chgo 840 South Wood St Chicago IL 60612 Personal E-mail: tohru630@gmail.com. Business E-Mail: tohru@uic.edu.

YAMADA, TORU, research scientist; b. Kanagawa, Japan, Jan. 2, 1963; BS, U. Tsukuba, 1986, PhD, 1991. Rsch. assoc. U. Tsukuba, Inst. Biol. Scis., 1991—92; rsch. scientist Ministry Internat. Trade and Industry, Agy. Indsl. Sci. and Tech., Electrotech. Lab., 1992—97, sr. rsch. scientist, 1997—2001; sr. rsch. scientist Neurosci. Rsch. Inst. Nat. Inst. Advanced Indsl. Sci. and Tech., 2001—10, sr. rsch. scientist Human Tech. Rsch. Inst., 2010—. Mem. peer rev. bd. Inst. Electronics, Info. and Communication Engrs., 2009. Mem.: Japan Neurosci. Soc., Japanese Soc. Med. and Biol. Engring., Optical Soc. America. Office: Central 2 1-1-1 Umezono Tsukuba Ibaraki 305-8568 Japan Business E-Mail: toru.yamada@aist.go.jp.

YAMAGATA, KENJI, dental educator; b. Ibaraki, Japan, Dec. 12, 1972; PhD, Hokkaido U., 1997. Asst. prof. dept. oral & maxillofacial surgery Inst. Clin. Medicine, U. Tsukuba, 2005—. Office: 1-1-1 Tennodai Tsukuba Ibaraki 305-8575 Japan Business E-Mail: y-kenji@md.tsukuba.ac.jp.

YAMAGISHI, KAZUMASA, epidemiologist, educator; b. Shimabara, Nagasaki-ken, Japan, Aug. 21, 1974; married. MD, U. Tsukuba, Ibaraki-ken, Japan, 2000, PhD, 2003. Postdoc. fellow U. Tsukuba, 2003—04, asst. prof., 2004—; vis. asst. prof. U. Minn., Mpls., 2007—09. Contbr. articles to numerous profl. jours. Rsch. grant, Ministry Edn., Culture, Sports, Sci. and Tech., Japan, 2005—07, 2010—, Health Care Sci. Inst., Japan, 2005, Kanae Found. Promotion Med. Scis., Japan, 2007—08, Ministry of Health, Labour & Welfare, Japan, 2009—, Uehara Meml. Found., 2009—10. Mem.: Am. Stroke Assn., Japan Stroke Assn., Japan Hypertension Assn., Japan Indsl. Health Assn., Japan Epidemiology Assn., Japan Hygiene Assn., Japan Pub. Health Assn., Am. Heart Assn. Office: University Tsukuba Dept Pub Health Med 1-1-1 Tennodai Tsukuba Ibaraki-ken 305-8575 Japan Office Fax: 81-29-853-2695. Business E-Mail: k-yamagishi@umin.net.

YAMAGUCHI, KEN, surgeon, educator; b. LA, Nov. 8, 1960; s. Hiroshi and Yoshiko Yamaguchi; m. Kathy Taeko Yamaguchi; children: Kelli Emiko, Kyle Kiyoshi. BS, UCLA, 1983, MA, 1985; MD, George Washington U., 1989. Diplomate Am. Bd. Orthopedic Surgery. Intern George Washington U., resident in orthopedic surgery; fellow shoulder and elbow surgery Columbia U.; assoc. prof. Washington U., St. Louis, 1995—; staff physician John Cochran VA Hosp., St. Louis, 1996—. Reviewer Am. Jour. Sports Medicine, 1996—; cons. reviewer Jour. Shoulder and Elbow Surgery, 1998—, assoc. editor Techniques in Shoulder and Elbow Surgery, 1999—, Jour. Bone and Joint Surgery, 1997—; contbr. articles to profl. jours. Recipient Emanual D. Kaplan award, 1997, Rsch. award Soc. Radiologists, 1998; N.Am. Travelling fellow, 1997. Mem. AMA, Am. Acad. Orthop. Surgeons, Mid.-Am. Orthop. Assn., St. Louis Orthop. Soc. Avocations: rollerblading, tennis, swimming. Office: Washington U Dept Orthop Surgery 1 Barnes Jewish Hosp Plz Saint Louis MO 63110 Office Phone: 314-742-2534. Business E-Mail: yamaguchik@wustl.edu.

YAMAGUCHI, KEN, medical association administrator; b. Kihoku cho, Mie, Japan, Mar. 2, 1950; MD, Keio U. Sch. Medicine, 1974; PhD, U. Tokyo, 1981. Chief Growth Factor Divsn., Nat. Cancer Ctr. Rsch. Inst., 1987—2002; dep. dir. Nat. Cancer Ctr. Rsch. Inst., 1999—2002; spl. advisor Imperial Household, 1999—2005; mem. sci. coun. Internat. Agy. Rsch. Cancer, 2000—03; pres. Shizuoka Cancer Ctr., 2002—. Bd. mem., selection designated cancer ctr. hosp. Ministry Health, Labour and Welfare, Japan, 2000—11; councilor Princess Takamatsu Cancer Rsch. Fund, 1996—2011, Found. Promotion Cancer Rsch., 2002—11, Japan Cancer Soc., 2001—11; bd. dirs. Found. Meml. to Yasushi Inoue, 2006—11. Recipient award, Princess Takamatsu Cancer Rsch. Fund. Mem.: Am. Assn. Cancer Rsch., Japanese Cancer Assn. Office: Shimonagakubo 1007 Nagaizumi-cho Sunto-gun Shizuoka 411-8777 Japan

YAMAGUCHI, MASARU, orthodontist; b. Kisarazu, Chiba, Japan, Mar. 11, 1963; DDS, Nihon U., Japan, 1989; PhD, Nihon U., 1994. Authorized dentist in orthodontics Japanese Orthodontic Soc., 1996, authorized orthodontic instr. Japanese Orthodontic Soc., 2003, cert. esthetic dentistry Japan Acad. Esthetic Dentistry, 2004. Rsch. resident Aging and Health from the Ministry Pub. Welfare Japan, Matsudo, Chiba, Japan, 1997—2000; asst. prof. Nihon U. Sch. Dentistry, Matsudo, 2000—01, sr. lectr. dept. orthodontics, 2001—. Lectr. Spl. Sch. Dental Hygiene Nihon U. Sch. Dentistry, Matsudo, 2001—04; rsch. fellow orthodontics faculty dentistry U. Sydney. Grantee, Japan Soc. for the Promotion of Sci., 2002—04; Suzuki Rsch. grantee, Nihon U. Sch. Dentistry, 2003, 2005. Mem.: World Fedn. Orthodontists (assoc.), Am. Assn. Orthodontists (assoc.), Internat. Assn. for Dental Rsch. (assoc.). Achievements include research in effects of mechanical stress in periodontal tissues; effects of low power laser irradiation on bone remodeling. Avocations: tennis, golf, reading. Office: 2-870-1 Sakaecho-nishi Matsudo Chiba 271-8587 Japan Office Fax: 81-47-364-6295. Business E-Mail: yamaguchi.masaru@nihon-u.ac.jp.

YAMAGUCHI, TORU, endocrinologist; b. Kobe, Japan, Mar. 7, 1958; MD, Kobe U., 1982, PhD, 1989. Lic. physician, Japan. Resident internal medicine Kobe U. Hosp., 1982-83, Uwajima City Hosp., 1983-85; sr. staff internal medicine Miki City Hosp., 1989, Seirankai Mima Hosp., 1989-91; clin. staff and asst. prof. medicine 3d divsn. dept. medicine Kobe U., 1991—94, 1999—2002; chief internal medicine Hattori Hosp., Hyogo, Japan, 1994-96; rsch. fellow Brigham & Women's Hosp., Boston, 1996-99; sr. staff internal medicine Takatsuki Gen. Hosp., 2002—05; assoc. prof. 1st divsn. dept. medicine Shimane U., Izumo-shi, Japan, 2005—. Contbr. articles to profl. jours. Japanese Soc. Osteoporosis award, 2002, Japanese Soc. Bone & Mineral Rsch. award, 2007. Fellow Japanese Soc. Internal Medicine; mem. Japan Endocrine Soc., Japanese Soc. Gastroenterology, Japanese Soc. Bone and Mineral Rsch., Am. Soc. Bone and Mineral Rsch.,

Japanese Soc. Osteoporosis, Endocrine Soc, Am. Diabetes Assn. Office: Shimane University Internal Medicine 1 Faculty Medicine 89-1 En-ya-cho Izumo-shi 693-8501 Japan

YAMAJI, SHUNSUKE, physical education educator, medical researcher; b. Tatsunokuchi, Japan, Oct. 29, 1973; s. Kikou and Mitsuko Yamaji; m. Sachiko Shima, Sept. 14, 1973; 1 child, Koushiro. Dr., Kanazawa U., 2001—03. Teacher's Special License (Physical And Health Education) Ministry of Edn., 1998. Asst. prof. Fukui Nat. Coll. Tech., Sabae, Japan, 1998—. Lectr. Assn. of Ishikawa Sports instr., Kanazawa, Japan, 2002—03. Home: 1-1-3 Hikime Fukui 918-8156 Japan Office: Fukui Nat Coll Tech Geshi Sabae Fukui 916-8507 Japan Office Fax: 81-77-862-3417. E-mail: yamaji@fukui-nct.ac.jp.

YAMAKADO, KOTARO, physician; b. Japan, Jan. 13, 1969; MD, Kanazawa U., 1994, PhD, 2002. Chief physician Fukui Gen. Hosp., 2005—. Office: 58-16-1 Egami Fukui 9108561 Japan Personal E-mail: yamakadok@hotmail.com.

YAMAKI, MASAO, dentist, educator; b. June 14, 1934; s. Shigeji and Shige Shirakawa Yamaki; m. Hiromi Yamashita, Dec. 18, 1963; children: Hiroshi, Mariko. DDS, Tokyo Med. and Dental U., 1960; D Med. Sci., Kyoto U., 1965. Rsch. fellow Eastman Dental Ctr., Rochester, NY, 1965—66, rsch. assoc., 1966—67; instr. Hiroshima U., Hiroshima, Japan, 1967—68, assoc. prof., 1968—77, prof., chmn. dept. dental materials sci., 1977—98, prof. emeritus, 1998—. Author: Standard Textbook of Dental Materials, 1995. Mem.: Japanese Soc. Dental Materials and Devices (hon.). Home: 1362-129 Katsugi Kabe-Cho Hiroshima 731-0235 Japan

YAMAKI, TAKASHI, plastic surgeon, researcher; b. Tokyo, Oct. 13, 1960; s. Kunio and Nobuko Yamaki. MD, Kagoshima U., Sch. Medicine, Japan, 1988. Registered plastic surgeon 1995. Asst. prof. Tokyo Women's Med. U., Dept. Plastic Reconstructive Surgery, 2008—. Contbr. to profl. jours., chapters to books. Mem. bd. exam com. Japanese Coll. Angiology, Tokyo. Recipient Sigvaris Travel Fellowship award, Am. Venous Forum, 2006, Travel award, Internat. Union Angiology, 1998, Young Investigator award, Internat. Coll. Angiology, 1999, Platinum award, Am. Coll. Phlebology, 2010. Mem.: AAAS, Internat. Soc. Endovascular Specialists, Internat. Soc. Thrombosis Haemostasis, Am. Venous Forum, Am. Coll. Phlebology (Platinum award 1997, Bronze Abstract award 2004, Platinum Abstract award 2005, Gold Abstract award 2007, Platinum award 2010), Japanese Soc. Phlebology (mem. Disease Surveillance Com., mem. Thromboembolism Com.). Office: Tokyo Women's Med Univ 8-1 Kawada-cho Shinjuku-ku Tokyo 162-8666 Japan Office Phone: 81-3-3353-8111. Personal E-mail: yamakiintokyo@aol.com. Business E-Mail: yamaki@prs.twmu.ac.jp.

YAMAMOTO, DAISUKE, medical educator; b. Osaka, Mar. 18, 1962; M in Pharm. Sci., Okayama U., 1987; PhD, OUPS, 1990. Lectr. to assoc. prof. Osaka Med. Coll., 1998—. Office: Osaka Med Coll 2-7 Daigakucho Takatsuki Osaka 569-8686 Japan Business E-Mail: center@art.osaka-med.ac.jp.

YAMAMOTO, KAZUHIRO, cardiologist; b. Hiroshima, Japan, Mar. 7, 1962; s. Tadao Yamamoto; m. Ryoko Suzuki, Apr. 7, 1965. MD, Osaka U., Suita, 1986, PhD, 1994. Lic. Ministry of Health, Labor and Welfare, Japan, 1986. Resident Osaka U. Hosp., Suita, 1986—87, Osaka Police Hosp., 1987—88, cardiology staff, 1988—90; rsch. fellow Mayo Clinic, Rochester, Minn., 1994—96; rsch. attendant Osaka U., 1996—98; cardiology staff Osaka U. Hosp., 1996—, dir. cardiovasc. care unit, 1998—2001, codir. echocarddiographic lab., 2001—. Asst. prof. Osaka U. Grad. Sch. Med., 1998—. Recipient Young Investigator's award, Japanese Soc. Echocardiography, 1997; grantee, Japanese Soc. for Promotion of Sci., 2003, Naito Found., 2000, Clin. Vascular Found., 2001, Takeda Sci. Found., 2002, Japan Cardiovasc. Rsch. Found., 2003, Salt Sci. Rsch. Found., 2003, Osaka Heart Club, 2003; fellow, Uehara Meml. Found., 1994, Japan Soc. for Promotion Sci., 1995. Fellow: Japanese Coll. Cardiology (tokyo), Am. Coll. Cardiology (bethesda), Japan Soc. Ultrasonics in Medicine (assoc.; tokyo); mem.: Japanese Soc. Internal Medicine (cert. 1991), Japanese Circulation Soc. (cert. 1993). Office: Osaka Univ Grad Sch Med 2-2 Yamadaoka Suita 565-0871 Japan Office Fax: +81-6-6879-6613. E-mail: kazuhiro@medone.med.osaka-u.ac.jp.

YAMAMOTO, MASAHIRO, neurologist; b. Chiba, Japan, Oct. 15, 1943; s. Shouichi and Reiko Yamamoto; m. Junko Hayashi, Dec. 3, 1977; children: Satoshi, Eriko, Mamiko. MB, Keio U., 1969, Dr. Med. Sciences, 1991. Lic. physician Ministry Health and Welfare, 1969, diplomate Japanese Soc. Internal Medicine, 1988, Japanese Soc. Neurology, 1988, Japan Stroke Soc., 2003, Japanese Headache Soc., 2005, cert. occupl. physician Japan Med. Assn., 1998. Rsch. asst. Tokai U. Sch. of Medicine, Isehara, Kanagawa, Japan, 1976—81; rsch. fellow Baylor Coll. of Medicine, Houston, Tex., 1977—80; vice-director Yokohama Stroke And Brain Ctr., Yokohama, Kanagawa, Japan, 1999—2003, dir., 2003—05, trustee, 2005—; asst. prof. Tokai U. Sch. of Medicine, Isehara, Kanagawa, Japan, 1981—92, assoc. prof., 1992—95; dir. Yokohama Yuai Hosp., Yokohama, Kanagawa, Japan, 1995—99; asst. (internal medicine) Keio U. Sch. of Medicine, Tokyo, Japan, 1969—75, instr. (internal medicine), 1975—76. Contbr. scientific papers to seminars, workshops, profl. groups. Mem.: Soc. Neurol. Japonica (mem. coun. 1989), Japanese Soc. Cerebral Blood Flow and Metabolism (coun. mem. 1988), Japan Stroke Soc. (mem. coun. 1982), Japanese Headache Soc. (mem. coun. 1996), Japanese Soc. Neurol. Therapeutics (councilor 1994). Avocations: fishing, travel, films. Home: 1-7-19 Noge Setagaya-ku Tokyo 158-0092 Japan Office: Yokohama Stroke & Brain Ctr 1-2-1 Takigashira Isogo-ku Yokohama Kanagawa 235-0012 Japan Office Fax: 81-45753-2859; Home Fax: 81-35752-5155. Personal E-mail: junco@h00.itscom.net.

YAMAMOTO, SEIICHI, engineering educator; b. Japan, Apr. 30, 1956; PhD, Nagoya U., 1993. Prof. Kobe City Coll. Tech., 2000—11. Office: 8-3 Gakuen-Higashi-machi Nishi-ku Kobe 651-2194 Japan Business E-Mail: s-yama@kobe-kose.ac.jp.

YAMAMOTO, SEIJI, neurosurgeon, educator; b. Wakayama, Japan, Apr. 12, 1954; m. Yoko Miyamoto Yamamoto, Apr. 15, 1978; children: Sayoko, Koh. MD, Hamamatsu U., Japan, 1980, PhD, 1994. Resident in neurosurgery Hamamatsu U. Hosp., 1980—84; chief of neurosurgery Yaizu (Japan) Mcpl. Hosp., 1985—88; rsch. assoc. Hamamatsu U. Med. Sch., 1988—2000, assoc. prof., 2000—. Mem.: Internat. Soc. Cerebral Blood Flow and Metabolism, Soc. Neurosci. Office: Photon Med Rsch Ctr Hamamatsu U Sch Medicine 1-20-1 Handayama Hamamatsu 431-3192 Japan E-mail: seijiy@hama-med.ac.jp.

YAMAMOTO, SHIRO, neurologist; MD, Mie U., 1999. Resident Osaka-Minami Nat. Hosp., Japan, 1999—2003; clin. fellow Kansai Rosai Hosp., Hyogo, Japan, 2003—06; staff physician Yodogawa Christian Hosp., Osaka, 2006—08, Kobe City Med. Ctr. Gen. Hosp., Hyogo, 2008—. Contbr. articles to profl. pubs. Mem.: Japan Stroke Soc. Office: Kobe City Med Ctr Gen Hosp 2-1-1 Minatojima Minamimachi Chuo Kobe 650-0046 Japan

YAMAMOTO, SHUICHIRO, physician; b. Fukuoka, Japan, Aug. 31, 1970; MD, U. Occupl. and Environ. Health, Japan; PhD, U. Occupl. and Environ. Health, 1997. Sr. head physician Hitachi Health Care Ctr., 2009—. Avocation: reading book. Office: 4-3-16 Ose-cho Hitachi Ibaraki 317-0076 Japan Business E-Mail: shuichiro.yamamoto.sr@hitachi.com.

YAMAMOTO, TATSUO, nephrologist, researcher; MD, Hamamatsu U. Sch. of Medicine, Japan, 1980, PhD, 1987. Bd. cert. Japanese Soc. of Nephrology, 1993, Japanese Soc. of Internal Medicine, 1990, bd. cert Japanese Soc. of Dialysis Therapy, 1994, bd. cert. Japanese Soc. of Dialysis Therapy, 1997, cert. attending nephrologist Japanese Soc. of Nephrology, 1995. Resident first dept. of medicine Hamamatsu U. Hosp., Japan, 1980—81; resident in internal medicine Enshu Gen. Hosp., Hamamatsu, Japan, 1981—82; physician in internal medicine Tenryu Nat. Hosp., 1982—83; instr. first dept. of medicine Hamamatsu U. Sch. of Medicine, 1987—90; post-doctoral rsch. fellow divsn. of nephrology U. of Utah, Salt Lake City, 1990—92; instr. in the first dept. of medicine Hamamatsu U. Sch. of Medicine, Japan, 1992—93, asst. prof. in the first dept. of medicine, 1993—96; head physician in the dept. of nephrology Seirei Hamamatsu Gen. Hosp., Japan, 1996—97, asst. chief in the dept. of nephrology, 1997—98, chief dept. of nephrology, 1998—99; asst. prof. first dept. of medicine Hamamatsu U. Sch. of Medicine, 1999—. Assoc. councilor Japanese Soc. of Nephrology, Tokyo, 1995—; councilor Tokai Br. Japanese Soc. of Internal Medicine, Japan, 1993—96, Nagoya, 1999—; sr. mem. Japanese Soc. Dialysis Therapy. Contbr. articles to profl. jours. Mem.: Japanese Soc. of Internal Medicine, Japanese Soc. of Nephrology, Internat. Soc. of Nephrology, Am. Soc. of Nephrology (corr.), Japanese Soc. of Dialysis Therapy (sr.). Office: Hamamatsu U Sch Medicine 1-20-1 Handayama Shizuoka Hamamatsu 431-3192 Japan E-mail: ytatsuo@hama-med.ac.jp.

YAMAMOTO, TOSHIYUKI, neurologist, educator; b. Aioi, Hyogo, Japan, Jan. 13, 1965; s. Yoshiaki and Kimiko Yamamoto; married. D, Tottori U., 1989. Asst. prof. Divsn. Child Neurology, Inst. Neurol. Scis., Faculty of Medicine, Tottori U., Yonago, Japan, 1993—95, Gene Rsch. Ctr., Tottori U., Yonago, 1995—2002; vis. fellow Women's and Children's Hosp., Adelaide U., Australia, 2002—03; med. chief Kanagawa Children's Med. Ctr., Yokohama, Japan, 2003—05; assoc. prof. Tokyo Women's Med. U., 2006—. Health & welfare Concierge of Chromosome and Genetics, Tokyo, 2008—, Kanagawa Down Syndrome Network, Yokohama, Japan, 2002—08. Fellowship, Kanae Found. Promotion Med. Sci., 2002, Japan Epilepsy Rsch. Found., 2002, Miyata Cardiac Rsch. Promotion Found., 2008, Rsch. grant, Uehara Meml. Found., 2003, grant, Yuumi Meml. Found. 200Home Health Care, 2004. Mem.: Japanese Soc. Child Neurology (Ann. award 2005). Achievements include research in human molecular cytogenetics for neurological disorders. Office: Tokyo Women's Med University Inst Integrated Med Sci 8-1 Kawada-cho Tokyo Shinjuku-ward 162-8666 Japan Office Fax: +81-3-3352-3088. Business E-Mail: toshiyuki.yamamoto@twmu.ac.jp.

YAMAMOTO, YUKIYA, medical educator; b. Tokyo, Dec. 28, 1968; MD, Nagoya U., 1993, PhD, 2002. Rsch. fellow Harvard U., 2002—04; asst. prof. Fujita Health U., 2005—. Recipient KYO award, Japanese Leukaemia Rsch. Fund, 2004; Med. Rsch. fellowship, Takeda Sci. Found., 2008. Master: Japanese Soc. Internal Medicine; fellow: Japanese Soc. Med. Oncology, Japanese Soc. Hematology; mem.: Japanese Cancer Assn., Am. Soc. Hematology. Office: 1-98 Dengakugakubo Kutsukake Toyoake Aichi 470-1192 Japan Business E-Mail: yyukiya@fujita-hu.ac.jp.

YAMAMURA, HIDEO, medical educator; b. Kumagaya, Japan, Jan. 23, 1920; s. Hisashi and Kimiko Yamamura; m. Miyoko Yamamura, Oct. 20, 1942; children: Akio, Nobuko, Shigeru. MD, Tokyo U., 1943, PhD, 1948. Resident Tokyo U., 1948-52, assoc. prof., 1952-56, prof., 1956-80, prof. emeritus, dean, 1978-79; pres. Tokyo Sembai Hosp. Japan Tobacco Co., Tokyo, 1980-90; pres. Kosaikai Hosp. Kosaika Med. Corp., Tokyo, 1990—99. Chmn. bd. dirs. Japan Found. Emerg. Med., Tokyo, 1991—99; prof. Teikyo U., Tokyo, 1980—2002; pres. Japan Soc. Acupuncture, Tokyo, 1989—98. Editor: Japanese Jour. of Anesthesiology. Decorated Commendatory medal with purple ribbon Japanese Govt., 1982, 2nd Class of the Order of Merit, 1990. Fellow Royal Coll. Anaesthetists; mem. Assn. Univ. Anesthesiologists (hon.), Internat. Assn. Study of Pain (hon.), Japan Soc. Anesthesiology, German Soc. Anesthesiology (hon.). Avocation: music. Home: 3-40-3 Hamacho Nihonbashi Chuoku Tokyo 103 Japan Office: Kosaikai Hosp 3-4-17 Koyama Shinagawaku Tokyo 142 Japan Office Phone: 03-3666-6716. E-mail: fwhv3032@nifty.com.

YAMAMURA, MITSUHIRO, vascular surgeon; b. Ashiya City, Japan, Feb. 1, 1964; s. Sohei and Yasuko (Sakaue) Y.; m. Haruyo Miyata, July 28, 1996. MD, Hyogo Coll. Medicine, 1988, PhD, 2001. Lic. physician Japanese Nat. Med. Bd.; cert. Japanese Bd. Cardiovasc. Surgeons. Resident Hyogo Coll. Medicine, Cardiovasc. Inst., Kansai Rosai Hosp., 1988—94; hon. fellow U. Wis., Madison, 1997—98, rsch. intern, 1998—99; asst. prof. Hyogo Coll. Medicine, Japan, 2002—08, assoc. prof. Nishinomiya City, 2010—, co-chmn. membership com. Recipient Morimura's award Hyogo Coll. Medicine, 1988. Fellow Internat. Coll. Angiology (Prof. Albert Senn Young Investigator award 2000); mem. Japanese Soc. Cardiovasc. Surgery, Japanese Assn. Thoracic Surgery, Japanese Soc. Vascular Surgery (councilor), Kansai Assn. Thoracic Surgery (councilor), Japanese Coll. Angiology (disting. fellow), Japanese Soc. Artificial Organs (councilor), Soc. Vascular Surgery

YAMAMURA, TAKASHI, neurologist, director; b. Nagoya, Japan, Oct. 18, 1955; MD, Kyoto U., PhD, 1980. Vis. scientist Max-Planck Inst. Multiple Sclerosis Rsch., 1987—89; rsch. fellow Harvard Med. Sch., 1989—90; chief, lab. demyelinating disease Nat. Inst. Neurosci. NCNP, 1990—99, dir., dept. immunology, 1999—; dir., multiple sclerosis ctr. Nat. Ctr. Neurology and Psychiatry, 2010—. Adj. prof. Waseda U., 2005, Sch. Medicine Chiba U., 2009; internat. adv. bd. mem. Internat. Soc. Neuroimmunology, 2006; co-chair Fedn. Clin. Immunology Socs., 2006—07. Fellow Alexander Von Humboldt Found. fellow; Uehara Meml. Found. grant, Rsch. grant, Japanese Govt. Master: Japanese Soc. Clin. Immunology, Japanese Soc. Neuroimmunology; mem.: Am. Assn. Immunologists. Avocations: piano, jazz, opera. Office: NCNP 4-1-1 Ogawahigashi Kodaira Tokyo 187-8502 Japan Office Fax: 81423461753.

YAMANAKA, SHINYA, stem cell scientist, educator; b. Higashiôsaka, Osaka, Japan, Sept. 4, 1962; MD, Kobe U., Japan, 1987; PhD, Osaka City U. Grad. Sch., 1993. Resident orthop. surgery Nat. Osaka Hosp., Japan, 1987—89; postdoc. fellow Gladstone Inst. Cardiovasc. Disease, San Francisco, 1993—95, staff rsch. investigator, 1995—96, sr. investigator, L.K. Whittier Found. investigator stem cell biology, 2007—; asst. prof. Osaka City U. Med. Sch., 1996—99; assoc. prof. Nara Inst. Sci. & Tech., Japan, 1999—2003, prof., 2003—05; prof. Inst. Frontier Med. Scis., Kyoto U., Japan, 2004—10, prof. Inst. Integrated Cell-Material Scis., 2007—, dir. Ctr. iPS Cell Rsch. & Application, 2008—; prof. anatomy U. Calif., San Francisco, 2007—. Recipient Meyenburg prize, Meyenburg Found./German Cancer Rsch. Ctr., 2007, JSPS prize, Japan Soc. Promotion of Sci., 2007, Asahi award, Asahi Newspaper Co., 2007, Inoue prize for sci., 2007, Yamazaki-Teiichi prize in biol. sci. & tech., Found. Promotion Material Sci. & Tech. Japan, 2008, Spl. prize for sci. & tech., Min. Edn., Culture, Sports, Sci. & Tech. Japan, 2008, Medal of Honor with Purple Ribbon, 2008, Robert Koch prize, 2008, Sankyo Takamine Meml. award, 2008, Gairdner Found. Internat. award, 2009, March of Dimes prize in devel. biology, 2010, Imperial prize, Japan Acad., 2010, Balzan prize for biology, Internat. Balzan Found., 2010, Kyoto Prize in advanced tech., Inamori Found., 2010, Albany Med. Ctr. prize, 2011, King Faisal Internat. prize for medicine, 2011, Frontier of Knowledge & Culture award in medicine, BBVA Found., 2011; co-recipient Shaw prize in life sci. & medicine, 2008, Albert Lasker Basic Med. Rsch. award, Lasker Found., 2009, Lewis S. Rosenstiel award for disting. work in basic med. rsch., 2009, Wolf prize in medicine, Israel, 2011; named one of The 100 Most Influential People in the World, TIME mag., 2008. Mem.: NAS (fgn. assoc.). Achievements include with his team of scientists in 2006, generated Induced Pluripotent Stem Cells- a type of pluripotent stem cell artificially derived from a non-pluripotent cell, typically an adult somatic cell, by inducing a "forced" expression of specific genes; this discovery profoundly changed the understanding of how cells develop and opened new possibilities in regenerative medicine. Office: Institute Integrated Cell Material Sciences Kyoto Univ Yoshida Ushinomiya cho Sakyo ku Kyoto 606 8501 Japan also: Gladstone Inst Cardiovascular Disease 1650 Owens St San Francisco CA 94158 Office Phone: 415-734-2710. Office Fax: 415-355-0960. E-mail: syamanaka@gladstone.ucsf.edu. *

YAMANE, STANLEY JOEL, retired optometrist, consultant; b. Lihue, Kauai, Hawaii, Mar. 13, 1943; s. Tooru and Yukiko (Miura) Y.; m. Joyce Mitsuko Tamura; children— Stanley Tooru Aiichi, Karen Margaret BS in Optometry, Pacific U., 1966, O.D., 1966, LHD (hon.); DS (hon.), Pa. Coll. Optometry. Diplomate Am. Acad. Optometry. Practice optometry, Waipahu, Hawaii, 1967-73; ptnr. with Dr. Dennis M. Kuwabara, 1973-81; ptnr. Drs. Kuwabara & Yamane, Optometrists, Inc., Waipahu, 1981-91, with br. office Honolulu; with DBA Eye Care Assocs. of Hawaii, Honolulu, 1989-91; dir. profl. affairs Vistakon, Inc., 1991-92; v.p. profl. affairs Vistakon Inc., 1992—2004, chair global profl. affairs coun., 1996-99; ret., 2004—05; v.p. profl. rels. VisionWeb, Inc., 2005—08; ret., 2008. Lectr., cons. in field; sec.-treas. Hawaii Bd. Examiners in Optometry, 1975-76, v.p., 1976-78, pres., 1978-80; mem. adj. faculty Coll. Optometry, Pacific U., 1977-91, Pa. Coll. Optometry, 1981-91, So. Coll. Optometry, 1982-91, U. Mo., St. Louis, 1990-91; bd. dirs. Hawaii Vision Svc. Plan, 1984-91. Cons. editor Optometric Mgmt. Jour., 1981-91, Contact Lens Forum Jour., 1987-91, editor, 1991; contbr. articles to profl. jours. Bd. mgrs. Leeward Oahu Br. YMCA, 1967-70, Hi-Y advisor, 1967-71, mem. Century Club, 1967-91, bd. mgrs. West Oahu Br., 1971-78, gen. chmn. sustaining membership, 1976; 2d v.p. August Ahrens Elem. Sch. PTA, 1969; mem. Leeward Mental Health Adv. Council, 1975-76, Friends of Waipahu Cultural Garden Park Found., 1976—, Aloha council Boy Scouts Am., 1976-91; mem. bus. adv. council Waipahu High Sch., 1976-81, Parent-Tchr.-Community Adv. Council, 1978-80; bd. dirs. Central/Leeward unit Am. Cancer Soc., 1977-80, pub. edn. dir., 1978-79, v.p., 1979-80, founder, chmn. Celebrity Auction, 1980, dir. Oahu Baseline Survey, 1978; bd. dirs. Barbers Point council Navy League Am., 1981-85; profl. bd. advisors U. Houston Inst. for Contact Lens Research. Recipient Merit award Nat. Eye Research Found., 1974, Disting. Service award, 1976, Founder's award Pacific U., 1996, Heart of Am. Contact Lens Soc. Vision Svc. award, 1998, Lifetime Achievement award, 2004. Fellow Am. Acad. Optometry (cornea and contact lens diplomate, vice chair cornea and contact lens sect. 1992-94, chair cornea and contact lens sect. 1994-96, immediate past chair, 1997-99, sec., 1990-92, vice chair ethics com. 1991-92, corp. support for Jour. com. 1981, chair diplomate awards com. 1988-90), AAAS, Am. Optometric Assn. (ann. congress del. 1978, pub. health com. 19738, optometric paraoptometric personnel com. 1978-79, contact lens project team 1979-80, task force on R&D 1984-87, contact lens sect. coun. 1988-92, sec., 1989-90, vice chair 1990-91, chair elect 1991-92, numerous coms.), Leeward Oahu Jaycees (Disting. Service award 1969, Top Outstanding Young Man award 1975), Hawaii State Jaycees, Am. Optometric Found. (bd. dirs. 1981-91, chmn. task force clin. research 1981-83, nominations com. 1982, treas. 1985-86, sec., 1987-88, pres.-elect, 1988-89, pres. 1989-90), Am. Pub. Health Assn. (recipient Disting. Svc. award, Vision Care Section, 2003), Better Vision Inst., Coll.

Optometrists in Vision Devel., Hawaii Optometric Assn. (corr. sec. 1968-70, state newsletter editor 1968-70, rec. sec. 1971, 2d v.p. 1972, pres. 1974-75; Man of Yr. 1975, Optometrist of Yr. 1979), Internat. Optometric & Optical League, Internat. Soc. Contact Lens Rsch., Brit. Contact Lens Assn., Japan Contact Lens Acad., Nat. Assn. of the Professions, Nat. Eye Research Found. (fellow Internat. Orthokeratology sect.; editorial bd. Contacto Jour. 1979, contact lens cert. com. 1981-85), Nat. Fedn. Ind. Bus., Optometric Cons. in Contact Lens Optometric Extension Program Found. (chmn. study group 1969-70, state dir. 1971-73), Optometric Hist. Soc., Optometric Polit. Action Coms., Soc. Contact Lens Specialists, Hawaii Assn. Children with Learning Disabilities, Hawaii Assn. Intellectually Gifted Children (pub. relations chmn. 1st Ann. State Conf. 1975, legis. lobbyist 1975-76), Waipahu Bus. Assn. (bd. dirs. 1974-78, chmn. pub. relations 1974-75, legis. lobbyist 1974-75, pres. 1974-75), Nat. Acad. Practice in Optometry (mem.-at-large on exec. com., disting. practitioner in optometry) Democrat. Baptist. Home: 8609 Autumn Green Dr Jacksonville FL 32256-9560 E-mail: sjyamane@comcast.net.

YAMAOKA-TOJO, MINAKO, physician, researcher; b. Matsumoto, Nagano, Japan, Apr. 22, 1969; d. Masashi and Kaoru Yamaoka; m. Taiki Tojo, Aug. 16, 2000; children: Risa Tojo, Erika Tojo. MD, Yamagata U., Japan, 1995, PhD, 1999. Prof. Kitasato U. Sch., Sagamihara, Kanagawa, Japan, 2002—03, asst. prof., 2005—; assoc. prof., dept. rehab. Kitasato U. Sch. Allied Health Scis. & Grad. Sch. Med. Sci., 2009—. Editor: Prevention of Heart Failure; contbr. articles to profl. jours. Grantee, Ministry Edn., Sci. and Culture, Japan, 2006—07, 2009—; fellow, Yamagata U. Sch. Medicine, Japan, 1999—2000, Kitasato U. Hosp., 2000—01, Emory U., Divsn. Cardiology, Atlanta, 2003—05, Am. Heart Assn., 2003—05. Mem.: ACP, Japanese Soc. Treatment Obesity, Japanese Heart Failure Soc., Japanese Assn. Cardiac Rehabilitation, Japanese Assn. for Cerebo-Cardiovas. Disease Prevention, Japanese Soc. Internal Medicine, Japanese Circulation Soc. Office: Kitasato Univ Sch Allied Health Scis 1-15-1 Kitasato Minami-Ku Sagamihara 252-0373 Japan Office Fax: 81.42.778.9696. E-mail: myamaoka@med.kitasato-u.ac.jp.

YAMASAKI, TAKAO, neuroscientist, educator; b. Nishisonogi, Nagasaki, Japan, Oct. 29, 1972; PhD, Kyushu U., 2005. Rsch. asst. prof., dept. clin. neurophysiology Neurol. Inst., Grad. Sch. Med. Scis., Kyushu U., 2007—. Office: 3-1-1 Maidashi Higashi-ku Fukuoka 812-8582 Japan Office Fax: 81-92-642-5545. Business E-Mail: yamasa@neurophy.med.kyushu-u.ac.jp.

YAMASAKI, TORU, retired agricultural studies educator; b. Fukuiken, Japan, July 28, 1944; Degree in Bioresource Agr., Gifu U., 1967; PhD in Bioresource Agr., Kyoto U., 1978. Adj. prof. Kagawa U., 1982—89, prof., 1989—2009, emeritus prof., 2009—. Mem.: Am. Chemical Soc., Japan Soc. Biosci., Biotech. and Agrochemistry, Japanese Soc. Pharmacognosy, Pharm. Soc. Japan. Avocations: bicycling, gardening. Home: Okamoto-cho 147-97 Takamatsu-shi Kagawa ken 761-8047 Japan E-mail: toruyama@pe.kagawa-u.ac.jp.

YAMASHITA, ATSUSHI, pharmacist, educator; b. Shimonoseki, Yamaguchi, Japan, Aug. 8, 1961; PhD in Pharm. Scis., Hiroshima U. Sch. Medicine, 1990. Rsch. asst. prof. Teikyo U. Faculty Pharm. Scis., 1990—2002, assoc. prof., 2002—09, prof., 2009—. Mem.: Pharm. Soc. Japan, Japanese Biochem. Soc., Japanese Conf. on Biochemistry Lipids. Office: 1091-1 Suwarochi Midori-ku Sagamihara Kanagawa 252-5195 Japan Office Fax: +81-42-685-1345. Business E-Mail: ayamashi@pharm.teikyo-u.ac.jp.

YAMASHITA, HIROSHI, physiologist, educator; b. Fukuoka, Japan, Feb. 4, 1935; s. Miroku and Ayako (Kawasumi) Y.; m. Fumiko Sakai; children: Takeshi, Yuri, Junko. MD, Kobe U., Japan, 1962, PhD, 1966. Asst. Kobe U., 1966-71, postdoc. fellow, SUNY, Bklyn., 1968—70, instr., 1970-71; assoc. prof. Kobe U., 1971—78; vis. assoc. prof. SUNY, Bklyn., 1976-77; prof. U. Occupational and Environ. Health, Kitakyushu, 1978-2000, prof. emeritus, 2000—. Vis. scholar Fitzwilliam Coll., Cambridge, Eng., 1984-85. Editor past Jour. Neuroendocrinology, Neuroendocrinology, Exptl. Physiology, Japanese Jour. Physiology; contbr. articles to profl. jours. Recipient medal of Sechenov Anokhin Inst. Normal Physiology of Russian Acad. Med. Scis., 1986, diploma of Union of Sci. Workers of Bulgaria, 1987. Mem Physiology Soc., Japanese Physiology Soc., Japanese Neuroendocrine Soc., Japanese Endocrine Soc., Soc. for Neurosci., Japan Neurosci. Soc., Japan Obesity Soc. Avocations: tennis, reading. Office: U Occup & Environ Health Sch Medicine Yahata Nishi-ku Iseigaoka 1-1 Kitakyushu Fukuoka 807 Japan Office Phone: 81-93-691-7420.

YAMASHITA, JUNRO, dental educator; b. Kyoto, Mar. 1, 1963; DDS, Hokkaido U., 1991; PhD, Tokyo Med. Dental U., 1997. Asst. prof. U. Mich., 2004—. Office: University Mich Dental 1011 N University Ave Ann Arbor MI 48109-1078 Business E-Mail: yamashit@umich.edu.

YAMASHITA, KOICHI, physician, educator; b. Toyonaka, Japan, Jan. 30, 1968; MD, Kochi Med. Sch., PhD, 1994. Assoc. prof. Kochi Med. Sch., 2004—. Office: Kohasu Oko-cho Nankoku Kochi 783-8505 Japan Office Fax: 81-88-880-2475. Business E-Mail: koichiya@kochi-u.ac.jp.

YAMASHITA, KOUWA, pharmacist, educator; b. Tokyo, Sept. 7, 1951; PhD, Tohoku U., 1976. Sr. rsch. scientist Nippon Kayaku Co., Ltd., 1976—2004; vis. scholar Vanderbilt U., 1987—89; assoc. prof. Tohoku Pharm. U., 2004—10, prof., 2010—. Editl. bd. Japan Soc. Analytical Chemistry, 2004—11; councilor Japanese Soc. Study Xenobiotics, 1989—2011. Grant, Ministry of Edn., Culture, Sports and Tech. Japan. Mem.: Am. Chem. Soc., Japanese Soc. Study Xenobiotics, Am. Soc. Mass Spectrometry, Japan Soc. Analytical Chemistry, Pharm. Soc. Japan. Avocations: gardening, movies. Office: 4-4-1Komatsushima Aoba-ku Sendai Miyagi 981-8558 Japan Office Phone: 81-22-727-0138. Office Fax: 81-22-727-0137. Business E-Mail: kyama@tohoku-pharm.ac.jp.

YAMASHITA, MASAKANE, research scientist, educator; b. Osaka, Japan, Nov. 15, 1956; DSc, Grad. Sch. Sci., 1984. Prof. Hokkaido U., Faculty Sci., 1998—, dean, 2011—. Mem.: Japanese Soc. Devel. Biologist, Japanese Soc. Zoology (Zool. Sci. award). Office: North 10 West 8 Kita-Ku Sapporo Hokkaido 060-0810 Japan Office Fax: 81-11-706-4456. Business E-Mail: myama@sci.hokudai.ac.jp.

YAMASHITA, YOSHIHISA, dental educator; b. Fukuoka, Japan, Nov. 25, 1957; DDS, Kyushu Dental Coll., 1982, PhD, 1986. Asst. prof. Kyushu Dental Coll., 1986—90, lectr., 1990—93; assoc. prof. Kyushu U. Faculty Dentistry, 1993—2000, prof., 2003—, vice dean, 2009—10; prof. Nihon U. Sch. Dentistry, 2000—03. Mem.: Japanese Assn. Oral Biology, Japanese Soc. Bacteriology, Japanese Soc. Dental Health, Internat. Assn. Dental Rsch., Am. Soc. Microbiolgy. Avocations: skiing, cooking, winemaking. Office: 3-1-1 Maidashi Higashi-ku Fukuoka 812-8582 Japan Office Phone: 81-92-642-6350. Office Fax: 81-92-642-6354. Business E-Mail: yoshi@dent.kyushu-u.ac.jp.

YAMAUCHI, HAYATO, physician; b. Japan, Nov. 17, 1978; MD, Gunma U., 2003. Physician Grad. Sch. Medicine Gunma U. Office: Gunma University 3-39-22 Showa-machi Maebashi Gunma 371-8511 Japan Business E-Mail: m07702048@gunma-u.ac.jp.

YAMAUCHI, YASUSHI, surgeon, educator; b. Fukuoka, Japan, July 18, 1966; s. Kiyoshi and Haruko Yamauchi; m. Junko Sei, May 22, 1993; children: Kento, Yuto, Takuto. DMS, Fukuoka U., 2002. Resident Osumikanoya Hosp., Kanoya, Kagoshima, Japan, 1991—93, sr. resident, 1993—95, Kishiwada Tokushukai Hosp., Osaka, 1995—95; chief physician dept. surgery Osumikanoya Hosp., Japan, 1995—99; tchg. fellow dept. surgery Fukuoka U. Sch. Medicine, 2005—. Grantee, Clin. Rsch. Found., 2004; fellow, Nat. Cancer Ctr. Hosp., Hepatobiliary and Pancreatic Divsn., Tokyo, 1999, Copenhagen U., Dept. Surg. Gastroent., 2002—03. Mem.: Japan Surg. Soc. (licentiate). Achievements include discovery of Molecular Biology Of Thrombospondin-1; research in Liver Transplantation. Office: Fukuoka U Sch Medicine Nanakuma 7-45-1 Jonan-ku Fukuoka 814-0180 Japan Personal E-mail: yyama@fukuoka-u.ac.jp.

YAMAZAKI, HIROSHI, medical educator, researcher; b. Osaka, Japan, Dec. 5, 1960; PhD, Osaka U., 1992. Rsch. scientist Osaka Prefectural Inst. Pub. Health, 1987—98; rsch. assoc. Vanderbilt U. Sch. Medicine, 1994; assoc. prof. Kanazawa U., 1998—2001, Hokkaido U., 2001—05; prof. Showa Pharm. U., 2005—. Recipient Young Scientists award, Pharm. Soc. Japan, 2000. Master: Japanese Soc. Study of Xenobiotics (fellow, Young Scientists award 2005), Internat. Soc. Study of Xenobiotics. Office: Higashi-tamagawa Gakuen Machida Tokyo 194-8543 Japan Business E-Mail: hyamazak@ac.shoyaku.ac.jp.

YAMAZAKI, YOSHITAKA, organizational educator; b. Niigata, Japan, July 9, 1956; s. Yoshiro and Koiko Yamazaki; m. Sachi Arima; children: Yusuke, Yumi. PhD, Case Western Res. U., Cleve., 2004. Mgr., supr. Citibank N.A., Tokyo, 1990—96; prof., orgnl. behavior Internat. U. Japan, Minami Uonuma, Niigata, 2004—. Assoc. dir. evaluation Case Western Res. U., 2002—03. Rsch. grant, Japan Soc. Promotion Sci., 2008. Mem.: Acad. Mgmt. Office: Internat Univ Japan 777 Kokusai-cho Minami Uonuma Niigata 949 7277 Japan

YAMAZAKI, YUU, physician; b. Japan, Jan. 3, 1978; MD, Hiroshima U., 2002. Staff physician Hiroshima U. Grad. Sch. Biomedical Scis., 2008—. Office: 1-2-3 Kasumi Minami-ku Hiroshima 734-0001 Japan Personal E-mail: yuu.yamazaki@gmail.com.

YAMINI, DANIEL, plastic surgeon; BA in Psychology, Stanford U., 1990, BS in Biology, 1990; MD, Med. Coll. Wis., 1994. Cert. Am. Bd. Plastic Surgery, Am. Bd. Surgery, lic. Calif. Bd. Medicine. Resident, gen. surgery UCLA, 1994—2000, Harbor Gen. Hosp., Torrance, Calif., 1994—2000; resident, plastic and reconstructive surgery Providence Hosp. and Med. Ctrs. & Inst. for Craniofacial and Reconstructive Plastic Surgery, Detroit, 2000—02; fellow in advanced cosmetic surgery Dr. Richard Ellenbogen, Beverly Hills, Calif., 2002; founding ptnr., plastic surgeon Sunset Cosmetic Surgery, LA. Presenter in field; hosp. affiliations include Century City Hosp., Midway Hosp. Contbr. articles to profl. jours., chapters to books, Abstracts; featured on Dr. 90210. Recipient Soc. Academic Surgery Student Rsch. award, 1994, First prize: Resident Rsch. award, Am. Coll. Surgeons, So. Calif. Conf., 1998, Providence Hosp. Rsch. Symposium, 2002. Fellow: Am. Coll. Surgeons; mem.: AMA, Am. Soc. Plastic Surgeons, Calif. Soc. Plastic Surgeons, Calif. Med. Assn. Office: Sunset Cosmetic Surgery 9201 Sunset Blvd Ste 805 Los Angeles CA 90069 Office Phone: 310-858-9100.

YAMUNA, SRINIVASAN, pediatrician; b. Chennai, Nov. 24, 1965; MBBS, Stanley Med. Coll., 1989; diploma in Child Health, Madras Med. Coll., 1996. Cert. DCH Madras Med. Coll., PGDAP Madras Med. Coll. Cons. paediatrician & adolescent physician Child and Adolescent Clinic, 2000. Mem.: Indian Acad. Paediatrics. Avocations: reading, writing. Office: H 110/S2 Waves First Seaward Rd Va Chennai Tamil Nadu 600041 India

YAN, GANGLIN, biology professor; b. Jiayuguan, Nov. 19, 1952; BS, Jilin U., China, 1977. Prof. Jilin U., 2007—. Home: Qian Jin Da Jie 2699 Changchun Jilin 130012 China Business E-Mail: ygl@jlu.edu.cn.

YAN, HEDE, surgeon; b. China, Feb. 8, 1973; MD, Zhejiang U., 2002. Surgeon 2nd affiliated Hosp. Wenzhou Med. Coll., 2007—. Office: W Xueyuan Rd 109 Wenzhou Zhejiang 325027 China Personal E-mail: yanhede@hotmail.com.

YAN, WEI HUA, medical researcher; b. China, Dec. 3, 1971; PhD, Shanghai Second Med. U., 2003. Dir. Med. Rsch. Ctr., Taizhou Hosp. Zhejiang Province, 2005. Mem.: Am. Soc. Histocompatibility and Immunogenetics. Office: 150 Ximen St Linhai Zhejiang 317000 China Office Fax: 86-576-85199876. Personal E-mail: yanwhcom@yahoo.com.

YAN, WING-WA, critical care physician, consultant; b. Hong Kong, Mar. 6, 1961; s. Wen Ko Yin and Tsui Ying Tai; m. Betty Chan Yan, Apr. 7, 1990; children: John, Tim. MB, BChir, U. Hong Kong, 1985. Med. officer Hosp. Authority, Hong Kong, 1986—91, sr. med. officer, 1991—95, cons., chief of svc., 1995—2003, cons., 2003—. Fellow: Royal Coll. Physicians (London), Royal Coll. Physicians (Edinburgh), Hong Kong Acad. Medicine, Hong Kong Coll. Physicians; mem.: Royal Coll. Physicians (U.K.). Avocations: badminton, football, ping pong/table tennis, fishing. Office: Rm 112 Block J Princess Margaret Hosp Lai Chi Kok Hong Kong Hong Kong Office Fax: (852) 2990 3477. E-mail: yanww@ha.org.hk.

YAN, XIN, statistician, educator; b. China, Nov. 11, 1955; PhD, U. Calif. Davis, 1998. Assoc. prof. U. Mo. Kans. City, 2006—. Mem.: Am. Statis. Assn. Office: 5100 Rockhii Rd Kansas City MO 64110 Business E-Mail: yanxi@umkc.edu.

YANAGAWA, YOSHIKI, pharmacist, educator; b. Nagoya, Japan, June 16, 1968; BS, Hokkaido U., 1991, PhD, 1999. Instr. Inst. Genetic Medicine, Hokkaido U., 2000—07, asst. prof., 2007—09, Faculty Pharm. Scis., Health Scis. U. Hokkaido, 2009—. Mem.: Japanese Pharmacological Soc., Japanese Soc. Immunology, Am. Assn. Immunologists. Office: Kanazawa 1757 Ishikari-Tobetsu Hokkaido 061-0293 Japan Office Fax: 81-133-23-1579. E-mail: yanagawa@hoku-iryo-u.ac.jp.

YANAGISAWA, EIJI, otolaryngologist, educator; b. Yokohama, Japan, May 12, 1930; came to U.S., 1955; s. Jiro and Sue Yanagisawa; m. June Yanagisawa, Sept. 16, 1960; children: Ken, Kay, Amy Ray. MD, Nihon U., Tokyo, 1955. Intern Hosp. of St. Raphael, New Haven, 1962, U.S. Tokyo Army Hosp., 1955—56; resident in otolaryngology Yale-New Haven Hosp., 1956—59; instr. otolaryngology Yale U. Sch. Medicine, New Haven, 1959-61, 63-64, clin. instr., 1964-67, asst. clin. prof., 1967-72, assoc. clin. prof., 1972-83, clin. prof., 1983—; pvt. practice New Haven, 1964—. Co-author (with G. Gardner): The Surgical Atlas of Otology and Neuro-0tology, 1983; co-author: (with D.A. Christmas and J.P. Mirante) Powered Instrumentation in Otolaryngology and Head and Neck Surgery, 2001; author: Color Atlas of Diagnostic Endoscopy in Otorhinolaryngology, 1997, Atlas of Rhinoscopy--Endoscopic Sinonasal Anatomy and Pathology, 2000; contbg. author more than 400 chpts. and jour. articles, Rhinoscopic Clinic editor Ear, Nose & Throat Jour., 1999—. Recipient Lifetime Achievement award, AAO, 2003, Pulitzer Soc. Meeting, Cleve., 2007. Mem.: AMA, ACS (presiding officer Clin. Congress, Otolaryngol. Movie Session 1984—2002), Biol. Photographic Assn. (John Muir Med. Film Festival award 1990, C. Graham Eddy Endoscopic award 1980), Am. Med. Writers Assn., Am. Rhinologic Soc., New Eng. Otolaryngol. Soc. (pres. 1992), Triological Soc. (v.p., chmn. ea. sect. 1990), Am. Otol. Soc., Am. Broncho-Esophagological Assn. (pres. 1994, Chevalier Jackson award 2000), Am. Laryngol. Assn., Am. Acad. Otolaryngology-Head and Neck Surgery (chmn. continuing edn. through TV subcom. 1988—98, co-chmn. interactive multimedia faculty 1998—2000), Japan Bronscho-Esphagological Assn. (hon.), Nihon U. Alumni Assn. (hon.). Avocations: photography, videography, digital imaging. Office: So New Eng ENT and Facial Plastic Surg Group 1 Long Wharf Dr Ste 302 New Haven CT 06511-5593 Home Phone: 203-397-1620; Office Phone: 203 777-2264.

YANAGISAWA, OSAMU, research scientist, educator; s. Nakao and Yoshiko Yanagisawa. BBA, Aoyama Gakuin U., Tokyo, 1997; M in Phys. Edn., U. Tsukuba, Ibaraki, Japan, 1999; MD, U. Tsukuba, 2003. Rschr. Japan Inst. Sports Scis., Kita-ku, 2003—. Mem. internat. reviewers panel Med. Sci. Monitor, NYC, 2005—. Contbr. articles to profl. jours. Grantee, Ministry of Edn., Culture, Sports, Sci. and Tech., 2004—. Mem.: Japanese Soc. Clin. Sports Medicine, Japanese Soc. Magnetic Resonance in Medicine, Japan Soc. Phys. Edn., Health and Sport Scis., Japanese Soc. Phys. Fitness and Sports Medicine, Am. Coll. Sports Medicine, European Coll. Sport Sci. Avocations: driving, baseball, exercise, aquariums, travel. Office: Japan Inst Sports Scis Nishigaoka 3-15-1 Kita 115-0056 Japan Office Fax: +81-3-5963-0232. E-mail: yanagisawa.osamu@jiss.naash.go.jp.

YANAGISAWA, SATOKO, nursing educator, researcher; MS, PhD, Grad. Sch. Medicine, U. Tokyo. RN Ministry of Health, Labour and Welfare, Japan, PHN, RM. Prof. Aichi U., Nagoya, Japan, 2004—. Achievements include cooperative projects and researches with developing countries. Office: Aichi Prefectural Univ Tougoku Kamishidami Moriyama-Ku Nagoya Aichi 463-8502 Japan Personal E-mail: sarahyana@hotmail.com. Business E-Mail: sayanagi@nrs.aichi-pu.ac.jp.

YANAGITA, SHIGEHIRO, oncologist; b. Kagoshima, Japan, Aug. 10, 1970; s. Koichi and Yoshiko Yanagita; m. Hiroyo Yanagita; children: Kodai, Haruka. MD, Kagoshima U., PhD, 1998. Digestive surgeon Kagoshima U., 1998—. Home: 8-35-1 Sakuragaoka Kagoshima 890-8520 Japan Office: Kagoshima Univ Dept Surg 8-35-1 Sakuragaoka Kagoshima 890-8520 Japan Office Fax: 81-99-265-7426. Personal E-mail: s0810y2003@yahoo.co.jp. Business E-Mail: y0810@m.kufm.kagoshima-u.ac.jp.

YANAI, HIDEKATSU, physician, educator, researcher; b. Iwaki, Fukushima, Japan, Jan. 14, 1969; s. Tadashi and Kikuko Yanai; m. Mie Yanai, Oct. 2, 2001; 1 child, Daiki. MD, Nat. Def. Med. Coll., Tokorozawa, Japan, 1995; PhD, Hokkaido U., Sapporo, Japan, 2002. Resident internal medicine Nat. Def. Med. Coll. Hosp., Tokorozawa, 1995—97; rsch. fellow Hokkaido U., 1997—2002; fellow, internal medicine Sapporo Self-Def. Force Hosp., 1999—2002; invited phd rsch. fellow Nat. Inst. Child Health and Human Devel., Bethesda, Md., 2002—04; asst. prof. internal medicine Jikei U. Sch. Medicine, Kashiwa, Chiba, Japan, 2004—07, lectr. internal medicine, 2007—09; med. dir. Nat. Ctr. Global Health & Medicine, Kohnodai Hosp., Chiba, Japan. Contbr. rsch articles to sci. jours. Vol.dr., Kashiwa, 2005—09; coord. dietary therapy, 2006—; lecture citizens 10th Med. Cooperation Forum, Kashiwa, 2007; vol. Maj. Med., 2003—04, Itami, Hyogo. Recipient Young Investigator award, Internat. Soc. Thrombosis Haemostasis, 2000; Travel grant, 5th Congress of Asian-Pacific Soc. Atherosclerosis and Vascular Diseases, 2006. Fellow: ACP, Japanese Acad. Primary Care Physicians, Japanese Soc. Internal Medicine; mem.: Japan Atherosclerosis Soc. Achievements include research in lipid metabolism. Office Fax: 81473721858. Business E-Mail: dyanai@hospk.ncgm.go.jp.

YANAI, SHLOMO, pharmaceutical company executive, retired military officer; BA in Polit. Sci. & Economics, Tel Aviv U.; MPA in Nat. Resources Mgmt., George Washington U. Advanced through ranks to maj. gen. Israel Def. Forces, commanding officer southern command, 1996—98, head divsn. strategic planning, 1998—2001; pres., CEO Makhteshim-Agan Industries Ltd., 2003—06, Teva Pharmaceuticals Industries Ltd., 2007—. Bd. mem. Lycord Natural Products Industries, 2003—08, Bank Leumi Le-Israel Ltd., 2004—07. Hon. bd. mem. Herzliya Interdisciplinary Inst. Policy and Strategy; mem. MBA program Ben-Gurion U. Decorated Disting. Svc. medal Israel Def. Forces; recipient Max Perlman award for Excellence in Global Bus. Mgmt., 2005, Dun & Bradstreet Leadership Excellence award, 2006; named one of Bus. People of Yr., Fortune mag., 2010. Office: Teva Pharmaceuticals 5, Basel St 49131 Petach Tikva Israel *

YANCEY, ASA G., SR., physician, educator; b. Atlanta, Aug. 19, 1916; s. Arthur H. and Daisy L. (Sherard) Yancey; m. Carolyn E. Dunbar, Dec. 28, 1944; children: Arthur H. II, Carolyn L., Caren L., Asa Greenwood Jr. BS, Morehouse Coll., Atlanta, 1937, ScD (hon.), 1991; MD, U. Mich., 1941; ScD (hon.), Howard U., Washington, DC, 1991. Diplomate Am. Bd. Surgery. Intern City Hosp., Cleve., 1941-42; resident Freedmen's Hosp., Washington, 1942-45, U.S. Marine Hosp., Boston, 1945; instr. surgery Meharry Med. Coll., 1946-48; chief surgery VA Hosp., Tuskegee, Ala., 1948-58; chief surgery of Hughes Spalding Pavilion, 1958-72; pvt. practice specializing in surgery Atlanta, 1958-86; from asst. prof. to assoc. prof. surgery Emory U., 1958—75, prof., 1975-86, prof. emeritus, 1986—, assoc. dean Sch. Medicine, 1972-89; med. dir. Grady Meml. Hosp., Atlanta, 1972-89, trustee, 1989—93; clin. prof. surgery Morehouse Sch. Medicine, 1985—; mem. staff Hughes Spalding Hosp., St. Joseph Hosp., Emory U. Hosp., 1986—88. Contbr. articles to profl. jours. Mem. Atlanta Bd. Edn., 1967—77, Fulton-De Kalb Hosp. Authority. 1st lt. M.C. US Army, 1942. Fellow: ACS, Am. Surg. Assn.; mem.: So. Surg. Assn., Inst. Medicine of NAS, Nat. Med. Assn. (1st v.p. 1988—89, trustee 1960—66, mem. editl. bd. jour. 1964—80). Baptist. Home and Office: 2845 Engle Rd NW Atlanta GA 30318-7216 Office Phone: 404-799-5045.

YANCHICK, VICTOR A., dean, educator; b. Joliet, Ill., Dec. 3, 1940; BS in Pharmacy, U. Iowa, 1962, MS in Pharmacy, 1966; PhD in Pharmacy, Purdue U., West Lafayette, Ind., 1968. Asst. chief pharmacist Silver Cross Hosp., Joliet, Ill., 1962-64; hosp. pharmacy resident Univs. Hosp., Iowa City, 1964-66; instr. clin. pharmacy Purdue U., 1966-68; asst. prof. pharmacy U. Tex., Austin, 1968-72, assoc. prof. pharmacy, 1972-78, prof. pharmacy, 1978-84, acting asst. dean, 1971-73, asst. dean academic affairs, 1973-81, assoc. dean, 1981-84; dean U. Okla. Coll. Pharmacy, Oklahoma City, 1985-96; prof. pharmacy, dean. Va. Commonwealth U. Sch. Pharmacy, Richmond, 1996—. Cons. Tex. Nursing Home Assn., Austin, 1978—84, Baylor Coll. Medicine, Houston, 1988—90; dir. Okla. Poison Ctr., Oklahoma City, 1994—96; mem. adv. bd. Nat. Assn. Retail Druggist Edn., Nat. Assn. Chain Drug Stores. Recipient Alumni Assn. award, U. Okla., 1989, Disting. Alumnus award, Purdue U., 1995. Mem.: Am. Assn. Colleges of Pharmacy. Avocations: tennis, racquetball, gardening, antique collecting. Office: VCU Sch Pharmacy Deans Office 410 N 12th St PO Box 980581 Richmond VA 23298-0581 Office Phone: 804-828-3006. Office Fax: 804-827-0002. Business E-Mail: vyanchick@vcu.edu.

YANCY, CLYDE WARREN, JR., cardiologist, educator; b. Baton Rouge, Jan. 2, 1958; MD, Tulane U. Sch. Medicine, 1982. Diplomate Am. Bd. Internal Medicine, Sub-specialty Cardiovascular Disease. Intern, internal medicine Parkland Meml. Hosp. and U. Tex. Southwestern Med. Ctr., Dallas, 1982—83, resident, internal medicine, 1983, dir., cardiology clinics, 1990—96; clin. rsch. assoc., dept. cardiovascular rsch. Tulane U. Sch. Medicine, New Orleans, 1985—86; staff physician, dept. internal medicine and ambulatory care New Orleans Vet. Adminstrn. Hosp., New Orleans, 1985—86; staff physician Gen. Hosp. Lakewood, Dallas, 1987—89; attending cardiologist, coronary care unit Parkland Meml. Hosp., Dallas, 1989, assoc. dir., cardiac rehabilitation program, 1990—93, cons. cardiologist, renal transplant program, 1990—92, acting med. dir., coronary care unit, 1992—93; attending cardiologist, coronary care unit Dallas Vet. Adminstrn. Hosp., Dallas, 1989; clin. cardiologist Zale-Lipshy U. Hosp., Dallas, 1989; assoc. attending staff, dept. medicine, divsn. cardiology St. Paul Med. Ctr., Dallas, 1993; fellow, cardiology U. Tex. Southwestern Med. Ctr., Dallas, 1986—89, attending cardiologist, 1989, asst. prof. medicine, divsn. cardiology, 1989—95, assoc. prof. medicine, divsn. cardiology, 1995—2004, prof. medicine, divsn. cardiology, 2004—06, Carl Westcott Disting. Chair, med. rsch., 1996, med. dir., Heart Failure/Heart Transplant Program, 1991—2006, assoc. dean, clin. affairs, 2002—06; med. dir., Baylor Heart & Vascular Inst. Baylor U. Med. Ctr., Dallas, 2006—, chief, cardiothoracic transplantation, 2006—. Rsch. asst., biomedical scis. dept. So. U., Baton Rouge, 1976; rsch. chemist Merck, Sharpe and Dohme Rsch. Lab., Rahway, NJ, 1978; camp counselor Am. Diabetes Assn., 1979; vis. tchg. staff dept., sect. medicine, cardiology St. Paul Med. Ctr., Dallas, 1989; advanced cardiac life support instr., 1990—93; cons. Ctr. for Disease Control, Vet. Affairs Med. Ctrs., NIH; mem., cardiovascular device panel Ctr. for Devices and Radiological Health; FDA; Integrity-Com. and Conf. Mgmt. Br., 2003—; mem., Nat. Immunization Program Adv. Com. Ctr. for Disease Control; FDA, 2003—05; mem., Circulatory Sys. Devices Panel of the Med. Devices Adv. Com., Dept. HHS, FDA, 2005—08; mem., physician health and recovery com. U. Tex. Southwestern Med. Ctr., Dallas, 2006; mem. scientific adv. bd. Internat. Acad. Cardiology and the World Congress, 2006—07; Newall Powell Vis. professorship Scott & White Clinic, Temple, Tex., 2004; invited lectr. in field. Contbr. chapters to books, several articles to profl. jours., web-based ednl. media, to several CD-Roms; assoc. editor Am. Jour. Cardiology, Congestive Heart Failure, mem. editl. bd., 2002—, Am. Heart Jour., Cardiology Review, Urban Cardiology, Jour. Cardiovascular Pharmacology and Therapeutics & Circulation, Progress in Transplantation, 2002—, Jour. Cardiac Failure, 2002—04, Current Heart Failure Reports, 2003—, Jour. Acute Cardiac Care, 2006—07, reviewer for major cardiovascular jours. Bd. dirs. Family Place. Named one of Top Doctors, D Mag., 1992, Top 330 Doctors in 2001, Top 381 Doctors in 2002 (Featured Top Doctor), Best Doctors, 2003—04, Top 572 Doctors of 2003 (Featured Top Doctor), Top 638 Doctors of 2004 (Featured Top Doctor), Best Doctors, 2005, Best Doctors in Am., 1998, 2000, America's Leading Physicians, Black Enterprise Mag., 2001, Tex. Super Docs, Tex. Monthly, 2004, Tex. Super Doctors 2005, America's Top Physicians, Guide to America's Top Physicians, e-book, 2006. Fellow: Internal. Soc. on Hypertension in Blacks (Outstanding Rsch. award 2001), ACP, Am. Heart Assn. (first v.p., Dallas Divsn. 1993—94, pres.-elect, Dallas Divsn 1994—95, pres., Dallas Divsn. 1995—96, first v.p., Tex. affiliate 1996—97, pres.-elect, Tex. affiliate 1997—98, pres., Tex. affiliate 1998—99, bd. dir., Tex. affiliate 2001—02, coun. clin. cardiology's heart failure and transplantation sub-com., mem. nat. bd. dirs. 2000—02, nat. spokesperson, bd. dirs. Dallas Divsn. and Tex. Affiliate, chmn., hypertension task force, Dallas Divsn., Douglas Perry Vol. Yr. award, Dallas Divsn. 1996, Walter M. Kirkendall, award for Outstanding Scientist/Educator Vol., Tex. affiliate 1996, Physician Vol. Yr., Tex. Affiliate 2001, Nat. Physician of Yr. 2003), ACS, Am. Coll. Cardiology (sec.-treas., Tex. chpt. 1993—95); mem.: Dallas County Med. Soc., Tex. Med. Assn., Tex. Transplatation Soc., Tex. Acad. Physician Assts. (hon.), Am. Soc. Transplantation, Am. Diabetes Assn. (minority initiative com., bd. dirs. 1990—92), Assn. Black Cardiologists, Inc. (chmn., organ transplatation com. 2002—03, heart failure com. chair 2002—03, editl. bd. Digest of Urban Cardiology 2002—04, Daniel Savage award for Scientific Merit 2002, Cardiologists-In-Tng. Hero award 2006), Heart Failure Soc. Am. (mem. exec. com., ex-officio 2001—03), Am. Soc. Hypertension, Internat. Soc. Heart and Lung Transplantation, Alpha Omega Alpha. Office: Baylor Heart & Vascular Inst Baylor U Med Ctr 3500 Gaston Ave Ste H-030 Dallas TX 75246 Office Phone: 214-820-7357. Office Fax: 214-820-7533. Business E-Mail: clydey@baylorhealth.edu.

YANDERS, ARMON FREDERICK, biological sciences educator, science administrator; b. Lincoln, Nebr., Apr. 12, 1928; s. Fred W. and Beatrice (Pate) Yanders; m. Evelyn Louise Gatz, Aug. 1, 1948; children: Mark Frederick, Kent Michael. AB, Nebr. State Coll., Peru, 1948; MS, U. Nebr., 1950, PhD, 1953. Rsch. asso. Oak Ridge Nat. Lab. and Northwestern U., 1953-54; biophysicist US Naval Radiol. Def. Lab., San Francisco, 1955-58; asso. geneticist Argonne Nat. Lab., Ill., 1958-59; with dept. zoology Mich. State U., 1959-69; prof., asst. dean Mich. State U. (Coll. Natural Sci.), 1963-69; prof. biol. scis. U. Mo., Columbia, 1969—, dean Coll. Arts and Scis., 1969-82, rsch. prof., dir. Environ. Trace Substances Rsch. Ctr., 1983-93, dir. Alzheimer's Disease and Related Disorders Program, 1994—, dir. Spinal Cord Injury Rsch. Program, 2002—, rsch. prof., dir. Environ. Trace Substances Rsch. Ctr. and Sinclair Comparative Medicine Rsch. Farm, 1984-94, prof. emeritus, 1994—; dean emeritus, 2007—. Trustee Argonne Univs. Assn., 1965-77, v.p., 1969-73, pres., 1973, 76-77, chmn. bd., 1973-75; bd. dirs. Coun. Colls. Arts and Scis., 1981-82; mem. adv. com. environ. hazards VA, Washington, 1985-2002, chmn. sci. coun., 1988-2000, chmn. of com., 1990-2002. Contbr. articles to profl. jours. Trustee Peru State Coll., 1992-2001. Served from ensign to lt. USNR, 1954-58. Recipient Disting. Svc. award Peru State Coll., 1989, U. Mo., 2007. Fellow AAAS; mem. AAUP (Robert W. Martin acad. freedom award 1971), Environ. Mutagen Soc., Genetics Soc. Am., Radiation Rsch. Soc., Soc. Environ. Toxicology and Chemistry. Home: 1204 Castle Bay Pl Columbia MO 65203-6257 Office: U Mo 521 Clark Hall Columbia MO 65211-4420 Office Phone: 573-882-1640. Business E-Mail: YandersA@umsystem.edu.

YAÑEZ SANTOS, JORGE ANTONIO, medical educator, researcher; s. Heraclio Yañez and Dolores Santos; m. Maria Lilia Cedillo Ramirez, Jan. 9, 1959; children: Adriana Patricia Yañez Cedillo, Jorge Antonio Yañez Cedillo. PhD in Microbiology, Escuela Nacional de Ciencias Biologicos, Instituto Politecnico Nacional, Mexico City, 1997. Vis. scientist dept. microbiology U. Ala., Birmingham, 1992—93; asst. rschr. Ea. Biomed. Rsch. Ctr., Instituto Mexicano del Seguro Social, Puebla City, Puebla, Mexico, 1993—2000; prof. and chmn. faculty stomatology Oral Microbiology Rsch. Lab., Puebla City, Puebla, Mexico, 2000—. Chmn. of the lab. of bacteriology Ea. Biomedical Rsch. Ctr., Instituto Mexicano del Seguro Social, Puebla City, Puebla, Mexico, 1993—2000; head of the exptl. pathology divsn. Ea. Biomedical Rsch. Ctr., IMSS, Puebla City, Puebla, Mexico, 1993—2000; chmn. oral microbiology rsch. lab. Faculty of Stomatology, Puebla City, Puebla, Mexico, 2000—. Recipient Travel Fellowship Award to attend the 12th Internat. Orgn. for Mycoplasmology Conf. in Sydney, Australia, Internat. Orgn. for Mycoplasmology, 1998. Mem.: Am. Soc. for Microbiology, Internat. Assn. for Dental Rsch. Catholic. Achievements include research in Isolation and identification of a Mycoplasma penetrans strain in an HIV negative patient with primary antiphospholipid syndrome. Avocations: jogging, swimming, travel. Office Fax: 52(222)229-5604. E-mail: jorge.yanez@festom.buap.mx.

YANG, BAOFENG, medical educator; b. Jilin, China, Nov. 27, 1957; PhD, Tongji Med. U., 1988. Postdoc. fellow Eisai Rsch. Inst. Tsukuba, Japan, 1990—92; prof. Harbin Med. U., 1994—, pres., 2001; vis. fellow Montreal Heart Inst., 1995—96. Vis. prof. W.Va. U., 2005, U. Mo., Kans. City, 2006, Nippon Med. Sch., 2007; hon. prof. Perm Pharm. Acad., 2006; academician Chinese Acad. Engring., 2009. Recipient Nat. prize, State Coun. People's Republic of China, Ministry of Edn., China, Nat. Excellent Tchg. award, State Sci. and Tech. award, Natural Sci. award. Master: Chinese Pharmacological Soc. Avocations: ping pong/table tennis, writing. Office: Dept Pharmacology Harbin Med University Harbin Heilongjiang 150081 China Office Fax: 86-451-86669482.

YANG, BIN, pathologist, molecular biologist; MD, Zhengzhou U., China, 1983, MS in Cancer Biology, 1986; PhD, Case Western Res. U., Cleve, Ohio, 1996. Diplomate Pathology Bd. Cert. for Anatomic Pathology and Cytopathology 2003. Instr. Henan Med. U., Zhengzhou, China, 1986—88; postdoctoral fellow Case Western Res. U., Cleve., 1988—90; pathology resident Cleve. Clinic Found., 1996—2000, staff pathologist, 2003—; surg. pathology fellow Wash. U., St. Louis, 2000—01; cytopathology fellow Johns Hopkins U., Balt., 2001—03. Dir. cancer epigenetics core lab. Cleve. Clinic Found., 2003—. Contbr. scientific papers pub. to profl. jour. and confs. Recipient George Hoffman award, 2000, Geno Saccomanno New Frontier in Cytology award, 2002, 2007, Hans Popper Outstanding Sci. award, 2003, Johns Hopkins Pathology Young Investigator's award, 2003, Innovation award, Cleveland Clin., 2006. Mem.: Chinese Am. Pathologists Assn. (pres. 2006—08). Avocations: tennis, golf, photography, gardening.

YANG, BING-SHIANG, engineering educator; BS in Mech. Engring. with honors, Nat. Taiwan U., 1994, MS in Mech. Engring., 1996; PhD in Mech. Engring. and Biomechanics, U. Mich., 2004. Cert. nat. refrigeration and air-conditioning profl. engr., ROC, 1995. Rsch. asst. Nat. Taiwan U., Taipei, 1993—96; engr. Tenkey Refrigeration MFG. Co. Ltd., Taipei, 1994; lectr. Tjing-Ling Indsl. Rsch. Ctr., Taipei, 1995—96; tchg. asst. Nat. Taiwan U., 1998—99; rsch. asst. U. Mich., 1999—2004; rsch. assoc. Rehab. Inst. of Chgo., 2005—06; postdoctoral fellow Northwestern U., Chgo., 2005—06; asst. prof. Nat. Chiao Tung U., 2006—11, assoc. prof., 2010—, dir. Biomechanics and Med. Application Lab., 2006—, cons. tech. lic. office, 2008—; smart gymnasium tech. organizer Integrated Smart Living Tech. Regional Ctr., 2008—; com. mem. Instl. Review Bd. Hsinchu Gen. Hosp., 2010—11, Instl. Review Bd. Nat. Taiwan U. Hosp. Hsinchu Br., 2011—. Mem. com. Internat. Conf. on Rehab. Robotics, Chgo., 2005; mem. award com. Nat. Sci. Coun., Taiwan, 2006, external grant reviewer, 07, 08, Nat. Med. Rsch. Coun., Singapore, 2007—; rsch. affiliate Brain Rsch. Ctr. Nat. Chiao Tung U., 2006—; organizer Internat. Conf. Mech. in Medicine and Biology, Singapore, 2006; spkr. in field; conf. chair Internat. Biomechanics Conf. & Annual Meeting Taiwanese Soc. Biomechanics, 2011. Contbr. articles to profl. pubs. Second lt. Armor, Army, 1996—98, Taiwan. Decorated Best Trainee award ROC Army Pre-Mil. Tng. Ctr., ranked 1st/250 second lt. ROC Army Armor Officer Tng. Ctr.; recipient Academic, Personal, Profl., and Leadership Devel. Cert., U. Mich., 2004, Sarah Baskin Rsch. Excellence award, Rehab. Inst. Chgo., 2006, Excellence Scholarship award, Nat. Chiao Tung U., 2008—10, NCTU Design Contest Gold & Silver medal, 2009, Outstanding mentor award, 2010; finalist Young Investigator award, Internat. Soc. Biomech., 2007, Clin. Biomechanics award, Internat. Soc. Biomechanics, 2009; Tchg. Fellow, U. Mich., 2004, Advanced Rehab. Rsch. Tng. Postdoctoral fellowship, US Nat. Inst. on Disability and Rehab. Rsch., 2005—06, Travel grant, Neural Control of Movement Soc. and Nat. Inst. on Disability and Rehab. Rsch., 2006, U Mich. Internat. Inst., 2002, U Mich. Rackham Grad. Sch., 2002, 2003, 2004. Mem.: Taiwanese Biomed. Engring. Soc., Biomed. Engring. Soc. ROC, Taiwanese Soc. Biomechanics (coun. mem. 2008—), Soc. for Neurosci., Soc. for Neural Control of Movement, Internat. Soc. of Biomechanics, Am. Soc. of Biomechanics, Am. Soc. for Mech. Engineers. Achievements include patents for self-guided drill jib for equal-distance holes, ROC utility model; research in simulation study of human balance control on raised rigid structures; experimental study of age and gender differences on stepping and balancing behavior on laterally-compliant raised structures; modelling of human balance control on raised structures with lateral structural compliance; sensory input-enhanced stroke rehabilitation; task-specific modulation arm/hand posture and stiffness; smart living technology, advanced vehicle technology; development of feedback fitness system. Avocations: martial arts (3d Dan-black belt), swimming, ping pong/table tennis, bicycling, travel. Home: 3582 Freldcrest Ln Ypsilanti MI 48197 Business E-Mail: bsyang@umich.edu.

YANG, CATHERINE FANGXIN, biochemist, educator, inventor; b. Hangzhou, June 1, 1960; PhD, Tufts U., 1993. Postdoc. fellow Harvard Med. Sch., 1995; prof. Rowan U., 1995—, chair, dept. chem. & biochem., 2007—; CEO, founder DNJ Pharm. Inc., 2011. V.p. AZKEF Found., 2008—. Named to Wall of Fame, Rowan U. Mem.: Am. Chem. Soc. Avocations: reading, travel, history, volleyball, tennis. Home: Rue Du Bois Cherry Hill NJ 08003 Home Fax: 856-256-4478. Business E-Mail: yang@rown.edu.

YANG, CHICH-HAUNG RICHARD, physical therapist, educator; b. Changhaw, Taiwan, Dec. 31, 1967; s. Wu-Fu Yang and Chiu-Hisang Hong; m. Yu-Ching Tiffany Ho, June 7, 1999. BSc In Phys. Therapy, Kaohsiung Med. U., Taiwan, 1992; MSc in Biomechanics, Nat. Cheng-Kung U., Taiwan, 1994; PhD in Physiotherapy, U. Queensland, Brisbane, Australia, 2011. Lic. phys. therapist Dept. Health, Taiwan, 1996. Phys. therapist Tzu-Chi Gen. Hosp., Hua-Lien, Taiwan, 1996—; sr. lectr. phys. therapy Tzu-Chi Coll. Tech., 1996—. Contbr. articles to profl. jours. Vol. Buddhist Compassion Relief Tzu-Chi Found., Hua-Lien, Taiwan, 2000—08. 2d lt. in med. svc. Taiwanese Army, 1994—96, Island of Machu. Recipient Best Tchg. award, Tzu-Chi College Tech., 2006. Mem.: Phys. Therapy Assn. (licentiate). Achievements include research in the injury of lower limbs, including the knee and ankle; patents related to the invention and design of devices for sports and rehabilitation. Office: Tzu-Chi Coll Tech 880 Sect 2 Jiangup Rd Hua-Lien 97005 Taiwan Home: 3 Ln 35 Jiezhi St Hualien City 97074 Taiwan Office Fax: 886 3 8561072. Personal E-mail: chichhaung.yang@gmail.com. Business E-Mail: r.chyang@mail.tcu.edu.tw.

YANG, CHI-CHIANG, medical educator, consultant; b. Miaoli, Taiwan, Aug. 29, 1965; s. Fu-Sow Yang and Tsai-May Lao. BSc, Chung Shan Med. & Dental Coll., 1987; PhD, U. Leeds, Eng., 1994. Intern Cathay Gen. Hosp., Taipei, Taiwan, 1987; rsch. asst. Academia Sinica, Taipei, 1989—90; assoc. prof. Sch. Med. Lab. and Biotech. Chung Shan Med. U., Taichung, Taiwan, 1994—2005, prof. Sch. Med. Lab. and Biotech., 2005—; vis. scientist Aaron Diamond AIDS Rsch. Ctr., NYC, 1997—98; vis. prof. Wuhan (China) U., Hubei Province, 2002—, hon. prof., 2003—; prof. Yunyang Med. Coll., Shiyan, Hubei Province, China, 2003—; rsch. cons. Xianfan City First Peoples' Hosp., Xianfan, Hubei Province, China, 2003—. Author: Introduction to Virology, Oral Virology. Recipient AIDS prevention award, Dept. of Health, Taiwan, R.O.C., 2000. Mem.: Chung Shan Med. U. Prof. Assn. (mem. com. 2002—), Taiwan AIDS Care Assn. (gen. sec. 1999—2003, vice chmn. 2003—), Assn. Lab. Medicine R.O.C., Am. Soc. Micobiology, Soc. Gen. Microbiology. Buddhist. Achievements include patents for pharmaceutical compositions and combinations for the treatment or prophylaxis of disorders related to HIV and retrovirus; pharmaceutical compositions and combinations for the cytokine modulation; pharmaceutical compositions and combinations for the treatment or prophylaxis of disorders related to cancer; patents pending for new strain of lactobacteria; novel rotaviruses and use thereof; pharmaceutical composition for use in the prevention and/or treatment of the oral cavity diseases caused by microorganisms; viral factors associated with breast cancer, thyroid tumor, and fibroadenoma and use and compositions against thereof. Avocations: travel, music, geography. Office: Chung Shan Med U Sch Med Lab and Biotech No 110 Sec 1 Chien-Kuo North Road Taichung 402 Taiwan Office Fax: 886-4-24727746; Home Fax: 886-4-23767469. Personal E-mail: yang1386@yahoo.com.tw. Business E-Mail: cyang@csmu.edu.tw.

YANG, CHIH-PING, pharmaceutical executive; b. Taipei, Taiwan, July 5, 1959; s. Ching-Tong and Yueh (Chou) Y.; m. Shir-Ly Huang, Nov. 7, 1992; children: Szu-Min, Hsin-Min. BS, Nat. Taiwan U., 1982; PhD, U. Tex., 1990; MBA, Nat. Cheng-Chi U., 1999. Postdoctoral rsch. scientist Upjohn Co., Kalamazoo, 1990-92; assoc. rsch. fellow Devel. Ctr. for Biotech., Taipei, 1992-94, rsch. fellow, 1995-96; med. dir. Bayer Taiwan, 1996-99; dir. med. affairs Schering-Plough Taiwan, Taipei, 1999-2000; v.p. Caleb Pharms., 2000-01, CEO, 2001—02; v.p. Vita Genomics Inc., Taipei, 2002—03; CEO Genetrol Brotherapeutics, 2002—04, CytoPharm Inc., Taipei, 2003—04; gen. mgr., COO Chugai Pharma Taiwan, 2005—. Contbr. articles to profl. jours. Recipient fellowship Robert A. Welch Found., 1984, Young Investigator grant Nat. Sci. Coun., Taipei, 1994. Mem. AAAS, Am. Chem. Soc., Chinese Soc. Biophysics (coun.), NY Acad. Scis., Internat. Union Pure and Applied Biology (coun.), Chinese Soc. Proteomics (coun. mem.), Internat. Rsch. Pharm. Mfr. Assn.(standing dir. & com. chmn.) Achievements include patents on anti-HIV drug; design and synthesis of U-96.988 as anti-HIV agents. Office: 3F No73 Zhouz St Neihu Dist Taipei 11493 Taiwan Office Phone: 886-2-2658-8800. Office Fax: 886 2 2658-8852. Business E-Mail: cp.yang@chugai.com.tw, chihpingyang@yam.com.

YANG, DAL-MO, radiologist, educator; b. Sang-Ju, Republic of Korea, Apr. 7, 1963; s. Won-Gab Yang and Sun-Do Kang; m. Kum-Hee Lee, May 23, 1964; children: Ko-Eun, Hee-Eun. M.S., In-Ha U., Incheon, Republic of Korea, 1999; MD, Kyung-Hee U., Seoul, Republic of Korea, 1988. Cert. Korean Bd. Diagnostic Radiology Ministry Health and Welfare, 1992, nat. med. lic. Ministry Health and Welfare, 1988. Radiology resident Kyung-Hee U., Seoul, 1989—92; dir. diagnostic radiology Gil Med. Ctr., Incheon, 1992—99; asst. prof. Gachon Med. Sch., Incheon, 1999—2001, assoc. prof., 2001—05; prof. diagnostic radiology East-West Neo Med. Ctr. Kyung Hee U. East-West Neo Med. Ctr., Seoul, 2006 . Contbr. articles to profl. jours. Recipient Cert. of Merit, Am. Roentgen Ray Soc., 2003, cum laude, European Congress Radiology, 2004, Radiological Soc. N.Am., 2003. Mem.: Korean Radiol. Soc., Korean Soc. Abdominal Radiology, Korean Soc. Med. Ultrasound (Internat. Work award 2002). Office: Kyung Hee U East West Neo Med Ctr Sangil-Dong 149 134-090 Seoul Seoul Republic of Korea Office Fax: 82-32-460-3065. Personal E-mail: dmy2988@yahoo.co.kr. Business E-Mail: dmy2988@paran.com.

YANG, DAVID CHANG-SUE, ophthalmologist, educator; b. Taipei, Taiwan, 1959; m. Melody Hsiao; children: Christine, Kevin, Stephen. MD, Taipei Med. U., 1984; MS in Hosp. Adminstrn., Nat. Yang-Ming U., Taipei, 2005. Internship Nat. Taiwan U. Hosp., Taipei, 1983—84; resident Dept. Ophthalmology, Taipei Veterans Gen. Hosp., 1987—91, attending physician, 1994—; asst. prof. Nat. Yang Ming U., 2006—. Dir. Dept. Ophthalmology, Taipei Mcpl. Chung-Hsing Hosp., 2001—03; clin. assoc. prof. Dept. Ophthalmology, Nat. Def. Med. Coll., Taipei, 2004—. Contbr. scientific papers to profl. jours. Recipient Disting. Rsch. award, Nat. Sci. Coun.; fellowship, Taipei Veterans Gen. Hosp., 1991—93, Duke U. Eye Ctr., Durham, NC, 1995—96. Mem.: Am. Soc. Retinal Specialists, Am. Acad. Ophthalmology. Office: Taipei Veterans Gen Hosp No 201 Sec 2 Shih-Pai Rd Taipei 11217 Taiwan

YANG, EUN BAE, medical educator; b. Gimcheonsi, Gyeongsangbukdo, Republic of Korea, Aug. 2, 1969; s. Heon Gon Yang and Dong Hee Kim; m. Eun Young Hwang, Oct. 29, 1995; children: Dong Gyun, Yu Jin. BA in Edn., Yonsei U., Seoul, Republic of Korea, 1994, BA in Theology, 1992, MA in Edn., 1996, PhD in Edn., 2001. Cert. tchr. Ministry Edn., 1994. Rsch. asst. Yonsei U. Coll. Medicine, 1996—99, rsch. fellow, 2000—02, instr., 2003—06, asst. prof., 2007—10, assoc. prof., 2010—; sec. Korean Inst. Med. Edn. & Evaluation, Seoul, 2004—. Bd. mem. Accreditatin Bd. Med. Edn., Seoul, 2001—03; vis. rschr. Inst. Edn., Yonsei U., 2004—07; sec. Korean Soc. Med. Edn., Seoul, 2005—08, editor, 2006—. Author: (book) The Accreditation for Medical Schools and The Quality of Medical Education, Future of Social Medicine and Medical Education; contbr. articles to profl. jours. Recipient Academic Rsch. Encouragement prize, Korean Soc. Med. Edn., 2005, award, 2007, Outstanding Rsch. award, Assn. Standardized Patient Educators, 2008, Hangok Med. Edn. prize, 2011. Office: Yonsei Univ Coll Medicine 250 Seongsanno Seoul Seadaemungu 120-752 Republic of Korea Office Fax: 822-364-5450.

YANG, EUN KYUNGG, biomedical researcher; b. Republic of Korea, Aug. 26, 1968; d. Chun Sang Yang and In Soon Jung; m. Jae Young Cho, Apr. 20, 1994; children: Woo Won Cho, Jung Won Cho. PHD, Dongguk U., Seoul, Republic of Korea, 1998. Diploma in tissue banking IAEA, Singapore, 2002. Rschr. KRIBB, Daejeon, Chungnam, Republic of Korea, 1993—95, Bioland Ltd., Cheonan, Chungnam, 2000—. Com. mem. Korea Bio Industry Orgn., Seoul, 2007—. Achievements include patents for dermal substitute. Office: Bioland Ltd Ochang Gak-Ri 644-6 Cheongwon-Gun Chung-Buk 363-883 Republic of Korea Home: Gs-XI Apt 106-302 2075 331-092 Cheonan Chungcheongnam-do Republic of Korea Office Phone: 82-43-240-8620. Office Fax: 82-43-240-8699. Personal E-mail: tissueng@dreamwiz.com. Business E-Mail: ekyang@biolandkorea.com, skin@biolandkorea.com.

YANG, GUO-YUAN, neuroscientist; s. Zhongwei and Yuzheng Yang; m. Yuming Chen, Sept. 25; 1 child, Yibo. MD, PhD, Shanghai Med. U., 1987. Vis. rsch. investigator U. Mich. Med. Ctr. Dept. Neurosurgery, Ann Arbor, 1991—92, rsch. investigator, 1992—95, asst. rsch. scientist, 1995—2001; assoc. prof. U. Calif. Depts. Anesthesia & Neurosurgery, San Francisco, 2001—06, prof., 2006—; nuerosurgeon Shanghai Med. U. HuaShan Hosp. Dept. Neurosurgery, 1982—89. Vis. prof. Fudan U., Shanghai, 1996—, Med-X Rsch. Inst., Shanghai Jiaotong U., 2008—. Recipient 2nd Pl. award, Sci. Tech. Devel. by Dept. Health, China, 1987, award, Sturge Weber Found., 2007; grantee Mechanisms Action IL-1 Ischemic Brain, NIH NINDS, 1997, Transgenic Murine Model Brain Vascular Malformation, 2003, Integrative Study Brain Vascular Malformation, 2003, BBB Protection During Treatment Transient Ischemia, 2005. Mem.: Am. Heart Assn., Am. Stroke Assn. (faha), Soc. Neurosci. (nsf), Internat. Soc. Cerebral Blood Flow & Metabolism. Achievements include development of suture induced middle cerebral artery occlusion in mice and this focal cerebral ischemia model is widely used; research in novel adenoviral gene transfer technique, induce IL-1 receptor antagonist over expression in the ischemic brain and reduce ischemia-induced brain injury.

YANG, GUOZHONG, information researcher; b. Taiyuan, Shanxi, China, July 9, 1939; s. Shuiqing Yang and Yuting Liu; m. Yanbin Chang, Oct. 1, 1967; 1 child, Yin. Student, Inst. of Fgn. Langs., Beijing, 1957-62. Rsch. prof. Inst. of Med. Info., Beijing, 1962—. Mem., sec., expert panel of biomed. engring. State Commn. of Sci. and Tech., Beijing, 1979-84. Author, co-editor: Medical Imaging Technology, 1987. Mem. Chinese Soc. of Biomed. Engring. (a founder, mem. coun.). Achievements include pioneering in set up of biomedical engineering as an independent discipline in China. Office: Inst of Med Info 3 Yabao Rd 100020 Beijing China Office Phone: 861052328724. Office Fax: 861052328610. Personal E-mail: laofuzi_6210@yahoo.cn.

YANG, HAI-SONG, orthopedist; b. Shandong Province, China, Sept. 21, 1981; Grad. with honors, Shanghai Municipality, 2010; MD, Second Mil. Med. U., 2010. Resident physician, orthops. Changzheng Hosp., 2006—10, physician, orthops., 2010—. Recipient Maj. award, Second Mil. Med. U., 2009, Changzheng Hosp., 2010. Avocations: ping pong/table tennis, swimming. Office: 415 Fengyang Rd Shanghai 86 200003 China E-mail: yanghs.spine@yahoo.com.cn.

YANG, HYUNWON, immunologist; b. Seoul, Republic of Korea, June 25, 1964; s. Moon Kyu Yang and Young Soon Choi; m. Insoon Lee; children: Jaeyoung, Hyeayoung. PhD in Biology, Hanyang U., Seoul, 1997. Asst. prof. Eulji U. Sch. Medicine, Seoul, 2002—04; instr. neuroendocrine Immunology Pennington Biomed. Rsch. Ctr., Baton Rouge, Md., 2007—. Recipient Fellows awards rsch. excellence, NIH, 2006; vis. fellowship, 2004. Mem.: AAAS, Am. Assn. Immunologists, Soc. Endocrinology, Soc. Study Reproduction. Roman Catholic. Achievements include research in aging and immune function; obesity and immune function. Office: Lab Endocrine Immunology Dept Biotechnology Seoul Womens University 126 Gongreung-Dong Nowon-Gu Seoul 139-774 Republic of Korea Office Phone: 8229705662. Personal E-mail: hyunwonyang@gmail.com. Business E-Mail: hwyang@swu.ac.kr.

YANG, JEONG SUN, health facility administrator, researcher; b. Seoul, Republic of Korea, Aug. 3, 1960; PhD, Seoul Nat. U., 1984. Rsch. scientist Occupl. Safety and Health Bd., 1993—2006, bd. dirs. Korea Occupl. Safety and Health Agy., 2006—. Fellow: NRC, Korean Soc. Indsl. Hygienist, Korean Soc. Analytical Chemistry, Korean Soc. Toxicology. Office: Korea Occupational Safety and Health Agency Yuseong-Gu Munji-dong 104-8 Daejeon 305-380 Republic of Korea Office Fax: 82-42-863-9001.

YANG, JEONG-IN, obstetrician, gynecologist, educator; b. Kwangju, Cheonranam-do, Republic of Korea, Jan. 17, 1963; d. Yoo-Keun Yang and Hee-Ho Yoon; m. Jai Hyun Park, Dec. 20, 1987; children: Ji-Ha Park, Ji-Won Park, Ji-Yoon Park, Joo-Han Park. Med. degree in Medicine, Ewha Woman's U. Sch. of Medicine, Seoul, 1981—86; M in Medicine, Yonsei U. Coll. of Medicine, Grad. Sch., Seoul, 1993—95; MD, Korea U. coll. of Medicine, Grad. Sch., Seoul, 1996—97. Diplomate Korea Assn. of Ob-Gyn., 1992. Intership & residency Yonsei U. Med. Ctr., Seoul, Republic of Korea, 1987—92; fellowship Yonsei U. YongDong Severance Hosp., Seoul, Republic of Korea, 1992—93; instr. Ajou U. Hosp., Suwon, Republic of Korea, 1994—97, asst. prof., 1997—2002, assoc. prof., present, 2003. Mem. Korea Psychosomatic Ob-Gyn, Sci. Com., Seoul, 2001. Mem.: Internat. Soc. Ultrasound in Ob-Gyn. (licentiate), Korea Soc. Perinatologists (licentiate), Korea Soc. Ultrasound in Ob-Gyn. (licentiate), Korea Assn. Ob-Gyn. (licentiate), Korea Med. Assn. (licentiate). Avocations: travel, golf, scuba diving. Office: Ajou Univ Hosp Dept Ob & Gyn San5 Wonchon-Dong Paldal-Gu 442-749 Suwon Kyunggi-do Republic of Korea Office Fax: 82 31 219 5245. Personal E-mail: santafei17@hotmail.com. Business E-Mail: yangji@ajou.ac.kr.

YANG, JIN HYANG, geriatric nurse practitioner, educator; b. Gyeongju, Republic Of Korea, Jan. 2, 1965; d. Chae Kyu Yang and Kwang Ja Ryu; m. Keon Soo Lee, Sept. 10, 1994; 1 child, Ju Myung Lee. PhD, Ewha Womans U., Seoul, Korea, 2001. Cert. nurse practitioner, Ministry Health, Welfare & Family Affairs, Korea, 2007. Assoc. prof. Inje U., Pusan, Republic of Korea, 2001—; cons. Pub. Health Ctr., Pusan, 2002—; editl. bd. mem. Korean Ctr. Qualitative Rsch., Seoul, Republic of Korea, 2004—, Korean Soc. Nursing Sci., Seoul, 2006—08; examiner Nat. Exam. Com. Nurses, Seoul, 2008—08. Med. vol. fgn. workers Nat. Red Cross, 2002—05. Active Korea Ctr. Disease Control and Prevention, Busan, 2004—08; med. vol., health educator Republic Korea Nat. Red Cross, Pusan, 2002—09; educator Social Welfare Ctr., 2007—. Mem.: Sigma Theta Tau Int'l Lambda Alpha Chapter-at-Large. Christian Ch. Achievements include research in complementary & alternative therapy for patients with chronic pain, and undergoing chemotherapy. Avocations: reading, travel. Home: 596 Kaegum-dong #107-1702 Pusanjin-gu Pusan 614-751 Republic of Korea Office Phone: 82-51-890-6839. Office Fax: 82-51-896-9740. Personal E-mail: yjh7552@hotmail.com. Business E-Mail: jhyang@inje.ac.kr.

YANG, JUNG-HYUN, surgeon, educator; b. Jungup, Chullabukdo, Republic of Korea, Aug. 9, 1949; s. Chong Eui Yang and Sook Nam Kim; married; children: Young Eun, Young Jae. MD, Seoul Nat. U., 1973, PhD, 1982. Registered Ministry Health and Social Affairs, 1973. Staff surgeon Nat. Med. Ctr., Seoul, Republic of Korea, 1981—94; prof. surgery Sungkyunkwan U. Sch. Medicine, Seoul, 1997—. Pres. Korean Breast Cancer Soc., Seoul, 2003—05. Author: (essay) A man falling in love with the breast. V.p. Korean Cancer Assn., Seoul, 2003—04. Maj. US Army, 1978—81, Seoul. Recipient award, Ministry Health and Social Affairs, 1992. Fellow: ACS, Chgo. Home: G-3304 Tower Palace Dogokdong Gangnamgu Seoul 135-281 Republic of Korea Office: Samsung Med Ctr 50 Ilwondong Gangnamgu Seoul 135-710 Republic of Korea Office Fax: 82-2-3410-6982. Business E-Mail: jhyang0809@skku.edu.

YANG, JUN-YOUNG, medical professor; b. Daejeon, Republic of Korea, June 3, 1965; s. Se-Woo Yang and Suk-Hee Kim; m. Mi-Jung Kim, May 29, 1965; children: Kyung-Jin, Myung-Jin. PhD, Chungnam Nat. U., Daejeon, 2002. Diplomate Korean Med. Assn., bd. orthopedics Korean Med. Assn. Prof. Chungnam Nat. U., Daejeon, Republic of Korea, 1999—. Recipient Best Basic Sci. award, Internat. Congress on Spinal Surgery, 2002, Cervical Spine Rsch. Soc., 2005, Korean Spine Assn., 2005, Korean Fracture Sssn., 2002; fellow, Korean Spine Assn., 2004. Mem.: Korena Cyber-orthopaedic assn. (assoc.), Korean Tissue Transplantation Soc. (assoc.), Korean Bone and Soft Tissue Tumor Soc. (assoc.), Korean Orthopaedic Assn. (assoc. Best Basic Sci. award 2005). Home: Garam Apt 7-807 Samcheon-Dong Seo-Gu Daejeon 301-721 Republic of Korea Office: 640 Daesa-Dong Jung-Gu Daejeon 301-721 Republic of Korea Office Phone: 82-42-280-7351. Office Fax: 82-42-252-7098; Home Fax: 82-42-252-7098. Personal E-mail: jyyang@cnu.ac.kr.

YANG, KE-PING AGNES, healthcare educator, researcher; b. Taichung, Taiwan, Aug. 20, 1946; d. Pei-Chen Yang and Chuan Lin; m. Kuo-Chih Albert Lee; children: Jimbo Lee, Mayer Lee. PhD, U. Mich., 1995. Registered nurse, Taipei, Taiwan, 1971, Mich., 1995. Pres. Cardinal Tien Coll. Healthcare & Mgmt., Sin-Dian, Taipei, 2001—. Editor Jour. Nursing Rsch., Taipei, 1997—. Mem.: Taiwan Nurses Assn., Taipei (mem. coun. 2003—, B. Braun Nursing Rsch. award 2004), Sigma Theta Tau Internat. Office: Cardinal Tien Coll Healthcare & Mgmt 112 Ming-Zu Rd Sin-Dian City Taipei 23143 Taiwan Office Fax: +886-2-2219-7718. Business E-Mail: oneness68@gmail.com.

YANG, LIN, science educator; b. Harbin, Heilongjiang Province, China, July 23, 1966; D, Niigata U., Japan, 2007. Assoc. prof. Harbin Inst. Tech., 2007—. Office: 73 Huanghe Rd Nangang Dist Harbin Heilongjiang Province 150090 China Office Fax: 86-451-8628-2906. Business E Mail: ly6617@hit.edu.cn.

YANG, LI-XIA, biomedical researcher, scientist, educator; arrived in US, 1999, permanent resident, 2007; d. Chun and Guizhen Yang; m. Lizhi Gu, Aug. 4, 1986; 1 child, Chunyang Gu. MD in Medicine with honors, Jiamusi U. Sch. Medicine, China, 1982, MS in Pathophysiology, 1987; PhD in Biochemistry and Molecular Biology/Genetics, Kochi Med. Sch., Japan, 1996. Asst. prof. pathology Jiamusi U. Sch. Medicine, 1982—86, lectr. pathology, 1987—94, prin. investigator, 1987—94, assoc. prof. medicine, 1994—96; postdoc. rschr. molecular neurobiology Inst. Phys. Chem. Rsch., Nagoya, Japan, 1996—99; postdoc. rsch. fellow molecular cellular devel. neurobiology Nat. Inst. Child Health and Human Devel., NIH, Bethesda, Md., 1999—2002; intramural rsch. fellow molecular cellular pathology Molecular Imaging Lab Clin. Ctr. NIH, Bethesda, Md., 2002—03; faculty rsch. assoc. functional genomics U. Pitts., 2003—; asst. prof. Hough Ear Inst. Bapt. Med. Ctr., Oklahoma, Okla., 2006—08, rsch. scientist hearing rsch., 2006—08; prin. scientist Ctr. Innovative Rsch. Banyan Biomarkers, Inc., Alachua, Fla., 2008—; staff scientist Found. Applied Molecular Evolution and The Westheimer Inst. Sci. and Tech., Gainesville, Fla., 2011—. Sci. judge NIH, Bethesda, Md., 2002. Contbr. articles to profl. jours. Rsch. grant, Ministry Edn. Sci. Culture, Japan, 1990—92. Mem.: AAAS (life), Nat. Neurotrauma Soc., Assn. Rsch. Otolaryngology, Soc. Neurosci., Chinese Soc. Medicine (life). Achievements include unique discoveries of three novel Isoreceptors, GFRa-1c, GFRa-1d and GFRa-1e in human and mouse; novel gene sequences deposited to the world GenBank for public access; discovery of neural cell adhesion molecule, NCAM as novel biomarker for traumatic brain injury and as the proteolytic substrate of calpain. Avocations: music, art, swimming, dance, yoga. Mailing: 813 Turkey Creek Alachua FL 32615 Office: Found Applied Molecular Evolution 720 SW 2nd Ave Ste 201 PO Box 13174 Gainesville FL 32601 Office Phone: 352-271-7005. Office Fax: 352-271-7076. Business E-Mail: lxyang@pitt.edu.

YANG, PHILLIP C., medical educator; b. Tokyo, Aug. 25, 1962; MD, Yale U., New Haven, 1989. Asst. prof. Stanford U., 2005—. Office: 300 Pasteur Dr H2157 Stanford CA 94305 Business E-Mail: phillip@stanford.edu.

YANG, SEONG-HO, medical researcher; b. Incheon, Republic of Korea, Oct. 7, 1971; M, Korea U., 2000. Rsch. dir. Maria Plus Fertility Hosp., 2010—. Office: 121-1 garak1 dong Sopagu Seoul 138-806 Republic of Korea Business E-Mail: shyang@mariababy.com.

YANG, SEUNG YEOB, medical educator; b. Seoul, Republic of Korea, Aug. 17, 1969; B, Seoul Nat. U., 1996, PhD, 2010. Prof. Dongguk U. Grad. Sch., 2007—. Mem.: Korean Med. Assn., Internat. Stereotactic Radiosurgery Soc., Korean Neurosurg. Soc. (47th Ann. Meeting Best Academic award), Am. Assn. Neurol. Surgeons, Congress Neurol. Surgeons. Office: 814 Sicsa-Dong Ilsandong-Gu Goyang Gyeonggi-Do 410-773 Republic of Korea Office Phone: 82-31-961-7323. Office Fax: 82-31-961-7327. Business E-Mail: soundofmusic@dumc.or.kr.

YANG, SEUNG-HO, medical educator; b. Cheuju Island, Mar. 3, 1772; PhD, Cath. U. Korea, 1997. Assoc. prof. Cath. U. Korea, 2011—. Office: 93-6 Chi-dong Paldal-gu Suwon Kunggido 442-723 Republic of Korea Business E-Mail: 72ysh@catholic.ac.kr.

YANG, SHANG-YOU, medical educator; m. Lei Liu, 1985. MD, Qingdao Med. Coll., Tsingdao, China, 1983; PhD, Thornhill U., London, 2001. Scholar Kansas Biosci. Authority; asst. prof. Wayne State U., Detroit, 2002—08; sr. scientist and assoc. prof. Orthop. Res. Inst., Wichita State U., U. Kans. Med. Ctr., 2008—. Grantee RO3, NIH, 2007—; Robbinson fellow, Arthritis Found., 2001—02. Mem.: Orthopaedic Rsch. Soc., Am. Coll. Rheumatology, Soc. Biomaterials. Achievements include research in novel murine models for aseptic loosening of joint arthroplasty; first to virus-mediated gene therapy for orthopaedic disorders. Office: ORI Via Christi Regional Med Ctr 929 N St francis Wichita KS 67214 Office Fax: 316-291-4998. Business E-Mail: syang-you.yang@wichita.edu.

YANG, SHU-HUA, surgeon, educator; b. Taipei City, Taiwan, Aug. 7, 1967; MD, Nat. Taiwan U., 1993, PhD, 2005. Resident, dept. orthops. Nat. Taiwan U. Hosp., 1993—98, attending surgeon, dept. orthops., 1999—; dir., dept. orthops. Nat. Taiwan U. Hosp. Yun-Lin Br., 2008—10; adj. asst. prof., dept. orthops. Coll. Medicine Nat. Taiwan U., 2006—09, asst. prof., dept. orthops., 2009—. Clin. fellow, dept. orthop. surgery Tohoku U., Sendai, Japan, 2002; rsch. fellow, dept. orthop. surgery Johns Hopkins Med. Inst., Balt., 2002—03; vis. scholar, dept. orthops. Rush U. Med. Ctr., Chgo., 2011—. Mem.: Asia Pacific Orthop. Assn., Taiwan Spine Soc., Taiwan Orthop. Assn., Orthop. Rsch. Soc. Avocations: travel, baseball. Office: 7 Jhong-Shan S Rd Dept Orthopedics Taipei City 10002 Taiwan Office Fax: 886-2-23224112. Business E-Mail: shuhuayang@ntu.edu.tw.

YANG, SHUNG-HAUR, colon and rectal surgeon; b. I-Lan county, Taiwan, Nov. 1, 1963; s. Yu-I and Kuei-Hsin Yang; m. Huei-Chen Huang, Mar. 17, 1991; children: Yueh-Chuan, Yu-Chieh, Cai-Rong, Mu-Ying. MD, Nat. Yang-Ming U., Taiwan, 1988; PhD, Nat. Yang-Ming U., 2005. Attending staff Divsn. of Colon & Rectal Surgery, Dept. of Surgery Taipei-Vets. Gen. Hosp., Taipei, Taiwan, 1998—; asst. prof. Nat. Yang-Ming U., Taipei, Taiwan, 2005—. 2d lt., med. officer Army, 1988—90, Don-In Islands, Taiwan. Mem.: Soc. of Colorectal Surgery, Taiwan (assoc.). Achievements include research in studys of colorectal surgery, cancer. Office: Taipei-Veterans General Hosp No 201 Sec 2 Shih-Pai Rd Taipei 11217 Taiwan Office Fax: #886-228757639. Business E-Mail: yangsh@vghtpe.gov.tw.

YANG, SUNG HOON, surgeon; b. Jeju, Republic Of Korea, Dec. 4, 1969; s. Young Jin Yang and Ko Im Saeng; m. Kim Kyung; children: Yu Jung, Su Jung. PhD, Chonbuk Nat. U., Jeonju, Korea, 2006. Cert. gen. surgeon Korean Surg. Soc., 2005. Gen. surgery resident Chonbuk Nat. U. Hosp., Jeonju, 2001—05; pancreato-biliary surgery and liver transplantation, fellowship Seoul Nat. U. Hosp., Republic of Korea, 2005—07; head third dept. surgery Incheon Med. Ctr., Republic of Korea, 2007—. Contbr. articles to profl. jours. Recipient Travel award, Joint Internat. Congress ILTS, 2006. Mem.: Korean Soc. Parenteral and Enteral Nutrition, Korean Soc. Clin. Oncology, Korean Assn. HBP Surgery, Korean Surg. Soc. Office: Incheon Med Ctr Dong-Gu 401-711 Incheon Incheon Republic of Korea Office Fax: 82-32-580-6460. E-mail: moljin@korea.com.

YANG, SUNG YEUL, biochemist, educator; b. Boseong County, Dec. 12, 1955; MD, Chonnam Nat. U., 1982, PhD, 1988. Prof. Chonnam Nat. U. Med. Sch., 1999—, vice-dean, 2008—10, chair dept. biochemistry, 2006—11, chair IRB, 2010—11. Mem.: Korean Soc. Gerontology, Korean Soc. Biochemistry and Molecular Biology. Avocations: archery, music. Office: Chonnam Nat University 5 Hakdong Donggu Gwangju 501-746 Republic of Korea Office Fax: 82-62-223-8321. Business E-Mail: syyang@jnu.ac.kr.

YANG, TAEYOUNG, physician; b. Republic of Korea, Nov. 24, 1966; PhD, Chonnam Med. Sch., 2006. Clin. fellow Samsung Med. Ctr., 1999—2001; rsch. fellow Harvard Med. Sch., 2009—10. Mem.: ADA, KES, KDA. Avocations: piano, writing. Office: 182-1 Haeri Haenam Chonnam 536-800 Republic of Korea Business E-Mail: ruru30@chol.com.

YANG, TSONG-TOH (T.T.), pharmacist, researcher; b. Taiwan, Mar. 1, 1949; s. Yen-Leng and Chhai-Shia Lin Yang; m. Lee-Ju Wu Yang, Aug. 26, 1951; children: Benson Pin-Sheng, Steven Shih-E. BS in Pharmacy, Kaohsiung Med. Coll., Taiwan, 1971; MS in Pharmacy, U. R.I., 1979; PhD in Pharm. Sci., U. So. Calif., 1984. Registered pharmacist Taiwan, 1971. Med. supply officer Chinese Army in Taiwan, 1971—73; prodn. supr. Sterling Products Internat. Inc., Taiwan, Taipei, 1973—77; tchg. asst. U. R.I., Kingston, 1977—79, U. So. Calif., LA, 1979—81, U. N.C., Chapel Hill, 1982—83; rsch. pharmacist Am. Cyanamid Co., Pearl River, NY, 1984—85; devel. fellow Schering-Plough Rsch. Inst., Kenilworth, NJ, 1985—2006; pharm. cons., 2007—. Vis. prof. Nat. Health Rsch. Inst., Taiwan, 2009—. Recipient Pres.'s award for Devel., Schering-Plough Rsch. Inst., 1994, 2002, 2005, DuPont Gold award for dry powder inhaler, 1998, Thomas Alva Edison Patent award, R&D Coun. NJ, 2005. Mem.: Am. Chinese Pharm. Assn., Controlled Release Soc., Am. Assn. for Pharm. Scientists. Achievements include patents for Preparation of powder agglomerates; inhaler for powdered medications; invention of Twisthaler dry powder inhaler- device and formulation. Home: 9 Old Farm Rd Warren NJ 07059 Office Phone: 732-563-0065. Personal E-mail: ttyangphd@yahoo.com.

YANG, VICTOR TING HSUN, retired gastroenterologist; b. Peikang, Taiwan, Apr. 9, 1931; s. Luh Hoh and Chih (Chen) Yang. MB, Nat. Taiwan U., Taipei, 1957. Intern dept. medicine Nat. Taiwan U. Hosp., Taipei, 1959, resident dept. medicine, 1959-63, fellow in gastroenterology, 1963-66, staff physician dept. medicine, 1966-92; fellow in gastroenterology dept. medicine Hosp. U. Pa./U. Pa. Sch. Medicine, Phila., 1971-72; instr. medicine Nat. Taiwan U. Coll. Medicine, 1969-92; ret., 1992. 2d lt. Taiwan Army (ROTC), 1957—59. Roman Catholic. Avocations: reading, listening to classical music, hospital work.

YANG, XILIN, epidemiologist, researcher; s. Liqing Yang and Cuiying Liu; m. Wei Sui, Sept. 3, 1990; 1 child, Xinyue. Diploma of Medicine, Chengde Med. Coll., China, 1980—83; M of Engring., Tianjin Inst. Light Industry, 1988—91; PhD, U. Melbourne, Australia, 2000—02. Rsch. assoc. Chinese U. Hong Kong, Shatin, 2003—05, postdoctoral fellow, 2005—07, asst. rsch. prof., 2007—. Recipient Significant Contbn. to Chinese Cmty. Health, Chinese Health Found. Australia, 1997. Mem. Christian Ch. Achievements include research in finding the prevalence of gestational diabetes in Tianjin and that pregnancy outcomes were poorer in Chinese women with impaired glucose tolerance during pregnancy; development of risk scores for prediction of major complications in type 2 diabetic patients; discovery of A or V-shaped relations between lipid components and cancer in type 2 diabetic patient; renin-angiotensin syatem and lipid metabolism cross talk may be involved in the elevated risks of cancer in type 2 diabetic patients; low LDL cholesterol has an interaction with albuminuria, which is related to cancer in diabetes; instead of increasing cancer risk, use of insulin may reduce cancer risk in type to diabetics; the anticancer effect of metformin is most evident in type 2 diabetic in type 2 diabetic patients with low HDL Cholesterol. Avocation: travel. Office: Room 507 LIHS Prince Wales Hosp NT Shatin Hong Kong Office Phone: 852 3763 6052. Office Fax: 852 2637 3852. Personal E-mail: yxl@hotmail.com. Business E-Mail: yang.xilin@cuhk.edu.hk.

YANG, YANG-MING, medical educator; d. Ming-ding Yang and Jian Song; m. C. Clifford Conaway, June 18, 1994. MD, Zhong Shan U., Med. Sch., Canton, China, 1977; PhD, NY Med. Coll., Valhalla, 1996. Rsch. scientist Am. Health Found., Valhalla, 1991—2003; rsch. asst. prof. NY Med. Coll., 2003—. Contbr. articles to profl. jours. Mem., adult fellowship Drew United Meth. Ch., Carmel, NY, 1998—. Rsch. grant, NIH, 2004. Mem.: Am. Assn. Cancer Rsch. Conservative. Avocations: gardening, swimming, travel, photography. Office: NY Med Coll 95 Grassland Reservation Valhalla NY 10595 Home: 80 Watermelon Hill Rd Mahopac NY 10541-3918 E-mail: yang-ming_yang@nymc.edu.

YANG, YIH-PEY, engineering educator; b. Taipei, Nov. 24, 1966; PhD, Nat. Yang-Ming U., 1998. Postdoc. rsch. fellow Academia Sinica, 1998—2002; asst. prof. Nat. Ilan U., 2002—. Mem.: Taiwanese Soc. Biomed. Engring. Office: 1 Shen-Lung Rd Sec 1 I-Lan 26047 Taiwan Business E-Mail: ypyang@niu.edu.tw.

YANG, YUN-SIK, ophthalmologist, educator; b. Namwon, Jeonbuk, Republic Of Korea, Oct. 25, 1961; s. Hae-Bang Yang and Young-Hee Kim; m. So-Young Kim, Dec. 21, 1986; children: Song-Wha, Ki-Hun, Ji-Yun. PhD, Chonnam U. Grad. Sch.Medicine, Gwangju, 1995; MD, Korean Min. Health and Welfare, 1986. Cert. ophthalmologist Korean Min. Health and Welfare, 1990. Rsch. fellow Wilmer Inst., Baltimore, 1996—97; prof. Wonkwang U. Sch. Medicine, Icksan, Jeonbuk, 1993—; head strategic & info. dept. Wonkwang U. Hosp., 2009—10; dir. Gunsan Med. Ctr., 2011—. Contbr. articles to numerous profl. jours. Capt. 6th Corp, Jinhae Mil. Hosp., 1990—93, Yeoncheon. Grant, Korean Min. Health and Welfare, 2002, 2004—06, Gene Rsch. Ctr. Immune Disease grant, 2004—11, Devel. Nr. Infrared Biomicroscope grant, Korea Min. Commerce, Industry and Energy, 2006—07. Mem.: European Assn. Vision and Eye Rsch., Am. Acad. Ohthalmology, Assn. Rsch. Vision Sci. and Ophthalmology, European Vitreo Retina Soc., Korea Retina Soc., Korean Ophthalmology Soc. Won Buddhist. Achievements include patents for three dimensional real time image apparatus of ocular retina (Japan patent No.3686589, 2005, 06, 10); patents pending for indirect ophthalmoscope with upright image (PCT/KR2007/002922); development of indirect ophthalmoscope with upright image from 2004-2007. Avocations: saxophone, golf, flying, travel. Home: Seosin-dong e-Comport World Apt 107/505 Jeonju Jeonbuk 560-821 Republic of Korea Office: Dept Ophthalmology Sinyong-dong 344-2 Wonkwang Univ Hosp Icksan Jeonbuk 570-711 Republic of Korea also: Gunsan Med Ctr Jigokdong 29-1 Jeonbuk Gunsan 573-390 Republic of Korea Office Phone: 82-63-859-1373. Business E-Mail: ysyang@wonkwang.ac.kr.

YANG, ZHULIN, medical educator; b. Luodi City, Hunan Province, China, Aug. 8, 1962; PhD, Hunan Med. Coll., 1998. Prof. Second Xiangya Hosp. Ctrl. South U., 2001—. Office: People'S Middle Rd 139 Changsha Hunan 410011 China Business E-Mail: yangzhulin8@sina.com.

YANKELEVITZ, DAVID F., radiologist, educator; MD, SUNY Health Sci. Ctr., Bklyn., 1981. Cert. diagnostic radiology, nuclear medicine. Intern Staten Island Hosp.; resident Long Island Coll. Hosp.; fellow Weill Cornell Med. Coll., prof. radiology & cardiothoracic surgery; attending radiologist NY-Presbyterian Hosp. Office: 525 E 68th St Box 586 New York NY 10021 Office Phone: 212-746-2526. Office Fax: 212-746-2811.

YANNAS, IOANNIS VASSILIOS, polymer science educator; b. Athens, Apr. 14, 1935; s. Vassilios Pavlos and Thalia (Sarafoglou) Yannas; m. Stamatia Frondistou (div. Oct. 1984); children: Tania, Alexis. AB, Harvard U., 1957; SM, MIT, 1959; MS, Princeton U., 1965, PhD, 1966. Asst. prof. mech. engring. MIT, Cambridge, 1966-68, duPont asst. prof., 1968-69, assoc. prof., 1969-78, prof. polymer sci. and engring. dept. mech. engring., 1978—, prof. dept. materials sci. and engring., 1983—; prof. Harvard-MIT Div. Health Scis. and Tech., Cambridge, 1978—. Vis. prof. Royal Inst. Tech., Stockholm, 1974. Author: Tissue and Organ Regeneration in Adults, 2001; editor: Regenerative Medicine, 2 vols., 2005; mem. editl. bd. Jour. Biomed. Materials Rsch., 1986—, Jour. Materials Sci. Materials Medicine, 1990—, Tissue Engring., 1994—, Interface, 2004, Biomed. Materials (China); contbr. articles to profl. jours. Recipient Founders award, Soc. Biomaterials, 1982, Clemson award, 1992, Fred O. Conley award, Soc. Plastics Engrs., 1982, award in medicine and genetics, Sci. Digest/Cutty Sark, 1982, Doolittle award, Am. Chem. Soc., 1988; fellow, Shriners Burns Inst., Mass. Gen. Hosp., 1980—81; Pub. Health Svc. fellow, Princeton U., 1963. Fellow: Biomaterials Sci. and Engring., Am. Inst. Med. and Biol. Engrs. (founding mem.), Am. Inst. Chemists; mem.: Inst. Medicine Nat. Acad Scis. Achievements include patents in field. Office: MIT Bldg 3-332 77 Mass Ave Cambridge MA 02139-4307

YANO, TOMONORI, gastroenterologist; b. Oita, Japan, Mar. 27, 1973; MD, Kansai Med. U., 1997. Chief dept. gastroenterology and GI oncology Nat. Cancer Ctr. Hosp. East, 2010—. Office: 6-5-1 Kashiwanoha Kashiwa Chiba 277-0882 Japan Business E-Mail: toyano@east.ncc.go.jp.

YANOFF, MYRON, ophthalmologist; b. Phila., Dec. 21, 1936; s. Jacob and Lillian S. (Fishman) Yanoff; m. Karin Michelle Lindblad, Aug. 8, 1980; 1 child, Alexis A.;children from previous marriage: Steven L., David A., Joanne M. AB, U. Pa., 1957, MD, 1961. Prof. ophthalmology and pathology U. Pa. Med. Sch., Phila.; William F. Norris and George E. de Schweinitz prof. ophthalmology, chmn. dept., dir. Scheie Eye Inst., 1977-86; chmn., prof. ophthalmology Drexel U., Phila., 1988—. 1st exch. vis. prof. U. Vienna, 1992. Author: Ocular Pathology, Textbook of Ophthalmology, 6th edit., Ophthalmology, 3rd edit.; contbr. articles to profl. jours. Served to maj. M.C. USAR. Recipient Humboldt award, 1988. Mem.: Am. Acad. Ophthalmology (Sr. Honor award 1995), Am. Ophthalmic Soc., Verhoeff Soc. Office: 219 N Broad St Fl 3 Philadelphia PA 19107 Mailing: PO Box 254 Gwynedd Valley PA 19437-0254 Office Phone: 215-762-3937. Business E-Mail: myanoff@drexelmed.edu, myanoffmd@aol.com.

YANOFSKY, CHARLES, retired biology professor; b. NYC, Apr. 17, 1925; s. Frank and Jennie (Kopatz) Y.; m. Carol Cohen, June 19, 1949, (dec. Dec. 1990); children: Stephen David, Robert Howard, Martin Fred; m. Edna Crawford, Jan. 4, 1992. BS, CCNY, 1948; MS, Yale U., 1950, PhD, 1951, DSc (hon.), 1981, U. Chgo., 1980. Rsch. asst. Yale U., 1951-54; asst. prof. microbiology Western Res. U. Med. Sch., 1954-57; mem. faculty Stanford U., 1958—2000, prof. biology, 1961—2000, Herzstein prof. biology, 1966—2000, prof. emeritus, 2000—; ret. Career investigator Am. Heart Assn., 1969-95. Served with AUS, 1944-46. Recipient Lederle Med. Faculty award, 1957, Eli Lilly award bacteriology, 1959, U.S. Steel Co. award molecular biology, 1964, Howard Taylor Ricketts award U. Chgo., 1966, Albert and Mary Lasker award, 1971, Townsend Harris medal Coll. City N.Y., 1973, Louisa Gross Horwitz prize in biology and biochemistry Columbia U., 1976, V.D. Mattia award Roche Inst., 1982, medal Genetics Soc. Am., 1983, Internat. award Gairdner Found., 1985, named Passano Laureate, Passano Found., 1992; recipient William C. Rose award in biochemistry and molecular biology, 1997, Abbott Lifetime Achievement award Am. Soc. Microbiology, 1998, Nat. medal of Sci., 2003. Mem. NAS (Selman A. Waksman award in microbiology 1972), Am. Acad. Arts and Scis., Genetics Soc. Am. (pres. 1969, Thomas Hunt Morgan medal 1990), Am. Soc. Biol. Chemists (pres. 1984), Royal Soc. (fgn. mem.), Japanese Biochem. Soc. (hon.) Home: 725 Mayfield Ave Stanford CA 94305-1016 Office: Stanford U Dept Of Biological Sci Stanford CA 94305 Business E-Mail: yanofsky@stanford.edu.

YAO, FRANCIS, physician, director; b. Hong Kong, Sept. 20, 1960; BS, U. Calif. Berkeley, 1983; MD, Albert Einstein Coll. Medicine, 1987. Prof. medicine surgery U. Calif., San Francisco, 1999—, med. dir. liver transplantation, 2009—. Named Best Drs. in Am., Best Drs. in Am. Database. Mem.: Am. Assn. Study Liver Disease. Office: 513 Parnassus Ave S 357 San Francisco CA 94143 Office Fax: 415-476-0659. Business E-Mail: francis.yao@ucsf.edu.

YAO, JOHN, physician; b. Honolulu, Aug. 1954; s. Hsin-Hung and D. Yao. MPH, Columbia U., 1978, MD, 1983; MBA, UCLA, 1998; MPA, Harvard U., 1999. Diplomate Am. Bd. Internal Medicine, Nat. Bd. Med. Examiners. Resident in internal medicine U. Calif.-San Francisco Med. Ctr., 1983-86, asst. clin. prof., 1988-94; chief med. officer USPHS, Calif., 1990-98; med. dir. Cigna Healthcare, inc., 1997-98; fellow in policy studies Harvard U., Cambridge, Mass., 1998—. Mem. exec. com. State of Calif. TB Control, 1994—; mem. steering com. Breast and Cervical Cancer Prevention, Stte of Calif., 1991-94; med. advisor State of Calif. Medicaid Reform com., 1994-95. Contbr. articles to profl. jours. Med. advisor Gov.'s Coun. on Exercise and Health, Calif., 19945; mem. Calif. HIV-AIDS Commn., 1990-93. Fellow ACP. Avocations: golf, tennis, skiing, classical music, opera. E-mail: jyaomd@jyaomd.com.

YAO, MAOSHENG, environmental engineer, educator; b. Inner Mongolia, China, Mar. 11, 1973; PhD in Environ Sci., Rutgers U., 2006. Postdoc. rschr. Yale U., 2006—07; prof. Peking U., 2007—. Recipient hon., Rutgers U. Grad. Sch. Mem.: Sci. Rsch. Soc., Am. Assn. Aerosol Rsch., Sigma Xi. Avocations: music, travel, reading. Office: Coll Environ Sci & Engineering Peking Beijing 100871 China Business E-Mail: yao@pku.edu.cn.

YAO, MICHAEL J., physician, educator; married; 2 children. MD/BS five-year cooperative program, Jefferson Med. Coll. and Penn. State U., 1987. Diplomate Am. Bd. Family Medicine, Am. Bd. Family Medicine-geriatric medicine. Resident Forbes Family Practice, 1990, dir. geriatric edn.; asst. prof. family medicine Drexel Univ.; clin. instr. medicine Lake Erie Coll.; med. dir. Golden Living Centers, divisional dir.; hosp. affiliation include Forbes Regional Hosp. Mem.: Pa. Geriatrics Soc. (bd. dirs.). Office: 2566 Haymaker Rd Monroeville PA 15146 Office Phone: 412-858-2765. Office Fax: 412-858-2765.

YAO, SONG, medical educator; b. Ankang, China, Sept. 8, 1981; PhD, Roswell Pk. Cancer Inst., 2009. Rsch. asst. prof. Roswell Pk. Cancer Inst., 2010—. Mem.: Am. Assn. Cancer Rsch., SW Oncology Group. Avocations: jogging, reading, travel. Office: Elm and Carlton Sts Buffalo NY 14263 Business E-Mail: song.yao@roswellpark.org.

YAO, TITO GO, pediatrician; b. Manila, May 30, 1943; arrived in U.S., 1970, naturalized, 1984; s. Vincente and Sin Keng (Go) Yao; m. Lilia Ytem, July 3, 1976; children: Robert, James, Richard. MD, Far Eastern U., Manila, 1969. Diplomate Am. Bd. Pediatrics, Am. Bd. Quality Assurance. Intern Evang. Deaconess Hosp., Milw., 1970-71; resident in pediatrics T.C. Thompson Children's Hosp., Chattanooga, 1971-72, Meth. Hosp., Bklyn., 1972-73; fellow St. Christopher Hosp. Children, Phila., 1973-74, Cook County Children's Hosp., Chgo., 1974-75; dir. GSK Med. Ctr., Chgo., 1976—; preceptor Rush Med. Coll., 2003—. Chmn. dept. pediat. St. Anne's Hosp., Chgo., 1986—88, Loretto Hosp., Chgo., 1988—; dir. RJ Med. Ctr., Chgo., 1980—; mem. staff Norwegian Am. Hosp., St. Anthony's Hosp., St. Mary Nazareth Hosp. Fellow: Am. Coll. Utilization Rev. Physicians, Am. Acad. Pediat. (life); mem.: AMA (life Physician Recognition award 1973—), Chgo. Pediatric Soc., Chgo. Med. Soc., Am. Assn. Individual Investors, Ill. Med. Assn., Assn. Philippine Physicians Practicing in Am. Home: 5140 W Chicago Ave Chicago IL 60651-2903 Office Phone: 773-287-0751, 773-287-0752. Personal E-mail: titogyao@aol.com.

YAOEDA, KIYOSHI, ophthalmologist; MD, Niigata U., Japan, 2001. Asst., dept. opthalmol. Niigata U., 2008—. Office: Niigata Univ Grad Sch Med Sci 1-757 Asahimachi-dori Niigata Niigata prefecture 951-8510 Japan Office Fax: 81-25-227-0785. Business E-Mail: yaoeda@med.niigata-u.ac.jp.

YAP, CLARENCE, biotechnology executive; 1 child. BS in Biomedical Engring., Northwestern U., Evanston, Ill., 2000; MD, Northwestern U. Feinberg Sch. Medicine, Chgo., 2004; MPH, Northwestern U., Chgo., 2004. Assoc. McKinsey & Co., NYC, 2004—06; dir. Biomarin Pharm., Novato, Calif., 2006—. Contbr. articles to profl. jours. Club pres. Chinatown Health Clinic, Northwestern U. Med. Sch., Chgo., 2001—02; vol. NY Cares, 2004—05. Recipient Govr. Gen.'s medal, Can., 1997, Best Published Paper award, Jour. Biomech. Engring., 2000; Summer Rsch. fellow, Sunnybrook Hosp., 1998, Inst. Med. Sci., 1999, Rsch. fellow, Alpha Omega Alpha, 2001.

Mem.: APHA, AMA, Soc. Gen. Internal Medicine, Am. Coll. Preventative Medicine, Sigma Xi, Tau Beta Pi. Achievements include research in analyzing dosing errors in patients with renal insufficiency in the ambulatory care setting; effectiveness of newly developed pharmaceuticals used in corneal preservation; the prevention of mechanical stretch-induced endothelial and smooth muscle cell injury in experimental vein grafts; development of of drug candidates in multiple cardiovascular indications including and orphan diseases. Avocations: travel, swimming, squash, golf. Office: BioMarin Pharm 105 Digital Dr Novato CA 94949

YAP, KEVIN YI-LWERN, medical educator; b. Singapore, Sept. 29, 1977; s. Lawrence Cheng Hai Yap and Annie Kim Eng Soh. BS in Pharmacy with honors, Nat. U. Singapore, 2002; specialist diploma in Digital Media Creation, Singapore Polytech., 2007; M in Engring., Nanyang Technol. U., Singapore, 2007; PhD, Nat. U. Singapore, 2011. Cert. traditional Chinese medicine and nutrition Nat. U. Singapore Ext., 2006, traditional Chinese medicine and health Nat. U. Singapore Ext., 2006. Pharmacy asst. Unity Healthcare Coop. Ltd., Singapore, 2000—02; pre-registration pharmacist Tan Tock Seng Hosp., Singapore, 2002—03; pharmacist Inst. Mental Health, Singapore, 2003; acad. staff Republic Poly., Singapore, 2003—06; project officer, biomed. engring. rsch. ctr. Nanyang Technol. U., Singapore, 2006; pharmacist Nat. Cancer Ctr., Singapore, 2011; asst. prof. Inst. Digital Healthcare WMG, Warwick U., 2011—. Contbr. articles to profl. journals. Recipient Sun Microsystems award, Sun Microsystems, 2007, Best Grad. Rschr. award, NUS Pharmacy Dept. and Sci. Faculty, 2011, Wang Gungwu medal and prize, 2011. Mem.: American Soc. Clin. Oncology, Healthcare Info. and Mgmt. Sys. Soc., American Chem. Soc., Healthcare Info. and Mgmt. Sys. Soc., Singapore Pharmacy Coun., Pharm. Soc. Singapore (assoc.). Avocations: bowling, volleyball, gym. Office: University Warwick Inst Digital Healthcare WMG Internat Digital Lab Coventry CV47AL England Personal E-mail: kevinyap.ehealth@gmail.com. Business E-Mail: k.yap@warwick.ac.uk.

YAPOR, WESLEY YAMIL, neurosurgeon; b. Chgo., July 3, 1955; s. Carlos and Eneida Yapor; children: Myles Prescott, Lance Nathaniel, Danielle Yvonne, Austin Conrad. BA in biology, Andrews U., 1977; MD, U. Ill., 1982; asst. prof. (hon.), Northwestern U., 2003. Resident U. Ill., Chgo., 1983—88; neurosurgeon Northwestern Neurosurgical Assn., Chgo., 1989—2003; chmn. neurosurgery St. Mary of Nazareth Hosp., Chgo., 2000—. Author: Essentials of Diving Safety, 2000, On-Site Management of Scuba Diving and Boating Emergencies, 2001. Achievements include patents in field of cerebral dilator in US, France, England, Japan, and Germany. Avocations: scuba diving, boating, skiing. Office: Northwestern Neurosurgical 7447 W Talcott Ave Ste 340 Chicago IL 60631-3714 Office Phone: 312-926-3490.

YAQOOB, MUHAMMAD MAGDI, nephrologist, educator; s. Ismail and Khadija Yaqoob; m. Rabia Lakhany; children: Khadija, Fatima, Ali. MBBS, Dow Med. Coll., Karachi, 1982, MD, Liverpool U., UK, 1994. Cert. in internal medicine and nephrology JCCMT, 1984. Prof. Barts and London NHS Trust and Sch. Medicine and Dentistry, 1995—, cons., 1995—. Dir. William Harvey Rsch. Ltd., London, 2003—. Contbr. articles to profl. jours. (Best Clin. Sci. Presentation, 2006). Recipient Young Investigator Yr. award, European Renal Assn., 1991. Master: RCP; fellow: RCP. Achievements include discovery of hydrocarbon exposure and renal disease, peritubular capillaries and diabetic nephropathy. Office: Royal London Hosp PO Box 59 E1 1BB London England Personal E-mail: m.m.yaqoob@qmul.ac.uk.

YARAGUDRI, VINOD K., neuroscientist, researcher; b. Belgaum, Karanataka, India, July 11, 1973; s. Kallappa V. and Ratna K. Yaragudri; m. Shilpa Sulebhavi, Apr. 3, 2003; 1 child, Nathan. BS, Karanatak U., Dharwad, India, 1994, MS, 1996; PhD, NIMH and Neuroscience, Bangalore, India, 2002. Rsch. scholar NIMH and Neuroscis., Banaglore, India, 1996—97, sr. rsch. scholar, 1997—2001; rsch. project mgr. Nathan S. Kline Inst. Psychiat. Rsch., Orangeburg, NY, 2002—03, asst. rsch. scientist, 2003—05, assoc. rsch. scientist, 2005—; rsch. project mgr. N.Y. State Psychiat. Inst., NYC, 2002—03, asst. rsch. scientist, 2003—05, assoc. rsch. scientist, 2005—; asst. prof. child & adolescent psychiatry NY Sch. Medicine, 2007—. Contbr. articles to profl. jours. Founder Narayana Rural Devel. Soc., Mudhol, India, 2003. Recipient Academic Excellence Gold medal, Karnatak U., Dharwad, India, 1997, Burswood Rsch. Poster award, Asian Pacific Congress Clin. Biochemistry, 2004; grantee, Am. Found. Suicide Prevention, 2004—06; fellow, Lady Tata Meml. Trust, India, 1998, Indian Coun. Med. Rsch., 1999—2001, Internat. Brain Rsch. Orgn., 2001, Rsch. Found. Mental Hygeine, 2002—; scholar, Karnataka State Tchr.'s Assn., Bangalore, India, 1991, Jindal Aluminium Trust, Bangalore, India, 1994—96; grant, NIH, 2007—. Mem.: Am. Found. Suicide Prevention (hon.), Soc. Biol. Psychiatry (assoc.), Internat. Cannabinoid Rsch. Soc. (assoc.), Rsch. Soc. Alcoholism (assoc.), Schizophrenia Rsch. Forum (life), Indian Acad. Neurosci. (life), Internat. Brain Rsch. Orgn. (life). Achievements include research in the implication of the role of the brain endocannabinoid system in major depressive disorder and suicide. Home: 120 Nottingham Ct Montvale NJ 07645 Office: Nathan Kline Inst 140 Old Orangeburg Rd Orangeburg NY 10962 Office Fax: 845-398-5451. Personal E-mail: ky_vinod@yahoo.com. Business E-Mail: vyaragudri@nki.rfmh.org.

YARBROUGH, KATHRYN DAVIS, public health nurse; b. Montrose, Colo., Aug. 31, 1947; d. L.O. and V. Jean (Dunn) Davis; m. James H. Yarbrough, Aug. 8, 1970; children: James, Jason. Diploma, Good Samaritan Hosp. Sch. Nursing, Phoenix, 1971; BSN, Kennesaw State Coll., 1996. RN, Ga.; cert. NAACOG. Supr. Cherokee County Health Dept., Canton, Ga., 1976-97. Den mother Boy Scouts Am., Canton, 1986-87; bd. dirs. Cancer soc., Canton, 1987—, Cherokee County Violence Ctr., 1990, First Steps Bd., 1993-97, Cherokee County Advocacy Ctr., 1994-97; HIV cons. ARC, Canton, 1988—, disaster vol., Cherokee County, 1993-99; co-chair Early Intervention Coun., Canton, 1991-93; mem. Leadership Cherokee, 1994, Interagy Coun., 1994; mem. Blue Ridge Jud. Cir. Domestic Violence Task Force, 1995. Mem.: ANA, Shepherd Ctr. Spinal Cord Rehab. Quad, CASA (bd. dirs. 2008), Without Reservation Luncheon Club, Ga. Nurses Assn., Svc. League Cherokee County (hon.). Methodist. Mailing: PO Box 408 Canton GA 30169 E-mail: Kyarbro216@aol.com.

YARBROUGH, TERRY PINCKNEY, physician; b. Columbia, SC, Apr. 2, 1940; s. Dabney Randolph and Frances Horton (Colcock) Y.; m. Alexandra Mayo, Aug. 28, 1965; children: Alexandra, Laurens. MD, Med. Coll. Va., 1965. Intern U. Tex. Med. Br., Galveston, 1965—66; resident in internal medicine Med. Coll. Va., Richmond, 1968—71; pvt. practice Internal Medicine of Portsmouth Ltd., 1971—. Capt. USAR, 1966-68. Named to America's Top Physician. Mem. ACP, Am. Coll. of Cardiology, Coun. Clin. Cardiology, Am. Heart Assn., Med. Soc. of Va. Episcopalian. Office: Internal Medicine Portsmouth Ltd 3300 High St Portsmouth VA 23707-3321

YARCHOAN, ROBERT, clinical immunologist, researcher; b. NYC, July 21, 1950; s. Zachary and Anne Mae (Veneroso) Y.; m. Giovana Tosato; children: Mark, John. BA magna cum laude, Amherst Coll., 1971; MD, U. Pa., 1975. Diplomate Am. Bd. Internal Medicine, Am. Bd. Allergy and Immunology. Resident in medicine U. Minn. Hosps., Mpls., 1975-78; clin. assoc. metabolism br. Nat. Cancer Inst., NIH, Bethesda, Md., 1978-80, investigator metabolism br., 1980-83, investigator clin. oncology program, 1983-87, sr. investigator clin. oncology program, 1988-91, chief retroviral diseases sect. medicine br., 1991-96, chief HIV and AIDS Malignancy Br., 1996—, AIDS coord., 2006—, dir. Office HIV and AIDS Malignancy, 2007—. Assoc. editor Jour. Immunology, 1985-89, AIDS Rsch. and Human Retroviruses, 1986-2004, AIDS, 1990-2000, Jour. AIDS, 2000-06, Jour. Human Virology, 2002-04, Infectious Agents and Cancer, 2006-; sect. editor Thymus, 1992-97; contbr. articles to sci. jours., chpts. to textbooks; patentee in field. Capt. USPHS, 1978—2008. Recipient Commendation medal USPHS, 1991, Asst. Sec. Health award US govt. Dept. Health & Human Svcs., 1989, Inventors award US Dept. Commerce, 1986, 87, Fed. Tech. Transfer Act award, 1999, 2000, 01, Outstanding Svc. medal USPHS, 2002, awarded NIH First World AIDS Day award, 2006, NCI HIV Aids Rsch. Excellence award, 2007, NCI Award of Merit, 2009. Fellow AAAS; mem. Am. Soc. Hematology, Am. Assn. Immunologists, Clin. Immunology Soc., Am. Soc. for Clin. Investigation, Phi Beta Kappa, Sigma Xi. Achievements include co-inventor of therapies for AIDS and AIDS malignancies including ddI (didanosine) and ddC (zalcitabine) for AIDS and IL-12 for Kaposi's sarcoma; co-developer of therapies for AIDS and AIDS malignancies including AZT (zidovudine) for AIDS and paclitaxel for Kaposi's sarcoma; research in interactions between viruses and the immune system, therapy of AIDS and virally induced tumors; pathogenesis of AIDS and viral-induced tumors.

YARKONY, GARY MICHAEL, physician, researcher; b. NYC, May 22, 1953; m. Kirsten Kohlmeyer; children: Judith, Rachel, Seth, Lauren. BA in Biology, SUNY, Buffalo, 1974; MD, SUNY, Syracuse, 1978; Master in Mgmt., Northwestern U., 1994. Intern, then resident in physical medicine, rehab. Northwestern U., Chgo., 1978—81, chief resident dept. rehab. medicine, 1980; asst. dir. head trauma program Rehab. Inc. Chgo., 1981—84, attending staff, 1981—94; chief of rehab. svcs. U. Chgo. Hosps. Rehab. Ctr., 1994—2000; clin. prof. sect. orthopaedic surgery and rehab. medicine U. Chgo. Med. Ctr., 1995—2000, clin. prof. dept. surgery and neurology, 1995—2000; clin. prof. dept. rehab. medicine Chgo. Med. Sch., 2000—. Attending physician Northwestern Meml. Hosp., Chgo., 1984-94, Provera St. Joseph's Hosp., Elgin, Ill., 2000—; assoc. prof. dept. rehab. medicine Northwestern U. Med. Sch., 1985-94; adj. prof. Pritzker Inst. for Med. Engring., Ill. Inst. Tech., 1991-97; dir. rehab. Midwest Regional Spinal Cord Injury Care Sys., Chgo., 1984-94; dir. rsch. Schwab Rehab. Hosp., 1997-2000. Contbr. articles to profl. jours. and chpts. to book. Fellow Am. Acad. Physical Medicine and Rehab.; mem. Assn. Academic Physiatrists, Am. Spinal Injury Assn., Internat. Med. Soc. Paraplegia, Internal Rehab. Medicine Assn., Phi Beta Kappa, Phi Eta Sigma. Office: 87 N Airlite St EG-16 Elgin IL 60123 Office Phone: 847-468-1511.

YARMUCH, JULIO GUTIERREZ, surgeon, educator; b. Santiago, Chile, June 22, 1945; Degree in Medicine, U. Chile, 1971, degree, 1980. Sub-dir. dept. surgery U. Chile. Clin. Hosp., 1996—2010, dir. dept. surgery, 2010—. Prof. titular U. Chile, 1995—; editor chief Revista Chilena de Cirugía, 2004—. Master: Soc. de Cirujanos de Chile. Avocations: fishing, golf, tennis. Office: Román Díaz 107 Dpto 401 Providencia Santiago 7500000 Chile Office Fax: 56 2 7370844. E-mail: jyarmuch9@gmail.com.

YAROM, NOAM, dentist; b. Ramat-Gan, Israel; married. DMD, Tel-Aviv U., 1999. Dir., oral medicine clinic Sheba Med. Ctr., Tel-Hashomer, Israel, 2002—; specialist oral pathology, oral medicine Sch. Dental Medicine, Tel Aviv U. Office: Sheba Med Ctr Tel-Hashomer Tel-Hashomer 11111 Israel Office Phone: 972-3-5303819. Business E-Mail: noamyar@post.tau.ac.il.

YARWOOD, BRUCE, former health science association administrator; b. Sacramento, Calif. 2 children; 2 stepchildren. Mgr. MediCal program Calif. Dept. Health; exec. v.p. Calif. Assn. Health Facilities; CEO Crestwood Hospitals, Inc.; ptnr. Helmsin Yarwood & Associates, 1989—2005; legis. counsel Am. Health Care Assn., Washington, acting pres., CEO, 2005, pres., CEO, 2005—10. Bd. dirs. Skilled Healthcare Group, Inc., 2011—. Mailing: c/o Skilled Healthcare Group Inc Board Directors 27442 Portola Pkwy Ste 200 Foothill Ranch CA 92610 Office Phone: 202-842-4444. Office Fax: 202-842-3860. E-mail: byarwood@ahca.org. *

YASHON, DAVID, neurosurgeon, educator; b. Chgo., May 13, 1935; s. Samuel and Dorothy (Cutler) Y.; children: Jaclyn, Lisa, Steven. BS in Medicine, U. Ill., 1958, MD, 1960. Diplomate Am. Bd. Neurol. Surgery. Intern U. Ill., 1961, resident, 1961-64, asst. in neuroanatomy, 1960; clin. instr. neurosurgery U. Chgo., 1965-66; asst. prof. neurosurgery Case Western Res U., Cleve., 1966-69; assoc. prof. neurosurgery Ohio State U., Columbus, 1969-74, prof., 1974-89, prof. emeritus, 1989—; mem. staff St. Ann's Hosp., Children's Hosp., Grant Med. Ctr., Ohio State U. East Med. Ctr. Cons. Med. Research and Devel. Command, U.S. Army; mem. Neurology B Study Sect NIH. Author: Spinal Injury; contbr. articles to med. jours. Served as capt. U.S. Army, 1960-68. Fellow Royal Coll. Surgeons Can. (cert.), A.C.S.; mem. AMA, Am. Physiol. Soc., Congress Neurol. Surgeons, Am. Assn. Anatomists, Canadian, Ohio neurosurg. socs., Am. Assn. Neurol. Surgeons, Research Soc. Neurol. Surgeons, Acad. Medicine Columbus and Franklin County, Soc. for Neurosci., Soc. Univ. Surgeons, Am. Acad. Neurology, Assn. for Acad. Surgery, Am. Acad. Neurol. Surgery, Am. Assn. for Surgery of Trauma, Central Surg. Soc., Ohio Med. Soc., Columbus Surg. Soc., Sigma Xi, Alpha Omega Alpha.

YASNOFF, WILLIAM ALAN, computer scientist, preventive medicine physician; b. Chgo., Apr. 7, 1953; s. Meyer Yasnoff and Doris Norwell; m. Joanene Lois Feldman; children: Cynthia Aggson, David, Rebecca. BS, Northwestern U., Evanston, Ill., 1974; MD, Northwestern U., Chgo., 1975; PhD in Computer Sci., Northwestern U., Evanston, Ill., 1980. Asst. prof., med. computer sci. dept. U. Tex. Health Sci. Ctr., Dallas, 1980—83; asst. prof., dir. cardiology image processing Med. Coll. Ohio, Toledo, 1983—85; v.p. rsch. Cell Analysis Sys., Inc., Lombard, Ill., 1985—86; pres., founder Morphometrix, Inc., Western Springs, Ill., 1986—87; med. dir. AMA/Net AMA, Chgo., 1987—90; assoc. dir., health network svcs. Oreg. Health Scis. U., Portland, 1990—93; dir. immunization registry and DOLPHIN network Oreg. Health Divsn., Portland, 1994—97; assoc. dir. for sci., pub. health practice program office Ctrs. for Disease Control and Prevention, Atlanta, 1997—2002; sr. adv. nat. health info. infrastructure U.S. Dept. HHS, Washington, 2002—05; mng. ptnr. NHII Advisors, Arlington, Va., 2005—. Assoc. editor Jour. of Biomed. Informatics, San Diego, 2000—; adj. prof. biostatistics Emory U., Atlanta, 2002—; cons. Compuserve, Inc., Columbus, OHIO, 1995, Ea. Va. Med. Sch., Norfolk, VA., 1995, Abbott Labs., Inc., San Jose, 1993—94, Columbine Venure Ptnrs., Englewood, 1989—91; prof. divsn. health scis. informatics Johns Hopkins U., 2003—. Author: (book) Public Health Informatics and Information Systems, 2003, Personal Health Records, 2009; contbr. articles to profl. jours. Grief recovery counselor NE Bapt. Ch., Atlanta, 2000. Fellow: Am. Coll. of Med. Informatics; mem.: Assn. for Computing Machinery, IEEE Computer Soc., Am. Med. Informatics Assn. (bd. dirs. 2003—04, sci. program chair spring meeting 2001). Avocation: tennis. Office: NHII Advisors 1854 Clarendon Blvd Arlington VA 22201 Business E-Mail: william.yasnoff@nhiiadvisors.com.

YASSIN, YASSIN MOHAMED, gut and hepatic surgeon, laparoendoscopic surgeon, gastroenterologist; b. Sohag, Egypt, July 3, 1938; s. Mohamed Yassin Mohamed Ibrahim Mahrous and Hamida Abdel-Rassoul Mohamed; m. Titinia Ali Hafez, June 30, 1966; children: Rania Yassin Mohamed, Tamer Yassin Mohamed, Sherif Yassin Mohamed. MB ChB, Alexandria U. Med. Coll., Egypt, 1961. Diploma of general surgery Cairo U. Med. Coll., 1965. Cons. surgeon Gastroenterology Unit, Kobri-El-Kobba Armed Forces Hosp., Cairo, 1975—85, dept. head and chmn. surgery, 1985—90; unit head and chief surgeon Exptl. Liver Transplantation Unit, Kobri-El-Kobba Armed Forces Hosp., 1985—90; prof. surgery Mil. Med. Acad., Cairo, 1987; sr. cons. surgeon Cairo Med. Ctr. - Pvt. Clinic, 2004—. Vis. prof. Suez Canal U. Med. Coll., 1982—90, Organ Transplantation Ctr., Presbyn. Hosp., Pitts., 1983, Liver Transplantation Unit, Baylor U. Med. Ctr., Dallas, 1987, Liver Transplantation Svc., Paul Brousse Hosp., Paris, 1988, Liver Transplantation Unit, Princess Alexandra Hosp., Brisbane, Australia, 1990, Liver Transplantation Unit, Asan Med. Ctr., Seoul, Republic of Korea, 2001, Liver Transplantation Unit, Jackson Meml. Hosp., Miami, 2002; sr. cons. surgeon Qatif Ctrl. Hosp., Dammam, Eastern Province, Saudi Arabia, 1990—99; chmn. surgery and med. dir. Khafji Joint Ops. Hosp., Al-Khafji, Eastern Province, 1999—2003. Contbr. chapters to books, articles to jours. Fellow, Profl. Unit Surgery and Transplantation, U. Cambridge Sch. Medicine, UK, 1982. Fellow: ACS, RCS; mem.: Internat. Assn. Study Liver, European Assn. Study Liver, European Neurogastroenterological Motility Soc., Brit. Soc. Gastroenterology, Assn. Surgeons Gt. Britain and Ireland, Egyptian Soc. Laparoscopic Surgery, Egyptian Soc. Hepatology, Egyptian Soc. Gastroenterology, Soc. Am. Gastrointestinal Endoscopic Surgeons, Soc. Organ Sharing, Transplantation Soc., World Orgn. Gastroenterology, Egyptian Soc. Surgeons. Achievements include first to 180 degrees antero-medial fundoplication for GERD & hiatal hernia, experimental live-donor liver transplantation, and eversion repair of ventral and large incisional hernia (hernio-abdomino-plasty); endoscopic sclerotherapy and highly selective devascularization for esophageal varices. Home: 78 Gomhouria St Apt 29 Cairo 11111 Egypt Office Phone: 00 202 25931373. Personal E-mail: ysemsem01@yahoo.com.

YASTER, MYRON, anesthesiologist, educator; b. Aug. 22, 1952; MD, SUNY Downstate Med. Ctr., 1977. Prof. Johns Hopkins U., 1982—. Mem.: IARS, SPA, ASA. Office: Johns Hopkins Hosp Blalock 935 Baltimore MD 21287 Business E-Mail: myasterl@jhmi.edu.

YASUDA, HIROSHI, internist, educator; b. Tokyo, Jan. 16, 1960; MD, PhD, Tohoku U., 1984. Prof., divsn. gastroenterology and hepatology St. Marianna U. Sch. Medicine, 2010. Fellow: Japanese Soc. Internal Medicine. Avocation: guitar. Office: 2-16-1 Sugao Miyamae-ku Kawasaki Kanagawa 216-8511 Japan Office Fax: 81-44-976-5805. Business E-Mail: hyasuda@marianna-u.ac.jp.

YASUDA, HIROYASU, oncologist, researcher, pulmonologist; b. Sapporo, Hokkaido, Japan, Feb. 20, 1970; s. Michihiro and Fusako Yasuda; m. Kanako Horikoshi, Aug. 23, 2008; 1 child, Atsuki. MD, Yamagata U. Sch. Medicine, 1997; PhD, Tohoku U. Sch. Medicine, Sendai, Miyagi, Japan, 2003. Diplomate Japanese Govt., 1997. Med. staff Tohoku U., Sendai, 2003—06; assoc. prof. Kyoto U. Hosp., 2006—08, Tohoku U. Translational Rsch. Ctr., 2008—. Contbr. articles to med. jours. Recipient, Kanae Found. Life & Socio-Med. Sci., 2007; Sci. Rsch. grant, Ministry Edn., Sci. Culture Japanese Govt., 2005—. Fellow: Japanese Respiratory Soc., Japanese Soc. Internal Medicine; mem.: Am. Thoracic Soc., Am. Assn. Cancer Rsch., Am. Soc. Clin. Oncology. Achievements include patents for inhibitory method of rhinovirus infection and prediction of chemosensitivity to cancer chemotherapy; increase in chemosensitivit to cancer cemotherapy with nitric oxide donors and prevention of chronic diseases. Home: 5-1-3 Murasakiyama Izumi-ku Sendai Miyagi 981-3205 Japan Office: Tohoku Univ Sch Medicine Translational Rsch Ctr

H Seiro-machi Aoba-ku Sendai 980-8574 Japan Office Phone: 81227177122. Office Fax: 81227177104. Personal E-mail: hirokana@msg.biglobe.ne.jp. Business E-Mail: yasuda@trc.med.tohoku.ac.jp.

YASUDA, YUZURU, neurologist; b. Kyoto, May 7, 1949; S. Saburo and Shigeko (Kuriyama) Terada; m. Hiroko Suwa, Jan. 15, 1983; children: Ken, Noriko. MD, Kyoto U., 1983. Diplomate Am. Bd. Neurology. Intern Kyoto U. Sch. Medicine, 1977—78, Kitano Hosp., Osaka, Japan, 1978-79; sub-chief dept. neurology Kyoto City Hosp., 1983-90; chief dept. neurology Otsu Red Cross Hosp., Japan, 1990—2003; guest rschr. Ctr. Neurol. and Cerebrovascular Diseases, Takeda Hosp., Kyoto, 2003—; chief Yasuda Clinic, 2003—. Mem. Japanese Soc. Neurology, Japanese Soc. Internal Medicine, Japanese Soc. Neuropathology. Home: 62-4 Takenokaido-cho Takehana Yamashina Kyoto 607-8080 Japan Office Phone: 0755832288. Personal E-mail: yuzuru-yasuda@mra.biglobe.ne.jp.

YASUI, YUKIHIKO, medical educator; b. Shiga, Japan, Nov. 9, 1952; BS in Dentistry, Hiroshima U., 1981; MD, Kyoto U., 2008. Prof. Shimane U. Sch. Medicine, 1993—. Mem.: Japan Neurosci. Soc., Japanese Assn. Anatomists, Soc. Neurosci. Office: Enya-cho 89-1 Izumo Shimane 693-8501 Japan Office Fax: 81-853-20-2105. Business E-Mail: yyasui@med.shimane-u.ac.jp.

YASUO, BUNAI, medical educator; b. Takaoka City, Toyama, Japan, Jan. 25, 1954; MD, Sch. Medicine, Gifu U., 1978; PhD, Grad. Sch. Medicine, Gifu U., 1985. Assoc. prof. Sch. Medicine Dept. Legal Medicine, Gifu U., 1991—2002, prof. Grad. Sch. Medicine, 2002—. Mem.: Japanese Assn. Legal Medicine. Office: 1-1 Yanagido Gifu 501-1194 Japan Office Fax: 81-230-6418. Business E-Mail: bunaiy@gifu-u.a.cjp.

YASUSHI, UDA, agricultural studies educator; b. Tottori,, Japan, Oct. 23, 1947; PhD, Grad. Sch. Agrl. Chemistry, Utsunomiya U., Tochigi, Japan, 1972. Lectr. Coll. Nutrition, Yanamashigakuin U., 1972—74; asst. prof. Faculty Agr., Utsunomiya U., 1974—84, assoc. prof., 1985—95, prof., 1986—. Councilor Utsunomiya U., 2007—09. Mem.: Japan Soc. Food Sci. and tech., Japan Soc. Biosci., Biotech. and Agrochemistry. Avocations: flute, hiking. Home: 3015-29 HIgashimine-cho Utsunomiya Tochigi 321-0499 Japan Home Fax: 81-28-662-3290. Business E-Mail: uda@cc.utsunomiya-u.ac.jp.

YATERA, KAZUHIRO, medical educator, researcher; s. Keiji and Noriko Yatera. MD, U. Occupl. and Environ. Health Japan, Fukuoka, 1994, PhD, 2001. Physician-in-chief Chubu Rousai Hosp., Nagoya City, Aichi, Japan, 2000—01; adjacent asst. prof. U. Occupl. and Environ. Health Japan, Kitakyushu City, 2000—. Author: (jour.) Increased expression of Clara cell ablated mice inhaling crystalline silica (Chair award 20th ann. meeting U. Occupl. and Environ. Health Japan, 2002). Recipient 17th Ichiro Kanehara Meml. Med. Found. Travel award, Ichiro Kanehara Meml. Med. Found., 2003; grantee Lung injury using Clara cell ablated mice, Found. Occupl. and Environ. Health Japan, 2001. Fellow: The Japanese Respiratory Soc., Japanese Soc. of Internal Medicine. Office: James Hogg iCAPTURE Centre/UBC St Paul's Hosp 1081 Burrard St Vancouver BC Canada V6Z1Y6 Personal E-mail: kyatera@mrl.ubc.ca. Business E-Mail: yatera@med.uoeh-u.ac.jp.

YATES, JAMES ARTHUR, plastic surgeon; b. Butler, Pa., June 5, 1935; s. Adolph Walter and Laura Marie (De Foggie) Y.; m. Debra Lynne Stringer, June 19, 1983; 1 child, Jamie Dale Yates Reynolds. BA, Cornell U., 1956; MD, U. Md., 1960. Diplomate Am. Bd. Plastic Surgery, Nat. Bd. Med. Examiners, Am. Bd. Surgery; lic. physician, Pa., Ohio, R.I. Intern Cleve. Clinic Hosp., 1960—61, resident in gen. surgery, 1961—62, U. Pitts. Med. Ctr., 1963—65; resident in plastic surgery R.I. Hosp., 1966—67, chief resident, 1967—68; pvt. practice Plastic Surgery Ctr. Ltd., Camp Hill, Pa., 1968—; med. dir. Grandview Surgery Ctr., Camp Hill, Pa. Tchg. fellow gen. surgery U. Pitts. Med. Ctr., 1963-65, instr. gen. surgery, 1965-66; clin. instr. plastic surgery Milton S. Hershey (Pa.) Med. Ctr., 1968—; staff maxillofacial and plastic surgery dept. Harrisburg (Pa.) Hosp., 1968—; chief plastic and aesthetic surgery dept. Holy Spirit Hosp., Camp Hill, 1968—; staff Mechanicsburg Rehab. Hosp., Carlisle (Pa.) Hosp., Pinnacle Health Sys. Hosps.; med. dir. Grandview Surgery and Laser Ctr., Camp Hill; cons. Harrisburg State Hosp.; physician surveyor Am. Assn. Ambulatory Health Care; physician trainer plastic surgery residency program Am. Coll. Osteo. Surgery; bd. dirs., pres. Am. Assn. Accreditatiion of Ambulatory Surgery Facilities. Contbr. articles to profl. jours.; adv. bd. Town and Country Mag. Police commr. West Shore Regional Police Dept.; pres. Boro Coun. Lemoyne Boro; mem. credentialling com. Keystone Health Plan; mem. task force on ambulatory surgery Pa. Dept. Health; mem. coun. Lemoyne (Pa.) Borough Coun., pres.; credentialing officer Freedom Health Care HMO; commr. West Shore Regional Police. Fellow ACS; mem. AMA, Pa. Med. Soc., Am. Burn Assn., Am. Soc. Plastic and Reconstructive Surgeons, Am. Burn Victim Found., Am. Soc. Aesthetic Plastic Surgery, Vail Cosmetic Surgery Soc., Pa. Plastic Surgery Soc. (past pres.), Am. Soc. Automobile Medicine, Northeastern Soc. Plastic Surgeons, Royal Soc. Medicine, Lipolysis Soc. N.Am., Internat. Soc. Clin. Plastic Surgeons, South Ctrl. Pa. Regional Med. Dirs., Am. Coll. Physician Execs. Republican. Roman Catholic. Avocations: bicycling, skiing, model building, sports cars. Home: 833 Kiehl Dr Lemoyne PA 17043-1201 Office: Plastic Surgery Ctr Ltd 205 Grandview Ave Camp Hill PA 17011-1708 Home Phone: 717-761-1281; Office Phone: 717-763-7814. Personal E-mail: jay5plas@msn.com.

YAVIN, EYLON, science educator; b. Jerusalem, July 3, 1969; PhD, Weizmann Inst. Sci., 2003. Asst. prof. Hebrew U., 2006—. Mem.: ACS. Office: Sch Pharmacy Hadassah Ein Karem Jerusalem 92110 Israel Business E-Mail: eylony@ekmd.huji.ac.il.

YAZAKI, YOSHIO, hospital administrator; b. 1938; MD, PhD, DMS, U. Tokyo. Med. sch. rsch. fellow Harvard Univ., 1971; rsch. fellow Tufts Univ., 1972—74; third dept. of internal medicine cardiovasc. divsn. chief Univ. of Tokyo, 1975, asst. prof. of medicine, 1984, assoc. prof. of medicine, 1988, third dept. of internal medicine prof., 1991—99, third dept. of internal medicine chmn., 1991—99, faculty of medicine dean, 1995; dir. Internat. Med. Ctr. Japan, 1999—, pres., 2000, Nat. Hosp. Orgn., Japan. Office: National Hospital Organization 152-8621 No 21 Higashigaoka 2-chome Tokyo Jamaica Office Phone: 0357125050. *

YAZDANI, SHAHRAM, pediatrician; b. July 20, 1967; MD, Tulane U. Sch. Medicine, New Orleans, 1995. Cert. Am. Bd. Pediat., 2006. Internship in pediat. UCLA Sch. Medicine, 1995—96, residency in pediat., 1996—98, physician, 1998—, asst. prof. pediat., 1998—, asst. clin. prof. gen. pediat., 1998—. Dir. resident med. edn. UCLA Med. Sch., site dir., 3rd yr. med. sch., mem. ambulatory medicine com., 2001—; med. coord., cons. Madisons Found., 2003—. Mem.: Assn. Pediatric Program Directors. Office: UCLA Children's Health Ctr 200 UCLA Med Plz Ste 265 Los Angeles CA 90095 Office Phone: 310-825-0867. Office Fax: 310-794-5066. Business E-Mail: syazdani@mednet.ucla.edu.

YAZGAN, IZZET CAGRI, psychiatrist; b. Izmir, Turkey, June 13, 1966; MD, Ege U., 1990. Geriat. psychiatrist Meridian Svcs., 2007—. Assoc. prof. Marmara U. Med. Sch., 1999—2007. Bristol Myers fellowship, Am. Assn. Geriatric Psychiatry. Mem.: Am. Psychiat. Assn. Office: 240 N Tillotson Ave Muncie IN 47304 Office Phone: 765-747-3281. E-mail: cgyazgan@yahoo.com.

YBERT, JEAN-PAUL GUSTAVE, occupational medicine physician, anthropologist; b. Angerville, L'Orcher, France, May 2, 1944; s. Paul Léon and Paulette Henriette (Cesarine). MD, Faculty of Medicine, Rouen, France, 1974; qualified in agrl. medicine, U. Tours, France, 1988; qualified in occupl. medicine, U. Paris, 1994. Physician Com. Inter-entreprises de Mé du Tra vail dela Nièvre, Nevers, France, 1976—78, Svc. de Médecine du Travail Inter-entreprises, Rouen, 1978—83, Assn. Inter-entreprises de Médecine du Travail de la Région d'Alençon, Alençon, France, 1988—91, Assn. Médico-Sociale inter-Entreprise d'Evreux et de sa Région, Louviers, France, 1991, Svc. Medico-Sociaux Inter-Entreprises, St. Quentin, 1996—98, Assn. Médicosociale Vernon et de sa Région, Vernon, France, 2000—. Adminstr. Ctr. de Recherches Archéologiques Val de Seine; med. coun. Fedn. Française des Fibromyalgiques. Contbr. papers to conf. procs. Mem.: AAAS, N.Y. Acad. Scis., Groupe des Paléopathologistes de langue française, Internat. Commn. Occupl. Health. Home: 25 Parc de Cerisy Rue du Pays de Caux 76130 Mont Saint Aignan France

YE, GANG, medical educator, director; b. MeiShan, China, June 2, 1963; PhD, MD, Third Mil. Med. U., 1998. Cons. urologist, Com. Family Planning, Chongqing; divisional clin. urologist, Cancer Svcs., China Charity Fedn., Beijing; vice dir. Ctr. Infertility and Reproduction PLA, Chongqing City; prof., co-dir. Ctr. Nephrology, Third Mil. Med. U., Chongqing; dir., prof., dept. urology Ctr. Nephrology, Xinqiao Hosp., Third Mil. Med. U., Chongqing, China, 2009—. Cons. prof. Com. Chongqing Sci. & Tech. Recipient Innovation Clinic award, Clin. Mgmt. Office and Academic Assn. TMMU, Clin. Achievement award, Ministry Health of PLA, Faculty Tchg. award, Xinqiao Hosp., Third Mil. Med. U., 2008; grant, Com. Nat. Sci. Fund, 2010, Com. Chongqing Nature and Sci. Fund. Master: Andrology Assn. Chongqing; mem.: Chinese Andrology Assn., Standing Com. PLA Urologic Assn., Chinese Urologic Assn. (Chongqing City Sect.), Chinese Med. Assn. Avocations: swimming, music, dance, badminton. Office: ShaPinBa Dist Xinqiao Main Ave Chongqing ChongQing 400037 China Office Fax: 86-023-65539436. Personal E-mail: goodocyeah@163.com.

YE, JIANPING, medical educator; b. Henan, China, Oct. 11, 1963; MD, Beijing U., 1989. Prof. Pennington Biomedical Rsch. Ctr., 2006—. Adj. prof., dept. biol. sci. LSU, 2006. Mem.: Am. Soc. Biochemistry and Molecular Biology, Am. Physiol. Soc., Am. Endocrinology Soc., Am. Diabetes Assn. Avocation: sports. Office: 6400 Perkins Rd Baton Rouge LA 70808 Business E-Mail: yej@pbrc.edu.

YE, LING, dental educator; b. China, Jan. 29, 1975; DDS, Sichuan U., PhD, 2003. Prof., assoc. dean, grad. edn. West China Sch. Stomatology Sichuan U., 2010—. Mem.: Internat. Assn. Dental Rsch. Office: 14 3rd Sect Renmin Nanlu Wuhou Dist Chengdu Sichuan 610041 China Personal E-mail: ling-ye@hotmail.com.

YE, QIXIANG, science educator; b. Henan, Oct. 18, 1978; PhD, Inst. Chinese Acad. Scis., 2006. Assoc. prof. Chinese Acad. Scis., 2009—11. Recipient Outstanding Paper award, Sony Corp. Office: Yuquan Rd 19A Beijing 100049 China Business E-Mail: qxye@gucas.ac.cn.

YE, SHENG-LONG, oncologist, educator; m. Wen-Di Zhao; 1 child, Xiao-Dan. MD, Shanghai Med. U., 1969, MSc, 1982, PhD, 1992. Attending physician and lectr. Zhongshan Hosp., Shanghai Med. U., 1982—88, prof. oncology, 1992—2000; vis. rsch. scientist New Eng. Deaconess Hosp., Harvard Med. Sch., Boston, 1988—92; prof. medicine and oncology Zhongshan Hosp., Fudan U., 2000—. Dep. dir. Liver Cancer Inst., Shanghai Med. U. and Fudan U., 1992—; exec. councilor Chinese Soc. Cancer Biotherapy, Beijing, 1994—, Chinese Soc. Hepatology, Beijing, 1997—; chmn. Dept. Hepatic Oncology, Zhongshan Hosp., Shanghai Med. U. and current Fudan U., Shanghai, 1998—; chief Key Lab. of Carcinogenesis and Cancer Invasion, Ministry Edn., China, Shanghai, 2000—; pres. Chinese Soc. Liver Cancer, Shanghai, 2005—09; mem. governing bd. Internat. Liver Cancer Assn., Brussels, 2007—; exec. councilor Chinese Anti-Cancer Assn., Beijing, 2007—. Recipient 1st prize, Sci. and Tech., China, 2006. Office: Zhongshan Hosp Fudan Univ 180 Ferglin Rd Shanghai 200032 China

YEAP, SWAN SIM, rheumatologist, consultant; m. Leslie Charles Lai, May 17, 1997; children: Mark Ken Hoe Lai, Paul Ken Chiew Lai. MBChB, U. of Dundee, Scotland, 1987; MD, U. Dundee, Scotland, 1997. CCST Joint Com. for Higher Specialist Med. Tng., UK, 1997, Royal Coll. of Physicians, London, 2007. Assoc. prof. in medicine U. Malaya, Kuala Lumpur, Malaysia, 2001—02, hon. cons., 2003—08; cons. rheumatologist Subang Jaya Med. Ctr., Subang Jaya, Selangor, Malaysia, 2004—. Editl. bd. mem. APLAR Jour. of Rheumatology, Australia, 2002—. Contbr. articles to profl. jours. Grantee, Royal Coll. Physicians, 2007; Rsch. grants, From U. and Pharm. Cos. for Rsch., 1997—2004. Fellow: RCP (Edinburg); mem.: RCP (Scotland), SLE Assn. Malaysia (v.p. 2008—), Asia-Pacific League Assns. for Rheumatology (v.p. 2004—06, treas. 2006—08, sec. gen. 2008—10, v.p. 2010—), Brit. Soc. Rheumatology, Malaysian Soc. Rheumatology (v.p. 2002—04, pres. 2004—08, sec. 1998—2000), Malaysian Med. Assn. (life), Malaysian Osteoporosis Soc. (life; treas. 2004—06, 2008—10, pres. 2010—, sec. 1998—2000, treas. 2000—02), Arthritis Found. Malaysia (com. mem. 1999—2011).

YEATMAN, HARRY CLAY, biologist, educator; b. Ashwood, Tenn., June 22, 1916; s. Trezevant Player and Mary (Wharton) Y.; m. Jean Hansford Anderson, Nov. 24, 1949; children— Henry Clay, Jean Hansford. AB, U. NC, Chapel Hill, 1939, MA, 1942, PhD, 1953; student, Cornell U., Ithaca, NY, summer 1937. Asst. prof. biology U. of South, Sewanee, Tenn., 1950-54, asso. prof., 1954-60, prof., 1960—, Kenan prof., 1980—, chmn. dept., 1972-76, elderhostel tchr., 1987-88. Vis. prof. marine biology Va. Inst. Marine Sci., Gloucester Point, summer 1967; cons. Smithsonian Instn., Sci. Applications, Inc., La Jolla, Calif., Ctrs. for Disease Control, Atlanta, WHO, Ecol. Analysts, Inc., Balt., Duke Power Co., Charlotte, N.C., Helminthic Disease Branch. Contbr. articles to profl. jours. Served with AUS, 1942-46. Gen. Edn. Bd. fellow, 1941-42; Brown Found. fellow, 1984, State Naturalist award Tenn. Dept. Environ. & Concervation. Fellow AAAS; mem. Soc. Systematic Biology (charter), Soc. Limnology and Oceanography (charter), Soc. Ichthyology and Herpetology, Tenn. Acad. Sci., Am. Micros. Soc., Am. Ornithologists Union, Tenn. Ornithol. Soc., Tenn. Archeol. Soc., Nat. Speleological Soc., Blue Key, Phi Beta Kappa, Sigma Xi, Omicron Delta Kappa, Sigma Nu. Republican. Episcopalian. Home: PO Box 356 199 Cloudcroft Pl Jumpoff Rd Sewanee TN 37375 Office: 735 University Ave Sewanee TN 37383-1000 Office Fax: 931-598-1145.

YEE, CASSIAN K., oncologist, researcher; BSc in Medicine, U. Manitoba, 1986, MD, 1986. Postdoctoral fellow Ontarion Cancer Inst., 1987—89; resident Stanford U., 1989—91; oncologist U. Wash. Sch. Medicine, 1993—, assoc. prof., 2004—; oncologist, scientist Fred Hutchinson Cancer Rsch. Ctr., 1998—, assoc. mem. clin. rsch. program in immunology, 1995—98, dir. immune monitoring lab, 2003—. Contbr. several articles to peer-reviewed publ. Mem.: Soc. for Biol. Therapy, Am. Assn. Immunologist, Am. Assn. for Cancer Rsch. Address: Seattle Cancer Care Alliance 825 Eastlake Ave E PO Box 19023 Seattle WA 98109-1023 Office: Fred Hutchinson Cancer Rsch Ctr 1100 Fairview Ave N PO Box 19024 D3-100 Seattle WA 98109-1024 Office Phone: 206-667-6287. Office Fax: 206-667-7983. Business E-Mail: cyee@fhcrc.org.

YEE, KUO CHIANG, neuroscientist, neurologist; b. Shanghai, Jan. 18, 1935; came to U.S., 1981; s. Hun and Wang J. Yee; m. Pei Ching Cai, Oct. 1, 1954; children: Hsiao Chiang, Hsiao Pei. MD, Zuzhen Med. Sch., Cheking, China, 1954; MS, U. Wash., 1983; PhD, U. B.C., Vancouver, Can., 1992. Prof. U. B.C., Vancouver, 1992-93; dir. Neurosci. Med. Ctr., Seattle, 1981—; pres. AmeriTek, Inc., Seattle, 1993—. Author: Biological Effects and Dosimetry of Nonionizing Radiation, 1982; contbr. numerous articles to profl. jours. Achievements include development of advanced rapid in-vitro immunodiagnostic and clinical chemical reagent systems diagnostic test kits. Home: 15205 3rd Dr Se Mill Creek WA 98012-5398 Office Phone: 425-379-2580. Business E-Mail: kcyee@ameritek.org.

YEE-MELICHAR, DARLENE, gerontological health educator; b. NYC, Sept. 19, 1958; d. Jimmy Tow and Yuen Hing (Chin) Y.; m. Joseph F. Melichar. BA in Biology, Barnard Coll., 1980; MS in Gerontology, Coll. New Rochelle, 1981; MS in Health Edn., Columbia U., 1984, EdD in Health Edn., 1985. Cert. Nat. Commn. Health Edn. Asst. dir. biology lab. Barnard Coll., NYC, 1980-83; rsch. assoc, safety rsch. and edn. project Columbia U. Tchrs. Coll., NYC, 1983-85; asst. prof. health and phys. edn. York Coll., NYC, 1985-88; cons. Transp. Rsch. Bd., NAS, Washington, 1987, N.Y. State Dept. Edn., Albany, 1987, U.S. Dept. Edn., Washington, 1991; assoc. prof. clin. gerontology, health edn. and promotion U. Tex. Med. Br., Galveston, 1988-90; assoc. prof. health edn. San Francisco State U., 1990-93; prof. health edn., 1994-95; dir., prof. gerontology San Francisco State U., 1995—. Contbr. articles to profl. jours. Mem. Am. Coll. Health Care Adminstrs., Gerontol. Soc. Am., Am. Soc. on Aging, Assn. for Advancement Health Edn., Nat. Coun. on Aging, Sigma Xi. Home: 1470 Tartan Trail Rd Hillsborough CA 94010-7220 Office Phone: 415-338-3558. E-mail: dyee@sfsu.edu.

YEH, CHARLOTTE SHAWING, emergency physician, nongovernmental organization executive; b. Ames, Iowa, Feb. 14, 1952; d. Charles Chia Ching and Sally Shing Shing (Liu) Y.; m. Frederick Murray Gale; children: Julianne Yulan Gale, Jessalyn Yulien Gale. BS, Northwestern U., Evanston, Ill., 1971; MD, Northwestern U., Chgo., 1975. Diplomate Am. Bd. Emergency Medicine. Intern gen. surgery U. Wash., Seattle, 1975-76; resident surgery UCLA, LA, 1976-77, emergency medicine resident, 1978-80; staff physician emergency dept. Newton-Wellesley Hosp., Mass., 1980-86, chief dept. emergency medicine Mass., 1986; physician-in-chief div. emergency medicine New Eng. Med. Ctr., Boston, 1990—98; med. dir. for medicare policy Nat. Heritage Ins. Co., Hingham, Mass., 1998—2003; regional adminstr., Boston and NY offices Centers for Medicare & Medicaid Services; chief med. officer AARP (American Assn. of Retired People). Asst. prof. dept. emergency medicine Tufts U. Sch. of Medicine; bd. dirs. Blue Cross Blue Shield of Mass. Found. Recipient Elliot Strom Meml. award Am. Coll. Emergency Physcians (Mass. chpt.), 1985, Outstanding Mem. of Yr. award, 1986, Emergency Med. Svcs. award Commonwealth of Mass., 1987, Individual of Yr. award for Outstanding Achievement in Field of Occupant Protection for Citizens of Mass., 1986; named Outstanding Resident II of Yr. UCLA, 1977. Fellow Am. Coll. Emergency Physicians (bd. dirs. 1988—, sec.-treas. 1991-92); mem. Alpha Lambda Delta, Alpha Omega Alpha. Office: AARP c/o Chief Medical Officer 601 E St NW Washington DC 20049 *

YEH, CHI-YUAN, hospital administrator; Grad., East U., Taipei Med. U. Dir. ctr. of radiation oncology Tungs Taichung MetroHarbor Hospital, Taiwan. Pluralistic clin. instr. Taipei Med. U. Office: Tungs Taichung MetroHarbor Hospital No 8 Cheng Gong W St Shalu Taichung Taiwan Office Phone: 886426626161. *

YEH, CHUN-YU, physical therapist, educator; b. Taiwan, Nov. 20, 1968; PhD, Nat. Cheng Kung U., 2004. Prof. Chung Shan Med. U.,

2004—. Office: 110 Sec 1 Jiangguo NRd Taichung 40201 Taiwan Business E-Mail: cyy@csmu.edu.tw.

YEH, CORY C., facial plastic surgeon, educator; grad., MD, Stanford U. Diplomate Am. Bd. Otolaryngology, cert. facial plastic and reconstructive surgery, lic. Calif., NY. Tchr. and lectr.; resident head and neck surgery Harvard Med. Sch.; fellow Am. Acad. of Facial Plastic and Reconstructive Surgery, NY; med. staff surgery dept. Saddleback Meml. Med. Ctr., San Clemente Meml. Med. Ctr., Laguna Hills Surgery Ctr.; hosp. appointments and affiliations include Mass. Gen. Hosp., Brigham and Women's Hosp., Beth Israel Deaconess Med. Ctr., Mass. Eye and Ear Infirmary, Albany Med. Ctr., Stratton Veteran Affairs Hosp., St. Peter's Hosp., Albany Meml. Hosp.; owner Yeh Facial Plastic Surgery. Co-author: Effect of FK506 on Functional Recovery After Facial Nerve injury in the Rat, 2007, Cosmetic and Functional Effects of Cephalic Malposition of the Lower Lateral Cartilages: A Facial Plastic Surgical Case Study, 2009, Fat Management in Lower Lid Blepharoplasty, 2009, Midface Restoration in the Management of the Lower Eyelid, 2010. Recipient Best Sci. Paper award, Facial Plastic and Reconstructive Surgery Ann. Meeting. Mem.: Phi Beta Kappa. Office: Yeh Facial Plastic Surgery Ste 350 24331 El Toro Rd Laguna Hills CA 92637 Office Phone: 949-916-7066.

YEH, EDWARD TU-HSING, cardiologist, educator, medical researcher; arrived in U.S., 1971; s. Jack and Pi-Lien Yeh; m. Hui-Ming Chang, Nov. 6, 1982; 1 child, Andrew Allen. MD, U. Calif., Davis, 1980. Diplomate Am. Bd. Cardiovascular Diseases. Asst. prof. Harvard Med. Sch., Boston, 1987—92; assoc. prof. U. Tex. Med. Sch., Houston, 1992—97, prof., 1997—2000; prof., chmn. cardiology MD Anderson Cancer Ctr., Houston, 2000—. Named Established Investigator, Am. Heart Assn., 1992. Mem.: Am. Heart Assn. (pres. Houston chpt. 2004—05), Assn. Am. Physicians (life). Achievements include patents in field; patents pending in field. Office: MD Anderson Cancer Ctr 1515 Holcombe 449 Houston TX 77030

YEH, HSU-CHONG, radiology educator; b. Taipei, Taiwan, Mar. 30, 1937; came to US, 1973; s. Ping-Hui and Ah-Chu (Chuang) Y.; m. Cha-Pying Yeh, Sept. 26, 1964; children: David, Benjamin. MD, Nat. Taiwan U., 1962. Diplomate Am. Bd. Radiology. Rotating intern U. Alberta Hosp., Edmonton, Canada, 1964—65; resident diagnostic radiology Montreal Gen. Hosp. McGill U., Canada, 1969—72, fellow diagnostic ultrasound Montreal Gen. Hosp., 1972—73; mem. active med. staff Soldier's Meml. Hosp., Campbellton, NB, Canada, 1967—69; assoc. Mt. Sinai Sch. Medicine, NYC, 1973—75, asst. prof. radiology, 1976—78, assoc. prof., 1979—86, prof., 1986—. Cons. radiology VA Hosp., Bronx, NY, 1977-87. Author: Radiology of the Adrenals, 1982; contbg. author: Progress in Liver Disease, 1979, Frontiers in Liver Disease, 1981, Ultrasound Annual, 1982, 85, Ultrasound in Urology, 1984, Ultrasonography of the Urinary Tract, 1991, Surgical Management of Urologic Disease, 1991; contbr. articles to med. jour. 2d lt. Armored Corps, Taiwan Army, 1962-63. Fellow Soc. Radiologists in Ultrasound; mem. Am. Inst. Ultrasound in Medicine (sr.), Radiol. Soc. N.Am. (sci. exhibit award 1988-2000), Computerized Radiology Soc., Am. Roentgen Ray Soc. (sci. exhibit award 1988), NY Roentgen Ray Soc. Avocations: painting, sculpting, jogging, movies. Office: Mt Sinai Med Ctr One Gustave L Levy Pl New York NY 10029-6574 Business E-Mail: hsu-chong.yeh@mountsinai.org.

YEH, MEI-LING, nursing educator, researcher, consultant; m. Hsing-Hsia Chen. PhD, U. Md., Balt., 1996, China Acad. Traditional Chinese Medicine, Beijing, 2005. Cert. in Traditional Chinese Medicine WHO, 2004; RN Taiwan, 1987, Md., 1995. RN Nat. Taiwan U. Hosp., Taipei, 1987—89; rsch. asst. U. Md., Balt., 1992—96; assoc. prof. Nat. Taipei Coll. Nursing, 1997—2004, prof., 2005—, dir. grad. inst., 2001—04. Recipient Excellent Rsch. award, Nat. Sci. Coun., 1997; grantee, 1997—2000, 2001—05, Com. Traditional Chinese Medicine and Pharmacy, Dept. Health, Exec. Yuan, 2003—04. Fellow: Taiwan Nursing Assn.; mem.: Formosan Med. Assn., Sigma Theta Tau (grantee Internat., Pi Chpt. 1995). Achievements include research in critical thinking and computer-assistant-instruction. Office: National Taipei Coll Nursing 365 Mingte Rd Peitou 112 Taipei 112 Taiwan Office Fax: 886-2-28212374. Business E-Mail: meiling@ntcn.edu.tw.

YEH, MING-LUN, pediatric surgeon; b. Tainan, Taiwan, Dec. 22, 1947; s. Tso-Shueh and Ai-Lien (Yen) Y.; m. Ya-Chuan Hu, Feb. 2, 1976; children: Jessica, Jeff. MD, Nat. Taiwan U., Taipei, 1974. Attending surgeon Mackay Meml. Hosp., Taipei, 1980-82, chief of pediat. surgery, 1983-90; fellow pediat. surgery Johns Hopkins U., Balt., 1982-83; chief pediat. surgery Shin Kong Hosp., Taipei, 1992—2005, Taipei Med. U. Hosp., 2006—07, E-Da Hosp., Kaohsiung, Taiwan, 2007—. Author: Concise Atlas of Pediatric Surgery, 2004, rev. edit., 2008; contbr. articles to profl. jours. including Asian Jour. Surgery, Jour. Pediat. Surgery, Pediat. Surgery Internat., and World Jour. Pediats. Mem. Taiwan Surg. Assn., Taiwanese Assn. Pediat. Surgs., Pacific Assn. Pediat. Surgeons. Avocation: tennis. Office: E-Da Hosp 1 E-Da Rd Yan-Chao Dist Kaohsiung 824 Taiwan Personal E-mail: alanmyeh@yahoo.com.tw.

YELIGAR, SAMANTHA M., medical researcher; b. Westwood, NJ, May 3, 1982; MS, U. Southern Calif., 2006, PhD, 2009. Rsch. asst. psychology dept. U. Southern Calif., Riverside, 2002—04, rsch. asst. Inst. Genetic Medicine, 2004—06, predoctoral fellow Rsch. Ctr. Alcoholic Liver & Pancreatic Diseases, 2006—09; bioinformatics cons. edn. Riverside Unified Sch. Dist., 2004—05; postdoc. fellow Alcohol & Lung Biology Ctr., Atlanta Va. Med. Ctr. Emory U., 2009—, social com. mem. Office Postdoc. Edn., 2009—. Rsch. asst. DaVita Dialysis Ctr., 2003, Drew U. Medicine and Sci., 2003; health scis. campus chair USC Grad. & Profl. Student Senate, 2005—06; v.p. USC Sch. Medicine Grad. Student Assn., 2007—08. Recipient award, Emory U., Alcohol and Lung Biology Ctr., Order of Arete, U. Southern Calif., Rsch. Ctr. Alcoholic Liver & Pancreatic Diseases award. Mem.: Am. Chem. Soc., Rsch. Soc. Alcoholism, Internat. Soc. Hepatic Sinusoidal Rsch. (Travel award), Soc. Free Radical Biology and Medicine (Travel award), Am. Physiol. Soc. Avocations: photography, kayaking, hiking. Home: 921 Briarvista Way NE Atlanta GA 30329 Personal E-mail: crimsontgress@yahoo.com.

YELLON, ROBERT FORREST, surgeon, medical educator; b. NYC, June 26, 1956; s. Pauline Yellon; m. Keely Ann Cofano, June 24, 2003; children: Jeremy Marc, Nathaniel Benjamin. AB in Biology, Princeton U., NJ, 1978; MD, SUNY Stony Brook, 1986. Diplomate Am. Bd. of Otolaryngolgoy, 1993. Dir. of clin. svcs. dept. otolaryngology Children's Hosp. of Pitts., 1997—; prof. otolaryngology U. Pitts., 2009—. Assoc. editor Laryngoscope Jour. Editor: (textbook) Pediatric Otolaryngology; contbr. articles to profl. jour. Recipient Best Doctors in Am., 2010; named to, 2006—08. Fellow: Am. Soc. of Pediat. Otolaryngology, Am. Acad. of Otolaryngology Head and Neck Surgery; mem.: Triologic Soc., Alpha Omega Alpha. Achievements include microtia surgery, aural atresia surgery, laryngotracheal reconstruction. Office: Children's Hospital of Pittsburgh 3705 5th Ave Pittsburgh PA 15213 also: Dept Pediat Otolarygology 4404 Penn Ave Pittsburgh PA 15224 Office Fax: 412-692-6074; Home Fax: 412-692-6074. E-mail: robert.yellon@chp.edu. *

YEN, CHUAN MIN, medical educator, medical researcher; s. Yen Yu Shan and Chou A. Tsui; m. Wang Ying Hui, Jan. 27, 1978; children: Yen Miao Ju, Yen Chih Ta. B in Pharmacy, Kaohsiung Med. Coll., Taiwan, 1976, M in Pharmacy, 1980; D in Pharmacy, Kaohsiung Med. U., Taiwan, 1988. Lic. Pharmacist Dept. of Health, Exec. Yuan, Taiwan. R.O.C., 1976. Tchg. asst. Kaohsiung Med. U., 1977—80, lectr., 1980—88; fellow Nat. Chiba U., Japan, 1985; assoc. prof. Kaohsiung Med. U., Kaohsiung, 1988—92, prof., 1992—. Dir. of dept. of parasitology Kaohsiung Med. U., Kaohsiung, 1991—; dir. Kaohsiung Med. U., Rsch. Ctr. Tropical Medicine, Kaohsiung, 1992—2004, Kaohsiung Med. U., Lab. Animal Ctr., Kaohsiung, 1996—2005. Translator: (book) Tropical Medicine and Parasitology (in Chinese). Donator Jan-Ai Found., Kaohsiung Med. U. Hosp., Kaohsiung, 2000, Tai Tung Christian Hosp., Taitung, Taiwan, 2005—06, Heng Chun Christian Hosp., Pingtung, Taiwan, 2005—06, Buddhist Compassion Relief Tzu Chi Found. Taiwan, Hualien, 2006. Recipient Outstanding Tchg. award, Ministry Edn., 1993; Rsch. grant, Nat. Sci. Coun., 1990—. Fellow: Formosan Med. Assn., Chinese Soc. Microbiology, Taiwan Soc. Parasitology (coun. mem. 1992—). Avocations: music, reading, chinese chess, mountain climbing, travel. Office: Kaohsiung Med Univ No 100 Shih Chuan 1st Rd Kaohsiung 807 Taiwan Office Fax: 886-7-3218309. Business E-Mail: chmiye@kmu.edu.tw.

YENDAMURI, SAI, medical educator; b. India, Mar. 1, 1974; MBBS, All India Inst. Med. Scis., 1997. Assoc. prof. Roswell Pk. Cancer Inst., 2007—. Office: Elm and Carlton Sts Carlton House R Buffalo NY 14228 Office Fax: 716-845-7692. Business E-Mail: sai.yendamuri@roswellpark.org.

YENIAD, BARIS, ophthalmologist; b. Istanbul, Oct. 17, 1974; MD, Cerrahpasa Faculty Medicine, 1998; degree in Ophthalmology, Istanbul Faculty Medicine, 2004. Cons. dept. ophthalmology Istanbul U., Istanbul Faculty Medicine, 2004—. Avocations: travel, sailing. Office: Ophthalmology Dept Istanbul Faculty Medicine Istanbul Fatih 34390 Turkey E-mail: byeniad@yahoo.com.

YEO, CHANG-YEOL, medical educator; b. Teegu, Republic of Korea, June 20, 1967; BSc, Kyungpook Nat. U., 1989; PhD, Harvard U., 2001. Assoc. prof. Ewha Womans U., 2002—. Office: 52 Ewhayeodae-gil Seodaemun gu Seoul 120-750 Republic of Korea Business E-Mail: cyeo@ewha.ac.kr.

YEO, EUI-JU, biochemist, educator; b. Youngkwang-Gun, Jeonranam-Do, Republic of Korea, Sept. 29, 1960; d. Doo-Shig Yeo and Kyung-Ae Lee; m. Boo-Shig Shin, Aug. 18, 1985; children: Mina Shin, Minseo Shin. Degree, Seoul Nat. U., Republic of Korea, 1982, degree, 1984; PhD, Vanderbilt U., Nashville, Tenn., 1992. Cert. nutritionist Ministry Health Welfare, 1982. Rsch. assoc. Vanderbilt U., 1992—93, Howard Hughes Med. Inst., Nashville, 1993—95; asst. prof. Seoul Nat. U. Sch. Medicine, 1995—98; asst. prof. to dep. dir. Cheju Nat. U., 1998—2001; assoc. prof. Gachon U. Medicine & Sci., Incheon, 2001—06; prof. Gachon U. Medicine Sci., Incheon, Republic of Korea, 2006—. Contbr. articles to jours. Vol. Korean Nat. Red Cross, Sieheung, Gyunggi-Do, 2004; working com. mem. Korean Fedn. Women's Sci. & Tech. Assns., Seoul, 2008—; planning com. mem. Women's Biosci. Forum, Seoul, 2008—08; adv. com. Sieheung Ctr. Devel.Women Resources, Sieheung, Gyunggi-Do, 2004. Recipient The Poster awards, Asia/Oceania Regional Congress Gerontology, 2003, Best Faculty award, Gachon U. Medicine & Sci., 2006; Grad. Rsch. Asst. fellowship, Vanderbilt U., 1988—92, Postdoc. Rsch. fellowship, 1992—93, Rsch. Assoc. fellowship, Howard Hughes Med. Inst., 1993—95, Rsch. grants, Health Tech. Planning & Evaluation Bd., 1995—98, Rsch. fellowship, Seoul Nat. U. Med. Ctr., 1996—98, Cheju Nat. U. Sch. Medicine, 1998—99, Rsch. grant, Health Tech. Planning & Evaluation Bd., 1998—2001, Korea Sci. Engring. Found., 2002—08. Mem.: Korean Soc. Gerontology(Seoul), Korean Soc. Med. Biochemistry and Molecular Biology(Seoul), Korean Soc. Molecular and Cellular Biology(Seoul). Buddhism. Achievements include patents for signals and molecular species involved in senescence; regulation of aging by adenylyl cyclase inhibitors. Avocations: travel, movies, music, violin. Office: Gachon Univ Medicine & Sci 534-2 Yeonsu 3-dong Yeonsu-gu Incheon 406-799 Republic of Korea Home: Cheong-Gu Apt 103-504 Daeya-Dong 429-717 Sieheung-Si Gyeonggi-do Republic of Korea Office Phone: 82-32-820-4742. Office Fax: 82-32-820-4744. Business E-Mail: euiju@gachon.ac.kr.

YEO, JAE CHEON, health facility administrator, consultant; b. Chun Cheon, Gangwon-Do, Republic of Korea, Oct. 16, 1962; s. Yong Hwan Yeo and Young Hui Park; m. Hyun Ju Park, Nov. 2, 1991; children: Chung Hyun, Ji Hyun. BS in Chem. Engring., Chungang U., Seoul, 1985; postgrad., Yonsei U., Seoul, 2004. Rank-holding judo expert Korea Judo Assn., 1984. Bur. dir. Korea Drug Rsch. Assn., Seoul, 1989—, prin. cons., 2000—, editor, 2001—. Expert advisor for pharm. devel. Health and Med. Devel. Spl. Com., Seoul, 2001; expert advisor MOST, Seoul, 2002—03, MOCIE, Seoul, 2005—, tech. planning com., 2004; rschr. KIPO, Seoul, 2005—; expert advisor KRIBB, Seoul, 2005—; inspection com. for new drug devel. fund Ministry Health and Welfare, Seoul, 2000—01; advisor Korea Health Industry Devel. Inst., Ministry Health and Welfare, Seoul, 2004—; ctrl. pharmacist inspection com. Advisor For New Drug R & D, Seoul, 2004—; tech. planning com. Ministry of Commerce, Industry and Energy Indsl., Seoul, 2005. Deacon, choir mem. Chungrangri Ch., Seoul, 1962—2005. Recipient Individual award 4th Indsl. Cooperation Conv., Fedn. Korea Industries, 2001, Commr. prize, Korea Food and Drug Adminstrn., 2003, Ministry prize, Ministry Health and Welfare, 2003, Ministry Commerce, Industry and Energy, 2006. Avocations: mountain climbing, music, travel. Home: 360-11 Namgaja-2dong Seodaemoon-Gu Seoul 120-807 Republic of Korea Office: Korea Drug Research Assn 474-15 Bangbae-Dong Seocho-Gu Seoul 137-060 Republic of Korea Office Fax: 02-525-3109; Home Fax: 02-525-3109. Personal E-mail: jcyeoid@naver.com. Business E-Mail: jcyeo@kdra.or.kr.

YEO, SEUNG-GU, oncologist, educator; b. Nonsan, Republic of Korea, Oct. 6, 1973; s. Unho Yeo and Deoksun Yoo; m. Min-Jeong Kim, May 22, 2005; children: Kyeong Seo, Eun Seo. PhD in Medicine Radiation Oncology, Chungnam Nat. U., 2011. Lic. med. physician 2003, in radiation oncology 2008. Clin. fellow Radiation Oncology Proton Therapy Ctr., Nat. Cancer Ctr., 2008; clin. lectr. Radiation Oncology Inje U. Sanggye Paik Hosp., 2009; instr. Radiation Oncology Soonchunhyang U. Coll. Medicine, 2010—. Contbr. articles to profl. jours. Recipient Academic award, Korean Rsch. Found. Oncology, 2009, Boryung Academic award, Korean Assn. Clin. Oncology, 2011. Mem.: Korean Assn. Clinical Oncology, Korean Cancer Assn., Korean Soc. Therapeutic Radiology and Oncology, Korean Med. Assn. Home: 101-407 Hyundai Apt Gwiin-dong Anyang-si Gyeonggi-do 431-756 Republic of Korea Home Phone: 82-10-5328-6630. Business E-Mail: md6630@daum.net.

YEOM, JIN SUP, orthopedist, educator; s. Dong Ho Yeom and Soon Ok Song; m. Kyung In Woo, Jan. 29, 1988; children: Arim, Eugene. MD, Seoul Nat. U., 1988, MS in Orthopaedic Surgery, 1998, PhD, 2000. Cert. in orthopaedic surgery Ministry Health, Welfare and Family Affairs, South Korea, 1993, ECFMG, 1998. Staff surgeon, dept. orthopedic surgery Kangnam Gen. Hosp., Seoul, 1993—96; asst. prof., dept. orthopedic surgery Gachon Med. Sch., Incheon, Republic of Korea, 1999—2000, Eulji U., Daejeon, Republic of Korea, 2000—03; vis. scholar Cervical Spine Inst., Wash. U. St. Louis, 2006—07; internship Seoul Nat. U. Hosp., Sugnam, Republic of Korea, 1988—89, residence, dept. orthopedic surgery, 1989—93, spine fellow, dept. orthopedic surgery, 1996—97, rsch. fellow, dept. orthopedic surgery, 1998—99, assoc. prof., dept. orthopedic surgery, coll. medicine, 2003—, asst. prof., dept. orthopedic surgery, coll medicine, 2003—. Contbr. articles to numerous profl. jours. Capt. Korean Army, 1993—96. Recipient Basic Sci. Rsch. award, 1997, 2001, Best Clin. Paper award, 1998, 2005, 2008, Poster award, 2005, 2001—02, First Pl. Clin. Poster award, 2006, First Pl. Clin. Paper award, 2006, Best Paper award, 2000, 2002, Paper award, 2004. Mem.: North Am. Spine Soc., Internat. Soc. Computer Assisted Orthopedic Surgery, Asian Soc. Computer Assisted Orthopedic Surgery, Korean Soc. Computer Assisted Orthopedic Surgery, Korean Orthopedic Assn., Korean Soc. Spine Surgery, Korean Orthopedic Rsch. Soc., Korean Orthopedic Cyber Soc., Am. Acad. Orthopedic Surgeons, Korean Soc. Med. and Biol. Engring.

YEOM, TAE-HO, physicist, researcher, educator; b. Eumsung, Chungbuk, Republic of Korea, Jan. 15, 1962; s. Jong-Won Yeom and Byung-Sik Yeom Seok; m. Hyun-Mee Yeom Reu, Feb. 14, 1962; children: Soo-Hye, Jee-Hye, Sang-Heon. BS in Physics, Korea U., Seoul, 1984, MSc in Solid State Physics, 1986, PhD, 1992. Postdoctoral staff dept. applied sci. City U. Hong Kong, 1992—93, postdoctoral staff divsn. electronics and info. Korea Inst. Sci. and Tech., Seoul, 1993—94; full time instr. dept. physics Seonam U., Republic of Korea, 1994—96; from asst. to full prof. dept. physics Cheongju U., Republic of Korea, 1996—. Vis. scientist dept. physics S.W. Inst. for Nationalities, China, 1999; rsch. assoc. prof. dept. physics Brown U., 2004—05; dir. Office Pub. Rels. Cheongin U., 2006—09; dir. Office Planning Cheongju U., 2010—. Contbr. articles to numerous profl. jours. Counselor Chungsamo, Cheongju, 2002—03. Recipient Young Scientist award, 1995. Mem.: Am. Phys. Soc., Korean Magnetic Resonance Soc., Korean Magnetic Soc., Groupment Ampere, Internat. Soc. Magnetic Resonance, Internat. Electron Paramagnetic Resonance/Electron Spin Resonance Soc., Korean Phys. Soc. Achievements include patents in field. Home: Woosong Apt 501-708 Seocho 2-dong Seo 137-072 Republic of Korea Office: Cheongju Univ 36 Naedok-dong Sangdang-gu Chungbuk Cheongju 360-764 Republic of Korea Office Fax: +82-43-229-8432. E-mail: thyeom@cju.ac.kr.

YEOMAN, LYNN CHALMERS, medical educator; b. Evanston, Ill., May 17, 1943; m. Carol J. Yeoman; children: Caroline, Christopher, Sarah. BA, DePauw U., Greencastle, 1965; PhD, U. Ill., Urbana, 1970. Instr. Baylor Coll. Medicine, Houston, 1972-73, asst. prof., 1973-76, assoc. prof., 1976-84, prof., 1984—; assoc. dir. Bristol-Baylor Lab, Houston, 1989-90; assoc. dir. anti-cancer drug discovery and cell and molecular biology Bristol-Myers Co., Wallingford, Conn., 1989—90; dir. curriculum database program Baylor Coll. Medicine, Houston, 1995—, dir. integrated problem solving program, 1997—, dir. ednl. resource ctr., 2009—, sr. dir. acad. computing, 2004—; owner Yeoman Consulting Svc., 2008—. Cons. Litton Bionetics, Ft. Detrick, Md., 1977-78, Colon Cancer Working Group, Houston, 1985-86, Oncos, Ltd., Houston, 1985-87, Bristol-Myers Co., Wallingford, Conn., 1985-89, Ubiquitex Tech. Corp., 1995-96, U. Tex. Med. Br., Galveston, 1998, ProteEx, Inc., 2001-03, Feedback Tech., Inc., 2004-09; mem. com. revision U.S. Pharmacopeial Conv., 1985-90, 1995—, chmn. expert com. on biols. and biotech.: proteins and polysaccharides, 2000—10, com. of experts exec. com., 2004—08, chmn. content devel. task force, CATCHUM Project, Galveston, 2004-08. Editor: Methods in Cancer Research, Vols. 19 and 20, 1982; mem. editl. bd. Frontiers in Biosci., rev. edit., Med. Edn. Online; contbr. articles to profl. jours. V.p. Marilyn Estates Assn., Houston, 2004-05; bd. mem. Baylor Coll. Medicine Fed. Credit Union, 2007-, vice chair, Baylor Coll. Medicine Fed. Credit Union, 2008-, chair, Assets & Liabilites Oversight Com., 2008-, Friends Houston Acad. Medicine-Tex. Med. Ctr. Libr. Bd., 2007-, treas. Friends of the HAM-TMC Libr. 2010-, bd.dir. Friends of the HAM-TMC Libr.; mem. cmty. outreach adv. com., Chapelwood UMC Foundation, 2009-. NCI grantee, 1987-2003. Mem. Group on Ednl. Affairs and Security Workgroup, AAMC Group on Info. Resources (security working group 2010-). Methodist. Achievements include patent for detection of antigen gp650 in sera and other specimens from cancer patients with anti-gp650 monoclonal antibody. Home: 5434 Rutherglenn Dr Houston TX 77096-4032 Office: 1 Baylor Plz Houston TX 77030-3411 Office Phone: 713-798-7336. Business E-Mail: lyeoman@bcm.edu.

YERGLER, WILLARD G., orthopedist; Grad., Purdue U.; MD, Ind. U. Sch. Medicine. Resident Ind. U. Med. Ctr.; team physician & dir. sports medicine U. Notre Dame; orthopedic surgeon South Bend Orthopaedic Surgery & Sports Medicine. Fellow: Am. Acad. Orthopaedic Surgeons; mem.: Am. Orthopaedic Soc. for Sports Medicine. Office: 53880 Carmichael Dr South Bend IN 46635 Office Phone: 574-247-9441.

YEUM, KYUNG-JIN, nutritionist; b. Republic of Korea, Jan. 24, 1964; PhD, Yonsei U., 1992. Scientist Jean Mayer USDA-Human Nutrition Rsch. Ctr. Aging, 1993—. Mem.: Am. Soc. Nutrition. Office: 711 Washington St Boston MA 02111 Office Fax: 617-556-3344.

YEUN, EUNJA, nursing educator, director; b. Incheon metro-city, Republic Of Korea, Sept. 4, 1956; d. Bockman Yeun and Heewhan Kim; m. Hanbeom Lee, Oct. 20, 1985; children: Haeri Lee, Haechan Lee. BSN, Chungang U., Seoul, 1979, MSN, 1981, PhD, 1995; postgrad., Case Western Res. U., Ohio, 2004. RN Ministry Health & Welfare, 1979, cert. health educator, Ministry Edn. & Human Resource Devel., 1979; child care tchr. Ministry Gender Equality and Family, 2006. Head nurse Chungang U. Hosp., Seoul, 1982—85, don, 1986—93; vis. observer sch. nursing U. Calif., San Francisco, 1995; dean, asst. prof., dept. nursing Konkuk U., Chungju, 1996—2001, assoc. prof., dept. nursing, 2001—06; vis. prof. FPB Sch. of Nursing, Case Western Res. U., Ohio, 2003—04; prof., dept. nursing Konkuk U., Seoul, 2006—, dean Coll. Biomed. & Health Sci., 2009—11. Com. Nat. Health Pers. Licensing Exam. Bd., Seoul, 2002. Author: (books) Medical-Surgical Nursing I, II, 6th.edit., 2010, Medical-Surgical Nursing I, II.III, 2007, Adult Nursing I, II, 2nd edit., 2006, Management of Elder Care I, II, Essentials of Clinical Nursing, 2003, Emergency Nursing, 2002, Adult Nursing Practice, 2001, Adult Nursing I, II, 2002, Introduction to Nursing, 2000, Qualitative Research Terminology Dictionary, 2003, Health and Safety Control in Infancy, 2002, Gerontological Nursing, 2008, (exhibition) The experience of Middle-aged women with Sauna, 2002, A study about desiring sexual and masturbation in married women, 2002, The experience of Smoking behavior in high school girls, Effectiveness of Video-Record Method of Fundamental Nursing Skill Education, A study on the health promoting lifestyle practices of middle-aged women in Korea, 2000, How People Understand Death: A co-orientational look, 1997, A Study on the Professional Nursing Image of Nursing Unit Manager: A Q-methodological approach, 1996, Attitudes of Elderly Korean Patients Toward Death and Dying, 2005, Verification of the Profile of Mood States-Brief: Cross Cultural Analysis, 2006, Application of the Transtheoretical Model to Identify Aspects Influencing Condom Use Among Korean Coll., 2008, Psychometric Testing of the Depressive Cognition Scale in Korean Adults, 2011, Cross-cultural Gelotophobia Study, Attitude Toward Life Sustaining Treatment in Korean Adults, 2011; contbr. numberous articles to profl. jours. Com. Policy devel. for Women, Chungju, Republic of Korea, 1997—2002; pub. health com. Pub. Health Coun., Chungju, 1998—2003; acad.advisor Aeorsinsarang, Seoul, 2004—. Rsch. grant, Konkuk U., 1996—97, 2004—05, 2008—, Study grant, Pacific Scholarship & Culture Found., 1998—99, 2001—02. Mem.: Applied Nursing Rsch. (reviewer 2011—), Korea Soc. Health Edn. and Promotion, Korean Soc. Sci. Study of Subjectivity, Korean Acad. of Adult Nursing Soc. (acad. com. 1998—2000, editor 2002—, editor-in-chief 2010—), Korean Acad. of Nursing Soc., Korean Nurse Assn. (academic com. edn. 1997—2000). Catholic. Achievements include development of an instrument to measure nursing professional values. Avocations: yoga, travel, mountain climbing, oil painting. Home: 787 Jayang-dong Kwangin-gu Seoul 143-882 Republic of Korea Office: Konkuk Univ Dept Nursing 322 Danwol-dong Chungju 380-701 Republic of Korea Office Fax: 82-43-840-3929. Business E-Mail: eunice@kku.ac.kr.

YEUNG, CECIL S.T., plastic surgeon; Grad., U. of Toronto, Med. Sch. U. Toronto. Intern Toronto Gen. Hosp.; resident otolaryngology head & neck surgery Univ. of Toronto; fellow head & neck plastic & microvascular reconstructive surgery Washington Univ.; asst. prof. otolaryngology Univ. of Texas Health Sci. Ctr., 1986—90, clin. asst. prof. otolaryngology, 1991; mem. ent collaborative com. St. Luke's Episcopal Hosp., 1996—; mem. msrdp quality assurance com. Univ. of Texas. Recipient Scholastic award, 1987, Residents award, 1987; grantee Biomedical Research Support grant. Mem.: ACS, Harris County Med. Assn., Texas Med. Assn., Am. Assn. of Advance Sci., Am. Acad. of Otolaryngology, Am. Acad. of Facial & Reconstructive Surgery. Office: Yeung Institute 1103 Banks St Houston TX 77006 Office Phone: 713-795-4885.

YEUNG, VICTOR HIP WO, surgeon, researcher; BA in Biophysics, Johns Hopkins U., Baltimore, MD, 2001; MBBS in Surgery, U. Hong Kong, 2006. Surgeon Queen Elizabeth Hosp., Hong Kong, 2006—. Mem.: Royal Coll. Surgeons, Edinburg, Johns Hopkins U. Hong Kong Alumni Assn. (pres. 2008). Achievements include research in thoracic actinomycosis in an adolescent mimicking chest wall tumor or pulmonary tuberculosis; computed tomographic appearance of Prolene Hernia System and polypropylene mesh plug inguinal hernia repair.

YEW, DAVID, physician, director; b. NYC, Oct. 5, 1970; MD, SUNY, 1996—99. Cert. Am. Bd. Emergency Medicine, 2003. Emergency medicine physician St. Luke's-Roosevelt Hosp., Columbia U., NYC, 1999—2001, Kaiser Permamente, Honolulu, 2002—03, Tripler Army Med. Ctr., Honolulu, 2003—; ship dr. Norwegian Cruise Line, Honolulu, 2005—; med. dir. AirMed Hawaii, Honolulu, 2006—. Disaster medicine physician Dept. Homeland Security FEMA/DMAT, Honolulu, 2003—; mcht. mariner US Coast Guard, Honolulu, 2004—; asst. clin. prof. dept. surgery U. Hawaii Med. Sch., Honolulu, 2005—. Contbr. chapters to books. Recipient Outstanding Staff Tchr. award/Jeffrey P. Kavolius award, Tripler Army Med. Ctr., 2005. Mem.: Fed. Physicians Assn. (assoc.), Air Med. Physicians Assn. (assoc.), Mensa (life). Achievements include development of virtual simulation education. Office: AirMed Hawaii 90 Nakolo Pl Ste 203 Honolulu HI 96817 Personal E-mail: yewdave@hotmail.com. Business E-Mail: dyew@airmed.com.

YEW HOONG, CHEAH, biomedical researcher, consultant; s. Lee Ah Fong; life ptnr. Chew Geok Chin. BS, Nat. U. Malaysia, Bangi, Selangor, 2004, MS, PhD student, Nat. U. Malaysia, Bangi, Selangor, 2007—. Rsch. officer Inst. Med. Rsch., Kuala Lumpur, 2004—. Cons. Insight Synergy Sdn. Bhd., Selangor, 2004—08, Caryn Personal Care Sdn. Bhd., Kuala Lumpur, Malaysia, 2005—09. Contbr. articles to profl. jours. Grantee, Ministry of Health Malaysia. Achievements include discovery of xanthorrhizol and combination with curcumin as potential antiproliferative agent for breast cancer cells, involved in animal study for antitumor, antimetastatic and toxicology investigation. Office: Inst Med Rsch Jalan Pahang 53000 Kuala Lumpur Malaysia Office Phone: 603 26162633, 60122350527. Personal E-mail: yhcheah@gmail.com.

YI, DONNA, psychiatrist, educator; MD, Meharry Med. Coll., 1983. Diplomate Am. Bd. Psychiatry and Neurology-psychiatry, 1989, Am. Bd. Psychiatry and Neurology-addiction psychiatry, 2004, lic. Tex., 2000. Resident psychiatry LA County - Univ. South Calif. Med. Ctr., 1984—86; resident addiction psychiatry UCLA Neuropsychiatric Inst, 1986—87; faculty Cornell Univ., Univ. South Calif., Baylor Univ.; dir. profl. assessments Menninger Clinic, assoc. chief of staff, eating disorders program med. dir.; psychiatrist Donna Yi MD PA, Houston. Office: Donna Yi MD PA Ste 950 2323 South Shepherd Dr Houston TX 77019 Office Phone: 832-900-2548. Office Fax: 832-582-8656.

YI, HYEONG-JOONG, medical educator; b. Busan, Republic Of Korea, Dec. 11, 1966; s. Young-Ja Choi and Eung-Cheol Yi; m. Eun-Sil Yoo, Jan. 16, 1994; 1 child, Jang-Hoon. MS, Hanyang U. Med. Coll., Seoul, Republic Of Korea, 2001, MD, PhD, Hanyang U. Med. Coll., Seoul, Republic Of Korea. Lic. in med. Ministry Health & Welfare, 1991. Residency neurosurgery Hanyang U. Med. Ctr., Seoul, 1991—96, fellowship neurosurgery, 1999—2001; instr. Hanyang U. Med. Coll., Seoul, 2001—02, asst. prof., 2002—05, assoc. prof., 2005—, chair person stroke inst., 2006—. Capt. 20th Inf. Divsn. Korean Army, 1996—99, Yangpyeong. Recipient Red-Ribbon award, 2003. Mem.: Korean Neurosurgical Soc. (Ann. Clin. Achievement 2007). Roman Catholic. Achievements include research in animal experiment for stroke. Office: Hanyang Univ Med Ctr Neurosurgery Dept Haengdang-dong Sungdong-gu Seoul 133-792 Republic of Korea Office Fax: 82-2-2281-0954. Business E-Mail: hjyi8499@hanyang.ac.kr.

YI, LEE S. H., educator; b. Seoul, Republic of Korea, July 29, 1957; BS, Seoul Nat. U., 1980; PhD, U. Ill., 1988. Prof. Sungkyunkwan U., Suwon, Republic of Korea, 1993—. Mem.: Soc. for the Study of Reproduction. Business E-Mail: shlee@yurim.skku.ac.kr.

YI, PING, engineering educator; b. Luoyang, Henan, July 13, 1969; PhD, Fudan U., 2005. Prof. Shanghai Jiao Tong U., 2005—. Mem.: IEEE. Avocation: badminton. Home: 101 Zhong Cao Rd Shanghai 200030 China Personal E-mail: yiping01@163.com.

YI, YOUNG-JOO, animal scientist; b. Daejeon, Republic of Korea, Nov. 25, 1975; PhD, Chungnam Nat. U., Republic of Korea, 2004. Rsch. prof. Chungnam Nat. U., 2004—08; postdoc. fellow U. Mo., 2004—06, 2008—11. Mem.: Soc. Study Reproduction. Office: University Mo S140 Animal Sci Rsch Ctr 920 E Campus Dr Columbia MO 65211-5300 Office Fax: 573-884-5540. Business E-Mail: yiyo@missouri.edu.

YIANNAKOPOULOS, CHRISTOS, orthopedist; b. Sparta, Greece, Oct. 6, 1967; s. Konstantinos Yiannakopoulos and Georgia Mavrogiannea; m. Athanasia Sokka, Dec. 15, 2002. MD, U. Athens, Greece, 1991. Orthop. surgeon Mayday U. Hosp., London, 2002—03; dir. Iaso Gen. Hosp., Athens. Contbr. articles to profl. jours. Capt. M.C., 1992—94. John Insall Travelling fellowship, Knee Soc., 2005. Achievements include patents pending for surgical techniques. Home: Byzantiou 2 Athens 17121 Greece Office: Evinou7 Athens 11525 Greece Business E-Mail: cky@ath.forthnet.gr.

YIELDING, K. LEMONE, physician; b. Auburn, Ala., Mar. 25, 1931; s. Riley Lafayette and Bertie (Dees) Y.; m. Lerena Wade Hauge, Dec. 8, 1973; children: K. Lemone, Michael Lafon, Teresa Louise, Riley Lafayette, Katrina Elizabeth, Elaine Louise Blodgett, Laura Carlen Blodgett. BS, Ala. Poly. Inst., 1949; MS, U. Ala., 1952, MD, 1954. Intern U. Ala. Med. Center, 1954-55; clin. assoc. Nat. Inst. Arthritis and Metabolic Diseases, NIH, 1955-57, sr. investigator, 1958-64; resident med. service USPHS Hosp., Balt., 1957-58; physician in practice of oncology and emergency medicine, 1995—. Adj. asst. prof. medicine Georgetown U. Med. Sch., 1958-64; cons. USPHS, 1964-68, 75—; prof. biochemistry, assoc. prof. medicine, chief lab. molecular biology U. Ala. Med. Ctr., Birmingham, 1964-80; prof., chmn. dept. anatomy, prof. medicine U. So. Ala. Coll. Medicine, Mobile, 1980-87; dean grad. sch. U. Tex. Med. Br., Galveston, 1987-95, dean emeritus, 1995—, v.p. for rsch., 1987-94; cons. Am. Heart Assn., Arthritis Found., NIH, NASA, EPA, FDA, NIOSH. Contbr. to profl. jours., books. Served with USPHS, 1955-64. Grantee USPHS, Am. Cancer Soc., Nat. Found.-March of Dimes, U.S. Army, Am. Inst. Cancer Research. Mem. Am. Soc. Biol. Chemistry, Am. Assn. Cancer Research, Am. Assn. Photobiology, Assn. Research Vision and Ophthalmology, Soc. Exptl. Biology and Medicine, Am. Soc. Pharm. and Exptl. Therapeutics, Am. Assn. Pathologists, So. Soc. Clin. Investigation, Am. Assn. Anatomy, Soc. Toxicology, Sigma Xi. Personal E-mail: lemoneyielding@hughes.net.

YIH, BONG-SOOK, nursing educator; b. Phychang Gun, Republic of Korea, July 19, 1972; d. Sang-Gue Yih and Gak-Soon Park. BSN, Latrobe U., Melbourne, 1999; MSN, LaTrobe U., Melbourne, Australia, 2001; PhD, Seoul Nat. U., 2007. Cert. nurse, Min. Health and Welfare Korea, 1993. Rschr. Rsch. Inst. Nursing Sci., Seoul Nat. U., Republic of Korea, 2004—06; lectr. Songgok Coll., Kangwon-do, Republic of Korea, 2006—09, chmn., nursing dept.; asst. prof., chmn. Daebul U., Jeonnam, Republic of Korea, 2009—. Contbr. articles to profl. jours. Cons. Youngam-Gun Health Ctr., Jeonnam, 2009—. Dementia grant, Korea Rsch. Found., 2005, Multicultural rsch. grant, Songgok Coll., 2008, Daebul U., 2010. Mem.: Korea Nurse Assn., Korean Soc. Nursing Sci. Buddhst. Achievements include research in methodological expansion in nursing using a narrative study method from sociology and humanities. Avocations: travel, writing, walking. Office: DaeBul University Sanho-Ri Samho-Up 72 526-702 Youngam-gun Jeollanam-do Republic of Korea Office Phone: 82-61-469-1309. Office Fax: 82-61-469-1317. Business E-Mail: yihjunga@naver.com, yihb@db.ac.kr.

YIH, WONHO, education educator; b. Gongjoo, Republic of Korea, Jan. 10, 1955; s. Nam Gyu Yih and Jae Shim Lim; m. Jee Eun Choi, Sept. 29, 1984; children: Jung Woo, Jo Eun. PhD, Seoul Nat. U., Republic of Korea, 1985. Prof. Kunsan Nat. U., Jeonbook, Republic of Korea, 1986—; rsch. assoc. Smithsonian Environ. Rsch. Ctr., Edgewater, Md., 2002—. Dir. Coastal Rsch. Ctr. Kunsan Nat. U., Jeonbook, Republic of Korea, 1993—95, dir. Red Tide Rsch. Ctr., 2000—02, v.p. for academic affairs, 2003—05; vis. rsch. scientist U. Miami, Fla., 1990—91. Contbr. articles to profl. jours. Program dir. Nat. Rsch. Lab., Kunsan, 2003—08. Sgt. Korean Army, 1979—81. Recipient The Luigi Provasali award, Phsycological Soc. Am.; fellow, Smithonian Instn., 1998—99. Mem.: Phycalogical Soc. America (The Luigi Provasoli award), Internat. Soc. Protistology (corr.), Internat. Soc. Yellow Sea Rsch. (corr.), Japanese Soc. Marine Biotechnology (corr.), Korean Soc. Oceanography (corr. award 2009). Presbyterian. Achievements include research in establishing lab strains of marine Myrionecta and Dinophysis. Home: 13-1003 Garam Apt Samcheon Dong Seo-Gu Daejon Republic of Korea Office: Kunsan Nat Univ San 68 Miryong-Dong 573-701 Kunsan Jeollabuk-do Republic of Korea Office Fax: 82-63-469-4990. Business E-Mail: ywonho@kunsan.ac.kr.

YIIN, LIH-MING, educator; arrived in U.S., 1993; s. Hsiang-Hour Yiin and Suh-Kuei Lee; m. Ming-Chi Lin, Sept. 25, 1997; children: Fan-Shiuan, Fan-Yu. Degree in Chemistry, Nat. Taiwan U., 1989; MS in Environ. Sci., Rutgers U., 1995, PhD, 1999. Rsch. tchg. specialist U. Medicine and Dentistry N.J., Piscataway, 1999—2001, asst. prof. exposure assessment Sch. Pub. Health, 2001—04; assoc. prof. Dept. Public Health Tzu-Chi U., Hualien, Taiwan, 2004—. With Taiwan Mil., 1989—91. Recipient Health Homes and Lead Tech. Studies award, U.S. Dept. Housing and Urban Devel., 2002. Mem.: APHA, AAUP (UMDNJ-Coun. of Chpts.), AAAS, N.J. Pub. Health Assn., Am. Chem. Soc., Internat. Soc. Exposure Analysis (Student award 1997). Office: Tzu Chi U 701 Chung Yang Rd Sec 3 Hualien Taiwan 970 Office Phone: 886-38565301 x7216. Business E-Mail: lmyiin@mail.tcu.edu.tw.

YILDIRIM, YAVUZ SELIM, physician; b. Turkey, Sept. 10, 1980; MD, Istanbul U., 2005. Physician Elbistan State Hosp., 2011—. Mem.: ERS. Home: Yesilyurt Mah Mimars Kahramanmaras Karaelbistan 34300 Turkey Personal E-mail: dryavuzselim@yahoo.com.

YILDIZHAN, AHMET, neurosurgeon, educator; b. Ladik-Samsun, Turkey, Feb. 24, 1956; s. Hasan and Fatma Yildizhan; m. Zeynep Sema Ugur; children: Saliha Elif, Fatma Esra, Abdullah Emir, Fatih Selim. MD, Ankara U., Turkey, 1980. Cert. Neurosurgeon Ministry of Health, 1986. Resident Faculty Medicine Erciyes U., Kayseri, Turkey, 1981—86; founder Dept. Neurosurgery SSK Hosp., Kayseri, Turkey, 1986—88; assoc. prof. Vakif Gureba Hosp., Istanbul, 1989—94; assoc. prof. Merter Vatan Hosp. and Istanbul Vatan Hosp. Universal Hosp. Group, 1994—. Adv. bd. Turkish Jour. Medicine, Ankara, 1994—2004; prin., owner Edn. and Sci. Mag., Istanbul, 1998—; vis. rschr. Harvard U., Cambridge, Mass., 1992; neurosurgeon Gulhane Mil. Med. Acad., Ankara, 1990—91; assoc. prof. Faculty Medicine Yeditepe U., Istanbul, 2003—. Author: Bel Fitigi ve Korunma Yollari, 1997, 2007, Lumbar Disc Herniation and Its Prevention (100 Recommendations for Low Back Health), 2005, 2007, Bilim Egitim ve Kultur Yazilari - Kuresel Problemler Nasil Cozulur? (Science Education and Cultural Essays - How are Global Problems Resolved?), 2007, Mutlulugun Denklemi (Equation of Happiness), 2007, Evrensel Bahceye (Didaktik Siirler) (Didactic Poems for the Universal Garden), 2007; mem. editl. bd.: Medikal Plus Mag., 2002—; contbr. 53 scientific papers in field, over 50 articles to profl. pubs. Mem. Yesilay, Istanbul, 1993; lifetime vol. mem. TEMA; supporter Neurosurgery Rsch. and Edn. Found., Provision for Clean Water in Africa, Engelliler ve Dostlari Kulubu, Campaign for Edn. of Girls in Antolia. Mem.: Turkish Neurosurgical Soc., Soc. Neuro-Oncology, Am. Assn. Neurol. Surgeons, Istanbul Chamber Medicine, Turkish Neurosurg. Soc. (Internat. Pub. award 1989, 1990, 1992), Yesilay, Nat. Geographic Soc. Muslim. Avocations: reading, writing, swimming, travel, thinking. Office Fax: 902122418121. Business E-Mail: ayildizhan@e-kolay.net.

YILMAZ, ISMET, medical educator; b. Malatya, Turkey, Feb. 1, 1965; Degree in Vet. Medicine, Firat U. Faculty Vet. Medicine, 1987. Adj. prof., dept. pharmacology Inonu U. Faculty Pharmacy, 2009—. Avocation: reading. Office: University Kampus Malatya Eastern Anatolia 44280 Turkey Office Fax: 90-04223411217.

YILMAZ, OMER FARUK, ophthalmologist, educator; b. Samsun, Nov. 9, 1949; Degree, Hacettepe U., 1973, degree, 1983. Chief prof. Beyoglu Eye Hosp., 1985—. Mem.: TCOD, TOD, ESCRA, ASCRS, AAO. Avocations: photography, travel, soccer. Office: Valikonagi Cad Akkavak Sok Polat 32 K2 Istanbul 34420 Turkey Office Fax: 0090 212 2404371. E-mail: ofyilmaz@superonline.com.

YIM, HYUNGSHIN, biomedical researcher, pharmacist; b. Kwang Ju, Jeon La Nam Do, Republic Of Korea, Apr. 15, 1972; d. Kwang Nam Yim and Kyung Ja Kim; m. Chun Soo Kim, Jan. 25, 1998; children: Doh Hyun Kim, Seung Hyun Kim. BS, Duksung Women's U., Seoul, Republic of Korea, 1995; MS, Seoul Nat. U., 1997, PhD, 2004. Lic. pharmaceutist Ministry Health and Welfare, Republic of Korea, 1995, cert. oriental medicine pharmaceutist Ministry Health and Welfare, Republic of Korea, 1997. Fellow Seoul Nat. U., Seoul, 2004—06, Harvard U., Cambridge, Mass., 2006—09, Harvard Med. Sch., Boston, 2009—. Reviewer Pharm. Soc. Korea, Seoul, 2005—06; lectr. Sookmyong Women's U., Seoul, 2005—06, Korea Nat. Open U., Seoul, 2005—06. Contbr. articles to profl. jours. Recipient NEBS award, Korean Soc. Molecular & Cellular Biology, Republic of Korea, 2009, Honor Highly Rated Papers, Am. Assn. Cancer Rsch., 2009, DCF award, Harvard U., 2009; Young Scientist fellowship, Ministry Sci. & Tech., Republic of Korea, 2004—05, Postdoc. fellowship, Basic Rsch. Promotion Fund, Korea Rsch. Found., 2006—07. Mem.: Pharm. Soc. Korea, Korean Soc. Biochemistry & Molecular Biology, Korean Soc. Molecular & Cellular Biology, Am. Soc. Microbiology, Am. Assn. Cancer Rsch. Achievements include patents for apoptotic inhibitor of uncleavable Cdc6 mutation protein and apoptotic inducer containing Cdc6 deleted protein. Office: Harvard Med Sch 77 Ave Louis Pasteur NRB-939 Boston MA 02115 Office Fax: 617-432-2689. Business E-Mail: hyim@fas.harvard.edu.

YIM, JIN HO, ophthalmologist, educator; b. Deajeon, Republic of Korea, Oct. 17, 1971; s. Go Bin Yim and Jung Ae Jang; m. Sun Young Song, Feb. 3, 2002; children: Dong Jin, Dong Hyun. Degree in Medicine, Chungnam Nat. U. Coll. Medicine, Deajeon, 2008. Diplomate Korean Bd. Ophthalmology, Ministry Health Welfare, 2003. Intern. Chungnam Nat. U. Hosp., Daejeon, 1998—99, resident ophthalmology, 1999—2003; dr. Jin San Pub. Health Ctr., Chungnam, 2003—04; dir. dept. ophthalmology Hong Seong Med. Ctr., Chungnam, Republic of Korea, 2004—06; fellow glaucoma Samsung Med. Ctr., Seoul, Republic of Korea, 2006—07; asst. prof. Ulsan U. Hosp., Coll. Medicine, Republic of Korea, 2007—. Reviewer Acta Pharmacologica Sinica, China, 2008—. Contbr. articles to jours. Scholar Rsch. fellowship, Taejoon-Santen found., 2008. Mem.: Korean Ophthal. Soc., Korean Med. Assn. (med. dr. ophthalmology 2008), Korea Glaucoma Soc. Achievements include research in glaucoma management. Avocations: travel, golf. Office: Ulsan University Hosp 290-3 Jeonha-Dong Dong-Gu 682-714 Ulsan Republic of Korea Office Phone: 82 52 250 7170. Office Fax: 82 52 250 7174. Business E-Mail: yimjinho@hanmail.net.

YIM, MAN BIN, neurosurgeon, educator; b. Hong Seung, Chung Nam, Republic of Korea, Feb. 29, 1948; s. Byung Soon Yim and Jeung Ok Kang; m. In Sook Kim, Dec. 4, 1974; children: Chang Ok, Chang Baek. PhD, KyungPook Nat. U., Daegu, Republic of Korea, 1988. Lic. med. practitioner Ministry Health and Welfare, Republic of Korea, 1973, cert. Korean Bd. of Neurosurgery, 1981. Instr. Keimyung U. Sch. of Medicine, Daegu, Republic of Korea, 1981—83, asst. prof., 1983—87, assoc. prof., 1988—93, head neurosurgery Dong San Med. Ctr., 1991—99, chmn. neurosurgery, 1993—99, prof. neurosurgery, 1993—; dir. brain rsch. inst. Keimyung U., 2000—05; dean Keimjung U. Sch. Medicine, 2005—. Sec. gen. 5th Japanese and Korean Friendship Conf. on Surgery for Cerebral Stroke, Cheju, Republic of Korea, 1996—99; v.p. 7th Japanese and Korean Friendship Conf. on Surgery for Cerebral Stroke, KyungJu, 2002—; sci. trustee The Korean Soc. of Cerebrovascular Surgery, Seoul, 1996—98, sec. gen., 1998—, mem. arrangement com. 6th internat. workshop, 2000, pres., 2003—04. Author: Text Book of Neurosurgery, contbr. articles to profl. jours. including Jour. Korean Neurosurg. Soc. (Best Sci. Article, Korean Soc. of Cerebrovascular Surgery, 2003, Best Sci. Article, Korean Soc. of Neurosurgery, 2003). Capt. Army, 1973—76, Republic of Korea. Recipient Encouragement award of Han-Mi Essay Lit., The Korean Doctors' Weekly, 2003; named Best Dr. in Cerebrovascular Disease, Shin Dong Ah monthly mag., 1999, Best Dr. in Cerebovascular Disease, Dong Ah Daily News, 2003. Mem.: Korean Neurosurgical Soc. (licentiate; bd. trustees 1995—99, pres. (Daegu and Kyung Pook local chapt.) 1996—97, mem. bd. exam. com. 1996—99, mem. scientific com. 2000—02, bd. trustees 2003—), Korean Med. Assn. (licentiate), World Fedn. of Neurosurgical Societies (assoc.). Avocations: tennis, essay writing. Home: 1502 202 Dong ManChon WooBang 2 Cha Ap Daegu 706-759 Republic of Korea Office: Keimyung Univ Neurosurgery Dongsan Dong Jung-Gu 194 700-712 Daegu Daegu Republic of Korea Office Fax: 82-53-250-7356. Business E-Mail: y760111@dsmc.or.kr.

YIM, SOO JAE, orthopedist, educator; b. Seoul, Republic of Korea, Sept. 27, 1961; s. Jongho Yim and Gayoung Lee; m. Mi Yeon Lee, Mar. 3, 1992; children: Seojin, Taehyung. MD, Soonchunhyang U., Seoul, 1998. Orthop. surgeon Soonchunhyang U. Hosp., Seoul, 1995—2008, mem. joint ctr., 1995—2008, mem. joint replacement, 2000; prof. Soonchunhyang U., 1995—. Sec. gen. Korean Orthop. Soc., Seoul, Republic Of Korea, 2004—08. Contbr. to profl. jour. Presbyter Herin Presbyn. Ch., Seoul, 2003—08. Capt. Capital Def. Divisional Hdqs., 1992—95, Seoul. Presbyterian. Achievements include research in ceramic property. Home: Mokdong Apt 234-106 Seoul 158-056 Republic of Korea Office: Soonchunhyang Univ Hosp Dept Os Jungdong 1174 420-020 Bucheon-Si Republic of Korea Office Fax: 82-32-621-5018. Business E-Mail: yimsj@chol.com.

YIN, CHANGSHIK, physician, educator, researcher; 1 child. MD in Korean Med. Sci., Kyung Hee U., Seoul, 1996, PhD, 2004. Cert. Korean physician Ministry Health and Welfare, 1996, applied kinesiology practitioner Internat. Coll. Applied Kinesiology, 2003, specialist physician in acupuncture medicine Ministry of Health and Welfare, 2005; neurology specialist Am. Coll. Functional Neurology, 2009. Resident Kyung Hee U. Hosp., Seoul, 2002—05; clin. prof. dept. applied kinesiology Temporomandibular Joint and Bee Venom Acupuncture Clinic, CHA Biomed. Ctr. Coll. Medicine, CHA U., Seoul, 2005—07; asst. prof. Acupuncture and Meridian Ctr., Kyung Hee U., Seoul, 2007—; functional neurologist Am. Coll. Functional Neurology FACFN, 2009; assoc. prof. Kyung Hee U., 2011—. Author: Veterinary Acupuncture in Oriental Medicine, 1999, Bee Venom Acupuncture Therapy, 2003, The Origin of Acupuncture Medicine, 2004; translator: The Rediscovery of Traditional Chinese Medicine - Mawangdui books on Medicine, 2000, DNA and I-Ching, 2002, Applied Kinesiology - Synopsis 2d ed., 2002, The Origin of Huangdineijing, 2003, Acupuncture Manipulation, 2004, Maffetone Method, 2004, Syndrome X, 2006; contbr. articles to profl. jours. Fellow: Am. Coll. Functional Neurology; mem.: Soc. Functional Cerebrospinal Therapy Instructor, Soc. Clin. Rsch. Bee Venom Acupuncture Therapy (instr.), Korean Acupuncture and Moxibustion Soc. (life), Internat. Coll. Applied Kinesiology. Achievements include research in functional neurology, bee venom acupuncture therapy; functional cerebrospinal therapy TMJ therapy; applied kinesiology; acupuncture and meridian. Office: Acupuncture and Meridian Sci Rsch Ctr Kyung Hee U 1 Hoegi-dong Dongdaemun-gu Seoul 130-701 Republic of Korea Business E-Mail: acuyin@paran.com.

YIN, CHUN, mathematics professor; b. Nanchong, Apr. 17, 1986; Attending, UESTC, 2011—. Educator UESTC, 2008—. Office: UESTC Chengdu Sichuan 611731 China Business E-Mail: yinchun.86416@163.com.

YIN, HUIYONG, medical educator, researcher; b. China, Dec. 31, 1968; PhD, Vanderbilt U., 2002. Assoc. prof., rschr. Vanderbilt Sch. Medicine, 2008—11. Dir., drug metabolism and pharmacokinetics Vanderbilt Program Drug Discovery, 2007—10. Recipient Young Investigator award, Soc. Free Radicals in Biology and Medicine. Mem.: Soc. Free Radicals in Biology and Medicine, Am. Chem. Soc. Achievements include research in lipid metabolism of human disease including cardiovascular diseases and neurodegenerative diseases. Avocations: tennis, ping pong/table tennis, travel. Home: 1132 Pin Oak Ln Brentwood TN 37027 Personal E-mail: huiyong.yin@vanderbilt.edu.

YIN, KAISHENG, pulmonologist; b. Chongqing, Apr. 16, 1946; Degree in Medicine, Nanfjing Med. Coll., 1969; MD, Nanfjing Med. U., 1983. Dir. Respiratory Assn. Jiangsu Med. Assn., 2003—10; mem. standing com. Respiratory Assn. Chinese Med. Assn., 2000—. Mem. bd. dirs. dept. respiratory medicine Jiangsu Province Hosp., 1992—2009. Recipient Chinese Physician award, Chinese Physician Assn., award, Chinese Respiratory Medicine Assn., Spl. Subsidy award, Sate Coun. China, 1st prize, Jiangsu, China. Fellow: Am. Coll. Chest Physicians. Avocation: gemology. Office: 300# Guangzhou Rd Nangjing Jiangsu 210029 China Office Fax: 025-83718836.

YIN, TOM CHI TIEN, neuroscientist, educator; b. Kunming, China, Jan. 7, 1945; BS in Engring., Princeton U., 1966; PhD, U. Mich., 1973. Postdoc. fellow Johns Hopkins U., 1974—77; prof., chair, dept. neurosci. U. Wis., 1977—. Dir. Neurosci. Tng. Program, 2006—11. Recipient Chancellor's Disting. Tchg. award, U. Wis. Tchg. Awards Com. Avocations: bicycling, sports. Office: University Wis Dept Neuroscience 290 Medical Sci Bldg Madison WI 53706 Office Fax: 608-265-5512. Business E-Mail: tcyin@wisc.edu.

YIN, WAY, physician, director; b. Apr. 1, 1961; MD, Coll. Physicians & Surgeons, Columbia U., 1987. Med. dir. Bellingham Spine Pain Specialists PC, 2000—. Pres. Internat. Spine Intervention Soc, 2009—11. Office: 2075 Barkley Blvd Ste 110 Bellingham WA 98226 Office Fax: 360-527-8115. Business E-Mail: wyin@nospinepain.com.

YING-FANG, YANG, research scientist; b. Taiwan, June 26, 1967; PhD, Nat. Hsing Hua U., 2009. Rschr. Biomed. Tech. and Device Rsch. Lab, Indsl. Tech. Rsch. Inst., 1998. Office: B53 R737 195-85 Chung-Hsin Rd Sec 4 Chutung HsinChu 310 Taiwan Business E-Mail: yingfang_yang@itri.org.tw.

YIOU, ERIC, physical education educator; b. Chevreuse, Aug. 6, 1971. Bachelor, Courcelles U., 1991, PhD, U. Paris 11, Orsay, Ile De France, 2001. Asst. prof. scis. and techniques phys. and sporting activities UFR-U. Paris sud 11, Orsay, 2002—. Avocations: tai chi, travel. Office: G Clémenceau Orsay Ile De France 91 405 France Personal E-mail: eric.yiou@u-psud.fr.

YIP, MICHAEL C. W., psycholinguist; BA, U. Hong Kong, 1995; MPhil, Chinese U. Hong Kong, 1997, PhD, 2000. Assoc. prof. Hong Kong Inst. Edn. Office Phone: 852-29488992. Business E-Mail: mcwyip@ied.edu.hk.

YITONG, MA, cardiologist, director; b. Hangzhou, Xinjiang Autonomous Region, China, Jan. 2, 1961; married. BS, Xinjiang Med. U., Urumqi, Xinjiang Autonomous Region, 1983, MS, 1990, PhD, 1996. Dir., heart ctr. 1st affiliated hosp. Xin Jiang Med. U., 1999—, dir., cardiac pacing and interventional treatment ctr., 1999—, dir., internal medicine dept., 2002—, dir., cardiovasc. disease, 2003—. Recipient 2nd Class Sci. and Tech. Progress award, Xinjiang, 2003, 2004, 3rd Class Sci. and Tech. Progress award, 2006, Outstanding Expert award, Autonomous Region Xinjiang, 2007. Mem.: Cardiovasc. Chinese Med. Assoc. (chinese med. assoc.). Communist. Avocations: tennis, badminton. Office: Xinjiang Med Univ NO8 Xinyi Rd Urumqi Xinjiang Autonomous Region 830054 China Office Phone: 86-0991-4362611. Office Fax: 86-0991-4365330. Business E-Mail: mytxj@163.com.

YLITALO, PAULI, pharmacologist, toxicologist and educator; b. Lavia, Finland, Apr. 27, 1944; s. Heikki and Saima (Kesti) Y.; m. Liisa Holma, 1966; 1 child, Ritva. MD, U. Helsinki, Finland, 1970, PhD, 1973, Docent in Pharmacology, 1975; Docent in Clin. Pharmacology, U. Tampere, Finland, 1986. Rsch. assoc. U. Helsinki, 1970-72, U. Heidelberg, Germany, 1973-74; chief asst. U. Tampere, 1974-82, prof. clin. pharmacology, 1992—2005, dir. Med. Sch., 2001—04; prof. toxicology U. Kuopio, Finland, 1983-92; specialist physician Tampere U. Hosp., 1980-83, head physician in clin. pharmacology, 1992—2005, prof. emeritus, 2005—. Editor Clin. Pharmacology, 1994, The Century of Healthcare, 1998, Clinical Pharmacology and Drug Treatment, 2002, 30-year War of Medical Faculty, 2003, Proceedings of 10th Int Congress Toxicology, 2005, Internat. Edit Bd. Brit. Jour. Clin. Pharmacol 2005-; contbr. articles to profl. jours. Grantee Acad. of Finland, 1986-91, Ministry of Def. of Finland, 1986-91. Mem. Finnish Soc. Clin. Pharmacology (pres. 2000-02), Finnish Med. Soc. (bd. dirs. 1999-2001), Tampere Med. Soc. (hon)(sec.-gen. 1980-81, v.p. 1996-97, pres. 1998-99), Finnish Soc. Toxicology (hon)(v.p. 1988-89, pres. 1990-91), Finnish Pharmacol. Soc. (v.p. 1989-93, pres. 1994-97), Solemn Confirment of Acad. Degrees U. Tampere (head officer 1982, chief marshall 1992). Sanitary captain, Finland Army. Office: Univ Tampere Medical Sch 33014 Tampere Finland Office Phone: 358-500-830822. Personal E-mail: pauli.ylitalo@fimnet.fi.

YODAIKEN, RALPH E., pathologist, occupational health physician, educator; b. Johannesburg, Aug. 22, 1928; arrived in US, 1964, naturalized, 1970; m. Naomi Baumslag Yodaiken; children: Victor, Barry D., Ruth T. MD, U. Witwatersrand, Republic of South Africa, 1956; MPH, Johns Hopkins U., 1976. Diplomate Am. Bd. Pathology, Am. Bd. Forensic Medicine. Intern Coronation Hosp., Johannesburg, 1956-57; resident U. Witwatersrand Med. Ctr., 1957-58, Johannesburg Gen. Hosp., 1958; assoc. pathologist Buffalo Gen. Hosp., 1965-67; mem. staff Cin. Gen. Hosp., 1968-71; rsch. assoc. Johns Hopkins U. Sch. Hygiene and Pub. Health, Balt., 1976—; sr. staff mem. Nat. Inst. Occupational Safety and Health, Washington, 1977—, chmn. sr. adv. staff, 1983; dir. office occupational medicine Occupational Safety and Health Adminstrn., U.S. Dept. Labor, Washington, 1983-91, sr. med. advisor, 1991—98; clin. prof. preventive medicine U. Health Scis., Washington, 1983—. Lectr. U. Witwatersrand, 1958-63; asst. prof. pathology, SUNY Buffalo, 1963-67; assoc. prof. pathology U. Cin., 1968-71; prof. pathology, assoc. prof. medicine Emory U., Atlanta, 1971-75; adj. clin. prof. George Washington U., 1975—; sr. assoc. Johns Hopkins Sch. Hygiene and Pub. Health; clin. prof. preventive medicine uniformed svcs. U. Health Scis. Bd. mem. Am. Jewish Com.; ret. bd. mem. Bradley Blvd. Citizens Assn., 1994—2006. With Israeli Commandos Israeli Army, 1948—50. Mem. Coll. Am. Pathologists. Democrat. Jewish. Office Phone: 301-728-4041.

YODER, MARY JANE WARWICK, psychotherapist; b. Corryton, Tenn., Nov. 20, 1933; d. Harry Alonzo and Mary Luzelle (Furches) Warwick; m. Edwin Milton Yoder, Jr., Nov. 1, 1958; children: Anne Daphne, Edwin Warwick. BA, U. N.C., Chapel Hill, 1956; MFA, U. N.C., Greensboro, 1969; MSW, Va. Commonwealth U., 1987; cert. individual psychotherapy, Smith Coll., 1991. Lic. clin. social worker, Va. Editorial asst. Harper & Bros., NYC, 1956-57; flight attendant Pan Am. Airlines, NYC, 1957-59; adj. faculty mem. in ballet Guilford Coll., Greensboro, 1961-64; ballet tchr., adminstr. Jane Yoder Sch. of Ballet, Greensboro, 1964-75; homilitics listener Va. Theol. Sem., Alexandria, 1978-80; social worker, dance therapist Woodbine Nursing Ctr., Alexandria, 1983-87; staff psychotherapist D.C. Inst. Mental Health, 1987-92; pvt. practice Capitol Hill Ctr. Individual and Family Therapy, 1992—2009. Ballet and book critic Greensboro Daily News, 1961-75. Dancer, choreographer Greensboro Civic Ballet, 1961-75. Mem. Nat. Assn. Social Workers, Greater Washington Soc. for Clin. Social Work, Inc., Washington Sch. Psychiatry, Washington Soc. for Jungian Psychology, Jungian Venture, Army-Navy Country Club, Phi Beta Kappa. Episcopalian. Avocations: ballet, modern dance, horseback riding, swimming, reading. Office: 4001 Harris Pl Alexandria VA 22304 Office Phone: 703-751-7836, 703-751-7836. Personal E-mail: yoder100@comcast.net.

YODER-WISE, PATRICIA SNYDER, nursing educator; d. Belford Grant and Leona Cora (Mohler) Snyder; m. Robert Thomas Wise, Feb. 17, 1973; children: Doreen Ellen Wise, Deborah Ann Wise. BSN, Ohio State U., 1963; MSN, Wayne State U., 1968; EdD, Tex. Tech. U., 1984. RN Tex., CNAA-BC. Interim assoc. dean practice program Tex. Tech. U. Health Sci. Ctr. Sch. Nursing, Lubbock, 1979—, interim dean, prof., 1991-93, dean, prof., 1993-2000; clin. prof. U. Tex. Health Sci. Ctr., San Antonio, 1993—2000; prof. Tex. Woman's U., 2004—. Mem. rev. panel Nursing Outlook, 1993—; mem. adv. com. GlaxoWellcome, 1996—2000; mem. Nat. Quality Forum Health Profls. Provide and Health Plans Panel, 2001—06. Author, editor: Leading and Managing in Nursing, 1994 (Book of Yr. award, 1996, 2003), 1998, 2002; co-author: Beyond Leading and Managing, 2006 (Book of Yr. award, 2007); peer reviewer Jour. Profl. Nursing, 1984—2003, mem. editl. bd. Jour. Continuing Edn. Nursing, 1978—; editor: Jour. Continuing Edn. Nursing, 1988—2007; editor-in-chief Jour. Continuing Edn. Nursing, 2008—. Mem. Leadership Am., 1999—2000; participant Leadership Tex.-Found. Women's Resources, 1997—98, mem. Leadership Tex., 1998—99. Recipient Women of Excellence in Medicine, YWCA, Lubbock, 1996, Woman of Excellence in Medicine, 1996, Nurse of Yr. Fellow: Acad. Nursing Edn. (treasurer 2007—), Am. Acad. Nursing (chair Inst. for Nursing Leadership 1999—2002, mem. planning com. 2004); mem.: ANCC (pres. 2005—07), ANA (del. 1995—2000, chair constituent assembly 1998—2000, sec. 2000—02, 1st v.p. 2002—05), Wise Group (pres.), Tex. Nurses Assn. (pres. 1995—99). Home: 7309 93d St Lubbock TX 79424 Office Phone: 806-559-5957, 806-790-4600. Personal E-mail: psywrn@aol.com.

YOGEV, SARA, psychologist; b. Tel Aviv, May 23, 1946; came to U.S., 1975; d. Israel and Cila (Fink) Frankel; m. Ram Yogev, Oct. 2, 1967; children: Eldad, Shelly, Tomer. BA, Hebrew U., 1969, MA, 1973; PhD, Northwestern U., Evanston, Ill., 1979. Cert. clin. psychologist, Ill. Clin. experience dist. sch. psychologist Office Edn. and Culture, Jerusalem, 1968-71; intern. Beer Yaakov Psychiatric Hosp., Israel, 1971-72; asst. dir. Dept. Psychology, Hebrew U., Jerusalem, 1972-73; psychotherapist Mental Health Ctr., Hebrew U., Jerusalem; clin. psychologist Inst. Psychoanalysis, Jerusalem, 1973-75; psychotherapist, supr. Youth and Family Services, Ill., 1977-80; pvt. practice Skokie and Chgo., 1981—. Academic experience instr. counseling psychology, 1977-79, asst. prof., Northwestern U., 1979-82, research psychologist at the rank asst. prof., 1983-86, visiting scholar, Ctr. Urban Affairs and Policy Research, 1987. Author: For Better or Worse But Not for Lunch: Making Your Marriage Work in Retirement, 2001; contbr. articles to profl. jours., chpts. to books Mem. American Assn. for Marriage and Family Therapy, American Psyhological Assn., Nat. Register Health Service. Jewish. Office: # 32 5225 Old Orchard Rd Skokie IL 60077-1027 also: 500 1 East Superior St Chicago IL 60611 also: 719 Milhigan Ave Evanston IL 60202 Office Phone: 847-470-1925. Business E-Mail: sarayogev@yahoo.com.

YOHANNES, ABEBAW MENGISTU, physical therapist, educator; b. Addis Ababa, Ethiopia, July 20, 1964; arrived in England, 1991; s. Hailu and Beletech Yohannes. Diploma in Physiotherapy, Evelyn Hone Coll., Lusaka, Zambia, 1988; MSc in Geriat. Medicine, U. Manchester, Eng., 1997, PhD in Geriat. Medicine, 2002. Physiotherapist Malawi Against Polio, Blantyre, Malawi, 1988—91; lectr. Manchester Sch. Physiotherapy, 1991—2003; sr. lectr. physiotherapy Manchester Met. U., 2003—. Rsch. fellow Manchester Sch. Physiotherapy, 1999—2001; reader in physiotherapy Manchester Me. U., 2007; presenter in field. Contbr. over 30 articles to profl. jours. Mem. parish coun. Holy Trinity Platt Ch., Manchester, 2004—07. Recipient Exemplary Rsch. award, Manchester Met. U., 2004. Mem.: Chartered Soc. Physiotherapy (licentiate). Labor. Achievements include design of the Manchester respiratory activities of daily living scale. Avocations: tennis, squash, travel, swimming, hiking. Home: 34 Monica Grove Manchester M19 2BN England Office: Manchester Met Univ Elizabeth Gaskell Campus Hathersage Road M13 0JA Manchester England Home Phone: 44 165 220 9053. Office Fax: 441612475671. Business E-Mail: a.yohannes@mmu.ac.uk.

YOHN, DAVID STEWART, virologist, retired science administrator; b. Shelby, Ohio, June 7, 1929; s. Joseph Van and Agnes (Tryon) Y.; m. Olivetta Kathleen McCoy, June 11, 1950; children: Linda Jean, Kathleen Ann, Joseph John, David McCoy, Kristine Renee (dec.). BS, Otterbein Coll., 1951; MS, Ohio State U., 1953, PhD, 1957; M.P.H., U. Pitts., 1960. Research fellow, scholar in microbiology Ohio State U., Columbus, 1952-56, prof. virology Coll. Veterinary Medicine, 1969-95, prof. emeritus, 1995—, dir. Comprehensive Cancer Ctr., 1973-88, dep. dir. Comprehensive Cancer Ctr., 1988-94, dir. emeritus Comprehensive Cancer Ctr., 1994—. Research assoc., asst. prof. microbiology U. Pitts., 1956-62; assoc. cancer research scientist Roswell Park Meml. Inst., Buffalo, 1962-69; mem. nat. med. and sci. adv. com. Leukemia Soc. Am., 1970-91, trustee, 1971-91; pres. Ohio Cancer Research Assocs., 1982—2008; mem. cancer research centers rev. com. Nat. Cancer Inst., 1972-77 Pres. bd. deacons North Presbyn. Ch., Williamsburg, N.Y., 1967-68. Recipient Pub. Service award Lions, 1968; named to Shelby H.S. Hall of Distinction, 2005, Outstanding Alumnus award, 2011. Mem. Am. Assn. Cancer Rsch., Am. Soc. Microbiology, Am. Assn. Immunologists, Internat. Assn. Comparative Rsch. on Leukemia and Related Diseases (sec.-gen. 1974-95), Ohio Valley-Lake Erie Assn. Cancer Ctrs. (sec. 1978-95), Sertoma (pres. 1992-93, chmn. bd. dirs. 1993-94, Dist. Sertoman of Yr. award 1987).

YOJI, NEISHI, cardiologist, researcher; b. Hiroshima, Japan, Aug. 31, 1971; s. Iwaji and Naoko Neishi; m. Masami Sawada, Oct. 11, 1999; children: Sho Neishi, Hinano Neishi. MD, Kawasaki Med. Sch., Kurashiki, Japan, 2005. Resident in internal medicine Kawasaki Med. Sch., Kurashiki, Japan, 1996—98, cardiologist, 1998—2000, Kojima Ctrl. Hosp., Kurashiki, 2005—. Rschr. Kawasaki Med. Sch., Kurashiki, 2000—05. Avocations: travel, tennis, baseball. Office: Kawasaki Med Sch 577 Matsushima Kurashiki 701-0192 Japan E-mail: neishi@med.kawasaki-m.ac.jp.

YOKOE, KIYOSHI, orthopedist, surgeon; b. Nagoya, Japan, Sept. 27, 1948; s. Masaaki and Shigeko Yokoe; married, June 15, 1980. MD, Nagoya U., Japan, 1974. Cert. orthopaedic surgeon Japanese Orthopaedic Assn., sports doctor Japan Amateur Athletic Fedn. Intern Nagoya Ekisaikai Hosp., 1974, staff, 1975—76, Mamamatsu Med. Ctr., 1976—79; fellow Pa. State U., Coll. Sta., Pa., 1979; mem. staff Kanto Rosai Hosp., Kawasaki, Japan, 1980—87; chief rschr. Inst. Sports Medicine and Sci., Aichi, Japan, 1987—98, dir., 1998—. Author: Running Injury, 1988. Mem.: Japanese Amateur Athletic Fedn. (mem. med. com.), Japanese Soc. Clin. Sports Medicine (councilor), Japanese Orthopaedic Soc. Sports Medicine (councilor). Avocations: jogging, mountain climbing. Office: Inst Sports Medicine and Science Agui 4702212 Japan Office Phone: 81-569-48-7266. Business E-Mail: yokoe@sorc.or.jp.

YOKOTANI, KUNIHIKO, pharmacologist, educator; b. Himeji, Japan, Aug. 24, 1947; s. Kaoru and Shigeko Yokotani; m. Keiko Okuda Yokotani, Jan. 9, 1984; children: Reiko, Mayuko. MD, Nagasaki U., Japan, 1972; PhD, Kyoto U., Japan, 1983. Resident dept. surgery Kyoto U., Kyoto, 1972—73; sr. resident dept. surgery Himeji Nat. Hosp., Hyogo, 1973—79; asst. prof. Kochi Med. Sch., Kochi; rsch. investigator gastroenterology internal medicine U. Mich., Ann Arbor, Mich., 1989—91; assoc. prof. dept. pharmacology Kochi Med. Sch., Kochi, Japan, 1995—99; prof. Kochi Med. Sch., 1999—. Avocation: reading. Home: Midori-ga-oka 2-2013 Nankoku 783-0086 Japan Office: Kochi Med Sch Nankoku Kochi 783-8505 Japan Office Phone: +81-88-880-2328. Business E-Mail: yokotani@med.kochi-u.ac.jp.

YOKOYAMA, TOSHIRO, biomedical engineer; b. Japan, Nov. 17, 1963; PhD, Kurume U. Sch. Medicine, 2005. With, dept. pathology Kurume U. Hosp., 1987—96, sub-chief engr., 1997—2003, chief engr., 2004—06, Kurume U. Med. ctr., 2007—. Exec. sec., info. com. Japanese Soc. Cytotechnologists' Fukuoka, 2004—. Rsch. grant, JST Japan Sci. & Tech. Agy. Mem.: Japanese Soc. Clin. Cytology, Internat. Acad. Cytology. Office: Kokubu 155-1 Kurume Fukuoka 839-0863 Japan Office Fax: 81-942-22-6533. Business E-Mail: ykymat@med.kurume-u.ac.jp.

YOKOYAMA, WAYNE MAKOTO, medical educator, researcher, rheumatologist; b. Wailuku Maui, Hawaii, July 1, 1952; BA, U. Rochester, NY, 1974; MD, U. Hawaii JA Burns Sch. Medicine, Honolulu, 1978. Cert. Internal Medicine, Rheumatology. Intern, internal medicine U. Iowa Hosp., Iowa City, 1978—79, resident, internal medicine, 1979—81, fellow, clin. rheumatology, 1982, fellow, rsch. rheumatology, 1982—85; fellow, rsch. immunology Nat. Inst. Allergy and Infectious Diseases/NIH, Bethesda, Md., 1985—89; asst. prof. medicine and rheumatology U. Calif., San Francisco, 1989—92; assoc. prof. medicine and microbiology Mt. Sinai Med. Sch., NYC, 1992—95; Sam and Audrey Loew Levin chair for rsch. in arthritis Wash. U. Sch. Medicine, St. Louis, 1995—, chief, rheumatology, divsn. dept. medicine, 1995—2007, prof. medicine and pathology and immunology, dir., Ctr. for Arthritis and Related Diseases, 1996—2007, dir., med. scientist tng. program. Assoc. investigator Howard Hughes Med. Inst., 1994—95, investigator, 1997—; mem. editl. bd. Immunity, Internat. Immunology, Immunogenetics. Contbr. articles to profl. jours.; mem. adv. bd. Immunity, assoc. editor Ann. Rev. Immunol, reviewer of severel peer-reviewed jours. Recipient Novartis prize for basic immunology, 2001. Mem.: NAS, Am. Acad. Arts & Sciences, Am. Soc. Clin. Investigation, Assn. Am. Physicians, Am. Acad. Microbiology. Address: Wash U Sch Medicine Dept Medicine 10058 Clinical Sciences Research Bldg Saint Louis MO 63110 Mailing: Wash U Sch Medicine Divsn Rheumatology Campus Box 8045 666 S Euclid Ave Campus Box 8045 Saint Louis MO 63110 Office Phone: 314-362-9075. Office Fax: 314-362-9257. Business E-Mail: yokoyama@dom.wustl.edu.

YOKOZAWA, TOSHIHARU, researcher; b. Japan, Sept. 13, 1976; PhD in Sports Scis., U. Tsukuba, 2005. Rschr. Japan Inst. Sports Scis., 2006—. Office: 3-15-1 Nishigaoka Kita-ku Tokyo 115-0056 Japan Office Fax: 81-3-5963-0232. Business E-Mail: yokozawa.toshiharu@jiss.naash.go.jp.

YOM, SUE SUN, physician; d. Syng Sup and Byong Hee Lee Yom. BA, Rice U., 1991; MD, PhD, U. Pa., 2002. Cert. EMT Tex., 1992, US med. lic. 2002, Am. Bd. Radiology, 2008. Resident physician MD Anderson Cancer Ctr., Houston, 2002—07; asst. prof. U. Calif. San Francisco, 2007—. Recipient Eleanor Montague Disting. Resident award, 2006; named one of Best Drs. in America, 2009—; Nat. Merit scholar, Nat. Merit Found., 1987, Mellon Humanities fellow, Andrew W. Mellon Found., 1992, Andrew W. Mellon Dissertation fellow, 1998. Mem.: Internat. Assn. Study Lung Cancer (internat. sci. com. 2010—), Radiation Therapy Oncology Group (health svcs. rsch. outcomes com. 2009—), Am. Radium Soc. (ednl. resources com. 2010—), Am. Soc. Therapeutic Radiation Oncologists (emerging tech. com. 2007—), Am. Coll. Radiology (appropriateness criteria expert panel 2009—), Am. Soc. Clin. Oncology. Office: University Calif San Francisco Dept Radiation Oncology 1600 Divisadero St Ste H 1031 San Francisco CA 94143-1708 Home Phone: 415-672-5959; Office Phone: 415-353-7175. Personal E-mail: suesunyom@gmail.com.

YOM, YOUNG-HEE, nursing educator; d. Bong Yong Yom and Oh Kab Kang; m. Kyung Hee Han, Dec. 17, 1980; children: Dong Kyu Han, Min Kyu Han. BSN, Korea U., Seoul, 1976; MPH, Seoul Nat. U., 1982; MS, Adelphi U., NY, 1992; PhD, U. Iowa, Iowa City, 1995. Registered nurse, Ministry Health, Welfare & Family Affairs, Seoul, 1976. Staff nurse Korea U. Hosp., Seoul, 1976—77; sch. nurse Shinil HS, Seoul, 1977—83; lectr. Dongnam Jr. Coll., Suwon, Republic of Korea, 1983—85; assoc. prof. Hallym U., Chunchon, Kangwon, Republic of Korea, 1997—2004; prof. Chung Ang U., Seoul, 2004—. Com., bd. rsch. Korean Nurses Polit. Soc., Seoul, 2003—06, com. bd.; pres. Korean Acad. Nursing Adminstrn., Seoul, 2004—05, v.p., 2002—03, reviewer, 2000—, auditor, 2006—07; exec. bd. Korean Soc. Health Info. & Health Stats., Seoul, 2007—, reviewer, 2007—; com., bd. edn. Korean Soc. Med. Informatics, Seoul, 2002—, reviewer, 2008—, Korean Acad. Nursing Sci., Seoul, 2000—06; com., bd. policy Korean Nurses Assn., Seoul, 2006—07; com. bd., licensing exam. nurse Nat. Health Personal Licensing Exam. Bd., Seoul, 2003—05; exec. bd. mem. Kangwon Nurses Soc., Chunchon, 2004. Translator: (transl.) Proceedings of NI 2006. Com. Dongjak-Gu, Seoul, 2004—08; advisor, sign lang. group Hallym U., Chunchon, 1998—2004. Recipient Course Ware Devel., Hallym U., 2000, Superior Achievement, U. Iowa, 1995; grantee Rsch. Grant, Hallym U., 1997, 2000, 2001, Korean Rsch. Found., 2002, 2003, 2008, Chung Ang U., 2005, 2007, Nat. Health Personal Licensing Exam. Bd., 2004, Ministery Edn., Republic of Korea, 2000. Mem.: Korean Nurses Assn., Korean Soc. Med. Informatics, Korean Acad. Fundamental Nursing, Korean Acad. Cmty. Nursing, Korean Acad. Adult Nursing, Korean Acad. Nursing Adminstrn., Korean Soc. Nursing Sci., Sigma Theta Tau Internat. Achievements include research in translation and validation of nursing interventions classification; review of minimum data sets and standardized nursing classifications; validation of the NIC taxonomy structure; development of effect analysis of an internet based nursing program: application to nursing informatics; research in analysis of nursing interventions performed by chosunjok nurses; effects on health information education for the deaf; knowledge, experience and attitude of nurses toward complementary and alternative therapies; comparison of disease-related knowledge between hearing impaired and normal hearing persons; empowerment experience of hospital nurses using focus group; evolution of theory development in nursing administration; korean older adults perception of the aging progress; development of standardized and competency based curriculum in nursing informatics. Avocations: jogging, reading, painting. Office: Dept Nursing Chung-Ang Univ 221 Heukseok-Dong Donjak-Gu Seoul 156-756 Republic of Korea Home Phone: 82-2-6279-9310; Office Phone: 82-2-820-5700. Office Fax: 82-2-824-7961. Business E-Mail: yhyom@cau.ac.kr.

YONEI, YOSHIKAZU, gastroenterologist; b. Tokyo, Jan. 18, 1958; s. Hidekazu and Chieko (Nakada) Y.; m. Keiko Nakatani, Dec. 15, 1985; children: Shoichiro, Lisa. MD, Keio U., Tokyo, 1982, PhD, 1986. Vis. rschr. Ctr. for Ulcer Rsch., LA, 1986-89; attending physician Nippon Kokan Hosp., Kawasaki, Japan, 1989—2005; prof. Anti-Aging Rsch. Ctr. Doshisha U., Kyoto, 2005—. Sec. gen. Japan Anti-Aging Soc., Tokyo, 2002-. Co-author: Mast Cell, 1990. Named Hon. Citizen Botucatu City, Sao Paulo, Brazil, 1981. Mem. Keio Sakura Reunion (pres. 1992—), Sympathy for H. Pylori Assn. (pres. 1999—), Keio Med. Sch. Yacht Club (bd. dirs. 1993-98). Avocation: sailing. Office: Doshisha Univ 1-3 Miyakodani Tatara Kyotanabe-shi Kyoto 610-0394 Japan Office Phone: 81-774-65-6394. Business E-Mail: yyonei@mail.doshisha.ac.jp.

YONG, YANG, epidemiologist, researcher; b. China, May 10, 1965; Degree in Medicine, Shanxi Med. U., 1986; PhD, Nat. U. Singapore, 2007. Epidemiologist Singapore Gen. Hosp., 2006—. Office: Outram Rd Singapore 169608 Singapore Office Fax: 65-663234370. Business E-Mail: yang.yong@sgh.com.sg.

YONGBO, LAI, engineering educator; b. Anhui, China., Sept. 30, 1975; MS, Jiangnan U., 2007. Lectr. Dept. Electric Engring., 2007. Office: 1 Qian Ou Lu Wuxi Jiangsu 214153 China Business E-Mail: lyb2004vip@163.com.

YONG-DAE, KWON, dental educator; b. Seoul, Republic of Korea, June 25, 1971; DMD, Kyung Hee U., 1996, PhD, 2006. Chief oral surgeon ROK Navy Med. Command, 2000—03; clin. instr. Kyung Hee U. Med. Ctr., 2004—05; clin. rschr. Johannes Gutenberg U. Mainz, 2005—06; asst. prof. Kyung Hee U. Sch. Dentistry, 2007—10, assoc. prof., 2011—. Rsch. grant, Osteology Found., 2011. Fellow: Korean Assn. Oral & Maxillofacial Implants, Internat. Team Implantology (Rsch. grant); mem.: Korean Soc. Bone Metabolism, Korean Assn. Oral & Maxillofacial Surgeons, Korean Assn. Maxillofacial Plastic Reconstructive Surgeons. Office: Kyung Hee University Sch Dentistry Hoegi-dong 1 Dongdaemun-ku Seoul 130701 Republic of Korea Office Fax: 82-2-966-4572. Business E-Mail: kwony@khu.ac.kr.

YONKER, RICHARD AARON, rheumatologist; b. Phila., Aug. 8, 1952; BA, George Washington U., 1974; DO, Des Moines U. Coll. Osteopathic Medicine, 1978. Diplomate Am. Bd. Internal Medicine, Am. Bd. Rheumatology. Rheumatologist Sarasota (Fla.) Arthritis Ctr., 1984—. Fellow Am. Coll. Rheumatology; mem. Am. Osteopathic Assn., Fla. Osteopathic Med. Assn., Fla. Rheumatology Soc. Office: Sarasota Arthritis Ctr 3500 S Tamiami Trl Sarasota FL 34239-6026 Home Phone: 941-922-0177; Office Phone: 941-365-0770. Personal E-mail: pandryonker@comcast.net.

YOO, BONG GOO, medical educator; b. Ulsan, Republic Of Korea, Apr. 18, 1967; s. Byung Lae Yoo and Duk Soon Jung; m. Soo Jeong Son, July 6, 1996; 1 child, Na Young. MD, Kosin U., Busan, South Korea, 1992; MS, Kosin U., 1997, PhD, 2003. Lic. South Korea, 1992, in neurology South Korea, 1997, cert. geriatrics specialist Korean Geriatric Soc., 2003. Intern Kosin U., Gospel Hosp., 1992, resident, 1993—97; chief resident Kosin U. Hosp., 1993—96; chief neurology Mil. Masan Hosp., Republic of Korea, 1998—2000; clin. fellow Kosin U. Hosp., 2000—01; instr. Kosin U. Coll. Medicine, 2001—03, asst. prof., 2003—07, assoc. prof., 2007—, dir. dept. neurology, 2010—; postdoc dept. neurology U. Calif. San Francisco, 2008—09. Dir. dept. neurology Kosin U. Coll. Medicine, 2004—05; dir. dept. quality improvement Kosin U. Hosp., 2007—; postdoc. fellow U. Calif. San Francisco, 2008—09. Contbr. articles to profl. jours. Internet health cons. Busan IIbo; mem. med. svc. com. Podowon Ch., Busan, 2001. Capt. Korean Army, 1997—2000, Wonju, Masan. Recipient Exellent Investigator Award, 2006, Dir. award, Masan Hosp., Excellent Paper award, Korean Dementia Assn., 2008; named Excellent Army Physician, 2000; grantee Rsch. grants, Kosin U., 2001—05, Yansen Pharms., 2004—05, Rsch. grant, Eisai Pharms., 2006, Norvatis Pharms., 2007. Mem.: Korean Neurocritical Care Soc. (dir. spl. com. 2008), Busan-Kyengnam Stroke Assn. (dir. fin. com. 2005—08), Busan-Kyeongnam Dementia Assn. (dir. planning com. 2005—), Korean Stroke Soc., Korean Geriatric Soc., Korean Neurol. Assn. (mem. planning com. 2006—08), European Stroke Conf., World Stroke Soc., Am. Stroke Assn. Avocations: travel, golf. Office: Kosin Univ Coll Medicine 34 Amnam-dong Seo-gu Busan 602-702 Republic of Korea Home Phone: 82519906364; Office Phone: 82519906461. Office Fax: 82 51 990 3077. Business E-Mail: ybgne@ns.kosinmed.or.kr, ybg99@naver.com.

YOO, CHEOL-IN, medical researcher; b. Pusan, Republic of Korea, Nov. 4, 1962; s. Jong-Tae Yoo and Bok-Nam Lee; m. So-Young Jang, Sept. 9, 1990; children: Jung-Min, Jung-Won, Seung-Min. SM, Pusan Nat. U., Republic Of Korea, 1989, MD, 1987, PhD, 1993. Diplomate Korean Bd. Preventive Medicine, 1991, Korea Bd. Occupl. and Environ. Medicine, 1996. Prof. Ulsan U. Hosp., Republic of Korea, 1997—. Voting membership Internatinal Assn. of Cancer Registries, Lyon, 2002—; dir. Ulsan Cancer Registry, Ulsan, Republic Of Korea, 2004—, Ulsan Assn. Smoking and Health, 2005—; vis. prof. U. Calif., Davis, 2003—04; chmn. dept. occupational and environ. medicine Ulsan U. Hosp., Republic of Korea, 2008—. Health cons. Ulsan Met. City, 2005—. Office: Ulsan U Hosp 290-3 Jeonha-Dong Dong-Gu 682-060 Ulsan Republic of Korea Office Phone: 82-52-250-8819. Office Fax: 82-52-250-7289. Business E-Mail: ciyoo62@hanmail.net.

YOO, HWA-SEUNG, oncologist, educator; b. Seoul, Republic of Korea, Feb. 20, 1971; m. Yeon-Yee Kang, Apr. 2, 2000; children: Hye-Won, Jun-Ho, Sung-Ho. MD, PhD, Daejeon U. Oriental Med. Sch., Republic of Korea. Lic. MD Korea Ministry Health and Welfare, 1998, cert. internal medicine Korea Ministry Health and Welfare, 2003, OM cert. NCCAOM, 2008. V.p. East-West Cancer Ctr., Daejeon, 2003—; prof. Daejeon U. Oriental Med. Sch., 2005—. Faculty mem. Korean Phamacopuncture Inst., Seoul, 2003—, Assn Korean Oriental Oncology, Seoul, 2003—; irb dir. Daejeon U. Dunsan Oriental Hosp., 2005—; rschr. Nat. Cancer Inst. Author: (book) Evidence Based Medicine for Korean Oriental Oncology, The Benefit of Korean Oriental Cancer Therapy; contbr. chapters to books. Grantee, Korean Ministry Health and Welfare, 2005. Mem.: Assn. Korean Pharmacopuncture Inst., Soc. Integrative Oncology, Assn. Korean Oriental Oncology. Buddhist. Achievements include research in mechanism of Hang-Am-Dan for cancer; mechanism of cultured wild ginseng pharmacopuncture for cancer. Home: 201 1804 Smart City Apt Doryong-dong Yusung-gu Daejeon 305-340 Republic of Korea Office: Daejeon Univ/Dunsan Oriental Hosp East-West Cancer Ctr Dunsan-Dong Seo-Gu 1136 302-122 Daejeon Republic of Korea Office Fax: 82424709006.

YOO, JIN-SAN, medical researcher, consultant; b. Seoul, Republic of Korea, Apr. 12, 1963; s. Seong-Soo Yoo and Shin-Ja Cho; m. Hyeon-Mi You, Sept. 10, 1987; 1 child, Alfred Francis. Diploma, Georg-August U., 1990, diploma in Biology, 1991, Dr. Rer. Nat, 1996. Rsch. fellow Howard Hughes Med. Inst., Stanford U. Med. Ctr., Palo Alto, Calif., 1996—98; sr. rsch. assoc. Scripps Rsch. Inst., La Jolla, Calif., 1998—2001; head, therapeutic antibody divsn. LG Life Scis. Rsch. Inst., Yuseong Gu, Daejeon, Republic of Korea, 2001—. Bd. mem. Korean Antibody Rsch. Assn., Seoul, Republic of Korea, 2002—. Contbr. articles to profl. jours. in field. Evaluator rsch. grant proposal Korean Govt., Seoul, 2004—. Fellow Cystic Fibrosis Rsch. fellowship, Novartis; grant, Korean Ministry of Health and Welfare, 2004—, fellowship, Howard Hughes Med. Inst., Max Planck Soc., Goettingen Protestant Student fellowship. Mem.: Therapeutic Antibody Devel. Assn. R&D Spl. Pk., Immunology Assn. Korea, Am. Assn. Cancer Rsch. Achievements include development of therapeutic antibody for cancer treament in preclinical study; patents in field. Home: Expo Apt 410 1004 Jeonmin Dong Daejeon Yuseong Gu 305 380 Republic of Korea Office: LG Life Sciences Research Inst 1 Moonji Dong Daejeon 104 305-380 Yuseong Gu Daejeon Republic of Korea Office Fax: 82-42-861-2566; Home Fax: 82-42-861-2566. Personal E-mail: wincancer@gmail.com. Business E-Mail: yoojs@lgls.co.kr.

YOO, JINYOUNG, pathologist, educator; b. Seoul, Republic of Korea, Jan. 22, 1956; MD, Ewha Women's U., 1980; PhD, Cath. U., 1996. Prof. Cath. U. Sch. Medicine, 1993—, chief in pathology, St. Vincent Hosp., 2004—. Recipient Excellent Achievement award, Cath. U., 2001, 2003. Mem.: Internat. Assn. Pathology, Korean Soc. Pathology (Academic award 2003, 2006). Avocation: travel. Office: Catholic University Saint Vincent Hosp Suwon Gyeonggi 442-723 Republic of Korea Office Fax: 8231-244-6786. Business E-Mail: jinyyoo@catholic.ac.kr.

YOO, JUNHWAN, medical researcher; b. Seoul, June 13, 1976; M in Gastroenterology, Ajou U. Sch. Medicine, 2007. Epidemiologic investigation svc. officer Divsn. Pub. Health Policy, Incheon Met. City Hall, Incheon, Republic of Korea, 2008—09; gastroenterologist, therapeutic endoscopist Ajou U., Sch. Medicine. Office: Ajou University Sch Medicine Dept Gastroenterology 164 Worldcup-ro Yoengtong-gu Suwon Kyunggi 443-721 Republic of Korea Office Fax: 031-219-5999. Business E-Mail: dubogi@hanmail.net.

YOO, JUN-HYUN, physician, educator; s. Chae-Ha Yoo and Jong-Bun Jeon; m. Tae-Sook Yoo, May 2, 1987; 1 child, Hyo-Kyung. MD, Seoul Nat. U., 1983, PhD cum laude, 1997. Resident Seoul Nat. U. Hosp., 1983—86, fellow, 1988—89; asst. prof. Hallym U. Coll. Medicine, Seoul, 1990—94; dept. chair Kangdang Sacred Heart Hosp., Seoul, 1990—94, Samsung Med. Ctr., Seoul, 1995—2001; assoc. prof. Sungkyunkwan U. Sch. Medicine, Seoul, 1995—. Rsch. scholar U. Calif., Berkeley, 2003. Reviewer: Stroke, Am. Stroke Assn., 2001—; contbr. articles to profl. jours. Pres. Han-Family med. Svc., Seoul, 1995—. Mem.: Am. Aging Assn., Korean Acad. Family Medicine (mem. adv. bd.), Korean Geriatrics Soc. (editor-in-chief jour. 2003—). Achievements include discovery of homocystinuria in Korea; introduced homocystem research and significance of folate nutrition in clinical medicine. Office: Samsung Med Ctr 50 Ilwon-dong Kangnam-ku Seoul 135-710 Republic of Korea Office Phone: 82-2-3410-2440. Business E-Mail: drjohn.yoo@samsung.com.

YOO, KEUN-YOUNG, epidemiologist, educator; s. Byung-Joo Yoo and Kap-Soon Kim; m. Joo-Young Lee, Mar. 6, 1980; children: Inwook, Inkee. PhD, Seoul Nat. U., Republic Of Korea, 1985. Cert. med. dr. Seoul, 1978. Prof. epidemiology Seoul Nat. U. Coll. Medicine, 1999—; pres. Nat. Cancer Ctr., Goyang City, Kyeonggi-do, Republic of Korea, 2006—08. Sec. gen. Asian Pacific Orgn. Cancer Prevention, Nagoya, Japan, 2006—; co-chair Asia Cohort Consortium. Capt. divsn. med. affairs, 1983—86, Hdqs. 3rd Republic of Korea Army. Fellow, Yale Univ. Dept. Epidemiology and Pub. Health, 1989—90. Office: Seoul Nat Univ Coll Med 103 Daehangno Chongno-gu Seoul 110-799 Republic of Korea Office Fax: 82-2-747-4830. Business E-Mail: kyyoo@plaza.snu.ac.kr.

YOO, KYUNG YEON, physician, anesthesiologist, researcher; b. Shinbuk-myun, Youngam-gun, Chonnam, Republic of Korea, June 5, 1950; s. Byung Youn and Sun Duck Yoo; m. Jeong Hee Lee; children: Hee-Joo, Shi-Hyun. MD, Chonnam Nat. U., Gwangju, Korea, 1976, MSc, 1979, PhD, 1982. Cert. Korean Board of Anesthesiology, Korean Board of Pain. Maj. Busan Army Hosp., Busan, Busan, Republic of Korea, 1982—85; instr. dept. anesthesiology Chonnam U. Med. Sch., Gwangju, Republic of Korea, 1985—87, asst. prof., 1988—91; vis. asst. prof. Georgetown U. Med. Sch., Washington, 1991—92; assoc. prof. Chonnam U. Med. Sch., Gwangju, 1992—96, prof., 1997—. Dir. ICU, Chonnam U. Hosp., Gwangju, 1993—97; dir. libr. Chonnam U. Med. Sch., Gwangju, 1997—99, sect. chief, cardiovasc. anesthesia, 1990—, chmn. dept. anesthesiology, 1999—2003; cons. Nat. Health Ins. Rev. Agy., Gwangju, 2001—02; dir. Cancer Rsch. Inst. Chonnam U. Hosp., 2004—06. Author: (book) Textbook of Anesthesiology, 2002; contbr. articles to profl. jours. Maj. Busan Army Hosp., 1982—85, Busan. Recipient Cmty. Svc., Korean Med. Assn., Chonnam Chpt., 1977. Mem.: Korean Soc. Cardiothoracic and Vascular Anesthesiologists (pres. 2006—08), Soc. Cardiovasc. Anesthesiologists, Internat. Anesthesia Rsch. Soc., Korean Soc. of Pain, Korean Soc. Anesthesiologists (chmn. 2003—04), Korean Med. Assn. Conservative. Avocation: baseball. Home: Pungam-dong Seo-gu Gwangju 501 Republic of Korea Office: Chonnam Nat U Hosp Hak Dong Dong Gu 8 501-757 Gwangju Chonnam Republic of Korea Home Phone: 82-62-681-5597; Office Phone: 82-62-220-6893. Office Fax: 82-62-232-6294. Business E-Mail: kyyoo@jnu.ac.kr.

YOO, SUN DONG, pharmacy educator; b. Ansung, Kyonggi-do, Republic of Korea, Apr. 13, 1954; s. Tae Seung Yoo and Young Ok Ahn; m. Eun Duk Choi, July 8, 1991; 1 child, Hee Sang. B.Sc., Sungkyunkwan U., Republic of Korea, 1980; M.Sc., U. Man., Can., 1984; PhD, U. BC, Can., 1989. Postdoctoral fellow U. Ky., Lexington; asst. prof. U. SC, Columbia; prof. Sungkyunkwan U., Suwon, Kyonggi-do, Republic of Korea, 1997—, dept. chair, 2002—04, dean Coll. Pharmacy, 2004—, dean grad. sch. clin. pharmacy, 2004—, dir. Rsch. Inst. Pharm. Scis., 2004—. Grantee Endocrine Disruptors Rsch., Korea Inst. Toxicological Rsch., Korea, 1998—2002, Brain Korea 21, Ministry of Edn., 1999—2002, Century 21 Frontier Project, Ministry Sci. and Tech., Republic of Korea, 2001—, Health and Med. Rsch., Ministry Health and Welfare, Korea, 2002—03; Rsch. and Productive scholar, U. SC, 1991. Mem.: Am. Pharm. Assn., Am. Assn. Colls. Pharmacy (new investigator's award 1992), Korean Soc. Pharmaceutics, Pharm. Soc. Korea, Am. Assn. Pharm. Scientists. Office: Sungkyunkwan Univ 300 Chonchon-dong Changan-gu Kyonggi-do Suwon 440-746 Republic of Korea Office Fax: +82-31-292-8800.

YOO, TAE MOO, medical association administrator; b. YeSan, Republic of Korea, Mar. 1, 1961; PhD, SungKyunKwan U., 1991. Dir. Korea Food Drug Adminstrn., 2009—. Adj. prof. SungKyunKwan U., 1994—2011. Recipient Pres. award, Korea Govt. Mem.: Regulatory Harmonization Steering Com., APEC Life Sci. Innovation Forum. Avocation: soccer. Office: Osong Health Technology Adminstrn Cheongwon-gun Chungcheongbuk-do 363-951 Republic of Korea Office Fax: 82-43-719-2900. Business E-Mail: taemoo@kfda.go.kr.

YOO, VAK YEONG, health facility administrator; b. Seoul, Republic of Korea, June 28, 1947; d. Jang Mun Yoo and So Ran Choi. MA, Ewha Women's U., Seoul, 1974, MD, 1980. Med. diplomate internal medicine. Founder pvt. med. exam. ctr., Seoul, 1981—; dir. Yoo-vakyeong Internal Medicine, Seoul, 1981-92; head Med. Exam. Ctr., Seoul, 1981—; dir. Cheong-Vak P.B. Hosp., Seoul, 1992—; head Women's Health Dx & Climacteric, Seoul, 1992—. Mem. menopause and osteoporosis unit, 1992—, YVY-QOL Inst., 1997, YVY-QOL osteoporosis leader NOF-PPN, 1997; mem. sci. com. Koran Soc. Menopause, 1997-99; creator, organizer YVY-QOL support group for meno/osteoporosis Nat. Osteoporosis Found., 1997. Author: Phytoestrogens, 1995, Quality of Midbeyond Womens Life, 1996, Aging and Gender Specific Quality of Life, 1997; editor Jour. Meno/Osteoporosis, 1998—; co-editor Jour. Menopause Soc. Korea, 1999—; inventor in field. Mem. N.Am. Menopause Soc., Internat. Menopause Soc., Korean Soc. Endoscopy, Christian Med. Assn. (planning dir. 1993-96), Am. Assn. Clin. Endocrinologists, AAAS, Am. Soc. for Microbiology, Korean Soc. Endocrinology, Korean Diabetes Assn., Korean Soc. Menopause (sci. com. 1996-98, editing com. 1999—), Korean Soc. Circulation, The Endocrine Soc., NY Acad. Scis., NOF-Profl. Ptnr. Network, Am. Soc. Bone and Mineral Rsch. Avocations: travel, listening to music, opera music. Office: Cheongvak Antiaging Hosp 582 Shinsa Dong Kangnam Ku Seoul 135-120 Republic of Korea Home: 138-60 Yongdu Dong 130-070 Seoul Seoul Republic of Korea

YOO, YON-SIK, orthopedist, educator; b. Seoul, Republic of Korea, Oct. 7, 1965; MD, Chung-ang Coll. Medicine, Seoul, 1990. Shoulder and elbow svc. chief dr. Pohang St Mary Hosp., 2001—05; rsch. assoc. U. Pitts. Med. Ctr., 2005—07; assoc. prof. Hallym U. Med. Ctr., 2007—. Contbr. articles to profl. jours. Capt. Air Force Korean Army, 1995—98. Recipient John Joyce award, Internat. Soc. Arthroscopy, Knee Surgery and Orthopedic Sports Medicine. Mem.: Am. Acad. Orthopedic Surgeons, Korean Shoulder and Elbow Soc. (editl. bd. mem.), Internat. Soc. Arthroscopy (assoc.). Republican. Presbyterian. Office: Hallym University Orthopedic Dept Gyodong 153 200-702 Chuncheon Gangwon-do Republic of Korea Office Phone: 82 33 253 5198. Personal E-mail: ybw1999@gmail.com.

YOOD, ROBERT A., rheumatologist; b. Ithaca, NY, Jan. 18, 1949; s. Bertram and Shirley (Saffran) Y.; m. Joan D. Schlachter, Aug. 3, 1975; children: Sara, David, Benjamin. BA, Yale U., 1970; MD, Oreg. Health and Sci. U., Portland, 1974. Rheumatologist Fallon Clinic, Worcester, Mass., 1979—, treas., 1988-96, acting med. dir., 1995-96, bd. dirs., 1984-98, 2002—, chair bd. trustees, 2009—. Med. dir. rsch. dept. St. Vincent Hosp., chair divsn. rheumatic diseases and musculoskeletal medicine; clin. prof. medicine U. Mass. Med. Sch. Contbr. articles to profl. jours. Fellow ACP, Am. Coll. Rheumatology; mem. New Eng. Rheumatism Soc., Am. Med. Group Assn., Arthritis Found. (former med. adv. bd. Mass. chpt.). Office: Fallon Clinic 425 N Lake Ave Worcester MA 01605

YOON, BUMCHUL, dean; b. Seoul, Republic of Korea, Oct. 26, 1957; PhD, Korea U., 2000. Assoc. dean Coll. Health Sci. Korea U., 2010—. Chief phys. therapy, lectr., dept. rehab. medicine Korea U. Med. Ctr. & Dept. Health Sci., Korea U., Seoul, 1983—96; assoc. prof., asst. prof., orthop pt, sports pt, therapeutic exercise etc, dept. phys. therapy Coll. Health Sci., Korea U., 1996—2005; courtesy prof., vis. prof., dept. radiogy, dept. phys. therapy Med. Sch. & Coll. Health Professions, U. Fla., 2002—04; prof., clin. neurorehab., clin. kinesiology, neurol. therapeutic exercise Inst. Health Scis., Korea U., 2006—08; vis. prof., dept. kinesiology Sch. Pub. Health, U. Md., Coll. Pk., Md., 2009—10. Recipient cert., Ministry of Edn., Sci. & Tech., Korea, Appreciation plaque, Dept. Biomed., Grad. Sch. Korea U. Fellow: Korean Soc. Phys. Therapy; mem.: Neurosci., Korean Soc. Toxicogenomics & Toxicoproteiomics, Korean Occupl. Therapy Assn., Korean Phys. Therapy Assn. Avocations: golf, literature. Office: JeongReung-Dong SungBuk-Gu Seoul 136-703 Republic of Korea Office Fax: 82-2-940-2830. E-mail: yoonbc@korea.ac.kr.

YOON, BYUNG-KOO, medical educator; b. Seoul, Republic of Korea, Sept. 16, 1957; s. Hurn-Sik Yoon and In-Hee Kim; m. Eun-Kyung Zong, Feb. 7, 1987; children: Sun-Kee, Jung-Kee. MD, Seoul Nat. U. Coll. Medicine, 1982, PhD, 1992. Lic. physician Korean Med. Assn., 1982, Korean Soc. of Obstetrics and Gynecology, 1986. Clin. fellow Seoul Nat. U. Hosp., Republic of Korea, 1989—91; rsch. fellow Mayo Clinic, Rochester, Minn., 1991—93, Beth Israel Hosp., Boston, 1993—94; clin. staff dept. obstetrics & gynecology Samsung Med. Ctr., Seoul, 1994—; assoc. prof. Sungkyunkwan U. Sch. Medicine, Suwon, Kyungki-do, Republic of Korea, 1997—2002, prof., 2002—. Dir. menopause rsch. Samsung Med. Ctr., Seoul, 1994—. Achievements include first to therapeutic efficacy of hormone replacement therapy in patients with Alzheimer's disease.

YOON, CHEONJAE, medical association administrator; b. Seoul, Republic of Korea, Jan. 26, 1969; B, Yonsei U., 1994, M, 2002. Dir., burn ctr. Bestian Seoul Hosp., 2002—10; dir. Bestian Buchon Hosp., 2011—. Mem.: Internat. Soc. Burn Injury, Korean Soc. Emergency Medicine, Am. Burn Assn., Korean Burn Soc. Avocations: golf, snowboarding. Office: 577-2 Songnae 2 dong Bucheon Gyeonggido 422-040 Republic of Korea Office Fax: 082-32-611-7877.

YOON, DAE YOUNG, radiologist, educator; b. Daegu, Republic of Korea, Sept. 25, 1962; s. Jong Doo Yoon and Kyung Sook Ok; m. Min Jin Lee, June 19, 1993; 1 child, Eun Hae. MD in Medicine, Seoul Nat. U., 1987, MS in Medicine, 1996, PhD in Radiology, 1998. Intern Seoul Nat. U. Hosp., 1987—88, resident, 1991—95; prof. Kangdong Seong-Sim Hosp., Seoul, 1995—2007. Co-author (with Kee Hyun Chang): Neuroradiology, 2000. 1st lt. Korean Mil., 1988—91. Mem.: Korean Radiol. Soc. (licentiate). Avocations: travel, sports. Home: 1-206 Yeoksam Woosung Apt Dogok-dong Seoul 135-270 Republic of Korea Office: Kangdong Seong-Sim Hosp 445 Gil-dong Kangdong-ku Seoul 134-701 Republic of Korea Office Fax: 82-2-488-7370. Personal E-mail: evee0914@hanmail.net. Business E-Mail: evee0914@chollian.net.

YOON, DOJUN, physician, educator; b. Seoul, Oct. 9, 1964; MD, PhD, Yonsei U., 1995. Prof. Kwandong U., 1999—. Office: Kwandong University Coll Medicine Gangneung Gangwon 210-701 Republic of Korea Business E-Mail: mozart@kd.ac.kr.

YOON, HYE-GYUNG HELENA, ecologist, educator; b. Seoul, Republic of Korea, Mar. 11, 1959; PhD, Yonsei U., 2000. Chief rschr. Yonsei U., 2000, sr. rsch. prof., 2008—. Fellow: Internat. Jour. Indoor and Built Environment. Avocations: gardening, yoga. Home: 103-807 Shin Hyundai Apt Apgujeongdong Seoul 135-786 Republic of Korea Business E-Mail: hg_yoon@yonsei.ac.kr.

YOON, HYE-RAN, biochemical geneticist, director, researcher; d. Suk-Man Yoon and Kum-Za Choi. BS, Sung-Kyun-Kwan U. Coll. Pharmacy, 1982—86; MS, Seoul Nat. U. Coll. Pharmacy, 1986—88, PhD, 1991—94. Postdoctoral fellow Seoul Nat. U., 1994—95, Yale U. Sch. Medicine, 1995—98; external lectr. Sung-Kyun-Kwan U., Suwon, 1998—99, 1994—95. Dep. directorship Seoul Med. Sci. Inst., Seoul Clin. Laboratories (SCL), 2003—. Belief tchr., Korea (South), 1972—2003. Recipient Honors of Min. Dept of Pub. Health Prize, Korea, 2002; grant, 2000—02, full scholarship, Sung-Kyun-Kwan U., 1982—86, fellowship, Korea Rsch. Found., 1995, Nat. Health Found., 1993, Korea Sci. and Engring. Found., 1992, Korea Inst. Dept. Pharm. Sci., 1987. Fellow: Korea Soc. Inherited Metabolic Disorders; mem.: Soc. Inherited Metabolic Disorder, Soc. the Study Inborn Errors Metabolism, Korea Soc. Med. Genetics, Korea Quality Assurance Program Newborn Screening. Achievements include patents for simultaneous analyses of organic acids, amino acids and glycines by GC/MS. Home: Socho gu Yangjedong 154-2 Woosung APT Seoul 131 Republic of Korea Office: Seoul Med Sci Inst Seoul Clin Lab B-Yang Bd 2d Fl 7-14 Dongbinggo Dong 140-809 Yongsan Gu Seoul Seoul Republic of Korea Office Fax: 82-2-790-6506.

YOON, HYUN JIN, physicist; b. Daegu, Jan. 1, 1968; PhD, Dong-A U., 1999. Rsch. prof. Busan Nat. U., 2006—09; physicist Dong -A U. Med. Ctr., 2009—. Postdoc. fellowship, Nat. Rsch. Found. Korea. Mem.: Korean Phys. Soc., Korean Soc. Med. Physics, Korean Soc. Human Brain Mapping, Korean Soc. Nuc. Medicine. Office: 1 3-Ga Dongdaeshin-dong Seo-gu Busan 602-715 Republic of Korea Personal E-mail: bnisee@yahoo.com.

YOON, HYUNJOONG, oral surgeon, educator; b. Republic of Korea, Mar. 29, 1964; DDS, Yonsei U., PhD, 1989. Chief, dept. oral and maxillofacial surgery Yeouido St. Mary's Hosp., 2009—. Prof. Med. Coll., Cath. U. Korea, 1999—2011. Office: Dept Oral & Maxillofacial Surgery Seoul 150-713 Republic of Korea Business E-Mail: omfsyhj@catholic.ac.kr.

YOON, HYUN-KI, medical educator; b. Republic of Korea, June 10, 1963; MD, Seoul Nat. U., PhD, 1988. Prof. radiology Asan Med. Ctr., 1995—. Mem.: Cardiovascular and Interventional Radiol. Soc. Europe. Avocation: travel. Office: 388-1 Poongnap-2-Dong Songpa-Gu Seoul 138-736 Republic of Korea Office Fax: 82-2-476-0090. Business E-Mail: hkyoon@amc.seoul.kr.

YOON, JEONG-JUN, microbiologist, educator; b. Seoul, Republic of Korea, Jan. 8, 1967; s. Jung Ja Shin; BS in Agrl. Sci, Kinki U., Japan, 1997, MA in Agrl. Chemistry, 1999; PhD in Applied Life Scis., Kyoto U., 2002. Post-doctoral fellow U. Tokyo, 2002—04; lectr. Kookmin U., Seoul, 2005—06; rsch. prof. Konkuk U., Seoul, 2006—08. Assoc. editor Mycoscience, 2005—; contbr. articles to profl. jours. Cpl. Republic of Korea Army, 1989—91. Recipient Excellent Paper award, Fedn. Korean Microbiol. Socs., 2006. Mem.: Japanese Soc. Mushroom Sci. Biotech. (Younger Rschr. award 2003), Mycological Soc. Japan, Korean Soc. Wood Sci. and Tech., Korean Soc. Microbiology. Presbyterian. Achievements include research in cellulase system related to lignocellulosic degradation by brown-rot fungi; enzymatic saccharification for woody bioethanol production from lignocellulosics; enzymatic studies on the glyoxylate and TCA cycles during fruit body formation of wood-decay fungi. Avocations: golf, travel, reading. Home: Seongwon Sangttevill Apt 202 1301 Eonnam Dong Yongin Si Gyeonggi Do 446 792 Republic of Korea Office: Korea Inst Indsl Tech 35-3 Hongchen Ipjangmyeon Cheonansi 330-825 Chungnam Chungnam Republic of Korea Personal E-mail: kinoko67@hanmail.net. Business E-Mail: jjyoon@kitech.re.kr.

YOON, JIN-SANG, medical educator; b. Hwasun County, Chonnam, Republic of Korea, Feb. 18, 1955; s. Tae-Won Yoon and Ye-Bi Kim; m. Suk Cho, May 30, 1955, children: Sue-Lin, Hee-Jung, Sue-Yoon, Hee-Chan. MD, Chonnam Nat. U. Med. Sch., Kwangju, 1980; PhD, Chonnam Nat. U., Kwangju, 1986. Intern Chonnam Nat. U. Hosp., Kwangju, 1980—81, resident neuropsychiatry, 1981—84; instr. Chonnam Nat. U. Med. Sch., Kwangju, Republic of Korea, 1986—90, asst. prof., 1990—94, assoc. prof., 1994—99, prof., 1999—; attending Nat. Naju Mental Hosp., Chonnam, Republic of Korea, 1984—86. Rsch fellow Henry Ford Hosp. Sleep Disorders Ctr., Detroit, 1988—89; rsch. fellow Human Psychopharmacology Rsch Unit U. Surrey, Guildford, England, 1992—93; chmn. Dept. Psychiatry Chonnam Nat. U. Med. Sch., Kwangju, 2002—. Author: (book) Human Psychopharmacology: Measures and Methods, vol. 4; contbr. articles to profl. jours. Mem. Roman Cath., Kwangju, 1996. Mem.: Korean Neurol. Assn. (licentiate), Korean Psychiat. Assn. (licentiate), Korean Med. Assn. (licentiate), Korean Soc. Biol. Psychiatry (corr.), Korean Soc. Sleep Rsch. (corr.), Am. Acad. Sleep Medicine (corr.), Korean Soc. Psychopharmacology (corr.). Office: Chonnam Nat Univ Med Sch Hack-Dong Dong-Ku 5 501-746 Gwangju Republic of Korea Office Fax: +82-62-225-2351. E-mail: jsyoon@chonnam.ac.kr.

YOON, JOON-KEE, medical educator; b. Seoul, Republic Of Korea, Oct. 11, 1970; s. Byung-Min Yoon and Kyung-Ja Lee; m. Hye-Jin Cho; children: Hyun-Bin, Hyun-Seo. MD, Seoul Nat. U., 1997; PhD, Sungkyunkwan U., Suwon, Republic of Korea, 2006. Cert. nuclear medicine physician Korean Ministry of Health, Welfare and Family Affairs, 2002. Resident dr. Dept. Nuc. Medicine, Samsung Med. Ctr., Seoul, 1998—2001, clin. fellow, 2002, Ajou U. Hosp., Suwon, Kyunggi-do, 2002—03; asst. prof. Ajou U. Sch. Medicine, 2003—. Contbr. scientific papers to profl. jours. Recipient Disting. Sci. prize, Korean Fedn. Sci. and Tech. Socs., 2007. Mem.: Korean PET Assn. (com. pub. rels. 2008), Korean Thyroid Assn., Korean Assn. Study of Lung Cancer, Korean Soc. Molecular Imaging, Korean Soc. Nuc. Medicine (com. tng. resident drs. 2003—04). Achievements include development of decision tree software for SELDI TOF mass spectrometry. Office: Ajou Univ Sch Medicine Youngtong-gu Wonchun-dong San 5 Suwon Kyunggi-do 443-721 Republic of Korea Personal E-mail: jkyoon3@paran.com. Business E-Mail: jkyoon3@ajou.ac.kr.

YOON, KYUNGLIM, physician; b. Seoul, Apr. 5, 1970; BS, Kyung Hee U., 1995, PhD, 2005. Fellow Asan Med. Ctr., 2001—02; instr. Seoul Eulji Hosp., 2002—06; asst. prof. Kyung Hee U. Hosp., Gangdong, 2006—09, assoc. prof., 2009—. Mem.: Korean Pediat. Heart Assn., Korean Soc. Cardiology, Korean Pediat. Soc. Office: #149 Sangil-dong Gangdong-gu Seoul 134-727 Republic of Korea Office Fax: 82/2/440/6295. Business E-Mail: ykr3215@hanmail.net.

YOON, KYUNG-SIK, molecular biologist; b. Seoul, Republic of Korea, Sept. 5, 1968; MD, KyungHee U., 1992, PhD, 1996. Organizing com. mem. Biochemistry & Molecular Biology, Republic of Korea, 2007—. Mem. Genetic Test Counseling, Ministry of Health &

Welfare, 2009—. Office: 1 hoegi-dong Kyunghee University Sch Medicine Seoul 130-701 Republic of Korea Office Fax: 82-2-965-6349. Business E-Mail: sky9999@khu.ac.kr.

YOON, RICHARD K., dentist, educator; b. NYC, Oct. 5, 1972; DDS, Columbia U., 1998, cert in Pediatric Dentistry, 2001. Program dir., assoc. prof. Columbia U., 2008—. Attending pediatric dentist NY Presbyn. Hosp., 2001. Recipient Biotene award, Yale-New Haven Hosp.; Samuel Harris grant, ADA Found. Fellow: Am. Acad. Pediatric Dentistry; mem.: ADA, Am. Bd. Pediatric Dentistry, Omicron Kappa Upsilon. Avocation: piano. Office: Columbia University CDM-Pediatrics 722 New York NY 10032 Business E-Mail: rky1@columbia.edu.

YOON, SANG JIN, medical educator; b. Suwon, Feb. 22, 1965; MD, Seoul Nat. U., 1990, PhD, 2007. Prof. Gachon U. Medicine & Sci., 1998—. Recipient Outstanding Intellectuals 21st Century award, Internat. Biographical Ctr., 2011, Med. Sci. of Excellence award, Am. Biographical Inst., 2011; named Man of the Yr., 2011, Top 100 Healthcare Profl., Internat. Biographical Ctr., 2011, Great Mins of 21th Century, Am. Biographical Inst., 2011; fellow, ABI, 2011. Mem.: Internat. Biographical Assn. (life). Achievements include patents for surgical suture appatus having sewing function, suturing instrument capable of selecting and supplying a suture thread, suturing instrument having a fixing mean, suture apparatus having sewing function; surgical device and medical needle module with pointing function. Office: Guwol-Dong Namdong-Gu 1198 405-760 Incheon Incheon Republic of Korea Office Phone: 82-10-4740-9691. Personal E-mail: uysjr@hanmail.net. Business E-Mail: ysj6245@gilhospital.com.

YOON, SANG-PIL, medical educator; s. Soon-Geol Yoon and Ok-O Ko; m. Ju-Won Ku, Nov. 8, 1997; 1 child, Chan-Woong. BS in Medicine, Chosun U., Gwangju, South Korea, 1997, MS, 1999, PhD, 2005. Asst. prof., dept. anatomy Seonam U. Med Sch., Namwon, Jeollabuk-Do, Republic of Korea, 2005—10; dir. Korean Assn. Anatomists, Republic of Korea, 2007—08; editor Islets, 2009—; assoc. prof., dept. anatomy Jeju Nat. U. Med. Sch., Republic of Korea, 2010. Contbr. articles to profl. jours. Capt. med. examiner, 1999—2002, Busan, Republic of Korea. Office: Jeju Nat University Med Sch 66 Jejudaehakno Jeju 690-756 Republic of Korea Office Fax: 82-64-725-2593. Business E-Mail: spyoon@jejunu.ac.kr. E-mail: samsoobag@korea.com.

YOON, SEONG KUK, radiologist, educator; b. Busan, Republic of Korea, July 17, 1970; s. Jin Heon Yoon and Jung Young Jang; m. Yun Kyung Rhee; children: Ho Jung children: Soo Bin. MB, Dong-A U., Busan, 1994; MS, Dong-A U., 2001, PhD, 2003. Med. diplomate Ministry of Health and Welfare, Korea, cert. Korean Bd. Diagnostic Radiology. Resident in diagnostic radiology Dong-A U. Hosp., Busan, 1996—2000, fellow dept. diagnostic radiology, 2000—02; instr. Coll. of Medicine, Dong-A U., 2002—04, asst. prof., 2004—09, assoc. prof., 2008—. Spkr. in field. Contbr. articles to profl. jours. Mem.: Internat. Soc. Magnetic Resonance in Medicine, Radiol. Soc. N.Am. (cert. of merit 83d Sci. Assembly and Ann. Meeting 1997, cert. of merit 89th Sci. Assembly and Ann. Meeting 2003, cert. of merit 94th Sci. Assembly and Ann. Meeting 2008), Korean Soc. Med. Ultrasound (reviewer 2004—), Korean Soc. Uroradiology (bd. dirs. 2002—), Korean Radiol. Soc., Dong-A U. Coll. Medicine Alumni Assn. (chief editor 2002—). Home: Dongnae SK View Apt #102-1702 Onchon-2 Busan 607-783 Republic of Korea Office: Dong-A U Hosp Dept Diagnostic Radiology 3-Ga Dongdaesin-Dong Seo-Gu 1 602-715 Busan Busan Republic of Korea Office Phone: 82-51-240-5367. Office Fax: 82-51-253-4931. Personal E-mail: cerub@chollian.net.

YOON, SEUNG-YONG, medical educator; b. Seoul, Sept. 27, 1976; MD, U. Ulsan, 2002, PhD, 2006. Asst. prof. U. Ulsan, 2009—. Recipient Basic Med. Rsch. award, Korean Med. Assn. Mem.: Soc. Neurosci. Achievements include research in alzheimer's disease, neuroanatomy, neurobiology, neurodegenerative diseases, schizophrenia. Office: Anatomy and Cell Biology 88 Olympic-ro Songpa-gu Seoul 138-736 Republic of Korea Business E-Mail: ysy@amc.seoul.kr.

YOON, TAE-YOUNG, dermatologist, educator; b. Seoul, Korea, Sept. 18, 1956; s. Il-Byeong and Soon-Hee (Lee) Y.; m. Mi-Kyeong Kim, Mar. 9, 1985; children: Young-Sik, Jae Hong. MB, Seoul Nat. U., 1982, MM, 1985, PhD in Medicine, 1990. Intern Seoul Nat. U. Hosp., 1982-83, resident in dermatology, 1983-86; from instr. to prof. Chungbuk (Republic of Korea) Nat. U., 1990—2002, prof., 2002—, dir. dept. dermatology, 1990—. Contbr. articles to profl. jours. including Brit. Jour. Dermatology, Jour. Am. Acad. Dermatology, Jour. Dermatology (Japan), Internat. Jour. Dermatology, Clin. and Exptl. Dermatology. Mem. Korean Derm. Assn. Avocations: travel, swimming. Office: Chungbuk Nat U Dept Dermatology Gaesin dong Cheongju Chungbuk 361-711 Republic of Korea Office Phone: 82-43-269-6369. Business E-Mail: tyyoon@chungbuk.ac.kr.

YOON, WAN-HEE, surgeon, educator; b. Yeonsan, Chungnam, Republic of Korea, Dec. 18, 1957; s. Ju-Chul Yoon and Hang-Sun Lim; m. Hae-Duck Park, Oct. 19, 1980; 1 child, Ki-Yeon. MD, Chungnam Nat. U., Daejon, Republic of Korea, 1981, MS, 1984, PhD, 1988. Postdoc. rsch. fellow U. Calif., San Francisco, 1986—88; instr. Chungnam Nat. U. Coll. Medicine, Daejon, 1988—92, 1992—97, assoc. prof., 1997—. Mem.: European Assn. Cancer Rsch., Am. Assn. Cancer Rsch., Am. Soc. Colorectal Surgery. Avocation: scuba diving. Office: Chungnam Nat U Dept Surgery 640 Daesa-Dong Joong-Ku Daejeon 301 744 Republic of Korea Home: 13-903 Karam Apt 302-222 Daejeon Daejeon Republic of Korea Office Phone: 42 361-5500.

YOON, YEO JOON, biotechnologist, educator; b. Seoul, Republic of Korea, May 12, 1969; s. Seok Myung Yoon and Bong Ja Bae; m. Yoon Joo Han; children: Seung Won children: Seung Jay. BS, Seoul Nat. U., 1992, PhD, 2000. Vis. scholar U. Wis., Madison, 1996—98; postdoctoral rschr. U. Minn., Mpls., 2000—02; asst. prof. U. Ulsan, Republic of Korea, 2002—04; assoc. prof. Ewha Woman's U., Seoul, 2004—. Contbr. articles to profl. jours. Mem.: Korean Soc. Biotech. and Bioengring. (life), Korean Soc. Microbiology and Biotech. (life). Office: Ewha Woman's U Dept Chemistry & Nano Sci 11-1 Daehyun-dong Seodaemun-gu Seoul 120-750 Republic of Korea Office Phone: 82-2-3277-4082. Office Fax: 82-2-3277-3419. Business E-Mail: joonyoon@ewha.ac.kr.

YOON, YONG BUM, medical educator; b. Seoul, Republic Of Korea, Feb. 28, 1948; s. Deok Rim Yoon and Soo Gil Kim; m. In Tack Kwon; children: Won Jae, In Jae. PhD, Seoul Nat. U., 1981. Bd. cert. internist Korean Assn. Internal Medicine, 1977. Prof. Med. Coll., Seoul Nat. U., 1981—. Pres. Korean Soc. Gastrointestinal Endoscopy, 2003—05, Korean Soc. Gastroenterology, Seoul, 2007—. Pres. Seoul Shinsa Rotary Club, 2001—02. Maj. Korean Army, 1977—80. Home: 2-707 Hannam Heights Apt Oksoo-dong Seoul 133-768 Republic of Korea Office: Seoul Nat Univ Hospital 101 Daehang-ro Jongno-gu Seoul 110-744 Republic of Korea Office Phone: 82-2-2072-3346. Office Fax: 82-2-765-8265. Business E-Mail: yyb10604@plaza.snu.ac.kr.

YOON, YOUNG CHEOL, medical educator; b. Busan, Republic of Korea, Apr. 25, 1968; m. Myung Sim Kim, Apr. 19, 1997; 1 child, Chae Ryung Yun. MD, Republic of Korea, 1993; D, Kangwon U., Republic of Korea, 2007. Assoc. prof. Coll. Medicine, Sungkyunkwan U., Seoul, 2004—. Contbr. articles to profl. jours. Office: Samsung Med Ctr 50 Ilwon-dong Kangnam-ku Seoul 135-710 Republic of Korea Office Phone: 822-3410-6454. Business E-Mail: ycyoon@skku.edu.

YORK, JOAN ELIZABETH SMITH, psychologist; b. Englewood, NJ, Jan. 18, 1940; d. Julius Freeman and Lottie Winfred (Mays) Smith. BA, W.Va. State Coll., 1962; MEd, Trenton State Coll., 1980; postgrad. in counseling psychology, Union Grad. Lic. drug and alcohol counselor. Sch. counselor Portsmouth (Va.) Child-Family Svc., 1972—73; dir. Richmond (Va.) City Jail-Work Release Program, 1974—75; counselor Employee Adv. Svc., Trenton, 1975—2002; part-time counselor Trenton State Prison Evening Sch., 1981—82; pvt. counselor Delaware Valley Psychol. Clinic, 1982—; pvt. therapist Mercer Consultation Assn., 1986—; drug and alcoholism counselor, 1987—; bd. mem. New Horizon Treatment Ctr., 1994—. Pvt. practice, 1980—; first v.p. NJ Task Force on Women and Alcohol., mem. exec. bd. Mem.: APA, NJ Alcoholism Assn., Nat. Black Alcoholism Counselors, Am. Assn. Counseling & Devel., Assn. Black Psychologists. Democrat. Baptist. Home Phone: 609-396-4887; Office Phone: 609-396-4887. Personal E-mail: jesy138@comcast.net.

YORK, MICHELE KLASWICK, medical educator; b. Md., Dec. 23, 1971; PhD, Vanderbilt U., 1998. Asst. prof., sect. head neuropsychology dept. neurology Baylor Coll. Medicine, 1998—, asst. prof. dept. neurosurgery, 2000—05, asst. prof. dept. psychiatry, 2003—11; neuropsychologist Michael E. DeBakey Vets. Affairs Med. Ctr., 2002—11. Med. adv. com. Houston Area Parkinson's Disease Soc., 2007—11. Recipient Roy H. Cullen Quality Life award, Houston Area Parkinson's Disease Soc., Herbert Hornung Achievement award, Alpha Lambda Delta; grant, Gillson-Logenbaugh Found., Nat. Inst. Neurol. Disorders and Stroke, NIH. Mem.: Functional Neurosurgery Working Group (co-chair), Cognitive and Behavioral Working Group, Parkinson's Study Group. Avocations: painting, drawing, reading. Office: Baylor Coll Medicine Neurology 6 Houston TX 77030 Office Phone: 713-798-8673. Business E-Mail: myork@bcm.edu.

YOSHIDA, GLEN YOSHIO, otolaryngologist; b. Honolulu, Feb. 20, 1955; s. Charles K. and Yoshiko Yoshida; m. Nancy Marie Gustafson, Apr. 22, 1989; 1 child, Michael B. BA, Lawrence U., Appleton, Wis., 1977; MD, Uniformed Svcs. U. Health Scis., Bethesda, Md., 1982. Diplomate Am. Bd. Otolaryngology, 1987. Commd. 2d lt. US Army, 1982, advanced through grades to lt. col., 1994; intern otolaryn.-head and neck surgery Tripler Army Med. Ctr., Honolulu, 1982—83, resident otolaryn.-head and neck surgery, 1983—87; chief otolaryn.-head and neck surgery 121 Evac Hosp., Seoul, Republic of Korea, 1987—88; fellow head and neck surgery Meth. Hosp., Indpls., 1988—89; asst. chief otolaryn.-head and neck surgery Fitzsimons Army Med. Ctr., Aurora, Colo., 1989—96; mem. otolaryngology staff Altru Health Sys., Grand Forks, ND, 1996—. Mem. adv. bd. Grand Forks Pharmacy, 2000—; cons. in field; asst. clin. prof., co-program dir. otolaryngology residency U. Colo. Health Scis. Ctr., 1990—96; asst. clin. prof. Uniformed Svcs. U. Health Scis., 1995—96, U. ND Sch. Medicine, 1998—; presenter in field. Contbr. articles to med. jours. Otolaryngologist med. mission trip SW Med. Teams, Romania, 1995, Internat. Relief Teams, Honduras, 2006; med. vol. mission trip Calvary Luth. Ch., Honduras, 2004; bd. dirs. Greater Grand Forks Symphony Orch., 2001—. Decorated Army Commendation medal, Nat. Def. medal, Meritorious Svc. medal; recipient Tchr. of Yr. award, U. Colo. otolaryngology-head and neck surgery dept., 1996. Fellow: ACS, Am. Acad. Facial Plastic and Reconstructive Surgery, Am. Head and Neck Soc., Am. Acad. Otolaryngology-Head and Neck Surgery (Honor award 1998); mem.: Am. Acad. Sleep Medicine, Fighting Souix Club. Lutheran. Avocations: running, horseback riding, sled dogs, photography, golf. Office: Altru Health Sys 1000 S Columbia Rd 4D Grand Forks ND 58201

YOSHIDA, HIROSHI, physician, educator, researcher; b. Sasebo, Nagasaki, Japan, Aug. 5, 1962; s. Sakae and Kinuko Yoshida; m. Mayumi Watanabe, Feb. 3, 1991; 1 child, Tomohiro. MD, Nat. Def. Med. Coll., Tokorozawa, Saitama, Japan, 1987, PhD, 1999. Rsch. fellow U. Calif. San Diego, La Jolla, 1996—98; maj. divsn. surgeon 13th Divsn. Hdqs. Ground Self-Def. Force, Kaitaichi, Hiroshima, Japan, 1998—99, lt. col. divsn. surgeon, 1999—2000; lt. col. Med. Dept. Plans and Adminstrn. Japan Def. Agy., Ichigaya, Tokyo, 2000—01; instr., asst. prof. Dept. Internal Medicine Kashiwa Hosp. Jikei U. Sch. Medicine, Nishi-Shinbashi, Tokyo, 2001, chief physician Dept. Gen. Medicine Kashiwa Hosp. Chiba, Japan, 2003—, lectr., asst. prof. Dept. Gen. Medicine, 2003—; interlocking asst. prof. Jikei Kashiwa Nursing Sch., 2003—. Lt. col. Japanese Def. Agy., 1994—2001. Decorated 3d Rank award Gorund Self-def. Force; recipient Award of Excellence, Nat. Def. Med. Soc., 2000. Fellow: Japanese Circulation Soc., Japan Soc. Internal Medicine; mem.: ACP, Japan Atherosclerosis Soc. (counciller 1999—). Achievements include research in measurement of cholesterol levels of the major serum lipoprotein classes by anion-exchange HPLC with perchlorate ion-containing eluent. Avocations: golf, art, travel, movies. Home: 949-42 Kashiwa Kashiwa 277-0005 Japan Office: Jikei U Sch Medicine Kashiwa Hosp 163-1 Kashiwashita Kashiwa 277-8567 Japan Office Fax: 81-4-7164-1126; Home Fax: 81-4-7162-0186. Personal E-mail: hiyoshida@jcom.home.ne.jp. Business E-Mail: hyoshida@jikei.ac.jp.

YOSHIDA, JUNICHI, surgeon; b. Nagoya, Japan, June 26, 1955; s. Shigeru and Ikuko (Masuda) Y.; m. Yukimi Izumi, Dec. 2, 1984; children: Masashi Christopher, Hiroki. MD, Kyushu U., Fukuoka, Japan, 1981; MS, U. Ill., Chgo., 1986. Bd. cert. in surgery. Resident Kyushu U., 1981-85; rsch. assoc. U. Ill., Chgo., 1985-88; house officer Kyushu U. Affiliated Hosp., 1988-93; asst. prof. Kyushu U., 1993-96; divsn. chief Shimonoseki City Ctrl. Hosp., 1996—. Contbr. articles to profl. jours. Fellow ACS, Infection Control Dr. Office: Shimonoseki City Hosp Surg 1-13-1 Koyo-cho 750-8520 Shimonoseki Japan Office Phone: 81 83 231 4111.

YOSHIDA, JUNJI, thoracic surgeon, consultant; b. Kushiro, Hokkaido, Japan, June 11, 1959; s. Saburo and Hisae Yoshida; m. Erika Hanamura; 1 child, Ai. MD, Sch. Medicine, U. Tokyo, 1984; PhD, Grad. Sch. Medicine, U. Tokyo, 1992. Cert. surgeon Japan Surg. Soc., 1989. Thoracic surgeon Nat. Cancer Ctr. Hosp. East, Kashiwa, Chiba, Japan, 1992—2002, sr. cons., 2002—. Office: Nat Cancer Ctr Hosp East 6-5-1 Kashiwanoha Kashiwa Chiba 277-8577 Japan Office Fax: 81-4-7131-4724. Business E-Mail: jyoshida@east.ncc.go.jp.

YOSHIDA, MAKOTO, pharmacologist, researcher; b. Funabashi, Japan, Aug. 12, 1963; B in Pharmacy, Tohoku U., 1985, PhD, 1999. Rsch. assoc. Tohoku U. Pharm. Inst, Sendai, Japan, 1987—90; asst. in biochemistry Vanderbilt U. Sch. of Medicine, Nashville, 1990—93; rsch. assoc. Tohoku U. Pharm. Inst., 1993—95; rsch. instr. Tohoku U. Grad. Sch. of Pharm. Sciences, 1995—2001, asst. prof., 2001—03, assoc. prof., 2003—06; prof. Takasaki U. Health Welfare Faculty Pharm., 2006—. Sci. councilor Japanese Pharm. Soc., Tokyo, 2000—. Author: (textbook) New Textbook of Pharmacology. Recipient award, Phamaceutical Soc. of Japan, 1999; Rsch. grant, Rsch. Found. for Pharm. Sciences, 2003, grant, Japan Soc. for the Promotion Sciences, 2002—03, 2005—. Mem.: Pharm. Soc. of Japan, Japanese Assn. of Cardiovasc. Pharmacology. Office: Faculty Pharm Takasaki U Health Welfare 60 Nakaohrui Takasaki 370-0033 Japan

YOSHIDA, MASASHI, surgeon, educator; b. Chiba, Japan, Feb. 1963; MD, Kyorin U., 1988; PhD, Keio U., 2002. Assoc. prof., chief dept. surgery Internat. U. Health and Welfare Mita Hosp., 2007—; rsch. fellow U. Calif. Irvine. Councilor Japanese Soc. Ulcer Rsch., 2005, Japan Surg. Assn., 2007; bd. dirs. Japanese Soc. Wound Healing, 2008; councilor Japanese Soc. Helicobacter Rsch., 2008, Japanese Soc. Gastro-surgical Pathophysiology, 2008. Recipient Histamine Receptor prize, Japanese Study Group Histamine Receptor, 1995, Ulcer Rsch. prize, Japanese Soc. Exptl. Ulcer, 2002, Organizer prize, Japanese Study Group for Ulcer Rsch. Fellow: ACS; mem.: Japanese Surg. Soc., Japan Soc. Endoscopic Surgery, Internat. Gastric Cancer Assn., Internat. Soc. Surgery. Avocation: baseball. Office: 1-4-3 Mita Minatoku Tokyo 1088329 Japan Office Fax: 81 3 3454 0067. Business E-Mail: masashi@iuhw.ac.jp.

YOSHIDA, MINORU, medical educator; b. Sapporo, Hokkaido, Japan, May 20, 1952; MD, Hokkaido U., 1977. Prof. Fourth Dept. Internal Medicine Teikyo U. Sch. Medicine, 2006—. Avocation: music. Office: 3-8-3 Mizonokuchi Takatsu-ku Kawasaki Kanagawa 213-8507 Japan Office Fax: 81-44-844-3546. Business E-Mail: myoshida@med.teikyo-u.ac.jp.

YOSHIDA, YOSHIO, medical educator; b. Japan, Aug. 17, 1960; MD, U. Fukui, PhD, 1987. Assoc. prof U. Fukui, 2002—. Office: Eiheiji-cho Matuoka Shimoaizuki 23-3 Yoshida-gun Fukui 910-1193 Japan Office Phone: 81-776-61-3111. Business E-Mail: yyoshida@u-fukui.ac.jp.

YOSHIDA, YUICHI, engineering educator; b. Japan, June 30, 1968; MD, Kyushu U., 1994, PhD, 1999. Assoc. prof. Tottori U., 2006—. Office: 86 Nishi-cho Yonago Tottori 683-8503 Japan Business E-Mail: yxy@grape.med.tottori-u.ac.jp.

YOSHIHARA, SHIGEMI, pediatrician; b. Tochigi, Japan, Oct. 24, 1958; married, 1984; 3 children. MD, Dokkyo Univ. Sch. of Medicine, 1983; PhD, Dokkyo Univ. Sch. of Graduate Course, 1989. Residentship, dept. pediat. Dokkyo Univ. Hosp., 1983—85; rsch. fellow Shizuoka Univ., Japan, 1985—86; instr. pediat. Dokkyo Univ. Sch. of Medicine, 1989—90, asst. prof. pediat., 1990—2003; rsch. fellow Divsn. pulmonary Medicine, cardiovascular Rsch. Inst. Univ. Calif., San Fransisco, Calif., 1993—95; dir. Allergy and Pulmonary disease dept. of pediat. Dokkyo Univ. Sch. of Medicine, 1999—, assoc. prof. pediat., 2004—. Mem.: European Respiratory Soc., Am. Thoracic Soc. Office: Dept Pediat Dokkyo Univ Sch of Medicine 880 Mibui Tochigi 321 0293 Japan Office Phone: 81 282 86 1111. Business E-Mail: shigemi@dokkyomed.ac.jp.

YOSHIHIRO, FUJIWARA, agriculturist; b. Okayama, Japan, Mar. 31, 1965; BAS, Kobe U., 1987; PhD, Nagoya U., 1993. Sr. scientist Preventec Inc., 2008—. Home: Grandmere Matshishiro B201 Matsushiro 2 Tsukuba Ibaragi 305-0035 Japan Personal E-mail: fwara@home.nifty.jp.

YOSHIKAWA, HIROMI, pharmaceutical executive; b. Tokyo; B in Bus., Waseda Univ. Computer sys. sect., fin. dept. Otsuka Pharm. Co. Ltd., 1976—77; acctg. mgr. Japan Immunoresearch Lab. (after acquisition by OPC), 1977—80; in charge of installation, integrated mgmt. sys. China Otsuka (OPC subs.), 1980; fin. dept., Tokyo office Otsuka, 1994—97, developer, bus. sys., Europe London, 1997—2000; chmn., CEO Otsuka Am. Pharm. Inc. (OAPI), Rockville, Md., 2000—09; also, chmn., CEO Otsuka Am. Inc. (OAI) holding co. Bd. dir. Pharm. Rsch. Mfr. Am. Office: Otsuka America Inc One Embarcadero Ctr Ste 2020 San Francisco CA 94111 Office Phone: 301-990-0030. Office Fax: 301-212-8647.

YOSHIKAWA, KUNIHIKO, dermatologist, educator, consultant, department chairman; b. Kyoto, May 16, 1939; s. Saburou and Yukiko (Nishino) Y.; m. Noriko Ohkido, Mar. 30, 1971; children: Momoko, Tadahiko, Yuko. BSc, Osaka U., Japan, 1960, MD, 1964, PhD, 1978.

Diplomate Japanese Dermatol. Assn., Japanese Nat. Bd. Instr. Sch. Medicine, Osaka U., Japan, 1970-71, prof., chmn. dept. dermatology, 1985—2003, prof. emeritus, 2003—; rsch. fellow dept. dermatology Sch. Medicine, U. Miami, Fla., 1972—75; assoc. prof. dept. dermatology Med. Sch., Nagoya City U., Japan, 1975—85; cons. dermatologist Kyoritsu Hosp., 2003—, Yukioka Hosp., 2003—, Maruho Corp., 2005—09, K.F.G. Corp., 2003—. Vis. scientist Oreg. Regional Primate Rsch. Ctr., Beaverton, 1971—72; expert panel mem. Rsch. Inst. Fragrance Materials, Hackensack, NJ, 1988—96; mem. exam. com. Japan Med. Bd., 1993—97; chmn. bd. dirs. Japan Com. Sunlight Protection, 2000—04, Keisaidan Found. Osaka U. Hosp., 2006—; cons. in field. Editor-in-chief Jour. Dermatol. Sci., 1993—97, Photomedicine and Photobiology, 1995—97; co-editor: Comprehensive Dermatology Series, 1986—90, Dermatology for non-Specialist Series, 1987—; mem. editl. bd. Environ. Dermatology, 1994—2003. Recipient Best Clin. Poster award, 17th World Congress Dermatology, 1987, Yasuda Sakamoto award, 2000, Photomed. Photobiol award, 2008. Mem.: Japan Allergy Found. (head Kansai divsn. 1996—2002, bd. dirs.), Japanese Soc. Connective Tissue Rsch. (auditor 1986—2003), Japanese Soc. Contact Dermatitis Rsch. (bd. dirs. 1987—2005), Japanese Soc. Psoriasis Rsch. (bd. dirs. 1989—2003), Japanese Soc. Photomedicine and Photobiology (bd. dirs. 1985—93, chmn. bd. dirs. 1994—97), Japanese Soc. Dermatoallergology (bd. dirs. 1990—2004), Japanese Med. Assn. (v.p. Osaka divsn. 1996—2002), Japanese Soc. Investigative Dermatology (hon.; exec. bd. dirs. 1988—96, v.p. 1997—98, insp. 1999—2001), Japanese Dermatol. Assn. (hon.; bd. dirs. 1988—2002, head ctrl. divsn. 1997—2002). Buddhist. Avocations: golf, gardening, sports. Home: 9-3-14 Higashitokiwadai Toyono Cho Osaka 563-0103 Japan Business E-Mail: yoshikawa@derma.med.osaka-u.ac.jp. *

YOSHIKAWA, YASUHIRO, agricultural studies educator; b. Nagano Prefecture, Japan, Nov. 19, 1946; Vet. Dr., Tokyo U., 1971, PhD in Agr., 1976. Govt. employee, dept. mealses virus NIH Japan, 1976—80, gen. dir., Tsukuba Primate Ctr., 1990—96; asst. prof., lectr., assoc. prof., Inst. Med. Sci. Tokyo U., 1980—90, prof., Grad. Sch. Agrl. and Life Scis., 1996—2010; pres. All Japan Coun. Vet. Schs., 2007—. Chmn., prion expert com. Food Safety Commn., Cabinet Office Japan, 2003—10; mem., WG wildlife diseases OIE, World Orgn. Animal Health, 2009. Recipient Tokyo Creation award, Japan Fashion Assn., Ochi award, Japan's Assn. Vet. Sci. Avocations: painting, reading, gardening. Home: Shimachi 2-9-7 Nishitokyo Tokyo 202-0023 Japan Personal E-mail: ayyoshi@mail.ecc.u-tokyo.ac.jp.

YOSHIKAZU, MIYAMOTO, anesthesiologist, educator; b. Tanabe, Wakayama Prefecture, Japan, Dec. 3, 1968; MD, Osaka U., Japan, 1993, PhD, 2000. Asst. prof., dept. anesthesiology and intensive care medicine Grad. Sch. Medicine, Osaka U., 2004—. Recipient Young Scientists award, Ministry of Edn., Culture, Sports, Sci. and Tech., Japan; Rsch. grant, fellowship, Japan Soc. Promotion Sci. Mem.: Japanese Soc. Pediat. Anesthesia (bd. dirs. 2011—), Japanese Soc. Intensive Care Medicine, Japanese Soc. Anesthesiologists, Am. Soc. Anesthesiologists. Office: 2-2 Yamadaoka Suita Osaka 565-0871 Japan Office Fax: 81-6-6879-3139.

YOSHIMOTO, KANJI, neuropharmacologist, educator; b. Hiroshima, Japan, Sept. 11, 1954; s. Takumi and Muneko Yoshimoto; m. Junko Yoshimoto, May 29, 1983; children: Mariko, Koki, Eki. BS, Yamaguchi U., 1977; PhD, Kyoto Prefectural U. Medicine, 1987. Instr. Shiga (Japan) U. Medicine, 1977-83; sr. asst. Kyoto (Japan) Prefectural U. Medicine, 1983-89, asst. prof., 1991—2003, assoc. prof., 2004—; rsch. assoc. inst. psychiat. rsch. Ind. U., Indpls., 1989-91. Contbr. articles and revs. to profl. jours. Avocations: painting, collecting beer labels. Home: 7-11-5 Ohginosato Higashi Ohtsu 520-0248 Japan Office: Kyoto Pref U Medicine Dept Legal Med Kawaramachi Kamigo-ku Kyoto 602-8566 Japan Office Phone: 81-75-251-5345. Office Fax: 81-75-251-5345. Business E-Mail: kyoshimo@koto.kpu-m.ac.jp.

YOSHIMURA, KAZUAKI, medical educator; b. Japan, Sept. 3, 1967; MD, U. Occupl. and Environ. Health, PhD, 1992. Asst. prof. U. Occupl. and Environ. Health, 2001—. Office: 1-1 Iseigaoka Yahatanishi-ku Kitakyushu 807-8555 Japan Business E-Mail: yoppy@med.uoeh-u.ac.jp.

YOSHIMURA, SHINICHI, neurosurgeon, educator; b. Gifu, Japan, May 23, 1963; MD, Gifu U., 1989, PhD, 1998. Clin. prof. Dept. Neurosurgery, Grad. Sch. Medicine, Gifu U., 2008—. Fellow: Japanese Soc. Neuroendovascular Therapy; mem.: Japan Stroke Soc., Japanese Congress Neurol. Surgeons, Japan Neurosurg. Soc. (Galenus award). Avocations: bicycling, travel, camping. Office: 1-1 Yanagido Gifu City Gifu Prefecture 501-1194 Japan Office Fax: 81-58-230-6272. E-mail: shinichiyoshimura@hotmail.com.

YOSHINO, ICHIRO, thoracic surgeon; b. Naha, Okinawa, Japan, Apr. 21, 1962; s. Sonji Amuro and Ayako Yoshino; m. Masayo Takeda, May 6, 1989; children: Yutaro, Akito, Haruka. MD, Kyushu U., Fukuoka, Japan, 1987, PhD, 1992. Rsch. fellow Harvard Med. Sch., Brigham & Woman's Hosp., Boston, 1992-94; asst. prof. U. Occupl. and Environ. Health, Kitakyushu, Japan, 1995—. Contbr. articles to profl. jours. Recipient grant Fujita Meml. Fund Med. Rsch., 1997. Mem. Am. Assn. Cancer Rsch. (corr.), Japan Surg. Soc., Japanese Assn. Chest Surgery. Office: U Occupl & Environ Health 1-1 Iselgaoka Yahata-Nishi Kitakyushu 807 Japan

YOSHINORI, MATSUOKA, medical educator, director; b. Japan, Feb. 16, 1979; MD, Saga U., 2003; PhD in Emergency Medicine, Kyushu U., 2010. Asst. prof., co-dir. critical care medicine Dept. Anesthesiology & Critical Care Medicine, Faculty Medicine, Saga U., 2011—. Fellow: Japanese Soc. Anesthesiologists, Japanese Soc. Intensive Care Medicine, Japanese Assn. Acute Medicine. Home: Nabeshima 5 chome 1 1 Saga 849 8501 Japan Home Phone: 81-90-7392-1881. Personal E-mail: yoshinori216@h2.dion.ne.jp.

YOSHIO, OGAWA, medical educator; b. Tokyo, May 23, 1955; MD, Showa U., 1981, PhD, 1985. Prof. Showa U., 2007—. Mem.: Am. Urol. Assn. Office: 15-8 Hatanodai Shinagawaku Tokyo 142-8666 Japan Business E-Mail: ogawayos@med.showa-u.ac.jp.

YOSHIO, TAKU, physician, educator; b. Toyama-Ken, Japan, Aug. 2, 1952; MD, PhD, Akita U., 1979. Prof. Jichi Med. U., 2010. Office: 3111-1 Yakushiji Shimotsuke Tochigi-Ken 3290498 Japan Office Fax: 81285448064. Business E-Mail: takuyosh@jichi.ac.jp.

YOSHIOKA, YASUNORI, chemistry professor; b. Kobe, July 19, 1950; Deng, Osaka U., 1978. Prof. dept. chemistry Mie U., Japan, 2001—. Office: Kurimamachiya1577 Tsu Mie 514-8507 Japan Business E-Mail: yyoshi@chem.mie-u.ac.jp.

YOSHIUCHI, ELLEN HAVEN, healthcare educator, clinical counselor; b. Newark, Apr. 15, 1949; d. Michael Joseph and Adeline V. (Lindblom) Haven; m. Takeshi Yoshiuchi, Dec. 1, 1973; children: Teri Takumi, Niki Noboru. BA summa cum laude, CUNY, 1980; M Profl. Studies in Human Rels., N.Y. Inst. Tech., 1991. Cert. bereavement svcs. counselor, cert. kidney early evaluation program. Pvt. practice childbirth edn., 1983—89; program asst. parent/family edn. St. Luke's/Roosevelt Hosp. Ctr., NYC, 1989—93, mem. faculty parent/family edn. program, 1990—2002; mem. faculty Family Ctr. at Riverdale Neighborhood House, Bronx, 1991—96; faculty mem. The Greater N.Y. March of Dimes, NYC, 1996—2001; mgr. patient svcs. N.Y.C. chpt. The Leukemia and Lymphoma Soc., 1998—2004; divsn. program dir. Nat. Kidney Found. of Greater N.Y., 2004—. Mem. perinatal bereavement com. St. Luke's/Roosevelt Hosp. Ctr., N.Y.C., 1989-95. Editor ASPO/N.Y.C. News, 1983-86; contbr. articles to profl. jours. Trustee Pan Asian Repertory Theatre, N.Y.C., 1996-2001. Fellow: Am. Coll. Childbirth Educators; mem.: NY Citizens' Com. on Health Care Decisions, Coun. Nephrology Social Workers, C.G. Jung Found. for Analytical Psychology, Lamaze Internat. (cert. tchr., pres. N.Y.C. chpt. 1987—91, nominating com. 1991—93, dir. ednl. program 1991—93). Office: 30 E 33d St New York NY 10016-6901 Office Phone: 212-889-2210.

YOSHIUCHI, ISSEI, physician, researcher; s. Michinori and Chizuko Yoshiuchi. MD, Hiroshima U., 1993, PhD, 2004. Cert. profl. sect. Am. Diabetes Assn. Mem. med. staff Social Ins. Kinan Gen. Hosp., Wakayama, 1993—95; rsch. assoc. U. Chgo., 2000—03; mem. med. staff Toyonaka Mcpl. Hosp., 2004—05, Ashiya St. Maria Hosp., 2006—07; dir. Yoshiuchi Med. Diabetes Inst., 2006—. Vis. rschr. Found. Biomed. Rsch. and Invention, 2005—06. Contbr. articles to profl. jours. Mem.: AAAS, Am. Soc. Human Genetics, NY Acad. Scis., Endocrine Soc., Am. Diabetes Assn. Avocations: running, music. Home: 2-16-41 Kawakurayama Kamakura Kanagawa 248-0031 Japan Business E-Mail: yoshiuchi@m9.dion.ne.jp.

YOSHIYAMA, MITSUHARU, physician, researcher; b. Sawara, Chiba, Japan, Aug. 26, 1964; s. Nobuharu and Tsuyako Yoshiyama. MD, Showa U. Sch. Medicine, Tokyo, 1989, PhD, 1993. Rsch. assoc. dept. pharmacology U. Pitts. Sch. Medicine, 1989—98, instr., 1998, rsch. asst. prof., 1990—, clin. fellow Showa U. Fujigaoka Hosp., Yokohama, Japan, 2000; clin. fellow dept. neurology Chiba-Higashi Nat. Hosp., Japan, 2000, Chiba U. Grad. Sch. Medicine, 2000—03, Asahi Hosp. for Neurol. Diseases, 2001—03, Yamanashi Onsen Hosp., 2003—06, Yamanashi Rehab. Hosp., 2006—. Panel evaluator Current Drugs Ltd., London, 1998—; cons. Eisai Pharm. Corp., Tsukuba, Japan, 1999—2002, Dynogen Pharms., Inc., Boston, 2002—, Toray Industries, Inc., Kamakura, Japan, 2001—; adj. asst. prof. dept. urology U. Yamanashi Interdisciplinary Grad. Sch. Med. & Engring., 2003—06, Yamanashi Rehab. Hosp., 2006—. Mem. med. rev. bd.: IMP Japanese Home Health Handbook, 2002—03. Avocations: music, guitar, singing. Home: A-101 330 37 Hatta Isawa-cho Fuefuki Yamanashi 406-0023 Japan Office Phone: 81 0 553 26 3030. Personal E-mail: pxn15164@nifty.ne.jp.

YOSHIZAWA, HIROHISA, medical educator; b. Osaka, Japan, May 22, 1959; MD, St. Marianna U. Sch. Medicine, 1974; PhD, Niigata U. Sch. Medicine, 1991. Prof. Niigata U. Med. and Dental Hosp., 2010—. Bd. dirs. NE Japan Treatment Group, 2010. Grant, Tsukada Meml. Found. Fellow: ACP, Japanese Soc. Med. Oncology, Japanese Respiratory Soc., Japanese Soc. Internal Medicine. Office: 1-754 Asahimachi-Dori Chuo-ku Niigata 951-8520 Japan Office Fax: 81-25-227-2517. Business E-Mail: nnys@med.niigata-u.ac.jp.

YOSHIZUMI, DONALD TETSURO, dentist; b. Honolulu, Feb. 18, 1930; s. Richard Kiyoshi and Hatsue (Tanouye) Yoshizumi; m. Barbara Fujiko Iwashita, June 25, 1955 (dec. Feb. 1998); children: Beth Ann E., Cara Leigh S., Erin Yuri. BS, U. Hawaii, 1952; DDS, U. Mo., 1960, grad. cert. prosthodontics, 1962, MS, 1963. Clin. instr. U. Mo. Sch. Dentistry, Kansas City, 1960—63; pvt. practice Santa Clara, Calif., 1963—70, San Jose, Calif., 1970—2008. Contbr. articles to profl. jours. With USAF, 1952—56. Mem.: ADA, Santa Clara County Dental Soc., Calif. Dental Assn., Delta Sigma Delta, Omicron Kappa Upsilon. Home: 683 Apricot Ct Los Banos CA 93635-9691

YOSHOR, DANIEL, neurosurgeon; b. Oct. 26, 1968; BA, Yeshiva U., 1989; MD with honors, U. Chgo. Pritzker Sch. Medicine, 1993. Assoc. prof., program dir. Baylor Coll. Medicine, 2008—. Chief neurosurgery St. Luke's Episcopal Hosp. Grant, NIH, VA. Fellow: Am. Assn. Neurol. Surgeons. Office: 1709 Dryden Ste 750 Houston TX 77096 Business E-Mail: dyoshor@bcm.edu.

YOU, YONG-OUK, dentist, educator; b. Seosan City, Chungnam, Republic of Korea, Aug. 17, 1966; s. Jeong-Gon and Geum-Ja (Her) You; m. Na-Young Choi, May 28, 1994; 1 child, Ju-Hyoung. Student, Wonkwang U., Republic of Korea, 1985—87, DDS, 1992; MS in Dentistry, Seoul Nat. U., Republic of Korea, 1994, PhD, 2000. Lic. dentist Ministry Health and Welfare, 1992. Rsch. and tchg. asst. Wonkwang U., Iksan, Jeonbuk, Republic of Korea, 1992—2004, prof. and chmn. dept. oral biochemistry Sch. Dentistry, 2000—; dentist Dental Clinic Seosan (Republic of Korea) Pub. Health Ctr., 1994—97; invited prof. dept. oral biochemistry Sch. Denistry Seoul Nat. U., 2000—02. Interviewer admissions office Sch. Dentistry Wonkwang U., Iksan, 2001—05; mem. Korea Dentist Licensing Exam. Bd., Seoul, 2001—; grant proposal reviewer Korea Rsch. Found., Seoul, 2002—; mem. acad. bd. Korean Assn. for Dental Rsch., Seoul, 2002—04; referee U. Indsl. Tech. Force (UNITEF) in Korea, Seoul, 2005. Vol. Med. Svc. Orgn., Sch. Dentistry Wonkwang U., Iksan, 2004; mem. Christian Med. Fellowship Korea, Seoul, 1985. Recipient Bum-Ho Young Scientist Acad. award, Korean Assn. Dental Rsch., 2000, Unilever Travel award, Internat. Assn. Dental Rsch., 2002; grantee, Korea Sci. and Engring. Found., 1996—98, 2001—04, 2002—, 2004—, Korea Rsch. Found., 2000—01, 2001—02. Mem.: Korean Acad. Prosthodontics, Korean Acad. Dental Health, Internat. Assn. for Dental Rsch., Korean Acad. Oral Biology. Achievements include patents for Composition For Inhibiting Gingival Hyperplasia That Comprising Retinol; Composition for inhibiting gingival hyperplasia that comprising ursolic acid; Composition for inhibiting gingival hyperplasia that comprising licorice acid; patents pending for Active essential oil extract isolated from Compositae Chrysanthemum boreale having inhibitory effects on growing medical pathogens; Antimicrobial drug composition against methicillin-resistant Staphylococcus aureus containing berberine; An Anti-inflammatory composition containing Tanshinone IIA; Antimicrobial drug composition against cariogenic pathogen containing Asarum sieboldii; Antimicrobial drug composition against cariogenic pathogen containing Caesalpinia sappan; A polyhydroxy-1.2.3.4-tetrahydroisoquinoline derivative and a process for the preparation thereof. Office: Wonkwang Univ Sch Dentistry 344-2 Shinyong-Dong 570-749 Iksan Jeollabuk-do Republic of Korea Office Fax: 82 63 850 7157; Home Fax: 82 63 831 4281. Business E-Mail: hope7788@wku.ac.kr.

YOUM, THOMAS, orthopedist, surgeon; b. New York, NY, Nov. 24, 1973; s. Kwang-Youl and Chung Ok Youm; m. Janet Kaye Han, Mar. 18, 2006. BA in History, Yale U., New Haven, 1995; MD, NYU Sch. Medicine, NYC, 1999. Clin. asst. prof. NYU Hosp. Joint Diseases, NYC, 2005—. Fellow: Alpha Omega Alpha; mem.: Am. Orthopaedic Soc. Sports Medicine, Arthroscopy Assn. N.Am., Am. Acad. Orthopaedic Surgeons. Office: Enrique Ergas & Thomas Youm MD PC 1056 Fifth Ave New York NY 10028

YOUMANS, JULIAN RAY, neurosurgeon, educator; b. Baxley, Ga., Jan. 2, 1928; s. John Edward and Jennie Lou (Milton) Y.; children—Reed Nesbit, John Edward, Julian Milton. BS, Emory U., 1949, MD, 1952; MS, U. Mich., 1955, PhD, 1957. Diplomate: Am. Bd. Neurol. Surgery. Intern U. Mich. Hosp., Ann Arbor, 1952-53, resident in neurol. surgery, 1953-55, 56-58; fellow in neurology U. London, 1955-56; asst. prof. neurosurgery U. Miss., 1959-62, assoc. prof., 1962-63, Med. U. S.C., 1963-65, prof., 1965-67, chief div. neurosurgery, 1963-67; prof. U. Calif., Davis, 1967-91; prof. emeritus, 1991—; chmn. dept. neurosurgery U. Calif., 1967-82. Cons. USAF, U.S. VA, NRC. Editor: Neurological Surgery, 1973; contbr. articles to profl. jours. No. vice chmn. Republican State Central Com. of Calif., 1979-81. Served with U.S. Navy, 1944-46. Mem. ACS (bd. govs. 1972-78), Congress of Neurol. Surgeons (exec. com. 1967-70), Am. Acad. Neurology, Am. Assn. Neurol. Surgeons, Am. Assn. Surgery of Trauma, Pan-Pacific Surg. Assn., Western Neurosurg. Soc., Neurosurg. Soc. Am., Soc. Neurol. Surgeons, Soc. Univ. Neurosurgeons, N. Pacific Soc. Neurology and Psychiatry, Royal Soc. Medicine, Am. Trauma Soc., U.S. C. of C., Bohemian Club, Rotary. Republican. Episcopalian. Office Phone: 530-756-6018. Business E-Mail: jryoumans@ucdavis.edu. *

YOUN, ANTHONY SUNGJIN, plastic surgeon; b. Greenville, Mich., Oct. 31, 1972; Grad. with high honors, Kalamazoo Coll.; MD, Mich. State U., 1998. Cert. Am. Bd. Plastic Surgery, 2005. Resident gen. surgery Mich. State U., Grand Rapids, 1998—2001, resident plastic surgery, 2001—03; advanced aesthetic surgery fellowship Dr. Richard Ellenbogen, LA, 2003—04; founder, surgeon Hills Plastic Surgery and Laser Centre, Rochester Hills, Mich. Ptnr. Eye Place, Bloomfield Hills, Mich.; hosp. affiliations include William Beaumont Hosp. of Troy, Crittenton Hosp. and Unasource Surgery Ctr.; cons. plastic surgeon for US Weekly, In Touch, Life and Style, OK! Mag., Pink, Jane, Plastic Surgery Products Mag., Hour Detroit, Troy Somerset Gazette, Suburban Lifestyles, Baltimore Sun, Women's Lifestyle Mag., Plastic & Reconstructive Surgery, Aesthetic Surgery Jour., Women's Healthy Style Mag., and Metro Parent Mag., among others; spkr. in field. Authored and co-authored (numerous papers and scientific manuscripts), featured on Dr. 90210, guest appearances (radio) Motor City Midday on Live 97.1 FM, 96.3 FM WDVD, host (online blog) Celebrity Cosmetic Surgery. Named Top Doctors, Hour Detroit. Mem.: AMA, Am. Soc. Plastic Surgeons, Oakland County Med. Soc., Mich. State Med. Soc. Office: Beverly Hills Plastic Surgery Centre 1349 S Rochester Rd Ste 100B Rochester MI 48307 Office Phone: 248-650-1900. Office Fax: 248-650-1967.

YOUN, BANG BU, hospital administrator; MD, Yonsei U., 1967, PhD, 1972. Family medicine resident U. Minn., 1975—78; physician UN, 1987—; founder, chief dir. Korean Acad. of Family Medicine, 1981—91; v.p. World Org. of Family Doctors, 1986—91; prof. Yonsei Univ., 1983—2008; hon. prof. Yonsei U., 2008; v.p. Gachon U., chair prof.; dir. Gachon Brain Ctr., Gil Hosp. Internat. Med. Ctr. Health columnist Radio Korea Broadcasting Station, LA, 2004—. Advisor, Goodwill Amb. to McDonals Korea, 2005—. Recipient Order of Svc. Merit. Red Stripes, 2008. Office: Gachon University Gil Medical Center 1198 Guwol-dong Namdong-Gu Incheon 405760 Republic of Korea Office Phone: 82324603213. *

YOUN, BYUNG-SOO, scientific association administrator, educator; s. Taeson Youn and Byunghyun Choi; m. Keumhee Lee, Sept. 17, 1987; children: Sup, Yeeun Christine. PhD, Ind. U., 1997. Rsch. asst. prof. Sch. of Medicine, Ind. U., 2000—01; v.p., sci. dir. KOMED Inst. for Life Sci., Seoul, Republic of Korea, 2001—03. Sci. dir. KOMED Inst. for Life Sci., Seoul, Korea (South), 2001—03; bd. mem. KOMED Ltd. Co., 2001. Author (reviewer) sci. journal. V.p. Young Christian Bus. Men's Com., Seoul, 2001—03. Achievements include discovery of several genes encoding chemokine and chemokine receptors. Office: KOMED Inst for Life Sci Korea Univ Rm 640 1 5-ka Anam-dong Sungbuk-ku Seoul 136-701 Republic of Korea Home: Woo Bang Apt 403-906 Gongneung-dong 180 Nowon-Ku Seoul Republic of Korea Office Fax: 82-2-926-1670. E-mail: bsyoun@komed.com.

YOUN, SANG-WOONG, dermatologist, educator; b. Seoul, Republic of Korea, Sept. 22, 1968; s. Myung-Koo Youn and Yong-Suk Lee; m. Won-Sun Jung, Sept. 14, 2002; 1 child, Sean Youn. MB, Seoul Nat. U., 1993, MMed in Dermatology, 1997, PhD in Dermatology, 2003. Cert. dermatologist Korean Bd. Dermatology, 1998, lic. physician Ministry Health and Welfare, 1993. Intern Seoul Nat. U. Hosp., 1993—94, resident dermatology, 1994—98; army surgeon Republic of Korea Army, 1998—2001; fellow Seoul Nat. U. Hosp., 2001—02; instr. Inje U. Coll. Medicine, 2002; clin. asst. prof. Seoul Nat. U. Bundang Hosp., Seongnam, 2002; asst. prof. Seoul Nat. U., Coll. Medicine, Seoul, 2004—. Author: (textbook) Dermatology for Medical College Students, 2006; contbr. articles to profl. jours. Capt. Republic of Korea Army, 1998—2001. Mem.: Korean Dermatol. Assn. (sec. gen. Gyeonggi divsn. 2004—05), Internat. Soc. Bioengrig. and Skin, Soc. Investigative Dermatology. Home: 5 907 Daekyo Apt Yoido-dong Youngdeungpo-gu Seoul 150889 Republic of Korea Office: Seoul Nat Univ Bundang Hosp Dept Dermatology Gumi-Dong Bundang-Gu 300 462-707 Seongnam Gyeonggi-do Republic of Korea E-mail: swyoun@snu.ac.kr, sangwoong.youn@gmail.com.

YOUN, TAE-JIN, medical educator; b. Seoul, Republic of Korea, Mar. 5, 1968; MD, Seoul Nat. U., 1992, PhD, 2004. Assoc. prof. Seoul Nat. U. Bundang Hosp. and Coll. Medicine, Seoul Nat. U., 2004—. Office: 166 Gumi-ro Bundang-gu Seongnam-si Gyeonggi-do 463-707 Republic of Korea Business E-Mail: ytjmd@snubh.org.

YOUNG, ALFRED BYRON, neurosurgeon; b. Nov. 6, 1939; s. Carlos Young and Margaret Louise (Rayburn) Stout; m. Judith Floy Gaines, Aug. 26, 1961; children: John Kevin, Alexander Bryce. BA, Transylvania U., 1961, D (hon.), 2006; MD, U. Ky., 1965; DSc honoris causa, Transylvania U., 2006. Diplomate Am. Bd. Neurol. Surgery (guest examiner 1980, 84, 94, 2005). Intern Vanderbilt U., Nashville, 1965-66, asst. resident in surgery, 1966-67, resident in neurosurgery, 1967-71; clin. instr. U. Ky., Lexington, Ky., 1973-74; pvt. practice Lexington, Ky., 1973-74; asst. prof. divsn. neurosurgery, dept. surgery U. Ky. Med. Ctr., Lexington, Ky., 1974—, prof., 1982—, acting chief, 1974-75, chief neurosurgery, 1977—2008; chief of staff U. Hosp., 2000—05, assoc. dean clin. affairs, 2000—05, sr. assoc. dean for clin. affairs, 2005—06, founding chair dept. neurosurgery, 2008—09; dir. Ky. Neurosci. Inst., 2000—. Chmn. dept. surgery U. Ky., 1986-96, chmn. operating rm. comm. 1986-96, hosp. clin. bd., 1986-96, VA dean's comm. 1986-96, press comm., 1991-96, hosp. bd. elected faculty rep., 1994-96, chmn. managed care comm., 1994-96, coun. clin. chair, 1995-96; vis. prof. U. Cin., 1981, U. Louisville, 1988, Vanderbilt U., 1988; chmn. Johnston-Wright Endowed chair, 1988-2007, chair dept. neurosurg., 2008-09; dir. Ky. Neuroscience Inst., 2004—; past bd. dirs. Ky. Organ Donor Affiliates; mem. exec. com., bd. trustees Transylvania U., bd. mem. North America Gaumma Knife Constorium; presenter in field. Contbr. articles to profl. jours. Adv. bd. Ctrl. Bank & Trust, 1999—2005; mem. liaison com. Shriner's Hosp., 1999—2005; bd. mem. North American Gamma Knife Consortium. Maj. US Army, 1971—73, Korea. Recipient Disting. Outstanding Alumnus award, Transylvania U., 2001, Disting. Alumnus award, 2001, Morrison Medallion awards, 2001, Irving E. Lunger award, 2011, Mahaley Clin. Rsch. award, Congress Neurol. Surgeons, Assn. Neurol Surgeons, 1998, William R Willard Deoris award, UK Coll Med., 2004, Disting. Alumni award, 2001, Irwin Elunger award, Tronsylvania U., 2011; named one of Am.'s Best Drs., 2005—11, Am.'s Top Drs. for Cancer, 2005, 2006—11; grantee NIH, 1987—95, 1988—99, Bowman Gray/Pfizer, 1992—96, Upjohn Pharm., 1992—94, Sterling Winthrop, 1992—95, Ciba-Geigy, 1993—97. Mem. ACS, AMA, NIH (advisory comm. 1991-95, monitoring comm. 1994—, com. mem.), Nat. Inst. Neurol. Disorders, Acad. Neurological Surgeons, Am. Surgical Assn., Soc. Neurological Surgeons, Neurosurgical Soc. Am., Am. Assn. Neurological Surgeons (bylaws comm. 1979-83, chmn. bylaws comm. 1982-83, rep. to Nat. Inst. Neurol and Comm. Disorders and Stroke 1987-2010), Congress Neurological Surgeons (rep. to NIH 1987—2010), Ky. Med. Assn., Fayette County Med. Soc., Southern Neurosurgical Soc. (pres. 1991-92, pres.-elect 1990, exec. coun. 1986-94, treas. 1986-89, chmn. fin. comm. 1986-89, long range planning comm. 1990—, chmn. long range planning comm. 1992-93, constn. and bylaws comm. 1989-90, comm. disting. practioner award, 1992—, chmn. comm. disting. practioner award, 1992-93, nominating comm. 1992—, chmn. nominating comm. 1992-93, residents award comm. 1981-82), Am. Soc. Stereotactic and Functional Neurosurgery, Ky. Neurosurgical Soc. (pres. 1990-91), Soc. Internat. Surgery, Internat. Stereotactic Radiosurgery Soc., Leksell Gamma Knife Soc., Neurotrauma Soc Achievements include patent (with others) in Multiple Function Intubation Apparatus and Method, 5,836,935 Implantable refillable controlled release device to deliver drugs directly to an internal portion of the body; research in zinc supplementation associated with improved neurologic recovery rate and visceral protein levels of patients with severe closed head-injury, nutritional and metabolic mgmt. of the head-injury patient, demographics of brain metastasis, neurosurgical diseases of aging patients, brain metastases, nutritional and metabolic variables correlate with amino acid forearm flux in patients with severe head injury, effect of lovastatin on early carotid atherosclerosis and cardiovascular events, cyclosporins- severe head injury and numerous others.

YOUNG, BARBARA, psychiatrist, educator, photographer, psychoanlyst; b. Chgo., Oct. 27, 1920; d. William Harvey and Blanche (DeBra) Y. AB, Knox Coll., 1942; MD, Johns Hopkins U., 1945; grad., Balt. Psychoanalytic Inst., 1953. Intern Univ. Hosps., Iowa City, 1945-46, asst. resident in neurology, 1946—47; asst. resident in psychiatry Phipps Clinic, Johns Hopkins U. Hosp., Balt., 1947-49; staff psychiatrist Perry Point (Md.) VA Hosp., 1949-51; practice medicine specializing in psychiatry/psychoanalysis Balt., 1951—; instr. Johns Hopkins U., 1953-69, asst. prof. psychiatry, 1969—, prof. emeritus, 1997—; freelance photographer, 1958—. Lectr. dept. psychiatry Johns Hopkins U.; lectr. Lucy Daniels Found., Carey, N.C., dept. humanities Yale U. Med. Sch., Boston Inst. for Psychotherapy, local psychiat. and social orgns. Works represented in Mus. Modern Art, N.Y.C., Balt. Mus. Art, Santa Barbara (Calif.) Mus. Art, Eastman House, Rochester, N.Y., Yale U. Gallery of Art; photographer: The Plop-A-Lop Tree, 1995, Tales of Courage: Recovering LIfe After Catastrophe, 2003; contbr. articles to profl. jours. Mem.: Am. Psychoanalytic Assn., Am. Psychiat. Assn., Balt.-Washington Ctr. for Psychoanalysis. Democrat. Address: 5307 Herring Run Dr Baltimore MD 21214-1937 Office Phone: 410-426-3583. Personal E-mail: barbarayoungmd@mac.com.

YOUNG, BENJAMIN, physician; b. Apr. 1, 1961; MD, PhD, U. Colo., 1992. Med. dir. Rocky Mountain CARES, 2009—. Office: 4545 E 9th Ave Ste 120 Denver CO 80220 Office Fax: 303-320-1953. Business E-Mail: byoung@rockymountaincares.org.

YOUNG, BRUCE KENNETH, obstetrician, gynecologist, educator; b. NYC, Aug. 11, 1938; s. Morton David and Cecile Barbara (Lebenson) Y.; m. Phyllis Ann Lipsius, Dec. 16, 1962; children: Kathryn Rachel, Caroline Sue. AB, Princeton U., 1959; MD, NYU, 1963. Diplomate Nat. Bd. Med. Examiners, 1964, Am. Bd. Ob-gyn., 1970; cert. spl. competence in maternal-fetal medicine Am. Bd. Ob-gyn., 1975. Intern Montefiore Hosp., Bronx, NY, 1963-64; resident ob-gyn. Bellevue Hosp. Ctr., NYC, 1964-68, NYU Hosp., 1964-68, rsch. fellow reproductive endocrinology, 1966—68, chief resident, 1967—68; maj. USAF, 1968—70; chief obstetrics Bellevue Hosp., NYC, 1970-95; dir. obstet. svcs. NYU Hosps. Network, 1995—2005; chief obstetrics, endocrine & infertility svc. Wilford Hall Hosp., San Antonio. Cons. NJ Health Sys. Agy., Hoffman LaRoche Co., Kimberly Clark, Litton Ind., Revlon Corp., 1975—85; dir. maternal and fetal medicine NYU Sch. Medicine Med. Ctr., NYC, 1975—2005; prof. ob-gyn. NYU Sch. Medicine, 1980—, Silverman prof. ob-gyn., 1996—; mem. sci. adv. bd. Grain Foods Found., 2005-. Author: Miscarriage, Medicine and Miracles, 2008, The Intellectual Devotional Health, 2009;editor: Perinatal Medicine Today, 1980, Problems in Perinatal Medicine, 1986, Jour. Maternal-Fetal Neonatal Medicine, 2007-09, Maternal Fetal Medicine Report, 2005-; Diagnostic Gynecology and Obstetrics, 1988-90, Jour. Perinatal Medicine, 1995-; contbr. chpts. to books and articles to profl. jours. Bd. dirs. N.Y. State Prenatal Diagnostic Ctr., 1977-87, Am. Bd. Ob-gyn. Div. Maternal Fetal Medicine 1980-90, dir. exams., 1984-; chair health professions bd. Greater N.Y. March of Dimes, N.Y.C., 1995—2005, v.p., dir., 1995-2005. Recipient Barton award, 1968, Disting. Svc. in Med. Edn. award March of Dimes, 1985, Voluntary Svc. award, 1990, Program Excellence award, 1991, Disting. Alumnus award Bellevue Obst. Gyn. Soc., 1998, Solomon A. Berson Med. Alumni Achievement award, NYU, 2005 Fellow ACOG (Outstanding Achievement award 1998), Am. Fertility Soc., Am. Gynecol. and Obstet. Soc., Am. Assn. Gynecol. Laparoscopists, Soc. Laparoendoscopic Surgeons, N.Y. Perinatal Soc. (pres. 1997-99), NY Obstet. Soc. (pres. 2001-02), Royal Soc. Medicine (Eng.); mem. AMA, Soc. Maternal-Fetal Medicine (bd. dirs., 1980-83), Soc. Gynecol. Investigation, Soc. Study Reproduction, Am. Inst. Ultrasound Medicine, NY Acad. Med., NY Acad. Scis., NYU Sch. Medicine Alumni Assn. (pres. 1995-96, citation 1996, NYU Faculty Senator, 2008-2010), Mar-a-Lago Club (Palm Beach, Fla.), Princeton Club NY, Alpha Omega Alpha Med. Honor. Soc., NYU Sch. Medicine. Achievements include NYU ob-gyn.dept annual research day named after him. Office: 530 1st Ave Ste 5G New York NY 10016-6402 Office Phone: 212-263-6359. Business E-Mail: bruce.young@nyumc.org.

YOUNG, DANIEL GREER, surgical pediatrics educator; b. Skipness, Scotland, Nov. 22, 1932; s. Gabriel and Julia McColl (McNair) Y.; m. Agnes Gilchrist Donald, Aug. 3, 1957; children: Rhoda Agnes, Kenneth Donald. MBChB, U. Glasgow, Scotland, 1956; diploma of tropical medicine and hygiene, U. Liverpool, Eng., 1959; MD (hon.), U. Wroclaw, 2008. Sr. registrar, resident asst. surgeon Hosp. for Sick Children, London, 1965-67; sr. lectr. Inst. Child Health, London, 1967-69; hon. cons. surgeon Gt. Ormond St. & Queen Elizabeth Hosps., London, 1967-69; head dept. surg. pediatrics U. Glasgow, 1969-98, reader in surg. pediatrics, 1983-92, prof. surg. pediatrics, 1992-98, hon. sr. rsch. fellow, 1999—. Hon. cons. surgeon Greater Glasgow Health Bd., 1979-98; chmn. nat. paramedic tng. bd. Scottish Ambulance Svc., 1990-98; profl. adv. group Scottish Ambulance Svc. Brit. Isles, 1988-98; vis. prof. Pilasganovich, 1998; hon. sr. rsch. fellow Glasgow U.; archivist Royal Hosp. Sick Children, Glasgow, 1998—. Co-author: Pediatric Surgery, 1972, Children's Medicine and Surgery, 1995, The History of Surgical Pediatrics, 2009; editor Jour. Pediat. Surgery, 1987—. Hon. sec. Soc. for Rsch. in Hydrocephalus and Spina Bifida, 1980-85, trustee, 1995—, hon. mem., 1998—, hon. mem. BAPS; pres. British Soc. for History of Pediat. and Child Health, 2007-; elder Sherbrooks, St. Gilbert's Ch. of Scotland, 1975-. Recipient Denis Browne Gold medal, 1999. Fellow Royal Coll. Surgeons, Edinburgh, Royal Coll. Surgeons, Royal Coll. Physicians and Surgeons (mem. coun. 1987-91), Royal Coll. Pediats. and Child Health; mem. Brit. Med. Assn., Brit. Assn. Pediat. Surgeons (pres. 1990-92, hon. 1998—), Brit. Urol. Assn., Royal Soc. Medicine, West of Scotland Surg. Assn. (pres. 1993-94), Royal Med. Chirurgical Soc. of Glasgow (pres. 1988-89), Hungarian Pediatric Surg. Assn. (hon.), South African Pediat. Surg. Assn. (hon.), Am. Pediat. Surg. Assn. (hon.), Polish Assn. Ped. Surg. (hon.), Scottish Spina Bifida Assn. (hon. pres. 1976—), Egyptian Pediatric Surg. Assn. (hon.), Ont Soc. Hist. Padiat. Child Health(pres. 2006-10, sec. 2010-11, hon. mem. 2011-). Presbyterian. Avocations: gardening, curling. Home: 49 Sherbrooke Ave Glasgow G41 4SE Scotland Office: Royal Hosp Sick Children Yorkhill Glasgow G3 8SJ Scotland Office Phone: 0044-141-201-0572. Business E-Mail: dgy1x@clinmed.gla.ac.uk, daniel.young@glasgow.ac.uk.

YOUNG, DARRIN JUN, engineering educator; b. Shanghai, July 31, 1967; PhD, U. Calif., Berkeley, 1999. Asst. prof. Case Western Res. U., 1999—2005, assoc. prof., 2005—09, Utah Sci. Tech. and Rsch., U. Utah, 2009—. Mem.: IEEE. Avocations: hiking, travel, reading. Office: University Utah 50 S Central Campus Dr Salt Lake City UT 84112 Business E-Mail: darrin.young@utah.edu.

YOUNG, DELANO VICTOR, cell biologist, pharmaceutical scientist, biochemist, educator; b. Honolulu, Nov. 17, 1945; s. Lum Fai and Gladys Sau Pung (Wong) Y.; m. Chin-Yi Caroline Yang, Jan. 31, 1970; 1 child, Heather Tien. BS, Stanford U., 1967; PhD, Columbia U., 1973. Postdoctoral fellow Salk Inst. for Biol. Studies, San Diego, 1973-75; asst. prof. dept. chemistry Boston U., 1975-83; asst. dir. Bioassay Systems Rsch. Corp., Woburn, Mass., 1984-86; sr. scientist Damon Biotech, Inc., Needham Heights, Mass., 1986-88, dir., 1988-90; head cell biology Abbott Biotech, Inc. (formerly Damon Biotech, Inc.), Needham Heights, 1990-92; group leader tissue culture Transkaryotic Therapies, Inc., Cambridge, Mass., 1992-94; sect. head, cell culture NitroMed, Inc., Boston, 1994—2006. Cons. D. Van Nostrand Pub., Boston, 1975-83, Allyn and Bacon Pub., Boston, 1975-83, Pearson Prentice Hall Pub., Upper Saddle River, NJ, 2010-; vis. scholar in biochemistry and molecular biology Harvard U., 1982-83; reviewer sci. jour. in biochemistry, 1973—; initial scientist several biotech. start-up cos., Boston area; adj. faculty mem. Mass. Bay CC, Wellesley, 2007-; part time lectr. Northeastern U., Boston, 2008-. Author: (chpt.) Inverted Microcarriers: Using Microencapsulation to Grow Anchorage-Dependent Cells, 1992, Fundamentals of Animal Cell Encapsulation and Immobilization, 1992, Culture of Anchorage Dependent Cells, 1999, Cell Encapsulation Technology and Therapeutics, 1999; contbr. over 30 articles to profl. jours. Eugene Higgins fellow Columbia U., 1967-68, Jane Coffin Childs fellow Salk Inst., 1973-75; GM scholar Stanford U., 1963-67. Mem. AAAS, Sigma Xi, Phi Beta Kappa, Phi Lambda Upsilon, Am. Soc. Cell Biology (emeritus mem.). Roman Catholic. Achievements include significant contributions to understanding of the biochemical role of polyamines, to nutritional requirements of cancer cells, to devel. of recombinant protein production in biotechnology, to cultivation of anchorage dependent cells in suspension and to nitric oxide pharmaceuticals. Home: 12 Dennis Rd Wellesley MA 02481 Personal E-mail: delyoung@verizon.net.

YOUNG, DONALD ALAN, former Federal Agency Administrator; b. Oakland, Calif., Feb. 8, 1939; s. Leo Alan and Pearl Anita (Walker) Y.; children: Jennifer, Karen BA, U. Calif., Berkeley, 1960, MD, 1964. Diplomate Am. Bd. Internal Medicine. Intern, then resident in internal medicine U. Calif. Hosp., San Francisco, 1964-66; resident in internal medicine Parkland Hosp., Dallas, 1966-67; fellow chest diseases U. Calif. Hosp., San Francisco, 1967-68; mem. staff Palo Alto (Calif.) Med. Clinic, 1970-75; med. dir. Am. Lung Assn., 1975-77; scholar adminstrv. scholars program VA, Washington, 1977-80; dep. dir. policy Bur. Program Policy Health Care Financing Adminstrn., HHS, Washington, 1980—84; exec. dir. Prospective Payment Assessment Commn., Washington, 1984—97; sr. v.p. Am. Assn. Health Plans, 1997—99; COO, med. dir., pres. Health Ins. Associates Am., 1999—2003; acting asst. sec. planning and evaluation HHS, Washington, 1999—2005; chmn. Md. Health Svcs. Cost Review Commn., 2007—. Clin. instr. U. Calif. Med. Sch., San Francisco, 1968—70, Stanford U. Med. Sch., 1970—75. Bd. visitors Ind. U. Served with M.C. AUS, 1968-70, mem. Md. Health Care Reform Coordinatory Coun., 2010- Decorated Commendation medal.; Recipient Borden award, 1964 Home: 6109 Trotter Ridge Ct Columbia MD 21044-4919

YOUNG, DONALD STIRLING, clinical pathology educator; b. Belfast, N. Ireland, Dec. 17, 1933; s. John Stirling and Ruth Muir (Whipple) Y.; m. Silja Meret; children: Gordon, Robert, Peter. MB, ChB, U. Aberdeen, Scotland, 1957; PhD in Chem. Pathology, U. London, 1962. Terminable lectr. materia medica U. Aberdeen, 1958-59; fellow Postgrad. Med. Sch., U. London, 1959-62, registrar, 1962-64; vis. scientist NIH, Bethesda, Md., 1965-66, chief clin. chemistry service, 1966-77; head clin. chemistry sect. Mayo Clinic, Rochester, Minn., 1977-84; prof. pathology and lab. medicine U. Pa., 1984—, vice chmn. lab. medicine dept. pathology and lab. medicine, 1994—2009; dir. William Pepper Lab. Hosp. of U. Pa., 1984—2009. Past bd. dirs. Nat. Com. Clin. Lab. Standards. Co-editor: Drug Interference and Drug Metabolism in Clinical Chemistry, 1976, Clinician and Chemist, 1979, Chemical Diagnosis of Disease, 1979, Drug Measurement and Drug Effects in Laboratory Health Science, 1980, Interpretation of Clinical Laboratory Tests, 1985, Effects of Preanalytical Variables on Clinical Laboratory Tests, 2007, Effects of Drugs on Clinical Laboratory Tests, 2000, Effects of Disease on Clinical Laboratory Tests, 2001. Recipient Dir.'s award NIH, 1977, Gerard B. Lambert award, 1974-75, MDS Health Group award Can. Soc. Clin. Chemists, 1978; Roman lectr. Australian Assn. Clin. Biochemists, 1979; Jendrassik award Hungarian Soc. Clin. Pathologists, 1985, ATB award Italian Soc. Clin. Biochemistry, 1987. Mem. Am. Assn. Clin. Chemistry (J.H. Roe award Capital sect. 1973, Bernard Gerulat award N.J. sect. 1977, Ames award 1977, Van Slyke award N.Y. met. sect. 1985, J.G. Reinhold award Phila. sect. 1993, past pres.), Internat. Fedn. Clin. Chemists (Distinguished Clin. Chemist award, 2008, past pres.), Acad. Clin. Lab. Physicians and Scientists (past exec. com.), Assn. Clin. Biochemists (Ciba-Corning lectr. 1985). Achievements include research in clinical chemistry, optimized use of the clinical laboratory. Office: Hosp U Pa 3400 Spruce St Philadelphia PA 19104-4283 Business E-Mail: donaldyo@mail.med.upenn.edu.

YOUNG, ESTELLE IRENE, dermatologist, educator; b. NYC, Nov. 2, 1945; d. Sidney D. and Blanche (Krosney) Young. BA magna cum laude, Mt. Holyoke Coll., 1967; MD, Downstate Med. Ctr., 1971. Intern Lenox Hill Hosp., NYC, 1971—72, resident in medicine, 1972—73; resident in dermatology Columbia Presbyn. Hosp., 1973—74, NYU Hosp., 1974—75, Boston U. Hosp., 1975—76; asst. dermatologist Harvard U. Health Svcs., Cambridge, 1975—76; assoc. staff mem. dermatology Boston U. Med. Ctr., 1975—77; pvt. practice medicine specializing in dermatology Petersburg, Va., 1976—97; mem. staff Poplar Springs Hosp., 1976—2002, Southside Regional Med. Ctr. (formerly Petersburg Gen. Hosp.), 1976—2002, Ctrl. State Hosp., 1984—2007. Clin. instr. dept. dermatology Med. Coll. Va., 1976-87, asst. clinic prof., 1988-94, assoc. clin. prof., 1994-2002; sec. med. staff Petersburg Gen. Hosp., 1982; dermatology cons. Cerebral Palsy Assn. N.Y. State, 1999-2005, 2007-08, Manhattan's Physician Group, 2008. Author: Visions of Mauna Kea; contbr. articles to profl. jours. Fellow: Am. Acad. Dermatology; mem.: Hawaii Dermatology Soc., Tidewater Dermatology Soc. (pres. 1982—83), Va. Dermatology Soc., Amateur Astronomers Assn., Physicians Social Responsibility Soc., Tidewater Physicians Social Responsibility (pres. 1990), Internat. Physicians Prevention of Nuclear War, Sigma Xi. Home and Office: PO Box 20182 New York NY 10021-0063 Office Fax: 212-249-5948. Personal E-mail: eiy112@aol.com.

YOUNG, FRANK EDWARD, retired federal agency and religious organization administrator; b. Mineola, NY, Sept. 1, 1931; s. Frank E. and Erma F. Y.; m. Leanne Hutchinson, Oct. 20, 1956; children: Lorrie, Debora, Peggy, Frank, Jonathan. MD, SUNY, 1956; PhD, Case Western Res. U., 1962; DSc (hon.), Roberts Wesleyan Coll., 1983, Houghton Coll., 1984, SUNY, 1986, L.I. U., 1986, Western Bapt. Coll., 1988. Asst. prof. pathology Western Res. U., Cleve., 1962-65; assoc. mem. microbiology Scripps Clinic & Rsch. Found., LaJolla, Calif., 1965-68; assoc. prof. biology U. Calif., San Diego, 1967-70; mem. microbiology & exptl. pathology Scripps Clinic & Rsch.

Found., LaJolla, Calif., 1968-70; prof. microbiology and chmn. dept., prof. pathology and radiation biology and biophysics U. Rochester, N.Y., 1970-79, dir. Med. Ctr., N.Y., 1979-81, dean Sch. Medicine and Dentistry, N.Y., 1979-84, v.p. for health affairs N.Y., 1981-84; commr. FDA, Rockville, Md., 1984-89, dep. asst. sec. for health sci. and environ., 1989-93; dir. office emergency preparedness, 1993-96; pastor adult ministries 4th Presbyn. Ch., Bethesda, Md., 1996—2002; exec. dir. Reformed Theol. Sem. Met. Washington, Bethesda, 1996-99; v.p. Reformed Theol. Sem., Bethesda, Md., 1999—2002; chmn., CEO Cosmos Alliance, 2002—08, chmn., 2009; ptnr. Essex Woodlands Health Ventures, 2006—. U.S. rep. WHO exec. bd., Geneva, 1985-88; bd. dirs. High Tech., Rochester, N.Y., 1983-84. Contbr. numerous articles on cloning, gene mapping, gene shuttle vectors, 1970-84; initiator Fed. Regulations rules to increase access to exptl. drugs to desperately ill, 1987-88. Lectr. Christian orgns., 1970—; mem. United Way, Rochester, N.Y., 1982-84, N.Y. State Statutory Adv. Com. on DNA, Albany, N.Y., 1978. Recipient sec.'s spl. citation Dept. Health and Human Svcs., 1989, Surgeon Gen.'s Exemplary Svc. medal, 1988, Disting. Svc. medal Pub. Health Svc., 1986, Edward Mott award, 1985, Surgeon Gen.'s Medallion, 1992, Disting. Alumnus Up state Med. U., 2006. Mem. Inst. Medicine of NAS, AAAS, Am. Acad. Microbiology (bd. govs.). Avocations: fishing, boating. Office Phone: 301-908-3182. Personal E-mail: frankcosmos@aol.com. Business E-Mail: fyoung@ewhv.com.

YOUNG, G. BRYAN, medical educator; b. Melfort, Sask., Can., May 21, 1946; s. William Gordon and Grace Marie Young; m. Ingrid Ann Hutchinson, July 22, 2006; children: Stewart Ross, Andrew Bryan, Megan Elizabeth, Zara Katarina Hutchinson. MD, U. Sask., Saskatoon, 1970. Prof. neurology U. Western Ont., London, Canada, 1981—. Editor Can. Jour. Neurol. Scis. Author books on coma and neurocritical care. Mem.: Royal Coll. Physicians and Surgeons Can. Home: 3-140 McGarrell Dr London ON Canada N6A5J1 Office: Univ Hosp 339 Winderemere Rd PO Box 5339 Stn B London ON N6A5A5 Canada Office Fax: 5196633753. Business E-Mail: bryan.young@lhsc.on.ca.

YOUNG, HENRY E., tissue engineering medical educator; b. Dayton, Ohio, Dec. 5, 1951; s. Henry O. and Lucille M. Y.; m. Valerie E. Achorn, May 16, 1976; 1 child, Katherine. BS in Biology, Ohio State U., 1974; MSc in Zoology, U. Ark., 1977; PhD, Tex. Tech. U., 1983, postdoc. in Carbohydrate Biochemistry, Case Western Res. U., Cleave. Instr.biochemistry Rush Presbyn.-St. Luke's Med. Ctr., Chgo., 1987—88; asst. prof. anatomy Mercer U. Sch. Medicine, Macon, Ga., 1988—95, asst. prof. surgery, 1988—94, assoc. prof. anatomy, pediat., 1995—2004, prof. anatomy, pediat., 2004—; prof. ob/gyn, 2007—; prof. anesthesiology, 2009—. Inventor in field. Recipient Hooding award for excellence in tchg. and rsch., Mercer U. Med. Sch., 1993, Merit award, 1993, Hooding award for excellence in tchg. and rsch., 1994, Gender Equity award, Am. Med. Women's Assn., 1997, Humanism in Medicine award, Arnold P. Gold Found., 2005, Internat. Einstein Iconic Achievement award, 2009, Tchg. award, 1993—94, Men Achievement award, 1996; nominee Man of Yr. award, 2010; NIH Postdoctoral fellow in biochemistry, Case We. Res. U., Cleve., 1983—85, postdoctoral fellow, Muscular Dystrophy Assn., 1985—87. Mem.: Internat. Cellular Medicine Soc., Am. Soc. Cell Biology, Stem Cells and Regen Medicine, Tissue Culture Soc., Am. Assn. Anatomists, Arnold P. Gold Found., Humanism Hon. Soc. Achievements include discovery of adult germ layer lineage stem cells, adult pluripotent stem cells, and adult near totipotent stem cells; invention of muscle morphogenetic protein and scar inhibitory factor; research in basic mechanisms of fetal alcohol syndrome, tissue regeneration and stem cell biology. Avocation: reading. Office: 1550 College Str Macon GA 31207 Office Phone: 478-301-4034, 478-301-4088. Office Fax: 478-301-5487. Personal E-mail: young.he@yahoo.com. Business E-Mail: young_he@mercer.edu.

YOUNG, JAMES BENARD, dean; b. Berkeley, Calif., Feb. 17, 1949; BS, U. Kans., 1971; MD, Baylor Coll. Medicine, 1974. Sect. head, heart failure and cardiac transplant medicine Cleve. Clinic Found., 1995—2003, chmn., divsn. medicine, 2003—09, exec. dean, Cleve. Clinic Lerner Coll. Medicine, 2009—. Prof., medicine Cleve. Clinic Lerner Coll. Medicine Case Western Res. U., 2003. Fellow: ACP, European Soc. Cardiology, Am. Heart Assn., Am. Coll. Cardiololgy. Office: Cleve Clinic Found 9500 Euclid Ave Cleveland OH 44195 Office Fax: 216-636-3206. Business E-Mail: youngj@ccf.org.

YOUNG, JAMES JULIUS, academic administrator, retired military officer; b. Ft. Ringgold, Tex., Nov. 28, 1926; s. John Cooper and Violet Thelma (Ohl) Y.; m. June Agnes Hillstead, Dec. 17, 1948; children: Robert Michael, Steven Andrew, Patrick James, Mary Frances. BS, U. Md., 1960; M.H.A., Baylor U., 1962; PhD in Hosp. and Health Adminstrn, U. Iowa, 1969. Commd. 2d lt. U.S. Army, 1947, advanced through grades to brig. gen., 1977, comdr., med. ops. officer, dir. tng. field med. units in European Command, 1949-53; comdr. Mil. Med. Leadership Sch., 1953-54; med. advisor (Nationalist Army of China), 1955-57; asst. adminstr. Fitzsimons Army Med. Center, 1957-60; med. plans and ops. officer (US Forces), Korea, 1962-63; sr. field med. instr., chief field med. service Med. Field Service Sch., 1963-66; dir. health care orgn. and mgmt. analysis Office of Surgeon Gen., 1969-71; dir. med. plans and ops. directorate Office of the Surgeon, Military Assistance Command, Vietnam, 1971-72; exec. officer, chief adminstrv. services Silas Hays Army Hosp., 1973-74; military health analyst, military health care study OMB, Exec. Office of Pres., 1974-76; dep. dir. resources mgmt. and cons. for health care adminstrn. Office of Surgeon Gen., 1976-77; chief med. svcs. corps U.S. Army, 1977-81; dir. resources mgmt. Office of Surgeon Gen., 1977-81; ret., 1981; instr. U. Iowa, 1967-69; asst. prof., preceptor Baylor U., 1973-74; vice chancellor for health affairs W.Va. Bd. Regents, Charleston, 1982-87; dean sch. of allied health scis. U. Tex. Health Sci. Ctr., San Antonio, 1987-90, interim dean Sch. Medicine, 1988-89, dean Sch. Medicine, 1989—, dean emeritus, 2000—. Cons. to Min. of Health, Republic of Vietnam, 1971-72, 1989-2000; adj. prof. Baylor U., 1977-81, George Washington U., 1975-76, W.Va. U., 1986; prof. U. Tex. health Sci. Ctr., San Antonio, 1989-2000. Contbr. articles to profl. jours. Decorated D.S.M., Legion of Merit, Meritorious Service medal, others; recipient Walter Reed medal, 1981; Army Med. Dept. medal for contbn. to health service, 1981, Order of Mil. Med. Merit, 1981, U. Tex. Health Scis. Ctr. Hon. medallion Fountains of Progress, 2000; recipient Humanism in Medicine medallion Health Care Foun. NJ, 2000; named to Hall of Fame, Infantry Sch. Officer Cand. Roman Catholic. Home: 1610 Anchor Dr San Antonio TX 78213-1943 Personal E-mail: jyoung51@satx.rr.com.

YOUNG, JAY ALFRED, chemical safety and health consultant, editor, writer; b. Huntington, Ind., Sept. 8, 1920; s. Jacob Phillip and Marie (Skully) Y.; m. Anne Elizabeth Neff, June 29, 1942 (dec. June 1962); children: John, Paul, Cecelia, Michael, Joseph, Andrea, Therese, Gregory, Thomas, Lucy, Margaret, Antonia; m. Mary Ann Owens, Aug. 15, 1962; children: James, Laurence; 4 stepchildren. BS, Ind. U., Bloomington, 1939; AM, Oberlin Coll., Ohio, 1940; PhD, U. Notre Dame, South Bend, Ind., 1950. Chief chemist Asbestos Mfg. Co., Huntington, Ind., 1941-42; ordnance engr. U.S. War Dept., Washington, 1942-44; from instr. to prof. chemistry King's Coll., Wilkes-Barre, Pa., 1949-69; vis. prof. Carleton U., Ottawa, Ont., Canada, 1969-70, Fla. State U., Tallahassee, 1975-77; Hudson prof. Auburn (Ala.) U., 1970-75; mgr. tech. publs. Chem. Mfrs. Assn., Washington, 1977-80; chem. safety and health cons. Silver Spring, Md., 1980—. Pro bono cons. OSHA, EPA, Consumer Product Safety Commn., Washington, 1980—; contributor Ency. Britannica, 1974-; lectr. in field. Author: Practice in Thinking, 1958, Elements of General Chemistry, 1960, Chemical Concepts, 1963, Selected Principles of Chemistry, 1963, Arithmetic for Students of Science, 1968, Instructor's Guide for Chemistry, a Cultural Approach, 1971, Study Guide for General Chemistry, 1974, Fire!, 1977, Actions and Reactions, 1978, Chemistry, A Human Concern, 1978, Kitchen Chemistry, 1980, Electron Microscopy Safety Handbook, 1985, Introduction to Toxicology, 2004; co-author: Study Guide for Continental Classroom Chemistry, NBC/TV, vols. I and II, 1959, 60, Keys to Chemistry, 1973, Chemistry Preparation Laboratory, 1973, Keys to Oxidation-Reduction, 1974, Things that Last, 1977, Principles of Laboratory Safety (with videotape), 1980, OSHA Hazard Communication Regulations, 1984, Chemical Safety Manual for Small Businesses, 1989, 2d edit., 1992, Developing a Chemical Hygiene Plan, 1990; editor: Guidelines and Recommendations for the Preparation and Continuing Education of Secondary School Teachers of Chemistry, 1977, Improving Safety in the Chemical Laboratory: A Practical Guide, 1989, 2d edit., 1992 (also contbr.), Safety in Academic Chemistry Laboratories, Vols. 1 and 2, 7th edit., 2002, Chemical Safety for Teachers and Their Supervisors, Grades 7-12, 2001; co-editor: Heath Chemistry Laboratory Experiments, 1987, Handbook of Chemical Health and Safety, 2001 (also contbr.), Chem. Lab. Info. Profiles, 2001—09; contbr. articles to profl. jours. Tech. resource person to media and expert witness regarding chem. hazards, precautions, transp. incidents involving chems.; mem. NSF Coll. Chemistry Commn., 1962-68. Lt. USNR, 1944-46. Recipient Disting. Chemistry Alumnus award U. Notre Dame, 1968, Excellence in Chemistry Tchg. award Mfg. Chemists Assn., 1970. Fellow AAAS; Fellow Am. Chem. Soc. (councilor 1963-87, policy com. 1970-81, sec. divsn. chem. edn. 1969-78, chmn. divsn. chem. health and safety 1979-80, mem. chem. safety com. 1982-2003, Chem. Health and Safety award 1991, Outstanding Svc. award 2003, 2007). Roman Catholic. Avocations: wood and metalworking, gardening. Home and Office: 12916 Allerton Ln Silver Spring MD 20904-3105 Office Phone: 301-384-1768. Personal E-mail: chemsafety@verizon.net.

YOUNG, JAY MAITLAND, health products executive, consultant; b. Louisville, Nov. 26, 1944; s. Clyde Dudley and Olive May (Tyas) Y. BA in Chemistry and Math. magna cum laude, Vanderbilt U., 1966; MS in Biochemistry, Yale U., 1967, MPhil in Phys. Chemistry, 1968, PhD in Chemistry, 1971. Cert. Am. Med. Writers Assn. Multidisciplinary Core, 1999. Asst. prof. chemistry Bryn Mawr (Pa.) Coll., 1970-76; rsch. biochemist Abbott Labs., Ill., 1977-78, project mgr. physiol. diagnostics Abbott Park, 1978-80, project mgr. cancer product devel., 1980-82, internat. clin. specialist sci. affairs, 1982-85, clin. project mgr. physiol. diagnostic quality and sci. support, 1986-90, staff quality assurance and sci. support, 1990-93, fertility, pregnancy, thyroid cancer mgr., quality and sci. support, 1993-95, 1995-97, staff noninfectious disease diagnostics sci. affairs, 1997—2001; cons. and med. writer diagnostic and pharm. areas, 2002—. Cons. Inst. for Cancer Rsch., Fox Chase, Phila., 1974, vis. scientist, 1975-76; honors examiner Swarthmore Coll., 1973, 74, mem. vis. evaluation com., 1975; presenter to med. groups on cancer markers, viral hepatitis and epidemiology of AIDS, 1982-84. Contbr. articles to profl. jours. Vol. Episcopal Ch. Outreach Commn. Named to Hon. Order Ky. Cols.; predoctoral fellow NSF, Yale U., 1966-70; postdoctoral fellow, NIH, U. Oxford, 1971-72; travel grantee NATO, 1974. Mem. Am. Med. Writers Assn. (Del. Valley chpt. program chair 2002-03, treas. 2003-06, cert mem. Multi-disciplinary Core 1999). Home Phone: 773-728-1386. E-mail: maitlandyoung@hotmail.com.

YOUNG, JEANINE, nursing director, researcher; b. Innisfail, Queensland, Australia, July 25, 1967; BSN, U. West Eng., 1995; PhD, Sch. Medicine, U. Bristol, 1999. E grade staff nurse, midwife St. Michaels Hosp., 1991—99, Southmead Hosp., 1991—95; rsch. assoc. U. Bristol, 1995—99; nursing dir., rsch. Royal Children's Hosp., Children's Health Svcs., 2000—. Adj. prof. Sch. Nursing and Midwifery, Faculty Health, Queensland U. Tech., 2007—11, Rsch. Ctr. Clin. and Cmty. Practice Innovation, Griffith U., 2008—11; adj. assoc. prof. Ctr. On-Line Health, U. Queensland, 2010—11, Sch. Nursing and Midwifery, U. Queensland, 2008—10; chair, sci. adv. group SIDS and Kids Nat., 2004. Recipient Red Nose Day Hero award, SIDS and Kids Queensland, Queensland Finalist, Hesta Australian Nursing award, Hesta Australia, 2007, Queensland Health Australia Day award, Queensland Health, 2011, ISPID Health Educator award, Internat. Soc. Study and Prevention Infant Death, 2011; finalist Leadership Nursing and Midwifery Finalist, Deakin U. and Health Super, 2010. Fellow: Royal Coll. Nursing Australia; mem.: Australian Coll. Children and Young People's Nurses, Queensland Honor Soc. Nursing, Australian Coll. Midwives. Avocations: mountain climbing, walking. Office: Royal Children's Hosp Herston Rd Brisbane Queensland 4029 Australia Office Fax: 61 7 3636 1224. Business E-Mail: jeanine_young@health.qld.gov.au.

YOUNG, JENNIFER BAXENDELL, former federal agency administrator; b. Bellevue, Ohio; m. J. T. Young. BA magna cum laude, Georgetown U. Exec. asst. Ohio Human Services Dept.; dir. health legis. Nat. Governors' Assn.; sr. adv. to Chmn. William V. Roth Senate Fin. Com.; sr. adv. on health care issues to Chmn. William Thomas House Com. on Ways and Means; exec. dir. pub. programs Am. Assn. Health Plans, 2002; dep. asst. sec. for legis. US Dept. Health & Human Services, Washington, asst. sec. for legis., 2003—05, acting sr. counselor for health policy, 2005; ptnr. Tarplin, Downs & Young LLC, 2006—.

YOUNG, JESS RAY, retired internist; b. Fairfield, Ill., Feb. 4, 1928; s. Edgar S. and Clara B. (Musgrave) Y.; m. Gloria Wynn, July 10, 1953; children— James C., Patricia A. BS, Franciscan U., 1951; MD, St. Louis U., 1955. Intern Highland Alameda County Hosp., Oakland, Calif., 1955-56; resident in internal medicine Cleve. Clinic Hosp., 1956-59, mem. staff dept. vascular medicine, 1959-97, chmn. dept., 1976-97; ret., 1998. Co-author: Leg Ulcer, 1975, Peripheral Vascular Diseases, 1991, 1996; contbr. articles to profl. jours., chpts. to books. Served with AUS, 1946-47. Mem. AMA, Am. Heart Assn. (stroke council), Am. Coll. Cardiology, Internat. Cardiovascular Soc., ACP, Am. Fedn. Clic. Research, Ohio Soc. Internal Medicine, Soc. for Vascular Medicine, Inter-Urban Club. Methodist. Home: 1503 Burlington Rd Cleveland OH 44118-1216 Personal E-mail: jesyoung@adelphia.net.

YOUNG, LAURENCE RETMAN, biomedical engineer, educator; b. NYC, Dec. 19, 1935; s. Benjamin and Bess (Retman) Y.; m. Joan Marie Fisher, June 12, 1960; children: Eliot Fisher, Leslie Ann, Robert Retman. AB, Amherst Coll., 1957; SB, MIT, 1957, SM, 1959, ScD, 1962; Certificat de License (French Govt. fellow), Faculty of Sci. U. of Paris, France, 1958. Registered profl. engr., Mass. Engr. Sperry Gyroscope Co., Great Neck, NY, 1957; engr. NASA Instrumentation Lab., MIT, 1958-60, asst. prof. aero. and astronautics, 1962-67, assoc. prof., 1967-70, prof., 1970—, payload specialist spacelab life sci., 1991-93; Apollo Program prof., chair in astronautics MIT, Cambridge, 1995—; prof. Baylor Coll. Medicine, Houston, 1996—2003; prof. of health sci. and tech. Harvard MIT, 2003—. Dir. Nat. Space Biomed. Rsch. Inst., 1997-01; summer lectr. U. Ala., Huntsville, 1966-68; lectr. Med. Sch. Harvard U., 1970-78; mem. tng. com. biomed. engring. NIH, 1971-73; mem. com. space medicine and biology Space Sci. Bd., NAS, 1974-77, chmn. vestibular panel summer study of life scis. in space, 1977; mem. com. engring. and clin. care NAE, 1970; mem. Air Force Sci. Adv. Bd., 1979-85; mem. Air Force Studies Bd., NRC, 1982, Aeros. and Space Engrs. Bd., 1982-87; mem. NRC Com. on Space Sta., 1987, 1991—, Com. on Human Exploration Space, 1990, Com. on Human Factors, 1990—; CHABA coun. NASA Task Force on Sci. Uses of Space Sta., 1982-85; vis. prof. Swiss Fed. Inst. Tech., Zurich, 1972-73, Conservatoire Nationale des Arts and Metiers, Paris, 1972-73, Stanford U., 1987-88; vis. scientist Kantonsspital Zurich, 1972-73; prin. investigator vestibular expts. on Spacelabs— 1, SLS-1, 2 and D-1, 1977—; cons. Applied Sci. Lab., NASA, Gulf & Western, Link div. Singer Co., Boeing, Lockheed, others; payload specialist Space Shuttle STS-58 (Spacelab SLS-2), NASA Johnson Space Ctr., 1992—; vis. prof. Coll. de France, Paris, 2003. Contbg. author: chpt. on vestibular system Medical Physiology, 1974, Handbook of Physiology, 1983, Encyclopedia of Neuroscience, 1987, editorial bd. chpt. on vestibular system Internat. Jour. Man-Machine Studies, 1966-75, Neurosci., 1976-92; contbr. numerous articles to profl. jours. Recipient Pub. Svc. Group Achievement award NASA, 1984, Exceptional Civilian Svc. award USAR, 1985, Koetser Found. prize, 1998. Fellow IEEE (Franklin V. Taylor award 1963, First Ann. Space Life Sci. lectr. 1990), AIAA (Dryden lectr. 1981), Aerospace Medical Assn. (Jeffries Medical Rsch. award 1992), Aerospace Human Factor Assn. (Paul Hensen award 1995), Am. Inst. Med. and Biol. Engring., US Ski Assn. (award of merit 1976), Explorers Club; mem. NAE, Inst. Medicine, Am. Physiol. Soc. (1st lectr. in aerospace life scis. 1990), Biomed. Engring. Soc. (founding/charter mem., dir. 1972-75, pres. 1979-80, Alza lectr. 1984), Aerospace Med. Assn., ASTM (com. on snow skiing 1975—, chmn. 1988-93), Internat. Soc. Skiing Safety (bd. dirs. 1977-85), Internat. Fedn. Automatic Control (tech. com. biomed. engring. 1975-85), AIAA (working group for simulator facilities 1976-80), Nat. Acad. Engrs., Inst. Medicine, Internat. Acad. Astronautics (corr.), Aerospace Medicine and Medicine Extreme Environments (standing com., nominated 2007), TU Delft (promotor, doctorate supr., 2007), Barany Soc., Cosmos Club, Tau Beta Pi. Achievements include research in instrumentation and basic and applied research in field of vestibular function; psychophysical work on semicircular canal and otolith function led to models which are applied to flight simulator motion control and are being extended to include visually-induced motion effects; ski injurys. Home: 217 Thorndike St Apt 108 Cambridge MA 02141-1504 Office: MIT Man-Vehicle Lab Rm 37-219 Cambridge MA 02139 Business E-Mail: lry@mit.edu.

YOUNG, LORRAINE, dermatologist, educator; children: Brian, Madeline children: Stephanie. MD, U. Calif., San Francisco, 1981. Clin. prof. UCLA, LA, 2004—, co-chief dermatology clin. svcs., 2004—. Fellow: Am. Acad. Dermatology; mem.: Women's Dermatologic Soc., LA Dermatology Soc., Assn. Profs. Dermatology. Office: UCLA Sch Medicine 200 Med Plz Ste 450 Los Angeles CA 90095

YOUNG, LUCIA PATAT, psychotherapist; b. Charleston, SC, Aug. 19, 1947; d. Leon Philip and Amelia (Wallace) P.; m. David Michael Young, Sept. 2, 1972 (dec. 2008); children: David Michael II, Allison Amelia. BS, U. S.C., 1969; MEd, EdS, U. Fla., 1991, PhD, 1996. Lic. clin. profl. counselor Nat. Bd. Cert. Counselors. Mental health assoc. Med. U. SC, Charleston, 1969; exec. sec. Mass. Gen. Hosp., Boston, 1969-73, sr. biol. and biochem. technician dept. neurology, summer 1974; adminstrv. asst. Harvard U., Cambridge, Mass., 1973-74; tchr. biology, anatomy and physiology Brimmer & May Sch., Chestnut Hill, Mass., 1974-76; mng. editl. asst. Molecular and Cellular Biochemistry, Gainesville, Fla., 1982-86; adminstrv. asst. U. Fla. Found., Gainesville, Fla., 1986-89; addictions counselor Bridge House Residential Ctr., Gainesville, 1990-91; family therapy internship; sch. guidance counselor Trenton Middle and HS, Fla., 1991-92; mental health counselor, children's outpatient dept. Mental Health Svcs., Gainesville, 1992-93; children's bereavement counselor, family counselor Hospice of N. Ctrl. Fla., Gainesville, 1993-96; pvt. practice Gainesville, 1996—2000, Gloucester, Mass., 2000—01, Ellsworth, Maine, 2002—; trauma therapist Arbour Trauma Counseling Ctr., Allston, Mass., 2000—01. Mem. AAAS, Am. Assn. Marriage and Family Therapy, Internat. Assn. Eating Disorders Profls., Nat. Bd.

Cert. Counselors, Eye Movement Desensitization and Reprocessing, Internat. Assn., Kappa Delta Pi, Chi Sigma Iota. Office: 210 Main St Ellsworth ME 04605 Home: Po Box 408 Sullivan ME 04664-0408 Office Phone: 207-667-4334. Personal E-mail: luciayoungly@yahoo.com.

YOUNG, LUCY CLEAVER, retired physician; b. Aug. 8, 1943; d. Oliver B. and Ada (Smith) Cleaver; m. Lynn H. Young, Feb. 4, 1968 (div. 1977); m. Lynn H. Young, Apr. 2, 1986; 1 child, Clinton Oliver. BS in Chemistry, Wheaton Coll., Ill., 1965; MD, Ohio State U., 1969. Diplomate Am. Bd. Family Practice, Bd. Ins. Medicine. Rotating intern Riverside Meth. Hosp., Columbus, Ohio, 1969—70; resident Trumbull Meml. Hosp., Warren, Ohio, 1970—71; practice medicine specializing in family practice West Chicago, Ill., 1971—73, Paw Paw and Mendota, Ill., 1973—78; co-founder, med. dir. Wholistic Health Ctr. of Mendota, 1976—78; asst. med. dir. Gt. Lakes head office Met. Life Ins. Co., Aurora, Ill., 1979—80; med. dir. Commonwealth Life Ins. Co., Louisville, 1980—85; locum tenens family practice Kron Med. Corp. of Chapel Hill, NC, 1986—89; physician Red Bird Mission & Med. Ctr., Beverly, Ky., 1989—90; family practice floater Ochsner Clinic satellites, New Orleans, 1990—2006; ret. Assoc. prof. U. Ill. Abraham Lincoln Sch. Medicine, 1976-79; faculty monitor MacNeal Meml. Hosp. Family Practice Ctr. (Ill.), 1979-80; faculty preceptor U. Louisville Family Practice Dept., 1981-85; clin. faculty preceptor La. State U. Sch. Medicine, 1992-2006; mem. staffs Ctrl. DuPage Hosp., Winfield, Ill., 1971-73, Mendota Cmty. Hosp., 1973-80, Ochsner Found. Hosp., New Orleans, 1991-2006; musician La. Via de Cristo, 2003-05. Vol. Red Bird Med. Ctr., 1985—2006; part-time worship coord. Hosanna Luth. Ch., Mandeville, La., 1996-97; musician, lay preacher, nursing home visitor, 1990—2006; musician, lay preacher, coun. mem., bible class tchr. St. Matthew, Lake Luth. Ch., Benton, Ky., 2006-; vol. H.P.O.E. Clinic Crisis Pregnancy Ctr., Benton, 2007-. Fellow Am. Acad. Family Practice; mem. Christian Med. and Dental Assns. (del. to Ho. 1995-2000). Lutheran. Home: PO Box 187 239 Jetty Dr #6-27 Grand Rivers KY 42045-0187

YOUNG, MARK PHILIP, allergist; b. NYC, May 30, 1954; MD, U. Ctrl. Del Caribe, 1982. Cert. Am. Bd. Allergy/Immunology. Resident pediat. Miami Children's Hosp., 1983—86, former assoc. dir. Department of Allergy/Immunology; fellowship allergy and immunology Emory U., Atlanta, 1986—87, Georgetown U., 1987—88; pvt. practice Asthma & Allergy Assocs. of Fla., PA, Miami. Fellow: Am. Coll. Allergy, Asthma and Immunology; mem.: Fla. Allergy Asthma and Immunology Soc. Office: Asthma & Allergy Assocs of Fla, PA 7800 SW 87th Ave, Ste C-340 Miami FL 33173 Office Phone: 305-595-0109. Office Fax: 305-595-7092.

YOUNG, MICHAEL CHUNG-EN, allergist, immunologist, pediatrician; b. Chgo., July 10, 1953; s. Koon C. and Siu Fun (Hui) Y.; m. Karen Lee Young, Apr. 7, 1979; 1 child, Liane. AB cum laude, Harvard Coll., 1975; MD, Yale U., 1979. Diplomate Am. Bd. Allergy and Immunology, Am. Bd. Pediatrics, Nat. Bd. Med. Examiners. Resident pediat. Children's Hosp., Boston, 1979—82, fellow in allergy and immunology, 1982—84, asst. in medicine (immunology), attending physician, 1984—; clin. instr. pediat. Harvard Med. Sch., Boston, 1985—2001, asst. clin. prof. pediat., 2002—. Mem. active staff South Shore Hosp., South Weymouth, Mass., 1985—. Author: Peanut Allergy Answer Book, 2001, 2d edit., 2006; contbr. articles to profl. jours. Recipient Nat. Rsch. Svc. award, NIH, 1982—84, Mariel C. Furlong award for Making a Difference, Food Allergy & Anaphylaxis Network, 2005; named physician honoree, Asthma and Allergy Found. Am., 2001; named to Guide to Top Doctors, Ctr. for the Study of Svcs. Fellow Am. Coll. Allergy and Immunology (Parke Davis Allergy Fellows award 1983), Am. Acad. Allergy and Immunology, Am. Coll. Chest Physicians, Am. Acad. Pediatrics; mem. New Eng. Soc. Allergy, Mass. Allergy Soc. (pres. 1992-94), Mass. Med. Soc. Office: South Shore Allergy & Asthma Specialists 851 Main St South Weymouth MA 02190-1612

YOUNG, MICHAEL WARREN, geneticist, educator; b. Miami, Fla., Mar. 28, 1949; s. Lloyd George and Mildred (Tillery) Y.; m. Laurel Ann Eckhardt, Dec. 27, 1978; children: Natalie, Arissa. BA, U. Tex., 1971, PhD, 1975. NIH postdoctoral fellow Stanford (Calif.) U. Med. Sch., 1975-77; asst. prof. genetics Rockefeller U., NYC, 1978—83, assoc. prof., 1984—88, prof., 1988—, Richard and Jeanne Fisher prof., 2004—. Investigator Howard Hughes Med. Inst., N.Y.C., 1987-96; adv. panel on genetic biology NSF, Washington, 1983-87; spl. advisor Am. Cancer Soc., N.Y.C., 1985—; spl. reviewer genetics study sect. NIH, Bethesda, Md., 1990—, cell biology study sect., 1993-97; head Rockefeller unit NSF Sci. and Tech. Ctr. Biol. Timing, 1991-2001; dir. Levy/White Ctr. Mind, Brain and Behavioral Studies Rockefeller U., N.Y.C., 2000-2002, v.p. academic affairs, 2004-. Contbr. articles to profl. jours. Meyer Found. fellow, N.Y.C., 1978-83. Fellow N.Y. Soc. Fellows, Am. Acad. Microbiology; mem. AAAS, Genetics Soc. Am., Am. Soc. Microbiologists, N.Y. Acad. Scis., Harvey Soc., Nat. Acad. Sci., Am. Chem. Soc., Gruber Found.(Neuroscis. prize, 2009) Achievements include research on transposable DNA elements, molecular genetics of nerve and muscle development, biological clocks, molecular control of circadian rhythms. Home: 51 Greenwoods Rd Old Tappan NJ 07675-7018 Office: The Rockefeller Univ 1230 York Ave New York NY 10021-6399

YOUNG, NOEL, medical educator; b. Sydney, Dec. 22, 1958; MBBS, U. NSW, 1983. Assoc. prof. Westmead Hosp., 1987—, U. Sydney, 1993—, Notre Dame U., Australia, 2007—, U. Western Sydney, 2007—, U. NSW, 2010—. Fellow: Royal Australian and New Zealand Coll. Radiologists; mem.: Cardiovasc. Radiol. Soc. Europe, Am. Roentgen Ray Soc. Avocations: reading, history. Office: Dept Radiology Westmead Hosp Sydney NSW 2111 Australia Office Fax: 61296872109.

YOUNG, PATRICIA JANEAN, speech pathology/audiology services professional; b. San Diego, Nov. 30, 1953; d. Bernarr E. and Janean Romig Young. AA, Palomar C.C., San Marcos, Calif., 1974; BA, Calif. State U., Chico, 1976; MA, Calif. State U., Long Beach, 1981. Cert. clin. competence Am. Speech-Lang.-Hearing Assn., lic. speech pathologist Calif., cert. tchr. Calif. Mgmt. trainee Robinson's Dept. Store, LA, 1976—78; speech and hearing screening coord. Riverview Hearing, Speech, Lang. Ctrs., Long Beach, 1978—81, speech pathologist, 1981—84, Lake Elsinore Unified Sch. Dist., Calif., 1998—; speech pathologist, dir. Speech Pathology Svcs., Carlsbad and Temecula, Calif., 1984—. Prodr. TV shows on comm. disorders Long Beach Cable TV, 1983; coord. pub. svc. announcement and interviewee for Disabilities Awareness Week ABC TV, San Diego, 1986, San Diego, 88. Game inventor: Match This!, 1995; author: (children's book) Bird Boy, 2006; contbr. poetry to lit. publs.;, author. Named to Outstanding Young Women Am. Mem.: Calif. Speech-Lang-Hearing Assn. (region rep., Outstanding Achievement award 1987), Am. Speech-Lang-Hearing Assn., Zeta Tau Alpha. Avocations: writing, theater, decorating. Home: 31935 Calle Espinoza Temecula CA 92592 Office: Lake Elsinore Unified Sch Dist 545 Chaney St Lake Elsinore CA 92530 Home Phone: 951-303-9422; Office Phone: 951-253-7000. Personal E-mail: pjyoung2000@aol.com.

YOUNG, PAUL ANDREW, anatomist; b. St. Louis, Oct. 3, 1926; s. Nicholas A. and Olive A. (Langford) Y.; m. Catherine Ann Hofmeister, May 14, 1949; children— Paul, Robert, David, Ann, Carol, Richard, James, Steven, Kevin, Michael. BS, St. Louis U., 1947, MS, 1953; PhD, U. Buffalo, 1957. Asst. in anatomy U. Buffalo, 1953, instr. anatomy, 1957; asst. prof. anatomy St. Louis U., 1957, assoc. prof., 1966, prof., 1972—, chmn. dept., 1973—2004, prof. anatomy in surgery, 2004, prof. and chair emeritus, dept. anatomy and neurobiology, 2006. Author: (with B.D. Bhagat and D.E. Biggerstaff) Fundamentals of Visceral Innervation, 1977, (with P.H. Young) Basic Clinical Neuroanatomy, 1996, (with P.H.Young and D.L.Tolbert) Basic Clinical Neuroscience, 2007, also computer assisted neurological anatomy tutorials; contbr. articles to profl. publs. Recipient Preclinical Golden Apple Tchg. award, St. Louis U. Sch. Medicine, 1974, 2000, Outstanding Preclinical, 1981, 1985, 1986, 1991, 1992, tchg. award, St. Louis Acad. Sci., 1993, Emerson Excellence for St. Louis U. faculty, 2001, Acad. Sci. Outstanding Sr. Louis Scientist award, 2008. Mem. Am. Assn. Anatomists, Am. Assn. Clin. Anatomists, Soc. Neurosci., Sigma Xi, Alpha Omega Alpha. Achievements include Paul A. Young Hall dedication in 2010. Office: St Louis Univ Ctr for Anatomical Science and Education 1402 S Grand Blvd Saint Louis MO 63104-1004 Home Phone: 636-225-1437; Office Phone: 314-977-8025. Personal E-mail: pay1957@gmail.com. Business E-Mail: youngpa@slu.edu.

YOUNG, PAUL RAY, medical association administrator, physician; b. Fairfield, Nebr., June 27, 1932; s. Earl Edward and Louisa May (Saunders) Young; m. Irene Marie Gray (div. 1971); children: Michael, Susan, Jean, James; m. Faye Elizabeth Hall, Oct. 28, 1972. BA, U. Nebr., Lincoln, 1953; MD, U. Nebr., Omaha, 1958. Diplomate Am. Bd. Family Practice. Intern Rsch. Hosp., Kansas City, Mo., 1958—59, dir. continuing med. edn., 1967—71; pvt. practice Raytown, Mo., 1961—67; assoc. prof. family practice U. Mo. Coll. Medicine, Columbia, 1971—75; chmn. dept. U. Nebr. Coll. Medicine, 1975—80, U. Tex. Med. Br., Galveston, 1980—88; dep. dir. Am. Bd. Family Practice, Lexington, Ky., 1988—90, exec. dir., 1990—97, sr. exec., 1998—2003, emeritus exec. dir., 2003—. Chmn. RRC for Family Practice, Chgo., 1979—87. Founding editor: Family Practice Recert, 1979, Jour. Am. Bd. Family Practice, 1987. Pres. Nicholas J. Piscano Meml. Found., 1990—97. Capt. M.C. USAF, 1959—61. Fellow: Am. Acad. Family Physicians; mem.: Soc. Tchrs. Family Medicine (bd. dirs. 1970—72), Alpha Omega Alpha. Office: Am Bd Family Medicine Inc 1648 McGrathiana Pkwy Fl5 Lexington KY 40511-1338 Office Phone: 859-269-5626. Business E-Mail: pyoung@theabfm.org.

YOUNG, ROBERT, research scientist; DPhil, Oxford U., 1988. Rsch. scientist Wellcome Found., Beckenham, UK, 1990—; rsch. scientist, investigator GlaxoWellcome, GlaxoSmithKline, Stevenage, UK, 1996. Hon. vis. lectr. U. St. Andrews, UK, 2001—. Author: (textbook) Antiviral Chemotherapy. Fellow: Royal Soc. Chemistry. Achievements include patents for antiviral nucleosides; nitric oxide syntheses inhibitors; anticoagulant serine protease inhibitors; expertise in physical methods in drug discovery and property based design.

YOUNG, ROBERT CRABILL, hospital administrator, medical researcher, educator; b. Columbus, Ohio, 1940; BS in zoology, Ohio State U., 1960; MD, Cornell U., 1965. Diplomate Am. Bd. Internal Medicine, subspecialty bds. hematology and med. oncology. Intern N.Y. Hosp., NYC, 1965-66, resident, 1966-67; sr. resident Yale-New Haven Med. Ctr., 1969-70; sr. investigator, attending physician med. br. Nat. Cancer Inst., Bethesda, Md., 1971—, chief med. br., 1974-88; chancellor Fox Chase Cancer Ctr., Phila., 1988—. Clin. prof. medicine Georgetown U., from 1974, assoc. prof., 1976-84; clin. prof. medicine George Washington U., 1984—; bd. Sci. Advisors, Nat. Cancer Inst., 1996—; bd. Nat. Cancer Policy, 1997-99; chmn. bd. Nat. Comprehensive Cancer Network. Assoc. editor Jour. Clin. Oncology; chmn. editl. bd. Oncology Times. Sr. surgeon USPHS, 1967-69. Fellow ACP; mem. Am. Soc. Hematology, Am. Assn. Cancer Rsch., Am. Soc. Clin. Oncology (pres. 1990), Am. Cancer Soc. (bd. dir. 1995-99, 1st v.p. 1999-2000, pres. 2002), Internat. Gynecol. Cancer Soc. (pres.-elect 1998, pres. 2000). Office: Fox Chase Cancer Ctr 333 Cottman Ave Philadelphia PA 19111-2497 Business E-Mail: robert.young@fccc.edu. *

YOUNG, ROGER CHARLES, gynecologist, educator; b. Honolulu, Sept. 2, 1950; BA, Western Md. Coll., 1972; MD, U. NC, Chapel Hill, 1982; PhD, U. NC. Asst. prof. ob-gyn. Duke U. Med. Ctr., 1986—88; prof. Med. Coll. SC, 1988—2001, Darthmouth-Hitchcock Med. Ctr., 2001—06, U. Vt., 2006—. Trustee Mar. Dimes, 2007—. Rsch. grant, NIH. Fellow: Am. Congress ob-gyn. (Resident's Tchg. award); mem.: Soc. Gynecologic Investigation. Office: 111 Colchester Ave Burlington VT 05403 Personal E-mail: youngschwarzenberger@gmail.com.

YOUNG, RONALD FREDERICK, neurosurgeon; b. Buffalo, Jan. 4, 1939; s. Frederick Earl and Ruth Henrietta (Cowan) Y.; m. Sheila Marie Young, June 23, 1962 (div. 1990); children: Scott Ronald, Anne Louise, Karen Lynn. BA, SUNY, Buffalo, 1961, MD, 1965. Diplomate Am. Bd. Neurol. Surgery. Intern U. Minn Hosp., Mpls., 1965-66; resident in neurosurgery VA Hosp., Longbeach, Calif., 1966-67, SUNY, Syracuse, 1969-73, asst. prof. neurosurgery, 1973-77; assoc. prof. UCLA, 1977-85; prof. neurosurgery U. Calif., Irvine, 1986-93; chief of neurosurgery U. Calif. Med. Ctr., Irvine, 1986-93; clin. prof. U. Calif., Irvine, 1993—98; dir. N.W. Gamma Knife Ctr. and N.W. Neurosci. Inst. Northwest Hosp., Seattle, 1993—2010; med. dir. Los Robles Hosp. Neuroscience Inst. GAMMA Knite Ctr., Thousand Oaks, Calif., 2006—, Rotating Gamma Inst., Anaheim, Calif., 2008—, Providence St. Joseph's Med. Ctr., Burbank, Calif., 2009—, Movement Disorder Ctr., 2010—, Gamma Knife Ctr. and DBS Program, Swedish Hosp., Seattle. Elizabeth Crosby Meml. lectr. U. Mich., Ann Arbor, 1990; mem. med. staff Northwest Hosp, Seattle, Los Robles Hosp., Thousand Oaks, Calif., Providence St. Joseph's Med. Ctr., Burbank, Calif., Swedish Hosp., Seattle. Author: Spinal Cord Injury, 1981; contbr. articles to profl. jours. Capt. USAF M.C., 1967-69. Recipient Kongress medal German Neurosurg. Soc., 1982. Fellow ACS; mem. Western Neurosurg. Soc. (v.p. 1990-91, pres. 1993-94), Am. Acad. Pain Medicine (sec. 1991-93), Am. Assn. Neurol. Surg., Congress Neurol. Surgery, Soc. Neurol. Surgeons, Internat. Leksell Gamma Knife Soc. (chmn. 1995). Avocations: travel, photography, french lessons, horseback riding. Office: Neuroscience Inst Med GRP 637 S Lucas Ave Ste 501 Los Angeles CA 90017 Office Phone: 206-320-7130, 626-716-1851. Personal E-mail: rfy127@hotmail.com.

YOUNG, VERNON LEROY, plastic surgeon, researcher; b. Oneida, Ky., Oct. 14, 1945; s. Roy Young and Susie Lou; m. Jill Marie Meyer, Mar. 12, 1988; children: Ann Elizabeth, Hunter, Chase, Hampton. BA, U. Ky., Lexington, 1966, MD, 1970. Cert. Am. Bd. Plastic Surgery, 1981. Intern Univ. Ky. Med. Ctr., Lexington, 1970—71, resident in surgery, 1973—77; resident in plastic surgery Barnes Hosp. Washington Univ., St. Louis, 1977—79; William G. Hamm prof. plastic surgery Washington Univ., St. Louis, 1979—2002; pres. Body Aesthetic Plastic Surgery, St. Louis, 2002—. Cons. Cook Biotech, Indpls., 2000—06, Ethicon, NJ, 2003—06; mem. adv. bd. Renovo, Manchester, England, 2006, Aovtech, Sydney, 2006; examiner Am. Bd. Plastic Surgery. Editor (assoc.): Aesthetic Surgery Jour., 2005. Capt. US Army, 1971—73. Mem.: Am. Assn. Plastic Surgery, Am. Soc. for Aesthetic Surgery, Am. Soc. Plastic Surgeons. Episcopalian. Avocation: gardening. Home: 18229 Melrose Rd Wildwood MO 63069 Office: Body Aesthetic Plastic Surgery 969 Mason Rd Saint Louis MO 63141 Office Phone: 314-628-8200. Office Fax: 314-628-9504. Business E-Mail: vlyoungmd@bodyaesthetic.com.

YOUNG, VICTORIA E., occupational health nurse, lawyer; b. Concord, Mich., Apr. 20, 1933; d. Arthur Raymond and Edith Louise (Hands) Y. Diploma, Mercy Sch. Nursing, Jackson, Mich., 1954; BSN, UCLA, 1960, MPH in Adminstrn., 1966; JD, U. West LA, Culver City, 1973. Bar: Calif., U.S. Dist. Ct., Calif.; RN, Calif.; cert. pub. health nurse, pediatric nurse practitioner. Pub. health nurse L.A. City and Los Angeles County Health Dept.; exec. dir. Santa Monica (Calif.) Vis. Nurse Assn.; sch. nurse practitioner L.A. Unified Schs.; relief nurse L.A. Times. Vol. Moorpark City Hall, Moorpark Sr. Ctr; mem. Disaster Assistance Response Team, Moorpark. Ret. capt. USNR, Desert Storm. Mem. Nat. Assn. Pediatric Nurse Assocs. and Practitioners, Calif. Bar Assn., Fleet Res. Assn., Moorpark Woman's Fortnightly Club (treas. 1998-99). Home: 4359 Brookdale Ln Moorpark CA 93021-2302

YOUNGDAHL, PAULA SUN, obstetrician, gynecologist; MD, U. Pa., 1985. Diplomate Am. Bd. Ob-Gyn, lic. Pa., 1986. Resident Western Pa. Hosp., 1989; hosp. affiliations include Ellwood City Hosp., Heritage Valley Beaver, Pa. Fellow: Am. Congress of Obstetricians and Gynecologists. Office: Heritage Valley Beaver 1000 Dutch Ridge Rd Beaver PA 15009 Office Phone: 724-843-0737.

YOUNG-JOON, JUN, plastic surgeon, educator; b. Seoul, Feb. 15, 1969; s. Chun Sung-kyu and Lee Gae-soon; m. Chung Jae-hee, Sept. 27, 2002. PhD in Med. Sci., Plastic and Reconstructive Surgery, Cath. U. Korea, Seoul, 2006. Cert. in plastic and reonstructive surgery Ministry Health Welfare and Family Affairs, 2003. Prof., plastic & reconstructive surgery Cath. U. Korea, Seoul, 2003—, chair, 2009—; prof., plastic & reconstructive surgery Bucheon St. Marys Hosp., Bucheon St., Kyunggi-Do, 2003—. Contbr. articles to profl. jours. Achievements include research in adipose-derived stem cells and peripheral nerve regeneration. Home: 1-1007 Kwangjang-APT Youido-Dong Yeungdeungpo Seoul 150-762 Republic of Korea Office: Plastic Surgery Bucheon St Marys Hosp Cath University Korea 2 Sosa-Dong Wonmi-Gu Bucheon Kyunggi-Do 420-717 Republic of Korea Personal E-mail: joony@catholic.ac.kr. Business E-Mail: psdoc@korea.com.

YOUNGKEUN, AHN, cardiologist; b. Gwangju, Republic of Korea, Nov. 10, 1964; s. Ahn Tae-Hew and Kim Jin-Ok; m. Ko Youngmin; children: Ahn Junhyuk, Ahn Haeji. MD, Chonnam Nat. U. Med. Sch., Gwangju, 1989, Master, 1992; PhD, Chonnam Nat. U., Gwangju, 1998. Asst. prof. Chonnam Nat. U., Gwangju, Republic of Korea, 2002—; intern Chonnam Nat. U. Hosp., 1989—90, resident internal medicine, 1990—94, full time clin. instr. Gwangju, 1998—2002. Clinician, rschr. Chonnam Nat. U. Hosp., Gwangju, Korea (South), 1998—. Capt. Korean Army, 1994—97. Fellow Postdoc. Rsch. fellow, Harvard U., 2000-2002. Mem.: Am. Soc. Gene Therapy, Am. Coll. Cardiology, Am. Heart Assn., Korean Soc. Molecular Biology, Korean Med. Assn. (grantee 2004), Korean Soc. Circulation (grantee 2002). Achievements include research in Gene therapy for coronary in-stent restenosis and myocardial protection; patents pending for Methods for treating ischemic reperfusion injury using I kappa B kinase-beta inhibitors. Home: #103-1301 Hyundai APT Munheu Gigu Buk Ku Gwangju 510-100 Republic of Korea Office: Chonnam Nat U Hosp Dept Cardiology Hak Dong Dong Ku 8 501-757 Gwangju Republic of Korea Personal E-mail: cecilyk@hanmail.net.

YOUNIS, RAMZI T., otolaryngologist, educator; b. El-Maten, Lebanon, Jan. 3, 1970; MD, Am. U. Beirut, 1985. Prof. chief divsn. pediat. otolaryngology Miller Sch. Medicine, U. Miami, 2002—. Named one of Best Doctors in Am. Fellow: Am. Acad. Otolaryngology Head & Neck Surgery, Am. Acad. Pediat. Office: 900 NW 17th St 3rd Fl Clinic Miami FL 33136 Office Fax: 305-547-3670. Business E-Mail: ryounis@med.miami.edu.

YOUSEF, MONA LEE, psychoanalyst; BS in Human Devel. and Family Studies, Cornell U.; MSW, NYU. Cert. psychoanalyst Psychoanalytic Psychotherapy Study Ctr, NY; lic. clin. social worker NY; credentialed alcoholism and substance abuse counselor NY, master addictions counselor, cert. alcohol and drug couselor, HIV counselor

NY. Psychoanalyst pvt. practice, NYC, 1993—. Mem. NASW, APA (Divsn. 39), Nat. Assn. Alcoholism and Drug Abuse Counselors-Assn. for Addiction Profls., Acad. Cert. Social Workers, Am. Assn. Psychoanalysis Clin. Social Work, Assn. Addiction Profls. of NY, Soc. Advancement Sexual Health, Nat. Assn. Anorexia Nervosa and Associated Disorders, Internat. Assn. Psychoanalytic Self Psychology, Internat. Soc. Study Trauma & Dissociation, NY State Soc. for Clin. Social Work, Stuyvesant HS Alumni Assn., Psi Chi (life). Democrat. Avocations: writing, dance, art. Office: 19 W 34th St Penthouse New York NY 10001

YOUSEFIPOUR, ZIVAR, medical educator; b. Abadone, Sept. 7, 1965; PhD, Tex. So. U., 2004. Asst. prof. Tex. So. U., 2008. Adj. prof. HCCS, 2002. Mem.: Am. Physiol. Soc. (Caroline Tum Sudan Profl. Opportunity award), Am. Heart Assn. Avocation: travel. Office: 3100 Cleburne Ave Houston TX 77004 Business E-Mail: yousefipour_zx@tsu.edu.

YOUSHENG, LIANG, lab administrator; b. Danyang, Jiangsu, China, Dec. 22, 1958; PhD, U. Bristol, 2001. Dep. head Jiangsu Provincial Key Lab. Molecular Biology Parasites, 1999—, Key Lab. Tech. Parasitic Disease Prevention and Control, 2005—; vice dir. Jiangsu Inst. Parasitic Diseases, 2004—. Vice dir. Jiangsu Assn. Schistosomiasis & other Parasitic Diseases Control, 2003—; adj. prof. Jiangsu U., 2005—; S & T cons. Jurong Mcpl. Govt., 2008—; vice dir. Chinese Assn. Schistosomiasis Control, 2011—; mem. Chinese Jour. Schistosomiasis Control, Internat. Jour. Med. Parasitic Diseases, Chinese Jour. Tropical Medicine; expert cons. Diseases Control, Ministry Health. Contbr. articles to profl. jours., chapters to books. Recipient Jiangsu Outstanding Returned Talents award, Jiangsu Provincial People's Govt., Jiangsu Outstanding Med. Talents award, Jiangsu Outstanding Experts award, Outstanding Med. Talents award, Ministry Health. Mem.: Chinese Soc. Malacology. Avocations: reading, travel. Office: 117 Yangxiang Meiyuan Wuxi Jiangsu 214064 China Office Fax: 8651085510263. E-mail: wxliangyousheng@yahoo.cn.

YOUSIF, MARIAM HASSAN MOHAMMAD, medical educator; b. Kuwait, May 18, 1964; PhD, U. Bath, Eng., 1996. Asst. prof., dept. pharmacology & toxicology Kuwait U. Faculty Medicine, 1999—2004, assoc. prof., dept. pharmacology & toxicology, 2004—, vice dean, rsch., 2007—09. Recipient Med. Scis. award, Kuwait Found. Advencement Scis., Best Young Rschr. award, Rsch. Adminstrn. Kuwait U., Best Tchr. award, Faculty of Medicine Kuwait U. Office: Al-Jabryia Kuwait 13110 Kuwait Business E-Mail: mariam@hsc.edu.kw.

YOUSSEF, NAGY A., psychiatrist; MD, Cairo U. Sch. Medicine, 1995. Diplomate Am. Bd. Psychiatry and Neurology, 2006, in psychosomatic medicine Am. Bd. Psychiatry and Neurology, 2009, Am. Bd. Disability Analysts. Sr. rsch. assoc. Duke U. Med. Ctr., Durham, NC, 2009—, Mid Atlantic Mental Illness Rsch., Edn. & Clin. Ctr., Durham VA Med. Ctr., 2009—; adj. asst. prof. U. S. Ala., Mobile. Editl. bd. Annals Clin. Psychiatry; mem. bd. dirs. Am. Acad. Clin. Psychiatrists, manuscript reviewer Am. Jour. Psychiatry; hon. mem. bd. dirs. Am. Bd. of Disability Analysts; chmn. electronic communication com. Am. Acad. Clin. Psychiatrists. Contbr. articles to profl. jours., chapters to books. Recipient Rolls of Honors, Cairo U. Sch. Medicine; named one of Top Psychiatrists, Consumers' Rsch. Coun. Am., 2009—10. Fellow: Am. Bd. Disability Analysts; mem.: Am. Assn. Psychiat. Medicine, Am. Acad. Health Care Providers Addictive Disorders, Am. Assn. Clin. Psychiatrists, Am. Psychiat. Assn.

YOUSUF, MUHAMMAD, internist, consultant; s. Mian Qamar Din and Wazir Begum; m. Naila Latif, Jan. 13, 1985; children: Fahad, Fouad, Anam. MBBS, King Edward Med. Coll., Lahore, 1978. Asst. prof. medicine and vis. physician Quaid-i-Azam Med. Coll. and Bahawal Victoria Hosp., Bahawalpur, Punjab, 1984—90; cons. internal medicine King Abdul Aziz Hosp., Madinah, Westen Region, Saudi Arabia, 1990—95; asst. prof. medicine and vis. physician King Edward Med. Coll. and Mayo Hosp., Lahore, 1995—96; assoc. prof. medicine and vis. prof. Quaid-i-Azam Med. Coll. and Bahawal Victoria Hosp., 1996—97; assoc. prof. medicine and vis. physician Post Grad. Med. Inst. and Lahore Gen. Hosp., 1997—2002; cons. internal medicine King Abdul Aziz Specialist Hosp., Taif, Wesern, 2002—07; cons., divsn. internal medicine, dept. medicine King Fahad N.G. Hosp., K.A.M.C., Riyadh, Central Province, Saudi Arabia, 2007—. Author: (medical book) Diagnostic Approach To History Taking. Master: RCP (Ireland); fellow: RCP (Ireland), RCP (Edinburgh); mem.: RCS (Eng.). Home: 324/1-K Phase 1 DHA Lahore Cantt Lahore Punjab 54792 Pakistan Office: King Fahad Nat Guard Hosp PO Box 22490 11495 Riyadh Saudi Arabia Personal E-mail: drmyousuf@hotmail.com.

YOVANOF, SILVANA, physician; b. Lubojno, Macedonia, Jan. 14, 1956; came to U.S., 1961; d. Peter and Nuna Yovanof. BS in Biology and Psychology, Loyola U., Chgo., 1978; MS, U. Ill., 1982; MD, Am. U. Caribbean, Montserrat, 1985. Diplomate Am. Bd. Internal Medicine. Intern Deaconess Hosp., St. Louis, 1986-87; resident in internal medicine St. Joseph Mercy Hosp., Pontiac, Mich., 1987-89, chief resident in medicine, 1989-90; fellow U. Ill. Med. Ctr., Chgo., 1990-92; chmn. dept. medicine Monongahela Valley Hosp., 2002—08. Mem. adv. panel Internal Medicine for the Specialist, 1988—; affiliated with hosps. Jefferson Hosp., Pitts., 1991, MonValley Hosp., Monongahela, Pa., 1993, Mercy Hosp., Pitts., 1995. Contbr. articles to profl. jours. including Neurosci. Letters. Mem.: ACP, Am. Assn. Clin. Endocrinologists, Allegheny County Med. Soc. (med. legal com. 1996—), Pa. State Med. Soc., Am. Diabetes Assn.

YTREHUS, KIRSTI, medical educator, heart researcher; b. Drammen, Norway, June 2, 1953; d. Kjell and Ingeborg (Ramm) Y.; m. Svein Ingvald Karoliussen; children: Ingvild, Torkel, Egil. MD, U. Oslo, 1980; PhD, U. Tromsø (Norway), 1988. Med. diplomate. Mem. staff Cmty. Hosp., Narvik, Norway, 1982-83, Cmty. Health Svc., Balsfjord, Norway, 1983; rsch. fellow U. Tromsø (Norway), 1982-87; assoc. prof. U. Tromsø, Norway, 1987-92; vis. assoc. prof. U. South Ala., Mobile, 1992-93; prof. U. Tromsø, 1994—, vice dean, 1998—2003, dean, faculty medicine, 2003—05; prof. U. Bergen, Norway, 1995-96. Cons. Norwegian Rsch. Coun., Oslo, 1989-96, 1998—2003; vis. rschr. Nat. Inst. Aging, NIH, 2001-02; mem. Norwegian Health Authorities Expert Group on Biomedicine, 2007-. Contbr. articles to profl. jours. Mem. Nordic Com. Arctic Med. Rsch., Oslo, 1989-96; bd. dirs. Nat. Inst. Occupl. Health, Oslo, 1995—2005. Mem. Norwegian Med. Assn., Norwegian Soc. Cardiology, Internat. Soc. Heart Rsch. Office: University Tromso Faculty Health Scis Dept Med Biology Cardiovascular Rsch Group Dept Med Physiology Tromso 9037 Norway Business E-Mail: kirsti.ytrehus@uit.no.

YU, ANDREW, minister; b. Fu-Yang, Chekian, China, Feb. 28, 1927; came to the U.S., 1972; s. Kung-Chu Yu and Mei-Chen Liu; m. Julie Yu, July 13, 1957; children: Peter, Ruth. BTh, Taiwan Bapt. Theol. Sem., Taipei, 1957; postgrad., Tanghai U., Taichung, Taiwan, 1965; MA in Ministry Studies, Moody Bible Inst., 1991; postgrad., Bibl. Archaeology Soc., 1993, Fuller Theol. Sem., 1996, Fuqua Internat. Sch. Christian Comm., 1998. Cert. pastoral counseling. Jour. clk. Bankers Trust Co., NYC, 1972-80; pastoral coounselor Am. Assn. Christian Counseling, Forest, Va., 1991—; minister Manhattan Chinese Bapt. Ch., NYC, 1980—, sr. pastor, 1986—. Author: Rekinling the Fires of Revial, 1993, A Master Piece of Spirituality, 1995, The Poem of Draw Wings, 2001, A Song of Harmonies, 2008; editor Chinese Christian Workers, 1999—; editor: Chinese Newsletter, NY, 1999-2002. Mem. Bapt. World Alliance 100th Anniversary Congress, Bermingham, England, 2005. Recipient Lifetime Royal Patronage status Kevin, Prince Regent Princepality of Hutt River Province, Australia, 1994, Cert. of Appreciation, Ronald Reagan Presdl. Found., 2003. Mem.: Poetry Soc. Am. Avocations: reading, writing, music, travel, collecting. Home: Apt 20E 675 Water St New York NY 10002 Office: Manhattan Chinese Bapt Ch 236 W 72nd St New York NY 10023 Office Phone: 212-496-1486. Personal E-mail: andreweyu@gmail.com, andrewyu236@hotmail.com.

YU, CHACK YUNG, pediatrics educator, molecular biologist; b. Guangdong, People Republic of China, Dec. 24, 1957; s. Hung Ho and Shui-Wo (Kwok) Y.; m. Lai-Chu, Apr. 23, 1987; children: Gayang Heidi, Gakit Richard. BS, Chinese U. Hong Kong, 1981, MPhil, 1983; DPhil, Oxford U., England, 1988. Asst. prof. Ohio State U., Columbus, 1990-96, assoc. prof., 1996—. Contbr. articles to profl. jours. Grantee NIH, Bethesda, Md., 1994—, March of Dimes, 1992-94; postdoctoral fellow Med. Rsch. Coun. Lab. Molecular Biology, Cambridge, England, 1987-90. Mem. AAAS, Am. Assn. Immunologists, Am. Soc. Human Genetics, Am. Soc. Microbiology, Am. Soc. Biochemistry and Molecular Biology, Soc. for Pediat. Rsch. Office: Children's Rsch Inst 700 Childrens Dr Columbus OH 43205-2664 E-mail: cyu@chi.osu.edu.

YU, EVAN YA-WEN, oncologist, educator; b. Bellevue, Wash., July 7, 1971; BS, U. Wash., 1994, MD, 1998. Asst. prof. U. Wash., 2004—10, assoc. prof., 2010—. Assoc. mem. Fred Hutchinson Cancer Rsch. Ctr. Office: Seattle Cancer Care Alliance 825 Eastlake Ave Seattle WA 98109 Office Fax: 206-288-2042. Business E-Mail: evanyu@u.washington.edu.

YU, FEI, internist; b. Beijing, Mar. 12, 1956; came to U.S., 1990; d. Longshan and Dan (Zheng) Y.; m. Xiangqun Fu, Jan. 7, 1984; 1 child, Danni. MD, Beijing Med. U., 1982; PhD in Med. Sci., Beijing Union Med. Coll., 1989. Diplomate Am. Bd. Internal Medicine, Am. Bd. Med. Acupuncture. Intern The People's Hosp., Beijing Med. U., 1981-82; resident in internal medicine Jishuitan Hosp., Beijing, 1983-84, Beijing Union Med. Coll. Hosp., 1984-87; clin. fellow hematology dept. internal medicine Beijing Union Med. Coll., Chinese Acad. Med. Scis., 1987-89; rsch. fellow dept. devel. cell biology Sloan-Ketterng Inst. Cancer Rsch., NYC, 1991-93; rsch. fellow dept. internal medicine Columbia U. Coll. Physicians and Surgeons, NYC, 1993—95; resident in medicine N.Y. Meth. Hosp., Bklyn., 1996-99; physician Regal Med. PC, Clifton, NJ, 2000—02, Clifton Med. & Rehab. Ctr., 2003; pvt. practice Englewood Cliffs, NJ, 2003—; attending physician Englewood Med. Ctr. & Hackensack Med. Ctr. Contbr. articles to profl. jours. Avocations: music, novel reading, travel, stamp collecting, ballroom dancing. Office: 385 Sylvan Ave 25 Englewood Cliffs NJ 07632 Office Phone: 201-567-0686. Personal E-mail: drfeiyu@aol.com.

YU, FU WING, structural engineer; B Engring. in Bldg. Svcs. Engring. with honors, Hong Kong Poly. U., 1999, PhD, 2004. Postdoctoral fellow bldg. svcs. engring. Hong Kong Poly. U., 2004—. Achievements include research in chiller system study. Office: Hong Kong Poly U Dept Bldg Svcs Engring Hong Kong Hong Kong

YU, HANRY, science educator; b. Chongqing, China, Apr. 4, 1964; s. Liangyi Yu and Chaixia Lee; m. Wing Chan; 1 child, Isabel. BSc with honors, Honors Coll., Mich. State U., East Lansing, 1987; MSc, Wash. U., St. Louis, 1990; PhD, Duke U., Durham, NC, 1994. Postdoc. fellow Duke U. Med. Ctr., 1994—95; sr. rsch. scientist Nat. U. Med. Inst., Singapore, 1997—2001; program coord. tissue engring. Inst. Materials Sci. and Engring., Singapore, 1998—2003; assoc. prof. Nat. U. Singapore, 2001—08; group leader Inst. Bioengring. and Nanotech., Singapore, 2003—; prof. Nat. U. Health Sys., Singapore, 2008—. Founding co-chairman NUS Grad. Program Bioengring., Singapore, 2001—05; sci. adv. bd. mem. CordLife Ltd., Singapore, 2002—, REGEA Inst. Regenerative Medicine, Tampere, Finland, 2007—; vice chair sci. adv. bd. Singapore-U. Wash. Alliance, Seattle, 2005—; program co-chair & chair grad. com., computation sys. biology Singapore-MIT Alliance, Cambridge, 2005—; vis. assoc. prof. MIT, 2008—09, vis. prof., 2009—10; grad. chair Mechanobiology Inst. Singapore Founding Scientist Histoindex Pvt. Ltd. Contbr. articles to profl. sci. jours. Deacon, principle Sunday sch. Chinese Christian Mission Ch., Durham, 1995; deacon Queenstown Chinese Meth. Ch., Singapore, 2003—. Recipient Outstanding Rschr. award, Nat. U. Singapore, 2002, Faculty Rsch. Excellence award, NY, 2008, NUHS, Singapore, 2009; HFSP Long Term Rsch. fellowship, European Molecular Biology Lab., Heidelberg, Germany, 1995—97, Rsch. grant, Singapore Govt. Agys., 1997—, HFSP Network grant, Internat. Human Frontier Sci. Program, 1998—2001. Mem.: Materials Rsch. Soc., Tissue Engring. and Regenerative Medicine Soc., Am. Soc. Biochemistry Molecular Biology, Am. Soc. Cell Biology, Golden Key Nat. Honor Soc. Achievements include patents for 3D cell culture technologies and in vitro drug testing models. Avocations: travel, photography. Office: Nat Univ Health System Md9 2 Med Dr #03-03 117597 Singapore Singapore Personal E-mail: nmiyuh@gmail.com. Business E-Mail: nanry_yu@nuhs.edu.sg.

YU, HWA-LUNG, environmental engineer, educator; b. Taipei, Taiwan, Oct. 18, 1976; PhD, U. NC, Chapel Hill, 2005. Asst. prof. Nat. Taiwan U., 2007—. Office: 1 Roosevelt Rd Sect 4 Taipei 10617 Taiwan Business E-Mail: hlyu@ntu.edu.tw.

YU, HYEONG GON, medical educator, researcher; s. Chong In Yu and Young Huh; m. So Ra Kang, Dec. 10, 1996; children: Sang-Yoon, Sang-Yup. MD, Seoul Nat. U., 1991, master degree, 2000, PhD, 2002. Lic. physician Ministry of Health and Welfare, diplomate ophthalmology Ministry of Health and Welfare. Asst. prof. Seoul Nat. U., 2001—04, assoc. prof., 2004—. Clin. fellow Seoul Nat. U. Hosp., Seoul, Korea (South), 1997—98; rsch. fellow Harvard Med. Sch., Boston, 2004—05; resident Seoul Nat. U. Hosp., Seoul, Korea (South), 1992—96; full-time rschr. Seoul Nat. U., Med. Rsch. Inst., Seoul, Korea (South), 1998—99. Contbr. articles to jour. Capt. US Army, 1996—96, Korea. Recipient Pres. award, Seoul Nat. U., 1992; named Resident of Yr., 1996. Mem.: Korean Retina Soc. (life Acad. award 2005). Achievements include research in safety and effectiveness of phacovitrectomy in complicated vitreoretinal diseases; natural killer T cells role in the pathogenesis of Behcet's uveitis. Office: Ophthalmology Seoul Natl Univ Hosp 28 Yongong Dong Chongno Gu Seoul 110 744 Republic of Korea Business E-Mail: hgonyu@snu.ac.kr.

YU, JEN, medical educator; b. Taipei, Taiwan, Jan. 23, 1943; came to U.S., 1969; s. Chin Chuan and Shiu Lan (Lin) Y.; m. Janet Chen, June 16, 1973; children: Benjamin, Christopher. MD, Nat. Taiwan U., 1968; PhD in Physiology, U. Pa., 1972. Diplomate Am. Bd. Phys. Medicine and Rehab. Intern Phila. Gen. Hosp., 1972-73; resident in phys. medicine and rehab. Hosps. of U. Pa., 1973-75; asst. prof. dept. phys. medicine and rehab. U. Pa. Sch. Medicine, Phila., 1975-76, U. Tex. Health Sci. Ctr., San Antonio, 1976-79, assoc. prof., 1979-81; prof. dept. phys. medicine and rehab. U. Calif. Irvine Coll. Medicine, 1981-82, prof., chmn. dept. phys. medicine and rehab., 1982—. Contbr. articles to profl. jours. Mem. Am. Acad. Phys. Medicine and Rehab., Am. Congress Rehab. Medicine, Assn. Acad. Physiatrists, Am. Assn. Anatomists, Soc. for Neurosci. Office: U Calif Irvine Med Ctr Dept Phys Medicine & Rehab 101 The City Dr Orange CA 92868 Office Phone: 714-456-6504. Business E-Mail: jyu@uci.edu.

YU, JEN-FANG, medical educator; s. Ming-Hsiung Yu and Tsui-Hsia Chiang; m. Ying-Chin Peng. BS, Chinese Culture U., Taiwan, 1993; MS, Chung Hua U., Taiwan, 1995; PhD, U. Tex., Arlington, 2001. EIT Tex., 1999. Postdoctoral rsch. fellow Nat. Taiwan U., Taipei, 2002—03; asst. prof. No. Taiwan Inst. Sci. and Tech., Taipei, 2003—05; prin. investigator Taiouan Interdisciplinary Otolaryngology Lab., Kweishan, Taiwan, 2003—; asst. prof. Chung San Med. U., Taichung, Taiwan, 2005—06, Chang Gung U., Kweishan, 2006—. Contbr. articles to med. jours. Mem. Earth Watch, Taipei, 2004—05. Recipient Outstanding Tchg. award, No. Taiwan Inst. Sci. and Tech., 2003; Rsch. grantee, Nat. Sci. Coun., Taiwan, 2006. Fellow: Am. Acad. Otolaryngology-Head and Neck Surgery; mem.: Speech-Lang.-Hearing Assn. Taiwan, Acoustical Soc. Taiwan (life), Taiwanese Soc. Biomechanics (life), Biomedical Engring. Soc. Taiwan (life). Avocations: swimming, boating. Office: Inst Med Mechatronics CGU No 259 Wen-Hwa 1st Rd Taoyuan 333 Taiwan Home: 4F No146 Changgung Guishan Taoyuan 333 Taiwan Office Fax: 886 3 2118050. Business E-Mail: dr.jfyu@gmail.com.

YU, JOHN SUN, neurosurgeon, immunologist; b. Seoul, Republic of Korea, Sept. 11, 1963; s. Victor Seung Jae Yu, Grace Eun Duk Yu; m. Helena Yoon; children: Jeffrey, Lauren. BA, BS, Stanford U., 1985; MD, Harvard U., 1990, MS in Genetics, 1990. Diplomate Am. Bd. Neurol. Surgery. Resident in neurosurgery Mass. Gen. Hosp., Boston, 1997; neurosurgeon Cedars-Sinai Med. Ctr., LA, 1997—, prof. vice chair, 2009—; med. dir. Gamma Knife, 2006—; chmn., chief sci. officer Immunocellular Therapeutics Ltd., Woodland Hills, Calif., 2006—; dir. surg. neuro-oncology Cedars-Sinai Med. Ctr., LA, 2007—. Editor: Current Stem Cell Rsch. and Therapy; contbr. articles to Lancet, Cancer Rsch., Human Gene Therapy, others.; patent for differentiation of whole bone marrow cells into neural progenitor cells, 2001. Recipient Acad. award, Am. Acad. Neurol. Surgery, 1998, Betty Lea Stone award, Am. Cancer Soc., 1986, Preuss Resident Rsch. award, AANS and CNS, 1995, Mahaley Clin. Rsch. award, 2005; grantee, NIH, 2001—. Mem.: Am Assn. Neurol. Surgeons (tumor sect.). Office: Cedars-Sinai Neurosurg Inst 8631 W Third St Ste 800E Los Angeles CA Office Phone: 310-423-7900. Business E-Mail: yuj@cshs.org.

YU, JUN, medical researcher; b. Anyi, Jiangxi, China, Jan. 17, 1979; MD, Gannan Med. U., 2003; PhD, Kyushu U., 2009. Postdoc. rsch. fellow Johns Hopkins Medicine Instns., 2010—. Recipient Chinese Govt. award, China Scholarship Coun., 2007, Young Investigator award, Am. Pancreatic Assn., Japan Pancreas Soc., 2009; Japanese Govt. scholarship, 2008—10. Mem.: AACR. Avocation: music. Office: 1550 Orleans St CRBII Rm 3M41 J Baltimore MD 21231 Business E-Mail: shun@surg1.med.kyushu-u.ac.jp.

YU, JUN, medical educator; b. Hebei, China, Feb. 13, 1963; PhD, Tongji Med. U., 1994. Sr. rsch. officer Storr Liver Unit, Westmead Millennium Inst., Dept. of Gastroenterology and Hepatology, The U. of Sydney at Westmead Hosp., Sydney, Australia, 2003—05; postdoc. rschr. Carl Gusta Carus Hosp., Tech. U. Dresden, Dept. Gastroenterology, Otto-von-Guericke, 1998—99, Chinese U. Hong Kong, 1999—2002, rsch. asst. prof. to assoc. prof. to prof., dept. medicine & therapeutics, 2005—. Clin. officer, resident, physician, dept. medicine 3rd Affiliated Hosp., Hebei Med. U., China, 1986—88; clin. officer, lectr., gastroenterologist, dept. Gastroenterology & Hepatology 2nd Affiliated Hosp. Beijing U., 1994—98; vis. prof. Hebei Med. U. Recipient 1st Class prize Natural Sci. award, Ministry of Edn., China, Rsch. Excellence award, Chinese U. Hong Kong, 1st Class Mil. Med. Achievement award, Chinese People's Liberation Army, 1st Class Sci. & Technol. Progress award, Health Bur. Hebei Province, 3rd prize Provincial award, People's Govt. Hebei. Master: Hong Kong Immunology Assn. (Coun. mem.); fellow: Beijing 302 Hosp. (vice-chmn.), Sun-Yat Sen U., Peking U. Cancer Hosp.; mem.: Australian Med.

Assn., Am. Gastroenterology Assn., Hong Kong Scientist Com. Office: Rm 707A Li Ka Shing Bldg PWH Shatin Hong Kong

YU, LU, microbiologist, educator; b. Gongzhuling, Jilin, China, June 14, 1970; PhD, U. Agr. and Animal Scis. PLA, 2003. Prof. Key Lab. Zoonosis Rsch., Ministry of Edn., Inst. Zoonosis, Jilin U., 2007—. Dir. Chinese Vet. Pharmacology and Toxicology, 2005—. Recipient prize, Sci. and Tech. Dept., Jilin. Fellow: Zoonoses Soc. Jilin Province. Avocations: reading, ping pong/table tennis. Office: Xian Rd 5333# Changchun Jilin 130062 China Business E-Mail: yulu225@126.com.

YU, PETER LEGASPI, rehabilitation physician; b. Jan. 31, 1957; BS, U. Santo Tomas, Manila, 1975, MD, 1979. Diplomate Am. Bd. Ind. Med. Examiners, U.S. Ednl. Coun. Fgn. Med. Grads., 1980, U.S. Fed. Lic. Examination, 1982, Philippine Med. Bd. Examination, 1980. Intern Vets. Meml. Med. Ctr., Quezon City, The Philippines, 1979-80; resident in gen. surgery St. Clare's Hosp., NYC, 1982-84; resident in phys. medicine U. Ala., Birmingham, 1984—87; pvt. practice South Bend, Ind., 1988—; lect., spasticity mgmt. closed head injury patient Ind. Head Injury Assn., 2000; with physiatric mgmt. arthritic pain Arthritis Found. Greater Chgo., 2004. Attending physiatrist Meth. Hosp., Gary, Ind., 1989—, Merrillville, 1989—, Porter Meml. Hosp., Ind., 1994-2000, Meml. Hosp., South Bend, 1988—, Lakeland Med. Ctr., Niles, 1995-2002, St. Anthony Med. Ctr., Crown Point, Ind., 1992—, St. Mary's Med. Ctr., Hobart, Ind., 1994—, St. Catherines Hosp., East Chgo., Ind., 1994—; rehab. dir. Healthwin Hosp., South Bend, 1999-2002, Cardinal Nursing and Rehab. Ctr., South Bend, 1999-2001, Silverbrook Manor, Niles, Mich., 1997-2001, Ironwood Health and Rehab. Ctr., 2004-08; rehab. dir. Hamilton Ctmtys., New Carlisle, Ind., 2006-; rehab. med. cons. Fountainview Nursing Home, Mishawaka, Ind., 2008-, Golden Living Ctrs., Merrillville, Ind., 2010-; lect., rehab. topics U. Ala., Northern Ind. Hosps., 1984-2008. Contbg. editor: US Thomasian Mag., 2006—. Vol., chmn. Philippine Centennial Celebration for South Bend, Ind., 1998, Philippine Centennial Celebration SW Mich.; lector St. Pius X Cath. Ch., Granger, Ind., 2006—. Recipient Youngest Grad. award, U. Santo Tomas, Faculty Medicine & Surgery, 1979, Cmty. Svc. award, St. Joseph Chapin Street Clinic, South Bend, 1989, Filipino-Am. Assn., South Bend, 1994—95, Provincial Bd. Resolution, Aklan Province Med. Mission, 2007, Twenty Outstanding Filipinos Abroad award, Filipino Image Mag., 2008; named Asian Leader in Ind., Asian Access Mag., 2007, Physician of Yr., Ind. Philippine Med. Assn., 2008; named one of Top Physiatrists, Nation Based on Press Gainey Orgn. Patient Satisfaction Survey, 2003, 2009. Mem. AMA, No. Ind. Rehab. Med. (pres.), Philippine Am. Physiatry Assn., (pres. 1999-2001), Asian Am. Med. Soc. (bd. dirs. 1999-02, 2006—), Am. Acad. Phys. Medicine and Rehab., Am. Congress Rehab. Medicine, Am. Acad. Electrodiagnostic Medicine, Am. Acad. Exec. Physicians, Ind. State Med. Assn., Ind. Soc. Phys. Medicine and Rehab., Ind. Philippine Med. Assn. (pres. 2008, chmn. med. and surg. mission to Aklan Province, Philippines 2007, co-chmn. med. mission 2009, Virac, Catanduanes, Philippines), St. Joseph County Med. Soc., U. Santo Tomas Med. Alumni Assn. America (lectr. chronic pain mgmt. 2008, auditor 2006-2008, bd. dirs. 2008-09, sec. 2009-10, v.p. 10-11, chmn. com. UST Med. Alumni Assn.2011-12, chmn. program com. 2011-), U. Santo Tomas Medicine Alumni Assn. America Found. (UST medicine class 1979 sec., USA chpt. 2003—, editor-in-chief newsletter, class website moderator). Address: 8127 Merrillville Rd Merrillville IN 46410-6158 Office Phone: 219-736-1266. Personal E-mail: nirm-mvl@sbcglobal.net.

YU, QINGZHAO, statistician, educator; b. China, Feb. 27, 1976; PhD, Ohio State U., 2006. Asst. prof. LSUHSC, 2006—. Mem.: ASA. Office: 2020 Gravier St 3rd Fl New Orleans LA 70112 Business E-Mail: qyu@lsuhsc.edu.

YU, QIUMING, research scientist; b. Nanjing, China, Aug. 8, 1963; PhD, Cornell U., 1995. Rsch. assoc. prof. U. Wash., 2009—. Mem.: SPIE, Am. Chem. Soc., Materials Rsch. Soc. Office: Dept Chemical Engring Box Seattle WA 98195 Business E-Mail: qyu@uw.edu.

YU, ROBERT KUAN-JEN, biochemistry professor; b. Chungking, China, Jan. 27, 1938; came to U.S., 1962; m. Helen Chow, July 1, 1972; children: David S., Jennifer S. BS, Tunghai U., Taiwan, 1960; PhD, U. Ill., 1967; Med.ScD. (hon.), Tokyo, 1980; MA (hon.), Yale U., 1985. Rsch. assoc., instr. Albert Einstein Coll. Medicine, Bronx, 1967-72; asst. prof. Yale U., New Haven, 1973-75, assoc. prof., 1975-82, prof., 1983-88; prof. biochemistry, chmn. dept. Med. Coll. Va. Va. Commonwealth U., Richmond, 1988-2000; dir. Inst. Mol. Med. Genetics Med. Coll. Ga, Augusta, 2000—09, prof., 2009—; dir. inst. neurosci. Ga. Health Scis. U., Med. Coll. Ga., Augusta, 2005. Mem. study sect. NIH, Washington, 1980-84, 96—; mem. Bd. Lab. Svcs., Va., 1994-98, Acadmician, Acad. Sinica ROC, 2004-, Ga. Comm. saving and Cure, 2007-, Editor: Gangioside Structure Function and Biomedical Potential, 1984, New Trends in Ganglioside Research, 1988; contbr. over 500 articles to profl. publs. Josiah Macy scholar, 1979; grantee NIH, 1975—, 84-91; recipient Va. Outstanding Scientist of Yr. award, 1995, Alexander von Humboldt award, 1990, GRA Eminent scholar, 2000, Dist. Alumnus award Tunghai U., 2003, Achievement award Chinese Assn. Engrs. and Scientists So. Calif., 2004, Outstanding Faculty award Sch. Medicine, Med. Coll. Ga., 2006, 2009, Lifetime Achievement award. Mem. AAAS, Am. Soc. Cell Biology, Am. Soc. Neurochemistry (mem. coun. 1983-86, 91-95, pres. 2001-03), Internat. Soc. Neurochemistry, Soc. Neurosci., Am. Soc. Biochemistry and Molecular Biology, Am. Chem. Soc., N.Y. Acad. Sci., Soc. Glybiol, Am. Soc. Cell Biol. Business E-Mail: ryu@georgiahealth.edu.

YU, WEN-CHUNG, cardiologist; b. Taipei, Taiwan, Nov. 25, 1961; s. Chien-Yen Yu and Hua-Zi Lee; m. Chao-Ti Ko, May 3, 1988; children: Tsung-Huan, Tsung-Yun. MD, Nat. Yang-Ming U., 1988. Lic. doctor internal medicine Dept. Health Taiwan, 1995. Intern Taichun Vets Gen. Hosp., Taiwan, 1986—87, Taipei Vets. Gen. Hosp., 1987—88, resident internal medicine, 1992—95, fellow cardiology, 1995—98, attending physician cardiology, 1998—; asst. prof. medicine Nat. Yang-Ming U., Taipei, 2002—. Contbr. articles to profl. jours. Recipient Ann. Best Resident Rsch. award, Chung Hua I.Hsueh Rsch. Found., 1998; named Best Clin. Tchr., Taipei Vets. Gen. Hosp., 2003. Fellow: European Soc. Cardiology; mem.: Taiwan Soc. Cardiology (assoc. sec. gen. 2001—05, Young Investigator award 1999). Office: Taipei Veterans General Hospital 201 Section 2 Shih-Pai Road Taipei 112 Taiwan Office Fax: 886-2-28771746. Business E-Mail: wcyu@vghtpe.gov.tw.

YU, WINNIE CLOTHING, engineering educator; b. Hong Kong; PhD, U. Leeds, 1996. Assoc. prof. Hong Kong Poly. U., 1989—. Recipient Silver medal, Internat. Exhbn. Inventors Geneva, Gold medal, Internat. Trade Fair-Ideas, Inventions, New Products, Nuremberg, Germany. Fellow: The Textile Inst. Avocations: hiking, badminton, swimming. Office: Hong Kong Polytechnic University Inst Textiles & Clothing Yuk Choi Rd Hung Hom Kowloon Hong Kong HK Hong Kong Business E-Mail: tcyuwm@inet.polyu.edu.hk.

YU, YING, medical researcher; b. China, July 4, 1968; MD, Soochow U., China, 1990; PhD, Showa U., Japan, 1998. Rsch. scientist Tokai U., Japan, 1999; rsch. fellow U. Calif., Irvine, 2000—05, project scientist, 2005—08; sr. scientist Alcon Labs., 2008—. Rsch. fellowship, Pulmonary Hypertension Assn., 2003—05. Mem.: Am. Heart Assn. (Scientist Devel. grant 2006—09, Rsch. fellowship 2003—05). Avocations: badminton, photography. Office: 6201 S Freeway Fort Worth TX 76134 Business E-Mail: ying.yu@alconlabs.com.

YU, YONG PENG, physician; b. Qingdao, Sept. 24, 1979; M, Qingdao U., 2009. Physician Wendeng Ctr. Hosp. Weihai, Affiliated Hosp. Weifang Med. Coll., 2009—. Recipient Nat. award, Edn. Dept. Shandong. Office: Mishan Rd West No 3 Wendeng Weihai Sandong 264400 China Business E-Mail: yypeng6688@126.com.

YU, ZHAO, surgeon, educator; b. Shen Yang, China, June 30, 1970; BS, Chinese Med. U., 1993; PhD, Peking Union Med. Coll., 2002. Assoc. prof. Peking Union Med. Coll. Hosp., 2006—. Fellowship, Ao Found. Mem.: Chinese Orthop. Assn. Avocations: reading, chess, badminton. Office: Shuai Fuyuan 1 Wang Fujing St Beijing 100730 China Personal E-mail: zhaoyupumch@hotmail.com.

YUAN, HENGJIE, pharmacist; b. Heilongjiang, China, June 22, 1973; PhD, Tianjin Med. U., 2009. Assoc. chief pharmacy Gen. Hosp., Tianjin Med. U., 2008—. Office: 154 Anshan Rd 154 Heping Dist Tianjin 300052 China E-mail: hengjieyuan@163.com.

YUAN, JIAN-MIN, epidemiologist; MD, Shanghai Med. U., 1983, MPH; PhD in epidemiology, U. Southern Calif., 1996. Rsch. fellow Shanghai Cancer Inst., 1986—88, asst. prof. epidemiology, 1989—92; rsch. asst. U. Southern Calif. Sch. Medicine, LA, 1992—96, rsch. assoc., 1996—99, asst. prof. preventive medicine, 1999—2005; assoc. prof. epidemiology and cmty. health U. Minn./Masonic Cancer Ctr., Mpls., 2005—, rschr. prevention and etiology, 2005—. Recipient Nat. Sci. and Tech. Achievement award, China, 1995. Office: U Minn Masonic Cancer Ctr Mayo Mail Code 806 420 Delaware St SE Minneapolis MN 55455 Office Phone: 612-625-8056. E-mail: jyuan@umn.edu.

YUAN, LIJUAN, virologist, immunologist, educator; arrived in USA, 1993, naturalized, 2006; PhD, Ohio State U., 2000. Rsch. scientist Ohio State U., Wooster, Va., 2002—07; asst. prof. Va. Poly. Inst. & State U., Blacksburg, 2007—. Rsch. grant R21, 2005, R01, 2009, NCCAM, NIH, R01 subcontract, 2010, NIAID, NIH. Mem.: ASM, ASV. Avocation: photography. Office: Viginia Tech 1981 Kraft Dr ILSB CRC Blacksburg VA 24061-0913 Business E-Mail: lyuan@vt.edu.

YUAN, LIJUN, physician, researcher; b. He Gang, China, June 5, 1972; d. Lianggui Yuan and Xiuhua Ma; m. Guodong Yang. PhD, 4th Mil. Med. U., Xi'an, China, 2003. Residual physician Jia Mu Si R.R. Hosp., China, 1995—97, Tangdu Hosp., Xi'an, 1997—2000, physician in charge, 2000—03; postdoctor 4th Mil. Med. U., Xi'an, 2004—. Cons. Tangdu Hosp., 2002—. Sci. Rsch. grantee, Mil. Med. U., 2004—05. Achievements include research in measuring intrathoracic pressure noninvasively. Office: Tangdu Hosp Xinsi Rd Baqiao Dist 710038 Xi'an Shanxisheng China E-mail: healthwealthhappy@yahoo.com.cn.

YUAN, ROBIN TSU-WANG, plastic surgeon; b. Boston, July 2, 1954; s. Robert Hsun-Piao and Grace I. (Chen) Y. AB, Harvard U., 1974, MD, 1978. Diplomate Am. Bd. Plastic Surgery. Resident in gen. surgery UCLA Med. Ctr., 1978-80, Cedars-Sinai Med. Ctr., LA, 1980-81, 83-84; resident in plastic surgery U. Miami (Fla.)-Jackson Meml. Hosp., 1985-87; pvt. practice LA, 1987—. Clin. instr. divsn. plastic surgery UCLA, 1987-98, asst. clin. prof., 1998—; vice-chief divsn. plastic surgery Cedars-Sinai Med. Ctr., LA, 1991—; pres., CEO, founder Family of Independent Reconstructive Surgery Teams, 1990—, pres. Millard Soc., 2003, Ethics Com., Calif. Soc. Plastic Surgeons, 2002-, plastic surgeon ABC's Extreme Makeover, 2004 Author: Cheer Up...You're Only Half Dead!, Reflections at Mid-Life, 1996; contbr. numerous articles to med. jours. Named LA's Super Dr., 2007—; named one of Am.'s Top Drs., Med. Castle Connolly Pub., 2006. Mem. Am. Soc. Plastic and Reconstructive Surgery, Am. Cleft Palate Assn., Calif. Med. Assn. (del.), LA County Med. Assn. (bd. govs. dist. 1), Phi Lambda (co-mgr. 1991—). Avocations: tennis, skiing, golf, creative writing, violin. Office: 462 N Linden Dr Ste 236 Beverly Hills CA 90212 Office Phone: 310-385-8425. Personal E-mail: robinpbhps@aol.com.

YUAN, ZHEN, biomedical researcher; b. Zibo City, Shandong, China, Dec. 16, 1972; s. Anzhe Yuan; children: Anzhe, Eddie; m. Guifen Yin. PhD, U. Sci. & Tech., Hefei, China, 2002. Engineering, U. Sci. and Tech., China, 2002. Rsch. asst. dept. modern mechanics U. Sci. and Tech., Hefei, 1996—2002; postdoctoral rsch. fellow Inst. High Performance Computing, Nat. U. Singapore, Singapore City, 2002—04; postdoctoral rsch. assoc. physics dept. Clemson Univ., 2004—05; postdoctoral rsch. scientist biomedical engring. dept. U. Fla., Gainesville, 2005—07, rsch. asst. prof. biomed. engring. dept., 2007—. Fellow, Nat. U. Singapore, 2003; scholar Lixue Pandeng, Chiense Acad. Scis., 2002. Mem.: BMES, SPIE, OSA. Achievements include research in biomedical imaging of cancer-related diseases; invention of finite-elment-based photoacoustic imaging; electric-sensitive BIOMEMS; first to hydrogel biomaterials development. Home: 1324 NW 16th Ave Apt 36 Gainesville FL 32605-4051 Office: Univ Florida Biomedical Engineering Gainesville FL 32611 Business E-Mail: yzhen@bme.ufl.edu.

YUAN, ZHI, chemist, educator; b. Tianjin, China, Apr. 3, 1961; d. Zuo Wen Yuan and Guizhi Li; m. Bin Liu; 1 child, Tong Liu. BS in Chemistry, Nankai U., China, 1983, MS in Chemistry, 1986, PhD in Chemistry, 1989. Instr. Inst. Polymer Chemistry, Nankai U., 1989, assoc. prof., 1993, prof., 1996. Contbr. articles to profl. jours. Commr. China Dem. League, 2003—; exec. commr. Tianjin Dem. League, 2003—, Tianjin People's Polit. Consultative Conf., 2007—. Recipient DuPont Innovation award, Ministry of Edn. China, 2000; named Outstanding Young Chemist, Chinese Chem. Soc., 1989. Mem.: Tianjin Biomed. Engring. Inst. (exec. dir.), China Biomed. Engring. Acad. (dir.), State Fund Com. Meeting (expert reviewer). Achievements include patents for adsorbent preparation for endotoxin hemoperfusion; nano liver targering drug carrier biodegradable materials. Office: Polymer Inst Nan Kai University Weijin St 94 # Nankai Zone Tianjin 300071 China Office Fax: 022 2350 3510. Business E-Mail: zhiy@nankai.edu.cn.

YUE, PATRICK YING-KIT, biology professor; b. Hong Kong, Dec. 15, 1945; PhD, Hong Kong Bapt. U., 2006. Lectr. dept. biology Hong Kong Bapt. U., 1999—. Contbr. articles to profl. publs. Avocations: hiking, rock climbing. Office: Waterloo Rd Kowloon Tong Hong Kong Hong Kong Office Fax: 852-3411-5995.

YUEN, MANTAK, psychologist, researcher; s. Tat and Miu-ling Yuen; m. Lai-mui Amy Ho; children: Ho-shun, Ho-wang Michael. PhD, Chinese U. of Hong Kong, 1995—2001; MSc, U. Coll. London, 1989—90; MA in Edn., Chinese U. of Hong Kong, 1986—89; BS, U. of Hong Kong, 1979—82. Chartered psychologist Brit. Psychol. Soc., 1992, registered psychologist Hong Kong Psychol. Soc., 1995, cert. counselor Hong Kong Profl. Counselling Assn. Tchr. Sai Kung Sung Tsun Cath. Secondary Sch., Hong Kong, 1982—85, Pentecostal Lam Hon Kwong Sch., Hong Kong, 1985—86; lectr. Northcote Coll. of Edn., Hong Kong, 1986—90; ednl. psychologist Hong Kong govt., 1990—95; sr. lectr. Hong Kong Inst. of Edn., 1995—96; assoc. prof. U. of Hong Kong, 1996—; coord. gifted edn. and talent devel. U. Hong Kong, 2002—, advisor, Acad. for Talented, 2011—, advisor Acad. Talented; hon. cons. gifted edn. Tung Wah Group Hosps. Divsn., 2005—; mem. sch. mgmt. com. Farm Rd. Govt. Primary Sch., 2008—; hon. cons. HKMLC Queen Maud Secondary Sch., 2003—; hon. cons. psychol. Svc. Po Leung Kuk Scondary Sch. & Spl. Sch., 2000—; hon. cons. Hong Kong Assn. Parents Gifted Children, 2011—; mem. steering com. Sch. Based Ednl. Psychol. Svc. Hong Kong Coun. Ch. Christ China; co-convener Ctr. Advancement in Spl. Edn., Spl. Interest Group for Gifted Edn., Creativity and Talent Devel.; dir. Ctr. Advancement Inclusive & Spl. Edn., 2011—. Vis. consulting psychologist Hong Kong Sea Sch., 1992—95, mem. adv. com. sch. guidance, discipline, and support svc., 1996—98, mem. com. spl. ednl. needs, 1999—2003, mem. working group on personal and social edn. curriculum for students with spl. ednl. needs, 1999—2002, mem. ad hoc com. guide curriculum for gifted/high ability students, 2000—03, mem. adv. panel on support measures for the exceptionally gifted students, 2001—03, mem. working group integrated edn., 2001—03, adv. panel disability discrimination ordinance, 2002—04, mem. action com. against Narcotics, sub-com. on rsch., 2002—05, mem. com. gifted edn., 2003—; project leader Life Skills Devel. Project, 2001—; convener, project learning to collaborate U. Hong Kong, 2006—08; cons. in field. Editor: (book) Life Skills Development and Comprehensive Guidance Program: theories and practices; author: Career development self-efficacy inventory: user's manual, Academic Development Self-Efficacy Inventory: user manual, Acculturation of young arrivals from the mainland China, Research on acculturation of young new arrivals from mainland China, Adaptation and needs of young new arrivals from mainland China in Sham Shui Po District, Personal-Social Development Self-efficacy Inventory: user's manual; mem. editl. bd.: Asian Jour. Counselling, 2001—; contbr. articles to profl. jours. (First Class Award, 2001). Bd. mem. Support Com. on Integrated Edn., Hong Kong, 1998; chairperson Ad Hoc Com. CDCC (GE) Devel. Identification Pamphlet, Povert Pamphlet and Povert Edn. in gifted edn., 2006—07. Grantee, Rsch. Grant Coun., 2003, 2006, Quality Edn. Fund, 2001; scholar Govt. Tng. Scholarship in Ednl. Psychology, Hong Kong Govt. Tng. Unit, 1989. Fellow: Hong Kong Psychol. Soc. (assoc.; registration bd. mem. 2000—03); mem.: ACA, APA, Hong Kong Profl. Counselling Assn., Internat. Sch. Psychology Assn. (rsch. com. mem. 2002—04), World Coun. Gifted and Talented Children, Am. Ednl. Rsch. Assn., Internat. Assn. Ednl. and Vocat. Guidance. Achievements include research in the development of the Chinese Career Development Self-efficacy Inventory; the development of the Chinese Academic Development Self-efficacy Inventory; the development of the Chinese Personal-Social Development Self-efficacy Inventory; development of career and talent development self-efficacy scale; comprehensive guidance and counseling program inventory. Office: Faculty of Education Univ Hong Kong Pokfulam Road Hong Kong China Office Phone: (852) 2857 8542. Office Fax: (852) 2858 5649. Business E-Mail: intyuen@hku.hk.

YUHUA, SUN, cardiologist, researcher; b. JiaXiang County, Shandong Province, China, Oct. 14, 1963; s. Sun Xianshu and Zhang Guier; m. Wang Cunming, Feb. 19, 1968; 1 child, Sun QinZhang. Diplomate Chinese Acad. Med. Scis. Physician, Zhaozhuang City, Shandong Province, China, 1982—87; assoc. prof. Cardiovasc. Inst., Beijing, 1990—. Dir. Sino-German Lab. Medicine Rsch., Beijing, 1998—2001. Contbr. scientific papers, articles to profl. jours. Achievements include research in cardiovascular disease and infection. Office: Cardiovasc Inst Fu Wai Heart Hosp Chinese Acad Med Sci Peking Union Med Co Beilishilu 167 Beijing 100037 China Office Fax: 8610-68351786. E-mail: sunyh0903@yahoo.com.

YUKI, NOBUKAZU, gastroenterologist, director; MD, Osaka U. Grad. Sch. Medicine, Suita, Japan, 1984. Diplomate Japanese Govt., 1984. Rsch. fellow Osaka U. Grad. Sch. Medicine, 1984—98; asst. dir. dept. gastroenterology Osaka Nat. Hosp., 1998—. Achievements include research in viral hepatitis. Office: Osaka Nat Hosp Hoenzaka 2-1-14 Chuo-ku Osaka 540-0006 Japan Office Phone: 6 6942 1331. Business E-Mail: yuki@onh.go.jp.

YUKIHIRO, NISHIO, gynecologist; b. Tokyo, Apr. 10, 1960; MD, Osaka U., 1986, PhD, 1994. Chief ob-gyn. Osaka Police Hosp., 2004—. Office: 10-31 Kitayama-cho Tennnoji Osaka 543-0035 Japan Office Fax: 81-6-6775-7551. Business E-Mail: chief_obgyn@oph.gr.jp.

YUKIMOTO, ISHII, physician, educator; b. Tokyo, May 7, 1957; MD, Nihon U. Sch. Medicine, 1986, PhD, 1989. Prof. Nihon U. Sch. Medicine, 2010—. Office: Ohyaguchi Itabashi-ku Tokyo 173-8610 Japan Office Fax: 81-3-3972-8180. Business E-Mail: ishii.yukimoto@nihon-u.ac.jp.

YUKIOKA, HIDEKAZU, anesthesiologist, educator; b. Osaka, Japan, Apr. 29, 1950; s. Yoshio and Nobuko Y.; m. Akiko Kuroda, Nov. 23, 1976; children: Daisuke, Tomoko, Mariko. BS, MB, Osaka City U., 1976, MD, 1987. Asst. dept. anesthesiology Osaka City U. Med. Sch., 1978—87, lectr. dept. anesthesiology and intensive care medicine, 1987—93, assoc. prof. divsn. critical care medicine, 1993—2005, vice chmn. critical care and ICU, 1993—2005; vice dir. dept. anesthesia, emergency and intensive care Yukioka Hosp., Osaka, Japan, 2005—. Rsch. assoc. dept. anaesthetics Wales U., Cardiff, 1984-85. Contbr. articles to profl. jours. Mem. Internat. Assn. for Study of Pain, Soc. Critical Care Medicine, European Soc. Intensive Care Medicine, Am. Soc. Regional Anesthesia, Internat. Anesthesia Rsch. Soc., European Resuscitation Coun. Japan Soc. Anesthesiology (councilor 1996-99), Japanese Soc. Intensive Care Medicine (councilor 1993—), Japanese Assn. Acute Medicine (councilor 1998—), Japanese Soc. Emergency Medicine (councilor 1998—), Japanese Soc. Reanimatology (councilor, 2002—), N.Y. Acad. Scis., Japanese Soc. Respiratory Care Medicine (councilor 2003-), Japan Soc. Circulation Control in Medicine (councilor 1996-), Japanese Soc. Cardiovascular Anesthesiologists (councilor 1996-). Avocations: reading, travel. Home: 1-14-5 Minase Shimamoto-cho Mishima-Gun Osaka 618-0014 Japan Office: Yukioka Hosp Dept Anesthesia Emergency and Intensive Care 2 2 3 Ukita Kita-ku Osaka 530-0021 Japan Business E-Mail: yukioka@msic.med.osaka-cu.ac.jp.

YUKO, INAGAKI, medical educator; b. Japan, Aug. 5, 1948; Grad, Med. Sch. Mie U., 1973; postgrad, Med. Sch. Kobe U., 1979. Prof. child devel. and behavior faculty human scis. Konan Women's U., 2000—. Office: 6-2-23 Morikita-machi Higashinada-ku Kobe Hyougo 658 0001 Japan Office Fax: 81-78-413-3093. Business E-Mail: yinagaki@konan-wu.ac.jp.

YUM, KEUN SANG, physician, educator; b. Seoul, Republic Of Korea, Mar. 25, 1963; s. Chang-hoon Yum and Ok-soon Han; m. Ho-Jeong Lee; children: Yun-a, Yun-jin, Ji-seung. Degree, UCLA, 2004. Cert. med. physician Cath. Med. Sch., Seoul, 1989. Chief prof. dep. family medicine St. Mary's Hosp., Seoul, 1996—2005, Uijeongbu St. Mary's Hosp., Republic of Korea. Cooperation dir. Korean Soc. Study Obesity, Seoul, 2009—. Contbr. articles. Vol. med. svc. Free-Foreinger Med. Svc. Cmty., Uijeonbu-si, 2007. Lt. Korean Army, 1990—93, Gang-won do. Grant, Korean Hanmi Pharmacy Co., 2008. Mem.: Korean Acad. Family Medicine. Achievements include research in the psychological characteristics of functional dyspepsia patients by MMPI; age associated changes in body mass index and body fat distribution, the association between obesity indices and physical fitness; the relationship between physical fitness and fatigue among female employees in general hospitals; validity analysis of four exercise tests in assessing aerobic capacity of young men; the association of influenza vaccination in high risk group; the association of hypercholesterolemia and cardiovascular disease in adult. Avocations: golf, mountain climbing. Office: Uijeongbu St Mary's Hosp #65-1 Geumo-dong Uijeongbu-si Gyeonggi-do 480-717 Republic of Korea Office Fax: 82-31-847-3941; Home Fax: 82-2-416-3790. Business E-Mail: yks6303@catholic.ac.kr.

YUN, MIJIN, medical educator; b. Kwangju, Nov. 23, 1968; MD, Yonsei U., 1993; PhD, Korea U., 2005. Assoc. prof. Yonsei U. Health Sys., 2008—. Bd. mem. Clin. Nuc. Medicine, 2011. Mem.: Soc. Nuc. Medicine. Avocations: tennis, gardening, golf. Office: 135 Shinhon-dong Seodaemun-ku Seoul 120-752 Republic of Korea Office Fax: 82-2-312-0578. Business E-Mail: yunmijin@yuhs.ac.

YUN, PIL-YOUNG, oral surgeon; b. Incheon, Republic of Korea, May 5, 1970; s. Byeong-Seok Yun and Jum-Rye Choi; m. Mi-Seon Ko, July 18, 1970; children: Lin, Geon. MS in Dentistry, Seoul Nat. U., Republic of Korea, 1998, PhD in Dentistry, 2005. Fellow Seoul Nat. U. Dental Hosp., 2002—03, Seoul Nat. U. Bundang Hosp., 2003—05, clin. asst. prof., 2005—. Author: (book) Osstem Implant System, 2006. Mil. dental officer UN Peace Keeping Operation, El Aaiun, Western Sahara, 2001—02. Mem.: Korean Assn. Maxillofacial Plastic and Reconstructive Surgeons (life), Korean Assn. Oral and Maxillofacial Surgeons (life). Avocations: Judo, basketball, ping pong/table tennis, travel, tennis. Home: 77 Gumi-dong Bundang-gu Seongnam 463-743 Republic of Korea Office: Seoul Nat Univ Bundang Hos Gumi-Dong Bundang-Gu 300 463-707 Seongnam Republic of Korea Personal E-mail: pilyounge@empal.com. Business E-Mail: pilyoung@snubh.org.

YUN, SANG PIL, oriental physician; s. Yun and Oh; m. Kim; children: Yun CW, Yun JW. PhD, Kyunghee U.; D, St. Paul's Oriental Med. Ctr., Seoul, Republic of Korea. Oriental physician Kyunghee Oriental Med. Ctr., Seoul, 1999—2000, 2002—05, St. Paul's Oriental Med. Ctr., 2005—09. Contbr. articles to profl. jours. Office: Kyunghee Bon Oriental Med Clinic 285-2 Dosun-dong Seongdong-gu Seoul 133-882 Republic of Korea Personal E-mail: yunpaul@yahoo.co.kr.

YUN, SEOK-KWEON, dermatologist, educator; b. Gokseong, Republic of Korea, June 6, 1967; s. Yun and Seo; m. Mi-Won Lee, May 7, 1994; children: Seong-Ih, Chi-Oh. MD, Chonbuk Nat. U., 1992, MS, 1995; PhD, Chonnam Nat. U., 2004. Diplomate Korean Bd. Dermatology, 1997, lic. physician Ministry Health and Welfare, Republic of Korea, 1992, fgn. med. practitioner Ministry Health, Labour and Welfare, Japan, 2004. Intern Chonbuk Nat. U. Hosp., Jeonju, Republic of Korea, 1992—93, resident Dept. Dermatology, 1993—97, fellow Dept. Dermatology, 2000; dir. Dept. Dermatology Namwon Med. Ctr., Republic of Korea, 1997—2000; lectr. Dept. Dermatology Med. Sch. Chonbuk Nat. U., 2000—02, asst. prof. Dept. Dermatology Med. Sch., 2002—. Capt. med. br. Republic of Korea Armay, 1997—2000. Scholar, Takeda Sci. Found., Japan, 2004. Mem.: The Korean Soc. Investigative Dermatology (licentiate), Korean Soc. Dermatologic Surgery (licentiate), Korean Dermatol. Assn. (licentiate; dir. 2003—), Korean Soc. Laser Medicine (assoc.), Korean Soc. Med. Mycology (assoc.), Am. Acad. Dermatology (assoc.), Korean Med. Assn. (assoc.). Office: Nat Univ Med Sch Dept of Derm Chonbuk 634-18 Geumam-Dong Deokjin-Gu 561-712 Jeonju Republic of Korea Office Fax: 82-63-250-1970. Business E-Mail: dermayun@chonbuk.ac.kr.

YUN, THOMAS WONKI, federal agency administrator, physician; b. May 3, 1949; BS, U. Va.; MS, U. Ga.; MD, Ea. Va. Med. Sch., 1980. Cert. Family Practice. Regional med. officer US Dept. State, Dhaka, Beijing, Jakarta, head medevac ops. London, Singapore, dep. med. dir. Office Med. Svcs., 2006—08, med. dir., 2008—. Office: US Department of State Office of Medical Services 2201 C St NW Washington DC 20520 *

YUN, YEO-MIN, physician, educator; b. Seoul, Republic of Korea, Feb. 20, 1969; MD, Coll. Medicine, Seoul Nat. U., 1993; PhD, Seoul Nat. U., 2005. Resident dept. lab. medicine Seoul Nat. U. Hosp., 1997—2001, fellow dept. lab. medicine, 2001—02; dir., assoc. prof. dept. lab. medicine Jeju Nat. U. Hosp. and Coll. Medicine, 2002—04, Konkuk U. Hosp. and Sch. Medicine, 2005—. Recipient Conf. Travel award, Am. Assn. Clin. Chemistry, 2002. Mem.: Korean Soc. Clin. Chemistry (dir. pub. relationships 2009—10), Korean Assn. Qaulity Assurance Clin. Lab. (sec. gen. 2006—11, Quality Assurance award 2009), Korean Soc. Lab. Medicine (dir. spl. affair 2010—11). Avocations: golf, tennis. Office: Konkuk University Hosp 4-12 Hawyang Seoul 143-729 Republic of Korea Office Fax: +822-2030-5587. Business E-Mail: doctory@paran.com.

YUN, YOUNGO HO, physician, researcher; b. Naju-si, Republic of Korea, July 1, 1964; m. Yoon Jung Choi; children: Sang Yeon, Seok Jin. MD, Seoul Nat. U., Republic of Korea, 1990, PhD, 2002. Chief Nat. Cancer Ctr., Goyang-si, Gyeonggi-do, Republic of Korea, 2000—. Capt. Republic of Korea Air Force, 1993—96. Grantee, Nat. Cancer Ctr., 2001—05. Office: Nat Cancer Ctr Madu1-Dong Ilsan-Gu 809 410-769 Goyang-sì Gyeonggi-do Republic of Korea Office Fax: 82-31-920-2199. Business E-Mail: lawyun08@ncc.re.kr.

YUNG, WAI KWAN ALFRED, neurology and neuro-oncology educator; b. Hong Kong; BS, U. Minn., 1971; MD, U. Chgo., 1975. Intern in neurology U. Calif., San Diego, 1975—76; asst. resident neurology UCSD, 1976—78, chief resident neurology, 1978, MSKCC, 1978—79, fellow neurology, 1978—81; clin. fellow neurology NY Hosp., 1979—81; prof. neurology Dept. Neurology, U. Tex. Med. Sch., Houston, 1992—, prof. of tumor biology dept. tumor biology M.D. Anderson Cancer Ctr., Houston, 1992—, prof. neurology dept. of neuro oncology, 1992—, chmn. dept. neuro-oncology, 1999—. Florence M. Thomas prof. of cancer rsch. M.D. Anderson Cancer Ctr., Houston, 1996-2002, chmn. Margaret and Ben Love chair in clin. cancer care, 2002—. Office: MD Anderson Cancer Ctr Box 431 1515 Holcombe Blvd Houston TX 77030-4009 Office Phone: 713-794-1285.

YUNJIN, KIM, biomedical researcher; b. Incheon, Republic Of Korea, Apr. 18, 1976; s. Kim TaeWoong and Jung YeonSoon. MD, Nanjing U. Traditional Chinese Medicine, 2003. Rschr. Dept. Physics Chung-Ang U., Seoul, 2000—05; rschr. Seoul Nat. U., Biomedical Physics Lab., Sch. Physics, Seoul, 2005—. Physician Tcm Med. Tk Sdn Bhd, Skudai, Johor Bahru, Malaysia, 2007—. Editor: Traditional Chinese Medicine Prescription Textbook. Scholar, NJUTCM, 2000—04. Mem.: Am. Acad. Neurology (assoc.). Home: 18/1 248-144 Sunguei 4 Dong Namku Incheon 402-014 Republic of Korea Office: Tcm Medical Tk Sdn Bhd 78 Jalan Indah1 Taman Bukit Indah Johor Bahru Skudai 81200 Malaysia Personal E-mail: neurokim@gmail.com.

YURT, ROGER WILLIAM, surgeon, educator; b. Louisville, June 8, 1945; s. Albert William and Mary Louise (McGrath) Yurt; m. Joan A. Terry, Sept. 3, 1971; children: Jennifer, Daniel, Gregory. BS in Biology, Loyola U., New Orleans, 1967; Md, U. Miami Sch. Medicine, 1972. Diplomate Am. Bd. Surgery, Nat. Bd. Med. Examiners. Intern surgery Parkland Meml. Hosp.-Southwestern Med. Sch., U. Tex., Dallas, 1972-73, resident surgery, 1973-74; postdoc. fellow Robert B. Brigham Hosp.-Harvard Med. Sch., Boston, 1974—77; resident, chief resident NY Presbyn. Hosp.-Weill Cornell Med. Ctr., NYC, 1977-79, acting dir. Burn Ctr., dir. rsch., 1982-83, vice chmn. dept. surgery, 1987—, acting chmn., 1991-93, dir. Trauma Ctr., 1992-99, attending surgeon, chief burn surgery, 1995—, dir. William Randolph Hearst Burn Ctr.; prof. surgery Weill Cornell Med. Coll., 1982—95, Johnson & Johnson disting. prof. surgery, 1995—. Clin. asst. prof. surgery Uniformed Svcs. U. Health Sci., Bethesda, Md., 1980—82, U. Tex. Health Sci. Ctr., San Antonio, 1981—82; chmn. burn com. Regional Emergency Med. Svcs., NY, 1982—84, mem. trauma ctr. adv. com., 1984—89, chmn., 1995—98, chmn. burn ctr. adv. com., 1996—2000. Editor: Infections in Surgery, 1981—88; contbr. articles to profl. jours., chapters to books. Maj. US Army, 1979—82. Recipient Hewitt award, Royal Soc. Medicine, 2003, Meritorious Humanitarian Recognition award, Am. Skin Assn., 2003, Physician of Yr. award, NY Presbyn. Hosp., 2006; named one of Best Doctors in America, Castle Connelly Med. Ltd., 1998—, NY's SuperDoctors, 2008; named to NY Mag.'s 'Best Doctors' issue, 1998—; grantee United Health Found., 1968—69, USPHS, 1973—75, NIH, 1984—87. Mem.: ACS (gov. 1990—96), Internat. Surg. Soc., Assn. Acad. Surgery, Am. Surg. Assn., Soc. Univ. Surgeons, Am. Surg. Infection Soc. (sec. 1987—90, pres. 1991—92, charter mem., chmn. membership com.), Am. Burn Assn. (v.p. bd. trustees 2004—06), Am. Assn. Med. Colleges (del. coun. academic societies 1985—87), Am. Assn. Surgery of Trauma, Omicron Delta Kappa, Alpha Omega Alpha. Roman Catholic. Office Phone: 212-746-5410. Office Fax: 212-746-8991.

YURTCU, MUSLIM, medical educator; b. Sanliurfa, June 1, 1960; Assoc. prof. Istanbul U. Cerrahpasa Med. Faculty, 1992, Selcuk U. Meram Med. Faculty, 1992—. Mem.: Turkish Pediatric Urology Assn., Turkish Pediatric Surgery Assn. Avocation: swimming. Home: Kizilirmak Konya Meram 42090 Turkey Home Fax: 0332 223 61 81. Business E-Mail: muslimyurtcu@selcuk.edu.tr.

YURY, MILOVANOV, physician; b. Ukraine, Aug. 1, 1944; MD, First Moscow Med. Inst., 1972, PhD, 1981. Physician First Moscow Med. Inst., 1972—, cons., 1984—2011. Mem.: Inst. Uronephrology. Home: Marshala Zakharova 10/2/351 Marshala ZA Moscow 115569 Russia Home Fax: 7-495-3932492. Personal E-mail: yuriymilovanov@mail.ru.

YUSONG, PAN, physics professor; b. An'qing City, Anhui, China, June 5, 1972; PhD, Nanjing U. Sci. and Tech., 2008. Tchr. Anhui U. Sci. and Tech., 2008—. Mem.: Inst. Biomaterials. Home: Shungeng Middle Rd 168 Huainan Anhui 232001 China Personal E-mail: yusongpan@163.com.

YUSPA, STUART HOWARD, oncologist, researcher; b. Balt., July 19, 1941; BS, Johns Hopkins U., 1962; MD, U. Md., 1966. Diplomate Am. Bd. Internal Medicine. Intern Hosp. of U. Pa., Phila., 1966-67, resident in internal medicine, 1970-72; rsch. assoc. Ctr. Cancer Rsch., Nat. Cancer Inst., NIH, Bethesda, Md., 1967-70, sr. investigator, 1972—, chief Lab. Cellular Carcinogenesis and Tumor Promotion, chief Lab. Cancer Biology and Genetics, head In Vitro Pathogenesis Sect. Assoc. editor Cancer Rsch., 1983—96; editor-in-chief Molecular Carcinogenesis, 1987—92. Recipient Lila Gruber Cancer Rsch. Award, Am. Acad. Dermatology, 1989, DSM, USPHS. Fellow AAAS; mem Am. Assn. Cancer Rsch. (G.H.A. Clowes Meml. Award 1993), Am. Soc. Cell Biology, Soc. Investigative Dermatology, USPHS Commd. Officers Assn. Achievements include research in determining mechanisms whereby chemicals initiate or promote malignant transformation of epithelial cells. Office: Lab Cellular Carcinogenesis and Tumor Promotion Ctr Cancer Rsch Bldg 37 Rm 4068A1 37 Convent Dr Bethesda MD 20892 Office Phone: 301-496-2162. Office Fax: 301-496-8709. E-mail: sy12j@nih.gov. *

YUSPEH, ALAN RALPH, lawyer, hospital administrator; b. New Orleans, June 13, 1949; s. Michel and Rose Fay (Rabenovitz) Y.; m. Janet Horn, June 8, 1975. B in Polit. Sci. & Economics magna cum laude with honors, Yale U., 1971; MBA with distinction, Harvard U., 1973; JD, Georgetown U., 1978. Bar: DC 1978. Editor, law & policy, internat. bus. Georgetown U.; mgmt. cons. McKinsey & Co., Washington, 1973-74; adminstrv. asst., legis. asst. to senator J. Bennett Johnston La., 1974-78; atty. Shaw, Pittman, Potts & Trowbridge, Washington, 1978-79, Ginsburg, Feldman, Weil & Bress, Washington, 1979-82; gen. counsel US Senate Com. on Armed Svcs., Washington, 1982-85; ptnr. Preston, Thorgrimson, Ellis & Holman, Washington, 1985-88, Miller & Chevalier, Washington, 1988-91, Howrey & Simon, Washington, 1991-97; sr. v.p., ethics, compliance & corp. responsibility HCA, Inc., 1997—2007, sr. v.p., chief ethics officer & chief compliance officer, 2007—. Coord. Def. Industry Initiative on Bus., Ethics and Conduct, 1987-97; pres. Health Care Compliance Assn., 2002. Editor Law and Policy in Internat. Bus. Jour., 1978-79, Nat. Contract Mgmt. Jour., 1988-92; assoc. editor Pub. Contract Law Jour., 1987-91. Chmn. bd. ethics, City of Balt., 1988-96, planning commn., 1996-97; chmn. bd. dirs. Tenn. Repertory Theater, 2002-05; bd. dirs. Balt. Housing Authority, 1996-97, Ethics Officer Assn., 2001-04, YMCA Mid. Tenn. Camp, 2002-, Tenn. Performing Arts Ctr., 2003-, Nashville Pub. Libr. Found., 2005-. 1st lt. USAR, 1971-77, nat. pres. Health Care Compliance Assn., 2004, bd. dirs. United Way of Nashville, Urban League of Middle Tenn., Nashville Alliance for Pu. Edn., Nashville Opera, chmn., Ctr., Bus. Ethics Belmont U., bd. adv. Vanderbilt Inst. for Global Health, Montgomery Bell Acad., mem., Citizens Adv. Comm. on Ethics Recipient Health Care Compliance Profl. of the Yr., Health Care Compliance Assn., 1999. Office: HCA Inc 1 Park Plz Nashville TN 37203 Home: 126 Third Ave N Franklin TN 37064 Office Phone: 615-344-9551. Business E-Mail: alan.yuspeh@hcahealthcare.com.

YUSUF, HARMAS YAZID, oral surgeon; b. Jakarta, Indonesia, July 18, 1957; s. Teuku and Maftuchah Yusuf; m. Nani Murniati Naceu; children: Mirza Ismail Yazid, Tasya Aniza Yazid. DDS, Padjadjaran U., Bandung, West Java, Indonesia, 1981, PhD, 2001. OMFS PABMI, Indonesian Assn. Oral and Maxillofacial Surgeos, Bandung, 1981. Sec. dept. oral and maxillofacial surgeon, faculty dentistry Padjadjaran U., 1996—98, sec. post grad. oral and maxillofacial surgeon trainee programme, 2006—. Mem.: Indonesian Assn. Oral and Maxillofacial Surgeon (mem. ethical commn. 2008—). Achievements include research in oral oncology. Home: Jln Cibogo 43 Bandung West Java 40164 Indonesia Office: Faculty Dentistry Padjadjaran Univ Jl Sekeloa Selatan I Bandung West Java 40132 Indonesia Office Phone: 62 22 2041196. Home Fax: 62 22 2036169. Business E-Mail: harmas@bdg.centrin.net.id.

YUSUKE, OKUMURA, medical technician; b. Ishikawa, Japan, Dec. 20, 1981; B in Health Sci., Kanazawa U., 2004, D in Health Edn., 2010. Radiol. technologist Ishikawaken Saiseikai Kanazawa Hosp., 2004—. Office: Akatsuchi Kanazawa Ishikawa 9200353 Japan Business E-Mail: oxson@mist.ocn.ne.jp.

YUTER, JOSHUA, rabbi; b. Albany, NY, Aug. 4, 1977; BA in Computer Sci., Yeshiva U., 1999; MA in Social Scis., U. Chgo., 2008. Programming analyst Info. Builders, 2005—07; assoc. applications developer JPMorgan Chase, 2007—08; rabbi Stanton St. Shul, 2008—. Recipient People's Choice award, Jewish and Israeli Blog Network. Mem.: Internat. Rabbinic Fellowship, Rabbinical Coun. Am. Office: Stanton St Shul PO Box 1008 New York NY 10002 Personal E-mail: jyuter@gmail.com.

YUTKIN, VLADIMIR, surgeon; b. Russia, June 13, 1970; MD, Hebrew U., 1998. Surgeon, urology dept. Hadassah and Hebrew U. Med. Ctr., 2000—. Mem.: Am. Urol. Assn. Office: Ein Karem Campus Urology Dept Jerusalem 91120 Israel Office Fax: 972-2-6778135. Business E-Mail: yutkin@hadassah.org.il.

YU-TZU, TSAO, nephrologist, educator; b. Kaohsiung, Taiwan, Sept. 9, 1976; married. MD, Nat. Def. Med. Ctr. Lic. physician R.O.C., 2001, cert. 2008, in aviation medicine 2004, in internal medicine 2006, nephrologist 2008. Flight surgeon air force Nat. Def.

R.O.C., Taipei, Taiwan, 2001—, instr., 2008—; attending physician nephrology Trisvc. Gen. Hosp., Taipei, 2008—. Contbr. scientific papers. Squadron leader Air Force, R.O.C. Grant, Trisvc. Gen. Hosp., Civilian Clin. Dept., 2007—08. Mem.: Soc. Aviation Medicine, Soc. Med. Ultrasound, Soc. Critical Care Medicine, Soc. Nephrology, Soc. Internal Medicine. Office: Nat Def Med Ctr N325 Sec 2 Cheng-Kung Rd Neihu Taipei 114 Taiwan Office Fax: 886-2-87927134. E-mail: tsaoyutzu@gmail.com.

ZABALA, MIKEL, physical education educator; b. Estella, Spain, Sept. 26, 1974; MSc, Faculty Phys. Activity and Sport Scis., 2000, PhD, 2004. Tech. dir. Spanish Cycling Fedn., 2005—08, dir. projects prevention doping, 2008—; sr. lectr. Faculty Phys. Activity and Sport Scis., 2005—, vice dean, 2008—. Mem.: Spanish Sports Medicine Assn. Avocations: bicycling, reading. Office: Carretera Alfacar s/n 18011 Granada 18011 Spain Office Fax: 34-958244369. Business E-Mail: mikelz@ugr.es.

ZABETAKIS, PAUL MICHAEL, nephrologist, educator; b. Washington, Pa., July 30, 1947; s. Michael G. and Rebecca A. (Banakas) Z.; m. Martha Robinson, Oct. 3, 1970; 1 child, Amy Shannon. BA, Washington & Jefferson Coll., 1969; mD, U. Tenn., 1972. Diplomate Am. Bd. Internal Medicine, Am. Bd. Nephrology. Intern in medicine U. Pitts., 1972-73, resident in medicine, 1973-75; fellow in nephrology Yale U., New Haven, 1975-77; asst. chief nephrology-hypertension Lenox Hill Hosp., NYC, 1977-82, assoc. chief nephrology-hypertension, 1978-99, dir. home peritoneal dialysis, 1985-99; asst. prof. clin. medicine NY Med. Coll., Valhalla, 1980-88, assoc. prof. clin. medicine, 1988-92; clin. asst. prof. medicine Cornell U., NYC, 1992-93; clin. assoc. prof. medicine NYU, 1993-99; exec. v.p., COO Everest Healthcare Svc., Oak Park, Ill., 1999-2001; CEO Extracorporeal Alliance Fresenius Med. Care, N.Am., 2001—06; pres. Renal Rsch. Inst., 2006—. Mem. editl. bd. Clinical Nephrology, 1979—, Clinical and Experimental Dialysis and Apheresis, 1983-86, Geriatric Nephrology and Urology, 1995—, Advances in Renal Replacement Therapy, 1999—; nephrology cons. Nicholas Inst. Sports Medicine and Athletic Trauma Lenox Hill Hosp., N.Y.C., 1978-99, rsch. physician, 1982-99; mem. hypertension svc. adv. com. ARC, N.Y.C., 1981-99; mem. exec. com. End Stage Renal Disease Network N.Y. Inc., 1986-99, treas., 1992-93, chmn. long-range planning com., 1994; bd. dirs. Physician Hosp. Orgn. Lenox Hill Hosp., chmn. bd. dirs., 1996-99, v.p. med. bd., 1997-99; vice-chmn. quality improvement, med. dir. Everest Healthcare Svcs., Chgo., 1996-99. Contbr. numerous chpts. to books; patentee in field; lectr. in field; contbr. articles to profl. jours. Fellow ACP, Am. Coll. Preventive Medicine, Am. Coll. Sports Medicine; mem. N.Y. County Med. Soc., Med. Soc. of State of N.Y., Am. Heart Assn., Westchester Heart Assn., N.Y. Soc. Nephrology, Am. Soc. Nephrology, Internat. Soc. Nephrology, N.Y. Acad. Scis., N.Y. State Fedn. Profl. Health Educators, Am. Fedn. Clin. Sch., Internat. Soc. Peritoneal Dialysis, Am. Soc. Artificial Internal Organs (program com. 1995-99), Soc. Critical Care Medicine, Am. Coll. Nutrition, Internat. Soc. for Renal Nutrition and Metabolism, Internat. Soc. Geriatric Nephrology and Urology (founding mem., sec-treas. 1994-99). Avocation: sailboat racing. Business E-Mail: paul.zabetakis@fmc-na.com.

ZABKA, TANJA SERENA, veterinarian; b. Ossining, NY, July 09; BA, Princeton U., 1996; DVM, U. Ga., 2001. Diplomate Am. Coll. Vet. Pathologists. Vet. pathologist Wildlife Health Ctr. U. Calif., Davis, Marine Mammal Ctr. Wildlife and Vet. Care Facility, 2005—07; sr. vet. pathologist, global safety biomarker lead Roche Pharms., 2007—. Mem.: IAMMM, ACVM, ACVP. Avocations: soccer, tennis, volleyball, skiing, hiking, piano, scuba diving. Home: 400 Chambers St 18F New York NY 10282 Personal E-mail: tszabka@yahoo.com.

ZACCARO, RONALDO POSELLA, engineering educator; b. São Paulo, Brazil, July 3, 1953; Degree in Agrl. Engring., FCAV Jaboticabal-UNESP, 1976, D in Agronomy, 2002. Prof. Centro Universitário Moura Lacerda, 2006—. Mem.: Internat. Citrus Virologists. Home: Sítio Manga Rosa Área Rural Bonfim Paulista São Paulo 14.110-970 Brazil Personal E-mail: rzaccaro@fcav.unesp.br.

ZACHARIAS, LEANDRO CABRAL, ophthalmologist; b. São Paulo, Brazil, Oct. 27, 1977; MD, U. São Paulo, 2000. Attending physician U. São Paulo, 2008—. Mem.: Conselho Brasileiro Oftalmologia, Soc. Brasileira Retina e Vítreo, ARVO, Am. Acad. Ophthalmology, Am. Soc. Retinal Specialists. Office: R Prof Carlos Carvalho 175 São Paulo 04531080 Brazil Office Fax: 5511-30784611. E-mail: lczacharias@gmail.com.

ZACHARIAS, NIKOLAOS MARIOS, obstetrician, gynecologist, perinatologist; b. Athens, Greece; s. Marios Nikolaos and Constantoula Marios Zacharias; m. Ioanna Dimitrios Athanassaki, May 12, 2000. MD, Nat. and Kapodistrian U., Athens, 1995. Cert. in ob-gyn. 2008. Gen. practitioner Greek Nat. Health Svc., Vassiliki, Greece, 1996-97; gen. surgery intern Laikon Gen. Hosp., Athens, 1997-98; chief resident in ob-gyn. Baylor Coll. Medicine, Houston, 1998—2002; fellow in maternal-fetal medicine U. Tex. Med. Br., Galveston, 2002—05; asst. prof. ob-gyn Baylor Coll. Medicine, Houston, 2005—; program dir. dist. prenatal ultrasound maternal fetal medicine Harris County Hosp., Houston, 2005—; med. dir. maternal fetal ultrasound unit Ben Taub Hosp. Undergrad. Ann. scholar Found. State Scholarships, 1990-94; Papadakis grantee Nat. and Kapodistrian U. Athens, 1990-95, Kontoleon grantee, 1998-2002, Acad. fellow U. Tex. Med. Br., 2002-. Fellow Am. Congress-Coll. & Obstetricians and Gynecologists; mem. AMA, Athens Med. Assn., Gen. Med. Coun., Tex. Med. Assn., Soc. for Maternal-Fetal Medicine. Avocations: swimming, basketball, travel. Home: 125 White Dr Bellaire TX 77401 Office: Baylor Coll Medicine 1709 Dryden Ste 1100 Houston TX 77030-2400 Office Phone: 713-873-3436, 713-870-6884. Business E-Mail: nmz@bcm.edu, nikolaos_zacharias@hchd.tmc.edu.

ZACHERT, VIRGINIA, retired psychologist; b. Jacksonville, Ala., Mar. 1, 1920; d. R.E. and Cora H. (Massee) Z. Student, Norman Jr. Coll., 1937; AB, Ga. State Woman's Coll., 1940; MA, Emory U., 1947; PhD, Purdue U., 1949. Diplomate Am. Bd. Profl. Psychologists. Statistician Davison-Paxon Co., Atlanta, 1941-44; research psychologist Mil. Contracts, Auburn Research Found., Ala. Poly. Inst.; indsl. and research psychologist Sturm & O'Brien (cons. engrs.), 1958-59; research project dir. Western Design, Biloxi, Miss., 1960-61; self-employed cons. psychologist Norman Park, Ga., 1961-71, Good Hope, Ga., 1971-99; ret. Rsch. assoc. med. edn. Med. Coll. Ga., Augusta, 1963-65, assoc. prof., 1965-70, rsch. prof., 1970-84, rsch. prof. emeritus, 1984—, chief learning materials divsn., 1973-84, faculty senate, 1976-84, acad. coun., 1976-82, pres. acad. coun., 1983, sec., 1978; mem. Ga. Bd. Examiners Psychologists, 1974-79, v.p., 1977, pres. 1978; adv. bd. Comdr. Gen. ATC USAF, 1967-70; cons. Ga. Silver Haired Legislature, 1980-86, senator, 1987-93, pres. protem, 1987-88, pres., 1989-93, rep., spkr. protem, 1993-96, spkr., 1997-98, Nat. Silver-Haired Congress rep., 1995—, spkr. 1997-99; govs. appointee White House Conf. on Aging, 1971, 96, Ga. Coun. on Aging, 1988-96; U.S. Senate mem. Fed. Coun. on the Aging, 1990-93; senator appointee White House Conf. on Aging, 1995; Ga. Health Decision's appointee to Ga. Coalition for Health, 1996-98. Author: (with P.L. Wilds) Essentials of Gynecology-Oncology, 1967, Applications of Gynecology-Oncology, 1967. Del. White House Conf. on Aging, 1981, 95. Served as aerologist USN, 1944-46; aviation psychologist, Lackland Air Force, San Antonio, USAF, 1949-55. Recipient Jane Kennedy Excellence Aging award, 1999. Fellow AAAS, Am. Psychol. Assn.; mem. AAUP (chpt. pres. 1977-80), Sigma Xi. (chpt. pres. 1980-81) Baptist. Home: 4275 Owens Rd # 403 Evans GA 30809

ZACHIAN, VICTOR A., gynecologist, obstetrician; MD, Thomas Jefferson U. Diplomate Am. Bd. Ob-Gyn., 1984. Intern Albert Einstein Med. Ctr.; resident Pa. Hosp.; attending physician Children's Hosp. of Phila. Named one of Top Doctors, Phila. mag., 2002, 2004, 2007—09, 2011, Best Doctors in America, 2005—06, 2007—08, 2009—10. Fellow: ACOG. Office: Children's Hospitalof Philadelphia 34th St and Civic Center Blvd Philadelphia PA 19104-4399 Office Phone: 215-590-1000.

ZACHOPOULOU, EVRIDIKI, physical education educator; b. Thessaloniki, Dec. 10, 1966; MSc, Democritus U. Thrace, 1996, PhD, 1998. Prof. Alexander Technol. Ednl. Inst. Thessaloniki, 2003—. Recipient Success Stories award, European Commn., Edn. & Tng. Avocation: tennis. Home: Vriantos 3 Thessaloniki 55131 Greece Personal E-mail: ezachopo@bc.teithe.gr.

ZAFFAGNINI, STEFANO, orthopedist; b. Lugo, Ravenna, Italy, Sept. 20, 1962; married. Degree in Medicine, U. Bologna, Italy, 1987; Specialization in Orthopedics & Traumatology, 1992. Cert. Inst. Ortopedic Rizzoli, 2008. Sr. orthopaedic surgeon Inst. Ortopedici Rizzoli, Bologna, 1997—. Clin. rschr. Biomechanics Lab. Inst. Ortopedici Rizzoli, 1992—; fellow sports medicine & orthopaedic rsch. U. Pitts., 1993—94; asst. prof. U. Bologna, 2005—08, rschr., 2008—. Contbr. articles to profl. jours. Ive Rotary Club Faenza, Italy, 1997—2008. Mem.: S.I.G.A.S.C.O.T., Italian Soc. Arthroscopy, Italian Soc. Orthopaedics & Traumatology, Magellan Soc., Internat. Soc. Arthroscopy, Knee & Orthopaedic Surgery, Internat. Cartilage Rsch. Soc., European Soc. Shoulder & Knee Arthroscopy, Am. Orthopaedic Soc. Sports Medicine, Italian Orthopaedic Rsch. Soc., Am. Acad. Orthopaedic surgeons. Roman Cath. Achievements include patents pending for surgical arthroscopic instrument for knee surgery. Avocations: swimming, travel. Office: Inst Ortopedic Rizzoli 10 Via di Barbiano 1 40136 Bologna BO Italy Office Fax: 0039 051 583789. Business E-Mail: s.zaffagnini@biomec.ior.it.

ZAFFARONI, ALEJANDRO C., retired biochemist, biotechnology entrepreneur; b. Montevideo, Uruguay, Feb. 27, 1923; arrived in U.S., 44; s. Carlos and Luisa (Alfaro) Zaffaroni; m. Lyda Russomanno, July 5, 1946; children: Alejandro A., Elisa. B., U. Montevideo, 1943; PhD in Biochemistry, U. Rochester, 1949; Doctorate (hon.), U. Republic, Montevideo, 1983; M.Divinity, Cen. Bapt. Seminary, 1987. Dir. biochem. research Syntex S.A., Mexico City, 1951—54, v.p., dir. research, 1954—56; exec. v.p., dir. Syntex Corp., Palo Alto, Calif., 1956—68; pres. Syntex Labs. Inc., Palo Alto, Calif., 1962—68, Syntex Research, Palo Alto, Calif., 1962—68; founder, co-chmn. ALZA Corp., Palo Alto, Calif., 1968—, also CEO, till 1998, founder, dir. emeritus, 1998—99, ret., 1999; founder, mem. policy bd. and exec. com. DNAX Research Inst. of Molecular and Cellular Biology, Inc. (acquired by Schering-Plough), Palo Alto, Calif., 1980—82, chmn., 1980—82, current mem. policy bd.; founder, chmn., chief exec. officer Affymax, N.V. (acquired by Glaxo plc), Palo Alto, 1988—95; founder Affymetrix, Inc., Santa Clara, Calif., 1991; co-founder Symyx Technologies, Inc., Santa Clara, Calif., 1994, Maxygen Inc., Redwood City, Calif., 1997—, mem. scientific adv. bd.; co-founder SurroMed, Inc., Mountain View, Calif., 1997, also bd. dir.; founder, chmn. Alexza Pharm., 2000—. Chmn. Internat. Psoriasis Research Found., Palo Alto; incorporator Neuroscis. Research Found. MIT, Brookline, Mass.; bd. govs. Weizmann Inst. Sci., Rehovot, Israel; mem. pharm. panel of com. on tech. and internat. econs. and trade issues Nat. Acad. Engring. Office of Fgn. Sec. and Assembly of Engring., Washington; hon. prof. biochemistry Nat. U. Mex., 1957, U. Montevideo, 1959; bd. dir. Perlegen Sciences, 2004—; founding investor Genospectra; mng. ptnr. Technogen Associates, L.P. Contbr. numerous articles to profl. jours.; patentee in field. Recipient Barren medal, Barren Found., Chgo., 1974, Pres.'s award, Weizmann Inst. Sci., 1978, Chem. Pioneer award, Am. Inst. Chemists, Inc., 1979, National Medal of Technology, 1995, Bower award for Bus. Leadership, Franklin Inst., 2005. Fellow: Am. Pharm. Assn., Am. Acad. Arts and Scis.; mem.: AAAS, NAE, Christian Legal Soc. (Mo. bd. dirs. 1973—), N.Y. Acad. Scis., Internat. Soc. Research in Biology of Reproduction, Endocrine Soc., Biochem. Soc. Eng., Sociedad Mexicana de Nutricion y Endocrinologia, Soc. Exptl. Biology and Medicine, Internat. Soc. Study of Biol. Rhythms, Internat. Soc. Chronobiology, Internat. Pharm. Fedn., Calif. Pharmacists Assn., Biomed. Engring. Soc., Am. Soc. Pharmacology and Exptl. Therapeutics, Am. Soc. Microbiology, Am. Soc. Biol. Chemists, Inc., Am. Inst. Chemists, Inc., Am. Found. Pharm. Edn., Am. Chem. Soc., Tau Kappa Epsilon (internat. pres. 1953—57).

ZAGALO, CARLOS, otolaryngologist; b. Angola, Sept. 5, 1960; MD, New U. Lisbon, Portugal, 1984; PhD, U. Porto, 2002. ENT specialist Portuguese Inst. Oncology, 1994—2011. Adj. prof. Egas Moniz, Health Sciences Inst., 1996—2011; conf. assoc. U. Paul Sabatier (formerly U. Toulouse III), 2006—06. Finalist Young Investigator award, Aerospace Med. Assn., Space Medicine Br., 2001. Home: Praceta Comércio 13 14 Esq Alfragide Amadora Lisbon 2610-042 Portugal Office Phone: 351 919350242. Personal E-mail: czagalo1@sapo.pt.

ZAGAR, MAJA, dentist; b. Zagreb, Feb. 10, 1980; D in Dental Medicine, Sch. Dental Medicine Zagreb, 2003, DDS, 2011. Dentist Sch. Dental Medicine Zagreb, 2004—. Office: Gunduliceva 5 Zagreb Hrvatska 10000 Croatia Business E-Mail: mpavic@sfzg.hr.

ZAGER, BERNARD SOLOMON, physician, consultant; b. Detroit, Nov. 3, 1926; s. Philip and Lena Zager; m. Denise Acheson, Sept. 11, 1953; children: Robert, Gerald, Martin. BA with distinction, Wayne State U., 1946; MD, Northwestern U., 1950. Diplomate Am. Bd. Preventive Medicine and Occpl. Medicine. Intern Detroit Grace Hosp., 1949-50, resident in surgery, 1952-56; chief physician AAD Ford Motor Co., Utica, Mich., 1964-68; med. dir. Nuc. Energy Divsn. GE, San Jose, Calif., 1968-87; occupl. medicine cons. Reno, 1987—. Capt. US Army, 1950—52, Korea. Mem.: Alpha Omega Alpha. Home and Office: 1210 Bridlewood Way Reno NV 89509-7116 Home Phone: 775-329-8940; Office Phone: 775-329-8940. Personal E-mail: bernzag@aol.com.

ZAGLIS, DIMITRIS, physician, neurologist; b. Athens, Dec. 28, 1958; s. Petros and Ioanna Z.; m. Euthima Agelopoulov, 1991; children: Ioanna, Sofia. MD, Med. Sch., Padova, Italy, 1985, specialization in neurology, 1989; specialization in accupuncture, Bologna, Italy, 1984; specialization in hemopathy, Greek Assn. for Homeopathy, 1994. Head Athens Headache and Pain Clinic, 1990—; head headache ctr. 1 Hosp. of Pub. Ins., Athens, 1994—; dir. headache dept. Met. Hosp., Athens, 2002—. Mem. Greek Assn. for Phyotherapy and Aromatherapy (v.p. 1995—), Hellenic Med. Assn. for Holistic Medicine (treas. 2000—), Greek Soc. for Headache, Greek Soc. for Neurology, Greek Homeopathy Assn., WASS. Office: Vlakhopoilu 2 114 71 Athens Greece Office Phone: 210-6432804.

ZAGON, IAN STUART, neuroscience and anatomy educator, researcher, inventor; s. Benjamin and Beatrice (Shaffer) Z.; m. Eileen Kostel, Nov. 26, 1964. BS, U. Wis., 1965; MS, U. Ill., Urbana, 1969; PhD, U. Colo., Denver, 1972. Asst. prof. biol. structure U. Miami, Fla., 1972-74; asst. prof. anatomy Pa. State U., Hershey, 1974-78, prof. genetics, 1975—, assoc. prof. anatomy, 1978-85, prof., 1985-91, prof. cell and molecular biology and neurosci., 1984—, prof. neurosci. and anatomy, 1991—2003, prof. neural and behavioral scis., 2003—, disting. educator, 2002—, disting. univ. prof., 2005—, program dir. on edn. in human structure, 2005—. Cons. Nat. Inst. on Drug Abuse, Rockville, Md., 1980—; cons., reviewer NIH, Bethesda, Md., 1984—; grant reviewer Am. Heart Assn. of Pa., 1985—, mem. rsch. com., 1988—, bd. dirs., 1992-97, v.p., 1993-96; founder ZoeGenics LLC. Author: Maternal Substance Abuse and the Developing Nervous System, 1992, Receptors in the Developing Nervous System, 1993; mem. editl. bd. Brain Rsch. Bull., 1980—, sect. editor for cellular and molecular neurobiology, 1994—; mem. editl. bd. Physiology and Behavior, 1987-97, Pharmacology, Biochemistry and Behavior, 1989—, Internat. Jour. Oncology, 1998—, Advances in Neuroimmunology, 1990, Internat. Jour. Devel. Neurosci., 1987-89, Brain Rsch., 1992-, Devel. Brain Rsch., 1992-2006, Cancer Therapy, 2003—09, Exptl. Biology and Medicine, 2006—, assoc. editor Anatomy & Pathology, 2009-, Open Acess Jour. Clin. Trials, 2009-, Jour. Anesthesia & Clin. Rsch., 2010-, Internat. Jour. Clin. Medicine, 2010-, Jour. Carcinogenesis & Mutagenesis, 2010-, Jour. Clin. & Exptl. Ophthalmology, 2010-, World Jour. Diabetes, 2010-, Jour. Clin. & Cellular Immunology, 2010-, Chinese Jour. Clinicians, 2010-; contbr. numerous articles to med. and profl. jours.; patentee on growth factors, receptors, devel., cancer, wound healing. Recipient Entrepreneurial Achievement award, Kutztown U., The John Marshall Soc., Franklin and Marshall Coll.; grantee NIH, Am. Cancer Soc., Nat. Inst. Drug Abuse, Philip Morris, Nat. Multiple Sclerosis Soc. Mem.: Soc. Exptl. Biology and Medicine (Disting. Scientist award), Am. Assn. Cancer Rsch., Am. Diabetes Assn., Assn. for Rsch. in Vision and Ophthalmology, Soc. for Neurosci., Am. Soc. Cell Biology. Achievements include discovery of low-dose naltrexone, topical naltrexone, and opioid growth factor therapies, non-erythroid spectrin, CCK-C receptor, and opioid growth factor receptor gene, endogenous opioids as regulators of cell proliferation. Office: Pa State U Coll Medicine PO Box 850 H109 500 University Dr Hershey PA 17033-0850 Business E-Mail: isz1@psu.edu.

ZAGOREN, JOY CARROLL, health facility director, researcher; b. NYC, Oct. 31, 1933; d. Murray Morris and Celia (Donner) Rossman; m. Robert H. Zagoren, June 29, 1958 (div. 1988); children: Glenn, Robin; m. Robert Henry Chester, Apr. 1, 1988 (dec. Mar. 1998); children: Peter Chester, Lisabeth Chester, Melinda Chester, Cecily Chester, Kate Chester. BS, NYU, 1957; MS, Adelphi U., Garden City, NY, 1969; PhD with distinction, NYU, 1981. Sec. sch. faculty Great Neck Pub. Schs., NY, 1957-71; rsch. scientist Inst. Psychobiol. Studies, Queens Village, NY, 1968-71; rsch. assoc. Albert Einstein Coll. Medicine, Bronx, NY, 1971-84; asst. prof. SUNY Sch. Medicine, Stony Brook, 1984-86; dir. Seriatum, NYC, 1991—; bd. mem. Owners Assoc., 2011—. Ptnr. Winter Tree Collection; chmn. Esrath Nashim Hosp., 1986—; med. bd. dir. Sarah Herzog Meml. Hosp.; lectr. in field. Editor: The Node of Ranvier, 1984; contbr. articles to profl. jours. Chair Peace Corps Svc. Coun., Tri-State, 1965-75; chair Homeland Security Upper East Side of Manhattan, OEM CERT program, 2004—; pres. Kidney Found. LI, NY, 1965-77; v.p. United Cmty. Fund LI, 1970-83; bd. dirs. Jerusalem Mental Health Ctr., NYC, 1986—; mem. med. bd. dirs. Sarah Herzog Meml. Hosp., hon. chair dinner, 1995, chair dinner, 1996, med. chair, 1998, chair membership cocktail party, 2000, chair bd. dirs., 2000—; chmn. mem. NY Acad. Scis., 2000, vice chair Lyceum Club, NY Acad. Scis., 2001; mem. med. adv. bd. www.hipforkids.org. Recipient Svc. awards, Kidney Found., Kiwanis, others, 1970—87; named Disting. Alumnus of Yr., Adelphi U., 1986; fellow NIH fellow, 1982-84, Svc. awards Kidney Found., Kiwanis, others, 1970-87, NIH, 1982—84; hon. lectr., N.Y. Acad. Scis., 2006. Mem. AAAS, Nat. Acad. Sci., Am. Assn. Neuropathology, NY Acad. Scis. (lectr. 2003, 06, v.p. Lyceum Soc. 2001—). Democrat. Jewish. Avocations: art, literature, piano, swimming, gardening. Home: 405 E 82nd St New York NY 10028-6038 Office: Seriatum 405 East 82d St New York NY 10028

ZAGUE, VIVIAN, pharmacist; b. Campinas, Sao Paulo, Brazil, Jan. 19, 1981; BS in Pharmacy, UNIMEP, 2003; PharmM, U. Sao Paulo, 2007. Rsch. scientist GELITA do Brasil, 2007—. Office: 200 Phillip Leiner Cotia Sao Paulo 06714-285 Brazil E-mail: vizague@hotmail.com.

ZAGZAG, DAVID, pathologist, educator; Attended, Lariboisiere St. Louis Med. Sch., 1984. Diplomate Am. Bd. Pathology-neuropathology, 1993, Am. Bd. Pathology, 1993. Intern in surgery Rothschild Found., 1981—82; resident in surg. pathology NYU Med. Ctr., 1988—90, clin. fellow in neuropathology, 1990—92; assoc. prof. pathology NYU Sch. Medicine; chief divsn. neuropathology NYU Langone Med. Ctr., dir. microvascular and molecular neuro-oncology lab.; dir. neurosurgery and pathology depts. Human Brain Tumor Bank. Co-author: (jour. articles) Schwannoma of the fourth ventricle presenting with hemifacial spasm, 1993, mRNA detection in cerebral vessels by nonradioactive in situ hybridization, 2003, Therapeutic targets in malignant glioblastoma microenvironment, 2009, numerous other jour. articles. Achievements include research in Mechanisms of Cerebral Vasculogenesis and Angiogenesis. Office: New York University Langone Medical Center Pathology Department 550 1st Ave New York NY 10016 Office Phone: 212-263-6449.

ZAHER, KAWTHER ALI, virologist, educator; b. Cairo, May 25, 1970; PhD in Virology, Alboun Pasteur Lang. Sch., 1992. Assoc. prof. Nat. Rsch. Ctr., 2009—. Cons. Military Force, 2010. Home: King Faisal St Cairo Giza 121112 Egypt Personal E-mail: zaherkus@yahoo.com.

ZAHKA, KENNETH GEORGE, pediatrician, cardiologist, educator; b. 1950; BA summa cum laude, Boston U., 1971; MD, Johns Hopkins U., 1975. Cert. Am. Bd. Pediat., 1980, Pediat. Cardiology, 1981. Intern pediat. Johns Hopkins Hosp., Balt., 1975—76, resident pediat., 1976—78, clin. fellow pediat. cardiology, 1978—81, dir. Pediat. Heart Station, 1983—90; asst. prof. pediat. Johns Hopkins U. Sch. Medicine, 1981—88, assoc. prof., 1988—90; dir. Divsn. Pediat. Cardiology Rainbow Babies and Children's Hosp., 1990—2004, vice chair subspecialty practices, vice chair clin. affairs, 1997—; dir. pediat. cardiology Case Western Reserve Sch. Medicine, 1990—2004, prof. pediat., 2004—. Assoc. staff MetroHealth Med. Ctr., 1991—97; cons. Lakewood Hosp., 1991—98; physician Dept. Pediat. Cons. Staff Mt. Sinai Med. Ctr., 1994—97; cons. staff St. Elizabeth Health Ctr., 1997—, Tod Children's Hosp., 1997—, S.W. Gen. Health Ctr., 1997—, Bedford Med. Ctr., 1997—; spkr. in field. Contbr. articles to med. jours. Recipient Presdl. Recognition Award, Republic of Armenia, 1994, Friend of Armenians Award, Diocese of Am. Ch. of Am., 1997. Fellow: Am. Coll. Cardiology (Hoechst Marion Roussel Ohio Chap. award 1997), Am. Acad. Pediat.; mem.: Am. Soc. Echocardiography, Am. Heart Assn., Southeastern Pediat. Cardiology Soc.

ZAHNER, VIVIANE, microbiologist; b. Rio de Janeiro, Sept. 10, 1962; Rsch. scientist Oswaldo Cruz Found., 1990; postdoc. fellow Can. Forest Ctr., 2004. Office: Ave Brasil 4365 Rio De Janeiro RJ 20045900 Brazil Office Fax: 55-21-25984277. Business E-Mail: vzahner@fiocruz.br

ZAHROWSKI, JAMES J., orthodontist; m. Sally H. Zahrowski, June 30, 1979; children: Kelly L., Mark T. BS, U. Calif., Riverside, 1974; PharmD, USC Sch. Pharmacy, LA, 1979; Dr. in Dental Medicine, U. Oreg., Portland, 1985; MS, UCLA, 1989. Diplomate Am. Bd. Orthodontics, 2006, cert. in orthodontic specialty UCLA, 1987. Orthodontic clin. instr. UCLA, 1992—98; pvt. practice Tustin, Calif., 1988—. Contbr. articles to profl. jours. Mem.: ADA, Pacific Coast Soc. Orthodontists, Edward H. Angle Orthodontic Soc., Orange County Dental Soc., Calif. Dental Soc., Am. Assn. Orthodontists. Office: James J Zahrowski DMD MS INC 13372 Newport Ave E Tustin CA 92780

ZAIBAK, ZACK, cosmetic dentist; BS, St. Xavier U., Chgo.; BSD with honors, DDS with honors, U. Ill.; MA. Cert. forensic dentistry US Navy, Lumineers, Invasalign, laser surgery. Resident advanced dentistry gen. practice Loyola Hosp.; trained Las Vegas Inst. Advanced Dental Studies; owner Zaibak Ctr. for Dentistry. Named one of Top Dentist, Consumer Rsch. Coun. America, 2009. Mem.: Am. Assn. Hosp. Dentists, Am. Soc. Forensic Odontology, Acad. Gen. Dentistry, ADA, Chgo. Dental Soc., Ill. State Dental Assn., THe Am. Acad. Cosmetic Dentistry. Office: Zaibak Center for Dentistry 6828 W 171st St Tinley Park IL 60477 Office Phone: 708-802-9600. Office Fax: 708-802-9826.

ZAIRIS, IGNATIOS S., thoracic surgeon; MD, U. Athens, Greece, 1973. Diplomate Am. Bd. Surgery, 2000, Am. Bd. Surgery-vascular surgery, cert. thoracic cardiovasc. surgery. Intern SUNY Downstate Med. Ctr., resident surgery Bklyn., 1977—84, resident cardiothoracic surgery, 1982—84; surgeon Englewood Hosp. and Med. Ctr., Englewood, NJ. Office: Englewood Hospital and Medical Center 741 Teaneck Rd Teaneck NJ 07666 Office Phone: 201-837-8282. Office Fax: 201-837-0010.

ZAITSEV, SERGEI VLADIMIROVICH, biochemist, educator; b. Ufa, Russia, July 12, 1951; PhD, Lomonosov Moscow State U., 1978, DSc, 1987. Prof. biochemistry Lomonosov Moscow State U., 1988—. Guest prof. Karolinska Inst., 1993. Recipient Internat. award, Juvenile Diabetes Rsch. Found.; fellowship, Wenner-Gren Found., STINT Found., grant, European Found. Study Diabetes. Mem.: Swedish Acad. Pharm. Scis., Swedish Soc. Medicine, European Peptide Soc. Avocation: travel. Office: Lomonosov Moscow State University Leninskie Gory 1 Moscow 119991 Russia Business E-Mail: sergei.zaitsev@ki.se.

ZAITZ, CLARISSE, dermatologist, researcher, writer; b. São Paulo, São Paulo, Brazil, June 23, 1952; d. Abram and Lea Merzel Bobrow; m. Mauro Zaitz, Apr. 7, 1973 (div. July 5, 2000); children: Daniela Zaitz Kolar, Marcio, Denis; life ptnr. Roberto Gheler. MD, Santa Casa Med. Sch. São Paulo, Brazil, 1975; M in Medicine, Universidade Fed. de São Paulo, 1988, PhD in Medicine, 1993. Cert. dermatologist Brazilian Soc. Dermatology, 1978. Prof. dermatology Santa Casa Med. Sch., São Paulo, 1993—, chief divsn. dermatology, 2000—03. Head coord. anual micology course Santa Casa Med. Sch., São Paulo, 1987—, thesis orienter, rev. bd. mem., 1993—; albaconazole adv. bd. Stiefel Labs., Coral-Gables, Fla., 2006—; tefin adv. bd. Mantecorp, São Paulo, 2007—; chairperson 21st World Congress Dermatology, Buenos Aires, 2007, Brazilian Congress of Dermatology, São Paulo, São Paulo, Brazil, 1997—; permanent mem. of the brazilian soc. of dermatolgy concil 1997 Brazilian Soc. of Dermatology, São Paulo, São Paulo, Brazil. Author: Medical Mycology, 1995, 2d edit., 2004, Textbook of Medical Mycology, 1998, History of Brazilian Dermatology, 1999; assoc. editor: Anais Brasileiros de Dermatologia, 1994—96; mem. rev. bd. Anais Brasileiros de Dermatologia, 1994—. Mem.: European Acad. Dermatology (assoc.), Am. Acad. Dermatology (assoc.), Brazilian Soc. Dermatology (assoc.; pres. 1997—98, dir. continual med. edn. 1998—99, chairperson, permanent mem. dermatology coun. 1997—). Office: R Padre João Manoel 1212 conj 113 São Paulo 01411-000 Brazil Business E-Mail: czaitz@uol.com.br.

ZAK, JODY ANN, nurse; b. Buffalo, Oct. 31, 1953; BSN, SUNY, Buffalo, 1975. Ptnr. neurosurg. ICU U. Md. Med. Ctr., 1990—92, ptnr. CCU, 1992—96, ptnr. EP lab., 1996—2009, supr. EP lab., 2009—. Author Critical Care Nurse, 2006—10. Contbr. articles to profl. publs. Named Pioneer Nurse, Dept. Medicine. Mem.: AACN. Avocations: reading, gardening, yoga. Home: 200 Windrush Farm Ln Severna Park MD 21146 Office Fax: 410-328-0977. Business E-Mail: jzak@medicine.umaryland.edu.

ZAKARIA, ZABARIAH, engineering educator; b. Seremban, July 3, 1983; BSc in Med. Physics, U. Sci. Malaysia, 2005, MSc in Med. Physics, 2006. Lectr. Brit. Malaysian Inst., U. Kuala Lumpur, 2006—. Short Term Rsch. grant. Mem.: Malaysian Sci. Engring. Tech. Avocation: swimming. Office: University Kuala Lumpur Brit Malaysia Gombak Selangor 53100 Malaysia Business E-Mail: zabariah@bmi.unikl.edu.my.

ZALAVRAS, CHARALAMPOS, orthopedic surgeon; arrived in U.S., 2000; s. Georgios Zalavras and Maria Zalavra. Attended, Aristoteleion U. Med. Sch., Greece, 1991; PhD, U. Ioannina, Greece, 2000. Cert. orthop. surgeon Ministry of Health, Greece, European Union, physician's cert. of registration Med. Bd. Calif. Resident dept. orthop. surgery U. Ioannina, Ioannina, Greece, 1996—2000; from clin. rsch. fellow to prof., dept. orthop. surgery U. So. Calif., LA, 2000—10, prof. dept. orthop. surgery, 2010—. Recipient Best Scientific Work award, Balkan Congress Orthops., 1997, Best Resident, Fellow Paper award, Arthroscopy Assn. No. Am., 2002, Marshall Urist Young Investigator award, Assn. Bone and Joint Surgeons, 2003. Mem.: ACS, Musculoskeletal Infection Soc. N.Am. (v.p., Scholar award 2009), Hellenic Soc. for Reconstructive Microsurgery, Hellenic Soc. for Surgery of Hand, Hellenic Assn. Orthop. Surgery and Traumatology, European Soc. Sports Traumatology, Knee Surgery and Arthroscopy. Western Orthop. Assn. Home: 106 Esperanza Ave Sierra Madre CA 91024 Office Fax: 323-226-4051. Business E-Mail: zalavras@usc.edu.

ZALD, DAVID H., cognitive neuroscientist; b. Nashville, Apr. 10, 1966; s. Mayer Nathan and Joan Khalila (Kadri) Z.; m. Mary Beth Early, Sept. 5, 1993; 1 child, Khalila Marie Early. BA, U. Mich., 1989; PhD in clin. psychology, U. Minn., 1997. Psychiatric interviewer, dept. family studies U. Minn., Mpls., 1991—94, tchg. asst., 1992—93, instr. psychology, 1994—96, 1999; intern in clin. neuropsychology Ann Arbor VA Med. Ctr./U. Mich. Hosp., 1995—96; rsch. fellow in neuroimaging U. Minn./Minn. VA Med. Ctr., Mpls., 1997—2000; asst. prof. psychology Vanderbilt U., Nashville, 2000—07, assoc. prof. psychology, 2007—, dir. undergraduate studies. Contbr. articles to profl. jours.; co-editor: The Orbitofrontal Cortex, 2006. Recipient Young Investigator award Am. Neuropsychiat. Assn., 1997, Nat. Rsch. Svc. award NIMH, 1997. Mem. APA, Assn. Chemoreceptor Sci. Avocation: music. Achievements include first neuroimaging studies of human amygdula activation during olfactory and gustatory stimulation; recognized expert on functions of human orbitofrontal cortex. Office: Vanderbilt U 301 David K Wilson Hall 2201 West End Ave Nashville TN 37240 also: Zald Lab 219 Wilson Hall 111 21st Ave S Nashville TN 37203 Office Phone: 615-343-6076, 615-322-2874, 614-343-1446. Office Fax: 615-343-8449. E-mail: david.zald@vanderbilt.edu.

ZALDIVAR, NIEVES M., health facility administrator; b. Cuba, Aug. 14, 1941; arrived in U.S., 1964; d. Armando Zaldivar and Luz Moran; 1 child, Sebastian C. MD, CUNY, 1971. Diplomate Am. Bd. Pediats., Nat. Bd. Med. Examiners. Pediat. intern Mt. Sinai Hosp., NYC, 1971—72, fellow in pediat. infectious diseases/host immune response, 1973—74; instr. dept. pediats. Mt. Sinai Sch. Medicine, CUNY, NYC, 1973—74; asst. prof. dept. pediats. U. Miami Sch. Medicine, 1974—75, dir. pediat. infectious diseases and immunology clinics, 1974—75, assoc. dir. divsn. pediat. infectious diseases and immunology, 1974—75; clin. instr. child health and devel. George Washington U. Sch. Medicine and Health Scis., Washington, 1979—83, asst. clin. prof. child health and devel., 1983—; clin. asst. prof. dept. pediats. Georgetown U. Sch. Medicine, Washington, 1984—; assoc. regional med. dir. Prince Georges region Group Health Assn., Washington, 1992—94, med. dir. Marlow Heights Ctr., 1992—94; v.p., bd. dirs. Mitchell-Trotman Med. Group, P.C., Washington, 1994—97; med. dir. Mary's Ctr. for Maternal and Child Care, Washington, 1998—2001; med. dir., exec. staff mem. Medicaid HMO Chartered Health Plan, Washington, 2002—; med. dir. Mt. Sinai Sch. Medicine, NYC, 2004—. Prin. investgator children's sentinel nutrition assessment program Boston U., 1999—2002; mem. mental health adv. com. Montgomery County (Md.) Coun., 2001—; mem. pharmacy and therapeutics com. D.C. Chartered Health Plan, Washington, 2001—, mem. network and ops. team, 2002—; mem. quality of care subcom. D.C. Healthcare Safety Net Dept. Health, Washington, 2002—; co-chmn. youth families and mental health subcom. D.C. Medicaid Med. Care Adv. Com., Washington, 2002—. Contbr. articles to profl. jours. Pres. Park View Citizens Assn., Chevy Chase, Md., 2001—; mem. mental health adv. com. Montgomery County (Md.) Coun., Md., 2001—. Comdr. M.C. USNR, 1975—79. Herman Muehlstein scholar, Muehlstein Found., N.Y.C., 1970—71. Fellow: Am. Acad. Pediats.; mem.: AMA, Am. Coll. Healthcare Execs., Am. Coll. Physician Execs., Mt. Sinai Alumni Assn., Alpha Omega Alpha. Office: Dc Chartered Health Plan 1025 15th St Nw Washington DC 20005-2601 Office Phone: 202-408-2039.

ZALENSKI, ROBERT JOSEPH, emergency physician, educator; b. NJ, Sept. 10, 1953; MD, U. Miami, 1984. Prof. Wayne State U., 1996—. Dir. palliative medicine Wayne State U., 2005. Recipient Crystal Rose award, Hospice Mich. Mem.: Am. Acad. Hospice & Palliative Medicine, Mich. Coll. Emergency Physicians, Soc. Academic Emergency Medicine, Am. Coll. Emergency Physicians. Avocations: golf, boating. Home: 3891 Forester Blvd Auburn Hills MI 48326 Home Fax: 313-966-3970. Business E-Mail: rzalensk@med.wayne.edu.

ZALESKI, JAN FRANCISZEK, biochemist; b. Bytom, Poland, Feb. 3, 1949; came to U.S., 1979; s. Stanislaw and Maria (Fliska) Z.; m. Margaret M. Toczkowska, Dec. 28, 1971; children: Marta, Monika. MS in Biochemistry, U. Warsaw, Poland, 1971, PhD in Biochemistry, 1978. Rsch. assoc., asst. prof., assoc. prof. U. Warsaw Inst. Biochemistry, 1971-82; vis. scientist Roswell Park Meml. Inst., Buffalo, 1979-82; assoc. scientist Okla. Med. Rsch. Found., Oklahoma City, 1982-85; rsch. assoc. U. Pa. Med. Sch., Phila., 1985-88; vis. scientist Great Lakes Lab., Buffalo, 1988; rsch. assoc. prof. Rutgers U. Sch. Pharmacy, New Brunswick, NJ, 1989-97. Cons. J.A. Haley Vets. Hosp., Tampa, 1985, Great Lakes Lab., Buffalo, 1988, Wyeth-Ayerst Rsch., Princeton, 1994. Contbr. articles to profl. jours., chpts. to books. Mem. Am. Soc. Biochemistry and Molecular Biology. Avocations: interior decorating, photography, art, printmaking. Personal E-mail: jmzaleski@comcast.net.

ZALEZNIK, ABRAHAM, psychoanalyst, management specialist, educator; b. Phila., Jan. 30, 1924; s. Isadore and Anna (Appelbaum) Z.; m. Elizabeth Ann Aron, June 24, 1945; children: Dori Faith, Ira Harry. AB in Econs., Alma Coll., 1945, DLitt (hon.), 1992; MBA, Harvard U., 1947, DCS, 1951; grad., Boston Psychoanalytic Soc. and Inst., 1965; D (hon.), U. Montreal, 1999; prof. (hon.), Haute Etude Commercial, France, 2001. Research asst. Harvard U. Grad. Sch. Bus. Adminstrn., 1947-48, instr., 1948-51, asst. prof., 1951-56, assoc. prof., 1956-61, prof., 1961—, Cahners-Rabb prof. social psychology of mgmt., 1967-83, Konosuke Matsushita prof. leadership, 1983-90, Konosuke Matsushita prof. leadership emeritus, 1990—; research fellow Boston Psychoanalytic Soc. and Inst., 1965-68, mem. faculty, 1972—; pvt. practice psychoanalysis Boston, 1968—. Cons. in field. Author: Human Dilemmas of Leadership, 1966, (with Manfred F.R. Kets de Vries) Power and the Corporate Mind, 1975, The Managerial Mystique, 1989, An Executive Guide to Motivating People, 1990, Learning Leadership, 1992; contbr. articles to profl. jours. Bd. overseers Beth Israel Hosp., Boston, 1968—. With USN, 1942-46. Mem. Boston Psychoanalytic Soc., Am. Psychoanalytic Assn. (cert.), Am. Sociol. Assn., Tavern Club (Boston), Belmont Country Club (Mass.). Home: 170 N Ocean Blvd Palm Beach FL 33480-3946 Office: Harvard University Business School Boston MA 02163 Home Phone: 561-832-5270; Office Phone: 617-495-6285. E-mail: azaleznik@hbs.edu.

ZALOM, MARTINA, medical researcher; b. Calif., Aug. 22, 1981; BS, U. Calif., Berkeley, 2003, MD, UCSD, 2007. Clin. fellow hematology, oncology UCLA Olive View Med. Ctr., 2010—. Clin. Rsch. fellow, Cedars-Sinai Sports Spectacular. Avocations: hiking, cooking, travel. Office: Dept Hematology & Oncology 2700 Beverly Blvd Los Angeles CA 90068 Business E-Mail: martina.zalom@cshs.org.

ZALTA, EDWARD, otolaryngologist, physician; b. Houston, Mar. 2, 1930; s. Nouri Louis and Marie Zahde (Lizmi) Zalta; m. Carolyn Mary Gordon, Oct. 8, 1971; 1 child, Ryan David;children from previous marriage: Nouri Allan, Lori Ann, Barry Thomas, Marci Louise. BS, Tulane U., 1952, MD, 1956. Diplomate Am. Bd. Quality Assurance and Utilization Rev. Physicians. Intern Brooke Army Hosp., San Antonio, 1956—57; resident otolaryngology U.S. Army Hosp., Ft. Campbell, Ky., 1957—60; practice medicine specializing in otolaryngology Glendora, West Covina and San Dimas, Calif., 1960—82. ENT cons. City of Hope Med. Ctr., 1961—76; mem. staff Foothill Presbyn.; past pres. L.A. Found. Cmty. Svc., L.A. Poison Info. Ctr., So. Calif. Physicians Coun., Inc.; founder, chmn. bd. dirs., CEO Health Solutions Internat.; founder, chmn. bd. dirs. CAPP CARE, Inc.; founder Inter-Hosp. Coun. Continuing Med. Edn.; trustee U.S. Pharmacopeial Conv., Inc.; mem. adv. bd. Global Health Sys., Inc. Author (with others): Medicine and Your Money; mem. editl. staff Jour. Assn. Managed Healthcare Orgns., Managed Care Interface, Mng. Employee Health Benefits, mem. editl. adv. bd. Inside Medicaid Managed Care, Disease Mgmt. News, Managed Care Outlook; contbr. articles to profl. jours. Pres. bd. govs. Glendora Unified Sch. Dist., 1965—71; mem. Calif. Cancer Adv. Coun., 1967—71, Commn. Californias, Los Angeles County Commn. Economy and Efficiency. Served to capt. Med. Corps US Army, 1957—60. Recipient award of Merit, Order St. Lazarus, 1981. Mem.: AMA, Los Angeles County Med. Assn., Am. Coll. Med. Quality, Am. Assn. Preferred Provider Orgns., Am. Coun. Otolaryngology, Am. Acad. Otolaryngology, Calif. Med. Assn., Pacific Golf Club (San Juan Capistrano), Glendora Country Club, Ctr. Club (Costa Mesa, Calif.), Sea Bluff Beach and Racquet Club, Centurion Club, Phi Delta Epsilon, Kappa Nu. Republican. Jewish. Home: 3 Morning Dove Laguna Niguel CA 92677 Office: Ste 1123 27136 B Paseo Espada San Juan Capistrano CA 92675 Office Phone: 949-292-1951. Personal E-mail: edzata@cox.net.

ZALUT, DAVID, physician, educator; BS, Penn State U., University Pk., 1973—77; MD, Med. Coll. Pa., Phila., 1978—82. Diplomate Am. Bd. Family Practice, 1985, recertified 1991, 1997, 2003. Resident family practice Abington Meml. Hosp., Pa., 1982—85, intern, chief resident, 1985; hosp. affiliations include West Jersey Hosp. Voorhees and Marlton, NJ, John F. Kennedy Hosp. Stratford, 1987—2000; med. dir. Meridian Nursing Home, 1986—97; assoc. med. dir. quality assurance US Healthcare, 1988—92; bd. dirs. parent West Jersey Hosp., 1998—2000, bd. dirs. exec., chmn. dept. family practice, 1998—; quality assurance com. mem. Aetna US Healthcare, 1994—2000; pres. West Jersey Primary Care Affiliates, 1997—99; chmn. West Jersey Physician Info. Tech. Counsel, 1998—2000; mem. info. tech. com. Virtua Hosp., 2003—; sec., treas. Virtua West Jersey Med. Staff, 2008—; asst. prof. Med. Coll. Pa.; clin. instr. Robert Wood Johnson Med. Sch. Sec., treas. camden divsn. NJ Acad. of Family Practice, 1993—98, del., 1994—2001. Recipient Physician Recognition award, Virtua Hosp., 2006; named Best Tchr. Family Medicine in 30 Years, Robert Wood Johnson Med. Sch., 1992, Top Doc NJ, South Jersey Mag., 2004, 2007, 2008, Top Doc for Pediats. chosen by doctors, 2008, Top Doc chosen by patients, 2009, Top Doc chosen by doctors, NJ Mag., 2008, Pa. Mag., 2010, Best Physician, Del. Valley Consumers Checkbook, 2007. Fellow: Am. Acad. Family Practice. Office: Glendale Executive Campus 1000 White Horse Rd Ste 806 Voorhees NJ 08043 Office Phone: 856-770-0022, 856-355-6000. Office Fax: 856-770-9194. E-mail: Fam_doc@fam-doc.com.

ZALVAN, CRAIG H., otolaryngologist, educator; MD, Yeshiva U., 1995. Diplomate Am. Bd. Otolaryngology. Resident in otolaryngology Manhattan Eye. Ear and Throat Hosp., 1997—99, NY Presbyn. Med. Ctr., 1999—2001; fellow ACS; fellow in laryngology St. Luke's Roosevelt Emd. Ctr., 2001—02; assoc. prof. otolaryngology NY Med. Coll.; med. dir. Inst. for Voice and Swallowing Disorders Phelps Meml. Hosp. Ctr., dir. of laryngology. Office: Phelps Memorial Hospital 701 N Broadway Tarrytown NY 10591 Office Phone: 914-366-3000. Office Fax: 914-366-1314.

ZAMAN, RAIYAN TRIPTI, biomedical engineer, researcher; d. Mohammad Amin Uz. Zaman and Mahjuza Khanam; m. Syed Mohiul Alam. BS in Engring., U. Tex. Austin, 2000, MSEE, 2006; PhD in Biomed. Engring., 2011; postdoc, Stanford U. Sch. Medicine. Undergrad. rsch. asst. dept. mech. engring. U. Tex. at Austin, 1996—97, undergrad. rsch. asst. dept. elec. and computer engring., 1999, lab. rsch. asst. II dept. physics, 1997—99, grader dept. math., tchg. asst. dept. elec. and computer engring., 2000, tchg. asst. dept. biomed. engring., 2005, rsch. asst. dept. biology, 2002—03; rsch. asst. biophotonics lab. Dept. Biomed. Engring., U. Tex. at Austin, 2006, rsch. asst. biomed. engring. laser lab., 2007—09, tchg. asst., 2010; sr. applications engr. Motorola Semiconductor and Freescale Semiconductor Inc., Austin, 2000—05; vol. dept. ophthalmology U. Tex. Health Sci. Ctr., San Antonio, 2004; rschr. Stanford Med. Sch., 2011. Contbr. articles to profl. jours. Recipient Newport Spectra Physics Rsch. Excellent award, BIOS Photonic West SPIE Conf., 2009, Profl. Devel. awards, U. Tex. Austin, 2008—09; named to Nat. Dean's List, 1995—99, 2003—06, Chancellor's List, 2004—06; Travel grant, USAF, 2010, Am. Soc. Laser Medicine & Surgery, 2009, USAF, 2009, U. Tex. Austin, 2007. Office: University Tex at Austin 1 University Sta C0800 Austin TX 78712 Office Phone: 512-471-1397.

ZAMBACOS, GEORGE, plastic surgeon; s. John and Chrysoula Zambacos; m. Georgette Alexandra Kanarachos, Sept. 28, 2002. MD, Med. Sch. U. Athens, Greece, 1992. Locum cons. plastic surgery Derriford Hosp., Plymouth, 2003—07; cons. plastic surgeon Surgery In Greece, Athens, 2004—; locum cons. plastic surgery Royal London Hosp., 2004; assoc. dermatologist U. Athens, 2005—; locum cons. plastic surgery Birmingham City Hosp., England, 2005. Contbr. chapters to books, articles to profl. jours. Mem.: Internat. Soc. Aesthetic Plastic Surgery, Brit. Assn. Plastic Reconstructive Aesthetic Surgeons (corr.), Internat. Confederation Plastic Reconstructive Aesthetic Surgery (assoc.), Fedn. European Soc. Surgery Hand (assoc.), European Assn. Plastic Surgeons (assoc.), Hellenic Senologic Soc. (life), Hellenic Soc. Microsurgery (life), Hellenic Soc. Plastic Aesthetic Reconstructive Surgery (life), Hellenic Melanoma Soc. (life). Achievements include research in field. Office: Surgery In Greece 27 Skoufa St Athens Attica 10673 Greece Business E-Mail: gz@surgeryingreece.com.

ZAMBELIS, NIKOLAUS, internist; b. Athens, Attika, Greece, July 7, 1936; s. Neofytos and Eleni (Karamiliotaki) Z.; children: Nikoletta, Marcella, Ekaterini; m. Ulla Goldgruber Waimann, Sept. 18, 1986. MD, U. Innsbruck, Austria, 1971; nuclear specialist, U. Klinik, Innsbruck; intern specialist, Gen. Hosp., Lienz, Austria, 1984; Dr. U. Med., Leopold-Franzes U., Innsbruck, Austria. Surgeon Inst. Exptl. Pathology, Innsbruck, 1966-74; asst., doctor Nuc. Medicine Clin., U. Innsbruck, 1974—79; ward physician Gen. Hosp., Lienz, 1979-89, sr. physician Zell am See, Austria, 1989—2001; pvt. practice specialist in gastroenterology and hepatology, 2000—. Commr. radiation protection Gen. Hosp., Zell am See, 1989. Editor Wiener Klinische Wochenschrift, 1971, Contraception, 1971, 72, Exptl. Pathology, 1974, Acta Endokrinologica, 1979 (höchst-Stiftung award 1980), Wiener Klinische Wochenschrift, 1981, Mem. works coun. Gen. Hosp., Zell am See, 1989. Mem. Osterrerchische Gesellschaft Nuklearmedizin, Deutsche Gesellschaft Nephrologie, Kiwanis (pres.-elect 1999—2000), Deutsche Gesellschaft Endokrinologie. Greek Orthodox. Personal E-mail: zambelis@aon.at.

ZAMBON, JOSEPH JAMES, periodontist, educator; b. Batavia, NY, Dec. 10, 1949; BS, St. John Fisher Coll., 1973; DDS, U. Buffalo, 1974, PhD, 1984. Dental officer USN, 1974—78; disting. tchg. prof. U. Buffalo, Sch. Dental Medicine, 1982—. Recipient Rsch. Career Devel. award, NIH, R. Earl Robinson Periodontal Regeneration award, Am. Acad. Periodontology, Clin. Rsch. award; named Dental Educator of the Yr., U. Buffalo, Sch. Dental Medicine. Fellow: Am. Coll. Dentists, Internat. Coll. Dentists; mem.: ADA, Eighth Dist. Dental Soc., NY State Dental Assn. Avocation: bicycling. Home: 133 Presidents Walk Buffalo NY 14221 Personal E-mail: zambon1147@roadrunner.com.

ZAMBRI, MELISSA MARIE, lawyer, educator; b. Albany, NY, Dec. 16, 1971; d. Zachary Edward and Donna Marie Zambri; life ptnr. Gina Marie Moran; children: Anthony, Sofia. BS in Fin., Siena Coll., 1994; MBA in Health Sys., Union Coll., 1998; JD, Albany Law Sch., 1998. Bar: NY 1999, US Dist. Ct. (no. dist.) NY 1999. Atty. Sherrin & Glasel, LLP, Albany, 1998—99; ptnr. Hiscock & Barclay, LLP, Albany, 1999—. Adj. prof. mgmt. Grad. Coll. Union U., 2005—; lectr. in field. Contbg. editor Health Care Law Guide, 2003—; exec. editor: Albany Law Jour. Sci. Tech., 1997—98. Mentor grad. program Union Coll., 2000—05; vol. coach Miss Shen Softball, Clifton Park, NY, 1990—2001, 2010—; health law sect. chair Com. Fraud Abuse & Compliance. Recipient Student Achievement award, The Wall St. Jour., 1994; Merit scholar, Albany Law Sch., 1994—97, Union Coll., 1995—96. Mem.: ABA, NY State Bar Assn., Am. Health Lawyers Assn. Home: 670 Riverview Rd Rexford NY 12148 Office: Hiscock & Barclay LLP 80 State St Albany NY 12207 Office Fax: 518-434-2621. Business E-Mail: mzambri@hblaw.com.

ZAMDBORG, YURY, internist; b. Kiev, USSR, Jan. 25, 1956; came to U.S., 1989; s. Leonid and Riva (Keselman) Z.; m. Ninel Reznik, Mar. 19, 1982; children: Leonid, Rebecca. MD, Ivano-Frankovsk Med. Sch., 1979; PhD in Med. Scis., U. Kiev, 1984. Diplomate Am. Bd. Internal Medicine. Intern United Hosps. Med. Ctr., Newark, 1991-92, resident, 1992-95; attending physician N.Y. Cmty. Hosp., 1997, N.Y. Meth. Hosp., Bklyn., 1997—; pvt. practice Bklyn. Author: Medical Ethics, 1988; contbr. articles to med. jours. Office: 2005 Ocean Ave Brooklyn NY 11230-6872 Office Phone: 718-375-8052.

ZÁMECNÍKOVA, ADRIANA, geneticist; b. Nitra, Slovakia, Jan. 8, 1961; d. Andrew and Maria Peter. Diploma in Biochemistry; RNDr in Natural Scis., Faculty Natural Scis., Czechoslovak Republic, 1986, PhD in Genetics, 2000; Specialization, in Med. Genetics, Czechoslovak Republic, 1989. Cert. in cloning recombinant molecules Czechoslovak Republic, 1986, European Sch Med. Genetics, Italy, 1995, gaslini-IARC in cancer genetics Italy, 1996, clin. scientist UK, 2006. Sr. specialist Faculty Hosp., Bratislava, Slovakia, 1986—93, Nat. Cancer Inst., Bratislava, 1993—97, dept. head, 1997—2000; sr. specialist, lab. supr. Kuwait Cancer Control Ctr., 2000—. Contbr. numerous sci. articles to profl. jours. Fellowship, Matsumae Internat., Japan, 2000. Home: 5 Granada 00965 Kuwait Office: Kuwait Cancer Control Ctr Po Box 42262 965 Shuwaikh Kuwait Office Fax: 00965 24810007. Personal E-mail: annaadria@yahoo.com.

ZAMMIT, GERARD VINCENT, podiatrist; b. Australia, Feb. 25, 1983; Degree in Podiatry with honors, La Trobe U., 2004, postgrad, 2011. Rschr. La Trobe U., 2005—. Clinician Med. Foot Care, 2007—11. Mem.: Australian Podiatry Assn. Avocations: bicycling, travel. Home: 5 Edward St Deer Pk Melbourne Victoria 3023 Australia Personal E-mail: g.zammit@latrobe.edu.au.

ZAMORA, ROLANDO, pediatrician, director; b. LA, Aug. 15, 1960; MD, U. de Monterrey, 1983. Prof. clin. pediat. U. Ariz., 1992—2003; med. dir. Pediat. Cardiology Assocs., 2003—. Fellow: Am. Acad. Pediat. Avocations: fishing, reading, travel. Office: 4499 Medical Dr Ste 29 San Antonio TX 78229 Office Fax: 210-615-0888. E-mail: zamorasalinas@aol.com.

ZAMPIERI, FABIO, medical researcher; b. Padua, Aug. 11, 1976; Degree in Philosophy, U. Padua, 2000; PhD in History of Medicine, U. Geneva, 2006. Rschr. med. humanities Padua U. Med. Sch., 2009—. Home: via Isabella Andreini 1 Padua 35141 Italy Personal E-mail: fabio.zampieri@unipd.it.

ZAMRAZIL, VÁCLAV, internist, endocrinologist, educator; b. Prague, Czech Republic, Sept. 28, 1936; s. Václav and Marie (Ružičková) Z.; m. Elvíra Šimková, Aug. 25, 1960; children: Václav, Hana. MD, Charles U., Prague, Czech Republic, 1960, PhD, 1972, DSc, 1989. Physician County Hosp., Písek, Czech Republic, 1960—65; rschr. Inst. Endocrinology, Prague, 1965—83, head clin. dept., 1983—2004. Cons. Tchg. Hosp. Prague Motol, 1978—; tchr. med. sch. Charles U., 1994—, prof. internal medicine, 1997, head dept. endocrinology Postgrad. Med. Sch., 1999—. Author: Diabetes and Thyroid disorders, 1985, Proceedings in Endocrinology, 1989, Iondine Deficiency in Czech Republic: Therapeutic Uses of Trace Elements, 1996, Early Stages of Diabetes Mellitus, 1997, Interdisciplinary endocrinology, 2006; co-author: Diseases of the Thyroid, 1995, Endocrinology, 1995, Diabetes Mellitus, 2000, Endocrinology for Internists, 2003, Management of Carcinoid, 2004, Thyroid Gland and Diabetes Mellitus, 2004, Clinical Endocrinology, 2005, Endowing Endocrine Emergencies, 2007; contbr. articles to profl. publs. With med. mil. svc. Czech Army, 1960—. Mem.: European Thyroid Assn., Czech Soc. Diabetologists, Czech Endocrine Soc., Internat. Com. for Control of Iodine Def. Disorders. Roman Catholic. Avocation: collecting ceramics and fine art articles. Office: Inst Endocrinology Národní 8 116 94 Prague Czech Republic Home: Pod Terebkou 3 140 00 Prague Czech Republic Office Phone: 420-2-24905-302, 4202224905312. Fax: 420-2-24905-325. E-mail: vzamrazil@endo.cz.

ZANARDELLI, JOHN JOSEPH, healthcare organization executive; b. Monongahela, Pa., July 27, 1950; s. John and Linda (Lazzari) Z.; m. Suzanne King, Jan. 29, 1972; children: Brandon John, Stephen William, Robyn Lynn. Student, Davis & Elkins Coll., 1968; AA, C.C. Allegheny Cty, Pitts., 1970; AS in Acctg., C.C. Allegheny Cty., Pitts., 1991; BS in Edn., California State Coll. Pa., 1972; MPH, U. Pitts., 1979, cert. acct., 1994; cert. non-profit mgmt., Harvard U., 1998; cert. gen. mgmt., Carnegie Mellon U., 1999. Cert. in evaluation pub. health promotion and health edn. programs U. Pitts., 2008. Rsch. asst. grad. sch. pub. health U. Pitts., 1973-78; adminstrv. resident Ctrl. Med. Ctr. and Hosp., Pitts., 1978-79; vice-chmn., sec., dir. Allegheny Mountain Health Enterprises, Inc., Oil City, Pa., 1985-88; exec. v.p. Oil City Area Health Ctr., Inc., 1979-88; exec. v.p., COO Grane Healthcare, Inc., Pitts., 1988-90; adminstr., COO Southwood Psychiat. Hosp., Inc., Pitts., 1990-91; exec. dir. Allegheny divsn. Presbyn. Sr.Care, Pitts., 1991-92; pres. & CEO United Meth. Svcs. for Aging, 1993—. Preceptor, mentor health adminstrn. program U. Pitts. Grad. Sch. Pub. Health, 1980—2006, vis. faculty, 1997—98; adj. asst. prof. health svcs. adminstrn. Grad. Sch. Pub. Health, 1998—2001, adj. assoc. prof. health policy and mgmt., 2001—05, adj. assoc. prof. behavioral and cmty. health scis., 2005—; pres. HCCP, Inc., Pitts., 1983—; bd. dirs. Faith-Based Network, Inc., 1998—2008; co-chair pub. rels. and mktg. com. Davis and Elkins Coll., 2000—02; co-chair exec.-in-residence com. U. Pitts. Grad. Sch. Pub. Health, 2001—02, exec. in residence, health adminstrn. program, 2001—03, fellow evaluation sci., dept. behavioral and cmty. health scis., 2004—08, sr. fellow evaluation sci., dept. behavioral and cmty. health scis., 2008—; fellow sponsor, initiative social enterprise Harvard Bus. Sch., 2001—; mem. planning com. and faculty longterm care program U. Pitts. Inst. Aging, 2002—05, 2007—08; mem. evidence based mgmt. collaborative Acad. Mgmt. and Carnegie Mellon U., 2007—. Fellow: Am. Coll. Healthcare Execs.; mem.: Delta Omega (Omicron chpt., pres. 2000—01). Home: 2997 Greenwald Rd Bethel Park PA 15102-1615 Office: Asbury Heights 700 Bower Hill Rd Pittsburgh PA 15243-2040 Office Phone: 412-571-5134. Business E-Mail: johnzan@alumni.pitt.edu, jzanardelli@asburyheights.org.

ZANDER, GAILLIENNE GLASHOW, psychologist; b. Bklyn., Apr. 7, 1932; d. Saul and Anna (Karasik) G.; m. A.J. Zander, Aug. 5, 1952; children: Elizabeth L., Caroline M., Catherine A. MusB, U. Wis., 1953, MS, 1970; PhD, Marquette U., 1984. Diplomate Am. Bd. Forensic Examiners, Am. Acad. Pain Mgmt.; cert. Am. Soc. Clin. Hypnosis; lic. sch. psychologist, clin. psychologist, Va., in pvt. practice sch. psychology, gen. psychology, WI. Music tchr. Wis. Sch. Systems, 1953-65; psychol. asst. Vernon Psychol. Labs., Chgo., 1965-70; psychologist Milw. Pub. Schs., 1970-92, CESA 19, Kenosha, Wis., 1977-78; pvt. practice psychology Milw., 1980—. Fellow Am. Orthopsychiat. Assn.; mem. APA, Wis. Psychol. Assn. also: A Healing Ctr 20860 Watertown Rd Waukesha WI 53186-1872 Home: 12153 Eddystone Ct Woodbridge VA 22192 Home Phone: 703-910-6440; Office Phone: 262-821-6117. Personal E-mail: zanderga@aol.com.

ZANDMAN-GODDARD, GISELE, science association director; b. Paris, Feb. 19, 1956; d. Felix and Ruta Zandman (Stepmother), Ruth Apfel; m. Eli Goddard, Mar. 28, 1985; children: Maya Abady, Shir Goddard, Yam Goddard, Tal Goddard. MD, Hadassah Med. Sch., Jerusalem, 1983. Specialist in internal medicine Israel, 1991, specialist in rheumatology Israel, 2002. Sr. physician, dept. medicine B Sheba Med. Ctr., Tel Hashomer, Israel, 1991—2006, head, Lupus Clinic, 2001—06; rheumatology fellow Albert Einstein Coll. Medicine, Bronx, NY, 1995—99; head, dept. medicine C Wolfson Med. Ctr., Holon, Israel, 2006—, dir., residency program, 2008—. Lectr., internal medicine & rheumatology dept. Sackler Faculty Medicine, Tel Aviv U., 2002—. Contbr. chapters to books, articles to numerous med. jours. Recipient Excellence award, Ministry Health, 1993, 2002. Mem.: Am. Coll. Rheumatology. Achievements include research in systemic lupus erythematosus. Home: 16 Agmon St Ramat Gan 52960 Israel Office: Dept Medicine C Wolfson Med Ctr 63 Halochamim St Holon 58100 Israel Office Fax: 972-5028810; Home Fax: 972-3-7369274. Personal E-mail: gisele@goddard.co.il. Business E-Mail: goddard@wolfson.health.gov.il.

ZANETTI, MICHELA, endocrinologist, educator; b. Pordenone, Aug. 1, 1966; MD, U. Padova, 1992; PhD, U. Genova, 2002. Rsch. fellow Mayo Clinic, 1998—2000; asst. prof., medicine U. Trieste, 2001—, cons. endocrinologist, 2001—, rep., med. faculty, 2009—, U. Lang. Ctrl. Rsch. fellowship, Am. Heart Assn. Mem.: Italian Soc. Parenteral Nutrition and Metabolism (bd. dirs. 2009—). Avocation: classical music. Office: Clinica Medica-Ospedale di Cattinara St Trieste 34100 Italy Office Fax: 39-0403994593. Business E-Mail: zanetti@units.it.

ZANG, DAE YOUNG, medical educator, researcher; MD, PhD, Hallym U. Coll. Medicine, Anyang, Republic of Korea, 1989. Rsch. assoc. Fred Hutchinson Cancer Rsch. Ctr., Seattle, 1998—2000; assoc. prof. Hallym U. Med. Ctr., 2000—, chmn. divsn. hematology and oncology, 2004—. Contbr. articles to profl. jours. Mem.: European Soc. Med. Oncology, Am. Soc. Hematology, Am. Soc. Clin. Oncology. Office: Hallym Univ Sacred Heart Hosp Pyeongchon-Dong Dongan-Gu 896 431-070 Anyang Republic of Korea Office Fax: 82-31-386-2269. Business E-Mail: fhdzang@hallym.or.kr.

ZANNA, MARTIN THOMAS, physician; b. Mpls., Apr. 2, 1947; s. Peter J. and Mary L. (Peck) Z. AB, Harvard U., 1969, MPH, 1976; MD, U. Minn., 1973. Diplomate Am. Bd. Preventive Medicine. Resident in pub. health N.J. State Dept. Health, 1974-77, acting dir. chronic disease svcs., 1976-79, dir. chronic disease svcs., 1979-81; med. adminstr. Fla. Dept. Health and Rehab. Svcs., Tallahassee, 1981-82; med. cons. N.J. Medicaid, Trenton, 1982—, chief med. cons., 1990-96; med. cons. N.J. State Dept. Health and Sr. Svcs., 1996—. Mem. Fla. Cancer Coun., 1981-82, Fla. Bd. Med. Examiners, 1982, N.J. Hypertension Study Group, 1977-81; chmn. grad. med. edn. com. N.J. State Dept. Health & Sr. Svcs., 1993—; diabetes adv. coun. exec. com. N.J. Dept. Health, 2001—. Contbr. articles to profl. jours. Participant Fla. Gov.'s Mission to Haiti, 1982; mem. divsn. profl. edn. Am. Cancer Soc., 1976-81. Fellow Am. Coll. Preventive Medicine; mem. APHA, Harvard Club (Boston), Harvard Faculty Club (Cambridge). Home: 104 Olympic Ct Apt 2 Princeton NJ 08540 Office: NJ State Dept Health & Sr Svcs PO Box 807 Trenton NJ 08625-0722

ZANORIA, MARIA DELFA TAN, cardiologist, consultant; b. Cebu, Philippines, Feb. 25, 1954; m. Martiniano Ceniza Zanoria, Jan. 6, 1982; children: Sheila, Catherine, Carla, Marlo. MD, Cebu Inst. Medicine, 1977. Postgrad. intern Siliman U. Med. Ctr., Dumaguete, Philippines, 1977—78; med. resident Perpetual Succour Hosp., Cebu City, 1979, med. dir., 2004—06; med. resident Metro Cebu Cmty. Med. Ctr., Cebu City, 1980—81, head intensive care, 1987—89, 1995—2000; fellow adult cardiology Philippine Heart Ctr., Manila, 1981—84; asst. profl. in medicine Cebu Dr.'s Coll. Medicine, 1985—87, Cebu Inst. Medicine, 1985—95; head ICU Cebu Velez Gen. Hosp., 1987—2000; chief cardiology sect. Cebu Heart Inst., 1995—2004. Chmn. dept. medicine Perpetual Succour Hosp., Cebu, 1987—89; pres. Christi Found. Fellow: Philippine Coll. Cardiology (diplomate), Am. Coll. Cardiology (diplomate), Philippine Heart Assn. (Cebu chpt.) (pres. 1995—96), Philippine Coll. Physicians (life; diplomate); mem.: Cebu Med. Soc., Philippine Med. Assn. (life). Roman Catholic. Avocation: reading. Office: Cebu Velez Gen Hosp Rm 207 F Ramos St Cebu City 6000 Philippines also: Perpetual Succour Hosp Specialty Ctr Rm 307 Gorordo Ave 6000 Cebu City Philippines Home: # 5 Paseo Antonio Ma Luisa Park Banilad 6000 Cebu City Central Visayas Philippines Office Phone: 032 2560674. E-mail: delfazanoria@yahoo.com.

ZAOSHENG, WANG, environmentalist, educator; b. Ganzhou, Jiangxi, Apr. 29, 1977; PhD, Shanghai Jiaotong U., 2007. Assoc. prof. Inst. Urban Environment, Chinese Acad. Scis., 2007—. Office: 1799 Jimei Blvd Xiamen Fujian 361021 China Business E-Mail: zswang@iue.ac.cn.

ZAPOLANSKI, ALEX J., thoracic surgeon; MD, Universidad De Buenos Aires, Argentina, 1973. Diplomate Am. Bd. Thoracic Surgery, 2004. Resident surgery Cleveland Clinic, Cleve., 1975—79; resident cardiothoracic surgery Toronto Gen. Hosp., Toronto, Canada, 1979—81; surgeon Valley Hosp., Ridgewood. Office: Valley Hospital Valley Columbia Heart Center 223 North Van Dien Ave Ridgewood NJ 07450 Office Phone: 201-447-8377.

ZAPPA, DESPINA, psychologist, writer; b. Athens, Attica, Greece, Mar. 10, 1972; d. Vassilios-Evangellos and Chrisoula-Georgiou Papadopoulos. BA in Psychology, Am. Coll. Greece, Athens, 1996; MA in Psychoanalytical Studies, U. London, 1999—; postgraduate studies in Psychology Pantion, U. Social and Polit. Scis., 2004—07. European Computing Driving Licence ECDL Found. Psychol. assessor, recruiter Sleetac Coll., London, 1997—99; sec. asst. Comet, Athens, 2000, Inter Ptnr. Assistance, Athens, 2001—03; pvt. practice Athens, 2003—; prof. in psychology Pantion U. Social and Polit. Scis. Vol. psychologist Lyrakus A. E. Neurol. and Psychiatric Clinic, Athens, 2001—03, Athens Euroclinic, 2008—. Author: A Critique of Psychoanalytical Accounts of Racism, 2003. Mem.: APA (assoc.), Greek Assn. Psychologists, Greek Psychological Assn., Greek-European Assn. Counselling. Democratical. Avocations: movies, reading, music, travel, stamp collecting/philately. Home and Office: Tzomerkon 13 St 156 69 Athens Greece Personal E-mail: deszap@hotmail.com.

ZAPPOLI THYRION, ROBERTO, retired neurologist, neurophysiologist; b. Sarezzano, Alessandria, Italy, Sept. 10, 1926; s. Federico Zappoli and Giorgia Bidone; m. Giuliana Laura Cuccodoro; children: Federico Zappoli, Erica Zappoli, Giorgia Donata Zappoli. MD in Medicine/Surgery, U. of Bologna, 1951; specialist in Neurology, U. of Padua, 1955. Asst. prof 2nd neurol. clinic U. Florence, Italy, 1960—74, dir. 2nd neurol. clinic, 1975—85, dir. inst. nervous and mental diseases, 1985—88, dir. dept. neurol., psychiat. sci., 1989—93. Lectr. in field. Contbr. over 300 articles/reviews in various nat./internat. jours. Recipient VIth Edit. A. Arrigo Award for Clin. Neurophysiology, U. of Pavia, 1996, 20th Anniversary (The Olympics of the Brain) of the IOP award for psychophysiology and related neurosciences, Internat. Organ. of Psychophysiology, 2002. Mem.: Italian Soc. Psychophysiology (founder/pres. 1990—98, hon. pres. 1999), Italian Soc. EEG and Clin. Neurophysiology (pres. 1978—83), Italian Clin. Neurophysiology Soc., Italian Soc. Clin. Neurophysiology, Italian Neurol. Soc., Internat. Org. Psychophysiology (bd. dirs. 1989). Achievements include research in important results concerning permanent or transitory effects of different brain diseases on neurocognitive components of the CNV complex. Avocations: skiing, snorkeling. Home: Via Bolognese 419 50139 Florence FI Italy Personal E-mail: giorgia.zappoli@infinito.it.

ZARAGOZA, CRISTÓBAL, general and digestive surgeon; b. El Palmar, Spain, Oct. 19, 1951; s. Agustín Zaragoza and Isabel Fernández; m. Mercedes Ninet, Jan. 9, 1987; children: Gora, Violeta, Cristóbal. Degree in anatomy, U. Valencia, Spain, 1978; degree in surgery, U. Valencia, 1980, BS in Medicine and Surgery, 1980, splty. degree in gen. and digestive surgery, 1985, PhD in Medicine and Surgery, 1990; MS in Laparoscopic Surgery, U. Montpellier, France, 2000. Intern resident surgeon Hosp. Gen. Universitario, Valencia, 1981—85, asst. surgeon, 1986—89, head sect. surgery, 1989—94, head maj. ambulatory surgery svc., 1997—; univ. lectr., mem. dept. surgery Faculty of Medicine U. Valencia, 1987—; univ. lectr. in surgery Faculty of Medicine U. Montpellier, 1993; head surgery svc. Hosp. Gen. de Requena, Spain, 1994—97; head Ambulatory Surgery Gen U. Hosp., 2005—; dir. Minimally Surgery U. Voiendo, 2005; rsch. fellow bd. advisor Am. Biographical Inst., 2005; head surgeon Va Lenoan Bullring, 2006. Academician of Royal Acad. Medicine U. Granada, Spain, 1981—, U. Barcelona, 1985—, U. Valladolid, Spain, 2000—, U. Valencia, 2001—; surgeon Press Soc., Valencia, 1989—; coord. gen. surgery Hosp. Bal-la Ahmed Zein, Rabuny, Algeria, 1995—2000; cloister mem. U. Valencia, 1989—93; surgeon of bull-fighting ring Regional Govt. Valencia, 1988—; chmn. Sixth Nat. Conf. Maj. Ambulatory Surgery, 2003; mem. rsch. bd. advisors Am. Biog. Inst., 2005; dir. Mag. of Ofcl. Drs. Assn. of Valencia; exec. com. mem. Digestive Pathology Soc., 2007—10; dir. Valencia Med. Assn., 2006—10; mem. continuous tng. com. Valencian Cmty. Health Professions Health Minister, 2008; lectr. Cath. U. SocVicemte Martir Cutaneous Intergrity Damage Ulcers & Wounds, 2008—11; mem. U. Advanced Senate, 2010; lectr. master dir. nursing care surgery Cath. U. Vicente Martir, 2010—11. Dir.: (CD-ROM) Major Ambulatory Surgery; author: (CD-ROM) La cure laparoscopique du reflux gastrooesophagien; editor: (book) Major Ambulatory Surgery Accreditation Book; contbr. articles to profl. jours. Recipient award, Inst. Federico Oloriz, 1979, Dr. Zumel, 1981, U. Sevilla, 1983, 1985, Best Surg. Video of Laparoscopic Surgery, 1993, award, Dr. Juan Peset Aleixandre, 1997, García Guijarro, 1998, Nat. Rsch. award in Health, award for best poster, 6th Internat. Congress on Ambulatory Surgery, Sevilla, Spain, 2005, Am. Medal of Honor, Am. Biog. Inst., 2005, Academician of the Spanish Royal Drs. Acad., 2006; named Internat. Scientist of Yr., Internat. Biographical Ctr. Cambridge, 2004; grantee, Spanish Ministry of Edn. and Sci., 1978—79, Spanish Ministry of Univs. and Rsch., 1981—83, Spanish Soc. of Digestive Pathology, 1993, Nat. Health Inst. (Spanish Ministry of Health), 1993, Leonardo da Vinci grantee for surg. rsch. and tchg., Head Office for Continual Tng. in the European Cmty., 1998—2000. Master: Euromediterranean Sch. Endoscopic Surgery (life); fellow: Surgery Assn. Valencia, Spanish Assn. Colo-proctology, European Assn. Endoscopic Surgery and Other Interventional Techniques, Soc. Digestive Pathology of Valencia, Spanish Soc. Digestive Pathology, Spanish Assn. Videosurgery, Spanish Soc. Maj. Ambulatory Surgery, Spanish Assn. Surgeons; mem.: Royal Acad. Drs. of Spain, Surg. Soc. Valencia (coord. surgery in No. Africa 1997—), Acad. Med. Sci. Mem. Progressive Party. Avocations: tennis, gardening. Office: Hosp Gen Universitario Ave Tres Cruces s/n 46014 Valencia Spain Office Fax: 00 34 961972192; Home Fax: 00 34 96 274 3177. Personal E-mail: gora.ninet@wanadoo.es. Business E-Mail: zaragoza_cri@gva.es.

ZARDINI, PIERO, retired cardiology educator; b. Verona, Italy, Oct. 16, 1934; s. Aurelio and Graziella (Toppan) Z.; m. Regina Grazia Lana, July 18, 1971; 1 child, Francesca. MD, U. Padova, Italy, 1959. Cert. in internal medicine with splty. in cardiology. Asst. prof. medicine U. Torino, Italy, 1962-70, full prof. cardiology, 1973-82; chmn. dept. medicine and clin. pharmacology Torino-Monrovia Med. Sch., Liberia, 1971-72; dir. Inst. Cardiology U. Verona, 1983—, chmn. dept. biomed. and surg. sci., 1998—. Contbr. 400 sci. articles to profl. jours. With mil. Sanita, Padova, 1961-62. Mem. Italian Soc. Cardiology (pres. 1988, past pres. 1989-90) Avocations: classic and opera music, pianoforte's player. Home Phone: 0039-045-8345124; Office Phone: 0039-045-8300100. E-mail: piero.zardini@univr.it.

ZAREM, HARVEY ALAN, plastic surgeon; b. Savannah, Ga., Feb. 13, 1932; s. Harry A. and Rose (Gold) Z.; m. Beth McCanghey, July 11, 1981; children: Harold, Allison, Melissa, Kathryn, Michael, Robert. BA, Yale U., 1953; MD, Columbia U. Coll. Physicians and Surgeons, 1957. Diplomate Am. Bd. Surgery, Am. Bd. Plastic Surgery; lic. physician, Md., Ill., Calif. Intern, surgery Johns Hopkins Hosp., Balt., 1957-58, resident, plastic surgery, 1964-66; rsch. fellow Peter Bent Brigham Hosp., Boston, 1958-59, asst. resident, surgery, 1959-61; resident, surgery then chief resident Boston City Hosp., 1961-63; postdoctoral fellow NYU, NYC, 1963-64; from asst. prof. to assoc. prof. surgery U. Chgo., 1966-73; head, sect. plastic surgery U. Chgo. Hosp. and Clinics; prof. surgery U. Calif., LA, 1973-87, prof. emeritus, 1987—, chief, divsn. plastic and reconstructive surgery, 1973—87; mem. med. staff Pacific Surgicenter, Santa Monica, Calif., 1987—. Physician Sepulveda (Calif.) VA Hosp., 1974—; mem. med. staff St. Johns Hosp., Santa Monica, Calif., 1987—, Santa Monica Hosp., 1988—; vis. prof. So. Ill. U., 1983, Lackaland AFB, 1986, Creighton U., 1987, Comesa, Milan, 1989, Baylor Coll. Medicine, 1990; Kazanjian vis. prof. Mass. Gen. Hosp., 1986, 88; cons. and presenter in field; cons. plastic surgery, Wadsworth VA Hosp., LA; surgeon, Extreme Makeover, ABC TV, 2003-. Contbr. numerous articles to profl. jours. Grantee NIH, 1964-75, NIH, 1967-72, Sheldon and Carol Appel Family Found., 1982—, Chantal Pharms., 1983-84, Mentor Corp./Heyer-Schulte Products, 1985—, Michael Jackson Burn Found., 1986-87. Fellow ACS; mem. AMA, Am. Soc. Plastic Reconstructive Sugeons, Inc., Am. Burn Assn., Am. Cleft Palat Assn., Am. Assn. Plastic Surgeons (trustee 1987, 1989), Am. Soc. Aesthetic Plastic Surgery, Inc., Am. Assn. Hand Surgery, Am. Assn. Surgery of Trauma, Calif. Med. Asssn., Calif. Soc. Plastic Surgeons, New Eng. Soc. Plastic Surgeons (hon.), L.A. County Med. Assn., Johns Hopkins Med. and Surg. Soc., Plastic Surgery Rsch. Coun., Soc. Head and Neck Surgeons (sr.), Soc. U. Surgeons, Lipoplasty Soc. N.Am., Bay Surgical Soc., N.W. Soc. Plastic Surgeons (hon.), Calif. Plastic Surgeon Assn. (pres.), Calif. Yacht Club, Beverly Hills Country Club, (bd. dirs.). Office: Pacific Surgicenter 1301 20th St Ste 350 Santa Monica CA 90404-2082 Home Phone: 310-474-3904; Office Phone: 310-315-0222, 310-586-0700. Business E-Mail: hzarem@ucla.edu, drzarem@drzarem.com.

ZAREMBA, JAROSLAW, neuroimmunologist; b. Poznan, Poland, Sept. 14, 1956; s. Eugeniusz Wojciech and Janina Zaremba. MD, Poznan Med. U., 1987, diploma in neurology, 1990, PhD, 2007. From asst. to lectr. dept. anatomy Poznan Med. U., 1981—89, lectr. dept. neurology, 1989—97, lectr. dept. clin. neuro-immunology, 1997—2007, prof. neurology, 2007—. Contbr. articles to med. jours. Fellow: European Fedn. Neurol. Socs., Polish Neurol. Soc. (sec. 1991—2002), World Fedn. Neurology. Achievements include research in studies of development of motor nuclei of cranial nerves; studies on inflammatory mediators in acute phase of human stroke. Avocation: art. Home: ul Bonin 12/7 60-658 Poznan Poland Office: Poznan Med U Clin Neuroimm ul Przybyszewskiego 49 60-355 Poznan Poland Business E-Mail: zarembastroke@esculap.pl. E-mail: jarosaw.3897069@pharmanet.com.pl.

ZARET, BARRY LEWIS, cardiologist, medical educator; b. NYC, Oct. 3, 1940; s. Irving Z. and Beatrice (Fader) Zaret; m. Myrna Zimmerman, June 23, 1963; children: Adam L., Elliot C., Owen M. BS, Queens Coll., Flushing, NY, 1962; MD, NYU, 1966; MA, Yale U., New Haven, Conn., 1982. Diplomate Am. Bd. Internal Medicine. Intern Bellevue Hosp., NYC, 1966-67, resident, 1967-79; rsch. fellow John Hopkins U., Balt., 1969-71; asst. prof. medicine Yale U., New Haven, 1973-76, assoc. prof. medicine and diagnostic radiology, 1976, chief sect. cardiology, 1978—2004, assoc. prof. medicine and diagnostic radiology, 1980-82, prof. medicine and diagnostic radiology, 1982-84, Robert W. Berliner prof. medicine, 1984—, assoc. chair clin. affairs dept. internal medicine, 1994—2004; mem. staff Yale-New Haven Med. Ctr.; med. dir. Yale-New Haven Med. Hosp. Heart Ctr., 1999—2004. Mem. cardiovasc. subsplty. bd. Am Bd. Internal Medicine, 2002—. Mem. editl. bd. Am. Jour. Cardiology, 1977—, Jour. Am. Coll. Cardiology, 1986-91, 92-97, Jour. Cardiac Imaging, 1986—, Circulation, 1993; assoc. editor: Yearbook of Nuc. Medicine, 1980-95; editor-in-chief Jour. Nuc. Cardiology, 1993-2004; contbr. articles to profl. jours. Recipient Casimir Funk award Soc. Mil. Surgeons, 1973; recipient Herrman Blumgart Pioneer award New Eng. chpt. Soc. Nuc. Medicine, 1978, Solomon Berson Alumni Achievement award in clin. sci. NYU Sch. Medicine, 1998, Ellis Island medal Honor, 2004, Disting. Svc. award Am. Soc. Nuc. Cardiology, 2006. Fellow Am. Coll. Cardiology, Coun. Clin. Cardiology, Am. Heart Assn., Coun. Circulation, Am. Heart Assn., Am. Physiology Soc.; mem. Am. Soc. Clin. Investigation, Am. Fedn. Clin. Rsch., Assn. Am. Physicians, Soc. Nuc. Medicine, Am. Soc. Nuc. Cardiology (Disting. Svc. award 2006), Assn. Univ. Cardiologists, Assn. Profs. Cardiology (pres. 1992), Phi Beta Kappa, Alpha Omega Alpha, Interurban Clin. Club. Jewish. Home: 15 Cassway Rd Woodbridge CT 06525-1214 Office: 333 Cedar St # 3 New Haven CT 06520-8017 Office Phone: 203-785-4127. Business E-Mail: barry.zaret@yale.edu.

ZARI, TALAL ALI, biologist, researcher; b. Mecca, Saudi Arabia, Apr. 8, 1951; s. Ali Abdulah and Monera Ibrahim Zari; m. Ahlam Mohammed Khatib, June 21, 1977; children: Shadi, Ali, Mohammed, Sarah. BS in Botany, Zoology, King Saud U., Riyadh, Saudi Arabia, 1974; MA in Biol. Scis., U. No. Colo., 1981; PhD in Thermal Biology and Energetics, U. Nottingham, Eng., 1987. Tchr. biology Secondary Faisal Sch., Riyadh, 1974-76; demonstrator dept. biol. scis. King Abdul Aziz U., Jeddah, Saudi Arabia, 1976-77, lectr. dept. biol. scis., 1982-84, asst. prof. dept. biol. scis., 1987-92, assoc. prof. dept. biol. scis., 1992-98, prof. dept. biol. scis., 1998—, head zoology group, 1999—2002. Mem. joint PhD supervision program King Abdul Aziz U., 1993—99, tchr., rschr. ecophysiology and behavior. Contbr. articles to profl. jours. Mem. AAAS, Saudi Biol. Soc., Egyptian German Soc., Zool. Soc. Egypt, Herpetological Soc. Japan. Islamic. Avocations: swimming, soccer, photography, computers, travel. Home: Mecca Rd 876 Prince Fawaz Housing Jeddah Saudi Arabia Office: King Abdul Aziz Univ Faculty Sci/Dept Biol Sciences PO Box 80203 21589 Jeddah Saudi Arabia Personal E-mail: talzari@yahoo.com.

ZARINS, BERTRAM, orthopedic surgeon; b. Latvia, June 22, 1942; came to U.S., 1946, naturalized, 1956; s. Richard Arthur and Maria (Rozenbergs) Z. AB in Chemistry, Lafayette Coll., 1963; MD, SUNY, Syracuse, 1967. Diplomate Am. Bd. Orthop. Surgery. Clin. instr. orthop. surgery Harvard Med. Sch., Boston, 1976—, asst. clin. prof., 1982—, assoc. clin. prof., 1996—, Harvard Thorndike prof. orthopaedic surgery, 2007—; orthop. surgeon Mass. Gen. Hosp., Boston, 1982-95, chief sports medicine svc., 1982—; team physician Boston Bruins Hockey Team, 1976—2008. Chmn. edn. com. Sports Medicine Coun., U.S. Olympic Com., 1980-92; team physician New England Patriots football team, 1982—2006; head physician USA Olympic teams XIV Winter Olympic Games, Sarajevo, Yugoslavia, 1984; cons. editor for sports medicine Jour. of Bone and Joint Surgery, 1999—2008. Contbr. articles to profl. jours. Team physician N.E. Revolution profl. soccer team, 1996—2010. Lt. comdr. M.C., USNR, 1973-75. Fellow ACS, Am. Acad. Orthop. Surgeons (chmn. com. on sports medicine 1993-97), mem. AMA, Internat. Arthroscopy Assn. (bd. dirs. 1991-95), N.Am. Trauma Assn. (pres. 1977), Internat. Soc. of Arthroscopy, Knee Surgery and Orthopaedic Sports Medicine, Am. Shoulder and Elbow Surgeons, Herodicus Soc., Brookline (Mass.) Country Club, Somerset Club. Home: 6 CRS Boston MA 02114 Office Phone: 617-726-3421. Business E-Mail: bzarins@partners.org.

ZARINS, CHRISTOPHER KRISTAPS, surgeon, educator; b. Tukums, Latvia, Dec. 2, 1943; came to U.S., 1946; s. Richard A. and Maria (Rozenbergs) Z.; m. Zinta Zarins, July 8, 1967; children: Daina, Sascha, Karina. BA, Lehigh U., 1964; MD, Johns Hopkins U., 1968; PhD (hon.), Riga Stradins U., Latvia, 2010. Surgery residency U. Mich., Ann Arbor, 1968-74; asst. prof. surgery U. Chgo., 1976-79, assoc. prof. surgery, 1979-82, prof. surgery, 1983-93, chief of vascular surgery, 1978-93; prof. surgery Stanford (Calif.) U., 1993—2010, chmn. divsn. vascular surgery, 1993—2005, acting chmn. dept. of surgery, 1995-97; clindester emeritus prof. surgery Stanford U., 2010. Author: Essays In Surgery, 1986, Atlas of Vascular Surgery, 1988; editor Jour. of Surg. Rsch., 1982-95; contbr. articles to profl. jours. Pres. Latvian Med. Found., Boston, 1991. Lt. comdr. USN, 1974-76. Grantee NIH, NSF. Mem. Am. Surg. Soc., Soc. for Clin. Surgery, Soc. for Vascular Surgery (pres. 1998-99), Internat. Soc. for Endovascular Surgery, Soc. of Univ. Surgeons, Latvian Nat. Acad. of Scis.(Three Star Order award 2003, Grand medal 2009), Latvian Vascular Surg. Soc. (pres. 1989), Soc. for Vascular Surgery (pres. 1998-99). Avocations: triathlons, skiing. Office: Stanford U Med Ctr Divsn Vascular Surgery 300 Pasteur Dr # H3642 Stanford CA 94304-2203 Office Phone: 650-725-7830.

ZARRELLA, RONALD L., retired pharmaceutical executive; b. Waterbury, Conn., 1949; BSEE, Worcester Poly. Inst., Worcester, Mass., 1971; student, NYU Grad. Sch. Bus., NYC. With Bristol Myers Co., Esmark Corp.; exec. Bausch & Lomb Inc., 1985—94; v.p., No. Am. Vehicle Sales GM Co., 1994—98, exec. v.p. GM N. Am., 1998—2001; chmn., CEO Bausch & Lomb Inc., Rochester, NY, 2001—08, chmn. emeritus, 2008—. Bd. dir. Avaya, Inc., FIRST (For Inspiration and Recognition of Science and Technology), Univ. Rochester Med. Ctr., NY. Mem.: Rochester Inst. Tech., Comm. for Econ. Devel., Nat. Italian Found. Office: c/o Bausch & Lomb Inc One Bausch & Lomb Place Rochester NY 14604

ZARRIN-KHAMEH, NEDA, pathologist; arrived in US, 1999; d. Hassan Zarrin-Khameh and Amirzadeh Amir-Ghazanfari; m. Hamed Jafar-Nejad, Aug. 18, 1994; 1 child, Neema Jafar-Nejad. MD, Tehran U. Med. Scis., 1994; MPH, U. Tex. Sch. Pub. Health, Houston, 2002. Lic. Tex. Med. Examiner, 2007. Internship Tehran U. Tchg. Hosps., 1992—94; supr. physician, blood donation sect. Iranian Blood Transfusion Services, Tehran, 1994—96; gen. practitioner, emergency dept. Shahriar Gen. Hosp., Tehran, 1994—97; gen. practitioner Ghadir Khom Clinic, Tehran, 1996—99; rsch. asst. Nat. Rsch. Ctr. Genetic Engring. & Biotech., Tehran, 1998—99; v.p. knowledge devel. Intelligent Diagnostics Inc., Houston, 2000—01; pathology resident Baylor Coll. Medicine, Houston, 2005—07, cytopathology fellow, 2007—; surg. pathology fellow Meth. Hosp., Houston, 2008—; asst. prof. Baylor Coll. Medicine; with Ben Tanb Gen. Hosp., Houston; asst. prof. Baylor Coll. Medicine, ben Tanb Gen. Hosp. Recipient Resident Good Citizen award, Baylor Coll. Medicine, 2007. Mem.: AMA, US and Can. Acad. Pathology, Tex. Med. Assn., Harris County Med. Soc., Tex. Soc. Pathologists. Achievements include patents for automated medical decision making utilization; research in the association of heat shock protein 70 gene polymorphism with risk of coronary heart disease and stroke; molecular studies in a sample of Iranian phenylketonuria patients; several case reports. Avocations: basketball, cooking, gardening. Office: Baylor Coll Med Dept Pathology One Baylor Plz Houston TX 77030

ZARTMAN, DAVID LESTER, retired zoology educator, researcher; b. Albuquerque, July 6, 1940; s. Lester Grant and Mary Elizabeth (Kitchel) Z.; m. Micheal Aline Plemmons, July 6, 1963; children: Kami Renee, Dalan Lee. BS cum laude in Dairy Husbandry, N.Mex. State U., 1962; MS in Genetics, Ohio State U., 1966, PhD in Genetics, 1968. Cert. dairy cattle specialist, Am. Registry Profl. Animal Scientists. Jr. ptnr. Marlea Guernsey Farm, Albuquerque, 1962-64; grad. rsch. assoc. Ohio State U., Columbus, 1964-68; asst. prof. dairy sci. N.Mex. State U., Las Cruces, 1968-71, assoc. prof., 1971-79, prof., 1979-84, Ohio State U., Columbus, 1984—2006, emeritus prof., 2006—. Chmn. dept. Ohio State U., Columbus, 1984-99; pres. Mary K. Zartman, Inc., Albuquerque, 1976-84; cons. Bio-Med. Electronics, Inc., San Diego, 1984-89, Zartemp, Inc., Northbrook, Ill., 1990, Recom Applied Solutions, 1993-2000, Am. Registry of Profl. Animal Scientists, 1996—, Midwest Univs. Consortium for Internat. Assistance, 2004. Contbr. articles to profl. jours.; patentee in field. Recipient State Regional Outstanding Young Farmer award Jaycees, 1963, Disting. Rsch. award N.Mex. State U. Coll. Agr. and Home Econs., 1983, Outstanding Svc. award Ohio Poultry Assn., 1999, Grazier of Yr. award Gt. Lakes Internat. Grazing Conf., 2001, hon. state degree Ohio FFA, 2000, The Jack Tucker Disting. Svc. award Ohio Forage and Grassland Coun., 2004; course acclaimed by Humane Soc. of U.S.; named one of Top 100 Agr. Alumni, N.Mex. State U. Centennial, 1987; spl. postdoctoral fellow NIH, New Zealand, 1973; Fulbright-Hayes lectr., Malaysia, 1976. Fellow AAAS; mem. Am. Dairy Sci. Assn., Am. Soc. Animal Sci., Dairy Shrine Club, Ohio Farm Bur., Sigma Xi, Gamma Sigma Delta, Alpha Gamma Rho

(1st Outstanding Alumnus N.Mex. chpt. 1985), Alpha Zeta, Phi Kappa Phi. Home: 7671 Deer Creek Dr Worthington OH 43085-1551 Office: Ohio State U 2027 Coffey Rd Columbus OH 43210-1043 Office Phone: 614-431-3479. Business E-Mail: zartman.3@osu.edu.

ZASADA, MARY EILEEN, nursing administrator; b. Waterbury, Conn., July 23, 1957; d. Walter Francis and Elizabeth Ann (Doyle) Lewis; m. Peter Pilkington Zasada, Sept. 8, 1984; children: Kathleen, Andrew. Diploma in nursing, St. Vincent's Med. Ctr., 1978; BS in Mgmt., Tiekyo Post U., 1983; MSN, Sacred Heart U., 1997. RN, Conn. Staff New Britian (Conn.) Gen. Hosp., 1978-79, St. Mary's Hosp., Waterbury, Conn., 1980-84, nurse analyst, 1984-98, project leader clin. applications, 1998—. Bd. dirs. Conn. Healthcare Informatics Network. Mem. Rotary Internat. (bd. dirs. 1990-98, Paul Harris fellow), Girls Inc. of Waterbury (bd. dirs. 1996-2001), Sigma Theta Tau (Mu Delta chpt.). Home: 122 Terrell Farm Rd Bethlehem CT 06751-1408 Office: St Marys Hosp 56 Franklin St Waterbury CT 06706-1238

ZASUKHINA, GALINA DMITRIEVNA, geneticist; b. Saratov, USSR, Apr. 20, 1932; d. Dmitriji Nicolaevich Zusukhin and Tatjana Eduardovna (Rauschenbach) Balandina; m. Igor Vasuljevich Petrojanov-Sokolov, July 19, 1989; 1 child, Tatjana Nicolaevna. Degree in medicine, 1 Moscow Med. Inst., 1955; MD, Inst. Virology, Moscow, 1958; D Med. Sci., Acad. Med. Sci., Moscow, 1968. Scientist Inst. Virology, Moscow, 1958-60; sr. scientist Inst. Poliomyelitis and Virus Encephalitis, Moscow, 1960-73; head lab. Inst. Gen. Genetics, Moscow, 1973—, vice dir., 1973-78, prof. genetics, 1975—. Mem. Biology Experts of Supreme Attestation Com., Moscow, 1974—. Mem. editl. bd. jour. Radiobiology, Radioecology, 1992—; author: (with N. Dubinin) Repair Mechanisms and Viruses, 1975, Repair Mechanisms and Problems of Environmental Pollutants, 1979; co-author monograph: Genetics and Evolution of Arboviruses, 1973; contbr. over 200 articles to profl. jours. Mem. Russian Genetic Soc., N.Y. Acad. Scis., Internat. Acad. Informatization. Avocations: reading, symphonic music, friends. Home: Vavilov Str 44-3-20 117333 Moscow Russia Office: Inst Gen Genetics Gubkin Str 3 117809 Moscow B-333 Russia Office Phone: 8 499 132 8967. Business E-Mail: zasukhina@vigg.ru.

ZATEYSHCHIKOV, DMITRY, medical educator; b. Russia, Sept. 24, 1961; PhD, Russian Med. U., 1984. Lectr. Ednl.-Sci. Med. Ctr. Russian Pres., 1993—2002, prof. cardiology, 2002—. Mem.: European Atherosclerosis Soc., European Soc. Cardiology. Home: Shvernika st 11-3-158 Moscow 117449 Russia Business E-Mail: dz@bk.ru.

ZATLIN, GABRIEL STANLEY, physician; b. NYC, Dec. 5, 1935; s. Samuel and Bernice (Morgenstern) Z.; m. Linda M. Gertner, Dec. 29, 1959 (div. 1973); children: Jonathan Reid, Andrew Evan; m. Lorna G. Schofield, May 14, 1983(div. 2006); 1 child, Sarah Schofield; m. Jane Suttell, June 30, 2009. BS, U. Miami, Coral Gables, Fla., 1956; MD, Washington U., St. Louis, 1960. Diplomate Am. Bd. Pediatrics, Am. Bd. Family Practice. Intern St. Louis Children's Hosp., 1960-61, resident, 1961-62, Children's Hosp. Med. Ctr., Boston, 1965-66, Downstate Med. Ctr., Bklyn., 1979-81; Epidemiologist Ctrs. for Disease Control, Atlanta, 1962-64; pvt. practice Atlanta, 1966-73; cons. Pertamina, Jakarta, Indonesia, 1974-76; field dir. African Health Tng. Project, Yaounde, Cameroun, 1976-77; assoc. dir. Brown U. Health Svcs., Providence, 1977-79; asst. prof. Downstate Med. Ctr., Bklyn., 1981-82; assoc. dir. St. Mary Hosp. Family Practice, Hoboken, NJ, 1982-88, dir., 1988-92; clin. assoc. prof. Downstate Med. Ctr., Bklyn., 1992-95, dir. family practice residency program, 1993-95; faculty family practice residency program Beth Israel Hosp., 1997—. Clin. asst. prof. Albert Einstein Sch. Medicine, 1997—. Contbr. articles to profl. jours. With USPHS, 1962-64. Fellow Am. Acad. Pediatrics; mem. Am. Acad. Family Practice. Avocation: gardening. Office: Inst for Urban Family Prac 16 E 16th St New York NY 10003-3105 Office Phone: 212-924-7744 x 1318.

ZAULI, GIORGIO, anatomist, researcher, educator; b. Forlì, Emilia-Romagna, Italy, Oct. 10, 1960; s. Menotto Zauli and Mirella Mengozzi; m. Francesca La Placa, Jan. 27, 1965; children: Federica, Enrico. MD, U. of Bologna, Bologna, Italy, 1985, PhD in Hematology, 1990, specialist in Oncology, 1992. Rsch. assoc. Calif. Pacific Med. Ctr., San Francisco, Calif., 1989—91; asst. prof. of human anatomy U. of Ferrara, Ferrara, Emilia-Romagna, Italy, 1992—98; assoc. prof. of human anatomy U. of Chieti, Chieti, Abruzzo, Italy, 1998—2001; full prof. of human anatomy U. of Trieste, Trieste, Friuli-Venezia Giulia, Italy. Cons. Area Sci. Pk., Trieste, Friuli-Venezia Giulia, Italy, 2002—. Contbr. articles to 148 scientific publs. Pres. Instn. for the Right to Univ. Studies, Trieste, Friuli-Venezia Giulia, Italy, 2003—. Tenent Air Force, 1986—87, Cervia-Italy. Grantee AIDS project on the role of HIV-1 Tat protein in AIDS pathogenesis, Italian Ministry of Health, 1999—2003, Mechanisms of survival/proliferation of human hematopoietic cells, Italian Min. of Univ. and Sci. Rsch., 2002—04, Potential role of TRAIL in the treatment of hematological malignancies, Italian Assn. for Cancer Rsch., 2000—03. Catholic. Achievements include research in prize for biomed. activity in 2000 from Univ.of Chieti. Office: Univ Trieste Via Manzoni 16 Trieste 34138 Italy Office Fax: 39-040-5586016. E-mail: zauli@units.it.

ZAVARONI, CARLO REMO, government agency administrator, educator; b. Montecchio Emilia, Italy, June 17, 1955; s. Adalberto and Marta Zavaroni. MD, U. of Parma, 1986, degree in Geriatrics & Gerontology, 1991. Med. mgr. of first level S. Maria dei Battuti Hosp., S. Vito al Tagliamento, Italy, 1991—95, Dist. Health Authority, Pordenone, Italy, 1995—2000, Regional Health Authority of Friuli-Venezia Giulia Region, Udine, Italy, 2000—03. Prof. Regional Nursing Sch., S. Vito al Tagliamento, 1992—96; cons. Regional Health Authority of Friuli-Venezia Giulia Region, 1994—2000, Regional Direction of UE & Fgn. Affairs, Trieste, Italy, 1994—96, Provincial Adminstrn., Pordenone, 1994, Dept. of Welfare of the Prime Minister's Office, Rome, 1997—2000; cons. health commn. & working group for elderly Alpe Adria working cmty.; in charge Sub-District Health Authority, Sacile, Italy, 1997; mem. working group for elderly Alpe Adria working cmty., Gyor, Hungary, 1998—2002; prof. geriatrics U. Udine, Udine, 1998—2004; cons. Italian Oncological Commn., Rome, 1999; prof. geriatric studies U. Trieste, Trieste, 2000—03. Contbr. chapters to books Assistenza Domiciliare Integrata (A.D.I.) - indagine conoscitiva sulla situazione nazionale, 1995, articles to profl. publs. Recipient award, Dept. of Pub. Affairs of the Prime Minister's Office, 1997, 2000, Triveneto award, 1991, award in Pub. Adminstrn., Nat. Pub. Adminstrn. Forum, 2002. Mem.: ALASS, Italian Soc. for Quality in Health Care (award 1997, 2000), Italian Soc. of Inpatient Geriatricians, Italian Soc. of Gerontology & Geriat. Avocation: trout fishing. Home: Via dei Mille 17 Montecchio Emilia (RE) 42027 Italy Office: Regional Health Authority Piazzale S Maria della Misericordia15 Udine 33100 Italy Office Fax: 0432 549280. Personal E-mail: carlo.zavaroni@sanita.fvg.it. E-mail: carlo.zavaroni@katamail.com.

ZAVOS, CHRISTOS, gastroenterologist, researcher; b. Larissa, Greece, July 1, 1974; s. Konstantinos Zavos and Sofia Sakellariou. MD, Aristotle U. Thessaloniki, Greece, 1999, PhD in Gastroenterology with honors, 2010. Cert. hellenic repub. and Dutch BIG-register, Gastroenterologist Hellenic Republic, European Union Med. Specialists European Bd. Gastroenterology & Hepatology; English Lang. tchr. Hellenic Republic. Rural dr. Health Ctr. Gonni, Greece, 1999—2000; resident Theagenio Cancer Hosp., Thessaloniki, 2003—04; rsch. assoc. gastroenterology Second Med. Clinic, Aristotle U. Thessaloniki, Ippokration Hosp., Thessaloniki, Greece, 2004—06; gastroenterology resident U. Hosp. Heraklion, Crete, Greece, 2006—10; rsch. assoc. gastroenterology Second Med. Clin. Aristotle U. Thessaloniki, Ippokration Hosp. Thessaloniki, Greece, 2011—; fellow gastroenterology U. Medisch Centrum, Utrecht, The Netherlands, 2011—. Clerk Albert Szent-Györgyi Med. U., Szeged, Hungary, 1996, U. Degli Studi di Roma "La Sapienza", Rome, Italy, 1999; cons. army pers. Greek Army, Mytilene & Larissa, 2001—02; acad. visitor St. Mary's Hosp., Imperial Coll. London, 2002; presenter in field. Contbr. articles to profl. jours. Recipient John Ioannovits award, Adjuvant Therapy Malignant Melanoma, Athens, 2004, Excellence Rsch. award, Hellenic Soc. Gastroenterology, 2007; Travel grant, GASTRO, 2009. Fellow: Hellenic Soc. Gastroenterology; mem.: Hellenic Soc. Study Cancer, Hellenic Helicobacter Pylori Study Group, Dutch Med. Assn., Med. Assn. Larissa Greece, European Bd. Gastroenterology & Hepatology. Achievements include research in pathophysiology of glaucoma, reporting for the first time that glaucoma may be associated with Helicobacter pylori infection. Avocations: travel, classical music, theater, reading. Mailing: PO Box 1457 710 01 Heraklion Greece Home: Ina Boudier-Bakkerlaan 32A Utrecht 3582 VA Netherlands Personal E-mail: czavos@hotmail.com, czavos@ymail.com.

ZAWACKI, BRUCE EDWIN, surgeon, educator, ethicist; b. Northampton, Mass., Dec. 6, 1935; BS, Coll. of Holy Cross, 1957; MD, Harvard U., 1961; MA, U. So. Calif., 1986. Diplomate Am. Bd. Surgery. Intern in surgery Mass. Gen. Hosp., 1961—62, resident in surgery, 1962—65; vis. scholar in trauma surgery Birmingham Accident Hosp., Birmingham, England, 1966; resident in surgery Mass. Gen. Hosp., 1967; gen. surgeon So. Calif. Permanente Med. Group, Panorama City, 1969-71; dir. burn ctr. L.A. County and U. So. Calif. Med. Ctr., LA, 1971-98; assoc. prof. surgery U. So. Calif. Sch. Medicine, LA, 1975-98, assoc. prof. emeritus, 1998—; assoc. prof. religion U. So. Calif. Sch. Religion, LA, 1992-98; assoc. for edn. Pacific Ctr. for Health Policy and Ethics, 1997—2010; adj. assoc. prof. religion U. So. Calif., 2001—02. Contbr. articles to profl. jours. Served to maj. U.S. Army, 1967-68. Mem. Am. Burn Assn. (2d v.p., bd. trustees 1992-93; Harvey Stuart Allen Disting. Svc. award 1996), Am. Soc. Bioethics and Humanities. Achievements include first to describe the natural history of reversible burn injury, the independence of burn hypermetabolism from evaporative water loss and an autonomous role for burn patients without precedent for survival.

ZAWILLA, NERMIN HAMDY, medical educator; b. Cairo, June 26, 1971; B, 1993; MD in Indsl. Medicine and Occupl. Diseases, Cairo U., 2002. Asst. prof., dept. indsl. medicine and occupl. diseases Facuty Medicine Cairo U., 2008—. Home: 500 Cairo Maadi 16599 Egypt Personal E-mail: nerhamdy71@hotmail.com.

ZAWISTOWSKI, STEPHEN LOUIS, psychologist, educator; b. Lackawanna, NY, July 28, 1955; s. Louis Henry and Alice Theresa (Bartus) Z.; m. Jane Elaine Clark, May 26, 1979; 1 child, Matthew. BA, Canisius Coll., 1977; AM, U. Ill., 1979, PhD, 1983. Cert. tech. animal rescue specialist, Am. Humane Assn./Rescue 3. Vis. asst. prof. Ind. U., Bloomington, 1983-84, postdoctoral fellow, 1984-85; asst. prof. St. John's U., NYC, 1985-88; exec. v.p. ASPCA, NYC, 1988—2010, sci. advisor, 2010—; adj. prof. Hunter Coll. Animal Behaviour & Cons. Program, 2008; adj. faculty Canisius Coll. Grad. Program Anthrozoology. Adj. prof. U. Ill. Vet. Coll., 2004; nat. rsch. coun. panel for rev. of the nat. zoo Nat. Rsch. Coun., 2003—04. Author: Animal Shelter Medicine for Veterinarians and Staff, 2004, Companion Animals in Soc., 2008; co-author: Animal Rights Handbook, 1990, Heritage of Care, 2008; editor Animal Behavior Cons. Newsletter, 2001; co-editor: For Kids Who Love Animals, 1991; contbg. editor Animal Watch Mag., 1990-2004; co-exec. prodr. (film) Question of Respect, 1990 (Silver Apple award 1990); writer, host ASPCA pet check segments, PBS; mem. bd. editors Psychologists for the Ethical Treatment of Animals, 1988-95; founding co-editor Jour. Applied Animal Welfare Sci.; contbg. editor, sci. advisor Animaland Mag., 1998-2000; script cons. Animal Rescue Kid, 1997; contbr. articles to profl. jours. Scoutmaster Boy Scouts Am., SI, 1988-98; asst. coach SI Youth Soccer, 1986-95; bd. dirs. Nat. Coun. on Pet Population Study and Policy, v.p., 1995-96, 99-2000, pres., 1996-97, advisor, 2004—; mem. steering com. NY State Watchable Wildlife Program; mem. Nat. Humane Dog Tng. Task Force; bd. dirs. United for Wildlife, 1999-2001, Harmony Inst. Cmty. Adv. Bd.; mem. sci. adv. com. Humane Farm Animal Care, 2003-08; bd. dirs., vice chair Alliance for the Contraception of Cats and Dogs, 2005, chmn. 2006-09. Recipient Stan Lesny scholarship Kosciuszki Found., 1977, U. Ill. Grad. fellowship, 1977, Postdoctoral fellowship NSF, 1984, Patrick Daley award for contbns. to edn. St. John's U.; named Psychologist of Yr., Psychologists for Ethical Treatment of Animals, 1989, ACCD Leadership award, 2010, Green Chimneys Gala award, 2009, Dept. Justice Public Svc. award 2008, USDA OI6 Excellence award, 2008. Mem. World Soc. for Protection of Animals (sci. adv. panel 2003—), Animal Behavior Soc. (cert. applied animal behaviorist, chmn. Issues in Applied Animal Behavior Com. 2007-, chmn. bd. profl. cert. 1998-2007, devel. com. 1995-98, animal welfare com. 1989-95), Order of Arrow (mem. exec. bd. 1996-98), Sigma Xi. Achievements include research in genetics and animal learning, animal behavior and welfare. Office: ASPCA 520 8th Ave 7th Fl New York NY 10018 Office Phone: 212-876-7700 ext. 4401. Business E-Mail: stevez@aspca.org.

ZAX, MELVIN, psychologist, educator; b. Cambridge, Mass., Apr. 14, 1928; s. Joseph and Sadie (Kirshner) Z.; m. Ruth Leah Vogel, Apr. 23, 1977; children: Jeffrey S., David B., Jonathan B. AB, Boston U., 1951, A.M., 1952; PhD, U. Tenn., 1955. Clin. psychologist U. Tenn., Knoxville, 1955-56; staff psychologist St. Elizabeths Hosp., Washington, 1956-57; asst. prof. psychology U. Rochester, NY, 1957-62, assoc. prof. psychology NY, 1962-67, prof. NY, 1967-93, prof. emeritus NY, 1993—; pvt. practice, 1973—. Chmn. exptl. and spl. tng. rev. com. NIMH, 1970-71. Author: (with G. Stricker) Patterns of Psychopathology, 1963, (with E.L. Cowen) Abnormal Psychology: Changing Conceptions, 1972, (with G.A. Specter) An Introduction to Community Psychology, 1974, (with M. Nichols) Catharsis in Psychotherapy, 1977; editor: (with Stricker) The Study of Abnormal Behavior: Selected Readings, 1964, (with Cowen and E.A. Gardner) Emergent Approaches to Mental Health Problems, 1967, (with D. Dorr and J. Bonner) The Psychology of Discipline, 1983; adv. editor Jour. Cons. and Clin. Psychology, 1965-81; contbr. articles to profl. jours. Served with AUS, 1946-47. NIMH spl. research fellow Psykologisk Inst., Copenhagen, 1966-67 Fellow Am. Psychol. Assn.; mem. Eastern Psychol. Assn., AAUP, Phi Beta Kappa, Sigma Xi, Phi Kappa Phi. Home: 27 Sky Ridge Dr Rochester NY 14625-2167 Office Phone: 585-385-6370.

ZAYDON, THOMAS JOHN, JR., plastic surgeon; b. Phila., Apr. 3, 1952; s. Thomas J. and Helen (Joseph) Z. BS, Fla. State U., 1974; MD with spl. honors, Hahnemann Med. U., 1978. Cert. Am. Bd. Plastic Surgery, 1982; diplomate Am. Bd. Surgery, 1991. Intern in gen. surgery Eastern Va. Med. Sch., Norfolk, 1978—79, resident in gen. surgery, 1979—80; jr. resident in gen. surgery Monmouth Med. Ctr., Long Beach, NJ, 1980-81, sr. resident in gen. surgery, 1981-82; resident in plastic surgery La. State U., New Orleans, 1982-83, chief resident in plastic surgery, 1983-84, clin. instr.; pvt. practice surgery Cosmetic Surgery Inst., Miami, 1984—; assoc. chief plastic surgery Miami Heart Inst., Fla., 1984—85; assoc. chief, plastic surgery Mercy Hosp., 2004—05, chief, plastic surgery, 2007—08; pvt. practice. Vol. clin. instr. plastic surgery U. Miami, Fla. 1986—. Author articles and book chpts. in field. Fellow ACS; mem. Dade County Med. Assn., John Rives Surg. Soc., Aesculapian Soc. Miami, Fla. Med. Assn., Fla. Soc. Plastic and Reconstructive Surgeons, Fla. Soc. Plastic Surgeons, Greater Miami Soc. Plastic Surgeons, Am. Soc. Plastic Surgeons, Am. Soc. Aesthetic Plastic Surgery, Southeastern Soc. Plastic Surgeons. Office: Cosmetic Surgery Inst Miami Mercy Hosp Profl Bldg 3661 S Miami Ave Ste 509 Miami FL 33133-4206 also: Dadeland Med Ctr 7400 N Kendall Dr Ste 502 Miami FL 33156 Office Phone: 305-856-3030. E-mail: tzaydon@pol.net.

ZAYED, RANIA AHMED, medical educator; b. Cairo, Aug. 2, 1973; MD, Kasr AlAiny, 1995. Lectr. Cairo U., 2004—10, asst. prof., 2010—11. Mem.: Egyptian Soc. Progenitor Cell Rsch., Egyptian Soc. Lab. Medicine. Home: 27 Elmaraghi St Agouza Cairo Giza 12411 Egypt Personal E-mail: raniaa_zayed@yahoo.com.

ZAZULIA, ALLYSON ROBYN, neurologist, educator; b. Perth Amboy, NJ, Dec. 19, 1967; d. Irwin Zazulia and Nina Foer; m. Michael Neil Diringer, June 3, 2001; 1 child, Daniel Diringer. BS in Psychology, U. Md., College Park, 1990; MD, Georgetown U., DC, 1994. Lic. dr. Nat. Bd. Med. Examiners, 1995, diplomate neurology Am. Bd. Psychiatry & Neurology, 1999, vascular neurology Am. Bd. Psychiatry & Neurology, 2006. Rsch. asst. NIH, Bethesda, Md., 1988—90; resident internal medicine Wash. U., St. Louis, 1994—95, resident neurology, 1995—98, fellow cerebrovascular disease, 1998—2000, instr. neurology, 1998—2001, asst. prof. neurology and radiology, 2001—08, assoc. prof. neurology and radiology, 2008—; attending neurologist Barnes-Jewish Hosp., St. Louis, 1998—. Dir. pre-clinical neurol. edn. Wash. U., 2001—, mem. editl. bd. Internet Stroke Ctr., 2005—. Recipient Coursemaster of Yr. award, Wash. U. Sch. Medicine, 2005, Samuel R. Goldstein Leadership award in med. student edn., 2006, Clin. Tchr. of Yr. award, 2008; grantee Patient-Oriented Rsch. Career Devel. award, NIH, 2003. Mem.: Am. Neurol. Assn., Am. Heart Assn. (assoc.), Am. Acad. Neurology (assoc.), Alpha Omega Alpha, Phi Beta Kappa. Office: Wash Univ Sch Medicine 660 S Euclid Ave Campus Box 8111 Saint Louis MO 63110

ZBAR, LLOYD IRWIN STANLEY, otolaryngologist, educator; b. Jersey City, June 2, 1939; m. Margo Wally, Mar. 25, 1965; children: Ross I.S., Brett I.W. MD, Queen's U., Kingston, Ont., Can., 1964. Cert. otolaryngologist. Intern Beth Israel/Harvard, Boston, 1964; resident surgery French Hosp., NYC, 1965—66; resident otolaryngology Bellevue Hosp. Ctr.-NYU, NYC, 1966—69, fellow otolaryngology, 1969—70; chmn. med. edn. com. Mountainside Hosp., Montclair, NJ, 1979—89, dir. otolaryngology, 1990—97, 1999—2009. Sec. med. bd. Mountainside Hosp., Glen Ridge, N.J., 1986-90, clin. assoc. prof. otolaryngology NYU Sch. Medicine Contbr. rev. to New Eng. Jour. Medicine, 1988 Mem. exec. bd. Boy Scouts Am., Essex County, N.J., 1984-95; pres. Mountainside Physicians Scholarship Loan Fund, 1972-85 With USAF. Named one of Top Dr. in NY Metro Area, 1998—2011. Fellow ACS, Am. Acad. Otolaryngology-Head and Neck Surgery, Royal Soc. Medicine Office: 200 Highland Ave Glen Ridge NJ 07028-1528 Office Phone: 973-744-2424. Office Fax: 973-743-3111. Personal E-mail: liszmd@yahoo.com.

ZDERIC, STEPHEN ANTHONY, urologist, surgeon; b. Detroit, July 2, 1956; s. John Anthony and Marie Alice Zderic; m. Kathleen (Kate) Marie Cronan, Dec. 6, 1953; children: Olivia Cronan, Colin Cronan, Natalie Sang Me. BS Chemistry and BioChemistry, U. Calif. Riverside, 1979; MD, UCLA, 1983. Cert. Urologist Am. Bd. of Urology, 1993. Asst. prof. surgery in urology Sch. Medicine U. Pa., Phila., 1991—99; attending surgeon Children's Hosp. Phila., 1991—; assoc. prof. surgery in urology Sch. Medicine Sch. Medicine U. Pa., 1999—2006, prof. surgery in urology, 2006—; John W. Duckett endowed chair pediat. urology Childrens Hosp. Phila., 2009. Editor: (sci. mongraph) Muscle Matrix and Bladder Function, Pediatric

Gender Assignment A Critical Reappraisal, (book) Pediatric Urology for the Primary Care Provider; cons. reviewer Jour. Urology, Brit. Jour. Urology; contbr. articles to profl. jours. Grantee, NIH, 1993—98, 1994—95, 2003—05, 1998—2003, 2003—; Rsch. Grant, Am. Found. Urologic Disease, 1989—90. Avocations: tennis, skiing, swimming. Office: Children's Hosp Philadelphia 34th & Civic Center Blvd Philadelphia PA 19104 Office Phone: 215-590-3766. Office Fax: 215-590-3985. Personal E-mail: zderic@email.chop.edu.

ZEAVIN, LYNNE, psychologist, educator; b. Calif., May 29, 1958; BA, U. Calif., Berkeley, 1978; PhD, Yeshiva U., Albert Einstein Coll. Medicine, 1985. Asst. clin. prof. NYU Sch. Medicine, 1998—. Pvt. practice in psychoanalysis, 1988. Contbr. articles to profl. jours. Mem.: Am. Psychoanalytic Assn. Avocations: classical music, piano. Office: 80 University Pl New York NY 10003 Office Fax: 212-929-6326. Business E-Mail: lynnezeavin@mindspring.com.

ZECKHAUSER, RICHARD JAY, economist, educator; b. Phila., Nov. 1, 1940; s. Julius Nathaniel and Estelle (Borgenicht) Zeckhauser; m. Nancy Mackell Hoover, Sept. 9, 1967; children: Bryn Gordon, Benjamin Rennell. AB, Harvard U., 1962, PhD, 1969. Jr. fellow Soc. Fellows Harvard U., Cambridge, Mass., 1965-68, mem. faculty, 1968—, prof. polit. econ. Kennedy Sch., 1972—, Frank P. Ramsey prof. polit. economy. Founder, bd. dirs. Niederhoffer, Cross & Zeckhauser, 1968—84; sr. advisor, prin. Equity Resource Investments, 2005—; bus. adv. bd. Tengion, Inc., 2006—. Co-author: A Primer for Policy Analysis, 1978, Demographic Dimensions of the New Republic, 1982, The Early Admissions Game: Joining the Elite, 2003; editor or co-editor: Benefit-Cost and Policy Analysis, 1974, What Role for Government, 1983, Principals and Agents: The Structure of Business, 1985, American Society: Public and Private Responsibilities, 1986, Privatization and State-Owned Enterprises: Lessons from the United States, Great Britain, and Canada, 1989, Strategy and Choice, 1991, Wise Choices: Games, Decisions, and Negotiations, 1996, Targeting in Social Programs: Avoiding Bad Bets, Removing Bad Apples, 2006; editor or co-editor The Patron's Payoff: Conspicuous Commissions in Italian Renaissance Art, 2008; contbr. 248 articles to profl. jours., chapters to books; rsch. fin., coll. admissions, climate change and healthcare. Bd. dirs. Commonwealth Sch. Recipient 2d pl., US Mixed-Teams Championship, 2003, 3d pl., US Open Pairs Championship, 2004, 1st Pl., US Mixed Pairs, 2007; named winner, numerous regional and nat. contract bridge competitions; finalist, World Paris Championship, 1998. Fellow: AAAS, Inst. Medicine/NAS, Assn. Pub. Policy and Mgmt., Econometric Soc. Office: Harvard U John F Kennedy Sch Govt 79 JFK St Cambridge MA 02138-5801 Business E-Mail: richard_zeckhauser@harvard.edu.

ZEC SAMBOL, SILVIJA, medical products executive, ozone therapist, vegetarianism researcher; b. Hrvatska, Croatia, June 13, 1973; Grad. with honors, 1998; MD, U. Rijeka, Croatia, MSc, 2004; PhD in Ozone Therapy. Med. rep. Schering-Plough, 2002—07; sr. med. rep. Sanofi Aventis, 2007—. Mem.: Croatian Bioethics Assn., Croatian Assn. Physicians. Avocation: aerobics. Home: Zametskog Korena 36 Rijeka 51 000 Croatia Home Fax: 0038551641057. Business E-Mail: silvijazecsambol@email.t-com.hr.

ZEDLITZ, ANN C., dermatologist; Grad., U. New Orleans; MD with honors, La. State U. Med. Ctr., 1996. Diplomate Am. Bd. Dermatology. Intern, emergency medicine La. State Univ., resident, dermatology, resident, emergency medicine, chief resident, 2009—10, asst. clin. prof. dermatology; diplomat Am. Bd. Dermatology, Am. Bd. Emergency Medicine; joined Dermatology Clinic, 2010—. Mem.: Our Lady of the Lake Hosp., Am. Soc. of Dermatologic Surgery, Women's Dermatol. Soc., Am. Soc. for Laser Medicine and Surgery, Alpha Omega Alpha Med. Honor Soc. Office: Dermatology Clinic 5326 O'Donovan Dr Baton Rouge LA 70808 Office Phone: 225-769-7546.

ZEGADA, LUIS FERNANDO, neurologist; b. La Paz, Bolivia, Jan. 31, 1940; s. Victor and Elena Zegada; m. Cristina Maria Cataldi, Jan. 29, 1971; children: Tatiana, Luis, Jan Pablo. MD, San Francisco Xavier, Sucre, 1968; specialist in neurology, Edinburgh U., Scotland, 1975. Medical diplomate. Clin. asst. W.G. Hosp., Edinburgh, Scotland, 1974-75; commd. 2d lt. Bolivia Air Force, 1977, advance through grades to lt. col., neurologist, head neurophysiology, 1977-94; assoc. prof. U. Mayor de San Andes, La Paz, 1978-94; med. neurologist, chief dept. neurology Social Security, La Paz, 1977—. Co-author: Tropical Neurology, 1970. British Coun. scholar, Scotland, 1974. Mem. N.Y. Acad. Sci., Am. Acad. Neurology (assoc.), Bolivian Soc. Neurology (pres. 1981), Queen Sq. Alumnus Assn. (London). Avocations: trekking, travel, music, history of neurology. Office: Edif Marischal de Ayacucho PO Box 2903 La Paz Bolivia Fax: 591-2-811921.

ZEGANS, LEONARD SAUL, psychiatry educator; b. NYC, Apr. 12, 1934; m. Susan S. Zegans; children: Marc, Michael. AB cum laude, Princeton U., 1955; MD, NYU, 1959; postgrad., Wash. Sch. Psychiatry, 1963-65. Diplomate Am. Bd. Psychiatry and Neurology. Intern Greenwich (Conn.) Hosp., 1959-60; psychiatric resident U. Mich., Ann Arbor, 1960-63; NIMH spl. postdoctorate rsch. fellow Tavistock Clinic, London, 1965-66; jr. clin. instr. U. Mich., Ann Arbor, 1962-63; instr. psychiatry Howard U., Washington, 1963-65; assoc. prof. dept. psychiatry Yale U., 1966-71, assoc. prof. clin. psychiatry dept. psychiatry, 1971-78, fellow Jonathan Edwards Coll., 1969-78; prof. psychiatry dept. psychiatry U. Calif., Sch. Medicine, San Francisco, 1978—. Staff psychiatrist USPHS, St. Elizabeth Hosp., Washington, 1963-65; staff physician Conn. Mental Health Ctr., New Haven, 1966-78; attending physician Yale New Haven (Conn.) Hosp., 1966-78, Langley Porter Psychiat. Inst., San Francisco, 1979—; dir. grad. and postgrad. edn. dept. psychiatry Yale U., 1971-78; dir. edn. and profl. stds., dept. psychiatry, U. Calif., Sch. Medicine, San Francisco, 1978—, dir. residency tng. program, 1980-89, acting dir. Ctr. Deafness dept. psychiatry, 1982-84, others. Editl. bd. U. Calif. San Francisco Mag., 1978—; editl. cons. Free Press, MacMillan Pub. Co., 1978, Grune & Stratton, Inc., 1980, Gastroentereology, 1986, Western Medicine, 1986; editl. reviewer Jour. AMA, 1989, Internat. Jour. Psychiatry in Medicine, 1989; series editor Mind & Medicine Series Grune & Stratton, Inc., 1983-88, Mind & Medicine Series Rutgers U. Press, 1989, others; contbr. articles to profl. jours. Cons. Com. on Re-Orgn., Butler Hosp., Providence, 1969-70, VA Med. Ctr., West Haven, Conn., 1972-78, Dept. Corrections, San Quentin Prison, 1978-82, Behavioral Medicine Clinic, Divsn. Gen. Internal Medicine, U. Calif. San Francisco, Langley Porter Psychiat. Inst., 1981—, NIMH AIDS Edn. Program, 1988-89, Napa State Hosp. Ednl. Planning, 1989, NIH Sect. on Alt. Medicine Grant Revs., 1993, others, Former chair UCSF Acad. Senate, 2004-08, UC Segston Wide Com., Health Edn. Com. Recipient Pawlowski Peace prize Pawlowski Peace Found., 1972; Tng. grantee NIMH, 1978-82, 81-82, 83-86, 86-89, 89-92; grantee Nat. Inst. Handicapped Rsch., 1983-87; Behavioral Sci. Rsch. grantee U. Calif. San Francisco, 1988-89; others. Fellow Am. Psychiat. Assn. (grad. edn. com. No. Calif. Psychiat. Soc. 1979), Royal Soc. Health; mem. AMA, AAAS, Am. Acad. Polit. and Social Scis., Am. Assn. Dirs. Psychiatric Residency Tng., Assn. for Acad. Psychiatry, Physicians for Social Responsibility. Office: Univ Calif San Francisco 401 Parnassus Ave San Francisco CA 94143-9911

ZEGEL, HARRY, diagnostic radiologist; MD, Jefferson Med. Coll. of Thomas Jefferson U., 1975. Diplomate Am. Bd. of Radiology-diagnostic radiology, 1979. Intern Thomas Jefferson Univ. Hosp., 1976, fellow, 1980; resident Pa. Hosp., 1979; hosp. affiliation include/s Bryn Mawr Hosp., 2000—, Lankenau Med. Ctr., 2000—, Paoli Hosp., 2000—, Riddle Hosp., 2009—; chmn. radiology dept. Main Line Health, 2005—. Office: Lankenau Hospital Radiology 100 Lancaster Ave Wynnewood PA 19096 Office Phone: 484-476-2802.

ZEHEL, WENDELL EVANS, surgeon; b. Brownsville, Pa., Mar. 6, 1934; s. Michael and Emma (Evans) Z.; m. Joan Leasure, Nov. 1, 1958 (dec. Jan. 17, 2008); children: Lori Ann, Wendell Charles. BA, Washington and Jefferson Coll., Pa., 1956; MD, U. Pitts., 1960; postgrad. in bioengring., Carnegie-Mellon U., Pitts., 1968-75. Diplomate Am. Bd. Surgery. Intern Shadyside Hosp., Pitts., 1960-61; resident in surgery U. Pitts., VA Hosp., 1963-66, Wilmington Med. Ctr., Del., 1966-68; pvt. practice Pitts., 1968—; surgeon St. Clair Hosp., Pitts., 1968—. Served with USAF, 1961-63. Fellow ACS; mem. Assn. Advancement of Med. Instrumentation. Home: 553 Harrogate Rd Pittsburgh PA 15241-2028 Office: 110 Fort Couch Rd Ste 3D Pittsburgh PA 15241-1030 Office Phone: 412-563-4800. Office Fax: 412-835-7159. Personal E-mail: wzehelagentsbuilding@aol.com.

ZEHENDER, HARTMUT HANS, pharmacologist; s. Johann and Elisabeth Balla; m. Genevieve Marguerite Kuntzelmann, Nov. 5, 1994; children: Yasmine Rhebecca Hack-Gross, Fabian. Dr. rer. nat., Germany, 1983; PhD, U. Tuebingen, Germany, 1983, U. Freiburg, 1983. Postdoc. fellow U. Heidelberg, Klinikum Mannheim, Germany, 1984—89; lab. head Sandoz Pharma AG, Basel, Switzerland, 1989—96, Novartis Pharma AG, Basel, 1996—2001, project team rep., clin. pharmacology expert oncology, 2007—; lab. head drug discovery Novartis Inst. Biomed. Rsch., Basel, 2001—07. Contbr. articles to profl. jours. Business E-Mail: hartmut.zehender@novartis.com.

ZEHETGRUBER, MANFRED H., cardiologist, educator; b. Linz, Austria, July 7, 1963; MD, U. Vienna, 1987, MSc. Prof. medicine, cardiology U. Vienna, 1991—. Recipient award, Austrian Soc. Cardiology. Fellow: European Soc. Cardiology; mem.: European Bifurcation Club. Avocation: sports. Office: Skodagasse 32 Vienna 1080 Austria Business E-Mail: manfred.zehetgruber@meduniwien.ac.at.

ZEHETNER, ANTHONY, pediatrician; b. Sydney, Aug. 10, 1973; MBBS, U. Sydney, 2001, diploma in Child Health, 2005. Cons. paediatrician Gosford Hosp., Ctrl. Coast Local Health Network, 2011—. Lectr. paediat. U. Newcastle, 2011; staff specialist adolescent medicine Children's Hosp. Westmead. Recipient New Investigator award, Wiley Blackwell Pub., World Congress Internal Medicine, 2010. Fellow: Royal Australasian Coll. Physicians. Office: Gosford Hosp Private Consulting Rm PO Box 361 Gosford NSW 2250 Australia Office Fax: 61243203508. Business E-Mail: anthony.zehetner@newcastle.edu.au.

ZEHNBAUER, BARBARA ANN, geneticist; b. St. Louis, Mar. 1, 1952; PhD, U. Chgo., 1979. Cert. in clin. molecular genetics Am. Bd. Med. Genetics, 1993, lab. insp. in molecular pathology Coll. Am. Pathologists, 2002. Asst. prof. Johns Hopkins Med. Instns., 1982—94; prof. Wash. U. Sch. Medicine, St. Louis, 1994—2009; br. chief Ctrs. Disease Control and Prevention, 2009; advisor to consensus com. molecular methods Clin. and Lab. Stds. Inst., 2011—. Sr. assoc. editor jour. molecular diagnostics Am. Soc. Investigative Pathology, 2009—; adj. prof. Emory U. Sch. Medicine, 2009. Fellow: Am. Coll. Med. Genetics; mem.: Am. Soc. Human Genetics, Am. Assn. Clin. Chemistry, Assn. Molecular Pathology. Achievements include research in development of best practices guidelines and laboratory standards in genetics, molecular pathology, and other laboratory medicine disciplines. Avocations: travel, movies, weightlifting. Office: CDC-OSELS-LSPPPO-DLSS 1600 Clifton Rd Atlanta GA 30329 Office Fax: 404-498-2372. Business E-Mail: bzehnbauer@cdc.gov.

ZEHNDER, JAMES L., laboratory director, medical educator; b. San Juan, Apr. 20, 1955; MD, Tufts U., 1984. Diplomate Am. Bd. Internal Medicine, Am. Bd. Oncology, Am. Bd. Hematology. Intern Stanford (Calif.) U. Hosp., 1984-85, resident, 1985-87, fellow in hematology, 1988-91, fellow in oncology, 1991-93, dir. lab., 1994—; asst. prof. pathology, asst. prof. hematology Sch. Medicine Stanford U., 1994—, prof. pathology and medicine, 2007—. Hematologist Coagulation and Molecular Genetic Pathology Labs., 1994—. Office: Stanford U Med Ctr Dept Pathology L235 Stanford CA 94305 Business E-Mail: zehnder@stanford.edu. *

ZE-HONG, MIAO, medical educator; b. Sichuan, China, Apr. 23, 1966; PhD, Chinese Acad. Scis., 2003. Prof. Shanghai Inst. Materia Medica, Chinese Acad. Scis., 2003. Office: 555 Zuchongzhi Rd Shanghai 201203 China Personal E-mail: zhmiao@mail.shcnc.ac.cn.

ZEISEL, STEVEN H., nutritionist, scientist, educator; b. NYC, July 16, 1950; BS in Life Sci., MIT, 1971; MD, Harvard Med. Sch., 1975; PhD in Nutrition, MIT, 1980. Asst. in medicine Children's Hosp., Boston, 1980-81; asst. prof. pathology and pediatrics Boston U. Sch. Medicine, 1982—90, assoc. prof., 1987-90, prof., 1990; prof. dept. pediatrics U. N.C., Chapel Hill, 1990—, prof. dept. nutrition, 1990—, chair dept. nutrition, 1990—2005; chair med. edn. com. Am. Soc. Clin. Nutrition, 1995—97. Chair joint membership com. AIN/ASCN, 1992-94; chmn. adv. bd. Gen. Clin. Rsch. Ctr., U. N.C., 1990-2000; mem. Inst. of Medicine panel on folate and B Vitamins, 1997-99; mem. sci. adv. bd. Monsanto Corp., 1998-2000; mem. sci. coun. Dannon Inst.; bd. dirs. Interactive Info; dir. U. NC Clin. Nutrition Rsch. Unit. Editor-in-chief Jour. Nutritional Biochemistry. Mem. Internat. Soc. for Rsch. on Human Milk and Lactation, Am. Soc. Nutritional Scis., Am. Soc. Clin. Nutrition (councilor 1991-94, chmn. residency edn. and subspecialty tng. com. 1995—), Am. Soc. Parenteral and Enteral Nutrition, Am. Coll. Nutrition, Am. Pub. Health Assn., Soc. Pediatric Rsch. Achievements include development of hippocampus is influenced by the availability of choline because of changes in mitosis and apoptosis in neuronal cells. Office: UNC Dept Nutrition #7461 Sch Pub Health/Sch Medicine 2115A Michael Hooker Rsch Ctr Chapel Hill NC 27599-7461 Office Phone: 919-843-4731. Office Fax: 919-843-8555. E-mail: steven_zeisel@unc.edu.

ZEITLER, KRISTEN, pharmacist; b. NYC, Sept. 23, 1984; B in Chemistry, Fairfield U., 2007; PharmD, U. Buffalo Sch. Pharmacy & Pharm. Scis., 2011. Pharmacy intern Buffalo Pharmacies, Inst., 2008—11; pharmacy resident Hosp. U. Pa., 2011—. Home: 352 Martin Dr West Islip NY 11795 Personal E-mail: zeitler.kristen@gmail.com.

ZEKAN, JOŠKO, obstetrician, gynecologist; b. Split, Dalmatia, Croatia, Nov. 29, 1956; s. Ante and Matuša Zekan; m. Karolina Kerezi, July 1, 1999; 1 child, Iva Antonia. Degree, Med. Faculty, Zagreb, Croatia, 1980, postgrad., 1982, specialist of Gynaecology and Obstetrics, 1990; MS, Faculty of Sci., Zagreb, Croatia, 1995. Intern Clin. Hosp. Ctr., Zagreb, 1981—82; asst. investigator dept. pharmacology Med. Faculty, 1983—84; surg. resident Mil. Med. Acad., Belgrade, Yugoslavia, 1985—86; resident in ob-gyn. Med. Faculty, Zagreb, 1986—90, specialist ob-gyn., 1990—96, 1996—, head preclin. cancer office, 2004, head outpatient dept., 2004. Investigator Dept. Health, Edn. and Welfare, Pub. Health Svc., U.S. and Med. Faculty, Zagreb, 1983—84; founder, dir. family planning and reproductive health course Inter-U. Ctr., Dubrovnik, Croatia, 1997—; coord. Nat. Program for Youth, Zagreb, 2001—. Editor: Drustvena Istrazivanja, 1999; guest editor Jour. Gen. Social Issues, 1999. Coord. Nat. Youth Program, Croatia, 2001—. Mem.: Internat. Fedn. Cervical Pathology and Colposcopy, NY Acad. Sci., Croatian Soc. Colposcopy and Cervicovaginal Pathology, Croatian Med. Assn. Avocations: diving, skiing. Home: Gruska 18 Zagreb 10000 Croatia Office: Sch Medicine Dept Gyn Oncology Petrova Ulica 13 10-000 Zagreb 10000 Croatia Office Phone: 38514604710, 385 14604714. Office Fax: 38514633512. Personal E-mail: josko.zekan@zg.t-com.hr.

ZELAC, RONALD EDWARD, physicist; b. Chgo., Jan. 22, 1941; BS in Engring. Physics summa cum laude, U. Ill., 1962, MS in Physics, 1964; MS in Environ. Health, U. Mich., 1965; PhD in Environ. Engring., U. Fla., 1970. Diplomate Am. Bd. Health Physics, Am. Bd. Medical Physics. Chief health physicist IIT Rsch. Inst., Chgo., 1965-68; radiation physicist Mercy Medical Ctr., Chgo., 1967-68; asst., assoc. prof. Temple U., Phila., 1970-92, radiation safety officer, 1970-91; adj. assoc. prof. U. Pa., Phila., 1980-86; assoc. vice provost Temple U., Phila., 1987-91; sr. physicist and exec. mgr. tech. Landauer Inc., Glenwood, Ill., 1991-97. Adj. prof. Northwestern U., Evanston, Ill., 1991-97, Temple U., 1992—, Purdue U., 1998—; health physicist, tech. asst., sr. asst. to chmn., sr. health physicist, US NRC, Rockville, Md., 1998—; cons. Wyeth-Ayerst Rsch., Radnor, Pa., Princeton, NJ, 1971-94, Presby. U. Pa. Med. Ctr., Phila., 1974-86, Mobil Rsch. Devel. Corp., Paulsboro, Princeton, 1977-95, Rhone-Poulenc Rorer Cen. Rsch., Ft. Washington, Collegeville, Pa., 1986-93, Smith, Kline and French Labs., Phila., 1979-86. Editor: A Guide to Personnel Monitoring, 1993; contbr. articles to profl. jours. Fellow Phi Kappa Phi, 1962-63, U.S. AEC, 1964-65, USPHS, 1968-70. Mem. Health Physics Soc. (com. mem. 1978-79), Campus Safety Assn., Am. Assn. Physicists in Medicine (com. mem. 1995—), Am. Coll. Medical Physics, Sigma Xi (v.p., pres. 1984-88). Home and Office: PO Box 26786 Elkins Park PA 19027-5773 Business E-Mail: ronald.zelac@nrc.gov.

ZELDIS, STEVEN MARTIN, cardiologist; b. Bklyn., June 11, 1946; s. Milton E. and Norma (Gratz) Z.; m. Roberta L. Weiss, June 8, 1974; children: Mark, Beth. BA, U. Rochester, 1968; MD, Yale U., 1972. Diplomate Am. Bd. Internal Medicine, Am. Bd. Cardiovascular Diseases. Intern Yale-New Haven (Conn.) Hosp., 1972-73, resident, 1973-75; cardiology fellow U. Pa., Phila., 1975-77; dir. non-invasive cardiology Long Island Jewish Med. Ctr., New Hyde Park, N.Y., 1977-81; asst. prof. medicine SUNY, Stony Brook, 1977-87, assoc. prof. medicine, 1987—; acting chief cardiology Nassau Hosp., Mineola, N.Y., 1981-84; chief cardiology Winthrop U. Hosp., Mineola, 1981-93, dir. med. edn., 1991—, firm chief, 2011. Pres. Temple Beth Sholom, Roslyn Heights, NY. Recipient Leadership award, Am. Heart Assn., Nassau, N.Y., Long Island Heart Coun. Fellow Clin. Coun. Am. Heart Assn., Am. Coll. of Physicians, Am. Coll. Cardiology (key contact com. 1991), Am. Coll. Chest Physicians. Avocations: computers, music, photography, outdoors. Office: Long Island Heart Assn 300 Old Country Rd Mineola NY 11051 Office Phone: 516-877-0977.

ZELENETZ, ANDREW DAVID, medical oncologist; BA, Harvard Coll.; PhD, Harvard U., MD, 1984. Diplomate Am. Bd. Internal Medicine-med. oncology, registered NY, 1991. Intern Stanford Hosp., Calif., 1985, resident, 1986, fellow, 1991; cons. MGI Pharma Inc., GlaxoSmithKline, Genentech Inc., Favrille, Cephalon Inc., Cell Therapeutics Inc., Abbott Labs.; medicine assoc. prof. Weil med. coll. Cornell Univ.; asoc. attending physician Meml. Hosp.; head lab. molecular hematology/oncology Meml. Sloan-Kettering Cancer Ctr., NY, chief lymphoma svc. in hematology/oncology divsn. medicine dept. Author: (articles) Pre-transplant functional imaging predicts outcome following autologous stem cell transplant for relapsed and refractory Hodgkin lymphoma, 2010, Risk-adapted dose-dense immunochemotherapy determined by interim FDG-PET in Advanced-stage diffuse large B-Cell lymphoma, 2010, NCCN Clinical Practice Guidelines in Oncology: non-Hodgkin's lymphomas, 2010, High-dose chemo-radiotherapy for relapsed or refractory Hodgkin lymphoma and the significance of pre-transplant functional imaging, 2010, Time to treatment response in patients with follicular lymphoma treated with bortezomib is longer compared with other histologic subtypes, 2010, various others. Recipient Meml. Sloan-Kettering Fellowship Tchg. Excellence award; named one of Best Doctors, NY Mag., 2010. Mem.: Lymphoma Rsch. Found. Sci. Adv. (bd. dirs.), Leukemia and Lymphoma Soc. (bd. dirs.), Nat. Comprehensive Cancer Network (chairperson), Cancer and Leukemia Group B Lymphoma Core Com. (vice chairperson), Am. Coll. of Physicians, Am. Soc. of Clin. Oncology, Am. Soc. of Hematology. Achievements include development of number of agents now approved to treat lymphoma including 131I-tosituomab/tositumomab, bortezomib, and pralatrexate; research in improving the prognostic value of patients' pathology specimens using computer-aided image analysis. Office: Memorial Sloan-Kettering Cancer Center 1275 York Ave New York NY 10065 Office Phone: 212-639-2656.

ZELIS, ROBERT FELIX, cardiologist, educator; b. Perth Amboy, NJ, Aug. 5, 1939; s. Felix Andrew and Rita Marie (Jurasz) Z.; m. Gail Ann Heelon, Sept. 10, 1960; children: Robert Felix, Kathleen, Karen, David. BS cum laude, U. Mass., 1960; MD with honors, U. Chgo., 1964. Diplomate: Am. Bd. Internal Medicine (cardiovascular disease). Intern, then asst. resident in medicine Beth Israel Hosp., Harvard U. Med. Sch., 1964-66; clin. assoc. (lt. comdr. USPHS) cardiology br. Nat. Heart Inst., NIH, Bethesda, Md., 1966-68; mem. faculty U. Calif. Med. Sch., Davis, 1968-74, asst. assoc. prof. medicine, 1972-74, chief lab. clin. physiology, 1968-74, asst. chief sect. cardiovasc. medicine, 1970-74; prof. medicine and cellular/molecular physiology Milton S. Hershey (Pa.) Med. Ctr., Pa. State U. Coll. Medicine, 1974—, chief divsn. cardiology, 1974-84, dir. cardiology rsch., 1984—2002. Editor: The Peripheral Circulations, 1975; co-editor: Calcium Blockers, 1982; mem. editorial bd. Annals Internal Medicine, 1976-79, Am. Jour. Physiology, 1976-79, Circulation, 1979-82, Am. Heart Jour., 1980-90, Am. Jour. Cardiology, 1983-86, Jour. Cardiovasc. Pharmacology, 1991-2001, Jour. Am. Coll. Cardiology, 1994-99; contbr. articles to profl. jours. Walter S. Barr fellow, 1960-64; recipient Borden Rsch. award, 1964, Palmer award for Faculty Mentoring Pa. State U., 1997, Disting. Educator award Pa. State U. Coll. Medicine, 2003, Disting. Svc. award U. Chgo. Med. and Biol. Scis. Alumni Assn., 2004. Fellow A.C.P., Am. Coll. Chest Physicians, Am. Coll. Cardiology (gov. Eastern Pa. 1977-80); mem. Am. Fedn. Clin. Research (pres. 1977-78), Am. Soc. Clin. Investigation (nat. council 1981-85, v.p. 1984-85), Am. Physiol. Soc., Assn. Am. Physicians, Assn. Univ. Cardiologists, Am. Soc. Pharmacology and Exptl. Therapeutics, Am. Heart Assn. (nat. fellow councils circulation, arteriosclerosis, clin. cardiology and epidemiology, v.p. for community programs 1979-81, award of merit 1983 v.p., exec. com. Pa. 1976-79, pres. Pa. affiliate 1979-80, Charles T. Mears Humanitarian award 1984), Western Soc. Clin. Research, Sigma Xi, Alpha Omega Alpha, Phi Eta Sigma. Roman Catholic. Home: 815 Verden Dr Hummelstown PA 17036-9700 Office: MS Hershey Med Ctr Cardiology Divsn HO-47 PO Box 850 Hershey PA 17033-0850 Home Phone: 717-533-7512.

ZELLER, MICHAEL JAMES, psychologist, educator; b. Des Moines, Dec. 3, 1939; s. George and Lila (Fitch) Zeller. BS, Iowa State U., 1962, MS, 1967. Instr. psychology Minn. State U., Mankato, 1967—73, asst. prof., 1974—89, assoc. prof., 1990—2001, prof. emeritus, 2001—. Mem. social sci. edn. Mankato State U., 1976—; ednl. cons. Random Ho., Scott Foresman, West Pub. Co-author: (book) Unit Mastery Workbook, 1974, Test Item File to Accompany Psychology, 1974, 2d edit., 1976, Unit Mastery Workbook, 2d edit., 1976, Psychology: A Personal Approach, 1982, 2d edit., 1984, Test File for Psychology, 3d edit., 1988, Test Item File to Accompany Introduction to Psychology, 5th edit., 1989; editor: Test Item File to Accompany Introduction to Psychology, 6th edit., 1992; contbr. chapters to books. With USAR, 1964—70. Mem.: APA (life), Assn. for Psychol. Sci. (u. tchr.), Psi Chi (award 1988). Achievements include research in educational materials, methods of instruction and career opportunities for psychology majors. Home and Office: 209 Deveraux Pt Mc Cormick SC 29835 Personal E-mail: mzeller39@yahoo.com.

ZELNICK, RONALD STUART, surgeon; b. NYC, Dec. 6, 1958; BS, George Washington U., 1980; MD, Albany Med. Coll., 1984. Diplomate Am. Bd. Surgery, Am. Bd. Colon Rectal Surgery. Resident gen. surgery L.I. Jewish Hosp., New Hyde Park, N.Y., 1984-89; fellowship colon and rectal surgery Henry Ford Hosp., Detroit, 1989-90; pvt. practice Jupiter, Fla., 1991—. Fellow ACS, Am. Soc. Colon Rectal Surgeons; mem. Fla. Surg. Soc., Fla. Colon Rectal Surgery Soc. Office: Ste 105 210 Jupiter Lakes Blvd #3105 Jupiter FL 33458 Office Phone: 561-575-7875.

ZELTZER, LONNIE K., pediatrician, educator; b. Passaic, NJ, Oct. 4, 1944; m. Paul Zeltzer; 3 children. BA, Rutgers U., 1966; MD, U. Cin., 1970. Bd. cert. Am. Bd. Pediats., Nat. Bd. Med. Examiners; lic. physician, Tex., Calif. Intern pediat. UCLA, 1970—71; resident pediat. U. Ariz., 1971—72, chief resident, 1972—73; adolescent medicine fellow Children's Hosp. of LA, 1975—76; asst. prof. dept. pediat. U. So. Calif. Sch. Medicine, 1976—78; from asst. prof. to assoc. prof. dept. pediat. U. Tex. Health Sci. Ctr., San Antonio, 1978—86; assoc. prof. dept. pediat. U. So. Calif. Sch. Medicine, 1986—88; prof. pediat. Dept. Pediat. UCLA Sch. Medicine, 1988—. Med. dir. LA Job Corps, 1975-78; head divsn. adolescent medicine dept. pediats. U. Tex. Health Sci. Ctr., San Antonio, 1978-86; dir. behavioral sci. sect. divsn. hematology-oncology Children's Hosp. of L.A., 1986-88, dir. psychology fellowship and internship program; head divsn. child devel. and biobehavioral pediats. UCLA Sch. Medicine, 1988-81, dir. pediat. pain program dept. pediats., 1989—; assoc. dir. patients and survivors divsn. prevention and control rsch. br. UCLA Jonsson Comprehensive Cancer Ctr., 1996; Jour. of Pediats. vis. prof. dept. pediats. U. Iowa, 1982; con. in field. Mem. editl. bd.: Clin. Pediats., 1982-90, Pediats. Update, 1985-88, Jour. Pediat. Psychology, Topics in Pain Mgmt., 1990-96, others; outside reviewer: Jour. Adolescent Health Care, 1980-82, Health Psychology, 1985—, Pain, 1992—, Jour. Adolescent Health, 1992—, others; contbr. numerous articles to profl. jours. Mem. adv. bd. Comty. Guidance Ctr., San Antonio, 1980-82; mem. med. adv. bd. Vital Options, L.A., 1987-91; camp physician Ronald McDonald Camp Goodtimes, 1988; mem. med. adv. bd. Starbright Pediat. Network, 1993-96; med. advisor Cancervive, 1995-96 Recipient W.T. Grant Found. Faculty Scholars award, 1985-91, Rsch. Career Devel. award Nat. Cancer Inst., 1985-90; Health Professions scholar USPHS, 1966-70; also numerous rsch. grants. Fellow Am. Acad. Pediats., Soc. Clin. and Exptl. Hypnosis, Soc. for Clin. and Exptl. Hypnosis; mem. APA (sect. on clin. child psychology, sect. on pediat. psychology), Internat. Assn. for Study of Pain, Internat. Soc. Pediat. Oncology, Am. Pain Soc., Am. Pediat. Soc., Am. Soc. Clin. Hypnosis, Am. Soc. Clin. Oncology, Western Soc. for Pediat. Rsch., So. Soc. for Pediat. Rsch., Soc. for Adolescent Medicine, L.A. Pediat. Soc., Soc. for Rsch. in Adolescence, Soc. for Behavioral Medicine, Soc. for Pediat. Rsch., Soc. for Devel. and Behavioral Pediats., Ambulatory Pediat. Assn., San Antonio Pediat. Soc. Office: Mattel Children's Hosp at UCLA Pediat Pain Program 22-464 MDCC, 10833 Le Conte Ave Los Angeles CA 90095-1752 Office Phone: 310-825-0731. Office Fax: 310-794-2104. E-mail: lzeltzer@pediatrics.medsch.ucla.edu.

ZEMAN, HERBERT DAVID, biomedical engineer; b. NYC, Mar. 17, 1944; s. Mark Waldo and Adele (Cohen) Zemansky. AB magna cum laude, Oberlin Coll., 1965; MS, Stanford U., 1966, PhD, 1972. Fellow U. Muenster, Fed. Republic Germany, 1972-74; physicist SRI Internat., Menlo Park, Calif., 1974-76; rsch. assoc. Stanford U., Calif., 1976-78, sr. rsch. assoc. Calif., 1980-87; staff scientist Xerox Med. Systems, Palo Alto, Calif., 1978-80; med. physicist Nat. Synchrotron Light Source Brookhaven Nat. Labs., Upton, NY, 1987-90; assoc. prof. biomed. engring. and radiology U. Tenn., Memphis, 1990—2005; founder Luminetx Corp., Memphis, 2001, chief scientist, 2005—08. Contbr. articles to profl. jours. Chmn. Charleston Meadows Neighborhood Orgn., Palo Alto, 1977-84; founder Palo Alto Coalition for Equal Rights, 1981; steering com. mem. Palo Alto Civic League, 1983-84, Oberlin Lamda Alumni, 2007—; sec. AIDS/KS Found., Santa Clara County, 1983-84; bd. dirs. Nat. Stonewall Democrats, 2007—09; bd. dirs. NSD-PAC, 2009-10, Tenn. Equality Project, 2011-; second tenor Memphis Symphony Chorus, 1994-2004, Memphis Vocal Arts Ensemble, 2006—08, Memphis Men's Chorale, 2006—10, Rhodes MasterSingers, 2007—, Addms Ave. Camerata, 2009-10. Fellow NSF, Woodrow Wilson Found., Alexander von Humboldt Found. Mem. IEEE, Soc. Photo-Optical Instrument Engring., Am. Phys. Soc., Am. Assn. Physicists in Medicine, Optical Soc. Am.PFP Investment Club (sec. 1983-87), Phi Beta Kappa, Sigma Xi. Democrat. Jewish. Achievements include invention of the Vein-Viewer, 1995. Home and Office: 435 S Front St #401 Memphis TN 38103 Office Phone: 901-229-0508. Personal E-mail: herbzeman@gmail.com.

ZEMBLES, TRACY, pharmacist; b. Rockford, Ill., Oct. 12, 1976; PharmD, Drake U., 2000. Clin. pharmacist Truman Med. Ctr., 2000—02, St. Luke's Med. Ctr., 2002—05, Children's Hosp. Wis., 2005—. Bd. cert. pharmacotherapy specialist Bd. Pharmacy Specialties, 2006. Mem.: Am. Soc. Health Sys. Pharmacists. Avocations: reading, photography, exercise. Home: W173N4874 Crabapple Ct Menomonee Falls WI 53051 Personal E-mail: tzembles@chw.org.

ZEMLICKA, JIRI, medical educator, researcher; b. Prague, Czech Republic, July 31, 1933; arrived in U.S., 1968; s. Vojtech Zemlicka and Otilie Zemlickova; m. Helena Zvarova, Mar. 30, 1961; children: Helena, George. MS, Charles U., Prague, 1956, Rerum Naturarum Dr., 1966; PhD, Czech Acad. Scis., Prague, 1959. Rsch. scientist Czech Acad. Scis., Prague, 1959—69; vis. scientist Mich. Cancer Found., Detroit, 1968—69, rsch. scientist, 1969—83, mem., 1983—94, Karmanos Cancer Inst., Detroit, 1994—2009. Assoc. prof. Wayne State U., Detroit, 1971—85, prof., 1985—2009, emeritus prof., 2009—; cons. Microbiotix, Inc., Worcester, Mass., 2002, 2010—, Therapeutic Sys. Rsch. Lab., Inc., Ann Arbor, Mich., 2005—. Mem. editl. bd.: Nucleosides, Nucleotides & Nucleic Acids, 1982—2010, Antiviral Chemistry and Chemotherapy, 2000—; contbr. chapters to books, articles to profl. jours. Emeritus mem. Am. Chem. Soc. Grant, NIH, 1972—81, 1984—2009. Achievements include patents in field. Home: 2025 Common Warren MI 48092 Business E-Mail: ac6051@wayne.edu.

ZEMLYANAYA, ANNA, psychiatrist; b. Moscow Region, Apr. 14, 1972; MD, RMSU, 1994; PhD, Moscow Rsch. Inst. Psychiatry, 2006. Sr. scientist Moscow Rsch. Inst. Psychiatry, 2008—. Office: Poteshnaya 3 Moscow 107076 Russia Business E-Mail: a_zemlyanaya@mail.ru.

ZENDA, TAKAHIRO, gastroenterologist; b. Hakusan, Ishikawa, Japan, Oct. 17, 1961; s. Shoichi and Tokie Zenda; m. Keiko Emura; children: Takuto, Shirou. MD, Tsukuba U. Sch. Medicine, 1988. Cert. hepatologist Japan Soc. Hepatology, Tokyo, 2006. Gen. physician Kanazawa U. 2nd Dept. Internal Medicine, Ishikawa, 1988—94; divison chief gastroenterology Himi Mcpl. Hosp., Toyama, Japan, 1995—99; divsn. chief gastroenterology Kanazawa Social Ins. Hosp., 2001—06, Kinjyo Hosp., Kanazawa City, 2007—, Tsurugi Mpcl. Hosp., 2009—. Contbr. articles to profl. sci. jours. Fellow: Japan Gastroent. Endoscopy Soc., Japanese Soc. Gastroenterology, Japanese Soc. Internal Medicine. Avocations: mountain climbing, travel, reading. Home: Masuizumi 1-20-25 Kanazawa Ishikawa 921-8025 Japan Office: Tsurugi Mpcl Hosp 1 Tsurugi-Mito Machi Hakusan Ishikawa 920-2134 Japan Home Phone: 81-76-244-8150; Office Phone: 81762721250. Office Fax: 81762723144; Home Fax: 81-76-244-8150. Personal E-mail: zenzen@spacelan.ne.jp. Business E-Mail: t-zenda@tsurugihp.jp.

ZENDEJAS, GREGORIO HERNANDEZ, plastic surgeon, educator; b. Celaya, Guanajuato, Mexico, Dec. 29, 1961; MD, Leon (Mex.) Sch. Med., 1986. Diplomate Mexican Bd. Med. Examiners, Mexican Bd. Gen. Surgery, Mexican Bd. Plastic Surgery. Intern Leon (Mex.) Gen. Hosp., 1984—85; chief resident in gen. surgery Leon (Mex.) Med. Ctr., 1988—89; resident in plastic surgery Inst. for Plastic Surgery, Guadalajara, Mexico, 1989—92, asst. prof., 1992—94, chief. in dept. Microsurgery, 1994—96, assoc. prof., 1994—, chief in ednl. divsn., 1999—2000, chief in divsn. micorsurgery, 1999—. Dir. rsch. ctr. Inst. for Plastic Surgery, 1996, dir. postgrad. thesis, 97. Editor: Worldplast Jour., 1996—; contbr. articles to profl. jours. Recipient Best Paper and Ann. award, Sr. Resident Conf., 1992, Acknowledgement, Pres. of U.S. of Mex., 1992. Fellow: ACS, Internat. Soc. Aesthetic Plastic Surgery, Mexican Assn. Plastic Surgery. Roman Catholic. Achievements include invention of surgical techniques and device. Avocation: sports. Office: Plastic Surgery Ruben Dario 420 44680 Guadalajara Jalisco Mexico Office Fax: (33) 36154179.

ZENG, STEVE, insurance company executive; b. 1968; married; 3 children. MBA, 2006. Auditor, 1989—98; joined Health Ins. Plan of Greater NY (subs. EmblemHealth, Inc.), 1998, v.p., corp. devel., 2006—. Named one of 40 Under 40, Crain's NY Bus., 2007. Office: Health Insurance Plan of Greater New York 55 Water St New York NY 10041-8190 Office Phone: 646-447-5000. Office Fax: 646-447-3011. Business E-Mail: szeng@emblemhealth.com.

ZENG, WENBIN, medical educator, researcher; b. Hunan, China, Aug. 18, 1975; PhD, U. Muenster, Germany, 2004. Shenghua scholar Ctrl. South U., 2009—, prof., 2009—. Editor Anti-Cancer Agents Med. Chem., 2009—, Internat. Jour. Drug Devel., 2010—. Recipient New Century Excellent award. Avocations: reading, travel. Office: 172 Tongzipo Rd Changsha HuNan 410013 China Personal E-mail: wbzeng@hotmail.com.

ZENG, XIAORONG, medical association administrator; b. Mianyang, Sichuan, China, May 1, 1955; B, Luzhou Med. Coll., 1978. Dir., inst. cardiovasology Luzhou Med. Coll., 1998, v.p., 2001—. Adj. prof. Shantou U., 1997, Chengdu U. Info. Tech., 2010. Recipient Academic Tech. Leaders award, Govt. of Sichuan. Master: Profl. Com. Circulation Physiology Chinese Assn. Physiol. Scis. Avocations: calligraphy, music. Office: Zhongshan Rd Luzhou Sichuan 646000 China Office Fax: 86-830-3160619. Business E-Mail: zxr8818@vip.sina.com.

ZENG, ZHENG, physician; b. Yulin, China, June 29, 1964; MD, Peking U. Heath Sci. Ctr., PhD, 2000. Chief Peking U. First Hosp., 2004—. Grant, Nat. Cancer Inst., NIH, Rsch. grant, Nat. Nature Sci. Found. China. Mem.: Chinese Med. Assn., Beijing Med. Assn. (com. devel. sci. and tech., com. experts clin. pharmacy), Chinese Assn. Hepatology (com. drug-induced liver injury). Office: 8 Xishiku St Xicheng Dist Beijing 100034 China Business E-Mail: zeng@bjmu.edu.cn.

ZENN, MICHAEL ROBERT, plastic and reconstructive surgeon; b. NYC, Feb. 28, 1962; s. Renee Schwam; m. Susan Speer; children: Andrew, Erica. BA summa cum laude, U. Pa., 1984; MD, Cornell U., 1988. Diplomate Am. Bd. Gen. Surgery, 1994, Am. Bd. Plastic Surgery, 1998. Resident in gen. surgery NY Hosp. Cornell Med. Ctr., NYC, 1988—92, chief surgical resident, 1992—93; resident in plastic surgery Mass. Gen. Hosp., Boston, 1993-95; fellow in microsurgery Meml. Sloan-Kettering Cancer Ctr., NYC, 1995; asst. prof. plastic surgery U. N.C., Chapel Hill, 1996-2000, Duke Univ. Med. Ctr., Durham, NC, 2000—05, assoc. prof. plastic surgery, program dir. plastic surgery residency, 2005—. Contbr. articles to profl. jours. Named a Best Doctor for Women-Southeast Region, Ladies Home Jour., 2002, Best Doctor, Redbook mag., 2001; recipient NC Med. Soc. Tobacco Control award, 1999; named Best Cosmetic Surgeon in the Triangle, News and Observer, 1997. Fellow ACS (assoc.); mem. AMA, Am. Soc. Plastic Surgeons, Am. Soc. Reconstructive Microsurgery, World Soc. Reconstructive Microsurgery, Plastic Surgery Rsch. Coun., NC Med. Soc., NC Soc. Plastic and Reconstructive Surgeons (v.p., 2001-02, pres., 2002-03), Nathan A. Womack Surg. Soc., Alpha Omega Alpha Avocations: painting, golf. Office: Plastic Surgery 3358 Duke Univ Med Ctr Durham NC 27710 Office Fax: 919-684-4954. Business E-Mail: michael.zenn@duke.edu.

ZENTALL, THOMAS R., psychologist, educator; b. Bezier, Herault, France, Sept. 29, 1940; came to the US, 1942; s. Robert Sigmund and Elizabeth Aigner Zentall; m. Sydney Snider, Aug. 29, 1965 (div.); m. Melodie Rae, June 4, 1988; children: Gabriel Clay, Shannon Rae. BA, BSEE, Union Coll., 1963; PhD, U. Calif., Berkeley, 1969. Asst. prof. U. Pitts., 1969-75; prof. U. Ky., Lexington, 1975—. Editor: Social Learning, 1988, Animal Cognition, 1993, 2006, Stimulus Class Formation, 1996; assoc. editor Psychonomic Bull. and Rev., 1998-2002, Animal Learning & Behavior, 2002-08, Comparative Cognition, 2006. Fellow APA (exec. com. divsn. 6 1998-2001, pres. 2005-06, exec. com. divsn. 3 1999—2002, pres. 2005-06, exec. com. divsn. 25 2006-), Am. Psychol. Soc., Midwestern Psychol. Assn. (sec.-treas. 1998-2001, pres. 2002-03), Ea. Psychol. Assn. (bd. dirs. 2006—), Psychonomic Soc. (governing bd. 2001—, chair 2006-07), Comparative Cognition Soc. (pres. 2004-06). Office: Dept Psychology Univ Ky Lexington KY 40506-0044 Business E-Mail: zentall@uky.edu. *

ZENTY, THOMAS F., III, hospital administrator; BS in Health Planning and Adminstrn., Pa. State U.; MPA, NY U.; M in Health Administn., Xavier U., Cin.; completed exec. edn. program in competition & strategy and audit committees in the new era of governance, Harvard U., Mass. Career health systems adminstr., Ariz., NJ, Conn.; exec. v.p. clin. care services, COO Cedars-Sinai Health Sys., LA; CEO Univ. Hospitals, Cleve., 2003—. Mem. Sustain Cleve. 2019 Coun.; co-chmn. Cleve. Foodbank Harvest Hunger Campaign; bd. mem. Greater Cleve. Partnership, United Way Northeast Ohio, Urban League, BioEnterprise, Invest in Children, Cuyahoga CC Found., Ohio Bus. Roundtable. Recipient Nat. Healthcare award, B'nai B'rith Internat., 2010; named one of Power 100 Leaders in Northeast Ohio; named to Northeast Ohio Bus. Hall of Fame. Mem.: American Hosp. Assn. (bd. trustees), Beta Sigma Gamma Internat. Honor Soc. (hon.). Office: University Hospitals 11100 Euclid Ave Cleveland OH 44106 *

ZEQUI, STÊNIO DE CÁSSIO, medical educator; b. São Paulo, Brazil, 1967; Grad. in Medicine, ABC Found., 90; MD, Faculdade de Medicina do ABC, 1990; PhD, AC Camargo Fundação Antônio Prudente, 2008. Gen. surgery and urology resident, faculty medical scis. Santa Casa de São Paulo, 1991—95; prof. Hosp. AC Camargo-Fundação Antônio Prudente, 1995—. Recipient Prêmio Nylceo Marques de Castro, Faculdade de Madicina do ABC. Mem.: Sociedade Brasileira de Urologia, Societe Internationaller D'Urologie, Am. Urol. Assn. Avocations: jogging, history. Office: Rua Batataes 391 4o andar Rua Profe São Paulo 01423010 Brazil Office Fax: 551138877088. Personal E-mail: steniozequi@gmail.com.

ZERBE, KATHRYN JANE, psychiatrist; b. Harrisburg, Pa., Oct. 17, 1951; d. Grover Franklin and Ethel (Schreckengaust) Z. BS with BA equivalent cum laude, Duke U., Durham, NC, 1973; MD, Temple U.,

Phila., 1978. Diplomate Am. Bd. Psychiatry. Resident Karl Menninger Sch. Psychiatry, Topeka, 1982, dean, dir. edn. and rsch., 1992-97; staff psychiatrist Menninger Found., Topeka, 1982-2001; v.p. edn. and rsch. The Menninger Clinic, Topeka, 1993-97, prof., 1997-2001, Jack Aron chair in psychiat. edn., 1997-2001, apptd. tng. and supr. analyst, 1995—; prof. psychiatry, prof. ob-gyn. Oreg. Health Scis. Univ., Portland, 2001—, dir. outpatient clinic, 2003—08, vice chair for psychotherapy, 2003—08; tng. and supr. analyst Oreg. Psychoanalytic Inst., 2002—, dir., 2008—. Instr. numerous seminars and courses; mem. Ctr. Advanced Psychoanalytic Studies, Princeton, 2009—11. Author: (book) The Body Betrayed: Women, Eating Disorders and Treatment, 1993, Women's Mental Health in Primary Care, 1999, Eating Disorders for Ob-Gyns, 2007, Integrated Tretment of Eating Disorder, 2008, numerous articles profl. rsch. papers; editor: Womens Mental Health: Primary Care Clinics, 2001; assoc. editor:, 1996—98; editor: Bull. of Menninger Clinic, 1998;; mem. editl. bd.: Eating Disorders Rev., Eating Disorders: The Jour. of Treatment and Prevention Postgrad. Medicine, 2001; editor (sect.): Current Women's Health; contbr. book revs. and articles to profl. jours. Probation officer Juvenile divsn. Dauphin County, Pa., 1973. Recipient Ann. Laughlin Merit award The Nat. Psychiat. Endowment Fund, 1982, Outstanding Paper of Profl. Programs award The Menninger Found. Alumni Assn., 1982, Writing award Topeka Inst. for Psychoanalysis, 1985, 90, Mentorship award, 1997, Women Helping Women award, 1995, Tchr. of Yr. award Psychiatry Residents, 1988, 96, 99, 03, 05, 06, 08, 09; named one of Outstanding Young Women in Am., 1986, 88, Portland's Top Drs., 2007, 2011, Best Drs. in America, 2007-11; Seeley fellow, 1979-82; Hilde Bruch lectureship, 1996. Fellow Am. Psychiat. Assn. (Alexandra Symonds award 2005, Edith Sabshin award 2007); mem. AMA, APA, Am. Coll. Psychiatrists, Am. Med. Women's Assn., Oreg. Med. Assn., Ctr. Advanced Psychoanalytic Studies, Am. Coll. Psychoanalyst, Oreg. Psychiat. Assn., Sigma Xi, Alpha Omega Alpha. Avocations: writing, reading, art history, travel. Office: 4800 SW Macadam Ave Portland OR 97239 Office Phone: 503-295-9909. Personal E-mail: kzbone@comcast.net. Business E-Mail: zerbek@ohsu.edu.

ZERBIB, ERIC, nuclear medicine physician; b. Paris, Feb. 7, 1963; MS, U. Paris 13, 1994; Nuclear Medicine Specialist, Cochin U., Paris, 1992; Med. Statis. Cert., Paris, 1993. Asst. Univ. Hosps. AP/HP, Paris, 1992-95; hosp. physician Marie Lannelongue Medecine Nucleaire, Le Plessis Robinson, France, 1995—. Med. reporter Impact Medecin, Paris, 1988-92; med. dir. JBH Santé, Paris, 1996-97. Author: Hepatic and Biliary Tract Scintigraphies, 1998, Radio isotpic investigation for cardiology (French), Eng Medico-dur, 2001; editor in chief: Octreographies, 1997; editor in chief Radio-isotropic investigations for digestive pathology (in French, Ency. Medico-Chirurgicale, 1998, 2003, Kryptographics, 2002, mem. editor bd. PCM, 1992—95; coord.: Nuclear Medicine and Gastroeuterology, 2000; coord. Isotopes, 2001; contbr. articles to profl. jours. Mem. French Soc. Biophysics and Nuclear Medicine, European Assn. Nuclear Medicine, Assn. Physicians Paris (pres. 2004—), Nuc. Medicine Physicians Assn., Parisian Assn. Nuclear Medicine (pres. 2004—), French Nuc. Medicine Syndicate (v.p. 2009-). Office: Ctre Chir Val d Or 14 rue Pasteur 92210 Saint Cloud France

ZERBIN-RUEDIN, EDITH, retired psychiatric geneticist, educator; b. Munich, May 2, 1921; d. Ernst and Edith (Senger) Ruedin; m. Adolf Zerbin, May 30, 1956. Interpreter, Translator Grade B, Mcpl. Lang. Sch., Munich, 1946; Translator I and II, Munich Translator Sem., 1947; MD magna cum laude, Ludwig-Maximilian U., Munich, 1950. Med. diplomate. Clin. asst. Psychiat. U. Clinic, Munich, 1950-51; rsch. worker Max-Planck-Inst. Psychiatrie, Munich, 1947-58, head rsch. group psychiat. genetics, 1958-86; lectr. med. genetics Bavarian Ministry Edn. and Culture, Munich, 1972-86, extraordinary prof. med. genetics, 1978—. Lectr. nat. and internat. congresses, symposia and seminaries, Austria, Denmark, France, Germany, Italy, Japan, Mexico, Norway, Switzerland, U.S.A. Co-editor Archiv für Psychiatrie und Nervenkrankheiten, 1975-86, European Archives of Psychiatry and Neurol. Scis., 1986-88, Neuropsychobiology, 1975-91; translator 4 med. books and book chpts.; author; Nature and Nurture in the Origin of Psychiatric Disturbances, Schizophrenia; contbr. articles to profl. jours., chpts. to books. Mem. Am. Soc. Human Genetics, Am. Behavior Genetics Assn., Soc. for Study Social Biology. Avocations: theater visits, study of history, skiing, mountain climbing, gardening. Home: Besselstr. 1 A 81679 Munich Germany Home Phone: 49-089-989910.

ZEREN, KARL JOSEPH, dentist, educator; children: Sarah, Lindsey, Kurt. BS in Psychology, U. Md., College Park, 1969; DDS, U. Md., Balt., 1975. Diplomate Am. Bd. Periodontology, 1986. Attending in periodontics Johns Hopkins Med. Instn., Balt., 1980—2008. Asst. clin. prof. U. Md., Sch. Dentistry, Balt., 1987—. Contbr. scientific papers. Lay chaliscist Trinity Episcopal Ch., Towson, Md., 2005—07. Lt. U.S. Navy, 1976—77. Named one of, Top Dentists in the Am., 2005. Mem.: Am. Coll. Dentists, Internat. Coll. Dentists, Md. Soc. Periodontists (pres. 1988—90), Am. Acad. Periodontology. Independent-Republican. Episcopalian. Achievements include research in human allograft block gfafting in dento-alveolar ridge augmentation. Avocations: golf, skiing, travel. Office: Karl J Zeren DDS LLC 9515 Deereco Rd Ste 308 Timonium MD 21093 E-mail: kjzeren@verizon.net.

ZERHOUNI, ELIAS ADAM, pharmaceutical executive, radiologist; b. Nedroma, Algeria, Apr. 12, 1951; arrived in US, 1975; s. Mohamed and Yamna (Raahmouni) Zerhouni; m. Nadia Azza, Oct. 25, 1975; children: Djillali, Yasmin, Adam. MD, U. Algiers, 1975. Diplomate American Bd. Radiology. Resident diagnostic radiology John Hopkins U. Sch. Medicine, Balt., 1974—75, chief resident diagnostic radiology, 1975—78, instr., 1978—79, asst. prof. radiology, 1979—81, assoc. prof. radiology, 1985—92, Martin Donner prof. radiology, 1992, prof. biomedical engring., 1995, chmn. Russell H. Morgan dept. radiology & radiol. sci., 1996, exec. vice dean, vice dean clin. affairs, 1996—99, vice dean rsch., 1999—2000, exec. vice dean, 2000—02, sr. adv., prof. radiology & biomedical engring., 2009—; asst. dir. body CT Johns Hopkins Hosp., Balt., 1978—81, radiologist-in-chief, 1996—2002; asst. prof. radiology Eastern Va. Med. Sch., Norfolk, Va., 1981—83, assoc. prof. radiology, 1983—85; vice chmn., dir. body imaging De Paul Hosp., Norfolk, Va., 1982—85; dir. Advanced Med. Imaging Inst., Norfolk, Va., 1991—92, NIH, Bethesda, Md., 2002—08; sr. fellow for global health The Bill & Melinda Gates Found., Seattle, 2009—; founder, pres. Zerhouni Group, LLC, Columbia, Md., 2010—; pres. global rsch & devel. Sanofi-Aventis SA, Paris, 2011—, mem. exec. & mgmt. com., 2011—. Mem. bd. sci. advisors Nat. Cancer Inst., 1998—2002; bd. dirs. Lasker Found., Research!America; bd. trustees Mayo Clinic; advisor to CEO Sanofi-Aventis; chmn. Md. Econ. Devel. Commn., 2009—. Assoc. editor Jour. Surg. & Radiol. Anatomy, 1980—86, Radiology, 1983—90, Jour. Thoracic Imaging, 1990—97; chief scientific advisor Science-Translational Medicine; contbr. articles to profl. jours. Bd. trustees King Abdullah U. Sci. & Tech. (KAUST), 2009—. Recipient Lauterbur award for MRI rsch., 1989, 1993, Hounsfield award for CT imaging, 1991, Legion of Honor medal, French Nat. Order, 2008; named Hon. Dr. Emeritus, U. Algiers, 2005. Mem.: AAAS, French Acad. Medicine, Inst. Medicine, Soc. Cardiovasc. Magnetic Resonance, North American Soc. Cardiac Imaging, Balt. City Med. Soc., American Coll. Radiology, American Heart Assn., Internat. Soc. Magnetic Resonance in Medicine (bd. trustees 1995—98), Assn. Univ. Radiologists, Soc. Computed Body Tomography, Soc. Thoracic Radiology (founding mem.), Radiol. Soc. of North America, American Roentgen Ray Soc. Achievements include research in magnetic resonance imaging (MRI); development of imaging methods used for diagnosing cancer and cardiovascular disease; discovery of magnetic tagging, a non-invasive method of using MRI to track the motions of a heart in three dimensions; design of an imaging technique called computed tomographic (CT) densitometry that helps discriminate between non-cancerous and cancerous nodules in the lung; patents in field. Avocations: swimming, windsurfing, music. Office: Sanofi-Aventis SA 174 Avenue de France 75013 Paris France also: Zerhouni Group, LLC Ste 710 10500 Little Patuxent Parkway Columbia MD 21044 also: Johns Hopkins U 601 N Caroline St Baltimore MD 21287-0006 Office Phone: 443-518-7200. Office Fax: 443-430-0121. E-mail: Elias.Zerhouni@zerhounigroup.com. *

ZERNICKA-GOETZ, MAGDALENA, biologist; b. Warsaw, Aug. 30, 1963; d. Boguslaw Zernicki and Danuta Zernicka; m. David Moore Glover, Apr. 1, 2000; children: Natasha, Simon. MSc, U.Warsaw, 1988, PhD, 1993. EMBO rsch. fellow U. Cambridge, England, 1995—97; sr. rsch. fellow Lister Inst., Cambridge, 1997—2002; Stanley Elmore sr. rsch. fellow U. Cambridge, 1997—2002, prof. stem cell & devel. biology; sr. rsch. fellow The Wellcome Trust/Cancer Rsch. UK Gurdon Inst., Cambridge, 2002—. Adv. bd. Faculty Of 1000, 2001—. Contbr. articles to profl. jours. Mem.: European Molecular Biology Orgn. (Young Investigator award 2001—04). Achievements include patent for RNA interference in mammalian cells; discovery of importance of early polarity in mammalian embryos. Avocations: painting, creative arts, tennis. Office: Wellcome Trust Cancer Rsch UK Gurdon Inst Tennis Court Rd Cambridge CB2 1QN England Office Fax: 00 44 1223 334089. Business E-Mail: mzg@mole.bio.cam.ac.uk.

ZERVAS, NICHOLAS THEMISTOCLES, neurosurgeon; b. Lynn, Mass., Mar. 9, 1929; s. Themistocles and Demetra P. (Stasinopoulos) Z.; m. Thalia Poleway, Feb. 15, 1959; children: T. Nicholas, Christopher Louis, Rhea. AB, Harvard U., 1950; MD, U. Chgo., 1954. Intern N.Y. Hosp., 1955; resident in neurology Montreal Neurol. Inst., 1956; resident in neurosurgery Mass. Gen. Hosp., Boston, 1958-62; fellow in stereotaxic cerebral surgery U. Paris, 1960 61; asst. attending surgeon, asso. neurosurgery Jefferson Med. Coll., Phila., 1962-67; asso. prof. surgery Harvard U., 1971-77; also chief neurosurg. service Beth Israel Hosp., Boston, 1967-77; prof. surgery Harvard U., 1977-200; also chief neurosurg. service Mass. Gen. Hosp., 1977-2000; Higgins prof. neurosurgery Harvard U., 1986-2000. Contbr. numerous articles to sci. jours. Chmn. Mass. Coun. Arts and Humanities, 1983-91; trustee Boston Symphony Orch., 1990—, vice chmn., 1993—, pres., 1994-2002; bd. dirs. Medical Edn. South African Blacks, 2004-. Capt. M.C. AUS, 1956-58, 87-2002. Fellow Am. Acad. Arts and Scis.; mem. Am. Acad. Neurol. Surgery (pres. 1990-91), Am. Assn. Neurol. Surgeons, Soc. Neurol. Surgeons, Am. Neurol. Assn., Am. Bd. Neurol. Surgery (chmn. 1990-91), Inst. Medicine Nat. Acad. Scis., Sigma Xi. Home: 100 Canton Ave Milton MA 02186-3507 Business E-Mail: nzervas@partners.org.

ZERVOUDIS, STEPHANE, surgeon, gynecologist; b. Toulouse, France, Oct. 14, 1958; s. Nicolas Zervoudis and Jacqueline Martin; m. Anastasia Kyriazopoulou, Feb. 10, 2001; 1 child, Zervoudis Alexia. MD, Toulouse Faculty Medicine, 1987. Assoc. prof. ob-gyn. Faculty Medicine, Bucarest, 2000—. Vis. prof. ob-gyn. Faculty Medicine, Ioannina, Greece, 2002—; co-dir. breast dept. Lito Hosp., Athens, 1996—; pres. Mobile U. Mastology, Ioannina, 2002—. Co-author: Quality in Mastology, 2001, Radiobiology, 2003. Mem.: European Soc. Mastology, Greek Soc. Mastology, Greek Assn. Laser Therapy, Romanian Soc. Mastology, European Union Ob-gyn. Avocations: tennis, classical music, history, archaeology, astronomy. Office: Metaxa St 16674 Glyfada Greece Home: Vasileos Pailu 2-4 166 73 Voula Greece Office Phone: 30 6944308777. Business E-Mail: szervoud@otenet.gr.

ZETIN, MARK I., psychiatrist; b. Seattle, June 19, 1948; m. Lynda Bjornson PhD, Pomona Coll., 1970; MS, Stanford U., 1971; MD, U. Calif., Irvine, 1975. Diplomate Am. Bd. Psychiatry & Neurology. Clin. prof. psychiatry U. Calif., Irvine, 1979-94; pvt. practive psychiatry Garden Grove, Calif., 1994—; adj. prof. psychology Chapman U., 2009—. Author: (book) Challenging Depression, Norton, 2010. Fellow: APA (disting.). Office: PO Box 879 Orange CA 92856-6879 Office Phone: 714-971-8103. Personal E-mail: mzetinmd@pacbell.net.

ZETTERMAN, ROWEN KENT, gastroenterologist, hepatologist, dean; b. York, Nebr., July 30, 1944; s. Verlie L. and Maurine E. Z.; m. Emily Joan Clark, June 4, 1966; children: David, Justin, Corey. BA, Nebr. Wesleyan U., 1966; MD, U. Nebr., 1969. Diplomate Am. Bd. Internal Medicine, Am. Bd. Gastroenterology. Intern U. Nebr. Med. Ctr., Omaha, 1969-70, resident, 1970-71, resident gastroenterology, 1971-72, gastroenterologist, 1976—, sect. chief digestive diseases, 1984-91, vice chair internal medicine, 1996; hepatology fellow NJ Med. Sch., Newark, 1972-74; gastroenterologist Walter Reed Army Med. Ctr., Washington, 1974-76; chief medicine dept. Omaha VA Med. Ctr., 1998—2002; chief of staff for vet. affairs Nebr.-Western Iowa Health Care Sys., 2002—09; dean Creighton U. Sch. Medicine, 2009—. Faculty mem. Dept. Internal Medicine Creighton U., 1977, clin. prof. internal medicine. Editor Digestive Diseases, 1981-92, Am. Jour. Gastroenterology, 1991-97; contbr. 110 articles to med. jours. Troop chmn. Boy Scouts Am., 1980-90; active 1st United Meth. Ch., Omaha, 1976—. Fellow ACP (bd. govs. 1992-96, 96-97, chair-elect bd. govs. 1995-96, regent 1997—), Am. Coll. Gastroenterology (gov. 1990-92, v.p. 1998-99, Berk/Fise Clinical Achievement Award, 2008). Office: Creighton U Sch Medicine 2500 California Plaza Omaha NE 68178 Office Fax: 402-280-2600. Business E-Mail: rze63323@creighton.edu. *

ZEUTHEN, JESPER, biologist, researcher, venture capitalist, consultant; b. Copenhagen, Apr. 27, 1947; s. Erik and Elisabeth Zeuthen; m. Natalia I. Misuno. MSc, U. Copenhagen, 1971, DSc, 1984. Rsch. fellow Karolinska Inst., Sweden, 1972-74; assoc. prof. U. Aarhus, Denmark, 1974-82; mem. Basel Inst. Immunology, Switzerland, 1980-81; head dept. Novo Industri A/S, Denmark, 1982-83, rsch. dir., 1983-88; head of dept. Danish Cancer Soc., 1988-2000; mng. dir. BI Technology, Inc., BankInvest Group, Copenhagen, 2000—09. Cons. BankInvest Biotech, Copenhagen, 1989-2000; chmn. Fibiger Inst., Denmark, 1989-93, Genmab A/S, Copenhagen, 1999-2003, 06, Pantheco A/S, 2002-03, Santaris Pharma A/S, 2003-06, Borean Pharma A/S, 2004-07, LiPlasome Pharma A/S, 2008-09, Dandrit Biotech A/S, 2009-10; adj. prof. U. Copenhagen, 1987-92; sec. Com. on Basic Cancer Rsch. of Danish Rsch. Coun., Copenhagen, 1980-82; mem. biotech. sect. Swedish Tech. Rsch. Coun., 1996-98; Nordic guest prof. Karolinska Inst., Sweden, 1997-2000; adv. bd. BankInvest Biomed. Devel., 1998-2000; bd.dirs. Nereus Pharmaceuticals, San Diego, 2006-09; bd. dirs. Topo Target A/S, Copenhagen, 2006-09; vice chmn. Biotech Rsch. & Innovation Ctr., U. Copenhagen, 2005—09. Author: Epstein-Barr Virus, 1984; editor: Gene Expression, 1978, T-Cell Hybridomas, 1982. Recipient Cancer Rsch. prize Boel Found., Copenhagen, 1981, Internat. prize Found. E. Nuti, Rome, 1992. Mem. Danish Biol. Soc. (sec. 1989-92), Danish Soc. for Cancer Rsch. (treas. 1989-92, Hon. Cancer Rsch. prize 1996), Danish Soc. Immunology (treas. 1995-98), Scandinavian Soc. Immunology (pres. 1998-2001), Royal Physiographic Soc. (Lund, Sweden). Achievements include patents in field. Office Phone: 45-42757900. Personal E-mail: jzeuthen@hotmail.com.

ZEWAIL, AHMED HASSAN, physics and chemistry professor; b. Damanhour, Egypt, Feb. 26, 1946; arrived in U.S., 1969, naturalized, 1982; s. Hassan A. Zewail and Rawhia Dar; m. Dema Zewail, children: Maha, Amani, Nabeel, Hani. BS, Alexandria U., Egypt, 1967, MS, 1969; PhD, U. Pa., 1974; MA (hon.), Oxford U., 1991; DSc (hon.), Am. U., Cairo, 1993, U. Lausanne, 1997, U. New Brunswick, 2000, Jadavpur U., 2001, Heriot-Watt U., 2002, Trinity Coll., U. Dublin, 2004, Mansoura U., 2007, U. Malaya, 2007, U. Tech. Malaysia, 2007, U. Jordan, 2009. Tchg. asst. U. Pa., Phila., 1969—70; IBM fellow U. Calif., Berkeley, 1974—76; asst. prof. chem. physics Calif. Inst. Tech., Pasadena, 1976—78, assoc. prof., 1978—82, prof., 1982—89, Linus Pauling prof. chem. physics, 1990—94, Linus Pauling prof. chemistry, prof. physics, 1995—, dir. NSF Lab. Molecular Scis., 1996—2007, dir. Phys. Biology Ctr. Ultrafast Sci. & Tech., 2005—. Cons. Xerox Corp., Webster, NY, 1977—80, ARCO Solar, Inc., Calif., 1978—81; mem. Pres.'s Coun. of Advisors on Sci. and Tech. (PCAST), 2009—. Editor: Laser Chemistry, 1980—85, Jour. Phys. Chemistry, 1985—90, Chem. Physics Letters, 1991—, International Series Monographs on Chemistry, 1992—, Advances in Laser Spectroscopy, 1977—, 1978—, Photochemistry and Photobiology, 1983—, Ultrafast Phenomena, 1990—, 1993—, 1994—, The Chemical Bond: Structure and Dynamics, 1992, Femtochemistry-Ultrafst Dynamics of the Chemical Bond, 1994; contbr. numerous articles to sci. jours. Recipient Tchr.-Scholar award, Dreyfus Found., 1979—85, Sr. US Scientist award, Alexander von Humboldt Found., 1983, King Faisal Internat. prize in sci., 1989, NASA award, 1991, Nobel Laureate Signature award, 1992, U. Qatar medal, 1993, Wolf prize in chemistry, Wolf Found., Israel, 1993, Order of Merit first class, Egypt, 1995, Coll. de France medal, Leonardo Da Vinci award of excellence, France, 1995, J.G. Kirwood medal, Yale U., 1996, Beijing U. medal, 1996, Robert A. Welch award in chemistry, 1997, Pitts. Spectroscopy award, 1997, Benjamin Franklin medal, 1999, Paul Karrer Gold medal, Zurich, 1999, Roentgen prize, Germany, 1999, E.O. Lawrence award, US Govt., 1999, Merski award, U. Nebr., 1999, Nobel prize in chemistry, 1999, Order of Zayed, United Arab Emirates, 2000, Order of Cedar, Lebanon, 2000, Order of ISESCO 1st class, Saudi Arabia, 2000, Order of merit, Tunisia, 2000, Albert Einstein World award of sci., 2006; fellow John Simon Guggenheim Meml. Found., 1987. Mem.: NAS (Chem. Scis. award 1996), AAAS, Third World Acad. Scis., European Acad. Arts, Scis. & Humanities, Royal Danish Acad. Scis. & Letters, Pontifical Acad. Sci., Am. Phys. Soc. (Herbert P. Broida prize 1995), Am. Philos. Soc., Am. Chem. Soc. (Buck-Whitney medal 1985, Harrison-Howe award 1989, Hoechst prize 1990, Peter Debye award 1997, E.B. Wilson award 1997, Linus Pauling medal 1997, William H. Nichols award 1998, Richard C. Tolman medal 1998), Am. Acad. Arts & Scis., Sigma Xi (Earle K. Plyler prize 1993). Office: Arthur Amos Noyes Lab Chem Physics Calif Inst Tech MC 127 72 1200 E California Blvd Pasadena CA 91125 Business E-Mail: zewail@caltech.edu. *

ZGLICZYNSKI, STEFAN, endocrinologist, medical educator; b. Plock, Poland, Jan. 10, 1935; s. Stanslaw and Maria (Goscicka) Z.; m. Barbara Bojanowska, July 18, 1956; children: Wojciech, Joanna, Piotr, Stefan. MD, Med. Acad. Warsaw, Poland, 1957. Diplomate in internal medicine and endocrinology. Fellow in internal medicine and gen. practice Med. Acad. Warsaw, 1957-60; prof. asst., sr. asst. dept. internal medicine Med. Ctr. Postgrad. Edn., Warsaw, 1960-67, adj., 1967-74, assoc. prof. dept. endocrinology, 1974-80, prof. medicine, dir. dept. endocrinology, 1980—2005. Editor-in-chief Polish Jour. Endocrinology, 2002—05, Antyaging, 2003—05. Contbr. numerous articles to Jour. Clin. Endocrinology and Metabolism, Hormone and Metabolic Rsch., Clin. and Exptl. Hypertension, others. Mem. NY Acad. Sci., Internat. Endocrine Soc., European Endocrine Soc., European Neuroendocrine Assn., N.Am. Menopause Soc., Internat. Menopause Soc., Polish Soc. Endocrinology (pres. 2002-05), Nat. Found. Endocrinology (founder), Polish Menopause and Andropause Soc. (founder), European Menopause and Andropause Soc., Internat.

Soc. for Study of Aging Male, Polish Soc. Preventive and Antiaging Medicine (founder, pres. 2007). Home: 10 Ciolkowskiego 01-480 Warsaw Poland Office: Med Ctr Postgrad Edn Dept Endocrinology 01-809 Warsaw Poland Home Phone: 48 22 666 7090; Office Phone: 48 22 834 3131. Business E-Mail: klinendo@cmkp.edu.pl.

ZGODA, JAMES CHRISTOPHER, veterinarian; b. Buffalo, July 24, 1958; BA, U. Pa., 1980; MS, Rutgers U., 1981; DVM, Cornell Coll. Vet. Medicine, 1985. Assoc. veterinarian Westfield Vet. Group, 1985—91, Morristown Animal Hosp., 1991—95; owner, hosp. dir. Otterkill Animal Hosp., 1995—. Asst. scoutmaster Boy Scouts America; mng. dir. Classic Choral Soc.; veterinarian Humane Soc. Named Veterinarian of Yr., Hartz Co. Mem.: AAHA, AVMA, Soc. Theriogenology, HVVMS, NYSVMS. Office: 258 Maybrook Rd Campbell Hall NY 10916 Office Fax: 845-427-2344. Business E-Mail: doctors@otterkill.com.

ZHANG, AMY YANYUN, cancer and health services researcher; arrived in U.S., 1989; d. Xiangnan Zhang and Yusheng Chen. BA, Peking U., Beijing, 1982; MS, Pa. State U., 1992, PhD, 1995. Agy. for Health Care Policy Rsch. NIMH postdoctoral fellow Sch. Pub. Health, U. Calif., Berkeley, 1996—98; sr. rsch. assoc. Case Western Res. U. Med. Sch., Cleve., 1999—2000, asst. prof. medicine, 2001—03, asst. prof. nursing, 2004—09, assoc. prof. nursing, 2009—. Translator: The Psychology of Emotion, 1986, The Interpretation of Dreams, 1987; contbr. articles to profl. jours. Grantee, Am. Cancer Soc., NIH, Nat. Cancer Inst. Office: Case Western Res Univ Sch Nursing 10900 Euclid Ave Cleveland OH 44106-4904 Business E-Mail: amy.zhang@case.edu.

ZHANG, CHENGGANG, nuclear medicine physician, educator; b. Jinan, Shandong, China, Nov. 16, 1936; s. Jingjiang and Yanfang (Wang) Zhang; m. Huimin Liang, Aug. 20, 1960; children: Weina, Tong, Jin. MD, Shanxi Med. Coll., Taiyuan, China, 1959. Assoc. prof. Shanxi Med. U., Shanxi Province, China, 1986—93, prof. Taiyuan, China, 1993—. Cons. prof. No. 3 Hosp. Shanxi Med. U., Taiyuan, 1997—. Editor: (monograph) Practical Nuclear Medicine, 1984, Radionuclide Therapy of Thyroid Diseases, 2003, Clinical Nuclear Medicine, 1995, (book) Question and Answers of Nuclear Medicine, 1984, Nuclear Medicine Procedure Manual of Shanxi Province, 2004, Genitourinary Nuclear Medicine, 2006; author: The Quality Control and Reference Procedure of SPECT and Gamma Camera, 2010; contbr. articles to profl. jours. Recipient Ministerial Sci. and Tech. Progress prize, 1979, 1980, 1984, 1999, 2010. Mem.: Chinese Med. Soc. (mem. nuc. medicine specialist com. Shanxi br. 1964—2005), Soc. Chinese Med. Imaging (coun. mem. 2003—05), Soc. of Nuc. Medicine. Avocations: travel, classical music. Home: 59 Xin Jian South Rd Shanxi Province Taiyuan 030001 China Office: PO Box 155 No 1 Hospital Shanxi Med Univ 85 Jie Fang South Rd Shanxi Province Taiyuan 030001 China Office Phone: 86 351 6134282. Office Fax: 86-351-6134282. Personal E-mail: zcg1936@163.com.

ZHANG, DA, medical educator; b. China, May 27, 1963; MD, Shandong Med. U., 1985; MS, Chinese Acad. Med. Sci., 1990. Assoc. prof. U. Kans. Med. Ctr., 2005—. Fellow: Coll. Am. Pathologists. Office: 3901 Rainbow Blvd MS3045 Kansas City KS 66160 Business E-Mail: dzhang@kumc.edu.

ZHANG, DEPING, physician, director; b. Chiina, June 6, 1962; MD, Sun-Yatsun U. Med. Sci., 1990. Dir. Nanjing Drum Tower Hosp., Nanjing U., 1998. Mem.: CMA. Office: 321 Zhogshan Rd Nanjing Jiangsu 210008 China Office Fax: 0086-25-83308069. Business E-Mail: dpzhang207@yahoo.com.cn.

ZHANG, HAIZHOU, physician; b. Binhai, Jiangsu, China, July 3, 1977; D, Shandong U., 2005. Assoc. chief physician Provincial Hosp. Affiliated Shandong U., 2005—. Office: 324 Jingwu Rd Jinan Shandong 250021 China Business E-Mail: zhz_doctor@163.com.

ZHANG, JAMES XUEJIE, healthcare educator; s. Wudong Zhang and Xinde Huang; m. Cindy Zhang. BA, Fudan U., Shanghai, 1988; PhD, Northern Ill. U., DeKalb, 1999. Assoc. prof. Chinese U. of Hong Kong, 2001—03; dir. health econometrics U. Chgo., 2003—06, rsch. assoc., asst. prof., 2006—. Contbr. articles to profl. jours. Grantee, NIH, 1998—99, 2000—03, 2001—05. Mem.: Internat. Health Econs. Assn. (sci. com. 2006—), Acad. Health (Paper of Yr. Award com. 2007—, interest group adv. bd. 2006—). Office: U Chgo 5841 S Maryland Ave MC 2007 Chicago IL 60521 Office Fax: 773-834-2238. Personal E-mail: ktmg_chicago@yahoo.com.

ZHANG, JIANBIN, medical educator; b. JiangXi, China, Feb. 6, 1975; D, ChongQing Med. U., 2010. Prof. First Hosp. Nanchang City, 2007—. Office: 128 XiangShan Rd NanChang JiangXi 330008 China Personal E-mail: zxg0233@126.com.

ZHANG, JING, research scientist; b. China, Nov. 5, 1975; PhD, Nat. U. Singapore, 2009. Scientist I Inst. Infocomm Rsch., 2009—. Mem.: IEEE, SSAGSG, PREMIA. Home: Clementi West St 2 Singapore 120729 Singapore Business E-Mail: jzhang@i2r.a-star.edu.sg.

ZHANG, JINSONG, radiologist, educator; b. Xi'an, Shaanxi, China, Apr. 27, 1970; MD, Fourth Mil. Med. U., 2005. Assoc. prof. dept. radiology Xijing Hosp., Xi'an, 2005—. Vice dir. dept radiology, 2010—. Recipient Third prize, China, 2002, Second prize, 2008, First prize, Shaanxi, China, 2003. Mem.: Chinese Med. Assn. Office: Xijing Hosp Dept Radiology Xi'an Shaanxi 710032 China Business E-Mail: zhangjs@tom.com.

ZHANG, JOHN J., obstetrician, gynecologist, reproductive endocrinologist; b. Oct. 16, 1961; MD, Zhejiang U. Sch. Medicine, China, 1984; MA, Birmingham U., Eng., 1985; PhD in Embryology, Cambridge U., Eng., 1991. Diplomate American Bd. Obstetrics & Gynecology. Resident dept. ob-gyn. NYU Sch. Medicine, fellow divsn. reproductive endocrinology & infertility, 2001; founder, fertility physician New Hope Fertility Ctr., NYC, 2004—. Achievements include research in he biology of mammalian reproduction, human embryology and In-Vitro Fertilization (IVF). Office: New Hope Fertility Center 784 Park Ave. New York NY 10021 also: New Hope Fertility Center 4 Columbus Cir New York NY 10019 *

ZHANG, JUN, pathologist, researcher; b. Shijiazhuang, China, Mar. 11, 1937; came to U.S., 1987; became citizen, 1999; s. Jing-Chen and Jing-Fang (Liang) Z.; m. Da-Ai-Liu Zhang, Sept. 21, 1972; children: Hua, Paul P. Chang. MD, Beijing Med. U., 1961, MS in Med. Scis., 1964. Asst. Beijing Med. U., 1964-65; assoc. prof. Xinjiang Med. Coll., Urumqi, China, 1985-87; sr. staff fellow Ctr. for Drug Evaluation & Rsch. FDA, Laurel, Md., 1988-2000, pharmacologist, 2000—. Coun. mem. Xinjiang subcom., Chinese Electron Microscope, Urumqi, China, 1985-87; mem. editl. bd. Chinese Jour. Pathology, Beijing, China, 1986-87. Author: Recent Development of Electron Microscopy, 1985. Recipient Rsch. award Xinjiang Sci. and Tech. Coun., 1984-88, FDA award, 1997-2000, 2003, 06, 07; named Outstanding Scientist Chinese Nat. Sci. and Tech. Com., Beijing, 1986. Achievements include research in biomarkers for drug-induced cardiovascular and renal injury in animal experiments. Office: Divsn Drug Safety Rsch FDA (HFD-910) 10903 New Hampshire Ave Silver Spring MD 20993 Office Phone: 301-796-0084. Business E-Mail: jun.zhang@fda.hhs.gov.

ZHANG, LEI, thoracic surgeon; b. Yichang, Hubei, China, July 28, 1977; MD, Ctrl. South U., 2000, PhD, 2007. Surgeon, dept. thoracic surgery Tianjin Cancer Instn. and Hosp., 2007—. Recipient New Century Talents award, Tianjin Cancer Instn. and Hosp.; fellowship, Meml. U. Newfoundland. Office: Huanhuxi Rd Tianjin Cancer Hosp Tianjin 300060 China Personal E-mail: chinaray728@gmail.com.

ZHANG, LILI, medical educator; b. Harbin, Apr. 27, 1973; MD, Harbin Med. U., 2003. Assoc. prof. 4th Affiliated Hosp., 2003—. Office: Yiyuan Harbin Heilongjiang 150001 China E-mail: drzhanglili@163.com.

ZHANG, WENJIAN, dental educator; b. China, July 13, 1971; DDS, Xian Jiaotong U., 1994; PhD, U. Conn. Health Ctr., 2006. Asst. prof. U. Tex. Dental Br., Houston, 2007—. Dentist 2nd Hosp. Affiliated to Wuhan U., 1997—2000; oral session chair Dentin-Devel. and Pathology, Internat. Am.-Can. Assn. Dental Rsch., 2011. Grantee, NIH-NIDCR. Mem.: Am. Dental Edn. Assn., Internat. Assn. Dental Rsch., Am. Assn. Dental Rsch., Am. Acad. Oral and Maxillofacial Radiology. Avocations: music, walking, cooking. Office: 6516 MD Anderson Blvd Rm 1076 Houston TX 77030 Office Fax: 713-500-0412. Business E-Mail: wenjian.zhang@uth.tmc.edu.

ZHANG, XIAOLIANG, professor, scientist; b. Xi'an, China, Mar. 18, 1963; PhD, U. Minn., Mpls., 2002. Rsch. assoc. Ohio State U., Columbus, 1996—99; engr. Philips Med. Sys. (formerly Picker Internat.), 1999; asst. prof. U. Minn., Mpls., 2002—06; assoc. prof., dir., Parallel Imaging and High Field MR Tech. Lab. U. Calif., San Francisco, 2006—. Recipient QB3 Rsch. award, Calif. Inst. for Quantitative Bioscis.; Rsch. grant, NIH. Office: Byers Hall 102D 1700 4th St San Francisco CA 94158 Business E-Mail: xiaoliang.zhang@ucsf.edu.

ZHANG, YEJIA (ZHANG YEJIA), physiatrist; MD, Second Mil. Med. Univ., Shanghai, P.R. China, 1989; PhD, Univ. Penn., Phila, Pa., 1997. Rsch. asst., dept. parasitology Second Mil. Med. Univ., Shanghai, P.R. China, 1989—91, Univ. Penn., 1991—93, rsch. asst., grad. group cell and devel. bio., 1993—97; intern, transitional residency St. Francis Hosp., Evanston, Ill., 1997—98; post-doctoral fell., dept. pathology, dept. dermatology Northwestern Univ., 1998—99; resident, dept. phys. medicine, rehab. Univ. Rochester, 2000—02, chief resident, 2001; resident, dept. phys. medicine, rehab. Rush Univ., 1999—2000, instr., dept. phys. medicine, rehab., 2002—. Tchg. asst. Second Mil. Med. Univ., Shanghai, P.R. China, 1989—91; rschr. Thomas Jefferson Univ., Phila., 2006—08. Contbr. articles to numerous profl. jours. Named to Top Doctor's, Chgo. Mag., 2009; Rsch. fellow, NIH, 1998—99, 2002—05. Mem.: Am. Acad. Phys. Medicine and Rehab., Am. Acad. Academic Psychiatrists. Office: Midwest Orthopaedics at Rush 1 Westbrook Corp Ctr Ste 240 Westchester IL 60154 Business E-Mail: yejia_zhang@rush.edu.

ZHANG, YINGMEI, zoologist, educator; b. Shanxi, China, July 20, 1963; PhD, Lanzhou U., 1996. Vice dir., Sch. Life Sci. Lanzhou U., 1999—2004, dir., sci. and tech. dept., 2007—. Chair Coun. Gansu Zool. Soc., 2005—; editl. bd. mem. Jour. Lanzhou U. Named one of Excellent Young U. Tchr., Gansu Province. Achievements include research in toxicity effects and mechanisms of environmental pollution on animals. Avocation: ping pong/table tennis. Office: 222 S Tianshui Rd Lanzhou Gansu 730000 China Office Fax: 0931-8913631. Business E-Mail: ymzhang@lzu.edu.cn.

ZHANG, YONGHUI, health facility administrator; MBA. Chief physician; dir. Guangdong Provincial Disease Prevention and Control Centre. With 10th standing com. Guangdong Province Legis. Counsel; with Ministry of Health; v.p. Nutrition Soc. Recipient Nat. Patriotic Health Advanced Individual, Nat. Advanced Individual Health Supervision, Standards for the 5th Advanced Individual, Ministry of Health. Mem.: China Preventive Medicine Assn., Assn. of Preventive Medicine (chmn. food safety products sub com. standards). Achievements include research in Food hygiene and safety, public health management. Office: Guangdong Provincial Disease Prevention and Control Centre Number 176 Xingang W Rd Haizhu Dist Guangzhou China *

ZHANG, YU, materials scientist, educator, physicist; s. De-yong Zhang and Tian-juan Wu; m. Josette Vella, Apr. 25, 1993; children: Denzil Suo, Elyzia. PhD, Monash U., Melbourne, Australia, 2002. Postdoc. fellow NIST, Gaithersburg, Md., 2002—05; asst. prof. NY U. Coll. Dentistry, NYC, 2005—. Rsch. fellow Monash U., Clayton, Victoria, Australia, 2001—02. Contbr. scientific papers. RO1 grant, NIH, 2007—, NIDCR, 2007—, grant, NSF, 2008—, CMMI, 2008—. Mem.: Internat. Assn. Dental Rsch. (Arthur R. Frechette award 2007), MRS, AADR. Achievements include research in novel bioceramics. Office: NY Univ Coll Dentistry 345 E 24th St New York NY 10010 Office Phone: 212-998-9637. Office Fax: 212-995-4244. Business E-Mail: yz21@nyu.edu.

ZHANG, ZHI GUANG, dentist; b. Guangdong, Jan. 9, 1955; B, Sun Yat-Sen U. Med. Scis., 1977; M, Sun Yat-Sen U., 2005. Dr., tchg. asst. dept. stomatology Sun Yat-Sen Meml. Hosp., Sun Yat-Sen U. Med. Scis., 1977—85, dep. dir. dept. stomatology, 1988—94, assoc. prof., assoc. chief physician dept. oral and maxillofacial surgery, 1991—95, vice dean Ling Nan Med. Coll., 1992—97; vice dean, dep. dir., prof. Guanghua Sch. Stomatology, Hosp. Stomatology, Sun Yat-Sen U., 1997—. Vis. pr Sch. Dentistry, Karolinska Inst., Sweden. Recipient 2nd prize, People's Govt. of Guangdong Province; named Spl. Allowance Expert, State Coun. China. Master: Guangdong Stomatological Assn. (v.p.), Chinese Assn. Plastics and Aesthetics, Chinese Soc. TMD & Occlusion; mem.: Nat. Natural Sci. Found. (mem. com. peer-reviewed experts), Chinese Stomatological Assn. (mem. divsn. oral & maxillofacial trauma). Avocations: swimming, ping pong/table tennis. Office: 56 Ling Yuan Rd W Guangzhou Guangdong 510055 China Office Fax: 00-86-20-83822807. Business E-Mail: drzhangzg@163.com.

ZHANG, ZHONGHENG, physician; b. Jinhua, Zhejiang, China, Nov. 11, 1984; MS in Medicine, Zhejiang U., 2009. Physician Jinhua Mcpl. Ctrl. Hosp., 2009—11. Master: Jinhua Ctrl. Hosp. Avocations: stamp collecting/philately, swimming, literature, jogging. Office: 351# Mingyue Rd Jinhua Zhejiang 321000 China Personal E-mail: zh_zhang1984@hotmail.com.

ZHANLI, WANG, medical educator; b. Shanghai, May 9, 1974; D, Peking U., 2004. Assoc. prof. Coll. Pharm. Sci., Zhejiang U. Tech., 2009—10; prof. Affiliated 1st People's Hosp., Baotou Med. Coll., 2010—. Home: 20 Zhentai Rd Shanghai 201901 China Personal E-mail: wang.zhanli@hotmail.com.

ZHAO, CHANGLING, agricultural studies educator; b. Dujiangyan, Sichuan, China, Nov. 30, 1969; D, Nanjing Agrl. U., 2005. Prof. Yunnan Agrl. U., 1994—. Office: Heilongtan Kunming Yunnan 650201 China Personal E-mail: zhaoplumblossom7@163.com.

ZHAO, CHONGHAO, neurologist, educator; MD, Guangzhou Med. Coll., China, 1986; PhD, Med. Coll. Va., 1994. Diplomate Am. Bd. Neurology, Ill., 2004, Am. Bd. Med. Acupuncture, Calif., 2002. Sr. lectr. UCLA, LA, 2001—; pres. Calif. Headache and Pain Ctr., Burbank; staff physician Providence St. Joseph Med. Ctr. Contbr. articles to profl. jours. Hon. chmn. physicians' adv. bd. Nat. Rep. Congl. Com., Washington, 2005—05; pres. So-Sue-Fang Ednl. Found., Guangzhou, China, 2003—05. Recipient Ronald Reagan Rep. Gold medal, Nat. Rep. Congl. Com., 2005; fellow, Cleve. Clinic Found., 2003. Mem.: Am. Acad. Pain Medicine, Am. Pain Soc., Am. Acad. Neurology, Am. Headache Soc. Achievements include research in Superficial cervical plexus block as an acute abortive therapy for intractable headache. Office: Calif Headache and Pain Ctr 201 S Buena Vista St Ste 238 Burbank CA 91505 Office Fax: 818-842-1638. E-mail: drzhao@chpci.com.

ZHAO, GANG, engineering educator; b. Tongshan County, Jiangsu, Apr. 25, 1977; PhD, U. Sci. & Tech. China, 2004. Postdoc. rschr., dept. modern mechanics USTC, 2004—06, assoc. prof., 2006—10, prof., dept. electronic sci., tech., 2010—; JSPS rsch. fellow Kyushu U., Japan, 2008—10. Vice dir. Biomed. Engring. Rsch. Ctr., USTC, 2011, Inst. Cryo-Biomed. Engring., 2011. Recipient Progress award, Anhui Sci. & Tech. Dept. Fellow: Chinese Assn. Refrigeration. Avocations: movies, cooking. Office: 96 Rd JinZhai Hefei Anhui 230027 China Business E-Mail: zhaog@ustc.edu.cn.

ZHAO, GANG, orthopedist; b. Qingzhou, Shandong, China, Oct. 18, 1963; MS, 3rd Mil. Med. U., 1992. High-energy trauma patients savior, dept. orthop. trauma Gen. Hosp. Jinan Mil. Region and Traumatic Orthop. Ctr., 1982—2011. Mem. Trauma Com. Jinan Mil. Region, 2003—11. Named Outstanding Profl. Talent, Polit. Dept. Jinan Mil. Region. Office: 46 Shifan Rd Tianqiao Dist Jinan Shandong 250031 China Business E-Mail: zhaogang198@163.com.

ZHAO, LIZI, medical researcher; b. Henan, China, Aug. 18, 1970; PhD, Sun Yat-sen U., 2005. Rsch. scientist Sch. Pharm. Scis., 2005—, Clin. Trial Ctr. Sun Yat-sen U., 2010—11. Fellow: Guangdong Pharmacology Soc., Clin. Pharmacology Assn.; mem.: Internat. Soc. for Study Xenobiotics, Chinese Pharmacology Soc. Avocations: reading, painting, swimming. Office: 132 Waihuan E Rd University City Guangzhou Guangdong 510006 China Office Fax: 020-39943034. Business E-Mail: zhaolizi@mail.sysu.edu.cn.

ZHAO, PING, medical educator; b. Dalian, China, July 9, 1956; MD, Liaoning U. Chinese Medicine, China, 1983; M in Medicine, PLA 4th Mil. Med. U., 1991. Physician, rehab. dept. PLA 470 Hosp., 1983—88; postgrad. rschr. PLA Ctr. TCM Manipulative Orthopedics, 1988—97, assoc. prof. to prof., 1997—, dep. dir. to dir., 1999—2005. Master: China Assn. TCM Spinal Manipulative Therapy, China Assn. TCM Tui Na. Avocation: swimming. Office: Fu Shi Lu 30 Beijing 100142 China Business E-Mail: kzzp@sina.com.

ZHAO, QIUQU, medical association administrator; b. Qu Zhou, China, Oct. 29, 1956; MD, Zhejiang Med. U., 1983, PhD, 1991. Med. dir. Bklyn. Chinese Family Health Ctr., Luth. Med. Ctr., 2007—. Mem.: Am. Acad. Family Physician. Home: 2100 Linwood Ave 19 N Fort Lee NJ 07024 Office Phone: 718-210-1030. Business E-Mail: qzhao@lmcmc.com.

ZHAO, WEI-GUANG, chemistry professor; b. Hebei Province, Nov. 9, 1971; BS, Nankai U., 1994, PhD, 2001. Prof. Nankai U., 2001. Recipient 2nd award, State Technol. Invention, China State Coun. Office: Weijin Rd 94# Tianjin 300071 China Office Fax: 00812223505948. Business E-Mail: zwg@nankai.edu.cn.

ZHAO, WEIGUO, neurosurgeon, educator; b. Shanghai, Aug. 6, 1957; MD, Shanghai Second Med. U., 1984; PhD, Tokyo Women's Med. U., 1999. Prof., chmn. dept neurosurgery Ruijin Hosp., Shanghai Jiaotong U. Sch. Medicine, 2008—. Mem.: China Assn. Neurosurgery, Congress Neurol. Surgeon. Avocations: swimming, travel, golf. Home: Rm 401 3 Ln 269 Fenglin Rd Shanghai 200032 China Personal E-mail: rjneurosurgery@yahoo.com.cn.

ZHAO, WU-SHU, immunologist, researcher; b. Lai Shi City, Shandong, China, Oct. 29, 1940; s. Ji-Quan and Rui-Lan (Gao) Z.; m. Hui-Zhen Ma, Feb. 6, 1973; children: Ya-Li, Lu-Ting. BS, Peking U., Beijing, 1964; MS, Peking Union of Med. Coll., Beijing, 1980. Asst. rschr. Chinese Acad. Med. Scis., Beijing, 1964-75, assoc. rschr., 1976-82; vis. prof. Osaka City U., Japan, 1983-85; assoc. prof. China

Japan Friendship Inst. of Clin. Med. Scis., Beijing, 1985-93, prof., 1993—, dep. dir. dept. immunology, 1986-89, dir. dept. immunology, 1990—2003. Author: Basis of Molecular Biology, 1990; editor: Modern Clinical Immunology, 1994, Study on Immune Balance and Its Clinical Significance, 2005, The Immunity Protects Your Health, 2008. Mem. china Biochemistry Molecular Biology Soc., NY Acad. Scis., Chinese Microbiology and Immunology Soc. (com. mem. 1991—). Office: China Japan Friendship Hosp Ying Hua East Rd 100029 Beijing China Office Phone: (86-010)64221122. Business E-Mail: zhaowushu@sino.com.

ZHAO, YUAN, biologist; d. Yuanshen Zhao and Qiong Qiong Tan; children: Nicole Ying, Mimi Yue. MSc, Zhongshan U., Guangzhou, China, 1982; PhD, Manchester U., Eng., 1991. Postdoctoral scientist John Radcliff Hosp., Oxford U., England, 1991—95; sr. scientist Chester Beatty Lab., London, 1996—98, U. Coll. London, 1999—2001; prin. scientist NIBSC, London, 2001—. Grantee Oversea scholarship, Academia Sinica. Achievements include patents for application of proteomics in product testing. Office: NIBSC Blache Ln Potters Bar EN6 3QG England Business E-Mail: yzhao@nibsc.ac.uk, yuan.zhao@nibsc.hpa.org.uk.

ZHAO, ZHENGUO, medical educator, department chairman; b. Inner Mongulia, Dec. 25, 1963; M, Tianjin Med. Sch., 1990. Prof., chmn. Pudong People Hosp., Shanghai, 2000—. Prof. Anhui Med. U., 2011. Recipient Precede Talented Man, Pudong Med. Bur., Shanghai. Mem.: Chinese Med. Assn. Avocations: tennis, swimming. Office: Chuanghuan Nanlu 490 Pudong Shanghai 201200 China Office Fax: 021-58902950. Business E-Mail: zhaozhenguo1@sina.com.

ZHAO-FAN, XIA, surgeon, educator; b. Fujian, Mar. 16, 1954; CM, Second Mil. Med. U., 1985, D in Surgery, 1988. Instr., indication surgeon burn surgery U. Affiliated Shanghai Hosp., Second Mil. Med. U., 1988—89, assoc. prof., assoc. chief surgeon burn surgery, 1989—94, prof., chief surgeon burn surgery, 1994—, dir. burn surgery, 1999; vis. scholar Shriners Burns Inst., U. Tex. Med. Br. Galveston, 1990—92, U. Tex. Southwesten Med. Ctr., Dallas, 1992—94. Dir. Burns Rsch. Inst. PLA, 2006, Emergency Burn Care Ctr. Shanghai City, 2009; assoc. chief editor Chinese Jour. Burns, 2008; editor English edit. Chinese Med. Jour., 2010. Recipient Bai-Yu-Lan award, Sci. and Tech. Com. Shanghai City, Shanghai Ten Sci. and Technol. Elites; Yangtze River scholar, Chinese Ministry of Edn., grant, Chinese Nat. Nature Sci. Fundation, Chinese Ministry of Pers. Master: Internat. Burn Assn., Shanghai Burn Assn., Chinese Burn Assn.; mem.: Internat. Shock Soc., Chinese Med. Assn. Avocations: reading, swimming, travel. Office: 168 Changhai Rd Shanghai 200433 China Office Fax: 021-65589829. E-mail: xiazhaofan@163.com.

ZHARIKOV, GENNADY ALEKSEEVICH, research scientist; b. Tula, Russia, Aug. 20, 1956; PhD in Biology, Obolensk, 1988; DSc in Biology, Moscow, 1999. Head, divsn. environ. biotech. State Fed. Enterprise Sci. Rsch. Ctr. Toxicology and Hygienic Regulation Biopreparations Fed. Medico-Biol. Agy., 1994—. Prof. Internat. U. Nature, Soc. and Human 'Dubna', 'Protvino' Br., 2000—. Recipient Star Scientist award, Internat. Acad. Ecology & Life Protection Scis., medal, Pres. Russian Fedn. Master: Internat. Acad. Ecology and Life Protection Scis. (actual mem., academician). Avocation: farming. Home: St Biologov Bld 1 -311 Obolensk Moscow Region 142279 Russia Home Fax: 7 (4967) 39-97-38. Personal E-mail: zharikov@toxicbio.ru.

ZHELEZNOVA, ELENA, psychiatrist, researcher; b. Moscow, Nov. 21, 1964; MD, Moscow State Med. Stomatological Inst., PhD, 1991; DMS, 2006. Leading rschr. Moscow Rsch. Inst. Psychiatry, 2004—. Mem.: Russian League Against Epilepsy. Office: 3 Poteshnaya Moscow 107076 Russia Office Fax: 7 495 963 76 37.

ZHENG, MIN, medical educator; b. Hunan, China, Nov. 24, 1963; D, Zurich U., 2003. Prof. Tomor Ctr., Sun Yat-sen U., 1988—. Office: Dongfeng Rd East 651 Guangzhou Guangdong 510060 China Personal E-mail: zheng_min_2006@yahoo.com.cn.

ZHENG, X. LONG, hematologist, educator; b. Guangfeng, China, Jan. 8, 1982; MD, Nanchang U., 2005; PhD, Med. U. Vienna, 2009. Fellow Wash. U., St. Louis, 1999—2003; asst. prof. U. Pa., 2003—11, assoc. prof., 2011—. Med. dir. Children's Hosp. Phila., 2003—11. Mem.: Internat. Soc. Thrombosis and Hemostasis, Am. Soc. Hematology. Office: 816G Abramson Research Ctr 34th St and Civic Center Blvd Philadelphia PA 19104 Business E-Mail: zheng@email.chop.edu.

ZHEN-GANG, WANG, medical educator; b. June 2, 1923; MD, Cheeloo U. Cons. Shanzhan Jian An Pharm. Co. Ltd. Contbr. scientific papers. Mem.: Chinese Pharmacological Soc. (pres. 1984—93, hon. pres. 1993—2002). Home: Yo An Men Wai Yu Lin Xi Li Bldg 61-804 Feng Tai Dist Beijing 100069 China Home Phone: 86-010-63058779. Personal E-mail: drwangzhengang@126.com.

ZHENYU, DING, oncologist; b. China, Mar. 1, 1979; MD, Third Mil. Med. U., PhD, 2008. Attending physician Gen. Hosp. Shenyang Mil. Region, 2008—. Mem.: Com. Tumor Marker, Liaoning Provincial Anti-cancer Assn. Avocations: badminton, computers. Office: 83 Wenhua Rd Shenhe District Shenyang Liaoning 110840 China Personal E-mail: dingdzy@yahoo.com.cn.

ZHEN-YU, GONG, physician, educator; b. Hangzhou, China, Nov. 21, 1969; MPH, Zhejiang U., 2006. Prof. Zhejiang CDC, 2010. Home: Huancheng Dong Rd 108 Hangzhou Zhejiang 310009 China Personal E-mail: 87235011@163.com.

ZHONG, LIANG JUN, dental educator; b. Xinjiang, China, Apr. 12, 1964; B in Stomatology, Second Med. U., Shanghai, 1988; PhD, Sichuan U., 2001. Commr. Chinese Stomatological Assn. Profl. Com. Periodontal Disease, 2003—, Chinese Stomatological Assn. Profl. Com. Integration of Traditional and Western Medicine, 2007—; coun. mem. Chinese Stomatological Assn. Coun., 2006—; chief commr. Xinjiang Med. Assn. Stomatology, 2007—; prof. Internat. Coll. Dentists, 2011—. Expert peer rev. Nat. Natural Sci. Found. China, 2004—; editl. mem. Yearbook Chinese Stomatology, 2005—, Shanghai Jour. Stomatology, 2008—; evaluation expert Ministry of Health Sci. Rsch. Projects, 2006—; commr. Second Sector Chinese Med. Sci. and Tech. Awards Rev. Com., 2007—10. Recipient Outstanding Postdoc. award, Govt. of Xinjiang Uygur Autonomous Region of China, 2006, 3rd prize, Govt. of Urumqi, Xinjiang Uygur Autonomous Region of China, 2006, 2nd prize, Govt. of Xinjiang Uygur Autonomous Region of China, 2008, Bur. Health, Xinjiang Uygur Autonomous Region of China, 2005, Highest Reputation prize, All China Fedn. Trade Unions, 2009. Master: Xinjiang Med. Assn. Stomatology; mem.: Internat. Coll. Dentists. Avocations: swimming, travel, reading. Office: 126 Wenzhou Rd Hangzhou Zhejiang 310015 China Office Phone: 86571-88303551. Office Fax: 8657128865621. Personal E-mail: zymdxx@163.com.

ZHONGCHEN, BAI, research scientist; b. Harbin, China, Dec. 1, 1979; M, Guizhou U., 2009. Rsch. scientist, biosensor & microfluidic Guizhou U., 2006—. Engr. Guomai Group Heilongjiang Telecommunication, 2003—06. Office: Sci Coll Guozhou University Guiyang Guizhou 550025 China Personal E-mail: yufengvc@163.com.

ZHONGYUANG, JIANG, hospital administrator; Grad., Tsinghua U.; M in Life Sciences, Nat. Tsinghua U.; grad., Nat. Taiwan U. Chief resident Nat. Taiwan U. Hosp., physician; dir. of surgery Provincial Hsinchu Hosp.; v.p. dept. of health Taoyuan Med. Hosp., Hsinchu Gen. Hosp. Office: Hsin Chu General Hospital No 25 Lane 442 Sec 1 Jingguo Rd Hsinchu 30059 Taiwan Office Phone: 88635326151. E-mail: hch21001@hch.doh.gov.tw. *

ZHOU, DE-QING, microbiologist; b. Zhenhai, China, Dec. 7, 1935; s. Bing-cai and A-ju (Wang) Z.; m. Shi-ju Xu; children: Ren-ling, Ren-gang. Grad., Fudan U., 1957. Assoc. prof. Fudan U., Shanghai, 1980-88, prof., 1988—. Author: Dictionary of Microbiology, 2005; Course of Microbiology, 1993 (1st award State Edn. Com. China 1995), 3rd ed., 2011; co-author: Microbiology, 1987 (1st award State Edn. Com. China 1988); editor-in-chief: Experimental Handbook of Microbiology, 1987; contbr. articles to profl. jours. Recipient 1st award Outstanding Tchg. Achievement, Shanghai Mcpl. Govt., 1996, 2d award, 1995, 2d award Outstanding Tchg. Achievement, State Grade of China, 1997, 2d award Sci. and Tech. Progress, State Ednl. Com. of China, 1997. Mem. Chinese Soc. for Microbiology (coun. 1987 96). Personal E-mail: zrl689@sina.com.

ZHOU, LI, research scientist; m. Ning Xu, Feb. 5, 1960; 1 child, Yuancheng Xu. PhD, Lunds U., Lund, Sweden, 1994—99; MD, Shanghai Med. U., Shanghai, China, 1978—83. Rsch. assoc. BMC, Lunds U., Lund, Skane, Sweden, 2002—, post doc, 2000—01; Phd student Lunds U., Lund, Sweden, 1994—99; lectr. Shanghai Med. U., Sg, Shanghai, 1989—91. Lipid metabolism (basic research) Sources of eicosanoid precursor fatty acid pools in tissues. Achievements include research in Biochemistry. E-mail: li.zhou@med.lu.se.

ZHOU, QIAO, pathologist, educator, researcher; b. Yichang, Hubei, China, June 4, 1963; s. Guangyu Pan and Lianhui Zhou; m. Yingli Kou, Aug. 8, 1987; 1 child, Shenmin. MD, West China Med. Sch., Chengdu, 1984; PhD in Pathology, Duke U., 1998. Lic. in pathology Min. Health, China, 1999. Intern West China Hosp., 1983—84, resident dept. pathology, 1985—89, pathologist, 1990—94, prof., assoc. chair pathology dept., 2001—. Dir. Rsch. Labs. Patholgy West China Hosp., 2000—; fellow Dept. Pathology Med. Ctr. Duke U., Durham, NC, 1994—98; rsch. assoc. Children's Hosp. Harvard U., Boston, 1999—2000; prof. Med. Sch. West China U., Chengdu, 2001—, Sichuan U., 2001—. Contbr. chapters to books, articles to profl. jours. Grantee Rsch. grants, Min. of Edn., 2001—04, Natural Sci. Found. China, 2002—, Rsch. grant, Min. Sci. & Tech. China, 2002—05; fellow, Duke U. Med. Ctr., 1994—98; Fellowship, G. Harold & Leila Y. Mathers Charitable Found., 1997. Mem.: Chinese Med. Assn., Assn. Dirs. Pathology China, Asia Pacific Assn. Socs. Pathologists, Internat. Acad. Pathology. Achievements include research in interaction of caspases and apoptosis inhibitors, diagnostic pathology and tissue microarrays. Avocations: languages, collecting books, history. Office: W China Hosp Pathology Dept W China Med Sch Sichuan U Chengdu 610041 China

ZHOU, SHENG NIAN, neurologist; b. Ji Nan, China, Aug. 1, 1958; M, Shandong U., 1987, PhD, 2004. Neurology Qilu Hosp. Shandong U., 1982—. Office: West Wen Hua Rd 44 Ji Nan Shan Dong 250012 China Personal E-mail: zhoushengnian126@126.com.

ZHOU, SHI NING, microbiologist, researcher; s. Xue Zhao Zhou and Jin Di Lin; m. Hui Zhen Wen, Dec. 26, 1971; children: Geng Shan, Wei (Maggie). Student, Zhongshan U., China, 1965—70, MS, 1982. V.p. Guangdong Soc. for Microbiology, Guangzhou, Guangdong, China, 1991—2003; vice dean of dept. Zhongshan(Sun Yat-sen) U., Guangdong, 1991—97, dept. dean, 2000—04; v.p. Guangzhou Soc. for Microbiology, Guangzhou, Guangdong, China, 1995—2003; prof. Zhongshan(Sun Yat-sen) U., Guangzhou, Guangdong, China, 1998—. Mem. of dir. com. (br.) of higher edn. Edn. Ministry of China, Beijing, 2001—. Grantee Rsch. Fund For Natural Scis., Ministry of Sci. & Tech., 1996—98, 1999—2001, 2004—08, Rsch. Fund For High Tech. Rsch. & Devel., Ministry of Sci. & Tech., China, 2001—05, Rsch. Fund, Dept. Sci. & Tech., China, 1999—2001, 2002—04, Rsch. fund, Dept. of Sci. & Tech., Guangdong Province, 2006—09, Fund Further Study Abroad, Edn. Minstry of China, 1984—87; Rsch. Fund For High Tech. Rsch. & Devel., Ministry of Sci. & Tech., China, 2007—. Master: China Soc. Microbiology (assoc.; committeeman marine microbiology branch); mem.: Chinese Soc. Microbiology. Achievements include patents for methods for preparation of anti-hypertension and anti-tumor compounds; anti-tumor compounds and their preparation and application; patents pending for method for preparation of extract from a marine fungus and its application; anti-tumor compound and its preparation and application for drugs; a strain of Rhodomarinobacter and its application for drug production; application and preparation of a novel compound; a strain of endophytic bacterium of bananas and its application; application of Chinese medicines as bacterial guorum sensing inhibitors. Avocations: table tennis, swimming, travel. Office: Zhongshan(Sun Yat-sen) U Coll Life Scis 135 Xingangxil 510275 Guangzhou Yandongsheng China Business E-Mail: lsszsl@mail.sysu.edu.cn.

ZHOU, TIAN-BIAO, pediatrician; b. Shantou, Guangdong, China, Sept. 13, 1983; MD, Guangxi Med. U., 2008. Physician First Affiliated Hosp. Guangxi Med. U., 2008—. Contbr. articles to profl. jours. Office: Shuang-Yong Rd 6 Nanning Guangxi 530021 China Business E-Mail: a126tianbiao@126.com.

ZHOU, WEN-LIANG, physiologist, educator; b. Jiangxi, China, Jan. 26, 1967; BS, Sun Yat-Sen U., 1988; PhD, Chinese U. Hong Kong, 1997. Postdoc. assoc. MIT, 1999—2000; instr. Harvard Med. Sch., 2000—03; prof. Sun Yat-Sen U., 2003—. Mem.: Am. Soc. Physiology. Avocations: reading, ping pong/table tennis, running. Office: Sun Yat-Sen University Sch Life Sci Guangzhou Guangdong 510275 China Office Fax: 86-20-84110060. Personal E-mail: wenliangzhou@yahoo.com.

ZHOU, YINGQUN, physician; b. Anhui Province, Oct. 8, 1971; MD, Fudan U., 2004; PhD, Tongji U. Physician dept. gastroenterology Shanghai Tenth People's Hosp., 1995—. Office: Yanchang Rd 301 Zhabei dist Shanghai 200072 China E-mail: yqzh02@163.com.

ZHOU, ZHI-HUA, information science educator; b. Guangzhou, China, Nov. 20, 1973; BSc, Nanjing U., China, 1996, MSc, 1998, PhD, 2000. Asst. prof. Nanjing U., 2001—02, assoc. prof., 2002—03, dir. artificial intelligence lab., 2002—, prof., 2003—, Cheung Kong prof., 2007—. Grant reviewer Rsch. Coun. Hong Kong, Nat. Sci. Found., Netherlands, grant review panelist, China. Assoc. editor-in-chief: Chinese Sci. Bulletin, assoc. editor: IEEE Transactions on Knowledge and Data Engring., mem. editl. bd.: Artificial Intelligence in Medicine, Internat. Jour. Data Warehousing and Mining, Intelligent Data Analysis, Jour. Computer Sci. and Tech., Jour. of Software; author: publs. in areas of artificial intelligence, machine learning and data mining, pattern recognition and information retrieval. Recipient Nat. Excellent Doctoral Dissertation award, China, 2003, Disting. Young Scholar of China award, Nat. Sci. Fund, 2003, Nat. Sci. and Tech. award for young scholars of China, 2006, Microsoft Professorship award, 2006. Mem.: ACM, AAAI, IEEE Computer Soc. (sr.), IEEE (sr.), Chinese Assn. Artificial Intelligence, China Computer Fedn. (sr.). Achievements include patents in field. Office: Nanjing U Nat Key Lab for Novel Software Technol 22 Hankou Rd 210093 Nanjing China Business E-Mail: zhouzh@nju.edu.cn.

ZHU, DONGBIN, research scientist; b. China, Sept. 16, 1975; D, Hebei U. Tech., 2009. Rschr. Hebei U. Tech., 2009. Avocations: sports, music, reading. Office: Hebei University Tech Sch Material and Engring 8 Dingzigu 1 Rd Hongqiao Dist Tianjin 300130 China Business E-Mail: zhudongbin@hebut.edu.cn.

ZHU, FRANK XIANG, medical researcher, internist; b. Nanjing, China, Mar. 1, 1958; m. Dexi and Lijuan (Qian) Z., m. Juliet Dui Hu, May 16, 1986; children: David Hemu, Serena Hui Zhu. MB, 2d Mil. Med. U., Shanghai, 1983, M in Med. Sci., 1989. Resident, asst. tutor Changhai Hosp/2d Mil. Med. U., Shanghai, 1983-89, physician in charge, lectr., 1989-92, dep. dir., physician, assoc. prof., 1992-95; rsch. fellow Royal Marsden Hosp./Inst. Cancer Rsch., London, 1995-97; rsch. scientist Baker Med. Rsch. Inst., Melbourne, Australia, 1997-99; med. doctor Latrobe Regional Hosp., Victoria, Australia, 2000—02, Frankston Hosp., Victoria, Australia, 2002—04, Maroondah Hosp., Victoria, Australia, 2004—05, Kempsy Hosp., 2005—, Hastings Med. Ctr., 2007—. Mem. com. hosp. infection adminstrn. Changhai Hosp., 1993-95. Editor-in-chief: Handbook of Practical Anti-infection Therapy, 1993; editor: Yearbook of Medicine of China, 1991—94; contbr. articles to profl. jours. Recipient award for sci. and tech. achievement Gen. Logistics Dept. of PLA, 1991; named Grade A Tchr., 2d Mil. Med. U., 1991; Marie Curie fellow, London, 1995; Prostate Cancer Rsch. Fund grantee, London, 1996. Mem. Soc. Internal Medicine, Chinese Med. Assn. (Shanghai br.), Australian Soc. for Med. Rsch., Australian Med. Assn. Avocations: swimming, stamp collecting/philately. Office: Kempsey Hosp River St Kempsey NSW 2440 Australia Home: 816/1-3 Owen St Port Macquarie NSW 2444 Australia Office Phone: 61 2 65620250. Business E-Mail: zhufrank@gmail.com.

ZHU, JIN, chemistry professor; b. Shangrao, China, Feb. 2, 1971; PhD, Northwestern U., Evanston, Ill., 1999. Prof. Nanjing U., 2005—. Office: 22 Hankou Rd Nanjing University Nanjing Jiangsu 210093 China Business E-Mail: jinz@nju.edu.cn.

ZHU, JUN, health science association administrator, director; b. Sichuan, China, Jan. 24, 1964; M, Zhongqing Med. U., 1988. Dir. Nat. Ctr. Birth Defects Monitoring, Nat. Office Maternal and Children Health Surveillance, 1996—. Cons. expert com. prenatal diagnosis & newborn screening Ministry Health China, 2003—. Office: 17 Sec 3 Renmin Lanlu Chengdu Sichuan 610041 China Office Fax: 86-28-85501386. Business E-Mail: zhu_jun1@163.com.

ZHU, ZHENGGANG, hospital administrator; Pres. Rui Jin Hosp., Shanghai. Author: (publ.) Efficacy and Safety of Intraoperative Peritoneal Hyperthermic Chemotherapy for Advanced Gastric Cancer Patients with Serosal Invasion. Office: Rui Jin Hospital Shanghai Jiao Tong University School of Medicine 197 Rui Jin Er Rd Shanghai 200025 China Office Phone: 862164313054. E-mail: yzbgs@rjh.com.cn. *

ZHUK, OLGA VIKTOROVNA, pharmacologist, educator; b. Inza, Russia, Aug. 28, 1952; d. Viktor Petroich Bogdanov and Zoia Vasilievna Bogdanova; m. Sergei Konstantinovich Zhuk; 1 child, Maksim Sergeivich. BSc, Odessa U., Ukraine, DSc, 1996, MSc, 1974. Jr. rsch. assoc. U. Odessa, 1974—79, rsch. assoc., 1979—89, sr. rsch. assoc., 1989—2004, prof., 1994—2001, U. Opole, 2001—. Expert Pharmacol. Com., Kiev, Ukraine, 1994—2004. Mem.: Polish Pharmacol. Soc. Achievements include research in modeling of pharmacokinetics and metabolism of the new derivatives of 1, 4-benzdiazepines, new antiviral drug-amixin; relationship of pharmacodynamics and pharmacokinetics. Home: Senkevich 33 apt 108 Opole 45-037 Poland Office: Univ Opole Kominka 4 Opole 45-035 Poland Business E-Mail: olga_zhuk@uni.opole.pl, kbsie@uni.opole.pl.

ZHURAVENKO, IGOR N., health services administrator, physician; b. Lvov, Ukraine, Mar. 6, 1959; came to U.S., 1992; s. Naum and Raisa Zhuravenko; m. Svetlana Zhuravenko, Dec. 1, 1990; children: Dimitri, Gary, Richard, Gabrielle. MD, Lvov Med. Sch., 1983. Diplomate Am. Bd. Internal Medicine. Physician Gen. Hosp., Rovno, Ukraine, 1984-88, Diagnostic Ctr., Lvov, 1989-92; clin. instr. ultrasound Med. Sch., Lvov, 1990-92; resident in internal medicine SUNY, Buffalo, 1995-98, clin. asst. instr. medicine, 1995-98; physician Ocean Med. Plz., 2003—07; pres. IZNY Med. PC, 2007—. Physician MEDEX, Forest Hills, NY, 1998—99; med. dir. Adult Home Sites/CHS, NYC, 1999—; mem. sci. adv. bd. Nutrition Superstores, Inc., West Palm Beach, Fla., 1999—; pres. Z Best Med. Care, P.C., 1999—2003; med. dir. Privilege Care a Diagnostic and Treatment Ctr., 1999—2001. Contbr. articles to profl. jours. Named one of America's Top Physicians, 2003—10. Mem. ACP, AMA (Physician's Recognition award 1998, 2002, 03, 04, 05, 06, 07, 08, 08, 09), Am. Thyroid Assn. Avocations: chess, reading, computers. Office Phone: 718-375-1777. Personal E-mail: izbest@aol.com.

ZIEGLER, DEWEY KIPER, neurologist, educator; b. Omaha, May 31, 1920; s. Isidor and Pearl (Kiper) Z.; Mar. 30, 1954; children: Amy, Laura, Sara. BA, Harvard U., 1941, MD, 1945. Diplomate Am. Bd. Psychiatry and Neurology (bd. dirs. 1974-83, exec. com. 1978-82). Intern in medicine Boston City Hosp., 1945-46; asst. resident then chief resident in neurology N.Y. Neurol. Inst.-Columbia U. Coll. Physicians and Surgeons, 1948-51; resident in psychiatry Boston Psychopathic Hosp., 1951-53; asst. chief neurol. service Montefiore Hosp., NYC; and asst. prof. neurology Columbia U., 1953-55; asst. prof. U. Minn., 1955-56; asso. clin. prof. U. Kans. Med. Sch., 1956-64, chief dept. neurology, 1968-85; prof. U. Kans. Med. Center, 1964-89, prof. emeritus, 1989—. Cons. Social Security Adminstrn., 1975—; mem. com. on certification and co-certification Am. Bd. Med. Specialties, 1979-82 Author: In Divided and Distinguished Worlds, 1942; Contbr. numerous articles to profl. jours. Served to lt., j.g., M.C. USNR, 1946-48. Fellow Am. Acad. Neurology (pres. 1979-81); mem. AMA, Am. Neurol. Assn. (v.p. 1972-73), Am. Headache Assn. Jewish. Home: 8347 Delmar Ln Shawnee Mission KS 66207-1821 Office: Kans U Med Ctr 3900 Rainbow Blvd Kansas City KS 66103-2918 Home Phone: 913-648-7244.

ZIEGLER, EKHARD ERICH, pediatrics educator; b. Saalfelden, Austria, Apr. 12, 1940; children: Stefan, Gabriele, Lena. MD, U. Innsbruck, Austria, 1964. Diplomate: Am. Bd. Pediatrics. Intern U. Innsbruck, 1966-67, resident in pediatrics, 1967-68 70-71, resident in pharmacology, 1964-66, asst. dept. pediatrics, 1970-73; vis. instr. pediatrics U. Iowa, Iowa City, 1968-70, asst. prof. pediatrics, 1973-76, assoc. prof., 1976-81, prof., 1981—. Mem. nutrition study sect. NIH, 1988-92. Recipient Nutrition award Am. Acad. Pediactrics, 1988. Mem. Am. Soc. Clin. Nutrition, Soc. Pediatric Research, Soc. Exptl. Biology and Medicine, N.Am. Soc. Pediatric Gastroenterology, Midwest Soc. Pediatric Research, Am. Pediatric Soc., The Nutrition Soc., N.Y. Acad. Scis., Am. Acad. Pediatrics., Am. Dietetic Assn. (hon.). Office: A136 MTF 2501 Crosspark Rd Coralville IA 52241 Office Phone: 319-335-4570. Business E-Mail: ekhard-ziegler@uiowa.edu.

ZIEGLER, JAN L., dentist; Dentist Miami Cosmetic Ctr. for Cosmetic and Implant Dentistry. Mem.: South Fla. Dist. Dental Assn., Fla Dental Assn., Dental Orgn. for Conscious Sedation, Fla. Acad. of Cosmetic Dentistry, Am. Acad. of Cosmetic Dentistry, ADA. Office: Miami Center for Cosmetic and Implant Dentistry 13840 SW 56th St Miami FL 33175 Office Phone: 305-387-6453.

ZIEGLER, PENELOPE, psychiatrist, educator; MD, George Wash. U., Washington, DC, 1978. Diplomate Am. Bd. Psychiatry and Neurology-psychiatry, 1986, Am. Bd. Psychiatry and Neurology-addiction psychiatry, 2003. Resident psychiatry Sheppard Enoch Pratt Hosp., Balt., 1978—82; assoc. prof. dept. psychiatry Virginia Commonwealth Univ., dir. health practitioners' intervention program dept. psychiatry. Office: Virginia Commonwealth University PO Box 980109 Richmond VA 23298-0109 Office Phone: 757-565-0106. E-mail: ppziegle@vcu.edu.

ZIEGLER, RICHARD J., medical educator, former dean; BS in biology, Muhlenberg Coll., 1965; PhD in microbiology, Temple U., 1970. Rsch. assoc. in microbiology Rockefeller U., 1970—71; asst. prof. microbiology U. Minn.-Duluth, 1971—77, assoc. prof. microbiology, 1977—89; prof. microbiology Sch. Medicine, U. Minn.-Duluth, 1989—, interim dean, 1997—98, dean, 1998—2008. Recipient James H. Sova award, Minn. Med. Found., 2000. Office: UMD Sch Medicine 1035 Univ Dr Duluth MN 55812 Office Phone: 218-726-7280. Business E-Mail: rziegler@umn.edu. *

ZIENIEWICZ, STEPHEN, hospital administrator; BS in Biology, St. John's U.; MPH, Columbia U. Staff role to mgmt. then sr. mgmt. positions North Shore U. Hosp., Manhasset, NY; adminstr. Winthrop-University Hosp.; asst. v.p. Long Island Health Network; v.p. NY Methodist Hosp., Bklyn.; v.p. support and ancillary services, South Nassau Hosp. Winthrop South Nassau U. Health System, 1999—2004; COO Saint Louis U. Hosp., 2004—07, Tenet Healthcare Corp., 2004—07; exec. dir. U. Wash. Medical Ctr., 2007—. Former adj. prof. health mgmt. and policy Saint Louis U. Sch. Public Health; former chmn. Statewide Disaster Preparedness Com. Mo. Dept. Health, Division of Health and Sr. Services. Fellow: American Coll. Healthcare Executives.

ZIERDT, CHARLES HENRY, retired microbiologist; b. Pitts., Apr. 24, 1922; s. Conrad Henry and Nancy Leora (Harshberger) Zierdt; m. Margaret May Wise, June 1, 1942 (div. 1962); children: Charles Henry Jr., Carolyn, Douglas, Richard; m. Willadene Smith, Sept. 30, 1967. BS, Pa. State U., 1943; MS, U. Mich., 1945; PhD, George Washington U., 1967. Rsch. assoc. Parke-Davis & Co., Detroit, 1945—48; microbiologist Henry Ford Hosp., Detroit, 1948—53, USPHS, Detroit, 1953—56; rsch. microbiologist NIH, Bethesda, Md., 1956—93, ret., 1993. Scientist sponsor U. Md., 1975—; instr. Found. Advanced Edn. Scis., Bethesda, Md., 1978—. Author: Glucose Nonfermenting Gram Negative Bacteria in Clinical Microbiology, 1978, Non-fermentative Gram Negative Rods: Laboratory Identification and Clinical Aspects, 1985, McGraw-Hill Yearbook of Science and Technology, 1986, Diagnostic Procedures for Bacterial Infections, 1987; contbr. articles to profl. jours. Fellow: Am. Acad. Microbiology; mem.: Mensa, Avanti Owners Assn. Internat., U.S. Fedn. Culture Collections (membership chmn. 1985), Am. Soc. Microbiology (chpt. pres. 1976), Antique Auto Club Am. (pres. Sugar Loaf Mountain region 1997), Model T Ford Club Internat., Model A Ford Club Am. (Fairfax, Va. chpt. pres. 1985), Sigma Xi. Achievements include the classification and pathogenesis of Blastocystis Hominis, an intestinal protozoan parasite of man; description of non-oxidative (anaerobic) mitochondria. Avocations: gardening, antique car restoration, church historian. Office: NIH Bethesda MD 20816 Home: 4707 Coachway Dr Rockville MD 20852-2339

ZIERSKI, JAN TOMASZ, neurosurgeon; b. Lwow, Poland, Oct. 10, 1940; arrived in Eng., 1969. s. Marian and Lina Hermine (Unger) Z.; m. Zofia Barbara Grochowska, Dec. 27, 1969; 1 child, Anne-Catherine. MD, Med. Acad., Lodz, Poland, 1969; Priv Doz, Giessen U., Germany, 1986. Asst. Dept. Neurosurgery, Lodz, Poland, 1965-69, resident Lyon, France, 1967-68, registrar Hull, Eng., 1969-72, asst. rsch. Giessen, Germany, 1972-85, dep. head, 1985-87; head dept. neurosurgery Hosp. Neukoelln, Berlin, 1987—; prof. neurosurgery Giessen, Germany, 1987. Editor: Cerebral Aneurysms, 1979, Spontaneous Cerebral Haematomas, 1980, Intrathecal Treatment of Spasticity, 1986, Mrjaras, The Spive, 2007; contbr. articles to profl. jours. Decorated Officers Cross of Merit Pres. Polish Republic, 1996. Mem. German-Polish Med. Soc. (pres. 1994-96), German Soc. Neurosurgery, Polish Soc. Neurosurgery (hon.), Austrian Soc. Neurosurgery. Avocations: theater, languages. Home: Nelkenweg 1 14532 Stahnsdorf Germany Office: Neurosurg Offices Schlueterstr 38 10629 Berlin Germany Office Phone: 00480 88326090. Personal E-mail: j.zierski@t-online.de.

ZIESSMAN, HARVEY A., nuclear medicine physician, medical association administrator; BS, Indiana U., MD, 1969; MBA, Georgetown U. Joined faculty Georgetown U., 1984, dir. nuclear medicine, 1991—2003; prof. radiology, divsn. nuclear medicine Johns Hopkins U., 2003—. Author: Nuclear Medicine, The Requisites. Mem.: American Bd. Nuclear Medicine (chair 2009). Office: Johns Hopkins Nuclear Medicine Ste 3223 600 N Caroline St Baltimore MD 21287

ZIGIOTTI, GIAN LUIGI, plastic surgeon; b. Argenta, Aug. 3, 1946; MB BS, U. Bologna, Italy, 1971. Cert. specialist in plastic surgery U. Catania, Italy. Specialist plastic surgery, plastic surgery unit U. Hosp. S. Orsola-Malpighi, Bologna, 2003—. Aggregate prof. ophthalmology U. Bologna, 2001—11. Mem.: GMC. Avocations: motorcycling, mountain climbing. Office: Via S Gervasio 6 Bologna 40121 Italy E-mail: gian.zigiotti@gmail.com.

ZIKOS, ANTONIOS, pulmonologist, educator; MD, Philadelphia Coll. of Osteopathic Medicine. Diplomate Am. Bd. Internal Medicine-pulmonary, Am. Bd. Internal Medicine-critical care medicine. Practice Integrated pulmonary Physicians Ltd.; intern Allegheny Gen. Hosp., resident, med. dir. neuro-intensive care unit; fellow Temple Univ. Hosp.; clin. asst. prof. dept. of medicine Drexel Univ. Named one of Top Doctors, Pitts. mag., 2011. Office: Allegheny General Hospital 320 E N Ave Pittsburgh PA 15212 Office Phone: 412-359-3131. Office Fax: 412-359-4108.

ZILBERBERG, MARYA, epidemiologist, researcher; MD, Boston U. Sch. Medicine, 1992; MPH in Epidemiology, U. Mass., Amherst, 2008. Resident & fellow Tufts U. Sch. Medicine, 1992—98; intensivist Winchester Hosp., 1996—98; outcomes rsch. Johnson & Johnson, 2001—07; founder & pres. EviMed Research Group LLC, 2007; physician & researcher U. Mass. Office: University of Massachusetts School of Public Health 715 N Pleasant St Amherst MA 01003-9304 also: 421 N Main St Leeds MA 01053 Office Phone: 413-268-3414. E-mail: MZilberb@schoolph.umass.edu, Marya@EviMedGroup.org.

ZILVETI, CARLOS BENJAMIN, preventive medicine physician, pediatrician; b. Sucre, Bolivia, June 14, 1928; arrived in USA, 1956; s. Carlos and Marina (De La Reza) Z.; m. Halina J. Daszewski, Sept. 8, 1957 (div. Sept. 1976); 1 child: Carlos Joseph III; m. Vita Palazzolo, Sept. 5, 1987. BS, Sacred Heart Coll., Sucre, Bolivia, 1946; MD, U. San Francisco Xavier, Sucre, Bolivia, 1954; MPH, Yale U., New Haven, Conn., 1966. Physician in rural medicine Bolivian Power Co., La Paz, 1955; intern Hosp. Obrero Victor Paz Estenssoro, La Paz, 1956; asst. resident in pediats. St. Luke's Hosp., Meml. Cancer Ctr., Woman's Hosp., NYC, 1957-58; resident and chief resident in pediats. Hosp. of St. Raphael, New Haven, 1958-59; pvt. practice New Haven and Branford, Conn., 1960-63; dir. maternal-child health New Haven Dept. Health, 1964-74; regional med. officer South and Ctrl. Am. Peace Corps, Bogota, Colombia, 1975-76; regional med. officer, sci. attache in West Africa U.S. Dept. of State, Liberia, Ghana, Togo, Sierra Leone, 1976-79; reserve appt. of maj., advanced to col. USAF, San Antonio, 1979-91, chief environ. medicine Wilford Hall Med. Ctr., 1979-83, cons. preventive and occupl. medicine, 1983-91, cons. aerospace-preventive medicine Wilford Hall Med. Ctr. Lackland AFB, Tex., 1984-91, ret. col., 1991. Cons. FDA, HEW, Washington, 1966-75; cons. to Headstart Am. Acad. Pediats., Stanford-Norwalk, Conn., 1968-75; regional med. officer, sci. attache West Africa U.S. Dept. State. Contbr. articles to profl. jours. Chmn. gov.'s task force Conn. State Dept. Health, Hartford, 1969-75. Fellow Am. Acad. Pediats. (emeritus), Am. Coll. Preventive Medicine (emeritus); mem. APHA, AMA, New Eng. Pub. Health Assn., Conn. Acad. Preventive Medicine, Am. Occupl. Med. Assn. Avocations: swimming, tennis, golf, travel, classical music. Home: 9222 Dover Rdg San Antonio TX 78250-3557

ZIMET, CARL NORMAN, retired psychologist, educator; b. Vienna, June 3, 1925; came to U.S., 1943, naturalized, 1945; s. Leon and Gisela (Kosser) Z.; m. Sara F. Goodman, June 4, 1950; children: Andrew, Gregory. BA, Cornell U., 1949; PhD, Syracuse U., 1953; postdoctoral fellow, Stanford U., 1953-55. Diplomate in clin. psychology Am. Bd. Profl. Psychology (trustee 1966-74). Instr., then asst. prof. psychology and psychiatry Yale U., 1955-63; mem. faculty U. Colo. Med. Center, 1963—, prof. clin. psychology, 1965—2007, head div., 1963—2006, prof. emeritus, 2008—, U. Colo. Med. Sch., 2007—. Mem. Colo. Bd. Psychol. Examiners, 1966-72, Colo. Mental Health Planning Commn., 1964-66; mem. acad. adv. com. John F. Kennedy Child Devel. Center, U. Colo., 1966-68; chmn. Council for Nat. Register of Health Service Providers in Psychology, 1975-85, pres., mem. exec. bd. div. psychotherapy, 1970-89; chair exec. com. Assn. Psychol. Internship Ctrs., 1988-91. Bd. editors: Jour. Clin. Psychology, 1962-91, Jour. Clin. and Cons. Psychology, 1964-73, Psychotherapy, 1967—, Profl. Psychology, 1969-75. With USNR, 1943-46. Recipient Disting. Service award Colo. Psychol. Assn., 1976 Fellow: APA (coun. reps. 1969—72, 1973—76, bd. dirs. 1985—88, Disting. award for profl. contbn., div. psychotherapy and div. clin. psychology 1987), Soc. Personality Assessment (pres. 1975—76, 1975—76, chair gen. psychol. svcs. 1987—97, bd. dirs.); mem.: Med. Sch. Profs. Psychology (pres. 1992—94, bd. dirs. 2004—06), Denver Psychoanalytic (trustee 1968—71), Am. Acad. Clin. Psychology (pres. 1993—2001). Home: 400 E 3rd Ave # 901 Denver CO 80203 Office Phone: 303-724-9128. Business E-Mail: carl.zimet@ucdenver.edu.

ZIMET, LLOYD, sport psychologist, health educator, author, program planner and administrator; b. Bklyn., 1951; s. Victor R. and Marcia Z. BA, Whittier Coll., Calif., 1973; MA, U. Md., 1983, PhD, 1984; MPH, NYU, 1989; DD, U. Life Ch. Monastery, 2007. Diplomate Coll. Health Behavior & Coll. Advocacy Edn., AAIM, bd. cert. health behavior Am. Assn. Integrative Medicine; ordained min. Universal Life Ch., 2007; cert. in sport psychology Nat. Inst. Sport Profl., 2008. Head basketball coach Aarhus U., Denmark, 1973—78, 1980—82, 1985—86; resident dir. U. Md., College Park, 1978—80; sports supr. Montgomery County Dept. Recreation, Md., 1978, 1982—84; dir. health promotion Optimal Fitness Inc., NYC, 1986—91; internat. cons. cmty. and occupational health, 1984—; dir. World of Discovery Day Camp, Bklyn., 1997—2000. Dir. edn. AIDS Ctr. of Queens County, NY, 1989-90; bd. dirs. Patricia Manning Meml. Fund childhood cancer Am. Cancer Soc., Queens, 1988-95; mem. AIDS med. adv. com. NYC Bd. Edn., 1989-90; mem. adv. bd. Adolescent Health Network, Queens, 1989-90; keynote speaker NYU Health Edn. Alumni, 1990, USPHS Region II Conf., 1991; prevention specialist Hillsborough County Sch. Dist., Fla., 2004-08, mem. sch. health adv. com., 2004, staff & program developer, 2005; program dir. HIV/STD/Pregnancy Prevention Program, Youth Risk Behavior Survery, Fla. Youth Surveys, 2005-08; mem. AIDS adv. com. Dept. Edn., State of Fla., 2004-08, Dist. Wellness Task Force, 2005-08. Bd. govs. US Amateur Boxing Fedn., Colorado Springs, Colo., 1988-91; bd. dirs. Met. Amateur Boxing Fedn., NYC, 1988-91; mem. USA Boxing Nat. Scholarship com., 1984-88. Fellow: Am. Inst. Stress, Am. Assn. Intergrative Medicine, Soc. Pub. Health Educators; mem.: APHA, APA.

ZIMMER, PAUL GERALD, II, retired community care licensing professional; b. Detroit, Oct. 2, 1946; s. Paul Gerald and Beatrice Mae (Mitchell) Z.; m. Shelly Mardell Hallier, May 23, 1980; children: Paul Gerald III, Carrie Lea. BA in Religion/Social Work, Azusa Pacific U., Calif., 1973. Ordained to ministry So. Bapt. Conf., 1985. Vocat. rehab. counselor dept. vocat. rehab. State of Calif., Riverside, 1986-88, intake specialist social svc. cmty. care licensing, 1988-91, licensing program supr. dept. social svc. cmty. care licensing, 1991-2001; ret., 2001. Instr., adv. bd. mem. Riverside County Office Edn.-Family-to-Family, 1993—; mem. Riverside County Dept. Pub. Social Svcs. Child Advocacy Coun., 1994—; co-chair RICKI com. Riverside County Dept. Health-Immunizations, 1996-98; monthly music evangelist LA Union Rescue Mission, 1984-2005, Christian Concert Assn., 2005-; mem. Fontana chpt. Am. Red Cross, 1983-87. Author (booklet): The Age of Becoming, 1977, Spiritually Broke, 2003; author (books): Prodigal Daze, 2004, Thorn Daze, 2006, Final Daze, 2011; author (music album) Day-A-Comin', 1989, (lyrics) Flashback Music, 1996. Dist. exec. Boy Scouts Am., Redlands/Victorville, Calif., 1981-83, mem. Order of Arrow, 1963—; mem./instr. Riverside County Office Edn. Child Care Initiative Project for Spanish Speaking Care Providers Indio, 1994—; appointed mem. State of Calif. Equal Employment Opportunity Adv. Com.-Disability Adv. Com., Sacramento, 1997-2000; min. Ch. in the Park, Hemet, Calif., 1996-2001; bd. dirs. Christian Concert Assn., 2005—. With US Army, 1967-68. Recipient Youth Adv. of Yr. award Riverside County Office Edn., 1993. Mem. Inland Empire Parents Anonymous (group facilitator, crisis counselor 1990-93). Avocations: writing/performing christian music, fitness walking, coin collecting/numismatics. Home: 1188 Wilson Ave Perris CA 92571-4926 Home Phone: 951-657-0500. Personal E-mail: airskypony@aol.com.

ZIMMER, ROSS R., cardiologist; Attended, Temple U. Diplomate Am. Bd. Internal Medicine, Am. Bd. Internal Medicine-cardiovasc. medicine, 1995. Intern Temple Univ. Hosp., resident, fellow; clin. asst. prof. of medicine Univ. of Pa.; dir. heart failure program Penn Presbyn. Med. Ctr. Named one of Top Doctors, Del. Valley Consumers Checkbook, 2003, Phila. Mag., 2010—11, Best Doctors in America, 2003—04, 2005—06, 2009—10. Fellow: Heart Failure Soc. of America, Am. Heart Assn. (adv. coun.); mem.: Internat. Soc. of Heart and Lung Transplantation, Am. Coll. of Cardiology. Office: Penn Presbyterian Medical Center Philadelphia Heart Institute 4th Fl Ste 400 51 N 39th St Philadelphia PA 19104 Office Phone: 800-789-7366.

ZIMMERMAN, ANDREW, pediatrician, neurologist; AB, Princeton U.; MD, Columbia U., 1970. Diplomate Am. Bd. Pediatrics, Am. Bd. Psychiatry & Neurology. Clinical assoc. Devel. & Metabolic Neurology Branch NIH; fellow Johns Hopkins U. Sch. Medicine, 1974, assoc. prof. neurology & psychiatry; faculty U. Conn. Sch. Medicine, 1977—83; pvt. practice Knoxville Neurology Clinic; pediatric neurologist Kennedy Krieger Inst. Ctr. for Autism & Related Disorders, dir. med. rsch. Recipient Disting. Svc. award, Autism Soc. America East Tenn. Chpt. Mem.: AMA, Soc. for Neuroscience, Child Neurology Soc., Am. Acad. Neurology, Am. Acad. Pediatrics. Office: Kennedy Krieger Institute 707 N Broadway Baltimore MD 21205 Office Phone: 443-923-9150. Office Fax: 443-923-9160.

ZIMMERMAN, EARL ABRAM, neurologist, educator; b. Harrisburg, Pa., May 5, 1937; s. Earl Beckley and Hazel Marie (Myers) Z. BS in Chemistry, Franklin and Marshall Coll., 1959; MD, U. Pa., 1963. Diplomate Am. Bd. Psychiatry and Neurology, Am. Bd. Internal Medicine. Intern Presbyn. Hosp., NYC, 1963-64, resident, 1964-65, Neurol. Inst. CPMC, NYC, 1965-68, research fellow endocrinology, 1970-72; asst. prof. to prof. neurology Columbia U., NYC, 1972-85; prof., chmn. dept. neurology Oreg. Health Sci. U., Portland, 1985-

2000; chmn. dept. neurology Albany (N.Y.) Med. Coll., 2000—04; clin. dir. neuroscis. Advanced Imaging Rsch. Ctr., dir. Alzheimer's Ctr., Albany Med. Ctr./GE Global Rsch., 2002—. Dir. neurology Helen Hayes Hosp., Haverstraw, N.Y., 1982-83 Mem. editl. bd. Jour. Histochem. Cytochemistry, 1980-85, 87, Neuroendocrinology, 1985-88, Annals of Neurology, 1985-91, Western Jour. Medicine, 1993-98, Jour. Clin. Endocrinal Metabolism, 1995-99; contbr. numerous articles to profl. jours. Maj. USAF, 1968-70 Rsch. grantee NIH, 1977—. Mem. Am. Neurol. Assn. (program chmn. 1980-82), Am. Acad. Neurology (Wartenber lectr. 1985), Endocrine Soc. Democrat. Mem. United Ch. of Christ Avocations: woodworking, gardening, theater, music, art, skiing, tennis. Office: Albany Med Coll Dept Neurology 47 New Scotland Ave MC-65 Albany NY 12208 Home Phone: 518-785-3638; Office Phone: 518-262-0801. Business E-Mail: zimmere@mail.amc.edu.

ZIMMERMAN, FREDERICK J., health services professor; BA in Economics, U. Notre Dame, Ind., 1985; MS in Economics, U. Wis., Madison, 1989, PhD in Economics, 1994. Asst. prof. Food Rsch. Inst., Stanford U., Calif., 1994—99; biostatistician/health economist Child Care Inst., U. Wash., Seattle, 1999—2000, acting asst. prof. dept. healrh svcs., 2000—02, asst. prof., 2002—05, assoc. prof., 2005—08; assoc. prof. dept. health svcs. UCLA, 2008—, Fred W. & Pamela K. Wasserman chair health svcs. Vis. scholar, agrl. & cultural economics U. Calif., Berkeley, 1996—97; biostatistician/health economist Child Care Inst., U. Wash., 1999—2000, co-dir., 2002—06. Author: Development at a Crossroads: Uncertain Paths to Sustainability, 1998, The Elephant in the Living Room: Make TV Work for Your Kids, 2006; contbr. articles to profl. jours. Mem.: Soc. Devel. & Behavioral Pediat., Soc. Rsch. in Child Devel., Am. Soc. Health Economics, Internat. Health Economics Assn., Am. Econ. Assn. Achievements include research in economic influences on population health, with a particular focus the effects of advertising and economic structure on child obesity; studies of how child obesity is framed and what effect that framing has on attempts to find solutions to the problems of poor diet and inadequate physical activity among children. Office: UCLA Sch Pub Health Dept Health Scis Box 951772 41 295D CHS Los Angeles CA 90095 Office Phone: 310-825-1971. Office Fax: 310-825-3317. E-mail: fredzimmerman@ucla.edu. *

ZIMMERMAN, GUY ALEXANDER, internist, educator, research scientist; b. Decatur, Ga., July 10, 1946; s. Edgar Alexander and Helen (Summerour) Z.; m. Mary Frances Bonner, Aug. 19, 1972; children: Anne, Patrick. BA, Emory U., 1968; MS, MD, Baylor Coll. Medicine, 1973. Intern, resident and fellow U. Utah Med. Ctr., Salt Lake City, 1973-78; resident U. Wash. Med. Ctr., Seattle, 1978-80; asst. prof. U. Utah Sch. Medicine, Salt Lake City, 1980-85, assoc. prof., 1985-90, prof., 1991—, assoc. chair, 1998—2001, 2009—. Dir. program in cardiovasc. pharmacology, cell biology Nora Eccles Harrison Cardiovasc. Rsch. and Tng. Inst., Salt Lake City, 1985-99, dir. Program Human Molecular Biology and Genetics, 1999-2009; cons. NIH, Am. Heart Assn., internat. granting orgns.; cons. to industry, lectr. in field. Assoc. editor Am. Jour. Respiratory Cell and Molecular Biology; mem. editorial bd. Jour. Clin. Investigation, numerous others; contbr. articles to profl. jours. NIH grantee; recipient Clin. Investigator award NIH, 1980, Established Investigator award Am. Heart Assn., 1985, Merit award NIH, 2004, Rsch. Achievement award, 2009 Mem. Am. Fedn. for Clin. Rsch., Am. Soc. for Clin. Investigation, Am. Soc. Cell Biology, Am. Soc. Biol. Chemistry, Assn. Am. Physicians, Royal Coll. Physicians (Ireland). Office: U Utah Med Ctr Rm 4220 Eccles Inst Human Genetics 15 North 2030 East Salt Lake City UT 84112 Office Phone: 801-585-0950. Business E-Mail: guy.zimmerman@hmbg.utah.edu.

ZIMMERMAN, JERALD R., physiatrist; MD, U. Ill., 1982. Diplomate Am. Bd. Physical Medicine and Rehab., 1989. Resident orthopedic surgery Univ. of Minn. Med. Ctr., Mpls., 1983—85; fellow physical medicine & rehab. Columbia-Presbyn. Med. Ctr., NYC, 1985—88; attending phycisian Englewood Hosp. and Med. Ctr., NJ. Office: Englewood Hospital and Medical Center 370 Grand Ave Ste 102 Englewood NJ 07631 Office Phone: 201-567-3370. Office Fax: 201-816-1265.

ZIMMERMAN, JO ANN, retired health science association administrator, educator, retired lieutenant governor; b. Van Buren County, Iowa, Dec. 24, 1936; d. Russell and Hazel (Ward) McIntosh; m. A. Tom Zimmerman, Aug. 26, 1956; children: Andrew, Lisa, Don and Ron (twins), Beth. Diploma, Broadlawns Sch. of Nursing, Des Moines, 1958; BA with honors, Drake U., 1973; postgrad., Iowa State U., 1973—75. RN, Iowa. Asst. head nurse maternity dept. Broadlawns Med. Ctr., Des Moines, 1958—59, weekend supr. nursing svcs., 1960—61, supr. maternity dept., 1966—68; instr. maternity nursing Broadlawns Sch. Nursing, 1968—71; health planner, community rels. assoc. Iowa Health Systems Agy., Des Moines, 1978—82; mem. Iowa Ho. Reps., 1982—86; lt. gov., pres. of Senate, State of Iowa, 1987—91; cons. health svcs., grant writing and continuing edn. Zimmerman & Assocs., Des Moines, 1991—2000; dir. patient care svcs. Nursing Svcs. Iowa, 1996—98; nurse case mgr. Olsten Health Svcs. (now Gentiva Health Svcs.), 1998—2004; founder JAZ Tours, 2002—04, ret., 2004, 2004. Ops. dir. Medlink Svcs., Inc., Des Moines, 1992-96. Contbr. articles to profl. jours. Mem. advanced registered nurse practioner task force on cert. nurse mid-wives Iowa Bd. Nursing, 1980-81, Waukee, Polk County, Iowa Health Edn. Coord. Coun., Iowa Women's Polit. Caucus, Dallas County Women's Polit. Caucus; chmn. Des Moines Area Maternity Nursing Conf. Group. 1969-70, task force on sch. health svcs. Iowa Dept. Health, 1982, task force health edn. Iowa Dept. Pub. Instruction, 1979, adv. com. health edn. assessment tool, 1980-81, Nat. Lt. Govs., chair com. on Agrl. and Rural Devel., 1989; Dallas County Dem. Ctrl. Com., 1972-84, 98—; bd. dirs. Waukee Cmty. Sch. Bd., 1976-79, pres. 1978-79; bd. dirs. Iowa PTA, 1979-83, chair Health Com., 1980-84; mem. steering com. ERA, Iowa, 1991-92; founder Dem. Activist Women's Network (DAWN), 1992; mem. Disciples of Christ Mission Group to El Salvadore, 2003, 04; founder health ministry First Christian Ch., Des Moines, Iowa, 2004. Recipient Woman Achievement award, YWCA Greater Des Moines, 2005, Search Your Heart award, Am. Heart Assn., 2007; named to Iowa Women's Hall of Fame, 2005. Mem. ANA, LWV (health chmn. met. Des Moines chpt.), Iowa Nurses Assn., Iowa League for Nursing (bd. dirs. 1979-83), Family Centered Childbirth Edn. Assn. (childbirth instr., advisor), Iowa Cattleman's Assn., Am. Lung Assn. (bd. dirs. Iowa 1988-92), Dem. Activist Women's Network (founder 1992), State Hist. Soc. Iowa (bd. mem. 2007-), First Christian Ch. Des Moines (pres. elect 2008, pres. 2009), Dallas County Master Gardeners (pres. 2008-10). Mem. Christian Ch. Avocations: gardening, sewing, reading, bridge.

ZIMMERMAN, JOSEPH, physician, researcher; b. Tel Aviv, June 25, 1948; s. Dov and Miriam (Matz) Z.; m. Shoshana Comforty, Oct. 21, 1971; children: Donna, Tal. MD, Hebrew U., Hadassah Med. Sch., Jerusalem, 1977. Cert. in internal medicine and gastroenterology Israel; lic. in medicine, Ill. Resident in internal medicine Hadassah U. Hosp., Jerusalem, 1977-82, fellow in gastroenterology, 1982-84; Fogarty fellow U. Chgo., 1984-86; sr. lectr. Hadanah U. Hosp., Jerusalem, 1986-94, assoc. prof. internal medicine, 1994—; chmn. Inst. Postgrad. Studies Hebrew U.-Hadassah Med. Sch., 1995-97. Capt. Israeli Defense Force, 1966-68, 75-77. Mem. Am. Gastroenterological Assn., Israeli Gastroenterological Assn., Israeli Soc. Clin. and Experimental Hypnosis, 1988—. Office: Hadassah U Hosp-Gastro Unit PO Box 12000 91120 Jerusalem Israel E-mail: zimmerj@vms.huji.ac.il.

ZIMMERMAN, ROBERT A., neuroradiologist, educator; BA in Biology, Temple U., Phila., 1960; MD, Georgetown U., Washington DC, 1964. Diplomate Am. Bd. Radiology, Am. Bd. Radiology-neuroradiology. Radiology residency and fellowship in special procedures Hosp. of the Univ. of Pa., Phila., prof. radiology, The Children's Hosp. of Phila., chief neuroradiology divsn./MRI. With Pediatric Brain Tumor Consortium; brain tumor strategy group and tumor imaging steering com. The Children's Cancer Study Group; cons. vaccine compensation program US Dept. of Jusice; cons. STOP sickle cell study NIH. Editor-in-chief: USA, Neuroradiology, 1989—, reviewer: sci. articles, editor: Annals of Neurology, Cancer, Am. Jour. of Neuroradiology, Am. Jour. of Roentgenology, Med. and Pediatric Oncology, Neuro-Oncology, Pediatric Emergency Medicine, Pediatric Radiology, Pediatrics, author/co-author: numerous sci. publs. Recipient Endowed Chair in Pediatric Neuroradiology, The Children's Hosp. of Phila., 2007—09. Fellow: Am. Coll. of Radiology; mem.: Coll. of Physicians of Phila., Phila. Roentgen Ray Soc., Pa. Radiologic Soc., Am. Soc. of Pediatric Neurology (pres. 1995—96), Am. Soc. of Spinal Radiology, Soc. of Magnetic Resonance in Magnetic, Belgian Radiologic Soc. (hon.), Am. Soc. of Neuroradiology (sr.), European Soc. of Neuroradiology (hon.), The Soc. for Pediatric Radiology, Am. Soc. of Head & Neck Radiology, Radiol. Soc. of N.Am., Assn. of Univ. Radiologists, Internat. Soc. of Pediatric Neurosurgery, Brit. Inst. of Radiology. Office: The Childrens Hospital of Philadelphia 34th St and Civic Center Blvd Philadelphia PA 19104 Office Phone: 215-590-2569. Office Fax: 215-590-1345.

ZIMMERMANN-GORSKA, IRENA TERESA, rheumatologist, educator; b. Lwow, Poland, May 19, 1935; d. Marian Michal and Zofia Aleksandra Zimmermann; 1 child, Ewa Gorska Tatarkiewicz, Grad., U. Med. Scis., Poznan, Poland, 1957, MD, 1963, grad. in Philosophy, 1963. Specialist internal medicine U. Med. Scis., Poznan, 1964; specialist rheumatology Inst. Rheumatology, Warsaw, 1970, prof. rheumatology U. Med. Scis., Poznan, 1985. Cons. internal medicine and rheumatology Poznan Region, 1970—. Author: (book) Essentials of Rheumatology For Medical Studies, 2003. Mem.: European League Against Rheumatism, Polish Soc. Internal Medicine (hon.), European Fedn. Internal Medicine (hon.). Avocation: classical music. Office Phone: 4861 831 0317. Office Fax: 4861 831 0317. Personal E-mail: zimmermanngorska@hotmail.com.

ZIN, WALTER ARAUJO, physiology educator, researcher; b. Rio de Janeiro, June 16, 1952; s. Walter and Candida Augusta (Araujo) Z.; m. Andrea Araujo Zin, Dec. 19, 1986; children: Emilia Araujo Zin, Olivia Araujo Zin. MD, U. Fed. Rio de Janeiro, 1975; MSc, Fed. U. Rio de Janeiro, 1979, DSc, 1984. Instr. Fed. U. Rio de Janeiro, 1977-80, from asst. to assoc. prof., 1980—84, prof., 1993—, chief lab. respiratory physiology Inst. Biophysics, 1987—, dir. Inst. Biophysics, 2001—04, acad. dir. Univ. Libr., 1999-2001. Vis. asst. prof. McGill U., Montreal, Canada, 1980—84, vis. assoc. prof., 1985—86, vis. prof., 1994—95; vis. assoc. prof. U. Pitts, 1991—92, Univ.2 Pitts, 1998; vis. prof. Hosp. U. Bellvitge, Hosp. Llobregat, Spain, 1992, 95, 1998—2001, U. Rep. Montevideo, Uruguay, 1994—95, 1997, 2000, 06, U. Studies Trieste, Italy, 1996—97, 2003—09, 2011, U. Studies Florence, Italy, 1997, 1999—2005, U. Studies, Catania, Italy, 2010; cons. sci. com. Brazilian Coun. for Sci. and Tech. Devel., 1993—95, 1998—2001, 2008—; cons. Coun. for Grad. Studies and Rsch. Fed. U. Rio de Janeiro, 1990—97; life scis. area coord. Rio de Janeiro State Found. for Sci. Devel., 1998—2000, bd. councillors, 2000—06; mem. sci. and tech. com. nat. health coun. Min. Health, 2000—07; mem. multidisciplinary postgrad. courses Min. Edn., 2001—03; vis. prof. U. Barcelona, Spain, 2005, 07; coun. cons. Financing for Studies and Projects, 2008—. Contbr. articles to profl. jours. Named Knight of Nat. Order of Sci. Merit, Brazil, 2002, Ad Honorem prof. faculty medicine, U. de la Republice, Montevideo, 2006. Mem. Am. Thoracic Soc., European Respiratory Soc. (nomination com. 2005-06, Brazilian nat. del. 2005—08), Am. Physiol. Soc., Brazilian Acad. Scis., Am. Heart Assn. (cardiorespiratory and critical care coun.), Brazilian Soc. Pneumology (pres. dept. pathophysiology 1992-98), Brazilian Soc. Cardiology (pres. dept. cardiovasc. and respiratory physiology 1987-91), Brazilian Physiol. Soc. (treas. 1988-91, steering com. 1994-2003, 06—08, v.p. 2002-04, pres. 2004-06), Fedn. Brazilian Socs. for Exptl. Biology (v.p. 1995-2001, 2007-). Office: U Fed Rio de Janeiro Inst de Biofisica 21949900 Rio de Janeiro Brazil

ZINCZENKO, DAVID, publishing executive, editor-in-chief, editorial director, author; b. Dec. 13, 1969; s. Bohdan Zinczenko and Janice Sobieski. Grad., Moravian Coll., Bethlehem, Pa. Assoc. editor Men's Jour., 1991—93; editl. dir. Men's Health Internat.; editor-in-chief Men's Health mag. Rodale Inc., 2000—, editl. dir. Best Life mag., 2004—09, editl. dir. Women's Health mag., 2008—, editl. dir. organic gardening, editl. dir. prevention, 2011—. Chmn. Am. Mag. Conf., 2007. Author: (books) The Abs Diet series, 2004—06 (NY Times Bestsellers), Men, Love & Sex: The Complete User's Guide for Women, 2006; co-author (with Matt Goulding): Eat This, Not That!, 2007, Eat This, Not That! For Kids, 2008, Eat This, Not That! Supermarket Survival Guide, 2008, Eat This Not That! The Best (& Worst!) Foods in America, 2009, Eat This, Not That! Restaurant Survival Guide, 2009, Cook This, Not That! Kitchen Survival Guide, 2010; author: (web logs) Eat This, Not That!, Mysteries of the Sexes Explained; regular contbr. Today Show, NY Times, LA Times, USA Today, TV appearances include Ellen, 20/20, Biggest Loser, Oprah, Rachael Ray, Good Morning America; co-author: The Eat This Not That No Diet Diet, 2011, The Worlds Easiest Weight loss plan; author: Yahoo! Eat This Not That Blog. Served with USNR. Recipient Nat. Mag. award for gen. excellence, American Soc. Mag. Editors, 2010, Nat. Mag. award for personal svc., 2011, Nat. Mag. award for gen. excellence, 2011; named Editor of Yr., Ad Week, 2008; named one of Thirty Under 30, Folio mag., 1999, 50 Most Eligible Bachelors, People mag., 2002, 2007, 21 Most Intriguing People, MIN mag., 2003, Ten Best-Dressed in Media, Ad Age, 2005, 40 Under 40, Crain's NY Bus., 2005. Achievements include helping pass legislation in 1994 establishing the week of Father's Day as National Men's Health Week; launching FitSchools in 2007, a national campaign to reinvigorate physical education programs in America's elementary schools and get children in healthy, active living. Office: Men's Health 733 Third Ave New York NY 10017 also: Men's Health Rodale 33 E Minor St Emmaus PA 18098 Office Phone: 212-808-1324, 610-967-5171. Office Fax: 610-967-8963. Business E-Mail: david.zinczenko@rodale.com.

ZINDRICK, MICHAEL R., orthopedist; MD, Loyola Univ. Stritch Sch. Med. Cert. Am. Bd. Orthopaedic Examiners, Am. Bd. Spinal Surgery Examiners. Internship & residency Loyola Univ. Med. Ctr., Maywood, Ill.; fellowship in spine surgery Long Beach Meml. Hosp., Calif.; ptnr. Hinsdale Orthopaedic Assoc., S.C., 1985—; staff physician Hinsdale Hosp. and Good Samaritan Hosp.; clin. assoc. prof., dept. orthopaedic surgery Loyola Univ. Clin. dir. Rsch. and Spinal Surgery Fellowship Program; examiner Am. Bd. Orthopaedic Surgery; v.p. Am. Bd. Spinal Surgery, 2005—08. Contbr. articles to profl. jours. Mem.: Am. Acad. Orthopaedic Surgeons, Am. Orthopaedic Assn., Assn. Bone and Joint Surgeons, North Am. Spine Soc., Internat. Soc. the Study of the Lumbar Spine, Ill. State Med. Soc. Office: Hinsdale Orthopaedics 550 W Ogden Ave Hinsdale IL 60521

ZINGALE, DONALD PAUL, academic administrator, educator; b. Bklyn., Aug. 3, 1946; s. Charles and Helen (Puglisi) Z. BS in Health, Phys. Edn., Bklyn. Coll., 1967; MS in Phys. Edn., U. Mass., 1969; PhD in Phys. Edn., Ohio State U., 1973; MSW, Calif. State U., Sacramento, 1984. Lic. clin. social worker, Calif.; lic. marriage and family counselor, Calif.; cert. health and phys. edn. instr. secondary schs., N.Y.C., N.Y.; cert. Alpine ski instr. Prof., assoc. dean health, human svcs. Calif. State U., Sacramento, 1973-93, assoc. v.p. rsch. and grad. studies, 1993-95, dean LA, 1995—96; dean Coll. Health and Human Svcs. San Francisco State U., 1996—2004; v.p. acad. affairs Calif. Maritime Acad., 2004—08; pres. SUNY Cobleskill, 2008—. Contbr. articles to profl. jours. and publs. Mem.: APHA, ACE, AASCU, Nat. Coun. U. Rsch. Adminstrs., Am. Assn. Higher Edn., Am. Assn. Health Phys. Edn., Recreation and Dance, Profl. Ski Instrs. Am. Roman Catholic. Avocations: alpine skiing, sailing, travel, cooking, home renovation. Office: SUNY Cobleskill 106 Suffolk Cir Knapp Hall Cobleskill NY 12043

ZINGALE, ROBERT G., surgeon; b. Bklyn., Feb. 9, 1957; s. Joseph and Theresa Zingale; m. Christine A. Smith, Oct. 4, 1986; children-:Jillian, Kara, Alec. BS cum laude, Pace U., 1979; MD, SUNY, Bklyn., 1983. Diplomate Am. Bd. Surgery, Surg. Crit. Care, Nat. Bd. Med. Examiners. Resident Maimonides Med. Ctr., Bklyn., 1983-88; trauma fellow Coney Island Hosp, Bklyn., 1988-89; attending physician, dir. trauma, pres. med. staff Huntington (N.Y.) Hosp., 1989—; attending physician Nassau County Med. Ctr., East Meadow, NY, 1991—; clin. instr. SUNY, Stony Brook, 1991—; assoc. clin. prof. surgery N.Y. Med. Coll./North Shore U. Hosp., Valhalla, 1993—; pres. med. staff Huntington Hosp. Dir. surg. svcs. Dolan Health Ctr. Contbr. articles to profl. jours. Fellow ACS, Suffolk Acad. Medicine; mem. AMA, Soc. Laparoendoscopic Surgeons, Am. Soc. Gen. Surgeons, N.Y. Met. Breast Cancer Grop, Med. Soc. N.Y., Suffolk County Med. Soc. Office: 158 E Main St Huntington NY 11743 Office Phone: 631-271-1822.

ZINK, HARRY A., ophthalmologist; MD, Univ. Pa., 1971. Resident, rsch. fellow, glaucoma Barnes Hosp.-Washington Univ. Sch. Med., St. Louis, 1976; asst. clin. prof. Case Western Res. Univ.; pvt. practice Wooster, Ohio. Mem.: Ohio Ophthalmological Soc., Am. Acad. Ophthalmology (mem. coun. from Ohio Ophthalmological Soc. 1993—95, trustee-at-large 1995—97, sec. mem. svcs. 1998—2004, pres. 2005—06, chmn. membership adv. com., ad hoc com. on primary eye care). Office: Wooster Eye Ctr 3519 Friendsville Rd Wooster OH 44691 Office Phone: 330-345-7200.

ZINKERNAGEL, ROLF MARTIN, immunologist, educator; b. Basle, Switzerland, Jan. 6, 1944; s. Robert W. and Suzanne (Staehlin) Zinkernagel; m. Kathrin G. Ludin, Mar. 11, 1968; children: Christine, Annelies, Martin. MD, U. Basel, 1968; PhD, Australian Nat. U., Canberra, 1975. Surg. intern St. Claraspital Hosp., Basel, 1968—69; postdoc. fellow, Lab. Electron Microscopy, Inst. Anatomy U. Basel, 1969—70; postdoc. fellow, Inst. Biochemistry U. Lausanne, 1971—73; vis. fellow dept. microbiology Australian Nat. U., 1973—75; asst. to assoc. prof. dept. immunopathology Scripps Rsch. Inst., La Jolla, Calif., 1975—79, prof., 1979; assoc. prof. dept. pathology U. Zurich, 1979—88, prof. dept. pathology, 1988—2008, prof. emeritus, 2008—; co-head Inst. Exptl. Immunology Inst. Exptl. Immunology, Zurich, 1992—2008. Adj. assoc. prof. dept. pathology U. Calif., San Diego, 1977—79. Mem. editl. bd. Exptl. Cell Biology, 1976—88, Immunogenetics, 1977—2008, Parasite Immunology, 1978—84, 1978—80, Thymus, 1979—89, Antiviral Rsch., 1980—88, Jour. Exptl. Medicine, 1981—84, European Jour. Immunology, 1981—2007, Jour. Environ. Pathology, Toxicology & Oncology, 1981—2007, Cellular Immunology, 1983—2007, Internat. Jour. Microbiology, 1983—2007, others; contbr. articles to profl. jours. Recipient Gairdner Found. Internat. award, Can., 1986, Christoforo Colombo award, Italy, 1992, Albert Lasker award for basic med. rsch., 1995, Nobel prize for physiology/medicine, 1996, Drew-Novartis award, 1997, Starzl prize, Pitts., 2001, Maharashi Sushruta award, India, 2002. Fellow: NAS (fgn.), Am. Acad. Microbiology, Am. Acad. Arts & Scis. (fgn.), Royal Soc. (fgn.), Australian Acad. Scis. (fgn.),

Am. Philos. Soc. (fgn.); mem.: Russian Acad. Scis. (fgn.), German Soc. Virology, German Soc. Immunology, Am. Assn. Immunologists (hon.), Swiss Soc. Allergy & Immunology (hon.; pres. 1993—94), Australian Soc. Immunology (hon.), Scandinavian Soc. Immunology (hon.), Internat. Soc. Antiviral Rsch., Acadmia Euopea, Swiss Soc. Cell & Molecular Biology, Swiss Soc. Microbiology, Swiss Soc. Pathology, Am. Assn. Pathologists. Achievements include discovery of of MHC-restricted T cell recognition; of the thymus role in determining MHC-restricted T-cell specficity; NK-cell activity in virus infections, T-cell epitope escape virus mutants, tolerances to viruses; research in on role of virus-specific T-cells in causing immunopathology. Office: University Zurich Dept Pathology Schmelzbergstr 12 8091 Zurich Switzerland Office Phone: 41 44 255 2989. Office Fax: 41 44 255 4420. Business E-Mail: Rolf.Zinkernagel@usz.ch. *

ZINN, KEITH MARSHALL, ophthalmologist, educator; b. Bklyn., Oct. 15, 1940; s. Victor Zinn and Eve (Lane) Z.; m. Elaine H. Kirban, Apr. 8, 1979. Student, NYU, Bronx, 1961; MD, SUNY, Bklyn., 1965. Diplomate Am. Bd. Ophthalmology; lic. physician, NY, Calif. Intern St. Lukes Hosp., NYC, 1965-66; research assoc. NIH, Bethesda, Md., 1966-68; post-doctoral fellow Retina Found., Boston, 1968-69; post-doctoral fellow dept. ophthalmology Harvard U. Med. Sch., Boston, 1968; asst. resident chief resident dept. ophthalmology Mount Sinai Hosp., NYC, 1969-71, ednl. fellow dept. ophthalmology, 1971-72; chief clin. fellow retina service Mass. Eye & Ear Infirmary, Harvard U. Med. Sch., Boston, 1972-73, Heed fellow dept. ophthalmology, 1972-73; research assoc. dept. retina research Retina Found., Boston, 1972-73; mem. faculty Lancaster Post-Grad. Course Ophthalmology, Harvard U. Med. Sch., Boston, 1970-90; consulting mng. dir. HT Capital Advisors, LLC, 2000—. Guest faculty dept. ophthalmology Harvard U. Med. Sch., Boston, 1969-84; asst. prof. dept. ophthalmology Mt. Sinai Sch. medicine, NYC, assoc. clin. prof., 1976-80, clin. prof., 1980—; attending ophthalmic surgeon NYC, 1980—; attending ophthalmic surgeon Manhattan Eye Ear & Throat Hosp., NYC, 1981—; surgeon cons. Hosp. Joint Diseases, NYC, 1975-83, Patrolmen's Benevolent Assn., NYC, 1977—; lectr. field. Author: The Pupil, 1972, Ocular Fine Structure for the Clinician, 1973, The Developing Visual System, 1975, The Retinal Pigment Epithelium, 1975; author-editor: The Retinal Epithelium, 1979, Clinical Atlas of Peripheral Retinal Disorders, 1988; numerous audio-visual teaching progs. in ophthalmology; contbg. editor Mt. Sinai Jour. Medicine, 1975—; assoc. mem. editorial bd. Ophthalmic Surgery, 1980-89; mem. faculty editorial bd. Clin. Opththalmology Update, 1982—; inventor field. Served lt. comdr. USPHS, 1966-68. Recipient numerous awards excellence medicine, including: Joseph Globus award Mount Sinai Jour. Medicine, 1979, Abraham Kornzweig Teaching award Mount Sinai Sch. Medicine, 1982. Fellow Am. Acad. Ophthalmology, Otolaryngology, ACS, Internat. Coll. Surgeons, Internat. Eye Found., Soc. Eye Surgeons, NY Acad. Medicine, NY Diabetes Assn., NY Heart Assn., NY Soc. Clin. Ophthalmology, Soc. Heed Fellows, Retina Soc., Ophthalmic Soc. UK, Oxford Ophthal. Congress, Brit. Am. Retinal Group; mem. AMA (Physicians Recognition award 1971, 76, 81, 82, 85), Ophthalmic Laser Surg. Soc. (v.p. 1986-88, pres. 1988-90), Am. Intraocular Lens Implant Soc., NY Acad. Medicine (trustee 1989-90, sec. 1985-86, chmn. ophthalmology sect. 1987-88, David Warfield fellowship com. 1990-92), Am. Bd. Laser Surgery (bd. dir. 1987—). Home: 125 E 87th St Apt 14C New York NY 10128 Office Phone: 646-895-9045.

ZINNERT, MICHELLE, medical association administrator; BA in Polit. Sci., Ind. U., Pa., 1991. Dir. mktg. and corp. rels. Am. Assn. Blood Banks; sr. mgr. corp. rels. Am. Urol. Assn.; assn. exec. SmithBucklin, 2007—; exec. dir. Internat. Soc. Exptl. Hematology, Washington, 2007—, Am. Urogynecologic Assn., Washington, 2007—. Mem.: Am. Soc. Assn. Execs., Ctr. Assn. Leadership. Office: Am Urogynecologic Assn 2025 M St NW Ste 800 Washington DC 20036 Office Phone: 202-367-1167. Office Fax: 202-367-2167. Business E-Mail: mzinnert@smithbucklin.com. *

ZINZOW, HEIDI, psychologist; b. Decatur, Ga., Apr. 7, 1976; PhD, U. Ga., 2007. Rsch. assoc. Caliber Assocs., 1999—2002; psychology intern dept. vet. affairs Med. U. SC, 2005—06; postdoc. rsch. fellow Nat. Crime Victims Rsch. & Treatment Ctr., 2007—08; asst. prof. Clemson U., 2008—11; pvt. practice clin. psychologist, 2009—. Recipient Outstanding Faculty Publ. award, Clemson U.; grant, Army Med. Rsch. and Material Command, Postdoc. fellowship, Med. U. SC. Mem.: Assn. Advancement Behavioral and Cognitive Therapies. Office: 400-4 Coll Ave Clemson SC 29631 Business E-Mail: hzinzow@clemson.edu.

ZIPES, DOUGLAS PETER, cardiologist, researcher; b. White Plains, NY, Feb. 27, 1939; s. Robert Samuel Zipes and Josephine Helen Weber; m. Marilyn Joan Jacobus, Feb. 18, 1961; children: Debra, Jeffrey, David. BA cum laude, Dartmouth Coll., 1961, B of Med. Sci., 1962; MD cum laude, Harvard Med. Sch., 1964. Diplomate Internal Medicine 1970, Cardiovascular Disease 1972. Intern, medicine Duke U. Med. Ctr., Durham, NC, 1964—65, resident, cardiology, 1965—66, fellow, 1966—68; joined Ind. U. Sch. Medicine, Indpls., 1970, prof. medicine, 1976—94, disting. prof., medicine, pharmacology and toxicology, 1994—2007, disting. prof. emeritus, 2007—, dir., cardiology divsn. and Krannert Inst. Cardiology, 1995—. Bd. dirs. Inst. for Clin. Evaluation; cardiology adv. com NIH, 1991—94; mem. med. adv. bd. ABCNews.com, 2000—; mem. dean's coun. Dartmouth Med. Sch., Ind. Med. Sch. Contbr. articles to profl. jours., chapters to books in medicine; founding editor-in-chief Jour. Cardiovascular Electrophysiology, founding editor Heart Rhythm, N.Am. Soc. Pacing and Electrophysiology/Heart Rhythm Soc., mem. of several editl. bds. of peer-reviewed jours.; author: (novels) The Black Widows. Past pres. Indpls. Opera. Recipient Sagamore of Wabash, Gov. of Ind., 2001, Disting. Alumnus award, Duke U. Med. Ctr., 2007, Pres. medal, Ind. U., 2010. Master: Am. Coll. Cardiology (past pres., Disting. Scientist award 1996); fellow: Heart Rhythm Soc. (past pres., Disting. Scientist award 1995); mem.: Am. Bd. Internal Medicine (past chair), Assn. U. Cardiologists (past pres.), Cardiac Electrophysiology Soc. (past pres.), Argentine Cardiology Soc. (hon.), Am. Heart Assn. (Disting. Achievement award 1989, James B. Herrick award 1997, Cor Vitae award 2004), Assn. Am. Physicians, Am. Soc. Clin. Investigation. Home: 10614 Winterwood Carmel IN 46032-9688 Office: Krannert Inst Cardiology Rm E474 1801 N Capitol Ave Ste E400 Indianapolis IN 46202-1228 Office Phone: 317-962-0555, 317-962-0556. Office Fax: 317-962-0568. Business E-Mail: dzipes@iupui.edu.

ZIPPIN, CALVIN, epidemiologist, educator; b. Albany, NY, July 17, 1926; s. Samuel and Jennie (Perkel) Z.; m. Patricia Jayne Schubert, Feb. 9, 1964; children: David Benjamin, Jennifer Dorothy. AB magna cum laude, SUNY, Albany, 1947; ScD, Johns Hopkins U., Balt., 1953. Rsch. asst. Sterling-Winthrop Rsch. Inst., Rensselaer, NY, 1947-50, Johns Hopkins U., Balt., 1950—53; instr. biostats. Sch. Pub. Health, U. Calif., Berkeley, 1953-55; asst. to full rsch. biostatistician Sch. Medicine U. Calif., San Francisco, 1955-67, asst. prof. preventive medicine, 1958-60; post doctoral fellow London Sch. Hygiene and Tropical Medicine, 1964-65; prof. epidemiology U. Calif., San Francisco, 1967-91, prof. emeritus, 1991—. Vis. assoc. prof. stats. Stanford U., 1962; adv. WHO, 1969—; vis rsch. worker Middlesex Hosp. Med. Sch., London, 1975; com. mem. Am. Cancer Soc. and Nat. Cancer Inst., 1956—; faculty adviser Regional Cancer Centre, Trivandrum, India, 1983—; cons., lectr., vis. prof. in field. Co-author book, book chpts.; author or co-author papers primarily on biometry and epidemiology of cancer; editl. advisor Jour. Stats. in Medicine, 1981-86. Mem., alt. mem. Dem. Ctrl. Com., Marin County, Calif., 1987-96. Recipient Disting. Alumnus award SUNY, Albany, 1969, Lifetime Achievement and Leadership award Nat. Cancer Inst., 2003, also awards, fellowships and grants for work in cancer biometry and epidemiology. Fellow Am. Statis. Assn., Am. Coll. Epidemiology, Royal Statis. Soc. Gt. Britain; mem. Biometric Soc. (mem. internat. coun. 1978-81, pres. Western N.Am. region 1979-80), Calif. Cancer Registrars Assn. (hon.), Internat. Assn. Cancer Registries (hon.), B'nai B'rith (pres. Golden Gate lodge 1970-71, pres. Greater San Francisco unit 21 2003-06, internat. bd. govs. 2005—07, greater San Francisco Man of Yr., 2009), Phi Beta Kappa, Sigma Xi, Delta Omega.

ZISLIN, JOSEF, psychiatrist, researcher; b. St. Petersburg, Russia, Jan. 25, 1961; arrived in Israel, 1991; s. Meir Natan and Mara Josef Zislin; children: Jakob, Asia, Eden, Mey. Lic. psychiatrist. Resident in psychiatry Ezrat Nashim Hosp., 1991-97; sr. psychiatrist Kfar Shaul Mental Hosp., Jerusalem, 1997—. Contbr. articles to profl. jours. Achievements include research in psychopharmacology:-marked evaluation of serum creatinine kinase associated with olanzapine therapy; Cultural psychiatry-Male self-mutilation and Jerusalem Syndrome; psychiatric nosology and biological taxonomy; neuropragmatics-the generation of psychosis: a pragmatic approach; toward the structuralist approach to the diagnosis, Semiotic approach to the Psychiatric Diagnosis; ego dystonic Delusions as a predictor of Dangerous Behaviour Damp Crows behavior; wavelet analysis of the frontal auditory evoked potentials in schizophrenia, Imagination of Body tation can induced eye movements, theory of unitary psychosis and nostitatis language theory. Office: Kfar Shaul Mental Hosp Givat shaul B Jerusalem Israel Home: Mavo Tamar 121/5 Zur Hadassa Israel Office Phone: 972 2 6551 512, 97226551524. Personal E-mail: jozislin@yahoo.com.

ZISSELMAN, MARC, geriatric psychiatry, director; MD, NYU. Diplomate Am. Bd. Psychiatry and Neurology-geriatric psychiatry, cert. electroconvulsive therapy (ETC). Resident Albert Einstein/Montefiore Med. Ctr., NY; geriatric psychiatrist Albert Einstein Med. Ctr., Phila., med. dir. geriatric psychiatry divsn., med. dir. inpatient and geriatric psychiatry, assoc. chair psychiatry dept. Office: MossRehab 4th Fl 1200 W Tabor Rd Philadelphia PA 19141 Office Phone: 215-456-9472. Office Fax: 215-456-9186.

ZITRIN, ARTHUR, physician; b. Bklyn., Apr. 10, 1918; s. William and Lillian (Elbaum) Z.; m. Charlotte Marker, Oct. 4, 1942; children— Richard Alan, Elizabeth Ann. BS, City Coll. N.Y., 1938; MS, N.Y. U., 1941, MD, 1945; certificate psychoanalytic medicine, Columbia, 1955. Diplomate: Am. Bd. Psychiatry and Neurology. Research fellow animal behavior Am. Museum Natural History, 1939-42; intern King County Hosp., 1945-46; resident psychiatry Bellevue Hosp., 1948-51; instr. physiology Hunter Coll., NYC, 1948-49; mem. faculty N.Y.U. Sch. Medicine, 1949-97, prof. psychiatry, 1967-97, prof. emeritus, 1997—; mem. staff Bellevue Hosp., NYC, 1951—, dir. psychiatry, 1955-68, N.Y.C. Dept. Hosps., 1962-64; pvt. practice, 1949—; attending psychiatrist Univ. Hosp., NYC. Cons. psychiatrist Manhattan Va Hosp. Author papers in field. Served to capt., M.C. AUS, 1946- 48. Fellow Am. Psychiat. Assn. (life), N.Y. Acad. Medicine; mem. AMA, N.Y. Soc. Clin. Psychiatry (pres. 1966-67), Am. Psychoanalytic Assn. (life), Sigma Xi, Alpha Omega Alpha. Home: 56 Ruxton Rd Great Neck NY 11023-1529 Office: 550 1st Ave New York NY 10016-6402 Office Phone: 212-683-1560. Personal E-mail: azitrin@aol.com.

ZIVKO-BABIC, JASENKA, dentist, prosthodontist, researcher; d. Stjepan and Mandica Zivko; 1 child, Ivan Babic. DDS, Zagreb, 1973. Cert. full prof. prosthodontics Sch. Dental Medicine, Croatia, 2002, sci. cons./adviser Sch. Dental Medicine, 2002. Sci. asst. Sch. Dental Medicine, Zagreb, 1982—87, sci. assoc., 1987—88, asst. prof., 1988—97, higher sci. assoc., 1997, assoc. prof., 1997—2002, prof., 2002—, head clin. dept., 2001—03. Author: (textbook) Metals in Prosthodontics. Office: Sch Dental Medicine Gunduliceva Ulica 5 10-000 Zagreb Croatia Office Phone: 38514802135. Personal E-mail: zivko@sfzg.hr.

ZLATOHLAVKOVA, BLANKA, pediatrician; b. Prague, Czech Republic, Dec. 13, 1954; MD, Charles U. Prague, 1983. Asst. prof.-ethics, Inst. Med. Humanities Gen. U. Hosp. and 1st Faculty Medicine, Charles U. Medicine, 1991, asst. prof. pediats., dept. pediats. and adolescent medicine, 1991, head, intermediate care unit, divsn. neonatology, dept. ob-gyn., 1999—. Mem.: Rsch. Group Pediat., Czech Neonatology Soc. JEP, Czech Pediat. Soc. JEP. Office: Apolinarska 18 Prague 12808 Czech Republic Business E-Mail: b.zlatohlavkova@seznam.cz.

ZLOTNIK, ALEXANDER, anesthesiologist, researcher; b. Kiev, Ukraine, Dec. 5, 1971; MD, Stavropol Med. Acad., Russia, 1997; PhD, Ben Gurion U. Negev, Israel, 2009. Attending anesthesiologist, dir. rsch. unit in dept. anesthesiology and critical care Soroka Med. Ctr., Beer Sheva, Israel, 2008—. Sr. lectr. Ben Gurion U. Negev, Beer Sheva, Israel, 2011. Rsch. grant, European Soc. Anesthesiologists. Mem.: Soc. Neurosurg. Anesthesiology and Critical Care (New Investigator award). Avocation: photography. Office: Soroka Med Ctr Reiger St Beer-Sheva 84005 Israel Business E-Mail: zlotnika@bgu.ac.il.

ZLOTOWSKI, MARTIN, psychologist; b. Lodz, Poland, Aug. 10, 1934; s. Pawel and Helen Zlotowski; m. Judith Ann Lifschitz, May 17, 1974; children: David, Steven, Laura. BA, NYU, 1955; MA, Mich. State U., 1958, PhD, 1960. Rsch. assoc. Grad. Sch. Pub. Health U. Pitts., 1960-61; rsch. assoc., lectr. Boston U., 1961-62; staff psychologist VA Hosp., Coatesville, Pa., 1962-65, unit chief, 1965-73; clin. dir. St. Mary Providence, 1966-70; assoc. prof. spl. edn. West Chester (Pa.) U., 1973—2003. Grad. coord., 1987-2000; dir. Counseling Assocs., Paoli, Pa., 1973-85, exec. dir., 1985—. Pres. Chester County Family Acad., 1999-2002, bd. trustees 2002-04; v.p. Victim Witness Svcs. Chester County, 1976-77. Fellow: Phila. Psychol. Assn., Phila. Soc. Clin. Psychologists (pres. 1978—79, sec. human svcs. ctr. 1982), Am. Orthopyschiat. Assn. (life); mem.: APA, Pa. Fedn. Coun. Exceptional Children (pres. Pa. divsn. behavior disorders 2000—04). Democrat. Jewish. Home: 23101 Shannondell Dr Audubon PA 19403 Personal E-mail: martinzlot@comcast.net.

ZLOTY, PETER, ophthalmologist; b. Apr. 16, 1960; BS, Rensselaer Polytechnic Inst., Troy, NY, 1980; MD, Albany Med. Coll., Union Univ., 1984. Cert. Ophthalmology 1993. Intern, categorical diversified medicine Albany Med. Ctr. Hosp., resident, ophthalmology; fellowship in corneal and external disease Albany Med. Coll., NY, 1991; ophthalmologist Southeast Eye Clinic, Dothan, Ala.; dir., cornea and external disease and anterior segment surgery, Eye Ctr. South, Dothan. Spkr. in field. Published (articles concerning advances in glaucoma therapy, pterygium surgery, and infectious diseases of the eye), featured on Miracle Workers (ABC), 2006. Active mem. Mt. Gilead Baptist Ch. and enjoys participating in mission trips. Emergency room physician USN, 1985—88, Newport Naval Hosp. Fellow: Am. Acad. Ophthalomolgy; mem.: Am. Soc. Cataract and Refractive Surgeons, Sigma Xi Rsch. Soc. (assoc.). Office: Southeast Eye Clinic 102 Doctors Dr Dothan AL 36301-2911 also: Eye Ctr South 103 Creek Ridge Rd Dothan AL 36301 Office Phone: 334-794-1968. Business E-Mail: DrZolty@SoutheastEyeClinic.com.

ZNAOR, LJUBO, physician; b. Jan. 19, 1976; s. Marko and Adriana (Ignjatovic) Znaor. MD, Med. Sch. Padova, 2001; PhD, Med. Sch. Split, 2007. Croatian med. lic., Italian med. lic. Physician U. Hosp. Ctr., 2003—. Asst., dept. sci. methodology U. Split Sch. Medicine, 2009—. Mem.: Croatian Ophthal. Soc., Am. Acad. Ophthalmology. Roman Catholic. Avocations: languages, painting. Home: Istarska 10 Split 21000 Croatia Home Phone: 38521345462; Office Phone: 38521 556 752. Home Fax: 38521345462. Personal E-mail: ljuboznaor@hotmail.com, ljuboznaor@gmail.com.

ZOCHLING, JANE, rheumatologist, researcher; b. Hobart, Australia, June 17, 1968; MBBS, U. Tasmania, 1991; M.Med. in Clinical Epidemiology, U. Sydney, PhD, 2004. Registrar rheumatologist Royal North Shore Hosp., 1999—2000; rsch. fellow Rheumatology Dept., Royal North Shore Hosp., Sydney, 2000—04, Rheumazentrum-Ruhrgebiet, St Josef's Krankenhaus, Herne, 2004—06; Buttfield rsch. fellow Menzies Rsch. Inst. Tasmania, Hobart, Australia, 2006—; pvt. practice Hobart. Contbr. articles to profl. publs. Grant, Nat. Health and Med. Rsch. Coun., Australia, Ascent Arthritis - Kilimanjaro, Arthritis Australia, Royal Hobart Hosp. Rsch. Found., Travel grant, Arthritis Australia, NSW Br. Fellow: Royal Australasian Coll. Physicians; mem.: Group Rsch. Psoriasis and Psoriatic Arthritis, Assessments SpondyloArthritis Internat. Soc., Australian Rheumatology Assn. Office: University Tasmania Menzies Rsch Inst Tasmania 17 Liverpool St Hobart Tasmania 7000 Australia Office Fax: 61 3 6226 7704. Business E-Mail: jane.zochling@utas.edu.au.

ZOGHBI, WILLIAM ANTOINE, cardiologist, educator; b. Beirut, Oct. 28, 1955; arrived in US, 1977; m. Huda El Hibri, Sept. 17, 1983; children: Roula Maya, Anthony William. BS, Am. U., Beirut, 1975; postgrad., Am. U., 1975-77; MD, Meharry Med. Coll., 1979. Diplomate Internal Medicine 1982, Cardiovascular Diseases Am. Bd. Internal Medicine, 1985. Intern, internal med. U. Tex. Med. Br. Hosps., Galveston, 1979-80; resident, cardiology Baylor Coll. Affiliated Hosps., Houston, 1980-82; fellow, electrocardiogram Baylor Coll. Medicine, Houston, 1982-85, instr., asst. prof., 1985-91, assoc. prof., 1991-98, prof. medicine, 1998—, dir., echocardiography rsch.; assoc. dir., echocardiography lab. Methodist DeBakey Heart Ctr., Tex., dir., Cardiovascular Imaging Inst. Tex.; William Williams Chair in Cardiovascular Imaging Methodist Hosp., Tex. Dir. medicine Meth Hosp., Houston, 1990—. Contbr. articles to profl. jours.; reviewer (of sci. jours.). Fellow: Coun. on Clin. Cardiology, Am. Coll. Cardiology (chmn. scientific sessions 2000, bd. trustee (five-year) 2002—07, bd. trustee 2008—09, treas., v.p. 2010); mem.: Harris County Med. Soc., Tex. Med. Assn., Am. Heart Assn. (prog. com. 1991—94), Am. Soc. Echocardiography (v.p. 2006—07, pres.-elect 2007—08, pres. 2008—, bd. dirs.), Alpha Omega Alpha. Home: 6618 Sewanee St Houston TX 77005-3750 Office: Methodist Hosp 6550 Fannin St SM 677 Houston TX 77030-2717 also: Methodist Hosp 6550 Fannin Ste 1901 Smith Tower Houston TX 77030 Office Phone: 713-441-4342, 713-441-1100.

ZOGRAFOS, GEORGE, surgeon, educator; b. Athens, Oct. 7, 1955; s. Konstantinos Zografos and Eleni Zografou; children: Eleni Zografou, Konstantinos. MD, U. Athens, Greece, 1980, PhD, 1988. Lic. gen. surgeon. Asst. surgeon Greek Army, Alexandropolis, Greece, 1980—83; fellow 1st surg. clinic Hippokration U. Hosp., Athens, 1983—86; jr. attending Red Cross Hosp., 1986—89; hon. attending Hammersmith Royal Postgraduate Med. Sch., London, 1989—90; sr. attending Red Cross Hosp., Athens, 1990—91; fellow surg. oncology Roswell Pk. Meml. Hosp., Buffalo, 1991; from lectr. to assoc. prof. surgery Hippokration U. Hosp., Athens, 1992—. Mem. adv. com. U. Athens, Greece, 2000—05; mem. rsch. adv. com. European Union, Brussels, 2001—02; head breast unit Med. Sch. U. Athens, 2002—, hon. assoc. prof. surgery; mem. adv. bds. Greek Ministry Health, 2002—04; mem. exec. com. Regional Health Authority, Greece, 2005. Author: General Surgery, 2002; contbr. scientific papers to profl. jours. Recipient hons., Onassis Found., 1989, U. Athens, 2004—05; grantee, Nat. Grant Found., 1990. Fellow: ACS (instr. com. on trauma 1993);

mem.: Hellenic Surg. Soc. (gen. sec. 2004—05). Democrat. Greek Orthodox. Achievements include research in surgical techniques. Avocations: tennis, swimming. Home: Litous 4 Vouliagmeni 16571 Athens Greece Office: Vasilissis Sofias 1031 115 21 Athens Greece Office Phone: 00306932524836. Office Fax: 0030 210-6426390. E-mail: gzografo@med.uoa.gr.

ZOHER, MERAD-BOUDIA, oncologist, researcher; b. Tremblay en France, France, Oct. 27, 1960; s. Boudia Merad and Djenat Khrelil; m. Merad Boudia Soumia, Sept. 11, 1990; children: Merad Boudia Nassim, Merad Boudia Walid. MD in Oncology, Paris, 1989. Cons. Hosp., Paris, 1989—. Home: Allee Jacques Monod 62200 Boulogne France Home Fax: 03/21/99/38/26. Personal E-mail: z.merad@ch-boulogne-mer.fr.

ZOLI, GIORGIO, gastroenterologist, educator; b. Russ, Italy, Feb. 9, 1954; Degree in Medicine & Surgery, U. Bologna, Italy, 1978, degree in Gastroenterology, Internal Medicine, 1982. Prof., head dept. internal medicine Azienda USL Ferrara, SS. Annunziata Hosp., Cento, 1999—. Assoc. prof. internal medicine U. Bologna, 2000. Recipient Giuseppe Rizzi prize, U. Bologna, 1986; Sr. Rsch. fellowship, Centro Nazionale Ricerca, 1990. Mem.: Italian Group IBD, Brit. Soc. Gastroenterology, Italian Soc. Gastroenterology, Italian Soc. Internal Medicine (Squibb prize 1987), Rotary Internat. Avocations: horseback riding, bicycling, scuba diving. Home: Via Vincenzo Toffano 15 Bologna 40125 Italy Home Fax: 39051390599. Business E-Mail: g.zoli@ausl.fe.it.

ZOLLE, ILSE MARTHA, nuclear pharmacist, researcher; MS, Johns Hopkins Med. Insts., Balt., 1970; PharmM, DSc, U. Vienna, 1958; habil, Nuc. Medicine U., 1997. Cert. Bd. Austrian Chamber Of Pharmacy, 1960. Radiopharmacist U. Vienna, 1970—97. Author: (text book) Technetium-99m Pharmaceuticals. Chairperson, Cost B3 Eur. Sci. Cooperative, 1993—98. Grantee, Austrian Ministry Of Sci., 1992—98, Austrian Nat. Bank, 2003—07. Mem.: Austrian Soc. Nuc. Medicine, European Soc. Nuc. Medicine, Soc. Nuc. Medicine, Johns Hopkins Alumni Assn. Achievements include patents for radiolabelled phenylethyl imidazole carboxylic acid ester derivatives. Office: Univ Vienna Althanstrasse 14 Vienna 1090 Austria Business E-Mail: ilse.zolle@univie.ac.at.

ZOLLER, MICHAEL, otolaryngologist, head and neck surgeon, educator; b. New Orleans, July 21, 1947; s. Harry and Mildred (Daitch) Z.; m. Linda Kramer, Dec. 21, 1974; children: Rebecca, Jonathan. BS, U. New Orleans, 1971; MD, Tulane U., 1972. Resident in gen. surgery Jewish Hosp., St. Louis, Washington U. Sch. Medicine, 1972—74; resident in otolaryngology Mass. Eye and Ear Infirmary, Harvard U. Med. Sch., Boston, 1974—77; pres. Ear, Nose and Throat Assocs., Savannah, Ga., 1977—; chmn. eye, ear, nose and throat dept. Candler Hosp., 1996—98; clin. prof. otolaryngology, head neck surgery Med. Coll. Ga., Augusta, 2009—. Asst. clin. prof. otolaryngology, head and neck surgery Med. Coll. Ga., Augusta, 1982—96, assoc. clin. prof. otolaryngology, head and neck surgery, 1996—2009; assoc. prof. surgery Mercer Med. Sch., 2000—09, clin. prof. surgery, 2009—; dir. otology otoncurology dept. St. Joseph's Hosp., Savannah, 1994—; bd. dirs. Darby Bank and Trust, 2007—10. Chmn. med. divsn. United Way, Savannah, 1990, chmn. profl. divsn., 1991, 94-2001, vice chmn. campaign, 2002, chmn. campaign, 2003, bd. dirs., 2002-07, vice chmn. bd. dirs., 2004-05, chmn. bd. dirs., 2005-2006; allocation panel, 1997-2002; bd. dirs. Am. Cancer Soc., Savannah, 1993-2000, pres. Chatham County unit, 1996-97, chmn. bd., 1997-98; bd. dirs. Savannah Country Day Sch., 1993-97, chmn. ann. campaign, 1995-96; bd. dirs. St. Joseph's Candler Found., 2001-; pres. Savannah Jewish Fedn., 1991-93; active Savannah Jewish Fedn. Endowment Bd., 1995-99; mem. med. adv. bd. South Coll., 1996-2000; mem. parents coun. Washington U., St. Louis, 1997-2001, Tulane U., 2002-05, Tulane Med. Sch., 2005-06, Tulane Med. Alumni Assn, 2007-2010; bd. dirs. Leadership Savannah, 1996-98. Recipient Young Leadership award Savannah Jewish Fedn., 1985, Boss of Yr. award Savannah Jaycees, 1993, Celebrate Savannah award for outstanding contbns. to Savannah, Ga. Guardian, 1996; Harvard U. Med. Sch. fellow, 1976-77, C.G. Taylor Alumnus award Tulane Med. Alumny, 2009. Fellow: ACS; mem.: Ga. Soc. Otolaryngology (pres. bd. trustees 1997—98, editor newsletter 1998—2001, Lester Brown Lifetime Achievement award 2005), Med. Assn. Ga. (mem. ho. of dels. 1990—2005, bd. dirs. 1995—2004, editl. bd. mem. 2001—, Ga. Cup award 1993, Ayest-Wyeth Cmty. Svc. award 1996, Cmty. Svc. award 2001), 1st Dist. Med. Assn. (pres. 1987—88), Ga. Med. Soc. (pres. 1992, chmn. bd. trustees 1997, chmn. endowment fund 2004—, John B. Rabun Cmty. Svc. award 1995, Hero's award 2001), Am. Neurotology Soc., Am. Soc. Head and Neck Surgery, Am. Acad. Otolaryngology and Head and Neck Surgery (tonsils and adenoids com. 1996—99, sleep disorders com. 1996—2002, pediat. otolaryngology com. 2003—09, equilibrium com. 2005—). Office: Ear Nose and Throat Assocs Savannah 5201 Frederick St Savannah GA 31405-4501 Personal E-mail: MZ47ent@aol.com.

ZÖLLNER, EKKEHARD WERNER, pediatrician; b. Pretoria, South Africa, Apr. 24, 1957; MBBCh, U. Cape Town, 1982, M in Med., 1996. Physician Tygerberg Children's Hosp., 2006—. Head paediat. endocrine and diabetes unit U. Stellenbosch, 2006. Recipient AstraZeneca SATS Rsch. award, South African Thoracic Soc.; Rsch. grants, Med. Rsch. Coun. South Africa. Mem.: South African Thoracic Soc., Allergy Soc. South Africa, Paediat. and Adolescent Endocrinology and Diabetes Soc. (South Africa), South African Med. Assn., Soc. Endocrinology, Metabolism and Diabetes (South Africa). Avocations: running, hiking, water sports. Office: PO Box 19063 Tygerberg Cape Town Western Cape 7505 South Africa Office Fax: 27219389138. Business E-Mail: zollner@sun.ac.za.

ZOLLO, RAYMOND ANTHONY, physician; b. Rochester, NY, May 9, 1967; MD, U. Rochester, 1994. Dir. Ctr. Innovation in Perioperative Medicine U. Rochester Med. Ctr., 2005—. Grant, Found. Anesthesia Edn. and Rsch. Avocations: hiking, boating, bicycling. Office: Box 604 601 Elmwood Ave Rochester NY 14642 Business E-Mail: raymond_zollo@urmc.rochester.edu.

ZOLOTAREV, VASILIY, lab administrator; b. Leningrad, Russia, Aug. 18, 1961; MS in Biology, Leningrad State U., Russia, 1983; PhD, Pavlov Inst. Physiology, St. Petersburg, Russia, 1990. Chief, lab. Pavlov Inst. Physiology, 2011—. INTAS Devel. grant, grant, US Civilian Rsch. Devel. Found., 1996—, FIRCA grant, NIH, 2007—09, Hon. scholarship, Gov. of St. Petersburg Region, 2005—06. Fellow: Monell Chem. Senses Ctr. (affiliated rschr.). Office: 6 Makarova Nab Saint Petersburg 199034 Russia Personal E-mail: vasiliy_zolotarev@hotmail.com.

ZON, LEONARD IRA, pediatrics educator, researcher; b. Hartford, Conn. BS in Chemistry and Natural Sciences, Muhlenberg Coll., Allentown, Pa., 1979; MD, Jefferson Med. Coll., 1983. Diplomate Am. Bd. Internal Medicine; lic. physician, Mass. Rsch. asst. Jefferson Med. Coll., Phila., 1980-82; intern New Eng. Deaconess Hosp., Boston, 1983-84, from jr. to sr. resident in internal medicine, 1984-86; rsch. fellow Children's Hosp., Boston, 1987-90, founder, dir. Stem Cell Rsch. Program, Grousbeck prof. hematology/oncology; instr. Harvard Med. Sch., Boston, 1989-91, asst. prof. pediatrics, 1991—, mem. faculty grad. program biol. and biomed. scis., 1994—, prof. pediat. medicine, Children's Hosp. Boston; investigator Howard Hughes Med. Inst., 1993—. Guest faculty Okla. Health Scis. Ctr., 1993; lectr. in field. Contbr. articles to Am. Jour. Physiology, Jour. Clin. Microbiology, Lancet, Am. Jour. Medicine, Br. Jour. Haematology, Nature, Biotechniques, Molecular Cell Biology, Biology of Hematopoiesis, Jour. Biol. Chemistry. Recipient Hyman Menduke Rsch. awrd, 1983; Friends of the Farber fellow, 1987, Dana-Farber Cancer Inst. fellow, med. oncology, 1986-89; grantee NSF, 1978, NIH, 1980, 89—, Chalres H. Hood Found., 1990-92, Hoffmann-La Roche, 1991-94. Mem. AMA, ACP, Am. Soc. Clin. Oncology, Am. Soc. Hematology, Am. Fisheries Soc., Mass. Med. Soc., Inst. Medicine., Internat. Soc. for Stem Cell Rsch. (founder, past pres.), Am. Soc. for Cln. Investigation;fellow AAAS, Am. Acad. Arts & Scis. Achievements include research in hematopoiesis, development, genetics. Office: Childrens Hosp Boston 300 Longwood Ave Karp-7 Boston MA 02115 also: Howard Hughes Med Inst New Rsch Bldg Rm 7211 1 Blackfan Cir Boston MA 02115 Office Phone: 617-919-2069. Office Fax: 617-730-0222. E-mail: zpn@enders.tch.harvard.edu.

ZONENSHAYN, MARTIN, neurosurgeon, educator; MD, NYU, 1996. Diplomate Am. Bd. Neurol. Surgery. Intern Presbyn. hosp. Weill med. coll. Cornell Univ., resident Presbyn. hosp. Weill med. coll., 1997—2002, asst. prof. dept. neurol. surgery; fellow NYU Hosp., 2002—03; chief divsn. of neurosurgery NY Meth. Office. New York Methodist Hospital Ste 4B 263 Seventh Ave Brooklyn NY 11215 Office Phone: 718-246-8660.

ZONSZEIN, JOEL, endocrinologist; b. Mexico City, Mex., Mar. 15, 1945; came to U.S., 1970; s. Szepsel and Elena (Sheinberg) Z.; m. Anat Arad Zonszein, Aug. 24, 1976; children: Yonatan, Matrav. MD, U. Nacional Autonoma de Mex., 1969. Cert. diabetes educator. Chief endocrinology Bronx (N.Y.) Lebanon Hosp., 1980-93; prof. clin. medicine Albert Einstein Coll. Medicine, Bronx, 1986-2000, dir. Clin. Diabetes Ctr., 1993—, prof. clin. medicine, 2000—. Contbr. articles to profl. jours. Fellow ACP, Am. Coll. Endocrinology; mem. Am. Diabetes Assn., Endocrine Soc. Office: 1575 Blondell Ave Bronx NY 10461 Office Phone: 718-904-2883. Business E-Mail: joel.zonszein@einstein.yu.edu.

ZOOK, ELVIN GLENN, plastic surgeon, educator; b. Huntington County, Ind., Mar. 21, 1937; s. Glenn Hardman and Ruth (Barton) Z.; m. Sharon Kay Neher, Dec. 11, 1960; children— Tara E., Leigh A., Nicole L. BA, Manchester Coll., 1959; MD, Ind. U., 1963. Diplomate Am. Bd. Surgery, 1970, Am. Bd. Thoracic Surgery, 1970, Am. Bd. Plastic Surgery, 1972, Am. Bd. Plastic Surgery, Hand Surgery, 1989. Intern Meth. Hosp., Indpls., 1963-64; resident in gen. and thoracic surgery Ind. U. Med. Center, Indpls., 1964-69; resident in plastic surgery Ind. U. Hosp., Indpls., 1969-71, asst. prof. plastic surgery, 1971-73; asso. prof. surgery So. Ill. U., Springfield, 1973-75, prof. plastic surgery, 1975—2006, chmn. div. plastic surgery, 1973—2006, prof. emeritus of plastic surgery, 2006—. Mem. staff Meml. Med. Center, St. Johns Hosp., Springfield. Author of five books, contbr. over 100 articles to med. jours., contbr. to over 40 books. Mem. Ind. Nat. Guard 1963-71. Recipient Michael J. Caey Meml. Svc. award, McCaskey award, Mem. Assn. Acad. Surgery, Am. Soc. Plastic Surgery (sec. 1988-91, v.p. 1991-92, pres.-elect 1992-93, pres. 1993-94), Midwestern Soc. Plastic Surgery (pres. 1986-87), ACS, Sangamon County Med. Soc. (pres. 1987), Am. Cleft Palate Assn., Am. Assn. Plastic Surgery (trustee 1987-90), Plastic Surgery Rsch. Coun. (chmn. 1981), Am. Burn Assn., Ill. Surg. Soc., Am. Soc. Surgery Hand (coun.), Am. Bd. of Plastic Surgery (sec.-treas. 1988-91, chmn. 1991-92), Am. Soc. Aesthetic Plastic Surgery, Am. Soc. Surgery of Trauma, Assn. Acad. Chmn. Plastic Surgery (pres. 1986-87), Am. Surg. Assn., RRC for Plastic Surgery, Sangamo Club, Springfield Med. Club, Island Bay Yacht Club. Clubs: Sangamo, Springfield Med, Island Bay Yacht. Presbyterian. Office: Div of Plastic Surgery 747 N Rutledge St Springfield IL 62702-6700 Office Phone: 217-545-6314. Office Fax: 217-545-2588. E-mail: ezook@siumed.edu.

ZOOK, JOHN EDWIN, surgeon; b. Tabor, Iowa, Oct. 3, 1924; s. Abram Eyster Zook and Eunice (Francis) Brenneman; m. Jeanne Pierson, Sept. 7, 1952; children: Rebecca Clair, Daniel John, Paul Michael. BA, Lewis and Clark Coll., 1950; MD, U. Oreg., 1954. Cert. in tropical medicine Antwerp Sch. Tropical Medicine, Belgium, 1956, diplomate Am. Bd. Surgery. Intern Emanuel Hosp., Portland, Oreg., 1954—55; dir. med. activities Africa Intermennonite Mission, Republic of the Congo, 1961—65, surgeon, 1969—77; resident surgery Good Samaritan Hosp., Portland, 1965—69; pvt. practice medicine specializing in gen. surgery Portland, 1977—2005; chief staff Mt. Hood Med. Ctr., 1982; exchange physician China Ednl. Exchange Program, Chungquin Med. Coll., 1984—90; chief staff Woodland Pk. Hosp., 1989. Mem. bd. dirs., 1988—91. Ednl. missionary Unevangelized Tribes Mission, Republic of the Congo, 1943—46; med. missionary Congo Inland Mission, 1955—65; v.p. Mennonite Men of Mennonite Ch., 1982—. Fellow: ACS; mem.: Portland Surg. Soc., Internat. Coll. Surgeons (Oreg. regent 1980—84, v.p. 1985). Republican. Office: E Portland Surg Clinic 25500 SE Stark St Gresham OR 97030 Home Phone: 503-257-5190. Personal E-mail: jeannezook123@msn.com.

ZOON, KATHRYN CHRISTINE, biochemist; b. Yonkers, NY, Nov. 6, 1948; d. August R. and Violet T. (Pollock) Egloff; m. Robert A. Zoon, Aug. 22, 1970; children: Christine K., Jennifer R. BS, Rensselaer Poly. Inst., 1970; PhD, Johns Hopkins U., 1976. Rsch. chemist divsn. biochem. biophys. Bur. Biologics FDA, Bethesda, Md., 1980-84, rsch. chemist divsn. virology, 1984-88, rsch. chemist divsn. cytokine biology Ctr. Biologics, 1988—92, divsn. dir., 1989-92; dir. Ctr. Biologics Evaluation and Rsch., 1992—2003; dep. dir. Ctr. for Cancer Rsch. Nat. Cancer Inst., NIH, 2003—04; dep. dir. planning and devel. divsn. intramural rsch. NIAID, NIH, 2004—06, dir. divsn. intramural rsch., 2006—; sci. dir. NIAD. Chmn. expert com. on biol. standardization WHO, 1997-98, 99, 2000, 01; mem. adv. com. of CMR, 2000-03; mem. adhoc expert on biology standardization WHO, 2004—; dir. NIH, NIAID, DIR; lectr. in field. Contbr. articles to rsch. in biol. chemistry to sci. jours.; assoc. editor Jour. Interferon and Cytokine Rsch., 1980—. Bd. dirs. Found. Advanced Edn. Scis., 1996-2004, 1st v.p., 1999-03; mem. adv. bd. Def. Advance Rsch. Projects Agy., 1998-00, Inst. Medicine Nat. Acad. Sci., 2002-. Recipient Person of the Yr. award Biopharm, 1992, Pub. Svc. and Genetic Engring. News award, 1995, Presdl. Meritorious Exec. Rank award, 1994, Grateful Patient award Nat. Assn. Cancer Patients, 1997, Rensselaer Alumni Assn. award, 1997, Sec.'s award for disting. svc. Dept. Health and Human Svcs., 2001, 03, Disting. Alumnus award Johns Hopkins U., 2003; NY State Regents fellow, 1970, Interferon rsch. fellow NIH, Bethesda, 1975-77, staff fellow, 1979-80. Mem. Am. Soc. Biochem. and Molecular Biology, Intenat. Soc. Interferon and Cytokine Rsch. (pres. elect 1998-99, pres. 2000-01), Internat. Assn. Biol. Standardization (govt. liason adv. coun. 2000—) Roman Catholic. Office: NIAID/NIH Bldg 33 Rm 2NN05 10 Center Dr Bethesda MD 20892 Office Phone: 301-496-3006. Business E-Mail: kzoon@niaid.nih.gov.

ZOROWITZ, RICHARD DAVID, physiatrist, educator; b. Teaneck, NJ, Nov. 23, 1958; s. Irving Monroe and Selma Doris Zorowitz; children: Samuel, Joel. BS, Northwestern U., Evanston, IL, 1977—81; MD, Tulane U., New Orleans, 1981—85. Diplomate Am. Bd. Phys. Medicine and Rehab., Spinal Cord Injury Medicine. Internal medicine intern L.I. Jewish Med. Ctr., 1986; resident in phys. medicine and rehab. Northwestern U., 1986-89; asst. prof. phys. medicine and rehab. U. Medicine Dentistry N.J.-N.J. Med. Sch., Newark, 1991-95; asst. prof. rehab. medicine U. Pa., Phila., 1995—2006, assoc. prof. phys. medicine & rehab., 2001—06, Johns Hopkins Bayview Med. Ctr., Balt., 2006—, vis. assoc. prof. phys. medicine and rehab., 2006—08, assoc. prof. phys. medicine & rehab., 2008—. Med. dir. Piersol rehab. unit Hosp. U. Pa., 1997—2006. Cubmaster pack 36 Cub Scouts Am., Cherry Hill, N.J., 1999-2005. Recipient career achievement award for stroke caregiving Nat. Stroke and Quality of Life Med. Edn. Inst., 1996. Mem. Am. Acad. Phys. Medicine and Rehab., Assn. Acad. Physiatrists, Am. Heart Assn. (fellow stroke coun., Operation Stroke Inst. award S.E. Pa. region 2001, Outstanding Leadership award Pa.-Del. affiliate 2002), Nat. Stroke Assn., (Visionary in Practice Soc. award 2002, Excellence in Stroke Edn. award 2001), Phi Eta Sigma, Tau Beta Pi. Democrat. Jewish. Avocations: swimming, music, theater. Home: 7444 Park Heights Ave Pikesville MD 21208 Office: Bldg AA Rm 1654 4940 Eastern Ave Baltimore MD 21224 Personal E-mail: rdzorowitz@pol.net. Business E-Mail: rzorowi1@jhmi.edu.

ZORRON, RICARDO, surgeon, educator; b. Hannover, Germany, July 21, 1962; m. Milene Charles Charles, Nov. 4, 1999; 1 child, Beatriz. MD, U. Fed. Rio de Janeiro, 1987, MS, 1995, PhD, 2005. Cert. in gen. and digestive surgery U. Hosp. HUCFF-UFRJ, Brazil, 1991. Surgeon Divsn. Trauma and Emergency Surgery, Gen. Hosp. Nova Iguacu, Rio de Janeiro, 1987—95, U. Hosp. HUCFF-UFRJ, Rio de Janeiro, 1995—2005; surgeon, coord. residency in gen. surgery Divsn. Gen. and Digestive Surgery, Lourenco Jorge Hosp., Rio de Janeiro, 1997—; prof. and chmn. U. Hosp. Teresopolis HCTCO-FESO, Rio de Janeiro, 2005—; dir., postgrad. course minimally invasive surgery U. Teresopolis FESO, Rio de Janeiro, 2005—. Sages fellow Soc. Am. Gastrointestinal Endoscopic Surgeons, 1997—. Contbr. articles to profl. med. jours. Recipient Title Recognition Outstanding Sci. award, Mcpl. Dep. Congress Teresopolis Rio de Janeiro, 2006, Best Oral Presentation award, Brazilian Coll. Surgeons Congress CBC, 2007, Outstanding Achievements Original Rsch. in Ofcl. Congresses awards, 2007; fellowship, Nürnberg U., Erlangen, Germany, 1995, Humboldt U., Berlin, 1997, grant, U. Estadual Norte Fluminense, 2006, Rsch. grant, SAGES- Soc. Am. Gastrointestinal and Endoscopic Surgeons, 2008. Fellow: SAGES- Soc. Am. Gastrointestinal Endoscopic Surgeons, Brazilian Soc. Laparoscopic Surgery SOBRACIL (Brazil) (pres., sci. comission 2003—05); mem.: Brazilian Coll. Surgeons (pres., spl. comission notes 1997—). Achievements include patents pending for new natural orifice surgery conductors and endoscopic instruments; first to perform robotic surgery in Brazil in 2003. Avocations: windsurfing, reading, travel, films, fishing. Office: Univ Hosp Teresopolis FESO Av do Alto Teresopolis Rio de Janeiro 22790-700 Brazil Business E-Mail: rzorron@terra.com.br.

ZORZOU, MARKELA PAGONITSA, physician; b. Athens, Greece, Oct. 3, 1972; MD, Med. Sch. Athens, 1998, PhD, 2003. Cons. Gen. Hosp. Chios, Greece, 2007—. Home: 11 Patelida St Chios 82100 Greece Home Fax: 302271020186. Business E-Mail: pzorzou@med.uoa.gr.

ZOUNTSAS, BASILIOS, neurosurgeon, director; b. Tuebingen, Germany, Oct. 12, 1968; s. Georgios Zountsas and Mary Zountsa; m. Katerina Kantziou, Jan. 2, 1999; children: Mary Zountsa, Georgios, Anny Zountsa. MD, Arisotel's Med. Sch., Thessaloniki, 1992; PhD, Charite U. Medizin, Berlin, 2005. Cert. neurosurgeon Greece, 2001. Consulting neurosurgeon Evangelisches Krankenhaus Bielefeld-Bethel, Germany, 2001—05; dir., neurosurg. dept. St. Lukes Hosp., Panorama Thessaloniki, Greece, 2006—. Mem.: Hellenic Inst. Neuroscis., Hellenic Spine Soc., European Neurosurg. Soc., German Neurosurg. Soc., Hellenic Neurosurg. Soc. Office: St Lukes Hosp Panorama Thessaloniki 55236 Greece Office Fax: 302310390655; Home Fax: 302310810814. Personal E-mail: zountsas@otenet.gr. Business E-Mail: zountsas@neurogroup.gr.

ZUBILLAGA, GABRIEL GARMENDIA, internist, educator; b. Tolosa, Spain, Apr. 11, 1946; s. Ceferino G. Zubillaga and Cecilia O. Garmendia; m. Maria Visitacion Galarza Azpiroz, Oct. 14, 1972; children: Gabriel, David, Elena. MD, Univ. de Navarra, Pamplona, Spain, 1969; PhD, U. del Pais Vasco, Bilbao, Spain, 1979. Diplomate Am. Bd. Internal Medicine, Am. Bd. Pulmonary Medicine. Medicine residency U. Ill., Chgo., 1971-76; med. dir. Hosp. de Guipuzcoa, San Sebastian, Spain, 1977-80; head internal medicine svc. Hosp. de Donostia, San Sebastian, Spain, 1977—; prof. medicine U. del Pais Vasco, San Sebastian, Spain, 1987—. Fellow Am. Coll. Chest Physicians; mem. Internal Medicine Soc., Respiratory Soc. Avocations: tennis, bicycling. Home: 141 Calzada Vieja de Ategorrieta 20013 San Sebastian Spain Office: Hosp Donostia c/Camino 6 20004 San Sebastian Spain

ZUBOWSKI, ROBERT, plastic surgeon, educator; Diplomate Am. Bd. Plastic Surgery, cert. gen. surgery. Resident gen. surgery NY Med. Coll., assoc. prof. plastic surgery; resident Cleve. Clinic Found.; former assoc. dir. plastic surgery The Valley Hosp. Plastic surgery splty. dir. Cleve. Clinic Found. Alumni Assn. Fellow: ACS; mem.: AMA, Am. Soc. for Plastic Surgery, Am. Soc. of Plastic Surgeons. Office: 1 Sears Drive Paramus NJ 07652 Office Phone: 201-261-7550. Office Fax: 201-261-7515.

ZUBRIN, JAY ROSS, surgeon; b. Phila., June 11, 1936; m. Bonnie Zubrin; children: Larry, Sandy Cruttenden. BS, Dickinson Coll., 1959; MD, Temple U., 1963. Diplomate Am. Bd. Surgery. Intern San Francisco Gen. Hosp., 1963—64; resident in gen. surgery U. Calif. Med. Ctr., 1964—69; pvt. practice; chief staff Hoag Meml. Hosp. Presbyn., Newport Beach, Calif. Maj. Med. Corp US Army, 1969—71. Mem. ACS, AMA, Calif. Med Assn., Orange County Med. Assn. (pres. 2005-06). Republican. Avocation: golf. Office: Ste 601 351 Hospital Rd Newport Beach CA 92663-3500 Office Phone: 949-548-2264. Office Fax: 949-650-3606. Business E-Mail: jzubrin@hoag.org. *

ZUBROW, ALAN B., neonatologist; MD, U. Pa. Diplomate Am. Bd. Pediatrics-neonatal-perinatal medicine. Resident Children's Hosp. of Phila., Pa.; fellow columbia presbyn. Med. Ctr., NYC; prof. pediatrics Drexel Univ.; attending neonatologist St. Christopher's Hosp. for Children, dir. neonatal-perinatal medicine fellowship program. Named one of Top Doctors, Phila. mag., 2011. Office: St. Christopher's Hospital for Children 3601 A St Philadelphia PA 19134 Office Phone: 215-427-5202.

ZUCARO, ALDO CHARLES, insurance company executive; b. Grenoble, France, Apr. 2, 1939; s. Louis and Lucy Zucaro; m. Gloria J. Ward, Oct. 12, 1963; children: Lucy, Louis, Faye. BS in Acctg, Queens Coll., NYC, 1962. C.P.A., N.Y., Ill. Ptnr. Coopers & Lybrand (and predecessor), Chgo. and NYC, 1962-76; exec. v.p., chief fin. officer Old Republic Internat. Corp., Chgo., 1976-81; pres. Old Republic International Corp., Chgo., 1981—; CEO Old Republic Internat. Corp., Chgo., 1990—93; chmn., CEO Old Republic International Corp., Chgo., 1993—. Pres., bd. dirs. Old Republic Life Ins. Co., Old Republic Life of N.Y., Old Republic Ins. Co., Internat. Bus. and Merc. Reassurance Co., Republic Mortgage Ins. Co., Old Republic Nat. Title Ins. Co., Home Owners Life Ins. Co. Editor: Financial Accounting Practices of the Insurance Industry, 1975, 76. Mem. AICPAs. Roman Catholic. Office: Old Republic Internat Corp 307 N Michigan Ave Chicago IL 60601-5311 *

ZUCCO, RONDA KAY, healthcare business development & administration professional; b. Peoria, Ill., Apr. 3, 1960; d. Richard Leon Zucco. BA, So. Ill. U., 1981; MBA, Fla. Southern Coll., 2009. Cert. addiction profl.; cert. relapse prevention specialist. Dir. continuing care Parkside Lodge Fla. (merged with Fla. Hosp. Ctr. Psychiatry), Orlando, Fla., 1989-95; program dir. Charter Behavioral Health Sys., Kissimmee, Fla., 1995-97; dir. outpatient svcs. Heart of Fla. Behavioral Ctr., Lakeland, Fla., 1997-99; bus. devel. account mgr. Lakeland Regional Med. Ctr., 1999—2011; dir. bus. devel., admissions & patient satisfaction Brunswick Hosp. Ctr. Behavioral Health & Wellness, Amityville, NY, 2011—. Vol. ARC, Carbondale, Ill., 1978—81, Alliance for Mentally Ill of Greater Orlando, Fla., 1995—97, Coalition for Homeless, Orlando, 1995—97, Spl. Olympics, 1999—; crisis hotline vol. Jackson County Cmty. Mental Health Ctr., Carbondale, Ill., 1981; mem. AIDS spkrs. bur. BroMenn Healthcare, Bloomington, Ill., 1986—89; adv. bd. Inner Act Alliance (formerly Drug Prevention Resource Ctr.), Lakeland, Fla., 1998—; sustainer Jr. League of Greater Lakeland, 2000—; torch bearer Salt Lake City Olympics, 2002, Leadership Lakeland XX, 2004; adv. bd. Imperial Symphony Orch., Lakeland, 2001—, Word Alive Ministries Cmty. Svc. Corp., 2006—. Recipient State of Ill. scholar, Gen. Assembly, 1977—81, Outstanding Coll. Sr. in Sociology, 1981; named Outstanding Profl. of Yr., Fla. Sch. Addiction Studies, 1999. Mem. Am. Mktg. Assn., Am. Assn. for Counseling and Devel., Am. Mental Health Counselors Assn., Fla. Alcohol and Drug Abuse Assn., Fla. Prevention Assn., Nat. Businesswomen's Leadership Assn., Am. Bus. Women's Assn., C. of C. Greater Lakeland, Fla. Coun. on Crime and Delinquency, Phi Kappa Phi, Kappa Delta Pi, Chi Sigma Iota. Avocations: reading, swimming, travel, the arts. Home: 10 Dixon Ave Apt 25 Amityville NY 11701 Office Phone: 631-789-7276.

ZUCKER, HOWARD ALAN, pediatric cardiologist, anesthesiologist, government agency administrator; b. NYC, Sept. 6, 1959; s. Saul and Phyllis (Goldblatt) Zucker. BS, McGill U., Montreal, 1979; MD, George Washington U., 1982; JD, Fordham U., 2000; LLM, Columbia U., 2001. Bar: U.S. Supreme Ct. Pediatric intern Johns Hopkins Hosp., Balt., 1982-83, pediatric resident, 1983-85; anesthesiology resident Hosp. of U. Pa., Phila., 1985-87; pediatric critical care fellow Children's Hosp. of Phila., 1987-88; asst. prof. anesthesiology and pediatrics Yale U. Sch. Medicine, New Haven, 1988-90; pediatric cardiology fellow Children's Hosp., Harvard Med. Sch., Boston, 1990-92; assoc. prof. clin. pediat. and clin. anesthesiology N.Y. Presbyn. Hosp. and Children's Hosp., NYC, 1992—2001; dir. pediatric transport Columbia Presbyn. Med. Ctr. Babies and Children's Hosp. N.Y., NYC, 1992—2001; White House fellow Washington, 2001—02; dep. asst. sec. for health U.S. Dept. HHS, 2002—05; asst. dir.-gen. WHO, Geneva, 2005—08, Hervard Kennedy Sch., 2009; sr. adv. Mass. Gen. Hosp., 2009—; dir. Global Health, World Economic Forum, 2010. Adj. assoc. prof. pediat. Cornell U. Weill Coll. Medicine, 2000—01; involved with crew tng. NASA Space Shuttle STS-1 Mission, 1978—80; rsch. affiliate Man-vehicle Lab MIT; White House fellow, 2001—02; coun. on fgn. relations, 2003—. Participant med. missions to China Children China Pediat. Found.; chmn. bd. Terre Verte Found., Inc.; bd. dirs. Little Hearts Pediat. Found. Named Person of the Week, ABC World News Tonight, 1993; fellow, White House, 2001—02. Fellow: Am. Coll. Critical Care Medicine, Am. Coll. Legal Medicine, Am. Coll. Cardiology, Am. Coll. Chest Physicians, Am. Acad. Pediat.; mem.: AMA, Soc. Critical Care Medicine, Am. Heart Assn., Am. Soc. Anesthesiologists (mem. coun. fgn. rels. 2003—), Coun. Fgn. Rels. Jewish. Achievements include research in adaptation to zero gravity, cardiac critical care. Home: 100 Winston Dr Apt 12G Cliffside Park NJ 07010-3240

ZUCKER, ROBERT A(LPERT), psychologist; b. NYC, Dec. 9, 1935; s. Morris and Sophie (Alpert) Z.; m. Martine Latil; children: Lisa, Alex, Eleanor; m. Kristine Ellen Freeark, Mar. 10, 1979; 1 child, Katherine. B.C.E., CCNY, 1956; postgrad., UCLA, 1956-58; PhD, Harvard U., 1966. Diplomate Am. Bd. Profl. Psychology (clin.); lic. psychologist, Mich. From instr. to asst. prof. psychology Rutgers U., 1963-68; from asst. prof. to assoc. prof. to prof. Mich. State U., 1968-94; prof. psychology in psychiatry and psychology U. Mich., 1994—, dir. Addiction Rsch. Ctr., 1994—, dir. substance abuse sect. Dept. Psychiatry, 1994—, faculty assoc. RCGD Inst. for Social Rsch., 1996—. Vis. prof. U. Tex., Austin, 1975; vis. rsch. prof. psychology in psychiatry U. Mich., 1990-91; vis. scholar Nat. Inst. Alcohol Abuse and Alcoholism, 1980; dir. clin. tng. Mich. State U., 1982-94; lectr. Nebr. Symposium on Motivation, 1986; cons. in field. Co-author, editor: Further Explorations in Personality, 1981, Personality and the Prediction of Behavior, 1984, The Emergence of Personality, 1987, Studying Persons and Lives, 1990, Personality Structure in the Life Course, 1992, The Development of Alcohol Problems: Exploring the Biopsychosocial Matrix of Risk, 1994, Alcohol Problems Among Adolescents: Current Directions in Prevention Research, 1995, Alcohol Problems and Aging, 1998, Multiproblem Youth: Intervention and Treatment, 2004; contbr. chpts. and articles to profl. publs. Bd. dirs. Nat. Coun. on Alcoholism-Mich., 1978-82; mem. Psychosocial Initial Rev. Group, Nat. Inst. Alcohol Abuse and Alcoholism, 1989-92; mem. HPRB study sect. Ctr. for Sci. Rev., NIH, 1998-2000; mem. League of Rsch. Excellence U. Mich. Med. Sch., 2011-. Recipient Fellow's award, Inst. Children Youth and Families, Mich. State U., 1993, Excellence in Clin. Rsch. award, Blue Cross-Blue Shield Mich. Found., 1997, Method Extend Rsch. Time Merit award, NIH, 2003—. Fellow AAAS, APA (pres. Soc. Addiction Psychology 1997-98), APS, Am. Orthopsychiat. Assn.; mem. Midwestern Psychol. Assn., Rsch. Soc. on Alcoholism (sec., bd. dirs. 2000-03, bd. dirs. 2007—11), Polish Soc. Addictions Rsch. (hon.; founding mem. 2006), Polish Psychiat. Soc.(hon., named to Hall Fame 2007), Rsch. Soc. Alcoholism (Disting. Rschr. award, 2010). Office: Univ Mich Addiction Rsch Ctr 4250 Plymouth Rd Ann Arbor MI 48109-2700 Office Phone: 734-232-0280. Business E-Mail: zuckerra@umich.edu.

ZUCKER, ROBERT STEPHEN, neuroscientist, educator; b. Phila., Apr. 18, 1945; s. Irving Aaron and Dorothy Ruth (Pittenturf) Z.; m. Glenda Anita Teal, Sept. 1, 1968 (div. Apr. 1982); 1 child, David Aaron; m. Susan Henrietta Schwartz, Jan. 3, 1983; children: Mark Daniel Isaac, Ariel Dana. SB in Physics, MIT, 1966; PhD in Neurol. Sci., Stanford U., 1971. Asst. prof. physiology U. Calif., Berkeley, 1974-80, assoc. prof., 1980-85, prof., 1985-90, prof. neurobiology, 1990—. Vis. investigator Univ. Coll., London, 1971-73, Nat. Ctr. Sci. Rsch., Gif-sur-Yvette, France, 1973-74; corp. mem. Marine Biology Lab., Woods Hole, Mass., 1981—; mem. bd. sci. counselors Nat. Inst. Neurol. and Communicative Disorders and Stroke, Washington, 1982; mem. NIH Reviewers' Res., 1994-99; Nachshen meml. lectr. U. Md., 1992. Mem. editl. bd. Jour. Neurobiology, 1982-86, Jour. Neurosci., 1988-94, Neuron, 1997—; contbr. articles to profl. jours. Recipient Jacob Javits award, 1987-94; Helen Hay Whitney Found. fellow; NATO fellow; Alfred P. Sloan Found. fellow; grantee NIH, NSF, 1976—. Mem. AAAS, AAUP, ACLU, Soc. Neurosci., Biophys. Sci., Union Concerned Scientists, Fedn. Am. Scientists, Sierra Club, Sigma Xi. Democrat. Jewish. Achievements include research in mechanisms of synaptic function and plasticity, regulation of ion channels, control of neuronal excitability, egg fertilization, neurobiological bases of behavior, and methods of measurement, control and simulation of diffusion of calcium in neurons and spectroscopic measures of protein interactions. Home: 1236 Oxford St Berkeley CA 94709-1423 Office: U Calif Dept Molecular Cell Biology Berkeley CA 94720-3200 Office Phone: 510-642-3407. Business E-Mail: zucker@berkeley.edu.

ZUCKER-FRANKLIN, DOROTHEA, internist, educator; b. Berlin, Aug. 9, 1930; came to U.S., 1949; d. Julian J. and Gertrude Zucker; m. Edward C. Franklin (dec.); 1 child, Deborah Julie. BA, CUNY, 1952, PhD in Sci. (hon.), 1996; MD, N.Y. Med. Coll., 1956. Diplomate Am. Bd. Medicine. Intern Phila. Gen. Hosp., 1956-57; resident in internal medicine Montefiore Hosp., NYC, 1957-59, postdoctoral fellow in hematology, 1959-61; postdoctoral fellow in electron microscopy NYU Sch. Medicine, NYC, 1961-63, asst. prof. medicine, 1963-67, assoc. prof., 1968-74, prof. medicine, 1974—; assoc. attending physician Bellevue Hosp., 1968-74, attending physician, 1974—. Assoc. attending physician Univ. Hosp., Tisch Hosp., 1968—74, attending physician, 1974—; cons. physician Manhattan VA Hosp., 1970—; meml. editl. bd. numerous publs., including Blood, 1963—76, 1980—86, Am. Jour. Pathology, 1979—, Ultrastructure Pathology, 1979—, Blood Cells, 1980, Am. Jour. Medicine, 1981—87, Hematology Oncology, 1982—, Jour. AIDS Rsch., 1987—, Hematopathology and Molecular Hematology, 1987—, others; meml. bd. reviewing editors Jour. Lab. and Clin. Medicine, 1990—; mem. hematology panel Health Rsch. Coun. City of N.Y., 1971—74; mem. pathology tng. com. Nat. Inst. Med. Scis., 1971—74; mem. allergy and immunology rsch. com. Nat. Inst. Allergy and Infectious Diseases, 1974—81; mem. U.S.-Israel Binat. Sci. Found., 1980—; mem. ad hoc promotion com. Harvard Med. Sch., 1981, 83; mem. blood products adv. com. FDA, 1981—86; mem. sci. adv. bd. and sci. rev. panel Israel Cancer Rsch. Found., 1982—90; mem. grant rev. panel VA AIDS Ctr., 1988—89; vis. fellow Assn. Claude Bernard, 1974—75. Co-author: The Physiology and Pathology of Leukocytes, 1962, Amyloidosis, 1986, Atlas of Blood Cells: Function and Pathology, 2 vols., 1981, 3d edit., 2003, Thrombopoiesis and Thrombopoietins: Molecular, Cellular, Preclinical and Clinical Biology, 1996; contbr. over 300 articles to profl. jours. Bd. dirs. Henry M. and Lillian Stratton Found., Inc., 1987-95. Named to Hall of Fame, Hunter Coll., 1977, Internat. Profl. and Bus. Women, 1994. Fellow: AAAS, N.Y. Acad. Scis.; mem.: NTLV and Related Viruses, Internat. Retrovirology Assn., N.Y. Soc. Study of Blood (chair program com. 1976—80, pres. 1981—82), N.Y. Soc. Electron Microscopists (program chair 1984, pres. 1984—85), Am. Soc. Cell Biology (program com. internat. congress 1976), Am. Soc. Exptl. Pathology, Am. Assn. Immunologists, Am. Acad. Arts and Scis., Reticuloendothelial Soc. (life; program com. 1974—76, nominating com. 1976—78, pres. 1984—85), Am. Soc. Physiology, Federated Socs. Exptl. Biology and Medicine, Am. Soc. Hematology (program com. 1973, edn. com. 1974—78, chair subcom. on leukocyte physiology 1977, chair subcom. on immunohematology 1984, com. on advanced learning resources 1986—, exec. coun. 1987—91, pres.-elect 1992, v.p. 1993, pres. 1994—95, chair adv. bd. 1996, com. on govt. affairs 2001), Am. Soc. Clin. Investigation, Am. Fedn. Clin. Rsch., Am. Assn. Physicians, Inst. Medicine NAS, Alpha Omega Alpha, Phi Beta Kappa. Office: NYU Med Ctr 550 1st Ave New York NY 10016-6402 Office Phone: 212-263-5634. Business E-Mail: dorothea.zucker-franklin@med.nyu.edu.

ZUCKERMAN, DARRYL, radiologist, educator; b. NYC, Dec. 4, 1957; MD, SUNY, 1983. Asst. prof. radiology Wash. U., 2008—. Office: Mallinckrodt Inst Radiology 510 South Kingshighway Saint Louis MO 63110 Business E-Mail: zuckermand@mir.wustl.edu.

ZUCKERMAN, JOSEPH D., orthopedist, surgeon; b. Bronx, NY, Jan. 25, 1952; s. Morris and Lee Zuckerman; m. Janet Rivkin, July 1, 1984; children: Scott, Matthew. BS, Cornell U., Ithaca, NY, 1973; MD, Med. Coll. Wis., Milw., 1978. Diplomate Am. Bd. Orthop. Surgery (mem.), 1986, Am. Bd. Orthop. Surgery (mem.), 1996. Intern and resident U. Wash., Seattle, 1978—83; fellow Brigham and Women's Hosp., Havard Med. Sch., Boston, 1983—84, Mayo Clinic, Rochester, Minn., 1984; vice chmn.dept. orthop surgery Hosp. for Joint Diseases, NYC, 1990—94, chmn. dept. orthop. surgery, 1994—97; Walter A.L. Thompson prof., chmn. dept. orthop. surgery N.Y.U. Med. Ctr. /Hosp. for Joint Diseases, 1997—. Co-author (editor): Comprehensive Care of Orthopaedic Injuries in the Elderly, 1990; co-author: Fractures and Dislocations.Hospital for Joint Diseases, 1995; co-editor: Fractures in the Elderly, 1998, A Comprehensive Review Text of Orthopaedic Surgery, 1999; co-author: Fractures of the Hip: A Practical Guide to Management, 1999. Recipient Clin. Rsch. award, Orthop. Rsch. and Edn. Found., 1987; fellow Mary and David Hoar fellowship in Musculoskeletal /Trauma Rsch., 1987. Mem.: Orthop. Rsch. Soc., Shoulder and Elbow Surgeons, Am. Acad. Orthop. Surgeons (pres. 2009—), Am. Orthop. Assn. (N. Am. traveling fellowship 1985), Alpha Omega Alpha. Office: Hosp for Joint Diseases 301 E 17th St New York NY 10003 Office Phone: 212-598-6674. Office Fax: 212-598-6793. E-mail: joseph.zuckerman@med.nyu.edu.

ZUCKERMAN, MARVIN, retired psychologist; b. Chgo., Mar. 21, 1928; s. Eli and Sophia (Pilder) Z.; children: April B. Zuckerman Schanoes, Steven H. BA, NYU, 1949, PhD, 1954. Rsch. assoc. Inst. Psychiat. Rsch., Ind. U. Med. Ctr., 1956-59; asst. prof. psychology Bklyn. Coll., 1959-62; rsch. assoc. Albert Einstein Med. Ctr., Phila., 1963-69; prof. psychology U. Del., Newark, 1969—2002, prof. emeritus, 2002—, ret., 2002. Author: (with C.D. Spielberger) Emotions and Anxiety, 1976, Sensation Seeking: Beyond the Optimal Level of Arousal, 1979, Biological Bases of Sensation Seeking, Impulsivity and Anxiety, 1983, Psychobiology of Personality, 1991, 2d edit. 2005, Behavioral Expressions and Biosocial Bases of Sensation Seeking, 1994, Vulnerability to Psychopathology, 1999, Sensation Seeking and Risky Behavior, 2007, Personality Science: Three Approaches, 2011. Fellow APA, Assn. Psychol. Sci.; mem. Internat. Soc. Study Individual Differences (past pres.). Home: 1500 Locust St Apt 4013 Philadelphia PA 19102-4326 Home Phone: 215-732-2408. Business E-Mail: zuckerma@udel.edu.

ZUIDEMA, GEORGE DALE, surgeon, educator; b. Holland, Mich., Mar. 8, 1928; s. Jacob and Reka (Dalman) Z.; m. Joan K. Houtman, June 2, 1953; children: Karen Sue, David Jay, Nancy Ruth, Sarah Kay. AB, Hope Coll., 1949, D.Sc. (hon.), 1969; MD, Johns Hopkins U., 1953. Diplomate: Am. Bd. Surgery. Intern Mass. Gen. Hosp., 1953-54, asst. resident surgeon, then chief resident surgeon, 1954, 57, 58, 59; asst. prof. surgery, then assoc. prof. U. Mich. Sch. Medicine, 1960-64; prof. surgery, dir. dept. Johns Hopkins Sch. Medicine; also surgeon in chief Johns Hopkins Hosp., 1964-84; prof. surgery, vice provost med. affairs U. Mich., 1984-94. Cons. Walter Reed Army Med. Center, Sinai Hosp., Balt., Balt. City Hosp., Clin. Center of NIH; chmn. Study on Surg. Svcs. for U.S., 1970-75 Editor: (with O.H. Gauer) Gravitational Stress in Aerospace Medicine, 1961; (with G.L. Nardi) Surgery-A Concise Guide to Clinical Practice, 1961, 4th edit., 1982; (with R.D. Judge and F. Fitzgerald) Physical Diagnosis, 1963, 6th edit., 1997; (with W.F. Ballinger and R.B. Rutherford) Management of Trauma, 1968, 4th edit., 1985; (with L. Schlossberg) Atlas of Human Functional Anatomy, 1977, 4th edit., 1997, Shackelford's Surgery of the Alimentary Tract, 5th edit., 2001; editor Jour. Surg. Rsch., 1966-72, assoc. editor, mem. editl. bd., 1972—; mem. editl. bd. Surgery Ann., 1968-75, Surgery, 1970-97, co-editor in chief, 1975-97. Bd. dirs. Md. divsn. Am. Cancer Soc., 1964-68; trustee William Beaumont Hosp., Royal Oak, Mich., 1984-94, Hope Coll., Holland, Mich, 1987—. Capt. M.C., USAF, 1954-56. John and Mary R. Markle scholar academic medicine, 1961-66; recipient Henry Russell award U. Mich., 1963 Fellow ACS, Royal Coll. Surgeons Ireland (hon.); mem. Assn. Am. Med. Colls., Ctrl. Soc. Clin. Rsch., Soc. Univ. Surgeons, Am. Surg. Assn., So. Surg. Assn., Soc. Clin. Surgery, Soc. Vascular Surgery, Internat. Cardiovascular Surgery, Halsted Soc., Nat. Inst. Medicine, Assn. Acad. Surgeons (pres. 1967-69), Allen O. Whipple Soc., Coun. on Grad. Med. Edn., Ft. Del. Soc. (dir., 2006—), Del. Acad. Soc. (pres., 1994-1996, 2004—, dir., 1990—), Phi Beta Kappa, Tri Beta, Alpha Omega Alpha.

ZUK, CARMEN VEIGA, psychiatrist; b. Buenos Aires, Mar. 5, 1939; arrived in USA, 1971, naturalized, 1979; d. Carlos and Carmen Villella Veiga; m. Gerald Harvey, May 7, 1974; children: Cary Elizabeth and Gabrielle Anne. MD, U. Buenos Aires, 1964, cert.

psychiatry, 1969. Diplomate Am. Bd. Psychiatry and Neurology. Intern Med. Coll. Pa., Phila., 1974—75; resident in psychiatry Norristown State Hosp., Norristown, Pa., 1977—79; child psychiatry fellowship Med. Coll. Pa. and Ea. Pa. Psychiat. Inst., Phila., 1979—81; dir. child and adolescent unit Hosp. of Med. Coll. Ga., Augusta, 1981—83; dir. treatment team New Orleans Adolescent Hosp., 1983—85; assoc. Psychiatry Med. Group, Calif., 1985—86; mental health psychiatrist L.A. County Dept. Mental Health San Fernando Mental Health Svcs., 1986—88; psychiatrist-ptnr. So. Calif. Permanente Med. Group, Van Nuys, 1988—98, ptnr., 1988—98; staff psychiatrist Santa Clarita Child and Family Ctr., 1999—2002; ret., 2006. Asst. prof. dept. psychiatry Med. Coll. Ga., 1981-83; clin. asst. prof. dept. psychiatry and neurology Tulane U., 1983-85. Co-author: Psychology of Delusion, 2005; contbr. articles to profl. jours. Mem. AMA, Internat. Soc. for Adolescent Psychiatry. Avocations: reading, cooking, gardening, swimming, music. Home: 2140 Santa Cruz Ave Apt E-102 Menlo Park CA 94025 Personal E-mail: carmenzuk@msn.com.

ZUK, GERALD HARVEY, retired psychologist, consultant; b. Chgo., Oct. 25, 1929; s. Albert and Gladys (Gross) Z.; m. Carmen Veiga, May 7, 1974; children: Cary and Gabrielle (twins). BA, L.A. State Coll., 1951; PhD, U. Chgo., 1955. Lic. psychologist, Calif. Asst. rsch. psychologist Inst. Child Welfare/U. Calif., Berkeley, 1955-56; clin. psychologist Pacific State Hosp., Pomona, Calif., 1956-57; chief psychologist St. Christopher's Hosp. for Children, Phila., 1957-61; assoc. dir., dir. tng. program dept. family psychiatry Ea. Pa. Psychiat. Inst., Phila., 1961-80; prof. dept. psychiatry, dir. family therapy program Med. Coll. Ga., 1981-83; clin. prof. dept. psychiatry and neurology Tulane U. Sch. Medicine, New Orleans, 1983-85; assoc. and dir. family therapy tng. program Beck Psychiat. Med. Group, Los Angeles County, 1985-86; pvt. practice Calif., 1986—. Cons. and presenter in field. Author: Family Therapy: A Triadic-Based Approach, 1972, 2d edit., 1981, Process and Practice in Family Therapy, 1975, 2d edit., 1986; co-author: The Psychology of Delusion, 2005; editor: Family Therapy Approaches for Adolescents, 1985; co-editor: Family Therapy and Disturbed Families, 1967; founding editor Internat. Jour., 1979-86, Contemporary Family Therapy Dall painting and Female Life Cycle, 2010, Prevalence Childhood Autism; mem. editl. bd. Family Process, Psychotherapy: Theory, Rsch. and Practice, Jour. Marriage and Family Counseling, Terapia Familiar; contbr. articles to profl. jours. Fellow APA. Avocation: classical music. Home and Office: 2140 Santa Cruz Ave Apt # E102 Menlo Park CA 94025 Personal E-mail: geraldzuk@msn.com. *

ZULEY, MARGARITA, radiologist, educator; Grad., U. Notre Dame; MD, U. Pitts. Resident & fellow U. Pitts.; assoc. prof. dept. radiology Magee-Women's Hosp. U. Pitts. Med. Ctr., dir. breast imaging. Office: Magee-Women's Hospital 300 Halket St Pittsburgh PA 15213 Office Phone: 412-641-5591. E-mail: zuleyml@upmc.edu.

ZUMO, BILLIE THOMAS, retired biologist; b. Cheyenne, Wyo., Sept. 25, 1936; d. Thomas Elias and Katherine A. (Pappas); m. Charles Vincent, Aug. 21, 1959; 1 child, Thomas J. BA, U. Wyo., Laramie, 1958; MA, U. No. Colo., Greeley, 1963. Cert. tchr. Tchr. Carey Jr. H.S., Cheyenne, 1958-61, 61-63; English lang. tchr. McCormick Jr. H.S., Cheyenne, 1961; biology tchr. Laramie County C.C., Cheyenne; tchr. Ctrl. H.S., Cheyenne, 1963—99; ret., 1999. Exec. bd. Sch. Dist. curriculum adv., 1982-85; chmn. sci. dept., 1990—; mem. faculty adv. com. Ctrl. H.S., 1988—, mem. prin. screening com., 1990-91. Editor: (newsletter) Philogramma. Football statistician Ctrl. Football Team, Cheyenne, 1976—; lay mem. rsch. com. of the Pharmacy Theraputics Com., 1985; judge sch. dist. sci. fair, Cheyenne, 1987-88; ch. choir dir., Cheyenne; judge Nat. Oratorical Contest, Greek Orthodox Archdiocese Am.; chmn. Nicholas G. Cledon Scholarship award. Recipient Disting. Svc. award Sts. Constandine and Helen Orthodox Ch., 1979, Disting. Svc. award as choir dir. Archbishop Iakovas, NY, 1988, Disting. Svc. award as choir dir. Patriarch Athenagoras, 2006. Mem. Nat. Assn. Biology Tchrs. (state rep. 1992-99), NEA, Cheyenne Tchrs. Edn. Assn., Wyo. Edn. Assn., Nat. Forum of Greek Orthodox Musicians, Ladies Philoptochos Soc. of Denver Diocese (treas. 1989-93, 1st v.p. 1993-95, pres. 1995-99, diocese adv. 1999-2003, diocese philoptochos bd., 2003—, editor newsletter, 1997—, apptd. to nat. philoptochos bd. 1997-99, 2000—, ch. heritage com., nat. philoptochos chmn. Support A Mission Priest), AAUW, Phi Delta Kappa, Laramie County Hist. Soc. Democrat. Ea. Greek Orthodox. Avocations: reading, walking, music, golf. Home: 900 Ranger Dr Cheyenne WY 82009-2535 Personal E-mail: bczoom2@bresnan.net.

ZUMWALT, ROGER CARL, healthcare accreditation surveyor, consultant; b. Eugene, Oreg., Oct. 26, 1943; s. Robert Walter and Jean Elaine (Adams) Z.; children: Kathryn Nicole Zumwalt DeWeber, Timothy Robert Zumwalt. Student, Boise State U., 1963—65; BA, We. Oreg. U., 1969; postgrad., U. Iowa, 1969—71; MA cum laude, Oreg. State U., 1973. Adminstr. Coulee Cmty. Hosp., Grand Coulee, Wash., 1973-75; exec. dir. Eastmoreland Hosp., Portland, Oreg., 1975—81, Cmty. Hosp., Grand Junction, Colo., 1981-97; pres., healthcare accreditation surveyor, cons. Salem, Oreg., 1997—2008; dir. adminstrv. svcs. divsn. SAIF Corp., Salem, 1998—2008. Chmn., bd. dirs. Alphabet House Pediat. Rehab. and Edn., 1998—2000, Castle Rock Med. Group, Inc., Denver, 1998—2003; part owner, chmn. bd. dirs. Castle Rock Med. Ctr., Colo., 1998—, N.W. Okla. Regional Med. Ctr. Cherokee, 2000; spkr. numerous local and nat. presentations, subjects including healthcare, hosp. mktg./success/costs, 1981—97; guest lectr. Mesa State Coll., 1992—98, Colo. Christian Coll., 1996—98. Newspaper columnist, 1973-75; contbr. articles, presentations to profl. publs. Commr. Multnomah County Health Care Commn., Portland, Oreg., 1978-81; health cons. Grant County Housing Auth., Grand Coulee, 1974-75; mem. pk. bd. City of Tigard, Oreg., 1976-78; caucus rep. Mesa County Rep. Party, Grand Junction, 1988; mem. adv. com., pres.'s office Mesa State Coll., Grand Junction, 1989; bd. dirs. Hospice of Grand Valley, Grand Junction, 1992-97, mem. devel. com., 1993-97, vice chmn. bd. dirs., 1994-97; bd. dirs. Grand Valley Hospice, 1992-96; com. mem. Salem Coalition on Youth Literacy, 2000—. Fellow Coll. Osteo. Healthcare Execs. (bd. dirs. 1985-88, pres. 1987, examiner 1989—, Disting. Svc. award 1989); mem. Am. Osteo. Healthcare Assn. (bd. dirs. 1987-98, treas. 1992-93, 1st v.p. 1994-95, 2d v.p. 1993-94, vice chairperson 1994-95, chmn. 1996-97, chairperson 1997-98, past chmn. 1998), Am. Osteo. Assn. (ex-officio mem. bd. dirs. 1996), Bur. Healthcare Facilities Accreditation (v.p. 1994, advisor 1995-98, accreditation cons. 1995—, accreditation surveyer 1978—, accreditation survey instr. 1994—), Joint Commn. on Am. Healthcare Orgn. (task force on small and rural hosps. 1994-98), Colo. Hosp. Assn. (bd. dirs. 1987-92), Mountain States Vol. Hosp. Assn. (bd. dirs. 1984-98, exec. com. 1991-98, v.p. 1993, vice chmn. bd. dirs. 1992-98), We. Coll. Ind. Practice Assn. (Medicine Mauls Measles com., fin. com. 1991-92), We. Colo. Health Care Alliance (bd. dirs. 1989-94, v.p. 1992, chmn. bd. dirs. 1993), Mesa County Mental Health Assn. (bd. dirs. 1988-89, 91-92), Grand Junction C. of C. (bd. dirs. 1991-93), Rotary (Grand Coolee, Wash. 1973-75, Portland 1975-81, Grand Junction 1981-98, Salem 1998—, chmn. fund raising com. 2000-01, bd. dirs. 2001-02), Western Oreg. U. Alumni Assn. (bd. dirs. 2006—10, v.p. bd. dirs. 2006-07, pres.-elect 2007-08, pres., 2008-09, past pres. 2009), Western Oreg. U. Found. (bd. dir. 2009-, exec. com. 2010-), Masons, Shriners (pres. Grand Junction club 1989, bd. dirs. El Jebel 1986-90, 1st v.p. Western Colo. club 1989, pres. 1990-91), Knights of Columbus (3rd degree Knight) Republican. Roman Catholic. Avocations: golf, camping, fishing, travel. Home and Office: 592 Meadowbrook Ln Stayton OR 97383-1465 Office Phone: 503-769-1661. *

ZUMWALT, ROSS EUGENE, forensic pathologist, educator; b. Goodrich, Mich., July 18, 1943; s. Paul Lawrence and Lila Ann (Birky) Z.; m. Theresa Ann Schar, Sept. 12, 1970 (div. Apr. 1988); children: Christopher Todd, Tenley Ann; m. Cheryl Lynn Willman, Sept. 4, 1988; 1 child, David Willman Zumwalt. BA, Wabash Coll., 1967; MD, U. Ill., 1971. Diplomate in anat. and forensic pathology Am. Bd. Pathology. Intern, resident in pathology Mary Bassett Hosp., Cooperstown, NY, 1971-73; resident in anat. and forensic pathology Southwestern Med. Sch., Dallas, 1973-76; asst. med. examiner Dallas County, Dallas, 1974-76; staff pathologist, dir. labs. Naval Regional Med. Ctr., Camp Lejeune, NC, 1976-78; dep. coroner Cuyahoga County, Cleve., 1978-80, Hamilton County, Cin., 1980-86; assoc. prof. pathology U. Cin. Sch. Medicine, 1980-86; prof. pathology U. N.Mex. Sch. Medicine, Albuquerque, 1987—; chief med. investigator Office of Med. Investigator, Albuquerque, 1991—; pres. Am. Bd. of Pathology, Tampa, 2000—01. Trustee Am. Bd. Pathology, Tampa, Fla., 1993-2004. Lt. comdr. USN, 1976-78. Fellow Am. Acad. Forensic Scis., Coll. Am. Pathologists; mem. AMA, Nat. Assn. Med. Examiners (bd. dirs. 1984-96, pres. 1995-96), Am. Soc. Clin. Pathologists, Am. and Can. Acad. Pathologists. Avocation: golf. Home Phone: 505-344-7480, Office Phone: 505-272-0710. Business E-Mail: rzumwalt@salud.unm.edu.

ZUNDEL, NATAN, surgeon, educator; b. Bogota, Colombia, Jan. 16, 1960; MD, U. Javeriana, 1982, degree in Gen. Surgery, 1988. Cert. Am. Bd. Surgery. Prof. surgery FIU Herbert Wertheim Coll. Medicine, 2007—. Fellow: ACS; mem.: ALACE, FELAC, ASMBS, SAGES. Avocations: reading, music, theater. Office: 17038 W Dixie Hwy Ste 210 North Miami Beach FL 33160 Office Fax: 305-466-4970. Personal E-mail: drnazuma99@yahoo.com.

ZUNINO, NATALIA, psychologist; b. NYC, Nov. 23, 1937; d. Frank Anthony and Elizabeth (Delafield) Zunino; m. Philip Puschel, June 29, 1974 (div. 1978). BA, Mt. Holyoke Coll., Mass., 1959; MA, Columbia U., 1962, NYU, 1975, PhD, 1982. Rschr. Time-Life Books, NYC, 1962-67; sr. editor Harcourt Brace Jovanovich, NYC, 1967-80; staff psychotherapist Met. Ctr. for Mental Health, NYC, 1983-85; pvt. practice, 1984—; staff psychotherapist Washington Sq. Inst., NYC, 1984-87; supr. Met. Inst. Tng. in Psychoanalytic Psychotherapy, NYC, 1985—; supr., staff psychotherapist Eating Disorder Resource Ctr., NYC, 1986—2004; mem. faculty Ctr. for Study of Anorexia and Bulimia, NYC, 1987—96, supr., 1995—; psychotherapist family and couple treatment Inst. Contemporary Psychotherapy, NYC, 1988—90; participant intensive-extern program Family Inst. Westchester, Harrison, NY, 1990—94; participant Ea. Group Psychotherapy Tng. Program, 1997—98. Mem. intake com. Ctr. Study Anorexia and Bulimia, 1997—, exec. com., 2006—; adj. asst. prof. Coll. S.I., NY, 1984—86. Editor: Psychology: Its Principles and Applications, 1969, 8th edit. 1984, Sociology: The Study of Human Relationships, 1972, 2nd edit. 1977; contbr. articles to profl. jours. Mem. APA, Acad. for Eating Disorders, Nat. Eating Disorders Assn. Avocations: horseback riding, gardening. Home: 115 4th Ave #7G New York NY 10003-4909 Office Phone: 212-677-0804.

ZUO, GUO-YING, pharmacist, researcher; b. Yunnan, China, July 27, 1963; PhD, Kunming Inst. Botany, 2001. Rschr., Ctr. Natural Medicines Kunming Gen. Hosp., PLA, 2001—. Office: 212 Daguan Rd Kunming Yunnan 650032 China Business E-Mail: zuoguoying@263.net.

ZURAWSKI, JEANETTE, rehabilitation services professional; b. June 30, 1951; Student, U. Wis., 1969-70, Portland CC, 1974-78; BS in Chemistry, Portland State U., 1981; MD, Oreg. Health Scis. U., 1985; postgrad. in Acupuncture, UCLA, 2000. Diplomate Am. Bd. Phys. Medicine and Rehab. Resident U. Kans. Med. Ctr., Kansas City, 1985-89; med. dir. rehab. svcs. North Miss Med. Ctr., Tupelo, 1989-97; pvt. practice Tupelo, Miss. Past mem. adv. com. Medicare Carrier; presenter in field; bd. dirs. Gilbert's Home Health Care Agy. Past chair pers. com., exec. bd. mem., co-chair fund raising com. Big Brothers/Big Sisters, Lee County, Miss. Mem. AMA, Am. Acad. Phys. Medicine and Rehab. (chairperson edn. com., mem. exec. coun. resident physician sect.), Am. Med. Women's Assn., Am. Bus. Women's Assn. (chair membership com., treas., recipient Woman of the Year), Miss. State Med. Assn., Assn. Acad. Physiatrists, Am. Med. Acupuncture Assn. (bd. eligible), Iota Sigma Pi. Home: 637 W Main St Tupelo MS 38804-3732 *

ZUR HAUSEN, HARALD, virologist, research center executive; b. Gelsenkirchen, Germany, Mar. 11, 1936; s. Eduard and Melanie zur Hausen; m. Ethel-Michele de Villiers; children from previous marriage: Jan Dirk, Axel, Gerrit. MD, U. Düsseldorf, Germany, 1960; DSc (hon.), U. Chgo., 1984; PhD (hon.), U. Umea, Sweden, 1992, Charles U., Prague, 1994, U. Salford, England, 1997, U. Helsinki, Finland, 2000, U. Erlangen, 2005, U. Würzburg, 2008. Rsch. fellow Inst. Hygiene & Microbiology, U. Düsseldorf, 1962—65; rsch. fellow divsn. virology Children's Hosp. Phila., 1966-69; sr. scientist Inst. Virology, U. Würzburg, Germany, 1969-72; chmn., prof. Inst. Clin. Virology, U. Erlangen-Nuremberg, Bavaria, Germany, 1972-77, Inst. Virology, U. Freiburg, Germany, 1977-83; sci. dir., chmn. mgmt. bd. German Cancer Rsch. Ctr., Heidelberg, 1983—2003, prof. emeritus, 2003—. Coun. mem. Internat. Union Against Cancer, Geneva, 1986—94, bd. dirs., 2006—; chmn. Assn. Nat. Rsch. Centers, 1989—91; vice chmn. Orgn. European Cancer Institutes, 1990—93, pres., 1993—96; mem. exec. bd. Swiss Cancer Inst., Lausanne, 1990—95; mem. sci. adv. bd. Imperial Cancer Rsch. Ctr., London, 1994—98, Vienna Sci. Rsch. & Tech. Fund, 2007—; mem. governing coun. Internat. Network Cancer Treatment & Rsch., Brussels, 1999—; mem. health rsch. coun. German Ministry Sci. & Tech., 2003—05; mem. internat. adv. com. French Nat. Cancer Inst., Paris, 2005—, Nat. Sci. & Tech. Devel. Agy., Bangkok, 2007—. Contbr. articles to profl. jours. Recipient Wilhelm-Warner prize, U. Hamburg, 1974, Robert-Koch prize, Germany, 1975, Lila Gruber award, Am. Acad. Dermatology, 1985, Charles S. Mott prize, GM Cancer Rsch. Found., 1986, Sebatia prize, Italy, 1992, Clin. Rsch. award, Fedn. European Cancer Societies, 1993, Martinus Willem Beijerinck Medal, Nederlands Acad. Scis., 1996, Paul Ehrlich-Ludwig Darmstätter prize, Germany, 1994, Ernst Jung prize, 1996, Charles Rodolphe Brupacher prize, Switzerland, 1999, Arthur Burkhardt prize, Germany, 2001, Parram Thomas prize, Am. Soc. Sexually Transmitted Diseases, 2001, San Marino prize for medicine, 2002, Prince Mahidol award, Bangkok, 2006, Raymond Bourgin award, Paris, 2006, Loeffler-Frosch Medal, German Virological Soc., 2007, German Cancer prize, 2007, Lifetime Achievement award, Am. Assn. Cancer Rsch., 2008, Warren Alpert Found. prize, Harvard U., 2008, Gairdner Found. Internat. award, Can., 2008, Nobel prize in physiology/medicine, 2008. Fellow: World Acad. Arts & Scis. (hon.); mem.: Acad. Cancer Immunology, Am. Philos. Soc., Venezuelan Nat. Acad. Medicine, Polish Acad. Scis. (fgn.), Academia Europaea (v.p. 1991—93), Human Genome Orgn., German Acad. Natural Scis. Leopoldina, Heidelberg Acad. Scis., European Molecular Biology Orgn., Polish Soc. Dermatology (hon.), Japanese Cancer Soc. (hon.), South African Soc. Dermatology (hon.), Czechoslovak Soc. Microbiology (hon.), Hungarian Cancer Soc. (hon.), Italian Soc. Virology (hon.), German Soc. Virology (hon.), German Dermatological Soc. (hon.). Achievements include discovery of the causative role of papilloma viruses in cancer of the cervix which led to the development of a successful HPV vaccine. Office: German Cancer Rsch Ctr Im Neuenheimer Feld 280 69120 Heidelberg Germany *

ZUSMAN, EDIE ELLEN, neurosurgeon; b. El Paso, Oct. 29, 1963; d. Sidney Harold and Sandra Phyllis Zusman; m. Stephen Roy Pratt, Feb. 17, 1991; children: Adam, Abby. BS, Northwestern U., 1985, MD, 1987. Diplomate Am. Bd. Neurol. Surgery, Nat. Bd. Med. Examiners. With U. Calif., San Francisco, 1993-94, clin. instr., 1994-97, molecular med. rsch. fellow, 1994-96; staff neurosurgeon Kaiser Permanent, Sacramento, 1997-99; asst. prof. U Calif. Davis Sch. Medicine, Sacramento, 1999—; dir. adult neurosurgery Sutter Neuroscience Inst., Sacramento. Mem. exec. com. Coun. State Neurol. Socs., 1997—; adj. asst. prof. neurol. surgery U. Calif., Davis; prin. investigator Ctr. for Biophotonics Sci. and Tech. Author: The Outcome Following Traumatic Spinal Cord Injuries, 1992; contbr. articles to profl. jours. Participant Habitat for Humanity, Oakland, Calif., 1997—. Mem. AMA, Am. Assn. Neurol. Surgeons (bd. dirs.), Congress Neurol. Surgeons, Calif. Assn. Neurol. Surgeons, Northwestern U. Alumni Assn., Women in Neurological Surgery (past pres.), Coun. of State Neurosurgical Soc., Am. Epilepsy Soc. Avocations: tennis, opera. Office: Sutter Neuroscience Med Group Ste 500 2800 L St Sacramento CA 95816 Office Phone: 916-454-6936. Business E-Mail: zusmane@sutterhealth.org.

ZUSMAN, JOSE ALBERTO, psychiatrist, educator; b. Rio de Janeiro, Aug. 17, 1960, MD, Fluminense Fed. U., 1985; PhD in Psychoanalysis, Feferal U. Rio de Janeiro, 2000. Physician, psychotherapy supr. Fed. U. Rio de Janeiro, 1989; trainning analist Intrnat. Psychoalyyical Assn., 2002—. Psychoanalysis prof., 2000. Mem.: FEPAL. Avocation: music, running. Home: Rua Itaipava 124/101 Rua Jardim Botanic Rio de Janeiro 22461-030 Brazil Home Fax: 55 21 2529-8739. Personal E-mail: jazusman@infolink.com.br.

ZWANGER, JEROME, physician; b. NYC, Apr. 4, 1923; m. Bernice E. Lomazov, May 22, 1955 (dec.); children: Susan, Roberta (dec.), Melissa, Betsy. AB, U. Pa., 1943; MD, Chgo. Med. Sch., 1947. Diplomate Am. Bd. Radiology. Intern Wyckoff Heights Hosp., Bklyn., 1947-49; resident L.I. Coll. Hosp., Bklyn., 1949-52; practice medicine specializing in radiology; asst. dir. dept. radiology L.I. Coll. Hosp., NYC, 1953-54; radiologist L.I. Jewish Hosp., 1955-60; dir. radiology North Shore U. Hosp., Plainview, NY, 1961—92, also bd. dirs. Asst. prof. clin. radiology SUNY, Stony Brook, 1974-80; governing bd. Nassau-Suffolk Health Systems Agy., 1974-94; mem. N.Y. State Bd. Medicine, Bd. Profl. Med. Conduct N.Y. State Dept. Health. Mem. vis. com. Met. Mus. Art; bd. overseers Sch. Arts and Scis., U. Pa. Fellow: Nassau Acad. Medicine (founding fellow, past pres.), Am. Coll. Radiology (councilor 1975—); mem.: AMA, Soc. for Breast Imaging, L.I. Radiol. Soc. (past pres.), N.Y. State Radiol. Soc. (pres. 1986—87), Radiol. Soc. N.Am., Nassau County Med. Soc. (past pres.), Med. Soc. N.Y., U. Pa. Alumni Assn. (bd. overseers 1997). Office: 126 Hicksville Rd Massapequa NY 11758-5822

ZWAS, SHIFRA TZILA, nuclear medicine physician, educator; d. Pinchas and Genia Czerniak; m. Gideon Zwas, Sept. 6, 1966 (dec. Jan. 16, 2000); children: Gila, Eyal. MD, Hebrew U./Tel-Aviv U., 1971. Lic. Ministry Health, Israel, 1971. Fellow dept. nuc. medicine L.I.-Hillside Med. Ctr., NYC, 1971—72; resident dept. nuc. medicine Sheba Med. Ctr., Tel-Hashomer, Ramat-Gan, Israel, 1973—77; sr. fellow nuc. medicine NYU Hosp., NYC, 1977—79; acting dir., assoc. dept. nuc. medicine Sheba Med. Ctr., Tel-Hashomer, Ramat Gan, Israel, 1980—92, dir. dept. nuc. medicine Tel-Hashomer, Ramat-Gan, Israel, 1992—; assoc. prof. nuc. medicine Sackler Sch. Medicine, Tel-Aviv U., 1990—, vice chairperson divsn. imaging, 2004—. Mem. regulatory com. quality assurance in nuc. medicine Ministry Health/State of Israel, Jerusalem, 1991—2000, chairperson ad-hoc regulatory com. on hospitals radiation safety, 1992—94, mem. adv. regulatory profl. com. in nuc. medicine. Mem. editl. bd.: Jour. Nuc. Medicine, 1987—, Turkish Jour. Nuc. Medicine, 2002—. Recipient First prize, Ahavat Zion Found. Nuc. Medicine and Radiopharmacology, Tel-Aviv, 1976, Second prize, 1986; grantee, Deepbreeze Co., Israel, 2004—, IAEA, Vienna, 1991—93, 1994—97, Mallincrodt Med.Co., Nuc. Medicine Dept., The Netherlands, 1993—97, Pfizer Pharm. Divsn. Inc., 1994—97, Adams Brain Ctr., Tel-Aviv U., 2001—, Shering Co., 2003—. Mem.: Israel Endocrine Soc. (assoc.), European Assn. Nuc. Medicine (assoc.; mem. task group com. edn. 1991—97), Am. Soc. Nuc. Medicine (assoc. Second award Ann. Conv. Sci. Exhibit 1983), Israel Soc. Nuc. Medicine (assoc.; pres. 1990—2000), Israel Med. Assn. (assoc.; head nuc. medicine bd. 1990—2000). Achievements include development of radioiodinated toluidine blue and use of innovative radiotracers for Parathyroidal per-operative localization scanning and new methodologies; functional brain scanning in brain trauma and psychiatric disorders; research in role of bone scan in stress fracture injuries in soldiers. Office: Sheba Med Ctr Tel- Hashomer 52621 Ramat Gan Israel Business E-Mail: zwast@post.tau.ac.il.

ZWEBACK, STANLEY, psychologist, educator; s. Harry and Belle Zweback; m. Dianne Barbara Fain, Dec. 24, 1964; children: Franklin Edward, Jessica Ellen. PhD, U. Md., 1972; BA, Coll. N.J., 1964. Diplomate Am. Bd. Profl. Disability Consultants. Assoc. prof. psychology Towson U., Md., 1970—; dir. svcs. Pers. Screening Sys., Severna Park, Md., 1985—. Cons. Balt. City Pub. Sch. Sys., 1999—2003; dir. svcs. Drs. Zweback, Driscoll and Assocs., Severna Park, 1989—98; psychol. cons. Arthur Slade Regional Sch., Glen Burnie, Md., 1973—2010. Contbr. articles to profl. jours., chapters to books. Pres. Bello Machre, Inc., Pasadena, Md., 1987—96. Experienced Tchr. fellow in sch. psychology, U.S. Office Edn., 1967—68. Office: Towson U 8000 York Rd Towson MD 21252 Home: 914 Main St Unit 809 Houston TX 77002 Office Phone: 410-704-3210. Personal E-mail: stanzwe@yahoo.com. Business E-Mail: zweback@towson.edu.

ZWEIMAN, BURTON, allergist, immunologist, educator; b. NYC, June 7, 1931; s. Charles and Gertrude (Levine) Z.; m. Claire Traig, Dec. 30, 1962; children: Amy Beth, Diane Susan. AB, U. Pa., 1952, MD, 1956. Diplomate Am. Bd. Internal Medicine, Am. Bd. Allergy & Immunology. Intern Mt. Sinai Hosp., NYC; Hosp. U. Pa., Bellevue Hosp. Ctr. Hosp. U. Pa., Bellevue Hosp. Center, 1957-60; fellow NYU Sch. Medicine, 1960-61; mem. faculty dept. medicine U. Pa. Sch. Medicine, Phila., 1963—, prof. medicine, chief allergy and immunology divsn., 1975-98. Cons. U.S. Army, NIH; co-chmn. Am. Bd. Allergy and Immunology, 1979-81. Editor Jour. Allergy Clin. Immunology, 1988-93; editor Allergy and Asthma: Disease Management Center, 1998—, now med. editor; contbr. articles to med. jours. Served with M.C., USNR, 1961-63. Allergy Found. Am. fellow, 1959-61 Fellow ACP, Am. Acad. Allergy, Asthma and Immunology (past pres.); mem. Am. Assn. Immunologists, Am. Fedn. Clin. Rsch., Phi Beta Kappa, Alpha Omega Alpha. Office: PA Presbyn Med Ctr 518 Mutch Bldg 38th Market St Philadelphia PA 19104 Business E-Mail: bzweiman@mail.med.upenn.edu.

ZWILLENBERG, DAVID, pediatric otolaryngologist; MD, U. of Toledo Coll. of Medicine, 1976. Diplomate Am. Bd. of Pediatrics-pediatric otolaryngology. Intern Grad. Hosp., 1977, resident, 1978, Pa. Hosp., 1981. Fellow: ACS; mem.: Am. Acad. of Otolaryngology - Head and Neck Surgery, Am. Broncho-Esophagological Assn. Office: St Christophers Hospital for Children 3601 A St Philadelphia PA 19134 Office Phone: 215-427-8915.

ZWISLOCKI, JOZEF JOHN, neuroscience educator, researcher; b. Lwow, Poland, Mar. 19, 1922; arrived in U.S., 1951; s. Tadeusz and Helena (Moscicki) Z.; m. Ruth Gerber, Oct. 29, 1945 (div. May 1954); m. Sylvia Claire Goldman, July 11, 1954 (dec. July 17, 1992); m. Jadwiga M. Morrison, Dec. 2, 1993. Diploma, Fed. Tech. Inst., Zurich, Switzerland, 1944, ScD, 1948; D honoris causa, U. Adam Mickiewicz, Poznán, Poland, 1991, Syracuse U., NY, 2004. Head electroacoustic lab. dept. otolaryngology U. Basel, Basel, Switzerland, 1945-51; rsch. fellow, Psychoacoustics Lab. Harvard U., Cambridge, Mass., 1951-57; dir. Bioacoustic Lab. Syracuse U., 1958-63, founder, dir. Lab. of Sensory Communication, 1963-73, founder dir. Inst. for Sensory Rsch., 1973—84, prof. neurosci., 1984—88, disting. prof. neurosci., 1988—92, disting. prof. emeritus, 1992—; prof. communicative disorders dept. spl. edn. Syracuse U. Sch. Edn., 1982—92; rsch. prof. SUNY Health Sci. Ctr., Syracuse, 1967—. Affiliate prof. bioengring. L.C. Smith Coll. Engring., Syracuse U., 1986-92; Carhart Meml. lectr. Am. Auditory Soc., 1992; Richard C. Heyser Meml. lectr. Audio Engring. Soc., 2005; mem. exec. coun. Com. Hearing, Bioacoustics and Biomechanics, NRC, Washington, 1965-68, chmn., 1967-68; mem. rev. panel on communicative scis.

NIH, Bethesda, Md., 1966-70, chmn., 1969-70; mem. Communicative Disorders Program Project rev. com. NIH, Bethesda, 1971-75; chmn. Bd. Sci. Advs. Ctr. Health Scis., U. Wis., Madison, 1975-78. Inventor acoustic ear simulator, acoustic bridge, several types of ear defenders; contbr. articles to profl. jours.; author: Auditory Sound Transmission: An Autobiographical Perspective, 2002, Sensory Neuroscience: Four Laws of Psychophysics, 2009. Recipient Faculty Rsch. award Syracuse chpt. Sigma Xi, 1973, Internat. Ctr. Ricerche e Studi Amplifon prize, 1976, Chancellor's citation for exceptional acad. achievement Syracuse U., 1980, Javits Neurosci. Investigator award NIH, 1984, Kwiek medal Acoustics Inst., A. Mickiewicz U., Poland, 1991, medal Acoustical Soc. Poland, 1991, Hugh Knowles prize Northwestern U., 1992, Life Achievement award, Am. Auditory Soc., 2007, Legend of Auditory Sci., Am. Acad. Audiology, 2006. Fellow Acoustical Soc. Am. (chmn. tech. com. on psychol. and physiol. acoustics 1962, 63, exec. coun. 1982-85, recipient 1st of Bekesy medal 1985, chmn. long-range planning com. 1983-86, nominating com. 1986-87, mem. com. on tutorials 1988-91, com. on meetings 1988-91, chmn. spring meeting, 1989), Am. Speech and Hearing Assn., The Polish Inst. Arts and Scis. Am.; mem. NAS, Polish Acad. Scis., Internat. Soc. Audiology (v.p. 1967-72), Internat. Union of Physiol. Scis. (commn. on auditory physiology 1982-89), Internat. Union Pure and Applied Physics (Commn. on Acoustics 1982-89), Collegium Oto Rhino Laryngologicum Amicitiae Sacrum, Assn. for Rsch. in Otolaryngology (award of merit 1988), Am. Otol. Soc. (assoc.), Hearing Rsch. (editl. bd.). Avocations: skiing, tennis, trout fishing, inventions.

ZYGMUNT, STEFAN CAROL, neurosurgeon; b. Sept. 14, 1949; MD, U. Linköping, Sweden, 1977; PhD, U. Lund, Sweden, 1992. Cert. in neurosurgery Nat. Swedish Bd. Health Welfare, 1986, in orthops. Nat. Swedish Bd. Health Welfare, 1990. Cons., orthops.; assoc. prof., neurosurgery U. Lund, 1995; cons., neurosurgeon U. Hosp. Northern Sweden, Umea, 1990—96, U. Hosp. Birmingham, England, 1996—; hon. sr. lectr. U. Birmingham, 1996—. Mem.: World Federation Neurol. Soc., Scandinavian Neurosurg. Soc., Swedish Neurosurg. Soc., Swedish Med. Assoc., Swedish Med. Soc., Brit. Med. Assoc., Soc. Brit. Neurol. Surgeons. Office: Priory Rd Edgbaston B5 7UG Birmingham England Office Phone: 44 121 6978243. Office Fax: 44 121 4544697.